# STUDENT STUDY BIBLE

• • •

Presented To

By

On

THOMAS NELSON

NEW KING JAMES VERSION®

# STUDENT STUDY BIBLE

A GUIDE TO KNOWING AND LIVING GOD'S WORD

Thomas Nelson
NKJV

# STUDENT STUDY BIBLE

A GUIDE TO KNOWING AND LIVING GOD'S WORD

Thomas Nelson
*Since 1798*

www.ThomasNelsonBibles.com

*Student Study Bible*, NKJV





Published in Nashville, TN, by Thomas Nelson. Thomas Nelson is a registered trademark of HarperCollins Christian Publishing, Inc.

Library of Congress Control Number: 2025930747



*Printed in South Korea*

25 26 27 28 29 30 31 32 33 34 /SWK/ 15 14 13 12 11 10 9 8 7 6 5 4 3 2 1

# CONTENTS

Abbreviations .... vii
How to Use the *Student Study Bible* .... ix
How to Study the Bible .... xii
Bible Facts .... xv
The Story of the New King James Version .... xviii

## THE OLD TESTAMENT

### THE BEGINNING OF ISRAEL (THE BOOKS OF THE LAW)

*Introduction to the Books of the Law* .... *2*
Genesis .... 4
Exodus .... 59
Leviticus .... 106
Numbers .... 135
Deuteronomy .... 176

### THE STORY OF ISRAEL (THE BOOKS OF HISTORY)

*Introduction to the Books of History* .... *214*
Joshua .... 216
Judges .... 240
Ruth .... 266
1 Samuel .... 272
2 Samuel .... 304
1 Kings .... 332
2 Kings .... 364
1 Chronicles .... 395
2 Chronicles .... 423
Ezra .... 458
Nehemiah .... 471
Esther .... 487

### THE WRITINGS OF ISRAEL (THE BOOKS OF POETRY AND WISDOM)

*Introduction to the Books of Poetry and Wisdom* .... *496*
Job .... 498
Psalms .... 530
Proverbs .... 624
Ecclesiastes .... 657
Song of Solomon .... 668

### THE MAJOR PROPHETS OF ISRAEL (BOOKS OF PROPHECY)

*Introduction to the Books of Prophecy* .... *676*
Isaiah .... 678
Jeremiah .... 744
Lamentations .... 805
Ezekiel .... 813
Daniel .... 862

### THE MINOR PROPHETS OF ISRAEL (BOOKS OF PROPHECY)

Hosea .... 880
Joel .... 891
Amos .... 897
Obadiah .... 906
Jonah .... 909
Micah .... 913
Nahum .... 920
Habakkuk .... 924
Zephaniah .... 928
Haggai .... 932
Zechariah .... 935
Malachi .... 947
*Between the Testaments* .... *953*

# THE NEW TESTAMENT

## THE STORY OF JESUS (THE GOSPELS)

*Introduction to the Gospels and the Book of History* . . . . . . *958*
Matthew . . . . . . 960
Mark . . . . . . 1002
Luke . . . . . . 1029
John . . . . . . 1068

## THE STORY OF THE CHURCH (BOOK OF HISTORY)

Acts . . . . . . 1103

## THE PAULINE EPISTLES (EPISTLES)

*Introduction to the Epistles and the Book of Apocalypse* . . . . . . *1144*
Romans . . . . . . 1146
1 Corinthians . . . . . . 1165
2 Corinthians . . . . . . 1182
Galatians . . . . . . 1193
Ephesians . . . . . . 1201
Philippians . . . . . . 1208
Colossians . . . . . . 1213
1 Thessalonians . . . . . . 1219
2 Thessalonians . . . . . . 1224
1 Timothy . . . . . . 1227
2 Timothy . . . . . . 1233
Titus . . . . . . 1238
Philemon . . . . . . 1241

## THE GENERAL EPISTLES (EPISTLES)

Hebrews . . . . . . 1244
James . . . . . . 1259
1 Peter . . . . . . 1265
2 Peter . . . . . . 1272
1 John . . . . . . 1276
2 John . . . . . . 1282
3 John . . . . . . 1284
Jude . . . . . . 1286

## THE VICTORY OF JESUS (APOCALYPSE)

Revelation . . . . . . 1289

Table of Monies, Weights, and Measures . . . . . . 1312
The Jewish Calendar . . . . . . 1314
30 Days of Getting to Know God . . . . . . 1315
60 Days with Paul . . . . . . 1316
90 Days Through the Gospels Chronologically . . . . . . 1317
365 Days Through the Bible Chronologically . . . . . . 1321
The Prophecies of Jesus . . . . . . 1325
The Miracles of Jesus . . . . . . 1333
The Parables of Jesus . . . . . . 1335
Features Index . . . . . . 1337
Topical Index . . . . . . 1345
Dictionary-Concordance . . . . . . 1352
Index to Maps . . . . . . 1388

# ABBREVIATIONS

## BOOK ABBREVIATIONS

in alphabetical order by abbreviation
OT = Old Testament
NT = New Testament

| Abbreviation | Book | Testament | Page |
|---|---|---|---|
| Acts | Acts | NT | 1103 |
| Amos | Amos | OT | 897 |
| 1 Chr. | 1 Chronicles | OT | 395 |
| 2 Chr. | 2 Chronicles | OT | 423 |
| Col. | Colossians | NT | 1213 |
| 1 Cor. | 1 Corinthians | NT | 1165 |
| 2 Cor. | 2 Corinthians | NT | 1182 |
| Dan. | Daniel | OT | 862 |
| Deut. | Deuteronomy | OT | 176 |
| Eccl. | Ecclesiastes | OT | 657 |
| Eph. | Ephesians | NT | 1201 |
| Esth. | Esther | OT | 487 |
| Ex. | Exodus | OT | 59 |
| Ezek. | Ezekiel | OT | 813 |
| Ezra | Ezra | OT | 458 |
| Gal. | Galatians | NT | 1193 |
| Gen. | Genesis | OT | 4 |
| Hab. | Habakkuk | OT | 924 |
| Hag. | Haggai | OT | 932 |
| Heb. | Hebrews | NT | 1244 |
| Hos. | Hosea | OT | 880 |
| Is. | Isaiah | OT | 678 |
| James | James | NT | 1259 |
| Jer. | Jeremiah | OT | 744 |
| Job | Job | OT | 498 |
| Joel | Joel | OT | 891 |
| John | John | NT | 1068 |
| 1 John | 1 John | NT | 1276 |
| 2 John | 2 John | NT | 1282 |
| 3 John | 3 John | NT | 1284 |
| Jon. | Jonah | OT | 909 |
| Josh. | Joshua | OT | 216 |
| Jude | Jude | NT | 1286 |
| Judg. | Judges | OT | 240 |
| 1 Kin. | 1 Kings | OT | 332 |
| 2 Kin. | 2 Kings | OT | 364 |
| Lam. | Lamentations | OT | 805 |
| Lev. | Leviticus | OT | 106 |
| Luke | Luke | NT | 1029 |
| Mal. | Malachi | OT | 947 |
| Mark | Mark | NT | 1002 |
| Matt. | Matthew | NT | 960 |
| Mic. | Micah | OT | 913 |
| Nah. | Nahum | OT | 920 |
| Neh. | Nehemiah | OT | 471 |
| Num. | Numbers | OT | 135 |
| Obad. | Obadiah | OT | 906 |
| 1 Pet. | 1 Peter | NT | 1265 |
| 2 Pet. | 2 Peter | NT | 1272 |
| Phil. | Philippians | NT | 1208 |
| Philem. | Philemon | NT | 1241 |
| Prov. | Proverbs | OT | 624 |
| Ps. | Psalms | OT | 530 |
| Rev. | Revelation | NT | 1289 |
| Rom. | Romans | NT | 1146 |
| Ruth | Ruth | OT | 266 |
| 1 Sam. | 1 Samuel | OT | 272 |
| 2 Sam. | 2 Samuel | OT | 304 |
| Song | Song of Solomon | OT | 668 |
| 1 Thess. | 1 Thessalonians | NT | 1219 |
| 2 Thess. | 2 Thessalonians | NT | 1224 |
| 1 Tim. | 1 Timothy | NT | 1227 |
| 2 Tim. | 2 Timothy | NT | 1233 |
| Titus | Titus | NT | 1238 |
| Zech. | Zechariah | OT | 935 |
| Zeph. | Zephaniah | OT | 928 |

## SPECIAL ABBREVIATIONS

- Arab. . . . Arabic
- Aram. . . . Aramaic
- Bg. . . . . . Blomberg, the 1524–25 edition of the Hebrew Old Testament published by Daniel Bomberg
- c. . . . . . . approximately
- cf. . . . . . compare
- ch., chs. . . chapter, chapters
- DSS . . . . Dead Sea Scrolls
- e.g. . . . . for example
- f., ff. . . . . following verse, following verses
- fem. . . . . feminine
- Gr. . . . . . Greek
- Heb. . . . . Hebrew
- i.e. . . . . . that is
- Kt. . . . . . Kethib (literally, in Aramaic, "written"), the written words of the Hebrew Old Testament preserved by the Masoretes (see "Qr." below)

Lat. . . . . Latin
lit. . . . . . literally
LXX . . . . Septuagint, an ancient translation of the Old Testament into Greek
M . . . . . . Majority Text
masc. . . masculine
ms., mss. . . manuscript, manuscripts
MT . . . . . Masoretic Text, the traditional Hebrew Old Testament
NU . . . . . the modern eclectic, or "critical," text of the Greek New Testament, published in the twenty-seventh edition of the Nestle-Aland Greek New Testament (N) and in the fourth edition of the United Bible Societies' Greek New Testament (U)
pl. . . . . . plural
Qr. . . . . . Qere (literally, in Aramaic, "read")—certain words read aloud, differing from the written words, in the Masoretic tradition of the Hebrew Old Testament (see "Kt." above)
Sam. . . . . Samaritan Pentateuch, a variant Hebrew edition of the books of Moses used by the Samaritan community
sing. . . . singular
Syr. . . . . Syriac
Tg. . . . . . Targum, ancient Aramaic interpretations of the Old Testament
TR . . . . . Textus Receptus or Received Text
v., vv. . . . verse, verses
vss. . . . . versions, ancient translations of the Bible
Vg. . . . . . Vulgate, an ancient translation of the Bible into Latin, translated and edited by Jerome

## CONTRIBUTORS

**Joel Evrist** provided the *Know the Truth* articles. Joel was born in California and became a Christian when he was seven years old. He has served for over fifteen years in student, young adult, and teaching ministries in Tennessee.

**Nate Gallagher** provided the *Apply the Truth* articles. Nate was born in California and became a Christian when he was eighteen years old. He has served for over twelve years in student ministry in Florida.

**Shaq Hardy** provided the *Seeing Jesus* notes. Shaq was born in Georgia and became a Christian when he was seventeen years old. He has served for over seven years in student ministry and family ministries in Tennessee and North Carolina.

**Ross Harvey** provided the *Live the Truth* articles. Ross was born in North Carolina and became a Christian when he was seven years old. He has served for over ten years in student and children ministry in Tennessee.

**Zak Shellabarger** provided the *Story of Scripture* devotions. Zak was born in California and became a Christian when he was ten years old. He has served for over fifteen years in teaching ministries in California.

# HOW TO USE THE *STUDENT STUDY BIBLE*

Whether you're curious about the Christian faith and just beginning to explore it, you've recently placed your faith in Christ, or you've been a follower of Jesus for some time, the *Student Study Bible* you hold in your hands can help you take the next steps of your journey. God gave us the Bible not just so we would read it, but also so we would understand it, come to know Him, and discover how He wants us to live each day. While reading the Scriptures with the Holy Spirit's guidance is more than enough to do this, God has given us a wonderful gift in other believers who can help us as well. This is what we saw in the early church in Acts, as Philip explained the Scriptures to the Ethiopian official (see Acts 8:26–35) and Aquila and Pricilla explained the gospel more clearly to Apollos (see Acts 18:24–28). The *Student Study Bible* has been designed to be your Philip or Aquila and Pricilla. While it cannot take the place of faithful believers in your life, its features are designed to help you study God's Word and draw deeply from its well of life-giving waters.

## THE ROMANS ROAD

Perhaps the most important feature in this Bible and the one you would want to begin with is the Romans Road. This popular explanation of the gospel—the saving message of faith in Jesus—uses five passages in Paul's letter to the church at Rome. Beginning with Romans 3:23 on page 1149, you will find a brief reading explaining that verse and how it relates to God's plan of salvation. The reading ends with a prompt of where to turn from there. You can use the Romans Road for your own understanding of the gospel and to share it with others.

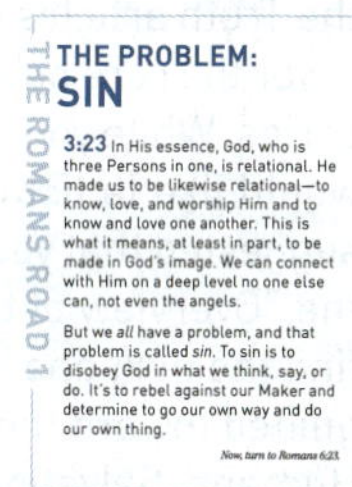

THE ROMANS ROAD 1

THE PROBLEM: SIN

3:23 In His essence, God, who is three Persons in one, is relational. He made us to be likewise relational—to know, love, and worship Him and to know and love one another. This is what it means, at least in part, to be made in God's image. We can connect with Him on a deep level no one else can, not even the angels.

But we *all* have a problem, and that problem is called *sin*. To sin is to disobey God in what we think, say, or do. It's to rebel against our Maker and determine to go our own way and do our own thing.

*Now, turn to Romans 6:23.*

## SECTION AND BOOK INTRODUCTIONS

An introduction is provided for each of the six major sections of the Bible and for each book. The section introductions are designed to acclimate you to the big ideas and genres of each part of Scripture. Think of these as giving you the big picture of a larger portion of the Bible. The book introductions are intended to familiarize you with the more specific details of each book. Combined, these introductions provide important and helpful context to what you read in Scripture.

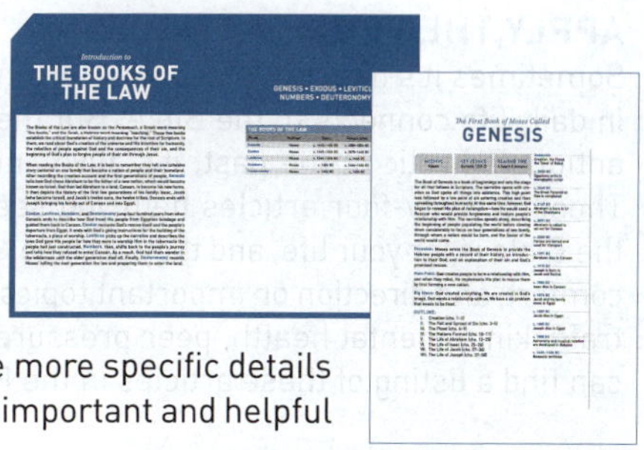


## THE STORY OF SCRIPTURE DEVOTIONS

These sixty brief readings have two goals. First, they provide an overview of the big story arc—often called the metanarrative—of the Bible's one story of Jesus. If you've ever been confused about how the different stories, people, and events of the Bible fit together, this is what you've been looking for. Second, these devotions help train you how to read the Bible on your own. They provide a consistent framework for reading the Bible that you can use for any passage.

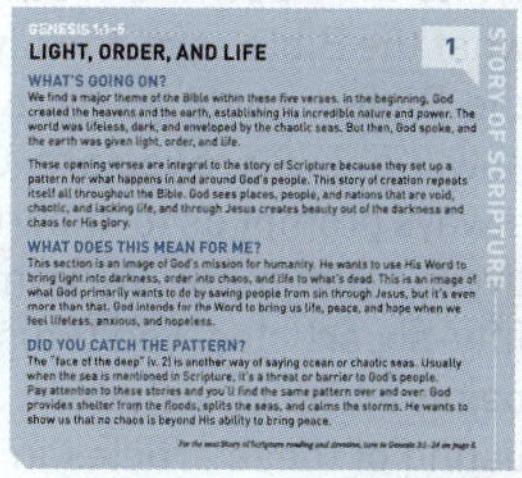

STORY OF SCRIPTURE 1

GENESIS 1:1–5

LIGHT, ORDER, AND LIFE

WHAT'S GOING ON?

We find a major theme of the Bible within these five verses. In the beginning, God created the heavens and the earth, establishing His incredible nature and power. The world was lifeless, dark, and enveloped by the chaotic seas. But then, God spoke, and the earth was given light, order, and life.

These opening verses are integral to the story of Scripture because they set up a pattern for what happens in and around God's people. This story of creation repeats itself all throughout the Bible. God sees places, people, and nations that are void, chaotic, and lacking life, and through Jesus creates beauty out of the darkness and chaos for His glory.

WHAT DOES THIS MEAN FOR ME?

This section is an image of God's mission for humanity. He wants to use His Word to bring light into darkness, order into chaos, and life to what's dead. This is an image of what God primarily wants to do by saving people from sin through Jesus, but it's even more than that. God intends for the Word to bring us life, peace, and hope when we feel lifeless, anxious, and hopeless.

DID YOU CATCH THE PATTERN?

The "face of the deep" (v. 2) is another way of saying ocean or chaotic seas. Usually when the sea is mentioned in Scripture, it's a threat or barrier to God's people. Pay attention to these stories and you'll find the same pattern over and over. God provides shelter from the floods, splits the seas, and calms the storms. He wants to show us that no chaos is beyond His ability to bring peace.

*For the next Story of Scripture reading and devotion, turn to Genesis 3:1–24 on page 5.*

You will find the first devotion, "Light, Order, and Life" based on Genesis 1:1–5 on page 5. A prompt will point you to the next devotion. While these devotions are designed to be completed in order, a list of all sixty is included in the Features Index in the back of this Bible that you can use to complete them in any order you like.

## STUDY NOTES

While much of the Bible is somewhat easy to understand, some parts can be more difficult—even the apostle Peter understood this (see 2 Pet. 3:16). This is why over 500 study notes have been included to help you grasp concepts, terms, and cultural contexts that might be easy to miss.

> **1:26** Because God is spirit (John 4:24), there can be no **image** or **likeness** of Him in a physical sense. Instead, God's image in people is more likely to consist of specific moral, ethical, and intellectual abilities and/or specific roles. In ancient times an emperor might command statues of himself to be placed in remote parts of his empire. These symbols would declare these areas were under his power and reign. God placed humans as image-bearers, or living symbols of Himself, on earth to represent His reign.

## SEEING JESUS NOTES

Throughout the features of this Bible, you'll see the recurring theme of Jesus. That's intentional. He's the center of the Bible's story and the one we look for in whatever we read. To help you with this, over 300 Seeing Jesus notes have been provided showing how Jesus is present through prophecy, typology, pictures, foreshadowing, and more. You can find a list of these notes in the Features Index.

> **SEEING JESUS IN THE SCRIPTURE**
>
> **3:15** From the beginning, God had a plan to save people from sin. Here's the first mention of that plan. This verse points to the crushing blow delivered to Satan when Jesus rose from the dead, a blow that will be completed when Jesus returns (see Rom. 16:20).

## KNOW THE TRUTH ARTICLES

Good doctrine—beliefs about God—is the foundation of our faith. Lay this foundation well, and what you build upon it will be strong and lasting. That's where the Know the Truth articles come in. These seventy-seven articles cover the core beliefs of our faith in eight linked doctrinal series. While you can read these articles in any order you would like (a list is provided in the Features Index), it's suggested that you explore them in order, beginning with the "Overview of the Doctrine of Scripture" on page 479. That article will prompt you where to find the next one in the Doctrine of Scripture series. Once that series is completed, you will be guided toward the next of the seven doctrinal series: God, Jesus, the Holy Spirit, Creation and Humans, Salvation, the Church, and the Future.

> KNOW THE TRUTH
>
> **THE DOCTRINE OF CREATION AND HUMANS**
>
> PART 8: THE FALL OF HUMANS
>
> **5:1–5** A significant event happened here that sometimes goes unnoticed: Adam *died*. The Hebrew word for *died* in this verse had been used only three times before. It's used first as a loving warning (Gen. 2:17) and next as a reminder against eating what a good God hadn't permitted (Gen. 3:3). Then, in Genesis 3:4 it's used by the serpent who said, "You will not surely die." Finally, we come to Genesis 5:5, "Adam lived . . . and he died." Clearly, God didn't create humans to die. Why then do we die?
>
> In the beginning, when God made all that was made, He declared it all to be "good" (Gen. 1:31). But people with freewill to love God used it instead to rebel against God's perfect rule and attempted self-rule. This historical event is often called *the Fall*. While physical death is the most notable consequence of the Fall, its main consequence was separation from the sinless, life-giving Creator. Spiritual separation from God resulted in humanity being corrupted with sin, evil, sickness, disease, death, and more. Only in the sin-forgiving, sickness-healing, demon-dominating, resurrected Savior Jesus Christ can we find hope to receive the prized gift of eternal life with God for which we were originally designed to enjoy.
>
> *For* **THE DOCTRINE OF CREATION AND HUMANS: PART 9: THE SIN AND EVIL IN HUMANS**, *turn to Genesis 6:5 on page 12.* • • •

## APPLY THE TRUTH ARTICLES

Sometimes it's difficult to see how what we experience in daily life connects to the Bible. But the Bible isn't an antiquated relic of the past; it's alive and active today. These seventy-four articles help you see how relevant the Bible is for your life, and they provide understanding, comfort, and direction on important topics like abuse, bullying, dating, depression, fame, human trafficking, mental health, peer pressure, pornography, racism, social media, and more. You can find a listing of these articles in the Features Index.

> APPLY THE TRUTH
>
> **BULLYING**
>
> **16:1–6** When you think of a bullying, you might think of someone getting stuffed in a locker or having his lunch money taken by force. This still happens, but a new form of virtual bullying is on the rise: blocking, spamming, and shaming others online. Bullying in both forms is a problem for many people. Some people just seem to enjoy putting others down or trying to intimidate them. Sometimes no matter how much you avoid or ignore them, it persists. What causes this behavior? Why does it seem like some people only want to put others down?
>
> In this passage we get insight into why people target others. For Sarai, it was insecurity about her infertility and jealousy of her maid Hagar's pregnancy. Thus Sarai aimed to ruin Hagar's life. How did Hagar respond? She didn't retaliate; she simply avoided Sarai. Ultimately God dealt with both. Jesus tells us to respond to our enemies with love and kindness (see Matt. 5:43–44). In doing so, we show our trust in God and represent Him well.

## LIVE THE TRUTH ARTICLES

While the Apply the Truth articles start with life to see what the Bible says, the Live the Truth articles start with the Bible to help you see how you can live it out right now, right where you are. Our time in God's Word should always prompt us to know God more, love Him more, and live for Him more. We can't miss this last part. In these fifty-six articles, you'll discover how Jesus connects to being a friend, a student, a part of your family, a part of the church, and more. You can find a listing of these articles in the Features Index.

> LIVE THE TRUTH
>
> **BEING A GOOD FRIEND**
>
> **19:18** Friendships can be tricky and difficult to navigate. People can seem one way one day and totally different the next. Friends sometimes get along with great ease; at other times they don't seem to like each other at all. Sometimes you do everything right and your friends still don't accept you. And it doesn't get easier; these problems are common for teens and adults.
>
> God knows all about friendship. He invented relationships, created marriage, and designed us for community. Even more, God the Father, God the Son, and God the Spirit maintain a perfect relationship within the one Godhead. Because of this, God knows best how we should navigate friendships: loving others is the key. That includes loving our friends even when they're difficult to love. When anyone wrongs us—an enemy or a friend—we shouldn't try to get even or hold a grudge. Rather, God says we're to love them like we love ourselves. We forgive them. We do what's best for them. We don't quit on them. We may not always like or agree with our friends' actions (just like they may not always like ours), but God calls us to persist in loving them and wanting the best for them. That's how we make friendship work.

## OTHER FEATURES

The *Student Study Bible* includes several other features to help you engage God's Word more deeply on a regular basis. Articles, such as "About the Bible," "How to Study the Bible," and "Between the Testaments"; charts and tables, such as Bible Facts and the Prophecies, Miracles, and Parables of Jesus; reading plans; a Topical Index; and a Dictionary-Concordance can be found in the front, back, and throughout this Bible.

## CROSS REFERENCES AND TRANSLATOR NOTES

As you read the Bible, you will notice *italic* type at times and superscript letters and numbers. Here's what they mean.

**Italic type** in the text indicates words that the original texts do not contain but which English requires for clarity.

### *Cross References*

A **superior letter** before or after a word or phrase in the text indicates a cross reference is provided. Each verse's cross reference identifiers begin with *a*. There are two types of cross references.

1. A Scripture reference indicates that the word or phrase noted in the text also appears in the cross-referenced verse.
2. A Scripture reference in square brackets indicates that the concept or idea noted in the text also appears in the cross-referenced verse.

### *Translator Notes*

A **superior number** before or after a word or phrase in the text indicates a translator note is provided. Each verse's translator note identifiers begin with *1*. There are six types of translator notes.

1. An equivalent translation provides a synonymous word or phrase to what is in the text to deepen your understanding of what is meant.
2. An alternative translation is introduced by "or" and provides a different meaning from what is in the text, but one that could have been justified by the original languages.
3. An explanatory note provides an explanation of the word or phrase but is not based on the original languages.
4. A literal translation is introduced by "Lit." and gives the literal meaning of a word or phrase.
5. A language note is introduced by "Arab.," "Aram.," "Heb.," or "Gr." and provides the Arabic, Aramaic, Hebrew, or Greek word or phrase that underlies the English translation.
6. A textual note is introduced by a manuscript name or abbreviation and points out significant textual variants concerning the text found in the verse.

The **bold number** in the cross references and translator notes field indicates the verse to which an entry applies.

# HOW TO STUDY THE BIBLE

There is no other book in the world quite like the Bible. It is an exceptional piece of literature featuring narrative, poetry, history, gospels, prophecy, and epistles that you can enjoy reading for its diversity and quality alone. You can look to the Bible for comfort, guidance, inspiration, knowledge, or enjoyment.

But the Bible is much more than a book. It's also God's special revelation, teaching us about God and ourselves and pointing the way to salvation and eternal life found only in Jesus Christ. As God's Word, the Bible speaks authoritatively to all our needs and desires and calls on us to listen and obey.

You can read the Bible just as you do other books, skimming off the surface meaning of various passages. But to get to the heart of what God is saying, you also must *study* the Bible. This is a vital part of growing in spiritual maturity. Studying may sound more challenging than reading, and it certainly requires effort, but the rewards are well worth the time and energy you spend. Because the Bible is God's revelation of Himself, learning more about the Bible will ultimately lead to increased knowledge of God. This doesn't mean just knowing about God—though certainly that is important. It means personally knowing God and developing a close relationship with Him through faith in Jesus Christ.

Studying the Bible will also make you more aware of God's will for your life. The Bible explains why you exist, what God expects of you, and how you can have an abundant and meaningful life. Eventually you will probably experience a wonderful cycle in your life: As you study the Bible and pray, you will come to know God better and love Him more. Then, as you know and love God more, you will respond to Him and follow His will for your life with joy and gratitude. As you do this, you will draw even closer to God and want to spend more time with Him by praying and studying the Bible. The cycle will then repeat itself with your enjoyment of studying the Bible growing fuller as time goes on. As your relationship with God grows, your Bible study will become less an act of work and more an act of worship and enjoyment.

## GETTING STARTED

So how can you get started? While there's no one proper way to study the Bible, some basic guidelines will help. First, be patient with yourself. The Bible is a fairly large book of roughly 770,000 words. The average adult would need about fifty to sixty-five hours to read it all the way through. And while much of the Bible is easy to read and understand, some of it can be challenging. Give yourself enough time to read at a comfortable pace, and don't get frustrated with yourself as you begin reading.

Second, know that you don't have to study the Bible alone. Actually, it's best not to. Before you begin to study the Bible, pray that the Holy Spirit will give you understanding. Remember that God wants you to understand the Bible, and He will help you do just that. There are also various tools such as commentaries and concordances to help you study. Because you are learning to study the Bible yourself, you shouldn't rely too heavily on commentaries to explain passages to you but don't neglect these helpful tools either. A good approach is to read a portion of Scripture and work through it, trying to understand it on your own. Then consult other resources to answer any lingering questions you might have and to confirm or correct what you discovered.

Third, focus first on learning and practicing basic Bible study skills, such as considering the context of what you're reading. Know as much of the literary and historical context of the book and passage as possible. Studying poetry is different from studying history. And studying a parable of Jesus in a Gospel is different from studying a narrative account in that same Gospel. Important questions to keep in mind are:

- Who wrote the book?
- Whom was it written to?
- What is its purpose?
- What came before this passage? What comes after it? Can I learn anything about this passage from that?
- What does this passage tell me about God or Jesus?
- How does this passage help me love God and serve Him more?

Consider the general point of a passage before looking for a specific application. As you develop ideas about what you are studying, test them against other passages. Is your idea supported elsewhere? Is it discounted somewhere else? The Bible is its own best commentary.

Finally, you should have a plan to follow. Consider when, where, and how you will study the Bible. Studying the Bible at the same time each day or week can help you develop a routine. Consistency over time is key. To further cement the habit, you might want to study the Bible in the same location each time too. Choose a place where you will be comfortable with as few distractions as possible. It's also a good idea to record what you learn each time in a journal. Finally, choose an approach to studying the Bible. No one method is best. Pick one you feel most comfortable with or use more than one for variety. No matter which method you use, always follow three basic steps:

1. **Observation:** What does this passage say? What is it about?
2. **Interpretation:** What does this passage mean? Why was it written?
3. **Application:** What does this passage do? What difference should it make in my life?

What follows is a variety of Bible study methods for you to consider.

## BOOK STUDY

Read through a book of the Bible. Learn the book's background by reading the book introduction, a Bible dictionary, or commentary. As you read ask *who*, *what*, *where*, *when*, *why*, and *how* questions about everything you encounter. Record your insights, thoughts, and lingering questions. Try to outline the book to see its development and flow and identify its theme and what it teaches you about God, Jesus, yourself, and life.

## NARRATIVE STUDY

Study the storyline of Scripture. The Bible is made up of sixty-six books that each tell part of one cohesive story that runs throughout it. This true story is one of God creating people to have a relationship with Him, their rebellion, and His plan to redeem them through Jesus. As you read, note how what you are studying advances this narrative. What can you learn about God's intention for people? About sin's effects? About people's failed attempts to make things right on their own? About God's plan to provide Jesus? About what it means to live in relationship with Jesus? About God's plans to conclude the story?

## CHRONOLOGICAL STUDY

Read the Bible according to the timing of its events. Much of the Bible isn't organized by chronology, but rather by genres and themes. Using a chronological reading plan, study how events happened over time to understand how God's plan of salvation progressed. Note how different books of the Bible fit together and how God's people came to understand more of the plan of salvation as it progressed.

## CHARACTER STUDY

Study the life of a person in the Bible. Choose a person in the Bible such as Moses, David, Ruth, Mary, or Peter and look up all the passages featuring that person by using a cross reference system, concordance, or Bible dictionary. As you study each passage, record insights about the person. In what ways did this person love and obey God? In what ways did he or she fail? What can you learn from that person about how you might live today?

## THEME STUDY

Trace a theme or concept throughout the Bible. Choose a theme such as prayer, sacrifice, forgiveness, or family and use a concordance, cross reference system, or Bible dictionary to trace it throughout Scripture. Consider how the theme is developed in the Bible. What seems to be constant about the theme for all people, places, and times? What differs? How does the theme relate to your life?

## WORD STUDY

Study how a word is used throughout the Bible. Choose a word such as *grace*, *mercy*, or *love* and use a concordance, Bible dictionary, or cross reference system to find each passage in which it occurs. Note where the word occurs more often and where it is absent. Has the meaning of the word remained consistent over time? Does it have differing uses? How does that word help you understand God, the Bible, and His plan for your life?

## THEOLOGICAL STUDY

Follow the development of a theological theme in Scripture. Choose a theological theme, such as salvation, God's attributes, or the Bible itself. Use a theology text, concordance, or Bible dictionary to find and read the passages that address the theme. Note what you can learn about that theological theme, how it has been developed, and what questions arise as you read.

# BIBLE FACTS

**40** Human writers of the Bible

**1,600** Years it took to write the Bible (~1500 BC to ~ AD 100)

**3** Languages the Bible was written in (Hebrew, Aramaic, and Greek)

**3** Continents the Bible was written on (Asia, Africa, and Europe)

**1,200+** Languages the Bible has been translated into

**5,000,000,000+** Bibles that have been sold[1]

## SIGNIFICANT YEARS IN BIBLE PUBLISHING

- **1228** Chapter numbers added to the Bible
- **1388** First Bible in English published
- **1448** Old Testament verse numbers added to the Bible
- **1551** New Testament verse numbers added to the Bible
- **1752** First Bible in America published
- **1901** Red letters of Jesus added to the Bible
- **1982** New King James Version published

## BOOKS, CHAPTERS, AND VERSES OF THE BIBLE

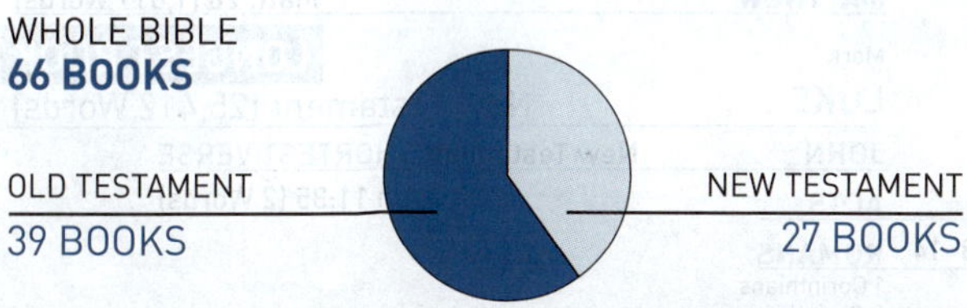


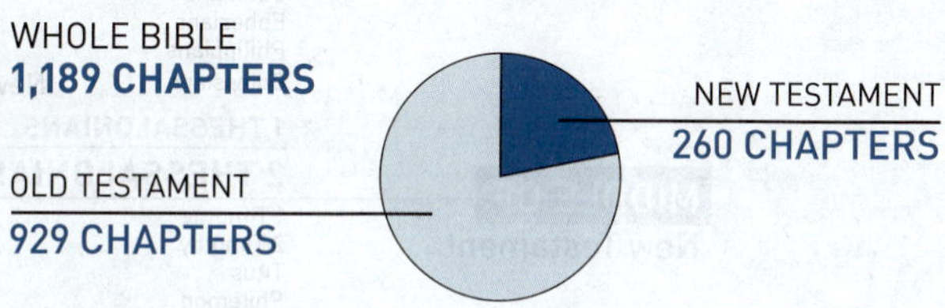


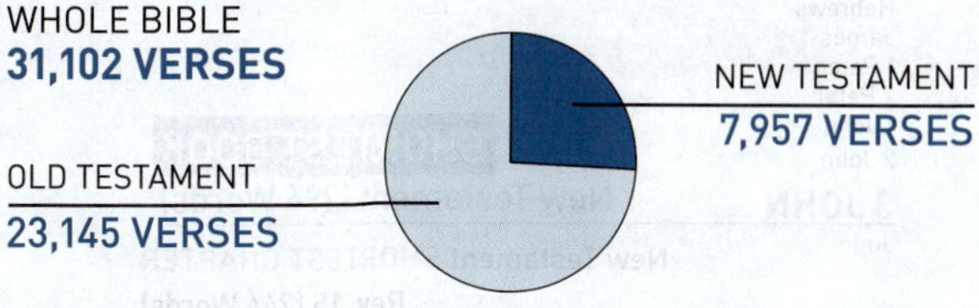


1 Guinness World Records, "Best selling book of non-fiction," Guinness World Records, http://www.guinnessworldrecords.com/world-records/best-selling-book-of-non-fiction/.

**GENESIS** — Old Testament **SHORTEST VERSE** Gen.10:27 + 90 Others (3 Words)

Exodus
Leviticus
Numbers
Deuteronomy
Joshua
Judges
Ruth
1 Samuel
2 Samuel
1 Kings
2 Kings
1 Chronicles

Old Testament **MIDDLE VERSE** 2 Chr. 18:30 — **2 CHRONICLES**

Ezra
Nehemiah

**ESTHER** — Old Testament **LONGEST VERSE** Esth. 8:9 (81 Words)

Old Testament **MIDDLE CHAPTER** Job 29 — **JOB** — Old Testament **SHORTEST CHAPTER** Ps. 17 (30 Words)

Whole Bible **MIDDLE CHAPTER** Ps. 117 — **PSALMS**

Whole Bible **MIDDLE VERSE** Ps. 103:1–2

**LONGEST BOOK** Old Testament (42,023 Words)

Old Testament **LONGEST CHAPTER** Ps. 119 (2,386 Words)

**MIDDLE OF** Old Testament — **PROVERBS**

Ecclesiastes
Song of Solomon
Isaiah
Jeremiah
Lamentations
Ezekiel
Daniel
Hosea
Joel
Amos

**OBADIAH** — **SHORTEST BOOK** Old Testament (646 Words)

Jonah

**MIDDLE OF** Whole Bible — **MICAH**

**NAHUM**

Habakkuk
Zephaniah
Haggai
Zechariah
Malachi

**MATTHEW** — New Testament **LONGEST CHAPTER** Matt. 26 (1,619 Words)

Mark

**LUKE** — **LONGEST BOOK** New Testament (25,412 Words)

**JOHN** — New Testament **SHORTEST VERSE** John 11:35 (2 Words)

New Testament **MIDDLE VERSE** Acts 7:7 — **ACTS**

New Testament **MIDDLE CHAPTER** Rom. 13–14 — **ROMANS**

1 Corinthians
2 Corinthians
Galatians
Ephesians
Philippians
Colossians

**1 THESSALONIANS** — New Testament **SHORTEST VERSE** 1Thess. 5:16 (2 Words)

**MIDDLE OF** New Testament — **2 THESSALONIANS**

1 Timothy
2 Timothy
Titus
Philemon
Hebrews
James
1 Peter
2 Peter
1 John
2 John

**3 JOHN** — **SHORTEST BOOK** New Testament (296 Words)

Jude

New Testament **SHORTEST CHAPTER** Rev. 15 (244 Words)

**REVELATION** — New Testament **LONGEST VERSE** Rev. 20:4 (70 Words)

# WORDS IN THE BIBLE

WHOLE BIBLE
**769,296 WORDS**

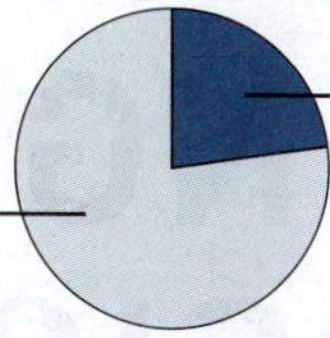

NEW TESTAMENT
**177,976 WORDS**

OLD TESTAMENT
**591,320 WORDS**

## MIDDLE WORDS

| | |
|---|---|
| **MIDDLE OF WHOLE BIBLE** | "the inward" (Psalm 64:6) |
| **MIDDLE OLD TESTAMENT** | "soldiers of" (1 Chronicles 19:18) |
| **MIDDLE NEW TESTAMENT** | "me, that" (Acts 8:24) |

Maher-Shalal-Hash-Baz **LONGEST WORD** (18 letters)

**9,706** Appearances of *a/an*

**61,650** Appearances of *the*

**4,425** Appearances of *God* or *god*

**7,909** Appearances of *lord*, *Lord*, or *Lord*

**981** Appearances of *Jesus*

**361** Appearances of *love*

**158** Appearances of *joy*

# LETTERS IN THE BIBLE

WHOLE BIBLE
**3,124,782 LETTERS**

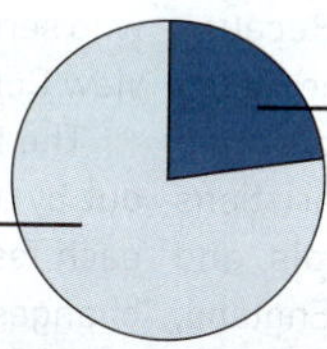

NEW TESTAMENT
**721,840 LETTERS**

OLD TESTAMENT
**2,402,942 LETTERS**

## MIDDLE LETTERS

| | |
|---|---|
| **MIDDLE OF WHOLE BIBLE** | *fl* in "flesh" (Psalm 63:1) |
| **MIDDLE OLD TESTAMENT** | *at* in "that" (1 Chronicles 22:12) |
| **MIDDLE NEW TESTAMENT** | *n a* in "heaven again" (Acts 10:16) |

Verse that contains all the letters of the alphabet: **Ezekiel 28:13**

Verse that contains all the letters of the alphabet except "j": **Ezra 7:21**

Verses that contain all the letters of the alphabet except "q": **Genesis 34:30**; **Joshua 7:24**; **1 Chronicles 12:40**; **1 Kings 1:9**; **Haggai 1:1**

Verses that contain all the letters of the alphabet except "x": **2 Kings 1:2**; **2 Kings 16:15**; **1 Chronicles 4:10**

Verses that contain all the letters of the alphabet except "z": **1 Kings 19:21**; **Jeremiah 21:12**; **Ezekiel 18:17**

# THE STORY OF THE NEW KING JAMES VERSION®

In the latter part of the nineteenth century, F. H. A. Scrivener observed that the King James Bible, "so laborious, so generally accurate, so close, so abhorrent of paraphrase, so grave and weighty in word and rhythm, so intimately bound up with the religious convictions of the English people, will never yield its hard-earned supremacy, save to some reverential and well-considered revision of which it has been adapted as the basis, that shall be happy enough to retain its characteristic excellence, while amending its venial [trifling] errors and supplying its unavoidable defects."[1]

In 1975, Thomas Nelson Publishers, successor to the British firm that had first published the English Revised Version in 1885, the American Standard Version in 1901, and the Revised Standard Version (1952), determined to evaluate interest in a possible new revision of the King James Version. Because any revision of the Scriptures must meet the needs of public worship, Christian education, and personal reading and study, leading clergy and lay Christians were invited to meetings in Chicago, Illinois, and Nashville, Tennessee, in 1975, and London, England, in 1976, to discuss the need for revision. Almost 100 church leaders from a broad spectrum of Christian churches strongly supported the commencement of a new revision.

Work began immediately. Biblical scholars representing a cross-section of evangelical Christendom were selected to work on this major project. They came from England, Scotland, Canada, New Zealand, Australia, the Netherlands, Taiwan, and the United States, so that the New King James Version would reflect internationally accepted English usage.

Each translator worked privately and independently recommended changes in the King James text. Translators of the Old Testament used the *Biblia Hebraica Stuttgartensia*, while the *Scrivener Greek Text* was the basis of the New Testament. The 1769 revision of the King James Version, the edition in general use today, was the English language text that guided the new revision process. The translator's work was then submitted to the Executive Editor for the Old or New Testament. Word studies of the English, Greek, and Hebrew and an elaborate concordance were prepared especially for this revision by the Executive Editors and their associates. Using the original texts, the King James Bible, and carefully established guidelines, the Executive Editor for the Old or New Testament reviewed each scholar's work. Where necessary, they made recommendations for further changes or, in some cases, for restoration of the King James reading.

Each book was then submitted to the English Editor to be checked for grammatical accuracy, literary beauty, and the effective communication of the content.

Throughout the entire editorial process, the work was regularly reviewed by the clergy and lay advisors who served on the British and North American Overview Committees.

The final exhaustive review process was carried out by a separate Executive Review Committee for each Testament over a four-year period. All proposed changes by translators, editors, and reviewers were considered during this time, including final alterations proposed by committee members. The review process was completed in July 1981 at St. Andrews University in northeast Scotland, not far from Stirling Castle, King James' historic residence. During part of this time, the North American Committee was joined in its activity by the distinguished members of the British Overview Committee.

The New King James Version was thus prepared with profound reverence for the Word of God and with a deep appreciation of the wise traditions established by the translators of 1611. It was the prayer of the revisers that the work in which they labored may indeed be, as Dr. Scrivener said years before, a "reverential and well-considered revision" retaining the characteristic excellencies of the King James Bible.



---

1 F. H. A. Scrivener, *The Authorized Edition of the English Bible (1611): Its Subsequent Reprints and Modern Representatives* (University Press: Cambridge, 1884), 135–36.

# THE OLD TESTAMENT

*Introduction to*

# THE BOOKS OF THE LAW

The Books of the Law are also known as the *Pentateuch*, a Greek word meaning "five books," and the *Torah*, a Hebrew word meaning "teaching." These five books establish the critical foundation of history and doctrine for the rest of Scripture. In them, we read about God's creation of the universe and His intention for humanity, the rebellion of people against God and the consequences of their sin, and the beginning of God's plan to forgive people of their sin through Jesus.

When reading the Books of the Law, it is best to remember they tell one cohesive story centered on one family that became a nation of people and their homeland. After recording the creation account and the first generations of people, **Genesis** tells how God chose Abraham to be the father of a new nation, which would become known as Israel. God then led Abraham to a land, Canaan, to become his new home. It then depicts the history of the first few generations of his family: Isaac, Jacob (who became Israel), and Jacob's twelve sons, the twelve tribes. Genesis ends with Joseph bringing his family out of Canaan and into Egypt.

**Exodus**, **Leviticus**, **Numbers**, and **Deuteronomy** jump four hundred years from when Genesis ends to describe how God freed His people from Egyptian bondage and guided them back to Canaan. **Exodus** recounts God's rescue itself and the people's departure from Egypt. It ends with God's giving instructions for the building of the tabernacle, a place of worship. **Leviticus** picks up the narrative and describes the laws God gave His people for how they were to worship Him in the tabernacle the people had just constructed. **Numbers**, then, shifts back to the people's journey and tells how they refused to enter Canaan. As a result, God had them wander in the wilderness until the older generation died off. Finally, **Deuteronomy** records Moses' telling the next generation the law and preparing them to enter the land.

# GENESIS • EXODUS • LEVITICUS NUMBERS • DEUTERONOMY

## THE BOOKS OF THE LAW

| Book | Author | Date | Timeframe | Theme |
|---|---|---|---|---|
| **Genesis** | Moses | c. 1445–1406 BC | c. 4000–1804 BC | Beginnings |
| **Exodus** | Moses | c. 1445–1406 BC | c. 1875–1445 BC | Deliverance |
| **Leviticus** | Moses | c. 1444–1406 BC | c. 1444 BC | Worship |
| **Numbers** | Moses | c. 1406 BC | c. 1444–1406 BC | Disobedience |
| **Deuteronomy** | Moses | c. 1406 BC | c. 1406 BC | Obedience |

*The First Book of Moses Called*

# GENESIS

| AUTHOR | KEY VERSES | READING TIME |
| --- | --- | --- |
| Moses | Genesis 12:2–3 | 4 hours 8 minutes |

The Book of Genesis is a book of beginnings and sets the stage for all that follows in Scripture. The narrative opens with creation as God spoke all things into existence. This high point was followed by a low point of sin entering creation and then spreading throughout humanity. At this same time, however, God began to reveal His plan of redemption—how He would send a Rescuer who would provide forgiveness and restore people's relationship with Him. The narrative speeds along, describing the beginning of people populating the world before slowing down considerably to focus on four generations of one family, through whom a nation would be born, and the Savior of the world would come.

**Occasion:** Moses wrote the Book of Genesis to provide the Hebrew people with a record of their history, an introduction to their God, and an explanation of their sin and God's promised rescue.

**Main Point:** God creates people to be in a relationship with Him, and when they rebel, He implements His plan to rescue them by first forming a new nation.

**Big Ideas:** God created everything. We are created in God's image. God wants a relationship with us. We have a sin problem that needs to be fixed.

## OUTLINE:

I. Creation (chs. 1–2)
II. The Fall and Spread of Sin (chs. 3–5)
III. The Flood (chs. 6–9)
IV. The Nations Formed (chs. 10–11)
V. The Life of Abraham (chs. 12–25)
VI. The Life of Isaac (chs. 25–26)
VII. The Life of Jacob (chs. 27–36)
VIII. The Life of Joseph (chs. 37–50)

**Undatable**
Creation, the Flood, the Tower of Babel

**c. 3000 BC**
Egyptians write in hieroglyphic script

**c. 2560 BC**
The Great Pyramid at Giza is completed

**c. 2167 BC**
Abraham is born in Ur of the Chaldeans

**c. 2091 BC**
Abraham is called to set out for Canaan

**c. 2000 BC**
Horses are tamed and used for transport

**c. 1991 BC**
Abraham dies in Canaan

**c. 1915 BC**
Joseph is born to Jacob and Rachel

**c. 1886 BC**
Isaac dies in Canaan

**c. 1876 BC**
Jacob and his family move to Egypt

**c. 1859 BC**
Jacob dies in Egypt

**c. 1805 BC**
Joseph dies in Egypt

**c. 1800 BC**
Astronomy and musical notation are developed in Babylon

**c. 1445–1406 BC**
**Genesis written**

### *THE HISTORY OF CREATION*
*(Gen. 2:4–9; Job 38:4–11; John 1:1–5)*

1 In the [a]beginning [b]God created the heavens
and the earth. 2 The earth was [a]without form,
and void; and darkness *was*[1] on the face of the
deep. [b]And the Spirit of God was hovering over
the face of the waters.
3 [a]Then God said, [b]"Let there be [c]light"; and
there was light. 4 And God saw the light, that *it*
*was* good; and God divided the light from the
darkness. 5 God called the light Day, and the
[a]darkness He called Night. So the evening and
the morning were the first day.
6 Then God said, [a]"Let there be a firmament
in the midst of the waters, and let it divide the
waters from the waters." 7 Thus God made the
firmament, [a]and divided the waters which *were*
under the firmament from the waters which
*were* [b]above the firmament; and it was so. 8 And
God called the firmament Heaven. So the eve-
ning and the morning were the second day.
9 Then God said, [a]"Let the waters under the
heavens be gathered together into one place, and
[b]let the dry *land* appear"; and it was so. 10 And
God called the dry *land* Earth, and the gathering
together of the waters He called Seas. And God
saw that *it was* good.
11 Then God said, "Let the earth [a]bring forth
grass, the herb *that* yields seed, *and* the [b]fruit
tree *that* yields fruit according to its kind, whose
seed *is* in itself, on the earth"; and it was so. 12 And
the earth brought forth grass, the herb *that*
yields seed according to its kind, and the tree
*that* yields fruit, whose seed *is* in itself according
to its kind. And God saw that *it was* good. 13 So
the evening and the morning were the third day.
14 Then God said, "Let there be [a]lights in the
firmament of the heavens to divide the day from
the night; and let them be for signs and [b]seasons,
and for days and years; 15 and let them be for
lights in the firmament of the heavens to give
light on the earth"; and it was so. 16 Then God
made two great lights: the [a]greater light to rule
the day, and the [b]lesser light to rule the night.
*He made* [c]the stars also. 17 God set them in the
firmament of the [a]heavens to give light on the
earth, 18 and to [a]rule over the day and over the
night, and to divide the light from the darkness.

**1:1** [a] [John 1:1–3] [b] Acts 17:24 **1:2** [a] Jer. 4:23 [b] Is. 40:13, 14 [1] Words in italic type have been added for clarity. They are not found in the original Hebrew or Aramaic. **1:3** [a] Ps. 33:6, 9 [b] 2 Cor. 4:6 [c] [Heb. 11:3] **1:5** [a] Ps. 19:2; 33:6; 74:16; 104:20; 136:5 **1:6** [a] Jer. 10:12 **1:7** [a] Prov. 8:27–29 [b] Ps. 148:4 **1:9** [a] Job 26:10 [b] Ps. 24:1, 2; 33:7; 95:5 **1:11** [a] Heb. 6:7 [b] 2 Sam. 16:1 **1:14** [a] Ps. 74:16; 136:5–9 [b] Ps. 104:19 **1:16** [a] Ps. 136:8 [b] Ps. 8:3 [c] Job 38:7 **1:17** [a] Gen. 15:5 **1:18** [a] Jer. 31:35

GENESIS 1:1–5

## LIGHT, ORDER, AND LIFE

1

STORY OF SCRIPTURE

### WHAT'S GOING ON?

We find a major theme of the Bible within these five verses. In the beginning, God created the heavens and the earth, establishing His incredible nature and power. The world was lifeless, dark, and enveloped by the chaotic seas. But then, God spoke, and the earth was given light, order, and life.

These opening verses are integral to the story of Scripture because they set up a pattern for what happens in and around God's people. This story of creation repeats itself all throughout the Bible. God sees places, people, and nations that are void, chaotic, and lacking life, and through Jesus creates beauty out of the darkness and chaos for His glory.

### WHAT DOES THIS MEAN FOR ME?

This section is an image of God's mission for humanity. He wants to use His Word to bring light into darkness, order into chaos, and life to what's dead. This is an image of what God primarily wants to do by saving people from sin through Jesus, but it's even more than that. God intends for the Word to bring us life, peace, and hope when we feel lifeless, anxious, and hopeless.

### DID YOU CATCH THE PATTERN?

The "face of the deep" (v. 2) is another way of saying ocean or chaotic seas. Usually when the sea is mentioned in Scripture, it's a threat or barrier to God's people. Pay attention to these stories and you'll find the same pattern over and over. God provides shelter from the floods, splits the seas, and calms the storms. He wants to show us that no chaos is beyond His ability to bring peace.

*For the next* Story of Scripture *reading and devotion, turn to Genesis 3:1–24 on page 8.*

And God saw that *it was* good. 19 So the evening and the morning were the fourth day.

20 Then God said, "Let the waters abound with an abundance of living creatures, and let birds fly above the earth across the face of the firmament of the heavens." 21 So [a]God created great sea creatures and every living thing that moves, with which the waters abounded, according to their kind, and every winged bird according to its kind. And God saw that *it was* good. 22 And God blessed them, saying, [a]"Be fruitful and multiply, and fill the waters in the seas, and let birds multiply on the earth." 23 So the evening and the morning were the fifth day.

24 Then God said, "Let the earth bring forth the living creature according to its kind: cattle and creeping thing and beast of the earth, *each* according to its kind"; and it was so. 25 And God made the beast of the earth according to its kind, cattle according to its kind, and everything that creeps on the earth according to its kind. And God saw that *it was* good.

26 Then God said, [a]"Let Us make man in Our image, according to Our likeness; [b]let them have dominion over the fish of the sea, over the birds of the air, and over the cattle, over all[1] the earth and over every creeping thing that creeps on the earth." 27 So God created man [a]in His *own* image; in the image of God He created him; [b]male and female He created them. 28 Then God blessed them, and God said to them, [a]"Be fruitful and multiply; fill the earth and [b]subdue it; have dominion over the fish of the sea, over the birds of the air, and over every living thing that moves on the earth."

> **1:26** Because God is spirit (John 4:24), there can be no **image** or **likeness** of Him in a physical sense. Instead, God's image in people is more likely to consist of specific moral, ethical, and intellectual abilities and/or specific roles. In ancient times an emperor might command statues of himself to be placed in remote parts of his empire. These symbols would declare these areas were under his power and reign. God placed humans as image-bearers, or living symbols of Himself, on earth to represent His reign.

29 And God said, "See, I have given you every herb *that* yields seed which *is* on the face of all the earth, and every tree whose fruit yields seed; [a]to you it shall be for food. 30 Also, to [a]every beast of the earth, to every [b]bird of the air, and to everything that creeps on the earth, in which *there is* life, *I have given* every green herb for food"; and it was so. 31 Then [a]God saw everything that He had made, and indeed *it was* very good. So the evening and the morning were the sixth day.

2 Thus the heavens and the earth, and [a]all the host of them, were finished. 2 [a]And on the seventh day God ended His work which He had done, and He rested on the seventh day from all His work which He had done. 3 Then God [a]blessed the seventh day and sanctified it, because in it He rested from all His work which God had created and made.

4 [a]This *is* the history[1] of the heavens and the earth when they were created, in the day that the LORD God made the earth and the heavens, 5 before any [a]plant of the field was in the earth and before any herb of the field had grown. For the LORD God had not [b]caused it to rain on the earth, and *there was* no man [c]to till the ground; 6 but a mist went up from the earth and watered the whole face of the ground.

7 And the LORD God formed man *of* the [a]dust of the ground, and [b]breathed into his [c]nostrils the breath of life; and [d]man became a living being.

### *LIFE IN GOD'S GARDEN*

8 The LORD God planted [a]a garden [b]eastward in [c]Eden, and there He put the man whom He had formed. 9 And out of the ground the LORD God made [a]every tree grow that is pleasant to the sight and good for food. [b]The tree of life *was* also in the midst of the garden, and the tree of the knowledge of good and [c]evil.

10 Now a river went out of Eden to water the garden, and from there it parted and became four riverheads. 11 The name of the first *is* Pishon; it *is* the one which skirts [a]the whole land of Havilah, where *there is* gold. 12 And the gold of that land *is* good. [a]Bdellium and the onyx stone *are* there. 13 The name of the second river *is* Gihon; it *is* the one which goes around the whole land of Cush. 14 The name of the third river *is* [a]Hiddekel;[1] it *is* the one which goes toward the east of Assyria. The fourth river *is* the Euphrates.

15 Then the LORD God took the man and put him in the garden of Eden to tend and keep it. 16 And the LORD God commanded the man, saying, "Of every tree of the garden you may freely eat; 17 but of the tree of the knowledge of good and evil [a]you shall not eat, for in the day that you eat of it [b]you shall surely [c]die."

18 And the LORD God said, "*It is* not good that man should be alone; [a]I will make him a helper

1:21 [a] Ps. 104:25–28 1:22 [a] Gen. 8:17 1:26 [a] Gen. 9:6; Ps. 100:3; Eccl. 7:29; [Eph. 4:24]; James 3:9 [b] Gen. 9:2; Ps. 8:6–8 [1] Syriac reads *all the wild animals of.* 1:27 [a] Gen. 5:2; 1 Cor. 11:7 [b] Matt. 19:4; [Mark 10:6–8] 1:28 [a] Gen. 9:1, 7; Lev. 26:9 [b] 1 Cor. 9:27 1:29 [a] Gen. 9:3; Ps. 104:14, 15 1:30 [a] Ps. 145:15 [b] Job 38:41 1:31 [a] [Ps. 104:24; 1 Tim. 4:4] 2:1 [a] Ps. 33:6 2:2 [a] Ex. 20:9–11; 31:17; Heb. 4:4, 10 2:3 [a] [Is. 58:13] 2:4 [a] Gen. 1:1; Ps. 90:1, 2 [1] Hebrew *toledoth,* literally *generations* 2:5 [a] Gen. 1:11, 12 [b] Gen. 7:4; Job 5:10; 38:26–28 [c] Gen. 3:23 2:7 [a] Gen. 3:19, 23; Ps. 103:14 [b] Job 33:4 [c] Gen. 7:22 [d] 1 Cor. 15:45 2:8 [a] Is. 51:3 [b] Gen. 3:23, 24 [c] Gen. 4:16 2:9 [a] Ezek. 31:8 [b] [Gen. 3:22; Rev. 2:7; 22:2, 14] [c] [Deut. 1:39] 2:11 [a] Gen. 25:18 2:12 [a] Num. 11:7 2:14 [a] Dan. 10:4 [1] Or *Tigris* 2:17 [a] Gen. 3:1, 3, 11, 17 [b] Gen. 3:3, 19; [Rom. 6:23] [c] Rom. 5:12; 1 Cor. 15:21, 22 2:18 [a] 1 Cor. 11:8, 9; 1 Tim. 2:13

KNOW THE TRUTH

## THE DOCTRINE OF GOD

### PART 2: GOD THE CREATOR

**2:4** God is the uncreated Creator of the "heavens and the earth." *Heavens* summarizes every galaxy, star, and planet, and everything else in the universe. Space, time, energy, and matter came into being because God created it. *Earth* summarizes every element, plant, animal, and person, and everything else on the earth. The smallest strand of DNA within the nucleus of a cell to the largest mountain range on earth are created by God. God's creation of everything extends even into the spiritual realm, including angels (see Col. 1:16–17). Angels were created to serve, worship, and assist God in His plans (see Pss. 91:11; 103:11; 104:4). All of God's creation is amazing, but people are its pinnacle. God created every person, including you (see Ps. 139:13–16; Acts 17:24–28). All human life has immeasurable value because each person is a unique creation of God, made in His image (see Gen. 1:26–28).

God not only has the power to create, but He also has the power to recreate. When a person repents of sin and trusts in Jesus Christ, God makes that person a new creation—an eternal child of God (see John 1:12–13). Although the heavens and the earth that God created are presently affected by sin, God will create new heavens and a new earth fit for His perfect eternal kingdom of sons and daughters (see Rev. 21:1, 5).

*For* **THE DOCTRINE OF GOD: PART 3: GOD THE SPIRIT**, *turn to John 4:24 on page 1075.*

comparable to him." 19 [a]Out of the ground the
LORD God formed every beast of the field and
every bird of the air, and [b]brought *them* to Adam
to see what he would call them. And whatever
Adam called each living creature, that *was* its
name. 20 So Adam gave names to all cattle, to
the birds of the air, and to every beast of the
field. But for Adam there was not found a helper
comparable to him.
21 And the LORD God caused a [a]deep sleep
to fall on Adam, and he slept; and He took one
of his ribs, and closed up the flesh in its place.
22 Then the rib which the LORD God had taken
from man He made into a woman, [a]and He
[b]brought her to the man.
23 And Adam said:

"This *is* now [a]bone of my bones
And flesh of my flesh;
She shall be called Woman,
Because she was [b]taken out of Man."

**2:17** God's declaration that Adam and Eve eating of the **tree** would lead to their death does not mean that death had to happen instantaneously, but rather that it would surely happen—there would be no escape (see Heb. 9:27).

24 [a]Therefore a man shall leave his father and
mother and [b]be joined to his wife, and they shall
become one flesh.
25 [a]And they were both naked, the man and
his wife, and were not [b]ashamed.

### *THE TEMPTATION AND FALL OF MAN*

*(Rom. 5:12–21)*

3 Now [a]the serpent was [b]more cunning than
any beast of the field which the LORD God
had made. And he said to the woman, "Has God
indeed said, 'You shall not eat of every tree of
the garden'?"
2 And the woman said to the serpent, "We
may eat the [a]fruit of the trees of the garden; 3 but
of the fruit of the tree which *is* in the midst of
the garden, God has said, 'You shall not eat it,
nor shall you [a]touch it, lest you die.'"
4 [a]Then the serpent said to the woman, "You
will not surely die. 5 For God knows that in the
day you eat of it your eyes will be opened, and
you will be like God, knowing good and evil."
6 So when the woman [a]saw that the tree *was*
good for food, that it *was* pleasant to the eyes,
and a tree desirable to make *one* wise, she took
of its fruit [b]and ate. She also gave to her husband
with her, and he ate. 7 Then the eyes of both of
them were opened, [a]and they knew that they
*were* naked; and they sewed fig leaves together
and made themselves coverings.
8 And they heard [a]the sound of the LORD

**2:19** [a] Gen. 1:20, 24 [b] Ps. 8:6 **2:21** [a] Gen. 15:12; 1 Sam. 26:12 **2:22** [a] Gen. 3:20; 1 Tim. 2:13 [b] Heb. 13:4 **2:23** [a] Gen. 29:14 [b] 1 Cor. 11:8, 9 **2:24** [a] Matt. 19:5 [b] Mark 10:6–8 **2:25** [a] Gen. 3:7, 10 [b] Is. 47:3 **3:1** [a] 1 Chr. 21:1 [b] 2 Cor. 11:3 **3:2** [a] Gen. 2:16, 17 **3:3** [a] Ex. 19:12, 13 **3:4** [a] [2 Cor. 11:3] **3:6** [a] 1 John 2:16 [b] 1 Tim. 2:14 **3:7** [a] Gen. 2:25 **3:8** [a] Job 38:1

GENESIS 3:1–24

## A PROMISE OF REDEMPTION

STORY OF SCRIPTURE 2

### WHAT'S GOING ON?

God gave Adam and Eve one restriction: they weren't to eat from the tree of the knowledge of good and evil (see Gen. 1:15–17). Influenced by the serpent and enticed by the idea of being just like God they rebelled against their Creator and did just that. Amid the judgment of sin that followed, God gave a wonderful promise (3:15). One day, a descendant of Eve would rise up and crush the serpent's head. But first He would be bruised. This foreshadowed Jesus, the One who defeated sin, death, and Satan through His death on the cross. The rest of the Old Testament builds up to this promise, as God prepares His people for the arrival of the Rescuer.

### WHAT DOES THIS MEAN FOR ME?

Like Adam and Eve, we may feel like we're wandering east of Eden, longing for an abundant life. Every person in Scripture after Adam and Eve felt this same pining after paradise but often looked for it in the wrong places. The temptation for us is to look for Eden in people, devices, and activities. However, the Bible shows us true life is found only in Jesus. Everything else is counterfeit.

### DID YOU CATCH THE PATTERN?

Originally, Adam and Eve were naked and unashamed (see Gen. 2:25). After the Fall, though, they realized they were naked and felt ashamed (3:17). Adam and Eve tried to cover themselves with fig leaves, but it didn't work. Instead, God covered Adam and Eve with an animal's hide (3:21). This can be considered the first animal sacrifice offered to cover the effect of sin. Many more animal sacrifices followed in the Old Testament. Eventually, though, Jesus' sacrifice dealt with sin once and for all. When you see animals being sacrificed in the Bible, look back to this moment in Genesis, and look forward to the sacrifice of Jesus.

*For the next* Story of Scripture *reading and devotion, turn to Genesis 4:1–8 on page 10.*

God walking in the garden in the cool of the
day, and Adam and his wife [b]hid themselves
from the presence of the LORD God among the
trees of the garden.
9 Then the LORD God called to Adam and
said to him, "Where *are* you?"
10 So he said, "I heard Your voice in the gar-
den, [a]and I was afraid because I was naked; and
I hid myself."
11 And He said, "Who told you that you *were*
naked? Have you eaten from the tree of which
I commanded you that you should not eat?"
12 Then the man said, [a]"The woman whom
You gave *to be* with me, she gave me of the tree,
and I ate."
13 And the LORD God said to the woman,
"What *is* this you have done?"
The woman said, [a]"The serpent deceived
me, and I ate."
14 So the LORD God said to the serpent:

"Because you have done this,
You *are* cursed more than all cattle,
And more than every beast of the field;
On your belly you shall go,
And [a]you shall eat dust
All the days of your life.
15 And I will put enmity
Between you and the woman,
And between [a]your seed and [b]her Seed;
[c]He shall bruise your head,
And you shall bruise His heel."

**SEEING JESUS IN THE SCRIPTURE**

**3:15** From the beginning, God had a plan to save people from sin. Here's the first mention of that plan. This verse points to the crushing blow delivered to Satan when Jesus rose from the dead, a blow that will be completed when Jesus returns (see Rom. 16:20).

16 To the woman He said:

"I will greatly multiply your sorrow and
your conception;
[a]In pain you shall bring forth children;

**3:8** [b] Job 31:33 **3:10** [a] Gen. 2:25 **3:12** [a] [Prov. 28:13] **3:13** [a] 2 Cor. 11:3 **3:14** [a] Deut. 28:15–20 **3:15** [a] John 8:44 [b] Is. 7:14 [c] Rom. 16:20 **3:16** [a] John 16:21

[b]Your desire *shall be* for your husband,
And he shall [c]rule over you."

17 Then to Adam He said, [a]"Because you have
heeded the voice of your wife, and have eaten
from the tree [b]of which I commanded you, say-
ing, 'You shall not eat of it':

[c]"Cursed *is* the ground for your sake;
[d]In toil you shall eat *of* it
All the days of your life.
18 Both thorns and thistles it shall bring
forth for you,
And [a]you shall eat the herb of the field.
19 [a]In the sweat of your face you shall eat
bread
Till you return to the ground,
For out of it you were taken;
[b]For dust you *are,*
And [c]to dust you shall return."

20 And Adam called his wife's name [a]Eve,
because she was the mother of all living.
21 Also for Adam and his wife the LORD God
made tunics of skin, and clothed them.

**4:3** Genesis doesn't explain how the practice of sacrificial worship began, but it's clear that Adam and Eve's two sons understood this practice to some degree. Some people believe Cain's **offering** was unsuitable because it wasn't a blood offering, and blood is required for the forgiveness of sins (Heb. 9:22). But nothing in this chapter indicates Cain and Abel were coming to God for forgiveness. Their offerings were acts of worship, and as such a bloodless offering wasn't necessarily inappropriate (see Lev. 6:14–23). Apparently, the deficiency was in Cain's heart, not in the actual offering. Abel's offering was "more excellent" than Cain's because of his faith in the Lord (Heb. 11:4).

**SEEING JESUS IN THE SCRIPTURE**

**3:21** An innocent animal died in Eden to cover Adam and Eve's shame. That sacrifice pictures what Jesus did for the sins of the world. His sacrifice was sufficient to cover all sin and shame (see Rom. 5:15).

22 Then the LORD God said, "Behold, the man
has become like one of Us, to know good and
evil. And now, lest he put out his hand and take
also of the tree of life, and eat, and live forever"—
23 therefore the LORD God sent him out of the
garden of Eden [a]to till the ground from which
he was taken. 24 So [a]He drove out the man; and
He placed [b]cherubim [c]at the east of the garden
of Eden, and a flaming sword which turned
every way, to guard the way to the tree of [d]life.

### *CAIN MURDERS ABEL*
*(Luke 11:51; Heb. 11:4; 12:24)*

**4** Now Adam knew Eve his wife, and she con-
ceived and bore Cain, and said, "I have ac-
quired a man from the LORD." 2 Then she bore
again, this time his brother Abel. Now [a]Abel was
a keeper of sheep, but Cain was a tiller of the
ground. 3 And in the process of time it came to
pass that Cain brought an offering of the fruit [a]of
the ground to the LORD. 4 Abel also brought of
[a]the firstborn of his flock and of [b]their fat. And
the LORD [c]respected Abel and his offering, 5 but
He did not respect Cain and his offering. And
Cain was very angry, and his countenance fell.
6 So the LORD said to Cain, "Why are you
angry? And why has your countenance fallen?
7 If you do well, will you not be accepted? And if
you do not do well, sin lies at the door. And its
desire *is* for you, but you should rule over it."
8 Now Cain talked with Abel his brother;[1] and it
came to pass, when they were in the field, that Cain
rose up against Abel his brother and [a]killed him.
9 Then the LORD said to Cain, "Where *is* Abel
your brother?"
He said, [a]"I do not know. *Am* I [b]my brother's
keeper?"
10 And He said, "What have you done? The
voice of your brother's blood [a]cries out to Me
from the ground. 11 So now [a]you *are* cursed from
the earth, which has opened its mouth to receive
your brother's blood from your hand. 12 When
you till the ground, it shall no longer yield its
strength to you. A fugitive and a vagabond you
shall be on the earth."
13 And Cain said to the LORD, "My punishment
*is* greater than I can bear! 14 Surely You have driv-
en me out this day from the face of the ground;
[a]I shall be [b]hidden from Your face; I shall be a
fugitive and a vagabond on the earth, and it will
happen *that* [c]anyone who finds me will kill me."
15 And the LORD said to him, "Therefore,[1]
whoever kills Cain, vengeance shall be taken on
him [a]sevenfold." And the LORD set a [b]mark on
Cain, lest anyone finding him should kill him.

### *THE FAMILY OF CAIN*

16 Then Cain [a]went out from the [b]presence
of the LORD and dwelt in the land of Nod on the

3:16 [b] Gen. 4:7 [c] 1 Cor. 11:3 3:17 [a] 1 Sam. 15:23 [b] Gen. 2:17 [c] Rom. 8:20–22 [d] Eccl. 2:23 3:18 [a] Ps. 104:14 3:19 [a] 2 Thess. 3:10 [b] Gen. 2:7; 5:5 [c] Job 21:26 3:20 [a] 2 Cor. 11:3 3:23 [a] Gen. 4:2; 9:20 3:24 [a] Ezek. 31:3, 11 [b] Ps. 104:4 [c] Gen. 2:8 [d] Gen. 2:9 4:2 [a] Luke 11:50, 51 4:3 [a] Num. 18:12 4:4 [a] Num. 18:17 [b] Lev. 3:16 [c] Heb. 11:4 4:8 [a] [1 John 3:12–15] [1] Samaritan Pentateuch, Septuagint, Syriac, and Vulgate add *"Let us go out to the field."* 4:9 [a] John 8:44 [b] 1 Cor. 8:11–13 4:10 [a] Heb. 12:24 4:11 [a] Gen. 3:14 4:14 [a] Ps. 51:11 [b] Is. 1:15 [c] Num. 35:19, 21, 27 4:15 [a] Gen. 4:24 [b] Ezek. 9:4, 6 [1] Following Masoretic Text and Targum; Septuagint, Syriac, and Vulgate read *Not so.* 4:16 [a] 2 Kin. 13:23; 24:20 [b] Jon. 1:3

GENESIS 4:1–8

## BROTHERS AT WAR

STORY OF SCRIPTURE 3

### WHAT'S GOING ON?

Cain and Abel both brought sacrifices before God. Cain, a farmer, brought crops from the field. Abel, a shepherd, brought the firstborn of his flock. God accepted Abel's offering but not Cain's, although the Bible isn't clear as to why. Perhaps it was because Abel brought the best of what he had and Cain didn't. No matter, the emphasis of the story is Cain's reaction to rejection. He teems with anger and contempt, which boiled over into murder. Humanity had gone from perfection to fratricide in a single generation. God's warning that sin would result in death was tragically proven true.

### WHAT DOES THIS MEAN FOR ME?

Cain, like his parents before him, was offered a choice to rise above pride and temptation and do the right thing. God encouraged Cain that he could rule over the temptation to sin. James 4:7 tells us if we resist the devil, he will flee from us. Sin often feels most natural to us, and we must fight it with decisive force to go in the right direction. God always provides a way out, but we must have the strength of character to step in that direction.

### DID YOU CATCH THE PATTERN?

This story is the first of a pattern throughout the Biblical narrative that goes something like this: God blesses the younger brother over the older and the older becomes jealous and lashes out in violence. This usually creates a cycle of division and hardship, but the younger brother usually prevails. We see this pattern in the stories of Jacob and Esau and Joseph and his brothers, and by extension with King Saul and David. These stories foreshadow the old religious system of the Pharisees being replaced by the new covenant of Jesus. Like Cain, the religious leaders lashed out and killed Jesus, but Jesus was ultimately victorious.

*For the next* Story of Scripture *reading and devotion, turn to Genesis 12:1–9 on page 17.*

east of Eden. 17 And Cain knew his wife, and she
conceived and bore Enoch. And he built a city,
[a]and called the name of the city after the name
of his son—Enoch. 18 To Enoch was born Irad;
and Irad begot Mehujael, and Mehujael begot
Methushael, and Methushael begot Lamech.
19 Then Lamech took for himself [a]two wives:
the name of one *was* Adah, and the name of the
second *was* Zillah. 20 And Adah bore Jabal. He was
the father of those who dwell in tents and have
livestock. 21 His brother's name *was* Jubal. He
was the father of all those who play the harp and
flute. 22 And as for Zillah, she also bore Tubal-Cain,
an instructor of every craftsman in bronze and
iron. And the sister of Tubal-Cain *was* Naamah.
23 Then Lamech said to his wives:

"Adah and Zillah, hear my voice;
Wives of Lamech, listen to my speech!
For I have killed a man for wounding me,
Even a young man for hurting me.
24 [a]If Cain shall be avenged sevenfold,
Then Lamech seventy-sevenfold."

### *A NEW SON*

25 And Adam knew his wife again, and she
bore a son and [a]named him Seth, "For God has
appointed another seed for me instead of Abel,
whom Cain killed." 26 And as for Seth, [a]to him
also a son was born; and he named him Enosh.[1]
Then *men* began [b]to call on the name of the
LORD.

### *THE FAMILY OF ADAM*

*(1 Chr. 1:1–4; Luke 3:36–38)*

5 This is the book of the [a]genealogy of Adam.
In the day that God created man, He made
him in [b]the likeness of God. 2 He created them
[a]male and female, and [b]blessed them and called
them Mankind in the day they were created.
3 And Adam lived one hundred and thirty years,
and begot *a son* [a]in his own likeness, after his
image, and [b]named him Seth. 4 After he begot
Seth, [a]the days of Adam were eight hundred
years; [b]and he had sons and daughters. 5 So all
the days that Adam lived were nine hundred
and thirty years; [a]and he died.

4:17 [a] Ps. 49:11 4:19 [a] Gen. 2:24; 16:3 4:24 [a] Gen. 4:15 4:25 [a] Gen. 5:3 4:26 [a] Gen. 5:6 [b] Zeph. 3:9 [1] Greek *Enos* 5:1 [a] Gen. 2:4; 6:9 [b] Gen. 1:26; 9:6 5:2 [a] Mark 10:6 [b] Gen. 1:28; 9:1 5:3 [a] 1 Cor. 15:48, 49 [b] Gen. 4:25 5:4 [a] Luke 3:36–38 [b] Gen. 1:28; 4:25 5:5 [a] [Heb. 9:27]

KNOW THE TRUTH

# THE DOCTRINE OF CREATION AND HUMANS

## PART 8: THE FALL OF HUMANS

**5:1–5** A significant event happened here that sometimes goes unnoticed: Adam *died*. The Hebrew word for *died* in this verse had been used only three times before. It's used first as a loving warning (Gen. 2:17) and next as a reminder against eating what a good God hadn't permitted (Gen. 3:3). Then, in Genesis 3:4 it's used by the serpent who said, "You will not surely die." Finally, we come to Genesis 5:5, "Adam lived . . . and he died." Clearly, God didn't create humans to die. Why then do we die?

In the beginning, when God made all that was made, He declared it all to be "good" (Gen. 1:31). But people with freewill to love God used it instead to rebel against God's perfect rule and attempted self-rule. This historical event is often called *the Fall*. While physical death is the most notable consequence of the Fall, its main consequence was separation from the sinless, life-giving Creator. Spiritual separation from God resulted in humanity being corrupted with sin, evil, sickness, disease, death, and more. Only in the sin-forgiving, sickness-healing, demon-dominating, resurrected Savior Jesus Christ can we find hope to receive the prized gift of eternal life with God for which we were originally designed to enjoy.

*For* **THE DOCTRINE OF CREATION AND HUMANS: PART 9: THE SIN AND EVIL IN HUMANS,** *turn to Genesis 6:5 on page 12.* • • •

6 Seth lived one hundred and five years, and
begot [a]Enosh. 7 After he begot Enosh, Seth lived
eight hundred and seven years, and had sons
and daughters. 8 So all the days of Seth were
nine hundred and twelve years; and he died.
9 Enosh lived ninety years, and begot Cai-
nan.[1] 10 After he begot Cainan, Enosh lived eight
hundred and fifteen years, and had sons and
daughters. 11 So all the days of Enosh were nine
hundred and five years; and he died.
12 Cainan lived seventy years, and begot Ma-
halalel. 13 After he begot Mahalalel, Cainan lived
eight hundred and forty years, and had sons and
daughters. 14 So all the days of Cainan were nine
hundred and ten years; and he died.
15 Mahalalel lived sixty-five years, and begot
Jared. 16 After he begot Jared, Mahalalel lived
eight hundred and thirty years, and had sons
and daughters. 17 So all the days of Mahalalel were
eight hundred and ninety-five years; and he died.
18 Jared lived one hundred and sixty-two
years, and begot [a]Enoch. 19 After he begot Enoch,
Jared lived eight hundred years, and had sons
and daughters. 20 So all the days of Jared were
nine hundred and sixty-two years; and he died.
21 Enoch lived sixty-five years, and begot Me-
thuselah. 22 After he begot Methuselah, Enoch
[a]walked with God three hundred years, and had
sons and daughters. 23 So all the days of Enoch
were three hundred and sixty-five years. 24 And
[a]Enoch walked with God; and he *was* not, for
God [b]took him.

**5:21–24** Only **Enoch** and Elijah (2 Kin. 2:11) were taken by God without experiencing death. As the refrain, "and he died" echoes throughout this chapter, reminding us of God's promised judgment to Adam and Eve, the account of Enoch provides a jarring break to that cadence. The point is there is a way to escape death—not by our actions, though, but rather by God's grace.

25 Methuselah lived one hundred and eighty-
seven years, and begot Lamech. 26 After he begot
Lamech, Methuselah lived seven hundred and
eighty-two years, and had sons and daughters.
27 So all the days of Methuselah were nine hun-
dred and sixty-nine years; and he died.
28 Lamech lived one hundred and eighty-
two years, and had a son. 29 And he called his
name [a]Noah, saying, "This *one* will comfort us
concerning our work and the toil of our hands,
because of the ground [b]which the LORD has
cursed." 30 After he begot Noah, Lamech lived
five hundred and ninety-five years, and had
sons and daughters. 31 So all the days of Lamech
were seven hundred and seventy-seven years;
and he died.
32 And Noah was five hundred years old, and
Noah begot [a]Shem, Ham, [b]and Japheth.

**5:6** [a] Gen. 4:26 **5:9** [1] Hebrew *Qenan* **5:18** [a] Jude 14, 15 **5:22** [a] Gen. 6:9; 17:1; 24:40; 48:15 **5:24** [a] 2 Kin. 2:11 [b] Heb. 11:5 **5:29** [a] Luke 3:36 [b] Gen. 3:17–19; 4:11 **5:32** [a] Gen. 6:10; 7:13 [b] Gen. 10:21

### THE WICKEDNESS AND JUDGMENT OF MAN

6 Now it came to pass, [a]when men began to
multiply on the face of the earth, and daugh-
ters were born to them, 2 that the sons of God saw
the daughters of men, that they *were* beautiful;
and they [a]took wives for themselves of all whom
they chose.

> **6:2** This verse is difficult to interpret. Some believe the **sons of God** were the men of the righteous line of Seth, while the **daughters of men** were Cain's offspring. A second view is the "sons of God" were some of the rebellious angels who had joined Satan and here took on human form to take women for themselves, resulting in their immediate imprisonment by God (2 Pet. 2:4; Jude v. 6). Either way, it's clear what happened here was corrupt and one of the reasons for the flood.

3 And the LORD said, [a]"My Spirit shall not
[b]strive[1] with man forever, [c]for he *is* indeed flesh;
yet his days shall be one hundred and twenty
years." 4 There were giants on the earth in those
[a]days, and also afterward, when the sons of God
came in to the daughters of men and they bore
*children* to them. Those *were* the mighty men
who *were* of old, men of renown.

5 Then the LORD[1] saw that the wickedness
of man *was* great in the earth, and *that* every
[a]intent of the thoughts of his heart *was* only
evil continually. 6 And [a]the LORD was sorry that
He had made man on the earth, and [b]He was
grieved in His [c]heart. 7 So the LORD said, "I will
[a]destroy man whom I have created from the
face of the earth, both man and beast, creeping
thing and birds of the air, for I am sorry that I
have made them." 8 But Noah [a]found grace in
the eyes of the LORD.

### NOAH PLEASES GOD

9 This is the genealogy of Noah. [a]Noah was
a just man, perfect in his generations. Noah
[b]walked with God. 10 And Noah begot three sons:
[a]Shem, Ham, and Japheth.
11 The earth also was corrupt [a]before God,
and the earth was [b]filled with violence. 12 So
God [a]looked upon the earth, and indeed it was
corrupt; for [b]all flesh had corrupted their way
on the earth.

### THE ARK PREPARED

*(Heb. 11:7; 1 Pet. 3:20)*

13 And God said to Noah, [a]"The end of all
flesh has come before Me, for the earth is filled
with violence through them; [b]and behold, [c]I will
destroy them with the earth. 14 Make yourself
an ark of gopherwood; make rooms in the ark,
and cover it inside and outside with pitch. 15 And

**6:1** [a] Gen. 1:28 **6:2** [a] Deut. 7:3, 4 **6:3** [a] [Gal. 5:16, 17] [b] 2 Thess. 2:7 [c] Ps. 78:39 [1] Septuagint, Syriac, Targum, and Vulgate read *abide.* **6:4** [a] Num. 13:32, 33 **6:5** [a] Gen. 8:21 [1] Following Masoretic Text and Targum; Vulgate reads *God;* Septuagint reads *LORD God.* **6:6** [a] 1 Sam. 15:11, 29 [b] Is. 63:10 [c] Mark 3:5 **6:7** [a] Gen. 7:4, 23 **6:8** [a] Gen. 19:19 **6:9** [a] 2 Pet. 2:5 [b] Gen. 5:22, 24 **6:10** [a] Gen. 5:32; 7:13 **6:11** [a] Rom. 2:13 [b] Ezek. 8:17 **6:12** [a] Ps. 14:2; 53:2, 3 [b] Ps. 14:1–3 **6:13** [a] 1 Pet. 4:7 [b] Gen. 6:17 [c] 2 Pet. 2:4–10

KNOW THE TRUTH

## THE DOCTRINE OF CREATION AND HUMANS

### PART 9: THE SIN AND EVIL IN HUMANS

**6:5** Hardly anyone denies sin and evil fill our world. But sin and evil weren't created by God. Everything He made was "good" (Gen. 1:31). Where then do sin and evil come from? Because God is Creator of everything, He has authority over everything and has the right to rule over everything. His will and plans are the flawless "bullseye" of creation's aim. But instead of submitting to God's rule and obeying His commands, we have rebelled against Him and acted unlike Him. Our attempt to self-rule apart from God produced sin, which is a word that has to do with missing the bullseye of God's perfect plan. The original miss of the bullseye in Eden has produced unending misses from people ever since.

Sin has then produced evil. In its essence, evil is that which ought *not* to be, that which is crooked and immoral in comparison to God's good plans for creation. Simply put, people are responsible for the existence of evil because of our choice to sin. Because of our hardness of heart and mind, we intentionally live counter to God's ways and plans at times. However, God's plan is to destroy sin and evil without destroying people who sin and produce evil. Only Jesus can provide forgiveness, judge and remove evil, and restore creation to its intended goodness.

*For* **THE DOCTRINE OF CREATION AND HUMANS: PART 10: THE DEATH OF HUMANS**, *turn to Job 19:25–26 on page 512.*

this is how you shall make it: The length of the ark *shall be* three hundred cubits, its width fifty cubits, and its height thirty cubits. 16 You shall make a window for the ark, and you shall finish it to a cubit from above; and set the door of the ark in its side. You shall make it *with* lower, second, and third *decks.* 17 [a]And behold, I Myself am bringing [b]floodwaters on the earth, to destroy from under heaven all flesh in which *is* the breath of life; everything that *is* on the earth shall [c]die. 18 But I will establish My [a]covenant with you; and [b]you shall go into the ark—you, your sons, your wife, and your sons' wives with you. 19 And of every living thing of all flesh you shall bring [a]two of every *sort* into the ark, to keep *them* alive with you; they shall be male and female. 20 Of the birds after their kind, of animals after their kind, and of every creeping thing of the earth after its kind, two of every *kind* [a]will come to you to keep *them* alive. 21 And you shall take for yourself of all food that is eaten, and you shall gather *it* to yourself; and it shall be food for you and for them."

22 [a]Thus Noah did; [b]according to all that [c]God commanded him, so he did.

### *THE GREAT FLOOD*
*(Luke 17:26, 27)*

**7** Then the [a]LORD said to Noah, [b]"Come into the ark, you and all your household, because I have seen *that* [c]you *are* righteous before Me in this generation. 2 You shall take with you seven each of every [a]clean animal, a male and his female; [b]two each of animals that *are* unclean, a male and his female; 3 also seven each of birds of the air, male and female, to keep the species alive on the face of all the earth. 4 For after [a]seven more days I will cause it to rain on the earth [b]forty days and forty nights, and I will destroy from the face of the earth all living things that I have made." 5 [a]And Noah did according to all that the LORD commanded him. 6 Noah *was* [a]six hundred years old when the floodwaters were on the earth.

> **7:2** God instructed Noah to take additional **clean** animals onto the ark for eating (Gen. 9:3) and sacrifice.

7 [a]So Noah, with his sons, his wife, and his sons' wives, went into the ark because of the waters of the flood. 8 Of clean animals, of animals that *are* unclean, of birds, and of everything that creeps on the earth, 9 two by two they went into the ark to Noah, male and female, as God had commanded Noah. 10 And it came to pass after seven days that the waters of the flood were on the earth. 11 In the six hundredth year of Noah's life, in the second month, the seventeenth day of the month, on [a]that day all [b]the fountains of the great deep were broken up, and the [c]windows of heaven were opened. 12 [a]And the rain was on the earth forty days and forty nights.

13 On the very same day Noah and Noah's sons, Shem, Ham, and Japheth, and Noah's wife and the three wives of his sons with them, entered the ark— 14 [a]they and every beast after its kind, all cattle after their kind, every creeping thing that creeps on the earth after its kind, and every bird after its kind, every bird of every [b]sort. 15 And they [a]went into the ark to Noah, two by two, of all flesh in which *is* the breath of life. 16 So those that entered, male and female of all flesh, went in [a]as God had commanded him; and the LORD shut him in.

> **7:16** God shutting the door was a symbol of closure, safety, and God's deliverance by His hand.

17 [a]Now the flood was on the earth forty days. The waters increased and lifted up the ark, and it rose high above the earth. 18 The waters prevailed and greatly increased on the earth, [a]and the ark moved about on the surface of the waters. 19 And the waters prevailed exceedingly on the earth, and all the high hills under the whole heaven were covered. 20 The waters prevailed fifteen cubits upward, and the mountains were covered. 21 [a]And all flesh died that moved on the earth: birds and cattle and beasts and every creeping thing that creeps on the earth, and every man. 22 All in [a]whose nostrils *was* the breath of the spirit[1] of life, all that *was* on the dry *land,* died. 23 So He destroyed all living things which were on the face of the ground: both man and cattle, creeping thing and bird of the air. They were destroyed from the earth. Only [a]Noah and those who *were* with him in the ark remained *alive.* 24 [a]And the waters prevailed on the earth one hundred and fifty days.

### *NOAH'S DELIVERANCE*

**8** Then God [a]remembered Noah, and every living thing, and all the animals that *were* with him in the ark. [b]And God made a wind to pass over the earth, and the waters subsided. 2 [a]The fountains of the deep and the windows of heaven were also [b]stopped, and [c]the rain from heaven was restrained. 3 And the waters receded

**6:17** [a] 2 Pet. 2:5 [b] 2 Pet. 3:6 [c] Luke 16:22 **6:18** [a] Gen. 8:20—9:17; 17:7 [b] Gen. 7:1, 7, 13 **6:19** [a] Gen. 7:2, 8, 9, 14–16 **6:20** [a] Gen. 7:9, 15 **6:22** [a] Gen. 7:5; 12:4, 5 [b] Gen. 7:5, 9, 16 [c] [1 John 5:3] **7:1** [a] Matt. 11:28 [b] Matt. 24:38 [c] Gen. 6:9 **7:2** [a] Lev. 11 [b] Lev. 10:10 **7:4** [a] Gen. 7:10 [b] Gen. 7:12, 17 **7:5** [a] Gen. 6:22 **7:6** [a] Gen. 5:4, 32 **7:7** [a] Matt. 24:38 **7:11** [a] Matt. 24:39 [b] Gen. 8:2 [c] Ps. 78:23 **7:12** [a] Gen. 7:4, 17 **7:14** [a] Gen. 6:19 [b] Gen. 1:21 **7:15** [a] Gen. 6:19, 20; 7:9 **7:16** [a] Gen. 7:2, 3 **7:17** [a] Gen. 7:4, 12; 8:6 **7:18** [a] Ps. 104:26 **7:21** [a] Gen. 6:7, 13, 17; 7:4 **7:22** [a] Gen. 2:7 [1] Septuagint and Vulgate omit *of the spirit.* **7:23** [a] 2 Pet. 2:5 **7:24** [a] Gen. 8:3, 4 **8:1** [a] Gen. 19:29 [b] Ex. 14:21; 15:10 **8:2** [a] Gen. 7:11 [b] Deut. 11:17 [c] Job 38:37

continually from the earth. At the end [a]of the
hundred and fifty days the waters decreased.
4 Then the ark rested in the seventh month, the
seventeenth day of the month, on the mountains
of Ararat. 5 And the waters decreased continu-
ally until the tenth month. In the tenth *month,*
on the first *day* of the month, the tops of the
mountains were seen.
6 So it came to pass, at the end of forty days,
that Noah opened [a]the window of the ark which
he had made. 7 Then he sent out a raven, which
kept going to and fro until the waters had dried
up from the earth. 8 He also sent out from him-
self a dove, to see if the waters had receded from
the face of the ground. 9 But the dove found no
resting place for the sole of her foot, and she
returned into the ark to him, for the waters *were*
on the face of the whole earth. So he put out his
hand and took her, and drew her into the ark
to himself. 10 And he waited yet another seven
days, and again he sent the dove out from the
ark. 11 Then the dove came to him in the evening,
and behold, a freshly plucked olive leaf *was*
in her mouth; and Noah knew that the waters
had receded from the earth. 12 So he waited yet
another seven days and sent out the dove, which
did not return again to him anymore.
13 And it came to pass in the six hundred and
first year, in the first *month,* the first *day* of the
month, that the waters were dried up from the
earth; and Noah removed the covering of the ark
and looked, and indeed the surface of the ground
was dry. 14 And in the second month, on the twenty-
seventh day of the month, the earth was dried.
15 Then God spoke to Noah, saying, 16 "Go out
of the ark, [a]you and your wife, and your sons and
your sons' wives with you. 17 Bring out with you
every living thing of all flesh that *is* with you:
birds and cattle and every creeping thing that
creeps on the earth, so that they may abound
on the earth, and [a]be fruitful and multiply on
the earth." 18 So Noah went out, and his sons and
his wife and his sons' wives with him. 19 Every
animal, every creeping thing, every bird, *and*
whatever creeps on the earth, according to their
families, went out of the ark.

### GOD'S COVENANT WITH CREATION

20 Then Noah built an [a]altar to the LORD, and
took of [b]every clean animal and of every clean
bird, and offered [c]burnt offerings on the altar.
21 And the LORD smelled [a]a soothing aroma.
Then the LORD said in His heart, "I will never
again [b]curse the ground for man's sake, although
the [c]imagination of man's heart *is* evil from his
youth; [d]nor will I again destroy every living thing
as I have done.

22 "While the earth [a]remains,
Seedtime and harvest,
Cold and heat,
Winter and summer,
And [b]day and night
Shall not cease."

9 So God blessed Noah and his sons, and said
to them: [a]"Be fruitful and multiply, and fill
the earth.[1] 2 [a]And the fear of you and the dread of
you shall be on every beast of the earth, on every
bird of the air, on all that move *on* the earth, and
on all the fish of the sea. They are given into your
hand. 3 [a]Every moving thing that lives shall be
food for you. I have given you [b]all things, even
as the [c]green herbs. 4 [a]But you shall not eat flesh
with its life, *that is,* its blood. 5 Surely for your
lifeblood I will demand *a reckoning;* [a]from the
hand of every beast I will require it, and [b]from
the hand of man. From the hand of every [c]man's
brother I will require the life of man.

6 "Whoever [a]sheds man's blood,
By man his blood shall be shed;
[b]For in the image of God
He made man.
7 And as for you, [a]be fruitful and multiply;
Bring forth abundantly in the earth
And multiply in it."

8 Then God spoke to Noah and to his sons
with him, saying: 9 "And as for Me, [a]behold, I
establish [b]My covenant with you and with your
descendants[1] after you, 10 [a]and with every living
creature that *is* with you: the birds, the cattle,
and every beast of the earth with you, of all
that go out of the ark, every beast of the earth.
11 Thus [a]I establish My covenant with you: Never
again shall all flesh be cut off by the waters of
the flood; never again shall there be a flood to
destroy the earth."
12 And God said: [a]"This *is* the sign of the
covenant which I make between Me and you,
and every living creature that *is* with you, for
perpetual generations: 13 I set [a]My rainbow in
the cloud, and it shall be for the sign of the
covenant between Me and the earth. 14 It shall
be, when I bring a cloud over the earth, that the
rainbow shall be seen in the cloud; 15 and [a]I will
remember My covenant which *is* between Me
and you and every living creature of all flesh;
the waters shall never again become a flood to

**8:3** [a] Gen. 7:24 **8:6** [a] Gen. 6:16 **8:16** [a] Gen. 7:13 **8:17** [a] Gen. 1:22, 28; 9:1, 7 **8:20** [a] Gen. 12:7; Ex. 29:18, 25 [b] Gen. 7:2; Lev. 11 [c] Gen. 22:2; Ex. 10:25 **8:21** [a] Ex. 29:18, 25; Lev. 1:9; Ezek. 20:41; 2 Cor. 2:15; Eph. 5:2 [b] Gen. 3:17; 6:7, 13, 17; Is. 54:9 [c] Gen. 6:5; 11:6; Job 14:4; Ps. 51:5; Jer. 17:9; Rom. 1:21; 3:23; Eph. 2:1–3 [d] Gen. 9:11, 15 **8:22** [a] Is. 54:9 [b] Ps. 74:16; Jer. 33:20, 25 **9:1** [a] Gen. 1:28, 29; 8:17; 9:7, 19; 10:32 [1] Compare Genesis 1:28 **9:2** [a] Gen. 1:26, 28; Ps. 8:6 **9:3** [a] Deut. 12:15; 14:3, 9, 11; Acts 10:12, 13 [b] Rom. 14:14, 20; 1 Cor. 10:23, 26; Col. 2:16; [1 Tim. 4:3, 4] [c] Gen. 1:29 **9:4** [a] Lev. 7:26; 17:10–16; 19:26; Deut. 12:16, 23; 15:23; 1 Sam. 14:33, 34; Acts 15:20, 29 **9:5** [a] Ex. 21:28 [b] Gen. 4:9, 10; Ps. 9:12 [c] Acts 17:26 **9:6** [a] Ex. 21:12–14; Lev. 24:17; Num. 35:33; Matt. 26:52 [b] Gen. 1:26, 27 **9:7** [a] Gen. 9:1, 19 **9:9** [a] Gen. 6:18 [b] Is. 54:9 [1] Literally *seed* **9:10** [a] Ps. 145:9 **9:11** [a] Gen. 8:21; Is. 54:9 **9:12** [a] Gen. 9:13, 17; 17:11 **9:13** [a] Ezek. 1:28; Rev. 4:3 **9:15** [a] Lev. 26:42, 45; Deut. 7:9; Ezek. 16:60

KNOW THE TRUTH

## THE DOCTRINE OF CREATION AND HUMANS

### PART 6: THE IMAGE OF GOD IN HUMANS

**9:6–7** Only humans are made in the image of God. As such, human life is unique and of the highest value to God. Being made in God's image, or likeness, means He has placed certain characteristics of who He is within us. While we're like God in certain ways, we aren't in any way God (or "gods"). For example, we have intellect like God, but we aren't all-knowing as He is. Both male and female, young and old, and all ethnicities, nationalities, tribes, and tongues are beautiful, special, and equal expressions of God's image in the world. Human life is also unique in its function in the world (see Gen. 1:26–28). God created people to reign with Him, relate to Him, and worship Him (see Rev. 20:4; 21:1–4).

Because of our rebellion against God's rule and the resulting power of sin, we've corrupted our function as image-bearers although while retaining our intrinsic value as image-bearers. We have been destroying ourselves, our relationships, and the earth for all of history. Through Christ, the perfect image of God (see Col. 1:15–17), we recover our full identity as image-bearing, co-laboring, caring, holy sons and daughters of God (see Eph. 4:20–24). What we lost through sin and rebellion, we gain back as the Spirit makes us more like Christ.

*For* **THE DOCTRINE OF CREATION AND HUMANS: PART 7: THE PURPOSE OF HUMANS**, *turn to Jude vv. 24–25 on page 1288.*

destroy all flesh. 16 The rainbow shall be in the
cloud, and I will look on it to remember [a]the
everlasting covenant between God and every
living creature of all flesh that *is* on the earth."
17 And God said to Noah, "This *is* the sign of the
covenant which I have established between Me
and all flesh that *is* on the earth."

### *NOAH AND HIS SONS*

18 Now the sons of Noah who went out of the
ark were Shem, Ham, and Japheth. [a]And Ham
*was* the father of Canaan. 19 [a]These three *were*
the sons of Noah, [b]and from these the whole
earth was populated.

20 And Noah began *to be* [a]a farmer, and he
planted a vineyard. 21 Then he drank of the wine
[a]and was drunk, and became uncovered in his
tent. 22 And Ham, the father of Canaan, saw
the nakedness of his father, and told his two
brothers outside. 23 [a]But Shem and Japheth took
a garment, laid *it* on both their shoulders, and
went backward and covered the nakedness of
their father. Their faces *were* turned away, and
they did not see their father's nakedness.

24 So Noah awoke from his wine, and knew
what his younger son had done to him. 25 Then
he said:

[a]"Cursed *be* Canaan;
A [b]servant of servants
He shall be to his brethren."

26 And he said:

[a]"Blessed *be* the LORD,
The God of Shem,
And may Canaan be his servant.
27 May God [a]enlarge Japheth,
[b]And may he dwell in the tents of Shem;
And may Canaan be his servant."

28 And Noah lived after the flood three hun-
dred and fifty years. 29 So all the days of Noah
were nine hundred and fifty years; and he died.

### *NATIONS DESCENDED FROM NOAH*

*(1 Chr. 1:5–27)*

**10** Now this *is* the genealogy of the sons of
Noah: Shem, Ham, and Japheth. [a]And sons
were born to them after the flood.

2 [a]The sons of Japheth *were* Gomer, Magog,
Madai, Javan, Tubal, Meshech, and Tiras. 3 The
sons of Gomer *were* Ashkenaz, Riphath,[1] and
Togarmah. 4 The sons of Javan *were* Elishah,
Tarshish, Kittim, and Dodanim.[1] 5 From these
[a]the coastland *peoples* of the Gentiles were sep-
arated into their lands, everyone according to
his language, according to their families, into
their nations.

6 [a]The sons of Ham *were* Cush, Mizraim,
Put,[1] and Canaan. 7 The sons of Cush *were* Seba,
Havilah, Sabtah, Raamah, and Sabtechah; and
the sons of Raamah *were* Sheba and Dedan.

**9:16** [a] Gen. 17:13, 19; 2 Sam. 23:5; Is. 55:3; Jer. 32:40; Heb. 13:20 **9:18** [a] Gen. 9:25–27; 10:6 **9:19** [a] Gen. 5:32 [b] Gen. 9:1, 7; 10:32; 1 Chr. 1:4 **9:20** [a] Gen. 3:19, 23; 4:2; Prov. 12:11; Jer. 31:24 **9:21** [a] Prov. 20:1; Eph. 5:18 **9:23** [a] Ex. 20:12; Gal. 6:1 **9:25** [a] Deut. 27:16; Josh. 9:23, 27 [b] Josh. 9:23; 1 Kin. 9:20, 21 **9:26** [a] Gen. 14:20; 24:27; Ps. 144:15; Heb. 11:16 **9:27** [a] Gen. 10:2–5; 39:3; Is. 66:19 [b] Luke 3:36; John 1:14; Eph. 2:13, 14; 3:6 **10:1** [a] Gen. 9:1, 7, 19 **10:2** [a] 1 Chr. 1:5–7 **10:3** [1] Spelled *Diphath* in 1 Chronicles 1:6 **10:4** [1] Spelled *Rodanim* in Samaritan Pentateuch and 1 Chronicles 1:7 **10:5** [a] Gen. 11:8; Ps. 72:10; Jer. 2:10; 25:22 **10:6** [a] 1 Chr. 1:8–16 [1] Or *Phut*

8 Cush begot [a]Nimrod; he began to be a mighty one on the earth. 9 He was a mighty [a]hunter [b]before the LORD; therefore it is said, "Like Nimrod the mighty hunter before the LORD." 10 [a]And the beginning of his kingdom was [b]Babel, Erech, Accad, and Calneh, in the land of Shinar. 11 From that land he went [a]to Assyria and built Nineveh, Rehoboth Ir, Calah, 12 and Resen between Nineveh and Calah (that *is* the principal city).

13 Mizraim begot Ludim, Anamim, Lehabim, Naphtuhim, 14 Pathrusim, and Casluhim [a](from whom came the Philistines and Caphtorim).

15 Canaan begot Sidon his firstborn, and [a]Heth; 16 [a]the Jebusite, the Amorite, and the Girgashite; 17 the Hivite, the Arkite, and the Sinite; 18 the Arvadite, the Zemarite, and the Hamathite. Afterward the families of the Canaanites were dispersed. 19 [a]And the border of the Canaanites was from Sidon as you go toward Gerar, as far as Gaza; then as you go toward Sodom, Gomorrah, Admah, and Zeboiim, as far as Lasha. 20 These *were* the sons of Ham, according to their families, according to their languages, in their lands *and* in their nations.

21 And *children* were born also to Shem, the father of all the children of Eber, the brother of Japheth the elder. 22 The [a]sons of Shem *were* Elam, Asshur, [b]Arphaxad, Lud, and Aram. 23 The sons of Aram *were* Uz, Hul, Gether, and Mash.[1] 24 Arphaxad begot [a]Salah,[1] and Salah begot Eber. 25 [a]To Eber were born two sons: the name of one *was* Peleg, for in his days the earth was divided; and his brother's name *was* Joktan. 26 Joktan begot Almodad, Sheleph, Hazarmaveth, Jerah, 27 Hadoram, Uzal, Diklah, 28 Obal,[1] Abimael, Sheba, 29 Ophir, Havilah, and Jobab. All these *were* the sons of Joktan. 30 And their dwelling place was from Mesha as you go toward Sephar, the mountain of the east. 31 These *were* the sons of Shem, according to their families, according to their languages, in their lands, according to their nations.

32 [a]These *were* the families of the sons of Noah, according to their generations, in their nations; [b]and from these the nations were divided on the earth after the flood.

### *THE TOWER OF BABEL*

**11** Now the whole earth had one language and one speech. 2 And it came to pass, as they journeyed from the east, that they found a plain in the land [a]of Shinar, and they dwelt there. 3 Then they said to one another, "Come, let us make bricks and bake *them* thoroughly." They had brick for stone, and they had asphalt for mortar. 4 And they said, "Come, let us build ourselves a city, and a tower [a]whose top *is* in the heavens; let us make a [b]name for ourselves, lest we [c]be scattered abroad over the face of the whole earth."

5 [a]But the LORD came down to see the city and the tower which the sons of men had built. 6 And the LORD said, "Indeed [a]the people *are* one and they all have [b]one language, and this is what they begin to do; now nothing that they [c]propose to do will be withheld from them. 7 Come, [a]let Us go down and there [b]confuse their language, that they may not understand one another's speech." 8 So [a]the LORD scattered them abroad from there [b]over the face of all the earth, and they ceased building the city. 9 Therefore its name is called Babel, [a]because there the LORD confused the language of all the earth; and from there the LORD scattered them abroad over the face of all the earth.

> **11:7** God divided people into different language groups because they refused to obey His command to fill the earth and became united for an evil purpose. This doesn't mean God wants the world to remain divided. Christ came to reconcile the world to God (2 Cor. 5:19), and when we are in Christ we are reconciled not only to God but also to one another (see Eph. 2:11–19). The unity God destroyed by judgment at Babel was restored by grace on the Day of Pentecost (see Acts 2:4–12). On that day people from different nations came together to hear the gospel in their own languages.

### *SHEM'S DESCENDANTS*

*(1 Chr. 1:17–27; Luke 3:34–36)*

10 [a]This *is* the genealogy of Shem: Shem *was* one hundred years old, and begot Arphaxad two years after the flood. 11 After he begot Arphaxad, Shem lived five hundred years, and begot sons and daughters.

12 Arphaxad lived thirty-five years, [a]and begot Salah. 13 After he begot Salah, Arphaxad lived four hundred and three years, and begot sons and daughters.

14 Salah lived thirty years, and begot Eber. 15 After he begot Eber, Salah lived four hundred and three years, and begot sons and daughters.

16 [a]Eber lived thirty-four years, and begot [b]Peleg. 17 After he begot Peleg, Eber lived four hundred and thirty years, and begot sons and daughters.

**10:8** [a] Mic. 5:6 **10:9** [a] Jer. 16:16; Mic. 7:2 [b] Gen. 21:20 **10:10** [a] Mic. 5:6 [b] Gen. 11:9 **10:11** [a] Gen. 25:18; 2 Kin. 19:36; Mic. 5:6 **10:14** [a] 1 Chr. 1:12 **10:15** [a] Gen. 23:3 **10:16** [a] Gen. 14:7; 15:19–21; Deut. 7:1; Neh. 9:8 **10:19** [a] Gen. 13:12, 14, 15, 17; 15:18–21; Num. 34:2–12 **10:22** [a] Gen. 11:10–26; 1 Chr. 1:17–28 [b] Gen. 10:24; 11:10; Luke 3:36 **10:23** [1] Called *Meshech* in Septuagint and 1 Chronicles 1:17 **10:24** [a] Gen. 11:12; Luke 3:35 [1] Following Masoretic Text, Vulgate, and Targum; Septuagint reads *Arphaxad begot Cainan, and Cainan begot Salah* (compare Luke 3:35, 36). **10:25** [a] 1 Chr. 1:19 **10:28** [1] Spelled *Ebal* in 1 Chronicles 1:22 **10:32** [a] Gen. 10:1 [b] Gen. 9:19; 11:8 **11:2** [a] Gen. 10:10; 14:1; Dan. 1:2 **11:4** [a] Deut. 1:28; 9:1; Ps. 107:26 [b] Gen. 6:4; 2 Sam. 8:13 [c] Deut. 4:27 **11:5** [a] Gen. 18:21; Ex. 3:8; 19:11, 18, 20 **11:6** [a] Gen. 9:19; Acts 17:26 [b] Gen. 11:1 [c] Deut. 31:21; Ps. 2:1 **11:7** [a] Gen. 1:26 [b] Gen. 42:23; Ex. 4:11; Deut. 28:49; Is. 33:19; Jer. 5:15 **11:8** [a] Gen. 11:4; Deut. 32:8; Ps. 92:9; [Luke 1:51] [b] Gen. 10:25, 32 **11:9** [a] 1 Cor. 14:23 **11:10** [a] Gen. 10:22–25; 1 Chr. 1:17 **11:12** [a] Luke 3:35 **11:16** [a] 1 Chr. 1:19 [b] Luke 3:35

18 Peleg lived thirty years, and begot Reu.
19 After he begot Reu, Peleg lived two hundred
and nine years, and begot sons and daughters.
20 Reu lived thirty-two years, and begot [a]Serug.
21 After he begot Serug, Reu lived two hundred
and seven years, and begot sons and daughters.
22 Serug lived thirty years, and begot Nahor.
23 After he begot Nahor, Serug lived two hundred
years, and begot sons and daughters.
24 Nahor lived twenty-nine years, and begot
[a]Terah. 25 After he begot Terah, Nahor lived one
hundred and nineteen years, and begot sons
and daughters.
26 Now Terah lived seventy years, and [a]begot
Abram, Nahor, and Haran.

### *TERAH'S DESCENDANTS*

27 This *is* the genealogy of Terah: Terah begot
[a]Abram, Nahor, and Haran. Haran begot Lot.
28 And Haran died before his father Terah in
his native land, in Ur of the Chaldeans. 29 Then
Abram and Nahor took wives: the name of
Abram's wife *was* [a]Sarai, and the name of Nahor's
wife, [b]Milcah, the daughter of Haran the father
of Milcah and the father of Iscah. 30 But [a]Sarai
was barren; she had no child.
31 And Terah [a]took his son Abram and his
grandson Lot, the son of Haran, and his daughter-
in-law Sarai, his son Abram's wife, and they went
out with them from [b]Ur of the Chaldeans to go
to [c]the land of Canaan; and they came to Haran
and dwelt there. 32 So the days of Terah were two
hundred and five years, and Terah died in Haran.

### *PROMISES TO ABRAM*

*(Acts 7:2–5)*

12 Now the [a]LORD had said to Abram:

"Get [b]out of your country,
From your family
And from your father's house,
To a land that I will show you.
2 [a]I will make you a great nation;
[b]I will bless you
And make your name great;
[c]And you shall be a blessing.

**11:20** [a] Luke 3:35 **11:24** [a] Gen. 11:31; Josh. 24:2; Luke 3:34 **11:26** [a] Josh. 24:2; 1 Chr. 1:26 **11:27** [a] Gen. 11:31; 17:5 **11:29** [a] Gen. 17:15; 20:12 [b] Gen. 22:20, 23; 24:15 **11:30** [a] Gen. 16:1, 2 **11:31** [a] Gen. 12:1 [b] Acts 7:4 [c] Gen. 10:19 **12:1** [a] Acts 7:2, 3 [b] Gen. 13:9 **12:2** [a] Deut. 26:5 [b] Gen. 22:17; 24:35 [c] Gen. 28:4

STORY OF SCRIPTURE 4

GENESIS 12:1–9

## STEPPING OUT IN FAITH

### WHAT'S GOING ON?

God called Abram on a grand adventure: "Get out of your country . . . to a land that I will show you." Through Abram and his lineage, God would bless the whole earth. Abram, in faith, responded to God's call. He accepted the Lord's invitation, left his home, and embarked on a life-changing journey of faith and failure, tragedy and triumph. Later, God sealed His promise to Abram by making a covenant with him—an unbreakable bond of faithfulness and provision. Through every peak and valley, the Lord's promise sustained Abram.

### WHAT DOES THIS MEAN FOR ME?

Although God assured Abram this unknown journey would be bountiful, it still took faith for Abram to leave his comfort zone and make the first move. Likewise, God calls each of us to step out of what's familiar and into the unknown. These giant steps of faith will ultimately set a course for the rest of our lives. The question for us to consider is: Will we faithfully respond to God's call despite our fears?

### DID YOU CATCH THE PATTERN?

Before this encounter with God, Abram was unknown and seemingly unremarkable. But God didn't choose Abram because he was great. God chose Abram and *made* him great. This pattern is repeated throughout Scripture. God chose people not because they were wise, strong, or charismatic. Instead, He called the weak and anonymous to follow Him, and empowered them to live up to their calling. This is especially evident in David, the least impressive in his family who became king of his people. It was also repeated in Jesus' call of His disciples: "Follow Me, and I will make you fishers of men" (Matt. 4:19). Jesus didn't call fishers of men. Rather, as normal men followed Him, they *became* fishers of men. God doesn't call the qualified, He qualifies the called.

*For the next* Story of Scripture *reading and devotion, turn to Genesis 22:1–19 on page 27.*

3 [a]I will bless those who bless you,
And I will curse him who curses you;
And in [b]you all the families of the earth
shall be [c]blessed."

**SEEING JESUS IN THE SCRIPTURE**

**12:3** God's covenant with Abram was both a promise and a picture of Jesus' salvation. As promised, Jesus came from Abraham's lineage (see Matt. 1:1). As pictured, everyone in Christ is blessed with the gift of salvation.

4So Abram departed as the LORD had spoken
to him, and Lot went with him. And Abram *was*
seventy-five years old when he departed from
Haran. 5Then Abram took Sarai his wife and Lot
his brother's son, and all their possessions that
they had gathered, and [a]the people whom they
had acquired [b]in Haran, and they [c]departed to
go to the land of Canaan. So they came to the
land of Canaan. 6Abram [a]passed through the
land to the place of Shechem, [b]as far as the
terebinth tree of Moreh.[1] [c]And the Canaanites
*were* then in the land.
7[a]Then the LORD appeared to Abram and
said, [b]"To your descendants I will give this land."
And there he built an [c]altar to the LORD, who had
appeared to him. 8And he moved from there to
the mountain east of Bethel, and he pitched his
tent *with* Bethel on the west and Ai on the east;
there he built an altar to the LORD and [a]called
on the name of the LORD. 9So Abram journeyed,
[a]going on still toward the South.[1]

### *ABRAM IN EGYPT*

10Now there was [a]a famine in the land, and
Abram [b]went down to Egypt to dwell there,
for the famine *was* [c]severe in the land. 11And
it came to pass, when he was close to entering
Egypt, that he said to Sarai his wife, "Indeed I
know that you *are* [a]a woman of beautiful coun-
tenance. 12Therefore it will happen, when the
Egyptians see you, that they will say, 'This *is* his
wife'; and they [a]will kill me, but they will let you
live. 13[a]Please say you *are* my [b]sister, that it may
be well with me for your sake, and that I[1] may
live because of you."
14So it was, when Abram came into Egypt,
that the Egyptians saw the woman, that she *was*
very beautiful. 15The princes of Pharaoh also
saw her and commended her to Pharaoh. And
the woman was taken to Pharaoh's house. 16He
[a]treated Abram well for her sake. He [b]had sheep,
oxen, male donkeys, male and female servants,
female donkeys, and camels.
17But the LORD [a]plagued Pharaoh and his
house with great plagues because of Sarai,
Abram's wife. 18And Pharaoh called Abram
and said, [a]"What *is* this you have done to me?
Why did you not tell me that she *was* your wife?
19Why did you say, 'She *is* my sister'? I might have
taken her as my wife. Now therefore, here is your
wife; take *her* and go your way." 20[a]So Pharaoh
commanded *his* men concerning him; and they
sent him away, with his wife and all that he had.

### *ABRAM INHERITS CANAAN*

13 Then Abram went up from Egypt, he and
his wife and all that he had, and [a]Lot with
him, [b]to the South.[1] 2[a]Abram *was* very rich in
livestock, in silver, and in gold. 3And he went on
his journey [a]from the South as far as Bethel, to
the place where his tent had been at the begin-
ning, between Bethel and Ai, 4to the [a]place of
the altar which he had made there at first. And
there Abram [b]called on the name of the LORD.
5Lot also, who went with Abram, had flocks
and herds and tents. 6Now [a]the land was not able
to support them, that they might dwell together,
for their possessions were so great that they
could not dwell together. 7And there was [a]strife
between the herdsmen of Abram's livestock and
the herdsmen of Lot's livestock. [b]The Canaanites
and the Perizzites then dwelt in the land.
8So Abram said to Lot, [a]"Please let there
be no strife between you and me, and between
my herdsmen and your herdsmen; for we *are*
brethren. 9[a]*Is* not the whole land before you?
Please [b]separate from me. [c]If *you take* the left,
then I will go to the right; or, if *you go* to the
right, then I will go to the left."
10And Lot lifted his eyes and saw all [a]the plain
of Jordan, that it *was* well watered everywhere
(before the LORD [b]destroyed Sodom and Gomor-
rah) [c]like the garden of the LORD, like the land of
Egypt as you go toward [d]Zoar. 11Then Lot chose for
himself all the plain of Jordan, and Lot journeyed
east. And they separated from each other. 12Abram
dwelt in the land of Canaan, and Lot [a]dwelt in
the cities of the plain and [b]pitched *his* tent even
as far as Sodom. 13But the men of Sodom [a]*were*
exceedingly wicked and [b]sinful against the LORD.
14And the LORD said to Abram, after Lot [a]had
separated from him: "Lift your eyes now and
look from the place where you are—[b]northward,
southward, eastward, and westward; 15for all
the land which you see [a]I give to you and [b]your

12:3 [a] Num. 24:9 [b] Acts 3:25 [c] Is. 41:27 12:5 [a] Gen. 14:14 [b] Gen. 11:31 [c] Gen. 13:18 12:6 [a] Heb. 11:9 [b] Deut. 11:30 [c] Gen. 10:18, 19 [1] Hebrew *Alon Moreh* 12:7 [a] Gen. 17:1; 18:1 [b] Gen. 13:15; 15:18; 17:8 [c] Gen. 13:4, 18; 22:9 12:8 [a] Gen. 4:26; 13:4; 21:33 12:9 [a] Gen. 13:1, 3; 20:1; 24:62 [1] Hebrew *Negev* 12:10 [a] Gen. 26:1 [b] Ps. 105:13 [c] Gen. 43:1 12:11 [a] Gen. 12:14; 26:7; 29:17 12:12 [a] Gen. 20:11; 26:7 12:13 [a] Gen. 20:1–18; 26:6–11 [b] Gen. 20:12 [1] Literally *my soul* 12:16 [a] Gen. 20:14 [b] Gen. 13:2 12:17 [a] 1 Chr. 16:21 12:18 [a] Gen. 20:9, 10; 26:10 12:20 [a] [Prov. 21:1] 13:1 [a] Gen. 12:4; 14:12, 16 [b] Gen. 12:9 [1] Hebrew *Negev* 13:2 [a] Gen. 24:35; 26:14 13:3 [a] Gen. 12:8, 9 13:4 [a] Gen. 12:7, 8; 21:33 [b] Ps. 116:17 13:6 [a] Gen. 36:7 13:7 [a] Gen. 26:20 [b] Gen. 12:6; 15:20, 21 13:8 [a] 1 Cor. 6:7 13:9 [a] Gen. 20:15; 34:10 [b] Gen. 13:11, 14 [c] [Rom. 12:18] 13:10 [a] Gen. 19:17–29 [b] Gen. 19:24 [c] Gen. 2:8, 10 [d] Deut. 34:3 13:12 [a] Gen. 19:24, 25, 29 [b] Gen. 14:12; 19:1 13:13 [a] Gen. 18:20, 21 [b] Gen. 6:11; 39:9 13:14 [a] Gen. 13:11 [b] Gen. 28:14 13:15 [a] Acts 7:5 [b] 2 Chr. 20:7

descendants[1] forever. 16 And [a]I will make your
descendants as the dust of the earth; so that
if a man could number the dust of the earth,
*then* your descendants also could be numbered.
17 Arise, walk in the land through its length and
its width, for I give it to you."
18 [a]Then Abram moved *his* tent, and went and
[b]dwelt by the terebinth trees of Mamre,[1] [c]which *are*
in Hebron, and built an [d]altar there to the LORD.

### *LOT'S CAPTIVITY AND RESCUE*

**14** And it came to pass in the days of Amraphel king [a]of Shinar, Arioch king of Ellasar,
Chedorlaomer king of [b]Elam, and Tidal king of
nations,[1] 2 *that* they made war with Bera king of
Sodom, Birsha king of Gomorrah, Shinab king
of [a]Admah, Shemeber king of Zeboiim, and the
king of Bela (that is, [b]Zoar). 3 All these joined
together in the Valley of Siddim [a](that is, the Salt
Sea). 4 Twelve years [a]they served Chedorlaomer,
and in the thirteenth year they rebelled.
5 In the fourteenth year Chedorlaomer and the
kings that *were* with him came and attacked [a]the
Rephaim in Ashteroth Karnaim, [b]the Zuzim in
Ham, [c]the Emim in Shaveh Kiriathaim, 6 [a]and the
Horites in their mountain of Seir, as far as El Paran,
which *is* by the wilderness. 7 Then they turned back
and came to En Mishpat (that *is,* Kadesh), and
attacked all the country of the Amalekites, and
also the Amorites who dwelt [a]in Hazezon Tamar.
8 And the king of Sodom, the king of Gomorrah, the king of Admah, the king of Zeboiim,
and the king of Bela (that *is,* Zoar) went out and
joined together in battle in the Valley of Siddim
9 against Chedorlaomer king of Elam, Tidal king
of nations,[1] Amraphel king of Shinar, and Arioch
king of Ellasar—four kings against five. 10 Now
the Valley of Siddim *was full of* [a]asphalt pits;
and the kings of Sodom and Gomorrah fled;
*some* fell there, and the remainder fled [b]to the
mountains. 11 Then they took [a]all the goods of
Sodom and Gomorrah, and all their provisions,
and went their way. 12 They also took Lot, Abram's
[a]brother's son [b]who dwelt in Sodom, and his
goods, and departed.
13 Then one who had escaped came and told
Abram the [a]Hebrew, for [b]he dwelt by the terebinth trees of Mamre[1] the Amorite, brother of
Eshcol and brother of Aner; [c]and they *were* allies
with Abram. 14 Now [a]when Abram heard that [b]his
brother was taken captive, he armed his three
hundred and eighteen trained *servants* who were
[c]born in his own house, and went in pursuit [d]as
far as Dan. 15 He divided his forces against them
by night, and he and his servants [a]attacked them
and pursued them as far as Hobah, which *is* north
of Damascus. 16 So he [a]brought back all the goods,
and also brought back his brother Lot and his
goods, as well as the women and the people.
17 And the king of Sodom [a]went out to meet
him at the Valley of Shaveh (that *is,* the [b]King's
Valley), [c]after his return from the defeat of Chedorlaomer and the kings who *were* with him.

### *ABRAM AND MELCHIZEDEK*

*(Heb. 7:1, 2)*

18 Then [a]Melchizedek king of Salem brought
out [b]bread and wine; he *was* [c]the priest of [d]God
Most High. 19 And he blessed him and said:

[a]"Blessed be Abram of God Most High,
[b]Possessor of heaven and earth;
20 And [a]blessed be God Most High,
Who has delivered your enemies into
your hand."

And he [b]gave him a tithe of all.
21 Now the king of Sodom said to Abram,
"Give me the persons, and take the goods for
yourself."
22 But Abram [a]said to the king of Sodom, "I
[b]have raised my hand to the LORD, God Most High,
[c]the Possessor of heaven and earth, 23 that [a]I *will
take* nothing, from a thread to a sandal strap, and
that I will not take anything that *is* yours, lest you
should say, 'I have made Abram rich'— 24 except
only what the young men have eaten, and the
portion of the men who went with me: Aner,
Eshcol, and Mamre; let them take their portion."

### *GOD'S COVENANT WITH ABRAM*

*(Heb. 11:8–10)*

**15** After these things the word of the LORD came to Abram [a]in a vision, saying, [b]"Do
not be afraid, Abram. I *am* your [c]shield, your
exceedingly [d]great reward."
2 [a]But Abram said, "Lord GOD, what will You
give me, [b]seeing I go childless, and the heir of

**SEEING JESUS IN THE SCRIPTURE**

**14:18** *Melchizedek* means "king of righteousness." He was king and priest of Salem, which means "peace." As priest and the king of righteousness and of peace, Melchizedek points ahead to Jesus, the Prince of Peace and only other person God appointed as both king and priest (see Heb. 5:5–11; 7:1–10).

**13:15** [1] Literally *seed,* and so throughout the book **13:16** [a] Gen. 22:17 **13:18** [a] Gen. 26:17 [b] Gen. 14:13 [c] Gen. 23:2; 35:27 [d] Gen. 8:20; 22:8, 9 [1] Hebrew *Alon Mamre* **14:1** [a] Gen. 10:10; 11:2 [b] Is. 11:11; 21:2 [1] Hebrew *goyim* **14:2** [a] Deut. 29:23 [b] Gen. 13:10; 19:22 **14:3** [a] Num. 34:12 **14:4** [a] Gen. 9:26 **14:5** [a] Gen. 15:20 [b] Deut. 2:20 [c] Deut. 2:10 **14:6** [a] Deut. 2:12, 22 **14:7** [a] 2 Chr. 20:2 **14:9** [1] Hebrew *goyim* **14:10** [a] Gen. 11:3 [b] Gen. 19:17, 30 **14:11** [a] Gen. 14:16, 21 **14:12** [a] Gen. 11:27; 12:5 [b] Gen. 13:12 **14:13** [a] Gen. 39:14; 40:15 [b] Gen. 13:18 [c] Gen. 14:24; 21:27, 32 [1] Hebrew *Alon Mamre* **14:14** [a] Gen. 19:29 [b] Gen. 13:8; 14:12 [c] Gen. 12:5; 15:3; 17:27 [d] Deut. 34:1 **14:15** [a] Is. 41:2, 3 **14:16** [a] Gen. 31:18 **14:17** [a] 1 Sam. 18:6 [b] 2 Sam. 18:18 [c] Heb. 7:1 **14:18** [a] Heb. 7:1–10 [b] Gen. 18:5 [c] Ps. 110:4 [d] Acts 16:17 **14:19** [a] Ruth 3:10 [b] Gen. 14:22 **14:20** [a] Gen. 24:27 [b] Heb. 7:4 **14:22** [a] Gen. 14:2, 8, 10 [b] Dan. 12:7 [c] Gen. 14:19 **14:23** [a] 2 Kin. 5:16 **15:1** [a] Dan. 10:1 [b] Gen. 21:17; 26:24 [c] Deut. 33:29 [d] Prov. 11:18 **15:2** [a] Gen. 17:18 [b] Acts 7:5

my house *is* Eliezer of Damascus?" 3 Then Abram
said, "Look, You have given me no offspring;
indeed [a]one born in my house is my heir!"
4 And behold, the word of the LORD *came* to
him, saying, "This one shall not be your heir, but
one who [a]will come from your own body shall be
your heir." 5 Then He brought him outside and
said, "Look now toward heaven, and [a]count the
[b]stars if you are able to number them." And He
said to him, [c]"So shall your [d]descendants be."
6 And he [a]believed in the LORD, and He [b]ac-
counted it to him for righteousness.

> **15:6** Almost ten years had passed since God made His promise to Abram. As Abram grew older and still had no children, he wondered more about how God's promises could be fulfilled. In answer to Abram's questions, God, who had revealed Himself in word, and who had faithfully protected him and sustained him, again pledged His word of promise. Abram **believed** and his faith was **accounted** to him as **righteousness**. Some have thought in Old Testament times people were saved by their good deeds or offering animal sacrifices rather than by faith, but this idea is mistaken. Abram wasn't saved because of righteous living or obedience, but rather by believing in God and so being declared righteous by Him. The only valid work is the work of faith (see John 6:28–29; James 2:2).

7 Then He said to him, "I *am* the LORD, who
[a]brought you out of [b]Ur of the Chaldeans, [c]to
give you this land to inherit it."
8 And he said, "Lord GOD, [a]how shall I know
that I will inherit it?"
9 So He said to him, "Bring Me a three-year-
old heifer, a three-year-old female goat, a three-
year-old ram, a turtledove, and a young pigeon."
10 Then he brought all these to Him and [a]cut
them in two, down the middle, and placed each
piece opposite the other; but he did not cut [b]the
birds in two. 11 And when the vultures came down
on the carcasses, Abram drove them away.
12 Now when the sun was going down, [a]a deep
sleep fell upon Abram; and behold, horror *and*
great darkness fell upon him. 13 Then He said to
Abram: "Know certainly [a]that your descendants
will be strangers in a land *that is* not theirs, and
will serve them, and [b]they will afflict them four
hundred years. 14 And also the nation whom they
serve [a]I will judge; afterward [b]they shall come
out with great possessions. 15 Now as for you,
[a]you shall go [b]to your fathers in peace; [c]you
shall be buried at a good old age. 16 But [a]in the
fourth generation they shall return here, for the
iniquity [b]of the Amorites [c]*is* not yet complete."
17 And it came to pass, when the sun went
down and it was dark, that behold, there ap-
peared a smoking oven and a burning torch that
[a]passed between those pieces. 18 On the same day
the LORD [a]made a covenant with Abram, saying:
[b]"To your descendants I have given this land,
from the river of Egypt to the great river, the River
Euphrates— 19 the Kenites, the Kenezzites, the
Kadmonites, 20 the Hittites, the Perizzites, the
Rephaim, 21 the Amorites, the Canaanites, the
Girgashites, and the Jebusites."

### *HAGAR AND ISHMAEL*

16 Now Sarai, Abram's wife, [a]had borne him no
*children.* And she had [b]an Egyptian maid-
servant whose name was [c]Hagar. 2 [a]So Sarai said
to Abram, "See now, the LORD [b]has restrained me
from bearing *children.* Please, [c]go in to my maid;
perhaps I shall obtain children by her." And Abram
[d]heeded the voice of Sarai. 3 Then Sarai, Abram's
wife, took Hagar her maid, the Egyptian, and gave
her to her husband Abram to be his wife, after
Abram [a]had dwelt ten years in the land of Canaan.
4 So he went in to Hagar, and she conceived. And
when she saw that she had conceived, her mistress
became [a]despised in her eyes.

> **16:2** In Old Testament times, for a couple to be childless was considered tragic. Children were seen as a sign of God's blessing. Female servants were expected to bear their master's children if the master's wife could not.

5 Then Sarai said to Abram, "My wrong *be*
upon you! I gave my maid into your embrace;
and when she saw that she had conceived, I
became despised in her eyes. [a]The LORD judge
between you and me."
6 [a]So Abram said to Sarai, "Indeed your maid
*is* in your hand; do to her as you please." And
when Sarai dealt harshly with her, [b]she fled
from her presence.
7 Now the [a]Angel of the LORD found her by a
spring of water in the wilderness, [b]by the spring
on the way to [c]Shur. 8 And He said, "Hagar, Sarai's
maid, where have you come from, and where
are you going?"

15:3 [a] Gen. 14:14 15:4 [a] 2 Sam. 7:12 15:5 [a] Ps. 147:4 [b] Jer. 33:22 [c] Ex. 32:13 [d] Gen. 17:19 15:6 [a] Rom. 4:3, 9, 22 [b] Ps. 32:2; 106:31 15:7 [a] Gen. 12:1 [b] Gen. 11:28, 31 [c] Ps. 105:42, 44 15:8 [a] Luke 1:18 15:10 [a] Jer. 34:18 [b] Lev. 1:17 15:12 [a] Gen. 2:21; 28:11 15:13 [a] Ex. 1:11 [b] Ex. 12:40 15:14 [a] Ex. 6:6 [b] Ex. 12:36 15:15 [a] Job 5:26 [b] Gen. 25:8; 47:30 [c] Gen. 25:8 15:16 [a] Ex. 12:41 [b] 1 Kin. 21:26 [c] Matt. 23:32 15:17 [a] Jer. 34:18, 19 15:18 [a] Gen. 24:7 [b] Gen. 12:7; 17:8 16:1 [a] Gen. 11:30; 15:2, 3 [b] Gen. 12:16; 21:9 [c] Gal. 4:24 16:2 [a] Gen. 30:3 [b] Gen. 20:18 [c] Gen. 30:3, 9 [d] Gen. 3:17 16:3 [a] Gen. 12:4, 5 16:4 [a] [Prov. 30:21, 23] 16:5 [a] Gen. 31:53 16:6 [a] 1 Pet. 3:7 [b] Ex. 2:15 16:7 [a] Gen. 21:17, 18; 22:11, 15; 31:11 [b] Gen. 20:1; 25:18 [c] Ex. 15:22

APPLY THE TRUTH

## BULLYING

**16:1–6** When you think of a bullying, you might think of someone getting stuffed in a locker or having his lunch money taken by force. This still happens, but a new form of virtual bullying is on the rise: blocking, spamming, and shaming others online. Bullying in both forms is a problem for many people. Some people just seem to enjoy putting others down or trying to intimidate them. Sometimes no matter how much you avoid or ignore them, it persists. What causes this behavior? Why does it seem like some people only want to put others down?

In this passage we get insight into why people target others. For Sarai, it was insecurity about her infertility and jealousy of her maid Hagar's pregnancy. Thus Sarai aimed to ruin Hagar's life. How did Hagar respond? She didn't retaliate; she simply avoided Sarai. Ultimately God dealt with both. Jesus tells us to respond to our enemies with love and kindness (see Matt. 5:43–44). In doing so, we show our trust in God and represent Him well.

She said, "I am fleeing from the presence
of my mistress Sarai."
9 The Angel of the LORD said to her, "Return
to your mistress, and [a]submit yourself under her
hand." 10 Then the Angel of the LORD said to her,
[a]"I will multiply your descendants exceedingly,
so that they shall not be counted for multitude."
11 And the Angel of the LORD said to her:

"Behold, you *are* with child,
[a]And you shall bear a son.
You shall call his name Ishmael,
Because the LORD has heard your
affliction.
12 [a]He shall be a wild man;
His hand *shall be* against every man,
And every man's hand against him.
[b]And he shall dwell in the presence of all
his brethren."

13 Then she called the name of the LORD who
spoke to her, You-Are-the-God-Who-Sees; for
she said, "Have I also here seen Him [a]who sees
me?" 14 Therefore the well was called [a]Beer Lahai
Roi;[1] observe, *it is* [b]between Kadesh and Bered.
15 So [a]Hagar bore Abram a son; and Abram
named his son, whom Hagar bore, Ishmael.
16 Abram *was* eighty-six years old when Hagar
bore Ishmael to Abram.

### *THE SIGN OF THE COVENANT*

*(Ex. 12:43—13:2)*

**17** When Abram was ninety-nine years old,
the LORD [a]appeared to Abram and said
to him, [b]"I *am* Almighty God; [c]walk before Me
and be [d]blameless. 2 And I will make My [a]cov-
enant between Me and you, and [b]will multiply
you exceedingly." 3 Then Abram fell on his face,
and God talked with him, saying: 4 "As for Me,
behold, My covenant is with you, and you shall
be [a]a father of many nations. 5 No longer shall
[a]your name be called Abram, but your name
shall be Abraham; [b]for I have made you a father
of many nations. 6 I will make you exceedingly
fruitful; and I will make [a]nations of you, and
[b]kings shall come from you. 7 And I will [a]estab-
lish My covenant between Me and you and your
descendants after you in their generations, for
an everlasting covenant, [b]to be God to you and
[c]your descendants after you. 8 Also [a]I give to
you and your descendants after you the land
[b]in which you are a stranger, all the land of Ca-
naan, as an everlasting possession; and [c]I will
be their God."

**SEEING JESUS IN THE SCRIPTURE**

**17:7** The covenant established with Abraham was everlasting. God's covenant with Abraham and his descendants wasn't just for them; it was for the whole world. Through Jesus, God the Father fulfilled His covenant promise to Abraham and everyone who receives Jesus' salvation (see Gal. 3:7).

9 And God said to Abraham: "As for you, [a]you
shall keep My covenant, you and your descen-
dants after you throughout their generations.
10 This *is* My covenant which you shall keep,
between Me and you and your descendants after
you: [a]Every male child among you shall be cir-
cumcised; 11 and you shall be circumcised in the
flesh of your foreskins, and it shall be [a]a sign of
the covenant between Me and you. 12 He who is

**16:9** [a] [Titus 2:9] **16:10** [a] Gen. 17:20 **16:11** [a] Luke 1:13, 31 **16:12** [a] Gen. 21:20 [b] Gen. 25:18 **16:13** [a] Gen. 31:42 **16:14** [a] Gen. 24:62 [b] Num. 13:26 [1] Literally *Well of the One Who Lives and Sees Me* **16:15** [a] Gal. 4:22 **17:1** [a] Gen. 12:7; 18:1 [b] Gen. 28:3; 35:11 [c] 2 Kin. 20:3 [d] Deut. 18:13 **17:2** [a] Gen. 15:18 [b] Gen. 12:2; 13:16; 15:5; 18:18 **17:4** [a] [Rom. 4:11, 12, 16] **17:5** [a] Neh. 9:7 [b] Rom. 4:17 **17:6** [a] Gen. 17:16; 35:11 [b] Matt. 1:6 **17:7** [a] [Gal. 3:17] [b] Gen. 26:24; 28:13 [c] Rom. 9:8 **17:8** [a] Acts 7:5 [b] Gen. 23:4; 28:4 [c] Lev. 26:12 **17:9** [a] Ex. 19:5 **17:10** [a] Acts 7:8 **17:11** [a] Ex. 12:13, 48

eight days old among you [a]shall be circumcised,
every male child in your generations, he who is
born in your house or bought with money from
any foreigner who is not your descendant. 13 He
who is born in your house and he who is bought
with your money must be circumcised, and
My covenant shall be in your flesh for an ever-
lasting covenant. 14 And the uncircumcised male
child, who is not circumcised in the flesh of his
foreskin, that person [a]shall be cut off from his
people; he has broken My covenant."
15 Then God said to Abraham, "As for Sarai
your wife, you shall not call her name Sarai, but
Sarah *shall be* her name. 16 And I will bless her
[a]and also give you a son by her; then I will bless
her, and she shall be *a mother* [b]*of* nations; [c]kings
of peoples shall be from her."
17 Then Abraham fell on his face [a]and
laughed, and said in his heart, "Shall *a child* be
born to a man who is one hundred years old?
And shall Sarah, who is ninety years old, bear
*a child?*" 18 And Abraham [a]said to God, "Oh, that
Ishmael might live before You!"
19 Then God said: "No, [a]Sarah your wife shall
bear you a son, and you shall call his name Isaac;
I will establish My [b]covenant with him for an
everlasting covenant, *and* with his descendants
after him. 20 And as for Ishmael, I have heard
you. Behold, I have blessed him, and will make
him fruitful, and [a]will multiply him exceedingly.
He shall beget [b]twelve princes, [c]and I will make
him a great nation. 21 But My [a]covenant I will
establish with Isaac, [b]whom Sarah shall bear
to you at this [c]set time next year." 22 Then He
finished talking with him, and God went up
from Abraham.

### SEEING JESUS IN THE SCRIPTURE

**17:19** *Isaac* means "he laughs." God re-establishing His covenant with Abraham including the command to name his son Isaac, points ahead to the joy the birth of Jesus, the ultimate Son of promise, brings to the world (see John 15:11).

23 So Abraham took Ishmael his son, all who
were born in his house and all who were bought
with his money, every male among the men of
Abraham's house, and circumcised the flesh of
their foreskins that very same day, as God had
said to him. 24 Abraham *was* ninety-nine years
old when he was circumcised in the flesh of his
foreskin. 25 And Ishmael his son *was* thirteen
years old when he was circumcised in the flesh
of his foreskin. 26 That very same day Abraham
was circumcised, and his son Ishmael; 27 and
[a]all the men of his house, born in the house
or bought with money from a foreigner, were
circumcised with him.

### *THE SON OF PROMISE*
*(Heb. 13:2)*

**18** Then the LORD appeared to him by the
[a]terebinth trees of Mamre,[1] as he was sit-
ting in the tent door in the heat of the day. 2 [a]So
he lifted his eyes and looked, and behold, three
men were standing by him; [b]and when he saw
*them,* he ran from the tent door to meet them,
and bowed himself to the ground, 3 and said, "My
Lord, if I have now found favor in Your sight, do
not pass on by Your servant. 4 Please let [a]a little
water be brought, and wash your feet, and rest
yourselves under the tree. 5 And [a]I will bring
a morsel of bread, that [b]you may refresh your
hearts. After that you may pass by, [c]inasmuch
as you have come to your servant."
They said, "Do as you have said."

**18:1–5** In the biblical period, hospitality wasn't a courtesy; it was a duty. People were expected to welcome travelers into their homes and care for their needs. It was considered rude for a host to ask his guests questions or carry on a conversation with them before they were given a chance to clean up and eat. Verse 1 states that **the LORD appeared** to Abraham, then the next verse refers to **three men**. It seems clear from verses 1, 13, and 17 that one of the three was the Lord Himself and the other two were angels. Apparently all three were in human form and were able to eat the meal Abraham had prepared. Many have speculated this was an appearance of the preincarnate Christ.

6 So Abraham hurried into the tent to Sarah
and said, "Quickly, make ready three measures
of fine meal; knead *it* and make cakes." 7 And
Abraham ran to the herd, took a tender and
good calf, gave *it* to a young man, and he has-
tened to prepare it. 8 So [a]he took butter and milk
and the calf which he had prepared, and set *it*
before them; and he stood by them under the
tree as they ate.
9 Then they said to him, "Where *is* Sarah
your wife?"
So he said, "Here, [a]in the tent."
10 And He said, "I will certainly return to
you [a]according to the time of life, and behold,
[b]Sarah your wife shall have a son."
(Sarah was listening in the tent door which

**17:12** [a] Lev. 12:3 **17:14** [a] Ex. 4:24–26 **17:16** [a] Gen. 18:10 [b] Gen. 35:11 [c] Gen. 17:6; 36:31 **17:17** [a] Gen. 17:3; 18:12; 21:6 **17:18** [a] Gen. 18:23 **17:19** [a] Gen. 18:10; 21:2 [b] Gen. 22:16 **17:20** [a] Gen. 16:10 [b] Gen. 25:12–16 [c] Gen. 21:13, 18 **17:21** [a] Gen. 26:2–5 [b] Gen. 21:2 [c] Gen. 18:14 **17:27** [a] Gen. 18:19 **18:1** [a] Gen. 13:18; 14:13 [1] Hebrew *Alon Mamre* **18:2** [a] Heb. 13:2 [b] Gen. 19:1 **18:4** [a] Gen. 19:2; 24:32; 43:24 **18:5** [a] Judg. 6:18, 19; 13:15, 16 [b] Judg. 19:5 [c] Gen. 19:8; 33:10 **18:8** [a] Gen. 19:3 **18:9** [a] Gen. 24:67 **18:10** [a] 2 Kin. 4:16 [b] Rom. 9:9

*was* behind him.) 11 Now [a]Abraham and Sarah
were old, well advanced in age; *and* Sarah [b]had
passed the age of childbearing.[1] 12 Therefore
Sarah [a]laughed within herself, saying, [b]"After I
have grown old, shall I have pleasure, my [c]lord
being old also?"

13 And the LORD said to Abraham, "Why did
Sarah laugh, saying, 'Shall I surely bear *a child,*
since I am old?' 14 [a]Is anything too hard for the
LORD? [b]At the appointed time I will return to
you, according to the time of life, and Sarah
shall have a son."

15 But Sarah denied *it,* saying, "I did not
laugh," for she was afraid.

And He said, "No, but you did laugh!"

### ABRAHAM INTERCEDES FOR SODOM

16 Then the men rose from there and looked
toward Sodom, and Abraham went with them
[a]to send them on the way. 17 And the LORD said,
[a]"Shall I hide from Abraham what I am doing,
18 since Abraham shall surely become a great and
mighty nation, and all the nations of the earth
shall be [a]blessed in him? 19 For I have known him,
in order [a]that he may command his children and
his household after him, that they keep the way
of the LORD, to do righteousness and justice, that
the LORD may bring to Abraham what He has
spoken to him." 20 And the LORD said, "Because
[a]the outcry against Sodom and Gomorrah is
great, and because their [b]sin is very grave, 21 [a]I
will go down now and see whether they have
done altogether according to the outcry against
it that has come to Me; and if not, [b]I will know."

22 Then the men turned away from there
[a]and went toward Sodom, but Abraham still
stood before the LORD. 23 And Abraham [a]came
near and said, [b]"Would You also [c]destroy the
[d]righteous with the wicked? 24 Suppose there
were fifty righteous within the city; would You
also destroy the place and not spare *it* for the fif-
ty righteous that were in it? 25 Far be it from You
to do such a thing as this, to slay the righteous
with the wicked, so [a]that the righteous should
be as the wicked; far be it from You! [b]Shall not
the Judge of all the earth do right?"

26 So the LORD said, [a]"If I find in Sodom fifty
righteous within the city, then I will spare all the
place for their sakes."

27 Then Abraham answered and said, "In-
deed now, I who *am* [a]*but* dust and ashes have
taken it upon myself to speak to the Lord: 28 Sup-
pose there were five less than the fifty righteous;
would You destroy all of the city for *lack of* five?"

So He said, "If I find there forty-five, I will
not destroy *it.*"

29 And he spoke to Him yet again and said,
"Suppose there should be forty found there?"

So He said, "I will not do *it* for the sake of
forty."

30 Then he said, "Let not the Lord be angry,
and I will speak: Suppose thirty should be found
there?"

So He said, "I will not do *it* if I find thirty there."

31 And he said, "Indeed now, I have taken
it upon myself to speak to the Lord: Suppose
twenty should be found there?"

So He said, "I will not destroy *it* for the sake
of twenty."

32 Then he said, [a]"Let not the Lord be angry,
and I will speak but once more: Suppose ten
should be found there?"

[b]And He said, "I will not destroy *it* for the
sake of ten." 33 So the LORD went His way as soon
as He had finished speaking with Abraham; and
Abraham returned to his place.

### SODOM'S DEPRAVITY

19 Now [a]the two angels came to Sodom in
the evening, and [b]Lot was sitting in the
gate of Sodom. When Lot saw *them,* he rose to
meet them, and he bowed himself with his face
toward the ground. 2 And he said, "Here now, my
lords, please [a]turn in to your servant's house and
spend the night, and [b]wash your feet; then you
may rise early and go on your way."

And they said, [c]"No, but we will spend the
night in the open square."

3 But he insisted strongly; so they turned in to
him and entered his house. [a]Then he made them a
feast, and baked [b]unleavened bread, and they ate.
4 Now before they lay down, the men of the
city, the men of Sodom, both old and young, all the
people from every quarter, surrounded the house.
5 [a]And they called to Lot and said to him, "Where
are the men who came to you tonight? [b]Bring
them out to us that we [c]may know them *carnally.*"
6 So [a]Lot went out to them through the
doorway, shut the door behind him, 7 and said,
"Please, my brethren, do not do so wickedly!
8 [a]See now, I have two daughters who have not
known a man; please, let me bring them out to
you, and you may do to them as you wish; only
do nothing to these men, [b]since this is the reason
they have come under the shadow of my roof."
9 And they said, "Stand back!" Then they said,
"This one [a]came in to stay *here,* [b]and he keeps
acting as a judge; now we will deal worse with you
than with them." So they pressed hard against
the man Lot, and came near to break down the
door. 10 But the men reached out their hands
and pulled Lot into the house with them, and

**18:11** [a] Gen. 17:17 [b] Gen. 31:35 [1] Literally *the manner of women had ceased to be with Sarah* **18:12** [a] Gen. 17:17 [b] Luke 1:18 [c] 1 Pet. 3:6 **18:14** [a] Jer. 32:17 [b] Gen. 17:21; 18:10 **18:16** [a] Rom. 15:24 **18:17** [a] Ps. 25:14 **18:18** [a] [Acts 3:25, 26] **18:19** [a] [Deut. 4:9, 10; 6:6, 7] **18:20** [a] Gen. 4:10; 19:13 [b] Gen. 13:13 **18:21** [a] Gen. 11:5 [b] Deut. 8:2; 13:3 **18:22** [a] Gen. 18:16; 19:1 **18:23** [a] [Heb. 10:22] [b] Num. 16:22 [c] Job 9:22 [d] Gen. 20:4 **18:25** [a] Is. 3:10, 11 [b] Deut. 1:16, 17; 32:4 **18:26** [a] Jer. 5:1 **18:27** [a] [Gen. 3:19] **18:32** [a] Judg. 6:39 [b] James 5:16 **19:1** [a] Gen. 18:2, 16, 22 [b] Gen. 18:1–5 **19:2** [a] Gen. 24:31; [Heb. 13:2] [b] Gen. 18:4; 24:32 [c] Luke 24:28 **19:3** [a] Gen. 18:6–8; Ex. 23:15; Num. 9:11; 28:17 [b] Ex. 12:8 **19:5** [a] Is. 3:9 [b] Judg. 19:22 [c] Gen. 4:1; Rom. 1:24, 27; Jude 7 **19:6** [a] Judg. 19:23 **19:8** [a] Judg. 19:24 [b] Gen. 18:5 **19:9** [a] 2 Pet. 2:7, 8 [b] Ex. 2:14

shut the door. 11 And they [a]struck the men who
*were* at the doorway of the house with blindness,
both small and great, so that they became weary
*trying* to find the door.

### SODOM AND GOMORRAH DESTROYED

*(Matt. 11:23, 24; Luke 17:28–32)*

12 Then the men said to Lot, "Have you
anyone else here? Son-in-law, your sons, your
daughters, and whomever you have in the
city—[a]take *them* out of this place! 13 For we will
destroy this place, because the [a]outcry against
them has grown great before the face of the
LORD, and [b]the LORD has sent us to destroy it."
14 So Lot went out and spoke to his sons-in-
law, [a]who had married his daughters, and said,
[b]"Get up, get out of this place; for the LORD will
destroy this city!" [c]But to his sons-in-law he
seemed to be joking.
15 When the morning dawned, the angels
urged Lot to hurry, saying, [a]"Arise, take your wife
and your two daughters who are here, lest you be
consumed in the punishment of the city." 16 And
while he lingered, the men [a]took hold of his hand,
his wife's hand, and the hands of his two daugh-
ters, the [b]LORD being merciful to him, [c]and they
brought him out and set him outside the city. 17 So
it came to pass, when they had brought them out-
side, that he[1] said, [a]"Escape for your life! [b]Do not
look behind you nor stay anywhere in the plain.
Escape [c]to the mountains, lest you be destroyed."
18 Then Lot said to them, "Please, [a]no, my
lords! 19 Indeed now, your servant has found
favor in your sight, and you have increased your
mercy which you have shown me by saving my
life; but I cannot escape to the mountains, lest
some evil overtake me and I die. 20 See now, this
city *is* near *enough* to flee to, and it *is* a little one;
please let me escape there (*is* it not a little one?)
and my soul shall live."
21 And he said to him, "See, [a]I have favored
you concerning this thing also, in that I will not
overthrow this city for which you have spoken.
22 Hurry, escape there. For [a]I cannot do anything
until you arrive there."
Therefore [b]the name of the city was called Zoar.
23 The sun had risen upon the earth when
Lot entered Zoar. 24 Then the LORD rained [a]brim-
stone and [b]fire on Sodom and Gomorrah, from
the LORD out of the heavens. 25 So He overthrew
those cities, all the plain, all the inhabitants of
the cities, and [a]what grew on the ground.
26 But his wife looked back behind him, and
she became [a]a pillar of salt.
27 And Abraham went early in the morning to
the place where [a]he had stood before the LORD.

> **19:26** Numerous rock **salt** formations, including pillars about the size of a human, are near the Dead Sea, which is believed to cover the site of Sodom and Gomorrah now. Jesus referred to the fate of Lot's wife as a historical fact (Luke 17:32).

28 Then he looked toward Sodom and Gomor-
rah, and toward all the land of the plain; and he
saw, and behold, [a]the smoke of the land which
went up like the smoke of a furnace. 29 And it
came to pass, when God destroyed the cities of
the plain, that God [a]remembered Abraham, and
sent Lot out of the midst of the overthrow, when
He overthrew the cities in which Lot had dwelt.

### THE DESCENDANTS OF LOT

30 Then Lot went up out of Zoar and [a]dwelt
in the mountains, and his two daughters were
with him; for he was afraid to dwell in Zoar. And
he and his two daughters dwelt in a cave. 31 Now
the firstborn said to the younger, "Our father *is*
old, and *there is* no man on the earth [a]to come
in to us as is the custom of all the earth. 32 Come,
let us make our father drink wine, and we will
lie with him, that we [a]may preserve the lineage
of our father." 33 So they made their father drink
wine that night. And the firstborn went in and
lay with her father, and he did not know when
she lay down or when she arose.
34 It happened on the next day that the first-
born said to the younger, "Indeed I lay with my fa-
ther last night; let us make him drink wine tonight
also, and you go in *and* lie with him, that we may
preserve the lineage of our father." 35 Then they
made their father drink wine that night also. And
the younger arose and lay with him, and he did
not know when she lay down or when she arose.
36 Thus both the daughters of Lot were with
child by their father. 37 The firstborn bore a son
and called his name Moab; [a]he *is* the father of the
Moabites to this day. 38 And the younger, she also
bore a son and called his name Ben-Ammi; [a]he
*is* the father of the people of Ammon to this day.

### ABRAHAM AND ABIMELECH

20 And Abraham journeyed from [a]there to
the South, and dwelt between [b]Kadesh
and Shur, and [c]stayed in Gerar. 2 Now Abraham
said of Sarah his wife, [a]"She *is* my sister." And
Abimelech king of Gerar sent and [b]took Sarah.
3 But [a]God came to Abimelech [b]in a dream
by night, and said to him, [c]"Indeed you *are* a

**19:11** [a] Gen. 20:17 **19:12** [a] Gen. 7:1; 2 Pet. 2:7, 9 **19:13** [a] Gen. 18:20 [b] Lev. 26:30–33; Deut. 4:26; 28:45; 1 Chr. 21:15 **19:14** [a] Matt. 1:18 [b] Num. 16:21, 24, 26, 45; Rev. 18:4 [c] Ex. 9:21; Jer. 43:1, 2; Luke 17:28; 24:11 **19:15** [a] Ps. 37:2; Rev. 18:4 **19:16** [a] Deut. 5:15; 6:21; 7:8; 2 Pet. 2:7 [b] Ex. 34:7; Ps. 32:10; 33:18, 19; Luke 18:13 [c] Ps. 34:22 **19:17** [a] 1 Kin. 19:3; Jer. 48:6 [b] Gen. 19:26; Matt. 24:16–18; Luke 9:62; Phil. 3:13, 14 [c] Gen. 14:10 [1] Septuagint, Syriac, and Vulgate read *they*. **19:18** [a] Acts 10:14 **19:21** [a] Job 42:8, 9; Ps. 145:19 **19:22** [a] Ex. 32:10; Deut. 9:14 [b] Gen. 13:10; 14:2 **19:24** [a] Deut. 29:23 [b] Lev. 10:2 **19:25** [a] Ps. 107:34 **19:26** [a] Luke 17:32 **19:27** [a] Gen. 18:22 **19:28** [a] Rev. 9:2; 18:9 **19:29** [a] Gen. 8:1; 18:23 **19:30** [a] Gen. 19:17, 19 **19:31** [a] Gen. 16:2, 4; 38:8, 9 **19:32** [a] [Mark 12:19] **19:37** [a] Deut. 2:9 **19:38** [a] Deut. 2:19 **20:1** [a] Gen. 18:1 [b] Gen. 12:9; 16:7, 14 [c] Gen. 26:1, 6 **20:2** [a] Gen. 12:11–13; 26:7 [b] Gen. 12:15 **20:3** [a] Ps. 105:14 [b] Job 33:15 [c] Gen. 20:7

dead man because of the woman whom you
have taken, for she *is* a man's wife."
4 But Abimelech had not come near her; and
he said, "Lord, [a]will You slay a righteous nation
also? 5 Did he not say to me, 'She *is* my sister'?
And she, even she herself said, 'He *is* my brother.'
[a]In the integrity of my heart and innocence of
my hands I have done this."
6 And God said to him in a dream, "Yes, I
know that you did this in the integrity of your
heart. For [a]I also withheld you from sinning
[b]against Me; therefore I did not let you touch
her. 7 Now therefore, restore the man's wife; [a]for
he *is* a prophet, and he will pray for you and you
shall live. But if you do not restore *her,* [b]know that
you shall surely die, you [c]and all who *are* yours."
8 So Abimelech rose early in the morning,
called all his servants, and told all these things
in their hearing; and the men were very much
afraid. 9 And Abimelech called Abraham and
said to him, "What have you done to us? How
have I offended you, [a]that you have brought on
me and on my kingdom a great sin? You have
done deeds to me [b]that ought not to be done."
10 Then Abimelech said to Abraham, "What did
you have in view, that you have done this thing?"
11 And Abraham said, "Because I thought,
surely [a]the fear of God *is* not in this place; and
[b]they will kill me on account of my wife. 12 But
indeed [a]*she is* truly my sister. She *is* the daughter
of my father, but not the daughter of my mother;
and she became my wife. 13 And it came to pass,
when [a]God caused me to wander from my father's
house, that I said to her, 'This *is* your kindness
that you should do for me: in every place, wher-
ever we go, [b]say of me, "He *is* my brother." ' "
14 Then Abimelech [a]took sheep, oxen, and male
and female servants, and gave *them* to Abraham;
and he restored Sarah his wife to him. 15 And Abim-
elech said, "See, [a]my land *is* before you; dwell where
it pleases you." 16 Then to Sarah he said, "Behold, I
have given your brother a thousand *pieces* of silver;
[a]indeed this vindicates you[1] [b]before all who *are* with
you and before everybody." Thus she was rebuked.
17 So Abraham [a]prayed to God; and God
[b]healed Abimelech, his wife, and his female
servants. Then they bore *children;* 18 for the LORD
[a]had closed up all the wombs of the house of
Abimelech because of Sarah, Abraham's wife.

### ISAAC IS BORN
*(Heb. 11:11)*

**21** And the LORD [a]visited Sarah as He had
said, and the LORD did for Sarah [b]as He had
spoken. 2 For Sarah [a]conceived and bore Abraham
a son in his old age, [b]at the set time of which God
had spoken to him. 3 And Abraham called the
name of his son who was born to him—whom
Sarah bore to him—[a]Isaac. 4 Then Abraham [a]cir-
cumcised his son Isaac when he was eight days
old, [b]as God had commanded him. 5 Now [a]Abra-
ham was one hundred years old when his son
Isaac was born to him. 6 And Sarah said, [a]"God
has made me laugh, *and* all who hear [b]will laugh
with me." 7 She also said, "Who would have said to
Abraham that Sarah would nurse children? [a]For
I have borne *him* a son in his old age."

### HAGAR AND ISHMAEL DEPART
*(Gal. 4:21–30)*

8 So the child grew and was weaned. And
Abraham made a great feast on the same day
that Isaac was weaned.
9 And Sarah saw the son of Hagar [a]the Egyp-
tian, whom she had borne to Abraham, [b]scoffing.
10 Therefore she said to Abraham, [a]"Cast out this
bondwoman and her son; for the son of this bond-
woman shall not be heir with my son, *namely* with
Isaac." 11 And the matter was very displeasing in
Abraham's sight [a]because of his son.
12 But God said to Abraham, "Do not let it be
displeasing in your sight because of the lad or
because of your bondwoman. Whatever Sarah
has said to you, listen to her voice; for [a]in Isaac
your seed shall be called. 13 Yet I will also make
[a]a nation of the son of the bondwoman, because
he *is* your seed."

> **SEEING JESUS IN THE SCRIPTURE**
>
> **21:12** The promised birth of Isaac points to something far greater than Abraham's physical offspring; the lineage of Jesus can be traced through Isaac. In Jesus, even those not of Jewish descent can be part of God's family (see Rom. 9:7–8).

14 So Abraham rose early in the morning, and
took bread and a skin of water; and putting *it* on
her shoulder, he gave *it* and the boy to Hagar, and
[a]sent her away. Then she departed and wandered
in the Wilderness of Beersheba. 15 And the water
in the skin was used up, and she placed the boy
under one of the shrubs. 16 Then she went and
sat down across from *him* at a distance of about
a bowshot; for she said to herself, "Let me not
see the death of the boy." So she sat opposite
*him,* and lifted her voice and wept.
17 And [a]God heard the voice of the lad. Then
the [b]angel of God called to Hagar out of heaven,

**20:4** [a] Gen. 18:23–25 **20:5** [a] 2 Kin. 20:3 **20:6** [a] 1 Sam. 25:26, 34 [b] Gen. 39:9 **20:7** [a] 1 Sam. 7:5 [b] Gen. 2:17 [c] Num. 16:32, 33 **20:9** [a] Gen. 26:10; 39:9 [b] Gen. 34:7 **20:11** [a] Prov. 16:6 [b] Gen. 12:12; 26:7 **20:12** [a] Gen. 11:29 **20:13** [a] Gen. 12:1–9, 11 [b] Gen. 12:13; 20:5 **20:14** [a] Gen. 12:16 **20:15** [a] Gen. 13:9; 34:10; 47:6 **20:16** [a] Gen. 26:11 [b] Mal. 2:9 [1] Literally *it is a covering of the eyes for you* **20:17** [a] Job 42:9 [b] Gen. 21:2 **20:18** [a] Gen. 12:17 **21:1** [a] 1 Sam. 2:21 [b] [Gal. 4:23, 28] **21:2** [a] Heb. 11:11, 12 [b] Gen. 17:21; 18:10, 14 **21:3** [a] Gen. 17:19, 21 **21:4** [a] Acts 7:8 [b] Gen. 17:10, 12 **21:5** [a] Gen. 17:1, 17 **21:6** [a] Is. 54:1 [b] Luke 1:58 **21:7** [a] Gen. 18:11, 12 **21:9** [a] Gen. 16:1, 4, 15 [b] [Gal. 4:29] **21:10** [a] Gal. 3:18; 4:30 **21:11** [a] Gen. 17:18 **21:12** [a] [Rom. 9:7, 8] **21:13** [a] Gen. 16:10; 17:20; 21:18; 25:12–18 **21:14** [a] John 8:35 **21:17** [a] Ex. 3:7 [b] Gen. 22:11

and said to her, "What ails you, Hagar? Fear not,
for God has heard the voice of the lad where
he *is*. 18 Arise, lift up the lad and hold him with
your hand, for [a]I will make him a great nation."
19 Then [a]God opened her eyes, and she saw
a well of water. And she went and filled the skin
with water, and gave the lad a drink. 20 So God
[a]was with the lad; and he grew and dwelt in the
wilderness, [b]and became an archer. 21 He dwelt
in the Wilderness of Paran; and his mother [a]took
a wife for him from the land of Egypt.

### A COVENANT WITH ABIMELECH

22 And it came to pass at that time that
[a]Abimelech and Phichol, the commander of his
army, spoke to Abraham, saying, [b]"God *is* with
you in all that you do. 23 Now therefore, [a]swear
to me by God that you will not deal falsely with
me, with my offspring, or with my posterity;
but that according to the kindness that I have
done to you, you will do to me and to the land
in which you have dwelt."
24 And Abraham said, "I will swear."
25 Then Abraham rebuked Abimelech be-
cause of a well of water which Abimelech's ser-
vants [a]had seized. 26 And Abimelech said, "I do
not know who has done this thing; you did not
tell me, nor had I heard *of it* until today." 27 So
Abraham took sheep and oxen and gave them
to Abimelech, and the two of them [a]made a cov-
enant. 28 And Abraham set seven ewe lambs of
the flock by themselves.
29 Then Abimelech asked Abraham, [a]"What
*is the meaning of* these seven ewe lambs which
you have set by themselves?"
30 And he said, "You will take *these* seven
ewe lambs from my hand, that [a]they may be my
witness that I have dug this well." 31 Therefore he
[a]called that place Beersheba,[1] because the two
of them swore an oath there.
32 Thus they made a covenant at Beersheba.
So Abimelech rose with Phichol, the commander
of his army, and they returned to the land of the
Philistines. 33 Then *Abraham* planted a tamarisk
tree in Beersheba, and [a]there called on the name
of the LORD, [b]the Everlasting God. 34 And Abraham
stayed in the land of the Philistines many days.

### ABRAHAM'S FAITH CONFIRMED

*(Heb. 11:17–19)*

22 Now it came to pass after these things
that [a]God tested Abraham, and said to
him, "Abraham!"
And he said, "Here I am."
2 Then He said, "Take now your son, [a]your
only *son* Isaac, whom you [b]love, and go [c]to the
land of Moriah, and offer him there as a [d]burnt
offering on one of the mountains of which I
shall tell you."
3 So Abraham rose early in the morning and
saddled his donkey, and took two of his young
men with him, and Isaac his son; and he split
the wood for the burnt offering, and arose and
went to the place of which God had told him.
4 Then on the third day Abraham lifted his eyes
and saw the place afar off. 5 And Abraham said
to his young men, "Stay here with the donkey;
the lad[1] and I will go yonder and worship, and
we will [a]come back to you."
6 So Abraham took the wood of the burnt
offering and [a]laid *it* on Isaac his son; and he
took the fire in his hand, and a knife, and the
two of them went together. 7 But Isaac spoke to
Abraham his father and said, "My father!"
And he said, "Here I am, my son."
Then he said, "Look, the fire and the wood,
but where *is* the lamb for a burnt offering?"
8 And Abraham said, "My son, God will pro-
vide for Himself the [a]lamb for a [b]burnt offering."
So the two of them went together.
9 Then they came to the place of which God
had told him. And Abraham built an altar there
and placed the wood in order; and he bound
Isaac his son and [a]laid him on the altar, upon
the wood. 10 And Abraham stretched out his hand
and took the knife to slay his son.
11 But the [a]Angel of the LORD called to him
from heaven and said, "Abraham, Abraham!"
So he said, "Here I am."
12 And He said, [a]"Do not lay your hand on
the lad, or do anything to him; for [b]now I know
that you fear God, since you have not [c]withheld
your son, your only *son,* from Me."
13 Then Abraham lifted his eyes and looked,
and there behind *him was* a ram caught in a
thicket by its horns. So Abraham went and took
the ram, and offered it up for a burnt offering
instead of his son. 14 And Abraham called the
name of the place, The-LORD-Will-Provide;[1] as
it is said *to* this day, "In the Mount of the LORD
it shall be provided."
15 Then the Angel of the LORD called to Abra-
ham a second time out of heaven, 16 and said:
[a]"By Myself I have sworn, says the LORD, be-
cause you have done this thing, and have not
withheld your son, your only *son*— 17 blessing I
will [a]bless you, and multiplying I will multiply
your descendants [b]as the stars of the heaven
[c]and as the sand which *is* on the seashore; and
[d]your descendants shall possess the gate of
their enemies. 18 [a]In your seed all the nations
of the earth shall be blessed, [b]because you have

**21:18** [a] Gen. 16:10; 21:13; 25:12–16 **21:19** [a] Num. 22:31 **21:20** [a] Gen. 28:15; 39:2, 3, 21 [b] Gen. 16:12 **21:21** [a] Gen. 24:4 **21:22** [a] Gen. 20:2, 14; 26:26 [b] Gen. 26:28 **21:23** [a] Josh. 2:12 **21:25** [a] Gen. 26:15, 18, 20–22 **21:27** [a] Gen. 26:31; 31:44 **21:29** [a] Gen. 33:8 **21:30** [a] Gen. 31:48, 52 **21:31** [a] Gen. 21:14; 26:33 [1] Literally *Well of the Oath* or *Well of the Seven* **21:33** [a] Gen. 4:26; 12:8; 13:4; 26:25 [b] Deut. 32:40; 33:27 **22:1** [a] Heb. 11:17 **22:2** [a] Gen. 22:12, 16 [b] John 5:20 [c] 2 Chr. 3:1 [d] Gen. 8:20; 31:54 **22:5** [a] [Heb. 11:19] [1] Or *young man* **22:6** [a] John 19:17 **22:8** [a] John 1:29, 36 [b] Ex. 12:3–6 **22:9** [a] [Heb. 11:17–19] **22:11** [a] Gen. 16:7–11; 21:17, 18; 31:11 **22:12** [a] 1 Sam. 15:22 [b] James 2:21, 22 [c] Gen. 22:2, 16 **22:14** [1] Hebrew *YHWH Yireh* **22:16** [a] Ps. 105:9 **22:17** [a] Gen. 17:16; 26:3, 24 [b] Gen. 15:5; 26:4 [c] Gen. 13:16; 32:12 [d] Gen. 24:60 **22:18** [a] Gen. 12:3; 18:18; 26:4 [b] Gen. 18:19; 22:3, 10; 26:5

GENESIS 22:1–19

## THE TEST

STORY OF SCRIPTURE 5

### WHAT'S GOING ON?

God commanding Abraham to sacrifice Isaac as a burnt offering was a significant test of love and faith for Abraham. Imagine how heartbreaking this must have been. Isaac was the son Abraham waited years for and the symbol of God's favor. More than that, Isaac was the future of the nation God had promised. Nevertheless, Abraham obeyed God and took Isaac to Moriah. Isaac carried the wood up the mountain, and Abraham lifted the blade to do the unthinkable. Right before Abraham drove the blade down, an angel stopped him and provided a replacement sacrifice—a ram caught in the thicket.

### WHAT DOES THIS MEAN FOR ME?

Being commanded by God to sacrifice his son must have been confusing for Abraham. Despite Abraham's feelings, he obeyed. The same was true for Isaac, who willingly let his father set him on the altar and bind him. Both Abraham and Isaac displayed faith and obedience despite their confusion. They may not have grasped God's plans, but they were clear on God's faithfulness. That was enough. We all face frustrations, doubts, and confusion. Ultimately, trusting in God's *character* will help us when we're unsure about his *commands*.

### DID YOU CATCH THE PATTERN?

Although Jesus isn't mentioned by name in the Old Testament, shadows of His life, death, and resurrection run throughout it, including two here. First, Isaac obeyed his father by carrying wood up a mountain, ready to be sacrificed. Jesus, in obedience to His heavenly Father, carried a wooden cross up a hill to be sacrificed. Second, the ram caught in the thicket died in Isaac's place. Jesus died in our place. He is the sacrificial lamb slain on behalf of humanity. Pay close attention to references to lambs and sheep throughout the Bible.

*For the next* Story of Scripture *reading and devotion, turn to Genesis 32:22–32 on page 39.*

### SEEING JESUS IN THE SCRIPTURE

**22:18** Centuries after this, Paul affirmed God's promise to bless the nations through Abraham's seed was realized through the coming of the Messiah, Jesus (see Gal. 3:8). The gospel began not in the advent of Jesus, but in the promise of Jesus.

obeyed My voice." 19 So Abraham returned to his
young men, and they rose and went together to
[a]Beersheba; and Abraham dwelt at Beersheba.

### *THE FAMILY OF NAHOR*

20 Now it came to pass after these things that
it was told Abraham, saying, "Indeed [a]Milcah
also has borne children to your brother Nahor:
21 [a]Huz his firstborn, Buz his brother, Kemuel
the father [b]of Aram, 22 Chesed, Hazo, Pildash,
Jidlaph, and Bethuel." 23 And [a]Bethuel begot
Rebekah.[1] These eight Milcah bore to Nahor,
Abraham's brother. 24 His concubine, whose
name was Reumah, also bore Tebah, Gaham,
Thahash, and Maachah.

### *SARAH'S DEATH AND BURIAL*

23 Sarah lived one hundred and twenty-
seven years; *these were* the years of the life
of Sarah. 2 So Sarah died in [a]Kirjath Arba (that *is,*
[b]Hebron) in the land of Canaan, and Abraham
came to mourn for Sarah and to weep for her.
3 Then Abraham stood up from before his
dead, and spoke to the sons of [a]Heth, saying, 4 [a]"I
*am* a foreigner and a visitor among you. [b]Give
me property for a burial place among you, that
I may bury my dead out of my sight."
5 And the sons of Heth answered Abraham,
saying to him, 6 "Hear us, my lord: You *are* [a]a
mighty prince among us; bury your dead in the
choicest of our burial places. None of us will
withhold from you his burial place, that you
may bury your dead."
7 Then Abraham stood up and bowed himself
to the people of the land, the sons of Heth. 8 And

**22:19** [a] Gen. 21:31 **22:20** [a] Gen. 11:29; 24:15 **22:21** [a] Job 1:1 [b] Job 32:2 **22:23** [a] Gen. 24:15 [1] Spelled *Rebecca* in Romans 9:10
**23:2** [a] Josh. 14:15; 15:13; 21:11 [b] Gen. 13:18; 23:19 **23:3** [a] Gen. 10:15; 15:20 **23:4** [a] [Gen. 17:8] [b] Acts 7:5, 16 **23:6** [a] Gen. 13:2; 14:14; 24:35

he spoke with them, saying, "If it is your wish
that I bury my dead out of my sight, hear me,
and meet with Ephron the son of Zohar for me,
9 that he may give me the cave of [a]Machpelah
which he has, which *is* at the end of his field. Let
him give it to me at the full price, as property
for a burial place among you."
10 Now Ephron dwelt among the sons of
Heth; and Ephron the Hittite answered Abra-
ham in the presence of the sons of Heth, all who
[a]entered at the gate of his city, saying, 11 [a]"No,
my lord, hear me: I give you the field and the
cave that *is* in it; I give it to you in the presence
of the sons of my people. I give it to you. Bury
your dead!"
12 Then Abraham bowed himself down be-
fore the people of the land; 13 and he spoke to
Ephron in the hearing of the people of the land,
saying, "If you *will give it,* please hear me. I will
give you money for the field; take *it* from me
and I will bury my dead there."
14 And Ephron answered Abraham, saying to
him, 15 "My lord, listen to me; the land *is worth* four
hundred [a]shekels of silver. What *is* that between
you and me? So bury your dead." 16 And Abraham
listened to Ephron; and Abraham [a]weighed out
the silver for Ephron which he had named in the
hearing of the sons of Heth, four hundred shekels
of silver, currency of the merchants.
17 So [a]the field of Ephron which *was* in Mach-
pelah, which *was* before Mamre, the field and
the cave which *was* in it, and all the trees that
*were* in the field, which *were* within all the sur-
rounding borders, were deeded 18 to Abraham
as a possession in the presence of the sons of
Heth, before all who went in at the gate of his city.
19 And after this, Abraham buried Sarah
his wife in the cave of the field of Machpelah,
before Mamre (that *is,* Hebron) in the land of
Canaan. 20 So the field and the cave that *is* in it
[a]were deeded to Abraham by the sons of Heth
as property for a burial place.

### *A BRIDE FOR ISAAC*

24 Now Abraham [a]was old, well advanced in
age; and the LORD [b]had blessed Abraham
in all things. 2 So Abraham said [a]to the oldest
servant of his house, who [b]ruled over all that
he had, "Please, [c]put your hand under my thigh,
3 and I will make you [a]swear by the LORD, the God
of heaven and the God of the earth, that [b]you will
not take a wife for my son from the daughters
of the Canaanites, among whom I dwell; 4 [a]but
you shall go [b]to my country and to my family,
and take a wife for my son Isaac."

> **24:4** The **family** unit included everyone from grandparents to multiple wives, from widowed daughters to servants. God used the family structure to spread His message from generation to generation. Abraham wanted Isaac's wife to come from among his family to keep his family unified.

5 And the servant said to him, "Perhaps the
woman will not be willing to follow me to this
land. Must I take your son back to the land from
which you came?"
6 But Abraham said to him, "Beware that you
do not take my son back there. 7 The LORD God of
heaven, who [a]took me from my father's house and
from the land of my family, and who spoke to me
and swore to me, saying, [b]'To your descendants[1] I
give this land,' [c]He will send His angel before you,
and you shall take a wife for my son from there.
8 And if the woman is not willing to follow you,
then [a]you will be released from this oath; only do
not take my son back there." 9 So the servant put
his hand under the thigh of Abraham his master,
and swore to him concerning this matter.
10 Then the servant took ten of his master's
camels and departed, [a]for all his master's goods
*were in* his hand. And he arose and went to Mes-
opotamia, to [b]the city of Nahor. 11 And he made
his camels kneel down outside the city by a well
of water at evening time, the time [a]when women
go out to draw *water.* 12 Then he [a]said, "O LORD
God of my master Abraham, please [b]give me
success this day, and show kindness to my mas-
ter Abraham. 13 Behold, *here* [a]I stand by the well
of water, and [b]the daughters of the men of the
city are coming out to draw water. 14 Now let it
be that the young woman to whom I say, 'Please
let down your pitcher that I may drink,' and she
says, 'Drink, and I will also give your camels a
drink'—*let* her *be the one* You have appointed
for Your servant Isaac. And [a]by this I will know
that You have shown kindness to my master."
15 And it happened, [a]before he had finished
speaking, that behold, [b]Rebekah, who was born
to Bethuel, son of [c]Milcah, the wife of Nahor,
Abraham's brother, came out with her pitcher
on her shoulder. 16 Now the young woman [a]*was*
very beautiful to behold, a virgin; no man had
known her. And she went down to the well, filled
her pitcher, and came up. 17 And the servant ran
to meet her and said, "Please let me drink a little
water from your pitcher."

**23:9** [a] Gen. 25:9 **23:10** [a] Gen. 23:18; 34:20, 24; Ruth 4:1, 4, 11 **23:11** [a] 2 Sam. 24:21–24 **23:15** [a] Ex. 30:13; Ezek. 45:12 **23:16** [a] 2 Sam. 14:26; Jer. 32:9, 10; Zech. 11:12 **23:17** [a] Gen. 25:9; 49:29–32; 50:13; Acts 7:16 **23:20** [a] Jer. 32:10, 11 **24:1** [a] Gen. 18:11; 21:5 [b] Gen. 12:2; 13:2; 24:35; Ps. 112:3; Prov. 10:22; [Gal. 3:9] **24:2** [a] Gen. 15:2 [b] Gen. 24:10; 39:4–6 [c] Gen. 47:29; 1 Chr. 29:24 **24:3** [a] Gen. 14:19, 22 [b] Gen. 26:35; 28:2; Ex. 34:16; Deut. 7:3; 2 Cor. 6:14–17 **24:4** [a] Gen. 28:2 [b] Gen. 12:1; Heb. 11:15 **24:7** [a] Gen. 12:1; 24:3 [b] Gen. 12:7; 13:15; 15:18; 17:8; Ex. 32:13; Deut. 1:8; 34:4; Acts 7:5 [c] Gen. 16:7; 21:17; 22:11; Ex. 23:20, 23; 33:2; Heb. 1:4, 14 [1] Literally *seed* **24:8** [a] Josh. 2:17–20 **24:10** [a] Gen. 24:2, 22 [b] Gen. 11:31, 32; 22:20; 27:43; 29:5 **24:11** [a] Ex. 2:16; 1 Sam. 9:11 **24:12** [a] Gen. 24:27, 42, 48; 26:24; 32:9; Ex. 3:6, 15 [b] Gen. 27:20; Neh. 1:11; Ps. 37:5 **24:13** [a] Gen. 24:43 [b] Ex. 2:16 **24:14** [a] Judg. 6:17, 37; 1 Sam. 14:10; 16:7; 20:7; 2 Kin. 20:9; Prov. 16:33; Acts 1:26 **24:15** [a] Is. 65:24 [b] Gen. 24:45; 25:20 [c] Gen. 22:20, 23 **24:16** [a] Gen. 12:11; 26:7; 29:17

18 [a]So she said, "Drink, my lord." Then she quickly let her pitcher down to her hand, and gave him a drink. 19 And when she had finished giving him a drink, she said, "I will draw *water* for your camels also, until they have finished drinking." 20 Then she quickly emptied her pitcher into the trough, ran back to the well to draw *water,* and drew for all his camels. 21 And the man, wondering at her, remained silent so as to know whether [a]the LORD had made his journey prosperous or not.

22 So it was, when the camels had finished drinking, that the man took a golden [a]nose ring weighing half a shekel, and two bracelets for her wrists weighing ten *shekels* of gold, 23 and said, "Whose daughter *are* you? Tell me, please, is there room *in* your father's house for us to lodge?"

24 So she said to him, [a]"I *am* the daughter of Bethuel, Milcah's son, whom she bore to Nahor." 25 Moreover she said to him, "We have both straw and feed enough, and room to lodge."

26 Then the man [a]bowed down his head and worshiped the LORD. 27 And he said, [a]"Blessed *be* the LORD God of my master Abraham, who has not forsaken [b]His mercy and His truth toward my master. As for me, being on the way, the LORD [c]led me to the house of my master's brethren." 28 So the young woman ran and told her mother's household these things.

29 Now Rebekah had a brother whose name *was* [a]Laban, and Laban ran out to the man by the well. 30 So it came to pass, when he saw the nose ring, and the bracelets on his sister's wrists, and when he heard the words of his sister Rebekah, saying, "Thus the man spoke to me," that he went to the man. And there he stood by the camels at the well. 31 And he said, "Come in, [a]O blessed of the LORD! Why do you stand outside? For I have prepared the house, and a place for the camels."

32 Then the man came to the house. And he unloaded the camels, and [a]provided straw and feed for the camels, and water to [b]wash his feet and the feet of the men who *were* with him. 33 *Food* was set before him to eat, but he said, [a]"I will not eat until I have told about my errand."

And he said, "Speak on."

34 So he said, "I *am* Abraham's servant. 35 The LORD [a]has blessed my master greatly, and he has become great; and He has given him flocks and herds, silver and gold, male and female servants, and camels and donkeys. 36 And Sarah my master's wife [a]bore a son to my master when she was old; and [b]to him he has given all that he has. 37 Now my master [a]made me swear, saying, 'You shall not take a wife for my son from the daughters of the Canaanites, in whose land I dwell; 38 [a]but you shall go to my father's house and to my family, and take a wife for my son.' 39 [a]And I said to my master, 'Perhaps the woman will not follow me.' 40 [a]But he said to me, 'The LORD, [b]before whom I walk, will send His angel with you and prosper your way; and you shall take a wife for my son from my family and from my father's house. 41 [a]You will be clear from this oath when you arrive among my family; for if they will not give *her* to you, then you will be released from my oath.'

42 "And this day I came to the well and said, [a]'O LORD God of my master Abraham, if You will now prosper the way in which I go, 43 [a]behold, I stand by the well of water; and it shall come to pass that when the virgin comes out to draw *water,* and I say to her, "Please give me a little water from your pitcher to drink," 44 and she says to me, "Drink, and I will draw for your camels also,"—*let* her *be* the woman whom the LORD has appointed for my master's son.'

45 [a]"But before I had finished [b]speaking in my heart, there was Rebekah, coming out with her pitcher on her shoulder; and she went down to the well and drew *water.* And I said to her, 'Please let me drink.' 46 And she made haste and let her pitcher down from her *shoulder,* and said, 'Drink, and I will give your camels a drink also.' So I drank, and she gave the camels a drink also. 47 Then I asked her, and said, 'Whose daughter *are* you?' And she said, 'The daughter of Bethuel, Nahor's son, whom Milcah bore to him.' So I put the nose ring on her nose and the bracelets on her wrists. 48 [a]And I bowed my head and worshiped the LORD, and blessed the LORD God of my master Abraham, who had led me in the way of truth to [b]take the daughter of my master's brother for his son. 49 Now if you will [a]deal kindly and truly with my master, tell me. And if not, tell me, that I may turn to the right hand or to the left."

50 Then Laban and Bethuel answered and said, [a]"The thing comes from the LORD; we cannot [b]speak to you either bad or good. 51 [a]Here *is* Rebekah before you; take *her* and go, and let her be your master's son's wife, as the LORD has spoken."

52 And it came to pass, when Abraham's servant heard their words, that [a]he worshiped the LORD, *bowing himself* to the earth. 53 Then the servant brought out [a]jewelry of silver, jewelry of gold, and clothing, and gave *them* to Rebekah. He also gave [b]precious things to her brother and to her mother.

54 And he and the men who *were* with him ate and drank and stayed all night. Then they arose in the morning, and he said, [a]"Send me away to my master."

**24:18** [a] Gen. 24:14, 46; [1 Pet. 3:8, 9] **24:21** [a] Gen. 24:12–14, 27, 52 **24:22** [a] Gen. 24:47; Ex. 32:2, 3; Is. 3:19–21 **24:24** [a] Gen. 22:23; 24:15 **24:26** [a] Gen. 24:48, 52; Ex. 4:31 **24:27** [a] Gen. 24:12, 42, 48; Ex. 18:10; Ruth 4:14; 1 Sam. 25:32, 39; 2 Sam. 18:28; Luke 1:68 [b] Gen. 32:10; Ps. 98:3 [c] Gen. 24:21, 48 **24:29** [a] Gen. 29:5, 13 **24:31** [a] Gen. 26:29; Judg. 17:2; Ruth 3:10; Ps. 115:15 **24:32** [a] Gen. 43:24; Judg. 19:21 [b] Gen. 19:2; John 13:5, 13–15 **24:33** [a] Job 23:12; John 4:34; Eph. 6:5–7 **24:35** [a] Gen. 13:2; 24:1 **24:36** [a] Gen. 21:1–7 [b] Gen. 21:10; 25:5 **24:37** [a] Gen. 24:2–4 **24:38** [a] Gen. 24:4 **24:39** [a] Gen. 24:5 **24:40** [a] Gen. 24:7 [b] Gen. 5:22, 24; 17:1; 1 Kin. 8:23 **24:41** [a] Gen. 24:8 **24:42** [a] Gen. 24:12 **24:43** [a] Gen. 24:13 **24:45** [a] Gen. 24:15 [b] 1 Sam. 1:13 **24:48** [a] Gen. 24:26, 52 [b] Gen. 22:23; 24:27; Ps. 32:8; 48:14; Is. 48:17 **24:49** [a] Gen. 47:29; Josh. 2:14 **24:50** [a] Ps. 118:23; Matt. 21:42; Mark 12:11 [b] Gen. 31:24, 29 **24:51** [a] Gen. 20:15 **24:52** [a] Gen. 24:26, 48 **24:53** [a] Gen. 24:10, 22; Ex. 3:22; 11:2; 12:35 [b] 2 Chr. 21:3; Ezra 1:6 **24:54** [a] Gen. 24:56, 59; 30:25

55 But her brother and her mother said, "Let
the young woman stay with us *a few* days, at
least ten; after that she may go."
56 And he said to them, "Do not hinder me,
since the LORD has prospered my way; send me
away so that I may go to my master."
57 So they said, "We will call the young
woman and ask her personally." 58 Then they
called Rebekah and said to her, "Will you go
with this man?"
And she said, "I will go."

> **24:57** Asking Rebekah's opinion about the marriage plans was an unusual courtesy. Marriages were generally arranged by young people's families. Few men, and even fewer women, were allowed to give their opinion, let alone make their own choice.

59 So they sent away Rebekah their sister [a]and
her nurse, and Abraham's servant and his men.
60 And they blessed Rebekah and said to her:

"Our sister, *may* you *become*
[a]*The mother of* thousands of ten thousands;
[b]And may your descendants possess
The gates of those who hate them."

61 Then Rebekah and her maids arose, and
they rode on the camels and followed the man.
So the servant took Rebekah and departed.
62 Now Isaac came from the way of [a]Beer
Lahai Roi, for he dwelt in the South. 63 And Isaac
went out [a]to meditate in the field in the evening;
and he lifted his eyes and looked, and there, the
camels *were* coming. 64 Then Rebekah lifted her
eyes, and when she saw Isaac [a]she dismounted
from her camel; 65 for she had said to the ser-
vant, "Who *is* this man walking in the field to
meet us?"
The servant said, "It *is* my master." So she
took a veil and covered herself.
66 And the servant told Isaac all the things
that he had done. 67 Then Isaac brought her into
his mother Sarah's tent; and he [a]took Rebekah
and she became his wife, and he loved her. So
Isaac [b]was comforted after his mother's *death.*

### *ABRAHAM AND KETURAH*
*(1 Chr. 1:32, 33)*

**25** Abraham again took a wife, and her name
*was* [a]Keturah. 2 And [a]she bore him Zim-
ran, Jokshan, Medan, Midian, Ishbak, and Shuah.
3 Jokshan begot Sheba and Dedan. And the sons
of Dedan were Asshurim, Letushim, and Leum-
mim. 4 And the sons of Midian *were* Ephah,
Epher, Hanoch, Abidah, and Eldaah. All these
*were* the children of Keturah.
5 And [a]Abraham gave all that he had to Isaac.
6 But Abraham gave gifts to the sons of the con-
cubines which Abraham had; and while he was
still living he [a]sent them eastward, away from
Isaac his son, to [b]the country of the east.

### *ABRAHAM'S DEATH AND BURIAL*

7 This *is* the sum of the years of Abraham's
life which he lived: one hundred and seventy-
five years. 8 Then Abraham breathed his last and
[a]died in a good old age, an old man and full *of
years,* and [b]was gathered to his people. 9 And
[a]his sons Isaac and Ishmael buried him in the
cave of [b]Machpelah, which *is* before Mamre, in
the field of Ephron the son of Zohar the Hittite,
10 [a]the field which Abraham purchased from
the sons of Heth. [b]There Abraham was buried,
and Sarah his wife. 11 And it came to pass, after
the death of Abraham, that God blessed his son
Isaac. And Isaac dwelt at [a]Beer Lahai Roi.

### *THE FAMILIES OF ISHMAEL AND ISAAC*
*(1 Chr. 1:29–31)*

12 Now this *is* the [a]genealogy of Ishmael,
Abraham's son, whom Hagar the Egyptian,
Sarah's maidservant, bore to Abraham. 13 And
[a]these *were* the names of the sons of Ishmael,
by their names, according to their generations:
The firstborn of Ishmael, Nebajoth; then Kedar,
Adbeel, Mibsam, 14 Mishma, Dumah, Massa,
15 Hadar,[1] Tema, Jetur, Naphish, and Kedemah.
16 These *were* the sons of Ishmael and these
*were* their names, by their towns and their set-
tlements, [a]twelve princes according to their
nations. 17 These *were* the years of the life of
Ishmael: one hundred and thirty-seven years;
and [a]he breathed his last and died, and was
gathered to his people. 18 [a](They dwelt from
Havilah as far as Shur, which *is* east of Egypt as
you go toward Assyria.) He died [b]in the presence
of all his brethren.
19 This *is* the [a]genealogy of Isaac, Abraham's
son. [b]Abraham begot Isaac. 20 Isaac was forty
years old when he took Rebekah as wife, [a]the
daughter of Bethuel the Syrian of Padan Aram,
[b]the sister of Laban the Syrian. 21 Now Isaac
pleaded with the LORD for his wife, because she
*was* barren; [a]and the LORD granted his plea, [b]and
Rebekah his wife conceived. 22 But the children
struggled together within her; and she said, "If
*all is* well, why *am I like* this?" [a]So she went to
inquire of the LORD.

**24:59** [a] Gen. 35:8 **24:60** [a] Gen. 17:16 [b] Gen. 22:17; 28:14 **24:62** [a] Gen. 16:14; 25:11 **24:63** [a] Josh. 1:8; Ps. 1:2; 77:12; 119:15, 27, 48; 143:5; 145:5 **24:64** [a] Josh. 15:18 **24:67** [a] Gen. 25:20; 29:20; Prov. 18:22 [b] Gen. 23:1, 2; 38:12 **25:1** [a] 1 Chr. 1:32, 33 **25:2** [a] 1 Chr. 1:32, 33 **25:5** [a] Gen. 24:35, 36 **25:6** [a] Gen. 21:14 [b] Judg. 6:3 **25:8** [a] Gen. 15:15; 47:8, 9 [b] Gen. 25:17; 35:29; 49:29, 33 **25:9** [a] Gen. 35:29; 50:13 [b] Gen. 23:9, 17; 49:30 **25:10** [a] Gen. 23:3–16 [b] Gen. 49:31 **25:11** [a] Gen. 16:14 **25:12** [a] Gen. 11:10, 27; 16:15 **25:13** [a] 1 Chr. 1:29–31 **25:15** [1] Masoretic Text reads *Hadad.* **25:16** [a] Gen. 17:20 **25:17** [a] Gen. 25:8; 49:33 **25:18** [a] 1 Sam. 15:7 [b] Gen. 16:12 **25:19** [a] Gen. 36:1, 9 [b] Matt. 1:2 **25:20** [a] Gen. 22:23; 24:15, 29, 67 [b] Gen. 24:29 **25:21** [a] 1 Chr. 5:20 [b] Rom. 9:10–13 **25:22** [a] 1 Sam. 1:15; 9:9; 10:22

23 And the LORD said to her:

[a]"Two nations *are* in your womb,
Two peoples shall be separated from your body;
*One* people shall be stronger than [b]the other,
[c]And the older shall serve the younger."

**25:23** The ancient custom was for sons to inherit their father's possessions upon his death, divided evenly between them, only with the oldest brother receiving a double portion. The oldest son also assumed the leadership role in the family. A **younger** son ruling over his older brother was unheard of and shocking.

24 So when her days were fulfilled *for her* to give birth, indeed *there were* twins in her womb. 25 And the first came out red. *He was* [a]like a hairy garment all over; so they called his name Esau.[1] 26 Afterward his brother came out, and [a]his hand took hold of Esau's heel; so [b]his name was called Jacob.[1] Isaac *was* sixty years old when she bore them.

27 So the boys grew. And Esau was [a]a skillful hunter, a man of the field; but Jacob was [b]a mild man, [c]dwelling in tents. 28 And Isaac loved Esau because he [a]ate *of his* game, [b]but Rebekah loved Jacob.

### *ESAU SELLS HIS BIRTHRIGHT*

*(Heb. 12:16)*

29 Now Jacob cooked a stew; and Esau came in from the field, and he *was* weary. 30 And Esau said to Jacob, "Please feed me with that same red *stew,* for I *am* weary." Therefore his name was called Edom.[1]

31 But Jacob said, "Sell me your birthright as of this day."

32 And Esau said, "Look, I *am* about to die; so [a]what *is* this birthright to me?"

33 Then Jacob said, "Swear to me as of this day."

So he swore to him, and [a]sold his birthright to Jacob. 34 And Jacob gave Esau bread and stew of lentils; then [a]he ate and drank, arose, and went his way. Thus Esau [b]despised *his* birthright.

### *ISAAC AND ABIMELECH*

**26** There was a famine in the land, besides [a]the first famine that was in the days of Abraham. And Isaac went to [b]Abimelech king of the Philistines, in Gerar.

2 Then the LORD appeared to him and said: [a]"Do not go down to Egypt; live in [b]the land of which I shall tell you. 3 [a]Dwell in this land, and [b]I will be with you and [c]bless you; for to you and your descendants [d]I give all these lands, and I will perform [e]the oath which I swore to Abraham your father. 4 And [a]I will make your descendants multiply as the stars of heaven; I will give to your descendants all these lands; [b]and in your seed all the nations of the earth shall be blessed; 5 [a]because Abraham obeyed My voice and kept My charge, My commandments, My statutes, and My laws."

**SEEING JESUS IN THE SCRIPTURE**

**26:4** God promised Isaac what He promised Abraham: God would bless all the nations through a coming descendant (see Gen. 12:3; 22:18). Isaac wasn't the fulfillment of this promise. Jesus, who came through Abraham and Isaac's lineage, is the one through whom all the nations are blessed (see Gal. 3:8).

6 So Isaac dwelt in Gerar. 7 And the men of the place asked about his wife. And [a]he said, "She *is* my sister"; for [b]he was afraid to say, "*She is* my wife," *because he thought,* "lest the men of the place kill me for Rebekah, because she *is* [c]beautiful to behold." 8 Now it came to pass, when he had been there a long time, that Abimelech king of the Philistines looked through a window, and saw, and there was Isaac, showing endearment to Rebekah his wife. 9 Then Abimelech called Isaac and said, "Quite obviously she *is* your wife; so how could you say, 'She *is* my sister'?"

Isaac said to him, "Because I said, 'Lest I die on account of her.' "

10 And Abimelech said, "What *is* this you have done to us? One of the people might soon have lain with your wife, and [a]you would have brought guilt on us." 11 So Abimelech charged all *his* people, saying, "He who [a]touches this man or his wife shall surely be put to death."

12 Then Isaac sowed in that land, and reaped in the same year [a]a hundredfold; and the LORD [b]blessed him. 13 The man [a]began to prosper, and continued prospering until he became very prosperous; 14 for he had possessions of flocks and possessions of herds and a great number of servants. So the Philistines [a]envied him. 15 Now the Philistines had stopped up all the wells [a]which his father's servants had dug in the days of Abraham his father, and they had filled them with earth. 16 And Abimelech said

**25:23** [a] Gen. 17:4–6, 16; 24:60 [b] 2 Sam. 8:14 [c] Rom. 9:12 **25:25** [a] Gen. 27:11, 16, 23 [1] Literally *Hairy* **25:26** [a] Hos. 12:3 [b] Gen. 27:36 [1] Literally *Supplanter* **25:27** [a] Gen. 27:3, 5 [b] Job 1:1, 8 [c] Heb. 11:9 **25:28** [a] Gen. 27:4, 19, 25, 31 [b] Gen. 27:6–10 **25:30** [1] Literally *Red* **25:32** [a] Mark 8:36, 37 **25:33** [a] Heb. 12:16 **25:34** [a] Eccl. 8:15 [b] Heb. 12:16, 17 **26:1** [a] Gen. 12:10 [b] Gen. 20:1, 2 **26:2** [a] Gen. 12:7; 17:1; 18:1; 35:9 [b] Gen. 12:1 **26:3** [a] Heb. 11:9 [b] Gen. 28:13, 15 [c] Gen. 12:2 [d] Gen. 12:7; 13:15; 15:18 [e] Gen. 22:16 **26:4** [a] Gen. 15:5; 22:17 [b] Gen. 12:3; 22:18 **26:5** [a] Gen. 22:16, 18 **26:7** [a] Gen. 12:13; 20:2, 12, 13 [b] Prov. 29:25 [c] Gen. 12:11; 24:16; 29:17 **26:10** [a] Gen. 20:9 **26:11** [a] Ps. 105:15 **26:12** [a] Matt. 13:8, 23 [b] Gen. 24:1; 25:8, 11; 26:3 **26:13** [a] Gen. 24:35; [Prov. 10:22] **26:14** [a] Gen. 37:11; Eccl. 4:4 **26:15** [a] Gen. 21:25, 30

to Isaac, "Go away from us, for [a]you are much
mightier than we."
17 Then Isaac departed from there and
pitched his tent in the Valley of Gerar, and dwelt
there. 18 And Isaac dug again the wells of water
which they had dug in the days of Abraham his
father, for the Philistines had stopped them up
after the death of Abraham. [a]He called them by
the names which his father had called them.
19 Also Isaac's servants dug in the valley,
and found a well of running water there. 20 But
the herdsmen of Gerar [a]quarreled with Isaac's
herdsmen, saying, "The water *is* ours." So he
called the name of the well Esek,[1] because they
quarreled with him. 21 Then they dug another
well, and they quarreled over that *one* also. So
he called its name Sitnah.[1] 22 And he moved from
there and dug another well, and they did not
quarrel over it. So he called its name Rehoboth,[1]
because he said, "For now the LORD has made
room for us, and we shall [a]be fruitful in the land."

> **26:17–20 Wells** were dug in solid limestone, using primitive tools. The job was time-consuming and backbreaking. Considering the work it took to dig a well and with water in short supply, it's no wonder that the diggers were eager to protect their well.

23 Then he went up from there to Beersheba.
24 And the LORD [a]appeared to him the same
night and said, [b]"I *am* the God of your father
Abraham; [c]do not fear, for [d]I *am* with you. I
will bless you and multiply your descendants
for My servant Abraham's sake." 25 So he [a]built
an altar there and [b]called on the name of the
LORD, and he pitched his tent there; and there
Isaac's servants dug a well.
26 Then Abimelech came to him from Gerar
with Ahuzzath, one of his friends, [a]and Phichol
the commander of his army. 27 And Isaac said
to them, "Why have you come to me, [a]since you
hate me and have [b]sent me away from you?"
28 But they said, "We have certainly seen that
the LORD [a]is with you. So we said, 'Let there now
be an oath between us, between you and us; and
let us make a covenant with you, 29 that you will
do us no harm, since we have not touched you,
and since we have done nothing to you but good
and have sent you away in peace. [a]You *are* now
the blessed of the LORD.' "
30 [a]So he made them a feast, and they ate and
drank. 31 Then they arose early in the morning and
[a]swore an oath with one another; and Isaac sent
them away, and they departed from him in peace.
32 It came to pass the same day that Isaac's
servants came and told him about the well which
they had dug, and said to him, "We have found
water." 33 So he called it Shebah.[1] [a]Therefore the
name of the city *is* Beersheba[2] to this day.
34 [a]When Esau was forty years old, he took as
wives Judith the daughter of Beeri the Hittite,
and Basemath the daughter of Elon the Hittite.
35 And [a]they were a grief of mind to Isaac and
Rebekah.

### *ISAAC BLESSES JACOB*

27 Now it came to pass, when Isaac was [a]old
and [b]his eyes were so dim that he could
not see, that he called Esau his older son and
said to him, "My son."

And he answered him, "Here I am."
2 Then he said, "Behold now, I am old. I [a]do
not know the day of my death. 3 [a]Now therefore,
please take your weapons, your quiver and your
bow, and go out to the field and hunt game for
me. 4 And make me savory food, such as I love,
and bring *it* to me that I may eat, that my soul
[a]may bless you before I die."

> **27:4** To **bless** someone was to request God's favor and goodness upon them and often included speaking prophetic words about the individual. Abraham, Isaac, and Jacob each blessed their sons in Genesis.

5 Now Rebekah was listening when Isaac
spoke to Esau his son. And Esau went to the field
to hunt game and to bring *it*. 6 So Rebekah spoke
to Jacob her son, saying, "Indeed I heard your
father speak to Esau your brother, saying, 7 'Bring
me game and make savory food for me, that I may
eat it and bless you in the presence of the LORD
before my death.' 8 Now therefore, my son, [a]obey
my voice according to what I command you. 9 Go
now to the flock and bring me from there two
choice kids of the goats, and I will make [a]savory
food from them for your father, such as he loves.
10 Then you shall take *it* to your father, that he may
eat *it*, and that he [a]may bless you before his death."
11 And Jacob said to Rebekah his mother,
"Look, [a]Esau my brother *is* a hairy man, and I
*am* a smooth-*skinned* man. 12 Perhaps my father
will [a]feel me, and I shall seem to be a deceiver
to him; and I shall bring [b]a curse on myself and
not a blessing."

**26:16** [a] Ex. 1:9 **26:18** [a] Gen. 21:31 **26:20** [a] Gen. 21:25 [1] Literally *Quarrel* **26:21** [1] Literally *Enmity* **26:22** [a] Gen. 17:6; 28:3; 41:52; Ex. 1:7 [1] Literally *Spaciousness* **26:24** [a] Gen. 26:2 [b] Gen. 17:7, 8; 24:12; Ex. 3:6; Acts 7:32 [c] Gen. 15:1 [d] Gen. 26:3, 4 **26:25** [a] Gen. 12:7, 8; 13:4, 18; 22:9; 33:20 [b] Gen. 21:33; Ps. 116:17 **26:26** [a] Gen. 21:22 **26:27** [a] Judg. 11:7 [b] Gen. 26:16 **26:28** [a] Gen. 21:22, 23 **26:29** [a] Gen. 24:31; Ps. 115:15 **26:30** [a] Gen. 19:3 **26:31** [a] Gen. 21:31 **26:33** [a] Gen. 21:31; 28:10 [1] Literally *Oath* or *Seven* [2] Literally *Well of the Oath* or *Well of the Seven* **26:34** [a] Gen. 28:8; 36:2 **26:35** [a] Gen. 27:46; 28:1, 8 **27:1** [a] Gen. 35:28 [b] Gen. 48:10; 1 Sam. 3:2 **27:2** [a] [Prov. 27:1; James 4:14] **27:3** [a] Gen. 25:27, 28 **27:4** [a] Gen. 27:19, 25, 27, 31; 48:9, 15, 16; 49:28; Deut. 33:1; Heb. 11:20 **27:8** [a] Gen. 27:13, 43 **27:9** [a] Gen. 27:4 **27:10** [a] Gen. 27:4; 48:16 **27:11** [a] Gen. 25:25 **27:12** [a] Gen. 27:21, 22 [b] Gen. 9:25; Deut. 27:18

13 But his mother said to him, [a]“*Let* your curse
*be* on me, my son; only obey my voice, and go,
get *them* for me.” 14 And he went and got *them*
and brought *them* to his mother, and his mother
[a]made savory food, such as his father loved.
15 Then Rebekah took [a]the choice clothes of her
elder son Esau, which *were* with her in the house,
and put them on Jacob her younger son. 16 And
she put the skins of the kids of the goats on his
hands and on the smooth part of his neck. 17 Then
she gave the savory food and the bread, which
she had prepared, into the hand of her son Jacob.
18 So he went to his father and said, “My
father.”

And he said, “Here I am. Who *are* you, my son?”
19 Jacob said to his father, “I *am* Esau your
firstborn; I have done just as you told me; please
arise, sit and eat of my game, [a]that your soul
may bless me.”
20 But Isaac said to his son, “How *is it* that
you have found *it* so quickly, my son?”

And he said, “Because the LORD your God
brought *it* to me.”
21 Isaac said to Jacob, “Please come near, that
I [a]may feel you, my son, whether you *are* really
my son Esau or not.” 22 So Jacob went near to
Isaac his father, and he felt him and said, “The
voice *is* Jacob’s voice, but the hands *are* the
hands of Esau.” 23 And he did not recognize him,
because [a]his hands were hairy like his brother
Esau’s hands; so he blessed him.
24 Then he said, “*Are* you really my son Esau?”

He said, “I *am.*”
25 He said, “Bring *it* near to me, and I will eat
of my son’s game, so [a]that my soul may bless
you.” So he brought *it* near to him, and he ate;
and he brought him wine, and he drank. 26 Then
his father Isaac said to him, “Come near now
and kiss me, my son.” 27 And he came near and
[a]kissed him; and he smelled the smell of his
clothing, and blessed him and said:

“Surely, [b]the smell of my son
*Is* like the smell of a field
Which the LORD has blessed.
28 Therefore may [a]God give you
Of [b]the dew of heaven,
Of [c]the fatness of the earth,
And [d]plenty of grain and wine.
29 [a]Let peoples serve you,
And nations bow down to you.
Be master over your brethren,
And [b]let your mother’s sons bow down to
you.
[c]Cursed *be* everyone who curses you,
And blessed *be* those who bless you!”

### ESAU’S LOST HOPE

*(Heb. 12:17)*

30 Now it happened, as soon as Isaac had
finished blessing Jacob, and Jacob had scarcely
gone out from the presence of Isaac his father,
that Esau his brother came in from his hunting.
31 He also had made savory food, and brought
it to his father, and said to his father, “Let my
father arise and [a]eat of his son’s game, that your
soul may bless me.”
32 And his father Isaac said to him, “Who
*are* you?”

So he said, “I *am* your son, your firstborn,
Esau.”
33 Then Isaac trembled exceedingly, and said,
“Who? Where *is* the one who hunted game and
brought *it* to me? I ate all *of it* before you came,
and I have blessed him—[a]*and* indeed he shall
be blessed.”
34 When Esau heard the words of his father,
[a]he cried with an exceedingly great and bitter
cry, and said to his father, “Bless me—me also,
O my father!”
35 But he said, “Your brother came with de-
ceit and has taken away your blessing.”
36 And *Esau* said, [a]“Is he not rightly named
Jacob? For he has supplanted me these two
times. He took away my birthright, and now
look, he has taken away my blessing!” And he
said, “Have you not reserved a blessing for me?”
37 Then Isaac answered and said to Esau,
[a]“Indeed I have made him your master, and all
his brethren I have given to him as servants;
with [b]grain and wine I have sustained him. What
shall I do now for you, my son?”
38 And Esau said to his father, “Have you only
one blessing, my father? Bless me—me also, O my
father!” And Esau lifted up his voice [a]and wept.
39 Then Isaac his father answered and said
to him:

“Behold, [a]your dwelling shall be of the
fatness of the earth,
And of the dew of heaven from above.
40 By your sword you shall live,
And [a]you shall serve your brother;
And [b]it shall come to pass, when you
become restless,
That you shall break his yoke from your
neck.”

### JACOB ESCAPES FROM ESAU

41 So Esau [a]hated Jacob because of the blessing
with which his father blessed him, and Esau said
in his heart, [b]“The days of mourning for my father
are at hand; [c]then I will kill my brother Jacob.”

**27:13** [a] Gen. 43:9; 1 Sam. 25:24; 2 Sam. 14:9; Matt. 27:25 **27:14** [a] Prov. 23:3; Luke 21:34 **27:15** [a] Gen. 27:27 **27:19** [a] Gen. 27:4 **27:21** [a] Gen. 27:12 **27:23** [a] Gen. 27:16 **27:25** [a] Gen. 27:4, 10, 19, 31 **27:27** [a] Gen. 29:13 [b] Song 4:11; Hos. 14:6 **27:28** [a] Heb. 11:20 [b] Gen. 27:39; Deut. 33:13, 28; 2 Sam. 1:21; Ps. 133:3; Prov. 3:20; Mic. 5:7; Zech. 8:12 [c] Gen. 45:18; Num. 18:12 [d] Deut. 7:13; 33:28 **27:29** [a] Gen. 9:25; 25:23; Is. 45:14; 49:7; 60:12, 14 [b] Gen. 37:7, 10; 49:8 [c] Gen. 12:2, 3; Zeph. 2:8, 9 **27:31** [a] Gen. 27:4 **27:33** [a] Gen. 25:23; 28:3, 4; Num. 23:20; Rom. 11:29 **27:34** [a] [Heb. 12:17] **27:36** [a] Gen. 25:26, 32–34 **27:37** [a] 2 Sam. 8:14 [b] Gen. 27:28, 29 **27:38** [a] Heb. 12:17 **27:39** [a] Gen. 27:28; Heb. 11:20 **27:40** [a] Gen. 25:23; 27:29; 2 Sam. 8:14; [Obad. 18–20] [b] 2 Kin. 8:20–22 **27:41** [a] Gen. 26:27; 32:3–11; 37:4, 5, 8 [b] Gen. 50:2–4, 10 [c] Obad. 10

42 And the words of Esau her older son were
told to Rebekah. So she sent and called Jacob
her younger son, and said to him, "Surely your
brother Esau [a]comforts himself concerning you
*by intending* to kill you. 43 Now therefore, my son,
obey my voice: arise, flee to my brother Laban
[a]in Haran. 44 And stay with him a [a]few days, un-
til your brother's fury turns away, 45 until your
brother's anger turns away from you, and he
forgets what you have done to him; then I will
send and bring you from there. Why should I be
bereaved also of you both in one day?"

46 And Rebekah said to Isaac, [a]"I am weary
of my life because of the daughters of Heth; [b]if
Jacob takes a wife of the daughters of Heth, like
these *who are* the daughters of the land, what
good will my life be to me?"

**28** Then Isaac called Jacob and [a]blessed
him, and charged him, and said to him:
[b]"You shall not take a wife from the daughters
of Canaan. 2 [a]Arise, go to [b]Padan Aram, to the
house of [c]Bethuel your mother's father; and take
yourself a wife from there of the daughters of
[d]Laban your mother's brother.

3 "May [a]God Almighty bless you,
And make you [b]fruitful and multiply you,
That you may be an assembly of peoples;
4 And give you [a]the blessing of Abraham,
To you and your descendants with you,
That you may inherit the land
[b]In which you are a stranger,
Which God gave to Abraham."

5 So Isaac sent Jacob away, and he went to Padan
Aram, to Laban the son of Bethuel the Syrian, the
brother of Rebekah, the mother of Jacob and Esau.

### *ESAU MARRIES MAHALATH*

6 Esau saw that Isaac had blessed Jacob and
sent him away to Padan Aram to take himself a
wife from there, *and that* as he blessed him he
gave him a charge, saying, "You shall not take a
wife from the daughters of Canaan," 7 and that
Jacob had obeyed his father and his mother
and had gone to Padan Aram. 8 Also Esau saw
[a]that the daughters of Canaan did not please
his father Isaac. 9 So Esau went to Ishmael and
[a]took [b]Mahalath the daughter of Ishmael, Abra-
ham's son, [c]the sister of Nebajoth, to be his wife
in addition to the wives he had.

### *JACOB'S VOW AT BETHEL*

10 Now Jacob [a]went out from Beersheba and
went toward [b]Haran. 11 So he came to a certain
place and stayed there all night, because the sun
had set. And he took one of the stones of that
place and put it at his head, and he lay down in
that place to sleep. 12 Then he [a]dreamed, and
behold, a ladder *was* set up on the earth, and
its top reached to heaven; and there [b]the angels
of God were ascending and descending on it.

> **SEEING JESUS IN THE SCRIPTURE**
>
> **28:10–12** This ladder reminds us of Jesus' words about the angels "ascending and descending upon the Son of Man" (John 1:51), vividly depicting Himself as the Way into the heavenlies.

13 [a]And behold, the LORD stood above it and
said: [b]"I *am* the LORD God of Abraham your
father and the God of Isaac; [c]the land on which
you lie I will give to you and your descendants.
14 Also your [a]descendants shall be as the dust of
the earth; you shall spread abroad [b]to the west
and the east, to the north and the south; and in
you and [c]in your seed all the families of the earth
shall be blessed. 15 Behold, [a]I *am* with you and
will [b]keep you wherever you go, and will [c]bring
you back to this land; for [d]I will not leave you
[e]until I have done what I have spoken to you."

16 Then Jacob awoke from his sleep and said,
"Surely the LORD is in [a]this place, and I did not
know *it.*" 17 And he was afraid and said, "How
awesome *is* this place! This *is* none other than
the house of God, and this *is* the gate of heaven!"

18 Then Jacob rose early in the morning, and
took the stone that he had put at his head, [a]set it
up as a pillar, [b]and poured oil on top of it. 19 And
he called the name of [a]that place Bethel;[1] but
the name of that city had been Luz previously.
20 [a]Then Jacob made a vow, saying, "If [b]God will
be with me, and keep me in this way that I am
going, and give me [c]bread to eat and clothing
to put on, 21 so that [a]I come back to my father's
house in peace, [b]then the LORD shall be my God.
22 And this stone which I have set as a pillar [a]shall
be God's house, [b]and of all that You give me I
will surely give a tenth to You."

### *JACOB MEETS RACHEL*

**29** So Jacob went on his journey [a]and came to
the land of the people of the East. 2 And he
looked, and saw a [a]well in the field; and behold,
there *were* three flocks of sheep lying by it; for
out of that well they watered the flocks. A large

**27:42** [a]Ps. 64:5 **27:43** [a]Gen. 11:31; 25:20; 28:2, 5 **27:44** [a]Gen. 31:41 **27:46** [a]Gen. 26:34, 35; 28:8 [b]Gen. 24:3 **28:1** [a]Gen. 27:33 [b]Gen. 24:3 **28:2** [a]Hos. 12:12 [b]Gen. 25:20 [c]Gen. 22:23 [d]Gen. 24:29; 27:43; 29:5 **28:3** [a]Gen. 17:16; 35:11; 48:3 [b]Gen. 26:4, 24 **28:4** [a]Gen. 12:2, 3; 22:17 [b]Gen. 17:8; 23:4; 36:7 **28:8** [a]Gen. 24:3; 26:34, 35; 27:46 **28:9** [a]Gen. 26:34, 35 [b]Gen. 36:2, 3 [c]Gen. 25:13 **28:10** [a]Hos. 12:12 [b]Gen. 12:4, 5; 27:43; 29:4 **28:12** [a]Gen. 31:10; 41:1 [b]John 1:51 **28:13** [a]Gen. 35:1; 48:3 [b]Gen. 26:24 [c]Gen. 13:15, 17; 26:3; 35:12 **28:14** [a]Gen. 13:16; 22:17 [b]Gen. 13:14, 15 [c]Gen. 12:3; 18:18; 22:18; 26:4 **28:15** [a]Gen. 26:3, 24; 31:3 [b]Gen. 48:16 [c]Gen. 35:6; 48:21 [d]Deut. 7:9; 31:6, 8 [e]Num. 23:19 **28:16** [a]Ex. 3:5 **28:18** [a]Gen. 31:13, 45 [b]Lev. 8:10–12 **28:19** [a]Judg. 1:23, 26 [1]Literally *House of God* **28:20** [a]Judg. 11:30 [b]Gen. 28:15 [c]1 Tim. 6:8 **28:21** [a]Judg. 11:31 [b]Deut. 26:17 **28:22** [a]Gen. 35:7, 14 [b]Gen. 14:20 **29:1** [a]Num. 23:7 **29:2** [a]Gen. 24:10, 11

stone *was* on the well's mouth. 3 Now all the flocks would be gathered there; and they would roll the stone from the well's mouth, water the sheep, and put the stone back in its place on the well's mouth.

4 And Jacob said to them, "My brethren, where *are* you from?"

And they said, "We *are* from [a]Haran."

5 Then he said to them, "Do you know [a]Laban the son of Nahor?"

And they said, "We know him."

6 So he said to them, [a]"Is he well?"

And they said, "*He is* well. And look, his daughter Rachel [b]is coming with the sheep."

7 Then he said, "Look, *it is* still high day; *it is* not time for the cattle to be gathered together. Water the sheep, and go and feed *them*."

8 But they said, "We cannot until all the flocks are gathered together, and they have rolled the stone from the well's mouth; then we water the sheep."

9 Now while he was still speaking with them, [a]Rachel came with her father's sheep, for she was a shepherdess. 10 And it came to pass, when Jacob saw Rachel the daughter of Laban his mother's brother, and the sheep of Laban his mother's brother, that Jacob went near and [a]rolled the stone from the well's mouth, and watered the flock of Laban his mother's brother. 11 Then Jacob [a]kissed Rachel, and lifted up his voice and wept. 12 And Jacob told Rachel that he *was* [a]her father's relative and that he *was* Rebekah's son. [b]So she ran and told her father.

13 Then it came to pass, when Laban heard the report about Jacob his sister's son, that [a]he ran to meet him, and embraced him and kissed him, and brought him to his house. So he told Laban all these things. 14 And Laban said to him, [a]"Surely you *are* my bone and my flesh." And he stayed with him for a month.

## JACOB MARRIES LEAH AND RACHEL

15 Then Laban said to Jacob, "Because you *are* my relative, should you therefore serve me for nothing? Tell me, [a]what *should* your wages *be?*" 16 Now Laban had two daughters: the name of the elder *was* Leah, and the name of the younger *was* Rachel. 17 Leah's eyes *were* delicate, but Rachel was [a]beautiful of form and appearance.

18 Now Jacob loved Rachel; so he said, [a]"I will serve you seven years for Rachel your younger daughter."

19 And Laban said, "*It is* better that I give her to you than that I should give her to another man. Stay with me." 20 So Jacob [a]served seven years for Rachel, and they seemed *only* a few days to him because of the love he had for her.

21 Then Jacob said to Laban, "Give *me* my wife, for my days are fulfilled, that I may [a]go in to her." 22 And Laban gathered together all the men of the place and [a]made a feast. 23 Now it came to pass in the evening, that he took Leah his daughter and brought her to Jacob; and he went in to her. 24 And Laban gave his maid [a]Zilpah to his daughter Leah *as* a maid. 25 So it came to pass in the morning, that behold, it *was* Leah. And he said to Laban, "What is this you have done to me? Was it not for Rachel that I served you? Why then have you [a]deceived me?"

26 And Laban said, "It must not be done so in our country, to give the younger before the firstborn. 27 [a]Fulfill her week, and we will give you this one also for the service which you will serve with me still another seven years."

28 Then Jacob did so and fulfilled her week. So he gave him his daughter Rachel as wife also. 29 And Laban gave his maid [a]Bilhah to his daughter Rachel as a maid. 30 Then *Jacob* also went in to Rachel, and he also [a]loved Rachel more than Leah. And he served with Laban [b]still another seven years.

## THE CHILDREN OF JACOB

31 When the LORD [a]saw that Leah *was* unloved, He [b]opened her womb; but Rachel *was* barren. 32 So Leah conceived and bore a son, and she called his name Reuben;[1] for she said, "The LORD has surely [a]looked on my affliction. Now therefore, my husband will love me." 33 Then she conceived again and bore a son, and said, "Because the LORD has heard that I *am* unloved, He has therefore given me this *son* also." And she called his name Simeon.[1] 34 She conceived again and bore a son, and said, "Now this time my husband will become attached to me, because I have borne him three sons." Therefore his name was called Levi.[1] 35 And she conceived again and bore a son, and said, "Now I will praise the LORD." Therefore she called his name [a]Judah.[1] Then she stopped bearing.

**29:31** God was kind to Leah. Even though she was the unloved wife, it was through her son Judah that the messianic line was carried out.

**30** Now when Rachel saw that [a]she bore Jacob no children, Rachel [b]envied her sister, and said to Jacob, "Give me children, [c]or else I die!"

2 And Jacob's anger was aroused against

**29:4** [a] Gen. 11:31; 28:10 **29:5** [a] Gen. 24:24, 29; 28:2 **29:6** [a] Gen. 43:27 [b] Gen. 24:11; Ex. 2:16, 17 **29:9** [a] Ex. 2:16 **29:10** [a] Ex. 2:17 **29:11** [a] Gen. 33:4; 45:14, 15 **29:12** [a] Gen. 13:8; 14:14, 16; 28:5 [b] Gen. 24:28 **29:13** [a] Gen. 24:29–31; Luke 15:20 **29:14** [a] Gen. 2:23; 37:27; Judg. 9:2; 2 Sam. 5:1; 19:12, 13 **29:15** [a] Gen. 30:28; 31:41 **29:17** [a] Gen. 12:11, 14; 26:7 **29:18** [a] Gen. 31:41; 2 Sam. 3:14; Hos. 12:12 **29:20** [a] Gen. 30:26; Hos. 12:12 **29:21** [a] Judg. 15:1 **29:22** [a] Judg. 14:10; John 2:1, 2 **29:24** [a] Gen. 30:9, 10 **29:25** [a] Gen. 27:35; 31:7; 1 Sam. 28:12 **29:27** [a] Gen. 31:41; Judg. 14:2 **29:29** [a] Gen. 30:3–5 **29:30** [a] Gen. 29:17–20; Deut. 21:15–17 [b] Gen. 30:26; 31:41; Hos. 12:12 **29:31** [a] Ps. 127:3 [b] Gen. 30:1 **29:32** [a] Gen. 16:11; 31:42; Ex. 3:7; 4:31; Deut. 26:7; Ps. 25:18 [1] Literally *See, a Son* **29:33** [1] Literally *Heard* **29:34** [1] Literally *Attached* **29:35** [a] Gen. 49:8; Matt. 1:2 [1] Literally *Praise* **30:1** [a] Gen. 16:1, 2; 29:31 [b] Gen. 37:11 [c] 1 Sam. 1:5, 6; [Job 5:2]

Rachel, and he said, [a]"*Am* I in the place of God, who has withheld from you the fruit of the womb?"

3 So she said, "Here is [a]my maid Bilhah; go in to her, [b]and she will bear *a child* on my knees, [c]that I also may have children by her." 4 Then she gave him Bilhah her maid [a]as wife, and Jacob went in to her. 5 And Bilhah conceived and bore Jacob a son. 6 Then Rachel said, "God has [a]judged my case; and He has also heard my voice and given me a son." Therefore she called his name Dan.[1] 7 And Rachel's maid Bilhah conceived again and bore Jacob a second son. 8 Then Rachel said, "With great wrestlings I have wrestled with my sister, *and* indeed I have prevailed." So she called his name Naphtali.[1]

9 When Leah saw that she had stopped bearing, she took Zilpah her maid and [a]gave her to Jacob as wife. 10 And Leah's maid Zilpah bore Jacob a son. 11 Then Leah said, "A troop comes!"[1] So she called his name Gad.[2] 12 And Leah's maid Zilpah bore Jacob a second son. 13 Then Leah said, "I am happy, for the daughters [a]will call me blessed." So she called his name Asher.[1]

14 Now Reuben went in the days of wheat harvest and found mandrakes in the field, and brought them to his mother Leah. Then Rachel said to Leah, [a]"Please give me *some* of your son's mandrakes."

15 But she said to her, [a]"*Is it* a small matter that you have taken away my husband? Would you take away my son's mandrakes also?"

And Rachel said, "Therefore he will lie with you tonight for your son's mandrakes."

16 When Jacob came out of the field in the evening, Leah went out to meet him and said, "You must come in to me, for I have surely hired you with my son's mandrakes." And he lay with her that night.

> **30:14–16 Mandrakes** were prescribed to increase fertility. A mandrake is a fruit-producing plant with dark green leaves and small blue flowers. The yellow fruit of this plant is small, sweet, and fragrant.

17 And God listened to Leah, and she conceived and bore Jacob a fifth son. 18 Leah said, "God has given me my wages, because I have given my maid to my husband." So she called his name Issachar.[1] 19 Then Leah conceived again and bore Jacob a sixth son. 20 And Leah said, "God has endowed me *with* a good endowment; now my husband will dwell with me, because I have borne him six sons." So she called his name Zebulun.[1] 21 Afterward she bore a [a]daughter, and called her name Dinah.

22 Then God [a]remembered Rachel, and God listened to her and [b]opened her womb. 23 And she conceived and bore a son, and said, "God has taken away [a]my reproach." 24 So she called his name Joseph,[1] and said, [a]"The LORD shall add to me another son."

### JACOB'S AGREEMENT WITH LABAN

25 And it came to pass, when Rachel had borne Joseph, that Jacob said to Laban, [a]"Send me away, that I may go to [b]my own place and to my country. 26 Give *me* my wives and my children [a]for whom I have served you, and let me go; for you know my service which I have done for you."

27 And Laban said to him, "Please *stay,* if I have found favor in your eyes, *for* [a]I have learned by experience that the LORD has blessed me for your sake." 28 Then he said, [a]"Name me your wages, and I will give *it.*"

29 So *Jacob* said to him, [a]"You know how I have served you and how your livestock has been with me. 30 For what you had before I *came was* little, and it has increased to a great amount; the LORD has blessed you since my coming. And now, when shall I also [a]provide for my own house?"

31 So he said, "What shall I give you?"

And Jacob said, "You shall not give me anything. If you will do this thing for me, I will again feed and keep your flocks: 32 Let me pass through all your flock today, removing from there all the speckled and spotted sheep, and all the brown ones among the lambs, and the spotted and speckled among the goats; and [a]*these* shall be my wages. 33 So my [a]righteousness will answer for me in time to come, when the subject of my wages comes before you: every one that *is* not speckled and spotted among the goats, and brown among the lambs, will be considered stolen, if *it is* with me."

34 And Laban said, "Oh, that it were according to your word!" 35 So he removed that day the male goats that were [a]speckled and spotted, all the female goats that were speckled and spotted, every one that had *some* white in it, and all the brown ones among the lambs, and gave *them* into the hand of his sons. 36 Then he put three days' journey between himself and Jacob, and Jacob fed the rest of Laban's flocks.

37 Now [a]Jacob took for himself rods of green poplar and of the almond and chestnut trees, peeled white strips in them, and exposed the white which *was* in the rods. 38 And the rods which he had peeled, he set before the flocks in the gutters, in the watering troughs where the flocks

**30:2** [a] Gen. 16:2; 1 Sam. 1:5 **30:3** [a] Gen. 16:2 [b] Gen. 50:23; Job 3:12 [c] Gen. 16:2, 3 **30:4** [a] Gen. 16:3, 4 **30:6** [a] Gen. 18:25; Ps. 35:24; 43:1; Lam. 3:59 [1] Literally *Judge* **30:8** [1] Literally *My Wrestling* **30:9** [a] Gen. 30:4 **30:11** [1] Following Qere, Syriac, and Targum; Kethib, Septuagint, and Vulgate read *in fortune.* [2] Literally *Troop* or *Fortune* **30:13** [a] Prov. 31:28; Luke 1:48 [1] Literally *Happy* **30:14** [a] Gen. 25:30 **30:15** [a] [Num. 16:9, 13] **30:18** [1] Literally *Wages* **30:20** [1] Literally *Dwelling* **30:21** [a] Gen. 34:1 **30:22** [a] Gen. 19:29; 1 Sam. 1:19, 20 [b] Gen. 29:31 **30:23** [a] 1 Sam. 1:6; Is. 4:1; Luke 1:25 **30:24** [a] Gen. 35:16–18 [1] Literally *He Will Add* **30:25** [a] Gen. 24:54, 56 [b] Gen. 18:33 **30:26** [a] Gen. 29:18–20, 27, 30; Hos. 12:12 **30:27** [a] Gen. 26:24; 39:3; Is. 61:9 **30:28** [a] Gen. 29:15; 31:7, 41 **30:29** [a] Gen. 31:6, 38–40; Matt. 24:45; Titus 2:10 **30:30** [a] [1 Tim. 5:8] **30:32** [a] Gen. 31:8 **30:33** [a] Ps. 37:6 **30:35** [a] Gen. 31:9–12 **30:37** [a] Gen. 31:9–12

came to drink, so that they should conceive when
they came to drink. 39 So the flocks conceived
before the rods, and the flocks brought forth
streaked, speckled, and spotted. 40 Then Jacob
separated the lambs, and made the flocks face
toward the streaked and all the brown in the flock
of Laban; but he put his own flocks by themselves
and did not put them with Laban's flock.
41 And it came to pass, whenever the stronger
livestock conceived, that Jacob placed the rods
before the eyes of the livestock in the gutters,
that they might conceive among the rods. 42 But
when the flocks were feeble, he did not put *them*
in; so the feebler were Laban's and the stronger
Jacob's. 43 Thus the man [a]became exceedingly
prosperous, and [b]had large flocks, female and
male servants, and camels and donkeys.

### *JACOB FLEES FROM LABAN*

**31** Now *Jacob* heard the words of Laban's
sons, saying, "Jacob has taken away all
that was our father's, and from what was our
father's he has acquired all this [a]wealth." 2 And
Jacob saw the [a]countenance of Laban, and in-
deed it *was* not [b]*favorable* toward him as before.
3 Then the LORD said to Jacob, [a]"Return to the
land of your fathers and to your family, and I
will [b]be with you."
4 So Jacob sent and called Rachel and Leah to
the field, to his flock, 5 and said to them, [a]"I see
your father's countenance, that it *is* not *favorable*
toward me as before; but the God of my father [b]has
been with me. 6 And [a]you know that with all my
might I have served your father. 7 Yet your father
has deceived me and [a]changed my wages [b]ten
times, but God [c]did not allow him to hurt me. 8 If
he said thus: [a]'The speckled shall be your wages,'
then all the flocks bore speckled. And if he said
thus: 'The streaked shall be your wages,' then all

> **31:7** Jacob had **deceived** his father and tricked his brother out of the birthright. But in Laban he met his match. The consequences of dishonesty reach both ways. Because of his own trickery, Jacob had to flee from his home. He apparently never saw his mother again and his relationship with his father and his only brother was broken. Lying not only harms the liar, but it also affects those he lies to. Because of Laban's trickery, Jacob was affected by an unloved wife, quarreling sons, and constant domestic strife.

the flocks bore streaked. 9 So God has [a]taken away
the livestock of your father and given *them* to me.
10 "And it happened, at the time when the
flocks conceived, that I lifted my eyes and saw
in a dream, and behold, the rams which leaped
upon the flocks *were* streaked, speckled, and
gray-spotted. 11 Then [a]the Angel of God spoke to
me in a dream, saying, 'Jacob.' And I said, 'Here
I am.' 12 And He said, 'Lift your eyes now and see,
all the rams which leap on the flocks *are* streaked,
speckled, and gray-spotted; for [a]I have seen all
that Laban is doing to you. 13 I *am* the God of Beth-
el, [a]where you anointed the pillar *and* where you
made a vow to Me. Now [b]arise, get out of this land,
and return to the land of your family.' "
14 Then Rachel and Leah answered and said
to him, [a]"Is there still any portion or inheri-
tance for us in our father's house? 15 Are we not
considered strangers by him? For [a]he has sold
us, and also completely consumed our money.
16 For all these riches which God has taken from
our father are *really* ours and our children's;
now then, whatever God has said to you, do it."
17 Then Jacob rose and set his sons and his
wives on camels. 18 And he carried away all his
livestock and all his possessions which he had
gained, his acquired livestock which he had
gained in Padan Aram, to go to his father Isaac
in the land of [a]Canaan. 19 Now Laban had gone
to shear his sheep, and Rachel had stolen the
[a]household idols that were her father's. 20 And
Jacob stole away, unknown to Laban the Syrian,
in that he did not tell him that he intended to
flee. 21 So he fled with all that he had. He arose
and crossed the river, and [a]headed toward the
mountains of Gilead.

### *LABAN PURSUES JACOB*

22 And Laban was told on the third day that
Jacob had fled. 23 Then he took [a]his brethren with
him and pursued him for seven days' journey,
and he overtook him in the mountains of Gil-
ead. 24 But God [a]had come to Laban the Syrian
in a dream by night, and said to him, "Be careful
that you [b]speak to Jacob neither good nor bad."
25 So Laban overtook Jacob. Now Jacob had
pitched his tent in the mountains, and Laban with
his brethren pitched in the mountains of Gilead.
26 And Laban said to Jacob: "What have you
done, that you have stolen away unknown to me,
and [a]carried away my daughters like captives
*taken* with the sword? 27 Why did you flee away
secretly, and steal away from me, and not tell
me; for I might have sent you away with joy and
songs, with timbrel and harp? 28 And you did not
allow me [a]to kiss my sons and my daughters.
Now [b]you have done foolishly in *so* doing. 29 It

**30:43** [a] Gen. 12:16; 30:30 [b] Gen. 13:2; 24:35; 26:13, 14 **31:1** [a] Ps. 49:16 **31:2** [a] Gen. 4:5 [b] Deut. 28:54 **31:3** [a] Gen. 28:15, 20, 21; 32:9 [b] Gen. 46:4 **31:5** [a] Gen. 31:2, 3 [b] Is. 41:10 **31:6** [a] Gen. 30:29; 31:38–41 **31:7** [a] Gen. 29:25; 31:41 [b] Num. 14:22 [c] Job 1:10 **31:8** [a] Gen. 30:32 **31:9** [a] Gen. 31:1, 16 **31:11** [a] Gen. 16:7–11; 22:11, 15; 31:13; 48:16 **31:12** [a] Ex. 3:7 **31:13** [a] Gen. 28:16–22; 35:1, 6, 15 [b] Gen. 31:3; 32:9 **31:14** [a] Gen. 2:24 **31:15** [a] Gen. 29:15, 20, 23, 27 **31:18** [a] Gen. 17:8; 33:18; 35:27 **31:19** [a] Judg. 17:5 **31:21** [a] 2 Kin. 12:17 **31:23** [a] Gen. 13:8 **31:24** [a] Gen. 20:3; 31:29; 46:2–4 [b] Gen. 24:50; 31:7, 29 **31:26** [a] 1 Sam. 30:2 **31:28** [a] Gen. 31:55; Ruth 1:9, 14; 1 Kin. 19:20; Acts 20:37 [b] 1 Sam. 13:13

is in my power to do you harm, but the [a]God of
your father spoke to me [b]last night, saying, 'Be
careful that you speak to Jacob neither good nor
bad.' 30 And now you have surely gone because
you greatly long for your father's house, *but* why
did you [a]steal my gods?"

31 Then Jacob answered and said to Laban,
"Because I was [a]afraid, for I said, 'Perhaps you
would take your daughters from me by force.'
32 With whomever you find your gods, [a]do not
let him live. In the presence of our brethren,
identify what I have of yours and take *it* with
you." For Jacob did not know that Rachel had
stolen them.

33 And Laban went into Jacob's tent, into
Leah's tent, and into the two maids' tents, but
he did not find *them.* Then he went out of Leah's
tent and entered Rachel's tent. 34 Now Rachel
had taken the household idols, put them in the
camel's saddle, and sat on them. And Laban
searched all about the tent but did not find *them.*
35 And she said to her father, "Let it not displease
my lord that I cannot [a]rise before you, for the
manner of women *is* with me." And he searched
but did not find the household idols.

36 Then Jacob was angry and rebuked Laban,
and Jacob answered and said to Laban: "What
*is* my trespass? What *is* my sin, that you have
so hotly pursued me? 37 Although you have
searched all my things, what part of your house-
hold things have you found? Set *it* here before
my brethren and your brethren, that they may
judge between us both! 38 These twenty years I
*have been* with you; your ewes and your female
goats have not miscarried their young, and I
have not eaten the rams of your flock. 39 [a]That
which was torn *by beasts* I did not bring to you;
I bore the loss of it. [b]You required it from my
hand, *whether* stolen by day or stolen by night.
40 *There* I was! In the day the drought consumed
me, and the frost by night, and my sleep depart-
ed from my eyes. 41 Thus I have been in your
house twenty years; I [a]served you fourteen years
for your two daughters, and six years for your
flock, and [b]you have changed my wages ten
times. 42 [a]Unless the God of my father, the God
of Abraham and [b]the Fear of Isaac, had been
with me, surely now you would have sent me
away empty-handed. [c]God has seen my afflic-
tion and the labor of my hands, and [d]rebuked
*you* last night."

### *LABAN'S COVENANT WITH JACOB*

43 And Laban answered and said to Jacob,
"*These* daughters *are* my daughters, and *these*
children *are* my children, and *this* flock *is* my
flock; all that you see *is* mine. But what can I do
this day to these my daughters or to their chil-
dren whom they have borne? 44 Now therefore,
come, [a]let us make a covenant, [b]you and I, and
let it be a witness between you and me."

45 So Jacob [a]took a stone and set it up *as* a
pillar. 46 Then Jacob said to his brethren, "Gather
stones." And they took stones and made a heap,
and they ate there on the heap. 47 Laban called
it Jegar Sahadutha,[1] but Jacob called it Galeed.[2]
48 And Laban said, [a]"This heap *is* a witness be-
tween you and me this day." Therefore its name
was called Galeed, 49 also [a]Mizpah,[1] because he
said, "May the LORD watch between you and me
when we are absent one from another. 50 If you
afflict my daughters, or if you take *other* wives
besides my daughters, *although* no man *is* with
us—see, God *is* witness between you and me!"

51 Then Laban said to Jacob, "Here is this
heap and here is *this* pillar, which I have placed
between you and me. 52 This heap *is* a witness,
and *this* pillar *is* a witness, that I will not pass
beyond this heap to you, and you will not pass
beyond this heap and this pillar to me, for harm.
53 The God of Abraham, the God of Nahor, and
the God of their father [a]judge between us." And
Jacob [b]swore by [c]the Fear of his father Isaac.
54 Then Jacob offered a sacrifice on the moun-
tain, and called his brethren to eat bread. And
they ate bread and stayed all night on the moun-
tain. 55 And early in the morning Laban arose,
and [a]kissed his sons and daughters and [b]blessed
them. Then Laban departed and [c]returned to
his place.

### *ESAU COMES TO MEET JACOB*

32 So Jacob went on his way, and [a]the angels
of God met him. 2 When Jacob saw them,
he said, "This *is* God's [a]camp." And he called the
name of that place Mahanaim.[1]

3 Then Jacob sent messengers before him
to Esau his brother [a]in the land of Seir, [b]the
country of Edom. 4 And he commanded them,
saying, [a]"Speak thus to my lord Esau, 'Thus your
servant Jacob says: "I have dwelt with Laban and
stayed there until now. 5 [a]I have oxen, donkeys,
flocks, and male and female servants; and I
have sent to tell my lord, that [b]I may find favor
in your sight." ' "

6 Then the messengers returned to Jacob,
saying, "We came to your brother Esau, and [a]he
also is coming to meet you, and four hundred
men *are* with him." 7 So Jacob was greatly afraid
and [a]distressed; and he divided the people that
*were* with him, and the flocks and herds and
camels, into two companies. 8 And he said, "If

**31:29** [a] Gen. 28:13; 31:5, 24, 42, 53 [b] Gen. 31:24 **31:30** [a] Gen. 31:19; Josh. 24:2; Judg. 17:5; 18:24 **31:31** [a] Gen. 26:7; 32:7, 11 **31:32** [a] Gen. 44:9 **31:35** [a] Ex. 20:12; Lev. 19:32 **31:39** [a] Ex. 22:10 [b] Ex. 22:10–13 **31:41** [a] Gen. 29:20, 27–30 [b] Gen. 31:7 **31:42** [a] Gen. 31:5, 29, 53; Ps. 124:1, 2 [b] Gen. 31:53; Is. 8:13 [c] Gen. 29:32; Ex. 3:7 [d] Gen. 31:24, 29; 1 Chr. 12:17 **31:44** [a] Gen. 21:27, 32; 26:28 [b] Josh. 24:27 **31:45** [a] Gen. 28:18; 35:14; Josh. 24:26, 27 **31:47** [1] Literally, in Aramaic, *Heap of Witness* [2] Literally, in Hebrew, *Heap of Witness* **31:48** [a] Josh. 24:27 **31:49** [a] Judg. 10:17; 11:29; 1 Sam. 7:5, 6 [1] Literally *Watch* **31:53** [a] Gen. 16:5 [b] Gen. 21:23 [c] Gen. 31:42 **31:55** [a] Gen. 29:11, 13; 31:28, 43 [b] Gen. 28:1 [c] Gen. 18:33; 30:25; Num. 24:25 **32:1** [a] Num. 22:31 **32:2** [a] Josh. 5:14 [1] Literally *Double Camp* **32:3** [a] Gen. 14:6; 33:14, 16 [b] Gen. 25:30; 36:6–9 **32:4** [a] Prov. 15:1 **32:5** [a] Gen. 30:43 [b] Gen. 33:8, 15 **32:6** [a] Gen. 33:1 **32:7** [a] Gen. 32:11; 35:3

Esau comes to the one company and attacks
it, then the other company which is left will
escape."
9 [a]Then Jacob said, [b]"O God of my father
Abraham and God of my father Isaac, the LORD
[c]who said to me, 'Return to your country and to
your family, and I will deal well with you': 10 I am
not worthy of the least of all the [a]mercies and of
all the truth which You have shown Your servant;
for I crossed over this Jordan with [b]my staff, and
now I have become two companies. 11 [a]Deliver
me, I pray, from the hand of my brother, from
the hand of Esau; for I fear him, lest he come
and attack me *and* [b]the mother with the children.
12 For [a]You said, 'I will surely treat you well, and
make your descendants as the [b]sand of the sea,
which cannot be numbered for multitude.' "
13 So he lodged there that same night, and
took what came to his hand as [a]a present for
Esau his brother: 14 two hundred female goats and
twenty male goats, two hundred ewes and twenty
rams, 15 thirty milk camels with their colts, forty
cows and ten bulls, twenty female donkeys and
ten foals. 16 Then he delivered *them* to the hand
of his servants, every drove by itself, and said to
his servants, "Pass over before me, and put some
distance between successive droves." 17 And he
commanded the first one, saying, "When Esau
my brother meets you and asks you, saying, 'To
whom do you belong, and where are you going?
Whose *are* these in front of you?' 18 then you shall
say, 'They *are* your servant Jacob's. It *is* a present
sent to my lord Esau; and behold, he also *is* be-
hind us.' " 19 So he commanded the second, the
third, and all who followed the droves, saying, "In
this manner you shall speak to Esau when you
find him; 20 and also say, 'Behold, your servant
Jacob *is* behind us.' " For he said, "I will [a]appease
him with the present that goes before me, and
afterward I will see his face; perhaps he will accept
me." 21 So the present went on over before him,
but he himself lodged that night in the camp.

### WRESTLING WITH GOD

22 And he arose that night and took his two
wives, his two female servants, and his eleven

32:9 [a] [Ps. 50:15] [b] Gen. 28:13; 31:42 [c] Gen. 31:3, 13 32:10 [a] Gen. 24:27 [b] Job 8:7 32:11 [a] Ps. 59:1, 2 [b] Hos. 10:14 32:12 [a] Gen. 28:13–15 [b] Gen. 22:17 32:13 [a] Gen. 43:11 32:20 [a] [Prov. 21:14]

GENESIS 32:22–32

## WRESTLING WITH GOD

6

STORY OF SCRIPTURE

### WHAT'S GOING ON?

Isaac gave Abraham two grandsons, Jacob and Esau. Jacob, the younger, lied and swindled to get ahead in life. Years before, he persuaded Esau to give up his family birthright—a double-portion of the family inheritance—for a bowl of stew (see Gen. 25:29–34). Later, he tricked his father into blessing him over Esau, an act that caused him to flee for years. When Jacob returned home, he wasn't sure if Esau would seek revenge or reconciliation. In distress, Jacob prayed to God for His favor. But Jacob couldn't gain that favor through trickery or smooth-talking. This time, it would come by struggle. A mysterious Man, perhaps the Lord Himself, wrestled with Jacob until dawn. Jacob held on, refusing to let go of the Man until he was blessed. This is when Jacob was given a new name: Israel, which means "wrestles with God" or "God is victorious." Jacob was given this new name because he wrestled with God and discovered victory is God's alone.

### WHAT DOES THIS MEAN FOR ME?

Through Jacob's struggle, we glimpse our relationships with God. We wrestle with God in some way. We struggle with doubt, fear, pride, or something else. And just as Jacob experienced victory through his struggle, if we diligently cling to God, we will experience true victory in Him.

### DID YOU CATCH THE PATTERN?

Jacob became Israel, and his children bore the name Israelites. Through Jacob's sons, the twelve tribes of the nation of Israel formed. This nation demonstrated a pattern of wrestling with God. They struggled repeatedly with idolatry, doubt, disobedience, and fear. But even through their struggles and rebellion, God's love was fixed on them, and He was unwavering in His promise to provide victory for them, victory realized in Christ Jesus.

*For the next* Story of Scripture *reading and devotion, turn to Genesis 41:37–57 on page 49.*

sons, [a]and crossed over the ford of Jabbok. 23 He took them, sent them over the brook, and sent over what he had. 24 Then Jacob was left alone; and [a]a Man wrestled with him until the breaking of day. 25 Now when He saw that He did not prevail against him, He touched the socket of his hip; and [a]the socket of Jacob's hip was out of joint as He wrestled with him. 26 And [a]He said, "Let Me go, for the day breaks."

But he said, [b]"I will not let You go unless You bless me!"

27 So He said to him, "What *is* your name?"

He said, "Jacob."

28 And He said, [a]"Your name shall no longer be called Jacob, but Israel;[1] for you have [b]struggled with God and [c]with men, and have prevailed."

29 Then Jacob asked, saying, "Tell *me* Your name, I pray."

And He said, [a]"Why *is* it *that* you ask about My name?" And He [b]blessed him there.

30 So Jacob called the name of the place Peniel:[1] "For [a]I have seen God face to face, and my life is preserved." 31 Just as he crossed over Penuel[1] the sun rose on him, and he limped on his hip. 32 Therefore to this day the children of Israel do not eat the muscle that shrank, which *is* on the hip socket, because He touched the socket of Jacob's hip in the muscle that shrank.

## *JACOB AND ESAU MEET*

**33** Now Jacob lifted his eyes and looked, and there, [a]Esau was coming, and with him were four hundred men. So he divided the children among Leah, Rachel, and the two maidservants. 2 And he put the maidservants and their children in front, Leah and her children behind, and Rachel and Joseph last. 3 Then he crossed over before them and [a]bowed himself to the ground seven times, until he came near to his brother.

4 [a]But Esau ran to meet him, and embraced him, [b]and fell on his neck and kissed him, and they wept. 5 And he lifted his eyes and saw the women and children, and said, "Who *are* these with you?"

So he said, "The children [a]whom God has graciously given your servant." 6 Then the maidservants came near, they and their children, and bowed down. 7 And Leah also came near with her children, and they bowed down. Afterward Joseph and Rachel came near, and they bowed down.

8 Then Esau said, "What *do* you *mean by* [a]all this company which I met?"

And he said, "*These are* [b]to find favor in the sight of my lord."

9 But Esau said, "I have enough, my brother; keep what you have for yourself."

10 And Jacob said, "No, please, if I have now found favor in your sight, then receive my present from my hand, inasmuch as I [a]have seen your face as though I had seen the face of God, and you were pleased with me. 11 Please, take [a]my blessing that is brought to you, because God has dealt [b]graciously with me, and because I have enough." [c]So he urged him, and he took *it*.

12 Then Esau said, "Let us take our journey; let us go, and I will go before you."

13 But Jacob said to him, "My lord knows that the children *are* weak, and the flocks and herds which are nursing *are* with me. And if the men should drive them hard one day, all the flock will die. 14 Please let my lord go on ahead before his servant. I will lead on slowly at a pace which the livestock that go before me, and the children, are able to endure, until I come to my lord [a]in Seir."

15 And Esau said, "Now let me leave with you *some* of the people who *are* with me."

But he said, "What need is there? [a]Let me find favor in the sight of my lord." 16 So Esau returned that day on his way to Seir. 17 And Jacob journeyed to [a]Succoth, built himself a house, and made booths for his livestock. Therefore the name of the place is called Succoth.[1]

## *JACOB COMES TO CANAAN*

18 Then Jacob came safely to [a]the city of [b]Shechem, which *is* in the land of Canaan, when he came from Padan Aram; and he pitched his tent before the city. 19 And [a]he bought the parcel of land, where he had pitched his tent, from the children of Hamor, Shechem's father, for one hundred pieces of money. 20 Then he erected an altar there and called it [a]El Elohe Israel.[1]

## *THE DINAH INCIDENT*

**34** Now [a]Dinah the daughter of Leah, whom she had borne to Jacob, went out to see the daughters of the land. 2 And when Shechem the son of Hamor the Hivite, prince of the country, saw her, he [a]took her and lay with her, and violated her. 3 His soul was strongly attracted to Dinah the daughter of Jacob, and he loved the young woman and spoke kindly to the young woman. 4 So Shechem [a]spoke to his father Hamor, saying, "Get me this young woman as a wife."

5 And Jacob heard that he had defiled Dinah his daughter. Now his sons were with his livestock in the field; so Jacob [a]held his peace until they came. 6 Then Hamor the father of Shechem went out to Jacob to speak with him. 7 And the sons of Jacob came in from the field when they

**32:22** [a] Deut. 3:16 **32:24** [a] Hos. 12:2–4 **32:25** [a] 2 Cor. 12:7 **32:26** [a] Luke 24:28 [b] Hos. 12:4 **32:28** [a] Gen. 35:10 [b] Hos. 12:3, 4 [c] Gen. 25:31; 27:33 [1] Literally *Prince with God* **32:29** [a] Judg. 13:17, 18 [b] Gen. 35:9 **32:30** [a] Gen. 16:13 [1] Literally *Face of God* **32:31** [1] Same as *Peniel,* verse 30 **33:1** [a] Gen. 32:6 **33:3** [a] Gen. 18:2; 42:6 **33:4** [a] Gen. 32:28 [b] Gen. 45:14, 15 **33:5** [a] Gen. 48:9; [Ps. 127:3]; Is. 8:18 **33:8** [a] Gen. 32:13–16 [b] Gen. 32:5 **33:10** [a] Gen. 43:3; 2 Sam. 3:13; 14:24, 28, 32 **33:11** [a] Judg. 1:15; 1 Sam. 25:27; 30:26 [b] Gen. 30:43; Ex. 33:19 [c] 2 Kin. 5:23 **33:14** [a] Gen. 32:3; 36:8 **33:15** [a] Gen. 34:11; 47:25; Ruth 2:13 **33:17** [a] Josh. 13:27; Judg. 8:5; Ps. 60:6 [1] Literally *Booths* **33:18** [a] John 3:23 [b] Gen. 12:6; 35:4; Josh. 24:1; Judg. 9:1; Ps. 60:6 **33:19** [a] Josh. 24:32; John 4:5 **33:20** [a] Gen. 35:7 [1] Literally *God, the God of Israel* **34:1** [a] Gen. 30:21 **34:2** [a] Gen. 20:2 **34:4** [a] Judg. 14:2 **34:5** [a] 2 Sam. 13:22

heard *it;* and the men were grieved and very angry, because he [a]had done a disgraceful thing in Israel by lying with Jacob's daughter, [b]a thing which ought not to be done. 8 But Hamor spoke with them, saying, "The soul of my son Shechem longs for your daughter. Please give her to him as a wife. 9 And make marriages with us; give your daughters to us, and take our daughters to yourselves. 10 So you shall dwell with us, and the land shall be before you. Dwell and trade in it, and acquire possessions for yourselves in it."

11 Then Shechem said to her father and her brothers, "Let me find favor in your eyes, and whatever you say to me I will give. 12 Ask me ever so much [a]dowry and gift, and I will give according to what you say to me; but give me the young woman as a wife."

13 But the sons of Jacob answered Shechem and Hamor his father, and spoke [a]deceitfully, because he had defiled Dinah their sister. 14 And they said to them, "We cannot do this thing, to give our sister to one who is [a]uncircumcised, for [b]that *would be* a reproach to us. 15 But on this *condition* we will consent to you: If you will become as we *are,* if every male of you is circumcised, 16 then we will give our daughters to you, and we will take your daughters to us; and we will dwell with you, and we will become one people. 17 But if you will not heed us and be circumcised, then we will take our daughter and be gone."

18 And their words pleased Hamor and Shechem, Hamor's son. 19 So the young man did not delay to do the thing, because he delighted in Jacob's daughter. He *was* [a]more honorable than all the household of his father.

20 And Hamor and Shechem his son came to the [a]gate of their city, and spoke with the men of their city, saying: 21 "These men *are* at peace with us. Therefore let them dwell in the land and trade in it. For indeed the land *is* large enough for them. Let us take their daughters to us as wives, and let us give them our daughters. 22 Only on this *condition* will the men consent to dwell with us, to be one people: if every male among us is circumcised as they *are* circumcised. 23 *Will* not their livestock, their property, and every animal of theirs *be* ours? Only let us consent to them, and they will dwell with us." 24 And all who went out of the gate of his city heeded Hamor and Shechem his son; every male was circumcised, all who [a]went out of the gate of his city.

25 Now it came to pass on the third day, when they were in pain, that two of the sons of Jacob, [a]Simeon and Levi, Dinah's brothers, each took his sword and came boldly upon the city and killed all the males. 26 And they [a]killed Hamor and Shechem his son with the edge of the sword, and took Dinah from Shechem's house, and went out. 27 The sons of Jacob came upon the slain, and plundered the city, because their sister had been defiled. 28 They took their sheep, their oxen, and their donkeys, what *was* in the city and what *was* in the field, 29 and all their wealth. All their little ones and their wives they took captive; and they plundered even all that *was* in the houses.

30 Then Jacob said to Simeon and Levi, [a]"You have [b]troubled me [c]by making me obnoxious among the inhabitants of the land, among the Canaanites and the Perizzites; [d]and since I *am* few in number, they will gather themselves together against me and kill me. I shall be destroyed, my household and I."

31 But they said, "Should he treat our sister like a harlot?"

### JACOB'S RETURN TO BETHEL

**35** Then God said to Jacob, "Arise, go up to [a]Bethel and dwell there; and make an altar there to God, [b]who appeared to you [c]when you fled from the face of Esau your brother."

2 And Jacob said to his [a]household and to all who *were* with him, "Put away [b]the foreign gods that *are* among you, [c]purify yourselves, and change your garments. 3 Then let us arise and go up to Bethel; and I will make an altar there to God, [a]who answered me in the day of my distress [b]and has been with me in the way which I have gone." 4 So they gave Jacob all the foreign gods which *were* in their hands, and the [a]earrings which *were* in their ears; and Jacob hid them under [b]the terebinth tree which *was* by Shechem.

5 And they journeyed, and [a]the terror of God was upon the cities that *were* all around them, and they did not pursue the sons of Jacob. 6 So Jacob came to [a]Luz (that *is,* Bethel), which *is* in the land of Canaan, he and all the people who *were* with him. 7 And he [a]built an altar there and called the place El Bethel,[1] because [b]there God appeared to him when he fled from the face of his brother.

8 Now [a]Deborah, Rebekah's nurse, died, and she was buried below Bethel under the terebinth tree. So the name of it was called Allon Bachuth.[1]

9 Then [a]God appeared to Jacob again, when he came from Padan Aram, and [b]blessed him. 10 And God said to him, "Your name *is* Jacob; [a]your name shall not be called Jacob anymore, [b]but Israel shall be your name." So He called his name Israel. 11 Also God said to him: [a]"I *am* God Almighty. [b]Be fruitful and multiply; [c]a nation and a company of nations shall proceed from

**34:7** [a] Deut. 22:20–30; Josh. 7:15; Judg. 20:6 [b] Deut. 23:17; 2 Sam. 13:12 **34:12** [a] Ex. 22:16, 17; Deut. 22:29 **34:13** [a] Gen. 31:7; Ex. 8:29 **34:14** [a] Ex. 12:48 [b] Josh. 5:2–9 **34:19** [a] 1 Chr. 4:9 **34:20** [a] Ruth 4:1, 11 **34:24** [a] Gen. 23:10, 18 **34:25** [a] Gen. 29:33, 34; 42:24; 49:5–7 **34:26** [a] Gen. 49:5, 6 **34:30** [a] Gen. 49:6 [b] Josh. 7:25 [c] Ex. 5:21 [d] Deut. 4:27 **35:1** [a] Gen. 28:19; 31:13 [b] Gen. 28:13 [c] Gen. 27:43 **35:2** [a] Josh. 24:15 [b] Josh. 24:2, 14, 23 [c] Ex. 19:10, 14 **35:3** [a] Gen. 32:7, 24 [b] Gen. 28:15, 20; 31:3, 42 **35:4** [a] Hos. 2:13 [b] Josh. 24:26 **35:5** [a] Ex. 15:16; 23:27 **35:6** [a] Gen. 28:19, 22; 48:3 **35:7** [a] Eccl. 5:4 [b] Gen. 28:13 [1] Literally *God of the House of God* **35:8** [a] Gen. 24:59 [1] Literally *Terebinth of Weeping* **35:9** [a] Josh. 5:13 [b] Gen. 32:29 **35:10** [a] Gen. 17:5 [b] Gen. 32:28 **35:11** [a] Ex. 6:3 [b] Gen. 9:1, 7 [c] Gen. 17:5, 6, 16; 28:3; 48:4

**35:10–12** The renewal of God's covenant with Jacob was introduced by confirming Jacob's change of name to **Israel**, the one who "wrestled with God and prevailed." The promises made to Abraham and Isaac were once again repeated, underscoring the continuity of the covenant. Furthermore, a rather significant phrase is added, **be fruitful and multiply**, which incorporated the creation ordinance, thus exhibiting the continuity with the covenant of creation.

you, and kings shall come from your body. 12 The
[a]land which I gave Abraham and Isaac I give to
you; and to your descendants after you I give
this land." 13 Then God [a]went up from him in
the place where He talked with him. 14 So Jacob
[a]set up a pillar in the place where He talked with
him, a pillar of stone; and he poured a drink
offering on it, and he poured oil on it. 15 And
Jacob called the name of the place where God
spoke with him, [a]Bethel.

### *DEATH OF RACHEL*

16 Then they journeyed from Bethel. And
when there was but a little distance to go to
Ephrath, Rachel labored *in childbirth,* and she
had hard labor. 17 Now it came to pass, when
she was in hard labor, that the midwife said to
her, "Do not fear; [a]you will have this son also."
18 And so it was, as her soul was departing (for
she died), that she called his name Ben-Oni;[1] but
his father called him Benjamin.[2] 19 So [a]Rachel
died and was buried on the way to [b]Ephrath
(that *is,* Bethlehem). 20 And Jacob set a pillar on
her grave, which *is* the pillar of Rachel's grave
[a]to this day.
21 Then Israel journeyed and pitched his tent
beyond [a]the tower of Eder. 22 And it happened,
when Israel dwelt in that land, that Reuben went
and [a]lay with Bilhah his father's concubine; and
Israel heard *about it.*

### *JACOB'S TWELVE SONS*

Now the sons of Jacob were twelve: 23 the
sons of Leah *were* [a]Reuben, Jacob's firstborn,
and Simeon, Levi, Judah, Issachar, and Zebulun;
24 the sons of Rachel *were* Joseph and Benjamin;
25 the sons of Bilhah, Rachel's maidservant, *were*
Dan and Naphtali; 26 and the sons of Zilpah,
Leah's maidservant, *were* Gad and Asher. These
*were* the sons of Jacob who were born to him
in Padan Aram.

### *DEATH OF ISAAC*

27 Then Jacob came to his father Isaac at
[a]Mamre, or [b]Kirjath Arba[1] (that *is,* Hebron),
where Abraham and Isaac had dwelt. 28 Now
the days of Isaac were one hundred and eighty
years. 29 So Isaac breathed his last and died, and
[a]was gathered to his people, *being* old and full of
days. And [b]his sons Esau and Jacob buried him.

### *THE FAMILY OF ESAU*

*(1 Chr. 1:35–42)*

36 Now this *is* the genealogy of Esau, [a]who
is Edom. 2 [a]Esau took his wives from the
daughters of Canaan: Adah the daughter of
Elon the [b]Hittite; [c]Aholibamah the daughter
of Anah, the daughter of Zibeon the Hivite;
3 and [a]Basemath, Ishmael's daughter, sister of
Nebajoth. 4 Now [a]Adah bore Eliphaz to Esau,
and Basemath bore Reuel. 5 And Aholibamah
bore Jeush, Jaalam, and Korah. These *were* the
sons of Esau who were born to him in the land
of Canaan.
6 Then Esau took his wives, his sons, his
daughters, and all the persons of his household,
his cattle and all his animals, and all his goods
which he had gained in the land of Canaan, and
went to a country away from the presence of his
brother Jacob. 7 [a]For their possessions were too
great for them to dwell together, and [b]the land
where they were strangers could not support
them because of their livestock. 8 So Esau dwelt
in [a]Mount Seir. [b]Esau *is* Edom.
9 And this *is* the genealogy of Esau the father
of the Edomites in Mount Seir. 10 These *were* the
names of Esau's sons: [a]Eliphaz the son of Adah
the wife of Esau, and Reuel the son of Basemath
the wife of Esau. 11 And the sons of Eliphaz were
Teman, Omar, Zepho,[1] Gatam, and Kenaz.
12 Now Timna was the concubine of Eliphaz,
Esau's son, and she bore [a]Amalek to Eliphaz.
These *were* the sons of Adah, Esau's wife.
13 These *were* the sons of Reuel: Nahath,
Zerah, Shammah, and Mizzah. These were the
sons of Basemath, Esau's wife.
14 These were the sons of Aholibamah, Esau's
wife, the daughter of Anah, the daughter of
Zibeon. And she bore to Esau: Jeush, Jaalam,
and Korah.

### *THE CHIEFS OF EDOM*

15 These *were* the chiefs of the sons of Esau.
The sons of Eliphaz, the firstborn *son* of Esau,
were Chief Teman, Chief Omar, Chief Zepho,
Chief Kenaz, 16 Chief Korah,[1] Chief Gatam, *and*
Chief Amalek. These *were* the chiefs of Eliphaz
in the land of Edom. They *were* the sons of Adah.

35:12 [a] Gen. 12:7; 13:15; 26:3, 4; 28:13; 48:4 35:13 [a] Gen. 17:22; 18:33 35:14 [a] Gen. 28:18, 19; 31:45 35:15 [a] Gen. 28:19 35:17 [a] Gen. 30:24; 1 Sam. 4:20 35:18 [1] Literally *Son of My Sorrow* [2] Literally *Son of the Right Hand* 35:19 [a] Gen. 48:7 [b] Ruth 1:2; 4:11; Mic. 5:2; Matt. 2:6 35:20 [a] 1 Sam. 10:2 35:21 [a] Mic. 4:8 35:22 [a] Gen. 49:4; 1 Chr. 5:1 35:23 [a] Gen. 29:31–35; 30:18–20; 46:8; Ex. 1:1–4 35:27 [a] Gen. 13:18; 18:1; 23:19 [b] Josh. 14:15 [1] Literally *Town of Arba* 35:29 [a] Gen. 15:15; 25:8; 49:33 [b] Gen. 25:9; 49:31 36:1 [a] Gen. 25:30 36:2 [a] Gen. 26:34; 28:9 [b] 2 Kin. 7:6 [c] Gen. 36:25 36:3 [a] Gen. 28:9 36:4 [a] 1 Chr. 1:35 36:7 [a] Gen. 13:6, 11 [b] Gen. 17:8; 28:4; Heb. 11:9 36:8 [a] Gen. 32:3; Deut. 2:5; Josh. 24:4 [b] Gen. 36:1, 19 36:10 [a] 1 Chr. 1:35 36:11 [1] Spelled *Zephi* in 1 Chronicles 1:36 36:12 [a] Ex. 17:8–16; Num. 24:20; Deut. 25:17–19; 1 Sam. 15:2, 3 36:16 [1] Samaritan Pentateuch omits *Chief Korah.*

17 These *were* the sons of Reuel, Esau's son: Chief Nahath, Chief Zerah, Chief Shammah, and Chief Mizzah. These *were* the chiefs of Reuel in the land of Edom. These *were* the sons of Basemath, Esau's wife.

18 And these *were* the sons of Aholibamah, Esau's wife: Chief Jeush, Chief Jaalam, and Chief Korah. These *were* the chiefs *who descended* from Aholibamah, Esau's wife, the daughter of Anah. 19 These *were* the sons of Esau, who is Edom, and these *were* their chiefs.

### *THE SONS OF SEIR*

20 [a]These *were* the sons of Seir [b]the Horite who inhabited the land: Lotan, Shobal, Zibeon, Anah, 21 Dishon, Ezer, and Dishan. These *were* the chiefs of the Horites, the sons of Seir, in the land of Edom.

22 And the sons of Lotan were Hori and Hemam.[1] Lotan's sister *was* Timna.

23 These *were* the sons of Shobal: Alvan,[1] Manahath, Ebal, Shepho,[2] and Onam.

24 These *were* the sons of Zibeon: both Ajah and Anah. This *was the* Anah who found the water[1] in the wilderness as he pastured [a]the donkeys of his father Zibeon. 25 These *were* the children of Anah: Dishon and Aholibamah the daughter of Anah.

26 These *were* the sons of Dishon:[1] Hemdan,[2] Eshban, Ithran, and Cheran. 27 These *were* the sons of Ezer: Bilhan, Zaavan, and Akan.[1] 28 These *were* the sons of Dishan: [a]Uz and Aran.

29 These *were* the chiefs of the Horites: Chief Lotan, Chief Shobal, Chief Zibeon, Chief Anah, 30 Chief Dishon, Chief Ezer, and Chief Dishan. These *were* the chiefs of the Horites, according to their chiefs in the land of Seir.

### *THE KINGS OF EDOM*

31 [a]Now these *were* the kings who reigned in the land of Edom before any king reigned over the children of Israel: 32 Bela the son of Beor reigned in Edom, and the name of his city *was* Dinhabah. 33 And when Bela died, Jobab the son of Zerah of Bozrah reigned in his place. 34 When Jobab died, Husham of the land of the Temanites reigned in his place. 35 And when Husham died, Hadad the son of Bedad, who attacked Midian in the field of Moab, reigned in his place. And the name of his city *was* Avith. 36 When Hadad died, Samlah of Masrekah reigned in his place. 37 And when Samlah died, Saul of [a]Rehoboth-*by*-the-River reigned in his place. 38 When Saul died, Baal-Hanan the son of Achbor reigned in his place. 39 And when Baal-Hanan the son of Achbor died, Hadar[1] reigned in his place; and the name of his city *was* Pau.[2] His wife's name *was* Mehetabel, the daughter of Matred, the daughter of Mezahab.

### *THE CHIEFS OF ESAU*

40 And these *were* the names of the chiefs of Esau, according to their families and their places, by their names: Chief Timnah, Chief Alvah,[1] Chief Jetheth, 41 Chief Aholibamah, Chief Elah, Chief Pinon, 42 Chief Kenaz, Chief Teman, Chief Mibzar, 43 Chief Magdiel, and Chief Iram. These *were* the chiefs of Edom, according to their dwelling places in the land of their possession. Esau *was* the father of the Edomites.

### *JOSEPH DREAMS OF GREATNESS*

**37** Now Jacob dwelt in the land [a]where his father was a stranger, in the land of Canaan. 2 This *is* the history of Jacob.

Joseph, *being* seventeen years old, was feeding the flock with his brothers. And the lad *was* with the sons of Bilhah and the sons of Zilpah, his father's wives; and Joseph brought [a]a bad report of them to his father.

3 Now Israel loved Joseph more than all his children, because he *was* [a]the son of his old age. Also he [b]made him a tunic of *many* colors. 4 But when his brothers saw that their father loved him more than all his brothers, they [a]hated him and could not speak peaceably to him.

5 Now Joseph had a dream, and he told *it* to his brothers; and they hated him even more. 6 So he said to them, "Please hear this dream which I have dreamed: 7 [a]There we were, binding sheaves in the field. Then behold, my sheaf arose and also stood upright; and indeed your sheaves stood all around and bowed down to my sheaf."

8 And his brothers said to him, "Shall you indeed reign over us? Or shall you indeed have dominion over us?" So they hated him even more for his dreams and for his words.

9 Then he dreamed still another dream and told it to his brothers, and said, "Look, I have dreamed another dream. And this time, [a]the sun, the moon, and the eleven stars bowed down to me."

10 So he told *it* to his father and his brothers; and his father rebuked him and said to him, "What *is* this dream that you have dreamed? Shall your mother and I and [a]your brothers indeed come to bow down to the earth before you?" 11 And [a]his brothers envied him, but his father [b]kept the matter *in mind.*

**36:20** [a] 1 Chr. 1:38–42 [b] Gen. 14:6; Deut. 2:12, 22 **36:22** [1] Spelled *Homam* in 1 Chronicles 1:39 **36:23** [1] Spelled *Alian* in 1 Chronicles 1:40 [2] Spelled *Shephi* in 1 Chronicles 1:40 **36:24** [a] Lev. 19:19 [1] Following Masoretic Text and Vulgate (*hot springs*); Septuagint reads *Jamin;* Targum reads *mighty men;* Talmud interprets as *mules.* **36:26** [1] Hebrew *Dishan* [2] Spelled *Hamran* in 1 Chronicles 1:41 **36:27** [1] Spelled *Jaakan* in 1 Chronicles 1:42 **36:28** [a] Job 1:1 **36:31** [a] Gen. 17:6, 16; 35:11; 1 Chr. 1:43 **36:37** [a] Gen. 10:11 **36:39** [1] Spelled *Hadad* in Samaritan Pentateuch, Syriac, and 1 Chronicles 1:50 [2] Spelled *Pai* in 1 Chronicles 1:50 **36:40** [1] Spelled *Aliah* in 1 Chronicles 1:51 **37:1** [a] Gen. 17:8; 23:4; 28:4; 36:7; Heb. 11:9 **37:2** [a] Gen. 35:25, 26; 1 Sam. 2:22–24 **37:3** [a] Gen. 44:20 [b] Gen. 37:23, 32; Judg. 5:30; 1 Sam. 2:19 **37:4** [a] Gen. 27:41; 49:23; 1 Sam. 17:28; John 15:18–20 **37:7** [a] Gen. 42:6, 9; 43:26; 44:14 **37:9** [a] Gen. 46:29; 47:25 **37:10** [a] Gen. 27:29 **37:11** [a] Matt. 27:17, 18; Acts 7:9 [b] Dan. 7:28; Luke 2:19, 51

### *JOSEPH SOLD BY HIS BROTHERS*

12 Then his brothers went to feed their fa-
ther's flock in [a]Shechem. 13 And Israel said to
Joseph, "Are not your brothers feeding *the flock*
in Shechem? Come, I will send you to them."
So he said to him, "Here I am."
14 Then he said to him, "Please go and see if
it is well with your brothers and well with the
flocks, and bring back word to me." So he sent
him out of the Valley of [a]Hebron, and he went
to Shechem.
15 Now a certain man found him, and there he
was, wandering in the field. And the man asked
him, saying, "What are you seeking?"
16 So he said, "I am seeking my brothers.
[a]Please tell me where they are feeding *their
flocks.*"
17 And the man said, "They have departed
from here, for I heard them say, 'Let us go to
Dothan.'" So Joseph went after his brothers and
found them in [a]Dothan.
18 Now when they saw him afar off, even before
he came near them, [a]they conspired against him
to kill him. 19 Then they said to one another, "Look,
this dreamer is coming! 20 [a]Come therefore, let
us now kill him and cast him into some pit; and
we shall say, 'Some wild beast has devoured him.'
We shall see what will become of his dreams!"
21 But [a]Reuben heard *it*, and he delivered him
out of their hands, and said, "Let us not kill him."
22 And Reuben said to them, "Shed no blood, *but*
cast him into this pit which *is* in the wilderness,
and do not lay a hand on him"—that he might
deliver him out of their hands, and bring him
back to his father.
23 So it came to pass, when Joseph had come
to his brothers, that they [a]stripped Joseph *of* his
tunic, the tunic of *many* colors that *was* on him.
24 Then they took him and cast him into a pit.
And the pit *was* empty; *there was* no water in it.
25 [a]And they sat down to eat a meal. Then
they lifted their eyes and looked, and there was
a company of [b]Ishmaelites, coming from Gil-
ead with their camels, bearing spices, [c]balm,
and myrrh, on their way to carry *them* down to
Egypt. 26 So Judah said to his brothers, "What
profit *is there* if we kill our brother and [a]conceal
his blood? 27 Come and let us sell him to the Ish-
maelites, and [a]let not our hand be upon him,
for he *is* [b]our brother *and* [c]our flesh." And his
brothers listened. 28 Then [a]Midianite traders
passed by; so *the brothers* pulled Joseph up and
lifted him out of the pit, [b]and sold him to the
Ishmaelites for [c]twenty *shekels* of silver. And
they took Joseph to Egypt.
29 Then Reuben returned to the pit, and in-
deed Joseph *was* not in the pit; and he [a]tore his
clothes. 30 And he returned to his brothers and
said, "The lad [a]*is* no *more;* and I, where shall I go?"
31 So they took [a]Joseph's tunic, killed a kid
of the goats, and dipped the tunic in the blood.
32 Then they sent the tunic of *many* colors, and
they brought *it* to their father and said, "We have
found this. Do you know whether it *is* your son's
tunic or not?"
33 And he recognized it and said, "*It is* my
son's tunic. A [a]wild beast has devoured him.
Without doubt Joseph is torn to pieces." 34 Then
Jacob [a]tore his clothes, put sackcloth on his waist,
and [b]mourned for his son many days. 35 And all

**37:12** [a] Gen. 33:18–20 **37:14** [a] Gen. 13:18; 23:2, 19; 35:27; Josh. 14:14, 15; Judg. 1:10 **37:16** [a] Song 1:7 **37:17** [a] 2 Kin. 6:13 **37:18** [a] 1 Sam. 19:1; Ps. 31:13; 37:12, 32; Matt. 21:38; 26:3, 4; 27:1; Mark 14:1; John 11:53; Acts 23:12 **37:20** [a] Gen. 37:22; Prov. 1:11 **37:21** [a] Gen. 42:22 **37:23** [a] Matt. 27:28 **37:25** [a] Prov. 30:20 [b] Gen. 16:11, 12; 37:28, 36; 39:1 [c] Jer. 8:22 **37:26** [a] Gen. 37:20 **37:27** [a] 1 Sam. 18:17 [b] Gen. 42:21 [c] Gen. 29:14 **37:28** [a] Gen. 37:25; Judg. 6:1–3; 8:22, 24 [b] Gen. 45:4, 5; Ps. 105:17; Acts 7:9 [c] Matt. 27:9 **37:29** [a] Gen. 37:34; 44:13; Job 1:20 **37:30** [a] Gen. 42:13, 36 **37:31** [a] Gen. 37:3, 23 **37:33** [a] Gen. 37:20 **37:34** [a] Gen. 37:29; 2 Sam. 3:31 [b] Gen. 50:10

APPLY THE TRUTH

## HUMAN TRAFFICKING

**37:25–27** People are creative in our capacity for evil. In this story, Joseph was sold by his brothers into slavery. This act would eventually lead to all of Israel's descendants being bound in slavery to the Egyptians. It would be four hundred years until God set them free through Moses. How could people in that day be this corrupt? Tragically, this behavior still happens as millions of people are modern-day slaves.

So, where is God in all this? First, we must recognize that human trafficking is a sin problem that God has ultimately addressed. Joseph's brothers sold him not to make money, but rather to get even. They had a heart problem. God provided Jesus to heal the hearts of sinners. Through Christ, slavery can and will come to an end.

Second, we can know that God never abandons the slave. He was faithful to Joseph. Later, He heard the cries of His people and raised up Moses to bring freedom. God works the same way today. He remains faithful during difficult situations, listens to people's cries, and raises up people to bring about deliverance. Pause and pray for those who are in slavery.

**37:34 Sackcloth** was a coarse, uncomfortable material made from camel or goat hair, worn during times of sorrow and mourning.

his sons and all his daughters [a]arose to comfort him; but he refused to be comforted, and he said, "For [b]I shall go down into the grave to my son in mourning." Thus his father wept for him.

36 Now [a]the Midianites[1] had sold him in Egypt to Potiphar, an officer of Pharaoh *and* captain of the guard.

### *JUDAH AND TAMAR*

**38** It came to pass at that time that Judah departed from his brothers, and [a]visited a certain Adullamite whose name *was* Hirah. 2 And Judah [a]saw there a daughter of a certain Canaanite whose name *was* [b]Shua, and he married her and went in to her. 3 So she conceived and bore a son, and he called his name [a]Er. 4 She conceived again and bore a son, and she called his name [a]Onan. 5 And she conceived yet again and bore a son, and called his name [a]Shelah. He was at Chezib when she bore him.

6 Then Judah [a]took a wife for Er his firstborn, and her name *was* [b]Tamar. 7 But [a]Er, Judah's firstborn, was wicked in the sight of the LORD, [b]and the LORD killed him. 8 And Judah said to Onan, "Go in to [a]your brother's wife and marry her, and raise up an heir to your brother." 9 But Onan knew that the heir would not be [a]his; and it came to pass, when he went in to his brother's wife, that he emitted on the ground, lest he should give an heir to his brother. 10 And the thing which he did displeased the LORD; therefore He killed [a]him also.

11 Then Judah said to Tamar his daughter-in-law, [a]"Remain a widow in your father's house till my son Shelah is grown." For he said, "Lest he also die like his brothers." And Tamar went and dwelt [b]in her father's house.

12 Now in the process of time the daughter of Shua, Judah's wife, died; and Judah [a]was comforted, and went up to his sheepshearers at Timnah, he and his friend Hirah the Adullamite. 13 And it was told Tamar, saying, "Look, your father-in-law is going up [a]to Timnah to shear his sheep." 14 So she took off her widow's garments, covered *herself* with a veil and wrapped herself, and [a]sat in an open place which *was* on the way to Timnah; for she saw [b]that Shelah was grown, and she was not given to him as a wife. 15 When Judah saw her, he thought she *was* a harlot, because she had covered her face. 16 Then he turned to her by the way, and said, "Please let me come in to you"; for he did not know that she *was* his daughter-in-law.

So she said, "What will you give me, that you may come in to me?"

17 And he said, [a]"I will send a young goat from the flock."

So she said, [b]"Will you give *me* a pledge till you send *it?*"

18 Then he said, "What pledge shall I give you?"

So she said, [a]"Your signet and cord, and your staff that *is* in your hand." Then he gave *them* to her, and went in to her, and she conceived by him. 19 So she arose and went away, and [a]laid aside her veil and put on the garments of her widowhood.

20 And Judah sent the young goat by the hand of his friend the Adullamite, to receive *his* pledge from the woman's hand, but he did not find her. 21 Then he asked the men of that place, saying, "Where is the harlot who *was* openly by the roadside?"

And they said, "There was no harlot in this *place.*"

22 So he returned to Judah and said, "I cannot find her. Also, the men of the place said there was no harlot in this *place.*"

23 Then Judah said, "Let her take *them* for herself, lest we be shamed; for I sent this young goat and you have not found her."

24 And it came to pass, about three months after, that Judah was told, saying, "Tamar your daughter-in-law has [a]played the harlot; furthermore she *is* with child by harlotry."

So Judah said, "Bring her out [b]and let her be burned!"

25 When she *was* brought out, she sent to her father-in-law, saying, "By the man to whom these belong, I *am* with child." And she said, [a]"Please determine whose these *are*—the signet and cord, and staff."

26 So Judah [a]acknowledged *them* and said, [b]"She has been more righteous than I, because [c]I did not give her to Shelah my son." And he [d]never knew her again.

27 Now it came to pass, at the time for giving birth, that behold, twins *were* in her womb. 28 And so it was, when she was giving birth, that *the one* put out *his* hand; and the midwife took a scarlet *thread* and bound it on his hand, saying,

**38:1–30** At first glance it appears the story of Judah and Tamar is an intrusion into the story of Joseph, but it's here for a reason. It provides a stunning contrast between the morals of Judah and Joseph.

**37:35** [a] 2 Sam. 12:17 [b] Gen. 25:8; 35:29; 42:38; 44:29, 31 **37:36** [a] Gen. 39:1 [1] Masoretic Text reads *Medanites.* **38:1** [a] 2 Kin. 4:8 **38:2** [a] Gen. 34:2 [b] 1 Chr. 2:3 **38:3** [a] Gen. 46:12; Num. 26:19 **38:4** [a] Gen. 46:12; Num. 26:19 **38:5** [a] Num. 26:20 **38:6** [a] Gen. 21:21 [b] Ruth 4:12 **38:7** [a] Gen. 46:12; Num. 26:19 [b] 1 Chr. 2:3 **38:8** [a] Deut. 25:5, 6; Matt. 22:24 **38:9** [a] Deut. 25:6 **38:10** [a] Gen. 46:12; Num. 26:19 **38:11** [a] Ruth 1:12, 13 [b] Lev. 22:13 **38:12** [a] 2 Sam. 13:39 **38:13** [a] Josh. 15:10, 57; Judg. 14:1 **38:14** [a] Prov. 7:12 [b] Gen. 38:11, 26 **38:17** [a] Judg. 15:1; Ezek. 16:33 [b] Gen. 38:20 **38:18** [a] Gen. 38:25; 41:42 **38:19** [a] Gen. 38:14 **38:24** [a] Judg. 19:2 [b] Lev. 20:14; 21:9; Deut. 22:21 **38:25** [a] Gen. 37:32; 38:18 **38:26** [a] Gen. 37:33 [b] 1 Sam. 24:17 [c] Gen. 38:14 [d] Job 34:31, 32

"This one came out first." 29 Then it happened, as
he drew back his hand, that his brother came out
unexpectedly; and she said, "How did you break
through? *This* breach *be* upon you!" Therefore
his name was called [a]Perez.[1] 30 Afterward his
brother came out who had the scarlet *thread*
on his hand. And his name was called [a]Zerah.

### *JOSEPH A SLAVE IN EGYPT*

**39** Now Joseph had been taken [a]down to
Egypt. And [b]Potiphar, an officer of Phar-
aoh, captain of the guard, an Egyptian, [c]bought
him from the Ishmaelites who had taken him
down there. 2 [a]The LORD was with Joseph, and he
was a successful man; and he was in the house
of his master the Egyptian. 3 And his master saw
that the LORD *was* with him and that the LORD
[a]made all he did to prosper in his hand. 4 So Jo-
seph [a]found favor in his sight, and served him.
Then he made him [b]overseer of his house, and all
*that* he had he put under his authority. 5 So it was,
from the time *that* he had made him overseer
of his house and all that he had, that [a]the LORD
blessed the Egyptian's house for Joseph's sake;
and the blessing of the LORD was on all that he
had in the house and in the field. 6 Thus he left all
that he had in Joseph's hand, and he did not know
what he had except for the bread which he ate.

Now Joseph [a]was handsome in form and
appearance.

7 And it came to pass after these things that
his master's wife cast longing eyes on Joseph,
and she said, [a]"Lie with me."

8 But he refused and said to his master's wife,
"Look, my master does not know what *is* with me
in the house, and he has committed all that he has
to my hand. 9 *There is* no one greater in this house
than I, nor has he kept back anything from me
but you, because you *are* his wife. [a]How then can
I do this great wickedness, and [b]sin against God?"

10 So it was, as she spoke to Joseph day by
day, that he [a]did not heed her, to lie with her *or*
to be with her.

11 But it happened about this time, when
Joseph went into the house to do his work, and
none of the men of the house *was* inside, 12 that
she [a]caught him by his garment, saying, "Lie
with me." But he left his garment in her hand,
and fled and ran outside. 13 And so it was, when
she saw that he had left his garment in her hand
and fled outside, 14 that she called to the men of
her house and spoke to them, saying, "See, he
has brought in to us a [a]Hebrew to mock us. He
came in to me to lie with me, and I cried out with
a loud voice. 15 And it happened, when he heard
that I lifted my voice and cried out, that he left
his garment with me, and fled and went outside."

16 So she kept his garment with her until his
master came home. 17 Then she [a]spoke to him
with words like these, saying, "The Hebrew ser-
vant whom you brought to us came in to me to
mock me; 18 so it happened, as I lifted my voice
and cried out, that he left his garment with me
and fled outside."

19 So it was, when his master heard the words
which his wife spoke to him, saying, "Your servant
did to me after this manner," that his [a]anger was
aroused. 20 Then Joseph's master took him and
[a]put him into the [b]prison, a place where the king's
prisoners *were* confined. And he was there in the

**38:29** [a] Gen. 46:12; Num. 26:20; Ruth 4:12; 1 Chr. 2:4; Matt. 1:3 [1] Literally *Breach* or *Breakthrough* **38:30** [a] Gen. 46:12; 1 Chr. 2:4; Matt. 1:3 **39:1** [a] Gen. 12:10; 43:15 [b] Gen. 37:36; Ps. 105:17 [c] Gen. 37:28; 45:4 **39:2** [a] Gen. 26:24, 28; 28:15; 35:3; 39:3, 21, 23; 1 Sam. 16:18; 18:14, 28; Acts 7:9 **39:3** [a] Ps. 1:3 **39:4** [a] Gen. 18:3; 19:19; 39:21 [b] Gen. 24:2, 10; 39:8, 22; 41:40 **39:5** [a] Gen. 18:26; 30:27; 2 Sam. 6:11 **39:6** [a] Gen. 29:17; 1 Sam. 16:12 **39:7** [a] 2 Sam. 13:11 **39:9** [a] Lev. 20:10; Prov. 6:29, 32 [b] Gen. 20:6; 42:18; 2 Sam. 12:13; Ps. 51:4 **39:10** [a] Prov. 1:10 **39:12** [a] Prov. 7:13 **39:14** [a] Gen. 14:13; 41:12 **39:17** [a] Ex. 23:1; Ps. 120:3; Prov. 26:28 **39:19** [a] Prov. 6:34, 35 **39:20** [a] Ps. 105:18; [1 Pet. 2:19] [b] Gen. 40:3, 15; 41:14

APPLY THE TRUTH

## TRIALS AND TRIBULATIONS

**39:19–23** One thing after another! Have you ever felt like that? You just can't seem to catch a break. Everything that *could* go wrong *goes* wrong. That's likely how Joseph felt. He had gone from being in a pit, to being someone's property, to being thrown into prison. Problem after problem.

Like Joseph we may constantly walk through trials, but God often uses these trials to grow us. Joseph ultimately would be lifted from the prison to the palace where he would be used to save his family and entire nations. And at least in the end, Joseph recognized that although his trials were surely hard, God used them for good.

We have a choice: we can let trials make us bitter, or we can use trials to make us better—we can grow and serve God through them. Remember God loves you and will give you His strength to endure. Look for opportunities for God to use you for His glory during your trials. If you simply look for ways to escape or survive trials, you'll likely miss all God wants to do in and through you.

prison. 21 But the LORD was with Joseph and showed
him mercy, and He [a]gave him favor in the sight of
the keeper of the prison. 22 And the keeper of the
prison [a]committed to Joseph's hand all the pris-
oners who *were* in the prison; whatever they did
there, it was his doing. 23 The keeper of the prison
did not look into anything *that was* under *Joseph's*
authority,[1] because [a]the LORD was with him; and
whatever he did, the LORD made *it* prosper.

### THE PRISONERS' DREAMS

**40** It came to pass after these things *that*
the [a]butler and the baker of the king of
Egypt offended their lord, the king of Egypt.
2 And Pharaoh was [a]angry with his two officers,
the chief butler and the chief baker. 3 [a]So he put
them in custody in the house of the captain of
the guard, in the prison, the place where Joseph
*was* confined. 4 And the captain of the guard
charged Joseph with them, and he served them;
so they were in custody for a while.
5 Then the butler and the baker of the king
of Egypt, who *were* confined in the prison, [a]had
a dream, both of them, each man's dream in
one night *and* each man's dream with its *own*
interpretation. 6 And Joseph came in to them in
the morning and looked at them, and saw that
they *were* sad. 7 So he asked Pharaoh's officers
who *were* with him in the custody of his lord's
house, saying, [a]"Why do you look *so* sad today?"
8 And they said to him, [a]"We each have had
a dream, and *there is* no interpreter of it."
So Joseph said to them, [b]"Do not interpre-
tations belong to God? Tell *them* to me, please."
9 Then the chief butler told his dream to Jo-
seph, and said to him, "Behold, in my dream a
vine *was* before me, 10 and in the vine *were* three
branches; it *was* as though it budded, its blossoms
shot forth, and its clusters brought forth ripe
grapes. 11 Then Pharaoh's cup *was* in my hand;
and I took the grapes and pressed them into Phar-
aoh's cup, and placed the cup in Pharaoh's hand."
12 And Joseph said to him, [a]"This *is* the in-
terpretation of it: The three branches [b]*are* three
days. 13 Now within three days Pharaoh will [a]lift
up your head and restore you to your place, and
you will put Pharaoh's cup in his hand according
to the former manner, when you were his butler.
14 But [a]remember me when it is well with you,
and [b]please show kindness to me; make mention
of me to Pharaoh, and get me out of this house.
15 For indeed I was [a]stolen away from the land
of the Hebrews; [b]and also I have done nothing
here that they should put me into the dungeon."
16 When the chief baker saw that the interpre-
tation was good, he said to Joseph, "I also *was*
in my dream, and there *were* three white baskets
on my head. 17 In the uppermost basket *were* all
kinds of baked goods for Pharaoh, and the birds
ate them out of the basket on my head."
18 So Joseph answered and said, [a]"This *is*
the interpretation of it: The three baskets *are*
three days. 19 [a]Within three days Pharaoh will
lift off your head from you and [b]hang you on a
tree; and the birds will eat your flesh from you."
20 Now it came to pass on the third day, *which
was* Pharaoh's [a]birthday, that he [b]made a feast
for all his servants; and he [c]lifted up the head of
the chief butler and of the chief baker among his
servants. 21 Then he [a]restored the chief butler to
his butlership again, and [b]he placed the cup in
Pharaoh's hand. 22 But he [a]hanged the chief baker,
as Joseph had interpreted to them. 23 Yet the chief
butler did not remember Joseph, but [a]forgot him.

### PHARAOH'S DREAMS

**41** Then it came to pass, at the end of two full
years, that [a]Pharaoh had a dream; and be-
hold, he stood by the river. 2 Suddenly there came
up out of the river seven cows, fine looking and
fat; and they fed in the meadow. 3 Then behold,
seven other cows came up after them out of the
river, ugly and gaunt, and stood by the *other* cows
on the bank of the river. 4 And the ugly and gaunt
cows ate up the seven fine looking and fat cows.
So Pharaoh awoke. 5 He slept and dreamed a
second time; and suddenly seven heads of grain
came up on one stalk, plump and good. 6 Then
behold, seven thin heads, blighted by the [a]east
wind, sprang up after them. 7 And the seven thin
heads devoured the seven plump and full heads.
So Pharaoh awoke, and indeed, *it was* a dream.
8 Now it came to pass in the morning [a]that his
spirit was troubled, and he sent and called for

> **41:8** ***Magicians*** is related to the word for stylus, a writing instrument. Thus, magicians were associated in some manner with writing and knowledge, no doubt of the occult. Wise men were a class of scholars associated with the courts of the ancient Near East. They were either practitioners of pagan religions or merely observers and interpreters of life. Ancient kings often used astrologers and magicians as advisors to help them make important decisions. They tried to predict the future by "reading" the body parts of the sacrificed animals they used in pagan worship.

**39:21** [a] Gen. 39:2; Ex. 3:21; Ps. 105:19; [Prov. 16:7]; Dan. 1:9; Acts 7:9, 10 **39:22** [a] Gen. 39:4; 40:3, 4 **39:23** [a] Gen. 39:2, 3 [1] Literally *his hand* **40:1** [a] Gen. 40:11, 13; Neh. 1:11 **40:2** [a] Prov. 16:14 **40:3** [a] Gen. 39:1, 20, 23; 41:10 **40:5** [a] Gen. 37:5; 41:1 **40:7** [a] Neh. 2:2 **40:8** [a] Gen. 41:15 [b] [Gen. 41:16; Dan. 2:11, 20–22, 27, 28, 47] **40:12** [a] Gen. 40:18; 41:12, 25; Judg. 7:14; Dan. 2:36; 4:18, 19 [b] Gen. 40:18; 42:17 **40:13** [a] 2 Kin. 25:27; Ps. 3:3; Jer. 52:31 **40:14** [a] 1 Sam. 25:31; Luke 23:42 [b] Gen. 24:49; 47:29; Josh. 2:12; 1 Sam. 20:14, 15; 2 Sam. 9:1; 1 Kin. 2:7 **40:15** [a] Gen. 37:26–28 [b] Gen. 39:20 **40:18** [a] Gen. 40:12 **40:19** [a] Gen. 40:13 [b] Deut. 21:22 **40:20** [a] Matt. 14:6–10 [b] Mark 6:21 [c] Gen. 40:13, 19 **40:21** [a] Gen. 40:13 [b] Neh. 2:1 **40:22** [a] Gen. 40:19 **40:23** [a] Eccl. 9:15, 16 **41:1** [a] Gen. 40:5 **41:6** [a] Ex. 10:13 **41:8** [a] Dan. 2:1, 3; 4:5, 19

all [b]the magicians of Egypt and all its [c]wise men. And Pharaoh told them his dreams, but *there was* no one who could interpret them for Pharaoh.

9 Then the [a]chief butler spoke to Pharaoh, saying: "I remember my faults this day. 10 When Pharaoh was [a]angry with his servants, [b]and put me in custody in the house of the captain of the guard, *both* me and the chief baker, 11 [a]we each had a dream in one night, he and I. Each of us dreamed according to the interpretation of his *own* dream. 12 Now there *was* a young [a]Hebrew man with us there, a [b]servant of the captain of the guard. And we told him, and he [c]interpreted our dreams for us; to each man he interpreted according to his *own* dream. 13 And it came to pass, just [a]as he interpreted for us, so it happened. He restored me to my office, and he hanged him."

14 [a]Then Pharaoh sent and called Joseph, and they [b]brought him quickly [c]out of the dungeon; and he shaved, [d]changed his clothing, and came to Pharaoh. 15 And Pharaoh said to Joseph, "I have had a dream, and *there is* no one who can interpret it. [a]But I have heard it said of you *that* you can understand a dream, to interpret it."

16 So Joseph answered Pharaoh, saying, [a]"*It is* not in me; [b]God will give Pharaoh an answer of peace."

17 Then Pharaoh said to Joseph: "Behold, [a]in my dream I stood on the bank of the river. 18 Suddenly seven cows came up out of the river, fine looking and fat; and they fed in the meadow. 19 Then behold, seven other cows came up after them, poor and very ugly and gaunt, such ugliness as I have never seen in all the land of Egypt. 20 And the gaunt and ugly cows ate up the first seven, the fat cows. 21 When they had eaten them up, no one would have known that they had eaten them, for they *were* just as ugly as at the beginning. So I awoke. 22 Also I saw in my dream, and suddenly seven heads came up on one stalk, full and good. 23 Then behold, seven heads, withered, thin, *and* blighted by the east wind, sprang up after them. 24 And the thin heads devoured the seven good heads. So [a]I told *this* to the magicians, but *there was* no one who could explain *it* to me."

25 Then Joseph said to Pharaoh, "The dreams of Pharaoh *are* one; [a]God has shown Pharaoh what He *is* about to do: 26 The seven good cows *are* seven years, and the seven good heads *are* seven years; the dreams *are* one. 27 And the seven thin and ugly cows which came up after them *are* seven years, and the seven empty heads blighted by the east wind are [a]seven years of famine. 28 [a]This *is* the thing which I have spoken to Pharaoh. God has shown Pharaoh what He *is* about to do. 29 Indeed [a]seven years of great plenty will come throughout all the land of Egypt; 30 but after them seven years of famine will [a]arise, and all the plenty will be forgotten in the land of Egypt; and the famine [b]will deplete the land. 31 So the plenty will not be known in the land because of the famine following, for it *will be* very severe. 32 And the dream was repeated to Pharaoh twice because the [a]thing *is* established by God, and God will shortly bring it to pass.

33 "Now therefore, let Pharaoh select a discerning and wise man, and set him over the land of Egypt. 34 Let Pharaoh do *this,* and let him appoint officers over the land, [a]to collect one-fifth *of the produce* of the land of Egypt in the seven plentiful years. 35 And [a]let them gather all the food of those good years that are coming, and store up grain under the authority of Pharaoh, and let them keep food in the cities. 36 Then that food shall be as a reserve for the land for the seven years of famine which shall be in the land of Egypt, that the land [a]may not perish during the famine."

## *JOSEPH'S RISE TO POWER*

37 So [a]the advice was good in the eyes of Pharaoh and in the eyes of all his servants. 38 And Pharaoh said to his servants, "Can we find *such a one* as this, a man [a]in whom *is* the Spirit of God?"

39 Then Pharaoh said to Joseph, "Inasmuch as God has shown you all this, *there is* no one as discerning and wise as you. 40 [a]You shall be over my house, and all my people shall be ruled according to your word; only in regard to the throne will I be greater than you." 41 And Pharaoh said to Joseph, "See, I have [a]set you over all the land of Egypt."

42 Then Pharaoh [a]took his signet ring off his hand and put it on Joseph's hand; and he [b]clothed him in garments of fine linen [c]and put a gold chain around his neck. 43 And he had him ride in the second [a]chariot which he had; [b]and they cried out before him, "Bow the knee!" So he set him [c]over all the land of Egypt. 44 Pharaoh also said to Joseph, "I *am* Pharaoh, and without your consent no man may lift his hand or foot in all the land of Egypt." 45 And Pharaoh called Joseph's name Zaphnath-Paaneah. And he gave him as a wife [a]Asenath, the daughter of Poti-Pherah priest of On. So Joseph went out over *all* the land of Egypt.

46 Joseph was thirty years old when he [a]stood before Pharaoh king of Egypt. And Joseph went out from the presence of Pharaoh, and went throughout all the land of Egypt. 47 Now in the seven plentiful years the ground brought forth abundantly. 48 So he gathered up all the food of the seven years which were in the land of Egypt, and laid up the food in the cities; he laid up in every city the food of the fields which surrounded them. 49 Joseph gathered very much grain, [a]as the sand of the sea, until he stopped counting, for *it was* immeasurable.

41:8 [b] Ex. 7:11, 22 [c] Matt. 2:1 41:9 [a] Gen. 40:1, 14, 23 41:10 [a] Gen. 40:2, 3 [b] Gen. 39:20 41:11 [a] Gen. 40:5 41:12 [a] Gen. 39:14; 43:32 [b] Gen. 37:36 [c] Gen. 40:12 41:13 [a] Gen. 40:21, 22 41:14 [a] Ps. 105:20 [b] Dan. 2:25 [c] [1 Sam. 2:8] [d] 2 Kin. 25:27–29 41:15 [a] Dan. 5:16 41:16 [a] Dan. 2:30 [b] Dan. 2:22, 28, 47 41:17 [a] Gen. 41:1 41:24 [a] Is. 8:19 41:25 [a] Dan. 2:28, 29, 45 41:27 [a] 2 Kin. 8:1 41:28 [a] [Gen. 41:25, 32] 41:29 [a] Gen. 41:47 41:30 [a] Gen. 41:54, 56 [b] Gen. 47:13 41:32 [a] Num. 23:19 41:34 [a] [Prov. 6:6–8] 41:35 [a] Gen. 41:48 41:36 [a] Gen. 47:15, 19 41:37 [a] Acts 7:10 41:38 [a] Num. 27:18 41:40 [a] Ps. 105:21 41:41 [a] Dan. 6:3 41:42 [a] Esth. 3:10 [b] Esth. 8:2, 15 [c] Dan. 5:7, 16, 29 41:43 [a] Gen. 46:29 [b] Esth. 6:9 [c] Gen. 42:6 41:45 [a] Gen. 46:20 41:46 [a] 1 Sam. 16:21 41:49 [a] Gen. 22:17

GENESIS 41:37–57

# FROM THE PRISON TO THE PALACE

7

STORY OF SCRIPTURE

## WHAT'S GOING ON?

Joseph was Israel's favored son. Out of jealousy, Joseph's brothers sold him into slavery for a sack of silver. Joseph became a slave in Potiphar's house in Egypt. But God was with Joseph and the slave rose to become head of that household. Then Joseph was accused of a crime he didn't commit and was thrown into a dark prison. But God was with Joseph and the prisoner rose to become head over that prison. Years later, Joseph stood before Pharaoh and became the second most powerful person in Egypt. In this role, he was able to save his family from certain starvation. No family of Israel would have meant no nation of Israel. No nation of Israel would have meant no Messiah.

## WHAT DOES THIS MEAN FOR ME?

Joseph didn't have a linear path to success. His life was filled with highs and lows, peaks and valleys. It's easy to think if we follow God, our lives will be easy and carefree. That simply isn't true. God intends to refine us and use us in all circumstances. Whether we are in the palace or in the prison, there are always opportunities to glorify God and find purpose.

## DID YOU CATCH THE PATTERN?

Joseph was sold for a few pieces of silver, wrongly declared guilty, and thrown into prison. But Joseph eventually rose out of the prison to save the very people who had betrayed him. Joseph's story is an image of Jesus, a shadow of the gospel. Jesus was sold out by Judas for a few pieces of silver, declared guilty although innocent, and thrown into the grave. But Jesus rose again to save the very people who had betrayed Him. These shadows are everywhere, and they repeat in the Bible's most famous heroes like Moses, Joshua, David, and Daniel.

*For the next* Story of Scripture *reading and devotion, turn to Exodus 1:8—2:10 on page 61.*

50 [a]And to Joseph were born two sons before the years of famine came, whom Asenath, the daughter of Poti-Pherah priest of On, bore to him. 51 Joseph called the name of the firstborn Manasseh:[1] "For God has made me forget all my toil and all my [a]father's house." 52 And the name of the second he called Ephraim:[1] "For God has caused me to be [a]fruitful in the land of my affliction."

53 Then the seven years of plenty which were in the land of Egypt ended, 54 [a]and the seven years of famine began to come, [b]as Joseph had said. The famine was in all lands, but in all the land of Egypt there was bread. 55 So when all the land of Egypt was famished, the people cried to Pharaoh for bread. Then Pharaoh said to all the Egyptians, "Go to Joseph; [a]whatever he says to you, do." 56 The famine was over all the face of the earth, and Joseph opened all the storehouses[1] and [a]sold to the Egyptians. And the famine became severe in the land of Egypt. 57 [a]So all countries came to Joseph in Egypt to [b]buy *grain,* because the famine was severe in all lands.

### *JOSEPH'S BROTHERS GO TO EGYPT*

**42** When [a]Jacob saw that there was grain in Egypt, Jacob said to his sons, "Why do you look at one another?" 2 And he said, "Indeed I have heard that there is grain in Egypt; go down to that place and buy for us there, that we may [a]live and not die."

3 So Joseph's ten brothers went down to buy grain in Egypt. 4 But Jacob did not send Joseph's brother Benjamin with his brothers, for he said, [a]"Lest some calamity befall him." 5 And the sons of Israel went to buy *grain* among those who journeyed, for the famine was [a]in the land of Canaan.

6 Now Joseph *was* governor [a]over the land; and it was he who sold to all the people of the

**42:6** God fulfilled this dream He gave to Joseph at the age of seventeen (see Gen. 37:5–11).

**41:50** [a] Gen. 46:20; 48:5 **41:51** [a] Ps. 45:10 [1] Literally *Making Forgetful* **41:52** [a] Gen. 17:6; 28:3; 49:22 [1] Literally *Fruitfulness* **41:54** [a] Acts 7:11 [b] Gen. 41:30 **41:55** [a] John 2:5 **41:56** [a] Gen. 42:6 [1] Literally *all that was in them* **41:57** [a] Ezek. 29:12 [b] Gen. 27:28, 37; 42:3 **42:1** [a] Acts 7:12 **42:2** [a] Gen. 43:8; Ps. 33:18, 19; Is. 38:1 **42:4** [a] Gen. 42:38 **42:5** [a] Gen. 12:10; 26:1; 41:57; Acts 7:11 **42:6** [a] Gen. 41:41, 55

land. And Joseph's brothers came and [b]bowed
down before him with *their* faces to the earth.
7 Joseph saw his brothers and recognized them,
but he acted as [a]a stranger to them and spoke
roughly to them. Then he said to them, "Where
do you come from?"

And they said, "From the land of Canaan
to buy food."

8 So Joseph recognized his brothers, but
they did not recognize him. 9 Then Joseph [a]re-
membered the dreams which he had dreamed
about them, and said to them, "You *are* spies!
You have come to see the nakedness of the land!"

10 And they said to him, "No, my lord, but
your servants have come to buy food. 11 We *are*
all one man's sons; we *are* honest *men;* your
servants are not spies."

12 But he said to them, "No, but you have
come to see the nakedness of the land."

13 And they said, "Your servants *are* twelve
brothers, the sons of one man in the land of
Canaan; and in fact, the youngest *is* with our
father today, and one [a]*is* no more."

14 But Joseph said to them, "It *is* as I spoke
to you, saying, 'You *are* spies!' 15 In this *manner*
you shall be tested: [a]By the life of Pharaoh, you
shall not leave this place unless your youngest
brother comes here. 16 Send one of you, and let
him bring your brother; and you shall be kept
in prison, that your words may be tested to see
whether *there is* any truth in you; or else, by
the life of Pharaoh, surely you *are* spies!" 17 So
he put them all together in prison [a]three days.

18 Then Joseph said to them the third day,
"Do this and live, [a]*for* I fear God: 19 If you *are*
honest *men,* let one of your brothers be confined
to your prison house; but you, go and carry grain
for the famine of your houses. 20 And [a]bring your
youngest brother to me; so your words will be
verified, and you shall not die."

And they did so. 21 Then they said to one
another, [a]"We *are* truly guilty concerning our
brother, for we saw the anguish of his soul when
he pleaded with us, and we would not hear;
[b]therefore this distress has come upon us."

22 And Reuben answered them, saying,
[a]"Did I not speak to you, saying, 'Do not sin
against the boy'; and you would not listen?
Therefore behold, his blood is now [b]required
of us." 23 But they did not know that Joseph
understood *them,* for he spoke to them through
an interpreter. 24 And he turned himself away
from them and [a]wept. Then he returned to
them again, and talked with them. And he took
[b]Simeon from them and bound him before
their eyes.

### *THE BROTHERS RETURN TO CANAAN*

25 Then Joseph [a]gave a command to fill their
sacks with grain, to [b]restore every man's money
to his sack, and to give them provisions for the
journey. [c]Thus he did for them. 26 So they loaded
their donkeys with the grain and departed from
there. 27 But as [a]one *of them* opened his sack to
give his donkey feed at the encampment, he saw
his money; and there it was, in the mouth of his
sack. 28 So he said to his brothers, "My money
has been restored, and there it is, in my sack!"
Then their hearts failed *them* and they were
afraid, saying to one another, "What *is* this *that*
God has done to us?"

29 Then they went to Jacob their father in the
land of Canaan and told him all that had happened
to them, saying: 30 "The man *who is* lord of the land
[a]spoke roughly to us, and took us for spies of the
country. 31 But we said to him, 'We *are* honest *men;*
we are not spies. 32 We *are* twelve brothers, sons
of our father; one *is* no *more,* and the youngest
*is* with our father this day in the land of Canaan.'
33 Then the man, the lord of the country, said to
us, [a]'By this I will know that you *are* honest *men:*
Leave one of your brothers *here* with me, take *food*
*for* the famine of your households, and be gone.
34 And bring your [a]youngest brother to me; so I
shall know that you *are* not spies, but *that* you *are*
honest *men.* I will grant your brother to you, and
you may [b]trade in the land.' "

35 Then it happened as they emptied their
sacks, that surprisingly [a]each man's bundle of
money *was* in his sack; and when they and their
father saw the bundles of money, they were
afraid. 36 And Jacob their father said to them,
"You have [a]bereaved me: Joseph is no *more,*
Simeon is no *more,* and you want to take [b]Ben-
jamin. All these things are against me."

37 Then Reuben spoke to his father, saying, "Kill
my two sons if I do not bring him *back* to you; put
him in my hands, and I will bring him back to you."

38 But he said, "My son shall not go down
with you, for [a]his brother is dead, and he is left
alone. [b]If any calamity should befall him along
the way in which you go, then you would [c]bring
down my gray hair with sorrow to the grave."

### *JOSEPH'S BROTHERS RETURN WITH BENJAMIN*

43 Now the famine *was* [a]severe in the land.
2 And it came to pass, when they had eat-
en up the grain which they had brought from
Egypt, that their father said to them, "Go [a]back,
buy us a little food."

3 But Judah spoke to him, saying, "The man
solemnly warned us, saying, 'You shall not see

42:6 [b] Gen. 37:7–10; 41:43; Is. 60:14 42:7 [a] Gen. 45:1, 2 42:9 [a] Gen. 37:5–9 42:13 [a] Gen. 37:30; 42:32; 44:20; Lam. 5:7 42:15 [a] 1 Sam. 1:26; 17:55 42:17 [a] Gen. 40:4, 7, 12 42:18 [a] Gen. 22:12; 39:9; Ex. 1:17; Lev. 25:43; Neh. 5:15; Prov. 1:7; 9:10 42:20 [a] Gen. 42:34; 43:5; 44:23 42:21 [a] Gen. 37:26–28; 44:16; 45:3; Job 36:8, 9; Hos. 5:15 [b] Prov. 21:13; Matt. 7:2 42:22 [a] Gen. 37:21, 22, 29 [b] Gen. 9:5, 6; 1 Kin. 2:32; 2 Chr. 24:22; Ps. 9:12; Luke 11:50, 51 42:24 [a] Gen. 43:30; 45:14, 15 [b] Gen. 34:25, 30; 43:14, 23 42:25 [a] Gen. 44:1 [b] Gen. 43:12 [c] [Matt. 5:44; Rom. 12:17, 20, 21; 1 Pet. 3:9] 42:27 [a] Gen. 43:21, 22 42:30 [a] Gen. 42:7 42:33 [a] Gen. 42:15, 19, 20 42:34 [a] Gen. 42:20; 43:3, 5 [b] Gen. 34:10 42:35 [a] Gen. 43:12, 15, 21 42:36 [a] Gen. 43:14 [b] Gen. 35:18; [Rom. 8:28, 31] 42:38 [a] Gen. 37:22; 42:13; 44:20, 28 [b] Gen. 42:4; 44:29 [c] Gen. 37:35; 44:31 43:1 [a] Gen. 41:54, 57; 42:5; 45:6, 11 43:2 [a] Gen. 42:2; 44:25

my face unless your [a]brother *is* with you.' 4 If you
send our brother with us, we will go down and buy
you food. 5 But if you will not send *him,* we will
not go down; for the man said to us, 'You shall
not see my face unless your brother *is* with you.' "
6 And Israel said, "Why did you deal *so*
wrongfully with me *as* to tell the man whether
you had still *another* brother?"
7 But they said, "The man asked us pointedly
about ourselves and our family, saying, '*Is* your
father still alive? Have you *another* brother?' And
we told him according to these words. Could we
possibly have known that he would say, 'Bring
your brother down'?"
8 Then Judah said to Israel his father, "Send
the lad with me, and we will arise and go, that
we may [a]live and not die, both we and you *and*
also our little ones. 9 I myself will be surety for
him; from my hand you shall require him. [a]If I
do not bring him *back* to you and set him before
you, then let me bear the blame forever. 10 For
if we had not lingered, surely by now we would
have returned this second time."
11 And their father Israel said to them, "If *it*
*must be* so, then do this: Take some of the best

**43:8** Judah promised he would keep Benjamin safe. Judah had changed tremendously (see Gen. 38:1–30). Instead of leaving the family, he protected his brother and was concerned about his father's welfare.

fruits of the land in your vessels and [a]carry down
a present for the man—a little [b]balm and a little
honey, spices and myrrh, pistachio nuts and
almonds. 12 Take double money in your hand,
and take back in your hand the money [a]that was
returned in the mouth of your sacks; perhaps it
was an oversight. 13 Take your brother also, and
arise, go back to the man. 14 And may God [a]Al-
mighty [b]give you mercy before the man, that he
may release your other brother and Benjamin.
[c]If I am bereaved, I am bereaved!"
15 So the men took that present and Ben-
jamin, and they took double money in their
hand, and arose and went [a]down to Egypt; and
they stood before Joseph. 16 When Joseph saw
Benjamin with them, he said to the [a]steward of
his house, "Take *these* men to my home, and
slaughter an animal and make ready; for *these*
men will dine with me at noon." 17 Then the man
did as Joseph ordered, and the man brought the
men into Joseph's house.
18 Now the men were [a]afraid because they
were brought into Joseph's house; and they said,
"*It is* because of the money, which was returned
in our sacks the first time, that we are brought
in, so that he may make a case against us and
seize us, to take us as slaves with our donkeys."
19 When they drew near to the steward of
Joseph's house, they talked with him at the
door of the house, 20 and said, "O sir, [a]we indeed
came down the first time to buy food; 21 but [a]it
happened, when we came to the encampment,
that we opened our sacks, and there, *each* man's
money *was* in the mouth of his sack, our money
in full weight; so we have brought it back in our
hand. 22 And we have brought down other money
in our hands to buy food. We do not know who
put our money in our sacks."
23 But he said, "Peace *be* with you, do not
be afraid. Your God and the God of your father
has given you treasure in your sacks; I had your
money." Then he brought [a]Simeon out to them.
24 So the man brought the men into Jo-
seph's house and [a]gave *them* water, and they
washed their feet; and he gave their donkeys
feed. 25 Then they made the present ready for
Joseph's coming at noon, for they heard that
they would eat bread there.
26 And when Joseph came home, they
brought him the present which *was* in their hand
into the house, and [a]bowed down before him
to the earth. 27 Then he asked them about *their*
well-being, and said, "*Is* your father well, the
old man [a]of whom you spoke? *Is* he still alive?"
28 And they answered, "Your servant our father
*is* in good health; he *is* still alive." [a]And they bowed
their heads down and prostrated themselves.
29 Then he lifted his eyes and saw his brother
Benjamin, [a]his mother's son, and said, "*Is* this your
younger brother [b]of whom you spoke to me?"
And he said, "God be gracious to you, my son."
30 Now [a]his heart yearned for his brother; so Jo-
seph made haste and sought *somewhere* to weep.
And he went into *his* chamber and [b]wept there.
31 Then he washed his face and came out; and he
restrained himself, and said, "Serve the [a]bread."
32 So they set him a place by himself, and
them by themselves, and the Egyptians who ate

**43:32** Eating with another person was one of the highest forms of hospitality. The Egyptians, however, refused to eat at the same table as the Israelites because they saw the Israelites as a lower class of people.

**43:3** [a] Gen. 42:20; 43:5; 44:23 **43:8** [a] Gen. 42:2; 47:19 **43:9** [a] Gen. 42:37; 44:32 **43:11** [a] Gen. 32:20; 33:10; 43:25, 26; [Prov. 18:16] [b] Gen. 37:25; Jer. 8:22; Ezek. 27:17 **43:12** [a] Gen. 42:25, 35; 43:21, 22 **43:14** [a] Gen. 17:1; 28:3; 35:11; 48:3 [b] Gen. 39:21; Ps. 106:46 [c] Gen. 42:36; Esth. 4:16 **43:15** [a] Gen. 39:1; 46:3, 6 **43:16** [a] Gen. 24:2; 39:4; 44:1 **43:18** [a] Gen. 42:28 **43:20** [a] Gen. 42:3, 10 **43:21** [a] Gen. 42:27, 35 **43:23** [a] Gen. 42:24 **43:24** [a] Gen. 18:4; 19:2; 24:32 **43:26** [a] Gen. 37:7, 10; 42:6; 44:14 **43:27** [a] Gen. 29:6; 42:11, 13; 43:7; 45:3; 2 Kin. 4:26 **43:28** [a] Gen. 37:7, 10 **43:29** [a] Gen. 35:17, 18 [b] Gen. 42:13 **43:30** [a] 1 Kin. 3:26 [b] Gen. 42:24; 45:2, 14, 15; 46:29 **43:31** [a] Gen. 43:25

with him by themselves; because the Egyptians
could not eat food with the [a]Hebrews, for that *is*
[b]an abomination to the Egyptians. 33 And they
sat before him, the firstborn according to his
[a]birthright and the youngest according to his
youth; and the men looked in astonishment at
one another. 34 Then he took servings to them
from before him, but Benjamin's serving was
[a]five times as much as any of theirs. So they
drank and were merry with him.

### JOSEPH'S CUP

44 And he commanded the [a]steward of his
house, saying, [b]"Fill the men's sacks with
food, as much as they can carry, and put each
man's money in the mouth of his sack. 2 Also put
my cup, the silver cup, in the mouth of the sack
of the youngest, and his grain money." So he did
according to the word that Joseph had spoken.
3 As soon as the morning dawned, the men were
sent away, they and their donkeys. 4 When they
had gone out of the city, *and* were not *yet* far
off, Joseph said to his steward, "Get up, follow
the men; and when you overtake them, say to
them, 'Why have you [a]repaid evil for good? 5 *Is*
not this *the one* from which my lord drinks, and
with which he indeed practices divination? You
have done evil in so doing.' "

6 So he overtook them, and he spoke to them
these same words. 7 And they said to him, "Why
does my lord say these words? Far be it from
us that your servants should do such a thing.
8 Look, we brought back to you from the land
of Canaan [a]the money which we found in the
mouth of our sacks. How then could we steal
silver or gold from your lord's house? 9 With
whomever of your servants it is found, [a]let him
die, and we also will be my lord's slaves."

10 And he said, "Now also *let* it *be* accord-
ing to your words; he with whom it is found
shall be my slave, and you shall be blameless."
11 Then each man speedily let down his sack to
the ground, and each opened his sack. 12 So he
searched. He began with the oldest and left off
with the youngest; and the cup was found in
Benjamin's sack. 13 Then they [a]tore their clothes,
and each man loaded his donkey and returned
to the city.

14 So Judah and his brothers came to Joseph's
house, and he *was* still there; and they [a]fell
before him on the ground. 15 And Joseph said
to them, "What deed *is* this you have done? Did
you not know that such a man as I can certainly
practice divination?"

16 Then Judah said, "What shall we say to
my lord? What shall we speak? Or how shall we
clear ourselves? God has [a]found out the iniquity
of your servants; here [b]we are, my lord's slaves,
both we and *he* also with whom the cup was
found."

17 But he said, [a]"Far be it from me that I
should do so; the man in whose hand the cup
was found, he shall be my slave. And as for you,
go up in peace to your father."

### JUDAH INTERCEDES FOR BENJAMIN

18 Then Judah came near to him and said:
"O my lord, please let your servant speak a word
in my lord's hearing, and [a]do not let your anger
burn against your servant; for you *are* even like
Pharaoh. 19 My lord asked his servants, saying,
'Have you a father or a brother?' 20 And we said
to my lord, 'We have a father, an old man, and
[a]a child of *his* old age, *who is* young; his brother
is [b]dead, and he [c]alone is left of his mother's
children, and his [d]father loves him.' 21 Then you
said to your servants, [a]'Bring him down to me,
that I may set my eyes on him.' 22 And we said
to my lord, 'The lad cannot leave his father, for
*if* he should leave his father, *his father* would
die.' 23 But you said to your servants, [a]'Unless
your youngest brother comes down with you,
you shall see my face no more.'

24 "So it was, when we went up to your ser-
vant my father, that we told him the words of
my lord. 25 And [a]our father said, 'Go back *and*
buy us a little food.' 26 But we said, 'We cannot go
down; if our youngest brother is with us, then we
will go down; for we may not see the man's face
unless our youngest brother *is* with us.' 27 Then
your servant my father said to us, 'You know that
[a]my wife bore me two sons; 28 and the one went
out from me, and I said, [a]"Surely he is torn to
pieces"; and I have not seen him since. 29 But if
you [a]take this one also from me, and calamity
befalls him, you shall bring down my gray hair
with sorrow to the grave.'

30 "Now therefore, when I come to your
servant my father, and the lad *is* not with us,
since [a]his life is bound up in the lad's life, 31 it
will happen, when he sees that the lad *is* not *with
us,* that he will die. So your servants will bring
down the gray hair of your servant our father
with sorrow to the grave. 32 For your servant
became surety for the lad to my father, saying,
[a]'If I do not bring him *back* to you, then I shall
bear the blame before my father forever.' 33 Now
therefore, please [a]let your servant remain in-
stead of the lad as a slave to my lord, and let
the lad go up with his brothers. 34 For how shall
I go up to my father if the lad *is* not with me,
lest perhaps I see the evil that would come
upon my father?"

**43:32** [a] Gen. 41:12; Ex. 1:15 [b] Gen. 46:34; Ex. 8:26 **43:33** [a] Gen. 27:36; 42:7; Deut. 21:16, 17 **43:34** [a] Gen. 35:24; 45:22 **44:1** [a] Gen. 43:16 [b] Gen. 42:25 **44:4** [a] 1 Sam. 25:21 **44:8** [a] Gen. 43:21 **44:9** [a] Gen. 31:32 **44:13** [a] Gen. 37:29, 34; Num. 14:6; 2 Sam. 1:11 **44:14** [a] Gen. 37:7, 10 **44:16** [a] [Num. 32:23] [b] Gen. 44:9 **44:17** [a] Prov. 17:15 **44:18** [a] Gen. 18:30, 32; Ex. 32:22 **44:20** [a] Gen. 37:3; 43:8; 44:30 [b] Gen. 42:38 [c] Gen. 46:19 [d] Gen. 42:4 **44:21** [a] Gen. 42:15, 20 **44:23** [a] Gen. 43:3, 5 **44:25** [a] Gen. 43:2 **44:27** [a] Gen. 30:22–24; 35:16–18; 46:19 **44:28** [a] Gen. 37:31–35 **44:29** [a] Gen. 42:36, 38; 44:31 **44:30** [a] [1 Sam. 18:1; 25:29] **44:32** [a] Gen. 43:9 **44:33** [a] Ex. 32:32

### *JOSEPH REVEALED TO HIS BROTHERS*

**45** Then Joseph could not restrain himself
before all those who stood by him, and
he cried out, "Make everyone go out from me!"
So no one stood with him [a]while Joseph made
himself known to his brothers. 2 And he [a]wept
aloud, and the Egyptians and the house of Phar-
aoh heard *it*.
3 Then Joseph said to his brothers, [a]"I *am* Jo-
seph; does my father still live?" But his brothers
could not answer him, for they were dismayed in
his presence. 4 And Joseph said to his brothers,
"Please come near to me." So they came near.
Then he said: "I *am* Joseph your brother, [a]whom
you sold into Egypt. 5 But now, do not therefore be
grieved or angry with yourselves because you sold
me here; [a]for God sent me before you to preserve
life. 6 For these two years the [a]famine *has been* in
the land, and *there are* still five years in which *there
will be* neither plowing nor harvesting. 7 And God
[a]sent me before you to preserve a posterity for
you in the earth, and to save your lives by a great
deliverance. 8 So now *it was* not you *who* sent me
here, but [a]God; and He has made me [b]a father to
Pharaoh, and lord of all his house, and a [c]ruler
throughout all the land of Egypt.
9 "Hurry and go up to my father, and say to
him, 'Thus says your son Joseph: "God has made
me lord of all Egypt; come down to me, do not
tarry. 10 [a]You shall dwell in the land of Goshen,
and you shall be near to me, you and your chil-
dren, your children's children, your flocks and
your herds, and all that you have. 11 There I will
[a]provide for you, lest you and your household,
and all that you have, come to poverty; for *there
are* still five years of famine." '
12 "And behold, your eyes and the eyes of my
brother Benjamin see that *it is* [a]my mouth that
speaks to you. 13 So you shall tell my father of
all my glory in Egypt, and of all that you have
seen; and you shall hurry and [a]bring my father
down here."
14 Then he fell on his brother Benjamin's neck
and wept, and Benjamin wept on his neck. 15 More-
over he [a]kissed all his brothers and wept over
them, and after that his brothers talked with him.
16 Now the report of it was heard in Pharaoh's
house, saying, "Joseph's brothers have come." So
it pleased Pharaoh and his servants well. 17 And
Pharaoh said to Joseph, "Say to your brothers,
'Do this: Load your animals and depart; go to
the land of Canaan. 18 Bring your father and your
households and come to me; I will give you the
best of the land of Egypt, and you will eat [a]the fat
of the land. 19 Now you are commanded—do this:
Take carts out of the land of Egypt for your little
ones and your wives; bring your father and come.
20 Also do not be concerned about your goods,
for the best of all the land of Egypt *is* yours.' "
21 Then the sons of Israel did so; and Joseph
gave them [a]carts, according to the command of
Pharaoh, and he gave them provisions for the
journey. 22 He gave to all of them, to each man,
[a]changes of garments; but to Benjamin he gave
three hundred *pieces* of silver and [b]five changes
of garments. 23 And he sent to his father these
*things:* ten donkeys loaded with the good things
of Egypt, and ten female donkeys loaded with
grain, bread, and food for his father for the
journey. 24 So he sent his brothers away, and they
departed; and he said to them, "See that you do
not become troubled along the way."
25 Then they went up out of Egypt, and came
to the land of Canaan to Jacob their father. 26 And
they told him, saying, "Joseph *is* still alive, and
he *is* governor over all the land of Egypt." [a]And
Jacob's heart stood still, because he did not
believe them. 27 But when they told him all the
words which Joseph had said to them, and when
he saw the carts which Joseph had sent to carry
him, the spirit [a]of Jacob their father revived.
28 Then Israel said, "*It is* enough. Joseph my son
*is* still alive. I will go and see him before I die."

### *JACOB'S JOURNEY TO EGYPT*

*(Ex. 6:14–25)*

**46** So Israel took his journey with all that he
had, and came to [a]Beersheba, and offered
sacrifices [b]to the God of his father Isaac. 2 Then
God spoke to Israel [a]in the visions of the night,
and said, "Jacob, Jacob!"
And he said, "Here I am."
3 So He said, "I *am* God, [a]the God of your
father; do not fear to go down to Egypt, for I
will [b]make of you a great nation there. 4 [a]I will
go down with you to Egypt, and I will also surely
[b]bring you up *again;* and [c]Joseph will put his
hand on your eyes."
5 Then [a]Jacob arose from Beersheba; and the
sons of Israel carried their father Jacob, their
little ones, and their wives, in the carts [b]which
Pharaoh had sent to carry him. 6 So they took
their livestock and their goods, which they had
acquired in the land of Canaan, and went to
Egypt, [a]Jacob and all his descendants with him.
7 His sons and his sons' sons, his daughters and
his sons' daughters, and all his descendants he
brought with him to Egypt.
8 Now [a]these *were* the names of the children
of Israel, Jacob and his sons, who went to Egypt:
[b]Reuben *was* Jacob's firstborn. 9 The [a]sons of
Reuben *were* Hanoch, Pallu, Hezron, and Carmi.

45:1 [a] Acts 7:13 45:2 [a] Gen. 43:30; 46:29 45:3 [a] Gen. 43:27; Acts 7:13 45:4 [a] Gen. 37:28; 39:1; Ps. 105:17 45:5 [a] Gen. 45:7, 8; 50:20; Ps. 105:16, 17 45:6 [a] Gen. 43:1; 47:4, 13 45:7 [a] Gen. 45:5; 50:20 45:8 [a] [Rom. 8:28] [b] Judg. 17:10; Is. 22:21 [c] Gen. 41:43; 42:6 45:10 [a] Gen. 46:28, 34; 47:1, 6; Ex. 9:26 45:11 [a] Gen. 47:12 45:12 [a] Gen. 42:23 45:13 [a] Gen. 46:6–28; Acts 7:14 45:15 [a] Gen. 48:10 45:18 [a] Gen. 27:28; 47:6; Deut. 32:9–14 45:21 [a] Gen. 45:19; 46:5 45:22 [a] 2 Kin. 5:5 [b] Gen. 43:34 45:26 [a] Job 29:24 45:27 [a] Judg. 15:19 46:1 [a] Gen. 21:31, 33; 26:32, 33; 28:10 [b] Gen. 26:24, 25; 28:13; 31:42; 32:9 46:2 [a] Gen. 15:1; 22:11; 31:11 46:3 [a] Gen. 17:1; 28:13 [b] Deut. 26:5 46:4 [a] Gen. 28:15; 31:3; 48:21 [b] Gen. 15:16; 50:12, 24, 25 [c] Gen. 50:1 46:5 [a] Acts 7:15 [b] Gen. 45:19–21 46:6 [a] Deut. 26:5 46:8 [a] Ex. 1:1–4 [b] Num. 26:4, 5 46:9 [a] Ex. 6:14

10 [a]The sons of Simeon *were* Jemuel,[1] Jamin, Ohad, Jachin,[2] Zohar,[3] and Shaul, the son of a Canaanite woman. 11 The sons of [a]Levi *were* Gershon, Kohath, and Merari. 12 The sons of [a]Judah *were* [b]Er, Onan, Shelah, Perez, and Zerah (but Er and Onan died in the land of Canaan). [c]The sons of Perez were Hezron and Hamul. 13 The sons of Issachar *were* Tola, Puvah,[1] Job,[2] and Shimron. 14 The [a]sons of Zebulun *were* Sered, Elon, and Jahleel. 15 These *were* the [a]sons of Leah, whom she bore to Jacob in Padan Aram, with his daughter Dinah. All the persons, his sons and his daughters, *were* thirty-three.

16 The sons of Gad *were* Ziphion,[1] Haggi, Shuni, Ezbon,[2] Eri, Arodi,[3] and Areli. 17 [a]The sons of Asher *were* Jimnah, Ishuah, Isui, Beriah, and Serah, their sister. And the sons of Beriah *were* Heber and Malchiel. 18 [a]These *were* the sons of Zilpah, [b]whom Laban gave to Leah his daughter; and these she bore to Jacob: sixteen persons.

19 The [a]sons of Rachel, [b]Jacob's wife, *were* Joseph and Benjamin. 20 [a]And to Joseph in the land of Egypt were born Manasseh and Ephraim, whom Asenath, the daughter of Poti-Pherah priest of On, bore to him. 21 [a]The sons of Benjamin *were* Belah, Becher, Ashbel, Gera, Naaman, [b]Ehi, Rosh, [c]Muppim, Huppim,[1] and Ard. 22 These *were* the sons of Rachel, who were born to Jacob: fourteen persons in all.

23 The son of Dan *was* Hushim.[1] 24 [a]The sons of Naphtali *were* Jahzeel,[1] Guni, Jezer, and Shillem.[2] 25 [a]These *were* the sons of Bilhah, [b]whom Laban gave to Rachel his daughter, and she bore these to Jacob: seven persons in all.

26 [a]All the persons who went with Jacob to Egypt, who came from his body, [b]besides Jacob's sons' wives, *were* sixty-six persons in all. 27 And the sons of Joseph who were born to him in Egypt *were* two persons. [a]All the persons of the house of Jacob who went to Egypt were seventy.

### *JACOB SETTLES IN GOSHEN*

28 Then he sent Judah before him to Joseph, [a]to point out before him *the way* to Goshen. And they came [b]to the land of Goshen. 29 So Joseph made ready his [a]chariot and went up to Goshen to meet his father Israel; and he presented himself to him, and [b]fell on his neck and wept on his neck a good while.

30 And Israel said to Joseph, [a]"Now let me die, since I have seen your face, because you *are* still alive."

31 Then Joseph said to his brothers and to his father's household, [a]"I will go up and tell Pharaoh, and say to him, 'My brothers and those of my father's house, who *were* in the land of Canaan, have come to me. 32 And the men *are* [a]shepherds, for their occupation has been to feed livestock; and they have brought their flocks, their herds, and all that they have.' 33 So it shall be, when Pharaoh calls you and says, [a]'What is your occupation?' 34 that you shall say, 'Your servants' [a]occupation has been with livestock [b]from our youth even till now, both we *and* also our fathers,' that you may dwell in the land of Goshen; for every shepherd *is* [c]an abomination to the Egyptians."

47 Then Joseph [a]went and told Pharaoh, and said, "My father and my brothers, their flocks and their herds and all that they possess, have come from the land of Canaan; and indeed they *are* in [b]the land of Goshen." 2 And he took five men from among his brothers and [a]presented them to Pharaoh. 3 Then Pharaoh said to his brothers, [a]"What *is* your occupation?"

And they said to Pharaoh, [b]"Your servants *are* shepherds, both we *and* also our fathers." 4 And they said to Pharaoh, [a]"We have come to dwell in the land, because your servants have no pasture for their flocks, [b]for the famine *is* severe in the land of Canaan. Now therefore, please let your servants [c]dwell in the land of Goshen."

5 Then Pharaoh spoke to Joseph, saying, "Your father and your brothers have come to you. 6 [a]The land of Egypt *is* before you. Have your father and brothers dwell in the best of the land; let them dwell [b]in the land of Goshen. And if you know *any* competent men among them, then make them chief herdsmen over my livestock."

7 Then Joseph brought in his father Jacob and set him before Pharaoh; and Jacob [a]blessed Pharaoh. 8 Pharaoh said to Jacob, "How old *are* you?"

9 And Jacob said to Pharaoh, [a]"The days of the years of my pilgrimage *are* [b]one hundred and thirty years; [c]few and evil have been the days of the years of my life, and [d]they have not attained to the days of the years of the life of my fathers in the days of their pilgrimage." 10 So Jacob [a]blessed Pharaoh, and went out from before Pharaoh.

11 And Joseph situated his father and his brothers, and gave them a possession in the land of Egypt, in the best of the land, in the land of [a]Rameses, [b]as Pharaoh had commanded. 12 Then

**46:10** [a] Ex. 6:15 [1] Spelled *Nemuel* in 1 Chronicles 4:24 [2] Called *Jarib* in 1 Chronicles 4:24 [3] Called *Zerah* in 1 Chronicles 4:24 **46:11** [a] 1 Chr. 6:1, 16 **46:12** [a] 1 Chr. 2:3; 4:21 [b] Gen. 38:3, 7, 10 [c] Gen. 38:29 **46:13** [1] Spelled *Puah* in 1 Chronicles 7:1 [2] Same as *Jashub* in Numbers 26:24 and 1 Chronicles 7:1 **46:14** [a] Num. 26:26 **46:15** [a] Gen. 35:23; 49:31 **46:16** [1] Spelled *Zephon* in Samaritan Pentateuch, Septuagint, and Numbers 26:15 [2] Called *Ozni* in Numbers 26:16 [3] Spelled *Arod* in Numbers 26:17 **46:17** [a] 1 Chr. 7:30 **46:18** [a] Gen. 30:10; 37:2 [b] Gen. 29:24 **46:19** [a] Gen. 35:24 [b] Gen. 44:27 **46:20** [a] Gen. 41:45, 50–52; 48:1 **46:21** [a] 1 Chr. 7:6; 8:1 [b] Num. 26:38 [c] Num. 26:39 [1] Called *Hupham* in Numbers 26:39 **46:23** [1] Called *Shuham* in Numbers 26:42 **46:24** [a] Num. 26:48 [1] Spelled *Jahziel* in 1 Chronicles 7:13 [2] Spelled *Shallum* in 1 Chronicles 7:13 **46:25** [a] Gen. 30:5, 7 [b] Gen. 29:29 **46:26** [a] Ex. 1:5 [b] Gen. 35:11 **46:27** [a] Deut. 10:22 **46:28** [a] Gen. 31:21 [b] Gen. 47:1 **46:29** [a] Gen. 41:43 [b] Gen. 45:14, 15 **46:30** [a] Luke 2:29, 30 **46:31** [a] Gen. 47:1 **46:32** [a] Gen. 47:3 **46:33** [a] Gen. 47:2, 3 **46:34** [a] Gen. 47:3 [b] Gen. 30:35; 34:5; 37:17 [c] Gen. 43:32; Ex. 8:26 **47:1** [a] Gen. 46:31 [b] Gen. 45:10; 46:28; 50:8 **47:2** [a] Acts 7:13 **47:3** [a] Gen. 46:33; Jon. 1:8 [b] Gen. 46:32, 34; Ex. 2:17, 19 **47:4** [a] Gen. 15:13; Deut. 26:5; Ps. 105:23 [b] Gen. 43:1; Acts 7:11 [c] Gen. 46:34 **47:6** [a] Gen. 20:15; 45:10, 18; 47:11 [b] Gen. 47:4 **47:7** [a] Gen. 47:10; 48:15, 20; 2 Sam. 14:22; 1 Kin. 8:66; Heb. 7:7 **47:9** [a] Ps. 39:12; [Heb. 11:9, 13] [b] Gen. 47:28 [c] [Job 14:1] [d] Gen. 5:5; 11:10, 11; 25:7, 8; 35:28 **47:10** [a] Gen. 47:7 **47:11** [a] Ex. 1:11; 12:37 [b] Gen. 47:6, 27

Joseph provided [a]his father, his brothers, and all his father's household with bread, according to the number in *their* families.

### *JOSEPH DEALS WITH THE FAMINE*

13 Now *there was* no bread in all the land; for the famine *was* very severe, [a]so that the land of Egypt and the land of Canaan languished because of the famine. 14 [a]And Joseph gathered up all the money that was found in the land of Egypt and in the land of Canaan, for the grain which they bought; and Joseph brought the money into Pharaoh's house.

15 So when the money failed in the land of Egypt and in the land of Canaan, all the Egyptians came to Joseph and said, "Give us bread, for [a]why should we die in your presence? For the money has failed."

16 Then Joseph said, "Give your livestock, and I will give you *bread* for your livestock, if the money is gone." 17 So they brought their livestock to Joseph, and Joseph gave them bread *in exchange* for the horses, the flocks, the cattle of the herds, and for the donkeys. Thus he fed them with bread *in exchange* for all their livestock that year.

18 When that year had ended, they came to him the next year and said to him, "We will not hide from my lord that our money is gone; my lord also has our herds of livestock. There is nothing left in the sight of my lord but our bodies and our lands. 19 Why should we die before your eyes, both we and our land? Buy us and our land for bread, and we and our land will be servants of Pharaoh; give *us* seed, that we may [a]live and not die, that the land may not be desolate."

20 Then Joseph [a]bought all the land of Egypt for Pharaoh; for every man of the Egyptians sold his field, because the famine was severe upon them. So the land became Pharaoh's. 21 And as for the people, he moved them into the cities,[1] from *one* end of the borders of Egypt to the *other* end. 22 [a]Only the land of the [b]priests he did not buy; for the priests had rations *allotted to them* by Pharaoh, and they ate their rations which Pharaoh gave them; therefore they did not sell their lands.

23 Then Joseph said to the people, "Indeed I have bought you and your land this day for Pharaoh. Look, *here is* seed for you, and you shall sow the land. 24 And it shall come to pass in the harvest that you shall give one-fifth to Pharaoh. Four-fifths shall be your own, as seed for the field and for your food, for those of your households and as food for your little ones."

25 So they said, "You have saved [a]our lives; let us find favor in the sight of my lord, and we will be Pharaoh's servants." 26 And Joseph made it a law over the land of Egypt to this day, *that* Pharaoh should have one-fifth, [a]except for the land of the priests only, *which* did not become Pharaoh's.

### *JOSEPH'S VOW TO JACOB*

27 So Israel [a]dwelt in the land of Egypt, in the country of Goshen; and they had possessions there and [b]grew and multiplied exceedingly. 28 And Jacob lived in the land of Egypt seventeen years. So the length of Jacob's life was one hundred and forty-seven years. 29 When the time [a]drew near that Israel must die, he called his son Joseph and said to him, "Now if I have found favor in your sight, please [b]put your hand under my thigh, and [c]deal kindly and truly with me. [d]Please do not bury me in Egypt, 30 but [a]let me lie with my fathers; you shall carry me out of Egypt and [b]bury me in their burial place."

And he said, "I will do as you have said."

31 Then he said, "Swear to me." And he swore to him. So [a]Israel bowed himself on the head of the bed.

### *JACOB BLESSES JOSEPH'S SONS*

*(Heb. 11:21)*

**48** Now it came to pass after these things that Joseph was told, "Indeed your father *is* sick"; and he took with him his two sons, [a]Manasseh and Ephraim. 2 And Jacob was told, "Look, your son Joseph is coming to you"; and Israel strengthened himself and sat up on the bed. 3 Then Jacob said to Joseph: "God [a]Almighty appeared to me at [b]Luz in the land of Canaan and blessed me, 4 and said to me, 'Behold, I will [a]make you fruitful and multiply you, and I will make of you a multitude of people, and [b]give this land to your descendants after you [c]*as an* everlasting possession.' 5 And now your [a]two sons, Ephraim and Manasseh, who were born to you in the land of Egypt before I came to you in Egypt, *are* mine; as Reuben and Simeon, they shall be mine. 6 Your offspring whom you beget after them shall be yours; they will be called by the name of their brothers in their inheritance. 7 But as for me, when I came from Padan, [a]Rachel died beside me in the land of Canaan on

> **48:5–7** As firstborn, **Reuben** should have received a double portion of the inheritance, but he had forfeited his birthright by his sins (see Gen. 35:22). By adopting **Ephraim and Manasseh** as his sons, Jacob gave the double portion to Joseph.

**47:12** [a] Gen. 45:11; 50:21 **47:13** [a] Gen. 41:30; Acts 7:11 **47:14** [a] Gen. 41:56; 42:6 **47:15** [a] Gen. 47:19 **47:19** [a] Gen. 43:8 **47:20** [a] Jer. 32:43 **47:21** [1] Following Masoretic Text and Targum; Samaritan Pentateuch, Septuagint, and Vulgate read *made the people virtual slaves.* **47:22** [a] Lev. 25:34; Ezra 7:24 [b] Gen. 41:45 **47:25** [a] Gen. 33:15 **47:26** [a] Gen. 47:22 **47:27** [a] Gen. 47:11 [b] Gen. 17:6; 26:4; 35:11; 46:3; Ex. 1:7; Deut. 26:5; Acts 7:17 **47:29** [a] Deut. 31:14; 1 Kin. 2:1 [b] Gen. 24:2–4 [c] Gen. 24:49; Josh. 2:14 [d] Gen. 50:25 **47:30** [a] 2 Sam. 19:37 [b] Gen. 49:29; 50:5–13; Heb. 11:21 **47:31** [a] Gen. 48:2; 1 Kin. 1:47; Heb. 11:21 **48:1** [a] Gen. 41:51, 56; 46:20; 50:23; Josh. 14:4 **48:3** [a] Gen. 43:14; 49:25 [b] Gen. 28:13, 19; 35:6, 9 **48:4** [a] Gen. 46:3 [b] Gen. 35:12; Ex. 6:8 [c] Gen. 17:8 **48:5** [a] Gen. 41:50; 46:20; 48:8; Josh. 13:7; 14:4 **48:7** [a] Gen. 35:9, 16, 19, 20

the way, when *there was* but a little distance to
go to Ephrath; and I buried her there on the way
to Ephrath (that is, Bethlehem)."
8 Then Israel saw Joseph's sons, and said,
"Who *are* these?"
9 Joseph said to his father, "They *are* my sons,
whom God has given me in this *place*."
And he said, "Please bring them to me, and
[a]I will bless them." 10 Now [a]the eyes of Israel were
dim with age, *so that* he could not see. Then
Joseph brought them near him, and he [b]kissed
them and embraced them. 11 And Israel said to
Joseph, [a]"I had not thought to see your face; but
in fact, God has also shown me your offspring!"
12 So Joseph brought them from beside his
knees, and he bowed down with his face to the
earth. 13 And Joseph took them both, Ephraim
with his right hand toward Israel's left hand,
and Manasseh with his left hand toward Israel's
right hand, and brought *them* near him. 14 Then
Israel stretched out his right hand and [a]laid *it*
on Ephraim's head, who *was* the younger, and
his left hand on Manasseh's head, [b]guiding his
hands knowingly, for Manasseh *was* the [c]first-
born. 15 And [a]he blessed Joseph, and said:

"God, [b]before whom my fathers Abraham
and Isaac walked,
The God who has fed me all my life long to
this day,
16 The Angel [a]who has redeemed me from
all evil,
Bless the lads;
Let [b]my name be named upon them,
And the name of my fathers Abraham and
Isaac;
And let them [c]grow into a multitude in
the midst of the earth."

17 Now when Joseph saw that his father [a]laid
his right hand on the head of Ephraim, it dis-
pleased him; so he took hold of his father's hand
to remove it from Ephraim's head to Manasseh's
head. 18 And Joseph said to his father, "Not so,
my father, for this *one is* the firstborn; put your
right hand on his head."
19 But his father refused and said, [a]"I know,
my son, I know. He also shall become a people,
and he also shall be great; but truly [b]his younger
brother shall be greater than he, and his descen-
dants shall become a multitude of nations."
20 So he blessed them that day, saying, [a]"By
you Israel will bless, saying, 'May God make you
as Ephraim and as Manasseh!' " And thus he set
Ephraim before Manasseh.
21 Then Israel said to Joseph, "Behold, I am
dying, but [a]God will be with you and bring you
back to the land of your fathers. 22 Moreover
[a]I have given to you one portion above your
brothers, which I took from the hand [b]of the
Amorite with my sword and my bow."

### JACOB'S LAST WORDS TO HIS SONS

49 And Jacob called his sons and said, "Gath-
er together, that I may [a]tell you what shall
befall you [b]in the last days:

2 "Gather together and hear, you sons of
Jacob,
And listen to Israel your father.

3 "Reuben, you are [a]my firstborn,
My might and the beginning of my
strength,
The excellency of dignity and the
excellency of power.
4 Unstable as water, you shall not excel,
Because you [a]went up to your father's bed;
Then you defiled *it*—
He went up to my couch.

5 "Simeon and Levi *are* brothers;
Instruments of cruelty *are in* their
dwelling place.
6 [a]Let not my soul enter their council;
Let not my honor be united [b]to their
assembly;
[c]For in their anger they slew a man,
And in their self-will they hamstrung an
ox.
7 Cursed *be* their anger, for *it is* fierce;
And their wrath, for it is cruel!
[a]I will divide them in Jacob
And scatter them in Israel.

8 "Judah,[a] you *are he* whom your brothers
shall praise;
[b]Your hand *shall be* on the neck of your
enemies;
[c]Your father's children shall bow down
before you.
9 Judah *is* [a]a lion's whelp;
From the prey, my son, you have gone up.
[b]He bows down, he lies down as a lion;
And as a lion, who shall rouse him?
10 [a]The scepter shall not depart from Judah,
Nor [b]a lawgiver from between his feet,
[c]Until Shiloh comes;
[d]And to Him *shall be* the obedience of the
people.
11 Binding his donkey to the vine,
And his donkey's colt to the choice vine,
He washed his garments in wine,
And his clothes in the blood of grapes.

**48:9** [a] Gen. 27:4; 47:15 **48:10** [a] Gen. 27:1; 1 Sam. 3:2 [b] Gen. 27:27; 45:15; 50:1 **48:11** [a] Gen. 45:26 **48:14** [a] Matt. 19:15; Mark 10:16 [b] Gen. 48:19 [c] Gen. 41:51, 52; Josh. 17:1 **48:15** [a] Gen. 47:7, 10; 49:24; [Heb. 11:21] [b] Gen. 17:1; 24:40; 2 Kin. 20:3 **48:16** [a] Gen. 22:11, 15–18; 28:13–15; 31:11; [Ps. 34:22; 121:7] [b] Amos 9:12; Acts 15:17 [c] Num. 26:34, 37 **48:17** [a] Gen. 48:14 **48:19** [a] Gen. 48:14 [b] Num. 1:33, 35; Deut. 33:17 **48:20** [a] Ruth 4:11, 12 **48:21** [a] Gen. 28:15; 46:4; 50:24 **48:22** [a] Josh. 24:32 [b] Gen. 34:28 **49:1** [a] Deut. 33:1, 6–25 [b] Is. 2:2; 39:6 **49:3** [a] Gen. 29:32 **49:4** [a] Gen. 35:22 **49:6** [a] Prov. 1:15, 16 [b] Ps. 26:9 [c] Gen. 34:26 **49:7** [a] Josh. 19:1, 9; 21:1–42 **49:8** [a] Deut. 33:7 [b] Ps. 18:40 [c] 1 Chr. 5:2 **49:9** [a] [Rev. 5:5] [b] Num. 23:24; 24:9 **49:10** [a] Num. 24:17 [b] Ps. 60:7 [c] Is. 11:1 [d] Ps. 2:6–9; 72:8–11

**SEEING JESUS IN THE SCRIPTURE**

**49:10** God revealed through Jacob that Judah's line would be the kingly line, and the people would obey one particular king. Jesus is the ultimate king of Judah who reigns victorious over His people forevermore (see Rev. 5:5).

12 His eyes *are* darker than wine,
And his teeth whiter than milk.

13 "Zebulun[a] shall dwell by the haven of the sea;
He *shall become* a haven for ships,
And his border shall [b]adjoin Sidon.

14 "Issachar[a] is a strong donkey,
Lying down between two burdens;
15 He saw that rest *was* good,
And that the land *was* pleasant;
He bowed [a]his shoulder to bear *a burden*,
And became a band of slaves.

16 "Dan[a] shall judge his people
As one of the tribes of Israel.
17 [a]Dan shall be a serpent by the way,
A viper by the path,
That bites the horse's heels
So that its rider shall fall backward.
18 [a]I have waited for your salvation, O LORD!

19 "Gad,[a] a troop shall tramp upon him,
But he shall triumph at last.

20 "Bread from [a]Asher *shall be* rich,
And he shall yield royal dainties.

21 "Naphtali[a] *is* a deer let loose;
He uses beautiful words.

22 "Joseph *is* a fruitful bough,
A fruitful bough by a well;
His branches run over the wall.
23 The archers have [a]bitterly grieved him,
Shot *at him* and hated him.
24 But his [a]bow remained in strength,
And the arms of his hands were made strong
By the hands of [b]the Mighty *God* of Jacob
[c](From there [d]*is* the Shepherd, [e]the Stone of Israel),
25 [a]By the God of your father who will help you,
[b]And by the Almighty [c]who will bless you
*With* blessings of heaven above,
Blessings of the deep that lies beneath,
Blessings of the breasts and of the womb.
26 The blessings of your father
Have excelled the blessings of my ancestors,
[a]Up to the utmost bound of the everlasting hills.
[b]They shall be on the head of Joseph,
And on the crown of the head of him who was separate from his brothers.

27 "Benjamin is a [a]ravenous wolf;
In the morning he shall devour the prey,
[b]And at night he shall divide the spoil."

28 All these *are* the twelve tribes of Israel,
and this *is* what their father spoke to them. And
he blessed them; he blessed each one according
to his own blessing.

### JACOB'S DEATH AND BURIAL

29 Then he charged them and said to them:
"I [a]am to be gathered to my people; [b]bury me
with my fathers [c]in the cave that *is* in the field
of Ephron the Hittite, 30 in the cave that *is* in the
field of Machpelah, which *is* before Mamre in the
land of Canaan, [a]which Abraham bought with
the field of Ephron the Hittite as a possession
for a burial place. 31 [a]There they buried Abraham
and Sarah his wife, [b]there they buried Isaac and
Rebekah his wife, and there I buried Leah. 32 The
field and the cave that *is* there *were* purchased
from the sons of Heth." 33 And when Jacob had
finished commanding his sons, he drew his feet
up into the bed and breathed his last, and was
gathered to his people.

50 Then Joseph [a]fell on his father's face and
[b]wept over him, and kissed him. 2 And Jo-
seph commanded his servants the physicians to
[a]embalm his father. So the physicians embalmed
Israel. 3 Forty days were required for him, for
such are the days required for those who are
embalmed; and the Egyptians [a]mourned for
him seventy days.

4 Now when the days of his mourning were
past, Joseph spoke to [a]the household of Pharaoh,
saying, "If now I have found favor in your eyes,
please speak in the hearing of Pharaoh, saying,
5 [a]'My father made me swear, saying, "Behold, I
am dying; in my grave [b]which I dug for myself
in the land of Canaan, there you shall bury me."
Now therefore, please let me go up and bury my
father, and I will come back.'"

6 And Pharaoh said, "Go up and bury your
father, as he made you swear."

7 So Joseph went up to bury his father; and
with him went up all the servants of Pharaoh,

**49:13** [a] Deut. 33:18, 19 [b] Gen. 10:19 **49:14** [a] 1 Chr. 12:32 **49:15** [a] 1 Sam. 10:9 **49:16** [a] Deut. 33:22 **49:17** [a] Judg. 18:27 **49:18** [a] Is. 25:9 **49:19** [a] Deut. 33:20 **49:20** [a] Deut. 33:24 **49:21** [a] Deut. 33:23 **49:23** [a] Gen. 37:4, 24 **49:24** [a] Job 29:20 [b] Ps. 132:2, 5 [c] Gen. 45:11; 47:12 [d] [Ps. 23:1; 80:1] [e] Is. 28:16 **49:25** [a] Gen. 28:13; 32:9; 35:3; 43:23; 50:17 [b] Gen. 17:1; 35:11 [c] Deut. 33:13 **49:26** [a] Deut. 33:15 [b] Deut. 33:16 **49:27** [a] Judg. 20:21, 25 [b] Zech. 14:1 **49:29** [a] Gen. 15:15; 25:8; 35:29 [b] Gen. 47:30 [c] Gen. 23:16–20; 50:13 **49:30** [a] Gen. 23:3–20 **49:31** [a] Gen. 23:19, 20; 25:9 [b] Gen. 35:29; 50:13 **50:1** [a] Gen. 46:4, 29 [b] 2 Kin. 13:14 **50:2** [a] Gen. 50:26 **50:3** [a] Deut. 34:8 **50:4** [a] Esth. 4:2 **50:5** [a] Gen. 47:29–31 [b] Is. 22:16

the elders of his house, and all the elders of the land of Egypt, [8]as well as all the house of Joseph, his brothers, and his father's house. Only their little ones, their flocks, and their herds they left in the land of Goshen. [9]And there went up with him both chariots and horsemen, and it was a very great gathering.

[10]Then they came to the threshing floor of Atad, which *is* beyond the Jordan, and they [a]mourned there with a great and very solemn lamentation. [b]He observed seven days of mourning for his father. [11]And when the inhabitants of the land, the Canaanites, saw the mourning at the threshing floor of Atad, they said, "This *is* a deep mourning of the Egyptians." Therefore its name was called Abel Mizraim,[1] which *is* beyond the Jordan.

[12]So his sons did for him just as he had commanded them. [13]For [a]his sons carried him to the land of Canaan, and buried him in the cave of the field of Machpelah, before Mamre, which Abraham [b]bought with the field from Ephron the Hittite as property for a burial place. [14]And after he had buried his father, Joseph returned to Egypt, he and his brothers and all who went up with him to bury his father.

## *JOSEPH REASSURES HIS BROTHERS*

[15]When Joseph's brothers saw that their father was dead, [a]they said, "Perhaps Joseph will hate us, and may actually repay us for all the evil which we did to him." [16]So they sent *messengers* to Joseph, saying, "Before your father died he commanded, saying, [17]'Thus you shall say to Joseph: "I beg you, please forgive the trespass of your brothers and their sin; [a]for they did evil to you."' Now, please, forgive the trespass of the servants of [b]the God of your father." And Joseph wept when they spoke to him.

[18]Then his brothers also went and [a]fell down before his face, and they said, "Behold, we *are* your servants."

[19]Joseph said to them, [a]"Do not be afraid, [b]for *am* I in the place of God? [20][a]But as for you, you meant evil against me; *but* [b]God meant it for good, in order to bring it about as *it is* this day, to save many people alive. [21]Now therefore, do not be afraid; [a]I will provide for you and your little ones." And he comforted them and spoke kindly to them.

### SEEING JESUS IN THE SCRIPTURE

**50:20** God used the brothers' evil for an exceedingly great work. Joseph not only saved numerous lives, but he also testified to the power and goodness of the living God. Later, God used the greatest evil ever, the cross, to bring about the greatest good (see Acts 2:22–24).

## *DEATH OF JOSEPH*

*(Heb. 11:22)*

[22]So Joseph dwelt in Egypt, he and his father's household. And Joseph lived one hundred and ten years. [23]Joseph saw Ephraim's children [a]to the third *generation.* [b]The children of Machir, the son of Manasseh, [c]were also brought up on Joseph's knees.

[24]And Joseph said to his brethren, "I am dying; but [a]God will surely visit you, and bring you out of this land to the land [b]of which He swore to Abraham, to Isaac, and to Jacob." [25]Then [a]Joseph took an oath from the children of Israel, saying, "God will surely visit you, and [b]you shall carry up my [c]bones from here." [26]So Joseph died, *being* one hundred and ten years old; and they embalmed him, and he was put in a coffin in Egypt.

**50:10** [a] Acts 8:2 [b] 1 Sam. 31:13 **50:11** [1] Literally *Mourning of Egypt* **50:13** [a] Acts 7:16 [b] Gen. 23:16–20 **50:15** [a] [Job 15:21] **50:17** [a] [Prov. 28:13] [b] Gen. 49:25 **50:18** [a] Gen. 37:7–10; 41:43; 44:14 **50:19** [a] Gen. 45:5 [b] 2 Kin. 5:7 **50:20** [a] Ps. 56:5 [b] [Acts 3:13–15] **50:21** [a] [Matt. 5:44] **50:23** [a] Job 42:16 [b] Num. 26:29; 32:39 [c] Gen. 30:3 **50:24** [a] Ex. 3:16, 17 [b] Gen. 26:3; 35:12; 46:4 **50:25** [a] Ex. 13:19 [b] Deut. 1:8; 30:1–8 [c] Ex. 13:19

# The Second Book of Moses Called
# EXODUS

**AUTHOR**
Moses

**KEY VERSE**
Exodus 19:5

**READING TIME**
3 hours 33 minutes

Exodus continues the narrative of the Book of Genesis. This book traces the next steps of God's promise to form a nation through Abraham's family and provide a Savior to the world through it. Several generations had passed since Joseph rose to prominence in Egypt and his family had grown from a modest size of about seventy to upwards of two to three million. Posing a threat to Egypt, they had become slaves in a nation that was not their home. But God heard their cries for deliverance and freedom and provided an unlikely rescuer in a man named Moses. After a series of mighty works, God led the Hebrews out of Egypt back toward the land He had promised to their ancestors. Along the way, He gave the Hebrews the law so they would know what He expected of them.

**Occasion:** Moses wrote the Book of Exodus to preserve the account of the Hebrews' deliverance from Egyptian bondage by God's mighty works and the giving of God's law.

**Main Point:** God delivers His people from bondage in Egypt and prepares them to be His chosen people as He leads them back toward the Land of Promise.

**Big Ideas:** God has provided a Rescuer to free us from sin like He provided a rescuer to free the Hebrews from slavery. The Ten Commandments are God's instructions for honoring Him and living well. We must remember all God has done for us.

## OUTLINE:

I. The Captivity in Egypt (ch. 1)
II. The Calling Moses (chs. 2–4)
III. The First Nine Plagues (chs. 5–10)
IV. The Final Plague and First Passover (chs. 11–13)
V. The Crossing of the Red Sea (chs. 14–15)
VI. The People Travel to Mount Sinai (chs. 16–18)
VII. The Ten Commandments and the Law (chs. 19–24)
VIII. The Tabernacle and Priesthood (chs. 25–31)
IX. The Gold Calf (ch. 32)
X. The People's Response and Building of the Tabernacle (chs. 33–40)

**c. 1915 BC**
Joseph is born to Jacob and Rachel

**c. 1898 BC**
Joseph is sold into slavery

**c. 1876 BC**
Jacob and his family move to Egypt

**c. 1800 BC**
Astronomy and musical notation are developed in Babylon

**c. 1730 BC**
The Israelites are enslaved in Egypt

**c. 1700 BC**
Phoenicians develop a consonantal alphabet

**c. 1625 BC**
Chariots used by the Hittites

**c. 1527 BC**
Moses is born

**c. 1487 BC**
Moses flees Egypt for Midian

**c. 1450 BC**
Earliest Egyptian shadow clock

**c. 1446 BC**
Moses leads the Israelites out of Egypt

**c. 1445 BC**
The Law is given on Mount Sinai

**c. 1445–1406 BC**
**Exodus written**

**c. 1406 BC**
Forty years of wilderness wandering end

## *ISRAEL'S SUFFERING IN EGYPT*

**1** Now [a]these *are* the names of the children of Israel who came to Egypt; each man and his household came with Jacob: 2 Reuben, Simeon, Levi, and Judah; 3 Issachar, Zebulun, and Benjamin; 4 Dan, Naphtali, Gad, and Asher. 5 All those who were descendants[1] of Jacob were [a]seventy[2] persons (for Joseph was in Egypt *already*). 6 And [a]Joseph died, all his brothers, and all that generation. 7 [a]But the children of Israel were fruitful and increased abundantly, multiplied and grew exceedingly mighty; and the land was filled with them.

8 Now there arose a new king over Egypt, [a]who did not know Joseph. 9 And he said to his people, "Look, the people of the children of Israel *are* more and [a]mightier than we; 10 [a]come, let us [b]deal shrewdly with them, lest they multiply, and it happen, in the event of war, that they also join our enemies and fight against us, and *so* go up out of the land." 11 Therefore they set taskmasters over them [a]to afflict them with their [b]burdens. And they built for Pharaoh [c]supply cities, Pithom [d]and Raamses. 12 But the more they afflicted them, the more they multiplied and grew. And they were in dread of the children of Israel. 13 So the Egyptians made the children of Israel [a]serve with rigor. 14 And they [a]made their lives bitter with hard bondage— [b]in mortar, in brick, and in all manner of service in the field. All their service in which they made them serve *was* with rigor.

15 Then the king of Egypt spoke to the [a]Hebrew midwives, of whom the name of one *was* Shiphrah and the name of the other Puah; 16 and he said, "When you do the duties of a midwife for the Hebrew women, and see *them* on the birthstools, if it *is* a [a]son, then you shall kill him; but if it *is* a daughter, then she shall live." 17 But the midwives [a]feared God, and did not do [b]as the king of Egypt commanded them, but saved the male children alive. 18 So the king of Egypt called for the midwives and said to them, "Why have you done this thing, and saved the male children alive?"

> **SEEING JESUS IN THE SCRIPTURE**
>
> **1:15** Centuries after the Egyptian king ordered the execution of Hebrew boys, King Herod did the same in his attempt to kill Jesus (see Matt. 2:16–18). Just as the Egyptian king failed to stop Israel's growth, Herod failed to kill baby Jesus.

19 And [a]the midwives said to Pharaoh, "Because the Hebrew women *are* not like the Egyptian women; for they *are* lively and give birth before the midwives come to them."

20 [a]Therefore God dealt well with the midwives, and the people multiplied and grew very mighty. 21 And so it was, because the midwives feared God, [a]that He provided households for them.

22 So Pharaoh commanded all his people, saying, [a]"Every son who is born[1] you shall cast into the river, and every daughter you shall save alive."

## *MOSES IS BORN*

*(Heb. 11:23)*

**2** And [a]a man of the house of Levi went and took *as wife* a daughter of Levi. 2 So the woman conceived and bore a son. And [a]when she saw that he *was* a beautiful *child,* she hid him three months. 3 But when she could no longer hide him, she took an ark of [a]bulrushes for him, daubed it with [b]asphalt and [c]pitch, put the child in it, and laid *it* in the reeds [d]by the river's bank. 4 [a]And his sister stood afar off, to know what would be done to him.

5 Then the [a]daughter of Pharaoh came down to bathe at the river. And her maidens walked along the riverside; and when she saw the ark among the reeds, she sent her maid to get it. 6 And when she opened *it,* she saw the child, and behold, the baby wept. So she had compassion on him, and said, "This is one of the Hebrews' children."

7 Then his sister said to Pharaoh's daughter, "Shall I go and call a nurse for you from the Hebrew women, that she may nurse the child for you?"

8 And Pharaoh's daughter said to her, "Go." So the maiden went and called the child's mother. 9 Then Pharaoh's daughter said to her, "Take this child away and nurse him for me, and I will give *you* your wages." So the woman took the child and nursed him. 10 And the child grew, and she brought him to Pharaoh's daughter, and he became [a]her son. So she called his name Moses,[1] saying, "Because I drew him out of the water."

## *MOSES FLEES TO MIDIAN*

*(Heb. 11:24, 25)*

11 Now it came to pass in those days, [a]when Moses was grown, that he went out to his brethren and looked at their burdens. And he saw an Egyptian beating a Hebrew, one of his brethren. 12 So he looked this way and that way, and when he saw no one, he [a]killed the Egyptian and hid him in the sand. 13 And [a]when he went out the second day, behold, two Hebrew men [b]were fighting, and he said to the one who did the wrong, "Why are you striking your companion?"

**1:1** [a] Gen. 46:8–27 **1:5** [a] Gen. 46:26, 27 [1] Literally *who came from the loins of* [2] Dead Sea Scrolls and Septuagint read *seventy-five* (compare Acts 7:14). **1:6** [a] Gen. 50:26 **1:7** [a] Acts 7:17 **1:8** [a] Acts 7:18, 19 **1:9** [a] Gen. 26:16 **1:10** [a] Ps. 83:3, 4 [b] Acts 7:19 **1:11** [a] Ex. 3:7; 5:6 [b] Ex. 1:14; 2:11; 5:4–9; 6:6 [c] 1 Kin. 9:19 [d] Gen. 47:11 **1:13** [a] Gen. 15:13 **1:14** [a] Num. 20:15 [b] Ps. 81:6 **1:15** [a] Ex. 2:6 **1:16** [a] Acts 7:19 **1:17** [a] Prov. 16:6 [b] Dan. 3:16, 18 **1:19** [a] Josh. 2:4 **1:20** [a] [Prov. 11:18] **1:21** [a] 1 Sam. 2:35 **1:22** [a] Acts 7:19 [1] Samaritan Pentateuch, Septuagint, and Targum add *to the Hebrews.* **2:1** [a] Ex. 6:16–20 **2:2** [a] Acts 7:20 **2:3** [a] Is. 18:2 [b] Gen. 14:10 [c] Gen. 6:14 [d] Is. 19:6 **2:4** [a] Num. 26:59 **2:5** [a] Acts 7:21 **2:10** [a] Acts 7:21 [1] Literally *Drawn Out* **2:11** [a] Heb. 11:24–26 **2:12** [a] Acts 7:24, 25 **2:13** [a] Acts 7:26–28 [b] Prov. 25:8

STORY OF SCRIPTURE 8

EXODUS 1:8—2:10

## DRAWN FROM WATER

### WHAT'S GOING ON?

Three hundred years after Joseph brought his family to Egypt, the Israelites were slaves. A large workforce is an advantage; *too* large of a workforce is a threat. So, Pharaoh did the unthinkable to control Israel's population: he commanded all newborn Hebrew boys to be thrown into the Nile. In desperation, one woman from the tribe of Levi placed her son in a basket and floated him along the Nile. This baby was found by Pharaoh's daughter, who named the child Moses. Moses's mother became his nurse. Therefore, Moses grew up with a dual identity. Not entirely Hebrew because of his upbringing, but not entirely Egyptian because of his birth. Moses, cut from two cloths, would be the one God would use to free His people.

### WHAT DOES THIS MEAN FOR ME?

Great things often happen under intense circumstances. The Hebrews multiplied under the pressure of persecution. The Hebrew midwives were blessed while their lives were at risk. Moses was spared because of the kindness of the daughter of the very one who ordered his death. Harsh circumstances don't prevent God from doing great things. In fact, these dark moments can be the perfect places for God's light to shine brightest.

### DID YOU CATCH THE PATTERN?

Moses's name means "drawn from water," which was both literally and figuratively true of him. Water played a key role in his life. He met his wife by a well (see Ex. 2:15–21). The first plague was the Nile turning into blood (see Ex. 7:14–25). He held up his hand and watched God part of the Red Sea (see Ex. 14:21). And he struck a rock and water poured out for Israel (see Ex. 17:5–6). As you continue to read about Moses's life, look for what God wants to teach you through water.

*For the next* Story of Scripture *reading and devotion, turn to Exodus 3:1–22 on page 63.*

**2:11** The years of Moses's experience in the pharaoh's court are not detailed. Yet Stephen, the New Testament martyr, reported the long-held and surely accurate tradition: "Moses was learned in all the wisdom of the Egyptians, and was mighty in words and deeds" (Acts 7:22). The training Moses received was the best education the world had to offer at the time. He would have learned three languages: Egyptian, Akkadian, and Hebrew. When Moses came into the presence of Pharaoh to demand freedom for his people, he was no uneducated slave; he had received an education on a par with the king's.

14 Then he said, [a]"Who made you a prince
and a judge over us? Do you intend to kill me
as you killed the Egyptian?"
So Moses [b]feared and said, "Surely this thing
is known!" 15 When Pharaoh heard of this matter,
he sought to kill Moses. But [a]Moses fled from
the face of Pharaoh and dwelt in the land of
[b]Midian; and he sat down by [c]a well.
16 [a]Now the priest of Midian had seven
daughters. [b]And they came and drew water,
and they filled the [c]troughs to water their father's
flock. 17 Then the [a]shepherds came and [b]drove
them away; but Moses stood up and helped
them, and [c]watered their flock.
18 When they came to [a]Reuel their father, [b]he
said, "How *is it that* you have come so soon today?"
19 And they said, "An Egyptian delivered us
from the hand of the shepherds, and he also
drew enough water for us and watered the flock."
20 So he said to his daughters, "And where
*is* he? Why *is* it *that* you have left the man? Call
him, that he may [a]eat bread."
21 Then Moses was content to live with the
man, and he gave [a]Zipporah his daughter to
Moses. 22 And she bore *him* a son. He called his
name [a]Gershom,[1] for he said, "I have been [b]a
stranger in a foreign land."
23 Now it happened [a]in the process of time
that the king of Egypt died. Then the children

**2:14** [a] Acts 7:27, 28 [b] Judg. 6:27 **2:15** [a] Acts 7:29 [b] Ex. 3:1 [c] Gen. 24:11; 29:2 **2:16** [a] Ex. 3:1; 4:18; 18:12 [b] Gen. 24:11, 13, 19; 29:6–10 [c] Gen. 30:38 **2:17** [a] Gen. 47:3 [b] Gen. 26:19–21 [c] Gen. 29:3, 10 **2:18** [a] Num. 10:29 [b] Ex. 3:1; 4:18 **2:20** [a] Gen. 31:54; 43:25 **2:21** [a] Ex. 4:25; 18:2 **2:22** [a] Ex. 4:20; 18:3, 4 [b] Acts 7:29 [1] Literally *Stranger There* **2:23** [a] Acts 7:34

of Israel [b]groaned because of the bondage, and
they cried out; and [c]their cry came up to God
because of the bondage. 24 So God [a]heard their
groaning, and God [b]remembered His [c]covenant
with Abraham, with Isaac, and with Jacob. 25 And
God [a]looked upon the children of Israel, and
God [b]acknowledged *them.*

### *MOSES AT THE BURNING BUSH*

*(Ex. 6:2—7:7; 11:1–4; 12:35, 36)*

**3** Now Moses was tending the flock of [a]Jethro
his father-in-law, [b]the priest of Midian. And
he led the flock to the back of the desert, and
came to [c]Horeb, [d]the mountain of God. 2 And [a]the
Angel of the LORD appeared to him in a flame
of fire from the midst of a bush. So he looked,
and behold, the bush was burning with fire, but
the bush *was* not consumed. 3 Then Moses said,
"I will now turn aside and see this [a]great sight,
why the bush does not burn."

> **3:2** *Angel* simply means "messenger" (Mal. 1:1). In the Old Testament, **the Angel of the LORD** is used numerous times, and seems to be a unique being who often spoke and acted as God. The Angel of the Lord commanded Hagar (Gen. 16:7–12); made promises to Abraham (Gen. 22:11–13, 15–18); confronted Balaam (Num. 22:22–35); corrected the people of Israel (Judg. 2:1–4); called Gideon (Judg. 6:11–24); and told of Samson's birth (Judg. 13:2ff). In this passage, having mentioned the Angel of the Lord appeared to Moses, it is immediately established it was the Lord Himself (see Ex. 3:4).

4 So when the LORD saw that he turned aside
to look, God called [a]to him from the midst of the
bush and said, "Moses, Moses!"
And he said, "Here I am."
5 Then He said, "Do not draw near this place.
[a]Take your sandals off your feet, for the place
where you stand *is* holy ground." 6 Moreover He
said, [a]"I *am* the God of your father—the God of
Abraham, the God of Isaac, and the God of Jacob."
And Moses hid his face, for [b]he was afraid
to look upon God.
7 And the LORD said: [a]"I have surely seen the
oppression of My people who *are* in Egypt, and
have heard their cry [b]because of their taskmasters,
[c]for I know their sorrows. 8 So [a]I have come down
to [b]deliver them out of the hand of the Egyptians,
and to bring them up from that land [c]to a good and
large land, to a land [d]flowing with milk and honey,
to the place of [e]the Canaanites and the Hittites and
the Amorites and the Perizzites and the Hivites
and the Jebusites. 9 Now therefore, behold, [a]the
cry of the children of Israel has come to Me, and
I have also seen the [b]oppression with which the
Egyptians oppress them. 10 [a]Come now, therefore,
and I will send you to Pharaoh that you may bring
My people, the children of Israel, out of Egypt."
11 But Moses said to God, [a]"Who *am* I that I
should go to Pharaoh, and that I should bring
the children of Israel out of Egypt?"
12 So He said, [a]"I will certainly be with you.
And this *shall be* a [b]sign to you that I have sent
you: When you have brought the people out of
Egypt, you shall serve God on this mountain."
13 Then Moses said to God, "Indeed, *when* I
come to the children of Israel and say to them,
'The God of your fathers has sent me to you,'
and they say to me, 'What *is* His name?' what
shall I say to them?"
14 And God said to Moses, "I AM WHO I AM."
And He said, "Thus you shall say to the children of
Israel, [a]'I AM has sent me to you.'" 15 Moreover God
said to Moses, "Thus you shall say to the children
of Israel: 'The LORD God of your fathers, the God
of Abraham, the God of Isaac, and the God of Jacob,
has sent me to you. This *is* [a]My name forever,
and this *is* My memorial to all generations.' 16 Go
and [a]gather the elders of Israel together, and say
to them, 'The LORD God of your fathers, the God
of Abraham, of Isaac, and of Jacob, appeared to
me, saying, [b]"I have surely visited you and *seen*
what is done to you in Egypt; 17 and I have said [a]I
will bring you up out of the affliction of Egypt to
the land of the Canaanites and the Hittites and
the Amorites and the Perizzites and the Hivites
and the Jebusites, to a land flowing with milk and
honey."' 18 Then [a]they will heed your voice; and
[b]you shall come, you and the elders of Israel, to
the king of Egypt; and you shall say to him, 'The
LORD God of the Hebrews has [c]met with us; and

> **SEEING JESUS IN THE SCRIPTURE**
>
> **3:14** When Moses asked for God's name, God said it's "I AM," a name meaning timeless existence. God has always been, always is, and always will be. Jesus said the same about Himself, revealing He is fully God (see John 8:58).

**2:23** [b] Deut. 26:7 [c] James 5:4 **2:24** [a] Ex. 6:5 [b] Gen. 15:13; 22:16–18; 26:2–5; 28:13–15 [c] Gen. 12:1–3; 15:14; 17:1–14 **2:25** [a] Ex. 4:31 [b] Ex. 3:7 **3:1** [a] Ex. 4:18 [b] Ex. 2:16 [c] Ex. 17:6 [d] Ex. 18:5 **3:2** [a] Deut. 33:16 **3:3** [a] Acts 7:31 **3:4** [a] Deut. 33:16 **3:5** [a] Josh. 5:15 **3:6** [a] [Matt. 22:32] [b] 1 Kin. 19:13 **3:7** [a] Ex. 2:23–25 [b] Ex. 1:11 [c] Gen. 18:21; Ex. 2:25 **3:8** [a] Gen. 15:13–16; 46:4; 50:24, 25 [b] Ex. 6:6–8; 12:51 [c] Num. 13:27; Deut. 1:25; 8:7–9; Josh. 3:17 [d] Ex. 3:17; 13:5; Jer. 11:5; Ezek. 20:6 [e] Gen. 15:19–21; Josh. 24:11 **3:9** [a] Ex. 2:23 [b] Ex. 1:11, 13, 14 **3:10** [a] Gen. 15:13, 14; Ex. 12:40, 41; [Mic. 6:4]; Acts 7:6, 7 **3:11** [a] Ex. 4:10; 6:12; 1 Sam. 18:18 **3:12** [a] Gen. 31:3; Ex. 4:12, 15; 33:14–16; Deut. 31:23; Josh. 1:5; Is. 43:2; Rom. 8:31 [b] Ex. 4:8; 19:3 **3:14** [a] [Ex. 6:3; John 8:24, 28, 58; Heb. 13:8; Rev. 1:8; 4:8] **3:15** [a] Ps. 30:4; 97:12; 102:12; 135:13; [Hos. 12:5] **3:16** [a] Ex. 4:29 [b] Gen. 50:24; Ex. 2:25; 4:31; Ps. 33:18; Luke 1:68 **3:17** [a] Gen. 15:13–21; 46:4; 50:24, 25 **3:18** [a] Ex. 4:31 [b] Ex. 5:1, 3 [c] Num. 23:3, 4, 15, 16

EXODUS 3:1–22

## GOD IS NEAR

STORY OF SCRIPTURE 9

### WHAT'S GOING ON?

After killing a man, Moses fled Egypt and became a shepherd in the wilderness where he came across a bush on fire but not consumed. God called out from the flames and commissioned Moses to lead His people out of slavery. This account sets the stage for the rest of the exodus story, but most importantly, it introduces God's divine name: I AM. This phrase is often used as an expression of existence, but in Hebrew it means more than that. It's a declaration by God that He is not only here, there, and everywhere, but He is also *nearby*. He is near His people. Near Moses. Near the suffering and the weak. Near anyone in need of salvation.

### WHAT DOES THIS MEAN FOR ME?

Of the many profound truths in this passage, two stand out. First, Moses wasn't the most eloquent or qualified leader. He was a murderer with a speech impediment. That would undoubtedly disqualify any of us from leading millions of people. Yet, anyone yielded to God can do great things. Second, God's name, I AM, declares He is near us. He is near to you even in life's darkest moments.

### DID YOU CATCH THE PATTERN?

What was Moses doing before he encountered God? Tending sheep. He's far from the only notable shepherd in Scripture. Abraham, Jacob, David, and Amos were all shepherds. Furthermore, a group of shepherds were among the first people to see the newborn Jesus. This all foreshadows Jesus, the Good Shepherd. You will encounter shepherds and shepherding in many other places in the Bible. Pay close attention when you come across them.

*For the next* Story of Scripture *reading and devotion, turn to Exodus 12:1–32 on page 71.*

now, please, let us go three days' journey into the
wilderness, that we may sacrifice to the LORD our
God.' 19 But I am sure that the king of Egypt [a]will
not let you go, no, not even by a mighty hand.
20 So I will [a]stretch out My hand and strike Egypt
with [b]all My wonders which I will do in its midst;
and [c]after that he will let you go. 21 And [a]I will give
this people favor in the sight of the Egyptians;
and it shall be, when you go, that you shall not
go empty-handed. 22 [a]But every woman shall ask
of her neighbor, namely, of her who dwells near
her house, [b]articles of silver, articles of gold, and
clothing; and you shall put *them* on your sons
and on your daughters. So [c]you shall plunder
the Egyptians."

### *MIRACULOUS SIGNS FOR PHARAOH*

4 Then Moses answered and said, "But suppose they will not believe me or listen to
my voice; suppose they say, 'The LORD has not
appeared to you.' "
2 So the LORD said to him, "What *is* that in
your hand?"
He said, "A rod."
3 And He said, "Cast it on the ground." So he
cast it on the ground, and it became a serpent;
and Moses fled from it. 4 Then the LORD said to
Moses, "Reach out your hand and take *it* by the
tail" (and he reached out his hand and caught
it, and it became a rod in his hand), 5 "that they
may [a]believe that the [b]LORD God of their fathers,
the God of Abraham, the God of Isaac, and the
God of Jacob, has appeared to you."
6 Furthermore the LORD said to him, "Now
put your hand in your bosom." And he put his
hand in his bosom, and when he took it out,
behold, his hand *was* leprous, [a]like snow. 7 And
He said, "Put your hand in your bosom again."
So he put his hand in his bosom again, and drew
it out of his bosom, and behold, [a]it was restored
like his *other* flesh. 8 "Then it will be, if they do not
believe you, nor heed the message of the [a]first
sign, that they may believe the message of the
latter sign. 9 And it shall be, if they do not believe
even these two signs, or listen to your voice, that
you shall take water from the river[1] and pour *it*
on the dry *land*. [a]The water which you take from
the river will become blood on the dry *land*."
10 Then Moses said to the LORD, "O my Lord,
I *am* not eloquent, neither before nor since You
have spoken to Your servant; but [a]I *am* slow of
speech and slow of tongue."

**3:19** [a] Ex. 5:2 **3:20** [a] Ex. 6:6; 9:15 [b] Deut. 6:22; Neh. 9:10; Ps. 105:27; 135:9; Jer. 32:20; Acts 7:36 [c] Ex. 11:1; 12:31–37 **3:21** [a] Ex. 11:3; 12:36; 1 Kin. 8:50; Ps. 105:37; 106:46; [Prov. 16:7] **3:22** [a] Ex. 11:2 [b] Ex. 33:6 [c] Job 27:17; Prov. 13:22; [Ezek. 39:10] **4:5** [a] Ex. 4:31; 19:9 [b] Gen. 28:13; 48:15; Ex. 3:6, 15 **4:6** [a] Num. 12:10; 2 Kin. 5:27 **4:7** [a] Num. 12:13–15; Deut. 32:39 **4:8** [a] Ex. 7:6–13 **4:9** [a] Ex. 7:19, 20 [1] That is, the Nile **4:10** [a] Ex. 3:11; 4:1; 6:12

11 So the LORD said to him, [a]"Who has made
man's mouth? Or who makes the mute, the deaf,
the seeing, or the blind? *Have* not I, the LORD?
12 Now therefore, go, and I will be [a]with your
mouth and teach you what you shall say."
13 But he said, "O my Lord, [a]please send by
the hand of whomever *else* You may send."
14 So [a]the anger of the LORD was kindled
against Moses, and He said: "Is not Aaron the
Levite your [b]brother? I know that he can speak
well. And look, [c]he is also coming out to meet
you. When he sees you, he will be glad in his
heart. 15 Now [a]you shall speak to him and [b]put
the words in his mouth. And I will be with your
mouth and with his mouth, and [c]I will teach you
what you shall do. 16 So he shall be your spokes-
man to the people. And he himself shall be as a
mouth for you, and [a]you shall be to him as God.
17 And you shall take this rod in your hand, with
which you shall do the signs."

### *MOSES GOES TO EGYPT*

18 So Moses went and returned to [a]Jethro his
father-in-law, and said to him, "Please let me go
and return to my brethren who *are* in Egypt, and
see whether they are still alive."
And Jethro said to Moses, [b]"Go in peace."
19 Now the LORD said to Moses in [a]Midi-
an, "Go, return to [b]Egypt; for all the men who
[c]sought your life are dead." 20 Then Moses [a]took
his wife and his sons and set them on a donkey,
and he returned to the land of Egypt. And Moses
took [b]the rod of God in his hand.
21 And the LORD said to Moses, "When you go
back to Egypt, see that you do all those [a]wonders
before Pharaoh which I have put in your hand.
But [b]I will harden his heart, so that he will not
let the people go. 22 Then you shall [a]say to Phar-
aoh, 'Thus says the LORD: [b]"Israel *is* My son, [c]My
firstborn. 23 So I say to you, let My son go that he
may serve Me. But if you refuse to let him go,
indeed [a]I will kill your son, your firstborn." ' "
24 And it came to pass on the way, at the [a]en-
campment, that the LORD [b]met him and sought
to [c]kill him. 25 Then [a]Zipporah took [b]a sharp
stone and cut off the foreskin of her son and
cast *it* at *Moses'*[1] feet, and said, "Surely you *are*
a husband of blood to me!" 26 So He let him go.
Then she said, "*You are* a husband of blood!"—
because of the circumcision.
27 And the LORD said to Aaron, "Go into the
wilderness [a]to meet Moses." So he went and met
him on [b]the mountain of God, and kissed him.
28 So Moses [a]told Aaron all the words of the LORD
who had sent him, and all the [b]signs which He
had commanded him. 29 Then Moses and Aaron
[a]went and gathered together all the elders of the
children of Israel. 30 [a]And Aaron spoke all the
words which the LORD had spoken to Moses.
Then he did the signs in the sight of the people.
31 So the people [a]believed; and when they heard
that the LORD had [b]visited the children of Israel
and that He [c]had looked on their affliction, then
[d]they bowed their heads and worshiped.

> **4:21** Some interpret God saying He would **harden** Pharaoh's **heart** to mean He would confirm what Pharaoh had stubbornly determined to do. In the first five plagues, the hardening was attributed to Pharaoh (Ex. 7:13, 22; 8:15, 19, 32; 9:7). Then for the sixth plague, God hardened a heart that had already rejected Him (Ex. 9:12). Others insist God had determined Pharaoh's negative response to Moses long before Pharaoh could harden his heart. These interpreters point to this verse and to Exodus 9:16, in which God says He raised up Pharaoh for the purpose of demonstrating His power.

### *FIRST ENCOUNTER WITH PHARAOH*

5 Afterward Moses and Aaron went in and told
Pharaoh, "Thus says the LORD God of Israel:
'Let My people go, that they may hold [a]a feast
to Me in the wilderness.' "
2 And Pharaoh said, [a]"Who *is* the LORD, that
I should obey His voice to let Israel go? I do not
know the LORD, [b]nor will I let Israel go."
3 So they said, [a]"The God of the Hebrews
has [b]met with us. Please, let us go three days'
journey into the desert and sacrifice to the LORD
our God, lest He fall upon us with [c]pestilence or
with the sword."
4 Then the king of Egypt said to them, "Moses
and Aaron, why do you take the people from
their work? Get *back* to your [a]labor." 5 And Phar-
aoh said, "Look, the people of the land *are* [a]many
now, and you make them rest from their labor!"
6 So the same day Pharaoh commanded the
[a]taskmasters of the people and their officers,
saying, 7 "You shall no longer give the people straw
to make [a]brick as before. Let them go and gather
straw for themselves. 8 And you shall lay on them
the quota of bricks which they made before. You
shall not reduce it. For they are idle; therefore they
cry out, saying, 'Let us go *and* sacrifice to our God.'
9 Let more work be laid on the men, that they may
labor in it, and let them not regard false words."

**4:11** [a] Ps. 94:9; 146:8 **4:12** [a] Is. 50:4 **4:13** [a] Jon. 1:3 **4:14** [a] Num. 11:1, 33 [b] Num. 26:59 [c] Ex. 4:27 **4:15** [a] Ex. 4:12, 30; 7:1, 2 [b] Num. 23:5, 12 [c] Deut. 5:31 **4:16** [a] Ex. 7:1, 2 **4:18** [a] Ex. 2:21; 3:1; 4:18 [b] Judg. 18:6 **4:19** [a] Ex. 3:1; 18:1 [b] Gen. 46:3, 6 [c] Ex. 2:15, 23 **4:20** [a] Ex. 18:2–5 [b] Num. 20:8, 9, 11 **4:21** [a] Ex. 3:20; 11:9, 10 [b] John 12:40 **4:22** [a] Ex. 5:1 [b] Hos. 11:1 [c] Jer. 31:9 **4:23** [a] Ex. 11:5; 12:29 **4:24** [a] Gen. 42:27 [b] Num. 22:22 [c] Gen. 17:14 **4:25** [a] Ex. 2:21; 18:2 [b] Josh. 5:2, 3 [1] Literally *his* **4:27** [a] Ex. 4:14 [b] Ex. 3:1; 18:5; 24:13 **4:28** [a] Ex. 4:15, 16 [b] Ex. 4:8, 9 **4:29** [a] Ex. 3:16; 12:21 **4:30** [a] Ex. 4:15, 16 **4:31** [a] Ex. 3:18; 4:8, 9; 19:9 [b] Gen. 50:24 [c] Ex. 2:25; 3:7 [d] Gen. 24:26 **5:1** [a] Ex. 3:18; 7:16; 10:9 **5:2** [a] 2 Kin. 18:35 [b] Ex. 3:19; 7:14 **5:3** [a] Ex. 3:18; 7:16 [b] Num. 23:3 [c] Ex. 9:15 **5:4** [a] Ex. 1:11; 2:11; 6:6 **5:5** [a] Ex. 1:7, 9 **5:6** [a] Ex. 1:11; 3:7; 5:10, 13, 14 **5:7** [a] Ex. 1:14

> **5:7** Trees were scarce in Egypt. With little wood available, Egyptian builders used huge stones to construct their pyramids and temples. For houses and common buildings, they used bricks made of straw and mud.

10 And the taskmasters of the people and
their officers went out and spoke to the people,
saying, "Thus says Pharaoh: 'I will not give you
straw. 11 Go, get yourselves straw where you can
find it; yet none of your work will be reduced.'"
12 So the people were scattered abroad through-
out all the land of Egypt to gather stubble instead
of straw. 13 And the taskmasters forced *them*
to hurry, saying, "Fulfill your work, *your* daily
quota, as when there was straw." 14 Also the [a]of-
ficers of the children of Israel, whom Pharaoh's
taskmasters had set over them, were [b]beaten
*and* were asked, "Why have you not fulfilled
your task in making brick both yesterday and
today, as before?"

15 Then the officers of the children of Is-
rael came and cried out to Pharaoh, saying,
"Why are you dealing thus with your servants?
16 There is no straw given to your servants, and
they say to us, 'Make brick!' And indeed your
servants *are* beaten, but the fault *is* in your
*own* people."

17 But he said, "You *are* idle! Idle! Therefore
you say, 'Let us go *and* sacrifice to the LORD.'
18 Therefore go now *and* work; for no straw shall
be given you, yet you shall deliver the quota of
bricks." 19 And the officers of the children of
Israel saw *that* they *were* in trouble after it was
said, "You shall not reduce *any* bricks from your
daily quota."

20 Then, as they came out from Pharaoh,
they met Moses and Aaron who stood there to
meet them. 21 [a]And they said to them, "Let the
LORD look on you and judge, because you have
made us abhorrent in the sight of Pharaoh and
in the sight of his servants, to put a sword in
their hand to kill us."

### *ISRAEL'S DELIVERANCE ASSURED*

*(Ex. 3:1—4:17)*

22 So Moses returned to the LORD and said,
"Lord, why have You brought trouble on this
people? Why *is* it You have sent me? 23 For since
I came to Pharaoh to speak in Your name, he
has done evil to this people; neither have You
delivered Your people at all."

6 Then the LORD said to Moses, "Now you
shall see what I will do to Pharaoh. For [a]with
a strong hand he will let them go, and with a
strong hand [b]he will drive them out of his land."

2 And God spoke to Moses and said to him:
"I *am* the LORD. 3 [a]I appeared to Abraham, to
Isaac, and to Jacob, as [b]God Almighty, but *by* My
name [c]LORD[1] I was not known to them. 4 [a]I have
also established My covenant with them, [b]to
give them the land of Canaan, the land of their
pilgrimage, [c]in which they were strangers. 5 And
[a]I have also heard the groaning of the children
of Israel whom the Egyptians keep in bondage,
and I have remembered My covenant. 6 Therefore
say to the children of Israel: [a]'I *am* the LORD; [b]I
will bring you out from under the burdens of the
Egyptians, I will [c]rescue you from their bondage,
and I will redeem you with an outstretched arm
and with great judgments. 7 I will [a]take you as My
people, and [b]I will be your God. Then you shall
know that I *am* the LORD your God who brings
you out [c]from under the burdens of the Egyp-
tians. 8 And I will bring you into the land which
I [a]swore to give to Abraham, Isaac, and Jacob;
and I will give it to you *as* a heritage: I *am* the
LORD.'" 9 So Moses spoke thus to the children of
Israel; [a]but they did not heed Moses, because of
[b]anguish of spirit and cruel bondage.

10 And the LORD spoke to Moses, saying, 11 "Go
in, tell Pharaoh king of Egypt to let the children
of Israel go out of his land."

12 And Moses spoke before the LORD, saying,
"The children of Israel have not heeded me.
How then shall Pharaoh heed me, for [a]I *am* of
uncircumcised lips?"

13 Then the LORD spoke to Moses and Aaron,
and gave them a [a]command for the children of
Israel and for Pharaoh king of Egypt, to bring
the children of Israel out of the land of Egypt.

### *THE FAMILY OF MOSES AND AARON*

*(Gen. 46:8–27)*

14 These *are* the heads of their fathers' hous-
es: [a]The sons of Reuben, the firstborn of Israel,
*were* Hanoch, Pallu, Hezron, and Carmi. These
are the families of Reuben. 15 [a]And the sons
of Simeon *were* Jemuel,[1] Jamin, Ohad, Jachin,
Zohar, and Shaul the son of a Canaanite woman.
These *are* the families of Simeon. 16 These *are*
the names of [a]the sons of Levi according to their
generations: Gershon, Kohath, and Merari. And
the years of the life of Levi *were* one hundred and
thirty-seven. 17 [a]The sons of Gershon *were* Libni
and Shimi according to their families. 18 And [a]the
sons of Kohath *were* Amram, Izhar, Hebron,

**5:14** [a] Ex. 5:6 [b] Is. 10:24 **5:21** [a] Ex. 6:9; 14:11; 15:24; 16:2 **6:1** [a] Ex. 3:19 [b] Ex. 12:31, 33, 39 **6:3** [a] Gen. 17:1; 35:9; 48:3 [b] Gen. 28:3; 35:11 [c] Ex. 3:14, 15; 15:3; Ps. 68:4; 83:18; Is. 52:6; Jer. 16:21; Ezek. 37:6, 13; John 8:58 [1] Hebrew *YHWH*, traditionally *Jehovah* **6:4** [a] Gen. 12:7; 15:18; 17:4, 7, 8; 26:3; 28:4, 13 [b] Gen. 47:9; Lev. 25:23 [c] Gen. 28:4 **6:5** [a] Ex. 2:24; [Job 34:28]; Acts 7:34 **6:6** [a] Ex. 13:3, 14; 20:2; Deut. 6:12 [b] Ex. 3:17; 7:4; 12:51; 16:6; 18:1; Deut. 26:8; Ps. 136:11 [c] Ex. 15:13; Deut. 7:8; 1 Chr. 17:21; Neh. 1:10 **6:7** [a] Ex. 19:5; Deut. 4:20; 7:6; 2 Sam. 7:24 [b] Gen. 17:7; Ex. 29:45, 46; Lev. 26:12, 13, 45; Deut. 29:13; Rev. 21:7 [c] Ex. 5:4, 5 **6:8** [a] Gen. 15:18; 26:3; Num. 14:30; Neh. 9:15; Ezek. 20:5, 6 **6:9** [a] Ex. 5:21 [b] Ex. 2:23; Num. 21:4 **6:12** [a] Ex. 4:10; 6:30; Jer. 1:6 **6:13** [a] Num. 27:19, 23; Deut. 31:14 **6:14** [a] Gen. 46:9; Num. 26:5–11; 1 Chr. 5:3 **6:15** [a] Gen. 46:10; Num. 26:12–14; 1 Chr. 4:24 [1] Spelled *Nemuel* in Numbers 26:12 **6:16** [a] Gen. 46:11; Num. 3:17; 1 Chr. 6:16–30 **6:17** [a] 1 Chr. 6:17 **6:18** [a] 1 Chr. 6:2, 18

and Uzziel. And the years of the life of Kohath *were* one hundred and thirty-three. 19 [a]The sons of Merari *were* Mahli and Mushi. These *are* the families of Levi according to their generations.

20 Now [a]Amram took for himself [b]Jochebed, his father's sister, as wife; and she bore him [c]Aaron and Moses. And the years of the life of Amram *were* one hundred and thirty-seven. 21 [a]The sons of Izhar *were* Korah, Nepheg, and Zichri. 22 And [a]the sons of Uzziel *were* Mishael, Elzaphan, and Zithri. 23 Aaron took to himself Elisheba, daughter of [a]Amminadab, sister of Nahshon, as wife; and she bore him [b]Nadab, Abihu, [c]Eleazar, and Ithamar. 24 And [a]the sons of Korah *were* Assir, Elkanah, and Abiasaph. These are the families of the Korahites. 25 Eleazar, Aaron's son, took for himself one of the daughters of Putiel as wife; and [a]she bore him Phinehas. These *are* the heads of the fathers' houses of the Levites according to their families.

26 These *are the same* Aaron and Moses to whom the LORD said, "Bring out the children of Israel from the land of Egypt according to their [a]armies." 27 These *are* the ones who spoke to Pharaoh king of Egypt, [a]to bring out the children of Israel from Egypt. These *are the same* Moses and Aaron.

### *AARON IS MOSES' SPOKESMAN*

28 And it came to pass, on the day the LORD spoke to Moses in the land of Egypt, 29 that the LORD spoke to Moses, saying, "I *am* the LORD. [a]Speak to Pharaoh king of Egypt all that I say to you."

30 But Moses said before the LORD, "Behold, [a]I *am* of uncircumcised lips, and how shall Pharaoh heed me?"

**7** So the LORD said to Moses: "See, I have made you [a]*as* God to Pharaoh, and Aaron your brother shall be [b]your prophet. 2 You [a]shall speak all that I command you. And Aaron your brother shall tell Pharaoh to send the children of Israel out of his land. 3 And [a]I will harden Pharaoh's heart, and [b]multiply My [c]signs and My wonders in the land of Egypt. 4 But [a]Pharaoh will not heed you, so [b]that I may lay My hand on Egypt and bring My armies *and* My people, the children of Israel, out of the land of Egypt [c]by great judgments. 5 And the Egyptians [a]shall know that I *am* the LORD, when I [b]stretch out My hand on Egypt and [c]bring out the children of Israel from among them."

6 Then Moses and Aaron [a]did *so;* just as the LORD commanded them, so they did. 7 And Moses *was* [a]eighty years old and [b]Aaron eighty-three years old when they spoke to Pharaoh.

### *AARON'S MIRACULOUS ROD*

*(Ex. 4:1–5)*

8 Then the LORD spoke to Moses and Aaron, saying, 9 "When Pharaoh speaks to you, saying, [a]'Show a miracle for yourselves,' then you shall say to Aaron, [b]'Take your rod and cast *it* before Pharaoh, *and* let it become a serpent.' " 10 So Moses and Aaron went in to Pharaoh, and they did so, just [a]as the LORD commanded. And Aaron cast down his rod before Pharaoh and before his servants, and it [b]became a serpent.

11 But Pharaoh also [a]called the wise men and [b]the sorcerers; so the magicians of Egypt, they also [c]did in like manner with their enchantments. 12 For every man threw down his rod, and they became serpents. But Aaron's rod swallowed up their rods. 13 And Pharaoh's heart grew hard, and he did not heed them, as the LORD had said.

### *THE FIRST PLAGUE: WATERS BECOME BLOOD*

14 So the LORD said to Moses: [a]"Pharaoh's heart *is* hard; he refuses to let the people go. 15 Go to Pharaoh in the morning, when he goes out to the [a]water, and you shall stand by the river's bank to meet him; and [b]the rod which was turned to a serpent you shall take in your hand. 16 And you shall say to him, [a]'The LORD God of the Hebrews has sent me to you, saying, "Let My people go, [b]that they may serve Me in the wilderness"; but indeed, until now you would not hear! 17 Thus says the LORD: "By this [a]you shall know that I *am* the LORD. Behold, I will strike the waters which *are* in the river with the rod that *is* in my hand, and [b]they shall be turned [c]to blood. 18 And the fish that *are* in the river shall die, the river shall stink, and the Egyptians will [a]loathe to drink the water of the river." ' "

19 Then the LORD spoke to Moses, "Say to Aaron, 'Take your rod and [a]stretch out your hand over the waters of Egypt, over their streams, over their rivers, over their ponds, and over all their pools of water, that they may become blood. And there shall be blood throughout all the land of Egypt, both in *buckets of* wood and *pitchers of* stone.' " 20 And Moses and Aaron did so, just as the LORD commanded. So he [a]lifted up the rod and struck the waters that *were* in the river, in the sight of Pharaoh and in the sight of his servants. And all the [b]waters that *were* in the river were turned to blood. 21 The fish that *were* in the river died, the river stank, and the Egyptians [a]could not drink the water of the river. So there was blood throughout all the land of Egypt.

22 [a]Then the magicians of Egypt did [b]so with

**6:19** [a] 1 Chr. 6:19; 23:21 **6:20** [a] Ex. 2:1, 2; Num. 3:19 [b] Num. 26:59 [c] Num. 26:59 **6:21** [a] Num. 16:1; 1 Chr. 6:37, 38 **6:22** [a] Lev. 10:4 **6:23** [a] Ruth 4:19, 20; 1 Chr. 2:10; Matt. 1:4 [b] Lev. 10:1; Num. 3:2; 26:60 [c] Ex. 28:1 **6:24** [a] Num. 26:11 **6:25** [a] Num. 25:7, 11; Josh. 24:33 **6:26** [a] Ex. 7:4; 12:17, 51; Num. 33:1 **6:27** [a] Ex. 6:13; 32:7; 33:1; Ps. 77:20 **6:29** [a] Ex. 6:11; 7:2 **6:30** [a] Ex. 4:10; 6:12; Jer. 1:6 **7:1** [a] Ex. 4:16; Jer. 1:10 [b] Ex. 4:15, 16 **7:2** [a] Ex. 4:15; Deut. 18:18 **7:3** [a] Ex. 4:21; 9:12 [b] Ex. 11:9; Acts 7:36 [c] Ex. 4:7; Deut. 4:34 **7:4** [a] Ex. 3:19, 20; 10:1; 11:9 [b] Ex. 9:14 [c] Ex. 6:6; 12:12 **7:5** [a] Ex. 7:17; 8:22; 14:4, 18; Ps. 9:16 [b] Ex. 9:15 [c] Ex. 3:20; 6:6; 12:51 **7:6** [a] Ex. 7:2 **7:7** [a] Deut. 29:5; 31:2; 34:7; Acts 7:23, 30 [b] Num. 33:39 **7:9** [a] Ex. 10:1; Is. 7:11; John 2:18; 6:30 [b] Ex. 4:2, 3, 17 **7:10** [a] Ex. 7:9 [b] Ex. 4:3 **7:11** [a] Gen. 41:8 [b] Dan. 2:2; 2 Tim. 3:8 [c] Ex. 7:22; 8:7, 18; 2 Tim. 3:9; Rev. 13:13, 14 **7:14** [a] Ex. 8:15; 10:1, 20, 27 **7:15** [a] Ex. 2:5; 8:20 [b] Ex. 4:2, 3; 7:10 **7:16** [a] Ex. 3:13, 18; 4:22 [b] Ex. 3:12, 18; 4:23; 5:1, 3; 8:1 **7:17** [a] Ex. 5:2; 7:5; 10:2; Ps. 9:16; Ezek. 25:17 [b] Ex. 4:9; 7:20 [c] Rev. 11:6; 16:4, 6 **7:18** [a] Ex. 7:24 **7:19** [a] Ex. 8:5, 6, 16; 9:22; 10:12, 21; 14:21, 26 **7:20** [a] Ex. 17:5 [b] Ps. 78:44; 105:29, 30 **7:21** [a] Ex. 7:18 **7:22** [a] Ex. 7:11 [b] Ex. 8:7

their enchantments; and Pharaoh's heart grew
hard, and he did not heed them, [c]as the LORD
had said. 23 And Pharaoh turned and went into
his house. Neither was his heart moved by this.
24 So all the Egyptians dug all around the river
for water to drink, because they could not drink
the water of the river. 25 And seven days passed
after the LORD had struck the river.

### THE SECOND PLAGUE: FROGS

8 And the LORD spoke to Moses, "Go to Phar-
aoh and say to him, 'Thus says the LORD: "Let
My people go, [a]that they may serve Me. 2 But if
you [a]refuse to let *them* go, behold, I will smite
all your territory with [b]frogs. 3 So the river shall
bring forth frogs abundantly, which shall go up
and come into your house, into your [a]bedroom,
on your bed, into the houses of your servants,
on your people, into your ovens, and into your
kneading bowls. 4 And the frogs shall come up on
you, on your people, and on all your servants." ' "
5 Then the LORD spoke to Moses, "Say to
Aaron, [a]'Stretch out your hand with your rod
over the streams, over the rivers, and over the
ponds, and cause frogs to come up on the land of
Egypt.' " 6 So Aaron stretched out his hand over
the waters of Egypt, and [a]the frogs came up and
covered the land of Egypt. 7 [a]And the magicians
did so with their enchantments, and brought up
frogs on the land of Egypt.
8 Then Pharaoh called for Moses and Aaron,
and said, [a]"Entreat the LORD that He may take
away the frogs from me and from my people;
and I will let the people [b]go, that they may sac-
rifice to the LORD."
9 And Moses said to Pharaoh, "Accept the
honor of saying when I shall intercede for you,
for your servants, and for your people, to destroy
the frogs from you and your houses, *that* they
may remain in the river only."
10 So he said, "Tomorrow." And he said, "*Let
it be* according to your word, that you may know
that [a]*there is* no one like the LORD our God. 11 And
the frogs shall depart from you, from your hous-
es, from your servants, and from your people.
They shall remain in the river only."
12 Then Moses and Aaron went out from
Pharaoh. And Moses [a]cried out to the LORD
concerning the frogs which He had brought
against Pharaoh. 13 So the LORD did according
to the word of Moses. And the frogs died out of
the houses, out of the courtyards, and out of the
fields. 14 They gathered them together in heaps,
and the land stank. 15 But when Pharaoh saw that
there was [a]relief, [b]he hardened his heart and did
not heed them, as the LORD had said.

### THE THIRD PLAGUE: LICE

16 So the LORD said to Moses, "Say to Aaron,
'Stretch out your rod, and strike the dust of the
land, so that it may become lice throughout all
the land of Egypt.' " 17 And they did so. For Aaron
stretched out his hand with his rod and struck
the dust of the earth, and [a]it became lice on man
and beast. All the dust of the land became lice
throughout all the land of Egypt.
18 Now [a]the magicians so worked with their
enchantments to bring forth lice, but they [b]could
not. So there were lice on man and beast. 19 Then
the magicians said to Pharaoh, "This *is* [a]the fin-
ger of God." But Pharaoh's [b]heart grew hard, and
he did not heed them, just as the LORD had said.

### THE FOURTH PLAGUE: FLIES

20 And the LORD said to Moses, [a]"Rise early
in the morning and stand before Pharaoh as he
comes out to the water. Then say to him, 'Thus
says the LORD: [b]"Let My people go, that they may
serve Me. 21 Or else, if you will not let My people go,
behold, I will send swarms *of flies* on you and your
servants, on your people and into your houses. The
houses of the Egyptians shall be full of swarms
*of flies,* and also the ground on which they *stand.*
22 And in that day [a]I will set apart the land of [b]Go-
shen, in which My people dwell, that no swarms
*of flies* shall be there, in order that you may [c]know
that I *am* the LORD in the midst of the [d]land. 23 I will
make a difference[1] between My people and your
people. Tomorrow this [a]sign shall be." ' " 24 And the
LORD did so. [a]Thick swarms *of flies* came into the
house of Pharaoh, *into* his servants' houses, and
into all the land of Egypt. The land was corrupted
because of the swarms *of flies.*
25 Then Pharaoh called for Moses and Aaron,
and said, "Go, sacrifice to your God in the land."
26 And Moses said, "It is not right to do so, for
we would be sacrificing [a]the abomination of the
Egyptians to the LORD our God. If we sacrifice the
abomination of the Egyptians before their eyes,
then will they not stone us? 27 We will go [a]three
days' journey into the wilderness and sacrifice
to the LORD our God as [b]He will command us."
28 So Pharaoh said, "I will let you go, that
you may sacrifice to the LORD your God in the
wilderness; only you shall not go very far away.
[a]Intercede for me."
29 Then Moses said, "Indeed I am going out
from you, and I will entreat the LORD, that the
swarms *of flies* may depart tomorrow from Phar-
aoh, from his servants, and from his people. But
let Pharaoh not [a]deal deceitfully anymore in not
letting the people go to sacrifice to the LORD."
30 So Moses went out from Pharaoh and

**7:22** [c] Ex. 3:19; 7:3 **8:1** [a] Ex. 3:12, 18; 4:23; 5:1, 3 **8:2** [a] Ex. 7:14; 9:2 [b] Rev. 16:13 **8:3** [a] Ps. 105:30 **8:5** [a] Ex. 7:19 **8:6** [a] Ps. 78:45; 105:30 **8:7** [a] Ex. 7:11, 22 **8:8** [a] Ex. 8:28; 9:28; 10:17; Num. 21:7; 1 Kin. 13:6 [b] Ex. 10:8, 24 **8:10** [a] Ex. 9:14; 15:11; Deut. 4:35, 39; 33:26; 2 Sam. 7:22; 1 Chr. 17:20; Ps. 86:8; Is. 46:9; [Jer. 10:6, 7] **8:12** [a] Ex. 8:30; 9:33; 10:18; 32:11; [James 5:16–18] **8:15** [a] Eccl. 8:11 [b] Ex. 7:14, 22; 9:34; 1 Sam. 6:6 **8:17** [a] Ps. 105:31 **8:18** [a] Ex. 7:11, 12; 8:7 [b] Dan. 5:8; 2 Tim. 3:8, 9 **8:19** [a] Ex. 7:5; 10:7; 1 Sam. 6:3, 9; Ps. 8:3; Luke 11:20 [b] Ex. 8:15 **8:20** [a] Ex. 7:15; 9:13 [b] Ex. 3:18; 4:23; 5:1, 3; 8:1 **8:22** [a] Ex. 9:4, 6, 26; 10:23; 11:6, 7; 12:13 [b] Gen. 50:8 [c] Ex. 7:5, 17; 10:2; 14:4 [d] Ex. 9:29 **8:23** [a] Ex. 4:8 [1] Literally *set a ransom* (compare Exodus 9:4 and 11:7) **8:24** [a] Ps. 78:45; 105:31 **8:26** [a] Gen. 43:32; 46:34; [Deut. 7:25, 26; 12:31] **8:27** [a] Ex. 3:18; 5:3 [b] Ex. 3:12 **8:28** [a] Ex. 8:8, 15, 29, 32; 9:28; 1 Kin. 13:6 **8:29** [a] Ex. 8:8, 15

[a]entreated the LORD. 31 And the LORD did ac-
cording to the word of Moses; He removed the
swarms *of flies* from Pharaoh, from his servants,
and from his people. Not one remained. 32 But
Pharaoh [a]hardened his heart at this time also;
neither would he let the people go.

### THE FIFTH PLAGUE: LIVESTOCK DISEASED

9 Then the LORD said to Moses, [a]"Go in to Phar-
aoh and tell him, 'Thus says the LORD God of
the Hebrews: "Let My people go, that they may
[b]serve Me. 2 For if you [a]refuse to let *them* go, and
still hold them, 3 behold, the [a]hand of the LORD
will be on your cattle in the field, on the horses,
on the donkeys, on the camels, on the oxen, and
on the sheep—a very severe pestilence. 4 And
[a]the LORD will make a difference between the
livestock of Israel and the livestock of Egypt.
So nothing shall die of all *that* belongs to the
children of Israel." ' " 5 Then the LORD appointed
a set time, saying, "Tomorrow the LORD will do
this thing in the land."

6 So the LORD did this thing on the next day,
and [a]all the livestock of Egypt died; but of the
livestock of the children of Israel, not one died.
7 Then Pharaoh sent, and indeed, not even one
of the livestock of the Israelites was dead. But
the [a]heart of Pharaoh became hard, and he did
not let the people go.

### THE SIXTH PLAGUE: BOILS

*(Deut. 28:27)*

8 So the LORD said to Moses and Aaron, "Take
for yourselves handfuls of ashes from a furnace,
and let Moses scatter it toward the heavens in
the sight of Pharaoh. 9 And it will become fine
dust in all the land of Egypt, and it will cause
[a]boils that break out in sores on man and beast
throughout all the land of Egypt." 10 Then they
took ashes from the furnace and stood before
Pharaoh, and Moses scattered *them* toward heav-
en. And *they* caused [a]boils that break out in sores
on man and beast. 11 And the [a]magicians could
not stand before Moses because of the [b]boils, for
the boils were on the magicians and on all the
Egyptians. 12 But the LORD hardened the heart
of Pharaoh; and he [a]did not heed them, just [b]as
the LORD had spoken to Moses.

### THE SEVENTH PLAGUE: HAIL

13 Then the LORD said to Moses, [a]"Rise early
in the morning and stand before Pharaoh, and
say to him, 'Thus says the LORD God of the He-
brews: "Let My people go, that they may [b]serve
Me, 14 for at this time I will send all My plagues
to your very heart, and on your servants and
on your people, [a]that you may know that *there*
*is* none like Me in all the earth. 15 Now if I had
[a]stretched out My hand and struck you and your
people with [b]pestilence, then you would have
been cut off from the earth. 16 But indeed for
[a]this *purpose* I have raised you up, that I may
[b]show My power *in* you, and that My [c]name may
be declared in all the earth. 17 As yet you exalt
yourself against My people in that you will not
let them go. 18 Behold, tomorrow about this time
I will cause very heavy hail to rain down, such
as has not been in Egypt since its founding until
now. 19 Therefore send now *and* gather your live-
stock and all that you have in the field, for the
hail shall come down on every man and every
animal which is found in the field and is not
brought home; and they shall die." ' "

20 He who [a]feared the word of the LORD
among the [b]servants of Pharaoh made his ser-
vants and his livestock flee to the houses. 21 But
he who did not regard the word of the LORD left
his servants and his livestock in the field.

22 Then the LORD said to Moses, "Stretch out
your hand toward heaven, that there may be [a]hail
in all the land of Egypt—on man, on beast, and
on every herb of the field, throughout the land
of Egypt." 23 And Moses stretched out his rod
toward heaven; and [a]the LORD sent thunder and
hail, and fire darted to the ground. And the LORD
rained hail on the land of Egypt. 24 So there was
hail, and fire mingled with the hail, so very heavy
that there was none like it in all the land of Egypt
since it became a nation. 25 And the [a]hail struck
throughout the whole land of Egypt, all that *was* in
the field, both man and beast; and the hail struck
every herb of the field and broke every tree of the
field. 26 [a]Only in the land of Goshen, where the
children of Israel *were,* there was no hail.

27 And Pharaoh sent and [a]called for Moses
and Aaron, and said to them, [b]"I have sinned
this time. [c]The LORD *is* righteous, and my peo-
ple and I *are* wicked. 28 [a]Entreat the LORD, that
there may be no *more* mighty thundering and
hail, for *it is* enough. I will let you [b]go, and you
shall stay no longer."

29 So Moses said to him, "As soon as I have
gone out of the city, I will [a]spread out my hands
to the LORD; the thunder will cease, and there
will be no more hail, that you may know that
the [b]earth *is* the LORD's. 30 But as for you and
your servants, [a]I know that you will not yet fear
the LORD God."

31 Now the flax and the barley were struck,
[a]for the barley *was* in the head and the flax *was*
in bud. 32 But the wheat and the spelt were not
struck, for they *are* late crops.

33 So Moses went out of the city from Phar-
aoh and [a]spread out his hands to the LORD; then

8:30 [a] Ex. 8:12 8:32 [a] Ex. 4:21; 8:8, 15; Ps. 52:2 9:1 [a] Ex. 4:23; 8:1 [b] Ex. 7:16 9:2 [a] Ex. 8:2 9:3 [a] Ex. 7:4; 1 Sam. 5:6; Ps. 39:10; Acts 13:11 9:4 [a] Ex. 8:22 9:6 [a] Ex. 9:19, 20, 25; Ps. 78:48, 50 9:7 [a] Ex. 7:14; 8:32 9:9 [a] Deut. 28:27; Rev. 16:2 9:10 [a] Deut. 28:27 9:11 [a] [Ex. 8:18, 19; 2 Tim. 3:9] [b] Deut. 28:27; Job 2:7; Rev. 16:1, 2 9:12 [a] Ex. 7:13 [b] Ex. 4:21 9:13 [a] Ex. 8:20 [b] Ex. 9:1 9:14 [a] Ex. 8:10 9:15 [a] Ex. 3:20; 7:5 [b] Ex. 5:3 9:16 [a] [Rom. 9:17, 18] [b] Ex. 7:4, 5; 10:1; 11:9; 14:17 [c] 1 Kin. 8:43 9:20 [a] [Prov. 13:13] [b] Ex. 8:19; 10:7 9:22 [a] Rev. 16:21 9:23 [a] Josh. 10:11 9:25 [a] Ps. 78:47, 48; 105:32, 33 9:26 [a] Ex. 8:22, 23; 9:4, 6; 10:23; 11:7; 12:13 9:27 [a] Ex. 8:8 [b] Ex. 9:34; 10:16, 17 [c] 2 Chr. 12:6 9:28 [a] Ex. 8:8, 28; 10:17 [b] Ex. 8:25; 10:8, 24 9:29 [a] Is. 1:15 [b] Ps. 24:1 9:30 [a] [Is. 26:10] 9:31 [a] Ruth 1:22; 2:23 9:33 [a] Ex. 8:12; 9:29

the thunder and the hail ceased, and the rain was not poured on the earth. 34 And when Pharaoh saw that the rain, the hail, and the thunder had ceased, he sinned yet more; and he hardened his heart, he and his servants. 35 So [a]the heart of Pharaoh was hard; neither would he let the children of Israel go, as the LORD had spoken by Moses.

### *THE EIGHTH PLAGUE: LOCUSTS*

*(Joel 1:2–4)*

**10** Now the LORD said to Moses, "Go in to Pharaoh; [a]for I have hardened his heart and the hearts of his servants, [b]that I may show these signs of Mine before him, 2 and that [a]you may tell in the hearing of your son and your son's son the mighty things I have done in Egypt, and My signs which I have done among them, that you may [b]know that I *am* the LORD."

3 So Moses and Aaron came in to Pharaoh and said to him, "Thus says the LORD God of the Hebrews: 'How long will you refuse to [a]humble yourself before Me? Let My people go, that they may [b]serve Me. 4 Or else, if you refuse to let My people go, behold, tomorrow I will bring [a]locusts into your territory. 5 And they shall cover the face of the earth, so that no one will be able to see the earth; and [a]they shall eat the residue of what is left, which remains to you from the hail, and they shall eat every tree which grows up for you out of the field. 6 They shall [a]fill your houses, the houses of all your servants, and the houses of all the Egyptians—which neither your fathers nor your fathers' fathers have seen, since the day that they were on the earth to this day.'" And he turned and went out from Pharaoh.

> **10:4 Locusts** are still a major problem in North Africa and the Middle East. A large swarm can destroy entire crops and block off sunlight to an entire region.

7 Then Pharaoh's [a]servants said to him, "How long shall this man be [b]a snare to us? Let the men go, that they may serve the LORD their God. Do you not yet know that Egypt is destroyed?"

8 So Moses and Aaron were brought again to Pharaoh, and he said to them, "Go, serve the LORD your God. Who *are* the ones that are going?"

9 And Moses said, "We will go with our young and our old; with our sons and our daughters, with our flocks and our herds we will go, for [a]we must hold a feast to the LORD."

10 Then he said to them, "The LORD had better be with you when I let you and your little ones go! Beware, for evil is ahead of you. 11 Not so! Go now, you *who are* men, and serve the LORD, for that is what you desired." And they were driven [a]out from Pharaoh's presence.

12 Then the LORD said to Moses, [a]"Stretch out your hand over the land of Egypt for the locusts, that they may come upon the land of Egypt, and [b]eat every herb of the land—all that the hail has left." 13 So Moses stretched out his rod over the land of Egypt, and the LORD brought an east wind on the land all that day and all *that* night. When it was morning, the east wind brought the locusts. 14 And [a]the locusts went up over all the land of Egypt and rested on all the territory of Egypt. *They were* very severe; [b]previously there had been no such locusts as they, nor shall there be such after them. 15 For they [a]covered the face of the whole earth, so that the land was darkened; and they [b]ate every herb of the land and all the fruit of the trees which the hail had left. So there remained nothing green on the trees or on the plants of the field throughout all the land of Egypt.

16 Then Pharaoh called [a]for Moses and Aaron in haste, and said, [b]"I have sinned against the LORD your God and against you. 17 Now therefore, please forgive my sin only this once, and [a]entreat the LORD your God, that He may take away from me this death only." 18 So he [a]went out from Pharaoh and entreated the LORD. 19 And the LORD turned a very strong west wind, which took the locusts away and blew them [a]into the Red Sea. There remained not one locust in all the territory of Egypt. 20 But the LORD [a]hardened Pharaoh's heart, and he did not let the children of Israel go.

### *THE NINTH PLAGUE: DARKNESS*

21 Then the LORD said to Moses, [a]"Stretch out your hand toward heaven, that there may be darkness over the land of Egypt, darkness *which* may even be felt." 22 So Moses stretched out his hand toward heaven, and there was [a]thick darkness in all the land of Egypt [b]three days. 23 They did not see one another; nor did anyone rise from his place for three days. [a]But all the children of Israel had light in their dwellings.

24 Then Pharaoh called to Moses and [a]said, "Go, serve the LORD; only let your flocks and your herds be kept back. Let your [b]little ones also go with you."

25 But Moses said, "You must also give us sacrifices and burnt offerings, that we may sacrifice to the LORD our God. 26 Our [a]livestock also shall go with us; not a hoof shall be left behind. For

9:35 [a] Ex. 4:21 10:1 [a] John 12:40 [b] Ex. 7:4; 9:16 10:2 [a] Joel 1:3 [b] Ex. 7:5, 17; 8:22 10:3 [a] [1 Kin. 21:29] [b] Ex. 4:23; 8:1; 9:1 10:4 [a] Rev. 9:3 10:5 [a] Ex. 9:32 10:6 [a] Ex. 8:3, 21 10:7 [a] Ex. 7:5; 8:19; 9:20; 12:33 [b] Ex. 23:33; Josh. 23:13; 1 Sam. 18:21; Eccl. 7:26; 1 Cor. 7:35 10:9 [a] Ex. 5:1; 7:16 10:11 [a] Ex. 10:28 10:12 [a] Ex. 7:19 [b] Ex. 10:5, 15 10:14 [a] Deut. 28:38; Ps. 78:46; 105:34 [b] Joel 1:4, 7; 2:1–11; Rev. 9:3 10:15 [a] Ex. 10:5 [b] Ps. 105:35 10:16 [a] Ex. 8:8 [b] Ex. 9:27 10:17 [a] Ex. 8:8, 28; 9:28; 1 Kin. 13:6 10:18 [a] Ex. 8:30 10:19 [a] Joel 2:20 10:20 [a] Ex. 4:21; 10:1; 11:10 10:21 [a] Ex. 9:22 10:22 [a] Ps. 105:28; Rev. 16:10 [b] Ex. 3:18 10:23 [a] Ex. 8:22, 23 10:24 [a] Ex. 8:8, 25; 10:8 [b] Ex. 10:10 10:26 [a] Ex. 10:9

we must take some of them to serve the LORD
our God, and even we do not know with what
we must serve the LORD until we arrive there."
27 But the LORD [a]hardened Pharaoh's heart,
and he would not let them go. 28 Then Pharaoh
said to him, [a]"Get away from me! Take heed to
yourself and see my face no more! For in the
day you see my face you shall die!"
29 So Moses said, "You have spoken well. [a]I
will never see your face again."

### *DEATH OF THE FIRSTBORN ANNOUNCED*

*(Ex. 3:21, 22; 12:35, 36)*

**11** And the LORD said to Moses, "I will bring
one more plague on Pharaoh and on Egypt.
[a]Afterward he will let you go from here. [b]When
he lets *you* go, he will surely drive you out of
here altogether. 2 Speak now in the hearing of the
people, and let every man ask from his neighbor
and every woman from her neighbor, [a]articles of
silver and articles of gold." 3 [a]And the LORD gave
the people favor in the sight of the Egyptians.
Moreover the man [b]Moses *was* very great in the
land of Egypt, in the sight of Pharaoh's servants
and in the sight of the people.
4 Then Moses said, "Thus says the LORD:
[a]'About midnight I will go out into the midst of
Egypt; 5 and [a]all the firstborn in the land of Egypt
shall die, from the firstborn of Pharaoh who sits
on his throne, even to the firstborn of the female
servant who *is* behind the handmill, and all the
firstborn of the animals. 6 [a]Then there shall be a
great cry throughout all the land of Egypt, [b]such
as was not like it *before,* nor shall be like it again.
7 [a]But against none of the children of Israel [b]shall
a dog move its tongue, against man or beast, that
you may know that the LORD does make a dif-
ference between the Egyptians and Israel.' 8 And
[a]all these your servants shall come down to me
and bow down to me, saying, 'Get out, and all the
people who follow you!' After that I will go out."
[b]Then he went out from Pharaoh in great anger.
9 But the LORD said to Moses, [a]"Pharaoh
will not heed you, so that [b]My wonders may be
multiplied in the land of Egypt." 10 So Moses
and Aaron did all these wonders before Phar-
aoh; [a]and the LORD hardened Pharaoh's heart,
and he did not let the children of Israel go out
of his land.

### *THE PASSOVER INSTITUTED*

*(Num. 9:1–14; Deut. 16:1–8; Ezek. 45:21–25)*

**12** Now the LORD spoke to Moses and Aaron
in the land of Egypt, saying, 2 [a]"This month
*shall be* your beginning of months; it *shall be* the
first month of the year to you. 3 Speak to all the
congregation of Israel, saying: 'On the [a]tenth
of this month every man shall take for himself
a lamb, according to the house of *his* father, a
lamb for a household. 4 And if the household is
too small for the lamb, let him and his neighbor
next to his house take *it* according to the number
of the persons; according to each man's need you
shall make your count for the lamb. 5 Your lamb
shall be [a]without blemish, a male of the first year.
You may take *it* from the sheep or from the goats.
6 Now you shall keep it until the [a]fourteenth day
of the same month. Then the whole assembly of
the congregation of Israel shall kill it at twilight.
7 And they shall take *some* of the blood and put
*it* on the two doorposts and on the lintel of the
houses where they eat it. 8 Then they shall eat the
flesh on that [a]night; [b]roasted in fire, with [c]unleav-
ened bread *and* with bitter *herbs* they shall eat
it. 9 Do not eat it raw, nor boiled at all with water,
but [a]roasted in fire—its head with its legs and its
entrails. 10 [a]You shall let none of it remain until
morning, and what remains of it until morning
you shall burn with fire. 11 And thus you shall eat
it: *with* a belt on your waist, your sandals on your
feet, and your staff in your hand. So you shall eat
it in haste. [a]It *is* the LORD's Passover.
12 'For I [a]will pass through the land of Egypt
on that night, and will strike all the firstborn
in the land of Egypt, both man and beast; and
[b]against all the gods of Egypt I will execute
judgment: [c]I *am* the LORD. 13 Now the blood shall
be a sign for you on the houses where you *are.*
And when I see the blood, I will pass over you;
and the plague shall not be on you to destroy
*you* when I strike the land of Egypt.
14 'So this day shall be to you [a]a memorial;
and you shall keep it as a [b]feast to the LORD
throughout your generations. You shall keep it
as a feast [c]by an everlasting ordinance. 15 [a]Seven
days you shall eat unleavened bread. On the first
day you shall remove leaven from your houses.
For whoever eats leavened bread from the first
day until the seventh day, [b]that person shall be
cut off from Israel. 16 On the first day *there shall
be* [a]a holy convocation, and on the seventh day
there shall be a holy convocation for you. No
manner of work shall be done on them; but

**SEEING JESUS IN THE SCRIPTURE**

**12:14** God's people celebrated the Passover meal to remember His work to free them from Egypt. Likewise, God's people today observe the Lord's Supper (or Communion) to remember Jesus' death on the cross to free us from sin (see Luke 22:19-20).

**10:27** [a] Ex. 4:21; 10:1, 20; 14:4, 8 **10:28** [a] Ex. 10:11 **10:29** [a] Ex. 11:8; Heb. 11:27 **11:1** [a] Ex. 12:31, 33, 39 [b] Ex. 6:1; 12:39 **11:2** [a] Ex. 3:22; 12:35, 36 **11:3** [a] Ex. 3:21; 12:36; Ps. 106:46 [b] Deut. 34:10–12; 2 Sam. 7:9; Esth. 9:4 **11:4** [a] Ex. 12:12, 23, 29 **11:5** [a] Ex. 4:23; 12:12, 29; Ps. 78:51; 105:36; 135:8; 136:10; Amos 4:10 **11:6** [a] Ex. 12:30; Amos 5:17 [b] Ex. 10:14 **11:7** [a] Ex. 8:22 [b] Josh. 10:21 **11:8** [a] Ex. 12:31–33 [b] Heb. 11:27 **11:9** [a] Ex. 3:19; 7:4; 10:1 [b] Ex. 7:3; 9:16 **11:10** [a] Rom. 2:5 **12:2** [a] Deut. 16:1 **12:3** [a] Josh. 4:19 **12:5** [a] [1 Pet. 1:19] **12:6** [a] Lev. 23:5 **12:8** [a] Num. 9:12 [b] Deut. 16:7 [c] 1 Cor. 5:8 **12:9** [a] Deut. 16:7 **12:10** [a] Ex. 16:19; 23:18; 34:25 **12:11** [a] Ex. 12:13, 21, 27, 43 **12:12** [a] Ex. 11:4, 5 [b] Num. 33:4 [c] Ex. 6:2 **12:14** [a] Ex. 13:9 [b] Lev. 23:4, 5 [c] Ex. 12:17, 24; 13:10 **12:15** [a] Lev. 23:6 [b] Gen. 17:14 **12:16** [a] Lev. 23:2, 7, 8

EXODUS 12:1–32

# THE BLOOD OF THE LAMB

10

STORY OF SCRIPTURE

## WHAT'S GOING ON?

Egypt had experienced nine plagues, yet Pharaoh stubbornly refused to release the Hebrews. One last plague would convince him. God would move through the land and strike down every firstborn son, including those of the Hebrews. Unless, that is, they heeded God's instructions regarding the Passover. Each family was to select a flawless lamb, sacrifice it, and place its blood around their doors. The lamb symbolized innocence, foreshadowing *the* sacrificial Lamb of God—Jesus. When God moved through the land that night, He passed over the homes protected by the lamb's blood but took the life of the firstborn males otherwise. This tragic moment was a reversal of Pharaoh's decree to kill every Hebrew baby boy (see Ex. 1:22). This event is about justice, the cost of freedom, and an epic foreshadowing of Christ's ultimate redemption of humanity as the Lamb of God (see John 1:29).

## WHAT DOES THIS MEAN FOR ME?

Just as anyone who didn't have the blood of the lamb on their doorposts met a fateful end, so is the destiny of anyone without the blood of Jesus. His sacrifice on the cross and our declaration of faith in Him serves as the blood covering our doorposts. Under that blood, you are completely safe.

## DID YOU CATCH THE PATTERN?

In the Old Testament, unblemished lambs were sacrificed to atone for sins. When we shift to the New Testament, John the Baptist identifies Jesus as the "Lamb of God who takes away the sin of the world" (John 1:29). Jesus was unblemished, being without sin. His sacrifice is both a fulfillment and a transcendence of the sacrificial system, offering grace and redemption to all who believe. Just as you should keep an eye out for shepherd imagery throughout Scripture, keep a close eye on the presence of sheep and lambs. Any time you come across one in your reading, stop and see if it points to Jesus.

*For the next* Story of Scripture *reading and devotion, turn to Exodus 13:17—14:31 on page 75.*

*that* which everyone must eat—that only may
be prepared by you. 17 So you shall observe *the*
*Feast of* Unleavened Bread, for [a]on this same
day I will have brought your armies [b]out of the
land of Egypt. Therefore you shall observe this
day throughout your generations as an ever-
lasting ordinance. 18 [a]In the first *month,* on the
fourteenth day of the month at evening, you
shall eat unleavened bread, until the twenty-
first day of the month at evening. 19 For [a]seven
days no leaven shall be found in your houses,
since whoever eats what is leavened, that same
person shall be cut off from the congregation
of Israel, whether *he is* a stranger or a native of
the land. 20 You shall eat nothing leavened; in all
your dwellings you shall eat unleavened bread.' "
21 Then [a]Moses called for all the [b]elders of Is-
rael and said to them, [c]"Pick out and take lambs
for yourselves according to your families, and
kill the Passover *lamb.* 22 [a]And you shall take
a bunch of hyssop, dip *it* in the blood that *is*
in the basin, and [b]strike the lintel and the two
doorposts with the blood that *is* in the basin.
And none of you shall go out of the door of his
house until morning. 23 [a]For the LORD will pass
through to strike the Egyptians; and when He
sees the [b]blood on the lintel and on the two
doorposts, the LORD will pass over the door
and [c]not allow [d]the destroyer to come into your
houses to strike *you.* 24 And you shall [a]observe
this thing as an ordinance for you and your
sons forever. 25 It will come to pass when you
come to the land which the LORD will give you,
[a]just as He promised, that you shall keep this
service. 26 [a]And it shall be, when your children
say to you, 'What do you mean by this service?'
27 that you shall say, [a]'It *is* the Passover sacrifice
of the LORD, who passed over the houses of the
children of Israel in Egypt when He struck the
Egyptians and delivered our households.' " So
the people [b]bowed their heads and worshiped.
28 Then the children of Israel went away and [a]did
*so;* just as the LORD had commanded Moses and
Aaron, so they did.

**12:17** [a] Ex. 12:14; 13:3, 10 [b] Num. 33:1 **12:18** [a] Lev. 23:5–8 **12:19** [a] Ex. 12:15; 23:15; 34:18 **12:21** [a] [Heb. 11:28] [b] Ex. 3:16 [c] Num. 9:4 **12:22** [a] Heb. 11:28 [b] Ex. 12:7 **12:23** [a] Ex. 11:4; 12:12, 13 [b] Ex. 24:8 [c] Rev. 7:3; 9:4 [d] Heb. 11:28 **12:24** [a] Ex. 12:14, 17; 13:5, 10 **12:25** [a] Ex. 3:8, 17 **12:26** [a] Ex. 10:2; 13:8, 14, 15 **12:27** [a] Ex. 12:11 [b] Ex. 4:31 **12:28** [a] [Heb. 11:28]

### *THE TENTH PLAGUE: DEATH OF THE FIRSTBORN*

*(Ex. 11:1–10)*

29 [a]And it came to pass at midnight that [b]the LORD struck all the firstborn in the land of Egypt, from the firstborn of Pharaoh who sat on his throne to the firstborn of the captive who *was* in the dungeon, and all the firstborn of [c]livestock. 30 So Pharaoh rose in the night, he, all his servants, and all the Egyptians; and there was a great cry in Egypt, for *there was* not a house where *there was* not one dead.

### *THE EXODUS*

31 Then he [a]called for Moses and Aaron by night, and said, "Rise, go out from among my people, [b]both you and the children of Israel. And go, serve the LORD as you have [c]said. 32 [a]Also take your flocks and your herds, as you have said, and be gone; and bless me also."

33 [a]And the Egyptians [b]urged the people, that they might send them out of the land in haste. For they said, "We *shall* all *be* dead." 34 So the people took their dough before it was leavened, having their kneading bowls bound up in their clothes on their shoulders. 35 Now the children of Israel had done according to the word of Moses, and they had asked from the Egyptians [a]articles of silver, articles of gold, and clothing. 36 [a]And the LORD had given the people favor in the sight of the Egyptians, so that they granted them *what they requested.* Thus [b]they plundered the Egyptians.

37 Then [a]the children of Israel journeyed from [b]Rameses to Succoth, about [c]six hundred thousand men on foot, besides children. 38 A [a]mixed multitude went up with them also, and flocks and herds—a great deal of [b]livestock. 39 And they baked unleavened cakes of the dough which they had brought out of Egypt; for it was not leavened, because [a]they were driven out of Egypt and could not wait, nor had they prepared provisions for themselves.

**12:37 Six hundred thousand men** would indicate a total population of perhaps three million men, women, and children.

40 Now the sojourn of the children of Israel who lived in Egypt[1] *was* [a]four hundred and thirty years. 41 And it came to pass at the end of the four hundred and thirty years—on that very same day—it came to pass that [a]all the armies of the LORD went out from the land of Egypt. 42 It *is* [a]a night of solemn observance to the LORD for bringing them out of the land of Egypt. This *is* that night of the LORD, a solemn observance for all the children of Israel throughout their generations.

### *PASSOVER REGULATIONS*

*(Gen. 17:9–14; Ex. 12:1–13)*

43 And the LORD said to Moses and Aaron, "This *is* [a]the ordinance of the Passover: No foreigner shall eat it. 44 But every man's servant who is bought for money, when you have [a]circumcised him, then he may eat it. 45 [a]A sojourner and a hired servant shall not eat it. 46 In one house it shall be eaten; you shall not carry any of the flesh outside the house, [a]nor shall you break one of its bones. 47 [a]All the congregation of Israel shall keep it. 48 And [a]when a stranger dwells with you *and wants* to keep the Passover to the LORD, let all his males be circumcised, and then let him come near and keep it; and he shall be as a native of the land. For no uncircumcised person shall eat it. 49 [a]One law shall be for the native-born and for the stranger who dwells among you."

50 Thus all the children of Israel did; as the LORD commanded Moses and Aaron, so they did. 51 [a]And it came to pass, on that very same day, that the LORD brought the children of Israel out of the land of Egypt [b]according to their armies.

### *THE FIRSTBORN CONSECRATED*

13 Then the LORD spoke to Moses, saying, 2 [a]"Consecrate to Me all the firstborn, whatever opens the womb among the children of Israel, *both* of man and beast; it is Mine."

**SEEING JESUS IN THE SCRIPTURE**

**13:2** God's command to consecrate all the firstborn of Israel reminded Israel that God had spared their firstborn in Egypt. Jesus was consecrated to God after His birth, but unlike the Israelites, He wasn't spared from death (see Luke 2:23).

### *THE FEAST OF UNLEAVENED BREAD*

*(Ex. 12:14–20)*

3 And Moses said to the people: [a]"Remember this day in which you went out of Egypt, out of the house of bondage; for [b]by strength of hand the LORD brought you out of this *place.* [c]No leavened bread shall be eaten. 4 [a]On this day you are going out, in the month Abib. 5 And it shall be, when the LORD [a]brings you into the [b]land of the Canaanites and the Hittites and the Amorites and the Hivites and the Jebusites,

**12:29** [a] Ex. 11:4, 5 [b] Num. 8:17; 33:4 [c] Ex. 9:6 **12:31** [a] Ex. 10:28, 29 [b] Ex. 8:25; 11:1 [c] Ex. 10:9 **12:32** [a] Ex. 10:9, 26 **12:33** [a] Ex. 10:7 [b] Ps. 105:38 **12:35** [a] Ex. 3:21, 22; 11:2, 3 **12:36** [a] Ex. 3:21 [b] Gen. 15:14 **12:37** [a] Num. 33:3, 5 [b] Gen. 47:11 [c] Ex. 38:26 **12:38** [a] Num. 11:4 [b] Deut. 3:19 **12:39** [a] Ex. 6:1; 11:1; 12:31–33 **12:40** [a] Acts 7:6 [1] Samaritan Pentateuch and Septuagint read *Egypt and Canaan.* **12:41** [a] Ex. 3:8, 10; 6:6; 7:4 **12:42** [a] Deut. 16:1, 6 **12:43** [a] Num. 9:14 **12:44** [a] Gen. 17:12, 13 **12:45** [a] Lev. 22:10 **12:46** [a] [John 19:33, 36] **12:47** [a] Ex. 12:6 **12:48** [a] Num. 9:14 **12:49** [a] Num. 15:15, 16 **12:51** [a] Ex. 12:41; 20:2 [b] Ex. 6:26 **13:2** [a] Luke 2:23 **13:3** [a] Deut. 16:3 [b] Ex. 3:20; 6:1 [c] Ex. 12:8, 19 **13:4** [a] Ex. 12:2; 23:15; 34:18 **13:5** [a] Ex. 3:8, 17 [b] Gen. 17:8

## THE EXODUS

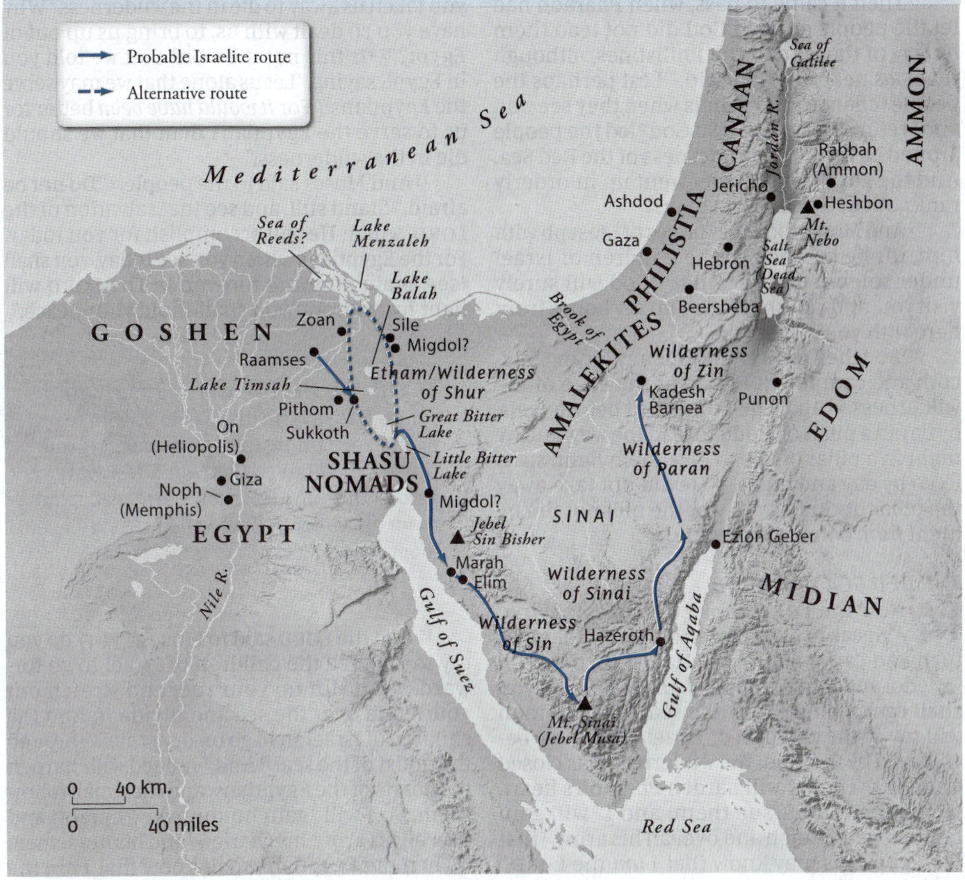


which He [c]swore to your fathers to give you, a
land flowing with milk and honey, [d]that you
shall keep this service in this month. 6 [a]Seven
days you shall eat unleavened bread, and on the
seventh day *there shall be* a feast to the LORD.
7 Unleavened bread shall be eaten seven days.
And [a]no leavened bread shall be seen among
you, nor shall leaven be seen among you in all
your quarters. 8 And you shall [a]tell your son in
that day, saying, '*This is done* because of what the
LORD did for me when I came up from Egypt.'
9 It shall be as [a]a sign to you on your hand and as
a memorial between your eyes, that the LORD's
law may be in your mouth; for with a strong
hand the LORD has brought you out of Egypt.
10 [a]You shall therefore keep this ordinance in its
season from year to year.

### THE LAW OF THE FIRSTBORN

11 "And it shall be, when the LORD [a]brings
you into the land of the [b]Canaanites, as He
swore to you and your fathers, and gives it to
you, 12 [a]that you shall set apart to the LORD all
that open the womb, that is, every firstborn
that comes from an animal which you have; the
males *shall be* the LORD's. 13 But [a]every firstborn
of a donkey you shall redeem with a lamb; and
if you will not redeem *it*, then you shall break
its neck. And all the firstborn of man among
your sons [b]you shall redeem. 14 [a]So it shall be,
when your son asks you in time to come, say-
ing, 'What *is* this?' that you shall say to him,
[b]'By strength of hand the LORD brought us out
of Egypt, out of the house of bondage. 15 And
it came to pass, when Pharaoh was stubborn
about letting us go, that [a]the LORD killed all
the firstborn in the land of Egypt, both the
firstborn of man and the firstborn of beast.
Therefore I sacrifice to the LORD all males
that open the womb, but all the firstborn of
my sons I redeem.' 16 It shall be as [a]a sign on
your hand and as frontlets between your eyes,
for by strength of hand the LORD brought us
out of Egypt."

**13:5** [c] Ex. 6:8 [d] Ex. 12:25, 26 **13:6** [a] Ex. 12:15–20 **13:7** [a] Ex. 12:19 **13:8** [a] Ex. 10:2; 12:26; 13:14 **13:9** [a] Deut. 6:8; 11:18 **13:10** [a] Ex. 12:14, 24 **13:11** [a] Ex. 13:5 [b] Num. 21:3 **13:12** [a] Lev. 27:26 **13:13** [a] Ex. 34:20 [b] Num. 3:46, 47; 18:15, 16 **13:14** [a] Deut. 6:20 [b] Ex. 13:3, 9 **13:15** [a] Ex. 12:29 **13:16** [a] Ex. 13:9

### *THE WILDERNESS WAY*

*(Ex. 40:34–38; Num. 9:15–23; 1 Kin. 8:10, 11)*

17 Then it came to pass, when Pharaoh had let the people go, that God did not lead them *by* way of the land of the Philistines, although that *was* near; for God said, "Lest perhaps the people [a]change their minds when they see war, and [b]return to Egypt." 18 So God [a]led the people around *by* way of the wilderness of the Red Sea. And the children of Israel went up in orderly ranks out of the land of Egypt.

19 And Moses took the [a]bones of [b]Joseph with him, for he had placed the children of Israel under solemn oath, saying, [c]"God will surely visit you, and you shall carry up my bones from here with you."[1]

20 So [a]they took their journey from [b]Succoth and camped in Etham at the edge of the wilderness. 21 And [a]the LORD went before them by day in a pillar of cloud to lead the way, and by night in a pillar of fire to give them light, so as to go by day and night. 22 He did not take away the pillar of cloud by day or the pillar of fire by night *from* before the people.

### *THE RED SEA CROSSING*

**14** Now the LORD spoke to Moses, saying: 2 "Speak to the children of Israel, [a]that they turn and camp before [b]Pi Hahiroth, between [c]Migdol and the sea, opposite Baal Zephon; you shall camp before it by the sea. 3 For Pharaoh will say of the children of Israel, [a]'They *are* bewildered by the land; the wilderness has closed them in.' 4 Then [a]I will harden Pharaoh's heart, so that he will pursue them; and I [b]will gain honor over Pharaoh and over all his army, [c]that the Egyptians may know that I *am* the LORD." And they did so.

5 Now it was told the king of Egypt that the people had fled, and [a]the heart of Pharaoh and his servants was turned against the people; and they said, "Why have we done this, that we have let Israel go from serving us?" 6 So he made ready his chariot and took his people with him. 7 Also, he took [a]six hundred choice chariots, and all the chariots of Egypt with captains over every one of them. 8 And the LORD [a]hardened the heart of Pharaoh king of Egypt, and he pursued the children of Israel; and [b]the children of Israel went out with boldness. 9 So the [a]Egyptians pursued them, all the horses *and* chariots of Pharaoh, his horsemen and his army, and overtook them camping by the sea beside Pi Hahiroth, before Baal Zephon.

10 And when Pharaoh drew near, the children of Israel lifted their eyes, and behold, the Egyptians marched after them. So they were very afraid, and the children of Israel [a]cried out to the LORD. 11 [a]Then they said to Moses, "Because *there were* no graves in Egypt, have you taken us away to die in the wilderness? Why have you so dealt with us, to bring us up out of Egypt? 12 [a]*Is* this not the word that we told you in Egypt, saying, 'Let us alone that we may serve the Egyptians'? For *it would have been* better for us to serve the Egyptians than that we should die in the wilderness."

13 And Moses said to the people, [a]"Do not be afraid. [b]Stand still, and see the [c]salvation of the LORD, which He will accomplish for you today. For the Egyptians whom you see today, you shall [d]see again no more forever. 14 [a]The LORD will fight for you, and you shall [b]hold your peace."

> **14:13** The Hebrew word for ***salvation*** comes from a term that has to do with room or space. The people were under great pressure, squeezed between the waters before them and Pharaoh's armies behind them. Salvation relieved the pressure in a most dramatic way.

15 And the LORD said to Moses, "Why do you cry to Me? Tell the children of Israel to go forward. 16 But [a]lift up your rod, and stretch out your hand over the sea and divide it. And the children of Israel shall go on dry *ground* through the midst of the sea. 17 And I indeed will [a]harden the hearts of the Egyptians, and they shall follow them. So I will [b]gain honor over Pharaoh and over all his army, his chariots, and his horsemen. 18 Then the Egyptians shall know that I *am* the LORD, when I have gained honor for Myself over Pharaoh, his chariots, and his horsemen." 19 And the Angel of God, [a]who went before the camp of Israel, moved and went behind them; and the pillar of cloud went from before them and stood behind them. 20 So it came between the camp of the Egyptians and the camp of Israel. Thus it was a cloud and darkness *to the one,* and it gave light by night *to the other,* so that the one did not come near the other all that night.

21 Then Moses stretched out his hand over the sea; and the LORD caused the sea to go *back* by a strong east wind all that night, and [a]made the sea into dry *land,* and the waters were [b]divided. 22 So [a]the children of Israel went into the midst of the sea on the dry *ground,* and the waters *were* [b]a wall to them on their right hand and on their left. 23 And the Egyptians pursued and went after them into the midst of the sea, all Pharaoh's horses, his chariots, and his horsemen.

13:17 [a] Ex. 14:11 [b] Deut. 17:16 13:18 [a] Num. 33:6 13:19 [a] Gen. 50:24, 25 [b] Ex. 1:6; Deut. 33:13–17 [c] Ex. 4:31 [1] Genesis 50:25 13:20 [a] Num. 33:6–8 [b] Ex. 12:37 13:21 [a] Deut. 1:33 14:2 [a] Ex. 13:18 [b] Num. 33:7 [c] Jer. 44:1 14:3 [a] Ps. 71:11 14:4 [a] Ex. 4:21; 7:3; 14:17 [b] Ex. 9:16; 14:17, 18, 23 [c] Ex. 7:5; 14:25 14:5 [a] Ps. 105:25 14:7 [a] Ex. 15:4 14:8 [a] Ex. 14:4 [b] Num. 33:3 14:9 [a] Josh. 24:6 14:10 [a] Neh. 9:9 14:11 [a] Ps. 106:7, 8 14:12 [a] Ex. 5:21; 6:9 14:13 [a] 2 Chr. 20:15, 17 [b] Ps. 46:10, 11 [c] Ex. 14:30; 15:2 [d] Deut. 28:68 14:14 [a] Deut. 1:30; 3:22 [b] [Is. 30:15] 14:16 [a] Num. 20:8, 9, 11 14:17 [a] Ex. 14:8 [b] Ex. 14:4 14:19 [a] [Is. 63:9] 14:21 [a] Ps. 66:6; 106:9; 136:13, 14 [b] Is. 63:12, 13 14:22 [a] Ex. 15:19 [b] Ex. 14:29; 15:8

EXODUS 13:17—14:31

## GOD PARTS THE SEA

11

STORY OF SCRIPTURE

### WHAT'S GOING ON?

Newly freed and led by Moses, the Israelites embarked on their journey out of Egypt. As they approached the Red Sea, Pharaoh changed his mind about letting them go and sent his army after them. Trapped between the army and the sea, the Israelites feared for their lives. Moses, under God's instruction, stretched out his hand over the sea and the waters parted, allowing the Israelites to cross on dry land. When the Egyptian army followed, the sea returned to its normal level, drowning them. The Israelites witnessed this miracle and awed at God's power. God's guidance was displayed through the flame and smoke, and His redemption was displayed through the parting sea and conquering of Pharaoh.

### WHAT DOES THIS MEAN FOR ME?

In a cinematic moment of boldness, Moses declared, "Do not be afraid. Stand still, and see the salvation of the LORD, which He will accomplish for you today. For the Egyptians whom you see today, you shall see again no more forever. The LORD will fight for you, and you shall hold your peace" (Ex. 14:13–14). This declaration is also true of the sin, shame, and evil that pursue us. Just as the Egyptians drowned in pursuit of the Israelites, so was our sin buried in the grave with Jesus.

### DID YOU CATCH THE PATTERN?

This is another time in Moses's life when water played a significant role. The Red Sea represented several things. First, the waters closing on top of Pharaoh and his armies could be seen as judgment—something the Israelites were saved by walking through, with God's protection. Second, the parting of the Red Sea can be seen as a foreshadowing of baptism, a picture of believers passing from death to life, like how the Israelites passed from slavery to freedom.

*For the next* Story of Scripture *reading and devotion, turn to Exodus 16:1—17:7 on page 78.*

24 Now it came to pass, in the morning [a]watch, that [b]the LORD looked down upon the army of the Egyptians through the pillar of fire and cloud, and He troubled the army of the Egyptians. 25 And He took off[1] their chariot wheels, so that they drove them with difficulty; and the Egyptians said, "Let us flee from the face of Israel, for the LORD [a]fights for them against the Egyptians."

26 Then the LORD said to Moses, "Stretch out your hand over the sea, that the waters may come back upon the Egyptians, on their chariots, and on their horsemen." 27 And Moses stretched out his hand over the sea; and when the morning appeared, the sea [a]returned to its full depth, while the Egyptians were fleeing into it. So the LORD [b]overthrew the Egyptians in the midst of the sea. 28 Then [a]the waters returned and covered the chariots, the horsemen, *and* all the army of Pharaoh that came into the sea after them. Not so much as one of them remained. 29 But [a]the children of Israel had walked on dry *land* in the midst of the sea, and the waters *were* a wall to them on their right hand and on their left.

30 So the LORD [a]saved Israel that day out of the hand of the Egyptians, and Israel [b]saw the Egyptians dead on the seashore. 31 Thus Israel saw the great work which the LORD had done in Egypt; so the people feared the LORD, and [a]believed the LORD and His servant Moses.

### *THE SONG OF MOSES*

*(Ex. 14:13, 14; Ps. 78:12–14)*

15 Then [a]Moses and the children of Israel sang this song to the LORD, and spoke, saying:

"I will [b]sing to the LORD,
For He has triumphed gloriously!
The horse and its rider
He has thrown into the sea!

2 The LORD *is* my strength and [a]song,
And He has become my salvation;
He *is* my God, and [b]I will praise Him;
My [c]father's God, and I [d]will exalt Him.

3 The LORD *is* a man of [a]war;
The LORD *is* His [b]name.

14:24 [a] Judg. 7:19 [b] Ex. 13:21 14:25 [a] Ex. 7:5; 14:4, 14, 18 [1] Samaritan Pentateuch, Septuagint, and Syriac read *bound.* 14:27 [a] Josh. 4:18 [b] Ex. 15:1, 7 14:28 [a] Ps. 78:53; 106:11 14:29 [a] Ps. 66:6; 78:52, 53 14:30 [a] Ps. 106:8, 10 [b] Ps. 58:10; 59:10 14:31 [a] John 2:11; 11:45 15:1 [a] Ps. 106:12 [b] Is. 12:1–6 15:2 [a] Is. 12:2 [b] Gen. 28:21, 22 [c] Ex. 3:6, 15, 16 [d] Is. 25:1 15:3 [a] Rev. 19:11 [b] Ps. 24:8; 83:18

APPLY THE TRUTH

## WAR

**15:3** People always seem to be at war. Many are conflicts over land or religions; others are ways power-hungry rulers expand their kingdoms. Some are small; others involve regions or even the whole world. It's not surprising, then, that the Bible is filled with conflict and war. We'd expect to see this conduct from ungodly nations, but it doesn't take long to see it from God's people too. In this verse, it's shocking that Moses called God "a man of war." How? Why?

Here, Moses celebrated the Israelites' victory over the Egyptians, ensuring their release from captivity. In saying God is "a man of war," Moses poetically thanked God for bringing their oppressors to justice. God is opposed to violence, but He is *for* justice. He is merciful, but He doesn't sweep evil under the rug. He does not allow it to go unpunished. The Israelites were at the center of God's plan for redeeming the world. Without Israel, we wouldn't have Jesus. Thus, to save the world, God saved Israel. And to save Israel, He warred against the Egyptians. Ultimately, God is a God of peace. This act of war was a channel for bringing ultimate peace through the gospel of Jesus Christ.

4 [a]Pharaoh's chariots and his army He has cast into the sea;
[b]His chosen captains also are drowned in the Red Sea.
5 The depths have covered them;
[a]They sank to the bottom like a stone.

6 "Your [a]right hand, O LORD, has become glorious in power;
Your right hand, O LORD, has dashed the enemy in pieces.
7 And in the greatness of Your [a]excellence
You have overthrown those who rose against You;
You sent forth [b]Your wrath;
It [c]consumed them [d]like stubble.
8 And [a]with the blast of Your nostrils
The waters were gathered together;
[b]The floods stood upright like a heap;
The depths congealed in the heart of the sea.
9 [a]The enemy said, 'I will pursue,
I will overtake,
I will [b]divide the spoil;
My desire shall be satisfied on them.
I will draw my sword,
My hand shall destroy them.'
10 You blew with Your wind,
The sea covered them;
They sank like lead in the mighty waters.

11 "Who[a] *is* like You, O LORD, among the gods?
Who *is* like You, [b]glorious in holiness,
Fearful in [c]praises, [d]doing wonders?
12 You stretched out Your right hand;
The earth swallowed them.
13 You in Your mercy have [a]led forth
The people whom You have redeemed;
You have guided *them* in Your strength
To [b]Your holy habitation.

14 "The [a]people will hear *and* be afraid;
[b]Sorrow will take hold of the inhabitants of Philistia.
15 [a]Then [b]the chiefs of Edom will be dismayed;
[c]The mighty men of Moab,
Trembling will take hold of them;
[d]All the inhabitants of Canaan will [e]melt away.
16 [a]Fear and dread will fall on them;
By the greatness of Your arm
They will be [b]*as* still as a stone,
Till Your people pass over, O LORD,
Till the people pass over
[c]Whom You have purchased.
17 You will bring them in and [a]plant them
In the [b]mountain of Your inheritance,
*In* the place, O LORD, *which* You have made
For Your own dwelling,
The [c]sanctuary, O Lord, *which* Your hands have established.

18 "The[a] LORD shall reign forever and ever."

19 For the [a]horses of Pharaoh went with his
chariots and his horsemen into the sea, and
[b]the LORD brought back the waters of the sea
upon them. But the children of Israel went on
dry *land* in the midst of the sea.

### *THE SONG OF MIRIAM*

*(Num. 26:59)*

20 Then Miriam [a]the prophetess, [b]the sister
of Aaron, [c]took the timbrel in her hand; and all

**15:4** [a] Ex. 14:28 [b] Ex. 14:7 **15:5** [a] Neh. 9:11 **15:6** [a] Ps. 17:7; 118:15 **15:7** [a] Deut. 33:26 [b] Ps. 78:49, 50 [c] Ps. 59:13 [d] Is. 5:24 **15:8** [a] Ex. 14:21, 22, 29 [b] Ps. 78:13 **15:9** [a] Judg. 5:30 [b] Is. 53:12 **15:11** [a] 1 Kin. 8:23 [b] Is. 6:3 [c] 1 Chr. 16:25 [d] Ps. 77:11, 14 **15:13** [a] [Ps. 77:20] [b] Ps. 78:54 **15:14** [a] Josh. 2:9 [b] Ps. 48:6 **15:15** [a] Gen. 36:15, 40 [b] Deut. 2:4 [c] Num. 22:3, 4 [d] Josh. 5:1 [e] Josh. 2:9–11, 24 **15:16** [a] Josh. 2:9 [b] 1 Sam. 25:37 [c] Jer. 31:11 **15:17** [a] Ps. 44:2; 80:8, 15 [b] Ps. 2:6; 78:54, 68 [c] Ps. 68:16; 76:2; 132:13, 14 **15:18** [a] Is. 57:15 **15:19** [a] Ex. 14:23 [b] Ex. 14:28 **15:20** [a] Judg. 4:4 [b] Num. 26:59 [c] 1 Sam. 18:6

the women went out after her [d]with timbrels
and with dances. 21 And Miriam [a]answered them:

[b]"Sing to the LORD,
For He has triumphed gloriously!
The horse and its rider
He has thrown into the sea!"

> **15:20** Although there is no record of women serving as priests in ancient Israel, women did serve as prophets, such as Miriam here, Deborah (Judg. 4:4), Huldah (2 Kin. 22:14), and Isaiah's wife (Is. 8:3).

### *BITTER WATERS MADE SWEET*

22 So Moses brought Israel from the Red Sea;
then they went out into the Wilderness of [a]Shur.
And they went three days in the wilderness
and found no [b]water. 23 Now when they came
to [a]Marah, they could not drink the waters of
Marah, for they *were* bitter. Therefore the name
of it was called Marah.[1] 24 And the people [a]com-
plained against Moses, saying, "What shall we
drink?" 25 So he cried out to the LORD, and the
LORD showed him a tree. [a]When he cast *it* into
the waters, the waters were made sweet.
There He [b]made a statute and an ordinance
for them, and there [c]He tested them, 26 and said,
[a]"If you diligently heed the voice of the LORD
your God and do what is right in His sight, give
ear to His commandments and keep all His
statutes, I will put none of the [b]diseases on you
which I have brought on the Egyptians. For I *am*
the LORD [c]who heals you."
27 [a]Then they came to Elim, where there *were*
twelve wells of water and seventy palm trees; so
they camped there by the waters.

### *BREAD FROM HEAVEN*

16 And they [a]journeyed from Elim, and all
the congregation of the children of Is-
rael came to the Wilderness of Sin, which is
between Elim and [b]Sinai, on the fifteenth day

> **16:1** The location of the **Wilderness of Sin** is uncertain; its position **between Elim and Sinai** depends on the location of Mount Sinai. The name ***Sin*** has nothing to do with the English word "sin."

of the second month after they departed from
the land of Egypt. 2 Then the whole congregation
of the children of Israel [a]complained against
Moses and Aaron in the wilderness. 3 And the
children of Israel said to them, [a]"Oh, that we
had died by the hand of the LORD in the land
of Egypt, [b]when we sat by the pots of meat *and*
when we ate bread to the full! For you have
brought us out into this wilderness to kill this
whole assembly with hunger."
4 Then the LORD said to Moses, "Behold, I will
rain [a]bread from heaven for you. And the people
shall go out and gather a certain quota every day,
that I may [b]test them, whether they will [c]walk in
My law or not. 5 And it shall be on the sixth day
that they shall prepare what they bring in, and
[a]it shall be twice as much as they gather daily."
6 Then Moses and Aaron said to all the chil-
dren of Israel, [a]"At evening you shall know that
the LORD has brought you out of the land of
Egypt. 7 And in the morning you shall see [a]the
glory of the LORD; for He [b]hears your complaints
against the LORD. But [c]what *are* we, that you
complain against us?" 8 Also Moses said, "*This*
*shall be seen* when the LORD gives you meat to
eat in the evening, and in the morning bread
to the full; for the LORD hears your complaints
which you make against Him. And what *are* we?
Your complaints *are* not against us but [a]against
the LORD."
9 Then Moses spoke to Aaron, "Say to all the
congregation of the children of Israel, [a]'Come
near before the LORD, for He has heard your
complaints.' " 10 Now it came to pass, as Aaron
spoke to the whole congregation of the children
of Israel, that they looked toward the wilderness,
and behold, the glory of the LORD [a]appeared in
the cloud.
11 And the LORD spoke to Moses, saying, 12 [a]"I
have heard the complaints of the children of
Israel. Speak to them, saying, [b]'At twilight you
shall eat meat, and [c]in the morning you shall
be filled with bread. And you shall know that I
*am* the LORD your God.' "
13 So it was that [a]quail came up at evening
and covered the camp, and in the morning [b]the
dew lay all around the camp. 14 And when the
layer of dew lifted, there, on the surface of the
wilderness, was [a]a small round [b]substance, *as*
fine as frost on the ground. 15 So when the chil-
dren of Israel saw *it*, they said to one another,
"What is it?" For they did not know what it *was*.
And Moses said to them, [a]"This *is* the bread
which the LORD has given you to eat. 16 This is
the thing which the LORD has commanded: 'Let
every man gather it [a]according to each one's

**15:20** [d] Judg. 11:34; 21:21 **15:21** [a] 1 Sam. 18:7 [b] Ex. 15:1 **15:22** [a] Gen. 16:7; 20:1; 25:18 [b] Num. 20:2 **15:23** [a] Num. 33:8 [1] Literally *Bitter* **15:24** [a] Ex. 14:11; 16:2 **15:25** [a] 2 Kin. 2:21 [b] Josh. 24:25 [c] Deut. 8:2, 16 **15:26** [a] Deut. 7:12, 15 [b] Deut. 28:27, 58, 60 [c] Ex. 23:25 **15:27** [a] Num. 33:9 **16:1** [a] Num. 33:10, 11 [b] Ex. 12:6, 51; 19:1 **16:2** [a] 1 Cor. 10:10 **16:3** [a] Lam. 4:9 [b] Num. 11:4, 5 **16:4** [a] [John 6:31–35] **16:4** [b] Ex. 15:25; Deut. 8:2, 16 [c] Judg. 2:22 **16:5** [a] Ex. 16:22, 29; Lev. 25:21 **16:6** [a] Ex. 6:7 **16:7** [a] Ex. 16:10, 12; Is. 35:2; 40:5; John 11:4, 40 [b] Num. 14:27; 17:5 [c] Num. 16:11 **16:8** [a] 1 Sam. 8:7; Luke 10:16; [Rom. 13:2]; 1 Thess. 4:8 **16:9** [a] Num. 16:16 **16:10** [a] Ex. 13:21; 16:7; Num. 16:19; 1 Kin. 8:10 **16:12** [a] Ex. 16:8; Num. 14:27 [b] Ex. 16:6 [c] Ex. 16:7; 1 Kin. 20:28; Joel 3:17 **16:13** [a] Num. 11:31; Ps. 78:27–29; 105:40 [b] Num. 11:9 **16:14** [a] Ex. 16:31; Num. 11:7, 8; Deut. 8:3; Neh. 9:15; Ps. 78:24; 105:40 [b] Ps. 147:16 **16:15** [a] Ex. 16:4; Neh. 9:15; Ps. 78:24; [John 6:31, 49, 58]; 1 Cor. 10:3 **16:16** [a] Ex. 12:4

EXODUS 16:1—17:7

# SKY BREAD AND STONE WATER

12

STORY OF SCRIPTURE

## WHAT'S GOING ON?

Having passed through the waters of the Red Sea, the Israelites were free of the Egyptians, but their journey was far from over. As they traveled through the wilderness, their hunger and thirst caused them to grumble and even question the wisdom of leaving Egypt. Food and water in bondage were preferred over hunger and thirst in freedom. God responded to their complaints by providing manna and quail to eat. Then, He instructed Moses to strike a rock with his staff and water miraculously flowed. And with that, their choice was simplified to bondage without God or freedom with God.

## WHAT DOES THIS MEAN FOR ME?

These events demonstrate God's provision and care for His people. God led the Israelites out of Egypt. After delivering them from Pharaoh, there was no way He was going to let them perish in the wilderness. This ought to be an encouragement to us. Philippians 1:6 says, "Being confident of this very thing, that He who has begun a good work in you will complete it until the day of Jesus Christ." God doesn't start what He doesn't finish. When God leads you somewhere, He won't leave you high and dry. He'll be faithful to complete the work He began in You.

## DID YOU CATCH THE PATTERN?

We see two important images and patterns in this passage. First is the manna from heaven. This miraculous sustenance, which was loosely compared to bread, foreshadows Jesus, who called Himself the "Bread of Life" in John 6:35. Just as manna sustained the Israelites physically, Jesus sustains us spiritually. Second is the water that came from the rock, which serves as a type of Jesus, the "Living Water" who satisfies spiritual thirst (John 4:14). The rock had to be stricken to give water, just as Jesus had to be stricken for us to experience life.

*For the next* Story of Scripture *reading and devotion, turn to Exodus 19:16—20:21 on page 81.*

need, one [b]omer for each person, *according to*
*the* number of persons; let every man take for
*those* who *are* in his tent.' "
17 Then the children of Israel did so and gath-
ered, some more, some less. 18 So when they
measured *it* by omers, [a]he who gathered much
had nothing left over, and he who gathered little
had no lack. Every man had gathered according
to each one's need. 19 And Moses said, "Let no
one [a]leave any of it till morning." 20 Notwith-
standing they did not heed Moses. But some of
them left part of it until morning, and it bred
worms and stank. And Moses was angry with
them. 21 So they gathered it every morning, every
man according to his need. And when the sun
became hot, it melted.
22 And so it was, on the sixth day, *that* they
gathered twice as much bread, two omers for
each one. And all the rulers of the congregation
came and told Moses. 23 Then he said to them,
"This *is what* the LORD has said: 'Tomorrow *is* [a]a
Sabbath rest, a holy Sabbath to the LORD. Bake
what you will bake *today,* and boil what you will
boil; and lay up for yourselves all that remains,
to be kept until morning.' " 24 So they laid it up till
morning, as Moses commanded; and it did not
[a]stink, nor were there any worms in it. 25 Then
Moses said, "Eat that today, for today *is* a Sabbath
to the LORD; today you will not find it in the
field. 26 [a]Six days you shall gather it, but on the
seventh day, the Sabbath, there will be none."
27 Now it happened *that some* of the people
went out on the seventh day to gather, but they
found none. 28 And the LORD said to Moses, "How
long [a]do you refuse to keep My commandments
and My laws? 29 See! For the LORD has given you
the Sabbath; therefore He gives you on the sixth
day bread for two days. Let every man remain
in his place; let no man go out of his place on
the seventh day." 30 So the people rested on the
seventh day.
31 And the house of Israel called its name
Manna.[1] And [a]it *was* like white coriander seed, and
the taste of it *was* like wafers *made* with honey.
32 Then Moses said, "This *is* the thing which
the LORD has commanded: 'Fill an omer with it,

**16:16** [b] Ex. 16:32, 36 **16:18** [a] 2 Cor. 8:15 **16:19** [a] Ex. 12:10; 16:23; 23:18 **16:23** [a] Gen. 2:3; Ex. 20:8–11; 23:12; 31:15; 35:2; Lev. 23:3; Neh. 9:13, 14 **16:24** [a] Ex. 16:20 **16:26** [a] Ex. 20:9, 10 **16:28** [a] 2 Kin. 17:14; Ps. 78:10; 106:13 **16:31** [a] Num. 11:7–9; Deut. 8:3, 16

[1] Literally *What?* (compare Exodus 16:15)

to be kept for your generations, that they may see
the bread with which I fed you in the wilderness,
when I brought you out of the land of Egypt.' "
33 And Moses said to Aaron, [a]"Take a pot and
put an omer of manna in it, and lay it up before
the LORD, to be kept for your generations." 34 As
the LORD commanded Moses, so Aaron laid it
up [a]before the Testimony, to be kept. 35 And the
children of Israel [a]ate manna [b]forty years, [c]until
they came to an inhabited land; they ate manna
until they came to the border of the land of Canaan.
36 Now an omer *is* one-tenth of an ephah.

### WATER FROM THE ROCK
*(Num. 20:1–13)*

**17** Then [a]all the congregation of the children
of Israel set out on their journey from the
Wilderness of [b]Sin, according to the commandment
of the LORD, and camped in Rephidim;
but *there was* no water for the people to [c]drink.
2 [a]Therefore the people contended with Moses,
and said, "Give us water, that we may drink."

So Moses said to them, "Why do you contend
with me? Why do you [b]tempt the LORD?"

3 And the people thirsted there for water,
and the people [a]complained against Moses,
and said, "Why *is* it you have brought us up out
of Egypt, to kill us and our children and our
[b]livestock with thirst?"

4 So Moses [a]cried out to the LORD, saying,
"What shall I do with this people? They are almost
ready to [b]stone me!"

5 And the LORD said to Moses, [a]"Go on before
the people, and take with you some of the elders
of Israel. Also take in your hand your rod with
which [b]you struck the river, and go. 6 [a]Behold, I
will stand before you there on the rock in Horeb;
and you shall strike the rock, and water will come
out of it, that the people may drink."

> **SEEING JESUS IN THE SCRIPTURE**
>
> **17:5–6** God had Moses strike a rock to bring forth water, thus preserving the lives of His people. This points to Jesus, the Son of God who was struck down on the cross so we can find life in Him (see 1 Cor. 10:4).

And Moses did so in the sight of the elders
of Israel. 7 So he called the name of the place
[a]Massah[1] and Meribah,[2] because of the contention
of the children of Israel, and because they
tempted the LORD, saying, "Is the LORD among
us or not?"

### VICTORY OVER THE AMALEKITES
*(Gen. 14:7; Num. 13:29; 14:25)*

8 [a]Now Amalek came and fought with Israel
in Rephidim. 9 And Moses said to Joshua,
"Choose us some men and go out, fight with
Amalek. Tomorrow I will stand on the top of
the hill with [a]the rod of God in my hand." 10 So
Joshua did as Moses said to him, and fought with
Amalek. And Moses, Aaron, and Hur went up to
the top of the hill. 11 And so it was, when Moses
[a]held up his hand, that Israel prevailed; and
when he let down his hand, Amalek prevailed.
12 But Moses' hands *became* heavy; so they took
a stone and put *it* under him, and he sat on it.
And Aaron and Hur supported his hands, one
on one side, and the other on the other side; and
his hands were steady until the going down of
the sun. 13 So Joshua defeated Amalek and his
people with the edge of the sword.

14 Then the LORD said to Moses, [a]"Write this
*for* a memorial in the book and recount *it* in the
hearing of Joshua, that [b]I will utterly blot out the
remembrance of Amalek from under heaven."
15 And Moses built an altar and called its name,
The-LORD-Is-My-Banner;[1] 16 for he said, "Because
the LORD has [a]sworn: the LORD *will have* war
with Amalek from generation to generation."

### JETHRO'S ADVICE
*(Deut. 1:9–18)*

**18** And [a]Jethro, the priest of Midian, Moses'
father-in-law, heard of all that [b]God had
done for Moses and for Israel His people—that
the LORD had brought Israel out of Egypt. 2 Then
Jethro, Moses' father-in-law, took [a]Zipporah,
Moses' wife, after he had sent her back, 3 with
her [a]two sons, of whom the name of one *was*
Gershom (for he said, [b]"I have been a stranger
in a foreign land")[1] 4 and the name of the other
*was* Eliezer[1] (for *he said,* "The God of my father
*was* my [a]help, and delivered me from the sword
of Pharaoh"); 5 and Jethro, Moses' father-in-law,
came with his sons and his wife to Moses in the
wilderness, where he was encamped at [a]the
mountain of God. 6 Now he had said to Moses,
"I, your father-in-law Jethro, am coming to you
with your wife and her two sons with her."

7 So Moses [a]went out to meet his father-in-law,
bowed down, and [b]kissed him. And they
asked each other about *their* well-being, and they
went into the tent. 8 And Moses told his father-in-law
all that the LORD had done to Pharaoh
and to the Egyptians for Israel's sake, all the
hardship that had come upon them on the way,
and *how* the LORD had [a]delivered them. 9 Then
Jethro rejoiced for all the [a]good which the LORD

**16:33** [a] Heb. 9:4; Rev. 2:17 **16:34** [a] Num. 17:10 **16:35** [a] Deut. 8:3, 16 [b] Num. 33:38 [c] Josh. 5:12
**17:1** [a] Ex. 16:1 [b] Num. 33:11–15 [c] Ex. 15:22 **17:2** [a] Num. 20:2, 3, 13 [b] [Deut. 6:16] **17:3** [a] Ex. 16:2, 3 [b] Ex. 12:38 **17:4** [a] Ex. 14:15 [b] John 8:59; 10:31 **17:5** [a] Ezek. 2:6 [b] Num. 20:8 **17:6** [a] Num. 20:10, 11 **17:7** [a] Num. 20:13, 24; 27:14 [1] Literally *Tempted* [2] Literally *Contention* **17:8** [a] Gen. 36:12 **17:9** [a] Ex. 4:20 **17:11** [a] [James 5:16] **17:14** [a] Ex. 24:4; 34:27 [b] 1 Sam. 15:3
**17:15** [1] Hebrew *YHWH Nissi* **17:16** [a] Gen. 22:14–16 **18:1** [a] Ex. 2:16, 18; 3:1 [b] [Ps. 106:2, 8] **18:2** [a] Ex. 2:21; 4:20–26 **18:3** [a] Acts 7:29 [b] Ex. 2:22 [1] Compare Exodus 2:22 **18:4** [a] Gen. 49:25 [1] Literally *My God Is Help* **18:5** [a] Ex. 3:1, 12; 4:27; 24:13 **18:7** [a] Gen. 18:2 [b] Ex. 4:27 **18:8** [a] Ex. 15:6, 16 **18:9** [a] [Is. 63:7–14]

had done for Israel, whom He had delivered out
of the hand of the Egyptians. 10 And Jethro said,
[a]"Blessed *be* the LORD, who has delivered you
out of the hand of the Egyptians and out of the
hand of Pharaoh, *and* who has delivered the
people from under the hand of the Egyptians.
11 Now I know that the LORD *is* [a]greater than all
the gods; [b]for in the very thing in which they
behaved [c]proudly, *He was* above them." 12 Then
Jethro, Moses' father-in-law, took[1] a burnt [a]of-
fering and *other* sacrifices *to offer* to God. And
Aaron came with all the elders of Israel [b]to eat
bread with Moses' father-in-law before God.

13 And so it was, on the next day, that Moses
[a]sat to judge the people; and the people stood
before Moses from morning until evening. 14 So
when Moses' father-in-law saw all that he did
for the people, he said, "What *is* this thing that
you are doing for the people? Why do you alone
sit, and all the people stand before you from
morning until evening?"

15 And Moses said to his father-in-law, "Be-
cause [a]the people come to me to inquire of God.
16 When they have [a]a difficulty, they come to me,
and I judge between one and another; and I
make known the statutes of God and His laws."

17 So Moses' father-in-law said to him, "The
thing that you do *is* not good. 18 Both you and
these people who *are* with you will surely wear
yourselves out. For this thing *is* too much for
you; [a]you are not able to perform it by yourself.
19 Listen now to my voice; I will give you counsel,
and God will be with you: Stand [a]before God for
the people, so that you may [b]bring the difficul-
ties to God. 20 And you shall [a]teach them the
statutes and the laws, and show them the way
in which they must walk and [b]the work they
must do. 21 Moreover you shall select from all
the people [a]able men, such as [b]fear God, [c]men
of truth, [d]hating covetousness; and place *such*
over them *to be* rulers of thousands, rulers of
hundreds, rulers of fifties, and rulers of tens.
22 And let them judge the people at all times.
[a]Then it will be *that* every great matter they
shall bring to you, but every small matter they
themselves shall judge. So it will be easier for
you, for [b]they will bear *the burden* with you.
23 If you do this thing, and God *so* commands
you, then you will be able to endure, and all
this people will also go to their [a]place in peace."

24 So Moses heeded the voice of his father-
in-law and did all that he had said. 25 And [a]Moses
chose able men out of all Israel, and made them
heads over the people: rulers of thousands,
rulers of hundreds, rulers of fifties, and rulers
of tens. 26 So they judged the people at all times;
the [a]hard cases they brought to Moses, but they
judged every small case themselves.

27 Then Moses let his father-in-law depart,
and [a]he went his way to his own land.

### *ISRAEL AT MOUNT SINAI*

19 In the third month after the children of
Israel had gone out of the land of Egypt,
on the same day, [a]they came *to* the Wilderness
of Sinai. 2 For they had departed from [a]Rephi-
dim, had come *to* the Wilderness of Sinai, and
camped in the wilderness. So Israel camped
there before [b]the mountain.

3 And [a]Moses went up to God, and the LORD
[b]called to him from the mountain, saying, "Thus
you shall say to the house of Jacob, and tell
the children of Israel: 4 [a]'You have seen what
I did to the Egyptians, and *how* [b]I bore you on
eagles' wings and brought you to Myself. 5 Now
[a]therefore, if you will indeed obey My voice and
[b]keep My covenant, then [c]you shall be a special
treasure to Me above all people; for all the earth
*is* [d]Mine. 6 And you shall be to Me a [a]kingdom of
priests and a [b]holy nation.' These *are* the words
which you shall speak to the children of Israel."

7 So Moses came and called for the [a]elders of
the people, and laid before them all these words
which the LORD commanded him. 8 Then [a]all the
people answered together and said, "All that the
LORD has spoken we will do." So Moses brought
back the words of the people to the LORD. 9 And
the LORD said to Moses, "Behold, I come to you
[a]in the thick cloud, [b]that the people may hear
when I speak with you, and believe you forever."

So Moses told the words of the people to
the LORD.

10 Then the LORD said to Moses, "Go to the
people and [a]consecrate them today and tomor-
row, and let them wash their clothes. 11 And let
them be ready for the third day. For on the third
day the LORD will come down upon Mount Sinai
in the sight of all the people. 12 You shall set
bounds for the people all around, saying, 'Take
heed to yourselves *that* you do *not* go up to the
mountain or touch its base. [a]Whoever touches
the mountain shall surely be put to death. 13 Not
a hand shall touch him, but he shall surely be
stoned or shot *with an arrow;* whether man or
beast, he shall not live.' When the trumpet sounds
long, they shall come near the mountain."

14 So Moses went down from the mountain
to the people and sanctified the people, and
they washed their clothes. 15 And he said to the
people, "Be ready for the third day; [a]do not come
near *your* wives."

16 Then it came to pass on the third day, in the

18:10 [a] Gen. 14:20 18:11 [a] 2 Chr. 2:5 [b] Ex. 1:10, 16, 22; 5:2, 7 [c] Luke 1:51 18:12 [a] Ex. 24:5 [b] Deut. 12:7 [1] Following Masoretic Text and Septuagint; Syriac, Targum, and Vulgate read *offered.* 18:13 [a] Matt. 23:2 18:15 [a] Lev. 24:12 18:16 [a] Ex. 24:14 18:18 [a] Num. 11:14, 17 18:19 [a] Ex. 4:16; 20:19 [b] Num. 9:8; 27:5 18:20 [a] Deut. 5:1 [b] Deut. 1:18 18:21 [a] Acts 6:3 [b] 2 Sam. 23:3 [c] Ezek. 18:8 [d] Deut. 16:19 18:22 [a] Deut. 1:17 [b] Num. 11:17 18:23 [a] Ex. 16:29 18:25 [a] Deut. 1:15 18:26 [a] Job 29:16 18:27 [a] Num. 10:29, 30 19:1 [a] Num. 33:15 19:2 [a] Ex. 17:1 [b] Ex. 3:1, 12; 18:5 19:3 [a] Acts 7:38 [b] Ex. 3:4 19:4 [a] Deut. 29:2 [b] Is. 63:9 19:5 [a] Ex. 15:26; 23:22 [b] Deut. 5:2 [c] Ps. 135:4 [d] Ex. 9:29 19:6 [a] [1 Pet. 2:5, 9] [b] Deut. 7:6; 14:21; 26:19 19:7 [a] Ex. 4:29, 30 19:8 [a] Deut. 5:27; 26:17 19:9 [a] Ex. 19:16; 20:21; 24:15 [b] Deut. 4:12, 36 19:10 [a] Lev. 11:44, 45 19:12 [a] Heb. 12:20 19:15 [a] [1 Cor. 7:5]

morning, that there were [a]thunderings and light-
nings, and a thick cloud on the mountain; and
the sound of the trumpet was very loud, so that
all the people who *were* in the camp [b]trembled.
17 And [a]Moses brought the people out of the camp
to meet with God, and they stood at the foot of the
mountain. 18 Now [a]Mount Sinai *was* completely in
smoke, because the LORD descended upon [b]it in
fire. [c]Its smoke ascended like the smoke of a fur-
nace, and the [d]whole mountain[1] quaked greatly.
19 And when the blast of the trumpet sounded long
and became louder and louder, [a]Moses spoke, and
[b]God answered him by voice. 20 Then the LORD
came down upon Mount Sinai, on the top of the
mountain. And the LORD called Moses to the top
of the mountain, and Moses went up.
21 And the LORD said to Moses, "Go down
and warn the people, lest they break through
[a]to gaze at the LORD, and many of them perish.
22 Also let the [a]priests who come near the LORD
[b]consecrate themselves, lest the LORD [c]break
out against them."
23 But Moses said to the LORD, "The people
cannot come up to Mount Sinai; for You warned
us, saying, [a]'Set bounds around the mountain
and consecrate it.' "
24 Then the LORD said to him, "Away! Get
down and then come up, you and Aaron with
you. But do not let the priests and the people
break through to come up to the LORD, lest He
break out against them." 25 So Moses went down
to the people and spoke to them.

### *THE TEN COMMANDMENTS*

*(Deut. 5:1–22)*

20 And God spoke [a]all these words, saying:
2 [a]"I *am* the LORD your God, who brought you
out of the land of Egypt, [b]out of the house
of bondage.
3 [a]"You shall have no other gods before Me.
4 [a]"You shall not make for yourself a carved
image—any likeness *of anything* that *is*
in heaven above, or that *is* in the earth

19:16 [a] Heb. 12:18, 19 [b] Heb. 12:21 19:17 [a] Deut. 4:10 19:18 [a] Deut. 4:11 [b] Ex. 3:2; 24:17 [c] Gen. 15:17; 19:28 [d] Ps. 68:8 [1] Septuagint reads *all the people.* 19:19 [a] Heb. 12:21 [b] Ps. 81:7 19:21 [a] 1 Sam. 6:19 19:22 [a] Ex. 19:24; 24:5 [b] Lev. 10:3; 21:6–8 [c] 2 Sam. 6:7, 8 19:23 [a] Ex. 19:12 20:1 [a] Deut. 5:22 20:2 [a] Hos. 13:4 [b] Ex. 13:3 20:3 [a] Jer. 25:6; 35:15 20:4 [a] Deut. 4:15–19; 27:15

STORY OF SCRIPTURE

EXODUS 19:16—20:21

## PROMISES AND COVENANTS

13

### WHAT'S GOING ON?

Midway through their journey, the Israelites arrived at Mount Sinai, where God summoned Moses to receive a new covenant. God began this covenant by reminding Israel He had saved them and a wealth of promises was available if they sought and obeyed Him. God reminded them they were chosen for a special purpose—to be a nation of priests and ambassadors of His character to the world. The Ten Commandments are more than laws or moral guidelines; they outline the essence of what it means to display the character of God to the world and to one another. They guided the Israelites, and they guide us, in how to live.

### WHAT DOES THIS MEAN FOR ME?

Before giving the Israelites any commands, God emphasized they were redeemed, loved, and called to a higher purpose. This tells us God prefers to tell us who we are before He tells us what to do. God saved the Israelites; therefore, they were to worship only Him. They were chosen for a higher purpose; therefore, they weren't to do anything to compromise their character. The same is true of you. *Who you are* is to drive *what you do*. You obey because you are loved; you aren't loved because you obey. You worship God because you've been accepted; you aren't accepted because you worship.

### DID YOU CATCH THE PATTERN?

God connects with His chosen people through covenants. This specific covenant is known as the Mosaic Covenant. We've seen three so far: the one God made with Adam and Eve in Eden (Gen. 1:28–31; 2:16–17), the one He made with Noah after the Flood (Gen. 9:8–17), and the covenant between God and Abraham (Gen. 12:1–3; 17:1–14; 22:16–28). All these covenants lead to the ultimate covenant God made with us through Jesus.

*For the next* Story of Scripture *reading and devotion, turn to Exodus 35:30–35 on page 100.*

APPLY THE TRUTH

## CRIME

**20:2–17** During the exodus, God shaped Israel in two major ways. First, He established them as a nation. Second, He preserved them and providing for them to make good on His promise to bring the Messiah through them. The Ten Commandments advanced both these essential works, not only providing core laws for a nation, but also showing the vital connection between the heart and hands.

The first commandments are about putting God first, glorifying His name, and remembering who He is and what He does. They teach our need to have a right heart—God's heart. If we have this heart, we will please God in how we live. From there, the commandments focus on what we do with our hands—how we act toward one another. Don't murder, commit adultery, steal, lie, or covet. If we get the first commands right, we'll get these right too.

So, what does this have to do with crime? Every crime is ultimately an act of the heart, not the hands. People commit horrendous crimes because they reflect the broken condition of the heart. The justice system matters, but the gospel is the true answer for crime. Jesus came into the world not to condemn it but to save it by renewing people's hearts. If people have the heart of God, it will change how they treat others.

beneath, or that *is* in the water under
the earth; 5 [a]you shall not bow down to
them nor serve them. [b]For I, the LORD
your God, *am* a jealous God, [c]visiting the
iniquity of the fathers upon the children
to the third and fourth *generations* of
those who hate Me, 6 but [a]showing mercy
to thousands, to those who love Me and
keep My commandments.
7 [a]"You shall not take the name of the LORD your
God in vain, for the LORD [b]will not hold
*him* guiltless who takes His name in vain.
8 [a]"Remember the Sabbath day, to keep it holy.
9 [a]Six days you shall labor and do all your
work, 10 but the [a]seventh day *is* the Sabbath
of the LORD your God. *In it* you shall do no
work: you, nor your son, nor your daughter,
nor your male servant, nor your female
servant, nor your cattle, [b]nor your stranger
who *is* within your gates. 11 For [a]*in* six days
the LORD made the heavens and the earth,
the sea, and all that *is* in them, and rest-
ed the seventh day. Therefore the LORD
blessed the Sabbath day and hallowed it.
12 [a]"Honor your father and your mother, that
your days may be [b]long upon the land
which the LORD your God is giving you.
13 [a]"You shall not murder.
14 [a]"You shall not commit [b]adultery.
15 [a]"You shall not steal.
16 [a]"You shall not bear false witness against your
neighbor.
17 [a]"You shall not covet your neighbor's house;
[b]you shall not covet your neighbor's wife,
nor his male servant, nor his female ser-
vant, nor his ox, nor his donkey, nor any-
thing that *is* your neighbor's."

### *THE PEOPLE AFRAID OF GOD'S PRESENCE*

18 Now [a]all the people [b]witnessed the thun-
derings, the lightning flashes, the sound of the
trumpet, and the mountain [c]smoking; and when
the people saw *it,* they trembled and stood afar
off. 19 Then they said to Moses, [a]"You speak with
us, and we will hear; but [b]let not God speak with
us, lest we die."
20 And Moses said to the people, [a]"Do not
fear; [b]for God has come to test you, and [c]that
His fear may be before you, so that you may not
sin." 21 So the people stood afar off, but Moses
drew near [a]the thick darkness where God *was.*

### *THE LAW OF THE ALTAR*

22 Then the LORD said to Moses, "Thus you
shall say to the children of Israel: 'You have seen
that I have talked with you [a]from heaven. 23 You

**SEEING JESUS IN THE SCRIPTURE**

**20:13** The law wasn't given to save; our heart problem prevents us from fully obeying. The law was given to show our need for a savior. When Jesus came as that Savior, He didn't throw out the law. Rather, He upheld it and focused on the heart change we need (see Matt. 5:21–22).

**20:5** [a] Is. 44:15, 19 [b] Deut. 4:24 [c] Num. 14:18, 33 **20:6** [a] Deut. 7:9 **20:7** [a] Lev. 19:12 [b] Mic. 6:11 **20:8** [a] Lev. 26:2 **20:9** [a] Luke 13:14 **20:10** [a] Gen. 2:2, 3 [b] Neh. 13:16–19 **20:11** [a] Ex. 31:17 **20:12** [a] Lev. 19:3 [b] Deut. 5:16, 33; 6:2; 11:8, 9 **20:13** [a] Rom. 13:9 **20:14** [a] Matt. 5:27 [b] Deut. 5:18 **20:15** [a] Lev. 19:11, 13 **20:16** [a] Deut. 5:20 **20:17** [a] [Eph. 5:3, 5] [b] [Matt. 5:28] **20:18** [a] Heb. 12:18, 19 [b] Rev. 1:10, 12 [c] Ex. 19:16, 18 **20:19** [a] Heb. 12:19 [b] Deut. 5:5, 23–27 **20:20** [a] [Is. 41:10, 13] [b] [Deut. 13:3] [c] Is. 8:13 **20:21** [a] Ex. 19:16 **20:22** [a] Deut. 4:36; 5:24, 26

shall not make *anything to be* [a]with Me—gods of silver or gods of gold you shall not make for yourselves. 24 An altar of [a]earth you shall make for Me, and you shall sacrifice on it your burnt offerings and your peace offerings, [b]your sheep and your oxen. In every [c]place where I record My name I will come to you, and I will [d]bless you. 25 And [a]if you make Me an altar of stone, you shall not build it of hewn stone; for if you [b]use your tool on it, you have profaned it. 26 Nor shall you go up by steps to My altar, that your [a]nakedness may not be exposed on it.'

### THE LAW CONCERNING SERVANTS
*(Deut. 15:12–18)*

**21** "Now these *are* the judgments which you shall [a]set before them: 2 [a]If you buy a Hebrew servant, he shall serve six years; and in the seventh he shall go out free and pay nothing. 3 If he comes in by himself, he shall go out by himself; if he *comes in* married, then his wife shall go out with him. 4 If his master has given him a wife, and she has borne him sons or daughters, the wife and her children shall be her master's, and he shall go out by himself. 5 [a]But if the servant plainly says, 'I love my master, my wife, and my children; I will not go out free,' 6 then his master shall bring him to the [a]judges. He shall also bring him to the door, or to the doorpost, and his master shall pierce his ear with an awl; and he shall serve him forever.

7 "And if a man [a]sells his daughter to be a female slave, she shall not go out as the male slaves do. 8 If she does not please her master, who has betrothed her to himself, then he shall let her be redeemed. He shall have no right to sell her to a foreign people, since he has dealt deceitfully with her. 9 And if he has betrothed her to his son, he shall deal with her according to the custom of daughters. 10 If he takes another *wife,* he shall not diminish her food, her clothing, [a]and her marriage rights. 11 And if he does not do these three for her, then she shall go out free, without *paying* money.

### THE LAW CONCERNING VIOLENCE

12 [a]"He who strikes a man so that he dies shall surely be put to death. 13 However, [a]if he did not lie in wait, but God [b]delivered *him* into his hand, then [c]I will appoint for you a place where he may flee.

14 "But if a man acts with [a]premeditation against his neighbor, to kill him by treachery, [b]you shall take him from My altar, that he may die.

15 "And he who strikes his father or his mother shall surely be put to death.

16 [a]"He who kidnaps a man and [b]sells him, or if he is [c]found in his hand, shall surely be put to death.

17 "And [a]he who curses his father or his mother shall surely be put to death.

18 "If men contend with each other, and one strikes the other with a stone or with *his* fist, and he does not die but is confined to *his* bed, 19 if he rises again and walks about outside [a]with his staff, then he who struck *him* shall be acquitted. He shall only pay *for* the loss of his time, and shall provide *for him* to be thoroughly healed.

20 "And if a man beats his male or female servant with a rod, so that he dies under his hand, he shall surely be punished. 21 Notwithstanding, if he remains alive a day or two, he shall not be punished; for he *is* his [a]property.

22 "If men fight, and hurt a woman with child, so that she gives birth prematurely, yet no harm follows, he shall surely be punished accordingly as the woman's husband imposes on him; and he shall [a]pay as the judges *determine.* 23 But if *any* harm follows, then you shall give life for life, 24 [a]eye for eye, tooth for tooth, hand for hand, foot for foot, 25 burn for burn, wound for wound, stripe for stripe.

> **21:24** Here we encounter the best-known statement of the "law of retaliation." The idea here is not to foster revenge but to curtail it. The natural, sinful human response is "a head for an eye, a jaw for a tooth, an arm for a hand." This law intends, "*no more than* **eye for eye, tooth for tooth**."

26 "If a man strikes the eye of his male or female servant, and destroys it, he shall let him go free for the sake of his eye. 27 And if he knocks out the tooth of his male or female servant, he shall let him go free for the sake of his tooth.

### ANIMAL CONTROL LAWS

28 "If an ox gores a man or a woman to death, then [a]the ox shall surely be stoned, and its flesh shall not be eaten; but the owner of the ox *shall be* acquitted. 29 But if the ox tended to thrust with its horn in times past, and it has been made known to his owner, and he has not kept it confined, so that it has killed a man or a woman, the ox shall be stoned and its owner also shall be put to death. 30 If there is imposed on him a sum of money, then he shall pay [a]to redeem his life, whatever is imposed on him. 31 Whether it has gored a son or gored a daughter, according to this judgment it shall be done to him. 32 If the ox gores a male or female servant, he shall give to their master [a]thirty shekels of silver, and the [b]ox shall be stoned.

**20:23** [a] Ex. 32:1, 2, 4 **20:24** [a] Ex. 20:25; 27:1–8 [b] Ex. 24:5 [c] 2 Chr. 6:6 [d] Gen. 12:2 **20:25** [a] Deut. 27:5 [b] Josh. 8:30, 31 **20:26** [a] Ex. 28:42, 43 **21:1** [a] Deut. 4:14; 6:1 **21:2** [a] Jer. 34:14 **21:5** [a] Deut. 15:16, 17 **21:6** [a] Ex. 12:12; 22:8, 9 **21:7** [a] Neh. 5:5 **21:10** [a] [1 Cor. 7:3, 5] **21:12** [a] [Matt. 26:52] **21:13** [a] Deut. 19:4, 5 [b] 1 Sam. 24:4, 10, 18 [c] Num. 35:11 **21:14** [a] Deut. 19:11, 12 [b] 1 Kin. 2:28–34 **21:16** [a] Deut. 24:7 [b] Gen. 37:28 [c] Ex. 22:4 **21:17** [a] Mark 7:10 **21:19** [a] 2 Sam. 3:29 **21:21** [a] Lev. 25:44–46 **21:22** [a] Ex. 18:21, 22; 21:30 **21:24** [a] Lev. 24:20 **21:28** [a] Gen. 9:5 **21:30** [a] Ex. 21:22; Num. 35:31 **21:32** [a] Zech. 11:12, 13; Matt. 26:15; 27:3, 9 [b] Ex. 21:28

[33]"And if a man opens a pit, or if a man digs a pit and does not cover it, and an ox or a donkey falls in it, [34]the owner of the pit shall make *it* good; he shall give money to their owner, but the dead *animal* shall be his.

[35]"If one man's ox hurts another's, so that it dies, then they shall sell the live ox and divide the money from it; and the dead *ox* they shall also divide. [36]Or if it was known that the ox tended to thrust in time past, and its owner has not kept it confined, he shall surely pay ox for ox, and the dead animal shall be his own.

### RESPONSIBILITY FOR PROPERTY

**22** "If a man steals an ox or a sheep, and slaughters it or sells it, he shall [a]restore five oxen for an ox and four sheep for a sheep. [2]If the thief is found [a]breaking in, and he is struck so that he dies, *there shall be* [b]no guilt for his bloodshed. [3]If the sun has risen on him, *there shall be* guilt for his bloodshed. He should make full restitution; if he has nothing, then he shall be [a]sold for his theft. [4]If the theft is certainly [a]found alive in his hand, whether it is an ox or donkey or sheep, he shall [b]restore double.

[5]"If a man causes a field or vineyard to be grazed, and lets loose his animal, and it feeds in another man's field, he shall make restitution from the best of his own field and the best of his own vineyard.

[6]"If fire breaks out and catches in thorns, so that stacked grain, standing grain, or the field is consumed, he who kindled the fire shall surely make restitution.

[7]"If a man [a]delivers to his neighbor money or articles to keep, and it is stolen out of the man's house, [b]if the thief is found, he shall pay double. [8]If the thief is not found, then the master of the house shall be brought to the [a]judges *to see* whether he has put his hand into his neighbor's goods.

[9]"For any kind of trespass, *whether it concerns* an ox, a donkey, a sheep, or clothing, *or* for any kind of lost thing which *another* claims to be his, the [a]cause of both parties shall come before the judges; *and* whomever the judges condemn shall pay double to his neighbor. [10]If a man delivers to his neighbor a donkey, an ox, a sheep, or any animal to keep, and it dies, is hurt, or driven away, no one seeing *it,* [11]*then* an [a]oath of the LORD shall be between them both, that he has not put his hand into his neighbor's goods; and the owner of it shall accept *that,* and he shall not make *it* good. [12]But [a]if, in fact, it is stolen from him, he shall make restitution to the owner of it. [13]If it is [a]torn to pieces *by a beast, then* he shall bring it as evidence, *and* he shall not make good what was torn.

[14]"And if a man borrows *anything* from his neighbor, and it becomes injured or dies, the owner of it not *being* with it, he shall surely make *it* good. [15]If its owner *was* with it, he shall not make *it* good; if it *was* hired, it came for its hire.

### MORAL AND CEREMONIAL PRINCIPLES

[16][a]"If a man entices a virgin who is not betrothed, and lies with her, he shall surely pay the bride-price for her *to be* his wife. [17]If her father utterly refuses to give her to him, he shall pay money according to the [a]bride-price of virgins.

[18][a]"You shall not permit a sorceress to live.

[19][a]"Whoever lies with an animal shall surely be put to death.

[20][a]"He who sacrifices to *any* god, except to the LORD only, he shall be utterly destroyed.

[21][a]"You shall neither mistreat a stranger nor oppress him, for you were strangers in the land of Egypt.

[22][a]"You shall not afflict any widow or fatherless child. [23]If you afflict them in any way, *and* they [a]cry at all to Me, I will surely [b]hear their cry; [24]and My [a]wrath will become hot, and I will kill you with the sword; [b]your wives shall be widows, and your children fatherless.

[25][a]"If you lend money to *any of* My people *who are* poor among you, you shall not be like a moneylender to him; you shall not charge him [b]interest. [26][a]If you ever take your neighbor's garment as a pledge, you shall return it to him before the sun goes down. [27]For that *is* his only covering, it *is* his garment for his skin. What will he sleep in? And it will be that when he cries to Me, I will hear, for I *am* [a]gracious.

[28][a]"You shall not revile God, nor curse a [b]ruler of your people.

[29]"You shall not delay *to offer* [a]the first of your ripe produce and your juices. [b]The firstborn of your sons you shall give to Me. [30][a]Likewise you shall do with your oxen *and* your sheep. It shall be with its mother [b]seven days; on the eighth day you shall give it to Me.

[31]"And you shall be [a]holy men to Me: [b]you shall not eat meat torn *by beasts* in the field; you shall throw it to the dogs.

### JUSTICE FOR ALL

**23** "You [a]shall not circulate a false report. Do not put your hand with the wicked to be an [b]unrighteous witness. [2][a]You shall not follow a crowd to do evil; [b]nor shall you testify

**22:1** [a] 2 Sam. 12:6; Prov. 6:31; Luke 19:8 **22:2** [a] Job 24:16; Matt. 6:19; 24:43; 1 Pet. 4:15 [b] Num. 35:27 **22:3** [a] Ex. 21:2; Matt. 18:25 **22:4** [a] Ex. 21:16 [b] Prov. 6:31 **22:7** [a] Lev. 6:1–7 [b] Ex. 22:4 **22:8** [a] Ex. 21:6, 22; 22:28; Deut. 17:8, 9; 19:17 **22:9** [a] Deut. 25:1; 2 Chr. 19:10 **22:11** [a] Heb. 6:16 **22:12** [a] Gen. 31:39 **22:13** [a] Gen. 31:39 **22:16** [a] Deut. 22:28, 29 **22:17** [a] Gen. 34:12; 1 Sam. 18:25 **22:18** [a] Lev. 19:31; 20:6, 27; Deut. 18:10, 11; 1 Sam. 28:3–10; Jer. 27:9, 10 **22:19** [a] Lev. 18:23; 20:15, 16; Deut. 27:21 **22:20** [a] Ex. 32:8; 34:15; Lev. 17:7; Num. 25:2; Deut. 17:2, 3, 5; 1 Kin. 18:40; 2 Kin. 10:25 **22:21** [a] Ex. 23:9; Deut. 10:19; Zech. 7:10 **22:22** [a] Deut. 24:17, 18; Prov. 23:10, 11; Jer. 7:6, 7; [James 1:27] **22:23** [a] [Luke 18:7] [b] Deut. 10:17, 18; Ps. 18:6 **22:24** [a] Ps. 69:24 [b] Ps. 109:9 **22:25** [a] Lev. 25:35–37 [b] Ps. 15:5 **22:26** [a] Deut. 24:6, 10–13 **22:27** [a] Ex. 34:6, 7 **22:28** [a] Eccl. 10:20 [b] Acts 23:5 **22:29** [a] Ex. 23:16, 19 [b] Ex. 13:2, 12, 15 **22:30** [a] Deut. 15:19 [b] Lev. 22:27 **22:31** [a] Lev. 11:44; 19:2 [b] Ezek. 4:14 **23:1** [a] Ps. 101:5 [b] Deut. 19:16–21 **23:2** [a] Gen. 7:1 [b] Lev. 19:15

APPLY THE TRUTH

## ABUSE

**22:22–24** God doesn't take abuse of helpless people lightly. In fact, the Book of Exodus is about God rescuing the oppressed because His wrath is hot against oppression. These verses tell us God cares about the oppressed and acts on their behalf too.

We live in a world where outrage over injustices like domestic violence, sexual abuse, child abuse, and child neglect is common, but actions taken against these sins is rare. While people can be slow to act, God isn't. His heart remains fixed on the abused and His wrath remains hot against the abuse they endure.

God also continues to act on behalf of the abused. First, He provides comfort. God can heal even the deepest, darkest wounds a person might experience. His love and care are a balm to the soul. Second, He won't allow these sins to go unpunished. Unless abusers repent, they will face God's judgment. Third, He raises up a people—the church—with the culture of heaven to be His hands of compassion. The culture of heaven turns the world's power upside down. To be great in God's kingdom is to care about the least of these. Acts of compassion and mercy are part of what defines God's people, which is why so many hospitals, relief agencies, and shelters were started by Christians.

in a dispute so as to turn aside after many to pervert *justice.* 3 You shall not show partiality to a [a]poor man in his dispute.

4 [a]"If you meet your enemy's ox or his donkey going astray, you shall surely bring it back to him again. 5 [a]If you see the donkey of one who hates you lying under its burden, and you would refrain from helping it, you shall surely help him with it.

6 [a]"You shall not pervert the judgment of your poor in his dispute. 7 [a]Keep yourself far from a false matter; [b]do not kill the innocent and righteous. For [c]I will not justify the wicked. 8 And [a]you shall take no bribe, for a bribe blinds the discerning and perverts the words of the righteous.

9 "Also [a]you shall not oppress a stranger, for you know the heart of a stranger, because you were strangers in the land of Egypt.

### *THE LAW OF SABBATHS*

10 [a]"Six years you shall sow your land and gather in its produce, 11 but the seventh *year* you shall let it rest and lie fallow, that the poor of your people may eat; and what they leave, the beasts of the field may eat. In like manner you shall do with your vineyard *and* your olive grove. 12 [a]Six days you shall do your work, and on the seventh day you shall rest, that your ox and your donkey may rest, and the son of your female servant and the stranger may be refreshed.

13 "And in all that I have said to you, [a]be circumspect and [b]make no mention of the name of other gods, nor let it be heard from your mouth.

### *THREE ANNUAL FEASTS*

*(Ex. 34:18–26; Deut. 16:1–17)*

14 [a]"Three times you shall keep a feast to Me in the year: 15 [a]You shall keep the Feast of Unleavened Bread (you shall eat unleavened bread seven days, as I commanded you, at the time appointed in the month of Abib, for in it you came out of Egypt; [b]none shall appear before Me empty); 16 [a]and the Feast of Harvest, the firstfruits of your labors which you have sown in the field; and [b]the Feast of Ingathering at the end of the year, when you have gathered in *the fruit of* your labors from the field.

17 [a]"Three times in the year all your males shall appear before the Lord GOD.[1]

18 [a]"You shall not offer the blood of My sacrifice with leavened [b]bread; nor shall the fat of My sacrifice remain until morning. 19 [a]The first of the firstfruits of your land you shall bring into the house of the LORD your God. [b]You shall not boil a young goat in its mother's milk.

### *THE ANGEL AND THE PROMISES*

20 [a]"Behold, I send an Angel before you to keep you in the way and to bring you into the place which I have prepared. 21 Beware of Him and obey His voice; [a]do not provoke Him, for He will [b]not pardon your transgressions; for [c]My name *is* in Him. 22 But if you indeed obey His voice and do all that I speak, then [a]I will be an enemy to your enemies and an adversary to your adversaries. 23 [a]For My Angel will go before you and [b]bring you in to the Amorites and the Hittites and the Perizzites and the Canaanites and the Hivites and the Jebusites; and I will cut

**23:3** [a] Deut. 1:17; 16:19 **23:4** [a] [Rom. 12:20] **23:5** [a] Deut. 22:4 **23:6** [a] Eccl. 5:8 **23:7** [a] Eph. 4:25 [b] Matt. 27:4 [c] Rom. 1:18 **23:8** [a] Prov. 15:27; 17:8, 23 **23:9** [a] Ex. 22:21 **23:10** [a] Lev. 25:1–7 **23:12** [a] Luke 13:14 **23:13** [a] 1 Tim. 4:16 [b] Josh. 23:7 **23:14** [a] Ex. 23:17; 34:22–24 **23:15** [a] Ex. 12:14–20 [b] Ex. 22:29; 34:20 **23:16** [a] Ex. 34:22 [b] Deut. 16:13 **23:17** [a] Deut. 16:16 [1] Hebrew *YHWH*, usually translated *LORD* **23:18** [a] Ex. 34:25 [b] Deut. 16:4 **23:19** [a] Deut. 26:2, 10 [b] Deut. 14:21 **23:20** [a] Ex. 3:2; 13:15; 14:19 **23:21** [a] Ps. 78:40, 56 [b] Deut. 18:19 [c] Is. 9:6 **23:22** [a] Deut. 30:7 **23:23** [a] Ex. 23:20 [b] Josh. 24:8, 11

them off. 24 You shall not [a]bow down to their
gods, nor serve them, [b]nor do according to their
works; [c]but you shall utterly overthrow them
and completely break down their *sacred* pillars.
25 "So you shall [a]serve the LORD your God, and
[b]He will bless your bread and your water. And [c]I
will take sickness away from the midst of you.
26 [a]No one shall suffer miscarriage or be barren in
your land; I will [b]fulfill the number of your days.
27 "I will send [a]My fear before you, I will
[b]cause confusion among all the people to whom
you come, and will make all your enemies turn
*their* backs to you. 28 And [a]I will send hornets
before you, which shall drive out the Hivite,
the Canaanite, and the Hittite from before you.
29 [a]I will not drive them out from before you in
one year, lest the land become desolate and the
beasts of the field become too numerous for
you. 30 Little by little I will drive them out from
before you, until you have increased, and you
inherit the land. 31 And [a]I will set your bounds
from the Red Sea to the sea, Philistia, and from
the desert to the River.[1] For I will [b]deliver the
inhabitants of the land into your hand, and you
shall drive them out before you. 32 [a]You shall
make no covenant with them, nor with their
gods. 33 They shall not dwell in your land, lest
they make you sin against Me. For *if* you serve
their gods, [a]it will surely be a snare to you."

## ISRAEL AFFIRMS THE COVENANT

24 Now He said to Moses, "Come up to the
LORD, you and Aaron, [a]Nadab and Abihu,
[b]and seventy of the elders of Israel, and worship
from afar. 2 And Moses alone shall come near the
LORD, but they shall not come near; nor shall
the people go up with him."
3 So Moses came and told the people all the
words of the LORD and all the judgments. And all
the people answered with one voice and said, [a]"All
the words which the LORD has said we will do."
4 And Moses [a]wrote all the words of the LORD. And
he rose early in the morning, and built an altar at
the foot of the mountain, and twelve [b]pillars ac-
cording to the twelve tribes of Israel. 5 Then he sent
young men of the children of Israel, who offered
[a]burnt offerings and sacrificed peace offerings
of oxen to the LORD. 6 And Moses [a]took half the
blood and put *it* in basins, and half the blood he
sprinkled on the altar. 7 Then he [a]took the Book of
the Covenant and read in the hearing of the people.
And they said, "All that the LORD has said we will
do, and be obedient." 8 And Moses took the blood,
sprinkled *it* on the people, and said, "This is [a]the
blood of the covenant which the LORD has made
with you according to all these words."

**24:8** The sprinkling of **blood** as a covenant promise symbolized the people entering into it saying, "We would rather die than break our promise."

## ON THE MOUNTAIN WITH GOD

9 Then Moses went up, also Aaron, Nadab,
and Abihu, and seventy of the elders of Israel,
10 and they [a]saw the God of Israel. And *there was*
under His feet as it were a paved work of [b]sap-
phire stone, and it was like the [c]very heavens
in *its* clarity. 11 But on the nobles of the children
of Israel He [a]did not lay His hand. So [b]they saw
God, and they [c]ate and drank.
12 Then the LORD said to Moses, [a]"Come up
to Me on the mountain and be there; and I will
give you [b]tablets of stone, and the law and com-
mandments which I have written, that you may
teach them."
13 So Moses arose with [a]his assistant Joshua,
and Moses went up to the mountain of God.
14 And he said to the elders, "Wait here for us
until we come back to you. Indeed, Aaron and
[a]Hur *are* with you. If any man has a difficulty, let
him go to them." 15 Then Moses went up into the
mountain, and [a]a cloud covered the mountain.
16 Now [a]the glory of the LORD rested on Mount
Sinai, and the cloud covered it six days. And on
the seventh day He called to Moses out of the
midst of the cloud. 17 The sight of the glory of the
LORD *was* like [a]a consuming fire on the top of the
mountain in the eyes of the children of Israel.
18 So Moses went into the midst of the cloud and
went up into the mountain. And [a]Moses was on
the mountain forty days and forty nights.

## OFFERINGS FOR THE SANCTUARY

*(Ex. 35:4–9)*

25 Then the LORD spoke to Moses, saying:
2 "Speak to the children of Israel, that they
bring Me an offering. [a]From everyone who gives it
willingly with his heart you shall take My offering.
3 And this *is* the offering which you shall take from
them: gold, silver, and bronze; 4 blue, purple, and
scarlet *thread,* fine linen, and goats' *hair;* 5 ram
skins dyed red, badger skins, and acacia wood; 6 [a]oil
for the light, and [b]spices for the anointing oil and
for the sweet incense; 7 onyx stones, and stones to
be set in the [a]ephod and in the breastplate. 8 And
let them make Me a [a]sanctuary, that [b]I may dwell
among them. 9 According to all that I show you, *that
is,* the pattern of the tabernacle and the pattern of
all its furnishings, just so you shall make *it.*

**23:24** [a] Ex. 20:5; 23:13, 33 [b] Deut. 12:30, 31 [c] Num. 33:52 **23:25** [a] Deut. 6:13 [b] Deut. 28:5 [c] Ex. 15:26 **23:26** [a] Deut. 7:14; 28:4 [b] 1 Chr. 23:1 **23:27** [a] Ex. 15:16 [b] Deut. 7:23 **23:28** [a] Josh. 24:12 **23:29** [a] Deut. 7:22 **23:31** [a] Gen. 15:18 [b] Josh. 21:44 [1] Hebrew *Nahar,* the Euphrates **23:32** [a] Ex. 34:12, 15 **23:33** [a] Ps. 106:36 **24:1** [a] Lev. 10:1, 2 [b] Num. 11:16 **24:3** [a] Ex. 19:8; 24:7 **24:4** [a] Deut. 31:9 [b] Gen. 28:18 **24:5** [a] Ex. 18:12; 20:24 **24:6** [a] Heb. 9:18 **24:7** [a] Heb. 9:19 **24:8** [a] [Luke 22:20] **24:10** [a] [John 1:18; 6:46] [b] Ezek. 1:26 [c] Matt. 17:2 **24:11** [a] Ex. 19:21 [b] Gen. 32:30 [c] 1 Cor. 10:18 **24:12** [a] Ex. 24:2, 15 [b] Ex. 31:18; 32:15 **24:13** [a] Ex. 32:17 **24:14** [a] Ex. 17:10, 12 **24:15** [a] Ex. 19:9 **24:16** [a] Ex. 16:10; 33:18 **24:17** [a] Deut. 4:26, 36; 9:3 **24:18** [a] Ex. 34:28 **25:2** [a] Ex. 35:4–9, 21 **25:6** [a] Ex. 27:20 [b] Ex. 30:23 **25:7** [a] Ex. 28:4, 6–14 **25:8** [a] Ex. 36:1, 3, 4; Lev. 4:6; 10:4; 21:12; Heb. 9:1, 2 [b] Ex. 29:45; 1 Kin. 6:13; [2 Cor. 6:16; Heb. 3:6; Rev. 2:13]

**25:8–22** The **tabernacle** measured 15 by 45 feet and had two main sections: the outer room, known as "the holy place," and the inner room called the Most Holy Place (see Ex. 26:33). The only person who went into the Most Holy Place was the high priest, who entered once a year to offer a sacrifice for his sins and the sins of all the people. There was only one item in this place: **the ark of the Testimony**, also called the ark of the covenant, a box almost four feet long, two feet wide, and two feet tall. It was made from **acacia wood** with **two rings** on each side so **poles** could be slid through to carry it without touching it. Inside the ark, the Israelites kept the tablets of the Ten Commandments, a golden jar of manna, and Aaron's rod that had budded. The lid was called the **mercy seat**, the noun form of a Hebrew verb meaning "to atone for," "to cover over," or "to make propitiation." It was located on the lid of the ark of the Testimony, between the two winged creatures on each end of the lid.

The Israelites used the tabernacle as their place of worship until Solomon built the temple in Jerusalem. Hebrews 9:1–24 explains that the tabernacle pictured Jesus. In describing the incarnation (the Son of God coming to earth in human form), John used the word for "dwelt" that can be translated as "tabernacled." Just as God dwelled in a tent in the wilderness, so the Son of God dwelled in a human body.

### *THE ARK OF THE TESTIMONY*
*(Ex. 37:1–9)*

10 [a]"And they shall make an ark of acacia
wood; two and a half cubits *shall be* its length, a
cubit and a half its width, and a cubit and a half
its height. 11 And you shall overlay it with pure
gold, inside and out you shall overlay it, and
shall make on it a molding of [a]gold all around.
12 You shall cast four rings of gold for it, and put
*them* in its four corners; two rings *shall be* on
one side, and two rings on the other side. 13 And
you shall make poles *of* acacia wood, and overlay
them with gold. 14 You shall put the poles into the
rings on the sides of the ark, that the ark may
be carried by them. 15 [a]The poles shall be in the
rings of the ark; they shall not be taken from it.
16 And you shall put into the ark [a]the Testimony
which I will give you.

17 [a]"You shall make a mercy seat of pure gold;
two and a half cubits *shall be* its length and a
cubit and a half its width. 18 And you shall make
two cherubim of gold; of hammered work you
shall make them at the two ends of the mercy
seat. 19 Make one cherub at one end, and the
other cherub at the other end; you shall make
the cherubim at the two ends of it *of one piece*
with the mercy seat. 20 And [a]the cherubim shall
stretch out *their* wings above, covering the mercy
seat with their wings, and they shall face one
another; the faces of the cherubim *shall be* to-
ward the mercy seat. 21 [a]You shall put the mercy
seat on top of the ark, and [b]in the ark you shall
put the Testimony that I will give you. 22 And
[a]there I will meet with you, and I will speak with
you from above the mercy seat, from [b]between
the two cherubim which *are* on the ark of the
Testimony, about everything which I will give
you in commandment to the children of Israel.

### *THE TABLE FOR THE SHOWBREAD*
*(Ex. 37:10–16)*

23 [a]"You shall also make a table of acacia
wood; two cubits *shall be* its length, a cubit its
width, and a cubit and a half its height. 24 And
you shall overlay it with pure gold, and make a
molding of gold all around. 25 You shall make
for it a frame of a handbreadth all around, and
you shall make a gold molding for the frame all
around. 26 And you shall make for it four rings of
gold, and put the rings on the four corners that
*are* at its four legs. 27 The rings shall be close to
the frame, as holders for the poles to bear the
table. 28 And you shall make the poles of acacia
wood, and overlay them with gold, that the table
may be carried with them. 29 You shall make
[a]its dishes, its pans, its pitchers, and its bowls
for pouring. You shall make them of pure gold.
30 And you shall set the [a]showbread on the table
before Me always.

### *THE GOLD LAMPSTAND*
*(Ex. 37:17–24)*

31 [a]"You shall also make a lampstand of pure
gold; the lampstand shall be of hammered work.
Its shaft, its branches, its bowls, its *ornamental*
knobs, and flowers shall be *of one piece*. 32 And
six branches shall come out of its sides: three
branches of the lampstand out of one side, and
three branches of the lampstand out of the other
side. 33 [a]Three bowls *shall be* made like almond
*blossoms* on one branch, *with* an *ornamental* knob
and a flower, and three bowls made like almond
*blossoms* on the other branch, *with* an *ornamental*
knob and a flower—and so for the six branches
that come out of the lampstand. 34 [a]On the lamp-
stand itself four bowls *shall be* made like almond

**25:10** [a] Ex. 37:1–9; Deut. 10:3; Heb. 9:4 **25:11** [a] Ex. 37:2; Heb. 9:4 **25:15** [a] Num. 4:6; 1 Kin. 8:8 **25:16** [a] Ex. 16:34; 31:18; Deut. 10:2; 31:26; 1 Kin. 8:9; Heb. 9:4 **25:17** [a] Ex. 37:6; Heb. 9:5 **25:20** [a] 1 Kin. 8:7; 1 Chr. 28:18; Heb. 9:5 **25:21** [a] Ex. 26:34; 40:20 [b] Ex. 25:16 **25:22** [a] Ex. 29:42, 43; 30:6, 36; Lev. 16:2; Num. 17:4 [b] Num. 7:89; 1 Sam. 4:4; 2 Sam. 6:2; 2 Kin. 19:15; Ps. 80:1; Is. 37:16 **25:23** [a] Ex. 37:10–16; 1 Kin. 7:48; 2 Chr. 4:8; Heb. 9:2 **25:29** [a] Ex. 37:16; Num. 4:7 **25:30** [a] Ex. 39:36; 40:23; Lev. 24:5–9 **25:31** [a] Ex. 37:17–24; 1 Kin. 7:49; Zech. 4:2; Heb. 9:2; Rev. 1:12 **25:33** [a] Ex. 37:19 **25:34** [a] Ex. 37:20–22

# THE TABERNACLE AND TABERNACLE FURNISHINGS

The symbolism of God's redemptive covenant was preserved in the tabernacle, making each element an object lesson for the worshiper. Likely reconstructions of the furnishings are based on the detailed descriptions and precise measurements recorded in Exodus 25–40. The bronze basin is not shown here.

**1 Ark of the Covenant (Testimony)** The only article of furniture in the innermost room, the Most Holy Place. The ark was made of acacia wood overlaid with gold. The gold cover was called the "mercy seat" (Ex. 25:17–22) because on the Day of Atonement, the sacrificed animal's blood was applied to it to signify God had extended mercy and forgiven sin. A cherub was positioned at each end of the mercy seat facing the other with its wings outstretched and their faces bowed. Within the ark were two stone tablets containing the Ten Commandments (Ex. 25:16, 21), a gold pot of manna (Ex. 16:32–34), and Aaron's rod that budded (Num. 17:1–11).

**2 Incense Altar** Here, incense was burned every morning and evening, symbolizing the prayers of the people. The priest sprinkled blood on this altar to make atonement for his sins and those of the people.

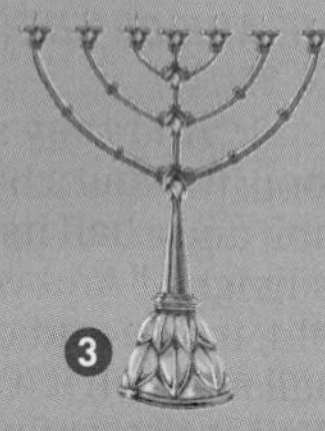


**3 Lampstand** This furnishing was made of solid gold with decorations modeled after an almond blossom (Ex. 25:33). The lampstand itself resembled a tree. Its purpose was to give light in the tabernacle, but it symbolized God's giving light to His people.

**4 Table of Showbread** Twelve loaves of holy bread were placed on this table each sabbath to symbolize God's presence and provision. The old bread was removed and eaten by the priests and any leftovers were burned with incense as an offering.

**5 Bronze Altar** The altar of burnt offering was made of wood overlaid with bronze and was the largest furnishing. It was placed in the outer court (Ex. 40:6) and was used for making daily sacrifices. The fire was to be kept burning perpetually (Lev. 6:13).

*blossoms, each with* its *ornamental* knob and flower. 35 And *there shall be* a knob under the *first* two branches of the same, a knob under the *second* two branches of the same, and a knob under the *third* two branches of the same, according to the six branches that extend from the lampstand. 36 Their knobs and their branches *shall be of one piece;* all of it *shall be* one hammered piece of pure gold. 37 You shall make seven lamps for it, and [a]they shall arrange its lamps so that they [b]give light in front of it. 38 And its wick-trimmers and their trays *shall be* of pure gold. 39 It shall be made of a talent of pure gold, with all these utensils. 40 And [a]see to it that you make *them* according to the pattern which was shown you on the mountain.

## THE TABERNACLE

*(Ex. 36:8–38)*

**26** "Moreover [a]you shall make the tabernacle *with* ten curtains *of* fine woven linen and blue, purple, and scarlet *thread;* with artistic designs of cherubim you shall weave them. 2 The length of each curtain *shall be* twenty-eight cubits, and the width of each curtain four cubits. And every one of the curtains shall have the same measurements. 3 Five curtains shall be coupled to one another, and *the other* five curtains *shall be* coupled to one another. 4 And you shall make loops of blue *yarn* on the edge of the curtain on the selvedge of *one* set, and likewise you shall do on the outer edge of *the other* curtain of the second set. 5 Fifty loops you shall make in the one curtain, and fifty loops you shall make on the edge of the curtain that *is* on the end of the second set, that the loops may be clasped to one another. 6 And you shall make fifty clasps of gold, and couple the curtains together with the clasps, so that it may be one tabernacle.

7 [a]"You shall also make curtains of goats' *hair,* to be a tent over the tabernacle. You shall make eleven curtains. 8 The length of each curtain *shall be* thirty cubits, and the width of each curtain four cubits; and the eleven curtains shall all have the same measurements. 9 And you shall couple five curtains by themselves and six curtains by themselves, and you shall double over the sixth curtain at the forefront of the tent. 10 You shall make fifty loops on the edge of the curtain that is outermost in *one* set, and fifty loops on the edge of the curtain of the second set. 11 And you shall make fifty bronze clasps, put the clasps into the loops, and couple the tent together, that it may be one. 12 The remnant that remains of the curtains of the tent, the half curtain that remains, shall hang over the back of the tabernacle. 13 And a cubit on one side and a cubit on the other side, of what remains of the length of the curtains of the tent, shall hang over the sides of the tabernacle, on this side and on that side, to cover it.

14 [a]"You shall also make a covering of ram skins dyed red for the tent, and a covering of badger skins above that.

15 "And for the tabernacle you shall [a]make the boards of acacia wood, standing upright. 16 Ten cubits *shall be* the length of a board, and a cubit and a half *shall be* the width of each board. 17 Two tenons *shall be* in each board for binding one to another. Thus you shall make for all the boards of the tabernacle. 18 And you shall make the boards for the tabernacle, twenty boards for the south side. 19 You shall make forty sockets of silver under the twenty boards: two sockets under each of the boards for its two tenons. 20 And for the second side of the tabernacle, the north side, *there shall be* twenty boards 21 and their forty sockets of silver: two sockets under each of the boards. 22 For the far side of the tabernacle, westward, you shall make six boards. 23 And you shall also make two boards for the two back corners of the tabernacle. 24 They shall be coupled together at the bottom and they shall be coupled together at the top by one ring. Thus it shall be for both of them. They shall be for the two corners. 25 So there shall be eight boards with their sockets of silver—sixteen sockets—two sockets under each of the boards.

26 "And you shall make bars of acacia wood: five for the boards on one side of the tabernacle, 27 five bars for the boards on the other side of the tabernacle, and five bars for the boards of the side of the tabernacle, for the far side westward. 28 The [a]middle bar shall pass through the midst of the boards from end to end. 29 You shall overlay the boards with gold, make their rings of gold *as* holders for the bars, and overlay the bars with gold. 30 And you shall raise up the tabernacle [a]according to its pattern which you were shown on the mountain.

31 [a]"You shall make a veil woven of blue, purple, and scarlet *thread,* and fine woven linen. It shall be woven with an artistic design of cherubim. 32 You shall hang it upon the four pillars of acacia *wood* overlaid with gold. Their hooks *shall be* gold, upon four sockets of silver. 33 And you shall hang the veil from the clasps. Then you shall bring [a]the ark of the Testimony in there, behind the veil. The veil shall be a divider for you between [b]the holy *place* and the Most

### SEEING JESUS IN THE SCRIPTURE

**26:33** Because of their sin, God's people couldn't come into God's presence, so a veil blocked off the Most Holy Place. This veil, or curtain, was torn in two when Jesus died, marking how we now have full access to God through Jesus (see Mark 15:38).

**25:37** [a] Ex. 27:21; 30:8; Lev. 24:3, 4; 2 Chr. 13:11 [b] Num. 8:2 **25:40** [a] Ex. 25:9; 26:30; Num. 8:4; 1 Chr. 28:11, 19; Acts 7:44; [Heb. 8:5] **26:1** [a] Ex. 36:8–19 **26:7** [a] Ex. 36:14 **26:14** [a] Ex. 35:7, 23; 36:19 **26:15** [a] Ex. 36:20–34 **26:28** [a] Ex. 36:33 **26:30** [a] Ex. 25:9, 40; 27:8; 39:32; Num. 8:4; Acts 7:44; [Heb. 8:2, 5] **26:31** [a] Ex. 27:21; 36:35–38; Lev. 16:2; 2 Chr. 3:14; Matt. 27:51; Heb. 9:3; 10:20 **26:33** [a] Ex. 25:10–16; 40:21 [b] Lev. 16:2; Heb. 9:2, 3

Holy. 34 [a]You shall put the mercy seat upon the ark of the Testimony in the Most Holy. 35 [a]You shall set the table outside the veil, and [b]the lampstand across from the table on the side of the tabernacle toward the south; and you shall put the table on the north side.

36 [a]"You shall make a screen for the door of the tabernacle, *woven of* blue, purple, and scarlet *thread,* and fine woven linen, made by a weaver. 37 And you shall make for the screen [a]five pillars of acacia *wood,* and overlay them with gold; their hooks *shall be* gold, and you shall cast five sockets of bronze for them.

### THE ALTAR OF BURNT OFFERING
*(Ex. 38:1–7)*

**27** "You shall make [a]an altar of acacia wood, five cubits long and five cubits wide—the altar shall be square—and its height *shall be* three cubits. 2 You shall make its horns on its four corners; its horns shall be of one piece with it. And you shall overlay it with bronze. 3 Also you shall make its pans to receive its ashes, and its shovels and its basins and its forks and its firepans; you shall make all its utensils of bronze. 4 You shall make a grate for it, a network of bronze; and on the network you shall make four bronze rings at its four corners. 5 You shall put it under the rim of the altar beneath, that the network may be midway up the altar. 6 And you shall make poles for the altar, poles of acacia wood, and overlay them with bronze. 7 The poles shall be put in the rings, and the poles shall be on the two sides of the altar to bear it. 8 You shall make it hollow with boards; [a]as it was shown you on the mountain, so shall they make *it.*

### THE COURT OF THE TABERNACLE
*(Ex. 38:9–20)*

9 [a]"You shall also make the court of the tabernacle. For the south side *there shall be* hangings for the court *made of* fine woven linen, one hundred cubits long for one side. 10 And its twenty pillars and their twenty sockets *shall be* bronze. The hooks of the pillars and their bands *shall be* silver. 11 Likewise along the length of the north side *there shall be* hangings one hundred *cubits* long, with its twenty pillars and their twenty sockets of bronze, and the hooks of the pillars and their bands of silver.

12 "And along the width of the court on the west side *shall be* hangings of fifty cubits, with their ten pillars and their ten sockets. 13 The width of the court on the east side *shall be* fifty cubits. 14 The hangings on *one* side *of the gate shall be* fifteen cubits, *with* their three pillars and their three sockets. 15 And on the other side *shall be* hangings of fifteen *cubits, with* their three pillars and their three sockets.

16 "For the gate of the court *there shall be* a screen twenty cubits long, *woven of* blue, purple, and scarlet *thread,* and fine woven linen, made by a weaver. It *shall have* four pillars and four sockets. 17 All the pillars around the court shall have bands of silver; their [a]hooks *shall be* of silver and their sockets of bronze. 18 The length of the court *shall be* one hundred cubits, the width fifty throughout, and the height five cubits, *made of* fine woven linen, and its sockets of bronze. 19 All the utensils of the tabernacle for all its service, all its pegs, and all the pegs of the court, *shall be* of bronze.

### THE CARE OF THE LAMPSTAND
*(Lev. 24:1–4)*

20 "And [a]you shall command the children of Israel that they bring you pure oil of pressed olives for the light, to cause the lamp to burn continually. 21 In the tabernacle of meeting, [a]outside the veil which *is* before the Testimony, [b]Aaron and his sons shall tend it from evening until morning before the LORD. [c]*It shall be* a statute forever to their generations on behalf of the children of Israel.

### GARMENTS FOR THE PRIESTHOOD
*(Ex. 39:1–7)*

**28** "Now take [a]Aaron your brother, and his sons with him, from among the children of Israel, that he may minister to Me as [b]priest, Aaron *and* Aaron's sons: [c]Nadab, Abihu, [d]Eleazar, and Ithamar. 2 And [a]you shall make holy garments for Aaron your brother, for glory and for beauty. 3 So [a]you shall speak to all *who are* gifted artisans, [b]whom I have filled with the spirit of wisdom, that they may make Aaron's garments, to consecrate him, that he may minister to Me as priest. 4 And these *are* the garments which they shall make: [a]a breastplate, [b]an ephod,[1] [c]a robe, [d]a skillfully woven tunic, a turban, and [e]a sash. So they shall make holy garments for Aaron your brother and his sons, that he may minister to Me as priest.

### THE EPHOD

5 "They shall take the gold, blue, purple, and scarlet *thread,* and the fine linen, 6 [a]and they shall make the ephod of gold, blue, purple, *and* scarlet *thread,* and fine woven linen, artistically worked. 7 It shall have two shoulder straps joined at its two edges, and *so* it shall be joined together. 8 And the intricately woven band of the ephod, which *is* on it, shall be of the same workmanship, *made of* gold, blue, purple, and scarlet *thread,* and fine woven linen.

**26:34** [a] Ex. 25:17–22; 40:20; Heb. 9:5 **26:35** [a] Ex. 40:22; Heb. 9:2 [b] Ex. 40:24 **26:36** [a] Ex. 36:37 **26:37** [a] Ex. 36:38 **27:1** [a] Ex. 38:1; Ezek. 43:13 **27:8** [a] Ex. 25:40; 26:30; Acts 7:44; [Heb. 8:5] **27:9** [a] Ex. 38:9–20 **27:17** [a] Ex. 38:19 **27:20** [a] Ex. 35:8, 28; Lev. 24:1–4 **27:21** [a] Ex. 26:31, 33 [b] Ex. 30:8; 1 Sam. 3:3; 2 Chr. 13:11 [c] Ex. 28:43; 29:9; Lev. 3:17; 16:34; Num. 18:23; 19:21; 1 Sam. 30:25 **28:1** [a] Num. 3:10; 18:7 [b] Ps. 99:6; Heb. 5:4 [c] Ex. 24:1, 9; Lev. 10:1 [d] Ex. 6:23; Lev. 10:6, 16 **28:2** [a] Ex. 29:5, 29; 31:10; 39:1–31; Lev. 8:7–9, 30 **28:3** [a] Ex. 31:6; 36:1 [b] Ex. 31:3; 35:30, 31; Is. 11:2; Eph. 1:17 **28:4** [a] Ex. 28:15 [b] Ex. 28:6 [c] Ex. 28:31 [d] Ex. 28:39 [e] Lev. 8:7 [1] That is, an ornamented vest **28:6** [a] Ex. 39:2–7; Lev. 8:7

9 "Then you shall take two onyx [a]stones and
engrave on them the names of the sons of Israel:
10 six of their names on one stone and six names
on the other stone, in order of their [a]birth. 11 With
the work of an [a]engraver in stone, *like* the en-
gravings of a signet, you shall engrave the two
stones with the names of the sons of Israel. You
shall set them in settings of gold. 12 And you shall
put the two stones on the shoulders of the ephod
*as* memorial stones for the sons of Israel. So
[a]Aaron shall bear their names before the LORD
on his two shoulders [b]as a memorial. 13 You shall
also make settings of gold, 14 and you shall make
two chains of pure gold like braided cords, and
fasten the braided chains to the settings.

### *THE BREASTPLATE*
*(Ex. 39:8–21)*

15 [a]"You shall make the breastplate of judg-
ment. Artistically woven according to the work-
manship of the ephod you shall make it: of gold,
blue, purple, and scarlet *thread,* and fine woven
linen, you shall make it. 16 It shall be doubled into
a square: a span *shall be* its length, and a span
*shall be* its width. 17 [a]And you shall put settings
of stones in it, four rows of stones: *The first* row
*shall be* a sardius, a topaz, and an emerald; *this
shall be* the first row; 18 the second row *shall be* a
turquoise, a sapphire, and a diamond; 19 the third
row, a jacinth, an agate, and an amethyst; 20 and
the fourth row, a beryl, an onyx, and a jasper.
They shall be set in gold settings. 21 And the stones
shall have the names of the sons of Israel, twelve
according to their names, *like* the engravings of
a signet, each one with its own name; they shall
be according to the twelve tribes.

22 "You shall make chains for the breast-
plate at the end, like braided cords of pure gold.
23 And you shall make two rings of gold for the
breastplate, and put the two rings on the two
ends of the breastplate. 24 Then you shall put
the two braided *chains* of gold in the two rings
which are on the ends of the breastplate; 25 and
the *other* two ends of the two braided *chains* you
shall fasten to the two settings, and put them on
the shoulder straps of the ephod in the front.

26 "You shall make two rings of gold, and put
them on the two ends of the breastplate, on the
edge of it, which is on the inner side of the ephod.
27 And two *other* rings of gold you shall make, and
put them on the two shoulder straps, underneath
the ephod toward its front, right at the seam
above the intricately woven band of the ephod.
28 They shall bind the breastplate by means of
its rings to the rings of the ephod, using a blue
cord, so that it is above the intricately woven
band of the ephod, and so that the breastplate
does not come loose from the ephod.

29 "So Aaron shall [a]bear the names of the
sons of Israel on the breastplate of judgment
over his heart, when he goes into the holy *place,*
as a memorial before the LORD continually.
30 And [a]you shall put in the breastplate of judg-
ment the Urim and the Thummim,[1] and they
shall be over Aaron's heart when he goes in be-
fore the LORD. So Aaron shall bear the judgment
of the children of Israel over his heart before
the LORD continually.

> **28:30** The **Urim and the Thummim** can be translated as "Lights" and "Perfections." Together their names may mean "perfect knowledge" or a similar idea. It's not known exactly what the Urim and Thummim were, or how they were used. Some have suggested that they were two stones used for the casting of lots.

### *OTHER PRIESTLY GARMENTS*
*(Ex. 39:22–31)*

31 [a]"You shall make the robe of the ephod
all of blue. 32 There shall be an opening for his
head in the middle of it; it shall have a woven
binding all around its opening, like the opening
in a coat of mail, so that it does not tear. 33 And
upon its hem you shall make pomegranates of
blue, purple, and scarlet, all around its hem,
and bells of gold between them all around: 34 a
golden bell and a pomegranate, a golden bell
and a pomegranate, upon the hem of the robe
all around. 35 And it shall be upon Aaron when
he ministers, and its sound will be heard when
he goes into the holy *place* before the LORD and
when he comes out, that he may not die.

36 [a]"You shall also make a plate of pure gold
and engrave on it, *like* the engraving of a signet:

HOLINESS TO THE LORD.

37 And you shall put it on a blue cord, that it may
be on the turban; it shall be on the front of the
turban. 38 So it shall be on Aaron's forehead, that
Aaron may [a]bear the iniquity of the holy things
which the children of Israel hallow in all their
holy gifts; and it shall always be on his forehead,
that they may be [b]accepted before the LORD.

39 "You shall [a]skillfully weave the tunic of fine
linen *thread,* you shall make the turban of fine
linen, and you shall make the sash of woven work.

40 [a]"For Aaron's sons you shall make tunics,
and you shall make sashes for them. And you
shall make hats for them, for glory and [b]beauty.
41 So you shall put them on Aaron your brother

**28:9** [a] Ex. 35:27 **28:10** [a] Gen. 29:31—30:24; 35:16–18 **28:11** [a] Ex. 35:35 **28:12** [a] Ex. 28:29, 30; 39:6, 7 [b] Lev. 24:7; Num. 31:54; Josh. 4:7; Zech. 6:14; 1 Cor. 11:24 **28:15** [a] Ex. 39:8–21 **28:17** [a] Ex. 39:10 **28:29** [a] Ex. 28:12 **28:30** [a] Lev. 8:8; Num. 27:21; Deut. 33:8; 1 Sam. 28:6; Ezra 2:63; Neh. 7:65 [1] Literally *the Lights and the Perfections* (compare Leviticus 8:8) **28:31** [a] Ex. 39:22–26 **28:36** [a] Ex. 39:30, 31; Lev. 8:9; Zech. 14:20 **28:38** [a] Ex. 28:43; Lev. 10:17; 22:9, 16; Num. 18:1; [Is. 53:11]; Ezek. 4:4–6; [John 1:29; Heb. 9:28; 1 Pet. 2:24] [b] Lev. 1:4; 22:27; 23:11; Is. 56:7 **28:39** [a] Ex. 35:35; 39:27–29 **28:40** [a] Ex. 28:4; 39:27–29, 41; Ezek. 44:17, 18 [b] Ex. 28:2

and on his sons with him. You shall [a]anoint
them, [b]consecrate them, and sanctify them,
that they may minister to Me as priests. 42 And
you shall make [a]for them linen trousers to cover
their nakedness; they shall reach from the waist
to the thighs. 43 They shall be on Aaron and on
his sons when they come into the tabernacle of
meeting, or when they come near [a]the altar to
minister in the holy *place,* that they [b]do not incur
iniquity and die. [c]*It shall be* a statute forever to
him and his descendants after him.

### *AARON AND HIS SONS CONSECRATED*

*(Lev. 8:1–36)*

**29** "And this is what you shall do to them to hal-
low them for ministering to Me as priests:
[a]Take one young bull and two rams without blem-
ish, 2 and [a]unleavened bread, unleavened cakes
mixed with oil, and unleavened wafers anointed
with oil (you shall make them of wheat flour). 3 You
shall put them in one basket and bring them in
the basket, with the bull and the two rams.
4 "And Aaron and his sons you shall bring
to the door of the tabernacle of meeting, [a]and
you shall wash them with water. 5 [a]Then you
shall take the garments, put the tunic on Aaron,
and the robe of the ephod, the ephod, and the
breastplate, and gird him with [b]the intricately
woven band of the ephod. 6 [a]You shall put the
turban on his head, and put the holy crown on
the turban. 7 And you shall take the anointing
[a]oil, pour *it* on his head, and anoint him. 8 Then
[a]you shall bring his sons and put tunics on them.
9 And you shall gird them with sashes, Aaron
and his sons, and put the hats on them. [a]The
priesthood shall be theirs for a perpetual statute.
So you shall [b]consecrate Aaron and his sons.
10 "You shall also have the bull brought be-
fore the tabernacle of meeting, and [a]Aaron and
his sons shall put their hands on the head of
the bull. 11 Then you shall kill the bull before the
LORD, *by* the door of the tabernacle of meeting.
12 You shall take *some* of the blood of the bull and
put *it* on [a]the horns of the altar with your finger,
and [b]pour all the blood beside the base of the
altar. 13 And [a]you shall take all the fat that covers
the entrails, the fatty lobe *attached* to the liver,
and the two kidneys and the fat that *is* on them,
and burn *them* on the altar. 14 But [a]the flesh of
the bull, with its skin and its offal, you shall burn
with fire outside the camp. It *is* a sin offering.
15 [a]"You shall also take one ram, and Aaron
and his sons shall [b]put their hands on the head
of the ram; 16 and you shall kill the ram, and you
shall take its blood and [a]sprinkle *it* all around
on the altar. 17 Then you shall cut the ram in
pieces, wash its entrails and its legs, and put
*them* with its pieces and with its head. 18 And
you shall burn the whole ram on the altar. It *is* a
[a]burnt offering to the LORD; it *is* a sweet aroma,
an offering made by fire to the LORD.
19 [a]"You shall also take the other ram, and
Aaron and his sons shall put their hands on
the head of the ram. 20 Then you shall kill the
ram, and take some of its blood and put *it* on
the tip of the right ear of Aaron and on the tip of
the right ear of his sons, on the thumb of their
right hand and on the big toe of their right foot,
and sprinkle the blood all around on the altar.
21 And you shall take some of the blood that is
on the altar, and some of [a]the anointing oil, and
sprinkle *it* on Aaron and on his garments, on
his sons and on the garments of his sons with
him; and [b]he and his garments shall be hallowed,
and his sons and his sons' garments with him.
22 "Also you shall take the fat of the ram, the
fat tail, the fat that covers the entrails, the fatty
lobe *attached to* the liver, the two kidneys and
the fat on them, the right thigh (for it *is* a ram
of consecration), 23 [a]one loaf of bread, one cake
*made with* oil, and one wafer from the basket of
the unleavened bread that *is* before the LORD;
24 and you shall put all these in the hands of
Aaron and in the hands of his sons, and you
shall [a]wave them *as* a wave offering before the
LORD. 25 [a]You shall receive them back from their
hands and burn *them* on the altar as a burnt
offering, as a sweet aroma before the LORD. It
*is* an offering made by fire to the LORD.
26 "Then you shall take [a]the breast of the ram
of Aaron's consecration and wave it *as* a wave
offering before the LORD; and it shall be your
portion. 27 And from the ram of the consecration
you shall consecrate [a]the breast of the wave of-
fering which is waved, and the thigh of the heave
offering which is raised, of *that* which *is* for Aaron
and of *that* which is for his sons. 28 It shall be from
the children of Israel *for* Aaron and his sons [a]by a
statute forever. For it is a heave offering; [b]it shall
be a heave offering from the children of Israel
from the sacrifices of their peace offerings, *that
is,* their heave offering to the LORD.
29 "And the [a]holy garments of Aaron [b]shall
be his sons' after him, [c]to be anointed in them
and to be consecrated in them. 30 [a]That son who
becomes priest in his place shall put them on
for [b]seven days, when he enters the tabernacle
of meeting to minister in the holy *place.*
31 "And you shall take the ram of the con-
secration and [a]boil its flesh in the holy place.

**28:41** [a] Ex. 29:7–9; 30:30; 40:15; Lev. 10:7 [b] Ex. 29:9; Lev. 8; Heb. 7:28 **28:42** [a] Ex. 39:28; Lev. 6:10; 16:4; Ezek. 44:18 **28:43** [a] Ex. 20:26 [b] Lev. 5:1, 17; 20:19, 20; 22:9; Num. 9:13; 18:22 [c] Ex. 27:21; Lev. 17:7 **29:1** [a] Lev. 8; [Heb. 7:26–28] **29:2** [a] Lev. 2:4; 6:19–23 **29:4** [a] Ex. 40:12; Lev. 8:6; [Heb. 10:22] **29:5** [a] Ex. 28:2; Lev. 8:7 [b] Ex. 28:8 **29:6** [a] Ex. 28:36, 37; Lev. 8:9 **29:7** [a] Ex. 25:6; 30:25–31; Lev. 8:12; 10:7; 21:10; Num. 35:25; Ps. 133:2 **29:8** [a] Ex. 28:39, 40; Lev. 8:13 **29:9** [a] Ex. 40:15; Num. 3:10; 18:7; 25:13; Deut. 18:5 [b] Ex. 28:41; Lev. 8 **29:10** [a] Lev. 1:4; 8:14 **29:12** [a] Lev. 8:15 [b] Ex. 27:2; 30:2; Lev. 4:7 **29:13** [a] Lev. 1:8; 3:3, 4 **29:14** [a] Lev. 4:11, 12, 21; Heb. 13:11 **29:15** [a] Lev. 8:18 [b] Lev. 1:4–9 **29:16** [a] Ex. 24:6; Lev. 1:5, 11 **29:18** [a] Ex. 20:24 **29:19** [a] Lev. 8:22 **29:21** [a] Ex. 30:25, 31; Lev. 8:30 [b] Ex. 28:41; 29:1; [Heb. 9:22] **29:23** [a] Lev. 8:26 **29:24** [a] Lev. 7:30; 10:14 **29:25** [a] Lev. 8:28 **29:26** [a] Lev. 7:31, 34; 8:29 **29:27** [a] Lev. 7:31, 34; Num. 18:11, 18; Deut. 18:3 **29:28** [a] Lev. 10:15 [b] Lev. 3:1; 7:34 **29:29** [a] Ex. 28:2 [b] Num. 20:26, 28 [c] Ex. 28:41; 30:30; Num. 18:8 **29:30** [a] Num. 20:28 [b] Lev. 8:35 **29:31** [a] Lev. 8:31

32 Then Aaron and his sons shall eat the flesh of
the ram, and the [a]bread that *is* in the basket, *by*
the door of the tabernacle of meeting. 33 [a]They
shall eat those things with which the atonement
was made, to consecrate *and* to sanctify them;
[b]but an outsider shall not eat *them,* because they
*are* holy. 34 And if any of the flesh of the conse-
cration offerings, or of the bread, remains until
the morning, then [a]you shall burn the remainder
with fire. It shall not be eaten, because it *is* holy.
35 "Thus you shall do to Aaron and his sons,
according to all that I have commanded you.
[a]Seven days you shall consecrate them. 36 And
you [a]shall offer a bull every day *as* a sin offering
for atonement. [b]You shall cleanse the altar when
you make atonement for it, and you shall anoint
it to sanctify it. 37 Seven days you shall make
atonement for the altar and sanctify it. And the
altar shall be most holy. [a]Whatever touches the
altar must be holy.[1]

### *THE DAILY OFFERINGS*
*(Num. 28:1–8)*

38 "Now this *is* what you shall offer on the
altar: [a]two lambs of the first year, [b]day by day
continually. 39 One lamb you shall offer [a]in the
morning, and the other lamb you shall offer at
twilight. 40 With the one lamb shall be one-tenth
*of an ephah* of flour mixed with one-fourth of a
hin of pressed oil, and one-fourth of a hin of wine
*as* a drink offering. 41 And the other lamb you
shall [a]offer at twilight; and you shall offer with
it the grain offering and the drink offering, as in
the morning, for a sweet aroma, an offering made
by fire to the LORD. 42 *This shall be* [a]a continual
burnt offering throughout your generations *at*
the door of the tabernacle of meeting before
the LORD, [b]where I will meet you to speak with
you. 43 And there I will meet with the children of
Israel, and *the tabernacle* [a]shall be sanctified by
My glory. 44 So I will consecrate the tabernacle of
meeting and the altar. I will also [a]consecrate both
Aaron and his sons to minister to Me as priests.
45 [a]I will dwell among the children of Israel and
will [b]be their God. 46 And they shall know that [a]I
*am* the LORD their God, who [b]brought them up
out of the land of Egypt, that I may dwell among
them. I *am* the LORD their God.

### *THE ALTAR OF INCENSE*
*(Ex. 37:25–28)*

**30** "You shall make [a]an altar to burn incense
on; you shall make it of acacia wood. 2 A
cubit *shall be* its length and a cubit its width—
it shall be square—and two cubits *shall be* its

> **30:1** ***Altar*** is derived from a word meaning "to slaughter for sacrifice." Altars made of earth, wood, stones, or bronze were used in sacrificial worship. The ritual slaughtering of animals to God was central to Hebrew worship at the tabernacle and temple, but throughout the Bible, God warned that righteousness, justice, and a humble heart submitted to Him were more important than bringing sacrificial gifts to the altar. Sacrifices in the tabernacle and temple were demonstrations of faith by the Israelites and a sign that God had forgiven their sins, ultimately pointing to the sacrifice Jesus would make on the cross.

height. Its horns *shall be* of one piece with it.
3 And you shall overlay its top, its sides all around,
and its horns with pure gold; and you shall make
for it a molding of gold all around. 4 Two gold
rings you shall make for it, under the molding
on both its sides. You shall place *them* on its two
sides, and they will be holders for the poles with
which to bear it. 5 You shall make the poles of
acacia wood, and overlay them with gold. 6 And
you shall put it before the [a]veil that *is* before the
ark of the Testimony, before the [b]mercy seat that
*is* over the Testimony, where I will meet with you.
7 "Aaron shall burn on it [a]sweet incense every
morning; when [b]he tends the lamps, he shall
burn incense on it. 8 And when Aaron lights the
lamps at twilight, he shall burn incense on it, a
perpetual incense before the LORD throughout
your generations. 9 You shall not offer [a]strange
incense on it, or a burnt offering, or a grain
offering; nor shall you pour a drink offering on
it. 10 And [a]Aaron shall make atonement upon
its horns once a year with the blood of the sin
offering of atonement; once a year he shall make
atonement upon it throughout your genera-
tions. It *is* most holy to the LORD."

### *THE RANSOM MONEY*

11 Then the LORD spoke to Moses, saying:
12 [a]"When you take the census of the children of
Israel for their number, then every man shall
give [b]a ransom for himself to the LORD, when
you number them, that there may be no [c]plague
among them when *you* number them. 13 [a]This is
what everyone among those who are numbered
shall give: half a shekel according to the shekel
of the sanctuary [b](a shekel *is* twenty gerahs).

**29:32** [a] Matt. 12:4 **29:33** [a] Lev. 10:14, 15, 17 [b] Ex. 12:43; Lev. 22:10 **29:34** [a] Ex. 12:10; 23:18; 34:25; Lev. 7:18; 8:32 **29:35** [a] Lev. 8:33–35 **29:36** [a] Heb. 10:11 [b] Ex. 30:26–29; 40:10, 11 **29:37** [a] Num. 4:15; Hag. 2:11–13; Matt. 23:19 [1] Compare Numbers 4:15 and Haggai 2:11–13 **29:38** [a] Num. 28:3–31; 29:6–38; 1 Chr. 16:40; Ezra 3:3 [b] Dan. 12:11 **29:39** [a] Ezek. 46:13–15 **29:41** [a] 1 Kin. 18:29, 36; 2 Kin. 16:15; Ezra 9:4, 5; Ps. 141:2 **29:42** [a] Ex. 30:8 [b] Ex. 25:22; 33:7, 9; Num. 17:4 **29:43** [a] Ex. 40:34; 1 Kin. 8:11; 2 Chr. 5:14; Ezek. 43:5; Hag. 2:7, 9 **29:44** [a] Lev. 21:15 **29:45** [a] Ex. 25:8; Lev. 26:12; Num. 5:3; Deut. 12:11; Zech. 2:10; [John 14:17, 23; Rev. 21:3] [b] Gen. 17:8; Lev. 11:45 **29:46** [a] Ex. 16:12; 20:2; Deut. 4:35 [b] Lev. 11:45 **30:1** [a] Ex. 37:25–29 **30:6** [a] Ex. 26:31–35 [b] Ex. 25:21, 22 **30:7** [a] Ex. 30:34; 1 Sam. 2:28; 1 Chr. 23:13; Luke 1:9 [b] Ex. 27:20, 21 **30:9** [a] Lev. 10:1 **30:10** [a] Lev. 16:3–34 **30:12** [a] Ex. 38:25, 26; Num. 1:2; 26:2; 2 Sam. 24:2 [b] Num. 31:50; [Matt. 20:28; 1 Pet. 1:18, 19] [c] 2 Sam. 24:15 **30:13** [a] Matt. 17:24 [b] Lev. 27:25; Num. 3:47; Ezek. 45:12

[c]The half-shekel *shall be* an offering to the LORD.
14 Everyone included among those who are num-
bered, from twenty years old and above, shall
give an offering to the LORD. 15 The [a]rich shall
not give more and the poor shall not give less
than half a shekel, when *you* give an offering to
the LORD, to make atonement for yourselves.
16 And you shall take the atonement money of the
children of Israel, and [a]shall appoint it for the
service of the tabernacle of meeting, that it may
be [b]a memorial for the children of Israel before
the LORD, to make atonement for yourselves."

### *THE BRONZE LAVER*

17 Then the LORD spoke to Moses, saying:
18 [a]"You shall also make a laver of bronze, with
its base also of bronze, for washing. You shall
[b]put it between the tabernacle of meeting and
the altar. And you shall put water in it, 19 for
Aaron and his sons [a]shall wash their hands and
their feet in water from it. 20 When they go into
the tabernacle of meeting, or when they come
near the altar to minister, to burn an offering
made by fire to the LORD, they shall wash with
water, lest they die. 21 So they shall wash their
hands and their feet, lest they die. And [a]it shall
be a statute forever to them—to him and his
descendants throughout their generations."

### *THE HOLY ANOINTING OIL*

*(Ex. 37:29)*

22 Moreover the LORD spoke to Moses, saying:
23 "Also take for yourself [a]quality spices—five
hundred *shekels* of liquid [b]myrrh, half as much
sweet-smelling cinnamon (two hundred and fifty
*shekels*), two hundred and fifty *shekels* of sweet-
smelling [c]cane, 24 five hundred *shekels* of [a]cassia,
according to the shekel of the sanctuary, and a
[b]hin of olive oil. 25 And you shall make from these
a holy anointing oil, an ointment compounded
according to the art of the perfumer. It shall be [a]a
holy anointing oil. 26 [a]With it you shall anoint the
tabernacle of meeting and the ark of the Testimo-
ny; 27 the table and all its utensils, the lampstand
and its utensils, and the altar of incense; 28 the
altar of burnt offering with all its utensils, and the
laver and its base. 29 You shall consecrate them,
that they may be most holy; [a]whatever touches
them must be holy.[1] 30 [a]And you shall anoint
Aaron and his sons, and consecrate them, that
*they* may minister to Me as priests.
31 "And you shall speak to the children of Is-
rael, saying: 'This shall be a holy anointing oil to
Me throughout your generations. 32 It shall not
be poured on man's flesh; nor shall you make
*any other* like it, according to its composition.
[a]It *is* holy, *and* it shall be holy to you. 33 [a]Whoever
compounds *any* like it, or whoever puts *any* of it
on an outsider, [b]shall be cut off from his people.'"

### *THE INCENSE*

*(Ex. 37:29)*

34 And the LORD said to Moses: [a]"Take sweet
spices, stacte and onycha and galbanum, and pure
frankincense with *these* sweet spices; there shall
be equal amounts of each. 35 You shall make of
these an incense, a compound [a]according to the
art of the perfumer, salted, pure, *and* holy. 36 And
you shall beat *some* of it very fine, and put some
of it before the Testimony in the tabernacle of
meeting [a]where I will meet with you. [b]It shall be
most holy to you. 37 But *as for* the incense which
you shall make, [a]you shall not make any for your-
selves, according to its composition. It shall be to
you holy for the LORD. 38 [a]Whoever makes *any* like
it, to smell it, he shall be cut off from his people."

### *ARTISANS FOR BUILDING THE TABERNACLE*

*(Ex. 35:30—36:1)*

31 Then the LORD spoke to Moses, saying:
2 [a]"See, I have called by name Bezalel the
[b]son of Uri, the son of Hur, of the tribe of Judah.
3 And I have [a]filled him with the Spirit of God, in
wisdom, in understanding, in knowledge, and in
all *manner of* workmanship, 4 to design artistic
works, to work in gold, in silver, in bronze, 5 in
cutting jewels for setting, in carving wood, and
to work in all *manner of* workmanship.
6 "And I, indeed I, have appointed with him
[a]Aholiab the son of Ahisamach, of the tribe of
Dan; and I have put wisdom in the hearts of
all the [b]gifted artisans, that they may make all
that I have commanded you: 7 [a]the tabernacle
of meeting, [b]the ark of the Testimony and [c]the
mercy seat that *is* on it, and all the furniture of
the tabernacle— 8 [a]the table and its utensils, [b]the
pure *gold* lampstand with all its utensils, the altar
of incense, 9 [a]the altar of burnt offering with all
its utensils, and [b]the laver and its base— 10 [a]the
garments of ministry,[1] the holy garments for
Aaron the priest and the garments of his sons,
to minister as priests, 11 [a]and the anointing oil
and [b]sweet incense for the holy *place*. According
to all that I have commanded you they shall do."

### *THE SABBATH LAW*

12 And the LORD spoke to Moses, saying,
13 "Speak also to the children of Israel, saying:
[a]'Surely My Sabbaths you shall keep, for it *is* a sign
between Me and you throughout your generations,

**30:13** [c] Ex. 38:26 **30:15** [a] Job 34:19; Prov. 22:2; [Eph. 6:9] **30:16** [a] Ex. 38:25–31 [b] Num. 16:40 **30:18** [a] Ex. 38:8; 1 Kin. 7:38 [b] Ex. 40:30 **30:19** [a] Ex. 40:31, 32; Ps. 26:6; Is. 52:11; John 13:8, 10; Heb. 10:22 **30:21** [a] Ex. 28:43 **30:23** [a] Song 4:14; Ezek. 27:22 [b] Ps. 45:8; Prov. 7:17 [c] Song 4:14 **30:24** [a] Ps. 45:8 [b] Ex. 29:40 **30:25** [a] Ex. 37:29; 40:9 **30:26** [a] Lev. 8:10 **30:29** [a] Ex. 29:37; Num. 4:15; Hag. 2:11–13 [1] Compare Numbers 4:15 and Haggai 2:11–13 **30:30** [a] Lev. 8:12 **30:32** [a] Ex. 30:25, 37 **30:33** [a] Ex. 30:38 [b] Gen. 17:14 **30:34** [a] Ex. 25:6; 37:29 **30:35** [a] Ex. 30:25 **30:36** [a] Ex. 29:42 [b] Lev. 2:3 **30:37** [a] Ex. 30:32 **30:38** [a] Ex. 30:33 **31:2** [a] Ex. 35:30—36:1 [b] 1 Chr. 2:20 **31:3** [a] 1 Kin. 7:14 **31:6** [a] Ex. 35:34 [b] Ex. 28:3; 35:10, 35; 36:1 **31:7** [a] Ex. 36:8 [b] Ex. 37:1–5 [c] Ex. 37:6–9 **31:8** [a] Ex. 37:10–16 [b] Ex. 37:17–24 **31:9** [a] Ex. 38:1–7 [b] Ex. 38:8 **31:10** [a] Ex. 39:1, 41 [1] Or *woven garments* **31:11** [a] Ex. 30:23–33 [b] Ex. 30:34–38 **31:13** [a] Ezek. 20:12, 20

that *you* may know that I *am* the LORD who [b]sanctifies you. 14 [a]You shall keep the Sabbath, therefore, for *it is* holy to you. Everyone who profanes it shall surely be put to death; for [b]whoever does *any* work on it, that person shall be cut off from among his people. 15 Work shall be done for [a]six days, but the [b]seventh *is* the Sabbath of rest, holy to the LORD. Whoever does *any* work on the Sabbath day, he shall surely be put to death. 16 Therefore the children of Israel shall keep the Sabbath, to observe the Sabbath throughout their generations *as* a perpetual covenant. 17 It *is* [a]a sign between Me and the children of Israel forever; for [b]*in* six days the LORD made the heavens and the earth, and on the seventh day He rested and was refreshed.' "

18 And when He had made an end of speaking with him on Mount Sinai, He gave Moses [a]two tablets of the Testimony, tablets of stone, written with the finger of God.

### *THE GOLD CALF*

*(Deut. 9:6–29)*

**32** Now when the people saw that Moses [a]delayed coming down from the mountain, the people [b]gathered together to Aaron, and said to him, [c]"Come, make us gods that shall [d]go before us; for *as for* this Moses, the man who [e]brought us up out of the land of Egypt, we do not know what has become of him."

2 And Aaron said to them, "Break off the [a]golden earrings which *are* in the ears of your wives, your sons, and your daughters, and bring *them* to me." 3 So all the people broke off the golden earrings which *were* in their ears, and brought *them* to Aaron. 4 [a]And he received *the gold* from their hand, and he fashioned it with an engraving tool, and made a molded calf.

Then they said, "This *is* your god, O Israel, that [b]brought you out of the land of Egypt!"

> **32:4** This **molded calf** was an ominous worship symbol. Not only were the cow and the bull worshiped in Egypt, but the bull was a familiar embodiment of Baal seen in Canaan. It appears the worship of the Lord had been blended with the symbols of Baal and other fertility gods. In this one action, the people broke the first three of God's commandments.

5 So when Aaron saw *it,* he built an altar before it. And Aaron made a [a]proclamation and said, "Tomorrow *is* a feast to the LORD." 6 Then they rose early on the next day, offered burnt offerings, and brought peace offerings; and the people [a]sat down to eat and drink, and rose up to play.

7 And the LORD said to Moses, [a]"Go, get down! For your people whom you brought out of the land of Egypt [b]have corrupted *themselves.* 8 They have turned aside quickly out of the way which [a]I commanded them. They have made themselves a molded calf, and worshiped it and sacrificed to it, and said, [b]'This *is* your god, O Israel, that brought you out of the land of Egypt!' " 9 And the LORD said to Moses, [a]"I have seen this people, and indeed it *is* a stiff-necked people! 10 Now therefore, [a]let Me alone, that [b]My wrath may burn hot against them and I may consume them. And [c]I will make of you a great nation."

11 [a]Then Moses pleaded with the LORD his God, and said: "LORD, why does Your wrath burn hot against Your people whom You have brought out of the land of Egypt with great power and with a mighty hand? 12 [a]Why should the Egyptians speak, and say, 'He brought them out to harm them, to kill them in the mountains, and to consume them from the face of the earth'? Turn from Your fierce wrath, and [b]relent from this harm to Your people. 13 Remember Abraham, Isaac, and Israel, Your servants, to whom You [a]swore by Your own self, and said to them, [b]'I will multiply your descendants as the stars of heaven; and all this land that I have spoken of I give to your descendants, and they shall inherit *it* forever.' "[1] 14 So the LORD [a]relented from the harm which He said He would do to His people.

15 And [a]Moses turned and went down from the mountain, and the two tablets of the Testimony *were* in his hand. The tablets *were* written on both sides; on the one *side* and on the other they were written. 16 Now the [a]tablets *were* the work of God, and the writing *was* the writing of God engraved on the tablets.

17 And when Joshua heard the noise of the people as they shouted, he said to Moses, "*There is* a noise of war in the camp."

18 But he said:

"*It is* not the noise of the shout of victory,
Nor the noise of the cry of defeat,
*But* the sound of singing I hear."

19 So it was, as soon as he came near the camp, that [a]he saw the calf *and* the dancing. So Moses' anger became hot, and he cast the

**31:13** [b] Lev. 20:8 **31:14** [a] Ex. 20:8 [b] Num. 15:32–36 **31:15** [a] Ex. 20:9–11 [b] Gen. 2:2 **31:17** [a] Ex. 31:13 [b] Gen. 1:31; 2:2, 3 **31:18** [a] [Ex. 24:12; 32:15, 16; Deut. 4:13; 5:22; 2 Cor. 3:3] **32:1** [a] Ex. 24:18; Deut. 9:9–12 [b] Ex. 17:1–3 [c] Acts 7:40 [d] Ex. 13:21 [e] Ex. 32:8 **32:2** [a] Ex. 11:2; 35:22; Judg. 8:24–27 **32:4** [a] Ex. 20:3, 4, 23; Deut. 9:16; Judg. 17:3, 4; 1 Kin. 12:28; Neh. 9:18; Ps. 106:19; Acts 7:41 [b] Ex. 29:45, 46 **32:5** [a] Lev. 23:2, 4, 21, 37; 2 Kin. 10:20; 2 Chr. 30:5 **32:6** [a] Ex. 32:17–19; Num. 25:2; 1 Cor. 10:7 **32:7** [a] Deut. 9:8–21; Dan. 9:14 [b] Gen. 6:11, 12 **32:8** [a] Ex. 20:3, 4, 23; Deut. 32:17 [b] 1 Kin. 12:28 **32:9** [a] Ex. 33:3, 5; 34:9; Deut. 9:6; 2 Chr. 30:8; Is. 48:4; [Acts 7:51] **32:10** [a] Deut. 9:14, 19 [b] Ex. 22:24 [c] Num. 14:12 **32:11** [a] Deut. 9:18, 26–29 **32:12** [a] Num. 14:13–19; Deut. 9:28; Josh. 7:9 [b] Ex. 32:14 **32:13** [a] Gen. 22:16–18; [Heb. 6:13] [b] Gen. 12:7; 13:15; 15:7, 18; 22:17; 26:4; 35:11, 12; Ex. 13:5, 11; 33:1 [1] Genesis 13:15 and 22:17 **32:14** [a] 2 Sam. 24:16 **32:15** [a] Deut. 9:15 **32:16** [a] Ex. 31:18 **32:19** [a] Deut. 9:16, 17

tablets out of his hands and broke them at the
foot of the mountain. 20 [a]Then he took the calf
which they had made, burned *it* in the fire, and
ground *it* to powder; and he scattered *it* on the
water and made the children of Israel drink
*it.* 21 And Moses said to Aaron, [a]"What did this
people do to you that you have brought *so* great
a sin upon them?"
22 So Aaron said, "Do not let the anger of my
lord become hot. [a]You know the people, that they
*are set* on evil. 23 For they said to me, 'Make us
gods that shall go before us; *as for* this Moses,
the man who brought us out of the land of Egypt,
we do not know what has become of him.' 24 And
I said to them, 'Whoever has any gold, let them
break *it* off.' So they gave *it* to me, and I cast it
into the fire, and this calf came out."
25 Now when Moses saw that the people *were*
[a]unrestrained (for Aaron [b]had not restrained
them, to *their* shame among their enemies),
26 then Moses stood in the entrance of the camp,
and said, "Whoever *is* on the LORD's side—
*come* to me!" And all the sons of Levi gathered
themselves together to him. 27 And he said to
them, "Thus says the LORD God of Israel: 'Let
every man put his sword on his side, and go in
and out from entrance to entrance throughout
the camp, and [a]let every man kill his brother,
every man his companion, and every man his
neighbor.' " 28 So the sons of Levi did according
to the word of Moses. And about three thou-
sand men of the people fell that day. 29 [a]Then
Moses said, "Consecrate yourselves today to the
LORD, that He may bestow on you a blessing
this day, for every man has opposed his son
and his brother."
30 Now it came to pass on the next day that
Moses said to the people, [a]"You have commit-
ted a great sin. So now I will go up to the LORD;
[b]perhaps I can [c]make atonement for your sin."
31 Then Moses [a]returned to the LORD and said,
"Oh, these people have committed a great sin,
and have [b]made for themselves a god of gold!
32 Yet now, if You will forgive their sin—but if
not, I pray, [a]blot me [b]out of Your book which
You have written."
33 And the LORD said to Moses, [a]"Whoever
has sinned against Me, I will [b]blot him out of My
book. 34 Now therefore, go, lead the people to *the
place* of which I have [a]spoken to you. [b]Behold,
My Angel shall go before you. Nevertheless, [c]in
the day when I [d]visit for punishment, I will visit
punishment upon them for their sin."
35 So the LORD plagued the people because of
[a]what they did with the calf which Aaron made.

### *THE COMMAND TO LEAVE SINAI*

33 Then the LORD said to Moses, "Depart
*and* go up from here, you [a]and the peo-
ple whom you have brought out of the land of
Egypt, to the land of which I swore to Abraham,
Isaac, and Jacob, saying, [b]'To your descendants
I will give it.' 2 [a]And I will send *My* Angel before
you, [b]and I will drive out the Canaanite and the
Amorite and the Hittite and the Perizzite and
the Hivite and the Jebusite. 3 *Go up* [a]to a land
flowing with milk and honey; for I will not go up
in your midst, lest [b]I consume you on the way,
for you *are* a [c]stiff-necked people."
4 And when the people heard this bad news,
[a]they mourned, [b]and no one put on his orna-
ments. 5 For the LORD had said to Moses, "Say
to the children of Israel, 'You *are* a stiff-necked
people. I could come up into your midst in one
moment and consume you. Now therefore, take
off your ornaments, that I may [a]know what to
do to you.' " 6 So the children of Israel stripped
themselves of their ornaments by Mount Horeb.

### *MOSES MEETS WITH THE LORD*

7 Moses took his tent and pitched it outside
the camp, far from the camp, and [a]called it the
tabernacle of meeting. And it came to pass *that*
everyone who [b]sought the LORD went out to
the tabernacle of meeting which *was* outside
the camp. 8 So it was, whenever Moses went out
to the tabernacle, *that* all the people rose, and
each man stood [a]*at* his tent door and watched
Moses until he had gone into the tabernacle.
9 And it came to pass, when Moses entered the
tabernacle, that the pillar of cloud descended
and stood *at* the door of the tabernacle, and *the
LORD* [a]talked with Moses. 10 All the people saw
the pillar of cloud standing *at* the tabernacle
door, and all the people rose and [a]worshiped,
each man *in* his tent door. 11 So [a]the LORD spoke
to Moses face to face, as a man speaks to his
friend. And he would return to the camp, but
[b]his servant Joshua the son of Nun, a young
man, did not depart from the tabernacle.

### *THE PROMISE OF GOD'S PRESENCE*

12 Then Moses said to the LORD, "See, [a]You
say to me, 'Bring up this people.' But You have
not let me know whom You will send with me.
Yet You have said, [b]'I know you by name, and
you have also found grace in My sight.' 13 Now
therefore, I pray, [a]if I have found grace in Your
sight, [b]show me now Your way, that I may know
You and that I may find grace in Your sight. And
consider that this nation *is* [c]Your people."

**32:20** [a] Num. 5:17, 24; Deut. 9:21 **32:21** [a] Gen. 26:10 **32:22** [a] Ex. 14:11; Deut. 9:24 **32:25** [a] Ex. 33:4, 5 [b] 2 Chr. 28:19 **32:27** [a] Num. 25:5–13 **32:29** [a] Ex. 28:41; 1 Sam. 15:18, 22; Prov. 21:3; Zech. 13:3 **32:30** [a] 1 Sam. 12:20, 23 [b] 2 Sam. 16:12 [c] Num. 25:13 **32:31** [a] Deut. 9:18 [b] Ex. 20:23 **32:32** [a] Ps. 69:28; Is. 4:3; Mal. 3:16; Rom. 9:3 [b] Dan. 12:1; Phil. 4:3; Rev. 3:5; 21:27 **32:33** [a] Lev. 23:30; [Ezek. 18:4; 33:2, 14, 15] [b] Ex. 17:14; Deut. 29:20; Ps. 9:5; Rev. 3:5; 21:27 **32:34** [a] Ex. 3:17 [b] Ex. 23:20; Josh. 5:14 [c] Deut. 32:35; Rom. 2:5, 6 [d] Ps. 89:32 **32:35** [a] Neh. 9:18 **33:1** [a] Ex. 32:1, 7, 13; Josh. 3:17 [b] Gen. 12:7 **33:2** [a] Ex. 32:34; Josh. 5:14 [b] Ex. 23:27–31; Josh. 24:11 **33:3** [a] Ex. 3:8 [b] Num. 16:21, 45 [c] Ex. 32:9; 33:5 **33:4** [a] Num. 14:1, 39 [b] Ezra 9:3; Esth. 4:1, 4; Ezek. 24:17, 23 **33:5** [a] [Ps. 139:23] **33:7** [a] Ex. 29:42, 43 [b] Deut. 4:29 **33:8** [a] Num. 16:27 **33:9** [a] Ex. 25:22; 31:18; Ps. 99:7 **33:10** [a] Ex. 4:31 **33:11** [a] Num. 12:8; Deut. 34:10 [b] Ex. 24:13 **33:12** [a] Ex. 3:10; 32:34 [b] Ex. 33:17; John 10:14, 15; 2 Tim. 2:19 **33:13** [a] Ex. 34:9 [b] Ps. 25:4; 27:11; 86:11; 119:33 [c] Deut. 9:26, 29

14 And He said, [a]"My Presence will go *with*
*you,* and I will give you [b]rest."
15 Then he said to Him, [a]"If Your Presence
does not go *with us,* do not bring us up from
here. 16 For how then will it be known that Your
people and I have found grace in Your sight,
[a]except You go with us? So we [b]shall be separate,
Your people and I, from all the people who *are*
upon the face of the earth."
17 So the LORD said to Moses, [a]"I will also
do this thing that you have spoken; for you
have found grace in My sight, and I know you
by name."
18 And he said, "Please, show me [a]Your
glory."
19 Then He said, "I will make all My [a]goodness
pass before you, and I will proclaim the name
of the LORD before you. [b]I will be gracious to
whom I will be [c]gracious, and I will have com-
passion on whom I will have compassion." 20 But
He said, "You cannot see My face; for [a]no man
shall see Me, and live." 21 And the LORD said,
"Here is a place by Me, and you shall stand on
the rock. 22 So it shall be, while My glory passes
by, that I will put you [a]in the cleft of the rock,
and will [b]cover you with My hand while I pass
by. 23 Then I will take away My hand, and you
shall see My back; but My face shall [a]not be
seen."

## *MOSES MAKES NEW TABLETS*

*(Deut. 10:1–5)*

34 And the LORD said to Moses, [a]"Cut two
tablets of stone like the first *ones,* and [b]I
will write on *these* tablets the words that were on
the first tablets which you broke. 2 So be ready
in the morning, and come up in the morning to
Mount Sinai, and present yourself to Me there
[a]on the top of the mountain. 3 And no man shall
[a]come up with you, and let no man be seen
throughout all the mountain; let neither flocks
nor herds feed before that mountain."
4 So he cut two tablets of stone like the first
*ones.* Then Moses rose early in the morning and
went up Mount Sinai, as the LORD had com-
manded him; and he took in his hand the two
tablets of stone.
5 Now the LORD descended in the [a]cloud
and stood with him there, and [b]proclaimed the
name of the LORD. 6 And the LORD passed be-
fore him and proclaimed, "The LORD, the LORD
[a]God, merciful and gracious, longsuffering, and
abounding in [b]goodness and [c]truth, 7 [a]keeping
mercy for thousands, [b]forgiving iniquity and
transgression and sin, [c]by no means clearing *the*
*guilty,* visiting the iniquity of the fathers upon
the children and the children's children to the
third and the fourth generation."
8 So Moses made haste and [a]bowed his head

**33:14** [a] Is. 63:9 [b] Josh. 21:44; 22:4 **33:15** [a] Ex. 33:3 **33:16** [a] Num. 14:14 [b] Ex. 34:10 **33:17** [a] [James 5:16] **33:18** [a] [1 Tim. 6:16] **33:19** [a] Ex. 34:6, 7 [b] [Rom. 9:15, 16, 18] [c] [Rom. 4:4, 16] **33:20** [a] [Gen. 32:30] **33:22** [a] Is. 2:21 [b] Ps. 91:1, 4 **33:23** [a] [John 1:18] **34:1** [a] [Ex. 24:12; 31:18; 32:15, 16, 19] [b] Deut. 10:2, 4 **34:2** [a] Ex. 19:11, 18, 20 **34:3** [a] Ex. 19:12, 13; 24:9–11 **34:5** [a] Ex. 19:9 [b] Ex. 33:19 **34:6** [a] Neh. 9:17 [b] Rom. 2:4 [c] Ps. 108:4 **34:7** [a] Ex. 20:6 [b] Ps. 103:3, 4 [c] Job 10:14 **34:8** [a] Ex. 4:31

KNOW THE TRUTH

# THE DOCTRINE OF GOD

## PART 14: THE GOODNESS AND BENEVOLENCE OF GOD

**34:6–7** When Moses asked to see God's "glory" (weighty splendor), the Lord gave Moses this gift (Ex. 33:18–23). First, though, He prepared Moses by explaining what the Israelite leader would see and hear during the coming encounter. Moses would hear the Lord proclaim the beauty and wonder of His name. Moses would see God's goodness pass before him. The word *goodness* in Exodus 33:19 comes from a verb that means to be good, pleasant, or delightful, and to be as something ought to be. God is indeed good according to this full definition. He's what one ought to be in every way. He's limitlessly beautiful, lovely, pure, and radiant. He's of the highest possible quality. He's virtuous, noble, trustworthy, upright, and the standard of moral perfection.

When the Lord passed by Moses and proclaimed His name, He described Himself as "abounding" in goodness. This means God is bountifully spilling over with good, kind, faithful love He wants to shower upon others. In 2 Chronicles 7:1–3, when God made known the glory of His presence at the temple's dedication, the people fell on their faces and shouted to God, "For He is good, for His mercy endures forever." Put another way, that phrase could mean the Lord is everlasting, relentless goodness and lovingkindness. At all times and in all ways, God is perfectly good.

*For* **THE DOCTRINE OF GOD: PART 15: THE FAITHFULNESS AND TRUTHFULNESS OF GOD,** *turn to Deuteronomy 32:3–4 on page 209.*

toward the earth, and worshiped. 9 Then he said, "If now I have found grace in Your sight, O Lord, [a]let my Lord, I pray, go among us, even though we *are* a [b]stiff-necked people; and pardon our iniquity and our sin, and take us as [c]Your inheritance."

### *THE COVENANT RENEWED*

*(Ex. 23:14–19; Deut. 7:1–6; 16:1–17)*

10 And He said: "Behold, [a]I make a covenant. Before all your people I will [b]do marvels such as have not been done in all the earth, nor in any nation; and all the people among whom you *are* shall see the work of the LORD. For it *is* [c]an awesome thing that I will do with you. 11 [a]Observe what I command you this day. Behold, [b]I am driving out from before you the Amorite and the Canaanite and the Hittite and the Perizzite and the Hivite and the Jebusite. 12 [a]Take heed to yourself, lest you make a covenant with the inhabitants of the land where you are going, lest it be a snare in your midst. 13 But you shall [a]destroy their altars, break their *sacred* pillars, and [b]cut down their wooden images 14 (for you shall worship [a]no other god, for the LORD, whose [b]name *is* Jealous, *is* a [c]jealous God), 15 lest you make a covenant with the inhabitants of the land, and they [a]play the harlot with their gods and make sacrifice to their gods, and *one of them* [b]invites you and you [c]eat of his sacrifice, 16 and you take of [a]his daughters for your sons, and his daughters [b]play the harlot with their gods and make your sons play the harlot with their gods.

17 [a]"You shall make no molded gods for yourselves.

18 "The Feast of [a]Unleavened Bread you shall keep. Seven days you shall eat unleavened bread, as I commanded you, in the appointed time of the month of Abib; for in the [b]month of Abib you came out from Egypt.

19 [a]"All that open the womb *are* Mine, and every male firstborn among your livestock, *whether* ox or sheep. 20 But [a]the firstborn of a donkey you shall redeem with a lamb. And if you will not redeem *him,* then you shall break his neck. All the firstborn of your sons you shall redeem.

"And none shall appear before Me [b]empty-handed.

21 [a]"Six days you shall work, but on the seventh day you shall rest; in plowing time and in harvest you shall rest.

22 "And you shall observe the Feast of Weeks, of the firstfruits of wheat harvest, and the Feast of Ingathering at the year's end.

23 [a]"Three times in the year all your men shall appear before the Lord, the LORD God of Israel. 24 For I will [a]cast out the nations before you and enlarge your borders; neither will any man covet your land when you go up to appear before the LORD your God three times in the year.

25 "You shall not offer the blood of My sacrifice with leaven, [a]nor shall the sacrifice of the Feast of the Passover be left until morning.

26 [a]"The first of the firstfruits of your land you shall bring to the house of the LORD your God. You shall not boil a young goat in its mother's milk."

27 Then the LORD said to Moses, "Write [a]these words, for according to the tenor of these words I have made a covenant with you and with Israel." 28 [a]So he was there with the LORD forty days and forty nights; he neither ate bread nor drank water. And [b]He wrote on the tablets the words of the covenant, the Ten Commandments.[1]

### *THE SHINING FACE OF MOSES*

29 Now it was so, when Moses came down from Mount Sinai (and the [a]two tablets of the Testimony *were* in Moses' hand when he came down from the mountain), that Moses did not know that [b]the skin of his face shone while he talked with Him. 30 So when Aaron and all the children of Israel saw Moses, behold, the skin of his face shone, and they were afraid to come near him. 31 Then Moses called to them, and Aaron and all the rulers of the congregation returned to him; and Moses talked with them. 32 Afterward all the children of Israel came near, [a]and he gave them as commandments all that the LORD had spoken with him on Mount Sinai. 33 And when Moses had finished speaking with them, he put [a]a veil on his face. 34 But [a]whenever Moses went in before the LORD to speak with Him, he would take the veil off until he came out; and he would come out and speak to the children of Israel whatever he had been commanded. 35 And whenever the children of Israel saw the face of Moses, that the skin of Moses' face shone, then Moses would put the veil on his face again, until he went in to speak with Him.

### *SABBATH REGULATIONS*

**35** Then Moses gathered all the congregation of the children of Israel together, and said to them, [a]"These *are* the words which the LORD has commanded *you* to do: 2 Work shall be done for [a]six days, but the seventh day shall be a holy day for you, a Sabbath of rest to the LORD. Whoever does any work on it shall be put to [b]death. 3 [a]You shall kindle no fire throughout your dwellings on the Sabbath day."

**34:9** [a] Ex. 33:12–16 [b] Ex. 33:3 [c] Ps. 33:12; 94:14 **34:10** [a] Deut. 5:2 [b] Ps. 77:14 [c] Ps. 145:6 **34:11** [a] Deut. 6:25 [b] Ex. 23:20–33; 33:2 **34:12** [a] Ex. 23:32, 33 **34:13** [a] Deut. 12:3 [b] 2 Kin. 18:4 **34:14** [a] [Ex. 20:3–5] [b] [Is. 9:6; 57:15] [c] [Deut. 4:24] **34:15** [a] Judg. 2:17 [b] Num. 25:1, 2 [c] 1 Cor. 8:4, 7, 10 **34:16** [a] Gen. 28:1 [b] Num. 25:1, 2 **34:17** [a] Ex. 20:4, 23; 32:8 **34:18** [a] Ex. 12:15, 16 [b] Ex. 12:2; 13:4 **34:19** [a] Ex. 13:2; 22:29 **34:20** [a] Ex. 13:13 [b] Ex. 22:29; 23:15; Deut. 16:16 **34:21** [a] Ex. 20:9; 23:12; 31:15; 35:2; Lev. 23:3; Deut. 5:13 **34:23** [a] Ex. 23:14–17 **34:24** [a] [Ex. 33:2]; Josh. 11:23; 1 Kin. 4:21; 2 Chr. 36:14–16; Ps. 78:55 **34:25** [a] Ex. 12:10 **34:26** [a] Ex. 23:19; Deut. 26:2 **34:27** [a] Ex. 17:14; 24:4; Deut. 31:9 **34:28** [a] Ex. 24:18 [b] Ex. 34:1, 4; Deut. 4:31; 10:2, 4 [1] Literally *Ten Words* **34:29** [a] Ex. 32:15 [b] Matt. 17:2; 2 Cor. 3:7 **34:32** [a] Ex. 24:3 **34:33** [a] [2 Cor. 3:13, 14] **34:34** [a] [2 Cor. 3:13–16] **35:1** [a] Ex. 34:32 **35:2** [a] Ex. 20:9, 10; Lev. 23:3; Deut. 5:13 [b] Num. 15:32–36 **35:3** [a] Ex. 12:16; 16:23

### *OFFERINGS FOR THE TABERNACLE*

*(Ex. 25:1–9; 39:32–43)*

4 And Moses spoke to all the congregation of the children of Israel, saying, [a]"This *is* the thing which the LORD commanded, saying: 5 'Take from among you an offering to the LORD. [a]Whoever *is* of a willing heart, let him bring it as an offering to the LORD: [b]gold, silver, and bronze; 6 [a]blue, purple, and scarlet *thread,* fine linen, and [b]goats' *hair;* 7 ram skins dyed red, badger skins, and acacia wood; 8 oil for the light, [a]and spices for the anointing oil and for the sweet incense; 9 onyx stones, and stones to be set in the ephod and in the breastplate.

### *ARTICLES OF THE TABERNACLE*

10 [a]'All *who are* gifted artisans among you shall come and make all that the LORD has commanded: 11 [a]the tabernacle, its tent, its covering, its clasps, its boards, its bars, its pillars, and its sockets; 12 [a]the ark and its poles, *with* the mercy seat, and the veil of the covering; 13 the [a]table and its poles, all its utensils, [b]and the showbread; 14 also [a]the lampstand for the light, its utensils, its lamps, and the oil for the light; 15 [a]the incense altar, its poles, [b]the anointing oil, [c]the sweet incense, and the screen for the door at the entrance of the tabernacle; 16 [a]the altar of burnt offering with its bronze grating, its poles, all its utensils, *and* the laver and its base; 17 [a]the hangings of the court, its pillars, their sockets, and the screen for the gate of the court; 18 the pegs of the tabernacle, the pegs of the court, and their cords; 19 [a]the garments of ministry,[1] for ministering in the holy *place*—the holy garments for Aaron the priest and the garments of his sons, to minister as priests.' "

### *THE TABERNACLE OFFERINGS PRESENTED*

20 And all the congregation of the children of Israel departed from the presence of Moses. 21 Then everyone came [a]whose heart was stirred, and everyone whose spirit was willing, *and* they [b]brought the LORD's offering for the work of the tabernacle of meeting, for all its service, and for the holy garments. 22 They came, both men and women, as many as had a willing heart, *and* brought [a]earrings and nose rings, rings and necklaces, all [b]jewelry of gold, that is, every man who *made* an offering of gold to the LORD. 23 And [a]every man, with whom was found blue, purple, and scarlet *thread,* fine linen, and goats' *hair,* red skins of rams, and badger skins, brought *them.* 24 Everyone who offered an offering of silver or bronze brought the LORD's offering. And everyone with whom was found acacia wood for any work of the service, brought *it.* 25 All the women *who were* [a]gifted artisans spun yarn with their hands, and brought what they had spun, of blue, purple, *and* scarlet, and fine linen. 26 And all the women whose hearts stirred with wisdom spun yarn of goats' *hair.* 27 [a]The rulers brought onyx stones, and the stones to be set in the ephod and in the breastplate, 28 and [a]spices and oil for the light, for the anointing oil, and for the sweet incense. 29 The children of Israel brought a [a]freewill offering to the LORD, all the men and women whose hearts were willing to bring *material* for all kinds of work which the LORD, by the hand of Moses, had commanded to be done.

### *THE ARTISANS CALLED BY GOD*

*(Ex. 31:1–11)*

30 And Moses said to the children of Israel, "See, [a]the LORD has called by name Bezalel the son of Uri, the son of Hur, of the tribe of Judah; 31 and He has filled him with the Spirit of God, in wisdom and understanding, in knowledge and all manner of workmanship, 32 to design artistic works, to work in gold and silver and bronze, 33 in cutting jewels for setting, in carving wood, and to work in all manner of artistic workmanship.

34 "And He has put in his heart the ability to teach, *in* him and [a]Aholiab the son of Ahisamach, of the tribe of Dan. 35 He has [a]filled them with skill to do all manner of work of the engraver and the designer and the tapestry maker, in blue, purple, and scarlet *thread,* and fine linen, and of the weaver—those who do every work and those who design artistic works.

36 "And Bezalel and Aholiab, and every [a]gifted artisan in whom the LORD has put wisdom and understanding, to know how to do all manner of work for the service of the [b]sanctuary, shall do according to all that the LORD has commanded."

### *THE PEOPLE GIVE MORE THAN ENOUGH*

2 Then Moses called Bezalel and Aholiab, and every gifted artisan in whose heart the LORD had put wisdom, everyone [a]whose heart was stirred, to come and do the work. 3 And they received from Moses all the [a]offering which the children of Israel [b]had brought for the work of the service of making the sanctuary. So they continued bringing to him freewill offerings every morning. 4 Then all the craftsmen who were doing all the work of the sanctuary came, each from the work he was doing, 5 and they spoke to Moses, saying, [a]"The people bring much more than enough for the service of the work which the LORD commanded *us* to do."

**35:4** [a] Ex. 25:1, 2 **35:5** [a] Ex. 25:2; 1 Chr. 29:14; Mark 12:41–44; 2 Cor. 8:10–12; 9:7 [b] Ex. 38:24 **35:6** [a] Ex. 36:8 [b] Ex. 36:14 **35:8** [a] Ex. 25:6; 30:23–25 **35:10** [a] Ex. 31:2–6; 36:1, 2 **35:11** [a] Ex. 26:1, 2; 36:14 **35:12** [a] Ex. 25:10–22 **35:13** [a] Ex. 25:23 [b] Ex. 25:30; Lev. 24:5, 6 **35:14** [a] Ex. 25:31 **35:15** [a] Ex. 30:1 [b] Ex. 30:25 [c] Ex. 30:34–38 **35:16** [a] Ex. 27:1–8 **35:17** [a] Ex. 27:9–18 **35:19** [a] Ex. 31:10; 39:1, 41 [1] Or *woven garments* **35:21** [a] Ex. 25:2; 35:5, 22, 26, 29; 36:2 [b] Ex. 35:24 **35:22** [a] Ex. 32:2, 3 [b] Ex. 11:2 **35:23** [a] 1 Chr. 29:8 **35:25** [a] Ex. 28:3; 31:6; 36:1 **35:27** [a] 1 Chr. 29:6; Ezra 2:68 **35:28** [a] Ex. 30:23 **35:29** [a] Ex. 35:5, 21; 36:3; 1 Chr. 29:9 **35:30** [a] Ex. 31:1–6 **35:34** [a] Ex. 31:6 **35:35** [a] Ex. 31:3, 6; 35:31; 1 Kin. 7:14; 2 Chr. 2:14; Is. 28:26 **36:1** [a] Ex. 28:3; 31:6; 35:10, 35 [b] Ex. 25:8 **36:2** [a] Ex. 35:21, 26; 1 Chr. 29:5, 9, 17 **36:3** [a] Ex. 35:5 [b] Ex. 35:27 **36:5** [a] 2 Chr. 24:14; 31:6–10; [2 Cor. 8:2, 3]

EXODUS 35:30–35

## THE SPIRIT AND THE TABERNACLE

14 STORY OF SCRIPTURE

### WHAT'S GOING ON?

The Israelites had lived four hundred years in a foreign land following the Egyptian's laws and knowing only the Egyptian gods. God had given His people their own laws on Mount Sinai. Now, He showed them what true worship was. The center of their worship would be the tabernacle, a portable tent where God dwelled among His people. God chose Bezalel and Aholiab to lead the work of constructing the tabernacle. They were endowed with divine wisdom, understanding, and skills in all kinds of craftsmanship. This is one of the first times we see God empowering people for a task with His Holy Spirit. The tabernacle was made up of various components such as the ark of the covenant, the table of showbread, the gold lampstand, and the altar of burnt offering. Each of these elements had specific purposes and symbolic meanings in the Israelites' worship.

### WHAT DOES THIS MEAN FOR ME?

Bezalel and Aholiab were called and equipped by God for a holy task. God equips all of us with unique gifts and skills for His purpose. Recognize your gifts and how you can use them to serve God. When you feel inadequate or unprepared for the tasks God has set before you, remember the same Spirit who filled Bezalel and Aholiab will empower you.

### DID YOU CATCH THE PATTERN?

The theme of God dwelling among His people is crucial throughout the Bible. First, He dwelled in the garden of Eden with Adam and Eve. Then, He followed the family of Abraham, Isaac, and Jacob. Here, we see Him dwell among the Israelites in the tabernacle. After this, it will be the temple. Ultimately, God's mission to dwell with His people culminated in the incarnation of Jesus (Immanuel, meaning "God with us") and the coming of the Holy Spirit to dwell within believers.

*For the next* Story of Scripture *reading and devotion, turn to Leviticus 25:1–34 on page 130.*

6 So Moses gave a commandment, and they
caused it to be proclaimed throughout the camp,
saying, "Let neither man nor woman do any
more work for the offering of the sanctuary."
And the people were restrained from bringing,
7 for the material they had was sufficient for all
the work to be done—indeed too [a]much.

### *BUILDING THE TABERNACLE*

*(Ex. 26:1–37)*

8 [a]Then all the gifted artisans among them
who worked on the tabernacle made ten curtains
woven of fine linen, and of blue, purple, and
scarlet *thread; with* artistic designs of cherubim
they made them. 9 The length of each curtain
*was* twenty-eight cubits, and the width of each
curtain four cubits; the curtains *were* all the
same size. 10 And he coupled five curtains to one
another, and *the other* five curtains he coupled
to one another. 11 He made loops of blue *yarn* on
the edge of the curtain on the selvedge of one
set; likewise he did on the outer edge of *the other*
curtain of the second set. 12 [a]Fifty loops he made
on one curtain, and fifty loops he made on the
edge of the curtain on the end of the second
set; the loops held one *curtain* to another. 13 And
he made fifty clasps of gold, and coupled the
curtains to one another with the clasps, that it
might be one tabernacle.

14 [a]He made curtains of goats' *hair* for the
tent over the tabernacle; he made eleven cur-
tains. 15 The length of each curtain *was* thirty
cubits, and the width of each curtain four cubits;
the eleven curtains *were* the same size. 16 He cou-
pled five curtains by themselves and six curtains
by themselves. 17 And he made fifty loops on the
edge of the curtain that is outermost in one
set, and fifty loops he made on the edge of the
curtain of the second set. 18 He also made fifty
bronze clasps to couple the tent together, that
it might be one. 19 [a]Then he made a covering for
the tent of ram skins dyed red, and a covering
of badger skins above *that.*

20 For the tabernacle [a]he made boards of
acacia wood, standing upright. 21 The length
of each board *was* ten cubits, and the width of
each board a cubit and a half. 22 Each board had
two tenons [a]for binding one to another. Thus
he made for all the boards of the tabernacle.
23 And he made boards for the tabernacle, twenty

**36:7** [a] 1 Kin. 8:64 **36:8** [a] Ex. 26:1–14 **36:12** [a] Ex. 26:5 **36:14** [a] Ex. 26:7 **36:19** [a] Ex. 26:14 **36:20** [a] Ex. 26:15–29 **36:22** [a] Ex. 26:17

boards for the south side. 24 Forty sockets of
silver he made to go under the twenty boards:
two sockets under each of the boards for its two
tenons. 25 And for the other side of the taber-
nacle, the north side, he made twenty boards
26 and their forty sockets of silver: two sockets
under each of the boards. 27 For the west side of
the tabernacle he made six boards. 28 He also
made two boards for the two back corners of
the tabernacle. 29 And they were coupled at the
bottom and coupled together at the top by one
ring. Thus he made both of them for the two
corners. 30 So there were eight boards and their
sockets—sixteen sockets of silver—two sockets
under each of the boards.

31 And he made [a]bars of acacia wood: five for
the boards on one side of the tabernacle, 32 five
bars for the boards on the other side of the tab-
ernacle, and five bars for the boards of the tab-
ernacle on the far side westward. 33 And he made
the middle bar to pass through the boards from
one end to the other. 34 He overlaid the boards
with gold, made their rings of gold *to be* holders
for the bars, and overlaid the bars with gold.

35 And he made [a]a veil of blue, purple, and
scarlet *thread,* and fine woven linen; it was
worked *with* an artistic design of cherubim.
36 He made for it four pillars of acacia *wood,*
and overlaid them with gold, with their hooks of
gold; and he cast four sockets of silver for them.

37 He also made a [a]screen for the tabernacle
door, of blue, purple, and scarlet *thread,* and fine
woven linen, made by a weaver, 38 and its five
pillars with their hooks. And he overlaid their
capitals and their rings with gold, but their five
sockets *were* bronze.

### *MAKING THE ARK OF THE TESTIMONY*

*(Ex. 25:10–22)*

**37** Then [a]Bezalel made [b]the ark of acacia
wood; two and a half cubits *was* its length,
a cubit and a half its width, and a cubit and a half
its height. 2 He overlaid it with pure gold inside
and outside, and made a molding of gold all
around it. 3 And he cast for it four rings of gold
*to be set* in its four corners: two rings on one
side, and two rings on the other side of it. 4 He
made poles of acacia wood, and overlaid them
with gold. 5 And he put the poles into the rings
at the sides of the ark, to bear the ark. 6 He also
made the [a]mercy seat of pure gold; two and a
half cubits *was* its length and a cubit and a half
its width. 7 He made two cherubim of beaten
gold; he made them of one piece at the two
ends of the mercy seat: 8 one cherub at one end
on this side, and the other cherub at the *other*
end on that side. He made the cherubim at the
two ends *of one piece* with the mercy seat. 9 The
cherubim spread out *their* wings above, *and*
covered the [a]mercy seat with their wings. They
faced one another; the faces of the cherubim
were toward the mercy seat.

### *MAKING THE TABLE FOR THE SHOWBREAD*

*(Ex. 25:23–30)*

10 He made [a]the table of acacia wood; two
cubits *was* its length, a cubit its width, and a
cubit and a half its height. 11 And he overlaid it
with pure gold, and made a molding of gold all
around it. 12 Also he made a frame of a hand-
breadth all around it, and made a molding of
gold for the frame all around it. 13 And he cast
for it four rings of gold, and put the rings on
the four corners that *were* at its four legs. 14 The
rings were close to the frame, as holders for the
poles to bear the table. 15 And he made the poles
of acacia wood to bear the table, and overlaid
them with gold. 16 He made of pure gold the
utensils which were on the table: its [a]dishes,
its cups, its bowls, and its pitchers for pouring.

### *MAKING THE GOLD LAMPSTAND*

*(Ex. 25:31–40)*

17 He also made the [a]lampstand of pure gold;
of hammered work he made the lampstand.
Its shaft, its branches, its bowls, its *ornamental*
knobs, and its flowers were of the same piece.
18 And six branches came out of its sides: three
branches of the lampstand out of one side, and
three branches of the lampstand out of the other
side. 19 There were three bowls made like almond
*blossoms* on one branch, with an *ornamental*
knob and a flower, and three bowls made like
almond *blossoms* on the other branch, with an
*ornamental* knob and a flower—and so for the six
branches coming out of the lampstand. 20 And on
the lampstand itself *were* four bowls made like
almond *blossoms, each with* its *ornamental* knob
and flower. 21 *There was* a knob under the *first* two
branches of the same, a knob under the *second*
two branches of the same, and a knob under the
*third* two branches of the same, according to the
six branches extending from it. 22 Their knobs
and their branches were of one piece; all of it
*was* one hammered piece of pure gold. 23 And he
made its seven lamps, its [a]wick-trimmers, and
its trays of pure gold. 24 Of a talent of pure gold
he made it, with all its utensils.

### *MAKING THE ALTAR OF INCENSE*

*(Ex. 30:1–5)*

25 [a]He made the incense altar of acacia wood.
Its length *was* a cubit and its width a cubit—*it
was* square—and two cubits *was* its height. Its
horns were *of one piece* with it. 26 And he overlaid
it with pure gold: its top, its sides all around,
and its horns. He also made for it a molding of
gold all around it. 27 He made two rings of gold
for it under its molding, by its two corners on
both sides, as holders for the poles with which

**36:31** [a] Ex. 26:26–29 **36:35** [a] Ex. 26:31–37 **36:37** [a] Ex. 26:36 **37:1** [a] Ex. 35:30; 36:1 [b] Ex. 25:10–20 **37:6** [a] Ex. 25:17 **37:9** [a] Ex. 25:20 **37:10** [a] Ex. 25:23–29 **37:16** [a] Ex. 25:29 **37:17** [a] Ex. 25:31–39 **37:23** [a] Num. 4:9 **37:25** [a] Ex. 30:1–5

to bear it. 28 And he [a]made the poles of acacia wood, and overlaid them with gold.

### *MAKING THE ANOINTING OIL AND THE INCENSE*

*(Ex. 30:22–38)*

29 He also made [a]the holy anointing oil and the pure incense of sweet spices, according to the work of the perfumer.

### *MAKING THE ALTAR OF BURNT OFFERING*

*(Ex. 27:1–8)*

**38** He made [a]the altar of burnt offering of acacia wood; five cubits *was* its length and five cubits its width—*it was* square—and its height *was* three cubits. 2 He made its horns on its four corners; the horns were *of one piece* with it. And he overlaid it with bronze. 3 He made all the utensils for the altar: the pans, the shovels, the basins, the forks, and the firepans; all its utensils he made of bronze. 4 And he made a grate of bronze network for the altar, under its rim, midway from the bottom. 5 He cast four rings for the four corners of the bronze grating, *as* holders for the poles. 6 And he made the poles of acacia wood, and overlaid them with bronze. 7 Then he put the poles into the rings on the sides of the altar, with which to bear it. He made the altar hollow with boards.

### *MAKING THE BRONZE LAVER*

8 He made [a]the laver of bronze and its base of bronze, from the bronze mirrors of the serving women who assembled at the door of the tabernacle of meeting.

### *MAKING THE COURT OF THE TABERNACLE*

*(Ex. 27:9–19)*

9 Then he made [a]the court on the south side; the hangings of the court *were of* fine woven linen, one hundred cubits long. 10 There *were* twenty pillars for them, with twenty bronze sockets. The hooks of the pillars and their bands *were* silver. 11 On the north side *the hangings were* one hundred cubits *long,* with twenty pillars and their twenty bronze sockets. The hooks of the pillars and their bands *were* silver. 12 And on the west side *there were* hangings of fifty cubits, with ten pillars and their ten sockets. The hooks of the pillars and their bands *were* silver. 13 For the east side *the hangings were* fifty cubits. 14 The hangings of one side *of the gate were* fifteen cubits *long, with* their three pillars and their three sockets, 15 and the same for the other side of the court gate; on this side and that *were* hangings of fifteen cubits, *with* their three pillars and their three sockets. 16 All the hangings of the court all around *were of* fine woven linen. 17 The sockets for the pillars *were* bronze, the hooks of the pillars and their bands *were* silver, and the overlay of their capitals *was* silver; and all the pillars of the court had bands of silver. 18 The screen for the gate of the court *was* woven of blue, purple, and scarlet *thread,* and of fine woven linen. The length *was* twenty cubits, and the height along its width *was* five cubits, corresponding to the hangings of the court. 19 And *there were* four pillars *with* their four sockets of bronze; their hooks *were* silver, and the overlay of their capitals and their bands *was* silver. 20 All the [a]pegs of the tabernacle, and of the court all around, *were* bronze.

### *MATERIALS OF THE TABERNACLE*

21 This is the inventory of the tabernacle, [a]the tabernacle of the Testimony, which was counted according to the commandment of Moses, for the service of the Levites, [b]by the hand of [c]Ithamar, son of Aaron the priest.

22 [a]Bezalel the son of Uri, the son of Hur, of the tribe of Judah, made all that the LORD had commanded Moses. 23 And with him *was* [a]Aholiab the son of Ahisamach, of the tribe of Dan, an engraver and designer, a weaver of blue, purple, and scarlet *thread,* and of fine linen.

24 All the gold that was used in all the work of the holy *place,* that is, the gold of the [a]offering, was twenty-nine talents and seven hundred and thirty shekels, according to [b]the shekel of the sanctuary. 25 And the silver from those who were [a]numbered of the congregation *was* one hundred talents and one thousand seven hundred and seventy-five shekels, according to the shekel of the sanctuary: 26 [a]a bekah for each man (*that is,* half a shekel, according to the shekel of the sanctuary), for everyone included in the numbering from twenty years old and above, for [b]six hundred and three thousand, five hundred and fifty *men.* 27 And from the hundred talents of silver were cast [a]the sockets of the sanctuary and the bases of the veil: one hundred sockets from the hundred talents, one talent for each socket. 28 Then from the one thousand seven hundred and seventy-five *shekels* he made hooks for the pillars, overlaid their capitals, and [a]made bands for them.

29 The offering of bronze *was* seventy talents and two thousand four hundred shekels. 30 And with it he made the sockets for the door of the

> **38:21–31** Only **gold** and **silver**, the finest and most expensive metals, were good enough to be used as decorations for the holy area. The outer area of the tabernacle was decorated with **bronze**, a less expensive metal.

37:28 [a] Ex. 30:5 37:29 [a] Ex. 30:23–25 38:1 [a] Ex. 27:1–8 38:8 [a] Ex. 30:18 38:9 [a] Ex. 27:9–19 38:20 [a] Ex. 27:19
38:21 [a] Num. 1:50, 53; 9:15; 10:11; 17:7, 8; 2 Chr. 24:6; Acts 7:44 [b] Num. 4:28, 33 [c] Ex. 28:1; Lev. 10:6, 16 38:22 [a] Ex. 31:2, 6; 1 Chr. 2:18–20
38:23 [a] Ex. 31:6; 36:1 38:24 [a] Ex. 35:5, 22 [b] Ex. 30:13, 24; Lev. 5:15; 27:3, 25; Num. 3:47; 18:16 38:25 [a] Ex. 30:11–16; Num. 1:2
38:26 [a] Ex. 30:13, 15 [b] Ex. 12:37; Num. 1:46; 26:51 38:27 [a] Ex. 26:19, 21, 25, 32 38:28 [a] Ex. 27:17

tabernacle of meeting, the bronze altar, the bronze grating for it, and all the utensils for the altar, 31 the sockets for the court all around, the bases for the court gate, all the pegs for the tabernacle, and all the pegs for the court all around.

### *MAKING THE GARMENTS OF THE PRIESTHOOD*

*(Ex. 28:1–43)*

**39** Of the [a]blue, purple, and scarlet *thread* they made [b]garments of ministry,[1] for ministering in the holy *place,* and made the holy garments for Aaron, [c]as the LORD had commanded Moses.

### *MAKING THE EPHOD*

2 [a]He made the [b]ephod of gold, blue, purple, and scarlet *thread,* and of fine woven linen. 3 And they beat the gold into thin sheets and cut *it into* threads, to work *it* in *with* the blue, purple, and scarlet *thread,* and the fine linen, *into* artistic designs. 4 They made shoulder straps for it to couple *it* together; it was coupled together at its two edges. 5 And the intricately woven band of his ephod that *was* on it *was* of the same workmanship, *woven of* gold, blue, purple, and scarlet *thread,* and *of* fine woven linen, as the LORD had commanded Moses.

6 [a]And they set onyx stones, enclosed in settings of gold; they were engraved, as signets are engraved, with the names of the sons of Israel. 7 He put them on the shoulders of the ephod *as* [a]memorial stones for the sons of Israel, as the LORD had commanded Moses.

### *MAKING THE BREASTPLATE*

8 [a]And he made the breastplate, artistically woven like the workmanship of the ephod, of gold, blue, purple, and scarlet *thread,* and of fine woven linen. 9 They made the breastplate square by doubling it; a span *was* its length and a span its width when doubled. 10 [a]And they set in it four rows of stones: a row with a sardius, a topaz, and an emerald was the first row; 11 the second row, a turquoise, a sapphire, and a diamond; 12 the third row, a jacinth, an agate, and an amethyst; 13 the fourth row, a beryl, an onyx, and a jasper. *They were* enclosed in settings of gold in their mountings. 14 *There were* [a]twelve stones according to the names of the sons of Israel: according to their names, *engraved like* a signet, each one with its own name according to the twelve tribes. 15 And they made chains for the breastplate at the ends, like braided cords of pure gold. 16 They also made two settings of gold and two gold rings, and put the two rings on the two ends of the breastplate. 17 And they put the two braided *chains* of gold in the two rings on the ends of the breastplate. 18 The two ends of the two braided *chains* they fastened in the two settings, and put them on the shoulder straps of the ephod in the front. 19 And they made two rings of gold and put *them* on the two ends of the breastplate, on the edge of it, which *was* on the inward side of the ephod. 20 They made two *other* gold rings and put them on the two shoulder straps, underneath the ephod toward its front, right at the seam above the intricately woven band of the ephod. 21 And they bound the breastplate by means of its rings to the rings of the ephod with a blue cord, so that it would be above the intricately woven band of the ephod, and that the breastplate would not come loose from the ephod, as the LORD had commanded Moses.

### *MAKING THE OTHER PRIESTLY GARMENTS*

22 [a]He made the [b]robe of the ephod of woven work, all of blue. 23 And *there was* an opening in the middle of the robe, like the opening in a coat of mail, *with* a woven binding all around the opening, so that it would not tear. 24 They made on the hem of the robe pomegranates of blue, purple, and scarlet, and of fine woven *linen.* 25 And they made [a]bells of pure gold, and put the bells between the pomegranates on the hem of the robe all around between the pomegranates: 26 a bell and a pomegranate, a bell and a pomegranate, all around the hem of the robe to minister in, as the LORD had commanded Moses.

> **39:24–26** In ancient times, **purple** was worn only by the wealthy. The dye came from a shellfish that lived in the Mediterranean Sea. Preparing it was difficult and expensive. **Scarlet** and **blue** dyes were also very valuable.

27 [a]They made tunics, artistically woven of fine linen, for Aaron and his sons, 28 [a]a turban of fine linen, exquisite hats of fine linen, [b]short trousers of fine woven linen, 29 [a]and a sash of fine woven linen with blue, purple, and scarlet *thread,* made by a weaver, as the LORD had commanded Moses.

30 [a]Then they made the plate of the holy crown of pure gold, and wrote on it an inscription *like* the engraving of a signet:

[b]HOLINESS TO THE LORD.

31 And they tied to it a blue cord, to fasten *it* above on the turban, as the LORD had commanded Moses.

**39:1** [a] Ex. 25:4; 35:23 [b] Ex. 31:10; 35:19 [c] Ex. 28:4 [1] Or *woven garments* **39:2** [a] Ex. 28:6–14 [b] Lev. 8:7 **39:6** [a] Ex. 28:9–11 **39:7** [a] Ex. 28:12, 29; Josh. 4:7 **39:8** [a] Ex. 28:15–30 **39:10** [a] Ex. 28:17 **39:14** [a] Rev. 21:12 **39:22** [a] Ex. 28:31–35 [b] Ex. 29:5; Lev. 8:7 **39:25** [a] Ex. 28:33 **39:27** [a] Ex. 28:39, 40 **39:28** [a] Ex. 28:4, 39; Lev. 8:9; Ezek. 44:18 [b] Ex. 28:42; Lev. 6:10 **39:29** [a] Ex. 28:39 **39:30** [a] Ex. 28:36, 37 [b] Zech. 14:20

### *THE WORK COMPLETED*
*(Ex. 35:10–19)*

32 Thus all the work of the tabernacle of the
tent of meeting was [a]finished. And the children
of Israel did [b]according to all that the LORD
had commanded Moses; so they did. 33 And
they brought the tabernacle to Moses, the tent
and all its furnishings: its clasps, its boards, its
bars, its pillars, and its sockets; 34 the covering
of ram skins dyed red, the covering of badger
skins, and the veil of the covering; 35 the ark of
the Testimony with its poles, and the mercy seat;
36 the table, all its utensils, and the [a]showbread;
37 the pure *gold* lampstand with its lamps (the
lamps set in order), all its utensils, and the oil
for light; 38 the gold altar, the anointing oil, and
the sweet incense; the screen for the tabernacle
door; 39 the bronze altar, its grate of bronze, its
poles, and all its utensils; the laver with its base;
40 the hangings of the court, its pillars and its
sockets, the screen for the court gate, its cords,
and its pegs; all the utensils for the service of
the tabernacle, for the tent of meeting; 41 and the
garments of ministry,[1] to minister in the holy
*place:* the holy garments for Aaron the priest,
and his sons' garments, to minister as priests.
42 According to all that the LORD had com-
manded Moses, so the children of Israel [a]did
all the work. 43 Then Moses looked over all the
work, and indeed they had done it; as the LORD
had commanded, just so they had done it. And
Moses [a]blessed them.

### *THE TABERNACLE ERECTED AND ARRANGED*

**40** Then the LORD [a]spoke to Moses, saying:
2 "On the first day of the [a]first month you
shall set up [b]the tabernacle of the tent of meet-
ing. 3 [a]You shall put in it the ark of the Testimony,
and partition off the ark with the veil. 4 [a]You shall
bring in the table and [b]arrange the things that
are to be set in order on it; [c]and you shall bring
in the lampstand and light its lamps. 5 [a]You shall
also set the altar of gold for the incense before
the ark of the Testimony, and put up the screen
for the door of the tabernacle. 6 Then you shall
set the [a]altar of the burnt offering before the
door of the tabernacle of the tent of meeting.
7 And [a]you shall set the laver between the tab-
ernacle of meeting and the altar, and put water
in it. 8 You shall set up the court all around, and
hang up the screen at the court gate.
9 "And you shall take the anointing oil, and
[a]anoint the tabernacle and all that *is* in it; and
you shall hallow it and all its utensils, and it
shall be holy. 10 You shall [a]anoint the altar of
the burnt offering and all its utensils, and con-
secrate the altar. [b]The altar shall be most holy.
11 And you shall anoint the laver and its base,
and consecrate it.
12 [a]"Then you shall bring Aaron and his sons
to the door of the tabernacle of meeting and
wash them with water. 13 You shall put the holy
[a]garments on Aaron, [b]and anoint him and con-
secrate him, that he may minister to Me as priest.
14 And you shall bring his sons and clothe them
with tunics. 15 You shall anoint them, as you
anointed their father, that they may minister
to Me as priests; for their anointing shall surely
be [a]an everlasting priesthood throughout their
generations."
16 Thus Moses did; according to all that the
LORD had commanded him, so he did.
17 And it came to pass in the first month of
the second year, on the first *day* of the month,
*that* the [a]tabernacle was raised up. 18 So Moses
raised up the tabernacle, fastened its sockets,
set up its boards, put in its bars, and raised up
its pillars. 19 And he spread out the tent over the
tabernacle and put the covering of the tent on
top of it, as the LORD had commanded Moses.
20 He took [a]the Testimony and put *it* into the ark,
inserted the poles through the rings of the ark,
and put the mercy seat on top of the ark. 21 And
he brought the ark into the tabernacle, [a]hung
up the veil of the covering, and partitioned
off the ark of the Testimony, as the LORD had
commanded Moses.
22 [a]He put the table in the tabernacle of meet-
ing, on the north side of the tabernacle, outside
the veil; 23 [a]and he set the bread in order upon it
before the LORD, as the LORD had commanded
Moses. 24 [a]He put the lampstand in the taber-
nacle of meeting, across from the table, on the
south side of the tabernacle; 25 and [a]he lit the
lamps before the LORD, as the LORD had com-
manded Moses. 26 [a]He put the gold altar in the
tabernacle of meeting in front of the veil; 27 [a]and
he burned sweet incense on it, as the LORD had
commanded Moses. 28 [a]He hung up the screen
*at* the door of the tabernacle. 29 [a]And he put the
altar of burnt offering *before* the door of the
tabernacle of the tent of meeting, and [b]offered
upon it the burnt offering and the grain offering,
as the LORD had commanded Moses. 30 [a]He set
the laver between the tabernacle of meeting
and the altar, and put water there for washing;
31 and Moses, Aaron, and his sons would [a]wash
their hands and their feet *with water* from it.
32 Whenever they went into the tabernacle of

39:32 [a] Ex. 40:17 [b] Ex. 25:40; 39:42, 43 39:36 [a] Ex. 23—30 39:41 [1] Or *woven garments* 39:42 [a] Ex. 35:10 39:43 [a] Lev. 9:22, 23; Num. 6:23–26; Josh. 22:6; 2 Sam. 6:18; 1 Kin. 8:14; 2 Chr. 30:27 40:1 [a] Ex. 25:1—31:18 40:2 [a] Ex. 12:2; 13:4 [b] Ex. 26:1, 30; 40:17 40:3 [a] Ex. 26:33; 40:21; Lev. 16:2; Num. 4:5 40:4 [a] Ex. 26:35; 40:22 [b] Ex. 25:30; 40:23 [c] Ex. 40:24, 25 40:5 [a] Ex. 40:26 40:6 [a] Ex. 39:39 40:7 [a] Ex. 30:18; 40:30 40:9 [a] Ex. 30:26; Lev. 8:10 40:10 [a] Ex. 30:26–30 [b] Ex. 29:36, 37 40:12 [a] Ex. 29:4–9; Lev. 8:1–13 40:13 [a] Ex. 29:5; 39:1, 41 [b] [Ex. 28:41]; Lev. 8:12 40:15 [a] Ex. 29:9; Num. 25:13 40:17 [a] Ex. 40:2; Num. 7:1 40:20 [a] Ex. 25:16; Deut. 10:5; 1 Kin. 8:9; 2 Chr. 5:10; Heb. 9:4 40:21 [a] Ex. 26:33 40:22 [a] Ex. 26:35 40:23 [a] Ex. 40:4; Lev. 24:5, 6 40:24 [a] Ex. 26:35 40:25 [a] Ex. 25:37; 30:7, 8; 40:4; Lev. 24:3, 4 40:26 [a] Ex. 30:1, 6; 40:5 40:27 [a] Ex. 30:7 40:28 [a] Ex. 26:36; 40:5 40:29 [a] Ex. 40:6 [b] Ex. 29:38–42 40:30 [a] Ex. 30:18; 40:7 40:31 [a] Ex. 30:19, 20; John 13:8

meeting, and when they came near the altar, they
washed, [a]as the LORD had commanded Moses.
33 [a]And he raised up the court all around the
tabernacle and the altar, and hung up the screen
of the court gate. So Moses [b]finished the work.

### *THE CLOUD AND THE GLORY*

*(Ex. 13:21, 22; Num. 9:15–23)*

34 [a]Then the [b]cloud covered the tabernacle
of meeting, and the [c]glory of the LORD filled the
tabernacle. 35 And Moses [a]was not able to enter
the tabernacle of meeting, because the cloud
rested above it, and the glory of the LORD filled
the tabernacle. 36 [a]Whenever the cloud was taken
up from above the tabernacle, the children of
Israel would go onward in all their journeys.
37 But [a]if the cloud was not taken up, then they
did not journey till the day that it was taken
up. 38 For [a]the cloud of the LORD *was* above the
tabernacle by day, and fire was over it by night,
in the sight of all the house of Israel, throughout
all their journeys.

**40:32** [a] Ex. 30:19 **40:33** [a] Ex. 27:9–18; 40:8 [b] [Heb. 3:2–5] **40:34** [a] Ex. 29:43; Lev. 16:2; Num. 9:15; 2 Chr. 5:13; Is. 6:4 [b] 1 Kin. 8:10, 11 [c] Lev. 9:6, 23 **40:35** [a] [Lev. 16:2]; 1 Kin. 8:11; 2 Chr. 5:13, 14 **40:36** [a] Ex. 13:21, 22; Num. 9:17; Neh. 9:19 **40:37** [a] Num. 9:19–22 **40:38** [a] Ex. 13:21; Num. 9:15; Ps. 78:14; Is. 4:5

*The Third Book of Moses Called*

# LEVITICUS

| AUTHOR | KEY VERSE | READING TIME |
|---|---|---|
| Moses | Leviticus 20:7 | 2 hours 33 minutes |

The Book of Exodus ends with the Hebrews, constructing the tabernacle according to God's plans and then God's glory occupying it. The Book of Leviticus picks up the account there, with Moses receiving instructions for what God wanted proper worship using that tabernacle to be like. The Hebrews had lived in Egypt—a land of false gods—for generations. As a result, they had no idea how to worship the one true God. Proper worship is what God taught them in Leviticus. While God set apart some of His people as a formal priesthood, He set apart all the Hebrews to be a kingdom of priests and a holy nation. In Leviticus, God taught His people how they were to fulfill this priestly calling.

**Occasion:** Moses wrote the Book of Leviticus as a continuation of the Book of Exodus, giving detail about what worship in the tabernacle should look like.

**Main Point:** God's people are to be a holy nation of priests, living differently from the nations around them.

**Big Ideas:** God is holy. God deserves our worship. We are to be holy and worship God because we love Him.

## OUTLINE:

I. The Rules for Offerings (chs. 1–7)
II. The Rules for Priests (chs. 8–10)
III. The Rules for Pure Living (chs. 11–15)
IV. The Day of Atonement (chs. 16–17)
V. More Rules for the People (chs. 18–20)
VI. More Rules for Priests (chs. 21–22)
VII. The Rules for Feasts (chs. 23–25)
VIII. The Blessings and Curses (ch. 26)
IX. The Rules for Vows (ch. 27)

**c. 1779 BC**
Earliest evidence of spoke wheel

**c. 1730 BC**
The Israelites are enslaved in Egypt

**c. 1660 BC**
Horses are used in Nubia in southern Egypt

**c. 1600 BC**
Beginning of the Shang Dynasty in China

**c. 1527 BC**
Moses is born

**c. 1487 BC**
Moses flees Egypt for Midian

**c. 1446 BC**
Moses leads the Israelites out of Egypt

**c. 1445 BC**
The Law is given on Mount Sinai

**c. 1444–1406 BC**
**Leviticus written**

**c. 1406 BC**
Forty years of wilderness wandering end

**c. 1405–1400 BC**
The conquest of Canaan

**c. 1400 BC**
Mycenaean Greeks invade Crete, destroying the palace at Knossos

### *THE BURNT OFFERING*

**1** Now the LORD [a]called to Moses, and spoke to him [b]from the tabernacle of meeting, saying, 2 "Speak to the children of Israel, and say to them: [a]'When any one of you brings an offering to the LORD, you shall bring your offering of the livestock—of the herd and of the flock.

3 'If his offering *is* a burnt sacrifice of the herd, let him offer a male [a]without blemish; he shall offer it of his own free will at the door of the tabernacle of meeting before the LORD. 4 [a]Then he shall put his hand on the head of the burnt offering, and it will be [b]accepted on his behalf [c]to make atonement for him. 5 He shall kill the [a]bull before the LORD; [b]and the priests, Aaron's sons, shall bring the blood [c]and sprinkle the blood all around on the altar that *is by* the door of the tabernacle of meeting. 6 And he shall [a]skin the burnt offering and cut it into its pieces. 7 The sons of Aaron the priest shall put [a]fire on the altar, and [b]lay the wood in order on the fire. 8 Then the priests, Aaron's sons, shall lay the parts, the head, and the fat in order on the wood that *is* on the fire upon the altar; 9 but he shall wash its entrails and its legs with water. And the priest shall burn all on the altar as a burnt sacrifice, an offering made by fire, a [a]sweet aroma to the LORD.

> **1:1–4** The animal being sacrificed represented the person who was offering it to God. The death of the animal was payment for the person's sins. Touching the animal on the head was one of many symbolic gestures included in the sacrifice.

10 'If his offering *is* of the flocks—of the sheep or of the goats—as a burnt sacrifice, he shall bring a male [a]without blemish. 11 [a]He shall kill it on the north side of the altar before the LORD; and the priests, Aaron's sons, shall sprinkle its blood all around on the altar. 12 And he shall cut it into its pieces, with its head and its fat; and the priest shall lay them in order on the wood that *is* on the fire upon the altar; 13 but he shall wash the entrails and the legs with water. Then the priest shall bring *it* all and burn *it* on the altar; it *is* a burnt sacrifice, an [a]offering made by fire, a sweet aroma to the LORD.

14 'And if the burnt sacrifice of his offering to the LORD *is* of birds, then he shall bring his offering of [a]turtledoves or young pigeons. 15 The priest shall bring it to the altar, wring off its head, and burn *it* on the altar; its blood shall be drained out at the side of the altar. 16 And he shall remove its crop with its feathers and cast it [a]beside the altar on the east side, into the place for ashes. 17 Then he shall split it at its wings, *but* [a]shall not divide *it* completely; and the priest shall burn it on the altar, on the wood that *is* on the fire. [b]It *is* a burnt sacrifice, an offering made by fire, a sweet aroma to the LORD.

### *THE GRAIN OFFERING*

**2** 'When anyone offers [a]a grain offering to the LORD, his offering shall be *of* fine flour. And he shall pour oil on it, and put [b]frankincense on it. 2 He shall bring it to Aaron's sons, the priests, one of whom shall take from it his handful of fine flour and oil with all the frankincense. And the priest shall burn [a]*it as* a memorial on the altar, an offering made by fire, a sweet aroma to the LORD. 3 [a]The rest of the grain offering *shall be* Aaron's and his [b]sons'. [c]*It is* most holy of the offerings to the LORD made by fire.

4 'And if you bring as an offering a grain offering baked in the oven, *it shall be* unleavened cakes of fine flour mixed with oil, or unleavened wafers [a]anointed with oil. 5 But if your offering *is* a grain offering *baked* in a pan, *it shall be of* fine flour, unleavened, mixed with oil. 6 You shall break it in pieces and pour oil on it; it *is* a grain offering.

7 'If your offering *is* a grain offering *baked* in a [a]covered pan, it shall be made *of* fine flour with oil. 8 You shall bring the grain offering that is made of these things to the LORD. And when it is presented to the priest, he shall bring it to the altar. 9 Then the priest shall take from the grain offering [a]a memorial portion, and burn *it* on the altar. *It is* an [b]offering made by fire, a sweet aroma to the LORD. 10 And [a]what is left of the grain offering *shall be* Aaron's and his sons'. *It is* most holy of the offerings to the LORD made by fire.

11 'No grain offering which you bring to the LORD shall be made with [a]leaven, for you shall burn no leaven nor any honey in any offering to the LORD made by fire. 12 [a]As for the offering of the firstfruits, you shall offer them to the LORD, but they shall not be burned on the altar for a sweet aroma. 13 And every offering of your grain offering [a]you shall season with salt; you shall not allow [b]the salt of the covenant of your God to be lacking from your grain offering. [c]With all your offerings you shall offer salt.

14 'If you offer a grain offering of your firstfruits to the LORD, [a]you shall offer for the grain offering of your firstfruits green heads of grain roasted on the fire, grain beaten from [b]full heads. 15 And [a]you shall put oil on it, and lay

**1:1** [a] Ex. 19:3; 25:22 [b] Ex. 40:34 **1:2** [a] Lev. 22:18, 19 **1:3** [a] Eph. 5:27 **1:4** [a] Lev. 3:2, 8, 13; 4:15 [b] [Rom. 12:1] [c] 2 Chr. 29:23, 24 **1:5** [a] Mic. 6:6 [b] 2 Chr. 35:11 [c] [Heb. 12:24] **1:6** [a] Lev. 7:8 **1:7** [a] Mal. 1:10 [b] Gen. 22:9 **1:9** [a] Gen. 8:21 **1:10** [a] Lev. 1:3 **1:11** [a] Lev. 1:5 **1:13** [a] Num. 15:4–7; 28:12–14 **1:14** [a] Lev. 5:7, 11; 12:8 **1:16** [a] Lev. 6:10 **1:17** [a] Gen. 15:10; Lev. 5:8 [b] Lev. 1:9, 13 **2:1** [a] Lev. 6:14; 9:17; Num. 15:4 [b] Lev. 5:11 **2:2** [a] Lev. 2:9; 5:12; 6:15; 24:7; Acts 10:4 **2:3** [a] Lev. 7:9 [b] Lev. 6:6; 10:12, 13 [c] Ex. 29:37; Num. 18:9 **2:4** [a] Ex. 29:2 **2:7** [a] Lev. 7:9 **2:9** [a] Lev. 2:2, 16; 5:12; 6:15 [b] Ex. 29:18 **2:10** [a] Lev. 2:3; 6:16 **2:11** [a] Ex. 23:18; 34:25; Lev. 6:16, 17; [Matt. 16:12; Mark 8:15; Luke 12:1; 1 Cor. 5:8; Gal. 5:9] **2:12** [a] Ex. 22:29; 34:22; Lev. 23:10, 11, 17, 18 **2:13** [a] [Mark 9:49, 50; Col. 4:6] [b] Num. 18:19; 2 Chr. 13:5 [c] Ezek. 43:24 **2:14** [a] Lev. 23:10, 14 [b] 2 Kin. 4:42 **2:15** [a] Lev. 2:1

## CHRIST IN THE LEVITICAL SACRIFICES

| Offering | Reference | Meaning |
|---|---|---|
| **The Burnt Offering** | Leviticus 1 | Christ offering Himself to the Father in complete obedience and dedication |
| **The Grain Offering** | Leviticus 2 | The pure, beautiful aroma of Christ's perfect life offered |
| **The Peace Offering** | Leviticus 3 | The reconciliation accomplished by Christ's work on the cross |
| **The Sin Offering** | Leviticus 4 | The atoning nature of Christ's sacrifice to save people |
| **The Trespass Offering** | Leviticus 5 | The atoning nature of Christ's sacrifice to save people |

frankincense on it. It *is* a grain offering. 16 Then the priest shall burn [a]the memorial portion: *part* of its beaten grain and *part* of its oil, with all the frankincense, as an offering made by fire to the LORD.

### THE PEACE OFFERING

**3** 'When his offering *is* a [a]sacrifice of a peace offering, if he offers *it* of the herd, whether male or female, he shall offer it [b]without blemish before the LORD. 2 And [a]he shall lay his hand on the head of his offering, and kill it *at* the door of the tabernacle of meeting; and Aaron's sons, the priests, shall [b]sprinkle the blood all around on the altar. 3 Then he shall offer from the sacrifice of the peace offering an offering made by fire to the LORD. [a]The fat that covers the entrails and all the fat that *is* on the entrails, 4 the two kidneys and the fat that *is* on them by the flanks, and the fatty lobe *attached* to the liver above the kidneys, he shall remove; 5 and Aaron's sons [a]shall burn it on the altar upon the [b]burnt sacrifice, which *is* on the wood that *is* on the fire, *as* an [c]offering made by fire, a [d]sweet aroma to the LORD.

6 'If his offering as a sacrifice of a peace offering to the LORD *is* of the flock, *whether* male or female, [a]he shall offer it without blemish. 7 If he offers a [a]lamb as his offering, then he shall [b]offer it [c]before the LORD. 8 And he shall lay his hand on the head of his offering, and kill it before the tabernacle of meeting; and Aaron's sons shall sprinkle its blood all around on the altar.

9 'Then he shall offer from the sacrifice of the peace offering, as an offering made by fire to the LORD, its fat *and* the whole fat tail which he shall remove close to the backbone. And the fat that covers the entrails and all the fat that *is* on the entrails, 10 the two kidneys and the fat that *is* on them by the flanks, and the fatty lobe *attached* to the liver above the kidneys, he shall remove; 11 and the priest shall burn *them* on the altar *as* [a]food, an offering made by fire to the LORD.

12 'And if his [a]offering *is* a goat, then [b]he shall offer it before the LORD. 13 He shall lay his hand on its head and kill it before the tabernacle of meeting; and the sons of Aaron shall sprinkle its blood all around on the altar. 14 Then he shall offer from it his offering, as an offering made by fire to the LORD. The fat that covers the entrails and all the fat that *is* on the entrails, 15 the two kidneys and the fat that *is* on them by the flanks, and the fatty lobe *attached* to the liver above the kidneys, he shall remove; 16 and the priest shall burn them on the altar *as* food, an offering made by fire for a sweet aroma; [a]all the fat *is* the LORD's.

17 '*This shall be* a [a]perpetual statute throughout your generations in all your dwellings: you shall eat neither fat nor [b]blood.' "

### THE SIN OFFERING

**4** Now the LORD spoke to Moses, saying, 2 "Speak to the children of Israel, saying: [a]'If a person sins unintentionally against any of the commandments of the LORD *in anything* which ought not to be done, and does any of them, 3 [a]if the anointed priest sins, bringing guilt on the people, then let him offer to the LORD for his sin which he has sinned [b]a young bull without blemish as a [c]sin offering. 4 He shall bring the bull [a]to the door of the tabernacle of meeting before the LORD, lay his hand on the bull's head, and kill the bull before the LORD. 5 Then the anointed priest [a]shall take some of the bull's blood and bring it to the tabernacle of meeting. 6 The priest shall dip his finger in the blood and sprinkle some of the blood seven times before the LORD, in front of the [a]veil of the sanctuary. 7 And the priest shall [a]put some of the blood on the horns of the altar of sweet incense before the LORD, which is in the tabernacle of meeting; and he shall pour [b]the remaining blood of the bull at the base of the altar of the burnt offering, which is at the door of the tabernacle of meeting. 8 He shall take from it all the fat of the bull as the sin offering. The fat that covers the entrails and all the fat which *is* on the

**2:16** [a] Lev. 2:2 **3:1** [a] Lev. 7:11, 29 [b] Lev. 1:3; 22:20–24 **3:2** [a] Ex. 29:10, 11, 16, 20; Lev. 1:4, 5; 16:21 [b] Lev. 1:5 **3:3** [a] Ex. 29:13, 22; Lev. 1:8; 3:16; 4:8, 9 **3:5** [a] Ex. 29:13; Lev. 6:12; 7:28–34 [b] 2 Chr. 35:14 [c] Num. 28:3–10 [d] Num. 15:8–10 **3:6** [a] Lev. 3:1; 22:20–24 **3:7** [a] Num. 15:4, 5 [b] 1 Kin. 8:62 [c] Lev. 17:8, 9 **3:11** [a] Lev. 21:6, 8, 17, 21, 22; 22:25; Num. 28:2; [Ezek. 44:7; Mal. 1:7, 12] **3:12** [a] Num. 15:6–11 [b] Lev. 3:1, 7 **3:16** [a] Lev. 7:23–25; 1 Sam. 2:15; 2 Chr. 7:7 **3:17** [a] Lev. 6:18; 7:36; 17:7; 23:14 [b] Gen. 9:4; Lev. 7:23, 26; 17:10, 14; 1 Sam. 14:33 **4:2** [a] Lev. 5:15–18; Num. 15:22–30; 1 Sam. 14:27; Acts 3:17 **4:3** [a] Ex. 40:15; Lev. 8:12 [b] Lev. 3:1; 9:2 [c] Lev. 9:7 **4:4** [a] Lev. 1:3, 4; 4:15; Num. 8:12 **4:5** [a] Lev. 16:14; Num. 19:4 **4:6** [a] Ex. 40:21, 26 **4:7** [a] Lev. 4:18, 25, 30, 34; 8:15; 9:9; 16:18 [b] Ex. 40:5, 6; Lev. 5:9

entrails, 9 the two kidneys and the fat that *is* on them by the flanks, and the fatty lobe *attached* to the liver above the kidneys, he shall remove, 10 [a]as it was taken from the bull of the sacrifice of the peace offering; and the priest shall burn them on the altar of the burnt offering. 11 [a]But the bull's hide and all its flesh, with its head and legs, its entrails and offal— 12 the whole bull he shall carry outside the camp to a clean place, [a]where the ashes are poured out, and [b]burn it on wood with fire; where the ashes are poured out it shall be burned.

13 'Now [a]if the whole congregation of Israel sins unintentionally, [b]and the thing is hidden from the eyes of the assembly, and they have done *something against* any of the commandments of the LORD *in anything* which should not be done, and are guilty; 14 when the sin which they have committed becomes known, then the assembly shall offer a young bull for the sin, and bring it before the tabernacle of meeting. 15 And the elders of the congregation [a]shall lay their hands on the head of the bull before the LORD. Then the bull shall be killed before the LORD. 16 [a]The anointed priest shall bring some of the bull's blood to the tabernacle of meeting. 17 Then the priest shall dip his finger in the blood and sprinkle *it* seven times before the LORD, in front of the veil. 18 And he shall put *some* of the blood on the horns of the altar which *is* before the LORD, which *is* in the tabernacle of meeting; and he shall pour the remaining blood at the base of the altar of burnt offering, which is at the door of the tabernacle of meeting. 19 He shall take all the fat from it and burn *it* on the altar. 20 And he shall do [a]with the bull as he did with the bull as a sin offering; thus he shall do with it. [b]So the priest shall make atonement for them, and it shall be forgiven them. 21 Then he shall carry the bull outside the camp, and burn it as he burned the first bull. It *is* a sin offering for the assembly.

22 'When a ruler has sinned, and [a]done *something* unintentionally *against* any of the commandments of the LORD his God *in anything* which should not be done, and is guilty, 23 or [a]if his sin which he has committed comes to his knowledge, he shall bring as his offering a kid of the goats, a male without blemish. 24 And [a]he shall lay his hand on the head of the goat, and kill it at the place where they kill the burnt offering before the LORD. It *is* a sin offering. 25 [a]The priest shall take some of the blood of the sin offering with his finger, put *it* on the horns of the altar of burnt offering, and pour its blood at the base of the altar of burnt offering. 26 And he shall burn all its fat on the altar, like [a]the fat of the sacrifice of the peace offering. [b]So the priest shall make atonement for him concerning his sin, and it shall be forgiven him.

27 [a]'If anyone of the common people sins unintentionally by doing *something against* any of the commandments of the LORD *in anything* which ought not to be done, and is guilty, 28 or [a]if his sin which he has committed comes to his knowledge, then he shall bring as his offering a kid of the goats, a female without blemish, for his sin which he has committed. 29 [a]And he shall lay his hand on the head of the sin offering, and kill the sin offering at the place of the burnt offering. 30 Then the priest shall take *some* of its blood with his finger, put *it* on the horns of the altar of burnt offering, and pour all *the remaining* blood at the base of the altar. 31 [a]He shall remove all its fat, [b]as fat is removed from the sacrifice of the peace offering; and the priest shall burn it on the altar for a [c]sweet aroma to the LORD. [d]So the priest shall make atonement for him, and it shall be forgiven him.

32 'If he brings a lamb as his sin offering, [a]he shall bring a female without blemish. 33 Then he shall [a]lay his hand on the head of the sin offering, and kill it as a sin offering at the place where they kill the burnt offering. 34 The priest shall take *some* of the blood of the sin offering with his finger, put *it* on the horns of the altar of burnt offering, and pour all *the remaining* blood at the base of the altar. 35 He shall remove all its fat, as the fat of the lamb is removed from the sacrifice of the peace offering. Then the priest shall burn it on the altar, [a]according to the offerings made by fire to the LORD. [b]So the priest shall make atonement for his sin that he has committed, and it shall be forgiven him.

### *THE TRESPASS OFFERING*

**5** 'If a person sins in [a]hearing the utterance of an oath, and *is* a witness, whether he has seen or known *of the matter*—if he does not tell *it*, he [b]bears guilt.

2 'Or [a]if a person touches any unclean thing, whether *it is* the carcass of an unclean beast, or the carcass of unclean livestock, or the carcass of unclean creeping things, and he is unaware of it, he also shall be unclean and [b]guilty. 3 Or if he touches [a]human uncleanness—whatever uncleanness with which a man may be defiled, and he is unaware of it—when he realizes *it*, then he shall be guilty.

4 'Or if a person swears, speaking thoughtlessly with *his* lips [a]to do evil or [b]to do good, whatever *it is* that a man may pronounce by an oath, and he is unaware of it—when he realizes *it*, then he shall be guilty in any of these *matters*.

**4:10** [a] Lev. 3:3–5 **4:11** [a] Ex. 29:14; Lev. 9:11; Num. 19:5 **4:12** [a] Lev. 4:21; 6:10, 11; 16:27 [b] [Heb. 13:11, 12] **4:13** [a] Num. 15:24–26; Josh. 7:11 [b] Lev. 5:2–4, 17 **4:15** [a] Lev. 1:3, 4 **4:16** [a] Lev. 4:5; [Heb. 9:12–14] **4:20** [a] Lev. 4:3 [b] Num. 15:25 **4:22** [a] Lev. 4:2, 13, 27 **4:23** [a] Lev. 4:14; 5:4 **4:24** [a] Lev. 4:4; [Is. 53:6] **4:25** [a] Lev. 4:7, 18, 30, 34 **4:26** [a] Lev. 3:3–5 [b] Lev. 4:20; Num. 15:28 **4:27** [a] Lev. 4:2; Num. 15:27 **4:28** [a] Lev. 4:23 **4:29** [a] Lev. 1:4; 4:4, 24 **4:31** [a] Lev. 3:14 [b] Lev. 3:3, 4 [c] Gen. 8:21; Ex. 29:18; Lev. 1:9, 13; 2:2, 9, 12 [d] Lev. 4:26 **4:32** [a] Lev. 4:28 **4:33** [a] Lev. 1:4; Num. 8:12 **4:35** [a] Lev. 3:5 [b] Lev. 4:26, 31 **5:1** [a] Prov. 29:24; [Jer. 23:10] [b] Lev. 5:17; 7:18; 17:16; 19:8; 20:17; Num. 9:13 **5:2** [a] Lev. 11:24, 28, 31, 39; Num. 19:11–16; Deut. 14:8 [b] Lev. 5:17 **5:3** [a] Lev. 5:12, 13, 15 **5:4** [a] 1 Sam. 25:22; Acts 23:12 [b] [Matt. 5:33–37]; Mark 6:23; [James 5:12]

5 ‘And it shall be, when he is guilty in any
of these *matters*, that he shall [a]confess that he
has sinned in that *thing;* 6 and he shall bring his
trespass offering to the LORD for his sin which he
has committed, a female from the flock, a lamb
or a kid of the goats as a sin offering. So the priest
shall make atonement for him concerning his sin.
7 [a]‘If he is not able to bring a lamb, then he
shall bring to the LORD, for his trespass which he
has committed, two [b]turtledoves or two young
pigeons: one as a sin offering and the other as a
burnt offering. 8 And he shall bring them to the
priest, who shall offer *that* which *is* for the sin
offering first, and [a]wring off its head from its
neck, but shall not divide *it* completely. 9 Then
he shall sprinkle *some* of the blood of the sin
offering on the side of the altar, and the [a]rest
of the blood shall be drained out at the base of
the altar. It *is* a sin offering. 10 And he shall offer
the second *as* a burnt offering according to the
[a]prescribed manner. So [b]the priest shall make
atonement on his behalf for his sin which he
has committed, and it shall be forgiven him.
11 ‘But if he is [a]not able to bring two turtledoves
or two young pigeons, then he who sinned shall
bring for his offering one-tenth of an ephah of fine
flour as a sin offering. [b]He shall put no oil on it,
nor shall he put frankincense on it, for it *is* a sin
offering. 12 Then he shall bring it to the priest, and
the priest shall take his handful of it [a]as a memo-
rial portion, and burn *it* on the altar [b]according
to the offerings made by fire to the LORD. It *is* a
sin offering. 13 [a]The priest shall make atonement
for him, for his sin that he has committed in any
of these matters; and it shall be forgiven him.
[b]*The rest* shall be the priest’s as a grain offering.’ ”

### *OFFERINGS WITH RESTITUTION*

14 Then the LORD spoke to Moses, saying:
15 [a]“If a person commits a trespass, and sins
unintentionally in regard to the holy things of
the LORD, then [b]he shall bring to the LORD as
his trespass offering a ram without blemish
from the flocks, with your valuation in shekels
of silver according to [c]the shekel of the sanctu-
ary, as a trespass offering. 16 And he shall make
restitution for the harm that he has done in
regard to the holy thing, [a]and shall add one-fifth
to it and give it to the priest. [b]So the priest shall
make atonement for him with the ram of the
trespass offering, and it shall be forgiven him.
17 “If a person sins, and commits any of these
things which are forbidden to be done by the
commandments of the LORD, [a]though he does
not know *it*, yet he is [b]guilty and shall bear his
iniquity. 18 [a]And he shall bring to the priest a ram

> **5:17** Ignorance doesn’t make an offense harmless. The offender was still guilty and bore responsibility for his or her sin.

without blemish from the flock, with your valu-
ation, as a trespass offering. So the priest shall
make atonement for him regarding his ignorance
in which he erred and did not know *it*, and it
shall be forgiven him. 19 It is a trespass offering;
[a]he has certainly trespassed against the LORD.”

**6** And the LORD spoke to Moses, saying: 2 “If a
person sins and [a]commits a trespass against
the LORD by [b]lying to his neighbor about [c]what
was delivered to him for safekeeping, or about a
pledge, or about a robbery, or if he has [d]extorted
from his neighbor, 3 or if he [a]has found what was
lost and lies concerning it, and [b]swears falsely—
in any one of these things that a man may do in
which he sins: 4 then it shall be, because he has
sinned and is guilty, that he shall restore [a]what
he has stolen, or the thing which he has extorted,
or what was delivered to him for safekeeping, or
the lost thing which he found, 5 or all that about
which he has sworn falsely. He shall [a]restore its
full value, add one-fifth more to it, *and* give it to
whomever it belongs, on the day of his trespass
offering. 6 And he shall bring his trespass offering
to the LORD, [a]a ram without blemish from the
flock, with your valuation, as a trespass offering,
to the priest. 7 [a]So the priest shall make atone-
ment for him before the LORD, and he shall be
forgiven for any one of these things that he may
have done in which he trespasses.”

### *THE LAW OF THE BURNT OFFERING*

8 Then the LORD spoke to Moses, saying,
9 “Command Aaron and his sons, saying, ‘This *is*
the [a]law of the burnt offering: The burnt offering
*shall be* on the hearth upon the altar all night
until morning, and the fire of the altar shall be
kept burning on it. 10 [a]And the priest shall put
on his linen garment, and his linen trousers he
shall put on his body, and take up the ashes of
the burnt offering which the fire has consumed
on the altar, and he shall put them [b]beside the
altar. 11 Then [a]he shall take off his garments, put
on other garments, and carry the ashes outside
the camp [b]to a clean place. 12 And the fire on the
altar shall be kept burning on it; it shall not be
put out. And the priest shall burn wood on it
every morning, and lay the burnt offering in
order on it; and he shall burn on it [a]the fat of the
peace offerings. 13 A fire shall always be burning
on the [a]altar; it shall never go out.

**5:5** [a] Lev. 16:21; 26:40; Num. 5:7; Ezra 10:11, 12; Ps. 32:5; Prov. 28:13 **5:7** [a] Lev. 12:6, 8; 14:21 [b] Lev. 1:14 **5:8** [a] Lev. 1:15–17 **5:9** [a] Lev. 4:7, 18, 30, 34 **5:10** [a] Lev. 1:14–17 [b] Lev. 4:20, 26; 5:13, 16 **5:11** [a] Lev. 14:21–32 [b] Lev. 2:1, 2; 6:15; Num. 5:15 **5:12** [a] Lev. 2:2 [b] Lev. 4:35 **5:13** [a] Lev. 4:26 [b] Lev. 2:3; 6:17, 26 **5:15** [a] Lev. 4:2; 22:14; Num. 5:5–8 [b] Ezra 10:19 [c] Ex. 30:13; Lev. 27:25 **5:16** [a] Lev. 6:5; 22:14; 27:13, 15, 27, 31; Num. 5:7 [b] Lev. 4:26 **5:17** [a] Lev. 4:2, 13, 22, 27 [b] Lev. 5:1, 2 **5:18** [a] Lev. 5:15 **5:19** [a] Ezra 10:2 **6:2** [a] Num. 5:6 [b] Lev. 19:11; Acts 5:4; Col. 3:9 [c] Ex. 22:7, 10 [d] Prov. 24:28 **6:3** [a] Ex. 23:4; Deut. 22:1–4 [b] Ex. 22:11; Lev. 19:12; Jer. 7:9; Zech. 5:4 **6:4** [a] Lev. 24:18, 21 **6:5** [a] Lev. 5:16; Num. 5:7, 8; 2 Sam. 12:6 **6:6** [a] Lev. 1:3; 5:15 **6:7** [a] Lev. 4:26 **6:9** [a] Ex. 29:38–42; Num. 28:3–10 **6:10** [a] Ex. 28:39–43; Lev. 16:4; Ezek. 44:17, 18 [b] Lev. 1:16 **6:11** [a] Ezek. 44:19 [b] Lev. 4:12 **6:12** [a] Lev. 3:3, 5, 9, 14 **6:13** [a] Lev. 1:7

### THE LAW OF THE GRAIN OFFERING

14 'This *is* the law of the grain offering: The
sons of Aaron shall offer it on the altar before
the LORD. 15 He shall take from it his handful of
the fine flour of the grain offering, with its oil,
and all the frankincense which *is* on the grain
offering, and shall burn *it* on the altar *for* a sweet
aroma, as a memorial to the LORD. 16 And the
remainder of it Aaron and his sons shall eat;
with unleavened bread it shall be eaten in a
holy place; in the court of the tabernacle of
meeting they shall eat it. 17 It shall not be baked
with leaven. I have given it *as* their portion
of My offerings made by fire; it *is* most holy,
like the sin offering and the [a]trespass offering.
18 [a]All the males among the children of Aaron
may eat it. [b]*It shall be* a statute forever in your
generations concerning the offerings made by
fire to the LORD. [c]Everyone who touches them
must be holy.' "[1]
19 And the LORD spoke to Moses, saying,
20 [a]"This *is* the offering of Aaron and his sons,
which they shall offer to the LORD, *beginning*
on the day when he is anointed: one-tenth of
an [b]ephah of fine flour as a daily grain offering,
half of it in the morning and half of it at night.
21 It shall be made in a [a]pan with oil. *When it is*
mixed, you shall bring it in. The baked pieces
of the grain offering you shall offer *for* a sweet
aroma to the LORD. 22 The priest from among his
sons, [a]who is anointed in his place, shall offer
it. *It is* a statute forever to the LORD. [b]It shall
be wholly burned. 23 For every grain offering
for the priest shall be wholly burned. It shall
not be eaten."

### THE LAW OF THE SIN OFFERING

24 Also the LORD spoke to Moses, saying,
25 "Speak to Aaron and to his sons, saying, 'This
*is* the law of the sin offering: [a]In the place where
the burnt offering is killed, the sin offering
shall be killed before the LORD. It *is* most holy.
26 [a]The priest who offers it for sin shall eat it. In
a holy place it shall be eaten, in the court of the
tabernacle of meeting. 27 [a]Everyone who touches
its flesh must be holy.[1] And when its blood is
sprinkled on any garment, you shall wash that
on which it was sprinkled, in a holy place. 28 But
the earthen vessel in which it is boiled [a]shall be
broken. And if it is boiled in a bronze pot, it shall
be both scoured and rinsed in water. 29 All the
males among the priests may eat it. It *is* most
holy. 30 [a]But no sin offering from which *any*
of the blood is brought into the tabernacle of
meeting, to make atonement in the holy [b]*place*,[1]
shall be [c]eaten. It shall be [d]burned in the fire.

### THE LAW OF THE TRESPASS OFFERING

7 'Likewise [a]this *is* the law of the trespass of-
fering (it *is* most holy): 2 In the place where
they kill the burnt offering they shall kill the
trespass offering. And its blood he shall sprinkle
all around on the altar. 3 And he shall offer from
it all its fat. The fat tail and the fat that covers the
entrails, 4 the two kidneys and the fat that *is* on
them by the flanks, and the fatty lobe *attached*
to the liver above the kidneys, he shall remove;
5 and the priest shall burn them on the altar *as*
an offering made by fire to the LORD. It *is* a tres-
pass offering. 6 [a]Every male among the priests
may eat it. It shall be eaten in a holy place. [b]It
*is* most holy. 7 [a]The trespass offering *is* like the
sin offering; *there is* one law for them both: the
priest who makes atonement with it shall have
*it*. 8 And the priest who offers anyone's burnt
offering, that priest shall have for himself the
skin of the burnt offering which he has offered.
9 Also [a]every grain offering that is baked in the
oven and all that is prepared in the covered pan,
or in a pan, shall be the priest's who offers it.
10 Every grain offering, *whether* mixed with oil
or dry, shall belong to all the sons of Aaron, to
one *as much* as the other.

### THE LAW OF PEACE OFFERINGS

11 [a]'This *is* the law of the sacrifice of peace
offerings which he shall offer to the LORD: 12 If
he offers it for a thanksgiving, then he shall
offer, with the sacrifice of thanksgiving, unleav-
ened cakes mixed with oil, unleavened wafers
[a]anointed with oil, or cakes of blended flour
mixed with oil. 13 Besides the cakes, *as* his of-
fering he shall offer [a]leavened bread with the
sacrifice of thanksgiving of his peace offering.
14 And from it he shall offer one cake from each
offering *as* a heave offering to the LORD. [a]It shall
belong to the priest who sprinkles the blood of
the peace offering.
15 [a]'The flesh of the sacrifice of his peace
offering for thanksgiving shall be eaten the
same day it is offered. He shall not leave any
of it until morning. 16 But [a]if the sacrifice of
his offering *is* a vow or a voluntary offering, it
shall be eaten the same day that he offers his
sacrifice; but on the next day the remainder
of it also may be eaten; 17 the remainder of the
flesh of the sacrifice on the third day must be
burned with fire. 18 And if *any* of the flesh of the
sacrifice of his peace offering is eaten at all on
the third day, it shall not be accepted, nor shall it
be [a]imputed to him; it shall be an [b]abomination
*to* him who offers it, and the person who eats
of it shall bear guilt.

**6:17** [a] Lev. 7:7 **6:18** [a] Lev. 6:29; 7:6; Num. 18:10; 1 Cor. 9:13 [b] Lev. 3:17 [c] Ex. 29:37; Lev. 22:3–7; Num. 4:15; Hag. 2:11–13 [1] Compare Numbers 4:15 and Haggai 2:11–13 **6:20** [a] Ex. 29:2 [b] Ex. 16:36 **6:21** [a] Lev. 2:5; 7:9 **6:22** [a] Lev. 4:3 [b] Ex. 29:25 **6:25** [a] Lev. 1:1, 3, 5, 11 **6:26** [a] [Lev. 10:17, 18]; Num. 18:9, 10; [Ezek. 44:28, 29] **6:27** [a] Ex. 29:37; Num. 4:15; Hag. 2:11–13 [1] Compare Numbers 4:15 and Haggai 2:11–13 **6:28** [a] Lev. 11:33; 15:12 **6:30** [a] Lev. 4:7, 11, 12, 18, 21; 10:18; 16:27; [Heb. 13:11, 12] [b] Ex. 26:33 [c] Lev. 6:16, 23, 26 [d] Lev. 16:27 [1] The Most Holy Place when capitalized **7:1** [a] Lev. 5:14—6:7 **7:6** [a] Lev. 6:16–18, 29; Num. 18:9 [b] Lev. 2:3 **7:7** [a] Lev. 6:24–30; 14:13 **7:9** [a] Lev. 2:3, 10; Num. 18:9; Ezek. 44:29 **7:11** [a] Lev. 3:1; 22:18, 21; Ezek. 45:15 **7:12** [a] Lev. 2:4; Num. 6:15 **7:13** [a] Lev. 2:12; 23:17, 18; Amos 4:5 **7:14** [a] Num. 18:8, 11, 19 **7:15** [a] Lev. 22:29, 30 **7:16** [a] Lev. 19:5–8 **7:18** [a] Num. 18:27 [b] Lev. 11:10, 11, 41; 19:7; [Prov. 15:8]

19 'The flesh that touches any unclean thing shall not be eaten. It shall be burned with fire. And as for the *clean* flesh, all who are clean may eat of it. 20 But the person who eats the flesh of the sacrifice of the peace offering that *belongs* to the [a]LORD, [b]while he is unclean, that person [c]shall be cut off from his people. 21 Moreover the person who touches any unclean thing, *such as* [a]human uncleanness, *an* [b]unclean animal, or any [c]abominable unclean thing,[1] and who eats the flesh of the sacrifice of the peace offering that *belongs* to the LORD, that person [d]shall be cut off from his people.' "

### FAT AND BLOOD MAY NOT BE EATEN

22 And the LORD spoke to Moses, saying, 23 "Speak to the children of Israel, saying: [a]'You shall not eat any fat, of ox or sheep or goat. 24 And the fat of an animal that dies *naturally*, and the fat of what is torn by wild beasts, may be used in any other way; but you shall by no means eat it. 25 For whoever eats the fat of the animal of which men offer an offering made by fire to the LORD, the person who eats *it* shall be cut off from his people. 26 [a]Moreover you shall not eat any blood in any of your dwellings, *whether* of bird or beast. 27 Whoever eats any blood, that person shall be cut off from his people.' "

### THE PORTION OF AARON AND HIS SONS

28 Then the LORD spoke to Moses, saying, 29 "Speak to the children of Israel, saying: [a]'He who offers the sacrifice of his peace offering to the LORD shall bring his offering to the LORD from the sacrifice of his peace offering. 30 [a]His own hands shall bring the offerings made by fire to the LORD. The fat with the breast he shall bring, that the [b]breast may be waved *as* a wave offering before the LORD. 31 [a]And the priest shall burn the fat on the altar, but the [b]breast shall be Aaron's and his sons'. 32 [a]Also the right thigh you shall give to the priest *as* a heave offering from the sacrifices of your peace offerings. 33 He among the sons of Aaron, who offers the blood of the peace offering and the fat, shall have the right thigh for *his* part. 34 For [a]the breast of the wave offering and the thigh of the heave offering I have taken from the children of Israel, from the sacrifices of their peace offerings, and I have given them to Aaron the priest and to his sons from the children of Israel by a statute forever.' "

35 This *is* the consecrated portion for Aaron and his sons, from the offerings made by fire to the LORD, on the day when *Moses* presented them to minister to the LORD as priests. 36 The LORD commanded this to be given to them by the children of Israel, [a]on the day that He anointed them, *by* a statute forever throughout their generations.

37 This *is* the law [a]of the burnt offering, [b]the grain offering, [c]the sin offering, [d]the trespass offering, [e]the consecrations, and [f]the sacrifice of the peace offering, 38 which the LORD commanded Moses on Mount Sinai, on the day when He commanded the children of Israel [a]to offer their offerings to the LORD in the Wilderness of Sinai.

### AARON AND HIS SONS CONSECRATED

*(Ex. 29:1–37)*

**8** And the LORD spoke to Moses, saying: 2 [a]"Take Aaron and his sons with him, and [b]the garments, [c]the anointing oil, a [d]bull as the sin offering, two [e]rams, and a basket of unleavened bread; 3 and gather all the congregation together at the door of the tabernacle of meeting."

4 So Moses did as the LORD commanded him. And the congregation was gathered together at the door of the tabernacle of meeting. 5 And Moses said to the congregation, "This *is* what the LORD commanded to be done."

6 Then Moses brought Aaron and his sons and [a]washed them with water. 7 And he [a]put the tunic on him, girded him with the sash, clothed him with the robe, and put the ephod on him; and he girded him with the intricately woven band of the ephod, and with it tied *the ephod* on him. 8 Then he put the breastplate on him, and he [a]put the Urim and the Thummim[1] in the breastplate. 9 [a]And he put the turban on his head. Also on the turban, on its front, he put the golden plate, the holy crown, as the LORD had commanded Moses.

> **8:8** The **Urim and the Thummim** can be translated as "Lights" and "Perfections." Together their names may mean "perfect knowledge" or a similar idea. It's not known exactly what the Urim and Thummim were, or how they were used. Some have suggested they were two stones used for the casting of lots.

10 [a]Also Moses took the anointing oil, and anointed the tabernacle and all that *was* in it, and consecrated them. 11 He sprinkled some of it on the altar seven times, anointed the altar and all its utensils, and the laver and its base,

**7:20** [a] [Heb. 2:17] [b] Lev. 5:3; 15:3; 22:3–7; Num. 19:13; [1 Cor. 11:28] [c] Gen. 17:14; Ex. 31:14 **7:21** [a] Lev. 5:2, 3, 5 [b] Lev. 11:24, 28 [c] Ezek. 4:14 [d] Lev. 7:20 [1] Following Masoretic Text, Septuagint, and Vulgate; Samaritan Pentateuch, Syriac, and Targum read *swarming thing* (compare 5:2). **7:23** [a] Lev. 3:17; 17:10–15; Deut. 14:21; Ezek. 4:14; 44:31 **7:26** [a] Acts 15:20, 29 **7:29** [a] Lev. 3:1; 22:21; Ezek. 45:15 **7:30** [a] Lev. 3:3, 4, 9, 14 [b] Ex. 29:24, 27; Lev. 8:27; 9:21; Num. 6:20 **7:31** [a] Lev. 3:5, 11, 16 [b] Num. 18:11; Deut. 18:3 **7:32** [a] Ex. 29:27; Lev. 7:34; 9:21; Num. 6:20 **7:34** [a] Ex. 29:28; Lev. 10:14, 15; Num. 18:18, 19; Deut. 18:3 **7:36** [a] Ex. 40:13–15; Lev. 8:12, 30 **7:37** [a] Lev. 6:9 [b] Lev. 6:14 [c] Lev. 6:25 [d] Lev. 7:1 [e] Ex. 29:1; Lev. 6:20 [f] Lev. 7:11 **7:38** [a] Lev. 1:1, 2; Deut. 4:5 **8:2** [a] Ex. 29:1–3 [b] Ex. 28:2, 4 [c] Ex. 30:24, 25 [d] Ex. 29:10 [e] Ex. 29:15, 19 **8:6** [a] Ex. 30:20; Heb. 10:22 **8:7** [a] Ex. 39:1–31 **8:8** [a] Ex. 28:30; Num. 27:21; Deut. 33:8; 1 Sam. 28:6; Ezra 2:63; Neh. 7:65 [1] Literally *the Lights and the Perfections* (compare Exodus 28:30) **8:9** [a] Ex. 28:36, 37; 29:6 **8:10** [a] Ex. 30:26–29; 40:10, 11; Lev. 8:2

to consecrate them. 12 And he [a]poured some of
the anointing oil on Aaron's head and anointed
him, to consecrate him.

13 [a]Then Moses brought Aaron's sons and
put tunics on them, girded them with sashes,
and put hats on them, as the LORD had com-
manded Moses.

14 [a]And he brought the bull for the sin offer-
ing. Then Aaron and his sons [b]laid their hands
on the head of the bull for the sin offering, 15 and
Moses killed *it.* [a]Then he took the blood, and put
*some* on the horns of the altar all around with his
finger, and purified the altar. And he poured the
blood at the base of the altar, and consecrated
it, to make atonement for it. 16 [a]Then he took all
the fat that *was* on the entrails, the fatty lobe
*attached to* the liver, and the two kidneys with
their fat, and Moses burned *them* on the altar.
17 But the bull, its hide, its flesh, and its offal, he
burned with fire outside the camp, as the LORD
[a]had commanded Moses.

18 [a]Then he brought the ram as the burnt
offering. And Aaron and his sons laid their hands
on the head of the ram, 19 and Moses killed *it.*
Then he sprinkled the blood all around on the
altar. 20 And he cut the ram into pieces; and
Moses [a]burned the head, the pieces, and the fat.
21 Then he washed the entrails and the legs in
water. And Moses burned the whole ram on the
altar. It *was* a burnt sacrifice for a sweet aroma,
an offering made by fire to the LORD, [a]as the
LORD had commanded Moses.

22 And [a]he brought the second ram, the ram
of consecration. Then Aaron and his sons laid
their hands on the head of the ram, 23 and Moses
killed *it.* Also he took *some* of [a]its blood and put
it on the tip of Aaron's right ear, on the thumb of
his right hand, and on the big toe of his right foot.
24 Then he brought Aaron's sons. And Moses put
*some* of the [a]blood on the tips of their right ears,
on the thumbs of their right hands, and on the
big toes of their right feet. And Moses sprinkled
the blood all around on the altar. 25 [a]Then he took
the fat and the fat tail, all the fat that *was* on the
entrails, the fatty lobe *attached to* the liver, the two
kidneys and their fat, and the right thigh; 26 [a]and
from the basket of unleavened bread that was
before the LORD he took one unleavened cake,
a cake of bread *anointed with* oil, and one wafer,
and put *them* on the fat and on the right thigh;
27 and he put all *these* [a]in Aaron's hands and in his
sons' hands, and waved them *as* a wave offering
before the LORD. 28 [a]Then Moses took them from
their hands and burned *them* on the altar, on the
burnt offering. They *were* consecration offerings
for a sweet aroma. That *was* an offering made by
fire to the LORD. 29 And [a]Moses took the [b]breast
and waved it *as* a wave offering before the LORD.
It was Moses' [c]part of the ram of consecration,
as the LORD had commanded Moses.

30 Then [a]Moses took some of the anointing
oil and some of the blood which *was* on the altar,
and sprinkled *it* on Aaron, on his garments, on
his sons, and on the garments of his sons with
him; and he consecrated Aaron, his garments,
his sons, and the garments of his sons with him.

31 And Moses said to Aaron and his sons,
[a]"Boil the flesh *at* the door of the tabernacle of
meeting, and eat it there with the bread that *is*
in the basket of consecration offerings, as I com-
manded, saying, 'Aaron and his sons shall eat it.'
32 [a]What remains of the flesh and of the bread
you shall burn with fire. 33 And you shall not go
outside the door of the tabernacle of meeting *for*
seven days, until the days of your consecration
are ended. For [a]seven days he shall consecrate
you. 34 [a]As he has done this day, *so* the LORD has
commanded to do, to make atonement for you.
35 Therefore you shall stay *at* the door of the
tabernacle of meeting day and night for seven
days, and [a]keep the charge of the LORD, so that
you may not die; for so I have been commanded."
36 So Aaron and his sons did all the things that
the LORD had commanded by the hand of Moses.

## THE PRIESTLY MINISTRY BEGINS

9 It came to pass on the [a]eighth day that Moses
called Aaron and his sons and the elders of
Israel. 2 And he said to Aaron, "Take for yourself a
young [a]bull as a sin offering and a ram as a burnt
offering, without blemish, and offer *them* before
the LORD. 3 And to the children of Israel you shall
speak, saying, [a]'Take a kid of the goats as a sin
offering, and a calf and a lamb, *both* of the first
year, without blemish, as a burnt offering, 4 also
a bull and a ram as peace offerings, to sacrifice
before the LORD, and [a]a grain offering mixed
with oil; for [b]today the LORD will appear to you.'"

5 So they brought what Moses commanded
before the tabernacle of meeting. And all the
congregation drew near and stood before the
LORD. 6 Then Moses said, "This *is* the thing which
the LORD commanded you to do, and the glory
of the LORD will appear to you." 7 And Moses said
to Aaron, "Go to the altar, [a]offer your sin offering
and your burnt offering, and make atonement
for yourself and for the people. [b]Offer the of-
fering of the people, and make atonement for
them, as the LORD commanded."

8 Aaron therefore went to the altar and killed
the calf of the sin offering, which *was* for him-
self. 9 Then the sons of Aaron brought the blood

**8:12** [a] Ex. 29:7; 30:30; Lev. 21:10, 12; Ps. 133:2 **8:13** [a] Ex. 29:8, 9 **8:14** [a] Ex. 29:10; Ps. 66:15; Ezek. 43:19 [b] Lev. 4:4 **8:15** [a] Ex. 29:12, 36; Lev. 4:7; Ezek. 43:20, 26; [Heb. 9:22] **8:16** [a] Ex. 29:13; Lev. 4:8 **8:17** [a] Ex. 29:14; Lev. 4:11, 12 **8:18** [a] Ex. 29:15 **8:20** [a] Lev. 1:8 **8:21** [a] Ex. 29:18 **8:22** [a] Ex. 29:19, 31; Lev. 8:2 **8:23** [a] Ex. 29:20, 21; Lev. 14:14 **8:24** [a] [Heb. 9:13, 14, 18–23] **8:25** [a] Ex. 29:22 **8:26** [a] Ex. 29:23 **8:27** [a] Ex. 29:24; Lev. 7:30, 34 **8:28** [a] Ex. 29:25 **8:29** [a] Ps. 99:6 [b] Ex. 29:27 [c] Ex. 29:26 **8:30** [a] Ex. 29:21; 30:30; Num. 3:3 **8:31** [a] Ex. 29:31, 32 **8:32** [a] Ex. 29:34 **8:33** [a] Ex. 29:30, 35; Lev. 10:7; Ezek. 43:25, 26 **8:34** [a] [Heb. 7:16] **8:35** [a] Num. 1:53; 3:7; 9:19; Deut. 11:1; 1 Kin. 2:3; Ezek. 48:11 **9:1** [a] Ezek. 43:27 **9:2** [a] Ex. 29:21; Lev. 4:1–12 **9:3** [a] Lev. 4:23, 28; Ezra 6:17; 10:19 **9:4** [a] Lev. 2:4 [b] Ex. 29:43; Lev. 9:6, 23 **9:7** [a] Lev. 4:3; 1 Sam. 3:14; [Heb. 5:3–5; 7:27] [b] Lev. 4:16, 20; Heb. 5:1

to him. And he dipped his finger in the blood, put *it* on the horns of the altar, and poured the blood at the base of the altar. 10 [a]But the fat, the kidneys, and the fatty lobe from the liver of the sin offering he burned on the altar, as the LORD had commanded Moses. 11 [a]The flesh and the hide he burned with fire outside the camp.

12 And he killed the burnt offering; and Aaron's sons presented to him the blood, [a]which he sprinkled all around on the altar. 13 [a]Then they presented the burnt offering to him, with its pieces and head, and he burned *them* on the altar. 14 [a]And he washed the entrails and the legs, and burned *them* with the burnt offering on the altar.

15 [a]Then he brought the people's offering, and took the goat, which *was* the sin offering for the people, and killed it and offered it for sin, like the first one. 16 And he brought the burnt offering and offered it [a]according to the prescribed manner. 17 Then he brought the grain offering, took a handful of it, and burned *it* on the altar, [a]besides the burnt sacrifice of the morning.

18 He also killed the bull and the ram *as* [a]sacrifices of peace offerings, which *were* for the people. And Aaron's sons presented to him the blood, which he sprinkled all around on the altar, 19 and the fat from the bull and the ram—the fatty tail, what covers *the entrails* and the kidneys, and the fatty lobe *attached to* the liver; 20 and they put the fat on the breasts. [a]Then he burned the fat on the altar; 21 but the breasts and the right thigh Aaron waved [a]*as* a wave offering before the LORD, as Moses had commanded.

22 Then Aaron lifted his hand toward the people, [a]blessed them, and came down from offering the sin offering, the burnt offering, and peace offerings. 23 And Moses and Aaron went into the tabernacle of meeting, and came out and blessed the people. Then the glory of the LORD appeared to all the people, 24 and [a]fire came out from before the LORD and consumed the burnt offering and the fat on the altar. When all the people saw *it*, they [b]shouted and fell on their [c]faces.

### *THE PROFANE FIRE OF NADAB AND ABIHU*

**10** Then [a]Nadab and Abihu, the sons of Aaron, [b]each took his censer and put fire in it, put incense on it, and offered [c]profane fire before the LORD, which He had not commanded them. 2 So [a]fire went out from the LORD and devoured them, and they died before the LORD. 3 And Moses said to Aaron, "This is what the LORD spoke, saying:

'By those [a]who come near Me
I must be regarded as holy;

> **10:1–2** Aaron and his sons served the Lord as high priests in the worship of the tabernacle. They had been properly appointed, purified, clothed, anointed, and ordained. Initially they did everything the Lord commanded through Moses. But when **Nadab and Abihu** disobeyed God in the performance of their duties, the Lord swiftly punished them with a consuming fire. Being blessed with a thriving ministry is no excuse to go off and do things our own way. God doesn't take such actions lightly, and neither should we.

And before all the people
I must be glorified.' "

So Aaron held his peace.

4 Then Moses called Mishael and Elzaphan, the sons of Uzziel the uncle of Aaron, and said to them, "Come near, [a]carry your brethren from before the sanctuary out of the camp." 5 So they went near and carried them by their tunics out of the camp, as Moses had said.

6 And Moses said to Aaron, and to Eleazar and Ithamar, his sons, "Do not uncover your heads nor tear your clothes, lest you die, and [a]wrath come upon all the people. But let your brethren, the whole house of Israel, bewail the burning which the LORD has kindled. 7 [a]You shall not go out from the door of the tabernacle of meeting, lest you die, [b]for the anointing oil of the LORD *is* upon you." And they did according to the word of Moses.

### *CONDUCT PRESCRIBED FOR PRIESTS*

8 Then the LORD spoke to Aaron, saying: 9 [a]"Do not drink wine or intoxicating drink, you, nor your sons with you, when you go into the tabernacle of meeting, lest you die. *It shall be* a statute forever throughout your generations, 10 that you may [a]distinguish between holy and unholy, and between unclean and clean, 11 [a]and that you may teach the children of Israel all the statutes which the LORD has spoken to them by the hand of Moses."

12 And Moses spoke to Aaron, and to Eleazar and Ithamar, his sons who were left: [a]"Take the grain offering that remains of the offerings made by fire to the LORD, and eat it without leaven beside the altar; [b]for it *is* most holy. 13 You shall eat it in a [a]holy place, because it *is* your due and your sons' due, of the sacrifices made by fire to the LORD; for [b]so I have been commanded.

**9:10** [a] Ex. 23:18; Lev. 8:16 **9:11** [a] Lev. 4:11, 12; 8:17 **9:12** [a] Lev. 1:5; 8:19 **9:13** [a] Lev. 8:20 **9:14** [a] Lev. 8:21 **9:15** [a] [Is. 53:10; Heb. 2:17; 5:3] **9:16** [a] Lev. 1:1–13 **9:17** [a] Ex. 29:38, 39 **9:18** [a] Lev. 3:1–11 **9:20** [a] Lev. 3:5, 16 **9:21** [a] Ex. 29:24, 26, 27; Lev. 7:30–34 **9:22** [a] Num. 6:22–26; Deut. 21:5; Luke 24:50 **9:24** [a] Gen. 4:4; Judg. 6:21; 2 Chr. 7:1; Ps. 20:3 [b] Ezra 3:11 [c] 1 Kin. 18:38, 39 **10:1** [a] Ex. 24:1, 9; Num. 3:2–4; 1 Chr. 24:2 [b] Lev. 16:12 [c] Ex. 30:9; 1 Sam. 2:17 **10:2** [a] Gen. 19:24; Num. 11:1; 16:35; Rev. 20:9 **10:3** [a] Ex. 19:22; Lev. 21:6; Is. 52:11; Ezek. 20:41 **10:4** [a] Acts 5:6, 10 **10:6** [a] Num. 1:53; 16:22, 46; 18:5; Josh. 7:1; 22:18, 20; 2 Sam. 24:1 **10:7** [a] Lev. 8:33; 21:12 [b] Lev. 8:30 **10:9** [a] Gen. 9:21; [Prov. 20:1; 31:5]; Is. 28:7; Ezek. 44:21; Hos. 4:11; Luke 1:15; [Eph. 5:18]; 1 Tim. 3:3; Titus 1:7 **10:10** [a] Lev. 11:47; 20:25; Ezek. 22:26; 44:23 **10:11** [a] Deut. 24:8; Neh. 8:2, 8; Jer. 18:18; Mal. 2:7 **10:12** [a] Num. 18:9 [b] Lev. 21:22 **10:13** [a] Num. 18:10 [b] Lev. 2:3; 6:16

14 [a]The breast of the wave offering and the thigh
of the heave offering you shall eat in a clean place,
you, your sons, and your [b]daughters with you; for
*they are* your due and your sons' [c]due, *which* are
given from the sacrifices of peace offerings of
the children of Israel. 15 [a]The thigh of the heave
offering and the breast of the wave offering they
shall bring with the offerings of fat made by fire,
to offer *as* a wave offering before the LORD. And
it shall be yours and your sons' with you, by a
statute forever, as the LORD has commanded."
16 Then Moses made careful inquiry about
[a]the goat of the sin offering, and there it was—
burned up. And he was angry with Eleazar and
Ithamar, the sons of Aaron *who were* left, saying,
17 [a]"Why have you not eaten the sin offering in
a holy place, since it *is* most holy, and *God* has
given it to you to bear [b]the guilt of the congre-
gation, to make atonement for them before the
LORD? 18 See! [a]Its blood was not brought inside
the holy *place;*[1] indeed you should have eaten
it in a holy *place,* [b]as I commanded."
19 And Aaron said to Moses, "Look, [a]this day
they have offered their sin offering and their
burnt offering before the LORD, and such things
have befallen me! *If* I had eaten the sin offering
today, [b]would it have been accepted in the sight
of the LORD?" 20 So when Moses heard *that,* he
was content.

### *FOODS PERMITTED AND FORBIDDEN*

*(Deut. 14:3–21)*

**11** Now the LORD spoke to Moses and Aaron,
saying to them, 2 "Speak to the children of
Israel, saying, [a]'These *are* the animals which
you may eat among all the animals that *are*
on the earth: 3 Among the animals, whatever
divides the hoof, having cloven hooves *and*
chewing the cud—that you may eat. 4 Never-
theless these you shall [a]not eat among those
that chew the cud or those that have cloven
hooves: the camel, because it chews the cud
but does not have cloven hooves, is unclean to
you; 5 the rock hyrax, because it chews the cud
but does not have cloven hooves, *is* unclean to
you; 6 the hare, because it chews the cud but does
not have cloven hooves, *is* unclean to you; 7 and
the swine, though it divides the hoof, having
cloven hooves, yet does not chew the cud, [a]*is*
unclean to you. 8 Their flesh you shall not eat,
and their carcasses you shall not touch. [a]They
*are* unclean to you.
9 [a]'These you may eat of all that *are* in the
water: whatever in the water has fins and scales,
whether in the seas or in the rivers—that you
may eat. 10 But all in the seas or in the rivers that
do not have fins and scales, all that move in the
water or any living thing which *is* in the water,
they *are* an [a]abomination to you. 11 They shall be an
abomination to you; you shall not eat their flesh,
but you shall regard their carcasses as an abomi-
nation. 12 Whatever in the water does not have fins
or scales—that *shall be* an abomination to you.
13 [a]'And these you shall regard as an abomi-
nation among the birds; they shall not be eaten,
they *are* an abomination: the eagle, the vulture,
the buzzard, 14 the kite, and the falcon after its
kind; 15 every raven after its kind, 16 the ostrich,
the short-eared owl, the sea gull, and the hawk
after its kind; 17 the little owl, the fisher owl, and
the screech owl; 18 the white owl, the jackdaw,
and the carrion vulture; 19 the stork, the heron
after its kind, the hoopoe, and the bat.
20 'All flying insects that creep on *all* fours
*shall be* an abomination to you. 21 Yet these you
may eat of every flying insect that creeps on *all*
fours: those which have jointed legs above their
feet with which to leap on the earth. 22 These you
may eat: [a]the locust after its kind, the destroying
locust after its kind, the cricket after its kind, and
the grasshopper after its kind. 23 But all *other*
flying insects which have four feet *shall be* an
abomination to you.

### *UNCLEAN ANIMALS*

24 'By these you shall become unclean; who-
ever touches the carcass of any of them shall be
unclean until evening; 25 whoever carries part of
the carcass of any of them [a]shall wash his clothes
and be unclean until evening: 26 *The carcass* of any
animal which divides the foot, but is not cloven-
hoofed or does not chew the cud, *is* unclean to
you. Everyone who touches it shall be unclean.
27 And whatever goes on its paws, among all kinds
of animals that go on *all* fours, those *are* unclean
to you. Whoever touches any such carcass shall
be unclean until evening. 28 Whoever carries *any*
*such* carcass shall wash his clothes and be unclean
until evening. It *is* unclean to you.
29 'These also *shall be* unclean to you among
the creeping things that creep on the earth: the
mole, [a]the mouse, and the large lizard after its
kind; 30 the gecko, the monitor lizard, the sand
reptile, the sand lizard, and the chameleon.
31 These *are* unclean to you among all that creep.
Whoever [a]touches them when they are dead shall
be unclean until evening. 32 Anything on which
*any* of them falls, when they are dead shall be
unclean, whether *it is* any item of wood or clothing
or skin or sack, whatever item *it is,* in which *any*
work is done, [a]it must be put in water. And it shall
be unclean until evening; then it shall be clean.

**10:14** [a] Ex. 29:24, 26, 27; Lev. 7:30–34; Num. 18:11 [b] Lev. 22:13 [c] Num. 18:10 **10:15** [a] Lev. 7:29, 30, 34 **10:16** [a] Lev. 9:3, 15 **10:17** [a] Lev. 6:24–30 [b] Ex. 28:38; Lev. 22:16; Num. 18:1 **10:18** [a] Lev. 6:30 [b] Lev. 6:26, 30 [1] The Most Holy Place when capitalized **10:19** [a] Lev. 9:8, 12 [b] [Is. 1:11–15]; Jer. 6:20; 14:12; Hos. 9:4; [Mal. 1:10, 13; 3:1–4] **11:2** [a] Deut. 14:4; Ezek. 4:14; Dan. 1:8; [Matt. 15:11]; Acts 10:12, 14; [Rom. 14:14; Heb. 9:10; 13:9] **11:4** [a] Acts 10:14 **11:7** [a] Is. 65:4; 66:3, 17; Mark 5:1–17 **11:8** [a] Is. 52:11; [Mark 7:2, 15, 18]; Acts 10:14, 15; 15:29 **11:9** [a] Deut. 14:9 **11:10** [a] Lev. 7:18, 21; Deut. 14:3 **11:13** [a] Deut. 14:12–19; Is. 66:17 **11:22** [a] Matt. 3:4; Mark 1:6 **11:25** [a] Lev. 14:8; 15:5; Num. 19:10, 21, 22; 31:24; Zech. 13:1; [Heb. 9:10; 10:22; Rev. 7:14] **11:29** [a] Is. 66:17 **11:31** [a] Hag. 2:13 **11:32** [a] Lev. 15:12

33 Any [a]earthen vessel into which *any* of them
falls [b]you shall break; and whatever *is* in it shall
be unclean: 34 in such a vessel, any edible food
upon which water falls becomes unclean, and
any drink that may be drunk from it becomes
unclean. 35 And everything on which *a part* of *any*
*such* carcass falls shall be unclean; *whether it is* an
oven or cooking stove, it shall be broken down;
*for* they *are* unclean, and shall be unclean to you.
36 Nevertheless a spring or a cistern, *in which there*
*is* plenty of water, shall be clean, but whatever
touches any such carcass becomes unclean. 37 And
if a part of *any such* carcass falls on any planting
seed which is to be sown, it *remains* clean. 38 But
if water is put on the seed, and if *a part* of *any*
*such* carcass falls on it, it *becomes* unclean to you.
39 'And if any animal which you may eat dies,
he who touches its carcass shall be [a]unclean
until evening. 40 [a]He who eats of its carcass shall
wash his clothes and be unclean until evening.
He also who carries its carcass shall wash his
clothes and be unclean until evening.
41 'And every creeping thing that creeps on the
earth *shall be* an abomination. It shall not be eat-
en. 42 Whatever crawls on its belly, whatever goes
on *all* fours, or whatever has many feet among all
creeping things that creep on the earth—these
you shall not eat, for they *are* an abomination.
43 [a]You shall not make yourselves abominable
with any creeping thing that creeps; nor shall you
make yourselves unclean with them, lest you be
defiled by them. 44 For I *am* the LORD your [a]God.
You shall therefore consecrate yourselves, and
[b]you shall be holy; for I *am* holy. Neither shall you
defile yourselves with any creeping thing that
creeps on the earth. 45 [a]For I *am* the LORD who
brings you up out of the land of Egypt, to be your
God. [b]You shall therefore be holy, for I *am* holy.

**SEEING JESUS IN THE SCRIPTURE**

**11:44** God, who is holy, calls His people to be likewise holy. No matter how hard we try, we cannot live up to this standard. But when we trust in Christ, we're made new in His perfect, holy image, and thus we *become* God's holy people (see Col. 1:15).

46 'This *is* the law of the animals and the
birds and every living creature that moves in the
waters, and of every creature that creeps on the
earth, 47 [a]to distinguish between the unclean and
the clean, and between the animal that may be
eaten and the animal that may not be eaten.' "

## *THE RITUAL AFTER CHILDBIRTH*
*(cf. Luke 2:22–24)*

12 Then the LORD spoke to Moses, saying,
2 "Speak to the children of Israel, saying:
'If a [a]woman has conceived, and borne a male
child, then [b]she shall be unclean seven days; [c]as
in the days of her customary impurity she shall
be unclean. 3 And on the [a]eighth day the flesh
of his foreskin shall be circumcised. 4 She shall
then continue in the blood of *her* purification
thirty-three days. She shall not touch any hal-
lowed thing, nor come into the sanctuary until
the days of her purification are fulfilled.
5 'But if she bears a female child, then she
shall be unclean two weeks, as in her customary
impurity, and she shall continue in the blood of
*her* purification sixty-six days.
6 [a]'When the days of her purification are
fulfilled, whether for a son or a daughter, she
shall bring to the priest a [b]lamb of the first year
as a burnt offering, and a young pigeon or a
turtledove as a [c]sin offering, to the door of the
tabernacle of meeting. 7 Then he shall offer it
before the LORD, and make atonement for her.
And she shall be clean from the flow of her
blood. This *is* the law for her who has borne a
male or a female.
8 [a]'And if she is not able to bring a lamb, then
she may bring two turtledoves or two young
pigeons—one as a burnt offering and the other
as a sin offering. [b]So the priest shall make atone-
ment for her, and she will be clean.' "

## *THE LAW CONCERNING LEPROSY*

13 And the LORD spoke to Moses and Aaron,
saying: 2 "When a man has on the skin of
his body a swelling, [a]a scab, or a bright spot,
and it becomes on the skin of his body *like* a
leprous[1] sore, [b]then he shall be brought to Aaron
the priest or to one of his sons the priests. 3 The
priest shall examine the sore on the skin of the
body; and if the hair on the sore has turned
white, and the sore appears *to be* deeper than
the skin of his body, it *is* a leprous sore. Then
the priest shall examine him, and pronounce
him unclean. 4 But if the bright spot *is* white on
the skin of his body, and does not appear *to be*
deeper than the skin, and its hair has not turned
white, then the priest shall isolate *the one who*
*has* the sore [a]seven days. 5 And the priest shall
examine him on the seventh day; and indeed
*if* the sore appears to be as it was, *and* the sore
has not spread on the skin, then the priest shall
isolate him another seven days. 6 Then the priest
shall examine him again on the seventh day;
and indeed *if* the sore has faded, *and* the sore

**11:33** [a] Lev. 6:28 [b] Lev. 15:12; Ps. 2:9; Jer. 48:38; [2 Tim. 2:21]; Rev. 2:27 **11:39** [a] Hag. 2:11–13 **11:40** [a] Ex. 22:31; Lev. 17:15; 22:8; Deut. 14:21; Ezek. 4:14; 44:31 **11:43** [a] Lev. 20:25 **11:44** [a] Ex. 6:7; Lev. 22:33; 25:38; 26:45 [b] Ex. 19:6; Lev. 19:2; 20:7, 26; [Amos 3:3]; Matt. 5:48; 1 Thess. 4:7; 1 Pet. 1:15, 16; [Rev. 22:11, 14] **11:45** [a] Ex. 6:7; 20:2; Lev. 22:33; 25:38; 26:45; Ps. 105:43–45; Hos. 11:1 [b] Lev. 11:44 **11:47** [a] Lev. 10:10; Ezek. 44:23; Mal. 3:18 **12:2** [a] Lev. 15:19; [Job 14:4; Ps. 51:5] [b] Ex. 22:30; Lev. 8:33; 13:4; Luke 2:22 [c] Lev. 18:19 **12:3** [a] Gen. 17:12; Luke 1:59; 2:21; John 7:22, 23; Gal. 5:3 **12:6** [a] Luke 2:22 [b] [John 1:29; 1 Pet. 1:18, 19] [c] Lev. 5:7 **12:8** [a] Lev. 5:7; Luke 2:22–24 [b] Lev. 4:26 **13:2** [a] Deut. 28:27; Is. 3:17 [b] Deut. 17:8, 9; 24:8; Mal. 2:7; Luke 17:14 [1] Hebrew *saraath,* disfiguring skin diseases, including leprosy, and so in verses 2–46 and 14:2–32 **13:4** [a] Lev. 14:8

has not spread on the skin, then the priest shall pronounce him clean; it *is only* a scab, and he [a]shall wash his clothes and be clean. 7 But if the scab should at all spread over the skin, after he has been seen by the priest for his cleansing, he shall be seen by the priest again. 8 And *if* the priest sees that the scab has indeed spread on the skin, then the priest shall pronounce him unclean. It *is* leprosy.

9 "When the leprous sore is on a person, then he shall be brought to the priest. 10 [a]And the priest shall examine *him;* and indeed *if* the swelling on the skin *is* white, and it has turned the hair white, and *there is* a spot of raw flesh in the swelling, 11 it *is* an old leprosy on the skin of his body. The priest shall pronounce him unclean, and shall not isolate him, for he *is* unclean.

12 "And if leprosy breaks out all over the skin, and the leprosy covers all the skin of *the one who has* the sore, from his head to his foot, wherever the priest looks, 13 then the priest shall consider; and indeed *if* the leprosy has covered all his body, he shall pronounce *him* clean *who has* the sore. It has all turned [a]white. He *is* clean. 14 But when raw flesh appears on him, he shall be unclean. 15 And the priest shall examine the raw flesh and pronounce him to be unclean; *for* the raw flesh *is* unclean. It *is* leprosy. 16 Or if the raw flesh changes and turns white again, he shall come to the priest. 17 And the priest shall examine him; and indeed *if* the sore has turned white, then the priest shall pronounce *him* clean *who has* the sore. He *is* clean.

18 "If the body develops a [a]boil in the skin, and it is healed, 19 and in the place of the boil there comes a white swelling or a bright spot, reddish-white, then it shall be shown to the priest; 20 and *if,* when the priest sees it, it indeed appears deeper than the skin, and its hair has turned white, the priest shall pronounce him unclean. It *is* a leprous sore which has broken out of the boil. 21 But if the priest examines it, and indeed *there are* no white hairs in it, and it *is* not deeper than the skin, but has faded, then the priest shall isolate him seven days; 22 and if it should at all spread over the skin, then the priest shall pronounce him unclean. It *is* a leprous sore. 23 But if the bright spot stays in one place, *and* has not spread, it *is* the scar of the boil; and the priest shall pronounce him clean.

24 "Or if the body receives a [a]burn on its skin by fire, and the raw *flesh* of the burn becomes a bright spot, reddish-white or white, 25 then the priest shall examine it; and indeed *if* the hair of the bright spot has turned white, and it appears deeper than the skin, it *is* leprosy broken out in the burn. Therefore the priest shall pronounce him unclean. It *is* a leprous sore. 26 But if the priest examines it, and indeed *there are* no white hairs in the bright spot, and it *is* not deeper than the skin, but has faded, then the priest shall isolate him seven days. 27 And the priest shall examine him on the seventh day. If it has at all spread over the skin, then the priest shall pronounce him unclean. It *is* a leprous sore. 28 But if the bright spot stays in one place, *and* has not spread on the skin, but has faded, it *is* a swelling from the burn. The priest shall pronounce him clean, for it *is* the scar from the burn.

29 "If a man or woman has a sore on the head or the beard, 30 then the priest shall examine the sore; and indeed if it appears deeper than the skin, *and there is* in it thin yellow hair, then the priest shall pronounce him unclean. It *is* a scaly leprosy of the head or beard. 31 But if the priest examines the scaly sore, and indeed it does not appear deeper than the skin, and *there is* no black hair in it, then the priest shall isolate *the one who has* the scale seven days. 32 And on the seventh day the priest shall examine the sore; and indeed *if* the scale has not spread, and there is no yellow hair in it, and the scale does not appear deeper than the skin, 33 he shall shave himself, but the scale he shall not shave. And the priest shall isolate *the one who has* the scale another seven days. 34 On the seventh day the priest shall examine the scale; and indeed *if* the scale has not spread over the skin, and does not appear deeper than the skin, then the priest shall pronounce him clean. He shall wash his clothes and be clean. 35 But if the scale should at all spread over the skin after his cleansing, 36 then the priest shall examine him; and indeed *if* the scale has spread over the skin, the priest need not seek for yellow hair. He *is* unclean. 37 But if the scale appears to be at a standstill, and there is black hair grown up in it, the scale has healed. He *is* clean, and the priest shall pronounce him clean.

38 "If a man or a woman has bright spots on the skin of the body, *specifically* white bright spots, 39 then the priest shall look; and indeed *if* the bright spots on the skin of the body *are* dull white, it *is* a white spot *that* grows on the skin. He *is* clean.

40 "As for the man whose hair has fallen from his head, he *is* bald, *but* he *is* clean. 41 He whose hair has fallen from his forehead, he *is* bald on the forehead, *but* he *is* clean. 42 And if there is on the bald head or bald [a]forehead a reddish-white sore, it *is* leprosy breaking out on his bald head or his bald forehead. 43 Then the priest shall examine it; and indeed *if* the swelling of the sore *is* reddish-white on his bald head or on his bald forehead, as the appearance of leprosy on the skin of the body, 44 he is a leprous man. He *is* unclean. The priest shall surely pronounce him unclean; his sore *is* on his [a]head.

45 "Now the leper on whom the sore *is,* his

13:6 [a] Lev. 11:25; 14:8; [John 13:8, 10] 13:10 [a] Num. 12:10, 12; 2 Kin. 5:27; 2 Chr. 26:19, 20 13:13 [a] Ex. 4:6 13:18 [a] Ex. 9:9; 15:26 13:24 [a] Is. 3:24 13:42 [a] 2 Chr. 26:19 13:44 [a] Is. 1:5

clothes shall be torn and his head [a]bare; and he
shall [b]cover his mustache, and cry, [c]'Unclean!
Unclean!' 46 He shall be unclean. All the days he
has the sore he shall be unclean. He *is* unclean,
and he shall dwell alone; his dwelling *shall be*
[a]outside the camp.

### *THE LAW CONCERNING LEPROUS GARMENTS*

47 "Also, if a garment has a leprous plague[1]
in it, *whether it is* a woolen garment or a linen
garment, 48 whether *it is* in the warp or woof of
linen or wool, whether in leather or in anything
made of leather, 49 and if the plague is greenish
or reddish in the garment or in the leather,
whether in the warp or in the woof, or in any-
thing made of leather, it *is* a leprous plague and
shall be shown to the priest. 50 The priest shall
examine the plague and isolate *that which has*
the plague seven days. 51 And he shall examine
the plague on the seventh day. If the plague has
spread in the garment, either in the warp or in
the woof, in the leather *or* in anything made
of leather, the plague *is* [a]an active leprosy. It *is*
unclean. 52 He shall therefore burn that garment
in which is the plague, whether warp or woof, in
wool or in linen, or anything of leather, for it *is*
an active leprosy; *the garment* shall be burned
in the fire.

53 "But if the priest examines *it,* and indeed
the plague has not spread in the garment, either
in the warp or in the woof, or in anything made
of leather, 54 then the priest shall command that
they wash *the thing* in which *is* the plague; and
he shall isolate it another seven days. 55 Then
the priest shall examine the plague after it has
been washed; and indeed *if* the plague has not
changed its color, though the plague has not
spread, it *is* unclean, and you shall burn it in
the fire; it continues eating away, *whether* the
damage *is* outside or inside. 56 If the priest ex-
amines *it,* and indeed the plague has faded
after washing it, then he shall tear it out of the
garment, whether out of the warp or out of the
woof, or out of the leather. 57 But if it appears
again in the garment, either in the warp or in
the woof, or in anything made of leather, it *is* a
spreading *plague;* you shall burn with fire that
in which is the plague. 58 And if you wash the
garment, either warp or woof, or whatever is
made of leather, if the plague has disappeared
from it, then it shall be washed a second time,
and shall be clean.

59 "This *is* the law of the leprous plague in
a garment of wool or linen, either in the warp
or woof, or in anything made of leather, to pro-
nounce it clean or to pronounce it unclean."

### *THE RITUAL FOR CLEANSING HEALED LEPERS*

*(cf. Matt. 8:1–4; Luke 5:12–14)*

14 Then the LORD spoke to Moses, saying,
2 "This shall be the law of the leper for the
day of his cleansing: He [a]shall be brought to the
priest. 3 And the priest shall go out of the camp,
and the priest shall examine *him;* and indeed,
*if* the leprosy is healed in the leper, 4 then the
priest shall command to take for him who is to
be cleansed two living *and* clean birds, [a]cedar
wood, [b]scarlet, and [c]hyssop. 5 And the priest shall
command that one of the birds be killed in an
earthen vessel over running water. 6 As for the
living bird, he shall take it, the cedar wood and
the scarlet and the hyssop, and dip them and the
living bird in the blood of the bird *that was* killed
over the running water. 7 And he shall [a]sprinkle it
[b]seven times on him who is to be cleansed from
the leprosy, and shall pronounce him clean, and
shall let the living bird loose in the open field.
8 He who is to be cleansed [a]shall wash his clothes,
shave off all his hair, and [b]wash himself in water,
that he may be clean. After that he shall come
into the camp, and [c]shall stay outside his tent
seven days. 9 But on the [a]seventh day he shall
shave all the hair off his head and his beard and
his eyebrows—all his hair he shall shave off.
He shall wash his clothes and wash his body in
water, and he shall be clean.

10 "And on the eighth day [a]he shall take two
male lambs without blemish, one ewe lamb of
the first year without blemish, three-tenths *of*
*an ephah* of fine flour mixed with oil as [b]a grain
offering, and one log of oil. 11 Then the priest who
makes *him* clean shall present the man who is
to be made clean, and those things, before the
LORD, *at* the door of the tabernacle of meeting.
12 And the priest shall take one male lamb and
[a]offer it as a trespass offering, and the log of oil,
and [b]wave them *as* a wave offering before the
LORD. 13 Then he shall kill the lamb [a]in the place
where he kills the sin offering and the burnt of-
fering, in a holy place; for [b]as the sin offering *is*
the priest's, so *is* the trespass offering. [c]It *is* most
holy. 14 The priest shall take *some* of the blood of
the trespass offering, and the priest shall put *it*
[a]on the tip of the right ear of him who is to be

**14:14** After making his sacrifice, the unclean person received a dab of blood on his **ear**, his **thumb**, and his **toe**. These three places symbolized the three main activities of life: thinking, working, and walking.

**13:45** [a] Lev. 10:6; 21:10 [b] Ezek. 24:17, 22; Mic. 3:7 [c] Is. 6:5; 64:6; Lam. 4:15; Luke 5:8 **13:46** [a] Num. 5:1–4; 12:14; 2 Kin. 7:3; 15:5; 2 Chr. 26:21; Ps. 38:11; Luke 17:12 **13:47** [1] A mold, fungus, or similar infestation, and so in verses 47–59 **13:51** [a] Lev. 14:44 **14:2** [a] Matt. 8:2, 4; Mark 1:40, 44; Luke 5:12, 14; 17:14 **14:4** [a] Lev. 14:6, 49, 51, 52; Num. 19:6; Heb. 9:19 [b] Ex. 25:4 [c] Ex. 12:22; Ps. 51:7 **14:7** [a] Num. 19:18, 19; [Heb. 9:13, 21; 12:24] [b] 2 Kin. 5:10, 14; Ps. 51:2 **14:8** [a] Lev. 11:25; 13:6; Num. 8:7 [b] Lev. 11:25; [Eph. 5:26; Heb. 10:22; Rev. 1:5, 6] [c] Lev. 13:5; Num. 5:2, 3; 12:14, 15; 2 Chr. 26:21 **14:9** [a] Num. 19:19 **14:10** [a] Matt. 8:4; Mark 1:44; Luke 5:14 [b] Lev. 2:1; Num. 15:4 **14:12** [a] Lev. 5:6, 18; 6:6; 14:19 [b] Ex. 29:22–24, 26 **14:13** [a] Ex. 29:11; Lev. 1:5, 11; 4:4, 24 [b] Lev. 6:24–30; 7:7 [c] Lev. 2:3; 7:6; 21:22 **14:14** [a] Ex. 29:20; Lev. 8:23, 24

cleansed, on the thumb of his right hand, and
on the big toe of his right foot. 15 And the priest
shall take *some* of the log of oil, and pour *it* into
the palm of his own left hand. 16 Then the priest
shall dip his right finger in the oil that *is* in his
left hand, and shall [a]sprinkle some of the oil
with his finger seven times before the LORD.
17 And of the rest of the oil in his hand, the priest
shall put *some* on the tip of the right ear of him
who is to be cleansed, on the thumb of his right
hand, and on the big toe of his right foot, on the
blood of the trespass offering. 18 The rest of the
oil that *is* in the priest's hand he shall put on the
head of him who is to be cleansed. [a]So the priest
shall make atonement for him before the LORD.

19 "Then the priest shall offer [a]the sin offer-
ing, and make atonement for him who is to be
cleansed from his uncleanness. Afterward he
shall kill the burnt offering. 20 And the priest
shall offer the burnt offering and the grain of-
fering on the altar. So the priest shall make
atonement for him, and he shall be [a]clean.

21 "But [a]if he *is* poor and cannot afford it,
then he shall take one male lamb *as* a trespass
offering to be waved, to make atonement for
him, one-tenth *of an ephah* of fine flour mixed
with oil as a grain offering, a log of oil, 22 [a]and two
turtledoves or two young pigeons, such as he is
able to afford: one shall be a sin offering and the
other a burnt offering. 23 [a]He shall bring them
to the priest on the eighth day for his cleansing,
to the door of the tabernacle of meeting, before
the LORD. 24 [a]And the priest shall take the lamb
of the trespass offering and the log of oil, and
the priest shall wave them *as* a wave offering
before the LORD. 25 Then he shall kill the lamb of
the trespass offering, [a]and the priest shall take
*some* of the blood of the trespass offering and
put *it* on the tip of the right ear of him who is to
be cleansed, on the thumb of his right hand, and
on the big toe of his right foot. 26 And the priest
shall pour some of the oil into the palm of his
own left hand. 27 Then the priest shall sprinkle
with his right finger *some* of the oil that *is* in his
left hand seven times before the LORD. 28 And
the priest shall put *some* of the oil that *is* in his
hand on the tip of the right ear of him who is
to be cleansed, on the thumb of the right hand,
and on the big toe of his right foot, on the place
of the blood of the trespass offering. 29 The rest
of the oil that *is* in the priest's hand he shall
put on the head of him who is to be cleansed,
to make atonement for him before the LORD.
30 And he shall offer one of [a]the turtledoves or
young pigeons, such as he can afford— 31 such
as he is able to afford, the one *as* a sin offering
and the other *as* a burnt offering, with the grain
offering. So the priest shall make atonement
for him who is to be cleansed before the LORD.
32 This *is* the law *for one* who had a leprous sore,
who cannot afford [a]the usual cleansing."

## THE LAW CONCERNING LEPROUS HOUSES

33 And the LORD spoke to Moses and Aaron,
saying: 34 [a]"When you have come into the land of
Canaan, which I give you as a possession, and [b]I
put the leprous plague[1] in a house in the land of
your possession, 35 and he who owns the house
comes and tells the priest, saying, 'It seems to me
that *there is* [a]some plague in the house,' 36 then
the priest shall command that they empty the
house, before the priest goes *into it* to exam-
ine the plague, that all that *is* in the house may
not be made unclean; and afterward the priest
shall go in to examine the house. 37 And he shall
examine the plague; and indeed *if* the plague *is*
on the walls of the house with ingrained streaks,
greenish or reddish, which appear to be deep
in the wall, 38 then the priest shall go out of the
house, to the door of the house, and shut up the
house seven days. 39 And the priest shall come
again on the seventh day and look; and indeed *if*
the plague has spread on the walls of the house,
40 then the priest shall command that they take
away the stones in which *is* the plague, and they
shall cast them into an unclean place outside the
city. 41 And he shall cause the house to be scraped
inside, all around, and the dust that they scrape
off they shall pour out in an unclean place outside
the city. 42 Then they shall take other stones and
put *them* in the place of *those* stones, and he shall
take other mortar and plaster the house.

43 "Now if the plague comes back and breaks
out in the house, after he has taken away the
stones, after he has scraped the house, and after
it is plastered, 44 then the priest shall come and
look; and indeed *if* the plague has spread in the
house, it *is* [a]an active leprosy in the house. It *is*
unclean. 45 And he shall break down the house,
its stones, its timber, and all the plaster of the
house, and he shall carry *them* outside the city
to an unclean place. 46 Moreover he who goes
into the house at all while it is shut up shall be
unclean [a]until evening. 47 And he who lies down
in the house shall [a]wash his clothes, and he who
eats in the house shall wash his clothes.

48 "But if the priest comes in and examines
*it,* and indeed the plague has not spread in the
house after the house was plastered, then the
priest shall pronounce the house clean, because
the plague is healed. 49 And [a]he shall take, to
cleanse the house, two birds, cedar wood, scarlet,
and hyssop. 50 Then he shall kill one of the birds
in an earthen vessel over running water; 51 and
he shall take the cedar wood, the hyssop, the
scarlet, and the living bird, and dip them in the

**14:16** [a] Lev. 4:6 **14:18** [a] Lev. 4:26; 5:6; Num. 15:28; [Heb. 2:17] **14:19** [a] Lev. 5:1, 6; 12:7; [2 Cor. 5:21] **14:20** [a] Lev. 14:8, 9 **14:21** [a] Lev. 5:7, 11; 12:8; 27:8 **14:22** [a] Lev. 12:8; 15:14, 15 **14:23** [a] Lev. 14:10, 11 **14:24** [a] Lev. 14:12 **14:25** [a] Lev. 14:14, 17 **14:30** [a] Lev. 14:22; 15:14, 15 **14:32** [a] Lev. 14:10 **14:34** [a] Gen. 12:7; 13:17; 17:8; Num. 32:22; Deut. 7:1; 32:49 [b] [Prov. 3:33] [1] Decomposition by mildew, mold, dry rot, etc., and so in verses 34–53 **14:35** [a] [Ps. 91:9, 10; Prov. 3:33; Zech. 5:4] **14:44** [a] Lev. 13:51; [Zech. 5:4] **14:46** [a] Lev. 11:24; 15:5 **14:47** [a] Lev. 14:8 **14:49** [a] Lev. 14:4

blood of the slain bird and in the running water,
and sprinkle the house seven times. 52 And he
shall cleanse the house with the blood of the
bird and the running water and the living bird,
with the cedar wood, the hyssop, and the scarlet.
53 Then he shall let the living bird loose outside
the city in the open field, and [a]make atonement
for the house, and it shall be clean.
54 "This *is* the law for any [a]leprous sore and
scale, 55 for the [a]leprosy of a garment [b]and of a
house, 56 [a]for a swelling and a scab and a bright
spot, 57 to [a]teach when *it is* unclean and when *it*
*is* clean. This *is* the law of leprosy."

### THE LAW CONCERNING BODILY DISCHARGES

**15** And the LORD spoke to Moses and Aaron,
saying, 2 "Speak to the children of Israel, and
say to them: [a]'When any man has a discharge from
his body, his discharge *is* unclean. 3 And this shall
be his uncleanness in regard to his discharge—
whether his body runs with his discharge, or
his body is stopped up by his discharge, it *is* his
uncleanness. 4 Every bed is unclean on which
he who has the discharge lies, and everything
on which he sits shall be unclean. 5 And whoev-
er [a]touches his bed shall [b]wash his clothes and
[c]bathe in water, and be unclean until evening.
6 He who sits on anything on which he who has
the [a]discharge sat shall wash his clothes and
bathe in water, and be unclean until evening.
7 And he who touches the body of him who has
the discharge shall wash his clothes and bathe in
water, and be unclean until evening. 8 If he who
has the discharge [a]spits on him who is clean, then
he shall wash his clothes and bathe in water, and
be unclean until evening. 9 Any saddle on which
he who has the discharge rides shall be unclean.
10 Whoever touches anything that was under him
shall be unclean until evening. He who carries
*any of* those things shall wash his clothes and
bathe in water, and be unclean until evening.
11 And whomever the one who has the discharge
touches, and has not rinsed his hands in water, he
shall wash his clothes and bathe in water, and be
unclean until evening. 12 The [a]vessel of earth that
he who has the discharge touches shall be broken,
and every vessel of wood shall be rinsed in water.
13 'And when he who has a discharge is
cleansed of his discharge, then [a]he shall count
for himself seven days for his cleansing, wash
his clothes, and bathe his body in running water;
then he shall be clean. 14 On the eighth day he shall
take for himself [a]two turtledoves or two young
pigeons, and come before the LORD, to the door
of the tabernacle of meeting, and give them to
the priest. 15 Then the priest shall offer them, [a]the
one *as* a sin offering and the other *as* a burnt
offering. [b]So the priest shall make atonement for
him before the LORD because of his discharge.
16 [a]'If any man has an emission of semen,
then he shall wash all his body in water, and be
unclean until evening. 17 And any garment and
any leather on which there is semen, it shall be
washed with water, and be unclean until evening.
18 Also, when a woman lies with a man, and *there*
*is* an emission of semen, they shall bathe in
water, and [a]be unclean until evening.
19 [a]'If a woman has a discharge, *and* the dis-
charge from her body is blood, she shall be set
apart seven days; and whoever touches her shall
be unclean until evening. 20 Everything that she
lies on during her impurity shall be unclean;
also everything that she sits on shall be unclean.
21 Whoever touches her bed shall wash his clothes
and bathe in water, and be unclean until evening.
22 And whoever touches anything that she sat on
shall wash his clothes and bathe in water, and be
unclean until evening. 23 If *anything* is on *her* bed
or on anything on which she sits, when he touches
it, he shall be unclean until evening. 24 And [a]if any
man lies with her at all, so that her impurity is on
him, he shall be unclean seven days; and every
bed on which he lies shall be unclean.
25 'If [a]a woman has a discharge of blood for
many days, other than at the time of her *custom-*
*ary* impurity, or if it runs beyond her *usual time*
*of* impurity, all the days of her unclean discharge
shall be as the days of her *customary* impurity.
She *shall be* unclean. 26 Every bed on which she
lies all the days of her discharge shall be to her
as the bed of her impurity; and whatever she
sits on shall be unclean, as the uncleanness of
her impurity. 27 Whoever touches those things
shall be unclean; he shall wash his clothes and
bathe in water, and be unclean until evening.
28 'But [a]if she is cleansed of her discharge,
then she shall count for herself seven days, and
after that she shall be clean. 29 And on the eighth
day she shall take for herself two turtledoves or
two young pigeons, and bring them to the priest,
to the door of the tabernacle of meeting. 30 Then
the priest shall offer the one *as* a sin offering
and the other *as* a [a]burnt offering, and the priest
shall make atonement for her before the LORD
for the discharge of her uncleanness.
31 'Thus you shall [a]separate the children of Is-
rael from their uncleanness, lest they die in their
uncleanness when they [b]defile My tabernacle that
*is* among them. 32 [a]This *is* the law for one who has
a discharge, [b]and *for him* who emits semen and is
unclean thereby, 33 [a]and for her who is indisposed
because of her *customary* impurity, and for one
who has a discharge, either man [b]or woman,
[c]and for him who lies with her who is unclean.' "

**14:53** [a] Lev. 14:20 **14:54** [a] Lev. 13:30; 26:21 **14:55** [a] Lev. 13:47–52 [b] Lev. 14:34 **14:56** [a] Lev. 13:2 **14:57** [a] Lev. 11:47; 20:25; Deut. 24:8; Ezek. 44:23 **15:2** [a] Lev. 22:4; Num. 5:2; 2 Sam. 3:29 **15:5** [a] Lev. 5:2; 14:46 [b] Lev. 14:8, 47 [c] Lev. 11:25; 17:15 **15:6** [a] Lev. 15:10; Deut. 23:10 **15:8** [a] Num. 12:14 **15:12** [a] Lev. 6:28; 11:32, 33 **15:13** [a] Lev. 14:8; 15:28; Num. 19:11, 12 **15:14** [a] Lev. 14:22, 23, 30, 31 **15:15** [a] Lev. 14:30, 31 [b] Lev. 14:19, 31 **15:16** [a] Lev. 22:4; Deut. 23:10, 11 **15:18** [a] [Ex. 19:15; 1 Sam. 21:4; 1 Cor. 6:18] **15:19** [a] Lev. 12:2 **15:24** [a] Lev. 18:19; 20:18 **15:25** [a] Matt. 9:20; Mark 5:25; Luke 8:43 **15:28** [a] Lev. 15:13–15 **15:30** [a] Lev. 5:7 **15:31** [a] Lev. 11:47; 14:57; 22:2; Deut. 24:8; Ezek. 44:23; [Heb. 12:15] [b] Lev. 20:3; Num. 5:3; 19:13, 20; Ezek. 5:11; 23:38; 36:17 **15:32** [a] Lev. 15:2 [b] Lev. 15:16 **15:33** [a] Lev. 15:19 [b] Lev. 15:25 [c] Lev. 15:24

## THE DAY OF ATONEMENT

16 Now the LORD spoke to Moses after [a]the
death of the two sons of Aaron, when they
offered *profane fire* before the LORD, and died;
2 and the LORD said to Moses: "Tell Aaron your
brother [a]not to come at *just* any time into the
Holy *Place* inside the veil, before the mercy seat
which *is* on the ark, lest he die; for [b]I will appear
in the cloud above the mercy seat.
3 "Thus Aaron shall [a]come into the Holy
*Place:* [b]with *the blood of* a young bull as a sin
offering, and *of* a ram as a burnt offering. 4 He
shall put the [a]holy linen tunic and the linen
trousers on his body; he shall be girded with a
linen sash, and with the linen turban he shall
be attired. These *are* holy garments. Therefore
[b]he shall wash his body in water, and put them
on. 5 And he shall take from [a]the congregation
of the children of Israel two kids of the goats as
a sin offering, and one ram as a burnt offering.
6 "Aaron shall offer the bull as a sin offering,
which *is* for himself, and [a]make atonement for
himself and for his house. 7 He shall take the two
goats and present them before the LORD *at* the
door of the tabernacle of meeting. 8 Then Aaron
shall cast lots for the two goats: one lot for the
LORD and the other lot for the scapegoat. 9 And
Aaron shall bring the goat on which the LORD's
lot fell, and offer it *as* a sin offering. 10 But the
goat on which the lot fell to be the scapegoat
shall be presented alive before the LORD, to
make [a]atonement upon it, *and* to let it go as the
scapegoat into the wilderness.
11 "And Aaron shall bring the bull of the sin
offering, which is for [a]himself, and make atone-
ment for himself and for his house, and shall kill
the bull as the sin offering which *is* for himself.
12 Then he shall take [a]a censer full of burning
coals of fire from the altar before the LORD,
with his hands full of [b]sweet incense beaten
fine, and bring *it* inside the veil. 13 [a]And he shall
put the incense on the fire before the LORD, that
the cloud of incense may cover the [b]mercy seat
that *is* on the Testimony, lest he [c]die. 14 [a]He shall
take some of the blood of the bull and [b]sprinkle
*it* with his finger on the mercy seat on the east
*side;* and before the mercy seat he shall sprinkle
some of the blood with his finger seven times.
15 [a]"Then he shall kill the goat of the sin offer-
ing, which *is* for the people, bring its blood [b]inside
the veil, do with that blood as he did with the blood
of the bull, and sprinkle it on the mercy seat and
before the mercy seat. 16 So he shall [a]make atone-
ment for the Holy *Place,* because of the unclean-
ness of the children of Israel, and because of their
transgressions, for all their sins; and so he shall
do for the tabernacle of meeting which remains
among them in the midst of their uncleanness.
17 There shall be [a]no man in the tabernacle of
meeting when he goes in to make atonement in
the Holy *Place,* until he comes out, that he may
make atonement for himself, for his household,
and for all the assembly of Israel. 18 And he shall go
out to the altar that *is* before the LORD, and make
atonement for [a]it, and shall take some of the blood
of the bull and some of the blood of the goat, and
put it on the horns of the altar all around. 19 Then
he shall sprinkle some of the blood on it with his
finger seven times, cleanse it, and [a]consecrate it
from the uncleanness of the children of Israel.
20 "And when he has made an end of atoning
for the Holy *Place,* the tabernacle of meeting, and
the altar, he shall bring the live goat. 21 Aaron shall
lay both his hands on the head of the live goat,
[a]confess over it all the iniquities of the children of
Israel, and all their transgressions, concerning all
their sins, [b]putting them on the head of the goat,
and shall send *it* away into the wilderness by the
hand of a suitable man. 22 The goat shall [a]bear on
itself all their iniquities to an uninhabited land;
and he shall [b]release the goat in the wilderness.

### SEEING JESUS IN THE SCRIPTURE

**16:22** This scapegoat represented the removal of the sin of God's people. This goat was sent into the wilderness, picturing how their sins were carried away. The death, burial, and resurrection of Jesus removed sin once and for all (see Heb. 9:28).

23 "Then Aaron shall come into the taberna-
cle of meeting, [a]shall take off the linen garments
which he put on when he went into the Holy
*Place,* and shall leave them there. 24 And he
shall wash his body with water in a holy place,
put on his garments, come out and offer his
burnt offering and the burnt offering of the
people, and make atonement for himself and
for the people. 25 [a]The fat of the sin offering he
shall burn on the altar. 26 And he who released
the goat as the scapegoat shall wash his clothes
[a]and bathe his body in water, and afterward he
may come into the camp. 27 [a]The bull *for* the sin
offering and the goat *for* the sin offering, whose
blood was brought in to make atonement in the
Holy *Place,* shall be carried outside the camp.
And they shall burn in the fire their skins, their

**16:1** [a] Lev. 10:1, 2; 2 Sam. 6:6–8 **16:2** [a] Ex. 30:10; Lev. 16:34; 23:27; [Heb. 6:19; 9:7, 8, 12; 10:19] [b] Ex. 25:21, 22; 40:34; 1 Kin. 8:10–12 **16:3** [a] Lev. 4:1–12; 16:6; [Heb. 9:7, 12, 24, 25] [b] Lev. 4:3 **16:4** [a] Ex. 28:39, 42, 43; Lev. 6:10; Ezek. 44:17, 18 [b] Ex. 30:20; Lev. 8:6, 7 **16:5** [a] Lev. 4:14; Num. 29:11; 2 Chr. 29:21; Ezra 6:17; Ezek. 45:22, 23 **16:6** [a] Lev. 9:7; [Heb. 5:3; 7:27, 28; 9:7] **16:10** [a] [Is. 53:5, 6; Rom. 3:25; Heb. 7:27; 9:23, 24; 1 John 2:2] **16:11** [a] [Heb. 7:27; 9:7] **16:12** [a] Lev. 10:1; Num. 16:7, 18; Is. 6:6, 7; Rev. 8:5 [b] Ex. 30:34–38 **16:13** [a] Ex. 30:7, 8; Num. 16:7, 18, 46 [b] Ex. 25:21 [c] Ex. 28:43; Lev. 22:9; Num. 4:15, 20 **16:14** [a] Lev. 4:5; [Heb. 9:25; 10:4] [b] Lev. 4:6, 17 **16:15** [a] [Heb. 2:17] [b] [Heb. 6:19; 7:27; 9:3, 7, 12] **16:16** [a] Ex. 29:36; 30:10; Ezek. 45:18; [Heb. 9:22–24] **16:17** [a] Ex. 34:3; Luke 1:10 **16:18** [a] Ex. 29:36 **16:19** [a] Lev. 16:14; Ezek. 43:20 **16:21** [a] Lev. 5:5; 26:40 [b] [Is. 53:6] **16:22** [a] Lev. 8:14; [Is. 53:6, 11, 12; John 1:29; Heb. 9:28; 1 Pet. 2:24] [b] Lev. 14:7 **16:23** [a] Lev. 6:11; 16:4; Ezek. 42:14; 44:19 **16:25** [a] Lev. 1:8; 4:10 **16:26** [a] Lev. 15:5 **16:27** [a] Lev. 4:12, 21; 6:30; Heb. 13:11

## CHRIST IN THE JEWISH FEASTS

| Feast | Reference | Meaning | Reference |
|---|---|---|---|
| **The Passover** | Exodus 12; Numbers 9:1–14; 28:16–25; Deuteronomy 16:1–6 | Redemption accomplished on the cross | 1 Peter 1:18–19 |
| **Unleavened Bread** | Exodus 12:15–17 | Our justification and sanctification accomplished by Christw | 2 Corinthians 5:21; 1 Corinthians 5:7 |
| **Firstfruits** | Leviticus 23:9–14 | Christ's resurrection | 1 Corinthians 5:7 |
| **Pentecost** | Exodus 23:16; 34:22; Leviticus 23:15–22; Numbers 28:26–31; Deuteronomy 16:9–12 | Christ sending the Holy Spirit | Acts 2:1–41 |
| **Trumpets** | Leviticus 23:23–25; Numbers 29:1–6 | When Christ returns | 1 Corinthians 15:52; 1 Thessalonians 4:16–17 |
| **Day of Atonement** | Leviticus 16:1–34; 23:26–32; 25:9; Numbers 29:7–11 | Cross and Return | Zechariah 12:10; 13:1 |
| **Tabernacles** | Leviticus 23:33–43; Numbers 29:12–38; Deuteronomy 16:13–15 | Christ's kingdom on earth | Zechariah 14:16 |

flesh, and their offal. 28 Then he who burns them
shall wash his clothes and bathe his body in water, and afterward he may come into the camp.
29 "*This* shall be a statute forever for you:
[a]In the seventh month, on the tenth *day* of the month, you shall afflict your souls, and do no work at all, *whether* a native of your own country or a stranger who dwells among you.
30 For
on that day *the priest* shall make atonement for you, to [a]cleanse you, *that* you may be clean from
all your sins before the LORD.
31 [a]It *is* a sabbath
of solemn rest for you, and you shall afflict your
souls. *It is* a statute forever.
32 [a]And the priest,
who is anointed and [b]consecrated to minister as priest in his father's place, shall make atonement, and put on the linen clothes, the holy garments;
33 then he shall make atonement for the Holy
Sanctuary,[1] and he shall make atonement for the tabernacle of meeting and for the altar, and he shall make atonement for the priests and for all
the people of the assembly.
34 [a]This shall be an
everlasting statute for you, to make atonement for the children of Israel, for all their sins, [b]once a year." And he did as the LORD commanded Moses.

### THE SANCTITY OF BLOOD

17 And the LORD spoke to Moses, saying,
2 "Speak to Aaron, to his sons, and to all the
children of Israel, and say to them, 'This *is* the thing which the LORD has commanded, saying:
3 "Whatever man of the house of Israel who [a]kills
an ox or lamb or goat in the camp, or who kills *it*
outside the camp,
4 and does not bring it to the
door of the tabernacle of meeting to offer an offering to the LORD before the tabernacle of the LORD, the guilt of bloodshed shall be [a]imputed to that man. He has shed blood; and that man
shall be cut off from among his people,
5 to the
end that the children of Israel may bring their sacrifices [a]which they offer in the open field, that they may bring them to the LORD at the door of the tabernacle of meeting, to the priest, and offer
them *as* peace offerings to the LORD.
6 And the
priest [a]shall sprinkle the blood on the altar of the LORD *at* the door of the tabernacle of meeting, and [b]burn the fat for a sweet aroma to the
LORD.
7 They shall no more offer their sacrifices
[a]to demons, after whom they [b]have played the harlot. This shall be a statute forever for them throughout their generations." '
8 "Also you shall say to them: 'Whatever man
of the house of Israel, or of the strangers who dwell among you, [a]who offers a burnt offering
or sacrifice,
9 and does not [a]bring it to the door
of the tabernacle of meeting, to offer it to the LORD, that man shall be cut off from among his people.
10 [a]'And whatever man of the house of Israel,
or of the strangers who dwell among you, who eats any blood, [b]I will set My face against that

**16:29** [a] Ex. 30:10; Lev. 23:27–32; Num. 29:7 **16:30** [a] Ps. 51:2; Jer. 33:8; [Eph. 5:26; Heb. 9:13, 14; 1 John 1:7, 9] **16:31** [a] Lev. 23:27, 32; Ezra 8:21; Is. 58:3, 5; Dan. 10:12 **16:32** [a] Lev. 4:3, 5, 16; 21:10 [b] Ex. 29:29, 30; Num. 20:26, 28 **16:33** [1] That is, *the Most Holy Place* **16:34** [a] Lev. 23:31; Num. 29:7 [b] Ex. 30:10; [Heb. 9:7, 25, 28] **17:3** [a] Deut. 12:5, 15, 21 **17:4** [a] Rom. 5:13 **17:5** [a] Gen. 21:33; 22:2; 31:54; Deut. 12:1–27; Ezek. 20:28 **17:6** [a] Lev. 3:2 [b] Ex. 29:13, 18; Num. 18:17 **17:7** [a] Ex. 22:20; 32:8; 34:15; Deut. 32:17; 2 Chr. 11:15; Ps. 106:37; 1 Cor. 10:20 [b] Ex. 34:15; Deut. 31:16; Ezek. 23:8 **17:8** [a] Lev. 1:2, 3; 18:26 **17:9** [a] Lev. 14:23 **17:10** [a] Gen. 9:4; Lev. 3:17; 7:26, 27; Deut. 12:16, 23–25; 15:23; 1 Sam. 14:33 [b] Lev. 20:3, 5, 6

person who eats blood, and will cut him off from
among his people. 11 For the [a]life of the flesh *is*
in the blood, and I have given it to you upon the
altar [b]to make atonement for your souls; for [c]it
*is* the blood *that* makes atonement for the soul.'
12 Therefore I said to the children of Israel, 'No
one among you shall eat blood, nor shall any
stranger who dwells among you eat blood.'
13 "Whatever man of the children of Israel,
or of the strangers who dwell among you, who
[a]hunts and catches any animal or bird that may
be eaten, he shall [b]pour out its blood and [c]cover
it with dust; 14 [a]for *it is* the life of all flesh. Its
blood sustains its life. Therefore I said to the
children of Israel, 'You shall not eat the blood
of any flesh, for the life of all flesh is its blood.
Whoever eats it shall be cut off.'
15 [a]"And every person who eats what died
*naturally* or what was torn *by beasts*, *whether he*
*is* a native of your own country or a stranger, [b]he
shall both wash his clothes and [c]bathe in water,
and be unclean until evening. Then he shall be
clean. 16 But if he does not wash *them* or bathe
his body, then [a]he shall bear his guilt."

### LAWS OF SEXUAL MORALITY

**18** Then the LORD spoke to Moses, saying,
2 "Speak to the children of Israel, and say to
them: [a]'I am the LORD your God. 3 [a]According to
the doings of the land of Egypt, where you dwelt,
you shall not do; and [b]according to the doings
of the land of Canaan, where I am bringing you,
you shall not do; nor shall you walk in their
ordinances. 4 [a]You shall observe My judgments
and keep My ordinances, to walk in them: I *am*
the LORD your God. 5 You shall therefore keep
My statutes and My judgments, which if a man
does, he shall live by them: I *am* the LORD.

> **SEEING JESUS IN THE SCRIPTURE**
>
> **18:5** Paul explained the law is "cursed" because it's unable to give anyone life (see Gal. 3:12–13). Jesus, however, has provided life by keeping God's law and then becoming cursed in a different way—by hanging on the cross to pay our sin penalty.

6 'None of you shall approach anyone who
is near of kin to him, to uncover his nakedness:
I *am* the LORD. 7 The nakedness of your father
or the nakedness of your mother you shall not
uncover. She *is* your mother; you shall not un-
cover her nakedness. 8 The nakedness of your
[a]father's wife you shall not uncover; it *is* your
father's nakedness. 9 [a]The nakedness of your
sister, the daughter of your father, or the daughter
of your mother, *whether* born at home or else-
where, their nakedness you shall not uncover.
10 The nakedness of your son's daughter or your
daughter's daughter, their nakedness you shall
not uncover; for theirs *is* your own nakedness.
11 The nakedness of your father's wife's daughter,
begotten by your father—she *is* your sister—you
shall not uncover her nakedness. 12 [a]You shall not
uncover the nakedness of your father's sister;
she *is* near of kin to your father. 13 You shall not
uncover the nakedness of your mother's sister, for
she *is* near of kin to your mother. 14 [a]You shall not
uncover the nakedness of your father's brother.
You shall not approach his wife; she *is* your aunt.
15 You shall not uncover the nakedness of your
daughter-in-law—she *is* your son's wife—you
shall not uncover her nakedness. 16 You shall not
uncover the nakedness of your brother's wife; it *is*
your brother's nakedness. 17 You shall not uncover
the nakedness of a woman and her [a]daughter, nor
shall you take her son's daughter or her daughter's
daughter, to uncover her nakedness. They *are*
near of kin to her. It *is* wickedness. 18 Nor shall you
take a woman [a]as a rival to her sister, to uncover
her nakedness while the other is alive.
19 'Also you shall not approach a woman to
uncover her nakedness as [a]long as she is in her
[b]*customary* impurity. 20 [a]Moreover you shall
not lie carnally with your [b]neighbor's wife, to
defile yourself with her. 21 And you shall not let
any of your descendants [a]pass through [b]*the fire*
to [c]Molech, nor shall you profane the name of
your God: I *am* the LORD. 22 You shall not lie with
[a]a male as with a woman. It *is* an abomination.
23 Nor shall you mate with any [a]animal, to defile
yourself with it. Nor shall any woman stand be-
fore an animal to mate with it. It *is* perversion.
24 [a]'Do not defile yourselves with any of these
things; [b]for by all these the nations are defiled,
which I am casting out before you. 25 For [a]the
land is defiled; therefore I [b]visit the punishment
of its iniquity upon it, and the land [c]vomits out
its inhabitants. 26 [a]You shall therefore keep My
statutes and My judgments, and shall not commit
*any* of these abominations, *either* any of your
own nation or any stranger who dwells among
you 27 (for all these abominations the men of the
land have done, who *were* before you, and thus the
land is defiled), 28 lest [a]the land vomit you out also
when you defile it, as it vomited out the nations
that *were* before you. 29 For whoever commits any
of these abominations, the persons who commit
*them* shall be cut off from among their people.

**17:11** [a] Gen. 9:4; Lev. 17:14 [b] [Matt. 26:28; Rom. 3:25; Eph. 1:7; Col. 1:14, 20; 1 Pet. 1:2; 1 John 1:7] [c] [Heb. 9:22] **17:13** [a] Lev. 7:26 [b] Deut. 12:16, 24 [c] Ezek. 24:7 **17:14** [a] Gen. 9:4; Lev. 17:11; Deut. 12:23 **17:15** [a] Ex. 22:31; Lev. 7:24; 22:8; Deut. 14:21; Ezek. 4:14; 44:31 [b] Lev. 11:25 [c] Lev. 15:5 **17:16** [a] Lev. 5:1 **18:2** [a] Ex. 6:7; Lev. 11:44, 45; 19:3; Ezek. 20:5, 7, 19, 20 **18:3** [a] Josh. 24:14; Ezek. 20:7, 8 [b] Ex. 23:24; Lev. 18:24–30; 20:23; Deut. 12:30, 31 **18:4** [a] Ezek. 20:19 **18:8** [a] Gen. 35:22 **18:9** [a] Lev. 18:11; 20:17; Deut. 27:22 **18:12** [a] Lev. 20:19 **18:14** [a] Lev. 20:20 **18:17** [a] Lev. 20:14 **18:18** [a] 1 Sam. 1:6, 8 **18:19** [a] Ezek. 18:6 [b] Lev. 15:24; 20:18 **18:20** [a] [Prov. 6:25–33] [b] Lev. 20:10 **18:21** [a] Lev. 20:2–5 [b] 2 Kin. 16:3 [c] 1 Kin. 11:7, 33 **18:22** [a] Lev. 20:13 **18:23** [a] Ex. 22:19 **18:24** [a] Matt. 15:18–20 [b] Deut. 18:12 **18:25** [a] Num. 35:33, 34 [b] Jer. 5:9 [c] Lev. 18:28; 20:22 **18:26** [a] Lev. 18:5, 30 **18:28** [a] Jer. 9:19

30 'Therefore you shall keep My ordinance,
so [a]that *you* do not commit *any* of these abom-
inable customs which were committed before
you, and that you do not defile yourselves by
them: [b]I *am* the LORD your God.' "

### *MORAL AND CEREMONIAL LAWS*

**19** And the LORD spoke to Moses, saying,
2 "Speak to all the congregation of the chil-
dren of Israel, and say to them: [a]'You shall be
holy, for I the LORD your God *am* holy.
3 [a]'Every one of you shall revere his mother
and his father, and [b]keep My Sabbaths: I *am* the
LORD your God.
4 [a]'Do not turn to idols, [b]nor make for your-
selves molded gods: I *am* the LORD your God.
5 'And [a]if you offer a sacrifice of a peace of-
fering to the LORD, you shall offer it of your
own free will. 6 It shall be eaten the same day
you offer *it,* and on the next day. And if any re-
mains until the third day, it shall be burned in
the fire. 7 And if it is eaten at all on the third day,
it *is* an abomination. It shall not be accepted.
8 Therefore *everyone* who eats it shall bear his
iniquity, because he has profaned the hallowed
*offering* of the LORD; and that person shall be
cut off from his people.
9 [a]'When you reap the harvest of your land,
you shall not wholly reap the corners of your
field, nor shall you gather the gleanings of your
harvest. 10 And you shall not glean your vineyard,
nor shall you gather *every* grape of your vine-
yard; you shall leave them for the poor and the
stranger: I *am* the LORD your God.
11 [a]'You shall not steal, nor deal falsely, [b]nor
lie to one another. 12 And you shall not [a]swear
by My name falsely, [b]nor shall you profane the
name of your God: I *am* the LORD.
13 [a]'You shall not cheat your neighbor, nor
rob *him.* [b]The wages of him who is hired shall not
remain with you all night until morning. 14 You
shall not curse the deaf, [a]nor put a stumbling
block before the blind, but shall fear your God:
I *am* the LORD.
15 'You shall do no injustice in [a]judgment.
You shall not [b]be partial to the poor, nor honor
the person of the mighty. In righteousness you
shall judge your neighbor. 16 You shall not go
about *as* a [a]talebearer among your people; nor
shall you [b]take a stand against the life of your
neighbor: I *am* the LORD.
17 [a]'You shall not hate your brother in your
heart. [b]You shall surely rebuke your neighbor,
and not bear sin because of him. 18 [a]You shall not
take vengeance, nor bear any grudge against the
children of your people, [b]but you shall love your
neighbor as yourself: I *am* the LORD.
19 'You shall keep My statutes. You shall not
let your livestock breed with another kind. You

**SEEING JESUS IN THE SCRIPTURE**

**19:18** When we're wronged, instead of seeking vengeance, we're to love. This is what Jesus did. He came to earth not to punish us, but to love us by laying down His life for us (see John 15:12–13). When we trust in Jesus, we're forgiven the sins we committed against Him.

**18:30** [a] Lev. 18:3; 22:9 [b] Lev. 18:2 **19:2** [a] Lev. 11:44; 20:7, 26 **19:3** [a] Ex. 20:12 [b] Ex. 16:23; 20:8; 31:13 **19:4** [a] Ex. 20:4 [b] Ex. 34:17 **19:5** [a] Lev. 7:16 **19:9** [a] Deut. 24:19–22 **19:11** [a] Ex. 20:15, 16 [b] Eph. 4:25 **19:12** [a] Deut. 5:11 [b] Lev. 18:21 **19:13** [a] Ex. 22:7–15, 21–27 [b] Deut. 24:15 **19:14** [a] Deut. 27:18 **19:15** [a] Deut. 16:19 [b] Ex. 23:3, 6 **19:16** [a] Prov. 11:13; 18:8; 20:19 [b] 1 Kin. 21:7–19 **19:17** [a] [1 John 2:9, 11; 3:15] [b] Matt. 18:15 **19:18** [a] [Deut. 32:35] [b] Mark 12:31

LIVE THE TRUTH

## BEING A GOOD FRIEND

**19:18** Friendships can be tricky and difficult to navigate. People can seem one way one day and totally different the next. Friends sometimes get along with great ease; at other times they don't seem to like each other at all. Sometimes you do everything right and your friends still don't accept you. And it doesn't get easier; these problems are common for teens and adults.

God knows all about friendship. He invented relationships, created marriage, and designed us for community. Even more, God the Father, God the Son, and God the Spirit maintain a perfect relationship within the one Godhead. Because of this, God knows best how we should navigate friendships: loving others is the key. That includes loving our friends even when they're difficult to love. When anyone wrongs us—an enemy or a friend—we shouldn't try to get even or hold a grudge. Rather, God says we're to love them like we love ourselves. We forgive them. We do what's best for them. We don't quit on them. We may not always like or agree with our friends' actions (just like they may not always like ours), but God calls us to persist in loving them and wanting the best for them. That's how we make friendship work.

shall not sow your field with mixed seed. Nor shall a garment of mixed linen and wool come upon you.

20 'Whoever lies carnally with a woman who *is* [a]betrothed to a man as a concubine, and who has not at all been redeemed nor given her freedom, for this there shall be scourging; *but* they shall not be put to death, because she was not free. 21 And he shall bring his trespass offering to the LORD, to the door of the tabernacle of meeting, a ram as a trespass offering. 22 The priest shall make atonement for him with the ram of the trespass offering before the LORD for his sin which he has committed. And the sin which he has committed shall be forgiven him.

23 'When you come into the land, and have planted all kinds of trees for food, then you shall count their fruit as uncircumcised. Three years it shall be as uncircumcised to you. *It* shall not be eaten. 24 But in the fourth year all its fruit shall be holy, a praise to the LORD. 25 And in the fifth year you may eat its fruit, that it may yield to you its increase: I *am* the LORD your God.

26 'You shall not eat *anything* with the blood, nor shall you practice divination or soothsaying. 27 You shall not shave around the sides of your head, nor shall you disfigure the edges of your beard. 28 You shall not [a]make any cuttings in your flesh for the dead, nor tattoo any marks on you: I *am* the LORD.

29 [a]'Do not prostitute your daughter, to cause her to be a harlot, lest the land fall into harlotry, and the land become full of wickedness.

30 'You shall keep My Sabbaths and [a]reverence My sanctuary: I *am* the LORD.

31 'Give no regard to mediums and familiar spirits; do not seek after [a]them, to be defiled by them: I *am* the LORD your God.

32 [a]'You shall rise before the gray headed and honor the presence of an old man, and [b]fear your God: I *am* the LORD.

33 'And [a]if a stranger dwells with you in your land, you shall not mistreat him. 34 [a]The stranger who dwells among you shall be to you as one born among you, and [b]you shall love him as yourself; for you were strangers in the land of Egypt: I *am* the LORD your God.

35 'You shall do no injustice in judgment, in measurement of length, weight, or volume. 36 You shall have [a]honest scales, honest weights, an honest ephah, and an honest hin: I *am* the LORD your God, who brought you out of the land of Egypt.

37 [a]'Therefore you shall observe all My statutes and all My judgments, and perform them: I *am* the LORD.' "

### *PENALTIES FOR BREAKING THE LAW*

**20** Then the LORD spoke to Moses, saying, 2 [a]"Again, you shall say to the children of Israel: [b]'Whoever of the children of Israel, or of the strangers who dwell in Israel, who gives *any* of his descendants to Molech, he shall surely be put to death. The people of the land shall [c]stone him with stones. 3 [a]I will set My face against that man, and will cut him off from his people, because he has given *some* of his descendants to Molech, to defile My sanctuary and profane My holy name. 4 And if the people of the land should in any way hide their eyes from the man, when he gives *some* of his descendants to Molech, and they do not kill him, 5 then I will set My face against that man and against his family; and I will cut him off from his people, and all who prostitute themselves with him to commit harlotry with Molech.

> **20:2–5** The penalty for child sacrifice, whether carried out by a citizen of Israel or a foreigner, was death. Offenders were taken outside the camp where the men of the community threw rocks at them until they died. Children are a trust and blessing from God and killing them in a pagan ritual is a wickedness that God will not tolerate.

6 'And [a]the person who turns to mediums and familiar spirits, to prostitute himself with them, I will set My face against that person and cut him off from his people. 7 [a]Consecrate yourselves therefore, and be holy, for I *am* the LORD your God. 8 And you shall keep [a]My statutes, and perform them: [b]I *am* the LORD who sanctifies you.

9 'For [a]everyone who curses his father or his mother shall surely be put to death. He has cursed his father or his mother. [b]His blood *shall be* upon him.

10 [a]'The man who commits adultery with *another* man's wife, *he* who commits adultery with his neighbor's wife, the adulterer and the adulteress, shall surely be put to death. 11 The man who lies with his [a]father's wife has uncovered his father's nakedness; both of them shall surely be put to death. Their blood *shall be* upon them. 12 If a man lies with his [a]daughter-in-law, both of them shall surely be put to death. They have committed perversion. Their blood *shall be* upon them. 13 [a]If a man lies with a male as he lies with a woman, both of

**19:20** [a] Deut. 22:23–27 **19:28** [a] 1 Kin. 18:28; Jer. 16:6 **19:29** [a] Lev. 21:9; Deut. 22:21; 23:17, 18 **19:30** [a] Lev. 26:2; Eccl. 5:1 **19:31** [a] Lev. 20:6, 27; Deut. 18:11; 1 Sam. 28:3; Is. 8:19 **19:32** [a] Prov. 23:22; Lam. 5:12; 1 Tim. 5:1 [b] Lev. 19:14 **19:33** [a] Ex. 22:21; Deut. 24:17, 18 **19:34** [a] Ex. 12:48 [b] Deut. 10:19 **19:36** [a] Deut. 25:13–15; Prov. 20:10 **19:37** [a] Lev. 18:4, 5; Deut. 4:5, 6; 5:1; 6:25 **20:2** [a] Lev. 18:2 [b] Lev. 18:21; 2 Kin. 23:10; 2 Chr. 33:6; Jer. 7:31 [c] Deut. 17:2–5 **20:3** [a] Lev. 17:10 **20:6** [a] Lev. 19:31; 1 Sam. 28:7–25 **20:7** [a] Lev. 19:2; Heb. 12:14 **20:8** [a] Lev. 19:19, 37 [b] Ex. 31:13; Deut. 14:2; Ezek. 37:28 **20:9** [a] Ex. 21:17; Deut. 27:16; Prov. 20:20; Matt. 15:4 [b] 2 Sam. 1:16 **20:10** [a] Ex. 20:14; Lev. 18:20; Deut. 5:18; 22:22; John 8:4, 5 **20:11** [a] Lev. 18:7, 8; Deut. 27:20 **20:12** [a] Lev. 18:15 **20:13** [a] Lev. 18:22; Deut. 23:17; Judg. 19:22

them have committed an abomination. They
shall surely be put to death. Their blood *shall
be* upon them. 14 If a man marries a woman
and her [a]mother, it *is* wickedness. They shall be
burned with fire, both he and they, that there
may be no wickedness among you. 15 If a man
mates with an [a]animal, he shall surely be put
to death, and you shall kill the animal. 16 If a
woman approaches any animal and mates with
it, you shall kill the woman and the animal.
They shall surely be put to death. Their blood
*is* upon them.

17 'If a man takes his [a]sister, his father's
daughter or his mother's daughter, and sees
her nakedness and she sees his nakedness, it
*is* a wicked thing. And they shall be cut off in
the sight of their people. He has uncovered his
sister's nakedness. He shall bear his guilt. 18 [a]If
a man lies with a woman during her sickness
and uncovers her nakedness, he has exposed
her flow, and she has uncovered the flow of
her blood. Both of them shall be cut off from
their people.

19 'You shall not uncover the nakedness of
your [a]mother's sister nor of your [b]father's sister,
for that would uncover his near of kin. They shall
bear their guilt. 20 If a man lies with his [a]uncle's
wife, he has uncovered his uncle's nakedness.
They shall bear their sin; they shall die child-
less. 21 If a man takes his [a]brother's wife, it *is* an
unclean thing. He has uncovered his brother's
nakedness. They shall be childless.

22 'You shall therefore keep all My [a]statutes
and all My judgments, and perform them, that
the land where I am bringing you to dwell [b]may
not vomit you out. 23 [a]And you shall not walk in
the statutes of the nation which I am casting out
before you; for they commit all these things, and
[b]therefore I abhor them. 24 But [a]I have said to
you, "You shall inherit their land, and I will give
it to you to possess, a land flowing with milk
and honey." I *am* the LORD your God, [b]who has
separated you from the peoples. 25 [a]You shall
therefore distinguish between clean animals
and unclean, between unclean birds and clean,
[b]and you shall not make yourselves abomina-
ble by beast or by bird, or by any kind of living
thing that creeps on the ground, which I have
separated from you as unclean. 26 And you shall
be holy to Me, [a]for I the LORD *am* holy, and
have separated you from the peoples, that you
should be Mine.

27 [a]'A man or a woman who is a medium, or
who has familiar spirits, shall surely be put to
death; they shall stone them with stones. Their
blood *shall be* upon them.' "

### *REGULATIONS FOR CONDUCT OF PRIESTS*
*(cf. Ezek. 44:15–31)*

21 And the LORD said to Moses, "Speak to the
priests, the sons of Aaron, and say to them:
[a]'None shall defile himself for the dead among
his people, 2 except for his relatives who are
nearest to him: his mother, his father, his son, his
daughter, and his brother; 3 also his virgin sister
who is near to him, who has had no husband, for
her he may defile himself. 4 *Otherwise* he shall
not defile himself, *being* a chief man among his
people, to profane himself.

5 [a]'They shall not make any bald *place* on
their heads, nor shall they shave the edges of
their beards nor make any cuttings in their flesh.
6 They shall be [a]holy to their God and not profane
the name of their God, for they offer the offer-
ings of the LORD made by fire, *and* the [b]bread of
their God; [c]therefore they shall be holy. 7 [a]They
shall not take a wife *who is* a harlot or a defiled
woman, nor shall they take a woman [b]divorced
from her husband; for *the priest*[1] is holy to his
God. 8 Therefore you shall consecrate him, for
he offers the bread of your God. He shall be holy
to you, for [a]I the LORD, who [b]sanctify you, *am*
holy. 9 The daughter of any priest, if she profanes
herself by playing the harlot, she profanes her
father. She shall be [a]burned with fire.

10 '*He who is* the high priest among his breth-
ren, on whose head the anointing oil was [a]poured
and who is consecrated to wear the garments,
shall not [b]uncover his head nor tear his clothes;
11 nor shall he go [a]near any dead body, nor defile
himself for his father or his mother; 12 [a]nor shall
he go out of the sanctuary, nor profane the sanc-
tuary of his God; for the [b]consecration of the
anointing oil of his God *is* upon him: I *am* the
LORD. 13 And he shall take a wife in her virginity.
14 A widow or a divorced woman or a defiled
woman *or* a harlot—these he shall not marry;
but he shall take a virgin of his own people as
wife. 15 Nor shall he profane his posterity among
his people, for I the LORD sanctify him.' "

16 And the LORD spoke to Moses, saying,
17 "Speak to Aaron, saying: 'No man of your de-
scendants in *succeeding* generations, who has
*any* defect, may approach to offer the bread of
his God. 18 For any man who has a [a]defect shall not
approach: a man blind or lame, who has a marred
*face* or any *limb* [b]too long, 19 a man who has a bro-
ken foot or broken hand, 20 or is a hunchback or
a dwarf, or *a man* who has a defect in his eye, or
eczema or scab, or is a eunuch. 21 No man of the
descendants of Aaron the priest, who has a defect,
shall come near to offer the offerings made by fire
to the LORD. He has a defect; he shall not come

**20:14** [a] Lev. 18:17 **20:15** [a] Lev. 18:23; Deut. 27:21 **20:17** [a] Lev. 18:9; Deut. 27:22 **20:18** [a] Lev. 15:24; 18:19 **20:19** [a] Lev. 18:13 [b] Lev. 18:12 **20:20** [a] Lev. 18:14 **20:21** [a] Lev. 18:16; Matt. 14:3, 4 **20:22** [a] Lev. 18:26; 19:37 [b] Lev. 18:25, 28; 2 Chr. 36:14–16 **20:23** [a] Lev. 18:3, 24 [b] Deut. 9:5 **20:24** [a] Ex. 3:17; 6:8; 13:5; 33:1–3 [b] Ex. 19:5; 33:16; Lev. 20:26; Deut. 7:6; 14:2; 1 Kin. 8:53 **20:25** [a] Lev. 10:10; 11:1–47; Deut. 14:3–21 [b] Lev. 11:43 **20:26** [a] Lev. 19:2; 1 Pet. 1:16 **20:27** [a] Lev. 19:31; 1 Sam. 28:9 **21:1** [a] Lev. 19:28; Ezek. 44:25 **21:5** [a] Lev. 19:27; Deut. 14:1; Ezek. 44:20 **21:6** [a] Ex. 22:31 [b] Lev. 3:11 [c] Is. 52:11 **21:7** [a] Ezek. 44:22 [b] Deut. 24:1, 2 [1] Literally *he* **21:8** [a] Lev. 11:44, 45 [b] Lev. 8:12, 30 **21:9** [a] Deut. 22:21 **21:10** [a] Lev. 8:12 [b] Lev. 10:6, 7 **21:11** [a] Num. 19:14 **21:12** [a] Lev. 10:7 [b] Ex. 29:6, 7 **21:18** [a] Lev. 22:19–25 [b] Lev. 22:23

near to offer the bread of his God. 22 He may eat the bread of his God, *both* the most holy and the holy; 23 only he shall not go near the [a]veil or approach the altar, because he has a defect, lest [b]he profane My sanctuaries; for I the LORD sanctify them.' "

24 And Moses told *it* to Aaron and his sons, and to all the children of Israel.

**22** Then the LORD spoke to Moses, saying, 2 "Speak to Aaron and his sons, that they [a]separate themselves from the holy things of the children of Israel, and that they [b]do not profane My holy name *by* what they [c]dedicate to Me: I *am* the LORD. 3 Say to them: 'Whoever of all your descendants throughout your generations, who goes near the holy things which the children of Israel dedicate to the LORD, [a]while he has uncleanness upon him, that person shall be cut off from My presence: I *am* the LORD.

4 'Whatever man of the descendants of Aaron, who *is* a [a]leper or has [b]a discharge, shall not eat the holy offerings [c]until he is clean. And [d]whoever touches anything made unclean *by* a corpse, or [e]a man who has had an emission of semen, 5 or [a]whoever touches any creeping thing by which he would be made unclean, or [b]any person by whom he would become unclean, whatever his uncleanness may be— 6 the person who has touched any such thing shall be unclean until evening, and shall not eat the holy *offerings* unless he [a]washes his body with water. 7 And when the sun goes down he shall be clean; and afterward he may eat the holy *offerings*, because [a]it *is* his food. 8 [a]Whatever dies *naturally* or is torn *by beasts* he shall not eat, to defile himself with it: I *am* the LORD.

9 'They shall therefore keep [a]My ordinance, [b]lest they bear sin for it and die thereby, if they profane it: I the LORD sanctify them.

10 [a]'No outsider shall eat the holy *offering;* one who dwells with the priest, or a hired servant, shall not eat the holy thing. 11 But if the priest [a]buys a person with his money, he may eat it; and one who is born in his house may eat his food. 12 If the priest's daughter is married to an outsider, she may not eat of the holy offerings. 13 But if the priest's daughter is a widow or divorced, and has no child, and has returned to her father's house as in her youth, she may eat her father's food; but no outsider shall eat it.

14 'And if a man eats the holy *offering* unintentionally, then he shall restore a holy *offering* to the priest, and add one-fifth to it. 15 They shall not profane the [a]holy *offerings* of the children of Israel, which they offer to the LORD, 16 or allow them to bear the guilt of trespass when they eat their holy *offerings;* for I the LORD sanctify them.' "

### *OFFERINGS ACCEPTED AND NOT ACCEPTED*

17 And the LORD spoke to Moses, saying, 18 "Speak to Aaron and his sons, and to all the children of Israel, and say to them: [a]'Whatever man of the house of Israel, or of the strangers in Israel, who offers his sacrifice for any of his vows or for any of his freewill offerings, which they offer to the LORD as a burnt offering— 19 [a]*you shall offer* of your own free will a male without blemish from the cattle, from the sheep, or from the goats. 20 [a]Whatever has a defect, you shall not offer, for it shall not be acceptable on your behalf. 21 And [a]whoever offers a sacrifice of a peace offering to the LORD, [b]to fulfill *his* vow, or a freewill offering from the cattle or the sheep, it must be perfect to be accepted; there shall be no defect in it. 22 [a]Those *that are* blind or broken or maimed, or have an ulcer or eczema or scabs, you shall not offer to the LORD, nor make [b]an offering by fire of them on the altar to the LORD. 23 Either a bull or a lamb that has any limb [a]too long or too short you may offer *as* a freewill offering, but for a vow it shall not be accepted.

24 'You shall not offer to the LORD what is bruised or crushed, or torn or cut; nor shall you make *any offering of them* in your land. 25 Nor [a]from a foreigner's hand shall you offer any of these as [b]the bread of your God, because their [c]corruption *is* in them, *and* defects *are* in them. They shall not be accepted on your behalf.' "

26 And the LORD spoke to Moses, saying: 27 [a]"When a bull or a sheep or a goat is born, it shall be seven days with its mother; and from the eighth day and thereafter it shall be accepted as an offering made by fire to the LORD. 28 *Whether it is* a cow or ewe, do not kill both her [a]and her young on the same day. 29 And when you [a]offer a sacrifice of thanksgiving to the LORD, offer *it* of your own free will. 30 On the same day it shall be eaten; you shall leave [a]none of it until morning: I *am* the LORD.

31 [a]"Therefore you shall keep My commandments, and perform them: I *am* the LORD. 32 [a]You shall not profane My holy name, but [b]I will be hallowed among the children of Israel. I *am* the LORD who [c]sanctifies you, 33 [a]who brought you out of the land of Egypt, to be your God: I *am* the LORD."

### *FEASTS OF THE LORD*

**23** And the LORD spoke to Moses, saying, 2 "Speak to the children of Israel, and say to them: 'The feasts of the LORD, which you shall proclaim *to be* [a]holy convocations, these *are* My feasts.

**21:23** [a] Lev. 16:2 [b] Lev. 21:12 **22:2** [a] Num. 6:3 [b] Lev. 18:21 [c] Ex. 28:38; Lev. 16:19; 25:10; Num. 18:32; Deut. 15:19 **22:3** [a] Lev. 7:20, 21; Num. 19:13 **22:4** [a] Num. 5:2 [b] Lev. 15:2 [c] Lev. 14:2; 15:13 [d] Lev. 11:24–28, 39, 40; Num. 19:11 [e] Lev. 15:16, 17 **22:5** [a] Lev. 11:23–28 [b] Lev. 15:7, 19 **22:6** [a] Lev. 15:5 **22:7** [a] Lev. 21:22; Num. 18:11, 13 **22:8** [a] Ex. 22:31; Lev. 7:24; 11:39, 40; 17:15; Ezek. 44:31 **22:9** [a] Lev. 18:30 [b] Ex. 28:43; Lev. 22:16; Num. 18:22 **22:10** [a] Ex. 29:33; Lev. 22:13; Num. 3:10 **22:11** [a] Ex. 12:44 **22:15** [a] Num. 18:32 **22:18** [a] Lev. 1:2, 3, 10 **22:19** [a] Lev. 1:3; Deut. 15:21 **22:20** [a] Deut. 15:21; 17:1; Mal. 1:8, 14; [Eph. 5:27; Heb. 9:14; 1 Pet. 1:19] **22:21** [a] Lev. 3:1, 6 [b] Num. 15:3, 8; Ps. 61:8; 65:1; Eccl. 5:4, 5 **22:22** [a] Lev. 22:20; Mal. 1:8 [b] Lev. 1:9, 13; 3:3, 5 **22:23** [a] Lev. 21:18 **22:25** [a] Num. 15:15, 16 [b] Lev. 21:6, 17 [c] Mal. 1:14 **22:27** [a] Ex. 22:30 **22:28** [a] Deut. 22:6, 7 **22:29** [a] Lev. 7:12; Ps. 107:22; 116:17; Amos 4:5 **22:30** [a] Lev. 7:15 **22:31** [a] Lev. 19:37; Num. 15:40; Deut. 4:40 **22:32** [a] Lev. 18:21 [b] Lev. 10:3; Matt. 6:9; Luke 11:2 [c] Lev. 20:8 **22:33** [a] Lev. 19:36, 37; Num. 15:40; Deut. 4:40 **23:2** [a] Ex. 12:16

### *THE SABBATH*

3 [a]'Six days shall work be done, but the sev-
enth day *is* a Sabbath of solemn rest, a holy
convocation. You shall do no work *on it;* it *is*
the Sabbath of the LORD in all your dwellings.

### *THE PASSOVER AND UNLEAVENED BREAD*

*(Num. 28:16–25)*

4 [a]'These *are* the feasts of the LORD, holy con-
vocations which you shall proclaim at their ap-
pointed times. 5 [a]On the fourteenth *day* of the first
month at twilight *is* the LORD's Passover. 6 And on
the fifteenth day of the same month *is* the Feast
of Unleavened Bread to the LORD; seven days you
must eat unleavened bread. 7 [a]On the first day
you shall have a holy convocation; you shall do
no customary work on it. 8 But you shall offer an
offering made by fire to the LORD for seven days.
The seventh day *shall be* a holy convocation; you
shall do no customary work *on it.*' "

### *THE FEAST OF FIRSTFRUITS*

9 And the LORD spoke to Moses, saying,
10 "Speak to the children of Israel, and say to
them: [a]'When you come into the land which I give
to you, and reap its harvest, then you shall bring
a sheaf of [b]the firstfruits of your harvest to the
priest. 11 He shall [a]wave the sheaf before the LORD,
to be accepted on your behalf; on the day after
the Sabbath the priest shall wave it. 12 And you
shall offer on that day, when you wave the sheaf,
a male lamb of the first year, without blemish, as
a burnt offering to the LORD. 13 Its grain offering
*shall be* two-tenths *of an ephah* of fine flour mixed
with oil, an offering made by fire to the LORD, for
a sweet aroma; and its drink offering *shall be* of
wine, one-fourth of a hin. 14 You shall eat neither
bread nor parched grain nor fresh grain until the
same day that you have brought an offering to
your God; *it shall be* a statute forever throughout
your generations in all your dwellings.

### *THE FEAST OF WEEKS*

*(Ex. 34:22; Num. 28:26–31; Deut. 16:9, 10)*

15 'And you shall count for yourselves from
the day after the Sabbath, from the day that you
brought the sheaf of the wave offering: seven
Sabbaths shall be completed. 16 Count [a]fifty days
to the day after the seventh Sabbath; then you
shall offer [b]a new grain offering to the LORD.
17 You shall bring from your dwellings two wave
*loaves* of two-tenths *of an ephah.* They shall be
of fine flour; they shall be baked with leaven.
*They are* [a]the firstfruits to the LORD. 18 And you
shall offer with the bread seven lambs of the first
year, without blemish, one young bull, and two
rams. They shall be *as* a burnt offering to the
LORD, with their grain offering and their drink
offerings, an offering made by fire for a sweet
aroma to the LORD. 19 Then you shall sacrifice
[a]one kid of the goats as a sin offering, and two
male lambs of the first year as a sacrifice of a
[b]peace offering. 20 The priest shall wave them
with the bread of the firstfruits *as* a wave offering
before the LORD, with the two lambs. [a]They shall
be holy to the LORD for the priest. 21 And you
shall proclaim on the same day *that* it is a holy
convocation to you. You shall do no customary
work *on it. It shall be* a statute forever in all your
dwellings throughout your generations.

22 [a]'When you reap the harvest of your land,
you shall not wholly reap the corners of your
field when you reap, nor shall you gather any
gleaning from your harvest. You shall leave
them for the poor and for the stranger: I *am*
the LORD your God.' "

### *THE FEAST OF TRUMPETS*

*(Num. 29:1–6)*

23 Then the LORD spoke to Moses, saying,
24 "Speak to the children of Israel, saying: 'In the
[a]seventh month, on the first *day* of the month,
you shall have a sabbath-*rest,* [b]a memorial of
blowing of trumpets, a holy convocation. 25 You
shall do no customary work *on it;* and you shall
offer an offering made by fire to the LORD.' "

### *THE DAY OF ATONEMENT*

*(Num. 29:7–11)*

26 And the LORD spoke to Moses, saying:
27 [a]"Also the tenth *day* of this seventh month
*shall be* the Day of Atonement. It shall be a holy
convocation for you; you shall afflict your souls,
and offer an offering made by fire to the LORD.
28 And you shall do no work on that same day,
for it *is* the Day of Atonement, [a]to make atone-
ment for you before the LORD your God. 29 For
any person who is not [a]afflicted *in soul* on that
same day [b]shall be cut off from his people. 30 And
any person who does any work on that same
day, [a]that person I will destroy from among
his people. 31 You shall do no manner of work;
*it shall be* a statute forever throughout your
generations in all your dwellings. 32 It *shall be*
to you a sabbath of *solemn* rest, and you shall
afflict your souls; on the ninth *day* of the month
at evening, from evening to evening, you shall
celebrate your sabbath."

### *THE FEAST OF TABERNACLES*

*(Num. 29:12–40; Deut. 16:13–17)*

33 Then the LORD spoke to Moses, saying,
34 "Speak to the children of Israel, saying: [a]'The
fifteenth day of this seventh month *shall be*

**23:3** [a] Ex. 20:9; 23:12; 31:15; Lev. 19:3; Deut. 5:13, 14; Luke 13:14 **23:4** [a] Ex. 23:14–16; Lev. 23:2, 37 **23:5** [a] Ex. 12:1–28; Num. 9:1–5; 28:16–25; Deut. 16:1–8; Josh. 5:10 **23:7** [a] Ex. 12:16; Num. 28:18, 25 **23:10** [a] Ex. 23:19; 34:26 [b] [Rom. 11:16]; James 1:18; Rev. 14:4 **23:11** [a] Ex. 29:24 **23:16** [a] Acts 2:1 [b] Num. 28:26 **23:17** [a] Ex. 23:16, 19; Num. 15:17–21 **23:19** [a] Lev. 4:23, 28; Num. 28:30; [2 Cor. 5:21] [b] Lev. 3:1 **23:20** [a] Lev. 14:13; Num. 18:12; Deut. 18:4 **23:22** [a] Lev. 19:9, 10; Deut. 24:19–22; Ruth 2:2, 15 **23:24** [a] Num. 29:1 [b] Lev. 25:9 **23:27** [a] Lev. 16:1–34; 25:9; Num. 29:7 **23:28** [a] Lev. 16:34 **23:29** [a] Is. 22:12; Jer. 31:9; Ezek. 7:16 [b] Gen. 17:14; Lev. 13:46; Num. 5:2 **23:30** [a] Lev. 20:3–6 **23:34** [a] Ex. 23:16; Num. 29:12; Deut. 16:13–16; Ezra 3:4; Neh. 8:14; Zech. 14:16–19; John 7:2

the Feast of Tabernacles *for* seven days to the LORD. 35 On the first day *there shall be* a holy convocation. You shall do no customary work *on it.* 36 *For* seven days you shall offer an [a]offering made by fire to the LORD. [b]On the eighth day you shall have a holy convocation, and you shall offer an offering made by fire to the LORD. It *is* a [c]sacred assembly, *and* you shall do no customary work *on it.*

37 [a]'These *are* the feasts of the LORD which you shall proclaim *to be* holy convocations, to offer an offering made by fire to the LORD, a burnt offering and a grain offering, a sacrifice and drink offerings, everything on its day— 38 [a]besides the Sabbaths of the LORD, besides your gifts, besides all your vows, and besides all your freewill offerings which you give to the LORD.

39 'Also on the fifteenth day of the seventh month, when you have [a]gathered in the fruit of the land, you shall keep the feast of the LORD *for* seven days; on the first day *there shall be* a sabbath-*rest,* and on the eighth day a sabbath-*rest.* 40 And [a]you shall take for yourselves on the first day the fruit of beautiful trees, branches of palm trees, the boughs of leafy trees, and willows of the brook; [b]and you shall rejoice before the LORD your God for seven days. 41 [a]You shall keep it as a feast to the LORD for seven days in the year. *It shall be* a statute forever in your generations. You shall celebrate it in the seventh month. 42 [a]You shall dwell in booths for seven days. [b]All who are native Israelites shall dwell in booths, 43 [a]that your generations may [b]know that I made the children of Israel dwell in booths when [c]I brought them out of the land of Egypt: I *am* the LORD your God.' "

44 So Moses [a]declared to the children of Israel the feasts of the LORD.

### CARE OF THE TABERNACLE LAMPS

*(Ex. 27:20, 21)*

**24** Then the LORD spoke to Moses, saying: 2 [a]"Command the children of Israel that they bring to you pure oil of pressed olives for the light, to make the lamps burn continually. 3 Outside the veil of the Testimony, in the tabernacle of meeting, Aaron shall be in charge of it from evening until morning before the LORD continually; *it shall be* a statute forever in your generations. 4 He shall be in charge of the lamps on [a]the pure *gold* lampstand before the LORD continually.

### THE BREAD OF THE TABERNACLE

5 "And you shall take fine flour and bake twelve [a]cakes with it. Two-tenths *of an ephah* shall be in each cake. 6 You shall set them in two rows, six in a row, [a]on the pure *gold* table before the LORD. 7 And you shall put pure frankincense on *each* row, that it may be on the bread for a [a]memorial, an offering made by fire to the LORD. 8 [a]Every Sabbath he shall set it in order before the LORD continually, *being taken* from the children of Israel by an everlasting covenant. 9 And [a]it shall be for Aaron and his sons, [b]and they shall eat it in a holy place; for it *is* most holy to him from the offerings of the LORD made by fire, by a perpetual statute."

### THE PENALTY FOR BLASPHEMY

10 Now the son of an Israelite woman, whose father *was* an Egyptian, went out among the children of Israel; and this Israelite *woman's* son and a man of Israel fought each other in the camp. 11 And the Israelite woman's son [a]blasphemed the name *of the LORD* and [b]cursed; and so they [c]brought him to Moses. (His mother's name *was* Shelomith the daughter of Dibri, of the tribe of Dan.) 12 Then they [a]put him in custody, [b]that the mind of the LORD might be shown to them.

13 And the LORD spoke to Moses, saying, 14 "Take outside the camp him who has cursed; then let all who heard *him* [a]lay their hands on his head, and let all the congregation stone him.

15 "Then you shall speak to the children of Israel, saying: 'Whoever curses his God [a]shall bear his sin. 16 And whoever [a]blasphemes the name of the LORD shall surely be put to death. All the congregation shall certainly stone him, the stranger as well as him who is born in the land. When he blasphemes the name *of the LORD,* he shall be put to death.

17 [a]'Whoever kills any man shall surely be put to death. 18 [a]Whoever kills an animal shall make it good, animal for animal.

19 'If a man causes disfigurement of his neighbor, as [a]he has done, so shall it be done to him— 20 fracture for [a]fracture, [b]eye for eye, tooth for tooth; as he has caused disfigurement of a man, so shall it be done to him. 21 And whoever kills an animal shall restore it; but whoever kills a man shall be put to death. 22 You shall have [a]the same law for the stranger and for one from your own country; for I *am* the LORD your God.' "

23 Then Moses spoke to the children of Israel; and they took outside the camp him who had cursed, and stoned him with stones. So the children of Israel did as the LORD commanded Moses.

### THE SABBATH OF THE SEVENTH YEAR

*(Deut. 15:1–11)*

**25** And the LORD spoke to Moses on Mount [a]Sinai, saying, 2 "Speak to the children of Israel, and say to them: 'When you come into the land which I give you, then the land shall [a]keep

**23:36** [a] Num. 29:12–34 [b] Num. 29:35–38; Neh. 8:18; John 7:37 [c] Deut. 16:8; 2 Chr. 7:8 **23:37** [a] Lev. 23:2, 4 **23:38** [a] Num. 29:39 **23:39** [a] Ex. 23:16; Deut. 16:13 **23:40** [a] Neh. 8:15 [b] Deut. 12:7; 16:14, 15 **23:41** [a] Num. 29:12; Neh. 8:18 **23:42** [a] [Is. 4:6] [b] Neh. 8:14–16 **23:43** [a] Deut. 31:13 [b] Ex. 10:2 [c] Lev. 22:33 **23:44** [a] Lev. 23:2 **24:2** [a] Ex. 27:20, 21 **24:4** [a] Ex. 25:31; 31:8; 37:17 **24:5** [a] Ex. 25:30; 39:36; 40:23 **24:6** [a] 1 Kin. 7:48 **24:7** [a] Lev. 2:2, 9, 16 **24:8** [a] 1 Chr. 9:32 **24:9** [a] Matt. 12:4 [b] Ex. 29:33 **24:11** [a] Ex. 22:28 [b] Is. 8:21 [c] Ex. 18:22, 26 **24:12** [a] Num. 15:34 [b] Num. 27:5 **24:14** [a] Deut. 13:9; 17:7 **24:15** [a] Lev. 20:17 **24:16** [a] [Mark 3:28, 29] **24:17** [a] Ex. 21:12 **24:18** [a] Lev. 24:21 **24:19** [a] Ex. 21:24 **24:20** [a] Ex. 21:23 [b] [Matt. 5:38, 39] **24:22** [a] Ex. 12:49 **25:1** [a] Lev. 26:46 **25:2** [a] Lev. 26:34, 35

LEVITICUS 25:1–34

# REST SETS US FREE

15

STORY OF SCRIPTURE

## WHAT'S GOING ON?

As slaves in Egypt, work preserved the Israelites' lives and was the means to garner favor with their masters. Here in Leviticus, God made it clear this was no longer the case. Since the very beginning, rest has been important to God. He even rested on the seventh day, although not because He was tired. God made this seventh day holy for His people. It was to be a day to rest and worship God. Furthermore, God embedded rest in the rhythm of the Biblical calendar. Every seventh year was designated as a Sabbath year, during which the land was to lie fallow and debts were forgiven. The fiftieth year, following seven cycles of seven years, was the Year of Jubilee. In this year, slaves were set free, ancestral lands that had been sold were returned to their original families, and all debts were canceled. The laws aimed to create a just and sustainable society by preventing land and wealth accumulating in a few hands. It also illustrates a radical trust in God's provision.

## WHAT DOES THIS MEAN FOR ME?

Although we may not adhere to the precise details of the Sabbath, there's still something profound about taking a day to unplug, reset, rest, and worship. Life can become chaotic and sap us of joy. Forcing ourselves to slow down and rest renews our trust in God and restores our minds, bodies, and souls. Furthermore, it reminds us of our acceptance by God because of Jesus' work, not the work we do.

## DID YOU CATCH THE PATTERN?

In this passage, we see the pattern of seven, symbolizing divine completeness or perfection, which recurs throughout the Bible. The seven-day week of creation, the seven years of plenty and famine in Joseph's story, the seven feasts for Israel, and the seven churches in Revelation are a few examples of where else we see this in Scripture.

*For the next* Story of Scripture *reading and devotion, turn to Numbers 21:4–9 on page 159.*

a sabbath to the LORD. 3 Six years you shall sow
your field, and six years you shall prune your
vineyard, and gather its fruit; 4 but in the [a]seventh
year there shall be a sabbath of solemn [b]rest for
the land, a sabbath to the LORD. You shall neither
sow your field nor prune your vineyard. 5 [a]What
grows of its own accord of your harvest you shall
not reap, nor gather the grapes of your untended
vine, *for* it is a year of rest for the land. 6 And the
sabbath *produce* of the land shall be food for you:
for you, your male and female servants, your
hired man, and the stranger who dwells with
you, 7 for your livestock and the beasts that *are*
in your land—all its produce shall be for food.

### *THE YEAR OF JUBILEE*

8 'And you shall count seven sabbaths of
years for yourself, seven times seven years;
and the time of the seven sabbaths of years
shall be to you forty-nine years. 9 Then you shall
cause the trumpet of the Jubilee to sound on
the tenth *day* of the seventh month; [a]on the
Day of Atonement you shall make the trumpet
to sound throughout all your land. 10 And you
shall consecrate the fiftieth year, and [a]proclaim
liberty throughout *all* the land to all its inhab-
itants. It shall be a Jubilee for you; [b]and each of
you shall return to his possession, and each of
you shall return to his family. 11 That fiftieth year
shall be a Jubilee to you; in it [a]you shall neither
sow nor reap what grows of its own accord, nor
gather *the grapes* of your untended vine. 12 For it
*is* the Jubilee; it shall be holy to you; [a]you shall
eat its produce from the field.

## SEEING JESUS IN THE SCRIPTURE

**25:10** The year of Jubilee was a time of restoration when people received back their inheritance. In Jesus, we receive freedom from sin and death and a restored relationship with God, our true inheritance as His children (see Luke 4:18–19).

13 [a]'In this Year of Jubilee, each of you shall
return to his possession. 14 And if you sell

**25:4** [a] Deut. 15:1 [b] [Heb. 4:9] **25:5** [a] 2 Kin. 19:29 **25:9** [a] Lev. 23:24, 27 **25:10** [a] Is. 61:2; 63:4; Jer. 34:8, 15, 17; [Luke 4:19] [b] Lev. 25:13, 28, 54; Num. 36:4 **25:11** [a] Lev. 25:5 **25:12** [a] Lev. 25:6, 7 **25:13** [a] Lev. 25:10; 27:24; Num. 36:4

anything to your neighbor or buy from your neighbor's hand, you shall not [a]oppress one another. 15 [a]According to the number of years after the Jubilee you shall buy from your neighbor, and according to the number of years of crops he shall sell to you. 16 According to the multitude of years you shall increase its price, and according to the fewer number of years you shall diminish its price; for he sells to you *according* to the number *of the years* of the crops. 17 Therefore [a]you shall not oppress one another, [b]but you shall fear your God; for I *am* the LORD your God.

### PROVISIONS FOR THE SEVENTH YEAR

18 [a]'So you shall observe My statutes and keep My judgments, and perform them; [b]and you will dwell in the land in safety. 19 Then the land will yield its fruit, and [a]you will eat your fill, and dwell there in safety.

20 'And if you say, [a]"What shall we eat in the seventh year, since [b]we shall not sow nor gather in our produce?" 21 Then I will [a]command My blessing on you in the [b]sixth year, and it will bring forth produce enough for three years. 22 [a]And you shall sow in the eighth year, and eat [b]old produce until the ninth year; until its produce comes in, you shall eat *of* the old *harvest.*

### REDEMPTION OF PROPERTY

23 'The land shall not be sold permanently, for [a]the land *is* Mine; for you *are* [b]strangers and sojourners with Me. 24 And in all the land of your possession you shall grant redemption of the land.

25 [a]'If one of your brethren becomes poor, and has sold *some* of his possession, and if [b]his redeeming relative comes to redeem it, then he may redeem what his brother sold. 26 Or if the man has no one to redeem it, but he himself becomes able to redeem it, 27 then [a]let him count the years since its sale, and restore the remainder to the man to whom he sold it, that he may return to his possession. 28 But if he is not able to have *it* restored to himself, then what was sold shall remain in the hand of him who bought it until the Year of Jubilee; [a]and in the Jubilee it shall be released, and he shall return to his possession.

29 'If a man sells a house in a walled city, then he may redeem it within a whole year after it is sold; *within* a full year he may redeem it. 30 But if it is not redeemed within the space of a full year, then the house in the walled city shall belong permanently to him who bought it, throughout his generations. It shall not be released in the Jubilee. 31 However the houses of villages which have no wall around them shall be counted as the fields of the country. They may be redeemed, and they shall be released in the Jubilee. 32 Nevertheless [a]the cities of the Levites, *and* the houses in the cities of their possession, the Levites may redeem at any time. 33 And if a man purchases a house from the Levites, then the house that was sold in the city of his possession shall be released in the Jubilee; for the houses in the cities of the Levites *are* their possession among the children of Israel. 34 But [a]the field of the common-land of their cities may not be [b]sold, for it *is* their perpetual possession.

### LENDING TO THE POOR

35 'If one of your brethren becomes poor, and falls into poverty among you, then you shall [a]help him, like a stranger or a sojourner, that he may live with you. 36 [a]Take no usury or interest from him; but [b]fear your God, that your brother may live with you. 37 You shall not lend him your money for usury, nor lend him your food at a profit. 38 [a]I *am* the LORD your God, who brought you out of the land of Egypt, to give you the land of Canaan *and* to be your God.

### THE LAW CONCERNING SLAVERY

39 'And if *one of* your brethren *who dwells* by you becomes poor, and sells himself to you, you shall not compel him to serve as a slave. 40 As a hired servant *and* a sojourner he shall be with you, *and* shall serve you until the Year of Jubilee. 41 And *then* he shall depart from you—he and his children [a]with him—and shall return to his own family. He shall return to the possession of his fathers. 42 For they *are* [a]My servants, whom I brought out of the land of Egypt; they shall not be sold as slaves. 43 [a]You shall not rule over him [b]with rigor, but you [c]shall fear your God. 44 And as for your male and female slaves whom you may have—from the nations that are around you, from them you may buy male and female slaves. 45 Moreover you may buy [a]the children of the strangers who dwell among you, and their families who are with you, which they beget in your land; and they shall become your property. 46 And [a]you may take them as an inheritance for your children after you, to inherit *them as* a possession; they shall be your permanent slaves. But regarding your brethren, the children of Israel, you shall not rule over one another with rigor.

47 'Now if a sojourner or stranger close to you becomes rich, and *one of* your brethren *who dwells* by him becomes poor, and sells himself to the stranger *or* sojourner close to you, or to a member of the stranger's family, 48 after he is sold

**25:14** [a] Lev. 19:13 **25:15** [a] Lev. 27:18, 23 **25:17** [a] Lev. 25:14; Prov. 14:31; 22:22; Jer. 7:5, 6; 1 Thess. 4:6 [b] Lev. 19:14, 32; 25:43 **25:18** [a] Lev. 19:37 [b] Lev. 26:5; Deut. 12:10; Ps. 4:8; Jer. 23:6 **25:19** [a] Lev. 26:5; Ezek. 34:25 **25:20** [a] Matt. 6:25, 31 [b] Lev. 25:4, 5 **25:21** [a] Deut. 28:8 [b] Ex. 16:29 **25:22** [a] 2 Kin. 19:29 [b] Lev. 26:10; Josh. 5:11 **25:23** [a] Ex. 19:5; 2 Chr. 7:20 [b] Gen. 23:4; Ex. 6:4; 1 Chr. 29:15; Ps. 39:12; Heb. 11:13; 1 Pet. 2:11 **25:25** [a] Ruth 2:20; 4:4, 6 [b] Num. 5:8; Ruth 3:2, 9, 12; [Job 19:25]; Jer. 32:7, 8 **25:27** [a] Lev. 25:50–52 **25:28** [a] Lev. 25:10, 13 **25:32** [a] Num. 35:1–8; Josh. 21:2 **25:34** [a] Num. 35:2–5 [b] Acts 4:36, 37 **25:35** [a] Deut. 15:7–11; 24:14, 15; Luke 6:35; 1 John 3:17 **25:36** [a] Ex. 22:25; Deut. 23:19, 20 [b] Neh. 5:9 **25:38** [a] Lev. 11:45; 22:32, 33 **25:41** [a] Ex. 21:3 **25:42** [a] Lev. 25:55; [Rom. 6:22; 1 Cor. 7:22, 23] **25:43** [a] Eph. 6:9; Col. 4:1 [b] Ex. 1:13, 14; Lev. 25:46, 53; Ezek. 34:4 [c] Ex. 1:17; Deut. 25:18; Mal. 3:5 **25:45** [a] [Is. 56:3, 6, 7] **25:46** [a] Is. 14:2

he may be redeemed again. One of his brothers
may redeem him; 49 or his uncle or his uncle's
son may redeem him; or *anyone* who is near of
kin to him in his family may redeem him; or if he
is able he may redeem himself. 50 Thus he shall
reckon with him who bought him: The price of
his release shall be according to the number
of years, from the year that he was sold to him
until the Year of Jubilee; *it shall be* [a]according to
the time of a hired servant for him. 51 If *there are*
still many years *remaining*, according to them he
shall repay the price of his redemption from the
money with which he was bought. 52 And if there
remain but a few years until the Year of Jubilee,
then he shall reckon with him, *and* according
to his years he shall repay him the price of his
redemption. 53 He shall be with him as a yearly
hired servant, and he shall not rule with rigor
over him in your sight. 54 And if he is not re-
deemed in these *years*, then he shall be released
in the Year of Jubilee—he and his children with
him. 55 For the children of Israel *are* servants to
Me; they *are* My servants whom I brought out
of the land of Egypt: I *am* the LORD your God.

### *PROMISE OF BLESSING AND RETRIBUTION*

*(Deut. 7:12–24; 28:1–68)*

**26** 'You shall [a]not make idols for yourselves;
neither a carved image nor a *sacred* pillar
shall you rear up for yourselves;
nor shall you set up an engraved stone in
your land, to bow down to it;
for I *am* the LORD your God.
2 [a]You shall keep My Sabbaths and reverence
My sanctuary:
I *am* the LORD.

3 [a]'If you walk in My statutes and keep My com-
mandments, and perform them,
4 [a]then I will give you rain in its season, [b]the
land shall yield its produce, and the trees
of the field shall yield their fruit.
5 [a]Your threshing shall last till the time of
vintage, and the vintage shall last till the
time of sowing;
you shall eat your bread to the full, and
[b]dwell in your land safely.
6 [a]I will give peace in the land, and [b]you shall
lie down, and none will make *you* afraid;
I will rid the land of [c]evil beasts,
and [d]the sword will not go through your land.
7 You will chase your enemies, and they shall
fall by the sword before you.
8 [a]Five of you shall chase a hundred, and a hun-
dred of you shall put ten thousand to flight;
your enemies shall fall by the sword before
you.
9 'For I will [a]look on you favorably and [b]make
you fruitful, multiply you and confirm My
[c]covenant with you.
10 You shall eat the [a]old harvest, and clear out
the old because of the new.
11 [a]I will set My tabernacle among you, and My
soul shall not abhor you.

**SEEING JESUS IN THE SCRIPTURE**

**26:11** God's promise to set His tabernacle among His people was the promise of His presence. This promise was fulfilled by Jesus, who came and dwelt among us (see John 1:14). Jesus promised to return one day and make His permanent dwelling with us (see John 14:1–3).

12 [a]I will walk among you and be your God, and
you shall be My people.
13 I *am* the LORD your God, who brought you
out of the land of Egypt, that *you* should
not be their slaves;
I have broken the bands of your [a]yoke and
made you walk upright.

14 'But if you do not obey Me, and do not ob-
serve all these commandments,
15 and if you despise My statutes, or if your
soul abhors My judgments, so that you
do not perform all My commandments,
*but* break My covenant,
16 I also will do this to you:
I will even appoint terror over you,
[a]wasting disease and fever which shall
[b]consume the eyes and [c]cause sorrow
of heart.
And [d]you shall sow your seed in vain, for
your enemies shall eat it.
17 I will set [a]My face against you, and [b]you shall
be defeated by your enemies.
[c]Those who hate you shall reign over you,
and you shall [d]flee when no one pursues
you.

18 'And after all this, if you do not obey Me, then
I will punish you [a]seven times more for
your sins.
19 I will [a]break the pride of your power;
I [b]will make your heavens like iron and your
earth like bronze.
20 And your [a]strength shall be spent in vain;
for your [b]land shall not yield its produce,
nor shall the trees of the land yield their
fruit.

**25:50** [a] Job 7:1; Is. 16:14 **26:1** [a] Ex. 20:4, 5; Deut. 4:15–18; 5:8 **26:2** [a] Lev. 19:30 **26:3** [a] Deut. 28:1–14 **26:4** [a] Is. 30:23 [b] Ps. 67:6 **26:5** [a] Deut. 11:15; Joel 2:19, 26; Amos 9:13 [b] Lev. 25:18, 19; Ezek. 34:25 **26:6** [a] Is. 45:7 [b] Job 11:19; Ps. 4:8; Zeph. 3:13 [c] 2 Kin. 17:25; Hos. 2:18 [d] Ezek. 14:17 **26:8** [a] Deut. 32:30; Judg. 7:7–12 **26:9** [a] Ex. 2:25; 2 Kin. 13:23 [b] Gen. 17:6, 7; Ps. 107:38 [c] Gen. 17:1–7 **26:10** [a] Lev. 25:22 **26:11** [a] Ex. 25:8; 29:45, 46; Josh. 22:19; Ps. 76:2; Ezek. 37:26; Rev. 21:3 **26:12** [a] Deut. 23:14; [2 Cor. 6:16] **26:13** [a] Gen. 27:40 **26:16** [a] Deut. 28:22 [b] 1 Sam. 2:33 [c] Ezek. 24:23; 33:10 [d] Judg. 6:3–6 **26:17** [a] Ps. 34:16 [b] Deut. 28:25 [c] Ps. 106:41 [d] Prov. 28:1 **26:18** [a] 1 Sam. 2:5 **26:19** [a] Is. 25:11 [b] Deut. 28:23 **26:20** [a] Ps. 127:1 [b] Gen. 4:12

21 'Then, if you walk contrary to Me, and are not willing to obey Me, I will bring on you seven times more plagues, according to your sins.
22 [a]I will also send wild beasts among you, which shall rob you of your children, destroy your livestock, and make you few in number;
and [b]your highways shall be desolate.

23 'And if [a]by these things you are not reformed by Me, but walk contrary to Me,
24 [a]then I also will walk contrary to you, and I will punish you yet seven times for your sins.
25 And [a]I will bring a sword against you that will execute the vengeance of the covenant;
when you are gathered together within your cities [b]I will send pestilence among you;
and you shall be delivered into the hand of the enemy.
26 [a]When I have cut off your supply of bread, ten women shall bake your bread in one oven, and they shall bring back your bread by weight, [b]and you shall eat and not be satisfied.

27 'And after all this, if you do not obey Me, but walk contrary to Me,
28 then I also will walk contrary to you in fury;
and I, even I, will chastise you seven times for your sins.
29 [a]You shall eat the flesh of your sons, and you shall eat the flesh of your daughters.
30 [a]I will destroy your high places, cut down your incense altars, and cast your carcasses on the lifeless forms of your idols;
and My soul shall abhor you.
31 I will lay your [a]cities waste and [b]bring your sanctuaries to desolation, and I will not [c]smell the fragrance of your sweet aromas.
32 [a]I will bring the land to desolation, and your enemies who dwell in it shall be astonished at it.
33 [a]I will scatter you among the nations and draw out a sword after you;
your land shall be desolate and your cities waste.
34 [a]Then the land shall enjoy its sabbaths as long as it lies desolate and you *are* in your enemies' land;
then the land shall rest and enjoy its sabbaths.
35 As long as *it* lies desolate it shall rest—
for the time it did not rest on your [a]sabbaths when you dwelt in it.

36 'And as for those of you who are left, I will send [a]faintness into their hearts in the lands of their enemies;
the sound of a shaken leaf shall cause them to flee;
they shall flee as though fleeing from a sword, and they shall fall when no one pursues.
37 [a]They shall stumble over one another, as it were before a sword, when no one pursues;
and [b]you shall have no *power* to stand before your enemies.
38 You shall [a]perish among the nations, and the land of your enemies shall eat you up.
39 And those of you who are left [a]shall waste away in their iniquity in your enemies' lands;
also in their [b]fathers' iniquities, which are with them, they shall waste away.

40 '*But* [a]if they confess their iniquity and the iniquity of their fathers, with their unfaithfulness in which they were unfaithful to Me, and that they also have walked contrary to Me,
41 and *that* I also have walked contrary to them and have brought them into the land of their enemies;
if their [a]uncircumcised hearts are [b]humbled, and they [c]accept their guilt—
42 then I will [a]remember My covenant with Jacob, and My covenant with Isaac and My covenant with Abraham I will remember;
I will [b]remember the land.
43 [a]The land also shall be left empty by them, and will enjoy its sabbaths while it lies desolate without them;
they will accept their guilt, because they [b]despised My judgments and because their soul abhorred My statutes.
44 Yet for all that, when they are in the land of their enemies, [a]I will not cast them away, nor shall I abhor them, to utterly destroy them and break My covenant with them;
for I *am* the LORD their God.
45 But [a]for their sake I will remember the covenant of their ancestors, [b]whom I brought out of the land of Egypt [c]in the sight of the nations, that I might be their God:
I *am* the LORD.' "

46 [a]These *are* the statutes and judgments and laws which the LORD made between Himself and the children of Israel [b]on Mount Sinai by the hand of Moses.

26:22 [a] Deut. 32:24 [b] Judg. 5:6 26:23 [a] Amos 4:6–12 26:24 [a] Lev. 26:28, 41 26:25 [a] Ezek. 5:17 [b] Deut. 28:21 26:26 [a] Ps. 105:16 [b] Mic. 6:14 26:29 [a] 2 Kin. 6:28, 29 26:30 [a] 2 Chr. 34:3 26:31 [a] 2 Kin. 25:4, 10 [b] Ps. 74:7 [c] Is. 1:11–15 26:32 [a] Jer. 9:11; 18:16 26:33 [a] Deut. 4:27 26:34 [a] 2 Chr. 36:21 26:35 [a] Lev. 25:2 26:36 [a] Ezek. 21:7, 12, 15 26:37 [a] 1 Sam. 14:15, 16 [b] Josh. 7:12, 13 26:38 [a] Deut. 4:26 26:39 [a] Ezek. 4:17; 33:10 [b] Ex. 34:7 26:40 [a] Neh. 9:2 26:41 [a] Acts 7:51 [b] 2 Chr. 12:6, 7, 12 [c] Dan. 9:7 26:42 [a] Ex. 2:24; 6:5 [b] Ps. 136:23 26:43 [a] Lev. 26:34, 35 [b] Lev. 26:15 26:44 [a] Deut. 4:31; 2 Kin. 13:23; Jer. 30:11; [Rom. 11:1–36] 26:45 [a] [Rom. 11:28] [b] Lev. 22:33; 25:38 [c] Ps. 98:2; Ezek. 20:9, 14, 22 26:46 [a] Lev. 27:34; Deut. 6:1; 12:1; [John 1:17] [b] Lev. 25:1

### *REDEEMING PERSONS AND PROPERTY DEDICATED TO GOD*

**27** Now the LORD spoke to Moses, saying, 2 "Speak to the children of Israel, and say to them: [a]'When a man consecrates by a vow certain persons to the LORD, according to your valuation, 3 if your valuation is of a male from twenty years old up to sixty years old, then your valuation shall be fifty shekels of silver, [a]according to the shekel of the sanctuary. 4 If it *is* a female, then your valuation shall be thirty shekels; 5 and if from five years old up to twenty years old, then your valuation for a male shall be twenty shekels, and for a female ten shekels; 6 and if from a month old up to five years old, then your valuation for a male shall be five shekels of silver, and for a female your valuation shall be three shekels of silver; 7 and if from sixty years old and above, if *it is* a male, then your valuation shall be fifteen shekels, and for a female ten shekels.

8 'But if he is too poor to pay your valuation, then he shall present himself before the priest, and the priest shall set a value for [a]him; according to the ability of him who vowed, the priest shall value him.

9 'If *it is* an animal that men may bring as an offering to the LORD, all that *anyone* gives to the LORD shall be holy. 10 He shall not substitute it or exchange it, good for bad or bad for good; and if he at all exchanges animal for animal, then both it and the one exchanged for it shall be [a]holy. 11 If *it is* an unclean animal which they do not offer as a sacrifice to the LORD, then he shall present the animal before the priest; 12 and the priest shall set a value for it, whether it is good or bad; as you, the priest, value it, so it shall be. 13 [a]But if he *wants* at all *to* redeem it, then he must add one-fifth to your valuation.

14 'And when a man dedicates his house *to be* holy to the LORD, then the priest shall set a value for it, whether it is good or bad; as the priest values it, so it shall stand. 15 If he who dedicated it *wants to* redeem his house, then he must add one-fifth of the money of your valuation to it, and it shall be his.

16 'If a man dedicates to the LORD *part* of a field of his possession, then your valuation shall be according to the seed for it. A homer of barley seed *shall be valued* at fifty shekels of silver. 17 If he dedicates his field from the Year of Jubilee, according to your valuation it shall stand. 18 But if he dedicates his field after the Jubilee, then the priest shall [a]reckon to him the money due according to the years that remain till the Year of Jubilee, and it shall be deducted from your valuation. 19 And if he who dedicates the field ever wishes to redeem it, then he must add one-fifth of the money of your valuation to it, and it shall belong to him. 20 But if he does not want to redeem the field, or if he has sold the field to another man, it shall not be redeemed anymore; 21 but the field, [a]when it is released in the Jubilee, shall be holy to the LORD, as a [b]devoted field; it shall be [c]the possession of the priest.

22 'And if a man dedicates to the LORD a field which he has bought, which is not the field of [a]his possession, 23 then the priest shall reckon to him the worth of your valuation, up to the Year of Jubilee, and he shall give your valuation on that day *as* a holy *offering* to the LORD. 24 [a]In the Year of Jubilee the field shall return to him from whom it was bought, to the one who *owned* the land as a possession. 25 And all your valuations shall be according to the shekel of the sanctuary: [a]twenty gerahs to the shekel.

26 'But the [a]firstborn of the animals, which should be the LORD's firstborn, no man shall dedicate; whether *it is* an ox or sheep, it *is* the LORD's. 27 And if *it is* an unclean animal, then he shall redeem *it* according to your valuation, and [a]shall add one-fifth to it; or if it is not redeemed, then it shall be sold according to your valuation.

28 [a]'Nevertheless no devoted *offering* that a man may devote to the LORD of all that he has, *both* man and beast, or the field of his possession, shall be sold or redeemed; every devoted *offering* *is* most holy to the LORD. 29 [a]No person under the ban, who may become doomed to destruction among men, shall be redeemed, *but* shall surely be put to death. 30 And [a]all the tithe of the land, *whether* of the seed of the land *or* of the fruit of the tree, *is* the LORD's. It *is* holy to the LORD. 31 [a]If a man wants at all to redeem *any* of his tithes, he shall add one-fifth to it. 32 And concerning the tithe of the herd or the flock, of whatever [a]passes under the rod, the tenth one shall be holy to the LORD. 33 He shall not inquire whether it is good or bad, [a]nor shall he exchange it; and if he exchanges it at all, then both it and the one exchanged for it shall be holy; it shall not be redeemed.' "

34 [a]These *are* the commandments which the LORD commanded Moses for the children of Israel on Mount [b]Sinai.

**27:2** [a] Lev. 7:16; Num. 6:2; Deut. 23:21–23; Judg. 11:30, 31, 39 **27:3** [a] Ex. 30:13; Lev. 27:25; Num. 3:47; 18:16 **27:8** [a] Lev. 5:11; 14:21–24 **27:10** [a] Lev. 27:33 **27:13** [a] Lev. 6:5; 22:14; 27:15, 19 **27:18** [a] Lev. 25:15, 16, 28 **27:21** [a] Lev. 25:10, 28, 31 [b] Lev. 27:28 [c] Num. 18:14; Ezek. 44:29 **27:22** [a] Lev. 25:10, 25 **27:24** [a] Lev. 25:10–13, 28 **27:25** [a] Ex. 30:13; Lev. 27:3; Num. 3:47; 18:16; Ezek. 45:12 **27:26** [a] Ex. 13:2, 12; 22:30 **27:27** [a] Lev. 27:11, 12 **27:28** [a] Lev. 27:21; Num. 18:14; Josh. 6:17–19 **27:29** [a] Num. 21:2 **27:30** [a] Gen. 28:22; Num. 18:21, 24; 2 Chr. 31:5, 6, 12; Neh. 13:12; Mal. 3:8 **27:31** [a] Lev. 27:13 **27:32** [a] Jer. 33:13; Ezek. 20:37; Mic. 7:14 **27:33** [a] Lev. 27:10 **27:34** [a] Lev. 26:46; Deut. 4:5; Mal. 4:4 [b] Ex. 19:1–6, 25; [Heb. 12:18–29]

# *The Fourth Book of Moses Called*
# NUMBERS

| AUTHOR | KEY VERSES | READING TIME |
|---|---|---|
| Moses | Numbers 14:30–31 | 3 hours 28 minutes |

**c. 1527 BC**
Moses is born

**c. 1498–1483 BC**
Hatshepsut, female Pharaoh, reigns in Egypt

**c. 1487 BC**
Moses flees Egypt for Midian

**c. 1470 BC**
Massive volcanic eruption on the Aegean island of Thera

**c. 1446 BC**
Moses leads the Israelites out of Egypt

**c. 1445 BC**
The Law is given on Mount Sinai

**c. 1445–1406 BC**
Events in Numbers

**c. 1406 BC**
**Numbers written**

**c. 1405–1400 BC**
The conquest of Canaan

Numbers is the book of wanderings. At the book's opening, the Hebrews were encamped at Sinai (Num. 1:1—10:10) before they began moving toward the Promised Land (10:11—12:16). When they arrived at the land's borders at Kadesh, Moses sent in twelve spies on a scouting mission. But when ten of the spies gave a negative report, the Hebrews disobeyed God by refusing to enter the land (13:1—20:13). In response, God forced the people to wander for forty years, during which time the first generation, save the two faithful spies, died off (20:14—25:18). Numbers closes with the second generation's march back toward the Promised Land. During this journey, Moses reminded the Hebrews of God's covenant and prepared them to enter the land (26:1—36:13). For Israel, an eleven-day journey had become a forty-year agony.

**Occasion:** Moses wrote the Book of Numbers to preserve a record of Israel's experiences for future generations and serve as an "instruction manual" to the second generation about to enter the Promised Land.

**Main Point:** God takes the unfaithfulness of His people seriously.

**Big Ideas:** God provides all we need. We are to trust God in every situation, knowing He cares for us. Our sin always has consequences.

## OUTLINE:

I. The First Generation Is Counted (chs. 1–4)
II. The Laws and Cleansing of the Levites (chs. 5–8)
III. The Passover Is Celebrated (ch. 9)
IV. The First Generation Travels to Kadesh (chs. 10–12)
V. The First Generation Refuses to Enter the Land (chs. 13–14)
VI. The First Generation Wanders and Dies in the Wilderness (chs. 15–25)
VII. The Second Generation Is Counted (ch. 26)
VIII. The Second Generation Prepares to Enter the Land (chs. 27–30)
IX. The Second Generation Arrives at the Promised Land (chs. 31–36)

### *THE FIRST CENSUS OF ISRAEL*
*(cf. 2 Sam. 24:1–9; 1 Chr. 21:1–6)*

1 Now the LORD spoke to Moses [a]in the Wilder-
ness of Sinai, [b]in the tabernacle of meeting,
on the [c]first *day* of the second month, in the
second year after they had come out of the land
of Egypt, saying: 2 [a]"Take a census of all the
congregation of the children of Israel, by their
families, by their fathers' houses, according to
the number of names, every male [b]individually,
3 from [a]twenty years old and above—all who *are*
*able to* go to war in Israel. You and Aaron shall
number them by their armies. 4 And with you
there shall be a man from every tribe, each one
the head of his father's house.

5 "These are the names of the men who shall
stand with you: from Reuben, Elizur the son of
Shedeur; 6 from Simeon, Shelumiel the son of
Zurishaddai; 7 from Judah, Nahshon the son
of Amminadab; 8 from Issachar, Nethanel the
son of Zuar; 9 from Zebulun, Eliab the son of
Helon; 10 from the sons of Joseph: from Ephraim,
Elishama the son of Ammihud; from Manasseh,
Gamaliel the son of Pedahzur; 11 from Benjamin,
Abidan the son of Gideoni; 12 from Dan, Ahiezer
the son of Ammishaddai; 13 from Asher, Pagiel
the son of Ocran; 14 from Gad, Eliasaph the son of
[a]Deuel;[1] 15 from Naphtali, Ahira the son of Enan."
16 [a]These *were* [b]chosen from the congregation,
leaders of their fathers' tribes, [c]heads of the
divisions in Israel.

17 Then Moses and Aaron took these men
who had been mentioned [a]by name, 18 and they
assembled all the congregation together on the
first *day* of the second month; and they recited
their [a]ancestry by families, by their fathers'
houses, according to the number of names,
from twenty years old and above, each one in-
dividually. 19 As the LORD commanded Moses, so
he numbered them in the Wilderness of Sinai.

20 Now the [a]children of Reuben, Israel's old-
est son, their genealogies by their families, by
their fathers' house, according to the number
of names, every male individually, from twenty
years old and above, all who *were able to* go to
war: 21 those who were numbered of the tribe of
Reuben *were* forty-six thousand five hundred.

22 From the [a]children of Simeon, their geneal-
ogies by their families, by their fathers' house,
of those who were numbered, according to the
number of names, every male individually, from
twenty years old and above, all who *were able to* go
to war: 23 those who were numbered of the tribe of
Simeon *were* fifty-nine thousand three hundred.

24 From the [a]children of Gad, their geneal-
ogies by their families, by their fathers' house,
according to the number of names, from twenty
years old and above, all who *were able to* go to war:
25 those who were numbered of the tribe of Gad
*were* forty-five thousand six hundred and fifty.

26 From the [a]children of Judah, their geneal-
ogies by their families, by their fathers' house,
according to the number of names, from twenty
years old and above, all who *were able to* go to
war: 27 those who were numbered of the tribe of
Judah *were* [a]seventy-four thousand six hundred.

28 From the [a]children of Issachar, their ge-
nealogies by their families, by their fathers'
house, according to the number of names, from
twenty years old and above, all who *were able to* go
to war: 29 those who were numbered of the tribe of
Issachar *were* fifty-four thousand four hundred.

30 From the [a]children of Zebulun, their ge-
nealogies by their families, by their fathers'
house, according to the number of names, from
twenty years old and above, all who *were able to* go
to war: 31 those who were numbered of the tribe of
Zebulun *were* fifty-seven thousand four hundred.

32 From the sons of Joseph, the [a]children of
Ephraim, their genealogies by their families, by
their fathers' house, according to the number
of names, from twenty years old and above, all
who *were able to* go to war: 33 those who were
numbered of the tribe of Ephraim *were* forty
thousand five hundred.

34 From the [a]children of Manasseh, their ge-
nealogies by their families, by their fathers' house,
according to the number of names, from twenty
years old and above, all who *were able to* go to
war: 35 those who were numbered of the tribe of
Manasseh *were* thirty-two thousand two hundred.

36 From the [a]children of Benjamin, their
genealogies by their families, by their fathers'
house, according to the number of names, from
twenty years old and above, all who *were able to*
go to war: 37 those who were numbered of the
tribe of Benjamin *were* thirty-five thousand
four hundred.

38 From the [a]children of Dan, their geneal-
ogies by their families, by their fathers' house,
according to the number of names, from twenty
years old and above, all who *were able to* go to
war: 39 those who were numbered of the tribe of
Dan *were* sixty-two thousand seven hundred.

**1:20–46** The 603,550 people counted in the census were all men. Including women and children probably meant a total population of three million or more.

1:1 [a] Ex. 19:1; Num. 10:11, 12 [b] Ex. 25:22 [c] Ex. 40:2, 17; Num. 9:1; 10:11 1:2 [a] Ex. 30:12; Num. 26:2, 63, 64; 2 Sam. 24:2; 1 Chr. 21:2 [b] Ex. 30:12, 13; 38:26 1:3 [a] Ex. 30:14; 38:26 1:14 [a] Num. 7:42 [1] Spelled *Reuel* in 2:14 1:16 [a] Ex. 18:21; Num. 7:2; 1 Chr. 27:16–22 [b] Num. 16:2 [c] Ex. 18:21, 25; Jer. 5:5; Mic. 3:1, 9; 5:2 1:17 [a] Is. 43:1 1:18 [a] Ezra 2:59; Heb. 7:3 1:20 [a] Num. 2:10, 11; 26:5–11; 32:6, 15, 21, 29 1:22 [a] Num. 2:12, 13; 26:12–14 1:24 [a] Gen. 30:11; Num. 26:15–18; Josh. 4:12; Jer. 49:1 1:26 [a] Gen. 29:35; Num. 26:19–22; 2 Sam. 24:9; Ps. 78:68; Matt. 1:2 1:27 [a] 2 Chr. 17:14 1:28 [a] Num. 2:5, 6 1:30 [a] Num. 2:7, 8; 26:26, 27 1:32 [a] Gen. 48:1–22; Num. 26:28–37; Deut. 33:13–17; Jer. 7:15; Obad. 19 1:34 [a] Num. 2:20, 21; 26:28–34 1:36 [a] Gen. 49:27; Num. 26:38–41; 2 Chr. 17:17; Rev. 7:8 1:38 [a] Gen. 30:6; 46:23; Num. 2:25, 26; 26:42, 43

40 From the [a]children of Asher, their geneal-
ogies by their families, by their fathers' house,
according to the number of names, from twenty
years old and above, all who *were able to* go to
war: 41 those who were numbered of the tribe of
Asher *were* forty-one thousand five hundred.

42 From the children of Naphtali, their geneal-
ogies by their families, by their fathers' house,
according to the number of names, from twenty
years old and above, all who *were able to* go to
war: 43 those who were numbered of the tribe of
Naphtali *were* fifty-three thousand four hundred.

44 [a]These are the ones who were numbered,
whom Moses and Aaron numbered, with the
leaders of Israel, twelve men, each one repre-
senting his father's house. 45 So all who were
numbered of the children of Israel, by their fa-
thers' houses, from twenty years old and above,
all who *were able to* go to war in Israel— 46 all
who were numbered were [a]six hundred and
three thousand five hundred and fifty.

47 But [a]the Levites were not numbered
among them by their fathers' tribe; 48 for the
LORD had spoken to Moses, saying: 49 [a]"Only the
tribe of Levi you shall not number, nor take a
census of them among the children of Israel;
50 [a]but you shall appoint the Levites over the
tabernacle of the Testimony, over all its furnish-
ings, and over all things that belong to it; they
shall carry the tabernacle and all its furnishings;
they shall attend to it [b]and camp around the
tabernacle. 51 [a]And when the tabernacle is to go
forward, the Levites shall take it down; and when
the tabernacle is to be set up, the Levites shall
set it [b]up. [c]The outsider who comes near shall
be put to death. 52 The children of Israel shall
pitch their tents, [a]everyone by his own camp,
everyone by his own standard, according to their
armies; 53 [a]but the Levites shall camp around the
tabernacle of the Testimony, that there may be
no [b]wrath on the congregation of the children
of Israel; and the Levites shall [c]keep charge of
the tabernacle of the Testimony."

54 Thus the children of Israel did; accord-
ing to all that the LORD commanded Moses,
so they did.

## *THE TRIBES AND LEADERS BY ARMIES*

**2** And the LORD spoke to Moses and Aaron,
saying: 2 [a]"Everyone of the children of Is-
rael shall camp by his own standard, beside
the emblems of his father's house; they shall
camp [b]some distance from the tabernacle of
meeting. 3 On the [a]east side, toward the rising
of the sun, those of the standard of the forces
with Judah shall camp according to their armies;
and [b]Nahshon the son of Amminadab *shall be*
the leader of the children of Judah." 4 And his
army was numbered at seventy-four thousand
six hundred.

5 "Those who camp next to him *shall be* the
tribe of Issachar, and Nethanel the son of Zuar
*shall be* the leader of the children of Issachar."
6 And his army was numbered at fifty-four thou-
sand four hundred.

7 "Then *comes* the tribe of Zebulun, and Eliab
the son of Helon *shall be* the leader of the children
of Zebulun." 8 And his army was numbered at
fifty-seven thousand four hundred. 9 "All who were
numbered according to their armies of the forces
with Judah, one hundred and eighty-six thousand
four hundred—[a]these shall break camp first.

10 "On the [a]south side *shall be* the standard
of the forces with Reuben according to their
armies, and the leader of the children of Reu-
ben *shall be* Elizur the son of Shedeur." 11 And
his army was numbered at forty-six thousand
five hundred.

12 "Those who camp next to him *shall be* the
tribe of Simeon, and the leader of the children of
Simeon *shall be* Shelumiel the son of Zurishad-
dai." 13 And his army was numbered at fifty-nine
thousand three hundred.

14 "Then *comes* the tribe of Gad, and the lead-
er of the children of Gad *shall be* Eliasaph the
son of Reuel."[1] 15 And his army was numbered at
forty-five thousand six hundred and fifty. 16 "All
who were numbered according to their armies of
the forces with Reuben, one hundred and fifty-
one thousand four hundred and fifty—[a]they
shall be the second to break camp.

17 [a]"And the tabernacle of meeting shall move
out with the camp of the Levites [b]in the middle
of the camps; as they camp, so they shall move
out, everyone in his place, by their standards.

18 "On the west side *shall be* the standard
of the forces with Ephraim according to their
armies, and the leader of the children of Ephra-
im *shall be* Elishama the son of Ammihud."
19 And his army was numbered at forty thousand
five hundred.

20 "Next to him *comes* the tribe of Manas-
seh, and the leader of the children of Manasseh
*shall be* Gamaliel the son of Pedahzur." 21 And
his army was numbered at thirty-two thousand
two hundred.

22 "Then *comes* the tribe of Benjamin, and
the leader of the children of Benjamin *shall be*
Abidan the son of Gideoni." 23 And his army was
numbered at thirty-five thousand four hundred.
24 "All who were numbered according to their
armies of the forces with Ephraim, one hundred
and eight thousand one hundred—[a]they shall
be the third to break camp.

**1:40** [a] Num. 2:27, 28; 26:44–47 **1:44** [a] Num. 26:64 **1:46** [a] Ex. 12:37; 38:26; Num. 2:32; 26:51, 63; Heb. 11:12; Rev. 7:4–8 **1:47** [a] Num. 2:33; 3:14–22; 26:57–62; 1 Chr. 6:1–47; 21:6 **1:49** [a] Num. 2:33; 26:62 **1:50** [a] Ex. 38:21; Num. 3:7, 8; 4:15, 25–27, 33 [b] Num. 3:23, 29, 35, 38 **1:51** [a] Num. 4:5–15; 10:17, 21 [b] Num. 10:21 [c] Num. 3:10, 38; 4:15, 19, 20; 18:22 **1:52** [a] Num. 2:2, 34; 24:2 **1:53** [a] Num. 1:50 [b] Lev. 10:6; Num. 8:19; 16:46; 18:5; 1 Sam. 6:19 [c] Num. 8:24; 18:2–4; 1 Chr. 23:32 **2:2** [a] Num. 1:52; 24:2 [b] Josh. 3:4 **2:3** [a] Num. 10:5 [b] Num. 1:7; 7:12; 10:14; Ruth 4:20; 1 Chr. 2:10; Matt. 1:4; Luke 3:32, 33 **2:9** [a] Num. 10:14 **2:10** [a] Num. 10:6 **2:14** [1] Spelled *Deuel* in 1:14 and 7:42 **2:16** [a] Num. 10:18 **2:17** [a] Num. 10:17, 21 [b] Num. 1:53 **2:24** [a] Num. 10:22

25"The standard of the forces with Dan *shall*
*be* on the north side according to their armies,
and the leader of the children of Dan *shall be* Ahie-
zer the son of Ammishaddai." 26 And his army was
numbered at sixty-two thousand seven hundred.
27"Those who camp next to him *shall be* the
tribe of Asher, and the leader of the children of
Asher *shall be* Pagiel the son of Ocran." 28 And
his army was numbered at forty-one thousand
five hundred.
29"Then *comes* the tribe of Naphtali, and
the leader of the children of Naphtali *shall be*
Ahira the son of Enan." 30 And his army was
numbered at fifty-three thousand four hundred.
31"All who were numbered of the forces with
Dan, one hundred and fifty-seven thousand
six hundred—[a]they shall break camp last, with
their standards."
32 These *are* the ones who were numbered
of the children of Israel by their fathers' hous-
es. [a]All who were numbered according to their
armies of the forces *were* six hundred and three
thousand five hundred and fifty. 33 But [a]the Le-
vites were not numbered among the children
of Israel, just as the LORD commanded Moses.
34 Thus the children of Israel [a]did according
to all that the LORD commanded Moses; [b]so they
camped by their standards and so they broke
camp, each one by his family, according to their
fathers' houses.

### *THE SONS OF AARON*
*(Lev. 10:1-7)*

3 Now these *are* the [a]records of Aaron and
Moses when the LORD spoke with Moses on
Mount Sinai. 2 And these *are* the names of the
sons of Aaron: Nadab, the [a]firstborn, and [b]Abihu,
Eleazar, and Ithamar. 3 These *are* the names of
the sons of Aaron, [a]the anointed priests, whom
he consecrated to minister as priests. 4 [a]Nadab
and Abihu had died before the LORD when they
offered profane fire before the LORD in the
Wilderness of Sinai; and they had no children.
So Eleazar and Ithamar ministered as priests in
the presence of Aaron their father.

### *THE LEVITES SERVE IN THE TABERNACLE*

5 And the LORD spoke to Moses, saying:
6 [a]"Bring the tribe of Levi near, and present them
before Aaron the priest, that they may serve him.
7 And they shall attend to his needs and the needs
of the whole congregation before the tabernacle
of meeting, to do [a]the work of the tabernacle.
8 Also they shall attend to all the furnishings
of the tabernacle of meeting, and to the needs
of the children of Israel, to do the work of the

> **3:1–10** The **Levites** could care for the holy things, but only the **priests**, who ministered in the tabernacle, drew near to God. In the New Covenant this access is no longer confined to a particular group of God's people. All Christians comprise God's new temple and constitute "a holy priesthood, to offer up spiritual sacrifices acceptable to God through Jesus Christ" (1 Pet. 2:5).

tabernacle. 9 And [a]you shall give the Levites to
Aaron and his sons; they *are* given entirely to
him[1] from among the children of Israel. 10 So you
shall appoint Aaron and his sons, [a]and they shall
attend to their priesthood; [b]but the outsider who
comes near shall be put to death."
11 Then the LORD spoke to Moses, saying:
12"Now behold, [a]I Myself have taken the Levites
from among the children of Israel instead of
every firstborn who opens the womb among
the children of Israel. Therefore the Levites
shall be [b]Mine, 13 because [a]all the firstborn *are*
Mine. [b]On the day that I struck all the firstborn
in the land of Egypt, I sanctified to Myself all the
firstborn in Israel, both man and beast. They
shall be Mine: I *am* the LORD."

### *CENSUS OF THE LEVITES COMMANDED*
*(cf. Num. 1:47-54)*

14 Then the LORD spoke to Moses in the Wil-
derness of Sinai, saying: 15"Number the children
of Levi by their fathers' houses, by their families;
you shall number [a]every male from a month
old and above."
16 So Moses numbered them according to
the word of the LORD, as he was commanded.
17 [a]These were the sons of Levi by their names:
Gershon, Kohath, and Merari. 18 And these *are*
the names of the sons of [a]Gershon by their
families: [b]Libni and Shimei. 19 And the sons of
[a]Kohath by their families: [b]Amram, Izehar, He-
bron, and Uzziel. 20 [a]And the sons of Merari by
their families: Mahli and Mushi. These *are* the
families of the Levites by their fathers' houses.
21 From Gershon *came* the family of the Lib-
nites and the family of the Shimites; these *were*
the families of the Gershonites. 22 Those who were
numbered, according to the number of all the
males from a month old and above—of those who
were numbered *there were* seven thousand five
hundred. 23 [a]The families of the Gershonites were
to camp behind the tabernacle westward. 24 And

2:31 [a] Num. 10:25 2:32 [a] Ex. 38:26; Num. 1:46; 11:21 2:33 [a] Num. 1:47; 26:57–62 2:34 [a] Num. 1:54 [b] Num. 24:2, 5, 6 3:1 [a] Ex. 6:16–27 3:2 [a] Ex. 6:23 [b] Lev. 10:1, 2; Num. 26:60, 61; 1 Chr. 24:2 3:3 [a] Ex. 28:41; Lev. 8 3:4 [a] Lev. 10:1, 2; Num. 26:61; 1 Chr. 24:2 3:6 [a] Num. 8:6–22; 18:1–7; Deut. 10:8; 33:8–11 3:7 [a] Num. 1:50; 8:11, 15, 24, 26 3:9 [a] Num. 8:19; 18:6, 7 [1] Samaritan Pentateuch and Septuagint read *Me.* 3:10 [a] Ex. 29:9; Num. 18:7 [b] Num. 1:51; 3:38; 16:40 3:12 [a] Num. 3:41; 8:16; 18:6 [b] Ex. 13:2; Num. 3:45; 8:14 3:13 [a] Ex. 13:2; Lev. 27:26; Num. 8:16, 17; Neh. 10:36; Luke 2:23 [b] Ex. 13:12, 15; Num. 8:17 3:15 [a] Num. 3:39; 26:62 3:17 [a] Gen. 46:11; Ex. 6:16–22; Num. 26:57; 1 Chr. 6:1, 16; 23:6 3:18 [a] Num. 4:38–41 [b] Ex. 6:17 3:19 [a] Num. 4:34–37 [b] Ex. 6:18 3:20 [a] Ex. 6:19; Num. 4:42–45 3:23 [a] Num. 1:53

the leader of the father's house of the Gershon-
ites *was* Eliasaph the son of Lael. 25 [a]The duties
of the children of Gershon in the tabernacle of
meeting *included* [b]the tabernacle, [c]the tent with
[d]its covering, [e]the screen for the door of the tab-
ernacle of meeting, 26 [a]the screen for the door of
the court, [b]the hangings of the court which *are*
around the tabernacle and the altar, and [c]their
cords, according to all the work relating to them.
27 [a]From Kohath *came* the family of the Am-
ramites, the family of the Izharites, the family of
the Hebronites, and the family of the Uzzielites;
these *were* the families of the Kohathites. 28 Ac-
cording to the number of all the males, from a
month old and above, *there were* eight thousand
six[1] hundred keeping charge of the sanctuary.
29 [a]The families of the children of Kohath were
to camp on the south side of the tabernacle.
30 And the leader of the fathers' house of the
families of the Kohathites *was* Elizaphan the son
of [a]Uzziel. 31 [a]Their duty *included* [b]the ark, [c]the
table, [d]the lampstand, [e]the altars, the utensils
of the sanctuary with which they ministered,
[f]the screen, and all the work relating to them.
32 And Eleazar the son of Aaron the priest *was
to be* chief over the leaders of the Levites, *with* over-
sight of those who kept charge of the sanctuary.
33 From Merari *came* the family of the Mah-
lites and the family of the Mushites; these *were*
the families of Merari. 34 And those who were
numbered, according to the number of all the
males from a month old and above, *were* six
thousand two hundred. 35 The leader of the fa-
thers' house of the families of Merari *was* Zuriel
the son of Abihail. [a]These *were* to camp on the
north side of the tabernacle. 36 And [a]the ap-
pointed duty of the children of Merari *included*
the boards of the tabernacle, its bars, its pillars,
its sockets, its utensils, all the work relating to
them, 37 and the pillars of the court all around,
with their sockets, their pegs, and their cords.
38 [a]Moreover those who were to camp before
the tabernacle on the east, before the tabernacle
of meeting, *were* Moses, Aaron, and his sons,
[b]keeping charge of the sanctuary, [c]to meet the
needs of the children of Israel; but [d]the outsider
who came near was to be put to death. 39 [a]All who
were numbered of the Levites, whom Moses
and Aaron numbered at the commandment of
the LORD, by their families, all the males from a
month old and above, *were* twenty-two thousand.

### LEVITES DEDICATED INSTEAD OF THE FIRSTBORN

40 Then the LORD said to Moses: [a]"Number all
the firstborn males of the children of Israel from
a month old and above, and take the number of
their names. 41 [a]And you shall take the Levites for
Me—I *am* the LORD—instead of all the firstborn
among the children of Israel, and the livestock of
the Levites instead of all the firstborn among the
livestock of the children of Israel." 42 So Moses
numbered all the firstborn among the children
of Israel, as the LORD commanded him. 43 And
all the firstborn males, according to the number
of names from a month old and above, of those
who were numbered of them, were twenty-two
thousand two hundred and seventy-three.
44 Then the LORD spoke to Moses, saying:
45 [a]"Take the Levites instead of all the firstborn
among the children of Israel, and the livestock
of the Levites instead of their livestock. The
Levites shall be Mine: I *am* the LORD. 46 And
for [a]the redemption of the two hundred and
seventy-three of the firstborn of the children
of Israel, [b]who are more than the number of
the Levites, 47 you shall take [a]five shekels for
each one [b]individually; you shall take *them* in
the currency of the shekel of the sanctuary, [c]the
shekel of twenty gerahs. 48 And you shall give the
money, with which the excess number of them
is redeemed, to Aaron and his sons."
49 So Moses took the redemption money
from those who were over and above those who
were redeemed by the Levites. 50 From the first-
born of the children of Israel he took the money,
[a]one thousand three hundred and sixty-five
*shekels,* according to the shekel of the sanctuary.
51 And Moses [a]gave their redemption money to
Aaron and his sons, according to the word of the
LORD, as the LORD commanded Moses.

### DUTIES OF THE SONS OF KOHATH

4 Then the LORD spoke to Moses and Aaron,
saying: 2 "Take a census of the sons of [a]Ko-
hath from among the children of Levi, by their
families, by their fathers' house, 3 [a]from thirty
years old and above, even to fifty years old,
all who enter the service to do the work in the
tabernacle of meeting.
4 [a]"This *is* the service of the sons of Kohath
in the tabernacle of meeting, *relating to* [b]the
most holy things: 5 When the camp prepares to
journey, Aaron and his sons shall come, and they
shall take down [a]the covering veil and cover the
[b]ark of the Testimony with it. 6 Then they shall
put on it a covering of badger skins, and spread
over *that* a cloth entirely of [a]blue; and they shall
insert [b]its poles.
7 "On the [a]table of showbread they shall
spread a blue cloth, and put on it the dishes,
the pans, the bowls, and the pitchers for pouring;

**3:25** [a] Num. 4:24–26 [b] Ex. 25:9 [c] Ex. 26:1 [d] Ex. 26:7, 14 [e] Ex. 26:36 **3:26** [a] Ex. 27:9, 12, 14, 15 [b] Ex. 27:16 [c] Ex. 35:18 **3:27** [a] 1 Chr. 26:23 **3:28** [1] Some manuscripts of the Septuagint read *three.* **3:29** [a] Ex. 6:18; Num. 1:53 **3:30** [a] Lev. 10:4 **3:31** [a] Num. 4:15 [b] Ex. 25:10 [c] Ex. 25:23 [d] Ex. 25:31 [e] Ex. 27:1; 30:1 [f] Ex. 26:31–33 **3:35** [a] Num. 1:53; 2:25 **3:36** [a] Num. 4:31, 32 **3:38** [a] Num. 1:53 [b] Num. 18:5 [c] Num. 3:7, 8 [d] Num. 3:10 **3:39** [a] Num. 3:43; 4:48; 26:62 **3:40** [a] Num. 3:15 **3:41** [a] Num. 3:12, 45 **3:45** [a] Num. 3:12, 41 **3:46** [a] Ex. 13:13, 15; Num. 18:15, 16 [b] Num. 3:39, 43 **3:47** [a] Lev. 27:6; Num. 18:16 [b] Num. 1:2, 18, 20 [c] Ex. 30:13 **3:50** [a] Num. 3:46, 47 **3:51** [a] Num. 3:48 **4:2** [a] Num. 3:27–32 **4:3** [a] Num. 4:23, 30, 35; 8:24; 1 Chr. 23:3, 24, 27; Ezra 3:8 **4:4** [a] Num. 4:15 [b] Num. 4:19 **4:5** [a] Ex. 26:31; Heb. 9:3 [b] Ex. 25:10, 16 **4:6** [a] Ex. 39:1 [b] Ex. 25:13; 1 Kin. 8:7, 8 **4:7** [a] Ex. 25:23, 29, 30

and the [b]showbread[1] shall be on it. 8 They shall
spread over them a scarlet cloth, and cover the
same with a covering of badger skins; and they
shall insert its poles. 9 And they shall take a blue
cloth and cover the [a]lampstand of the light, [b]with
its lamps, its wick-trimmers, its trays, and all its
oil vessels, with which they service it. 10 Then
they shall put it with all its utensils in a covering
of badger skins, and put *it* on a carrying beam.
11 "Over [a]the golden altar they shall spread a
blue cloth, and cover it with a covering of badger
skins; and they shall insert its poles. 12 Then they
shall take all the [a]utensils of service with which
they minister in the sanctuary, put *them* in a
blue cloth, cover them with a covering of badger
skins, and put *them* on a carrying beam. 13 Also
they shall take away the ashes from the altar, and
spread a purple cloth over it. 14 They shall put on
it all its implements with which they minister
there—the firepans, the forks, the shovels, the
basins, and all the utensils of the altar—and they
shall spread on it a covering of badger skins,
and insert its poles. 15 And when Aaron and his
sons have finished covering the sanctuary and
all the furnishings of the sanctuary, when the
camp is set to go, then [a]the sons of Kohath shall
come to carry *them;* [b]but they shall not touch
any holy thing, lest they die.

"[c]These *are* the things in the tabernacle of
meeting which the sons of Kohath are to carry.

16 "The appointed duty of Eleazar the son of
Aaron the priest *is* [a]the oil for the light, the [b]sweet
incense, [c]the daily grain offering, the [d]anointing
oil, the oversight of all the tabernacle, of all that
*is* in it, with the sanctuary and its furnishings."

17 Then the LORD spoke to Moses and Aaron,
saying: 18 "Do not cut off the tribe of the fami-
lies of the Kohathites from among the Levites;
19 but do this in regard to them, that they may
live and not die when they approach [a]the most
holy things: Aaron and his sons shall go in and
appoint each of them to his service and his
task. 20 [a]But they shall not go in to watch while
the holy things are being covered, lest they die."

### DUTIES OF THE SONS OF GERSHON

21 Then the LORD spoke to Moses, saying:
22 "Also take a census of the sons of [a]Gershon, by
their fathers' house, by their families. 23 [a]From
thirty years old and above, even to fifty years
old, you shall number them, all who enter to
perform the service, to do the work in the tab-
ernacle of meeting. 24 This *is* the [a]service of
the families of the Gershonites, in serving and
carrying: 25 [a]They shall carry the [b]curtains of the
tabernacle and the tabernacle of meeting *with*
its covering, the covering of [c]badger skins that
*is* on it, the screen for the door of the tabernacle
of meeting, 26 the screen for the door of the gate
of the court, the hangings of the court which *are*
around the tabernacle and altar, and their cords,
all the furnishings for their service and all that
is made for these things: so shall they serve.

27 "Aaron and his sons shall assign all the
service of the sons of the Gershonites, all their
tasks and all their service. And you shall appoint
to them all their tasks as their duty. 28 This *is* the
service of the families of the sons of Gershon
in the tabernacle of meeting. And their duties
*shall be* [a]under the authority[1] of Ithamar the son
of Aaron the priest.

### DUTIES OF THE SONS OF MERARI

29 "*As for* the sons of [a]Merari, you shall num-
ber them by their families and by their fathers'
house. 30 [a]From thirty years old and above, even
to fifty years old, you shall number them, every-
one who enters the service to do the work of the
tabernacle of meeting. 31 And [a]this *is* [b]what they
must carry as all their service for the tabernacle
of meeting: [c]the boards of the tabernacle, its bars,
its pillars, its sockets, 32 and the pillars around the
court with their sockets, pegs, and cords, with all
their furnishings and all their service; and you
shall [a]assign *to each man* by name the items he
must carry. 33 This *is* the service of the families
of the sons of Merari, as all their service for the
tabernacle of meeting, under the authority[1] of
Ithamar the son of Aaron the priest."

### CENSUS OF THE LEVITES

34 [a]And Moses, Aaron, and the leaders of the
congregation numbered the sons of the Kohath-
ites by their families and by their fathers' house,
35 from thirty [a]years old and above, even to fifty
years old, everyone who entered the service for
work in the tabernacle of meeting; 36 and those
who were numbered by their families were two
thousand seven hundred and fifty. 37 These *were*
the ones who were numbered of the families
of the Kohathites, all who might serve in the
tabernacle of meeting, whom Moses and Aaron
numbered according to the commandment of
the LORD by the hand of Moses.

38 And those who were numbered of the
sons of Gershon, by their families and by their
fathers' house, 39 from thirty years old and above,
even to fifty years old, everyone who entered the
service for work in the tabernacle of meeting—
40 those who were numbered by their families,
by their fathers' house, were two thousand six
hundred and thirty. 41 [a]These *are* the ones who
were numbered of the families of the sons of
Gershon, of all who might serve in the tabernacle

**4:7** [b] Lev. 24:5–9 [1] Literally *the continual bread* **4:9** [a] Ex. 25:31 [b] Ex. 25:37, 38 **4:11** [a] Ex. 30:1–5 **4:12** [a] Ex. 25:9; 1 Chr. 9:29 **4:15** [a] Num. 7:9; 10:21; Deut. 31:9; Josh. 4:10; 2 Sam. 6:13; 1 Chr. 15:2, 15 [b] 2 Sam. 6:6, 7; 1 Chr. 13:9, 10 [c] Num. 3:31 **4:16** [a] Ex. 25:6; Lev. 24:2 [b] Ex. 30:34 [c] Ex. 29:38 [d] Ex. 30:23–25 **4:19** [a] Num. 4:4 **4:20** [a] Ex. 19:21; 1 Sam. 6:19 **4:22** [a] Num. 3:22 **4:23** [a] Num. 4:3; 1 Chr. 23:3, 24, 27 **4:24** [a] Num. 7:7 **4:25** [a] Num. 3:25, 26 [b] Ex. 36:8 [c] Ex. 26:14 **4:28** [a] Num. 4:33 [1] Literally *hand* **4:29** [a] Num. 3:33–37 **4:30** [a] Num. 4:3; 8:24–26 **4:31** [a] Num. 3:36, 37 [b] Num. 7:8 [c] Ex. 26:15 **4:32** [a] Ex. 25:9; 38:21 **4:33** [1] Literally *hand* **4:34** [a] Num. 4:2 **4:35** [a] Num. 4:47 **4:41** [a] Num. 4:22

of meeting, whom Moses and Aaron numbered according to the commandment of the LORD.

42 Those of the families of the sons of Merari who were numbered, by their families, by their fathers' house, 43 from thirty years old and above, even to fifty years old, everyone who entered the service for work in the tabernacle of meeting— 44 those who were numbered by their families were three thousand two hundred. 45 These *are* the ones who were numbered of the families of the sons of Merari, whom Moses and Aaron numbered [a]according to the word of the LORD by the hand of Moses.

46 All who were [a]numbered of the Levites, whom Moses, Aaron, and the leaders of Israel numbered, by their families and by their fathers' houses, 47 [a]from thirty years old and above, even to fifty years old, everyone who came to do the work of service and the work of bearing burdens in the tabernacle of meeting— 48 those who were numbered were eight thousand five hundred and eighty.

49 According to the commandment of the LORD they were numbered by the hand of Moses, [a]each according to his service and according to his task; thus were they numbered by him, [b]as the LORD commanded Moses.

### CEREMONIALLY UNCLEAN PERSONS ISOLATED

*(cf. Lev. 15:1–33)*

5 And the LORD spoke to Moses, saying: 2 "Command the children of Israel that they put out of the camp every [a]leper, everyone who has a [b]discharge, and whoever becomes [c]defiled by a corpse. 3 You shall put out both male and female; you shall put them outside the camp, that they may not defile their camps [a]in the midst of which I dwell." 4 And the children of Israel did so, and put them outside the camp; as the LORD spoke to Moses, so the children of Israel did.

### CONFESSION AND RESTITUTION

*(Lev. 6:1–7)*

5 Then the LORD spoke to Moses, saying, 6 "Speak to the children of Israel: [a]'When a man or woman commits any sin that men commit in unfaithfulness against the LORD, and that person is guilty, 7 [a]then he shall confess the sin which he has committed. He shall make restitution for his trespass [b]in full, plus one-fifth of it, and give *it* to the one he has wronged. 8 But if the man has no relative to whom restitution may be made for the wrong, the restitution for the wrong *must go* to the LORD for the priest, in addition to [a]the ram of the atonement with which atonement is made for him. 9 Every [a]offering of all the holy things of the children of Israel, which they bring to the priest, shall be [b]his. 10 And every man's holy things shall be his; whatever any man gives the priest shall be [a]his.' "

### CONCERNING UNFAITHFUL WIVES

11 And the LORD spoke to Moses, saying, 12 "Speak to the children of Israel, and say to them: 'If any man's wife goes astray and behaves unfaithfully toward him, 13 and a man [a]lies with her carnally, and it is hidden from the eyes of her husband, and it is concealed that she has defiled herself, and *there was* no witness against her, nor was she [b]caught— 14 if the spirit of jealousy comes upon him and he becomes [a]jealous of his wife, who has defiled herself; or if the spirit of jealousy comes upon him and he becomes jealous of his wife, although she has not defiled herself— 15 then the man shall bring his wife to the priest. He shall [a]bring the offering required for her, one-tenth of an ephah of barley meal; he shall pour no oil on it and put no frankincense on it, because it *is* a grain offering of jealousy, an offering for remembering, for [b]bringing iniquity to remembrance.

16 'And the priest shall bring her near, and set her before the LORD. 17 The priest shall take holy water in an earthen vessel, and take some of the dust that is on the floor of the tabernacle and put *it* into the water. 18 Then the priest shall stand the woman before the [a]LORD, uncover the woman's head, and put the offering for remembering in her hands, which *is* the grain offering of jealousy. And the priest shall have in his hand the bitter water that brings a curse. 19 And the priest shall put her under oath, and say to the woman, "If no man has lain with you, and if you have not gone astray to uncleanness *while* under your husband's *authority,* be free from this bitter water that brings a curse. 20 But if you have gone astray *while* under your husband's *authority,* and if you have defiled yourself and some man other than your husband has lain with you"— 21 then the priest shall [a]put the woman under the oath of the curse, and he shall say to the woman— [b]"the LORD make you a curse and an oath among your people, when the LORD makes your thigh rot and your belly swell; 22 and may this water that causes the curse [a]go into your stomach, and make *your* belly swell and *your* thigh rot."

'[b]Then the woman shall say, "Amen, so be it."

23 'Then the priest shall write these curses in a book, and he shall scrape *them* off into the bitter water. 24 And he shall make the woman drink the bitter water that brings a curse, and the water that brings the curse shall enter her *to become* bitter. 25 [a]Then the priest shall take

**4:45** [a] Num. 4:29 **4:46** [a] Num. 3:39; 26:57–62; 1 Chr. 23:3–23 **4:47** [a] Num. 4:3, 23, 30 **4:49** [a] Num. 4:15, 24, 31 [b] Num. 4:1, 21 **5:2** [a] Lev. 13:3, 8, 46; Num. 12:10, 14, 15 [b] Lev. 15:2 [c] Lev. 21:1; Num. 9:6, 10; 19:11, 13; 31:19 **5:3** [a] Lev. 26:11, 12; Num. 35:34; [2 Cor. 6:16] **5:6** [a] Lev. 5:14—6:7 **5:7** [a] Lev. 5:5; 26:40, 41; Josh. 7:19; Ps. 32:5; 1 John 1:9 [b] Lev. 6:4, 5 **5:8** [a] Lev. 5:15; 6:6, 7; 7:7 **5:9** [a] Ex. 29:28; Lev. 6:17, 18, 26; 7:6–14 [b] Lev. 7:32–34; 10:14, 15 **5:10** [a] Lev. 10:13 **5:13** [a] Lev. 18:20; 20:10 [b] John 8:4 **5:14** [a] Prov. 6:34; Song 8:6 **5:15** [a] Lev. 5:11 [b] 1 Kin. 17:18; Ezek. 29:16; Heb. 10:3 **5:18** [a] Heb. 13:4 **5:21** [a] Josh. 6:26; 1 Sam. 14:24; Neh. 10:29 [b] Jer. 29:22 **5:22** [a] Ps. 109:18 [b] Deut. 27:15–26 **5:25** [a] Lev. 8:27

the grain offering of jealousy from the woman's hand, shall [b]wave the offering before the LORD, and bring it to the altar; 26 and the priest shall take a handful of the offering, [a]as its memorial portion, burn *it* on the altar, and afterward make the woman drink the water. 27 When he has made her drink the water, then it shall be, if she has defiled herself and behaved unfaithfully toward her husband, that the water that brings a [a]curse will enter her *and become* bitter, and her belly will swell, her thigh will rot, and the woman [b]will become a curse among her people. 28 But if the woman has not defiled herself, and is clean, then she shall be free and may conceive children.

29 'This *is* the law of jealousy, when a wife, *while* under her husband's *authority,* [a]goes astray and defiles herself, 30 or when the spirit of jealousy comes upon a man, and he becomes jealous of his wife; then he shall stand the woman before the LORD, and the priest shall execute all this law upon her. 31 Then the man shall be free from iniquity, but that woman [a]shall bear her guilt.' "

## THE LAW OF THE NAZIRITE

**6** Then the LORD spoke to Moses, saying, 2 "Speak to the children of Israel, and say to them: 'When either a man or woman consecrates an offering to take the vow of a Nazirite, [a]to separate himself to the LORD, 3 [a]he shall separate himself from wine and *similar* drink; he shall drink neither vinegar made from wine nor vinegar made from *similar* drink; neither shall he drink any grape juice, nor eat fresh grapes or raisins. 4 All the days of his separation he shall eat nothing that is produced by the grapevine, from seed to skin.

5 'All the days of the vow of his separation no [a]razor shall come upon his head; until the days are fulfilled for which he separated himself to the LORD, he shall be holy. *Then* he shall let the locks of the hair of his head grow. 6 All the days that he separates himself to the LORD [a]he shall not go near a dead body. 7 [a]He shall not make himself unclean even for his father or his mother, for his brother or his sister, when they die, because his separation to God *is* on his head. 8 [a]All the days of his separation he shall be holy to the LORD.

9 'And if anyone dies very suddenly beside him, and he defiles his consecrated head, then he shall [a]shave his head on the day of his cleansing; on the seventh day he shall shave it. 10 Then [a]on the eighth day he shall bring two turtledoves or two young pigeons to the priest, to the door of the tabernacle of meeting; 11 and the priest shall offer one as a sin offering and *the* other as a burnt offering, and make atonement for him, because he sinned in regard to the corpse; and

> **6:2–12** Not to be confused with a Nazarene (a person from Nazareth), the vow to become a **Nazirite** was like a contract to dedicate a portion of one's life specifically to serving God. All Israelites were free to make the vow. The only people we know of in the Bible who were Nazirites were Samson (Judg. 13:2–7), Samuel (1 Sam. 1:11), and John the Baptist (Luke 1:15).

he shall sanctify his head that same day. 12 He shall consecrate to the LORD the days of his separation, and bring a male lamb in its first year [a]as a trespass offering; but the former days shall be lost, because his separation was defiled.

13 'Now this *is* the law of the Nazirite: [a]When the days of his separation are fulfilled, he shall be brought to the door of the tabernacle of meeting. 14 And he shall present his offering to the LORD: one male lamb in its first year without blemish as a burnt offering, one ewe lamb in its first year without blemish [a]as a sin offering, one ram without blemish [b]as a peace offering, 15 a basket of unleavened bread, [a]cakes of fine flour mixed with oil, unleavened wafers [b]anointed with oil, and their grain offering with their [c]drink offerings.

16 'Then the priest shall bring *them* before the LORD and offer his sin offering and his burnt offering; 17 and he shall offer the ram as a sacrifice of a peace offering to the LORD, with the basket of unleavened bread; the priest shall also offer its grain offering and its drink offering. 18 [a]Then the Nazirite shall shave his consecrated head *at* the door of the tabernacle of meeting, and shall take the hair from his consecrated head and put *it* on the fire which is under the sacrifice of the peace offering.

19 'And the priest shall take the [a]boiled shoulder of the ram, one [b]unleavened cake from the basket, and one unleavened wafer, and [c]put *them* upon the hands of the Nazirite after he has shaved his consecrated *hair,* 20 and the priest shall wave them as a wave offering before the LORD; [a]they *are* holy for the priest, together with the breast of the wave offering and the thigh of the heave offering. After that the Nazirite may drink wine.'

21 "This is the law of the Nazirite who vows to the LORD the offering for his separation, and besides that, whatever else his hand is able to provide; according to the vow which he takes, so he must do according to the law of his separation."

## THE PRIESTLY BLESSING

22 And the LORD spoke to Moses, saying: 23 "Speak to Aaron and his sons, saying, 'This is

**5:25** [b] Lev. 2:2, 9 **5:26** [a] Lev. 2:2, 9 **5:27** [a] Deut. 28:37; Is. 65:15; Jer. 24:9; 29:18, 22; 42:18 [b] Num. 5:21 **5:29** [a] Num. 5:19 **5:31** [a] Lev. 20:17, 19, 20 **6:2** [a] Lev. 27:2; Judg. 13:5; [Lam. 4:7; Amos 2:11, 12]; Acts 21:23; Rom. 1:1 **6:3** [a] Lev. 10:9; Amos 2:12; Luke 1:15 **6:5** [a] Judg. 13:5; 16:17; 1 Sam. 1:11 **6:6** [a] Lev. 21:1–3, 11; Num. 19:11–22 **6:7** [a] Lev. 21:1, 2, 11; Num. 9:6 **6:8** [a] [2 Cor. 6:17, 18] **6:9** [a] Lev. 14:8, 9; Acts 18:18; 21:24 **6:10** [a] Lev. 5:7; 14:22; 15:14, 29 **6:12** [a] Lev. 5:6 **6:13** [a] Acts 21:26 **6:14** [a] Lev. 4:2, 27, 32 [b] Lev. 3:6 **6:15** [a] Lev. 2:4 [b] Ex. 29:2 [c] Num. 15:5, 7, 10 **6:18** [a] Num. 6:9; Acts 21:23, 24 **6:19** [a] 1 Sam. 2:15 [b] Ex. 29:23, 24 [c] Lev. 7:30 **6:20** [a] Ex. 29:27, 28

the way you shall bless the children of Israel. Say to them:

24 "The LORD [a]bless you and [b]keep you;
25 The LORD [a]make His face shine upon you,
And [b]be gracious to you;
26 [a]The LORD lift up His countenance upon you,
And [b]give you peace." '

27 [a]"So they shall put My name on the children of Israel, and [b]I will bless them."

## OFFERINGS OF THE LEADERS

7 Now it came to pass, when Moses had finished [a]setting up the tabernacle, that he [b]anointed it and consecrated it and all its furnishings, and the altar and all its utensils; so he anointed them and consecrated them. 2 Then [a]the leaders of Israel, the heads of their fathers' houses, who *were* the leaders of the tribes and over those who were numbered, made an offering. 3 And they brought their offering before the LORD, six covered carts and twelve oxen, a cart for *every* two of the leaders, and for each one an ox; and they presented them before the tabernacle.

4 Then the LORD spoke to Moses, saying, 5 "Accept *these* from them, that they may be used in doing the work of the tabernacle of meeting; and you shall give them to the Levites, *to* every man according to his service." 6 So Moses took the carts and the oxen, and gave them to the Levites. 7 Two carts and four oxen [a]he gave to the sons of Gershon, according to their service; 8 [a]and four carts and eight oxen he gave to the sons of Merari, according to their service, under the authority[1] of Ithamar the son of Aaron the priest. 9 But to the sons of Kohath he gave none, because theirs *was* [a]the service of the holy things, [b]*which* they carried on their shoulders.

10 Now the leaders offered [a]the dedication *offering* for the altar when it was anointed; so the leaders offered their offering before the altar. 11 For the LORD said to Moses, "They shall offer their offering, one leader each day, for the dedication of the altar."

12 And the one who offered his offering on the first day *was* [a]Nahshon the son of Amminadab, from the tribe of Judah. 13 His offering *was* one silver platter, the weight of which *was* one hundred and thirty *shekels,* and one silver bowl of seventy shekels, according to [a]the shekel of the sanctuary, both of them full of fine flour mixed with oil as a [b]grain offering; 14 one gold pan of ten *shekels,* full of [a]incense; 15 [a]one young bull, one ram, and one male lamb [b]in its first year, as a burnt offering; 16 one kid of the goats as a [a]sin offering; 17 and for [a]the sacrifice of peace offerings: two oxen, five rams, five male goats, and five male lambs in their first year. This *was* the offering of Nahshon the son of Amminadab.

18 On the second day Nethanel the son of Zuar, leader of Issachar, presented *an offering.* 19 *For* his offering he offered one silver platter, the weight of which *was* one hundred and thirty *shekels,* and one silver bowl of seventy shekels, according to the shekel of the sanctuary, both of them full of fine flour mixed with oil as a grain offering; 20 one gold pan of ten *shekels,* full of incense; 21 one young bull, one ram, and one male lamb in its first year, as a burnt offering; 22 one kid of the goats as a sin offering; 23 and as the sacrifice of peace offerings: two oxen, five rams, five male goats, and five male lambs in their first year. This *was* the offering of Nethanel the son of Zuar.

24 On the third day Eliab the son of Helon, leader of the children of Zebulun, *presented an offering.* 25 His offering *was* one silver platter, the weight of which *was* one hundred and thirty *shekels,* and one silver bowl of seventy shekels, according to the shekel of the sanctuary, both of them full of fine flour mixed with oil as a grain offering; 26 one gold pan of ten *shekels,* full of incense; 27 one young bull, one ram, and one male lamb in its first year, as a burnt offering; 28 one kid of the goats as a sin offering; 29 and for the sacrifice of peace offerings: two oxen, five rams, five male goats, and five male lambs in their first year. This *was* the offering of Eliab the son of Helon.

30 On the fourth day [a]Elizur the son of Shedeur, leader of the children of Reuben, *presented an offering.* 31 His offering *was* one silver platter, the weight of which *was* one hundred and thirty *shekels,* and one silver bowl of seventy shekels, according to the shekel of the sanctuary, both of them full of fine flour mixed with oil as a grain offering; 32 one gold pan of ten *shekels,* full of incense; 33 one young bull, one ram, and one male lamb in its first year, as a burnt offering; 34 one kid of the goats as a sin offering; 35 and as the sacrifice of peace offerings: two oxen, five rams, five male goats, and five male lambs in their first year. This *was* the offering of Elizur the son of Shedeur.

36 On the fifth day [a]Shelumiel the son of Zurishaddai, leader of the children of Simeon, *presented an offering.* 37 His offering *was* one silver platter, the weight of which *was* one hundred and thirty *shekels,* and one silver bowl of seventy shekels, according to the shekel of the sanctuary, both of them full of fine flour mixed with oil as a grain offering; 38 one gold pan of ten *shekels,* full of incense; 39 one young bull, one ram, and one male lamb in its first

6:24 [a] Deut. 28:3–6 [b] Ps. 121:7; John 7:11 6:25 [a] Ps. 31:16; 67:1; 80:3, 7, 19; 119:135; Dan. 9:17 [b] Gen. 43:29; Ex. 33:19; Mal. 1:9 6:26 [a] Ps. 4:6; 89:15 [b] Lev. 26:6; Is. 26:3, 12; John 14:27; Phil. 4:7 6:27 [a] Deut. 28:10; 2 Sam. 7:23; 2 Chr. 7:14; Is. 43:7; Dan. 9:18, 19 [b] Ex. 20:24; Num. 23:20; Ps. 5:12; 67:7; 115:12, 13; Eph. 1:3 7:1 [a] Ex. 40:17–33 [b] Lev. 8:10, 11 7:2 [a] Num. 1:4 7:7 [a] Num. 4:24–28 7:8 [a] Num. 4:29–33 [1] Literally *hand* 7:9 [a] Num. 4:15 [b] Num. 4:6–14 7:10 [a] Num. 7:1; Deut. 20:5; 1 Kin. 8:63; 2 Chr. 7:5, 9; Ezra 6:16; Neh. 12:27 7:12 [a] Num. 2:3 7:13 [a] Ex. 30:13 [b] Lev. 2:1 7:14 [a] Ex. 30:34 7:15 [a] Lev. 1:2 [b] Ex. 12:5 7:16 [a] Lev. 4:23 7:17 [a] Lev. 3:1 7:30 [a] Num. 1:5; 2:10 7:36 [a] Num. 1:6; 2:12; 7:41

year, as a burnt offering; 40 one kid of the goats
as a sin offering; 41 and as the sacrifice of peace
offerings: two oxen, five rams, five male goats,
and five male lambs in their first year. This *was*
the offering of Shelumiel the son of Zurishaddai.
42 On the sixth day [a]Eliasaph the son of
Deuel,[1] leader of the children of Gad, *presented*
*an offering.* 43 His offering *was* one silver platter,
the weight of which *was* one hundred and thirty
*shekels,* and one silver bowl of seventy shekels,
according to the shekel of the sanctuary, both of
them full of fine flour mixed with oil as a grain
offering; 44 one gold pan of ten *shekels,* full of
incense; 45 one young bull, one ram, and one
male lamb in its first year, as [a]a burnt offering;
46 one kid of the goats as a sin offering; 47 and as
the sacrifice of peace offerings: two oxen, five
rams, five male goats, and five male lambs in
their first year. This *was* the offering of Eliasaph
the son of Deuel.
48 On the seventh day [a]Elishama the son
of Ammihud, leader of the children of Ephra-
im, *presented an offering.* 49 His offering *was*
one silver platter, the weight of which *was* one
hundred and thirty *shekels,* and one silver bowl
of seventy shekels, according to the shekel of
the sanctuary, both of them full of fine flour
mixed with oil as a grain offering; 50 one gold
pan of ten *shekels,* full of incense; 51 one young
bull, one ram, and one male lamb in its first
year, as a burnt offering; 52 one kid of the goats
as a sin offering; 53 and as the sacrifice of peace
offerings: two oxen, five rams, five male goats,
and five male lambs in their first year. This *was*
the offering of Elishama the son of Ammihud.
54 On the eighth day [a]Gamaliel the son of
Pedahzur, leader of the children of Manasseh,
*presented an offering.* 55 His offering *was* one
silver platter, the weight of which *was* one hun-
dred and thirty *shekels,* and one silver bowl of
seventy shekels, according to the shekel of the
sanctuary, both of them full of fine flour mixed
with oil as a grain offering; 56 one gold pan of
ten *shekels,* full of incense; 57 one young bull,
one ram, and one male lamb in its first year,
as a burnt offering; 58 one kid of the goats as
a sin offering; 59 and as the sacrifice of peace
offerings: two oxen, five rams, five male goats,
and five male lambs in their first year. This *was*
the offering of Gamaliel the son of Pedahzur.
60 On the ninth day [a]Abidan the son of Gideo-
ni, leader of the children of Benjamin, *presented*
*an offering.* 61 His offering *was* one silver platter,
the weight of which *was* one hundred and thirty
*shekels,* and one silver bowl of seventy shekels,
according to the shekel of the sanctuary, both of
them full of fine flour mixed with oil as a grain
offering; 62 one gold pan of ten *shekels,* full of in-
cense; 63 one young bull, one ram, and one male
lamb in its first year, as a burnt offering; 64 one kid
of the goats as a sin offering; 65 and as the sacrifice
of peace offerings: two oxen, five rams, five male
goats, and five male lambs in their first year. This
*was* the offering of Abidan the son of Gideoni.
66 On the tenth day [a]Ahiezer the son of Am-
mishaddai, leader of the children of Dan, *pre-*
*sented an offering.* 67 His offering *was* one silver
platter, the weight of which *was* one hundred
and thirty *shekels,* and one silver bowl of seventy
shekels, according to the shekel of the sanctuary,
both of them full of fine flour mixed with oil as a
grain offering; 68 one gold pan of ten *shekels,* full
of incense; 69 one young bull, one ram, and one
male lamb in its first year, as a burnt offering;
70 one kid of the goats as a sin offering; 71 and as
the sacrifice of peace offerings: two oxen, five
rams, five male goats, and five male lambs in
their first year. This *was* the offering of Ahiezer
the son of Ammishaddai.
72 On the eleventh day [a]Pagiel the son of
Ocran, leader of the children of Asher, *presented*
*an offering.* 73 His offering *was* one silver platter,
the weight of which *was* one hundred and thirty
*shekels,* and one silver bowl of seventy shekels,
according to the shekel of the sanctuary, both of
them full of fine flour mixed with oil as a grain
offering; 74 one gold pan of ten *shekels,* full of
incense; 75 one young bull, one ram, and one
male lamb in its first year, as a burnt offering;
76 one kid of the goats as a sin offering; 77 and as
the sacrifice of peace offerings: two oxen, five
rams, five male goats, and five male lambs in
their first year. This *was* the offering of Pagiel
the son of Ocran.
78 On the twelfth day [a]Ahira the son of Enan,
leader of the children of Naphtali, *presented an*
*offering.* 79 His offering *was* one silver platter,
the weight of which *was* one hundred and thirty
*shekels,* and one silver bowl of seventy shekels,
according to the shekel of the sanctuary, both of
them full of fine flour mixed with oil as a grain
offering; 80 one gold pan of ten *shekels,* full of
incense; 81 one young bull, one ram, and one male
lamb in its first year, as a burnt offering; 82 one kid
of the goats as a sin offering; 83 and as the sacrifice
of peace offerings: two oxen, five rams, five male
goats, and five male lambs in their first year. This
*was* the offering of Ahira the son of Enan.
84 This *was* [a]the dedication *offering* for the
altar from the leaders of Israel, when it was
anointed: twelve silver platters, twelve silver
bowls, and twelve gold pans. 85 Each silver platter
*weighed* one hundred and thirty *shekels* and
each bowl seventy *shekels.* All the silver of the
vessels *weighed* two thousand four hundred
*shekels,* according to the shekel of the sanctuary.
86 The twelve gold pans full of incense *weighed*
ten *shekels* apiece, according to the shekel of the
sanctuary; all the gold of the pans *weighed* one
hundred and twenty *shekels.* 87 All the oxen for

7:42 [a] Num. 1:14; 2:14; 10:20 [1] Spelled *Reuel* in 2:14 7:45 [a] Ps. 40:6 7:48 [a] Num. 1:10; 2:18; 1 Chr. 7:26 7:54 [a] Num. 1:10; 2:20
7:60 [a] Num. 1:11; 2:22 7:66 [a] Num. 1:12; 2:25 7:72 [a] Num. 1:13; 2:27 7:78 [a] Num. 1:15; 2:29 7:84 [a] Num. 7:10

> **8:10–12** The children of Israel who were to **lay their hands on the Levites** were showing their support for, and agreement with, the special role the Levites had been set aside for. Everyone could look back on this event surrounding this ancient symbol of dedication and remember it as an important, solemn time of dedication and asking for God's blessing.

the burnt offering *were* twelve young bulls, the rams twelve, the male lambs in their first year twelve, with their grain offering, and the kids of the goats as a sin offering twelve. 88 And all the oxen for the sacrifice of peace offerings were twenty-four bulls, the rams sixty, the male goats sixty, and the lambs in their first year sixty. This *was* the dedication *offering* for the altar after it was [a]anointed.

89 Now when Moses went into the tabernacle of meeting [a]to speak with Him, he heard [b]the voice of One speaking to him from above the mercy seat that *was* on the ark of the Testimony, from [c]between the two cherubim; thus He spoke to him.

### *ARRANGEMENT OF THE LAMPS*
*(Ex. 25:31–40)*

**8** And the LORD spoke to Moses, saying: 2 "Speak to Aaron, and say to him, 'When you [a]arrange the lamps, the seven [b]lamps shall give light in front of the lampstand.' " 3 And Aaron did so; he arranged the lamps to face toward the front of the lampstand, as the LORD commanded Moses. 4 [a]Now this workmanship of the lampstand *was* hammered gold; from its shaft to its flowers it *was* [b]hammered work. [c]According to the pattern which the LORD had shown Moses, so he made the lampstand.

### *CLEANSING AND DEDICATION OF THE LEVITES*

5 Then the LORD spoke to Moses, saying: 6 "Take the Levites from among the children of Israel and cleanse them *ceremonially.* 7 Thus you shall do to them to cleanse them: Sprinkle [a]water of purification on them, and [b]let them shave all their body, and let them wash their clothes, and *so* make themselves clean. 8 Then let them take a young bull with [a]its grain offering of fine flour mixed with oil, and you shall take another young bull as a sin offering. 9 [a]And you shall bring the Levites before the tabernacle of meeting, [b]and you shall gather together the whole congregation of the children of Israel. 10 So you shall bring the Levites before the LORD, and the children of Israel [a]shall lay their hands on the Levites; 11 and Aaron shall offer the Levites before the LORD *like* a [a]wave offering from the children of Israel, that they may perform the work of the LORD. 12 [a]Then the Levites shall lay their hands on the heads of the young bulls, and you shall offer one as a sin offering and the other as a burnt offering to the LORD, to make atonement for the Levites.

13 "And you shall stand the Levites before Aaron and his sons, and then offer them *like* a wave offering to the LORD. 14 Thus you shall [a]separate the Levites from among the children of Israel, and the Levites shall be [b]Mine. 15 After that the Levites shall go in to service the tabernacle of meeting. So you shall cleanse them and [a]offer them *like* a wave offering. 16 For they *are* [a]wholly given to Me from among the children of Israel; I have taken them for Myself [b]instead of all who open the womb, the firstborn of all the children of Israel. 17 [a]For all the firstborn among the children of Israel *are* Mine, *both* man and beast; on the day that I struck all the firstborn in the land of Egypt I sanctified them to Myself. 18 I have taken the Levites instead of all the firstborn of the children of Israel. 19 And [a]I have given the Levites as a gift to Aaron and his sons from among the children of Israel, to do the work for the children of Israel in the tabernacle of meeting, and to make atonement for the children of Israel, [b]that there be no plague among the children of Israel when the children of Israel come near the sanctuary."

20 Thus Moses and Aaron and all the congregation of the children of Israel did to the Levites; according to all that the LORD commanded Moses concerning the Levites, so the children of Israel did to them. 21 [a]And the Levites purified themselves and washed their clothes; then Aaron presented them *like* a wave offering before the LORD, and Aaron made atonement for them to cleanse them. 22 [a]After that the Levites went in to do their work in the tabernacle of meeting before Aaron and his sons; [b]as the LORD commanded Moses concerning the Levites, so they did to them.

23 Then the LORD spoke to Moses, saying, 24 "This *is* what *pertains* to the Levites: [a]From twenty-five years old and above one may enter to perform service in the work of the tabernacle of meeting; 25 and at the age of fifty years they must cease performing this work, and shall work no more. 26 They may minister with their brethren in the tabernacle of meeting, [a]to attend to needs, but they *themselves* shall do no work. Thus you shall do to the Levites regarding their duties."

**7:88** [a] Num. 7:1, 10 **7:89** [a] [Ex. 33:9, 11]; Num. 12:8 [b] Ex. 25:21, 22 [c] Ps. 80:1; 99:1 **8:2** [a] Lev. 24:2–4 [b] Ex. 25:37; 40:25 **8:4** [a] Ex. 25:31 [b] Ex. 25:18 [c] Ex. 25:40; Acts 7:44 **8:7** [a] Num. 19:9, 13, 17, 20; Ps. 51:2, 7; [Heb. 9:13, 14] [b] Lev. 14:8, 9 **8:8** [a] Lev. 2:1; Num. 15:8–10 **8:9** [a] Ex. 29:4; 40:12 [b] Lev. 8:3 **8:10** [a] Lev. 1:4 **8:11** [a] Num. 18:6 **8:12** [a] Ex. 29:10 **8:14** [a] Num. 16:9 [b] Num. 3:12, 45; 16:9 **8:15** [a] Num. 8:11, 13 **8:16** [a] Num. 3:9 [b] Ex. 13:2; Num. 3:12, 45 **8:17** [a] Ex. 12:2, 12, 13, 15; Num. 3:13; Luke 2:23 **8:19** [a] Num. 3:9 [b] Num. 1:53; 16:46; 18:5; 2 Chr. 26:16 **8:21** [a] Num. 8:7 **8:22** [a] Num. 8:15 [b] Num. 8:5 **8:24** [a] Num. 4:3; 1 Chr. 23:3, 24, 27 **8:26** [a] Num. 1:53

### *THE SECOND PASSOVER*
*(Ex. 12:1–20)*

**9** Now the LORD spoke to Moses in the Wilderness of Sinai, in the first month of the
second year after they had come out of the land
of Egypt, saying: 2 "Let the children of Israel keep
[a]the Passover at its appointed [b]time. 3 On the
fourteenth day of this month, at twilight, you
shall keep it at its appointed time. According
to all its rites and ceremonies you shall keep
it." 4 So Moses told the children of Israel that
they should keep the Passover. 5 And [a]they kept
the Passover on the fourteenth day of the first
month, at twilight, in the Wilderness of Sinai;
according to all that the LORD commanded
Moses, so the children of Israel did.
6 Now there were *certain* men who were [a]defiled by a human corpse, so that they could not
keep the Passover on that day; [b]and they came
before Moses and Aaron that day. 7 And those
men said to him, "We *became* defiled by a human corpse. Why are we kept from presenting
the offering of the LORD at its appointed time
among the children of Israel?"
8 And Moses said to them, "Stand still, that
[a]I may hear what the LORD will command concerning you."
9 Then the LORD spoke to Moses, saying,
10 "Speak to the children of Israel, saying: 'If
anyone of you or your posterity is unclean because of a corpse, or *is* far away on a journey,
he may still keep the LORD's Passover. 11 On [a]the
fourteenth day of the second month, at twilight,
they may keep it. They shall [b]eat it with unleavened bread and bitter herbs. 12 [a]They shall leave
none of it until morning, [b]nor break one of its
bones. [c]According to all the ordinances of the
Passover they shall keep it. 13 But the man who
*is* clean and is not on a journey, and ceases to
keep the Passover, that same person [a]shall be cut
off from among his people, because he [b]did not
bring the offering of the LORD at its appointed
time; that man shall [c]bear his sin.

> **SEEING JESUS IN THE SCRIPTURE**
>
> **9:12** Not breaking any of the Passover lamb's bones and fully consuming it points to Jesus' sacrifice. On the cross, Jesus gave Himself fully as our substitute, holding nothing back, and none of His bones were broken (see John 19:36).

14 'And if a stranger dwells among you, and
would keep the LORD's Passover, he must do so
according to the rite of the Passover and according
to its ceremony; [a]you shall have one ordinance,
both for the stranger and the native of the land.' "

### *THE CLOUD AND THE FIRE*
*(Ex. 13:21, 22; 40:34–38)*

15 Now [a]on the day that the tabernacle was
raised up, the cloud [b]covered the tabernacle,
the tent of the Testimony; [c]from evening until
morning it was above the tabernacle like the
appearance of fire. 16 So it was always: the cloud
covered it *by day,* and the appearance of fire by
night. 17 Whenever the cloud [a]was taken up from
above the tabernacle, after that the children of
Israel would journey; and in the place where
the cloud settled, there the children of Israel
would pitch their tents. 18 At the command of
the LORD the children of Israel would journey,
and at the command of the LORD they would
camp; [a]as long as the cloud stayed above the
tabernacle they remained encamped. 19 Even
when the cloud continued long, many days above
the tabernacle, the children of Israel [a]kept the
charge of the LORD and did not journey. 20 So it
was, when the cloud was above the tabernacle a
few days: according to the command of the LORD
they would remain encamped, and according to
the command of the LORD they would journey.
21 So it was, when the cloud remained only from
evening until morning: when the cloud was taken
up in the morning, then they would journey;
whether by day or by night, whenever the cloud
was taken up, they would journey. 22 *Whether it
was* two days, a month, or a year that the cloud
remained above the tabernacle, the children of
Israel [a]would remain encamped and not journey;
but when it was taken up, they would journey.
23 At the command of the LORD they remained
encamped, and at the command of the LORD they
journeyed; they [a]kept the charge of the LORD, at
the command of the LORD by the hand of Moses.

### *TWO SILVER TRUMPETS*

**10** And the LORD spoke to Moses, saying:
2 "Make two silver trumpets for yourself;
you shall make them of hammered work; you
shall use them for [a]calling the congregation
and for directing the movement of the camps.
3 When [a]they blow both of them, all the congregation shall gather before you at the door of the
tabernacle of meeting. 4 But if they blow *only* one,
then the leaders, the [a]heads of the divisions of
Israel, shall gather to you. 5 When you sound the
[a]advance, [b]the camps that lie on the east side shall
then begin their journey. 6 When you sound the
advance the second time, then the camps that
lie [a]on the south side shall begin their journey;

**9:2** [a] Ex. 12:1–16; Lev. 23:5; Num. 28:16; Deut. 16:1, 2 [b] 2 Chr. 30:1–15; Luke 22:7; [1 Cor. 5:7, 8] **9:5** [a] Josh. 5:10 **9:6** [a] Num. 5:2; 19:11–22; John 18:28 [b] Ex. 18:15, 19, 26; Num. 27:2 **9:8** [a] Ex. 18:22; Num. 27:5 **9:11** [a] 2 Chr. 30:2, 15 [b] Ex. 12:8 **9:12** [a] Ex. 12:10 [b] Ex. 12:46; [John 19:36] [c] Ex. 12:43 **9:13** [a] Gen. 17:14; Ex. 12:15, 47 [b] Num. 9:7 [c] Num. 5:31 **9:14** [a] Ex. 12:49; Lev. 24:22; Num. 15:15, 16, 29 **9:15** [a] Ex. 40:33, 34; Neh. 9:12, 19; Ps. 78:14 [b] Is. 4:5 [c] Ex. 13:21, 22; 40:38 **9:17** [a] Ex. 40:36–38; Num. 10:11, 12, 33, 34; Ps. 80:1 **9:18** [a] 1 Cor. 10:1 **9:19** [a] Num. 1:53; 3:8 **9:22** [a] Ex. 40:36, 37 **9:23** [a] Num. 9:19 **10:2** [a] Is. 1:13 **10:3** [a] Jer. 4:5; Joel 2:15 **10:4** [a] Ex. 18:21; Num. 1:16; 7:2 **10:5** [a] Joel 2:1 [b] Num. 2:3 **10:6** [a] Num. 2:10

they shall sound the call for them to begin their
journeys. 7 And when the assembly is to be gath-
ered together, [a]you shall blow, but not [b]sound the
advance. 8 [a]The sons of Aaron, the priests, shall
blow the trumpets; and these shall be to you as an
ordinance forever throughout your generations.
9 [a]"When you go to war in your land against
the enemy who [b]oppresses you, then you shall
sound an alarm with the trumpets, and you will
be [c]remembered before the LORD your God, and
you will be saved from your enemies. 10 Also
[a]in the day of your gladness, in your appointed
feasts, and at the beginning of your months,
you shall blow the trumpets over your burnt
offerings and over the sacrifices of your peace
offerings; and they shall be [b]a memorial for
you before your God: I *am* the LORD your God."

### DEPARTURE FROM SINAI

11 Now it came to pass on the twentieth *day* of
the second month, in the second year, that the
cloud [a]was taken up from above the tabernacle
of the Testimony. 12 And the children of Israel
set out from the [a]Wilderness of Sinai on [b]their
journeys; then the cloud settled down in the
[c]Wilderness of Paran. 13 So they started out for
the first time [a]according to the command of the
LORD by the hand of Moses.
14 The standard of the camp of the children
of Judah [a]set out first according to their armies;
over their army was [b]Nahshon the son of Am-
minadab. 15 Over the army of the tribe of the
children of Issachar *was* Nethanel the son of
Zuar. 16 And over the army of the tribe of the
children of Zebulun *was* Eliab the son of Helon.
17 Then [a]the tabernacle was taken down; and
the sons of Gershon and the sons of Merari set
out, [b]carrying the tabernacle.
18 And [a]the standard of the camp of Reuben
set out according to their armies; over their
army *was* Elizur the son of Shedeur. 19 Over the
army of the tribe of the children of Simeon *was*
Shelumiel the son of Zurishaddai. 20 And over
the army of the tribe of the children of Gad *was*
Eliasaph the son of Deuel.
21 Then the Kohathites set out, carrying the
[a]holy things. (The tabernacle would be prepared
for their arrival.)
22 And [a]the standard of the camp of the chil-
dren of Ephraim set out according to their armies;
over their army *was* Elishama the son of Ammi-
hud. 23 Over the army of the tribe of the children
of Manasseh *was* Gamaliel the son of Pedahzur.
24 And over the army of the tribe of the children
of Benjamin *was* Abidan the son of Gideoni.
25 Then [a]the standard of the camp of the
children of Dan (the rear guard of all the camps)
set out according to their armies; over their
army *was* Ahiezer the son of Ammishaddai.
26 Over the army of the tribe of the children of
Asher *was* Pagiel the son of Ocran. 27 And over
the army of the tribe of the children of Naphtali
*was* Ahira the son of Enan.
28 [a]Thus *was* the order of march of the chil-
dren of Israel, according to their armies, when
they began their journey.
29 Now Moses said to [a]Hobab the son of
[b]Reuel[1] the Midianite, Moses' father-in-law, "We
are setting out for the place of which the LORD
said, [c]'I will give it to you.' Come with us, and [d]we
will treat you well; for [e]the LORD has promised
good things to Israel."
30 And he said to him, "I will not go, but I
will depart to my *own* land and to my relatives."
31 So *Moses* said, "Please do not leave, inas-
much as you know how we are to camp in the
wilderness, and you can be our [a]eyes. 32 And it
shall be, if you go with us—indeed it shall be—
that [a]whatever good the LORD will do to us, the
same we will do to you."
33 So they departed from [a]the mountain of the
LORD on a journey of three days; and the ark of the
covenant of the LORD [b]went before them for the
three days' journey, to search out a resting place
for them. 34 And [a]the cloud of the LORD *was* above
them by day when they went out from the camp.
35 So it was, whenever the ark set out, that
Moses said:

[a]"Rise up, O LORD!
Let Your enemies be scattered,
And let those who hate You flee before You."

36 And when it rested, he said:

"Return, O LORD,
*To* the many thousands of Israel."

### THE PEOPLE COMPLAIN

11 Now [a]*when* the people complained, it dis-
pleased the LORD; [b]for the LORD heard *it,*
and His anger was aroused. So the [c]fire of the
LORD burned among them, and consumed *some*
in the outskirts of the camp. 2 Then the people
[a]cried out to Moses, and when Moses [b]prayed to
the LORD, the fire was quenched. 3 So he called
the name of the place Taberah,[1] because the fire
of the LORD had burned among them.
4 Now the [a]mixed multitude who were among
them yielded to [b]intense craving; so the children

10:7 [a] Num. 10:3 [b] Joel 2:1 10:8 [a] Num. 31:6; Josh. 6:4; 1 Chr. 15:24; 2 Chr. 13:12 10:9 [a] Num. 31:6; Josh. 6:5; 2 Chr. 13:14 [b] Judg. 2:18; 4:3; 6:9; 10:8, 12 [c] Gen. 8:1; Ps. 106:4 10:10 [a] Lev. 23:24; Num. 29:1; 1 Chr. 15:24; 2 Chr. 5:12; Ps. 81:3 [b] Lev. 23:24; Num. 10:9 10:11 [a] Num. 9:17 10:12 [a] Ex. 19:1; Num. 1:1; 9:5 [b] Ex. 40:36 [c] Gen. 21:21; Num. 12:16; Deut. 1:1 10:13 [a] Num. 10:5, 6 10:14 [a] Num. 2:3–9 [b] Num. 1:7 10:17 [a] Num. 1:51 [b] Num. 4:21–32; 7:7–9 10:18 [a] Num. 2:10–16 10:21 [a] Num. 4:4–20; 7:9 10:22 [a] Num. 2:18–24 10:25 [a] Num. 2:25–31; Josh. 6:9 10:28 [a] Num. 2:34 10:29 [a] Judg. 4:11 [b] Ex. 2:18; 3:1; 18:12 [c] Gen. 12:7; Ex. 6:4–8 [d] Judg. 1:16 [e] Gen. 32:12; Ex. 3:8 [1] Septuagint reads *Raguel* (compare Exodus 2:18). 10:31 [a] Job 29:15 10:32 [a] Ex. 18:9; Lev. 19:34; Judg. 1:16 10:33 [a] Ex. 3:1; Deut. 1:6 [b] Deut. 1:33; Josh. 3:3–6; Ezek. 20:6 10:34 [a] Ex. 13:21; Neh. 9:12, 19 10:35 [a] Ps. 68:1, 2; 132:8; Is. 17:12–14 11:1 [a] Num. 14:2; 16:11; 17:5; Deut. 9:22 [b] Ps. 78:21 [c] Lev. 10:2; 2 Kin. 1:12 11:2 [a] Num. 12:11, 13; 21:7 [b] [James 5:16] 11:3 [1] Literally *Burning* 11:4 [a] Ex. 12:38 [b] 1 Cor. 10:6

of Israel also wept again and said: [c]"Who will give us meat to eat? 5 [a]We remember the fish which we ate freely in Egypt, the cucumbers, the melons, the leeks, the onions, and the garlic; 6 but now [a]our whole being *is* dried up; *there is* nothing at all except this manna *before* our eyes!"

7 Now [a]the manna *was* like coriander seed, and its color like the color of bdellium. 8 The people went about and gathered *it,* ground *it* on millstones or beat *it* in the mortar, cooked *it* in pans, and made cakes of it; and [a]its taste was like the taste of pastry prepared with oil. 9 And [a]when the dew fell on the camp in the night, the manna fell on it.

> **SEEING JESUS IN THE SCRIPTURE**
>
> **11:7–9** God fed the Israelites manna, or bread from heaven, while they wandered in the wilderness. Jesus later told His followers He is "the true bread from heaven," sent by God to give us life (John 6:32–33).

10 Then Moses heard the people weeping throughout their families, everyone at the door of his tent; and [a]the anger of the LORD was greatly aroused; Moses also was displeased. 11 [a]So Moses said to the LORD, "Why have You afflicted Your servant? And why have I not found favor in Your sight, that You have laid the burden of all these people on me? 12 Did I conceive all these people? Did I beget them, that You should say to me, [a]'Carry them in your bosom, as a [b]guardian carries a nursing child,' to the land which You [c]swore to their fathers? 13 [a]Where am I to get meat to give to all these people? For they weep all over me, saying, 'Give us meat, that we may eat.' 14 [a]I am not able to bear all these people alone, because the burden *is* too heavy for me. 15 If You treat me like this, please kill me here and now—if I have found favor in Your sight—and [a]do not let me see my wretchedness!"

### *THE SEVENTY ELDERS*

16 So the LORD said to Moses: "Gather to Me [a]seventy men of the elders of Israel, whom you know to be the elders of the people and [b]officers over them; bring them to the tabernacle of meeting, that they may stand there with you. 17 Then I will come down and talk with you there. [a]I will take of the Spirit that *is* upon you and will put *the same* upon them; and they shall bear the burden of the people with you, that you may not bear *it* yourself alone. 18 Then you shall say to the people, 'Consecrate yourselves for tomorrow, and you shall eat meat; for you have wept [a]in the hearing of the LORD, saying, "Who will give us meat to eat? For *it was* well with us in Egypt." Therefore the LORD will give you meat, and you shall eat. 19 You shall eat, not one day, nor two days, nor five days, nor ten days, nor twenty days, 20 [a]but *for* a whole month, until it comes out of your nostrils and becomes loathsome to you, because you have [b]despised the LORD who is among you, and have wept before Him, saying, [c]"Why did we ever come up out of Egypt?" ' "

21 And Moses said, [a]"The people whom I *am* among *are* six hundred thousand men on foot; yet You have said, 'I will give them meat, that they may eat *for* a whole month.' 22 [a]Shall flocks and herds be slaughtered for them, to provide enough for them? Or shall all the fish of the sea be gathered together for them, to provide enough for them?"

23 And the LORD said to Moses, [a]"Has the LORD's arm been shortened? Now you shall see whether [b]what I say will happen to you or not."

24 So Moses went out and told the people the words of the LORD, and he [a]gathered the seventy men of the elders of the people and placed them around the tabernacle. 25 Then the LORD came down in the cloud, and spoke to him, and took of the Spirit that *was* upon him, and placed *the same* upon the seventy elders; and it happened, [a]when the Spirit rested upon them, that [b]they prophesied, although they never did *so* again.[1]

26 But two men had remained in the camp: the name of one *was* Eldad, and the name of the other Medad. And the Spirit rested upon them. Now they *were* among those listed, but who [a]had not gone out to the tabernacle; yet they prophesied in the camp. 27 And a young man ran and told Moses, and said, "Eldad and Medad are prophesying in the camp."

28 So Joshua the son of Nun, Moses' assistant, *one* of his choice men, answered and said, "Moses my lord, [a]forbid them!"

29 Then Moses said to him, "Are you zealous for my sake? [a]Oh, that all the LORD's people were prophets *and* that the LORD would put His Spirit upon them!" 30 And Moses returned to the camp, he and the elders of Israel.

### *THE LORD SENDS QUAIL*

31 Now a [a]wind went out from the LORD, and it brought quail from the sea and left *them* fluttering near the camp, about a day's journey on this side and about a day's journey on the other side, all around the camp, and about two cubits above the surface of the ground. 32 And the people stayed up all that day, all night, and all the next day, and gathered the quail (he who gathered least gathered ten [a]homers); and they spread *them* out

**11:4** [c] [Ps. 78:18] **11:5** [a] Ex. 16:3 **11:6** [a] Num. 21:5 **11:7** [a] Ex. 16:14, 31 **11:8** [a] Ex. 16:31 **11:9** [a] Ex. 16:13, 14 **11:10** [a] Ps. 78:21 **11:11** [a] Ex. 5:22; Deut. 1:12 **11:12** [a] Is. 40:11 [b] Is. 49:23; 1 Thess. 2:7 [c] Gen. 26:3 **11:13** [a] Matt. 15:33; Mark 8:4 **11:14** [a] Ex. 18:18; Deut. 1:12 **11:15** [a] Rev. 3:17 **11:16** [a] Ex. 18:25; 24:1, 9 [b] Deut. 16:18 **11:17** [a] 1 Sam. 10:6; 2 Kin. 2:15; [Joel 2:28] **11:18** [a] Ex. 16:7 **11:20** [a] Ps. 78:29; 106:15 [b] 1 Sam. 10:19 [c] Num. 21:5 **11:21** [a] Gen. 12:2; Ex. 12:37; Num. 1:46; 2:32 **11:22** [a] 2 Kin. 7:2 **11:23** [a] Is. 50:2; 59:1 [b] Num. 23:19 **11:24** [a] Num. 11:16 **11:25** [a] 2 Kin. 2:15 [b] 1 Sam. 10:5, 6, 10; Joel 2:28; Acts 2:17, 18; 1 Cor. 14:1 [1] Targum and Vulgate read *did not cease.* **11:26** [a] Jer. 36:5 **11:28** [a] [Mark 9:38–40; Luke 9:49] **11:29** [a] 1 Cor. 14:5 **11:31** [a] Ex. 16:13; Ps. 78:26–28; 105:40 **11:32** [a] Ex. 16:36; Ezek. 45:11

for themselves all around the camp. 33 But while the [a]meat *was* still between their teeth, before it was chewed, the wrath of the LORD was aroused against the people, and the LORD struck the people with a very great plague. 34 So he called the name of that place Kibroth Hattaavah,[1] because there they buried the people who had yielded to craving.

35 [a]From Kibroth Hattaavah the people moved to Hazeroth, and camped at Hazeroth.

### DISSENSION OF AARON AND MIRIAM

**12** Then [a]Miriam and Aaron spoke [b]against Moses because of the Ethiopian woman whom he had married; for [c]he had married an Ethiopian woman. 2 So they said, "Has the LORD indeed spoken only through [a]Moses? [b]Has He not spoken through us also?" And the LORD [c]heard *it.* 3 (Now the man Moses *was* very humble, more than all men who *were* on the face of the earth.)

4 [a]Suddenly the LORD said to Moses, Aaron, and Miriam, "Come out, you three, to the tabernacle of meeting!" So the three came out. 5 [a]Then the LORD came down in the pillar of cloud and stood *in* the door of the tabernacle, and called Aaron and Miriam. And they both went forward. 6 Then He said,

"Hear now My words:
If there is a prophet among you,
*I,* the LORD, make Myself known to him
[a]in a vision;
I speak to him [b]in a dream.
7 Not so with [a]My servant Moses;
[b]He *is* faithful in all [c]My house.
8 I speak with him [a]face to face,
Even [b]plainly, and not in dark sayings;
And he sees [c]the form of the LORD.
Why then [d]were you not afraid
To speak against My servant Moses?"

9 So the anger of the LORD was aroused against them, and He departed. 10 And when the cloud departed from above the tabernacle, [a]suddenly Miriam *became* [b]leprous, as *white as* snow. Then Aaron turned toward Miriam, and there she was, a leper. 11 So Aaron said to Moses, "Oh, my lord! Please [a]do not lay *this* sin on us, in which we have done foolishly and in which we have sinned. 12 Please [a]do not let her be as one dead, whose flesh is half consumed when he comes out of his mother's womb!"

13 So Moses cried out to the LORD, saying, "Please [a]heal her, O God, I pray!"

14 Then the LORD said to Moses, "If her father had but [a]spit in her face, would she not be shamed seven days? Let her be [b]shut out of the camp seven days, and afterward she may be received *again.*" 15 [a]So Miriam was shut out of the camp seven days, and the people did not journey till Miriam was brought in *again.* 16 And afterward the people moved from [a]Hazeroth and camped in the Wilderness of Paran.

### SPIES SENT INTO CANAAN

*(Deut. 1:19–33)*

**13** And the LORD spoke to Moses, saying, 2 [a]"Send men to spy out the land of Canaan, which I am giving to the children of Israel; from each tribe of their fathers you shall send a man, every one a leader among them."

3 So Moses sent them [a]from the Wilderness of Paran according to the command of the LORD, all of them men who *were* heads of the children of Israel. 4 Now these *were* their names: from the tribe of Reuben, Shammua the son of Zaccur; 5 from the tribe of Simeon, Shaphat the son of Hori; 6 [a]from the tribe of Judah, [b]Caleb the son of Jephunneh; 7 from the tribe of Issachar, Igal the son of Joseph; 8 from the tribe of Ephraim, Hoshea[1] the son of Nun; 9 from the tribe of Benjamin, Palti the son of Raphu; 10 from the tribe of Zebulun, Gaddiel the son of Sodi; 11 from the tribe of Joseph, *that is,* from the tribe of Manasseh, Gaddi the son of Susi; 12 from the tribe of Dan, Ammiel the son of Gemalli; 13 from the tribe of Asher, Sethur the son of Michael; 14 from the tribe of Naphtali, Nahbi the son of Vophsi; 15 from the tribe of Gad, Geuel the son of Machi.

16 These *are* the names of the men whom Moses sent to spy out the land. And Moses called [a]Hoshea[1] the son of Nun, Joshua.

> **13:16** ***Hoshea*** means "salvation." ***Joshua*** means "the Lord saves." Moses may have changed Joshua's name to emphasize that it was the Lord, not any particular leader, that the Israelites were dependent on. *Jesus* is a form of the name Joshua.

17 Then Moses sent them to spy out the land of Canaan, and said to them, "Go up this *way* into the South, and go up to [a]the mountains, 18 and see what the land is like: whether the people who dwell in it *are* strong or weak, few or many; 19 whether the land they dwell in *is* good or bad; whether the cities they inhabit *are* like camps or strongholds; 20 whether the land *is* rich or poor; and whether there are forests there or not. [a]Be of good courage. And bring some of the fruit of the land." Now the time *was* the season of the first ripe grapes.

**11:33** [a] Ps. 78:29–31; 106:15 **11:34** [1] Literally *Graves of Craving* **11:35** [a] Num. 33:17 **12:1** [a] Num. 20:1 [b] Num. 11:1 [c] Ex. 2:21 **12:2** [a] Num. 16:3 [b] Mic. 6:4 [c] Ezek. 35:12, 13 **12:4** [a] [Ps. 76:9] **12:5** [a] Ex. 19:9; 34:5 **12:6** [a] Gen. 46:2 [b] Gen. 31:10 **12:7** [a] Josh. 1:1 [b] Heb. 3:2, 5 [c] 1 Tim. 1:12 **12:8** [a] Deut. 34:10 [b] [1 Cor. 13:12] [c] Ex. 33:19–23 [d] 2 Pet. 2:10 **12:10** [a] Deut. 24:9 [b] 2 Kin. 5:27; 15:5 **12:11** [a] 2 Sam. 19:19; 24:10 **12:12** [a] Ps. 88:4 **12:13** [a] Ps. 103:3 **12:14** [a] Deut. 25:9 [b] Lev. 13:46 **12:15** [a] Deut. 24:9 **12:16** [a] Num. 11:35; 33:17, 18 **13:2** [a] Deut. 1:22; 9:23 **13:3** [a] Num. 12:16; 32:8 **13:6** [a] Num. 34:19 [b] Josh. 14:6, 7 **13:8** [1] Septuagint and Vulgate read *Oshea.* **13:16** [a] Ex. 17:9 [1] Septuagint and Vulgate read *Oshea.* **13:17** [a] Judg. 1:9 **13:20** [a] Deut. 31:6, 7, 23

21 So they went up and spied out the land [a]from
the Wilderness of Zin as far as [b]Rehob, near the
entrance of [c]Hamath. 22 And they went up through
the South and came to [a]Hebron; Ahiman, Sheshai,
and Talmai, the descendants of [b]Anak, *were* there.
(Now Hebron was built seven years before Zoan in
Egypt.) 23 [a]Then they came to the Valley of Eshcol,
and there cut down a branch with one cluster of
grapes; they carried it between two of them on a
pole. *They* also *brought* some of the pomegran-
ates and figs. 24 The place was called the Valley of
Eshcol,[1] because of the cluster which the men of
Israel cut down there. 25 And they returned from
spying out the land after forty days.
26 Now they departed and came back to Moses
and Aaron and all the congregation of the chil-
dren of Israel in the Wilderness of Paran, at [a]Ka-
desh; they brought back word to them and to all
the congregation, and showed them the fruit of
the land. 27 Then they told him, and said: "We went
to the land where you sent us. It truly flows with
[a]milk and honey, [b]and this *is* its fruit. 28 Neverthe-
less the [a]people who dwell in the land *are* strong;
the cities *are* fortified *and* very large; moreover
we saw the descendants of [b]Anak there. 29 [a]The
Amalekites dwell in the land of the South; the
Hittites, the Jebusites, and the Amorites dwell in
the mountains; and the Canaanites dwell by the
sea and along the banks of the Jordan."
30 Then [a]Caleb quieted the people before
Moses, and said, "Let us go up at once and take
possession, for we are well able to overcome it."
31 [a]But the men who had gone up with him
said, "We are not able to go up against the peo-
ple, for they *are* stronger than we." 32 And they
[a]gave the children of Israel a bad report of the
land which they had spied out, saying, "The land
through which we have gone as spies *is* a land that
devours its inhabitants, and [b]all the people whom
we saw in it *are* men of *great* stature. 33 There we
saw the giants[1] ([a]the descendants of Anak came
from the giants); and we were [b]like grasshoppers
in our own sight, and so we were [c]in their sight."

### *ISRAEL REFUSES TO ENTER CANAAN*

**14** So all the congregation lifted up their
voices and cried, and the people [a]wept
that night. 2 [a]And all the children of Israel com-
plained against Moses and Aaron, and the whole
congregation said to them, "If only we had died
in the land of Egypt! Or if only we had died in
this wilderness! 3 Why has the LORD brought us
to this land to fall by the sword, that our wives
and [a]children should become victims? Would
it not be better for us to return to Egypt?" 4 So
they said to one another, [a]"Let us select a leader
and [b]return to Egypt."
5 Then Moses and Aaron fell on their faces
before all the assembly of the congregation of
the children of Israel.
6 But Joshua the son of Nun and Caleb the son
of Jephunneh, *who were* among those who had
spied out the land, tore their clothes; 7 and they
spoke to all the congregation of the children of
Israel, saying: [a]"The land we passed through to
spy out *is* an exceedingly good land. 8 If the LORD
[a]delights in us, then He will bring us into this
land and give it to us, [b]'a land which flows with
milk and honey.'[1] 9 Only [a]do not rebel against the
LORD, [b]nor fear the people of the land, for [c]they
*are* our bread; their protection has departed from
them, [d]and the LORD *is* with us. Do not fear them."

**13:21** [a] Num. 20:1; 27:14; 33:36 [b] Josh. 19:28 [c] Josh. 13:5 **13:22** [a] Josh. 15:13, 14 [b] Josh. 11:21, 22 **13:23** [a] Deut. 1:24, 25 **13:24** [1] Literally *Cluster* **13:26** [a] Deut. 1:19 **13:27** [a] Ex. 3:8, 17; 13:5; 33:3 [b] Deut. 1:25 **13:28** [a] Deut. 1:28; 9:1, 2 [b] Josh. 11:21, 22 **13:29** [a] Judg. 6:3 **13:30** [a] Num. 14:6, 24 **13:31** [a] Deut. 1:28; 9:1–3 **13:32** [a] Num. 14:36, 37 [b] Amos 2:9 **13:33** [a] Deut. 1:28; 9:2 [b] Is. 40:22 [c] 1 Sam. 17:42 [1] Hebrew *nephilim* **14:1** [a] Deut. 1:45 **14:2** [a] Ex. 16:2; 17:3 **14:3** [a] Deut. 1:39 **14:4** [a] Neh. 9:17 [b] Acts 7:39 **14:7** [a] Num. 13:27 **14:8** [a] Deut. 10:15 [b] Num. 13:27 [1] Exodus 3:8 **14:9** [a] Deut. 1:26; 9:7, 23, 24 [b] Deut. 7:18 [c] Num. 24:8 [d] Deut. 20:1, 3, 4; 31:6–8

LIVE THE TRUTH

## BEING COURAGEOUS

**13:30** Courage is the mental and moral strength and conviction to preserve despite fear, danger, or difficulty. It's one of the hardest qualities to summon. When ten of the twelve spies returned from Canaan with a bad report, Caleb showed tremendous courage by calling on the people to trust God and take possession of the land. God gave this land to their ancestor Abraham and to them. The land was bountiful and beautiful. Yes, the inhabitants were big and powerful, but God is bigger and more powerful. In the end, the people didn't believe they could conquer the land and refused to listen to Caleb and Joshua's positive report.

What set Caleb apart? Why could he believe what so many others couldn't? Caleb knew it wasn't about the Israelites' or Canaanites' strength. What mattered was the strength and promise of God. This is what gave him courage to speak up in faith. God doesn't call us to find courage in ourselves, but rather in Him. We can go wherever God leads and do whatever He commands because we trust in Him. As we see over and over in the Scriptures and our lives, God is faithful. He will never leave you or forsake you. Have courage!

10 [a]And all the congregation said to stone them with stones. Now [b]the glory of the LORD appeared in the tabernacle of meeting before all the children of Israel.

### *MOSES INTERCEDES FOR THE PEOPLE*

11 Then the LORD said to Moses: "How long will these people [a]reject Me? And how long will they not [b]believe Me, with all the signs which I have performed among them? 12 I will strike them with the pestilence and disinherit them, and I will [a]make of you a nation greater and mightier than they."

13 And [a]Moses said to the LORD: [b]"Then the Egyptians will hear *it,* for by Your might You brought these people up from among them, 14 and they will tell *it* to the inhabitants of this land. They have [a]heard that You, LORD, *are* among these people; that You, LORD, are seen face to face and Your cloud stands above them, and You go before them in a pillar of cloud by day and in a pillar of fire by night. 15 Now *if* You kill these people as one man, then the nations which have heard of Your fame will speak, saying, 16 'Because the LORD was not [a]able to bring this people to the land which He swore to give them, therefore He killed them in the wilderness.' 17 And now, I pray, let the power of my Lord be great, just as You have spoken, saying, 18 [a]'The LORD is longsuffering and abundant in mercy, forgiving iniquity and transgression; but He by no means clears *the guilty,* [b]visiting the iniquity of the fathers on the children to the third and fourth *generation.*'[1] 19 [a]Pardon the iniquity of this people, I pray, [b]according to the greatness of Your mercy, just [c]as You have forgiven this people, from Egypt even until now."

20 Then the LORD said: "I have pardoned, [a]according to your word; 21 but truly, as I live, [a]all the earth shall be filled with the glory of the LORD— 22 [a]because all these men who have seen My glory and the signs which I did in Egypt and in the wilderness, and have put Me to the test now [b]these ten times, and have not heeded My voice, 23 they certainly shall not [a]see the land of which I swore to their fathers, nor shall any of those who rejected Me see it. 24 But My servant [a]Caleb, because he has a different spirit in him and [b]has followed Me fully, I will bring into the land where he went, and his descendants shall inherit it. 25 Now the Amalekites and the Canaanites dwell in the valley; tomorrow turn and [a]move out into the wilderness by the Way of the Red Sea."

### *DEATH SENTENCE ON THE REBELS*

26 And the LORD spoke to Moses and Aaron, saying, 27 [a]"How long *shall I bear with* this evil congregation who complain against Me? [b]I have heard the complaints which the children of Israel make against Me. 28 Say to them, [a]'As I live,' says the LORD, 'just as you have spoken in My hearing, so I will do to you: 29 The carcasses of you who have complained against Me shall fall in this wilderness, [a]all of you who were numbered, according to your entire number, from twenty years old and above. 30 [a]Except for Caleb the son of Jephunneh and Joshua the son of Nun, you shall by no means enter the land which I swore I would make you dwell in. 31 [a]But your little ones, whom you said would be victims, I will bring in, and they shall know the land which [b]you have despised. 32 But *as for* you, [a]your carcasses shall fall in this wilderness. 33 And your sons shall [a]be shepherds in the wilderness [b]forty years, and [c]bear the brunt of your infidelity, until your carcasses are consumed in the wilderness. 34 [a]According to the number of the days in which you spied out the land, [b]forty days, for each day you shall bear your guilt one year, *namely* forty years, [c]and you shall know My rejection. 35 [a]I the LORD have spoken this. I will surely do so to all [b]this evil congregation who are gathered together against Me. In this wilderness they shall be consumed, and there they shall die.' "

36 Now the men whom Moses sent to spy out the land, who returned and made all the congregation complain against him by bringing a bad report of the land, 37 those very men who brought the evil report about the land, [a]died by the plague before the LORD. 38 [a]But Joshua the son of Nun and Caleb the son of Jephunneh remained alive, of the men who went to spy out the land.

### *A FUTILE INVASION ATTEMPT*

*(Deut. 1:41–45)*

39 Then Moses told these words to all the children of Israel, [a]and the people mourned greatly. 40 And they rose early in the morning and went up to the top of the mountain, saying, [a]"Here we are, and we will go up to the place which the LORD has promised, for we have sinned!"

41 And Moses said, "Now why do you transgress the command of the LORD? For this will not succeed. 42 [a]Do not go up, lest you be defeated by your enemies, for the LORD *is* not among you. 43 For the Amalekites and the Canaanites *are* there before you, and you shall fall by the sword; [a]because you have turned away from the LORD, the LORD will not be with you."

44 [a]But they presumed to go up to the mountaintop. Nevertheless, neither the ark of the covenant of the LORD nor Moses departed from the camp. 45 Then the Amalekites and the Canaanites who dwelt in that mountain came down and attacked them, and drove them back as far as [a]Hormah.

**14:10** [a] Ex. 17:4 [b] Ex. 16:10 **14:11** [a] Heb. 3:8 [b] Deut. 9:23 **14:12** [a] Ex. 32:10 **14:13** [a] Ps. 106:23 [b] Ex. 32:12 **14:14** [a] Deut. 2:25 **14:16** [a] Deut. 9:28 **14:18** [a] Ex. 34:6, 7 [b] Ex. 20:5 [1] Exodus 34:6, 7 **14:19** [a] Ex. 32:32; 34:9 [b] Ps. 51:1; 106:45 [c] Ps. 78:38 **14:20** [a] Mic. 7:18–20 **14:21** [a] Ps. 72:19 **14:22** [a] Deut. 1:35 [b] Gen. 31:7 **14:23** [a] Num. 26:65; 32:11 **14:24** [a] Josh. 14:6, 8, 9 [b] Num. 32:12 **14:25** [a] Deut. 1:40 **14:27** [a] Ex. 16:28 [b] Ex. 16:12 **14:28** [a] Heb. 3:16–19 **14:29** [a] Num. 1:45, 46; 26:64 **14:30** [a] Deut. 1:36–38 **14:31** [a] Deut. 1:39 [b] Ps. 106:24 **14:32** [a] Num. 26:64, 65; 32:13 **14:33** [a] Ps. 107:40 [b] Deut. 2:14 [c] Ezek. 23:35 **14:34** [a] Num. 13:25 [b] Ezek. 4:6 [c] [Heb. 4:1] **14:35** [a] Num. 23:19 [b] 1 Cor. 10:5 **14:37** [a] [1 Cor. 10:10] **14:38** [a] Josh. 14:6, 10 **14:39** [a] Ex. 33:4 **14:40** [a] Deut. 1:41–44 **14:42** [a] Deut. 1:42; 31:17 **14:43** [a] 2 Chr. 15:2 **14:44** [a] Deut. 1:43 **14:45** [a] Num. 21:3

### *LAWS OF GRAIN AND DRINK OFFERINGS*

15 And the LORD spoke to Moses, saying, 2 [a]"Speak to the children of Israel, and say to them: 'When you have come into the land you are to inhabit, which I am giving to you, 3 and you [a]make an offering by fire to the LORD, a burnt offering or a sacrifice, [b]to fulfill a vow or as a freewill offering or [c]in your appointed feasts, to make a [d]sweet aroma to the LORD, from the herd or the flock, 4 then [a]he who presents his offering to the LORD shall bring [b]a grain offering of one-tenth *of an ephah* of fine flour mixed [c]with one-fourth of a hin of oil; 5 [a]and one-fourth of a hin of wine as a drink offering you shall prepare with the burnt offering or the sacrifice, for each [b]lamb. 6 [a]Or for a ram you shall prepare as a grain offering two-tenths *of an ephah* of fine flour mixed with one-third of a hin of oil; 7 and as a drink offering you shall offer one-third of a hin of wine as a sweet aroma to the LORD. 8 And when you prepare a young bull as a burnt offering, or as a sacrifice to fulfill a vow, or as a [a]peace offering to the LORD, 9 then shall be offered [a]with the young bull a grain offering of three-tenths *of an ephah* of fine flour mixed with half a hin of oil; 10 and you shall bring as the drink offering half a hin of wine as an offering made by fire, a sweet aroma to the LORD.

11 [a]'Thus it shall be done for each young bull, for each ram, or for each lamb or young goat. 12 According to the number that you prepare, so you shall do with everyone according to their number. 13 All who are native-born shall do these things in this manner, in presenting an offering made by fire, a sweet aroma to the LORD. 14 And if a stranger dwells with you, or whoever *is* among you throughout your generations, and would present an offering made by fire, a sweet aroma to the LORD, just as you do, so shall he do. 15 [a]One ordinance *shall be* for you of the assembly and for the stranger who dwells *with you,* an ordinance forever throughout your generations; as you are, so shall the stranger be before the LORD. 16 One law and one custom shall be for you and for the stranger who dwells with you.' "[1]

17 Again the LORD spoke to Moses, saying, 18 [a]"Speak to the children of Israel, and say to them: 'When you come into the land to which I bring you, 19 then it will be, when you eat of [a]the bread of the land, that you shall offer up a heave offering to the LORD. 20 [a]You shall offer up a cake of the first of your ground meal *as* a heave offering; as [b]a heave offering of the threshing floor, so shall you offer it up. 21 Of the first of your ground meal you shall give to the LORD a heave offering throughout your generations.

### *LAWS CONCERNING UNINTENTIONAL SIN*

22 [a]'If you sin unintentionally, and do not observe all these commandments which the LORD has spoken to Moses— 23 all that the LORD has commanded you by the hand of Moses, from the day the LORD gave commandment and onward throughout your generations— 24 then it will be, [a]if it is unintentionally committed, without the knowledge of the congregation, that the whole congregation shall offer one young bull as a burnt offering, as a sweet aroma to the LORD, [b]with its grain offering and its drink offering, according to the ordinance, and [c]one kid of the goats as a sin offering. 25 [a]So the priest shall make atonement for the whole congregation of the children of Israel, and it shall be forgiven them, for it was unintentional; they shall bring their offering, an offering made by fire to the LORD, and their sin offering before the LORD, for their unintended sin. 26 It shall be forgiven the whole congregation of the children of Israel and the stranger who dwells among them, because all the people *did it* unintentionally.

27 'And [a]if a person sins unintentionally, then he shall bring a female goat in its first year as a sin offering. 28 [a]So the priest shall make atonement for the person who sins unintentionally, when he sins unintentionally before the LORD, to make atonement for him; and it shall be forgiven him. 29 [a]You shall have one law for him who sins unintentionally, *for* him who is native-born among the children of Israel and for the stranger who dwells among them.

### *LAW CONCERNING PRESUMPTUOUS SIN*

30 [a]'But the person who does *anything* presumptuously, *whether he is* native-born or a stranger, that one brings reproach on the LORD, and he shall be cut off from among his people. 31 Because he has [a]despised the word of the LORD, and has broken His commandment, that person shall be completely cut off; his guilt *shall be* upon him.' "

### *PENALTY FOR VIOLATING THE SABBATH*

*(Ex. 31:12–17)*

32 Now while the children of Israel were in the wilderness, [a]they found a man gathering sticks on the Sabbath day. 33 And those who found him gathering sticks brought him to Moses and Aaron, and to all the congregation. 34 They put him [a]under guard, because it had not been explained what should be done to him.

35 Then the LORD said to Moses, [a]"The man must surely be put to death; all the congregation shall [b]stone him with stones outside the camp."

15:2 [a] Lev. 23:10; Num. 15:18; Deut. 7:1 15:3 [a] Lev. 1:2, 3 [b] Lev. 7:16; 22:18, 21 [c] Lev. 23:2, 8, 12, 38; Num. 28:18, 19, 27; Deut. 16:10 [d] Gen. 8:21; Ex. 29:18; Lev. 1:9 15:4 [a] Lev. 2:1; 6:14 [b] Ex. 29:40; Lev. 23:13 [c] Lev. 14:10; Num. 28:5 15:5 [a] Num. 28:7, 14 [b] Lev. 1:10; 3:6; Num. 15:11; 28:4, 5 15:6 [a] Num. 28:12, 14 15:8 [a] Lev. 7:11 15:9 [a] Num. 28:12, 14 15:11 [a] Num. 28 15:15 [a] Ex. 12:49; Num. 9:14; 15:29 15:16 [1] Compare Exodus 12:49 15:18 [a] Num. 15:2; Deut. 26:1 15:19 [a] Josh. 5:11, 12 15:20 [a] Ex. 34:26; Lev. 23:10, 14, 17; Deut. 26:2, 10; Prov. 3:9, 10 [b] Lev. 2:14; 23:10, 16 15:22 [a] Lev. 4:2 15:24 [a] Lev. 4:13 [b] Num. 15:8–10 [c] Lev. 4:23 15:25 [a] Lev. 4:20; [Heb. 2:17] 15:27 [a] Lev. 4:27–31 15:28 [a] Lev. 4:35 15:29 [a] Num. 15:15 15:30 [a] Num. 14:40–44; Deut. 1:43; 17:12; Ps. 19:13; Heb. 10:26 15:31 [a] 2 Sam. 12:9; Prov. 13:13 15:32 [a] Ex. 31:14, 15; 35:2, 3 15:34 [a] Lev. 24:12 15:35 [a] Ex. 31:14, 15 [b] Lev. 24:14; Deut. 21:21; 1 Kin. 21:13; Acts 7:58

36 So, as the LORD commanded Moses, all the
congregation brought him outside the camp
and stoned him with stones, and he died.

### *TASSELS ON GARMENTS*

37 Again the LORD spoke to Moses, saying,
38 "Speak to the children of Israel: Tell [a]them to
make tassels on the corners of their garments
throughout their generations, and to put a blue
thread in the tassels of the corners. 39 And you
shall have the tassel, that you may look upon
it and [a]remember all the commandments of
the LORD and do them, and that you [b]*may* not
[c]follow the harlotry to which your own heart and
your own eyes are inclined, 40 and that you may
remember and do all My commandments, and
be [a]holy for your God. 41 I *am* the LORD your God,
who brought you out of the land of Egypt, to be
your God: I *am* the LORD your God."

### *REBELLION AGAINST MOSES AND AARON*

**16** Now [a]Korah the son of Izhar, the son of
Kohath, the son of Levi, with [b]Dathan and
Abiram the sons of Eliab, and On the son of
Peleth, sons of Reuben, took *men;* 2 and they
rose up before Moses with some of the children
of Israel, two hundred and fifty leaders of the
congregation, [a]representatives of the congrega-
tion, men of renown. 3 [a]They gathered together
against Moses and Aaron, and said to them,
"*You take* too much upon yourselves, for [b]all the
congregation *is* holy, every one of them, [c]and
the LORD *is* among them. Why then do you exalt
yourselves above the assembly of the LORD?"

> **16:1 Korah** was already set aside in a special position; he was a Levite. His sin was greater than jealousy of his cousins, the priests. He had set himself against God and led others to do the same.

4 So when Moses heard *it,* he [a]fell on his face;
5 and he spoke to Korah and all his company,
saying, "Tomorrow morning the LORD will show
who *is* [a]His and *who is* [b]holy, and will cause *him*
to come near to Him. That one whom He chooses
He will cause to [c]come near to Him. 6 Do this:
Take censers, Korah and all your company; 7 put
fire in them and put incense in them before the
LORD tomorrow, and it shall be *that* the man
whom the LORD chooses *is* the holy one. *You take*
too much upon yourselves, you sons of Levi!"
8 Then Moses said to Korah, "Hear now, you
sons of Levi: 9 *Is it* [a]a small thing to you that the
God of Israel has [b]separated you from the con-
gregation of Israel, to bring you near to Himself,
to do the work of the tabernacle of the LORD, and
to stand before the congregation to serve them;
10 and that He has brought you near *to Himself,*
you and all your brethren, the sons of Levi,
with you? And are you seeking the priesthood
also? 11 Therefore you and all your company *are*
gathered together against the LORD. [a]And what
*is* Aaron that you complain against him?"
12 And Moses sent to call Dathan and Abiram
the sons of Eliab, but they said, "We will not come
up! 13 *Is it* a small thing that you have brought us
up out of [a]a land flowing with milk and honey, to
kill us in the wilderness, that you should [b]keep
acting like a prince over us? 14 Moreover [a]you
have not brought us into [b]a land flowing with
milk and honey, nor given us inheritance of
fields and vineyards. Will you put out the eyes
of these men? We will not come up!"
15 Then Moses was very angry, and said to the
LORD, [a]"Do not respect their offering. [b]I have
not taken one donkey from them, nor have I
hurt one of them."
16 And Moses said to Korah, "Tomorrow, you
and all your company be present [a]before the
LORD—you and they, as well as Aaron. 17 Let each
take his censer and put incense in it, and each
of you bring his censer before the LORD, two
hundred and fifty censers; both you and Aaron,
each *with* his censer." 18 So every man took his
censer, put fire in it, laid incense on it, and stood
at the door of the tabernacle of meeting with
Moses and Aaron. 19 And Korah gathered all the
congregation against them at the door of the
tabernacle of meeting. Then [a]the glory of the
LORD appeared to all the congregation.
20 And the LORD spoke to Moses and Aaron,
saying, 21 [a]"Separate yourselves from among
this congregation, that I may [b]consume them
in a moment."
22 Then they [a]fell on their faces, and said,
"O God, [b]the God of the spirits of all flesh, shall
one man sin, and You be angry with all the
[c]congregation?"
23 So the LORD spoke to Moses, saying,
24 "Speak to the congregation, saying, 'Get away
from the tents of Korah, Dathan, and Abiram.'"
25 Then Moses rose and went to Dathan and
Abiram, and the elders of Israel followed him.
26 And he spoke to the congregation, saying,
[a]"Depart now from the tents of these wicked
men! Touch nothing of theirs, lest you be con-
sumed in all their sins." 27 So they got away from
around the tents of Korah, Dathan, and Abiram;

**15:38** [a] Deut. 22:12; Matt. 23:5 **15:39** [a] Ps. 103:18 [b] Deut. 29:19 [c] Ps. 73:27; 106:39; James 4:4 **15:40** [a] [Lev. 11:44, 45; Rom. 12:1; Col. 1:22; 1 Pet. 1:15, 16] **16:1** [a] Ex. 6:21 [b] Num. 26:9; Deut. 11:6 **16:2** [a] Num. 1:16; 26:9 **16:3** [a] Num. 12:2; 14:2; Ps. 106:16 [b] Ex. 19:6 [c] Ex. 29:45 **16:4** [a] Num. 14:5; 20:6 **16:5** [a] [2 Tim. 2:19] [b] Lev. 21:6–8, 12 [c] Ezek. 40:46; 44:15, 16 **16:9** [a] 1 Sam. 18:23; Is. 7:13 [b] Num. 3:41, 45; 8:13–16; Deut. 10:8 **16:11** [a] Ex. 16:7, 8 **16:13** [a] Ex. 16:3; Num. 11:4–6 [b] Ex. 2:14; Acts 7:27, 35 **16:14** [a] Num. 14:1–4 [b] Ex. 3:8; Lev. 20:24 **16:15** [a] Gen. 4:4, 5 [b] 1 Sam. 12:3; Acts 20:33 **16:16** [a] 1 Sam. 12:3, 7 **16:19** [a] Ex. 16:7, 10; Lev. 9:6, 23; Num. 14:10 **16:21** [a] Gen. 19:17; Jer. 51:6 [b] Ex. 32:10; 33:5 **16:22** [a] Num. 14:5 [b] Num. 27:16; Job 12:10; Eccl. 12:7; Heb. 12:9 [c] Gen. 18:23–32; 20:4 **16:26** [a] Gen. 19:12, 14, 15, 17

and Dathan and Abiram came out and stood at
the door of their tents, with their wives, their
sons, and their little [a]children.
28 And Moses said: [a]"By this you shall know
that the LORD has sent me to do all these works,
for *I have* not *done them* [b]of my own will. 29 If
these men die naturally like all men, or if they
are [a]visited by the common fate of all men,
*then* the LORD has not sent me. 30 But if the
LORD creates [a]a new thing, and the earth opens
its mouth and swallows them up with all that
belongs to them, and they [b]go down alive into
the pit, then you will understand that these men
have rejected the LORD."
31 [a]Now it came to pass, as he finished speak-
ing all these words, that the ground split apart
under them, 32 and the earth opened its mouth
and swallowed them up, with their households
and [a]all the men with Korah, with all *their* goods.
33 So they and all those with them went down alive
into the pit; the earth closed over them, and they
perished from among the assembly. 34 Then all
Israel who *were* around them fled at their cry,
for they said, "Lest the earth swallow us up *also!*"
35 And [a]a fire came out from the LORD and
consumed the two hundred and fifty men who
were offering incense.
36 Then the LORD spoke to Moses, saying:
37 "Tell Eleazar, the son of Aaron the priest, to pick
up the censers out of the blaze, for [a]they are holy,
and scatter the fire some distance away. 38 The
censers of [a]these men who sinned against their
own souls, let them be made into hammered
plates as a covering for the altar. Because they
presented them before the LORD, therefore they
are holy; [b]and they shall be a sign to the children
of Israel." 39 So Eleazar the priest took the bronze
censers, which those who were burned up had
presented, and they were hammered out as a
covering on the altar, 40 *to be* a memorial to the
children of Israel [a]that no outsider, who *is* not
a descendant of Aaron, should come near to
offer incense before the LORD, that he might not
become like Korah and his companions, just as
the LORD had said to him through Moses.

### *COMPLAINTS OF THE PEOPLE*

41 On the next day [a]all the congregation of
the children of Israel complained against Moses
and Aaron, saying, "You have killed the peo-
ple of the LORD." 42 Now it happened, when the
congregation had gathered against Moses and
Aaron, that they turned toward the tabernacle
of meeting; and suddenly [a]the cloud covered
it, and the glory of the LORD appeared. 43 Then
Moses and Aaron came before the tabernacle
of meeting.
44 And the LORD spoke to Moses, saying,
45 "Get away from among this congregation, that
I may consume them in a moment."
And they fell on their faces.
46 So Moses said to Aaron, "Take a censer and
put fire in it from the altar, put incense *on it,* and
take it quickly to the congregation and make
atonement for them; [a]for wrath has gone out
from the LORD. The plague has begun." 47 Then
Aaron took *it* as Moses commanded, and ran
into the midst of the assembly; and already the
plague had begun among the people. So he put
in the incense and made atonement for the peo-
ple. 48 And he stood between the dead and the
living; so [a]the plague was stopped. 49 Now those
who died in the plague were fourteen thousand
seven hundred, besides those who died in the
Korah incident. 50 So Aaron returned to Moses
at the door of the tabernacle of meeting, for the
plague had stopped.

### *THE BUDDING OF AARON'S ROD*

17 And the LORD spoke to Moses, saying:
2 "Speak to the children of Israel, and get
from them a rod from each father's house, all
their leaders according to their fathers' houses—
twelve rods. Write each man's name on his rod.
3 And you shall write Aaron's name on the rod
of Levi. For there shall be one rod for the head
of *each* father's house. 4 Then you shall place
them in the tabernacle of meeting before [a]the
Testimony, [b]where I meet with you. 5 And it
shall be *that* the rod of the man [a]whom I choose
will blossom; thus I will rid Myself of the com-
plaints of the children of Israel, [b]which they
make against you."
6 So Moses spoke to the children of Israel,
and each of their leaders gave him a rod apiece,
for each leader according to their fathers' hous-
es, twelve rods; and the rod of Aaron *was* among
their rods. 7 And Moses placed the rods before
the LORD in [a]the tabernacle of witness.
8 Now it came to pass on the next day that
Moses went into the tabernacle of witness, and
behold, the [a]rod of Aaron, of the house of Levi,
had sprouted and put forth buds, had produced
blossoms and yielded ripe almonds. 9 Then
Moses brought out all the rods from before
the LORD to all the children of Israel; and they
looked, and each man took his rod.
10 And the LORD said to Moses, "Bring [a]Aar-
on's rod back before the Testimony, to be kept [b]as
a sign against the rebels, [c]that you may put their
complaints away from Me, lest they die." 11 Thus
did Moses; just as the LORD had commanded
him, so he did.
12 So the children of Israel spoke to Moses,

16:27 [a] Ex. 20:5; Num. 26:11 16:28 [a] Ex. 3:12; John 5:36 [b] Num. 24:13; John 5:30 16:29 [a] Ex. 20:5; Job 35:15; Is. 10:3 16:30 [a] Job 31:3; Is. 28:21 [b] [Ps. 55:15] 16:31 [a] Num. 26:10; Ps. 106:17 16:32 [a] Num. 26:11; 1 Chr. 6:22, 37 16:35 [a] Lev. 10:2; Num. 11:1–3; 26:10; Ps. 106:18 16:37 [a] Lev. 27:28 16:38 [a] Prov. 20:2; Hab. 2:10 [b] Num. 17:10; Ezek. 14:8 16:40 [a] Num. 3:10; 2 Chr. 26:18 16:41 [a] Num. 14:2; Ps. 106:25 16:42 [a] Ex. 40:34 16:46 [a] Lev. 10:6; Num. 18:5 16:48 [a] Num. 25:8; Ps. 106:30 17:4 [a] Ex. 25:16 [b] Ex. 25:22; 29:42, 43; 30:36; Num. 17:7 17:5 [a] Num. 16:5 [b] Num. 16:11 17:7 [a] Ex. 38:21; Num. 1:50, 51; 9:15; 18:2; Acts 7:44 17:8 [a] [Ezek. 17:24]; Heb. 9:4 17:10 [a] Heb. 9:4 [b] Num. 16:38; Deut. 9:7, 24 [c] Num. 17:5

saying, "Surely we die, we perish, we all perish! 13 [a]Whoever even comes near the tabernacle of the LORD must die. Shall we all utterly die?"

### DUTIES OF PRIESTS AND LEVITES

**18** Then the LORD said to Aaron: [a]"You and your sons and your father's house with you shall [b]bear the iniquity *related to* the sanctuary, and you and your sons with you shall bear the iniquity *associated with* your priesthood. 2 Also bring with you your brethren of the [a]tribe of Levi, the tribe of your father, that they may be [b]joined with you and serve you while you and your sons *are* with you before the tabernacle of witness. 3 They shall attend to your needs and [a]all the needs of the tabernacle; [b]but they shall not come near the articles of the sanctuary and the altar, [c]lest they die—they and you also. 4 They shall be joined with you and attend to the needs of the tabernacle of meeting, for all the work of the tabernacle; [a]but an outsider shall not come near you. 5 And you shall attend to [a]the duties of the sanctuary and the duties of the altar, [b]that there *may* be no more wrath on the children of Israel. 6 Behold, I Myself have [a]taken your brethren the Levites from among the children of Israel; [b]*they are* a gift to you, given by the LORD, to do the work of the tabernacle of meeting. 7 Therefore [a]you and your sons with you shall attend to your priesthood for everything at the altar and [b]behind the veil; and you shall serve. I give your priesthood *to you* as a [c]gift for service, but the outsider who comes near shall be put to death."

### OFFERINGS FOR SUPPORT OF THE PRIESTS

8 And the LORD spoke to Aaron: "Here, [a]I Myself have also given you charge of My heave offerings, all the holy gifts of the children of Israel; I have given them [b]as a portion to you and your sons, as an ordinance forever. 9 This shall be yours of the most holy things *reserved* from the fire: every offering of theirs, every [a]grain offering and every [b]sin offering and every [c]trespass offering which they render to Me, *shall be* most holy for you and your sons. 10 [a]In a most holy *place* you shall eat it; every male shall eat it. It shall be holy to you.

11 "This also *is* yours: [a]the heave offering of their gift, with all the wave offerings of the children of Israel; I have given them to you, and your sons and daughters with you, as an ordinance forever. [b]Everyone who is clean in your house may eat it.

12 [a]"All the best of the oil, all the best of the new wine and the grain, [b]their firstfruits which they offer to the LORD, I have given them to you. 13 Whatever first ripe fruit is in their land, [a]which they bring to the LORD, shall be yours. Everyone who is clean in your house may eat it.

14 [a]"Every devoted thing in Israel shall be yours.

15 "Everything that first opens [a]the womb of all flesh, which they bring to the LORD, whether man or beast, shall be yours; nevertheless [b]the firstborn of man you shall surely redeem, and the firstborn of unclean animals you shall redeem. 16 And those redeemed of the devoted things you shall redeem when one month old, [a]according to your valuation, for five shekels of silver, according to the shekel of the sanctuary, which *is* [b]twenty gerahs. 17 [a]But the firstborn of a cow, the firstborn of a sheep, or the firstborn of a goat you shall not redeem; they *are* holy. [b]You shall sprinkle their blood on the altar, and burn their fat *as* an offering made by fire for a sweet aroma to the LORD. 18 And their flesh shall be yours, just as the [a]wave breast and the right thigh are yours.

19 "All the heave offerings of the holy things, which the children of Israel offer to the LORD, I have given to you and your sons and daughters with you as an ordinance forever; [a]it *is* a covenant of salt forever before the LORD with you and your descendants with you."

20 Then the LORD said to Aaron: "You shall have [a]no inheritance in their land, nor shall you have any portion among them; [b]I *am* your portion and your inheritance among the children of Israel.

### TITHES FOR SUPPORT OF THE LEVITES

21 "Behold, [a]I have given the children of Levi all the tithes in Israel as an inheritance in return for the work which they perform, [b]the work of the tabernacle of meeting. 22 [a]Hereafter the children of Israel shall not come near the tabernacle of meeting, [b]lest they bear sin and die. 23 But the Levites shall perform the work of the tabernacle of meeting, and they shall bear their iniquity; *it shall be* a statute forever, throughout your generations, that among the children of Israel they shall have no inheritance. 24 For the tithes of the children of Israel, which they offer up *as* a heave offering to the LORD, I have given to the Levites as an inheritance; therefore I have said to them, 'Among the children of Israel they shall have no inheritance.' "

**17:13** [a] Num. 1:51, 53; 18:4, 7 **18:1** [a] Num. 17:13 [b] Ex. 28:38; Lev. 10:17; 22:16 **18:2** [a] Gen. 29:34; Num. 1:47 [b] Num. 3:5–10 **18:3** [a] Num. 3:25, 31, 36 [b] Num. 16:40 [c] Num. 4:15 **18:4** [a] Num. 3:10 **18:5** [a] Ex. 27:21; 30:7; Lev. 24:3 [b] Num. 8:19; 16:46 **18:6** [a] Num. 3:12, 45 [b] Num. 3:9 **18:7** [a] Num. 3:10; 18:5 [b] Heb. 9:3, 6 [c] Matt. 10:8; 1 Pet. 5:2, 3 **18:8** [a] Lev. 6:16, 18; 7:28–34; Num. 5:9 [b] Ex. 29:29; 40:13, 15 **18:9** [a] Lev. 2:2, 3; 10:12, 13 [b] Lev. 6:25, 26 [c] Lev. 7:7; Num. 5:8–10 **18:10** [a] Lev. 6:16, 26 **18:11** [a] Ex. 29:27, 28; Deut. 18:3–5 [b] Lev. 22:1–16 **18:12** [a] Ex. 23:19; Neh. 10:35, 36 [b] Ex. 22:29; Lev. 23:20 **18:13** [a] Ex. 22:29; 23:19; 34:26 **18:14** [a] Lev. 27:1–33 **18:15** [a] Ex. 13:2 [b] Ex. 13:12–15; Num. 3:46; Luke 2:22–24 **18:16** [a] Lev. 27:6 [b] Ex. 30:13 **18:17** [a] Deut. 15:19 [b] Lev. 3:2, 5 **18:18** [a] Ex. 29:26–28; Lev. 7:31–36 **18:19** [a] Lev. 2:13; 2 Chr. 13:5; [Mark 9:49, 50] **18:20** [a] Deut. 10:8, 9; 12:12; 14:27–29; 18:1, 2; Josh. 13:14, 33 [b] Ps. 16:5; Ezek. 44:28 **18:21** [a] Lev. 27:30–33; Deut. 14:22–29; Neh. 10:37; 12:44; Mal. 3:8–10; [Heb. 7:4–10] [b] Num. 3:7, 8 **18:22** [a] Num. 1:51 [b] Lev. 22:9

### THE TITHE OF THE LEVITES

25 Then the LORD spoke to Moses, saying, 26 "Speak thus to the Levites, and say to them: 'When you take from the children of Israel the tithes which I have given you from them as your inheritance, then you shall offer up a heave offering of it to the LORD, [a]a tenth of the tithe. 27 And your heave offering shall be reckoned to you as though *it were* the grain of the [a]threshing floor and as the fullness of the winepress. 28 Thus you shall also offer a heave offering to the LORD from all your tithes which you receive from the children of Israel, and you shall give the LORD's heave offering from it to Aaron the priest. 29 Of all your gifts you shall offer up every heave offering due to the LORD, from all the best of them, the consecrated part of them.' 30 Therefore you shall say to them: 'When you have lifted up the best of it, then *the rest* shall be accounted to the Levites as the produce of the threshing floor and as the produce of the winepress. 31 You may eat it in any place, you and your households, for it *is* [a]your reward for your work in the tabernacle of meeting. 32 And you shall [a]bear no sin because of it, when you have lifted up the best of it. But you shall not [b]profane the holy gifts of the children of Israel, lest you die.' "

### LAWS OF PURIFICATION

**19** Now the LORD spoke to Moses and Aaron, saying, 2 "This *is* the ordinance of the law which the LORD has commanded, saying: 'Speak to the children of Israel, that they bring you a red heifer without blemish, in which there *is* no [a]defect [b]*and* on which a yoke has never come. 3 You shall give it to Eleazar the priest, that he may take it [a]outside the camp, and it shall be slaughtered before him; 4 and Eleazar the priest shall take some of its blood with his finger, and [a]sprinkle some of its blood seven times directly in front of the tabernacle of meeting. 5 Then the heifer shall be burned in his sight: [a]its hide, its flesh, its blood, and its offal shall be burned. 6 And the priest shall take [a]cedar wood and [b]hyssop and scarlet, and cast *them* into the midst of the fire burning the heifer. 7 [a]Then the priest shall wash his clothes, he shall bathe in water, and afterward he shall come into the camp; the priest shall be unclean until evening. 8 And the one who burns it shall wash his clothes in water, bathe in water, and shall be unclean until evening. 9 Then a man *who is* clean shall gather up [a]the ashes of the heifer, and store *them* outside the camp in a clean place; and they shall be kept for the congregation of the children of Israel [b]for the water of purification;[1] it *is* for purifying from sin. 10 And the one who gathers the ashes of the heifer shall wash his clothes, and be unclean until evening. It shall be a statute forever to the children of Israel and to the stranger who dwells among them.

11 [a]'He who touches the dead body of anyone shall be unclean seven days. 12 [a]He shall purify himself with the water on the third day and on the seventh day; *then* he will be clean. But if he does not purify himself on the third day and on the seventh day, he will not be clean. 13 Whoever touches the body of anyone who has died, and [a]does not purify himself, [b]defiles the tabernacle of the LORD. That person shall be cut off from Israel. He shall be unclean, because [c]the water of purification was not sprinkled on him; [d]his uncleanness *is* still on him.

14 'This *is* the law when a man dies in a tent: All who come into the tent and all who *are* in the tent shall be unclean seven days; 15 and every [a]open vessel, which has no cover fastened on it, *is* unclean. 16 [a]Whoever in the open field touches one who is slain by a sword or who has died, or a bone of a man, or a grave, shall be unclean seven days.

17 'And for an unclean *person* they shall take some of the [a]ashes of the heifer burnt for purification from sin, and running water shall be put on them in a vessel. 18 A clean person shall take [a]hyssop and dip *it* in the water, sprinkle *it* on the tent, on all the vessels, on the persons who were there, or on the one who touched a bone, the slain, the dead, or a grave. 19 The clean *person* shall sprinkle the unclean on the third day and on the seventh day; [a]and on the seventh day he shall purify himself, wash his clothes, and bathe in water; and at evening he shall be clean.

20 'But the man who is unclean and does not purify himself, that person shall be cut off from among the assembly, because he has [a]defiled the sanctuary of the LORD. The water of purification has not been sprinkled on him; he *is* unclean. 21 It shall be a perpetual statute for them. He who sprinkles the water of purification shall

> **19:9** It's not that this **water** held any special powers, but it was prepared in obedience to God's commands and was an outward symbol of the inner work that God does to remove impurity. God designed these rituals and celebrations to create an awareness in His people of their spiritual needs, and ultimately to prepare them for Christ. All the washings and sacrifices were still powerless to change hearts. That is a spiritual work done by God alone.

**18:26** [a] Neh. 10:38 **18:27** [a] Num. 15:20; [2 Cor. 8:12] **18:31** [a] [Matt. 10:10; Luke 10:7]; 1 Cor. 9:13; [1 Tim. 5:18] **18:32** [a] Lev. 19:8; 22:16; Ezek. 22:26 [b] Lev. 22:2, 15 **19:2** [a] Lev. 22:20–25 [b] Deut. 21:3; 1 Sam. 6:7 **19:3** [a] Lev. 4:12, 21; Num. 19:9; Heb. 13:11 **19:4** [a] Lev. 4:6; Heb. 9:13 **19:5** [a] Ex. 29:14; Lev. 4:11, 12; 9:11 **19:6** [a] Lev. 14:4, 6, 49 [b] Ex. 12:22; 1 Kin. 4:33 **19:7** [a] Lev. 11:25; 15:5; 16:26, 28 **19:9** [a] [Heb. 9:13, 14] [b] Num. 19:13, 20, 21 [1] Literally *impurity* **19:11** [a] Lev. 21:1, 11; Num. 5:2; 6:6; 9:6, 10; 31:19; Lam. 4:14; Hag. 2:13 **19:12** [a] Num. 19:19; 31:19 **19:13** [a] Lev. 22:3–7 [b] Lev. 15:31 [c] Num. 8:7; 19:9 [d] Lev. 7:20; 22:3 **19:15** [a] Lev. 11:32; Num. 31:20 **19:16** [a] Num. 19:11; 31:19 **19:17** [a] Num. 19:9 **19:18** [a] Ps. 51:7 **19:19** [a] Lev. 14:9 **19:20** [a] Num. 19:13

wash his clothes; and he who touches the water of purification shall be unclean until evening. 22 [a]Whatever the unclean *person* touches shall be unclean; and [b]the person who touches *it* shall be unclean until evening.' "

### *MOSES' ERROR AT KADESH*
*(Ex. 17:1–7)*

**20** Then[a] the children of Israel, the whole congregation, came into the Wilderness of Zin in the first month, and the people stayed in [b]Kadesh; and [c]Miriam died there and was buried there.

2 [a]Now there was no water for the congregation; [b]so they gathered together against Moses and Aaron. 3 And the people [a]contended with Moses and spoke, saying: "If only we had died [b]when our brethren died before the LORD! 4 [a]Why have you brought up the assembly of the LORD into this wilderness, that we and our animals should die here? 5 And why have you made us come up out of Egypt, to bring us to this evil place? It *is* not a place of grain or figs or vines or pomegranates; nor *is* there any water to drink." 6 So Moses and Aaron went from the presence of the assembly to the door of the tabernacle of meeting, and [a]they fell on their faces. And [b]the glory of the LORD appeared to them.

7 Then the LORD spoke to Moses, saying, 8 [a]"Take the rod; you and your brother Aaron gather the congregation together. Speak to the rock before their eyes, and it will yield its water; thus [b]you shall bring water for them out of the rock, and give drink to the congregation and their animals." 9 So Moses took the rod [a]from before the LORD as He commanded him.

10 And Moses and Aaron gathered the assembly together before the rock; and he said to them, [a]"Hear now, you rebels! Must we bring water for you out of this rock?" 11 Then Moses lifted his hand and struck the rock twice with his rod; [a]and water came out abundantly, and the congregation and their animals drank.

12 Then the LORD spoke to Moses and Aaron, "Because [a]you did not believe Me, to [b]hallow Me in the eyes of the children of Israel, therefore you shall not bring this assembly into the land which I have given them."

13 [a]This *was* the water of Meribah,[1] because the children of Israel contended with the LORD, and He was hallowed among them.

### *PASSAGE THROUGH EDOM REFUSED*

14 [a]Now Moses sent messengers from Kadesh to the king of [b]Edom. [c]"Thus says your brother Israel: 'You know all the hardship that has befallen us, 15 [a]how our fathers went down to Egypt, [b]and we dwelt in Egypt a long time, [c]and the Egyptians afflicted us and our fathers. 16 [a]When we cried out to the LORD, He heard our voice and [b]sent the Angel and brought us up out of Egypt; now here we are in Kadesh, a city on the edge of your border. 17 Please [a]let us pass through your country. We will not pass through fields or vineyards, nor will we drink water from wells; we will go along the King's Highway; we will not turn aside to the right hand or to the left until we have passed through your territory.' "

18 Then [a]Edom said to him, "You shall not pass through my *land,* lest I come out against you with the sword."

19 So the children of Israel said to him, "We

**19:22** [a] Hag. 2:11–13 [b] Lev. 15:5 **20:1** [a] Num. 13:21; 33:36 [b] Num. 13:26 [c] Ex. 15:20; Num. 26:59 **20:2** [a] Ex. 17:1 [b] Num. 16:19, 42 **20:3** [a] Ex. 17:2; Num. 14:2 [b] Num. 11:1, 33; 14:37; 16:31–35, 49 **20:4** [a] Ex. 17:3 **20:6** [a] Num. 14:5; 16:4, 22, 45 [b] Num. 14:10 **20:8** [a] Ex. 4:17, 20; 17:5, 6 [b] Neh. 9:15; Ps. 78:15, 16; 105:41; Is. 43:20; 48:21; [1 Cor. 10:4] **20:9** [a] Num. 17:10 **20:10** [a] Ps. 106:33 **20:11** [a] Ex. 17:6; Deut. 8:15; Ps. 78:16; Is. 48:21; [1 Cor. 10:4] **20:12** [a] Num. 20:28; 27:14; Deut. 1:37; 3:26, 27; 34:5 [b] Lev. 10:3; Ezek. 20:41; 36:23; 1 Pet. 3:15 **20:13** [a] Deut. 33:8; Ps. 106:32 [1] Literally *Contention* **20:14** [a] Judg. 11:16, 17 [b] Gen. 36:31–39 [c] Deut. 2:4; Obad. 10–12 **20:15** [a] Gen. 46:6; Acts 7:15 [b] Ex. 12:40 [c] Ex. 1:11; Deut. 26:6; Acts 7:19 **20:16** [a] Ex. 2:23; 3:7 [b] Ex. 3:2; 14:19 **20:17** [a] Num. 21:22 **20:18** [a] Num. 24:18; Ps. 137:7; Ezek. 25:12, 13; Obad. 10–15

APPLY THE TRUTH

## ANGER

**20:7–13** When anger grips us, it can feel like there's no other option but to yell, scream, or punch. We're like a tea kettle about to release its white, hot steam. Often these emotions seem unavoidable. How can we move past them? Where do we channel them? Do we bury them or let them out?

This is what Moses faced. The people of Israel were rebelling and complaining, his sister had just died, and now the people were blaming *him* for their situation. He was boiling. Unfortunately for Moses, he let his anger get the best of him, and he disobeyed God. He struck the rock in anger when he was supposed to speak to it in faith.

Feelings aren't bad unless they're calling the shots. Control is the key. We need to control our emotions instead of allowing them to control us. That's why we need to do what Moses failed to do in this moment: channel those feelings toward something productive. Convert anger's energy into an energy that you can use to bless God and others. When you feel anger how can you direct those feelings into something positive?

will go by the Highway, and if I or my livestock
drink any of your water, [a]then I will pay for it; let
me only pass through on foot, nothing *more.*"
20 Then he said, [a]"You shall not pass
through." So Edom came out against them with
many men and with a strong hand. 21 Thus Edom
[a]refused to give Israel passage through his ter-
ritory; so Israel [b]turned away from him.

### *DEATH OF AARON*

22 Now the children of Israel, the whole
congregation, journeyed from [a]Kadesh [b]and
came to Mount Hor. 23 And the LORD spoke to
Moses and Aaron in Mount Hor by the border
of the land of Edom, saying: 24 "Aaron shall be
[a]gathered to his people, for he shall not enter
the land which I have given to the children of
Israel, because you rebelled against My word at
the water of Meribah. 25 [a]Take Aaron and Elea-
zar his son, and bring them up to Mount Hor;
26 and strip Aaron of his garments and put them
on Eleazar his son; for Aaron shall be gathered
*to his people* and die there." 27 So Moses did just
as the LORD commanded, and they went up to
Mount Hor in the sight of all the congregation.
28 [a]Moses stripped Aaron of his garments and
put them on Eleazar his son; and [b]Aaron died
there on the top of the mountain. Then Moses
and Eleazar came down from the mountain.
29 Now when all the congregation saw that Aaron
was dead, all the house of Israel mourned for
Aaron [a]thirty days.

### *CANAANITES DEFEATED AT HORMAH*

21 The [a]king of Arad, the Canaanite, who
dwelt in the South, heard that Israel was
coming on the road to Atharim. Then he fought
against Israel and took *some* of them prisoners.
2 [a]So Israel made a vow to the LORD, and said,
"If You will indeed deliver this people into my
hand, then [b]I will utterly destroy their cities."
3 And the LORD listened to the voice of Israel and
delivered up the Canaanites, and they utterly
destroyed them and their cities. So the name
of that place was called Hormah.[1]

### *THE BRONZE SERPENT*

4 Then they journeyed from Mount Hor by
the Way of the Red Sea, to [a]go around the land
of Edom; and the soul of the people became
very discouraged on the way. 5 And the people
[a]spoke against God and against Moses: "Why

20:19 [a] Deut. 2:6, 28 20:20 [a] Judg. 11:17 20:21 [a] Deut. 2:27, 30 [b] Deut. 2:8; Judg. 11:18 20:22 [a] Num. 33:37 [b] Num. 21:4 20:24 [a] Gen. 25:8; Deut. 32:50 20:25 [a] Num. 33:38; Deut. 32:50 20:28 [a] Ex. 29:29, 30; Deut. 10:6 [b] Num. 33:38 20:29 [a] Gen. 50:3, 10; Deut. 34:8 21:1 [a] Num. 33:40; Josh. 12:14; Judg. 1:16 21:2 [a] Gen. 28:20; Judg. 11:30 [b] Deut. 2:34 21:3 [1] Literally *Utter Destruction* 21:4 [a] Judg. 11:18 21:5 [a] Num. 20:4, 5

## THE WILDERNESS WANDERINGS

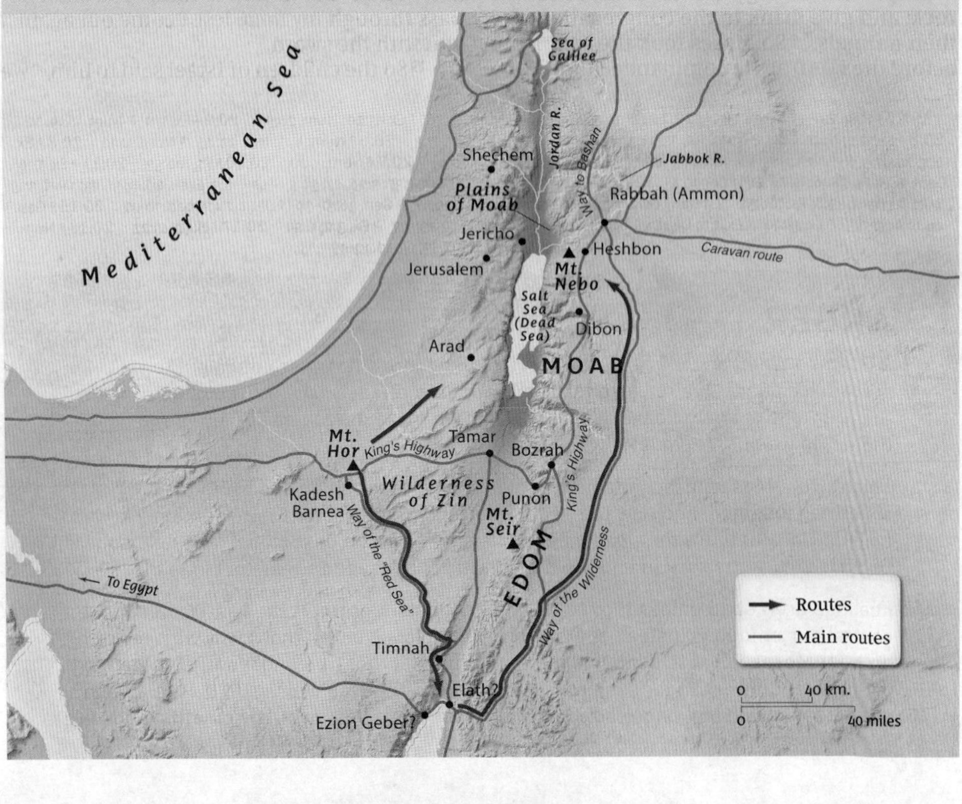

STORY OF SCRIPTURE 16

NUMBERS 21:4–9

## THE BRONZE SERPENT

### WHAT'S GOING ON?

The Israelites' journey through the wilderness wasn't just physical; it was also a spiritual sojourn marked by faith and faltering. In Numbers 21:4–9, the people of Israel fell into a familiar pattern of impatience and ingratitude. They spoke against God and Moses, despising the miraculous gift of manna. God's response was immediate and terrifying: a swarm of venomous snakes. The serpents brought death but also mercy, as their deadly presence led the Israelites toward repentance.

When Moses interceded for his people, God instructed him to create a bronze serpent and raise it on a pole; those who looked upon it after being bitten would live. In this divine directive, there's a shadow of the cross, where Jesus would be lifted up as a remedy for a far deadlier poison: sin (see John 3:14–15).

### WHAT DOES THIS MEAN FOR ME?

In looking at the bronze serpent, the Israelites acted in faith, acknowledging their sin and need for God's deliverance. For us, it's Christ on the cross we must look to in faith for salvation. Our "serpents" may not have fangs, but they are far fiercer: sin, despair, and death. Yet, the answer remains the same: look up and be saved.

### DID YOU CATCH THE PATTERN?

This pattern of judgment and mercy intertwined is a divine dance where love ultimately leads. The serpents were deadly, but they drove the Israelites to seek deliverance from God, just as our recognition of sin's deadliness should drive us to the foot of the cross. The pole in the wilderness was a foreshadowing of Calvary, where all who look to Jesus, acknowledging their need for Him, find eternal life.

*For the next* Story of Scripture *reading and devotion, turn to Deuteronomy 6:1—7:26 on page 185.*

have you brought us up out of Egypt to die in
the wilderness? For *there is* no food and no wa-
ter, and our soul loathes this worthless bread."
6 So [a]the LORD sent [b]fiery serpents among the
people, and they bit the people; and many of
the people of Israel died.
7 [a]Therefore the people came to Moses, and
said, "We have [b]sinned, for we have spoken
against the LORD and against you; [c]pray to the
LORD that He take away the serpents from us."
So Moses prayed for the people.
8 Then the LORD said to Moses, [a]"Make a
[b]fiery *serpent,* and set it on a pole; and it shall be
that everyone who is bitten, when he looks at it,
shall live." 9 So [a]Moses made a bronze serpent,
and put it on a pole; and so it was, if a serpent
had bitten anyone, when he looked at the bronze
serpent, he lived.

### SEEING JESUS IN THE SCRIPTURE

**21:8** The bronze serpent Moses made pictures Jesus. Just like the Israelites had to look to the serpent to be saved from death, we must look to Jesus to be saved from sin (see John 3:14–16).

### *FROM MOUNT HOR TO MOAB*

10 Now the children of Israel moved on and
[a]camped in Oboth. 11 And they journeyed from
Oboth and camped at Ije Abarim, in the wilder-
ness which *is* east of Moab, toward the sunrise.
12 [a]From there they moved and camped in the
Valley of Zered. 13 From there they moved and
camped on the other side of the Arnon, which *is*
in the wilderness that extends from the border
of the Amorites; for [a]the Arnon *is* the border of
Moab, between Moab and the Amorites. 14 There-
fore it is said in the Book of the Wars of the LORD:

"Waheb in Suphah,[1]
The brooks of the Arnon,
15 And the slope of the brooks
That reaches to the dwelling of [a]Ar,
And lies on the border of Moab."

16 From there *they went* [a]to Beer, which *is*
the well where the LORD said to Moses, "Gather

**21:6** [a] 1 Cor. 10:9 [b] Deut. 8:15 **21:7** [a] Num. 11:2; Ps. 78:34; Is. 26:16; Hos. 5:15 [b] Lev. 26:40 [c] Ex. 8:8; 1 Sam. 12:19; 1 Kin. 13:6; Acts 8:24 **21:8** [a] [John 3:14, 15] [b] Is. 14:29; 30:6 **21:9** [a] 2 Kin. 18:4; John 3:14, 15 **21:10** [a] Num. 33:43, 44 **21:12** [a] Deut. 2:13 **21:13** [a] Num. 22:36; Judg. 11:18 **21:14** [1] Ancient unknown places; Vulgate reads *What He did in the Red Sea.* **21:15** [a] Num. 21:28; Deut. 2:9, 18, 29 **21:16** [a] Judg. 9:21

the people together, and I will give them water." 17 [a]Then Israel sang this song:

"Spring up, O well!
All of you sing to it—
18 The well the leaders sank,
Dug by the nation's nobles,
By the [a]lawgiver, with their staves."

And from the wilderness *they went* to Mattanah, 19 from Mattanah to Nahaliel, from Nahaliel to Bamoth, 20 and from Bamoth, *in* the valley that *is* in the country of Moab, to the top of Pisgah which looks [a]down on the wasteland.[1]

### *KING SIHON DEFEATED*

*(Deut. 2:26–37)*

21 Then [a]Israel sent messengers to Sihon king of the Amorites, saying, 22 [a]"Let me pass through your land. We will not turn aside into fields or vineyards; we will not drink water from wells. We will go by the King's Highway until we have passed through your territory." 23 [a]But Sihon would not allow Israel to pass through his territory. So Sihon gathered all his people together and went out against Israel in the wilderness, [b]and he came to Jahaz and fought against Israel. 24 Then [a]Israel defeated him with the edge of the sword, and took possession of his land from the Arnon to the Jabbok, as far as the people of Ammon; for the border of the people of Ammon *was* fortified. 25 So Israel took all these cities, and Israel [a]dwelt in all the cities of the Amorites, in Heshbon and in all its villages. 26 For Heshbon *was* the city of Sihon king of the Amorites, who had fought against the former king of Moab, and had taken all his land from his hand as far as the Arnon. 27 Therefore those who speak in proverbs say:

"Come to Heshbon, let it be built;
Let the city of Sihon be repaired.

28 "For [a]fire went out from Heshbon,
A flame from the city of Sihon;
It consumed [b]Ar of Moab,
The lords of the [c]heights of the Arnon.
29 Woe to you, [a]Moab!
You have perished, O people of [b]Chemosh!
He has given his [c]sons as fugitives,
And his [d]daughters into captivity,
To Sihon king of the Amorites.

30 "But we have shot at them;
Heshbon has perished [a]as far as Dibon.
Then we laid waste as far as Nophah,
Which *reaches* to [b]Medeba."

31 Thus Israel dwelt in the land of the Amorites. 32 Then Moses sent to spy out [a]Jazer; and they took its villages and drove out the Amorites who *were* there.

### *KING OG DEFEATED*

*(Deut. 3:1–22)*

33 [a]And they turned and went up by the way to [b]Bashan. So Og king of Bashan went out against them, he and all his people, to battle [c]at Edrei. 34 Then the LORD said to Moses, [a]"Do not fear him, for I have delivered him into your hand, with all his people and his land; and [b]you shall do to him as you did to Sihon king of the Amorites, who dwelt at Heshbon." 35 [a]So they defeated him, his sons, and all his people, until there was no survivor left him; and they took possession of his land.

### *BALAK SENDS FOR BALAAM*

**22** Then [a]the children of Israel moved, and camped in the plains of Moab on the side of the Jordan *across from* Jericho.

2 Now [a]Balak the son of Zippor saw all that Israel had done to the Amorites. 3 And [a]Moab was exceedingly afraid of the people because they *were* many, and Moab was sick with dread because of the children of Israel. 4 So Moab said to [a]the elders of Midian, "Now this company will lick up everything around us, as an ox licks up the grass of the field." And Balak the son of Zippor *was* king of the Moabites at that time. 5 Then [a]he sent messengers to Balaam the son of Beor at [b]Pethor, which *is* near the River[1] in the land of the sons of his people,[2] to call him, saying: "Look, a people has come from Egypt. See, they cover the face of the earth, and are settling next to me! 6 [a]Therefore please come at once, [b]curse this people for me, for they *are* too mighty for me. Perhaps I shall be able to defeat them and drive them out of the land, for I know that he whom you bless *is* blessed, and he whom you curse is cursed."

7 So the elders of Moab and the elders of Midian departed with [a]the diviner's fee in their hand, and they came to Balaam and spoke to him the words of Balak. 8 And he said to them, [a]"Lodge here tonight, and I will bring back word to you, as the LORD speaks to me." So the princes of Moab stayed with Balaam.

9 [a]Then God came to Balaam and said, "Who *are* these men with you?"

10 So Balaam said to God, "Balak the son of

**21:17** [a]Ex. 15:1 **21:18** [a]Is. 33:22 **21:20** [a]Num. 23:28 [1]Hebrew *Jeshimon* **21:21** [a]Num. 32:33; Deut. 2:26–37; Judg. 11:19 **21:22** [a]Num. 20:16, 17 **21:23** [a]Deut. 29:7 [b]Deut. 2:32; Judg. 11:20 **21:24** [a]Deut. 2:33; Josh. 12:1; Neh. 9:22; Ps. 135:10; 136:19; Amos 2:9 **21:25** [a]Amos 2:10 **21:28** [a]Jer. 48:45, 46 [b]Deut. 2:9, 18; Is. 15:1 [c]Num. 22:41; 33:52 **21:29** [a]Jer. 48:46 [b]Judg. 11:24; 1 Kin. 11:33; 2 Kin. 23:13 [c]Is. 15:2, 5 [d]Is. 16:2 **21:30** [a]Num. 32:3, 34; Jer. 48:18, 22 [b]Is. 15:2 **21:32** [a]Num. 32:1, 3, 35; Jer. 48:32 **21:33** [a]Deut. 29:7 [b]Deut. 3:1 [c]Josh. 13:12 **21:34** [a]Deut. 3:2 [b]Num. 21:24; Ps. 135:10; 136:20 **21:35** [a]Deut. 3:3, 4; 29:7; Josh. 13:12 **22:1** [a]Num. 33:48, 49 **22:2** [a]Josh. 24:9; Judg. 11:25; Mic. 6:5; Rev. 2:14 **22:3** [a]Ex. 15:15 **22:4** [a]Num. 25:15–18; 31:1–3; Josh. 13:21 **22:5** [a]Num. 31:8, 16; Deut. 23:4; Josh. 13:22; 24:9; Neh. 13:1, 2; Mic. 6:5; 2 Pet. 2:15; Jude 11; Rev. 2:14 [b]Deut. 23:4 [1]That is, the Euphrates [2]Or *the people of Amau* **22:6** [a]Num. 22:17; 23:7, 8 [b]Num. 22:12; 24:9 **22:7** [a]1 Sam. 9:7, 8 **22:8** [a]Num. 22:19 **22:9** [a]Gen. 20:3

Zippor, king of Moab, has sent to me, *saying,*
11 'Look, a people has come out of Egypt, and
they cover the face of the earth. Come now,
curse them for me; perhaps I shall be able to
overpower them and drive them out.' "

12 And God said to Balaam, "You shall not go
with them; you shall not curse the people, for
[a]they *are* blessed."

13 So Balaam rose in the morning and said
to the princes of Balak, "Go back to your land,
for the LORD has refused to give me permission
to go with you."

14 And the princes of Moab rose and went to
Balak, and said, "Balaam refuses to come with us."

15 Then Balak again sent princes, more numer-
ous and more honorable than they. 16 And they
came to Balaam and said to him, "Thus says Balak
the son of Zippor: 'Please let nothing hinder you
from coming to me; 17 for I will certainly [a]honor
you greatly, and I will do whatever you say to me.
[b]Therefore please come, curse this people for me.' "

18 Then Balaam answered and said to the
servants of Balak, [a]"Though Balak were to give
me his house full of silver and gold, [b]I could not
go beyond the word of the LORD my God, to do
less or more. 19 Now therefore, please, you also
[a]stay here tonight, that I may know what more
the LORD will say to me."

20 [a]And God came to Balaam at night and
said to him, "If the men come to call you, rise
*and* go with them; but [b]only the word which I
speak to you—that you shall do." 21 So Balaam
rose in the morning, saddled his donkey, and
went with the princes of Moab.

### *BALAAM, THE DONKEY, AND THE ANGEL*

22 Then God's anger was aroused because
he went, [a]and the Angel of the LORD took His
stand in the way as an adversary against him.
And he was riding on his donkey, and his two
servants *were* with him. 23 Now [a]the donkey saw
the Angel of the LORD standing in the way with
His drawn sword in His hand, and the donkey
turned aside out of the way and went into the
field. So Balaam struck the donkey to turn her
back onto the road. 24 Then the Angel of the LORD
stood in a narrow path between the vineyards,
*with* a wall on this side and a wall on that side.
25 And when the donkey saw the Angel of the
LORD, she pushed herself against the wall and
crushed Balaam's foot against the wall; so he
struck her again. 26 Then the Angel of the LORD
went further, and stood in a narrow place where
there *was* no way to turn either to the right hand
or to the left. 27 And when the donkey saw the
Angel of the LORD, she lay down under Balaam;
so Balaam's anger was aroused, and he struck
the donkey with his staff.

28 Then the LORD [a]opened the mouth of the
donkey, and she said to Balaam, "What have
I done to you, that you have struck me these
three times?"

29 And Balaam said to the donkey, "Because
you have abused me. I wish there were a sword
in my hand, [a]for now I would kill you!"

30 [a]So the donkey said to Balaam, "*Am* I not
your donkey on which you have ridden, ever
since *I became* yours, to this day? Was I ever
disposed to do this to you?"

And he said, "No."

31 Then the LORD [a]opened Balaam's eyes,
and he saw the Angel of the LORD standing
in the way with His drawn sword in His hand;
and he bowed his head and fell flat on his face.
32 And the Angel of the LORD said to him, "Why
have you struck your donkey these three times?
Behold, I have come out to stand against you,
because *your* way is [a]perverse before Me. 33 The
donkey saw Me and turned aside from Me these
three times. If she had not turned aside from
Me, surely I would also have killed you by now,
and let her live."

34 And Balaam said to the Angel of the LORD,
[a]"I have sinned, for I did not know You stood in
the way against me. Now therefore, if it displeas-
es You, I will turn back."

35 Then the Angel of the LORD said to Ba-
laam, "Go with the men, [a]but only the word that
I speak to you, that you shall speak." So Balaam
went with the princes of Balak.

36 Now when Balak heard that Balaam was
coming, [a]he went out to meet him at the city of
Moab, [b]which *is* on the border at the Arnon, the
boundary of the territory. 37 Then Balak said to
Balaam, "Did I not earnestly send to you, calling
for you? Why did you not come to me? Am I not
able [a]to honor you?"

38 And Balaam said to Balak, "Look, I have
come to you! Now, have I any power at all to say
anything? [a]The word that God puts in my mouth,
that I must speak." 39 So Balaam went with Balak,
and they came to Kirjath Huzoth. 40 Then Balak
offered oxen and sheep, and he sent *some* to
Balaam and to the princes who *were* with him.

### *BALAAM'S FIRST PROPHECY*

41 So it was, the next day, that Balak took
Balaam and brought him up to the [a]high places
of Baal, that from there he might observe the
extent of the people.

23 Then Balaam said to Balak, [a]"Build seven
altars for me here, and prepare for me
here seven bulls and seven rams."

2 And Balak did just as Balaam had spoken,
and Balak and Balaam [a]offered a bull and a
ram on *each* altar. 3 Then Balaam said to Balak,

22:12 [a] Num. 23:20; [Rom. 11:28] 22:17 [a] Num. 24:11 [b] Num. 22:6 22:18 [a] Num. 22:38; 24:13 [b] 1 Kin. 22:14; 2 Chr. 18:13 22:19 [a] Num. 22:8 22:20 [a] Num. 22:9 [b] Num. 22:35; 23:5, 12, 16, 26; 24:13 22:22 [a] Ex. 4:24 22:23 [a] Josh. 5:13; 2 Kin. 6:17; Dan. 10:7; Acts 22:9 22:28 [a] 2 Pet. 2:16 22:29 [a] [Prov. 12:10; Matt. 15:19] 22:30 [a] 2 Pet. 2:16 22:31 [a] Gen. 21:19; 2 Kin. 6:17; Luke 24:16, 31 22:32 [a] [2 Pet. 2:14, 15] 22:34 [a] 1 Sam. 15:24, 30; 26:21; 2 Sam. 12:13 22:35 [a] Num. 22:20 22:36 [a] Gen. 14:17 [b] Num. 21:13 22:37 [a] Num. 22:17; 24:11 22:38 [a] Num. 23:26; 24:13; 1 Kin. 22:14; 2 Chr. 18:13 22:41 [a] Num. 21:28; Deut. 12:2 23:1 [a] Num. 23:29 23:2 [a] Num. 23:14, 30

[a]"Stand by your burnt offering, and I will go;
perhaps the LORD will come [b]to meet me, and
whatever He shows me I will tell you." So he
went to a desolate height. 4 [a]And God met Ba-
laam, and he said to Him, "I have prepared the
seven altars, and I have offered on *each* altar a
bull and a ram."
5 Then the LORD [a]put a word in Balaam's
mouth, and said, "Return to Balak, and thus you
shall speak." 6 So he returned to him, and there
he was, standing by his burnt offering, he and
all the princes of Moab.
7 And he [a]took up his oracle and said:

"Balak the king of Moab has brought me
from Aram,
From the mountains of the east.
[b]'Come, curse Jacob for me,
And come, [c]denounce Israel!'

8 "How[a] shall I curse whom God has not
cursed?
And how shall I denounce *whom* the
LORD has not denounced?
9 For from the top of the rocks I see him,
And from the hills I behold him;
There! [a]A people dwelling alone,
[b]Not reckoning itself among the nations.

10 "Who[a] can count the dust[1] of Jacob,
Or number one-fourth of Israel?
Let me die [b]the death of the righteous,
And let my end be like his!"

11 Then Balak said to Balaam, "What have you
done to me? [a]I took you to curse my enemies,
and look, you have blessed *them* bountifully!"
12 So he answered and said, [a]"Must I not
take heed to speak what the LORD has put in
my mouth?"

### BALAAM'S SECOND PROPHECY

13 Then Balak said to him, "Please come with
me to another place from which you may see
them; you shall see only the outer part of them,
and shall not see them all; curse them for me
from there." 14 So he brought him to the field of
Zophim, to the top of Pisgah, [a]and built seven
altars, and offered a bull and a ram on *each* altar.
15 And he said to Balak, "Stand here by your
burnt offering while I meet[1] *the LORD* over there."
16 Then the LORD met Balaam, and [a]put a
word in his mouth, and said, "Go back to Balak,
and thus you shall speak." 17 So he came to him,
and there he was, standing by his burnt offering,
and the princes of Moab were with him. And
Balak said to him, "What has the LORD spoken?"
18 Then he took up his oracle and said:

[a]"Rise up, Balak, and hear!
Listen to me, son of Zippor!

19 "God[a] *is* not a man, that He should lie,
Nor a son of man, that He should repent.
Has He [b]said, and will He not do?
Or has He spoken, and will He not make it
good?
20 Behold, I have received *a command* to bless;
[a]He has blessed, and I cannot reverse it.

21 "He[a] has not observed iniquity in Jacob,
Nor has He seen wickedness in Israel.
The LORD his God *is* with him,
[b]And the shout of a King *is* among them.
22 [a]God brings them out of Egypt;
He has [b]strength like a wild ox.

23 "For *there is* no sorcery against Jacob,
Nor any divination against Israel.
It now must be said of Jacob
And of Israel, 'Oh, [a]what God has done!'
24 Look, a people rises [a]like a lioness,
And lifts itself up like a lion;
[b]It shall not lie down until it devours the
prey,
And drinks the blood of the slain."

25 Then Balak said to Balaam, "Neither curse
them at all, nor bless them at all!"
26 So Balaam answered and said to Balak,
"Did I not tell you, saying, [a]'All that the LORD
speaks, that I must do'?"

### BALAAM'S THIRD PROPHECY

27 Then Balak said to Balaam, "Please come,
I will take you to another place; perhaps it will
please God that you may curse them for me
from there." 28 So Balak took Balaam to the top
of Peor, that [a]overlooks the wasteland.[1] 29 Then
Balaam said to Balak, "Build for me here seven
altars, and prepare for me here seven bulls and
seven rams." 30 And Balak did as Balaam had
said, and offered a bull and a ram on *every* altar.

**24** Now when Balaam saw that it pleased the
LORD to bless Israel, he did not go as at
[a]other times, to seek to use sorcery, but he set
his face toward the wilderness. 2 And Balaam
raised his eyes, and saw Israel [a]encamped ac-
cording to their tribes; and [b]the Spirit of God
came upon him.

**23:3** [a] Num. 23:15 [b] Num. 23:4, 16 **23:4** [a] Num. 23:16 **23:5** [a] Num. 22:20, 35, 38; 23:16; Deut. 18:18; Jer. 1:9 **23:7** [a] Deut. 23:4; Job 27:1; 29:1; Ps. 78:2 [b] Num. 22:6, 11, 17 [c] 1 Sam. 17:10 **23:8** [a] Num. 22:12 **23:9** [a] Deut. 32:8; 33:28; Josh. 11:23 [b] Ex. 33:16; Ezra 9:2; [Eph. 2:14] **23:10** [a] Gen. 13:16; 22:17; 28:14; 2 Chr. 1:9 [b] Ps. 116:15 [1] Or *dust cloud* **23:11** [a] Num. 22:11 **23:12** [a] Num. 22:38 **23:14** [a] Num. 23:1, 2 **23:15** [1] Following Masoretic Text, Targum, and Vulgate; Syriac reads *call;* Septuagint reads *go and ask God.* **23:16** [a] Num. 22:35; 23:5 **23:18** [a] Judg. 3:20 **23:19** [a] 1 Sam. 15:29; Mal. 3:6; James 1:17 [b] Num. 11:23; 1 Kin. 8:56 **23:20** [a] Gen. 12:2; 22:17; Num. 22:12 **23:21** [a] Ps. 32:2; [Rom. 4:7, 8] [b] Ps. 89:15–18 **23:22** [a] Num. 24:8 [b] Deut. 33:17; Job 39:10 **23:23** [a] Ps. 31:19; 44:1 **23:24** [a] Gen. 49:9 [b] Gen. 49:27; Josh. 11:23 **23:26** [a] Num. 22:38 **23:28** [a] Num. 21:20 [1] Hebrew *Jeshimon* **24:1** [a] Num. 23:3, 15 **24:2** [a] Num. 2:2, 34 [b] Num. 11:25; 1 Sam. 10:10; 19:20, 23; 2 Chr. 15:1

3 [a]Then he took up his oracle and said:

"The utterance of Balaam the son of Beor,
The utterance of the man whose eyes are
opened,
4 The utterance of him who hears the words
of God,
Who sees the vision of the Almighty,
Who [a]falls down, with eyes wide open:

5 "How lovely are your tents, O Jacob!
Your dwellings, O Israel!
6 Like valleys that stretch out,
Like gardens by the riverside,
[a]Like aloes [b]planted by the LORD,
Like cedars beside the waters.
7 He shall pour water from his buckets,
And his seed *shall be* [a]in many waters.

"His king shall be higher than [b]Agag,
And his [c]kingdom shall be exalted.

8 "God[a] brings him out of Egypt;
He has strength like a wild ox;
He shall [b]consume the nations, his
enemies;
He shall [c]break their bones
And [d]pierce *them* with his arrows.
9 'He[a] bows down, he lies down as a lion;
And as a lion, who shall rouse him?'[1]

[b]"Blessed *is* he who blesses you,
And cursed *is* he who curses you."

10 Then Balak's anger was aroused against
Balaam, and he [a]struck his hands together; and
Balak said to Balaam, [b]"I called you to curse my
enemies, and look, you have bountifully blessed
*them* these three times! 11 Now therefore, flee to
your place. [a]I said I would greatly honor you, but
in fact, the LORD has kept you back from honor."
12 So Balaam said to Balak, "Did I not also
speak to your messengers whom you sent to
me, saying, 13 'If Balak were to give me his house
full of silver and gold, I could not go beyond the
word of the LORD, to do good or bad of my own
will. What the LORD says, that I must speak'?
14 And now, indeed, I am going to my people.
Come, [a]I will advise you what this people will
do to your people in the [b]latter days."

### *BALAAM'S FOURTH PROPHECY*

15 So he took up his oracle and said:

"The utterance of Balaam the son of Beor,
And the utterance of the man whose eyes
are opened;
16 The utterance of him who hears the words
of God,
And has the knowledge of the Most High,
*Who* sees the vision of the Almighty,
*Who* falls down, with eyes wide open:

17 "I[a] see Him, but not now;
I behold Him, but not near;
[b]A Star shall come out of Jacob;
[c]A Scepter shall rise out of Israel,
And batter the brow of Moab,
And destroy all the sons of tumult.[1]

**SEEING JESUS IN THE SCRIPTURE**

**24:17** Both the "Star" and the "Scepter" represent Jesus (see Matt. 2:2). This prophecy points to the rule and reign of King Jesus over His people. But before that reign could come in full, Jesus had to defeat Israel's greatest enemy, sin.

18 "And [a]Edom shall be a possession;
Seir also, his enemies, shall be a
possession,
While Israel does valiantly.
19 [a]Out of Jacob One shall have dominion,
And destroy the remains of the city."

20 Then he looked on Amalek, and he took
up his oracle and said:

"Amalek *was* first among the nations,
But *shall be* last until he perishes."

21 Then he looked on the Kenites, and he
took up his oracle and said:

"Firm is your dwelling place,
And your nest is set in the rock;
22 Nevertheless Kain shall be burned.
How long until Asshur carries you away
captive?"

23 Then he took up his oracle and said:

"Alas! Who shall live when God does this?
24 But ships *shall come* from the coasts of
[a]Cyprus,[1]
And they shall afflict Asshur and afflict
[b]Eber,
And so shall *Amalek*,[2] until he perishes."

25 So Balaam rose and departed and [a]re-
turned to his place; Balak also went his way.

**24:3** [a] Num. 23:7, 18 **24:4** [a] Ezek. 1:28 **24:6** [a] Ps. 1:3; Jer. 17:8 [b] Ps. 104:16 **24:7** [a] Jer. 51:13; Rev. 17:1, 15 [b] 1 Sam. 15:8, 9 [c] 2 Sam. 5:12; 1 Chr. 14:2 **24:8** [a] Num. 23:22 [b] Num. 14:9; 23:24 [c] Ps. 2:9; Jer. 50:17 [d] Ps. 45:5 **24:9** [a] Gen. 49:9; Num. 23:24 [b] Gen. 12:3; 27:29 [1] Genesis 49:9 **24:10** [a] Ezek. 21:14, 17 [b] Num. 23:11; Neh. 13:2 **24:11** [a] Num. 22:17, 37 **24:14** [a] [Mic. 6:5] [b] Gen. 49:1; Deut. 4:30; Dan. 2:28 **24:17** [a] Rev. 1:7; Matt. 1:2; Luke 3:34 [b] Matt. 2:2 [c] Gen. 49:10 [1] Hebrew *Sheth* (compare Jeremiah 48:45) **24:18** [a] 2 Sam. 8:14 **24:19** [a] Gen. 49:10; Amos 9:11, 12 **24:24** [a] Gen. 10:4; Ezek. 27:6; Dan. 11:30 [b] Gen. 10:21, 25 [1] Hebrew *Kittim* [2] Literally *he* or *that one* **24:25** [a] Num. 22:5; 31:8

### *ISRAEL'S HARLOTRY IN MOAB*

**25** Now Israel remained in [a]Acacia Grove,[1] and the [b]people began to commit harlotry with the women of Moab. 2 [a]They invited the people to [b]the sacrifices of their gods, and the people ate and [c]bowed down to their gods. 3 So Israel was joined to Baal of Peor, and [a]the anger of the LORD was aroused against Israel.

4 Then the LORD said to Moses, [a]"Take all the leaders of the people and hang the offenders before the LORD, out in the sun, [b]that the fierce anger of the LORD may turn away from Israel."

5 So Moses said to [a]the judges of Israel, [b]"Every one of you kill his men who were joined to Baal of Peor."

> **25:3–5** Baal, which means "lord" or "master," was a fertility god worshiped by the Canaanites. Because Baal was worshiped throughout Canaan, the Canaanites added the names of their towns to his name. **Baal of Peor**, or "Baal Peor" (Deut. 4:3), is an example of this.

6 And indeed, one of the children of Israel came and presented to his brethren a Midianite woman in the sight of Moses and in the sight of all the congregation of the children of Israel, [a]who *were* weeping at the door of the tabernacle of meeting. 7 Now [a]when Phinehas [b]the son of Eleazar, the son of Aaron the priest, saw *it,* he rose from among the congregation and took a javelin in his hand; 8 and he went after the man of Israel into the tent and thrust both of them through, the man of Israel, and the woman through her body. So [a]the plague was [b]stopped among the children of Israel. 9 And [a]those who died in the plague were twenty-four thousand.

10 Then the LORD spoke to Moses, saying: 11 [a]"Phinehas the son of Eleazar, the son of Aaron the priest, has turned back My wrath from the children of Israel, because he was zealous with My zeal among them, so that I did not consume the children of Israel in [b]My zeal. 12 Therefore say, [a]'Behold, I give to him My [b]covenant of peace; 13 and it shall be to him and [a]his descendants after him a covenant of [b]an everlasting priesthood, because he was [c]zealous for his God, and [d]made atonement for the children of Israel.' "

14 Now the name of the Israelite who was killed, who was killed with the Midianite woman, *was* Zimri the son of Salu, a leader of a father's house among the Simeonites. 15 And the name of the Midianite woman who was killed *was* Cozbi the daughter of [a]Zur; he *was* head of the people of a father's house in Midian.

16 Then the LORD spoke to Moses, saying: 17 [a]"Harass the Midianites, and attack them; 18 for they harassed you with their [a]schemes by which they seduced you in the matter of Peor and in the matter of Cozbi, the daughter of a leader of Midian, their sister, who was killed in the day of the plague because of Peor."

### *THE SECOND CENSUS OF ISRAEL*

**26** And it came to pass, after the [a]plague, that the LORD spoke to Moses and Eleazar the son of Aaron the priest, saying: 2 [a]"Take a census of all the congregation of the children of Israel [b]from twenty years old and above, by their fathers' houses, all who are able to go to war in Israel." 3 So Moses and Eleazar the priest spoke with them [a]in the plains of Moab by the Jordan, *across from* Jericho, saying: 4 "*Take a census of the people* from twenty years old and above, just as the LORD [a]commanded Moses and the children of Israel who came out of the land of Egypt."

5 [a]Reuben *was* the firstborn of Israel. The children of Reuben *were: of* Hanoch, the family of the Hanochites; *of* Pallu, the family of the Palluites; 6 *of* Hezron, the family of the Hezronites; *of* Carmi, the family of the Carmites. 7 These *are* the families of the Reubenites: those who were numbered of them were forty-three thousand seven hundred and thirty. 8 And the son of Pallu *was* Eliab. 9 The sons of Eliab *were* Nemuel, Dathan, and Abiram. These *are* the Dathan and Abiram, [a]representatives of the congregation, who contended against Moses and Aaron in the company of Korah, when they contended against the LORD; 10 [a]and the earth opened its mouth and swallowed them up together with Korah when that company died, when the fire devoured two hundred and fifty men; [b]and they became a sign. 11 Nevertheless [a]the children of Korah did not die.

12 The sons of Simeon according to their families *were: of* Nemuel,[1] the family of the Nemuelites; *of* Jamin, the family of the Jaminites; *of* Jachin,[2] the family of the Jachinites; 13 *of* Zerah,[1] the family of the Zarhites; *of* Shaul, the family of the Shaulites. 14 These *are* the families of the Simeonites: twenty-two thousand two hundred.

15 The sons of Gad according to their families *were: of* Zephon,[1] the family of the Zephonites; *of* Haggi, the family of the Haggites; *of* Shuni, the

**25:1** [a] Num. 33:49; Josh. 2:1 [b] Rev. 2:14 [1] Hebrew *Shittim* **25:2** [a] Josh. 22:17; Hos. 9:10 [b] Ex. 34:15; Deut. 32:38; 1 Cor. 10:20 [c] Ex. 20:5 **25:3** [a] Ps. 106:28, 29 **25:4** [a] Deut. 4:3 [b] Num. 25:11; Deut. 13:17 **25:5** [a] Ex. 18:21 [b] Deut. 13:6, 9 **25:6** [a] Joel 2:17 **25:7** [a] Ps. 106:30 [b] Ex. 6:25 **25:8** [a] Ps. 106:30 [b] Num. 16:46–48 **25:9** [a] Deut. 4:3 **25:11** [a] Ps. 106:30 [b] [Ex. 20:5]; Deut. 32:16, 21; 1 Kin. 14:22; Ps. 78:58; Ezek. 16:38 **25:12** [a] [Mal. 2:4, 5; 3:1] [b] Is. 54:10; Ezek. 34:25; 37:26; Mal. 2:5 **25:13** [a] 1 Chr. 6:4 [b] Ex. 40:15 [c] Acts 22:3 [d] [Heb. 2:17] **25:15** [a] Num. 31:8; Josh. 13:21 **25:17** [a] Num. 31:1–3 **25:18** [a] Num. 31:16; Rev. 2:14 **26:1** [a] Num. 25:9 **26:2** [a] Ex. 30:12; 38:25, 26; Num. 1:2; 14:29 [b] Num. 1:3 **26:3** [a] Num. 22:1; 31:12; 33:48; 35:1 **26:4** [a] Num. 1:1 **26:5** [a] Gen. 46:8; Ex. 6:14; 1 Chr. 5:1–3 **26:9** [a] Num. 1:16; 16:1, 2 **26:10** [a] Num. 16:32–35 [b] Num. 16:38–40; 1 Cor. 10:6; 2 Pet. 2:6 **26:11** [a] Ex. 6:24; 1 Chr. 6:22, 23 **26:12** [1] Spelled *Jemuel* in Genesis 46:10 and Exodus 6:15 [2] Called *Jarib* in 1 Chronicles 4:24 **26:13** [1] Called *Zohar* in Genesis 46:10 **26:15** [1] Called *Ziphion* in Genesis 46:16

family of the Shunites; 16 *of* Ozni,[1] the family of the Oznites; *of* Eri, the family of the Erites; 17 *of* Arod,[1] the family of the Arodites; *of* Areli, the family of the Arelites. 18 These *are* the families of the sons of Gad according to those who were numbered of them: forty thousand five hundred.

19 [a]The sons of Judah *were* Er and Onan; and Er and Onan died in the land of Canaan. 20 And [a]the sons of Judah according to their families were: *of* Shelah, the family of the Shelanites; *of* Perez, the family of the Parzites; *of* Zerah, the family of the Zarhites. 21 And the sons of Perez were: *of* Hezron, the family of the Hezronites; *of* Hamul, the family of the Hamulites. 22 These *are* the families of Judah according to those who were numbered of them: seventy-six thousand five hundred.

23 The sons of Issachar according to their families *were: of* Tola, the family of the Tolaites; of Puah,[1] the family of the Punites;[2] 24 of Jashub, the family of the Jashubites; of Shimron, the family of the Shimronites. 25 These *are* the families of Issachar according to those who were numbered of them: sixty-four thousand three hundred.

26 [a]The sons of Zebulun according to their families *were:* of Sered, the family of the Sardites; of Elon, the family of the Elonites; of Jahleel, the family of the Jahleelites. 27 These *are* the families of the Zebulunites according to those who were numbered of them: sixty thousand five hundred.

28 [a]The sons of Joseph according to their families, by Manasseh and Ephraim, *were:* 29 The sons of [a]Manasseh: of [b]Machir, the family of the Machirites; and Machir begot Gilead; of Gilead, the family of the Gileadites. 30 These *are* the sons of Gilead: *of* Jeezer,[1] the family of the Jeezerites; of Helek, the family of the Helekites; 31 *of* Asriel, the family of the Asrielites; *of* Shechem, the family of the Shechemites; 32 *of* Shemida, the family of the Shemidaites; *of* Hepher, the family of the Hepherites. 33 Now [a]Zelophehad the son of Hepher had no sons, but daughters; and the names of the daughters of Zelophehad *were* Mahlah, Noah, Hoglah, Milcah, and Tirzah. 34 These *are* the families of Manasseh; and those who were numbered of them *were* fifty-two thousand seven hundred.

35 These *are* the sons of Ephraim according to their families: of Shuthelah, the family of the Shuthalhites; of Becher,[1] the family of the Bachrites; of Tahan, the family of the Tahanites. 36 And these *are* the sons of Shuthelah: of Eran, the family of the Eranites. 37 These *are* the families of the sons of Ephraim according to those who were numbered of them: thirty-two thousand five hundred.

These *are* the sons of Joseph according to their families.

38 [a]The sons of Benjamin according to their families were: of Bela, the family of the Belaites; of Ashbel, the family of the Ashbelites; of [b]Ahiram, the family of the Ahiramites; 39 of [a]Shupham,[1] the family of the Shuphamites; of Hupham,[2] the family of the Huphamites. 40 And the sons of Bela were Ard[1] and Naaman: [a]*of Ard,* the family of the Ardites; of Naaman, the family of the Naamites. 41 These *are* the sons of Benjamin according to their families; and those who were numbered of them *were* forty-five thousand six hundred.

42 These *are* the sons of Dan according to their families: of Shuham,[1] the family of the Shuhamites. These *are* the families of Dan according to their families. 43 All the families of the Shuhamites, according to those who were numbered of them, *were* sixty-four thousand four hundred.

44 [a]The sons of Asher according to their families *were:* of Jimna, the family of the Jimnites; of Jesui, the family of the Jesuites; of Beriah, the family of the Beriites. 45 Of the sons of Beriah: of Heber, the family of the Heberites; of Malchiel, the family of the Malchielites. 46 And the name of the daughter of Asher *was* Serah. 47 These *are* the families of the sons of Asher according to those who were numbered of them: fifty-three thousand four hundred.

48 [a]The sons of Naphtali according to their families *were:* of Jahzeel,[1] the family of the Jahzeelites; of Guni, the family of the Gunites; 49 of Jezer, the family of the Jezerites; of [a]Shillem, the family of the Shillemites. 50 These *are* the families of Naphtali according to their families; and those who were numbered of them *were* forty-five thousand four hundred.

51 [a]These *are* those who were numbered of the children of Israel: six hundred and one thousand seven hundred and thirty.

52 Then the LORD spoke to Moses, saying: 53 [a]"To these the land shall be [b]divided as an inheritance, according to the number of names. 54 [a]To a large *tribe* you shall give a larger inheritance, and to a small *tribe* you shall give a smaller inheritance. Each shall be given its inheritance according to those who were numbered of them. 55 But the land shall be [a]divided by lot; they shall inherit according to the names of the tribes

26:16 [1] Called *Ezbon* in Genesis 46:16 26:17 [1] Spelled *Arodi* in Samaritan Pentateuch, Syriac, and Genesis 46:16 26:19 [a] Gen. 38:2; 46:12 26:20 [a] 1 Chr. 2:3 26:23 [1] Hebrew *Puvah* (compare Genesis 46:13 and 1 Chronicles 7:1); Samaritan Pentateuch, Septuagint, Syriac, and Vulgate read *Puah.* [2] Samaritan Pentateuch, Septuagint, Syriac, and Vulgate read *Puaites.* 26:26 [a] Gen. 46:14 26:28 [a] Gen. 46:20; Deut. 33:16 26:29 [a] Josh. 17:1 [b] 1 Chr. 7:14, 15 26:30 [1] Called *Abiezer* in Joshua 17:2 26:33 [a] Num. 27:1; 36:11 26:35 [1] Called *Bered* in 1 Chronicles 7:20 26:38 [a] Gen. 46:21; 1 Chr. 7:6 [b] Gen. 46:21; 1 Chr. 8:1, 2 26:39 [a] 1 Chr. 7:12 [1] Masoretic Text reads *Shephupham,* spelled *Shephuphan* in 1 Chronicles 8:5. [2] Called *Huppim* in Genesis 46:21 26:40 [a] 1 Chr. 8:3 [1] Called *Addar* in 1 Chronicles 8:3 26:42 [1] Called *Hushim* in Genesis 46:23 26:44 [a] Gen. 46:17; 1 Chr. 7:30 26:48 [a] Gen. 46:24; 1 Chr. 7:13 [1] Spelled *Jahziel* in 1 Chronicles 7:13 26:49 [a] 1 Chr. 7:13 26:51 [a] Ex. 12:37; 38:26; Num. 1:46; 11:21 26:53 [a] Josh. 11:23; 14:1 [b] Num. 33:54 26:54 [a] Num. 33:54 26:55 [a] Num. 33:54; 34:13; Josh. 11:23; 14:2

of their fathers. 56 According to the lot their inheritance shall be divided between the larger and the smaller."

> **26:55–56** Dividing by **lot** was an ancient way of selecting, much like flipping a coin or drawing a straw today. The difference was the Israelites believed God influenced the outcome of the lots. Therefore, it was His will, and not blind luck, that determined the results. Lots were often used to make important decisions including choosing the scapegoat (Lev. 16:8–10), dividing the land (Num. 26:55–56; Josh. 14:2), dividing Jesus' garments (Matt. 27:35), and choosing Judas's replacement (Acts 1:24–26).

57 [a]And these *are* those who were numbered of the Levites according to their families: of Gershon, the family of the Gershonites; of Kohath, the family of the Kohathites; of Merari, the family of the Merarites. 58 These *are* the families of the Levites: the family of the Libnites, the family of the Hebronites, the family of the Mahlites, the family of the Mushites, and the family of the Korathites. And Kohath begot Amram. 59 The name of Amram's wife *was* [a]Jochebed the daughter of Levi, who was born to Levi in Egypt; and to Amram she bore Aaron and Moses and their sister Miriam. 60 [a]To Aaron were born Nadab and Abihu, Eleazar and Ithamar. 61 And [a]Nadab and Abihu died when they offered profane fire before the LORD.

62 [a]Now those who were numbered of them were twenty-three thousand, every male from a month old and above; [b]for they were not numbered among the other children of Israel, because there was [c]no inheritance given to them among the children of Israel.

63 These *are* those who were numbered by Moses and Eleazar the priest, who numbered the children of Israel [a]in the plains of Moab by the Jordan, *across from* Jericho. 64 [a]But among these there was not a man of those who were numbered by Moses and Aaron the priest when they numbered the children of Israel in the [b]Wilderness of Sinai. 65 For the LORD had said of them, "They [a]shall surely die in the wilderness." So there was not left a man of them, [b]except Caleb the son of Jephunneh and Joshua the son of Nun.

### *INHERITANCE LAWS*

**27** Then came the daughters of [a]Zelophehad the son of Hepher, the son of Gilead, the son of Machir, the son of Manasseh, from the families of Manasseh the son of Joseph; and these *were* the names of his daughters: Mahlah, Noah, Hoglah, Milcah, and Tirzah. 2 And they stood before Moses, before Eleazar the priest, and before the leaders and all the congregation, *by* the doorway of the tabernacle of meeting, saying: 3 "Our father [a]died in the wilderness; but he was not in the company of those who gathered together against the LORD, [b]in company with Korah, but he died in his own sin; and he had no sons. 4 Why should the name of our father be [a]removed from among his family because he had no son? [b]Give us a possession among our father's brothers."

> **27:3–4** Women were not allowed to inherit land in ancient Israelite society. The only exceptions were situations like the one facing Zelophehad's daughters. With no male in the family to take over their father's responsibilities, they were faced with the possibility of losing their land and, therefore, their means of supporting themselves.

5 So Moses [a]brought their case before the LORD.

6 And the LORD spoke to Moses, saying: 7 "The daughters of Zelophehad speak *what is* right; [a]you shall surely give them a possession of inheritance among their father's brothers, and cause the inheritance of their father to pass to them. 8 And you shall speak to the children of Israel, saying: 'If a man dies and has no son, then you shall cause his inheritance to pass to his daughter. 9 If he has no daughter, then you shall give his inheritance to his brothers. 10 If he has no brothers, then you shall give his inheritance to his father's brothers. 11 And if his father has no brothers, then you shall give his inheritance to the relative closest to him in his family, and he shall possess it.' " And it shall be to the children of Israel [a]a statute of judgment, just as the LORD commanded Moses.

### *JOSHUA THE NEXT LEADER OF ISRAEL*

*(Deut. 31:1–8)*

12 Now the LORD said to Moses: [a]"Go up into this Mount Abarim, and see the land which I have given to the children of Israel. 13 And when you have seen it, you also [a]shall be gathered to your people, as Aaron your brother was gathered. 14 For in the Wilderness of Zin, during the strife of the congregation, you [a]rebelled against My command to hallow Me at the waters before their eyes." (These *are* the [b]waters of Meribah, at Kadesh in the Wilderness of Zin.)

15 Then Moses spoke to the LORD, saying:

**26:57** [a] Gen. 46:11; Ex. 6:16–19; Num. 3:15; 1 Chr. 6:1, 16 **26:59** [a] Ex. 2:1, 2; 6:20 **26:60** [a] Num. 3:2 **26:61** [a] Lev. 10:1, 2; Num. 3:3, 4; 1 Chr. 24:2 **26:62** [a] Num. 3:39 [b] Num. 1:49 [c] Num. 18:20, 23, 24 **26:63** [a] Num. 26:3 **26:64** [a] Num. 14:29–35; Deut. 2:14–16; Heb. 3:17 [b] Num. 1:1–46 **26:65** [a] Num. 14:26–35; [1 Cor. 10:5, 6] [b] Num. 14:30 **27:1** [a] Num. 26:33; 36:1, 11; Josh. 17:3 **27:3** [a] Num. 14:35; 26:64, 65 [b] Num. 16:1, 2 **27:4** [a] Deut. 25:6 [b] Josh. 17:4 **27:5** [a] Ex. 18:13–26 **27:7** [a] Num. 36:2; Josh. 17:4 **27:11** [a] Num. 35:29 **27:12** [a] Num. 33:47; Deut. 3:23–27; 32:48–52; 34:1–4 **27:13** [a] Num. 20:12, 24, 28; 31:2; Deut. 10:6; 34:5, 6 **27:14** [a] Num. 20:12, 24; Deut. 1:37; 32:51; Ps. 106:32, 33 [b] Ex. 17:7

## APPLY THE TRUTH

### AUTHORITY

**27:20** "You're not the boss of me!" We've all said that to someone. Everyone, though, has a boss. But often, those in authority aren't perfect. This is why we must learn how to submit to authority, even when we disagree with it. How do we handle that unfair teacher, boss who doesn't notice our hard work, or coach who starts his child over us?

Here in the Book of Numbers, Joshua was being raised up from being Moses's assistant to becoming Israel's leader. This change didn't happen overnight; Joshua went through years of preparation before becoming the "boss." To be good at exercising authority, we must first be good at submitting to authority. Good leaders are made of good followers.

Most of us are under authority more than we have authority. When you're young, everyone else is in charge: your parents, teachers, coaches, and pastors. This is the time to learn how to be faithful under good authority so you can learn how to exercise good authority one day. And when you find yourself under difficult leaders, it isn't the time to rebel. Rather, it's the time to grow in humility and patience, essential leadership qualities.

16 "Let the LORD, [a]the God of the spirits of all flesh, set a man over the congregation, 17 [a]who may go out before them and go in before them, who may lead them out and bring them in, that the congregation of the LORD may not be [b]like sheep which have no shepherd."

18 And the LORD said to Moses: "Take Joshua the son of Nun with you, a man [a]in whom *is* the Spirit, and [b]lay your hand on him; 19 set him before Eleazar the priest and before all the congregation, and [a]inaugurate him in their sight. 20 And [a]you shall give *some* of your authority to him, that all the congregation of the children of Israel [b]may be obedient. 21 [a]He shall stand before Eleazar the priest, who shall inquire before the LORD for him [b]by the judgment of the Urim. [c]At his word they shall go out, and at his word they shall come in, he and all the children of Israel with him—all the congregation."

22 So Moses did as the LORD commanded him. He took Joshua and set him before Eleazar the priest and before all the congregation. 23 And he laid his hands on him [a]and inaugurated him, just as the LORD commanded by the hand of Moses.

### DAILY OFFERINGS
*(Ex. 29:38–46)*

**28** Now the LORD spoke to Moses, saying, 2 "Command the children of Israel, and say to them, 'My offering, [a]My food for My offerings made by fire as a sweet aroma to Me, you shall be careful to offer to Me at their appointed time.'

3 "And you shall say to them, [a]'This *is* the offering made by fire which you shall offer to the LORD: two male lambs in their first year without blemish, day by day, as a regular burnt offering. 4 The one lamb you shall offer in the morning, the other lamb you shall offer in the evening, 5 and [a]one-tenth of an ephah of fine flour as a [b]grain offering mixed with one-fourth of a hin of pressed oil. 6 *It is* [a]a regular burnt offering which was ordained at Mount Sinai for a sweet aroma, an offering made by fire to the LORD. 7 And its drink offering *shall be* one-fourth of a hin for each lamb; [a]in a holy *place* you shall pour out the drink to the LORD as an offering. 8 The other lamb you shall offer in the evening; as the morning grain offering and its drink offering, you shall offer *it* as an offering made by fire, a sweet aroma to the LORD.

### SABBATH OFFERINGS

9 'And on the Sabbath day two lambs in their first year, without blemish, and two-tenths *of an ephah* of fine flour as a grain offering, mixed with oil, with its drink offering— 10 *this is* [a]the burnt offering for every Sabbath, besides the regular burnt offering with its drink offering.

### MONTHLY OFFERINGS

11 [a]'At the beginnings of your months you shall present a burnt offering to the LORD: two young bulls, one ram, and seven lambs in their first year, without blemish; 12 [a]three-tenths *of an ephah* of fine flour as a grain offering, mixed with oil, for each bull; two-tenths *of an ephah* of fine flour as a grain offering, mixed with oil, for the one ram; 13 and one-tenth *of an ephah* of fine flour, mixed with oil, as a grain offering for each lamb, as a burnt offering of sweet aroma,

**27:16** [a] Num. 16:22; Heb. 12:9 **27:17** [a] Deut. 31:2; 1 Sam. 8:20; 18:13; 2 Chr. 1:10 [b] 1 Kin. 22:17; Zech. 10:2; Matt. 9:36; Mark 6:34 **27:18** [a] Gen. 41:38; Judg. 3:10; 1 Sam. 16:13, 18 [b] Deut. 34:9 **27:19** [a] Deut. 3:28; 31:3, 7, 8, 23 **27:20** [a] Num. 11:17 [b] Josh. 1:16–18 **27:21** [a] Judg. 20:18, 23, 26; 1 Sam. 23:9; 30:7 [b] Ex. 28:30; 1 Sam. 28:6 [c] Josh. 9:14; 1 Sam. 22:10 **27:23** [a] Deut. 3:28; 31:7, 8 **28:2** [a] Lev. 3:11; 21:6, 8; [Mal. 1:7, 12] **28:3** [a] Ex. 29:38–42 **28:5** [a] Ex. 16:36; Num. 15:4 [b] Lev. 2:1 **28:6** [a] Ex. 29:42; Amos 5:25 **28:7** [a] Ex. 29:42 **28:10** [a] Ezek. 46:4 **28:11** [a] Num. 10:10; 1 Sam. 20:5; 1 Chr. 23:31; 2 Chr. 2:4; Ezra 3:5; Neh. 10:33; Is. 1:13, 14; Ezek. 45:17; 46:6, 7; Hos. 2:11; Col. 2:16 **28:12** [a] Num. 15:4–12

an offering made by fire to the LORD. 14 Their
drink offering shall be half a hin of wine for a
bull, one-third of a hin for a ram, and one-fourth
of a hin for a lamb; this *is* the burnt offering for
each month throughout the months of the year.
15 Also [a]one kid of the goats as a sin offering to
the LORD shall be offered, besides the regular
burnt offering and its drink offering.

### *OFFERINGS AT PASSOVER*

*(Lev. 23:5–14)*

16 [a]'On the fourteenth day of the first month *is*
the Passover of the LORD. 17 [a]And on the fifteenth
day of this month *is* the feast; unleavened bread
shall be eaten for seven days. 18 On the [a]first day
*you shall have* a holy convocation. You shall do
no customary work. 19 And you shall present an
offering made by fire as a burnt offering to the
LORD: two young bulls, one ram, and seven lambs
in their first year. [a]Be sure they are without blem-
ish. 20 Their grain offering shall be of fine flour
mixed with oil: three-tenths *of an ephah* you shall
offer for a bull, and two-tenths for a ram; 21 you
shall offer one-tenth *of an ephah* for each of the
seven lambs; 22 also [a]one goat *as* a sin offering, to
make atonement for you. 23 You shall offer these
besides the burnt offering of the morning, which
*is* for a regular burnt offering. 24 In this manner
you shall offer the food of the offering made by
fire daily for seven days, as a sweet aroma to the
LORD; it shall be offered besides the regular burnt
offering and its drink offering. 25 And [a]on the
seventh day you shall have a holy convocation.
You shall do no customary work.

### *OFFERINGS AT THE FEAST OF WEEKS*

*(Lev. 23:15–22)*

26 'Also [a]on the day of the firstfruits, when
you bring a new grain offering to the LORD at
your *Feast of* Weeks, you shall have a holy con-
vocation. You shall do no customary work. 27 You
shall present a burnt offering as a sweet aroma
to the LORD: [a]two young bulls, one ram, and
seven lambs in their first year, 28 with their grain
offering of fine flour mixed with oil: three-tenths
*of an ephah* for each bull, two-tenths for the one
ram, 29 and one-tenth for each of the seven lambs;
30 *also* one kid of the goats, to make atonement for
you. 31 [a]Be sure they are without blemish. You shall
present *them* with their drink offerings, besides
the regular burnt offering with its grain offering.

### *OFFERINGS AT THE FEAST OF TRUMPETS*

*(Lev. 23:23–25)*

**29** 'And in the seventh month, on the first
*day* of the month, you shall have a holy
convocation. You shall do no customary work.
For you [a]it is a day of blowing the trumpets. 2 You
shall offer a burnt offering as a sweet aroma to
the LORD: one young bull, one ram, *and* seven
lambs in their first year, without blemish. 3 Their
grain offering *shall be* fine flour mixed with oil:
three-tenths *of an ephah* for the bull, two-tenths
for the ram, 4 and one-tenth for each of the seven
lambs; 5 also one kid of the goats *as* a sin offer-
ing, to make atonement for you; 6 besides [a]the
burnt offering with its grain offering for the New
Moon, [b]the regular burnt offering with its grain
offering, and their drink offerings, [c]according to
their ordinance, as a sweet aroma, an offering
made by fire to the LORD.

### *OFFERINGS ON THE DAY OF ATONEMENT*

*(Lev. 23:26–32)*

7 [a]'On the tenth *day* of this seventh month
you shall have a holy convocation. You shall
[b]afflict your souls; you shall not do any work.
8 You shall present a burnt offering to the LORD
*as* a sweet aroma: one young bull, one ram, *and*
seven lambs in their first year. [a]Be sure they are
without blemish. 9 Their grain offering *shall be*
*of* fine flour mixed with oil: three-tenths *of an*
*ephah* for the bull, two-tenths for the one ram,
10 and one-tenth for each of the seven lambs;
11 also one kid of the goats *as* a sin offering, be-
sides [a]the sin offering for atonement, the regular
burnt offering with its grain offering, and their
drink offerings.

### *OFFERINGS AT THE FEAST OF TABERNACLES*

*(Lev. 23:33–44)*

12 [a]'On the fifteenth day of the seventh month
you shall have a holy convocation. You shall do
no customary work, and you shall keep a feast
to the LORD seven days. 13 [a]You shall present a
burnt offering, an offering made by fire as a
sweet aroma to the LORD: thirteen young bulls,
two rams, *and* fourteen lambs in their first year.
They shall be without blemish. 14 Their grain
offering *shall be of* fine flour mixed with oil:
three-tenths *of an ephah* for each of the thirteen
bulls, two-tenths for each of the two rams, 15 and
one-tenth for each of the fourteen lambs; 16 also
one kid of the goats *as* a sin offering, besides
the regular burnt offering, its grain offering,
and its drink offering.

17 'On the [a]second day *present* twelve young
bulls, two rams, fourteen lambs in their first
year without blemish, 18 and their grain offer-
ing and their drink offerings for the bulls, for
the rams, and for the lambs, by their number,
[a]according to the ordinance; 19 also one kid of
the goats *as* a sin offering, besides the regular
burnt offering with its grain offering, and their
drink offerings.

28:15 [a] Num. 15:24; 28:3, 22 28:16 [a] Ex. 12:1–20; Lev. 23:5–8; Num. 9:2–5; Deut. 16:1–8; Ezek. 45:21 28:17 [a] Lev. 23:6 28:18 [a] Ex. 12:16; Lev. 23:7 28:19 [a] Lev. 22:20; Num. 28:31; 29:8; Deut. 15:21 28:22 [a] Num. 28:15 28:25 [a] Ex. 12:16; 13:6; Lev. 23:8 28:26 [a] Ex. 23:16; 34:22; Lev. 23:10–21; Deut. 16:9–12; Acts 2:1 28:27 [a] Lev. 23:18, 19 28:31 [a] Num. 28:3, 19 29:1 [a] Ex. 23:16; 34:22; Lev. 23:23–25 29:6 [a] Num. 28:11–15 [b] Num. 28:3 [c] Num. 15:11, 12 29:7 [a] Lev. 16:29–34; 23:26–32 [b] Ps. 35:13; Is. 58:5 29:8 [a] Num. 28:19 29:11 [a] Lev. 16:3, 5 29:12 [a] Lev. 23:33–35; Deut. 16:13–15; Ezek. 45:25 29:13 [a] Ezra 3:4 29:17 [a] Lev. 23:36 29:18 [a] Num. 15:12; 28:7, 14; 29:3, 4, 9, 10

20 'On the third day *present* eleven bulls, two
rams, fourteen lambs in their first year without
blemish, 21 and their grain offering and their
drink offerings for the bulls, for the rams, and
for the lambs, by their number, [a]according to
the ordinance; 22 also one goat *as* a sin offering,
besides the regular burnt offering, its grain
offering, and its drink offering.

23 'On the fourth day *present* ten bulls, two
rams, *and* fourteen lambs in their first year,
without blemish, 24 and their grain offering and
their drink offerings for the bulls, for the rams,
and for the lambs, by their number, according
to the ordinance; 25 also one kid of the goats *as* a
sin offering, besides the regular burnt offering,
its grain offering, and its drink offering.

26 'On the fifth day *present* nine bulls, two
rams, *and* fourteen lambs in their first year
without blemish, 27 and their grain offering and
their drink offerings for the bulls, for the rams,
and for the lambs, by their number, according to
the ordinance; 28 also one goat *as* a sin offering,
besides the regular burnt offering, its grain
offering, and its drink offering.

29 'On the sixth day *present* eight bulls, two
rams, *and* fourteen lambs in their first year
without blemish, 30 and their grain offering and
their drink offerings for the bulls, for the rams,
and for the lambs, by their number, according to
the ordinance; 31 also one goat *as* a sin offering,
besides the regular burnt offering, its grain
offering, and its drink offering.

32 'On the seventh day *present* seven bulls,
two rams, *and* fourteen lambs in their first year
without blemish, 33 and their grain offering and
their drink offerings for the bulls, for the rams,
and for the lambs, by their number, according to
the ordinance; 34 also one goat *as* a sin offering,
besides the regular burnt offering, its grain
offering, and its drink offering.

35 'On the eighth day you shall have a [a]sa-
cred assembly. You shall do no customary
work. 36 You shall present a burnt offering,
an offering made by fire as a sweet aroma to
the LORD: one bull, one ram, seven lambs in
their first year without blemish, 37 and their
grain offering and their drink offerings for
the bull, for the ram, and for the lambs, by
their number, according to the ordinance;
38 also one goat *as* a sin offering, besides the
regular burnt offering, its grain offering, and
its drink offering.

39 'These you shall present to the LORD at
your [a]appointed feasts (besides your [b]vowed
offerings and your freewill offerings) as
your burnt offerings and your grain offer-
ings, as your drink offerings and your peace
offerings.' "

40 So Moses told the children of Israel every-
thing, just as the LORD commanded Moses.

### *THE LAW CONCERNING VOWS*

30 Then Moses spoke to [a]the heads of the
tribes concerning the children of Israel,
saying, "This *is* the thing which the LORD has
commanded: 2 [a]If a man makes a vow to the
LORD, or [b]swears an oath to bind himself by
some agreement, he shall not break his word;
he shall [c]do according to all that proceeds out
of his mouth.

3 "Or if a woman makes a vow to the LORD,
and binds *herself* by some agreement while in
her father's house in her youth, 4 and her father
hears her vow and the agreement by which she
has bound herself, and her father holds his
peace, then all her vows shall stand, and every
agreement with which she has bound herself
shall stand. 5 But if her father overrules her on
the day that he hears, then none of her vows
nor her agreements by which she has bound
herself shall stand; and the LORD will release
her, because her father overruled her.

6 "If indeed she takes a husband, while
bound by her vows or by a rash utterance from
her lips by which she bound herself, 7 and her
husband hears *it,* and makes no response to
her on the day that he hears, then her vows
shall stand, and her agreements by which she
bound herself shall stand. 8 But if her husband
[a]overrules her on the day that he hears *it,* he
shall make void her vow which she took and
what she uttered with her lips, by which she
bound herself, and the LORD will release her.

9 "Also any vow of a widow or a divorced
woman, by which she has bound herself, shall
stand against her.

10 "If she vowed in her husband's house, or
bound herself by an agreement with an oath,
11 and her husband heard *it,* and made no re-
sponse to her *and* did not overrule her, then
all her vows shall stand, and every agreement
by which she bound herself shall stand. 12 But if
her husband truly made them void on the day
he heard *them,* then whatever proceeded from
her lips concerning her vows or concerning the
agreement binding her, it shall not stand; her
husband has made them void, and the LORD will
release her. 13 Every vow and every binding oath
to afflict her soul, her husband may confirm it,
or her husband may make it void. 14 Now if her
husband makes no response whatever to her
from day to day, then he confirms all her vows
or all the agreements that bind her; he confirms
them, because he made no response to her on
the day that he heard *them.* 15 But if he does
make them void after he has heard *them,* then
he shall bear her guilt."

16 These *are* the statutes which the LORD
commanded Moses, between a man and his
wife, and between a father and his daughter in
her youth in her father's house.

29:21 [a] Num. 29:18 29:35 [a] Lev. 23:36 29:39 [a] Lev. 23:1–44; 1 Chr. 23:31; 2 Chr. 31:3; Ezra 3:5; Neh. 10:33; Is. 1:14 [b] Lev. 7:16; 22:18, 21, 23; 23:38 30:1 [a] Num. 1:4, 16; 7:2 30:2 [a] Lev. 27:2; Deut. 23:21–23; Judg. 11:30, 31, 35; Eccl. 5:4 [b] Lev. 5:4; Matt. 14:9; Acts 23:14 [c] Job 22:27; Ps. 22:25; 50:14; 66:13, 14; Nah. 1:15 30:8 [a] [Gen. 3:16]

### VENGEANCE ON THE MIDIANITES

31 And the LORD spoke to Moses, saying: 2 [a]"Take vengeance on the Midianites for the children of Israel. Afterward you shall [b]be gathered to your people."

3 So Moses spoke to the people, saying, "Arm some of yourselves for war, and let them go against the Midianites to take vengeance for the LORD on [a]Midian. 4 A thousand from each tribe of all the tribes of Israel you shall send to the war."

5 So there were recruited from the divisions of Israel one thousand from *each* tribe, twelve thousand armed for war. 6 Then Moses sent them to the war, one thousand from *each* tribe; he sent them to the war with Phinehas the son of Eleazar the priest, with the holy articles and [a]the signal trumpets in his hand. 7 And they warred against the Midianites, just as the LORD commanded Moses, and [a]they killed all the [b]males. 8 They killed the kings of Midian with *the rest of* those who were killed—[a]Evi, Rekem, [b]Zur, Hur, and Reba, the five kings of Midian. [c]Balaam the son of Beor they also killed with the sword.

9 And the children of Israel took the women of Midian captive, with their little ones, and took as spoil all their cattle, all their flocks, and all their goods. 10 They also burned with fire all the cities where they dwelt, and all their forts. 11 And [a]they took all the spoil and all the booty—of man and beast.

### RETURN FROM THE WAR

12 Then they brought the captives, the booty, and the spoil to Moses, to Eleazar the priest, and to the congregation of the children of Israel, to the camp in the plains of Moab by the Jordan, *across from* Jericho. 13 And Moses, Eleazar the priest, and all the leaders of the congregation, went to meet them outside the camp. 14 But Moses was angry with the officers of the army, *with* the captains over thousands and captains over hundreds, who had come from the battle.

15 And Moses said to them: "Have you kept [a]all the women alive? 16 Look, [a]these *women* caused the children of Israel, through the [b]counsel of Balaam, to trespass against the LORD in the incident of Peor, and [c]there was a plague among the congregation of the LORD. 17 Now therefore, [a]kill every male among the little ones, and kill every woman who has known a man intimately. 18 But keep alive [a]for yourselves all the young girls who have not known a man intimately. 19 And as for you, [a]remain outside the camp seven days; whoever has killed any person, and [b]whoever has touched any slain, purify yourselves and your captives on the third day and on the seventh day. 20 Purify every garment, everything made of leather, everything woven of goats' *hair,* and everything made of wood."

21 Then Eleazar the priest said to the men of war who had gone to the battle, "This *is* the ordinance of the law which the LORD commanded Moses: 22 Only the gold, the silver, the bronze, the iron, the tin, and the lead, 23 everything that can endure fire, you shall put through the fire, and it shall be clean; and it shall be purified [a]with the water of purification. But all that cannot endure fire you shall put through water. 24 [a]And you shall wash your clothes on the seventh day and be clean, and afterward you may come into the camp."

### DIVISION OF THE PLUNDER

25 Now the LORD spoke to Moses, saying: 26 "Count up the plunder that was taken—of man and beast—you and Eleazar the priest and the chief fathers of the congregation; 27 and [a]divide the plunder into two parts, between those who took part in the war, who went out to battle, and all the congregation. 28 And levy a tribute for the LORD on the men of war who went out to battle: [a]one of every five hundred of the persons, the cattle, the donkeys, and the sheep; 29 take *it* from their half, and [a]give *it* to Eleazar the priest as a heave offering to the LORD. 30 And from the children of Israel's half you shall take [a]one of every fifty, drawn from the persons, the cattle, the donkeys, and the sheep, from all the livestock, and give them to the Levites [b]who keep charge of the tabernacle of the LORD." 31 So Moses and Eleazar the priest did as the LORD commanded Moses.

32 The booty remaining from the plunder, which the men of war had taken, was six hundred and seventy-five thousand sheep, 33 seventy-two thousand cattle, 34 sixty-one thousand donkeys, 35 and thirty-two thousand persons in all, of women who had not known a man intimately. 36 And the half, the portion for those who had gone out to war, was in number three hundred and thirty-seven thousand five hundred sheep; 37 and the LORD's tribute of the sheep was six hundred and seventy-five. 38 The cattle *were* thirty-six thousand, of which the LORD's tribute *was* seventy-two. 39 The donkeys *were* thirty thousand five hundred, of which the LORD's tribute *was* sixty-one. 40 The persons *were* sixteen thousand, of which the LORD's tribute *was* thirty-two persons. 41 So Moses gave the tribute *which was* the LORD's heave offering to Eleazar the priest, [a]as the LORD commanded Moses.

42 And from the children of Israel's half, which Moses separated from the men who fought— 43 now the half belonging to the congregation was three hundred and thirty-seven thousand five hundred sheep, 44 thirty-six thousand cattle, 45 thirty thousand five hundred donkeys, 46 and sixteen thousand persons— 47 and [a]from the

31:2 [a] Num. 25:17 [b] Num. 27:12, 13 31:3 [a] Josh. 13:21 31:6 [a] Num. 10:9 31:7 [a] Deut. 20:13; Judg. 21:11; 1 Sam. 27:9; 1 Kin. 11:15, 16 [b] Gen. 34:25 31:8 [a] Josh. 13:21 [b] Num. 25:15 [c] Num. 31:16; Josh. 13:22 31:11 [a] Deut. 20:14 31:15 [a] Deut. 20:14 31:16 [a] Num. 25:2 [b] Num. 24:14; 2 Pet. 2:15; Rev. 2:14 [c] Num. 25:9 31:17 [a] Deut. 7:2; 20:16–18; Judg. 21:11 31:18 [a] Deut. 21:10–14 31:19 [a] Num. 5:2 [b] Num. 19:11–22 31:23 [a] Num. 19:9, 17 31:24 [a] Lev. 11:25 31:27 [a] Josh. 22:8; 1 Sam. 30:24 31:28 [a] Num. 31:30, 47 31:29 [a] Deut. 18:1–5 31:30 [a] Num. 31:42–47 [b] Num. 3:7, 8, 25, 31, 36; 18:3, 4 31:41 [a] Num. 5:9, 10; 18:8, 19 31:47 [a] Num. 31:30

children of Israel's half Moses took one of every
fifty, drawn from man and beast, and gave them
to the Levites, who kept charge of the tabernacle
of the LORD, as the LORD commanded Moses.
48 Then the officers who *were* over thou-
sands of the army, the captains of thousands
and captains of hundreds, came near to Moses;
49 and they said to Moses, "Your servants have
taken a count of the men of war who *are* under
our command, and not a man of us is missing.
50 Therefore we have brought an offering for the
LORD, what every man found of ornaments of
gold: armlets and bracelets and signet rings and
earrings and necklaces, [a]to make atonement for
ourselves before the LORD." 51 So Moses and Ele-
azar the priest received the gold from them, all
the fashioned ornaments. 52 And all the gold of
the offering that they offered to the LORD, from
the captains of thousands and captains of hun-
dreds, was sixteen thousand seven hundred and
fifty shekels. 53 [a](The men of war had taken spoil,
every man for himself.) 54 And Moses and Eleazar
the priest received the gold from the captains
of thousands and of hundreds, and brought it
into the tabernacle of meeting [a]as a memorial
for the children of Israel before the LORD.

### *THE TRIBES SETTLING EAST OF THE JORDAN*

*(Deut. 3:12–22)*

32 Now the children of Reuben and the chil-
dren of Gad had a very great multitude of
livestock; and when they saw the land of [a]Jazer
and the land of [b]Gilead, that indeed the region
*was* a place for livestock, 2 the children of Gad
and the children of Reuben came and spoke to
Moses, to Eleazar the priest, and to the leaders of
the congregation, saying, 3 "Ataroth, Dibon, Jazer,
[a]Nimrah, [b]Heshbon, Elealeh, [c]Shebam, Nebo, and
[d]Beon, 4 the country [a]which the LORD defeated
before the congregation of Israel, *is* a land for
livestock, and your servants have livestock."
5 Therefore they said, "If we have found favor in
your sight, let this land be given to your servants
as a possession. Do not take us over the Jordan."
6 And Moses said to the children of Gad and
to the children of Reuben: "Shall your brethren
go to war while you sit here? 7 Now why will you
[a]discourage the heart of the children of Israel
from going over into the land which the LORD has
given them? 8 Thus your fathers did [a]when I sent
them away from Kadesh Barnea [b]to see the land.
9 For [a]when they went up to the Valley of Eshcol
and saw the land, they discouraged the heart of
the children of Israel, so that they did not go into
the land which the LORD had given them. 10 [a]So
the LORD's anger was aroused on that day, and He
swore an oath, saying, 11 'Surely none of the men
who came up from Egypt, [a]from twenty years old
and above, shall see the land of which I swore to
Abraham, Isaac, and Jacob, because [b]they have
not wholly followed Me, 12 except Caleb the son
of Jephunneh, the Kenizzite, and Joshua the son
of Nun, [a]for they have wholly followed the LORD.'
13 So the LORD's anger was aroused against Israel,
and He made them [a]wander in the wilderness
forty years, until [b]all the generation that had
done evil in the sight of the LORD was gone.
14 And look! You have risen in your fathers' place,
a brood of sinful men, to increase still more the
[a]fierce anger of the LORD against Israel. 15 For if
you [a]turn away from following Him, He will once
again leave them in the wilderness, and you will
destroy all these people."
16 Then they came near to him and said: "We
will build sheepfolds here for our livestock, and
cities for our little ones, 17 but [a]we ourselves will
be armed, ready *to go* before the children of Is-
rael until we have brought them to their place;
and our little ones will dwell in the fortified cities
because of the inhabitants of the land. 18 [a]We will
not return to our homes until every one of the
children of Israel has received his inheritance.
19 For we will not inherit with them on the other
side of the Jordan and beyond, [a]because our
inheritance has fallen to us on this eastern side
of the Jordan."
20 Then [a]Moses said to them: "If you do this
thing, if you arm yourselves before the LORD for
the war, 21 and all your armed men cross over the
Jordan before the LORD until He has driven out
His enemies from before Him, 22 and [a]the land is
subdued before the LORD, then afterward [b]you
may return and be blameless before the LORD and
before Israel; and [c]this land shall be your posses-
sion before the LORD. 23 But if you do not do so,
then take note, you have sinned against the LORD;
and be sure [a]your sin will find you out. 24 [a]Build
cities for your little ones and folds for your sheep,
and do what has proceeded out of your mouth."
25 And the children of Gad and the children
of Reuben spoke to Moses, saying: "Your ser-
vants will do as my lord commands. 26 [a]Our
little ones, our wives, our flocks, and all our
livestock will be there in the cities of Gilead;
27 [a]but your servants will cross over, every man
armed for war, before the LORD to battle, just
as my lord says."
28 So Moses gave command [a]concerning
them to Eleazar the priest, to Joshua the son
of Nun, and to the chief fathers of the tribes
of the children of Israel. 29 And Moses said to

**31:50** [a] Ex. 30:12–16 **31:53** [a] Num. 31:32; Deut. 20:14 **31:54** [a] Ex. 30:16 **32:1** [a] Num. 21:32; Josh. 13:25; 2 Sam. 24:5 [b] Deut. 3:13 **32:3** [a] Num. 32:36 [b] Josh. 13:17, 26 [c] Num. 32:38 [d] Num. 32:38 **32:4** [a] Num. 21:24, 34, 35 **32:7** [a] Num. 13:27—14:4 **32:8** [a] Num. 13:3, 26 [b] Deut. 1:19–25 **32:9** [a] Num. 13:24, 31; Deut. 1:24, 28 **32:10** [a] Num. 14:11; Deut. 1:34–36 **32:11** [a] Num. 14:28, 29; 26:63–65; Deut. 1:35 [b] Num. 14:24, 30 **32:12** [a] Num. 14:6–9, 24, 30; Deut. 1:36; Josh. 14:8, 9 **32:13** [a] Num. 14:33–35 [b] Num. 26:64, 65 **32:14** [a] Num. 11:1; Deut. 1:34 **32:15** [a] Deut. 30:17, 18; Josh. 22:16–18; 2 Chr. 7:19; 15:2 **32:17** [a] Josh. 4:12, 13 **32:18** [a] Josh. 22:1–4 **32:19** [a] Josh. 12:1; 13:8 **32:20** [a] Deut. 3:18; Josh. 1:14 **32:22** [a] Deut. 3:20; Josh. 11:23 [b] Josh. 22:4 [c] Deut. 3:12, 15, 16, 18; Josh. 1:15; 13:8, 32; 22:4, 9 **32:23** [a] Gen. 4:7; 44:16; Josh. 7:1–26; Is. 59:12; [Gal. 6:7] **32:24** [a] Num. 32:16 **32:26** [a] Josh. 1:14 **32:27** [a] Josh. 4:12 **32:28** [a] Josh. 1:13

them: "If the children of Gad and the children of Reuben cross over the Jordan with you, every man armed for battle before the LORD, and the land is subdued before you, then you shall give them the land of Gilead as a possession. 30 But if they do not cross over armed with you, they shall have possessions among you in the land of Canaan."

31 Then the children of Gad and the children of Reuben answered, saying: "As the LORD has said to your servants, so we will do. 32 We will cross over armed before the LORD into the land of Canaan, but the possession of our inheritance *shall remain* with us on this side of the Jordan."

33 So [a]Moses gave to the children of Gad, to the children of Reuben, and to half the tribe of Manasseh the son of Joseph, [b]the kingdom of Sihon king of the Amorites and the kingdom of Og king of Bashan, the land with its cities within the borders, the cities of the surrounding country. 34 And the children of Gad built [a]Dibon and Ataroth and [b]Aroer, 35 Atroth and Shophan and [a]Jazer and Jogbehah, 36 [a]Beth Nimrah and Beth Haran, [b]fortified cities, and folds for sheep. 37 And the children of Reuben built [a]Heshbon and Elealeh and Kirjathaim, 38 [a]Nebo and [b]Baal Meon [c](*their* names being changed) and Shibmah; and they gave *other* names to the cities which they built.

39 And the children of [a]Machir the son of Manasseh went to Gilead and took it, and dispossessed the Amorites who *were* in it. 40 So Moses [a]gave Gilead to Machir the son of Manasseh, and he dwelt in it. 41 Also [a]Jair the son of Manasseh went and took its small towns, and called them [b]Havoth Jair.[1] 42 Then Nobah went and took Kenath and its villages, and he called it Nobah, after his own name.

## *ISRAEL'S JOURNEY FROM EGYPT REVIEWED*

**33** These *are* the journeys of the children of Israel, who went out of the land of Egypt by their armies under the [a]hand of Moses and Aaron. 2 Now Moses wrote down the starting points of their journeys at the command of the LORD. And these *are* their journeys according to their starting points:

3 They [a]departed from Rameses in [b]the first month, on the fifteenth day of the first month; on the day after the Passover the children of Israel went out [c]with boldness in the sight of all the Egyptians. 4 For the Egyptians were burying all *their* firstborn, [a]whom the LORD had killed among them. Also [b]on their gods the LORD had executed judgments.

5 [a]Then the children of Israel moved from Rameses and camped at Succoth. 6 They departed from [a]Succoth and camped at Etham, which *is* on the edge of the wilderness. 7 [a]They moved from Etham and turned back to Pi Hahiroth, which *is* east of Baal Zephon; and they camped near Migdol. 8 They departed from before Hahiroth[1] and [a]passed through the midst of the sea into the wilderness, went three days' journey in the Wilderness of Etham, and camped at Marah. 9 They moved from Marah and [a]came to Elim. At Elim *were* twelve springs of water and seventy palm trees; so they camped there.

10 They moved from Elim and camped by the Red Sea. 11 They moved from the Red Sea and camped in the [a]Wilderness of Sin. 12 They journeyed from the Wilderness of Sin and camped at Dophkah. 13 They departed from Dophkah and camped at Alush. 14 They moved from Alush and camped at [a]Rephidim, where there was no water for the people to drink.

15 They departed from Rephidim and camped in the [a]Wilderness of Sinai. 16 They moved from the Wilderness of Sinai and camped [a]at Kibroth Hattaavah. 17 They departed from Kibroth Hattaavah and [a]camped at Hazeroth. 18 They departed from Hazeroth and camped at [a]Rithmah. 19 They departed from Rithmah and camped at Rimmon Perez. 20 They departed from Rimmon Perez and camped at Libnah. 21 They moved from Libnah and camped at Rissah. 22 They journeyed from Rissah and camped at Kehelathah. 23 They went from Kehelathah and camped at Mount Shepher. 24 They moved from Mount Shepher and camped at Haradah. 25 They moved from Haradah and camped at Makheloth. 26 They moved from Makheloth and camped at Tahath. 27 They departed from Tahath and camped at Terah. 28 They moved from Terah and camped at Mithkah. 29 They went from Mithkah and camped at Hashmonah. 30 They departed from Hashmonah and [a]camped at Moseroth. 31 They departed from Moseroth and camped at Bene Jaakan. 32 They moved from [a]Bene Jaakan and [b]camped at Hor Hagidgad. 33 They went from Hor Hagidgad and camped at Jotbathah. 34 They moved from Jotbathah and camped at Abronah. 35 They departed from Abronah [a]and camped at Ezion Geber. 36 They moved from Ezion Geber and camped in the [a]Wilderness of Zin, which *is* Kadesh. 37 They moved from [a]Kadesh and camped at Mount Hor, on the boundary of the land of Edom.

38 Then [a]Aaron the priest went up to Mount Hor at the command of the LORD, and died there in the fortieth year after the children of

**32:33** [a] Deut. 3:8–17; 29:8; Josh. 12:1–6; 13:8–31; 22:4 [b] Num. 21:24, 33, 35 **32:34** [a] Num. 33:45, 46 [b] Deut. 2:36 **32:35** [a] Num. 32:1, 3 **32:36** [a] Num. 32:3 [b] Num. 32:24 **32:37** [a] Num. 21:27 **32:38** [a] Is. 46:1 [b] Ezek. 25:9 [c] Ex. 23:13; Josh. 23:7 **32:39** [a] Gen. 50:23; Num. 27:1; 36:1 **32:40** [a] Deut. 3:12, 13, 15; Josh. 13:31 **32:41** [a] Deut. 3:14; Josh. 13:30 [b] Judg. 10:4; 1 Kin. 4:13 [1] Literally *Towns of Jair* **33:1** [a] Ps. 77:20 **33:3** [a] Ex. 12:37 [b] Ex. 12:2; 13:4 [c] Ex. 14:8 **33:4** [a] Ex. 12:29 [b] [Ex. 12:12; 18:11]; Is. 19:1 **33:5** [a] Ex. 12:37 **33:6** [a] Ex. 13:20 **33:7** [a] Ex. 14:1, 2, 9 **33:8** [a] Ex. 14:22; 15:22, 23 [1] Many Hebrew manuscripts, Samaritan Pentateuch, Syriac, Targum, and Vulgate read *from Pi Hahiroth* (compare verse 7). **33:9** [a] Ex. 15:27 **33:11** [a] Ex. 16:1 **33:14** [a] Ex. 17:1; 19:2 **33:15** [a] Ex. 16:1; 19:1, 2 **33:16** [a] Num. 11:34 **33:17** [a] Num. 11:35 **33:18** [a] Num. 12:16 **33:30** [a] Deut. 10:6 **33:32** [a] Deut. 10:6 [b] Deut. 10:7 **33:35** [a] Deut. 2:8; 1 Kin. 9:26; 22:48 **33:36** [a] Num. 20:1; 27:14 **33:37** [a] Num. 20:22, 23; 21:4 **33:38** [a] Num. 20:25, 28; Deut. 10:6; 32:50

Israel had come out of the land of Egypt, on the first *day* of the fifth month. 39 Aaron *was* one hundred and twenty-three years old when he died on Mount Hor.

40 Now [a]the king of Arad, the Canaanite, who dwelt in the South in the land of Canaan, heard of the coming of the children of Israel.

41 So they departed from Mount Hor and camped at Zalmonah. 42 They departed from Zalmonah and camped at Punon. 43 They departed from Punon and [a]camped at Oboth. 44 [a]They departed from Oboth and camped at Ije Abarim, at the border of Moab. 45 They departed from Ijim[1] and camped [a]at Dibon Gad. 46 They moved from Dibon Gad and camped at [a]Almon Diblathaim. 47 They moved from Almon Diblathaim [a]and camped in the mountains of Abarim, before Nebo. 48 They departed from the mountains of Abarim and [a]camped in the plains of Moab by the Jordan, *across from* Jericho. 49 They camped by the Jordan, from Beth Jesimoth as far as the [a]Abel Acacia Grove[1] in the plains of Moab.

### INSTRUCTIONS FOR THE CONQUEST OF CANAAN

50 Now the LORD spoke to Moses in the plains of Moab by the Jordan, *across from* Jericho, saying, 51 "Speak to the children of Israel, and say to them: [a]'When you have crossed the Jordan into the land of Canaan, 52 [a]then you shall drive out all the inhabitants of the land from before you, destroy all their engraved stones, destroy all their molded images, and demolish all their high places; 53 you shall dispossess *the inhabitants of* the land and dwell in it, for I have given you the land to [a]possess. 54 And [a]you shall divide the land by lot as an inheritance among your families; to the larger you shall give a larger inheritance, and to the smaller you shall give a smaller inheritance; there everyone's *inheritance* shall be whatever falls to him by lot. You shall inherit according to the tribes of your fathers. 55 But if you do not drive out the inhabitants of the land from before you, then it shall be that those whom you let remain *shall be* [a]irritants in your eyes and thorns in your sides, and they shall harass you in the land where you dwell. 56 Moreover it shall be *that* I will do to you as I thought to do to them.' "

### THE APPOINTED BOUNDARIES OF CANAAN

34 Then the LORD spoke to Moses, saying, 2 "Command the children of Israel, and say to them: 'When you come into [a]the land of Canaan, this *is* the land that shall fall to you as an inheritance—the land of Canaan to its boundaries. 3 [a]Your southern border shall be from the Wilderness of Zin along the border of Edom; then your southern border shall extend eastward to the end of [b]the Salt Sea; 4 your border shall turn from the southern side of [a]the Ascent of Akrabbim, continue to Zin, and be on the south of [b]Kadesh Barnea; then it shall go on to [c]Hazar Addar, and continue to Azmon; 5 the border shall turn from Azmon [a]to the Brook of Egypt, and it shall end at the Sea.

6 'As for the [a]western border, you shall have the Great Sea for a border; this shall be your western border.

7 'And this shall be your northern border: From the Great Sea you shall mark out your *border* line to [a]Mount Hor; 8 from Mount Hor you shall mark out *your border* [a]to the entrance of Hamath; then the direction of the border shall be toward [b]Zedad; 9 the border shall proceed to Ziphron, and it shall end at [a]Hazar Enan. This shall be your northern border.

10 'You shall mark out your eastern border from Hazar Enan to Shepham; 11 the border shall go down from Shepham [a]to Riblah on the east side of Ain; the border shall go down and reach to the eastern side of the Sea [b]of Chinnereth; 12 the border shall go down along the Jordan, and it shall end at [a]the Salt Sea. This shall be your land with its surrounding boundaries.' "

13 Then Moses commanded the children of Israel, saying: [a]"This *is* the land which you shall inherit by lot, which the LORD has commanded to give to the nine tribes and to the half-tribe. 14 [a]For the tribe of the children of Reuben according to the house of their fathers, and the tribe of the children of Gad according to the house of their fathers, have received *their inheritance;* and the half-tribe of Manasseh has received its inheritance. 15 The two tribes and the half-tribe have received their inheritance on this side of the Jordan, *across from* Jericho eastward, toward the sunrise."

### THE LEADERS APPOINTED TO DIVIDE THE LAND

16 And the LORD spoke to Moses, saying, 17 "These *are* the names of the men who shall divide the land among you as an inheritance: [a]Eleazar the priest and Joshua the son of Nun. 18 And you shall take one [a]leader of every tribe to divide the land for the inheritance. 19 These *are* the names of the men: from the tribe of Judah, Caleb the son of Jephunneh; 20 from the tribe of the children of Simeon, Shemuel the

33:40 [a] Num. 21:1 33:43 [a] Num. 21:10 33:44 [a] Num. 21:11 33:45 [a] Num. 32:34 [1] Same as *Ije Abarim,* verse 44 33:46 [a] Jer. 48:22; Ezek. 6:14 33:47 [a] Num. 21:20; Deut. 32:49 33:48 [a] Num. 22:1; 31:12; 35:1 33:49 [a] Num. 25:1; Josh. 2:1 [1] Hebrew *Abel Shittim* 33:51 [a] Deut. 7:1, 2; 9:1; Josh. 3:17 33:52 [a] Ex. 23:24, 33; 34:13; Deut. 7:2, 5; 12:3; Judg. 2:2; Ps. 106:34–36 33:53 [a] Deut. 11:31; Josh. 21:43 33:54 [a] Num. 26:53–56 33:55 [a] Josh. 23:13; Judg. 2:3 34:2 [a] Gen. 17:8; Deut. 1:7, 8; Ps. 78:54, 55; 105:11 34:3 [a] Josh. 15:1–3; Ezek. 47:13, 19 [b] Gen. 14:3; Josh. 15:2 34:4 [a] Josh. 15:3 [b] Num. 13:26; 32:8 [c] Josh. 15:3, 4 34:5 [a] Gen. 15:18; Josh. 15:4, 47; 1 Kin. 8:65; Is. 27:12 34:6 [a] Ex. 23:31; Josh. 15:12; Ezek. 47:20 34:7 [a] Num. 33:37 34:8 [a] Num. 13:21; Josh. 13:5; 2 Kin. 14:25 [b] Ezek. 47:15 34:9 [a] Ezek. 47:17 34:11 [a] 2 Kin. 23:33; Jer. 39:5, 6 [b] Deut. 3:17; Josh. 11:2; 12:3; 13:27; 19:35; Matt. 14:34; Luke 5:1 34:12 [a] Num. 34:3 34:13 [a] Gen. 15:18; Num. 26:52–56; Deut. 11:24; Josh. 14:1–5 34:14 [a] Num. 32:33 34:17 [a] Josh. 14:1, 2; 19:51 34:18 [a] Num. 1:4, 16

son of Ammihud; 21 from the tribe of Benjamin, Elidad the son of Chislon; 22 a leader from the tribe of the children of Dan, Bukki the son of Jogli; 23 from the sons of Joseph: a leader from the tribe of the children of Manasseh, Hanniel the son of Ephod, 24 and a leader from the tribe of the children of Ephraim, Kemuel the son of Shiphtan; 25 a leader from the tribe of the children of Zebulun, Elizaphan the son of Parnach; 26 a leader from the tribe of the children of Issachar, Paltiel the son of Azzan; 27 a leader from the tribe of the children of Asher, Ahihud the son of Shelomi; 28 and a leader from the tribe of the children of Naphtali, Pedahel the son of Ammihud."

29 These *are* the ones the LORD commanded to divide the inheritance among the children of Israel in the land of Canaan.

### *CITIES FOR THE LEVITES*

**35** And the LORD spoke to Moses in [a]the plains of Moab by the Jordan *across from* Jericho, saying: 2 [a]"Command the children of Israel that they give the Levites cities to dwell in from the inheritance of their possession, and you shall *also* give the Levites [b]common-land around the cities. 3 They shall have the cities to dwell in; and their common-land shall be for their cattle, for their herds, and for all their animals. 4 The common-land of the cities which you will give the Levites *shall extend* from the wall of the city outward a thousand cubits all around. 5 And you shall measure outside the city on the east side two thousand cubits, on the south side two thousand cubits, on the west side two thousand cubits, and on the north side two thousand cubits. The city *shall be* in the middle. This shall belong to them as common-land for the cities.

6 "Now among the cities which you will give to the Levites *you shall appoint* [a]six cities of refuge, to which a manslayer may flee. And to these you shall add forty-two cities. 7 So all the cities you will give to the Levites *shall be* [a]forty-eight; these *you shall give* with their common-land. 8 And the cities which you will give *shall be* [a]from the possession of the children of Israel; [b]from the larger *tribe* you shall give many, from the smaller you shall give few. Each shall give some of its cities to the Levites, in proportion to the inheritance that each receives."

### *CITIES OF REFUGE*

*(Deut. 19:1–13; Josh. 20:1–9)*

9 Then the LORD spoke to Moses, saying, 10 "Speak to the children of Israel, and say to them: [a]'When you cross the Jordan into the land of Canaan, 11 then [a]you shall appoint cities to be cities of refuge for you, that the manslayer who kills any person accidentally may flee there. 12 [a]They shall be cities of refuge for you from the avenger, that the manslayer may not die until he stands before the congregation in judgment. 13 And of the cities which you give, you shall have [a]six cities of refuge. 14 [a]You shall appoint three cities on this side of the Jordan, and three cities you shall appoint in the land of Canaan, *which* will be cities of refuge. 15 These six cities shall be for refuge for the children of Israel, [a]for the stranger, and for the sojourner among them, that anyone who kills a person accidentally may flee there.

16 [a]'But if he strikes him with an iron implement, so that he dies, he *is* a murderer; the murderer shall surely be put to death. 17 And if he strikes him with a stone in the hand, by which one could die, and he does die, he *is* a murderer; the murderer shall surely be put to death. 18 Or *if* he strikes him with a wooden hand weapon, by which one could die, and he does die, he *is* a murderer; the murderer shall surely be put to death. 19 [a]The avenger of blood himself shall put the murderer to death; when he meets him, he shall put him to death. 20 [a]If he pushes him out of hatred or, [b]while lying in wait, hurls something at him so that he dies, 21 or in enmity he strikes him with his hand so that he dies, the one who struck *him* shall surely be put to death. He *is* a murderer. The avenger of blood shall put the murderer to death when he meets him.

22 'However, if he pushes him suddenly [a]without enmity, or throws anything at him without lying in wait, 23 or uses a stone, by which a man could die, throwing *it* at him without seeing *him,* so that he dies, while he was not his enemy or seeking his harm, 24 then [a]the congregation shall judge between the manslayer and the avenger of blood according to these judgments. 25 So the congregation shall deliver the manslayer from the hand of the avenger of blood, and the congregation shall return him to the city of refuge where he had fled, and [a]he shall remain there until the death of the high priest [b]who was anointed with the holy oil. 26 But if the manslayer at any time goes outside the limits of the city of refuge where he fled, 27 and the avenger of blood finds him outside the limits of his city of refuge, and the avenger of blood kills the manslayer, he shall not be guilty of blood, 28 because he should have remained in his city of refuge until the death of the high priest. But after the death of the high priest the manslayer may return to the land of his possession.

29 'And these *things* shall be [a]a statute of judgment to you throughout your generations in all your dwellings. 30 Whoever kills a person,

**35:1** [a] Num. 33:50 **35:2** [a] Josh. 14:3, 4; 21:2, 3 [b] Lev. 25:32–34 **35:6** [a] Deut. 4:41; Josh. 20:2, 7, 8; 21:3, 13 **35:7** [a] Josh. 21:41 **35:8** [a] Josh. 21:3 [b] Num. 26:54; 33:54 **35:10** [a] Deut. 19:2; Josh. 20:1–9 **35:11** [a] Ex. 21:13; Num. 35:22–25; Deut. 19:1–13 **35:12** [a] Deut. 19:6; Josh. 20:3, 5, 6 **35:13** [a] Num. 35:6 **35:14** [a] Deut. 4:41; Josh. 20:8 **35:15** [a] Num. 15:16 **35:16** [a] Ex. 21:12, 14; Lev. 24:17; Deut. 19:11, 12 **35:19** [a] Num. 35:21, 24, 27; Deut. 19:6, 12 **35:20** [a] Gen. 4:8; 2 Sam. 3:27; 20:10; 1 Kin. 2:31, 32 [b] Ex. 21:14; Deut. 19:11, 12 **35:22** [a] Ex. 21:13 **35:24** [a] Num. 35:12; Josh. 20:6 **35:25** [a] Josh. 20:6 [b] Ex. 29:7; Lev. 4:3; 21:10 **35:29** [a] Num. 27:11

the murderer shall be put to death on the [a]tes-
timony of witnesses; but one witness is not *suf-
ficient* testimony against a person for the death
*penalty.* 31 Moreover you shall take no ransom
for the life of a murderer who *is* guilty of death,
but he shall surely be put to death. 32 And you
shall take no ransom for him who has fled to
his city of refuge, that he may return to dwell
in the land before the death of the priest. 33 So
you shall not pollute the land where you *are;* for
blood [a]defiles the land, and no atonement can
be made for the land, for the blood that is shed
on it, except [b]by the blood of him who shed it.
34 Therefore [a]do not defile the land which you
inhabit, in the midst of which I dwell; for [b]I the
LORD dwell among the children of Israel.' "

### *MARRIAGE OF FEMALE HEIRS*

**36** Now the chief fathers of the families of
the [a]children of Gilead the son of Machir,
the son of Manasseh, of the families of the sons
of Joseph, came near and [b]spoke before Moses
and before the leaders, the chief fathers of the
children of Israel. 2 And they said: [a]"The LORD
commanded my lord *Moses* to give the land as
an inheritance by lot to the children of Israel,
and [b]my lord was commanded by the LORD to
give the inheritance of our brother Zelophehad
to his daughters. 3 Now if they are married to any
of the sons of the *other* tribes of the children
of Israel, then their inheritance will be [a]taken
from the inheritance of our fathers, and it will be
added to the inheritance of the tribe into which
they marry; so it will be taken from the lot of
our inheritance. 4 And when [a]the Jubilee of the
children of Israel comes, then their inheritance
will be added to the inheritance of the tribe into
which they marry; so their inheritance will be
taken away from the inheritance of the tribe of
our fathers."

5 Then Moses commanded the children of
Israel according to the word of the LORD, saying:
[a]"What the tribe of the sons of Joseph speaks is
right. 6 This *is* what the LORD commands con-
cerning the daughters of Zelophehad, saying,
'Let them marry whom they think best, [a]but
they may marry only within the family of their
father's tribe.' 7 So the inheritance of the children
of Israel shall not change hands from tribe to
tribe, for every one of the children of Israel
shall [a]keep the inheritance of the tribe of his
fathers. 8 And [a]every daughter who possesses
an inheritance in any tribe of the children of
Israel shall be the wife of one of the family of
her father's tribe, so that the children of Israel
each may possess the inheritance of his fathers.
9 Thus no inheritance shall change hands from
*one* tribe to another, but every tribe of the chil-
dren of Israel shall keep its own inheritance."

10 Just as the LORD commanded Moses, so
did the daughters of Zelophehad; 11 [a]for Mahlah,
Tirzah, Hoglah, Milcah, and Noah, the daughters
of Zelophehad, were married to the sons of their
father's brothers. 12 They were married into the
families of the children of Manasseh the son of
Joseph, and their inheritance remained in the
tribe of their father's family.

13 These *are* the commandments and the
judgments which the LORD commanded the
children of Israel by the hand of Moses [a]in
the plains of Moab by the Jordan, *across from*
Jericho.

35:30 [a] Deut. 17:6; 19:15; Matt. 18:16; John 7:51; 8:17, 18; 2 Cor. 13:1; Heb. 10:28 35:33 [a] Deut. 21:7, 8; Ps. 106:38 [b] Gen. 9:6 35:34 [a] Lev. 18:24, 25; Deut. 21:23 [b] Ex. 29:45, 46 36:1 [a] Num. 26:29 [b] Num. 27:1–11 36:2 [a] Num. 26:55; 33:54; Josh. 17:4 [b] Num. 27:1, 5–7 36:3 [a] Num. 27:4 36:4 [a] Lev. 25:10 36:5 [a] Num. 27:7 36:6 [a] Num. 36:11, 12 36:7 [a] 1 Kin. 21:3 36:8 [a] 1 Chr. 23:22 36:11 [a] Num. 26:33; 27:1 36:13 [a] Num. 26:3; 33:50

*The Fifth Book of Moses Called*

# DEUTERONOMY

| AUTHOR | KEY VERSES | READING TIME |
|---|---|---|
| Moses | Deuteronomy 32:45–47 | 2 hours 46 minutes |

The Book of Deuteronomy records a series of farewell messages Moses, Israel's 120-year-old leader, gave to his people. In his final days, Moses addressed the second generation of Hebrews—those who had survived the forty years of wilderness wandering—destined to possess the Land of Promise. While Moses spoke his parting words, he also wrote them so those who were about to enter the land and their future generations would remember them. Like Leviticus, Deuteronomy contains a vast amount of legal detail, but its emphasis is on the layperson rather than the priest. Deuteronomy means "second law," but it is not a different law. Instead, this giving of the law is a restatement of the original law God had given on Mount Sinai. In sharing the law again, Moses reminded the new generation of their need to obey God, a lesson they could have learned from the sad failure of their parents.

**Occasion:** Moses wrote the Book of Deuteronomy just before the end of his life in about 1405 BC to record the series of farewell speeches he gave to the people of Israel.

**Main Point:** God's people are to be faithful and trust Him as He guides them into the Land of Promise.

**Big Ideas:** God is a good God, always caring for His people. We always are to remember what God has done for us. When we need courage, we can look to God.

## OUTLINE:

I. Moses's First Speech: What God Has Done for Israel (chs. 1–4)

II. Moses's Second Speech: What God Expects of Israel (chs. 5–28)

III. Moses's Third Speech: What God Will Do for Israel (chs. 29–30)

IV. Moses's Song (chs. 31–32)

V. Moses's Blessing and Death (chs. 33–34)

**c. 1446 BC**
Moses leads the Israelites out of Egypt

**c. 1445 BC**
The Law is given on Mount Sinai

**c. 1446–1406 BC**
Forty years of wilderness wandering

**c. 1406 BC**
Moses presents the Law to the second generation

**c. 1406 BC**
**Deuteronomy written**

**c. 1405–1400 BC**
The conquest of Canaan

**c. 1405–1380 BC**
Joshua leads the Israelites

**c. 1380 BC**
First canal built linking the Nile and the Red Sea

**c. 1360 BC**
Fire destroys royal archives in the palace of Canaanite city of Ugarit

### *THE PREVIOUS COMMAND TO ENTER CANAAN*

**1** These *are* the words which Moses spoke to all Israel [a]on this side of the Jordan in the wilderness, in the plain[1] opposite Suph,[2] between Paran, Tophel, Laban, Hazeroth, and Dizahab. 2 *It is* eleven days' *journey* from Horeb by way of Mount Seir [a]to Kadesh Barnea. 3 Now it came to pass [a]in the fortieth year, in the eleventh month, on the first *day* of the month, *that* Moses spoke to the children of Israel according to all that the LORD had given him as commandments to them, 4 [a]after he had killed Sihon king of the Amorites, who dwelt in Heshbon, and Og king of Bashan, who dwelt at Ashtaroth [b]in[1] Edrei.

5 On this side of the Jordan in the land of Moab, Moses began to explain this law, saying, 6 "The LORD our God spoke to us [a]in Horeb, saying: 'You have dwelt long [b]enough at this mountain. 7 Turn and take your journey, and go to the mountains of the Amorites, to all the neighboring *places* in the plain,[1] in the mountains and in the lowland, in the South and on the seacoast, to the land of the Canaanites and to Lebanon, as far as the great river, the River Euphrates. 8 See, I have set the land before you; go in and possess the land which the LORD swore to your fathers—to [a]Abraham, Isaac, and Jacob—to give to them and their descendants after them.'

### *TRIBAL LEADERS APPOINTED*

*(Ex. 18:13–27)*

9 "And [a]I spoke to you at that time, saying: 'I alone am not able to bear you. 10 The LORD your God has multiplied you, [a]and here you *are* today, as the stars of heaven in multitude. 11 [a]May the LORD God of your fathers make you a thousand times more numerous than you are, and bless you [b]as He has promised you! 12 [a]How can I alone bear your problems and your burdens and your complaints? 13 Choose wise, understanding, and knowledgeable men from among your tribes, and I will make them heads over you.' 14 And you answered me and said, 'The thing which you have told *us* to do *is* good.' 15 So I took [a]the heads of your tribes, wise and knowledgeable men, and made them heads over you, leaders of thousands, leaders of hundreds, leaders of fifties, leaders of tens, and officers for your tribes.

16 "Then I commanded your judges at that time, saying, 'Hear *the cases* between your brethren, and [a]judge righteously between a man and his [b]brother or the stranger who is with him. 17 [a]You shall not show partiality in judgment; you shall hear the small as well as the great; you shall not be afraid in any man's presence, for [b]the judgment *is* God's. The case that is too hard for you, [c]bring to me, and I will hear it.' 18 And I commanded you at that time all the things which you should do.

**1:16** In most places in the ancient Near East, a **stranger** (foreigner) had no legal rights. The land of the Israelites, however, was different. God's people were expected to treat strangers just as they would treat each other. They were to show that God's law applied to everyone.

### *ISRAEL'S REFUSAL TO ENTER THE LAND*

*(Num. 13:1–33)*

19 "So we departed from Horeb, [a]and went through all that great and terrible wilderness which you saw on the way to the mountains of the Amorites, as the LORD our God had commanded us. Then [b]we came to Kadesh Barnea. 20 And I said to you, 'You have come to the mountains of the Amorites, which the LORD our God is giving us. 21 Look, the LORD your God has set the land before you; go up *and* possess *it,* as the LORD God of your fathers has spoken to you; [a]do not fear or be discouraged.'

22 "And every one of you came near to me and said, 'Let us send men before us, and let them search out the land for us, and bring back word to us of the way by which we should go up, and of the cities into which we shall come.'

23 "The plan pleased me well; so [a]I took twelve of your men, one man from *each* tribe. 24 [a]And they departed and went up into the mountains, and came to the Valley of Eshcol, and spied it out. 25 They also took *some* of the fruit of the land in their hands and brought *it* down to us; and they brought back word to us, saying, '*It is* a [a]good land which the LORD our God is giving us.'

26 [a]"Nevertheless you would not go up, but rebelled against the command of the LORD your God; 27 and you [a]complained in your tents, and said, 'Because the LORD [b]hates us, He has brought us out of the land of Egypt to deliver us into the hand of the Amorites, to destroy us. 28 Where can we go up? Our brethren have discouraged our hearts, saying, [a]"The people *are* greater and taller than we; the cities *are* great and fortified up to heaven; moreover we have seen the sons of the [b]Anakim there." '

29 "Then I said to you, 'Do not be terrified, [a]or afraid of them. 30 [a]The LORD your God, who goes before you, He will fight for you, according

**1:1** [a] Deut. 4:44–46; Josh. 9:1, 10 [1] Hebrew *arabah* [2] One manuscript of the Septuagint, also Targum and Vulgate, read *Red Sea.* **1:2** [a] Num. 13:26; 32:8; Deut. 9:23 **1:3** [a] Num. 33:38 **1:4** [a] Num. 21:23, 24, 33–35; Deut. 2:26–35; Josh. 13:10; Neh. 9:22 [b] Josh. 13:12 [1] Septuagint, Syriac, and Vulgate read *and* (compare Joshua 12:4). **1:6** [a] Ex. 3:1, 12 [b] Ex. 19:1, 2 **1:7** [1] Hebrew *arabah* **1:8** [a] Gen. 12:7; 15:5; 22:17; 26:3; 28:13 **1:9** [a] Ex. 18:18, 24 **1:10** [a] Gen. 15:5; 22:17 **1:11** [a] 2 Sam. 24:3 [b] Gen. 15:5 **1:12** [a] 1 Kin. 3:8, 9 **1:15** [a] Ex. 18:25 **1:16** [a] Deut. 16:18 [b] Lev. 24:22 **1:17** [a] Prov. 24:23–26 [b] 2 Chr. 19:6 [c] Ex. 18:22, 26 **1:19** [a] Deut. 2:7; 8:15; 32:10 [b] Num. 13:26 **1:21** [a] Josh. 1:6, 9 **1:23** [a] Num. 13:2, 3 **1:24** [a] Num. 13:21–25 **1:25** [a] Num. 13:27 **1:26** [a] Num. 14:1–4 **1:27** [a] Ps. 106:25 [b] Deut. 9:28 **1:28** [a] Deut. 9:1, 2 [b] Num. 13:28 **1:29** [a] Num. 14:9 **1:30** [a] Ex. 14:14

to all He did for you in Egypt before your eyes,
31 and in the wilderness where you saw how the
LORD your God carried you, as a [a]man carries
his son, in all the way that you went until you
came to this place.' 32 Yet, for all that, [a]you did not
believe the LORD your God, 33 [a]who went in the
way before you [b]to search out a place for you to
pitch your tents, to show you the way you should
go, in the fire by night and in the cloud by day.

### *THE PENALTY FOR ISRAEL'S REBELLION*

*(Num. 14:20–45)*

34 "And the LORD heard the sound of your
words, and was angry, [a]and took an oath, saying,
35 [a]'Surely not one of these men of this evil genera-
tion shall see that good land of which I swore to give
to your fathers, 36 [a]except Caleb the son of Jephun-
neh; he shall see it, and to him and his children I
am giving the land on which he walked, because
[b]he wholly followed the LORD.' 37 [a]The LORD was
also angry with me for your sakes, saying, 'Even you
shall not go in there. 38 [a]Joshua the son of Nun, [b]who
stands before you, he shall go in there. [c]Encourage
him, for he shall cause Israel to inherit it.

39 [a]'Moreover your little ones and your chil-
dren, who [b]you say will be victims, who today [c]have
no knowledge of good and evil, they shall go in
there; to them I will give it, and they shall possess
it. 40 [a]But *as for* you, turn and take your journey
into the wilderness by the Way of the Red Sea.'

41 "Then you answered and said to me, [a]'We
have sinned against the LORD; we will go up and
fight, just as the LORD our God commanded us.'
And when everyone of you had girded on his
weapons of war, you were ready to go up into
the mountain.

42 "And the LORD said to me, 'Tell them, [a]"Do
not go up nor fight, for I *am* not among you; lest
you be defeated before your enemies." ' 43 So I
spoke to you; yet you would not listen, but [a]re-
belled against the command of the LORD, and [b]pre-
sumptuously went up into the mountain. 44 And
the Amorites who dwelt in that mountain came
out against you and chased you [a]as bees do, and
drove you back from Seir to Hormah. 45 Then you
returned and wept before the LORD, but the LORD
would not listen to your voice nor give ear to you.

46 [a]"So you remained in Kadesh many days,
according to the days that you spent *there.*

### *THE DESERT YEARS*

2 "Then we turned and [a]journeyed into the
wilderness of the Way of the Red Sea, [b]as
the LORD spoke to me, and we skirted Mount
Seir for many days.

2 "And the LORD spoke to me, saying: 3 'You
have skirted this mountain [a]long enough; turn
northward. 4 And command the people, saying,
[a]"You *are about to* pass through the territory of
[b]your brethren, the descendants of Esau, who
live in Seir; and they will be afraid of you. There-
fore watch yourselves carefully. 5 Do not meddle
with them, for I will not give you *any* of their
land, no, not so much as one footstep, [a]because
I have given Mount Seir to Esau *as* a possession.
6 You shall buy food from them with money, that
you may eat; and you shall also buy water from
them with money, that you may drink.

7 "For the LORD your God has blessed you
in all the work of your hand. He knows your
trudging through this great wilderness. [a]These
forty years the LORD your God *has been* with you;
you have lacked nothing." '

8 "And when we passed beyond our brethren,
the descendants of Esau who dwell in Seir, away
from the road of the plain, away from [a]Elath and
Ezion Geber, we [b]turned and passed by way of
the Wilderness of Moab. 9 Then the LORD said
to me, 'Do not harass Moab, nor contend with
them in battle, for I will not give you *any* of their
land *as* a possession, because I have given [a]Ar
to [b]the descendants of Lot *as* a possession.' "

10 [a](The Emim had dwelt there in times past,
a people as great and numerous and tall as [b]the
Anakim. 11 They were also regarded as giants,[1] like
the Anakim, but the Moabites call them Emim.
12 [a]The Horites formerly dwelt in Seir, but the
descendants of Esau dispossessed them and
destroyed them from before them, and dwelt
in their place, just as Israel did to the land of
their possession which the LORD gave them.)

13 " 'Now rise and cross over [a]the Valley of
the Zered.' So we crossed over the Valley of the
Zered. 14 And the time we took to come [a]from
Kadesh Barnea until we crossed over the Valley
of the Zered *was* thirty-eight years, [b]until all the
generation of the men of war was consumed
from the midst of the camp, [c]just as the LORD
had sworn to them. 15 For indeed the hand of the
LORD was against them, to destroy them from
the midst of the camp until they were consumed.

16 "So it was, when all the men of war had
finally perished from among the people, 17 that
the LORD spoke to me, saying: 18 'This day you are
to cross over at Ar, the boundary of Moab. 19 And
*when* you come near the people of Ammon, do
not harass them or meddle with them, for I will
not give you *any* of the land of the people of
Ammon *as* a possession, because I have given
it to [a]the descendants of Lot *as* a possession.' "

**1:31** [a] Is. 46:3, 4; 63:9 **1:32** [a] Jude 5 **1:33** [a] Ex. 13:21 [b] Num. 10:33 **1:34** [a] Deut. 2:14, 15 **1:35** [a] Num. 14:22, 23 **1:36** [a] [Josh. 14:9] [b] Num. 32:11, 12 **1:37** [a] Deut. 3:26; 4:21; 34:4 **1:38** [a] Num. 14:30 [b] 1 Sam. 16:22 [c] Deut. 31:7, 23 **1:39** [a] Num. 14:31 [b] Num. 14:3 [c] Is. 7:15, 16 **1:40** [a] Num. 14:25 **1:41** [a] Num. 14:40 **1:42** [a] Num. 14:41–43 **1:43** [a] Num. 14:44 [b] Deut. 17:12, 13 **1:44** [a] Num. 14:45; Ps. 118:12 **1:46** [a] Num. 13:25; 20:1, 22; Deut. 2:7, 14 **2:1** [a] Deut. 1:40 [b] Num. 14:25 **2:3** [a] Deut. 2:7, 14 **2:4** [a] Num. 20:14–21 [b] Deut. 23:7 **2:5** [a] Gen. 36:8; Josh. 24:4 **2:7** [a] Deut. 8:2–4; [Matt. 6:8, 32] **2:8** [a] Judg. 11:18; 1 Kin. 9:26 [b] Num. 21:4 **2:9** [a] Num. 21:15, 28; Deut. 2:18, 29 [b] Gen. 19:36–38 **2:10** [a] Gen. 14:5 [b] Num. 13:22, 33; Deut. 9:2 **2:11** [1] Hebrew *rephaim* **2:12** [a] Gen. 14:6; 36:20; Deut. 2:22 **2:13** [a] Num. 21:12 **2:14** [a] Num. 13:26 [b] Num. 14:33; 26:64; Deut. 1:34, 35 [c] Num. 14:35; Ezek. 20:15 **2:19** [a] Gen. 19:38; Num. 21:24

20 (That was also regarded as a land of gi-
ants;[1] giants formerly dwelt there. But the Am-
monites call them [a]Zamzummim, 21 [a]a people
as great and numerous and tall as the Anakim.
But the LORD destroyed them before them, and
they dispossessed them and dwelt in their place,
22 just as He had done for the descendants of
Esau, [a]who dwelt in Seir, when He destroyed [b]the
Horites from before them. They dispossessed
them and dwelt in their place, even to this day.
23 And [a]the Avim, who dwelt in villages as far as
Gaza—[b]the Caphtorim, who came from Caph-
tor, destroyed them and dwelt in their place.)
24 " 'Rise, take your journey, and [a]cross over
the River Arnon. Look, I have given into your
hand [b]Sihon the Amorite, king of Heshbon, and
his land. Begin to possess *it,* and engage him in
battle. 25 [a]This day I will begin to put the dread
and fear of you upon the nations under the whole
heaven, who shall hear the report of you, and
shall [b]tremble and be in anguish because of you.'

### KING SIHON DEFEATED
*(Num. 21:21–32)*

26 "And I [a]sent messengers from the Wilder-
ness of Kedemoth to Sihon king of Heshbon,
[b]with words of peace, saying, 27 [a]'Let me pass
through your land; I will keep strictly to the
road, and I will turn neither to the right nor to
the left. 28 You shall sell me food for money, that
I may eat, and give me water for money, that I
may drink; [a]only let me pass through on foot,
29 [a]just as the descendants of Esau who dwell in
Seir and the Moabites who dwell in Ar did for
me, until I cross the Jordan to the land which
the LORD our God is giving us.'
30 [a]"But Sihon king of Heshbon would not
let us pass through, for [b]the LORD your God
[c]hardened his spirit and made his heart obsti-
nate, that He might deliver him into your hand,
as *it is* this day.
31 "And the LORD said to me, 'See, I have begun
to [a]give Sihon and his land over to you. Begin to
possess *it,* that you may inherit his land.' 32 [a]Then
Sihon and all his people came out against us to
fight at Jahaz. 33 And [a]the LORD our God delivered
him over to us; so [b]we defeated him, his sons, and
all his people. 34 We took all his cities at that time,
and we [a]utterly destroyed the men, women, and
little ones of every city; we left none remaining.
35 We took only the livestock as plunder for our-
selves, with the spoil of the cities which we took.
36 [a]From Aroer, which *is* on the bank of the River
Arnon, and *from* [b]the city that *is* in the ravine, as
far as Gilead, there was not one city too strong for
us; [c]the LORD our God delivered all to us. 37 Only
you did not go near the land of the people of
Ammon—anywhere along the River [a]Jabbok, or
to the cities of the mountains, or [b]wherever the
LORD our God had forbidden us.

### KING OG DEFEATED
*(Num. 21:33–35)*

3 "Then we turned and went up the road to
Bashan; and [a]Og king of Bashan came out
against us, he and all his people, to battle [b]at
Edrei. 2 And the LORD said to me, 'Do not fear
him, for I have delivered him and all his people
and his land into your hand; you shall do to him
as you did to [a]Sihon king of the Amorites, who
dwelt at Heshbon.'
3 "So the LORD our God also delivered into
our hands Og king of Bashan, with all his people,
and we attacked him until he had no survivors
remaining. 4 And we took all his cities at that time;
there was not a city which we did not take from
them: sixty cities, [a]all the region of Argob, the
kingdom of Og in Bashan. 5 All these cities *were*
fortified with high walls, gates, and bars, besides a
great many rural towns. 6 And we utterly destroyed
them, as we did to Sihon king [a]of Heshbon, utterly
destroying the men, women, and children of
every city. 7 But all the livestock and the spoil of
the cities we took as booty for ourselves.
8 "And at that time we took the [a]land from
the hand of the two kings of the Amorites who
*were* on this side of the Jordan, from the River
Arnon to Mount [b]Hermon 9 (the Sidonians call
[a]Hermon Sirion, and the Amorites call it Senir),
10 [a]all the cities of the plain, all Gilead, and [b]all
Bashan, as far as Salcah and Edrei, cities of the
kingdom of Og in Bashan.
11 [a]"For only Og king of Bashan remained of the
remnant of [b]the giants.[1] Indeed his bedstead *was*
an iron bedstead. (*Is* it not in [c]Rabbah of the peo-
ple of Ammon?) Nine cubits *is* its length and four
cubits its width, according to the standard cubit.

### THE LAND EAST OF THE JORDAN DIVIDED
*(Num. 32:25–41)*

12 "And this [a]land, *which* we possessed at that
time, [b]from Aroer, which *is* by the River Arnon,
and half the mountains of Gilead and [c]its cities,
I gave to the Reubenites and the Gadites. 13 [a]The
rest of Gilead, and all Bashan, the kingdom of Og,
I gave to half the tribe of Manasseh. (All the region
of Argob, with all Bashan, was called the land of
the giants.[1] 14 [a]Jair the son of Manasseh took all

**2:20** [a] Gen. 14:5 [1] Hebrew *rephaim* **2:21** [a] Deut. 2:10 **2:22** [a] Gen. 36:8; Deut. 2:5 [b] Gen. 14:6; 36:20–30 **2:23** [a] Josh. 13:3 [b] Gen. 10:14; 1 Chr. 1:12; Jer. 47:4; Amos 9:7 **2:24** [a] Num. 21:13, 14; Judg. 11:18 [b] Deut. 1:4 **2:25** [a] Ex. 23:27; Deut. 11:25; Josh. 2:9 [b] Ex. 15:14–16 **2:26** [a] Num. 21:21–32; Deut. 1:4; Judg. 11:19–21 [b] Deut. 20:10 **2:27** [a] Num. 21:21, 22; Judg. 11:19 **2:28** [a] Num. 20:19 **2:29** [a] Num. 20:18; Deut. 23:3, 4; Judg. 11:17 **2:30** [a] Num. 21:23 [b] Josh. 11:20 [c] Ex. 4:21 **2:31** [a] Deut. 1:3, 8 **2:32** [a] Num. 21:23 **2:33** [a] Ex. 23:31; Deut. 7:2 [b] Num. 21:24 **2:34** [a] Lev. 27:28 **2:36** [a] Deut. 3:12; 4:48; Josh. 13:9 [b] Josh. 13:9, 16 [c] Ps. 44:3 **2:37** [a] Gen. 32:22; Num. 21:24; Deut. 3:16 [b] Deut. 2:5, 9, 19 **3:1** [a] Num. 21:33–35; Deut. 29:7 [b] Deut. 1:4 **3:2** [a] Num. 21:34; Josh. 13:21 **3:4** [a] Deut. 3:13, 14 **3:6** [a] Deut. 2:24, 34, 35 **3:8** [a] Josh. 12:6; 13:8–12 [b] 1 Chr. 5:23 **3:9** [a] 1 Chr. 5:23 **3:10** [a] Deut. 4:49 [b] Josh. 12:5; 13:11 **3:11** [a] Amos 2:9 [b] Gen. 14:5; Deut. 2:11, 20 [c] 2 Sam. 12:26; Jer. 49:2; Ezek. 21:20 [1] Hebrew *rephaim* **3:12** [a] Num. 32:33; Josh. 12:6; 13:8–12 [b] Deut. 2:36; Josh. 12:2 [c] Num. 34:14 **3:13** [a] Josh. 13:29–31; 17:1 [1] Hebrew *rephaim* **3:14** [a] 1 Chr. 2:22

the region of Argob, [b]as far as the border of the Geshurites and the Maachathites, and [c]called Bashan after his own name, Havoth Jair,[1] to this day.)

15 “Also I gave [a]Gilead to Machir. 16 And to the Reubenites [a]and the Gadites I gave from Gilead as far as the River Arnon, the middle of the river as *the* border, as far as the River Jabbok, [b]the border of the people of Ammon; 17 the plain also, with the Jordan as *the* border, from Chinnereth [a]as far as the east side of the Sea of the Arabah [b](the Salt Sea), below the slopes of Pisgah.

18 “Then I commanded you at that time, saying: ‘The LORD your God has given you this land to possess. [a]All you men of valor shall cross over armed before your brethren, the children of Israel. 19 But your wives, your little ones, and your livestock (I know that you have much livestock) shall stay in your cities which I have given you, 20 until the LORD has given [a]rest to your brethren as to you, and they also possess the land which the LORD your God is giving them beyond the Jordan. Then each of you may [b]return to his possession which I have given you.’

21 “And [a]I commanded Joshua at that time, saying, ‘Your eyes have seen all that the LORD your God has done to these two kings; so will the LORD do to all the kingdoms through which you pass. 22 You must not fear them, for [a]the LORD your God Himself fights for you.’

## MOSES FORBIDDEN TO ENTER THE LAND

23 “Then [a]I pleaded with the LORD at that time, saying: 24 ‘O Lord GOD, You have begun to show Your servant [a]Your greatness and Your mighty hand, for [b]what god *is there* in heaven or on earth who can do *anything* like Your works and Your mighty *deeds?* 25 I pray, let me cross over and see [a]the good land beyond the Jordan, those pleasant mountains, and Lebanon.’

26 “But the LORD [a]was angry with me on your account, and would not listen to me. So the LORD said to me: ‘Enough of that! Speak no more to Me of this matter. 27 [a]Go up to the top of Pisgah, and lift your eyes toward the west, the north, the south, and the east; behold *it* with your eyes, for you shall not cross over this Jordan. 28 But [a]command Joshua, and encourage him and strengthen him; for he shall go over before this people, and he shall cause them to inherit the land which you will see.’

29 “So we stayed in [a]the valley opposite Beth Peor.

## MOSES COMMANDS OBEDIENCE

4 “Now, O Israel, listen to [a]the statutes and the judgments which I teach you to observe, that you may live, and go in and possess the land which the LORD God of your fathers is giving you. 2 [a]You shall not add to the word which I command you, nor take from it, that you may keep the commandments of the LORD your God which I command you. 3 Your eyes have seen what the LORD did at [a]Baal Peor; for the LORD your God has destroyed from among you all the men who followed Baal of Peor. 4 But you who held fast to the LORD your God *are* alive today, every one of you.

5 “Surely I have taught you statutes and judgments, just as the LORD my God commanded me, that you should act according *to them* in the land which you go to possess. 6 Therefore be careful to observe *them;* for this *is* [a]your wisdom and your understanding in the sight of the peoples who will hear all these statutes, and say, ‘Surely this great nation *is* a wise and understanding people.’

7 “For [a]what great nation *is there* that has [b]God *so* near to it, as the LORD our God *is* to us, for whatever *reason* we may call upon Him? 8 And what great nation *is there* that has *such* statutes and righteous judgments as are in all this law which I set before you this day? 9 Only take heed to yourself, and diligently [a]keep yourself, lest you [b]forget the things your eyes have seen, and lest they depart from your heart all the days of your life. And [c]teach them to your children and your grandchildren, 10 *especially concerning* [a]the day you stood before the LORD your God in Horeb, when the LORD said to me, ‘Gather the people to Me, and I will let them hear My words, that they may learn to fear Me all the days they live on the earth, and *that* they may teach their children.’

11 “Then you came near and stood at the foot of the mountain, and the mountain burned with fire to the midst of heaven, with darkness, cloud, and thick darkness. 12 [a]And the LORD spoke to you out of the midst of the fire. You heard the sound of the words, but saw no form; [b]*you* only *heard* a voice. 13 [a]So He declared to you His covenant which He commanded you to perform, [b]the Ten Commandments; and [c]He wrote them on two tablets of stone. 14 And [a]the LORD commanded me at that time to teach you statutes and judgments, that you might observe them in the land which you cross over to possess.

## BEWARE OF IDOLATRY

15 [a]“Take careful heed to yourselves, for you saw no [b]form when the LORD spoke to you at Horeb out of the midst of the fire, 16 lest you [a]act corruptly and [b]make for yourselves a carved image in the form of any figure: [c]the likeness of male or female, 17 the likeness of any animal that *is* on the earth or the likeness of any winged bird that flies in the air, 18 the likeness of anything that creeps on the ground or the likeness of any fish

3:14 [b]Josh. 13:13 [c]Num. 32:41 [1]Literally *Towns of Jair* 3:15 [a]Num. 32:39, 40 3:16 [a]2 Sam. 24:5 [b]Num. 21:24 3:17 [a]Num. 34:11, 12 [b]Gen. 14:3 3:18 [a]Num. 32:20 3:20 [a]Deut. 12:9, 10 [b]Josh. 22:4 3:21 [a][Num. 27:22, 23] 3:22 [a]Ex. 14:14 3:23 [a][2 Cor. 12:8, 9] 3:24 [a]Deut. 5:24; 11:2 [b]2 Sam. 7:22 3:25 [a]Deut. 4:22 3:26 [a]Num. 20:12; 27:14 3:27 [a]Num. 23:14; 27:12 3:28 [a]Num. 27:18, 23 3:29 [a]Deut. 4:46; 34:6 4:1 [a][Rom. 10:5] 4:2 [a]Prov. 30:6 4:3 [a]Num. 25:1–9 4:6 [a][2 Tim. 3:15] 4:7 [a][2 Sam. 7:23] [b][Is. 55:6] 4:9 [a]Prov. 4:23 [b]Deut. 29:2–8 [c]Gen. 18:19 4:10 [a]Ex. 19:9, 16, 17 4:12 [a]Deut. 5:4, 22 [b]1 Kin. 19:11–18 4:13 [a]Deut. 9:9, 11 [b]Ex. 34:28 [c]Ex. 24:12 4:14 [a]Ex. 21:1 4:15 [a]Josh. 23:11 [b]Is. 40:18 4:16 [a]Deut. 9:12; 31:29 [b]Ex. 20:4, 5 [c]Rom. 1:23

that *is* in the water beneath the earth. 19 And *take heed,* lest you [a]lift your eyes to heaven, and *when* you see the sun, the moon, and the stars, [b]all the host of heaven, you feel driven to [c]worship them and serve them, which the LORD your God has given to all the peoples under the whole heaven as a heritage. 20 But the LORD has taken you and [a]brought you out of the iron furnace, out of Egypt, to be [b]His people, an inheritance, as you are this day. 21 Furthermore [a]the LORD was angry with me for your sakes, and swore that [b]I would not cross over the Jordan, and that I would not enter the good land which the LORD your God is giving you as an inheritance. 22 But [a]I must die in this land, [b]I must not cross over the Jordan; but you shall cross over and possess [c]that good land. 23 Take heed to yourselves, lest you forget the covenant of the LORD your God which He made with you, [a]and make for yourselves a carved image in the form of anything which the LORD your God has forbidden you. 24 For [a]the LORD your God *is* a consuming fire, [b]a jealous God.

25 "When you beget children and grandchildren and have grown old in the land, and act corruptly and make a carved image in the form of anything, and [a]do evil in the sight of the LORD your God to provoke Him to anger, 26 [a]I call heaven and earth to witness against you this day, that you will soon utterly perish from the land which you cross over the Jordan to possess; you will not prolong *your* days in it, but will be utterly destroyed. 27 And the LORD [a]will scatter you among the peoples, and you will be left few in number among the nations where the LORD will drive you. 28 And [a]there you will serve gods, the work of men's hands, wood and stone, [b]which neither see nor hear nor eat nor smell. 29 [a]But from there you will seek the LORD your God, and you will find *Him* if you seek Him with all your heart and with all your soul. 30 When you are in distress, and all these things come upon you in the [a]latter days, when you [b]turn to the LORD your God and obey His voice 31 (for the LORD your God *is* a merciful God), He will not forsake you nor [a]destroy you, nor forget the covenant of your fathers which He swore to them.

32 "For [a]ask now concerning the days that are past, which were before you, since the day that God created man on the earth, and *ask* [b]from one end of heaven to the other, whether *any* great *thing* like this has happened, or *anything* like it has been heard. 33 [a]Did *any* people *ever* hear the voice of God speaking out of the midst of the fire, as you have heard, and live? 34 Or did God *ever* try to go *and* take for Himself a nation from the midst of *another* nation, [a]by trials, [b]by signs, by wonders, by war, [c]by a mighty hand and [d]an outstretched arm, [e]and by great terrors, according to all that the LORD your God did for you in Egypt before your eyes? 35 To you it was shown, that you might know that the LORD Himself *is* God; [a]*there is* none other besides Him.

**4:19** [a] Deut. 17:3 [b] 2 Kin. 21:3 [c] [Rom. 1:25] **4:20** [a] Jer. 11:4 [b] Deut. 7:6; 27:9 **4:21** [a] Num. 20:12 [b] Num. 27:13, 14 **4:22** [a] 2 Pet. 1:13–15 [b] Deut. 3:27 [c] Deut. 3:25 **4:23** [a] Deut. 4:16 **4:24** [a] Deut. 9:3 [b] Ex. 20:5; 34:14 **4:25** [a] 2 Kin. 17:17 **4:26** [a] Deut. 30:18, 19 **4:27** [a] Deut. 28:62 **4:28** [a] Jer. 16:13 [b] Ps. 115:4–7; 135:15–17 **4:29** [a] [2 Chr. 15:4] **4:30** [a] Hos. 3:5 [b] Joel 2:12 **4:31** [a] Jer. 30:11 **4:32** [a] Job 8:8 [b] Matt. 24:31 **4:33** [a] Deut. 5:24–26 **4:34** [a] Deut. 7:19 [b] Ex. 7:3 [c] Ex. 13:3 [d] Ex. 6:6 [e] Deut. 26:8 **4:35** [a] Mark 12:32

KNOW THE TRUTH

## THE DOCTRINE OF GOD

### PART 1: OVERVIEW OF THE DOCTRINE OF GOD

**4:24–40** The most important question we can ask is, "Who is God?" The answer shapes all of life's meaning and purpose. As Moses prepared the people for his approaching death and their upcoming journey into the Promise Land, he gave them a theology lesson. *Theology* means to study and explain God. If the nation of Israel wanted to thrive in the Promise Land, they would have to obey God. And if they were to obey Him, they first would have to know Him. The same is true of us; theology is critical.

Perhaps the most essential quality we must understand about God is, "the LORD Himself is God in heaven above and on the earth beneath; there is no other" (v. 39). The God who reveals Himself in the Bible is the *only* true God. There is no other but Him. He is Creator of all. From the stars above you to the cells within you, God created and sustains it all (see Gen. 1:1; Ps. 139:13–16). In addition to being the Creator, God has revealed a breathtakingly complex set of His personal attributes in the Bible. He is infinitely good and only thinks, says, and does what is good (see Ps. 34:8). He is infinitely strong (see Jer. 32:27). He is infinitely loving and compassionate (see Ps. 86:15). He is perfectly righteous and eternally just (see Deut. 32:3–4). The list goes on and on!

*For* **THE DOCTRINE OF GOD: PART 2: GOD THE CREATOR,** *turn to Genesis 2:4 on page 7.*

36 [a]Out of heaven He let you hear His voice, that
He might instruct you; on earth He showed you
His great fire, and you heard His words out of
the midst of the fire. 37 And because [a]He loved
your fathers, therefore He chose their descen-
dants after them; and [b]He brought you out of
Egypt with His Presence, with His mighty power,
38 [a]driving out from before you nations greater
and mightier than you, to bring you in, to give
you their land *as* an inheritance, as *it is* this
day. 39 Therefore know this day, and consider *it*
in your heart, that [a]the LORD Himself *is* God in
heaven above and on the earth beneath; *there is*
no other. 40 [a]You shall therefore keep His statutes
and His commandments which I command you
today, that it may go well with you and with your
children after you, and that you may prolong
*your* days in the land which the LORD your God
is giving you for all time."

### *CITIES OF REFUGE EAST OF THE JORDAN*

41 Then Moses [a]set apart three cities on this
side of the Jordan, toward the rising of the sun,
42 [a]that the manslayer might flee there, who kills
his neighbor unintentionally, without having
hated him in time past, and that by fleeing to
one of these cities he might live: 43 [a]Bezer in the
wilderness on the plateau for the Reubenites,
Ramoth in Gilead for the Gadites, and Golan in
Bashan for the Manassites.

### *INTRODUCTION TO GOD'S LAW*

44 Now this *is* the law which Moses set be-
fore the children of Israel. 45 These *are* the
testimonies, the statutes, and the judgments
which Moses spoke to the children of Israel
after they came out of Egypt, 46 on this side of
the Jordan, [a]in the valley opposite Beth Peor,
in the land of Sihon king of the Amorites, who
dwelt at Heshbon, whom Moses and the chil-
dren of Israel [b]defeated after they came out of
Egypt. 47 And they took possession of his land
and the land [a]of Og king of Bashan, two kings
of the Amorites, who *were* on this side of the
Jordan, toward the rising of the sun, 48 [a]from
Aroer, which *is* on the bank of the River Arnon,
even to Mount Sion[1] (that is, [b]Hermon), 49 and
all the plain on the east side of the Jordan as
far as the Sea of the Arabah, below the [a]slopes
of Pisgah.

### *THE TEN COMMANDMENTS REVIEWED*

*(Ex. 20:1–17)*

5 And Moses called all Israel, and said to them:
"Hear, O Israel, the statutes and judgments
which I speak in your hearing today, that you
may learn them and be careful to observe them.
2 [a]The LORD our God made a covenant with us in
Horeb. 3 The LORD [a]did not make this covenant
with our fathers, but with us, those who *are* here
today, all of us who *are* alive. 4 [a]The LORD talked
with you face to face on the mountain from the
midst of the fire. 5 [a]I stood between the LORD and
you at that time, to declare to you the word of the
LORD; for [b]you were afraid because of the fire,
and you did not go up the mountain. *He* said:

6 [a]'I *am* the LORD your God who brought you
out of the land of Egypt, out of the house
of bondage.

7 [a]'You shall have no other gods before Me.

8 [a]'You shall not make for yourself a carved
image—any likeness *of anything* that *is*
in heaven above, or that *is* in the earth
beneath, or that *is* in the water under the
earth; 9 you shall not [a]bow down to them
nor serve them. For I, the LORD your God,
*am* a jealous God, visiting the iniquity of
the fathers upon the children to the third
and fourth *generations* of those who hate
Me, 10 [a]but showing mercy to thousands,
to those who love Me and keep My com-
mandments.

11 [a]'You shall not take the name of the LORD
your God in vain, for the LORD will not
hold *him* guiltless who takes His name
in vain.

12 [a]'Observe the Sabbath day, to keep it holy,
as the LORD your God commanded you.
13 [a]Six days you shall labor and do all your
work, 14 but the seventh day *is* the [a]Sab-
bath of the LORD your God. *In it* you shall
do no work: you, nor your son, nor your
daughter, nor your male servant, nor
your female servant, nor your ox, nor
your donkey, nor any of your cattle, nor
your stranger who *is* within your gates,
that your male servant and your female
servant may rest as well as you. 15 [a]And
remember that you were a slave in the
land of Egypt, and the LORD your God
brought you out from there [b]by a mighty
hand and by an outstretched arm; there-
fore the LORD your God commanded you
to keep the Sabbath day.

16 [a]'Honor your father and your mother, as the
LORD your God has commanded you,
[b]that your days may be long, and that it
may be well with [c]you in the land which
the LORD your God is giving you.

17 [a]'You shall not murder.

18 [a]'You shall not commit adultery.

19 [a]'You shall not steal.

20 [a]'You shall not bear false witness against your
neighbor.

4:36 [a] Heb. 12:19, 25 4:37 [a] Deut. 7:7, 8; 10:15; 33:3 [b] Ex. 13:3, 9, 14 4:38 [a] Deut. 7:1 4:39 [a] Josh. 2:11 4:40 [a] Lev. 22:31 4:41 [a] Num. 35:6 4:42 [a] Deut. 19:4 4:43 [a] Josh. 20:8 4:46 [a] Deut. 3:29 [b] Num. 21:24 4:47 [a] Num. 21:33–35 4:48 [a] Deut. 2:36; 3:12 [b] Deut. 3:9 [1] Syriac reads *Sirion* (compare 3:9). 4:49 [a] Deut. 3:17 5:2 [a] Ex. 19:5 5:3 [a] Heb. 8:9 5:4 [a] Ex. 19:9 5:5 [a] Gal. 3:19 [b] Ex. 19:16 5:6 [a] Ex. 20:2–17 5:7 [a] Hos. 13:4 5:8 [a] Ex. 20:4 5:9 [a] Ex. 34:7, 14–16 5:10 [a] Dan. 9:4 5:11 [a] Ex. 20:7 5:12 [a] Ex. 20:8 5:13 [a] Ex. 23:12; 35:2 5:14 [a] [Heb. 4:4] 5:15 [a] Deut. 15:15 [b] Deut. 4:34, 37 5:16 [a] Lev. 19:3 [b] Deut. 6:2 [c] Deut. 4:40 5:17 [a] Matt. 5:21 5:18 [a] Ex. 20:14 5:19 [a] [Rom. 13:9] 5:20 [a] Ex. 20:16; 23:1; Matt. 19:18

# THE TEN COMMANDMENTS THROUGHOUT SCRIPTURE

| | Commandment | Practical Application | OT References | NT References |
|---|---|---|---|---|
| | **The First Table** | | | |
| | Vertical commandments between a person and God | | | |
| 1 | **You shall have no other gods before Me** (Exodus 20:3, 23; 34:14) | Show respect to God and to those He has placed in authority over you | Deuteronomy 5:7; 6:4, 14; 13:6–10; 2 Kings 17:35; Psalm 81:9; Jeremiah 25:6; 35:15 | Matthew 4:10; 22:37–38; Mark 12:29–30; Luke 4:8 |
| 2 | **You shall not make for yourself a carved image** (Exodus 20:4–6) | Live your life in wholehearted devotion to God | Exodus 34:17; Leviticus 19:4; 26:1; Deuteronomy 4:15–20; 5:8–10; 7:25; Psalm 115:4–8; Isaiah 44:9–20 | Romans 1:22–23; 1 John 5:21; Revelation 14:9–11 |
| 3 | **You shall not take the name of the Lord your God in vain** (Exodus 20:7) | Guard your speech and strive to communicate effectively and respectfully | Leviticus 18:21; 19:12; 22:2; 24:16; Deuteronomy 5:11; 6:13; Ezekiel 39:7 | Matthew 5:33–37; James 5:12 |
| 4 | **Remember the Sabbath day, to keep it holy** (Exodus 20:8–11) | Allow time for meditation with proper rest and relaxation | Genesis 2:3; Exodus 16:23–30; 31:13–16; 35:2–3; Leviticus 19:3, 30; Deuteronomy 5:12–15; Jeremiah 17:21–27; Ezekiel 20:12 | Mark 2:27–28 |
| | **The Second Table** | | | |
| | Horizontal commandments between a person and other people | | | |
| 5 | **Honor your father and your mother** (Exodus 20:12; 21:17) | Treat parents with respect | Leviticus 19:3; Deuteronomy 5:16; 27:16; Proverbs 6:20–22 | Matthew 15:4–9; 19:19; Mark 7:10–13; 10:19; Luke 18:20; Ephesians 6:1–3; Colossians 3:20 |
| 6 | **You shall not murder** (Exodus 20:13) | Recognize God's control over life and death | Genesis 9:5–6; Leviticus 24:17; Deuteronomy 5:17 | Matthew 5:21–22; 19:18; Mark 10:19; Luke 18:20; Romans 13:9 |
| 7 | **You shall not commit adultery** (Exodus 20:14) | Honor the vow of faithfulness to spouse and God | Leviticus 18:20; 20:10; Deuteronomy 5:18; 22:22; Proverbs 6:29, 32 | Matthew 5:27–28; Mark 10:19; Luke 18:20; Romans 13:9; James 2:11 |
| 8 | **You shall not steal (Exodus 20:15)** | Guard against taking what is not yours | Exodus 21:16; Leviticus 19:11, 13; Deuteronomy 5:19 | Matthew 19:18; Romans 13:9; Ephesians 4:28 |
| 9 | **You shall not bear false witness against your neighbor** (Exodus 20:16) | Respond to others in integrity and respect | Exodus 23:1, 7; Deuteronomy 5:20; Psalm 101:5; Proverbs 6:16–19; 19:5; Zechariah 8:16 | Matthew 19:18; Mark 10:19; Luke 18:20; Romans 13:9; Ephesians 4:25; Colossians 3:9 |
| 10 | **You shall not covet** (Exodus 20:17) | Be satisfied with your own possessions and resources | Deuteronomy 5:21; 7:25; Proverbs 28:16 | Luke 12:15; Romans 7:7; 13:9; Ephesians 5:3, 5; Hebrews 13:5 |

LIVE THE TRUTH

## HONORING PARENTS

**5:16** One of the most important relationships is the one between parents (or parental figures) and children. But these relationships can be among the hardest too. In this verse, God instructs children on how to relate to their parents: with honor. This means children are to treat their parents with ultimate love, respect, and deference. Children are to listen to and obey their parents, even when they don't understand and even when they don't agree. There's no statute of limitations on God's command. Even when we're grown, we're to honor our parents.

Parents are sources of love, nurture, and provision, picturing God, our loving Father, in the home. As God oversees us, parents oversee their children. As God cares for us, parents care for their children. As God lovingly disciplines us, parents lovingly discipline their children. As such, the goal of parenting is to help a child come to know, love, and be like God. Parents aren't perfect; they aren't sinless. Children should never follow their parents into sin, but they should honor them, nonetheless, praying for them in these times and being quick to offer forgiveness and grace. Obeying this command comes with a promise of blessing. Even when it's difficult, honor the parental figures in your life and trust God to keep His promise.

21 [a]'You shall not covet your neighbor's wife;
and you shall not desire your neighbor's
house, his field, his male servant, his
female servant, his ox, his donkey, or
anything that *is* your neighbor's.'

22 "These words the LORD spoke to all your assembly, in the mountain from the midst of the fire, the cloud, and the thick darkness, with a loud voice; and He added no more. And [a]He wrote them on two tablets of stone and gave them to me.

### *THE PEOPLE AFRAID OF GOD'S PRESENCE*

*(Ex. 20:18–21)*

23 [a]"So it was, when you heard the voice from the midst of the darkness, while the mountain was burning with fire, that you came near to me, all the heads of your tribes and your elders. 24 And you said: 'Surely the LORD our God has shown us His glory and His greatness, and [a]we have heard His voice from the midst of the fire. We have seen this day that God speaks with man; yet he [b]*still* lives. 25 Now therefore, why should we die? For this great fire will consume us; [a]if we hear the voice of the LORD our God anymore, then we shall die. 26 [a]For who *is there* of all flesh who has heard the voice of the living God speaking from the midst of the fire, as we *have,* and lived? 27 You go near and hear all that the LORD our God may say, and [a]tell us all that the LORD our God says to you, and we will hear and do *it.*'

28 "Then the LORD heard the voice of your words when you spoke to me, and the LORD said to me: 'I have heard the voice of the words of this people which they have spoken to you. [a]They are right *in* all that they have spoken. 29 [a]Oh, that they had such a heart in them that they would fear Me and [b]always keep all My commandments, [c]that it might be well with them and with their children forever! 30 Go and say to them, "Return to your tents." 31 But as for you, stand here by Me, [a]and I will speak to you all the commandments, the statutes, and the judgments which you shall teach them, that they may observe *them* in the land which I am giving them to possess.'

32 "Therefore you shall be careful to do as the LORD your God has commanded you; [a]you shall not turn aside to the right hand or to the left. 33 You shall walk in [a]all the ways which the LORD your God has commanded you, that you may live [b]and *that it may be* well with you, and *that* you may prolong *your* days in the land which you shall possess.

### *THE GREATEST COMMANDMENT*

**6** "Now this *is* [a]the commandment, *and these are* the statutes and judgments which the LORD your God has commanded to teach you, that you may observe *them* in the land which you are crossing over to possess, 2 [a]that you may fear the LORD your God, to keep all His statutes and His commandments which I command you, you and your son and your grandson, all the days of your life, [b]and that your days may be prolonged. 3 Therefore hear, O Israel, and be careful to observe *it,* that it may be well with you, and that you may [a]multiply greatly [b]as the LORD God of your fathers has promised you—[c]'a land flowing with milk and honey.'[1]

5:21 [a] Ex. 20:17; [Rom. 7:7; 13:9] 5:22 [a] Ex. 24:12; 31:18; Deut. 4:13 5:23 [a] Ex. 20:18, 19 5:24 [a] Ex. 19:19 [b] Deut. 4:33; Judg. 13:22 5:25 [a] Ex. 20:18, 19; Deut. 18:16 5:26 [a] Deut. 4:33 5:27 [a] Ex. 20:19; Heb. 12:19 5:28 [a] Deut. 18:17 5:29 [a] Deut. 32:29; Ps. 81:13; Is. 48:18 [b] Deut. 11:1 [c] Deut. 4:40 5:31 [a] [Gal. 3:19] 5:32 [a] Deut. 17:20; 28:14; Josh. 1:7; 23:6; Prov. 4:27 5:33 [a] Deut. 10:12; Ps. 119:3; Jer. 7:23; Luke 1:6 [b] Deut. 4:40; Eph. 6:3 6:1 [a] Deut. 12:1 6:2 [a] Ex. 20:20; Deut. 10:12, 13; [Ps. 111:10; 128:1; Eccl. 12:13] [b] Deut. 4:40 6:3 [a] Deut. 7:13 [b] Gen. 22:17 [c] Ex. 3:8, 17 [1] Exodus 3:8

DEUTERONOMY 6:1—7:26

# GOD'S SPECIAL PEOPLE

17

STORY OF SCRIPTURE

## WHAT'S GOING ON?

These chapters in Deuteronomy are Moses's heartfelt plea to the Israelites, urging them to love God wholeheartedly and to obey His commandments. Moses knew Israel's prosperity and survival hinged not on their military strength or wisdom, but on their loyalty to God. Perhaps the central command of this passage is the Shema: "Hear, O Israel: The LORD our God, the LORD is one! You shall love the LORD your God with all your heart, with all your soul, and with all your strength" (Deut. 6:4–5). This isn't a call merely to engage one's emotions, but rather to engage in a lifestyle of love in action—obedience.

Moses also spoke of nations greater and mightier than Israel that God would dispossess before them, warning the Israelites not to be ensnared by these nation's gods but to remain steadfast in their commitment to the Lord. In this, there's a powerful reminder of God's covenant love and His desire for a people set apart for His purposes.

## WHAT DOES THIS MEAN FOR ME?

Like the Israelites, our love for God is proven by our obedience to His word. When we love God with all our heart, soul, and strength, our lives naturally align with His will. We show we are His special people in the way we obey and reflect His word to the world.

## DID YOU CATCH THE PATTERN?

God called Israel His "holy people" who were set apart for His purposes (Deut. 7:6). This intimate relationship with Israel is a continuation of the promises He made to Abraham, Isaac, and Jacob long before, and one He would forge with the church much later (see 1 Pet. 2:9).

*For the next* Story of Scripture *reading and devotion, turn to Joshua 2:18–19 on page 218.*

**4**[a]"Hear, O Israel: The LORD our God, the
LORD *is* one![1] **5**[a]You shall love the LORD your
God with all your heart, [b]with all your soul, and
with all your strength.

### SEEING JESUS IN THE SCRIPTURE

**6:4–5** These verses, known as the Shema, provide the foundation for all the commands in Scripture (see Matt. 22:34–40). Jesus perfectly demonstrated the partnership of loving God and loving people by coming to earth and laying down His life for our good and God's glory.

**6:8–9** Many Jews interpreted these instructions literally and wore phylacteries (boxes containing Scripture) between their **eyes** when they prayed and attached a small vessel called a mezuzah, which contained these verses, to their **doorposts**. More likely, however, God intends for these instructions to be symbolic. The gospel is to frame all we do (hands) and think (foreheads) and should define our homes much like a street address does.

**6**"And [a]these words which I command you
today shall be in your heart. **7**[a]You shall teach
them diligently to your children, and shall talk
of them when you sit in your house, when you
walk by the way, when you lie down, and when
you rise up. **8**[a]You shall bind them as a sign
on your hand, and they shall be as frontlets
between your eyes. **9**[a]You shall write them on
the doorposts of your house and on your gates.

### *CAUTION AGAINST DISOBEDIENCE*

**10**"So it shall be, when the LORD your God
brings you into the land of which He swore to
your fathers, to Abraham, Isaac, and Jacob, to
give you large and beautiful cities [a]which you
did not build, **11**houses full of all good things,
which you did not fill, hewn-out wells which you
did not dig, vineyards and olive trees which you
did not plant—[a]when you have eaten and are
full— **12***then* beware, lest you forget the [a]LORD
who brought you out of the land of Egypt, from

**6:4** [a] Deut. 4:35; Mark 12:29; John 17:3; [1 Cor. 8:4, 6] [1] Or *The LORD is our God, the LORD alone* (that is, the only one) **6:5** [a] Matt. 22:37; Mark 12:30; Luke 10:27 [b] 2 Kin. 23:25 **6:6** [a] Deut. 11:18–20; Ps. 119:11, 98 **6:7** [a] Deut. 4:9; 11:19; [Eph. 6:4] **6:8** [a] Ex. 12:14; 13:9, 16; Deut. 11:18; Prov. 3:3; 6:21; 7:3 **6:9** [a] Deut. 11:20; Is. 57:8 **6:10** [a] Deut. 9:1; 19:1; Josh. 24:13; Ps. 105:44 **6:11** [a] Deut. 8:10; 11:15; 14:29 **6:12** [a] Deut. 8:11–18

the house of bondage. 13 You shall [a]fear the LORD your God and serve Him, and [b]shall take oaths in His name. 14 You shall not go after other gods, [a]the gods of the peoples who *are* all around you 15 (for [a]the LORD your God *is* a jealous God [b]among you), lest the anger of the LORD your God be aroused against you and destroy you from the face of the earth.

16 [a]"You shall not tempt the LORD your God [b]as you tempted *Him* in Massah. 17 You shall [a]diligently keep the commandments of the LORD your God, His testimonies, and His statutes which He has commanded you. 18 And you [a]shall do *what is* right and good in the sight of the LORD, that it may be well with you, and that you may go in and possess the good land of which the LORD swore to your fathers, 19 [a]to cast out all your enemies from before you, as the LORD has spoken.

20 [a]"When your son asks you in time to come, saying, 'What *is the meaning of* the testimonies, the statutes, and the judgments which the LORD our God has commanded you?' 21 then you shall say to your son: 'We were slaves of Pharaoh in Egypt, and the LORD brought us out of Egypt [a]with a mighty hand; 22 and the LORD showed signs and wonders before our eyes, great and severe, against Egypt, Pharaoh, and all his household. 23 Then He brought us out from there, that He might bring us in, to give us the land of which He swore to our fathers. 24 And the LORD commanded us to observe all these statutes, [a]to fear the LORD our God, [b]for our good always, that [c]He might preserve us alive, as *it is* this day. 25 Then [a]it will be righteousness for us, if we are careful to observe all these commandments before the LORD our God, as He has commanded us.'

## *A CHOSEN PEOPLE*

*(Ex. 34:10–16)*

7 "When the LORD your God brings you into the land which you go to [a]possess, and has cast out many [b]nations before you, [c]the Hittites and the Girgashites and the Amorites and the Canaanites and the Perizzites and the Hivites and the Jebusites, seven nations greater and mightier than you, 2 and when the LORD your God delivers [a]them over to you, you shall conquer them *and* utterly destroy them. [b]You shall make no covenant with them nor show mercy to them. 3 [a]Nor shall you make marriages with them. You shall not give your daughter to their son, nor take their daughter for your son. 4 For they will turn your sons away from following Me, to serve other gods; [a]so the anger of the LORD will be aroused against you and destroy you suddenly. 5 But thus you shall deal with them: you shall [a]destroy their altars, and break down their *sacred* pillars, and cut down their wooden images,[1] and burn their carved images with fire.

6 "For you *are* a holy people to the LORD your God; [a]the LORD your God has chosen you to be a people for Himself, a special treasure above all the peoples on the face of the earth. 7 The LORD did not set His [a]love on you nor choose you because you were more in number than any other people, for you were [b]the least of all peoples; 8 but [a]because the LORD loves you, and because He would keep [b]the oath which He swore to your fathers, [c]the LORD has brought you out with a mighty hand, and redeemed you from the house of bondage, from the hand of Pharaoh king of Egypt.

9 "Therefore know that the LORD your God, He *is* God, [a]the faithful God [b]who keeps covenant and mercy for a thousand generations with those who love Him and keep His commandments; 10 and He repays those who hate Him to their face, to destroy them. He will not be [a]slack with him who hates Him; He will repay him to his face. 11 Therefore you shall keep the commandment, the statutes, and the judgments which I command you today, to observe them.

## *BLESSINGS OF OBEDIENCE*

*(Lev. 26:1–13; Deut. 28:1–14)*

12 "Then it shall come to pass, because you listen to these judgments, and keep and do them, that the LORD your God will keep with you the covenant and the mercy which He swore to your fathers. 13 And He will [a]love you and bless you and multiply you; [b]He will also bless the fruit of your womb and the fruit of your land, your grain and your new wine and your oil, the increase of your cattle and the offspring of your flock, in the land of which He swore to your fathers to give you. 14 You shall be blessed above all peoples; there shall not be a male or female [a]barren among you or among your livestock. 15 And the LORD will take away from you all sickness, and will afflict you with none of the [a]terrible diseases of Egypt which you have known, but will lay *them* on all those who hate you. 16 Also you shall destroy all the peoples whom the LORD your God delivers over to you; your eye shall have no pity on them; nor shall you serve their gods, for that *will* [a]*be* a snare to you.

17 "If you should say in your heart, 'These nations are greater than I; how can I dispossess them?'— 18 you shall not be afraid of them, *but*

6:13 [a] Deut. 13:4; Matt. 4:10; Luke 4:8 [b] Deut. 5:11; [Is. 45:23; Jer. 4:2] 6:14 [a] Deut. 13:7 6:15 [a] Ex. 20:5; Deut. 4:24 [b] Ex. 33:3 6:16 [a] Matt. 4:7; Luke 4:12 [b] [1 Cor. 10:9] 6:17 [a] Deut. 11:22; Ps. 119:4 6:18 [a] Ex. 15:26; Deut. 8:7–10 6:19 [a] Num. 33:52, 53 6:20 [a] Ex. 13:8, 14 6:21 [a] Ex. 13:3 6:24 [a] Deut. 6:2 [b] Deut. 10:12, 13; Job 35:7, 8; Jer. 32:39 [c] Deut. 4:1 6:25 [a] Deut. 24:13; [Rom. 10:3, 5] 7:1 [a] Deut. 6:10 [b] Gen. 15:19–21 [c] Ex. 33:2 7:2 [a] Num. 31:17; Deut. 20:16–18 [b] Ex. 23:32, 33; Josh. 2:14 7:3 [a] Ex. 34:15, 16; Josh. 23:12; 1 Kin. 11:2; Ezra 9:2 7:4 [a] Deut. 6:15 7:5 [a] Ex. 23:24; 34:13; Deut. 12:3 [1] Hebrew *Asherim*, Canaanite deities 7:6 [a] Ex. 19:5, 6; Amos 3:2; 1 Pet. 2:9 7:7 [a] Deut. 4:37 [b] Deut. 10:22 7:8 [a] Deut. 10:15 [b] Luke 1:55, 72, 73 [c] Ex. 13:3, 14 7:9 [a] 1 Cor. 1:9; 2 Thess. 3:3; 2 Tim. 2:13 [b] Ex. 20:6; Deut. 5:10; Neh. 1:5; Dan. 9:4 7:10 [a] [2 Pet. 3:10] 7:13 [a] Ps. 146:8; Prov. 15:9; John 14:21 [b] Deut. 28:4 7:14 [a] Ex. 23:26 7:15 [a] Ex. 9:14; 15:26; Deut. 28:27, 60 7:16 [a] Ex. 23:33; Judg. 8:27; Ps. 106:36

you shall [a]remember well what the LORD your God did to Pharaoh and to all Egypt: 19 [a]the great trials which your eyes saw, the signs and the wonders, the mighty hand and the outstretched arm, by which the LORD your God brought you out. So shall the LORD your God do to all the peoples of whom you are afraid. 20 [a]Moreover the LORD your God will send the hornet among them until those who are left, who hide themselves from you, are destroyed. 21 You shall not be terrified of them; for the LORD your God, the great and awesome God, *is* among you. 22 And the LORD your God will drive out those nations before you [a]little by little; you will be unable to destroy them at once, lest the beasts of the field become *too* numerous for you. 23 But the LORD your God will deliver them over to you, and will inflict defeat upon them until they are destroyed. 24 And [a]He will deliver their kings into your hand, and you will destroy their name from under heaven; [b]no one shall be able to stand against you until you have destroyed them. 25 You shall burn the carved images of their gods with fire; you shall not [a]covet the silver or gold *that is* on them, nor take *it* for yourselves, lest you be snared by it; for it *is* an abomination to the LORD your God. 26 Nor shall you bring an abomination into your house, lest you be doomed to destruction like it. You shall utterly detest it and utterly abhor it, [a]for it *is* an accursed thing.

### REMEMBER THE LORD YOUR GOD

**8** "Every commandment which I command you today [a]you must be careful to observe, that you may live and [b]multiply, and go in and possess the land of which the LORD swore to your fathers. 2 And you shall remember that the LORD your God [a]led you all the way these forty years in the wilderness, to humble you *and* [b]test you, [c]to know what *was* in your heart, whether you would keep His commandments or not. 3 So He humbled you, [a]allowed you to hunger, and [b]fed you with manna which you did not know nor did your fathers know, that He might make you know that man shall [c]not live by bread alone; but man lives by every *word* that proceeds from the mouth of the LORD. 4 [a]Your garments did not wear out on you, nor did your foot swell these forty years. 5 [a]You should know in your heart that as a man chastens his son, *so* the LORD your God chastens you.

6 "Therefore you shall keep the commandments of the LORD your God, [a]to walk in His ways and to fear Him. 7 For the LORD your God is bringing you into a good land, [a]a land of brooks of water, of fountains and springs, that flow out of valleys and hills; 8 a land of wheat and barley, of vines and fig trees and pomegranates, a land of olive oil and honey; 9 a land in which you will eat bread without scarcity, in which you will lack nothing; a land whose stones *are* iron and out of whose hills you can dig copper. 10 [a]When you have eaten and are full, then you shall bless the LORD your God for the good land which He has given you.

11 "Beware that you do not forget the LORD your God by not keeping His commandments, His judgments, and His statutes which I command you today, 12 [a]lest—*when* you have eaten and are full, and have built beautiful houses and dwell *in them;* 13 and *when* your herds and your flocks multiply, and your silver and your gold are multiplied, and all that you have is multiplied; 14 [a]when your heart is lifted up, and you [b]forget the LORD your God who brought you out of the land of Egypt, from the house of bondage; 15 who [a]led you through that great and terrible wilderness, [b]*in which were* fiery serpents and scorpions and thirsty land where there was no water; [c]who brought water for you out of the flinty rock; 16 who fed you in the wilderness with [a]manna, which your fathers did not know, that He might humble you and that He might test you, [b]to do you good in the end— 17 then you say in your heart, 'My power and the might of my hand have gained me this wealth.'

18 "And you shall remember the LORD your God, [a]for *it is* He who gives you power to get wealth, [b]that He may establish His covenant which He swore to your fathers, as *it is* this day. 19 Then it shall be, if you by any means forget the LORD your God, and follow other gods, and serve them and worship them, [a]I testify against you this day that you shall surely perish. 20 As the nations which the LORD destroys before you, [a]so you shall perish, because you would not be obedient to the voice of the LORD your God.

> **SEEING JESUS IN THE SCRIPTURE**
>
> **8:3** When Jesus was tempted in the wilderness, He used these words to rebuke Satan (see Luke 4:1–4). God's Word which points to Jesus, the Word (see John 1:1), is our only wisdom and hope.

### ISRAEL'S REBELLIONS REVIEWED
*(Ex. 32:1–35)*

**9** "Hear, O Israel: You *are* to cross over the Jordan today, and go in to dispossess nations greater and mightier than yourself, cities great and fortified up to heaven, 2 a people great and tall, the [a]descendants of the Anakim, whom you

**7:18** [a] Ps. 105:5 **7:19** [a] Deut. 4:34; 29:3 **7:20** [a] Ex. 23:28; Josh. 24:12 **7:22** [a] Ex. 23:29, 30 **7:24** [a] Josh. 10:24, 42; 12:1–24 [b] Josh. 23:9 **7:25** [a] Prov. 23:6 **7:26** [a] Deut. 13:17 **8:1** [a] Deut. 4:1; 6:24 [b] Deut. 30:16 **8:2** [a] Deut. 1:3; 2:7; 29:5; Ps. 136:16; Amos 2:10 [b] Ex. 16:4 [c] [John 2:25] **8:3** [a] Ex. 16:2, 3 [b] Ex. 16:12, 14, 35 [c] Matt. 4:4; Luke 4:4 **8:4** [a] Deut. 29:5; Neh. 9:21 **8:5** [a] 2 Sam. 7:14; Ps. 89:30–33; Prov. 3:11, 12; Heb. 12:5–11; Rev. 3:19 **8:6** [a] [Deut. 5:33] **8:7** [a] Deut. 11:9–12; Jer. 2:7 **8:10** [a] Deut. 6:11, 12 **8:12** [a] Deut. 28:47; Prov. 30:9; Hos. 13:6 **8:14** [a] 1 Cor. 4:7 [b] Deut. 8:11; Ps. 106:21 **8:15** [a] Is. 63:12–14 [b] Num. 21:6 [c] Ex. 17:6; Num. 20:11 **8:16** [a] Ex. 16:15 [b] Jer. 24:5, 6; [Heb. 12:11] **8:18** [a] Prov. 10:22; Hos. 2:8 [b] Deut. 7:8, 12 **8:19** [a] Deut. 4:26; 30:18 **8:20** [a] [Dan. 9:11, 12] **9:2** [a] Num. 13:22, 28, 33; Josh. 11:21, 22

know, and *of whom* you heard *it said,* ‘Who can
stand before the descendants of Anak?’ 3 There-
fore understand today that the LORD your God *is*
He who [a]goes over before you *as* a [b]consuming
fire. [c]He will destroy them and bring them down
before you; [d]so you shall drive them out and de-
stroy them quickly, as the LORD has said to you.
4 [a]“Do not think in your heart, after the LORD
your God has cast them out before you, saying,
‘Because of my righteousness the LORD has
brought me in to possess this land’; but *it is*
[b]because of the wickedness of these nations
*that* the LORD is driving them out from before
you. 5 [a]*It is* not because of your righteousness or
the uprightness of your heart *that* you go in to
possess their land, but because of the wickedness
of these nations *that* the LORD your God drives
them out from before you, and that He may
fulfill the [b]word which the LORD swore to your
fathers, to Abraham, Isaac, and Jacob. 6 Therefore
understand that the LORD your God is not giving
you this good land to possess because of your
righteousness, for you *are* a [a]stiff-necked people.
7 “Remember! Do not forget how you [a]pro-
voked the LORD your God to wrath in the wilder-
ness. [b]From the day that you departed from the
land of Egypt until you came to this place, you have
been rebellious against the LORD. 8 Also [a]in Horeb
you provoked the LORD to wrath, so that the LORD
was angry *enough* with you to have destroyed you.
9 [a]When I went up into the mountain to receive
the tablets of stone, the tablets of the covenant
which the LORD made with you, then I stayed
on the mountain forty days and [b]forty nights. I
neither ate bread nor drank water. 10 [a]Then the
LORD delivered to me two tablets of stone written
with the finger of God, and on them *were* all the
words which the LORD had spoken to you on the
mountain from the midst of the fire [b]in the day of
the assembly. 11 And it came to pass, at the end of
forty days and forty nights, *that* the LORD gave me
the two tablets of stone, the tablets of the covenant.
12 “Then the LORD said to me, [a]‘Arise, go
down quickly from here, for your people whom
you brought out of Egypt have acted corruptly;
they have [b]quickly turned aside from the way
which I commanded them; they have made
themselves a molded image.’
13 “Furthermore [a]the LORD spoke to me, say-
ing, ‘I have seen this people, and indeed [b]they
are a stiff-necked people. 14 [a]Let Me alone, that
I may destroy them and [b]blot out their name
from under heaven; [c]and I will make of you a
nation mightier and greater than they.’
15 [a]“So I turned and came down from the
mountain, and [b]the mountain burned with fire;
and the two tablets of the covenant *were* in my two
hands. 16 And [a]I looked, and behold, you had sinned
against the LORD your God—had made for your-
selves a molded calf! You had turned aside quickly
from the way which the LORD had commanded
you. 17 Then I took the two tablets and threw them
out of my two hands and [a]broke them before your
eyes. 18 And I [a]fell down before the LORD, as at the
first, forty days and forty nights; I neither ate bread
nor drank water, because of all your sin which you
committed in doing wickedly in the sight of the
LORD, to provoke Him to anger. 19 [a]For I was afraid
of the anger and hot displeasure with which the
LORD was angry with you, to destroy you. [b]But
the LORD listened to me at that time also. 20 And
the LORD was very angry with Aaron *and* would
have destroyed him; so I prayed for Aaron also
at the same time. 21 Then I took your sin, the calf
which you had made, and burned it with fire and
crushed it *and* ground *it* very small, until it was as
fine as dust; and I [a]threw its dust into the brook
that descended from the mountain.
22 “Also at [a]Taberah and [b]Massah and [c]Kib-
roth Hattaavah you provoked the LORD to wrath.
23 Likewise, [a]when the LORD sent you from Ka-
desh Barnea, saying, ‘Go up and possess the
land which I have given you,’ then you rebelled
against the commandment of the LORD your
God, and [b]you did not believe Him nor obey His
voice. 24 [a]You have been rebellious against the
LORD from the day that I knew you.
25 [a]“Thus I prostrated myself before the LORD;
forty days and forty nights I kept prostrating
myself, because the LORD had said He would
destroy you. 26 Therefore I prayed to the LORD,
and said: ‘O Lord GOD, do not destroy Your people
and [a]Your inheritance whom You have redeemed
through Your greatness, whom You have brought
out of Egypt with a mighty hand. 27 Remember
Your servants, Abraham, Isaac, and Jacob; do
not look on the stubbornness of this people, or
on their wickedness or their sin, 28 lest the land
from which You brought us should say, “Because
the LORD was not able to bring them to the land
which He promised them, and because He hated
them, He has brought them out to kill them in
the wilderness.” 29 Yet they *are* Your people and
Your inheritance, whom You brought out by Your
mighty power and by Your outstretched arm.’

### *THE SECOND PAIR OF TABLETS*

*(Ex. 34:1–9)*

10 “At that time the LORD said to me, ‘Hew
for yourself two tablets of stone like the
first, and come up to Me on the mountain and
make yourself an [a]ark of wood. 2 And I will write

9:3 [a] Deut. 1:33; 31:3; Josh. 3:11; 5:14; John 10:4 [b] Deut. 4:24; Heb. 12:29 [c] Deut. 7:24 [d] Ex. 23:31 9:4 [a] Deut. 8:17; [Rom. 11:6, 20; 1 Cor. 4:4, 7] [b] Gen. 15:16; Lev. 18:3, 24–30; Deut. 12:31; 18:9–14 9:5 [a] [Titus 3:5] [b] Gen. 50:24 9:6 [a] Ex. 34:9; Deut. 31:27 9:7 [a] Num. 14:22 [b] Ex. 14:11 9:8 [a] Ex. 32:1–8; Ps. 106:19 9:9 [a] Ex. 24:12, 15; Deut. 5:2–22 [b] Ex. 24:18 9:10 [a] Ex. 31:18; Deut. 4:13 [b] Ex. 19:17 9:12 [a] Ex. 32:7, 8 [b] Deut. 31:29 9:13 [a] Ex. 32:9 [b] Deut. 9:6 9:14 [a] Ex. 32:10 [b] Deut. 29:20 [c] Num. 14:12 9:15 [a] Ex. 32:15–19 [b] Ex. 19:18 9:16 [a] Ex. 32:19 9:17 [a] Ex. 32:19 9:18 [a] Ex. 34:28; Ps. 106:23 9:19 [a] Ex. 32:10, 11; Heb. 12:21 [b] Ex. 32:14 9:21 [a] Ex. 32:20 9:22 [a] Num. 11:1, 3 [b] Ex. 17:7 [c] Num. 11:4, 34 9:23 [a] Num. 13:3 [b] Ps. 106:24, 25 9:24 [a] Deut. 9:7; 31:27 9:25 [a] Deut. 9:18 9:26 [a] Deut. 32:9 10:1 [a] Ex. 25:10

on the tablets the words that were on the first
tablets, which you broke; and [a]you shall put
them in the ark.’
3 “So I made an ark of acacia wood, hewed
two tablets of stone like the first, and went up the
mountain, having the two tablets in my hand.
4 And He wrote on the tablets according to the
first writing, the Ten Commandments, [a]which
the LORD had spoken to you in the mountain
from the midst of the fire in the day of the as-
sembly; and the LORD gave them to me. 5 Then I
turned and [a]came down from the mountain, and
[b]put the tablets in the ark which I had made; [c]and
there they are, just as the LORD commanded me.”
6 (Now the children of Israel journeyed from
the wells of Bene Jaakan to Moserah, where
Aaron [a]died, and where he was buried; and El-
eazar his son ministered as priest in his stead.
7 [a]From there they journeyed to Gudgodah, and
from Gudgodah to Jotbathah, a land of rivers of
water. 8 At that time [a]the LORD separated the
tribe of Levi [b]to bear the ark of the covenant of
the LORD, [c]to stand before the LORD to minister
to Him and [d]to bless in His name, to this day.
9 [a]Therefore Levi has no portion nor inheritance
with his brethren; the LORD *is* his inheritance,
just as the LORD your God promised him.)
10 “As at the first time, [a]I stayed in the moun-
tain forty days and forty nights; [b]the LORD also
heard me at that time, *and* the LORD chose not to
destroy you. 11 [a]Then the LORD said to me, ‘Arise,
begin *your* journey before the people, that they
may go in and possess the land which I swore
to their fathers to give them.’

## THE ESSENCE OF THE LAW

12 “And now, Israel, [a]what does the LORD your
God require of you, but to fear the LORD your
God, to walk in all His ways and to [b]love Him,
to serve the LORD your God with all your heart
and with all your soul, 13 *and* to keep the com-
mandments of the LORD and His statutes which
I command you today [a]for your good? 14 Indeed
heaven and the highest heavens belong to the
[a]LORD your God, *also* the earth with all that *is*
in it. 15 The LORD delighted only in your fathers,
to love them; and He chose their descendants
after them, you above all peoples, as *it is* this
day. 16 Therefore circumcise the foreskin of your
[a]heart, and be [b]stiff-necked no longer. 17 For
the LORD your God *is* [a]God of gods and [b]Lord
of lords, the great God, [c]mighty and awesome,
who [d]shows no partiality nor takes a bribe. 18 [a]He
administers justice for the fatherless and the
widow, and loves the stranger, giving him food
and clothing. 19 Therefore love the stranger, for

> **10:18** In the ancient Near East, women who did not have a father or husband faced a very difficult situation. They had no one to protect them, no one to provide for them, and very few rights. Fortunately for them, the Lord cares about the well-being of widows and orphans. This is why He ordered His people to do the same.

you were strangers in the land of Egypt. 20 [a]You
shall fear the LORD your God; you shall serve
Him, and to Him you shall hold fast, and take
oaths in His name. 21 He *is* your praise, and He
*is* your God, who has done for you these great
and awesome things which your eyes have seen.
22 Your fathers went down to Egypt with seventy
persons, and now the LORD your God has made
you as the stars of heaven in multitude.

## LOVE AND OBEDIENCE REWARDED

11 “Therefore you shall love the LORD your
God, and keep His charge, His statutes,
His judgments, and His commandments al-
ways. 2 Know today that *I do* not *speak* with your
children, who have not known and who have
not seen the chastening of the LORD your God,
His greatness and His mighty hand and His
outstretched arm— 3 His signs and His acts
which He did in the midst of Egypt, to Pharaoh
king of Egypt, and to all his land; 4 what He did
to the army of Egypt, to their horses and their
chariots: [a]how He made the waters of the Red
Sea overflow them as they pursued you, and *how*
the LORD has destroyed them to this day; 5 what
He did for you in the wilderness until you came
to this place; 6 and [a]what He did to Dathan and
Abiram the sons of Eliab, the son of Reuben:
how the earth opened its mouth and swallowed
them up, their households, their tents, and all
the substance that *was* in their possession, in
the midst of all Israel— 7 but your eyes have
[a]seen every great act of the LORD which He did.
8 “Therefore you shall keep every command-
ment which I command you today, that you may
[a]be strong, and go in and possess the land which
you cross over to possess, 9 and [a]that you may
prolong *your* days in the land [b]which the LORD
swore to give your fathers, to them and their de-
scendants, [c]‘a land flowing with milk and honey.’[1]
10 For the land which you go to possess *is* not like
the land of Egypt from which you have come,
where you sowed your seed and watered *it* by foot,
as a vegetable garden; 11 [a]but the land which you

10:2 [a] Ex. 25:16, 21 10:4 [a] Ex. 20:1; 34:28 10:5 [a] Ex. 34:29 [b] Ex. 40:20 [c] 1 Kin. 8:9 10:6 [a] Num. 20:25–28; 33:38 10:7 [a] Num. 33:32–34 10:8 [a] Num. 3:6 [b] Num. 4:5, 15; 10:21 [c] Deut. 18:5 [d] Num. 6:23 10:9 [a] Num. 18:20, 24; Deut. 18:1, 2; Ezek. 44:28 10:10 [a] Ex. 34:28; Deut. 9:18 [b] Ex. 32:14 10:11 [a] Ex. 33:1 10:12 [a] Mic. 6:8 [b] Deut. 6:5; Matt. 22:37; 1 Tim. 1:5 10:13 [a] Deut. 6:24 10:14 [a] [Neh. 9:6; Ps. 68:33; 115:16] 10:16 [a] Lev. 26:41; Deut. 30:6; Jer. 4:4; Rom. 2:28, 29 [b] Deut. 9:6, 13 10:17 [a] Deut. 4:35, 39; Is. 44:8; 46:9; Dan. 2:47; 1 Cor. 8:5, 6 [b] Rev. 19:16 [c] Deut. 7:21 [d] Acts 10:34 10:18 [a] Ex. 22:22–24; Ps. 68:5; 146:9 10:20 [a] Matt. 4:10 11:4 [a] Ex. 14:28; Ps. 106:11 11:6 [a] Num. 16:1–35; Ps. 106:16–18 11:7 [a] Deut. 10:21; 29:2 11:8 [a] Deut. 31:6, 7, 23; Josh. 1:6, 7 11:9 [a] Deut. 4:40; 5:16, 33; 6:2; Prov. 10:27 [b] Deut. 9:5 [c] Ex. 3:8 [1] Exodus 3:8 11:11 [a] Deut. 8:7

cross over to possess *is* a land of hills and valleys,
which drinks water from the rain of heaven, 12 a
land for which the LORD your God cares; [a]the eyes
of the LORD your God *are* always on it, from the
beginning of the year to the very end of the year.
13 'And it shall be that if you earnestly obey
My commandments which I command you
today, to love the LORD your God and serve
Him with all your heart and with all your soul,
14 then [a]I[1] will give *you* the rain for your land in
its season, [b]the early rain and the latter rain, that
you may gather in your grain, your new wine,
and your oil. 15 [a]And I will send grass in your
fields for your livestock, that you may [b]eat and
be filled.' 16 Take heed to yourselves, [a]lest your
heart be deceived, and you turn aside and [b]serve
other gods and worship them, 17 lest [a]the LORD's
anger be aroused against you, and He [b]shut up
the heavens so that there be no rain, and the
land yield no produce, and [c]you perish quickly
from the good land which the LORD is giving you.

## SEEING JESUS IN THE SCRIPTURE

**11:16–17** God warned the Israelites not to be deceived by the gods of the land. Believing their deception would only lead to disaster. Jesus likewise warned the Jews many would arise claiming to be Him. Following them only leads to destruction (see Luke 21:8).

18 "Therefore [a]you shall lay up these words
of mine in your heart and in your [b]soul, and
[c]bind them as a sign on your hand, and they
shall be as frontlets between your eyes. 19 [a]You
shall teach them to your children, speaking of
them when you sit in your house, when you
walk by the way, when you lie down, and when
you rise up. 20 [a]And you shall write them on
the doorposts of your house and on your gates,
21 that [a]your days and the days of your children
may be multiplied in the land of which the LORD
swore to your fathers to give them, like [b]the days
of the heavens above the earth.
22 "For if [a]you carefully keep all these com-
mandments which I command you to do—to
love the LORD your God, to walk in all His ways,
and [b]to hold fast to Him— 23 then the LORD will
[a]drive out all these nations from before you,
and you will [b]dispossess greater and mightier
nations than yourselves. 24 [a]Every place on which
the sole of your foot treads shall be yours: [b]from
the wilderness and Lebanon, from the river,
the River Euphrates, even to the Western Sea,[1]
shall be your territory. 25 No man shall be able to
[a]stand against you; the LORD your God will put
the [b]dread of you and the fear of you upon all the
land where you tread, just as He has said to you.
26 [a]"Behold, I set before you today a bless-
ing and a curse: 27 [a]the blessing, if you obey the
commandments of the LORD your God which
I command you today; 28 and the [a]curse, if you
do not obey the commandments of the LORD
your God, but turn aside from the way which I
command you today, to go after other gods which
you have not known. 29 Now it shall be, when the
LORD your God has brought you into the land
which you go to possess, that you shall put the
[a]blessing on Mount Gerizim and the [b]curse on
Mount Ebal. 30 *Are* they not on the other side of
the Jordan, toward the setting sun, in the land of
the Canaanites who dwell in the plain opposite
Gilgal, [a]beside the terebinth trees of Moreh? 31 For
you will cross over the Jordan and go in to possess
the land which the LORD your God is giving you,
and you will possess it and dwell in it. 32 And you
shall be careful to observe all the statutes and
judgments which I set before you today.

### *A PRESCRIBED PLACE OF WORSHIP*

12 "These [a]*are* the statutes and judgments
which you shall be careful to observe in the
land which the LORD God of your fathers is giving
you to possess, [b]all the days that you live on the
earth. 2 [a]You shall utterly destroy all the places
where the nations which you shall dispossess
served their gods, [b]on the high mountains and on
the hills and under every green tree. 3 And [a]you
shall destroy their altars, break their *sacred* pillars,
and burn their wooden images with fire; you shall
cut down the carved images of their gods and
destroy their names from that place. 4 You shall
not [a]worship the LORD your God *with* such *things.*
5 "But you shall seek the [a]place where the
LORD your God chooses, out of all your tribes, to
put His name for His [b]dwelling place; and there
you shall go. 6 [a]There you shall take your burnt
offerings, your sacrifices, your tithes, the heave
offerings of your hand, your vowed offerings,
your freewill offerings, and the [b]firstborn of
your herds and flocks. 7 And [a]there you shall
eat before the LORD your God, and [b]you shall
rejoice in all to which you have put your hand,
you and your households, in which the LORD
your God has blessed you.

**11:12** [a]1 Kin. 9:3 **11:14** [a]Lev. 26:4; Deut. 28:12 [b]Joel 2:23; James 5:7 [1]Following Masoretic Text and Targum; Samaritan Pentateuch, Septuagint, and Vulgate read *He.* **11:15** [a]Ps. 104:14 [b]Deut. 6:11; Joel 2:19 **11:16** [a]Deut. 29:18; Job 31:27 [b]Deut. 8:19 **11:17** [a]Deut. 6:15; 9:19 [b]Deut. 28:24; 1 Kin. 8:35; 2 Chr. 6:26; 7:13 [c]Deut. 4:26; 2 Chr. 36:14–20 **11:18** [a]Deut. 6:6–9 [b]Ps. 119:2, 34 [c]Deut. 6:8 **11:19** [a]Deut. 4:9, 10; 6:7; Prov. 22:6 **11:20** [a]Deut. 6:9 **11:21** [a]Deut. 4:40 [b]Ps. 72:5; 89:29; Prov. 3:2; 4:10; 9:11 **11:22** [a]Deut. 11:1 [b]Deut. 10:20 **11:23** [a]Deut. 4:38 [b]Deut. 9:1 **11:24** [a]Josh. 1:3; 14:9 [b]Gen. 15:18; Ex. 23:31; Deut. 1:7, 8 [1]That is, the Mediterranean **11:25** [a]Deut. 7:24 [b]Ex. 23:27; Deut. 2:25; Josh. 2:9–11 **11:26** [a]Deut. 30:1, 15, 19 **11:27** [a]Deut. 28:1–14 **11:28** [a]Deut. 28:15–68 **11:29** [a]Deut. 27:12, 13; Josh. 8:33 [b]Deut. 27:13–26 **11:30** [a]Gen. 12:6 **12:1** [a]Deut. 6:1 [b]Deut. 4:9, 10; 1 Kin. 8:40 **12:2** [a]Ex. 34:13 [b]2 Kin. 16:4; 17:10, 11 **12:3** [a]Num. 33:52; Deut. 7:5; Judg. 2:2 **12:4** [a]Deut. 12:31 **12:5** [a]Ex. 20:24 [b]Ex. 15:13; 1 Sam. 2:29 **12:6** [a]Lev. 17:3, 4 [b]Deut. 14:23 **12:7** [a]Deut. 14:26 [b]Deut. 12:12, 18

**SEEING JESUS IN THE SCRIPTURE**

**12:7** The Israelites were to sacrifice with sobriety *and* joy. Worship is always to be taken seriously, but that doesn't mean it isn't also to be joyful. Likewise, our worship—especially the Lord's Supper—is to be a joyful celebration and proclamation of Jesus' sacrifice on our behalf (see 1 Cor. 11:26).

8"You shall not at all do as we are doing here
today—[a]every man doing whatever *is* right in his
own eyes— 9for as yet you have not come to the
[a]rest and the inheritance which the LORD your
God is giving you. 10But *when* you cross over the
Jordan and dwell in the land which the LORD
your God is giving you to inherit, and He gives
you [a]rest from all your enemies round about,
so that you dwell in safety, 11then there will be
the place where the LORD your God chooses to
make His name abide. There you shall bring all
that I command you: your burnt offerings, your
sacrifices, your tithes, the heave offerings of your
hand, and all your choice offerings which you
vow to the LORD. 12And [a]you shall rejoice before
the LORD your God, you and your sons and your
daughters, your male and female servants, and
the [b]Levite who *is* within your gates, since he
has no portion nor inheritance with you. 13Take
heed to yourself that you do not offer your burnt
offerings in every place that you see; 14but in the
place which the LORD chooses, in one of your
tribes, there you shall offer your burnt offerings,
and there you shall do all that I command you.
15"However, [a]you may slaughter and eat
meat within all your gates, whatever your heart
desires, according to the blessing of the LORD
your God which He has given you; [b]the unclean
and the clean may eat of it, [c]of the gazelle and the
deer alike. 16[a]Only you shall not eat the blood;
you shall pour it on the earth like water. 17You
may not eat within your gates the tithe of your
grain or your new wine or your oil, of the first-
born of your herd or your flock, of any of your
offerings which you vow, of your freewill offer-
ings, or of the heave offering of your hand. 18But
you must eat them before the LORD your God
in the place which the LORD your God chooses,
you and your son and your daughter, your male
servant and your female servant, and the Levite
who *is* within your gates; and you shall rejoice
before the LORD your God in all to which you
put your hands. 19Take heed to yourself that
you do not forsake the Levite as long as you
live in your land.

20"When the LORD your God [a]enlarges your
border as He has promised you, and you say, 'Let
me eat meat,' because you long to eat meat, you
may eat as much meat as your heart desires. 21If
the place where the LORD your God chooses to
put His name is too far from [a]you, then you may
slaughter from your herd and from your flock
which the LORD has given you, just as I have com-
manded you, and you may eat within your gates as
much as your heart desires. 22Just as the gazelle
and the deer are eaten, so you may eat them; the
unclean and the clean alike may eat them. 23Only
be sure that you do not eat the blood, [a]for the
blood *is* the life; you may not eat the life with the
meat. 24You shall not eat it; you shall pour it on
the earth like water. 25You shall not eat it, [a]that
it may go well with you and your children after
you, [b]when you do *what is* right in the sight of the
LORD. 26Only the [a]holy things which you have, and
your vowed offerings, you shall take and go to the
place which the LORD chooses. 27And [a]you shall
offer your burnt offerings, the meat and the blood,
on the altar of the LORD your God; and the blood
of your sacrifices shall be poured out on the altar
of the LORD your God, and you shall eat the meat.
28Observe and obey all these words which I com-
mand you, [a]that it may go well with you and your
children after you forever, when you do *what is*
good and right in the sight of the LORD your God.

### *BEWARE OF FALSE GODS*

29"When [a]the LORD your God cuts off from
before you the nations which you go to dispos-
sess, and you displace them and dwell in their
land, 30take heed to yourself that you are not
ensnared to follow them, after they are destroyed
from before you, and that you do not inquire after
their gods, saying, 'How did these nations serve
their gods? I also will do likewise.' 31[a]You shall
not worship the LORD your God in that way; for
every abomination to the LORD which He hates
they have done to their gods; for [b]they burn even
their sons and daughters in the fire to their gods.
32"Whatever I command you, be careful
to observe it; [a]you shall not add to it nor take
away from it.

### *PUNISHMENT OF APOSTATES*

13 "If there arises among you a prophet or a
[a]dreamer of dreams, [b]and he gives you a
sign or a wonder, 2and [a]the sign or the wonder
comes to pass, of which he spoke to you, saying,
'Let us go after other gods'—which you have
not known—'and let us serve them,' 3you shall
not listen to the words of that prophet or that
dreamer of dreams, for the LORD your God [a]is
testing you to know whether you love the LORD

**12:8** [a] Judg. 17:6; 21:25 **12:9** [a] Deut. 3:20; 25:19; Ps. 95:11 **12:10** [a] Josh. 11:23 **12:12** [a] Deut. 12:18; 26:11 [b] Deut. 10:9; 14:29 **12:15** [a] Deut. 12:21 [b] Deut. 12:22 [c] Deut. 14:5 **12:16** [a] Gen. 9:4; Lev. 7:26; 17:10–12; 1 Sam. 14:33; Acts 15:20, 29 **12:20** [a] Gen. 15:18; Ex. 34:24; Deut. 11:24; 19:8 **12:21** [a] Deut. 14:24 **12:23** [a] Gen. 9:4; Lev. 17:10–14; Deut. 12:16 **12:25** [a] Deut. 4:40; 6:18; Is. 3:10 [b] Ex. 15:26; 1 Kin. 11:38 **12:26** [a] Num. 5:9, 10; 18:19 **12:27** [a] Lev. 1:5, 9, 13, 17 **12:28** [a] Deut. 12:25 **12:29** [a] Ex. 23:23; Deut. 19:1; Josh. 23:4 **12:31** [a] Lev. 18:3, 26, 30; 20:1, 2 [b] Deut. 18:10; Ps. 106:37; Jer. 32:35 **12:32** [a] Deut. 4:2; 13:18; Josh. 1:7; Prov. 30:6; Rev. 22:18, 19 **13:1** [a] Num. 12:6; Jer. 23:28; Zech. 10:2 [b] Matt. 24:24; Mark 13:22; 2 Thess. 2:9 **13:2** [a] Deut. 18:22 **13:3** [a] Ex. 20:20; Deut. 8:2, 16

your God with all your heart and with all your
soul. 4 You shall [a]walk after the LORD your God
and fear Him, and keep His commandments and
obey His voice; you shall serve Him and [b]hold
fast to Him. 5 But [a]that prophet or that dreamer
of dreams shall be put to death, because he has
spoken in order to turn *you* away from the LORD
your God, who brought you out of the land of
Egypt and redeemed you from the house of
bondage, to entice you from the way in which
the LORD your God commanded you to walk.
[b]So you shall put away the evil from your midst.
6 [a]"If your brother, the son of your mother,
your son or your daughter, [b]the wife of your
bosom, or your friend [c]who is as your own soul,
secretly entices you, saying, 'Let us go and serve
other gods,' which you have not known, neither
you nor your fathers, 7 of the gods of the people
which *are* all around you, near to you or far
off from you, from *one* end of the earth to the
*other* end of the earth, 8 you shall [a]not consent
to him or listen to him, nor shall your eye pity
him, nor shall you spare him or conceal him;
9 but you shall surely kill him; your hand shall
be first against him to put him to [a]death, and
afterward the hand of all the people. 10 And
you shall stone him with stones until he dies,
because he sought to entice you away from the
LORD your God, who brought you out of the
land of Egypt, from the house of bondage. 11 So
all Israel shall hear and [a]fear, and not again do
such wickedness as this among you.
12 [a]"If you hear someone in one of your
cities, which the LORD your God gives you to
dwell in, saying, 13 'Corrupt men have gone out
from among you and enticed the inhabitants
of their city, saying, "Let us go and serve other
gods" '—which you have not known— 14 then
you shall inquire, search out, and ask diligently.
And *if it is* indeed true *and* certain *that* such an
abomination was committed among you, 15 you
shall surely strike the inhabitants of that city with
the edge of the sword, utterly destroying it, all
that is in it and its livestock—with the edge of
the sword. 16 And you shall gather all its plunder
into the middle of the street, and completely
[a]burn with fire the city and all its plunder, for the
LORD your God. It shall be [b]a heap forever; it shall
not be built again. 17 [a]So none of the accursed
things shall remain in your hand, that the LORD
may [b]turn from the fierceness of His anger and
show you mercy, have compassion on you and
multiply you, just as He swore to your fathers,
18 because you have listened to the voice of the
LORD your God, [a]to keep all His commandments
which I command you today, to do *what is* right
in the eyes of the LORD your God.

### IMPROPER MOURNING

14 "You *are* [a]the children of the LORD your
God; [b]you shall not cut yourselves nor
shave the front of your head for the dead. 2 [a]For
you *are* a holy people to the LORD your God,
and the LORD has chosen you to be a people for
Himself, a special treasure above all the peoples
who *are* on the face of the earth.

### CLEAN AND UNCLEAN MEAT

*(Lev. 11:1–47)*

3 [a]"You shall not eat any detestable thing.
4 [a]These *are* the animals which you may eat: the
ox, the sheep, the goat, 5 the deer, the gazelle, the
roe deer, the wild goat, the mountain goat,[1] the
antelope, and the mountain sheep. 6 And you may
eat every animal with cloven hooves, having the
hoof split into two parts, *and that* chews the cud,
among the animals. 7 Nevertheless, of those that
chew the cud or have cloven hooves, you shall not
eat, *such as* these: the camel, the hare, and the
rock hyrax; for they chew the cud but do not have
cloven hooves; they *are* unclean for you. 8 Also the
swine is unclean for you, because it has cloven
hooves, yet *does* not *chew* the cud; you shall not
eat their flesh [a]or touch their dead carcasses.
9 [a]"These you may eat of all that *are* in the
waters: you may eat all that have fins and scales.
10 And whatever does not have fins and scales
you shall not eat; it *is* unclean for you.
11 "All clean birds you may eat. 12 [a]But these
you shall not eat: the eagle, the vulture, the
buzzard, 13 the red kite, the falcon, and the kite
after their kinds; 14 every raven after its kind;
15 the ostrich, the short-eared owl, the sea gull,
and the hawk after their kinds; 16 the little owl,
the screech owl, the white owl, 17 the jackdaw, the
carrion vulture, the fisher owl, 18 the stork, the
heron after its kind, and the hoopoe and the bat.
19 "Also [a]every creeping thing that flies is
unclean for you; [b]they shall not be eaten.
20 "You may eat all clean birds.
21 [a]"You shall not eat anything that dies *of itself;*
you may give it to the alien who *is* within your gates,
that he may eat it, or you may sell it to a foreigner;
[b]for you *are* a holy people to the LORD your God.
"[c]You shall not boil a young goat in its
mother's milk.

**14:21** Unlike the Canaanites who would **boil a** live **young goat in its mother's milk** as a sacrifice to fertility gods, Israel was to practice a more humane method of animal sacrifice.

**13:4** [a] Deut. 10:12, 20; 2 Kin. 23:3 [b] Deut. 30:20 **13:5** [a] Deut. 18:20; Jer. 14:15 [b] Deut. 17:5, 7; 1 Cor. 5:13 **13:6** [a] Deut. 17:2 [b] Gen. 16:5 [c] 1 Sam. 18:1, 3 **13:8** [a] Deut. 7:16; Prov. 1:10 **13:9** [a] Lev. 24:14; Deut. 17:7 **13:11** [a] Deut. 17:13 **13:12** [a] Judg. 20:1–48 **13:16** [a] Josh. 6:24 [b] Josh. 8:28; Is. 17:1; 25:2; Jer. 49:2 **13:17** [a] Josh. 6:18 [b] Josh. 7:26 **13:18** [a] Deut. 12:25, 28, 32 **14:1** [a] [Rom. 8:16; Gal. 3:26] [b] Lev. 19:28; 21:1–5 **14:2** [a] Lev. 20:26; Deut. 7:6; [Rom. 12:1] **14:3** [a] Ezek. 4:14 **14:4** [a] Lev. 11:2–45 **14:5** [1] Or *addax* **14:8** [a] Lev. 11:26, 27 **14:9** [a] Lev. 11:9 **14:12** [a] Lev. 11:13 **14:19** [a] Lev. 11:20 [b] Lev. 11:23 **14:21** [a] Lev. 17:15; 22:8; Ezek. 4:14; 44:31 [b] Deut. 14:2 [c] Ex. 23:19; 34:26

### *TITHING PRINCIPLES*

[22] [a]"You shall truly tithe all the increase of your grain that the field produces year by year. [23] [a]And you shall eat before the LORD your God, in the place where He chooses to make His name abide, the tithe of your grain and your new wine and your oil, of [b]the firstborn of your herds and your flocks, that you may learn to fear the LORD your God always. [24] But if the journey is too long for you, so that you are not able to carry *the tithe, or* [a]if the place where the LORD your God chooses to put His name is too far from you, when the LORD your God has blessed you, [25] then you shall exchange *it* for money, take the money in your hand, and go to the place which the LORD your God chooses. [26] And you shall spend that money for whatever your heart desires: for oxen or sheep, for wine or similar drink, for whatever your heart desires; you shall eat there before the LORD your God, and you shall [a]rejoice, you and your household. [27] You shall not forsake the [a]Levite who *is* within your gates, for he has no part nor inheritance with you.

[28] [a]"At the end of *every* third year you shall bring out the [b]tithe of your produce of that year and store *it* up within your gates. [29] And the Levite, because he has no portion nor inheritance with you, and the stranger and the fatherless and the widow who *are* within your gates, may come and eat and be satisfied, that the LORD your God may bless you in all the work of your hand which you do.

### *DEBTS CANCELED EVERY SEVEN YEARS*

*(Ex. 21:1–11; Lev. 25:1–7)*

**15** "At the end of [a]*every* seven years you shall grant a release *of debts.* [2] And this *is* the form of the release: Every creditor who has lent *anything* to his neighbor shall release *it;* he shall not require *it* of his neighbor or his brother, because it is called the LORD's release. [3] Of a foreigner you may require *it;* but you shall give up your claim to what is owed by your brother, [4] except when there may be no poor among you; for the LORD will greatly [a]bless you in the land which the LORD your God is giving you to possess *as* an inheritance— [5] only if you carefully obey the voice of the LORD your God, to observe with care all these commandments which I command you today. [6] For the LORD your God will bless you just as He promised you; [a]you shall lend to many nations, but you shall not borrow; you shall reign over many nations, but they shall not reign over you.

### *GENEROSITY TO THE POOR*

[7] "If there is among you a poor man of your brethren, within any of the gates in your land which the LORD your God is giving you, [a]you shall not harden your heart nor shut your hand from your poor brother, [8] but [a]you shall open your hand wide to him and willingly lend him sufficient for his need, whatever he needs. [9] Beware lest there be a wicked thought in your heart, saying, 'The seventh year, the year of release, is at hand,' and your [a]eye be evil against your poor brother and you give him nothing, and [b]he cry out to the LORD against you, and [c]it become sin among you. [10] You shall surely give to him, and [a]your heart should not be grieved when you give to him, because [b]for this thing the LORD your God will bless you in all your works and in all to which you put your hand. [11] For [a]the poor will never cease from the land; therefore I command you, saying, 'You shall open your hand wide to your brother, to your poor and your needy, in your land.'

### *THE LAW CONCERNING BONDSERVANTS*

[12] [a]"If your brother, a Hebrew man, or a Hebrew woman, is [b]sold to you and serves you six years, then in the seventh year you shall let him go free from you. [13] And when you send him away free from you, you shall not let him go away empty-handed; [14] you shall supply him liberally from your flock, from your threshing floor, and from your winepress. *From what* the LORD your God has [a]blessed you with, you shall give to him. [15] [a]You shall remember that you were a slave in the land of Egypt, and the LORD your God redeemed you; therefore I command you this thing today. [16] And [a]if it happens that he says to you, 'I will not go away from you,' because he loves you and your house, since he prospers with you, [17] then you shall take an awl and thrust *it* through his ear to the door, and he shall be your servant forever. Also to your female servant you shall do likewise. [18] It shall not seem hard to you when you send him away free from you; for he has been worth [a]a double hired servant in serving you six years. Then the LORD your God will bless you in all that you do.

### *THE LAW CONCERNING FIRSTBORN ANIMALS*

[19] [a]"All the firstborn males that come from your herd and your flock you shall sanctify to the LORD your God; you shall do no work with the firstborn of your herd, nor shear the firstborn of your flock. [20] [a]You and your household shall eat *it* before the LORD your God year by year in the place which the LORD chooses. [21] [a]But if there is a defect in it, *if it is* lame or blind *or has* any serious defect, you shall not sacrifice it to the LORD your God. [22] You may eat it within your gates; [a]the unclean and the clean *person* alike *may eat it,* as *if it were* a gazelle or a deer. [23] Only you shall not eat its blood; you shall pour it on the ground like water.

**14:22** [a] Lev. 27:30; Deut. 12:6, 17; Neh. 10:37 **14:23** [a] Deut. 12:5–7 [b] Deut. 15:19, 20 **14:24** [a] Deut. 12:5, 21 **14:26** [a] Deut. 12:7 **14:27** [a] Deut. 12:12 **14:28** [a] Deut. 26:12; Amos 4:4 [b] Num. 18:21–24 **15:1** [a] Ex. 21:2; 23:10, 11; Lev. 25:4; Jer. 34:14 **15:4** [a] Deut. 7:13 **15:6** [a] Deut. 28:12, 44 **15:7** [a] Ex. 23:6; Lev. 25:35–37; Deut. 24:12–14; [1 John 3:17] **15:8** [a] Matt. 5:42; Gal. 2:10 **15:9** [a] Deut. 28:54, 56 [b] Ex. 22:23; Deut. 24:15; Job 34:28; Ps. 12:5; James 5:4 [c] [Matt. 25:41, 42] **15:10** [a] 2 Cor. 9:5, 7 [b] Deut. 14:29; Ps. 41:1; Prov. 22:9 **15:11** [a] Matt. 26:11; Mark 14:7; John 12:8 **15:12** [a] Ex. 21:2–6; Jer. 34:14 [b] Lev. 25:39–46 **15:14** [a] Prov. 10:22 **15:15** [a] Deut. 5:15 **15:16** [a] Ex. 21:5, 6 **15:18** [a] Is. 16:14 **15:19** [a] Ex. 13:2, 12 **15:20** [a] Lev. 7:15–18; Deut. 12:5; 14:23 **15:21** [a] Lev. 22:19–25; Deut. 17:1 **15:22** [a] Deut. 12:15, 16, 22

### *THE PASSOVER REVIEWED*
*(Ex. 12:1–20; 23:14–19; 34:18–26)*

**16** "Observe the [a]month of Abib, and keep
the Passover to the LORD your God, for [b]in
the month of Abib the LORD your God brought
you out of Egypt by night. 2 Therefore you shall
sacrifice the Passover to the LORD your God, from
the flock and [a]the herd, in the [b]place where the
LORD chooses to put His name. 3 You shall eat
no leavened bread with it; [a]seven days you shall
eat unleavened bread with it, *that is,* the bread of
affliction (for you came out of the land of Egypt in
haste), that you may [b]remember the day in which
you came out of the land of Egypt all the days of
your life. 4 [a]And no leaven shall be seen among
you in all your territory for seven days, nor shall
*any* of the meat which you sacrifice the first day
at twilight remain overnight until [b]morning.
5 "You may not sacrifice the Passover within
any of your gates which the LORD your God gives
you; 6 but at the place where the LORD your God
chooses to make His name abide, there you shall
sacrifice the Passover [a]at twilight, at the going
down of the sun, at the time you came out of
Egypt. 7 And you shall roast and eat *it* [a]in the
place which the LORD your God chooses, and
in the morning you shall turn and go to your
tents. 8 Six days you shall eat unleavened bread,
and [a]on the seventh day there *shall be* a sacred
assembly to the LORD your God. You shall do
no work *on it.*

### *THE FEAST OF WEEKS REVIEWED*
*(Ex. 34:22; Lev. 23:15–21; Num. 28:26–31)*

9 "You shall count seven weeks for yourself;
begin to count the seven weeks from *the time*
you begin *to put* the sickle to the grain. 10 Then
you shall keep the [a]Feast of Weeks to the LORD
your God with the tribute of a freewill offering
from your hand, which you shall give [b]as the
LORD your God blesses you. 11 [a]You shall rejoice
before the LORD your God, you and your son
and your daughter, your male servant and your
female servant, the Levite who *is* within your
gates, the stranger and the fatherless and the
widow who *are* among you, at the place where
the LORD your God chooses to make His name
abide. 12 [a]And you shall remember that you were
a slave in Egypt, and you shall be careful to
observe these statutes.

### *THE FEAST OF TABERNACLES REVIEWED*
*(Lev. 23:33–43; Num. 29:12–40)*

13 [a]"You shall observe the Feast of Tabernacles
seven days, when you have gathered from your
threshing floor and from your winepress. 14 And
[a]you shall rejoice in your feast, you and your son
and your daughter, your male servant and your
female servant and the Levite, the stranger and
the fatherless and the widow, who *are* within
your gates. 15 [a]Seven days you shall keep a sacred
feast to the LORD your God in the place which the
LORD chooses, because the LORD your God will
bless you in all your produce and in all the work
of your hands, so that you surely rejoice.
16 [a]"Three times a year all your males shall
appear before the LORD your God in the place
which He chooses: at the Feast of Unleavened
Bread, at the Feast of Weeks, and at the Feast of
Tabernacles; and [b]they shall not appear before
the LORD empty-handed. 17 Every man *shall give*
as he is able, [a]according to the blessing of the
LORD your God which He has given you.

### *JUSTICE MUST BE ADMINISTERED*

18 "You shall appoint [a]judges and officers in
all your gates, which the LORD your God gives
you, according to your tribes, and they shall
judge the people with just judgment. 19 [a]You
shall not pervert justice; [b]you shall not show
partiality, [c]nor take a bribe, for a bribe blinds
the eyes of the wise and twists the words of the
righteous. 20 You shall follow what is altogether
just, that you may [a]live and inherit the land
which the LORD your God is giving you.
21 [a]"You shall not plant for yourself any tree,
as a wooden image, near the altar which you
build for yourself to the LORD your God. 22 [a]You
shall not set up a *sacred* pillar, which the LORD
your God hates.

**17** "You [a]shall not sacrifice to the LORD your
God a bull or sheep which has any blem-
ish *or* defect, for that *is* an abomination to the
LORD your God.
2 [a]"If there is found among you, within any of
your gates which the LORD your God gives you,
a man or a woman who has been wicked in the
sight of the LORD your God, [b]in transgressing
His covenant, 3 who has gone and served other
gods and worshiped them, either [a]the sun or
moon or any of the host of heaven, [b]which I
have not commanded, 4 [a]and it is told you, and
you hear *of it,* then you shall inquire diligently.
And if *it is* indeed true *and* certain that such
an abomination has been committed in Israel,
5 then you shall bring out to your gates that man
or woman who has committed that wicked thing,
and [a]shall stone [b]to death that man or woman
with stones. 6 Whoever is deserving of death
shall be put to death on the testimony of two
or three [a]witnesses; he shall not be put to death
on the testimony of one witness. 7 The hands

**16:1** [a] Ex. 12:2 [b] Ex. 13:4 **16:2** [a] Num. 28:19 [b] Deut. 12:5, 26; 15:20 **16:3** [a] Num. 29:12 [b] Ex. 13:3; Deut. 4:9 **16:4** [a] Ex. 13:7 [b] Num. 9:12 **16:6** [a] Ex. 12:7–10 **16:7** [a] 2 Kin. 23:23 **16:8** [a] Ex. 12:16; 13:6; Lev. 23:8, 36 **16:10** [a] Ex. 34:22; Lev. 23:15, 16; Num. 28:26 [b] 1 Cor. 16:2 **16:11** [a] Deut. 16:14 **16:12** [a] Deut. 15:15 **16:13** [a] Ex. 23:16 **16:14** [a] Neh. 8:9 **16:15** [a] Lev. 23:39–41 **16:16** [a] Ex. 23:14–17; 34:22–24 [b] Ex. 23:15 **16:17** [a] Lev. 14:30, 31; Deut. 16:10 **16:18** [a] Ex. 23:1–8; Deut. 1:16, 17; John 7:24 **16:19** [a] Ex. 23:2, 6 [b] Deut. 1:17 [c] Ex. 23:8 **16:20** [a] Ezek. 18:5–9 **16:21** [a] Ex. 34:13 **16:22** [a] Lev. 26:1 **17:1** [a] Deut. 15:21; Mal. 1:8, 13 **17:2** [a] Deut. 13:6 [b] Josh. 7:11 **17:3** [a] Deut. 4:19 [b] Jer. 7:22 **17:4** [a] Deut. 13:12, 14 **17:5** [a] Lev. 24:14–16; Josh. 7:25 [b] Deut. 13:6–18 **17:6** [a] Num. 35:30; Deut. 19:15; Matt. 18:16; John 8:17; 2 Cor. 13:1; 1 Tim. 5:19; Heb. 10:28

of the witnesses shall be the first against him to put him to death, and afterward the hands of all the people. So you shall put away the evil from among [a]you.

**17:5–7** Stoning was the death penalty handed down to convicted murderers. When a person was convicted, he was immediately taken outside the camp and stoned to death.

8 [a]"If a matter arises which is too hard for you to judge, between degrees of guilt for bloodshed, between one judgment or another, or between one punishment or another, matters of controversy within your gates, then you shall arise and go up to the [b]place which the LORD your God chooses. 9 And [a]you shall come to the priests, the Levites, and [b]to the judge *there* in those days, and inquire *of them;* [c]they shall pronounce upon you the sentence of judgment. 10 You shall do according to the sentence which they pronounce upon you in that place which the LORD chooses. And you shall be careful to do according to all that they order you. 11 According to the sentence of the law in which they instruct you, according to the judgment which they tell you, you shall do; you shall not turn aside *to* the right hand or *to* the left from the sentence which they pronounce upon you. 12 Now [a]the man who acts presumptuously and will not heed the priest who stands to minister there before the LORD your God, or the judge, that man shall die. So you shall put away the evil from Israel. 13 [a]And all the people shall hear and fear, and no longer act presumptuously.

### *PRINCIPLES GOVERNING KINGS*

14 "When you come to the land which the LORD your God is giving you, and possess it and dwell in it, and say, [a]'I will set a king over me like all the nations that *are* around me,' 15 you shall surely set a king over you [a]whom the LORD your God chooses; *one* [b]from among your brethren you shall set as king over you; you may not set a foreigner over you, who *is* not your brother. 16 But he shall not multiply [a]horses for himself, nor cause the people [b]to return to Egypt to multiply horses, for [c]the LORD has said to you, [d]'You shall not return that way again.' 17 Neither shall he multiply wives for himself, lest his heart turn away; nor shall he greatly multiply silver and [a]gold for himself.

18 "Also it shall be, when he sits on the throne of his kingdom, that he shall write for himself a copy of this law in a book, from *the one* [a]before the priests, the Levites. 19 And [a]it shall be with him, and he shall read it all the days of his life, that he may learn to fear the LORD his God and be careful to observe all the words of this law and these statutes, 20 that his heart may not be lifted above his brethren, that he [a]may not turn aside from the commandment *to* the right hand or *to* the left, and that he may prolong *his* days in his kingdom, he and his children in the midst of Israel.

### *THE PORTION OF THE PRIESTS AND LEVITES*

**18** "The priests, the Levites—all the tribe of Levi—shall have no part nor [a]inheritance with Israel; they shall eat the offerings of the LORD made by fire, and His portion. 2 Therefore they shall have no inheritance among their brethren; the LORD is their inheritance, as He said to them.

3 "And this shall be the priest's [a]due from the people, from those who offer a sacrifice, whether *it is* bull or sheep: they shall give to the priest the shoulder, the cheeks, and the stomach. 4 [a]The firstfruits of your grain and your new wine and your oil, and the first of the fleece of your sheep, you shall give him. 5 For [a]the LORD your God has chosen him out of all your tribes [b]to stand to minister in the name of the LORD, him and his sons forever.

6 "So if a Levite comes from any of your gates, from where he [a]dwells among all Israel, and comes with all the desire of his mind [b]to the place which the LORD chooses, 7 then he may serve in the name of the LORD his God [a]as all his brethren the Levites *do,* who stand there before the LORD. 8 They shall have equal [a]portions to eat, besides what comes from the sale of his inheritance.

### *AVOID WICKED CUSTOMS*

9 "When you come into the land which the LORD your God is giving you, [a]you shall not learn to follow the abominations of those nations. 10 There shall not be found among you *anyone* who makes his son or his daughter [a]pass through the fire, [b]*or one* who practices witchcraft, *or* a soothsayer, or one who interprets omens, or a sorcerer, 11 [a]or one who conjures spells, or a medium, or a spiritist, or [b]one who calls up the dead. 12 For all who do these things *are* an abomination to the LORD, and [a]because of these abominations the LORD your God drives them out from before you. 13 You shall be blameless before the LORD your God. 14 For these nations which you will dispossess listened to soothsayers and diviners; but as for you, the LORD your God has not appointed such for you.

**17:7** [a] Deut. 13:5; 19:19; 1 Cor. 5:13 **17:8** [a] Deut. 1:17; 2 Chr. 19:10 [b] Deut. 12:5; 16:2 **17:9** [a] Jer. 18:18 [b] Deut. 19:17–19 [c] Ezek. 44:24 **17:12** [a] Num. 15:30; Deut. 1:43 **17:13** [a] Deut. 13:11 **17:14** [a] 1 Sam. 8:5, 19, 20; 10:19 **17:15** [a] 1 Sam. 9:15, 16; 10:24; 16:12, 13; 1 Chr. 22:8–10; Hos. 8:4 [b] Jer. 30:21 **17:16** [a] 1 Kin. 4:26; 10:26–29; Ps. 20:7 [b] Is. 31:1; Ezek. 17:15 [c] Ex. 13:17, 18; Hos. 11:5 [d] Deut. 28:68 **17:17** [a] 1 Kin. 10:14 **17:18** [a] Deut. 31:24–26 **17:19** [a] Ps. 119:97, 98 **17:20** [a] Deut. 5:32; 1 Kin. 15:5 **18:1** [a] Deut. 10:9; 1 Cor. 9:13 **18:3** [a] Lev. 7:32–34; Num. 18:11, 12; 1 Sam. 2:13–16, 29 **18:4** [a] Ex. 22:29 **18:5** [a] Ex. 28:1 [b] Deut. 10:8 **18:6** [a] Num. 35:2 [b] Deut. 12:5; 14:23 **18:7** [a] Num. 1:50; 2 Chr. 31:2 **18:8** [a] Lev. 27:30–33; Num. 18:21–24; 2 Chr. 31:4; Neh. 12:44 **18:9** [a] Lev. 18:26, 27, 30; Deut. 12:29, 30; 20:16–18 **18:10** [a] Lev. 18:21; Deut. 12:31 [b] Ex. 22:18; Lev. 19:26, 31; 20:6, 27; Is. 8:19 **18:11** [a] Lev. 20:27 [b] 1 Sam. 28:7 **18:12** [a] Lev. 18:24; Deut. 9:4

APPLY THE TRUTH

## WORLDVIEWS

**18:9** Your worldview is your perception and philosophy of life. Many aspects influence our worldview: spirituality, morality, ethics, politics, economics, and even entertainment. But what is it that most shapes our view of the world and makes sense of all these aspects? For some, it's their parents or upbringing. For others, it's the classroom or books they've read. For many people, however, their worldview has been shaped most by social media, shows, or celebrities. In other words, culture shapes their worldview. These people are building worldview "sandcastles" though. Beautiful and elaborate, but unable to withstand the crashing tides of opinions and trends.

This is what God warned the Israelites against. When they came into the Promised Land, they weren't to allow the nations around them to shape their views and behaviors. Instead, the Word of God and the ways of God were to inform their views and actions, which, in turn, were to influence those nations.

The Word of God is a sure foundation that can withstand the world's complexity and the rising tide of change. What foundation are you building your worldview upon? Are you building sandcastles? Or are you standing on the solid rock of God's Word?

### *A NEW PROPHET LIKE MOSES*

15 [a]"The LORD your God will raise up for you
a Prophet like me from your midst, from your
brethren. Him you shall hear, 16 according to all
you desired of the LORD your God in Horeb [a]in
the day of the assembly, saying, [b]'Let me not
hear again the voice of the LORD my God, nor
let me see this great fire anymore, lest I die.'

### SEEING JESUS IN THE SCRIPTURE

**18:15** Jesus is the Prophet like Moses, whom God raised for His people's salvation (see Luke 7:16). Jesus is more than a great prophet though. Jesus is the Son of God who came from heaven to save people from sin.

17 "And the LORD said to me: [a]'What they have
spoken is good. 18 [a]I will raise up for them a Proph-
et like you from among their brethren, and [b]will
put My words in His mouth, [c]and He shall speak
to them all that I command Him. 19 [a]And it shall
be *that* whoever will not hear My words, which He
speaks in My name, I will require *it* of him. 20 But
[a]the prophet who presumes to speak a word in My
name, which I have not commanded him to speak,
or [b]who speaks in the name of other gods, that
prophet shall die.' 21 And if you say in your heart,
'How shall we know the word which the LORD
has not spoken?'— 22 [a]when a prophet speaks
in the name of the LORD, [b]if the thing does not
happen or come to pass, that *is* the thing which the
LORD has not spoken; the prophet has spoken it
[c]presumptuously; you shall not be afraid of him.

### *THREE CITIES OF REFUGE*

*(Num. 35:9–28; Josh. 20:1–9)*

19 "When the LORD your God [a]has cut off the
nations whose land the LORD your God is
giving you, and you dispossess them and dwell
in their cities and in their houses, 2 [a]you shall
separate three cities for yourself in the midst of
your land which the LORD your God is giving you
to possess. 3 You shall prepare roads for yourself,
and divide into three parts the territory of your
land which the LORD your God is giving you to
inherit, that any manslayer may flee there.
4 "And [a]this *is* the case of the manslayer who
flees there, that he may live: Whoever kills his
neighbor unintentionally, not having hated
him in time past— 5 as when *a man* goes to the
woods with his neighbor to cut timber, and his
hand swings a stroke with the ax to cut down
the tree, and the head slips from the handle and
strikes his neighbor so that he dies—he shall flee
to one of these cities and live; 6 [a]lest the aveng-
er of blood, while his anger is hot, pursue the
manslayer and overtake him, because the way is
long, and kill him, though he *was* not deserving
of death, since he had not hated the victim in
time past. 7 Therefore I command you, saying,
'You shall separate three cities for yourself.'
8 "Now if the LORD your God [a]enlarges your
territory, as He swore to [b]your fathers, and gives
you the land which He promised to give to your
fathers, 9 and if you keep all these command-
ments and do them, which I command you
today, to love the LORD your God and to walk
always in His ways, [a]then you shall add three
more cities for yourself besides these three,
10 [a]lest innocent blood be shed in the midst of

**18:15** [a] Matt. 21:11; Luke 1:76; 2:25–34; 7:16; 24:19; Acts 3:22 **18:16** [a] Deut. 5:23–27 [b] Ex. 20:18, 19; Heb. 12:19 **18:17** [a] Deut. 5:28 **18:18** [a] John 1:45; 6:14; Acts 3:22 [b] Is. 49:2; 51:16; John 17:8 [c] [John 4:25; 8:28] **18:19** [a] Acts 3:23; [Heb. 12:25] **18:20** [a] Deut. 13:5; Jer. 14:14, 15; Zech. 13:2–5 [b] Deut. 13:1–3; Jer. 2:8 **18:22** [a] Jer. 28:9 [b] Deut. 13:2 [c] Deut. 18:20 **19:1** [a] Deut. 12:29 **19:2** [a] Ex. 21:13; Num. 35:10–15; Deut. 4:41; Josh. 20:2 **19:4** [a] Num. 35:9–34; Deut. 4:42 **19:6** [a] Num. 35:12 **19:8** [a] Deut. 12:20 [b] Gen. 15:18–21 **19:9** [a] Josh. 20:7–9 **19:10** [a] Num. 35:33; Deut. 21:1–9

your land which the LORD your God is giving you *as* an inheritance, and *thus* guilt of bloodshed be upon you.

11 "But [a]if anyone hates his neighbor, lies in wait for him, rises against him and strikes him mortally, so that he dies, and he flees to one of these cities, 12 then the elders of his city shall send and bring him from there, and deliver him over to the hand of the avenger of blood, that he may die. 13 [a]Your eye shall not pity him, [b]but you shall put away *the guilt of* innocent blood from Israel, that it may go well with you.

### PROPERTY BOUNDARIES

14 [a]"You shall not remove your neighbor's landmark, which the men of old have set, in your inheritance which you will inherit in the land that the LORD your God is giving you to possess.

### THE LAW CONCERNING WITNESSES

15 [a]"One witness shall not rise against a man concerning any iniquity or any sin that he commits; by the mouth of two or three witnesses the matter shall be established. 16 If a false witness [a]rises against any man to testify against him of wrongdoing, 17 then both men in the controversy shall stand before the LORD, [a]before the priests and the judges who serve in those days. 18 And the judges shall make careful inquiry, and indeed, *if* the witness *is* a false witness, who has testified falsely against his brother, 19 [a]then you shall do to him as he thought to have done to his brother; so [b]you shall put away the evil from among you. 20 [a]And those who remain shall hear and fear, and hereafter they shall not again commit such evil among you. 21 [a]Your eye shall not pity: [b]life *shall be* for life, eye for eye, tooth for tooth, hand for hand, foot for foot.

### PRINCIPLES GOVERNING WARFARE

20 "When you go out to battle against your enemies, and see [a]horses and chariots *and* people more numerous than you, do not be [b]afraid of them; for the LORD your God *is* [c]with you, who brought you up from the land of Egypt. 2 So it shall be, when you are on the verge of battle, that the priest shall approach and speak to the people. 3 And he shall say to them, 'Hear, O Israel: Today you are on the verge of battle with your enemies. Do not let your heart faint, do not be afraid, and do not tremble or be terrified because of them; 4 for the LORD your God *is* He who goes with you, [a]to fight for you against your enemies, to save you.'

5 "Then the officers shall speak to the people, saying: 'What man *is there* who has built a new house and has not [a]dedicated it? Let him go and return to his house, lest he die in the battle and another man dedicate it. 6 Also what man *is there* who has planted a vineyard and has not eaten of it? Let him go and return to his house, lest he die in the battle and another man eat of it. 7 [a]And what man *is there* who is betrothed to a woman and has not married her? Let him go and return to his house, lest he die in the battle and another man marry her.'

8 "The officers shall speak further to the people, and say, [a]'What man *is there who is* fearful and fainthearted? Let him go and return to his house, lest the heart of his brethren faint[1] like his heart.' 9 And so it shall be, when the officers have finished speaking to the people, that they shall make captains of the armies to lead the people.

10 "When you go near a city to fight against it, [a]then proclaim an offer of peace to it. 11 And it shall be that if they accept your offer of peace, and open to you, then all the people *who are* found in it shall be placed under tribute to you, and serve you. 12 Now if *the city* will not make peace with you, but war against you, then you shall besiege it. 13 And when the LORD your God delivers it into your hands, [a]you shall strike every male in it with the edge of the sword. 14 But the women, the little ones, [a]the livestock, and all that is in the city, all its spoil, you shall plunder for yourself; and [b]you shall eat the enemies' plunder which the LORD your God gives you. 15 Thus you shall do to all the cities *which are* very far from you, which *are* not of the cities of these nations.

16 "But [a]of the cities of these peoples which the LORD your God gives you *as* an inheritance, you shall let nothing that breathes remain alive, 17 but you shall utterly destroy them: the Hittite and the Amorite and the Canaanite and the Perizzite and the Hivite and the Jebusite, just as the LORD your God has commanded you, 18 lest [a]they teach you to do according to all their abominations which they have done for their gods, and you [b]sin against the LORD your God.

19 "When you besiege a city for a long time, while making war against it to take it, you shall not destroy its trees by wielding an ax against them; if you can eat of them, do not cut them down to use in the siege, for the tree of the field *is* man's *food*. 20 Only the trees which you know *are* not trees for food you may destroy and cut down, to build siegeworks against the city that makes war with you, until it is subdued.

19:11 [a] Num. 35:16, 24; Deut. 27:24; [1 John 3:15] 19:13 [a] Deut. 13:8 [b] Num. 35:33, 34; 1 Kin. 2:31 19:14 [a] Deut. 27:17; Job 24:2; Prov. 22:28; Hos. 5:10 19:15 [a] Num. 35:30; Deut. 17:6; Matt. 18:16; John 8:17; 2 Cor. 13:1; 1 Tim. 5:19; Heb. 10:28 19:16 [a] Ex. 23:1; Ps. 27:12; 35:11 19:17 [a] Deut. 17:8–11; 21:5 19:19 [a] Prov. 19:5; Dan. 6:24 [b] Deut. 13:5; 17:7; 21:21; 22:21 19:20 [a] Deut. 17:13; 21:21 19:21 [a] Deut. 19:13 [b] Ex. 21:23, 24; Lev. 24:20; Matt. 5:38, 39 20:1 [a] Ps. 20:7; Is. 31:1 [b] Deut. 7:18 [c] Num. 23:21; Deut. 5:6; 31:6, 8; 2 Chr. 13:12; 32:7, 8; Ps. 23:4; Is. 41:10 20:4 [a] Deut. 1:30; 3:22; Josh. 23:10 20:5 [a] Neh. 12:27 20:7 [a] Deut. 24:5 20:8 [a] Judg. 7:3 [1] Following Masoretic Text and Targum; Samaritan Pentateuch, Septuagint, Syriac, and Vulgate read *lest he make his brother's heart faint.* 20:10 [a] 2 Sam. 10:19 20:13 [a] Num. 31:7 20:14 [a] Josh. 8:2 [b] 1 Sam. 14:30 20:16 [a] Ex. 23:31–33; Num. 21:2, 3; Deut. 7:1–5; Josh. 11:14 20:18 [a] Ex. 34:12–16; Deut. 7:4; 12:30; 18:9 [b] Ex. 23:33; 2 Kin. 21:3–15; Ps. 106:34–41

### *THE LAW CONCERNING UNSOLVED MURDER*

**21** "If *anyone* is found slain, lying in the field in
the land which the LORD your God is giving
you to possess, *and* it is not known who killed
him, 2 then your elders and your judges shall go
out and measure *the distance* from the slain man
to the surrounding cities. 3 And it shall be *that* the
elders of the city nearest to the slain man will take
a heifer which has not been worked *and* which
has not pulled with a [a]yoke. 4 The elders of that
city shall bring the heifer down to a valley with
flowing water, which is neither plowed nor sown,
and they shall break the heifer's neck there in the
valley. 5 Then the priests, the sons of Levi, shall
come near, for [a]the LORD your God has chosen
them to minister to Him and to bless in the name
of the LORD; [b]by their word every controversy
and every assault shall be *settled.* 6 And all the
elders of that city nearest to the slain *man* [a]shall
wash their hands over the heifer whose neck was
broken in the valley. 7 Then they shall answer and
say, 'Our hands have not shed this blood, nor have
our eyes seen *it.* 8 Provide atonement, O LORD, for
Your people Israel, whom You have redeemed,
[a]and do not lay innocent blood to the charge
of Your people Israel.' And atonement shall be
provided on their behalf for the blood. 9 So [a]you
shall put away the *guilt of* innocent blood from
among you when you do *what is* right in the
sight of the LORD.

### *FEMALE CAPTIVES*

10 "When you go out to war against your ene-
mies, and the LORD your God delivers them into
your hand, and you take them captive, 11 and you
see among the captives a beautiful woman, and
desire her and would take her for your [a]wife,
12 then you shall bring her home to your house,
and she shall [a]shave her head and trim her nails.
13 She shall put off the clothes of her captivity,
remain in your house, and [a]mourn her father and
her mother a full month; after that you may go in
to her and be her husband, and she shall be your
wife. 14 And it shall be, if you have no delight in
her, then you shall set her free, but you certainly
shall not sell her for money; you shall not treat
her brutally, because you have [a]humbled her.

### *FIRSTBORN INHERITANCE RIGHTS*

15 "If a man has two wives, one loved [a]and the
other unloved, and they have borne him children,
*both* the loved and the unloved, and *if* the first-
born son is of her who is unloved, 16 then it shall
be, [a]on the day he bequeaths his possessions to
his sons, *that* he must not bestow firstborn status
on the son of the loved wife in preference to the
son of the unloved, the *true* firstborn. 17 But he
shall acknowledge the son of the unloved wife
*as* the firstborn [a]by giving him a double portion
of all that he has, for he [b]*is* the beginning of his
strength; [c]the right of the firstborn *is* his.

### *THE REBELLIOUS SON*

18 "If a man has a stubborn and rebellious
son who will not obey the voice of his father or
the voice of his mother, and *who,* when they
have chastened him, will not heed them, 19 then
his father and his mother shall take hold of him
and bring him out to the elders of his city, to
the gate of his city. 20 And they shall say to the
elders of his city, 'This son of ours is stubborn
and rebellious; he will not obey our voice; he is
a glutton and a drunkard.' 21 Then all the men
of his city shall stone him to death with stones;
[a]so you shall put away the evil from among you,
[b]and all Israel shall hear and fear.

### *MISCELLANEOUS LAWS*

22 "If a man has committed a sin [a]deserving
of death, and he is put to death, and you hang
him on a tree, 23 [a]his body shall not remain over-
night on the tree, but you shall surely bury him
that day, so that [b]you do not defile the land which
the LORD your God is giving you *as* an inheri-
tance; for [c]he who is hanged *is* accursed of God.

> **21:22–23** The hanging of a dead body on a tree was a warning to other would-be criminals. As such, some dead bodies were left hanging for several days. The Israelites were forbidden by God to leave a body hanging overnight.

**22** "You [a]shall not see your brother's ox or
his sheep going astray, and hide yourself
from them; you shall certainly bring them back
to your brother. 2 And if your brother *is* not near
you, or if you do not know him, then you shall
bring it to your own house, and it shall remain
with you until your brother seeks it; then you
shall restore it to him. 3 You shall do the same
with his donkey, and so shall you do with his
garment; with any lost thing of your brother's,
which he has lost and you have found, you shall
do likewise; you must not hide yourself.
4 [a]"You shall not see your brother's donkey
or his ox fall down along the road, and hide
yourself from them; you shall surely help him
lift *them* up again.
5 "A woman shall not wear anything that per-
tains to a man, nor shall a man put on a woman's
garment, for all who do so *are* an abomination
to the LORD your God.

21:3 [a] Num. 19:2 21:5 [a] Deut. 10:8; 1 Chr. 23:13 [b] Deut. 17:8, 9 21:6 [a] Ps. 19:12; 26:6; Matt. 27:24 21:8 [a] Deut. 19:10, 13; Jon. 1:14 21:9 [a] Deut. 19:13 21:11 [a] Num. 31:18 21:12 [a] Lev. 14:8, 9; Num. 6:9 21:13 [a] Ps. 45:10 21:14 [a] Gen. 34:2; Deut. 22:29; Judg. 19:24 21:15 [a] Gen. 29:33 21:16 [a] 1 Chr. 5:2; 26:10 21:17 [a] 2 Kin. 2:9 [b] Gen. 49:3 [c] Gen. 25:31, 33 21:21 [a] Deut. 13:5; 19:19, 20; 22:21, 24 [b] Deut. 13:11 21:22 [a] Deut. 22:26; Matt. 26:66; Mark 14:64; Acts 23:29 21:23 [a] Josh. 8:29; 10:26, 27; John 19:31 [b] Lev. 18:25; Num. 35:34 [c] Gal. 3:13 22:1 [a] Ex. 23:4 22:4 [a] Ex. 23:5

6 “If a bird’s nest happens to be before you
along the way, in any tree or on the ground, with
young ones or eggs, with the mother sitting on
the young or on the eggs, [a]you shall not take
the mother with the young; 7 you shall surely let
the mother go, and take the young for yourself,
[a]that it may be well with you and *that* you may
prolong *your* days.
8 “When you build a new house, then you
shall make a parapet for your roof, that you may
not bring guilt of bloodshed on your household
if anyone falls from it.
9 [a]“You shall not sow your vineyard with
different kinds of seed, lest the yield of the seed
which you have sown and the fruit of your vine-
yard be defiled.
10 [a]“You shall not plow with an ox and a don-
key together.
11 [a]“You shall not wear a garment of different
sorts, *such as* wool and linen mixed together.
12 “You shall make [a]tassels on the four
corners of the clothing with which you cover
*yourself.*

### LAWS OF SEXUAL MORALITY

13 “If any man takes a wife, and goes in to her,
and [a]detests her, 14 and charges her with shameful
conduct, and brings a bad name on her, and says,
‘I took this woman, and when I came to her I
found she *was* not a virgin,’ 15 then the father and
mother of the young woman shall take and bring
out *the evidence of* the young woman’s virginity to
the elders of the city at the gate. 16 And the young
woman’s father shall say to the elders, ‘I gave my
daughter to this man as wife, and he detests her.
17 Now he has charged her with shameful conduct,
saying, “I found your daughter *was* not a virgin,”
and yet these *are the evidences of* my daughter’s
virginity.’ And they shall spread the cloth before
the elders of the city. 18 Then the elders of that
city shall take that man and punish him; 19 and
they shall fine him one hundred *shekels* of silver
and give *them* to the father of the young woman,
because he has brought a bad name on a virgin
of Israel. And she shall be his wife; he cannot
divorce her all his days.
20 “But if the thing is true, *and evidences of*
virginity are not found for the young woman,
21 then they shall bring out the young woman to
the door of her father’s house, and the men of
her city shall stone her to death with [a]stones,
because she has [b]done a disgraceful thing in
Israel, to play the harlot in her father’s house.
[c]So you shall put away the evil from among you.
22 [a]“If a man is found lying with a woman
married to a husband, then both of them shall
die—the man that lay with the woman, and the
woman; so you shall put away the evil from
Israel.
23 “If a young woman *who is* a virgin is [a]be-
trothed to a husband, and a man finds her in
the city and lies with her, 24 then you shall bring
them both out to the gate of that city, and you
shall stone them to death with stones, the young
woman because she did not cry out in the city,
and the man because he [a]humbled his neigh-
bor’s wife; [b]so you shall put away the evil from
among you.
25 “But if a man finds a betrothed young
woman in the countryside, and the man forces
her and lies with her, then only the man who lay
with her shall die. 26 But you shall do nothing to
the young woman; *there is* in the young woman
no sin *deserving* of death, for just as when a man
rises against his neighbor and kills him, even so
*is* this matter. 27 For he found her in the country-
side, *and* the betrothed young woman cried out,
but *there was* no one to save her.
28 [a]“If a man finds a young woman *who is* a
virgin, who is not betrothed, and he seizes her
and lies with her, and they are found out, 29 then
the man who lay with her shall give to the young
woman’s father [a]fifty *shekels* of silver, and she
shall be his wife [b]because he has humbled her; he
shall not be permitted to divorce her all his days.
30 [a]“A man shall not take his father’s wife,
nor [b]uncover his father’s bed.

### THOSE EXCLUDED FROM THE CONGREGATION

23 “He who is emasculated by crushing or
mutilation shall [a]not enter the assembly
of the LORD.
2 “One of illegitimate birth shall not enter
the assembly of the LORD; even to the tenth
generation none of his *descendants* shall enter
the assembly of the LORD.
3 [a]“An Ammonite or Moabite shall not enter
the assembly of the LORD; even to the tenth
generation none of his *descendants* shall enter
the assembly of the LORD forever, 4 [a]because they
did not meet you with bread and water on the
road when you came out of Egypt, and [b]because
they hired against you Balaam the son of Beor
from Pethor of Mesopotamia,[1] to curse you. 5 Nev-
ertheless the LORD your God would not listen
to Balaam, but the LORD your God turned the
curse into a blessing for you, because the LORD
your God [a]loves you. 6 [a]You shall not seek their
peace nor their prosperity all your days forever.
7 “You shall not abhor an Edomite, [a]for he *is*
your brother. You shall not abhor an Egyptian,
because [b]you were an alien in his land. 8 The
children of the third generation born to them
may enter the assembly of the LORD.

22:6 [a] Lev. 22:28 22:7 [a] Deut. 4:40 22:9 [a] Lev. 19:19 22:10 [a] [2 Cor. 6:14–16] 22:11 [a] Lev. 19:19 22:12 [a] Num. 15:37–41; Matt. 23:5 22:13 [a] Deut. 21:15; 24:3 22:21 [a] Deut. 21:21 [b] Gen. 34:7; Judg. 20:5–10; 2 Sam. 13:12, 13 [c] Deut. 13:5 22:22 [a] Lev. 20:10; Num. 5:22–27; Ezek. 16:38; [Matt. 5:27, 28]; John 8:5; [1 Cor. 6:9; Heb. 13:4] 22:23 [a] Lev. 19:20–22; Matt. 1:18, 19 22:24 [a] Deut. 21:14 [b] Deut. 22:21, 22; 1 Cor. 5:2, 13 22:28 [a] Ex. 22:16, 17 22:29 [a] Ex. 22:16, 17 [b] Deut. 22:24 22:30 [a] Lev. 18:8; 20:11; Deut. 27:20; 1 Cor. 5:1 [b] Ruth 3:9; Ezek. 16:8 23:1 [a] Lev. 21:20; 22:24 23:3 [a] Neh. 13:1, 2 23:4 [a] Deut. 2:27–30 [b] Num. 22:5, 6; 23:7; Josh. 24:9; 2 Pet. 2:15; Jude 11 [1] Hebrew *Aram Naharaim* 23:5 [a] Deut. 4:37 23:6 [a] Ezra 9:12 23:7 [a] Gen. 25:24–26; Deut. 2:4, 8; Amos 1:11; Obad. 10, 12 [b] Ex. 22:21; 23:9; Lev. 19:34; Deut. 10:19

### CLEANLINESS OF THE CAMPSITE

9 "When the army goes out against your enemies, then keep yourself from every wicked thing. 10 [a]If there is any man among you who becomes unclean by some occurrence in the night, then he shall go outside the camp; he shall not come inside the camp. 11 But it shall be, when evening comes, that [a]he shall wash with water; and when the sun sets, he may come into the camp.

12 "Also you shall have a place outside the camp, where you may go out; 13 and you shall have an implement among your equipment, and when you sit down outside, you shall dig with it and turn and cover your refuse. 14 For the LORD your God [a]walks in the midst of your camp, to deliver you and give your enemies over to you; therefore your camp shall be holy, that He may see no unclean thing among you, and turn away from you.

### MISCELLANEOUS LAWS

15 [a]"You shall not give back to his master the slave who has escaped from his master to you. 16 He may dwell with you in your midst, in the place which he chooses within one of your gates, where it seems best to him; [a]you shall not oppress him.

> **23:15** Many ancient Near Eastern cultures allowed masters to kill **slaves** who **escaped**. Here, we see God's respect for human life in His command for the Israelites to protect escaped slaves.

17 "There shall be no *ritual* harlot[1] [a]of the daughters of Israel, or a [b]perverted[2] one of the sons of Israel. 18 You shall not bring the wages of a harlot or the price of a dog to the house of the LORD your God for any vowed offering, for both of these *are* an abomination to the LORD your God.

19 [a]"You shall not charge interest to your brother—interest on money *or* food *or* anything that is lent out at interest. 20 [a]To a foreigner you may charge interest, but to your brother you shall not charge interest, [b]that the LORD your God may bless you in all to which you set your hand in the land which you are entering to possess.

21 [a]"When you make a vow to the LORD your God, you shall not delay to pay it; for the LORD your God will surely require it of you, and it would be sin to you. 22 But if you abstain from vowing, it shall not be sin to you. 23 [a]That which has gone from your lips you shall keep and perform, for you voluntarily vowed to the LORD your God what you have promised with your mouth.

24 "When you come into your neighbor's vineyard, you may eat your fill of grapes at your pleasure, but you shall not put *any* in your container. 25 When you come into your neighbor's standing grain, [a]you may pluck the heads with your hand, but you shall not use a sickle on your neighbor's standing grain.

### LAW CONCERNING DIVORCE

**24** "When a [a]man takes a wife and marries her, and it happens that she finds no favor in his eyes because he has found some uncleanness in her, and he writes her a [b]certificate of divorce, puts *it* in her hand, and sends her out of his house, 2 when she has departed from his house, and goes and becomes another man's *wife,* 3 *if* the latter husband detests her and writes her a certificate of divorce, puts *it* in her hand, and sends her out of his house, or if the latter husband dies who took her as his wife, 4 [a]*then* her former husband who divorced her must not take her back to be his wife after she has been defiled; for that *is* an abomination before the LORD, and you shall not bring sin on the land which the LORD your God is giving you *as* an inheritance.

> **24:1–4** God created marriage and intended it to be a union of one man and one woman for life (see Gen. 2:24). And yet, the Mosaic law allowed **divorce**. When the Pharisees asked Jesus about divorce, He explained it hadn't been God's design, but Moses allowed it "because of the hardness of your hearts" (Matt. 19:8). Because sin can be so grievous, it seems God would rather a couple divorce—even though it isn't His design nor desire—than experience something even worse in a broken marriage. Jesus indicated unrepentant adultery might be grounds for such a divorce (Matt. 5:31–32; 19:1–12) while Paul shared abandonment by an unbeliever could be too (1 Cor. 7:12–15). Some see these as the only two reasons for a biblical divorce. Others believe they are two examples, and other situations, such as abuse, could also be grounds.

### MISCELLANEOUS LAWS

5 [a]"When a man has taken a new wife, he shall not go out to war or be charged with any business; he shall be free at home one year, and [b]bring happiness to his wife whom he has taken.

6 "No man shall take the lower or the upper millstone in pledge, for he takes *one's* living in pledge.

**23:10** [a] Lev. 15:16 **23:11** [a] Lev. 15:5 **23:14** [a] Lev. 26:12; Deut. 7:21 **23:15** [a] 1 Sam. 30:15 **23:16** [a] Ex. 22:21; Prov. 22:22 **23:17** [a] Lev. 19:29; Deut. 22:21 [b] Gen. 19:5; 2 Kin. 23:7 [1] Hebrew *qedeshah,* feminine of *qadesh* (see next note) [2] Hebrew *qadesh,* that is, one practicing sodomy and prostitution in religious rituals **23:19** [a] Ex. 22:25; Lev. 25:35–37; Neh. 5:2–7; Ps. 15:5 **23:20** [a] Deut. 15:3 [b] Deut. 15:10 **23:21** [a] Num. 30:1, 2; Job 22:27; Ps. 61:8; Eccl. 5:4, 5; Matt. 5:33 **23:23** [a] Num. 30:2; Ps. 66:13, 14 **23:25** [a] Matt. 12:1; Mark 2:23; Luke 6:1 **24:1** [a] [Matt. 5:31; 19:7; Mark 10:4] [b] [Jer. 3:8] **24:4** [a] [Jer. 3:1] **24:5** [a] Deut. 20:7 [b] Prov. 5:18

7 "If a man is [a]found kidnapping any of his
brethren of the children of Israel, and mistreats
him or sells him, then that kidnapper shall die;
[b]and you shall put away the evil from among you.
8 "Take heed in [a]an outbreak of leprosy, that
you carefully observe and do according to all
that the priests, the Levites, shall teach you; just
as I commanded them, *so* you shall be careful to
do. 9 [a]Remember what the LORD your God did [b]to
Miriam on the way when you came out of Egypt!
10 "When you [a]lend your brother anything,
you shall not go into his house to get his pledge.
11 You shall stand outside, and the man to whom
you lend shall bring the pledge out to you. 12 And
if the man *is* poor, you shall not keep his pledge
overnight. 13 [a]You shall in any case return the
pledge to him again when the sun goes down,
that he may sleep in his own garment and [b]bless
you; and [c]it shall be righteousness to you before
the LORD your God.
14 "You shall not [a]oppress a hired servant *who
is* poor and needy, *whether* one of your brethren
or one of the aliens who *is* in your land within
your gates. 15 Each day [a]you shall give *him* his
wages, and not let the sun go down on it, for he
*is* poor and has set his heart on it; [b]lest he cry
out against you to the LORD, and it be sin to you.
16 [a]"Fathers shall not be put to death for *their*
children, nor shall children be put to death for
*their* fathers; a person shall be put to death for
his own sin.
17 [a]"You shall not pervert justice due the
stranger or the fatherless, [b]nor take a widow's
garment as a pledge. 18 But [a]you shall remember
that you were a slave in Egypt, and the LORD
your God redeemed you from there; therefore
I command you to do this thing.
19 [a]"When you reap your harvest in your field,
and forget a sheaf in the field, you shall not go
back to get it; it shall be for the stranger, the
fatherless, and the widow, that the LORD your
God may [b]bless you in all the work of your hands.
20 When you beat your olive trees, you shall not go
over the boughs again; it shall be for the strang-
er, the fatherless, and the widow. 21 When you
gather the grapes of your vineyard, you shall
not glean *it* afterward; it shall be for the stranger,
the fatherless, and the widow. 22 And you shall
remember that you were a slave in the land of
Egypt; therefore I command you to do this thing.
25 "If there is a [a]dispute between men, and
they come to court, that *the judges* may
judge them, and they [b]justify the righteous and
condemn the wicked, 2 then it shall be, if the
wicked man [a]deserves to be beaten, that the
judge will cause him to lie down [b]and be beaten
in his presence, according to his guilt, with a
certain number of blows. 3 [a]Forty blows he may
give him *and* no more, lest he should exceed
this and beat him with many blows above these,
and your brother [b]be humiliated in your sight.
4 [a]"You shall not muzzle an ox while it treads
out *the grain.*

**25:4** Wheat and other grains had to be crushed so the grain could be separated from the leaves and stems of the plant. One of the best crushing methods was to spread the grain on the ground and have an **ox** pull a heavy piece of wood over it. As a reward for its hard work, the ox's mouth was left unmuzzled so it could eat some of the grain while it worked.

### *MARRIAGE DUTY OF THE SURVIVING BROTHER*

5 [a]"If brothers dwell together, and one of
them dies and has no son, the widow of the dead
man shall not be *married* to a stranger outside
*the family;* her husband's brother shall go in to
her, take her as his wife, and perform the duty of
a husband's brother to her. 6 And it shall be *that*
the firstborn son which she bears [a]will succeed
to the name of his dead brother, that [b]his name
may not be blotted out of Israel. 7 But if the man
does not want to take his brother's wife, then
let his brother's wife go up to the [a]gate to the
elders, and say, 'My husband's brother refuses to
raise up a name to his brother in Israel; he will
not perform the duty of my husband's brother.'
8 Then the elders of his city shall call him and
speak to him. But *if* he stands firm and says,
[a]'I do not want to take her,' 9 then his brother's
wife shall come to him in the presence of the
elders, [a]remove his sandal from his foot, spit in
his face, and answer and say, 'So shall it be done
to the man who will not [b]build up his brother's
house.' 10 And his name shall be called in Israel,
'The house of him who had his sandal removed.'

### *MISCELLANEOUS LAWS*

11 "If *two* men fight together, and the wife of
one draws near to rescue her husband from the
hand of the one attacking him, and puts out her
hand and seizes him by the genitals, 12 then you
shall cut off her hand; [a]your eye shall not pity *her.*
13 [a]"You shall not have in your bag differing
weights, a heavy and a light. 14 You shall not
have in your house differing measures, a large

**24:7** [a] Ex. 21:16 [b] Deut. 19:19 **24:8** [a] Lev. 13:2; 14:2 **24:9** [a] [1 Cor. 10:6] [b] Num. 12:10 **24:10** [a] Matt. 5:42 **24:13** [a] Ex. 22:26; Ezek. 18:7 [b] Job 29:11; 2 Tim. 1:18 [c] Deut. 6:25; Ps. 106:31; Dan. 4:27 **24:14** [a] Lev. 19:13; Deut. 15:7–18; [Prov. 14:31]; Amos 4:1; [Mal. 3:5; 1 Tim. 5:18] **24:15** [a] Lev. 19:13; Jer. 22:13 [b] Ex. 22:23; Deut. 15:9; Job 35:9; James 5:4 **24:16** [a] 2 Kin. 14:6; 2 Chr. 25:4; Jer. 31:29, 30; Ezek. 18:20 **24:17** [a] Ex. 23:6 [b] Ex. 22:26 **24:18** [a] Deut. 24:22 **24:19** [a] Lev. 19:9, 10 [b] Deut. 15:10; Ps. 41:1; Prov. 19:17 **25:1** [a] Deut. 17:8–13; 19:17; Ezek. 44:24 [b] Prov. 17:15 **25:2** [a] Prov. 19:29; Luke 12:48 [b] Matt. 10:17 **25:3** [a] 2 Cor. 11:24 [b] Job 18:3 **25:4** [a] [Prov. 12:10; 1 Cor. 9:9; 1 Tim. 5:18] **25:5** [a] Matt. 22:24; Mark 12:19; Luke 20:28 **25:6** [a] Gen. 38:9 [b] Ruth 4:5, 10 **25:7** [a] Ruth 4:1, 2 **25:8** [a] Ruth 4:6 **25:9** [a] Ruth 4:7, 8 [b] Ruth 4:11 **25:12** [a] Deut. 7:2; 19:13 **25:13** [a] Lev. 19:35–37; Prov. 11:1; 20:23; Ezek. 45:10; Mic. 6:11

and a small. 15 You shall have a perfect and just
weight, a perfect and just measure, [a]that your
days may be lengthened in the land which the
LORD your God is giving you. 16 For [a]all who do
such things, all who behave unrighteously, *are*
an abomination to the LORD your God.

### DESTROY THE AMALEKITES

17 [a]"Remember what Amalek did to you on
the way as you were coming out of Egypt, 18 how
he met you on the way and attacked your rear
ranks, all the stragglers at your rear, when you
*were* tired and weary; and he [a]did not fear God.
19 Therefore it shall be, [a]when the LORD your
God has given you rest from your enemies all
around, in the land which the LORD your God
is giving you to possess *as* an inheritance, *that*
you will [b]blot out the remembrance of Amalek
from under heaven. You shall not forget.

### OFFERINGS OF FIRSTFRUITS AND TITHES

**26** "And it shall be, when you come into the
land which the LORD your God is giving
you *as* an inheritance, and you possess it and
dwell in it, 2 [a]that you shall take some of the first
of all the produce of the ground, which you shall
bring from your land that the LORD your God
is giving you, and put *it* in a basket and [b]go to
the place where the LORD your God chooses to
make His name abide. 3 And you shall go to the
one who is priest in those days, and say to him, 'I
declare today to the LORD your[1] God that I have
come to the country which the LORD swore to
our fathers to give us.'

4 "Then the priest shall take the basket out
of your hand and set it down before the altar of
the LORD your God. 5 And you shall answer and
say before the LORD your God: 'My father *was*
[a]a Syrian,[1] [b]about to perish, and [c]he went down
to Egypt and dwelt there, [d]few in number; and
there he became a nation, [e]great, mighty, and
populous. 6 But the [a]Egyptians mistreated us,
afflicted us, and laid hard bondage on us. 7 [a]Then
we cried out to the LORD God of our fathers, and
the LORD heard our voice and looked on our
affliction and our labor and our oppression. 8 So
[a]the LORD brought us out of Egypt with a mighty
hand and with an outstretched arm, [b]with great
terror and with signs and wonders. 9 He has
brought us to this place and has given us this
land, [a]"a land flowing with milk and honey";[1]
10 and now, behold, I have brought the firstfruits
of the land which you, O LORD, have given me.'

"Then you shall set it before the LORD your
God, and worship before the LORD your God.
11 So [a]you shall rejoice in every good *thing* which
the LORD your God has given to you and your
house, you and the Levite and the stranger who
*is* among you.

12 "When you have finished laying aside all
the [a]tithe of your increase in the third year—[b]the
year of tithing—and have given *it* to the Levite,
the stranger, the fatherless, and the widow, so
that they may eat within your gates and be filled,
13 then you shall say before the LORD your God:
'I have removed the holy *tithe* from *my* house,
and also have given them to the Levite, the
stranger, the fatherless, and the widow, accord-
ing to all Your commandments which You have
commanded me; I have not transgressed Your
commandments, [a]nor have I forgotten *them.*
14 [a]I have not eaten any of it when in mourning,
nor have I removed *any* of it for an unclean *use,*
nor given *any* of it for the dead. I have obeyed
the voice of the LORD my God, and have done
according to all that You have commanded me.
15 [a]Look down from Your holy habitation, from
heaven, and bless Your people Israel and the land
which You have given us, just as You swore to our
fathers, [b]"a land flowing with milk and honey."'[1]

### A SPECIAL PEOPLE OF GOD

16 "This day the LORD your God commands
you to observe these statutes and judgments;
therefore you shall be careful to observe them
with all your heart and with all your soul. 17 Today
you have [a]proclaimed the LORD to be your God,
and that you will walk in His ways and keep His
statutes, His commandments, and His judg-
ments, and that you will [b]obey His voice. 18 Also
today [a]the LORD has proclaimed you to be His
special people, just as He promised you, that *you*
should keep all His commandments, 19 and that
He will set you [a]high above all nations which He
has made, in praise, in name, and in honor, and
that you may be [b]a holy people to the LORD your
God, just as He has spoken."

### THE LAW INSCRIBED ON STONES

**27** Now Moses, with the elders of Israel, com-
manded the people, saying: "Keep all the
commandments which I command you today.
2 And it shall be, on the day [a]when you cross over
the Jordan to the land which the LORD your God
is giving you, that [b]you shall set up for yourselves
large stones, and whitewash them with lime.
3 You shall write on them all the words of this
law, when you have crossed over, that you may
enter the land which the LORD your God is giving
you, [a]'a land flowing with milk and honey,'[1] just

25:15 [a] Ex. 20:12 25:16 [a] Prov. 11:1; [1 Thess. 4:6] 25:17 [a] Ex. 17:8–16; 1 Sam. 15:1–3 25:18 [a] [Ps. 36:1]; Rom. 3:18 25:19 [a] 1 Sam. 15:3 [b] Ex. 17:14 26:2 [a] Ex. 22:29; 23:16, 19; Num. 18:13; Deut. 16:10; Prov. 3:9 [b] Deut. 12:5 26:3 [1] Septuagint reads *my.* 26:5 [a] Gen. 25:20; Hos. 12:12 [b] Gen. 43:1, 2; 45:7, 11 [c] Gen. 46:1, 6; Acts 7:15 [d] Gen. 46:27; Deut. 10:22 [e] Deut. 1:10 [1] Or *Aramean* 26:6 [a] Ex. 1:8–11, 14 26:7 [a] Ex. 2:23–25; 3:9; 4:31 26:8 [a] Ex. 12:37, 51; 13:3, 14, 16; Deut. 5:15 [b] Deut. 4:34; 34:11, 12 26:9 [a] Ex. 3:8, 17 [1] Exodus 3:8 26:11 [a] Deut. 12:7; 16:11; Eccl. 3:12, 13; 5:18–20 26:12 [a] Lev. 27:30; Num. 18:24 [b] Deut. 14:28, 29 26:13 [a] Ps. 119:141, 153, 176 26:14 [a] Lev. 7:20; Jer. 16:7; Hos. 9:4 26:15 [a] Ps. 80:14; Is. 63:15; Zech. 2:13 [b] Ex. 3:8 [1] Exodus 3:8 26:17 [a] Ex. 20:19 [b] Deut. 15:5 26:18 [a] Ex. 6:7; 19:5; Deut. 7:6; 14:2; 28:9; [Titus 2:14; 1 Pet. 2:9] 26:19 [a] Deut. 4:7, 8; 28:1 [b] Ex. 19:6; Deut. 7:6; 28:9; Is. 62:12; [1 Pet. 2:9] 27:2 [a] Josh. 4:1 [b] Josh. 8:32 27:3 [a] Ex. 3:8 [1] Exodus 3:8

as the LORD God of your fathers promised you.
4 Therefore it shall be, when you have crossed over
the Jordan, *that* [a]on Mount Ebal you shall set up
these stones, which I command you today, and
you shall whitewash them with lime. 5 And there
you shall build an altar to the LORD your God, an
altar of stones; [a]you shall not use an iron *tool* on
them. 6 You shall build with whole stones the altar
of the LORD your God, and offer burnt offerings
on it to the LORD your God. 7 You shall offer peace
offerings, and shall eat there, and [a]rejoice before
the LORD your God. 8 And you shall [a]write very
plainly on the stones all the words of this law."
9 Then Moses and the priests, the Levites,
spoke to all Israel, saying, "Take heed and lis-
ten, O Israel: [a]This day you have become the
people of the LORD your God. 10 Therefore you
shall obey the voice of the LORD your God, and
observe His commandments and His statutes
which I command you today."

### CURSES PRONOUNCED FROM MOUNT EBAL

11 And Moses commanded the people on
the same day, saying, 12 "These shall stand [a]on
Mount Gerizim to bless the people, when you
have crossed over the Jordan: Simeon, Levi,
Judah, Issachar, Joseph, and Benjamin; 13 and
[a]these shall stand on Mount Ebal to curse: Reu-
ben, Gad, Asher, Zebulun, Dan, and Naphtali.
14 "And [a]the Levites shall speak with a loud
voice and say to all the men of Israel: 15 [a]'Cursed
*is* the one who makes a carved or molded image,
an abomination to the LORD, the work of the
hands of the craftsman, and sets *it* up in secret.'

[b]"And all the people shall answer and say,
'Amen!'

16 [a]'Cursed *is* the one who treats his father
or his mother with contempt.'

"And all the people shall say, 'Amen!'

17 [a]'Cursed *is* the one who moves his neigh-
bor's landmark.'

"And all the people shall say, 'Amen!'

18 [a]'Cursed *is* the one who makes the blind
to wander off the road.'

"And all the people shall say, 'Amen!'

19 [a]'Cursed *is* the one who perverts the justice
due the stranger, the fatherless, and widow.'

"And all the people shall say, 'Amen!'

20 [a]'Cursed *is* the one who lies with his father's
wife, because he has uncovered his father's bed.'

"And all the people shall say, 'Amen!'

21 [a]'Cursed *is* the one who lies with any kind
of animal.'

"And all the people shall say, 'Amen!'

22 [a]'Cursed *is* the one who lies with his sister,
the daughter of his father or the daughter of
his mother.'

"And all the people shall say, 'Amen!'

23 [a]'Cursed *is* the one who lies with his
mother-in-law.'

"And all the people shall say, 'Amen!'

24 [a]'Cursed *is* the one who attacks his neigh-
bor secretly.'

"And all the people shall say, 'Amen!'

25 [a]'Cursed *is* the one who takes a bribe to
slay an innocent person.'

"And all the people shall say, 'Amen!'

26 [a]'Cursed *is* the one who does not confirm
*all* the words of this law by observing them.'

"And all the people shall say, 'Amen!' "

### BLESSINGS ON OBEDIENCE

*(Lev. 26:1–13; Deut. 7:12–24)*

28 "Now it shall come to pass, [a]if you diligent-
ly obey the voice of the LORD your God, to
observe carefully all His commandments which
I command you today, that the LORD your God
[b]will set you high above all nations of the earth.
2 And all these blessings shall come upon you
and [a]overtake you, because you obey the voice
of the LORD your God:

3 [a]"Blessed *shall* you *be* in the city, and
blessed *shall* you *be* [b]in the country.

4 "Blessed *shall be* [a]the fruit of your body,
the produce of your ground and the increase
of your herds, the increase of your cattle and
the offspring of your flocks.

5 "Blessed *shall be* your basket and your
kneading bowl.

6 [a]"Blessed *shall* you *be* when you come in,
and blessed *shall* you *be* when you go out.

7 "The LORD [a]will cause your enemies who
rise against you to be defeated before your face;
they shall come out against you one way and
flee before you seven ways.

8 "The LORD will [a]command the blessing on
you in your storehouses and in all to which you
[b]set your hand, and He will bless you in the land
which the LORD your God is giving you.

9 [a]"The LORD will establish you as a holy
people to Himself, just as He has sworn to you, if
you keep the commandments of the LORD your
God and walk in His ways. 10 Then all peoples of
the earth shall see that you are [a]called by the
name of the LORD, and they shall be [b]afraid of
you. 11 And [a]the LORD will grant you plenty of
goods, in the fruit of your body, in the increase
of your livestock, and in the produce of your
ground, in the land of which the LORD swore to
your fathers to give you. 12 The LORD will open
to you His good treasure, the heavens, [a]to give
the rain to your land in its season, and [b]to bless
all the work of your hand. [c]You shall lend to
many nations, but you shall not borrow. 13 And

27:4 [a] Deut. 11:29; Josh. 8:30, 31 27:5 [a] Ex. 20:25; Josh. 8:31 27:7 [a] Deut. 26:11 27:8 [a] Josh. 8:32 27:9 [a] Deut. 26:18 27:12 [a] Josh. 8:33 27:13 [a] Deut. 11:29 27:14 [a] Deut. 33:10 27:15 [a] Ex. 20:4, 23; 34:17 [b] Num. 5:22 27:16 [a] Ezek. 22:7 27:17 [a] Deut. 19:14 27:18 [a] Lev. 19:14 27:19 [a] Ex. 22:21, 22; 23:9 27:20 [a] Deut. 22:30 27:21 [a] Lev. 18:23; 20:15, 16 27:22 [a] Lev. 18:9 27:23 [a] Lev. 18:17; 20:14 27:24 [a] Ex. 20:13; 21:12 27:25 [a] Ex. 23:7 27:26 [a] Gal. 3:10 28:1 [a] Ex. 15:26 [b] Deut. 26:19 28:2 [a] Deut. 28:15 28:3 [a] Ps. 128:1, 4 [b] Gen. 39:5 28:4 [a] Gen. 22:17 28:6 [a] Ps. 121:8 28:7 [a] Lev. 26:7, 8 28:8 [a] Lev. 25:21 [b] Deut. 15:10 28:9 [a] Ex. 19:5, 6 28:10 [a] Num. 6:27 [b] Deut. 11:25 28:11 [a] Deut. 30:9 28:12 [a] Lev. 26:4 [b] Deut. 14:29 [c] Deut. 15:6

the LORD will make [a]you the head and not the tail; you shall be above only, and not be beneath, if you heed the commandments of the LORD your God, which I command you today, and are careful to observe *them.* 14 [a]So you shall not turn aside from any of the words which I command you this day, *to* the right or the left, to go after other gods to serve them.

### *CURSES ON DISOBEDIENCE*

*(Lev. 26:14–46)*

15 "But it shall come to pass, [a]if you do not obey the voice of the LORD your God, to observe carefully all His commandments and His statutes which I command you today, that all these curses will come upon you and overtake you:

16 "Cursed *shall* you *be* in the city, and cursed *shall* you *be* in the country.

17 "Cursed *shall be* your basket and your kneading bowl.

18 "Cursed *shall be* the fruit of your body and the produce of your land, the increase of your cattle and the offspring of your flocks.

19 "Cursed *shall* you *be* when you come in, and cursed *shall* you *be* when you go out.

20 "The LORD will send on you [a]cursing, [b]confusion, and [c]rebuke in all that you set your hand to do, until you are destroyed and until you perish quickly, because of the wickedness of your doings in which you have forsaken Me. 21 The LORD will make the plague cling to you until He has consumed you from the land which you are going to possess. 22 [a]The LORD will strike you with consumption, with fever, with inflammation, with severe burning fever, with the sword, with [b]scorching, and with mildew; they shall pursue you until you perish. 23 And [a]your heavens which *are* over your head shall be bronze, and the earth which is under you *shall be* iron. 24 The LORD will change the rain of your land to powder and dust; from the heaven it shall come down on you until you are destroyed.

25 [a]"The LORD will cause you to be defeated before your enemies; you shall go out one way against them and flee seven ways before them; and you shall become troublesome to all the kingdoms of the earth. 26 [a]Your carcasses shall be food for all the birds of the air and the beasts of the earth, and no one shall frighten *them* away. 27 The LORD will strike you with [a]the boils of Egypt, with [b]tumors, with the scab, and with the itch, from which you cannot be healed. 28 The LORD will strike you with madness and blindness and [a]confusion of heart. 29 And you shall [a]grope at noonday, as a blind man gropes in darkness; you shall not prosper in your ways; you shall be only oppressed and plundered continually, and no one shall save *you.*

30 [a]"You shall betroth a wife, but another man shall lie with her; [b]you shall build a house, but you shall not dwell in it; [c]you shall plant a vineyard, but shall not gather its grapes. 31 Your ox *shall be* slaughtered before your eyes, but you shall not eat of it; your donkey *shall be* violently taken away from before you, and shall not be restored to you; your sheep *shall be* given to your enemies, and you shall have no one to rescue *them.* 32 Your sons and your daughters *shall be* given to [a]another people, and your eyes shall look and [b]fail *with longing* for them all day long; and *there shall be* no strength in your [c]hand. 33 A nation whom you have not known shall eat [a]the fruit of your land and the produce of your labor, and you shall be only oppressed and crushed continually. 34 So you shall be driven mad because of the sight which your eyes see. 35 The LORD will strike you in the knees and on the legs with severe boils which cannot be healed, and from the sole of your foot to the top of your head.

36 "The LORD will [a]bring you and the king whom you set over you to a nation which neither you nor your fathers have known, and [b]there you shall serve other gods—wood and stone. 37 And you shall become [a]an astonishment, a proverb, [b]and a byword among all nations where the LORD will drive you.

38 [a]"You shall carry much seed out to the field but gather little in, for [b]the locust shall consume it. 39 You shall plant vineyards and tend *them,* but you shall neither drink *of* the [a]wine nor gather the *grapes;* for the worms shall eat them. 40 You shall have olive trees throughout all your territory, but you shall not anoint *yourself* with the oil; for your olives shall drop off. 41 You shall beget sons and daughters, but they shall not be yours; for [a]they shall go into captivity. 42 Locusts shall consume all your trees and the produce of your land.

43 "The alien who *is* among you shall rise higher and higher above you, and you shall come down lower and lower. 44 He shall lend to you, but you shall not lend to him; he shall be the head, and you shall be the tail.

45 "Moreover all these curses shall come upon you and pursue and overtake you, until you are destroyed, because you did not obey the voice of the LORD your God, to keep His commandments and His statutes which He commanded you. 46 And they shall be upon [a]you for a sign and a wonder, and on your descendants forever.

47 [a]"Because you did not serve the LORD your God with joy and gladness of heart, [b]for the

**28:13** [a] [Is. 9:14, 15] **28:14** [a] Deut. 5:32; Josh. 1:7 **28:15** [a] Lev. 26:14–39; Josh. 23:15; Dan. 9:10–14; Mal. 2:2 **28:20** [a] Mal. 2:2 [b] Is. 65:14 [c] Ps. 80:16; Is. 30:17 **28:22** [a] Lev. 26:16 [b] Amos 4:9 **28:23** [a] Lev. 26:19 **28:25** [a] Deut. 32:30 **28:26** [a] 1 Sam. 17:44; Ps. 79:2 **28:27** [a] Ex. 15:26 [b] 1 Sam. 5:6 **28:28** [a] Jer. 4:9 **28:29** [a] Job 5:14 **28:30** [a] 2 Sam. 12:11; Job 31:10; Jer. 8:10 [b] Amos 5:11; Zeph. 1:13 [c] Deut. 20:6; Job 31:8; Jer. 12:13; Mic. 6:15 **28:32** [a] 2 Chr. 29:9 [b] Ps. 119:82 [c] Neh. 5:5 **28:33** [a] Lev. 26:16; Jer. 5:15, 17 **28:36** [a] 2 Kin. 17:4, 6; 24:12, 14; 25:7, 11; 2 Chr. 36:1–21; Jer. 39:1–9 [b] Deut. 4:28; Jer. 16:13 **28:37** [a] 1 Kin. 9:7, 8; Jer. 24:9; 25:9 [b] Ps. 44:14 **28:38** [a] Mic. 6:15; Hag. 1:6 [b] Ex. 10:4; Joel 1:4 **28:39** [a] Zeph. 1:13 **28:41** [a] Lam. 1:5 **28:46** [a] Num. 26:10; Is. 8:18; Ezek. 14:8 **28:47** [a] Deut. 12:7; Neh. 9:35–37 [b] Deut. 32:15

abundance of everything, 48 therefore you shall
serve your enemies, whom the LORD will send
against you, in [a]hunger, in thirst, in nakedness,
and in need of everything; and He [b]will put a
yoke of iron on your neck until He has destroyed
you. 49 [a]The LORD will bring a nation against you
from afar, from the end of the earth, [b]*as swift*
as the eagle flies, a nation whose language you
will not understand, 50 a nation of fierce coun-
tenance, [a]which does not respect the elderly nor
show favor to the young. 51 And they shall eat
the increase of your livestock and the produce
of your land, until you are destroyed; they shall
not leave you grain or new wine or oil, *or* the
increase of your cattle or the offspring of your
flocks, until they have destroyed you.

52 "They shall [a]besiege you at all your gates
until your high and fortified walls, in which you
trust, come down throughout all your land; and
they shall besiege you at all your gates through-
out all your land which the LORD your God has
given you. 53 [a]You shall eat the fruit of your own
body, the flesh of your sons and your daughters
whom the LORD your God has given you, in the
siege and desperate straits in which your ene-
my shall distress you. 54 The sensitive and very
refined man among you [a]will be hostile toward
his brother, toward [b]the wife of his bosom, and
toward the rest of his children whom he leaves
behind, 55 so that he will not give any of them the
flesh of his children whom he will eat, because he
has nothing left in the siege and desperate straits
in which your enemy shall distress you at all your
gates. 56 The tender and delicate woman among
you, who would not venture to set the sole of her
foot on the ground because of her delicateness
and sensitivity, will refuse[1] to the husband of
her bosom, and to her son and her daughter,
57 her placenta which comes out [a]from between
her feet and her children whom she bears; for
she will eat them secretly for lack of everything
in the siege and desperate straits in which your
enemy shall distress you at all your gates.

58 "If you do not carefully observe all the
words of this law that are written in this book, that
you may fear [a]this glorious and awesome name,
THE LORD YOUR GOD, 59 then the LORD will bring
upon you and your descendants [a]extraordinary
plagues—great and prolonged plagues—and
serious and prolonged sicknesses. 60 Moreover He
will bring back on you all [a]the diseases of Egypt, of
which you were afraid, and they shall cling to you.
61 Also every sickness and every plague, which *is*
not written in this Book of the Law, will the LORD
bring upon you until you are destroyed. 62 You
[a]shall be left few in number, whereas you were
[b]as the stars of heaven in multitude, because you
would not obey the voice of the LORD your God.
63 And it shall be, *that* just as the LORD [a]rejoiced
over you to do you good and multiply you, so the
LORD [b]will rejoice over you to destroy you and
bring you to nothing; and you shall be [c]plucked
from off the land which you go to possess.

64 "Then the LORD [a]will scatter you among all
peoples, from one end of the earth to the other,
and [b]there you shall serve other gods, which
neither you nor your fathers have known—
wood and stone. 65 And [a]among those nations
you shall find no rest, nor shall the sole of your
foot have a resting place; [b]but there the LORD
will give you a trembling heart, failing eyes,
and [c]anguish of soul. 66 Your life shall hang in
doubt before you; you shall fear day and night,
and have no assurance of life. 67 [a]In the morning
you shall say, 'Oh, that it were evening!' And at
evening you shall say, 'Oh, that it were morning!'
because of the fear which terrifies your heart,
and [b]because of the sight which your eyes see.

68 "And the LORD [a]will take you back to Egypt
in ships, by the way of which I said to you, [b]'You
shall never see it again.' And there you shall be
offered for sale to your enemies as male and
female slaves, but no one will buy *you.*"

### THE COVENANT RENEWED IN MOAB

**29** These *are* the words of the covenant which
the LORD commanded Moses to make
with the children of Israel in the land of Moab,
besides the [a]covenant which He made with
them in Horeb.

2 Now Moses called all Israel and said to them:
[a]"You have seen all that the LORD did before your
eyes in the land of Egypt, to Pharaoh and to all
his servants and to all his land— 3 [a]the great trials
which your eyes have seen, the signs, and those
great wonders. 4 Yet [a]the LORD has not given you a
heart to perceive and eyes to see and ears to hear,
to this *very* day. 5 [a]And I have led you forty years in
the wilderness. [b]Your clothes have not worn out
on you, and your sandals have not worn out on
your feet. 6 [a]You have not eaten bread, nor have
you drunk wine or *similar* drink, that you may
know that I *am* the LORD your God. 7 And when you
came to this place, [a]Sihon king of Heshbon and
Og king of Bashan came out against us to battle,
and we conquered them. 8 We took their land
and [a]gave it as an inheritance to the Reubenites,
to the Gadites, and to half the tribe of Manasseh.
9 Therefore [a]keep the words of this covenant, and
do them, that you may [b]prosper in all that you do.

28:48 [a] Lam. 4:4–6 [b] Jer. 28:13, 14 28:49 [a] Is. 5:26–30; 7:18–20; Jer. 5:15 [b] Jer. 48:40; 49:22; Lam. 4:19; Hos. 8:1 28:50 [a] 2 Chr. 36:17 28:52 [a] 2 Kin. 25:1, 2, 4 28:53 [a] Lev. 26:29; 2 Kin. 6:28, 29; Jer. 19:9; Lam. 2:20; 4:10 28:54 [a] Deut. 15:9 [b] Deut. 13:6 28:56 [1] Literally *her eye shall be evil toward* 28:57 [a] Gen. 49:10 28:58 [a] Ex. 6:3 28:59 [a] Dan. 9:12 28:60 [a] Deut. 7:15 28:62 [a] Deut. 4:27 [b] Deut. 10:22; Neh. 9:23 28:63 [a] Deut. 30:9; Jer. 32:41 [b] Prov. 1:26; [Is. 1:24] [c] Jer. 12:14; 45:4 28:64 [a] Lev. 26:33; Deut. 4:27, 28; Neh. 1:8; Jer. 16:13; Amos 9:9 [b] Deut. 28:36 28:65 [a] Lam. 1:3; Amos 9:4 [b] Lev. 26:36 [c] Lev. 26:16 28:67 [a] Job 7:4 [b] Deut. 28:34 28:68 [a] Jer. 43:7; Hos. 8:13 [b] Deut. 17:16 29:1 [a] Lev. 26:46; Deut. 5:2, 3 29:2 [a] Ex. 19:4; Deut. 11:7 29:3 [a] Deut. 4:34; 7:19 29:4 [a] [Is. 6:9, 10; Ezek. 12:2]; Matt. 13:14; [Acts 28:26, 27]; Rom. 11:8; [Eph. 4:18] 29:5 [a] Deut. 1:3; 8:2 [b] Deut. 8:4 29:6 [a] Ex. 16:12; Deut. 8:3 29:7 [a] Num. 21:23, 24; Deut. 2:26—3:3 29:8 [a] Num. 32:33; Deut. 3:12, 13 29:9 [a] Deut. 4:6; 1 Kin. 2:3 [b] Josh. 1:7

10 "All of you stand today before the LORD your God: your leaders and your tribes and your elders and your officers, all the men of Israel, 11 your little ones and your wives—also the stranger who *is* in your camp, from [a]the one who cuts your wood to the one who draws your water— 12 that you may enter into covenant with the LORD your God, and [a]into His oath, which the LORD your God makes with you today, 13 that He may [a]establish you today as a people for Himself, and *that* He may be God to you, [b]just as He has spoken to you, and [c]just as He has sworn to your fathers, to Abraham, Isaac, and Jacob.

14 "I make this covenant and this oath, [a]not with you alone, 15 but with *him* who stands here with us today before the LORD our God, [a]as well as with *him* who *is* not here with us today 16 (for you know that we dwelt in the land of Egypt and that we came through the nations which you passed by, 17 and you saw their abominations and their idols which *were* among them—wood and stone and silver and gold); 18 so that there may not be among you man or woman or family or tribe, [a]whose heart turns away today from the LORD our God, to go *and* serve the gods of these nations, [b]and that there may not be among you a root bearing [c]bitterness or wormwood; 19 and so it may not happen, when he hears the words of this curse, that he blesses himself in his heart, saying, 'I shall have peace, even though I follow the [a]dictates[1] of my heart'—[b]as though the drunkard could be included with the sober.

20 [a]"The LORD would not spare him; for then [b]the anger of the LORD and [c]His jealousy would burn against that man, and every curse that is written in this book would settle on him, and the LORD [d]would blot out his name from under heaven. 21 And the LORD [a]would separate him from all the tribes of Israel for adversity, according to all the curses of the covenant that are written in this Book of the [b]Law, 22 so that the coming generation of your children who rise up after you, and the foreigner who comes from a far land, would say, when they [a]see the plagues of that land and the sicknesses which the LORD has laid on it:

23 'The whole land *is* brimstone, [a]salt, and burning; it is not sown, nor does it bear, nor does any grass grow there, [b]like the overthrow of Sodom and Gomorrah, Admah, and Zeboiim, which the LORD overthrew in His anger and His wrath.' 24 All nations would say, [a]'Why has the LORD done so to this land? What does the heat of this great anger mean?' 25 Then *people* would say: 'Because they have forsaken the covenant of the LORD God of their fathers, which He made with them when He brought them out of the land of Egypt; 26 for they went and served other gods and worshiped them, gods that they did not know and that He had not given to them. 27 Then the anger of the LORD was aroused against this land, [a]to bring on it every curse that is written in this book. 28 And the LORD [a]uprooted them from their land in anger, in wrath, and in great indignation, and cast them into another land, as *it is* this day.'

29 "The secret *things belong* to the LORD our God, but those *things which are* revealed *belong* to us and to our children forever, that *we* may do all the words of this law.

> **29:29** Divine revelation is God giving us truths we wouldn't know otherwise. The details of creation in Genesis 1–2 are an example. Because humans weren't created until the sixth day, there was no way for us to know about what happened on the first five days apart from God telling us. God revealed these creation facts to Moses.

### *THE BLESSING OF RETURNING TO GOD*

**30** "Now [a]it shall come to pass, when [b]all these things come upon you, the blessing and the [c]curse which I have set before you, and [d]you call *them* to mind among all the nations where the LORD your God drives you, 2 and you [a]return to the LORD your God and obey His voice, according to all that I command you today, you and your children, with all your heart and with all your soul, 3 [a]that the LORD your God will bring you back from captivity, and have compassion on you, and [b]gather you again from all the nations where the LORD your God has scattered you. 4 [a]If *any* of you are driven out to the farthest *parts* under heaven, from there the LORD your God will gather you, and from there He will bring you. 5 Then the LORD your God will bring you to the land which your fathers possessed, and you shall possess it. He will prosper you and multiply you more than your fathers. 6 And [a]the LORD your God will circumcise your heart and the heart of your descendants, to love the LORD your God with all your heart and with all your soul, that you may live.

7 "Also the LORD your God will put all these [a]curses on your enemies and on those who hate you, who persecuted you. 8 And you will [a]again obey the voice of the LORD and do all His commandments which I command you today. 9 [a]The LORD your God will make you abound in all the work of your hand, in the fruit of your body, in the increase of your livestock, and in the produce

**29:11** [a]Josh. 9:21, 23, 27 **29:12** [a]Neh. 10:29 **29:13** [a]Deut. 28:9 [b]Ex. 6:7 [c]Gen. 17:7, 8 **29:14** [a][Jer. 31:31; Heb. 8:7, 8] **29:15** [a]Acts 2:39 **29:18** [a]Deut. 11:16 [b]Heb. 12:15 [c]Deut. 32:32; Acts 8:23 **29:19** [a]Jer. 3:17; 7:24 [b]Is. 30:1 [1]Or *stubbornness* **29:20** [a]Ezek. 14:7 [b]Ps. 74:1 [c]Ps. 79:5; Ezek. 23:25 [d]Ex. 32:33; Deut. 9:14; 2 Kin. 14:27 **29:21** [a][Matt. 24:51] [b]Deut. 30:10 **29:22** [a]Jer. 19:8; 49:17; 50:13 **29:23** [a]Jer. 17:6; Zeph. 2:9 [b]Gen. 19:24, 25; Is. 1:9; Jer. 20:16; Hos. 11:8 **29:24** [a]1 Kin. 9:8; Jer. 22:8 **29:27** [a]Dan. 9:11 **29:28** [a]1 Kin. 14:15; 2 Chr. 7:20; Ps. 52:5; Prov. 2:22 **30:1** [a]Lev. 26:40 [b]Deut. 28:2 [c]Deut. 28:15–45 [d]Deut. 4:29, 30 **30:2** [a]Deut. 4:29, 30; Neh. 1:9; Is. 55:7; Lam. 3:40; Joel 2:12 **30:3** [a]Ps. 106:45; Jer. 29:14; Lam. 3:22, 32 [b]Ps. 147:2; Jer. 32:37; Ezek. 34:13 **30:4** [a]Deut. 28:64; Neh. 1:9; Is. 62:11 **30:6** [a]Deut. 10:16; Jer. 32:39; Ezek. 11:19 **30:7** [a]Is. 54:15–17; Jer. 30:16, 20 **30:8** [a]Zeph. 3:20 **30:9** [a]Deut. 28:11

of your land for good. For the LORD will again [b]rejoice over you for good as He rejoiced over your fathers, 10 if you obey the voice of the LORD your God, to keep His commandments and His statutes which are written in this Book of the Law, *and* if you turn to the LORD your God with all your heart and with all your soul.

### THE CHOICE OF LIFE OR DEATH

11 "For this commandment which I command you today [a]*is* not *too* mysterious for you, nor *is* it far off. 12 [a]It *is* not in heaven, that you should say, 'Who will ascend into heaven for us and bring it to us, that we may hear it and do it?' 13 Nor *is* it beyond the sea, that you should say, 'Who will go over the sea for us and bring it to us, that we may hear it and do it?' 14 But the word *is* very near you, [a]in your mouth and in your heart, that you may do it.

15 "See, [a]I have set before you today life and good, death and evil, 16 in that I command you today to love the LORD your God, to walk in His ways, and to keep His commandments, His statutes, and His judgments, that you may live and multiply; and the LORD your God will bless you in the land which you go to possess. 17 But if your heart turns away so that you do not hear, and are drawn away, and worship other gods and serve them, 18 [a]I announce to you today that you shall surely perish; you shall not prolong *your* days in the land which you cross over the Jordan to go in and possess. 19 [a]I call heaven and earth as witnesses today against you, *that* [b]I have set before you life and death, blessing and cursing; therefore choose life, that both you and your descendants may live; 20 that you may love the LORD your God, that you may obey His voice, and that you may cling to Him, for He *is* your [a]life and the length of your days; and that you may dwell in the land which the LORD swore to your fathers, to Abraham, Isaac, and Jacob, to give them."

### JOSHUA THE NEW LEADER OF ISRAEL

*(Num. 27:12–23)*

**31** Then Moses went and spoke these words to all Israel. 2 And he said to them: "I [a]*am* one hundred and twenty years old today. I can no longer [b]go out and come in. Also the LORD has said to me, [c]'You shall not cross over this Jordan.' 3 The LORD your God [a]Himself crosses over before you; He will destroy these nations from before you, and you shall dispossess them. [b]Joshua himself crosses over before you, just [c]as the LORD has said. 4 [a]And the LORD will do to them [b]as He did to Sihon and Og, the kings of the Amorites and their land, when He destroyed them. 5 [a]The LORD will give them over to you, that you may do to them according to every commandment which I have commanded you. 6 [a]Be strong and of good courage, [b]do not fear nor be afraid of them; for the LORD your God, [c]He *is* the One who goes with you. [d]He will not leave you nor forsake you."

7 Then Moses called Joshua and said to him in the sight of all Israel, [a]"Be strong and of good courage, for you must go with this people to the land which the LORD has sworn to their fathers to give them, and you shall cause them to inherit it. 8 And the LORD, [a]He *is* the One who goes before you. [b]He will be with you, He will not leave you nor forsake you; do not fear nor be dismayed."

### THE LAW TO BE READ EVERY SEVEN YEARS

9 So Moses wrote this law [a]and delivered it to the priests, the sons of Levi, [b]who bore the ark of the covenant of the LORD, and to all the elders of Israel. 10 And Moses commanded them, saying: "At the end of *every* seven years, at the appointed time in the [a]year of release, [b]at the Feast of Tabernacles, 11 when all Israel comes to [a]appear before the LORD your God in the [b]place which He chooses, [c]you shall read this law before all Israel in their hearing. 12 [a]Gather the people together, men and women and little ones, and the stranger who *is* within your gates, that they may hear and that they may learn to fear the LORD your God and carefully observe all the words of this law, 13 and *that* their children, [a]who have not known it, [b]may hear and learn to fear the LORD your God as long as you live in the land which you cross the Jordan to possess."

### PREDICTION OF ISRAEL'S REBELLION

14 Then the LORD said to Moses, [a]"Behold, the days approach when you must die; call Joshua, and present yourselves in the tabernacle of meeting, that [b]I may inaugurate him."

So Moses and Joshua went and presented themselves in the tabernacle of meeting. 15 Now [a]the LORD appeared at the tabernacle in a pillar of cloud, and the pillar of cloud stood above the door of the tabernacle.

16 And the LORD said to Moses: "Behold, you will rest with your fathers; and this people will [a]rise and [b]play the harlot with the gods of the foreigners of the land, where they go *to be* among them, and they will [c]forsake Me and [d]break My covenant which I have made with them. 17 Then My anger shall be [a]aroused against them in that day, and [b]I will forsake them, and I will [c]hide My face from them, and they shall be devoured. And many evils and troubles shall befall them, so that

**30:9** [b] Deut. 28:63; Jer. 32:41 **30:11** [a] Is. 45:19 **30:12** [a] Prov. 30:4; Rom. 10:6–8 **30:14** [a] Rom. 10:8 **30:15** [a] Deut. 30:1, 19 **30:18** [a] Deut. 4:26; 8:19 **30:19** [a] Deut. 4:26 [b] Deut. 30:15 **30:20** [a] Ps. 27:1; [John 11:25; 14:6; Col. 3:4] **31:2** [a] Ex. 7:7; Deut. 34:7 [b] Num. 27:17; 1 Kin. 3:7 [c] Num. 20:12 **31:3** [a] Deut. 9:3; Josh. 11:23 [b] Num. 27:18 [c] Num. 27:21 **31:4** [a] Deut. 3:21 [b] Num. 21:24, 33 **31:5** [a] Deut. 7:2; 20:10–20 **31:6** [a] Josh. 10:25; 1 Chr. 22:13 [b] Deut. 1:29 [c] Deut. 20:4 [d] Josh. 1:5; Heb. 13:5 **31:7** [a] Num. 27:19; Deut. 31:23; Josh. 1:6 **31:8** [a] Ex. 13:21 [b] Deut. 31:6; Josh. 1:5; 1 Chr. 28:20; Heb. 13:5 **31:9** [a] Deut. 17:18; 31:25, 26 [b] Num. 4:5, 6, 15; Deut. 10:8; 31:25, 26; Josh. 3:3 **31:10** [a] Deut. 15:1, 2 [b] Lev. 23:34; Deut. 16:13 **31:11** [a] Deut. 16:16 [b] Deut. 12:5 [c] Josh. 8:34; 2 Kin. 23:2 **31:12** [a] Deut. 4:10 **31:13** [a] Deut. 11:2 [b] Ps. 78:6, 7 **31:14** [a] Num. 27:13 [b] Num. 27:19; Deut. 3:28 **31:15** [a] Ex. 33:9 **31:16** [a] Deut. 29:22 [b] Ex. 34:15; Deut. 4:25–28; Judg. 2:11, 12, 17 [c] Deut. 32:15 [d] Judg. 2:20 **31:17** [a] Judg. 2:14; 6:13 [b] 2 Chr. 15:2 [c] Deut. 32:20

KNOW THE TRUTH

## THE DOCTRINE OF SCRIPTURE

### PART 2: THE PURPOSE OF SCRIPTURE

**31:9–13** God instructed Moses write the law so His people could honor Him and prosper in the land He promised them. This captures the Bible's purpose: to reveal who God is and His plans for His creation, and to explain how people can know, obey, and glorify Him.

Of first importance is understanding the Bible isn't a book primarily about people; it's a book primarily about God. The Bible is God's special revelation of Himself to us (see John 5:39). The Bible teaches who God is, what His will is, and how He operates. We study the Word of God to know and understand the God of the Word.

The Bible also reveals who we are in Christ and how we can glorify Him (see Heb. 13:20–21). It teaches us we are loved by God so much that He sent His Son to pay the price for our sins (see 1 John 4:9–10). It teaches we can be forgiven of our sins through faith in Christ Jesus (see Eph. 2:4–10). It teaches we show our love for God by obeying His commands (see 1 John 5:2–3). The Bible reveals God's plans for restoring His creation and equips us for every good work in His plans (see 2 Tim. 3:16–17). It also gives us constant hope that everyone in Christ, no matter what, will spend eternity with Him (see Rev. 21:3–4).

*For* **THE DOCTRINE OF SCRIPTURE: PART 3: THE CONTENT OF SCRIPTURE**, *turn to John 5:39 on page 1077.*

they will say in that day, [d]'Have not these evils
come upon us because our God *is* [e]not among
us?' 18 And [a]I will surely hide My face in that day
because of all the evil which they have done, in
that they have turned to other gods.
19 "Now therefore, write down this song for
yourselves, and teach it to the children of Is-
rael; put it in their mouths, that this song may
be [a]a witness for Me against the children of Is-
rael. 20 When I have brought them to the land
flowing with milk and honey, of which I swore
to their fathers, and they have eaten and filled
themselves [a]and grown fat, [b]then they will turn
to other gods and serve them; and they will pro-
voke Me and break My covenant. 21 Then it shall
be, [a]when many evils and troubles have come
upon them, that this song will testify against
them as a witness; for it will not be forgotten
in the mouths of their descendants, for [b]I know
the inclination [c]of their behavior today, even
before I have brought them to the land of which
I swore *to give them*."
22 Therefore Moses wrote this song the
same day, and taught it to the children of Isra-
el. 23 [a]Then He inaugurated Joshua the son of
Nun, and said, [b]"Be strong and of good courage;
for you shall bring the children of Israel into
the land of which I swore to them, and I will
be with you."
24 So it was, when Moses had completed
writing the words of this law in a book, when
they were finished, 25 that Moses commanded
the Levites, who bore the ark of the covenant of
the LORD, saying: 26 "Take this Book of the Law,
[a]and put it beside the ark of the covenant of the
LORD your God, that it may be there [b]as a witness
against you; 27 [a]for I know your rebellion and your
[b]stiff neck. *If* today, while I am yet alive with you,
you have been rebellious against the LORD, then
how much more after my death? 28 Gather to me
all the elders of your tribes, and your officers,
that I may speak these words in their hearing
[a]and call heaven and earth to witness against
them. 29 For I know that after my death you will
[a]become utterly corrupt, and turn aside from
the way which I have commanded you. And [b]evil
will befall you [c]in the latter days, because you
will do evil in the sight of the LORD, to provoke
Him to anger through the work of your hands."

### *THE SONG OF MOSES*

30 Then Moses spoke in the hearing of all the
assembly of Israel the words of this song until
they were ended:

**32** "Give [a]ear, O heavens, and I will speak;
And hear, O [b]earth, the words of my
mouth.
2 Let [a]my teaching drop as the rain,
My speech distill as the dew,
[b]As raindrops on the tender herb,
And as showers on the grass.

**31:17** [d] Judg. 6:13 [e] Num. 14:42 **31:18** [a] Deut. 31:17; [Is. 1:15, 16] **31:19** [a] Deut. 31:22, 26 **31:20** [a] Deut. 32:15–17 [b] Deut. 31:16 **31:21** [a] Deut. 31:17 [b] Hos. 5:3 [c] Amos 5:25, 26 **31:23** [a] Num. 27:23; Deut. 31:14 [b] Deut. 31:7 **31:26** [a] 2 Kin. 22:8 [b] Deut. 31:19 **31:27** [a] Deut. 9:7, 24 [b] Ex. 32:9; Deut. 9:6, 13 **31:28** [a] Deut. 30:19 **31:29** [a] Judg. 2:19 [b] Deut. 28:15 [c] Gen. 49:1 **32:1** [a] Deut. 4:26 [b] Jer. 6:19 **32:2** [a] Is. 55:10, 11 [b] Ps. 72:6

3 For I proclaim the [a]name of the LORD:
[b]Ascribe greatness to our God.
4 *He is* [a]the Rock, [b]His work *is* perfect;
For all His ways *are* justice,
[c]A God of truth and [d]without injustice;
Righteous and upright *is* He.

5 "They[a] have corrupted themselves;
*They are* not His children,
Because of their blemish:
A [b]perverse and crooked generation.
6 Do you thus [a]deal with the LORD,
O foolish and unwise people?
*Is* He not [b]your Father, *who* [c]bought you?
Has He not [d]made you and established you?

7 "Remember[a] the days of old,
Consider the years of many generations.
[b]Ask your father, and he will show you;
Your elders, and they will tell you:
8 When the Most High [a]divided their inheritance to the nations,
When He [b]separated the sons of Adam,
He set the boundaries of the peoples
According to the number of the children of Israel.
9 For [a]the LORD's portion *is* His people;
Jacob *is* the place of His inheritance.

10 "He found him [a]in a desert land
And in the wasteland, a howling wilderness;
He encircled him, He instructed him,
He [b]kept him as the apple of His eye.
11 [a]As an eagle stirs up its nest,
Hovers over its young,
Spreading out its wings, taking them up,
Carrying them on its wings,
12 *So* the LORD alone led him,
And *there was* no foreign god with him.

13 "He[a] made him ride in the heights of the earth,
That he might eat the produce of the fields;
He made him draw honey from the rock,
And oil from the flinty rock;
14 Curds from the cattle, and milk of the flock,
[a]With fat of lambs;
And rams of the breed of Bashan, and goats,
With the choicest wheat;
And you drank wine, the [b]blood of the grapes.

15 "But Jeshurun grew fat and kicked;
[a]You grew fat, you grew thick,
You are obese!
Then he [b]forsook God *who* [c]made him,
And scornfully esteemed the [d]Rock of his salvation.

**32:3** [a] Deut. 28:58 [b] 1 Chr. 29:11 **32:4** [a] Ps. 18:2 [b] 2 Sam. 22:31 [c] Is. 65:16 [d] Job 34:10 **32:5** [a] Deut. 4:25; 31:29 [b] Phil. 2:15 **32:6** [a] Ps. 116:12 [b] Is. 63:16 [c] Ps. 74:2 [d] Deut. 32:15 **32:7** [a] Ps. 44:1 [b] Ps. 78:5–8 **32:8** [a] Acts 17:26 [b] Gen. 11:8 **32:9** [a] Ex. 19:5 **32:10** [a] Jer. 2:6 [b] Ps. 17:8 **32:11** [a] Is. 31:5 **32:13** [a] Is. 58:14 **32:14** [a] Ps. 81:16 [b] Gen. 49:11 **32:15** [a] Deut. 31:20 [b] Is. 1:4 [c] Is. 51:13 [d] Ps. 95:1

KNOW THE TRUTH

# THE DOCTRINE OF GOD

## PART 15: THE FAITHFULNESS AND TRUTHFULNESS OF GOD

**32:3–4** Moses lived in an unpredictable world filled with impulsive, unfaithful, inconsistent people. Yet, he could gladly and confidently proclaim the consistency of God. In verse 4, Moses declared the Lord is "a God of truth" whose "work is perfect." In essence, Moses proclaimed God is steady and reliable ("truth"), and He is complete and lacks nothing ("perfect"). Or put another way, Moses stated God is totally reliable and only does what is entirely complete with zero deficiencies.

In Psalm 100:5, the psalmist pronounced that God's goodness, lovingkindness, and faithfulness is everlasting and available to all generations—including us. Simply put, you can count on God! He never changes. He *is* truth (John 14:6). He only speaks what is entirely true and presently helpful. His promises can be trusted because they come from the One who is trustworthy. It's impossible for God to be mistaken. His understanding of all reality is limitless. He instantly, effortlessly knows everything always. It's impossible for God to lie (Heb. 6:18). Thus, we can count on God to speak what's entirely true and act in a reliable, steadfast way in all situations for all people in all ages. That includes to you today.

*For* **THE DOCTRINE OF GOD: PART 16: THE PERFECTION OF GOD**, *turn to Psalm 18:30 on page 541.*

16 [a]They provoked Him to jealousy with
foreign *gods;*
With abominations they provoked Him to
anger.
17 [a]They sacrificed to demons, not to God,
*To gods* they did not know,
To new *gods,* new arrivals
That your fathers did not fear.
18 [a]Of the Rock *who* begot you, you are
unmindful,
And have [b]forgotten the God who fathered
you.

19 "And[a] when the LORD saw *it,* He spurned
*them,*
Because of the provocation of His sons
and His daughters.
20 And He said: 'I will hide My face from
them,
I will see what their end *will be,*
For they *are* a perverse generation,
[a]Children in whom *is* no faith.
21 [a]They have provoked Me to jealousy by
*what* is not God;
They have moved Me to anger [b]by their
foolish idols.
But [c]I will provoke them to jealousy by
*those who are* not a nation;
I will move them to anger by a foolish
nation.
22 For [a]a fire is kindled in My anger,
And shall burn to the lowest hell;
It shall consume the earth with her
increase,
And set on fire the foundations of the
mountains.

23 'I will [a]heap disasters on them;
[b]I will spend My arrows on them.
24 *They shall be* wasted with hunger,
Devoured by pestilence and bitter
destruction;
I will also send against them the [a]teeth of
beasts,
With the poison of serpents of the
dust.
25 The sword shall destroy outside;
*There shall be* terror within
For the young man and virgin,
The nursing child with the man of gray
hairs.
26 [a]I would have said, "I will dash them in
pieces,
I will make the memory of them to cease
from among men,"
27 Had I not feared the wrath of the enemy,
Lest their adversaries should
misunderstand,
Lest they should say, [a]"Our hand *is* high;
And it is not the LORD who has done all
this." '

28 "For they *are* a nation void of counsel,
Nor *is there any* understanding in them.
29 [a]Oh, that they were wise, *that* they
understood this,
*That* they would consider their [b]latter
end!
30 How could one chase a thousand,
And two put ten thousand to flight,
Unless their Rock [a]had sold them,
And the LORD had surrendered them?
31 For their rock *is* not like our Rock,
[a]Even our enemies themselves *being*
judges.
32 For [a]their vine *is* of the vine of Sodom
And of the fields of Gomorrah;
Their grapes *are* grapes of gall,
Their clusters *are* bitter.
33 Their wine *is* [a]the poison of serpents,
And the cruel [b]venom of cobras.

34 '*Is* this not [a]laid up in store with Me,
Sealed up among My treasures?
35 [a]Vengeance is Mine, and recompense;
Their foot shall slip in *due* time;
[b]For the day of their calamity *is* at hand,
And the things to come hasten upon
them.'

36 "For[a] the LORD will judge His people
[b]And have compassion on His servants,
When He sees that *their* power is gone,
And [c]*there is* no one *remaining,* bond or
free.
37 He will say: [a]'Where *are* their gods,
The rock in which they sought refuge?
38 Who ate the fat of their sacrifices,
*And* drank the wine of their drink
offering?
Let them rise and help you,
*And* be your refuge.

39 'Now see that [a]I, *even* I, *am* He,
And [b]*there is* no God besides Me;
[c]I kill and I make alive;
I wound and I heal;
Nor *is there any* who can deliver from
My hand.
40 For I raise My hand to heaven,
And say, "As I live forever,
41 [a]If I whet My glittering sword,
And My hand takes hold on judgment,
I will render vengeance to My
enemies,
And repay those who hate Me.

**32:16** [a] 1 Cor. 10:22 **32:17** [a] Rev. 9:20 **32:18** [a] Is. 17:10 [b] Jer. 2:32 **32:19** [a] Judg. 2:14 **32:20** [a] Matt. 17:17 **32:21** [a] Ps. 78:58 [b] Ps. 31:6 [c] Rom. 10:19 **32:22** [a] Lam. 4:11 **32:23** [a] Ex. 32:12 [b] Ps. 7:12, 13 **32:24** [a] Lev. 26:22 **32:26** [a] Ezek. 20:23 **32:27** [a] Is. 10:12–15 **32:29** [a] [Luke 19:42] [b] Deut. 31:29 **32:30** [a] Judg. 2:14 **32:31** [a] [1 Sam. 4:7, 8] **32:32** [a] Is. 1:8–10 **32:33** [a] Ps. 58:4 [b] Rom. 3:13 **32:34** [a] [Jer. 2:22] **32:35** [a] Heb. 10:30 [b] 2 Pet. 2:3 **32:36** [a] Ps. 135:14 [b] Jer. 31:20 [c] 2 Kin. 14:26 **32:37** [a] Judg. 10:14 **32:39** [a] Is. 41:4; 43:10 [b] Is. 45:5 [c] 1 Sam. 2:6 **32:41** [a] Is. 1:24; 66:16

42 I will make My arrows drunk with blood,
And My sword shall devour flesh,
With the blood of the slain and the captives,
From the heads of the leaders of the enemy." '

43 "Rejoice,[a] O Gentiles, *with* His people;[1]
For He will [b]avenge the blood of His servants,
And render vengeance to His adversaries;
He [c]will provide atonement for His land *and* His people."

44 So Moses came with Joshua[1] the son of
Nun and spoke all the words of this song in
the hearing of the people. 45 Moses finished
speaking all these words to all Israel, 46 and he
said to them: [a]"Set your hearts on all the words
which I testify among you today, which you
shall command your [b]children to be careful to
observe—all the words of this law. 47 For it *is* not
a futile thing for you, because it *is* your [a]life, and
by this word you shall prolong *your* days in the
land which you cross over the Jordan to possess."

### *MOSES TO DIE ON MOUNT NEBO*

48 Then the LORD spoke to Moses that very
same day, saying: 49 [a]"Go up this mountain of
the Abarim, Mount Nebo, which *is* in the land
of Moab, across from Jericho; view the land of
Canaan, which I give to the children of Israel as
a possession; 50 and die on the mountain which
you ascend, and be gathered to your people,
just as [a]Aaron your brother died on Mount Hor
and was gathered to his people; 51 because [a]you
trespassed against Me among the children of
Israel at the waters of Meribah Kadesh, in the
Wilderness of Zin, because you [b]did not hallow
Me in the midst of the children of Israel. 52 [a]Yet
you shall see the land before *you,* though you
shall not go there, into the land which I am
giving to the children of Israel."

### *MOSES' FINAL BLESSING ON ISRAEL*

**33** Now this *is* [a]the blessing with which Moses
[b]the man of God blessed the children of
Israel before his death. 2 And he said:

[a]"The LORD came from Sinai,
And dawned on them from [b]Seir;
He shone forth from [c]Mount Paran,
And He came with [d]ten thousands of saints;
From His right hand
*Came* a fiery law for them.

3 Yes, [a]He loves the people;
[b]All His saints *are* in Your hand;
They [c]sit down at Your feet;
*Everyone* [d]receives Your words.
4 [a]Moses commanded a law for us,
[b]A heritage of the congregation of Jacob.
5 And He was [a]King in [b]Jeshurun,
When the leaders of the people were gathered,
All the tribes of Israel together.

6 "Let [a]Reuben live, and not die,
*Nor* let his men be few."

7 And this he said of [a]Judah:

"Hear, LORD, the voice of Judah,
And bring him to his people;
[b]Let his hands be sufficient for him,
And may You be [c]a help against his enemies."

8 And of [a]Levi he said:

[b]"*Let* Your Thummim and Your Urim *be* with Your holy one,
[c]Whom You tested at Massah,
And with whom You contended at the waters of Meribah,
9 [a]Who says of his father and mother,
'I have not [b]seen them';
[c]Nor did he acknowledge his brothers,
Or know his own children;
For [d]they have observed Your word
And kept Your covenant.
10 [a]They shall teach Jacob Your judgments,
And Israel Your law.
They shall put incense before You,
[b]And a whole burnt sacrifice on Your altar.
11 Bless his substance, LORD,
And [a]accept the work of his hands;
Strike the loins of those who rise against him,
And of those who hate him, that they rise not again."

> **33:8 Massah** and **Meribah** were the places where God gave the Israelites water to stop their grumbling and complaining. They were remembered as places where the people of Israel had gone too far in questioning and challenging God.

**32:43** [a] Rom. 15:10 [b] Rev. 6:10; 19:2 [c] Ps. 65:3; 79:9; 85:1 [1] A Dead Sea Scroll fragment adds *And let all the gods (angels) worship Him* (compare Septuagint and Hebrews 1:6). **32:44** [1] Hebrew *Hoshea* (compare Numbers 13:8, 16) **32:46** [a] Ezek. 40:4; 44:5 [b] Deut. 11:19 **32:47** [a] Deut. 8:3; 30:15–20 **32:49** [a] Num. 27:12–14 **32:50** [a] Num. 20:25, 28; 33:38 **32:51** [a] Num. 20:11–13 [b] Lev. 10:3 **32:52** [a] Deut. 34:1–5 **33:1** [a] Gen. 49:28 [b] Ps. 90 **33:2** [a] Ps. 68:8, 17 [b] Deut. 2:1, 4 [c] Num. 10:12 [d] Dan. 7:10 **33:3** [a] Hos. 11:1 [b] 1 Sam. 2:9 [c] [Luke 10:39] [d] Prov. 2:1 **33:4** [a] John 1:17; 7:19 [b] Ps. 119:111 **33:5** [a] Ex. 15:18 [b] Deut. 32:15 **33:6** [a] Gen. 49:3, 4 **33:7** [a] Gen. 49:8–12 [b] Gen. 49:8 [c] Ps. 146:5 **33:8** [a] Gen. 49:5 [b] Ex. 28:30 [c] Ps. 81:7 **33:9** [a] [Num. 25:5–8] [b] [Gen. 29:32] [c] Ex. 32:26–28 [d] Mal. 2:5, 6 **33:10** [a] Lev. 10:11; Deut. 31:9–13; Mal. 2:7 [b] Lev. 1:9; Ps. 51:19 **33:11** [a] 2 Sam. 24:23; Ezek. 20:40

12 Of Benjamin he said:

"The beloved of the LORD shall dwell in
safety by Him,
*Who* shelters him all the day long;
And he shall dwell between His
shoulders."

13 And of Joseph he said:

[a]"Blessed of the LORD *is* his land,
With the precious things of heaven, with
the [b]dew,
And the deep lying beneath,
14 With the precious fruits of the sun,
With the precious produce of the months,
15 With the best things of [a]the ancient
mountains,
With the precious things [b]of the
everlasting hills,
16 With the precious things of the earth and
its fullness,
And the favor of [a]Him who dwelt in the
bush.
Let *the blessing* come [b]'on the head of
Joseph,
And on the crown of the head of him *who
was* separate from his brothers.'[1]
17 His glory *is like* a [a]firstborn bull,
And his horns *like* the [b]horns of the wild
ox;
Together with them
[c]He shall push the peoples
To the ends of the earth;
[d]They *are* the ten thousands of Ephraim,
And they *are* the thousands of
Manasseh."

18 And of Zebulun he said:

[a]"Rejoice, Zebulun, in your going out,
And Issachar in your tents!
19 They shall [a]call the peoples *to* the
mountain;
There [b]they shall offer sacrifices of
righteousness;
For they shall partake *of* the abundance of
the seas
And *of* treasures hidden in the sand."

20 And of Gad he said:

"Blessed *is* he who [a]enlarges Gad;
He dwells as a lion,
And tears the arm and the crown of his
head.
21 [a]He provided the first *part* for himself,
Because a lawgiver's portion was reserved
there.
[b]He came *with* the heads of the people;
He administered the justice of the LORD,
And His judgments with Israel."

22 And of Dan he said:

"Dan *is* a lion's whelp;
[a]He shall leap from Bashan."

23 And of Naphtali he said:

"O Naphtali, [a]satisfied with favor,
And full of the blessing of the LORD,
[b]Possess the west and the south."

24 And of Asher he said:

[a]"Asher *is* most blessed of sons;
Let him be favored by his brothers,
And let him [b]dip his foot in oil.
25 Your sandals *shall be* [a]iron and bronze;
As your days, *so shall* your strength *be*.

26 "*There is* [a]no one like the God of [b]Jeshurun,
[c]*Who* rides the heavens to help you,
And in His excellency on the clouds.
27 The eternal God *is your* [a]refuge,
And underneath *are* the everlasting arms;
[b]He will thrust out the enemy from before
you,
And will say, 'Destroy!'
28 Then [a]Israel shall dwell in safety,
[b]The fountain of Jacob [c]alone,
In a land of grain and new wine;
His [d]heavens shall also drop dew.
29 [a]Happy *are* you, O Israel!
[b]Who *is* like you, a people saved by the
LORD,
[c]The shield of your help
And the sword of your majesty!
Your enemies [d]shall submit to you,
And [e]you shall tread down their high
places."

### *MOSES DIES ON MOUNT NEBO*

**34** Then Moses went up from the plains
of Moab [a]to Mount Nebo, to the top of
Pisgah, which is across from Jericho. And the
LORD showed him all the land of Gilead as far
as Dan, 2 all Naphtali and the land of Ephraim
and Manasseh, all the land of Judah as far as
the Western Sea,[1] 3 the South, and the plain of
the Valley of Jericho, [a]the city of palm trees, as

33:13 [a] Gen. 49:22–26 [b] Gen. 27:28 33:15 [a] Gen. 49:26 [b] Hab. 3:6 33:16 [a] Ex. 3:2–4; Acts 7:30–35 [b] Gen. 49:26 [1] Genesis 49:26 33:17 [a] 1 Chr. 5:1 [b] Num. 23:22 [c] 1 Kin. 22:11; Ps. 44:5 [d] Gen. 48:19 33:18 [a] Gen. 49:13–15 33:19 [a] Ex. 15:17; Ps. 2:6; Is. 2:3 [b] Ps. 4:5; 51:19 33:20 [a] 1 Chr. 12:8 33:21 [a] Num. 32:16, 17 [b] Josh. 4:12 33:22 [a] Gen. 49:16, 17; Josh. 19:47 33:23 [a] Gen. 49:21 [b] Josh. 19:32 33:24 [a] Gen. 49:20 [b] Job 29:6 33:25 [a] Deut. 8:9 33:26 [a] Ex. 15:11; Deut. 4:35; Ps. 86:8; Jer. 10:6 [b] Deut. 32:15 [c] Deut. 10:14; Ps. 68:3, 33, 34; 104:3 33:27 [a] [Ps. 90:1; 91:2, 9] [b] Deut. 9:3–5 33:28 [a] Deut. 33:12; Jer. 23:6; 33:16 [b] Deut. 8:7, 8 [c] Num. 23:9 [d] Gen. 27:28 33:29 [a] Ps. 144:15 [b] Deut. 4:32–34; 2 Sam. 7:23 [c] Gen. 15:1; Ps. 115:9 [d] Ps. 18:44; 66:3 [e] Num. 33:52 34:1 [a] Num. 27:12; Deut. 32:49 34:2 [1] That is, the Mediterranean 34:3 [a] 2 Chr. 28:15

far as Zoar. 4 Then the LORD said to him, [a]"This
*is* the land of which I swore to give Abraham,
Isaac, and Jacob, saying, 'I will give it to your
descendants.' [b]I have caused you to see *it* with
your eyes, but you shall not cross over there."
5 [a]So Moses the servant of the LORD died
there in the land of Moab, according to the word
of the LORD. 6 And He buried him in a valley in
the land of Moab, opposite Beth Peor; but [a]no
one knows his grave to this day. 7 [a]Moses *was*
one hundred and twenty years old when he
died. [b]His eyes were not dim nor his natural
vigor diminished. 8 And the children of Israel
wept for Moses in the plains of Moab [a]thirty
days. So the days of weeping *and* mourning for
Moses ended.
9 Now Joshua the son of Nun was full of the
[a]spirit of wisdom, for [b]Moses had laid his hands
on him; so the children of Israel heeded him,
and did as the LORD had commanded Moses.
10 But since then there [a]has not arisen in Is-
rael a prophet like Moses, [b]whom the LORD knew
face to face, 11 in all [a]the signs and wonders which
the LORD sent him to do in the land of Egypt,
before Pharaoh, before all his servants, and in
all his land, 12 and by all that mighty power and
all the great terror which Moses performed in
the sight of all Israel.

**34:4** [a] Gen. 12:7 [b] Deut. 3:27 **34:5** [a] Num. 20:12; Deut. 32:50; Josh. 1:1, 2 **34:6** [a] Jude 9 **34:7** [a] Deut. 31:2 [b] Gen. 27:1; 48:10 **34:8** [a] Gen. 50:3, 10 **34:9** [a] Is. 11:2 [b] Num. 27:18, 23 **34:10** [a] Deut. 18:15, 18 [b] Ex. 33:11; Num. 12:8; Deut. 5:4 **34:11** [a] Deut. 7:19

*Introduction to*

# THE BOOKS OF HISTORY

These books continue the true story of God's people where the Pentateuch ends. **Joshua** outlines Israel's entrance into and conquest of Canaan as well as the Israelites' dividing up the land to determine where everyone would live. **Judges** and **Ruth** describe a period of several hundred years after the conquest, a time during which the Israelites were plagued by the sin of idolatry. **First** and **2 Samuel** and **1–2 Kings** tell of the period after the judges when Israel was ruled by kings. Saul, David, and Solomon reign over all of Israel before the kingdom divides in two: Israel (or Samaria) and Judah. These accounts end with both kingdoms being taken into exile because of the people's ongoing idolatry. The two Books of **Chronicles** retell 1–2 Samuel and 1–2 Kings and was written after the exile ends. **Ezra** and **Nehemiah** recount God's people returning to their land after the exile, and **Esther** describes how God preserved His people during exile.

When reading the books of history, it is important to recognize these books do more than describe real events that happened to real people. We don't read these books just to learn facts, although those facts are important and helpful. And, like the Pentateuch, we're to keep the bigger story in mind as we read. But we also read these books primarily so we can understand more clearly our sinfulness as people and God's patience, grace, and mercy. The themes of God's judgment and redemption run through these books. Because of sin, God's judgment would come. But because of God's mercy and grace, He never abandoned His plan to rescue people from sin.

# JOSHUA • JUDGES • RUTH • 1–2 SAMUEL 1–2 KINGS • 1–2 CHRONICLES EZRA • NEHEMIAH • ESTHER

## THE BOOKS OF HISTORY (IN CHRONOLOGICAL ORDER)

| Book | Author | Date | Timeframe | Theme |
|---|---|---|---|---|
| **Joshua** | Joshua | c. 1406–1391 BC | c. 1406–1391 BC | Conquest |
| **Judges** | Samuel | c. 1040–1020 BC | c. 1380–1045 BC | Rescue |
| **Ruth** | Samuel | c. 1011–971 BC | c. 1370–1041 BC | Redemption |
| **1 Samuel** | Samuel; Nathan; Gad | c. 1105–1011 BC | c. 1105–1011 BC | Leadership |
| **2 Samuel** | Unknown | c. 1011–971 BC | c. 1011–971 BC | Kingship |
| **1 Chronicles** | Ezra | c. 450–400 BC | 1004–971 BC | Heritage |
| **1 Kings** | Unknown | c. 561–538 BC | c. 971–851 BC | Division |
| **2 Kings** | Unknown | c. 561–538 BC | c. 851–565 BC | Exile |
| **2 Chronicles** | Ezra | c. 450–400 BC | 971–538 BC | Hope |
| **Ezra** | Ezra | c. 457–444 BC | c. 538–516 BC / c. 458–457 BC | Renewal |
| **Esther** | Unknown | c. 470–424 BC | c. 483–473 BC | Preservation |
| **Nehemiah** | Nehemiah | c. 444–425 BC | c. 444–425 BC | Rebuilding |

*The Book of*

# JOSHUA

**AUTHOR**
Joshua

**KEY VERSE**
Joshua 1:9

**READING TIME**
2 hours 2 minutes

Moses was dead, and Joshua was Israel's new leader. The Book of Joshua opens with the people standing at the border of the Promised Land once again. This time, however, it was a new generation. This generation, unlike their parents forty years earlier, chose to obey God and enter. The nation of Israel was without a trained military and faced the challenge of uprooting foes in heavily fortified cities. But God went before His people in battle to secure the victory. The Israelites conquered the land over the course of three major military campaigns involving more than thirty enemy armies. Through it all, the Israelites learned a crucial lesson under Joshua's capable leadership: victory comes through faith in God and obedience to His word rather than through numerical superiority or military strength.

**Occasion:** Joshua records the second generation of Israelites after the exodus entering and conquering the Promised Land.

**Main Point:** When the people of Israel trust in God, He fulfills His promise to give them the land of their ancestors.

**Big Ideas:** God makes good on all His promises. We have nothing to fear because God goes before us. Our faith is an active faith, requiring us to act in obedience to whatever God calls us to do.

**OUTLINE:**

I. The People Enter the Land (chs. 1–5)
II. The Victory at Jericho (ch. 6)
III. The Setback at Ai (chs. 7–8)
IV. The Treaty with the Gibeonites (chs. 9–10)
V. The Land Is Conquered (chs. 11–12)
VI. The Lands East of the Jordan (ch. 13)
VII. The Lands West of the Jordan (chs. 14–19)
VIII. The Cities of Refuge (ch. 20)
IX. The Cities for the Levites (ch. 21)
X. The Conditions for Living in the Land (chs. 22–24)

**c. 1446–1406 BC**
Forty years of wilderness wandering

**c. 1405 BC**
Joshua succeeds Moses

**c. 1405–1400 BC**
The conquest of Canaan

**c. 1398 BC**
Canaan is apportioned to the tribes

**c. 1380 BC**
Joshua dies

**c. 1380–1050 BC**
Judges rule in Israel

**c. 1349 BC**
King Tut buried at Thebes

**c. 1200 BC**
Iron Age begins with the rise of iron technology

**c. 1050 BC**
Saul becomes king of Israel

## *GOD'S COMMISSION TO JOSHUA*

1 After the death of Moses the servant of the
LORD, it came to pass that the LORD spoke
to Joshua the son of Nun, Moses' [a]assistant,
saying: 2 [a]"Moses My servant is dead. Now
therefore, arise, go over this Jordan, you and
all this people, to the land which I am giving
to them—the children of Israel. 3 [a]Every place

> **SEEING JESUS IN THE SCRIPTURE**
>
> **1:1–2** *Joshua* and *Jesus* mean "the Lord saves." Both Joshua and Jesus led their people to a Promised Land—Joshua led the Hebrews into the land of Canaan while Jesus leads believers into the eternal Promised Land, heaven (see Matt. 1:21).

that the sole of your foot will tread upon I
have given you, as I said to Moses. 4 [a]From the
wilderness and this Lebanon as far as the great
river, the River Euphrates, all the land of the
Hittites, and to the Great Sea toward the going
down of the sun, shall be your territory. 5 [a]No
man shall *be able to* stand before you all the
days of your life; [b]as I was with Moses, *so* [c]I will
be with you. [d]I will not leave you nor forsake
you. 6 [a]Be strong and of good courage, for to
this people you shall divide as an inheritance
the land which I swore to their fathers to give
them. 7 Only be strong and very courageous,
that you may observe to do according to all
the law [a]which Moses My servant commanded
you; [b]do not turn from it to the right hand or to
the left, that you may prosper wherever you go.
8 [a]This Book of the Law shall not depart from
your mouth, but [b]you shall meditate in it day
and night, that you may observe to do accord-
ing to all that is written in it. For then you will
make your way prosperous, and then you will
have good success. 9 [a]Have I not commanded
you? Be strong and of good courage; [b]do not
be afraid, nor be dismayed, for the LORD your
God *is* with you wherever you go."

> **1:8** Unlike some forms of meditation that attempt to empty the mind, to **meditate** on Scripture seeks to fill the mind with truth. It's to think deeply about God's Word and consider how it should affect your life. Meditation, then, begins with thinking but doesn't end with it; it ends with acting.

## *THE ORDER TO CROSS THE JORDAN*

10 Then Joshua commanded the officers of
the people, saying, 11 "Pass through the camp and
command the people, saying, 'Prepare provi-
sions for yourselves, for [a]within three days you
will cross over this Jordan, to go in to possess
the land which the LORD your God is giving you
to possess.' "
12 And to the Reubenites, the Gadites, and
half the tribe of Manasseh Joshua spoke, saying,
13 "Remember [a]the word which Moses the servant
of the LORD commanded you, saying, 'The LORD
your God is giving you rest and is giving you this
land.' 14 Your wives, your little ones, and your
livestock shall remain in the land which Moses
gave you on this side of the Jordan. But you shall
pass before your brethren armed, all your mighty
men of valor, and help them, 15 until the LORD has
given your brethren rest, as He *gave* you, and they
also have taken possession of the land which the
LORD your God is giving them. [a]Then you shall
return to the land of your possession and enjoy
it, which Moses the LORD's servant gave you on
this side of the Jordan toward the sunrise."
16 So they answered Joshua, saying, "All that
you command us we will do, and wherever you
send us we will go. 17 Just as we heeded Moses
in all things, so we will heed you. Only the LORD
your God [a]be with you, as He was with Moses.
18 Whoever rebels against your command and
does not heed your words, in all that you com-
mand him, shall be put to death. Only be strong
and of good courage."

## *RAHAB HIDES THE SPIES*

*(Heb. 11:31)*

2 Now Joshua the son of Nun sent out two men
[a]from Acacia Grove[1] to spy secretly, saying,
"Go, view the land, especially Jericho."
So they went, and [b]came to the house of a
harlot named [c]Rahab, and lodged there. 2 And
[a]it was told the king of Jericho, saying, "Behold,
men have come here tonight from the children
of Israel to search out the country."
3 So the king of Jericho sent to Rahab, saying,
"Bring out the men who have come to you, who
have entered your house, for they have come to
search out all the country."
4 [a]Then the woman took the two men and
hid them. So she said, "Yes, the men came to me,
but I did not know where they *were* from. 5 And it
happened as the gate was being shut, when it was
dark, that the men went out. Where the men went
I do not know; pursue them quickly, for you may
overtake them." 6 (But [a]she had brought them
up to the roof and hidden them with the stalks
of flax, which she had laid in order on the roof.)
7 Then the men pursued them by the road to the

**1:1** [a] Ex. 24:13; Num. 13:16; 14:6, 29, 30, 37, 38; Deut. 1:38; Acts 7:45 **1:2** [a] Num. 12:7; Deut. 34:5 **1:3** [a] Deut. 11:24; Josh. 11:23 **1:4** [a] Gen. 15:18; Ex. 23:31; Num. 34:3–12 **1:5** [a] Deut. 7:24 [b] Ex. 3:12 [c] Deut. 31:8, 23 [d] Deut. 31:6, 7; Heb. 13:5 **1:6** [a] Deut. 31:7, 23 **1:7** [a] Num. 27:23; Deut. 31:7; Josh. 11:15 [b] Deut. 5:32 **1:8** [a] Deut. 17:18, 19; 31:24, 26; Josh. 8:34 [b] Deut. 29:9; Ps. 1:1–3 **1:9** [a] Deut. 31:7 [b] Ps. 27:1 **1:11** [a] Deut. 9:1; Josh. 3:17 **1:13** [a] Num. 32:20–28 **1:15** [a] Josh. 22:1–4 **1:17** [a] 1 Sam. 20:13; 1 Kin. 1:37 **2:1** [a] Num. 25:1; Josh. 3:1 [b] Heb. 11:31; James 2:25 [c] Matt. 1:5 [1] Hebrew *Shittim* **2:2** [a] Josh. 2:22 **2:4** [a] 2 Sam. 17:19, 20 **2:6** [a] Ex. 1:17; 2 Sam. 17:19

Jordan, to the fords. And as soon as those who
pursued them had gone out, they shut the gate.

> **2:3–7** Ancient houses were built with flat roofs that were used like modern decks or porches. Crops and clothes were often laid out on the roof to dry. When visitors stopped by, extra beds might have been provided on the roof to accommodate them.

8 Now before they lay down, she came up to
them on the roof, 9 and said to the men: [a]"I know
that the LORD has given you the land, that [b]the
terror of you has fallen on us, and that all the
inhabitants of the land [c]are fainthearted because
of you. 10 For we have heard how the LORD [a]dried
up the water of the Red Sea for you when you
came out of Egypt, and [b]what you did to the two
kings of the Amorites who *were* on the other side
of the Jordan, Sihon and Og, whom you [c]utterly
destroyed. 11 And as soon as we [a]heard *these things,*
[b]our hearts melted; neither did there remain any
more courage in anyone because of you, for [c]the
LORD your God, He *is* God in heaven above and on
earth beneath. 12 Now therefore, I beg you, [a]swear to
me by the LORD, since I have shown you kindness,
that you also will show kindness to [b]my father's
house, and [c]give me a true token, 13 and [a]spare my
father, my mother, my brothers, my sisters, and all
that they have, and deliver our lives from death."
14 So the men answered her, "Our lives for
yours, if none of you tell this business of ours.
And it shall be, when the LORD has given us the
land, that [a]we will deal kindly and truly with you."
15 Then she [a]let them down by a rope through
the window, for her house *was* on the city wall;
she dwelt on the wall. 16 And she said to them,
"Get to the mountain, lest the pursuers meet
you. Hide there three days, until the pursuers
have returned. Afterward you may go your way."
17 So the men said to her: "We *will be* [a]blame-
less of this oath of yours which you have made
us swear, 18 [a]unless, *when* we come into the land,
you bind this line of scarlet cord in the window
through which you let us down, [b]and unless you

**2:9** [a] Deut. 1:8 [b] Gen. 35:5; Ex. 23:27; Deut. 2:25; 11:25; Josh. 9:9, 10 [c] Ex. 15:15; Josh. 5:1 **2:10** [a] Ex. 14:21; Josh. 4:23 [b] Num. 21:21–35 [c] Deut. 20:17; Josh. 6:21 **2:11** [a] Ex. 15:14, 15 [b] Josh. 5:1; 7:5; Ps. 22:14; Is. 13:7 [c] Deut. 4:39 **2:12** [a] 1 Sam. 20:14, 15, 17 [b] 1 Tim. 5:8 [c] Ex. 12:13; Josh. 2:18 **2:13** [a] Josh. 6:23–25 **2:14** [a] Gen. 47:29; Judg. 1:24; [Matt. 5:7] **2:15** [a] Acts 9:25 **2:17** [a] Ex. 20:7 **2:18** [a] Josh. 2:12 [b] Josh. 6:23

STORY OF SCRIPTURE

18

JOSHUA 2:18–19

## THE SCARLET CORD

### WHAT'S GOING ON?

Rahab's story is woven with themes of faith, redemption, and divine providence. Having hidden the Israelite spies from certain death, Rahab was given a lifeline, a scarlet cord. When hung from her window, this cord ensured her safety and that of her household amid Jericho's impending destruction. The scarlet cord was a symbol of Rahab's pact with the spies and, more importantly, her faith in Israel's God. It's an emblem of salvation, set against the backdrop of a city marked for judgment. Rahab's actions, driven by faith in a God she had only heard of, speak to the universal search for hope and salvation. Her home, perched on the city wall, stands as a metaphor for the thin line between destruction and deliverance.

### WHAT DOES THIS MEAN FOR ME?

Rahab's story is a fascinating case study of ethics and moral ambiguity. Rahab was a prostitute with a checkered past who lied to save the Israelite spies. This story isn't a license to live or lie like Rahab but rather serves as another example of how God works despite sin, brokenness, and challenging situations.

### DID YOU CATCH THE PATTERN?

Rahab found refuge in a singular act of faith represented by a scarlet cord. The color scarlet appears throughout Scripture, from the blood of the sacrifices in the Levitical law to Jesus' ultimate sacrifice on Calvary. It signals both a cost and a covenant. The cord, meanwhile, is a clue to the lineage of Jesus. Rahab would go on to marry a man from the tribe of Judah named Salmon. Together, they would have a child named Boaz, who would marry Ruth and have a son named Obed. Obed would be the father of Jesse, the father of David. Through David's lineage, Jesus would be born (see Matt. 1:5).

*For the next* Story of Scripture *reading and devotion, turn to Joshua 3:1–17 on page 219.*

bring your father, your mother, your brothers, and all your father's household to your own home. 19 So it shall be *that* whoever goes outside the doors of your house into the street, his blood *shall be* on his own head, and we *will be* guiltless. And whoever is with you in the house, [a]his blood *shall be* on our head if a hand is laid on him. 20 And if you tell this business of ours, then we will be free from your oath which you made us swear."

21 Then she said, "According to your words, so *be* it." And she sent them away, and they departed. And she bound the scarlet cord in the window.

22 They departed and went to the mountain, and stayed there three days until the pursuers returned. The pursuers sought *them* all along the way, but did not find *them.* 23 So the two men returned, descended from the mountain, and crossed over; and they came to Joshua the son of Nun, and told him all that had befallen them. 24 And they said to Joshua, "Truly [a]the LORD has delivered all the land into our hands, for indeed all the inhabitants of the country are fainthearted because of us."

## *ISRAEL CROSSES THE JORDAN*

3 Then Joshua rose early in the morning; and they set out [a]from Acacia Grove[1] and came to the Jordan, he and all the children of Israel, and lodged there before they crossed over. 2 So it was, [a]after three days, that the officers went through the camp; 3 and they commanded the people, saying, [a]"When you see the ark of the covenant of the LORD your God, [b]and the priests, the Levites, bearing it, then you shall set out from your place and go after it. 4 [a]Yet there shall be a space between you and it, about two thousand cubits by measure. Do not come near it, that you may know the way by which you must go, for you have not passed *this* way before."

5 And Joshua said to the people, [a]"Sanctify yourselves, for tomorrow the LORD will do wonders among you." 6 Then Joshua spoke to the priests, saying, [a]"Take up the ark of the covenant and cross over before the people."

So they took up the ark of the covenant and went before the people.

7 And the LORD said to Joshua, "This day I will begin to [a]exalt you in the sight of all Israel, that they may know that, [b]as I was with Moses,

**2:19** [a] 1 Kin. 2:32; Matt. 27:25 **2:24** [a] Ex. 23:31; Josh. 6:2; 21:44 **3:1** [a] Josh. 2:1 [1] Hebrew *Shittim* **3:2** [a] Josh. 1:10, 11 **3:3** [a] Num. 10:33 [b] Deut. 31:9, 25 **3:4** [a] Ex. 19:12 **3:5** [a] Ex. 19:10, 14, 15; Lev. 20:7; Num. 11:18; Josh. 7:13; 1 Sam. 16:5; Job 1:5; Joel 2:16 **3:6** [a] Num. 4:15 **3:7** [a] Josh. 4:14; 1 Chr. 29:25; 2 Chr. 1:1 [b] Josh. 1:5, 9

JOSHUA 3:1–17

# CROSSING THE JORDAN

19

STORY OF SCRIPTURE

### WHAT'S GOING ON?

In Joshua 3, the Israelites were at a monumental moment: crossing the Jordan River into the Promised Land. It's a scene rich with symbolism and significance. The river represents not just a physical barrier but also a spiritual one. This miraculous event echoes the Red Sea crossing under Moses (see Ex. 14) and signifies a new chapter in Israel's history. This moment marks a key transition in the story of Scripture, moving from the wilderness wanderings to taking possession of the Promised Land, from a generation that knew only barrenness to one that would know the abundance of God's promises.

### WHAT DOES THIS MEAN FOR ME?

This story challenges us to consider our own faith journey. Are we standing at the edge of our own Jordan River, hesitant to take that step of faith into what God has promised us? This passage reminds us God's good works often follow our steps of obedience. We are called to trust and act, even when the path ahead seems uncertain.

### DID YOU CATCH THE PATTERN?

The parting of the Jordan River is part of a recurring theme in the Bible where God makes a way where there seems to be no way. From the parting of the Red Sea to Jesus calming the storm, the Bible is filled with stories where God intervenes in seemingly impossible situations. This pattern teaches us about God's nature—He is a God who saves, delivers, and opens paths for His people. This theme culminates in Jesus Christ, who is the ultimate expression of God making a way for humanity. Through His life, death, and resurrection, Jesus bridges the ultimate divide—sin—reconciling us to God and leading us into the "Promised Land" of eternal life.

*For the next* Story of Scripture *reading and devotion, turn to Judges 2:11–23 on page 243.*

*so* I will be with you. 8 You shall command [a]the
priests who bear the ark of the covenant, saying,
'When you have come to the edge of the water
of the Jordan, [b]you shall stand in the Jordan.' "
9 So Joshua said to the children of Israel,
"Come here, and hear the words of the LORD
your God." 10 And Joshua said, "By this you shall
know that [a]the living God *is* among you, and *that*
He will without fail [b]drive out from before you
the [c]Canaanites and the Hittites and the Hivites
and the Perizzites and the Girgashites and the
Amorites and the Jebusites: 11 Behold, the ark
of the covenant of [a]the Lord of all the earth is
crossing over before you into the Jordan. 12 Now
therefore, [a]take for yourselves twelve men from
the tribes of Israel, one man from every tribe.
13 And it shall come to pass, [a]as soon as the soles
of the feet of the priests who bear the ark of the
LORD, [b]the Lord of all the earth, shall rest in the
waters of the Jordan, *that* the waters of the Jor-
dan shall be cut off, the waters that come down
from upstream, and they [c]shall stand as a heap."
14 So it was, when the people set out from
their camp to cross over the Jordan, with the
priests bearing the [a]ark of the covenant before
the people, 15 and as those who bore the ark came
to the Jordan, and [a]the feet of the priests who
bore the ark dipped in the edge of the water (for
the [b]Jordan overflows all its banks [c]during the
whole time of harvest), 16 that the waters which
came down from upstream stood *still, and* rose
in a heap very far away at Adam, the city that *is*
beside [a]Zaretan. So the waters that went down
[b]into the Sea of the Arabah, [c]the Salt Sea, failed,
*and* were cut off; and the people crossed over
opposite Jericho. 17 Then the priests who bore the
ark of the covenant of the LORD stood firm on
dry ground in the midst of the Jordan; [a]and all
Israel crossed over on dry ground, until all the
people had crossed completely over the Jordan.

### THE MEMORIAL STONES

4 And it came to pass, when all the people
had completely crossed [a]over the Jordan,
that the LORD spoke to Joshua, saying: 2 [a]"Take
for yourselves twelve men from the people, one
man from every tribe, 3 and command them,
saying, 'Take for yourselves twelve stones from
here, out of the midst of the Jordan, from the
place where [a]the priests' feet stood firm. You
shall carry them over with you and leave them
in [b]the lodging place where you lodge tonight.' "
4 Then Joshua called the twelve men whom
he had appointed from the children of Israel,
one man from every tribe; 5 and Joshua said to
them: "Cross over before the ark of the LORD
your God into the midst of the Jordan, and each
one of you take up a stone on his shoulder, ac-
cording to the number of the tribes of the chil-
dren of Israel, 6 that this may be [a]a sign among
you [b]when your children ask in time to come,
saying, 'What do these stones *mean* to you?'
7 Then you shall answer them that [a]the waters
of the Jordan were cut off before the ark of the
covenant of the LORD; when it crossed over the
Jordan, the waters of the Jordan were cut off.
And these stones shall be for [b]a memorial to
the children of Israel forever."
8 And the children of Israel did so, just as
Joshua commanded, and took up twelve stones
from the midst of the Jordan, as the LORD had
spoken to Joshua, according to the number of
the tribes of the children of Israel, and carried
them over with them to the place where they
lodged, and laid them down there. 9 Then Joshua
set up twelve stones in the midst of the Jordan,
in the place where the feet of the priests who
bore the ark of the covenant stood; and they
are there to this day.
10 So the priests who bore the ark stood in the
midst of the Jordan until everything was finished
that the LORD had commanded Joshua to speak
to the people, according to all that Moses had
commanded Joshua; and the people hurried
and crossed over. 11 Then it came to pass, when
all the people had completely crossed over, that
the [a]ark of the LORD and the priests crossed over
in the presence of the people. 12 And [a]the men
of Reuben, the men of Gad, and half the tribe
of Manasseh crossed over armed before the
children of Israel, as Moses had spoken to them.
13 About forty thousand prepared for war crossed
over before the LORD for battle, to the plains of
Jericho. 14 On that day the LORD [a]exalted Joshua
in the sight of all Israel; and they feared him, as
they had feared Moses, all the days of his life.
15 Then the LORD spoke to Joshua, saying,
16 "Command the priests who bear [a]the ark of
the Testimony to come up from the Jordan."
17 Joshua therefore commanded the priests,
saying, "Come up from the Jordan." 18 And it
came to pass, when the priests who bore the ark
of the covenant of the LORD had come from the
midst of the Jordan, *and* the soles of the priests'
feet touched the dry land, that the waters of the
Jordan returned to their place [a]and overflowed
all its banks as before.
19 Now the people came up from the Jordan
on the tenth *day* of the first month, and they
camped [a]in Gilgal on the east border of Jericho.
20 And [a]those twelve stones which they took out
of the Jordan, Joshua set up in Gilgal. 21 Then he

3:8 [a] Josh. 3:3 [b] Josh. 3:17 3:10 [a] Deut. 5:26; Josh. 11:23; 1 Sam. 17:26; 2 Kin. 19:4; Hos. 1:10; Matt. 16:16; 1 Thess. 1:9 [b] Ex. 33:2; Deut. 7:1; 18:12; Ps. 44:2 [c] Acts 13:19 3:11 [a] Josh. 3:13; Job 41:11; Ps. 24:1; Mic. 4:13; Zech. 4:14; 6:5 3:12 [a] Josh. 4:2, 4 3:13 [a] Josh. 3:15, 16 [b] Josh. 3:11 [c] Ps. 78:13; 114:3 3:14 [a] Ps. 132:8; Acts 7:44, 45 3:15 [a] Josh. 3:13 [b] 1 Chr. 12:15; Jer. 12:5; 49:19 [c] Josh. 4:18; 5:10, 12 3:16 [a] 1 Kin. 4:12; 7:46 [b] Deut. 3:17 [c] Gen. 14:3; Num. 34:3 3:17 [a] Gen. 50:24; Ex. 3:8; 6:1–8; 14:21, 22, 29; 33:1; Deut. 6:10; Heb. 11:29 4:1 [a] Deut. 27:2; Josh. 3:17 4:2 [a] Josh. 3:12 4:3 [a] Josh. 3:13 [b] Josh. 4:19, 20 4:6 [a] Deut. 27:2; Ps. 103:2 [b] Ex. 12:26; 13:14; Deut. 6:20 4:7 [a] Josh. 3:13, 16 [b] Ex. 12:14; Num. 16:40 4:11 [a] Josh. 3:11; 6:11 4:12 [a] Num. 32:17, 20, 27, 28; Josh. 1:14 4:14 [a] Josh. 3:7; 1 Chr. 29:25 4:16 [a] Ex. 25:16, 22 4:18 [a] Josh. 3:15; 1 Chr. 12:15 4:19 [a] Josh. 5:9 4:20 [a] Deut. 11:30; Josh. 4:3; 5:9, 10

spoke to the children of Israel, saying: [a]"When your children ask their fathers in time to come, saying, 'What *are* these stones?' 22 then you shall let your children know, saying, [a]'Israel crossed over this Jordan on [b]dry land'; 23 for the LORD your God dried up the waters of the Jordan before you until you had crossed over, as the LORD your God did to the Red Sea, [a]which He dried up before us until we had crossed over, 24 [a]that all the peoples of the earth may know the hand of the LORD, that it *is* [b]mighty, that you may [c]fear the LORD your God forever."

### THE SECOND GENERATION CIRCUMCISED

**5** So it was, when all the kings of the Amorites who *were* on the west side of the Jordan, and all the kings of the Canaanites [a]who *were* by the sea, [b]heard that the LORD had dried up the waters of the Jordan from before the children of Israel until we[1] had crossed over, that their heart melted; [c]and there was no spirit in them any longer because of the children of Israel.

2 At that time the LORD said to Joshua, "Make [a]flint knives for yourself, and circumcise the sons of Israel again the second time." 3 So Joshua made flint knives for himself, and circumcised the sons of Israel at the hill of the foreskins.[1] 4 And this *is* the reason why Joshua circumcised them: [a]All the people who came out of Egypt *who were* males, all the men of war, had died in the wilderness on the way, after they had come out of Egypt. 5 For all the people who came out had been circumcised, but all the people born in the wilderness, on the way as they came out of Egypt, had not been circumcised. 6 For the children of Israel walked [a]forty years in the wilderness, till all the people *who were* men of war, who came out of Egypt, were consumed, because they did not obey the voice of the LORD—to whom the LORD swore that [b]He would not show them the land which the LORD had sworn to their fathers that He would give us, [c]"a land flowing with milk and honey."[1] 7 Then Joshua circumcised [a]their sons *whom* He raised up in their place; for they were uncircumcised, because they had not been circumcised on the way.

8 So it was, when they had finished circumcising all the people, that they stayed in their places in the camp [a]till they were healed. 9 Then the LORD said to Joshua, "This day I have rolled away [a]the reproach of Egypt from you." Therefore the name of the place is called [b]Gilgal[1] to this day.

10 Now the children of Israel camped in Gilgal, and kept the Passover [a]on the fourteenth day of the month at twilight on the plains of Jericho. 11 And they ate of the produce of the land on the day after the Passover, unleavened bread and parched grain, on the very same day. 12 Then [a]the manna ceased on the day after they had eaten the produce of the land; and the children of Israel no longer had manna, but they ate the food of the land of Canaan that year.

> **5:2** The generation that left Egypt had been circumcised. However, that generation had died in the wilderness and for some reason they had neglected to circumcise their sons, the generation which would enter the Promised Land. Here, to **circumcise the sons of Israel** wasn't only an act of obedience, but one of faith, considering they waited to do so until after they crossed the Jordan River, where they might have been vulnerable to the land's occupants.

### THE COMMANDER OF THE ARMY OF THE LORD

13 And it came to pass, when Joshua was by Jericho, that he lifted his eyes and looked, and behold, [a]a Man stood opposite him [b]with His sword drawn in His hand. And Joshua went to Him and said to Him, "*Are* You for us or for our adversaries?"

14 So He said, "No, but *as* Commander of the army of the LORD I have now come."

And Joshua [a]fell on his face to the earth and [b]worshiped, and said to Him, "What does my Lord say to His servant?"

15 Then the Commander of the LORD's army said to Joshua, [a]"Take your sandal off your foot, for the place where you stand *is* holy." And Joshua did so.

### THE DESTRUCTION OF JERICHO

**6** Now [a]Jericho was securely shut up because of the children of Israel; none went out, and none came in. 2 And the LORD said to Joshua: "See! [a]I have given Jericho into your hand, its [b]king, *and* the mighty men of valor. 3 You shall march around the city, all *you* men of war; you shall go all around the city once. This you shall do six days. 4 And seven priests shall bear seven [a]trumpets of rams' horns before the ark. But the seventh day you shall march around the city [b]seven times, and [c]the priests shall blow the trumpets. 5 It shall come to pass, when they make a long *blast* with the ram's horn, *and* when you hear the sound of the trumpet, that all the people shall shout with a great shout; then the

**4:21** [a] Josh. 4:6 **4:22** [a] Ex. 12:26, 27; 13:8–14; Deut. 26:5–9 [b] Josh. 3:17 **4:23** [a] Ex. 14:21 **4:24** [a] 1 Kin. 8:42; 2 Kin. 19:19; Ps. 106:8 [b] Ex. 15:16; 1 Chr. 29:12; Ps. 89:13 [c] Ex. 14:31; Deut. 6:2; Ps. 76:7; Jer. 10:7 **5:1** [a] Num. 13:29 [b] Ex. 15:14, 15 [c] Josh. 2:10, 11; 9:9; 1 Kin. 10:5 [1] Following Kethib; Qere, some Hebrew manuscripts and editions, Septuagint, Syriac, Targum, and Vulgate read *they*. **5:2** [a] Ex. 4:25 **5:3** [1] Hebrew *Gibeath Haaraloth* **5:4** [a] Num. 14:29; 26:64, 65; Deut. 2:14–16 **5:6** [a] Num. 14:33; Deut. 1:3; 29:5 [b] Num. 14:23, 29–35; 26:23–65; Heb. 3:11 [c] Ex. 3:8 [1] Exodus 3:8 **5:7** [a] Num. 14:31; Deut. 1:39 **5:8** [a] Gen. 34:25 **5:9** [a] Gen. 34:14 [b] Josh. 4:19 [1] Literally *Rolling* **5:10** [a] Ex. 12:6; Num. 9:5 **5:12** [a] Ex. 16:35 **5:13** [a] Gen. 18:1, 2; 32:24, 30; Ex. 23:23; Num. 22:31; Zech. 1:8; Acts 1:10 [b] Num. 22:23; 1 Chr. 21:16 **5:14** [a] Gen. 17:3; Num. 20:6 [b] Ex. 34:8 **5:15** [a] Ex. 3:5; Acts 7:33 **6:1** [a] Josh. 2:1 **6:2** [a] Josh. 2:9, 24; 8:1 [b] Deut. 7:24 **6:4** [a] Lev. 25:9; Judg. 7:16, 22 [b] 1 Kin. 18:43; 2 Kin. 4:35; 5:10 [c] Num. 10:8

wall of the city will fall down flat. And the people shall go up every man straight before him."

6 Then Joshua the son of Nun called the priests and said to them, "Take up the ark of the covenant, and let seven priests bear seven trumpets of rams' horns before the ark of the LORD." 7 And he said to the people, "Proceed, and march around the city, and let him who is armed advance before the ark of the LORD."

8 So it was, when Joshua had spoken to the people, that the seven priests bearing the seven trumpets of rams' horns before the LORD advanced and blew the trumpets, and the ark of the covenant of the LORD followed them. 9 The armed men went before the priests who blew the trumpets, [a]and the rear guard came after the ark, while *the priests* continued blowing the trumpets. 10 Now Joshua had commanded the people, saying, "You shall not shout or make any noise with your voice, nor shall a word proceed out of your mouth, until the day I say to you, 'Shout!' Then you shall shout." 11 So he had [a]the ark of the LORD circle the city, going around *it* once. Then they came into the camp and lodged in the camp.

12 And Joshua rose early in the morning, [a]and the priests took up the ark of the LORD. 13 Then seven priests bearing seven trumpets of rams' horns before the ark of the LORD went on continually and blew with the trumpets. And the armed men went before them. But the rear guard came after the ark of the LORD, while *the priests* continued blowing the trumpets. 14 And the second day they marched around the city once and returned to the camp. So they did six days.

15 But it came to pass on the seventh day that they rose early, about the dawning of the day, and marched around the city seven times in the same manner. On that day only they marched around the city seven times. 16 And the seventh time it happened, when the priests blew the trumpets, that Joshua said to the people: "Shout, for the LORD has given you the city! 17 Now the city shall be [a]doomed by the LORD to destruction, it and all who *are* in it. Only [b]Rahab the harlot shall live, she and all who *are* with her in the house, because [c]she hid the messengers that we sent. 18 And you, [a]by all means abstain from the accursed things, lest you become accursed when you take of the accursed things, and make the camp of Israel a curse, [b]and trouble it. 19 But all the silver and gold, and vessels of bronze and iron, *are* consecrated to the LORD; they shall come into the treasury of the LORD."

20 So the people shouted when *the priests* blew the trumpets. And it happened when the people heard the sound of the trumpet, and the people shouted with a great shout, that [a]the wall fell down flat. Then the people went up into the city, every man straight before him, and they took the city. 21 And they [a]utterly destroyed all that *was* in the city, both man and woman, young and old, ox and sheep and donkey, with the edge of the sword.

22 But Joshua had said to the two men who had spied out the country, "Go into the harlot's house, and from there bring out the woman and all that she has, [a]as you swore to her." 23 And the young men who had been spies went in and brought out Rahab, [a]her father, her mother, her brothers, and all that she had. So they brought out all her relatives and left them outside the camp of Israel. 24 But they burned the city and all that *was* in it with fire. Only the silver and gold, and the vessels of bronze and iron, they put into the treasury of the house of the LORD. 25 And Joshua spared Rahab the harlot, her father's household, and all that she had. So [a]she dwells in Israel to this day, because she hid the messengers whom Joshua sent to spy out Jericho.

26 Then Joshua charged *them* at that time, saying, [a]"Cursed *be* the man before the LORD who rises up and builds this city Jericho; he shall lay its foundation with his firstborn, and with his youngest he shall set up its gates."

27 So the LORD was with Joshua, and his fame spread throughout all the country.

## SEEING JESUS IN THE SCRIPTURE

**6:17** Rahab and her household were saved from Jericho's destruction, just as promised. Rehab, a Gentile prostitute, was welcomed into the people of Israel, even becoming an ancestor of Jesus (see Matt. 1:5). This points to how Jesus came to provide salvation for everyone who believes.

## *DEFEAT AT AI*

**7** But the children of Israel committed a [a]trespass regarding the [b]accursed things, for [c]Achan the son of Carmi, the son of Zabdi,[1] the son of Zerah, of the tribe of Judah, took of the accursed things; so the anger of the LORD burned against the children of Israel.

2 Now Joshua sent men from Jericho to Ai, which *is* beside Beth Aven, on the east side of Bethel, and spoke to them, saying, "Go up and spy out the country." So the men went up and spied out Ai. 3 And they returned to Joshua and said to him, "Do not let all the people go up, but let about two or three thousand men go up and attack Ai. Do not weary all the people there, for *the people of Ai are* few." 4 So about three thousand men went up there from the people, [a]but they fled before the men of Ai. 5 And the men of Ai struck down about thirty-six men, for they chased them *from* before the gate as

**6:9** [a] Num. 10:25 **6:11** [a] Josh. 4:11 **6:12** [a] Deut. 31:25 **6:17** [a] Deut. 13:17; Josh. 7:1 [b] Josh. 2:1; Matt. 1:5 [c] Josh. 2:4, 6 **6:18** [a] Deut. 7:26 [b] Josh. 7:1, 12, 25; 1 Kin. 18:17, 18; [Jon. 1:12] **6:20** [a] Heb. 11:30 **6:21** [a] Deut. 7:2; 20:16, 17 **6:22** [a] Josh. 2:12–19; Heb. 11:31 **6:23** [a] Josh. 2:13 **6:25** [a] [Matt. 1:5] **6:26** [a] 1 Kin. 16:34 **7:1** [a] Josh. 7:20, 21 [b] Josh. 6:17–19 [c] Josh. 22:20 [1] Called *Zimri* in 1 Chronicles 2:6 **7:4** [a] Lev. 26:17; Deut. 28:25

far as Shebarim, and struck them down on the descent; therefore [a]the hearts of the people melted and became like water.

6 Then Joshua [a]tore his clothes, and fell to the earth on his face before the ark of the LORD until evening, he and the elders of Israel; and they [b]put dust on their heads. 7 And Joshua said, "Alas, Lord GOD, [a]why have You brought this people over the Jordan at all—to deliver us into the hand of the Amorites, to destroy us? Oh, that we had been content, and dwelt on the other side of the Jordan! 8 O Lord, what shall I say when Israel turns its back before its enemies? 9 For the Canaanites and all the inhabitants of the land will hear *it,* and surround us, and [a]cut off our name from the earth. Then [b]what will You do for Your great name?"

### THE SIN OF ACHAN

10 So the LORD said to Joshua: "Get up! Why do you lie thus on your face? 11 Israel has sinned, and they have also transgressed My covenant which I commanded them. [a]For they have even taken some of the accursed things, and have both stolen and [b]deceived; and they have also put *it* among their own stuff. 12 [a]Therefore the children of Israel could not stand before their enemies, *but* turned *their* backs before their enemies, because [b]they have become doomed to destruction. Neither will I be with you anymore, unless you destroy the accursed from among you. 13 Get up, [a]sanctify the people, and say, [b]'Sanctify yourselves for tomorrow, because thus says the LORD God of Israel: "*There is* an accursed thing in your midst, O Israel; you cannot stand before your enemies until you take away the accursed thing from among you." 14 In the morning therefore you shall be brought according to your tribes. And it shall be *that* the tribe which [a]the LORD takes shall come according to families; and the family which the LORD takes shall come by households; and the household which the LORD takes shall come man by man. 15 [a]Then it shall be *that* he who is taken with the accursed thing shall be burned with fire, he and all that he has, because he has [b]transgressed the covenant of the LORD, and because he [c]has done a disgraceful thing in Israel.' "

16 So Joshua rose early in the morning and brought Israel by their tribes, and the tribe of Judah was taken. 17 He brought the clan of Judah, and he took the family of the Zarhites; and he brought the family of the Zarhites man by man, and Zabdi was taken. 18 Then he brought his household man by man, and Achan the son of Carmi, the son of Zabdi, the son of Zerah, of the tribe of Judah, [a]was taken.

19 Now Joshua said to Achan, "My son, I beg you, [a]give glory to the LORD God of Israel, [b]and make confession to Him, and [c]tell me now what you have done; do not hide *it* from me."

20 And Achan answered Joshua and said, "Indeed [a]I have sinned against the LORD God of Israel, and this is what I have done: 21 When I saw among the spoils a beautiful Babylonian garment, two hundred shekels of silver, and a wedge of gold weighing fifty shekels, I coveted them and took them. And there they are, hidden in the earth in the midst of my tent, with the silver under it."

22 So Joshua sent messengers, and they ran to the tent; and there it was, hidden in his tent, with the silver under it. 23 And they took them from the midst of the tent, brought them to Joshua and to all the children of Israel, and laid them out before the LORD. 24 Then Joshua, and all Israel with him, took Achan the son of Zerah, the silver, the garment, the wedge of gold, his sons, his daughters, his oxen, his donkeys, his sheep, his tent, and [a]all that he had, and they brought them to [b]the Valley of Achor. 25 And Joshua said, [a]"Why have you troubled us? The LORD will trouble you this day." [b]So all Israel stoned him with stones; and they burned them with fire after they had stoned them with stones.

> **7:25** Achan's punishment seems severe and might be hard to understand. But it illustrated God's firm insistence on holiness, which was especially important for the Israelites to understand as they began the conquest. God's concern was that, if left unchecked, sin could spread throughout His people like a virus. It's sobering to remember that our sins don't affect only ourselves; they often cause others to stumble and fall.

26 Then they [a]raised over him a great heap of stones, still there to this day. So [b]the LORD turned from the fierceness of His anger. Therefore the name of that place has been called [c]the Valley of Achor[1] to this day.

### THE FALL OF AI

**8** Now the LORD said to Joshua: [a]"Do not be afraid, nor be dismayed; take all the people of war with you, and arise, go up to Ai. See, [b]I have given into your hand the king of Ai, his people, his city, and his land. 2 And you shall do to Ai and its king as you did to [a]Jericho and its king. Only [b]its spoil and its cattle you shall take as booty for yourselves. Lay an ambush for the city behind it."

**7:5** [a] Lev. 26:36; Josh. 2:9, 11 **7:6** [a] Gen. 37:29, 34 [b] 1 Sam. 4:12 **7:7** [a] Ex. 17:3; Num. 21:5 **7:9** [a] Deut. 32:26 [b] Ex. 32:12; Num. 14:13 **7:11** [a] Josh. 6:17–19 [b] Acts 5:1, 2 **7:12** [a] Judg. 2:14 [b] Deut. 7:26; [Hag. 2:13, 14] **7:13** [a] Ex. 19:10 [b] Josh. 3:5 **7:14** [a] [Prov. 16:33] **7:15** [a] 1 Sam. 14:38, 39 [b] Josh. 7:11 [c] Gen. 34:7; Judg. 20:6 **7:18** [a] 1 Sam. 14:42 **7:19** [a] 1 Sam. 6:5; Jer. 13:16; John 9:24 [b] Num. 5:6, 7; 2 Chr. 30:22; Ezra 10:10, 11; Ps. 32:5; Prov. 28:13; Jer. 3:12, 13; Dan. 9:4 [c] 1 Sam. 14:43 **7:20** [a] Num. 22:34; 1 Sam. 15:24 **7:24** [a] Num. 16:32, 33; Dan. 6:24 [b] Josh. 7:26; 15:7 **7:25** [a] Josh. 6:18; 1 Chr. 2:7; [Gal. 5:12] [b] Deut. 17:5 **7:26** [a] Josh. 8:29; 2 Sam. 18:17; Lam. 3:53 [b] Deut. 13:17 [c] Josh. 7:24; Is. 65:10; Hos. 2:15 [1] Literally *Trouble* **8:1** [a] Deut. 1:21; 7:18; 31:8; Josh. 1:9; 10:8 [b] Josh. 6:2 **8:2** [a] Josh. 6:21 [b] Deut. 20:14; Josh. 8:27

3 So Joshua arose, and all the people of war, to
go up against Ai; and Joshua chose thirty thou-
sand mighty men of valor and sent them away
by night. 4 And he commanded them, saying:
"Behold, [a]you shall lie in ambush against the city,
behind the city. Do not go very far from the city,
but all of you be ready. 5 Then I and all the people
who *are* with me will approach the city; and it will
come about, when they come out against us as
at the first, that [a]we shall flee before them. 6 For
they will come out after us till we have drawn
them from the city, for they will say, '*They are*
fleeing before us as at the first.' Therefore we will
flee before them. 7 Then you shall rise from the
ambush and seize the city, for the LORD your God
will deliver it into your hand. 8 And it will be, when
you have taken the city, *that* you shall set the city
on fire. According to the commandment of the
LORD you shall do. [a]See, I have commanded you."
9 Joshua therefore sent them out; and they
went to lie in ambush, and stayed between Beth-
el and Ai, on the west side of Ai; but Joshua
lodged that night among the people. 10 Then
Joshua rose up early in the morning and mus-
tered the people, and went up, he and the elders
of Israel, before the people to Ai. 11 [a]And all the
people of war who *were* with him went up and
drew near; and they came before the city and
camped on the north side of Ai. Now a valley *lay*
between them and Ai. 12 So he took about five
thousand men and set them in ambush between
Bethel and Ai, on the west side of the city. 13 And
when they had set the people, all the army that
*was* on the north of the city, and its rear guard
on the west of the city, Joshua went that night
into the midst of the valley.
14 Now it happened, when the king of Ai saw
*it,* that the men of the city hurried and rose early
and went out against Israel to battle, he and all
his people, at an appointed place before the plain.
But he [a]did not know that *there was* an ambush
against him behind the city. 15 And Joshua and all
Israel [a]made as if they were beaten before them,
and fled by the way of the wilderness. 16 So all the
people who *were* in Ai were called together to
pursue them. And they pursued Joshua and were
drawn away from the city. 17 There was not a man
left in Ai or Bethel who did not go out after Isra-
el. So they left the city open and pursued Israel.
18 Then the LORD said to Joshua, "Stretch out
the spear that *is* in your hand toward Ai, for I will
give it into your hand." And Joshua stretched out
the spear that *was* in his hand toward the city.
19 So *those in* ambush arose quickly out of their
place; they ran as soon as he had stretched out
his hand, and they entered the city and took it,
and hurried to set the city on fire. 20 And when
the men of Ai looked behind them, they saw,
and behold, the smoke of the city ascended to
heaven. So they had no power to flee this way
or that way, and the people who had fled to the
wilderness turned back on the pursuers.
21 Now when Joshua and all Israel saw that
the ambush had taken the city and that the
smoke of the city ascended, they turned back
and struck down the men of Ai. 22 Then the
others came out of the city against them; so
they were *caught* in the midst of Israel, some
on this side and some on that side. And they
struck them down, so that they [a]let none of them
remain or escape. 23 But the king of Ai they took
alive, and brought him to Joshua.
24 And it came to pass when Israel had made
an end of slaying all the inhabitants of Ai in
the field, in the wilderness where they pursued
them, and when they all had fallen by the edge
of the sword until they were consumed, that all
the Israelites returned to Ai and struck it with
the edge of the sword. 25 So it was *that* all who
fell that day, both men and women, *were* twelve
thousand—all the people of Ai. 26 For Joshua did
not draw back his hand, with which he stretched
out the spear, until he had [a]utterly destroyed all
the inhabitants of Ai. 27 [a]Only the livestock and
the spoil of that city Israel took as booty for
themselves, according to the word of the LORD
which He had [b]commanded Joshua. 28 So Joshua
burned Ai and made it [a]a heap forever, a desola-
tion to this day. 29 [a]And the king of Ai he hanged
on a tree until evening. [b]And as soon as the sun
was down, Joshua commanded that they should
take his corpse down from the tree, cast it at the
entrance of the gate of the city, and [c]raise over it
a great heap of stones *that remains* to this day.

### *JOSHUA RENEWS THE COVENANT*
*(cf. Deut. 27:4, 5)*

30 Now Joshua built an altar to the LORD God
of Israel [a]in Mount Ebal, 31 as Moses the servant
of the LORD had commanded the children of
Israel, as it is written in the Book of the Law of
Moses: [a]"an altar of whole stones over which no
man has wielded an iron *tool.*"[1] And [b]they offered
on it burnt offerings to the LORD, and sacrificed
peace offerings. 32 And there, in the presence of
the children of Israel, [a]he wrote on the stones a
copy of the law of Moses, which he had written.
33 Then all Israel, with their elders and officers
and judges, stood on either side of the ark before
the priests, the Levites, [a]who bore the ark of the
covenant of the LORD, [b]the stranger as well as he
who was born among them. Half of them *were* in
front of Mount Gerizim and half of them in front
of Mount Ebal, [c]as Moses the servant of the LORD
had commanded before, that they should bless the
people of Israel. 34 And afterward [a]he read all the
words of the law, [b]the blessings and the cursings,
according to all that is written in the [c]Book of the

8:4 [a] Judg. 20:29 8:5 [a] Josh. 7:5; Judg. 20:32 8:8 [a] 2 Sam. 13:28 8:11 [a] Josh. 8:5 8:14 [a] Judg. 20:34; Eccl. 9:12 8:15 [a] Judg. 20:36 8:22 [a] Deut. 7:2 8:26 [a] Josh. 6:21 8:27 [a] Num. 31:22, 26 [b] Josh. 8:2 8:28 [a] Deut. 13:16 8:29 [a] Josh. 10:26 [b] Deut. 21:22, 23; Josh. 10:27 [c] Josh. 7:26; 10:27 8:30 [a] Deut. 27:4–8 8:31 [a] Ex. 20:25; Deut. 27:5, 6 [b] Ex. 20:24 [1] Deuteronomy 27:5, 6 8:32 [a] Deut. 27:2, 3, 8 8:33 [a] Deut. 31:9, 25 [b] Deut. 31:12 [c] Deut. 11:29; 27:12 8:34 [a] Deut. 31:11; Neh. 8:3 [b] Deut. 28:2, 15, 45; 29:20, 21; 30:19 [c] Josh. 1:8

Law. 35 There was not a word of all that Moses had
commanded which Joshua did not read before
all the assembly of Israel, [a]with the women, the
little ones, [b]and the strangers who were living
among them.

### *THE TREATY WITH THE GIBEONITES*

9 And it came to pass when [a]all the kings who
*were* on this side of the Jordan, in the hills
and in the lowland and in all the coasts of [b]the
Great Sea toward Lebanon—[c]the Hittite, the
Amorite, the Canaanite, the Perizzite, the Hi-
vite, and the Jebusite—heard *about it,* 2 that
they [a]gathered together to fight with Joshua
and Israel with one accord.
3 But when the inhabitants of [a]Gibeon [b]heard
what Joshua had done to Jericho and Ai, 4 they
worked craftily, and went and pretended to be
ambassadors. And they took old sacks on their
donkeys, old wineskins torn and mended, 5 old
and patched sandals on their feet, and old gar-
ments on themselves; and all the bread of their
provision was dry *and* moldy. 6 And they went to
Joshua, [a]to the camp at Gilgal, and said to him and
to the men of Israel, "We have come from a far
country; now therefore, make a covenant with us."
7 Then the men of Israel said to the [a]Hivites,
"Perhaps you dwell among us; so [b]how can we
make a covenant with you?"
8 But they said to Joshua, [a]"We *are* your
servants."
And Joshua said to them, "Who *are* you, and
where do you come from?"
9 So they said to him: [a]"From a very far country
your servants have come, because of the name
of the LORD your God; for we have [b]heard of His
fame, and all that He did in Egypt, 10 and [a]all that
He did to the two kings of the Amorites who *were*
beyond the Jordan—to Sihon king of Heshbon,

> **9:14** Significantly, the Israelites didn't ask **counsel of the LORD** about making peace with the Gibeonites, contrary to God's explicit instructions to Joshua (Num. 27:21).

and Og king of Bashan, who was at Ashtaroth.
11 Therefore our elders and all the inhabitants of
our country spoke to us, saying, 'Take provisions
with you for the journey, and go to meet them, and
say to them, "We *are* your servants; now therefore,
make a covenant with us." ' 12 This bread of ours
we took hot *for* our provision from our houses
on the day we departed to come to you. But now
look, it is dry and moldy. 13 And these wineskins
which we filled *were* new, and see, they are torn;
and these our garments and our sandals have
become old because of the very long journey."
14 Then the men of Israel took some of their
provisions; [a]but they did not ask counsel of the
LORD. 15 So Joshua [a]made peace with them, and
made a covenant with them to let them live; and
the rulers of the congregation swore to them.
16 And it happened at the end of three days,
after they had made a covenant with them, that
they heard that they *were* their neighbors who
dwelt near them. 17 Then the children of Israel
journeyed and came to their cities on the third
day. Now their cities *were* [a]Gibeon, Chephirah,
Beeroth, and Kirjath Jearim. 18 But the children
of Israel did not attack them, [a]because the rulers
of the congregation had sworn to them by the
LORD God of Israel. And all the congregation
complained against the rulers.
19 Then all the rulers said to all the congrega-
tion, "We have sworn to them by the LORD God
of Israel; now therefore, we may not touch them.

**8:35** [a] Ex. 12:38; Deut. 31:12 [b] Josh. 8:33 **9:1** [a] Num. 13:29; Josh. 3:10 [b] Num. 34:6 [c] Ex. 3:17; 23:23 **9:2** [a] Josh. 10:5; Ps. 83:3, 5 **9:3** [a] Josh. 9:17, 22; 10:2; 21:17; 2 Sam. 21:1, 2 [b] Josh. 6:27 **9:6** [a] Josh. 5:10 **9:7** [a] Josh. 9:1; 11:19 [b] Ex. 23:32; Deut. 7:2 **9:8** [a] Deut. 20:11; 2 Kin. 10:5 **9:9** [a] Deut. 20:15 [b] Ex. 15:14; Josh. 2:9, 10; 5:1 **9:10** [a] Num. 21:24, 33 **9:14** [a] Num. 27:21; Is. 30:1 **9:15** [a] 2 Sam. 21:2 **9:17** [a] Josh. 18:25 **9:18** [a] Ps. 15:4

**APPLY THE TRUTH**

## DECEPTION

**9:1–27** Pretending was fun when we were children. We became anything we wanted: a pirate, a pilot, an astronaut, or even a superhero. It's peculiar, however, when a kid doesn't stop pretending. As we get older, we would think we'd leave costumes behind. But sometimes we still play dress up. Rather than being true to ourselves and who God made us to be, we attempt to be something or someone else. It's no longer pretending, though. It's now deception.

Here, the Gibeonites deceived the Israelites by pretending to be nomads. They were afraid, unsure of how they'd be treated, and unhappy with who they were, so they pretended to be someone else. They tricked the Israelites, but they didn't trick God.

Maybe fear, uncertainty, or unhappiness has caused you to attempt to be someone you aren't. God knows who you really are. And He loves you—the real you. Jesus gives us a new identity, but He doesn't give us a whole new personality. He wants you to be who He made you to be and live the calling He gave you.

20 This we will do to them: We will let them live,
lest [a]wrath be upon us because of the oath which
we swore to them." 21 And the rulers said to them,
"Let them live, but let them be [a]woodcutters
and water carriers for all the congregation, as
the rulers had [b]promised them."

22 Then Joshua called for them, and he spoke
to them, saying, "Why have you deceived us, saying,
[a]'We *are* very far from you,' when [b]you dwell
near us? 23 Now therefore, you *are* [a]cursed, and
none of you shall be freed from being slaves—
woodcutters and water carriers for the house
of my God."

24 So they answered Joshua and said, "Because
your servants were clearly told that the
LORD your God [a]commanded His servant Moses
to give you all the land, and to destroy all the
inhabitants of the land from before you; therefore
[b]we were very much afraid for our lives
because of you, and have done this thing. 25 And
now, here we are, [a]in your hands; do with us as
it seems good and right to do to us." 26 So he did
to them, and delivered them out of the hand of
the children of Israel, so that they did not kill
them. 27 And that day Joshua made them [a]woodcutters
and water carriers for the congregation
and for the altar of the LORD, [b]in the place which
He would choose, even to this day.

### *THE SUN STANDS STILL*

**10** Now it came to pass when Adoni-Zedek
king of Jerusalem [a]heard how Joshua had
taken [b]Ai and had utterly destroyed it—[c]as he
had done to Jericho and its king, so he had done
to [d]Ai and its king—and [e]how the inhabitants
of Gibeon had made peace with Israel and were
among them, 2 that they [a]feared greatly, because
Gibeon *was* a great city, like one of the royal cities,
and because it *was* greater than Ai, and all its
men *were* mighty. 3 Therefore Adoni-Zedek king
of Jerusalem sent to Hoham king of Hebron,
Piram king of Jarmuth, Japhia king of Lachish,
and Debir king of Eglon, saying, 4 "Come up to
me and help me, that we may attack Gibeon, for
[a]it has made peace with Joshua and with the
children of Israel." 5 Therefore the five kings of
the [a]Amorites, the king of Jerusalem, the king of
Hebron, the king of Jarmuth, the king of Lachish,
*and* the king of Eglon, [b]gathered together and
went up, they and all their armies, and camped
before Gibeon and made war against it.

6 And the men of Gibeon sent to Joshua at
the camp [a]at Gilgal, saying, "Do not forsake your
servants; come up to us quickly, save us and
help us, for all the kings of the Amorites who
dwell in the mountains have gathered together
against us."

7 So Joshua ascended from Gilgal, he and [a]all
the people of war with him, and all the mighty
men of valor. 8 And the LORD said to Joshua,
[a]"Do not fear them, for I have delivered them
into your hand; [b]not a man of them shall [c]stand
before you." 9 Joshua therefore came upon them
suddenly, having marched all night from Gilgal.
10 So the LORD [a]routed them before Israel, killed
them with a great slaughter at Gibeon, chased
them along the road that goes [b]to Beth Horon,
and struck them down as far as [c]Azekah and
Makkedah. 11 And it happened, as they fled before
Israel *and* were on the descent of Beth Horon,
[a]that the LORD cast down large hailstones from
heaven on them as far as Azekah, and they died.
*There were* more who died from the hailstones
than the children of Israel killed with the sword.

12 Then Joshua spoke to the LORD in the
day when the LORD delivered up the Amorites
before the children of Israel, and he said in the
sight of Israel:

[a]"Sun, stand still over Gibeon;
And Moon, in the Valley of [b]Aijalon."
13 So the sun stood still,
And the moon stopped,
Till the people had revenge
Upon their enemies.

[a]*Is* this not written in the Book of Jasher? So the
sun stood still in the midst of heaven, and did
not hasten to go *down* for about a whole day.
14 And there has been [a]no day like that, before
it or after it, that the LORD heeded the voice of
a man; for [b]the LORD fought for Israel.

15 [a]Then Joshua returned, and all Israel with
him, to the camp at Gilgal.

### *THE AMORITE KINGS EXECUTED*

16 But these five kings had fled and hidden
themselves in a cave at Makkedah. 17 And it was
told Joshua, saying, "The five kings have been
found hidden in the cave at Makkedah."

18 So Joshua said, "Roll large stones against
the mouth of the cave, and set men by it to
guard them. 19 And do not stay *there* yourselves,
*but* pursue your enemies, and attack their rear
*guard.* Do not allow them to enter their cities,
for the LORD your God has delivered them into
your hand." 20 Then it happened, while Joshua
and the children of Israel made an end of slaying
them with a very great slaughter, till they
had finished, that those who escaped entered
fortified cities. 21 And all the people returned
to the camp, to Joshua at Makkedah, in peace.

[a]No one moved his tongue against any of
the children of Israel.

**9:20** [a] 2 Sam. 21:1, 2, 6; Ezek. 17:13, 15 **9:21** [a] Deut. 29:11 [b] Josh. 9:15 **9:22** [a] Josh. 9:6, 9 [b] Josh. 9:16 **9:23** [a] Gen. 9:25 **9:24** [a] Ex. 23:31–33; Deut. 7:1, 2 [b] Ex. 15:14 **9:25** [a] Gen. 16:6 **9:27** [a] Josh. 9:21, 23 [b] Deut. 12:5 **10:1** [a] Josh. 9:1 [b] Josh. 8:1 [c] Josh. 6:21 [d] Josh. 8:22, 26, 28 [e] Josh. 9:15 **10:2** [a] Ex. 15:14–16; Deut. 11:25; 1 Chr. 14:17 **10:4** [a] Josh. 9:15; 10:1 **10:5** [a] Num. 13:29 [b] Josh. 9:2 **10:6** [a] Josh. 5:10; 9:6 **10:7** [a] Josh. 8:1 **10:8** [a] Josh. 11:6; Judg. 4:14 [b] Josh. 1:5, 9 [c] Josh. 21:44 **10:10** [a] Judg. 4:15; 1 Sam. 7:10, 12; Is. 28:21 [b] Josh. 16:3, 5 [c] Josh. 15:35 **10:11** [a] Is. 30:30; Rev. 16:21 **10:12** [a] Is. 28:21; Hab. 3:11 [b] Judg. 12:12 **10:13** [a] 2 Sam. 1:18 **10:14** [a] Is. 38:7, 8 [b] Ex. 14:14; Deut. 1:30; 20:4; Josh. 10:42; 23:3 **10:15** [a] Josh. 10:43 **10:21** [a] Ex. 11:7

22 Then Joshua said, "Open the mouth of the cave, and bring out those five kings to me from the cave." 23 And they did so, and brought out those five kings to him from the cave: the king of Jerusalem, the king of Hebron, the king of Jarmuth, the king of Lachish, *and* the king of Eglon.

24 So it was, when they brought out those kings to Joshua, that Joshua called for all the men of Israel, and said to the captains of the men of war who went with him, "Come near, put your feet on the necks of these kings." And they drew near and [a]put their feet on their necks. 25 Then Joshua said to them, [a]"Do not be afraid, nor be dismayed; be strong and of good courage, for [b]thus the LORD will do to all your enemies against whom you fight." 26 And afterward Joshua struck them and killed them, and hanged them on five trees; and they [a]were hanging on the trees until evening. 27 So it was at the time of the going down of the sun *that* Joshua commanded, and they [a]took them down from the trees, cast them into the cave where they had been hidden, and laid large stones against the cave's mouth, *which remain* until this very day.

### SEEING JESUS IN THE SCRIPTURE

**10:24** As the Israelites continued their conquest of Canaan, God literally put their enemies under their feet. Their victories point ahead to Jesus' future rule and reign on earth when all His enemies will be under His feet for good (see 1 Cor. 15:25).

### *CONQUEST OF THE SOUTHLAND*

28 On that day Joshua took Makkedah, and struck it and its king with the edge of the sword. He utterly [a]destroyed them[1]—all the people who *were* in it. He let none remain. He also did to the king of Makkedah [b]as he had done to the king of Jericho.

29 Then Joshua passed from Makkedah, and all Israel with him, to [a]Libnah; and they fought against Libnah. 30 And the LORD also delivered it and its king into the hand of Israel; he struck it and all the people who *were* in it with the edge of the sword. He let none remain in it, but did to its king as he had done to the king of Jericho.

31 Then Joshua passed from Libnah, and all Israel with him, to Lachish; and they encamped against it and fought against it. 32 And the LORD delivered Lachish into the hand of Israel, who took it on the second day, and struck it and all the people who *were* in it with the edge of the sword, according to all that he had done to Libnah. 33 Then Horam king of Gezer came up to help Lachish; and Joshua struck him and his people, until he left him none remaining.

34 From Lachish Joshua passed to Eglon, and all Israel with him; and they encamped against it and fought against it. 35 They took it on that day and struck it with the edge of the sword; all the people who *were* in it he utterly destroyed that day, according to all that he had done to Lachish.

36 So Joshua went up from Eglon, and all Israel with him, to [a]Hebron; and they fought against it. 37 And they took it and struck it with the edge of the sword—its king, all its cities, and all the people who *were* in it; he left none remaining, according to all that he had done to Eglon, but utterly destroyed it and all the people who *were* in it.

38 Then Joshua returned, and all Israel with him, to [a]Debir; and they fought against it. 39 And he took it and its king and all its cities; they struck them with the edge of the sword and utterly destroyed all the people who *were* in it. He left none remaining; as he had done to Hebron, so he did to Debir and its king, as he had done also to Libnah and its king.

40 So Joshua conquered all the land: the [a]mountain country and the South[1] and the lowland and the wilderness slopes, and [b]all their kings; he left none remaining, but [c]utterly destroyed all that breathed, as the LORD God of Israel had commanded. 41 And Joshua conquered them from [a]Kadesh Barnea as far as [b]Gaza, [c]and all the country of Goshen, even as far as Gibeon. 42 All these kings and their land Joshua took at one time, [a]because the LORD God of Israel fought for Israel. 43 Then Joshua returned, and all Israel with him, to the camp at Gilgal.

### *THE NORTHERN CONQUEST*

11 And it came to pass, when Jabin king of Hazor heard *these things,* that he [a]sent to Jobab king of Madon, to the king [b]of Shimron, to the king of Achshaph, 2 and to the kings who *were* from the north, in the mountains, in the plain south of [a]Chinneroth, in the lowland, and in the heights [b]of Dor on the west, 3 to the Canaanites in the east and in the west, the [a]Amorite, the Hittite, the Perizzite, the Jebusite in the mountains, [b]and the Hivite below [c]Hermon [d]in the land of Mizpah. 4 So they went out, they and all their armies with them, *as* many people [a]*as* the sand that *is* on the seashore in multitude, with very many horses and chariots. 5 And when all these kings had met together, they came and camped together at the waters of Merom to fight against Israel.

**10:24** [a] Ps. 107:40; Is. 26:5, 6; Mal. 4:3 **10:25** [a] Deut. 31:6–8; Josh. 1:9 [b] Deut. 3:21; 7:19 **10:26** [a] Josh. 8:29; 2 Sam. 21:9 **10:27** [a] Deut. 21:22, 23; Josh. 8:29 **10:28** [a] Deut. 7:2, 16 [b] Josh. 6:21 [1] Following Masoretic Text and most authorities; many Hebrew manuscripts, some manuscripts of the Septuagint, and some manuscripts of the Targum read *it.* **10:29** [a] Josh. 15:42; 21:13; 2 Kin. 8:22; 19:8 **10:36** [a] Num. 13:22; Josh. 14:13–15; 15:13; Judg. 1:10, 20; 2 Sam. 5:1, 3, 5, 13; 2 Chr. 11:10 **10:38** [a] Josh. 15:15; Judg. 1:11; 1 Chr. 6:58 **10:40** [a] Deut. 1:7 [b] Deut. 7:24 [c] Deut. 20:16, 17 [1] Hebrew *Negev,* and so throughout this book **10:41** [a] Num. 13:26; Deut. 9:23 [b] Gen. 10:19; Josh. 11:22 [c] Josh. 11:16; 15:51 **10:42** [a] Josh. 10:14 **11:1** [a] Josh. 10:3 [b] Josh. 19:15 **11:2** [a] Num. 34:11 [b] Josh. 17:11; Judg. 1:27; 1 Kin. 4:11 **11:3** [a] Josh. 9:1 [b] Deut. 7:1; Judg. 3:3, 5; 1 Kin. 9:20 [c] Josh. 11:17; 13:5, 11 [d] Gen. 31:49 **11:4** [a] Gen. 22:17; 32:12; Judg. 7:12; 1 Sam. 13:5

6 But the LORD said to Joshua, [a]"Do not be
afraid because of them, for tomorrow about this
time I will deliver all of them slain before Israel.
You shall [b]hamstring their horses and burn their
chariots with fire." 7 So Joshua and all the people
of war with him came against them suddenly by
the waters of Merom, and they attacked them.
8 And the LORD delivered them into the hand of
Israel, who defeated them and chased them to
Greater [a]Sidon, to the Brook [b]Misrephoth,[1] and
to the Valley of Mizpah eastward; they attacked
them until they left none of them remaining.
9 So Joshua did to them as the LORD had told
him: he hamstrung their horses and burned
their chariots with fire.

10 Joshua turned back at that time and took
Hazor, and struck its king with the sword; for
Hazor was formerly the head of all those king-
doms. 11 And they struck all the people who *were*
in it with the edge of the sword, [a]utterly destroy-
ing *them*. There was none left [b]breathing. Then
he burned Hazor with fire.

12 So all the cities of those kings, and all their
kings, Joshua took and struck with the edge of
the sword. He utterly destroyed them, [a]as Moses
the servant of the LORD had commanded. 13 But
*as for* the cities that stood on their mounds,[1] Is-
rael burned none of them, except Hazor only,
*which* Joshua burned. 14 And all the [a]spoil of
these cities and the livestock, the children of
Israel took as booty for themselves; but they
struck every man with the edge of the sword
until they had destroyed them, and they left
none breathing. 15 [a]As the LORD had commanded
Moses His servant, so [b]Moses commanded Josh-
ua, and [c]so Joshua did. He left nothing undone
of all that the LORD had commanded Moses.

## SUMMARY OF JOSHUA'S CONQUESTS

16 Thus Joshua took all this land: [a]the moun-
tain country, all the South, [b]all the land of Go-
shen, the lowland, and the Jordan plain[1]—the
mountains of Israel and its lowlands, 17 [a]from
Mount Halak and the ascent to Seir, even as far
as Baal Gad in the Valley of Lebanon below Mount
Hermon. He captured [b]all their kings, and struck
them down and killed them. 18 Joshua made war
a long time with all those kings. 19 There was not
a city that made peace with the children of Israel,
except [a]the Hivites, the inhabitants of Gibeon.
All *the others* they took in battle. 20 For [a]it was of
the LORD to harden their hearts, that they should
come against Israel in battle, that He might ut-
terly destroy them, *and* that they might receive
no mercy, but that He might destroy them, [b]as
the LORD had commanded Moses.

21 And at that time Joshua came and cut off
[a]the Anakim from the mountains: from Hebron,
from Debir, from Anab, from all the mountains
of Judah, and from all the mountains of Israel;
Joshua utterly destroyed them with their cities.
22 None of the Anakim were left in the land of
the children of Israel; they remained only [a]in
Gaza, in Gath, [b]and in Ashdod.
23 So Joshua took the whole land, [a]according
to all that the LORD had said to Moses; and Josh-
ua gave it as an inheritance to Israel [b]according
to their divisions by their tribes. Then the land
[c]rested from war.

## THE KINGS CONQUERED BY MOSES
*(cf. Num. 21:21–35)*

12 These *are* the kings of the land whom the
children of Israel defeated, and whose land
they possessed on the other side of the Jordan
toward the rising of the sun, [a]from the River
Arnon [b]to Mount Hermon, and all the eastern
Jordan plain: 2 *One king was* [a]Sihon king of the
Amorites, who dwelt in Heshbon *and* ruled half
of Gilead, from Aroer, which is on the bank of
the River Arnon, from the middle of that river,
even as far as the River Jabbok, *which is* the
border of the Ammonites, 3 and [a]the eastern
Jordan plain from the Sea of Chinneroth as far
as the Sea of the Arabah (the Salt Sea), [b]the road
to Beth Jeshimoth, and southward below [c]the
slopes of Pisgah. 4 *The other king was* [a]Og king
of Bashan and his territory, *who was* of [b]the
remnant of the giants, [c]who dwelt at Ashtaroth
and at Edrei, 5 and reigned over [a]Mount Her-
mon, [b]over Salcah, over all Bashan, [c]as far as the
border of the Geshurites and the Maachathites,
and over half of Gilead *to* the border of Sihon
king of Heshbon.

6 [a]These Moses the servant of the LORD
and the children of Israel had conquered; and
[b]Moses the servant of the LORD had given it *as*
a possession to the Reubenites, the Gadites, and
half the tribe of Manasseh.

## THE KINGS CONQUERED BY JOSHUA

7 And these *are* the kings of the country
[a]which Joshua and the children of Israel con-
quered on this side of the Jordan, on the west,
from Baal Gad in the Valley of Lebanon as far
as Mount Halak and the ascent to [b]Seir, which
Joshua [c]gave to the tribes of Israel *as* a pos-
session according to their divisions, 8 [a]in the
mountain country, in the lowlands, in the *Jordan*
plain, in the slopes, in the wilderness, and in the
South—[b]the Hittites, the Amorites, the Canaan-
ites, the Perizzites, the Hivites, and the Jebusites:

11:6 [a] Josh. 10:8 [b] 2 Sam. 8:4 11:8 [a] Gen. 49:13 [b] Josh. 13:6 [1] Hebrew *Misrephoth Maim* 11:11 [a] Deut. 20:16 [b] Josh. 10:40 11:12 [a] Num. 33:50–56 11:13 [1] Hebrew *tel*, a heap of successive city ruins 11:14 [a] Deut. 20:14–18 11:15 [a] Ex. 34:10–17 [b] Deut. 31:7, 8 [c] Josh. 1:7 11:16 [a] Josh. 12:8 [b] Josh. 10:40, 41 [1] Hebrew *arabah* 11:17 [a] Josh. 12:7 [b] Deut. 7:24 11:19 [a] Josh. 9:3–7 11:20 [a] Deut. 2:30 [b] Deut. 20:16, 17 11:21 [a] Num. 13:22, 33 11:22 [a] 1 Sam. 17:4 [b] Josh. 15:46 11:23 [a] Num. 34:2–15 [b] Num. 26:53 [c] Deut. 12:9, 10; 25:19 12:1 [a] Num. 21:24 [b] Deut. 3:8 12:2 [a] Deut. 2:24–27 12:3 [a] Deut. 3:17 [b] Josh. 13:20 [c] Deut. 3:17; 4:49 12:4 [a] Num. 21:33 [b] Deut. 3:11 [c] Deut. 1:4 12:5 [a] Deut. 3:8 [b] Deut. 3:10 [c] Deut. 3:14 12:6 [a] Num. 21:24, 35 [b] Num. 32:29–33 12:7 [a] Josh. 11:17 [b] Gen. 14:6; 32:3 [c] Josh. 11:23 12:8 [a] Josh. 10:40; 11:16 [b] Ex. 3:8; 23:23

9 [a]the king of Jericho, one; [b]the king of Ai, which *is* beside Bethel, one; 10 [a]the king of Jerusalem, one; the king of Hebron, one; 11 the king of Jarmuth, one; the king of Lachish, one; 12 the king of Eglon, one; [a]the king of Gezer, one; 13 [a]the king of Debir, one; the king of Geder, one; 14 the king of Hormah, one; the king of Arad, one; 15 [a]the king of Libnah, one; the king of Adullam, one; 16 [a]the king of Makkedah, one; [b]the king of Bethel, one; 17 the king of Tappuah, one; [a]the king of Hepher, one; 18 the king of Aphek, one; the king of Lasharon, one; 19 the king of Madon, one; [a]the king of Hazor, one; 20 the king of [a]Shimron Meron, one; the king of Achshaph, one; 21 the king of Taanach, one; the king of Megiddo, one; 22 [a]the king of Kedesh, one; the king of Jokneam in Carmel, one; 23 the king of Dor in the [a]heights of Dor, one; the king of [b]the people of Gilgal, one; 24 the king of Tirzah, one—[a]all the kings, thirty-one.

### REMAINING LAND TO BE CONQUERED

**13** Now Joshua [a]was old, advanced in years. And the LORD said to him: "You are old, advanced in years, and there remains very much land yet to be possessed. 2 [a]This is the land that yet remains: [b]all the territory of the Philistines and all [c]*that of* the Geshurites, 3 [a]from Sihor, which *is* east of Egypt, as far as the border of Ekron northward (*which* is counted as Canaanite); the [b]five lords of the Philistines—the Gazites, the Ashdodites, the Ashkelonites, the Gittites, and the Ekronites; also [c]the Avites; 4 from the south, all the land of the Canaanites, and Mearah that belongs to the Sidonians [a]as far as Aphek, to the border of [b]the Amorites; 5 the land of [a]the Gebalites,[1] and all Lebanon, toward the sunrise, [b]from Baal Gad below Mount Hermon as far as the entrance to Hamath; 6 all the inhabitants of the mountains from Lebanon as far as [a]the Brook Misrephoth,[1] *and* all the Sidonians—them [b]I will drive out from before the children of Israel; only [c]divide it by lot to Israel as an inheritance, as I have commanded you. 7 Now therefore, divide this land as an inheritance to the nine tribes and half the tribe of Manasseh."

### THE LAND DIVIDED EAST OF THE JORDAN

8 With the other half-tribe the Reubenites and the Gadites received their inheritance, [a]which Moses had given them, [b]beyond the Jordan eastward, as Moses the servant of the LORD had given them: 9 from Aroer which *is* on the bank of the River Arnon, and the town that *is* in the midst of the ravine, [a]and all the plain of Medeba as far as Dibon; 10 [a]all the cities of Sihon king of the Amorites, who reigned in Heshbon, as far as the border of the children of Ammon; 11 [a]Gilead, and the border of the Geshurites and Maachathites, all Mount Hermon, and all Bashan as far as Salcah; 12 all the kingdom of Og in Bashan, who reigned in Ashtaroth and Edrei, who remained of [a]the remnant of the giants; [b]for Moses had defeated and cast out these.

13 Nevertheless the children of Israel [a]did not drive out the Geshurites or the Maachathites, but the Geshurites and the Maachathites dwell among the Israelites until this day.

14 [a]Only to the tribe of Levi he had given no inheritance; the sacrifices of the LORD God of Israel made by fire *are* their inheritance, [b]as He said to them.

### THE LAND OF REUBEN

15 [a]And Moses had given to the tribe of the children of Reuben *an inheritance* according to their families. 16 Their territory was [a]from Aroer, which *is* on the bank of the River Arnon, [b]and the city that *is* in the midst of the ravine, [c]and all the plain by Medeba; 17 [a]Heshbon and all its cities that *are* in the plain: Dibon, Bamoth Baal, Beth Baal Meon, 18 [a]Jahaza, Kedemoth, Mephaath, 19 [a]Kirjathaim, [b]Sibmah, Zereth Shahar on the mountain of the valley, 20 Beth Peor, [a]the slopes of Pisgah, and Beth Jeshimoth— 21 [a]all the cities of the plain and all the kingdom of Sihon king of the Amorites, who reigned in Heshbon, [b]whom Moses had struck [c]with the princes of Midian: Evi, Rekem, Zur, Hur, and Reba, who *were* princes of Sihon dwelling in the country. 22 The children of Israel also killed with the sword [a]Balaam the son of Beor, the soothsayer, among those who were killed by them. 23 And the border of the children of Reuben was the bank of the Jordan. This *was* the inheritance of the children of Reuben according to their families, the cities and their villages.

### THE LAND OF GAD

24 [a]Moses also had given *an inheritance* to the tribe of Gad, to the children of Gad according to their families. 25 [a]Their territory was Jazer, and all the cities of Gilead, [b]and half the land of the Ammonites as far as Aroer, which *is* before [c]Rabbah, 26 and from Heshbon to Ramath Mizpah and Betonim, and from Mahanaim to the border of Debir, 27 and in the valley [a]Beth Haram, Beth Nimrah, [b]Succoth, and Zaphon, the rest of the kingdom of Sihon king of Heshbon, with the Jordan as *its* border, as far as the edge [c]of the Sea of Chinnereth, on the other side of the Jordan eastward. 28 This *is* the inheritance of the children of Gad according to their families, the cities and their villages.

**12:9** [a] Josh. 6:2 [b] Josh. 8:29 **12:10** [a] Josh. 10:23 **12:12** [a] Josh. 10:33 **12:13** [a] Josh. 10:38, 39 **12:15** [a] Josh. 10:29, 30 **12:16** [a] Josh. 10:28 [b] Judg. 1:22 **12:17** [a] 1 Kin. 4:10 **12:19** [a] Josh. 11:10 **12:20** [a] Josh. 11:1; 19:15 **12:22** [a] Josh. 19:37; 20:7; 21:32 **12:23** [a] Josh. 11:2 [b] Is. 9:1 **12:24** [a] Deut. 7:24 **13:1** [a] Josh. 14:10; 23:1, 2 **13:2** [a] Judg. 3:1–3 [b] Joel 3:4 [c] 2 Sam. 3:3 **13:3** [a] Jer. 2:18 [b] Judg. 3:3 [c] Deut. 2:23 **13:4** [a] Josh. 12:18; 19:30 [b] Judg. 1:34 **13:5** [a] 1 Kin. 5:18; Ezek. 27:9 [b] Josh. 12:7 [1] Or *Giblites* **13:6** [a] Josh. 11:8 [b] Josh. 23:13 [c] Josh. 14:1, 2 [1] Hebrew *Misrephoth Maim* **13:8** [a] Num. 32:33 [b] Josh. 12:1–6 **13:9** [a] Num. 21:30 **13:10** [a] Num. 21:24, 25 **13:11** [a] Josh. 12:5 **13:12** [a] Deut. 3:11 [b] Num. 21:24, 34, 35 **13:13** [a] Josh. 13:11 **13:14** [a] Josh. 14:3, 4 [b] Josh. 13:33 **13:15** [a] Num. 34:14 **13:16** [a] Josh. 12:2 [b] Num. 21:28 [c] Num. 21:30 **13:17** [a] Num. 21:28, 30 **13:18** [a] Num. 21:23 **13:19** [a] Num. 32:37 [b] Num. 32:38 **13:20** [a] Deut. 3:17 **13:21** [a] Deut. 3:10 [b] Num. 21:24 [c] Num. 31:8 **13:22** [a] Num. 22:5; 31:8 **13:24** [a] Num. 34:14; 1 Chr. 5:11 **13:25** [a] Num. 32:1, 35 [b] Judg. 11:13, 15 [c] Deut. 3:11; 2 Sam. 11:1; 12:26 **13:27** [a] Num. 32:36 [b] Gen. 33:17; 1 Kin. 7:46 [c] Num. 34:11; Deut. 3:17

### HALF THE TRIBE OF MANASSEH (EAST)

29 [a]Moses also had given *an inheritance* to half the tribe of Manasseh; it was for half the tribe of the children of Manasseh according to their families: 30 Their territory was from Mahanaim, all Bashan, all the kingdom of Og king of Bashan, and [a]all the towns of Jair which are in Bashan, sixty cities; 31 half of Gilead, and [a]Ashtaroth and Edrei, cities of the kingdom of Og in Bashan, *were* for the [b]children of Machir the son of Manasseh, for half of the children of Machir according to their families.

32 These *are the areas* which Moses had distributed as an inheritance in the plains of Moab on the other side of the Jordan, by Jericho eastward. 33 [a]But to the tribe of Levi Moses had given no inheritance; the LORD God of Israel *was* their inheritance, [b]as He had said to them.

### THE LAND DIVIDED WEST OF THE JORDAN

**14** These *are the areas* which the children of Israel inherited in the land of Canaan, [a]which Eleazar the priest, Joshua the son of Nun, and the heads of the fathers of the tribes of the children of Israel distributed as an inheritance to them. 2 Their inheritance *was* [a]by lot, as the LORD had commanded by the hand of Moses, for the nine tribes and the half-tribe. 3 [a]For Moses had given the inheritance of the two tribes and the half-tribe on the other side of the Jordan; but to the Levites he had given no inheritance among them. 4 For [a]the children of Joseph were two tribes: Manasseh and Ephraim. And they gave no part to the Levites in the land, except [b]cities to dwell *in,* with their common-lands for their livestock and their property. 5 [a]As the LORD had commanded Moses, so the children of Israel did; and they divided the land.

### CALEB INHERITS HEBRON

6 Then the children of Judah came to Joshua in Gilgal. And Caleb the son of Jephunneh the [a]Kenizzite said to him: "You know [b]the word which the LORD said to Moses the man of God concerning [c]you and me in Kadesh Barnea. 7 I *was* forty years old when Moses the servant of the LORD [a]sent me from Kadesh Barnea to spy out the land, and I brought back word to him as *it was* in my heart. 8 Nevertheless [a]my brethren who went up with me made the heart of the people melt, but I wholly [b]followed the LORD my God. 9 So Moses swore on that day, saying, [a]'Surely the land [b]where your foot has trodden shall be your inheritance and your children's forever, because you have wholly followed the LORD my God.' 10 And now, behold, the LORD has kept me [a]alive, [b]as He said, these forty-five years, ever since the LORD spoke this word to Moses while Israel wandered in the wilderness; and now, here I am this day, eighty-five years old. 11 [a]As yet I *am as* strong this day as on the day that Moses sent me; just as my strength *was* then, so now *is* my strength for war, both [b]for going out and for coming in. 12 Now therefore, give me this mountain of which the LORD spoke in that day; for you heard in that day how [a]the Anakim *were* there, and *that* the cities *were* great *and* fortified. [b]It may be that the LORD *will be* with me, and [c]I shall be able to drive them out as the LORD said."

13 And Joshua [a]blessed him, [b]and gave Hebron to Caleb the son of Jephunneh as an inheritance. 14 [a]Hebron therefore became the inheritance of Caleb the son of Jephunneh the Kenizzite to this day, because he [b]wholly followed the LORD God of Israel. 15 And [a]the name of Hebron formerly was Kirjath Arba (*Arba was* the greatest man among the Anakim).

[b]Then the land had rest from war.

### THE LAND OF JUDAH

**15** So *this* was the lot of the tribe of the children of Judah according to their families:

[a]The border of Edom at the [b]Wilderness of Zin southward *was* the extreme southern boundary. 2 And their [a]southern border began at the shore of the Salt Sea, from the bay that faces southward. 3 Then it went out to the southern side of [a]the Ascent of Akrabbim, passed along to Zin, ascended on the south side of Kadesh Barnea, passed along to Hezron, went up to Adar, and went around to Karkaa. 4 *From there* it passed [a]toward Azmon and went out to the Brook of Egypt; and the border ended at the sea. This shall be your southern border.

5 The east border *was* the Salt Sea as far as the mouth of the Jordan.

And the [a]border on the northern quarter *began* at the bay of the sea at the mouth of the Jordan. 6 The border went up to [a]Beth Hoglah and passed north of Beth Arabah; and the border went up [b]to the stone of Bohan the son of Reuben. 7 Then the border went up toward [a]Debir from [b]the Valley of Achor, and it turned northward toward Gilgal, which *is* before the Ascent of Adummim, which *is* on the south side of the valley. The border continued toward the waters of En Shemesh and ended at [c]En Rogel. 8 And the border went up [a]by the Valley of the Son of Hinnom to the southern slope of the [b]Jebusite *city* (which *is* Jerusalem). The border went up to the top of the mountain

**13:29** [a] Num. 34:14; 1 Chr. 5:23 **13:30** [a] Num. 32:41; 1 Chr. 2:23 **13:31** [a] Josh. 9:10; 12:4; 13:12; 1 Chr. 6:71 [b] Num. 32:39, 40; Josh. 17:1 **13:33** [a] Deut. 18:1; Josh. 13:14; 18:7 [b] Num. 18:20; Deut. 10:9; 18:1, 2 **14:1** [a] Num. 34:16–29 **14:2** [a] Num. 26:55; 33:54; 34:13; Ps. 16:5 **14:3** [a] Num. 32:33; Josh. 13:8, 32, 33 **14:4** [a] Gen. 41:51; 46:20; 48:1, 5; Num. 26:28; 2 Chr. 30:1 [b] Num. 35:2–8; Josh. 21:1–42 **14:5** [a] Num. 35:2; Josh. 21:2 **14:6** [a] Num. 32:11, 12 [b] Num. 14:24, 30 [c] Num. 13:26 **14:7** [a] Num. 13:6, 17; 14:6 **14:8** [a] Num. 13:31, 32; Deut. 1:28 [b] Num. 14:24; Deut. 1:36 **14:9** [a] Num. 14:23, 24 [b] Num. 13:22; Deut. 1:36 **14:10** [a] Num. 14:24, 30, 38 [b] Josh. 5:6; Neh. 9:21 **14:11** [a] Deut. 34:7 [b] Deut. 31:2 **14:12** [a] Num. 13:28, 33 [b] Rom. 8:31 [c] Josh. 15:14; Judg. 1:20 **14:13** [a] Josh. 22:6 [b] Josh. 10:37; 15:13 **14:14** [a] Josh. 21:12 [b] Josh. 14:8, 9 **14:15** [a] Gen. 23:2; Josh. 15:13 [b] Josh. 11:23 **15:1** [a] Num. 34:3 [b] Num. 33:36 **15:2** [a] Num. 34:3, 4 **15:3** [a] Num. 34:4 **15:4** [a] Num. 34:5 **15:5** [a] Josh. 18:15–19 **15:6** [a] Josh. 18:19, 21 [b] Josh. 18:17 **15:7** [a] Josh. 13:26 [b] Josh. 7:26 [c] 2 Sam. 17:17; 1 Kin. 1:9 **15:8** [a] Josh. 18:16; 2 Kin. 23:10; Jer. 19:2, 6 [b] Josh. 15:63; 18:28; Judg. 1:21; 19:10

that *lies* before the Valley of Hinnom westward,
which *is* at the end of the Valley [c]of Rephaim[1]
northward. 9 Then the border went around from
the top of the hill to [a]the fountain of the water of
Nephtoah, and extended to the cities of Mount
Ephron. And the border went around [b]to Baal-
ah (which *is* [c]Kirjath Jearim). 10 Then the border
turned westward from Baalah to Mount Seir,
passed along to the side of Mount Jearim on the
north (which *is* Chesalon), went down to Beth
Shemesh, and passed on to [a]Timnah. 11 And the
border went out to the side of [a]Ekron northward.
Then the border went around to Shicron, passed
along to Mount Baalah, and extended to Jabneel;
and the border ended at the sea.
12 The west border *was* [a]the coastline of the
Great Sea. This *is* the boundary of the children
of Judah all around according to their families.

### *CALEB OCCUPIES HEBRON AND DEBIR*

*(Judg. 1:11–15)*

13 [a]Now to Caleb the son of Jephunneh he
gave a share among the children of [b]Judah,
according to the commandment of the LORD to
Joshua, *namely,* [c]Kirjath Arba, which *is* Hebron
(*Arba was* the father of Anak). 14 Caleb drove
out [a]the three sons of Anak from there: [b]She-
shai, Ahiman, and Talmai, the children of Anak.
15 Then [a]he went up from there to the inhab-
itants of Debir (formerly the name of Debir *was*
Kirjath Sepher).
16 [a]And Caleb said, "He who attacks Kirjath
Sepher and takes it, to him I will give Achsah
my daughter as wife." 17 So [a]Othniel the [b]son of
Kenaz, the brother of Caleb, took it; and he gave
him [c]Achsah his daughter as wife. 18 [a]Now it was
so, when she came *to him,* that she persuaded
him to ask her father for a field. So [b]she dis-
mounted from *her* donkey, and Caleb said to her,
"What do you wish?" 19 She answered, "Give me
a [a]blessing; since you have given me land in the
South, give me also springs of water." So he gave
her the upper springs and the lower springs.

### *THE CITIES OF JUDAH*

20 This *was* the inheritance of the tribe of the
children of Judah according to their families:
21 The cities at the limits of the tribe of the
children of Judah, toward the border of Edom in
the South, were Kabzeel, [a]Eder, Jagur, 22 Kinah,
Dimonah, Adadah, 23 Kedesh, Hazor, Ithnan,
24 [a]Ziph, Telem, Bealoth, 25 Hazor, Hadattah, Ke-
rioth, Hezron (which *is* Hazor), 26 Amam, Shema,
Moladah, 27 Hazar Gaddah, Heshmon, Beth Pelet,
28 Hazar Shual, [a]Beersheba, Bizjothjah, 29 Baalah,
Ijim, Ezem, 30 Eltolad, Chesil, [a]Hormah, 31 [a]Ziklag,
Madmannah, Sansannah, 32 Lebaoth, Shilhim,
Ain, and [a]Rimmon: all the cities *are* twenty-nine,
with their villages.
33 In the lowland: [a]Eshtaol, Zorah, Ashnah,
34 Zanoah, En Gannim, Tappuah, Enam, 35 Jar-
muth, [a]Adullam, Socoh, Azekah, 36 Sharaim,
Adithaim, Gederah, and Gederothaim: fourteen
cities with their villages; 37 Zenan, Hadashah,
Migdal Gad, 38 Dilean, Mizpah, [a]Joktheel, 39 [a]La-
chish, Bozkath, [b]Eglon, 40 Cabbon, Lahmas,[1]
Kithlish, 41 Gederoth, Beth Dagon, Naamah, and
Makkedah: sixteen cities with their villages;
42 [a]Libnah, Ether, Ashan, 43 Jiphtah, Ashnah,
Nezib, 44 Keilah, Achzib, and Mareshah: nine
cities with their villages; 45 Ekron, with its towns
and villages; 46 from Ekron to the sea, all that
*lay* near [a]Ashdod, with their villages; 47 Ashdod
with its towns and villages, Gaza with its towns
and villages—as far as [a]the Brook of Egypt and
[b]the Great Sea with *its* coastline.
48 And in the mountain country: Shamir,
Jattir, Sochoh, 49 Dannah, Kirjath Sannah (which
*is* Debir), 50 Anab, Eshtemoh, Anim, 51 [a]Goshen,
Holon, and Giloh: eleven cities with their vil-
lages; 52 Arab, Dumah, Eshean, 53 Janum, Beth
Tappuah, Aphekah, 54 Humtah, [a]Kirjath Arba
(which *is* Hebron), and Zior: nine cities with
their villages; 55 [a]Maon, Carmel, Ziph, Juttah,
56 Jezreel, Jokdeam, Zanoah, 57 Kain, Gibeah, and
Timnah: ten cities with their villages; 58 Halhul,
Beth Zur, Gedor, 59 Maarath, Beth Anoth, and
Eltekon: six cities with their villages; 60 [a]Kirjath
Baal (which *is* Kirjath Jearim) and Rabbah: two
cities with their villages.
61 In the wilderness: Beth Arabah, Middin,
Secacah, 62 Nibshan, the City of Salt, and [a]En
Gedi: six cities with their villages.
63 As for the Jebusites, the inhabitants of
Jerusalem, [a]the children of Judah could not
drive them out; [b]but the Jebusites dwell with
the children of Judah at Jerusalem to this day.

### *EPHRAIM AND WEST MANASSEH*

16 The lot fell to the children of Joseph from
the Jordan, by Jericho, to the waters of Jer-
icho on the east, to the [a]wilderness that goes up
from Jericho through the mountains to Bethel,
2 then went out from [a]Bethel to Luz,[1] passed
along to the border of the Archites at Ataroth,
3 and went down westward to the boundary of
the Japhletites, [a]as far as the boundary of Lower
Beth Horon to [b]Gezer; and it ended at the sea.
4 [a]So the children of Joseph, Manasseh and
Ephraim, took their inheritance.

**15:8** [c] Josh. 18:16 [1] Literally *Giants* **15:9** [a] Josh. 18:15 [b] 1 Chr. 13:6 [c] Judg. 18:12 **15:10** [a] Gen. 38:13; Judg. 14:1 **15:11** [a] Josh. 19:43 **15:12** [a] Num. 34:6, 7; Josh. 15:47 **15:13** [a] Josh. 14:13 [b] Num. 13:6 [c] Josh. 14:15 **15:14** [a] Judg. 1:10, 20 [b] Num. 13:22 **15:15** [a] Josh. 10:38; Judg. 1:11 **15:16** [a] Judg. 1:12 **15:17** [a] Judg. 1:13; 3:9 [b] Num. 32:12; Josh. 14:6 [c] Judg. 1:12 **15:18** [a] Judg. 1:14 [b] Gen. 24:64; 1 Sam. 25:23 **15:19** [a] Gen. 33:11 **15:21** [a] Gen. 35:21 **15:24** [a] 1 Sam. 23:14 **15:28** [a] Gen. 21:31; Josh. 19:2 **15:30** [a] Josh. 19:4 **15:31** [a] Josh. 19:5; 1 Sam. 27:6; 30:1 **15:32** [a] Judg. 20:45, 47 **15:33** [a] Judg. 13:25; 16:31 **15:35** [a] 1 Sam. 22:1 **15:38** [a] 2 Kin. 14:7 **15:39** [a] 2 Kin. 14:19 [b] Josh. 10:3 **15:40** [1] Or *Lahmam* **15:42** [a] Josh. 21:13 **15:46** [a] Josh. 11:22 **15:47** [a] Josh. 15:4 [b] Num. 34:6 **15:51** [a] Josh. 10:41; 11:16 **15:54** [a] Josh. 14:15 **15:55** [a] 1 Sam. 23:24, 25 **15:60** [a] Josh. 18:14; 1 Sam. 7:1, 2 **15:62** [a] 1 Sam. 23:29; Ezek. 47:10 **15:63** [a] Judg. 1:8, 21; 2 Sam. 5:6; 1 Chr. 11:4 [b] Judg. 1:21 **16:1** [a] Josh. 8:15; 18:12 **16:2** [a] Josh. 18:13; Judg. 1:26 [1] Septuagint reads *Bethel* (that is, Luz). **16:3** [a] Josh. 18:13; 1 Kin. 9:17; 2 Chr. 8:5 [b] Josh. 21:21; 1 Kin. 9:15; 1 Chr. 7:28 **16:4** [a] Josh. 17:14

### *THE LAND OF EPHRAIM*

5[a]The border of the children of Ephraim,
according to their families, was *thus:* The border
of their inheritance on the east side was [b]Ataroth
Addar [c]as far as Upper Beth Horon.
6And the border went out toward the sea on
the north side of [a]Michmethath; then the border
went around eastward to Taanath Shiloh, and
passed by it on the east of Janohah. 7Then it
went down from Janohah to Ataroth and Naarah,[1]
reached to Jericho, and came out at the Jordan.
8The border went out from [a]Tappuah west-
ward to the [b]Brook Kanah, and it ended at the
sea. This *was* the inheritance of the tribe of the
children of Ephraim according to their families.
9[a]The separate cities for the children of Ephra-
im *were* among the inheritance of the children
of Manasseh, all the cities with their villages.
10[a]And they did not drive out the Canaanites
who dwelt in Gezer; but the Canaanites dwell
among the Ephraimites to this day and have
become forced laborers.

### *THE OTHER HALF-TRIBE OF MANASSEH (WEST)*

**17** There was also a lot for the tribe of Manas-
seh, for he *was* the [a]firstborn of Joseph:
*namely* for [b]Machir the firstborn of Manasseh,
the father of Gilead, because he was a man of
war; therefore he was given [c]Gilead and Bashan.
2And there was *a lot* for [a]the rest of the children
of Manasseh according to their families: [b]for the
children of Abiezer,[1] the children of Helek, [c]the
children of Asriel, the children of Shechem, [d]the
children of Hepher, and the children of Shemi-
da; these *were* the male children of Manasseh
the son of Joseph according to their families.
3But [a]Zelophehad the son of Hepher, the son
of Gilead, the son of Machir, the son of Manas-
seh, had no sons, but only daughters. And these
*are* the names of his daughters: Mahlah, Noah,
Hoglah, Milcah, and Tirzah. 4And they came near
before [a]Eleazar the priest, before Joshua the son
of Nun, and before the rulers, saying, [b]"The LORD
commanded Moses to give us an inheritance
among our brothers." Therefore, according to
the commandment of the LORD, he gave them an
inheritance among their father's brothers. 5Ten
shares fell to [a]Manasseh, besides the land of Gil-
ead and Bashan, which *were* on the other side of
the Jordan, 6because the daughters of Manasseh
received an inheritance among his sons; and the
rest of Manasseh's sons had the land of Gilead.
7And the territory of Manasseh was from
Asher to [a]Michmethath, that *lies* east of She-
chem; and the border went along south to the
inhabitants of En Tappuah. 8Manasseh had the
land of Tappuah, but [a]Tappuah on the border of
Manasseh *belonged* to the children of Ephraim.
9And the border descended to the Brook Kanah,
southward to the brook. [a]These cities of Ephraim
*are* among the cities of Manasseh. The border of
Manasseh *was* on the north side of the brook;
and it ended at the sea.
10Southward *it was* Ephraim's, northward *it
was* Manasseh's, and the sea was its border. Ma-
nasseh's territory was adjoining Asher on the north
and Issachar on the east. 11And in Issachar and in
Asher, [a]Manasseh had [b]Beth Shean and its towns,
Ibleam and its towns, the inhabitants of Dor and
its towns, the inhabitants of En Dor and its towns,
the inhabitants of Taanach and its towns, and the
inhabitants of Megiddo and its towns—three hilly
regions. 12Yet [a]the children of Manasseh could
not drive out *the inhabitants of* those cities, but
the Canaanites were determined to dwell in that
land. 13And it happened, when the children of Is-
rael grew strong, that they put the Canaanites to
[a]forced labor, but did not utterly drive them out.

> **17:3–6** This account shows the theme of the Book of Joshua—God is faithful to keep His promises. Joshua was faithful to carry out the commands of God concerning His promise through Moses for the daughters of **Zelophehad** (see Num. 26:33; 27:1–11).

### *MORE LAND FOR EPHRAIM AND MANASSEH*

14[a]Then the children of Joseph spoke to Joshua,
saying, "Why have you given us *only* [b]one lot and
one share to inherit, since we *are* [c]a great people,
inasmuch as the LORD has blessed us until now?"
15So Joshua answered them, "If you *are* a
great people, *then* go up to the forest *country* and
clear a place for yourself there in the land of the
Perizzites and the giants, since the mountains
of Ephraim are too confined for you."
16But the children of Joseph said, "The
mountain country is not enough for us; and
all the Canaanites who dwell in the land of the
valley have [a]chariots of iron, *both those* who *are*
of Beth Shean and its towns and *those* who *are*
[b]of the Valley of Jezreel."
17And Joshua spoke to the house of Joseph—
to Ephraim and Manasseh—saying, "You *are* a
great people and have great power; you shall not
have *only* one lot, 18but the mountain country
shall be yours. Although it *is* wooded, you shall
cut it down, and its farthest extent shall be yours;
for you shall drive out the Canaanites, [a]though
they have iron chariots *and* are strong."

**16:5** [a] Judg. 1:29; 1 Chr. 7:28, 29 [b] Josh. 18:13 [c] 2 Chr. 8:5 **16:6** [a] Josh. 17:7 **16:7** [1] Or *Naaran* (compare 1 Chronicles 7:28) **16:8** [a] Josh. 17:8 [b] Josh. 17:9 **16:9** [a] Josh. 17:9 **16:10** [a] Josh. 15:63; 17:12, 13; Judg. 1:29; 1 Kin. 9:16 **17:1** [a] Gen. 41:51; 46:20; 48:18 [b] Gen. 50:23; Judg. 5:14 [c] Deut. 3:15 **17:2** [a] Num. 26:29–33 [b] 1 Chr. 7:18 [c] Num. 26:31 [d] Num. 26:32 [1] Called *Jeezer* in Numbers 26:30 **17:3** [a] Num. 26:33; 27:1; 36:2 **17:4** [a] Josh. 14:1 [b] Num. 27:2–11 **17:5** [a] Josh. 22:7 **17:7** [a] Josh. 16:6 **17:8** [a] Josh. 16:8 **17:9** [a] Josh. 16:9 **17:11** [a] 1 Chr. 7:29 [b] Judg. 1:27; 1 Sam. 31:10; 1 Kin. 4:12 **17:12** [a] Judg. 1:19, 27, 28 **17:13** [a] Josh. 16:10 **17:14** [a] Josh. 16:4 [b] Gen. 48:22 [c] Gen. 48:19; Num. 26:34, 37 **17:16** [a] Josh. 17:18; Judg. 1:19; 4:3 [b] Josh. 19:18; 1 Kin. 4:12 **17:18** [a] Deut. 20:1

### *THE REMAINDER OF THE LAND DIVIDED*

**18** Now the whole congregation of the children of Israel assembled together [a]at Shiloh, and [b]set up the tabernacle of meeting there. And the land was subdued before them. 2 But there remained among the children of Israel seven tribes which had not yet received their inheritance.

3 Then Joshua said to the children of Israel: [a]"How long will you neglect to go and possess the land which the LORD God of your fathers has given you? 4 Pick out from among you three men for *each* tribe, and I will send them; they shall rise and go through the land, survey it according to their inheritance, and come *back* to me. 5 And they shall divide it into seven parts. [a]Judah shall remain in their territory on the south, and the [b]house of Joseph shall remain in their territory on the north. 6 You shall therefore survey the land in seven parts and bring *the survey* here to me, [a]that I may cast lots for you here before the LORD our God. 7 [a]But the Levites have no part among you, for the priesthood of the LORD *is* their inheritance. [b]And Gad, Reuben, and half the tribe of Manasseh have received their inheritance beyond the Jordan on the east, which Moses the servant of the LORD gave them."

8 Then the men arose to go away; and Joshua charged those who went to survey the land, saying, "Go, walk [a]through the land, survey it, and come back to me, that I may cast lots for you here before the LORD in Shiloh." 9 So the men went, passed through the land, and wrote the survey in a book in seven parts by cities; and they came to Joshua at the camp in Shiloh. 10 Then Joshua cast [a]lots for them in Shiloh before the LORD, and there [b]Joshua divided the land to the children of Israel according to their divisions.

### *THE LAND OF BENJAMIN*

11 [a]Now the lot of the tribe of the children of Benjamin came up according to their families, and the territory of their lot came out between the children of Judah and the children of Joseph. 12 [a]Their border on the north side began at the Jordan, and the border went up to the side of Jericho on the north, and went up through the mountains westward; it ended at the Wilderness of Beth Aven. 13 The border went over from there toward Luz, to the side of Luz [a](which *is* Bethel) southward; and the border descended to Ataroth Addar, near the hill that *lies* on the south side [b]of Lower Beth Horon.

14 Then the border extended around the west side to the south, from the hill that *lies* before Beth Horon southward; and it ended at [a]Kirjath Baal (which *is* Kirjath Jearim), a city of the children of Judah. This *was* the west side.

15 The south side *began* at the end of Kirjath Jearim, and the border extended on the west and went out to [a]the spring of the waters of Nephtoah. 16 Then the border came down to the end of the mountain that *lies* before [a]the Valley of the Son of Hinnom, which *is* in the Valley of the Rephaim[1] on the north, descended to the Valley of Hinnom, to the side of the Jebusite *city* on the south, and descended to [b]En Rogel. 17 And it went around from the north, went out to En Shemesh, and extended toward Geliloth, which is before the Ascent of Adummim, and descended to [a]the stone of Bohan the son of Reuben. 18 Then it passed along toward the north side of Arabah,[1] and went down to Arabah. 19 And the border passed along to the north side of Beth Hoglah; then the border ended at the north bay at the [a]Salt Sea, at the south end of the Jordan. This *was* the southern boundary.

20 The Jordan was its border on the east side. This *was* the inheritance of the children of Benjamin, according to its boundaries all around, according to their families.

21 Now the cities of the tribe of the children of Benjamin, according to their families, were Jericho, Beth Hoglah, Emek Keziz, 22 Beth Arabah, Zemaraim, Bethel, 23 Avim, Parah, Ophrah, 24 Chephar Haammoni, Ophni, and Gaba: twelve cities with their villages; 25 [a]Gibeon, [b]Ramah, Beeroth, 26 Mizpah, Chephirah, Mozah, 27 Rekem, Irpeel, Taralah, 28 Zelah, Eleph, [a]Jebus (which *is* Jerusalem), Gibeath, *and* Kirjath: fourteen cities with their villages. This was the inheritance of the children of Benjamin according to their families.

### *SIMEON'S INHERITANCE WITH JUDAH*

**19** The [a]second lot came out for Simeon, for the tribe of the children of Simeon according to their families. [b]And their inheritance was within the inheritance of the children of Judah. 2 [a]They had in their inheritance Beersheba (Sheba), Moladah, 3 Hazar Shual, Balah, Ezem, 4 Eltolad, Bethul, Hormah, 5 Ziklag, Beth Marcaboth, Hazar Susah, 6 Beth Lebaoth, and Sharuhen: thirteen cities and their villages; 7 Ain, Rimmon, Ether, and Ashan: four cities and their villages; 8 and all the villages that *were* all around these cities as far as Baalath Beer, [a]Ramah of the South. This *was* the inheritance of the tribe of the children of Simeon according to their families.

9 The inheritance of the children of Simeon *was included* in the share of the children of Judah, for the share of the children of Judah was too much for them. [a]Therefore the children of Simeon had *their* inheritance within the inheritance of that people.

18:1 [a]Josh. 19:51; 21:2; 22:9; Jer. 7:12 [b]Judg. 18:31; 1 Sam. 1:3, 24; 4:3, 4 18:3 [a]Judg. 18:9 18:5 [a]Josh. 15:1 [b]Josh. 16:1—17:18 18:6 [a]Josh. 14:2; 18:10 18:7 [a]Num. 18:7, 20; Josh. 13:33 [b]Josh. 13:8 18:8 [a]Gen. 13:17 18:10 [a]Acts 13:19 [b]Num. 34:16–29; Josh. 19:51 18:11 [a]Judg. 1:21 18:12 [a]Josh. 16:1 18:13 [a]Gen. 28:19; Josh. 16:2; Judg. 1:23 [b]Josh. 16:3 18:14 [a]Josh. 15:9 18:15 [a]Josh. 15:9 18:16 [a]Josh. 15:8 [b]Josh. 15:7 [1]Literally *Giants* 18:17 [a]Josh. 15:6 18:18 [1]Or *Beth Arabah* (compare 15:6 and 18:22) 18:19 [a]Josh. 15:2, 5 18:25 [a]Josh. 11:19; 21:17; 1 Kin. 3:4, 5 [b]Jer. 31:15 18:28 [a]Josh. 15:8, 63 19:1 [a]Judg. 1:3 [b]Josh. 19:9 19:2 [a]1 Chr. 4:28 19:8 [a]1 Sam. 30:27 19:9 [a]Josh. 19:1

### THE LAND OF ZEBULUN

10 The third lot came out for the children
of Zebulun according to their families, and the
border of their inheritance was as far as Sarid.
11 [a]Their border went toward the west and to Mara-
lah, went to Dabbasheth, and extended along the
brook that is [b]east of Jokneam. 12 Then from Sarid
it went eastward toward the sunrise along the
border of Chisloth Tabor, and went out toward
[a]Daberath, bypassing Japhia. 13 And from there
it passed along on the east of [a]Gath Hepher, to-
ward Eth Kazin, and extended to Rimmon, which
borders on Neah. 14 Then the border went around
it on the north side of Hannathon, and it ended
in the Valley of Jiphthah El. 15 Included were Kat-
tath, Nahallal, Shimron, Idalah, and Bethlehem:
twelve cities with their villages. 16 This *was* the
inheritance of the children of Zebulun according
to their families, these cities with their villages.

### THE LAND OF ISSACHAR

17 The fourth lot came out to Issachar, for the
children of Issachar according to their families.
18 And their territory went to Jezreel, and *included*
Chesulloth, Shunem, 19 Haphraim, Shion, Ana-
harath, 20 Rabbith, Kishion, Abez, 21 Remeth, En
Gannim, En Haddah, and Beth Pazzez. 22 And the
border reached to Tabor, Shahazimah, and [a]Beth
Shemesh; their border ended at the Jordan: sixteen
cities with their villages. 23 This *was* the inheritance
of the tribe of the children of Issachar according
to their families, the cities and their villages.

### THE LAND OF ASHER

24 [a]The fifth lot came out for the tribe of the
children of Asher according to their families.
25 And their territory included Helkath, Hali,
Beten, Achshaph, 26 Alammelech, Amad, and
Mishal; it reached to [a]Mount Carmel westward,
along *the Brook* Shihor Libnath. 27 It turned to-
ward the sunrise to Beth Dagon; and it reached
to Zebulun and to the Valley of Jiphthah El, then
northward beyond Beth Emek and Neiel, by-
passing [a]Cabul *which was* on the left, 28 including
Ebron,[1] Rehob, Hammon, and Kanah, [a]as far
as Greater Sidon. 29 And the border turned to
Ramah and to the fortified city of Tyre; then the
border turned to Hosah, and ended at the sea by
the region of [a]Achzib. 30 Also Ummah, Aphek,
and Rehob *were included:* twenty-two cities with
their villages. 31 This *was* the inheritance of the
tribe of the children of Asher according to their
families, these cities with their villages.

### THE LAND OF NAPHTALI

32 [a]The sixth lot came out to the children of
Naphtali, for the children of Naphtali according
to their families. 33 And their border began at He-
leph, enclosing the territory from the terebinth
tree in Zaanannim, Adami Nekeb, and Jabneel, as
far as Lakkum; it ended at the Jordan. 34 [a]From
Heleph the border extended westward to Aznoth
Tabor, and went out from there toward Hukkok;
it adjoined Zebulun on the south side and Asher
on the west side, and ended at Judah by the Jor-
dan toward the sunrise. 35 And the fortified cities
*are* Ziddim, Zer, Hammath, Rakkath, Chinnereth,
36 Adamah, Ramah, Hazor, 37 [a]Kedesh, Edrei, En
Hazor, 38 Iron, Migdal El, Horem, Beth Anath,
and Beth Shemesh: nineteen cities with their
villages. 39 This *was* the inheritance of the tribe
of the children of Naphtali according to their
families, the cities and their villages.

### THE LAND OF DAN

40 [a]The seventh lot came out for the tribe of
the children of Dan according to their families.
41 And the territory of their inheritance was
Zorah, [a]Eshtaol, Ir Shemesh, 42 [a]Shaalabbin,
[b]Aijalon, Jethlah, 43 Elon, Timnah, [a]Ekron, 44 El-
tekeh, Gibbethon, Baalath, 45 Jehud, Bene Berak,
Gath Rimmon, 46 Me Jarkon, and Rakkon, with
the region near Joppa. 47 And the [a]border of the
children of Dan went beyond these, because the
children of Dan went up to fight against Leshem
and took it; and they struck it with the edge of
the sword, took possession of it, and dwelt in
it. They called Leshem, [b]Dan, after the name of
Dan their father. 48 This *is* the inheritance of the
tribe of the children of Dan according to their
families, these cities with their villages.

### JOSHUA'S INHERITANCE

49 When they had made an end of dividing
the land as an inheritance according to their
borders, the children of Israel gave an inher-
itance among them to Joshua the son of Nun.
50 According to the word of the LORD they gave
him the city which he asked for, [a]Timnath [b]Serah
in the mountains of Ephraim; and he built the
city and dwelt in it.

51 [a]These *were* the inheritances which Eleazar
the priest, Joshua the son of Nun, and the heads
of the fathers of the tribes of the children of Israel
divided as an inheritance by lot [b]in Shiloh before
the LORD, at the door of the tabernacle of meeting.
So they made an end of dividing the country.

### THE CITIES OF REFUGE

*(Num. 35:9–28; Deut. 19:1–13)*

20 The LORD also spoke to Joshua, saying,
2 "Speak to the children of Israel, saying:
[a]'Appoint for yourselves cities of refuge, of which
I spoke to you through Moses, 3 that the slayer

19:11 [a] Gen. 49:13 [b] Josh. 12:22 19:12 [a] 1 Chr. 6:72 19:13 [a] 2 Kin. 14:25 19:22 [a] Josh. 15:10; Judg. 1:33 19:24 [a] Judg. 1:31, 32
19:26 [a] 1 Sam. 15:12; 1 Kin. 18:20; Is. 33:9; 35:2; Jer. 46:18 19:27 [a] 1 Kin. 9:13 19:28 [a] Gen. 10:19; Josh. 11:8; Judg. 1:31; Acts 27:3

[1] Following Masoretic Text, Targum, and Vulgate; a few Hebrew manuscripts read *Abdon* (compare 21:30 and 1 Chronicles 6:74).

19:29 [a] Judg. 1:31 19:32 [a] Josh. 19:32–39; Judg. 1:33 19:34 [a] Deut. 33:23 19:37 [a] Josh. 20:7 19:40 [a] Josh. 19:40–48; Judg. 1:34–36
19:41 [a] Josh. 15:33 19:42 [a] Judg. 1:35; 1 Kin. 4:9 [b] Josh. 10:12; 21:24 19:43 [a] Josh. 15:11; Judg. 1:18 19:47 [a] Judg. 18 [b] Judg. 18:29
19:50 [a] Josh. 24:30 [b] 1 Chr. 7:24 19:51 [a] Num. 34:17; Josh. 14:1 [b] Josh. 18:1, 10 20:2 [a] Ex. 21:13; Num. 35:6–34; Deut. 19:2, 9

who kills a person accidentally *or* unintentionally may flee there; and they shall be your refuge from the avenger of blood. 4 And when he flees to one of those cities, and stands at the entrance of the gate of the city, and declares his case in the hearing of the elders of that city, they shall take him into the city as one of them, and give him a place, that he may dwell among them. 5 [a]Then if the avenger of blood pursues him, they shall not deliver the slayer into his hand, because he struck his neighbor unintentionally, but did not hate him beforehand. 6 And he shall dwell in that city [a]until he stands before the congregation for judgment, *and* until the death of the one who is high priest in those days. Then the slayer may return and come to his own city and his own house, to the city from which he fled.' "

7 So they appointed [a]Kedesh in Galilee, in the mountains of Naphtali, [b]Shechem in the mountains of Ephraim, and [c]Kirjath Arba (which *is* Hebron) in [d]the mountains of Judah. 8 And on the other side of the Jordan, by Jericho eastward, they assigned [a]Bezer in the wilderness on the plain, from the tribe of Reuben, [b]Ramoth in Gilead, from the tribe of Gad, and [c]Golan in Bashan, from the tribe of Manasseh. 9 [a]These were the cities appointed for all the children of Israel and for the stranger who dwelt among them, that whoever killed a person accidentally might flee there, and not die by the hand of the avenger of blood [b]until he stood before the congregation.

### *CITIES OF THE LEVITES*

*(1 Chr. 6:54–81)*

**21** Then the heads of the fathers' *houses* of the [a]Levites came near to [b]Eleazar the priest, to Joshua the son of Nun, and to the heads of the fathers' *houses* of the tribes of the children of Israel. 2 And they spoke to them at [a]Shiloh in the land of Canaan, saying, [b]"The LORD commanded through Moses to give us cities to dwell in, with their common-lands for our livestock." 3 So the children of Israel gave to the Levites from their inheritance, at the commandment of the LORD, these cities and their common-lands:

4 Now the lot came out for the families of the Kohathites. And [a]the children of Aaron the priest, *who were* of the Levites, [b]had thirteen cities by lot from the tribe of Judah, from the tribe of Simeon, and from the tribe of Benjamin. 5 [a]The rest of the children of Kohath had ten cities by lot from the families of the tribe of Ephraim, from the tribe of Dan, and from the half-tribe of Manasseh.

6 And [a]the children of Gershon had thirteen cities by lot from the families of the tribe of Issachar, from the tribe of Asher, from the tribe of Naphtali, and from the half-tribe of Manasseh in Bashan.

7 [a]The children of Merari according to their families had twelve cities from the tribe of Reuben, from the tribe of Gad, and from the tribe of Zebulun.

8 [a]And the children of Israel gave these cities with their common-lands by lot to the Levites, [b]as the LORD had commanded by the hand of Moses.

9 So they gave from the tribe of the children of Judah and from the tribe of the children of Simeon these cities which are designated by name, 10 which were for the children of Aaron, one of the families of the Kohathites, *who were* of the children of Levi; for the lot was theirs first. 11 [a]And they gave them Kirjath Arba (*Arba was* the father of [b]Anak), [c]which *is* Hebron, in the mountains of Judah, with the common-land surrounding it. 12 But [a]the fields of the city and its villages they gave to Caleb the son of Jephunneh as his possession.

13 Thus [a]to the children of Aaron the priest they gave [b]Hebron with its common-land (a city of refuge for the slayer), [c]Libnah with its common-land, 14 [a]Jattir with its common-land, [b]Eshtemoa with its common-land, 15 [a]Holon with its common-land, [b]Debir with its common-land, 16 [a]Ain with its common-land, [b]Juttah with its common-land, and [c]Beth Shemesh with its common-land: nine cities from those two tribes; 17 and from the tribe of Benjamin, [a]Gibeon with its common-land, [b]Geba with its common-land, 18 Anathoth with its common-land, and [a]Almon with its common-land: four cities. 19 All the cities of the children of Aaron, the priests, *were* thirteen cities with their common-lands.

20 [a]And the families of the children of Kohath, the Levites, the rest of the children of Kohath, even they had the cities of their lot from the tribe of Ephraim. 21 For they gave them [a]Shechem with its common-land in the mountains of Ephraim (a city of refuge for the slayer), [b]Gezer with its common-land, 22 Kibzaim with its common-land, and Beth Horon with its common-land: four cities; 23 and from the tribe of Dan, Eltekeh with its common-land, Gibbethon with its common-land, 24 [a]Aijalon with its common-land, *and* Gath Rimmon with its common-land: four cities; 25 and from the half-tribe of Manasseh, Tanach with its common-land and Gath Rimmon with its common-land: two cities. 26 All the ten cities with their common-lands were for the rest of the families of the children of Kohath.

27 [a]Also to the children of Gershon, of the families of the Levites, from the *other* half-tribe of Manasseh, *they gave* [b]Golan in Bashan with its

**20:5** [a] Num. 35:12 **20:6** [a] Num. 35:12, 24, 25 **20:7** [a] Josh. 21:32; 1 Chr. 6:76 [b] Josh. 21:21; 2 Chr. 10:1 [c] Josh. 14:15; 21:11, 13 [d] Luke 1:39 **20:8** [a] Deut. 4:43; Josh. 21:36; 1 Chr. 6:78 [b] Josh. 21:38; 1 Kin. 22:3 [c] Josh. 21:27 **20:9** [a] Num. 35:15 [b] Josh. 20:6 **21:1** [a] Num. 35:1–8 [b] Num. 34:16–29; Josh. 14:1; 17:4 **21:2** [a] Josh. 18:1 [b] Num. 35:2 **21:4** [a] Josh. 21:8, 19 [b] Josh. 19:51 **21:5** [a] Josh. 21:20 **21:6** [a] Josh. 21:27 **21:7** [a] Josh. 21:34 **21:8** [a] Josh. 21:3 [b] Num. 35:2 **21:11** [a] Josh. 20:7; 1 Chr. 6:55 [b] Josh. 14:15; 15:13, 14 [c] Josh. 20:7; Luke 1:39 **21:12** [a] Josh. 14:14; 1 Chr. 6:56 **21:13** [a] 1 Chr. 6:57 [b] Josh. 15:54; 20:2, 7 [c] Josh. 15:42; 2 Kin. 8:22 **21:14** [a] Josh. 15:48 [b] Josh. 15:50 **21:15** [a] 1 Chr. 6:58 [b] Josh. 15:49 **21:16** [a] 1 Chr. 6:59 [b] Josh. 15:55 [c] Josh. 15:10 **21:17** [a] Josh. 18:25 [b] Josh. 18:24 **21:18** [a] 1 Chr. 6:60 **21:20** [a] 1 Chr. 6:66 **21:21** [a] Josh. 20:7 [b] Judg. 1:29 **21:24** [a] Josh. 10:12 **21:27** [a] Josh. 21:6; 1 Chr. 6:71 [b] Josh. 20:8

common-land (a city of refuge for the slayer), and
Be Eshterah with its common-land: two cities;
28 and from the tribe of Issachar, Kishion with its
common-land, Daberath with its common-land,
29 Jarmuth with its common-land, *and* En Gannim
with its common-land: four cities; 30 and from
the tribe of Asher, Mishal with its common-land,
Abdon with its common-land, 31 Helkath with its
common-land, and Rehob with its common-land:
four cities; 32 and from the tribe of Naphtali,
[a]Kedesh in Galilee with its common-land (a city
of refuge for the slayer), Hammoth Dor with its
common-land, and Kartan with its common-land:
three cities. 33 All the cities of the Gershonites
according to their families *were* thirteen cities
with their common-lands.

34 [a]And to the families of the children of
Merari, the rest of the Levites, from the tribe
of Zebulun, Jokneam with its common-land,
Kartah with its common-land, 35 Dimnah with
its common-land, *and* Nahalal with its common-
land: four cities; 36 and from the tribe of Reuben,
[a]Bezer with its common-land, Jahaz with its
common-land, 37 Kedemoth with its common-
land, and Mephaath with its common-land: four
cities;[1] 38 and from the tribe of Gad, [a]Ramoth in
Gilead with its common-land (a city of refuge for
the slayer), Mahanaim with its common-land,
39 Heshbon with its common-land, *and* Jazer
with its common-land: four cities in all. 40 So all
the cities for the children of Merari according
to their families, the rest of the families of the
Levites, were *by* their lot twelve cities.

41 [a]All the cities of the Levites within the pos-
session of the children of Israel *were* forty-eight
cities with their common-lands. 42 Every one of
these cities had its common-land surrounding
it; thus *were* all these cities.

### THE PROMISE FULFILLED

43 So the LORD gave to Israel [a]all the land of
which He had sworn to give to their fathers, and
they [b]took possession of it and dwelt in it. 44 [a]The
LORD gave them [b]rest all around, according to all
that He had sworn to their fathers. And [c]not a man
of all their enemies stood against them; the LORD
delivered all their enemies into their hand. 45 [a]Not
a word failed of any good thing which the LORD
had spoken to the house of Israel. All came to pass.

### EASTERN TRIBES RETURN TO THEIR LANDS

22 Then Joshua called the Reubenites, the
Gadites, and half the tribe of Manasseh,
2 and said to them: "You have kept [a]all that Moses
the servant of the LORD commanded you, [b]and
have obeyed my voice in all that I commanded
you. 3 You have not left your brethren these many
days, up to this day, but have kept the charge
of the commandment of the LORD your God.
4 And now the LORD your God has given [a]rest
to your brethren, as He promised them; now
therefore, return and go to your tents *and* to
the land of your possession, [b]which Moses the
servant of the LORD gave you on the other side
of the Jordan. 5 But [a]take careful heed to do the
commandment and the law which Moses the
servant of the LORD commanded you, [b]to love
the LORD your God, to walk in all His ways, to
keep His commandments, to hold fast to Him,
and to serve Him with all your heart and with
all your soul." 6 So Joshua [a]blessed them and
sent them away, and they went to their tents.

> **SEEING JESUS IN THE SCRIPTURE**
>
> **22:4–5** Before Joshua sent the people to take possession of the land, he reminded them of their need to obey God to experience true rest. Jesus came into the world in full obedience to the Father so that by trusting in Him, we will have eternal rest (see Phil. 2:8; Heb. 4:8–10).

7 Now to half the tribe of Manasseh Moses had
given a possession in Bashan, [a]but to the *other*
half of it Joshua gave *a possession* among their
brethren on this side of the Jordan, westward.
And indeed, when Joshua sent them away to their
tents, he blessed them, 8 and spoke to them, saying,
"Return with much riches to your tents, with very
much livestock, with silver, with gold, with bronze,
with iron, and with very much clothing. [a]Divide
the spoil of your enemies with your brethren."

9 So the children of Reuben, the children of
Gad, and half the tribe of Manasseh returned,
and departed from the children of Israel at Shi-
loh, which *is* in the land of Canaan, to go to [a]the
country of Gilead, to the land of their possession,
which they had obtained according to the word
of the LORD by the hand of Moses.

### AN ALTAR BY THE JORDAN

10 And when they came to the region of the
Jordan which *is* in the land of Canaan, the chil-
dren of Reuben, the children of Gad, and half
the tribe of Manasseh built an altar there by
the Jordan—a great, impressive altar. 11 Now the
children of Israel [a]heard *someone* say, "Behold,
the children of Reuben, the children of Gad, and
half the tribe of Manasseh have built an altar on
the frontier of the land of Canaan, in the region
of the Jordan—on the children of Israel's side."

**21:32** [a] Josh. 20:7 **21:34** [a] Josh. 21:7; 1 Chr. 6:77–81 **21:36** [a] Deut. 4:43; Josh. 20:8 **21:37** [1] Following Septuagint and Vulgate (compare 1 Chronicles 6:78, 79); Masoretic Text, Bomberg, and Targum omit verses 36 and 37. **21:38** [a] Josh. 20:8 **21:41** [a] Num. 35:7 **21:43** [a] Gen. 12:7; 26:3, 4; 28:4, 13, 14 [b] Num. 33:53; Josh. 1:11 **21:44** [a] Deut. 7:23, 24; Josh. 11:23; 22:4 [b] Josh. 1:13, 15; 11:23 [c] Deut. 7:24 **21:45** [a] [Num. 23:19]; Josh. 23:14; 1 Kin. 8:56 **22:2** [a] Num. 32:20–22; Deut. 3:18 [b] Josh. 1:12–18 **22:4** [a] Josh. 21:44 [b] Num. 32:33 **22:5** [a] Deut. 6:6, 17; 11:22; Jer. 12:16 [b] Deut. 10:12; 11:13, 22 **22:6** [a] Gen. 47:7; Ex. 39:43; Josh. 14:13; 2 Sam. 6:18; Luke 24:50 **22:7** [a] Josh. 17:1–13 **22:8** [a] Num. 31:27; 1 Sam. 30:24 **22:9** [a] Num. 32:1, 26, 29 **22:11** [a] Deut. 13:12–18; Judg. 20:12, 13

12 And when the children of Israel heard *of it,* [a]the whole congregation of the children of Israel gathered together at Shiloh to go to war against them.

13 Then the children of Israel [a]sent [b]Phinehas the son of Eleazar the priest to the children of Reuben, to the children of Gad, and to half the tribe of Manasseh, into the land of Gilead, 14 and with him ten rulers, one ruler each from the chief house of every tribe of Israel; and [a]each one *was* the head of the house of his father among the divisions[1] of Israel. 15 Then they came to the children of Reuben, to the children of Gad, and to half the tribe of Manasseh, to the land of Gilead, and they spoke with them, saying, 16 "Thus says the whole congregation of the LORD: 'What [a]treachery *is* this that you have committed against the God of Israel, to turn away this day from following the LORD, in that you have built for yourselves an altar, [b]that you might rebel this day against the LORD? 17 *Is* the iniquity [a]of Peor not enough for us, from which we are not cleansed till this day, although there was a plague in the congregation of the LORD, 18 but that you must turn away this day from following the LORD? And it shall be, if you rebel today against the LORD, that tomorrow [a]He will be angry with the whole congregation of Israel. 19 Nevertheless, if the land of your possession *is* unclean, *then* cross over to the land of the possession of the LORD, [a]where the LORD's tabernacle stands, and take possession among us; but do not rebel against the LORD, nor rebel against us, by building yourselves an altar besides the altar of the LORD our God. 20 [a]Did not Achan the son of Zerah commit a trespass in the accursed thing, and wrath fell on all the congregation of Israel? And that man did not perish alone in his iniquity.' "

21 Then the children of Reuben, the children of Gad, and half the tribe of Manasseh answered and said to the heads of the divisions[1] of Israel: 22 "The LORD [a]God of gods, the LORD God of gods, He [b]knows, and let Israel itself know—if *it is* in rebellion, or if in treachery against the LORD, do not save us this day. 23 If we have built ourselves an altar to turn from following the LORD, or if to offer on it burnt offerings or grain offerings, or if to offer peace offerings on it, let the LORD Himself [a]require *an account.* 24 But in fact we have done it for fear, for a reason, saying, 'In time to come your descendants may speak to our descendants, saying, "What have you to do with the LORD God of Israel? 25 For the LORD has made the Jordan a border between you and us, *you* children of Reuben and children of Gad. You have no part in the LORD." So your descendants would make our descendants cease fearing the LORD.' 26 Therefore we said, 'Let us now prepare to build ourselves an altar, not for burnt offering nor for sacrifice, 27 but *that* it *may be* [a]a witness between you and us and our generations after us, that we may [b]perform the service of the LORD before Him with our burnt offerings, with our sacrifices, and with our peace offerings; that your descendants may not say to our descendants in time to come, "You have no part in the LORD." ' 28 Therefore we said that it will be, when they say *this* to us or to our generations in time to come, that we may say, 'Here is the replica of the altar of the LORD which our fathers made, though not for burnt offerings nor for sacrifices; but it *is* a witness between you and us.' 29 Far be it from us that we should rebel against the LORD, and turn from following the LORD this day, [a]to build an altar for burnt offerings, for grain offerings, or for sacrifices, besides the altar of the LORD our God which *is* before His tabernacle."

30 Now when Phinehas the priest and the rulers of the congregation, the heads of the divisions[1] of Israel who *were* with him, heard the words that the children of Reuben, the children of Gad, and the children of Manasseh spoke, it pleased them. 31 Then Phinehas the son of Eleazar the priest said to the children of Reuben, the children of Gad, and the children of Manasseh, "This day we perceive that the LORD *is* [a]among us, because you have not committed this treachery against the LORD. Now you have delivered the children of Israel out of the hand of the LORD."

32 And Phinehas the son of Eleazar the priest, and the rulers, returned from the children of Reuben and the children of Gad, from the land of Gilead to the land of Canaan, to the children of Israel, and brought back word to them. 33 So the thing pleased the children of Israel, and the children of Israel [a]blessed God; they spoke no more of going against them in battle, to destroy the land where the children of Reuben and Gad dwelt.

34 The children of Reuben and the children of Gad[1] called the altar, *Witness,* "For *it is* a witness between us that the LORD *is* God."

### *JOSHUA'S FAREWELL ADDRESS*

**23** Now it came to pass, a long time after the LORD [a]had given rest to Israel from all their enemies round about, that Joshua [b]was old, advanced in age. 2 And Joshua [a]called for all Israel, for their elders, for their heads, for their judges, and for their officers, and said to them:

"I am old, advanced in age. 3 You have seen all that the [a]LORD your God has done to all

22:12 [a] Josh. 18:1; Judg. 20:1 22:13 [a] Deut. 13:14; Judg. 20:12 [b] Ex. 6:25; Num. 25:7, 11–13 22:14 [a] Num. 1:4 [1] Literally *thousands* 22:16 [a] Deut. 12:5–14 [b] Lev. 17:8, 9 22:17 [a] Num. 25:1–9; Deut. 4:3 22:18 [a] Num. 16:22 22:19 [a] Josh. 18:1 22:20 [a] Josh. 7:1–26 22:21 [1] Literally *thousands* 22:22 [a] Deut. 4:35; 10:17; Is. 44:8; 45:5; 46:9; [1 Cor. 8:5, 6] [b] [Job 10:7; 23:10; Jer. 12:3; 2 Cor. 11:11, 31] 22:23 [a] Deut. 18:19; 1 Sam. 20:16 22:27 [a] Gen. 31:48; Josh. 22:34; 24:27 [b] Deut. 12:5, 14 22:29 [a] Deut. 12:13, 14 22:30 [1] Literally *thousands* 22:31 [a] Ex. 25:8; Lev. 26:11, 12; 2 Chr. 15:2; Zech. 8:23 22:33 [a] 1 Chr. 29:20; Neh. 8:6; Dan. 2:19; Luke 2:28 22:34 [1] Septuagint adds *and half the tribe of Manasseh.* 23:1 [a] Josh. 21:44; 22:4 [b] Josh. 13:1; 24:29 23:2 [a] Deut. 31:28 23:3 [a] Ps. 44:3

these nations because of you, for the [b]LORD
your God *is* He who has fought for you. 4 See,
[a]I have divided to you by lot these nations that
remain, to be an inheritance for your tribes,
from the Jordan, with all the nations that I
have cut off, as far as the Great Sea westward.
5 And the LORD your God [a]will expel them from
before you and drive them out of your sight.
So you shall possess their land, [b]as the LORD
your God promised you. 6 [a]Therefore be very
courageous to keep and to do all that is written
in the Book of the Law of Moses, [b]lest you turn
aside from it to the right hand or to the left,
7 *and* lest you [a]go among these nations, these
who remain among you. You shall not [b]make
mention of the name of their gods, nor cause
*anyone* to [c]swear *by them;* you shall not [d]serve
them nor bow down to them, 8 but you shall
[a]hold fast to the LORD your God, as you have
done to this day. 9 [a]For the LORD has driven
out from before you great and strong nations;
but *as for* you, no one has been able to stand
against you to this day. 10 [a]One man of you
shall chase a thousand, for the LORD your God
*is* He who fights for you, [b]as He promised you.
11 [a]Therefore take careful heed to yourselves,
that you love the LORD your God. 12 Or else,
if indeed you do [a]go back, and cling to the
remnant of these nations—these that remain
among you—and [b]make marriages with them,
and go in to them and they to you, 13 know for
certain that [a]the LORD your God will no lon-
ger drive out these nations from before you.
[b]But they shall be snares and traps to you, and
scourges on your sides and thorns in your eyes,
until you perish from this good land which the
LORD your God has given you.

14 "Behold, this day [a]I *am* going the way of all
the earth. And you know in all your hearts and in
all your souls that [b]not one thing has failed of all
the good things which the LORD your God spoke
concerning you. All have come to pass for you;
not one word of them has failed. 15 [a]Therefore
it shall come to pass, that as all the good things
have come upon you which the LORD your God
promised you, so the LORD will bring upon you
[b]all harmful things, until He has destroyed you
from this good land which the LORD your God
has given you. 16 When you have transgressed
the covenant of the LORD your God, which He
commanded you, and have gone and served
other gods, and bowed down to them, then the
[a]anger of the LORD will burn against you, and
you shall perish quickly from the good land
which He has given you."

## *THE COVENANT AT SHECHEM*

*(cf. Ex. 24:9–18)*

24 Then Joshua gathered all the tribes of Is-
rael to [a]Shechem and [b]called for the elders
of Israel, for their heads, for their judges, and for
their officers; and they [c]presented themselves
before God. 2 And Joshua said to all the people,
"Thus says the LORD God of Israel: [a]'Your fathers,
*including* Terah, the father of Abraham and the
father of Nahor, dwelt on the other side of the
River[1] in old times; and [b]they served other gods.
3 [a]Then I took your father Abraham from the
other side of the River, led him throughout all the
land of Canaan, and multiplied his descendants
and [b]gave him Isaac. 4 To Isaac I gave [a]Jacob and
Esau. To [b]Esau I gave the mountains of Seir to
possess, [c]but Jacob and his children went down
to Egypt. 5 [a]Also I sent Moses and Aaron, and [b]I
plagued Egypt, according to what I did among
them. Afterward I brought you out.

6 'Then I [a]brought your fathers out of Egypt,
and you came to the sea; and the Egyptians pur-
sued your fathers with chariots and horsemen
to the Red Sea. 7 So they cried out to the LORD;
and He put [a]darkness between you and the Egyp-
tians, brought the sea upon them, and covered
them. And [b]your eyes saw what I did in Egypt.
Then you dwelt in the wilderness [c]a long time.
8 And I brought you into the land of the Amorites,
who dwelt on the other side of the Jordan, [a]and
they fought with you. But I gave them into your
hand, that you might possess their land, and I
destroyed them from before you. 9 Then [a]Balak
the son of Zippor, king of Moab, arose to make
war against Israel, and [b]sent and called Balaam
the son of Beor to curse you. 10 [a]But I would not
listen to Balaam; [b]therefore he continued to bless
you. So I delivered you out of his hand. 11 Then
[a]you went over the Jordan and came to Jericho.
And [b]the men of Jericho fought against you—
*also* the Amorites, the Perizzites, the Canaanites,
the Hittites, the Girgashites, the Hivites, and the
Jebusites. But I delivered them into your hand.
12 [a]I sent the hornet before you which drove them
out from before you, *also* the two kings of the
Amorites, *but* [b]not with your sword or with your
bow. 13 I have given you a land for which you did
not labor, and [a]cities which you did not build, and
you dwell in them; you eat of the vineyards and
olive groves which you did not plant.'

14 [a]"Now therefore, fear the LORD, serve Him
in [b]sincerity and in truth, and [c]put away the gods
which your fathers served on the other side of
the River and [d]in Egypt. Serve the LORD! 15 And
if it seems evil to you to serve the LORD, [a]choose

**23:3** [b] Ex. 14:14; Deut. 1:30; Josh. 10:14, 42 **23:4** [a] Josh. 13:2, 6; 18:10 **23:5** [a] Ex. 23:30; 33:2 [b] Num. 33:53 **23:6** [a] Josh. 1:7 [b] Deut. 5:32 **23:7** [a] Deut. 7:2, 3 [b] Ex. 23:13 [c] Deut. 6:13; 10:20 [d] Ex. 20:5 **23:8** [a] Deut. 10:20 **23:9** [a] Deut. 7:24; 11:23 **23:10** [a] Lev. 26:8 [b] Ex. 14:14 **23:11** [a] Josh. 22:5 **23:12** [a] [2 Pet. 2:20, 21] [b] Deut. 7:3, 4 **23:13** [a] Judg. 2:3 [b] Ex. 23:33; 34:12 **23:14** [a] 1 Kin. 2:2 [b] Josh. 21:45 **23:15** [a] Deut. 28:63 [b] Deut. 28:15–68 **23:16** [a] Deut. 4:24–28 **24:1** [a] Gen. 35:4 [b] Josh. 23:2 [c] 1 Sam. 10:19 **24:2** [a] Gen. 11:7–32 [b] Josh. 24:14 [1] Hebrew *Nahar,* the Euphrates, and so in verses 3, 14, and 15 **24:3** [a] Gen. 12:1; Acts 7:2, 3 [b] [Ps. 127:3] **24:4** [a] Gen. 25:24–26 [b] Deut. 2:5 [c] Gen. 46:1, 3, 6 **24:5** [a] Ex. 3:10 [b] Ex. 7—10 **24:6** [a] Ex. 12:37, 51; 14:2–31 **24:7** [a] Ex. 14:20 [b] Deut. 4:34 [c] Josh. 5:6 **24:8** [a] Num. 21:21–35 **24:9** [a] Judg. 11:25 [b] Num. 22:2–14 **24:10** [a] Deut. 23:5 [b] Num. 23:11, 20; 24:10 **24:11** [a] Josh. 3:14, 17 [b] Josh. 6:1; 10:1 **24:12** [a] Ex. 23:28 [b] Ps. 44:3 **24:13** [a] Deut. 6:10, 11 **24:14** [a] 1 Sam. 12:24 [b] 2 Cor. 1:12 [c] Ezek. 20:18 [d] Ezek. 20:7, 8 **24:15** [a] 1 Kin. 18:21

LIVE THE TRUTH

## BEING ENGAGED AT HOME

**24:14–15** God has established the home to be central for the flourishing of humanity and the development of communities. It's been God's plan since the beginning and always will be. Think about your family—the people God has placed in your life—and how they have affected your life. God put these people around you to help you become the person He wants you to be. That means your siblings, parents or guardians, grandparents, and other family members are all God's gift to you. Even if it doesn't always feel that way, your homelife is part of God's perfect plan.

Joshua announced the purpose of homelife is loving and serving the Lord together. No matter what the people around you are doing, help guide your home toward increasing love for God and trust in Him. Avoid disconnecting from others at home; instead, engage in God's purposes for your family. Your family is one of the most important parts of your life. Each member of your family has something to give you or teach you that no one else can. The inverse is also true. When you see yourself as an invaluable part of your family and step into the role God has for you, you'll be able to help them as well.

for yourselves this day whom you will serve,
whether [b]the gods which your fathers served that
*were* on the other side of the River, or [c]the gods
of the Amorites, in whose land you dwell. [d]But
as for me and my house, we will serve the LORD."
16 So the people answered and said: "Far be
it from us that we should forsake the LORD to
serve other gods; 17 for the LORD our God *is* He
who brought us and our fathers up out of the
land of Egypt, from the house of bondage, who
did those great signs in our sight, and preserved
us in all the way that we went and among all the
people through whom we passed. 18 And the
LORD drove out from before us all the people,
including the Amorites who dwelt in the land.
[a]We also will serve the LORD, for He *is* our God."
19 But Joshua said to the people, [a]"You can-
not serve the LORD, for He *is* a [b]holy God. He *is*
[c]a jealous God; [d]He will not forgive your trans-
gressions nor your sins. 20 [a]If you forsake the
LORD and serve foreign gods, [b]then He will turn
and do you harm and consume you, after He
has done you good."
21 And the people said to Joshua, "No, but
we will serve the LORD!"
22 So Joshua said to the people, "You *are*
witnesses against yourselves that [a]you have
chosen the LORD for yourselves, to serve Him."
And they said, "*We are* witnesses!"
23 "Now therefore," *he said,* [a]"put away the
foreign gods which *are* among you, and [b]incline
your heart to the LORD God of Israel."
24 And the people [a]said to Joshua, "The LORD
our God we will serve, and His voice we will
obey!"
25 So Joshua [a]made a covenant with the
people that day, and made for them a statute
and an ordinance [b]in Shechem.
26 Then Joshua [a]wrote these words in the
Book of the Law of God. And he took [b]a large
stone, and [c]set it up there [d]under the oak that
*was* by the sanctuary of the LORD. 27 And Josh-
ua said to all the people, "Behold, this stone
shall be [a]a witness to us, for [b]it has heard all the
words of the LORD which He spoke to us. It shall
therefore be a witness to you, lest you deny your
God." 28 So [a]Joshua let the people depart, each
to his own inheritance.

### *DEATH OF JOSHUA AND ELEAZAR*

29 [a]Now it came to pass after these things
that Joshua the son of Nun, the servant of the
LORD, died, *being* one hundred and ten years
old. 30 And they buried him within the border
of his inheritance at [a]Timnath Serah, which *is*
in the mountains of Ephraim, on the north side
of Mount Gaash.
31 [a]Israel served the LORD all the days of Josh-
ua, and all the days of the elders who outlived
Joshua, who had [b]known all the works of the
LORD which He had done for Israel.
32 [a]The bones of Joseph, which the children
of Israel had brought up out of Egypt, they bur-
ied at Shechem, in the plot of ground [b]which
Jacob had bought from the sons of Hamor the
father of Shechem for one hundred pieces of
silver, and which had become an inheritance
of the children of Joseph.
33 And [a]Eleazar the son of Aaron died. They
buried him in a hill *belonging to* [b]Phinehas his
son, which was given to him in the mountains
of Ephraim.

24:15 [b] Josh. 24:2 [c] Ex. 23:24, 32 [d] Gen. 18:19 24:18 [a] Ps. 116:16 24:19 [a] Matt. 6:24 [b] 1 Sam. 6:20 [c] Ex. 20:5 [d] Ex. 23:21 24:20 [a] Ezra 8:22 [b] Deut. 4:24–26 24:22 [a] Ps. 119:173 24:23 [a] Gen. 35:2 [b] 1 Kin. 8:57, 58 24:24 [a] Deut. 5:24–27 24:25 [a] Ex. 15:25 [b] Josh. 24:1 24:26 [a] Deut. 31:24 [b] Judg. 9:6 [c] Gen. 28:18 [d] Gen. 35:4 24:27 [a] Gen. 31:48 [b] Deut. 32:1 24:28 [a] Judg. 2:6, 7 24:29 [a] Judg. 2:8 24:30 [a] Josh. 19:50 24:31 [a] Judg. 2:7 [b] Deut. 11:2 24:32 [a] Gen. 50:25 [b] Gen. 33:19 24:33 [a] Ex. 28:1 [b] Ex. 6:25

# *The Book of*
# JUDGES

**AUTHOR**
Samuel, likely

**KEY VERSES**
Judges 2:11–12

**READING TIME**
2 hours 4 minutes

The Book of Judges stands in stark contrast to the Book of Joshua. In Joshua, an obedient people conquered the land because of their trust in God. In Judges, an idolatrous people were conquered time and time again because of their rebellion against God. In seven distinct cycles of sin to salvation, Judges shows how the Israelites set aside God's law and substituted "what was right in [their] own eyes" (Judg. 21:25) in its place. But each time they did, internal corruption and external oppression followed. During the nearly four centuries spanned by this book, God raised military champions called judges to throw off the yoke of bondage and restore the nation to worship the one true God. But then after the judge was gone, the people rebelled yet again, and the cycle of sin began all over.

**Occasion:** The Book of Judges reveals the struggles of the Israelites in the Promised Land when they were without godly leaders and sets the stage for God's provision of the prophet Samuel's leadership.

**Main Point:** Generations of Israelites rebel against God and experience His discipline and judgment to bring them to repentance.

**Big Ideas:** Our sinful hearts long for independence from God. God is patient, but because He loves us, He will not leave us in our sin. The answer we need for our sin cannot be found anywhere but in God.

**OUTLINE:**

I. The People Sin (chs. 1–2)
II. Othniel, Ehud, and Shamgar (ch. 3)
III. Deborah, Barak, and Jael (chs. 4–5)
IV. Gideon (chs. 6–8)
V. Abimelech (ch. 9)
VI. Tola, Jair, Jephthah, Ibzan, Elon, and Abdon (chs. 10–12)
VII. Samson (chs. 13–16)
VIII. The People Continue to Sin (chs. 17–19)
IX. The People Fight Themselves (chs. 20–21)

**c. 1405–1400 BC**
The conquest of Canaan

**c. 1398 BC**
Canaan is apportioned to the tribes

**c. 1380 BC**
Joshua dies

**c. 1370 BC**
Othniel is judge over Israel

**c. 1310 BC**
Ehud is judge over Israel

**c. 1230 BC**
Deborah is victorious over Sisera

**c. 1200 BC**
Troy falls to the Greeks

**c. 1190 BC**
Gideon is judge over Israel

**c. 1100 BC**
Samson is judge over Israel

**c. 1100 BC**
Lumber trade by sea between Lebanon and Egypt thrives

**c. 1100–1010 BC**
Samuel's prophetic ministry

**c. 1050 BC**
Saul becomes king of Israel

**c. 1040–1020 BC**
**Judges written**

### *THE CONTINUING CONQUEST OF CANAAN*

*(Josh. 15:13–19)*

**1** Now after the [a]death of Joshua it came to pass that the children of Israel [b]asked the LORD, saying, "Who shall be first to go up for us against the [c]Canaanites to fight against them?"

2 And the LORD said, [a]"Judah shall go up. Indeed I have delivered the land into his hand."

3 So Judah said to [a]Simeon his brother, "Come up with me to my allotted territory, that we may fight against the Canaanites; and [b]I will likewise go with you to your allotted territory." And Simeon went with him. 4 Then Judah went up, and the LORD delivered the Canaanites and the Perizzites into their hand; and they killed ten thousand men at [a]Bezek. 5 And they found Adoni-Bezek in Bezek, and fought against him; and they defeated the Canaanites and the Perizzites. 6 Then Adoni-Bezek fled, and they pursued him and caught him and cut off his thumbs and big toes. 7 And Adoni-Bezek said, "Seventy kings with their thumbs and big toes cut off used to gather *scraps* under my table; [a]as I have done, so God has repaid me." Then they brought him to Jerusalem, and there he died.

8 Now [a]the children of Judah fought against Jerusalem and took it; they struck it with the edge of the sword and set the city on fire. 9 [a]And afterward the children of Judah went down to fight against the Canaanites who dwelt in the mountains, in the South,[1] and in the lowland. 10 Then Judah went against the Canaanites who dwelt in [a]Hebron. (Now the name of Hebron *was* formerly [b]Kirjath Arba.) And they killed Sheshai, Ahiman, and Talmai.

11 [a]From there they went against the inhabitants of Debir. (The name of Debir *was* formerly Kirjath Sepher.)

12 [a]Then Caleb said, "Whoever attacks Kirjath Sepher and takes it, to him I will give my daughter Achsah as wife." 13 And Othniel the son of Kenaz, [a]Caleb's younger brother, took it; so he gave him his daughter Achsah as wife. 14 [a]Now it happened, when she came *to him,* that she urged him[1] to ask her father for a field. And she dismounted from *her* donkey, and Caleb said to her, "What do you wish?" 15 So she said to him, [a]"Give me a blessing; since you have given me land in the South, give me also springs of water."

And Caleb gave her the upper springs and the lower springs.

16 [a]Now the children of the Kenite, Moses' father-in-law, went up [b]from the City of Palms with the children of Judah into the Wilderness of Judah, which *lies* in the South *near* [c]Arad; [d]and they went and dwelt among the people. 17 [a]And Judah went with his brother Simeon, and they attacked the Canaanites who inhabited Zephath, and utterly destroyed it. So the name of the city was called [b]Hormah. 18 Also Judah took [a]Gaza with its territory, Ashkelon with its territory, and Ekron with its territory. 19 So the LORD was with Judah. And they drove out the mountaineers, but they could not drive out the inhabitants of the lowland, because they had [a]chariots of iron. 20 [a]And they gave Hebron to Caleb, as Moses had said. Then he expelled from there the [b]three sons of Anak. 21 [a]But the children of Benjamin did not drive out the Jebusites who inhabited Jerusalem; so the Jebusites dwell with the children of Benjamin in Jerusalem to this day.

> **1:21** This verse duplicates Joshua 15:63 almost exactly, except in Joshua, the tribe of Judah was held responsible. **Jerusalem** lay on the border between Judah and **Benjamin**; either or both tribes were responsible for driving out the **Jebusites**. Jerusalem was captured and burned, but not settled. Their failure to do so was not because the task was too hard, but because they didn't really take God's commands and promises seriously. Jerusalem was not claimed for Israel until David's day (see 2 Sam. 5:6–10).

22 And the house of Joseph also went up against Bethel, [a]and the LORD *was* with them. 23 So the house of Joseph [a]sent men to spy out Bethel. (The name of the city *was* formerly [b]Luz.) 24 And when the spies saw a man coming out of the city, they said to him, "Please show us the entrance to the city, and [a]we will show you mercy." 25 So he showed them the entrance to the city, and they struck the city with the edge of the sword; but they let the man and all his family go. 26 And the man went to the land of the Hittites, built a city, and called its name Luz, which *is* its name to this day.

### *INCOMPLETE CONQUEST OF THE LAND*

27 [a]However, Manasseh did not drive out *the inhabitants of* Beth Shean and its villages, or [b]Taanach and its villages, or the inhabitants of [c]Dor and its villages, or the inhabitants of Ibleam and its villages, or the inhabitants of Megiddo and its villages; for the Canaanites were determined to dwell in that land. 28 And it came to pass, when Israel was strong, that they put the Canaanites under tribute, but did not completely drive them out.

**1:1** [a] Josh. 24:29 [b] Num. 27:21; Judg. 20:18 [c] Josh. 17:12, 13 **1:2** [a] Gen. 49:8, 9; Rev. 5:5 **1:3** [a] Josh. 19:1 [b] Judg. 1:17 **1:4** [a] 1 Sam. 11:8 **1:7** [a] Lev. 24:19; 1 Sam. 15:33; [James 2:13] **1:8** [a] Josh. 15:63; Judg. 1:21 **1:9** [a] Josh. 10:36; 11:21; 15:13 [1] Hebrew *Negev,* and so throughout this book **1:10** [a] Josh. 15:13–19 [b] Josh. 14:15 **1:11** [a] Josh. 15:15 **1:12** [a] Josh. 15:16, 17 **1:13** [a] Judg. 3:9 **1:14** [a] Josh. 15:18, 19 [1] Septuagint and Vulgate read *he urged her.* **1:15** [a] Gen. 33:11 **1:16** [a] Num. 10:29–32; Judg. 4:11, 17; 1 Sam. 15:6; 1 Chr. 2:55 [b] Deut. 34:3; Judg. 3:13 [c] Josh. 12:14 [d] 1 Sam. 15:6 **1:17** [a] Judg. 1:3 [b] Num. 21:3; Josh. 19:4 **1:18** [a] Josh. 11:22 **1:19** [a] Josh. 17:16, 18; Judg. 4:3, 13 **1:20** [a] Num. 14:24; Josh. 14:9, 14 [b] Josh. 15:14; Judg. 1:10 **1:21** [a] Josh. 15:63; Judg. 1:8 **1:22** [a] Judg. 1:19 **1:23** [a] Josh. 2:1; 7:2 [b] Gen. 28:19 **1:24** [a] Josh. 2:12, 14 **1:27** [a] Josh. 17:11–13 [b] Josh. 21:25 [c] Josh. 17:11

29 [a]Nor did Ephraim drive out the Canaanites
who dwelt in Gezer; so the Canaanites dwelt in
Gezer among them.

30 Nor did [a]Zebulun drive out the inhabitants
of Kitron or the inhabitants of Nahalol; so the
Canaanites dwelt among them, and were put
under tribute.

31 [a]Nor did Asher drive out the inhabitants
of Acco or the inhabitants of Sidon, or of Ahlab,
Achzib, Helbah, Aphik, or Rehob. 32 So the Asher-
ites [a]dwelt among the Canaanites, the inhab-
itants of the land; for they did not drive them out.

33 [a]Nor did Naphtali drive out the inhabitants
of Beth Shemesh or the inhabitants of Beth
Anath; but they dwelt among the Canaanites,
the inhabitants of the land. Nevertheless the
inhabitants of Beth Shemesh and Beth Anath
were put under tribute to them.

34 And the Amorites forced the children of
Dan into the mountains, for they would not
allow them to come down to the valley; 35 and
the Amorites were determined to dwell in Mount
Heres, [a]in Aijalon, and in Shaalbim;[1] yet when
the strength of the house of Joseph became
greater, they were put under tribute.

36 Now the boundary of the Amorites *was*
[a]from the Ascent of Akrabbim, from Sela, and
upward.

### *ISRAEL'S DISOBEDIENCE*

2 Then the Angel of the LORD came up from
Gilgal to Bochim, and said: [a]"I led you up
from Egypt and [b]brought you to the land of
which I swore to your fathers; and [c]I said, 'I will
never break My covenant with you. 2 And [a]you
shall make no covenant with the inhabitants of
this land; [b]you shall tear down their altars.' [c]But
you have not obeyed My voice. Why have you
done this? 3 Therefore I also said, 'I will not drive
them out before you; but they shall be [a]*thorns*
in your side,[1] and [b]their gods shall be a [c]snare
to you.' " 4 So it was, when the Angel of the LORD
spoke these words to all the children of Israel,
that the people lifted up their voices and wept.

5 Then they called the name of that place
Bochim;[1] and they sacrificed there to the LORD.
6 And when [a]Joshua had dismissed the people,
the children of Israel went each to his own in-
heritance to possess the land.

### *DEATH OF JOSHUA*

*(Josh. 24:29–31)*

7 [a]So the people served the LORD all the days
of Joshua, and all the days of the elders who out-
lived Joshua, who had seen all the great works
of the LORD which He had done for Israel. 8 Now
[a]Joshua the son of Nun, the servant of the LORD,
died *when he was* one hundred and ten years old.
9 [a]And they buried him within the border of his
inheritance at [b]Timnath Heres, in the mountains
of Ephraim, on the north side of Mount Gaash.
10 When all that generation had been gathered
to their fathers, another generation arose after
them who [a]did not know the LORD nor the work
which He had done for Israel.

### *ISRAEL'S UNFAITHFULNESS*

11 Then the children of Israel did [a]evil in the
sight of the LORD, and served the Baals; 12 and
they [a]forsook the LORD God of their fathers, who
had brought them out of the land of Egypt; and
they followed [b]other gods from *among* the gods
of the people who *were* all around them, and
they [c]bowed down to them; and they provoked
the LORD to anger. 13 They forsook the LORD
[a]and served Baal and the Ashtoreths.[1] 14 [a]And the
anger of the LORD was hot against Israel. So He
[b]delivered them into the hands of plunderers
who despoiled them; and [c]He sold them into the
hands of their enemies all around, so that they
[d]could no longer stand before their enemies.
15 Wherever they went out, the hand of the LORD
was against them for calamity, as the LORD had
said, and as the LORD had [a]sworn to them. And
they were greatly distressed.

16 Nevertheless, [a]the LORD raised up judges
who delivered them out of the hand of those
who plundered them. 17 Yet they would not lis-
ten to their judges, but they [a]played the harlot
with other gods, and bowed down to them. They
turned quickly from the way in which their fa-
thers walked, in obeying the commandments of
the LORD; they did not do so. 18 And when the
LORD raised up judges for them, [a]the LORD was
with the judge and delivered them out of the
hand of their enemies all the days of the judge;
[b]for the LORD was moved to pity by their groan-
ing because of those who oppressed them and

**SEEING JESUS IN THE SCRIPTURE**

**2:16** When the Israelites' sins brought God's hand against them, He sent judges to save and rule over them. These judges could only deliver God's people from the effects of their sin. Jesus, the perfect Judge and Savior, rescues us from sin itself (see 2 Tim. 4:1).

1:29 [a] Josh. 16:10; 1 Kin. 9:16 1:30 [a] Josh. 19:10–16 1:31 [a] Josh. 19:24–31 1:32 [a] Ps. 106:34, 35 1:33 [a] Josh. 19:32–39 1:35 [a] Josh. 19:42 [1] Spelled *Shaalabbin* in Joshua 19:42 1:36 [a] Num. 34:4; Josh. 15:3 2:1 [a] Ex. 20:2; Judg. 6:8, 9 [b] Deut. 1:8 [c] Gen. 17:7, 8; Lev. 26:42, 44; Deut. 7:9; Ps. 89:34 2:2 [a] Ex. 23:32; Deut. 7:2 [b] Ex. 34:12, 13; Deut. 12:3 [c] Ps. 106:34 2:3 [a] Num. 33:55; Josh. 23:13 [b] Judg. 3:6 [c] Ex. 23:33; Deut. 7:16; Ps. 106:36 [1] Septuagint, Targum, and Vulgate read *enemies to you.* 2:5 [1] Literally *Weeping* 2:6 [a] Josh. 22:6; 24:28–31 2:7 [a] Josh. 24:31 2:8 [a] Josh. 24:29 2:9 [a] Josh. 24:30 [b] Josh. 19:49, 50 2:10 [a] Ex. 5:2; 1 Sam. 2:12; Gal. 4:8; [Titus 1:16] 2:11 [a] Judg. 3:7, 12; 4:1; 6:1 2:12 [a] Deut. 31:16; Judg. 8:33; 10:6 [b] Deut. 6:14 [c] Ex. 20:5 2:13 [a] Judg. 10:6; Ps. 106:36 [1] Canaanite goddesses 2:14 [a] Deut. 31:17; Judg. 3:8; Ps. 106:40–42 [b] 2 Kin. 17:20 [c] Is. 50:1 [d] Lev. 26:37; Josh. 7:12, 13 2:15 [a] Lev. 26:14–26; Deut. 28:15–68 2:16 [a] Judg. 3:9, 10, 15; Ps. 106:43–45 2:17 [a] Ex. 34:15 2:18 [a] Josh. 1:5 [b] Gen. 6:6

JUDGES 2:11–23

## ISRAEL'S SPIRAL OF SIN

20 STORY OF SCRIPTURE

### WHAT'S GOING ON?

Judges 2:11–23 presents a cyclical pattern that characterizes much of Israel's history during the time of the Judges. It's a cycle of rebellion, oppression, repentance, and deliverance. The Israelites, having settled in the land promised to them, repeatedly turned away from God to worship the idols of the surrounding nations. This rebellion led to their oppression by multiple nations. In their distress, the Israelites cried out to God, who, in His mercy, raised up judges to deliver them from their enemies. Yet, the cycle repeated as the nation continually fell back into sin after each deliverance.

### WHAT DOES THIS MEAN FOR ME?

The story of Israel in Judges prompts us to look for patterns of sin, complacency, or forgetfulness of God's faithfulness in our lives. It's easy to judge the Israelites for their repeated failings. Still, we often find ourselves in similar cycles, turning to God in times of need but drifting away when life is comfortable.

### DID YOU CATCH THE PATTERN?

The pattern in Judges is a microcosm of the Biblical narrative of sin and redemption. From the garden of Eden to the exiles of Israel and Judah, the Bible is filled with stories of humanity's rebellion against God and His gracious acts of redemption. This pattern reaches its climax in the New Testament, where Jesus Christ, the ultimate Judge and Savior, provides a final solution to the cycle of sin. Through Christ's life, death, and resurrection, we're offered a way out of our cycle of sin. Unlike the temporary deliverance by the judges, Jesus offers eternal redemption, breaking the power of sin and death. This story invites us to live in freedom and fullness through a relationship with Christ. Through the power of the Holy Spirit, we can break free of the cycle of sin.

*For the next* Story of Scripture *reading and devotion, turn to Judges 16:23–31 on page 259.*

harassed them. 19 And it came to pass, [a]when the
judge was dead, that they reverted and behaved
more corruptly than their fathers, by following
other gods, to serve them and bow down to them.
They did not cease from their own doings nor
from their stubborn way.
20 Then the anger of the LORD was hot
against Israel; and He said, "Because this nation has [a]transgressed My covenant which I
commanded their fathers, and has not heeded
My voice, 21 I also will no longer drive out before
them any of the nations which Joshua [a]left when
he died, 22 so [a]that through them I may [b]test
Israel, whether they will keep the ways of the
LORD, to walk in them as their fathers kept *them,*
or not." 23 Therefore the LORD left those nations,
without driving them out immediately; nor did
He deliver them into the hand of Joshua.

### *THE NATIONS REMAINING IN THE LAND*

3 Now these *are* [a]the nations which the LORD
left, that He might test Israel by them, *that
is,* all who had not known any of the wars in Canaan 2 (*this was* only so that the generations of
the children of Israel might be taught to know
war, at least those who had not formerly known
it), 3 *namely,* [a]five lords of the Philistines, all the
Canaanites, the Sidonians, and the Hivites who
dwelt in Mount Lebanon, from Mount Baal Hermon to the entrance of Hamath. 4 And they were
*left, that He might* test Israel by them, to know
whether they would obey the commandments
of the LORD, which He had commanded their
fathers by the hand of Moses.
5 [a]Thus the children of Israel dwelt among
the Canaanites, the Hittites, the Amorites, the
Perizzites, the Hivites, and the Jebusites. 6 And
[a]they took their daughters to be their wives,
and gave their daughters to their sons; and they
served their gods.

### *OTHNIEL*

7 So the children of Israel did [a]evil in the sight
of the LORD. They [b]forgot the LORD their God,
and served the Baals and Asherahs.[1] 8 Therefore
the anger of the LORD was hot against Israel,
and He [a]sold them into the hand of [b]Cushan-Rishathaim king of Mesopotamia; and the

**2:19** [a] Judg. 3:12 **2:20** [a] [Josh. 23:16] **2:21** [a] Josh. 23:4, 5, 13 **2:22** [a] Judg. 3:1, 4 [b] Deut. 8:2, 16; 13:3 **3:1** [a] Judg. 1:1; 2:21, 22 **3:3** [a] Josh. 13:3 **3:5** [a] Ps. 106:35 **3:6** [a] Ex. 34:15, 16; Deut. 7:3, 4; Josh. 23:12 **3:7** [a] Judg. 2:11 [b] Deut. 32:18 [1] Name or symbol for Canaanite goddesses **3:8** [a] Deut. 32:30; Judg. 2:14 [b] Hab. 3:7

children of Israel served Cushan-Rishathaim eight years. 9 When the children of Israel [a]cried out to the LORD, the LORD [b]raised up a deliverer for the children of Israel, who delivered them: [c]Othniel the son of Kenaz, Caleb's younger brother. 10 [a]The Spirit of the LORD came upon him, and he judged Israel. He went out to war, and the LORD delivered Cushan-Rishathaim king of Mesopotamia into his hand; and his hand prevailed over Cushan-Rishathaim. 11 So the land had rest for forty years. Then Othniel the son of Kenaz died.

### *EHUD*

12 [a]And the children of Israel again did evil in the sight of the LORD. So the LORD strengthened [b]Eglon king of Moab against Israel, because they had done evil in the sight of the LORD. 13 Then he gathered to himself the people of Ammon and [a]Amalek, went and defeated Israel, and took possession of [b]the City of Palms. 14 So the children of Israel [a]served Eglon king of Moab eighteen years.

15 But when the children of Israel [a]cried out to the LORD, the LORD raised up a deliverer for them: Ehud the son of Gera, the Benjamite, a [b]left-handed man. By him the children of Israel sent tribute to Eglon king of Moab. 16 Now Ehud made himself a dagger (it was double-edged and a cubit in length) and fastened it under his clothes on his right thigh. 17 So he brought the tribute to Eglon king of Moab. (Now Eglon *was* a very fat man.) 18 And when he had finished presenting the tribute, he sent away the people who had carried the tribute. 19 But he himself turned back [a]from the stone images that *were* at Gilgal, and said, "I have a secret message for you, O king."

He said, "Keep silence!" And all who attended him went out from him.

20 So Ehud came to him (now he was sitting upstairs in his cool private chamber). Then Ehud said, "I have a message from God for you." So he arose from *his* seat. 21 Then Ehud reached with his left hand, took the dagger from his right thigh, and thrust it into his belly. 22 Even the hilt went in after the blade, and the fat closed over the blade, for he did not draw the dagger out of his belly; and his entrails came out. 23 Then Ehud went out through the porch and shut the doors of the upper room behind him and locked them.

24 When he had gone out, *Eglon's*[1] servants came to look, and *to their* surprise, the doors of the upper room were locked. So they said, "He is probably [a]attending to his needs in the cool chamber." 25 So they waited till they were [a]embarrassed, and still he had not opened the doors of the upper room. Therefore they took the key and opened *them.* And there was their master, fallen dead on the floor.

26 But Ehud had escaped while they delayed, and passed beyond the stone images and escaped to Seirah. 27 And it happened, when he arrived, that [a]he blew the trumpet in the [b]mountains of Ephraim, and the children of Israel went down with him from the mountains; and he led them. 28 Then he said to them, "Follow *me,* for [a]the LORD has delivered your enemies the Moabites into your hand." So they went down after him, seized the [b]fords of the Jordan leading to Moab, and did not allow anyone to cross over. 29 And at that time they killed about ten thousand men of Moab, all stout men of valor; not a man escaped. 30 So Moab was subdued that day under the hand of Israel. And [a]the land had rest for eighty years.

### *SHAMGAR*

31 After him was [a]Shamgar the son of Anath, who killed six hundred men of the Philistines [b]with an ox goad; [c]and he also delivered [d]Israel.

### *DEBORAH*

4 When Ehud was dead, [a]the children of Israel again did [b]evil in the sight of the LORD. 2 So the LORD [a]sold them into the hand of Jabin king of Canaan, who reigned in [b]Hazor. The commander of his army *was* [c]Sisera, who dwelt in [d]Harosheth Hagoyim. 3 And the children of Israel cried out to the LORD; for Jabin had nine hundred [a]chariots of iron, and for twenty years [b]he had harshly oppressed the children of Israel.

4 Now Deborah, a prophetess, the wife of Lapidoth, was judging Israel at that time. 5 [a]And she would sit under the palm tree of Deborah between Ramah and Bethel in the mountains of Ephraim. And the children of Israel came up to her for judgment. 6 Then she sent and called for [a]Barak the son of Abinoam from [b]Kedesh in Naphtali, and said to him, "Has not the LORD God of Israel commanded, 'Go and deploy *troops* at Mount [c]Tabor; take with you ten thousand men

**4:4 Deborah** is shown in the best light of all the judges. She is called a **prophetess**, and many sought out her decisions (v. 5). For this reason, she is called "a mother in Israel" (Judg. 5:7). She is probably included among the leaders in Israel (5:2), and she instructed Barak in the strategy of the battle (4:9, 14). She was also a prominent author of the victory song (5:1) and gave her name to a place in Israel, the palm tree of Deborah (v. 5).

3:9 [a] Judg. 3:15 [b] Judg. 2:16 [c] Judg. 1:13 3:10 [a] Num. 27:18; 1 Sam. 11:6; 2 Chr. 15:1 3:12 [a] Judg. 2:19 [b] 1 Sam. 12:9 3:13 [a] Judg. 5:14 [b] Deut. 34:3; Judg. 1:16; 2 Chr. 28:15 3:14 [a] Deut. 28:48 3:15 [a] Ps. 78:34 [b] Judg. 20:16 3:19 [a] Josh. 4:20 3:24 [a] 1 Sam. 24:3 [1] Literally *his* 3:25 [a] 2 Kin. 2:17; 8:11 3:27 [a] Judg. 6:34; 1 Sam. 13:3 [b] Josh. 17:15 3:28 [a] Judg. 7:9, 15; 1 Sam. 17:47 [b] Josh. 2:7; Judg. 12:5 3:30 [a] Judg. 3:11 3:31 [a] Judg. 5:6 [b] 1 Sam. 17:47 [c] Judg. 2:16 [d] 1 Sam. 4:1 4:1 [a] Judg. 2:19 [b] Judg. 2:11 4:2 [a] Judg. 2:14 [b] Josh. 11:1, 10 [c] 1 Sam. 12:9; Ps. 83:9 [d] Judg. 4:13, 16 4:3 [a] Deut. 20:1; Judg. 1:19 [b] Ps. 106:42 4:5 [a] Gen. 35:8 4:6 [a] Heb. 11:32 [b] Josh. 19:37; 21:32 [c] Judg. 8:18

of the sons of Naphtali and of the sons of Zebulun; 7 and against you [a]I will deploy Sisera, the commander of Jabin's army, with his chariots and his multitude at the [b]River Kishon; and I will deliver him into your hand'?"

8 And Barak said to her, "If you will go with me, then I will go; but if you will not go with me, I will not go!"

9 So she said, "I will surely go with you; nevertheless there will be no glory for you in the journey you are taking, for the LORD will [a]sell Sisera into the hand of a woman." Then Deborah arose and went with Barak to Kedesh. 10 And Barak called [a]Zebulun and Naphtali to Kedesh; he went up with ten thousand men [b]under his command,[1] and Deborah went up with him.

11 Now Heber [a]the Kenite, of the children of [b]Hobab the father-in-law of Moses, had separated himself from the Kenites and pitched his tent near the terebinth tree at Zaanaim, [c]which *is* beside Kedesh.

12 And they reported to Sisera that Barak the son of Abinoam had gone up to Mount Tabor. 13 So Sisera gathered together all his chariots, nine hundred chariots of iron, and all the people who *were* with him, from Harosheth Hagoyim to the River Kishon.

14 Then Deborah said to Barak, "Up! For this *is* the day in which the LORD has delivered Sisera into your hand. [a]Has not the LORD gone out before you?" So Barak went down from Mount Tabor with ten thousand men following him. 15 And the LORD routed Sisera and all *his* chariots and all *his* army with the edge of the sword before Barak; and Sisera alighted from *his* chariot and fled away on foot. 16 But Barak pursued the chariots and the army as far as Harosheth Hagoyim, and all the army of Sisera fell by the edge of the sword; not a man was [a]left.

17 However, Sisera had fled away on foot to the tent of [a]Jael, the wife of Heber the Kenite; for *there was* peace between Jabin king of Hazor and the house of Heber the Kenite. 18 And Jael went out to meet Sisera, and said to him, "Turn aside, my lord, turn aside to me; do not fear." And when he had turned aside with her into the tent, she covered him with a blanket.

19 Then he said to her, "Please give me a little water to drink, for I am thirsty." So she opened [a]a jug of milk, gave him a drink, and covered him. 20 And he said to her, "Stand at the door of the tent, and if any man comes and inquires of you, and says, 'Is there any man here?' you shall say, 'No.' "

21 Then Jael, Heber's wife, [a]took a tent peg and took a hammer in her hand, and went softly to him and drove the peg into his temple, and it went down into the ground; for he was fast asleep and weary. So he died. 22 And then, as Barak pursued Sisera, Jael came out to meet him, and said to him, "Come, I will show you the man whom you seek." And when he went into her *tent,* there lay Sisera, dead with the peg in his temple.

23 So on that day God subdued Jabin king of Canaan in the presence of the children of Israel. 24 And the hand of the children of Israel grew stronger and stronger against Jabin king of Canaan, until they had destroyed Jabin king of Canaan.

## THE SONG OF DEBORAH

**5** Then Deborah and Barak the son of Abinoam [a]sang on that day, saying:

2 "When leaders [a]lead in Israel,
[b]When the people willingly offer themselves,
Bless the LORD!

3 "Hear,[a] O kings! Give ear, O princes!
I, *even* [b]I, will sing to the LORD;
I will sing praise to the LORD God of
Israel.

4 "LORD, [a]when You went out from Seir,
When You marched from [b]the field of
Edom,
The earth trembled and the heavens
poured,
The clouds also poured water;
5 [a]The mountains gushed before the LORD,
[b]This Sinai, before the LORD God of Israel.

6 "In the days of [a]Shamgar, son of Anath,
In the days of [b]Jael,
[c]The highways were deserted,
And the travelers walked along the
byways.
7 Village life ceased, it ceased in Israel,
Until I, Deborah, arose,
Arose a mother in Israel.
8 They chose [a]new gods;
Then *there was* war in the gates;
Not a shield or spear was seen among
forty thousand in Israel.
9 My heart *is* with the rulers of Israel
Who offered themselves willingly with the
people.
Bless the LORD!

10 "Speak, you who ride on white [a]donkeys,
Who sit in judges' attire,
And who walk along the road.
11 Far from the noise of the archers, among
the watering places,
There they shall recount the righteous
acts of the LORD,

4:7 [a] Ex. 14:4 [b] Judg. 5:21; 1 Kin. 18:40; Ps. 83:9, 10 4:9 [a] Judg. 2:14 4:10 [a] Judg. 5:18 [b] Ex. 11:8; 1 Kin. 20:10 [1] Literally *at his feet*
4:11 [a] Judg. 1:16 [b] Num. 10:29 [c] Judg. 4:6 4:14 [a] Deut. 9:3; 31:3; 2 Sam. 5:24; Ps. 68:7; Is. 52:12 4:16 [a] Ex. 14:28; Ps. 83:9
4:17 [a] Judg. 5:6 4:19 [a] Judg. 5:24–27 4:21 [a] Judg. 5:24–27 5:1 [a] Ex. 15:1; Judg. 4:4 5:2 [a] Ps. 18:47 [b] 2 Chr. 17:16
5:3 [a] Deut. 32:1, 3 [b] Ps. 27:6 5:4 [a] Deut. 33:2; Ps. 68:7 [b] Ps. 68:8 5:5 [a] Ps. 97:5 [b] Ex. 19:18 5:6 [a] Judg. 3:31 [b] Judg. 4:17 [c] Is. 33:8
5:8 [a] Deut. 32:17 5:10 [a] Judg. 10:4; 12:14

The righteous acts *for* His villagers in
Israel;
Then the people of the LORD shall go
down to the gates.

12 "Awake,[a] awake, Deborah!
Awake, awake, sing a song!
Arise, Barak, and lead your captives away,
O son of Abinoam!

13 "Then the survivors came down, the
people against the nobles;
The LORD came down for me against the
mighty.
14 From Ephraim *were* those whose roots
were in [a]Amalek.
After you, Benjamin, with your peoples,
From Machir rulers came down,
And from Zebulun those who bear the
recruiter's staff.
15 And the princes of Issachar[1] *were* with
Deborah;
As Issachar, so *was* Barak
Sent into the valley under his command;[2]
Among the divisions of Reuben
*There were* great resolves of heart.
16 Why did you sit among the sheepfolds,
To hear the pipings for the flocks?
The divisions of Reuben have great
searchings of heart.
17 [a]Gilead stayed beyond the Jordan,
And why did Dan remain on ships?[1]
[b]Asher continued at the seashore,
And stayed by his inlets.
18 [a]Zebulun *is* a people *who* jeopardized their
lives to the point of death,
Naphtali also, on the heights of the
battlefield.

19 "The kings came *and* fought,
Then the kings of Canaan fought
In [a]Taanach, by the waters of Megiddo;
They took no spoils of silver.
20 They fought from the heavens;
The stars from their courses fought
against Sisera.
21 [a]The torrent of Kishon swept them away,
That ancient torrent, the torrent of
Kishon.
O my soul, march on in strength!
22 Then the horses' hooves pounded,
The galloping, galloping of his steeds.
23 'Curse Meroz,' said the angel[1] of the
LORD,
'Curse its inhabitants bitterly,
Because they did not come to the help of
the LORD,
To the help of the LORD against the
mighty.'

24 "Most blessed among women is Jael,
The wife of Heber the Kenite;
[a]Blessed is she among women in tents.
25 He asked for water, she gave milk;
She brought out cream in a lordly bowl.
26 She stretched her hand to the tent peg,
Her right hand to the workmen's hammer;
She pounded Sisera, she pierced his head,
She split and struck through his temple.
27 At her feet he sank, he fell, he lay still;
At her feet he sank, he fell;
Where he sank, there he fell [a]dead.

28 "The mother of Sisera looked through the
window,
And cried out through the lattice,
'Why is his chariot *so* long in coming?
Why tarries the clatter of his chariots?'
29 Her wisest ladies answered her,
Yes, she answered herself,
30 'Are they not finding and dividing the spoil:
To every man a girl *or* two;
For Sisera, plunder of dyed garments,
Plunder of garments embroidered and
dyed,
Two pieces of dyed embroidery for the
neck of the looter?'

31 "Thus let all Your enemies [a]perish, O LORD!
But *let* those who love Him *be* [b]like the [c]sun
When it comes out in full [d]strength."

So the land had rest for forty years.

## MIDIANITES OPPRESS ISRAEL

6 Then the children of Israel did [a]evil in the
sight of the LORD. So the LORD delivered
them into the hand of [b]Midian for seven years,
2 and the hand of Midian prevailed against Israel.
Because of the Midianites, the children of Israel
made for themselves the dens, [a]the caves, and
the strongholds which *are* in the mountains. 3 So
it was, whenever Israel had sown, Midianites
would come up; also Amalekites and the [a]people
of the East would come up against them. 4 Then
they would encamp against them and [a]destroy
the produce of the earth as far as Gaza, and
leave no sustenance for Israel, neither sheep
nor ox nor [b]donkey. 5 For they would come up
with their livestock and their tents, coming in
as numerous as locusts; both they and their
camels were without number; and they would
enter the land to destroy it. 6 So Israel was greatly
impoverished because of the Midianites, and
the children of Israel [a]cried out to the LORD.
7 And it came to pass, when the children
of Israel cried out to the LORD because of the
Midianites, 8 that the LORD sent a prophet to
the children of Israel, who said to them, "Thus

5:12 [a] Ps. 57:8 5:14 [a] Judg. 3:13 5:15 [1] Following Septuagint, Syriac, Targum, and Vulgate; Masoretic Text reads *And my princes in Issachar.* [2] Literally *at his feet* 5:17 [a] Josh. 22:9 [b] Josh. 19:29, 31 [1] Or *at ease* 5:18 [a] Judg. 4:6, 10 5:19 [a] Judg. 1:27 5:21 [a] Judg. 4:7 5:23 [1] Or *Angel* 5:24 [a] [Luke 1:28] 5:27 [a] Judg. 4:18–21 5:31 [a] Ps. 92:9 [b] 2 Sam. 23:4 [c] Ps. 37:6; 89:36, 37 [d] Ps. 19:5 6:1 [a] Judg. 2:11 [b] Num. 22:4; 31:1–3 6:2 [a] 1 Sam. 13:6; Heb. 11:38 6:3 [a] Judg. 7:12 6:4 [a] Lev. 26:16 [b] Deut. 28:31 6:6 [a] Ps. 50:15; Hos. 5:15

says the LORD God of Israel: 'I brought you up
from Egypt and brought you out of the [a]house
of bondage; 9 and I delivered you out of the hand
of the Egyptians and out of the hand of all who
oppressed you, and [a]drove them out before you
and gave you their land. 10 Also I said to you, "I
*am* the LORD your God; [a]do not fear the gods of
the Amorites, in whose land you dwell." But you
have not obeyed My [b]voice.' "

### GIDEON

11 Now the Angel of the LORD came and sat
under the terebinth tree which *was* in Ophrah,
which *belonged* to Joash [a]the Abiezrite, while his
son [b]Gideon threshed wheat in the winepress,
in order to hide *it* from the Midianites. 12 And
the [a]Angel of the LORD appeared to him, and
said to him, "The LORD *is* [b]with you, you mighty
man of valor!"

13 Gideon said to Him, "O my lord,[1] if the LORD
is with us, why then has all this happened to
us? And [a]where *are* all His miracles [b]which our
fathers told us about, saying, 'Did not the LORD
bring us up from Egypt?' But now the LORD has
[c]forsaken us and delivered us into the hands of
the Midianites."

14 Then the LORD turned to him and said,
[a]"Go in this might of yours, and you shall save
Israel from the hand of the Midianites. [b]Have
I not sent you?"

15 So he said to Him, "O my Lord,[1] how can I
save Israel? Indeed [a]my clan *is* the weakest in Ma-
nasseh, and I *am* the least in my father's house."
16 And the LORD said to him, [a]"Surely I will
be with you, and you shall defeat the Midianites
as one man."

17 Then he said to Him, "If now I have found
favor in Your sight, then [a]show me a sign that it
is You who talk with me. 18 [a]Do not depart from
here, I pray, until I come to You and bring out
my offering and set *it* before You."

And He said, "I will wait until you come back."
19 [a]So Gideon went in and prepared a young
goat, and unleavened bread from an ephah of
flour. The meat he put in a basket, and he put the
broth in a pot; and he brought *them* out to Him
under the terebinth tree and presented *them.*
20 The Angel of God said to him, "Take the meat
and the unleavened bread and [a]lay *them* on this
rock, and [b]pour out the broth." And he did so.

21 Then the Angel of the LORD put out the end
of the staff that *was* in His hand, and touched
the meat and the unleavened bread; and [a]fire
rose out of the rock and consumed the meat
and the unleavened bread. And the Angel of
the LORD departed out of his sight.

22 Now Gideon [a]perceived that He *was* the An-
gel of the LORD. So Gideon said, "Alas, O Lord GOD!
[b]For I have seen the Angel of the LORD face to face."
23 Then the LORD said to him, [a]"Peace *be* with
you; do not fear, you shall not die." 24 So Gide-
on built an altar there to the LORD, and called
it The-LORD-*Is*-Peace.[1] To this day it *is* still [a]in
Ophrah of the Abiezrites.

25 Now it came to pass the same night that
the LORD said to him, "Take your father's young
bull, the second bull of seven years old, and [a]tear
down the altar of [b]Baal that your father has, and
[c]cut down the wooden image[1] that *is* beside it;
26 and build an altar to the LORD your God on top
of this rock in the proper arrangement, and take
the second bull and offer a burnt sacrifice with the
wood of the image which you shall cut down." 27 So
Gideon took ten men from among his servants and
did as the LORD had said to him. But because he
feared his father's household and the men of the
city too much to do *it* by day, he did *it* by night.

### GIDEON DESTROYS THE ALTAR OF BAAL

28 And when the men of the city arose early
in the morning, there was the altar of Baal, torn
down; and the wooden image that *was* beside it
was cut down, and the second bull was being of-
fered on the altar *which had been* built. 29 So they
said to one another, "Who has done this thing?"
And when they had inquired and asked, they said,
"Gideon the son of Joash has done this thing."
30 Then the men of the city said to Joash, "Bring
out your son, that he may die, because he has
torn down the altar of Baal, and because he has
cut down the wooden image that *was* beside it."

31 But Joash said to all who stood against
him, "Would you plead for Baal? Would you save
him? Let the one who would plead for him be
put to death by morning! If he *is* a god, let him
plead for himself, because his altar has been
torn down!" 32 Therefore on that day he called
him [a]Jerubbaal,[1] saying, "Let Baal plead against
him, because he has torn down his altar."

33 Then all [a]the Midianites and Amalekites, the
people of the East, gathered together; and they
crossed over and encamped in [b]the Valley of Jez-
reel. 34 But [a]the Spirit of the LORD came upon Gid-
eon; then he [b]blew the trumpet, and the Abiezrites
gathered behind him. 35 And he sent messengers
throughout all Manasseh, who also gathered be-
hind him. He also sent messengers to [a]Asher, [b]Zeb-
ulun, and Naphtali; and they came up to meet them.

### THE SIGN OF THE FLEECE

36 So Gideon said to God, "If You will save
Israel by my hand as You have said— 37 [a]look, I

6:8 [a] Josh. 24:17 6:9 [a] Ps. 44:2, 3 6:10 [a] 2 Kin. 17:35, 37, 38; Jer. 10:2 [b] Judg. 2:1, 2 6:11 [a] Josh. 17:2; Judg. 6:15 [b] Judg. 7:1; Heb. 11:32 6:12 [a] Judg. 13:3; Luke 1:11, 28 [b] Josh. 1:5 6:13 [a] [Is. 59:1] [b] Josh. 4:6, 21; Ps. 44:1 [c] Deut. 31:17; 2 Chr. 15:2; Ps. 44:9–16 [1] Hebrew *adoni,* used of man 6:14 [a] 1 Sam. 12:11 [b] Josh. 1:9 6:15 [a] 1 Sam. 9:21 [1] Hebrew *Adonai,* used of God 6:16 [a] Ex. 3:12; Josh. 1:5 6:17 [a] Judg. 6:36, 37; 2 Kin. 20:8; Ps. 86:17; Is. 7:11; 38:7, 8 6:18 [a] Gen. 18:3, 5 6:19 [a] Gen. 18:6–8 6:20 [a] Judg. 13:19 [b] 1 Kin. 18:33, 34 6:21 [a] Lev. 9:24 6:22 [a] Gen. 32:30; Ex. 33:20; Judg. 13:21, 22 [b] Gen. 16:13 6:23 [a] Dan. 10:19 6:24 [a] Judg. 8:32 [1] Hebrew *YHWH Shalom* 6:25 [a] Judg. 2:2 [b] Judg. 3:7 [c] Ex. 34:13; Deut. 7:5 [1] Hebrew *Asherah,* a Canaanite goddess 6:32 [a] Judg. 7:1; 1 Sam. 12:11; 2 Sam. 11:21 [1] Literally *Let Baal Plead* 6:33 [a] Judg. 6:3 [b] Josh. 17:16; Hos. 1:5 6:34 [a] Judg. 3:10; 1 Chr. 12:18; 2 Chr. 24:20 [b] Num. 10:3; Judg. 3:27 6:35 [a] Judg. 5:17; 7:23 [b] Judg. 4:6, 10; 5:18 6:37 [a] [Ex. 4:3–7]

KNOW THE TRUTH

# THE DOCTRINE OF THE HOLY SPIRIT

## PART 1: OVERVIEW OF THE DOCTRINE OF THE HOLY SPIRIT

**6:34–35** Gideon went from secretly threshing wheat to openly blowing a trumpet to gather a fighting force to defeat Midian. This shocking shift took place when the Spirit of God came upon him. All throughout the Bible, the Holy Spirit is at work in God's creation and in the lives of people. The third member of the Godhead is given many titles throughout Scripture: the Spirit of God, the Spirit of the Lord, the Holy Spirit, the Helper, and more.

In both Hebrew and Greek, the word *spirit* has to do with breath or wind. You can see someone breathe but can't see their breath. You can see things flail and flutter in the wind, but you can't see the wind. In a similar way, you can't see the Holy Spirit, but you can clearly see His work.

Like God the Father and God the Son, God the Holy Spirit is a Person, not an "it." The Bible refers to the Spirit as "He" in the same way it refers to the Father and the Son. Until Christ returns, the Holy Spirit is our step-by-step Teacher, Guide, and Comforter. The Spirit lives in the hearts of believers, empowering us to be witnesses for Christ, guiding our prayers, filling us with praise, progressively transforming us into Christ's image, leading us into freedom, and so much more.

*For* **THE DOCTRINE OF THE HOLY SPIRIT: PART 2: THE DEITY OF THE HOLY SPIRIT**, *turn to Zechariah 4:6–9 on page 938.*

shall put a fleece of wool on the threshing floor;
if there is dew on the fleece only, and *it is* dry on
all the ground, then I shall know that You will
save Israel by my hand, as You have said." 38 And
it was so. When he rose early the next morning
and squeezed the fleece together, he wrung the
dew out of the fleece, a bowlful of water. 39 Then
Gideon said to God, [a]"Do not be angry with me,
but let me speak just once more: Let me test, I
pray, just once more with the fleece; let it now
be dry only on the fleece, but on all the ground
let there be dew." 40 And God did so that night. It
was dry on the fleece only, but there was dew on
all the ground.

**6:39** Gideon's desire to confirm God's sign could have been a violation of the law which prohibited people from testing God (Deut. 6:16). In asking God not to be angry with him, apparently, Gideon knew he was doing something unwise, if not sinful.

### *GIDEON'S VALIANT THREE HUNDRED*

**7** Then [a]Jerubbaal (that *is,* Gideon) and all the
people who *were* with him rose early and
encamped beside the well of Harod, so that the
camp of the Midianites was on the north side of
them by the hill of Moreh in the valley.
2 And the LORD said to Gideon, "The people
who *are* with you *are* too many for Me to give the
Midianites into their hands, lest Israel [a]claim
glory for itself against Me, saying, 'My own hand
has saved me.' 3 Now therefore, proclaim in the
hearing of the people, saying, [a]'Whoever *is* fearful
and afraid, let him turn and depart at once from
Mount Gilead.'" And twenty-two thousand of the
people returned, and ten thousand remained.
4 But the LORD said to Gideon, "The people
*are* still *too* many; bring them down to the water,
and I will test them for you there. Then it will
be, *that* of whom I say to you, 'This one shall go
with you,' the same shall go with you; and of
whomever I say to you, 'This one shall not go
with you,' the same shall not go." 5 So he brought
the people down to the water. And the LORD said
to Gideon, "Everyone who laps from the water
with his tongue, as a dog laps, you shall set apart
by himself; likewise everyone who gets down on
his knees to drink." 6 And the number of those
who lapped, *putting* their hand to their mouth,
was three hundred men; but all the rest of the
people got down on their knees to drink water.
7 Then the LORD said to Gideon, [a]"By the three
hundred men who lapped I will save you, and
deliver the Midianites into your hand. Let all
the *other* people go, every man to his place." 8 So
the people took provisions and their trumpets
in their hands. And he sent away all *the rest of*
Israel, every man to his tent, and retained those
three hundred men. Now the camp of Midian
was below him in the valley.

**6:39** [a] Gen. 18:32 **7:1** [a] Judg. 6:32 **7:2** [a] Deut. 8:17; Is. 10:13 **7:3** [a] Deut. 20:8 **7:7** [a] 1 Sam. 14:6

**7:2–8** God reduced Gideon's army from 22,000 to 300 to emphasize who was really bringing victory. All the credit and glory—not just most of it—was to go to God.

9 It happened on the same [a]night that the
LORD said to him, "Arise, go down against the
camp, for I have delivered it into your hand.
10 But if you are afraid to go down, go down to
the camp with Purah your servant, 11 and you
shall [a]hear what they say; and afterward your
hands shall be strengthened to go down against
the camp." Then he went down with Purah his
servant to the outpost of the armed men who
*were* in the camp. 12 Now the Midianites and Am-
alekites, [a]all the people of the East, were lying
in the valley [b]as numerous as locusts; and their
camels *were* without number, as the sand by the
seashore in multitude.
13 And when Gideon had come, there was a
man telling a dream to his companion. He said,
"I have had a dream: *To my* surprise, a loaf of
barley bread tumbled into the camp of Midian;
it came to a tent and struck it so that it fell and
overturned, and the tent collapsed."
14 Then his companion answered and said,
"This *is* nothing else but the sword of Gideon
the son of Joash, a man of Israel! Into his hand
[a]God has delivered Midian and the whole camp."
15 And so it was, when Gideon heard the tell-
ing of the dream and its interpretation, that he
worshiped. He returned to the camp of Israel,
and said, "Arise, for the LORD has delivered
the camp of Midian into your hand." 16 Then he
divided the three hundred men *into* three com-
panies, and he put a trumpet into every man's
hand, with empty pitchers, and torches inside
the pitchers. 17 And he said to them, "Look at me
and do likewise; watch, and when I come to the
edge of the camp you shall do as I do: 18 When
I blow the trumpet, I and all who *are* with me,
then you also blow the trumpets on every side
of the whole camp, and say, '*The sword of* the
LORD and of Gideon!'"
19 So Gideon and the hundred men who *were*
with him came to the outpost of the camp at the
beginning of the middle watch, just as they had
posted the watch; and they blew the trumpets
and broke the pitchers that *were* in their hands.
20 Then the three companies blew the trumpets
and broke the pitchers—they held the torches in
their left hands and the trumpets in their right
hands for blowing—and they cried, "The sword
of the LORD and of Gideon!" 21 And [a]every man
stood in his place all around the camp; [b]and the
whole army ran and cried out and fled. 22 When
the three hundred [a]blew the trumpets, [b]the LORD
set [c]every man's sword against his companion
throughout the whole camp; and the army fled
to Beth Acacia,[1] toward Zererah, as far as the
border of [d]Abel Meholah, by Tabbath.
23 And the men of Israel gathered together
from [a]Naphtali, Asher, and all Manasseh, and
pursued the Midianites.
24 Then Gideon sent messengers throughout
all the [a]mountains of Ephraim, saying, "Come
down against the Midianites, and seize from them
the watering places as far as Beth Barah and the
Jordan." Then all the men of Ephraim gathered
together and [b]seized the watering places as far as
[c]Beth Barah and the Jordan. 25 And they captured
[a]two princes of the Midianites, [b]Oreb and Zeeb.
They killed Oreb at the rock of Oreb, and Zeeb
they killed at the winepress of Zeeb. They pursued
Midian and brought the heads of Oreb and Zeeb
to Gideon on the [c]other side of the Jordan.

## GIDEON SUBDUES THE MIDIANITES

8 Now [a]the men of Ephraim said to him, "Why
have you done this to us by not calling us
when you went to fight with the Midianites?"
And they reprimanded him sharply.
2 So he said to them, "What have I done now
in comparison with you? *Is* not the gleaning *of
the grapes* of Ephraim better than the vintage of
[a]Abiezer? 3 [a]God has delivered into your hands the
princes of Midian, Oreb and Zeeb. And what was
I able to do in comparison with you?" Then their
[b]anger toward him subsided when he said that.
4 When Gideon came [a]to the Jordan, he and
[b]the three hundred men who *were* with him
crossed over, exhausted but still in pursuit.
5 Then he said to the men of [a]Succoth, "Please
give loaves of bread to the people who follow
me, for they are exhausted, and I am pursuing
Zebah and Zalmunna, kings of Midian."
6 And the leaders of Succoth said, [a]"*Are* the
hands of Zebah and Zalmunna now in your
hand, that [b]we should give bread to your army?"
7 So Gideon said, "For this cause, when the
LORD has delivered Zebah and Zalmunna into my
hand, [a]then I will tear your flesh with the thorns
of the wilderness and with briers!" 8 Then he went
up from there [a]to Penuel and spoke to them in
the same way. And the men of Penuel answered
him as the men of Succoth had answered. 9 So he
also spoke to the men of Penuel, saying, "When I
[a]come back in peace, [b]I will tear down this tower!"
10 Now Zebah and Zalmunna *were* at Kar-
kor, and their armies with them, about fifteen
thousand, all who were left of [a]all the army of
the people of the East; for [b]one hundred and
twenty thousand men who drew the sword had

**7:9** [a] Gen. 46:2, 3; Judg. 6:25 **7:11** [a] Gen. 24:14; 1 Sam. 14:9, 10 **7:12** [a] Judg. 6:3, 33; 8:10 [b] Judg. 6:5 **7:14** [a] Judg. 6:14, 16 **7:21** [a] Ex. 14:13, 14; 2 Chr. 20:17 [b] 2 Kin. 7:7 **7:22** [a] Josh. 6:4, 16, 20 [b] Ps. 83:9; Is. 9:4 [c] 1 Sam. 14:20; 2 Chr. 20:23 [d] 1 Kin. 4:12 [1] Hebrew *Beth Shittah* **7:23** [a] Judg. 6:35 **7:24** [a] Judg. 3:27 [b] Judg. 3:28 [c] John 1:28 **7:25** [a] Judg. 8:3 [b] Ps. 83:11; Is. 10:26 [c] Judg. 8:4 **8:1** [a] Judg. 12:1; 2 Sam. 19:41 **8:2** [a] Judg. 6:11 **8:3** [a] Judg. 7:24, 25 [b] Prov. 15:1 **8:4** [a] Judg. 7:25 [b] Judg. 7:6 **8:5** [a] Gen. 33:17; Ps. 60:6 **8:6** [a] 1 Kin. 20:11; Judg. 8:15 [b] 1 Sam. 25:11 **8:7** [a] Judg. 8:16 **8:8** [a] Gen. 32:30, 31; 1 Kin. 12:25 **8:9** [a] 1 Kin. 22:27 [b] Judg. 8:17 **8:10** [a] Judg. 7:12 [b] Judg. 6:5

fallen. 11 Then Gideon went up by the road of those who dwell in tents on the east of [a]Nobah and Jogbehah; and he attacked the army while the camp felt [b]secure. 12 When Zebah and Zalmunna fled, he pursued them; and he [a]took the two kings of Midian, Zebah and Zalmunna, and routed the whole army.

13 Then Gideon the son of Joash returned from battle, from the Ascent of Heres. 14 And he caught a young man of the men of Succoth and interrogated him; and he wrote down for him the leaders of Succoth and its elders, seventy-seven men. 15 Then he came to the men of Succoth and said, "Here are Zebah and Zalmunna, about whom you [a]ridiculed me, saying, '*Are* the hands of Zebah and Zalmunna now in your hand, that we should give bread to your weary men?'" 16 [a]And he took the elders of the city, and thorns of the wilderness and briers, and with them he taught the men of Succoth. 17 [a]Then he tore down the tower of [b]Penuel and killed the men of the city.

18 And he said to Zebah and Zalmunna, "What kind of men *were they* whom you killed at [a]Tabor?"

So they answered, "As you *are,* so *were* they; each one resembled the son of a king."

19 Then he said, "They *were* my brothers, the sons of my mother. *As* the LORD lives, if you had let them live, I would not kill you." 20 And he said to Jether his firstborn, "Rise, kill them!" But the youth would not draw his sword; for he was afraid, because he *was* still a youth.

21 So Zebah and Zalmunna said, "Rise yourself, and kill us; for as a man *is, so is* his strength." So Gideon arose and [a]killed Zebah and Zalmunna, and took the crescent ornaments that *were* on their camels' necks.

### GIDEON'S EPHOD

22 Then the men of Israel said to Gideon, [a]"Rule over us, both you and your son, and your grandson also; for you have [b]delivered us from the hand of Midian."

23 But Gideon said to them, "I will not rule over you, nor shall my son rule over you; [a]the LORD shall rule over you." 24 Then Gideon said to them, "I would like to make a request of you, that each of you would give me the earrings from his plunder." For they had golden earrings, [a]because they *were* Ishmaelites.

25 So they answered, "We will gladly give *them.*" And they spread out a garment, and each man threw into it the earrings from his plunder. 26 Now the weight of the gold earrings that he requested was one thousand seven hundred *shekels* of gold, besides the crescent ornaments, pendants, and purple robes which *were* on the

> **8:23** From the time the Israelites left Egypt, God had been their only King. Human leaders like Moses, Joshua, Deborah, and Gideon were used simply to communicate God's will to the people. Gideon recognized only God had the right to be King of Israel.

kings of Midian, and besides the chains that *were* around their camels' necks. 27 Then Gideon [a]made it into an ephod and set it up in his city, [b]Ophrah. And all Israel [c]played the harlot with it there. It became [d]a snare to Gideon and to his house.

28 Thus Midian was subdued before the children of Israel, so that they lifted their heads no more. [a]And the country was quiet for forty years in the days of Gideon.

### DEATH OF GIDEON

29 Then [a]Jerubbaal the son of Joash went and dwelt in his own house. 30 Gideon had [a]seventy sons who were his own offspring, for he had many wives. 31 [a]And his concubine who *was* in Shechem also bore him a son, whose name he called Abimelech. 32 Now Gideon the son of Joash died [a]at a good old age, and was buried in the tomb of Joash his father, [b]in Ophrah of the Abiezrites.

33 So it was, [a]as soon as Gideon was dead, that the children of Israel again [b]played the harlot with the Baals, [c]and made Baal-Berith their god. 34 Thus the children of Israel [a]did not remember the LORD their God, who had delivered them from the hands of all their enemies on every side; 35 [a]nor did they show kindness to the house of Jerubbaal (Gideon) in accordance with the good he had done for Israel.

### ABIMELECH'S CONSPIRACY

9 Then Abimelech the son of Jerubbaal went to Shechem, to [a]his mother's brothers, and spoke with them and with all the family of the house of his mother's father, saying, 2 "Please speak in the hearing of all the men of Shechem: 'Which is better for you, that all [a]seventy of the sons of Jerubbaal reign over you, or that one reign over you?' Remember that I *am* your own flesh and [b]bone."

3 And his mother's brothers spoke all these words concerning him in the hearing of all the men of Shechem; and their heart was inclined to follow Abimelech, for they said, "He is our [a]brother." 4 So they gave him seventy *shekels* of silver from the temple of [a]Baal-Berith, with which Abimelech hired [b]worthless and reckless men; and they followed him. 5 Then he went to his

8:11 [a] Num. 32:35, 42 [b] Judg. 18:27; [1 Thess. 5:3] 8:12 [a] Ps. 83:11 8:15 [a] Judg. 8:6 8:16 [a] Judg. 8:7 8:17 [a] Judg. 8:9 [b] 1 Kin. 12:25 8:18 [a] Judg. 4:6; Ps. 89:12 8:21 [a] Ps. 83:11 8:22 [a] [Judg. 9:8] [b] Judg. 3:9; 9:17 8:23 [a] 1 Sam. 8:7; 10:19; 12:12; Ps. 10:16 8:24 [a] Gen. 37:25, 28 8:27 [a] Judg. 17:5 [b] Judg. 6:11, 24 [c] [Ps. 106:39] [d] Deut. 7:16 8:28 [a] Judg. 5:31 8:29 [a] Judg. 6:32; 7:1 8:30 [a] Judg. 9:2, 5 8:31 [a] Judg. 9:1 8:32 [a] Gen. 25:8; Job 5:26 [b] Judg. 6:24; 8:27 8:33 [a] Judg. 2:19 [b] Judg. 2:17 [c] Judg. 9:4, 46 8:34 [a] Deut. 4:9; Judg. 3:7; Ps. 78:11, 42; 106:13, 21 8:35 [a] Judg. 9:16–18 9:1 [a] Judg. 8:31, 35 9:2 [a] Judg. 8:30; 9:5, 18 [b] Gen. 29:14 9:3 [a] Gen. 29:15 9:4 [a] Judg. 8:33 [b] Judg. 11:3; 2 Chr. 13:7; Acts 17:5

> **9:4** Not only were temples used as places of worship in ancient cultures, but they were also used to store valuables for safekeeping. Using money from **the temple of Baal-Berith** made it look as though Abimelech was getting help from Baal and not just from his human supporters.

father's house [a]at Ophrah and [b]killed his brothers,
the seventy sons of Jerubbaal, on one stone. But
Jotham the youngest son of Jerubbaal was left,
because he hid himself. 6 And all the men of She-
chem gathered together, all of Beth Millo, and
they went and made Abimelech king beside the
terebinth tree at the pillar that *was* in Shechem.

### *THE PARABLE OF THE TREES*

7 Now when they told Jotham, he went and
stood on top of [a]Mount Gerizim, and lifted his
voice and cried out. And he said to them:

"Listen to me, you men of Shechem,
That God may listen to you!

8 "The[a] trees once went forth to anoint a
king over them.
And they said to the olive tree,
[b]'Reign over us!'
9 But the olive tree said to them,
'Should I cease giving my oil,
[a]With which they honor God and men,
And go to sway over trees?'

10 "Then the trees said to the fig tree,
'You come *and* reign over us!'
11 But the fig tree said to them,
'Should I cease my sweetness and my good
fruit,
And go to sway over trees?'

12 "Then the trees said to the vine,
'You come *and* reign over us!'
13 But the vine said to them,
'Should I cease my new wine,
[a]Which cheers *both* God and men,
And go to sway over trees?'
14 "Then all the trees said to the bramble,
'You come *and* reign over us!'
15 And the bramble said to the trees,
'If in truth you anoint me as king over you,
*Then* come *and* take shelter in my [a]shade;
But if not, [b]let fire come out of the bramble
And devour the [c]cedars of Lebanon!'

16 "Now therefore, if you have acted in truth
and sincerity in making Abimelech king, and if
you have dealt well with Jerubbaal and his house,
and have done to him [a]as he deserves— 17 for
my [a]father fought for you, risked his life, and
[b]delivered you out of the hand of Midian; 18 [a]but
you have risen up against my father's house this
day, and killed his seventy sons on one stone, and
made Abimelech, the son of his [b]female servant,
king over the men of Shechem, because he is your
brother— 19 if then you have acted in truth and sin-
cerity with Jerubbaal and with his house this day,
*then* [a]rejoice in Abimelech, and let him also rejoice
in you. 20 But if not, [a]let fire come from Abimelech
and devour the men of Shechem and Beth Millo;
and let fire come from the men of Shechem and
from Beth Millo and devour Abimelech!" 21 And
Jotham ran away and fled; and he went to [a]Beer
and dwelt there, for fear of Abimelech his brother.

### *DOWNFALL OF ABIMELECH*

22 After Abimelech had reigned over Isra-
el three years, 23 [a]God sent a [b]spirit of ill will
between Abimelech and the men of Shechem;
and the men of Shechem [c]dealt treacherously
with Abimelech, 24 [a]that the crime *done* to the
seventy sons of Jerubbaal might be settled and
their [b]blood be laid on Abimelech their brother,
who killed them, and on the men of Shechem,
who aided him in the killing of his brothers.
25 And the men of Shechem set men in ambush
against him on the tops of the mountains, and
they robbed all who passed by them along that
way; and it was told Abimelech.
26 Now Gaal the son of Ebed came with his
brothers and went over to Shechem; and the
men of Shechem put their confidence in him.
27 So they went out into the fields, and gathered
*grapes* from their vineyards and trod *them*, and
made merry. And they went into [a]the house of
their god, and ate and drank, and cursed Abim-
elech. 28 Then Gaal the son of Ebed said, [a]"Who *is*
Abimelech, and who *is* Shechem, that we should
serve him? *Is he* not the son of Jerubbaal, and *is*
*not* Zebul his officer? Serve the men of [b]Hamor the
father of Shechem; but why should we serve him?
29 [a]If only this people were under my authority![1]
Then I would remove Abimelech." So he[2] said to
Abimelech, "Increase your army and come out!"
30 When Zebul, the ruler of the city, heard
the words of Gaal the son of Ebed, his anger was
aroused. 31 And he sent messengers to Abime-
lech secretly, saying, "Take note! Gaal the son of
Ebed and his brothers have come to Shechem;
and here they are, fortifying the city against
you. 32 Now therefore, get up by night, you and
the people who *are* with you, and lie in wait in

**9:5** [a] Judg. 6:24 [b] Judg. 8:30; 9:2, 18; 2 Kin. 11:1, 2 **9:7** [a] Deut. 11:29; 27:12; Josh. 8:33; John 4:20 **9:8** [a] 2 Kin. 14:9 [b] Judg. 8:22, 23 **9:9** [a] [John 5:23] **9:13** [a] Ps. 104:15 **9:15** [a] Is. 30:2; Dan. 4:12; Hos. 14:7 [b] Num. 21:28; Judg. 9:20; Ezek. 19:14 [c] 2 Kin. 14:9; Is. 2:13; Ezek. 31:3 **9:16** [a] Judg. 8:35 **9:17** [a] Judg. 7 [b] Judg. 8:22 **9:18** [a] Judg. 8:30, 35; 9:2, 5, 6 [b] Judg. 8:31 **9:19** [a] Is. 8:6; [Phil. 3:3] **9:20** [a] Judg. 9:15, 45, 56, 57 **9:21** [a] Num. 21:16 **9:23** [a] 1 Kin. 12:15; Is. 19:14 [b] 1 Sam. 16:14; 18:9, 10; 1 Kin. 22:22; 2 Chr. 18:22 [c] Is. 33:1 **9:24** [a] 1 Kin. 2:32; Esth. 9:25; Matt. 23:35, 36 [b] Num. 35:33 **9:27** [a] Judg. 9:4 **9:28** [a] 1 Sam. 25:10; 1 Kin. 12:16 [b] Gen. 34:2, 6; Josh. 24:32 **9:29** [a] 2 Sam. 15:4 [1] Literally *hand* [2] Following Masoretic Text and Targum; Dead Sea Scrolls read *they;* Septuagint reads *I.*

the field. 33 And it shall be, as soon as the sun is up in the morning, *that* you shall rise early and rush upon the city; and *when* he and the people who are with him come out against you, you may then do to them as you find opportunity."

34 So Abimelech and all the people who *were* with him rose by night, and lay in wait against Shechem in four companies. 35 When Gaal the son of Ebed went out and stood in the entrance to the city gate, Abimelech and the people who *were* with him rose from lying in wait. 36 And when Gaal saw the people, he said to Zebul, "Look, people are coming down from the tops of the mountains!"

But Zebul said to him, "You see the shadows of the mountains as *if they were* men."

37 So Gaal spoke again and said, "See, people are coming down from the center of the land, and another company is coming from the Diviners'[1] Terebinth Tree."

38 Then Zebul said to him, "Where indeed *is* your mouth now, with which you [a]said, 'Who is Abimelech, that we should serve him?' *Are* not these the people whom you despised? Go out, if you will, and fight with them now."

39 So Gaal went out, leading the men of Shechem, and fought with Abimelech. 40 And Abimelech chased him, and he fled from him; and many fell wounded, to the *very* entrance of the gate. 41 Then Abimelech dwelt at Arumah, and Zebul drove out Gaal and his brothers, so that they would not dwell in Shechem.

42 And it came about on the next day that the people went out into the field, and they told Abimelech. 43 So he took his people, divided them into three companies, and lay in wait in the field. And he looked, and there were the people, coming out of the city; and he rose against them and attacked them. 44 Then Abimelech and the company that *was* with him rushed forward and stood at the entrance of the gate of the city; and the *other* two companies rushed upon all who *were* in the fields and killed them. 45 So Abimelech fought against the city all that day; [a]he took the city and killed the people who *were* in it; and he [b]demolished the city and sowed it with salt.

**9:45** Sowing **salt** was Abimelech's way of cursing the land and destroying its ability to produce crops.

46 Now when all the men of the tower of Shechem had heard *that,* they entered the stronghold of the temple [a]of the god Berith. 47 And it was told Abimelech that all the men of the tower of Shechem were gathered together. 48 Then Abimelech went up to Mount [a]Zalmon, he and all the people who *were* with him. And Abimelech took an ax in his hand and cut down a bough from the trees, and took it and laid *it* on his shoulder; then he said to the people who were with him, "What you have seen me do, make haste *and* do as I *have done.*" 49 So each of the people likewise cut down his own bough and followed Abimelech, put *them* against the stronghold, and set the stronghold on fire above them, so that all the people of the tower of Shechem died, about a thousand men and women.

50 Then Abimelech went to Thebez, and he encamped against Thebez and took it. 51 But there was a strong tower in the city, and all the men and women—all the people of the city—fled there and shut themselves in; then they went up to the top of the tower. 52 So Abimelech came as far as the tower and fought against it; and he drew near the door of the tower to burn it with fire. 53 But a certain woman [a]dropped an upper millstone on Abimelech's head and crushed his skull. 54 Then [a]he called quickly to the young man, his armorbearer, and said to him, "Draw your sword and kill me, lest men say of me, 'A woman killed him.'" So his young man thrust him through, and he died. 55 And when the men of Israel saw that Abimelech was dead, they departed, every man to his place.

56 [a]Thus God repaid the wickedness of Abimelech, which he had done to his father by killing his seventy brothers. 57 And all the evil of the men of Shechem God returned on their own heads, and on them came [a]the curse of Jotham the son of Jerubbaal.

## TOLA

10 After Abimelech there [a]arose to save Israel Tola the son of Puah, the son of Dodo, a man of Issachar; and he dwelt in Shamir in the mountains of Ephraim. 2 He judged Israel twenty-three years; and he died and was buried in Shamir.

## JAIR

3 After him arose Jair, a Gileadite; and he judged Israel twenty-two years. 4 Now he had thirty sons who [a]rode on thirty donkeys; they also had thirty towns, [b]which are called "Havoth Jair"[1] to this day, which *are* in the land of Gilead. 5 And Jair died and was buried in Camon.

## ISRAEL OPPRESSED AGAIN

6 Then [a]the children of Israel again did evil in the sight of the LORD, and [b]served the Baals and the Ashtoreths, [c]the gods of Syria, the gods of [d]Sidon, the gods of Moab, the gods of the people of Ammon, and the gods of the Philistines; and they forsook the LORD and did not serve

**9:37** [1] Hebrew *Meonenim* **9:38** [a] Judg. 9:28, 29 **9:45** [a] Judg. 9:20 [b] Deut. 29:23; 2 Kin. 3:25 **9:46** [a] Judg. 8:33 **9:48** [a] Ps. 68:14 **9:53** [a] 2 Sam. 11:21 **9:54** [a] 1 Sam. 31:4 **9:56** [a] Judg. 9:24; Job 31:3; Prov. 5:22 **9:57** [a] Judg. 9:20 **10:1** [a] Judg. 2:16 **10:4** [a] Judg. 5:10; 12:14 [b] Deut. 3:14 [1] Literally *Towns of Jair* (compare Numbers 32:41 and Deuteronomy 3:14) **10:6** [a] Judg. 2:11; 3:7; 6:1; 13:1 [b] Judg. 2:13 [c] Judg. 2:12 [d] 1 Kin. 11:33; Ps. 106:36

Him. 7 So the anger of the LORD was hot against
Israel; and He [a]sold them into the hands of the
[b]Philistines and into the hands of the people of
[c]Ammon. 8 From that year they harassed and
oppressed the children of Israel for eighteen
years—all the children of Israel who *were* on
the other side of the Jordan in the [a]land of the
Amorites, in Gilead. 9 Moreover the people of
Ammon crossed over the Jordan to fight against
Judah also, against Benjamin, and against the
house of Ephraim, so that Israel was severely
distressed.

10 [a]And the children of Israel cried out to
the LORD, saying, "We have [b]sinned against
You, because we have both forsaken our God
and served the Baals!"

11 So the LORD said to the children of Isra-
el, *"Did I* not *deliver you* [a]from the Egyptians
and [b]from the Amorites and [c]from the people
of Ammon and [d]from the Philistines? 12 Also
[a]the Sidonians [b]and Amalekites and Maonites[1]
[c]oppressed you; and you cried out to Me, and I
delivered you from their hand. 13 [a]Yet you have
forsaken Me and served other gods. Therefore
I will deliver you no more. 14 Go and [a]cry out to
the gods which you have chosen; let them deliver
you in your time of distress."

15 And the children of Israel said to the LORD,
"We have sinned! [a]Do to us whatever seems best
to You; only deliver us this day, we pray." 16 [a]So
they put away the foreign gods from among
them and served the LORD. And [b]His soul could
no longer endure the misery of Israel.

17 Then the people of Ammon gathered to-
gether and encamped in Gilead. And the children
of Israel assembled together and encamped in
[a]Mizpah. 18 And the people, the leaders of Gilead,
said to one another, "Who *is* the man who will
begin the fight against the people of Ammon? He
shall [a]be head over all the inhabitants of Gilead."

## *JEPHTHAH*

11 Now [a]Jephthah the Gileadite was [b]a mighty
man of valor, but he *was* the son of a har-
lot; and Gilead begot Jephthah. 2 Gilead's wife
bore sons; and when his wife's sons grew up,
they drove Jephthah out, and said to him, "You
shall have [a]no inheritance in our father's house,
for you *are* the son of another woman." 3 Then
Jephthah fled from his brothers and dwelt in
the land of [a]Tob; and [b]worthless men banded to-
gether with Jephthah and went out *raiding* with
him.

4 It came to pass after a time that the [a]people
of Ammon made war against Israel. 5 And so
it was, when the people of Ammon made war
against Israel, that the elders of Gilead went to
get Jephthah from the land of Tob. 6 Then they
said to Jephthah, "Come and be our commander,
that we may fight against the people of Ammon."
7 So Jephthah said to the elders of Gilead,
[a]"Did you not hate me, and expel me from my
father's house? Why have you come to me now
when you are in distress?"

8 [a]And the elders of Gilead said to Jephthah,
"That is why we have [b]turned again to you now,
that you may go with us and fight against the
people of Ammon, and be [c]our head over all the
inhabitants of Gilead."

9 So Jephthah said to the elders of Gilead,
"If you take me back home to fight against the
people of Ammon, and the LORD delivers them
to me, shall I be your head?"

10 And the elders of Gilead said to Jephthah,
[a]"The LORD will be a witness between us, if we do
not do according to your words." 11 Then Jeph-
thah went with the elders of Gilead, and the
people made him [a]head and commander over
them; and Jephthah spoke all his words [b]before
the LORD in Mizpah.

12 Now Jephthah sent messengers to the
king of the people of Ammon, saying, [a]"What
do you have against me, that you have come to
fight against me in my land?"

13 And the king of the people of Ammon an-
swered the messengers of Jephthah, [a]"Because
Israel took away my land when they came up out
of Egypt, from [b]the Arnon as far as [c]the Jabbok,
and to the Jordan. Now therefore, restore those
*lands* peaceably."

14 So Jephthah again sent messengers to the
king of the people of Ammon, 15 and said to him,
"Thus says Jephthah: [a]'Israel did not take away
the land of Moab, nor the land of the people
of Ammon; 16 for when Israel came up from
Egypt, they walked through the wilderness as
far as the Red Sea and [a]came to Kadesh. 17 Then
[a]Israel sent messengers to the king of Edom,
saying, "Please let me pass through your land."
[b]But the king of Edom would not heed. And in
like manner they sent to the [c]king of Moab, but
he would not *consent.* So Israel [d]remained in
Kadesh. 18 And they [a]went along through the
wilderness and [b]bypassed the land of Edom and
the land of Moab, came to the east side of the
land of Moab, and encamped on the other side
of the Arnon. But they did not enter the border
of Moab, for the Arnon *was* the border of Moab.
19 Then [a]Israel sent messengers to Sihon king of
the Amorites, king of Heshbon; and Israel said

10:7 [a]Judg. 2:14; 4:2; 1 Sam. 12:9 [b]Judg. 13:1 [c]Judg. 3:13 10:8 [a]Num. 32:33 10:10 [a]Judg. 6:6; 1 Sam. 12:10 [b]Deut. 1:41 10:11 [a]Ex. 14:30 [b]Num. 21:21, 24, 25 [c]Judg. 3:12, 13 [d]Judg. 3:31 10:12 [a]Judg. 1:31; 5:19 [b]Judg. 6:3; 7:12 [c]Ps. 106:42, 43 [1]Some Septuagint manuscripts read *Midianites.* 10:13 [a][Deut. 32:15; Judg. 2:12; Jer. 2:13] 10:14 [a]Deut. 32:37, 38 10:15 [a]1 Sam. 3:18; 2 Sam. 15:26 10:16 [a]2 Chr. 7:14; Jer. 18:7, 8 [b]Ps. 106:44, 45; Is. 63:9 10:17 [a]Gen. 31:49; Judg. 11:11, 29 10:18 [a]Judg. 11:8, 11 11:1 [a]Heb. 11:32 [b]Judg. 6:12; 2 Kin. 5:1 11:2 [a]Gen. 21:10; Deut. 23:2 11:3 [a]2 Sam. 10:6, 8 [b]1 Sam. 22:2 11:4 [a]Judg. 10:9, 17 11:7 [a]Gen. 26:27 11:8 [a]Judg. 10:18 [b][Luke 17:4] [c]Judg. 10:18 11:10 [a]Gen. 31:49, 50; Jer. 29:23; 42:5 11:11 [a]Judg. 11:8 [b]Judg. 10:17; 20:1; 1 Sam. 10:17 11:12 [a]2 Sam. 16:10 11:13 [a]Num. 21:24–26 [b]Josh. 13:9 [c]Gen. 32:22 11:15 [a]Deut. 2:9, 19 11:16 [a]Num. 13:26; 20:1 11:17 [a]Num. 20:14 [b]Num. 20:14–21 [c]Josh. 24:9 [d]Num. 20:1 11:18 [a]Deut. 2:9, 18, 19 [b]Num. 21:4 11:19 [a]Num. 21:21; Deut. 2:26–36

to him, "Please [b]let us pass through your land
into our place." 20 [a]But Sihon did not trust Israel
to pass through his territory. So Sihon gathered
all his people together, encamped in Jahaz, and
fought against Israel. 21 And the LORD God of Is-
rael [a]delivered Sihon and all his people into the
hand of Israel, and they [b]defeated them. Thus
Israel gained possession of all the land of the
Amorites, who inhabited that country. 22 They
took possession of [a]all the territory of the Am-
orites, from the Arnon to the Jabbok and from
the wilderness to the Jordan.
23 'And now the LORD God of Israel has dis-
possessed the Amorites from before His people
Israel; should you then possess it? 24 Will you
not possess whatever [a]Chemosh your god gives
you to possess? So whatever [b]the LORD our God
takes possession of before us, we will possess.
25 And now, *are* you any better than [a]Balak the
son of Zippor, king of Moab? Did he ever strive
against Israel? Did he ever fight against them?
26 While Israel dwelt in [a]Heshbon and its villages,
in [b]Aroer and its villages, and in all the cities
along the banks of the Arnon, for three hundred
years, why did you not recover *them* within that
time? 27 Therefore I have not sinned against you,
but you wronged me by fighting against me.
May the LORD, [a]the Judge, [b]render judgment
this day between the children of Israel and the
people of Ammon.' " 28 However, the king of the
people of Ammon did not heed the words which
Jephthah sent him.

### *JEPHTHAH'S VOW AND VICTORY*

29 Then [a]the Spirit of the LORD came upon
Jephthah, and he passed through Gilead and
Manasseh, and passed through Mizpah of Gilead;
and from Mizpah of Gilead he advanced *toward*
the people of Ammon. 30 And Jephthah [a]made
a vow to the LORD, and said, "If You will indeed
deliver the people of Ammon into my hands,
31 then it will be that whatever comes out of the
doors of my house to meet me, when I return
in peace from the people of Ammon, [a]shall
surely be the LORD's, [b]and I will offer it up as a
burnt offering."
32 So Jephthah advanced toward the people
of Ammon to fight against them, and the LORD
delivered them into his hands. 33 And he defeat-
ed them from Aroer as far as [a]Minnith—twenty
cities—and to Abel Keramim,[1] with a very great
slaughter. Thus the people of Ammon were
subdued before the children of Israel.

### *JEPHTHAH'S DAUGHTER*

34 When Jephthah came to his house at [a]Miz-
pah, there was [b]his daughter, coming out to
meet him with timbrels and dancing; and she
*was his* only child. Besides her he had neither
son nor daughter. 35 And it came to pass, when
he saw her, that he [a]tore his clothes, and said,
"Alas, my daughter! You have brought me very
low! You are among those who trouble me! For I
[b]have given my word to the LORD, and [c]I cannot
go back on it."
36 So she said to him, "My father, *if* you have
given your word to the LORD, [a]do to me accord-
ing to what has gone out of your mouth, because
[b]the LORD has avenged you of your enemies,
the people of Ammon." 37 Then she said to her
father, "Let this thing be done for me: let me
alone for two months, that I may go and wander
on the mountains and bewail my virginity, my
friends and I."
38 So he said, "Go." And he sent her away
*for* two months; and she went with her friends,
and bewailed her virginity on the mountains.
39 And it was so at the end of two months that
she returned to her father, and he [a]carried out
his vow with her which he had vowed. She knew
no man.
And it became a custom in Israel 40 *that* the
daughters of Israel went four days each year to
lament the daughter of Jephthah the Gileadite.

**11:30–39** The text doesn't explicitly say that **Jephthah** killed his **daughter**, and some believe that instead he "sacrificed" her by dedicating her to a life of temple service and virginity. Human sacrifice was contrary to the law of Moses (Lev. 18:21; 20:2–5; Deut. 12:31; 18:10). Until the wicked reigns of Ahaz and Manasseh centuries later (2 Kin. 16:3; 21:6), there is no record of human sacrifice in Israel, even by those who followed Baal. The great respect Jephthah had for God would surely have prevented him from making such a perverse offering. The several references to her virginity seem to support the idea of lifelong celibacy, and the Bible provides evidence that such devoted service for women existed (Ex. 38:8; 1 Sam. 2:22; Luke 2:36–37). Jephthah's vow in verse 31 could be translated **shall surely be the LORD's**, or **I will offer it up as a burnt offering**. Thus, his vow could be interpreted that if a person came out first, he would dedicate that person to the Lord, or if an animal came out first, he would offer the animal as a burnt sacrifice.

**11:19** [b]Num. 21:22; Deut. 2:27 **11:20** [a]Num. 21:23; Deut. 2:27 **11:21** [a]Josh. 24:8 [b]Num. 21:24, 25 **11:22** [a]Deut. 2:36, 37 **11:24** [a]Num. 21:29; 1 Kin. 11:7; Jer. 48:7 [b][Deut. 9:4, 5; Josh. 3:10] **11:25** [a]Num. 22:2; Josh. 24:9; Mic. 6:5 **11:26** [a]Num. 21:25, 26 [b]Deut. 2:36 **11:27** [a]Gen. 18:25 [b]Gen. 16:5; 31:53; [1 Sam. 24:12, 15] **11:29** [a]Judg. 3:10 **11:30** [a]Gen. 28:20; Num. 30:2; 1 Sam. 1:11 **11:31** [a]Lev. 27:2, 3, 28; 1 Sam. 1:11 [b]Ps. 66:13 **11:33** [a]Ezek. 27:17 [1]Literally *Plain of Vineyards* **11:34** [a]Judg. 10:17; 11:11 [b]Ex. 15:20; 1 Sam. 18:6; Ps. 68:25; Jer. 31:4 **11:35** [a]Gen. 37:29, 34 [b]Eccl. 5:2, 4, 5 [c]Num. 30:2 **11:36** [a]Num. 30:2 [b]2 Sam. 18:19, 31 **11:39** [a]Judg. 11:31

### *JEPHTHAH'S CONFLICT WITH EPHRAIM*

**12** Then [a]the men of Ephraim gathered together, crossed over toward Zaphon, and said to Jephthah, "Why did you cross over to fight against the people of Ammon, and did not call us to go with you? We will burn your house down on you with fire!"

2 And Jephthah said to them, "My people and I were in a great struggle with the people of Ammon; and when I called you, you did not deliver me out of their hands. 3 So when I saw that you would not deliver *me,* I [a]took my life in my hands and crossed over against the people of Ammon; and the LORD delivered them into my hand. Why then have you come up to me this day to fight against me?" 4 Now Jephthah gathered together all the men of Gilead and fought against Ephraim. And the men of Gilead defeated Ephraim, because they said, "You Gileadites [a]*are* fugitives of Ephraim among the Ephraimites *and* among the Manassites." 5 The Gileadites seized the [a]fords of the Jordan before the Ephraimites *arrived.* And when *any* Ephraimite who escaped said, "Let me cross over," the men of Gilead would say to him, "*Are* you an Ephraimite?" If he said, "No," 6 then they would say to him, "Then say, [a]'Shibboleth'!" And he would say, "Sibboleth," for he could not pronounce *it* right. Then they would take him and kill him at the fords of the Jordan. There fell at that time forty-two thousand Ephraimites.

7 And Jephthah judged Israel six years. Then Jephthah the Gileadite died and was buried among the cities of Gilead.

### *IBZAN, ELON, AND ABDON*

8 After him, Ibzan of Bethlehem judged Israel. 9 He had thirty sons. And he gave away thirty daughters in marriage, and brought in thirty daughters from elsewhere for his sons. He judged Israel seven years. 10 Then Ibzan died and was buried at Bethlehem.

11 After him, Elon the Zebulunite judged Israel. He judged Israel ten years. 12 And Elon the Zebulunite died and was buried at Aijalon in the country of Zebulun.

13 After him, Abdon the son of Hillel the Pirathonite judged Israel. 14 He had forty sons and thirty grandsons, who [a]rode on seventy young donkeys. He judged Israel eight years. 15 Then Abdon the son of Hillel the Pirathonite died and was buried in Pirathon in the land of Ephraim, [a]in the mountains of the Amalekites.

### *THE BIRTH OF SAMSON*

*(cf. Num. 6:1–21)*

**13** Again the children of Israel [a]did evil in the sight of the LORD, and the LORD delivered them [b]into the hand of the Philistines for forty years.

2 Now there was a certain man from [a]Zorah, of the family of the Danites, whose name *was* Manoah; and his wife *was* barren and had no children. 3 And the [a]Angel of the LORD appeared to the woman and said to her, "Indeed now, you are barren and have borne no children, but you shall conceive and bear a son. 4 Now therefore, please be careful [a]not to drink wine or *similar* drink, and not to eat anything unclean. 5 For behold, you shall conceive and bear a son. And no [a]razor shall come upon his head, for the child shall be [b]a Nazirite to God from the womb; and he shall [c]begin to deliver Israel out of the hand of the Philistines."

> **SEEING JESUS IN THE SCRIPTURE**
>
> **13:5** Samson pictures Jesus. Just as God called Samson, a Nazirite, to deliver the Israelites from their enemies, the Father sent Jesus, a Nazarene, to deliver the world from its greatest enemy, sin (see Matt. 2:23).

6 So the woman came and told her husband, saying, [a]"A Man of God came to me, and His [b]countenance *was* like the countenance of the Angel of God, very awesome; but I [c]did not ask Him where He *was* from, and He did not tell me His name. 7 And He said to me, 'Behold, you shall conceive and bear a son. Now drink no wine or *similar* drink, nor eat anything unclean, for the child shall be a Nazirite to God from the womb to the day of his death.' "

8 Then Manoah prayed to the LORD, and said, "O my Lord, please let the Man of God whom You sent come to us again and teach us what we shall do for the child who will be born."

9 And God listened to the voice of Manoah, and the Angel of God came to the woman again as she was sitting in the field; but Manoah her husband *was* not with her. 10 Then the woman ran in haste and told her husband, and said to him, "Look, the Man who came to me the *other* day has just now appeared to me!"

11 So Manoah arose and followed his wife. When he came to the Man, he said to Him, "Are You the Man who spoke to this woman?"

And He said, "I *am.*"

12 Manoah said, "Now let Your words come *to pass!* What will be the boy's rule of life, and his work?"

13 So the Angel of the LORD said to Manoah, "Of all that I said to the woman let her be careful. 14 She may not eat anything that comes from the vine, [a]nor may she drink wine or *similar* drink, nor eat anything unclean. All that I commanded her let her observe."

**12:1** [a] Judg. 8:1 **12:3** [a] 1 Sam. 19:5; 28:21; Job 13:14 **12:4** [a] 1 Sam. 25:10 **12:5** [a] Josh. 22:11 **12:6** [a] Ps. 69:2, 15 **12:14** [a] Judg. 5:10; 10:4 **12:15** [a] Judg. 3:13, 27; 5:14 **13:1** [a] Judg. 2:11 [b] Judg. 10:7; 1 Sam. 12:9 **13:2** [a] Josh. 19:41; Judg. 16:31 **13:3** [a] Judg. 6:12 **13:4** [a] Num. 6:2, 3, 20; Judg. 13:4; Luke 1:15 **13:5** [a] Num. 6:5; 1 Sam. 1:11 [b] Num. 6:2 [c] 1 Sam. 7:13; 2 Sam. 8:1; 1 Chr. 18:1 **13:6** [a] Gen. 32:24–30 [b] Matt. 28:3; Luke 9:29; Acts 6:15 [c] Judg. 13:17, 18 **13:14** [a] Num. 6:3, 4; Judg. 13:4

15 Then Manoah said to the Angel of the LORD, "Please [a]let us detain You, and we will prepare a young goat for You."

16 And the Angel of the LORD said to Manoah, "Though you detain Me, I will not eat your food. But if you offer a burnt offering, you must offer it to the LORD." (For Manoah did not know He *was* the Angel of the LORD.)

17 Then Manoah said to the Angel of the LORD, "What *is* Your name, that when Your words come *to pass* we may honor You?"

18 And the Angel of the LORD said to him, [a]"Why do you ask My name, seeing it *is* wonderful?"

19 So Manoah took the young goat with the grain offering, [a]and offered it upon the rock to the LORD. And He did a wondrous thing while Manoah and his wife looked on— 20 it happened as the flame went up toward heaven from the altar—the Angel of the LORD ascended in the flame of the altar! When Manoah and his wife saw *this,* they [a]fell on their faces to the ground. 21 When the Angel of the LORD appeared no more to Manoah and his wife, [a]then Manoah knew that He *was* the Angel of the LORD.

22 And Manoah said to his wife, [a]"We shall surely die, because we have seen God!"

23 But his wife said to him, "If the LORD had desired to kill us, He would not have accepted a burnt offering and a grain offering from our hands, nor would He have shown us all these *things,* nor would He have told us *such things* as these at this time."

24 So the woman bore a son and called his name [a]Samson; and [b]the child grew, and the LORD blessed him. 25 [a]And the Spirit of the LORD began to move upon him at Mahaneh Dan[1] [b]between Zorah and [c]Eshtaol.

## SAMSON'S PHILISTINE WIFE

**14** Now Samson went down [a]to Timnah, and [b]saw a woman in Timnah of the daughters of the Philistines. 2 So he went up and told his father and mother, saying, "I have seen a woman in Timnah of the daughters of the Philistines; now therefore, [a]get her for me as a wife."

3 Then his father and mother said to him, "*Is there* no woman among the daughters of [a]your brethren, or among all my people, that you must go and get a wife from the [b]uncircumcised Philistines?"

And Samson said to his father, "Get her for me, for she pleases me well."

4 But his father and mother did not know that it was [a]of the LORD—that He was seeking an occasion to move against the Philistines. For at that time [b]the Philistines had dominion over Israel.

5 So Samson went down to Timnah with his father and mother, and came to the vineyards of Timnah.

Now *to his* surprise, a young lion *came* roaring against him. 6 And [a]the Spirit of the LORD came mightily upon him, and he tore the lion apart as one would have torn apart a young goat, though *he had* nothing in his hand. But he did not tell his father or his mother what he had done.

7 Then he went down and talked with the woman; and she pleased Samson well. 8 After some time, when he returned to get her, he turned aside to see the carcass of the lion. And behold, a swarm of bees and honey *were* in the carcass of the lion. 9 He took some of it in his hands and went along, eating. When he came to his father and mother, he gave *some* to them, and they also ate. But he did not tell them that he had taken the honey out of the [a]carcass of the lion.

**13:15** [a] Gen. 18:5; Judg. 6:18 **13:18** [a] Gen. 32:29 **13:19** [a] Judg. 6:19–21 **13:20** [a] Lev. 9:24; 1 Chr. 21:16; Ezek. 1:28; Matt. 17:6 **13:21** [a] Judg. 6:22 **13:22** [a] Gen. 32:30; Ex. 33:20; Deut. 5:26; Judg. 6:22, 23 **13:24** [a] Heb. 11:32 [b] 1 Sam. 3:19; Luke 1:80 **13:25** [a] Judg. 3:10; 1 Sam. 11:6; Matt. 4:1 [b] Josh. 15:33; Judg. 18:11 [c] Judg. 16:31 [1] Literally *Camp of Dan* (compare 18:12) **14:1** [a] Gen. 38:13; Josh. 15:10, 57 [b] Gen. 34:2 **14:2** [a] Gen. 21:21 **14:3** [a] Gen. 24:3, 4 [b] Gen. 34:14; Ex. 34:16; Deut. 7:3 **14:4** [a] Josh. 11:20; 1 Kin. 12:15; 2 Kin. 6:33; 2 Chr. 10:15 [b] Deut. 28:48; Judg. 13:1 **14:6** [a] Judg. 3:10 **14:9** [a] Lev. 11:27

APPLY THE TRUTH

## SELFISHNESS

**14:1–3** Samson didn't even seem to know her name. Nonetheless, he commanded his parents to bring him the woman he saw to become his wife. His parents objected. Wasn't there someone from the Israelites he could marry? But Samson was convinced and didn't want to listen to anyone. He was going to get what he wanted, no matter the cost. It was all about him. This story didn't end well for Samson, though. He ended up divorced, attacked, and alone.

Selfishness is all about "me." It reduces our behavior down to an impulse or emotion centered on ourselves. We want to feed whatever hunger we have, no matter what. We think by getting what we want, we'll be pleased. But we're usually left with emptiness or desires for other things to fill the lingering void.

To find true fulfilment, we must take our eyes off ourselves and put them on God and others. That's the mark of humility, the antidote for selfishness. God is our greatest treasure, and He has given us others to enjoy. We'll find what our hearts yearn for when we focus outside of ourselves, rather than within.

**14:8–9** Touching the **carcass of the lion** violated Samson's Nazirite vow (Judg. 13:5).

10 So his father went down to the woman.
And Samson gave a feast there, for young men
used to do so. 11 And it happened, when they
saw him, that they brought thirty companions
to be with him.
12 Then Samson said to them, "Let me [a]pose
a riddle to you. If you can correctly solve and ex-
plain it to me [b]within the seven days of the feast,
then I will give you thirty linen garments and
thirty [c]changes of clothing. 13 But if you cannot
explain *it* to me, then you shall give me thirty
linen garments and thirty changes of clothing."

And they said to him, [a]"Pose your riddle,
that we may hear it."
14 So he said to them:

"Out of the eater came something to
eat,
And out of the strong came something
sweet."

Now for three days they could not explain the
riddle.
15 But it came to pass on the seventh[1] day
that they said to Samson's wife, [a]"Entice your
husband, that he may explain the riddle to us,
[b]or else we will burn you and your father's house
with fire. Have you invited us in order to take
what is ours? *Is that* not *so?*"
16 Then Samson's wife wept on him, and said,
[a]"You only hate me! You do not love me! You
have posed a riddle to the sons of my people,
but you have not explained *it* to me."

And he said to her, "Look, I have not ex-
plained *it* to my father or my mother; so should
I explain *it* to you?" 17 Now she had wept on him
the seven days while their feast lasted. And it
happened on the seventh day that he told her,
because she pressed him so much. Then she
explained the riddle to the sons of her people.
18 So the men of the city said to him on the sev-
enth day before the sun went down:

"What *is* sweeter than honey?
And what *is* stronger than a lion?"

And he said to them:

"If you had not plowed with my heifer,
You would not have solved my riddle!"

19 Then [a]the Spirit of the LORD came upon
him mightily, and he went down to Ashkelon and
killed thirty of their men, took their apparel, and
gave the changes *of clothing* to those who had
explained the riddle. So his anger was aroused,
and he went back up to his father's house. 20 And
Samson's wife [a]was *given* to his companion, who
had been [b]his best man.

## SAMSON DEFEATS THE PHILISTINES

15 After a while, in the time of wheat harvest,
it happened that Samson visited his wife
with a [a]young goat. And he said, "Let me go in
to my wife, into *her* room." But her father would
not permit him to go in.
2 Her father said, "I really thought that you
thoroughly [a]hated her; therefore I gave her to
your companion. *Is* not her younger sister better
than she? Please, take her instead."
3 And Samson said to them, "This time I shall
be blameless regarding the Philistines if I harm
them!" 4 Then Samson went and caught three hun-
dred foxes; and he took torches, turned *the foxes* tail
to tail, and put a torch between each pair of tails.
5 When he had set the torches on fire, he let *the
foxes* go into the standing grain of the Philistines,
and burned up both the shocks and the standing
grain, as well as the vineyards *and* olive groves.
6 Then the Philistines said, "Who has done
this?"

And they answered, "Samson, the son-in-law
of the Timnite, because he has taken his wife and
given her to his companion." [a]So the Philistines
came up and burned her and her father with fire.
7 Samson said to them, "Since you would do a
thing like this, I will surely take revenge on you,
and after that I will cease." 8 So he attacked them
hip and thigh with a great slaughter; then he went
down and dwelt in the cleft of the rock of [a]Etam.
9 Now the Philistines went up, encamped in
Judah, and deployed themselves [a]against Lehi.
10 And the men of Judah said, "Why have you
come up against us?"

So they answered, "We have come up to ar-
rest Samson, to do to him as he has done to us."
11 Then three thousand men of Judah went
down to the cleft of the rock of Etam, and said to
Samson, "Do you not know that the Philistines
[a]rule over us? What *is* this you have done to us?"

And he said to them, "As they did to me, so
I have done to them."
12 But they said to him, "We have come down
to arrest you, that we may deliver you into the
hand of the Philistines."

Then Samson said to them, "Swear to me
that you will not kill me yourselves."
13 So they spoke to him, saying, "No, but we
will tie you securely and deliver you into their
hand; but we will surely not kill you." And they
bound him with two [a]new ropes and brought
him up from the rock.

**14:12** [a] 1 Kin. 10:1; Ezek. 17:2 [b] Gen. 29:27 [c] Gen. 45:22; 2 Kin. 5:22 **14:13** [a] Ezek. 17:2 **14:15** [a] Judg. 16:5 [b] Judg. 15:6 [1] Following Masoretic Text, Targum, and Vulgate; Septuagint and Syriac read *fourth*. **14:16** [a] Judg. 16:15 **14:19** [a] Judg. 3:10; 13:25 **14:20** [a] Judg. 15:2 [b] John 3:29 **15:1** [a] Gen. 38:17 **15:2** [a] Judg. 14:20 **15:6** [a] Judg. 14:15 **15:8** [a] 2 Chr. 11:6 **15:9** [a] Judg. 15:19 **15:11** [a] Lev. 26:25; Deut. 28:43; Judg. 13:1; 14:4; Ps. 106:40–42 **15:13** [a] Judg. 16:11, 12

14 When he came to Lehi, the Philistines came
shouting against him. Then [a]the Spirit of the
LORD came mightily upon him; and the ropes
that *were* on his arms became like flax that is
burned with fire, and his bonds broke loose from
his hands. 15 He found a fresh jawbone of a don-
key, reached out his hand and took it, and [a]killed
a thousand men with it. 16 Then Samson said:

"With the jawbone of a donkey,
Heaps upon heaps,
With the jawbone of a donkey
I have slain a thousand men!"

17 And so it was, when he had finished speaking,
that he threw the jawbone from his hand, and
called that place Ramath Lehi.[1]
18 Then he became very thirsty; so he cried
out to the LORD and said, [a]"You have given this
great deliverance by the hand of Your servant;
and now shall I die of thirst and fall into the hand
of the uncircumcised?" 19 So God split the hollow
place that *is* in Lehi,[1] and water came out, and he
drank; and [a]his spirit returned, and he revived.
Therefore he called its name En Hakkore,[2] which
is in Lehi to this day. 20 And [a]he judged Israel
[b]twenty years [c]in the days of the Philistines.

### SAMSON AND DELILAH

16 Now Samson went to [a]Gaza and saw a har-
lot there, and went in to her. 2 *When* the
Gazites *were told,* "Samson has come here!" they
[a]surrounded *the place* and lay in wait for him
all night at the gate of the city. They were quiet
all night, saying, "In the morning, when it is
daylight, we will kill him." 3 And Samson lay *low*
till midnight; then he arose at midnight, took
hold of the doors of the gate of the city and the
two gateposts, pulled them up, bar and all, put
*them* on his shoulders, and carried them to the
top of the hill that faces Hebron.
4 Afterward it happened that he loved a
woman in the Valley of Sorek, whose name *was*
Delilah. 5 And the [a]lords of the Philistines came
up to her and said to her, [b]"Entice him, and find
out where his great strength *lies,* and by what
*means* we may overpower him, that we may bind
him to afflict him; and every one of us will give
you eleven hundred *pieces* of silver."
6 So Delilah said to Samson, "Please tell me
where your great strength *lies,* and with what
you may be bound to afflict you."
7 And Samson said to her, "If they bind me
with seven fresh bowstrings, not yet dried, then
I shall become weak, and be like any *other* man."
8 So the lords of the Philistines brought up
to her seven fresh bowstrings, not yet dried, and
she bound him with them. 9 Now *men were* lying
in wait, staying with her in the room. And she
said to him, "The Philistines *are* upon you, Sam-
son!" But he broke the bowstrings as a strand of
yarn breaks when it touches fire. So the secret
of his strength was not known.
10 Then Delilah said to Samson, "Look, you
have mocked me and told me lies. Now, please
tell me what you may be bound with."
11 So he said to her, "If they bind me securely
with [a]new ropes that have never been used, then
I shall become weak, and be like any *other* man."
12 Therefore Delilah took new ropes and
bound him with them, and said to him, "The
Philistines *are* upon you, Samson!" And *men*
*were* lying in wait, staying in the room. But he
broke them off his arms like a thread.
13 Delilah said to Samson, "Until now you
have mocked me and told me lies. Tell me what
you may be bound with."
And he said to her, "If you weave the seven
locks of my head into the web of the loom"—
14 So she wove *it* tightly with the batten of
the loom, and said to him, "The Philistines *are*
upon you, Samson!" But he awoke from his
sleep, and pulled out the batten and the web
from the loom.
15 Then she said to him, [a]"How can you say,
'I love you,' when your heart *is* not with me? You
have mocked me these three times, and have not
told me where your great strength *lies.*" 16 And it
came to pass, when she pestered him daily with
her words and pressed him, *so* that his soul was
vexed to death, 17 that he [a]told her all his heart,
and said to her, [b]"No razor has ever come upon
my head, for I *have been* a Nazirite to God from
my mother's womb. If I am shaven, then my
strength will leave me, and I shall become weak,
and be like any *other* man."
18 When Delilah saw that he had told her all
his heart, she sent and called for the lords of
the Philistines, saying, "Come up once more,
for he has told me all his heart." So the lords of
the Philistines came up to her and brought the
money in their hand. 19 [a]Then she lulled him to
sleep on her knees, and called for a man and had
him shave off the seven locks of his head. Then
she began to torment him,[1] and his strength left
him. 20 And she said, "The Philistines *are* upon
you, Samson!" So he awoke from his sleep, and
said, "I will go out as before, at other times, and
shake myself free!" But he did not know that the
LORD [a]had departed from him.
21 Then the Philistines took him and put out
his [a]eyes, and brought him down to Gaza. They
bound him with bronze fetters, and he became
a grinder in the prison. 22 However, the hair of
his head began to grow again after it had been
shaven.

15:14 [a] Judg. 3:10; 14:6 15:15 [a] Lev. 26:8; Josh. 23:10; Judg. 3:31 15:17 [1] Literally *Jawbone Height* 15:18 [a] Ps. 3:7 15:19 [a] Gen. 45:27; Is. 40:29 [1] Literally *Jawbone* (compare verse 14) [2] Literally *Spring of the Caller* 15:20 [a] Judg. 10:2; 12:7–14 [b] Judg. 16:31 [c] Judg. 13:1 16:1 [a] Josh. 15:47 16:2 [a] 1 Sam. 23:26; Ps. 118:10–12 16:5 [a] Josh. 13:3 [b] Judg. 14:15 16:11 [a] Judg. 15:13 16:15 [a] Judg. 14:16 16:17 [a] [Mic. 7:5] [b] Num. 6:5; Judg. 13:5 16:19 [a] Prov. 7:26, 27 [1] Following Masoretic Text, Targum, and Vulgate; Septuagint reads *he began to be weak.* 16:20 [a] Num. 14:9, 42, 43; [Josh. 7:12]; 1 Sam. 16:14; 18:12; 28:15, 16; 2 Chr. 15:2 16:21 [a] 2 Kin. 25:7

### *SAMSON DIES WITH THE PHILISTINES*

23 Now the lords of the Philistines gathered
together to offer a great sacrifice to [a]Dagon their
god, and to rejoice. And they said:

"Our god has delivered into our hands
Samson our enemy!"

24 When the people saw him, they [a]praised their
god; for they said:

"Our god has delivered into our hands our
enemy,
The destroyer of our land,
And the one who multiplied our dead."

25 So it happened, when their hearts were [a]mer-
ry, that they said, "Call for Samson, that he may
perform for us." So they called for Samson from
the prison, and he performed for them. And they
stationed him between the pillars. 26 Then Samson
said to the lad who held him by the hand, "Let me
feel the pillars which support the temple, so that I
can lean on them." 27 Now the temple was full of men
and women. All the lords of the Philistines *were*
there—about three thousand men and women
on the [a]roof watching while Samson performed.
28 Then Samson called to the LORD, saying,
"O Lord GOD, [a]remember me, I pray! Strengthen
me, I pray, just this once, O God, that I may with
one *blow* take vengeance on the Philistines for
my two eyes!" 29 And Samson took hold of the
two middle pillars which supported the temple,
and he braced himself against them, one on his
right and the other on his left. 30 Then Samson
said, "Let me die with the Philistines!" And he
pushed with *all his* might, and the temple fell
on the lords and all the people who *were* in it. So
the dead that he killed at his death were more
than he had killed in his life.
31 And his brothers and all his father's house-
hold came down and took him, and brought *him*
up and [a]buried him between Zorah and Eshtaol
in the tomb of his father Manoah. He had judged
Israel [b]twenty years.

### *MICAH'S IDOLATRY*

17 Now there was a man from the mountains
of Ephraim, whose name *was* [a]Micah. 2 And
he said to his mother, "The eleven hundred
*shekels* of silver that were taken from you, and
on which you [a]put a curse, even saying it in my
ears—here *is* the silver with me; I took it."
And his mother said, [b]"*May you be* blessed

**16:23** [a] 1 Sam. 5:2 **16:24** [a] Dan. 5:4 **16:25** [a] Judg. 9:27 **16:27** [a] Deut. 22:8 **16:28** [a] Jer. 15:15 **16:31** [a] Judg. 13:25 [b] Judg. 15:20 **17:1** [a] Judg. 18:2 **17:2** [a] Lev. 5:1 [b] Gen. 14:19

JUDGES 16:23–31

## SAMSON'S DEATH BRINGS LIFE

21

STORY OF SCRIPTURE

### WHAT'S GOING ON?

Samson's story is as tragic as it is epic. He was once a mighty judge of Israel, empowered by God with superhuman strength. However, Samson's downfall was his pride, selfishness, and disobedience. Captured and blinded, Samson was brought to the temple of Dagon to be mocked by the Philistines for their entertainment. In this moment of deep humiliation and defeat, Samson turned to God in prayer and repentance. He asked for strength one last time, not for personal vengeance but to fulfill his role as God's instrument against Israel's enemies. Pushing against the temple pillars, Samson brought down the building, killing himself and many Philistines, achieving in death what he struggled to accomplish in life.

### WHAT DOES THIS MEAN FOR ME?

Samson's story is a warning about the dangers of pride, disobedience, and selfishness. His story challenges us to think about where our true strength lies. It's a reminder that our greatest strengths, if not surrendered to God, can become our downfall. Yet, there's also hope in Samson's story. It shows that it's never too late to turn back to God.

### DID YOU CATCH THE PATTERN?

Samson, in a moment of selflessness, gave up his life and buried the Philistines under rubble. Samson was extremely strong, but he was unable to deliver Israel until he gave up his life. This moment is a foreshadowing of Jesus, who gave up His life, died on the cross, and buried sin in the grave. But, unlike Samson, Jesus rose again so we can have everlasting victory.

*For the next* Story of Scripture *reading and devotion, turn to Ruth 4:11–22 on page 270.*

by the LORD, my son!" 3 So when he had re-
turned the eleven hundred *shekels* of silver to
his mother, his mother said, "I had wholly ded-
icated the silver from my hand to the LORD for
my son, to [a]make a carved image and a molded
image; now therefore, I will return it to you."
4 Thus he returned the silver to his mother. Then
his mother [a]took two hundred *shekels* of silver
and gave them to the silversmith, and he made
it into a carved image and a molded image; and
they were in the house of Micah.

> **17:3–4** The priests, who were chosen from the descendants of Levi, handled the gifts and offerings according to God's law. **Micah** and his family were not descendants of Levi, so they were not qualified to handle the gifts. Beyond that, using the money to create an idol violated God's law.

5 The man Micah had a [a]shrine, and made an
[b]ephod and [c]household idols;[1] and he consecrat-
ed one of his sons, who became his priest. 6 [a]In
those days *there was* no king in Israel; [b]everyone
did *what was* right in his own eyes.

7 Now there was a young man from [a]Beth-
lehem in Judah, of the family of Judah; he *was*
a Levite, and [b]was staying there. 8 The man de-
parted from the city of Bethlehem in Judah to
stay wherever he could find *a place.* Then he
came to the mountains of Ephraim, to the house
of Micah, as he journeyed. 9 And Micah said to
him, "Where do you come from?"

So he said to him, "I *am* a Levite from Beth-
lehem in Judah, and I am on my way to find *a
place* to stay."

10 Micah said to him, "Dwell with me, [a]and be
a [b]father and a priest to me, and I will give you
ten *shekels* of silver per year, a suit of clothes, and
your sustenance." So the Levite went in. 11 Then
the Levite was content to dwell with the man;
and the young man became like one of his sons
to him. 12 So Micah [a]consecrated the Levite, and
the young man [b]became his priest, and lived in
the house of Micah. 13 Then Micah said, "Now I
know that the LORD will be good to me, since I
have a Levite as [a]priest!"

### *THE DANITES ADOPT MICAH'S IDOLATRY*

**18** In [a]those days *there was* no king in Israel.
And in those days [b]the tribe of the Danites
was seeking an inheritance for itself to dwell in;
for until that day *their* inheritance among the
tribes of Israel had not fallen to them. 2 So the
children of Dan sent five men of their family
from their territory, men of valor from [a]Zorah
and Eshtaol, [b]to spy out the land and search it.
They said to them, "Go, search the land." So they
went to the mountains of Ephraim, to the [c]house
of Micah, and lodged there. 3 While they *were* at
the house of Micah, they recognized the voice
of the young Levite. They turned aside and said
to him, "Who brought you here? What are you
doing in this *place?* What do you have here?"

4 He said to them, "Thus and so Micah did for
me. He has [a]hired me, and I have become his priest."

5 So they said to him, "Please [a]inquire [b]of
God, that we may know whether the journey on
which we go will be prosperous."

6 And the priest said to them, [a]"Go in peace.
The presence of the LORD *be* with you on your
way."

7 So the five men departed and went to
[a]Laish. They saw the people who *were* there,
[b]how they dwelt safely, in the manner of the Si-
donians, quiet and secure. *There were* no rulers
in the land who might put *them* to shame for
anything. They *were* far from the [c]Sidonians,
and they had no ties with anyone.[1]

8 Then *the spies* came back to their brethren
at [a]Zorah and Eshtaol, and their brethren said
to them, "What *is* your *report?*"

9 So they said, [a]"Arise, let us go up against
them. For we have seen the land, and indeed it *is*
very good. *Would* you [b]*do* nothing? Do not hesi-
tate to go, *and* enter to possess the land. 10 When
you go, you will come to a [a]secure people and a
large land. For God has given it into your hands,
[b]a place where *there is* no lack of anything that
*is* on the earth."

11 And six hundred men of the family of the
Danites went from there, from Zorah and Eshta-
ol, armed with weapons of war. 12 Then they went
up and encamped in [a]Kirjath Jearim in Judah.
(Therefore they call that place [b]Mahaneh Dan[1]
to this day. There *it is,* west of Kirjath Jearim.)
13 And they passed from there to the mountains
of Ephraim, and came to [a]the house of Micah.

14 [a]Then the five men who had gone to spy
out the country of Laish answered and said to
their brethren, "Do you know that [b]there are
in these houses an ephod, household idols, a
carved image, and a molded image? Now there-
fore, consider what you should do." 15 So they
turned aside there, and came to the house of the
young Levite man—to the house of Micah—and
greeted him. 16 The [a]six hundred men armed
with their weapons of war, who *were* of the chil-
dren of Dan, stood by the entrance of the gate.

**17:3** [a] Ex. 20:4, 23; 34:17; Lev. 19:4 **17:4** [a] Is. 46:6 **17:5** [a] Judg. 18:24 [b] Judg. 8:27; 18:14 [c] Gen. 31:19, 30; Hos. 3:4 [1] Hebrew *teraphim* **17:6** [a] Judg. 18:1; 19:1 [b] Deut. 12:8; Judg. 21:25 **17:7** [a] Josh. 19:15; Judg. 19:1; Ruth 1:1, 2; Mic. 5:2; Matt. 2:1, 5, 6 [b] Deut. 18:6 **17:10** [a] Judg. 18:19 [b] Gen. 45:8; Job 29:16 **17:12** [a] Judg. 17:5 [b] Judg. 18:30 **17:13** [a] Judg. 18:4 **18:1** [a] Judg. 17:6; 19:1; 21:25 [b] Josh. 19:40–48 **18:2** [a] Judg. 13:25 [b] Num. 13:17; Josh. 2:1 [c] Judg. 17:1 **18:4** [a] Judg. 17:10, 12 **18:5** [a] 1 Kin. 22:5; [Is. 30:1]; Hos. 4:12 [b] Judg. 1:1; 17:5; 18:14 **18:6** [a] 1 Kin. 22:6 **18:7** [a] Josh. 19:47 [b] Judg. 18:27–29 [c] Judg. 10:12 [1] Following Masoretic Text, Targum, and Vulgate; Septuagint reads *with Syria.* **18:8** [a] Judg. 18:2 **18:9** [a] Num. 13:30; Josh. 2:23, 24 [b] 1 Kin. 22:3 **18:10** [a] Judg. 18:7, 27 [b] Deut. 8:9 **18:12** [a] Josh. 15:60 [b] Judg. 13:25 [1] Literally *Camp of Dan* **18:13** [a] Judg. 18:2 **18:14** [a] 1 Sam. 14:28 [b] Judg. 17:5 **18:16** [a] Judg. 18:11

17 Then [a]the five men who had gone to spy out the land went up. Entering there, they took [b]the carved image, the ephod, the household idols, and the molded image. The priest stood at the entrance of the gate with the six hundred men *who were* armed with weapons of war.

18 When these went into Micah's house and took the carved image, the ephod, the household idols, and the molded image, the priest said to them, "What are you doing?"

19 And they said to him, "Be quiet, [a]put your hand over your mouth, and come with us; [b]be a father and a priest to us. *Is it* better for you to be a priest to the household of one man, or that you be a priest to a tribe and a family in Israel?" 20 So the priest's heart was glad; and he took the ephod, the household idols, and the carved image, and took his place among the people.

21 Then they turned and departed, and put the little ones, the livestock, and the goods in front of them. 22 When they were a good way from the house of Micah, the men who *were* in the houses near Micah's house gathered together and overtook the children of Dan. 23 And they called out to the children of Dan. So they turned around and said to Micah, [a]"What ails you, that you have gathered such a company?"

24 So he said, "You have [a]taken away my gods which I made, and the priest, and you have gone away. Now what more do I have? How can you say to me, 'What ails you?' "

25 And the children of Dan said to him, "Do not let your voice be heard among us, lest angry men fall upon you, and you lose your life, with the lives of your household!" 26 Then the children of Dan went their way. And when Micah saw that they *were* too strong for him, he turned and went back to his house.

## *DANITES SETTLE IN LAISH*

27 So they took *the things* Micah had made, and the priest who had belonged to him, and went to Laish, to a people quiet and secure; [a]and they struck them with the edge of the sword and burned the city with fire. 28 *There was* no deliverer, because it *was* [a]far from Sidon, and they had no ties with anyone. It was in the valley that belongs [b]to Beth Rehob. So they rebuilt the city and dwelt there. 29 And [a]they called the name of the city [b]Dan, after the name of Dan their father, who was born to Israel. However, the name of the city formerly *was* Laish.

30 Then the children of Dan set up for themselves the carved image; and Jonathan the son of Gershom, the son of Manasseh,[1] and his sons were priests to the tribe of Dan [a]until the day of the captivity of the land. 31 So they set up for themselves Micah's carved image which he made, [a]all the time that the house of God was in Shiloh.

> **18:31** At one time, the tabernacle was housed in **Shiloh**, making it the religious capital for the Israelites. This is where Samuel grew up and served the Lord. When Solomon built the temple in Jerusalem, Shiloh became somewhat unimportant and eventually faded into obscurity. Later, however, the Greeks and Romans rebuilt this city.

## *THE LEVITE'S CONCUBINE*

**19** And it came to pass in those days, [a]when *there was* no king in Israel, that there was a certain Levite staying in the remote mountains of Ephraim. He took for himself a concubine from [b]Bethlehem in Judah. 2 But his concubine played the harlot against him, and went away from him to her father's house at Bethlehem in Judah, and was there four whole months. 3 Then her husband arose and went after her, to [a]speak kindly to her *and* bring her back, having his servant and a couple of donkeys with him. So she brought him into her father's house; and when the father of the young woman saw him, he was glad to meet him. 4 Now his father-in-law, the young woman's father, detained him; and he stayed with him three days. So they ate and drank and lodged there.

5 Then it came to pass on the fourth day that they arose early in the morning, and he stood to depart; but the young woman's father said to his son-in-law, [a]"Refresh your heart with a morsel of bread, and afterward go your way."

6 So they sat down, and the two of them ate and drank together. Then the young woman's father said to the man, "Please be content to stay all night, and let your heart be merry." 7 And when the man stood to depart, his father-in-law urged him; so he lodged there again. 8 Then he arose early in the morning on the fifth day to depart, but the young woman's father said, "Please refresh your heart." So they delayed until afternoon; and both of them ate.

9 And when the man stood to depart—he and his concubine and his servant—his father-in-law, the young woman's father, said to him, "Look, the day is now drawing toward evening; please spend the night. See, the day is coming to an end; lodge here, that your heart may be merry. Tomorrow go your way early, so that you may get home."

10 However, the man was not willing to spend that night; so he rose and departed, and came opposite [a]Jebus (that *is,* Jerusalem). With him were the two saddled donkeys; his concubine

**18:17** [a] Judg. 18:2, 14 [b] Judg. 17:4, 5 **18:19** [a] Job 21:5; 29:9; 40:4; Mic. 7:16 [b] Judg. 17:10 **18:23** [a] 2 Kin. 6:28 **18:24** [a] Gen. 31:30; Judg. 17:5 **18:27** [a] Josh. 19:47 **18:28** [a] Judg. 18:7 [b] Num. 13:21; 2 Sam. 10:6 **18:29** [a] Josh. 19:47 [b] Judg. 20:1; 1 Kin. 12:29, 30; 15:20 **18:30** [a] 2 Kin. 15:29 [1] Septuagint and Vulgate read *Moses.* **18:31** [a] Deut. 12:1–32; Josh. 18:1, 8; Judg. 19:18; 21:12 **19:1** [a] Judg. 17:6; 18:1; 21:25 [b] Judg. 17:7; Ruth 1:1 **19:3** [a] Gen. 34:3; 50:21 **19:5** [a] Gen. 18:5; Judg. 19:8; Ps. 104:15 **19:10** [a] Josh. 18:28; 1 Chr. 11:4, 5

*was* also with him. 11 They *were* near Jebus, and the day was far spent; and the servant said to his master, "Come, please, and let us turn aside into this city [a]of the Jebusites and lodge in it."

12 But his master said to him, "We will not turn aside here into a city of foreigners, who *are* not of the children of Israel; we will go on [a]to Gibeah." 13 So he said to his servant, "Come, let us draw near to one of these places, and spend the night in Gibeah or in [a]Ramah." 14 And they passed by and went their way; and the sun went down on them near Gibeah, which belongs to Benjamin. 15 They turned aside there to go in to lodge in Gibeah. And when he went in, he sat down in the open square of the city, for no one would [a]take them into *his* house to spend the night.

16 Just then an old man came in from [a]his work in the field at evening, who also *was* from the mountains of Ephraim; he was staying in Gibeah, whereas the men of the place *were* Benjamites. 17 And when he raised his eyes, he saw the traveler in the open square of the city; and the old man said, "Where are you going, and where do you come from?"

18 So he said to him, "We *are* passing from Bethlehem in Judah toward the remote mountains of Ephraim; I *am* from there. I went to Bethlehem in Judah; *now* I am going to [a]the house of the LORD. But there *is* no one who will take me into his house, 19 although we have both straw and fodder for our donkeys, and bread and wine for myself, for your female servant, and for the young man *who is* with your servant; *there is* no lack of anything."

20 And the old man said, [a]"Peace *be* with you! However, *let* all your needs *be* my responsibility; [b]only do not spend the night in the open square." 21 [a]So he brought him into his house, and gave fodder to the donkeys. [b]And they washed their feet, and ate and drank.

### *GIBEAH'S CRIME*

22 As they were [a]enjoying themselves, suddenly [b]certain men of the city, [c]perverted men,[1] surrounded the house *and* beat on the door. They spoke to the master of the house, the old man, saying, [d]"Bring out the man who came to your house, that we may know him *carnally!*"

23 But [a]the man, the master of the house, went out to them and said to them, "No, my brethren! I beg you, do not act *so* wickedly! Seeing this man has come into my house, [b]do not commit this outrage. 24 [a]Look, *here is* my virgin daughter and *the man's*[1] concubine; let me bring them out now. [b]Humble them, and do with them as you please; but to this man do not do such a vile thing!" 25 But the men would not heed him. So the man took his concubine and brought *her* out to them. And they [a]knew her and abused her all night until morning; and when the day began to break, they let her go.

26 Then the woman came as the day was dawning, and fell down at the door of the man's house where her master *was,* till it was light.

27 When her master arose in the morning, and opened the doors of the house and went out to go his way, there was his concubine, fallen *at* the door of the house with her hands on the threshold. 28 And he said to her, "Get up and let us be going." But [a]there was no answer. So the man lifted her onto the donkey; and the man got up and went to his place.

29 When he entered his house he took a knife, laid hold of his concubine, and [a]divided her into twelve pieces, limb by limb,[1] and sent her throughout all the territory of Israel. 30 And so it was that all who saw it said, "No such deed has been done or seen from the day that the children of Israel came up from the land of Egypt until this day. Consider it, [a]confer, and speak up!"

### *ISRAEL'S WAR WITH THE BENJAMITES*

**20** So [a]all the children of Israel came out, from [b]Dan to [c]Beersheba, as well as from the land of Gilead, and the congregation gathered together as one man before the LORD [d]at Mizpah. 2 And the leaders of all the people, all the tribes of Israel, presented themselves in the assembly of the people of God, four hundred thousand foot soldiers [a]who drew the sword. 3 (Now the children of Benjamin heard that the children of Israel had gone up to Mizpah.)

Then the children of Israel said, "Tell *us,* how did this wicked deed happen?"

4 So the Levite, the husband of the woman who was murdered, answered and said, "My concubine and [a]I went into Gibeah, which belongs to Benjamin, to spend the night. 5 [a]And the men of Gibeah rose against me, and surrounded the house at night because of me. They intended to kill me, [b]but instead they ravished my concubine so that she died. 6 So [a]I took hold of my concubine, cut her in pieces, and sent her throughout all the territory of the inheritance of Israel, because they [b]committed lewdness and outrage in Israel. 7 Look! All of you *are* children of Israel; [a]give your advice and counsel here and now!"

8 So all the people arose as one man, saying, "None *of us* will go to his tent, nor will any turn back to his house; 9 but now this *is* the thing which we will do to Gibeah: *We will go up* [a]against

19:11 [a] Josh. 15:8, 63; Judg. 1:21; 2 Sam. 5:6 19:12 [a] Josh. 18:28 19:13 [a] Josh. 18:25 19:15 [a] Matt. 25:43 19:16 [a] Ps. 104:23 19:18 [a] Josh. 18:1; Judg. 18:31; 20:18; 1 Sam. 1:3, 7 19:20 [a] Gen. 43:23; Judg. 6:23; 1 Sam. 25:6 [b] Gen. 19:2 19:21 [a] Gen. 24:32; 43:24 [b] Gen. 18:4; John 13:5 19:22 [a] Judg. 16:25; 19:6, 9 [b] Gen. 19:4, 5; Judg. 20:5; Hos. 9:9; 10:9 [c] Deut. 13:13; 1 Sam. 2:12; 1 Kin. 21:10; [2 Cor. 6:15] [d] Gen. 19:5; [Rom. 1:26, 27] [1] Literally *sons of Belial* 19:23 [a] Gen. 19:6, 7 [b] Gen. 34:7; Deut. 22:21; Judg. 20:6, 10; 2 Sam. 13:12 19:24 [a] Gen. 19:8 [b] Gen. 34:2; Deut. 21:14 [1] Literally *his* 19:25 [a] Gen. 4:1 19:28 [a] Judg. 20:5 19:29 [a] Judg. 20:6; 1 Sam. 11:7 [1] Literally *with her bones* 19:30 [a] Judg. 20:7; Prov. 13:10 20:1 [a] Josh. 22:12; Judg. 20:11; 21:5 [b] Judg. 18:29; 1 Sam. 3:20; 2 Sam. 3:10; 24:2 [c] Josh. 19:2 [d] Judg. 10:17; 1 Sam. 7:5 20:2 [a] Judg. 8:10 20:4 [a] Judg. 19:15 20:5 [a] Judg. 19:22 [b] Judg. 19:25, 26 20:6 [a] Judg. 19:29 [b] Josh. 7:15 20:7 [a] Judg. 19:30 20:9 [a] Judg. 1:3

it by lot. 10 We will take ten men out of *every*
hundred throughout all the tribes of Israel, a
hundred out of *every* thousand, and a thousand
out of *every* ten thousand, to make provisions
for the people, that when they come to Gibeah
in Benjamin, they may repay all the vileness
that they have done in Israel." 11 So all the men
of Israel were gathered against the city, united
together as one man.

12 [a]Then the tribes of Israel sent men through
all the tribe of Benjamin, saying, "What *is* this
wickedness that has occurred among you? 13 Now
therefore, deliver up the men, [a]the perverted
men[1] who *are* in Gibeah, that we may put them
to death and [b]remove the evil from Israel!" But
the children of Benjamin would not listen to the
voice of their brethren, the children of Israel.
14 Instead, the children of Benjamin gathered
together from their cities to Gibeah, to go to
battle against the children of Israel. 15 And from
their cities at that time [a]the children of Benja-
min numbered twenty-six thousand men who
drew the sword, besides the inhabitants of Gib-
eah, who numbered seven hundred select men.
16 Among all this people *were* seven hundred
select men *who were* [a]left-handed; every one
could sling a stone at a hair's *breadth* and not
miss. 17 Now besides Benjamin, the men of Isra-
el numbered four hundred thousand men who
drew the sword; all of these *were* men of war.

**20:16** A **sling** was a leather strap designed to hold a rock. The strap was whirled around and around until the rock was released. Because of the whirling motion, the rock flew out of the sling with great force. Most people used small clay pebbles in their slings. Some warriors, though, used baseball-sized limestone or flint rocks.

18 Then the children of Israel arose and [a]went
up to the house of God[1] to [b]inquire of God. They
said, "Which of us shall go up first to battle
against the children of Benjamin?"

The LORD said, [c]"Judah first!"

19 So the children of Israel rose in the morn-
ing and encamped against Gibeah. 20 And the
men of Israel went out to battle against Ben-
jamin, and the men of Israel put themselves
in battle array to fight against them at Gibeah.
21 Then [a]the children of Benjamin came out of
Gibeah, and on that day cut down to the ground
twenty-two thousand men of the Israelites.
22 And the people, that is, the men of Israel,
encouraged themselves and again formed
the battle line at the place where they had put
themselves in array on the first day. 23 [a]Then the
children of Israel went up and wept before the
LORD until evening, and asked counsel of the
LORD, saying, "Shall I again draw near for battle
against the children of my brother Benjamin?"

And the LORD said, "Go up against him."

24 So the children of Israel approached the
children of Benjamin on the second day. 25 And
[a]Benjamin went out against them from Gibeah
on the second day, and cut down to the ground
eighteen thousand more of the children of Is-
rael; all these drew the sword.

26 Then all the children of Israel, that is, all
the people, [a]went up and came to the house of
God[1] and wept. They sat there before the LORD
and fasted that day until evening; and they of-
fered burnt offerings and peace offerings before
the LORD. 27 So the children of Israel inquired of
the LORD ([a]the ark of the covenant of God *was*
there in those days, 28 [a]and Phinehas the son
of Eleazar, the son of Aaron, [b]stood before it in
those days), saying, "Shall I yet again go out to
battle against the children of my brother Ben-
jamin, or shall I cease?"

And the LORD said, "Go up, for tomorrow I
will deliver them into your hand."

29 Then Israel [a]set men in ambush all around
Gibeah. 30 And the children of Israel went up
against the children of Benjamin on the third day,
and put themselves in battle array against Gibeah
as at the other times. 31 So the children of Benjamin
went out against the people, *and* were drawn away
from the city. They began to strike down *and* kill
some of the people, as at the other times, in the
highways [a](one of which goes up to Bethel and the
other to Gibeah) and in the field, about thirty men
of Israel. 32 And the children of Benjamin said,
"They *are* defeated before us, as at first."

But the children of Israel said, "Let us flee
and draw them away from the city to the high-
ways." 33 So all the men of Israel rose from their
place and put themselves in battle array at Baal
Tamar. Then Israel's men in ambush burst forth
from their position in the plain of Geba. 34 And
ten thousand select men from all Israel came
against Gibeah, and the battle was fierce. [a]But
*the Benjamites*[1] did not know that disaster *was*
upon them. 35 The LORD defeated Benjamin be-
fore Israel. And the children of Israel destroyed
that day twenty-five thousand one hundred
Benjamites; all these drew the sword.

36 So the children of Benjamin saw that they
were defeated. [a]The men of Israel had given
ground to the Benjamites, because they relied on
the men in ambush whom they had set against
Gibeah. 37 [a]And the men in ambush quickly
rushed upon Gibeah; the men in ambush spread

**20:12** [a] Deut. 13:14; Josh. 22:13, 16 **20:13** [a] Deut. 13:13; Judg. 19:22 [b] Deut. 17:12; 1 Cor. 5:13 [1] Literally *sons of Belial* **20:15** [a] Num. 1:36, 37; 2:23; 26:41 **20:16** [a] Judg. 3:15; 1 Chr. 12:2 **20:18** [a] Judg. 20:23, 26 [b] Num. 27:21 [c] Judg. 1:1, 2 [1] Or *Bethel* **20:21** [a] [Gen. 49:27] **20:23** [a] Judg. 20:26, 27 **20:25** [a] Judg. 20:21 **20:26** [a] Judg. 20:18, 23; 21:2 [1] Or *Bethel* **20:27** [a] Josh. 18:1; 1 Sam. 1:3; 3:3; 4:3, 4 **20:28** [a] Num. 25:7, 13; Josh. 24:33 [b] Deut. 10:8; 18:5 **20:29** [a] Josh. 8:4 **20:31** [a] Judg. 21:19 **20:34** [a] Josh. 8:14; Job 21:13; Is. 47:11 [1] Literally *they* **20:36** [a] Josh. 8:15 **20:37** [a] Josh. 8:19

out and struck the whole city with the edge of the
sword. 38 Now the appointed signal between the
men of Israel and the men in ambush was that
they would make a great cloud of [a]smoke rise
up from the city, 39 whereupon the men of Israel
would turn in battle. Now Benjamin had begun to
strike *and* kill about thirty of the men of Israel.
For they said, "Surely they are defeated before us,
as *in* the first battle." 40 But when the cloud began
to rise from the city in a column of smoke, the
Benjamites [a]looked behind them, and there was
the whole city going up *in smoke* to heaven. 41 And
when the men of Israel turned back, the men of
Benjamin panicked, for they saw that disaster had
come upon them. 42 Therefore they turned *their*
*backs* before the men of Israel in the direction of
the wilderness; but the battle overtook them, and
whoever *came* out of the cities they destroyed in
their midst. 43 They surrounded the Benjamites,
chased them, *and* easily trampled them down as
far as the front of Gibeah toward the east. 44 And
eighteen thousand men of Benjamin fell; all
these *were* men of valor. 45 Then they[1] turned
and fled toward the wilderness to the rock of
[a]Rimmon; and they cut down five thousand of
them on the highways. Then they pursued them
relentlessly up to Gidom, and killed two thousand
of them. 46 So all who fell of Benjamin that day
were twenty-five thousand men who drew the
sword; all these *were* men of valor.

47 [a]But six hundred men turned and fled
toward the wilderness to the rock of Rimmon,
and they stayed at the rock of Rimmon for four
months. 48 And the men of Israel turned back
against the children of Benjamin, and struck
them down with the edge of the sword—from
*every* city, men and beasts, all who were found.
They also set fire to all the cities they came to.

### *WIVES PROVIDED FOR THE BENJAMITES*

21 Now [a]the men of Israel had sworn an oath
at Mizpah, saying, "None of us shall give
his daughter to Benjamin as a wife." 2 Then the
people came [a]to the house of God,[1] and remained
there before God till evening. They lifted up their
voices and wept bitterly, 3 and said, "O LORD God
of Israel, why has this come to pass in Israel, that
today there should be one tribe *missing* in Israel?"

> **21:1** The **men of Israel** weren't required to make this **oath**, but once they did, they were bound by it.

4 So it was, on the next morning, that the
people rose early and [a]built an altar there, and
offered burnt offerings and peace offerings.
5 The children of Israel said, "Who *is there* among
all the tribes of Israel who did not come up with
the assembly to the LORD?" [a]For they had made
a great oath concerning anyone who had not
come up to the LORD at Mizpah, saying, "He
shall surely be put to death." 6 And the children
of Israel grieved for Benjamin their brother,
and said, "One tribe is cut off from Israel today.
7 What shall we do for wives for those who re-
main, seeing we have sworn by the LORD that
we will not give them our daughters as wives?"

8 And they said, "What one *is there* from the
tribes of Israel who did not come up to Mizpah
to the LORD?" And, in fact, no one had come to
the camp from [a]Jabesh Gilead to the assembly.
9 For when the people were counted, indeed,
not one of the inhabitants of Jabesh Gilead
*was* there. 10 So the congregation sent out there
twelve thousand of their most valiant men, and
commanded them, saying, [a]"Go and strike the
inhabitants of Jabesh Gilead with the edge of the
sword, including the women and children. 11 And
this *is* the thing that you shall do: [a]You shall
utterly destroy every male, and every woman
who has known a man intimately." 12 So they
found among the inhabitants of Jabesh Gilead
four hundred young virgins who had not known
a man intimately; and they brought them to the
camp at [a]Shiloh, which is in the land of Canaan.

13 Then the whole congregation sent *word* to
the children of Benjamin [a]who *were* at the rock
of Rimmon, and announced peace to them. 14 So
Benjamin came back at that time, and they gave
them the women whom they had saved alive of
the women of Jabesh Gilead; and yet they had
not found enough for them.

15 And the people [a]grieved for Benjamin,
because the LORD had made a void in the tribes
of Israel.

16 Then the elders of the congregation said,
"What shall we do for wives for those who re-
main, since the women of Benjamin have been
destroyed?" 17 And they said, "*There must be*
an inheritance for the survivors of Benjamin,
that a tribe may not be destroyed from Israel.
18 However, we cannot give them wives from our
daughters, [a]for the children of Israel have sworn
an oath, saying, 'Cursed *be* the one who gives a
wife to Benjamin.' " 19 Then they said, "In fact,
*there is* a yearly [a]feast of the LORD in [b]Shiloh,
which *is* north of Bethel, on the east side of the
[c]highway that goes up from Bethel to Shechem,
and south of Lebonah."

20 Therefore they instructed the children of
Benjamin, saying, "Go, lie in wait in the vine-
yards, 21 and watch; and just when the daughters
of Shiloh come out [a]to perform their dances,

20:38 [a] Josh. 8:20 20:40 [a] Josh. 8:20 20:45 [a] Josh. 15:32; 1 Chr. 6:77; Zech. 14:10 [1] Septuagint reads *the rest.* 20:47 [a] Judg. 21:13
21:1 [a] Judg. 20:1 21:2 [a] Judg. 20:18, 26 [1] Or *Bethel* 21:4 [a] Deut. 12:5; 2 Sam. 24:25 21:5 [a] Judg. 20:1–3 21:8 [a] 1 Sam. 11:1; 31:11
21:10 [a] Num. 31:17; Judg. 5:23; 1 Sam. 11:7 21:11 [a] Num. 31:17; Deut. 20:13, 14 21:12 [a] Josh. 18:1; Judg. 18:31 21:13 [a] Judg. 20:47
21:15 [a] Judg. 21:6 21:18 [a] Judg. 11:35; 21:1 21:19 [a] Lev. 23:2 [b] Deut. 12:5; Josh. 18:1; Judg. 18:31; 1 Sam. 1:3 [c] Judg. 20:31 21:21 [a] Ex.
15:20; Judg. 11:34; 1 Sam. 18:6

then come out from the vineyards, and every
man catch a wife for himself from the daugh-
ters of Shiloh; then go to the land of Benjamin.
22 Then it shall be, when their fathers or their
brothers come to us to complain, that we will say
to them, 'Be kind to them for our sakes, because
we did not take a wife for any of them in the war;
for *it is* not *as though* you have given the *women*
to them at this time, making yourselves guilty
of your oath.' "

23 And the children of Benjamin did so; they
took enough wives for their number from those
who danced, whom they caught. Then they went
and returned to their inheritance, and they [a]re-
built the cities and dwelt in them. 24 So the chil-
dren of Israel departed from there at that time,
every man to his tribe and family; they went
out from there, every man to his inheritance.
25 [a]In those days *there was* no king in Israel;
[b]everyone did *what was* right in his own eyes.

21:23 [a] Judg. 20:48 21:25 [a] Judg. 17:6; 18:1; 19:1 [b] Deut. 12:8; Judg. 17:6

# *The Book of* RUTH

| AUTHOR | KEY VERSES | READING TIME |
|---|---|---|
| Samuel, likely | Ruth 1:16–17 | 17 minutes |

Just as the Book of Judges contrasts the Book of Joshua, the Book of Ruth contrasts Judges. In Judges, we see the faithlessness of God's people, but in Ruth, we see the faithfulness of a Moabite woman. Ruth forsook her home and pagan heritage to cling to her mother-in-law, the people of Israel, and the God of Israel. The Book of Ruth, therefore, is a cameo story of love, devotion, and redemption set against the dark context of the days of the judges. Because of Ruth's faithfulness in a time of national unfaithfulness, God rewarded this Moabite by giving her a new husband (Boaz), a son (Obed), and a privileged position (the great-grandmother of David) in the lineage of Christ.

**Occasion:** The Book of Ruth provides a cameo of faithfulness to God amid the faithlessness during the period of the judges and provides further details concerning the lineage of Jesus.

**Main Point:** God is a redeeming God who welcomes, loves, and blesses all who are faithful.

**Big Ideas:** God welcomes all who come to Him in faith. We can trust God always, even in times of desperation. We are to be faithful to God even if everyone around us is not.

## OUTLINE:

I. Ruth's Loyalty to Naomi (ch. 1)
II. Ruth's Impact on Boaz (ch. 2)
III. Ruth's Request for Redemption (ch. 3)
IV. Ruth's Redemption and Reward (ch. 4)

**c. 1446–1406 BC**
Forty years of wilderness wandering

**c. 1405–1400 BC**
The conquest of Canaan

**c. 1380–1050 BC**
Judges rule in Israel

**c. 1100–1010 BC**
Samuel's prophetic ministry

**c. 1050 BC**
Saul becomes king of Israel

**c. 1050–1015 BC**
**Ruth written**

**1010 BC**
David begins to reign at Hebron

**1003 BC**
David becomes king over all Israel

**c. 1000 BC**
Hebrew and Greek alphabets develop from Phoenician

**c. 975 BC**
The temple of Hera is constructed at Olympia in Greece

**970 BC**
Solomon becomes king of Israel

### *ELIMELECH'S FAMILY GOES TO MOAB*

**1** Now it came to pass, in the days when [a]the judges ruled, that there was [b]a famine in the land. And a certain man of [c]Bethlehem, Judah, went to dwell in the country of [d]Moab, he and his wife and his two sons. 2 The name of the man *was* Elimelech, the name of his wife *was* Naomi, and the names of his two sons *were* Mahlon and Chilion—[a]Ephrathites of Bethlehem, Judah. And they went [b]to the country of Moab and remained there. 3 Then Elimelech, Naomi's husband, died; and she was left, and her two sons. 4 Now they took wives of the women of Moab: the name of the one *was* Orpah, and the name of the other Ruth. And they dwelt there about ten years. 5 Then both Mahlon and Chilion also died; so the woman survived her two sons and her husband.

> **1:1–2** The country of **Moab** was an enemy of Israel located about fifty miles away, on the eastern side of the Dead Sea. **Bethlehem** and Jerusalem are neighboring cities on the western side of the Dead Sea.

### *NAOMI RETURNS WITH RUTH*

6 Then she arose with her daughters-in-law that she might return from the country of Moab, for she had heard in the country of Moab that the LORD had [a]visited His people by [b]giving them bread. 7 Therefore she went out from the place where she was, and her two daughters-in-law with her; and they went on the way to return to the land of Judah. 8 And Naomi said to her two daughters-in-law, [a]"Go, return each to her mother's house. [b]The LORD deal kindly with you, as you have dealt [c]with the dead and with me. 9 The LORD grant that you may find [a]rest, each in the house of her husband."

So she kissed them, and they lifted up their voices and wept. 10 And they said to her, "Surely we will return with you to your people."

11 But Naomi said, "Turn back, my daughters; why will you go with me? *Are* there still sons in my womb, [a]that they may be your husbands? 12 Turn back, my daughters, go—for I am too old to have a husband. If I should say I have hope, *if* I should have a husband tonight and should also bear sons, 13 would you wait for them till they were grown? Would you restrain yourselves from having husbands? No, my daughters; for it grieves me very much for your sakes that [a]the hand of the LORD has gone out against me!"

14 Then they lifted up their voices and wept again; and Orpah kissed her mother-in-law, but Ruth [a]clung to her.

15 And she said, "Look, your sister-in-law has gone back to [a]her people and to her gods; [b]return after your sister-in-law."

16 But Ruth said:

[a]"Entreat me not to leave you,
*Or to* turn back from following after you;
For wherever you go, I will go;
And wherever you lodge, I will lodge;
[b]Your people *shall be* my people,
And your God, my God.
17 Where you die, I will die,
And there will I be buried.
[a]The LORD do so to me, and more also,
If *anything but* death parts you and me."

> **SEEING JESUS IN THE SCRIPTURE**
>
> **1:16–17** Ruth's commitment to her mother-in-law sealed her place in Jesus' lineage (see Matt. 1:5). Ruth, the Moabite, shows us Jesus' salvation is for all people, not just the Jews.

18 [a]When she saw that she was determined to go with her, she stopped speaking to her.

19 Now the two of them went until they came to Bethlehem. And it happened, when they had come to Bethlehem, that [a]all the city was excited because of them; and the women said, [b]"*Is* this Naomi?"

20 But she said to them, "Do not call me Naomi;[1] call me Mara,[2] for the Almighty has dealt very bitterly with me. 21 I went out full, [a]and the LORD has brought me home again empty. Why do you call me Naomi, since the LORD has testified against me, and the Almighty has afflicted me?"

22 So Naomi returned, and Ruth the Moabitess her daughter-in-law with her, who returned from the country of Moab. Now they came to Bethlehem [a]at the beginning of barley harvest.

### *RUTH MEETS BOAZ*

**2** There was a [a]relative of Naomi's husband, a man of great wealth, of the family of [b]Elimelech. His name *was* [c]Boaz. 2 So Ruth the Moabitess said to Naomi, "Please let me go to the [a]field, and glean heads of grain after *him* in whose sight I may find favor."

And she said to her, "Go, my daughter."

3 Then she left, and went and gleaned in the field after the reapers. And she happened to

**1:1** [a] Judg. 2:16–18 [b] Gen. 12:10; 26:1; 2 Kin. 8:1 [c] Judg. 17:8; Mic. 5:2 [d] Gen. 19:37 **1:2** [a] Gen. 35:19; 1 Sam. 1:1; 1 Kin. 11:26 [b] Judg. 3:30 **1:6** [a] Ex. 3:16; 4:31; Jer. 29:10; Zeph. 2:7; Luke 1:68 [b] Ps. 132:15; Matt. 6:11 **1:8** [a] Josh. 24:15 [b] 2 Tim. 1:16–18 [c] Ruth 2:20 **1:9** [a] Ruth 3:1 **1:11** [a] Gen. 38:11; Deut. 25:5 **1:13** [a] Judg. 2:15; Job 19:21; Ps. 32:4; 38:2 **1:14** [a] [Prov. 17:17] **1:15** [a] Judg. 11:24 [b] Josh. 1:15 **1:16** [a] 2 Kin. 2:2, 4, 6 [b] Ruth 2:11, 12 **1:17** [a] 1 Sam. 3:17; 2 Sam. 19:13; 2 Kin. 6:31 **1:18** [a] Acts 21:14 **1:19** [a] Matt. 21:10 [b] Is. 23:7; Lam. 2:15 **1:20** [1] Literally *Pleasant* [2] Literally *Bitter* **1:21** [a] Job 1:21 **1:22** [a] Ruth 2:23; 2 Sam. 21:9 **2:1** [a] Ruth 3:2, 12 [b] Ruth 1:2 [c] Ruth 4:21 **2:2** [a] Lev. 19:9, 10; 23:22; Deut. 24:19

> **2:1–3** When God gave His laws to the Israelites, He made sure everyone was taken care of. This was why the law of Moses allowed the poor to **glean** in the farmer's fields (Lev. 23:22), picking up the loose grain that fell from the sheaves as the reapers gathered them up.

come to the part of the field *belonging* to Boaz,
who *was* of the family of Elimelech.
4 Now behold, Boaz came from [a]Bethlehem,
and said to the reapers, [b]"The LORD *be* with you!"
And they answered him, "The LORD bless you!"
5 Then Boaz said to his servant who was in
charge of the reapers, "Whose young woman
*is* this?"
6 So the servant who was in charge of the
reapers answered and said, "It *is* the young Mo-
abite woman [a]who came back with Naomi from
the country of Moab. 7 And she said, 'Please let
me glean and gather after the reapers among
the sheaves.' So she came and has continued
from morning until now, though she rested a
little in the house."
8 Then Boaz said to Ruth, "You will listen,
my daughter, will you not? Do not go to glean in
another field, nor go from here, but stay close by
my young women. 9 *Let* your eyes *be* on the field
which they reap, and go after them. Have I not
commanded the young men not to touch you?
And when you are thirsty, go to the vessels and
drink from what the young men have drawn."
10 So she [a]fell on her face, bowed down to
the ground, and said to him, "Why have I found
[b]favor in your eyes, that you should take notice
of me, since I *am* a foreigner?"
11 And Boaz answered and said to her, "It has
been fully reported to me, [a]all that you have
done for your mother-in-law since the death of
your husband, and *how* you have left your father
and your mother and the land of your birth, and
have come to a people whom you did not know
before. 12 [a]The LORD repay your work, and a full
reward be given you by the LORD God of Israel,
[b]under whose wings you have come for refuge."
13 Then she said, [a]"Let me find favor in your
sight, my lord; for you have comforted me,
and have spoken kindly to your maidservant,
[b]though I am not like one of your maidservants."
14 Now Boaz said to her at mealtime, "Come
here, and eat of the bread, and dip your piece of
bread in the vinegar." So she sat beside the reap-
ers, and he passed parched *grain* to her; and she
ate and [a]was satisfied, and kept some back. 15 And
when she rose up to glean, Boaz commanded his
young men, saying, "Let her glean even among
the sheaves, and do not reproach her. 16 Also let
*grain* from the bundles fall purposely for her;
leave *it* that she may glean, and do not rebuke her."
17 So she gleaned in the field until evening,
and beat out what she had gleaned, and it was
about an ephah of [a]barley. 18 Then she took *it* up
and went into the city, and her mother-in-law
saw what she had gleaned. So she brought out
and gave to her [a]what she had kept back after
she had been satisfied.
19 And her mother-in-law said to her, "Where
have you gleaned today? And where did you work?
Blessed be the one who [a]took notice of you."
So she told her mother-in-law with whom
she had worked, and said, "The man's name
with whom I worked today *is* Boaz."
20 Then Naomi said to her daughter-in-law,
[a]"Blessed *be* he of the LORD, who [b]has not for-
saken His kindness to the living and the dead!"
And Naomi said to her, "This man *is* a relation
of ours, [c]one of our close relatives."
21 Ruth the Moabitess said, "He also said to
me, 'You shall stay close by my young men until
they have finished all my harvest.' "
22 And Naomi said to Ruth her daughter-in-
law, "*It is* good, my daughter, that you go out with
his young women, and that people do not meet
you in any other field." 23 So she stayed close by
the young women of Boaz, to glean until the
end of barley harvest and wheat harvest; and
she dwelt with her mother-in-law.

## RUTH'S REDEMPTION ASSURED

3 Then Naomi her mother-in-law said to her,
"My daughter, [a]shall I not seek [b]security for
you, that it may be well with you? 2 Now Boaz,
[a]whose young women you were with, *is he* not our
relative? In fact, he is winnowing barley tonight at
the threshing floor. 3 Therefore wash yourself and
[a]anoint yourself, put on your *best* garment and
go down to the threshing floor; *but* do not make
yourself known to the man until he has finished
eating and drinking. 4 Then it shall be, when he
lies down, that you shall notice the place where
he lies; and you shall go in, uncover his feet, and
lie down; and he will tell you what you should do."

> **3:4** For Ruth to **uncover** Boaz's **feet** in this manner showed her submission to him while also asking him to be her protector.

5 And she said to her, "All that you say to
me I will do."
6 So she went down to the threshing floor
and did according to all that her mother-in-law
instructed her. 7 And after Boaz had eaten and
drunk, and [a]his heart was cheerful, he went to

**2:4** [a] Ruth 1:1 [b] Ps. 129:7, 8; Luke 1:28; 2 Thess. 3:16 **2:6** [a] Ruth 1:22 **2:10** [a] 1 Sam. 25:23 [b] 1 Sam. 1:18 **2:11** [a] Ruth 1:14–18 **2:12** [a] 1 Sam. 24:19; Ps. 58:11 [b] Ruth 1:16; Ps. 17:8; 36:7; 57:1; 61:4; 63:7; 91:4 **2:13** [a] Gen. 33:15; 1 Sam. 1:18 [b] 1 Sam. 25:41 **2:14** [a] Ruth 2:18 **2:17** [a] Ruth 1:22 **2:18** [a] Ruth 2:14 **2:19** [a] Ruth 2:10; [Ps. 41:1] **2:20** [a] Ruth 3:10; 2 Sam. 2:5 [b] Prov. 17:17 [c] Ruth 3:9; 4:4, 6 **3:1** [a] 1 Cor. 7:36; 1 Tim. 5:8 [b] Ruth 1:9 **3:2** [a] Ruth 2:3, 8 **3:3** [a] 2 Sam. 14:2 **3:7** [a] Judg. 19:6, 9, 22; 2 Sam. 13:28; Esth. 1:10

APPLY THE TRUTH

## DATING

**3:1–18** We don't see dating in the Bible because back then they established relationships differently. Instead of dating, they arranged marriages, worked to earn the right to marry, or, like here, uncovered a person's feet to show availability. In our culture, people date. So, how can we turn to the Bible to find guidance for this important part of our lives?

Even though Ruth didn't date as we know it, we can learn a few things from her life to apply to dating. (1) **Above all, be faithful and obedient to God.** Jesus must be first in our lives. If He isn't first, all other relationships will be out of order. (2) **Look in the right place.** Following Jesus will lead you to the right place with the right people. If you're around the right people, you can find the right person. (3) **Listen to godly advice and create godly accountability.** Ruth was obedient to God, doing what God had called her to do and listening to the advice of her godly mother-in-law.

lie down at the end of the heap of grain; and she
came softly, uncovered his feet, and lay down.
8 Now it happened at midnight that the man
was startled, and turned himself; and there,
a woman was lying at his feet. 9 And he said,
"Who *are* you?"

So she answered, "I *am* Ruth, your maid-
servant. [a]Take your maidservant under your
wing,[1] for you are [b]a close relative."
10 Then he said, [a]"Blessed *are* you of the LORD,
my daughter! For you have shown more kindness
at the end than [b]at the beginning, in that you did
not go after young men, whether poor or rich.
11 And now, my daughter, do not fear. I will do for
you all that you request, for all the people of my
town know that you *are* a [a]virtuous woman. 12 Now
it is true that I *am* a [a]close relative; however, [b]there
is a relative closer than I. 13 Stay this night, and in
the morning it shall be *that* if he will [a]perform the
duty of a close relative for you—good; let him do
it. But if he does not want to perform the duty for
you, then I will perform the duty for you, [b]*as* the
LORD lives! Lie down until morning."
14 So she lay at his feet until morning, and
she arose before one could recognize another.
Then he said, [a]"Do not let it be known that the
woman came to the threshing floor." 15 Also
he said, "Bring the shawl that *is* on you and
hold it." And when she held it, he measured six
*ephahs* of barley, and laid *it* on her. Then she[1]
went into the city.
16 When she came to her mother-in-law, she
said, "*Is* that you, my daughter?"

Then she told her all that the man had done
for her. 17 And she said, "These six *ephahs* of
barley he gave me; for he said to me, 'Do not go
empty-handed to your mother-in-law.' "
18 Then she said, [a]"Sit still, my daughter, until
you know how the matter will turn out; for the
man will not rest until he has concluded the
matter this day."

### *BOAZ REDEEMS RUTH*

4 Now Boaz went up to the gate and sat down
there; and behold, [a]the close relative of
whom Boaz had spoken came by. So Boaz said,
"Come aside, friend,[1] sit down here." So he came
aside and sat down. 2 And he took ten men of [a]the
elders of the city, and said, "Sit down here." So
they sat down. 3 Then he said to the close relative,
"Naomi, who has come back from the country
of Moab, sold the piece of land [a]which *belonged*
to our brother Elimelech. 4 And I thought to in-
form you, saying, [a]'Buy *it* back [b]in the presence
of the inhabitants and the elders of my people.
If you will redeem *it*, redeem *it;* but if you[1] will
not redeem *it, then* tell me, that I may know;
[c]for *there is* no one but you to redeem *it*, and I
*am* next after you.' "

And he said, "I will redeem *it*."
5 Then Boaz said, "On the day you buy the
field from the hand of Naomi, you must also buy
*it* from Ruth the Moabitess, the wife of the dead,
[a]to perpetuate[1] the name of the dead through
his inheritance."
6 [a]And the close relative said, "I cannot re-
deem *it* for myself, lest I ruin my own inheri-
tance. You redeem my right of redemption for
yourself, for I cannot redeem *it*."
7 [a]Now this *was the custom* in former times
in Israel concerning redeeming and exchang-
ing, to confirm anything: one man took off his
sandal and gave *it* to the other, and this *was* a
confirmation in Israel.

**3:9** [a] Ezek. 16:8 [b] Ruth 2:20; 3:12 [1] Or *Spread the corner of your garment over your maidservant* **3:10** [a] Ruth 2:20 [b] Ruth 1:8 **3:11** [a] Prov. 12:4; 31:10–31 **3:12** [a] Ruth 3:9 [b] Ruth 4:1 **3:13** [a] Deut. 25:5–10; Ruth 4:5, 10; Matt. 22:24 [b] Judg. 8:19; Jer. 4:2; 12:16 **3:14** [a] [Rom. 12:17; 14:16; 1 Cor. 10:32; 2 Cor. 8:21; 1 Thess. 5:22] **3:15** [1] Many Hebrew manuscripts, Syriac, and Vulgate read *she;* Masoretic Text, Septuagint, and Targum read *he.* **3:18** [a] [Ps. 37:3, 5] **4:1** [a] Ruth 3:12 [1] Hebrew *peloni almoni;* literally *so and so* **4:2** [a] 1 Kin. 21:8; Prov. 31:23 **4:3** [a] Lev. 25:25 **4:4** [a] Jer. 32:7, 8 [b] Gen. 23:18 [c] Lev. 25:25 [1] Following many Hebrew manuscripts, Septuagint, Syriac, Targum, and Vulgate; Masoretic Text reads *he.* **4:5** [a] Gen. 38:8; Deut. 25:5, 6; Ruth 3:13; Matt. 22:24 [1] Literally *raise up* **4:6** [a] Ruth 3:12, 13; Job 19:14 **4:7** [a] Deut. 25:7–10

STORY OF SCRIPTURE 22

RUTH 4:11–22

## RUTH'S LEGACY

### WHAT'S GOING ON?

The marriage of Ruth, a Moabite widow, to Boaz, a relative of her deceased husband, is the culmination of an extraordinary story of loyalty, faith, and redemption. This union was blessed by the people and elders at the gate, who prayed for the couple to have a prosperous and famous family in Bethlehem. This passage is a beautiful tapestry of redemption and hope. Ruth, once a foreigner and outsider, was fully integrated into the community and became an ancestor of Israel's greatest king, David. It's a testament to God's inclusive plan of salvation, one that transcends nationality, ethnicity, and social-economic status.

### WHAT DOES THIS MEAN FOR ME?

Ruth's story is a powerful reminder that our background doesn't determine our destiny. Her faithfulness, even in the face of loss and uncertainty, led her to a place of honor in the history of God's people. It encourages us to remain steadfast in faith, even when the future seems uncertain.

### DID YOU CATCH THE PATTERN?

The story of Ruth is part of a pattern in Scripture in which God uses unlikely individuals to fulfill His purposes. This pattern is seen in Joseph, David, and even Jesus, who came from humble beginnings to fulfill God's salvation plan for humanity.

In Genesis 22:18, God promised all nations would be blessed through Israel. Ruth's inclusion in the lineage of Christ is a foreshadowing of the gospel extending to all nations. It shows God's plan of redemption is for all people, breaking down barriers and uniting us under His grace. Ruth's story invites us to be part of God's redemptive work in the world, serving as a reminder that in God's kingdom, there are no outsiders.

*For the next* Story of Scripture *reading and devotion, turn to 1 Samuel 10:1–27 on page 282.*

8 Therefore the close relative said to Boaz,
"Buy *it* for yourself." So he took off his sandal.
9 And Boaz said to the elders and all the people,
"You *are* witnesses this day that I have bought all
that was Elimelech's, and all that *was* Chilion's
and Mahlon's, from the hand of Naomi. 10 More-
over, Ruth the Moabitess, the widow of Mahlon,
I have acquired as my wife, to perpetuate the
name of the dead through his inheritance, [a]that
the name of the dead may not be cut off from
among his brethren and from his position at
the gate.[1] You *are* witnesses this day."

### SEEING JESUS IN THE SCRIPTURE

**4:9–11** Boaz's agreement to buy Naomi's land included accepting responsibility for her family and marrying Ruth. Boaz's redemption of Ruth and her mother-in-law point to Jesus, who purchased our redemption through His death on the cross (see Eph. 1:7).

11 And all the people who *were* at the gate,
and the elders, said, "*We are* witnesses. [a]The
LORD make the woman who is coming to your
house like Rachel and Leah, the two who [b]built
the house of Israel; and may you prosper in
[c]Ephrathah and be famous in [d]Bethlehem.
12 May your house be like the house of [a]Perez,
[b]whom Tamar bore to Judah, because of [c]the
offspring which the LORD will give you from
this young woman."

### *DESCENDANTS OF BOAZ AND RUTH*

*(Matt. 1:2–6)*

13 So Boaz [a]took Ruth and she became his
wife; and when he went in to her, [b]the LORD gave
her conception, and she bore a son. 14 Then [a]the
women said to Naomi, "Blessed *be* the LORD, who
has not left you this day without a close relative;
and may his name be famous in Israel! 15 And
may he be to you a restorer of life and a nour-
isher of your old age; for your daughter-in-law,
who loves you, who is [a]better to you than seven
sons, has borne him." 16 Then Naomi took the
child and laid him on her bosom, and became

4:10 [a] Deut. 25:6 [1] Probably his civic office 4:11 [a] Ps. 127:3; 128:3 [b] Gen. 29:25–30; Deut. 25:9 [c] Gen. 35:16–18 [d] 1 Sam. 16:4–13; Mic. 5:2; Matt. 2:1–8 4:12 [a] 1 Chr. 2:4; Matt. 1:3 [b] Gen. 38:6–29 [c] 1 Sam. 2:20 4:13 [a] Ruth 3:11 [b] Gen. 29:31; 33:5; Matt. 1:5 4:14 [a] Luke 1:58; [Rom. 12:15] 4:15 [a] 1 Sam. 1:8

a nurse to him. 17 [a]Also the neighbor women
gave him a name, saying, "There is a son born
to Naomi." And they called his name Obed. He
*is* the father of Jesse, the father of David.
18 [a]Now this *is* the genealogy of Perez: [b]Perez
begot Hezron; 19 Hezron begot Ram, and Ram
begot Amminadab; 20 Amminadab begot [a]Nah-
shon, and Nahshon begot [b]Salmon;[1] 21 Salmon
begot Boaz, and Boaz begot Obed; 22 Obed begot
Jesse, and Jesse begot [a]David.

4:17 [a] Luke 1:58 4:18 [a] 1 Chr. 2:4, 5; Matt. 1:1–7 [b] Num. 26:20, 21 4:20 [a] Num. 1:7 [b] Matt. 1:4 [1] Hebrew *Salmah*
4:22 [a] 1 Chr. 2:15; Matt. 1:6

# *The First Book of* SAMUEL

**AUTHOR**
Samuel, mostly, with perhaps Nathan and Gad

**KEY VERSES**
1 Samuel 8:6–7

**READING TIME**
2 hours 48 minutes

The Book of 1 Samuel describes Israel's transition from the leadership of judges to kings, but it does much more than advance the historical narrative of God's people. The book also reveals the continued stubbornness of the Israelites and their failure to acknowledge God's sovereignty. When the people demanded a king (1 Sam. 8), their mistake was not in wanting a king but rather in wanting the wrong kind of king. The people had failed to learn that no human would be a sufficient leader, a lesson they should have learned from the time of the judges. Instead, the Israelites raised the stakes by wanting to give increased power and authority to a human king so they could be like the nations around them. God, the true King, warned His people of the folly of their demand, but when they persisted, He gave them exactly what they wanted. Saul, a man who looked ideal for the role, became Israel's first king. But it wouldn't take long for God's warnings to be proven true.

**Occasion:** Samuel bridges the time of the judges ruling over Israel and the beginning of the monarchy.

**Main Point:** God is the true King of His people.

**Big Ideas:** God is the King we need. We are usually on dangerous ground when we choose to be like the people around us. God sees people differently than we often see one another. We are never too young or insignificant to be used mightily by God.

**OUTLINE:**

I. The Birth and Early Life of Samuel (chs. 1–3)
II. The Ark is Captured and Returned (chs. 4–6)
III. Samuel Judges Israel (ch. 7)
IV. Saul Becomes King (chs. 8–11)
V. Samuel's Farewell Speech (ch. 12)
VI. Saul Disobeys God (chs. 13–15)
VII. David Is Chosen to Be the Next King (ch. 16)
VIII. David Defeats Goliath (ch. 17)
IX. Saul Resents David (ch. 18)
X. Saul Tries to Kill David (chs. 19–30)
XI. Saul Dies in Battle (ch. 31)

**c. 1380–1050 BC**
Judges rule in Israel

**c. 1200 BC**
Philistines occupy the Mediterranean coast

**c. 1100–1010 BC**
Samuel's prophetic ministry

**c. 1050 BC**
Saul becomes king of Israel

**c. 1027 BC**
End of Shang Dynasty in China

**c. 1018 BC**
Samuel anoints David to be king

**1010 BC**
David begins to reign at Hebron

**1003 BC**
David becomes king over all Israel

**970 BC**
Solomon becomes king of Israel

### THE FAMILY OF ELKANAH

**1** Now there was a certain man of Ramathaim Zophim, of the [a]mountains of Ephraim, and his name *was* [b]Elkanah the son of Jeroham, the son of Elihu,[1] the son of Tohu,[2] the son of Zuph, [c]an Ephraimite. 2 And he had [a]two wives: the name of one *was* Hannah, and the name of the other Peninnah. Peninnah had children, but Hannah had no children. 3 This man went up from his city [a]yearly [b]to worship and sacrifice to the LORD of hosts in [c]Shiloh. Also the two sons of Eli, Hophni and Phinehas, the priests of the LORD, *were* there. 4 And whenever the time came for Elkanah to make an [a]offering, he would give portions to Peninnah his wife and to all her sons and daughters. 5 But to Hannah he would give a double portion, for he loved Hannah, [a]although the LORD had closed her womb. 6 And her rival also [a]provoked her severely, to make her miserable, because the LORD had closed her womb. 7 So it was, year by year, when she went up to the house of the LORD, that she provoked her; therefore she wept and did not eat.

### HANNAH'S VOW

8 Then Elkanah her husband said to her, "Hannah, why do you weep? Why do you not eat? And why is your heart grieved? *Am* I not [a]better to you than ten sons?"

9 So Hannah arose after they had finished eating and drinking in Shiloh. Now Eli the priest was sitting on the seat by the doorpost of [a]the tabernacle[1] of the LORD. 10 [a]And she *was* in bitterness of soul, and prayed to the LORD and wept in anguish. 11 Then she [a]made a vow and said, "O LORD of hosts, if You will indeed [b]look on the affliction of Your maidservant and [c]remember me, and not forget Your maidservant, but will give Your maidservant a male child, then I will give him to the LORD all the days of his life, and [d]no razor shall come upon his head."

12 And it happened, as she continued praying before the LORD, that Eli watched her mouth. 13 Now Hannah spoke in her heart; only her lips moved, but her voice was not heard. Therefore Eli thought she was drunk. 14 So Eli said to her, "How long will you be drunk? Put your wine away from you!"

15 But Hannah answered and said, "No, my lord, I *am* a woman of sorrowful spirit. I have drunk neither wine nor intoxicating drink, but have [a]poured out my soul before the LORD. 16 Do not consider your maidservant a [a]wicked woman,[1] for out of the abundance of my complaint and grief I have spoken until now."

17 Then Eli answered and said, [a]"Go in peace, and [b]the God of Israel grant your petition which you have asked of Him."

18 And she said, [a]"Let your maidservant find favor in your sight." So the woman [b]went her way and ate, and her face was no longer *sad.*

### SAMUEL IS BORN AND DEDICATED

19 Then they rose early in the morning and worshiped before the LORD, and returned and came to their house at Ramah. And Elkanah [a]knew Hannah his wife, and the LORD [b]remembered her. 20 So it came to pass in the process of time that Hannah conceived and bore a son, and called his name Samuel,[1] *saying,* "Because I have asked for him from the LORD."

21 Now the man Elkanah and all his house [a]went up to offer to the LORD the yearly sacrifice and his vow. 22 But Hannah did not go up, for she said to her husband, "*Not* until the child is weaned; then I will [a]take him, that he may appear before the LORD and [b]remain there [c]forever."

> **1:22–23** Hebrew children were normally **weaned** when they were two or three years old. Samuel was probably still a toddler when his parents took him to Shiloh to be raised and taught by Eli the priest.

23 So [a]Elkanah her husband said to her, "Do what seems best to you; wait until you have weaned him. Only let the LORD establish His[1] word." Then the woman stayed and nursed her son until she had weaned him.

24 Now when she had weaned him, she [a]took him up with her, with three bulls,[1] one ephah of flour, and a skin of wine, and brought him to [b]the house of the LORD in Shiloh. And the child *was* young. 25 Then they slaughtered a bull, and [a]brought the child to Eli. 26 And she said, "O my lord! [a]As your soul lives, my lord, I *am* the woman who stood by you here, praying to the LORD. 27 [a]For this child I prayed, and the LORD has granted me my petition which I asked of Him. 28 Therefore I also have lent him to the LORD; as long as he lives he shall be lent to the LORD." So they [a]worshiped the LORD there.

**1:1** [a] Josh. 17:17, 18; 24:33 [b] 1 Chr. 6:27, 33–38 [c] Ruth 1:2 [1] Spelled *Eliel* in 1 Chronicles 6:34 [2] Spelled *Toah* in 1 Chronicles 6:34 **1:2** [a] Deut. 21:15–17 **1:3** [a] Luke 2:41 [b] Deut. 12:5–7; 16:16 [c] Josh. 18:1 **1:4** [a] Deut. 12:17, 18 **1:5** [a] Gen. 16:1; 30:1, 2 **1:6** [a] Job 24:21 **1:8** [a] Ruth 4:15 **1:9** [a] 1 Sam. 3:3 [1] Hebrew *heykal,* palace or temple **1:10** [a] Job 7:11 **1:11** [a] Num. 30:6–11 [b] Ps. 25:18 [c] Gen. 8:1 [d] Num. 6:5 **1:15** [a] Ps. 42:4; 62:8 **1:16** [a] Deut. 13:13 [1] Literally *daughter of Belial* **1:17** [a] Mark 5:34 [b] Ps. 20:3–5 **1:18** [a] Ruth 2:13 [b] Rom. 15:13 **1:19** [a] Gen. 4:1 [b] Gen. 21:1; 30:22 **1:20** [1] Literally *Heard by God* **1:21** [a] 1 Sam. 1:3 **1:22** [a] Luke 2:22 [b] 1 Sam. 1:11, 28 [c] Ex. 21:6 **1:23** [a] Num. 30:7, 10, 11 [1] Following Masoretic Text, Targum, and Vulgate; Dead Sea Scrolls, Septuagint, and Syriac read *your.* **1:24** [a] Num. 15:9, 10 [b] Josh. 18:1 [1] Dead Sea Scrolls, Septuagint, and Syriac read *a three-year-old bull.* **1:25** [a] Luke 2:22 **1:26** [a] 2 Kin. 2:2, 4, 6; 4:30 **1:27** [a] [Matt. 7:7] **1:28** [a] Gen. 24:26, 52

### *HANNAH'S PRAYER*
*(cf. Luke 1:46–55)*

2 And Hannah [a]prayed and said:

[b]"My heart rejoices in the LORD;
[c]My horn[1] is exalted in the LORD.
I smile at my enemies,
Because I [d]rejoice in Your salvation.

2 "No[a] one is holy like the LORD,
For *there is* [b]none besides You,
Nor *is there* any [c]rock like our God.
3 "Talk no more so very proudly;
[a]Let no arrogance come from your mouth,
For the LORD *is* the God of [b]knowledge;
And by Him actions are weighed.

4 "The[a] bows of the mighty men *are* broken,
And those who stumbled are girded with strength.
5 *Those who were* full have hired themselves out for bread,
And the hungry have ceased *to hunger.*
Even [a]the barren has borne seven,
And [b]she who has many children has become feeble.

6 "The[a] LORD kills and makes alive;
He brings down to the grave and brings up.
7 The LORD [a]makes poor and makes rich;
[b]He brings low and lifts up.
8 [a]He raises the poor from the dust
*And* lifts the beggar from the ash heap,
[b]To set *them* among princes
And make them inherit the throne of glory.

[c]"For the pillars of the earth *are* the LORD's,
And He has set the world upon them.
9 [a]He will guard the feet of His saints,
But the [b]wicked shall be silent in darkness.

"For by strength no man shall prevail.
10 The adversaries of the LORD shall be [a]broken in pieces;
[b]From heaven He will thunder against them.
[c]The LORD will judge the ends of the earth.

[d]"He will give [e]strength to His king,
And [f]exalt the horn of His anointed."

11 Then Elkanah went to his house at Ramah.
But the child ministered to the LORD before
Eli the priest.

### *THE WICKED SONS OF ELI*

12 Now the sons of Eli *were* [a]corrupt;[1] [b]they
did not know the LORD. 13 And the priests' custom
with the people *was that* when any man offered
a sacrifice, the priest's servant would come with
a three-pronged fleshhook in his hand while
the meat was boiling. 14 Then he would thrust
*it* into the pan, or kettle, or caldron, or pot; and
the priest would take for himself all that the
fleshhook brought up. So they did in [a]Shiloh to
all the Israelites who came there. 15 Also, before
they [a]burned the fat, the priest's servant would
come and say to the man who sacrificed, "Give
meat for roasting to the priest, for he will not
take boiled meat from you, but raw."
16 And *if* the man said to him, "They should
really burn the fat first; *then* you may take *as
much* as your heart desires," he would then an-
swer him, "*No,* but you must give *it* now; and if
not, I will take *it* by force."
17 Therefore the sin of the young men was
very great [a]before the LORD, for men [b]abhorred
the offering of the LORD.

### *SAMUEL'S CHILDHOOD MINISTRY*

18 [a]But Samuel ministered before the LORD,
*even as* a child, [b]wearing a linen ephod. 19 More-
over his mother used to make him a little robe,
and bring *it* to him year by year when she [a]came
up with her husband to offer the yearly sacrifice.
20 And Eli [a]would bless Elkanah and his wife,
and say, "The LORD give you descendants from
this woman for the loan that was [b]given to the
LORD." Then they would go to their own home.
21 And the LORD [a]visited Hannah, so that
she conceived and bore three sons and two
daughters. Meanwhile the child Samuel [b]grew
before the LORD.

### *PROPHECY AGAINST ELI'S HOUSEHOLD*

22 Now Eli was very old; and he heard every-
thing his sons did to all Israel,[1] and how they lay
with [a]the women who assembled at the door of
the tabernacle of meeting. 23 So he said to them,
"Why do you do such things? For I hear of your
evil dealings from all the people. 24 No, my sons!
For *it is* not a good report that I hear. You make
the LORD's people transgress. 25 If one man sins
against another, [a]God will judge him. But if a man
[b]sins against the LORD, who will intercede for him?"
Nevertheless they did not heed the voice of their
father, [c]because the LORD desired to kill them.
26 And the child Samuel [a]grew in stature, and
[b]in favor both with the LORD and men.
27 Then a [a]man of God came to Eli and said
to him, "Thus says the LORD: [b]'Did I not clearly

2:1 [a] Phil. 4:6 [b] Luke 1:46–55 [c] Ps. 75:10; 89:17, 24; 92:10; 112:9 [d] Ps. 9:14; 13:5; 35:9 [1] That is, strength 2:2 [a] Ex. 15:11 [b] Deut. 4:35 [c] Deut. 32:4, 30, 31 2:3 [a] Ps. 94:4 [b] 1 Sam. 16:7 2:4 [a] Ps. 37:15; 46:9 2:5 [a] Ps. 113:9 [b] Is. 54:1 2:6 [a] Deut. 32:39 2:7 [a] Deut. 8:17, 18 [b] Ps. 75:7 2:8 [a] Luke 1:52 [b] Job 36:7 [c] Job 38:4–6 2:9 [a] [1 Pet. 1:5] [b] [Rom. 3:19] 2:10 [a] Ps. 2:9 [b] Ps. 18:13, 14 [c] Ps. 96:13; 98:9 [d] [Matt. 28:18] [e] Ps. 21:1, 7 [f] Ps. 89:24 2:12 [a] Deut. 13:13 [b] Judg. 2:10 [1] Literally *sons of Belial* 2:14 [a] 1 Sam. 1:3 2:15 [a] Lev. 3:3–5, 16 2:17 [a] Gen. 6:11 [b] [Mal. 2:7–9] 2:18 [a] 1 Sam. 2:11; 3:1 [b] Ex. 28:4 2:19 [a] 1 Sam. 1:3, 21 2:20 [a] Gen. 14:19 [b] 1 Sam. 1:11, 27, 28 2:21 [a] Gen. 21:1 [b] Judg. 13:24; 1 Sam. 2:26; 3:19–21; Luke 1:80; 2:40 2:22 [a] Ex. 38:8 [1] Following Masoretic Text, Targum, and Vulgate; Dead Sea Scrolls and Septuagint omit the rest of this verse. 2:25 [a] Deut. 1:17; 25:1, 2 [b] Num. 15:30 [c] Josh. 11:20 2:26 [a] 1 Sam. 2:21 [b] Prov. 3:4 2:27 [a] Deut. 33:1; Judg. 13:6; 1 Sam. 9:6; 1 Kin. 13:1 [b] Ex. 4:14–16; 12:1

reveal Myself to the house of your father when
they were in Egypt in Pharaoh's house? 28 Did I
not [a]choose him out of all the tribes of Israel *to be*
My priest, to offer upon My altar, to burn incense,
and to wear an ephod before Me? And [b]did I not
give to the house of your father all the offerings of
the children of Israel made by fire? 29 Why do you
[a]kick at My sacrifice and My offering which I have
commanded *in My* [b]dwelling place, and honor
your sons more than [c]Me, to make yourselves
fat with the best of all the offerings of Israel My
people?' 30 Therefore the LORD God of Israel says:
[a]'I said indeed *that* your house and the house of
your father would walk before Me forever.' But now
the LORD says: [b]'Far be it from Me; for those who
honor Me I will honor, and [c]those who despise Me
shall be lightly esteemed. 31 Behold, [a]the days are
coming that I will cut off your arm and the arm
of your father's house, so that there will not be
an old man in your house. 32 And you will see an
enemy *in My* dwelling place, *despite* all the good
which God does for Israel. And there shall not be
[a]an old man in your house forever. 33 But any of
your men *whom* I do not cut off from My altar shall
consume your eyes and grieve your heart. And
all the descendants of your house shall die in the
flower of their age. 34 Now this *shall be* [a]a sign to
you that will come upon your two sons, on Hophni
and Phinehas: [b]in one day they shall die, both of
them. 35 Then [a]I will raise up for Myself a faithful
priest *who* shall do according to what *is* in My heart
and in My mind. [b]I will build him a sure house, and
he shall walk before [c]My anointed forever. 36 [a]And
it shall come to pass that everyone who is left in
your house will come *and* bow down to him for
a piece of silver and a morsel of bread, and say,
"Please, put me in one of the priestly positions,
that I may eat a piece of bread." ' "

**SEEING JESUS IN THE SCRIPTURE**

**2:35** The faithful priest Samuel spoke of points to Jesus. Jesus is the faithful priest who stands between the Father and humanity and whose sacrifice of Himself paid for our sins once and for all (see Heb. 2:17).

### *SAMUEL'S FIRST PROPHECY*

**3** Now [a]the boy Samuel ministered to the LORD
before Eli. And [b]the word of the LORD was
rare in those days; *there was* no widespread
revelation. 2 And it came to pass at that time,
while Eli *was* lying down in his place, and when
his eyes had begun to grow [a]so dim that he could
not see, 3 and before [a]the lamp of God went out
in the tabernacle[1] of the LORD where the ark
of God *was,* and while Samuel was lying down,
4 that the LORD called Samuel. And he answered,
"Here I am!" 5 So he ran to Eli and said, "Here I
am, for you called me."

And he said, "I did not call; lie down again."
And he went and lay down.

6 Then the LORD called yet again, "Samuel!"

So Samuel arose and went to Eli, and said,
"Here I am, for you called me." He answered,
"I did not call, my son; lie down again." 7 (Now
Samuel [a]did not yet know the LORD, nor was the
word of the LORD yet revealed to him.)

8 And the LORD called Samuel again the third
time. So he arose and went to Eli, and said, "Here
I am, for you did call me."

Then Eli perceived that the LORD had called
the boy. 9 Therefore Eli said to Samuel, "Go, lie
down; and it shall be, if He calls you, that you
must say, [a]'Speak, LORD, for Your servant hears.' "
So Samuel went and lay down in his place.

10 Now the LORD came and stood and called
as at other times, "Samuel! Samuel!"

And Samuel answered, "Speak, for Your
servant hears."

11 Then the LORD said to Samuel: "Behold, I
will do something in Israel [a]at which both ears
of everyone who hears it will tingle. 12 In that day
I will perform against Eli [a]all that I have spoken
concerning his house, from beginning to end.
13 [a]For I have told him that I will [b]judge his house
forever for the iniquity which he knows, because
[c]his sons made themselves vile, and he [d]did not
restrain them. 14 And therefore I have sworn to the
house of Eli that the iniquity of Eli's house [a]shall
not be atoned for by sacrifice or offering forever."

15 So Samuel lay down until morning,[1] and
opened the doors of the house of the LORD. And
Samuel was afraid to tell Eli the vision. 16 Then
Eli called Samuel and said, "Samuel, my son!"

He answered, "Here I am."

17 And he said, "What *is* the word that *the
LORD* spoke to you? Please do not hide *it* from
me. [a]God do so to you, and more also, if you hide
anything from me of all the things that He said
to you." 18 Then Samuel told him everything, and
hid nothing from him. And he said, [a]"It *is* the
LORD. Let Him do what seems good to Him."

19 So Samuel [a]grew, and [b]the LORD was with
him [c]and let none of his words fall to the ground.
20 And all Israel [a]from Dan to Beersheba knew

**2:28** [a] Ex. 28:1, 4; Num. 16:5 [b] Lev. 2:3, 10; 6:16; 7:7, 8, 34, 35; Num. 5:9 **2:29** [a] Deut. 32:15 [b] Deut. 12:5; Ps. 26:8 [c] Matt. 10:37 **2:30** [a] Ex. 29:9; Num. 25:13 [b] Jer. 18:9, 10 [c] Ps. 91:14; Mal. 2:9–12 **2:31** [a] 1 Sam. 4:11–18; 22:18, 19; 1 Kin. 2:27, 35 **2:32** [a] Zech. 8:4 **2:34** [a] 1 Sam. 10:7–9; 1 Kin. 13:3 [b] 1 Sam. 4:11, 17 **2:35** [a] 1 Kin. 2:35; Ezek. 44:15; [Heb. 2:17; 7:26–28] [b] 2 Sam. 7:11, 27; 1 Kin. 11:38 [c] Ps. 18:50 **2:36** [a] 1 Kin. 2:27 **3:1** [a] 1 Sam. 2:11, 18 [b] Ps. 74:9; Ezek. 7:26; Amos 8:11, 12 **3:2** [a] Gen. 27:1; 48:10; 1 Sam. 4:15 **3:3** [a] Ex. 27:20, 21 [1] Hebrew *heykal,* palace or temple **3:7** [a] 1 Sam. 2:12; Acts 19:2; 1 Cor. 13:11 **3:9** [a] 1 Kin. 2:17 **3:11** [a] 2 Kin. 21:12; Jer. 19:3 **3:12** [a] 1 Sam. 2:27–36; Ezek. 12:25; Luke 21:33 **3:13** [a] 1 Sam. 2:29–31 [b] 1 Sam. 2:22; Ezek. 7:3; 18:30 [c] 1 Sam. 2:12, 17, 22 [d] 1 Sam. 2:23, 25 **3:14** [a] Num. 15:30, 31; Is. 22:14; Heb. 10:4, 26–31 **3:15** [1] Following Masoretic Text, Targum, and Vulgate; Septuagint adds *and he arose in the morning.* **3:17** [a] Ruth 1:17 **3:18** [a] Gen. 24:50; Ex. 34:5–7; Lev. 10:3; Is. 39:8; Acts 5:39 **3:19** [a] 1 Sam. 2:21 [b] Gen. 21:22; 28:15; 39:2, 21, 23 [c] 1 Sam. 9:6 **3:20** [a] Judg. 20:1

that Samuel *had been* established as a prophet
of the LORD. 21 Then the LORD appeared again in
Shiloh. For the LORD revealed Himself to Samuel
in Shiloh by [a]the word of the LORD.

4 And the word of Samuel came to all Israel.[1]

### THE ARK OF GOD CAPTURED

Now Israel went out to battle against the
Philistines, and encamped beside [a]Ebenezer;
and the Philistines encamped in Aphek. 2 Then
the [a]Philistines put themselves in battle array
against Israel. And when they joined battle, Is-
rael was defeated by the Philistines, who killed
about four thousand men of the army in the
field. 3 And when the people had come into the
camp, the elders of Israel said, "Why has the
LORD defeated us today before the Philistines?
[a]Let us bring the ark of the covenant of the LORD
from Shiloh to us, that when it comes among us it
may save us from the hand of our enemies." 4 So
the people sent to Shiloh, that they might bring
from there the ark of the covenant of the LORD
of hosts, [a]who dwells *between* [b]the cherubim.
And the [c]two sons of Eli, Hophni and Phinehas,
*were* there with the ark of the covenant of God.

5 And when the ark of the covenant of the
LORD came into the camp, all Israel shouted so
loudly that the earth shook. 6 Now when the Philis-
tines heard the noise of the shout, they said, "What
*does* the sound of this great shout in the camp of
the Hebrews *mean?*" Then they understood that
the ark of the LORD had come into the camp. 7 So
the Philistines were afraid, for they said, "God has
come into the camp!" And they said, [a]"Woe to us!
For such a thing has never happened before. 8 Woe
to us! Who will deliver us from the hand of these
mighty gods? These *are* the gods who struck the
Egyptians with all the plagues in the wilderness.
9 [a]Be strong and conduct yourselves like men, you
Philistines, that you do not become servants of
the Hebrews, [b]as they have been to you. Conduct
yourselves like men, and fight!"

10 So the Philistines fought, and [a]Israel was
defeated, and every man fled to his tent. There
was a very great slaughter, and there fell of
Israel thirty thousand foot soldiers. 11 Also [a]the
ark of God was captured; and [b]the two sons of
Eli, Hophni and Phinehas, died.

> **4:6–11** Apparently, the **Philistines** viewed the **ark** as some sort of idol. The loss of the ark, symbolic of God's presence among His people, was a great tragedy for Israel—even worse than the loss of life. The ark probably never returned to Shiloh.

### DEATH OF ELI

12 Then a man of Benjamin ran from the battle
line the same day, and [a]came to Shiloh with his
clothes torn and [b]dirt on his head. 13 Now when he
came, there was Eli, sitting on [a]a seat by the way-
side watching,[1] for his heart trembled for the ark
of God. And when the man came into the city and
told *it,* all the city cried out. 14 When Eli heard the
noise of the outcry, he said, "What *does* the sound
of this tumult *mean?*" And the man came quickly
and told Eli. 15 Eli was ninety-eight years old, and
[a]his eyes were so dim that he could not see.

16 Then the man said to Eli, "I *am* he who
came from the battle. And I fled today from
the battle line."

And he said, [a]"What happened, my son?"

17 So the messenger answered and said, "Is-
rael has fled before the Philistines, and there
has been a great slaughter among the people.
Also your two sons, Hophni and Phinehas, are
dead; and the ark of God has been captured."

18 Then it happened, when he made men-
tion of the ark of God, that Eli fell off the seat
backward by the side of the gate; and his neck
was broken and he died, for the man was old
and heavy. And he had judged Israel forty years.

### ICHABOD

19 Now his daughter-in-law, Phinehas' wife,
was with child, *due* to be delivered; and when she
heard the news that the ark of God was captured,
and that her father-in-law and her husband were
dead, she bowed herself and gave birth, for her
labor pains came upon her. 20 And about the
time of her death [a]the women who stood by her
said to her, "Do not fear, for you have borne a
son." But she did not answer, nor did she regard
*it.* 21 Then she named the child [a]Ichabod,[1] saying,
[b]"The glory has departed from Israel!" because
the ark of God had been captured and because
of her father-in-law and her husband. 22 And
she said, "The glory has departed from Israel,
for the ark of God has been captured."

### THE PHILISTINES AND THE ARK

5 Then the Philistines took the ark of God and
brought it [a]from Ebenezer to Ashdod. 2 When
the Philistines took the ark of God, they brought
it into the house of [a]Dagon[1] and set it by Dagon.
3 And when the people of Ashdod arose early
in the morning, there was Dagon, [a]fallen on its

**3:21** [a] 1 Sam. 3:1, 4 **4:1** [a] 1 Sam. 7:12 [1] Following Masoretic Text and Targum; Septuagint and Vulgate add *And it came to pass in those days that the Philistines gathered themselves together to fight;* Septuagint adds further *against Israel.* **4:2** [a] 1 Sam. 12:9 **4:3** [a] Num. 10:35; Josh. 6:6–21 **4:4** [a] Ex. 25:18–21; 1 Sam. 6:2; Ps. 80:1 [b] Num. 7:89 [c] 1 Sam. 2:12 **4:7** [a] Ex. 15:14 **4:9** [a] 1 Cor. 16:13 [b] Judg. 13:1; 1 Sam. 14:21 **4:10** [a] Lev. 26:17; Deut. 28:15, 25; 1 Sam. 4:2; 2 Sam. 18:17; 19:8; 2 Kin. 14:12; 2 Chr. 25:22 **4:11** [a] 1 Sam. 2:32; Ps. 78:60, 61 [b] 1 Sam. 2:34; Ps. 78:64 **4:12** [a] 2 Sam. 1:2 [b] Josh. 7:6; 2 Sam. 13:19; 15:32; Neh. 9:1; Job 2:12 **4:13** [a] 1 Sam. 1:9; 4:18 [1] Following Masoretic Text and Vulgate; Septuagint reads *beside the gate watching the road.* **4:15** [a] 1 Sam. 3:2; 1 Kin. 14:4 **4:16** [a] 2 Sam. 1:4 **4:20** [a] Gen. 35:16–19 **4:21** [a] 1 Sam. 14:3 [b] Ps. 26:8; 78:61; [Jer. 2:11] [1] Literally *Inglorious* **5:1** [a] 1 Sam. 4:1; 7:12 **5:2** [a] Judg. 16:23–30; 1 Chr. 10:8–10 [1] A Philistine idol **5:3** [a] Is. 19:1; 46:1, 2

APPLY THE TRUTH

## RELIGIONS

**5:1–12** "What works for you doesn't have to work for me." This is how many people view religion. It's like a diet or a workout plan. What works for one person may not work for someone else, and that's neither right nor wrong. There's not a one-size-fits-all option. Or religion is seen as a buffet where we pick and choose whatever we like. This doesn't work for Christianity though.

In this account, the Philistines thought their god had defeated the Lord because the Israelites had lost in battle (the Israelites lost because they disobeyed the Lord). In the end, God proved His power and authority over the Philistines and their false god. God has no rival or comparison. He doesn't coexist with any other. He's not one god among many. He's the one and only God. Other religions may permit their gods existing with God, but not Christianity.

In addition, a primary distinction between Christianity and all other major religions is its solution. Religions say we must work our way to God through good behavior, law keeping, and ceremony. Christianity says we cannot get to God; instead, God came to us. Jesus came as God in the flesh to make the way for us to have access to God.

face to the earth before the ark of the LORD. So
they took Dagon and [b]set it in its place again.
4 And when they arose early the next morning,
there was Dagon, fallen on its face to the ground
before the ark of the LORD. [a]The head of Dagon
and both the palms of its hands *were* broken off
on the threshold; only Dagon's *torso*[1] was left of
it. 5 Therefore neither the priests of Dagon nor
any who come into Dagon's house [a]tread on
the threshold of Dagon in Ashdod to this day.
6 But the [a]hand of the LORD was heavy on
the people of Ashdod, and He [b]ravaged them
and struck them with [c]tumors,[1] *both* Ashdod
and its [d]territory. 7 And when the men of Ash-
dod saw how *it was,* they said, "The ark of the
[a]God of Israel must not remain with us, for His
hand is harsh toward us and Dagon our god."
8 Therefore they sent and gathered to themselves
all the [a]lords of the Philistines, and said, "What
shall we do with the ark of the God of Israel?"
And they answered, "Let the ark of the God of
Israel be carried away to [b]Gath." So they carried
the ark of the God of Israel away. 9 So it was, after
they had carried it away, that [a]the hand of the
LORD was against the city with a very great de-
struction; and He struck the men of the city, both
small and great, and tumors broke out on them.
10 Therefore they sent the ark of God to
Ekron. So it was, as the ark of God came to Ekron,
that the Ekronites cried out, saying, "They have
brought the ark of the God of Israel to us, to kill
us and our people!" 11 So they sent and gathered
together all the lords of the Philistines, and said,
"Send away the ark of the God of Israel, and let
it go back to its own place, so that it does not
kill us and our people." For there was a deadly
destruction throughout all the city; the hand of
God was very heavy there. 12 And the men who
did not die were stricken with the tumors, and
the [a]cry of the city went up to heaven.

### THE ARK RETURNED TO ISRAEL

6 Now the ark of the LORD was in the country
of the Philistines seven months. 2 And the
Philistines [a]called for the priests and the divin-
ers, saying, "What shall we do with the ark of the
LORD? Tell us how we should send it to its place."
3 So they said, "If you send away the ark of the
God of Israel, do not send it [a]empty; but by all
means return *it* to Him *with* [b]a trespass offering.
Then you will be healed, and it will be known
to you why His hand is not removed from you."
4 Then they said, "What *is* the trespass offer-
ing which we shall return to Him?"
They answered, [a]"Five golden tumors and
five golden rats, *according to* the number of the
lords of the Philistines. For the same plague *was*
on all of you and on your lords. 5 Therefore you
shall make images of your tumors and images
of your rats that [a]ravage the land, and you shall
[b]give glory to the God of Israel; perhaps He will
[c]lighten His hand from you, from [d]your gods,
and from your land. 6 Why then do you harden
your hearts [a]as the Egyptians and Pharaoh hard-
ened their hearts? When He did mighty things
among them, [b]did they not let the people go,

**5:3** [b] Is. 46:7 **5:4** [a] Jer. 50:2; Ezek. 6:4, 6; Mic. 1:7 [1] Following Septuagint, Syriac, Targum, and Vulgate; Masoretic Text reads *Dagon.* **5:5** [a] Zeph. 1:9 **5:6** [a] Ex. 9:3; Deut. 2:15; 1 Sam. 5:7; 7:13; Ps. 32:4; 145:20; 147:6 [b] 1 Sam. 6:5 [c] Deut. 28:27; Ps. 78:66 [d] Josh. 15:46, 47 [1] Probably bubonic plague. Septuagint and Vulgate add here *And in the midst of their land rats sprang up, and there was a great death panic in the city.* **5:7** [a] 1 Sam. 6:5 **5:8** [a] 1 Sam. 6:4 [b] Josh. 11:22 **5:9** [a] Deut. 2:15; 1 Sam. 5:11; 7:13; 12:15 **5:12** [a] 1 Sam. 9:16; Jer. 14:2 **6:2** [a] Gen. 41:8; Ex. 7:11; Is. 2:6; 47:13; Dan. 2:2; 5:7 **6:3** [a] Ex. 23:15; Deut. 16:16 [b] Lev. 5:15, 16 **6:4** [a] 1 Sam. 5:6, 9, 12; 6:17 **6:5** [a] 1 Sam. 5:6 [b] Josh. 7:19; 1 Chr. 16:28, 29; Is. 42:12; Jer. 13:16; Mal. 2:2; Rev. 14:7 [c] 1 Sam. 5:6, 11; Ps. 39:10 [d] 1 Sam. 5:3, 4, 7 **6:6** [a] Ex. 7:13; 8:15; 9:34; 14:17 [b] Ex. 12:31

that they might depart? 7 Now therefore, make [a]a new cart, take two milk cows [b]which have never been yoked, and hitch the cows to the cart; and take their calves home, away from them. 8 Then take the ark of the LORD and set it on the cart; and put [a]the articles of gold which you are returning to Him *as* a trespass offering in a chest by its side. Then send it away, and let it go. 9 And watch: if it goes up the road to its own territory, to [a]Beth Shemesh, *then* He has done us this great evil. But if not, then [b]we shall know that *it is* not His hand *that* struck us—it happened to us by chance."

> **6:7–8** This seemed like a good test to the Philistines. The natural inclination of the **cows** would be to return home to **their calves**. If the cows went against their normal instincts, it would show that God was causing them to walk away from their calves.

10 Then the men did so; they took two milk cows and hitched them to the cart, and shut up their calves at home. 11 And they set the ark of the LORD on the cart, and the chest with the gold rats and the images of their tumors. 12 Then the cows headed straight for the road to Beth Shemesh, *and* went along the [a]highway, lowing as they went, and did not turn aside to the right hand or the left. And the lords of the Philistines went after them to the border of Beth Shemesh.

13 Now *the people of* Beth Shemesh *were* reaping their [a]wheat harvest in the valley; and they lifted their eyes and saw the ark, and rejoiced to see *it.* 14 Then the cart came into the field of Joshua of Beth Shemesh, and stood there; a large stone *was* there. So they split the wood of the cart and offered the cows as a burnt offering to the LORD. 15 The Levites took down the ark of the LORD and the chest that *was* with it, in which *were* the articles of gold, and put *them* on the large stone. Then the men of Beth Shemesh offered burnt offerings and made sacrifices the same day to the LORD. 16 So when [a]the five lords of the Philistines had seen *it,* they returned to Ekron the same day.

17 [a]These *are* the golden tumors which the Philistines returned *as* a trespass offering to the LORD: one for Ashdod, one for Gaza, one for Ashkelon, one for [b]Gath, one for Ekron; 18 and the golden rats, *according to* the number of all the cities of the Philistines *belonging* to the five lords, *both* fortified cities and country villages, even as far as the large *stone of* Abel on which they set the ark of the LORD, *which stone remains* to this day in the field of Joshua of Beth Shemesh.

19 Then [a]He struck the men of Beth Shemesh, because they had looked into the ark of the LORD. He [b]struck fifty thousand and seventy men[1] of the people, and the people lamented because the LORD had struck the people with a great slaughter.

### THE ARK AT KIRJATH JEARIM

20 And the men of Beth Shemesh said, [a]"Who is able to stand before this holy LORD God? And to whom shall it go up from us?" 21 So they sent messengers to the inhabitants of [a]Kirjath Jearim, saying, "The Philistines have brought back the ark of the LORD; come down *and* take it up with you."

**7** Then the men of [a]Kirjath Jearim came and took the ark of the LORD, and brought it into the house of [b]Abinadab on the hill, and [c]consecrated Eleazar his son to keep the ark of the LORD.

### SAMUEL JUDGES ISRAEL

2 So it was that the ark remained in Kirjath Jearim a long time; it was there twenty years. And all the house of Israel lamented after the LORD.

3 Then Samuel spoke to all the house of Israel, saying, "If you [a]return to the LORD with all your hearts, *then* [b]put away the foreign gods and the [c]Ashtoreths[1] from among you, and [d]prepare your hearts for the LORD, and [e]serve Him only; and He will deliver you from the hand of the Philistines." 4 So the children of Israel put away the [a]Baals and the Ashtoreths,[1] and served the LORD only.

5 And Samuel said, [a]"Gather all Israel to Mizpah, and [b]I will pray to the LORD for you." 6 So they gathered together at Mizpah, [a]drew water, and poured *it* out before the LORD. And they [b]fasted that day, and said there, [c]"We have sinned against the LORD." And Samuel judged the children of Israel at Mizpah.

7 Now when the Philistines heard that the children of Israel had gathered together at Mizpah, the lords of the Philistines went up against Israel. And when the children of Israel heard *of it,* they were afraid of the Philistines. 8 So the children of Israel said to Samuel, [a]"Do not cease to cry out to the LORD our God for us, that He may save us from the hand of the Philistines."

9 And Samuel took a [a]suckling lamb and offered *it as* a whole burnt offering to the LORD. Then [b]Samuel cried out to the LORD for Israel, and the LORD answered him. 10 Now as Samuel was offering up the burnt offering, the Philistines drew near to battle against Israel. [a]But the LORD thundered with a loud thunder upon the Philistines that day, and so confused them that they were overcome

6:7 [a] 2 Sam. 6:3 [b] Num. 19:2; Deut. 21:3, 4 6:8 [a] 1 Sam. 6:4, 5 6:9 [a] Josh. 15:10; 21:16 [b] 1 Sam. 6:3 6:12 [a] Num. 20:19 6:13 [a] 1 Sam. 12:17 6:16 [a] Josh. 13:3; Judg. 3:3 6:17 [a] 1 Sam. 6:4 [b] 1 Sam. 5:8 6:19 [a] Ex. 19:21; Num. 4:5, 15, 16, 20 [b] 2 Sam. 6:7 [1] Or *He struck seventy men of the people and fifty oxen of a man* 6:20 [a] Lev. 11:44, 45; Ps. 24:3, 4; Mal. 3:2; Rev. 6:17 6:21 [a] Josh. 9:17; 15:9, 60; 18:14; Judg. 18:12; 1 Chr. 13:5, 6 7:1 [a] 1 Sam. 6:21; Ps. 132:6 [b] 2 Sam. 6:3, 4 [c] Lev. 21:8 7:3 [a] Deut. 30:2–10 [b] Gen. 35:2 [c] Judg. 2:13 [d] Job 11:13 [e] Luke 4:8 [1] Canaanite goddesses 7:4 [a] Judg. 2:11; 10:16 [1] Canaanite goddesses 7:5 [a] Judg. 10:17; 20:1 [b] 1 Sam. 12:17–19 7:6 [a] 2 Sam. 14:14 [b] Neh. 9:1, 2 [c] 1 Sam. 12:10 7:8 [a] Is. 37:4 7:9 [a] Lev. 22:27 [b] 1 Sam. 12:18 7:10 [a] 2 Sam. 22:14, 15

before Israel. 11 And the men of Israel went out of
Mizpah and pursued the Philistines, and drove
them back as far as below Beth Car. 12 Then Sam-
uel [a]took a stone and set *it* up between Mizpah
and Shen, and called its name Ebenezer,[1] saying,
"Thus far the LORD has helped us."

13 [a]So the Philistines were subdued, and they
[b]did not come anymore into the territory of
Israel. And the hand of the LORD was against
the Philistines all the days of Samuel. 14 Then
the cities which the Philistines had taken from
Israel were restored to Israel, from Ekron to
Gath; and Israel recovered its territory from the
hands of the Philistines. Also there was peace
between Israel and the Amorites.

15 And Samuel [a]judged Israel all the days of
his life. 16 He went from year to year on a circuit
to Bethel, Gilgal, and Mizpah, and judged Israel
in all those places. 17 But [a]he always returned to
Ramah, for his home *was* there. There he judged
Israel, and there he [b]built an altar to the LORD.

### *ISRAEL DEMANDS A KING*

8 Now it came to pass when Samuel was [a]old
that he [b]made his [c]sons judges over Israel.
2 The name of his firstborn was Joel, and the
name of his second, Abijah; *they were* judges
in Beersheba. 3 But his sons [a]did not walk in his
ways; they turned aside [b]after dishonest gain,
[c]took bribes, and perverted justice.

4 Then all the elders of Israel gathered to-
gether and came to Samuel at Ramah, 5 and
said to him, "Look, you are old, and your sons
do not walk in your ways. Now [a]make us a king
to judge us like all the nations."

6 But the thing [a]displeased Samuel when
they said, "Give us a king to judge us." So Samuel

> **8:4–9** The reasons the **elders of Israel** gave for wanting a **king** were Samuel's age and his sons' unreliability. This is, in part, a sad commentary on Samuel's failure to raise his sons to honor and obey the Lord, particularly considering the example of Eli's sons. But this wasn't really a reason to ask for a king. The Israelite judges had always been appointed by God, rather than gaining their position by inheritance. There was no reason to think God wouldn't appoint someone to succeed Samuel. Rather, it seems the people's true motivation was to be **like all the nations** around them. Instead of being holy, they wanted to blend in. This fulfilled the prophecy in Deuteronomy 17:14–20.

[b]prayed to the LORD. 7 And the LORD said to Sam-
uel, "Heed the voice of the people in all that they
say to you; for [a]they have not rejected you, but
[b]they have rejected Me, that I should not reign
over them. 8 According to all the works which
they have done since the day that I brought them
up out of Egypt, even to this day—with which
they have forsaken Me and served other gods—
so they are doing to you also. 9 Now therefore,
heed their voice. However, you shall solemnly
forewarn them, and [a]show them the behavior
of the king who will reign over them."

10 So Samuel told all the words of the LORD
to the people who asked him for a king. 11 And he
said, [a]"This will be the behavior of the king who
will reign over you: He will take your [b]sons and
appoint *them* for his own [c]chariots and *to be* his
horsemen, and *some* will run before his chariots.
12 He will [a]appoint captains over his thousands
and captains over his fifties, *will set some* to plow
his ground and reap his harvest, and *some* to
make his weapons of war and equipment for his
chariots. 13 He will take your daughters *to be* per-
fumers, cooks, and bakers. 14 And [a]he will take the
best of your fields, your vineyards, and your olive
groves, and give *them* to his servants. 15 He will
take a tenth of your grain and your vintage, and
give it to his officers and servants. 16 And he will
take your male servants, your female servants,
your finest young men,[1] and your donkeys, and
put *them* to his work. 17 He will take a tenth of
your sheep. And you will be his servants. 18 And
you will cry out in that day because of your king
whom you have chosen for yourselves, and the
LORD [a]will not hear you in that day."

19 Nevertheless the people [a]refused to obey
the voice of Samuel; and they said, "No, but we
will have a king over us, 20 that we also may be
[a]like all the nations, and that our king may judge
us and go out before us and fight our battles."

21 And Samuel heard all the words of the
people, and he repeated them in the hearing of
the LORD. 22 So the LORD said to Samuel, [a]"Heed
their voice, and make them a king."

And Samuel said to the men of Israel, "Every
man go to his city."

### *SAUL CHOSEN TO BE KING*

9 There was a man of Benjamin whose name
*was* [a]Kish the son of Abiel, the son of Zeror,
the son of Bechorath, the son of Aphiah, a Ben-
jamite, a mighty man of power. 2 And he had a
choice and handsome son whose name *was* Saul.
*There was* not a more handsome person than he
among the children of Israel. [a]From his shoulders
upward *he was* taller than any of the people.

3 Now the donkeys of Kish, Saul's father,
were lost. And Kish said to his son Saul, "Please

**7:12** [a] Josh. 4:9; 24:26 [1] Literally *Stone of Help* **7:13** [a] Judg. 13:1 [b] 1 Sam. 13:5 **7:15** [a] 1 Sam. 12:11 **7:17** [a] 1 Sam. 8:4 [b] Judg. 21:4 **8:1** [a] 1 Sam. 12:2 [b] Deut. 16:18, 19 [c] Judg. 10:4 **8:3** [a] Jer. 22:15–17 [b] Ex. 18:21 [c] Ex. 23:6–8 **8:5** [a] Deut. 17:14, 15 **8:6** [a] 1 Sam. 12:17 [b] 1 Sam. 7:9 **8:7** [a] Ex. 16:8 [b] 1 Sam. 10:19 **8:9** [a] 1 Sam. 8:11–18 **8:11** [a] Deut. 17:14–20 [b] 1 Sam. 14:52 [c] 2 Sam. 15:1 **8:12** [a] 1 Sam. 22:7 **8:14** [a] 1 Kin. 21:7 **8:16** [1] Septuagint reads *cattle.* **8:18** [a] Prov. 1:25–28; Is. 1:15; Mic. 3:4 **8:19** [a] Is. 66:4; Jer. 44:16 **8:20** [a] 1 Sam. 8:5 **8:22** [a] 1 Sam. 8:7; Hos. 13:11 **9:1** [a] 1 Sam. 14:51; 1 Chr. 8:33; 9:36–39 **9:2** [a] 1 Sam. 10:23

take one of the servants with you, and arise, go and look for the donkeys." 4 So he passed through the mountains of Ephraim and through the land of [a]Shalisha, but they did not find *them.* Then they passed through the land of Shaalim, and *they were* not *there.* Then he passed through the land of the Benjamites, but they did not find *them.*

5 When they had come to the land of [a]Zuph, Saul said to his servant who *was* with him, "Come, let [b]us return, lest my father cease *caring* about the donkeys and become worried about us."

6 And he said to him, "Look now, *there is* in this city [a]a man of God, and *he is* an honorable man; [b]all that he says surely comes to pass. So let us go there; perhaps he can show us the way that we should go."

7 Then Saul said to his servant, "But look, *if* we go, [a]what shall we bring the man? For the bread in our vessels is all gone, and *there is* no present to bring to the man of God. What do we have?"

8 And the servant answered Saul again and said, "Look, I have here at hand one-fourth of a shekel of silver. I will give *that* to the man of God, to tell us our way." 9 (Formerly in Israel, when a man [a]went to inquire of God, he spoke thus: "Come, let us go to the seer"; for *he who is* now *called* a prophet was formerly called [b]a seer.)

10 Then Saul said to his servant, "Well said; come, let us go." So they went to the city where the man of God *was.*

11 As they went up the hill to the city, [a]they met some young women going out to draw water, and said to them, "Is the seer here?"

12 And they answered them and said, "Yes, there he is, just ahead of you. Hurry now; for today he came to this city, because [a]there is a sacrifice of the people today [b]on the high place. 13 As soon as you come into the city, you will surely find him before he goes up to the high place to eat. For the people will not eat until he comes, because he must bless the sacrifice; afterward those who are invited will eat. Now therefore, go up, for about this time you will find him." 14 So they went up to the city. As they were coming into the city, there was Samuel, coming out toward them on his way up to the high place.

15 [a]Now the LORD had told Samuel in his ear the day before Saul came, saying, 16 "Tomorrow about this time [a]I will send you a man from the land of Benjamin, [b]and you shall anoint him commander over My people Israel, that he may save My people from the hand of the Philistines; for I have [c]looked upon My people, because their cry has come to Me."

> **9:16** To **anoint** was to pour oil on a person's head as a way of announcing the Lord had chosen him for a specific position, whether it was king, priest, or prophet.

17 So when Samuel saw Saul, the LORD said to him, [a]"There he is, the man of whom I spoke to you. This one shall reign over My people." 18 Then Saul drew near to Samuel in the gate, and said, "Please tell me, where *is* the seer's house?" 19 Samuel answered Saul and said, "I *am* the seer. Go up before me to the high place, for you shall eat with me today; and tomorrow I will let you go and will tell you all that *is* in your heart. 20 But as for [a]your donkeys that were lost three days ago, do not be anxious about them, for they have been found. And on whom [b]*is* all the desire of Israel? *Is it* not on you and on all your father's house?"

21 And Saul answered and said, [a]"*Am* I not a Benjamite, of the [b]smallest of the tribes of Israel, and [c]my family the least of all the families of the tribe[1] of Benjamin? Why then do you speak like this to me?"

22 Now Samuel took Saul and his servant and brought them into the hall, and had them sit in the place of honor among those who were invited; there *were* about thirty persons. 23 And Samuel said to the cook, "Bring the portion which I gave you, of which I said to you, 'Set it apart.' " 24 So the cook took up [a]the thigh with its upper part and set *it* before Saul. And *Samuel* said, "Here it is, what was kept back. *It* was set apart for you. Eat; for until this time it has been kept for you, since I said I invited the people." So Saul ate with Samuel that day.

25 When they had come down from the high place into the city, *Samuel* spoke with Saul on [a]the top of the house.[1] 26 They arose early; and it was about the dawning of the day that Samuel called to Saul on the top of the house, saying, "Get up, that I may send you on your way." And Saul arose, and both of them went outside, he and Samuel.

### *SAUL ANOINTED KING*

27 As they were going down to the outskirts of the city, Samuel said to Saul, "Tell the servant to go on ahead of us." And he went on. "But you stand here awhile, that I may announce to you the word of God."

9:4 [a] 2 Kin. 4:42 9:5 [a] 1 Sam. 1:1 [b] 1 Sam. 10:2 9:6 [a] Deut. 33:1; 1 Kin. 13:1; 2 Kin. 5:8 [b] 1 Sam. 3:19 9:7 [a] Judg. 6:18; 13:17; 1 Kin. 14:3; 2 Kin. 4:42; 8:8 9:9 [a] Gen. 25:22 [b] 2 Sam. 24:11; 2 Kin. 17:13; 1 Chr. 26:28; 29:29; 2 Chr. 16:7, 10; Is. 30:10; Amos 7:12 9:11 [a] Gen. 24:11, 15; 29:8, 9; Ex. 2:16 9:12 [a] Gen. 31:54; 1 Sam. 16:2 [b] 1 Sam. 7:17; 10:5; 1 Kin. 3:2 9:15 [a] 1 Sam. 15:1 9:16 [a] Deut. 17:15 [b] 1 Sam. 10:1 [c] Ex. 2:23–25; 3:7, 9 9:17 [a] 1 Sam. 16:12; Hos. 13:11 9:20 [a] 1 Sam. 9:3 [b] 1 Sam. 8:5, 19; 12:13 9:21 [a] 1 Sam. 15:17 [b] Judg. 20:46–48; Ps. 68:27 [c] Judg. 6:15 [1] Literally *tribes* 9:24 [a] Ex. 29:22, 27; Lev. 7:32, 33; Num. 18:18; Ezek. 24:4 9:25 [a] Deut. 22:8; 2 Sam. 11:2; Luke 5:19; Acts 10:9 [1] Following Masoretic Text and Targum; Septuagint omits *He spoke with Saul on the top of the house;* Septuagint and Vulgate add *And he prepared a bed for Saul on the top of the house, and he slept.*

**10** Then [a]Samuel took a flask of oil and poured
*it* on his head, [b]and kissed him and said:
"*Is it* not because [c]the LORD has anointed you
commander over [d]His inheritance?[1] 2 When you
have departed from me today, you will find two
men by [a]Rachel's tomb in the territory of Ben-
jamin [b]at Zelzah; and they will say to you, 'The
donkeys which you went to look for have been
found. And now your father has ceased caring
about the donkeys and is worrying about [c]you,
saying, "What shall I do about my son?"' 3 Then
you shall go on forward from there and come
to the terebinth tree of Tabor. There three men
going up [a]to God at Bethel will meet you, one
carrying three young goats, another carrying
three loaves of bread, and another carrying a
skin of wine. 4 And they will greet you and give
you two *loaves* of bread, which you shall receive
from their hands. 5 After that you shall come to
the hill of God [a]where the Philistine garrison *is*.
And it will happen, when you have come there
to the city, that you will meet a group of proph-
ets coming down [b]from the high place with a
stringed instrument, a tambourine, a flute, and a
harp before them; [c]and they will be prophesying.
6 Then [a]the Spirit of the LORD will come upon
you, and [b]you will prophesy with them and be
turned into another man. 7 And let it be, when
these [a]signs come to you, *that* you do as the
occasion demands; for [b]God *is* with you. 8 You
shall go down before me [a]to Gilgal; and surely I
will come down to you to offer burnt offerings
*and* make sacrifices of peace offerings. [b]Seven
days you shall wait, till I come to you and show
you what you should do."

9 So it was, when he had turned his back to
go from Samuel, that God gave him another
heart; and all those signs came to pass that day.
10 [a]When they came there to the hill, there was [b]a
group of prophets to meet him; then the Spirit of
God came upon him, and he prophesied among
them. 11 And it happened, when all who knew
him formerly saw that he indeed prophesied
among the prophets, that the people said to one
another, "What *is* this *that* has come upon the
son of Kish? [a]*Is* Saul also among the prophets?"
12 Then a man from there answered and said,
"But [a]who *is* their father?" Therefore it became
a proverb: "*Is* Saul also among the prophets?"
13 And when he had finished prophesying, he
went to the high place.

14 Then Saul's [a]uncle said to him and his
servant, "Where did you go?"

So he said, "To look for the donkeys. When
we saw that *they were* nowhere *to be found*, we
went to Samuel."

15 And Saul's uncle said, "Tell me, please,
what Samuel said to you."

16 So Saul said to his uncle, "He told us plainly
that the donkeys had been [a]found." But about
the matter of the kingdom, he did not tell him
what Samuel had said.

### *SAUL PROCLAIMED KING*

17 Then Samuel called the people together [a]to
the LORD [b]at Mizpah, 18 and said to the children
of Israel, [a]"Thus says the LORD God of Israel: 'I
brought up Israel out of Egypt, and delivered
you from the hand of the Egyptians *and* from
the hand of all kingdoms and from those who
oppressed you.' 19 [a]But you have today rejected
your God, who Himself saved you from all your
adversities and your tribulations; and you have
said to Him, 'No, set a king over us!' Now there-
fore, present yourselves before the LORD by your
tribes and by your clans."[1]

20 And when Samuel had [a]caused all the
tribes of Israel to come near, the tribe of Ben-
jamin was chosen. 21 When he had caused the
tribe of Benjamin to come near by their families,
the family of Matri was chosen. And Saul the
son of Kish was chosen. But when they sought
him, he could not be found. 22 Therefore they
[a]inquired of the LORD further, "Has the man
come here yet?"

And the LORD answered, "There he is, hid-
den among the equipment."

23 So they ran and brought him from there;
and when he stood among the people, [a]he was
taller than any of the people from his shoulders
upward. 24 And Samuel said to all the people,
"Do you see him [a]whom the LORD has cho-
sen, that *there is* no one like him among all
the people?"

So all the people shouted and said, [b]"Long
live the king!"

25 Then Samuel explained to the people [a]the
behavior of royalty, and wrote *it* in a book and
laid *it* up before the LORD. And Samuel sent
all the people away, every man to his house.
26 And Saul also went home [a]to Gibeah; and
valiant *men* went with him, whose hearts God
had touched. 27 [a]But some [b]rebels said, "How
can this man save us?" So they despised him,
[c]and brought him no presents. But he held
his peace.

10:1 [a] Ex. 30:23–33; 1 Sam. 9:16; 16:13; 2 Kin. 9:3, 6 [b] Ps. 2:12 [c] 2 Sam. 5:2; Acts 13:21 [d] Ex. 34:9; Deut. 32:9; Ps. 78:71 [1] Following Masoretic Text, Targum, and Vulgate; Septuagint reads *His people Israel; and you shall rule the people of the Lord;* Septuagint and Vulgate add *And you shall deliver His people from the hands of their enemies all around them. And this shall be a sign to you, that God has anointed you to be a prince.* 10:2 [a] Gen. 35:16–20; 48:7 [b] Josh. 18:28 [c] 1 Sam. 9:3–5 10:3 [a] Gen. 28:22; 35:1, 3, 7 10:5 [a] 1 Sam. 13:2, 3 [b] 1 Sam. 19:12, 20; 2 Kin. 2:3, 5, 15 [c] Ex. 15:20, 21; 2 Kin. 3:15; 1 Chr. 25:1–6; 1 Cor. 14:1 10:6 [a] Num. 11:25, 29; Judg. 14:6; 1 Sam. 16:13 [b] 1 Sam. 10:10; 19:23, 24 10:7 [a] Ex. 4:8; Luke 2:12 [b] Josh. 1:5; Judg. 6:12; 1 Sam. 3:19; [Heb. 13:5] 10:8 [a] 1 Sam. 11:14, 15; 13:8 [b] 1 Sam. 13:8–10 10:10 [a] 1 Sam. 10:5 [b] 1 Sam. 19:20 10:11 [a] 1 Sam. 19:24; Amos 7:14, 15; Matt. 13:54–57; John 7:15; Acts 4:13 10:12 [a] John 5:30, 36 10:14 [a] 1 Sam. 14:50 10:16 [a] 1 Sam. 9:20 10:17 [a] Judg. 20:1 [b] 1 Sam. 7:5, 6 10:18 [a] Judg. 6:8, 9; 1 Sam. 8:8; 12:6, 8 10:19 [a] 1 Sam. 8:7, 19; 12:12 [1] Literally *thousands* 10:20 [a] Acts 1:24, 26 10:22 [a] 1 Sam. 23:2, 4, 10, 11 10:23 [a] 1 Sam. 9:2 10:24 [a] Deut. 17:15; 1 Sam. 9:16; 2 Sam. 21:6 [b] 1 Kin. 1:25, 39 10:25 [a] Deut. 17:14–20; 1 Sam. 8:11–18 10:26 [a] Judg. 20:14 10:27 [a] 1 Sam. 11:12 [b] Deut. 13:13; 1 Sam. 25:17 [c] 2 Sam. 8:2; 1 Kin. 4:21; 10:25; 2 Chr. 17:5; Matt. 2:11

1 SAMUEL 10:1–27

## SELF-RULE

23

STORY OF SCRIPTURE

### WHAT'S GOING ON?

This passage marks a significant shift in Israel's history in which they moved from being ruled by judges to a centralized monarchy. This moment is tragic though as it marks the people's rejection of God as their king, instead desiring to be led by a human king like the nations around them. Saul fit the classic description of a king. He was tall, strong, handsome, and from a prominent family. However, Saul represents humanity's attempt at self-governance apart from God. His anointing as Israel's king gives us flashbacks to the garden of Eden when Adam and Eve rejected God's rule and forged their own path. Despite Israel's sinful demand for a king, God worked within their desires to establish His purpose, leading the way for King David.

### WHAT DOES THIS MEAN FOR ME?

On the outside, this story seems like a happy one. A brave, new, charismatic leader was chosen for Israel. On the outside, Saul seemed to have everything it took to be a great king. However, things aren't always as they seem. At the heart of this passage is rebellion and selfishness. This story warns us that just because something looks good doesn't mean it is good. We must have eyes like Samuel, who saw what was happening beneath the surface.

### DID YOU CATCH THE PATTERN?

Since the garden of Eden, God's people have been enticed by autonomy. We saw this pattern repeated in the Tower of Babel and the Israelites rebelling repeatedly in the wilderness and will see it again when the Israelites refuse to repent of their ongoing idolatry. Most notably, though, we see this pattern in our own sinfulness that is marked by our own desire for self-rule.

*For the next* Story of Scripture *reading and devotion, turn to 1 Samuel 17:1–50 on page 290.*

### *SAUL SAVES JABESH GILEAD*

**11** Then [a]Nahash the Ammonite came up and encamped against [b]Jabesh Gilead; and all the men of Jabesh said to Nahash, [c]"Make a covenant with us, and we will serve you."

2 And Nahash the Ammonite answered them, "On this *condition* I will make *a covenant* with you, that I may put out all your right eyes, and bring [a]reproach on all Israel."

3 Then the elders of Jabesh said to him, "Hold off for seven days, that we may send messengers to all the territory of Israel. And then, if *there is* no one to save us, we will come out to you."

4 So the messengers came [a]to Gibeah of Saul and told the news in the hearing of the people. And [b]all the people lifted up their voices and wept. 5 Now there was Saul, coming behind the herd from the field; and Saul said, "What *troubles* the people, that they weep?" And they told him the words of the men of Jabesh. 6 [a]Then the Spirit of God came upon Saul when he heard this news, and his anger was greatly aroused. 7 So he took a yoke of oxen and [a]cut them in pieces, and sent *them* throughout all the territory of Israel by the hands of messengers, saying, [b]"Whoever does not go out with Saul and Samuel to battle, so it shall be done to his oxen."

And the fear of the LORD fell on the people, and they came out with one consent. 8 When he numbered them in [a]Bezek, the children [b]of Israel were three hundred thousand, and the men of Judah thirty thousand. 9 And they said to the messengers who came, "Thus you shall say to the men of Jabesh Gilead: 'Tomorrow, by *the time* the sun is hot, you shall have help.'" Then the messengers came and reported *it* to the men of Jabesh, and they were glad. 10 Therefore the men of Jabesh said, "Tomorrow we will come out to you, and you may do with us whatever seems good to you."

11 So it was, on the next day, that [a]Saul put the people [b]in three companies; and they came into the midst of the camp in the morning watch, and killed Ammonites until the heat of the day. And it happened that those who survived were scattered, so that no two of them were left together.

12 Then the people said to Samuel, [a]"Who *is* he who said, 'Shall Saul reign over us?' [b]Bring the men, that we may put them to death."

**11:1** [a] 1 Sam. 12:12 [b] Judg. 21:8; 1 Sam. 31:11 [c] Gen. 26:28; 1 Kin. 20:34; Job 41:4; Ezek. 17:13 **11:2** [a] Gen. 34:14; 1 Sam. 17:26; Ps. 44:13 **11:4** [a] 1 Sam. 10:26; 15:34; 2 Sam. 21:6 [b] Gen. 27:38; Judg. 2:4; 20:23, 26; 21:2; 1 Sam. 30:4 **11:6** [a] Judg. 3:10; 6:34; 11:29; 13:25; 14:6; 1 Sam. 10:10; 16:13 **11:7** [a] Judg. 19:29 [b] Judg. 21:5, 8, 10 **11:8** [a] Judg. 1:5 [b] 2 Sam. 24:9 **11:11** [a] 1 Sam. 31:11 [b] Judg. 7:16, 20 **11:12** [a] 1 Sam. 10:27 [b] Luke 19:27

13 But Saul said, [a]"Not a man shall be put to death this day, for today [b]the LORD has accomplished salvation in Israel."

14 Then Samuel said to the people, "Come, let us go [a]to Gilgal and renew the kingdom there." 15 So all the people went to Gilgal, and there they made Saul king [a]before the LORD in Gilgal. [b]There they made sacrifices of peace offerings before the LORD, and there Saul and all the men of Israel rejoiced greatly.

### SAMUEL'S ADDRESS AT SAUL'S CORONATION

**12** Now Samuel said to all Israel: "Indeed I have heeded [a]your voice in all that you said to me, and [b]have made a king over you. 2 And now here is the king, [a]walking before you; [b]and I am old and grayheaded, and look, my sons *are* with you. I have walked before you from my childhood to this day. 3 Here I am. Witness against me before the LORD and before [a]His anointed: [b]Whose ox have I taken, or whose donkey have I taken, or whom have I cheated? Whom have I oppressed, or from whose hand have I received *any* [c]bribe with which to [d]blind my eyes? I will restore *it* to you."

4 And they said, [a]"You have not cheated us or oppressed us, nor have you taken anything from any man's hand."

5 Then he said to them, "The LORD *is* witness against you, and His anointed *is* witness this day, [a]that you have not found anything [b]in my hand."

And they answered, "*He is* witness."

6 Then Samuel said to the people, [a]"*It is* the LORD who raised up Moses and Aaron, and who brought your fathers up from the land of Egypt. 7 Now therefore, stand still, that I may [a]reason with you before the LORD concerning all the [b]righteous acts of the LORD which He did to you and your fathers: 8 [a]When Jacob had gone into Egypt,[1] and your fathers [b]cried out to the LORD, then the LORD [c]sent Moses and Aaron, who brought your fathers out of Egypt and made them dwell in this place. 9 And when they [a]forgot the LORD their God, He sold them into the hand of [b]Sisera, commander of the army of Hazor, into the hand of the [c]Philistines, and into the hand of the king of [d]Moab; and they fought against them. 10 Then they cried out to the LORD, and said, [a]'We have sinned, because we have forsaken the LORD [b]and served the Baals and Ashtoreths;[1] but now deliver us from the hand of our enemies, and we will serve You.' 11 And the LORD sent Jerubbaal,[1] Bedan,[2] [a]Jephthah, and [b]Samuel,[3] and delivered you out of the hand of your enemies on every side; and you dwelt in safety. 12 And when you saw that [a]Nahash king of the Ammonites came against you, [b]you said to me, 'No, but a king shall reign over us,' when [c]the LORD your God *was* your king.

13 "Now therefore, [a]here is the king [b]whom you have chosen *and* whom you have desired. And take note, [c]the LORD has set a king over you. 14 If you [a]fear the LORD and serve Him and obey His voice, and do not rebel against the commandment of the LORD, then both you and the king who reigns over you will continue following the LORD your God. 15 However, if you do [a]not obey the voice of the LORD, but [b]rebel against the commandment of the LORD, then the hand of the LORD will be against you, as *it was* against your fathers.

16 "Now therefore, [a]stand and see this great thing which the LORD will do before your eyes: 17 *Is* today not the [a]wheat harvest? [b]I will call to the LORD, and He will send thunder and [c]rain, that you may perceive and see that [d]your wickedness *is* great, which you have done in the sight of the LORD, in asking a king for yourselves."

18 So Samuel called to the LORD, and the LORD sent thunder and rain that day; and [a]all the people greatly feared the LORD and Samuel.

19 And all the people said to Samuel, [a]"Pray for your servants to the LORD your God, that we may not die; for we have added to all our sins the evil of asking a king for ourselves."

20 Then Samuel said to the people, "Do not fear. You have done all this wickedness; [a]yet do not turn aside from following the LORD, but serve the LORD with all your heart. 21 And [a]do not turn aside; [b]for *then you would go* after empty things which cannot profit or deliver, for they *are* nothing. 22 For [a]the LORD will not forsake [b]His people, [c]for His great name's sake, because [d]it has pleased the LORD to make you His people. 23 Moreover, as for me, far be it from me that I should sin against the LORD [a]in ceasing to pray for you; but [b]I will teach you the [c]good and the right way. 24 [a]Only fear the LORD, and serve Him in truth with all your heart; for [b]consider what [c]great things He has done for you. 25 But if you still do wickedly, [a]you shall be swept away, [b]both you and your king."

### SAUL'S UNLAWFUL SACRIFICE

**13** Saul reigned one year; and when he had reigned two years over Israel,[1] 2 Saul chose for himself three thousand *men* of Israel. Two thousand were with Saul in [a]Michmash and in

11:13 [a] 1 Sam. 10:27; 2 Sam. 19:22 [b] Ex. 14:13, 30; 1 Sam. 19:5 11:14 [a] 1 Sam. 7:16; 10:8 11:15 [a] 1 Sam. 10:17 [b] Josh. 8:31; 1 Sam. 10:8
12:1 [a] 1 Sam. 8:5, 7, 9, 20, 22 [b] 1 Sam. 10:24; 11:14, 15 12:2 [a] Num. 27:17 [b] 1 Sam. 8:1, 5 12:3 [a] 1 Sam. 10:1; 24:6 [b] Num. 16:15 [c] Ex. 23:8 [d] Deut. 16:19 12:4 [a] Lev. 19:13 12:5 [a] Acts 23:9; 24:20 [b] Ex. 22:4 12:6 [a] Mic. 6:4 12:7 [a] Is. 1:18 [b] Judg. 5:11 12:8 [a] Gen. 46:5, 6 [b] Ex. 2:23–25 [c] Ex. 3:10; 4:14–16 [1] Following Masoretic Text, Targum, and Vulgate; Septuagint adds *and the Egyptians afflicted them.* 12:9 [a] Judg. 3:7 [b] Judg. 4:2 [c] Judg. 3:31; 10:7; 13:1 [d] Judg. 3:12–30 12:10 [a] Judg. 10:10 [b] Judg. 2:13; 3:7 [1] Canaanite goddesses 12:11 [a] Judg. 11:1 [b] 1 Sam. 7:13 [1] Syriac reads *Deborah;* Targum reads *Gideon.* [2] Septuagint and Syriac read *Barak;* Targum reads *Simson.* [3] Syriac reads *Simson.* 12:12 [a] 1 Sam. 11:1, 2 [b] 1 Sam. 8:5, 19, 20 [c] Judg. 8:23 12:13 [a] 1 Sam. 10:24 [b] 1 Sam. 8:5; 12:17, 19 [c] Hos. 13:11 12:14 [a] Josh. 24:14 12:15 [a] Deut. 28:15 [b] Is. 1:20 12:16 [a] Ex. 14:13, 31 12:17 [a] Gen. 30:14 [b] [James 5:16–18] [c] Ezra 10:9 [d] 1 Sam. 8:7 12:18 [a] Ex. 14:31 12:19 [a] Ex. 9:28 12:20 [a] Deut. 11:16 12:21 [a] 2 Chr. 25:15 [b] Is. 41:29 12:22 [a] Deut. 31:6 [b] Is. 43:21 [c] Jer. 14:21 [d] Deut. 7:6–11 12:23 [a] Rom. 1:9 [b] Ps. 34:11 [c] 1 Kin. 8:36 12:24 [a] Eccl. 12:13 [b] Is. 5:12 [c] Deut. 10:21 12:25 [a] Josh. 24:20 [b] Deut. 28:36 13:1 [1] The Hebrew is difficult (compare 2 Samuel 5:4; 2 Kings 14:2; see also 2 Samuel 2:10; Acts 13:21). 13:2 [a] 1 Sam. 14:5, 31

LIVE THE TRUTH

## PRAYING

**12:23** Prayer isn't as mysterious as it sometimes seems. It's simply talking with God. Communication is an essential part of any relationship. Just as friends, spouses, and teammates talk with one another to know each other, we need to talk with God to deepen our most important relationship. This was Samuel's message to the Israelites. Prayer isn't optional; it's essential.

While defining prayer is simple, practicing it can be far from it. Thankfully, Jesus taught us how to pray in Matthew 6:5–15. His model includes worshiping God, giving thanks to God, confessing sins to God, making reconciliation with others, and asking for your needs and the needs of others. Prayer also includes asking God questions and simply listening for Him to guide you. Don't miss that last part—it's what makes prayer so powerful. Prayer is not about us bending God's will to ours. It's the opposite. It's about us remembering God is in control, He loves us, and He is perfectly good. Prayer puts us in God's presence, and it puts us there in the right posture: kneeling in submission. This is why prayer is so important. Indeed, it's the key to the Christian life.

the mountains of Bethel, and a thousand were
with [b]Jonathan in [c]Gibeah of Benjamin. The rest
of the people he sent away, every man to his tent.
3 And Jonathan attacked [a]the garrison of the
Philistines that *was* in [b]Geba, and the Philistines
heard *of it.* Then Saul blew the trumpet throughout
all the land, saying, "Let the Hebrews hear!" 4 Now
all Israel heard it said *that* Saul had attacked a
garrison of the Philistines, and *that* Israel had also
become an abomination to the Philistines. And
the people were called together to Saul at Gilgal.
5 Then the Philistines gathered together to
fight with Israel, thirty[1] thousand chariots and
six thousand horsemen, and people [a]as the sand
which *is* on the seashore in multitude. And they
came up and encamped in Michmash, to the
east of [b]Beth Aven. 6 When the men of Israel
saw that they were in danger (for the people
were distressed), then the people [a]hid in caves,
in thickets, in rocks, in holes, and in pits. 7 And
*some of* the Hebrews crossed over the Jordan to
the [a]land of Gad and Gilead.
As for Saul, he *was* still in Gilgal, and all the
people followed him trembling. 8 [a]Then he waited
seven days, according to the time set by Samuel.
But Samuel did not come to Gilgal; and the people
were scattered from him. 9 So Saul said, "Bring
a burnt offering and peace offerings here to
me." And he offered the burnt offering. 10 Now it
happened, as soon as he had finished presenting
the burnt offering, that Samuel came; and Saul
went out to meet him, that he might greet him.
11 And Samuel said, "What have you done?"
Saul said, "When I saw that the people were
scattered from me, and *that* you did not come
within the days appointed, and *that* the Philis-
tines gathered together at Michmash, 12 then I
said, 'The Philistines will now come down on
me at Gilgal, and I have not made supplication
to the LORD.' Therefore I felt compelled, and
offered a burnt offering."
13 And Samuel said to Saul, [a]"You have done
foolishly. [b]You have not kept the commandment
of the LORD your God, which He commanded you.
For now the LORD would have established your
kingdom over Israel forever. 14 [a]But now your king-
dom shall not continue. [b]The LORD has sought
for Himself a man [c]after His own heart, and the
LORD has commanded him *to be* commander over
His people, because you have [d]not kept what the
LORD commanded you."
15 Then Samuel arose and went up from Gilgal
to Gibeah of Benjamin.[1] And Saul numbered the
people present with him, [a]about six hundred men.

### *NO WEAPONS FOR THE ARMY*

16 Saul, Jonathan his son, and the people
present with them remained in Gibeah of Benja-
min. But the Philistines encamped in Michmash.
17 Then raiders came out of the camp of the
Philistines in three companies. One company
turned onto the road to [a]Ophrah, to the land of
Shual, 18 another company turned to the road *to*
[a]Beth Horon, and another company turned *to*
the road of the border that overlooks the Valley
of [b]Zeboim toward the wilderness.
19 Now [a]there was no blacksmith to be found
throughout all the land of Israel, for the Philis-
tines said, "Lest the Hebrews make swords or
spears." 20 But all the Israelites would go down

**13:2** [b] 1 Sam. 14:1 [c] 1 Sam. 10:26 **13:3** [a] 1 Sam. 10:5 [b] 2 Sam. 5:25 **13:5** [a] Judg. 7:12 [b] Josh. 7:2; 1 Sam. 14:23 [1] Following Masoretic Text, Septuagint, Targum, and Vulgate; Syriac and some manuscripts of the Septuagint read *three.* **13:6** [a] Judg. 6:2; 1 Sam. 14:11 **13:7** [a] Num. 32:1–42 **13:8** [a] 1 Sam. 10:8 **13:13** [a] 2 Chr. 16:9 [b] 1 Sam. 15:11, 22, 28 **13:14** [a] 1 Sam. 15:28; 31:6 [b] 1 Sam. 16:1 [c] Ps. 89:20; Acts 7:46; 13:22 [d] 1 Sam. 15:11, 19 **13:15** [a] 1 Sam. 13:2, 6, 7; 14:2 [1] Following Masoretic Text and Targum; Septuagint and Vulgate add *And the rest of the people went up after Saul to meet the people who fought against them, going from Gilgal to Gibeah in the hill of Benjamin.* **13:17** [a] Josh. 18:23 **13:18** [a] Josh. 16:3; 18:13, 14 [b] Gen. 14:2; Neh. 11:34 **13:19** [a] Judg. 5:8; 2 Kin. 24:14; Jer. 24:1; 29:2

to the Philistines to sharpen each man's plowshare, his mattock, his ax, and his sickle; 21 and the charge for a sharpening was a pim[1] for the plowshares, the mattocks, the forks, and the axes, and to set the points of the goads. 22 So it came about, on the day of battle, that [a]there was neither sword nor spear found in the hand of any of the people who *were* with Saul and Jonathan. But they were found with Saul and Jonathan his son. 23 [a]And the garrison of the Philistines went out to the pass of Michmash.

### *JONATHAN DEFEATS THE PHILISTINES*

**14** Now it happened one day that Jonathan the son of Saul said to the young man who bore his armor, "Come, let us go over to the Philistines' garrison that *is* on the other side." But he did not tell his father. 2 And Saul was sitting in the outskirts of [a]Gibeah under a pomegranate tree which *is* in Migron. The people who *were* with him *were* about six hundred men. 3 [a]Ahijah the son of Ahitub, [b]Ichabod's brother, the son of Phinehas, the son of Eli, the LORD's priest in Shiloh, was [c]wearing an ephod. But the people did not know that Jonathan had gone.

4 Between the passes, by which Jonathan sought to go over [a]to the Philistines' garrison, *there was* a sharp rock on one side and a sharp rock on the other side. And the name of one *was* Bozez, and the name of the other Seneh. 5 The front of one faced northward opposite Michmash, and the other southward opposite Gibeah.

6 Then Jonathan said to the young man who bore his armor, "Come, let us go over to the garrison of these [a]uncircumcised; it may be that the LORD will work for us. For nothing restrains the LORD [b]from saving by many or by few."

7 So his armorbearer said to him, "Do all that is in your heart. Go then; here I am with you, according to your heart."

8 Then Jonathan said, "Very well, let us cross over to *these* men, and we will show ourselves to them. 9 If they say thus to us, 'Wait until we come to you,' then we will stand still in our place and not go up to them. 10 But if they say thus, 'Come up to us,' then we will go up. For the LORD has delivered them into our hand, and [a]this *will be* a sign to us."

11 So both of them showed themselves to the garrison of the Philistines. And the Philistines said, "Look, the Hebrews are coming out of the holes where they have [a]hidden." 12 Then the men of the garrison called to Jonathan and his armorbearer, and said, "Come up to us, and we will show you something."

Jonathan said to his armorbearer, "Come up after me, for the LORD has delivered them into the hand of Israel." 13 And Jonathan climbed up on his hands and knees with his armorbearer after him; and they [a]fell before Jonathan. And as he came after him, his armorbearer killed them. 14 That first slaughter which Jonathan and his armorbearer made was about twenty men within about half an acre of land.[1]

15 And [a]there was trembling in the camp, in the field, and among all the people. The garrison and [b]the raiders also trembled; and the earth quaked, so that it was [c]a very great trembling. 16 Now the watchmen of Saul in Gibeah of Benjamin looked, and *there* was the multitude, melting away; and they [a]went here and there. 17 Then Saul said to the people who *were* with him, "Now call the roll and see who has gone from us." And when they had called the roll, surprisingly, Jonathan and his armorbearer *were* not *there.* 18 And Saul said to Ahijah, "Bring the ark[1] of God here" (for at that time the ark[2] of God was with the children of Israel). 19 Now it happened, while Saul [a]talked to the priest, that the noise which *was* in the camp of the Philistines continued to increase; so Saul said to the priest, "Withdraw your hand." 20 Then Saul and all the people who *were* with him assembled, and they went to the battle; and indeed [a]every man's sword was against his neighbor, *and there was* very great confusion. 21 Moreover the Hebrews *who* were with the Philistines before that time, who went up with them into the camp *from the* surrounding *country,* they also joined the Israelites who *were* with Saul and Jonathan. 22 Likewise all the men of Israel who [a]had hidden in the mountains of Ephraim, *when* they heard that the Philistines fled, they also followed hard after them in the battle. 23 [a]So the LORD saved Israel that day, and the battle shifted [b]to Beth Aven.

### *SAUL'S RASH OATH*

24 And the men of Israel were distressed that day, for Saul had [a]placed the people under oath, saying, "Cursed *is* the man who eats *any* food until evening, before I have taken vengeance on my enemies." So none of the people tasted food. 25 [a]Now all *the people* of the land came to a forest; and there was [b]honey on the ground. 26 And when the people had come into the woods, there was the honey, dripping; but no one put his hand to his mouth, for the people feared the oath. 27 But Jonathan had not heard his father charge the people with the oath; therefore he stretched out the end of the rod that *was* in his hand and dipped it in a honeycomb, and put his hand to his mouth; and his countenance brightened. 28 Then one of the people said, "Your father strictly charged the people with an oath,

**13:21** [1] About two-thirds shekel weight **13:22** [a] Judg. 5:8 **13:23** [a] 1 Sam. 14:1, 4 **14:2** [a] 1 Sam. 13:15, 16 **14:3** [a] 1 Sam. 22:9, 11, 20 [b] 1 Sam. 4:21 [c] 1 Sam. 2:28 **14:4** [a] 1 Sam. 13:23 **14:6** [a] 1 Sam. 17:26, 36; Jer. 9:25, 26 [b] Judg. 7:4, 7; 1 Sam. 17:46, 47; 2 Chr. 14:11; [Ps. 115:3; 135:6; Zech. 4:6; Matt. 19:26; Rom. 8:31] **14:10** [a] Gen. 24:14; Judg. 6:36–40 **14:11** [a] 1 Sam. 13:6; 14:22 **14:13** [a] Lev. 26:8; Josh. 23:10 **14:14** [1] Literally *half the area plowed by a yoke* (of oxen in a day) **14:15** [a] Deut. 28:7; 2 Kin. 7:6, 7; Job 18:11 [b] 1 Sam. 13:17 [c] Gen. 35:5 **14:16** [a] 1 Sam. 14:20 **14:18** [1] Following Masoretic Text, Targum, and Vulgate; Septuagint reads *ephod.* [2] Following Masoretic Text, Targum, and Vulgate; Septuagint reads *ephod.* **14:19** [a] Num. 27:21 **14:20** [a] Judg. 7:22; 2 Chr. 20:23 **14:22** [a] 1 Sam. 13:6 **14:23** [a] Ex. 14:30; 2 Chr. 32:22; Hos. 1:7 [b] 1 Sam. 13:5 **14:24** [a] Josh. 6:26 **14:25** [a] Deut. 9:28; Matt. 3:5 [b] Ex. 3:8; Num. 13:27; Matt. 3:4

saying, 'Cursed *is* the man who eats food this day.' " And the people were faint.

29 But Jonathan said, "My father has troubled the land. Look now, how my countenance has brightened because I tasted a little of this honey. 30 How much better if the people had eaten freely today of the spoil of their enemies which they found! For now would there not have been a much greater slaughter among the Philistines?"

31 Now they had driven back the Philistines that day from Michmash to Aijalon. So the people were very faint. 32 And the people rushed on the spoil, and took sheep, oxen, and calves, and slaughtered *them* on the ground; and the people ate *them* [a]with the blood. 33 Then they told Saul, saying, "Look, the people are sinning against the LORD by eating with the blood!"

So he said, "You have dealt treacherously; roll a large stone to me this day." 34 Then Saul said, "Disperse yourselves among the people, and say to them, 'Bring me here every man's ox and every man's sheep, slaughter *them* here, and eat; and do not sin against the LORD by eating with the blood.' " So every one of the people brought his ox with him that night, and slaughtered *it* there. 35 Then Saul [a]built an altar to the LORD. This was the first altar that he built to the LORD.

36 Now Saul said, "Let us go down after the Philistines by night, and plunder them until the morning light; and let us not leave a man of them."

And they said, "Do whatever seems good to you."

Then the priest said, "Let us draw near to God here."

37 So Saul [a]asked counsel of God, "Shall I go down after the Philistines? Will You deliver them into the hand of Israel?" But [b]He did not answer him that day. 38 And Saul said, [a]"Come over here, all you chiefs of the people, and know and see what this sin was today. 39 For [a]*as* the LORD lives, who saves Israel, though it be in Jonathan my son, he shall surely die." But not a man among all the people answered him. 40 Then he said to all Israel, "You be on one side, and my son Jonathan and I will be on the other side."

And the people said to Saul, "Do what seems good to you."

41 Therefore Saul said to the LORD God of Israel, [a]"Give a perfect *lot*."[1] [b]So Saul and Jonathan were taken, but the people escaped. 42 And Saul said, "Cast *lots* between my son Jonathan and me." So Jonathan was taken. 43 Then Saul said to Jonathan, [a]"Tell me what you have done."

And Jonathan told him, and said, [b]"I only tasted a little honey with the end of the rod that *was* in my hand. So now I must die!"

44 Saul answered, [a]"God do so and more also; [b]for you shall surely die, Jonathan."

45 But the people said to Saul, "Shall Jonathan die, who has accomplished this great deliverance in Israel? Certainly not! [a]*As* the LORD lives, not one hair of his head shall fall to the ground, for he has worked [b]with God this day." So the people rescued Jonathan, and he did not die.

> **SEEING JESUS IN THE SCRIPTURE**
>
> **14:45** Even though Saul made a rash vow, not one hair on Jonathan's head was harmed because of his faithful work for God. Jesus used similar words when He spoke of believers who endure to the end (see Luke 21:18).

46 Then Saul returned from pursuing the Philistines, and the Philistines went to their own place.

## *SAUL'S CONTINUING WARS*

47 So Saul established his sovereignty over Israel, and fought against all his enemies on every side, against Moab, against the people of [a]Ammon, against Edom, against the kings of [b]Zobah, and against the Philistines. Wherever he turned, he harassed *them*.[1] 48 And he gathered an army and [a]attacked the Amalekites, and delivered Israel from the hands of those who plundered them.

49 [a]The sons of Saul were Jonathan, Jishui,[1] and Malchishua. And the names of his two daughters *were these:* the name of the firstborn Merab, and the name of the younger [b]Michal. 50 The name of Saul's wife *was* Ahinoam the daughter of Ahimaaz. And the name of the commander of his army *was* Abner the son of Ner, Saul's [a]uncle. 51 [a]Kish *was* the father of Saul, and Ner the father of Abner *was* the son of Abiel.

52 Now there was fierce war with the Philistines all the days of Saul. And when Saul saw any strong man or any valiant man, [a]he took him for himself.

## *SAUL SPARES KING AGAG*

**15** Samuel also said to Saul, [a]"The LORD sent me to anoint you king over His people, over Israel. Now therefore, heed the voice of the words of the LORD. 2 Thus says the LORD of

**14:32** [a] Gen. 9:4; Lev. 3:17; 17:10–14; 19:26; Deut. 12:16, 23, 24; Acts 15:20 **14:35** [a] 1 Sam. 7:12, 17; 2 Sam. 24:25 **14:37** [a] Judg. 20:18 [b] 1 Sam. 28:6 **14:38** [a] Josh. 7:14; 1 Sam. 10:19 **14:39** [a] 1 Sam. 14:24, 44; 2 Sam. 12:5 **14:41** [a] Prov. 16:33; Acts 1:24–26 [b] Josh. 7:16; 1 Sam. 10:20, 21 [1] Following Masoretic Text and Targum; Septuagint and Vulgate read *Why do You not answer Your servant today? If the injustice is with me or Jonathan my son, O LORD God of Israel, give proof; and if You say it is with Your people Israel, give holiness.* **14:43** [a] Josh. 7:19 [b] 1 Sam. 14:27 **14:44** [a] Ruth 1:17; 1 Sam. 25:22 [b] 1 Sam. 14:39 **14:45** [a] 2 Sam. 14:11; 1 Kin. 1:52; Luke 21:18; Acts 27:34 [b] [2 Cor. 6:1; Phil. 2:12, 13] **14:47** [a] 1 Sam. 11:1–13 [b] 2 Sam. 10:6 [1] Septuagint and Vulgate read *prospered.* **14:48** [a] Ex. 17:16; 1 Sam. 15:3–7 **14:49** [a] 1 Sam. 31:2; 1 Chr. 8:33 [b] 1 Sam. 18:17–20, 27; 19:12 [1] Called *Abinadab* in 1 Chronicles 8:33 and 9:39 **14:50** [a] 1 Sam. 10:14 **14:51** [a] 1 Sam. 9:1, 21 **14:52** [a] 1 Sam. 8:11 **15:1** [a] 1 Sam. 9:16; 10:1

hosts: 'I will punish Amalek *for* what he did to
Israel, [a]how he ambushed him on the way when
he came up from Egypt. 3 Now go and [a]attack
Amalek, and [b]utterly destroy all that they have,
and do not spare them. But kill both man and
woman, infant and nursing child, ox and sheep,
camel and donkey.' "
4 So Saul gathered the people together and
numbered them in Telaim, two hundred thou-
sand foot soldiers and ten thousand men of
Judah. 5 And Saul came to a city of Amalek, and
lay in wait in the valley.
6 Then Saul said to [a]the Kenites, [b]"Go, depart,
get down from among the Amalekites, lest I de-
stroy you with them. For [c]you showed kindness
to all the children of Israel when they came up
out of Egypt." So the Kenites departed from
among the Amalekites. 7 [a]And Saul attacked the
Amalekites, from [b]Havilah all the way to [c]Shur,
which is east of Egypt. 8 [a]He also took Agag king
of the Amalekites alive, and [b]utterly destroyed
all the people with the edge of the sword. 9 But
Saul and the people [a]spared Agag and the best
of the sheep, the oxen, the fatlings, the lambs,
and all *that was* good, and were unwilling to
utterly destroy them. But everything despised
and worthless, that they utterly destroyed.

### *SAUL REJECTED AS KING*

10 Now the word of the LORD came to Samuel,
saying, 11 [a]"I greatly regret that I have set up Saul *as*
king, for he has [b]turned back from following Me,
[c]and has not performed My commandments."
And it [d]grieved Samuel, and he cried out to the
LORD all night. 12 So when Samuel rose early in
the morning to meet Saul, it was told Samuel,
saying, "Saul went to [a]Carmel, and indeed, he
set up a monument for himself; and he has gone
on around, passed by, and gone down to Gilgal."
13 Then Samuel went to Saul, and Saul said to him,
[a]"Blessed *are* you of the LORD! I have performed
the commandment of the LORD."
14 But Samuel said, "What then *is* this bleat-
ing of the sheep in my ears, and the lowing of
the oxen which I hear?"
15 And Saul said, "They have brought them
from the Amalekites; [a]for the people spared the
best of the sheep and the oxen, to sacrifice to
the LORD your God; and the rest we have utterly
destroyed."
16 Then Samuel said to Saul, "Be quiet! And I
will tell you what the LORD said to me last night."
And he said to him, "Speak on."
17 So Samuel said, [a]"When you *were* little in
your own eyes, *were* you not head of the tribes of
Israel? And did not the LORD anoint you king over
Israel? 18 Now the LORD sent you on a mission,
and said, 'Go, and utterly destroy the sinners, the
Amalekites, and fight against them until they
are consumed.' 19 Why then did you not obey the
voice of the LORD? Why did you swoop down on
the spoil, and do evil in the sight of the LORD?"
20 And Saul said to Samuel, [a]"But I have
obeyed the voice of the LORD, and gone on the
mission on which the LORD sent me, and brought
back Agag king of Amalek; I have utterly de-
stroyed the Amalekites. 21 [a]But the people took
of the plunder, sheep and oxen, the best of the
things which should have been utterly destroyed,
to sacrifice to the LORD your God in Gilgal."
22 So Samuel said:

[a]"Has the LORD *as great* delight in burnt
offerings and sacrifices,
As in obeying the voice of the LORD?
Behold, [b]to obey is better than sacrifice,
*And* to heed than the fat of rams.
23 For rebellion *is as* the sin of witchcraft,
And stubbornness *is as* iniquity and
idolatry.
Because you have rejected the word of the
LORD,
[a]He also has rejected you from *being* king."

> **15:22** Saul thought he was doing something good for God when instead of killing the animals, he sacrificed them. They would still be dead, he likely reasoned, but sacrificing them would honor God at the same time. But God wasn't pleased. Partial obedience isn't enough. God wants us to **obey** completely, even when it might not make sense to us.

24 [a]Then Saul said to Samuel, "I have sinned,
for I have transgressed the commandment of
the LORD and your words, because I [b]feared the
people and obeyed their voice. 25 Now therefore,
please pardon my sin, and return with me, that
I may worship the LORD."
26 But Samuel said to Saul, "I will not return
with you, [a]for you have rejected the word of the
LORD, and the LORD has rejected you from being
king over Israel."
27 And as Samuel turned around to go away,
[a]*Saul* seized the edge of his robe, and it tore. 28 So
Samuel said to him, [a]"The LORD has torn the
kingdom of Israel from you today, and has given
it to a neighbor of yours, *who is* better than you.
29 And also the Strength of Israel [a]will not lie nor
relent. For He *is* not a man, that He should relent."

**15:2** [a] Ex. 17:8, 14; Num. 24:20; Deut. 25:17–19 **15:3** [a] Deut. 25:19 [b] Lev. 27:28, 29; Num. 24:20; Deut. 20:16–18; Josh. 6:17–21 **15:6** [a] Num. 24:21; Judg. 1:16; 4:11–22; 1 Chr. 2:55 [b] Gen. 18:25; 19:12, 14; Rev. 18:4 [c] Ex. 18:10, 19; Num. 10:29, 32 **15:7** [a] 1 Sam. 14:48 [b] Gen. 2:11; 25:17, 18 [c] Gen. 16:7; Ex. 15:22; 1 Sam. 27:8 **15:8** [a] 1 Sam. 15:32, 33 [b] 1 Sam. 27:8, 9 **15:9** [a] 1 Sam. 15:3, 15, 19 **15:11** [a] Gen. 6:6, 7 [b] 1 Kin. 9:6 [c] 1 Sam. 13:13; 15:3, 9 [d] 1 Sam. 15:35; 16:1 **15:12** [a] Josh. 15:55 **15:13** [a] Judg. 17:2 **15:15** [a] [Gen. 3:12, 13]; 1 Sam. 15:9, 21 **15:17** [a] 1 Sam. 9:21; 10:22 **15:20** [a] 1 Sam. 15:13 **15:21** [a] 1 Sam. 15:15 **15:22** [a] [Is. 1:11–17] [b] [Hos. 6:6] **15:23** [a] 1 Sam. 13:14; 16:1 **15:24** [a] Josh. 7:20 [b] [Is. 51:12, 13] **15:26** [a] 1 Sam. 2:30 **15:27** [a] 1 Kin. 11:30, 31 **15:28** [a] 1 Kin. 11:31 **15:29** [a] Num. 23:19

30 Then he said, "I have sinned; *yet* [a]honor
me now, please, before the elders of my people
and before Israel, and return with me, that I may
worship the LORD your God." 31 So Samuel turned
back after Saul, and Saul worshiped the LORD.
32 Then Samuel said, "Bring Agag king of
the Amalekites here to me." So Agag came to
him cautiously.
And Agag said, "Surely the bitterness of
death is past."
33 But Samuel said, [a]"As your sword has made
women childless, so shall your mother be child-
less among women." And Samuel hacked Agag
in pieces before the LORD in Gilgal.
34 Then Samuel went to [a]Ramah, and Saul
went up to his house at [b]Gibeah of Saul. 35 And
[a]Samuel went no more to see Saul until the day
of his death. Nevertheless Samuel mourned for
Saul, and the LORD regretted that He had made
Saul king over Israel.

### *DAVID ANOINTED KING*

16 Now the LORD said to Samuel, [a]"How long
will you mourn for Saul, seeing I have
rejected him from reigning over Israel? [b]Fill
your horn with oil, and go; I am sending you to
[c]Jesse the Bethlehemite. For [d]I have provided
Myself a king among his sons."
2 And Samuel said, "How can I go? If Saul
hears *it,* he will kill me."
But the LORD said, "Take a heifer with you,
and say, [a]'I have come to sacrifice to the LORD.'
3 Then invite Jesse to the sacrifice, and I will
show you what you shall do; you shall anoint
for Me the one I name to you."
4 So Samuel did what the LORD said, and
went to Bethlehem. And the elders of the town
[a]trembled at his coming, and said, [b]"Do you
come peaceably?"
5 And he said, "Peaceably; I have come to
sacrifice to the LORD. [a]Sanctify yourselves, and
come with me to the sacrifice." Then he conse-
crated Jesse and his sons, and invited them to
the sacrifice.
6 So it was, when they came, that he looked
at [a]Eliab and [b]said, "Surely the LORD's anointed
*is* before Him!"
7 But the LORD said to Samuel, [a]"Do not look
at his appearance or at his physical stature, be-
cause I have refused him. [b]For *the LORD does* not
*see* as man sees;[1] for man [c]looks at the outward
appearance, but the LORD looks at the [d]heart."
8 So Jesse called Abinadab, and made him
pass before Samuel. And he said, "Neither has
the LORD chosen this one." 9 Then Jesse made
Shammah pass by. And he said, "Neither has the
LORD chosen this one." 10 Thus Jesse made seven
of his sons pass before Samuel. And Samuel
said to Jesse, "The LORD has not chosen these."
11 And Samuel said to Jesse, "Are all the young
men here?" Then he said, "There remains yet the
youngest, and there he is, keeping the [a]sheep."
And Samuel said to Jesse, "Send and bring
him. For we will not sit down[1] till he comes here."
12 So he sent and brought him in. Now he *was*
[a]ruddy, [b]with bright eyes, and good-looking.
[c]And the LORD said, "Arise, anoint him; for this
*is* the one!" 13 Then Samuel took the horn of oil
and anointed him in the midst of his brothers;
and [a]the Spirit of the LORD came upon David
from that day forward. So Samuel arose and
went to Ramah.

### *A DISTRESSING SPIRIT TROUBLES SAUL*

14 [a]But the Spirit of the LORD departed from
Saul, and [b]a distressing spirit from the LORD
troubled him. 15 And Saul's servants said to him,
"Surely, a distressing spirit from God is trou-
bling you. 16 Let our master now command your
servants, *who are* before you, to seek out a man
*who is* a skillful player on the harp. And it shall
be that he will [a]play it with his hand when the
distressing spirit from God is upon you, and
you shall be well."

> **16:13–14** After **the Spirit of the LORD came upon David**, Saul was no longer empowered by the Spirit to serve as king. In the Old Testament, the Holy Spirit came upon people selectively and temporarily. It was only after the resurrection of Jesus that the Holy Spirit came to indwell all believers permanently (see John 16:5–11; Acts 2:4).

17 So Saul said to his servants, "Provide me now
a man who can play well, and bring *him* to me."
18 Then one of the servants answered and
said, "Look, I have seen a son of Jesse the Bethle-
hemite, *who is* skillful in playing, a mighty man
of valor, a man of war, prudent in speech, and a
handsome person; and [a]the LORD *is* with him."
19 Therefore Saul sent messengers to Jesse,
and said, "Send me your son David, who *is* with
the sheep." 20 And Jesse [a]took a donkey *loaded*
*with* bread, a skin of wine, and a young goat, and
sent *them* by his son David to Saul. 21 So David
came to Saul and [a]stood before him. And he

**15:30** [a] [John 5:44; 12:43] **15:33** [a] [Gen. 9:6] **15:34** [a] 1 Sam. 7:17 [b] 1 Sam. 11:4 **15:35** [a] 1 Sam. 19:24 **16:1** [a] 1 Sam. 15:23, 35 [b] 1 Sam. 9:16; 10:1 [c] Ruth 4:18–22 [d] Ps. 78:70, 71; Acts 13:22 **16:2** [a] 1 Sam. 9:12 **16:4** [a] 1 Sam. 21:1 [b] 1 Kin. 2:13; 2 Kin. 9:22 **16:5** [a] Gen. 35:2; Ex. 19:10 **16:6** [a] 1 Sam. 17:13, 28 [b] 1 Kin. 12:26 **16:7** [a] Ps. 147:10 [b] Is. 55:8, 9 [c] 2 Cor. 10:7 [d] 1 Kin. 8:39 [1] Septuagint reads *For God does not see as man sees;* Targum reads *It is not by the appearance of a man;* Vulgate reads *Nor do I judge according to the looks of a man.* **16:11** [a] 2 Sam. 7:8; Ps. 78:70–72 [1] Following Septuagint and Vulgate; Masoretic Text reads *turn around;* Targum and Syriac read *turn away.* **16:12** [a] 1 Sam. 17:42 [b] Gen. 39:6; Ex. 2:2; Acts 7:20 [c] 1 Sam. 9:17 **16:13** [a] Num. 27:18; 1 Sam. 10:6, 9, 10 **16:14** [a] Judg. 16:20; 1 Sam. 11:6; 18:12; 28:15 [b] Judg. 9:23; 1 Sam. 16:15, 16; 18:10; 19:9; 1 Kin. 22:19–22 **16:16** [a] 1 Sam. 18:10; 19:9; 2 Kin. 3:15 **16:18** [a] 1 Sam. 3:19; 18:12, 14 **16:20** [a] 1 Sam. 10:4, 27; Prov. 18:16 **16:21** [a] Gen. 41:46; Prov. 22:29

loved him greatly, and he became his armor-
bearer. 22 Then Saul sent to Jesse, saying, "Please
let David stand before me, for he has found favor
in my sight." 23 And so it was, whenever the spirit
from God was upon Saul, that David would take a
harp and play *it* with his hand. Then Saul would
become refreshed and well, and the distressing
spirit would depart from him.

### DAVID AND GOLIATH

**17** Now the Philistines gathered their armies
together to battle, and were gathered at
[a]Sochoh, which *belongs* to Judah; they encamped
between Sochoh and Azekah, in Ephes Dammim.
2 And Saul and the men of Israel were gathered
together, and they encamped in the Valley of
Elah, and drew up in battle array against the
Philistines. 3 The Philistines stood on a moun-
tain on one side, and Israel stood on a mountain
on the other side, with a valley between them.

4 And a champion went out from the camp
of the Philistines, named [a]Goliath, from [b]Gath,
whose height *was* six cubits and a span. 5 *He
had* a bronze helmet on his head, and he *was*
armed with a coat of mail, and the weight of
the coat *was* five thousand shekels of bronze.
6 And *he had* bronze armor on his legs and a
bronze javelin between his shoulders. 7 Now
the staff of his spear *was* like a weaver's beam,
and his iron spearhead *weighed* six hundred
shekels; and a shield-bearer went before him.
8 Then he stood and cried out to the armies of
Israel, and said to them, "Why have you come
out to line up for battle? *Am* I not a Philistine,
and you the [a]servants of Saul? Choose a man for
yourselves, and let him come down to me. 9 If
he is able to fight with me and kill me, then we
will be your servants. But if I prevail against him
and kill him, then you shall be our servants and
[a]serve us." 10 And the Philistine said, "I [a]defy the
armies of Israel this day; give me a man, that we
may fight together." 11 When Saul and all Israel
heard these words of the Philistine, they were
dismayed and greatly afraid.

12 Now David *was* [a]the son of that [b]Ephrath-
ite of Bethlehem Judah, whose name *was* Jesse,
and who had [c]eight sons. And the man was old,
advanced *in years,* in the days of Saul. 13 The
three oldest sons of Jesse had gone to follow
Saul to the battle. The [a]names of his three sons
who went to the battle *were* Eliab the firstborn,
next to him Abinadab, and the third Shammah.
14 David *was* the youngest. And the three oldest
followed Saul. 15 But David occasionally went and
returned from Saul [a]to feed his father's sheep
at Bethlehem.

16 And the Philistine drew near and present-
ed himself forty days, morning and evening.

17 Then Jesse said to his son David, "Take now
for your brothers an ephah of this dried *grain*
and these ten loaves, and run to your brothers
at the camp. 18 And carry these ten cheeses to
the captain of *their* thousand, and [a]see how your
brothers fare, and bring back news of them."
19 Now Saul and they and all the men of Israel *were*
in the Valley of Elah, fighting with the Philistines.

20 So David rose early in the morning, left the
sheep with a keeper, and took *the things* and went
as Jesse had commanded him. And he came to
the camp as the army was going out to the fight
and shouting for the battle. 21 For Israel and the
Philistines had drawn up in battle array, army
against army. 22 And David left his supplies in
the hand of the supply keeper, ran to the army,
and came and greeted his brothers. 23 Then as he
talked with them, there was the champion, the
Philistine of Gath, Goliath by name, coming up
from the armies of the Philistines; and he spoke
[a]according to the same words. So David heard
*them.* 24 And all the men of Israel, when they
saw the man, fled from him and were dreadfully
afraid. 25 So the men of Israel said, "Have you
seen this man who has come up? Surely he has
come up to defy Israel; and it shall be *that* the
man who kills him the king will enrich with great
riches, [a]will give him his daughter, and give his
father's house exemption *from taxes* in Israel."

26 Then David spoke to the men who stood
by him, saying, "What shall be done for the man
who kills this Philistine and takes away [a]the
reproach from Israel? For who *is* this [b]uncir-
cumcised Philistine, that he should [c]defy the
armies of [d]the living God?"

27 And the people answered him in this man-
ner, saying, [a]"So shall it be done for the man
who kills him."

28 Now Eliab his oldest brother heard when
he spoke to the men; and Eliab's [a]anger was
aroused against David, and he said, "Why did
you come down here? And with whom have you
left those few sheep in the wilderness? I know
your pride and the insolence of your heart, for
you have come down to see the battle."

29 And David said, "What have I done now? [a]*Is
there* not a cause?" 30 Then he turned from him
toward another and [a]said the same thing; and
these people answered him as the first ones *did.*

31 Now when the words which David spoke
were heard, they reported *them* to Saul; and he
sent for him. 32 Then David said to Saul, [a]"Let no
man's heart fail because of him; [b]your servant
will go and fight with this Philistine."

33 And Saul said to David, [a]"You are not able
to go against this Philistine to fight with him;
for you *are* a youth, and he a man of war from
his youth."

**17:1** [a] Josh. 15:35; 2 Chr. 28:18 **17:4** [a] 2 Sam. 21:19 [b] Josh. 11:21, 22 **17:8** [a] 1 Sam. 8:17 **17:9** [a] 1 Sam. 11:1 **17:10** [a] 1 Sam. 17:26, 36, 45; 2 Sam. 21:21 **17:12** [a] Ruth 4:22; 1 Sam. 16:1, 18; 17:58 [b] Gen. 35:19 [c] 1 Sam. 16:10, 11; 1 Chr. 2:13–15 **17:13** [a] 1 Sam. 16:6, 8, 9; 1 Chr. 2:13 **17:15** [a] 1 Sam. 16:11, 19; 2 Sam. 7:8 **17:18** [a] Gen. 37:13, 14 **17:23** [a] 1 Sam. 17:8–10 **17:25** [a] Josh. 15:16 **17:26** [a] 1 Sam. 11:2 [b] 1 Sam. 14:6; 17:36; Jer. 9:25, 26 [c] 1 Sam. 17:10 [d] Deut. 5:26; 2 Kin. 19:4; Jer. 10:10 **17:27** [a] 1 Sam. 17:25 **17:28** [a] Gen. 37:4, 8–36; [Prov. 18:19; Matt. 10:36] **17:29** [a] 1 Sam. 17:17 **17:30** [a] 1 Sam. 17:26, 27 **17:32** [a] Deut. 20:1–4 [b] 1 Sam. 16:18 **17:33** [a] Num. 13:31; Deut. 9:2

1 SAMUEL 17:1–50

## DAVID AND GOLIATH

STORY OF SCRIPTURE 24

### WHAT'S GOING ON?

We've arrived at the iconic story of David and Goliath. The Israelites were at war with the Philistines, and Goliath, a giant warrior, challenged the Israelites to send a champion to fight him. David, a young shepherd boy, stepped forward to face Goliath. Despite his youth and lack of battle experience, David's faith in God was unwavering. He refused the king's armor, instead choosing to face Goliath with a sling and a few stones—the tools of a lowly shepherd. David knew God was on his side, giving him the boldness to enter the battle. David defeated the giant with a single stone and secured Israel's triumph in the battle.

### WHAT DOES THIS MEAN FOR ME?

The story of David and Goliath encourages us to face our own "giants"—challenges, fears, or seemingly impossible situations—through faith in God. David's victory shows with God, all things are possible, and our limitations don't limit God. However, there's something deeper at work in this story. While it's easy to view ourselves as David and Goliath as our problems, the ultimate message is that Jesus is the greater David, and our sin is Goliath. We are the Israelites, paralyzed by fear and unable to save ourselves. Jesus, our hero and shepherd, rose up to defeat the giant of sin we couldn't beat.

### DID YOU CATCH THE PATTERN?

David's victory over Goliath fits into a pattern where God uses unlikely heroes, particularly shepherds, to accomplish His purposes. Throughout the Bible, we see God work through individuals who weren't powerful by worldly standards, but who God chose because of their faith and willingness to trust in Him. This pattern culminates in Jesus Christ, who, though appearing rather ordinary, was God's chosen instrument for the ultimate victory over sin and death.

*For the next* Story of Scripture *reading and devotion, turn to 2 Samuel 7:1–17 on page 311.*

34 But David said to Saul, "Your servant used
to keep his father's sheep, and when a [a]lion or a
bear came and took a lamb out of the flock, 35 I
went out after it and struck it, and delivered *the*
*lamb* from its mouth; and when it arose against
me, I caught *it* by its beard, and struck and killed
it. 36 Your servant has killed both lion and bear;
and this uncircumcised Philistine will be like
one of them, seeing he has defied the armies
of the living God." 37 Moreover David said, [a]"The
LORD, who delivered me from the paw of the lion
and from the paw of the bear, He will deliver me
from the hand of this Philistine."

And Saul said to David, [b]"Go, and the LORD
be with you!"

### SEEING JESUS IN THE SCRIPTURE

**17:34–35** David risked his life to protect his father's sheep. David pictures Jesus, the Good Shepherd who laid down His life to save His Father's sheep (see John 10:11).

38 So Saul clothed David with his armor, and
he put a bronze helmet on his head; he also
clothed him with a coat of mail. 39 David fastened
his sword to his armor and tried to walk, for he
had not tested *them.* And David said to Saul, "I
cannot walk with these, for I have not tested
*them.*" So David took them off.

40 Then he took his staff in his hand; and
he chose for himself five smooth stones from
the brook, and put them in a shepherd's bag, in
a pouch which he had, and his sling was in his
hand. And he drew near to the Philistine. 41 So
the Philistine came, and began drawing near to
David, and the man who bore the shield *went*
before him. 42 And when the Philistine looked
about and saw David, he [a]disdained him; for he
was *only* a youth, [b]ruddy and good-looking. 43 So
the Philistine [a]said to David, "*Am* I a dog, that
you come to me with sticks?" And the Philistine
cursed David by his gods. 44 And the Philistine
[a]said to David, "Come to me, and I will give
your flesh to the birds of the air and the beasts
of the field!"

45 Then David said to the Philistine, "You

**17:34** [a] Judg. 14:5 **17:37** [a] [2 Cor. 1:10; 2 Tim. 4:17, 18] [b] 1 Sam. 20:13; 1 Chr. 22:11, 16 **17:42** [a] [Ps. 123:4; Prov. 16:18; 1 Cor. 1:27, 28] [b] 1 Sam. 16:12 **17:43** [a] 1 Sam. 24:14; 2 Sam. 3:8; 9:8; 16:9; 2 Kin. 8:13 **17:44** [a] 1 Sam. 17:46; 1 Kin. 20:10, 11

come to me with a sword, with a spear, and
with a javelin. [a]But I come to you in the name
of the LORD of hosts, the God of the armies
of Israel, whom you have [b]defied. 46 This day
the LORD will deliver you into my hand, and I
will strike you and take your head from you.
And this day I will give [a]the carcasses of the
camp of the Philistines to the birds of the air
and the wild beasts of the earth, [b]that all the
earth may know that there is a God in Israel.
47 Then all this assembly shall know that the
LORD [a]does not save with sword and spear; for
[b]the battle *is* the LORD's, and He will give you
into our hands."

48 So it was, when the Philistine arose and
came and drew near to meet David, that David
hurried and [a]ran toward the army to meet the
Philistine. 49 Then David put his hand in his
bag and took out a stone; and he slung *it* and
struck the Philistine in his forehead, so that the
stone sank into his forehead, and he fell on his
face to the earth. 50 So David prevailed over the
Philistine with a [a]sling and a stone, and struck
the Philistine and killed him. But *there was* no
sword in the hand of David. 51 Therefore David
ran and stood over the Philistine, took his [a]sword
and drew it out of its sheath and killed him, and
cut off his head with it.

And when the Philistines saw that their
champion was dead, [b]they fled. 52 Now the men
of Israel and Judah arose and shouted, and
pursued the Philistines as far as the entrance
of the valley[1] and to the gates of Ekron. And the
wounded of the Philistines fell along the road
to [a]Shaaraim, even as far as Gath and Ekron.
53 Then the children of Israel returned from
chasing the Philistines, and they plundered
their tents. 54 And David took the head of the
Philistine and brought it to Jerusalem, but he
put his armor in his tent.

55 When Saul saw David going out against
the Philistine, he said to [a]Abner, the commander
of the army, "Abner, [b]whose son *is* this youth?"

And Abner said, "As your soul lives, O king,
I do not know."

56 So the king said, "Inquire whose son this
young man *is*."

57 Then, as David returned from the slaugh-
ter of the Philistine, Abner took him and brought
him before Saul [a]with the head of the Philistine
in his hand. 58 And Saul said to him, "Whose son
*are* you, young man?"

So David answered, [a]"*I am* the son of your
servant Jesse the Bethlehemite."

## *SAUL RESENTS DAVID*

**18** Now when he had finished speaking to
Saul, [a]the soul of Jonathan was knit to
the soul of David, [b]and Jonathan loved him
as his own soul. 2 Saul took him that day, [a]and
would not let him go home to his father's house
anymore. 3 Then Jonathan and David made a
[a]covenant, because he loved him as his own
soul. 4 And Jonathan took off the robe that *was*
on him and gave it to David, with his armor, even
to his sword and his bow and his belt.

5 So David went out wherever Saul sent him,
*and* behaved wisely. And Saul set him over the
men of war, and he was accepted in the sight
of all the people and also in the sight of Saul's
servants. 6 Now it had happened as they were
coming *home,* when David was returning from
the slaughter of the Philistine, that [a]the women
had come out of all the cities of Israel, singing
and dancing, to meet King Saul, with tambou-
rines, with joy, and with musical instruments.
7 So the women [a]sang as they danced, and said:

[b]"Saul has slain his thousands,
And David his ten thousands."

8 Then Saul was very angry, and the saying [a]dis-
pleased him; and he said, "They have ascribed
to David ten thousands, and to me they have
ascribed *only* thousands. Now *what* more can
he have but [b]the kingdom?" 9 So Saul eyed David
from that day forward.

10 And it happened on the next day that [a]the
distressing spirit from God came upon Saul,
[b]and he prophesied inside the house. So David
[c]played *music* with his hand, as at other times;
[d]but *there was* a spear in Saul's hand. 11 And Saul
[a]cast the spear, for he said, "I will pin David to
the wall!" But David escaped his presence twice.
12 Now Saul was [a]afraid of David, because [b]the
LORD was with him, but had [c]departed from Saul.
13 Therefore Saul removed him from his presence,
and made him his captain over a thousand; and
[a]he went out and came in before the people.
14 And David behaved wisely in all his ways, and
[a]the LORD *was* with him. 15 Therefore, when Saul
saw that he behaved very wisely, he was afraid
of him. 16 But [a]all Israel and Judah loved David,
because he went out and came in before them.

## *DAVID MARRIES MICHAL*

17 Then Saul said to David, "Here is my older
daughter Merab; [a]I will give her to you as a wife.
Only be valiant for me, and fight [b]the LORD's

**17:45** [a] 2 Sam. 22:33, 35; 2 Chr. 32:8; Ps. 124:8; [2 Cor. 10:4]; Heb. 11:33, 34 [b] 1 Sam. 17:10 **17:46** [a] Deut. 28:26 [b] Josh. 4:24; 1 Kin. 8:43; 18:36; 2 Kin. 19:19; Is. 52:10 **17:47** [a] 1 Sam. 14:6; 2 Chr. 14:11; 20:15; Ps. 44:6; Hos. 1:7; Zech. 4:6 [b] 2 Chr. 20:15 **17:48** [a] Ps. 27:3 **17:50** [a] Judg. 3:31; 15:15; 20:16 **17:51** [a] 1 Sam. 21:9; 2 Sam. 23:21 [b] Heb. 11:34 **17:52** [a] Josh. 15:36 [1] Following Masoretic Text, Syriac, Targum, and Vulgate; Septuagint reads *Gath.* **17:55** [a] 1 Sam. 14:50 [b] 1 Sam. 16:21, 22 **17:57** [a] 1 Sam. 17:54 **17:58** [a] 1 Sam. 17:12 **18:1** [a] Gen. 44:30 [b] Deut. 13:6; 1 Sam. 20:17; 2 Sam. 1:26 **18:2** [a] 1 Sam. 17:15 **18:3** [a] 1 Sam. 20:8–17 **18:6** [a] Ex. 15:20, 21; Judg. 11:34; Ps. 68:25; 149:3 **18:7** [a] Ex. 15:21 [b] 1 Sam. 21:11; 29:5 **18:8** [a] Eccl. 4:4 [b] 1 Sam. 15:28 **18:10** [a] 1 Sam. 16:14 [b] 1 Sam. 19:24; 1 Kin. 18:29; Acts 16:16 [c] 1 Sam. 16:23 [d] 1 Sam. 19:9, 10 **18:11** [a] 1 Sam. 19:10; 20:33 **18:12** [a] 1 Sam. 18:15, 29 [b] 1 Sam. 16:13, 18 [c] 1 Sam. 16:14; 28:15 **18:13** [a] Num. 27:17; 1 Sam. 18:16; 29:6; 2 Sam. 5:2 **18:14** [a] Gen. 39:2, 3, 23; Josh. 6:27; 1 Sam. 16:18 **18:16** [a] Num. 27:16, 17; 1 Sam. 18:5; 2 Sam. 5:2; 1 Kin. 3:7 **18:17** [a] 1 Sam. 14:49; 17:25 [b] Num. 32:20, 27, 29; 1 Sam. 25:28

battles." For Saul thought, [c]"Let my hand not be against him, but let the hand of the Philistines be against him."

18 So David said to Saul, [a]"Who *am* I, and what *is* my life *or* my father's family in Israel, that I should be son-in-law to the king?" 19 But it happened at the time when Merab, Saul's daughter, should have been given to David, that she was given to [a]Adriel the [b]Meholathite as a wife.

20 [a]Now Michal, Saul's daughter, loved David. And they told Saul, and the thing pleased him. 21 So Saul said, "I will give her to him, that she may be a snare to him, and that [a]the hand of the Philistines may be against him." Therefore Saul said to David a second time, [b]"You shall be my son-in-law today."

22 And Saul commanded his servants, "Communicate with David secretly, and say, 'Look, the king has delight in you, and all his servants love you. Now therefore, become the king's son-in-law.' "

23 So Saul's servants spoke those words in the hearing of David. And David said, "Does it seem to you *a* light *thing* to be a king's son-in-law, seeing I *am* a poor and lightly esteemed man?" 24 And the servants of Saul told him, saying, "In this manner David spoke."

25 Then Saul said, "Thus you shall say to David: 'The king does not desire any [a]dowry but one hundred foreskins of the Philistines, to take [b]vengeance on the king's enemies.' " But Saul [c]thought to make David fall by the hand of the Philistines. 26 So when his servants told David these words, it pleased David well to become the king's son-in-law. Now [a]the days had not expired; 27 therefore David arose and went, he and [a]his men, and killed two hundred men of the Philistines. And [b]David brought their foreskins, and they gave them in full count to the king, that he might become the king's son-in-law. Then Saul gave him Michal his daughter as a wife.

28 Thus Saul saw and knew that the LORD *was* with David, and *that* Michal, Saul's daughter, loved him; 29 and Saul was still more afraid of David. So Saul became David's enemy continually. 30 Then the princes of the Philistines [a]went out *to war.* And so it was, whenever they went out, *that* David [b]behaved more wisely than all the servants of Saul, so that his name became highly esteemed.

### *SAUL PERSECUTES DAVID*

**19** Now Saul spoke to Jonathan his son and to all his servants, that they should kill [a]David; but Jonathan, Saul's son, [b]delighted greatly in David. 2 So Jonathan told David, saying, "My father Saul seeks to kill you. Therefore please be on your guard until morning, and stay in a secret *place* and hide. 3 And I will go out and stand beside my father in the field where you *are,* and I will speak with my father about you. Then what I observe, I will tell [a]you."

4 Thus Jonathan [a]spoke well of David to Saul his father, and said to him, "Let not the king [b]sin against his servant, against David, because he has not sinned against you, and because his works *have been* very good toward you. 5 For he took his [a]life in his hands and [b]killed the Philistine, and [c]the LORD brought about a great deliverance for all Israel. You saw *it* and rejoiced. [d]Why then will you [e]sin against innocent blood, to kill David without a cause?"

6 So Saul heeded the voice of Jonathan, and Saul swore, "*As* the LORD lives, he shall not be killed." 7 Then Jonathan called David, and Jonathan told him all these things. So Jonathan brought David to Saul, and he was in his presence [a]as in times past.

> **SEEING JESUS IN THE SCRIPTURE**
>
> **19:6** Jonathan went before his father to intercede for David and spare his life. This pictures Jesus who goes before His Father to intercede for all who trust in Him, sparing their lives (see Rom. 8:34).

8 And there was war again; and David went out and fought with the Philistines, [a]and struck them with a mighty blow, and they fled from him.

9 Now [a]the distressing spirit from the LORD came upon Saul as he sat in his house with his spear in his hand. And David was playing *music* with *his* hand. 10 Then Saul sought to pin David to the wall with the spear, but he slipped away from Saul's presence; and he drove the spear into the wall. So David fled and escaped that night.

11 [a]Saul also sent messengers to David's house to watch him and to kill him in the morning. And Michal, David's wife, told him, saying, "If you do not save your life tonight, tomorrow you will be killed." 12 So Michal [a]let David down through a window. And he went and fled and escaped. 13 And Michal took an image and laid *it* in the bed, put a cover of goats' *hair* for his head, and covered *it* with clothes. 14 So when Saul sent messengers to take David, she said, "He *is* sick."

15 Then Saul sent the messengers *back* to see David, saying, "Bring him up to me in the bed, that I may kill him." 16 And when the messengers had come in, there was the image in the bed, with

**18:17** [c] 1 Sam. 18:21, 25; 2 Sam. 12:9 **18:18** [a] 1 Sam. 9:21; 18:23; 2 Sam. 7:18 **18:19** [a] 2 Sam. 21:8 [b] Judg. 7:22; 2 Sam. 21:8; 1 Kin. 19:16 **18:20** [a] 1 Sam. 18:28 **18:21** [a] 1 Sam. 18:17 [b] 1 Sam. 18:26 **18:25** [a] Gen. 34:12; Ex. 22:17 [b] 1 Sam. 14:24 [c] 1 Sam. 18:17 **18:26** [a] 1 Sam. 18:21 **18:27** [a] 1 Sam. 18:13 [b] 2 Sam. 3:14 **18:30** [a] 2 Sam. 11:1 [b] 1 Sam. 18:5 **19:1** [a] 1 Sam. 8:8, 9 [b] 1 Sam. 18:1 **19:3** [a] 1 Sam. 20:8–13 **19:4** [a] 1 Sam. 20:32; [Prov. 31:8, 9] [b] Gen. 42:22; [Prov. 17:13]; Jer. 18:20 **19:5** [a] Judg. 9:17; 12:3 [b] 1 Sam. 17:49, 50 [c] 1 Sam. 11:13; 1 Chr. 11:14 [d] 1 Sam. 20:32 [e] [Deut. 19:10–13] **19:7** [a] 1 Sam. 16:21; 18:2, 10, 13 **19:8** [a] 1 Sam. 18:27; 23:5 **19:9** [a] 1 Sam. 16:14; 18:10, 11 **19:11** [a] Judg. 16:2; Ps. 59:title **19:12** [a] Josh. 2:15; Acts 9:25; 2 Cor. 11:33

a cover of goats' *hair* for his head. 17 Then Saul said to Michal, "Why have you deceived me like this, and sent my enemy away, so that he has escaped?"

And Michal answered Saul, "He said to me, 'Let me go! [a]Why should I kill you?' "

18 So David fled and escaped, and went to [a]Samuel at [b]Ramah, and told him all that Saul had done to him. And he and Samuel went and stayed in Naioth. 19 Now it was told Saul, saying, "Take note, David *is* at Naioth in Ramah!" 20 Then [a]Saul sent messengers to take David. [b]And when they saw the group of prophets prophesying, and Samuel standing *as* leader over them, the Spirit of God came upon the messengers of Saul, and they also [c]prophesied. 21 And when Saul was told, he sent other messengers, and they prophesied likewise. Then Saul sent messengers again the third time, and they prophesied also. 22 Then he also went to Ramah, and came to the great well that *is* at Sechu. So he asked, and said, "Where *are* Samuel and David?"

And *someone* said, "Indeed *they are* at Naioth in Ramah." 23 So he went there to Naioth in Ramah. Then [a]the Spirit of God was upon him also, and he went on and prophesied until he came to Naioth in Ramah. 24 [a]And he also stripped off his clothes and prophesied before Samuel in like manner, and lay down [b]naked all that day and all that night. Therefore they say, [c]"*Is* Saul also among the prophets?"[1]

## *JONATHAN'S LOYALTY TO DAVID*

**20** Then David fled from Naioth in Ramah, and went and said to Jonathan, "What have I done? What *is* my iniquity, and what *is* my sin before your father, that he seeks my life?"

2 So Jonathan said to him, "By no means! You shall not die! Indeed, my father will do nothing either great or small without first telling me. And why should my father hide this thing from me? It *is* not *so!*"

3 Then David took an oath again, and said, "Your father certainly knows that I have found favor in your eyes, and he has said, 'Do not let Jonathan know this, lest he be grieved.' But [a]truly, *as* the LORD lives and *as* your soul lives, *there is* but a step between me and death."

4 So Jonathan said to David, "Whatever you yourself desire, I will do *it* for you."

5 And David said to Jonathan, "Indeed tomorrow *is* the [a]New Moon, and I should not fail to sit with the king to eat. But let me go, that I may [b]hide in the field until the third *day* at evening. 6 If your father misses me at all, then say, 'David earnestly asked *permission* of me that he might run over [a]to Bethlehem, his city, for *there is* a yearly sacrifice there for all the family.' 7 [a]If he says thus: '*It is* well,' your servant will be safe. But if he is very angry, be sure that [b]evil is determined by him. 8 Therefore you shall [a]deal kindly with your servant, for [b]you have brought your servant into a covenant of the LORD with you. Nevertheless, [c]if there is iniquity in me, kill me yourself, for why should you bring me to your father?"

9 But Jonathan said, "Far be it from you! For if I knew certainly that evil was determined by my father to come upon you, then would I not tell you?"

10 Then David said to Jonathan, "Who will tell me, or what *if* your father answers you roughly?"

11 And Jonathan said to David, "Come, let us go out into the field." So both of them went out into the field. 12 Then Jonathan said to David: "The LORD God of Israel *is witness!* When I have sounded out my father sometime tomorrow, *or* the third *day,* and indeed *there is* good toward David, and I do not send to you and tell you, 13 may [a]the LORD do so and much more to Jonathan. But if it pleases my father *to do* you evil, then I will report it to you and send you away, that you may go in safety. And [b]the LORD be with you as He has [c]been with my father. 14 And you shall not only show me the kindness of the LORD while I still live, that I may not die; 15 but [a]you shall not cut off your kindness from my house forever, no, not when the LORD has cut off every one of the enemies of David from the face of the earth." 16 So Jonathan made *a covenant* with the house of David, *saying,* [a]"Let the LORD require *it* at the hand of David's enemies."

17 Now Jonathan again caused David to vow, because he loved him; [a]for he loved him as he loved his own soul. 18 Then Jonathan said to David, [a]"Tomorrow *is* the New Moon; and you will be missed, because your seat will be empty. 19 And *when* you have stayed three days, go down quickly and come to [a]the place where you hid on the day of the deed; and remain by the stone Ezel. 20 Then I will shoot three arrows to the side, as though I shot at a target; 21 and there I will send a lad, *saying,* 'Go, find the arrows.' If I expressly say to the lad, 'Look, the arrows *are* on this side of you; get them and come'—then, [a]as the LORD lives, *there is* safety for you and

> **20:16–17 Jonathan**'s love and loyalty to David is unparalleled among human relationships in the Bible. In protecting David from the murderous plots of Saul, Jonathan, the rightful heir, closed the door to his own reign over Israel after his father's death.

19:17 [a] 2 Sam. 2:22 19:18 [a] 1 Sam. 16:13 [b] 1 Sam. 7:17 19:20 [a] 1 Sam. 19:11, 14; John 7:32 [b] 1 Sam. 10:5, 6, 10; [1 Cor. 14:3, 24, 25] [c] Num. 11:25; Joel 2:28 19:23 [a] 1 Sam. 10:10 19:24 [a] Is. 20:2 [b] Mic. 1:8 [c] 1 Sam. 10:10–12 [1] Compare 1 Samuel 10:12 20:3 [a] 1 Sam. 27:1; 2 Kin. 2:6 20:5 [a] Num. 10:10; 28:11–15 [b] 1 Sam. 19:2, 3 20:6 [a] 1 Sam. 16:4; 17:12; John 7:42 20:7 [a] Deut. 1:23; 2 Sam. 17:4 [b] 1 Sam. 25:17; Esth. 7:7 20:8 [a] Josh. 2:14 [b] 1 Sam. 18:3; 20:16; 23:18 [c] 2 Sam. 14:32 20:13 [a] Ruth 1:17; 1 Sam. 3:17 [b] Josh. 1:5; 1 Sam. 17:37; 18:12; 1 Chr. 22:11, 16 [c] 1 Sam. 10:7 20:15 [a] 1 Sam. 24:21; 2 Sam. 9:1, 3, 7; 21:7 20:16 [a] Deut. 23:21; 1 Sam. 25:22; 31:2; 2 Sam. 4:7; 21:8 20:17 [a] 1 Sam. 18:1 20:18 [a] 1 Sam. 20:5, 24 20:19 [a] 1 Sam. 19:2 20:21 [a] Jer. 4:2

no harm. 22 But if I say thus to the young man, 'Look, the arrows *are* beyond you'—go your way, for the LORD has sent you away. 23 And as for [a]the matter which you and I have spoken of, indeed the LORD *be* between you and me forever."

24 Then David hid in the field. And when the New Moon had come, the king sat down to eat the feast. 25 Now the king sat on his seat, as at other times, on a seat by the wall. And Jonathan arose,[1] and Abner sat by Saul's side, but David's place was empty. 26 Nevertheless Saul did not say anything that day, for he thought, "Something has happened to him; he *is* unclean, surely he *is* [a]unclean." 27 And it happened the next day, the second *day* of the month, that David's place was empty. And Saul said to Jonathan his son, "Why has the son of Jesse not come to eat, either yesterday or today?"

28 So Jonathan [a]answered Saul, "David earnestly asked *permission* of me *to go* to Bethlehem. 29 And he said, 'Please let me go, for our family has a sacrifice in the city, and my brother has commanded me *to be there.* And now, if I have found favor in your eyes, please let me get away and see my brothers.' Therefore he has not come to the king's table."

30 Then Saul's anger was aroused against Jonathan, and he said to him, "You son of a perverse, rebellious *woman!* Do I not know that you have chosen the son of Jesse to your own shame and to the shame of your mother's nakedness? 31 For as long as the son of Jesse lives on the earth, you shall not be established, nor your kingdom. Now therefore, send and bring him to me, for he shall surely die."

32 And Jonathan answered Saul his father, and said to him, [a]"Why should he be killed? What has he done?" 33 Then Saul [a]cast a spear at him to kill him, [b]by which Jonathan knew that it was determined by his father to kill David.

34 So Jonathan arose from the table in fierce anger, and ate no food the second day of the month, for he was grieved for David, because his father had treated him shamefully.

35 And so it was, in the morning, that Jonathan went out into the field at the time appointed with David, and a little lad *was* with him. 36 Then he said to his lad, "Now run, find the arrows which I shoot." As the lad ran, he shot an arrow beyond him. 37 When the lad had come to the place where the arrow was which Jonathan had shot, Jonathan cried out after the lad and said, "*Is* not the arrow beyond you?" 38 And Jonathan cried out after the lad, "Make haste, hurry, do not delay!" So Jonathan's lad gathered up the arrows and came back to his master. 39 But the lad did not know anything. Only Jonathan and David knew of the matter. 40 Then Jonathan gave his weapons to his lad, and said to him, "Go, carry *them* to the city."

41 As soon as the lad had gone, David arose from *a place* toward the south, fell on his face to the ground, and bowed down three times. And they kissed one another; and they wept together, but David more so. 42 Then Jonathan said to David, [a]"Go in peace, since we have both sworn in the name of the LORD, saying, 'May the LORD be between you and me, and between your descendants and my descendants, forever.' " So he arose and departed, and Jonathan went into the city.

### *DAVID AND THE HOLY BREAD*

**21** Now David came to Nob, to Ahimelech the priest. And [a]Ahimelech was [b]afraid when he met David, and said to him, "Why *are* you alone, and no one is with you?"

2 So David said to Ahimelech the priest, "The king has ordered me on some business, and said to me, 'Do not let anyone know anything about the business on which I send you, or what I have commanded you.' And I have directed *my* young men to such and such a place. 3 Now therefore, what have you on hand? Give *me* five *loaves of* bread in my hand, or whatever can be found."

4 And the priest answered David and said, "*There is* no common bread on hand; but there is [a]holy bread, [b]if the young men have at least kept themselves from women."

5 Then David answered the priest, and said to him, "Truly, women *have been* kept from us about three days since I came out. And the [a]vessels of the young men are holy, and *the bread is* in effect common, even though it was consecrated [b]in the vessel this day."

6 So the priest [a]gave him holy *bread;* for there was no bread there but the showbread [b]which had been taken from before the LORD, in order to put hot bread *in its place* on the day when it was taken away.

> **21:1–6** The **bread** used for worship was replaced with a fresh loaf every seven days. Usually, only priests were allowed to eat the old bread. In giving the bread to David, Ahimelech broke the law, yet in his compassion he kept the spirit of the law. Jesus referred to this incident when He explained to the Pharisees that it was permissible to pick grain to eat on the Sabbath (Matt. 12:2–4).

7 Now a certain man of the servants of Saul *was* there that day, detained before the LORD. And his name *was* [a]Doeg, an Edomite, the chief of the herdsmen who *belonged* to Saul.

20:23 [a]1 Sam. 20:14, 15 20:25 [1]Following Masoretic Text, Syriac, Targum, and Vulgate; Septuagint reads *he sat across from Jonathan.* 20:26 [a]Lev. 7:20, 21; 15:5 20:28 [a]1 Sam. 20:6 20:32 [a]Gen. 31:36; 1 Sam. 19:5; [Prov. 31:9]; Matt. 27:23; Luke 23:22 20:33 [a]1 Sam. 18:11; 19:10 [b]1 Sam. 20:7 20:42 [a]1 Sam. 1:17 21:1 [a]1 Sam. 14:3; Mark 2:26 [b]1 Sam. 16:4 21:4 [a]Ex. 25:30; Lev. 24:5–9; Matt. 12:4 [b]Ex. 19:15 21:5 [a]Ex. 19:14, 15; 1 Thess. 4:4 [b]Lev. 8:26 21:6 [a]Matt. 12:3, 4; Mark 2:25, 26; Luke 6:3, 4 [b]Lev. 24:8, 9 21:7 [a]1 Sam. 14:47; 22:9; Ps. 52:title

8 And David said to Ahimelech, "Is there
not here on hand a spear or a sword? For I have
brought neither my sword nor my weapons with
me, because the king's business required haste."
9 So the priest said, "The sword of Goliath
the Philistine, whom you killed in [a]the Valley of
Elah, [b]there it is, wrapped in a cloth behind the
ephod. If you will take that, take *it*. For *there is*
no other except that one here."
And David said, "*There is* none like it; give
it to me."

### DAVID FLEES TO GATH

10 Then David arose and fled that day from
before Saul, and went to Achish the king of Gath.
11 And [a]the servants of Achish said to him, "*Is*
this not David the king of the land? Did they not
sing of him to one another in dances, saying:

[b]'Saul has slain his thousands,
And David his ten thousands'?"[1]

12 Now David [a]took these words to heart,
and was very much afraid of Achish the king of
Gath. 13 So [a]he changed his behavior before them,
pretended madness in their hands, scratched
on the doors of the gate, and let his saliva fall
down on his beard. 14 Then Achish said to his
servants, "Look, you see the man is insane. Why
have you brought him to me? 15 Have I need of
madmen, that you have brought this *fellow* to
play the madman in my presence? Shall this
*fellow* come into my house?"

### DAVID'S FOUR HUNDRED MEN

*(1 Chr. 12:16–18)*

**22** David therefore departed from there and
[a]escaped [b]to the cave of Adullam. So when
his brothers and all his father's house heard *it*,
they went down there to him. 2 [a]And everyone
*who was* in distress, everyone who *was* in debt,
and everyone *who was* discontented gathered
to him. So he became captain over them. And
there were about [b]four hundred men with him.
3 Then David went from there to Mizpah of
[a]Moab; and he said to the king of Moab, "Please
let my father and mother come here with you,
till I know what God will do for me." 4 So he
brought them before the king of Moab, and

> **22:3** Like the Philistines, the people of **Moab** were continually at war with the Israelites. David must have assumed the safest places for him to hide were with Saul's enemies.

they dwelt with him all the time that David was
in the stronghold.
5 Now the prophet [a]Gad said to David, "Do
not stay in the stronghold; depart, and go to the
land of Judah." So David departed and went into
the forest of Hereth.

### SAUL MURDERS THE PRIESTS

6 When Saul heard that David and the men
who *were* with him had been discovered—now
Saul was staying in [a]Gibeah under a tamarisk tree
in Ramah, with his spear in his hand, and all his
servants standing about him— 7 then Saul said
to his servants who stood about him, "Hear now,
you Benjamites! Will the son of Jesse [a]give every
one of you fields and vineyards, *and* make you
all captains of thousands and captains of hun-
dreds? 8 All of you have conspired against me,
and *there is* no one who reveals to me that [a]my
son has made a covenant with the son of Jesse;
and *there is* not one of you who is sorry for me
or reveals to me that my son has stirred up my
servant against me, to lie in wait, as *it is* this day."
9 Then answered [a]Doeg the Edomite, who
was set over the servants of Saul, and said, "I
saw the son of Jesse going to Nob, to [b]Ahime-
lech the son of [c]Ahitub. 10 [a]And he inquired of
the LORD for him, [b]gave him provisions, and
gave him the sword of Goliath the Philistine."
11 So the king sent to call Ahimelech the
priest, the son of Ahitub, and all his father's
house, the priests who *were* in Nob. And they
all came to the king. 12 And Saul said, "Hear now,
son of Ahitub!"
He answered, "Here I am, my lord."
13 Then Saul said to him, "Why have you
conspired against me, you and the son of Jesse,
in that you have given him bread and a sword,
and have inquired of God for him, that he should
rise against me, to lie in wait, as it is this day?"
14 So Ahimelech answered the king and said,
"And who among all your servants *is as* [a]faith-
ful as David, who is the king's son-in-law, who
goes at your bidding, and is honorable in your
house? 15 Did I then begin to inquire of God for
him? Far be it from me! Let not the king impute
anything to his servant, *or* to any in the house
of my father. For your servant knew nothing of
all this, little or much."
16 And the king said, "You shall surely die,
Ahimelech, you and all [a]your father's house!"
17 Then the king said to the guards who stood
about him, "Turn and kill the priests of the
LORD, because their hand also *is* with David,
and because they knew when he fled and did
not tell it to me." But the servants of the king
[a]would not lift their hands to strike the priests
of the LORD. 18 And the king said to Doeg, "You

**21:9** [a] 1 Sam. 17:2, 50 [b] 1 Sam. 31:10 **21:11** [a] Ps. 56:title [b] 1 Sam. 18:6–8; 29:5 [1] Compare 1 Samuel 18:7 **21:12** [a] Luke 2:19 **21:13** [a] Ps. 34:title **22:1** [a] Ps. 57:title; 142:title [b] Josh. 12:15; 15:35; 2 Sam. 23:13 **22:2** [a] Judg. 11:3 [b] 1 Sam. 25:13 **22:3** [a] 2 Sam. 8:2 **22:5** [a] 2 Sam. 24:11; 1 Chr. 21:9; 29:29; 2 Chr. 29:25 **22:6** [a] 1 Sam. 15:34 **22:7** [a] 1 Sam. 8:14 **22:8** [a] 1 Sam. 18:3; 20:16, 30 **22:9** [a] 1 Sam. 21:7; 22:22; Ps. 52:title [b] 1 Sam. 21:1 [c] 1 Sam. 14:3 **22:10** [a] Num. 27:21; 1 Sam. 10:22 [b] 1 Sam. 21:6, 9 **22:14** [a] 1 Sam. 19:4, 5; 20:32; 24:11 **22:16** [a] Deut. 24:16 **22:17** [a] Ex. 1:17

turn and kill the priests!" So Doeg the Edomite turned and struck the priests, and [a]killed on that day eighty-five men who wore a linen ephod. 19 [a]Also Nob, the city of the priests, he struck with the edge of the sword, both men and women, children and nursing infants, oxen and donkeys and sheep—with the edge of the sword.

20 [a]Now one of the sons of Ahimelech the son of Ahitub, named Abiathar, [b]escaped and fled after David. 21 And Abiathar told David that Saul had killed the LORD's priests. 22 So David said to Abiathar, "I knew that day, when Doeg the Edomite *was* there, that he would surely tell Saul. I have caused *the death* of all the persons of your father's house. 23 Stay with me; do not fear. [a]For he who seeks my life seeks your life, but with me you *shall be* safe."

## DAVID SAVES THE CITY OF KEILAH

**23** Then they told David, saying, "Look, the Philistines are fighting against [a]Keilah, and they are robbing the threshing floors."

2 Therefore David [a]inquired of the LORD, saying, "Shall I go and attack these Philistines?"

And the LORD said to David, "Go and attack the Philistines, and save Keilah."

3 But David's men said to him, "Look, we are afraid here in Judah. How much more then if we go to Keilah against the armies of the Philistines?" 4 Then David inquired of the LORD once again.

And the LORD answered him and said, "Arise, go down to Keilah. For I will deliver the Philistines into your hand." 5 And David and his men went to Keilah and [a]fought with the Philistines, struck them with a mighty blow, and took away their livestock. So David saved the inhabitants of Keilah.

6 Now it happened, when Abiathar the son of Ahimelech [a]fled to David at Keilah, *that* he went down *with* an ephod in his hand.

7 And Saul was told that David had gone to Keilah. So Saul said, "God has delivered him into my hand, for he has shut himself in by entering a town that has gates and bars." 8 Then Saul called all the people together for war, to go down to Keilah to besiege David and his men.

9 When David knew that Saul plotted evil against him, [a]he said to Abiathar the priest, "Bring the ephod here." 10 Then David said, "O LORD God of Israel, Your servant has certainly heard that Saul seeks to come to Keilah [a]to destroy the city for my sake. 11 Will the men of Keilah deliver me into his hand? Will Saul come down, as Your servant has heard? O LORD God of Israel, I pray, tell Your servant."

And the LORD said, "He will come down."

12 Then David said, "Will the men of Keilah deliver me and my men into the hand of Saul?"

And the LORD said, "They will deliver *you*."

13 So David and his men, [a]about six hundred, arose and departed from Keilah and went wherever they could go. Then it was told Saul that David had escaped from Keilah; so he halted the expedition.

## DAVID IN WILDERNESS STRONGHOLDS

14 And David stayed in strongholds in the wilderness, and remained in [a]the mountains in the Wilderness of [b]Ziph. Saul [c]sought him every day, but God did not deliver him into his hand. 15 So David saw that Saul had come out to seek his life. And David *was* in the Wilderness of Ziph in a forest.[1] 16 Then Jonathan, Saul's son, arose and went to David in the woods and strengthened his hand in God. 17 And he said to him, [a]"Do not fear, for the hand of Saul my father shall not find you. You shall be king over Israel, and I shall be next to you. [b]Even my father Saul knows that." 18 So the two of them [a]made a covenant before the LORD. And David stayed in the woods, and Jonathan went to his own house.

19 Then the Ziphites [a]came up to Saul at Gibeah, saying, "Is David not hiding with us in strongholds in the woods, in the hill of Hachilah, which *is* on the south of Jeshimon? 20 Now therefore, O king, come down according to all the desire of your soul to come down; and [a]our part *shall be* to deliver him into the king's hand."

21 And Saul said, "Blessed *are* you of the LORD, for you have compassion on me. 22 Please go and find out for sure, and see the place where his hideout is, *and* who has seen him there. For I am told he is very crafty. 23 See therefore, and take knowledge of all the lurking places where he hides; and come back to me with certainty, and I will go with you. And it shall be, if he is in the land, that I will search for him throughout all the clans[1] of Judah."

24 So they arose and went to Ziph before Saul. But David and his men *were* in the Wilderness [a]of Maon, in the plain on the south of Jeshimon. 25 When Saul and his men went to seek *him*, they told David. Therefore he went down to the rock, and stayed in the Wilderness of Maon. And when Saul heard *that*, he pursued David in the Wilderness of Maon. 26 Then Saul went on one side of the mountain, and David and his men on the other side of the mountain. [a]So David made haste to get away from Saul, for Saul and his men [b]were encircling David and his men to take them.

27 [a]But a messenger came to Saul, saying, "Hurry and come, for the Philistines have invaded the land!" 28 Therefore Saul returned from pursuing David, and went against the Philistines; so they called that place the Rock of Escape.[1] 29 Then David went up from there and dwelt in strongholds at [a]En Gedi.

**22:18** [a] 1 Sam. 2:31 **22:19** [a] Josh. 21:1–45; 1 Sam. 22:9, 11 **22:20** [a] 1 Sam. 23:6, 9; 30:7; 1 Kin. 2:26, 27 [b] 1 Sam. 2:33 **22:23** [a] 1 Kin. 2:26 **23:1** [a] Josh. 15:44; Neh. 3:17, 18 **23:2** [a] 1 Sam. 22:10; 23:4, 6, 9; 28:6; 30:8; 2 Sam. 5:19, 23 **23:5** [a] 1 Sam. 19:8; 2 Sam. 5:20 **23:6** [a] 1 Sam. 22:20 **23:9** [a] Num. 27:21; 1 Sam. 23:6; 30:7 **23:10** [a] 1 Sam. 22:19 **23:13** [a] 1 Sam. 22:2; 25:13 **23:14** [a] Ps. 11:1 [b] Josh. 15:55; 2 Chr. 11:8 [c] Ps. 32:7; 54:3, 4 **23:15** [1] Or *in Horesh* **23:17** [a] [Ps. 27:1–3; Heb. 13:6] [b] 1 Sam. 20:31; 24:20 **23:18** [a] 1 Sam. 18:3; 20:12–17, 42; 2 Sam. 9:1; 21:7 **23:19** [a] 1 Sam. 26:1; Ps. 54:title **23:20** [a] Ps. 54:3 **23:23** [1] Literally *thousands* **23:24** [a] Josh. 15:55; 1 Sam. 25:2 **23:26** [a] Ps. 31:22 [b] Ps. 17:9 **23:27** [a] 2 Kin. 19:9 **23:28** [1] Hebrew *Sela Hammahlekoth* **23:29** [a] Josh. 15:62; 2 Chr. 20:2

### DAVID SPARES SAUL

**24** Now it happened, [a]when Saul had returned from following the Philistines, that it was told him, saying, "Take note! David *is* in the Wilderness of En Gedi." 2 Then Saul took three thousand chosen men from all Israel, and [a]went to seek David and his men on the Rocks of the Wild Goats. 3 So he came to the sheepfolds by the road, where there *was* a cave; and [a]Saul went in to [b]attend to his needs. ([c]David and his men were staying in the recesses of the cave.) 4 [a]Then the men of David said to him, "This is the day of which the LORD said to you, 'Behold, I will deliver your enemy into your hand, that you may do to him as it seems good to you.' " And David arose and secretly cut off a corner of Saul's robe. 5 Now it happened afterward that [a]David's heart troubled him because he had cut Saul's robe. 6 And he said to his men, [a]"The LORD forbid that I should do this thing to my master, the LORD's anointed, to stretch out my hand against him, seeing he *is* the anointed of the LORD." 7 So David [a]restrained his servants with *these* words, and did not allow them to rise against Saul. And Saul got up from the cave and went on *his* way.

8 David also arose afterward, went out of the cave, and called out to Saul, saying, "My lord the king!" And when Saul looked behind him, David stooped with his face to the earth, and bowed down. 9 And David said to Saul: [a]"Why do you listen to the words of men who say, 'Indeed David seeks your harm'? 10 Look, this day your eyes have seen that the LORD delivered you today into my hand in the cave, and *someone* urged *me* to kill you. But *my eye* spared you, and I said, 'I will not stretch out my hand against my lord, for he *is* the LORD's anointed.' 11 Moreover, my father, see! Yes, see the corner of your robe in my hand! For in that I cut off the corner of your robe, and did not kill you, know and see that *there is* [a]neither evil nor rebellion in my hand, and I have not sinned against you. Yet you [b]hunt my life to take it. 12 [a]Let the LORD judge between you and me, and let the LORD avenge me on you. But my hand shall not be against you. 13 As the proverb of the ancients says, [a]'Wickedness proceeds from the wicked.' But my hand shall not be against you. 14 After whom has the king of Israel come out? Whom do you pursue? [a]A dead dog? [b]A flea? 15 [a]Therefore let the LORD be judge, and judge between you and me, and [b]see and [c]plead my case, and deliver me out of your hand."

> **24:10–12** David knew that the Lord had anointed him to be the king to succeed Saul, and Saul knew it too. Saul, probably thinking of how he would have responded, was sure that David would seize power and oust him with trickery and violence. Here, though, David proved he wasn't going to harm Saul, even if Saul was trying to kill him. It was God's place, and His alone, to arrange the transfer of power from Saul to David.

16 So it was, when David had finished speaking these words to Saul, that Saul said, [a]"*Is* this your voice, my son David?" And Saul lifted up his voice and wept. 17 [a]Then he said to David: "You *are* [b]more righteous than I; for [c]you have rewarded me with good, whereas I have rewarded you with evil. 18 And you have shown this day how you have dealt well with me; for when [a]the LORD delivered me into your hand, you did not kill me. 19 For if a man finds his enemy, will he let him get away safely? Therefore may the LORD reward you with good for what you have done to me this day. 20 And now [a]I know indeed that you shall surely be king, and that the kingdom of Israel shall be established in your hand. 21 [a]Therefore swear now to me by the LORD [b]that you will not cut off my descendants after me, and that you will not destroy my name from my father's house."

22 So David swore to Saul. And Saul went home, but David and his men went up to [a]the stronghold.

### DEATH OF SAMUEL

**25** Then [a]Samuel died; and the Israelites gathered together and [b]lamented for him, and buried him at his home in Ramah. And David arose and went down [c]to the Wilderness of Paran.[1]

### DAVID AND THE WIFE OF NABAL

2 Now *there was* a man [a]in Maon whose business *was* in [b]Carmel, and the man *was* very rich. He had three thousand sheep and a thousand goats. And he was shearing his sheep in Carmel. 3 The name of the man *was* Nabal, and the name of his wife Abigail. And *she was* a woman of good understanding and beautiful appearance; but the man *was* harsh and evil in *his* doings. He *was of the house of* [a]Caleb.

4 When David heard in the wilderness that Nabal was [a]shearing his sheep, 5 David sent

**24:1** [a] 1 Sam. 23:19, 28, 29 **24:2** [a] 1 Sam. 26:2; Ps. 38:12 **24:3** [a] 1 Sam. 24:10 [b] Judg. 3:24 [c] Ps. 57:title; 142:title **24:4** [a] 1 Sam. 26:8–11 **24:5** [a] 2 Sam. 24:10 **24:6** [a] 1 Sam. 26:11 **24:7** [a] Ps. 7:4; [Matt. 5:44; Rom. 12:17, 19] **24:9** [a] Ps. 141:6; [Prov. 16:28; 17:9] **24:11** [a] Judg. 11:27; Ps. 7:3; 35:7 [b] 1 Sam. 26:20 **24:12** [a] Gen. 16:5; Judg. 11:27; 1 Sam. 26:10–23; Job 5:8 **24:13** [a] [Matt. 7:16–20] **24:14** [a] 1 Sam. 17:43; 2 Sam. 9:8 [b] 1 Sam. 26:20 **24:15** [a] 1 Sam. 24:12 [b] 2 Chr. 24:22 [c] Ps. 35:1; 43:1; 119:154; Mic. 7:9 **24:16** [a] 1 Sam. 26:17 **24:17** [a] 1 Sam. 26:21 [b] Gen. 38:26 [c] [Matt. 5:44] **24:18** [a] 1 Sam. 26:23 **24:20** [a] 1 Sam. 23:17 **24:21** [a] Gen. 21:23; 1 Sam. 20:14–17 [b] 2 Sam. 21:6–8 **24:22** [a] 1 Sam. 23:29 **25:1** [a] 1 Sam. 28:3 [b] Num. 20:29; Deut. 34:8 [c] Gen. 21:21; Num. 10:12; 13:3 [1] Following Masoretic Text, Syriac, Targum, and Vulgate; Septuagint reads *Maon.* **25:2** [a] 1 Sam. 23:24 [b] Josh. 15:55 **25:3** [a] Josh. 15:13; 1 Sam. 30:14 **25:4** [a] Gen. 38:13; 2 Sam. 13:23

ten young men; and David said to the young men, "Go up to Carmel, go to Nabal, and greet him in my name. 6 And thus you shall say to him who lives *in prosperity:* [a]'Peace *be* to you, peace to your house, and peace to all that you have! 7 Now I have heard that you have shearers. Your shepherds were with us, and we did not hurt them, [a]nor was there anything missing from them all the while they were in Carmel. 8 Ask your young men, and they will tell you. Therefore let *my* young men find favor in your eyes, for we come on [a]a feast day. Please give whatever comes to your hand to your servants and to your son David.' "

9 So when David's young men came, they spoke to Nabal according to all these words in the name of David, and waited.

10 Then Nabal answered David's servants, and said, [a]"Who *is* David, and who *is* the son of Jesse? There are many servants nowadays who break away each one from his master. 11 [a]Shall I then take my bread and my water and my meat that I have killed for my shearers, and give *it* to men when I do not know where they *are* from?"

12 So David's young men turned on their heels and went back; and they came and told him all these words. 13 Then David said to his men, "Every man gird on his sword." So every man girded on his sword, and David also girded on his sword. And about four hundred men went with David, and two hundred [a]stayed with the supplies.

14 Now one of the young men told Abigail, Nabal's wife, saying, "Look, David sent messengers from the wilderness to greet our master; and he reviled them. 15 But the men *were* very good to us, and [a]we were not hurt, nor did we miss anything as long as we accompanied them, when we were in the fields. 16 They were [a]a wall to us both by night and day, all the time we were with them keeping the sheep. 17 Now therefore, know and consider what you will do, for [a]harm is determined against our master and against all his household. For he *is such* a [b]scoundrel[1] that *one* cannot speak to him."

18 Then Abigail made haste and [a]took two hundred *loaves* of bread, two skins of wine, five sheep already dressed, five seahs of roasted *grain,* one hundred clusters of raisins, and two hundred cakes of figs, and loaded *them* on donkeys. 19 And she said to her servants, [a]"Go on before me; see, I am coming after you." But she did not tell her husband Nabal.

20 So it was, *as* she rode on the donkey, that she went down under cover of the hill; and there were David and his men, coming down toward her, and she met them. 21 Now David had said, "Surely in vain I have protected all that this *fellow* has in the wilderness, so that nothing was missed of all that *belongs* to him. And he has [a]repaid me evil for good. 22 [a]May God do so, and more also, to the enemies of David, if I [b]leave [c]one male of all who *belong* to him by morning light."

23 Now when Abigail saw David, she [a]dismounted quickly from the donkey, fell on her face before David, and bowed down to the ground. 24 So she fell at his feet and said: "On me, my lord, *on* me *let* this iniquity *be!* And please let your maidservant speak in your ears, and hear the words of your maidservant. 25 Please, let not my lord regard this scoundrel Nabal. For as his name *is,* so *is* he: Nabal[1] *is* his name, and folly *is* with him! But I, your maidservant, did not see the young men of my lord whom you sent. 26 Now therefore, my lord, [a]*as* the LORD lives and *as* your soul lives, since the LORD has [b]held you back from coming to bloodshed and from [c]avenging yourself with your own hand, now then, [d]let your enemies and those who seek harm for my lord be as Nabal. 27 And now [a]this present which your maidservant has brought to my lord, let it be given to the young men who follow my lord. 28 Please forgive the trespass of your maidservant. For [a]the LORD will certainly make for my lord an enduring house, because my lord [b]fights the battles of the LORD, [c]and evil is not found in you throughout your days. 29 Yet a man has risen to pursue you and seek your life, but the life of my lord shall be [a]bound in the bundle of the living with the LORD your God; and the lives of your enemies He shall [b]sling out, *as from* the pocket of a sling. 30 And it shall come to pass, when the LORD has done for my lord according to all the good that He has spoken concerning you, and has appointed you [a]ruler over Israel, 31 that this will be no grief to you, nor offense of heart to my lord, either that you have shed blood without cause, or that my lord has avenged himself. But when the LORD has dealt well with my lord, then remember your maidservant."

32 Then David said to Abigail: [a]"Blessed *is* the LORD God of Israel, who sent you this day to meet me! 33 And blessed *is* your advice and blessed *are* you, because you have [a]kept me this day from coming to bloodshed and from avenging myself with my own hand. 34 For indeed, *as* the LORD God of Israel lives, who has [a]kept me back from hurting you, unless you had hurried

25:6 [a] Judg. 19:20; 1 Chr. 12:18; Ps. 122:7; Luke 10:5 25:7 [a] 1 Sam. 25:15, 21 25:8 [a] Neh. 8:10–12; Esth. 8:17; 9:19, 22 25:10 [a] Judg. 9:28 25:11 [a] Judg. 8:6, 15 25:13 [a] 1 Sam. 30:24 25:15 [a] 1 Sam. 25:7, 21 25:16 [a] Ex. 14:22; Job 1:10 25:17 [a] 1 Sam. 20:7 [b] Deut. 13:13; Judg. 19:22 [1] Literally *son of Belial* 25:18 [a] Gen. 32:13; [Prov. 18:16; 21:14] 25:19 [a] Gen. 32:16, 20 25:21 [a] 1 Sam. 24:17; Ps. 109:5; [Prov. 17:13] 25:22 [a] Ruth 1:17; 1 Sam. 3:17; 20:13, 16 [b] 1 Sam. 25:34 [c] 1 Kin. 14:10; 21:21; 2 Kin. 9:8 25:23 [a] Josh. 15:18; Judg. 1:14 25:25 [1] Literally *Fool* 25:26 [a] 2 Kin. 2:2 [b] Gen. 20:6; 1 Sam. 25:33 [c] [Rom. 12:19] [d] 2 Sam. 18:32 25:27 [a] Gen. 33:11; 1 Sam. 30:26; 2 Kin. 5:15 25:28 [a] 2 Sam. 7:11–16, 27; 1 Kin. 9:5; 1 Chr. 17:10, 25 [b] 1 Sam. 18:17 [c] 1 Sam. 24:11; Ps. 7:3 25:29 [a] [Ps. 66:9; Col. 3:3] [b] Jer. 10:18 25:30 [a] 1 Sam. 13:14; 15:28 25:32 [a] Gen. 24:27; Ex. 18:10; 1 Kin. 1:48; Ps. 41:13; 72:18; 106:48; Luke 1:68 25:33 [a] 1 Sam. 25:26 25:34 [a] 1 Sam. 25:26

and come to meet me, surely [b]by morning light
no males would have been left to Nabal!" 35 So
David received from her hand what she had
brought him, and said to her, [a]"Go up in peace
to your house. See, I have heeded your voice
and [b]respected your person."
36 Now Abigail went to Nabal, and there he
was, [a]holding a feast in his house, like the feast
of a king. And Nabal's heart *was* merry within
him, for he *was* very drunk; therefore she told
him nothing, little or much, until morning light.
37 So it was, in the morning, when the wine had
gone from Nabal, and his wife had told him these
things, that his heart died within him, and he
became *like* a stone. 38 Then it happened, *after*
about ten days, that the LORD [a]struck Nabal,
and he died.
39 So when David heard that Nabal was dead,
he said, [a]"Blessed *be* the LORD, who has [b]plead-
ed the cause of my reproach from the hand of
Nabal, and has [c]kept His servant from evil! For
the LORD has [d]returned the wickedness of Nabal
on his own head."

And David sent and proposed to Abigail,
to take her as his wife. 40 When the servants of
David had come to Abigail at Carmel, they spoke
to her saying, "David sent us to you, to ask you
to become his wife."
41 Then she arose, bowed her face to the
earth, and said, "Here is your maidservant, a
servant to [a]wash the feet of the servants of my
lord." 42 So Abigail rose in haste and rode on a
donkey, attended by five of her maidens; and she
followed the messengers of David, and became
his wife. 43 David also took Ahinoam [a]of Jezreel,
[b]and so both of them were his wives.
44 But Saul had given [a]Michal his daughter,
David's wife, to Palti[1] the son of Laish, who *was*
from [b]Gallim.

### *DAVID SPARES SAUL A SECOND TIME*

26 Now the Ziphites came to Saul at Gibeah,
saying, [a]"Is David not hiding in the hill of
Hachilah, opposite Jeshimon?" 2 Then Saul arose
and went down to the Wilderness of Ziph, having
[a]three thousand chosen men of Israel with him,
to seek David in the Wilderness of Ziph. 3 And
Saul encamped in the hill of Hachilah, which
*is* opposite Jeshimon, by the road. But David
stayed in the wilderness, and he saw that Saul
came after him into the wilderness. 4 David
therefore sent out spies, and understood that
Saul had indeed come.
5 So David arose and came to the place where
Saul had encamped. And David saw the place
where Saul lay, and [a]Abner the son of Ner, the
commander of his army. Now Saul lay within the
camp, with the people encamped all around him.
6 Then David answered, and said to Ahimelech
the Hittite and to Abishai [a]the son of Zeruiah,
brother of [b]Joab, saying, "Who will [c]go down
with me to Saul in the camp?"

And [d]Abishai said, "I will go down with you."
7 So David and Abishai came to the people
by night; and there Saul lay sleeping within the
camp, with his spear stuck in the ground by his
head. And Abner and the people lay all around
him. 8 Then Abishai said to David, [a]"God has
delivered your enemy into your hand this day.
Now therefore, please, let me strike him at once
with the spear, right to the earth; and I will not
*have to strike* him a second time!"
9 But David said to Abishai, "Do not destroy
him; [a]for who can stretch out his hand against
the LORD's anointed, and be guiltless?" 10 David
said furthermore, "*As* the LORD lives, [a]the LORD
shall strike him, or [b]his day shall come to die, or
he shall [c]go out to battle and perish. 11 [a]The LORD
forbid that I should stretch out my hand against
the LORD's anointed. But please, take now the
spear and the jug of water that *are* by his head,
and let us go." 12 So David took the spear and the
jug of water *by* Saul's head, and they got away;
and no man saw or knew *it* or awoke. For they
*were* all asleep, because [a]a deep sleep from the
LORD had fallen on them.
13 Now David went over to the other side, and
stood on the top of a hill afar off, a great distance
*being* between them. 14 And David called out to
the people and to Abner the son of Ner, saying,
"Do you not answer, Abner?"

Then Abner answered and said, "Who *are*
you, calling out to the king?"
15 So David said to Abner, "*Are* you not a man?
And who *is* like you in Israel? Why then have you
not guarded your lord the king? For one of the
people came in to destroy your lord the king.
16 This thing that you have done *is* not good.
*As* the LORD lives, you deserve to die, because
you have not guarded your master, the LORD's
anointed. And now see where the king's spear
*is*, and the jug of water that *was* by his head."
17 Then Saul knew David's voice, and said,
[a]"*Is* that your voice, my son David?"

David said, "*It is* my voice, my lord, O king."
18 And he said, [a]"Why does my lord thus pursue
his servant? For what have I done, or what evil
*is* in my hand? 19 Now therefore, please, let my
lord the king hear the words of his servant: If
the LORD has [a]stirred you up against me, let
Him accept an offering. But if *it is* the children
of men, *may* they *be* cursed before the LORD,

**25:34** [b]1 Sam. 25:22 **25:35** [a]1 Sam. 20:42; 2 Sam. 15:9; 2 Kin. 5:19; Luke 7:50; 8:48 [b]Gen. 19:21 **25:36** [a]2 Sam. 13:28; Prov. 20:1; Is. 5:11; Dan. 5:1; [Hos. 4:11] **25:38** [a]1 Sam. 26:10; 2 Sam. 6:7; Ps. 104:29 **25:39** [a]1 Sam. 25:32 [b]1 Sam. 24:15; Prov. 22:23 [c]1 Sam. 25:26, 34 [d]1 Kin. 2:44 **25:41** [a][Prov. 15:33]; Luke 7:38, 44 **25:43** [a]Josh. 15:56 [b]1 Sam. 27:3; 30:5 **25:44** [a]1 Sam. 18:20; 2 Sam. 3:14 [b]Is. 10:30 [1]Spelled *Paltiel* in 2 Samuel 3:15 **26:1** [a]1 Sam. 23:19; Ps. 54:title **26:2** [a]1 Sam. 13:2; 24:2 **26:5** [a]1 Sam. 14:50, 51; 17:55 **26:6** [a]1 Chr. 2:16 [b]2 Sam. 2:13 [c]Judg. 7:10, 11 [d]2 Sam. 2:18, 24 **26:8** [a]1 Sam. 24:4 **26:9** [a]1 Sam. 24:6, 7; 2 Sam. 1:14, 16 **26:10** [a][Deut. 32:35]; 1 Sam. 25:26, 38; [Luke 18:7; Rom. 12:19; Heb. 10:30] [b]Gen. 47:29; Deut. 31:14; [Job 7:1; 14:5]; Ps. 37:13 [c]1 Sam. 31:6 **26:11** [a]1 Sam. 24:6–12; [Rom. 12:17, 19] **26:12** [a]Gen. 2:21; 15:12; Is. 29:10 **26:17** [a]1 Sam. 24:16 **26:18** [a]1 Sam. 24:9, 11–14 **26:19** [a]2 Sam. 16:11; 24:1

[b]for they have driven me out this day from shar-
ing in the [c]inheritance of the LORD, saying, 'Go,
serve other gods.' 20 So now, do not let my blood
fall to the earth before the face of the LORD. For
the king of Israel has come out to seek [a]a flea, as
when one hunts a partridge in the mountains."

**26:19** Shiloh, the city where the ark of the covenant was kept, was considered the official worship site of the Israelites. Banishing someone from Israel prevented that person from officially worshiping God. Because worship was so important to the Israelites, depriving someone of the opportunity to worship was considered cruel punishment and was reserved for serious criminals.

21 Then Saul said, [a]"I have sinned. Return, my
son David. For I will harm you no more, because
my life was precious in your eyes this day. Indeed
I have played the fool and erred exceedingly."
22 And David answered and said, "Here is
the king's spear. Let one of the young men come
over and get it. 23 [a]May the LORD [b]repay every
man *for* his righteousness and his faithfulness;
for the LORD delivered you into *my* hand today,
but I would not stretch out my hand against the
LORD's anointed. 24 And indeed, as your life was
valued much this day in my eyes, so let my life
be valued much in the eyes of the LORD, and let
Him deliver me out of all tribulation."
25 Then Saul said to David, "*May* you *be*
blessed, my son David! You shall both do great
things and also still [a]prevail."

So David went on his way, and Saul returned
to his place.

### DAVID ALLIED WITH THE PHILISTINES

**27** And David said in his heart, "Now I shall
perish someday by the hand of Saul. *There*
*is* nothing better for me than that I should speed-
ily escape to the land of the Philistines; and Saul
will despair of me, to seek me anymore in any
part of Israel. So I shall escape out of his hand."
2 Then David arose [a]and went over with the six
hundred men who *were* with him [b]to Achish the
son of Maoch, king of Gath. 3 So David dwelt with
Achish at Gath, he and his men, each man with his
household, *and* David [a]with his two wives, Ahin-
oam the Jezreelitess, and Abigail the Carmelitess,
Nabal's widow. 4 And it was told Saul that David
had fled to Gath; so he sought him no more.

5 Then David said to Achish, "If I have now
found favor in your eyes, let them give me a
place in some town in the country, that I may
dwell there. For why should your servant dwell
in the royal city with you?" 6 So Achish gave him
Ziklag that day. Therefore [a]Ziklag has belonged
to the kings of Judah to this day. 7 Now the time
that David [a]dwelt in the country of the Philis-
tines was one full year and four months.
8 And David and his men went up and raided
[a]the Geshurites, [b]the Girzites,[1] and the [c]Amalek-
ites. For those *nations* were the inhabitants of the
land from of old, [d]as you go to Shur, even as far as
the land of Egypt. 9 Whenever David attacked the
land, he left neither man nor woman alive, but
took away the sheep, the oxen, the donkeys, the
camels, and the apparel, and returned and came
to Achish. 10 Then Achish would say, "Where have
you made a raid today?" And David would say,
"Against the southern *area* of Judah, or against
the southern *area* of [a]the Jerahmeelites, or against
the southern *area* of [b]the Kenites." 11 David would
save neither man nor woman alive, to bring *news*
to Gath, saying, "Lest they should inform on us,
saying, 'Thus David did.' " And thus *was* his be-
havior all the time he dwelt in the country of the
Philistines. 12 So Achish believed David, saying,
"He has made his people Israel utterly abhor him;
therefore he will be my servant forever."

**28** Now [a]it happened in those days that the
Philistines gathered their armies together
for war, to fight with Israel. And Achish said to
David, "You assuredly know that you will go out
with me to battle, you and your men."
2 So David said to Achish, "Surely you know
what your servant can do."
And Achish said to David, "Therefore I will
make you one of my chief guardians forever."

### SAUL CONSULTS A MEDIUM

*(cf. Deut. 18:9–14)*

3 Now [a]Samuel had died, and all Israel had
lamented for him and buried him in [b]Ramah,
in his own city. And Saul had put [c]the mediums
and the spiritists out of the land.
4 Then the Philistines gathered together,
and came and encamped at [a]Shunem. So Saul
gathered all Israel together, and they encamped
at [b]Gilboa. 5 When Saul saw the army of the Phi-
listines, he was [a]afraid, and his heart trembled
greatly. 6 And when Saul inquired of the LORD,
[a]the LORD did not answer him, either by [b]dreams
or [c]by Urim or by the prophets.
7 Then Saul said to his servants, "Find me a
woman who is a medium, [a]that I may go to her
and inquire of her."

**26:19** [b] Deut. 4:27, 28 [c] 2 Sam. 14:16; 20:19 **26:20** [a] 1 Sam. 24:14 **26:21** [a] Ex. 9:27; 1 Sam. 15:24, 30; 24:17; 2 Sam. 12:13 **26:23** [a] 1 Sam. 24:19; Ps. 7:8; 18:20; 62:12 [b] 2 Sam. 22:21 **26:25** [a] Gen. 32:28; 1 Sam. 24:20 **27:2** [a] 1 Sam. 25:13 [b] 1 Sam. 21:10; 1 Kin. 2:39 **27:3** [a] 1 Sam. 25:42, 43 **27:6** [a] Josh. 15:31; 19:5; 1 Chr. 12:1; Neh. 11:28 **27:7** [a] 1 Sam. 29:3 **27:8** [a] Josh. 13:2, 13 [b] Josh. 16:10; Judg. 1:29 [c] Ex. 17:8, 16; 1 Sam. 15:7, 8 [d] Gen. 25:18; Ex. 15:22 [1] Or *Gezrites* **27:10** [a] 1 Chr. 2:9, 25 [b] Judg. 1:16 **28:1** [a] 1 Sam. 29:1, 2 **28:3** [a] 1 Sam. 25:1 [b] 1 Sam. 1:19 [c] Ex. 22:18; Lev. 19:31; 20:27; Deut. 18:10, 11; 1 Sam. 15:23; 28:9 **28:4** [a] Josh. 19:18; 1 Sam. 28:4; 1 Kin. 1:3; 2 Kin. 4:8 [b] 1 Sam. 31:1 **28:5** [a] Job 18:11; [Is. 57:20] **28:6** [a] 1 Sam. 14:37; Prov. 1:28; Lam. 2:9 [b] Num. 12:6; Joel 2:28 [c] Ex. 28:30; Num. 27:21; Deut. 33:8 **28:7** [a] 1 Chr. 10:13

And his servants said to him, "In fact, *there*
*is* a woman who is a medium at En Dor."
8 So Saul disguised himself and put on other
clothes, and he went, and two men with him; and
they came to the woman by night. And [a]he said,
"Please conduct a séance for me, and bring up
for me the one I shall name to you."
9 Then the woman said to him, "Look, you
know what Saul has done, how he has [a]cut off
the mediums and the spiritists from the land.
Why then do you lay a snare for my life, to cause
me to die?"
10 And Saul swore to her by the LORD, saying,
"*As* the LORD lives, no punishment shall come
upon you for this thing."
11 Then the woman said, "Whom shall I bring
up for you?"

And he said, "Bring up Samuel for me."
12 When the woman saw Samuel, she cried
out with a loud voice. And the woman spoke to
Saul, saying, "Why have you deceived me? For
you *are* Saul!"
13 And the king said to her, "Do not be afraid.
What did you see?"

And the woman said to Saul, "I saw [a]a spirit[1]
ascending out of the earth."
14 So he said to her, "What *is* his form?"

And she said, "An old man is coming up, and
he *is* covered with [a]a mantle." And Saul perceived
that it *was* Samuel, and he stooped with *his* face
to the ground and bowed down.
15 Now Samuel said to Saul, "Why have you
[a]disturbed me by bringing me up?"

And Saul answered, "I am deeply distressed;
for the Philistines make war against me, and
[b]God has departed from me and [c]does not answer me anymore, neither by prophets nor by
dreams. Therefore I have called you, that you
may reveal to me what I should do."
16 Then Samuel said: "So why do you ask me,
seeing the LORD has departed from you and has
become your enemy? 17 And the LORD has done
for Himself[1] [a]as He spoke by me. For the LORD
has torn the kingdom out of your hand and given
it to your neighbor, David. 18 [a]Because you did
not obey the voice of the LORD nor execute His
fierce wrath upon [b]Amalek, therefore the LORD
has done this thing to you this day. 19 Moreover
the LORD will also deliver Israel with you into
the hand of the Philistines. And tomorrow you
and your sons *will be* with [a]me. The LORD will
also deliver the army of Israel into the hand of
the Philistines."
20 Immediately Saul fell full length on the
ground, and was dreadfully afraid because of the
words of Samuel. And there was no strength in
him, for he had eaten no food all day or all night.
21 And the woman came to Saul and saw that
he was severely troubled, and said to him, "Look,
your maidservant has obeyed your voice, and I
have [a]put my life in my hands and heeded the
words which you spoke to me. 22 Now therefore,
please, heed also the voice of your maidservant,
and let me set a piece of bread before you; and
eat, that you may have strength when you go
on *your* way."
23 But he refused and said, "I will not eat."

So his servants, together with the woman,
urged him; and he heeded their voice. Then
he arose from the ground and sat on the bed.
24 Now the woman had a fatted calf in the house,
and she hastened to kill it. And she took flour
and kneaded *it*, and baked unleavened bread
from it. 25 So she brought *it* before Saul and his
servants, and they ate. Then they rose and went
away that night.

### THE PHILISTINES REJECT DAVID

29 Then [a]the Philistines gathered together all
their armies [b]at Aphek, and the Israelites
encamped by a fountain which *is* in Jezreel. 2 And
the [a]lords of the Philistines passed in review by
hundreds and by thousands, but [b]David and his
men passed in review at the rear with Achish.
3 Then the princes of the Philistines said, "What
*are* these Hebrews *doing here?*"

And Achish said to the princes of the Philistines, "*Is* this not David, the servant of Saul king
of Israel, who has been with me [a]these days, or
these years? And to this day I have [b]found no
fault in him since he defected *to me.*"
4 But the princes of the Philistines were angry with him; so the princes of the Philistines
said to him, [a]"Make this fellow return, that he
may go back to the place which you have appointed for him, and do not let him go down
with us to [b]battle, lest [c]in the battle he become
our adversary. For with what could he reconcile
himself to his master, if not with the heads of
these [d]men? 5 *Is* this not David, [a]of whom they
sang to one another in dances, saying:

[b]'Saul has slain his thousands,
And David his ten thousands'?"[1]

6 Then Achish called David and said to him,
"Surely, *as* the LORD lives, you have been upright,
and [a]your going out and your coming in with
me in the army *is* good in my sight. For to this
day [b]I have not found evil in you since the day
of your coming to me. Nevertheless the lords do
not favor you. 7 Therefore return now, and go in
peace, that you may not displease the lords of
the Philistines."

**28:8** [a] Deut. 18:10, 11; 1 Chr. 10:13; Is. 8:19 **28:9** [a] 1 Sam. 28:3 **28:13** [a] Ex. 22:28; Ps. 138:1 [1] Hebrew *elohim* **28:14** [a] 1 Sam. 15:27; 2 Kin. 2:8, 13 **28:15** [a] Is. 14:9 [b] 1 Sam. 16:14; 18:12 [c] 1 Sam. 28:6 **28:17** [a] 1 Sam. 15:28 [1] Or *him*, that is, David **28:18** [a] 1 Sam. 13:9–13; 15:1–26; 1 Kin. 20:42; 1 Chr. 10:13; Jer. 48:10 [b] 1 Sam. 15:3–9 **28:19** [a] 1 Sam. 31:1–6; Job 3:17–19 **28:21** [a] Judg. 12:3; 1 Sam. 19:5; Job 13:14 **29:1** [a] 1 Sam. 28:1 [b] Josh. 12:18; 19:30; 1 Sam. 4:1; 1 Kin. 20:30 **29:2** [a] 1 Sam. 6:4; 7:7 [b] 1 Sam. 28:1, 2 **29:3** [a] 1 Sam. 27:7 [b] 1 Sam. 27:1–6; 1 Chr. 12:19, 20; Dan. 6:5 **29:4** [a] 1 Sam. 27:6 [b] 1 Sam. 14:21 [c] 1 Sam. 29:9 [d] 1 Chr. 12:19, 20 **29:5** [a] 1 Sam. 21:11 [b] 1 Sam. 18:7 [1] Compare 1 Samuel 18:7 **29:6** [a] 2 Sam. 3:25; 2 Kin. 19:27 [b] 1 Sam. 29:3

8 So David said to Achish, "But what have I done? And to this day what have you found in your servant as long as I have been with you, that I may not go and fight against the enemies of my lord the king?"

9 Then Achish answered and said to David, "I know that you *are* as good in my sight [a]as an angel of God; nevertheless [b]the princes of the Philistines have said, 'He shall not go up with us to the battle.' 10 Now therefore, rise early in the morning with your master's servants [a]who have come with you.[1] And as soon as you are up early in the morning and have light, depart."

11 So David and his men rose early to depart in the morning, to return to the land of the Philistines. [a]And the Philistines went up to Jezreel.

## *DAVID'S CONFLICT WITH THE AMALEKITES*

30 Now it happened, when David and his men came to [a]Ziklag, on the third day, that the [b]Amalekites had invaded the South and Ziklag, attacked Ziklag and burned it with fire, 2 and had taken captive the [a]women and those who *were* there, from small to great; they did not kill anyone, but carried *them* away and went their way. 3 So David and his men came to the city, and there it was, burned with fire; and their wives, their sons, and their daughters had been taken captive. 4 Then David and the people who *were* with him lifted up their voices and wept, until they had no more power to weep. 5 And David's two [a]wives, Ahinoam the Jezreelitess, and Abigail the widow of Nabal the Carmelite, had been taken captive. 6 Now David was greatly distressed, for [a]the people spoke of stoning him, because the soul of all the people was grieved, every man for his sons and his daughters. [b]But David strengthened himself in the LORD his God.

7 [a]Then David said to Abiathar the priest, Ahimelech's son, "Please bring the ephod here to me." And [b]Abiathar brought the ephod to David. 8 [a]So David inquired of the LORD, saying, "Shall I pursue this troop? Shall I overtake them?"

And He answered him, "Pursue, for you shall surely overtake *them* and without fail recover *all.*"

9 So David went, he and the six hundred men who *were* with him, and came to the Brook Besor, where those stayed who were left behind. 10 But David pursued, he and four hundred men; [a]for two hundred stayed *behind,* who were so weary that they could not cross the Brook Besor.

11 Then they found an Egyptian in the field, and brought him to David; and they gave him bread and he ate, and they let him drink water. 12 And they gave him a piece of [a]a cake of figs and two clusters of raisins. So [b]when he had eaten, his strength came back to him; for he had eaten no bread nor drunk water for three days and three nights. 13 Then David said to him, "To whom do you *belong,* and where *are* you from?"

And he said, "I *am* a young man from Egypt, servant of an Amalekite; and my master left me behind, because three days ago I fell sick. 14 We made an invasion of the southern *area* of [a]the Cherethites, in the *territory* which *belongs* to Judah, and of the southern *area* [b]of Caleb; and we burned Ziklag with fire."

15 And David said to him, "Can you take me down to this troop?"

So he said, "Swear to me by God that you will neither kill me nor deliver me into the hands of my [a]master, and I will take you down to this troop."

16 And when he had brought him down, there they were, spread out over all the land, [a]eating and drinking and dancing, because of all the great spoil which they had taken from the land of the Philistines and from the land of Judah. 17 Then David attacked them from twilight until the evening of the next day. Not a man of them escaped, except four hundred young men who rode on camels and fled. 18 So David recovered all that the Amalekites had carried away, and David rescued his two wives. 19 And nothing of theirs was lacking, either small or great, sons or daughters, spoil or anything which they had taken from them; [a]David recovered all. 20 Then David took all the flocks and herds they had driven before those *other* livestock, and said, "This *is* David's spoil."

21 Now David came to the [a]two hundred men who had been so weary that they could not follow David, whom they also had made to stay at the Brook Besor. So they went out to meet David and to meet the people who *were* with him. And when David came near the people, he greeted them. 22 Then all the wicked and [a]worthless men[1] of those who went with David answered and said, "Because they did not go with us, we will not give them *any* of the spoil that we have recovered, except for every man's wife and children, that they may lead *them* away and depart."

23 But David said, "My brethren, you shall not do so with what the LORD has given us, who has preserved us and delivered into our hand the troop that came against us. 24 For who will heed you in this matter? But [a]as his part *is* who goes down to the battle, so *shall* his part *be* who stays by the supplies; they shall share alike." 25 So it was, from that day forward; he made it a statute and an ordinance for Israel to this day.

29:9 [a] 2 Sam. 14:17, 20; 19:27 [b] 1 Sam. 29:4 29:10 [a] 1 Chr. 12:19, 22 [1] Following Masoretic Text, Targum, and Vulgate; Septuagint adds *and go to the place which I have selected for you there; and set no bothersome word in your heart, for you are good before me. And rise on your way.* 29:11 [a] 2 Sam. 4:4 30:1 [a] 1 Sam. 27:6 [b] 1 Sam. 15:7; 27:8 30:2 [a] 1 Sam. 27:2, 3 30:5 [a] 1 Sam. 25:42, 43 30:6 [a] Ex. 17:4; John 8:59 [b] 1 Sam. 23:16; Is. 25:4; Hab. 3:17–19 30:7 [a] 1 Sam. 23:2–9 [b] 1 Sam. 23:6 30:8 [a] 1 Sam. 23:2, 4; Ps. 50:15; 91:15 30:10 [a] 1 Sam. 30:9, 21 30:12 [a] 1 Sam. 25:18; 1 Kin. 20:7 [b] Judg. 15:19; 1 Sam. 14:27 30:14 [a] 2 Sam. 8:18; 1 Kin. 1:38, 44; Ezek. 25:16; Zeph. 2:5 [b] Josh. 14:13; 15:13 30:15 [a] Deut. 23:15 30:16 [a] 1 Thess. 5:3 30:19 [a] 1 Sam. 30:8 30:21 [a] 1 Sam. 30:10 30:22 [a] Deut. 13:13; Judg. 19:22 [1] Literally *men of Belial* 30:24 [a] Num. 31:27; Josh. 22:8

26 Now when David came to Ziklag, he sent
*some* of the spoil to the elders of Judah, to his
friends, saying, "Here is a present for you from
the spoil of the enemies of the LORD"— 27 to *those*
who *were* in Bethel, *those* who *were* in [a]Ramoth
of the South, *those* who *were* in [b]Jattir, 28 *those*
who *were* in [a]Aroer, *those* who *were* in [b]Siph-
moth, *those* who *were* in [c]Eshtemoa, 29 *those* who
*were* in Rachal, *those* who *were* in the cities of
[a]the Jerahmeelites, *those* who *were* in the cities
of the [b]Kenites, 30 *those* who *were* in [a]Hormah,
*those* who *were* in Chorashan,[1] *those* who *were*
in Athach, 31 *those* who *were* in [a]Hebron, and to
all the places where David himself and his men
were accustomed to [b]rove.

### *THE TRAGIC END OF SAUL AND HIS SONS*

*(1 Chr. 10:1–14)*

**31** Now [a]the Philistines fought against Isra-
el; and the men of Israel fled from before
the Philistines, and fell slain on Mount [b]Gilboa.
2 Then the Philistines followed hard after Saul
and his sons. And the Philistines killed [a]Jona-
than, Abinadab, and Malchishua, Saul's sons.
3 [a]The battle became fierce against Saul. The
archers hit him, and he was severely wounded
by the archers.

4 [a]Then Saul said to his armorbearer, "Draw
your sword, and thrust me through with it, lest
[b]these uncircumcised men come and thrust me
through and abuse me."
But his armorbearer would not, [c]for he was
greatly afraid. Therefore Saul took a sword and
[d]fell on it. 5 And when his armorbearer saw that
Saul was dead, he also fell on his sword, and died
with him. 6 So Saul, his three sons, his armor-
bearer, and all his men died together that same
day.

7 And when the men of Israel who *were* on
the other side of the valley, and *those* who *were*
on the other side of the Jordan, saw that the men
of Israel had fled and that Saul and his sons were
dead, they forsook the cities and fled; and the
Philistines came and dwelt in them. 8 So it hap-
pened the next day, when the Philistines came
to strip the slain, that they found Saul and his
three sons fallen on Mount Gilboa. 9 And they
cut off his head and stripped off his armor, and
sent *word* throughout the land of the Philistines,
to [a]proclaim *it in* the temple of their idols and
among the people. 10 [a]Then they put his armor
in the temple of the [b]Ashtoreths, and [c]they fas-
tened his body to the wall of [d]Beth Shan.[1]

11 [a]Now when the inhabitants of Jabesh Gil-
ead heard what the Philistines had done to Saul,
12 [a]all the valiant men arose and traveled all
night, and took the body of Saul and the bod-
ies of his sons from the wall of Beth Shan; and
they came to Jabesh and [b]burned them there.
13 Then they took their bones and [a]buried *them*
under the tamarisk tree at Jabesh, [b]and fasted
seven days.

**30:27** [a] Josh. 19:8 [b] Josh. 15:48; 21:14 **30:28** [a] Josh. 13:16 [b] 1 Chr. 27:27 [c] Josh. 15:50 **30:29** [a] 1 Sam. 27:10 [b] Judg. 1:16; 1 Sam. 15:6; 27:10 **30:30** [a] Num. 14:45; 21:3; Josh. 12:14; 15:30; 19:4; Judg. 1:17 [1] Or *Borashan* **30:31** [a] Num. 13:22; Josh. 14:13–15; 21:11–13; 2 Sam. 2:1 [b] 1 Sam. 23:22 **31:1** [a] 1 Chr. 10:1–12 [b] 1 Sam. 28:4 **31:2** [a] 1 Sam. 14:49; 1 Chr. 8:33 **31:3** [a] 2 Sam. 1:6 **31:4** [a] Judg. 9:54; 1 Chr. 10:4 [b] Judg. 14:3; 1 Sam. 14:6; 17:26, 36 [c] 2 Sam. 1:14 [d] 2 Sam. 1:6, 10 **31:9** [a] Judg. 16:23, 24; 2 Sam. 1:20 **31:10** [a] 1 Sam. 21:9 [b] Judg. 2:13; 1 Sam. 7:3 [c] 2 Sam. 21:12 [d] Judg. 1:27 [1] Spelled *Beth Shean* in Joshua 17:11 and elsewhere **31:11** [a] 1 Sam. 11:1–13 **31:12** [a] 2 Sam. 2:4–7 [b] 2 Chr. 16:14 **31:13** [a] 2 Sam. 2:4, 5; 21:12–14 [b] Gen. 50:10

*The Second Book of*

# SAMUEL

| AUTHOR | KEY VERSES | READING TIME |
|---|---|---|
| Unknown | 2 Samuel 7:12–13 | 2 hours 19 minutes |

The Book of 1 Samuel ends with David on the run and Saul and Jonathan killed in battle. Second Samuel picks up with David learning of their demise and becoming the second king of Israel soon after. David proved to be a much better king than Saul (see 2 Sam. 1–10), but he also proved to be far from a perfect king (see chs. 11–24). David's grievous sins of immorality and murder brought shattering consequences upon his family and the nation. Like Saul, David's reign began well but then soon faded. Unlike Saul, David repented, preserving his throne and allowing the kingdom to pass to his son Solomon, according to the covenant that God had made with him.

**Occasion:** Second Samuel traces the reign of David as the second king of Israel.

**Main Point:** David is a better king than Saul, but he is still not the king God's people need.

**Big Ideas:** God loves His people even when they sin. God is always ready to forgive when we repent of our sin. We should strive to please God in all we do no matter what.

**OUTLINE:**

I. David's Political Victories (chs. 1–5)
II. David's Spiritual Victories (chs. 6–7)
III. David's Military Victories (chs. 8–10)
IV. David's Serious Sin (ch. 11)
V. David's Family Troubles (chs. 12–14)
VI. David's Kingdom Troubles (chs. 15–24)

**c. 1050 BC** Saul becomes king of Israel

**c. 1018 BC** Samuel anoints David to be king

**1010 BC** David begins to reign at Hebron

**1003 BC** David becomes king over all Israel

**990 BC** David sins against Bathsheba and Uriah

**988 BC** Solomon is born

**980 BC** Absalom revolts against David

**970 BC** Solomon becomes king of Israel

**c. 950 BC** Assyrians make armor with iron scales

**930 BC** The kingdom is divided

**c. 900 BC** Etruscans establish Italian towns

### *THE REPORT OF SAUL'S DEATH*

**1** Now it came to pass after the [a]death of Saul, when David had returned from [b]the slaughter of the Amalekites, and David had stayed two days in Ziklag, 2 on the third day, behold, it happened that [a]a man came from Saul's camp [b]with his clothes torn and dust on his head. So it was, when he came to David, that he [c]fell to the ground and prostrated himself.

3 And David said to him, "Where have you come from?"

So he said to him, "I have escaped from the camp of Israel."

4 Then David said to him, [a]"How did the matter go? Please tell me."

And he answered, "The people have fled from the battle, many of the people are fallen and dead, and Saul and [b]Jonathan his son are dead also."

5 So David said to the young man who told him, "How do you know that Saul and Jonathan his son are dead?"

6 Then the young man who told him said, "As I happened by chance *to be* on [a]Mount Gilboa, there was [b]Saul, leaning on his spear; and indeed the chariots and horsemen followed hard after him. 7 Now when he looked behind him, he saw me and called to me. And I answered, 'Here I am.' 8 And he said to me, 'Who *are* you?' So I answered him, 'I *am* an Amalekite.' 9 He said to me again, 'Please stand over me and kill me, for anguish has come upon me, but my life still *remains* in me.' 10 So I stood over him and [a]killed him, because I was sure that he could not live after he had fallen. And I took the crown that *was* on his head and the bracelet that *was* on his arm, and have brought them here to my lord."

11 Therefore David took hold of his own clothes and [a]tore them, and *so did* all the men who *were* with him. 12 And they [a]mourned and wept and [b]fasted until evening for Saul and for Jonathan his son, for the [c]people of the LORD and for the house of Israel, because they had fallen by the sword.

13 Then David said to the young man who told him, "Where *are* you from?"

And he answered, "I *am* the son of an alien, an Amalekite."

14 So David said to him, "How [a]was it you were not [b]afraid to [c]put forth your hand to destroy the LORD's anointed?" 15 Then [a]David called one of the young men and said, "Go near, *and* execute him!" And he struck him so that he died. 16 So David said to him, [a]"Your blood *is* on your own head, for [b]your own mouth has testified against you, saying, 'I have killed the LORD's anointed.' "

### *THE SONG OF THE BOW*

17 Then David lamented with this lamentation over Saul and over Jonathan his son, 18 [a]and he told *them* to teach the children of Judah *the Song of* the Bow; indeed *it is* written [b]in the Book of Jasher:

19 "The beauty of Israel is slain on your high places!
[a]How the mighty have fallen!
20 [a]Tell *it* not in Gath,
Proclaim *it* not in the streets of [b]Ashkelon—
Lest [c]the daughters of the Philistines rejoice,
Lest the daughters of [d]the uncircumcised triumph.

21 "O [a]mountains of Gilboa,
[b]*Let there be* no dew nor rain upon you,
Nor fields of offerings.
For the shield of the mighty is cast away there!
The shield of Saul, not [c]anointed with oil.
22 From the blood of the slain,
From the fat of the mighty,
[a]The bow of Jonathan did not turn back,
And the sword of Saul did not return empty.

23 "Saul and Jonathan *were* beloved and pleasant in their lives,
And in their [a]death they were not divided;
They were swifter than eagles,
They were [b]stronger than lions.

**1:18 The Book of Jasher** (cf. Josh. 10:13), which contained everything from Joshua's speech at the battle of Gibeon to David's tribute to Saul and Jonathan, has been lost for centuries. There are at least a dozen other books mentioned in Scripture that aren't part of the Bible either including the *Book of the Acts of Solomon* (1 Kin. 11:41), the *Book of Nathan the Prophet* (1 Chr. 29:29; 2 Chr. 9:29), the *Book of Gad the Seer* (1 Chr. 29:29), the *Visions of Iddo the Seer* (2 Chr. 9:29; 12:15), the *Prophecy of Abijah the Shilonite* (2 Chr. 9:29), the *Book of Shemaiah the Prophet* (2 Chr. 12:15), the *Acts of Uzziah* (2 Chr. 26:22), the *Sayings of Hozai* (2 Chr. 33:19), a third letter of Paul to the Corinthians (1 Cor. 5:9), a letter of Paul to the Laodiceans (Col. 4:16), another letter of John (3 John v. 9), and the *Book of Enoch* (Jude v. 14).

**1:1** [a]1 Sam. 31:6 [b]1 Sam. 30:1, 17, 26 **1:2** [a]2 Sam. 4:10 [b]1 Sam. 4:12 [c]1 Sam. 25:23 **1:4** [a]1 Sam. 4:16; 31:3 [b]1 Sam. 31:2 **1:6** [a]1 Sam. 31:1 [b]1 Sam. 31:2–4 **1:10** [a]Judg. 9:54; 2 Kin. 11:12 **1:11** [a]2 Sam. 3:31; 13:31 **1:12** [a]2 Sam. 3:31 [b]1 Sam. 31:13 [c]2 Sam. 6:21 **1:14** [a]Num. 12:8 [b]1 Sam. 31:4 [c]1 Sam. 24:6; 26:9 **1:15** [a]2 Sam. 4:10, 12 **1:16** [a]1 Sam. 26:9; 2 Sam. 3:28; 1 Kin. 2:32–37 [b]2 Sam. 1:10; Luke 19:22 **1:18** [a]1 Sam. 31:3 [b]Josh. 10:13 **1:19** [a]2 Sam. 1:27 **1:20** [a]1 Sam. 27:2; 31:8–13; Mic. 1:10 [b]1 Sam. 6:17; Jer. 25:20 [c]Ex. 15:20; Judg. 11:34; 1 Sam. 18:6 [d]1 Sam. 31:4 **1:21** [a]1 Sam. 31:1 [b]Ezek. 31:15 [c]1 Sam. 10:1 **1:22** [a]Deut. 32:42; 1 Sam. 18:4 **1:23** [a]1 Sam. 31:2–4 [b]Judg. 14:18

24 "O daughters of Israel, weep over Saul,
Who clothed you in scarlet, with luxury;
Who put ornaments of gold on your apparel.
25 "How the mighty have fallen in the midst of the battle!
Jonathan *was* slain in your high places.
26 I am distressed for you, my brother Jonathan;
You have been very pleasant to me;
[a]Your love to me was wonderful,
Surpassing the love of women.

27 "How[a] the mighty have fallen,
And the weapons of war perished!"

### DAVID ANOINTED KING OF JUDAH

**2** It happened after this that David [a]inquired of the LORD, saying, "Shall I go up to any of the cities of Judah?"

And the LORD said to him, "Go up."

David said, "Where shall I go up?"

And He said, "To [b]Hebron."

2 So David went up there, and his [a]two wives also, Ahinoam the Jezreelitess, and Abigail the widow of Nabal the Carmelite. 3 And David brought up [a]the men who *were* with him, every man with his household. So they dwelt in the cities of Hebron.

4 [a]Then the men of Judah came, and there they [b]anointed David king over the house of Judah. And they told David, saying, [c]"The men of Jabesh Gilead *were the ones* who buried Saul." 5 So David sent messengers to the men of Jabesh Gilead, and said to them, [a]"You *are* blessed of the LORD, for you have shown this kindness to your lord, to Saul, and have buried him. 6 And now may [a]the LORD show kindness and truth to you. I also will repay you this kindness, because you have done this thing. 7 Now therefore, let your hands be strengthened, and be valiant; for your master Saul is dead, and also the house of Judah has anointed me king over them."

### ISHBOSHETH MADE KING OF ISRAEL

8 But [a]Abner the son of Ner, commander of Saul's army, took Ishbosheth[1] the son of Saul and brought him over to [b]Mahanaim; 9 and he made him king over [a]Gilead, over the [b]Ashurites, over [c]Jezreel, over Ephraim, over Benjamin, and over all Israel. 10 Ishbosheth, Saul's son, *was* forty years old when he began to reign over Israel, and he reigned two years. Only the house of Judah followed David. 11 And [a]the time that David was king in Hebron over the house of Judah was seven years and six months.

### ISRAEL AND JUDAH AT WAR

12 Now Abner the son of Ner, and the servants of Ishbosheth the son of Saul, went out from Mahanaim to [a]Gibeon. 13 And [a]Joab the son of Zeruiah, and the servants of David, went out and met them by [b]the pool of Gibeon. So they sat down, one on one side of the pool and the other on the other side of the pool. 14 Then Abner said to Joab, "Let the young men now arise and compete before us."

And Joab said, "Let them arise."

15 So they arose and went over by number, twelve from Benjamin, *followers* of Ishbosheth the son of Saul, and twelve from the servants of David. 16 And each one grasped his opponent by the head and *thrust* his sword in his opponent's side; so they fell down together. Therefore that place was called the Field of Sharp Swords,[1] which *is* in Gibeon. 17 So there was a very fierce battle that day, and Abner and the men of Israel were beaten before the servants of David.

18 Now the [a]three sons of Zeruiah were there: Joab and Abishai and Asahel. And Asahel *was* [b]*as* fleet of foot [c]as a wild gazelle. 19 So Asahel pursued Abner, and in going he did not turn to the right hand or to the left from following Abner.

20 Then Abner looked behind him and said, "*Are* you Asahel?"

He answered, "I *am.*"

21 And Abner said to him, "Turn aside to your right hand or to your left, and lay hold on one of the young men and take his armor for yourself." But Asahel would not turn aside from following him. 22 So Abner said again to Asahel, "Turn aside from following me. Why should I strike you to the ground? How then could I face your brother Joab?" 23 However, he refused to turn aside. Therefore Abner struck him [a]in the stomach with the blunt end of the spear, so that the spear came out of his back; and he fell down there and died on the spot. So it was *that* as many as came to the place where Asahel fell down and died, stood [b]still.

24 Joab and Abishai also pursued Abner. And the sun was going down when they came to the hill of Ammah, which *is* before Giah by the road to the Wilderness of Gibeon. 25 Now the children of Benjamin gathered together behind Abner and became a unit, and took their stand on top of a hill. 26 Then Abner called to Joab and said, "Shall the sword devour forever? Do you not know that it will be bitter in the latter end? How long will it be then until you tell the people to return from pursuing their brethren?"

27 And Joab said, "As God lives, unless [a]you had spoken, surely then by morning all the people would have given up pursuing their brethren." 28 So Joab blew a trumpet; and all the

**1:26** [a] 1 Sam. 18:1–4; 19:2; 20:17 **1:27** [a] 2 Sam. 1:19, 25 **2:1** [a] Judg. 1:1; 1 Sam. 23:2, 4, 9; 30:7, 8 [b] 1 Sam. 30:31; 2 Sam. 2:11; 5:1–3; 1 Kin. 2:11 **2:2** [a] 1 Sam. 25:42, 43; 30:5 **2:3** [a] 1 Sam. 27:2, 3; 30:1; 1 Chr. 12:1 **2:4** [a] 1 Sam. 30:26; 2 Sam. 2:11; 5:5; 19:14, 41–43 [b] 1 Sam. 16:13; 2 Sam. 5:3 [c] 1 Sam. 31:11–13 **2:5** [a] Ruth 2:20; 3:10 **2:6** [a] Ex. 34:6; 2 Tim. 1:16, 18 **2:8** [a] 1 Sam. 14:50; 2 Sam. 3:6 [b] Gen. 32:2; Josh. 21:38; 2 Sam. 17:24 [1] Called *Esh-Baal* in 1 Chronicles 8:33 and 9:39 **2:9** [a] Josh. 22:9 [b] Judg. 1:32 [c] 1 Sam. 29:1 **2:11** [a] 2 Sam. 5:5; 1 Kin. 2:11 **2:12** [a] Josh. 10:2–12; 18:25 **2:13** [a] 1 Sam. 26:6; 2 Sam. 8:16; 1 Chr. 2:16; 11:6 [b] Jer. 41:12 **2:16** [1] Hebrew *Helkath Hazzurim* **2:18** [a] 1 Chr. 2:16 [b] 1 Chr. 12:8; Hab. 3:19 [c] Ps. 18:33 **2:23** [a] 2 Sam. 3:27; 4:6; 20:10 [b] 2 Sam. 20:12 **2:27** [a] 2 Sam. 2:14

people stood still and did not pursue Israel anymore, nor did they fight anymore. 29 Then Abner and his men went on all that night through the plain, crossed over the Jordan, and went through all Bithron; and they came to Mahanaim.

30 So Joab returned from pursuing Abner. And when he had gathered all the people together, there were missing of David's servants nineteen men and Asahel. 31 But the servants of David had struck down, of Benjamin and Abner's men, three hundred and sixty men who died. 32 Then they took up Asahel and buried him in his father's tomb, which *was in* [a]Bethlehem. And Joab and his men went all night, and they came to Hebron at daybreak.

**3** Now there was a long [a]war between the house of Saul and the house of David. But David grew stronger and stronger, and the house of Saul grew weaker and weaker.

### SONS OF DAVID

2 Sons were born [a]to David in Hebron: His firstborn was Amnon [b]by Ahinoam the Jezreelitess; 3 his second, Chileab, by Abigail the widow of Nabal the Carmelite; the third, [a]Absalom the son of Maacah, the daughter of Talmai, king [b]of Geshur; 4 the fourth, [a]Adonijah the son of Haggith; the fifth, Shephatiah the son of Abital; 5 and the sixth, Ithream, by David's wife Eglah. These were born to David in Hebron.

### ABNER JOINS FORCES WITH DAVID

6 Now it was so, while there was war between the house of Saul and the house of David, that Abner was strengthening *his hold* on the house of Saul.

7 And Saul had a concubine, whose name *was* [a]Rizpah, the daughter of Aiah. So *Ishbosheth* said to Abner, "Why have you [b]gone in to my father's concubine?"

8 Then Abner became very angry at the words of Ishbosheth, and said, "*Am* I [a]a dog's head that belongs to Judah? Today I show loyalty to the house of Saul your father, to his brothers, and to his friends, and have not delivered you into the hand of David; and you charge me today with a fault concerning this woman? 9 [a]May God do so to Abner, and more also, if I do not do for David [b]as the LORD has sworn to him— 10 to transfer the kingdom from the house of Saul, and set up the throne of David over Israel and over Judah, [a]from Dan to Beersheba." 11 And he could not answer Abner another word, because he feared him.

12 Then Abner sent messengers on his behalf to David, saying, "Whose *is* the land?" saying *also*, "Make your covenant with me, and indeed my hand *shall be* with you to bring all Israel to you."

> **3:10** The phrase **over Israel and over Judah** shows the division occurring among God's people. In this verse, **Judah** refers to David's tribe and his followers and **Israel** refers to the tribes who followed Saul and his descendants.

13 And *David* said, "Good, I will make a covenant with you. But one thing I require of you: [a]you shall not see my face unless you first bring [b]Michal, Saul's daughter, when you come to see my face." 14 So David sent messengers to [a]Ishbosheth, Saul's son, saying, "Give *me* my wife Michal, whom I betrothed to myself [b]for a hundred foreskins of the Philistines." 15 And Ishbosheth sent and took her from *her* husband, from Paltiel[1] the son of Laish. 16 Then her husband went along with her to [a]Bahurim, weeping behind her. So Abner said to him, "Go, return!" And he returned.

17 Now Abner had communicated with the elders of Israel, saying, "In time past you were seeking for David *to be* king over you. 18 Now then, do *it!* [a]For the LORD has spoken of David, saying, 'By the hand of My servant David, I[1] will save My people Israel from the hand of the Philistines and the hand of all their enemies.' " 19 And Abner also spoke in the hearing of [a]Benjamin. Then Abner also went to speak in the hearing of David in Hebron all that seemed good to Israel and the whole house of Benjamin.

20 So Abner and twenty men with him came to David at Hebron. And David made a feast for Abner and the men who *were* with him. 21 Then Abner said to David, "I will arise and go, and [a]gather all Israel to my lord the king, that they may make a covenant with you, and that you may [b]reign over all that your heart desires." So David sent Abner away, and he went in peace.

### JOAB MURDERS ABNER

22 At that moment the servants of David and Joab came from a raid and brought much spoil with them. But Abner *was* not with David in Hebron, for he had sent him away, and he had gone in peace. 23 When Joab and all the troops that *were* with him had come, they told Joab, saying, "Abner the son of Ner came to the king, and he sent him away, and he has gone in peace." 24 Then Joab came to the king and said, "What have you done? Look, Abner came to you; why *is* it *that* you sent him away, and he has already gone? 25 Surely you realize that Abner the son of Ner came to deceive you, to know [a]your going out and your coming in, and to know all that you are doing."

**2:32** [a]1 Sam. 20:6 **3:1** [a]1 Kin. 14:30; [Ps. 46:9] **3:2** [a]1 Chr. 3:1–4 [b]1 Sam. 25:42, 43 **3:3** [a]2 Sam. 15:1–10 [b]Josh. 13:13; 1 Sam. 27:8; 2 Sam. 13:37; 14:32; 15:8 **3:4** [a]1 Kin. 1:5 **3:7** [a]2 Sam. 21:8–11 [b]2 Sam. 16:21 **3:8** [a]Deut. 23:18; 1 Sam. 24:14; 2 Sam. 9:8; 16:9 **3:9** [a]Ruth 1:17; 1 Kin. 19:2 [b]1 Sam. 15:28; 16:1, 12; 28:17; 1 Chr. 12:23 **3:10** [a]Judg. 20:1; 1 Sam. 3:20; 2 Sam. 17:11; 1 Kin. 4:25 **3:13** [a]Gen. 43:3 [b]1 Sam. 18:20; 19:11; 25:44; 2 Sam. 6:16 **3:14** [a]2 Sam. 2:10 [b]1 Sam. 18:25–27 **3:15** [1]Spelled *Palti* in 1 Samuel 25:44 **3:16** [a]2 Sam. 16:5; 19:16 **3:18** [a]2 Sam. 3:9 [1]Following many Hebrew manuscripts, Septuagint, Syriac, and Targum; Masoretic Text reads *he*. **3:19** [a]1 Sam. 10:20, 21; 1 Chr. 12:29 **3:21** [a]2 Sam. 3:10, 12 [b]1 Kin. 11:37 **3:25** [a]Deut. 28:6; 1 Sam. 29:6; Is. 37:28

26 And when Joab had gone from David's
presence, he sent messengers after Abner, who
brought him back from the well of Sirah. But
David did not know *it.* 27 Now when Abner had
returned to Hebron, Joab [a]took him aside in
the gate to speak with him privately, and there
stabbed him [b]in the stomach, so that he died
for the blood of [c]Asahel his brother.
28 Afterward, when David heard *it,* he said,
"My kingdom and I *are* guiltless before the LORD
forever of the blood of Abner the son of Ner.
29 [a]Let it rest on the head of Joab and on all his
father's house; and let there never fail to be in
the house of Joab one [b]who has a discharge or is
a leper, who leans on a staff or falls by the sword,
or who lacks bread." 30 So Joab and Abishai his
brother killed Abner, because he had killed their
brother [a]Asahel at Gibeon in the battle.

### DAVID'S MOURNING FOR ABNER

31 Then David said to Joab and to all the peo-
ple who were with him, [a]"Tear your clothes,
[b]gird yourselves with sackcloth, and mourn
for Abner." And King David followed the coffin.
32 So they buried Abner in Hebron; and the king
lifted up his voice and wept at the grave of Abner,
and all the people wept. 33 And the king sang *a
lament* over Abner and said:

"Should Abner die as a [a]fool dies?
34 Your hands were not bound
Nor your feet put into fetters;
As a man falls before wicked men, *so* you fell."

Then all the people wept over him again.
35 And when all the people came [a]to persuade
David to eat food while it was still day, David took
an oath, saying, [b]"God do so to me, and more
also, if I taste bread or anything else [c]till the sun
goes down!" 36 Now all the people took note *of
it,* and it pleased them, since whatever the king
did pleased all the people. 37 For all the people
and all Israel understood that day that it had
not been the king's *intent* to kill Abner the son
of Ner. 38 Then the king said to his servants, "Do
you not know that a prince and a great man has
fallen this day in Israel? 39 And I *am* weak today,
though anointed king; and these men, the sons
of Zeruiah, [a]*are* too harsh for me. [b]The LORD shall
repay the evildoer according to his wickedness."

### ISHBOSHETH IS MURDERED

4 When Saul's son[1] heard that Abner had died
in Hebron, [a]he lost heart, and all Israel was
[b]troubled. 2 Now Saul's son *had* two men *who
were* captains of troops. The name of one *was*
Baanah and the name of the other Rechab, the
sons of Rimmon the Beerothite, of the children
of Benjamin. (For [a]Beeroth also was *part* of Ben-
jamin, 3 because the Beerothites fled to [a]Gittaim
and have been sojourners there until this day.)
4 [a]Jonathan, Saul's son, had a son *who was*
lame in *his* feet. He was five years old when the
news about Saul and Jonathan came [b]from
Jezreel; and his nurse took him up and fled.
And it happened, as she made haste to flee,
that he fell and became lame. His name *was*
[c]Mephibosheth.[1]
5 Then the sons of Rimmon the Beerothite,
Rechab and Baanah, set out and came at about
the heat of the day to the [a]house of Ishbosheth,
who was lying on his bed at noon. 6 And they
came there, all the way into the house, *as though*
to get wheat, and they stabbed him [a]in the stom-
ach. Then Rechab and Baanah his brother es-
caped. 7 For when they came into the house,
he was lying on his bed in his bedroom; then
they struck him and killed him, beheaded him
and took his head, and were all night escaping
through the plain. 8 And they brought the head
of Ishbosheth to David at Hebron, and said to
the king, "Here is the head of Ishbosheth, the
son of Saul your enemy, [a]who sought your life;
and the LORD has avenged my lord the king this
day of Saul and his descendants."
9 But David answered Rechab and Baanah
his brother, the sons of Rimmon the Beerothite,
and said to them, "*As* the LORD lives, [a]who has
redeemed my life from all adversity, 10 when
[a]someone told me, saying, 'Look, Saul is dead,'
thinking to have brought good news, I arrested
him and had him executed in Ziklag—the one
who *thought* I would give him a reward for *his*
news. 11 How much more, when wicked men have
killed a righteous person in his own house on
his bed? Therefore, shall I not now [a]require his
blood at your hand and remove you from the
earth?" 12 So David [a]commanded his young men,
and they executed them, cut off their hands and
feet, and hanged *them* by the pool in Hebron.
But they took the head of Ishbosheth and buried
*it* in the [b]tomb of Abner in Hebron.

### DAVID REIGNS OVER ALL ISRAEL

*(1 Chr. 11:1–3)*

5 Then all the tribes of Israel [a]came to David
at Hebron and spoke, saying, "Indeed [b]we
*are* your bone and your flesh. 2 Also, in time
past, when Saul was king over us, [a]you were the
one who led Israel out and brought them in;
and the LORD said to you, [b]'You shall shepherd
My people Israel, and be ruler over Israel.' "

3:27 [a]2 Sam. 20:9, 10; 1 Kin. 2:5 [b]2 Sam. 4:6 [c]2 Sam. 2:23 3:29 [a]Deut. 21:6–9; 1 Kin. 2:32, 33 [b]Lev. 15:2 3:30 [a]2 Sam. 2:23 3:31 [a]Josh. 7:6; 2 Sam. 1:2, 11 [b]Gen. 37:34 3:33 [a]2 Sam. 13:12, 13 3:35 [a]2 Sam. 12:17; Jer. 16:7, 8 [b]Ruth 1:17 [c]Judg. 20:26; 2 Sam. 1:12 3:39 [a]2 Sam. 19:5–7 [b]1 Kin. 2:5, 6, 32–34; 2 Tim. 4:14 4:1 [a]Ezra 4:4; Is. 13:7 [b]Matt. 2:3 [1]That is, Ishbosheth 4:2 [a]Josh. 18:25 4:3 [a]Neh. 11:33 4:4 [a]2 Sam. 9:3 [b]1 Sam. 29:1, 11 [c]2 Sam. 9:6 [1]Called *Merib-Baal* in 1 Chronicles 8:34 and 9:40 4:5 [a]2 Sam. 2:8, 9 4:6 [a]2 Sam. 2:23; 20:10 4:8 [a]1 Sam. 19:2, 10, 11; 23:15; 25:29 4:9 [a]Gen. 48:16; 1 Kin. 1:29; Ps. 31:7 4:10 [a]2 Sam. 1:2–16 4:11 [a][Gen. 9:5, 6; Ps. 9:12] 4:12 [a]2 Sam. 1:15 [b]2 Sam. 3:32 5:1 [a]1 Chr. 11:1–3 [b]Gen. 29:14; Judg. 9:2; 2 Sam. 19:12, 13 5:2 [a]1 Sam. 18:5, 13, 16 [b]1 Sam. 16:1

3 [a]Therefore all the elders of Israel came to the king at Hebron, [b]and King David made a covenant with them at Hebron [c]before the LORD. And they anointed David king over Israel. 4 David *was* [a]thirty years old when he began to reign, *and* [b]he reigned forty years. 5 In Hebron he reigned over Judah [a]seven years and six months, and in Jerusalem he reigned thirty-three years over all Israel and Judah.

> **5:3** This was the third time that David was **anointed** as **king**. The first time was in anticipation of his rule (1 Sam. 16:13). The second time acknowledged his rule over Judah (2:4). This third time acknowledged his rule over the entire nation.

### *THE CONQUEST OF JERUSALEM*
*(1 Chr. 11:4–9; 14:1–7)*

6 [a]And the king and his men went to Jerusalem against [b]the Jebusites, the inhabitants of the land, who spoke to David, saying, "You shall not come in here; but the blind and the lame will repel you," thinking, "David cannot come in here." 7 Nevertheless David took the stronghold of Zion [a](that *is,* the City of David).

8 Now David said on that day, "Whoever climbs up by way of the water shaft and defeats the Jebusites (the lame and the blind, *who are* hated by David's soul), [a]*he shall be chief and captain.*"[1] Therefore they say, "The blind and the lame shall not come into the house."

9 Then David dwelt in the stronghold, and called it [a]the City of David. And David built all around from the Millo[1] and inward. 10 So David went on and became great, and [a]the LORD God of hosts *was* with [b]him.

11 Then [a]Hiram [b]king of Tyre sent messengers to David, and cedar trees, and carpenters and masons. And they built David a house. 12 So David knew that the LORD had established him as king over Israel, and that He had [a]exalted His kingdom [b]for the sake of His people Israel.

13 And [a]David took more concubines and wives from Jerusalem, after he had come from Hebron. Also more sons and daughters were born to David. 14 Now [a]these *are* the names of those who were born to him in Jerusalem: Shammua,[1] Shobab, Nathan, [b]Solomon, 15 Ibhar, Elishua,[1] Nepheg, Japhia, 16 Elishama, Eliada, and Eliphelet.

### *THE PHILISTINES DEFEATED*
*(1 Chr. 14:8–17)*

17 [a]Now when the Philistines heard that they had anointed David king over Israel, all the Philistines went up to search for David. And David heard *of it* [b]and went down to the stronghold. 18 The Philistines also went and deployed themselves in [a]the Valley of Rephaim. 19 So David [a]inquired of the LORD, saying, "Shall I go up against the Philistines? Will You deliver them into my hand?"

And the LORD said to David, "Go up, for I will doubtless deliver the Philistines into your hand."

20 So David went to [a]Baal Perazim, and David defeated them there; and he said, "The LORD has broken through my enemies before me, like a breakthrough of water." Therefore he called the name of that place Baal Perazim.[1] 21 And they left their images there, and David and his men [a]carried them away.

22 [a]Then the Philistines went up once again and deployed themselves in the Valley of Rephaim. 23 Therefore [a]David inquired of the LORD, and He said, "You shall not go up; circle around behind them, and come upon them in front of the mulberry trees. 24 And it shall be, when you [a]hear the sound of marching in the tops of the mulberry trees, then you shall advance quickly. For then [b]the LORD will go out before you to strike the camp of the Philistines." 25 And David did so, as the LORD commanded him; and he drove back the Philistines from [a]Geba[1] as far as [b]Gezer.

### *THE ARK BROUGHT TO JERUSALEM*
*(1 Chr. 13:1–14; 15:25—16:3)*

6 Again David gathered all *the* choice *men* of Israel, thirty thousand. 2 And [a]David arose and went with all the people who *were* with him from Baale Judah to bring up from there the ark of God, whose name is called by the Name,[1] the LORD of Hosts, [b]who dwells *between* the cherubim. 3 So they set the ark of God on a new cart, and brought it out of the house of Abinadab, which *was* on [a]the hill; and Uzzah and Ahio, the sons of Abinadab, drove the new cart.[1] 4 And they brought it out of [a]the house of Abinadab, which *was* on the hill, accompanying the ark of God; and Ahio went before the ark. 5 Then David and all the house of Israel [a]played *music* before the LORD on all kinds of *instruments of* fir wood, on harps, on stringed instruments, on tambourines, on sistrums, and on cymbals.

6 And when they came to [a]Nachon's threshing floor, Uzzah put out *his* [b]*hand* to the ark of

**5:3** [a] 2 Sam. 3:17; 1 Chr. 11:3 [b] 2 Sam. 2:4; 3:21; 2 Kin. 11:17 [c] Judg. 11:11; 1 Sam. 23:18 **5:4** [a] Gen. 41:46; Num. 4:3; Luke 3:23 [b] 1 Kin. 2:11; 1 Chr. 26:31; 29:27 **5:5** [a] 2 Sam. 2:11; 1 Chr. 3:4; 29:27 **5:6** [a] Judg. 1:21 [b] Josh. 15:63; Judg. 1:8; 19:11, 12 **5:7** [a] 2 Sam. 6:12, 16; 1 Kin. 2:10; 8:1; 9:24 **5:8** [a] 1 Chr. 11:6–9 [1] Compare 1 Chronicles 11:6 **5:9** [a] 2 Sam. 5:7; 1 Kin. 9:15, 24 [1] Literally *The Landfill* **5:10** [a] 1 Sam. 17:45 [b] 1 Sam. 18:12, 28 **5:11** [a] 1 Kin. 5:1–18 [b] 1 Chr. 14:1 **5:12** [a] Num. 24:7 [b] Is. 45:4 **5:13** [a] [Deut. 17:17]; 1 Chr. 3:9 **5:14** [a] 1 Chr. 3:5–8 [b] 2 Sam. 12:24 [1] Spelled *Shimea* in 1 Chronicles 3:5 **5:15** [1] Spelled *Elishama* in 1 Chronicles 3:6 **5:17** [a] 1 Chr. 11:16 [b] 2 Sam. 23:14 **5:18** [a] Gen. 14:5; Josh. 15:8; 1 Chr. 11:15; Is. 17:5 **5:19** [a] 1 Sam. 23:2; 2 Sam. 2:1 **5:20** [a] 1 Chr. 14:11; Is. 28:21 [1] Literally *Master of Breakthroughs* **5:21** [a] Deut. 7:5, 25 **5:22** [a] 1 Chr. 14:13 **5:23** [a] 2 Sam. 5:19 **5:24** [a] 2 Kin. 7:6; 1 Chr. 14:15 [b] Judg. 4:14 **5:25** [a] 1 Chr. 14:16 [b] Josh. 16:10 [1] Following Masoretic Text, Targum, and Vulgate; Septuagint reads *Gibeon.* **6:2** [a] 1 Chr. 13:5, 6 [b] Ex. 25:22; 1 Sam. 4:4; Ps. 80:1 [1] Septuagint, Targum, and Vulgate omit *by the Name;* many Hebrew manuscripts and Syriac read *there.* **6:3** [a] 1 Sam. 26:1 [1] Septuagint adds *with the ark.* **6:4** [a] 1 Sam. 7:1; 1 Chr. 13:7 **6:5** [a] 1 Sam. 18:6, 7 **6:6** [a] 1 Chr. 13:9 [b] Num. 4:15, 19, 20

God and took hold of it, for the oxen stumbled.
7 Then the anger of the LORD was aroused against
Uzzah, and God struck him there for *his* error;
and he died there by the ark of God. 8 And David
became angry because of the LORD's outbreak
against Uzzah; and he called the name of the
place Perez Uzzah[1] to this day.

**6:6–8** Why did God strike down **Uzzah** merely for trying to keep the **ark** from falling? Uzzah's motives seem proper. Even if he did wrong, the punishment doesn't quite appear to fit the crime. What's important to remember, though, is that God had given instructions on how to handle the ark (see Num. 4:15, 19–20). Perhaps part of the problem was the Kohathites should have been carrying the ark with poles through its rings rather than it being carried on a cart. Or, perhaps, Uzzah's problem was thinking God needed his help. Either way, God's instructions were clear that no person was to touch the ark or else he would die. This account is a reminder to take God's holiness seriously.

9 [a]David was afraid of the LORD that day; and
he said, "How can the ark of the LORD come to
me?" 10 So David would not move the ark of the
LORD with him into the [a]City of David; but David
took it aside into the house of Obed-Edom the [b]Git-
tite. 11 [a]The ark of the LORD remained in the house
of Obed-Edom the Gittite three months. And the
LORD [b]blessed Obed-Edom and all his household.

12 Now it was told King David, saying, "The
LORD has blessed the house of Obed-Edom and
all that *belongs* to him, because of the ark of
God." [a]So David went and brought up the ark of
God from the house of Obed-Edom to the City
of David with gladness. 13 And so it was, when
[a]those bearing the ark of the LORD had gone six
paces, that he sacrificed [b]oxen and fatted sheep.
14 Then David [a]danced before the LORD with all
*his* might; and David *was* wearing [b]a linen ephod.
15 [a]So David and all the house of Israel brought
up the ark of the LORD with shouting and with
the sound of the trumpet.

16 Now as the ark of the LORD came into the
City of David, [a]Michal, Saul's daughter, looked
through a window and saw King David leaping
and whirling before the LORD; and she despised
him in her heart. 17 So [a]they brought the ark of
the LORD, and set it in [b]its place in the midst
of the tabernacle that David had erected for it.
Then David [c]offered burnt offerings and peace
offerings before the LORD. 18 And when David
had finished offering burnt offerings and peace
offerings, [a]he blessed the people in the name of
the LORD of hosts. 19 [a]Then he distributed among
all the people, among the whole multitude of
Israel, both the women and the men, to every-
one a loaf of bread, a piece *of meat,* and a cake
of raisins. So all the people departed, everyone
to his house.

20 [a]Then David returned to bless his house-
hold. And Michal the daughter of Saul came
out to meet David, and said, "How glorious was
the king of Israel today, [b]uncovering himself
today in the eyes of the maids of his servants,
as one of the [c]base fellows shamelessly uncov-
ers himself!"

6:8 [1] Literally *Outburst Against Uzzah* 6:9 [a] Deut. 9:19; Ps. 119:120; Luke 5:8 6:10 [a] 2 Sam. 5:7 [b] 1 Chr. 13:13; 26:4–8 6:11 [a] 1 Chr. 13:14 [b] Gen. 30:27; 39:5 6:12 [a] 1 Chr. 15:25—16:3 6:13 [a] Num. 4:15; Josh. 3:3; 1 Sam. 6:15; 2 Sam. 15:24; 1 Chr. 15:2, 15 [b] 1 Kin. 8:5 6:14 [a] Ps. 30:11; 149:3 [b] 1 Sam. 2:18, 28 6:15 [a] 1 Chr. 15:28 6:16 [a] 2 Sam. 3:14 6:17 [a] 1 Chr. 16:1 [b] 1 Chr. 15:1; 2 Chr. 1:4 [c] 1 Kin. 8:5, 62, 63 6:18 [a] 1 Kin. 8:14, 15, 55 6:19 [a] 1 Chr. 16:3 6:20 [a] Ps. 30:title [b] 2 Sam. 6:14, 16 [c] Judg. 9:4

LIVE THE TRUTH

## RESTING IN GOD'S APPROVAL

**6:14** Almost everyone wants to be thought well of, to have a good reputation. Unfortunately, chasing after a reputation is like chasing after a moving target; it's nearly impossible to catch. As soon as we know what gives us the approval of others, their demands change. What is loved and respected one day is despised and rejected the next. Instead of seeking people's approval, we should be concerned with what God thinks. Throughout the Bible, God tells us what He desires and loves. He wants our obedience. He wants our hearts to be pleased with what pleases Him. He wants us to love Jesus and live like Him. And here's the really good news: God's demands *never* change.

David rejoiced because the ark of the Lord had returned to Jerusalem. The ark symbolized God's presence, so this event was certainly worthy of an extravagant celebration. David was so enthused that he stopped what he was doing and danced in praise to God. But some, including his wife Michal, were less than pleased. Michal didn't believe it was befitting of the king to dance among the people. David, though, was more concerned with what God thought about him. Those who believe in Jesus should always consider what God thinks about us, not others. Living for God is always our chief objective.

21 So David said to Michal, "*It was* before
the LORD, [a]who chose me instead of your father
and all his house, to appoint me ruler over the
[b]people of the LORD, over Israel. Therefore I will
play *music* before the LORD. 22 And I will be even
more undignified than this, and will be humble
in my own sight. But as for the maidservants of
whom you have spoken, by them I will be held
in honor."
23 Therefore Michal the daughter of Saul had
no children [a]to the day of her death.

### *GOD'S COVENANT WITH DAVID*

*(1 Chr. 17:1–15)*

7 Now it came to pass [a]when the king was
dwelling in his house, and the LORD had
given him rest from all his enemies all around,
2 that the king said to Nathan the prophet, "See
now, I dwell in [a]a house of cedar, [b]but the ark
of God dwells inside tent [c]curtains."
3 Then Nathan said to the king, "Go, do all
that *is* in your [a]heart, for the LORD *is* with you."
4 But it happened that night that the word
of the LORD came to Nathan, saying, 5 "Go and
tell My servant David, 'Thus says the LORD:
[a]"Would you build a house for Me to dwell in?
6 For I have not dwelt in a house [a]since the time
that I brought the children of Israel up from
Egypt, even to this day, but have moved about
in [b]a tent and in a tabernacle. 7 Wherever I have
[a]moved about with all the children of Israel, have
I ever spoken a word to anyone from the tribes
of Israel, whom I commanded [b]to shepherd My
people Israel, saying, 'Why have you not built
Me a house of cedar?' " ' 8 Now therefore, thus
shall you say to My servant David, 'Thus says the
LORD of hosts: [a]"I took you from the sheepfold,
from following the sheep, to be ruler over My
people, over Israel. 9 And [a]I have been with you
wherever you have gone, [b]and have cut off all
your enemies from before you, and have made
you a great name, like the name of the great men
who *are* on the earth. 10 Moreover I will appoint a
place for My people Israel, and will [a]plant them,
that they may dwell in a place of their own and
move no more; [b]nor shall the sons of wickedness
oppress them anymore, as previously, 11 [a]since
the time that I commanded judges *to be* over
My people Israel, and have caused you to rest
from all your enemies. Also the LORD tells you
[b]that He will make you a house.[1]
12 [a]"When your days are fulfilled and you
[b]rest with your fathers, [c]I will set up your seed
after you, who will come from your body, and

**6:21** [a] 1 Sam. 13:14; 15:28 [b] 2 Kin. 11:17 **6:23** [a] Is. 22:14 **7:1** [a] 1 Chr. 17:1–27 **7:2** [a] 2 Sam. 5:11 [b] Acts 7:46 [c] Ex. 26:1 **7:3** [a] 1 Kin. 8:17, 18 **7:5** [a] 1 Kin. 5:3, 4; 8:19 **7:6** [a] 1 Kin. 8:16 [b] Ex. 40:18, 34 **7:7** [a] Lev. 26:11, 12 [b] 2 Sam. 5:2 **7:8** [a] 1 Sam. 16:11, 12 **7:9** [a] 2 Sam. 5:10 [b] 1 Sam. 31:6 **7:10** [a] Ps. 44:2; 80:8 [b] Ps. 89:22, 23 **7:11** [a] Judg. 2:14–16 [b] 2 Sam. 7:27 [1] That is, a royal dynasty **7:12** [a] 1 Kin. 2:1 [b] Deut. 31:16 [c] Ps. 132:11

2 SAMUEL 7:1–17

## GOD'S COVENANT WITH DAVID

25

STORY OF SCRIPTURE

### WHAT'S GOING ON?

This is a significant moment in Israel's history and the story of Scripture: God forged a covenant with David. When King David expressed a desire to build a temple for God, the Lord, through the prophet Nathan, delivered a message that established David's lineage and kingdom forever. Instead of David building a house (a temple) for God, God promised to establish David's house (a dynasty) permanently. This covenant includes the assurance that David's offspring would build the temple and that David's kingdom would endure forever, ultimately fulfilled in Jesus Christ, a descendant of David.

### WHAT DOES THIS MEAN FOR ME?

David had a noble idea to build a temple for God, but God's plan encompassed more than a building. God eyed an everlasting kingdom. God's rejection of David's wishes can encourage us to hold our plans loosely and trust in God's greater purpose for our lives. Just because we have a good idea, doesn't mean it's God's plan. We must be willing to submit our good intentions to God's Word.

### DID YOU CATCH THE PATTERN?

Covenants are promises made and sustained by God. God's covenant with David fits into a larger pattern of God's faithfulness and fulfilled promises throughout the Bible. From the covenants with Noah, Abraham, and the people of Israel in the wilderness, this moment adds another in the list of promises leading to Jesus Christ. Through David's lineage, Jesus was born to establish the everlasting covenant.

*For the next* Story of Scripture *reading and devotion, turn to 1 Chronicles 21:1–5 on page 415.*

> **SEEING JESUS IN THE SCRIPTURE**
>
> **7:12** God promised to establish David's kingdom forever through his offspring. Though this promise refers in part to Solomon, David's son, God ultimately fulfilled this covenant through Jesus. Jesus came from the line of David, and His kingdom has no end (see Luke 3:31).

I will establish his kingdom. 13 [a]He shall build a house for My name, and I will [b]establish the throne of his kingdom forever. 14 [a]I will be his Father, and he shall be [b]My son. If he commits iniquity, I will chasten him with the rod of men and with the blows of the sons of men. 15 But My mercy shall not depart from him, [a]as I took *it* from Saul, whom I removed from before you. 16 And [a]your house and your kingdom shall be established forever before you.[1] Your throne shall be established forever." ' "

17 According to all these words and according to all this vision, so Nathan spoke to David.

### DAVID'S THANKSGIVING TO GOD
*(1 Chr. 17:16–27)*

18 Then King David went in and sat before the LORD; and he said: [a]"Who *am* I, O Lord GOD? And what is my house, that You have brought me this far? 19 And yet this was a small thing in Your sight, O Lord GOD; and You have also spoken of Your servant's house for a great while to come. [a]*Is* this the manner of man, O Lord GOD? 20 Now what more can David say to You? For You, Lord GOD, [a]know Your servant. 21 For Your word's sake, and according to Your own heart, You have done all these great things, to make Your servant know *them.* 22 Therefore [a]You are great, O Lord GOD.[1] For [b]*there is* none like You, nor *is there any* God besides You, according to all that we have heard with our [c]ears. 23 And who *is* like Your people, like Israel, [a]the one nation on the earth whom God went to redeem for Himself as a people, to make for Himself a name—and to do for Yourself great and awesome deeds for Your land—before [b]Your people whom You redeemed for Yourself from Egypt, the nations, and their gods? 24 For [a]You have made Your people Israel Your very own people forever; [b]and You, LORD, have become their God.

25 "Now, O LORD God, the word which You have spoken concerning Your servant and concerning his house, establish *it* forever and do as You have said. 26 So let Your name be magnified forever, saying, 'The LORD of hosts *is* the God over Israel.' And let the house of Your servant David be established before You. 27 For You, O LORD of hosts, God of Israel, have revealed *this* to Your servant, saying, 'I will build you a house.' Therefore Your servant has found it in his heart to pray this prayer to You.

28 "And now, O Lord GOD, You are God, and [a]Your words are true, and You have promised this goodness to Your servant. 29 Now therefore, let it please You to bless the house of Your servant, that it may continue before You forever; for You, O Lord GOD, have spoken *it,* and with Your blessing let the house of Your servant be blessed [a]forever."

### DAVID'S FURTHER CONQUESTS
*(1 Chr. 18:1–13)*

**8** After this it came to pass that David attacked the Philistines and subdued them. And David took Metheg Ammah from the hand of the Philistines.

2 Then [a]he defeated Moab. Forcing them down to the ground, he measured them off with a line. With two lines he measured off those to be put to death, and with one full line those to be kept alive. So the Moabites became David's [b]servants, *and* [c]brought tribute.

3 David also defeated Hadadezer the son of Rehob, king of [a]Zobah, as he went to recover [b]his territory at the River Euphrates. 4 David took from him one thousand *chariots,* seven hundred[1] horsemen, and twenty thousand foot soldiers. Also David [a]hamstrung all the chariot *horses,* except that he spared *enough* of them for one hundred chariots.

5 [a]When the Syrians of Damascus came to help Hadadezer king of Zobah, David killed twenty-two thousand of the Syrians. 6 Then David put garrisons in Syria of Damascus; and the Syrians became David's servants, *and* brought tribute. So [a]the LORD preserved David wherever he went. 7 And David took [a]the shields of gold that had belonged to the servants of Hadadezer, and brought them to Jerusalem. 8 Also from Betah[1] and from [a]Berothai, cities of Hadadezer, King David took a large amount of bronze.

9 When Toi[1] king of [a]Hamath heard that David had defeated all the army of Hadadezer, 10 then Toi sent Joram[1] his son to King David, to greet him and bless him, because he had fought against Hadadezer and defeated him (for Hadadezer had been at war with Toi); and *Joram* brought with him articles of silver, articles of gold, and articles of bronze. 11 King David also [a]dedicated these to the LORD, along with the silver and gold that he had dedicated from all the nations which he had subdued— 12 from Syria,[1] from Moab, from the people of Ammon, from the [a]Philistines, from

**7:13** [a] 1 Kin. 5:5; 8:19 [b] [Is. 9:7; 49:8] **7:14** [a] [Heb. 1:5] [b] [Ps. 2:7; 89:26, 27, 30] **7:15** [a] 1 Sam. 15:23, 28; 16:14 **7:16** [a] 2 Sam. 7:13 [1] Septuagint reads *Me.* **7:18** [a] Ex. 3:11 **7:19** [a] [Is. 55:8, 9] **7:20** [a] John 21:17 **7:22** [a] Deut. 10:17 [b] Ex. 15:11 [c] Ex. 10:2 [1] Targum and Syriac read *O LORD God.* **7:23** [a] Ps. 147:20 [b] Deut. 9:26; 33:29 **7:24** [a] [Deut. 26:18] [b] Ps. 48:14 **7:28** [a] John 17:17 **7:29** [a] 2 Sam. 22:51 **8:2** [a] Num. 24:17 [b] 2 Sam. 12:31 [c] 1 Kin. 4:21 **8:3** [a] 1 Sam. 14:47 [b] 2 Sam. 10:15–19 **8:4** [a] Josh. 11:6, 9 [1] Or *seven thousand* (compare 1 Chronicles 18:4) **8:5** [a] 1 Kin. 11:23–25 **8:6** [a] 2 Sam. 7:9; 8:14 **8:7** [a] 1 Kin. 10:16 **8:8** [a] Ezek. 47:16 [1] Spelled *Tibhath* in 1 Chronicles 18:8 **8:9** [a] 1 Kin. 8:65 [1] Spelled *Tou* in 1 Chronicles 18:9 **8:10** [1] Spelled *Hadoram* in 1 Chronicles 18:10 **8:11** [a] 1 Kin. 7:51 **8:12** [a] 2 Sam. 5:17–25 [1] Septuagint, Syriac, and some Hebrew manuscripts read *Edom.*

Amalek, and from the spoil of Hadadezer the
son of Rehob, king of Zobah.
13 And David made *himself* a [a]name when he
returned from killing [b]eighteen thousand Syri-
ans[1] in [c]the Valley of Salt. 14 He also put garrisons
in Edom; throughout all Edom he put garrisons,
and [a]all the Edomites became David's servants.
And the LORD preserved David wherever he went.

### *DAVID'S ADMINISTRATION*

*(1 Chr. 18:14–17)*

15 So David reigned over all Israel; and David
administered judgment and justice to all his peo-
ple. 16 [a]Joab the son of Zeruiah *was* over the army;
[b]Jehoshaphat the son of Ahilud *was* recorder;
17 [a]Zadok the son of Ahitub and Ahimelech the
son of Abiathar *were* the priests; Seraiah[1] *was*
the scribe; 18 [a]Benaiah the son of Jehoiada *was*
*over* both the [b]Cherethites and the Pelethites;
and David's sons were chief ministers.

### *DAVID'S KINDNESS TO MEPHIBOSHETH*

9 Now David said, "Is there still anyone who
is left of the house of Saul, that I may [a]show
him kindness for Jonathan's sake?"
2 And *there was* a servant of the house of Saul
whose name *was* [a]Ziba. So when they had called
him to David, the king said to him, "*Are* you Ziba?"
He said, "At your service!"
3 Then the king said, "*Is* there not still some-
one of the house of Saul, to whom I may show
[a]the kindness of God?"
And Ziba said to the king, "There is still a son
of Jonathan *who is* [b]lame in *his* feet."
4 So the king said to him, "Where *is* he?"
And Ziba said to the king, "Indeed he *is* in the
house of [a]Machir the son of Ammiel, in Lo Debar."

> **SEEING JESUS IN THE SCRIPTURE**
>
> **9:7** Mephibosheth had nothing to offer David, yet David gave Mephibosheth everything. David's kindness mirrors God's kindness toward us through Jesus. While we had nothing to offer God, He gave us new life in Jesus (see Eph. 2:4–7).

5 Then King David sent and brought him
out of the house of Machir the son of Ammiel,
from Lo Debar.
6 Now when [a]Mephibosheth the son of Jona-
than, the son of Saul, had come to David, he fell
on his face and prostrated himself. Then David
said, "Mephibosheth?"
And he answered, "Here is your servant!"
7 So David said to him, "Do not fear, for I
will surely show you kindness for Jonathan
your father's sake, and will restore to you all the
land of Saul your grandfather; and you shall eat
bread at my table continually."
8 Then he bowed himself, and said, "What *is*
your servant, that you should look upon such
[a]a dead dog as I?"
9 And the king called to Ziba, Saul's servant,
and said to him, [a]"I have given to your mas-
ter's son all that belonged to Saul and to all his
house. 10 You therefore, and your sons and your
servants, shall work the land for him, and you
shall bring in *the harvest,* that your master's son
may have food to eat. But Mephibosheth your
master's son [a]shall eat bread at my table always."
Now Ziba had [b]fifteen sons and twenty servants.
11 Then Ziba said to the king, "According to

**8:13** [a] 2 Sam. 7:9 [b] 2 Kin. 14:7 [c] 1 Chr. 18:12 [1] Septuagint, Syriac, and some Hebrew manuscripts read *Edomites* (compare 1 Chronicles 18:12). **8:14** [a] Gen. 27:29, 37–40 **8:16** [a] 2 Sam. 19:13; 20:23 [b] 1 Kin. 4:3 **8:17** [a] 1 Chr. 6:4–8; 24:3 [1] Spelled *Shavsha* in 1 Chronicles 18:16 **8:18** [a] 1 Chr. 18:17 [b] 1 Sam. 30:14 **9:1** [a] 1 Sam. 18:3; 20:14–16 **9:2** [a] 2 Sam. 16:1–4; 19:17, 29 **9:3** [a] 1 Sam. 20:14 [b] 2 Sam. 4:4 **9:4** [a] 2 Sam. 17:27–29 **9:6** [a] 2 Sam. 16:4; 19:24–30 **9:8** [a] 2 Sam. 16:9 **9:9** [a] 2 Sam. 16:4; 19:29 **9:10** [a] 2 Sam. 9:7, 11, 13; 19:28 [b] 2 Sam. 19:17

LIVE THE TRUTH

## BEING KIND

**9:1–13** Kindness is showing generosity to others, expecting nothing in return. It's freely giving of our resources—money, time, energy, love—to another. Because kindness involves giving, it always costs something. Genuine kindness means the giver pays that cost. Being kind to Mephibosheth didn't benefit David but it did cost him. Mephibosheth was a grandson of David's former political enemy, Saul. Most kings would have killed all the former king's family so they wouldn't try to retake the throne. Leaving someone like Mephibosheth alive was risky. But David did more than that; he invited Mephibosheth and his family to eat at his table. He treated Mephibosheth like a son and gave him Saul's land.

In showing kindness, David pictured the kindness God shows us. Because of our sin, we were God's enemy (see Rom. 5:10), but out of His great kindness, God extended forgiveness to us through Christ Jesus (Eph. 2:4–7). Now, we're restored as God's children and He invites us to sit at His table forever. Because we have received such lavish kindness, it's only reasonable that we freely show kindness to others, especially those who cannot pay us back.

all that my lord the king has commanded his
servant, so will your servant do."
"As for Mephibosheth," *said the king,* "he
shall eat at my table[1] like one of the king's sons."
12 Mephibosheth had a young son [a]whose name
*was* Micha. And all who dwelt in the house of
Ziba *were* servants of Mephibosheth. 13 So Me-
phibosheth dwelt in Jerusalem, [a]for he ate con-
tinually at the king's table. And he [b]was lame in
both his feet.

### *THE AMMONITES AND SYRIANS DEFEATED*

*(1 Chr. 19:1–19)*

**10** It happened after this that the [a]king of the
people of Ammon died, and Hanun his son
reigned in his place. 2 Then David said, "I will
show [a]kindness to Hanun the son of [b]Nahash,
as his father showed kindness to me."
So David sent by the hand of his servants
to comfort him concerning his father. And Da-
vid's servants came into the land of the people
of Ammon. 3 And the princes of the people of
Ammon said to Hanun their lord, "Do you think
that David really honors your father because
he has sent comforters to you? Has David not
*rather* sent his servants to you to search the city,
to spy it out, and to overthrow it?"
4 Therefore Hanun took David's servants,
shaved off half of their beards, cut off their
garments in the middle, [a]at their buttocks, and
sent them away. 5 When they told David, he sent
to meet them, because the men were greatly
ashamed. And the king said, "Wait at Jericho
until your beards have grown, and *then* return."
6 When the people of Ammon saw that they
[a]had made themselves repulsive to David, the
people of Ammon sent and hired [b]the Syrians
of [c]Beth Rehob and the Syrians of Zoba, twenty
thousand foot soldiers; and from the king of
[d]Maacah one thousand men, and from [e]Ish-
Tob twelve thousand men. 7 Now when David
heard *of it,* he sent Joab and all the army of
[a]the mighty men. 8 Then the people of Ammon
came out and put themselves in battle array at
the entrance of the gate. And [a]the Syrians of
Zoba, Beth Rehob, Ish-Tob, and Maacah *were*
by themselves in the field.
9 When Joab saw that the battle line was
against him before and behind, he chose some of
Israel's best and put *them* in battle array against
the Syrians. 10 And the rest of the people he put
under the command of [a]Abishai his brother,
that he might set *them* in battle array against
the people of Ammon. 11 Then he said, "If the
Syrians are too strong for me, then you shall
help me; but if the people of Ammon are too
strong for you, then I will come and help you.
12 [a]Be of good courage, and let us [b]be strong for
our people and for the cities of our God. And
may [c]the LORD do *what is* good in His sight."
13 So Joab and the people who *were* with him
drew near for the battle against the Syrians,
and they fled before him. 14 When the people of
Ammon saw that the Syrians were fleeing, they
also fled before Abishai, and entered the city. So
Joab returned from the people of Ammon and
went to [a]Jerusalem.
15 When the Syrians saw that they had been
defeated by Israel, they gathered together.
16 Then Hadadezer[1] sent and brought out the
Syrians who *were* beyond the River,[2] and they
came to Helam. And Shobach the commander
of Hadadezer's army *went* before them. 17 When
it was told David, he gathered all Israel, crossed
over the Jordan, and came to Helam. And the
Syrians set themselves in battle array against
David and fought with him. 18 Then the Syr-
ians fled before Israel; and David killed sev-
en hundred charioteers and forty thousand
[a]horsemen of the Syrians, and struck Shobach
the commander of their army, who died there.
19 And when all the kings *who were* servants to
Hadadezer[1] saw that they were defeated by Is-
rael, they made peace with Israel and [a]served
them. So the Syrians were afraid to help the
people of Ammon anymore.

### *DAVID, BATHSHEBA, AND URIAH*

**11** It happened in the spring of the year, at
the [a]time when kings go out *to battle,* that
[b]David sent Joab and his servants with him,
and all Israel; and they destroyed the people
of Ammon and besieged [c]Rabbah. But David
remained at Jerusalem.
2 Then it happened one evening that David
arose from his bed [a]and walked on the roof of the
king's house. And from the roof he [b]saw a woman
bathing, and the woman *was* very beautiful to
behold. 3 So David sent and inquired about the
woman. And *someone* said, "*Is* this not Bathshe-
ba, the daughter of Eliam, the wife [a]of Uriah the

> **11:2** The typical **house** in ancient Israel was built with a flat **roof** surrounded by a low wall. The roof, which could be reached by an outside stairway, was used as everything from a sleeping area to a patio or deck. From this high roof, David saw Bathsheba, who was probably bathing in the enclosed courtyard of her house, a place of privacy, not visible from the street.

9:11 [1] Septuagint reads *David's table.* 9:12 [a] 1 Chr. 8:34 9:13 [a] 2 Sam. 9:7, 10, 11; 1 Kin. 2:7; 2 Kin. 25:29 [b] 2 Sam. 9:3
10:1 [a] 2 Sam. 11:1; 1 Chr. 19:1 10:2 [a] 2 Sam. 9:1; 1 Kin. 2:7 [b] 1 Sam. 11:1 10:4 [a] Is. 20:4; 47:2 10:6 [a] Gen. 34:30; Ex. 5:21 [b] 2 Sam. 8:3, 5 [c] Judg. 18:28 [d] Deut. 3:14; Josh. 13:11, 13 [e] Judg. 11:3, 5 10:7 [a] 2 Sam. 23:8 10:8 [a] 2 Sam. 10:6 10:10 [a] 1 Sam. 26:6; 2 Sam. 3:30
10:12 [a] Deut. 31:6; Josh. 1:6, 7, 9; Neh. 4:14 [b] 1 Sam. 4:9; 1 Cor. 16:13 [c] 1 Sam. 3:18 10:14 [a] 2 Sam. 11:1 10:16 [1] Hebrew *Hadarezer* [2] That is, the Euphrates 10:18 [a] 1 Chr. 19:18 10:19 [a] 2 Sam. 8:6 [1] Hebrew *Hadarezer* 11:1 [a] 1 Kin. 20:22–26 [b] 1 Chr. 20:1 [c] 2 Sam. 12:26; Jer. 49:2, 3; Amos 1:14 11:2 [a] Deut. 22:8; 1 Sam. 9:25; Matt. 24:17; Acts 10:9 [b] Gen. 34:2; [Ex. 20:17]; Job 31:1; [Matt. 5:28] 11:3 [a] 2 Sam. 23:39

[b]Hittite?" 4 Then David sent messengers, and took her; and she came to him, and [a]he lay with her, for she was [b]cleansed from her impurity; and she returned to her house. 5 And the woman conceived; so she sent and told David, and said, "I *am* with child."

6 Then David sent to Joab, *saying,* "Send me Uriah the Hittite." And Joab sent Uriah to David. 7 When Uriah had come to him, David asked how Joab was doing, and how the people were doing, and how the war prospered. 8 And David said to Uriah, "Go down to your house and [a]wash your feet." So Uriah departed from the king's house, and a gift *of food* from the king followed him. 9 But Uriah slept at the [a]door of the king's house with all the servants of his lord, and did not go down to his house. 10 So when they told David, saying, "Uriah did not go down to his house," David said to Uriah, "Did you not come from a journey? Why did you not go down to your house?"

11 And Uriah said to David, [a]"The ark and Israel and Judah are dwelling in tents, and [b]my lord Joab and the servants of my lord are encamped in the open fields. Shall I then go to my house to eat and drink, and to lie with my wife? *As* you live, and *as* your soul lives, I will not do this thing."

12 Then David said to Uriah, "Wait here today also, and tomorrow I will let you depart." So Uriah remained in Jerusalem that day and the next. 13 Now when David called him, he ate and drank before him; and he made him [a]drunk. And at evening he went out to lie on his bed [b]with the servants of his lord, but he did not go down to his house.

14 In the morning it happened that David [a]wrote a letter to Joab and sent *it* by the hand of Uriah. 15 And he wrote in the letter, saying, "Set Uriah in the forefront of the hottest battle, and retreat from him, that he may [a]be struck down and die." 16 So it was, while Joab besieged the city, that he assigned Uriah to a place where he knew there *were* valiant men. 17 Then the men of the city came out and fought with Joab. And *some* of the people of the servants of David fell; and Uriah the Hittite died also.

18 Then Joab sent and told David all the things concerning the war, 19 and charged the messenger, saying, "When you have finished telling the matters of the war to the king, 20 if it happens that the king's wrath rises, and he says to you: 'Why did you approach so near to the city when you fought? Did you not know that they would shoot from the wall? 21 Who struck [a]Abimelech the son of Jerubbesheth?[1] Was it not a woman who cast a piece of a millstone on him from the wall, so that he died in Thebez? Why did you go near the wall?'—then you shall say, 'Your servant Uriah the Hittite is dead also.' "

22 So the messenger went, and came and told David all that Joab had sent by him. 23 And the messenger said to David, "Surely the men prevailed against us and came out to us in the field; then we drove them back as far as the entrance of the gate. 24 The archers shot from the wall at your servants; and *some* of the king's servants are dead, and your servant Uriah the Hittite is dead also."

25 Then David said to the messenger, "Thus you shall say to Joab: 'Do not let this thing displease you, for the sword devours one as well as another. Strengthen your attack against the city, and overthrow it.' So encourage him."

26 When the wife of Uriah heard that Uriah her husband was dead, she mourned for her husband. 27 And when her mourning was over, David sent and brought her to his house, and she [a]became his wife and bore him a son. But the thing that David had done [b]displeased the LORD.

### *NATHAN'S PARABLE AND DAVID'S CONFESSION*

**12** Then the LORD sent Nathan to David. And [a]he came to him, and [b]said to him: "There were two men in one city, one rich and the other poor. 2 The rich *man* had exceedingly many flocks and herds. 3 But the poor *man* had nothing, except one little ewe lamb which he had bought and nourished; and it grew up together with him and with his children. It ate of his own food and drank from his own cup and lay in his bosom; and it was like a daughter to him. 4 And a traveler came to the rich man, who refused to take from his own flock and from his own herd to prepare one for the wayfaring man who had come to him; but he took the poor man's lamb and prepared it for the man who had come to him."

5 So David's anger was greatly aroused against the man, and he said to Nathan, "*As* the LORD lives, the man who has done this shall surely die! 6 And he shall restore [a]fourfold for the lamb, because he did this thing and because he had no pity."

7 Then Nathan said to David, "You *are* the man! Thus says the LORD God of Israel: 'I [a]anointed you king over Israel, and I delivered you from the hand of Saul. 8 I gave you your master's house and your master's wives into your keeping, and gave you the house of Israel and Judah. And if *that had been* too little, I also would have given you much more! 9 [a]Why have you [b]despised the commandment of the LORD, to do evil in His sight? [c]You have killed Uriah the Hittite with the sword; you have taken his wife *to be* your wife, and have killed him with the sword of the people of Ammon. 10 Now therefore, [a]the sword shall never depart from your house, because you have despised Me, and have taken the wife of Uriah

**11:3** [b] 1 Sam. 26:6 **11:4** [a] [Lev. 20:10; Deut. 22:22]; Ps. 51:title; [James 1:14, 15] [b] Lev. 15:19, 28 **11:8** [a] Gen. 18:4; 19:2 **11:9** [a] 1 Kin. 14:27, 28 **11:11** [a] 2 Sam. 7:2, 6 [b] 2 Sam. 20:6–22 **11:13** [a] Gen. 19:33, 35 [b] 2 Sam. 11:9 **11:14** [a] 1 Kin. 21:8, 9 **11:15** [a] 2 Sam. 12:9 **11:21** [a] Judg. 9:50–54 [1] Same as *Jerubbaal* (Gideon), Judges 6:32ff **11:27** [a] 2 Sam. 12:9 [b] 1 Chr. 21:7; [Heb. 13:4] **12:1** [a] Ps. 51:title [b] 1 Kin. 20:35–41 **12:6** [a] [Ex. 22:1]; Luke 19:8 **12:7** [a] 1 Sam. 16:13; 2 Sam. 5:3 **12:9** [a] 1 Sam. 15:19 [b] Num. 15:31 [c] 2 Sam. 11:14–17, 27 **12:10** [a] 2 Sam. 13:28; 18:14; 1 Kin. 2:25; [Amos 7:9]

APPLY THE TRUTH

## HYPOCRISY

**12:1–7** Hypocrisy isn't trying and failing. Neither is it knowing the right thing to do but doing the wrong thing instead. Hypocrisy is acting. Like a movie actor convincing the audience he or she is someone else, hypocrisy is pretending to be someone you're not while hiding who you really are. This can look like behaving one way on Friday night and a different way on Sunday morning. Or carrying your Bible around but never opening it. It can also look like condemning someone's sin while participating in a similar one. The sins we struggle with always look worse on someone else.

Here, King David was a hypocrite. He had just committed his biggest failure. He stole another man's wife and had him murdered to cover it up. When he heard about a man who stole someone's sheep, he wanted judgment rained down upon him, not realizing the story was about him. Like David, we want grace for our sins but judgment for those of others. We can stop playing the hypocrite when we recognize we all need grace and God is kind to meet us wherever we are.

the Hittite to be your wife.' 11 Thus says the LORD: 'Behold, I will raise up adversity against you from your own house; and I will [a]take your wives before your eyes and give *them* to your neighbor, and he shall lie with your wives in the sight of this sun. 12 For you did *it* secretly, [a]but I will do this thing before all Israel, before the sun.' "

13 [a]So David said to Nathan, [b]"I have sinned against the LORD."

And Nathan said to David, "The LORD also has [c]put away your sin; you shall not die. 14 However, because by this deed you have given great occasion to the enemies of the LORD [a]to blaspheme, the child also *who is* born to you shall surely die." 15 Then Nathan departed to his house.

### *THE DEATH OF DAVID'S SON*

And the [a]LORD struck the child that Uriah's wife bore to David, and it became ill. 16 David therefore pleaded with God for the child, and David fasted and went in and [a]lay all night on the ground. 17 So the elders of his house arose *and went* to him, to raise him up from the ground. But he would not, nor did he eat food with them. 18 Then on the seventh day it came to pass that the child died. And the servants of David were afraid to tell him that the child was dead. For they said, "Indeed, while the child was alive, we spoke to him, and he would not heed our voice. How can we tell him that the child is dead? He may do some harm!"

19 When David saw that his servants were whispering, David perceived that the child was dead. Therefore David said to his servants, "Is the child dead?"

And they said, "He is dead."

20 So David arose from the ground, washed and [a]anointed himself, and changed his clothes; and he went into the house of the LORD and [b]worshiped. Then he went to his own house; and when he requested, they set food before him, and he ate. 21 Then his servants said to him, "What *is* this that you have done? You fasted and wept for the child *while he was* alive, but when the child died, you arose and ate food."

22 And he said, "While the child was alive, I fasted and wept; [a]for I said, 'Who can tell *whether* the LORD[1] will be gracious to me, that the child may live?' 23 But now he is dead; why should I fast? Can I bring him back again? I shall go [a]to him, but [b]he shall not return to me."

### SEEING JESUS IN THE SCRIPTURE

**12:18** David's sin being placed on his innocent son points to Jesus. Jesus, who was innocent, died on the cross as the world's sin was placed on Him (see John 19:4; 2 Cor. 5:21). Jesus didn't deserve to die, but it was necessary for our salvation.

### *SOLOMON IS BORN*

24 Then David comforted Bathsheba his wife, and went in to her and lay with her. So [a]she bore a son, and [b]he[1] called his name Solomon. Now the LORD loved him, 25 and He sent *word* by the hand of Nathan the prophet: So he[1] called his name Jedidiah,[2] because of the LORD.

### *RABBAH IS CAPTURED*

*(1 Chr. 20:1–3)*

26 Now [a]Joab fought against [b]Rabbah of the people of Ammon, and took the royal city. 27 And

**12:11** [a] Deut. 28:30; 2 Sam. 16:21, 22 **12:12** [a] 2 Sam. 16:22 **12:13** [a] 1 Sam. 15:24 [b] 2 Sam. 24:10; Job 7:20; Ps. 51; Luke 18:13 [c] 2 Sam. 24:10; Job 7:21; [Ps. 32:1–5; Prov. 28:13; Mic. 7:18]; Zech. 3:4 **12:14** [a] Is. 52:5; [Ezek. 36:20, 23]; Rom. 2:24 **12:15** [a] 1 Sam. 25:38 **12:16** [a] 2 Sam. 13:31 **12:20** [a] Ruth 3:3; Matt. 6:17 [b] Job 1:20 **12:22** [a] Is. 38:1–5; Joel 2:14; Jon. 3:9 [1] A few Hebrew manuscripts and Syriac read *God.* **12:23** [a] Gen. 37:35 [b] Job 7:8–10 **12:24** [a] Matt. 1:6 [b] 1 Chr. 22:9 [1] Following Kethib, Septuagint, and Vulgate; Qere, a few Hebrew manuscripts, Syriac, and Targum read *she.* **12:25** [1] Qere, some Hebrew manuscripts, Syriac, and Targum read *she.* [2] Literally *Beloved of the LORD* **12:26** [a] 1 Chr. 20:1 [b] Deut. 3:11; 2 Sam. 11:1

Joab sent messengers to David, and said, "I have fought against Rabbah, and I have taken the city's water *supply.* 28 Now therefore, gather the rest of the people together and encamp against the city and take it, lest I take the city and it be called after my name." 29 So David gathered all the people together and went to Rabbah, fought against it, and took it. 30 [a]Then he took their king's crown from his head. Its weight *was* a talent of gold, with precious stones. And it was *set* on David's head. Also he brought out the spoil of the city in great abundance. 31 And he brought out the people who *were* in it, and put *them to work* with saws and iron picks and iron axes, and made them cross over to the brick works. So he did to all the cities of the people of Ammon. Then David and all the people returned to Jerusalem.

### *AMNON AND TAMAR*

**13** After this [a]Absalom the son of David had a lovely sister, whose name *was* [b]Tamar; and [c]Amnon the son of David loved her. 2 Amnon was so distressed over his sister Tamar that he became sick; for she *was* a virgin. And it was improper for Amnon to do anything to her. 3 But Amnon had a friend whose name *was* Jonadab [a]the son of Shimeah, David's brother. Now Jonadab *was* a very crafty man. 4 And he said to him, "Why *are* you, the king's son, becoming thinner day after day? Will you not tell me?"

Amnon said to him, "I love Tamar, my brother Absalom's sister."

5 So Jonadab said to him, "Lie down on your bed and pretend to be ill. And when your father comes to see you, say to him, 'Please let my sister Tamar come and give me food, and prepare the food in my sight, that I may see *it* and eat it from her hand.' " 6 Then Amnon lay down and pretended to be ill; and when the king came to see him, Amnon said to the king, "Please let Tamar my sister come and [a]make a couple of cakes for me in my sight, that I may eat from her hand."

7 And David sent home to Tamar, saying, "Now go to your brother Amnon's house, and prepare food for him." 8 So Tamar went to her brother Amnon's house; and he was lying down. Then she took flour and kneaded *it,* made cakes in his sight, and baked the cakes. 9 And she took the pan and placed *them* out before him, but he refused to eat. Then Amnon said, [a]"Have everyone go out from me." And they all went out from him. 10 Then Amnon said to Tamar, "Bring the food into the bedroom, that I may eat from your hand." And Tamar took the cakes which she had made, and brought *them* to Amnon her brother in the bedroom. 11 Now when she had brought *them* to him to eat, [a]he took hold of her and said to her, "Come, lie with me, my sister."

12 But she answered him, "No, my brother, do not force me, for [a]no such thing should be done in Israel. Do not do this [b]disgraceful thing! 13 And I, where could I take my shame? And as for you, you would be like one of the fools in Israel. Now therefore, please speak to the king; [a]for he will not withhold me from you." 14 However, he would not heed her voice; and being stronger than she, he [a]forced her and lay with her.

15 Then Amnon hated her exceedingly, so that the hatred with which he hated her *was* greater than the love with which he had loved her. And Amnon said to her, "Arise, be gone!"

16 So she said to him, "No, indeed! This evil of sending me away *is* worse than the other that you did to me."

But he would not listen to her. 17 Then he called his servant who attended him, and said, "Here! Put this *woman* out, away from me, and bolt the door behind her." 18 Now she had on [a]a robe of many colors, for the king's virgin daughters wore such apparel. And his servant put her out and bolted the door behind her.

19 Then Tamar put [a]ashes on her head, and tore her robe of many colors that *was* on her, and [b]laid her hand on her head and went away crying bitterly. 20 And Absalom her brother said to her, "Has Amnon your brother been with you? But now hold your peace, my sister. He *is* your brother; do not take this thing to heart." So Tamar remained desolate in her brother Absalom's house.

> **13:19** In ancient times, people's clothing told a lot about them. Apparently, the style, color, or design of Tamar's robe indicated she was the daughter of the king and a virgin as well. After she was raped, she **tore her robe** and **put ashes on her head** to show her grief. This was the same thing people did to mourn the death of a loved one.

21 But when King David heard of all these things, he was very angry. 22 And Absalom spoke to his brother Amnon [a]neither good nor bad. For Absalom [b]hated Amnon, because he had forced his sister Tamar.

### *ABSALOM MURDERS AMNON*

23 And it came to pass, after two full years, that Absalom [a]had sheepshearers in Baal Hazor, which *is* near Ephraim; so Absalom invited all the king's sons. 24 Then Absalom came to the king and said, "Kindly note, your servant has sheepshearers; please, let the king and his servants go with your servant."

**12:30** [a] 1 Chr. 20:2 **13:1** [a] 2 Sam. 3:2, 3; 1 Chr. 3:2 [b] 1 Chr. 3:9 [c] 2 Sam. 3:2 **13:3** [a] 1 Sam. 16:9 **13:6** [a] Gen. 18:6 **13:9** [a] Gen. 45:1 **13:11** [a] Gen. 39:12; [Deut. 27:22]; Ezek. 22:11 **13:12** [a] [Lev. 18:9–11; 20:17] [b] Gen. 34:7; Judg. 19:23; 20:6 **13:13** [a] Gen. 20:12 **13:14** [a] Lev. 18:9; [Deut. 22:25; 27:22]; 2 Sam. 12:11 **13:18** [a] Gen. 37:3; Judg. 5:30; Ps. 45:13–14 **13:19** [a] Josh. 7:6; 2 Sam. 1:2; Job 2:12; 42:6 [b] Jer. 2:37 **13:22** [a] Gen. 24:50; 31:24 [b] [Lev. 19:17, 18; 1 John 2:9, 11; 3:10, 12, 15] **13:23** [a] Gen. 38:12, 13; 1 Sam. 25:4

25 But the king said to Absalom, "No, my son, let us not all go now, lest we be a burden to you." Then he urged him, but he would not go; and he blessed him.

26 Then Absalom said, "If not, please let my brother Amnon go with us."

And the king said to him, "Why should he go with you?" 27 But Absalom urged him; so he let Amnon and all the king's sons go with him.

28 Now Absalom had commanded his servants, saying, "Watch now, when Amnon's [a]heart is merry with wine, and when I say to you, 'Strike Amnon!' then kill him. Do not be afraid. Have I not commanded you? Be courageous and valiant." 29 So the servants of Absalom [a]did to Amnon as Absalom had commanded. Then all the king's sons arose, and each one got on [b]his mule and fled.

30 And it came to pass, while they were on the way, that news came to David, saying, "Absalom has killed all the king's sons, and not one of them is left!" 31 So the king arose and [a]tore his garments and [b]lay on the ground, and all his servants stood by with their clothes torn. 32 Then [a]Jonadab the son of Shimeah, David's brother, answered and said, "Let not my lord suppose they have killed all the young men, the king's sons, for only Amnon is dead. For by the command of Absalom this has been determined from the day that he forced his sister Tamar. 33 Now therefore, [a]let not my lord the king take the thing to his heart, to think that all the king's sons are dead. For only Amnon is dead."

### *ABSALOM FLEES TO GESHUR*

34 [a]Then Absalom fled. And the young man who was keeping watch lifted his eyes and looked, and there, many people were coming from the road on the hillside behind him.[1] 35 And Jonadab said to the king, "Look, the king's sons are coming; as your servant said, so it is." 36 So it was, as soon as he had finished speaking, that the king's sons indeed came, and they lifted up their voice and wept. Also the king and all his servants wept very bitterly.

37 But Absalom fled and went to [a]Talmai the son of Ammihud, king of Geshur. And *David* mourned for his son every day. 38 So Absalom fled and went to [a]Geshur, and was there three years. 39 And King David[1] longed to go to[2] Absalom. For he had been [a]comforted concerning Amnon, because he was dead.

### *ABSALOM RETURNS TO JERUSALEM*

**14** So Joab the son of Zeruiah perceived that the king's heart *was* concerned [a]about Absalom. 2 And Joab sent to [a]Tekoa and brought from there a wise woman, and said to her, "Please pretend to be a mourner, [b]and put on mourning apparel; do not anoint yourself with oil, but act like a woman who has been mourning a long time for the dead. 3 Go to the king and speak to him in this manner." So Joab [a]put the words in her mouth.

4 And when the woman of Tekoa spoke[1] to the king, she [a]fell on her face to the ground and prostrated herself, and said, [b]"Help, O king!"

5 Then the king said to her, "What troubles you?"

And she answered, [a]"Indeed I *am* a widow, my husband is dead. 6 Now your maidservant had two sons; and the two fought with each other in the field, and *there was* no one to part them, but the one struck the other and killed him. 7 And now the whole family has risen up against your maidservant, and they said, 'Deliver him who struck his brother, that we may execute him [a]for the life of his brother whom he killed; and we will destroy the heir also.' So they would extinguish my ember that is left, and leave to my husband *neither* name nor remnant on the earth."

8 Then the king said to the woman, "Go to your house, and I will give orders concerning you."

9 And the woman of Tekoa said to the king, "My lord, O king, *let* [a]the iniquity *be* on me and on my father's house, [b]and the king and his throne *be* guiltless."

10 So the king said, "Whoever says *anything* to you, bring him to me, and he shall not touch you anymore."

11 Then she said, "Please let the king remember the LORD your God, and do not permit [a]the avenger of blood to destroy anymore, lest they destroy my son."

And he said, [b]"*As* the LORD lives, not one hair of your son shall fall to the ground."

12 Therefore the woman said, "Please, let your maidservant speak *another* word to my lord the king."

And he said, "Say on."

13 So the woman said: "Why then have you schemed such a thing against [a]the people of God? For the king speaks this thing as one who is guilty, *in that* the king does not bring [b]his banished one home again. 14 For we [a]will surely die and *become* like water spilled on the ground, which cannot be gathered up again. Yet God does not [b]take away a life; but He [c]devises means, so

13:28 [a] Judg. 19:6, 9, 22; Ruth 3:7; 1 Sam. 25:36; Esth. 1:10 13:29 [a] 2 Sam. 12:10 [b] 2 Sam. 18:9; 1 Kin. 1:33, 38 13:31 [a] 2 Sam. 1:11 [b] 2 Sam. 12:16 13:32 [a] 2 Sam. 13:3–5 13:33 [a] 2 Sam. 19:19 13:34 [a] 2 Sam. 13:37, 38 [1] Septuagint adds *And the watchman went and told the king, and said, "I see men from the way of Horonaim, from the regions of the mountains."* 13:37 [a] 2 Sam. 3:3; 1 Chr. 3:2 13:38 [a] 2 Sam. 14:23, 32; 15:8 13:39 [a] Gen. 38:12; 2 Sam. 12:19, 23 [1] Following Masoretic Text, Syriac, and Vulgate; Septuagint reads *the spirit of the king;* Targum reads *the soul of King David.* [2] Following Masoretic Text and Targum; Septuagint and Vulgate read *ceased to pursue after.* 14:1 [a] 2 Sam. 13:39 14:2 [a] 2 Sam. 23:26; 2 Chr. 11:6; Amos 1:1 [b] Ruth 3:3 14:3 [a] Ex. 4:15; 2 Sam. 14:19 14:4 [a] 1 Sam. 20:41; 25:23; 2 Sam. 1:2 [b] 2 Kin. 6:26, 28 [1] Many Hebrew manuscripts, Septuagint, Syriac, and Vulgate read *came.* 14:5 [a] [Zech. 7:10] 14:7 [a] Num. 35:19; Deut. 19:12, 13 14:9 [a] Gen. 27:13; 43:9; 1 Sam. 25:24; Matt. 27:25 [b] 2 Sam. 3:28, 29; 1 Kin. 2:33 14:11 [a] Num. 35:19, 21; [Deut. 19:4–10] [b] 1 Sam. 14:45; 1 Kin. 1:52; Matt. 10:30; Acts 27:34 14:13 [a] Judg. 20:2 [b] 2 Sam. 13:37, 38 14:14 [a] Job 30:23; 34:15; [Heb. 9:27] [b] Job 34:19; Matt. 22:16; Acts 10:34; Rom. 2:11 [c] Num. 35:15

that His banished ones are not expelled from Him. 15 Now therefore, I have come to speak of this thing to my lord the king because the people have made me afraid. And your maidservant said, 'I will now speak to the king; it may be that the king will perform the request of his maidservant. 16 For the king will hear and deliver his maidservant from the hand of the man *who would* destroy me and my son together from the [a]inheritance of God.' 17 Your maidservant said, 'The word of my lord the king will now be comforting; for [a]as the angel of God, so *is* my lord the king in [b]discerning good and evil. And may the LORD your God be with you.' "

18 Then the king answered and said to the woman, "Please do not hide from me anything that I ask you."

And the woman said, "Please, let my lord the king speak."

19 So the king said, "*Is* the hand of Joab with you in all this?" And the woman answered and said, "*As* you live, my lord the king, no one can turn to the right hand or to the left from anything that my lord the king has spoken. For your servant Joab commanded me, and [a]he put all these words in the mouth of your maidservant. 20 To bring about this change of affairs your servant Joab has done this thing; but my lord *is* wise, [a]according to the wisdom of the angel of God, to know everything that *is* in the earth."

21 And the king said to Joab, "All right, I have granted this thing. Go therefore, bring back the young man Absalom."

22 Then Joab fell to the ground on his face and bowed himself, and thanked the king. And Joab said, "Today your servant knows that I have found favor in your sight, my lord, O king, in that the king has fulfilled the request of his servant." 23 So Joab arose [a]and went to Geshur, and brought Absalom to Jerusalem. 24 And the king said, "Let him return to his own house, but [a]do not let him see my face." So Absalom returned to his own house, but did not see the king's face.

### DAVID FORGIVES ABSALOM

25 Now in all Israel there was no one who was praised as much as Absalom for his good looks. [a]From the sole of his foot to the crown of his head there was no blemish in him. 26 And when he cut the hair of his head—at the end of every year he cut *it* because it was heavy on him—when he cut it, he weighed the hair of his head at two hundred shekels according to the king's standard. 27 [a]To Absalom were born three sons, and one daughter whose name *was* Tamar. She was a woman of beautiful appearance.

28 And Absalom dwelt two full years in Jerusalem, [a]but did not see the king's face. 29 Therefore Absalom sent for Joab, to send him to the king, but he would not come to him. And when he sent again the second time, he would not come. 30 So he said to his servants, "See, Joab's field is near mine, and he has barley there; go and set it on fire." And Absalom's servants set the field on fire.

31 Then Joab arose and came to Absalom's house, and said to him, "Why have your servants set my field on fire?"

32 And Absalom answered Joab, "Look, I sent to you, saying, 'Come here, so that I may send you to the king, to say, "Why have I come from Geshur? *It would be* better for me *to be* there still." ' Now therefore, let me see the king's face; but [a]if there is iniquity in me, let him execute me."

33 So Joab went to the king and told him. And when he had called for Absalom, he came to the king and bowed himself on his face to the ground before the king. Then the king [a]kissed Absalom.

### ABSALOM'S TREASON

15 After this [a]it happened that Absalom [b]provided himself with chariots and horses, and fifty men to run before him. 2 Now Absalom would rise early and stand beside the way to the gate. *So* it was, whenever anyone who had a [a]lawsuit came to the king for a decision, that Absalom would call to him and say, "What city *are* you from?" And he would say, "Your servant *is* from such and such a tribe of Israel." 3 Then Absalom would say to him, "Look, your case *is* good and right; but *there is* no deputy of the king to hear you." 4 Moreover Absalom would say, [a]"Oh, that I were made judge in the land, and everyone who has any suit or cause would come to me; then I would give him justice." 5 And *so* it was, whenever anyone came near to bow down to him, that he would put out his hand and take him and [a]kiss him. 6 In this manner Absalom acted toward all Israel who came to the king for judgment. [a]So Absalom stole the hearts of the men of Israel.

7 Now it came to pass [a]after forty[1] years that Absalom said to the king, "Please, let me go to [b]Hebron and pay the vow which I made to the LORD. 8 [a]For your servant [b]took a vow [c]while I dwelt at Geshur in Syria, saying, 'If the LORD indeed brings me back to Jerusalem, then I will serve the LORD.' "

9 And the king said to him, "Go in peace." So he arose and went to Hebron.

10 Then Absalom sent spies throughout all the tribes of Israel, saying, "As soon as you hear the sound of the trumpet, then you shall say,

14:16 [a] Deut. 32:9; 1 Sam. 26:19; 2 Sam. 20:19 14:17 [a] 1 Sam. 29:9; 2 Sam. 19:27 [b] 1 Kin. 3:9 14:19 [a] 2 Sam. 14:3 14:20 [a] 2 Sam. 14:17; 19:27 14:23 [a] 2 Sam. 13:37, 38 14:24 [a] Gen. 43:3; 2 Sam. 3:13 14:25 [a] Deut. 28:35; Job 2:7; Is. 1:6 14:27 [a] 2 Sam. 13:1; 18:18 14:28 [a] 2 Sam. 14:24 14:32 [a] 1 Sam. 20:8; [Prov. 28:13] 14:33 [a] Gen. 33:4; 45:15; Luke 15:20 15:1 [a] 2 Sam. 12:11 [b] 1 Kin. 1:5 15:2 [a] Deut. 19:17 15:4 [a] Judg. 9:29 15:5 [a] 2 Sam. 14:33; 20:9 15:6 [a] [Rom. 16:18] 15:7 [a] [Deut. 23:21] [b] 2 Sam. 3:2, 3

[1] Septuagint manuscripts, Syriac, and Josephus read *four.* 15:8 [a] 1 Sam. 16:2 [b] Gen. 28:20, 21 [c] 2 Sam. 13:38

'Absalom [a]reigns in Hebron!' " 11 And with Absalom went two hundred men [a]invited from Jerusalem, and they [b]went along innocently and did not know anything. 12 Then Absalom sent for Ahithophel the Gilonite, [a]David's counselor, from his city—from [b]Giloh—while he offered sacrifices. And the conspiracy grew strong, for the people with Absalom [c]continually increased in number.

### *DAVID ESCAPES FROM JERUSALEM*

13 Now a messenger came to David, saying, [a]"The hearts of the men of Israel are with Absalom."

14 So David said to all his servants who *were* with him at Jerusalem, "Arise, and let us [a]flee, or we shall not escape from Absalom. Make haste to depart, lest he overtake us suddenly and bring disaster upon us, and strike the city with the edge of the sword."

15 And the king's servants said to the king, "We *are* your servants, *ready to do* whatever my lord the king commands." 16 Then [a]the king went out with all his household after him. But the king left [b]ten women, concubines, to keep the house. 17 And the king went out with all the people after him, and stopped at the outskirts. 18 Then all his servants passed before him; [a]and all the Cherethites, all the Pelethites, and all the Gittites, [b]six hundred men who had followed him from Gath, passed before the king.

19 Then the king said to [a]Ittai the Gittite, "Why are you also going with us? Return and remain with the king. For you *are* a foreigner and also an exile from your own place. 20 In fact, you came *only* yesterday. Should I make you wander up and down with us today, since I go [a]I know not where? Return, and take your brethren back. Mercy and truth *be* with you."

21 But Ittai answered the king and said, [a]"*As* the LORD lives, and *as* my lord the king lives, surely in whatever place my lord the king shall be, whether in death or life, even there also your servant will be."

22 So David said to Ittai, "Go, and cross over." Then Ittai the Gittite and all his men and all the little ones who *were* with him crossed over. 23 And all the country wept with a loud voice, and all the people crossed over. The king himself also crossed over the Brook Kidron, and all the people crossed over toward the way of the [a]wilderness.

24 There was [a]Zadok also, and all the Levites with him, bearing the [b]ark of the covenant of God. And they set down the ark of God, and [c]Abiathar went up until all the people had finished crossing over from the city. 25 Then the king said to Zadok, "Carry the ark of God back into the city. If I find favor in the eyes of the LORD, He [a]will bring me back and show me *both* it and [b]His dwelling place. 26 But if He says thus: 'I have no [a]delight in you,' here I am, [b]let Him do to me as seems good to Him." 27 The king also said to Zadok the priest, "*Are* you *not* a [a]seer? Return to the city in peace, and [b]your two sons with you, Ahimaaz your son, and Jonathan the son of Abiathar. 28 See, [a]I will wait in the plains of the wilderness until word comes from you to inform me." 29 Therefore Zadok and Abiathar carried the ark of God back to Jerusalem. And they remained there.

30 So David went up by the Ascent of the *Mount of* Olives, and wept as he went up; and he [a]had his head covered and went [b]barefoot. And all the people who *were* with him [c]covered their heads and went up, [d]weeping as they went up. 31 Then *someone* told David, saying, [a]"Ahithophel *is* among the conspirators with Absalom." And David said, "O LORD, I pray, [b]turn the counsel of Ahithophel into foolishness!"

32 Now it happened when David had come to the top *of the mountain,* where he worshiped God—there was Hushai the [a]Archite coming to meet him [b]with his robe torn and dust on his head. 33 David said to him, "If you go on with me, then you will become [a]a burden to me. 34 But if you return to the city, and say to Absalom, [a]'I will be your servant, O king; *as* I *was* your father's servant previously, so I *will* now also *be* your servant,' then you may defeat the counsel of Ahithophel for me. 35 And *do* you not *have* Zadok and Abiathar the priests with you there? Therefore it will be *that* whatever you hear from the king's house, you shall tell to [a]Zadok and Abiathar the priests. 36 Indeed *they have* there [a]with them their two sons, Ahimaaz, Zadok's *son,* and Jonathan, Abiathar's *son;* and by them you shall send me everything you hear."

37 So Hushai, [a]David's friend, went into the city. [b]And Absalom came into Jerusalem.

**15:24 The ark of the covenant** contained the two flat stones on which God wrote the Ten Commandments. The ark was the centerpiece of Israel's worship of God. It had been captured once before in a war against the Philistines. The result was disaster for both the Philistines and the Israelites. David did not want to risk losing it again.

**15:10** [a] 1 Kin. 1:34; 2 Kin. 9:13 **15:11** [a] 1 Sam. 16:3, 5 [b] Gen. 20:5 **15:12** [a] 2 Sam. 16:15; 1 Chr. 27:33; Ps. 41:9; 55:12–14 [b] Josh. 15:51 [c] Ps. 3:1 **15:13** [a] Judg. 9:3; 2 Sam. 15:6 **15:14** [a] 2 Sam. 12:11; Ps. 3:title **15:16** [a] Ps. 3:title [b] 2 Sam. 12:11; 16:21, 22 **15:18** [a] 2 Sam. 8:18 [b] 1 Sam. 23:13; 25:13; 30:1, 9 **15:19** [a] 2 Sam. 18:2 **15:20** [a] 1 Sam. 23:13 **15:21** [a] Ruth 1:16, 17; [Prov. 17:17] **15:23** [a] 2 Sam. 15:28; 16:2 **15:24** [a] 2 Sam. 8:17 [b] Num. 4:15; 1 Sam. 4:4 [c] 1 Sam. 22:20 **15:25** [a] [Ps. 43:3] [b] Ex. 15:13; Jer. 25:30 **15:26** [a] Num. 14:8; 2 Sam. 22:20; 1 Kin. 10:9; 2 Chr. 9:8; Is. 62:4 [b] 1 Sam. 3:18 **15:27** [a] 1 Sam. 9:6–9 [b] 2 Sam. 17:17–20 **15:28** [a] Josh. 5:10; 2 Sam. 17:16 **15:30** [a] 2 Sam. 19:4; Esth. 6:12; Ezek. 24:17, 23 [b] Is. 20:2–4 [c] Jer. 14:3, 4 [d] [Ps. 126:6] **15:31** [a] Ps. 3:1, 2; 55:12 [b] 2 Sam. 16:23; 17:14, 23 **15:32** [a] Josh. 16:2 [b] 2 Sam. 1:2 **15:33** [a] 2 Sam. 19:35 **15:34** [a] 2 Sam. 16:19 **15:35** [a] 2 Sam. 17:15, 16 **15:36** [a] 2 Sam. 15:27 **15:37** [a] 2 Sam. 16:16; 1 Chr. 27:33 [b] 2 Sam. 16:15

### *MEPHIBOSHETH'S SERVANT*

**16** When[a] David was a little past the top *of
the mountain,* there was [b]Ziba the servant
of Mephibosheth, who met him with a couple
of saddled donkeys, and on them two hundred
*loaves* of bread, one hundred clusters of raisins,
one hundred summer fruits, and a skin of wine.
2 And the king said to Ziba, "What do you mean
to do with these?"

So Ziba said, "The donkeys *are* for the king's
household to ride on, the bread and summer
fruit for the young men to eat, and the wine for
[a]those who are faint in the wilderness to drink."
3 Then the king said, "And where *is* your
[a]master's son?"

[b]And Ziba said to the king, "Indeed he is
staying in Jerusalem, for he said, 'Today the
house of Israel will restore the kingdom of my
father to me.'"

4 So the king said to Ziba, "Here, all that *be-
longs* to Mephibosheth *is* yours."

And Ziba said, "I humbly bow before you,
*that* I may find favor in your sight, my lord,
O king!"

### *SHIMEI CURSES DAVID*

5 Now when King David came to [a]Bahurim,
there was a man from the family of the house of
Saul, whose name *was* [b]Shimei the son of Gera,
coming from there. He came out, cursing con-
tinuously as he came. 6 And he threw stones at
David and at all the servants of King David. And
all the people and all the mighty men *were* on
his right hand and on his left. 7 Also Shimei said
thus when he cursed: "Come out! Come out! You
bloodthirsty man, [a]you rogue! 8 The LORD has
[a]brought upon you all [b]the blood of the house of
Saul, in whose place you have reigned; and the
LORD has delivered the kingdom into the hand of
Absalom your son. So now you *are caught* in your
own evil, because you are a bloodthirsty man!"
9 Then Abishai the son of Zeruiah said to
the king, "Why should this [a]dead dog [b]curse
my lord the king? Please, let me go over and
take off his head!"
10 But the king said, [a]"What have I to do with
you, you sons of Zeruiah? So let him curse, be-
cause [b]the LORD has said to him, 'Curse David.'
[c]Who then shall say, 'Why have you done so?'"
11 And David said to Abishai and all his ser-
vants, "See how [a]my son who [b]came from my
own body seeks my life. How much more now
*may this* Benjamite? Let him alone, and let him
curse; for so the LORD has ordered him. 12 It may
be that the LORD will look on my affliction,[1] and
that the LORD will [a]repay me with [b]good for his
cursing this day." 13 And as David and his men
went along the road, Shimei went along the hill-
side opposite him and cursed as he went, threw
stones at him and kicked up dust. 14 Now the king
and all the people who *were* with him became
weary; so they refreshed themselves there.

### *THE ADVICE OF AHITHOPHEL*

15 Meanwhile [a]Absalom and all the people,
the men of Israel, came to Jerusalem; and Ahith-
ophel *was* with him. 16 And so it was, when Hu-
shai the Archite, [a]David's friend, came to Absa-
lom, that [b]Hushai said to Absalom, "*Long* live
the king! *Long* live the king!"
17 So Absalom said to Hushai, "*Is* this your
loyalty to your friend? [a]Why did you not go with
your friend?"
18 And Hushai said to Absalom, "No, but
whom the LORD and this people and all the men
of Israel choose, his I will be, and with him I will
remain. 19 Furthermore, [a]whom should I serve?
*Should I* not *serve* in the presence of his son? As
I have served in your father's presence, so will
I be in your presence."
20 Then Absalom said to [a]Ahithophel, "Give
advice as to what we should do."
21 And Ahithophel said to Absalom, "Go in to
your father's [a]concubines, whom he has left to
keep the house; and all Israel will hear that you
[b]are abhorred by your father. Then [c]the hands
of all who are with you will be strong." 22 So
they pitched a tent for Absalom on the top of
the house, and Absalom went in to his father's
concubines [a]in the sight of all Israel.

> **16:21** The **concubines** David left behind to take care of the palace could have been more like servants than wives. Because they "belonged" to David, though, it was a tremendous insult for Absalom to sleep with them. It was also a way for Absalom to show he intended to take over his father's throne.

23 Now the advice of Ahithophel, which he
gave in those days, *was* as if one had inquired
at the oracle of God. So *was* all the advice of
Ahithophel [a]both with David and with Absalom.

**17** Moreover Ahithophel said to Absalom,
"Now let me choose twelve thousand men,
and I will arise and pursue David tonight. 2 I will
come upon him while he *is* [a]weary and weak,
and make him afraid. And all the people who

**16:1** [a] 2 Sam. 15:30, 32 [b] 2 Sam. 9:2; 19:17, 29 **16:2** [a] 2 Sam. 15:23; 17:29 **16:3** [a] 2 Sam. 9:9, 10 [b] 2 Sam. 19:27 **16:5** [a] 2 Sam. 3:16 [b] 2 Sam. 19:21; 1 Kin. 2:8, 9, 44–46 **16:7** [a] Deut. 13:13 **16:8** [a] Judg. 9:24, 56, 57; 1 Kin. 2:32, 33 [b] 2 Sam. 1:16; 3:28, 29; 4:11, 12 **16:9** [a] 1 Sam. 24:14; 2 Sam. 9:8 [b] Ex. 22:28 **16:10** [a] 2 Sam. 3:39; 19:22; [1 Pet. 2:23] [b] 2 Kin. 18:25; [Lam. 3:38] [c] [Rom. 9:20] **16:11** [a] 2 Sam. 12:11 [b] Gen. 15:4 **16:12** [a] Deut. 23:5; Neh. 13:2; Prov. 20:22 [b] Deut. 23:5; [Rom. 8:28; Heb. 12:10, 11] [1] Following Kethib, Septuagint, Syriac, and Vulgate; Qere reads *my eyes;* Targum reads *tears of my eyes.* **16:15** [a] 2 Sam. 15:12, 37 **16:16** [a] 2 Sam. 15:37 [b] 2 Sam. 15:34 **16:17** [a] 2 Sam. 19:25; [Prov. 17:17] **16:19** [a] 2 Sam. 15:34 **16:20** [a] 2 Sam. 15:12 **16:21** [a] 2 Sam. 15:16; 20:3 [b] Gen. 34:30; 1 Sam. 13:4 [c] 2 Sam. 2:7; Zech. 8:13 **16:22** [a] 2 Sam. 12:11, 12 **16:23** [a] 2 Sam. 15:12 **17:2** [a] Deut. 25:18; 2 Sam. 16:14

*are* with him will flee, and I will [b]strike only the king. 3 Then I will bring back all the people to you. When all return except the man whom you seek, all the people will be at peace." 4 And the saying pleased Absalom and all the [a]elders of Israel.

### *THE ADVICE OF HUSHAI*

5 Then Absalom said, "Now call Hushai the Archite also, and let us hear what he [a]says too." 6 And when Hushai came to Absalom, Absalom spoke to him, saying, "Ahithophel has spoken in this manner. Shall we do as he says? If not, speak up."

7 So Hushai said to Absalom: "The advice that Ahithophel has given *is* not good at this time. 8 For," said Hushai, "you know your father and his men, that they *are* mighty men, and they *are* enraged in their minds, like [a]a bear robbed of her cubs in the field; and your father *is* a man of war, and will not camp with the people. 9 Surely by now he is hidden in some pit, or in some *other* place. And it will be, when some of them are overthrown at the first, that whoever hears *it* will say, 'There is a slaughter among the people who follow Absalom.' 10 And even he *who is* valiant, whose heart *is* like the heart of a lion, will [a]melt completely. For all Israel knows that your father *is* a mighty man, and *those* who *are* with him *are* valiant men. 11 Therefore I advise that all Israel be fully gathered to you, [a]from Dan to Beersheba, [b]like the sand that *is* by the sea for multitude, and that you go to battle in person. 12 So we will come upon him in some place where he may be found, and we will fall on him as the dew falls on the ground. And of him and all the men who *are* with him there shall not be left so much as one. 13 Moreover, if he has withdrawn into a city, then all Israel shall bring ropes to that city; and we will [a]pull it into the river, until there is not one small stone found there."

14 So Absalom and all the men of Israel said, "The advice of Hushai the Archite *is* better than the advice of Ahithophel." For [a]the LORD had purposed to defeat the good advice of Ahithophel, to the intent that the LORD might bring disaster on Absalom.

### *HUSHAI WARNS DAVID TO ESCAPE*

15 [a]Then Hushai said to Zadok and Abiathar the priests, "Thus and so Ahithophel advised Absalom and the elders of Israel, and thus and so I have advised. 16 Now therefore, send quickly and tell David, saying, 'Do not spend this night [a]in the plains of the wilderness, but speedily cross over, lest the king and all the people who *are* with him be swallowed up.' " 17 [a]Now Jonathan and Ahimaaz [b]stayed at [c]En Rogel, for they dared not be seen coming into the city; so a female servant would come and tell them, and they would go and tell King David. 18 Nevertheless a lad saw them, and told Absalom. But both of them went away quickly and came to a man's house [a]in Bahurim, who had a well in his court; and they went down into it. 19 [a]Then the woman took and spread a covering over the well's mouth, and spread ground grain on it; and the thing was not known. 20 And when Absalom's servants came to the woman at the house, they said, "Where *are* Ahimaaz and Jonathan?"

So [a]the woman said to them, "They have gone over the water brook."

And when they had searched and could not find *them,* they returned to Jerusalem. 21 Now it came to pass, after they had departed, that they came up out of the well and went and told King David, and said to David, [a]"Arise and cross over the water quickly. For thus has Ahithophel advised against you." 22 So David and all the people who *were* with him arose and crossed over the Jordan. By morning light not one of them was left who had not gone over the Jordan.

23 Now when Ahithophel saw that his advice was not followed, he saddled a donkey, and arose and went home to [a]his house, to his city. Then he put his [b]household in order, and [c]hanged himself, and died; and he was buried in his father's tomb.

24 Then David went to [a]Mahanaim. And Absalom crossed over the Jordan, he and all the men of Israel with him. 25 And Absalom made [a]Amasa captain of the army instead of Joab. This Amasa *was* the son of a man whose name *was* Jithra,[1] an Israelite,[2] who had gone in to [b]Abigail the daughter of Nahash, sister of Zeruiah, Joab's mother. 26 So Israel and Absalom encamped in the land of Gilead.

27 Now it happened, when David had come to Mahanaim, that [a]Shobi the son of Nahash from Rabbah of the people of Ammon, [b]Machir the son of Ammiel from Lo Debar, and [c]Barzillai the Gileadite from Rogelim, 28 brought beds and basins, earthen vessels and wheat, barley and flour, parched *grain* and beans, lentils and parched *seeds,* 29 honey and curds, sheep and cheese of the herd, for David and the people who *were* with him to eat. For they said, "The people are hungry and weary and thirsty [a]in the wilderness."

**17:2** [b] Zech. 13:7 **17:4** [a] 2 Sam. 5:3; 19:11 **17:5** [a] 2 Sam. 15:32–34 **17:8** [a] Hos. 13:8 **17:10** [a] Josh. 2:11 **17:11** [a] Judg. 20:1; 2 Sam. 3:10 [b] Gen. 22:17; Josh. 11:4; 1 Kin. 20:10 **17:13** [a] Mic. 1:6 **17:14** [a] 2 Sam. 15:31, 34 **17:15** [a] 2 Sam. 15:35, 36 **17:16** [a] 2 Sam. 15:28 **17:17** [a] 2 Sam. 15:27, 36; 1 Kin. 1:42, 43 [b] Josh. 2:4–6 [c] Josh. 15:7; 18:16 **17:18** [a] 2 Sam. 3:16; 16:5 **17:19** [a] Josh. 2:4–6 **17:20** [a] Ex. 1:19; [Lev. 19:11]; Josh. 2:3–5 **17:21** [a] 2 Sam. 17:15, 16 **17:23** [a] 2 Sam. 15:12 [b] 2 Kin. 20:1 [c] Matt. 27:5 **17:24** [a] Gen. 32:2; Josh. 13:26; 2 Sam. 2:8; 19:32 **17:25** [a] 2 Sam. 19:13; 20:9–12; 1 Kin. 2:5, 32 [b] 1 Chr. 2:16 [1] Spelled *Jether* in 1 Chronicles 2:17 and elsewhere [2] Following Masoretic Text, some manuscripts of the Septuagint, and Targum; some manuscripts of the Septuagint read *Ishmaelite* (compare 1 Chronicles 2:17); Vulgate reads *of Jezrael.* **17:27** [a] 1 Sam. 11:1; 2 Sam. 10:1; 12:29 [b] 2 Sam. 9:4 [c] 2 Sam. 19:31, 32; 1 Kin. 2:7 **17:29** [a] 2 Sam. 16:2, 14

### *ABSALOM'S DEFEAT AND DEATH*

**18** And David numbered the people who *were*
with him, and [a]set captains of thousands
and captains of hundreds over them. 2 Then
David sent out one third of the people under
the hand of Joab, [a]one third under the hand of
Abishai the son of Zeruiah, Joab's brother, and
one third under the hand of [b]Ittai the Gittite. And
the king said to the people, "I also will surely go
out with you myself."

3 [a]But the people answered, "You shall not go
out! For if we flee away, they will not care about
us; nor if half of us die, will they care about us.
But *you are* worth ten thousand of us now. For
you are now more help to us in the city."

4 Then the king said to them, "Whatever
seems best to you I will do." So the king stood
beside the gate, and all the people went out by
hundreds and by thousands. 5 Now the king had
commanded Joab, Abishai, and Ittai, saying,
"*Deal* gently for my sake with the young man
Absalom." [a]And all the people heard when the
king gave all the captains orders concerning
Absalom.

6 So the people went out into the field of
battle against Israel. And the battle was in the
[a]woods of Ephraim. 7 The people of Israel were
overthrown there before the servants of David,
and a great slaughter of twenty thousand took
place there that day. 8 For the battle there was
scattered over the face of the whole countryside,
and the woods devoured more people that day
than the sword devoured.

9 Then Absalom met the servants of David.
Absalom rode on a mule. The mule went under
the thick boughs of a great terebinth tree, and
[a]his head caught in the terebinth; so he was
left hanging between heaven and earth. And
the mule which *was* under him went on. 10 Now
a certain man saw *it* and told Joab, and said, "I
just saw Absalom hanging in a terebinth tree!"

11 So Joab said to the man who told him, "You
just saw *him!* And why did you not strike him
there to the ground? I would have given you ten
*shekels* of silver and a belt."

12 But the man said to Joab, "Though I were to
receive a thousand *shekels* of silver in my hand,
I would not raise my hand against the king's
son. [a]For in our hearing the king commanded
you and Abishai and Ittai, saying, 'Beware lest
anyone *touch* the young man Absalom!'[1] 13 Oth-
erwise I would have dealt falsely against my
own life. For there is nothing hidden from the
king, and you yourself would have set yourself
against *me*."

14 Then Joab said, "I cannot linger with you."
And he took three spears in his hand and thrust
them through Absalom's heart, while he was *still*
alive in the midst of the terebinth tree. 15 And ten
young men who bore Joab's armor surrounded
Absalom, and struck and killed him.

16 So Joab blew the trumpet, and the people
returned from pursuing Israel. For Joab held
back the people. 17 And they took Absalom and
cast him into a large pit in the woods, and [a]laid
a very large heap of stones over him. Then all
Israel [b]fled, everyone to his tent.

18 Now Absalom in his lifetime had taken
and set up a pillar for himself, which *is* in [a]the
King's Valley. For he said, [b]"I have no son to keep
my name in remembrance." He called the pillar
after his own name. And to this day it is called
Absalom's Monument.

### *DAVID HEARS OF ABSALOM'S DEATH*

19 Then [a]Ahimaaz the son of Zadok said, "Let
me run now and take the news to the king, how
the LORD has avenged him of his enemies."

20 And Joab said to him, "You shall not take
the news this day, for you shall take the news
another day. But today you shall take no news,
because the king's son is dead." 21 Then Joab
said to the Cushite, "Go, tell the king what you
have seen." So the Cushite bowed himself to
Joab and ran.

22 And Ahimaaz the son of Zadok said again
to Joab, "But whatever happens, please let me
also run after the Cushite."

So Joab said, "Why will you run, my son,
since you have no news ready?"

23 "But whatever happens," *he said,* "let me
run."

So he said to him, "Run." Then Ahimaaz
ran by way of the plain, and outran the Cushite.

24 Now David was sitting between the [a]two
gates. And the watchman went up to the roof over
the gate, to the wall, lifted his eyes and looked,
and there was a man, running alone. 25 Then
the watchman cried out and told the king. And
the king said, "If he *is* alone, *there is* news in his
mouth." And he came rapidly and drew near.

26 Then the watchman saw *another* man run-
ning, and the watchman called to the gatekeeper
and said, "There is *another* man, running alone!"
And the king said, "He also brings news."

27 So the watchman said, "I think the running
of the first is like the running of Ahimaaz the
son of Zadok."

And the king said, "He *is* a good man, and
comes with [a]good news."

28 So Ahimaaz called out and said to the
king, "All is well!" Then he bowed down with
his face to the earth before the king, and said,
[a]"Blessed *be* the LORD your God, who has deliv-
ered up the men who raised their hand against
my lord the king!"

29 The king said, "Is the young man Absa-
lom safe?"

**18:1** [a] Ex. 18:25; Num. 31:14; 1 Sam. 22:7 **18:2** [a] Judg. 7:16; 1 Sam. 11:11 [b] 2 Sam. 15:19–22 **18:3** [a] 2 Sam. 21:17 **18:5** [a] 2 Sam. 18:12 **18:6** [a] Josh. 17:15, 18; 2 Sam. 17:26 **18:9** [a] 2 Sam. 14:26 **18:12** [a] 2 Sam. 18:5 [1] The ancient versions read *'Protect the young man Absalom for me!'* **18:17** [a] Deut. 21:20, 21; Josh. 7:26; 8:29 [b] 2 Sam. 19:8; 20:1, 22 **18:18** [a] Gen. 14:17 [b] 2 Sam. 14:27 **18:19** [a] 2 Sam. 15:36; 17:17 **18:24** [a] Judg. 5:11; 2 Sam. 13:34; 2 Kin. 9:17 **18:27** [a] 1 Kin. 1:42 **18:28** [a] 2 Sam. 16:12

APPLY THE TRUTH

## GRIEF

**18:19–33** What's the most difficult thing you've ever done in your life? Accomplishing a specific goal? Making a difficult decision? Resolving a conflict with someone? We all experience difficulty, but loss is probably the most challenging thing we face. Loss is usually accompanied by grief, a deep, sometimes prolonged, sorrow or sadness. Grief is painful because we know we will never get back what was lost. Grief wants to rob us of the joy we've experienced and convince us we'll never get it back. When we stare into the darkness of grief, how can we move forward? Will we ever not feel the sorrow?

King David had just lost another son. He was heartbroken. But, in time, he found joy again. Like David, we must allow time to grieve and process. We rejoice in what we had, be present with those around us, and trust that God is with us as we move forward. Difficult or even impossible things to face become possible when we trust that our good, loving God holds us in His hands. Sorrow may come in the night, but joy comes in the morning.

Ahimaaz answered, "When Joab sent the
king's servant and *me* your servant, I saw a great
tumult, but I did not know what *it was about.*"
30 And the king said, "Turn aside *and* stand
here." So he turned aside and stood still.
31 Just then the Cushite came, and the Cush-
ite said, "There is good news, my lord the king!
For the LORD has avenged you this day of all
those who rose against you."
32 And the king said to the Cushite, "Is the
young man Absalom safe?"

So the Cushite answered, "May the enemies
of my lord the king, and all who rise against you
to do harm, be like *that* young man!"

### DAVID'S MOURNING FOR ABSALOM

33 Then the king was deeply moved, and went
up to the chamber over the gate, and wept. And
as he went, he said thus: [a]"O my son Absalom—
my son, my son Absalom—if only I had died in
your place! O Absalom my son, [b]my son!"

19 And Joab was told, "Behold, the king is
weeping and [a]mourning for Absalom." 2 So
the victory that day was *turned* into [a]mourning
for all the people. For the people heard it said
that day, "The king is grieved for his son." 3 And
the people stole back [a]into the city that day, as
people who are ashamed steal away when they
flee in battle. 4 But the king [a]covered his face, and
the king cried out with a loud voice, [b]"O my son
Absalom! O Absalom, my son, my son!"

5 Then [a]Joab came into the house to the
king, and said, "Today you have disgraced all
your servants who today have saved your life,
the lives of your sons and daughters, the lives
of your wives and the lives of your concubines,
6 in that you love your enemies and hate your
friends. For you have declared today that you
regard neither princes nor servants; for today I
perceive that if Absalom had lived and all of us
had died today, then it would have pleased you
well. 7 Now therefore, arise, go out and speak
comfort to your servants. For I swear by the
LORD, if you do not go out, not one will stay with
you this night. And that will be worse for you
than all the evil that has befallen you from your
youth until now." 8 Then the king arose and sat
in the [a]gate. And they told all the people, saying,
"There is the king, sitting in the gate." So all the
people came before the king.

For everyone of Israel had [b]fled to his tent.

### DAVID RETURNS TO JERUSALEM

9 Now all the people were in a dispute
throughout all the tribes of Israel, saying, "The
king saved us from the hand of our [a]enemies, he
delivered us from the hand of the [b]Philistines,
and now he has [c]fled from the land because of
Absalom. 10 But Absalom, whom we anointed
over us, has died in battle. Now therefore, why do
you say nothing about bringing back the king?"
11 So King David sent to [a]Zadok and Abia-
thar the priests, saying, "Speak to the elders of
Judah, saying, 'Why are you the last to bring
the king back to his house, since the words
of all Israel have come to the king, to his *very*
house? 12 You *are* my brethren, you *are* [a]my
bone and my flesh. Why then are you the last to
bring back the king?' 13 [a]And say to Amasa, '*Are*
you not my bone and my flesh? [b]God do so to
me, and more also, if you are not commander
of the army before me continually in place of
Joab.' " 14 So he swayed the hearts of all the men
of Judah, [a]just as *the heart of* one man, so that
they sent *this word* to the king: "Return, you
and all your servants!"

15 Then the king returned and came to the
Jordan. And Judah came to [a]Gilgal, to go to meet
the king, to escort the king [b]across the Jordan.
16 And [a]Shimei the son of Gera, a Benjamite, who

18:33 [a] 2 Sam. 12:10 [b] 2 Sam. 19:4 19:1 [a] Jer. 14:2 19:2 [a] Esth. 4:3 19:3 [a] 2 Sam. 17:24, 27; 19:32 19:4 [a] 2 Sam. 15:30 [b] 2 Sam. 18:33 19:5 [a] 2 Sam. 18:14 19:8 [a] 2 Sam. 15:2; 18:24 [b] 2 Sam. 18:17 19:9 [a] 2 Sam. 8:1–14 [b] 2 Sam. 3:18 [c] 2 Sam. 15:14 19:11 [a] 2 Sam. 15:24 19:12 [a] 2 Sam. 5:1; 1 Chr. 11:1 19:13 [a] 2 Sam. 17:25; 1 Chr. 2:17 [b] Ruth 1:17 19:14 [a] Judg. 20:1 19:15 [a] Josh. 5:9; 1 Sam. 11:14, 15 [b] 2 Sam. 17:22 19:16 [a] 2 Sam. 16:5; 1 Kin. 2:8

*was* from Bahurim, hurried and came down with the men of Judah to meet King David. 17 *There were* a thousand men of [a]Benjamin with him, and [b]Ziba the servant of the house of Saul, and his fifteen sons and his twenty servants with him; and they went over the Jordan before the king. 18 Then a ferryboat went across to carry over the king's household, and to do what he thought good.

### DAVID'S MERCY TO SHIMEI

Now Shimei the son of Gera fell down before the king when he had crossed the Jordan. 19 Then he said to the king, [a]"Do not let my lord impute iniquity to me, or remember what [b]wrong your servant did on the day that my lord the king left Jerusalem, that the king should [c]take *it* to heart. 20 For I, your servant, know that I have sinned. Therefore here I am, the first to come today of all [a]the house of Joseph to go down to meet my lord the king."

21 But Abishai the son of Zeruiah answered and said, "Shall not Shimei be put to death for this, [a]because he [b]cursed the LORD's anointed?"

22 And David said, [a]"What have I to do with you, you sons of Zeruiah, that you should be adversaries to me today? [b]Shall any man be put to death today in Israel? For do I not know that today I *am* king over Israel?" 23 Therefore [a]the king said to Shimei, "You shall not die." And the king swore to him.

### DAVID AND MEPHIBOSHETH MEET

24 Now [a]Mephibosheth the son of Saul came down to meet the king. And he had not cared for his feet, nor trimmed his mustache, nor washed his clothes, from the day the king departed until the day he returned in peace. 25 So it was, when he had come to Jerusalem to meet the king, that the king said to him, [a]"Why did you not go with me, Mephibosheth?"

26 And he answered, "My lord, O king, my servant deceived me. For your servant said, 'I will saddle a donkey for myself, that I may ride on it and go to the king,' because your servant *is* lame. 27 And [a]he has slandered your servant to my lord the king, [b]but my lord the king *is* like the angel of God. Therefore do *what is* good in your eyes. 28 For all my father's house were but dead men before my lord the king. [a]Yet you set your servant among those who eat at your own table. Therefore what right have I still to cry out anymore to the king?"

29 So the king said to him, "Why do you speak anymore of your matters? I have said, 'You and Ziba divide the land.' "

30 Then Mephibosheth said to the king, "Rather, let him take it all, inasmuch as my lord the king has come back in peace to his own house."

### DAVID'S KINDNESS TO BARZILLAI

31 And [a]Barzillai the Gileadite came down from Rogelim and went across the Jordan with the king, to escort him across the Jordan. 32 Now Barzillai was a very aged man, eighty years old. And [a]he had provided the king with supplies while he stayed at Mahanaim, for he *was* a very rich man. 33 And the king said to Barzillai, "Come across with me, and I will provide for you while you are with me in Jerusalem."

34 But Barzillai said to the king, "How long have I to live, that I should go up with the king to Jerusalem? 35 I *am* today [a]eighty years old. Can I discern between the good and bad? Can your servant taste what I eat or what I drink? Can I hear any longer the voice of singing men and singing women? Why then should your servant be a further burden to my lord the king? 36 Your servant will go a little way across the Jordan with the king. And why should the king repay me *with* such a reward? 37 Please let your servant turn back again, that I may die in my own city, near the grave of my father and mother. But here is your servant [a]Chimham; let him cross over with my lord the king, and do for him what seems good to you."

38 And the king answered, "Chimham shall cross over with me, and I will do for him what seems good to you. Now whatever you request of me, I will do for you." 39 Then all the people went over the Jordan. And when the king had crossed over, the king [a]kissed Barzillai and blessed him, and he returned to his own place.

### THE QUARREL ABOUT THE KING

40 Now the king went on to Gilgal, and Chimham[1] went on with him. And all the people of Judah escorted the king, and also half the people of Israel. 41 Just then all the men of Israel came to the king, and said to the king, "Why have our brethren, the men of Judah, stolen you away and [a]brought the king, his household, and all David's men with him across the Jordan?"

42 So all the men of Judah answered the men of Israel, "Because the king *is* [a]a close relative of ours. Why then are you angry over this matter? Have we ever eaten at the king's *expense?* Or has he given us any gift?"

43 And the men of Israel answered the men of Judah, and said, "We have [a]ten shares in the king; therefore we also have more *right* to David than you. Why then do you despise us—were we not the first to advise bringing back our king?"

Yet [b]the words of the men of Judah were fiercer than the words of the men of Israel.

**19:17** [a] 2 Sam. 3:19; 1 Kin. 12:21 [b] 2 Sam. 9:2, 10; 16:1, 2 **19:19** [a] 1 Sam. 22:15 [b] 2 Sam. 16:5, 6 [c] 2 Sam. 13:33 **19:20** [a] Judg. 1:22; 1 Kin. 11:28 **19:21** [a] [Ex. 22:28] [b] [1 Sam. 26:9] **19:22** [a] 2 Sam. 3:39; 16:10 [b] 1 Sam. 11:13 **19:23** [a] 1 Kin. 2:8, 9, 37, 46 **19:24** [a] 2 Sam. 9:6; 21:7 **19:25** [a] 2 Sam. 16:17 **19:27** [a] 2 Sam. 16:3, 4 [b] 2 Sam. 14:17, 20 **19:28** [a] 2 Sam. 9:7–13 **19:31** [a] 2 Sam. 17:27–29; 1 Kin. 2:7 **19:32** [a] 2 Sam. 17:27–29 **19:35** [a] Ps. 90:10 **19:37** [a] 2 Sam. 19:40; Jer. 41:17 **19:39** [a] Gen. 31:55; Ruth 1:14; 2 Sam. 14:33 **19:40** [1] Masoretic Text reads *Chimhan.* **19:41** [a] 2 Sam. 19:15 **19:42** [a] 2 Sam. 19:12 **19:43** [a] 1 Kin. 11:30, 31 [b] Judg. 8:1; 12:1

### THE REBELLION OF SHEBA

**20** And there happened to be there a rebel,[1] whose name *was* Sheba the son of Bichri, a Benjamite. And he blew a trumpet, and said:

[a]"We have no share in David,
Nor do we have inheritance in the son of Jesse;
[b]Every man to his tents, O Israel!"

2 So every man of Israel deserted David, *and* followed Sheba the son of Bichri. But the [a]men of Judah, from the Jordan as far as Jerusalem, remained loyal to their king.

3 Now David came to his house at Jerusalem. And the king took the ten women, [a]his concubines whom he had left to keep the house, and put them in seclusion and supported them, but did not go in to them. So they were shut up to the day of their death, living in widowhood.

4 And the king said to Amasa, [a]"Assemble the men of Judah for me within three days, and be present here yourself." 5 So Amasa went to assemble *the men of* Judah. But he delayed longer than the set time which David had appointed him. 6 And David said to [a]Abishai, "Now Sheba the son of Bichri will do us more harm than Absalom. Take [b]your lord's servants and pursue him, lest he find for himself fortified cities, and escape us." 7 So Joab's men, with the [a]Cherethites, the Pelethites, and [b]all the mighty men, went out after him. And they went out of Jerusalem to pursue Sheba the son of Bichri. 8 When they *were* at the large stone which *is* in Gibeon, Amasa came before them. Now Joab was dressed in battle armor; on it was a belt *with* a sword fastened in its sheath at his hips; and as he was going forward, it fell out. 9 Then Joab said to Amasa, "*Are* you in health, my brother?" [a]And Joab took Amasa by the beard with his right hand to kiss him. 10 But Amasa did not notice the sword that *was* in Joab's hand. And [a]he struck him with it [b]in the stomach, and his entrails poured out on the ground; and he did not *strike* him again. Thus he died.

Then Joab and Abishai his brother pursued Sheba the son of Bichri. 11 Meanwhile one of Joab's men stood near Amasa, and said, "Whoever favors Joab and whoever *is* for David—follow Joab!" 12 But Amasa wallowed in *his* blood in the middle of the highway. And when the man saw that all the people stood still, he moved Amasa from the highway to the field and threw a garment over him, when he saw that everyone who came upon him halted. 13 When he was removed from the highway, all the people went on after Joab to pursue Sheba the son of Bichri.

14 And he went through all the tribes of Israel to [a]Abel and Beth Maachah and all the Berites. So they were gathered together and also went after *Sheba*.[1] 15 Then they came and besieged him in Abel of Beth Maachah; and they [a]cast up a siege mound against the city, and it stood by the rampart. And all the people who *were* with Joab battered the wall to throw it down.

16 Then a wise woman cried out from the city, "Hear, hear! Please say to Joab, 'Come nearby, that I may speak with you.'" 17 When he had come near to her, the woman said, "*Are* you Joab?"

He answered, "I *am*."

Then she said to him, "Hear the words of your maidservant."

And he answered, "I am listening."

18 So she spoke, saying, "They used to talk in former times, saying, 'They shall surely seek *guidance* at Abel,' and so they would end *disputes*. 19 I *am among the* peaceable *and* faithful in Israel. You seek to destroy a city and a mother in Israel. Why would you swallow up [a]the inheritance of the LORD?"

20 And Joab answered and said, "Far be it, far be it from me, that I should swallow up or destroy! 21 That *is* not so. But a man from the mountains of Ephraim, Sheba the son of Bichri by name, has raised his hand against the king, against David. Deliver him only, and I will depart from the city."

So the woman said to Joab, "Watch, his head will be thrown to you over the wall." 22 Then the woman [a]in her wisdom went to all the people. And they cut off the head of Sheba the son of Bichri, and threw *it* out to Joab. Then he blew a trumpet, and they withdrew from the city, every man to his tent. So Joab returned to the king at Jerusalem.

### DAVID'S GOVERNMENT OFFICERS

23 And [a]Joab *was* over all the army of Israel; Benaiah the son of Jehoiada *was* over the Cherethites and the Pelethites; 24 Adoram *was* [a]in charge of revenue; [b]Jehoshaphat the son of Ahilud *was* recorder; 25 Sheva *was* scribe; [a]Zadok and Abiathar *were* the priests; 26 [a]and Ira the Jairite was a chief minister under David.

### DAVID AVENGES THE GIBEONITES

**21** Now there was a famine in the days of David for three years, year after year; and David [a]inquired of the LORD. And the LORD answered, "*It is* because of Saul and *his* bloodthirsty house, because he killed the Gibeonites." 2 So the king called the Gibeonites and spoke to them. Now the Gibeonites *were* not of the children of Israel, but [a]of the remnant of the Amorites; the children of Israel had sworn protection to them, but Saul had sought to kill them [b]in his zeal for the children of Israel and Judah.

20:1 [a] 2 Sam. 19:43; 1 Kin. 12:16 [b] 1 Sam. 13:2; 2 Sam. 18:17; 2 Chr. 10:16 [1] Literally *man of Belial* 20:2 [a] 2 Sam. 19:14 20:3 [a] 2 Sam. 15:16; 16:21, 22 20:4 [a] 2 Sam. 17:25; 19:13 20:6 [a] 2 Sam. 21:17 [b] 2 Sam. 11:11; 1 Kin. 1:33 20:7 [a] 2 Sam. 8:18; 1 Kin. 1:38, 44 [b] 2 Sam. 15:18 20:9 [a] Matt. 26:49; Luke 22:47 20:10 [a] 2 Sam. 3:27; 1 Kin. 2:5 [b] 2 Sam. 2:23 20:14 [a] 1 Kin. 15:20; 2 Kin. 15:29; 2 Chr. 16:4 [1] Literally *him* 20:15 [a] 2 Kin. 19:32; Ezek. 4:2 20:19 [a] 1 Sam. 26:19; 2 Sam. 14:16; 21:3 20:22 [a] 2 Sam. 20:16; [Eccl. 9:13–16] 20:23 [a] 2 Sam. 8:16–18; 1 Kin. 4:3–6 20:24 [a] 1 Kin. 4:6 [b] 2 Sam. 8:16; 1 Kin. 4:3 20:25 [a] 2 Sam. 8:17; 1 Kin. 4:4 20:26 [a] 2 Sam. 8:18 21:1 [a] Num. 27:21; 2 Sam. 5:19 21:2 [a] Josh. 9:3, 15–20 [b] [Ex. 34:11–16]

3 Therefore David said to the Gibeonites, "What shall I do for you? And with what shall I make atonement, that you may bless [a]the inheritance of the LORD?"

4 And the Gibeonites said to him, "We will have no silver or gold from Saul or from his house, nor shall you kill any man in Israel for us."

So he said, "Whatever you say, I will do for you."

5 Then they answered the king, "As for the man who consumed us and plotted against us, *that* we should be destroyed from remaining in any of the territories of Israel, 6 let seven men of his descendants be delivered [a]to us, and we will hang them before the LORD [b]in Gibeah of Saul, [c]*whom* the LORD chose."

And the king said, "I will give *them*."

7 But the king spared [a]Mephibosheth the son of Jonathan, the son of Saul, because of [b]the LORD's oath that *was* between them, between David and Jonathan the son of Saul. 8 So the king took Armoni and Mephibosheth, the two sons of [a]Rizpah the daughter of Aiah, whom she bore to Saul, and the five sons of Michal[1] the daughter of Saul, whom she brought up for Adriel the son of Barzillai the Meholathite; 9 and he delivered them into the hands of the Gibeonites, and they hanged them on the hill [a]before the LORD. So they fell, *all* seven together, and were put to death in the days of harvest, in the first *days,* in the beginning of barley harvest.

10 Now [a]Rizpah the daughter of Aiah took sackcloth and spread it for herself on the rock, [b]from the beginning of harvest until the late rains poured on them from heaven. And she did not allow the birds of the air to rest on them by day nor the beasts of the field by night.

11 And David was told what Rizpah the daughter of Aiah, the concubine of Saul, had done. 12 Then David went and took the bones of Saul, and the bones of Jonathan his son, from the men of [a]Jabesh Gilead who had stolen them from the street of Beth Shan,[1] where the [b]Philistines had hung them up, after the Philistines had struck down Saul in Gilboa. 13 So he brought up the bones of Saul and the bones of Jonathan his son from there; and they gathered the bones of those who had been hanged. 14 They buried the bones of Saul and Jonathan his son in the country of Benjamin in [a]Zelah, in the tomb of Kish his father. So they performed all that the king commanded. And after that [b]God heeded the prayer for the land.

### *PHILISTINE GIANTS DESTROYED*

*(1 Chr. 20:4–8)*

15 When the Philistines were at war again with Israel, David and his servants with him went down and fought against the Philistines; and David grew faint. 16 Then Ishbi-Benob, who *was* one of the sons of the [a]giant, the weight of whose bronze spear *was* three hundred *shekels,* who was bearing a new *sword,* thought he could kill David. 17 But [a]Abishai the son of Zeruiah came to his aid, and struck the Philistine and killed him. Then the men of David swore to him, saying, [b]"You shall go out no more with us to battle, lest you quench the [c]lamp of Israel."

18 [a]Now it happened afterward that there was again a battle with the Philistines at Gob. Then [b]Sibbechai the Hushathite killed Saph,[1] who *was* one of the sons of the giant. 19 Again there was war at Gob with the Philistines, where [a]Elhanan the son of Jaare-Oregim[1] the Bethlehemite killed [b]*the brother of* Goliath the Gittite, the shaft of whose spear *was* like a weaver's beam.

20 Yet again [a]there was war at Gath, where there was a man of *great* stature, who had six fingers on each hand and six toes on each foot, twenty-four in number; and he also was born to the giant. 21 So when he [a]defied Israel, Jonathan the son of Shimea,[1] David's brother, killed him.

22 [a]These four were born to the giant in Gath, and fell by the hand of David and by the hand of his servants.

### *PRAISE FOR GOD'S DELIVERANCE*

*(Ps. 18:1–50)*

**22** Then David [a]spoke to the LORD the words of this song, on the day when the LORD had [b]delivered him from the hand of all his enemies, and from the hand of Saul. 2 And he [a]said:[1]

[b]"The LORD *is* my rock and my [c]fortress and my deliverer;
3 The God of my strength, [a]in whom I will trust;
My [b]shield and the [c]horn of my salvation,
My [d]stronghold and my [e]refuge;
My Savior, You save me from violence.
4 I will call upon the LORD, *who is worthy* to be praised;
So shall I be saved from my enemies.

**SEEING JESUS IN THE SCRIPTURE**

**22:3–4** When David was delivered from his enemies, he called upon the Lord in gratitude for His salvation. When we call upon Jesus for salvation, we receive deliverance from our greatest enemy, sin (see Rom. 10:13).

**21:3** [a] 1 Sam. 26:19; 2 Sam. 20:19 **21:6** [a] Num. 25:4 [b] 1 Sam. 10:26 [c] 1 Sam. 10:24; [Hos. 13:11] **21:7** [a] 2 Sam. 4:4; 9:10 [b] 1 Sam. 18:3; 20:12–17; 23:18; 2 Sam. 9:1–7 **21:8** [a] 2 Sam. 3:7 [1] Or *Merab* (compare 1 Samuel 18:19 and 25:44; 2 Samuel 3:14 and 6:23) **21:9** [a] 2 Sam. 6:17 **21:10** [a] 2 Sam. 3:7; 21:8 [b] Deut. 21:23 **21:12** [a] 1 Sam. 31:11–13 [b] 1 Sam. 31:8 [1] Spelled *Beth Shean* in Joshua 17:11 and elsewhere **21:14** [a] Josh. 18:28 [b] 2 Sam. 24:25 **21:16** [a] 2 Sam. 21:18–22 **21:17** [a] 2 Sam. 20:6–10 [b] 2 Sam. 18:3 [c] 1 Kin. 11:36 **21:18** [a] 1 Chr. 20:4–8 [b] 1 Chr. 11:29; 27:11 [1] Spelled *Sippai* in 1 Chronicles 20:4 **21:19** [a] 2 Sam. 23:24 [b] 1 Chr. 20:5 [1] Spelled *Jair* in 1 Chronicles 20:5 **21:20** [a] 1 Chr. 20:6 **21:21** [a] 1 Sam. 17:10 [1] Spelled *Shammah* in 1 Samuel 16:9 and elsewhere **21:22** [a] 1 Chr. 20:8 **22:1** [a] Ex. 15:1 [b] Ps. 18:title; 34:19 **22:2** [a] Ps. 18 [b] Deut. 32:4 [c] Ps. 91:2 [1] Compare Psalm 18 **22:3** [a] Heb. 2:13 [b] Gen. 15:1 [c] Luke 1:69 [d] Prov. 18:10 [e] Ps. 9:9; 46:1, 7, 11

5 "When the waves of death surrounded me,
The floods of ungodliness made me afraid.
6 The [a]sorrows of Sheol surrounded me;
The snares of death confronted me.
7 In my distress [a]I called upon the LORD,
And cried out to my God;
He [b]heard my voice from His temple,
And my cry *entered* His ears.

8 "Then [a]the earth shook and trembled;
[b]The foundations of heaven[1] quaked and
were shaken,
Because He was angry.
9 Smoke went up from His nostrils,
And devouring [a]fire from His mouth;
Coals were kindled by it.
10 He [a]bowed the heavens also, and came down
With [b]darkness under His feet.
11 He rode upon a cherub, and flew;
And He was seen[1] [a]upon the wings of the
wind.
12 He made [a]darkness canopies around Him,
Dark waters *and* thick clouds of the skies.
13 From the brightness before Him
Coals of fire were kindled.

14 "The LORD [a]thundered from heaven,
And the Most High uttered His voice.
15 He sent out [a]arrows and scattered them;
Lightning bolts, and He vanquished them.
16 Then the channels of the sea [a]were seen,
The foundations of the world were
uncovered,
At the [b]rebuke of the LORD,
At the blast of the breath of His nostrils.

17 "He[a] sent from above, He took me,
He drew me out of many waters.
18 He delivered me from my strong enemy,
From those who hated me;
For they were too strong for me.
19 They confronted me in the day of my
calamity,
But the LORD was my [a]support.
20 [a]He also brought me out into a broad place;
He delivered me because He [b]delighted
in me.

21 "The[a] LORD rewarded me according to my
righteousness;
According to the [b]cleanness of my hands
He has recompensed me.
22 For I have [a]kept the ways of the LORD,
And have not wickedly departed from my
God.
23 For all His [a]judgments *were* before me;
And *as for* His statutes, I did not depart
from them.
24 I was also [a]blameless before Him,
And I kept myself from my iniquity.
25 Therefore [a]the LORD has recompensed
me according to my righteousness,
According to my cleanness in His eyes.[1]

26 "With [a]the merciful You will show Yourself
merciful;
With a blameless man You will show
Yourself blameless;
27 With the pure You will show Yourself
pure;
And [a]with the devious You will show
Yourself shrewd.
28 You will save the [a]humble people;
But Your eyes *are* on [b]the haughty, *that*
You may bring *them* down.

29 "For You *are* my [a]lamp, O LORD;
The LORD shall enlighten my darkness.
30 For by You I can run against a troop;
By my God I can leap over a [a]wall.
31 *As for* God, [a]His way *is* perfect;
[b]The word of the LORD *is* proven;
He *is* a shield to all who trust in Him.

32 "For [a]who *is* God, except the LORD?
And who *is* a rock, except our God?
33 God *is* my [a]strength *and* power,[1]
And He [b]makes my[2] way [c]perfect.
34 He makes my[1] feet [a]like the *feet* of deer,
And [b]sets me on my high places.
35 He teaches my hands to make war,
So that my arms can bend a bow of
bronze.

36 "You have also given me the shield of Your
salvation;
Your gentleness has made me great.
37 You [a]enlarged my path under me;
So my feet did not slip.

38 "I have pursued my enemies and
destroyed them;
Neither did I turn back again till they were
destroyed.

22:6 [a] Ps. 116:3 22:7 [a] Ps. 116:4; 120:1 [b] Ex. 3:7 22:8 [a] Judg. 5:4 [b] Job 26:11 [1] Following Masoretic Text, Septuagint, and Targum; Syriac and Vulgate read *hills* (compare Psalm 18:7). 22:9 [a] Heb. 12:29 22:10 [a] Is. 64:1 [b] Ex. 20:21 22:11 [a] Ps. 104:3 [1] Following Masoretic Text and Septuagint; many Hebrew manuscripts, Syriac, and Vulgate read *He flew* (compare Psalm 18:10); Targum reads *He spoke with power*. 22:12 [a] Job 36:29 22:14 [a] Job 37:2–5 22:15 [a] Deut. 32:23 22:16 [a] Nah. 1:4 [b] Ex. 15:8 22:17 [a] Ps. 144:7 22:19 [a] Is. 10:20 22:20 [a] Ps. 31:8; 118:5 [b] 2 Sam. 15:26 22:21 [a] 1 Sam. 26:23 [b] Ps. 24:4 22:22 [a] Ps. 119:3 22:23 [a] [Deut. 6:6–9; 7:12] 22:24 [a] [Eph. 1:4] 22:25 [a] 2 Sam. 22:21 [1] Septuagint, Syriac, and Vulgate read *the cleanness of my hands in His sight* (compare Psalm 18:24); Targum reads *my cleanness before His word*. 22:26 [a] [Matt. 5:7] 22:27 [a] [Lev. 26:23, 24] 22:28 [a] Ps. 72:12 [b] Job 40:11 22:29 [a] Ps. 119:105; 132:17 22:30 [a] 2 Sam. 5:6–8 22:31 [a] [Matt. 5:48] [b] Ps. 12:6 22:32 [a] Is. 45:5, 6 22:33 [a] Ps. 27:1 [b] [Heb. 13:21] [c] Ps. 101:2, 6 [1] Dead Sea Scrolls, Septuagint, Syriac, and Vulgate read *It is God who arms me with strength* (compare Psalm 18:32); Targum reads *It is God who sustains me with strength*. [2] Following Qere, Septuagint, Syriac, Targum, and Vulgate (compare Psalm 18:32); Kethib reads *His*. 22:34 [a] 2 Sam. 2:18 [b] Is. 33:16 [1] Following Qere, Septuagint, Syriac, Targum, and Vulgate (compare Psalm 18:33); Kethib reads *His*. 22:37 [a] Prov. 4:12

39 And I have destroyed them and wounded
them,
So that they could not rise;
They have fallen [a]under my feet.
40 For You have [a]armed me with strength for
the battle;
You have subdued under me [b]those who
rose against me.
41 You have also given me the [a]necks of my
enemies,
So that I destroyed those who hated me.
42 They looked, but *there was* none to save;
*Even* [a]to the LORD, but He did not answer
them.
43 Then I beat them as fine [a]as the dust of
the earth;
I trod them [b]like dirt in the streets,
*And* I spread them out.

44 "You[a] have also delivered me from the
strivings of my people;
You have kept me as the [b]head of the nations.
[c]A people I have not known shall serve me.
45 The foreigners submit to me;
As soon as they hear, they obey me.
46 The foreigners fade away,
And come frightened[1] [a]from their
hideouts.

47 "The LORD lives!
Blessed *be* my Rock!
Let God be exalted,
The [a]Rock of my salvation!
48 *It is* God who avenges me,
And [a]subdues the peoples under me;
49 He delivers me from my enemies.
You also lift me up above those who rise
against me;
You have delivered me from the [a]violent
man.
50 Therefore I will give thanks to You,
O LORD, among [a]the Gentiles,
And sing praises to Your [b]name.

51 "*He*[a] *is* the tower of salvation to His king,
And shows mercy to His [b]anointed,
To David and [c]his descendants
forevermore."

### *DAVID'S LAST WORDS*

**23** Now these *are* the last words of David.

*Thus* says David the son of Jesse;
*Thus* says [a]the man raised up on high,
[b]The anointed of the God of Jacob,
And the sweet psalmist of Israel:

2 "The[a] Spirit of the LORD spoke by me,
And His word *was* on my tongue.
3 The God of Israel said,
[a]The Rock of Israel spoke to me:
'He who rules over men *must be* just,
Ruling [b]in the fear of God.
4 And [a]*he shall be* like the light of the
morning *when* the sun rises,
A morning without clouds,
*Like* the tender grass *springing* out of the
earth,
By clear shining after rain.'

5 "Although my house *is* not so with God,
[a]Yet He has made with me an everlasting
covenant,
Ordered in all *things* and secure.
For *this is* all my salvation and all *my*
desire;
Will He not make *it* increase?
6 But *the sons* of rebellion *shall* all *be* as
thorns thrust away,
Because they cannot be taken with hands.
7 But the man *who* touches them
Must be armed with iron and the shaft of
a spear,
And they shall be utterly burned with fire
in *their* place."

### *DAVID'S MIGHTY MEN*

*(1 Chr. 11:10–47)*

8 These *are* the names of the mighty men
whom David had: Josheb-Basshebeth[1] the Tach-
monite, chief among the captains.[2] He was called
Adino the Eznite, because he had killed eight
hundred men at one time. 9 And after him *was*
[a]Eleazar the son of Dodo,[1] the Ahohite, *one* of
the three mighty men with David when they
defied the Philistines *who* were gathered there
for battle, and the men of Israel had retreated.
10 He arose and attacked the Philistines until
his hand was [a]weary, and his hand stuck to the
sword. The LORD brought about a great victory
that day; and the people returned after him only
to [b]plunder. 11 And after him *was* [a]Shammah the

**23:8–39** The term ***mighty men*** suggests these were the elite of David's troops, possibly his personal bodyguards. These men were heroes in the full sense of the word. Of note is the final man listed, **Uriah the Hittite**, the husband of Bathsheba whom David had murdered.

**22:39** [a] Mal. 4:3 **22:40** [a] [Ps. 18:32] [b] [Ps. 44:5] **22:41** [a] Gen. 49:8 **22:42** [a] 1 Sam. 28:6 **22:43** [a] Ps. 18:42 [b] Is. 10:6 **22:44** [a] 2 Sam. 3:1 [b] Deut. 28:13 [c] [Is. 55:5] **22:46** [a] [Mic. 7:17] [1] Following Septuagint, Targum, and Vulgate (compare Psalm 18:45); Masoretic Text reads *gird themselves.* **22:47** [a] Ps. 89:26 **22:48** [a] Ps. 144:2 **22:49** [a] Ps. 140:1, 4, 11 **22:50** [a] 2 Sam. 8:1–14 [b] Rom. 15:9 **22:51** [a] Ps. 144:10 [b] Ps. 89:20 [c] 2 Sam. 7:12–16 **23:1** [a] 2 Sam. 7:8, 9 [b] 1 Sam. 16:12, 13 **23:2** [a] [2 Pet. 1:21] **23:3** [a] [Deut. 32:4] [b] Ex. 18:21 **23:4** [a] Ps. 89:36 **23:5** [a] Ps. 89:29 **23:8** [1] Literally *One Who Sits in the Seat* (compare 1 Chronicles 11:11) [2] Following Masoretic Text and Targum; Septuagint and Vulgate read *the three.* **23:9** [a] 1 Chr. 11:12; 27:4 [1] Spelled *Dodai* in 1 Chronicles 27:4 **23:10** [a] Judg. 8:4 [b] 1 Sam. 30:24, 25 **23:11** [a] 1 Chr. 11:27

son of Agee the Hararite. [b]The Philistines had
gathered together into a troop where there was
a piece of ground full of lentils. So the people
fled from the Philistines. 12 But he stationed
himself in the middle of the field, defended it,
and killed the Philistines. So the LORD brought
about a great victory.

13 Then [a]three of the thirty chief men went
down at harvest time and came to David at [b]the
cave of Adullam. And the troop of Philistines
encamped in [c]the Valley of Rephaim. 14 David
*was* then in [a]the stronghold, and the garrison
of the Philistines *was* then *in* Bethlehem. 15 And
David said with longing, "Oh, that someone
would give me a drink of the water from the
well of Bethlehem, which *is* by the gate!" 16 So
the three mighty men broke through the camp
of the Philistines, drew water from the well of
Bethlehem that *was* by the gate, and took it and
brought *it* to David. Nevertheless he would not
drink it, but poured it out to the LORD. 17 And he
said, "Far be it from me, O LORD, that I should
do this! Is *this not* [a]the blood of the men who
went in *jeopardy of* their lives?" Therefore he
would not drink it.

These things were done by the three mighty
men.

18 Now [a]Abishai the brother of Joab, the son
of Zeruiah, was chief of *another* three.[1] He lifted
his spear against three hundred *men,* killed
*them,* and won a name among *these* three. 19 Was
he not the most honored of three? Therefore
he became their captain. However, he did not
attain to the *first* three.

20 Benaiah *was* the son of Jehoiada, the son
of a valiant man from [a]Kabzeel, who had done
many deeds. [b]He had killed two lion-like heroes
of Moab. He also had gone down and killed a
lion in the midst of a pit on a snowy day. 21 And
he killed an Egyptian, a spectacular man. The
Egyptian *had* a spear in his hand; so he went
down to him with a staff, wrested the spear out
of the Egyptian's hand, and killed him with his
own spear. 22 These *things* Benaiah the son of
Jehoiada did, and won a name among three
mighty men. 23 He was more honored than the
thirty, but he did not attain to the *first* three. And
David appointed him [a]over his guard.

24 [a]Asahel the brother of Joab *was* one of the
thirty; Elhanan the son of Dodo of Bethlehem,
25 [a]Shammah the Harodite, Elika the Harodite,
26 Helez the Paltite, Ira the son of Ikkesh the
Tekoite, 27 Abiezer the Anathothite, Mebunnai
the Hushathite, 28 Zalmon the Ahohite, Maharai
the Netophathite, 29 Heleb the son of Baanah
(the Netophathite), Ittai the son of Ribai from
Gibeah of the children of Benjamin, 30 Bena-
iah a Pirathonite, Hiddai from the brooks of
[a]Gaash, 31 Abi-Albon the Arbathite, Azmaveth
the Barhumite, 32 Eliahba the Shaalbonite (of
the sons of Jashen), Jonathan, 33 [a]Shammah the
Hararite, Ahiam the son of Sharar the Hararite,
34 Eliphelet the son of Ahasbai, the son of the
Maachathite, Eliam the son of [a]Ahithophel the
Gilonite, 35 Hezrai[1] the Carmelite, Paarai the
Arbite, 36 Igal the son of Nathan of [a]Zobah, Bani
the Gadite, 37 Zelek the Ammonite, Naharai the
Beerothite (armorbearer of Joab the son of Zer-
uiah), 38 [a]Ira the Ithrite, Gareb the Ithrite, 39 *and*
[a]Uriah the Hittite: thirty-seven in all.

### *DAVID'S CENSUS OF ISRAEL AND JUDAH*
*(1 Chr. 21:1–6)*

24 Again [a]the anger of the LORD was aroused
against Israel, and He moved David
against them to say, [b]"Go, number Israel and
Judah."

2 So the king said to Joab the commander of
the army who *was* with him, "Now go throughout
all the tribes of Israel, [a]from Dan to Beersheba,
and count the people, that [b]I may know the
number of the people."

3 And Joab said to the king, "Now may the
LORD your God [a]add to the people a hundred
times more than there are, and may the eyes of
my lord the king see *it.* But why does my lord
the king desire this thing?" 4 Nevertheless the
king's word prevailed against Joab and against
the captains of the army. Therefore Joab and the
captains of the army went out from the presence
of the king to count the people of Israel.

5 And they crossed over the Jordan and
camped in [a]Aroer, on the right side of the town
which *is* in the midst of the ravine of Gad, and
toward [b]Jazer. 6 Then they came to Gilead and to
the land of Tahtim Hodshi; they came to [a]Dan
Jaan and around to [b]Sidon; 7 and they came to
the stronghold of [a]Tyre and to all the cities of
the [b]Hivites and the Canaanites. Then they went
out to South Judah *as far as* Beersheba. 8 So
when they had gone through all the land, they
came to Jerusalem at the end of nine months
and twenty days. 9 Then Joab gave the sum of
the number of the people to the king. [a]And there
were in Israel eight hundred thousand valiant
men who drew the sword, and the men of Judah
were five hundred thousand men.

### *THE JUDGMENT ON DAVID'S SIN*
*(1 Chr. 21:7–17)*

10 And [a]David's heart condemned him after
he had numbered the people. So [b]David said

23:11 [b] 1 Chr. 11:13, 14 **23:13** [a] 1 Chr. 11:15 [b] 1 Sam. 22:1 [c] 2 Sam. 5:18 **23:14** [a] 1 Sam. 22:4, 5 **23:17** [a] [Lev. 17:10] **23:18** [a] 2 Sam. 21:17; 1 Chr. 11:20 [1] Following Masoretic Text, Septuagint, and Vulgate; some Hebrew manuscripts and Syriac read *thirty;* Targum reads *the mighty men.* **23:20** [a] Josh. 15:21 [b] Ex. 15:15 **23:23** [a] 2 Sam. 8:18; 20:23 **23:24** [a] 2 Sam. 2:18; 1 Chr. 27:7 **23:25** [a] 1 Chr. 11:27 **23:30** [a] Judg. 2:9 **23:33** [a] 2 Sam. 23:11 **23:34** [a] 2 Sam. 15:12 **23:35** [1] Spelled *Hezro* in 1 Chronicles 11:37 **23:36** [a] 2 Sam. 8:3 **23:38** [a] 1 Chr. 2:53 **23:39** [a] 2 Sam. 11:3, 6 **24:1** [a] 2 Sam. 21:1, 2 [b] Num. 26:2; 1 Chr. 27:23, 24 **24:2** [a] Judg. 20:1; 2 Sam. 3:10 [b] [Jer. 17:5] **24:3** [a] Deut. 1:11 **24:5** [a] Deut. 2:36; Josh. 13:9, 16 [b] Num. 32:1, 3 **24:6** [a] Josh. 19:47; Judg. 18:29 [b] Josh. 19:28; Judg. 18:28 **24:7** [a] Josh. 19:29 [b] Josh. 11:3; Judg. 3:3 **24:9** [a] 1 Chr. 21:5 **24:10** [a] 1 Sam. 24:5 [b] 2 Sam. 23:1

**SEEING JESUS IN THE SCRIPTURE**

**24:17** When Israel encountered God's wrath because of David's sin, David asked God to spare Israel and hold only his house responsible. Unlike David, Jesus never sinned, yet He took the punishment for our sin upon Himself (see Luke 23:15–16).

to the LORD, [c]"I have sinned greatly in what I
have done; but now, I pray, O LORD, take away
the iniquity of Your servant, for I have [d]done
very foolishly."
11 Now when David arose in the morning,
the word of the LORD came to the prophet [a]Gad,
David's [b]seer, saying, 12 "Go and tell David, 'Thus
says the LORD: "I offer you three *things;* choose
one of them for yourself, that I may do *it* to
you." ' " 13 So Gad came to David and told him;
and he said to him, "Shall [a]seven[1] years of famine come to you in your land? Or shall you flee
three months before your enemies, while they
pursue you? Or shall there be three days' plague
in your land? Now consider and see what answer
I should take back to Him who sent me."
14 And David said to Gad, "I am in great distress. Please let us fall into the hand of the LORD,
[a]for His mercies *are* great; but [b]do not let me
fall into the hand of man."
15 So [a]the LORD sent a plague upon Israel
from the morning till the appointed time. From
Dan to Beersheba seventy thousand men of the
people died. 16 [a]And when the angel[1] stretched
out His hand over Jerusalem to destroy it, [b]the
LORD relented from the destruction, and said
to the angel who was destroying the people, "It
is enough; now restrain your hand." And the
angel of the LORD was by the threshing floor of
Araunah[2] the Jebusite.
17 Then David spoke to the LORD when he
saw the angel who was striking the people, and
said, "Surely [a]I have sinned, and I have done
wickedly; but these sheep, what have they done?
Let Your hand, I pray, be against me and against
my father's house."

### *THE ALTAR ON THE THRESHING FLOOR*

*(1 Chr. 21:18–27)*

18 And Gad came that day to David and said
to him, [a]"Go up, erect an altar to the LORD on the
threshing floor of Araunah the Jebusite." 19 So
David, according to the word of Gad, went up as
the LORD commanded. 20 Now Araunah looked,
and saw the king and his servants coming toward
him. So Araunah went out and bowed before the
king with his face to the ground.
21 Then Araunah said, "Why has my lord the
king come to his servant?"
[a]And David said, "To buy the threshing
floor from you, to build an altar to the LORD,
that [b]the plague may be withdrawn from the
people."
22 Now Araunah said to David, "Let my lord
the king take and offer up whatever *seems* good
to him. [a]Look, *here are* oxen for burnt sacrifice,
and threshing implements and the yokes of the
oxen for wood. 23 All these, O king, Araunah has
given to the king."
And Araunah said to the king, "May the LORD
your God [a]accept you."
24 Then the king said to Araunah, "No, but I
will surely buy *it* from you for a price; nor will I
offer burnt offerings to the LORD my God with
that which costs me nothing." So [a]David bought
the threshing floor and the oxen for fifty shekels
of silver. 25 And David built there an altar to the
LORD, and offered burnt offerings and peace
offerings. [a]So the LORD heeded the prayers
for the land, and [b]the plague was withdrawn
from Israel.

**24:10** [c] 2 Sam. 12:13 [d] 1 Sam. 13:13; [2 Chr. 16:9] **24:11** [a] 1 Sam. 22:5 [b] 1 Sam. 9:9; 1 Chr. 29:29 **24:13** [a] Ezek. 14:21 [1] Following Masoretic Text, Syriac, Targum, and Vulgate; Septuagint reads *three* (compare 1 Chronicles 21:12). **24:14** [a] [Ps. 51:1; 103:8, 13, 14; 119:156; 130:4, 7] [b] [Is. 47:6; Zech. 1:15] **24:15** [a] 1 Chr. 21:14 **24:16** [a] Ex. 12:23; 2 Kin. 19:35; Acts 12:23 [b] Gen. 6:6; 1 Sam. 15:11 [1] Or *Angel* [2] Spelled *Ornan* in 1 Chronicles 21:15 **24:17** [a] 2 Sam. 7:8; 1 Chr. 21:17; Ps. 74:1 **24:18** [a] 1 Chr. 21:18 **24:21** [a] Gen. 23:8–16 [b] Num. 16:48, 50 **24:22** [a] 1 Sam. 6:14; 1 Kin. 19:21 **24:23** [a] [Ezek. 20:40, 41] **24:24** [a] 1 Chr. 21:24, 25 **24:25** [a] 2 Sam. 21:14 [b] 2 Sam. 24:21

*The First Book of the*

# KINGS

**AUTHOR**
Perhaps Jeremiah, Ezra, or Ezekiel

**KEY VERSES**
1 Kings 9:4–7

**READING TIME**
2 hours 36 minutes

The first half of 1 Kings traces the life of David's son Solomon, the third king of Israel. Under Solomon's leadership, Israel rose to the peak of its glory in terms of its territorial borders and influence. Solomon's great wealth, wisdom, and accomplishments—including the unsurpassed splendor of the temple that he constructed in Jerusalem—brought him worldwide fame and respect. However, Solomon's zeal for God diminished in his later years as pagan wives turned his heart from the worship of God in the temple and toward the worship of idols on high places. As a result, the king with the divided heart left behind a kingdom about to be divided. The Book of 1 Kings then traces the histories of two sets of disobedient nations and their kings who grew increasingly indifferent to God's laws and prophets.

**Occasion:** The Book of 1 Kings depicts Israel's history from the ending of the united monarchy into the time of the divided monarchy. Beyond preserving a faithful recording of history, the author of 1 Kings wanted to show the failure of the kings and the Israelites that prompted God's righteous judgment and their need to repent.

**Main Point:** God's people plunge further into sin and idolatry, refusing to repent and ignoring God's warnings of coming judgment.

**Big Ideas:** God never gives up on His people. Faithfulness to God is more important than earthly power or treasures. We may not worship idols of stone, but we are quick to worship other idols. We should heed God's warnings and turn away from all sin.

## OUTLINE:

I. Solomon Becomes King (chs. 1–2)
II. Solomon Rules Wisely (chs. 3–4)
III. Solomon Builds the Temple (chs. 5–8)
IV. Solomon Rules Foolishly (chs. 9–11)
V. The Kingdom Splits in Two (chs. 12–14)
VI. The Kings of Judah and Israel (chs. 15–16)
VII. The Reign of Ahab (chs. 17–22)

**1003 BC**
David becomes king over all Israel

**988 BC**
Solomon is born

**980 BC**
Absalom revolts against David

**970 BC**
Solomon becomes king of Israel

**967 BC**
Solomon begins construction of the temple

**930 BC**
The kingdom is divided

**910 BC**
Asa becomes king in Judah

**909 BC**
Baasha becomes king in Israel

**c. 900 BC**
Phoenicians establish trading colonies as far away as Spain

**874 BC**
Ahab becomes king in Israel

**872 BC**
Jehoshaphat becomes king in Judah

**865 BC**
Elijah begins to prophesy against Ahab

**850 BC**
The royal inscription called the Moabite Stone is made

**c. 561–538 BC**
**1 Kings written**

## *ADONIJAH PRESUMES TO BE KING*

1 Now King David was [a]old, advanced in years;
and they put covers on him, but he could
not get warm. 2 Therefore his servants said to
him, "Let a young woman, a virgin, be sought
for our lord the king, and let her stand before
the king, and let her care for him; and let her
lie in your bosom, that our lord the king may
be warm." 3 So they sought for a lovely young
woman throughout all the territory of Israel, and
found [a]Abishag the [b]Shunammite, and brought
her to the king. 4 The young woman *was* very
lovely; and she cared for the king, and served
him; but the king did not know her.

5 Then [a]Adonijah the son of Haggith exalted
himself, saying, "I will be king"; and [b]he prepared
for himself chariots and horsemen, and fifty
men to run before him. 6 (And his father had not
rebuked him at any time by saying, "Why have
you done so?" He *was* also very good-looking.
[a]*His mother* had borne him after Absalom.)
7 Then he conferred with [a]Joab the son of Zer-
uiah and with [b]Abiathar the priest, and [c]they
followed and helped Adonijah. 8 But [a]Zadok the
priest, [b]Benaiah the son of Jehoiada, [c]Nathan
the prophet, [d]Shimei, Rei, and [e]the mighty men
who *belonged* to David were not with Adonijah.

9 And Adonijah sacrificed sheep and oxen
and fattened cattle by the stone of Zoheleth,
which *is* by [a]En Rogel; he also invited all his
brothers, the king's sons, and all the men of
Judah, the king's servants. 10 But he did not invite
Nathan the prophet, Benaiah, the mighty men,
or [a]Solomon his brother.

11 So Nathan spoke to Bathsheba the mother
of Solomon, saying, "Have you not heard that
Adonijah the son of [a]Haggith has become king,
and David our lord does not know *it?* 12 Come,
please, let me now give you advice, that you
may save your own life and the life of your son
Solomon. 13 Go immediately to King David and
say to him, 'Did you not, my lord, O king, swear
to your maidservant, saying, [a]"Assuredly your
son Solomon shall reign after me, and he shall sit
on my throne"? Why then has Adonijah become
king?' 14 Then, while you are still talking there
with the king, I also will come in after you and
confirm your words."

15 So Bathsheba went into the chamber to the
king. (Now the king was very old, and Abishag
the Shunammite was serving the king.) 16 And
Bathsheba bowed and did homage to the king.
Then the king said, "What is your wish?"

17 Then she said to him, "My lord, [a]you swore
by the LORD your God to your maidservant,
*saying,* 'Assuredly Solomon your son shall reign
after me, and he shall sit on my throne.' 18 So
now, look! Adonijah has become king; and now,
my lord the king, you do not know about *it.*
19 [a]He has sacrificed oxen and fattened cattle
and sheep in abundance, and has invited all the
sons of the king, Abiathar the priest, and Joab
the commander of the army; but Solomon your
servant he has not invited. 20 And as for you, my
lord, O king, the eyes of all Israel *are* on you, that
you should tell them who will sit on the throne
of my lord the king after him. 21 Otherwise it
will happen, when my lord the king [a]rests with
his fathers, that I and my son Solomon will be
counted as offenders."

22 And just then, while she was still talking
with the king, Nathan the prophet also came in.
23 So they told the king, saying, "Here is Nathan
the prophet." And when he came in before the
king, he bowed down before the king with his
face to the ground. 24 And Nathan said, "My lord,
O king, have you said, 'Adonijah shall reign after
me, and he shall sit on my throne'? 25 [a]For he has
gone down today, and has sacrificed oxen and
fattened cattle and sheep in abundance, and has
invited all the king's sons, and the commanders
of the army, and Abiathar the priest; and look!
They are eating and drinking before him; and
they say, [b]'*Long* live King Adonijah!' 26 But he has
not invited me—me your servant—nor Zadok
the priest, nor Benaiah the son of Jehoiada, nor
your servant Solomon. 27 Has this thing been
done by my lord the king, and you have not
told your servant who should sit on the throne
of my lord the king after him?"

## *DAVID PROCLAIMS SOLOMON KING*

*(1 Chr. 29:22–25)*

28 Then King David answered and said, "Call
Bathsheba to me." So she came into the king's
presence and stood before the king. 29 And the
king took an oath and said, [a]"*As* the LORD lives,
who has redeemed my life from every distress,
30 [a]just as I swore to you by the LORD God of Is-
rael, saying, 'Assuredly Solomon your son shall
be king after me, and he shall sit on my throne
in my place,' so I certainly will do this day."
31 Then Bathsheba bowed with *her* face to the
earth, and paid homage to the king, and said,
[a]"Let my lord King David live forever!"

32 And King David said, "Call to me Zadok
the priest, Nathan the prophet, and Benaiah the
son of Jehoiada." So they came before the king.
33 The king also said to them, [a]"Take with you
the servants of your lord, and have Solomon my
son ride on my own [b]mule, and take him down
to [c]Gihon. 34 There let Zadok the priest and Na-
than the prophet [a]anoint him king over Israel;
and [b]blow the horn, and say, '*Long* live King

**1:1** [a] 1 Chr. 23:1 **1:3** [a] 1 Kin. 2:17 [b] Josh. 19:18; 1 Sam. 28:4 **1:5** [a] 2 Sam. 3:4 [b] 2 Sam. 15:1 **1:6** [a] 2 Sam. 3:3, 4; 1 Chr. 3:2 **1:7** [a] 1 Chr. 11:6 [b] 2 Sam. 20:25 [c] 1 Kin. 2:22, 28 **1:8** [a] 1 Kin. 2:35 [b] 1 Kin. 2:25; 2 Sam. 8:18 [c] 2 Sam. 12:1 [d] 1 Kin. 4:18 [e] 2 Sam. 23:8 **1:9** [a] Josh. 15:7; 18:16; 2 Sam. 17:17 **1:10** [a] 2 Sam. 12:24 **1:11** [a] 2 Sam. 3:4 **1:13** [a] 1 Kin. 1:30; 1 Chr. 22:9–13 **1:17** [a] 1 Kin. 1:13, 30 **1:19** [a] 1 Kin. 1:7–9, 25 **1:21** [a] Deut. 31:16; 2 Sam. 7:12; 1 Kin. 2:10 **1:25** [a] 1 Kin. 1:9, 19 [b] 1 Sam. 10:24 **1:29** [a] 2 Sam. 4:9; 12:5 **1:30** [a] 1 Kin. 1:13, 17 **1:31** [a] Neh. 2:3; Dan. 2:4; 3:9 **1:33** [a] 2 Sam. 20:6 [b] Esth. 6:8 [c] 2 Chr. 32:30; 33:14 **1:34** [a] 1 Sam. 10:1; 16:3, 12; 2 Sam. 2:4; 5:3; 1 Kin. 19:16; 2 Kin. 9:3; 11:12; 1 Chr. 29:22 [b] 2 Sam. 15:10; 2 Kin. 9:13; 11:14

Solomon!' 35 Then you shall come up after him, and he shall come and sit on my throne, and he shall be king in my place. For I have appointed him to be ruler over Israel and Judah."

36 Benaiah the son of Jehoiada answered the king and said, [a]"Amen! May the LORD God of my lord the king say so *too.* 37 [a]As the LORD has been with my lord the king, even so may He be with Solomon, and [b]make his throne greater than the throne of my lord King David."

38 So Zadok the priest, Nathan the prophet, [a]Benaiah the son of Jehoiada, the [b]Cherethites, and the Pelethites went down and had Solomon ride on King David's mule, and took him to Gihon. 39 Then Zadok the priest took a horn of [a]oil from the tabernacle and [b]anointed Solomon. And they blew the horn, [c]and all the people said, "*Long* live King Solomon!" 40 And all the people went up after him; and the people played the flutes and rejoiced with great joy, so that the earth *seemed to* split with their sound.

41 Now Adonijah and all the guests who *were* with him heard *it* as they finished eating. And when Joab heard the sound of the horn, he said, "Why *is* the city in such a noisy uproar?" 42 While he was still speaking, there came [a]Jonathan, the son of Abiathar the priest. And Adonijah said to him, "Come in, for [b]you *are* a prominent man, and bring good news."

43 Then Jonathan answered and said to Adonijah, "No! Our lord King David has made Solomon king. 44 The king has sent with him Zadok the priest, Nathan the prophet, Benaiah the son of Jehoiada, the Cherethites, and the Pelethites; and they have made him ride on the king's mule. 45 So Zadok the priest and Nathan the prophet have anointed him king at Gihon; and they have gone up from there rejoicing, so that the city is in an uproar. This *is* the noise that you have heard. 46 Also Solomon [a]sits on the throne of the kingdom. 47 And moreover the king's servants have gone to bless our lord King David, saying, [a]'May God make the name of Solomon better than your name, and may He make his throne greater than your throne.' [b]Then the king bowed himself on the bed. 48 Also the king said thus, 'Blessed *be* the LORD God of Israel, who has [a]given *one* to sit on my throne this day, while my eyes see [b]*it!*' "

49 So all the guests who were with Adonijah were afraid, and arose, and each one went his way.

50 Now Adonijah was afraid of Solomon; so he arose, and went and [a]took hold of the horns of the altar. 51 And it was told Solomon, saying, "Indeed Adonijah is afraid of King Solomon; for look, he has taken hold of the horns of the altar, saying, 'Let King Solomon swear to me today that he will not put his servant to death with the sword.' "

52 Then Solomon said, "If he proves himself a worthy man, [a]not one hair of him shall fall to the earth; but if wickedness is found in him, he shall die." 53 So King Solomon sent them to bring him down from the altar. And he came and fell down before King Solomon; and Solomon said to him, "Go to your house."

### *DAVID'S INSTRUCTIONS TO SOLOMON*

**2** Now [a]the days of David drew near that he should die, and he charged Solomon his son, saying: 2 [a]"I go the way of all the earth; [b]be strong, therefore, and prove yourself a man. 3 And keep the charge of the LORD your God: to walk in His ways, to keep His statutes, His commandments, His judgments, and His testimonies, as it is written in the Law of Moses, that you may [a]prosper in all that you do and wherever you turn; 4 that the LORD may [a]fulfill His word which He spoke concerning me, saying, [b]'If your sons take heed to their way, to [c]walk before Me in truth with all their heart and with all their soul,' He said, [d]'you shall not lack a man on the throne of Israel.'

5 "Moreover you know also what Joab the son of Zeruiah [a]did to me, *and* what he did to the two commanders of the armies of Israel, to [b]Abner the son of Ner and [c]Amasa the son of Jether, whom he killed. And he shed the blood of war in peacetime, and put the blood of war on his belt that *was* around his waist, and on his sandals that *were* on his feet. 6 Therefore do [a]according to your wisdom, and do not let his gray hair go down to the grave in peace.

7 "But show kindness to the sons of [a]Barzillai the Gileadite, and let them be among those who [b]eat at your table, for so [c]they came to me when I fled from Absalom your brother.

8 "And see, *you have* with you [a]Shimei the son of Gera, a Benjamite from Bahurim, who cursed me with a malicious curse in the day when I went to Mahanaim. But [b]he came down to meet me at the Jordan, and [c]I swore to him by the LORD, saying, 'I will not put you to death with the sword.' 9 Now therefore, [a]do not hold him guiltless, for you *are* a wise man and know what you ought to do to him; but [b]bring his gray hair down to the grave with blood."

### *DEATH OF DAVID*

*(1 Chr. 3:4; 29:26–28)*

10 So [a]David rested with his fathers, and was buried in [b]the City of David. 11 The period that

1:36 [a]Jer. 28:6 1:37 [a]Josh. 1:5, 17; 1 Sam. 20:13 [b]1 Kin. 1:47 1:38 [a]2 Sam. 8:18; 23:20–23 [b]2 Sam. 20:7; 1 Chr. 18:17 1:39 [a]Ex. 30:23, 25, 32; Ps. 89:20 [b]1 Chr. 29:22 [c]1 Sam. 10:24 1:42 [a]2 Sam. 17:17, 20 [b]2 Sam. 18:27 1:46 [a]1 Kin. 2:12; 1 Chr. 29:23 1:47 [a]1 Kin. 1:37 [b]Gen. 47:31 1:48 [a]1 Kin. 3:6; [Ps. 132:11, 12] [b]2 Sam. 7:12 1:50 [a]Ex. 27:2; 30:10; 1 Kin. 2:28 1:52 [a]1 Sam. 14:45; 2 Sam. 14:11; Acts 27:34 2:1 [a]Gen. 47:29; Deut. 31:14 2:2 [a]Josh. 23:14 [b]Deut. 31:7, 23; 1 Chr. 22:13 2:3 [a][Deut. 29:9; Josh. 1:7]; 1 Chr. 22:12, 13 2:4 [a]2 Sam. 7:25 [b][Ps. 132:12] [c]2 Kin. 20:3 [d]2 Sam. 7:12, 13; 1 Kin. 8:25 2:5 [a]2 Sam. 3:39; 18:5, 12, 14 [b]2 Sam. 3:27; 1 Kin. 2:32 [c]2 Sam. 20:10 2:6 [a]1 Kin. 2:9; Prov. 20:26 2:7 [a]2 Sam. 19:31–39 [b]2 Sam. 9:7, 10; 19:28 [c]2 Sam. 17:17–29 2:8 [a]2 Sam. 16:5–13 [b]2 Sam. 19:18 [c]2 Sam. 19:23 2:9 [a]Ex. 20:7; Job 9:28 [b]Gen. 42:38; 44:31 2:10 [a]1 Kin. 1:21; Acts 2:29; 13:36 [b]2 Sam. 5:7; 1 Kin. 3:1

David [a]reigned over Israel *was* forty years; seven
years he reigned in Hebron, and in Jerusalem
he reigned thirty-three years. 12 [a]Then Solomon
sat on the throne of his father David; and his
kingdom was [b]firmly established.

### SOLOMON EXECUTES ADONIJAH

13 Now Adonijah the son of Haggith came to
Bathsheba the mother of Solomon. So she said,
[a]"Do you come peaceably?"
And he said, "Peaceably." 14 Moreover he said,
"I have something *to say* to you."
And she said, "Say it."
15 Then he said, "You know that the kingdom
was [a]mine, and all Israel had set their expecta-
tions on me, that I should reign. However, the
kingdom has been turned over, and has become
my brother's; for [b]it was his from the LORD.
16 Now I ask one petition of you; do not deny me."
And she said to him, "Say it."
17 Then he said, "Please speak to King Sol-
omon, for he will not refuse you, that he may
give me [a]Abishag the Shunammite as wife."
18 So Bathsheba said, "Very well, I will speak
for you to the king."
19 Bathsheba therefore went to King Sol-
omon, to speak to him for Adonijah. And the
king rose up to meet her and [a]bowed down
to her, and sat down on his throne and had a
throne set for the king's mother; [b]so she sat at
his right hand. 20 Then she said, "I desire one
small petition of you; do not refuse me."
And the king said to her, "Ask it, my mother,
for I will not refuse you."
21 So she said, "Let Abishag the Shunammite
be given to Adonijah your brother as wife."
22 And King Solomon answered and said to
his mother, "Now why do you ask Abishag the
Shunammite for Adonijah? Ask for him the
kingdom also—for he *is* my [a]older brother—for
him, and for [b]Abiathar the priest, and for Joab
the son of Zeruiah." 23 Then King Solomon swore
by the LORD, saying, [a]"May God do so to me, and
more also, if Adonijah has not spoken this word
against his own life! 24 Now therefore, *as* the
LORD lives, who has confirmed me and set me
on the throne of David my father, and who has
established a house[1] for me, as He [a]promised,
Adonijah shall be put to death today!"
25 So King Solomon sent by the hand of [a]Be-
naiah the son of Jehoiada; and he struck him
down, and he died.

### ABIATHAR EXILED, JOAB EXECUTED

26 And to Abiathar the priest the king said,
"Go to [a]Anathoth, to your own fields, for you
*are* deserving of death; but I will not put you
to death at this time, [b]because you carried the
ark of the Lord GOD before my father David, and
because you were afflicted every time my father
was afflicted." 27 So Solomon removed Abiathar
from being priest to the LORD, that he might
[a]fulfill the word of the LORD which He spoke
concerning the house of Eli at Shiloh.
28 Then news came to Joab, for Joab [a]had de-
fected to Adonijah, though he had not defected
to Absalom. So Joab fled to the tabernacle of the
LORD, and [b]took hold of the horns of the altar.
29 And King Solomon was told, "Joab has fled to
the tabernacle of the LORD; there *he is,* by the
altar." Then Solomon sent Benaiah the son of
Jehoiada, saying, "Go, [a]strike him down." 30 So
Benaiah went to the tabernacle of the LORD, and
said to him, "Thus says the king, [a]'Come out!' "
And he said, "No, but I will die here." And
Benaiah brought back word to the king, saying,
"Thus said Joab, and thus he answered me."
31 Then the king said to him, [a]"Do as he
has said, and strike him down and bury him,
[b]that you may take away from me and from
the house of my father the innocent blood
which Joab shed. 32 So the LORD [a]will return his
blood on his head, because he struck down two
men more righteous [b]and better than he, and
killed them with the sword—[c]Abner the son of
Ner, the commander of the army of Israel, and
[d]Amasa the son of Jether, the commander of
the army of Judah—though my father David
did not know *it.* 33 Their blood shall therefore
return upon the head of Joab and [a]upon the
head of his descendants forever. [b]But upon
David and his descendants, upon his house
and his throne, there shall be peace forever
from the LORD."
34 So Benaiah the son of Jehoiada went up
and struck and killed him; and he was buried in
his own house in the wilderness. 35 The king put
Benaiah the son of Jehoiada in his place over
the army, and the king put [a]Zadok the priest in
the place of [b]Abiathar.

**2:17–22 Abishag** served as a nurse and a companion to David in his old age. Part of her responsibility was to help David stay warm at night. She slept alongside David but that didn't mean she had a physical relationship with him. Even so, Adonijah's request to marry Abishag was a way of claiming what had been David's. Solomon recognized Adonijah's plan to use this as a steppingstone to claim the throne.

**2:11** [a] 2 Sam. 5:4, 5; 1 Chr. 3:4; 29:26, 27 **2:12** [a] 1 Kin. 1:46; 1 Chr. 29:23 [b] 1 Kin. 2:46; 2 Chr. 1:1 **2:13** [a] 1 Sam. 16:4, 5 **2:15** [a] 1 Kin. 1:11, 18 [b] 1 Chr. 22:9, 10; 28:5–7; [Dan. 2:21] **2:17** [a] 1 Kin. 1:3, 4 **2:19** [a] [Ex. 20:12] [b] Ps. 45:9 **2:22** [a] 1 Kin. 1:6; 2:15; 1 Chr. 3:2, 5 [b] 1 Kin. 1:7 **2:23** [a] Ruth 1:17 **2:24** [a] 2 Sam. 7:11, 13; 1 Chr. 22:10 [1] That is, a royal dynasty **2:25** [a] 2 Sam. 8:18; 1 Kin. 4:4 **2:26** [a] Josh. 21:18; Jer. 1:1 [b] 1 Sam. 22:23; 23:6; 2 Sam. 15:14, 29 **2:27** [a] 1 Sam. 2:31–35 **2:28** [a] 1 Kin. 1:7 [b] 1 Kin. 1:50 **2:29** [a] 1 Kin. 2:5, 6 **2:30** [a] [Ex. 21:14] **2:31** [a] [Ex. 21:14] [b] [Num. 35:33; Deut. 19:13; 21:8, 9] **2:32** [a] [Gen. 9:6]; Judg. 9:24, 57 [b] 2 Chr. 21:13, 14 [c] 2 Sam. 3:27 [d] 2 Sam. 20:9, 10 **2:33** [a] 2 Sam. 3:29 [b] [Prov. 25:5] **2:35** [a] 1 Sam. 2:35; 1 Kin. 4:4; 1 Chr. 6:53; 24:3; 29:22 [b] 1 Kin. 2:27

### *SHIMEI EXECUTED*

36 Then the king sent and called for [a]Shimei,
and said to him, "Build yourself a house in Jerusalem and dwell there, and do not go out from
there anywhere. 37 For it shall be, on the day you
go out and cross [a]the Brook Kidron, know for certain you shall surely die; [b]your blood shall be on your own head."
38 And Shimei said to the king, "The saying *is*
good. As my lord the king has said, so your servant will do." So Shimei dwelt in Jerusalem many days.
39 Now it happened at the end of three years,
that two slaves of Shimei ran away to [a]Achish the son of Maachah, king of Gath. And they told Shimei,
saying, "Look, your slaves *are* in Gath!" 40 So Shim-
ei arose, saddled his donkey, and went to Achish at Gath to seek his slaves. And Shimei went and
brought his slaves from Gath. 41 And Solomon was
told that Shimei had gone from Jerusalem to Gath
and had come back. 42 Then the king sent and called
for Shimei, and said to him, "Did I not make you swear by the LORD, and warn you, saying, 'Know for certain that on the day you go out and travel anywhere, you shall surely die'? And you said to me, 'The word I have heard *is* good.' 43 Why then
have you not kept the oath of the LORD and the commandment that I gave you?" 44 The king said
moreover to Shimei, "You know, as your heart acknowledges, [a]all the wickedness that you did to my father David; therefore the LORD will [b]return your wickedness on your own head. 45 But King Solomon
*shall be* blessed, and [a]the throne of David shall be established before the LORD forever."
46 So the king commanded Benaiah the son
of Jehoiada; and he went out and struck him down, and he died. Thus the [a]kingdom was established in the hand of Solomon.

### *SOLOMON REQUESTS WISDOM*

*(2 Chr. 1:2–13)*

3 Now [a]Solomon made a treaty with Pharaoh
king of Egypt, and married Pharaoh's daughter; then he brought her [b]to the City of David until he had finished building his [c]own house, and [d]the house of the LORD, and [e]the wall all around
Jerusalem. 2 [a]Meanwhile the people sacrificed
at the high places, because there was no house built for the name of the LORD until those days.
3 And Solomon [a]loved the LORD, [b]walking in
the statutes of his father David, except that he sacrificed and burned incense at the high places.
4 Now [a]the king went to Gibeon to sacrifice
there, [b]for that *was* the great high place: Solomon offered a thousand burnt offerings on
that altar. 5 [a]At Gibeon the LORD appeared to
Solomon [b]in a dream by night; and God said, "Ask! What shall I give you?"
6 [a]And Solomon said: "You have shown great
mercy to Your servant David my father, because he [b]walked before You in truth, in righteousness, and in uprightness of heart with You; You have continued this great kindness for him, and You [c]have given him a son to sit on his throne, as *it is*
this day. 7 Now, O LORD my God, You have made
Your servant king instead of my father David, but I *am* a [a]little child; I do not know *how* [b]to
go out or come in. 8 And Your servant *is* in the
midst of Your people whom You [a]have chosen, a great people, [b]too numerous to be numbered
or counted. 9 [a]Therefore give to Your servant
an understanding heart [b]to judge Your people, that I may [c]discern between good and evil. For who is able to judge this great people of Yours?"
10 The speech pleased the Lord, that Sol-
omon had asked this thing. 11 Then God said to
him: "Because you have asked this thing, and have [a]not asked long life for yourself, nor have asked riches for yourself, nor have asked the life of your enemies, but have asked for yourself understanding to discern justice, 12 [a]behold, I
have done according to your words; [b]see, I have given you a wise and understanding heart, so that there has not been anyone like you before you, nor shall any like you arise after you. 13 And
I have also [a]given you what you have not asked: both [b]riches and honor, so that there shall not be anyone like you among the kings all your days. 14 So [a]if you walk in My ways, to keep My
statutes and My commandments, [b]as your father David walked, then I will [c]lengthen your days."
15 Then Solomon [a]awoke; and indeed it had
been a dream. And he came to Jerusalem and stood before the ark of the covenant of the LORD, offered up burnt offerings, offered peace offerings, and [b]made a feast for all his servants.

### *SOLOMON'S WISE JUDGMENT*

16 Now two women *who were* harlots came
to the king, and [a]stood before him. 17 And one
woman said, "O my lord, this woman and I dwell in the same house; and I gave birth while she *was* in the house. 18 Then it happened, the third
day after I had given birth, that this woman also gave birth. And we *were* together; no one *was* with us in the house, except the two of us in the house. 19 And this woman's son died in the
night, because she lay on him. 20 So she arose in
the middle of the night and took my son from

**2:36** [a] 2 Sam. 16:5–13; 1 Kin. 2:8 **2:37** [a] 2 Sam. 15:23; 2 Kin. 23:6; John 18:1 [b] Lev. 20:9; Josh. 2:19; 2 Sam. 1:16; Ezek. 18:13 **2:39** [a] 1 Sam. 27:2 **2:44** [a] 2 Sam. 16:5–13 [b] 1 Sam. 25:39; 2 Kin. 11:1, 12–16; Ps. 7:16; Ezek. 17:19 **2:45** [a] 2 Sam. 7:13; [Prov. 25:5] **2:46** [a] 1 Kin. 2:12; 2 Chr. 1:1 **3:1** [a] 1 Kin. 7:8; 9:24 [b] 2 Sam. 5:7 [c] 1 Kin. 7:1 [d] 1 Kin. 6 [e] 1 Kin. 9:15, 19 **3:2** [a] [Deut. 12:2–5, 13, 14]; 1 Kin. 11:7; 22:43 **3:3** [a] [Rom. 8:28] [b] [1 Kin. 3:6, 14] **3:4** [a] 1 Kin. 9:2; 2 Chr. 1:3 [b] 1 Chr. 16:39; 21:29 **3:5** [a] 1 Kin. 9:2; 11:9; 2 Chr. 1:7 [b] Num. 12:6; Matt. 1:20; 2:13 **3:6** [a] 2 Chr. 1:8 [b] 1 Kin. 2:4; 9:4; 2 Kin. 20:3 [c] 2 Sam. 7:8–17; 1 Kin. 1:48 **3:7** [a] 1 Chr. 22:5; Jer. 1:6, 7 [b] Num. 27:17; 2 Sam. 5:2 **3:8** [a] [Ex. 19:6; Deut. 7:6] [b] Gen. 13:6; 15:5; 22:17 **3:9** [a] 2 Chr. 1:10; [James 1:5] [b] Ps. 72:1, 2 [c] 2 Sam. 14:17; Is. 7:15; [Heb. 5:14] **3:11** [a] [James 4:3] **3:12** [a] [1 John 5:14, 15] [b] 1 Kin. 4:29–31; 5:12; 10:24; Eccl. 1:16 **3:13** [a] [Matt. 6:33; Eph. 3:20] [b] 1 Kin. 4:21, 24; 10:23; 1 Chr. 29:12 **3:14** [a] [1 Kin. 6:12] [b] 1 Kin. 15:5 [c] Ps. 91:16; Prov. 3:2 **3:15** [a] Gen. 41:7 [b] Gen. 40:20; 1 Kin. 8:65; Esth. 1:3; Dan. 5:1; Mark 6:21 **3:16** [a] Num. 27:2

my side, while your maidservant slept, and laid him in her bosom, and laid her dead child in my bosom. 21 And when I rose in the morning to nurse my son, there he was, dead. But when I had examined him in the morning, indeed, he was not my son whom I had borne."

22 Then the other woman said, "No! But the living one *is* my son, and the dead one *is* your son."

And the first woman said, "No! But the dead one *is* your son, and the living one *is* my son."

Thus they spoke before the king.

23 And the king said, "The one says, 'This *is* my son, who lives, and your son *is* the dead one'; and the other says, 'No! But your son *is* the dead one, and my son *is* the living one.' " 24 Then the king said, "Bring me a sword." So they brought a sword before the king. 25 And the king said, "Divide the living child in two, and give half to one, and half to the other."

26 Then the woman whose son *was* living spoke to the king, for [a]she yearned with compassion for her son; and she said, "O my lord, give her the living child, and by no means kill him!"

But the other said, "Let him be neither mine nor yours, *but* divide *him*."

27 So the king answered and said, "Give the first woman the living child, and by no means kill him; she *is* his mother."

28 And all Israel heard of the judgment which the king had rendered; and they feared the king, for they saw that the [a]wisdom of God *was* in him to administer justice.

## SOLOMON'S ADMINISTRATION

4 So King Solomon was king over all Israel. 2 And these *were* his officials: Azariah the son of Zadok, the priest; 3 Elihoreph and Ahijah, the sons of Shisha, scribes; [a]Jehoshaphat the son of Ahilud, the recorder; 4 [a]Benaiah the son of Jehoiada, over the army; Zadok and [b]Abiathar, the priests; 5 Azariah the son of Nathan, over [a]the officers; Zabud the son of Nathan, [b]a priest *and* [c]the king's friend; 6 Ahishar, over the household; and [a]Adoniram the son of Abda, over the labor force.

7 And Solomon had twelve governors over all Israel, who provided food for the king and his household; each one made provision for one month of the year. 8 These *are* their names: Ben-Hur,[1] in the mountains of Ephraim; 9 Ben-Deker,[1] in Makaz, Shaalbim, Beth Shemesh, and Elon Beth Hanan; 10 Ben-Hesed,[1] in Arubboth; to him *belonged* Sochoh and all the land of Hepher; 11 Ben-Abinadab,[1] *in* all the regions of Dor; he had Taphath the daughter of Solomon as wife; 12 Baana the son of Ahilud, *in* Taanach, Megiddo, and all Beth Shean, which *is* beside Zaretan below Jezreel, from Beth Shean to Abel Meholah, as far as the other side of Jokneam; 13 Ben-Geber,[1] in Ramoth Gilead; to him *belonged* [a]the towns of Jair the son of Manasseh, in Gilead; to him *also belonged* [b]the region of Argob in Bashan—sixty large cities with walls and bronze gate-bars; 14 Ahinadab the son of Iddo, *in* Mahanaim; 15 [a]Ahimaaz, in Naphtali; he also took Basemath the daughter of Solomon as wife; 16 Baanah the son of [a]Hushai, in Asher and Aloth; 17 Jehoshaphat the son of Paruah, in Issachar; 18 [a]Shimei the son of Elah, in Benjamin; 19 Geber the son of Uri, in the land of Gilead, *in* [a]the country of Sihon king of the Amorites, and of Og king of Bashan. *He was* the only governor who *was* in the land.

## PROSPERITY AND WISDOM OF SOLOMON'S REIGN

20 Judah and Israel *were* as numerous [a]as the sand by the sea in multitude, [b]eating and drinking and rejoicing. 21 So [a]Solomon reigned over all kingdoms from [b]the River[1] *to* the land of the Philistines, as far as the border of Egypt. [c]*They* brought tribute and served Solomon all the days of his life.

22 [a]Now Solomon's provision for one day was thirty kors of fine flour, sixty kors of meal, 23 ten fatted oxen, twenty oxen from the pastures, and one hundred sheep, besides deer, gazelles, roebucks, and fatted fowl.

24 For he had dominion over all *the region* on this side of the River[1] from Tiphsah even to Gaza, namely over [a]all the kings on this side of the River; and [b]he had peace on every side all around him. 25 And Judah and Israel [a]dwelt safely, [b]each man under his vine and his fig tree, [c]from Dan as far as Beersheba, all the days of Solomon.

26 [a]Solomon had forty[1] thousand stalls of [b]horses for his chariots, and twelve thousand horsemen. 27 And [a]these governors, each man in his month, provided food for King Solomon and for all who came to King Solomon's table. There was no lack in their supply. 28 They also brought barley and straw to the proper place, for the horses and steeds, each man according to his charge.

29 And [a]God gave Solomon wisdom and exceedingly great understanding, and largeness of heart like the sand on the seashore. 30 Thus Solomon's wisdom excelled the wisdom of all the men [a]of the East and all [b]the wisdom of Egypt. 31 For he was [a]wiser than all men—[b]than Ethan the Ezrahite, [c]and Heman, Chalcol, and Darda, the sons of Mahol; and his fame was in all the surrounding nations. 32 [a]He spoke three

3:26 [a] Gen. 43:30; Is. 49:15; Jer. 31:20; Hos. 11:8 3:28 [a] 1 Kin. 3:9, 11, 12; 2 Chr. 1:12; Dan. 1:17; [Col. 2:2, 3] 4:3 [a] 2 Sam. 8:16; 20:24 4:4 [a] 1 Kin. 2:35 [b] 1 Kin. 2:27 4:5 [a] 1 Kin. 4:7 [b] 2 Sam. 8:18; 20:26 [c] 2 Sam. 15:37; 16:16; 1 Chr. 27:33 4:6 [a] 1 Kin. 5:14 4:8 [1] Literally *Son of Hur* 4:9 [1] Literally *Son of Deker* 4:10 [1] Literally *Son of Hesed* 4:11 [1] Literally *Son of Abinadab* 4:13 [a] Num. 32:41; 1 Chr. 2:22 [b] Deut. 3:4 [1] Literally *Son of Geber* 4:15 [a] 2 Sam. 15:27 4:16 [a] 2 Sam. 15:32; 1 Chr. 27:33 4:18 [a] 1 Kin. 1:8 4:19 [a] Deut. 3:8–10 4:20 [a] Gen. 22:17; 32:12; 1 Kin. 3:8; [Prov. 14:28] [b] Ps. 72:3, 7; Mic. 4:4 4:21 [a] Ex. 34:24; 2 Chr. 9:26; Ps. 72:8 [b] Gen. 15:18; Josh. 1:4 [c] Ps. 68:29 [1] That is, the Euphrates 4:22 [a] Neh. 5:18 4:24 [a] Ps. 72:11 [b] 1 Kin. 5:4; 1 Chr. 22:9 [1] That is, the Euphrates 4:25 [a] [Jer. 23:6] [b] [Mic. 4:4; Zech. 3:10] [c] Judg. 20:1 4:26 [a] 1 Kin. 10:26; 2 Chr. 1:14 [b] [Deut. 17:16] [1] Following Masoretic Text and most other authorities; some manuscripts of the Septuagint read *four* (compare 2 Chronicles 9:25). 4:27 [a] 1 Kin. 4:7 4:29 [a] 1 Kin. 3:12 4:30 [a] Gen. 25:6 [b] Is. 19:11, 12; Acts 7:22 4:31 [a] 1 Kin. 3:12 [b] 1 Chr. 15:19; Ps. 89:title [c] 1 Chr. 2:6; Ps. 88:title 4:32 [a] Prov. 1:1; 10:1; 25:1; Eccl. 12:9

thousand proverbs, and his [b]songs were one
thousand and five. 33 Also he spoke of trees, from
the cedar tree of Lebanon even to the hyssop
that springs out of the wall; he spoke also of
animals, of birds, of creeping things, and of fish.
34 And men of all nations, from all the kings of
the earth who had heard of his wisdom, [a]came
to hear the wisdom of Solomon.

### *SOLOMON PREPARES TO BUILD THE TEMPLE*

*(2 Chr. 2:1–18)*

**5** Now [a]Hiram king of Tyre sent his servants
to Solomon, because he heard that they had
anointed him king in place of his father, [b]for
Hiram had always loved David. 2 Then [a]Solomon
sent to Hiram, saying:

3 [a]You know how my father David could not
build a house for the name of the LORD
his God [b]because of the wars which were
fought against him on every side, until
the LORD put *his foes*[1] under the soles of
his feet.
4 But now the LORD my God has given
me [a]rest on every side; *there is* neither
adversary nor evil occurrence.
5 [a]And behold, I propose to build a house
for the name of the LORD my God, [b]as the
LORD spoke to my father David, saying,
"Your son, whom I will set on your throne
in your place, he shall build the house for
My name."
6 Now therefore, command that they cut
down [a]cedars for me from Lebanon; and
my servants will be with your servants,
and I will pay you wages for your servants
according to whatever you say. For you
know *there is* none among us who has
skill to cut timber like the Sidonians.

7 So it was, when Hiram heard the words
of Solomon, that he rejoiced greatly and said,

Blessed *be* the LORD this day, for He has
given David a wise son over this great
people!

8 Then Hiram sent to Solomon, saying:

I have considered *the message* which
you sent me, *and* I will do all you desire
concerning the cedar and cypress logs.
9 My servants shall bring *them* down [a]from
Lebanon to the sea; I will float them in rafts
by sea to the place you indicate to me, and
will have them broken apart there; then you
can take *them* away. And you shall fulfill my
desire [b]by giving food for my household.

10 Then Hiram gave Solomon cedar and cypress
logs *according to* all his desire. 11 [a]And Solomon gave
Hiram twenty thousand kors of wheat *as* food for
his household, and twenty[1] kors of pressed oil. Thus
Solomon gave to Hiram year by year.
12 So the LORD gave Solomon wisdom, [a]as
He had promised him; and there was peace
between Hiram and Solomon, and the two of
them made a treaty together.
13 Then King Solomon raised up a labor force
out of all Israel; and the labor force was thirty
thousand men. 14 And he sent them to Lebanon,
ten thousand a month in shifts: they were one
month in Lebanon *and* two months at home;
[a]Adoniram *was* in charge of the labor force.
15 [a]Solomon had seventy thousand who carried
burdens, and eighty thousand who quarried
*stone* in the mountains, 16 besides three thousand
three hundred[1] from the [a]chiefs of Solomon's
deputies, who supervised the people who la-
bored in the work. 17 And the king commanded
them to quarry large stones, costly stones, *and*
[a]hewn stones, to lay the foundation of the tem-
ple.[1] 18 So Solomon's builders, Hiram's builders,
and the Gebalites quarried *them;* and they pre-
pared timber and stones to build the temple.

### *SOLOMON BUILDS THE TEMPLE*

*(2 Chr. 3:1–14)*

**6** And [a]it came to pass in the four hundred
and eightieth[1] year after the children of Is-
rael had come out of the land of Egypt, in the
fourth year of Solomon's reign over Israel, in the
month of Ziv, which *is* the second month, [b]that
he began to build the house of the LORD. 2 Now
[a]the house which King Solomon built for the
LORD, its length *was* sixty cubits, its width twen-
ty, and its height thirty cubits. 3 The vestibule in
front of the sanctuary[1] of the house *was* twenty
cubits long across the width of the house, *and*

> **6:1** Many scholars use this date to establish the timeframe of the exodus. The division of the kingdom just after Solomon's death can be dated at 930 BC (1 Kin. 11:41–43). Allowing forty years for Solomon's rule (1 Kin. 11:42), **the fourth year of reign** would be 966 BC. If the exodus took place 480 years before 966 BC, its date was 1446 BC.

**4:32** [b] Song 1:1 **4:34** [a] 1 Kin. 10:1; 2 Chr. 9:1, 23 **5:1** [a] 1 Kin. 5:10, 18; 2 Chr. 2:3 [b] 2 Sam. 5:11; 1 Chr. 14:1 **5:2** [a] 2 Chr. 2:3 **5:3** [a] 1 Chr. 28:2, 3 [b] 1 Chr. 22:8; 28:3 [1] Literally *them* **5:4** [a] 1 Kin. 4:24; 1 Chr. 22:9 **5:5** [a] 2 Chr. 2:4 [b] 2 Sam. 7:12, 13; 1 Kin. 6:38; 1 Chr. 17:12; 22:10; 28:6; 2 Chr. 6:2 **5:6** [a] 2 Chr. 2:8, 10 **5:9** [a] Ezra 3:7 [b] Ezek. 27:17; Acts 12:20 **5:11** [a] 2 Chr. 2:10 [1] Following Masoretic Text, Targum, and Vulgate; Septuagint and Syriac read *twenty thousand.* **5:12** [a] 1 Kin. 3:12 **5:14** [a] 1 Kin. 12:18 **5:15** [a] 1 Kin. 9:20–22; 2 Chr. 2:17, 18 **5:16** [a] 1 Kin. 9:23 [1] Following Masoretic Text, Targum, and Vulgate; Septuagint reads *three thousand six hundred.* **5:17** [a] 1 Kin. 6:7; 1 Chr. 22:2 [1] Literally *house,* and so frequently throughout this book **6:1** [a] 2 Chr. 3:1, 2 [b] Acts 7:47 [1] Following Masoretic Text, Targum, and Vulgate; Septuagint reads *fortieth.* **6:2** [a] Ezek. 41:1 **6:3** [1] Hebrew *heykal;* here the main room of the temple, elsewhere called the holy place (compare Exodus 26:33 and Ezekiel 41:1)

the width of *the vestibule*[2] *extended* ten cubits
from the front of the house. 4 And he made for
the house [a]windows with beveled frames.
5 Against the wall of the temple he built [a]cham-
bers all around, *against* the walls of the temple, all
around the sanctuary [b]and the inner sanctuary.[1]
Thus he made side chambers all around it. 6 The
lowest chamber *was* five cubits wide, the middle
*was* six cubits wide, and the third *was* seven cu-
bits wide; for he made narrow ledges around the
outside of the temple, so that *the support beams*
would not be fastened into the walls of the temple.
7 And [a]the temple, when it was being built, was
built with stone finished at the quarry, so that no
hammer or chisel *or* any iron tool was heard in
the temple while it was being built. 8 The doorway
for the middle story[1] *was* on the right side of the
temple. They went up by stairs to the middle *story,*
and from the middle to the third.
9 [a]So he built the temple and finished it, and
he paneled the temple with beams and boards
of cedar. 10 And he built side chambers against
the entire temple, each five cubits high; they
were attached to the temple with cedar beams.
11 Then the word of the LORD came to Sol-
omon, saying: 12 "*Concerning* this temple which
you are building, [a]if you walk in My statutes,
execute My judgments, keep all My command-
ments, and walk in them, then I will perform
My word with you, [b]which I spoke to your father
David. 13 And [a]I will dwell among the children of
Israel, and will not [b]forsake My people Israel."
14 So Solomon built the temple and finished
it. 15 And he built the inside walls of the temple
with cedar boards; from the floor of the temple to
the ceiling he paneled the inside with wood; and
he covered the floor of the temple with planks of
cypress. 16 Then he built the twenty-cubit room
at the rear of the temple, from floor to ceiling,
with cedar boards; he built *it* inside as the inner
sanctuary, as the [a]Most Holy *Place.* 17 And in front
of it the temple sanctuary was forty cubits *long.*
18 The inside of the temple was cedar, carved
with ornamental buds and open flowers. All *was*
cedar; there was no stone *to be* seen.
19 And he prepared the inner sanctuary inside
the temple, to set the ark of the covenant of the
LORD there. 20 The inner sanctuary *was* twen-
ty cubits long, twenty cubits wide, and twenty
cubits high. He overlaid it with pure gold, and
overlaid the altar of cedar. 21 So Solomon over-
laid the inside of the temple with pure gold. He

**6:3** [2] Literally *it* **6:4** [a] Ezek. 40:16; 41:16 **6:5** [a] Ezek. 41:6 [b] 1 Kin. 6:16, 19–21, 31 [1] Hebrew *debir;* here the inner room of the temple, elsewhere called the Most Holy Place (compare verse 16) **6:7** [a] Ex. 20:25; Deut. 27:5, 6 **6:8** [1] Following Masoretic Text and Vulgate; Septuagint reads *upper story;* Targum reads *ground story.* **6:9** [a] 1 Kin. 6:14, 38 **6:12** [a] 1 Kin. 2:4; 9:4 [b] [2 Sam. 7:13; 1 Chr. 22:10] **6:13** [a] Ex. 25:8; Lev. 26:11; [2 Cor. 6:16; Rev. 21:3] [b] [Deut. 31:6] **6:16** [a] Ex. 26:33; Lev. 16:2; 1 Kin. 8:6; 2 Chr. 3:8; Ezek. 45:3; Heb. 9:3

STORY OF SCRIPTURE 27

1 KINGS 6:1–28

## THE TEMPLE

### WHAT'S GOING ON?

The construction of Solomon's Temple in Jerusalem is another significant event in the story of Scripture. This temple wasn't just a building; it was a symbol of God's presence among His people, a physical manifestation of His relationship with the Israelites. The temple also symbolized God's faithfulness in fulfilling His promise to David, as his son Solomon completed its construction. This passage is about more than architecture; it's about creating a sacred space where God and humanity can meet. It represents God dwelling among His people and the centrality of worship in the life of Israel.

### WHAT DOES THIS MEAN FOR ME?

Those who have put their faith in Jesus are temples of the Holy Spirit (see 1 Cor. 6:19). Just as the temple was built with care and purpose, we are called to build our lives on the foundation of God's Word, paying attention to the spiritual details and dedicating ourselves to His service.

### DID YOU CATCH THE PATTERN?

The building of the temple fits into a larger biblical theme of God desiring to dwell among His people. From the tabernacle in the wilderness to the incarnation of Jesus, the Bible consistently shows God's initiative to be close to His people. Therefore, the story of Solomon building the temple is a physical representation of a spiritual truth that resonates through time: God is with us, and He desires to make His home in our hearts. This truth invites us to live to honor His presence and reflect His love to the world around us.

*For the next* Story of Scripture *reading and devotion, turn to 1 Kings 11:1–19 on page 348.*

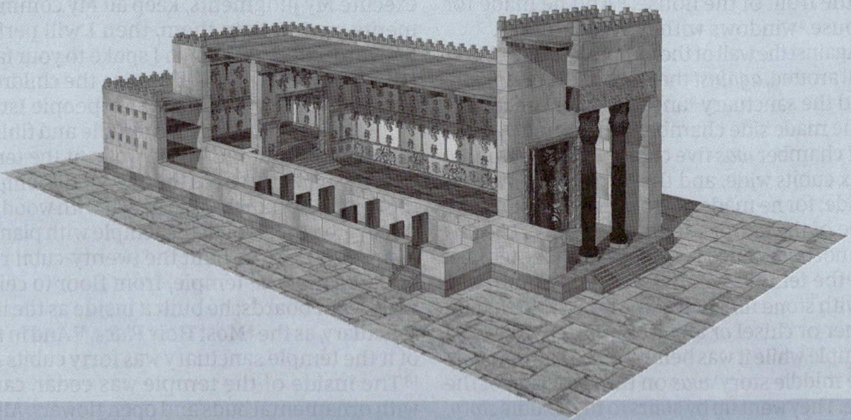

# SOLOMON'S TEMPLE AND TEMPLE FURNISHINGS

Temple source materials are subject to academic interpretation, and subsequent art reconstructions vary. This model recognizes influence from the wilderness tabernacle, accepts general Near Eastern cultural diffusion, and rejects overt pagan Canaanite symbols. It uses known archaeological parallels to supplement the text and assumes interior dimensions from 1 Kings 6:17–20. Glimpses of the rich ornamentation of Solomon's temple can be gained through recent discoveries that illumine the text of 1 Kings 6–7.

**1 Ark of the Covenant (Testimony)** The only article of furniture in the innermost room, the Most Holy Place. The ark was made of acacia wood overlaid with gold. The gold cover was called the "mercy seat" (Ex. 25:17–22) because on the Day of Atonement, the sacrificed animal's blood was applied to it to signify God had extended mercy and forgiven sin. A cherub was positioned at each end of the mercy seat facing the other with its wings outstretched and their faces bowed. Within the ark were two stone tablets containing the Ten Commandments (Ex. 25:16, 21), a gold pot of manna (Ex. 16:32–34), and Aaron's rod that budded (Num. 17:1–11).

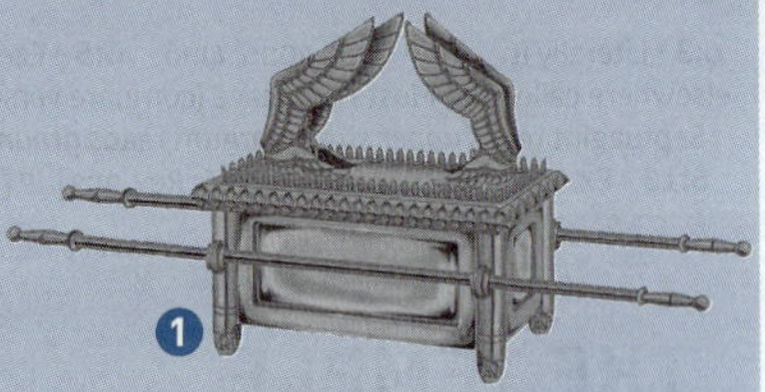


**2 Sea of Cast Bronze** The largest furnishing, the bronze sea was about fifteen feet in diameter. It was supported by twelve bulls. Its purpose was for the priests to wash in (2 Chr. 4:6).

**3 Incense Altar** Here, incense was burned every morning and evening, symbolizing the prayers of the people. The priest sprinkled blood on this altar to make atonement for his sins and those of the people.

**4 Table of Showbread** This furnishing was made of solid gold with decorations modeled after an almond blossom (Ex. 25:33). The lampstand itself resembled a tree. Its purpose was to give light in the tabernacle, but it symbolized God's giving light to His people.

**5 Lampstand** Ten lampstands were in the temple, five on each side of the sanctuary (1 Kin. 7:49), to which were added ten tables (2 Chr. 4:8). This furnishing was made of solid gold with decorations modeled after an almond blossom (Ex. 25:33). The lampstand itself resembled a tree. Its purpose was to give light in the temple, but it symbolized God's giving light to His people.

stretched gold chains across the front of the
inner sanctuary, and overlaid it with gold. 22 The
whole temple he overlaid with gold, until he had
finished all the temple; also he overlaid with gold
[a]the entire altar that *was* by the inner sanctuary.
23 Inside the inner sanctuary [a]he made two
cherubim *of* olive wood, *each* ten cubits high.
24 One wing of the cherub *was* five cubits, and the
other wing of the cherub five cubits: ten cubits
from the tip of one wing to the tip of the other.
25 And the other cherub *was* ten cubits; both
cherubim *were* of the same size and shape. 26 The
height of one cherub *was* ten cubits, and so *was*
the other cherub. 27 Then he set the cherubim
inside the inner room;[1] and [a]they stretched out
the wings of the cherubim so that the wing of the
one touched *one* wall, and the wing of the other
cherub touched the other wall. And their wings
touched each other in the middle of the room.
28 Also he overlaid the cherubim with gold.
29 Then he carved all the walls of the temple
all around, both the inner and outer *sanctuaries,*
with carved [a]figures of cherubim, palm trees,
and open flowers. 30 And the floor of the temple
he overlaid with gold, both the inner and outer
*sanctuaries.*
31 For the entrance of the inner sanctuary
he made doors *of* olive wood; the lintel *and*
doorposts *were* one-fifth *of the wall.* 32 The two
doors *were of* olive wood; and he carved on
them figures of cherubim, palm trees, and open
flowers, and overlaid *them* with gold; and he
spread gold on the cherubim and on the palm
trees. 33 So for the door of the sanctuary he also
made doorposts *of* olive wood, one-fourth *of the*
*wall.* 34 And the two doors *were of* cypress wood;
[a]two panels *comprised* one folding door, and
two panels *comprised* the other folding door.
35 Then he carved cherubim, palm trees, and
open flowers *on them,* and overlaid *them* with
gold applied evenly on the carved work.
36 And he built the [a]inner court with three
rows of hewn stone and a row of cedar beams.
37 [a]In the fourth year the foundation of the
house of the LORD was laid, in the month of
Ziv. 38 And in the eleventh year, in the month of
Bul, which is the eighth month, the house was
finished in all its details and according to all
its plans. So he was [a]seven years in building it.

## SOLOMON'S OTHER BUILDINGS

7 But Solomon took [a]thirteen years to build
his own house; so he finished all his house.
2 He also built the [a]House of the Forest of
Lebanon; its length *was* one hundred cubits,
its width fifty cubits, and its height thirty cubits,
with four rows of cedar pillars, and cedar beams
on the pillars. 3 And *it was* paneled with cedar

> **6:37** Solomon began work on the temple around 967 BC and completed it seven years later. In 586 BC, the Babylonians destroyed it completely. The Jewish people then built a second temple, which was completed in 516 BC (see Ezra, Haggai, and Zechariah). Herod was in the process of remodeling this temple in Jesus' day. Herod's temple was destroyed by the Romans in AD 70. It has never been rebuilt.

above the beams that *were* on forty-five pillars,
fifteen *to* a row. 4 *There were* windows *with beveled*
*frames in* three rows, and window *was* opposite
window *in* three tiers. 5 And all the doorways and
doorposts *had* rectangular frames; and window
*was* opposite window *in* three tiers.
6 He also made the Hall of Pillars: its length
*was* fifty cubits, and its width thirty cubits; and
in front of them *was* a portico with pillars, and
a canopy *was* in front of them.
7 Then he made a hall for the throne, the
Hall of Judgment, where he might judge; and
*it was* paneled with cedar from floor to ceiling.[1]
8 And the house where he dwelt *had* anoth-
er court inside the hall, of like workmanship.
Solomon also made a house like this hall for
Pharaoh's daughter, [a]whom he had taken *as wife.*
9 All these *were of* costly stones cut to size,
trimmed with saws, inside and out, from the foun-
dation to the eaves, and also on the outside to the
great court. 10 The foundation *was of* costly stones,
large stones, some ten cubits and some eight cu-
bits. 11 And above *were* costly stones, hewn to size,
and cedar wood. 12 The great court *was* enclosed
with three rows of hewn stones and a row of cedar
beams. So were the [a]inner court of the house of
the LORD [b]and the vestibule of the temple.

## HIRAM THE CRAFTSMAN

13 Now King Solomon sent and brought
Huram[1] from Tyre. 14 [a]He *was* the son of a widow
from the tribe of Naphtali, and [b]his father *was*
a man of Tyre, a bronze worker; [c]he was filled
with wisdom and understanding and skill in
working with all kinds of bronze work. So he
came to King Solomon and did all his work.

## THE BRONZE PILLARS FOR THE TEMPLE

*(2 Chr. 3:15–17)*

15 And he cast [a]two pillars of bronze, each one
eighteen cubits high, and a line of twelve cubits
measured the circumference of each. 16 Then he
made two capitals *of* cast bronze, to set on the
tops of the pillars. The height of one capital *was*

**6:22** [a] Ex. 30:1, 3, 6 **6:23** [a] Ex. 37:7–9; 2 Chr. 3:10–12 **6:27** [a] Ex. 25:20; 37:9; 1 Kin. 8:7; 2 Chr. 5:8 [1] Literally *house* **6:29** [a] Ex. 36:8, 35 **6:34** [a] Ezek. 41:23–25 **6:36** [a] 1 Kin. 7:12; Jer. 36:10 **6:37** [a] 1 Kin. 6:1 **6:38** [a] 2 Sam. 7:13; 1 Kin. 5:5; 6:1; 8:19 **7:1** [a] 1 Kin. 3:1; 9:10; 2 Chr. 8:1 **7:2** [a] 1 Kin. 10:17, 21; 2 Chr. 9:16 **7:7** [1] Literally *floor,* that is, of the upper level **7:8** [a] 1 Kin. 3:1; 9:24; 11:1; 2 Chr. 8:11 **7:12** [a] 1 Kin. 6:36 [b] John 10:23; Acts 3:11 **7:13** [1] Hebrew *Hiram* (compare 2 Chronicles 2:13, 14) **7:14** [a] 2 Chr. 2:14 [b] 2 Chr. 4:16 [c] Ex. 31:3; 36:1 **7:15** [a] 2 Kin. 25:17; 2 Chr. 3:15; 4:12; Jer. 52:21

five cubits, and the height of the other capital
*was* five cubits. 17 *He made* a lattice network, with
wreaths of chainwork, for the capitals which *were*
on top of the pillars: seven chains for one capital
and seven for the other capital. 18 So he made the
pillars, and two rows of pomegranates above the
network all around to cover the capitals that *were*
on top; and thus he did for the other capital.
19 The capitals which *were* on top of the pil-
lars in the hall *were* in the shape of lilies, four
cubits. 20 The capitals on the two pillars also
*had pomegranates* above, by the convex surface
which *was* next to the network; and there *were*
[a]two hundred such pomegranates in rows on
each of the capitals all around.
21 [a]Then he set up the pillars by the vestibule
of the temple; he set up the pillar on the right
and called its name Jachin, and he set up the
pillar on the left and called its name Boaz. 22 The
tops of the pillars were in the shape of lilies. So
the work of the pillars was finished.

### *THE SEA AND THE OXEN*

23 And he made [a]the Sea of cast bronze, ten
cubits from one brim to the other; *it was* com-
pletely round. Its height *was* five cubits, and a
line of thirty cubits measured its circumference.
24 Below its brim *were* ornamental buds en-
circling it all around, ten to a cubit, [a]all the way
around the Sea. The ornamental buds *were* cast
in two rows when it was cast. 25 It stood on [a]twelve
oxen: three looking toward the north, three
looking toward the west, three looking toward
the south, and three looking toward the east; the
Sea *was set* upon them, and all their back parts
*pointed* inward. 26 It *was* a handbreadth thick; and
its brim was shaped like the brim of a cup, *like* a
lily blossom. It contained two thousand[1] baths.

### *THE CARTS AND THE LAVERS*

27 He also made ten carts of bronze; four
cubits *was* the length of each cart, four cubits
its width, and three cubits its height. 28 And this
*was* the design of the carts: They had panels,
and the panels *were* between frames; 29 on the
panels that *were* between the frames *were* lions,
oxen, and cherubim. And on the frames *was* a
pedestal on top. Below the lions and oxen *were*
wreaths of plaited work. 30 Every cart had four
bronze wheels and axles of bronze, and its four
feet had supports. Under the laver *were* supports
of cast *bronze* beside each wreath. 31 Its opening
inside the crown at the top *was* one cubit in
diameter; and the opening *was* round, shaped
*like* a pedestal, one and a half cubits in outside
diameter; and also on the opening *were* engrav-
ings, but the panels were square, not round.
32 Under the panels *were* the four wheels, and
the axles of the wheels *were joined* to the cart.
The height of a wheel *was* one and a half cubits.
33 The workmanship of the wheels *was* like the
workmanship of a chariot wheel; their axle pins,
their rims, their spokes, and their hubs *were* all of
cast *bronze.* 34 And *there were* four supports at the
four corners of each cart; its supports *were* part
of the cart itself. 35 On the top of the cart, at the
height of half a cubit, *it was* perfectly round. And
on the top of the cart, its flanges and its panels
*were* of the same casting. 36 On the plates of its
flanges and on its panels he engraved cherubim,
lions, and palm trees, wherever there was a clear
space on each, with wreaths all around. 37 Thus
he made the ten carts. All of them were of the
same mold, one measure, *and* one shape.
38 Then [a]he made ten lavers of bronze; each
laver contained forty baths, *and* each laver *was*
four cubits. On each of the ten carts *was* a laver.
39 And he put five carts on the right side of the
house, and five on the left side of the house.
He set the Sea on the right side of the house,
toward the southeast.

### *FURNISHINGS OF THE TEMPLE*

*(2 Chr. 4:11–18)*

40 [a]Huram[1] made the lavers and the shovels
and the bowls. So Huram finished doing all the
work that he was to do for King Solomon *for* the
house of the LORD: 41 the two pillars, the *two* bowl-
shaped capitals that *were* on top of the two pillars;
the two [a]networks covering the two bowl-shaped
capitals which *were* on top of the pillars; 42 [a]four
hundred pomegranates for the two networks
(two rows of pomegranates for each network, to
cover the two bowl-shaped capitals that *were* on
top of the pillars); 43 the ten carts, and ten lavers
on the carts; 44 one Sea, and twelve oxen under
the Sea; 45 [a]the pots, the shovels, and the bowls.
All these articles which Huram[1] made for
King Solomon *for* the house of the LORD *were of*
burnished bronze. 46 [a]In the plain of Jordan the
king had them cast in clay molds, between [b]Suc-
coth and [c]Zaretan. 47 And Solomon did not weigh
all the articles, because *there were* so many;
the weight of the bronze was not [a]determined.
48 Thus Solomon had all the furnishings
made for the house of the LORD: [a]the altar of
gold, and [b]the table of gold on which *was* [c]the
showbread; 49 the lampstands of pure gold, five
on the right *side* and five on the left in front of the
inner sanctuary, with the flowers and the lamps
and the wick-trimmers of gold; 50 the basins, the
trimmers, the bowls, the ladles, and the censers
of pure gold; and the hinges of gold, *both* for the
doors of the inner room (the Most Holy *Place*)
*and* for the doors of the main hall of the temple.
51 So all the work that King Solomon had
done for the house of the LORD was finished;
and Solomon brought in the things [a]which his

7:20 [a] 2 Chr. 3:16; 4:13; Jer. 52:23 7:21 [a] 2 Chr. 3:17 7:23 [a] 2 Kin. 25:13; 2 Chr. 4:2; Jer. 52:17 7:24 [a] 2 Chr. 4:3 7:25 [a] 2 Chr. 4:4, 5; Jer. 52:20 7:26 [1] Or *three thousand* (compare 2 Chronicles 4:5) 7:38 [a] Ex. 30:18; 2 Chr. 4:6 7:40 [a] 2 Chr. 4:11—5:1 [1] Hebrew *Hiram* (compare 2 Chronicles 2:13, 14) 7:41 [a] 1 Kin. 7:17, 18 7:42 [a] 1 Kin. 7:20 7:45 [a] Ex. 27:3; 2 Chr. 4:16 [1] Hebrew *Hiram* (compare 2 Chronicles 2:13, 14) 7:46 [a] 2 Chr. 4:17 [b] Gen. 33:17; Josh. 13:27 [c] Josh. 3:16 7:47 [a] 1 Chr. 22:3, 14 7:48 [a] Ex. 37:25, 26; 2 Chr. 4:8 [b] Ex. 37:10, 11 [c] Lev. 24:5–8 7:51 [a] 2 Sam. 8:11; 1 Chr. 18:11; 2 Chr. 5:1

father David had dedicated: the silver and the
gold and the furnishings. He put them in the
treasuries of the house of the LORD.

### *THE ARK BROUGHT INTO THE TEMPLE*

*(2 Chr. 5:2–6:2)*

**8** Now [a]Solomon assembled the elders of Israel
and all the heads of the tribes, the chief fa-
thers of the children of Israel, to King Solomon in
Jerusalem, [b]that they might bring [c]up the ark of
the covenant of the LORD from the City of David,
which *is* Zion. 2 Therefore all the men of Israel
assembled with King Solomon at the [a]feast in the
month of Ethanim, which *is* the seventh month.
3 So all the elders of Israel came, [a]and the priests
took up the ark. 4 Then they brought up the ark
of the LORD, [a]the tabernacle of meeting, and all
the holy furnishings that *were* in the tabernacle.
The priests and the Levites brought them up.
5 Also King Solomon, and all the congregation
of Israel who were assembled with him, *were*
with him before the ark, [a]sacrificing sheep and
oxen that could not be counted or numbered for
multitude. 6 Then the priests [a]brought in the ark
of the covenant of the LORD to [b]its place, into the
inner sanctuary of the temple, to the Most Holy
*Place,* [c]under the wings of the cherubim. 7 For the
cherubim spread *their* two wings over the place
of the ark, and the cherubim overshadowed the
ark and its poles. 8 The poles [a]extended so that
the ends of the poles could be seen from the
holy *place,* in front of the inner sanctuary; but
they could not be seen from outside. And they
are there to this day. 9 [a]Nothing *was* in the ark
[b]except the two tablets of stone which Moses
[c]put there at Horeb, [d]when the LORD made *a*
*covenant* with the children of Israel, when they
came out of the land of Egypt.

10 And it came to pass, when the priests came
out of the holy *place,* that the cloud [a]filled the
house of the LORD, 11 so that the priests could not
continue ministering because of the cloud; for the
[a]glory of the LORD filled the house of the LORD.

12 [a]Then Solomon spoke:

"The LORD said He would dwell [b]in the
dark cloud.
13 [a]I have surely built You an exalted house,
[b]And a place for You to dwell in forever."

### *SOLOMON'S SPEECH AT COMPLETION OF THE WORK*

*(2 Chr. 6:3–11)*

14 Then the king turned around and [a]blessed
the whole assembly of Israel, while all the as-
sembly of Israel was standing. 15 And he said:
[a]"Blessed *be* the LORD God of Israel, who [b]spoke
with His mouth to my father David, and with His
hand has fulfilled *it,* saying, 16 'Since the day that
I brought My people Israel out of Egypt, I have
chosen no city from any tribe of Israel *in which*
to build a house, that [a]My name might be there;
but I chose [b]David to be over My people Israel.'
17 Now [a]it was in the heart of my father David to
build a temple[1] for the name of the LORD God of
Israel. 18 [a]But the LORD said to my father David,
'Whereas it was in your heart to build a temple for
My name, you did well that it was in your heart.
19 Nevertheless [a]you shall not build the temple,
but your son who will come from your body, he
shall build the temple for My name.' 20 So the
LORD has fulfilled His word which He spoke; and
I have filled the position of my father David, and
sit on the throne of Israel, [a]as the LORD promised;
and I have built a temple for the name of the
LORD God of Israel. 21 And there I have made a
place for the ark, in which *is* [a]the covenant of the
LORD which He made with our fathers, when He
brought them out of the land of Egypt."

### *SOLOMON'S PRAYER OF DEDICATION*

*(2 Chr. 6:12–39)*

22 Then Solomon stood before [a]the altar of
the LORD in the presence of all the assembly of
Israel, and [b]spread out his hands toward heaven;
23 and he said: "LORD God of Israel, [a]*there is* no
God in heaven above or on earth below like You,
[b]who keep *Your* covenant and mercy with Your
servants who [c]walk before You with all their
hearts. 24 You have kept what You promised
Your servant David my father; You have both
spoken with Your mouth and fulfilled *it* with
Your hand, as *it is* this day. 25 Therefore, LORD
God of Israel, now keep what You promised Your
servant David my father, saying, [a]'You shall not
fail to have a man sit before Me on the throne of
Israel, only if your sons take heed to their way,
that they walk before Me as you have walked
before Me.' 26 [a]And now I pray, O God of Israel,
let Your word come true, which You have spoken
to Your servant David my father.

27 "But [a]will God indeed dwell on the earth?
Behold, heaven and the [b]heaven of heavens
cannot contain You. How much less this temple
which I have built! 28 Yet regard the prayer of
Your servant and his supplication, O LORD my
God, and listen to the cry and the prayer which
Your servant is praying before You today: 29 that
Your eyes may be open toward this temple night
and day, toward the place of which You said, [a]'My
name shall be [b]there,' that You may hear the
prayer which Your servant makes [c]toward this

**8:1** [a] Num. 1:4; 7:2; 2 Chr. 5:2–14 [b] 2 Sam. 6:12–17; 1 Chr. 15:25–29 [c] 2 Sam. 5:7; 6:12, 16 **8:2** [a] Lev. 23:34; 1 Kin. 8:65; 2 Chr. 7:8–10 **8:3** [a] Num. 4:15; 7:9 **8:4** [a] 2 Chr. 1:3 **8:5** [a] 2 Sam. 6:13 **8:6** [a] 2 Sam. 6:17 [b] 1 Kin. 6:19 [c] 1 Kin. 6:27 **8:8** [a] Ex. 25:13–15; 37:4, 5 **8:9** [a] Ex. 25:21 [b] Deut. 10:5 [c] Ex. 24:7, 8; 40:20 [d] Ex. 34:27, 28 **8:10** [a] Ex. 40:34, 35 **8:11** [a] 2 Chr. 7:1, 2 **8:12** [a] 2 Chr. 6:1 [b] Ps. 18:11; 97:2 **8:13** [a] 2 Sam. 7:13 [b] Ps. 132:14 **8:14** [a] 2 Sam. 6:18 **8:15** [a] Luke 1:68 [b] 2 Sam. 7:2, 12, 13, 25 **8:16** [a] 1 Kin. 8:29 [b] 2 Sam. 7:8 **8:17** [a] 2 Sam. 7:2, 3 [1] Literally *house*, and so in verses 18–20 **8:18** [a] 2 Chr. 6:8, 9 **8:19** [a] 2 Sam. 7:5, 12, 13 **8:20** [a] 1 Chr. 28:5, 6 **8:21** [a] Deut. 31:26 **8:22** [a] 2 Chr. 6:12 [b] Ezra 9:5 **8:23** [a] Ex. 15:11 [b] [Neh. 1:5] [c] [Gen. 17:1] **8:25** [a] 1 Kin. 2:4; 9:5 **8:26** [a] 2 Sam. 7:25 **8:27** [a] [Acts 7:49; 17:24] [b] 2 Cor. 12:2 **8:29** [a] Deut. 12:11 [b] 1 Kin. 9:3 [c] Dan. 6:10

place. 30 [a]And may You hear the supplication of Your servant and of Your people Israel, when they pray toward this place. Hear in heaven Your dwelling place; and when You hear, forgive.

31 "When anyone sins against his neighbor, and is forced to take [a]an oath, and comes *and* takes an oath before Your altar in this temple, 32 then hear in heaven, and act, and judge Your servants, [a]condemning the wicked, bringing his way on his head, and justifying the righteous by giving him according to his righteousness.

33 [a]"When Your people Israel are defeated before an enemy because they have sinned against You, and [b]when they turn back to You and confess Your name, and pray and make supplication to You in this temple, 34 then hear in heaven, and forgive the sin of Your people Israel, and bring them back to the land which You gave to their [a]fathers.

35 [a]"When the heavens are shut up and there is no rain because they have sinned against You, when they pray toward this place and confess Your name, and turn from their sin because You afflict them, 36 then hear in heaven, and forgive the sin of Your servants, Your people Israel, that You may [a]teach them [b]the good way in which they should walk; and send rain on Your land which You have given to Your people as an inheritance.

37 [a]"When there is famine in the land, pestilence *or* blight *or* mildew, locusts *or* grasshoppers; when their enemy besieges them in the land of their cities; whatever plague or whatever sickness *there is;* 38 whatever prayer, whatever supplication is made by anyone, *or* by all Your people Israel, when each one knows the plague of his own heart, and spreads out his hands toward this temple: 39 then hear in heaven Your dwelling place, and forgive, and act, and give to everyone according to all his ways, whose heart You know (for You alone [a]know the hearts of all the sons of men), 40 [a]that they may fear You all the days that they live in the land which You gave to our fathers.

41 "Moreover, concerning a foreigner, who *is* not of Your people Israel, but has come from a far country for Your name's sake 42 (for they will hear of Your great name and Your [a]strong hand and Your outstretched arm), when he comes and prays toward this temple, 43 hear in heaven Your dwelling place, and do according to all for which the foreigner calls to You, [a]that all peoples of the earth may know Your name and [b]fear You, as *do* Your people Israel, and that they may know that this temple which I have built is called by Your name.

44 "When Your people go out to battle against their enemy, wherever You send them, and when they pray to the LORD toward the city which You have chosen and the temple which I have built for Your name, 45 then hear in heaven their prayer and their supplication, and maintain their cause.

46 "When they sin against You [a](for *there is* no one who does not sin), and You become angry with them and deliver them to the enemy, and they take them captive [b]to the land of the enemy, far or near; 47 [a]*yet* when they come to themselves in the land where they were carried captive, and repent, and make supplication to You in the land of those who took them captive, [b]saying, 'We have sinned and done wrong, we have committed wickedness'; 48 and *when* they [a]return to You with all their heart and with all their soul in the land of their enemies who led them away captive, and [b]pray to You toward their land which You gave to their fathers, the city which You have chosen and the temple which I have built for Your name: 49 then hear in heaven Your dwelling place their prayer and their supplication, and maintain their cause, 50 and forgive Your people who have sinned against You, and all their transgressions which they have transgressed against You; and [a]grant them compassion before those who took them captive, that they may have compassion on them 51 (for [a]they *are* Your people and Your inheritance, whom You brought out of Egypt, [b]out of the iron furnace), 52 [a]that Your eyes may be open to the supplication of Your servant and the supplication of Your people Israel, to listen to them whenever they call to You. 53 For You separated them from among all the peoples of the earth *to be* Your inheritance, [a]as You spoke by Your servant Moses, when You brought our fathers out of Egypt, O Lord GOD."

**8:46** In 586 BC, the Israelites, having rejected Solomon's warnings and openly worshiped idols, were punished by God. The Lord allowed the Babylonians to invade Israel, destroy the temple, and haul the people away as prisoners. For seventy years the people of Israel were held **captive** in a foreign land.

### *SOLOMON BLESSES THE ASSEMBLY*

*(2 Chr. 6:40–42)*

54 [a]And so it was, when Solomon had finished praying all this prayer and supplication to the LORD, that he arose from before the altar of the LORD, from kneeling on his knees with his hands spread up to heaven. 55 Then he stood

**8:30** [a] Neh. 1:6 **8:31** [a] Ex. 22:8–11 **8:32** [a] Deut. 25:1 **8:33** [a] Lev. 26:17; Deut. 28:25 [b] Lev. 26:39, 40 **8:34** [a] [Lev. 26:40–42; Deut. 30:1–3] **8:35** [a] Lev. 26:19; Deut. 28:23 **8:36** [a] Ps. 25:4; 27:11; 94:12 [b] 1 Sam. 12:23 **8:37** [a] Lev. 26:16, 25, 26; Deut. 28:21, 22, 27, 38, 42, 52 **8:39** [a] [1 Sam. 16:7; 1 Chr. 28:9; Jer. 17:10]; Acts 1:24 **8:40** [a] [Ps. 130:4] **8:42** [a] Ex. 13:3; Deut. 3:24 **8:43** [a] [Ex. 9:16; 1 Sam. 17:46; 2 Kin. 19:19] [b] Ps. 102:15 **8:46** [a] 2 Chr. 6:36; Ps. 130:3; Prov. 20:9; Eccl. 7:20; [Rom. 3:23; 1 John 1:8, 10] [b] Lev. 26:34, 44; Deut. 28:36, 64; 2 Kin. 17:6, 18; 25:21 **8:47** [a] [Lev. 26:40–42]; Neh. 9:2 [b] Ezra 9:6, 7; Neh. 1:6; Ps. 106:6; Dan. 9:5 **8:48** [a] Jer. 29:12–14 [b] Dan. 6:10; Jon. 2:4 **8:50** [a] [2 Chr. 30:9]; Ezra 7:6; Ps. 106:46; Acts 7:10 **8:51** [a] Ex. 32:11, 12; Deut. 9:26–29; Neh. 1:10; [Rom. 11:28, 29] [b] Deut. 4:20; Jer. 11:4 **8:52** [a] 1 Kin. 8:29 **8:53** [a] Ex. 19:5, 6 **8:54** [a] 2 Chr. 7:1

[a]and blessed all the assembly of Israel with a loud voice, saying: 56 "Blessed *be* the LORD, who has given [a]rest to His people Israel, according to all that He promised. [b]There has not failed one word of all His good promise, which He promised through His servant Moses. 57 May the LORD our God be with us, as He was with our fathers. [a]May He not leave us nor forsake us, 58 that He may [a]incline our hearts to Himself, to walk in all His ways, and to keep His commandments and His statutes and His judgments, which He commanded our fathers. 59 And may these words of mine, with which I have made supplication before the LORD, be near the LORD our God day and night, that He may maintain the cause of His servant and the cause of His people Israel, as each day may require, 60 [a]that all the peoples of the earth may know that [b]the LORD *is* God; *there is* no other. 61 Let your [a]heart therefore be loyal to the LORD our God, to walk in His statutes and keep His commandments, as at this day."

### SOLOMON DEDICATES THE TEMPLE

*(2 Chr. 7:4–11)*

62 Then [a]the king and all Israel with him offered sacrifices before the LORD. 63 And Solomon offered a sacrifice of peace offerings, which he offered to the LORD, twenty-two thousand bulls and one hundred and twenty thousand sheep. So the king and all the children of Israel dedicated the house of the LORD. 64 On [a]the same day the king consecrated the middle of the court that *was* in front of the house of the LORD; for there he offered burnt offerings, grain offerings, and the fat of the peace offerings, because the [b]bronze altar that *was* before the LORD *was* too small to receive the burnt offerings, the grain offerings, and the fat of the peace offerings.

65 At that time Solomon held [a]a feast, and all Israel with him, a great assembly from [b]the entrance of Hamath to [c]the Brook of Egypt, before the LORD our God, [d]seven days and seven *more* days—fourteen days. 66 [a]On the eighth day he sent the people away; and they blessed the king, and went to their tents joyful and glad of heart for all the good that the LORD had done for His servant David, and for Israel His people.

### GOD'S SECOND APPEARANCE TO SOLOMON

*(2 Chr. 7:12–22)*

9 And [a]it came to pass, when Solomon had finished building the house of the LORD [b]and the king's house, and [c]all Solomon's desire which he wanted to do, 2 that the LORD appeared to Solomon the second time, [a]as He had appeared to him at Gibeon. 3 And the LORD said to him: [a]"I have heard your prayer and your supplication that you have made before Me; I have consecrated this house which you have built [b]to put My name there forever, [c]and My eyes and My heart will be there perpetually. 4 Now if you [a]walk before Me [b]as your father David walked, in integrity of heart and in uprightness, to do according to all that I have commanded you, *and* if you [c]keep My statutes and My judgments, 5 then I will establish the throne of your kingdom over Israel forever, [a]as I promised David your father, saying, 'You shall not fail to have a man on the throne of Israel.' 6 [a]*But* if you or your sons at all turn from following Me, and do not keep My commandments *and* My statutes which I have set before you, but go and serve other gods and worship them, 7 [a]then I will cut off Israel from the land which I have given them; and this house which I have consecrated [b]for My name I will cast out of My sight. [c]Israel will be a proverb and a byword among all peoples. 8 And *as for* [a]this house, *which* is exalted, everyone who passes by it will be astonished and will hiss, and say, [b]'Why has the LORD done thus to this land and to this house?' 9 Then they will answer, 'Because they forsook the LORD their God, who brought their fathers out of the land of Egypt, and have embraced other gods, and worshiped them and served them; therefore the LORD has brought all this [a]calamity on them.' "

### SOLOMON AND HIRAM EXCHANGE GIFTS

10 Now [a]it happened at the end of twenty years, when Solomon had built the two houses, the house of the LORD and the king's house 11 [a](Hiram the king of Tyre had supplied Solomon with cedar and cypress and gold, as much as he desired), *that* King Solomon then gave Hiram twenty cities in the land of Galilee. 12 Then Hiram went from Tyre to see the cities which Solomon had given him, but they did not please him. 13 So he said, "What *kind of* cities *are* these which you have given me, my brother?" [a]And he called them the land of Cabul,[1] as they are to this day. 14 Then Hiram sent the king one hundred and twenty talents of gold.

### SOLOMON'S ADDITIONAL ACHIEVEMENTS

*(2 Chr. 8:3–16)*

15 And this *is* the reason for [a]the labor force which King Solomon raised: to build the house of the LORD, his own house, the [b]Millo,[1] the wall of Jerusalem, [c]Hazor, [d]Megiddo, and [e]Gezer. 16 (Pharaoh king of Egypt had gone up and taken Gezer and burned it with fire, [a]had killed the Canaanites who dwelt in the city, and had given it *as* a dowry to his daughter, Solomon's wife.) 17 And Solomon built Gezer, Lower [a]Beth Horon, 18 [a]Baalath, and

8:55 [a]2 Sam. 6:18 8:56 [a]1 Chr. 22:18 [b]Deut. 12:10 8:57 [a]Deut. 31:6 8:58 [a]Ps. 119:36 8:60 [a]1 Sam. 17:46 [b]Deut. 4:35, 39 8:61 [a]Deut. 18:13 8:62 [a]2 Chr. 7:4–10 8:64 [a]2 Chr. 7:7 [b]2 Chr. 4:1 8:65 [a]Lev. 23:34 [b]Num. 34:8 [c]Gen. 15:18 [d]2 Chr. 7:8 8:66 [a]2 Chr. 7:9 9:1 [a]2 Chr. 7:11 [b]1 Kin. 7:1 [c]2 Chr. 8:6 9:2 [a]1 Kin. 3:5; 11:9 9:3 [a]Ps. 10:17 [b]1 Kin. 8:29 [c]Deut. 11:12 9:4 [a]Gen. 17:1 [b]1 Kin. 11:4, 6; 15:5 [c]1 Kin. 8:61 9:5 [a]2 Sam. 7:12, 16 9:6 [a]2 Sam. 7:14–16 9:7 [a][Lev. 18:24–29] [b][Jer. 7:4–14] [c]Ps. 44:14 9:8 [a]2 Chr. 7:21 [b][Deut. 29:24–26] 9:9 [a][Deut. 29:25–28] 9:10 [a]2 Chr. 8:1 9:11 [a]1 Kin. 5:1 9:13 [a]Josh. 19:27 [1]Literally *Good for Nothing* 9:15 [a]1 Kin. 5:13 [b]2 Sam. 5:9; 1 Kin. 9:24 [c]Josh. 11:1; 19:36 [d]Josh. 17:11 [e]Josh. 16:10 [1]Literally *The Landfill* 9:16 [a]Josh. 16:10; Judg. 1:29 9:17 [a]Josh. 10:10; 16:3; 21:22; 2 Chr. 8:5 9:18 [a]Josh. 19:44; 2 Chr. 8:4

Tadmor in the wilderness, in the land *of Judah,*
19 all the storage cities that Solomon had, cities
for [a]his chariots and cities for his [b]cavalry, and
whatever Solomon [c]desired to build in Jerusalem,
in Lebanon, and in all the land of his dominion.
20 [a]All the people *who were* left of the Amo-
rites, Hittites, Perizzites, Hivites, and Jebusites,
who *were* not of the children of Israel— 21 that
is, their descendants [a]who were left in the land
after them, [b]whom the children of Israel had not
been able to destroy completely—[c]from these
Solomon raised [d]forced labor, as it is to this day.
22 But of the children of Israel Solomon [a]made
no forced laborers, because they *were* men of
war and his servants: his officers, his captains,
commanders of his chariots, and his cavalry.
23 Others *were* chiefs of the officials who *were*
over Solomon's work: [a]five hundred and fifty,
who ruled over the people who did the work.
24 But [a]Pharaoh's daughter came up from the
City of David to [b]her house which *Solomon*[1] had
built for her. [c]Then he built the Millo.
25 [a]Now three times a year Solomon offered
burnt offerings and peace offerings on the altar
which he had built for the LORD, and he burned
incense with them *on the altar* that *was* before
the LORD. So he finished the temple.
26 [a]King Solomon also built a fleet of ships at
[b]Ezion Geber, which *is* near Elath[1] on the shore
of the Red Sea, in the land of Edom. 27 [a]Then
Hiram sent his servants with the fleet, seamen
who knew the sea, to work with the servants
of Solomon. 28 And they went to [a]Ophir, and
acquired four hundred and twenty talents of
gold from there, and brought *it* to King Solomon.

### *THE QUEEN OF SHEBA'S PRAISE OF SOLOMON*

*(2 Chr. 9:1–28)*

10 Now when the [a]queen of Sheba heard of
the fame of Solomon concerning the name
of the LORD, she came [b]to test him with hard
questions. 2 She came to Jerusalem with a very
great retinue, with camels that bore spices, very
much gold, and precious stones; and when she
came to Solomon, she spoke with him about all
that was in her heart. 3 So Solomon answered
all her questions; there was nothing so difficult
for the king that he could not explain *it* to her.
4 And when the queen of Sheba had seen all the
wisdom of Solomon, the house that he had built,
5 the food on his table, the seating of his servants,
the service of his waiters and their apparel, his
cupbearers, [a]and his entryway by which he went
up to the house of the LORD, there was no more
spirit in her. 6 Then she said to the king: "It was a

> **SEEING JESUS IN THE SCRIPTURE**
>
> **10:4–5** Solomon built the temple just as God instructed. People from all over the world came to see its beauty and it took their breath away. The teaching of Jesus prompted a similar response (see Matt. 7:28–29).

true report which I heard in my own land about
your words and your wisdom. 7 However I did not
believe the words until I came and saw with my
own eyes; and indeed the half was not told me.
Your wisdom and prosperity exceed the fame of
which I heard. 8 [a]Happy *are* your men and happy
*are* these your servants, who stand continually
before you *and* hear your wisdom! 9 [a]Blessed be
the LORD your God, who [b]delighted in you, setting
you on the throne of Israel! Because the LORD
has loved Israel forever, therefore He made you
king, [c]to do justice and righteousness."
10 Then she [a]gave the king one hundred and
twenty talents of gold, spices in great quantity,
and precious stones. There never again came
such abundance of spices as the queen of Sheba
gave to King Solomon. 11 [a]Also, the ships of Hiram,
which brought gold from Ophir, brought great
quantities of almug[1] wood and precious stones
from Ophir. 12 [a]And the king made steps of the
almug wood for the house of the LORD and for the
king's house, also harps and stringed instruments
for singers. There never again came such [b]almug
wood, nor has the like been seen to this day.
13 Now King Solomon gave the queen of
Sheba all she desired, whatever she asked, be-
sides what Solomon had given her according to
the royal generosity. So she turned and went to
her own country, she and her servants.

### *SOLOMON'S GREAT WEALTH*

14 The weight of gold that came to Solomon
yearly was six hundred and sixty-six talents of
gold, 15 besides *that* from the [a]traveling merchants,
from the income of traders, [b]from all the kings of
Arabia, and from the governors of the country.
16 And King Solomon made two hundred large
shields *of* hammered gold; six hundred *shekels* of
gold went into each shield. 17 He also *made* [a]three
hundred shields *of* hammered gold; three minas
of gold went into each shield. The king put them
in the [b]House of the Forest of Lebanon.
18 [a]Moreover the king made a great throne
of ivory, and overlaid it with pure gold. 19 The
throne had six steps, and the top of the throne

**9:19** [a] 1 Kin. 10:26; 2 Chr. 1:14 [b] 1 Kin. 4:26 [c] 1 Kin. 9:1 **9:20** [a] 2 Chr. 8:7 **9:21** [a] Judg. 1:21–36; 3:1 [b] Josh. 15:63; 17:12, 13 [c] Judg. 1:28, 35 [d] Ezra 2:55, 58; Neh. 7:57 **9:22** [a] [Lev. 25:39] **9:23** [a] 2 Chr. 8:10 **9:24** [a] 1 Kin. 3:1 [b] 1 Kin. 7:8 [c] 2 Sam. 5:9; 1 Kin. 11:27; 2 Chr. 32:5 [1] Literally *he* (compare 2 Chronicles 8:11) **9:25** [a] Ex. 23:14–17; Deut. 16:16; 2 Chr. 8:12, 13 **9:26** [a] 2 Chr. 8:17, 18 [b] Num. 33:35; Deut. 2:8; 1 Kin. 22:48 [1] Hebrew *Eloth* (compare 2 Kings 14:22) **9:27** [a] 1 Kin. 5:6, 9; 10:11 **9:28** [a] Job 22:24 **10:1** [a] 2 Chr. 9:1; Matt. 12:42; Luke 11:31 [b] Judg. 14:12; Ps. 49:4; Prov. 1:6 **10:5** [a] 1 Chr. 26:16; 2 Chr. 9:4 **10:8** [a] Prov. 8:34 **10:9** [a] 1 Kin. 5:7 [b] 2 Sam. 22:20 [c] 2 Sam. 8:15; Ps. 72:2; [Prov. 8:15] **10:10** [a] Ps. 72:10, 15 **10:11** [a] 1 Kin. 9:27, 28; Job 22:24 [1] Or *algum* (compare 2 Chronicles 9:10, 11) **10:12** [a] 2 Chr. 9:11 [b] 2 Chr. 9:10 **10:15** [a] 2 Chr. 1:16 [b] 2 Chr. 9:24; Ps. 72:10 **10:17** [a] 1 Kin. 14:26 [b] 1 Kin. 7:2 **10:18** [a] 1 Kin. 10:22; 2 Chr. 9:17; Ps. 45:8

*was* round at the back; *there were* armrests on
either side of the place of the seat, and two lions
stood beside the armrests. 20 Twelve lions stood
there, one on each side of the six steps; nothing
like *this* had been made for any *other* kingdom.
21 [a]All King Solomon's drinking vessels *were*
gold, and all the vessels of the House of the Forest
of Lebanon *were* pure gold. Not *one was* silver, for
this was accounted as nothing in the days of Sol-
omon. 22 For the king had [a]merchant ships[1] at sea
with the fleet of Hiram. Once every three years the
merchant [b]ships came bringing gold, silver, ivory,
apes, and monkeys.[2] 23 So [a]King Solomon surpassed
all the kings of the earth in riches and wisdom.
24 Now all the earth sought the presence of
Solomon to hear his wisdom, which God had put
in his heart. 25 Each man brought his present:
articles of silver and gold, garments, armor, spic-
es, horses, and mules, at a set rate year by year.
26 [a]And Solomon [b]gathered chariots and
horsemen; he had one thousand four hundred
chariots and twelve thousand horsemen, whom
he stationed[1] in the chariot cities and with the
king at Jerusalem. 27 [a]The king made silver *as*
*common* in Jerusalem as stones, and he made
cedar trees as abundant as the sycamores which
*are* in the lowland.
28 [a]Also Solomon had horses imported from
Egypt and Keveh; the king's merchants bought
them in Keveh at the *current* price. 29 Now a
chariot that was imported from Egypt cost six
hundred *shekels* of silver, and a horse one hun-
dred and fifty; [a]and thus, through their agents,[1]
they exported *them* to all the kings of the Hittites
and the kings of Syria.

### *SOLOMON'S HEART TURNS FROM THE LORD*

11 But [a]King Solomon loved [b]many foreign
women, as well as the daughter of Pharaoh:
women of the Moabites, Ammonites, Edomites,
Sidonians, *and* Hittites— 2 from the nations of
whom the LORD had said to the children of Is-
rael, [a]"You shall not intermarry with them, nor
they with you. Surely they will turn away your
hearts after their gods." Solomon clung to these
in love. 3 And he had seven hundred wives, prin-
cesses, and three hundred concubines; and his
wives turned away his heart. 4 For it was so, when
Solomon was old, [a]that his wives turned his heart
after other gods; and his [b]heart was not loyal to
the LORD his God, [c]as *was* the heart of his father
David. 5 For Solomon went after [a]Ashtoreth the
goddess of the Sidonians, and after [b]Milcom the
abomination of the [c]Ammonites. 6 Solomon did
evil in the sight of the LORD, and did not fully
follow the LORD, as *did* his father David. 7 [a]Then
Solomon built a high place for [b]Chemosh the
abomination of Moab, on [c]the hill that *is* east
of Jerusalem, and for Molech the abomination
of the people of Ammon. 8 And he did likewise
for all his foreign wives, who burned incense
and sacrificed to their gods.
9 So the LORD became angry with Solomon,
because his heart had turned from the LORD God
of Israel, [a]who had appeared to him twice, 10 and
[a]had commanded him concerning this thing,
that he should not go after other gods; but he
did not keep what the LORD had commanded.
11 Therefore the LORD said to Solomon, "Because
you have done this, and have not kept My cov-
enant and My statutes, which I have commanded
you, [a]I will surely tear the kingdom away from
you and give it to your [b]servant. 12 Nevertheless
I will not do it in your days, for the sake of your
father David; I will tear it out of the hand of your
son. 13 [a]However I will not tear away the whole
kingdom; I will give [b]one tribe to your son [c]for
the sake of My servant David, and for the sake
of Jerusalem [d]which I have chosen."

### *ADVERSARIES OF SOLOMON*

14 Now the LORD [a]raised up an adversary
against Solomon, Hadad the Edomite; he *was* a
descendant of the king in Edom. 15 [a]For it hap-
pened, when David was in Edom, and Joab the
commander of the army had gone up to bury the
slain, [b]after he had killed every male in Edom
16 (because for six months Joab remained there
with all Israel, until he had cut down every male
in Edom), 17 that Hadad fled to go to Egypt, he
and certain Edomites of his father's servants

**11:1–4** Solomon was affected by the contemporary practices of the surrounding culture. Entering into a political marriage was a means to consolidate a relationship with a neighboring monarch, and Solomon followed this custom at the expense of obedience to God. Marrying **foreign women** violated the Lord's prohibition (Ex. 34:12–17; Deut. 7:1–3). Taking more than one wife violated the standard of monogamy established at the beginning (see Gen. 2:24–25), and resulted in rampant polygamy, something God had also forbidden Israel's kings, at least, from doing (see Deut. 17:17).

**10:21** [a] 2 Chr. 9:20 **10:22** [a] Gen. 10:4; 2 Chr. 20:36 [b] 1 Kin. 9:26–28; 22:48; Ps. 72:10 [1] Literally *ships of Tarshish,* deep-sea vessels [2] Or *peacocks* **10:23** [a] 1 Kin. 3:12, 13; 4:30; 2 Chr. 1:12 **10:26** [a] 1 Kin. 4:26; 2 Chr. 1:14; 9:25 [b] [Deut. 17:16]; 1 Kin. 9:19 [1] Following Septuagint, Syriac, Targum, and Vulgate (compare 2 Chronicles 9:25); Masoretic Text reads *led.* **10:27** [a] [Deut. 17:17]; 2 Chr. 1:15–17 **10:28** [a] [Deut. 17:16]; 2 Chr. 1:16; 9:28 **10:29** [a] Josh. 1:4; 2 Kin. 7:6, 7 [1] Literally *by their hands* **11:1** [a] [Neh. 13:26] [b] [Deut. 17:17]; 1 Kin. 3:1 **11:2** [a] Ex. 34:16; [Deut. 7:3, 4] **11:4** [a] [Deut. 17:17; Neh. 13:26] [b] 1 Kin. 8:61 [c] 1 Kin. 9:4 **11:5** [a] Judg. 2:13; 1 Kin. 11:33 [b] [Lev. 20:2–5] [c] 2 Kin. 23:13 **11:7** [a] Num. 33:52 [b] Num. 21:29; Judg. 11:24 [c] 2 Kin. 23:13 **11:9** [a] 1 Kin. 3:5; 9:2 **11:10** [a] 1 Kin. 6:12; 9:6, 7 **11:11** [a] 1 Kin. 11:31; 12:15, 16 [b] 1 Kin. 11:31, 37 **11:13** [a] 2 Sam. 7:15; 1 Chr. 17:13; Ps. 89:33 [b] 1 Kin. 12:20 [c] 2 Sam. 7:15, 16 [d] Deut. 12:11; 1 Kin. 9:3; 14:21 **11:14** [a] 1 Chr. 5:26 **11:15** [a] 2 Sam. 8:14; 1 Chr. 18:12, 13 [b] Num. 24:18, 19; [Deut. 20:13]

1 KINGS 11:1–9

## SOLOMON'S FALL

STORY OF SCRIPTURE 28

### WHAT'S GOING ON?

Despite his vast wisdom, Solomon disobeyed God by marrying many foreign women and worshiping their gods. Solomon built "high places" for the worship of these gods, directly violating God's commands. This passage highlights the tension between Solomon's wisdom and his failure to remain faithful to God. It shows how even the wisest and most powerful can fall into sin when they turn away from God's commandments. Solomon's actions affected his relationship with God and had lasting consequences for the kingdom of Israel. His disobedience led to the division of the kingdom after his death.

### WHAT DOES THIS MEAN FOR ME?

Solomon's story warns us about the friends we choose to spend time with. Solomon's ties to foreign nations that worshiped false gods ultimately influenced him for the worse. Sometimes, we hang out with ungodly people to influence them, but if we aren't careful, they'll end up influencing us instead.

### DID YOU CATCH THE PATTERN?

Solomon built "high places" to worship the false gods Chemosh, Ashtoreth, Molech, and Milcom. The garden of Eden was set in a high place, with rivers flowing down from it (see Gen. 2:10–14). Ever since the fall, people have tried to reclaim Eden by worshipping on high places, like the Tower of Babel, reaching high into the sky. Something in us longs to be closer to heaven. These "high places" where Solomon built altars were a sinful attempt at finding paradise again. But one day, paradise found us through Solomon's descendant. On a high place called Calvary, Jesus died on behalf of sinful people.

*For the next* Story of Scripture *reading and devotion, turn to 1 Kings 12:1–33 on page 350.*

with him. Hadad *was* still a little child. 18 Then they arose from Midian and came to Paran; and they took men with them from Paran and came to Egypt, to Pharaoh king of Egypt, who gave him a house, apportioned food for him, and gave him land. 19 And Hadad found great favor in the sight of Pharaoh, so that he gave him as wife the sister of his own wife, that is, the sister of Queen Tahpenes. 20 Then the sister of Tahpenes bore him Genubath his son, whom Tahpenes weaned in Pharaoh's house. And Genubath was in Pharaoh's household among the sons of Pharaoh.

21 [a]So when Hadad heard in Egypt that David rested with his fathers, and that Joab the commander of the army was dead, Hadad said to Pharaoh, "Let me depart, that I may go to my own country."

22 Then Pharaoh said to him, "But what have you lacked with me, that suddenly you seek to go to your own country?"

So he answered, "Nothing, but do let me go anyway."

23 And God raised up *another* adversary against him, Rezon the son of Eliadah, who had fled from his lord, [a]Hadadezer king of Zobah. 24 So he gathered men to him and became captain over a band *of raiders,* [a]when David killed those *of Zobah.* And they went to Damascus and dwelt there, and reigned in Damascus. 25 He was an adversary of Israel all the days of Solomon (besides the trouble that Hadad *caused*); and he abhorred Israel, and reigned over Syria.

### *JEROBOAM'S REBELLION*

26 Then Solomon's servant, [a]Jeroboam the son of Nebat, an Ephraimite from Zereda, whose mother's name *was* Zeruah, a widow, [b]also [c]rebelled against the king.

27 And this *is* what caused him to rebel against the king: [a]Solomon had built the Millo *and* repaired the damages to the City of David his father. 28 The man Jeroboam *was* a mighty man of valor; and Solomon, seeing that the young man was [a]industrious, made him the officer over all the labor force of the house of Joseph.

29 Now it happened at that time, when Jeroboam went out of Jerusalem, that the prophet [a]Ahijah the Shilonite met him on the way; and he had clothed himself with a new garment, and the two *were* alone in the field. 30 Then Ahijah took hold of the new garment that *was* on him, and [a]tore it *into* twelve pieces. 31 And he said to Jeroboam,

**11:21** [a] 1 Kin. 2:10, 34 **11:23** [a] 2 Sam. 8:3; 10:16 **11:24** [a] 2 Sam. 8:3; 10:8, 18 **11:26** [a] 1 Kin. 12:2 [b] 1 Kin. 11:11; 2 Chr. 13:6 [c] 2 Sam. 20:21 **11:27** [a] 1 Kin. 9:15, 24 **11:28** [a] [Prov. 22:29] **11:29** [a] 1 Kin. 12:15; 14:2; 2 Chr. 9:29 **11:30** [a] 1 Sam. 15:27, 28; 24:5

"Take for yourself ten pieces, for [a]thus says the
LORD, the God of Israel: 'Behold, I will tear the
kingdom out of the hand of Solomon and will give
ten tribes to you 32 (but he shall have one tribe for
the sake of My servant David, and for the sake of
Jerusalem, the city which I have chosen out of all
the tribes of Israel), 33 [a]because they have[1] forsaken
Me, and worshiped Ashtoreth the goddess of the
Sidonians, Chemosh the god of the Moabites, and
Milcom the god of the people of Ammon, and have
not walked in My ways to do *what is* right in My
eyes and *keep* My statutes and My judgments, as
*did* his father David. 34 However I will not take the
whole kingdom out of his hand, because I have
made him ruler all the days of his life for the sake
of My servant David, whom I chose because he
kept My commandments and My statutes. 35 But
[a]I will take the kingdom out of his son's hand and
give it to you—ten tribes. 36 And to his son I will
give one tribe, that [a]My servant David may always
have a lamp before Me in Jerusalem, the city
which I have chosen for Myself, to put My name
there. 37 So I will take you, and you shall reign
over all your heart desires, and you shall be king
over Israel. 38 Then it shall be, if you heed all that
I command you, walk in My ways, and do *what
is* right in My sight, to keep My statutes and My
commandments, as My servant David did, then
[a]I will be with you and [b]build for you an enduring
house, as I built for David, and will give Israel to
you. 39 And I will afflict the descendants of David
because of this, but not forever.' "

40 Solomon therefore sought to kill Jerobo-
am. But Jeroboam arose and fled to Egypt, to
[a]Shishak king of Egypt, and was in Egypt until
the death of Solomon.

### DEATH OF SOLOMON
*(2 Chr. 9:29–31)*

41 Now [a]the rest of the acts of Solomon, all that
he did, and his wisdom, *are* they not written in the
book of the acts of Solomon? 42 [a]And the period
that Solomon reigned in Jerusalem over all Israel
*was* forty years. 43 [a]Then Solomon rested with his
fathers, and was buried in the City of David his fa-
ther. And Rehoboam his son reigned in his [b]place.

### THE REVOLT AGAINST REHOBOAM
*(2 Chr. 10:1–19; 11:1–4)*

12 And [a]Rehoboam went to [b]Shechem, for all
Israel had gone to Shechem to make him
king. 2 So it happened, when [a]Jeroboam the son
of Nebat heard *it* (he was still in [b]Egypt, for he
had fled from the presence of King Solomon and
had been dwelling in Egypt), 3 that they sent and
called him. Then Jeroboam and the whole as-
sembly of Israel came and spoke to Rehoboam,
saying, 4 "Your father made our [a]yoke heavy;
now therefore, lighten the burdensome service
of your father, and his heavy yoke which he put
on us, and we will serve you."

5 So he said to them, "Depart *for* three days,
then come back to me." And the people departed.

6 Then King Rehoboam consulted the elders
who stood before his father Solomon while he
still lived, and he said, "How do you advise *me*
to answer these people?"

7 And they spoke to him, saying, [a]"If you will
be a servant to these people today, and serve
them, and answer them, and speak good words
to them, then they will be your servants forever."

8 But he rejected the advice which the elders
had given him, and consulted the young men
who had grown up with him, who stood before
him. 9 And he said to them, "What advice do you
give? How should we answer this people who
have spoken to me, saying, 'Lighten the yoke
which your father put on us'?"

10 Then the young men who had grown up
with him spoke to him, saying, "Thus you should
speak to this people who have spoken to you,
saying, 'Your father made our yoke heavy, but
you make *it* lighter on us'—thus you shall say
to them: 'My little *finger* shall be thicker than
my father's waist! 11 And now, whereas my father
put a heavy yoke on you, I will add to your yoke;
my father chastised you with whips, but I will
chastise you with scourges!' "[1]

12 So Jeroboam and all the people came to
Rehoboam the third day, as the king had di-
rected, saying, "Come back to me the third day."
13 Then the king answered the people roughly,
and rejected the advice which the elders had
given him; 14 and he spoke to them according
to the advice of the young men, saying, "My
father made your yoke heavy, but I will add to
your yoke; my father chastised you with whips,
but I will chastise you with scourges!"[1] 15 So the
king did not listen to the people; for [a]the turn *of
events* was from the LORD, that He might fulfill
His word, which the LORD had [b]spoken by Ahi-
jah the Shilonite to Jeroboam the son of Nebat.

16 Now when all Israel saw that the king did
not listen to them, the people answered the
king, saying:

[a]"What share have we in David?
*We have* no inheritance in the son of Jesse.
To your tents, O Israel!
Now, see to your own house, O David!"

So Israel departed to their tents. 17 But Reho-
boam reigned over [a]the children of Israel who
dwelt in the cities of Judah.

11:31 [a] 1 Kin. 11:11, 13 11:33 [a] 1 Sam. 7:3; 1 Kin. 11:5–8 [1] Following Masoretic Text and Targum; Septuagint, Syriac, and Vulgate read *he has.* 11:35 [a] 1 Kin. 12:16, 17 11:36 [a] [1 Kin. 15:4; 2 Kin. 8:19] 11:38 [a] Deut. 31:8; Josh. 1:5 [b] 2 Sam. 7:11, 27 11:40 [a] 1 Kin. 11:17; 14:25; 2 Chr. 12:2–9 11:41 [a] 2 Chr. 9:29 11:42 [a] 2 Chr. 9:30 11:43 [a] 1 Kin. 2:10; 2 Chr. 9:31 [b] 1 Kin. 14:21; 2 Chr. 10:1 12:1 [a] 2 Chr. 10:1 [b] Judg. 9:6 12:2 [a] 1 Kin. 11:26 [b] 1 Kin. 11:40 12:4 [a] 1 Sam. 8:11–18; 1 Kin. 4:7; 5:13–15 12:7 [a] 2 Chr. 10:7; [Prov. 15:1] 12:11 [1] Literally *scorpions* 12:14 [1] Literally *scorpions* 12:15 [a] Deut. 2:30; Judg. 14:4; 1 Kin. 12:24; 2 Chr. 10:15 [b] 1 Kin. 11:11, 29, 31 12:16 [a] 2 Sam. 20:1 12:17 [a] 1 Kin. 11:13, 36; 2 Chr. 11:14–17

1 KINGS 12:1–33

## A DIVIDED KINGDOM

29

STORY OF SCRIPTURE

### WHAT'S GOING ON?

This passage describes the division of the kingdom of Israel following Solomon's reign. Rehoboam, Solomon's son, ascended to the throne and faced immediate challenges. Ignoring the advice to lighten the burdens Solomon had placed on the people, Rehoboam instead threatened to increase the hardship, prompting ten tribes to revolt under Jeroboam's leadership. This resulted in the kingdom's split into Israel (northern kingdom) and Judah (southern kingdom). Jeroboam, fearful of losing his subjects if they continued to worship in Jerusalem, established new centers of worship in Bethel and Dan, introducing golden calves for worship, thus leading his people into idolatry.

### WHAT DOES THIS MEAN FOR ME?

Rehoboam rejected good advice, and he faced dire consequences because of it. We must never underestimate the power of good advice from our elders—people who have been there before us. It's good to have vision and do things your own way, but always consider the voices of wisdom God has placed around you.

### DID YOU CATCH THE PATTERN?

Israel split into two nations: Israel and Judah. Because of God's promise to David, He preserved Judah and David's lineage. Through the tribe of Judah and lineage of David, Jesus Christ was born. God preserving Judah isn't just an example of His faithfulness, but it's also a foreshadowing of the split between the Jews and Christ's followers that occurred in the Gospels and Acts.

*For the next* Story of Scripture *reading and devotion, turn to 1 Kings 18:17–40 on page 357.*

18 Then King Rehoboam [a]sent Adoram, who
*was* in charge of the revenue; but all Israel
stoned him with stones, and he died. Therefore
King Rehoboam mounted his chariot in haste
to flee to Jerusalem. 19 So [a]Israel has been in
rebellion against the house of David to this day.
20 Now it came to pass when all Israel heard
that Jeroboam had come back, they sent for him
and called him to the congregation, and made him
king over all [a]Israel. There was none who followed
the house of David, but the tribe of Judah [b]only.
21 And when [a]Rehoboam came to Jerusalem,
he assembled all the house of Judah with the
tribe of [b]Benjamin, one hundred and eighty
thousand chosen *men* who were warriors, to fight
against the house of Israel, that he might restore
the kingdom to Rehoboam the son of Solomon.
22 But [a]the word of God came to Shemaiah the
man of God, saying, 23 "Speak to Rehoboam the
son of Solomon, king of Judah, to all the house
of Judah and Benjamin, and to the rest of the
people, saying, 24 'Thus says the LORD: "You shall
not go up nor fight against your brethren the
children of Israel. Let every man return to his
house, [a]for this thing is from Me." ' " Therefore
they obeyed the word of the LORD, and turned
back, according to the word of the LORD.

### *JEROBOAM'S GOLD CALVES*

25 Then Jeroboam [a]built Shechem in the
mountains of Ephraim, and dwelt there. Also he
went out from there and built [b]Penuel. 26 And
Jeroboam said in his heart, "Now the kingdom
may return to the house of David: 27 If these
people [a]go up to offer sacrifices in the house
of the LORD at Jerusalem, then the heart of this
people will turn back to their lord, Rehoboam
king of Judah, and they will kill me and go back
to Rehoboam king of Judah."
28 Therefore the king asked advice, [a]made
two calves of gold, and said to the people, "It is
too much for you to go up to Jerusalem. [b]Here
are your gods, O Israel, which brought you up
from the land of Egypt!" 29 And he set up one in
[a]Bethel, and the other he put in [b]Dan. 30 Now this
thing became [a]a sin, for the people went *to worship*
before the one as far as Dan. 31 He made shrines[1]
on the high places, [a]and made priests from every
class of people, who were not of the sons of Levi.
32 Jeroboam ordained a feast on the fifteenth
day of the eighth month, like [a]the feast that *was*
in Judah, and offered sacrifices on the altar. So
he did at Bethel, sacrificing to the calves that
he had made. [b]And at Bethel he installed the
priests of the high places which he had made.

**12:18** [a] 1 Kin. 4:6; 5:14 **12:19** [a] 2 Kin. 17:21 **12:20** [a] 2 Kin. 17:21 [b] 1 Kin. 11:13, 32, 36 **12:21** [a] 2 Chr. 11:1–4 [b] 2 Sam. 19:17 **12:22** [a] 2 Chr. 11:2; 12:5–7 **12:24** [a] 1 Kin. 12:15 **12:25** [a] Gen. 12:6; Judg. 9:45–49; 1 Kin. 12:1 [b] Gen. 32:30, 31; Judg. 8:8, 17 **12:27** [a] [Deut. 12:5–7, 14] **12:28** [a] 2 Kin. 10:29; 17:16; [Hos. 8:4–7] [b] Ex. 32:4, 8 **12:29** [a] Gen. 28:19 [b] Judg. 18:26–31 **12:30** [a] 1 Kin. 13:34; 2 Kin. 17:21 **12:31** [a] [Num. 3:10; 17:1–11]; Judg. 17:5; 1 Kin. 13:33; 2 Kin. 17:32; 2 Chr. 11:14, 15 [1] Literally *a house* **12:32** [a] Lev. 23:33, 34; Num. 29:12; 1 Kin. 8:2, 5 [b] Amos 7:10–13

33 So he made offerings on the altar which he had made at Bethel on the fifteenth day of the eighth month, in the month which he had [a]devised in his own heart. And he ordained a feast for the children of Israel, and offered sacrifices on the altar and [b]burned incense.

### THE MESSAGE OF THE MAN OF GOD

**13** And behold, [a]a man of God went from Judah to Bethel by the word of the LORD, [b]and Jeroboam stood by the altar to burn incense. 2 Then he cried out against the altar by the word of the LORD, and said, "O altar, altar! Thus says the LORD: 'Behold, a child, [a]Josiah by name, shall be born to the house of David; and on you he shall sacrifice the priests of the high places who burn incense on you, and men's bones shall be [b]burned on you.' " 3 And he gave [a]a sign the same day, saying, "This *is* the sign which the LORD has spoken: Surely the altar shall split apart, and the ashes on it shall be poured out."

4 So it came to pass when King Jeroboam heard the saying of the man of God, who cried out against the altar in Bethel, that he stretched out his hand from the altar, saying, "Arrest him!" Then his hand, which he stretched out toward him, withered, so that he could not pull it back to himself. 5 The altar also was split apart, and the ashes poured out from the altar, according to the sign which the man of God had given by the word of the LORD. 6 Then the king answered and said to the man of God, "Please [a]entreat the favor of the LORD your God, and pray for me, that my hand may be restored to me."

So the man of God entreated the LORD, and the king's hand was restored to him, and became as before. 7 Then the king said to the man of God, "Come home with me and refresh yourself, and [a]I will give you a reward."

8 But the man of God said to the king, [a]"If you were to give me half your house, I would not go in with you; nor would I eat bread nor drink water in this place. 9 For so it was commanded me by the word of the LORD, saying, [a]'You shall not eat bread, nor drink water, nor return by the same way you came.' " 10 So he went another way and did not return by the way he came to Bethel.

### DEATH OF THE MAN OF GOD

11 Now an [a]old prophet dwelt in Bethel, and his sons came and told him all the works that the man of God had done that day in Bethel; they also told their father the words which he had spoken to the king. 12 And their father said to them, "Which way did he go?" For his sons had seen[1] which way the man of God went who came from Judah. 13 Then he said to his sons, "Saddle the donkey for me." So they saddled the donkey for him; and he rode on it, 14 and went after the man of God, and found him sitting under an oak. Then he said to him, "*Are* you the man of God who came from Judah?"

And he said, "I *am.*"

15 Then he said to him, "Come home with me and eat bread."

16 And he said, [a]"I cannot return with you nor go in with you; neither can I eat bread nor drink water with you in this place. 17 For I have been told [a]by the word of the LORD, 'You shall not eat bread nor drink water there, nor return by going the way you came.' "

18 He said to him, "I too *am* a prophet as you *are,* and an angel spoke to me by the word of the LORD, saying, 'Bring him back with you to your house, that he may eat bread and drink water.' " (He was lying to him.)

19 So he went back with him, and ate bread in his house, and drank water.

20 Now it happened, as they sat at the table, that the word of the LORD came to the prophet who had brought him back; 21 and he cried out to the man of God who came from Judah, saying, "Thus says the LORD: 'Because you have disobeyed the word of the LORD, and have not kept the commandment which the LORD your God commanded you, 22 but you came back, ate bread, and drank water in the [a]place of which *the LORD* said to you, "Eat no bread and drink no water," your corpse shall not come to the tomb of your fathers.' "

23 So it was, after he had eaten bread and after he had drunk, that he saddled the donkey for him, the prophet whom he had brought back. 24 When he was gone, [a]a lion met him on the road and killed him. And his corpse was thrown on the road, and the donkey stood by it. The lion also stood by the corpse. 25 And there, men passed by and saw the corpse thrown on the road, and the lion standing by the corpse. Then they went and told *it* in the city where the old prophet dwelt.

26 Now when the prophet who had brought him back from the way heard *it,* he said, "It *is* the man of God who was disobedient to the word of the LORD. Therefore the LORD has delivered him to the lion, which has torn him and killed him, according to the word of the LORD which He spoke to him." 27 And he spoke to his sons, saying, "Saddle the donkey for me." So they saddled *it.* 28 Then he went and found his corpse thrown on the road, and the donkey and the lion standing by the corpse. The lion had not eaten the corpse nor torn the donkey. 29 And the prophet took up the corpse of the man of God, laid it on the donkey, and brought it back. So the old prophet came to the city to mourn, and to bury him. 30 Then he laid the corpse in his own tomb; and they mourned over him, *saying,* [a]"Alas, my brother!" 31 So it was, after he had buried him, that he spoke to his sons, saying, "When I am dead, then bury me in the tomb where the man of God *is* buried; [a]lay my

**12:33** [a] Num. 15:39 [b] 1 Kin. 13:1 **13:1** [a] 2 Kin. 23:17 [b] 1 Kin. 12:32, 33 **13:2** [a] 2 Kin. 23:15, 16 [b] [Lev. 26:30] **13:3** [a] Ex. 4:1–5; Judg. 6:17; Is. 7:14; 38:7; John 2:18; 1 Cor. 1:22 **13:6** [a] [James 5:16] **13:7** [a] 1 Sam. 9:7; 2 Kin. 5:15 **13:8** [a] Num. 22:18; 24:13; 1 Kin. 13:16, 17 **13:9** [a] [1 Cor. 5:11] **13:11** [a] 1 Kin. 13:25 **13:12** [1] Septuagint, Syriac, Targum, and Vulgate read *showed him.* **13:16** [a] 1 Kin. 13:8, 9 **13:17** [a] 1 Kin. 20:35; 1 Thess. 4:15 **13:22** [a] 1 Kin. 13:9 **13:24** [a] 1 Kin. 20:36 **13:30** [a] Jer. 22:18 **13:31** [a] Ruth 1:17; 2 Kin. 23:17, 18

bones beside his bones. 32 [a]For the saying which he cried out by the word of the LORD against the altar in Bethel, and against all the shrines[1] on the high places which *are* in the cities of [b]Samaria, will surely come to pass."

33 [a]After this event Jeroboam did not turn from his evil way, but again he made priests from every class of people for the high places; whoever wished, he consecrated him, and he became *one* of the priests of the high places. 34 [a]And this thing was the sin of the house of Jeroboam, so as [b]to exterminate and destroy *it* from the face of the earth.

### *JUDGMENT ON THE HOUSE OF JEROBOAM*

**14** At that time Abijah the son of Jeroboam became sick. 2 And Jeroboam said to his wife, "Please arise, and disguise yourself, that they may not recognize you as the wife of Jeroboam, and go to Shiloh. Indeed, Ahijah the prophet *is* there, who told me that [a]*I would be* king over this people. 3 [a]Also take with you ten loaves, *some* cakes, and a jar of honey, and go to him; he will tell you what will become of the child." 4 And Jeroboam's wife did so; she arose [a]and went to Shiloh, and came to the house of Ahijah. But Ahijah could not see, for his eyes were glazed by reason of his age.

5 Now the LORD had said to Ahijah, "Here is the wife of Jeroboam, coming to ask you something about her son, for he *is* sick. Thus and thus you shall say to her; for it will be, when she comes in, that she will pretend *to be* another *woman*."

6 And so it was, when Ahijah heard the sound of her footsteps as she came through the door, he said, "Come in, wife of Jeroboam. Why do you pretend *to be* another *person*? For I *have been* sent to you *with* bad *news*. 7 Go, tell Jeroboam, 'Thus says the LORD God of Israel: [a]"Because I exalted you from among the people, and made you ruler over My people Israel, 8 and [a]tore the kingdom away from the house of David, and gave it to you; and *yet* you have not been as My servant David, [b]who kept My commandments and who followed Me with all his heart, to do only *what was* right in My eyes; 9 but you have done more evil than all who were before you, [a]for you have gone and made for yourself other gods and molded images to provoke Me to anger, and [b]have cast Me behind your back— 10 therefore behold! [a]I will bring disaster on the house of Jeroboam, and [b]will cut off from Jeroboam every male in Israel, [c]bond and free; I will take away the remnant of the house of Jeroboam, as one takes away refuse until it is all gone. 11 The dogs shall eat [a]whoever belongs to Jeroboam and dies in the city, and the birds of the air shall eat whoever dies in the field; for the LORD has spoken!"' 12 Arise therefore, go to your own house. [a]When your feet enter the city, the child shall die. 13 And all Israel shall mourn for him and bury him, for he is the only one of Jeroboam who shall come to the grave, because in him [a]there is found something good toward the LORD God of Israel in the house of Jeroboam.

14 [a]"Moreover the LORD will raise up for Himself a king over Israel who shall cut off the house of Jeroboam; this is the day. What? Even now! 15 For the LORD will strike Israel, as a reed is shaken in the water. He will [a]uproot Israel from this [b]good land which He gave to their fathers, and will scatter them [c]beyond the River,[1] [d]because they have made their wooden images,[2] provoking the LORD to anger. 16 And He will give Israel up because of the sins of Jeroboam, [a]who sinned and who made Israel sin."

17 Then Jeroboam's wife arose and departed, and came to [a]Tirzah. [b]When she came to the threshold of the house, the child died. 18 And they buried him; and all Israel mourned for him, [a]according to the word of the LORD which He spoke through His servant Ahijah the prophet.

### *DEATH OF JEROBOAM*

19 Now the rest of the acts of Jeroboam, how he [a]made war and how he reigned, indeed they *are* written in the book of the chronicles of the kings of Israel. 20 The period that Jeroboam reigned *was* twenty-two years. So he rested with his fathers. Then [a]Nadab his son reigned in his place.

### *REHOBOAM REIGNS IN JUDAH*

*(2 Chr. 11:5—12:16)*

21 And Rehoboam the son of Solomon reigned in Judah. [a]Rehoboam *was* forty-one years old when he became king. He reigned seventeen years in Jerusalem, the city [b]which the LORD had chosen out of all the tribes of Israel, to put His name there. [c]His mother's name *was* Naamah, an Ammonitess. 22 [a]Now Judah did evil in the sight of the LORD, and they [b]provoked Him to jealousy with their sins which they committed, more than all that their fathers had done. 23 For they also built for themselves [a]high places, [b]*sacred* pillars, and [c]wooden images on every high hill and [d]under every green tree. 24 [a]And there were also perverted persons[1] in the land. They did according to all the [b]abominations of the nations which the LORD had cast out before the children of [c]Israel.

**13:32** [a] 1 Kin. 13:2; 2 Kin. 23:16, 19 [b] 1 Kin. 16:24; John 4:5; Acts 8:14 [1] Literally *houses* **13:33** [a] 1 Kin. 12:31, 32; 2 Chr. 11:15; 13:9 **13:34** [a] 1 Kin. 12:30; 2 Kin. 17:21 [b] [1 Kin. 14:10; 15:29, 30] **14:2** [a] 1 Kin. 11:29–31 **14:3** [a] 1 Sam. 9:7, 8; 1 Kin. 13:7; 2 Kin. 4:42 **14:4** [a] 1 Kin. 11:29 **14:7** [a] 1 Kin. 16:2 **14:8** [a] 1 Kin. 11:31 [b] 1 Kin. 11:33, 38; 15:5 **14:9** [a] 1 Kin. 12:28 [b] Ps. 50:17 **14:10** [a] 1 Kin. 15:29 [b] 1 Kin. 21:21 [c] Deut. 32:36 **14:11** [a] 1 Kin. 16:4; 21:24 **14:12** [a] 1 Kin. 14:17 **14:13** [a] 2 Chr. 12:12; 19:3 **14:14** [a] 1 Kin. 15:27–29 **14:15** [a] 2 Kin. 17:6 [b] [Josh. 23:15, 16] [c] 2 Kin. 15:29 [d] [Ex. 34:13, 14] [1] That is, the Euphrates [2] Hebrew *Asherim*, Canaanite deities **14:16** [a] 1 Kin. 12:30; 13:34; 15:30, 34; 16:2 **14:17** [a] Song 6:4 [b] 1 Kin. 14:12 **14:18** [a] 1 Kin. 14:13 **14:19** [a] 2 Chr. 13:2–20 **14:20** [a] 1 Kin. 15:25 **14:21** [a] 2 Chr. 12:13 [b] 1 Kin. 11:32, 36 [c] 1 Kin. 14:31 **14:22** [a] 2 Chr. 12:1, 14 [b] Deut. 32:21 **14:23** [a] Deut. 12:2 [b] [Deut. 16:22] [c] [2 Kin. 17:9, 10] [d] Is. 57:5 **14:24** [a] Deut. 23:17 [b] Deut. 20:18 [c] [Deut. 9:4, 5] [1] Hebrew *qadesh*, that is, one practicing sodomy and prostitution in religious rituals

**14:23** The **high places** were a problem throughout the history of Judah and Israel (see Mic. 1:3). At times, the worship offered on them may have been done sincerely, in true worship of God (see 1 Kin. 3:2–4; 2 Kin. 12:3). But these were also the places in which Canaanite worship rites were practiced, and images set up to honor Baal and Asherah. Even when the worship on the high places was not mixed with pagan rituals, it was not in accord with the law of Moses (see 2 Chr. 1:3).

25[a]It happened in the fifth year of King Rehoboam *that* Shishak king of Egypt came up against Jerusalem. 26[a]And he took away the treasures of the house of the LORD and the treasures of the king's house; he took away everything. He also took away all the gold shields [b]which Solomon had made. 27Then King Rehoboam made bronze shields in their place, and committed *them* to the hands of the captains of the guard, who guarded the doorway of the king's house. 28And whenever the king entered the house of the LORD, the guards carried them, then brought them back into the guardroom.

29[a]Now the rest of the acts of Rehoboam, and all that he did, *are* they not written in the book of the chronicles of the kings of Judah? 30And there was [a]war between Rehoboam and Jeroboam all *their* days. 31[a]So Rehoboam rested with his fathers, and was buried with his fathers in the City of David. [b]His mother's name *was* Naamah, an Ammonitess. Then [c]Abijam[1] his son reigned in his place.

### *ABIJAM REIGNS IN JUDAH*

*(2 Chr. 13:1—14:1)*

**15** [a]In the eighteenth year of King Jeroboam the son of Nebat, Abijam became king over Judah. 2He reigned three years in Jerusalem. [a]His mother's name *was* [b]Maachah the granddaughter of [c]Abishalom. 3And he walked in all the sins of his father, which he had done before him; [a]his heart was not loyal to the LORD his God, as was the heart of his father David. 4Nevertheless [a]for David's sake the LORD his God gave him a lamp in Jerusalem, by setting up his son after him and by establishing Jerusalem; 5because David [a]did *what was* right in the eyes of the LORD, and had not turned aside from anything that He commanded him all the days of his life, [b]except in the matter of Uriah the Hittite. 6[a]And there was war between Rehoboam[1] and Jeroboam all the days of his life. 7[a]Now the rest of the acts of Abijam, and all that he did, *are* they not written in the book of the chronicles of the kings of Judah? And there was war between Abijam and Jeroboam.

8[a]So Abijam rested with his fathers, and they buried him in the City of David. Then Asa his son reigned in his place.

### *ASA REIGNS IN JUDAH*

*(2 Chr. 14:1—16:14)*

9In the twentieth year of Jeroboam king of Israel, Asa became king over Judah. 10And he reigned forty-one years in Jerusalem. His grandmother's name *was* Maachah the granddaughter of Abishalom. 11[a]Asa did *what was* right in the eyes of the LORD, as *did* his father David. 12[a]And he banished the perverted persons[1] from the land, and removed all the idols that his fathers had made. 13Also he removed [a]Maachah his grandmother from *being* queen mother, because she had made an obscene image of Asherah.[1] And Asa cut down her obscene image and [b]burned *it* by the Brook Kidron. 14[a]But the high places were not removed. Nevertheless Asa's [b]heart was loyal to the LORD all his days. 15He also brought into the house of the LORD the things which his father [a]had dedicated, and the things which he himself had dedicated: silver and gold and utensils.

16Now there was war between Asa and Baasha king of Israel all their days. 17And [a]Baasha king of Israel came up against Judah, and built [b]Ramah, [c]that he might let none go out or come in to Asa king of Judah. 18Then Asa took all the silver and gold *that was* left in the treasuries of the house of the LORD and the treasuries of the king's house, and delivered them into the hand of his servants. And King Asa sent them to [a]Ben-Hadad the son of Tabrimmon, the son of Hezion, king of Syria, who dwelt in [b]Damascus, saying, 19*"Let there be* a treaty between you and me, as there was between my father and your father. See, I have sent you a present of silver and gold. Come and break your treaty with Baasha king of Israel, so that he will withdraw from me."

20So Ben-Hadad heeded King Asa, and [a]sent the captains of his armies against the cities of Israel. He attacked [b]Ijon, [c]Dan, [d]Abel Beth Maachah, and all Chinneroth, with all the land of Naphtali. 21Now it happened, when Baasha heard *it,* that he stopped building Ramah, and remained in [a]Tirzah.

22[a]Then King Asa made a proclamation throughout all Judah; none *was* exempted. And they took away the stones and timber of Ramah, which Baasha had used for building;

**14:25** [a]1 Kin. 11:40 **14:26** [a]2 Chr. 12:9–11 [b]1 Kin. 10:17 **14:29** [a]2 Chr. 12:15, 16 **14:30** [a]1 Kin. 12:21–24; 15:6 **14:31** [a]2 Chr. 12:16 [b]1 Kin. 14:21 [c]2 Chr. 12:16 [1]Spelled *Abijah* in 2 Chronicles 12:16ff **15:1** [a]2 Chr. 13:1 **15:2** [a]2 Chr. 11:20–22 [b]2 Chr. 13:2 [c]2 Chr. 11:21 **15:3** [a]Ps. 119:80 **15:4** [a]2 Sam. 21:17 **15:5** [a]1 Kin. 9:4; 14:8 [b]2 Sam. 11:3, 15–17; 12:9, 10 **15:6** [a]1 Kin. 14:30 [1]Following Masoretic Text, Septuagint, Targum, and Vulgate; some Hebrew manuscripts and Syriac read *Abijam.* **15:7** [a]2 Chr. 13:2–22 **15:8** [a]2 Chr. 14:1 **15:11** [a]2 Chr. 14:2 **15:12** [a]1 Kin. 14:24; 22:46 [1]Hebrew *qedeshim,* that is, those practicing sodomy and prostitution in religious rituals **15:13** [a]2 Chr. 15:16–18 [b]Ex. 32:20 [1]A Canaanite goddess **15:14** [a]1 Kin. 3:2; 22:43 [b]1 Kin. 8:61; 15:3 **15:15** [a]1 Kin. 7:51 **15:17** [a]2 Chr. 16:1–6 [b]Josh. 18:25 [c]1 Kin. 12:26–29 **15:18** [a]2 Chr. 16:2 [b]1 Kin. 11:23, 24 **15:20** [a]1 Kin. 20:1 [b]2 Kin. 15:29 [c]Judg. 18:29 [d]2 Sam. 20:14, 15 **15:21** [a]1 Kin. 14:17; 16:15–18 **15:22** [a]2 Chr. 16:6

and with them King Asa built [b]Geba of Benjamin, and [c]Mizpah.

23 The rest of all the acts of Asa, all his might, all that he did, and the cities which he built, *are* they not written in the book of the chronicles of the kings of Judah? But [a]in the time of his old age he was diseased in his feet. 24 So Asa rested with his fathers, and was buried with his fathers in the City of David his father. [a]Then [b]Jehoshaphat his son reigned in his place.

### NADAB REIGNS IN ISRAEL

25 Now [a]Nadab the son of Jeroboam became king over Israel in the second year of Asa king of Judah, and he reigned over Israel two years. 26 And he did evil in the sight of the LORD, and walked in the way of his father, and in [a]his sin by which he had made Israel sin.

27 [a]Then Baasha the son of Ahijah, of the house of Issachar, conspired against him. And Baasha killed him at [b]Gibbethon, which *belonged* to the Philistines, while Nadab and all Israel laid siege to Gibbethon. 28 Baasha killed him in the third year of Asa king of Judah, and reigned in his place. 29 And it was so, when he became king, *that* he killed all the house of Jeroboam. He did not leave to Jeroboam anyone that breathed, until he had destroyed him, according to [a]the word of the LORD which He had spoken by His servant Ahijah the Shilonite, 30 [a]because of the sins of Jeroboam, which he had sinned and by which he had made Israel sin, because of his provocation with which he had provoked the LORD God of Israel to anger.

31 Now the rest of the acts of Nadab, and all that he did, *are* they not written in the book of the chronicles of the kings of Israel? 32 [a]And there was war between Asa and Baasha king of Israel all their days.

### BAASHA REIGNS IN ISRAEL

33 In the third year of Asa king of Judah, Baasha the son of Ahijah became king over all Israel in Tirzah, and *reigned* twenty-four years. 34 He did evil in the sight of the LORD, and walked in [a]the way of Jeroboam, and in his sin by which he had made Israel sin.

16 Then the word of the LORD came to [a]Jehu the son of [b]Hanani, against [c]Baasha, saying: 2 [a]"Inasmuch as I lifted you out of the dust and made you ruler over My people Israel, and [b]you have walked in the way of Jeroboam, and have made My people Israel sin, to provoke Me to anger with their sins, 3 surely I will [a]take away the posterity of Baasha and the posterity of his house, and I will make your house like [b]the house of Jeroboam the son of Nebat. 4 The dogs shall eat [a]whoever belongs to Baasha and dies in the city, and the birds of the air shall eat whoever dies in the fields."

5 Now the rest of the acts of Baasha, what he did, and his might, [a]*are* they not written in the book of the chronicles of the kings of Israel? 6 So Baasha rested with his fathers and was buried in [a]Tirzah. Then Elah his son reigned in his place.

7 And also the word of the LORD came by the prophet [a]Jehu the son of Hanani against Baasha and his house, because of all the evil that he did in the sight of the LORD in provoking Him to anger with the work of his hands, in being like the house of Jeroboam, and because [b]he killed them.

### ELAH REIGNS IN ISRAEL

8 In the twenty-sixth year of Asa king of Judah, Elah the son of Baasha became king over Israel, *and reigned* two years in Tirzah. 9 [a]Now his servant Zimri, commander of half *his* chariots, conspired against him as he was in Tirzah drinking himself drunk in the house of Arza, [b]steward of *his* house in Tirzah. 10 And Zimri went in and struck him and killed him in the twenty-seventh year of Asa king of Judah, and reigned in his place.

11 Then it came to pass, when he began to reign, as soon as he was seated on his throne, *that* he killed all the household of Baasha; he [a]did not leave him one male, neither of his relatives nor of his friends. 12 Thus Zimri destroyed all the household of Baasha, [a]according to the word of the LORD, which He spoke against Baasha by Jehu the prophet, 13 for all the sins of Baasha and the sins of Elah his son, by which they had sinned and by which they had made Israel sin, in provoking the LORD God of Israel to anger [a]with their idols.

14 Now the rest of the acts of Elah, and all that he did, *are* they not written in the book of the chronicles of the kings of Israel?

### ZIMRI REIGNS IN ISRAEL

15 In the twenty-seventh year of Asa king of Judah, Zimri had reigned in Tirzah seven days. And the people *were* encamped [a]against Gibbethon, which *belonged* to the Philistines. 16 Now the people *who were* encamped heard it said, "Zimri has conspired and also has killed the king." So all Israel made Omri, the commander of the army, king over Israel that day in the camp. 17 Then Omri and all Israel with him went up from Gibbethon, and they besieged Tirzah. 18 And it happened, when Zimri saw that the city was taken, that he went into the citadel of the king's house and burned the king's house down upon himself with fire, and died, 19 because of the sins which he had committed in doing evil in the sight of the LORD, [a]in walking in the [b]way of Jeroboam, and in his sin which he had committed to make Israel sin.

**15:22** [b] Josh. 21:17 [c] Josh. 18:26 **15:23** [a] 2 Chr. 16:11–14 **15:24** [a] 2 Chr. 17:1 [b] Matt. 1:8 **15:25** [a] 1 Kin. 14:20 **15:26** [a] 1 Kin. 12:28–33; 14:16 **15:27** [a] 1 Kin. 14:14 [b] Josh. 19:44; 21:23; 1 Kin. 16:15 **15:29** [a] 1 Kin. 14:10–14 **15:30** [a] 1 Kin. 14:9, 16 **15:32** [a] 1 Kin. 15:16 **15:34** [a] 1 Kin. 13:33; 14:16 **16:1** [a] 1 Kin. 16:7; 2 Chr. 19:2; 20:34 [b] 2 Chr. 16:7–10 [c] 1 Kin. 15:27 **16:2** [a] 1 Sam. 2:8; 1 Kin. 14:7 [b] 1 Kin. 12:25–33; 15:34 **16:3** [a] 1 Kin. 16:11; 21:21 [b] 1 Kin. 14:10; 15:29 **16:4** [a] 1 Kin. 14:11; 21:24 **16:5** [a] 2 Chr. 16:11 **16:6** [a] 1 Kin. 14:17; 15:21 **16:7** [a] 1 Kin. 16:1 [b] 1 Kin. 15:27, 29 **16:9** [a] 2 Kin. 9:30–33 [b] Gen. 24:2; 39:4; 1 Kin. 18:3 **16:11** [a] 1 Sam. 25:22 **16:12** [a] 1 Kin. 16:3 **16:13** [a] Deut. 32:21; 1 Sam. 12:21; [Is. 41:29; Jon. 2:8; 1 Cor. 8:4; 10:19] **16:15** [a] 1 Kin. 15:27 **16:19** [a] 1 Kin. 15:26, 34 [b] 1 Kin. 12:25–33

20 Now the rest of the acts of Zimri, and the treason he committed, *are* they not written in the book of the chronicles of the kings of Israel?

### *OMRI REIGNS IN ISRAEL*

21 Then the people of Israel were divided into two parts: half of the people followed Tibni the son of Ginath, to make him king, and half followed Omri. 22 But the people who followed Omri prevailed over the people who followed Tibni the son of Ginath. So Tibni died and Omri reigned. 23 In the thirty-first year of Asa king of Judah, Omri became king over Israel, *and reigned* twelve years. Six years he reigned in [a]Tirzah. 24 And he bought the hill of Samaria from Shemer for two talents of silver; then he built on the hill, and called the name of the city which he built, [a]Samaria, after the name of Shemer, owner of the hill. 25 [a]Omri did evil in the eyes of the LORD, and did worse than all who *were* before him. 26 For he [a]walked in all the ways of Jeroboam the son of Nebat, and in his sin by which he had made Israel sin, provoking the LORD God of Israel to anger with their [b]idols.

> **16:24** Omri, who turned out to be a powerful, successful, but evil king, set up his capital city in **Samaria**, thirty-five miles north of Jerusalem. Of the twelve tribes of Israel, Omri ruled ten. His kingdom was known as Israel or Samaria. The other two tribes were ruled by David's descendants. Their kingdom was called Judah.

27 Now the rest of the acts of Omri which he did, and the might that he showed, *are* they not written in the book of the chronicles of the kings of Israel?

28 So Omri rested with his fathers and was buried in Samaria. Then Ahab his son reigned in his place.

### *AHAB REIGNS IN ISRAEL*

29 In the thirty-eighth year of Asa king of Judah, Ahab the son of Omri became king over Israel; and Ahab the son of Omri reigned over Israel in Samaria twenty-two years. 30 Now Ahab the son of Omri did evil in the sight of the LORD, more than all who *were* before him. 31 And it came to pass, as though it had been a trivial thing for him to walk in the sins of Jeroboam the son of Nebat, [a]that he took as wife Jezebel the daughter of Ethbaal, king of the [b]Sidonians; [c]and he went and served Baal and worshiped him. 32 Then he set up an altar for Baal in [a]the temple of Baal, which he had built in Samaria. 33 [a]And Ahab made a wooden image.[1] Ahab [b]did more to provoke the LORD God of Israel to anger than all the kings of Israel who were before him. 34 In his days Hiel of Bethel built Jericho. He laid its foundation with Abiram his firstborn, and with his youngest *son* Segub he set up its gates, [a]according to the word of the LORD, which He had spoken through Joshua the son of Nun.[1]

### *ELIJAH PROCLAIMS A DROUGHT*

**17** And Elijah the Tishbite, of the [a]inhabitants of Gilead, said to Ahab, [b]"*As* the LORD God of Israel lives, [c]before whom I stand, [d]there shall not be dew nor rain [e]these years, except at my word."

2 Then the word of the LORD came to him, saying, 3 "Get away from here and turn eastward, and hide by the Brook Cherith, which flows into the Jordan. 4 And it will be *that* you shall drink from the brook, and I have commanded the [a]ravens to feed you there."

5 So he went and did according to the word of the LORD, for he went and stayed by the Brook Cherith, which flows into the Jordan. 6 The ravens brought him bread and meat in the morning, and bread and meat in the evening; and he drank from the brook. 7 And it happened after a while that the brook dried up, because there had been no rain in the land.

### *ELIJAH AND THE WIDOW*

8 Then the word of the LORD came to him, saying, 9 "Arise, go to [a]Zarephath, which *belongs* to [b]Sidon, and dwell there. See, I have commanded a widow there to provide for you." 10 So he arose and went to Zarephath. And when he came to the gate of the city, indeed a widow *was* there gathering sticks. And he called to her and said, "Please bring me a little water in a cup, that I may drink." 11 And as she was going to get *it,* he called to her and said, "Please bring me a morsel of bread in your hand."

12 So she said, "As the LORD your God lives, I do not have bread, only a handful of flour in a bin, and a little oil in a jar; and see, I *am* gathering a couple of sticks that I may go in and prepare it for myself and my son, that we may eat it, and [a]die."

13 And Elijah said to her, "Do not fear; go *and* do as you have said, but make me a small cake from it first, and bring *it* to me; and afterward make *some* for yourself and your son. 14 For thus says the LORD God of Israel: 'The bin of flour shall not be used up, nor shall the jar of oil run dry, until the day the LORD sends rain on the earth.'"

15 So she went away and did according to the word of Elijah; and she and he and her household ate for *many* days. 16 The bin of flour was not used up, nor did the jar of oil run dry, according to the word of the LORD which He spoke by Elijah.

**16:23** [a] 1 Kin. 15:21; 2 Kin. 15:14 **16:24** [a] 1 Kin. 13:32; 2 Kin. 17:24; John 4:4 **16:25** [a] Mic. 6:16 **16:26** [a] 1 Kin. 16:19 [b] 1 Kin. 16:13 **16:31** [a] Deut. 7:3 [b] Judg. 18:7; 1 Kin. 11:1–5 [c] 1 Kin. 21:25, 26; 2 Kin. 10:18; 17:16 **16:32** [a] 2 Kin. 10:21, 26, 27 **16:33** [a] 2 Kin. 13:6 [b] 1 Kin. 14:9; 16:29, 30; 21:25 [1] Hebrew *Asherah,* a Canaanite goddess **16:34** [a] Josh. 6:26 [1] Compare Joshua 6:26 **17:1** [a] Judg. 12:4 [b] 1 Kin. 18:10; 22:14; 2 Kin. 3:14; 5:20 [c] Deut. 10:8 [d] 1 Kin. 18:1; James 5:17 [e] Luke 4:25 **17:4** [a] Job 38:41 **17:9** [a] Obad. 20; Luke 4:25, 26 [b] 2 Sam. 24:6 **17:12** [a] Deut. 28:23, 24

### ELIJAH REVIVES THE WIDOW'S SON

17 Now it happened after these things *that*
the son of the woman who owned the house
became sick. And his sickness was so serious
that there was no breath left in him. 18 So she said
to Elijah, [a]"What have I to do with you, O man
of God? Have you come to me to bring my sin
to remembrance, and to kill my son?"
19 And he said to her, "Give me your son." So
he took him out of her arms and carried him
to the upper room where he was staying, and
laid him on his own bed. 20 Then he cried out to
the LORD and said, "O LORD my God, have You
also brought tragedy on the widow with whom
I lodge, by killing her son?" 21 [a]And he stretched
himself out on the child three times, and cried
out to the LORD and said, "O LORD my God, I pray,
let this child's soul come back to him." 22 Then
the LORD heard the voice of Elijah; and the soul
of the child came back to him, and he [a]revived.
23 And Elijah took the child and brought him
down from the upper room into the house, and
gave him to his mother. And Elijah said, "See,
your son lives!"
24 Then the woman said to Elijah, "Now by
this [a]I know that you *are* a man of God, *and* that
the word of the LORD in your mouth *is* the truth."

> **SEEING JESUS IN THE SCRIPTURE**
>
> **17:17–24** Elijah is one of two people in the Old Testament to raise someone from the dead. Jesus did it several times during His earthly ministry to show His power over death (see John 11:43–44).

### ELIJAH'S MESSAGE TO AHAB

18 And it came to pass *after* [a]many days that
the word of the LORD came to Elijah, in the
third year, saying, "Go, present yourself to Ahab,
and [b]I will send rain on the earth."
2 So Elijah went to present himself to Ahab;
and *there was* a severe famine in Samaria. 3 And
Ahab had called Obadiah, who *was* in charge of
*his* house. (Now Obadiah feared the LORD great-
ly. 4 For so it was, while Jezebel massacred the
prophets of the LORD, that Obadiah had taken
one hundred prophets and hidden them, fifty to
a cave, and had fed them with bread and water.)
5 And Ahab had said to Obadiah, "Go into the land
to all the springs of water and to all the brooks;
perhaps we may find grass to keep the horses
and mules alive, so that we will not have to kill
any livestock." 6 So they divided the land between
them to explore it; Ahab went one way by himself,
and Obadiah went another way by himself.
7 Now as Obadiah was on his way, suddenly
Elijah met him; and he [a]recognized him, and fell
on his face, and said, "*Is* that you, my lord Elijah?"
8 And he answered him, "*It is* I. Go, tell your
master, 'Elijah *is here*.' "
9 So he said, "How have I sinned, that you are
delivering your servant into the hand of Ahab, to
kill me? 10 *As* the LORD your God lives, there is no
nation or kingdom where my master has not sent
someone to hunt for you; and when they said, '*He
is* not *here*,' he took an oath from the kingdom or
nation that they could not find you. 11 And now you
say, 'Go, tell your master, "Elijah *is here*" '! 12 And it
shall come to pass, *as soon as* I am gone from you,
that [a]the Spirit of the LORD will carry you to a place
I do not know; so when I go and tell Ahab, and he
cannot find you, he will kill me. But I your servant
have feared the LORD from my youth. 13 Was it not
reported to my lord what I did when Jezebel killed
the prophets of the LORD, how I hid one hundred
men of the LORD's prophets, fifty to a cave, and fed
them with bread and water? 14 And now you say, 'Go,
tell your master, "Elijah *is here*." ' He will kill me!"
15 Then Elijah said, "*As* the LORD of hosts
lives, before whom I stand, I will surely present
myself to him today."
16 So Obadiah went to meet Ahab, and told
him; and Ahab went to meet Elijah.
17 Then it happened, when Ahab saw Elijah,
that Ahab said to him, [a]"*Is that* you, O [b]troubler
of Israel?"
18 And he answered, "I have not troubled
Israel, but you and your father's house *have*, [a]in
that you have forsaken the commandments of
the LORD and have followed the Baals. 19 Now
therefore, send *and* gather all Israel to me on
[a]Mount Carmel, the four hundred and fifty
prophets of Baal, [b]and the four hundred proph-
ets of Asherah,[1] who eat at Jezebel's table."

### ELIJAH'S MOUNT CARMEL VICTORY

20 So Ahab sent for all the children of Israel,
and [a]gathered the prophets together on Mount
Carmel. 21 And Elijah came to all the people, and
said, [a]"How long will you falter between two opin-
ions? If the LORD *is* God, follow Him; but if Baal,
[b]follow him." But the people answered him not a
word. 22 Then Elijah said to the people, [a]"I alone am
left a prophet of the LORD; [b]but Baal's prophets *are*
four hundred and fifty men. 23 Therefore let them
give us two bulls; and let them choose one bull
for themselves, cut it in pieces, and lay *it* on the
wood, but put no fire *under it*; and I will prepare
the other bull, and lay *it* on the wood, but put no
fire *under it*. 24 Then you call on the name of your
gods, and I will call on the name of the LORD; and
the God who [a]answers by fire, He is God."
So all the people answered and said, "It is
well spoken."
25 Now Elijah said to the prophets of Baal,

**17:18** [a] Luke 5:8 **17:21** [a] 2 Kin. 4:34, 35; Acts 20:10 **17:22** [a] Luke 7:14, 15; Heb. 11:35 **17:24** [a] John 2:11; 3:2; 16:30 **18:1** [a] 1 Kin. 17:1; Luke 4:25; James 5:17 [b] Deut. 28:12 **18:7** [a] 2 Kin. 1:6–8 **18:12** [a] 2 Kin. 2:16; Ezek. 3:12, 14; Matt. 4:1; Acts 8:39 **18:17** [a] 1 Kin. 21:20 [b] Josh. 7:25; Acts 16:20 **18:18** [a] 1 Kin. 16:30–33; [2 Chr. 15:2] **18:19** [a] Josh. 19:26; 2 Kin. 2:25 [b] 1 Kin. 16:33 [1] A Canaanite goddess **18:20** [a] 1 Kin. 22:6 **18:21** [a] 2 Kin. 17:41; [Matt. 6:24] [b] Josh. 24:15 **18:22** [a] 1 Kin. 19:10, 14 [b] 1 Kin. 18:19 **18:24** [a] 1 Kin. 18:38; 1 Chr. 21:26

"Choose one bull for yourselves and prepare *it*
first, for you *are* many; and call on the name of
your god, but put no fire *under it.*"
26 So they took the bull which was given them,
and they prepared *it,* and called on the name of Baal
from morning even till noon, saying, "O Baal, hear
us!" But *there was* [a]no voice; no one answered. Then
they leaped about the altar which they had made.
27 And so it was, at noon, that Elijah mocked
them and said, "Cry aloud, for he *is* a god; either he
is meditating, or he is busy, or he is on a journey,
*or* perhaps he is sleeping and must be awakened."
28 So they cried aloud, and [a]cut themselves, as was
their custom, with knives and lances, until the
blood gushed out on them. 29 And when midday
was past, [a]they prophesied until the *time* of the
offering of the *evening* sacrifice. But *there was* [b]no
voice; no one answered, no one paid attention.
30 Then Elijah said to all the people, "Come
near to me." So all the people came near to him.
[a]And he repaired the altar of the LORD *that was*
broken down. 31 And Elijah took twelve stones,
according to the number of the tribes of the
sons of Jacob, to whom the word of the LORD
had come, saying, [a]"Israel shall be your name."[1]
32 Then with the stones he built an altar [a]in the
name of the LORD; and he made a trench around
the altar large enough to hold two seahs of seed.
33 And he [a]put the wood in order, cut the bull in
pieces, and laid *it* on the wood, and said, "Fill four
waterpots with water, and [b]pour *it* on the burnt
sacrifice and on the wood." 34 Then he said, "Do
*it* a second time," and they did *it* a second time;
and he said, "Do *it* a third time," and they did *it*
a third time. 35 So the water ran all around the
altar; and he also filled [a]the trench with water.
36 And it came to pass, at *the time of* the offer-
ing of the *evening* sacrifice, that Elijah the proph-
et came near and said, "LORD [a]God of Abraham,
Isaac, and Israel, [b]let it be known this day that
You *are* God in Israel and I *am* Your servant, and
*that* [c]I have done all these things at Your word.
37 Hear me, O LORD, hear me, that this people
may know that You *are* the LORD God, and *that*
You have turned their hearts back *to You* again."
38 Then [a]the fire of the LORD fell and con-
sumed the burnt sacrifice, and the wood and the
stones and the dust, and it licked up the water

**18:26** [a] Ps. 115:5; Jer. 10:5; [1 Cor. 8:4] **18:28** [a] [Lev. 19:28; Deut. 14:1] **18:29** [a] Ex. 29:39, 41 [b] 1 Kin. 18:26 **18:30** [a] 1 Kin. 19:10, 14; 2 Chr. 33:16 **18:31** [a] Gen. 32:28; 35:10; 2 Kin. 17:34 [1] Genesis 32:28 **18:32** [a] [Ex. 20:25; Col. 3:17] **18:33** [a] Gen. 22:9; Lev. 1:6–8 [b] Judg. 6:20 **18:35** [a] 1 Kin. 18:32, 38 **18:36** [a] Gen. 28:13; Ex. 3:6; 4:5; [Matt. 22:32] [b] 1 Kin. 8:43; 2 Kin. 19:19 [c] Num. 16:28 **18:38** [a] Gen. 15:17; Lev. 9:24; 10:1, 2; Judg. 6:21; 2 Kin. 1:12; 1 Chr. 21:26; 2 Chr. 7:1; Job 1:16

1 KINGS 18:17–40

## ELIJAH'S BATTLE AND GOD'S VICTORY

30

STORY OF SCRIPTURE

### WHAT'S GOING ON?

This passage describes one of the most dramatic confrontations in the Bible: Elijah's challenge to the prophets of Baal on Mount Carmel. Israel was in a spiritual crisis under King Ahab and Queen Jezebel, who had led the people into Baal worship. In response, Elijah challenged four hundred fifty prophets of Baal to a test to prove who is the true God. The prophets of Baal failed to invoke any response from their god, while Elijah's prayer resulted in a miraculous fire from heaven consuming his offering that had been drenched with water. This event led the people of Israel acknowledging God as the true God and the execution of the prophets of Baal. There hadn't been such a stark contrast between God and other gods since the time of Moses.

### WHAT DOES THIS MEAN FOR ME?

In a world with many competing "gods"—ideologies, relationships, social media, possessions, fame—we're called to place our trust in the one true God above all else. Elijah's faith in the face of opposition reminds us true faith often requires courage, especially when it goes against the culture and what's considered trendy.

### DID YOU CATCH THE PATTERN?

The Old Testament is filled with moments when God shows Himself to be stronger than the gods of the world. This was demonstrated by the plagues He sent to Egypt, which were attacks against the gods of Egypt (see Ex. 7–11). He used Samson to destroy the Temple of Dagon (see Judg. 16). When the Philistines stole the ark of the Covenant, He cut off the head and hands of the statue of Dagon (see 1 Sam. 5). These examples remind us God is stronger than any ideology or dark force in this world; therefore, He is worthy of our worship.

*For the next* Story of Scripture *reading and devotion, turn to 2 Kings 17:5–23 on page 383.*

that *was* in the trench. 39 Now when all the people
saw *it,* they fell on their faces; and they said, [a]"The
LORD, He *is* God! The LORD, He *is* God!"
40 And Elijah said to them, [a]"Seize the proph-
ets of Baal! Do not let one of them escape!" So
they seized them; and Elijah brought them down
to the Brook [b]Kishon and [c]executed them there.

### THE DROUGHT ENDS

41 Then Elijah said to Ahab, "Go up, eat and
drink; for *there is* the sound of abundance of
rain." 42 So Ahab went up to eat and drink. And
Elijah went up to the top of Carmel; [a]then he
bowed down on the ground, and put his face
between his knees, 43 and said to his servant,
"Go up now, look toward the sea."
So he went up and looked, and said, "*There*
*is* nothing." And seven times he said, "Go again."
44 Then it came to pass the seventh *time,* that
he said, "There is a cloud, as small as a man's
hand, rising out of the sea!" So he said, "Go up,
say to Ahab, 'Prepare *your chariot,* and go down
before the rain stops you.' "
45 Now it happened in the meantime that
the sky became black with clouds and wind, and
there was a heavy rain. So Ahab rode away and
went to Jezreel. 46 Then the [a]hand of the LORD
came upon Elijah; and he [b]girded up his loins
and ran ahead of Ahab to the entrance of Jezreel.

### ELIJAH ESCAPES FROM JEZEBEL

19 And Ahab told Jezebel all that Elijah had
done, also how he had [a]executed all the
prophets with the sword. 2 Then Jezebel sent a
messenger to Elijah, saying, [a]"So let the gods do
*to me,* and more also, if I do not make your life as
the life of one of them by tomorrow about this
time." 3 And when he saw *that,* he arose and ran
for his life, and went to Beersheba, which *belongs*
to Judah, and left his servant there.

**19:3** We might ask why a man who had seen God's mighty power should give way to fear, but we must realize God didn't criticize Elijah for his reaction. Elijah was not a superhero but a man with a nature like ours (James 5:17). He had seen a great victory on Mount Carmel, but he also knew Jezebel was still in power, the faith of the people was still weak, at best, and his life truly was in danger.

4 But he himself went a day's journey into
the wilderness, and came and sat down under
a broom tree. And he [a]prayed that he might die,
and said, "It is enough! Now, LORD, take my life,
for I *am* no better than my fathers!"
5 Then as he lay and slept under a broom
tree, suddenly an angel[1] touched him, and said
to him, "Arise *and* eat." 6 Then he looked, and
there by his head *was* a cake baked on coals,
and a jar of water. So he ate and drank, and
lay down again. 7 And the angel[1] of the LORD
came back the second time, and touched him,
and said, "Arise *and* eat, because the journey
*is* too great for you." 8 So he arose, and ate and
drank; and he went in the strength of that food
forty days and [a]forty nights as far as [b]Horeb, the
mountain of God.
9 And there he went into a cave, and spent
the night in that place; and behold, the word
of the LORD *came* to him, and He said to him,
"What are you doing here, Elijah?"
10 So he said, [a]"I have been very [b]zealous for
the LORD God of hosts; for the children of Israel
have forsaken Your covenant, torn down Your
altars, and [c]killed Your prophets with the sword.
[d]I alone am left; and they seek to take my life."

**18:39** [a] 1 Kin. 18:21, 24 **18:40** [a] 2 Kin. 10:25 [b] Judg. 4:7; 5:21 [c] [Deut. 13:5; 18:20] **18:42** [a] James 5:17, 18 **18:46** [a] 2 Kin. 3:15; Is. 8:11; Ezek. 3:14 [b] 2 Kin. 4:29; 9:1; Jer. 1:17; 1 Pet. 1:13 **19:1** [a] 1 Kin. 18:40 **19:2** [a] Ruth 1:17; 1 Kin. 20:10; 2 Kin. 6:31 **19:4** [a] Num. 11:15; Jer. 20:14–18; Jon. 4:3, 8 **19:5** [1] Or *Angel* **19:7** [1] Or *Angel* **19:8** [a] Ex. 24:18; 34:28; Deut. 9:9–11, 18; Matt. 4:2 [b] Ex. 3:1; 4:27 **19:10** [a] Rom. 11:3 [b] Num. 25:11, 13; Ps. 69:9 [c] 1 Kin. 18:4 [d] 1 Kin. 18:22; Rom. 11:3

APPLY THE TRUTH

## MENTAL HEALTH

**19:4–10** One consistent aspect of life is its inconsistency. Friends move, plans change, feelings come and go. Life often feels like we're strapped into a roller coaster we never asked to be on. The result of this turmoil can be all sorts of emotional damage. To be healthy mentally is to remain present and consistent through the dramatic changes of life. It's to have emotional, phycological, and social well-being. But change, difficulty, and challenges can threaten the mental health of even the strongest, most faithful of us.

Elijah was a man God used in mighty ways. In the previous two chapters we see God use him to perform miracles and defeat hundreds of false prophets in front of His people. But here, Elijah wanted to die. It's a striking miniature of the ups and downs of life. For Elijah, the strength to keep going came from God's presence, rest, and a good meal. Like Elijah, we must first and foremost lean on the presence and power of God. But we're also to take healthy, practical steps that allow us to move forward. Go outside. Take a nap. Eat. Talk with a friend or professional. Do something that brings you joy.

### *GOD'S REVELATION TO ELIJAH*

11 Then He said, "Go out, and stand [a]on the
mountain before the LORD." And behold, the
LORD [b]passed by, and [c]a great and strong wind
tore into the mountains and broke the rocks in
pieces before the LORD, *but* the LORD *was* not
in the wind; and after the wind an earthquake,
*but* the LORD *was* not in the earthquake; 12 and
after the earthquake a fire, *but* the LORD *was* not
in the fire; and after the fire a still small voice.
13 So it was, when Elijah heard *it,* that [a]he
wrapped his face in his mantle and went out
and stood in the entrance of the cave. [b]Suddenly
a voice *came* to him, and said, "What are you
doing here, Elijah?"
14 [a]And he said, "I have been very zealous for
the LORD God of hosts; because the children of Is-
rael have forsaken Your covenant, torn down Your
altars, and killed Your prophets with the sword. I
alone am left; and they seek to take my life."
15 Then the LORD said to him: "Go, return on
your way to the Wilderness of Damascus; [a]and
when you arrive, anoint Hazael *as* king over
Syria. 16 Also you shall anoint [a]Jehu the son of
Nimshi *as* king over Israel. And [b]Elisha the son
of Shaphat of Abel Meholah you shall anoint *as*
prophet in your place. 17 [a]It shall be *that* whoever
escapes the sword of Hazael, Jehu will [b]kill; and
whoever escapes the sword of Jehu, [c]Elisha will
kill. 18 [a]Yet I have reserved seven thousand in
Israel, all whose knees have not bowed to Baal,
[b]and every mouth that has not kissed him."

### *ELISHA FOLLOWS ELIJAH*

19 So he departed from there, and found Eli-
sha the son of Shaphat, who *was* plowing *with*
twelve yoke *of oxen* before him, and he was with
the twelfth. Then Elijah passed by him and threw
his [a]mantle on him. 20 And he left the oxen and
ran after Elijah, and said, [a]"Please let me kiss my
father and my mother, and *then* I will follow you."

> **SEEING JESUS IN THE SCRIPTURE**
>
> **19:20** Elisha's urgency to follow Elijah after saying a quick goodbye to his parents is like what Jesus demanded of His disciples—He must become our greatest priority (see Matt. 8:21–22). We are to love our families, but not even they should be more important than Jesus.

And he said to him, "Go back again, for what
have I done to you?"
21 So *Elisha* turned back from him, and took a
yoke of oxen and slaughtered them and [a]boiled
their flesh, using the oxen's equipment, and gave
it to the people, and they ate. Then he arose and
followed Elijah, and became his servant.

### *AHAB DEFEATS THE SYRIANS*

**20** Now [a]Ben-Hadad the king of Syria gath-
ered all his forces together; thirty-two
kings *were* with him, with horses and chariots.
And he went up and besieged [b]Samaria, and
made war against it. 2 Then he sent messengers
into the city to Ahab king of Israel, and said to
him, "Thus says Ben-Hadad: 3 'Your silver and
your gold *are* mine; your loveliest wives and
children are mine.' "
4 And the king of Israel answered and said,
"My lord, O king, just as you say, I and all that I
have *are* yours."
5 Then the messengers came back and said,
"Thus speaks Ben-Hadad, saying, 'Indeed I have
sent to you, saying, "You shall deliver to me
your silver and your gold, your wives and your
children"; 6 but I will send my servants to you
tomorrow about this time, and they shall search
your house and the houses of your servants.
And it shall be, *that* whatever is pleasant in your
eyes, they will put *it* in their hands and take *it.*' "
7 So the king of Israel called all the elders of
the land, and said, "Notice, please, and see how
this *man* seeks trouble, for he sent to me for my
wives, my children, my silver, and my gold; and
I did not deny him."
8 And all the elders and all the people said
to him, "Do not listen or consent."
9 Therefore he said to the messengers of
Ben-Hadad, "Tell my lord the king, 'All that you
sent for to your servant the first time I will do,
but this thing I cannot do.' "
And the messengers departed and brought
back word to him.
10 Then Ben-Hadad sent to him and said,
[a]"The gods do so to me, and more also, if enough
dust is left of Samaria for a handful for each of
the people who follow me."
11 So the king of Israel answered and said,
"Tell *him,* 'Let not the one who puts on *his armor*
[a]boast like the one who takes *it off.*' "
12 And it happened when *Ben-Hadad* heard
this message, as he and the kings *were* [a]drinking
at the command post, that he said to his servants,
"Get ready." And they got ready to attack the city.
13 Suddenly a prophet approached Ahab king
of Israel, saying, "Thus says the LORD: 'Have
you seen all this great multitude? Behold, [a]I will
deliver it into your hand today, and you shall
know that I *am* the LORD.' "
14 So Ahab said, "By whom?"
And he said, "Thus says the LORD: 'By the
young leaders of the provinces.' "
Then he said, "Who will set the battle in order?"
And he answered, "You."

**19:11** [a] Ex. 19:20; 24:12, 18 [b] Ex. 33:21, 22 [c] Ezek. 1:4; 37:7 **19:13** [a] Ex. 3:6; Is. 6:2 [b] 1 Kin. 19:9 **19:14** [a] 1 Kin. 19:10 **19:15** [a] 2 Kin. 8:8–15 **19:16** [a] 2 Kin. 9:1–10 [b] 1 Kin. 19:19–21; 2 Kin. 2:9–15 **19:17** [a] 2 Kin. 8:12; 13:3, 22 [b] 2 Kin. 9:14—10:28 [c] [Hos. 6:5] **19:18** [a] Rom. 11:4 [b] Hos. 13:2 **19:19** [a] 1 Sam. 28:14; 2 Kin. 2:8, 13, 14 **19:20** [a] [Matt. 8:21, 22; Luke 9:61, 62]; Acts 20:37 **19:21** [a] 2 Sam. 24:22 **20:1** [a] 1 Kin. 15:18, 20; 2 Kin. 6:24 [b] 1 Kin. 16:24; 2 Kin. 6:24 **20:10** [a] 1 Kin. 19:2; 2 Kin. 6:31 **20:11** [a] Prov. 27:1; [Eccl. 7:8] **20:12** [a] 1 Kin. 20:16 **20:13** [a] 1 Kin. 20:28

15 Then he mustered the young leaders of the provinces, and there were two hundred and thirty-two; and after them he mustered all the people, all the children of Israel—seven thousand. 16 So they went out at noon. Meanwhile Ben-Hadad and the thirty-two kings helping him were [a]getting drunk at the command post. 17 The young leaders of the provinces went out first. And Ben-Hadad sent out *a patrol,* and they told him, saying, "Men are coming out of Samaria!" 18 So he said, "If they have come out for peace, take them alive; and if they have come out for war, take them alive."

19 Then these young leaders of the provinces went out of the city with the army which followed them. 20 And each one killed his man; so the Syrians fled, and Israel pursued them; and Ben-Hadad the king of Syria escaped on a horse with the cavalry. 21 Then the king of Israel went out and attacked the horses and chariots, and killed the Syrians with a great slaughter.

22 And the prophet came to the king of Israel and said to him, "Go, strengthen yourself; take note, and see what you should do, [a]for in the spring of the year the king of Syria will come up against you."

### THE SYRIANS AGAIN DEFEATED

23 Then the servants of the king of Syria said to him, "Their gods *are* gods of the hills. Therefore they were stronger than we; but if we fight against them in the plain, surely we will be stronger than they. 24 So do this thing: Dismiss the kings, each from his position, and put captains in their places; 25 and you shall muster an army like the army that you have lost, horse for horse and chariot for chariot. Then we will fight against them in the plain; surely we will be stronger than they."

And he listened to their voice and did so.

**20:23** The Canaanites believed each of their false gods controlled one specific area of the physical world. Ben-Hadad's officials believed Israel's God controlled the **hills**, so they figured if they moved the fight to flat land the Israelites would be helpless.

26 So it was, in the spring of the year, that Ben-Hadad mustered the Syrians and went up to [a]Aphek to fight against Israel. 27 And the children of Israel were mustered and given provisions, and they went against them. Now the children of Israel encamped before them like two little flocks of goats, while the Syrians filled the [a]countryside.

28 Then a [a]man of God came and spoke to the king of Israel, and said, "Thus says the LORD: 'Because the Syrians have said, "The LORD *is* God of the hills, but He *is* not God of the valleys," therefore [b]I will deliver all this great multitude into your hand, and you shall know that I *am* the LORD.' " 29 And they encamped opposite each other for seven days. So it was that on the seventh day the battle was joined; and the children of Israel killed one hundred thousand foot soldiers *of* the Syrians in one day. 30 But the rest fled to Aphek, into the city; then a wall fell on twenty-seven thousand of the men *who were* left.

And Ben-Hadad fled and went into the city, into an inner chamber.

### AHAB'S TREATY WITH BEN-HADAD

31 Then his servants said to him, "Look now, we have heard that the kings of the house of Israel *are* merciful kings. Please, let us [a]put sackcloth around our waists and ropes around our heads, and go out to the king of Israel; perhaps he will spare your life." 32 So they wore sackcloth around their waists and *put* ropes around their heads, and came to the king of Israel and said, "Your servant Ben-Hadad says, 'Please let me live.' "

And he said, "*Is* he still alive? He *is* my brother."

33 Now the men were watching closely to see whether *any sign of mercy would come* from him; and they quickly grasped *at this word* and said, "Your brother Ben-Hadad."

So he said, "Go, bring him." Then Ben-Hadad came out to him; and he had him come up into the chariot.

34 So *Ben-Hadad* said to him, [a]"The cities which my father took from your father I will restore; and you may set up marketplaces for yourself in Damascus, as my father did in Samaria."

Then *Ahab said,* "I will send you away with this treaty." So he made a treaty with him and sent him away.

### AHAB CONDEMNED

35 Now a certain man of [a]the sons of the prophets said to his neighbor [b]by the word of the LORD, "Strike me, please." And the man refused to strike him. 36 Then he said to him, "Because you have not obeyed the voice of the LORD, surely, as soon as you depart from me, a lion shall kill you." And as soon as he left him, [a]a lion found him and killed him.

37 And he found another man, and said, "Strike me, please." So the man struck him, inflicting a wound. 38 Then the prophet departed and waited for the king by the road, and disguised himself with a bandage over his eyes. 39 Now [a]as the king passed by, he cried out to the king and said, "Your servant went out into the midst of the battle; and there, a man came over and brought a man to me, and said, 'Guard this man; if by any means he is missing, [b]your life shall be for his life, or else you shall pay a talent of silver.' 40 While your servant was busy here and there, he was gone."

Then the king of Israel said to him, "So *shall* your judgment *be;* you yourself have decided *it.*"

20:16 [a] 1 Kin. 16:9; 20:12; [Prov. 20:1] 20:22 [a] 2 Sam. 11:1; 1 Kin. 20:26 20:26 [a] Josh. 13:4; 2 Kin. 13:17 20:27 [a] Judg. 6:3–5; 1 Sam. 13:5–8 20:28 [a] 1 Kin. 17:18 [b] 1 Kin. 20:13 20:31 [a] Gen. 37:34; 2 Sam. 3:31 20:34 [a] 1 Kin. 15:20 20:35 [a] 2 Kin. 2:3, 5, 7, 15 [b] 1 Kin. 13:17, 18 20:36 [a] 1 Kin. 13:24 20:39 [a] 2 Sam. 12:1 [b] 2 Kin. 10:24

41 And he hastened to take the bandage away
from his eyes; and the king of Israel recognized
him as one of the prophets. 42 Then he said to
him, "Thus says the LORD: [a]'Because you have let
slip out of *your* hand a man whom I appointed
to utter destruction, therefore your life shall
go for his life, and your people for his people.' "
43 So the king of Israel [a]went to his house
sullen and displeased, and came to Samaria.

### NABOTH IS MURDERED FOR HIS VINEYARD

21 And it came to pass after these things *that*
Naboth the Jezreelite had a vineyard which
*was* in [a]Jezreel, next to the palace of Ahab king
of Samaria. 2 So Ahab spoke to Naboth, saying,
"Give me your [a]vineyard, that I may have it for
a vegetable garden, because it *is* near, next to
my house; and for it I will give you a vineyard
better than it. *Or,* if it seems good to you, I will
give you its worth in money."
3 But Naboth said to Ahab, "The LORD for-
bid [a]that I should give the inheritance of my
fathers to you!"
4 So Ahab went into his house sullen and
displeased because of the word which Naboth
the Jezreelite had spoken to him; for he had
said, "I will not give you the inheritance of my
fathers." And he lay down on his bed, and turned
away his face, and would eat no food. 5 But [a]Jez-
ebel his wife came to him, and said to him, "Why
is your spirit so sullen that you eat no food?"
6 He said to her, "Because I spoke to Naboth
the Jezreelite, and said to him, 'Give me your
vineyard for money; or else, if it pleases you,
I will give you *another* vineyard for it.' And he
answered, 'I will not give you my vineyard.' "
7 Then Jezebel his wife said to him, "You now
exercise authority over Israel! Arise, eat food,
and let your heart be cheerful; I will give you
the vineyard of Naboth the Jezreelite."
8 And she wrote letters in Ahab's name, sealed
*them* with his seal, and sent the letters to the
elders and the nobles who *were* dwelling in the
city with Naboth. 9 She wrote in the letters, saying,

> Proclaim a fast, and seat Naboth with
> high honor among the people; 10 and seat
> two men, scoundrels, before him to bear
> witness against him, saying, "You have
> [a]blasphemed God and the king." *Then* take
> him out, and [b]stone him, that he may die.

11 So the men of his city, the elders and nobles
who were inhabitants of his city, did as Jezebel
had sent to them, as it *was* written in the letters
which she had sent to them. 12 [a]They proclaimed
a fast, and seated Naboth with high honor among
the people. 13 And two men, scoundrels, came
in and sat before him; and the scoundrels
[a]witnessed against him, against Naboth, in the
presence of the people, saying, "Naboth has
blasphemed God and the king!" [b]Then they took
him outside the city and stoned him with stones,
so that he died. 14 Then they sent to Jezebel,
saying, "Naboth has been stoned and is dead."
15 And it came to pass, when Jezebel heard
that Naboth had been stoned and was dead, that
Jezebel said to Ahab, "Arise, take possession of
the vineyard of Naboth the Jezreelite, which he
refused to give you for money; for Naboth is not
alive, but dead." 16 So it was, when Ahab heard
that Naboth was dead, that Ahab got up and
went down to take possession of the vineyard
of Naboth the Jezreelite.

### THE LORD CONDEMNS AHAB

17 [a]Then the word of the LORD came to [b]Elijah
the Tishbite, saying, 18 "Arise, go down to meet
Ahab king of Israel, [a]who *lives* in Samaria. There
*he is,* in the vineyard of Naboth, where he has gone
down to take possession of it. 19 You shall speak
to him, saying, 'Thus says the LORD: "Have you

**20:42** [a] 1 Kin. 22:31–37 **20:43** [a] 1 Kin. 21:4 **21:1** [a] Judg. 6:33; 1 Kin. 18:45, 46 **21:2** [a] 1 Sam. 8:14 **21:3** [a] [Lev. 25:23; Num. 36:7; Ezek. 46:18] **21:5** [a] 1 Kin. 19:1, 2 **21:10** [a] [Ex. 22:28; Lev. 24:15, 16]; Acts 6:11 [b] [Lev. 24:14] **21:12** [a] Is. 58:4 **21:13** [a] [Ex. 20:16; 23:1, 7] [b] 2 Kin. 9:26; 2 Chr. 24:21; Acts 7:58, 59; Heb. 11:37 **21:17** [a] [Ps. 9:12] [b] 1 Kin. 19:1 **21:18** [a] 1 Kin. 13:32; 2 Chr. 22:9

APPLY THE TRUTH

## GREED

**21:1–29** Have you ever tried to catch a bubble? It sure looks like something you could reach out and hold, but when you try, it usually pops. This is just like greed. Greed shows you something just out of reach and tells you to grab it. But when you reach out, it disappoints or disappears. King Ahab's story is filled with greed. He had a vineyard and was the king of a nation, and yet he wanted more! When he couldn't get what he wanted, he became distraught. He *needed* this vineyard. He couldn't go on without it.

Greed likes to make you think just a little more will be enough. What you currently have isn't making you happy, but if you only had *a little bit more*, then you'd be content. Greed also turns wants into needs. That want isn't a luxury; it's a necessity. The way we silence greed's lies is by learning to be content. If we aren't content with what we have, we won't be content with more. True joy and satisfaction come when we're content with Christ alone and view all other things as His favor and blessing upon our lives.

murdered and also taken possession?"' And you
shall speak to him, saying, 'Thus says the LORD:
[a]"In the place where dogs licked the blood of Na-
both, dogs shall lick your blood, even yours."'"
20 So Ahab said to Elijah, [a]"Have you found
me, O my enemy?"
And he answered, "I have found *you,* because
[b]you have sold yourself to do evil in the sight of
the LORD: 21 'Behold, [a]I will bring calamity on you. I
will take away your [b]posterity, and will cut off from
Ahab [c]every male in Israel, both [d]bond and free. 22 I
will make your house like the house of [a]Jeroboam
the son of Nebat, and like the house of [b]Baasha
the son of Ahijah, because of the provocation with
which you have provoked *Me* to anger, and made
Israel sin.' 23 And [a]concerning Jezebel the LORD
also spoke, saying, 'The dogs shall eat Jezebel by
the wall[1] of Jezreel.' 24 The dogs shall eat [a]whoever
belongs to Ahab and dies in the city, and the birds
of the air shall eat whoever dies in the field."
25 But [a]there was no one like Ahab who sold
himself to do wickedness in the sight of the
LORD, [b]because Jezebel his wife stirred him up.
26 And he behaved very abominably in following
idols, according to all [a]*that* the Amorites had
done, whom the LORD had cast out before the
children of Israel.
27 So it was, when Ahab heard those words,
that he tore his clothes and [a]put sackcloth on
his body, and fasted and lay in sackcloth, and
went about mourning.
28 And the word of the LORD came to Eli-
jah the Tishbite, saying, 29 "See how Ahab has
humbled himself before Me? Because he [a]has
humbled himself before Me, I will not bring the
calamity in his days. [b]In the days of his son I will
bring the calamity on his house."

### *MICAIAH WARNS AHAB*

*(2 Chr. 18:1–27)*

22 Now three years passed without war be-
tween Syria and Israel. 2 Then it came to
pass, in the third year, that [a]Jehoshaphat the king
of Judah went down to *visit* the king of Israel.
3 And the king of Israel said to his servants,
"Do you know that [a]Ramoth in Gilead *is* ours, but
we hesitate to take it out of the hand of the king
of Syria?" 4 So he said to Jehoshaphat, "Will you
go with me to fight at Ramoth Gilead?"
Jehoshaphat said to the king of Israel, [a]"I *am*
as you *are,* my people as your people, my horses
as your horses." 5 Also Jehoshaphat said to the
king of Israel, [a]"Please inquire for the word of
the LORD today."
6 Then the king of Israel [a]gathered the proph-
ets together, about four hundred men, and said to
them, "Shall I go against Ramoth Gilead to fight,
or shall I refrain?"
So they said, "Go up, for the Lord will deliver
*it* into the hand of the king."
7 And [a]Jehoshaphat said, "*Is there* not still a
prophet of the LORD here, that we may inquire
of Him?"[1]
8 So the king of Israel said to Jehoshaphat,
"*There is* still one man, Micaiah the son of Imlah,
by whom we may inquire of the LORD; but I
hate him, because he does not prophesy good
concerning me, but evil."
And Jehoshaphat said, "Let not the king
say such things!"
9 Then the king of Israel called an officer and
said, "Bring Micaiah the son of Imlah quickly!"
10 The king of Israel and Jehoshaphat the
king of Judah, having put on *their* robes, sat each
on his throne, at a threshing floor at the entrance
of the gate of Samaria; and all the prophets
prophesied before them. 11 Now Zedekiah the
son of Chenaanah had made [a]horns of iron for
himself; and he said, "Thus says the LORD: 'With
these you shall [b]gore the Syrians until they are
destroyed.'" 12 And all the prophets prophesied
so, saying, "Go up to Ramoth Gilead and prosper,
for the LORD will deliver *it* into the king's hand."
13 Then the messenger who had gone to call
Micaiah spoke to him, saying, "Now listen, the
words of the prophets with one accord encour-
age the king. Please, let your word be like the
word of one of them, and speak encouragement."
14 And Micaiah said, "*As* the LORD lives,
[a]whatever the LORD says to me, that I will speak."
15 Then he came to the king; and the king
said to him, "Micaiah, shall we go to war against
Ramoth Gilead, or shall we refrain?"
And he answered him, "Go and prosper, for
the LORD will deliver *it* into the hand of the king!"
16 So the king said to him, "How many times
shall I make you swear that you tell me nothing
but the truth in the name of the LORD?"
17 Then he said, "I saw all Israel [a]scattered on
the mountains, as sheep that have no shepherd.
And the LORD said, 'These have no master. Let
each return to his house in peace.'"
18 And the king of Israel said to Jehoshaphat,
"Did I not tell you he would not prophesy good
concerning me, but evil?"
19 Then *Micaiah* said, "Therefore hear the
word of the LORD: [a]I saw the LORD sitting on
His throne, [b]and all the host of heaven standing
by, on His right hand and on His left. 20 And the
LORD said, 'Who will persuade Ahab to go up, that
he may fall at Ramoth Gilead?' So one spoke in
this manner, and another spoke in that manner.

21:19 [a] 1 Kin. 22:38; 2 Kin. 9:26 21:20 [a] 1 Kin. 18:17 [b] 1 Kin. 21:25; 2 Kin. 17:17; [Rom. 7:14] 21:21 [a] 1 Kin. 14:10; 2 Kin. 9:8 [b] 2 Kin. 10:10 [c] 1 Sam. 25:22 [d] 1 Kin. 14:10 21:22 [a] 1 Kin. 15:29 [b] 1 Kin. 16:3, 11 21:23 [a] 2 Kin. 9:10, 30–37 [1] Following Masoretic Text and Septuagint; some Hebrew manuscripts, Syriac, Targum, and Vulgate read *plot of ground* (compare 2 Kings 9:36). 21:24 [a] 1 Kin. 14:11; 16:4 21:25 [a] 1 Kin. 16:30–33; 21:20 [b] 1 Kin. 16:31 21:26 [a] Gen. 15:16; [Lev. 18:25–30]; 2 Kin. 21:11 21:27 [a] Gen. 37:34; 2 Sam. 3:31; 2 Kin. 6:30 21:29 [a] [2 Kin. 22:19] [b] 2 Kin. 9:25; 10:11, 17 22:2 [a] 1 Kin. 15:24; 2 Chr. 18:2 22:3 [a] Deut. 4:43; Josh. 21:38; 1 Kin. 4:13 22:4 [a] 2 Kin. 3:7 22:5 [a] 2 Kin. 3:11 22:6 [a] 1 Kin. 18:19 22:7 [a] 2 Kin. 3:11 [1] Or *him* 22:11 [a] Zech. 1:18–21 [b] Deut. 33:17 22:14 [a] Num. 22:38; 24:13 22:17 [a] Num. 27:17; 1 Kin. 22:34–36; 2 Chr. 18:16; Matt. 9:36; Mark 6:34 22:19 [a] Is. 6:1; Ezek. 1:26–28; Dan. 7:9 [b] Job 1:6; 2:1; Ps. 103:20; Dan. 7:10; Zech. 1:10; [Matt. 18:10; Heb. 1:7, 14]

21 Then a spirit came forward and stood before the LORD, and said, 'I will persuade him.' 22 The LORD said to him, 'In what way?' So he said, 'I will go out and be a lying spirit in the mouth of all his prophets.' And the LORD said, [a]'You shall persuade *him,* and also prevail. Go out and do so.' 23 [a]Therefore look! The LORD has put a lying spirit in the mouth of all these prophets of yours, and the LORD has declared disaster against you."

24 Now Zedekiah the son of Chenaanah went near and [a]struck Micaiah on the cheek, and said, [b]"Which way did the spirit from the LORD go from me to speak to you?"

25 And Micaiah said, "Indeed, you shall see on that day when you go into an [a]inner chamber to hide!"

26 So the king of Israel said, "Take Micaiah, and return him to Amon the governor of the city and to Joash the king's son; 27 and say, 'Thus says the king: "Put this *fellow* in [a]prison, and feed him with bread of affliction and water of affliction, until I come in peace." ' "

28 But Micaiah said, "If you ever return in peace, [a]the LORD has not spoken by me." And he said, "Take heed, all you people!"

### *AHAB DIES IN BATTLE*

*(2 Chr. 18:28–34)*

29 So the king of Israel and Jehoshaphat the king of Judah went up to Ramoth Gilead. 30 And the king of Israel said to Jehoshaphat, "I will disguise myself and go into battle; but you put on your robes." So the king of Israel [a]disguised himself and went into battle.

31 Now the [a]king of Syria had commanded the thirty-two [b]captains of his chariots, saying, "Fight with no one small or great, but only with the king of Israel." 32 So it was, when the captains of the chariots saw Jehoshaphat, that they said, "Surely it *is* the king of Israel!" Therefore they turned aside to fight against him, and Jehoshaphat [a]cried out. 33 And it happened, when the captains of the chariots saw that it *was* not the king of Israel, that they turned back from pursuing him. 34 Now a *certain* man drew a bow at random, and struck the king of Israel between the joints of his armor. So he said to the driver of his chariot, "Turn around and take me out of the battle, for I am wounded."

35 The battle increased that day; and the king was propped up in his chariot, facing the Syrians, and died at evening. The blood ran out from the wound onto the floor of the chariot. 36 Then, as the sun was going down, a shout went throughout the army, saying, "Every man to his city, and every man to his own country!"

37 So the king died, and was brought to Samaria. And they buried the king in Samaria. 38 Then *someone* washed the chariot at a pool in Samaria, and the dogs licked up his blood while the harlots bathed,[1] according [a]to the word of the LORD which He had spoken.

39 Now the rest of the acts of Ahab, and all that he did, [a]the ivory house which he built and all the cities that he built, *are* they not written in the book of the chronicles of the kings of Israel? 40 So Ahab rested with his fathers. Then [a]Ahaziah his son reigned in his place.

### *JEHOSHAPHAT REIGNS IN JUDAH*

*(2 Chr. 20:31—21:1)*

41 [a]Jehoshaphat the son of Asa had become king over Judah in the fourth year of Ahab king of Israel. 42 Jehoshaphat *was* thirty-five years old when he became king, and he reigned twenty-five years in Jerusalem. His mother's name *was* Azubah the daughter of Shilhi. 43 And [a]he walked in all the ways of his father Asa. He did not turn aside from them, doing *what was* right in the eyes of the LORD. Nevertheless [b]the high places were not taken away, *for* the people offered sacrifices and burned incense on the high places. 44 Also [a]Jehoshaphat made [b]peace with the king of Israel.

45 Now the rest of the acts of Jehoshaphat, the might that he showed, and how he made war, *are* they not written [a]in the book of the chronicles of the kings of Judah? 46 [a]And the rest of the perverted persons,[1] who remained in the days of his father Asa, he banished from the land. 47 [a]*There was* then no king in Edom, only a deputy of the king.

48 [a]Jehoshaphat [b]made merchant ships[1] to go to [c]Ophir for gold; [d]but they never sailed, for the ships were wrecked at [e]Ezion Geber. 49 Then Ahaziah the son of Ahab said to Jehoshaphat, "Let my servants go with your servants in the ships." But Jehoshaphat would not.

50 And [a]Jehoshaphat rested with his fathers, and was buried with his fathers in the City of David his father. Then Jehoram his son reigned in his place.

### *AHAZIAH REIGNS IN ISRAEL*

51 [a]Ahaziah the son of Ahab became king over Israel in Samaria in the seventeenth year of Jehoshaphat king of Judah, and reigned two years over Israel. 52 He did evil in the sight of the LORD, and [a]walked in the way of his father and in the way of his mother and in the way of Jeroboam the son of Nebat, who had made Israel sin; 53 for [a]he served Baal and worshiped him, and provoked the LORD God of Israel to anger, [b]according to all that his father had done.

22:22 [a] Judg. 9:23; 1 Sam. 16:14; 18:10; 19:9; Job 12:16; [Ezek. 14:9; 2 Thess. 2:11] 22:23 [a] [Ezek. 14:9] 22:24 [a] Jer. 20:2 [b] 2 Chr. 18:23 22:25 [a] 1 Kin. 20:30 22:27 [a] 2 Chr. 16:10; 18:25–27 22:28 [a] Num. 16:29; Deut. 18:20–22 22:30 [a] 2 Chr. 35:22 22:31 [a] 1 Kin. 20:1 [b] 1 Kin. 20:24; 2 Chr. 18:30 22:32 [a] 2 Chr. 18:31 22:38 [a] 1 Kin. 21:19 [1] Syriac and Targum read *they washed his armor.* 22:39 [a] Amos 3:15 22:40 [a] 2 Kin. 1:2, 18 22:41 [a] 2 Chr. 20:31 22:43 [a] 2 Chr. 17:3; 20:32, 33 [b] 2 Kin. 12:3 22:44 [a] 2 Chr. 19:2 [b] 2 Chr. 18:1 22:45 [a] 2 Chr. 20:34 22:46 [a] 1 Kin. 14:24; 15:12 [1] Hebrew *qadesh,* that is, one practicing sodomy and prostitution in religious rituals 22:47 [a] 2 Sam. 8:14 22:48 [a] 2 Chr. 20:35–37 [b] 1 Kin. 10:22 [c] 1 Kin. 9:28 [d] 2 Chr. 20:37 [e] 1 Kin. 9:26 [1] Or *ships of Tarshish* 22:50 [a] 2 Chr. 21:1 22:51 [a] 1 Kin. 22:40 22:52 [a] 1 Kin. 15:26; 21:25 22:53 [a] Judg. 2:11 [b] 1 Kin. 16:30–32

# The Second Book of the
# KINGS

**AUTHOR**
Perhaps Jeremiah, Ezra, or Ezekiel

**KEY VERSES**
2 Kings 17:7–12

**READING TIME**
2 hours 30 minutes

The Book of 2 Kings continues the tragic history of two nations, each on a collision course with captivity that was begun in 1 Kings. Despite God's numerous warnings through the prophets, the people of both Israel and Judah refused to repent of their wicked ways, cast off their idols, and return to God. Through it all, God was patient, yet He would not relent on bringing judgment. It was not a matter of *if* judgment would come but *when*. In the northern kingdom of Israel, nineteen consecutive evil kings ruled, leading to that nation's captivity by Assyria. The picture was somewhat brighter in the southern kingdom of Judah, where godly kings occasionally emerged to reform the evils of their predecessors. In the end, however, sin outweighed righteousness and Judah was marched off to captivity in Babylonia.

**Occasion:** The Book of 2 Kings depicts the continued idolatry of God's people throughout the divided kingdom and their refusal to repent of their sin to avoid the coming judgment.

**Main Point:** Despite God's warnings, His people refuse to repent of their sins leading to judgment coming upon His unfaithful people.

**Big Ideas:** God is true to His promises, both those of blessing and those of discipline. Sin will always bring God's judgment, in some way at some time. We are to stay faithful to God, even if everybody around us is doing otherwise.

## OUTLINE:

I. The Prophetic Ministry of Elisha (chs. 1–8)
II. The Decline Rule of the Kings (chs. 9–16)
III. The Fall of Israel (ch. 17)
IV. The Rule of Hezekiah and Two Bad Kings (chs. 18–21)
V. The Rule of Josiah and Four Bad Kings (chs. 22–24)
VI. The Fall of Judah (ch. 25)

**872 BC**
Jehoshaphat becomes king in Judah

**865 BC**
Elijah begins to prophesy against Ahab

**850 BC**
Elijah is taken to heaven; Elisha prophesies

**825 BC**
The city of Carthage in northern Africa is founded

**755 BC**
Isaiah begins to prophesy in Judah

**c. 750 BC**
Homer's *Illiad* and *Odyssey* descend from oral tradition

**736 BC**
Ahaz becomes king in Judah

**722 BC**
The Assyrians defeat Israel

**c. 705 BC**
Earliest pin-tumbler lock mechanism used in Assyria

**697 BC**
Manasseh becomes king in Judah

**c. 650 BC**
Greeks start making clay objects using molds

**640 BC**
Josiah becomes king in Judah

**624 BC**
The Book of the law is found in Jerusalem

**612 BC**
The Babylonians conquer Assyria's capital Nineveh

**c. 594 BC**
Hanging Gardens of Babylon are built

**586 BC**
The Babylonians defeat Judah

**c. 565–538 BC**
**2 Kings written**

### GOD JUDGES AHAZIAH

**1** Moab [a]rebelled against Israel [b]after the death
of Ahab.
2 Now [a]Ahaziah fell through the lattice of his
upper room in Samaria, and was injured; so he
sent messengers and said to them, "Go, inquire
of [b]Baal-Zebub, the god of [c]Ekron, whether I shall
recover from this injury." 3 But the angel[1] of the
LORD said to Elijah the Tishbite, "Arise, go up
to meet the messengers of the king of Samaria,
and say to them, '*Is it* because *there is* no God
in Israel *that* you are going to inquire of Baal-
Zebub, the god of Ekron?' 4 Now therefore, thus
says the LORD: 'You shall not come down from
the bed to which you have gone up, but you shall
surely die.' " So Elijah departed.

> **1:1–2** The idol Baal was a god of many names. The people of Ekron, a Philistine city, called it **Baal-Zebub**, which means "Lord of Flies." Whatever its name, this pagan god was a stumbling block for the Israelites from the time they first arrived in Canaan.

5 And when the messengers returned to him,
he said to them, "Why have you come back?"
6 So they said to him, "A man came up to
meet us, and said to us, 'Go, return to the king
who sent you, and say to him, "Thus says the
LORD: '*Is it* because *there is* no God in Israel
*that* you are sending to inquire of Baal-Zebub,
the god of Ekron? Therefore you shall not come
down from the bed to which you have gone up,
but you shall surely die.' " ' "
7 Then he said to them, "What kind of man
*was it* who came up to meet you and told you
these words?"
8 So they answered him, [a]"A hairy man wear-
ing a leather belt around his waist."
And he said, [b]"It *is* Elijah the Tishbite."
9 Then the king sent to him a captain of fifty
with his fifty men. So he went up to him; and
there he was, sitting on the top of a hill. And he
spoke to him: "Man of God, the king has said,
'Come down!' "
10 So Elijah answered and said to the captain
of fifty, "If I *am* a man of God, then [a]let fire come
down from heaven and consume you and your
fifty men." And fire came down from heaven and
consumed him and his fifty. 11 Then he sent to
him another captain of fifty with his fifty men.
And he answered and said to him: "Man of
God, thus has the king said, 'Come down quickly!' "
12 So Elijah answered and said to them, "If
I *am* a man of God, let fire come down from
heaven and consume you and your fifty men."
And the fire of God came down from heaven
and consumed him and his fifty.
13 Again, he sent a third captain of fifty with his
fifty men. And the third captain of fifty went up,
and came and fell on his knees before Elijah, and
pleaded with him, and said to him: "Man of God,
please let my life and the life of these fifty servants
of yours [a]be precious in your sight. 14 Look, fire has
come down from heaven and burned up the first
two captains of fifties with their fifties. But let my
life now be precious in your sight."
15 And the angel[1] of the LORD said to Elijah,
"Go down with him; do not be afraid of him." So he
arose and went down with him to the king. 16 Then
he said to him, "Thus says the LORD: 'Because you
have sent messengers to inquire of Baal-Zebub,
the god of Ekron, *is it* because *there is* no God in
Israel to inquire of His word? Therefore you shall
not come down from the bed to which you have
gone up, but you shall surely die.' "
17 So *Ahaziah* died according to the word
of the LORD which Elijah had spoken. Because
he had no son, [a]Jehoram[1] became king in his
place, in the second year of Jehoram the son
of Jehoshaphat, king of Judah.
18 Now the rest of the acts of Ahaziah which
he did, *are* they not written in the book of the
chronicles of the kings of Israel?

### ELIJAH ASCENDS TO HEAVEN

**2** And it came to pass, when the LORD was
about to [a]take up Elijah into heaven by a
whirlwind, that Elijah went with [b]Elisha from
Gilgal. 2 Then Elijah said to Elisha, [a]"Stay here,
please, for the LORD has sent me on to Bethel."
But Elisha said, "As the LORD lives, and [b]*as*
your soul lives, I will not leave you!" So they
went down to Bethel.
3 Now [a]the sons of the prophets who *were*
at Bethel came out to Elisha, and said to him,
"Do you know that the LORD will take away your
master from over you today?"
And he said, "Yes, I know; keep silent!"
4 Then Elijah said to him, "Elisha, stay here,
please, for the LORD has sent me on to Jericho."
But he said, "*As* the LORD lives, and *as* your
soul lives, I will not leave you!" So they came
to Jericho.
5 Now the sons of the prophets who *were* at
Jericho came to Elisha and said to him, "Do you
know that the LORD will take away your master
from over you today?"
So he answered, "Yes, I know; keep silent!"
6 Then Elijah said to him, "Stay here, please,
for the LORD has sent me on to the Jordan."
But he said, "*As* the LORD lives, and *as* your
soul lives, I will not leave you!" So the two of
them went on. 7 And fifty men of the sons of

**1:1** [a] 2 Sam. 8:2 [b] 2 Kin. 3:5 **1:2** [a] 1 Kin. 22:40 [b] 2 Kin. 1:3, 6, 16; Matt. 10:25; Mark 3:22 [c] 1 Sam. 5:10 **1:3** [1] Or *Angel* **1:8** [a] Zech. 13:4; Matt. 3:4; Mark 1:6 [b] 1 Kin. 18:7 **1:10** [a] 1 Kin. 18:36–38; Luke 9:54 **1:13** [a] 1 Sam. 26:21; Ps. 72:14 **1:15** [1] Or *Angel* **1:17** [a] 1 Kin. 22:50; 2 Kin. 8:16; Matt. 1:8 [1] The son of Ahab king of Israel (compare 3:1) **2:1** [a] Gen. 5:24; [Heb. 11:5] [b] 1 Kin. 19:16–21 **2:2** [a] Ruth 1:15, 16 [b] 1 Sam. 1:26; 2 Kin. 2:4, 6; 4:30 **2:3** [a] 1 Kin. 20:35; 2 Kin. 2:5, 7, 15; 4:1, 38; 9:1

the prophets went and stood facing *them* at a distance, while the two of them stood by the Jordan. 8 Now Elijah took his mantle, rolled *it* up, and struck the water; and [a]it was divided this way and that, so that the two of them crossed over on dry [b]ground.

9 And so it was, when they had crossed over, that Elijah said to Elisha, "Ask! What may I do for you, before I am taken away from you?"

Elisha said, "Please let a double portion of your spirit be upon me."

10 So he said, "You have asked a hard thing. *Nevertheless,* if you see me *when I am* taken from you, it shall be so for you; but if not, it shall not be *so.*" 11 Then it happened, as they continued on and talked, that suddenly [a]a chariot of fire *appeared* with horses of fire, and separated the two of them; and Elijah [b]went up by a whirlwind into heaven.

**SEEING JESUS IN THE SCRIPTURE**

**2:11** When Elijah's work was completed and it was time for him to be with God, he was taken up into heaven. Elijah's ascension points to Jesus' ascension after He completed the work the Father gave Him to do (see Luke 24:51).

12 And Elisha saw *it,* and he cried out, [a]"My father, my father, the chariot of Israel and its horsemen!" So he saw him no more. And he took hold of his own clothes and tore them into two pieces. 13 He also took up the mantle of Elijah that had fallen from him, and went back and stood by the bank of the Jordan. 14 Then he took the mantle of Elijah that had fallen from him, and struck the water, and said, "Where *is* the LORD God of Elijah?" And when he also had struck the water, [a]it was divided this way and that; and Elisha crossed over.

15 Now when the sons of the prophets who *were* [a]from Jericho saw him, they said, "The spirit of Elijah rests on Elisha." And they came to meet him, and bowed to the ground before him. 16 Then they said to him, "Look now, there are fifty strong men with your servants. Please let them go and search for your master, [a]lest perhaps the Spirit of the LORD has taken him up and cast him upon some mountain or into some valley."

And he said, "You shall not send anyone."

17 But when they urged him till he was [a]ashamed, he said, "Send *them!*" Therefore they sent fifty men, and they searched for three days but did not find him. 18 And when they came back to him, for he had stayed in Jericho, he said to them, "Did I not say to you, 'Do not go'?"

### ELISHA PERFORMS MIRACLES

19 Then the men of the city said to Elisha, "Please notice, the situation of this city *is* pleasant, as my lord sees; but the water *is* bad, and the ground barren."

20 And he said, "Bring me a new bowl, and put salt in it." So they brought *it* to him. 21 Then he went out to the source of the water, and [a]cast in the salt there, and said, "Thus says the LORD: 'I have healed this water; from it there shall be no more death or barrenness.'" 22 So the water remains [a]healed to this day, according to the word of Elisha which he spoke.

23 Then he went up from there to Bethel; and as he was going up the road, some youths came from the city and mocked him, and said to him, "Go up, you baldhead! Go up, you baldhead!"

**2:23** In ancient Israel, baldness was considered shameful. The fact that certain pagans shaved their heads as part of their religion may have had something to do with the stigma.

24 So he turned around and looked at them, and [a]pronounced a curse on them in the name of the LORD. And two female bears came out of the woods and mauled forty-two of the youths. 25 Then he went from there to [a]Mount Carmel, and from there he returned to Samaria.

### MOAB REBELS AGAINST ISRAEL

**3** Now [a]Jehoram the son of Ahab became king over Israel at Samaria in the eighteenth year of Jehoshaphat king of Judah, and reigned twelve years. 2 And he did evil in the sight of the LORD, but not like his father and mother; for he put away the *sacred* pillar of Baal [a]that his father had made. 3 Nevertheless he persisted in [a]the sins of Jeroboam the son of Nebat, who had made Israel sin; he did not depart from them.

**3:1** Israel split into two kingdoms after King Solomon's reign. The southern part of the country was called **Judah**; the northern part kept the name **Israel**. Jerusalem was the capital of Judah; Samaria was the capital of Israel. David's descendants ruled Judah; a variety of kings ruled Israel.

4 Now Mesha king of Moab was a sheepbreeder, and he [a]regularly paid the king of Israel one hundred thousand [b]lambs and the wool of

2:8 [a] Ex. 14:21, 22; Josh. 3:16; 2 Kin. 2:14 [b] Josh. 3:17 2:11 [a] 2 Kin. 6:17; Ps. 104:4 [b] Gen. 5:24; Heb. 11:5 2:12 [a] 2 Kin. 13:14 2:14 [a] 2 Kin. 2:8 2:15 [a] 2 Kin. 2:7 2:16 [a] 1 Kin. 18:12; Ezek. 8:3; Acts 8:39 2:17 [a] 2 Kin. 8:11 2:21 [a] Ex. 15:25, 26; 2 Kin. 4:41; 6:6; John 9:6 2:22 [a] Ezek. 47:8, 9 2:24 [a] Deut. 27:13–26 2:25 [a] 1 Kin. 18:19, 20; 2 Kin. 4:25 3:1 [a] 2 Kin. 1:17 3:2 [a] 1 Kin. 16:31, 32 3:3 [a] 1 Kin. 12:28–32 3:4 [a] 2 Sam. 8:2 [b] Is. 16:1, 2

one hundred thousand rams. 5 But it happened,
when [a]Ahab died, that the king of Moab rebelled
against the king of Israel.
6 So King Jehoram went out of Samaria at
that time and mustered all Israel. 7 Then he went
and sent to Jehoshaphat king of Judah, saying,
"The king of Moab has rebelled against me. Will
you go with me to fight against Moab?"

And he said, "I will go up; [a]I *am* as you *are,* my
people as your people, my horses as your hors-
es." 8 Then he said, "Which way shall we go up?"

And he answered, "By way of the Wilderness
of Edom."
9 So the king of Israel went with the king of
Judah and the king of Edom, and they marched
on that roundabout route seven days; and there
was no water for the army, nor for the animals
that followed them. 10 And the king of Israel said,
"Alas! For the LORD has called these three kings
together to deliver them into the hand of Moab."
11 But [a]Jehoshaphat said, "*Is there* no prophet
of the LORD here, that we may inquire of the
LORD by him?"

So one of the servants of the king of Israel
answered and said, "Elisha the son of Shaphat *is*
here, who [b]poured water on the hands of Elijah."
12 And Jehoshaphat said, "The word of the LORD
is with him." So the king of Israel and Jehoshaphat
and the king of Edom [a]went down to him.
13 Then Elisha said to the king of Israel, [a]"What
have I to do with you? [b]Go to [c]the prophets of
your father and the [d]prophets of your mother."

But the king of Israel said to him, "No, for
the LORD has called these three kings *together*
to deliver them into the hand of Moab."
14 And Elisha said, [a]"*As* the LORD of hosts
lives, before whom I stand, surely were it not
that I regard the presence of Jehoshaphat king
of Judah, I would not look at you, nor see you.
15 But now bring me [a]a musician."

Then it happened, when the musician
[b]played, that [c]the hand of the LORD came upon
him. 16 And he said, "Thus says the LORD: [a]'Make
this valley full of ditches.' 17 For thus says the
LORD: 'You shall not see wind, nor shall you see
rain; yet that valley shall be filled with water, so
that you, your cattle, and your animals may drink.'
18 And this is a simple matter in the sight of the
LORD; He will also deliver the Moabites into your
hand. 19 Also you shall attack every fortified city
and every choice city, and shall cut down every
good tree, and stop up every spring of water,
and ruin every good piece of land with stones."
20 Now it happened in the morning, when
[a]the grain offering was offered, that suddenly
water came by way of Edom, and the land was
filled with water.
21 And when all the Moabites heard that the
kings had come up to fight against them, all
who were able to bear arms and older were
gathered; and they stood at the border. 22 Then
they rose up early in the morning, and the sun
was shining on the water; and the Moabites saw
the water on the other side *as* red as blood. 23 And
they said, "This is blood; the kings have surely
struck swords and have killed one another; now
therefore, Moab, to the spoil!"
24 So when they came to the camp of Israel, Is-
rael rose up and attacked the Moabites, so that they
fled before them; and they entered *their* land, kill-
ing the Moabites. 25 Then they destroyed the cities,
and each man threw a stone on every good piece
of land and filled it; and they stopped up all the
springs of water and cut down all the good trees.
But they left the stones of [a]Kir Haraseth *intact.*
However the slingers surrounded and attacked it.
26 And when the king of Moab saw that the
battle was too fierce for him, he took with him
seven hundred men who drew swords, to break
through to the king of Edom, but they could not.
27 Then [a]he took his eldest son who would have
reigned in his place, and offered him *as* a burnt
offering upon the wall; and there was great in-
dignation against Israel. [b]So they departed from
him and returned to *their own* land.

### ELISHA AND THE WIDOW'S OIL
*(cf. 1 Kin. 17:14–16)*

4 A certain woman of the wives of [a]the sons of
the prophets cried out to Elisha, saying, "Your
servant my husband is dead, and you know that
your servant feared the LORD. And the creditor
is coming [b]to take my two sons to be his slaves."
2 So Elisha said to her, "What shall I do for
you? Tell me, what do you have in the house?"
And she said, "Your maidservant has nothing
in the house but a jar of oil."
3 Then he said, "Go, borrow vessels from
everywhere, from all your neighbors—empty
vessels; [a]do not gather just a few. 4 And when you
have come in, you shall shut the door behind
you and your sons; then pour it into all those
vessels, and set aside the full ones."
5 So she went from him and shut the door
behind her and her sons, who brought *the vessels*
to her; and she poured *it* out. 6 Now it came to
pass, when the vessels were full, that she said
to her son, "Bring me another vessel."

And he said to her, "*There is* not another ves-
sel." So the oil ceased. 7 Then she came and told the
man of God. And he said, "Go, sell the oil and pay
your debt; and you *and* your sons live on the rest."

### ELISHA RAISES THE SHUNAMMITE'S SON
*(cf. 1 Kin. 17:17–24)*

8 Now it happened one day that Elisha went
to [a]Shunem, where there *was* a notable woman,
and she persuaded him to eat some food. So it

**3:5** [a] 2 Kin. 1:1 **3:7** [a] 1 Kin. 22:4 **3:11** [a] 1 Kin. 22:7 [b] 1 Kin. 19:21; [John 13:4, 5, 13, 14] **3:12** [a] 2 Kin. 2:25 **3:13** [a] [Ezek. 14:3] [b] Judg. 10:14; Ruth 1:15 [c] 1 Kin. 22:6–11 [d] 1 Kin. 18:19 **3:14** [a] 1 Kin. 17:1; 2 Kin. 5:16 **3:15** [a] 1 Sam. 10:5 [b] 1 Sam. 16:16, 23; 1 Chr. 25:1 [c] Ezek. 1:3; 3:14, 22; 8:1 **3:16** [a] Jer. 14:3 **3:20** [a] Ex. 29:39, 40 **3:25** [a] Is. 16:7, 11; Jer. 48:31, 36 **3:27** [a] [Deut. 18:10; Amos 2:1; Mic. 6:7] [b] 2 Kin. 8:20 **4:1** [a] 1 Kin. 20:35; 2 Kin. 2:3 [b] [Lev. 25:39–41, 48]; 1 Sam. 22:2; Neh. 5:2–5; Matt. 18:25 **4:3** [a] 2 Kin. 3:16 **4:8** [a] Josh. 19:18

was, as often as he passed by, he would turn in
there to eat some food. 9 And she said to her
husband, "Look now, I know that this *is* a holy
man of God, who passes by us regularly. 10 Please,
let us make a small upper room on the wall; and
let us put a bed for him there, and a table and a
chair and a lampstand; so it will be, whenever
he comes to us, he can turn in there."

11 And it happened one day that he came there,
and he turned in to the upper room and lay down
there. 12 Then he said to [a]Gehazi his servant, "Call
this Shunammite woman." When he had called
her, she stood before him. 13 And he said to him,
"Say now to her, 'Look, you have been concerned
for us with all this care. What *can I* do for you? Do
you want me to speak on your behalf to the king
or to the commander of the army?' "

She answered, "I dwell among my own people."
14 So he said, "What then *is* to be done for her?"

And Gehazi answered, "Actually, she has no
son, and her husband is old."

15 So he said, "Call her." When he had called her,
she stood in the doorway. 16 Then he said, "About
this time next year you shall embrace a son."

And she said, "No, my lord. Man of God, [a]do
not lie to your maidservant!"

17 But the woman conceived, and bore a son
when the appointed time had come, of which
Elisha had told her.

18 And the child grew. Now it happened one
day that he went out to his father, to the reapers.
19 And he said to his father, "My head, my head!"

So he said to a servant, "Carry him to his
mother." 20 When he had taken him and brought
him to his mother, he sat on her knees till noon,
and *then* died. 21 And she went up and laid him
on the bed of the man of God, shut *the door*
upon him, and went out. 22 Then she called to
her husband, and said, "Please send me one of
the young men and one of the donkeys, that I
may run to the man of God and come back."

23 So he said, "Why are you going to him to-
day? *It is* neither the [a]New Moon nor the Sabbath."

And she said, "*It is* well." 24 Then she saddled
a donkey, and said to her servant, "Drive, and go
forward; do not slacken the pace for me unless
I tell you." 25 And so she departed, and went to
the man of God [a]at Mount Carmel.

So it was, when the man of God saw her afar
off, that he said to his servant Gehazi, "Look, the
Shunammite woman! 26 Please run now to meet
her, and say to her, '*Is it* well with you? *Is it* well
with your husband? *Is it* well with the child?' "

And she answered, "*It is* well." 27 Now when
she came to the man of God at the hill, she
caught him by the feet, but Gehazi came near
to push her away. But the man of God said, "Let
her alone; for her soul *is* in deep distress, and
the LORD has hidden *it* from me, and has not
told me."

28 So she said, "Did I ask a son of my lord?
[a]Did I not say, 'Do not deceive me'?"

29 Then he said to Gehazi, [a]"Get yourself
ready, and take my staff in your hand, and be
on your way. If you meet anyone, [b]do not greet
him; and if anyone greets you, do not answer
him; but [c]lay my staff on the face of the child."

30 And the mother of the child said, [a]"*As* the
LORD lives, and *as* your soul lives, I will not [b]leave
you." So he arose and followed her. 31 Now Gehazi
went on ahead of them, and laid the staff on the
face of the child; but *there was* neither voice nor
hearing. Therefore he went back to meet him, and
told him, saying, "The child has [a]not awakened."

32 When Elisha came into the house, there
was the child, lying dead on his bed. 33 He [a]went
in therefore, shut the door behind the two of
them, [b]and prayed to the LORD. 34 And he went
up and lay on the child, and put his mouth on
his mouth, his eyes on his eyes, and his hands on
his hands; and [a]he stretched himself out on the
child, and the flesh of the child became warm.
35 He returned and walked back and forth in the
house, and again went up [a]and stretched himself
out on him; then [b]the child sneezed seven times,
and the child opened his eyes. 36 And he called
Gehazi and said, "Call this Shunammite woman."
So he called her. And when she came in to him,
he said, "Pick up your son." 37 So she went in, fell
at his feet, and bowed to the ground; then she
[a]picked up her son and went out.

### *ELISHA PURIFIES THE POT OF STEW*

38 And Elisha returned to [a]Gilgal, and *there
was* a [b]famine in the land. Now the sons of the
prophets *were* [c]sitting before him; and he said
to his servant, "Put on the large pot, and boil
stew for the sons of the prophets." 39 So one went
out into the field to gather herbs, and found a
wild vine, and gathered from it a lapful of wild
gourds, and came and sliced *them* into the pot
of stew, though they did not know *what they
were.* 40 Then they served it to the men to eat.
Now it happened, as they were eating the stew,
that they cried out and said, "Man of God, *there
is* [a]death in the pot!" And they could not eat *it.*

41 So he said, "Then bring some flour." And
[a]he put *it* into the pot, and said, "Serve *it* to
the people, that they may eat." And there was
nothing harmful in the pot.

### *ELISHA FEEDS ONE HUNDRED MEN*

*(cf. Matt. 14:13–21; 15:32–39)*

42 Then a man came from [a]Baal Shalisha,
[b]and brought the man of God bread of the first-
fruits, twenty loaves of barley bread, and newly

4:12 [a] 2 Kin. 4:29–31; 5:20–27; 8:4, 5 4:16 [a] 2 Kin. 4:28 4:23 [a] Num. 10:10; 28:11; 1 Chr. 23:31 4:25 [a] 2 Kin. 2:25 4:28 [a] 2 Kin. 4:16 4:29 [a] 1 Kin. 18:46; 2 Kin. 9:1 [b] Luke 10:4 [c] Ex. 7:19; 14:16; 2 Kin. 2:8, 14; Acts 19:12 4:30 [a] 2 Kin. 2:2 [b] 2 Kin. 2:4 4:31 [a] John 11:11 4:33 [a] 2 Kin. 4:4; [Matt. 6:6]; Luke 8:51 [b] 1 Kin. 17:20 4:34 [a] 1 Kin. 17:21–23; Acts 20:10 4:35 [a] 1 Kin. 17:21 [b] 2 Kin. 8:1, 5 4:37 [a] 1 Kin. 17:23; [Heb. 11:35] 4:38 [a] 2 Kin. 2:1 [b] 2 Kin. 8:1 [c] Luke 10:39; Acts 22:3 4:40 [a] Ex. 10:17 4:41 [a] Ex. 15:25; 2 Kin. 2:21 4:42 [a] 1 Sam. 9:4 [b] 1 Sam. 9:7; [1 Cor. 9:11; Gal. 6:6]

ripened grain in his knapsack. And he said, "Give
*it* to the people, that they may eat."
43 But his servant said, [a]"What? Shall I set
this before one hundred men?"
He said again, "Give it to the people, that
they may eat; for thus says the LORD: [b]'They
shall eat and have *some* left over.' " 44 So he set
*it* before them; and they ate [a]and had *some* left
over, according to the word of the LORD.

### SEEING JESUS IN THE SCRIPTURE

**4:42–44** Elisha's specific instructions and miraculous feeding of one hundred men is like Jesus' miracle of feeding five thousand men plus women and children. Jesus performed this miracle on a larger scale, leaving no doubt about His identity (see Matt. 14:1–21).

## NAAMAN'S LEPROSY HEALED

5 Now [a]Naaman, commander of the army of
the king of Syria, was [b]a great and honorable
man in the eyes of his master, because by him
the LORD had given victory to Syria. He was also
a mighty man of valor, *but* a leper. 2 And the Syr-
ians had gone out [a]on raids, and had brought
back captive a young girl from the land of Israel.
She waited on Naaman's wife. 3 Then she said to
her mistress, "If only my master *were* with the
prophet who *is* in Samaria! For he would heal
him of his leprosy." 4 And *Naaman* went in and
told his master, saying, "Thus and thus said the
girl who *is* from the land of Israel."
5 Then the king of Syria said, "Go now, and I
will send a letter to the king of Israel."

### SEEING JESUS IN THE SCRIPTURE

**5:3** Like Elijah, Elisha was a miracle worker, doing some of the same works: parting the Jordan, raising the dead, and increasing food supplies. Their work points to Jesus who performed greater miracles during His earthly ministry (see Mark 1:41).

So he departed and [a]took with him ten tal-
ents of silver, six thousand *shekels* of gold, and
ten changes of clothing. 6 Then he brought the
letter to the king of Israel, which said,

> Now be advised, when this letter comes to you, that I have sent Naaman my servant to you, that you may heal him of his leprosy.

7 And it happened, when the king of Israel read the
letter, that he tore his clothes and said, "*Am* I [a]God,
to kill and make alive, that this man sends a man
to me to heal him of his leprosy? Therefore please
consider, and see how he seeks a quarrel with me."
8 So it was, when Elisha the man of God heard
that the king of Israel had torn his clothes, that
he sent to the king, saying, "Why have you torn
your clothes? Please let him come to me, and
he shall know that there is a prophet in Israel."
9 Then Naaman went with his horses and
chariot, and he stood at the door of Elisha's house.
10 And Elisha sent a messenger to him, saying, "Go
and [a]wash in the Jordan seven times, and your
flesh shall be restored to you, and *you shall* be
clean." 11 But Naaman became furious, and went
away and said, "Indeed, I said to myself, 'He will
surely come out *to me,* and stand and call on the

**4:43** [a] Luke 9:13; John 6:9 [b] Luke 9:17; John 6:11 **4:44** [a] Matt. 14:20; 15:37; John 6:13 **5:1** [a] Luke 4:27 [b] Ex. 11:3 **5:2** [a] 2 Kin. 6:23; 13:20 **5:5** [a] 1 Sam. 9:8; 2 Kin. 8:8, 9 **5:7** [a] [Gen. 30:2; Deut. 32:39; 1 Sam. 2:6] **5:10** [a] 2 Kin. 4:41; John 9:7

LIVE THE TRUTH

# BEING COMPASSIONATE

**5:3** Naaman, a Syrian military officer, had contracted leprosy, a horrible skin disease with no known cure. His wife's servant was a young Israelite girl who had been kidnapped during a Syrian raid. It would have been easy for this girl to want harm and pain to come upon the Syrians, especially Naaman as the commander of their army. They had separated her from her home and family and made her a slave. Instead, this young girl offered hope of healing by suggesting that Nathan consult with God's prophet, Elisha. Her heart was one of compassion, not contempt. She wanted what was best for Naaman, even if he had taken her from what was best for her. As a result, Naaman was introduced to, and believed in, the one true God.

Compassion is personal empathy accompanied by action. To truly follow Jesus is to live with compassion; no one has ever felt more deeply and acted more boldly for others than Him. Jesus took on the flesh, lived within His creation, and gave up His life so we might live. He wanted our best, even while we despised Him. How can we then fail to live with compassion for others? No one is undeserving of it. No one is beyond its scope. Be scandalous with your compassion.

name of the LORD his God, and wave his hand
over the place, and heal the leprosy.' 12 *Are* not the
Abanah[1] and the Pharpar, the rivers of Damascus,
better than all the waters of Israel? Could I not
wash in them and be clean?" So he turned and
went away in a rage. 13 And his [a]servants came
near and spoke to him, and said, "My father, *if*
the prophet had told you *to do* something great,
would you not have done *it?* How much more
then, when he says to you, 'Wash, and be clean'?"
14 So he went down and dipped seven times in
the Jordan, according to the saying of the man
of God; and his [a]flesh was restored like the flesh
of a little child, and [b]he was clean.

15 And he returned to the man of God, he and
all his aides, and came and stood before him;
and he said, "Indeed, now I know that *there is*
[a]no God in all the earth, except in Israel; now
therefore, please take [b]a gift from your servant."

16 But he said, [a]"*As* the LORD lives, before
whom I stand, [b]I will receive nothing." And he
urged him to take *it,* but he refused.

17 So Naaman said, "Then, if not, please let your
servant be given two mule-loads of earth; for your
servant will no longer offer either burnt offering
or sacrifice to other gods, but to the LORD. 18 Yet
in this thing may the LORD pardon your servant:
when my master goes into the temple of Rimmon
to worship there, and [a]he leans on my hand, and
I bow down in the temple of Rimmon—when I
bow down in the temple of Rimmon, may the
LORD please pardon your servant in this thing."

19 Then he said to him, "Go in peace." So he
departed from him a short distance.

### *GEHAZI'S GREED*

20 But [a]Gehazi, the servant of Elisha the man
of God, said, "Look, my master has spared Na-
aman this Syrian, while not receiving from his
hands what he brought; but *as* the LORD lives, I
will run after him and take something from him."
21 So Gehazi pursued Naaman. When Naaman
saw *him* running after him, he got down from
the chariot to meet him, and said, "*Is* all well?"

22 And he said, "All *is* [a]well. My master has sent
me, saying, 'Indeed, just now two young men of
the sons of the prophets have come to me from
the mountains of Ephraim. Please give them a
talent of silver and two changes of garments.' "

23 So Naaman said, "Please, take two talents."
And he urged him, and bound two talents of
silver in two bags, with two changes of garments,
and handed *them* to two of his servants; and they
carried *them* on ahead of him. 24 When he came
to the citadel, he took *them* from their hand, and
stored *them* away in the house; then he let the
men go, and they departed. 25 Now he went in
and stood before his master. Elisha said to him,
"Where *did you go,* Gehazi?"

And he said, "Your servant did not go
anywhere."

26 Then he said to him, "Did not my heart go
*with you* when the man turned back from his
chariot to meet you? *Is it* [a]time to receive money
and to receive clothing, olive groves and vine-
yards, sheep and oxen, male and female servants?
27 Therefore the leprosy of Naaman [a]shall cling to
you and your descendants forever." And he went
out from his presence [b]leprous, *as white* as snow.

### *THE FLOATING AX HEAD*

6 And [a]the sons of the prophets said to Elisha,
"See now, the place where we dwell with you is
too small for us. 2 Please, let us go to the Jordan,
and let every man take a beam from there, and
let us make there a place where we may dwell."

So he answered, "Go."

3 Then one said, [a]"Please consent to go with
your servants."

And he answered, "I will go." 4 So he went with
them. And when they came to the Jordan, they cut
down trees. 5 But as one was cutting down a tree,
the iron *ax head* fell into the water; and he cried
out and said, "Alas, master! For it was [a]borrowed."

6 So the man of God said, "Where did it fall?"
And he showed him the place. So [a]he cut off a
stick, and threw *it* in there; and he made the iron
float. 7 Therefore he said, "Pick *it* up for yourself."
So he reached out his hand and took it.

### *THE BLINDED SYRIANS CAPTURED*

8 Now the [a]king of Syria was making war
against Israel; and he consulted with his ser-
vants, saying, "My camp *will be* in such and
such a place." 9 And the man of God sent to the
king of Israel, saying, "Beware that you do not
pass this place, for the Syrians are coming down
there." 10 Then the king of Israel sent *someone*
to the place of which the man of God had told
him. Thus he warned him, and he was watchful
there, not just once or twice.

11 Therefore the heart of the king of Syria was
greatly troubled by this thing; and he called his
servants and said to them, "Will you not show
me which of us *is* for the king of Israel?"

12 And one of his servants said, "None, my
lord, O king; but Elisha, the prophet who *is* in
Israel, tells the king of Israel the words that you
speak in your bedroom."

13 So he said, "Go and see where he *is,* that I
may send and get him."

And it was told him, saying, "Surely *he is*
in [a]Dothan."

14 Therefore he sent horses and chariots and
a great army there, and they came by night and
surrounded the city. 15 And when the servant of
the man of God arose early and went out, there
was an army, surrounding the city with horses

5:12 [1] Following Kethib, Septuagint, and Vulgate; Qere, Syriac, and Targum read *Amanah*. 5:13 [a] 1 Sam. 28:23 5:14 [a] 2 Kin. 5:10; Job 33:25 [b] Luke 4:27; 5:13 5:15 [a] Dan. 2:47; 3:29; 6:26, 27 [b] Gen. 33:11 5:16 [a] 2 Kin. 3:14 [b] Gen. 14:22, 23; 2 Kin. 5:20, 26; [Matt. 10:8]; Acts 8:18, 20 5:18 [a] 2 Kin. 7:2, 17 5:20 [a] 2 Kin. 4:12; 8:4, 5 5:22 [a] 2 Kin. 4:26 5:26 [a] [Eccl. 3:1, 6] 5:27 [a] [1 Tim. 6:10] [b] Ex. 4:6; Num. 12:10; 2 Kin. 15:5 6:1 [a] 2 Kin. 4:38 6:3 [a] 2 Kin. 5:23 6:5 [a] [Ex. 22:14] 6:6 [a] Ex. 15:25; 2 Kin. 2:21; 4:41 6:8 [a] 2 Kin. 8:28, 29 6:13 [a] Gen. 37:17

and chariots. And his servant said to him, "Alas, my master! What shall we do?"

16 So he answered, [a]"Do not fear, for [b]those who *are* with us *are* more than those who *are* with them." 17 And Elisha prayed, and said, "LORD, I pray, open his eyes that he may see." Then the LORD [a]opened the eyes of the young man, and he saw. And behold, the mountain *was* full of [b]horses and chariots of fire all around Elisha. 18 So when *the Syrians* came down to him, Elisha prayed to the LORD, and said, "Strike this people, I pray, with blindness." And [a]He struck them with blindness according to the word of Elisha.

19 Now Elisha said to them, "This *is* not the way, nor *is* this the city. Follow me, and I will bring you to the man whom you seek." But he led them to Samaria.

20 So it was, when they had come to Samaria, that Elisha said, "LORD, open the eyes of these *men,* that they may see." And the LORD opened their eyes, and they saw; and there *they were,* inside Samaria!

21 Now when the king of Israel saw them, he said to Elisha, "My [a]father, shall I kill *them?* Shall I kill *them?*"

22 But he answered, "You shall not kill *them.* Would you kill those whom you have taken captive with your sword and your bow? [a]Set food and water before them, that they may eat and drink and go to their master." 23 Then he prepared a great feast for them; and after they ate and drank, he sent them away and they went to their master. So [a]the bands of Syrian *raiders* came no more into the land of Israel.

### *SYRIA BESIEGES SAMARIA IN FAMINE*

24 And it happened after this that [a]Ben-Hadad king of Syria gathered all his army, and went up and besieged Samaria. 25 And there was a great [a]famine in Samaria; and indeed they besieged it until a donkey's head was *sold* for eighty *shekels* of silver, and one-fourth of a kab of dove droppings for five *shekels* of silver.

26 Then, as the king of Israel was passing by on the wall, a woman cried out to him, saying, "Help, my lord, O king!"

27 And he said, "If the LORD does not help you, where can I find help for you? From the threshing floor or from the winepress?" 28 Then the king said to her, "What is troubling you?"

And she answered, "This woman said to me, 'Give your son, that we may eat him today, and we will eat my son tomorrow.' 29 So [a]we boiled my son, and ate him. And I said to her on the next day, 'Give your son, that we may eat him'; but she has hidden her son."

30 Now it happened, when the king heard the words of the woman, that he [a]tore his clothes; and as he passed by on the wall, the people looked, and there underneath *he had* sackcloth on his body. 31 Then he said, [a]"God do so to me and more also, if the head of Elisha the son of Shaphat remains on him today!"

**6:30 Sackcloth** was a coarse, uncomfortable material made from camel or goat hair, worn during times of sorrow and mourning.

32 But Elisha was sitting in his house, and [a]the elders were sitting with him. And *the king* sent a man ahead of him, but before the messenger came to him, he said to the elders, [b]"Do you see how this son of [c]a murderer has sent someone to take away my head? Look, when the messenger comes, shut the door, and hold

6:16 [a] Ex. 14:13; 1 Kin. 17:13 [b] 2 Chr. 32:7; Ps. 55:18; [Rom. 8:31] 6:17 [a] Num. 22:31; Luke 24:31 [b] 2 Kin. 2:11; Ps. 34:7; 68:17; Zech. 1:8; 6:1–7 6:18 [a] Gen. 19:11; Acts 13:11 6:21 [a] 2 Kin. 2:12; 5:13; 8:9 6:22 [a] [Rom. 12:20] 6:23 [a] 2 Kin. 5:2; 6:8, 9 6:24 [a] 1 Kin. 20:1 6:25 [a] 2 Kin. 4:38; 8:1 6:29 [a] Lev. 26:27–29; Deut. 28:52–57; Lam. 4:10 6:30 [a] 1 Kin. 21:27 6:31 [a] Ruth 1:17; 1 Kin. 19:2 6:32 [a] Ezek. 8:1; 14:1; 20:1 [b] Luke 13:32 [c] 1 Kin. 18:4, 13, 14; 21:10, 13

APPLY THE TRUTH

## FEAR

**6:16** Fear can greatly affect our lives. It can come from past experiences, present feelings, or our minds and hearts casting shadows onto the future. Sometimes our fears are based on legitimate concerns or circumstances. Some fears can even be good, healthy, and helpful. The interesting thing is fear and faith aren't mutually exclusive. You can live with fear *and* with faith.

This chapter tells of a great army coming against God's people and bringing great fear with it. Notice that Elisha didn't pray for the enemy to go away; he prayed for his servant's eyes to be opened. Elisha told his servant not to fear, not because there wasn't a threat, but because God was at work even *with* the threat. This is how fear and faith can work together. Fear causes us to see we're not in control. We don't have all the answers. We can't do it alone. And that's where faith comes in. We need God to protect us: to bring us peace and to provide for us. The next time you feel fear, use it to drive you toward deeper faith in God.

him fast at the door. *Is* not the sound of his master's feet behind him?" 33 And while he was still talking with them, there was the messenger, coming down to him; and then *the king* said, "Surely this calamity *is* from the LORD; [a]why should I wait for the LORD any longer?"

**7** Then Elisha said, "Hear the word of the LORD. Thus says the LORD: [a]'Tomorrow about this time a seah of fine flour *shall be sold* for a shekel, and two seahs of barley for a shekel, at the gate of Samaria.'"

2 [a]So an officer on whose hand the king leaned answered the man of God and said, "Look, [b]*if* the LORD would make windows in heaven, could this thing be?"

And he said, "In fact, you shall see *it* with your eyes, but you shall not eat of it."

### THE SYRIANS FLEE

3 Now there were four leprous men [a]at the entrance of the gate; and they said to one another, "Why are we sitting here until we die? 4 If we say, 'We will enter the city,' the famine *is* in the city, and we shall die there. And if we sit here, we die also. Now therefore, come, let us surrender to the [a]army of the Syrians. If they keep us alive, we shall live; and if they kill us, we shall only die." 5 And they rose at twilight to go to the camp of the Syrians; and when they had come to the outskirts of the Syrian camp, to their surprise no one *was* there. 6 For the Lord had caused the army of the Syrians [a]to hear the noise of chariots and the noise of horses—the noise of a great army; so they said to one another, "Look, the king of Israel has hired against us [b]the kings of the Hittites and the kings of the Egyptians to attack us!" 7 Therefore they [a]arose and fled at twilight, and left the camp intact—their tents, their horses, and their donkeys—and they fled for their lives. 8 And when these lepers came to the outskirts of the camp, they went into one tent and ate and drank, and carried from it silver and gold and clothing, and went and hid *them;* then they came back and entered another tent, and carried *some* from there *also,* and went and hid *it.*

9 Then they said to one another, "We are not doing right. This day *is* a day of good news, and we remain silent. If we wait until morning light, some punishment will come upon us. Now therefore, come, let us go and tell the king's household." 10 So they went and called to the gatekeepers of the city, and told them, saying, "We went to the Syrian camp, and surprisingly no one *was* there, not a human sound—only horses and donkeys tied, and the tents intact." 11 And the gatekeepers called out, and they told *it* to the king's household inside.

12 So the king arose in the night and said to his servants, "Let me now tell you what the Syrians have done to us. They know that we *are* [a]hungry; therefore they have gone out of the camp to hide themselves in the field, saying, 'When they come out of the city, we shall catch them alive, and get into the city.'"

13 And one of his servants answered and said, "Please, let several *men* take five of the remaining horses which are left in the city. Look, they *may either become* like all the multitude of Israel that are left in it; or indeed, *I say,* they *may become* like all the multitude of Israel left from those who are consumed; so let us send them and see." 14 Therefore they took two chariots with horses; and the king sent them in the direction of the Syrian army, saying, "Go and see." 15 And they went after them to the Jordan; and indeed all the road *was* full of garments and weapons which the Syrians had thrown away in their haste. So the messengers returned and told the king. 16 Then the people went out and plundered the tents of the Syrians. So a seah of fine flour was *sold* for a shekel, and two seahs of barley for a shekel, [a]according to the word of the LORD.

17 Now the king had appointed the officer on whose hand he leaned to have charge of the gate. But the people trampled him in the gate, and he died, just [a]as the man of God had said, who spoke when the king came down to him. 18 So it happened just as the man of God had spoken to the king, saying, [a]"Two seahs of barley for a shekel, and a seah of fine flour for a shekel, shall be *sold* tomorrow about this time in the gate of Samaria."

19 Then that officer had answered the man of God, and said, "Now look, *if* the LORD would make windows in heaven, could such a thing be?"

And he had said, "In fact, you shall see *it* with your eyes, but you shall not eat of it." 20 And so it happened to him, for the people trampled him in the gate, and he died.

### THE KING RESTORES THE SHUNAMMITE'S LAND

**8** Then Elisha spoke to the woman [a]whose son he had restored to life, saying, "Arise and go, you and your household, and stay wherever you can; for the LORD [b]has called for a [c]famine, and furthermore, it will come upon the land for seven years." 2 So the woman arose and did according to the saying of the man of God, and she went with her household and dwelt in the land of the Philistines seven years.

3 It came to pass, at the end of seven years, that the woman returned from the land of the Philistines; and she went to make an appeal to the king for her house and for her land. 4 Then the king talked with [a]Gehazi, the servant of the man of God, saying, "Tell me, please, all the great things Elisha has done." 5 Now it happened, as he was telling the king how he had restored the dead to life, that there was the woman whose son he had [a]restored to life, appealing to the

6:33 [a] Job 2:9 7:1 [a] 2 Kin. 7:18, 19 7:2 [a] 2 Kin. 5:18; 7:17, 19, 20 [b] Gen. 7:11; Mal. 3:10 7:3 [a] [Lev. 13:45, 46; Num. 5:2–4; 12:10–14] 7:4 [a] 2 Kin. 6:24 7:6 [a] 2 Sam. 5:24; 2 Kin. 19:7; Job 15:21 [b] 1 Kin. 10:29 7:7 [a] Ps. 48:4–6; [Prov. 28:1] 7:12 [a] 2 Kin. 6:24–29 7:16 [a] 2 Kin. 7:1 7:17 [a] 2 Kin. 6:32; 7:2 7:18 [a] 2 Kin. 7:1 8:1 [a] 2 Kin. 4:18, 31–35 [b] Ps. 105:16; Hag. 1:11 [c] 2 Sam. 21:1; 1 Kin. 18:2; 2 Kin. 4:38; 6:25 8:4 [a] 2 Kin. 4:12; 5:20–27 8:5 [a] 2 Kin. 4:35

king for her house and for her land. And Gehazi
said, "My lord, O king, this *is* the woman, and this
*is* her son whom Elisha restored to life." 6And
when the king asked the woman, she told him.
So the king appointed a certain officer for
her, saying, "Restore all that *was* hers, and all
the proceeds of the field from the day that she
left the land until now."

### DEATH OF BEN-HADAD

7Then Elisha went to Damascus, and
[a]Ben-Hadad king of Syria was sick; and it was told
him, saying, "The man of God has come here."
8And the king said to [a]Hazael, [b]"Take a present
in your hand, and go to meet the man of God,
and [c]inquire of the LORD by him, saying, 'Shall I
recover from this disease?' " 9So [a]Hazael went to
meet him and took a present with him, of every
good thing of Damascus, forty camel-loads; and
he came and stood before him, and said, "Your
son Ben-Hadad king of Syria has sent me to
you, saying, 'Shall I recover from this disease?' "
10And Elisha said to him, "Go, say to him,
'You shall certainly recover.' However the LORD
has shown me that [a]he will really die." 11Then
he set his countenance in a stare until he was
ashamed; and the man of God [a]wept. 12And Haz-
ael said, "Why is my lord weeping?"
He answered, "Because I know [a]the evil that
you will do to the children of Israel: Their strong-
holds you will set on fire, and their young men you
will kill with the sword; and you [b]will dash their
children, and rip open their women with child."
13So Hazael said, "But what [a]*is* your ser-
vant—a dog, that he should do this gross thing?"
And Elisha answered, [b]"The LORD has shown
me that you *will become* king over Syria."
14Then he departed from Elisha, and came
to his master, who said to him, "What did Elisha
say to you?" And he answered, "He told me you
would surely recover." 15But it happened on the
next day that he took a thick cloth and dipped
*it* in water, and spread *it* over his face so that he
died; and Hazael reigned in his place.

### JEHORAM REIGNS IN JUDAH

*(2 Chr. 21:1–20)*

16Now [a]in the fifth year of Joram the son of
Ahab, king of Israel, Jehoshaphat *having been* king
of Judah, [b]Jehoram the son of Jehoshaphat began
to reign as king of Judah. 17He was [a]thirty-two
years old when he became king, and he reigned
eight years in Jerusalem. 18And he walked in the
way of the kings of Israel, just as the house of
Ahab had done, for [a]the daughter of Ahab was
his wife; and he did evil in the sight of the LORD.
19Yet the LORD would not destroy Judah, for the
sake of His servant David, [a]as He promised him
to give a lamp to him *and* his sons forever.
20In his days [a]Edom revolted against Judah's
authority, [b]and made a king over themselves. 21So
Joram[1] went to Zair, and all his chariots with him.
Then he rose by night and attacked the Edomites
who had surrounded him and the captains of the
chariots; and the troops fled to their tents. 22Thus
Edom has been in revolt against Judah's authority
to this day. [a]And Libnah revolted at that time.
23Now the rest of the acts of Joram, and all
that he did, *are* they not written in the book of
the chronicles of the kings of Judah? 24So Joram
rested with his fathers, and was buried with his
fathers in the City of David. Then [a]Ahaziah his
son reigned in his place.

### AHAZIAH REIGNS IN JUDAH

*(2 Chr. 22:1–6)*

25In the twelfth year of Joram the son of
Ahab, king of Israel, Ahaziah the son of Jehoram,
king of Judah, began to reign. 26Ahaziah *was*
[a]twenty-two years old when he became king, and
he reigned one year in Jerusalem. His mother's
name *was* Athaliah the granddaughter of Omri,
king of Israel. 27[a]And he walked in the way of
the house of Ahab, and did evil in the sight of
the LORD, like the house of Ahab, for he *was* the
son-in-law of the house of Ahab.
28Now he went [a]with Joram the son of Ahab
to war against Hazael king of Syria at [b]Ramoth
Gilead; and the Syrians wounded Joram. 29Then
[a]King Joram went back to Jezreel to recover from
the wounds which the Syrians had inflicted on
him at Ramah, when he fought against Hazael
king of Syria. [b]And Ahaziah the son of Jehoram,
king of Judah, went down to see Joram the son
of Ahab in Jezreel, because he was sick.

### JEHU ANOINTED KING OF ISRAEL

9 And Elisha the prophet called one of [a]the
sons of the prophets, and said to him, [b]"Get
yourself ready, take this flask of oil in your hand,
[c]and go to Ramoth Gilead. 2Now when you arrive
at that place, look there for Jehu the son of Je-
hoshaphat, the son of Nimshi, and go in and make
him rise up from among [a]his associates, and take
him to an inner room. 3Then [a]take the flask of
oil, and pour *it* on his head, and say, 'Thus says
the LORD: "I have anointed you king over Israel." '
Then open the door and flee, and do not delay."
4So the young man, the servant of the
prophet, went to Ramoth Gilead. 5And when
he arrived, there *were* the captains of the army
sitting; and he said, "I have a message for you,
Commander."
Jehu said, "For which *one* of us?"

**8:7** [a] 2 Kin. 6:24 **8:8** [a] 1 Kin. 19:15 [b] 1 Sam. 9:7; 1 Kin. 14:3; 2 Kin. 5:5 [c] 2 Kin. 1:2 **8:9** [a] 1 Kin. 19:15 **8:10** [a] 2 Kin. 8:15 **8:11** [a] Luke 19:41 **8:12** [a] 2 Kin. 10:32; 12:17; 13:3, 7; Amos 1:3, 4 [b] 2 Kin. 15:16; Hos. 13:16; Amos 1:13; Nah. 3:10 **8:13** [a] 1 Sam. 17:43; 2 Sam. 9:8 [b] 1 Kin. 19:15 **8:16** [a] 2 Kin. 1:17; 3:1 [b] 2 Chr. 21:3 **8:17** [a] 2 Chr. 21:5–10 **8:18** [a] 2 Kin. 8:26, 27 **8:19** [a] 2 Sam. 7:13; 1 Kin. 11:36; 15:4; 2 Chr. 21:7 **8:20** [a] Gen. 27:40; 2 Chr. 21:8–10 [b] 1 Kin. 22:47 **8:21** [1] Spelled *Jehoram* in verse 16 **8:22** [a] Josh. 21:13; 2 Kin. 19:8; 2 Chr. 21:10 **8:24** [a] 2 Chr. 22:1, 7 **8:26** [a] 2 Chr. 22:2 **8:27** [a] 2 Chr. 22:3, 4 **8:28** [a] 2 Chr. 22:5 [b] 1 Kin. 22:3, 29 **8:29** [a] 2 Kin. 9:15 [b] 2 Kin. 9:16; 2 Chr. 22:6, 7 **9:1** [a] 1 Kin. 20:35 [b] 2 Kin. 4:29; Jer. 1:17 [c] 2 Kin. 8:28, 29 **9:2** [a] 2 Kin. 9:5, 11 **9:3** [a] 1 Kin. 19:16

And he said, "For you, Commander." 6 Then he arose and went into the house. And he poured the oil on his head, and said to him, [a]"Thus says the LORD God of Israel: 'I have anointed you king over the people of the LORD, over Israel. 7 You shall strike down the house of Ahab your master, that I may [a]avenge the blood of My servants the prophets, and the blood of all the servants of the LORD, [b]at the hand of Jezebel. 8 For the whole house of Ahab shall perish; and [a]I will cut off from Ahab all [b]the males in Israel, both [c]bond and free. 9 So I will make the house of Ahab like the house of [a]Jeroboam the son of Nebat, and like the house of [b]Baasha the son of Ahijah. 10 [a]The dogs shall eat Jezebel on the plot *of ground* at Jezreel, and *there shall be* none to bury *her.*' " And he opened the door and fled.

11 Then Jehu came out to the servants of his master, and *one* said to him, "*Is* all well? Why did [a]this madman come to you?"

And he said to them, "You know the man and his babble."

12 And they said, "A lie! Tell us now."

So he said, "Thus and thus he spoke to me, saying, 'Thus says the LORD: "I have anointed you king over Israel." ' "

13 Then each man hastened [a]to take his garment and put *it* under him on the top of the steps; and they blew trumpets, saying, "Jehu is king!"

### JORAM OF ISRAEL KILLED

14 So Jehu the son of Jehoshaphat, the son of Nimshi, conspired against [a]Joram. (Now Joram had been defending Ramoth Gilead, he and all Israel, against Hazael king of Syria. 15 But [a]King Joram had returned to Jezreel to recover from the wounds which the Syrians had inflicted on him when he fought with Hazael king of Syria.) And Jehu said, "If you are so minded, let no one leave *or* escape from the city to go and tell *it* in Jezreel." 16 So Jehu rode in a chariot and went to Jezreel, for Joram was laid up there; [a]and Ahaziah king of Judah had come down to see Joram.

17 Now a watchman stood on the tower in Jezreel, and he saw the company of Jehu as he came, and said, "I see a company of men."

And Joram said, "Get a horseman and send him to meet them, and let him say, '*Is it* peace?' "

18 So the horseman went to meet him, and said, "Thus says the king: '*Is it* peace?' "

And Jehu said, "What have you to do with peace? Turn around and follow me."

So the watchman reported, saying, "The messenger went to them, but is not coming back."

19 Then he sent out a second horseman who came to them, and said, "Thus says the king: '*Is it* peace?' "

And Jehu answered, "What have you to do with peace? Turn around and follow me."

20 So the watchman reported, saying, "He went up to them and is not coming back; and the driving *is* like the driving of Jehu the son of Nimshi, for he drives furiously!"

21 Then Joram said, "Make ready." And his chariot was made ready. Then [a]Joram king of Israel and Ahaziah king of Judah went out, each in his chariot; and they went out to meet Jehu, and met him [b]on the property of Naboth the Jezreelite. 22 Now it happened, when Joram saw Jehu, that he said, "*Is it* peace, Jehu?"

So he answered, "What peace, as long as the harlotries of your mother Jezebel and her witchcraft *are so* many?"

23 Then Joram turned around and fled, and said to Ahaziah, "Treachery, Ahaziah!" 24 Now Jehu drew his bow with full strength and shot Jehoram between his arms; and the arrow came out at his heart, and he sank down in his chariot. 25 Then *Jehu* said to Bidkar his captain, "Pick *him* up, *and* throw him into the tract of the field of Naboth the Jezreelite; for remember, when you and I were riding together behind Ahab his father, that [a]the LORD laid this [b]burden upon him: 26 'Surely I saw yesterday the blood of Naboth and the blood of his sons,' says the LORD, [a]'and I will repay you in this plot,' says the LORD. Now therefore, take *and* throw him on the plot *of ground,* according to the word of the LORD."

### AHAZIAH OF JUDAH KILLED

*(2 Chr. 22:7–9)*

27 But when Ahaziah king of Judah saw *this,* he fled by the road to Beth Haggan.[1] So Jehu pursued him, and said, "Shoot him also in the chariot." *And they shot him* at the Ascent of Gur, which is by Ibleam. Then he fled to [a]Megiddo, and died there. 28 And his servants carried him in the chariot to Jerusalem, and buried him in his tomb with his fathers in the City of David. 29 In the eleventh year of Joram the son of Ahab, Ahaziah had become king over Judah.

### JEZEBEL'S VIOLENT DEATH

30 Now when Jehu had come to Jezreel, Jezebel heard *of it;* [a]and she put paint on her eyes and adorned her head, and looked through a window. 31 Then, as Jehu entered at the gate, she said, [a]"*Is it* peace, Zimri, murderer of your master?"

32 And he looked up at the window, and said, "Who *is* on my side? Who?" So two *or* three eunuchs looked out at him. 33 Then he said, "Throw her down." So they threw her down, and *some* of her blood spattered on the wall and on the horses; and he trampled her underfoot. 34 And

**9:6** [a] 1 Sam. 2:7, 8; 1 Kin. 19:16; 2 Kin. 9:3; 2 Chr. 22:7 **9:7** [a] [Deut. 32:35, 41] [b] 1 Kin. 18:4; 21:15 **9:8** [a] 1 Kin. 14:10; 21:21; 2 Kin. 10:17 [b] 1 Sam. 25:22 [c] Deut. 32:36; 2 Kin. 14:26 **9:9** [a] 1 Kin. 14:10; 15:29; 21:22 [b] 1 Kin. 16:3, 11 **9:10** [a] 1 Kin. 21:23; 2 Kin. 9:35, 36 **9:11** [a] Jer. 29:26; Hos. 9:7; Mark 3:21; John 10:20; Acts 26:24; [1 Cor. 4:10] **9:13** [a] Matt. 21:7, 8; Mark 11:7, 8 **9:14** [a] 2 Kin. 8:28 **9:15** [a] 2 Kin. 8:29 **9:16** [a] 2 Kin. 8:29 **9:21** [a] 1 Kin. 19:17; 2 Chr. 22:7 [b] 1 Kin. 21:1–14 **9:25** [a] 1 Kin. 21:19, 24–29 [b] Is. 13:1 **9:26** [a] 1 Kin. 21:13, 19 **9:27** [a] 2 Chr. 22:7, 9 [1] Literally *The Garden House* **9:30** [a] [Jer. 4:30]; Ezek. 23:40 **9:31** [a] 1 Kin. 16:9–20; 2 Kin. 9:18–22

when he had gone in, he ate and drank. Then
he said, "Go now, see to this accursed *woman,*
and bury her, for [a]she was a king's daughter."
35 So they went to bury her, but they found no
more of her than the skull and the feet and the
palms of *her* hands. 36 Therefore they came back
and told him. And he said, "This *is* the word of
the LORD, which He spoke by His servant Elijah
the Tishbite, saying, [a]'On the plot *of ground* at
Jezreel dogs shall eat the flesh of Jezebel;[1] 37 and
the corpse of Jezebel shall be [a]as refuse on the
surface of the field, in the plot at Jezreel, so that
they shall not say, "Here *lies* Jezebel." ' "

> **9:34–37** The Israelites considered it a tragedy not to be buried properly. Jehu didn't want to insult a member of the royal family—even someone as wicked as Jezebel—by not having someone **bury her** body. But before he could prepare a grave, Jezebel's body was eaten by **dogs**, in accordance with what Elijah had prophesied (1 Kin. 21:19). The Israelites considered dogs to be filthy scavengers, so what happened to Jezebel's corpse was particularly gruesome.

### *AHAB'S SEVENTY SONS KILLED*

**10** Now Ahab had seventy sons in Samaria.
And Jehu wrote and sent letters to Samar-
ia, to the rulers of Jezreel,[1] to the elders, and to
those who reared Ahab's *sons,* saying:

2 Now as soon as this letter comes to you,
since your master's sons *are* with you, and
you have chariots and horses, a fortified
city also, and weapons, 3 choose the best
qualified of your master's sons, set *him*
on his father's throne, and fight for your
master's house.

4 But they were exceedingly afraid, and said,
"Look, [a]two kings could not stand up to him; how
then can we stand?" 5 And he who *was* in charge
of the house, and he who *was* in charge of the
city, the elders also, and those who reared *the
sons,* sent to Jehu, saying, "We *are* your servants,
we will do all you tell us; but we will not make
anyone king. Do *what is* good in your sight."
6 Then he wrote a second letter to them, saying:

If you *are* for me and will obey my voice,
take the heads of the men, your master's
sons, and come to me at Jezreel by this
time tomorrow.

Now the king's sons, seventy persons, *were*
with the great men of the city, *who* were rearing
them. 7 So it was, when the letter came to them,
that they took the king's sons and [a]slaughtered
seventy persons, put their heads in baskets and
sent *them* to him at Jezreel.
8 Then a messenger came and told him,
saying, "They have brought the heads of the
king's sons."

And he said, "Lay them in two heaps at the
entrance of the gate until morning."
9 So it was, in the morning, that he went out
and stood, and said to all the people, "You *are* righ-
teous. Indeed [a]I conspired against my master and
killed him; but who killed all these? 10 Know now
that nothing shall [a]fall to the earth of the word of
the LORD which the LORD spoke concerning the
house of Ahab; for the LORD has done what He
spoke [b]by His servant Elijah." 11 So Jehu killed all
who remained of the house of Ahab in Jezreel,
and all his great men and his close acquaintances
and his priests, until he left him none remaining.

### *AHAZIAH'S FORTY-TWO BROTHERS KILLED*

12 And he arose and departed and went to
Samaria. On the way, at Beth Eked[1] of the Shep-
herds, 13 [a]Jehu met with the brothers of Ahaziah
king of Judah, and said, "Who *are* you?"

So they answered, "We *are* the brothers of
Ahaziah; we have come down to greet the sons
of the king and the sons of the queen mother."
14 And he said, "Take them alive!" So they took
them alive, and [a]killed them at the well of Beth
Eked, forty-two men; and he left none of them.

### *THE REST OF AHAB'S FAMILY KILLED*

15 Now when he departed from there, he
met [a]Jehonadab the son of [b]Rechab, *coming*
to meet him; and he greeted him and said to
him, "Is your heart right, as my heart *is* toward
your heart?"

And Jehonadab answered, "It is."

*Jehu said,* "If it is, [c]give *me* your hand." So he
gave *him* his hand, and he took him up to him
into the chariot. 16 Then he said, "Come with
me, and see my [a]zeal for the LORD." So they had
him ride in his chariot. 17 And when he came to
Samaria, [a]he killed all who remained to Ahab in
Samaria, till he had destroyed them, according to
the word of the LORD [b]which He spoke to Elijah.

### *WORSHIPERS OF BAAL KILLED*

18 Then Jehu gathered all the people together,
and said to them, [a]"Ahab served Baal a little, Jehu
will serve him much. 19 Now therefore, call to me all
the [a]prophets of Baal, all his servants, and all his
priests. Let no one be missing, for I have a great
sacrifice for Baal. Whoever is missing shall not

**9:34** [a] [Ex. 22:28]; 1 Kin. 16:31 **9:36** [a] 1 Kin. 21:23 [1] 1 Kings 21:23 **9:37** [a] Ps. 83:10 **10:1** [1] Following Masoretic Text, Syriac, and Targum; Septuagint reads *Samaria;* Vulgate reads *city.* **10:4** [a] 2 Kin. 9:24, 27 **10:7** [a] Judg. 9:5; 1 Kin. 21:21; 2 Kin. 11:1 **10:9** [a] 2 Kin. 9:14–24 **10:10** [a] 1 Sam. 3:19; 1 Kin. 8:56; Jer. 44:28 [b] 1 Kin. 21:17–24, 29 **10:12** [1] Or *The Shearing House* **10:13** [a] 2 Chr. 22:8 **10:14** [a] 2 Chr. 22:8 **10:15** [a] Jer. 35:6 [b] 1 Chr. 2:55 [c] Ezra 10:19; Ezek. 17:18 **10:16** [a] 1 Kin. 19:10 **10:17** [a] 2 Kin. 9:8; 2 Chr. 22:8 [b] 1 Kin. 21:21, 29 **10:18** [a] 1 Kin. 16:31, 32 **10:19** [a] 1 Kin. 18:19; 22:6

live." But Jehu acted deceptively, with the intent of destroying the worshipers of Baal. 20 And Jehu said, "Proclaim a solemn assembly for Baal." So they proclaimed *it.* 21 Then Jehu sent throughout all Israel; and all the worshipers of Baal came, so that there was not a man left who did not come. So they came into the temple[1] of Baal, and the [a]temple of Baal was full from one end to the other. 22 And he said to the one in charge of the wardrobe, "Bring out vestments for all the worshipers of Baal." So he brought out vestments for them. 23 Then Jehu and Jehonadab the son of Rechab went into the temple of Baal, and said to the worshipers of Baal, "Search and see that no servants of the LORD are here with you, but only the worshipers of Baal." 24 So they went in to offer sacrifices and burnt offerings. Now Jehu had appointed for himself eighty men on the outside, and had said, "*If* any of the men whom I have brought into your hands escapes, *whoever lets him escape, it shall be* [a]his life for the life of the other."

25 Now it happened, as soon as he had made an end of offering the burnt offering, that Jehu said to the guard and to the captains, "Go in *and* kill them; let no one come out!" And they killed them with the edge of the sword; then the guards and the officers threw *them* out, and went into the inner room of the temple of Baal. 26 And they brought the [a]*sacred* pillars out of the temple of Baal and burned them. 27 Then they broke down the *sacred* pillar of Baal, and tore down the temple of Baal and [a]made it a refuse dump to this day. 28 Thus Jehu destroyed Baal from Israel.

29 However Jehu did not turn away from the sins of Jeroboam the son of Nebat, who had made Israel sin, *that is,* from [a]the golden calves that *were* at Bethel and Dan. 30 And the LORD [a]said to Jehu, "Because you have done well in doing *what is* right in My sight, *and* have done to the house of Ahab all that *was* in My heart, [b]your sons shall sit on the throne of Israel to the fourth *generation.*" 31 But Jehu took no heed to walk in the law of the LORD God of Israel with all his heart; for he did not depart from [a]the sins of Jeroboam, who had made Israel sin.

### *DEATH OF JEHU*

32 In those days the LORD began to cut off *parts* of Israel; and [a]Hazael conquered them in all the territory of Israel 33 from the Jordan eastward: all the land of Gilead—Gad, Reuben, and Manasseh—from [a]Aroer, which *is* by the River Arnon, including [b]Gilead and Bashan.

34 Now the rest of the acts of Jehu, all that he did, and all his might, *are* they not written in the book of the chronicles of the kings of Israel? 35 So Jehu rested with his fathers, and they buried him in Samaria. Then [a]Jehoahaz his son reigned in his place. 36 And the period that Jehu reigned over Israel in Samaria *was* twenty-eight years.

### *ATHALIAH REIGNS IN JUDAH*

*(2 Chr. 22:10–12)*

**11** When [a]Athaliah [b]the mother of Ahaziah saw that her son was [c]dead, she arose and destroyed all the royal heirs. 2 But Jehosheba, the daughter of King Joram, sister of [a]Ahaziah, took Joash the son of Ahaziah, and stole him away from among the king's sons *who were* being murdered; and they hid him and his nurse in the bedroom, from Athaliah, so that he was not killed. 3 So he was hidden with her in the house of the LORD for six years, while Athaliah reigned over the land.

### *JOASH CROWNED KING OF JUDAH*

*(2 Chr. 23:1–11)*

4 In [a]the seventh year Jehoiada sent and brought the captains of hundreds—of the bodyguards and the escorts—and brought them into the house of the LORD to him. And he made a covenant with them and took an oath from them in the house of the LORD, and showed them the king's son. 5 Then he commanded them, saying, "This *is* what you shall do: One-third of you who come on duty [a]on the Sabbath shall be keeping watch over the king's house, 6 one-third *shall be* at the gate of Sur, and one-third at the gate behind the escorts. You shall keep the watch of the house, lest it be broken down. 7 The two contingents of you who go off duty on the Sabbath shall keep the watch of the house of the LORD for the king. 8 But you shall surround the king on all sides, every man with his weapons in his hand; and whoever comes within range, let him be put to death. You are to be with the king as he goes out and as he comes in."

9 [a]So the captains of the hundreds did according to all that Jehoiada the priest commanded. Each of them took his men who were to be on duty on the Sabbath, with those who were going off duty on the Sabbath, and came to Jehoiada the priest. 10 And the priest gave the captains of hundreds the spears and shields which *had belonged* to King David, [a]that were in the temple of the LORD. 11 Then the escorts stood, every man with his weapons in his hand, all around the king, from the right side of the temple to the left side of the temple, by the altar and the house. 12 And he brought out the king's son, put the crown on him, and *gave him* the [a]Testimony;[1] they made him king and anointed him, and they clapped their hands and said, [b]"Long live the king!"

**10:21** [a] 1 Kin. 16:32; 2 Kin. 11:18 [1] Literally *house,* and so elsewhere in this chapter **10:24** [a] 1 Kin. 20:39 **10:26** [a] [Deut. 7:5, 25]; 1 Kin. 14:23; 2 Kin. 3:2 **10:27** [a] Ezra 6:11; Dan. 2:5; 3:29 **10:29** [a] 1 Kin. 12:28–30; 13:33, 34 **10:30** [a] 2 Kin. 9:6, 7 [b] 2 Kin. 13:1, 10; 14:23; 15:8, 12 **10:31** [a] 1 Kin. 14:16 **10:32** [a] 1 Kin. 19:17; 2 Kin. 8:12; 13:22 **10:33** [a] Deut. 2:36 [b] Amos 1:3–5 **10:35** [a] 2 Kin. 13:1 **11:1** [a] 2 Chr. 22:10 [b] 2 Kin. 8:26 [c] 2 Kin. 9:27 **11:2** [a] 2 Kin. 8:25 **11:4** [a] 2 Kin. 12:2; 2 Chr. 23:1 **11:5** [a] 1 Chr. 9:25 **11:9** [a] 2 Chr. 23:8 **11:10** [a] 2 Sam. 8:7; 1 Chr. 18:7 **11:12** [a] Ex. 25:16; 31:18 [b] 1 Sam. 10:24 [1] That is, the Law (compare Exodus 25:16, 21 and Deuteronomy 31:9)

### *DEATH OF ATHALIAH*

*(2 Chr. 23:12—24:1)*

13 [a]Now when Athaliah heard the noise of the escorts *and* the people, she came to the people *in* the temple of the LORD. 14 When she looked, there was the king standing by [a]a pillar according to custom; and the leaders and the trumpeters were by the king. All the people of the land were rejoicing and blowing trumpets. So Athaliah tore her clothes and cried out, "Treason! Treason!"

15 And Jehoiada the priest commanded the captains of the hundreds, the officers of the army, and said to them, "Take her outside under guard, and slay with the sword whoever follows her." For the priest had said, "Do not let her be killed in the house of the LORD." 16 So they seized her; and she went by way of the horses' entrance *into* the king's house, and there she was killed.

17 [a]Then Jehoiada [b]made a covenant between the LORD, the king, and the people, that they should be the LORD's people, and *also* [c]between the king and the people. 18 And all the people of the land went to the [a]temple of Baal, and tore it down. They thoroughly [b]broke in pieces its altars and images, and [c]killed Mattan the priest of Baal before the altars. And [d]the priest appointed officers over the house of the LORD. 19 Then he took the captains of hundreds, the bodyguards, the escorts, and all the people of the land; and they brought the king down from the house of the LORD, and went by way of the gate of the escorts to the king's house. Then he sat on the throne of the kings. 20 So all the people of the land rejoiced; and the city was quiet, for they had slain Athaliah with the sword *in* the king's house. 21 Jehoash *was* [a]seven years old when he became king.

### *JEHOASH REPAIRS THE TEMPLE*

*(2 Chr. 24:1–14)*

**12** In the seventh year of Jehu, [a]Jehoash[1] became king, and he reigned forty years in Jerusalem. His mother's name *was* Zibiah of Beersheba. 2 Jehoash did *what was* right in the sight of the LORD all the days in which [a]Jehoiada the priest instructed him. 3 But [a]the high places were not taken away; the people still sacrificed and burned incense on the high places.

4 And Jehoash said to the priests, [a]"All the money of the dedicated gifts that are brought into the house of the LORD—each man's [b]census money, each man's [c]assessment money[1]—*and* all the money that a man [d]purposes in his heart to bring into the house of the LORD, 5 let the priests take *it* themselves, each from his constituency; and let them repair the damages of the temple, wherever any dilapidation is found."

6 Now it was so, by the twenty-third year of King Jehoash, [a]*that* the priests had not repaired the damages of the temple. 7 [a]So King Jehoash called Jehoiada the priest and the *other* priests, and said to them, "Why have you not repaired the damages of the temple? Now therefore, do not take *more* money from your constituency, but deliver it for repairing the damages of the temple." 8 And the priests agreed that they would neither receive *more* money from the people, nor repair the damages of the temple.

> **12:4** Once a year, every Israelite over the age of twenty donated a certain amount of **money** to be used for the temple. Other people gave gold and silver as gifts to show how much they appreciated what the Lord had done for them. These gifts and other valuables were stored in the temple.

9 Then Jehoiada the priest took [a]a chest, bored a hole in its lid, and set it beside the altar, on the right side as one comes into the house of the LORD; and the priests who kept the door put [b]there all the money brought into the house of the LORD. 10 So it was, whenever they saw that *there was* much money in the chest, that the king's [a]scribe and the high priest came up and put it in bags, and counted the money that was found in the house of the LORD. 11 Then they gave the money, which had been apportioned, into the hands of those who did the work, who had the oversight of the house of the LORD; and they paid it out to the carpenters and builders who worked on the house of the LORD, 12 and to masons and stonecutters, and for buying timber and hewn stone, to [a]repair the damage of the house of the LORD, and for all that was paid out to repair the temple. 13 However [a]there were not made for the house of the LORD basins of silver, trimmers, sprinkling-bowls, trumpets, any articles of gold or articles of silver, from the money brought into the house of the LORD. 14 But they gave that to the workmen, and they repaired the house of the LORD with it. 15 Moreover [a]they did not require an account from the men into whose hand they delivered the money to be paid to workmen, for they dealt faithfully. 16 [a]The money from the trespass offerings and the money from the sin offerings was not brought into the house of the LORD. [b]It belonged to the priests.

### *HAZAEL THREATENS JERUSALEM*

17 [a]Hazael king of Syria went up and fought against Gath, and took it; then [b]Hazael set his face to go up to Jerusalem. 18 And Jehoash king of Judah [a]took all the sacred things that his fathers,

**11:13** [a] 2 Kin. 8:26; 2 Chr. 23:12 **11:14** [a] 2 Kin. 23:3; 2 Chr. 34:31 **11:17** [a] 2 Chr. 23:16 [b] Josh. 24:24, 25; 2 Chr. 15:12–15 [c] 2 Sam. 5:3 **11:18** [a] 2 Kin. 10:26, 27 [b] [Deut. 12:3] [c] 1 Kin. 18:40; 2 Kin. 10:11 [d] 2 Chr. 23:18 **11:21** [a] 2 Chr. 24:1–14 **12:1** [a] 2 Chr. 24:1 [1] Spelled *Joash* in 11:2ff **12:2** [a] 2 Kin. 11:4 **12:3** [a] 1 Kin. 15:14; 22:43; 2 Kin. 14:4; 15:35 **12:4** [a] 2 Kin. 22:4 [b] Ex. 30:13–16 [c] Lev. 27:2–28 [d] Ex. 35:5; 1 Chr. 29:3–9 [1] Compare Leviticus 27:2ff **12:6** [a] 2 Chr. 24:5 **12:7** [a] 2 Chr. 24:6 **12:9** [a] 2 Chr. 23:1; 24:8 [b] Mark 12:41; Luke 21:1 **12:10** [a] 2 Sam. 8:17; 2 Kin. 19:2; 22:3, 4, 12 **12:12** [a] 2 Kin. 22:5, 6 **12:13** [a] 2 Chr. 24:14 **12:15** [a] 2 Kin. 22:7; [1 Cor. 4:2]; 2 Cor. 8:20 **12:16** [a] [Lev. 5:15, 18] [b] [Lev. 7:7; Num. 18:9] **12:17** [a] 2 Kin. 8:12 [b] 2 Chr. 24:23 **12:18** [a] 1 Kin. 15:18; 2 Kin. 16:8; 18:15, 16

Jehoshaphat and Jehoram and Ahaziah, kings of Judah, had dedicated, and his own sacred things, and all the gold found in the treasuries of the house of the LORD and in the king's house, and sent *them* to Hazael king of Syria. Then he went away from Jerusalem.

### *DEATH OF JOASH*
*(2 Chr. 24:23–27)*

19 Now the rest of the acts of Joash,[1] and all that he did, *are* they not written in the book of the chronicles of the kings of Judah?

20 And [a]his servants arose and formed a conspiracy, and killed Joash in the house of the Millo,[1] which goes down to Silla. 21 For Jozachar[1] the son of Shimeath and Jehozabad the son of Shomer,[2] his servants, struck him. So he died, and they buried him with his fathers in the City of David. Then [a]Amaziah his son reigned in his place.

### *JEHOAHAZ REIGNS IN ISRAEL*

**13** In the twenty-third year of [a]Joash[1] the son of Ahaziah, king of Judah, [b]Jehoahaz the son of Jehu became king over Israel in Samaria, *and reigned* seventeen years. 2 And he did evil in the sight of the LORD, and followed the [a]sins of Jeroboam the son of Nebat, who had made Israel sin. He did not depart from them.

3 Then [a]the anger of the LORD was aroused against Israel, and He delivered them into the hand of [b]Hazael king of Syria, and into the hand of [c]Ben-Hadad the son of Hazael, all *their* days. 4 So Jehoahaz [a]pleaded with the LORD, and the LORD listened to him; for [b]He saw the oppression of Israel, because the king of Syria oppressed them. 5 [a]Then the LORD gave Israel a deliverer, so that they escaped from under the hand of the Syrians; and the children of Israel dwelt in their tents as before. 6 Nevertheless they did not depart from the sins of the house of Jeroboam, who had made Israel sin, *but* walked in them; [a]and the wooden image[1] also remained in Samaria. 7 For He left of the army of Jehoahaz only fifty horsemen, ten chariots, and ten thousand foot soldiers; for the king of Syria had destroyed them [a]and made them [b]like the dust at threshing.

8 Now the rest of the acts of Jehoahaz, all that he did, and his might, *are* they not written in the book of the chronicles of the kings of Israel? 9 So Jehoahaz rested with his fathers, and they buried him in Samaria. Then Joash his son reigned in his place.

### *JEHOASH REIGNS IN ISRAEL*

10 In the thirty-seventh year of Joash king of Judah, Jehoash[1] the son of Jehoahaz became king over Israel in Samaria, *and reigned* sixteen years. 11 And he did evil in the sight of the LORD. He did not depart from all the sins of Jeroboam the son of Nebat, who made Israel sin, *but* walked in them.

12 [a]Now the rest of the acts of Joash, [b]all that he did, and [c]his might with which he fought against Amaziah king of Judah, *are* they not written in the book of the chronicles of the kings of Israel? 13 So Joash [a]rested with his fathers. Then Jeroboam sat on his throne. And Joash was buried in Samaria with the kings of Israel.

### *DEATH OF ELISHA*

14 Elisha had become sick with the illness of which he would die. Then Joash the king of Israel came down to him, and wept over his face, and said, "O my father, my father, [a]the chariots of Israel and their horsemen!"

15 And Elisha said to him, "Take a bow and some arrows." So he took himself a bow and some arrows. 16 Then he said to the king of Israel, "Put your hand on the bow." So he put his hand *on it,* and Elisha put his hands on the king's hands. 17 And he said, "Open the east window"; and he opened *it.* Then Elisha said, "Shoot"; and he shot. And he said, "The arrow of the LORD's deliverance and the arrow of deliverance from Syria; for you must strike the Syrians at [a]Aphek till you have destroyed *them.*" 18 Then he said, "Take the arrows"; so he took *them.* And he said to the king of Israel, "Strike the ground"; so he struck three times, and stopped. 19 And the man of God was angry with him, and said, "You should have struck five or six times; then you would have struck Syria till you had destroyed *it!* [a]But now you will strike Syria *only* three times."

20 Then Elisha died, and they buried him. And the [a]*raiding* bands from Moab invaded the land in the spring of the year. 21 So it was, as they were burying a man, that suddenly they spied a band *of raiders;* and they put the man in the tomb of Elisha; and when the man was let down and touched the bones of Elisha, he revived and stood on his feet.

### *ISRAEL RECAPTURES CITIES FROM SYRIA*

22 And [a]Hazael king of Syria oppressed Israel all the days of Jehoahaz. 23 But the LORD was [a]gracious to them, had compassion on them, and [b]regarded them, [c]because of His covenant with Abraham, Isaac, and Jacob, and would not yet destroy them or cast them from His presence.

24 Now Hazael king of Syria died. Then Ben-Hadad his son reigned in his place. 25 And Jehoash[1] the son of Jehoahaz recaptured from the hand of Ben-Hadad, the son of Hazael, the cities which he had taken out of the hand of

12:19 [1] Spelled *Jehoash* in 12:1ff 12:20 [a] 2 Kin. 14:5; 2 Chr. 24:25 [1] Literally *The Landfill* 12:21 [a] 2 Chr. 24:27 [1] Called *Zabad* in 2 Chronicles 24:26 [2] Called *Shimrith* in 2 Chronicles 24:26 13:1 [a] 2 Kin. 12:1 [b] 2 Kin. 10:35 [1] Spelled *Jehoash* in 12:1ff 13:2 [a] 1 Kin. 12:26–33 13:3 [a] Judg. 2:14 [b] 2 Kin. 8:12 [c] Amos 1:4 13:4 [a] [Ps. 78:34] [b] [Ex. 3:7, 9; Judg. 2:18]; 2 Kin. 14:26 13:5 [a] 2 Kin. 13:25; 14:25, 27; Neh. 9:27 13:6 [a] 1 Kin. 16:33 [1] Hebrew *Asherah,* a Canaanite goddess 13:7 [a] 2 Kin. 10:32 [b] [Amos 1:3] 13:10 [1] Spelled *Joash* in verse 9 13:12 [a] 2 Kin. 14:8–15 [b] 2 Kin. 13:14–19, 25 [c] 2 Kin. 14:9; 2 Chr. 25:17–25 13:13 [a] 2 Kin. 14:16 13:14 [a] 2 Kin. 2:12 13:17 [a] 1 Kin. 20:26 13:19 [a] 2 Kin. 13:25 13:20 [a] 2 Kin. 3:5; 24:2 13:22 [a] 2 Kin. 8:12, 13 13:23 [a] 2 Kin. 14:27 [b] [Ex. 2:24, 25] [c] Gen. 13:16, 17; 17:2–7; Ex. 32:13 13:25 [1] Spelled *Joash* in verses 12–14, 25

Jehoahaz his father by war. [a]Three times Joash defeated him and recaptured the cities of Israel.

## *AMAZIAH REIGNS IN JUDAH*

*(2 Chr. 25:1—26:2)*

**14** In [a]the second year of Joash the son of Jehoahaz, king of Israel, [b]Amaziah the son of Joash, king of Judah, became king. 2 He was twenty-five years old when he became king, and he reigned twenty-nine years in Jerusalem. His mother's name was Jehoaddan of Jerusalem. 3 And he did *what was* right in the sight of the LORD, yet not like his father David; he did everything [a]as his father Joash had done. 4 [a]However the high places were not taken away, and the people still sacrificed and burned incense on the high places.

5 Now it happened, as soon as the kingdom was established in his hand, that he executed his servants [a]who had murdered his father the king. 6 But the children of the murderers he did not execute, according to what is written in the Book of the Law of Moses, in which the LORD commanded, saying, [a]"Fathers shall not be put to death for their children, nor shall children be put to death for their fathers; but a person shall be put to death for his own sin."[1]

7 [a]He killed ten thousand Edomites in [b]the Valley of Salt, and took Sela by war, [c]and called its name Joktheel to this day.

8 [a]Then Amaziah sent messengers to Jehoash[1] the son of Jehoahaz, the son of Jehu, king of Israel, saying, "Come, let us face one another *in battle.*" 9 And Jehoash king of Israel sent to Amaziah king of Judah, saying, [a]"The thistle that *was* in Lebanon sent to the [b]cedar that *was* in Lebanon, saying, 'Give your daughter to my son as wife'; and a wild beast that *was* in Lebanon passed by and trampled the thistle. 10 You have indeed defeated Edom, and [a]your heart has lifted you up. Glory *in that,* and stay at home; for why should you meddle with trouble so that you fall—you and Judah with you?"

**14:9** The **cedar** trees of Lebanon might be compared to the redwood trees of California. Some cedars grow up to 100 feet tall, with trunks 45 feet in diameter. Jehoash insulted Amaziah by comparing the king of Judah's power and influence to a **thistle** and comparing his own power and influence to a cedar tree.

11 But Amaziah would not heed. Therefore Jehoash king of Israel went out; so he and Amaziah king of Judah faced one another at [a]Beth Shemesh, which *belongs* to Judah. 12 And Judah was defeated by Israel, and every man fled to his tent. 13 Then Jehoash king of Israel captured Amaziah king of Judah, the son of Jehoash, the son of Ahaziah, at Beth Shemesh; and he went to Jerusalem, and broke down the wall of Jerusalem from [a]the Gate of Ephraim to [b]the Corner Gate—four hundred cubits. 14 And he took all [a]the gold and silver, all the articles that were found in the house of the LORD and in the treasuries of the king's house, and hostages, and returned to Samaria.

15 [a]Now the rest of the acts of Jehoash which he did—his might, and how he fought with Amaziah king of Judah—*are* they not written in the book of the chronicles of the kings of Israel? 16 So Jehoash rested with his fathers, and was buried in Samaria with the kings of Israel. Then Jeroboam his son reigned in his place.

17 [a]Amaziah the son of Joash, king of Judah, lived fifteen years after the death of Jehoash the son of Jehoahaz, king of Israel. 18 Now the rest of the acts of Amaziah, *are* they not written in the book of the chronicles of the kings of Judah? 19 And [a]they formed a conspiracy against him in Jerusalem, and he fled to [b]Lachish; but they sent after him to Lachish and killed him there. 20 Then they brought him on horses, and he was buried at Jerusalem with his fathers in the City of David.

21 And all the people of Judah took [a]Azariah,[1] who *was* sixteen years old, and made him king instead of his father Amaziah. 22 He built [a]Elath and restored it to Judah, after the king rested with his fathers.

## *JEROBOAM II REIGNS IN ISRAEL*

23 In the fifteenth year of Amaziah the son of Joash, king of Judah, Jeroboam the son of Joash, king of Israel, became king in Samaria, *and reigned* forty-one years. 24 And he did evil in the sight of the LORD; he did not depart from all the [a]sins of Jeroboam the son of Nebat, who had made Israel sin. 25 He [a]restored the territory of Israel [b]from the entrance of Hamath to [c]the Sea of the Arabah, according to the word of the LORD God of Israel, which He had spoken through His servant [d]Jonah the son of Amittai, the prophet who *was* from [e]Gath Hepher. 26 For the LORD [a]saw *that* the affliction of Israel *was* very bitter; and whether bond or free, [b]there was no helper for Israel. 27 [a]And the LORD did not say that He would blot out the name of Israel from under heaven; but He saved them by the hand of Jeroboam the son of Joash.

**13:25** [a] 2 Kin. 13:18, 19 **14:1** [a] 2 Kin. 13:10 [b] 2 Chr. 25:1, 2 **14:3** [a] 2 Kin. 12:2 **14:4** [a] 2 Kin. 12:3 **14:5** [a] 2 Kin. 12:20 **14:6** [a] Deut. 24:16; [Jer. 31:30; Ezek. 18:4, 20] [1] Deuteronomy 24:16 **14:7** [a] 2 Chr. 25:5–16 [b] 2 Sam. 8:13; 1 Chr. 18:12; Ps. 60:title [c] Josh. 15:38 **14:8** [a] 2 Chr. 25:17, 18 [1] Spelled *Joash* in 13:12ff and 2 Chronicles 25:17ff **14:9** [a] Judg. 9:8–15 [b] 1 Kin. 4:33 **14:10** [a] Deut. 8:14; 2 Chr. 32:25; [Ezek. 28:2, 5, 17; Hab. 2:4] **14:11** [a] Josh. 19:38; 21:16 **14:13** [a] Neh. 8:16; 12:39 [b] Jer. 31:38; Zech. 14:10 **14:14** [a] 1 Kin. 7:51; 2 Kin. 12:18; 16:8 **14:15** [a] 2 Kin. 13:12, 13 **14:17** [a] 2 Chr. 25:25–28 **14:19** [a] 2 Chr. 25:27 [b] Josh. 10:31 **14:21** [a] 2 Kin. 15:13; 2 Chr. 26:1 [1] Called *Uzziah* in 2 Chronicles 26:1ff, Isaiah 6:1, and elsewhere **14:22** [a] 1 Kin. 9:26; 2 Kin. 16:6; 2 Chr. 8:17 **14:24** [a] 1 Kin. 12:26–33 **14:25** [a] 2 Kin. 10:32; 13:5, 25 [b] Num. 13:21; 34:8; 1 Kin. 8:65 [c] Deut. 3:17 [d] Jon. 1:1; Matt. 12:39, 40 [e] Josh. 19:13 **14:26** [a] Ex. 3:7; 2 Kin. 13:4; Ps. 106:44 [b] Deut. 32:36 **14:27** [a] [2 Kin. 13:5, 23]

28 Now the rest of the acts of Jeroboam, and all that he did—his might, how he made war, and how he recaptured for Israel, from [a]Damascus and Hamath, [b]*what had belonged* to Judah—*are* they not written in the book of the chronicles of the kings of Israel? 29 So Jeroboam rested with his fathers, the kings of Israel. Then [a]Zechariah his son reigned in his place.

### *AZARIAH REIGNS IN JUDAH*

*(2 Chr. 26:3–23)*

**15** In the twenty-seventh year of Jeroboam king of Israel, [a]Azariah the son of Amaziah, king of Judah, [b]became king. 2 He was sixteen years old when he became king, and he reigned fifty-two years in Jerusalem. His mother's name *was* Jecholiah of Jerusalem. 3 And he did *what was* right in the sight of the LORD, according to all that his father Amaziah had done, 4 [a]except that the high places were not removed; the people still sacrificed and burned incense on the high places. 5 Then the LORD [a]struck the king, so that he was a leper until the day of his [b]death; so he [c]dwelt in an isolated house. And Jotham the king's son *was* over the *royal* house, judging the people of the land.

6 Now the rest of the acts of Azariah, and all that he did, *are* they not written in the book of the chronicles of the kings of Judah? 7 So Azariah rested with his fathers, and [a]they buried him with his fathers in the City of David. Then Jotham his son reigned in his place.

### *ZECHARIAH REIGNS IN ISRAEL*

8 In the thirty-eighth year of Azariah king of Judah, [a]Zechariah the son of Jeroboam reigned over Israel in Samaria six months. 9 And he did evil in the sight of the LORD, [a]as his fathers had done; he did not depart from the sins of Jeroboam the son of Nebat, who had made Israel sin. 10 Then Shallum the son of Jabesh conspired against him, and [a]struck and killed him in front of the people; and he reigned in his place.

11 Now the rest of the acts of Zechariah, indeed they *are* written in the book of the chronicles of the kings of Israel.

12 This *was* the word of the LORD which He spoke to Jehu, saying, [a]"Your sons shall sit on the throne of Israel to the fourth *generation*."[1] And so it was.

### *SHALLUM REIGNS IN ISRAEL*

13 Shallum the son of Jabesh became king in the thirty-ninth year of Uzziah[1] king of Judah; and he reigned a full month in Samaria. 14 For Menahem the son of Gadi went up from [a]Tirzah, came to Samaria, and struck Shallum the son of Jabesh in Samaria and killed him; and he reigned in his place.

15 Now the rest of the acts of Shallum, and the conspiracy which he led, indeed they *are* written in the book of the chronicles of the kings of Israel.

16 Then from Tirzah, Menahem attacked [a]Tiphsah, all who *were* there, and its territory. Because they did not surrender, therefore he attacked *it*. All [b]the women there who were with child he ripped open.

### *MENAHEM REIGNS IN ISRAEL*

17 In the thirty-ninth year of Azariah king of Judah, Menahem the son of Gadi became king over Israel, *and reigned* ten years in Samaria. 18 And he did evil in the sight of the LORD; he did not depart all his days from the sins of Jeroboam the son of Nebat, who had made Israel sin. 19 [a]Pul[1] king of Assyria came against the land; and Menahem gave Pul a thousand talents of silver, that his hand might be with him to [b]strengthen the kingdom under his control. 20 And Menahem [a]exacted the money from Israel, from all the very wealthy, from each man fifty shekels of silver, to give to the king of Assyria. So the king of Assyria turned back, and did not stay there in the land.

21 Now the rest of the acts of Menahem, and all that he did, *are* they not written in the book of the chronicles of the kings of Israel? 22 So Menahem rested with his fathers. Then Pekahiah his son reigned in his place.

### *PEKAHIAH REIGNS IN ISRAEL*

23 In the fiftieth year of Azariah king of Judah, Pekahiah the son of Menahem became king over Israel in Samaria, *and reigned* two years. 24 And he did evil in the sight of the LORD; he did not depart from the sins of Jeroboam the son of Nebat, who had made Israel sin. 25 Then Pekah the son of Remaliah, an officer of his, conspired against him and killed him in Samaria, in the [a]citadel of the king's house, along with Argob and Arieh; and with him were fifty men of Gilead. He killed him and reigned in his place.

26 Now the rest of the acts of Pekahiah, and all that he did, indeed they *are* written in the book of the chronicles of the kings of Israel.

### *PEKAH REIGNS IN ISRAEL*

27 In the fifty-second year of Azariah king of Judah, [a]Pekah the son of Remaliah became king over Israel in Samaria, *and reigned* twenty years. 28 And he did evil in the sight of the LORD; he did not depart from the sins of Jeroboam the son of Nebat, who had made Israel sin. 29 In the days of Pekah king of Israel, Tiglath-Pileser king of Assyria [a]came and took [b]Ijon, Abel Beth Maachah, Janoah, Kedesh, Hazor, Gilead, and Galilee, all the land of Naphtali; and he [c]carried them captive to Assyria. 30 Then Hoshea the son of Elah led a conspiracy against Pekah the son of Remaliah, and

**14:28** [a] 1 Kin. 11:24 [b] 2 Sam. 8:6; 1 Kin. 11:24; 2 Chr. 8:3 **14:29** [a] 2 Kin. 15:8 **15:1** [a] 2 Kin. 15:13, 30 [b] 2 Kin. 14:21; 2 Chr. 26:1, 3, 4 **15:4** [a] 2 Kin. 12:3; 14:4; 15:35 **15:5** [a] 2 Chr. 26:19–23; Ps. 78:31 [b] Is. 6:1 [c] [Lev. 13:46]; Num. 12:14 **15:7** [a] 2 Chr. 26:23 **15:8** [a] 2 Kin. 14:29 **15:9** [a] 2 Kin. 14:24 **15:10** [a] Amos 7:9 **15:12** [a] 2 Kin. 10:30 [1] 2 Kings 10:30 **15:13** [1] Called *Azariah* in 14:21ff and 15:1ff **15:14** [a] 1 Kin. 14:17; Song 6:4 **15:16** [a] 1 Kin. 4:24 [b] 2 Kin. 8:12; Hos. 13:16 **15:19** [a] Hos. 8:9 [b] 2 Kin. 14:5 [1] That is, Tiglath-Pileser III (compare verse 29) **15:20** [a] 2 Kin. 23:35 **15:25** [a] 1 Kin. 16:18 **15:27** [a] 2 Chr. 28:6; Is. 7:1 **15:29** [a] 2 Kin. 16:7, 10; 1 Chr. 5:26 [b] 1 Kin. 15:20 [c] 2 Kin. 17:6

struck and killed him; so he [a]reigned in his place
in the twentieth year of Jotham the son of Uzziah.
31 Now the rest of the acts of Pekah, and all
that he did, indeed they *are* written in the book
of the chronicles of the kings of Israel.

### JOTHAM REIGNS IN JUDAH

*(2 Chr. 27:1–9)*

32 In the second year of Pekah the son of
Remaliah, king of Israel, [a]Jotham the son of
Uzziah, king of Judah, began to reign. 33 He was
twenty-five years old when he became king,
and he reigned sixteen years in Jerusalem. His
mother's name *was* Jerusha[1] the daughter of
Zadok. 34 And he did *what was* right in the sight
of the LORD; he did [a]according to all that his
father Uzziah had done. 35 [a]However the high
places were not removed; the people still sacri-
ficed and burned incense on the high places. [b]He
built the Upper Gate of the house of the LORD.
36 Now the rest of the acts of Jotham, and all
that he did, *are* they not written in the book of
the chronicles of the kings of Judah? 37 In those
days the LORD began to send [a]Rezin king of Syria
and [b]Pekah the son of Remaliah against Judah.
38 So Jotham rested with his fathers, and was
buried with his fathers in the City of David his
father. Then Ahaz his son reigned in his place.

### AHAZ REIGNS IN JUDAH

*(2 Chr. 28:1–27)*

**16** In the seventeenth year of Pekah the son of
Remaliah, Ahaz the son of Jotham, king of
Judah, began to reign. 2 Ahaz *was* twenty years
old when he became king, and he reigned sixteen
years in Jerusalem; and he did not do *what was*
right in the sight of the LORD his God, as his fa-
ther David *had done.* 3 But he walked in the way of
the kings of Israel; indeed [a]he made his son pass
through the fire, according to the [b]abominations
of the nations whom the LORD had cast out from
before the children of Israel. 4 And he sacrificed
and burned incense on the [a]high places, [b]on the
hills, and under every green tree.
5 [a]Then Rezin king of Syria and Pekah the
son of Remaliah, king of Israel, came up to Je-
rusalem to *make* war; and they besieged Ahaz
but could not overcome *him.* 6 At that time Rezin
king of Syria [a]captured Elath for Syria, and drove
the men of Judah from Elath. Then the Edom-
ites[1] went to Elath, and dwell there to this day.
7 So Ahaz sent messengers to [a]Tiglath-Pileser
king of Assyria, saying, "I *am* your servant and
your son. Come up and save me from the hand of
the king of Syria and from the hand of the king of
Israel, who rise up against me." 8 And Ahaz [a]took
the silver and gold that was found in the house of
the LORD, and in the treasuries of the king's house,
and sent *it as* a present to the king of Assyria. 9 So
the king of Assyria heeded him; for the king of
Assyria went up against [a]Damascus and [b]took it,
carried *its people* captive to [c]Kir, and killed Rezin.
10 Now King Ahaz went to Damascus to meet
Tiglath-Pileser king of Assyria, and saw an altar
that *was* at Damascus; and King Ahaz sent to
Urijah the priest the design of the altar and its
pattern, according to all its workmanship. 11 Then
[a]Urijah the priest built an altar according to all
that King Ahaz had sent from Damascus. So Uri-
jah the priest made *it* before King Ahaz came back
from Damascus. 12 And when the king came back
from Damascus, the king saw the altar; and [a]the
king approached the altar and made offerings
on it. 13 So he burned his burnt offering and his
grain offering; and he poured his drink offering
and sprinkled the blood of his peace offerings
on the altar. 14 He also brought [a]the bronze altar
which *was* before the LORD, from the front of
the temple—from between the *new* altar and the
house of the LORD—and put it on the north side
of the *new* altar. 15 Then King Ahaz commanded
Urijah the priest, saying, "On the great *new* altar
burn [a]the morning burnt offering, the evening
grain offering, the king's burnt sacrifice, and
his grain offering, with the burnt offering of all
the people of the land, their grain offering, and
their drink offerings; and sprinkle on it all the
blood of the burnt offering and all the blood of
the sacrifice. And the bronze altar shall be for
me to inquire *by.*" 16 Thus did Urijah the priest,
according to all that King Ahaz commanded.
17 [a]And King Ahaz cut off [b]the panels of the
carts, and removed the lavers from them; and
he took down [c]the Sea from the bronze oxen that
*were* under it, and put it on a pavement of stones.
18 Also he removed the Sabbath pavilion which
they had built in the temple, and he removed
the king's outer entrance from the house of the
LORD, on account of the king of Assyria.
19 Now the rest of the acts of Ahaz which
he did, *are* they not written in the book of the
chronicles of the kings of Judah? 20 So Ahaz
rested with his fathers, and [a]was buried with
his fathers in the City of David. Then Hezekiah
his son reigned in his place.

### HOSHEA REIGNS IN ISRAEL

**17** In the twelfth year of Ahaz king of Judah,
[a]Hoshea the son of Elah became king of
Israel in Samaria, *and he reigned* nine years.
2 And he did evil in the sight of the LORD, but
not as the kings of Israel who were before him.
3 [a]Shalmaneser king of Assyria came up against
him; and Hoshea [b]became his vassal, and paid

**15:30** [a] 2 Kin. 17:1; [Hos. 10:3, 7, 15] **15:32** [a] 2 Chr. 27:1 **15:33** [1] Spelled *Jerushah* in 2 Chronicles 27:1 **15:34** [a] 2 Kin. 15:3, 4; 2 Chr. 26:4, 5 **15:35** [a] 2 Kin. 15:4 [b] 2 Chr. 23:20; 27:3 **15:37** [a] 2 Kin. 16:5–9; Is. 7:1–17 [b] 2 Kin. 15:26, 27 **16:3** [a] [Lev. 18:21]; 2 Kin. 17:17; 2 Chr. 28:3; Ps. 106:37, 38; Is. 1:1 [b] [Deut. 12:31]; 2 Kin. 21:2, 11 **16:4** [a] 2 Kin. 15:34, 35 [b] [Deut. 12:2]; 1 Kin. 14:23 **16:5** [a] 2 Kin. 15:37; Is. 7:1, 4 **16:6** [a] 2 Kin. 14:22; 2 Chr. 26:2 [1] Some ancient authorities read *Syrians.* **16:7** [a] 2 Kin. 15:29; 1 Chr. 5:26; 2 Chr. 28:20 **16:8** [a] 2 Kin. 12:17, 18; 2 Chr. 28:21 **16:9** [a] 2 Kin. 14:28 [b] Amos 1:5 [c] Is. 22:6; Amos 9:7 **16:11** [a] Is. 8:2 **16:12** [a] 2 Chr. 26:16, 19 **16:14** [a] Ex. 27:1, 2; 40:6, 29; 2 Chr. 4:1 **16:15** [a] Ex. 29:39–41 **16:17** [a] 2 Chr. 28:24 [b] 1 Kin. 7:27–29 [c] 1 Kin. 7:23–25 **16:20** [a] 2 Chr. 28:27 **17:1** [a] 2 Kin. 15:30 **17:3** [a] 2 Kin. 18:9–12 [b] 2 Kin. 24:1

him tribute money. 4 And the king of Assyria un-
covered a conspiracy by Hoshea; for he had sent
messengers to So, king of Egypt, and brought
no tribute to the king of Assyria, as *he had done*
year by year. Therefore the king of Assyria shut
him up, and bound him in prison.

### *ISRAEL CARRIED CAPTIVE TO ASSYRIA*
*(2 Kin. 18:9–12)*

5 Now [a]the king of Assyria went throughout
all the land, and went up to Samaria and be-
sieged it for three years. 6 [a]In the ninth year of
Hoshea, the king of Assyria took Samaria and
[b]carried Israel away to Assyria, [c]and placed them
in Halah and by the Habor, the River of Gozan,
and in the cities of the Medes.

7 For [a]so it was that the children of Israel
had sinned against the LORD their God, who had
brought them up out of the land of Egypt, from
under the hand of Pharaoh king of Egypt; and
they had [b]feared other gods, 8 and [a]had walked
in the statutes of the nations whom the LORD
had cast out from before the children of Israel,
and of the kings of Israel, which they had made.
9 Also the children of Israel secretly did against
the LORD their God things that *were* not right,
and they built for themselves high places in all
their cities, [a]from watchtower to fortified city.
10 [a]They set up for themselves *sacred* pillars and
[b]wooden images[1] [c]on every high hill and under
every green tree. 11 There they burned incense
on all the high places, like the nations whom
the LORD had carried away before them; and
they did wicked things to provoke the LORD to
anger, 12 for they served idols, [a]of which the LORD
had said to them, [b]"You shall not do this thing."

13 Yet the LORD testified against Israel and
against Judah, by all of His [a]prophets, [b]every seer,
saying, [c]"Turn from your evil ways, and keep My
commandments *and* My statutes, according to
all the law which I commanded your fathers, and
which I sent to you by My servants the prophets."
14 Nevertheless they would not hear, but [a]stiff-
ened their necks, like the necks of their fathers,
who [b]did not believe in the LORD their God.
15 And they [a]rejected His statutes [b]and His cov-
enant that He had made with their fathers, and
His testimonies which He had testified against
them; they followed [c]idols, [d]became idolaters,
and *went* after the nations who *were* all around
them, *concerning* whom the LORD had charged
them that they should [e]not do like them. 16 So
they left all the commandments of the LORD
their God, [a]made for themselves a molded image
*and* two calves, [b]made a wooden image and wor-
shiped all the [c]host of heaven, [d]and served Baal.
17 [a]And they caused their sons and daughters to
pass through the fire, [b]practiced witchcraft and
soothsaying, and [c]sold themselves to do evil in
the sight of the LORD, to provoke Him to anger.
18 Therefore the LORD was very angry with Isra-
el, and removed them from His sight; there was
none left [a]but the tribe of Judah alone.

19 Also [a]Judah did not keep the command-
ments of the LORD their God, but walked in the
statutes of Israel which they made. 20 And the
LORD rejected all the descendants of Israel, af-
flicted them, and [a]delivered them into the hand
of plunderers, until He had cast them from His
[b]sight. 21 For [a]He tore Israel from the house of
David, and [b]they made Jeroboam the son of
Nebat king. Then Jeroboam drove Israel from
following the LORD, and made them commit a
great sin. 22 For the children of Israel walked in
all the sins of Jeroboam which he did; they did
not depart from them, 23 until the LORD removed
Israel out of His sight, [a]as He had said by all His
servants the prophets. [b]So Israel was carried away
from their own land to Assyria, *as it is* to this day.

### *ASSYRIA RESETTLES SAMARIA*

24 [a]Then the king of Assyria brought *people*
from Babylon, Cuthah, [b]Ava, Hamath, and from
Sepharvaim, and placed *them* in the cities of
Samaria instead of the children of Israel; and
they took possession of Samaria and dwelt in its
cities. 25 And it was so, at the beginning of their
dwelling there, *that* they did not fear the LORD;
therefore the LORD sent lions among them, which
killed *some* of them. 26 So they spoke to the king
of Assyria, saying, "The nations whom you have
removed and placed in the cities of Samaria do
not know the rituals of the God of the land; there-
fore He has sent lions among them, and indeed,
they are killing them because they do not know
the rituals of the God of the land." 27 Then the king
of Assyria commanded, saying, "Send there one
of the priests whom you brought from there; let
him go and dwell there, and let him teach them
the rituals of the God of the land." 28 Then one
of the priests whom they had carried away from
Samaria came and dwelt in Bethel, and taught
them how they should fear the LORD.

29 However every nation continued to make
gods of its own, and put *them* [a]in the shrines on
the high places which the Samaritans had made,
*every* nation in the cities where they dwelt. 30 The
men of [a]Babylon made Succoth Benoth, the men
of Cuth made Nergal, the men of Hamath made
Ashima, 31 [a]and the Avites made Nibhaz and
Tartak; and the Sepharvites [b]burned their chil-
dren in fire to Adrammelech and Anammelech,

17:5 [a]Hos. 13:16 17:6 [a]Hos. 1:4; 13:16 [b][Deut. 28:36, 64; 29:27, 28] [c]1 Chr. 5:26 17:7 [a][Josh. 23:16] [b]Judg. 6:10 17:8 [a][Lev. 18:3] 17:9 [a]2 Kin. 18:8 17:10 [a]Is. 57:5 [b][Ex. 34:12–14] [c][Deut. 12:2] [1]Hebrew *Asherim,* Canaanite deities 17:12 [a][Ex. 20:3–5] [b][Deut. 4:19] 17:13 [a]Neh. 9:29, 30 [b]1 Sam. 9:9 [c][Jer. 18:11; 25:5; 35:15] 17:14 [a][Acts 7:51] [b]Deut. 9:23 17:15 [a]Jer. 44:3 [b]Deut. 29:25 [c]Deut. 32:21 [d][Rom. 1:21–23] [e][Deut. 12:30, 31] 17:16 [a]1 Kin. 12:28 [b][1 Kin. 14:15] [c][Deut. 4:19] [d]1 Kin. 16:31; 22:53 17:17 [a]2 Kin. 16:3 [b][Deut. 18:10–12] [c]1 Kin. 21:20 17:18 [a]1 Kin. 11:13, 32 17:19 [a]Jer. 3:8 17:20 [a]2 Kin. 13:3; 15:29 [b]2 Kin. 24:20 17:21 [a]1 Kin. 11:11, 31 [b]1 Kin. 12:20, 28 17:23 [a]1 Kin. 14:16 [b]2 Kin. 17:6 17:24 [a]Ezra 4:2, 10 [b]2 Kin. 18:34 17:29 [a]1 Kin. 12:31; 13:32 17:30 [a]2 Kin. 17:24 17:31 [a]Ezra 4:9 [b][Lev. 18:21; Deut. 12:31]

2 KINGS 17:5–23

## ISRAEL'S FALL

31

STORY OF SCRIPTURE

### WHAT'S GOING ON?

This event marks the end of the northern kingdom of Israel due to its persistent disobedience and idolatry. The Israelites had forsaken the covenant with God, followed the practices of neighboring nations, and ignored God's prophets. Despite repeated warnings, they continued in their sinful ways, leading to their eventual conquest and exile. The people of Israel would one day return, but nothing would be the same. They would cease to be an autonomous nation. Instead, they would be ruled by other nations: Assyria, Babylon, Persia, and then Greece. Then, after a brief period of self-rule, they would be subjugated by the Romans. This history of captivity and oppression was the backdrop for Jesus coming and liberating God's people.

### WHAT DOES THIS MEAN FOR ME?

This passage challenges us to examine our lives for ways in which we might compromise our faith or ignore God's guidance. Additionally, this story highlights the importance of learning from the past. The Israelites ignored the lessons of their ancestors, leading to their downfall. It's crucial we remember the lessons of history and Scripture, allowing them to guide our choices and actions.

### DID YOU CATCH THE PATTERN?

The story of Israel's fall is part of a larger pattern in the Bible of God's justice and mercy. Time and again, we see God's people turn away from Him and face the consequences. Yet, God always offers a chance for repentance and restoration. This theme of justice and mercy culminates in the New Testament with the coming of Jesus. Through His life, death, and resurrection, Jesus provides the ultimate means for our restoration to God, offering forgiveness and new life to all who turn to Him. Thus, the northern kingdom's fall serves as a reminder of the need for faithfulness to God, while also pointing us to the hope and redemption found in Jesus Christ.

*For the next* Story of Scripture *reading and devotion, turn to 2 Chronicles 36:11–21 on page 456.*

the gods of Sepharvaim. 32 So they feared the
LORD, [a]and from every class they appointed for
themselves priests of the high places, who sacri-
ficed for them in the shrines of the high places.
33 [a]They feared the LORD, yet served their own
gods—according to the rituals of the nations
from among whom they were carried away.
34 To this day they continue practicing the
former rituals; they do not fear the LORD, nor
do they follow their statutes or their ordinances,
or the law and commandment which the LORD
had commanded the children of Jacob, [a]whom
He named Israel, 35 with whom the LORD had
made a covenant and charged them, saying:
[a]"You shall not fear other gods, nor [b]bow down to
them nor serve them nor sacrifice to them; 36 but
the LORD, who [a]brought you up from the land
of Egypt with great power and [b]an outstretched
arm, [c]Him you shall fear, Him you shall worship,
and to Him you shall offer sacrifice. 37 And the
statutes, the ordinances, the law, and the com-
mandment which He wrote for you, [a]you shall
be careful to observe forever; you shall not fear
other gods. 38 And the covenant that I have made
with you, [a]you shall not forget, nor shall you fear
other gods. 39 But the LORD your God you shall
fear; and He will deliver you from the hand of
all your enemies." 40 However they did not obey,
but they followed their former rituals. 41 [a]So these
nations feared the LORD, yet served their carved
images; also their children and their children's
children have continued doing as their fathers
did, even to this day.

### *HEZEKIAH REIGNS IN JUDAH*

*(2 Chr. 29:1, 2; 31:1)*

18 Now it came to pass in the third year of
[a]Hoshea the son of Elah, king of Israel, *that*
[b]Hezekiah the son of Ahaz, king of Judah, began
to reign. 2 He was twenty-five years old when he
became king, and he reigned twenty-nine years
in Jerusalem. His mother's name *was* [a]Abi[1] the
daughter of Zechariah. 3 And he did *what was*
right in the sight of the LORD, according to all
that his father David had done.
4 [a]He removed the high places and broke the
*sacred* pillars, cut down the wooden image[1] and
broke in pieces the [b]bronze serpent that Moses

**17:32** [a] 1 Kin. 12:31; 13:33 **17:33** [a] Zeph. 1:5 **17:34** [a] Gen. 32:28; 35:10 **17:35** [a] Judg. 6:10 [b] [Ex. 20:5] **17:36** [a] Ex. 14:15–30 [b] Ex. 6:6; 9:15 [c] [Deut. 10:20] **17:37** [a] Deut. 5:32 **17:38** [a] Deut. 4:23; 6:12 **17:41** [a] 2 Kin. 17:32, 33 **18:1** [a] 2 Kin. 17:1 [b] 2 Chr. 28:27; 29:1 **18:2** [a] Is. 38:5 [1] Called *Abijah* in 2 Chronicles 29:1ff **18:4** [a] 2 Chr. 31:1 [b] Num. 21:5–9 [1] Hebrew *Asherah*, a Canaanite goddess

had made; for until those days the children of
Israel burned incense to it, and called it Nehush-
tan.[2] 5 He [a]trusted in the LORD God of Israel, [b]so
that after him was none like him among all the
kings of Judah, nor who were before him. 6 For
he [a]held fast to the LORD; he did not depart from
following Him, but kept His commandments,
which the LORD had commanded Moses. 7 The
LORD [a]was with him; he [b]prospered wherever
he went. And he [c]rebelled against the king of
Assyria and did not serve him. 8 [a]He subdued
the Philistines, as far as Gaza and its territory,
[b]from watchtower to fortified city.
9 Now [a]it came to pass in the fourth year
of King Hezekiah, which *was* the seventh year
of Hoshea the son of Elah, king of Israel, *that*
Shalmaneser king of Assyria came up against Sa-
maria and besieged it. 10 And at the end of three
years they took it. In the sixth year of Hezekiah,
that *is,* [a]the ninth year of Hoshea king of Israel,
Samaria was taken. 11 [a]Then the king of Assyria
carried Israel away captive to Assyria, and put
them [b]in Halah and by the Habor, the River of
Gozan, and in the cities of the Medes, 12 because
they [a]did not obey the voice of the LORD their
God, but transgressed His covenant *and* all that
Moses the servant of the LORD had commanded;
and they would neither hear nor do *them.*
13 And [a]in the fourteenth year of King Hez-
ekiah, Sennacherib king of Assyria came up
against all the fortified cities of Judah and took
them. 14 Then Hezekiah king of Judah sent to
the king of Assyria at Lachish, saying, "I have
done wrong; turn away from me; whatever you
impose on me I will pay." And the king of Assyria
assessed Hezekiah king of Judah three hundred
talents of silver and thirty talents of gold. 15 So
Hezekiah [a]gave *him* all the silver that was found
in the house of the LORD and in the treasuries
of the king's house. 16 At that time Hezekiah
stripped *the gold from* the doors of the temple
of the LORD, and *from* the pillars which Heze-
kiah king of Judah had overlaid, and gave it to
the king of Assyria.

18:4 [2] Literally *Bronze Thing* 18:5 [a] 2 Kin. 19:10; [Job 13:15; Ps. 13:5] [b] 2 Kin. 23:25 18:6 [a] Deut. 10:20; Josh. 23:8 18:7 [a] [2 Chr. 15:2] [b] Gen. 39:2, 3; 1 Sam. 18:5, 14; Ps. 60:12 [c] 2 Kin. 16:7 18:8 [a] 1 Chr. 4:41; 2 Chr. 28:18; Is. 14:29 [b] 2 Kin. 17:9 18:9 [a] 2 Kin. 17:3 18:10 [a] 2 Kin. 17:6 18:11 [a] 2 Kin. 17:6; Hos. 1:4; Amos 4:2 [b] 1 Chr. 5:26 18:12 [a] 2 Kin. 17:7–18 18:13 [a] 2 Chr. 32:1; Is. 36:1—39:8 18:15 [a] 1 Kin. 15:18, 19; 2 Kin. 12:18; 16:8

## THE EXILE OF THE NORTHERN KINGDOM

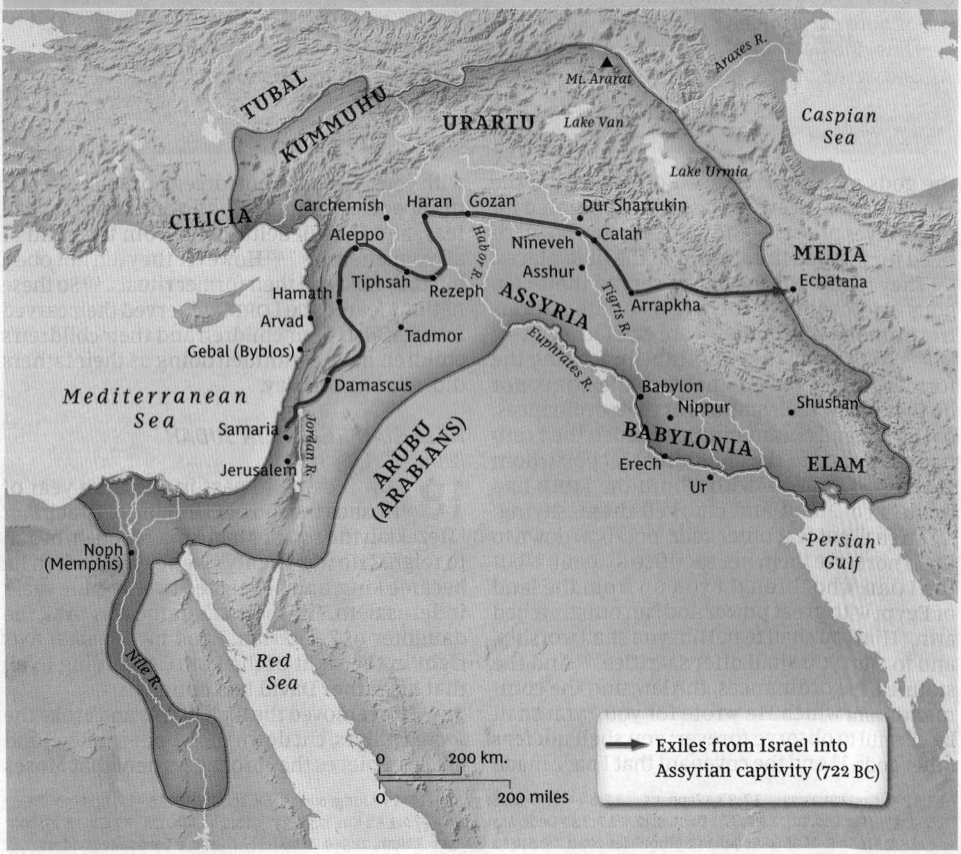

**18:14** Sennacherib, the king of Assyria, was so proud of his victory in **Lachish** that he had a scene of the battle recreated on one of the walls of his palace in Nineveh. The scene showed his Assyrian soldiers attacking with battering rams and other weapons while the inhabitants of Lachish tried to defend themselves with bows and arrows.

### *SENNACHERIB BOASTS AGAINST THE LORD*

*(Is. 36:2–22; 2 Chr. 32:9–15)*

17 Then the king of Assyria sent *the* Tartan,[1] *the* Rabsaris,[2] *and the* Rabshakeh[3] from Lachish, with a great army against Jerusalem, to King Hezekiah. And they went up and came to Jerusalem. When they had come up, they went and stood by the [a]aqueduct from the upper pool, [b]which *was* on the highway to the Fuller's Field. 18 And when they had called to the king, [a]Eliakim the son of Hilkiah, who *was* over the household, Shebna the scribe, and Joah the son of Asaph, the recorder, came out to them. 19 Then *the* Rabshakeh said to them, "Say now to Hezekiah, 'Thus says the great king, the king of Assyria: [a]"What confidence *is* this in which you trust? 20 You speak of *having* plans and power for war; but *they are* mere words. And in whom do you trust, that you rebel against me? 21 [a]Now look! You are trusting in the staff of this broken reed, Egypt, on which if a man leans, it will go into his hand and pierce it. So *is* Pharaoh king of Egypt to all who trust in him. 22 But if you say to me, 'We trust in the LORD our God,' *is* it not He [a]whose high places and whose altars Hezekiah has taken away, and said to Judah and Jerusalem, 'You shall worship before this altar in Jerusalem'?" ' 23 Now therefore, I urge you, give a pledge to my master the king of Assyria, and I will give you two thousand horses—if you are able on your part to put riders on them! 24 How then will you repel one captain of the least of my master's servants, and put your trust in Egypt for chariots and horsemen? 25 Have I now come up without the LORD against this place to destroy it? The LORD said to me, 'Go up against this land, and destroy it.' "

26 [a]Then Eliakim the son of Hilkiah, Shebna, and Joah said to *the* Rabshakeh, "Please speak to your servants in [b]Aramaic, for we understand *it;* and do not speak to us in Hebrew[1] in the hearing of the people who *are* on the wall."

27 But *the* Rabshakeh said to them, "Has my master sent me to your master and to you to speak these words, and not to the men who sit on the wall, who will eat and drink their own waste with you?"

28 Then *the* Rabshakeh stood and called out with a loud voice in Hebrew, and spoke, saying, "Hear the word of the great king, the king of Assyria! 29 Thus says the king: [a]'Do not let Hezekiah deceive you, for he shall not be able to deliver you from his hand; 30 nor let Hezekiah make you trust in the LORD, saying, "The LORD will surely deliver us; this city shall not be given into the hand of the king of Assyria." ' 31 Do not listen to Hezekiah; for thus says the king of Assyria: 'Make *peace* with me by a present and come out to me; and every one of you eat from his own [a]vine and every one from his own fig tree, and every one of you drink the waters of his own cistern; 32 until I come and take you away to a land like your own land, [a]a land of grain and new wine, a land of bread and vineyards, a land of olive groves and honey, that you may live and not die. But do not listen to Hezekiah, lest he persuade you, saying, "The LORD will deliver us." 33 [a]Has any of the gods of the nations at all delivered its land from the hand of the king of Assyria? 34 Where *are* the gods of [a]Hamath and Arpad? Where *are* the gods of Sepharvaim and Hena and [b]Ivah? Indeed, have they delivered Samaria from my hand? 35 Who among all the gods of the lands have delivered their countries from my hand, [a]that the LORD should deliver Jerusalem from my hand?' "

36 But the people held their peace and answered him not a word; for the king's commandment was, "Do not answer him." 37 Then Eliakim the son of Hilkiah, who *was* over the household, Shebna the scribe, and Joah the son of Asaph, the recorder, came to Hezekiah [a]with *their* clothes torn, and told him the words of *the* Rabshakeh.

### *ISAIAH ASSURES DELIVERANCE*

*(Is. 37:1–7)*

**19** And [a]so it was, when King Hezekiah heard *it,* that he tore his clothes, covered himself with [b]sackcloth, and went into the house of the LORD. 2 Then he sent Eliakim, who *was* over the household, Shebna the scribe, and the elders of the priests, covered with sackcloth, to Isaiah the prophet, the son of Amoz. 3 And they said to him, "Thus says Hezekiah: 'This day *is* a day of trouble, and rebuke, and blasphemy; for the children have come to birth, but *there is* no strength to bring them forth. 4 [a]It may be that the LORD your God will hear all the words of *the* Rabshakeh, whom his master the king of Assyria has sent to [b]reproach the living God, and will [c]rebuke the words which the LORD your God has heard. Therefore lift up *your* prayer for the remnant that is left.' "

5 So the servants of King Hezekiah came to Isaiah. 6 [a]And Isaiah said to them, "Thus you

**18:17** [a] 2 Kin. 20:20 [b] Is. 7:3 [1] A title, probably *Commander in Chief* [2] A title, probably *Chief Officer* [3] A title, probably *Chief of Staff* or *Governor* **18:18** [a] 2 Kin. 19:2; Is. 22:20 **18:19** [a] 2 Chr. 32:10; [Ps. 118:8, 9] **18:21** [a] Is. 30:2–7; Ezek. 29:6, 7 **18:22** [a] 2 Kin. 18:4; 2 Chr. 31:1; 32:12 **18:26** [a] Is. 36:11—39:8 [b] Ezra 4:7; Dan. 2:4 [1] Literally *Judean* **18:29** [a] 2 Chr. 32:15 **18:31** [a] 1 Kin. 4:20, 25 **18:32** [a] Deut. 8:7–9; 11:12 **18:33** [a] 2 Kin. 19:12; Is. 10:10, 11 **18:34** [a] 2 Kin. 19:13 [b] 2 Kin. 17:24 **18:35** [a] Dan. 3:15 **18:37** [a] Is. 33:7 **19:1** [a] 2 Kin. 18:13; 2 Chr. 32:20–22; Is. 37:1 [b] Ps. 69:11 **19:4** [a] 2 Sam. 16:12 [b] 2 Kin. 18:35 [c] Ps. 50:21 **19:6** [a] Is. 37:6

**19:2** The ministry of the prophet **Isaiah** had begun in the year that Uzziah (or Azariah) died (Is. 6:1), nearly four decades earlier (740 BC). Once Isaiah had sought out Judah's godless King Ahaz to minister to him (Is. 7:3); now the prophet was being sought by the godly Hezekiah (see Is. 36–39).

shall say to your master, 'Thus says the LORD:
"Do not be [b]afraid of the words which you have
heard, with which the [c]servants of the king of
Assyria have blasphemed Me. 7 Surely I will send
[a]a spirit upon him, and he shall hear a rumor
and return to his own land; and I will cause him
to fall by the sword in his own land." ' "

### *SENNACHERIB'S THREAT AND HEZEKIAH'S PRAYER*

*(Is. 37:8–20)*

8 Then *the* Rabshakeh returned and found
the king of Assyria warring against Libnah, for
he heard that he had departed [a]from Lachish.
9 And [a]the king heard concerning Tirhakah king
of Ethiopia, "Look, he has come out to make
war with you." So he again sent messengers to
Hezekiah, saying, 10 "Thus you shall speak to
Hezekiah king of Judah, saying: 'Do not let your
God [a]in whom you trust deceive you, saying,
"Jerusalem shall not be given into the hand of
the king of Assyria." 11 Look! You have heard what
the kings of Assyria have done to all lands by
utterly destroying them; and shall you be deliv-
ered? 12 [a]Have the gods of the nations delivered
those whom my fathers have destroyed, Gozan
and Haran and Rezeph, and the people of [b]Eden
who *were* in Telassar? 13 [a]Where *is* the king of
Hamath, the king of Arpad, and the king of the
city of Sepharvaim, Hena, and Ivah?' "

14 [a]And Hezekiah received the letter from
the hand of the messengers, and read it; and
Hezekiah went up to the house of the LORD,
and spread it before the LORD. 15 Then Hezeki-
ah prayed before the LORD, and said: "O LORD
God of Israel, *the One* [a]who dwells *between* the
cherubim, [b]You are God, You alone, of all the
kingdoms of the earth. You have made heaven
and earth. 16 [a]Incline Your ear, O LORD, and hear;
[b]open Your eyes, O LORD, and see; and hear
the words of Sennacherib, [c]which he has sent
to reproach the living God. 17 Truly, LORD, the
kings of Assyria have laid waste the nations and
their lands, 18 and have cast their gods into the
fire; for they *were* [a]not gods, but [b]the work of
men's hands—wood and stone. Therefore they
destroyed them. 19 Now therefore, O LORD our
God, I pray, save us from his hand, [a]that all the
kingdoms of the earth may [b]know that You *are*
the LORD God, You alone."

### *THE WORD OF THE LORD CONCERNING SENNACHERIB*

*(Is. 37:21–35)*

20 Then Isaiah the son of Amoz sent to Hez-
ekiah, saying, "Thus says the LORD God of Is-
rael: [a]'Because you have prayed to Me against
Sennacherib king of Assyria, [b]I have heard.'
21 This *is* the word which the LORD has spoken
concerning him:

'The virgin, [a]the daughter of Zion,
Has despised you, laughed you to scorn;
The daughter of Jerusalem
[b]Has shaken *her* head behind your back!

22 'Whom have you reproached and
blasphemed?
Against whom have you raised *your* voice,
And lifted up your eyes on high?
Against [a]the Holy *One* of Israel.
23 [a]By your messengers you have reproached
the Lord,
And said: [b]"By the multitude of my
chariots
I have come up to the height of the
mountains,
To the limits of Lebanon;
I will cut down its tall cedars
*And* its choice cypress trees;
I will enter the extremity of its borders,
*To* its fruitful forest.
24 I have dug and drunk strange water,
And with the soles of my feet I have
[a]dried up
All the brooks of defense."

25 'Did you not hear long ago
*How* [a]I made it,
From ancient times that I formed it?
Now I have brought it to pass,
That [b]you should be
For crushing fortified cities *into* heaps of
ruins.
26 Therefore their inhabitants had little
power;
They were dismayed and confounded;
They were *as* the grass of the field
And the green herb,
*As* [a]the grass on the housetops
And *grain* blighted before it is grown.

27 'But [a]I know your dwelling place,
Your going out and your coming in,
And your rage against Me.

19:6 [b] [Ps. 112:7] [c] 2 Kin. 18:17 19:7 [a] 2 Kin. 19:35–37; Jer. 51:1 19:8 [a] 2 Kin. 18:14, 17 19:9 [a] 1 Sam. 23:27; Is. 37:9 19:10 [a] 2 Kin. 18:5 19:12 [a] 2 Kin. 18:33, 34 [b] Ezek. 27:23 19:13 [a] 2 Kin. 18:34 19:14 [a] Is. 37:14 19:15 [a] Ex. 25:22; Ps. 80:1; Is. 37:16 [b] [Is. 44:6] 19:16 [a] Ps. 31:2; Is. 37:17 [b] 1 Kin. 8:29; 2 Chr. 6:40 [c] 2 Kin. 19:4 19:18 [a] [Is. 44:9–20; Jer. 10:3–5] [b] Ps. 115:4; Jer. 10:3; [Acts 17:29] 19:19 [a] Ps. 83:18 [b] 1 Kin. 8:42, 43 19:20 [a] Is. 37:21 [b] 2 Kin. 20:5; Ps. 65:2 19:21 [a] Jer. 14:17; Lam. 2:13 [b] Ps. 22:7, 8 19:22 [a] Jer. 51:5 19:23 [a] 2 Kin. 18:17 [b] Ps. 20:7 19:24 [a] Is. 19:6 19:25 [a] [Is. 45:7] [b] Is. 10:5, 6 19:26 [a] Ps. 129:6 19:27 [a] Ps. 139:1–3; Is. 37:28

28 Because your rage against Me and your
tumult
Have come up to My ears,
Therefore [a]I will put My hook in your
nose
And My bridle in your lips,
And I will turn you back
[b]By the way which you came.

29 'This *shall be* a [a]sign to you:

'You shall eat this year such as grows of
itself,
And in the second year what springs from
the same;
Also in the third year sow and reap,
Plant vineyards and eat the fruit of them.
30 [a]And the remnant who have escaped of the
house of Judah
Shall again take root downward,
And bear fruit upward.
31 For out of Jerusalem shall go a remnant,
And those who escape from Mount Zion.
[a]The zeal of the LORD of hosts[1] will do
this.'

32 "Therefore thus says the LORD concerning
the king of Assyria:

'He shall [a]not come into this city,
Nor shoot an arrow there,
Nor come before it with shield,
Nor build a siege mound against it.
33 By the way that he came,
By the same shall he return;
And he shall not come into this city,'
Says the LORD.
34 'For [a]I will [b]defend this city, to save it
For My own sake and [c]for My servant
David's sake.' "

### *SENNACHERIB'S DEFEAT AND DEATH*
*(Is. 37:36–38; 2 Chr. 32:20–23)*

35 And [a]it came to pass on a certain night
that the angel[1] of the LORD went out, and killed
in the camp of the Assyrians one hundred and
eighty-five thousand; and when *people* arose
early in the morning, there were the corpses—all
dead. 36 So Sennacherib king of Assyria departed
and went away, returned *home,* and remained
at [a]Nineveh. 37 Now it came to pass, as he was
worshiping in the temple of Nisroch his god, that
his sons [a]Adrammelech and Sharezer [b]struck
him down with the sword; and they escaped
into the land of Ararat. Then [c]Esarhaddon his
son reigned in his place.

### *HEZEKIAH'S LIFE EXTENDED*
*(2 Chr. 32:24–26; Is. 38:1–8)*

20 In [a]those days Hezekiah was sick and near
death. And Isaiah the prophet, the son of
Amoz, went to him and said to him, "Thus says
the LORD: 'Set your house in order, for you shall
die, and not live.' "
2 Then he turned his face toward the wall,
and prayed to the LORD, saying, 3 [a]"Remember
now, O LORD, I pray, how I have walked before
You in truth and with a loyal heart, and have
done *what was* good in Your sight." And Heze-
kiah wept bitterly.
4 And it happened, before Isaiah had gone
out into the middle court, that the word of the
LORD came to him, saying, 5 "Return and tell
Hezekiah [a]the leader of My people, 'Thus says
the LORD, the God of David your father: [b]"I have
heard your prayer, I have seen [c]your tears; surely
I will heal you. On the third day you shall go up
to the house of the LORD. 6 And I will add to your
days fifteen years. I will deliver you and this
city from the hand of the king of Assyria; and
[a]I will defend this city for My own sake, and for
the sake of My servant David." ' "

> **SEEING JESUS IN THE SCRIPTURE**
>
> **20:2–6** Hezekiah called to the Lord to save him from death. God heard his prayer and added fifteen years to his life. Today, when people call on the name of Jesus to save them, God hears and gives them eternal life (see Rom. 10:13).

7 Then [a]Isaiah said, "Take a lump of figs."
So they took and laid *it* on the boil, and he
recovered.
8 And Hezekiah said to Isaiah, [a]"What *is*
the sign that the LORD will heal me, and that I
shall go up to the house of the LORD the third
day?"
9 Then Isaiah said, [a]"This is the sign to you
from the LORD, that the LORD will do the thing
which He has spoken: *shall* the shadow go for-
ward ten degrees or go backward ten degrees?"
10 And Hezekiah answered, "It is an easy
thing for the shadow to go down ten de-
grees; no, but let the shadow go backward ten
degrees."
11 So Isaiah the prophet cried out to the LORD,
and [a]He brought the shadow ten degrees back-
ward, by which it had gone down on the sundial
of Ahaz.

**19:28** [a]Job 41:2; Ezek. 29:4; 38:4; Amos 4:2 [b]2 Kin. 19:33, 36 **19:29** [a]Ex. 3:12; 1 Sam. 2:34; 2 Kin. 20:8, 9; Is. 7:11–14; Luke 2:12 **19:30** [a]2 Kin. 19:4; 2 Chr. 32:22, 23 **19:31** [a]2 Kin. 25:26; Is. 9:7 [1]Following many Hebrew manuscripts and ancient versions (compare Isaiah 37:32); Masoretic Text omits *of hosts.* **19:32** [a]Is. 8:7–10 **19:34** [a]2 Kin. 20:6; 2 Chr. 32:21 [b]Is. 31:5 [c]1 Kin. 11:12, 13 **19:35** [a]Ex. 12:29; Is. 10:12–19; 37:36; Hos. 1:7 [1]Or *Angel* **19:36** [a]Gen. 10:11 **19:37** [a]2 Kin. 17:31 [b]2 Kin. 19:7; 2 Chr. 32:21 [c]Ezra 4:2 **20:1** [a]2 Kin. 18:13; 2 Chr. 32:24; Is. 38:1–22 **20:3** [a]2 Kin. 18:3–6; Neh. 13:22 **20:5** [a]1 Sam. 9:16; 10:1 [b]2 Kin. 19:20; Ps. 65:2 [c]Ps. 39:12; 56:8 **20:6** [a]2 Kin. 19:34; 2 Chr. 32:21 **20:7** [a]Is. 38:21 **20:8** [a]Judg. 6:17, 37, 39; Is. 7:11, 14; 38:22 **20:9** [a]Num. 23:19; Is. 38:7, 8 **20:11** [a]Josh. 10:12–14; Is. 38:8

### *THE BABYLONIAN ENVOYS*
*(Is. 39:1–8)*

12 [a]At that time Berodach-Baladan[1] the son of Baladan, king of Babylon, sent letters and a present to Hezekiah, for he heard that Hezekiah had been sick. 13 And [a]Hezekiah was attentive to them, and showed them all the house of his treasures—the silver and gold, the spices and precious ointment, and all[1] his armory—all that was found among his treasures. There was nothing in his house or in all his dominion that Hezekiah did not show them.

14 Then Isaiah the prophet went to King Hezekiah, and said to him, "What did these men say, and from where did they come to you?"

So Hezekiah said, "They came from a far country, from Babylon."

15 And he said, "What have they seen in your house?"

So Hezekiah answered, [a]"They have seen all that *is* in my house; there is nothing among my treasures that I have not shown them."

16 Then Isaiah said to Hezekiah, "Hear the word of the LORD: 17 'Behold, the days are coming when all that *is* in your house, and what your fathers have accumulated until this day, [a]shall be carried to Babylon; nothing shall be left,' says the LORD. 18 'And [a]they shall take away some of your sons who will descend from you, whom you will beget; [b]and they shall be [c]eunuchs in the palace of the king of Babylon.' "

19 So Hezekiah said to Isaiah, [a]"The word of the LORD which you have spoken *is* good!" For he said, "Will there not be peace and truth at least in my days?"

### *DEATH OF HEZEKIAH*
*(2 Chr. 32:32, 33)*

20 [a]Now the rest of the acts of Hezekiah—all his might, and how he [b]made a [c]pool and a tunnel and [d]brought water into the city—*are* they not written in the book of the chronicles of the kings of Judah? 21 So [a]Hezekiah rested with his fathers. Then Manasseh his son reigned in his place.

### *MANASSEH REIGNS IN JUDAH*
*(2 Chr. 33:1–20)*

**21** Manasseh [a]*was* twelve years old when he became king, and he reigned fifty-five years in Jerusalem. His mother's name *was* Hephzibah. 2 And he did evil in the sight of the LORD, [a]according to the abominations of the nations whom the LORD had cast out before the children of Israel. 3 For he rebuilt the high places [a]which Hezekiah his father had destroyed; he raised up altars for Baal, and made a wooden image,[1] [b]as Ahab king of Israel had done; and he [c]worshiped all the host of heaven[2] and served them. 4 [a]He also built altars in the house of the LORD, of which the LORD had said, [b]"In Jerusalem I will put My name." 5 And he built altars for all the host of heaven in the [a]two courts of the house of the LORD. 6 [a]Also he made his son pass through the fire, practiced [b]soothsaying, used witchcraft, and consulted spiritists and mediums. He did much evil in the sight of the LORD, to provoke *Him* to anger. 7 He even set a carved image of Asherah[1] that he had made, in the house of which the LORD had said to David and to Solomon his son, [a]"In this house and in Jerusalem, which I have chosen out of all the tribes of Israel, I will put My name forever; 8 [a]and I will not make the feet of Israel wander anymore from the land which I gave their fathers—only if they are careful to do according to all that I have commanded them, and according to all the law that My servant Moses commanded them." 9 But they paid no attention, and Manasseh [a]seduced them to do more evil than the nations whom the LORD had destroyed before the children of Israel.

10 And the LORD spoke [a]by His servants the prophets, saying, 11 [a]"Because Manasseh king of Judah has done these abominations ([b]he has acted more wickedly than all the [c]Amorites who *were* before him, and [d]has also made Judah sin with his idols), 12 therefore thus says the LORD God of Israel: 'Behold, *I* am bringing *such* calamity upon Jerusalem and Judah, that whoever hears of it, both [a]his ears will tingle. 13 And I will stretch over Jerusalem [a]the measuring line of Samaria and the plummet of the house of Ahab; [b]I will wipe Jerusalem as *one* wipes a dish, wiping *it* and turning *it* upside down. 14 So I will forsake the [a]remnant of My inheritance and deliver them into the hand of their enemies; and they shall become victims of plunder to all their enemies, 15 because they have done evil in My sight, and have provoked Me to anger since the day their fathers came out of Egypt, even to this day.' "

16 [a]Moreover Manasseh shed very much innocent blood, till he had filled Jerusalem from one end to another, besides his sin by which he made Judah sin, in doing evil in the sight of the LORD.

17 Now [a]the rest of the acts of [b]Manasseh—all that he did, and the sin that he committed—*are* they not written in the book of the chronicles of

20:12 [a] 2 Kin. 8:8, 9; 2 Chr. 32:31; Is. 39:1–8 [1] Spelled *Merodach-Baladan* in Isaiah 39:1 20:13 [a] 2 Kin. 16:9; 2 Chr. 32:27, 31 [1] Following many Hebrew manuscripts, Syriac, and Targum; Masoretic Text omits *all.* 20:15 [a] 2 Kin. 20:13 20:17 [a] Jer. 27:21, 22; 52:17 20:18 [a] 2 Kin. 24:12 [b] Dan. 1:3–7 [c] Dan. 1:11, 18 20:19 [a] 1 Sam. 3:18 20:20 [a] 2 Chr. 32:32 [b] Neh. 3:16 [c] Is. 7:3 [d] 2 Chr. 32:3, 30 20:21 [a] 2 Chr. 32:33 21:1 [a] 2 Chr. 33:1–9 21:2 [a] 2 Kin. 16:3 21:3 [a] 2 Kin. 18:4, 22 [b] 1 Kin. 16:31–33 [c] [Deut. 4:19; 17:2–5] [1] Hebrew *Asherah,* a Canaanite goddess [2] The gods of the Assyrians 21:4 [a] Jer. 7:30; 32:34 [b] 1 Kin. 11:13 21:5 [a] 1 Kin. 6:36; 7:12 21:6 [a] [Lev. 18:21; 20:2] [b] [Deut. 18:10–14] 21:7 [a] 1 Kin. 8:29; 9:3 [1] A Canaanite goddess 21:8 [a] 2 Sam. 7:10 21:9 [a] [Prov. 29:12] 21:10 [a] 2 Kin. 17:13 21:11 [a] 2 Kin. 23:26, 27; 24:3, 4 [b] 1 Kin. 21:26 [c] Gen. 15:16 [d] 2 Kin. 21:9 21:12 [a] Jer. 19:3 21:13 [a] Amos 7:7, 8 [b] 2 Kin. 22:16–19; 25:4–11 21:14 [a] Jer. 6:9 21:16 [a] 2 Kin. 24:4 21:17 [a] 2 Chr. 33:11–19 [b] 2 Kin. 20:21

> **21:16** Of all the kings who reigned in Israel and Judah, **Manasseh** held the throne longest. That's unfortunate because Manasseh was truly evil. He built altars to pagan gods, reintroduced astrology to the Israelites, and practiced witchcraft. Along the way, he also put many innocent people to death. As if that weren't enough, Jewish tradition says Manasseh put Isaiah to death by ordering that the prophet be sawed in half.

the kings of Judah? 18 So [a]Manasseh rested with
his fathers, and was buried in the garden of his
own house, in the garden of Uzza. Then his son
Amon reigned in his place.

### *AMON'S REIGN AND DEATH*

*(2 Chr. 33:21–25)*

19 [a]Amon *was* twenty-two years old when he
became king, and he reigned two years in Jerusa-
lem. His mother's name *was* Meshullemeth the
daughter of Haruz of Jotbah. 20 And he did evil
in the sight of the LORD, [a]as his father Manasseh
had done. 21 So he walked in all the ways that his
father had walked; and he served the idols that
his father had served, and worshiped them. 22 He
[a]forsook the LORD God of his fathers, and did
not walk in the way of the LORD.
23 [a]Then the servants of Amon [b]conspired
against him, and killed the king in his own
house. 24 But the people of the land [a]executed
all those who had conspired against King Amon.
Then the people of the land made his son Josiah
king in his place.
25 Now the rest of the acts of Amon which
he did, *are* they not written in the book of the
chronicles of the kings of Judah? 26 And he was
buried in his tomb in the garden of Uzza. Then
Josiah his son reigned in his place.

### *JOSIAH REIGNS IN JUDAH*

*(2 Chr. 34:1, 2)*

**22** Josiah [a]*was* eight years old when he be-
came king, and he reigned thirty-one
years in Jerusalem. His mother's name *was*
Jedidah the daughter of Adaiah of [b]Bozkath.
2 And he did *what was* right in the sight of the
LORD, and walked in all the ways of his father
David; he [a]did not turn aside to the right hand
or to the left.

### *HILKIAH FINDS THE BOOK OF THE LAW*

*(2 Chr. 34:8–28)*

3 [a]Now it came to pass, in the eighteenth year
of King Josiah, *that* the king sent Shaphan the
scribe, the son of Azaliah, the son of Meshullam,
to the house of the LORD, saying: 4 "Go up to Hilki-
ah the high priest, that he may count the money
which has been [a]brought into the house of the
LORD, which [b]the doorkeepers have gathered
from the people. 5 And let them [a]deliver it into
the hand of those doing the work, who are the
overseers in the house of the LORD; let them give
it to those who *are* in the house of the LORD doing
the work, to repair the damages of the house—
6 to carpenters and builders and masons—and to
buy timber and hewn stone to repair the house.
7 However [a]there need be no accounting made
with them of the money delivered into their
hand, because they deal faithfully."
8 Then Hilkiah the high priest said to Sha-
phan the scribe, [a]"I have found the Book of the
Law in the house of the LORD." And Hilkiah gave
the book to Shaphan, and he read it. 9 So Sha-
phan the scribe went to the king, bringing the
king word, saying, "Your servants have gathered
the money that was found in the house, and
have delivered it into the hand of those who do
the work, who oversee the house of the LORD."
10 Then Shaphan the scribe showed the king,
saying, "Hilkiah the priest has given me a book."
And Shaphan read it before the king.

> **22:8 The Book of the Law** may mean either parts of or all the Pentateuch. Although it was placed by the side of the ark of the covenant (see Deut. 31:26), it may have been lost, set aside, or hidden during the wicked reigns of Manasseh and Amon.

11 Now it happened, when the king heard the
words of the Book of the Law, that he tore his
clothes. 12 Then the king commanded Hilkiah the
priest, [a]Ahikam the son of Shaphan, Achbor[1] the
son of Michaiah, Shaphan the scribe, and Asaiah
a servant of the king, saying, 13 "Go, inquire of the
LORD for me, for the people and for all Judah,
concerning the words of this book that has been
found; for great *is* [a]the wrath of the LORD that is
aroused against us, because our fathers have not
obeyed the words of this book, to do according
to all that is written concerning us."
14 So Hilkiah the priest, Ahikam, Achbor,
Shaphan, and Asaiah went to Huldah the proph-
etess, the wife of Shallum the son of [a]Tikvah,
the son of Harhas, keeper of the wardrobe. (She
dwelt in Jerusalem in the Second Quarter.) And
they spoke with her. 15 Then she said to them,
"Thus says the LORD God of Israel, 'Tell the man
who sent you to Me, 16 "Thus says the LORD:

**21:18** [a] 2 Chr. 33:20 **21:19** [a] 2 Chr. 33:21–23 **21:20** [a] 2 Kin. 21:2–6, 11, 16 **21:22** [a] Judg. 2:12, 13; 1 Kin. 11:33; 1 Chr. 28:9 **21:23** [a] 1 Chr. 3:14; 2 Chr. 33:24, 25; Matt. 1:10 [b] 2 Kin. 12:20; 14:19 **21:24** [a] 2 Kin. 14:5 **22:1** [a] 2 Chr. 34:1 [b] Josh. 15:39 **22:2** [a] Deut. 5:32; Josh. 1:7 **22:3** [a] 2 Chr. 34:8 **22:4** [a] 2 Kin. 12:4 [b] 2 Kin. 12:9, 10 **22:5** [a] 2 Kin. 12:11–14 **22:7** [a] 2 Kin. 12:15; [1 Cor. 4:2] **22:8** [a] Deut. 31:24–26; 2 Chr. 34:14 **22:12** [a] 2 Kin. 25:22; Jer. 26:24 [1] *Abdon the son of Micah* in 2 Chronicles 34:20 **22:13** [a] [Deut. 29:23–28; 31:17, 18] **22:14** [a] 2 Chr. 34:22

'Behold, [a]I will bring calamity on this place and
on its inhabitants—all the words of the book
which the king of Judah has read— 17 [a]because
they have forsaken Me and burned incense to
other gods, that they might provoke Me to anger
with all the works of their hands. Therefore My
wrath shall be aroused against this place and
shall not be quenched.' " ' 18 But as for [a]the king
of Judah, who sent you to inquire of the LORD, in
this manner you shall speak to him, 'Thus says
the LORD God of Israel: "*Concerning* the words
which you have heard— 19 because your [a]heart
was tender, and you [b]humbled yourself before
the LORD when you heard what I spoke against
this place and against its inhabitants, that they
would become [c]a desolation and [d]a curse, and
you tore your clothes and wept before Me, I
also have heard *you*," says the LORD. 20 "Surely,
therefore, I will gather you to your fathers, and
you [a]shall be gathered to your grave in peace;
and your eyes shall not see all the calamity which
I will bring on this place." ' " So they brought
back word to the king.

### *JOSIAH RESTORES TRUE WORSHIP*

*(2 Chr. 34:29—35:19)*

23 Now [a]the king sent them to gather all the
elders of Judah and Jerusalem to him.
2 The king went up to the house of the LORD
with all the men of Judah, and with him all the
inhabitants of Jerusalem—the priests and the
prophets and all the people, both small and
great. And he [a]read in their hearing all the words
of the Book of the Covenant [b]which had been
found in the house of the LORD.

3 Then the king [a]stood by a pillar and made
a [b]covenant before the LORD, to follow the LORD
and to keep His commandments and His tes-
timonies and His statutes, with all *his* heart
and all *his* soul, to perform the words of this
covenant that were written in this book. And
all the people took a stand for the covenant.
4 And the king commanded Hilkiah the high
priest, the [a]priests of the second order, and the
doorkeepers, to bring [b]out of the temple of the
LORD all the articles that were made for Baal, for
Asherah,[1] and for all the host of heaven;[2] and he
burned them outside Jerusalem in the fields of
Kidron, and carried their ashes to Bethel. 5 Then
he removed the idolatrous priests whom the
kings of Judah had ordained to burn incense
on the high places in the cities of Judah and
in the places all around Jerusalem, and those
who burned incense to Baal, to the sun, to the
moon, to the constellations, and to [a]all the host
of heaven. 6 And he brought out the [a]wooden
image[1] from the house of the LORD, to the Brook
Kidron outside Jerusalem, burned it at the Brook
Kidron and ground *it* to [b]ashes, and threw its
ashes on [c]the graves of the common people.
7 Then he tore down the *ritual* booths [a]of the
perverted persons[1] that *were* in the house of the
LORD, [b]where the [c]women wove hangings for the
wooden image. 8 And he brought all the priests
from the cities of Judah, and defiled the high
places where the priests had burned incense,
from [a]Geba to Beersheba; also he broke down
the high places at the gates which *were* at the
entrance of the Gate of Joshua the governor of
the city, which *were* to the left of the city gate.
9 [a]Nevertheless the priests of the high places did
not come up to the altar of the LORD in Jeru-
salem, [b]but they ate unleavened bread among
their brethren.

10 And he defiled [a]Topheth, which *is* in [b]the
Valley of the Son[1] of Hinnom, [c]that no man might
make his son or his daughter [d]pass through the
fire to Molech. 11 Then he removed the horses
that the kings of Judah had dedicated to the
sun, at the entrance to the house of the LORD,
by the chamber of Nathan-Melech, the officer
who *was* in the court; and he burned the chariots
of the sun with fire. 12 The altars that *were* [a]on
the roof, the upper chamber of Ahaz, which the
kings of Judah had made, and the altars which
[b]Manasseh had made in the two courts of the
house of the LORD, the king broke down and
pulverized there, and threw their dust into the
Brook Kidron. 13 Then the king defiled the high
places that *were* east of Jerusalem, which *were*
on the south of the Mount of Corruption, which
[a]Solomon king of Israel had built for Ashtoreth
the abomination of the Sidonians, for Chemosh
the abomination of the Moabites, and for Mil-
com the abomination of the people of Ammon.
14 And he [a]broke in pieces the *sacred* pillars and
cut down the wooden images, and filled their
places with the bones of men.

> **23:11** Some ancient people believed the **sun**'s rays were pulled across the sky by a horse-drawn chariot driven by the sun god.

15 Moreover the altar that *was* at Bethel,
*and* the high place [a]which Jeroboam the son
of Nebat, who made Israel sin, had made, both
that altar and the high place he broke down;
and he burned the high place *and* crushed *it* to
powder, and burned the wooden image. 16 As

**22:16** [a] Deut. 29:27; [Dan. 9:11–14] **22:17** [a] Deut. 29:25–27; 2 Kin. 21:22 **22:18** [a] 2 Chr. 34:26 **22:19** [a] [Ps. 51:17] [b] 1 Kin. 21:29 [c] Lev. 26:31, 32 [d] Jer. 26:6; 44:22 **22:20** [a] [Is. 57:1, 2] **23:1** [a] 2 Chr. 34:29, 30 **23:2** [a] Deut. 31:10–13 [b] 2 Kin. 22:8 **23:3** [a] 2 Kin. 11:14 [b] 2 Kin. 11:17 **23:4** [a] 2 Kin. 25:18 [b] 2 Kin. 21:3–7 [1] A Canaanite goddess [2] The gods of the Assyrians **23:5** [a] 2 Kin. 21:3 **23:6** [a] 2 Kin. 21:7 [b] Ex. 32:20 [c] 2 Chr. 34:4 [1] Hebrew *Asherah,* a Canaanite goddess **23:7** [a] 1 Kin. 14:24; 15:12 [b] Ezek. 16:16 [c] Ex. 38:8 [1] Hebrew *qedeshim,* that is, those practicing sodomy and prostitution in religious rituals **23:8** [a] Josh. 21:17 **23:9** [a] [Ezek. 44:10–14] [b] 1 Sam. 2:36 **23:10** [a] Is. 30:33 [b] Josh. 15:8 [c] [Lev. 18:21] [d] 2 Kin. 21:6 [1] Kethib reads *Sons.* **23:12** [a] Jer. 19:13 [b] 2 Kin. 21:5 **23:13** [a] 1 Kin. 11:5–7 **23:14** [a] [Ex. 23:24] **23:15** [a] 1 Kin. 12:28–33

Josiah turned, he saw the tombs that *were* there on the mountain. And he sent and took the bones out of the tombs and burned *them* on the altar, and defiled it according to the [a]word of the LORD which the man of God proclaimed, who proclaimed these words. 17 Then he said, "What gravestone *is* this that I see?"

So the men of the city told him, "*It is* [a]the tomb of the man of God who came from Judah and proclaimed these things which you have done against the altar of Bethel."

18 And he said, "Let him alone; let no one move his bones." So they let his bones alone, with the bones of [a]the prophet who came from Samaria.

19 Now Josiah also took away all the shrines of the high places that *were* [a]in the cities of Samaria, which the kings of Israel had made to provoke the LORD[1] to anger; and he did to them according to all the deeds he had done in Bethel. 20 [a]He [b]executed all the priests of the high places who *were* there, on the altars, and [c]burned men's bones on them; and he returned to Jerusalem.

21 Then the king commanded all the people, saying, [a]"Keep the Passover to the LORD your God, [b]as *it is* written in this Book of the Covenant." 22 [a]Such a Passover surely had never been held since the days of the judges who judged Israel, nor in all the days of the kings of Israel and the kings of Judah. 23 But in the eighteenth year of King Josiah this Passover was held before the LORD in Jerusalem. 24 Moreover Josiah put away those who consulted mediums and spiritists, the household gods and idols, all the abominations that were seen in the land of Judah and in Jerusalem, that he might perform the words of [a]the law which were written in the book [b]that Hilkiah the priest found in the house of the LORD. 25 [a]Now before him there was no king like him, who turned to the LORD with all his heart, with all his soul, and with all his might, according to all the Law of Moses; nor after him did *any* arise like him.

### IMPENDING JUDGMENT ON JUDAH

26 Nevertheless the LORD did not turn from the fierceness of His great wrath, with which His anger was aroused against Judah, [a]because of all the provocations with which Manasseh had provoked Him. 27 And the LORD said, "I will also remove Judah from My sight, as [a]I have removed Israel, and will cast off this city Jerusalem which I have chosen, and the house of which I said, [b]'My name shall be there.' "[1]

### JOSIAH DIES IN BATTLE

*(2 Chr. 35:20—36:1)*

28 Now the rest of the acts of Josiah, and all that he did, *are* they not written in the book of the chronicles of the kings of Judah? 29 [a]In his days Pharaoh Necho king of Egypt went to the aid of the king of Assyria, to the River Euphrates; and King Josiah went against him. And *Pharaoh Necho* killed him at [b]Megiddo when he [c]confronted him. 30 [a]Then his servants moved his body in a chariot from Megiddo, brought him to Jerusalem, and buried him in his own tomb. And [b]the people of the land took Jehoahaz the son of Josiah, anointed him, and made him king in his father's place.

### THE REIGN AND CAPTIVITY OF JEHOAHAZ

*(2 Chr. 36:1–4)*

31 [a]Jehoahaz *was* twenty-three years old when he became king, and he reigned three months in Jerusalem. His mother's name *was* [b]Hamutal the daughter of Jeremiah of Libnah. 32 And he did evil in the sight of the LORD, according to all that his fathers had done. 33 Now Pharaoh Necho put him in prison [a]at Riblah in the land of Hamath, that he might not reign in Jerusalem; and he imposed on the land a tribute of one hundred talents of silver and a talent of gold. 34 Then [a]Pharaoh Necho made Eliakim the son of Josiah king in place of his father Josiah, and [b]changed his name to [c]Jehoiakim. And *Pharaoh* took Jehoahaz [d]and went to Egypt, and he[1] died there.

### JEHOIAKIM REIGNS IN JUDAH

*(2 Chr. 36:5–8)*

35 So Jehoiakim gave [a]the silver and gold to Pharaoh; but he taxed the land to give money according to the command of Pharaoh; he exacted the silver and gold from the people of the land, from every one according to his assessment, to give *it* to Pharaoh Necho. 36 [a]Jehoiakim *was* twenty-five years old when he became king, and he reigned eleven years in Jerusalem. His mother's name *was* Zebudah the daughter of Pedaiah of Rumah. 37 And he did evil in the sight of the LORD, according to all that his fathers had done.

### JUDAH OVERRUN BY ENEMIES

**24** In [a]his days Nebuchadnezzar king of [b]Babylon came up, and Jehoiakim became his vassal *for* three years. Then he turned and rebelled against him. 2 [a]And the LORD sent against him *raiding* bands of Chaldeans, bands

**23:16** [a]1 Kin. 13:2 **23:17** [a]1 Kin. 13:1, 30, 31 **23:18** [a]1 Kin. 13:11, 31 **23:19** [a]2 Chr. 34:6, 7 [1]Following Septuagint, Syriac, and Vulgate; Masoretic Text and Targum omit *the LORD*. **23:20** [a]1 Kin. 13:2 [b][Ex. 22:20]; 1 Kin. 18:40; 2 Kin. 10:25; 11:18 [c]2 Chr. 34:5 **23:21** [a]Num. 9:5; Josh. 5:10; 2 Chr. 35:1 [b]Ex. 12:3; Lev. 23:5; Num. 9:2; Deut. 16:2–8 **23:22** [a]2 Chr. 35:18, 19 **23:24** [a][Lev. 19:31; 20:27]; Deut. 18:11 [b]2 Kin. 22:8 **23:25** [a]2 Kin. 18:5 **23:26** [a]2 Kin. 21:11, 12; 24:3, 4; Jer. 15:4 **23:27** [a]2 Kin. 17:18, 20; 18:11; 21:13 [b]1 Kin. 8:29; 9:3; 2 Kin. 21:4, 7 [1]1 Kings 8:29 **23:29** [a]2 Chr. 35:20; Jer. 2:16; 46:2 [b]Judg. 5:19; Zech. 12:11 [c]2 Kin. 14:8 **23:30** [a]2 Chr. 35:24; 2 Kin. 22:20 [b]2 Chr. 36:1–4 **23:31** [a]1 Chr. 3:15; Jer. 22:11 [b]2 Kin. 24:18 **23:33** [a]2 Kin. 25:6; Jer. 52:27 **23:34** [a]2 Chr. 36:4 [b]2 Kin. 24:17; Dan. 1:7 [c]Matt. 1:11 [d]Jer. 22:11, 12; Ezek. 19:3, 4 [1]That is, Jehoahaz **23:35** [a]2 Kin. 23:33 **23:36** [a]2 Chr. 36:5; Jer. 22:18, 19; 26:1 **24:1** [a]2 Chr. 36:6; Jer. 25:1, 9; Dan. 1:1 [b]2 Kin. 20:14 **24:2** [a]Jer. 25:9; 32:28; 35:11; Ezek. 19:8

of Syrians, bands of Moabites, and bands of the people of Ammon; He sent them against Judah to destroy it, [b]according to the word of the LORD which He had spoken by His servants the prophets. 3 Surely at the commandment of the LORD *this* came upon Judah, to remove *them* from His sight [a]because of the sins of Manasseh, according to all that he had done, 4 [a]and also because of the innocent blood that he had shed; for he had filled Jerusalem with innocent blood, which the LORD would not pardon.

5 Now the rest of the acts of Jehoiakim, and all that he did, *are* they not written in the book of the chronicles of the kings of Judah? 6 [a]So Jehoiakim rested with his fathers. Then Jehoiachin his son reigned in his place.

7 And [a]the king of Egypt did not come out of his land anymore, for [b]the king of Babylon had taken all that belonged to the king of Egypt from the Brook of Egypt to the River Euphrates.

### *THE REIGN AND CAPTIVITY OF JEHOIACHIN*

*(2 Chr. 36:9, 10)*

8 [a]Jehoiachin *was* eighteen years old when he became king, and he reigned in Jerusalem three months. His mother's name *was* Nehushta the daughter of Elnathan of Jerusalem. 9 And he did evil in the sight of the LORD, according to all that his father had done.

10 [a]At that time the servants of Nebuchadnezzar king of Babylon came up against Jerusalem, and the city was besieged. 11 And Nebuchadnezzar king of Babylon came against the city, as his servants were besieging it. 12 [a]Then Jehoiachin king of Judah, his mother, his servants, his princes, and his officers went out to the king of Babylon; and the king of Babylon, [b]in the eighth year of his reign, took him prisoner.

> **24:11–16** In 597 BC, **Babylon** attacked and defeated **Jerusalem** and carried off thousands of people, including King **Jehoiachin**. The people's sense of national identity was bound to their land, the place God had given them, and to be torn from that land was the ultimate evidence that God had rejected them. The captivity lasted for seventy years, until after the Persians conquered Babylon. It was the Persian king, Cyrus, who eventually allowed the Jewish people to return to their homeland and rebuild the temple.

### *THE CAPTIVITY OF JERUSALEM*

13 [a]And he carried out from there all the treasures of the house of the LORD and the treasures of the king's house, and he [b]cut in pieces all the articles of gold which Solomon king of Israel had made in the temple of the LORD, [c]as the LORD had said. 14 Also [a]he carried into captivity all Jerusalem: all the captains and all the mighty men of valor, [b]ten thousand captives, and [c]all the craftsmen and smiths. None remained except [d]the poorest people of the land. 15 And [a]he carried Jehoiachin captive to Babylon. The king's mother, the king's wives, his officers, and the mighty of the land he carried into captivity from Jerusalem to Babylon. 16 [a]All the valiant men, seven thousand, and craftsmen and smiths, one thousand, all *who were* strong *and* fit for war, these the king of Babylon brought captive to Babylon.

### *ZEDEKIAH REIGNS IN JUDAH*

*(2 Chr. 36:11–14; Jer. 52:1–3)*

17 Then [a]the king of Babylon made Mattaniah, [b]*Jehoiachin's*[1] uncle, king in his place, and [c]changed his name to Zedekiah.

18 [a]Zedekiah *was* twenty-one years old when he became king, and he reigned eleven years in Jerusalem. His mother's name *was* [b]Hamutal the daughter of Jeremiah of Libnah. 19 [a]He also did evil in the sight of the LORD, according to all that Jehoiakim had done. 20 For because of the anger of the LORD *this* happened in Jerusalem and Judah, that He finally cast them out from His presence. [a]Then Zedekiah rebelled against the king of Babylon.

### *THE FALL AND CAPTIVITY OF JUDAH*

*(2 Chr. 36:15–21; Jer. 52:4–30)*

**25** Now it came to pass [a]in the ninth year of his reign, in the tenth month, on the tenth *day* of the month, *that* Nebuchadnezzar king of Babylon and all his army came against Jerusalem and encamped against it; and they built a siege wall against it all around. 2 So the city was besieged until the eleventh year of King Zedekiah. 3 By the ninth *day* of the [a]*fourth* month the famine had become so severe in the city that there was no food for the people of the land.

4 Then [a]the city wall was broken through, and all the men of war *fled* at night by way of the gate between two walls, which was by the king's garden, even though the Chaldeans *were* still encamped all around against the city. And [b]*the king*[1] went by way of the plain.[2] 5 But the army of the Chaldeans pursued the king, and they overtook him in the plains of Jericho. All his army

24:2 [b]2 Kin. 20:17; 21:12–14; 23:27 24:3 [a]2 Kin. 21:2, 11; 23:26 24:4 [a]2 Kin. 21:16 24:6 [a]2 Chr. 36:6, 8; Jer. 22:18, 19 24:7 [a]Jer. 37:5–7 [b]Jer. 46:2 24:8 [a]1 Chr. 3:16; 2 Chr. 36:9 24:10 [a]Dan. 1:1 24:12 [a]Jer. 22:24–30; 24:1; 29:1, 2; Ezek. 17:12 [b]2 Chr. 36:10 24:13 [a]2 Kin. 20:17; Is. 39:6 [b]Dan. 5:2, 3 [c]Jer. 20:5 24:14 [a]Is. 3:2, 3; Jer. 24:1 [b]2 Kin. 24:16; Jer. 52:28 [c]1 Sam. 13:19 [d]2 Kin. 25:12 24:15 [a]2 Chr. 36:10; Esth. 2:6; Jer. 22:24–28; Ezek. 17:12 24:16 [a]Jer. 52:28 24:17 [a]Jer. 37:1 [b]1 Chr. 3:15; 2 Chr. 36:10 [c]2 Chr. 36:4 [1]Literally *his* 24:18 [a]2 Chr. 36:11; Jer. 52:1 [b]2 Kin. 23:31 24:19 [a]2 Chr. 36:12 24:20 [a]2 Chr. 36:13; Ezek. 17:15 25:1 [a]2 Chr. 36:17; Jer. 6:6; 34:2; Ezek. 4:2; 24:1, 2; Hab. 1:6 25:3 [a]2 Kin. 6:24, 25; Is. 3:1; Jer. 39:2; Lam. 4:9, 10 25:4 [a]Jer. 39:2 [b]Jer. 39:4–7; Ezek. 12:12

[1]Literally *he* [2]Or *Arabah,* that is, the Jordan Valley

# THE EXILE OF THE SOUTHERN KINGDOM

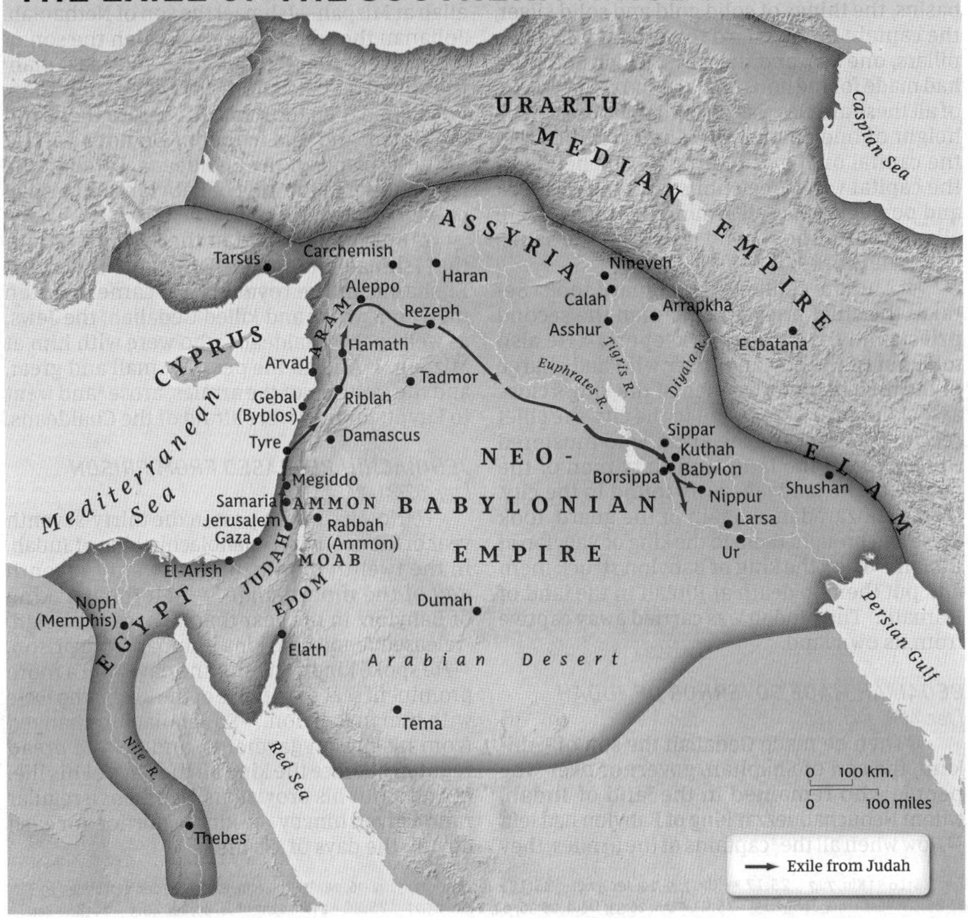


was scattered from him. 6 So they took the king
and brought him up to the king of Babylon [a]at
Riblah, and they pronounced judgment on him.
7 Then they killed the sons of Zedekiah before his
eyes, [a]put out the eyes of Zedekiah, bound him
with bronze fetters, and took him to Babylon.

8 And in the fifth month, [a]on the seventh
*day* of the month (which *was* [b]the nineteenth
year of King Nebuchadnezzar king of Babylon),
[c]Nebuzaradan the captain of the guard, a servant
of the king of Babylon, came to Jerusalem. 9 [a]He
burned the house of the LORD [b]and the king's
house; all the houses of Jerusalem, that is, all
the houses of the great, [c]he burned with fire.
10 And all the army of the Chaldeans who *were*
*with* the captain of the guard [a]broke down the
walls of Jerusalem all around.

11 Then Nebuzaradan the captain of the guard
carried away captive [a]the rest of the people *who*
remained in the city and the defectors who had
deserted to the king of Babylon, with the rest of
the multitude. 12 But the captain of the guard
[a]left *some* of the poor of the land as vinedressers
and farmers. 13 [a]The bronze [b]pillars that *were*
in the house of the LORD, and [c]the carts and
[d]the bronze Sea that *were* in the house of the
LORD, the Chaldeans broke in pieces, and [e]carried their bronze to Babylon. 14 They also took
away [a]the pots, the shovels, the trimmers, the

**25:13 The bronze Sea** was almost fifteen feet in diameter, more than seven feet deep, and three inches thick. It weighed more than ten tons and could hold about ten thousand gallons of water. The Sea, positioned in front of the temple, was used by the priest for ceremonial cleansing. The basin was supported by metal statues of twelve bulls.

25:6 [a] 2 Kin. 23:33; Jer. 52:9 25:7 [a] Jer. 39:7; Ezek. 17:16 25:8 [a] Jer. 52:12 [b] 2 Kin. 24:12 [c] Jer. 39:9 25:9 [a] 2 Kin. 25:13; 2 Chr. 36:19; Ps. 79:1; Jer. 7:14 [b] Jer. 39:8 [c] Jer. 17:27 25:10 [a] 2 Kin. 14:13; Neh. 1:3 25:11 [a] Is. 1:9; Jer. 5:19; 39:9 25:12 [a] 2 Kin. 24:14; Jer. 39:10; 40:7; 52:16 25:13 [a] Jer. 52:17 [b] 1 Kin. 7:15 [c] 1 Kin. 7:27 [d] 1 Kin. 7:23 [e] 2 Kin. 20:17; Jer. 27:19–22 25:14 [a] Ex. 27:3; 1 Kin. 7:45

spoons, and all the bronze utensils with which
the priests ministered. 15 The firepans and the
basins, the things of solid gold and solid silver,
the captain of the guard took away. 16 The two
pillars, one Sea, and the carts, which Solomon
had made for the house of the LORD, [a]the bronze
of all these articles was beyond measure. 17 [a]The
height of one pillar *was* eighteen cubits, and
the capital on it *was* of bronze. The height of
the capital was three cubits, and the network
and pomegranates all around the capital were
all of bronze. The second pillar was the same,
with a network.

18 [a]And the captain of the guard took [b]Se-
raiah the chief priest, [c]Zephaniah the second
priest, and the three doorkeepers. 19 He also
took out of the city an officer who had charge
of the men of war, [a]five men of the king's close
associates who were found in the city, the chief
recruiting officer of the army, who mustered
the people of the land, and sixty men of the
people of the land *who were* found in the city.
20 So Nebuzaradan, captain of the guard, took
these and brought them to the king of Babylon at
Riblah. 21 Then the king of Babylon struck them
and put them to death at Riblah in the land of
Hamath. [a]Thus Judah was carried away captive
from its own land.

### *GEDALIAH MADE GOVERNOR OF JUDAH*

*(Jer. 40:5—41:18)*

22 Then he made Gedaliah the son of [a]Ahi-
kam, the son of Shaphan, governor over [b]the
people who remained in the land of Judah,
whom Nebuchadnezzar king of Babylon had left.
23 Now when all the [a]captains of the armies, they
and *their* men, heard that the king of Babylon
had made Gedaliah governor, they came to Ged-
aliah at Mizpah—Ishmael the son of Nethaniah,
Johanan the son of Careah, Seraiah the son of
Tanhumeth the Netophathite, and Jaazaniah[1]
the son of a Maachathite, they and their men.
24 And Gedaliah took an oath before them and
their men, and said to them, "Do not be afraid
of the servants of the Chaldeans. Dwell in the
land and serve the king of Babylon, and it shall
be well with you."

25 But [a]it happened in the seventh month
that Ishmael the son of Nethaniah, the son of
Elishama, of the royal family, came with ten
men and struck and killed Gedaliah, the Jews,
as well as the Chaldeans who were with him at
Mizpah. 26 And all the people, small and great,
and the captains of the armies, arose [a]and went
to Egypt; for they were afraid of the Chaldeans.

### *JEHOIACHIN RELEASED FROM PRISON*

*(Jer. 52:31–34)*

27 [a]Now it came to pass in the thirty-seventh
year of the captivity of Jehoiachin king of Judah,
in the twelfth month, on the twenty-seventh
*day* of the month, *that* Evil-Merodach[1] king
of Babylon, in the year that he began to reign,
[b]released Jehoiachin king of Judah from prison.
28 He spoke kindly to him, and gave him a more
prominent seat than those of the kings who *were*
with him in Babylon. 29 So Jehoiachin changed
from his prison garments, and he [a]ate bread
regularly before the king all the days of his life.
30 And as for his provisions, *there was* a regular
ration given him by the king, a portion for each
day, all the days of his life.

25:16 [a] 1 Kin. 7:47 25:17 [a] 1 Kin. 7:15–22; Jer. 52:21 25:18 [a] Jer. 39:9–13; 52:12–16, 24 [b] 1 Chr. 6:14; Ezra 7:1 [c] Jer. 21:1; 29:25, 29 25:19 [a] Esth. 1:14; Jer. 52:25 25:21 [a] Lev. 26:33; Deut. 28:36, 64; 2 Kin. 23:27 25:22 [a] 2 Kin. 22:12 [b] Is. 1:9; Jer. 40:5 25:23 [a] Jer. 40:7–9 [1] Spelled *Jezaniah* in Jeremiah 40:8 25:25 [a] Jer. 41:1–3 25:26 [a] 2 Kin. 19:31; Jer. 43:4–7 25:27 [a] 2 Kin. 24:12, 15; Jer. 52:31–34 [b] Gen. 40:13, 20 [1] Literally *Man of Marduk* 25:29 [a] 2 Sam. 9:7

*The First Book of the*

# CHRONICLES

**AUTHOR**
Ezra, likely

**KEY VERSES**
1 Chronicles 17:11–14

**READING TIME**
2 hours 26 minutes

The books of 1 and 2 Chronicles cover the same period of history described in 2 Samuel through 2 Kings, only from a different perspective. Written after the captivity, 1 and 2 Chronicles provide a divine editorial on the history of God's people. While 2 Samuel and 1 and 2 Kings give a political history of Israel and Judah, 1 and 2 Chronicles present a religious history of the Davidic dynasty of Judah. The former were written from a prophetic and moral viewpoint and the latter from a priestly and spiritual perspective. The Book of 1 Chronicles begins with the royal line of David and then traces the spiritual significance of David's righteous reign, a reminder of the promise God had made to him—a promise that still stood.

**Occasion:** First Chronicles was written after the people had returned from foreign captivity to a much different Promised Land and provides a different perspective of the important events that had shaped Israel as a nation, for better or worse.

**Main Point:** The promise that God had made to David that Israel would be a great kingdom with an even greater King remains intact, even if it was difficult for the people to see it.

**Big Ideas:** God is faithful to His promises. Even when things are difficult and look down, we can trust that God is good, and He is at work for our good.

## OUTLINE:

I. David's Genealogy (chs. 1–3)
II. David's People's Genealogy (chs. 4–9)
III. David's Transition to Become King (chs. 10–12)
IV. David's Recovery of the Ark (chs. 13–17)
V. David's Military Victories (chs. 18–20)
VI. David's Preparations for the Temple (chs. 21–28)
VII. David's Final Days (ch. 29)

**c. 1900 BC**
Jacob and his family live in Canaan

**c. 1405–1400 BC**
The conquest of Canaan

**c. 1050 BC**
Saul becomes king of Israel

**c. 1018 BC**
Samuel anoints David to be king

**1010 BC**
David begins to reign at Hebron

**1003 BC**
David becomes king over all Israel

**997 BC**
The ark is brought to Jerusalem

**c. 990 BC**
David wars against the Ammonites

**c. 972 BC**
David stores up materials for the temple

**970 BC**
Solomon becomes king of Israel

**930 BC**
The kingdom is divided

**c. 450–400 BC**
**1 Chronicles written**

### *THE FAMILY OF ADAM—SETH TO ABRAHAM*
*(Gen. 5:1-32; 10:1-32; 11:10-26; Luke 3:34-38)*

1 Adam,[a] [b]Seth, Enosh, 2 Cainan,[1] Mahalalel,
Jared, 3 Enoch, Methuselah, Lamech, 4 [a]Noah,[1]
Shem, Ham, and Japheth.
5 [a]The sons of Japheth *were* Gomer, Magog,
Madai, Javan, Tubal, Meshech, and Tiras. 6 The
sons of Gomer *were* Ashkenaz, Diphath,[1] and
Togarmah. 7 The sons of Javan *were* Elishah,
Tarshishah,[1] Kittim, and Rodanim.[2]
8 [a]The sons of Ham *were* Cush, Mizraim,
Put, and Canaan. 9 The sons of Cush *were* Seba,
Havilah, Sabta,[1] Raama,[2] and Sabtecha. The sons
of Raama *were* Sheba and Dedan. 10 Cush [a]begot
Nimrod; he began to be a mighty one on the
earth. 11 Mizraim begot Ludim, Anamim, Leha-
bim, Naphtuhim, 12 Pathrusim, Casluhim (from
whom came the Philistines and the [a]Caphtorim).
13 [a]Canaan begot Sidon, his firstborn, and Heth;
14 the Jebusite, the Amorite, and the Girgashite;
15 the Hivite, the Arkite, and the Sinite; 16 the Ar-
vadite, the Zemarite, and the Hamathite.
17 The sons of [a]Shem *were* Elam, Asshur,
[b]Arphaxad, Lud, Aram, Uz, Hul, Gether, and
Meshech.[1] 18 Arphaxad begot Shelah, and She-
lah begot Eber. 19 To Eber were born two sons:
the name of one *was* Peleg,[1] for in his days the
earth was divided; and his brother's name *was*
Joktan. 20 [a]Joktan begot Almodad, Sheleph,
Hazarmaveth, Jerah, 21 Hadoram, Uzal, Diklah,
22 Ebal,[1] Abimael, Sheba, 23 Ophir, Havilah, and
Jobab. All these *were* the sons of Joktan.
24 [a]Shem, Arphaxad, Shelah, 25 [a]Eber, Peleg,
Reu, 26 Serug, Nahor, Terah, 27 and [a]Abram, who
*is* Abraham. 28 [a]The sons of Abraham *were* [b]Isaac
and [c]Ishmael.

> **1:24–27 Abraham** and the Israelites were descendants of Noah's oldest son, **Shem**. Rather than calling themselves "Shemites," they dropped the *h* and called themselves "Semites." Today, a person who holds a prejudice against Jewish people is known as an anti-Semite or anti-Semitic.

### *THE FAMILY OF ISHMAEL*
*(Gen. 25:12-16)*

29 These *are* their genealogies: The [a]firstborn
of Ishmael *was* Nebajoth; then Kedar, Adbeel,
Mibsam, 30 Mishma, Dumah, Massa, Hadad,[1]
Tema, 31 Jetur, Naphish, and Kedemah. These
*were* the sons of Ishmael.

### *THE FAMILY OF KETURAH*
*(Gen. 25:1-4)*

32 Now [a]the sons born to Keturah, Abraham's
concubine, *were* Zimran, Jokshan, Medan, Midi-
an, Ishbak, and Shuah. The sons of Jokshan *were*
Sheba and Dedan. 33 The sons of Midian *were*
Ephah, Epher, Hanoch, Abida, and Eldaah. All
these were the children of Keturah.

### *THE FAMILY OF ISAAC*
*(Gen. 36:10-14)*

34 And [a]Abraham begot Isaac. [b]The sons of
Isaac *were* Esau and Israel. 35 The sons of [a]Esau
*were* Eliphaz, Reuel, Jeush, Jaalam, and Korah.
36 And the sons of Eliphaz *were* Teman, Omar,
Zephi,[1] Gatam, *and* Kenaz; and *by* [a]Timna,[2] Am-
alek. 37 The sons of Reuel *were* Nahath, Zerah,
Shammah, and Mizzah.

### *THE FAMILY OF SEIR*
*(Gen. 36:20-28)*

38 [a]The sons of Seir *were* Lotan, Shobal, Zib-
eon, Anah, Dishon, Ezer, and Dishan. 39 And the
sons of Lotan *were* Hori and Homam; Lotan's
sister *was* Timna. 40 The sons of Shobal *were*
Alian,[1] Manahath, Ebal, Shephi,[2] and Onam. The
sons of Zibeon *were* Ajah and Anah. 41 The son
of Anah *was* [a]Dishon. The sons of Dishon *were*
Hamran,[1] Eshban, Ithran, and Cheran. 42 The
sons of Ezer *were* Bilhan, Zaavan, *and* Jaakan.[1]
The sons of Dishan *were* Uz and Aran.

### *THE KINGS OF EDOM*
*(Gen. 36:31-43)*

43 Now these *were* the [a]kings who reigned in
the land of Edom before a king reigned over the
children of Israel: Bela the son of Beor, and the
name of his city was Dinhabah. 44 And when Bela
died, Jobab the son of Zerah of Bozrah reigned
in his place. 45 When Jobab died, Husham of the
land of the Temanites reigned in his place. 46 And
when Husham died, Hadad the son of Bedad, who
attacked Midian in the field of Moab, reigned in
his place. The name of his city *was* Avith. 47 When
Hadad died, Samlah of Masrekah reigned in his
place. 48 [a]And when Samlah died, Saul of Reho-
both-by-the-River reigned in his place. 49 When
Saul died, Baal-Hanan the son of Achbor reigned
in his place. 50 And when Baal-Hanan died, Hadad[1]
reigned in his place; and the name of his city was
Pai.[2] His wife's name was Mehetabel the daughter

1:1 [a] Gen. 1:27; 2:7; 5:1, 2, 5 [b] Gen. 4:25, 26; 5:3–9 1:2 [1] Hebrew *Qenan* 1:4 [a] Gen. 5:28—10:1 [1] Following Masoretic Text and Vulgate; Septuagint adds *the sons of Noah.* 1:5 [a] Gen. 10:2–4 1:6 [1] Spelled *Riphath* in Genesis 10:3 1:7 [1] Spelled *Tarshish* in Genesis 10:4 [2] Spelled *Dodanim* in Genesis 10:4 1:8 [a] Gen. 10:6 1:9 [1] Spelled *Sabtah* in Genesis 10:7 [2] Spelled *Raamah* in Genesis 10:7 1:10 [a] Gen. 10:8–10, 13 1:12 [a] Deut. 2:23 1:13 [a] Gen. 9:18, 25–27; 10:15 1:17 [a] Gen. 10:22–29; 11:10 [b] Luke 3:36 [1] Spelled *Mash* in Genesis 10:23 1:19 [1] Literally *Division* 1:20 [a] Gen. 10:26 1:22 [1] Spelled *Obal* in Genesis 10:28 1:24 [a] Gen. 11:10–26; Luke 3:34–36 1:25 [a] Gen. 11:15 1:27 [a] Gen. 17:5 1:28 [a] Gen. 21:2, 3 [b] Gen. 21:2 [c] Gen. 16:11, 15 1:29 [a] Gen. 25:13–16 1:30 [1] Spelled *Hadar* in Genesis 25:15 1:32 [a] Gen. 25:1–4 1:34 [a] Gen. 21:2 [b] Gen. 25:9, 25, 26, 29; 32:28 1:35 [a] Gen. 36:10–19 1:36 [a] Gen. 36:12 [1] Spelled *Zepho* in Genesis 36:11 [2] Compare Genesis 36:12 1:38 [a] Gen. 36:20–28 1:40 [1] Spelled *Alvan* in Genesis 36:23 [2] Spelled *Shepho* in Genesis 36:23 1:41 [a] Gen. 36:25 [1] Spelled *Hemdan* in Genesis 36:26 1:42 [1] Spelled *Akan* in Genesis 36:27 1:43 [a] Gen. 36:31–43 1:48 [a] Gen. 36:37 1:50 [1] Spelled *Hadar* in Genesis 36:39 [2] Spelled *Pau* in Genesis 36:39

of Matred, the daughter of Mezahab. 51 Hadad died
also. And the chiefs of Edom were Chief Timnah,
Chief Aliah,[1] Chief Jetheth, 52 Chief Aholibamah,
Chief Elah, Chief Pinon, 53 Chief Kenaz, Chief
Teman, Chief Mibzar, 54 Chief Magdiel, and Chief
Iram. These *were* the chiefs of Edom.

### THE FAMILY OF ISRAEL

*(Gen. 35:23–26; 46:8–25)*

**2** These *were* the [a]sons of Israel: [b]Reuben, Sim-
eon, Levi, Judah, Issachar, Zebulun, 2 Dan,
Joseph, Benjamin, Naphtali, Gad, and Asher.

### FROM JUDAH TO DAVID

*(Ruth 4:18–22; Matt. 1:2–6; Luke 3:31–33)*

3 The sons of [a]Judah *were* Er, Onan, and
Shelah. *These* three were born to him by the
daughter of [b]Shua, the Canaanitess. [c]Er, the
firstborn of Judah, was wicked in the sight of
the LORD; so He killed him. 4 And [a]Tamar, his
daughter-in-law, [b]bore him Perez and Zerah. All
the sons of Judah *were* five.

5 The sons of [a]Perez *were* Hezron and Hamul.
6 The sons of Zerah *were* Zimri, [a]Ethan, Heman,
Calcol, and Dara—five of them in all.

7 The son of [a]Carmi *was* Achar,[1] the troubler of
Israel, who transgressed in the [b]accursed thing.

8 The son of Ethan *was* Azariah.

9 Also the sons of Hezron who were born to
him *were* Jerahmeel, Ram, and Chelubai.[1] 10 Ram
[a]begot Amminadab, and Amminadab begot Nah-
shon, [b]leader of the children of Judah; 11 Nahshon
begot Salma,[1] and Salma begot Boaz; 12 Boaz
begot Obed, and Obed begot Jesse; 13 [a]Jesse begot
Eliab his firstborn, Abinadab the second, Shim-
ea[1] the third, 14 Nethanel the fourth, Raddai the
fifth, 15 Ozem the sixth, *and* David the [a]seventh.

> **2:13–15 David**, who was of the tribe of Judah, was a descendant of Abraham. As the genealogies of the Gospels of Matthew and Luke show, David was also an ancestor of Jesus.

16 Now their sisters *were* Zeruiah and Abigail.
[a]And the sons of Zeruiah *were* Abishai, Joab,
and Asahel—three. 17 Abigail bore Amasa; and
the father of Amasa *was* Jether the Ishmaelite.[1]

### THE FAMILY OF HEZRON

18 Caleb the son of Hezron had children by
Azubah, *his* wife, and by Jerioth. Now these were
her sons: Jesher, Shobab, and Ardon. 19 When
Azubah died, Caleb took [a]Ephrath[1] as his wife,
who bore him Hur. 20 And Hur begot Uri, and
Uri begot [a]Bezalel.

21 Now afterward Hezron went in to the
daughter of [a]Machir the father of Gilead, whom
he married when he *was* sixty years old; and she
bore him Segub. 22 Segub begot [a]Jair, who had
twenty-three cities in the land of Gilead. 23 [a](Ge-
shur and Syria took from them the towns of Jair,
with Kenath and its towns—sixty towns.) All these
*belonged to* the sons of Machir the father of Gilead.
24 After Hezron died in Caleb Ephrathah, Hezron's
wife Abijah bore him [a]Ashhur the father of Tekoa.

### THE FAMILY OF JERAHMEEL

25 The sons of Jerahmeel, the firstborn of
Hezron, *were* Ram, the firstborn, and Bunah,
Oren, Ozem, *and* Ahijah. 26 Jerahmeel had an-
other wife, whose name was Atarah; she was the
mother of Onam. 27 The sons of Ram, the first-
born of Jerahmeel, were Maaz, Jamin, and Eker.
28 The sons of Onam were Shammai and Jada.
The sons of Shammai *were* Nadab and Abishur.
29 And the name of the wife of Abishur *was*
Abihail, and she bore him Ahban and Molid.
30 The sons of Nadab *were* Seled and Appaim;
Seled died without children. 31 The son of Ap-
paim *was* Ishi, the son of Ishi *was* Sheshan,
and [a]Sheshan's son *was* Ahlai. 32 The sons of
Jada, the brother of Shammai, *were* Jether and
Jonathan; Jether died without children. 33 The
sons of Jonathan *were* Peleth and Zaza. These
were the sons of Jerahmeel.

34 Now Sheshan had no sons, only daughters.
And Sheshan had an Egyptian servant whose
name *was* Jarha. 35 Sheshan gave his daughter
to Jarha his servant as wife, and she bore him
Attai. 36 Attai begot Nathan, and Nathan begot
[a]Zabad; 37 Zabad begot Ephlal, and Ephlal begot
[a]Obed; 38 Obed begot Jehu, and Jehu begot Az-
ariah; 39 Azariah begot Helez, and Helez begot
Eleasah; 40 Eleasah begot Sismai, and Sismai
begot Shallum; 41 Shallum begot Jekamiah, and
Jekamiah begot Elishama.

### THE FAMILY OF CALEB

42 The descendants of Caleb the brother of
Jerahmeel *were* Mesha, his firstborn, who was
the father of Ziph, and the sons of Mareshah the
father of Hebron. 43 The sons of Hebron *were*
Korah, Tappuah, Rekem, and Shema. 44 Shema
begot Raham the father of Jorkoam, and Rekem
begot Shammai. 45 And the son of Shammai *was*
Maon, and Maon *was* the father of Beth Zur.

46 Ephah, Caleb's concubine, bore Haran,
Moza, and Gazez; and Haran begot Gazez. 47 And

**1:51** [1] Spelled *Alvah* in Genesis 36:40 **2:1** [a] Gen. 29:32–35; 35:23, 26; 46:8–27 [b] Gen. 29:32; 35:22 **2:3** [a] Gen. 38:3–5; 46:12; Num. 26:19 [b] Gen. 38:2 [c] Gen. 38:7 **2:4** [a] Gen. 38:6 [b] Matt. 1:3 **2:5** [a] Gen. 46:12; Ruth 4:18 **2:6** [a] 1 Kin. 4:31 **2:7** [a] 1 Chr. 4:1 [b] Josh. 6:18 [1] Spelled *Achan* in Joshua 7:1 and elsewhere **2:9** [1] Spelled *Caleb* in 2:18, 42 **2:10** [a] Ruth 4:19–22; Matt. 1:4 [b] Num. 1:7; 2:3 **2:11** [1] Spelled *Salmon* in Ruth 4:21 and Luke 3:32 **2:13** [a] 1 Sam. 16:6 [1] Spelled *Shammah* in 1 Samuel 16:9 and elsewhere **2:15** [a] 1 Sam. 16:10, 11; 17:12 **2:16** [a] 2 Sam. 2:18 **2:17** [1] Compare 2 Samuel 17:25 **2:19** [a] 1 Chr. 2:50 [1] Spelled *Ephrathah* elsewhere **2:20** [a] Ex. 31:2; 38:22 **2:21** [a] Num. 27:1; Judg. 5:14; 1 Chr. 7:14 **2:22** [a] Judg. 10:3 **2:23** [a] Num. 32:41; Deut. 3:14; Josh. 13:30 **2:24** [a] 1 Chr. 4:5 **2:31** [a] 1 Chr. 2:34, 35 **2:36** [a] 1 Chr. 11:41 **2:37** [a] 2 Chr. 23:1

the sons of Jahdai *were* Regem, Jotham, Geshan, Pelet, Ephah, and Shaaph.

48 Maachah, Caleb's concubine, bore Sheber and Tirhanah. 49 She also bore Shaaph the father of Madmannah, Sheva the father of Machbenah and the father of Gibea. And the daughter of Caleb *was* [a]Achsah.

50 These were the descendants of Caleb: The sons of [a]Hur, the firstborn of Ephrathah, *were* Shobal the father of [b]Kirjath Jearim, 51 Salma the father of Bethlehem, *and* Hareph the father of Beth Gader.

52 And Shobal the father of Kirjath Jearim had descendants: Haroeh, *and* half of the *families of* Manuhoth.[1] 53 The families of Kirjath Jearim *were* the Ithrites, the Puthites, the Shumathites, and the Mishraites. From these came the Zorathites and the Eshtaolites.

54 The sons of Salma *were* Bethlehem, the Netophathites, Atroth Beth Joab, half of the Manahethites, and the Zorites.

55 And the families of the scribes who dwelt at Jabez *were* the Tirathites, the Shimeathites, *and* the Suchathites. These *were* the [a]Kenites who came from Hammath, the father of the house of [b]Rechab.

### THE FAMILY OF DAVID

*(Matt. 1:6)*

**3** Now these were the sons of David who were born to him in Hebron: The firstborn *was* [a]Amnon, by [b]Ahinoam the [c]Jezreelitess; the second, Daniel,[1] by [d]Abigail the Carmelitess; 2 the third, [a]Absalom the son of Maacah, the daughter of Talmai, king of Geshur; the fourth, [b]Adonijah the son of Haggith; 3 the fifth, Shephatiah, by Abital; the sixth, Ithream, by his wife [a]Eglah.

4 *These* six were born to him in Hebron. [a]There he reigned seven years and six months, and [b]in Jerusalem he reigned thirty-three years. 5 [a]And these were born to him in Jerusalem: Shimea,[1] Shobab, Nathan, and [b]Solomon—four by Bathshua[2] the daughter of Ammiel.[3] 6 Also *there* were Ibhar, Elishama,[1] Eliphelet,[2] 7 Nogah, Nepheg, Japhia, 8 Elishama, Eliada,[1] and Eliphelet—[a]nine *in all.* 9 *These were* all the sons of David, besides the sons of the concubines, and [a]Tamar their sister.

### THE FAMILY OF SOLOMON

*(Matt. 1:7–11)*

10 Solomon's son *was* [a]Rehoboam; Abijah[1] *was* his son, Asa his son, Jehoshaphat his son, 11 Joram[1] his son, Ahaziah his son, Joash[2] his son, 12 Amaziah his son, Azariah[1] his son, Jotham his son, 13 Ahaz his son, Hezekiah his son, Manasseh his son, 14 Amon his son, *and* Josiah his son. 15 The sons of Josiah *were* Johanan the firstborn, the second Jehoiakim, the third Zedekiah, and the fourth Shallum.[1] 16 The sons of [a]Jehoiakim *were* Jeconiah his son *and* Zedekiah[1] his son.

### THE FAMILY OF JECONIAH

17 And the sons of Jeconiah[1] *were* Assir,[2] Shealtiel [a]his son, 18 *and* Malchiram, Pedaiah, Shenazzar, Jecamiah, Hoshama, and Nedabiah. 19 The sons of Pedaiah *were* Zerubbabel and Shimei. The sons of Zerubbabel *were* Meshullam, Hananiah, Shelomith their sister, 20 and Hashubah, Ohel, Berechiah, Hasadiah, and Jushab-Hesed—five *in all.*

> **3:19 Zerubbabel** led the first group of Jewish exiles back to Jerusalem after they had spent seventy years as captives in Babylon. He became the governor of Judah and started the long, slow process of rebuilding the temple, which had been destroyed. Haggai and Zechariah, two prophets of God, encouraged Zerubbabel in his work.

21 The sons of Hananiah *were* Pelatiah and Jeshaiah, the sons of Rephaiah, the sons of Arnan, the sons of Obadiah, and the sons of Shechaniah. 22 The son of Shechaniah was Shemaiah. The sons of Shemaiah *were* [a]Hattush, Igal, Bariah, Neariah, and Shaphat—six *in all.* 23 The sons of Neariah *were* Elioenai, Hezekiah, and Azrikam—three *in all.* 24 The sons of Elioenai *were* Hodaviah, Eliashib, Pelaiah, Akkub, Johanan, Delaiah, and Anani—seven *in all.*

### THE FAMILY OF JUDAH

**4** The sons of Judah *were* [a]Perez, Hezron, Carmi, Hur, and Shobal. 2 And Reaiah the son of Shobal begot Jahath, and Jahath begot Ahumai and Lahad. These *were* the families of the Zorathites. 3 These *were the sons of* the father of Etam: Jezreel, Ishma, and Idbash; and the name of their sister *was* Hazelelponi; 4 and Penuel *was* the father of Gedor, and Ezer *was the* father of Hushah.

These *were* the sons of [a]Hur, the firstborn of Ephrathah the father of Bethlehem.

5 And [a]Ashhur the father of Tekoa had two wives, Helah and Naarah. 6 Naarah bore him Ahuzzam, Hepher, Temeni, and Haahashtari. These *were* the sons of Naarah. 7 The sons of

**2:49** [a] Josh. 15:17 **2:50** [a] 1 Chr. 4:4 [b] Josh. 9:17; 18:14 **2:52** [1] Same as *the Manahethites,* verse 54 **2:55** [a] Judg. 1:16 [b] Jer. 35:2 **3:1** [a] 2 Sam. 3:2–5 [b] 1 Sam. 25:43 [c] Josh. 15:56 [d] 1 Sam. 25:39–42 [1] Called *Chileab* in 2 Samuel 3:3 **3:2** [a] 2 Sam. 13:37; 15:1 [b] 1 Kin. 1:5 **3:3** [a] 2 Sam. 3:5 **3:4** [a] 2 Sam. 2:11 [b] 2 Sam. 5:5 **3:5** [a] 1 Chr. 14:4–7 [b] 2 Sam. 12:24, 25 [1] Spelled *Shammua* in 14:4 and 2 Samuel 5:14 [2] Spelled *Bathsheba* in 2 Samuel 11:3 [3] Called *Eliam* in 2 Samuel 11:3 **3:6** [1] Spelled *Elishua* in 14:5 and 2 Samuel 5:15 [2] Spelled *Elpelet* in 14:5 **3:8** [a] 2 Sam. 5:14–16 [1] Spelled *Beeliada* in 14:7 **3:9** [a] 2 Sam. 13:1 **3:10** [a] 1 Kin. 11:43 [1] Spelled *Abijam* in 1 Kings 15:1 **3:11** [1] Spelled *Jehoram* in 2 Kings 1:17 and 8:16 [2] Spelled *Jehoash* in 2 Kings 12:1 **3:12** [1] Called *Uzziah* in Isaiah 6:1 **3:15** [1] Called *Jehoahaz* in 2 Kings 23:31 **3:16** [a] Matt. 1:11 [1] Compare 2 Kings 24:17 **3:17** [a] Matt. 1:12 [1] Also called *Coniah* in Jeremiah 22:24 and *Jehoiachin* in 2 Kings 24:8 [2] Or *Jeconiah the captive were* **3:22** [a] Ezra 8:2 **4:1** [a] Gen. 38:29; 46:12 **4:4** [a] 1 Chr. 2:50 **4:5** [a] 1 Chr. 2:24

Helah *were* Zereth, Zohar, and Ethnan; 8 and
Koz begot Anub, Zobebah, and the families of
Aharhel the son of Harum.
9 Now Jabez was [a]more honorable than his
brothers, and his mother called his name Jabez,[1]
saying, "Because I bore *him* in pain." 10 And Jabez
called on the God of Israel saying, "Oh, that You
would bless me indeed, and enlarge my territory,
that Your hand would be with me, and that You
would keep *me* from evil, that I may not cause
pain!" So God granted him what he requested.
11 Chelub the brother of [a]Shuhah begot Mehir,
who *was* the father of Eshton. 12 And Eshton be-
got Beth-Rapha, Paseah, and Tehinnah the father
of Ir-Nahash. These *were* the men of Rechah.
13 The sons of Kenaz *were* [a]Othniel and Seraiah.
The sons of Othniel *were* Hathath,[1] 14 and Meono-
thai *who* begot Ophrah. Seraiah begot Joab the
father of [a]Ge Harashim,[1] for they were craftsmen.
15 The sons of [a]Caleb the son of Jephunneh *were* Iru,
Elah, and Naam. The son of Elah *was* Kenaz. 16 The
sons of Jehallelel *were* Ziph, Ziphah, Tiria, and Asa-
rel. 17 The sons of Ezrah *were* Jether, Mered, Epher,
and Jalon. And *Mered's wife*[1] bore Miriam, Sham-
mai, and Ishbah the father of Eshtemoa. 18 (His wife
Jehudijah[1] bore Jered the father of Gedor, Heber
the father of Sochoh, and Jekuthiel the father of
Zanoah.) And these were the sons of Bithiah the
daughter of Pharaoh, whom Mered took.
19 The sons of Hodiah's wife, the sister of
Naham, *were* the fathers of Keilah the Garmite
and of Eshtemoa the [a]Maachathite. 20 And the
sons of Shimon *were* Amnon, Rinnah, Ben-
Hanan, and Tilon. And the sons of Ishi *were*
Zoheth and Ben-Zoheth.
21 The sons of [a]Shelah [b]the son of Judah
*were* Er the father of Lecah, Laadah the father
of Mareshah, and the families of the house of
the linen workers of the house of Ashbea; 22 also
Jokim, the men of Chozeba, and Joash; Saraph,
who ruled in Moab, and Jashubi-Lehem. Now the
records are ancient. 23 These *were* the potters and
those who dwell at Netaim[1] and Gederah;[2] there
they dwelt with the king for his work.

### *THE FAMILY OF SIMEON*

*(Gen. 46:10)*

24 The [a]sons of Simeon *were* Nemuel, Jamin,
Jarib,[1] Zerah,[2] *and* Shaul, 25 Shallum his son, Mib-
sam his son, and Mishma his son. 26 And the sons
of Mishma *were* Hamuel his son, Zacchur his
son, and Shimei his son. 27 Shimei had sixteen
sons and six daughters; but his brothers did not
have many children, [a]nor did any of their fami-
lies multiply as much as the children of Judah.
28 They dwelt at Beersheba, Moladah, Hazar
Shual, 29 Bilhah, Ezem, Tolad, 30 Bethuel, Hor-
mah, Ziklag, 31 Beth Marcaboth, Hazar Susim,
Beth Biri, and at Shaaraim. These *were* their
cities until the reign of David. 32 And their vil-
lages *were* Etam, Ain, Rimmon, Tochen, and
Ashan—five cities— 33 and all the villages that
*were* around these cities as far as Baal.[1] These
*were* their dwelling places, and they maintained
their genealogy: 34 Meshobab, Jamlech, and Jo-
shah the son of Amaziah; 35 Joel, and Jehu the
son of Joshibiah, the son of Seraiah, the son of
Asiel; 36 Elioenai, Jaakobah, Jeshohaiah, Asaiah,
Adiel, Jesimiel, and Benaiah; 37 Ziza the son of
Shiphi, the son of Allon, the son of Jedaiah, the
son of Shimri, the son of Shemaiah— 38 these
mentioned by name *were* leaders in their fam-
ilies, and their father's house increased greatly.
39 So they went to the entrance of Gedor, as
far as the east side of the valley, to seek pasture
for their flocks. 40 And they found rich, good
pasture, and the land *was* broad, quiet, and
peaceful; for some Hamites formerly lived there.
41 These recorded by name came in the days of
Hezekiah king of Judah; and they [a]attacked their
tents and the Meunites who were found there,
and [b]utterly destroyed them, as it is to this day.
So they dwelt in their place, because *there was*
pasture for their flocks there. 42 Now *some* of them,
five hundred men of the sons of Simeon, went
to Mount Seir, having as their captains Pelatiah,
Neariah, Rephaiah, and Uzziel, the sons of Ishi.
43 And they defeated [a]the rest of the Amalekites
who had escaped. They have dwelt there to this day.

### *THE FAMILY OF REUBEN*

*(Gen. 46:8, 9)*

5 Now the sons of Reuben the firstborn of
Israel—[a]he *was* indeed the firstborn, but
because he [b]defiled his father's bed, [c]his birth-
right was given to the sons of Joseph, the son
of Israel, so that the genealogy is not listed ac-
cording to the birthright; 2 yet [a]Judah prevailed
over his brothers, and from him *came* a [b]ruler,
although the birthright was Joseph's— 3 the sons
of [a]Reuben the firstborn of Israel were Hanoch,
Pallu, Hezron, and Carmi.
4 The sons of Joel *were* Shemaiah his son, Gog
his son, Shimei his son, 5 Micah his son, Reaiah
his son, Baal his son, 6 and Beerah his son, whom
Tiglath-Pileser[1] king of Assyria [a]carried into cap-
tivity. He *was* leader of the Reubenites. 7 And his
brethren by their families, [a]when the genealogy of
their generations was registered: the chief, Jeiel,
and Zechariah, 8 and Bela the son of Azaz, the son
of Shema, the son of Joel, who dwelt in [a]Aroer, as
far as Nebo and Baal Meon. 9 Eastward they settled

4:9 [a] Gen. 34:19 [1] Literally *He Will Cause Pain* 4:11 [a] Job 8:1 4:13 [a] Josh. 15:17; Judg. 3:9, 11 [1] Septuagint and Vulgate add *and Meonothai.* 4:14 [a] Neh. 11:35 [1] Literally *Valley of Craftsmen* 4:15 [a] Josh. 14:6, 14; 15:13, 17; 1 Chr. 6:56 4:17 [1] Literally *she* 4:18 [1] Or *His Judean wife* 4:19 [a] 2 Kin. 25:23 4:21 [a] Gen. 38:11, 14 [b] Gen. 38:1–5; 46:12 4:23 [1] Literally *Plants* [2] Literally *Hedges* 4:24 [a] Num. 26:12–14 [1] Called *Jachin* in Genesis 46:10 [2] Called *Zohar* in Genesis 46:10 4:27 [a] Num. 2:9 4:33 [1] Or *Baalath Beer* (compare Joshua 19:8) 4:41 [a] 2 Kin. 18:8 [b] 2 Kin. 19:11 4:43 [a] Ex. 17:14; 1 Sam. 15:8; 30:17 5:1 [a] Gen. 29:32; 49:3 [b] Gen. 35:22; 49:4 [c] Gen. 48:15, 22 5:2 [a] Gen. 49:8, 10; Ps. 60:7; 108:8 [b] Mic. 5:2; Matt. 2:6 5:3 [a] Gen. 46:9; Ex. 6:14; Num. 26:5 5:6 [a] 2 Kin. 18:11 [1] Hebrew *Tilgath-Pilneser* 5:7 [a] 1 Chr. 5:17 5:8 [a] Num. 32:34; Josh. 12:2; 13:15, 16

as far as the entrance of the wilderness this side
of the River Euphrates, because their cattle had
multiplied [a]in the land of Gilead.
10 Now in the days of Saul they made war
[a]with the Hagrites, who fell by their hand; and
they dwelt in their tents throughout the entire
*area* east of Gilead.

### *THE FAMILY OF GAD*

11 And the [a]children of Gad dwelt next to them
in the land of [b]Bashan as far as [c]Salcah: 12 Joel
*was* the chief, Shapham the next, then Jaanai and
Shaphat in Bashan, 13 and their brethren of their
father's house: Michael, Meshullam, Sheba, Jorai,
Jachan, Zia, and Eber—seven *in all*. 14 These *were*
the children of Abihail the son of Huri, the son
of Jaroah, the son of Gilead, the son of Michael,
the son of Jeshishai, the son of Jahdo, the son of
Buz; 15 Ahi the son of Abdiel, the son of Guni, *was*
chief of their father's house. 16 And *the Gadites*
dwelt in Gilead, in Bashan and in its villages, and
in all the common-lands of [a]Sharon within their
borders. 17 All these were registered by genealo-
gies in the days of [a]Jotham king of Judah, and in
the days of [b]Jeroboam king of Israel.
18 The sons of Reuben, the Gadites, and half
the tribe of Manasseh *had* forty-four thousand
seven hundred and sixty valiant men, men
able to bear shield and sword, to shoot with the
bow, and skillful in war, who went to war. 19 They
made war with the Hagrites, [a]Jetur, Naphish, and
Nodab. 20 And [a]they were helped against them,
and the Hagrites were delivered into their hand,
and all who *were* with them, for they [b]cried out
to God in the battle. He heeded their prayer,
because they [c]put their trust in Him. 21 Then they
took away their livestock—fifty thousand of their
camels, two hundred and fifty thousand of their
sheep, and two thousand of their donkeys—also
one hundred thousand of their men; 22 for many
fell dead, because the war [a]*was* God's. And they
dwelt in their place until [b]the captivity.

### *THE FAMILY OF MANASSEH (EAST)*

23 So the children of the half-tribe of Manas-
seh dwelt in the land. Their *numbers* increased
from Bashan to Baal Hermon, that is, to [a]Senir,
or Mount Hermon. 24 These *were* the heads of
their fathers' houses: Epher, Ishi, Eliel, Azriel,
Jeremiah, Hodaviah, and Jahdiel. They were
mighty men of valor, famous men, *and* heads
of their fathers' houses.
25 And they were unfaithful to the God of
their fathers, and [a]played the harlot after the
gods of the peoples of the land, whom God had
destroyed before them. 26 So the God of Israel
stirred up the spirit of [a]Pul king of Assyria, that
is, [b]Tiglath-Pileser[1] king of Assyria. He carried
the Reubenites, the Gadites, and the half-tribe of
Manasseh into captivity. He took them to [c]Halah,
Habor, Hara, and the river of Gozan to this day.

> **5:26 Tiglath-Pileser** became **king of Assyria** in 745 BC. Rather than killing the leaders of the countries he defeated, Tiglath-Pileser took them captive and deported them. The conquered area then became a province of Assyria. **Halah**, **Habor**, and **Hara** were located near Nineveh, over 500 miles northeast of Jerusalem.

### *THE FAMILY OF LEVI*

*(Gen. 46:11)*

6 The sons of Levi *were* [a]Gershon, Kohath, and
Merari. 2 The sons of Kohath *were* Amram,
[a]Izhar, Hebron, and Uzziel. 3 The children of
Amram *were* Aaron, Moses, and Miriam. And the
sons of Aaron *were* [a]Nadab, Abihu, Eleazar, and
Ithamar. 4 Eleazar begot Phinehas, *and* Phinehas
begot Abishua; 5 Abishua begot Bukki, and Bukki
begot Uzzi; 6 Uzzi begot Zerahiah, and Zerahiah
begot Meraioth; 7 Meraioth begot Amariah, and
Amariah begot Ahitub; 8 [a]Ahitub begot [b]Zadok,
and Zadok begot Ahimaaz; 9 Ahimaaz begot Azari-
ah, and Azariah begot Johanan; 10 Johanan begot
Azariah (it was he [a]who ministered as priest in the
[b]temple that Solomon built in Jerusalem); 11 [a]Aza-
riah begot [b]Amariah, and Amariah begot Ahitub;
12 Ahitub begot Zadok, and Zadok begot Shallum;
13 Shallum begot Hilkiah, and Hilkiah begot Aza-
riah; 14 Azariah begot [a]Seraiah, and Seraiah begot
Jehozadak. 15 Jehozadak went *into captivity* [a]when
the LORD carried Judah and Jerusalem into cap-
tivity by the hand of Nebuchadnezzar.
16 The sons of Levi *were* [a]Gershon,[1] Kohath,
and Merari. 17 These are the names of the sons
of Gershon: Libni and Shimei. 18 The sons of Ko-
hath *were* Amram, Izhar, Hebron, and Uzziel.
19 The sons of Merari *were* Mahli and Mushi. Now
these *are* the families of the Levites according to
their fathers: 20 Of Gershon *were* Libni his son,
Jahath his son, [a]Zimmah his son, 21 Joah his son,
Iddo his son, Zerah his son, *and* Jeatherai his
son. 22 The sons of Kohath *were* Amminadab
his son, [a]Korah his son, Assir his son, 23 Elkanah his
son, Ebiasaph his son, Assir his son, 24 Tahath
his son, Uriel his son, Uzziah his son, and Shaul
his son. 25 The sons of Elkanah *were* [a]Amasai and
Ahimoth. 26 *As for* Elkanah,[1] the sons of Elkanah

**5:9** [a] Josh. 22:8, 9 **5:10** [a] Gen. 25:12 **5:11** [a] Num. 26:15–18 [b] Josh. 13:11, 24–28 [c] Deut. 3:10 **5:16** [a] 1 Chr. 27:29; Song 2:1; Is. 35:2; 65:10 **5:17** [a] 2 Kin. 15:5, 32 [b] 2 Kin. 14:16, 28 **5:19** [a] Gen. 25:15; 1 Chr. 1:31 **5:20** [a] [1 Chr. 5:22] [b] 2 Chr. 14:11–13 [c] Ps. 9:10; 20:7, 8; 22:4, 5 **5:22** [a] [Josh. 23:10; 2 Chr. 32:8; Rom. 8:31] [b] 2 Kin. 15:29; 17:6 **5:23** [a] Deut. 3:9 **5:25** [a] 2 Kin. 17:7 **5:26** [a] 2 Kin. 15:19 [b] 2 Kin. 15:29 [c] 2 Kin. 17:6; 18:11 [1] Hebrew *Tilgath-Pilneser* **6:1** [a] Gen. 46:11; Ex. 6:16; Num. 26:57; 1 Chr. 23:6 **6:2** [a] 1 Chr. 6:18, 22 **6:3** [a] Lev. 10:1, 2 **6:8** [a] 2 Sam. 8:17 [b] 2 Sam. 15:27 **6:10** [a] 2 Chr. 26:17, 18 [b] 1 Kin. 6:1; 2 Chr. 3:1 **6:11** [a] Ezra 7:3 [b] 2 Chr. 19:11 **6:14** [a] 2 Kin. 25:18–21; Neh. 11:11 **6:15** [a] 2 Kin. 25:21 **6:16** [a] Gen. 46:11; Ex. 6:16 [1] Hebrew *Gershom* (alternate spelling of *Gershon*, as in verses 1, 17, 20, 43, 62, and 71) **6:20** [a] 1 Chr. 6:42 **6:22** [a] Num. 16:1 **6:25** [a] 1 Chr. 6:35, 36 **6:26** [1] Compare verse 35

*were* Zophai[2] his son, Nahath[3] his son, 27 Eliab[1] his
son, Jeroham his son, *and* Elkanah his son. 28 The
sons of Samuel *were* Joel[1] the firstborn, and Abijah
the second.[2] 29 The sons of Merari *were* Mahli, Libni
his son, Shimei his son, Uzzah his son, 30 Shim-
ea his son, Haggiah his son, *and* Asaiah his son.

### MUSICIANS IN THE HOUSE OF THE LORD

31 Now these are [a]the men whom David ap-
pointed over the service of song in the house of
the LORD, after the [b]ark came to rest. 32 They were
ministering with music before the dwelling place
of the tabernacle of meeting, until Solomon had
built the house of the LORD in Jerusalem, and they
served in their office according to their order.
33 And these *are* the ones who ministered
with their sons: Of the sons of the [a]Kohathites
*were* Heman the singer, the son of Joel, the son
of Samuel, 34 the son of Elkanah, the son of Jero-
ham, the son of Eliel,[1] the son of Toah,[2] 35 the son
of Zuph, the son of Elkanah, the son of Mahath,
the son of Amasai, 36 the son of Elkanah, the son
of Joel, the son of Azariah, the son of Zephaniah,
37 the son of Tahath, the son of Assir, the son of
[a]Ebiasaph, the son of Korah, 38 the son of Izhar, the
son of Kohath, the son of Levi, the son of Israel.
39 And his brother [a]Asaph, who stood at his right
hand, *was* Asaph the son of Berachiah, the son of
Shimea, 40 the son of Michael, the son of Baaseiah,
the son of Malchijah, 41 the son of [a]Ethni, the son
of Zerah, the son of Adaiah, 42 the son of Ethan,
the son of Zimmah, the son of Shimei, 43 the son
of Jahath, the son of Gershon, the son of Levi.
44 Their brethren, the sons of Merari, on the
left hand, *were* Ethan the son of Kishi, the son
of Abdi, the son of Malluch, 45 the son of Hash-
abiah, the son of Amaziah, the son of Hilkiah,
46 the son of Amzi, the son of Bani, the son of
Shamer, 47 the son of Mahli, the son of Mushi,
the son of Merari, the son of Levi.
48 And their brethren, the Levites, *were* ap-
pointed to every [a]kind of service of the taber-
nacle of the house of God.

> **6:49** The rules and procedures for entering the Most Holy Place were strict and important to follow. Only the high priest was allowed to enter, once a year on the Day of Atonement, to ask God's forgiveness for Israel's sins. The only item in the Most Holy Place was the ark of the covenant, which the Israelites considered to be God's earthly throne.

### THE FAMILY OF AARON

49 [a]But Aaron and his sons offered sacrifices
[b]on the altar of burnt offering and [c]on the altar of
incense, for all the work of the Most Holy *Place,*
and to make atonement for Israel, according
to all that Moses the servant of God had com-
manded. 50 Now these *are* the [a]sons of Aaron:
Eleazar his son, Phinehas his son, Abishua his
son, 51 Bukki his son, Uzzi his son, Zerahiah his
son, 52 Meraioth his son, Amariah his son, Ahitub
his son, 53 Zadok his son, *and* Ahimaaz his son.

### DWELLING PLACES OF THE LEVITES

*(Josh. 21:1–42)*

54 [a]Now these *are* their dwelling places
throughout their settlements in their terri-
tory, for they were *given* by lot to the sons of
Aaron, of the family of the Kohathites: 55 [a]They
gave them Hebron in the land of Judah, with its
surrounding common-lands. 56 [a]But the fields
of the city and its villages they gave to Caleb the
son of Jephunneh. 57 And [a]to the sons of Aaron
they gave *one of* the cities of refuge, Hebron;
also Libnah with its common-lands, Jattir, Esh-
temoa with its common-lands, 58 Hilen[1] with its
common-lands, Debir with its common-lands,
59 Ashan[1] with its common-lands, and Beth She-
mesh with its common-lands. 60 And from the
tribe of Benjamin: Geba with its common-lands,
Alemeth[1] with its common-lands, and Anathoth
with its common-lands. All their cities among
their families *were* thirteen.
61 [a]To the rest of the family of the tribe of
the Kohathites *they gave* [b]by lot ten cities from
half the tribe of Manasseh. 62 And to the sons of
Gershon, throughout their families, *they gave*
thirteen cities from the tribe of Issachar, from
the tribe of Asher, from the tribe of Naphtali, and
from the tribe of Manasseh in Bashan. 63 To the
sons of Merari, throughout their families, *they
gave* [a]twelve cities from the tribe of Reuben,
from the tribe of Gad, and from the tribe of Zeb-
ulun. 64 So the children of Israel gave *these* cities
with their common-lands to the Levites. 65 And
they gave by lot from the tribe of the children of
Judah, from the tribe of the children of Simeon,
and from the tribe of the children of Benjamin
these cities which are called by *their* names.
66 Now [a]some of the families of the sons
of Kohath *were given* cities as their territory
from the tribe of Ephraim. 67 [a]And they gave
them *one of* the cities of refuge, Shechem
with its common-lands, in the mountains of
Ephraim, also Gezer with its common-lands,
68 [a]Jokmeam with its common-lands, Beth
Horon with its common-lands, 69 Aijalon with

**6:26** [2] Spelled *Zuph* in verse 35 and 1 Samuel 1:1 [3] Compare verse 34 **6:27** [1] Compare verse 34 **6:28** [1] Following Septuagint, Syriac, and Arabic (compare verse 33 and 1 Samuel 8:2) [2] Hebrew *Vasheni* **6:31** [a] 1 Chr. 15:16–22, 27; 16:4–6 [b] 2 Sam. 6:17; 1 Kin. 8:4; 1 Chr. 15:25—16:1 **6:33** [a] Num. 26:57 **6:34** [1] Spelled *Elihu* in 1 Samuel 1:1 [2] Spelled *Tohu* in 1 Samuel 1:1 **6:37** [a] Ex. 6:24 **6:39** [a] 2 Chr. 5:12 **6:41** [a] 1 Chr. 6:21 **6:48** [a] 1 Chr. 9:14–34 **6:49** [a] Ex. 28:1; [Num. 18:1–8] [b] Lev. 1:8, 9 [c] Ex. 30:7 **6:50** [a] 1 Chr. 6:4–8; Ezra 7:5 **6:54** [a] Josh. 21 **6:55** [a] Josh. 14:13; 21:11, 12 **6:56** [a] Josh. 14:13; 15:13 **6:57** [a] Josh. 21:13, 19 **6:58** [1] Spelled *Holon* in Joshua 21:15 **6:59** [1] Spelled *Ain* in Joshua 21:16 **6:60** [1] Spelled *Almon* in Joshua 21:18 **6:61** [a] 1 Chr. 6:66–70 [b] Josh. 21:5 **6:63** [a] Josh. 21:7, 34–40 **6:66** [a] 1 Chr. 6:61 **6:67** [a] Josh. 21:21 **6:68** [a] Josh. 21:22

its common-lands, and Gath Rimmon with its
common-lands. 70 And from the half-tribe of
Manasseh: Aner with its common-lands and
Bileam with its common-lands, for the rest of
the family of the sons of Kohath.
71 From the family of the half-tribe of Ma-
nasseh the sons of Gershon *were given* Golan in
Bashan with its common-lands and Ashtaroth
with its common-lands. 72 And from the tribe
of Issachar: Kedesh with its common-lands,
Daberath with its common-lands, 73 Ramoth
with its common-lands, and Anem with its
common-lands. 74 And from the tribe of Asher:
Mashal with its common-lands, Abdon with
its common-lands, 75 Hukok with its common-
lands, and Rehob with its common-lands. 76 And
from the tribe of Naphtali: Kedesh in Galilee with
its common-lands, Hammon with its common-
lands, and Kirjathaim with its common-lands.
77 From the tribe of Zebulun the rest of the
children of Merari *were given* Rimmon[1] with
its common-lands and Tabor with its common-
lands. 78 And on the other side of the Jordan,
across from Jericho, on the east side of the Jor-
dan, *they were given* from the tribe of Reuben:
Bezer in the wilderness with its common-lands,
Jahzah with its common-lands, 79 Kedemoth
with its common-lands, and Mephaath with
its common-lands. 80 And from the tribe of
Gad: Ramoth in Gilead with its common-lands,
Mahanaim with its common-lands, 81 Hesh-
bon with its common-lands, and Jazer with its
common-lands.

### THE FAMILY OF ISSACHAR
*(Gen. 46:13)*

**7** The sons of Issachar *were* [a]Tola, Puah,[1] Ja-
shub, and Shimron—four *in all.* 2 The sons of
Tola *were* Uzzi, Rephaiah, Jeriel, Jahmai, Jibsam,
and Shemuel, heads of their father's house. *The
sons* of Tola *were* mighty men of valor in their
generations; [a]their number in the days of David
*was* twenty-two thousand six hundred. 3 The son
of Uzzi *was* Izrahiah, and the sons of Izrahiah
*were* Michael, Obadiah, Joel, and Ishiah. All
five of them *were* chief men. 4 And with them,
by their generations, according to their fathers'
houses, *were* thirty-six thousand troops ready
for war; for they had many wives and sons.
5 Now their brethren among all the families
of Issachar *were* mighty men of valor, listed by
their genealogies, eighty-seven thousand in all.

### THE FAMILY OF BENJAMIN
*(Gen. 46:21)*

6 *The sons* of [a]Benjamin *were* Bela, Becher,
and Jediael—three *in all.* 7 The sons of Bela were
Ezbon, Uzzi, Uzziel, Jerimoth, and Iri—five *in
all.* They *were* heads of *their* fathers' houses, and
they were listed by their genealogies, twenty-two
thousand and thirty-four mighty men of valor.
8 The sons of Becher *were* Zemirah, Joash, El-
iezer, Elioenai, Omri, Jerimoth, Abijah, Anathoth,
and Alemeth. All these *are* the sons of Becher.
9 And they were recorded by genealogy accord-
ing to their generations, heads of their fathers'
houses, twenty thousand two hundred mighty
men of valor. 10 The son of Jediael *was* Bilhan, and
the sons of Bilhan *were* Jeush, Benjamin, Ehud,
Chenaanah, Zethan, Tharshish, and Ahishahar.
11 All these sons of Jediael *were* heads of their
fathers' houses; *there were* seventeen thousand
two hundred mighty men of valor fit to go out
for war *and* battle. 12 Shuppim and Huppim[1] *were*
the sons of Ir, *and* Hushim *was* the son of Aher.

### THE FAMILY OF NAPHTALI
*(Gen. 46:24)*

13 The [a]sons of Naphtali *were* Jahziel,[1] Guni,
Jezer, and Shallum,[2] the sons of Bilhah.

### THE FAMILY OF MANASSEH (WEST)

14 The [a]descendants of Manasseh: his Syr-
ian concubine bore him [b]Machir the father of
Gilead, the father of Asriel.[1] 15 Machir took as his
wife *the sister* of Huppim and Shuppim,[1] whose
name *was* Maachah. The name of *Gilead's* grand-
son[2] *was* [a]Zelophehad,[3] but Zelophehad begot
only daughters. 16 (Maachah the wife of Machir
bore a son, and she called his name Peresh. The
name of his brother *was* Sheresh, and his sons
*were* Ulam and Rakem. 17 The son of Ulam *was*
[a]Bedan.) These *were* the descendants of Gilead
the son of Machir, the son of Manasseh.

> **7:15** Usually, only sons inherited their father's land. Since **Zelophehad** had no sons, though, Moses allowed his land to be given to his **daughters**—on one condition. The daughters had to marry men in their own tribe. That way, Zelophehad's land would remain in the tribe of Manasseh.

18 His sister Hammoleketh bore Ishhod,
Abiezer, and Mahlah.
19 And the sons of Shemida were Ahian, She-
chem, Likhi, and Aniam.

### THE FAMILY OF EPHRAIM

20 [a]The sons of Ephraim *were* Shuthelah,
Bered his son, Tahath his son, Eladah his son,
Tahath his son, 21 Zabad his son, Shuthelah his
son, and Ezer and Elead. The men of Gath who
were born in *that* land killed *them* because they
came down to take away their cattle. 22 Then

6:77 [1] Hebrew *Rimmono,* alternate spelling of *Rimmon;* see 4:32 7:1 [a] Num. 26:23–25 [1] Spelled *Puvah* in Genesis 46:13 7:2 [a] 2 Sam. 24:1–9; 1 Chr. 27:1 7:6 [a] Gen. 46:21; Num. 26:38–41; 1 Chr. 8:1 7:12 [1] Called *Hupham* in Numbers 26:39 7:13 [a] Num. 26:48–50 [1] Spelled *Jahzeel* in Genesis 46:24 [2] Spelled *Shillem* in Genesis 46:24 7:14 [a] Num. 26:29–34 [b] 1 Chr. 2:21 [1] The son of Gilead (compare Numbers 26:30, 31) 7:15 [a] Num. 26:30–33; 27:1 [1] Compare verse 12 [2] Literally *the second* [3] Compare Numbers 26:30–33 7:17 [a] 1 Sam. 12:11 7:20 [a] Num. 26:35–37

Ephraim their father mourned many days, and
his brethren came to comfort him.
23 And when he went in to his wife, she con-
ceived and bore a son; and he called his name
Beriah,[1] because tragedy had come upon his
house. 24 Now his daughter *was* Sheerah, who
built Lower and Upper [a]Beth Horon and Uzzen
Sheerah; 25 and Rephah *was* his son, *as well*
as Resheph, and Telah his son, Tahan his son,
26 Laadan his son, Ammihud his son, [a]Elishama
his son, 27 Nun[1] his son, and [a]Joshua his son.
28 Now their [a]possessions and dwelling places
*were* Bethel and its towns: to the east Naaran, to
the west Gezer and its towns, and Shechem and its
towns, as far as Ayyah[1] and its towns; 29 and by the
borders of the children of [a]Manasseh *were* Beth
Shean and its towns, Taanach and its towns, [b]Me-
giddo and its towns, Dor and its towns. In these
dwelt the children of Joseph, the son of Israel.

### *THE FAMILY OF ASHER*
*(Gen. 46:17)*

30 [a]The sons of Asher *were* Imnah, Ishvah,
Ishvi, Beriah, and their sister Serah. 31 The sons
of Beriah *were* Heber and Malchiel, who was the
father of Birzaith.[1] 32 And Heber begot Japhlet,
Shomer,[1] Hotham,[2] and their sister Shua. 33 The
sons of Japhlet *were* Pasach, Bimhal, and Ashvath.
These *were* the children of Japhlet. 34 The sons of
[a]Shemer *were* Ahi, Rohgah, Jehubbah, and Aram.
35 And the sons of his brother Helem *were* Zophah,
Imna, Shelesh, and Amal. 36 The sons of Zophah
*were* Suah, Harnepher, Shual, Beri, Imrah, 37 Bezer,
Hod, Shamma, Shilshah, Jithran,[1] and Beera. 38 The
sons of Jether *were* Jephunneh, Pispah, and Ara.
39 The sons of Ulla *were* Arah, Haniel, and Rizia.
40 All these *were* the children of Asher, heads
of *their* fathers' houses, choice men, mighty men
of valor, chief leaders. And they were recorded
by genealogies among the army fit for battle;
their number *was* twenty-six thousand.

### *THE FAMILY TREE OF KING SAUL OF BENJAMIN*
*(Gen. 46:21)*

8 Now Benjamin begot [a]Bela his firstborn, Ash-
bel the second, Aharah[1] the third, 2 Nohah the
fourth, and Rapha the fifth. 3 The sons of Bela
*were* Addar,[1] Gera, Abihud, 4 Abishua, Naaman,
Ahoah, 5 Gera, Shephuphan, and Huram.
6 These *are* the sons of Ehud, who were the
heads of the fathers' *houses* of the inhabitants of
[a]Geba, and who forced them to move to [b]Man-
ahath: 7 Naaman, Ahijah, and Gera who forced
them to move. He begot Uzza and Ahihud.
8 Also Shaharaim had children in the country
of Moab, after he had sent away Hushim and Baara
his wives. 9 By Hodesh his wife he begot Jobab,
Zibia, Mesha, Malcam, 10 Jeuz, Sachiah, and Mirmah.
These *were* his sons, heads of their fathers' *houses*.
11 And by Hushim he begot Abitub and Elpa-
al. 12 The sons of Elpaal *were* Eber, Misham, and
Shemed, who built Ono and Lod with its towns;
13 and Beriah and [a]Shema, who *were* heads of
their fathers' *houses* of the inhabitants of Ai-
jalon, who drove out the inhabitants of Gath.
14 Ahio, Shashak, Jeremoth, 15 Zebadiah, Arad,
Eder, 16 Michael, Ispah, and Joha *were* the sons
of Beriah. 17 Zebadiah, Meshullam, Hizki, Heber,
18 Ishmerai, Jizliah, and Jobab *were* the sons of
Elpaal. 19 Jakim, Zichri, Zabdi, 20 Elienai, Zillethai,
Eliel, 21 Adaiah, Beraiah, and Shimrath *were* the
sons of Shimei. 22 Ishpan, Eber, Eliel, 23 Abdon,
Zichri, Hanan, 24 Hananiah, Elam, Antothijah,
25 Iphdeiah, and Penuel *were* the sons of Shashak.
26 Shamsherai, Shehariah, Athaliah, 27 Jaareshi-
ah, Elijah, and Zichri *were* the sons of Jeroham.
28 These *were* heads of the fathers' *houses*
by their generations, chief men. These dwelt
in Jerusalem.
29 Now the father of Gibeon, whose [a]wife's
name *was* Maacah, dwelt at Gibeon. 30 And his
firstborn son *was* Abdon, then Zur, Kish, Baal,
Nadab, 31 Gedor, Ahio, Zecher, 32 and Mikloth, *who*
begot Shimeah.[1] They also dwelt alongside their
relatives in Jerusalem, with their brethren. 33 [a]Ner[1]
begot Kish, Kish begot Saul, and Saul begot Jona-
than, Malchishua, Abinadab,[2] and Esh-Baal.[3] 34 The
son of Jonathan *was* Merib-Baal,[1] and Merib-Baal
begot [a]Micah. 35 The sons of Micah *were* Pithon,
Melech, Tarea, and Ahaz. 36 And Ahaz begot Jeho-
addah;[1] Jehoaddah begot Alemeth, Azmaveth, and
Zimri; and Zimri begot Moza. 37 Moza begot Binea,
Raphah[1] his son, Eleasah his son, *and* Azel his son.
38 Azel had six sons whose names *were* these:
Azrikam, Bocheru, Ishmael, Sheariah, Obadiah,
and Hanan. All these *were* the sons of Azel. 39 And
the sons of Eshek his brother *were* Ulam his first-
born, Jeush the second, and Eliphelet the third.
40 The sons of Ulam were mighty men of
valor—archers. *They* had many sons and grand-
sons, one hundred and fifty *in all*. These *were*
all sons of Benjamin.

9 So [a]all Israel was recorded by genealogies,
and indeed, they *were* inscribed in the book
of the kings of Israel. But Judah was carried away
captive to Babylon because of their unfaithful-
ness. 2 [a]And the first inhabitants who *dwelt* in
their possessions in their cities *were* Israelites,
priests, Levites, and [b]the Nethinim.

7:23 [1] Literally *In Tragedy* 7:24 [a] Josh. 16:3, 5; 2 Chr. 8:5 7:26 [a] Num. 10:22 7:27 [a] Ex. 17:9, 14; 24:13; 33:11 [1] Hebrew *Non* 7:28 [a] Josh. 16:1–10 [1] Many Hebrew manuscripts, Bomberg, Septuagint, Targum, and Vulgate read *Gazza*. 7:29 [a] Gen. 41:51; Josh. 17:7 [b] Josh. 17:11 7:30 [a] Gen. 46:17; Num. 26:44–47 7:31 [1] Or *Birzavith* or *Birzoth* 7:32 [1] Spelled *Shemer* in verse 34 [2] Spelled *Helem* in verse 35 7:34 [a] 1 Chr. 7:32 7:37 [1] Spelled *Jether* in verse 38 8:1 [a] Gen. 46:21; Num. 26:38; 1 Chr. 7:6 [1] Spelled *Ahiram* in Numbers 26:38 8:3 [1] Called *Ard* in Numbers 26:40 8:6 [a] 1 Chr. 6:60 [b] 1 Chr. 2:52 8:13 [a] 1 Chr. 8:21 8:29 [a] 1 Chr. 9:35–38 8:32 [1] Spelled *Shimeam* in 9:38 8:33 [a] 1 Sam. 14:51 [1] Also the son of Gibeon (compare 9:36, 39) [2] Called *Jishui* in 1 Samuel 14:49 [3] Called *Ishbosheth* in 2 Samuel 2:8 and elsewhere 8:34 [a] 2 Sam. 9:12 [1] Called *Mephibosheth* in 2 Samuel 4:4 8:36 [1] Spelled *Jarah* in 9:42 8:37 [1] Spelled *Rephaiah* in 9:43 9:1 [a] Ezra 2:59 9:2 [a] Ezra 2:70; Neh. 7:73 [b] Ezra 2:43; 8:20

### *DWELLERS IN JERUSALEM*

3 Now in [a]Jerusalem the children of Judah
dwelt, and some of the children of Benjamin,
and of the children of Ephraim and Manasseh:
4 Uthai the son of Ammihud, the son of Omri, the
son of Imri, the son of Bani, of the descendants
of Perez, the son of Judah. 5 Of the Shilonites:
Asaiah the firstborn and his sons. 6 Of the sons
of Zerah: Jeuel, and their brethren—six hundred
and ninety. 7 Of the sons of Benjamin: Sallu the
son of Meshullam, the son of Hodaviah, the son
of Hassenuah; 8 Ibneiah the son of Jeroham;
Elah the son of Uzzi, the son of Michri; Meshul-
lam the son of Shephatiah, the son of Reuel, the
son of Ibnijah; 9 and their brethren, according to
their generations—nine hundred and fifty-six.
All these men *were* heads of a father's *house* in
their fathers' houses.

### *THE PRIESTS AT JERUSALEM*

10 [a]Of the priests: Jedaiah, Jehoiarib, and
Jachin; 11 Azariah the son of Hilkiah, the son of
Meshullam, the son of Zadok, the son of Me-
raioth, the son of Ahitub, the [a]officer over the
house of God; 12 Adaiah the son of Jeroham, the
son of Pashur, the son of Malchijah; Maasai the
son of Adiel, the son of Jahzerah, the son of
Meshullam, the son of Meshillemith, the son
of Immer; 13 and their brethren, heads of their
fathers' houses—one thousand seven hundred
and sixty. *They were* very able men for the work
of the service of the house of God.

### *THE LEVITES AT JERUSALEM*

14 Of the Levites: Shemaiah the son of Has-
shub, the son of Azrikam, the son of Hashabi-
ah, of the sons of Merari; 15 Bakbakkar, Heresh,
Galal, and Mattaniah the son of Micah, the son
of [a]Zichri, the son of Asaph; 16 [a]Obadiah the
son of [b]Shemaiah, the son of Galal, the son of
Jeduthun; and Berechiah the son of Asa, the
son of Elkanah, who lived in the villages of the
Netophathites.

### *THE LEVITE GATEKEEPERS*

17 And the gatekeepers *were* Shallum, Akkub,
Talmon, Ahiman, and their brethren. Shallum
*was* the chief. 18 Until then *they had been* gate-
keepers for the camps of the children of Levi at
the King's Gate on the east.

19 Shallum the son of Kore, the son of Ebia-
saph, the son of Korah, and his brethren, from
his father's house, the Korahites, *were* in charge
of the work of the service, gatekeepers of the
tabernacle. Their fathers had been keepers of
the entrance to the camp of the LORD. 20 And
[a]Phinehas the son of Eleazar had been the offi-
cer over them in time past; the LORD *was* with
him. 21 [a]Zechariah the son of Meshelemiah *was*
keeper of the door of the tabernacle of meeting.

22 All those chosen as gatekeepers *were* two
hundred and twelve. [a]They were recorded by
their genealogy, in their villages. David and
Samuel [b]the seer had appointed them to their
trusted office. 23 So they and their children *were*
in charge of the gates of the house of the LORD,
the house of the tabernacle, by assignment.
24 The gatekeepers were assigned to the four
directions: the east, west, north, and south.
25 And their brethren in their villages *had* to
come with them from time to time [a]for seven
days. 26 For in this trusted office *were* four chief
gatekeepers; they were Levites. And they had
charge over the chambers and treasuries of the
house of God. 27 And they lodged *all* around the
house of God because they *had* the [a]responsi-
bility, and they *were* in charge of opening *it*
every morning.

### *OTHER LEVITE RESPONSIBILITIES*

28 Now *some* of them were in charge of the
serving vessels, for they brought them in and
took them out by count. 29 *Some* of them *were*
appointed over the furnishings and over all the
implements of the sanctuary, and over the [a]fine
flour and the wine and the oil and the incense
and the spices. 30 And *some* of the sons of the
priests made [a]the ointment of the spices.

31 Mattithiah of the Levites, the firstborn of
Shallum the Korahite, had the trusted office
[a]over the things that were baked in the pans.
32 And some of their brethren of the sons of
the Kohathites [a]*were* in charge of preparing the
showbread for every Sabbath.

33 These are [a]the singers, heads of the fa-
thers' *houses* of the Levites, *who lodged* in the
chambers, *and were* free *from other duties;* for
they were employed in *that* work day and night.
34 These heads of the fathers' *houses* of the Le-
vites *were* heads throughout their generations.
They dwelt at Jerusalem.

### *THE FAMILY OF KING SAUL*

35 Jeiel the father of Gibeon, whose wife's
name *was* [a]Maacah, dwelt at Gibeon. 36 His first-
born son *was* Abdon, then Zur, Kish, Baal, Ner,
Nadab, 37 Gedor, Ahio, Zechariah,[1] and Mikloth.
38 And Mikloth begot Shimeam.[1] They also dwelt
alongside their relatives in Jerusalem, with their
brethren. 39 [a]Ner begot Kish, Kish begot Saul,
and Saul begot Jonathan, Malchishua, Abina-
dab, and Esh-Baal. 40 The son of Jonathan *was*
Merib-Baal, and Merib-Baal begot Micah. 41 The
sons of Micah *were* Pithon, Melech, Tahrea,[1] [a]and
Ahaz.[2] 42 And Ahaz begot Jarah;[1] Jarah begot Al-
emeth, Azmaveth, and Zimri; and Zimri begot

9:3 [a] Neh. 11:1, 2 9:10 [a] Neh. 11:10–14 9:11 [a] 2 Chr. 31:13; Jer. 20:1 9:15 [a] Neh. 11:17 9:16 [a] Neh. 11:17 [b] Neh. 11:17 9:20 [a] Num. 25:6–13; 31:6 9:21 [a] 1 Chr. 26:2, 14 9:22 [a] 1 Chr. 26:1, 2 [b] 1 Sam. 9:9 9:25 [a] 2 Kin. 11:4–7; 2 Chr. 23:8 9:27 [a] 1 Chr. 23:30–32 9:29 [a] 1 Chr. 23:29 9:30 [a] Ex. 30:22–25 9:31 [a] Lev. 2:5; 6:21 9:32 [a] Lev. 24:5–8 9:33 [a] 1 Chr. 6:31; 25:1 9:35 [a] 1 Chr. 8:29–32 9:37 [1] Called *Zecher* in 8:31 9:38 [1] Spelled *Shimeah* in 8:32 9:39 [a] 1 Chr. 8:33–38 9:41 [a] 1 Chr. 8:35 [1] Spelled *Tarea* in 8:35 [2] Following Arabic, Syriac, Targum, and Vulgate (compare 8:35); Masoretic Text and Septuagint omit *and Ahaz.* 9:42 [1] Spelled *Jehoaddah* in 8:36

Moza; 43 Moza begot Binea, Rephaiah[1] his son, Eleasah his son, and Azel his son.

44 And Azel had six sons whose names *were* these: Azrikam, Bocheru, Ishmael, Sheariah, Obadiah, and Hanan; these *were* the sons of Azel.

### TRAGIC END OF SAUL AND HIS SONS

*(1 Sam. 31:1–13)*

**10** Now [a]the Philistines fought against Israel; and the men of Israel fled from before the Philistines, and fell slain on Mount Gilboa. 2 Then the Philistines followed hard after Saul and his sons. And the Philistines killed Jonathan, Abinadab, and Malchishua, Saul's sons. 3 The battle became fierce against Saul. The archers hit him, and he was wounded by the archers. 4 Then Saul said to his armorbearer, "Draw your sword, and thrust me through with it, lest these uncircumcised men come and abuse me." But his armorbearer would not, for he was greatly afraid. Therefore Saul took a sword and fell on it. 5 And when his armorbearer saw that Saul was dead, he also fell on his sword and died. 6 So Saul and his three sons died, and all his house died together. 7 And when all the men of Israel who *were* in the valley saw that they had fled and that Saul and his sons were dead, they forsook their cities and fled; then the Philistines came and dwelt in them.

8 So it happened the next day, when the Philistines came to strip the slain, that they found Saul and his sons fallen on Mount Gilboa. 9 And they stripped him and took his head and his armor, and sent word throughout the land of the Philistines to proclaim the news *in the temple* of their idols and among the people. 10 [a]Then they put his armor in the temple of their gods, and fastened his head in the temple of Dagon.

11 And when all Jabesh Gilead heard all that the Philistines had done to Saul, 12 all the [a]valiant men arose and took the body of Saul and the bodies of his sons; and they brought them to [b]Jabesh, and buried their bones under the tamarisk tree at Jabesh, and fasted seven days.

**10:11–12** Receiving a proper burial was very important in the Israelite culture. In fact, it was so important that Israelite law did not allow a body to be left out overnight. The people of **Jabesh Gilead** were insulted by the shameful and degrading way **the body of Saul** was being treated. Their courage and commitment to following proper burial procedures were rewarded by King David.

13 So Saul died for his unfaithfulness which he had committed against the LORD, [a]because he did not keep the word of the LORD, and also because [b]he consulted a medium for guidance. 14 But *he* did not inquire of the LORD; therefore He killed him, and [a]turned the kingdom over to David the son of Jesse.

### DAVID MADE KING OVER ALL ISRAEL

*(2 Sam. 5:1–3)*

**11** Then [a]all Israel came together to David at Hebron, saying, "Indeed we *are* your bone and your flesh. 2 Also, in time past, even when Saul was king, you *were* the one who led Israel out and brought them in; and the LORD your [a]God said to you, 'You shall [b]shepherd My people Israel, and be ruler over My people Israel.' " 3 Therefore all the elders of Israel came to the king at Hebron, and David made a covenant with them at Hebron before the LORD. And [a]they anointed David king over Israel, according to the word of the LORD by [b]Samuel.

### THE CITY OF DAVID

*(2 Sam. 5:6–10)*

4 And David and all Israel [a]went to Jerusalem, which is Jebus, [b]where the Jebusites *were,* the inhabitants of the land. 5 But the inhabitants of Jebus said to David, "You shall not come in here!" Nevertheless David took the stronghold of Zion (that is, the City of David). 6 Now David said, "Whoever attacks the Jebusites first shall be chief and captain." And Joab the son of Zeruiah went up first, and became chief. 7 Then David dwelt in the stronghold; therefore they called it the City of David. 8 And he built the city around it, from the Millo[1] to the surrounding area. Joab repaired the rest of the city. 9 So David [a]went on and became great, and the LORD of hosts *was* with [b]him.

### THE MIGHTY MEN OF DAVID

*(2 Sam. 23:8–39)*

10 Now [a]these *were* the heads of the mighty men whom David had, who strengthened themselves with him in his kingdom, with all Israel, to make him king, according to [b]the word of the LORD concerning Israel.

11 And this *is* the number of the mighty men whom David had: [a]Jashobeam the son of a Hachmonite, [b]chief of the captains;[1] he had lifted up his spear against three hundred, killed *by him* at one time.

12 After him *was* Eleazar the son of [a]Dodo, the Ahohite, who *was one* of the three mighty men. 13 He was with David at Pasdammim. Now there the Philistines were gathered for battle, and there was a piece of ground full of barley. So the people fled from the Philistines. 14 But

**9:43** [1] Spelled *Raphah* in 8:37 **10:1** [a] 1 Sam. 31:1, 2 **10:10** [a] 1 Sam. 31:10 **10:12** [a] 1 Sam. 14:52 [b] 2 Sam. 21:12 **10:13** [a] 1 Sam. 13:13, 14; 15:22–26 [b] [Lev. 19:31; 20:6]; 1 Sam. 28:7 **10:14** [a] 1 Sam. 15:28; 2 Sam. 3:9, 10; 5:3; 1 Chr. 12:23 **11:1** [a] 2 Sam. 5:1 **11:2** [a] 1 Sam. 16:1–3; Ps. 78:70–72 [b] 2 Sam. 7:7 **11:3** [a] 2 Sam. 5:3 [b] 1 Sam. 16:1, 4, 12, 13 **11:4** [a] 2 Sam. 5:6 [b] Josh. 15:8, 63; Judg. 1:21; 19:10, 11 **11:8** [1] Literally *The Landfill* **11:9** [a] 2 Sam. 3:1 [b] 1 Sam. 16:18 **11:10** [a] 2 Sam. 23:8 [b] 1 Sam. 16:1, 12 **11:11** [a] 1 Chr. 27:2 [b] 1 Chr. 12:18 [1] Following Qere; Kethib, Septuagint, and Vulgate read *the thirty* (compare 2 Samuel 23:8). **11:12** [a] 1 Chr. 27:4

they stationed themselves in the middle of *that*
field, defended it, and killed the Philistines. So
the LORD brought about a great victory.
15 Now three of the thirty chief men [a]went
down to the rock to David, into the cave of Adul-
lam; and the army of the Philistines encamped
[b]in the Valley of Rephaim. 16 David *was* then in
the stronghold, and the garrison of the Philis-
tines *was* then in Bethlehem. 17 And David said
with longing, "Oh, that someone would give me a
drink of water from the well of Bethlehem, which
is by the gate!" 18 So the three broke through the
camp of the Philistines, drew water from the well
of Bethlehem that *was* by the gate, and took *it*
and brought *it* to David. Nevertheless David
would not drink it, but poured it out to the LORD.
19 And he said, "Far be it from me, O my God, that
I should do this! Shall I drink the blood of these
men *who have put* their lives *in jeopardy?* For at
the risk of their lives they brought it." Therefore
he would not drink it. These things were done
by the three mighty men.

> **11:18** Even though he had been longing for a drink from his "home" **well**, David never considered sending any of his brave supporters to get it for him. When they risked their lives to bring it to him, David **poured it out to the LORD**, as if it were a blood offering. The Israelites were strictly forbidden to eat blood (Lev. 3:17; Deut. 12:23), and David considered this water to be in the same category. Only God could receive such a sacrifice (see Gen. 35:14).

20 [a]Abishai the brother of Joab was chief of
*another* three.[1] He had lifted up his spear against
three hundred *men,* killed *them,* and won a name
among *these* three. 21 [a]Of the three he was more
honored than the other two men. Therefore he
became their captain. However he did not attain
to the *first* three.
22 Benaiah was the son of Jehoiada, the son
of a valiant man from Kabzeel, who had done
many deeds. [a]He had killed two lion-like heroes
of Moab. He also had gone down and killed a lion
in the midst of a pit on a snowy day. 23 And he
killed an Egyptian, a man of *great* height, five
cubits tall. In the Egyptian's hand *there was* a
spear like a weaver's beam; and he went down
to him with a staff, wrested the spear out of the
Egyptian's hand, and killed him with his own
spear. 24 These *things* Benaiah the son of Jehoi-
ada did, and won a name among three mighty
men. 25 Indeed he was more honored than the
thirty, but he did not attain to the *first* three. And
David appointed him over his guard.
26 Also the mighty warriors *were* [a]Asahel the
brother of Joab, Elhanan the son of Dodo of Beth-
lehem, 27 Shammoth the Harorite,[1] [a]Helez the
Pelonite,[2] 28 [a]Ira the son of Ikkesh the Tekoite,
[b]Abiezer the Anathothite, 29 Sibbechai the Hu-
shathite, Ilai the Ahohite, 30 [a]Maharai the Netoph-
athite, Heled[1] the son of Baanah the Netophathite,
31 Ithai[1] the son of Ribai of Gibeah, of the sons of
Benjamin, [a]Benaiah the Pirathonite, 32 Hurai[1] of
the brooks of Gaash, Abiel[2] the Arbathite, 33 Az-
maveth the Baharumite,[1] Eliahba the Shaalbonite,
34 the sons of Hashem the Gizonite, Jonathan the
son of Shageh the Hararite, 35 Ahiam the son of
Sacar the Hararite, Eliphal the son of Ur, 36 Hepher
the Mecherathite, Ahijah the Pelonite, 37 Hezro
the Carmelite, Naarai the son of Ezbai, 38 Joel
the brother of Nathan, Mibhar the son of Hagri,
39 Zelek the Ammonite, Naharai the Berothite[1]
(the armorbearer of Joab the son of Zeruiah),
40 Ira the Ithrite, Gareb the Ithrite, 41 [a]Uriah the
Hittite, Zabad the son of Ahlai, 42 Adina the son
of Shiza the Reubenite (a chief of the Reubenites)
and thirty with him, 43 Hanan the son of Maachah,
Joshaphat the Mithnite, 44 Uzzia the Ashterathite,
Shama and Jeiel the sons of Hotham the Aroerite,
45 Jediael the son of Shimri, and Joha his brother,
the Tizite, 46 Eliel the Mahavite, Jeribai and Josh-
aviah the sons of Elnaam, Ithmah the Moabite,
47 Eliel, Obed, and Jaasiel the Mezobaite.

> **11:41** This is the same **Uriah** who was the husband of Bathsheba. That Uriah was one of the mighty men of valor, who did so much to establish David as king, makes David's sin against Bathsheba and Uriah doubly tragic (see 2 Sam. 11).

### *THE GROWTH OF DAVID'S ARMY*
*(1 Sam. 22:1, 2)*

**12** Now [a]these *were* the men who came to
David at [b]Ziklag while he was still a fugitive
from Saul the son of Kish; and they *were* among
the mighty men, helpers in the war, 2 armed
with bows, using both the right hand and [a]the
left in *hurling* stones and *shooting* arrows with
the bow. *They were* of Benjamin, Saul's brethren.
3 The chief *was* Ahiezer, then Joash, the sons of
Shemaah the Gibeathite; Jeziel and Pelet the sons
of Azmaveth; Berachah, and Jehu the Anathothite;
4 Ishmaiah the Gibeonite, a mighty man among
the thirty, and over the thirty; Jeremiah, Jahaziel,

**11:15** [a] 2 Sam. 23:13 [b] 2 Sam. 5:18; 1 Chr. 14:9 **11:20** [a] 2 Sam. 23:18; 1 Chr. 18:12 [1] Following Masoretic Text, Septuagint, and Vulgate; Syriac reads *thirty*. **11:21** [a] 2 Sam. 23:19 **11:22** [a] 2 Sam. 23:20 **11:26** [a] 2 Sam. 23:24 **11:27** [a] 2 Sam. 23:26; 1 Chr. 27:10 [1] Spelled *Harodite* in 2 Samuel 23:25 [2] Called *Paltite* in 2 Samuel 23:26 **11:28** [a] 1 Chr. 27:9 [b] 1 Chr. 27:12 **11:30** [a] 1 Chr. 27:13 [1] Spelled *Heleb* in 2 Samuel 23:29 and *Heldai* in 1 Chronicles 27:15 **11:31** [a] 1 Chr. 27:14 [1] Spelled *Ittai* in 2 Samuel 23:29 **11:32** [1] Spelled *Hiddai* in 2 Samuel 23:30 [2] Spelled *Abi-Albon* in 2 Samuel 23:31 **11:33** [1] Spelled *Barhumite* in 2 Samuel 23:31 **11:39** [1] Spelled *Beerothite* in 2 Samuel 23:37 **11:41** [a] 2 Sam. 11 **12:1** [a] 1 Sam. 27:2 [b] 1 Sam. 27:6 **12:2** [a] Judg. 3:15; 20:16

Johanan, and Jozabad the Gederathite; 5 Eluzai,
Jerimoth, Bealiah, Shemariah, and Shephatiah
the Haruphite; 6 Elkanah, Jisshiah, Azarel, Joezer,
and Jashobeam, the Korahites; 7 and Joelah and
Zebadiah the sons of Jeroham of Gedor.

8 *Some* Gadites joined David at the stronghold
in the wilderness, mighty men of valor, men
trained for battle, who could handle shield and
spear, whose faces *were like* the faces of lions, and
*were* [a]as swift as gazelles on the mountains: 9 Ezer
the first, Obadiah the second, Eliab the third,
10 Mishmannah the fourth, Jeremiah the fifth,
11 Attai the sixth, Eliel the seventh, 12 Johanan the
eighth, Elzabad the ninth, 13 Jeremiah the tenth,
and Machbanai the eleventh. 14 These *were* from
the sons of Gad, captains of the army; the least
was over a hundred, and the greatest was over a
[a]thousand. 15 These *are* the ones who crossed the
Jordan in the first month, when it had overflowed
all its [a]banks; and they put to flight all *those* in
the valleys, to the east and to the west.

16 Then some of the sons of Benjamin and
Judah came to David at the stronghold. 17 And
David went out to meet them, and answered
and said to them, "If you have come peaceably
to me to help me, my heart will be united with
you; but if to betray me to my enemies, since
*there is* no wrong in my hands, may the God of
our fathers look and bring judgment." 18 Then
the Spirit came upon [a]Amasai, chief of the cap-
tains, *and he said:*

"*We are* yours, O David;
We *are* on your side, O son of Jesse!
Peace, peace to you,
And peace to your helpers!
For your God helps you."

So David received them, and made them cap-
tains of the troop.

19 And *some* from Manasseh defected to Da-
vid [a]when he was going with the Philistines to
battle against Saul; but they did not help them,
for the lords of the Philistines sent him away
by agreement, saying, [b]"He may defect to his
master Saul *and endanger* our heads." 20 When he
went to Ziklag, those of Manasseh who defected
to him were Adnah, Jozabad, Jediael, Michael,
Jozabad, Elihu, and Zillethai, captains of the
thousands who *were* from Manasseh. 21 And
they helped David against [a]the bands *of raiders,*
for they *were* all mighty men of valor, and they
were captains in the army. 22 For at *that* time they
came to David day by day to help him, until *it*
*was* a great army, [a]like the army of God.

### *DAVID'S ARMY AT HEBRON*

23 Now these *were* the numbers of the divisions
*that were* equipped for war, *and* [a]came to David at
[b]Hebron to [c]turn *over* the kingdom of Saul to him,
[d]according to the word of the LORD: 24 of the sons
of Judah bearing shield and spear, six thousand
eight hundred armed for war; 25 of the sons of
Simeon, mighty men of valor fit for war, seven
thousand one hundred; 26 of the sons of Levi four
thousand six hundred; 27 Jehoiada, the leader of
the Aaronites, and with him three thousand seven
hundred; 28 [a]Zadok, a young man, a valiant warrior,
and from his father's house twenty-two captains;
29 of the sons of Benjamin, relatives of Saul, three
thousand (until then [a]the greatest part of them
had remained loyal to the house of Saul); 30 of the
sons of Ephraim twenty thousand eight hundred,
mighty men of valor, famous men throughout
their father's house; 31 of the half-tribe of Manas-
seh eighteen thousand, who were designated by
name to come and make David king; 32 of the sons
of Issachar [a]who had understanding of the times,
to know what Israel ought to do, their chiefs were
two hundred; and all their brethren were at their
command; 33 of Zebulun there were fifty thou-
sand who went out to battle, expert in war with
all weapons of war, [a]stouthearted men who could
keep ranks; 34 of Naphtali one thousand captains,
and with them thirty-seven thousand with shield
and spear; 35 of the Danites who could keep battle
formation, twenty-eight thousand six hundred;
36 of Asher, those who could go out to war, able to
keep battle formation, forty thousand; 37 of the
Reubenites and the Gadites and the half-tribe of
Manasseh, from the other side of the Jordan, one
hundred and twenty thousand armed for battle
with every *kind* of weapon of war.

38 All these men of war, who could keep
ranks, came to Hebron with a loyal heart, to
make David king over all Israel; and all the
rest of Israel *were* of [a]one mind to make David
king. 39 And they were there with David three
days, eating and drinking, for their brethren
had prepared for them. 40 Moreover those who
were near to them, from as far away as Issachar
and Zebulun and Naphtali, were bringing food
on donkeys and camels, on mules and oxen—
provisions of flour and cakes of figs and cakes
of raisins, wine and oil and oxen and sheep
abundantly, for *there was* joy in Israel.

### *THE ARK BROUGHT FROM KIRJATH JEARIM*
*(2 Sam. 6:1–11)*

**13** Then David consulted with the [a]captains of
thousands and hundreds, *and* with every
leader. 2 And David said to all the assembly of
Israel, "If *it seems* good to you, and if it is of the
LORD our God, let us send out to our brethren
everywhere *who are* [a]left in all the land of Is-
rael, and with them to the priests and Levites
*who are* in their cities *and* their common-lands,
that they may gather together to us; 3 and let us

12:8 [a] 2 Sam. 2:18 12:14 [a] 1 Sam. 18:13 12:15 [a] Josh. 3:15; 4:18, 19 12:18 [a] 2 Sam. 17:25 12:19 [a] 1 Sam. 29:2 [b] 1 Sam. 29:4
12:21 [a] 1 Sam. 30:1, 9, 10 12:22 [a] Gen. 32:2; Josh. 5:13–15 12:23 [a] 2 Sam. 2:1–4 [b] 1 Chr. 11:1 [c] 1 Chr. 10:14 [d] 1 Sam. 16:1–4
12:28 [a] 2 Sam. 8:17; 1 Chr. 6:8, 53 12:29 [a] 2 Sam. 2:8, 9 12:32 [a] Esth. 1:13 12:33 [a] Ps. 12:2; [James 1:8] 12:38 [a] 2 Chr. 30:12
13:1 [a] 1 Chr. 11:15; 12:34 13:2 [a] 1 Sam. 31:1; Is. 37:4

bring the ark of our God back to us, [a]for we have
not inquired at it since the days of Saul." 4 Then
all the assembly said that they would do so, for
the thing was right in the eyes of all the people.
5 So [a]David gathered all Israel together, from
[b]Shihor in Egypt to as far as the entrance of
Hamath, to bring the ark of God [c]from Kirjath
Jearim. 6 And David and all Israel went up to
[a]Baalah,[1] to Kirjath Jearim, which belonged to
Judah, to bring up from there the ark of God
the LORD, [b]who dwells *between* the cherubim,
where *His* name is proclaimed. 7 So they carried
the ark of God [a]on a new cart [b]from the house
of Abinadab, and Uzza and Ahio drove the cart.
8 Then [a]David and all Israel played *music* before
God with all *their* might, with singing, on harps,
on stringed instruments, on tambourines, on
cymbals, and with trumpets.
9 And when they came to Chidon's[1] threshing
floor, Uzza put out his hand to hold the ark,
for the oxen stumbled. 10 Then the anger of the
LORD was aroused against Uzza, and He struck
him [a]because he put his hand to the ark; and
he [b]died there before God. 11 And David became
angry because of the LORD's outbreak against
Uzza; therefore that place is called Perez Uzza[1]
to this day. 12 David was afraid of God that day,
saying, "How can I bring the ark of God to me?"

**SEEING JESUS IN THE SCRIPTURE**

**13:9–10** Uzza died when he touched the ark of the Covenant because it was holy. By providing forgiveness of sin, Jesus made it possible for us to be in God's holy presence without dying (see Heb. 10:19–20).

13 So David would not move the ark with him
into the City of David, but took it aside into the
house of Obed-Edom the Gittite. 14 [a]The ark of
God remained with the family of Obed-Edom in
his house three months. And the LORD blessed
[b]the house of Obed-Edom and all that he had.

### DAVID ESTABLISHED AT JERUSALEM
*(2 Sam. 5:11–16)*

**14** Now [a]Hiram king of Tyre sent messengers
to David, and cedar trees, with masons and
carpenters, to build him a house. 2 So David knew
that the LORD had established him as king over
Israel, for his kingdom was [a]highly exalted for
the sake of His people Israel.
3 Then David took more wives in Jerusalem,
and David begot more sons and daughters. 4 And
[a]these are the names of his children whom he
had in Jerusalem: Shammua,[1] Shobab, Nathan,
Solomon, 5 Ibhar, Elishua,[1] Elpelet,[2] 6 Nogah, Ne-
pheg, Japhia, 7 Elishama, Beeliada,[1] and Eliphelet.

### THE PHILISTINES DEFEATED
*(2 Sam. 5:17–25)*

8 Now when the Philistines heard that [a]David
had been anointed king over all Israel, all the
Philistines went up to search for David. And
David heard *of it* and went out against them.
9 Then the Philistines went and made a raid [a]on
the Valley of Rephaim. 10 And David [a]inquired
of God, saying, "Shall I go up against the Phi-
listines? Will You deliver them into my hand?"
The LORD said to him, "Go up, for I will de-
liver them into your hand."
11 So they went up to Baal Perazim, and David
defeated them there. Then David said, "God has
broken through my enemies by my hand like a
breakthrough of water." Therefore they called
the name of that place Baal Perazim.[1] 12 And
when they left their gods there, David gave a
commandment, and they were burned with fire.
13 [a]Then the Philistines once again made a
raid on the valley. 14 Therefore David inquired
again of God, and God said to him, "You shall not
go up after them; circle around them, [a]and come
upon them in front of the mulberry trees. 15 And
it shall be, when you hear a sound of marching
in the tops of the mulberry trees, then you shall
go out to battle, for God has gone out before you
to strike the camp of the Philistines." 16 So David
did as God commanded him, and they drove
back the army of the Philistines from Gibeon
as far as Gezer. 17 Then [a]the fame of David went
out into all lands, and the LORD [b]brought the
fear of him upon all nations.

### THE ARK BROUGHT TO JERUSALEM
*(2 Sam. 6:12–16)*

**15** *David* built houses for himself in the City
of David; and he prepared a place for the
ark of God, [a]and pitched a tent for it. 2 Then
David said, "No one may carry the [a]ark of God
but the Levites, for [b]the LORD has chosen them
to carry the ark of God and to minister before
Him forever." 3 And David [a]gathered all Israel
together at Jerusalem, to bring up the ark of
the LORD to its place, which he had prepared
for it. 4 Then David assembled the children of
Aaron and the Levites: 5 of the sons of Kohath,
Uriel the chief, and one hundred and twenty of
his brethren; 6 of the sons of Merari, Asaiah the

**13:3** [a] 1 Sam. 7:1, 2 **13:5** [a] 1 Sam. 7:5 [b] Josh. 13:3 [c] 1 Sam. 6:21; 7:1, 2 **13:6** [a] Josh. 15:9, 60 [b] Ex. 25:22; 1 Sam. 4:4; 2 Kin. 19:15 [1] Called *Baale Judah* in 2 Samuel 6:2 **13:7** [a] Num. 4:15; 1 Sam. 6:7 [b] 1 Sam. 7:1 **13:8** [a] 2 Sam. 6:5 **13:9** [1] Called *Nachon* in 2 Samuel 6:6 **13:10** [a] [Num. 4:15]; 1 Chr. 15:13, 15 [b] Lev. 10:2 **13:11** [1] Literally *Outburst Against Uzza* **13:14** [a] 2 Sam. 6:11 [b] [Gen. 30:27]; 1 Chr. 26:4–8 **14:1** [a] 2 Sam. 5:11; 1 Kin. 5:1 **14:2** [a] Num. 24:7 **14:4** [a] 1 Chr. 3:5–8 [1] Spelled *Shimea* in 3:5 **14:5** [1] Spelled *Elishama* in 3:6 [2] Spelled *Eliphelet* in 3:6 **14:7** [1] Spelled *Eliada* in 3:8 **14:8** [a] 2 Sam. 5:17–21 **14:9** [a] Josh. 17:15; 18:16; 1 Chr. 11:15; 14:13 **14:10** [a] 1 Sam. 23:2, 4; 30:8; 2 Sam. 2:1; 5:19, 23; 21:1 **14:11** [1] Literally *Master of Breakthroughs* **14:13** [a] 2 Sam. 5:22–25 **14:14** [a] 2 Sam. 5:23 **14:17** [a] Josh. 6:27; 2 Chr. 26:8 [b] [Ex. 15:14–16; Deut. 2:25; 11:25]; 2 Chr. 20:29 **15:1** [a] 1 Chr. 16:1 **15:2** [a] [Num. 4:15]; 2 Sam. 6:1–11 [b] Num. 4:2–15; Deut. 10:8; 31:9 **15:3** [a] Ex. 40:20, 21; 2 Sam. 6:12; 1 Kin. 8:1; 1 Chr. 13:5

chief, and two hundred and twenty of his brethren; 7 of the sons of Gershom, Joel the chief, and one hundred and thirty of his brethren; 8 of the sons of [a]Elizaphan, Shemaiah the chief, and two hundred of his brethren; 9 of the sons of [a]Hebron, Eliel the chief, and eighty of his brethren; 10 of the sons of Uzziel, Amminadab the chief, and one hundred and twelve of his brethren.

11 And David called for [a]Zadok and [b]Abiathar the priests, and for the Levites: for Uriel, Asaiah, Joel, Shemaiah, Eliel, and Amminadab. 12 He said to them, "You *are* the heads of the fathers' *houses* of the Levites; sanctify yourselves, you and your brethren, that you may bring up the ark of the LORD God of Israel to *the place* I have prepared for it. 13 For [a]because you *did* not *do it* the first *time,* [b]the LORD our God broke out against us, because we did not consult Him about the proper order."

14 So the priests and the Levites sanctified themselves to bring up the ark of the LORD God of Israel. 15 And the children of the Levites bore the ark of God on their shoulders, by its poles, as [a]Moses had commanded according to the word of the LORD.

16 Then David spoke to the leaders of the Levites to appoint their brethren *to be* the singers accompanied by instruments of music, stringed instruments, harps, and cymbals, by raising the voice with resounding joy. 17 So the Levites appointed [a]Heman the son of Joel; and of his brethren, [b]Asaph the son of Berechiah; and of their brethren, the sons of Merari, [c]Ethan the son of Kushaiah; 18 and with them their brethren of the second *rank:* Zechariah, Ben,[1] Jaaziel, Shemiramoth, Jehiel, Unni, Eliab, Benaiah, Maaseiah, Mattithiah, Elipheleh, Mikneiah, Obed-Edom, and Jeiel, the gatekeepers; 19 the singers, Heman, Asaph, and Ethan, *were* to sound the cymbals of bronze; 20 Zechariah, Aziel, Shemiramoth, Jehiel, Unni, Eliab, Maaseiah, and Benaiah, with strings according to [a]Alamoth; 21 Mattithiah, Elipheleh, Mikneiah, Obed-Edom, Jeiel, and Azaziah, to direct with harps on the [a]Sheminith; 22 Chenaniah, leader of the Levites, was instructor *in charge of* the music, because he *was* skillful; 23 Berechiah and Elkanah *were* doorkeepers for the ark; 24 Shebaniah, Joshaphat, Nethanel, Amasai, Zechariah, Benaiah, and Eliezer, the priests, [a]were to blow the trumpets before the ark of God; and [b]Obed-Edom and Jehiah, doorkeepers for the ark.

25 So [a]David, the elders of Israel, and the captains over thousands went to bring up the ark of the covenant of the LORD from the house of Obed-Edom with joy. 26 And so it was, when God helped the Levites who bore the ark of the covenant of the LORD, that they offered seven bulls and seven rams. 27 David was clothed with a robe of fine [a]linen, as were all the Levites who bore the ark, the singers, and Chenaniah the music master *with* the singers. David also wore a linen ephod. 28 [a]Thus all Israel brought up the ark of the covenant of the LORD with shouting and with the sound of the horn, with trumpets and with cymbals, making music with stringed instruments and harps.

29 And it happened, [a]*as* the ark of the covenant of the LORD came to the City of David, that Michal, Saul's daughter, looked through a window and saw King David whirling and playing music; and she despised him in her heart.

### *THE ARK PLACED IN THE TABERNACLE*

*(2 Sam. 6:17–19)*

**16** So [a]they brought the ark of God, and set it in the midst of the tabernacle that David had erected for it. Then they offered burnt offerings and peace offerings before God. 2 And when David had finished offering the burnt offerings and the peace offerings, [a]he blessed the people in the name of the LORD. 3 Then he distributed to everyone of Israel, both man and woman, to everyone a loaf of bread, a piece *of meat,* and a cake of raisins.

4 And he appointed some of the Levites to minister before the ark of the LORD, to [a]commemorate, to thank, and to praise the LORD God of Israel: 5 Asaph the chief, and next to him Zechariah, *then* [a]Jeiel, Shemiramoth, Jehiel, Mattithiah, Eliab, Benaiah, and Obed-Edom: Jeiel with stringed instruments and harps, but Asaph made music with cymbals; 6 Benaiah and Jahaziel the priests regularly *blew* the trumpets before the ark of the covenant of God.

### *DAVID'S SONG OF THANKSGIVING*

*(Ps. 96:1–13; 105:1–15; 106:1, 47, 48)*

7 On that day [a]David [b]first delivered *this psalm* into the hand of Asaph and his brethren, to thank the LORD:

8 [a]Oh, give thanks to the LORD!
Call upon His name;
Make known His deeds among the peoples!
9 Sing to Him, sing psalms to Him;
Talk of all His wondrous works!
10 Glory in His holy name;
Let the hearts of those rejoice who seek
the LORD!
11 Seek the LORD and His strength;
Seek His face evermore!
12 Remember His marvelous works which
He has done,
His wonders, and the judgments of His
mouth,
13 O seed of Israel His servant,
You children of Jacob, His chosen ones!

15:8 [a] Ex. 6:22 15:9 [a] Ex. 6:18 15:11 [a] 2 Sam. 8:17; 15:24–29, 35, 36; 18:19, 22, 27; 19:11; 20:25; 1 Chr. 12:28 [b] 1 Sam. 22:20–23; 23:6; 30:7; 1 Kin. 2:22, 26, 27; Mark 2:6 15:13 [a] 2 Sam. 6:3 [b] 1 Chr. 13:7–11 15:15 [a] Ex. 25:14; Num. 4:15; 7:9 15:17 [a] 1 Chr. 6:33; 25:1 [b] 1 Chr. 6:39 [c] 1 Chr. 6:44 15:18 [1] Following Masoretic Text and Vulgate; Septuagint omits *Ben.* 15:20 [a] Ps. 46:title 15:21 [a] Ps. 6:title 15:24 [a] [Num. 10:8]; Ps. 81:3 [b] 1 Chr. 13:13, 14 15:25 [a] 2 Sam. 6:12, 13; 1 Kin. 8:1 15:27 [a] 1 Sam. 2:18, 28 15:28 [a] Num. 23:21; Josh. 6:20; 1 Chr. 13:8; Zech. 4:7; 1 Thess. 4:16 15:29 [a] 1 Sam. 18:20, 27; 19:11–17; 2 Sam. 3:13, 14; 6:16, 20–23 16:1 [a] 2 Sam. 6:17; 1 Chr. 15:1 16:2 [a] 1 Kin. 8:14 16:4 [a] Ps. 38:title; 70:title 16:5 [a] 1 Chr. 15:18 16:7 [a] 2 Sam. 22:1; 23:1 [b] Ps. 105:1–15 16:8 [a] 1 Chr. 17:19, 20; Ps. 105:1–15

14 He *is* the LORD our God;
His [a]judgments *are* in all the earth.
15 Remember His covenant forever,
The word which He commanded, for a
thousand generations,
16 *The* [a]*covenant which* He made with
Abraham,
And His oath to Isaac,
17 And [a]confirmed it to [b]Jacob for a statute,
To Israel *for* an everlasting covenant,
18 Saying, "To you I will give the land of
Canaan
As the allotment of your inheritance,"
19 When you were [a]few in number,
Indeed very few, and strangers in it.

20 When they went from one nation to
another,
And from *one* kingdom to another
people,
21 He permitted no man to do them wrong;
Yes, He [a]rebuked kings for their sakes,
22 *Saying,* [a]"Do not touch My anointed ones,
And do My prophets no harm."[1]

23 [a]Sing to the LORD, all the earth;
Proclaim the good news of His salvation
from day to day.
24 Declare His glory among the nations,
His wonders among all peoples.

25 For the LORD *is* great and greatly to be
praised;
He *is* also to be feared above all gods.
26 For all the gods [a]of the peoples *are* idols,
But the LORD made the heavens.
27 Honor and majesty *are* before Him;
Strength and gladness are in His place.

28 Give to the LORD, O families of the
peoples,
Give to the LORD glory and strength.
29 Give to the LORD the glory *due* His name;
Bring an offering, and come before Him.
Oh, worship the LORD in the beauty of
holiness!
30 Tremble before Him, all the earth.
The world also is firmly established,
It shall not be moved.

31 Let the heavens rejoice, and let the earth
be glad;
And let them say among the nations, "The
LORD reigns."
32 Let the sea roar, and all its fullness;
Let the field rejoice, and all that *is* in it.
33 Then the [a]trees of the woods shall rejoice
before the LORD,
For He is [b]coming to judge the earth.[1]

34 [a]Oh, give thanks to the LORD, for *He is*
good!
For His mercy *endures* forever.[1]
35 [a]And say, "Save us, O God of our salvation;
Gather us together, and deliver us from
the Gentiles,
To give thanks to Your holy name,
To triumph in Your praise."

36 [a]Blessed *be* the LORD God of Israel
From everlasting to everlasting![1]

And all [b]the people said, "Amen!" and praised
the LORD.

### *REGULAR WORSHIP MAINTAINED*

37 So he left [a]Asaph and his brothers there
before the ark of the covenant of the LORD to
minister before the ark regularly, as every day's
work [b]required; 38 and [a]Obed-Edom with his
sixty-eight brethren, including Obed-Edom the
son of Jeduthun, and Hosah, *to be* gatekeepers;
39 and Zadok the priest and his brethren the
priests, [a]before the tabernacle of the LORD [b]at
the high place that *was* at Gibeon, 40 to offer
burnt offerings to the LORD on the altar of burnt
offering regularly [a]morning and evening, and
*to do* according to all that is written in the Law
of the LORD which He commanded Israel; 41 and
with them Heman and Jeduthun and the rest
who were chosen, who were designated by name,
to give thanks to the LORD, [a]because His mercy
*endures* forever; 42 and with them Heman and
Jeduthun, to sound aloud with trumpets and
cymbals and the musical instruments of God.
Now the sons of Jeduthun *were* gatekeepers.
43 [a]Then all the people departed, every man to
his house; and David returned to bless his house.

### *GOD'S COVENANT WITH DAVID*

*(2 Sam. 7:1–29)*

17 Now [a]it came to pass, when David was
dwelling in his house, that David said to
Nathan the prophet, "See now, I dwell in a house
of cedar, but the ark of the covenant of the LORD
*is* under tent curtains."
2 Then Nathan said to David, "Do all that *is*
in your heart, for God *is* with you."
3 But it happened that night that the word of
God came to Nathan, saying, 4 "Go and tell My ser-
vant David, 'Thus says the LORD: "You shall [a]not
build Me a house to dwell in. 5 For I have not dwelt

**16:14** [a] Ps. 48:10; [Is. 26:9] **16:16** [a] Gen. 17:2; 26:3; 28:13; 35:11 **16:17** [a] Gen. 35:11, 12 [b] Gen. 28:10–15 **16:19** [a] Gen. 34:30; Deut. 7:7 **16:21** [a] Gen. 12:17; 20:3; Ex. 7:15–18 **16:22** [a] Gen. 20:7; Ps. 105:15 [1] Compare verses 8–22 with Psalm 105:1–15 **16:23** [a] Ps. 96:1–13 **16:26** [a] Lev. 19:4; [1 Cor. 8:5, 6] **16:33** [a] Is. 55:12, 13 [b] [Joel 3:1–14]; Zech. 14:1–14; [Matt. 25:31–46] [1] Compare verses 23–33 with Psalm 96:1–13 **16:34** [a] 2 Chr. 5:13; 7:3; Ezra 3:11; Ps. 106:1; 107:1; 118:1; 136:1; Jer. 33:11 [1] Compare verse 34 with Psalm 106:1 **16:35** [a] Ps. 106:47, 48 **16:36** [a] 1 Kin. 8:15, 56; Ps. 72:18 [b] Deut. 27:15; Neh. 8:6 [1] Compare verses 35, 36 with Psalm 106:47, 48 **16:37** [a] 1 Chr. 16:4, 5 [b] 2 Chr. 8:14; Ezra 3:4 **16:38** [a] 1 Chr. 13:14 **16:39** [a] 1 Chr. 21:29; 2 Chr. 1:3 [b] 1 Kin. 3:4 **16:40** [a] [Ex. 29:38–42; Num. 28:3, 4] **16:41** [a] 1 Chr. 25:1–6; 2 Chr. 5:13; 7:3; Ezra 3:11; Jer. 33:11 **16:43** [a] 2 Sam. 6:18–20 **17:1** [a] 2 Sam. 7:1; 1 Chr. 14:1 **17:4** [a] [1 Chr. 28:2, 3]

## COVENANTS IN THE BIBLE

In biblical times the purpose of a covenant was to establish an agreement between two persons or groups. The elements of a covenant included a promise on the part of one person and the conditions that needed to be fulfilled on the part of the other person for the promises to be carried out by both parties to the covenant.

| Covenant | Parties | Description | Reference |
|---|---|---|---|
| **Edenic** | God and Adam | God gave Adam a place in His creation and charged him with the responsibility of caring for the garden. The only condition was that Adam could not eat of the fruit of the tree of the knowledge of good and evil. This covenant was terminated by Adam's disobedience which also resulted in humanity's spiritual and physical death. | Genesis 2:16–17 |
| **Adamic** | God and Adam and Eve | After the Edenic Covenant ended, God pronounced several curses on the serpent, Eve, and Adam for their respective roles in the fall. However, in His grace, He also declared the first promise of Jesus, the one who would bruise the serpent's head. | Genesis 3:16–19 |
| **Noahic** | God and Noah | After the flood, people were still responsible for governing the world for God. Under this covenant, humanity's relationship to the earth and to nature was confirmed, human government was established, and God promised never to use a universal flood again to judge the world. | Genesis 9:8–17 |
| **Abrahamic** | God and Abram | In this covenant, God promised to make Abram's family into a great nation, give them a land, and bring blessing to the world through him. This blessing would ultimately be fulfilled through the Messiah, Abraham's descendant Jesus. Jesus provides the blessing of salvation for all who believe. | Genesis 12:1–3; 15:9–21 |
| | Abraham and Eliezer | Abraham asked his servant, Eliezer, to promise he would find a wife for Isaac from among Abraham's people. | Genesis 24:2–3, 9, 41 |
| | Abimelech and Isaac | Abimelech asked Isaac to promise to bring him and his people no harm. | Genesis 26:28–30 |
| **Mosaic or Sinai** | God and Moses | Upon giving the Law to the people of Israel, God promised to bless them if they obeyed and curse them if they disobeyed. | Exodus 19–24 |
| **Land or Palestinian** | God and Moses | Near the end of Moses's life, God affirms his unconditional promise to give the people the land of Canaan. | Deuteronomy 27–30 |
| | David and Jonathan | David and Jonathan promised friendship and peace to one another. | 1 Samuel 18:3–4; 20:14–17, 42 |
| | David and Abner | Abner agreed to side with David and David demanded that his wife, Michal, be returned to him. | 2 Samuel 3:12–21 |
| **Davidic** | God and David | God promised David that a descendant would reign on the throne forever. This promise was fulfilled in Jesus, who came from David's lineage. | 2 Samuel 7:1–29; 1 Chronicles 17:11–14; 2 Chronicles 6:16 |
| | Solomon and Shimei | Solomon made Shimei promise to stay under house arrest in Jerusalem in exchange for sparing his life. | 1 Kings 2:36–46 |
| | Solomon and Hiram | Solomon and Hiram made a treaty of peace. | 1 Kings 5:12 |
| | Jehoida and the royal guard | Jehoida made the guard promise to fulfill its duties. | 2 Kings 11:4–8 |
| **New** | God and Israel | God promised to forgive sin and restore fellowship with people. This covenant would be mediated by Jesus Christ. | Jeremiah 31:31–34; Ezekiel 36:26–27 |

in a house since the time that I brought up Israel, even to this day, but have gone from tent to tent, and from *one* tabernacle *to another.* 6 Wherever I have moved about with all Israel, have I ever spoken a word to any of the judges of Israel, whom I commanded to shepherd My people, saying, 'Why have you not built Me a house of cedar?' " ' 7 Now therefore, thus shall you say to My servant David, 'Thus says the LORD of hosts: "I took you [a]from the sheepfold, from following the sheep, to be ruler over My people Israel. 8 And I have been with you wherever you have gone, and have cut off all your enemies from before you, and have made you a name like the name of the great men who *are* on the earth. 9 Moreover I will appoint a place for My people Israel, and will [a]plant them, that they may dwell in a place of their own and move no more; nor shall the sons of wickedness oppress them anymore, as previously, 10 since the time that I commanded judges *to be* over My people Israel. Also I will subdue all your enemies. Furthermore I tell you that the LORD will build you a house.[1] 11 And it shall be, when your days are [a]fulfilled, when you must go *to be* with your fathers, that I will set up your [b]seed after you, who will be of your sons; and I will establish his kingdom. 12 [a]He shall build Me a house, and I will establish his throne forever. 13 [a]I will be his Father, and he shall be My son; and I will not take My mercy away from him, [b]as I took *it* from *him* who was before you. 14 And [a]I will establish him in My house and in My kingdom forever; and his throne shall be established forever." ' "

## SEEING JESUS IN THE SCRIPTURE

**17:11** God's promise to establish the throne of David's son forever was fulfilled through Jesus (see Matt. 1:6). Both David and Solomon were "types" of Jesus. Their reign on earth was imperfect, but they pointed to the reign of the perfect Son, Jesus Christ.

15 According to all these words and according to all this vision, so Nathan spoke to David.

16 [a]Then King David went in and sat before the LORD; and he said: "Who *am* I, O LORD God? And what is my house, that You have brought me this far? 17 And *yet* this was a small thing in Your sight, O God; and You have *also* spoken of Your servant's house for a great while to come, and have regarded me according to the rank of a man of high degree, O LORD God. 18 What more can David *say* to You for the honor of Your servant? For You know Your servant. 19 O LORD, for Your servant's sake, and according to Your own heart, You have done all this greatness, in making known all these great things. 20 O LORD, *there is* none like You, nor *is there any* God besides You, according to all that we have heard with our ears. 21 [a]And who *is* like Your people Israel, the one nation on the earth whom God went to redeem for Himself *as* a people—to make for Yourself a name by great and awesome deeds, by driving out nations from before Your people whom You redeemed from Egypt? 22 For You have made Your people Israel Your very own people forever; and You, LORD, have become their God.

23 "And now, O LORD, the word which You have spoken concerning Your servant and concerning his house, *let it* be established forever, and do as You have said. 24 So let it be established, that Your name may be magnified forever, saying, 'The LORD of hosts, the God of Israel, *is* Israel's God.' And let the house of Your servant David be established before You. 25 For You, O my God, have revealed to Your servant that You will build him a house. Therefore Your servant has found it *in his heart* to pray before You. 26 And now, LORD, You are God, and have promised this goodness to Your servant. 27 Now You have been pleased to bless the house of Your servant, that it may continue before You forever; for You have blessed it, O LORD, and *it shall be* blessed forever."

### DAVID'S FURTHER CONQUESTS

*(2 Sam. 8:1–14)*

**18** After this [a]it came to pass that David attacked the Philistines, subdued them, and took Gath and its towns from the hand of the Philistines. 2 Then he defeated [a]Moab, and the Moabites became David's [b]servants, *and* brought tribute.

3 And [a]David defeated Hadadezer[1] king of Zobah *as far as* Hamath, as he went to establish his power by the River Euphrates. 4 David took from him one thousand chariots, seven thousand[1] horsemen, and twenty thousand foot soldiers. Also David hamstrung all the chariot *horses,* except that he spared enough of them for one hundred chariots.

5 When the [a]Syrians of Damascus came to help Hadadezer king of Zobah, David killed twenty-two thousand of the Syrians. 6 Then David put *garrisons* in Syria of Damascus; and the Syrians became David's servants, *and* brought tribute. So the LORD preserved David wherever he went. 7 And David took the shields of gold that were on the servants of Hadadezer, and brought them to Jerusalem. 8 Also from Tibhath[1] and from Chun, cities of Hadadezer, David brought a large amount of [a]bronze, with which [b]Solomon

**17:7** [a] 1 Sam. 16:11–13 **17:9** [a] [Deut. 30:1–9; Jer. 16:14–16; 23:5–8; 24:6; Ezek. 37:21–27]; Amos 9:14 **17:10** [1] That is, a royal dynasty **17:11** [a] 1 Kin. 2:10 [b] [1 Chr. 22:9–13; 28:20]; Matt. 1:6; Luke 3:31 **17:12** [a] [Ps. 89:20–37; Luke 1:33] **17:13** [a] Heb. 1:5 [b] [1 Sam. 15:23–28]; 1 Chr. 10:14 **17:14** [a] Matt. 19:28; 25:31; [Luke 1:31–33]; Acts 2:30 **17:16** [a] 2 Sam. 7:18 **17:21** [a] [Deut. 4:6–8, 33–38]; Ps. 147:20 **18:1** [a] 2 Sam. 8:1–18 **18:2** [a] 2 Sam. 8:2; Zeph. 2:9 [b] Ps. 60:8 **18:3** [a] 2 Sam. 8:3 [1] Hebrew *Hadarezer,* and so throughout chapters 18 and 19 **18:4** [1] Or *seven hundred* (compare 2 Samuel 8:4) **18:5** [a] 2 Sam. 8:5, 6; 1 Kin. 11:23–25 **18:8** [a] 2 Sam. 8:8 [b] 1 Kin. 7:15, 23; 2 Chr. 4:12, 15, 16 [1] Spelled *Betah* in 2 Samuel 8:8

**18:8 The bronze Sea** was almost fifteen feet in diameter, more than seven feet deep, and three inches thick. It weighed more than ten tons and could hold about ten thousand gallons of water. The Sea, positioned in front of the temple, was used by the priest for ceremonial cleansing. The basin was supported by metal statues of twelve bulls.

made the bronze Sea, the pillars, and the articles
of bronze.
9 Now when Tou[1] king of Hamath heard that
David had defeated all the army of Hadadezer
king of Zobah, 10 he sent Hadoram[1] his son to King
David, to greet him and bless him, because he had
fought against Hadadezer and defeated him (for
Hadadezer had been at war with Tou); and *Hado-
ram brought with him* all kinds of [a]articles of gold,
silver, and bronze. 11 King David also dedicated
these to the LORD, along with the silver and gold
that he had brought from all *these* nations—from
Edom, from Moab, from the [a]people of Ammon,
from the [b]Philistines, and from [c]Amalek.
12 Moreover [a]Abishai the son of Zeruiah
killed [b]eighteen thousand Edomites[1] in the Val-
ley of Salt. 13 [a]He also put garrisons in Edom, and
all the Edomites became David's servants. And
the LORD preserved David wherever he went.

### *DAVID'S ADMINISTRATION*
*(2 Sam. 8:15–18)*

14 So David reigned over all Israel, and ad-
ministered judgment and justice to all his peo-
ple. 15 Joab the son of Zeruiah *was* over the army;
Jehoshaphat the son of Ahilud *was* recorder;
16 Zadok the son of Ahitub and Abimelech the
son of Abiathar *were* the priests; Shavsha[1] *was*
the scribe; 17 [a]Benaiah the son of Jehoiada *was*
over the Cherethites and the Pelethites; and Da-
vid's sons *were* chief ministers at the king's side.

### *THE AMMONITES AND SYRIANS DEFEATED*
*(2 Sam. 10:1–19)*

19 It[a] happened after this that Nahash the king
of the people of Ammon died, and his son
reigned in his place. 2 Then David said, "I will show
kindness to Hanun the son of Nahash, because
his father showed kindness to me." So David sent
messengers to comfort him concerning his father.
And David's servants came to Hanun in the land
of the people of Ammon to comfort him.
3 And the princes of the people of Ammon
said to Hanun, "Do you think that David really
honors your father because he has sent com-
forters to you? Did his servants not come to
you to search and to overthrow and to spy out
the land?"
4 Therefore Hanun took David's servants,
shaved them, and cut off their garments in
the middle, at their [a]buttocks, and sent them
away. 5 Then *some* went and told David about
the men; and he sent to meet them, because the
men were greatly ashamed. And the king said,
"Wait at Jericho until your beards have grown,
and *then* return."

**19:4** Hebrew men were proud of their beards and scrupulously modest in their attire. The Ammonites had humiliated David's men in the most offensive way possible.

6 When the people of Ammon saw that they
had made themselves repulsive to David, Hanun
and the people of Ammon sent a thousand talents
of silver to hire for themselves chariots and horse-
men from Mesopotamia,[1] from Syrian Maacah,
[a]and from Zobah.[2] 7 So they hired for themselves
thirty-two thousand chariots, with the king of
Maacah and his people, who came and encamped
before Medeba. Also the people of Ammon gath-
ered together from their cities, and came to battle.
8 Now when David heard *of it,* he sent Joab and
all the army of the mighty men. 9 Then the people
of Ammon came out and put themselves in battle
array before the gate of the city, and the kings
who had come *were* by themselves in the field.
10 When Joab saw that the battle line was
against him before and behind, he chose some
of Israel's best and put *them* in battle array against
the Syrians. 11 And the rest of the people he put un-
der the command of Abishai his brother, and they
set *themselves* in battle array against the people
of Ammon. 12 Then he said, "If the Syrians are too
strong for me, then you shall help me; but if the
people of Ammon are too strong for you, then I
will help you. 13 Be of good courage, and let us be
strong for our people and for the cities of our God.
And may the LORD do *what is* good in His sight."
14 So Joab and the people who *were* with him
drew near for the battle against the Syrians,
and they fled before him. 15 When the people of
Ammon saw that the Syrians were fleeing, they
also fled before Abishai his brother, and entered
the city. So Joab went to Jerusalem.
16 Now when the Syrians saw that they had
been defeated by Israel, they sent messengers
and brought the Syrians who were beyond the
River,[1] and Shophach[2] the commander of Had-
adezer's army *went* before them. 17 When it was
told David, he gathered all Israel, crossed over the
Jordan and came upon them, and set up in battle
array against them. So when David had set up in

**18:9** [1] Spelled *Toi* in 2 Samuel 8:9, 10 **18:10** [a] 2 Sam. 8:10–12 [1] Spelled *Joram* in 2 Samuel 8:10 **18:11** [a] 2 Sam. 10:14 [b] 2 Sam. 5:17–25 [c] 2 Sam. 1:1 **18:12** [a] 2 Sam. 23:18; 1 Chr. 2:16 [b] 2 Sam. 8:13 [1] Or *Syrians* (compare 2 Samuel 8:13) **18:13** [a] Gen. 27:29–40; Num. 24:18; 2 Sam. 8:14 **18:16** [1] Spelled *Seraiah* in 2 Samuel 8:17 **18:17** [a] 2 Sam. 8:18 **19:1** [a] 1 Sam. 11:1; 2 Sam. 10:1–19 **19:4** [a] Is. 20:4 **19:6** [a] 1 Chr. 18:5, 9 [1] Hebrew *Aram Naharaim* [2] Spelled *Zoba* in 2 Samuel 10:6 **19:16** [1] That is, the Euphrates [2] Spelled *Shobach* in 2 Samuel 10:16

battle array against the Syrians, they fought with
him. 18 Then the Syrians fled before Israel; and
David killed seven thousand[1] charioteers and forty
thousand foot soldiers[2] of the Syrians, and killed
Shophach the commander of the army. 19 And
when the servants of Hadadezer saw that they were
defeated by Israel, they made peace with David
and became his servants. So the Syrians were not
willing to help the people of Ammon anymore.

### *RABBAH IS CONQUERED*

*(2 Sam. 11:1; 12:26–31)*

**20** It[a] happened in the spring of the year, at
the time kings go out *to battle,* that Joab
led out the armed forces and ravaged the country
of the people of Ammon, and came and besieged
Rabbah. But [b]David stayed at Jerusalem. And
[c]Joab defeated Rabbah and overthrew it. 2 Then
David [a]took their king's crown from his head, and
found it to weigh a talent of gold, and *there were*
precious stones in it. And it was set on David's
head. Also he brought out the spoil of the city
in great abundance. 3 And he brought out the
people who *were* in it, and put *them* to work[1] with
saws, with iron picks, and with axes. So David did
to all the cities of the people of Ammon. Then
David and all the people returned *to* Jerusalem.

### *PHILISTINE GIANTS DESTROYED*

*(2 Sam. 21:15–22)*

4 Now it happened afterward [a]that war broke
out at Gezer with the Philistines, at which time
[b]Sibbechai the Hushathite killed Sippai,[1] *who was
one* of the sons of the giant. And they were subdued.
5 Again there was war with the Philistines,
and Elhanan the son of Jair[1] killed Lahmi the
brother of Goliath the Gittite, the shaft of whose
spear *was* like a weaver's [a]beam.
6 Yet again [a]there was war at Gath, where
there was a man of *great* stature, with twenty-
four fingers and toes, six *on each hand* and six
*on each foot;* and he also was born to the giant.
7 So when he defied Israel, Jonathan the son of
Shimea,[1] David's brother, killed him.
8 These were born to the giant in Gath, and
they fell by the hand of David and by the hand
of his servants.

> **20:4–8** The men from **Gath** were ancestors of certain **Philistines** who lived during the time of David. Their most notable feature was their size. **Goliath**, the giant David killed, was from Gath.

### *THE CENSUS OF ISRAEL AND JUDAH*

*(2 Sam. 24:1–25)*

**21** Now [a]Satan stood up against Israel, and
moved David to number Israel. 2 So David
said to Joab and to the leaders of the people, "Go,
number Israel from Beersheba to Dan, [a]and bring
the number of them to me that I may know *it.*"
3 And Joab answered, "May the LORD make
His people a hundred times more than they are.
But, my lord the king, *are* they not all my lord's
servants? Why then does my lord require this
thing? Why should he be a cause of guilt in Israel?"
4 Nevertheless the king's word prevailed
against Joab. Therefore Joab departed and went
throughout all Israel and came to Jerusalem.
5 Then Joab gave the sum of the number of the
people to David. All Israel *had* one million one
hundred thousand men who drew the sword,
and Judah *had* four hundred and seventy thou-
sand men who drew the sword. 6 [a]But he did not
count Levi and Benjamin among them, for the
king's word was abominable to Joab.
7 And God was displeased with this thing;
therefore He struck Israel. 8 So David said to God,
[a]"I have sinned greatly, because I have done this
thing; [b]but now, I pray, take away the iniquity
of Your servant, for I have done very foolishly."
9 Then the LORD spoke to Gad, David's [a]seer,
saying, 10 "Go and tell David, [a]saying, 'Thus says
the LORD: "I offer you three *things;* choose one
of them for yourself, that I may do *it* to you." ' "
11 So Gad came to David and said to him,
"Thus says the LORD: 'Choose for yourself, 12 [a]ei-
ther three[1] years of famine, or three months to
be defeated by your foes with the sword of your
enemies overtaking *you,* or else for three days
the sword of the LORD—the plague in the land,
with the angel[2] of the LORD destroying through-
out all the territory of Israel.' Now consider what
answer I should take back to Him who sent me."
13 And David said to Gad, "I am in great dis-
tress. Please let me fall into the hand of the LORD,
for His [a]mercies *are* very great; but do not let
me fall into the hand of man."
14 So the LORD sent a [a]plague upon Israel,
and seventy thousand men of Israel fell. 15 And
God sent an [a]angel to Jerusalem to destroy it.
As he[1] was destroying, the LORD looked and
[b]relented of the disaster, and said to the angel
who was destroying, "It is enough; now restrain
your[2] hand." And the angel of the LORD stood
by the [c]threshing floor of Ornan[3] the Jebusite.
16 Then David lifted his eyes and [a]saw the angel
of the LORD standing between earth and heaven,
having in his hand a drawn sword stretched out
over Jerusalem. So David and the elders, clothed

**19:18** [1] Or *seven hundred* (compare 2 Samuel 10:18) [2] Or *horsemen* (compare 2 Samuel 10:18) **20:1** [a] 2 Sam. 11:1 [b] 2 Sam. 11:2—12:25 [c] 2 Sam. 12:26 **20:2** [a] 2 Sam. 12:30, 31 **20:3** [1] Septuagint reads *cut them.* **20:4** [a] 2 Sam. 21:18 [b] 1 Chr. 11:29 [1] Spelled *Saph* in 2 Samuel 21:18 **20:5** [a] 1 Sam. 17:7; 1 Chr. 11:23 [1] Spelled *Jaare-Oregim* in 2 Samuel 21:19 **20:6** [a] 1 Sam. 5:8; 2 Sam. 21:20 **20:7** [1] Spelled *Shimeah* in 2 Samuel 21:21 and *Shammah* in 1 Samuel 16:9 **21:1** [a] 2 Sam. 24:1–25; Job 1:6 **21:2** [a] 1 Chr. 27:23, 24 **21:6** [a] 1 Chr. 27:24 **21:8** [a] 2 Sam. 24:10 [b] 2 Sam. 12:13 **21:9** [a] 1 Sam. 9:9; 2 Kin. 17:13; 1 Chr. 29:29; 2 Chr. 16:7, 10; Is. 30:9, 10; Amos 7:12, 13 **21:10** [a] 2 Sam. 24:12–14 **21:12** [a] 2 Sam. 24:13 [1] Or *seven* (compare 2 Samuel 24:13) [2] Or *Angel,* and so elsewhere in this chapter **21:13** [a] Ps. 51:1; 130:4, 7 **21:14** [a] 1 Chr. 27:24 **21:15** [a] 2 Sam. 24:16 [b] Gen. 6:6 [c] 2 Chr. 3:1 [1] Or *He* [2] Or *Your* [3] Spelled *Araunah* in 2 Samuel 24:16 **21:16** [a] Josh. 5:13; 2 Chr. 3:1

1 CHRONICLES 21:1–5

# THE WAKE OF DAVID'S SIN

26 STORY OF SCRIPTURE

## WHAT'S GOING ON?

A census was normal to assess a nation's military might; God, however, hadn't commanded one. Despite Joab's warnings, King David insisted on conducting a census of his people, reflecting his pride and reliance on military strength rather than God's providence—a sad decline from his defeat over Goliath. This event led to a plague on Israel, highlighting the seriousness of relying on human wisdom over divine guidance. This story is important in the overarching narrative of Scripture because it showcases the decline of every king who wasn't named Jesus. Even David, for all his faithfulness, couldn't resist the draw of the flesh.

## WHAT DOES THIS MEAN FOR ME?

This passage challenges us to examine where our trust lies. Are we, like David, trusting our own abilities, resources, or achievements? This story encourages us to rely not on our own strength but on God's guidance and provision.

## DID YOU CATCH THE PATTERN?

The story of David's census aligns with a biblical pattern where God's people face consequences due to pride or disobedience but are also offered a chance for repentance and restoration. Like how God dealt with other leaders in the Bible, He used this incident to teach David a crucial lesson in humility and reliance upon Him. This pattern is seen throughout Scripture as a reminder of God's sovereignty and our need to submit to His will. It echoes the broader biblical narrative of redemption, where God, in His mercy, provides a way back to Him even when we stray.

*For the next* Story of Scripture *reading and devotion, turn to 1 Kings 6:1–28 on page 339.*

in sackcloth, fell on their faces.
17 And David said
to God, "Was it not I who commanded the people to be numbered? I am the one who has sinned and done evil indeed; but these [a]sheep, what have they done? Let Your hand, I pray, O LORD my God, be against me and my father's house, but not against Your people that they should be plagued."

### SEEING JESUS IN THE SCRIPTURE

**21:17** When David sinned and punishment was due, he interceded for his people to be spared. In a greater way, Jesus interceded for others when He was on the cross paying the punishment for the sins of the world (see Luke 23:34).

18 Therefore, the [a]angel of the LORD commanded Gad to say to David that David should go and erect an altar to the LORD on the threshing floor of Ornan the Jebusite.
19 So David went up at the word of Gad, which he had spoken in the name of the LORD.
20 Now Ornan turned and saw the angel; and his four sons *who were* with him hid themselves, but Ornan continued threshing wheat.
21 So David came to Ornan, and Ornan looked and saw David. And he went out from the threshing floor, and bowed before David with *his* face to the ground.
22 Then David said to Ornan, "Grant me the place of *this* threshing floor, that I may build an altar on it to the LORD. You shall grant it to me at the full price, that the plague may be withdrawn from the people."

23 But Ornan said to David, "Take *it* to yourself, and let my lord the king do *what is* good in his eyes. Look, I *also* give *you* the oxen for burnt offerings, the threshing implements for wood, and the wheat for the grain offering; I give *it* all."

24 Then King David said to Ornan, "No, but I will surely buy *it* for the full price, for I will not take what is yours for the LORD, nor offer burnt offerings with *that which* costs *me* nothing."
25 So
[a]David gave Ornan six hundred shekels of gold by weight for the place.
26 And David built there an altar to the LORD, and offered burnt offerings and peace offerings, and called on the LORD; and [a]He answered him from heaven by fire on the altar of burnt offering.

27 So the LORD commanded the angel, and he returned his sword to its sheath.

28 At that time, when David saw that the LORD had answered him on the threshing floor of Ornan the Jebusite, he sacrificed there.
29 [a]For the tabernacle of the LORD and the altar of the burnt

**21:17** [a] 2 Sam. 7:8; Ps. 74:1 **21:18** [a] 1 Chr. 21:11, 12; 2 Chr. 3:1 **21:25** [a] 2 Sam. 24:24 **21:26** [a] Lev. 9:24; Judg. 6:21; 1 Kin. 18:36–38; 2 Chr. 3:1; 7:1 **21:29** [a] 1 Kin. 3:4; 2 Chr. 1:3

offering, which Moses had made in the wilderness,
*were* at that time at the high place in [b]Gibeon. 30 But
David could not go before it to inquire of God, for
he was afraid of the sword of the angel of the LORD.

### *DAVID PREPARES TO BUILD THE TEMPLE*

22 Then David said, [a]"This *is* the house of the
LORD God, and this *is* the altar of burnt
offering for Israel." 2 So David commanded to
gather the [a]aliens who *were* in the land of Israel;
and he appointed masons to [b]cut hewn stones
to build the house of God. 3 And David prepared
iron in abundance for the nails of the doors
of the gates and for the joints, and bronze in
abundance [a]beyond measure, 4 and cedar trees
in abundance; for the [a]Sidonians and those
from Tyre brought much cedar wood to David.
5 Now David said, [a]"Solomon my son *is* young
and inexperienced, and the house to be built
for the LORD *must be* exceedingly magnificent,
famous and glorious throughout all countries.
I will now make preparation for it." So David
made abundant preparations before his death.
6 Then he called for his son Solomon, and
charged him to build a house for the LORD God
of Israel. 7 And David said to Solomon: "My son,
as for me, [a]it was in my mind to build a house [b]to
the name of the LORD my God; 8 but the word of
the LORD came to me, saying, [a]'You have shed
much blood and have made great wars; you shall
not build a house for My name, because you have
shed much blood on the earth in My sight. 9 [a]Be-
hold, a son shall be born to you, who shall be a
man of rest; and I will give him [b]rest from all his
enemies all around. His name shall be Solomon,[1]
for I will give peace and quietness to Israel in his
days. 10 [a]He shall build a house for My name, and
[b]he shall be My son, and I *will be* his Father; and
I will establish the throne of his kingdom over
Israel forever.' 11 Now, my son, may [a]the LORD be
with you; and may you prosper, and build the
house of the LORD your God, as He has said to you.
12 Only may the LORD [a]give you wisdom and under-
standing, and give you charge concerning Israel,
that you may keep the law of the LORD your God.
13 [a]Then you will prosper, if you take care to fulfill
the statutes and judgments with which the LORD
charged Moses concerning Israel. [b]Be strong and
of good courage; do not fear nor be dismayed.
14 Indeed I have taken much trouble to prepare
for the house of the LORD one hundred thousand
talents of gold and one million talents of silver,
and bronze and iron [a]beyond measure, for it is
so abundant. I have prepared timber and stone
also, and you may add to them. 15 Moreover *there*
*are* workmen with you in abundance: woodsmen
and stonecutters, and all types of skillful men
for every kind of work. 16 Of gold and silver and
bronze and iron *there is* no limit. Arise and begin
working, and [a]the LORD be with you."
17 David also commanded all the [a]leaders of
Israel to help Solomon his son, *saying,* 18 "*Is* not
the LORD your God with you? [a]And has He *not*
given you rest on every side? For He has given
the inhabitants of the land into my hand, and
the land is subdued before the LORD and before
His people. 19 Now set your heart and your soul
to seek the LORD your God. Therefore arise and
build the sanctuary of the LORD God, to [a]bring
the ark of the covenant of the LORD and the holy
articles of God into the house that is to be built
[b]for the name of the LORD."

**SEEING JESUS IN THE SCRIPTURE**

**22:10** God's promise of a son and an eternal throne wasn't focused on Solomon. It points ahead to the coming Messiah, Jesus, the Son of God, whose throne in God's kingdom is established forever (see Heb. 1:5).

### *THE DIVISIONS OF THE LEVITES*

23 So when David was old and full of days, he
made his son [a]Solomon king over Israel.
2 And he gathered together all the leaders of
Israel, with the priests and the Levites. 3 Now the
Levites were numbered from the age of [a]thirty
years and above; and the number of individual
males was thirty-eight thousand. 4 Of these,
twenty-four thousand *were* to [a]look after the
work of the house of the LORD, six thousand *were*
[b]officers and judges, 5 four thousand *were* gate-
keepers, and four thousand [a]praised the LORD
with *musical* instruments, [b]"which I made," *said*
*David,* "for giving praise."
6 Also [a]David separated them into divisions
among the sons of Levi: Gershon, Kohath, and
Merari.
7 Of the [a]Gershonites: Laadan[1] and Shimei.
8 The sons of Laadan: the first Jehiel, then Zetham
and Joel—three *in all.* 9 The sons of Shimei: She-
lomith, Haziel, and Haran—three *in all.* These
were the heads of the fathers' *houses* of Laadan.
10 And the sons of Shimei: Jahath, Zina,[1] Jeush,
and Beriah. These *were* the four sons of Shimei.
11 Jahath was the first and Zizah the second. But
Jeush and Beriah did not have many sons; there-
fore they were assigned as one father's house.

**21:29** [b] 1 Chr. 16:39 **22:1** [a] Deut. 12:5; 2 Sam. 24:18; 1 Chr. 21:18, 19, 26, 28; 2 Chr. 3:1 **22:2** [a] 1 Kin. 9:20, 21; 2 Chr. 2:17, 18 [b] 1 Kin. 5:17, 18 **22:3** [a] 1 Kin. 7:47; 1 Chr. 22:14 **22:4** [a] 1 Kin. 5:6–10 **22:5** [a] 1 Kin. 3:7; 1 Chr. 29:1, 2 **22:7** [a] 2 Sam. 7:1, 2; 1 Kin. 8:17; 1 Chr. 17:1; 28:2 [b] Deut. 12:5, 11 **22:8** [a] 2 Sam. 7:5–13; 1 Kin. 5:3; 1 Chr. 28:3 **22:9** [a] 1 Chr. 28:5 [b] 1 Kin. 4:20, 25; 5:4 [1] Literally *Peaceful* **22:10** [a] 1 Chr. 17:12, 13; 28:6 [b] Heb. 1:5 **22:11** [a] 1 Chr. 22:16 **22:12** [a] 1 Kin. 3:9–12; 2 Chr. 1:10 **22:13** [a] [Josh. 1:7, 8]; 1 Chr. 28:7 [b] [Deut. 31:7, 8; Josh. 1:6, 7, 9; 1 Chr. 28:20] **22:14** [a] 1 Chr. 22:3 **22:16** [a] 1 Chr. 22:11 **22:17** [a] 1 Chr. 28:1–6 **22:18** [a] Deut. 12:10; Josh. 22:4; 2 Sam. 7:1; [1 Kin. 5:4; 8:56] **22:19** [a] 1 Kin. 8:1–11; 2 Chr. 5:2–14 [b] 1 Kin. 5:3 **23:1** [a] 1 Kin. 1:33–40; 1 Chr. 28:4, 5 **23:3** [a] Num. 4:1–3 **23:4** [a] 2 Chr. 2:2, 18; Ezra 3:8, 9 [b] Deut. 16:18–20 **23:5** [a] 1 Chr. 15:16 [b] 2 Chr. 29:25–27 **23:6** [a] Ex. 6:16; Num. 26:57; 2 Chr. 8:14 **23:7** [a] 1 Chr. 26:21 [1] Spelled *Libni* in Exodus 6:17 **23:10** [1] Septuagint and Vulgate read *Zizah* (compare verse 11).

12 [a]The sons of Kohath: Amram, Izhar, He-
bron, and Uzziel—four *in all.* 13 The sons of
[a]Amram: Aaron and Moses; and [b]Aaron was
set apart, he and his sons forever, that he should
sanctify the most holy things, [c]to burn incense
before the LORD, [d]to minister to Him, and [e]to
give the blessing in His name forever. 14 Now [a]the
sons of Moses the man of God were reckoned
to the tribe of Levi. 15 [a]The sons of Moses *were*
Gershon[1] and Eliezer. 16 Of the sons of Gershon,
[a]Shebuel[1] *was* the first. 17 Of the descendants of
Eliezer, [a]Rehabiah was the first. And Eliezer had
no other sons, but the sons of Rehabiah were very
many. 18 Of the sons of Izhar, [a]Shelomith *was* the
first. 19 [a]Of the sons of Hebron, Jeriah *was* the
first, Amariah the second, Jahaziel the third, and
Jekameam the fourth. 20 Of the sons of Uzziel,
Michah *was* the first and Jesshiah the second.
21 [a]The sons of Merari *were* Mahli and Mushi.
The sons of Mahli *were* Eleazar and [b]Kish. 22 And
Eleazar died, and [a]had no sons, but only daugh-
ters; and their brethren, the sons of Kish, [b]took
them *as wives.* 23 [a]The sons of Mushi *were* Mahli,
Eder, and Jeremoth—three *in all.*
24 These *were* the sons of [a]Levi by their fa-
thers' houses—the heads of the fathers' *houses*
as they were counted individually by the number
of their names, who did the work for the service
of the house of the LORD, from the age of [b]twenty
years and above.
25 For David said, "The LORD God of Israel
[a]has given rest to His people, that they may dwell
in Jerusalem forever"; 26 and also to the Levites,
"They shall no longer [a]carry the tabernacle, or
any of the articles for its service." 27 For by the
[a]last words of David the Levites *were* numbered
from twenty years old and above; 28 because their
duty *was* to help the sons of Aaron in the service
of the house of the LORD, in the courts and in the
chambers, in the purifying of all holy things and
the work of the service of the house of God, 29 both
with [a]the showbread and [b]the fine flour for the
grain offering, with [c]the unleavened cakes and
[d]*what is baked in* the pan, with what is mixed and
with all kinds of [e]measures and sizes; 30 to stand
every morning to thank and praise the LORD, and
likewise at evening; 31 and at every presentation
of a burnt offering to the LORD [a]on the Sabbaths
and on the New Moons and on the [b]set feasts, by
number according to the ordinance governing
them, regularly before the LORD; 32 and that they
should [a]attend to the [b]needs of the tabernacle
of meeting, the needs of the holy *place,* and the
[c]needs of the sons of Aaron their brethren in the
work of the house of the LORD.

## THE DIVISIONS OF THE PRIESTS

24 Now *these are* the divisions of the sons of
Aaron. [a]The sons of Aaron *were* Nadab,
Abihu, Eleazar, and Ithamar. 2 And [a]Nadab and
Abihu died before their father, and had no chil-
dren; therefore Eleazar and Ithamar ministered
as priests. 3 Then David with Zadok of the sons
of Eleazar, and [a]Ahimelech of the sons of Ith-
amar, divided them according to the schedule
of their service.
4 There were more leaders found of the sons
of Eleazar than of the sons of Ithamar, and *thus*
they were divided. Among the sons of Eleazar *were*
sixteen heads of *their* fathers' houses, and eight
heads of their fathers' houses among the sons of
Ithamar. 5 Thus they were divided by lot, one group
as another, for there were officials of the sanctuary
and officials *of the house* of God, from the sons of
Eleazar and from the sons of Ithamar. 6 And the
scribe, Shemaiah the son of Nethanel, *one of* the
Levites, wrote them down before the king, the
leaders, Zadok the priest, Ahimelech the son of
Abiathar, and the heads of the fathers' *houses* of
the priests and Levites, one father's house taken
for Eleazar and *one* for Ithamar.
7 Now the first lot fell to Jehoiarib, the second
to Jedaiah, 8 the third to Harim, the fourth to Seo-
rim, 9 the fifth to Malchijah, the sixth to Mijamin,
10 the seventh to Hakkoz, the eighth to [a]Abijah, 11 the
ninth to Jeshua, the tenth to Shecaniah, 12 the
eleventh to Eliashib, the twelfth to Jakim,
13 the thirteenth to Huppah, the fourteenth to Je-
shebeab, 14 the fifteenth to Bilgah, the sixteenth to
Immer, 15 the seventeenth to Hezir, the eighteenth
to Happizzez,[1] 16 the nineteenth to Pethahiah,
the twentieth to Jehezekel,[1] 17 the twenty-first to
Jachin, the twenty-second to Gamul, 18 the twenty-
third to Delaiah, the twenty-fourth to Maaziah.
19 This *was* the schedule of their service [a]for
coming into the house of the LORD according to
their ordinance by the hand of Aaron their father,
as the LORD God of Israel had commanded him.

## OTHER LEVITES

20 And the rest of the sons of Levi: of the
sons of Amram, Shubael;[1] of the sons of Shu-
bael, Jehdeiah. 21 Concerning [a]Rehabiah, of the
sons of Rehabiah, the first *was* Isshiah. 22 Of
the Izharites, Shelomoth;[1] of the sons of Shelo-
moth, Jahath. 23 Of the sons *of* [a]*Hebron,*[1] Jeriah
*was the first,*[2] Amariah the second, Jahaziel the
third, *and* Jekameam the fourth. 24 *Of* the sons of
Uzziel, Michah; of the sons of Michah, Shamir.
25 The brother of Michah, Isshiah; of the sons of
Isshiah, Zechariah. 26 [a]The sons of Merari *were*

**23:12** [a] Ex. 6:18 **23:13** [a] Ex. 6:20 [b] Ex. 28:1; Heb. 5:4 [c] Ex. 30:7; 1 Sam. 2:28 [d] [Deut. 21:5] [e] Num. 6:23 **23:14** [a] 1 Chr. 26:20–24 **23:15** [a] Ex. 18:3, 4 [1] Hebrew *Gershom* (compare 6:16) **23:16** [a] 1 Chr. 26:24 [1] Spelled *Shubael* in 24:20 **23:17** [a] 1 Chr. 26:25 **23:18** [a] 1 Chr. 24:22 **23:19** [a] 1 Chr. 24:23 **23:21** [a] 1 Chr. 24:26 [b] 1 Chr. 24:29 **23:22** [a] 1 Chr. 24:28 [b] Num. 36:6 **23:23** [a] 1 Chr. 24:30 **23:24** [a] Num. 10:17, 21 [b] Num. 1:3; Ezra 3:8 **23:25** [a] 1 Chr. 22:18 **23:26** [a] Num. 4:5, 15; 7:9; Deut. 10:8 **23:27** [a] 2 Sam. 23:1 **23:29** [a] Ex. 25:30 [b] Lev. 6:20 [c] Lev. 2:1, 4 [d] Lev. 2:5, 7 [e] Lev. 19:35 **23:31** [a] Num. 10:10 [b] Lev. 23:2–4 **23:32** [a] 2 Chr. 13:10, 11 [b] [Num. 1:53]; 1 Chr. 9:27 [c] Num. 3:6–9, 38 **24:1** [a] Lev. 10:1–6; Num. 26:60, 61; 1 Chr. 6:3 **24:2** [a] Num. 3:1–4; 26:61 **24:3** [a] 1 Chr. 18:16 **24:10** [a] Neh. 12:4, 17; Luke 1:5 **24:15** [1] Septuagint and Vulgate read *Aphses.* **24:16** [1] Masoretic Text reads *Jehezkel.* **24:19** [a] 1 Chr. 9:25 **24:20** [1] Spelled *Shebuel* in 23:16 **24:21** [a] 1 Chr. 23:17 **24:22** [1] Spelled *Shelomith* in 23:18 **24:23** [a] 1 Chr. 23:19; 26:31 [1] Supplied from 23:19 (following some Hebrew manuscripts and Septuagint manuscripts) [2] Supplied from 23:19 (following some Hebrew manuscripts and Septuagint manuscripts) **24:26** [a] Ex. 6:19; 1 Chr. 23:21

Mahli and Mushi; the son of Jaaziah, Beno. 27 The sons of Merari by Jaaziah *were* Beno, Shoham, Zaccur, and Ibri. 28 Of Mahli: Eleazar, [a]who had no sons. 29 Of Kish: the son of Kish, Jerahmeel.

30 Also [a]the sons of Mushi *were* Mahli, Eder, and Jerimoth. These *were* the sons of the Levites according to their fathers' houses.

31 These also cast lots just as their brothers the sons of Aaron did, in the presence of King David, Zadok, Ahimelech, and the heads of the fathers' *houses* of the priests and Levites. The chief fathers *did* just as their younger brethren.

### THE MUSICIANS

**25** Moreover David and the captains of the army separated for the service *some* of the sons of [a]Asaph, of Heman, and of Jeduthun, who *should* prophesy with harps, stringed instruments, and cymbals. And the number of the skilled men performing their service was: 2 Of the sons of Asaph: Zaccur, Joseph, Nethaniah, and Asharelah;[1] the sons of Asaph *were* under the direction of Asaph, who prophesied according to the order of the king. 3 Of [a]Jeduthun, the sons of Jeduthun: Gedaliah, Zeri,[1] Jeshaiah, *Shimei,* Hashabiah, and Mattithiah, six,[2] under the direction of their father Jeduthun, who prophesied with a harp to give thanks and to praise the LORD. 4 Of Heman, the sons of Heman: Bukkiah, Mattaniah, Uzziel,[1] Shebuel,[2] Jerimoth,[3] Hananiah, Hanani, Eliathah, Giddalti, Romamti-Ezer, Joshbekashah, Mallothi, Hothir, *and* Mahazioth. 5 All these *were* the sons of Heman the king's seer in the words of God, to exalt his [a]horn.[1] For God gave Heman fourteen sons and three daughters.

6 All these *were* under the direction of their father for the music *in* the house of the LORD, with cymbals, stringed instruments, and [a]harps, for the service of the house of God. Asaph, Jeduthun, and Heman *were* [b]under the authority of the king. 7 So the [a]number of them, with their brethren who were instructed in the songs of the LORD, all who were skillful, *was* two hundred and eighty-eight.

8 And they cast lots for their duty, the small as well as the great, [a]the teacher with the student.

9 Now the first lot for Asaph came out for Joseph; the second for Gedaliah, him with his brethren and sons, twelve; 10 the third for Zaccur, his sons and his brethren, twelve; 11 the fourth for Jizri,[1] his sons and his brethren, twelve; 12 the fifth for Nethaniah, his sons and his brethren, twelve; 13 the sixth for Bukkiah, his sons and his brethren, twelve; 14 the seventh for Jesharelah,[1] his sons and his brethren, twelve; 15 the eighth for Jeshaiah, his sons and his brethren, twelve; 16 the ninth for Mattaniah, his sons and his brethren, twelve; 17 the tenth for Shimei, his sons and his brethren, twelve; 18 the eleventh for Azarel,[1] his sons and his brethren, twelve; 19 the twelfth for Hashabiah, his sons and his brethren, twelve; 20 the thirteenth for Shubael,[1] his sons and his brethren, twelve; 21 the fourteenth for Mattithiah, his sons and his brethren, twelve; 22 the fifteenth for Jeremoth,[1] his sons and his brethren, twelve; 23 the sixteenth for Hananiah, his sons and his brethren, twelve; 24 the seventeenth for Joshbekashah, his sons and his brethren, twelve; 25 the eighteenth for Hanani, his sons and his brethren, twelve; 26 the nineteenth for Mallothi, his sons and his brethren, twelve; 27 the twentieth for Eliathah, his sons and his brethren, twelve; 28 the twenty-first for Hothir, his sons and his brethren, twelve; 29 the twenty-second for Giddalti, his sons and his brethren, twelve; 30 the twenty-third for Mahazioth, his sons and his brethren, twelve; 31 the twenty-fourth for Romamti-Ezer, his sons and his brethren, twelve.

### THE GATEKEEPERS

**26** Concerning the divisions of the gatekeepers: of the Korahites, Meshelemiah the son of [a]Kore, of the sons of Asaph. 2 And the sons of Meshelemiah *were* [a]Zechariah the firstborn, Jediael the second, Zebadiah the third, Jathniel the fourth, 3 Elam the fifth, Jehohanan the sixth, Eliehoenai the seventh.

4 Moreover the sons of [a]Obed-Edom *were* Shemaiah the firstborn, Jehozabad the second, Joah the third, Sacar the fourth, Nethanel the fifth, 5 Ammiel the sixth, Issachar the seventh, Peulthai the eighth; for God blessed him.

6 Also to Shemaiah his son were sons born who governed their fathers' houses, because they *were* men of great ability. 7 The sons of Shemaiah *were* Othni, Rephael, Obed, and Elzabad, whose brothers Elihu and Semachiah *were* able men.

8 All these *were* of the sons of Obed-Edom, they and their sons and their brethren, [a]able men with strength for the work: sixty-two of Obed-Edom.

9 And Meshelemiah had sons and brethren, eighteen able men.

10 Also [a]Hosah, of the children of Merari, had sons: Shimri the first (for *though* he was not the firstborn, his father made him the first), 11 Hilkiah the second, Tebaliah the third, Zechariah the fourth; all the sons and brethren of Hosah *were* thirteen.

12 Among these *were* the divisions of the gatekeepers, among the chief men, *having* duties just like their brethren, to serve in the house of the LORD. 13 And they [a]cast lots for each gate, the small as well as the great, according to their father's

**24:28** [a] 1 Chr. 23:22 **24:30** [a] 1 Chr. 23:23 **25:1** [a] 1 Chr. 6:30, 33, 39, 44; 2 Chr. 5:12 **25:2** [1] Spelled *Jesharelah* in verse 14
**25:3** [a] 1 Chr. 16:41, 42 [1] Spelled *Jizri* in verse 11 [2] *Shimei,* appearing in one Hebrew and several Septuagint manuscripts, completes the total of six sons (compare verse 17). **25:4** [1] Spelled *Azarel* in verse 18 [2] Spelled *Shubael* in verse 20 [3] Spelled *Jeremoth* in verse 22
**25:5** [a] 1 Chr. 16:42 [1] That is, to increase his power or influence **25:6** [a] 1 Chr. 15:16 [b] 1 Chr. 15:19; 25:2 **25:7** [a] 1 Chr. 23:5 **25:8** [a] 2 Chr. 23:13 **25:11** [1] Spelled *Zeri* in verse 3 **25:14** [1] Spelled *Asharelah* in verse 2 **25:18** [1] Spelled *Uzziel* in verse 4 **25:20** [1] Spelled *Shebuel* in verse 4 **25:22** [1] Spelled *Jerimoth* in verse 4 **26:1** [a] Ps. 42:title **26:2** [a] 1 Chr. 9:21 **26:4** [a] 1 Chr. 15:18, 21
**26:8** [a] 1 Chr. 9:13 **26:10** [a] 1 Chr. 16:38 **26:13** [a] 1 Chr. 24:5, 31; 25:8

house. 14 The lot for the East *Gate* fell to Shelemiah. Then they cast lots *for* his son Zechariah, a wise counselor, and his lot came out for the North Gate; 15 to Obed-Edom the South Gate, and to his sons the storehouse.[1] 16 To Shuppim and Hosah *the lot came out* for the West Gate, with the Shallecheth Gate on the [a]ascending highway—watchman opposite watchman. 17 On the east *were* six Levites, on the north four each day, on the south four each day, and for the storehouse[1] two by two. 18 As for the Parbar[1] on the west, *there were* four on the highway *and* two at the Parbar. 19 These were the divisions of the gatekeepers among the sons of Korah and among the sons of Merari.

### THE TREASURIES AND OTHER DUTIES

20 Of the Levites, Ahijah *was* [a]over the treasuries of the house of God and over the treasuries of the [b]dedicated things. 21 The sons of Laadan, the descendants of the Gershonites of Laadan, heads of their fathers' *houses,* of Laadan the Gershonite: Jehieli. 22 The sons of Jehieli, Zetham and Joel his brother, *were* over the treasuries of the house of the LORD. 23 Of the [a]Amramites, the Izharites, the Hebronites, and the Uzzielites: 24 [a]Shebuel the son of Gershom, the son of Moses, *was* overseer of the treasuries. 25 And his brethren by Eliezer *were* Rehabiah his son, Jeshaiah his son, Joram his son, Zichri his son, and [a]Shelomith his son.

26 This Shelomith and his brethren *were* over all the treasuries of the dedicated things [a]which King David and the heads of fathers' *houses,* the captains over thousands and hundreds, and the captains of the army, had dedicated. 27 Some of the spoils won in battles they dedicated to maintain the house of the LORD. 28 And all that Samuel [a]the seer, Saul the son of Kish, Abner the son of Ner, and Joab the son of Zeruiah had dedicated, every dedicated *thing,* was under the hand of Shelomith and his brethren.

29 Of the Izharites, Chenaniah and his sons [a]*performed* duties as [b]officials and judges over Israel outside Jerusalem.

30 Of the Hebronites, [a]Hashabiah and his brethren, one thousand seven hundred able men, had the oversight of Israel on the west side of the Jordan for all the business of the LORD, and in the service of the king. 31 Among the Hebronites, [a]Jerijah *was* head of the Hebronites according to his genealogy of the fathers. In the fortieth year of the reign of David they were sought, and there were found among them capable men [b]at Jazer of Gilead. 32 And his brethren *were* two thousand seven hundred able men, heads of fathers' *houses,* whom King David made officials over the Reubenites, the Gadites, and the half-tribe of Manasseh, for every matter pertaining to God and the [a]affairs of the king.

> **26:20** All money and treasures that were taken in battle or dedicated to the Lord by grateful Israelites were kept in the temple **treasuries** for safekeeping. The money was used to maintain the temple and keep it properly furnished. For extra security, Solomon's temple had a courtyard with a wall and gates around it.

### THE MILITARY DIVISIONS

27 And the children of Israel, according to their number, the heads of fathers' *houses,* the captains of thousands and hundreds and their officers, served the king in every matter of the *military* divisions. *These divisions* came in and went out month by month throughout all the months of the year, each division *having* twenty-four thousand.

2 Over the first division for the first month *was* [a]Jashobeam the son of Zabdiel, and in his division *were* twenty-four thousand; 3 *he was* of the children of Perez, and the chief of all the captains of the army for the first month. 4 Over the division of the second month *was* Dodai[1] an Ahohite, and of his division Mikloth also *was* the leader; in his division *were* twenty-four thousand. 5 The third captain of the army for the third month *was* [a]Benaiah, the son of Jehoiada the priest, who was chief; in his division *were* twenty-four thousand. 6 This was the Benaiah *who was* [a]mighty *among* the thirty, and was over the thirty; in his division *was* Ammizabad his son. 7 The fourth *captain* for the fourth month *was* [a]Asahel the brother of Joab, and Zebadiah his son after him; in his division *were* twenty-four thousand. 8 The fifth captain for the fifth month *was* Shamhuth[1] the Izrahite; in his division were twenty-four thousand. 9 The sixth *captain* for the sixth month *was* [a]Ira the son of Ikkesh the Tekoite; in his division *were* twenty-four thousand. 10 The seventh *captain* for the seventh month *was* [a]Helez the Pelonite, of the children of Ephraim; in his division *were* twenty-four thousand. 11 The eighth *captain* for the eighth month *was* [a]Sibbechai the Hushathite, of the Zarhites; in his division *were* twenty-four thousand. 12 The ninth *captain* for the ninth month *was* [a]Abiezer the Anathothite, of the Benjamites; in his division *were* twenty-four thousand. 13 The tenth *captain* for the tenth month *was* [a]Maharai the Netophathite, of the Zarhites; in his division *were* twenty-four thousand. 14 The

**26:15** [1] Hebrew *asuppim* **26:16** [a] 1 Kin. 10:5; 2 Chr. 9:4 **26:17** [1] Hebrew *asuppim* **26:18** [1] Probably a court or colonnade extending west of the temple **26:20** [a] 1 Chr. 9:26 [b] 2 Sam. 8:11; 1 Chr. 26:22, 24, 26; 28:12; Ezra 2:69 **26:23** [a] Ex. 6:18; Num. 3:19 **26:24** [a] 1 Chr. 23:16 **26:25** [a] 1 Chr. 23:18 **26:26** [a] 2 Sam. 8:11 **26:28** [a] 1 Sam. 9:9 **26:29** [a] Neh. 11:16 [b] 1 Chr. 23:4 **26:30** [a] 1 Chr. 27:17 **26:31** [a] 1 Chr. 23:19 [b] Josh. 21:39 **26:32** [a] 2 Chr. 19:11 **27:2** [a] 1 Chr. 11:11 **27:4** [1] Hebrew *Dodai,* usually spelled *Dodo* (compare 2 Samuel 23:9) **27:5** [a] 1 Chr. 18:17 **27:6** [a] 2 Sam. 23:20–23 **27:7** [a] 2 Sam. 23:24; 1 Chr. 11:26 **27:8** [1] Spelled *Shammoth* in 11:27 and *Shammah* in 2 Samuel 23:11 **27:9** [a] 1 Chr. 11:28 **27:10** [a] 1 Chr. 11:27 **27:11** [a] 2 Sam. 21:18; 1 Chr. 11:29; 20:4 **27:12** [a] 1 Chr. 11:28 **27:13** [a] 2 Sam. 23:28; 1 Chr. 11:30

eleventh *captain* for the eleventh month *was* [a]Benaiah the Pirathonite, of the children of Ephraim; in his division *were* twenty-four thousand. 15 The twelfth *captain* for the twelfth month *was* Heldai[1] the Netophathite, of Othniel; in his division *were* twenty-four thousand.

### LEADERS OF TRIBES

16 Furthermore, over the tribes of Israel: the officer over the Reubenites *was* Eliezer the son of Zichri; over the Simeonites, Shephatiah the son of Maachah; 17 *over* the Levites, [a]Hashabiah the son of Kemuel; over the Aaronites, Zadok; 18 *over* Judah, [a]Elihu, *one* of David's brothers; *over* Issachar, Omri the son of Michael; 19 *over* Zebulun, Ishmaiah the son of Obadiah; *over* Naphtali, Jerimoth the son of Azriel; 20 *over* the children of Ephraim, Hoshea the son of Azaziah; *over* the half-tribe of Manasseh, Joel the son of Pedaiah; 21 *over* the half-*tribe* of Manasseh in Gilead, Iddo the son of Zechariah; *over* Benjamin, Jaasiel the son of Abner; 22 *over* Dan, Azarel the son of Jeroham. These *were* the leaders of the tribes of Israel.

23 But David did not take the number of those twenty years old and under, because [a]the LORD had said He would multiply Israel like the [b]stars of the heavens. 24 Joab the son of Zeruiah began a census, but he did not finish, for [a]wrath came upon Israel because of this census; nor was the number recorded in the account of the chronicles of King David.

### OTHER STATE OFFICIALS

25 And Azmaveth the son of Adiel *was* over the king's treasuries; and Jehonathan the son of Uzziah was over the storehouses in the field, in the cities, in the villages, and in the fortresses. 26 Ezri the son of Chelub was over those who did the work of the field for tilling the ground. 27 And Shimei the Ramathite *was* over the vineyards, and Zabdi the Shiphmite was over the produce of the vineyards for the supply of wine. 28 Baal-Hanan the Gederite was over the olive trees and the sycamore trees that *were* in the lowlands, and Joash *was* over the store of oil. 29 And Shitrai the Sharonite *was* over the herds that fed in Sharon, and Shaphat the son of Adlai was over the herds *that were* in the valleys. 30 Obil the Ishmaelite *was* over the camels, Jehdeiah the Meronothite *was* over the donkeys, 31 and Jaziz the [a]Hagrite *was* over the flocks. All these *were* the officials over King David's property.

32 Also Jehonathan, David's uncle, *was* a counselor, a wise man, and a scribe; and Jehiel the son of Hachmoni *was* with the king's sons. 33 [a]Ahithophel *was* the king's counselor, and [b]Hushai the Archite *was* the king's companion. 34 After Ahithophel *was* Jehoiada the son of Benaiah, then [a]Abiathar. And the general of the king's army *was* [b]Joab.

### SOLOMON INSTRUCTED TO BUILD THE TEMPLE

**28** Now David assembled at Jerusalem all [a]the leaders of Israel: the officers of the tribes and [b]the captains of the divisions who served the king, the captains over thousands and captains over hundreds, and [c]the stewards over all the substance and possessions of the king and of his sons, with the officials, the valiant men, and all [d]the mighty men of valor.

2 Then King David rose to his feet and said, "Hear me, my brethren and my people: [a]I *had* it in my heart to build a house of rest for the ark of the covenant of the LORD, and for [b]the footstool of our God, and had made preparations to build it. 3 But God said to me, [a]'You shall not build a house for My name, because you *have been* a man of war and have shed [b]blood.' 4 However the LORD God of Israel [a]chose me above all the house of my father to be king over Israel forever, for He has chosen [b]Judah *to be* the ruler. And of the house of Judah, [c]the house of my father, and [d]among the sons of my father, He was pleased with me to make *me* king over all Israel. 5 [a]And of all my sons (for the LORD has given me many sons) [b]He has chosen my son Solomon to sit on the throne of the kingdom of the LORD over Israel. 6 Now He said to me, 'It is [a]your son Solomon *who* shall build My house and My courts; for I have chosen him *to be* My son, and I will be his Father. 7 Moreover I will establish his kingdom forever, [a]if he is steadfast to

> **28:4–6** Through most of Israel's history four leadership roles can be seen: (1) The **king** was the Lord's representative who ruled the people, but only as the Lord's servant. He led in war (1 Sam. 8:20) and made judicial decisions (2 Sam. 15:2), but could not make law since he himself was under the law (Deut. 17:14–20). (2) The priest taught the Lord's laws and officiated at the offering of sacrifices (Lev. 1:5). (3) The prophet was the man of God who spoke for God and gave divine pronouncements for the present or the future. (4) The wise man produced literary works stressing practical wisdom (Prov. 1:1), taught discipline of character to the young (Prov. 22:17), and gave counsel to the king (2 Sam. 16:20).

**27:14** [a]1 Chr. 11:31 **27:15** [1]Spelled *Heled* in 11:30 and *Heleb* in 2 Samuel 23:29 **27:17** [a]1 Chr. 26:30 **27:18** [a]1 Sam. 16:6 **27:23** [a][Deut. 6:3] [b]Gen. 15:5; 22:17; 26:4; Ex. 32:13; Deut. 1:10 **27:24** [a]2 Sam. 24:12–15; 1 Chr. 21:1–7 **27:31** [a]1 Chr. 5:10 **27:33** [a]2 Sam. 15:12 [b]2 Sam. 15:32–37 **27:34** [a]1 Kin. 1:7 [b]1 Chr. 11:6 **28:1** [a]1 Chr. 27:16 [b]1 Chr. 27:1, 2 [c]1 Chr. 27:25 [d]2 Sam. 23:8–39; 1 Chr. 11:10–47 **28:2** [a]2 Sam. 7:2 [b]Ps. 99:5; 132:7; [Is. 66:1] **28:3** [a]2 Sam. 7:5, 13; 1 Kin. 5:3 [b][1 Chr. 17:4; 22:8] **28:4** [a]1 Sam. 16:6–13 [b]Gen. 49:8–10; 1 Chr. 5:2; Ps. 60:7 [c]1 Sam. 16:1 [d]1 Sam. 13:14; 16:12, 13; Acts 13:22 **28:5** [a]1 Chr. 3:1–9; 14:3–7; 23:1 [b]1 Chr. 22:9; 29:1 **28:6** [a]2 Sam. 7:13, 14; 1 Kin. 6:38; 1 Chr. 22:9, 10; 2 Chr. 1:9; 6:2 **28:7** [a]1 Chr. 22:13

observe My commandments and My judgments, as it is this day.' 8 Now therefore, in the sight of all Israel, the assembly of the LORD, and in the hearing of our God, be careful to seek out all the commandments of the LORD your God, that you may possess this good land, and leave *it* as an inheritance for your children after you forever.

9 "As for you, my son Solomon, [a]know the God of your father, and serve Him [b]with a loyal heart and with a willing mind; for [c]the LORD searches all hearts and understands all the intent of the thoughts. [d]If you seek Him, He will be found by you; but if you forsake Him, He will [e]cast you off forever. 10 Consider now, [a]for the LORD has chosen you to build a house for the sanctuary; be strong, and do it."

11 Then David gave his son Solomon [a]the plans for the vestibule, its houses, its treasuries, its upper chambers, its inner chambers, and the place of the mercy seat; 12 and the [a]plans for all that he had by the Spirit, of the courts of the house of the LORD, of all the chambers all around, [b]of the treasuries of the house of God, and of the treasuries for the dedicated things; 13 also for the division of the priests and the [a]Levites, for all the work of the service of the house of the LORD, and for all the articles of service in the house of the LORD. 14 *He gave* gold by weight for *things* of gold, for all articles used in every kind of service; also *silver* for all articles of silver by weight, for all articles used in every kind of service; 15 the weight for the [a]lampstands of gold, and their lamps of gold, by weight for each lampstand and its lamps; for the lampstands of silver by weight, for the lampstand and its lamps, according to the use of each lampstand. 16 And by weight *he gave* gold for the tables of the showbread, for each [a]table, and silver for the tables of silver; 17 also pure gold for the forks, the basins, the pitchers of pure gold, and the golden bowls—*he gave gold* by weight for every bowl; and for the silver bowls, *silver* by weight for every bowl; 18 and refined gold by weight for the [a]altar of incense, and for the construction of the chariot, that is, the gold [b]cherubim that spread *their wings* and overshadowed the ark of the covenant of the LORD. 19 "All *this," said David,* [a]"the LORD made me understand in writing, by *His* hand upon me, all the works of these plans."

20 And David said to his son Solomon, [a]"Be strong and of good courage, and do *it;* do not fear nor be dismayed, for the LORD God—my God—*will be* with you. [b]He will not leave you nor forsake you, until you have finished all the work for the service of the house of the LORD. 21 *Here are* [a]the divisions of the priests and the Levites for all the service of the house of God; and [b]every willing craftsman *will be* with you for all manner of workmanship, for every kind of service; also the leaders and all the people *will be* completely at your command."

### *OFFERINGS FOR BUILDING THE TEMPLE*

**29** Furthermore King David said to all the assembly: "My son Solomon, whom alone God has [a]chosen, *is* [b]young and inexperienced; and the work *is* great, because the temple[1] *is* not for man but for the LORD God. 2 Now for the house of my God I have prepared with all my might: gold for *things to be made of* gold, silver for *things of* silver, bronze for *things of* bronze, iron for *things of* iron, wood for *things of* wood, [a]onyx stones, *stones* to be set, glistening stones of various colors, all kinds of precious stones, and marble slabs in abundance. 3 Moreover, because I have set my affection on the house of my God, I have given to the house of my God, over and above all that I have prepared for the holy house, my own special treasure of gold and silver: 4 three thousand talents of gold, of the gold of [a]Ophir, and seven thousand talents of refined silver, to overlay the walls of the houses; 5 the gold for *things of* gold and the silver for *things of* silver, and for all kinds of work *to be done* by the hands of craftsmen. Who *then* is [a]willing to consecrate himself this day to the LORD?"

> **SEEING JESUS IN THE SCRIPTURE**
>
> **29:1–3** When Solomon was young, David left him treasures to be used to build the temple one day. When the wise men visited Jesus as a child, they gave Him gifts fit for the King who had come to tabernacle with us (see Matt. 2:11).

6 Then [a]the leaders of the fathers' *houses,* leaders of the tribes of Israel, the captains of thousands and of hundreds, with [b]the officers over the king's work, [c]offered willingly. 7 They gave for the work of the house of God five thousand talents and ten thousand darics of gold, ten thousand talents of silver, eighteen thousand talents of bronze, and one hundred thousand talents of iron. 8 And whoever had *precious* stones gave *them* to the treasury of the house of the LORD, into the hand of [a]Jehiel[1] the Gershonite. 9 Then the people rejoiced, for they had offered willingly, because with a loyal heart they had [a]offered willingly to the LORD; and King David also rejoiced greatly.

**28:9** [a] [1 Sam. 12:24]; Jer. 9:24; Hos. 4:1; [John 17:3] [b] 2 Kin. 20:3 [c] [1 Sam. 16:7; 1 Kin. 8:39; 1 Chr. 29:17]; Jer. 11:20; 17:10; 20:12; Rev. 2:23 [d] 2 Chr. 15:2; [Jer. 29:13] [e] Deut. 31:17 **28:10** [a] 1 Chr. 22:13; 28:6 **28:11** [a] 1 Kin. 6:3; 1 Chr. 28:19 **28:12** [a] Ex. 25:40; Heb. 8:5 [b] 1 Chr. 26:20, 28 **28:13** [a] 1 Chr. 23:6 **28:15** [a] Ex. 25:31–39; 1 Kin. 7:49 **28:16** [a] 1 Kin. 7:48 **28:18** [a] Ex. 30:1–10 [b] Ex. 25:18–22; 1 Sam. 4:4; 1 Kin. 6:23 **28:19** [a] Ex. 25:40; 1 Chr. 28:11, 12 **28:20** [a] Deut. 31:6, 7; [Josh. 1:6–9]; 1 Chr. 22:13 [b] Josh. 1:5; Heb. 13:5 **28:21** [a] 1 Chr. 24—26 [b] Ex. 35:25–35; 36:1, 2; 2 Chr. 2:13, 14 **29:1** [a] 1 Chr. 28:5 [b] 1 Kin. 3:7; 1 Chr. 22:5; Prov. 4:3 [1] Literally *palace* **29:2** [a] Is. 54:11, 12; Rev. 21:18 **29:4** [a] 1 Kin. 9:28 **29:5** [a] 2 Chr. 29:31; [2 Cor. 8:5, 12] **29:6** [a] 1 Chr. 27:1; 28:1 [b] 1 Chr. 27:25–31 [c] Ex. 35:21–35 **29:8** [a] 1 Chr. 23:8 [1] Possibly the same as *Jehieli* (compare 26:21, 22) **29:9** [a] Ex. 25:2; 1 Kin. 8:61; 2 Cor. 9:7

### *DAVID'S PRAISE TO GOD*

10 Therefore David blessed the LORD before
all the assembly; and David said:

"Blessed are You, LORD God of Israel, our
Father, forever and ever.
11 [a]Yours, O LORD, *is* the greatness,
The power and the glory,
The victory and the majesty;
For all *that is* in heaven and in earth *is*
*Yours;*
Yours *is* the kingdom, O LORD,
And You are exalted as head over all.
12 [a]Both riches and honor *come* from You,
And You reign over all.
In Your hand *is* power and might;
In Your hand *it is* to make great
And to give strength to all.

13 "Now therefore, our God,
We thank You
And praise Your glorious name.
14 But who *am* I, and who *are* my people,
That we should be able to offer so
willingly as this?
For all things *come* from You,
And of Your own we have given You.
15 For [a]we *are* aliens and pilgrims before
You,
As *were* all our fathers;
[b]Our days on earth *are* as a shadow,
And without hope.

16 "O LORD our God, all this abundance that
we have prepared to build You a house for Your
holy name is from Your hand, and *is* all Your
own. 17 I know also, my God, that You [a]test the
heart and [b]have pleasure in uprightness. As
for me, in the uprightness of my heart I have
willingly offered all these *things;* and now with
joy I have seen Your people, who are present
here to offer willingly to You. 18 O LORD God of
Abraham, Isaac, and Israel, our fathers, keep this
forever in the intent of the thoughts of the heart
of Your people, and fix their heart toward You.
19 And [a]give my son Solomon a loyal heart to keep
Your commandments and Your testimonies and
Your statutes, to do all *these things,* and to build
the temple[1] for which [b]I have made provision."
20 Then David said to all the assembly, "Now
bless the LORD your God." So all the assembly
blessed the LORD God of their fathers, and bowed
their heads and prostrated themselves before
the LORD and the king.

### *SOLOMON ANOINTED KING*

*(1 Kin. 1:38–40; 2:12)*

21 And they made sacrifices to the LORD and
offered burnt offerings to the LORD on the next
day: a thousand bulls, a thousand rams, a thou-
sand lambs, with their drink offerings, and [a]sac-
rifices in abundance for all Israel. 22 So they ate
and drank before the LORD with great gladness
on that day. And they made Solomon the son
of David king the second time, and [a]anointed
*him* before the LORD *to be* the leader, and Zadok
*to be* priest. 23 Then Solomon sat on the throne
of the LORD as king instead of David his father,
and prospered; and all Israel obeyed him. 24 All
the leaders and the mighty men, and also all the
sons of King David, [a]submitted themselves to
King Solomon. 25 So the LORD exalted Solomon
exceedingly in the sight of all Israel, and [a]be-
stowed on him *such* royal majesty as had not
been on any king before him in Israel.

### *THE CLOSE OF DAVID'S REIGN*

26 Thus David the son of Jesse reigned over
all Israel. 27 [a]And the period that he reigned over
Israel *was* forty years; [b]seven years he reigned
in Hebron, and thirty-three *years* he reigned in
Jerusalem. 28 So he [a]died in a good old age, [b]full
of days and riches and honor; and Solomon his
son reigned in his place. 29 Now the acts of King
David, first and last, indeed they *are* written
in the book of Samuel the seer, in the book of
Nathan the prophet, and in the book of Gad the
seer, 30 with all his reign and his might, [a]and the
events that happened to him, to Israel, and to
all the kingdoms of the lands.

29:11 [a] Matt. 6:13; 1 Tim. 1:17; Rev. 5:13 29:12 [a] Rom. 11:36 29:15 [a] Lev. 25:23; Ps. 39:12; Heb. 11:13, 14; 1 Pet. 2:11 [b] Job 14:2; Ps. 90:9
29:17 [a] [1 Sam. 16:7; 1 Chr. 28:9] [b] Prov. 11:20 29:19 [a] [1 Chr. 28:9]; Ps. 72:1 [b] 1 Chr. 29:1, 2 [1] Literally *palace* 29:21 [a] 1 Kin. 8:62, 63
29:22 [a] 1 Kin. 1:32–35, 39; 1 Chr. 23:1 29:24 [a] Eccl. 8:2 29:25 [a] 1 Kin. 3:13; 2 Chr. 1:12; Eccl. 2:9 29:27 [a] 2 Sam. 5:4; 1 Kin. 2:11
[b] 2 Sam. 5:5 29:28 [a] Gen. 25:8 [b] 1 Chr. 23:1 29:30 [a] Dan. 2:21; 4:23, 25

# *The Second Book of the*
# CHRONICLES

| AUTHOR | KEY VERSES | READING TIME |
|---|---|---|
| Ezra, likely | 2 Chronicles 7:13–14 | 2 hours 50 minutes |

The Book of 2 Chronicles parallels 1 and 2 Kings but virtually ignores the northern kingdom of Israel because of its idolatry and refusal to acknowledge the temple in Jerusalem. Instead, 2 Chronicles focuses on the kings who patterned their lives and reigns after the life and reign of godly King David. It gives extended treatment to the reforms of Asa, Jehoshaphat, Joash, Hezekiah, and Josiah. The temple and temple worship, central throughout the book, befit a nation whose worship of God was central to its very survival. The book begins with the construction of Solomon's glorious temple and concludes with Cyrus's edict to rebuild the temple more than four hundred years later.

**Occasion:** Like 1 Chronicles, the Book of 2 Chronicles was written to elicit hope in the returned exiles, made clear by the bookends concerning Solomon's construction of the temple and Cyrus's proclamation allowing for it to be rebuilt. Times were difficult, but God was ever faithful.

**Main Point:** Dark days may have been behind Israel, but brighter days were ahead as God was at work restoring His people in their land.

**Big Ideas:** God is faithful. We can find encouragement for today and tomorrow by remembering God's goodness in the past. God's presence no longer fills a physical structure; He is present in His people, the church.

## OUTLINE:

I. Solomon Becomes King (ch. 1)
II. Solomon Completes the Temple (chs. 2–7)
III. Solomon's Reign as King (chs. 8–9)
IV. The Kingdom Divides (chs. 10–13)
V. The Sins and Reforms of Judah's Kings (chs. 14–35)
VI. The Fall of Judah and Cyrus's Decree (ch. 36)

**1010 BC**
David begins to reign at Hebron

**970 BC**
Solomon becomes king of Israel

**967 BC**
Solomon begins construction of the temple

**930 BC**
The kingdom is divided

**910 BC**
Asa becomes king in Judah

**872 BC**
Jehoshaphat becomes king in Judah

**776 BC**
Athletic contests begin at Olympia

**755 BC**
Isaiah begins to prophesy in Judah

**722 BC**
The Assyrians defeat Israel

**624 BC**
The Book of the law is found in Jerusalem

**586 BC**
The Babylonians defeat Judah

**c. 450–400 BC**
**2 Chronicles written**

### *SOLOMON REQUESTS WISDOM*

*(1 Kin. 3:1–15)*

**1** Now [a]Solomon the son of David was strength-
ened in his kingdom, and [b]the LORD his God
*was* with him and [c]exalted him exceedingly.
2 And Solomon spoke to all Israel, to [a]the
captains of thousands and of hundreds, to the
judges, and to every leader in all Israel, the
heads of the fathers' *houses.* 3 Then Solomon,
and all the assembly with him, went to the high
place that *was* at [a]Gibeon; for the tabernacle of
meeting with God was there, which Moses the
servant of the LORD had [b]made in the wilder-
ness. 4 [a]But David had brought up the ark of
God from Kirjath Jearim to *the place* David had
prepared for it, for he had pitched a tent for it at
Jerusalem. 5 Now [a]the bronze altar that [b]Bezalel
the son of Uri, the son of Hur, had made, he put[1]
before the tabernacle of the LORD; Solomon and
the assembly sought Him *there.* 6 And Solomon
went up there to the bronze altar before the
LORD, which *was* at the tabernacle of meeting,
and [a]offered a thousand burnt offerings on it.
7 [a]On that night God appeared to Solomon,
and said to him, "Ask! What shall I give you?"
8 And Solomon said to God: "You have shown
great [a]mercy to David my father, and have made
me [b]king in his place. 9 Now, O LORD God, let Your
promise to David my father be established, [a]for
You have made me king over a people like the
[b]dust of the earth in multitude. 10 [a]Now give me
wisdom and knowledge, that I may [b]go out and
come in before this people; for who can judge
this great people of Yours?"
11 [a]Then God said to Solomon: "Because this
was in your heart, and you have not asked riches
or wealth or honor or the life of your enemies,
nor have you asked long life—but have asked
wisdom and knowledge for yourself, that you
may judge My people over whom I have made
you king— 12 wisdom and knowledge *are* granted
to you; and I will give you riches and wealth
and honor, such as [a]none of the kings have had
who *were* before you, nor shall any after you
have the like."

**SEEING JESUS IN THE SCRIPTURE**

**1:11** God gave Solomon great wisdom to rule Israel. But even that wasn't enough to keep Solomon from sinning and failing as king. Jesus is the greater Solomon. He is the wisdom of God and our perfect, sinless King (see 1 Cor. 1:30).

### *SOLOMON'S MILITARY AND ECONOMIC POWER*

*(1 Kin. 10:26–29; 2 Chr. 9:25–28)*

13 So Solomon came to Jerusalem from the
high place that *was* at Gibeon, from before the
tabernacle of meeting, and reigned over Israel.
14 [a]And Solomon gathered chariots and horse-
men; he had one thousand four hundred char-
iots and twelve thousand horsemen, whom he
stationed in the chariot cities and with the king
in Jerusalem. 15 [a]Also the king made silver and
gold as common in Jerusalem as stones, and
he made cedars as abundant as the sycamores
which *are* in the lowland. 16 [a]And Solomon had
horses imported from Egypt and Keveh; the
king's merchants bought them in Keveh at the
*current* price. 17 They also acquired and imported
from Egypt a chariot for six hundred *shekels* of
silver, and a horse for one hundred and fifty; thus,
through their agents,[1] they exported them to all
the kings of the Hittites and the kings of Syria.

### *SOLOMON PREPARES TO BUILD THE TEMPLE*

*(1 Kin. 5:1–18)*

**2** Then Solomon [a]determined to build a tem-
ple for the name of the LORD, and a royal
house for himself. 2 [a]Solomon selected seventy
thousand men to bear burdens, eighty thousand
to quarry *stone* in the mountains, and three
thousand six hundred to oversee them.
3 Then Solomon sent to Hiram[1] king of Tyre,
saying:

[a]As you have dealt with David my father,
and sent him cedars to build himself
a house to dwell in, *so deal with me.*
4 Behold, [a]I am building a temple for the
name of the LORD my God, to dedicate *it* to
Him, [b]to burn before Him sweet incense,
for [c]the continual showbread, for [d]the
burnt offerings morning and evening, on
the [e]Sabbaths, on the New Moons, and on
the set feasts of the LORD our God. This *is*
*an ordinance* forever to Israel.

5 And the temple which I build *will be*
great, for [a]our God is greater than all gods.
6 [a]But who is able to build Him a temple,
since heaven and the heaven of heavens
cannot contain Him? Who *am* I then, that
I should build Him a temple, except to
burn sacrifice before Him?

7 Therefore send me at once a man skillful to
work in gold and silver, in bronze and iron,
in purple and crimson and blue, who has

**1:1** [a] 1 Kin. 2:46 [b] Gen. 39:2 [c] 1 Chr. 29:25 **1:2** [a] 1 Chr. 27:1–34 **1:3** [a] 1 Kin. 3:4 [b] Ex. 25—27; 35:4—36:38 **1:4** [a] 2 Sam. 6:2–17 **1:5** [a] Ex. 27:1, 2; 38:1, 2 [b] Ex. 31:2 [1] Some authorities read *it was there.* **1:6** [a] 1 Kin. 3:4 **1:7** [a] 1 Kin. 3:5–14; 9:2 **1:8** [a] Ps. 18:50 [b] 1 Chr. 28:5 **1:9** [a] 2 Sam. 7:8–16; 1 Kin. 3:7, 8 [b] Gen. 13:16; Num. 23:10 **1:10** [a] 1 Kin. 3:9 [b] Num. 27:17; Deut. 31:2 **1:11** [a] 1 Kin. 3:11–13 **1:12** [a] 1 Kin. 10:23; 1 Chr. 29:25; 2 Chr. 9:22; Eccl. 2:9 **1:14** [a] 1 Kin. 10:26; 2 Chr. 9:25 **1:15** [a] 1 Kin. 10:27; 2 Chr. 9:27; Job 22:24 **1:16** [a] 1 Kin. 10:28; 22:36; 2 Chr. 9:28 **1:17** [1] Literally *by their hands* **2:1** [a] 1 Kin. 5:5 **2:2** [a] 1 Kin. 5:15, 16; 2 Chr. 2:18 **2:3** [a] 1 Chr. 14:1 [1] Hebrew *Huram* (compare 1 Kings 5:1) **2:4** [a] 2 Chr. 2:1 [b] Ex. 30:7 [c] Ex. 25:30; Lev. 24:8 [d] Ex. 29:38–42 [e] Num. 28:3, 9–11 **2:5** [a] Ps. 135:5; [1 Cor. 8:5, 6] **2:6** [a] 1 Kin. 8:27; 2 Chr. 6:18; Is. 66:1

skill to engrave with the skillful men who
are with me in Judah and Jerusalem, [a]whom
David my father provided. 8 [a]Also send me
cedar and cypress and algum logs from
Lebanon, for I know that your servants have
skill to cut timber in Lebanon; and indeed
my servants *will be* with your servants, 9 to
prepare timber for me in abundance, for the
temple which I am about to build *shall be*
great and wonderful.
10 [a]And indeed I will give to your servants,
the woodsmen who cut timber, twenty
thousand kors of ground wheat, twenty
thousand kors of barley, twenty thousand
baths of wine, and twenty thousand baths
of oil.

11 Then Hiram king of Tyre answered in writ-
ing, which he sent to Solomon:

[a]Because the LORD loves His people, He
has made you king over them.

12 Hiram[1] also said:

[a]Blessed *be* the LORD God of Israel, [b]who
made heaven and earth, for He has given
King David a wise son, endowed with
prudence and understanding, who will
build a temple for the LORD and a royal
house for himself!
13 And now I have sent a skillful man,
endowed with understanding, Huram[1] my
master[2] *craftsman* 14 [a](the son of a woman
of the daughters of Dan, and his father was
a man of Tyre), skilled to work in gold and
silver, bronze and iron, stone and wood,
purple and blue, fine linen and crimson,
and to make any engraving and to
accomplish any plan which may be given
to him, with your skillful men and with the
skillful men of my lord David your father.
15 Now therefore, the wheat, the barley,
the oil, and the wine which [a]my lord has
spoken of, let him send to his servants.
16 [a]And we will cut wood from Lebanon, as
much as you need; we will bring it to you
in rafts by sea to Joppa, and you will carry
it up to Jerusalem.

17 [a]Then Solomon numbered all the aliens
who *were* in the land of Israel, after the census
in which [b]David his father had numbered them;
and there were found to be one hundred and
fifty-three thousand six hundred. 18 And he made
[a]seventy thousand of them bearers of burdens,
eighty thousand stonecutters in the mountain,
and three thousand six hundred overseers to
make the people work.

### *SOLOMON BUILDS THE TEMPLE*
*(1 Kin. 6:1–22)*

3 Now [a]Solomon began to build the house of
the LORD at [b]Jerusalem on Mount Moriah,
where *the LORD*[1] had appeared to his father Da-
vid, at the place that David had prepared on the
threshing floor of [c]Ornan[2] the Jebusite. 2 And he
began to build on the second *day* of the second
month in the fourth year of his reign.

> **3:1 Mount Moriah** was the mountain where Abraham brought his son Isaac to sacrifice him but where the Lord provided a ram instead (see Gen. 22). It was suitable that this place where Abraham showed such incredible obedience should be the site of the temple that dealt with the issues of sacrifice and sin.

3 This is the foundation [a]which Solomon laid
for building the house of God: The length *was*
sixty cubits (by cubits according to the former
measure) and the width twenty cubits. 4 And the
[a]vestibule that *was* in front *of the sanctuary*[1] was
twenty cubits long across the width of the house,
and the height *was* one hundred and[2] twenty. He
overlaid the inside with pure gold. 5 [a]The larger
room[1] he [b]paneled with cypress which he over-
laid with fine gold, and he carved palm trees and
chainwork on it. 6 And he decorated the house with
precious stones for beauty, and the gold *was* gold
from Parvaim. 7 He also overlaid the house—the
beams and doorposts, its walls and doors—with
gold; and he carved cherubim on the walls.
8 And he made the [a]Most Holy Place. Its
length was according to the width of the house,
twenty cubits, and its width twenty cubits. He
overlaid it with six hundred talents of fine gold.

> **3:8 Six hundred talents of gold**, about twenty-five tons, coated the walls of the **Most Holy Place** in the temple. The coating was about one-fifth of an inch thick.

**2:7** [a] 1 Chr. 22:15 **2:8** [a] 1 Kin. 5:6 **2:10** [a] 1 Kin. 5:11 **2:11** [a] 1 Kin. 10:9; 2 Chr. 9:8 **2:12** [a] 1 Kin. 5:7 [b] Gen. 1; 2; Acts 4:24; 14:15; Rev. 10:6 [1] Hebrew *Huram* (compare 1 Kings 5:1) **2:13** [1] Spelled *Hiram* in 1 Kings 7:13 [2] Literally *father* (compare 1 Kings 7:13, 14) **2:14** [a] 1 Kin. 7:13, 14 **2:15** [a] 2 Chr. 2:10 **2:16** [a] 1 Kin. 5:8, 9 **2:17** [a] 1 Kin. 5:13; 2 Chr. 8:7, 8 [b] 1 Chr. 22:2 **2:18** [a] 2 Chr. 2:2 **3:1** [a] 1 Kin. 6:1 [b] Gen. 22:2–14 [c] 1 Chr. 21:18; 22:1 [1] Literally *He,* following Masoretic Text and Vulgate; Septuagint reads *the LORD;* Targum reads *the Angel of the LORD.* [2] Spelled *Araunah* in 2 Samuel 24:16ff **3:3** [a] 1 Kin. 6:2 **3:4** [a] 1 Kin. 6:3 [1] The main room of the temple; elsewhere called the holy place (compare 1 Kings 6:3) [2] Following Masoretic Text, Septuagint, and Vulgate; Arabic, some manuscripts of the Septuagint, and Syriac omit *one hundred and.* **3:5** [a] 1 Kin. 6:17 [b] 1 Kin. 6:15 [1] Literally *house* **3:8** [a] Ex. 26:33

9 The weight of the nails *was* fifty shekels of gold; and he overlaid the upper [a]area with gold. 10 [a]In the Most Holy Place he made two cherubim, fashioned by carving, and overlaid them with gold. 11 The wings of the cherubim *were* twenty cubits in *overall* length: one wing *of the one cherub was* five cubits, touching the wall of the room, and the other wing *was* five cubits, touching the wing of the other cherub; 12 *one* wing of the other cherub *was* five cubits, touching the wall of the room, and the other wing *also was* five cubits, touching the wing of the other cherub. 13 The wings of these cherubim spanned twenty cubits overall. They stood on their feet, and they faced inward. 14 And he made the [a]veil of blue, purple, crimson, and fine linen, and wove cherubim into it.

15 Also he made in front of the temple[1] [a]two pillars thirty-five[2] cubits high, and the capital that *was* on the top of each of *them* was five cubits. 16 He made wreaths of chainwork, as in the inner sanctuary, and put *them* on top of the pillars; and he made [a]one hundred pomegranates, and put *them* on the wreaths of chainwork. 17 Then he [a]set up the pillars before the temple, one on the right hand and the other on the left; he called the name of the one on the right hand Jachin, and the name of the one on the left Boaz.

> **3:14** The **veil** was a heavy curtain between the holy place and the Most Holy Place. Because God's presence was within the Most Holy Place, this veil symbolized how sin had formed a barrier between Him and people. This veil was torn in two, from top to bottom, when Jesus died on the cross (Matt. 27:51). This tearing is a symbol that through Jesus, believers have direct access to God (see Heb. 6:19; 9:1—10:20).

### *FURNISHINGS OF THE TEMPLE*

*(1 Kin. 6:23–38; 7:13–51)*

**4** Moreover he made [a]a bronze altar: twenty cubits was its length, twenty cubits its width, and ten cubits its height.

2 [a]Then he made the Sea of cast *bronze,* ten cubits from one brim to the other; *it was* completely round. Its height *was* five cubits, and a line of thirty cubits measured its circumference. 3 [a]And under it *was* the likeness of oxen encircling it all around, ten to a cubit, all the way around the Sea. The oxen *were* cast in two rows, when it was cast. 4 It stood on twelve [a]oxen: three looking toward the north, three looking toward the west, three looking toward the south, and three looking toward the east; the Sea *was set* upon them, and all their back parts *pointed* inward. 5 It *was* a handbreadth thick; and its brim was shaped like the brim of a cup, *like* a lily blossom. It contained three thousand[1] baths.

6 He also made [a]ten lavers, and put five on the right side and five on the left, to wash in them; such things as they offered for the burnt offering they would wash in them, but the Sea *was* for the [b]priests to wash in. 7 [a]And he made ten lampstands of gold [b]according to their design, and set *them* in the temple, five on the right side and five on the left. 8 [a]He also made ten tables, and placed *them* in the temple, five on the right side and five on the left. And he made one hundred [b]bowls of gold.

9 Furthermore [a]he made the court of the priests, and the [b]great court and doors for the court; and he overlaid these doors with bronze. 10 [a]He set the Sea on the right side, toward the southeast.

11 Then [a]Huram made the pots and the shovels and the bowls. So Huram finished doing the work that he was to do for King Solomon for the house of God: 12 the two pillars and [a]the bowl-shaped capitals *that were* on top of the two pillars; the two networks covering the two bowl-shaped capitals which *were* on top of the pillars; 13 [a]four hundred pomegranates for the two networks (two rows of pomegranates for each network, to cover the two bowl-shaped capitals that *were* on the pillars); 14 he also made [a]carts and the lavers on the carts; 15 one Sea and twelve oxen under it; 16 also the pots, the shovels, the forks—and all their articles [a]Huram his master[1] *craftsman* made of burnished bronze for King Solomon for the house of the LORD.

17 In the plain of Jordan the king had them cast in clay molds, between Succoth and Zeredah.[1] 18 [a]And Solomon had all these articles made in such great abundance that the weight of the bronze was not determined.

19 Thus [a]Solomon had all the furnishings made for the house of God: the altar of gold and the tables on which *was* [b]the showbread; 20 the lampstands with their lamps of pure gold, to burn [a]in the prescribed manner in front of the inner sanctuary, 21 with [a]the flowers and the lamps and the wick-trimmers of gold, of purest gold; 22 the trimmers, the bowls, the ladles, and the censers of pure gold. As for the entry of the sanctuary, its inner doors to the Most Holy *Place,* and the doors of the main hall of the temple, *were* gold.

**5** So [a]all the work that Solomon had done for the house of the LORD was finished; and Solomon brought in the things which his father David had dedicated: the silver and the gold and all the furnishings. And he put *them* in the treasuries of the house of God.

**3:9** [a] 1 Chr. 28:11 **3:10** [a] 1 Kin. 6:23–28 **3:14** [a] Ex. 26:31 **3:15** [a] 1 Kin. 7:15–20 [1] Literally *house* [2] Or *eighteen* (compare 1 Kings 7:15; 2 Kings 25:17; and Jeremiah 52:21) **3:16** [a] 1 Kin. 7:20 **3:17** [a] 1 Kin. 7:21 **4:1** [a] Ex. 27:1, 2 **4:2** [a] 1 Kin. 7:23–26 **4:3** [a] 1 Kin. 7:24–26 **4:4** [a] 1 Kin. 7:25 **4:5** [1] Or *two thousand* (compare 1 Kings 7:26) **4:6** [a] 1 Kin. 7:38, 40 [b] Ex. 30:19–21 **4:7** [a] 1 Kin. 7:49 [b] Ex. 25:31; 1 Chr. 28:12, 19 **4:8** [a] 1 Kin. 7:48 [b] 1 Chr. 28:17 **4:9** [a] 1 Kin. 6:36 [b] 2 Kin. 21:5 **4:10** [a] 1 Kin. 7:39 **4:11** [a] 1 Kin. 7:40–51 **4:12** [a] 1 Kin. 7:41 **4:13** [a] 1 Kin. 7:20 **4:14** [a] 1 Kin. 7:27, 43 **4:16** [a] 1 Kin. 7:45; 2 Chr. 2:13 [1] Literally *father* **4:17** [1] Spelled *Zaretan* in 1 Kings 7:46 **4:18** [a] 1 Kin. 7:47 **4:19** [a] 1 Kin. 7:48–50 [b] Ex. 25:30 **4:20** [a] Ex. 27:20, 21 **4:21** [a] Ex. 25:31 **5:1** [a] 1 Kin. 7:51

### *THE ARK BROUGHT INTO THE TEMPLE*

*(1 Kin. 8:1–13)*

2 [a]Now Solomon assembled the elders of Israel and all the heads of the tribes, the chief fathers of the children of Israel, in Jerusalem, that they might bring the ark of the covenant of the LORD up [b]from the City of David, which *is* Zion. 3 [a]Therefore all the men of Israel assembled with the king [b]at the feast, which *was* in the seventh month. 4 So all the elders of Israel came, and the [a]Levites took up the ark. 5 Then they brought up the ark, the tabernacle of meeting, and all the holy furnishings that *were* in the tabernacle. The priests and the Levites brought them up. 6 Also King Solomon, and all the congregation of Israel who were assembled with him before the ark, were sacrificing sheep and oxen that could not be counted or numbered for multitude. 7 Then the priests brought in the ark of the covenant of the LORD to its place, into the [a]inner sanctuary of the temple,[1] to the Most Holy *Place,* under the wings of the cherubim. 8 For the cherubim spread *their* wings over the place of the ark, and the cherubim overshadowed the ark and its poles. 9 The poles extended so that the ends of the [a]poles of the ark could be seen from *the holy place,* in front of the inner sanctuary; but they could not be seen from outside. And they are there to this day. 10 Nothing was in the ark except the two tablets which Moses [a]put *there* at Horeb, when the LORD made *a covenant* with the children of Israel, when they had come out of Egypt.

11 And it came to pass when the priests came out of the *Most* Holy *Place* (for all the priests who *were* present had sanctified themselves, without keeping to their [a]divisions), 12 [a]and the Levites *who were* the singers, all those of Asaph and Heman and Jeduthun, with their sons and their brethren, stood at the east end of the altar, clothed in white linen, having cymbals, stringed instruments and harps, [b]and with them one hundred and twenty priests sounding with trumpets— 13 indeed it came to pass, when the trumpeters and singers *were* as one, to make one sound to be heard in praising and thanking the LORD, and when they lifted up their voice with the trumpets and cymbals and instruments of music, and praised the LORD, *saying:*

[a]"*For He is* good,
For His mercy *endures* forever,"[1]

that the house, the house of the LORD, was filled with a cloud, 14 so that the priests could not continue ministering because of the cloud; [a]for the glory of the LORD filled the house of God.

6 Then [a]Solomon spoke:

"The LORD said He would dwell in the
[b]dark cloud.
2 I have surely built You an exalted house,
And [a]a place for You to dwell in forever."

### *SOLOMON'S SPEECH UPON COMPLETION OF THE WORK*

*(1 Kin. 8:14–21)*

3 Then the king turned around and [a]blessed the whole assembly of Israel, while all the assembly of Israel was standing. 4 And he said: "Blessed *be* the LORD God of Israel, who has fulfilled with His hands *what* He spoke with His mouth to my father David, [a]saying, 5 'Since the day that I brought My people out of the land of Egypt, I have chosen no city from any tribe of Israel *in which* to build a house, that My name might be there, nor did I choose any man to be a ruler over My people Israel. 6 [a]Yet I have chosen Jerusalem, that My name may be there, and I [b]have chosen David to be over My people Israel.' 7 Now [a]it was in the heart of my father David to build a temple[1] for the name of the LORD God of Israel. 8 But the LORD said to my father David, 'Whereas it was in your heart to build a temple for My name, you did well in that it was in your heart. 9 Nevertheless you shall not build the temple, but your son who will come from your body, he shall build the temple for My [a]name.' 10 So the LORD has fulfilled His word which He spoke, and I have filled the position of my father David, and [a]sit on the throne of Israel, as the LORD promised; and I have built the temple for the name of the LORD God of Israel. 11 And there I have put the ark, [a]in which *is* the covenant of the LORD which He made with the children of Israel."

### *SOLOMON'S PRAYER OF DEDICATION*

*(1 Kin. 8:22–53)*

12 [a]Then *Solomon*[1] stood before the altar of the LORD in the presence of all the assembly of Israel, and spread out his hands 13 (for Solomon had made a bronze platform five cubits long, five cubits wide, and three cubits high, and had set it in the midst of the court; and he stood on it, knelt down on his knees before all the assembly of Israel, and spread out his hands toward heaven); 14 and he said: "LORD God of Israel, [a]*there is* no God in heaven or on earth like You, who keep *Your* [b]covenant and mercy with Your servants who walk before You with all their hearts. 15 [a]You have kept what You promised Your servant David my father; You have both spoken with Your mouth and fulfilled *it* with

**5:2** [a] 1 Kin. 8:1–9; Ps. 47:9 [b] 2 Sam. 6:12 **5:3** [a] 1 Kin. 8:2 [b] Lev. 23:34; 2 Chr. 7:8–10 **5:4** [a] 1 Chr. 15:2, 15 **5:7** [a] 2 Chr. 4:20 [1] Literally *house* **5:9** [a] Ex. 25:13–15 **5:10** [a] Ex. 25:16; Deut. 10:2, 5; 2 Chr. 6:11; Heb. 9:4 **5:11** [a] 1 Chr. 24:1–5 **5:12** [a] Ex. 32:26; 1 Chr. 25:1–7 [b] 1 Chr. 13:8; 15:16, 24 **5:13** [a] 1 Chr. 16:34, 41; Ps. 100:5; 106:1; 136 [1] Compare Psalm 106:1 **5:14** [a] Ex. 40:35; 1 Kin. 8:11; 2 Chr. 7:2; Ezek. 43:5 **6:1** [a] Ex. 19:9; 20:21; 1 Kin. 8:12–21 [b] [Lev. 16:2]; Ps. 97:2 **6:2** [a] 2 Sam. 7:13; 1 Chr. 17:12; 2 Chr. 7:12 **6:3** [a] 2 Sam. 6:18 **6:4** [a] 1 Chr. 17:5 **6:6** [a] Deut. 12:5–7; 2 Chr. 12:13; Zech. 2:12 [b] 1 Sam. 16:7–13; 1 Chr. 28:4 **6:7** [a] 2 Sam. 7:2; 1 Chr. 17:1; 28:2; Ps. 132:1–5 [1] Literally *house,* and so in verses 8–10 **6:9** [a] 1 Chr. 28:3–6 **6:10** [a] 1 Kin. 2:12; 10:9 **6:11** [a] 2 Chr. 5:7–10 **6:12** [a] 1 Kin. 8:22; 2 Chr. 7:7–9 [1] Literally *he* (compare 1 Kings 8:22) **6:14** [a] [Ex. 15:11; Deut. 4:39] [b] [Deut. 7:9] **6:15** [a] 1 Chr. 22:9, 10

Your hand, as *it is* this day. 16 Therefore, LORD God of Israel, now keep what You promised Your servant David my father, saying, [a]'You shall not fail to have a man sit before Me on the throne of Israel, [b]only if your sons take heed to their way, that they walk in My law as you have walked before Me.' 17 And now, O LORD God of Israel, let Your word come true, which You have spoken to Your servant David.

18 "But will God indeed dwell with men on the earth? [a]Behold, heaven and the heaven of heavens cannot contain You. How much less this temple[1] which I have built! 19 Yet regard the prayer of Your servant and his supplication, O LORD my God, and listen to the cry and the prayer which Your servant is praying before You: 20 that Your eyes may be [a]open toward this temple day and night, toward the place where *You* said *You would* put Your name, that You may hear the prayer which Your servant makes [b]toward this place. 21 And may You hear the supplications of Your servant and of Your people Israel, when they pray toward this place. Hear from heaven Your dwelling place, and when You hear, [a]forgive.

22 "If anyone sins against his neighbor, and is forced to take an [a]oath, and comes *and* takes an oath before Your altar in this temple, 23 then hear from heaven, and act, and judge Your servants, bringing retribution on the wicked by bringing his way on his own head, and justifying the righteous by giving him according to his [a]righteousness.

24 "Or if Your people Israel are defeated before an [a]enemy because they have sinned against You, and return and confess Your name, and pray and make supplication before You in this temple, 25 then hear from heaven and forgive the sin of Your people Israel, and bring them back to the land which You gave to them and their fathers.

26 "When the [a]heavens are shut up and there is no rain because they have sinned against You, when they pray toward this place and confess Your name, and turn from their sin because You afflict them, 27 then hear *in* heaven, and forgive the sin of Your servants, Your people Israel, that You may teach them the good way in which they should walk; and send rain on Your land which You have given to Your people as an inheritance.

28 "When there [a]is famine in the land, pestilence or blight or mildew, locusts or grasshoppers; when their enemies besiege them in the land of their cities; whatever plague or whatever [b]sickness *there is;* 29 whatever prayer, whatever supplication is *made* by anyone, or by all Your people Israel, when each one knows his own burden and his own grief, and spreads out his hands to this temple: 30 then hear from heaven Your dwelling place, and forgive, and give to everyone according to all his ways, whose heart You know (for You alone [a]know the [b]hearts of the sons of men), 31 that they may fear You, to walk in Your ways as long as they live in the land which You gave to our fathers.

32 "Moreover, concerning a foreigner, [a]who is not of Your people Israel, but has come from a far country for the sake of Your great name and Your mighty hand and Your outstretched arm, when they come and pray in this temple; 33 then hear from heaven Your dwelling place, and do according to all for which the foreigner calls to You, that all peoples of the earth may know Your name and fear You, as *do* Your people Israel, and that they may know that this temple which I have built is called by Your name.

34 "When Your people go out to battle against their enemies, wherever You send them, and when they pray to You toward this city which You have chosen and the temple which I have built for Your name, 35 then hear from heaven their prayer and their supplication, and maintain their cause.

36 "When they sin against You (for *there is* [a]no one who does not sin), and You become angry with them and deliver them to the enemy, and they take them [b]captive to a land far or near; 37 *yet* when they come to themselves in the land where they were carried captive, and repent, and make supplication to You in the land of their captivity, saying, 'We have sinned, we have done wrong, and have committed wickedness'; 38 and *when* they return to You with all their heart and with all their soul in the land of their captivity, where they have been carried captive, and pray toward their land which You gave to their fathers, the [a]city which You have chosen, and toward the temple which I have built for Your name: 39 then hear from heaven Your dwelling place their prayer and their supplications, and maintain their cause, and forgive Your people who have sinned against You. 40 Now, my God, I pray, let Your eyes be [a]open and *let* Your ears *be* attentive to the prayer *made* in this place.

41 "Now[a] therefore,
Arise, O LORD God, to Your [b]resting place,
You and the ark of Your strength.
Let Your priests, O LORD God, be clothed
with salvation,
And let Your saints [c]rejoice in goodness.

42 "O LORD God, do not turn away the face of
Your Anointed;
[a]Remember the mercies of Your servant
David."[1]

6:16 [a] 2 Sam. 7:12, 16; 1 Kin. 2:4; 6:12; 2 Chr. 7:18 [b] Ps. 132:12 6:18 [a] [2 Chr. 2:6; Is. 66:1; Acts 7:49] [1] Literally *house* 6:20 [a] 2 Chr. 7:15 [b] Ps. 5:7; Dan. 6:10 6:21 [a] [Is. 43:25; 44:22; Mic. 7:18] 6:22 [a] Ex. 22:8–11 6:23 [a] [Job 34:11] 6:24 [a] 2 Kin. 21:14, 15 6:26 [a] Deut. 28:23, 24; 1 Kin. 17:1 6:28 [a] 2 Chr. 20:9 [b] [Mic. 6:13] 6:30 [a] [1 Chr. 28:9; Prov. 21:2; 24:12] [b] [1 Sam. 16:7] 6:32 [a] John 12:20; Acts 8:27 6:36 [a] Prov. 20:9; Eccl. 7:20; [Rom. 3:9, 19; 5:12; Gal. 3:10]; James 3:2; 1 John 1:8 [b] Deut. 28:63–68 6:38 [a] Dan. 6:10 6:40 [a] 2 Chr. 6:20 6:41 [a] Ps. 132:8–10, 16 [b] 1 Chr. 28:2 [c] Neh. 9:25 6:42 [a] 2 Sam. 7:15; Ps. 89:49; 132:1, 8–10; Is. 55:3 [1] Compare Psalm 132:8–10

### *SOLOMON DEDICATES THE TEMPLE*
*(1 Kin. 8:62–66)*

**7** When [a]Solomon had finished praying, [b]fire came down from heaven and consumed the burnt offering and the sacrifices; and [c]the glory of the LORD filled the temple.[1] 2 [a]And the priests could not enter the house of the LORD, because the glory of the LORD had filled the LORD's house. 3 When all the children of Israel saw how the fire came down, and the glory of the LORD on the temple, they bowed their faces to the ground on the pavement, and worshiped and praised the LORD, *saying:*

[a]"For *He is* good,
[b]For His mercy *endures* forever."[1]

4 [a]Then the king and all the people offered sacrifices before the LORD. 5 King Solomon offered a sacrifice of twenty-two thousand bulls and one hundred and twenty thousand sheep. So the king and all the people dedicated the house of God. 6 [a]And the priests attended to their services; the Levites also with instruments of the music of the LORD, which King David had made to praise the LORD, saying, "For His mercy *endures* forever,"[1] whenever David offered praise by their ministry. [b]The priests sounded trumpets opposite them, while all Israel stood.

7 Furthermore [a]Solomon consecrated the middle of the court that *was* in front of the house of the LORD; for there he offered burnt offerings and the fat of the peace offerings, because the bronze altar which Solomon had made was not able to receive the burnt offerings, the grain offerings, and the fat.

8 [a]At that time Solomon kept the feast seven days, and all Israel with him, a very great assembly [b]from the entrance of Hamath to [c]the Brook of Egypt.[1] 9 And on the eighth day they held a [a]sacred assembly, for they observed the dedication of the altar seven days, and the feast seven days. 10 [a]On the twenty-third day of the seventh month he sent the people away to their tents, joyful and glad of heart for the good that the LORD had done for David, for Solomon, and for His people Israel. 11 Thus [a]Solomon finished the house of the LORD and the king's house; and Solomon successfully accomplished all that came into his heart to make in the house of the LORD and in his own house.

### *GOD'S SECOND APPEARANCE TO SOLOMON*
*(1 Kin. 9:1–9)*

12 Then the LORD [a]appeared to Solomon by night, and said to him: "I have heard your prayer, [b]and have chosen this [c]place for Myself as a house of sacrifice. 13 [a]When I shut up heaven and there is no rain, or command the locusts to devour the land, or send pestilence among My people, 14 if My people who are [a]called by My name will [b]humble themselves, and pray and seek My face, and turn from their wicked ways, [c]then I will hear from heaven, and will forgive their sin and heal their land. 15 Now [a]My eyes will be open and My ears attentive to prayer *made* in this place. 16 For now [a]I have chosen and sanctified this house, that My name may be there forever; and My eyes and My heart will be there perpetually. 17 [a]As for you, if you walk before Me as your father David walked, and do according to all that I have commanded you, and if you keep My statutes and My judgments, 18 then I will establish the throne of your kingdom, as I covenanted with David your father, saying, [a]'You shall not fail *to have* a man as ruler in Israel.'

19 [a]"But if you turn away and forsake My statutes and My commandments which I have set before you, and go and serve other gods, and worship them, 20 [a]then I will uproot them from My land which I have given them; and this house which I have sanctified for My name I will cast out of My sight, and will make it a proverb and a [b]byword among all peoples.

21 "And *as for* [a]this house, which is exalted, everyone who passes by it will be [b]astonished and say, [c]'Why has the LORD done thus to this land and this house?' 22 Then they will answer, 'Because they forsook the LORD God of their fathers, who brought them out of the land of Egypt, and embraced other gods, and worshiped them and served them; therefore He has brought all this calamity on them.' "

**SEEING JESUS IN THE SCRIPTURE**

**7:14** God is gracious and merciful in the Old Testament just as He is in the New Testament. The only difference is in the New Testament, God's wrath toward sin has been poured out on Jesus, just as He promised (see 2 Cor. 5:21).

### *SOLOMON'S ADDITIONAL ACHIEVEMENTS*
*(1 Kin. 9:10–28)*

**8** It [a]came to pass at the end of [b]twenty years, when Solomon had built the house of the LORD and his own house, 2 that the cities which Hiram[1] had given to Solomon, Solomon built

**7:1** [a]1 Kin. 8:54 [b]Lev. 9:24; Judg. 6:21; 1 Kin. 18:38; 1 Chr. 21:26 [c]1 Kin. 8:10, 11 [1]Literally *house* **7:2** [a]2 Chr. 5:14 **7:3** [a]2 Chr. 5:13; Ps. 106:1; 136:1 [b]1 Chr. 16:41; 2 Chr. 20:21 [1]Compare Psalm 106:1 **7:4** [a]1 Kin. 8:62, 63 **7:6** [a]1 Chr. 15:16 [b]2 Chr. 5:12 [1]Compare Psalm 106:1 **7:7** [a]1 Kin. 8:64–66; 9:3 **7:8** [a]1 Kin. 8:65 [b]1 Kin. 4:21, 24; 2 Kin. 14:25 [c]Josh. 13:3 [1]That is, the Shihor (compare 1 Chronicles 13:5) **7:9** [a]Lev. 23:36 **7:10** [a]1 Kin. 8:66 **7:11** [a]1 Kin. 9:1 **7:12** [a]1 Kin. 3:5; 11:9 [b]Deut. 12:5, 11 [c]2 Chr. 6:20 **7:13** [a]Deut. 28:23, 24; 1 Kin. 17:1; 2 Chr. 6:26–28 **7:14** [a]Deut. 28:10; [Is. 43:7] [b]2 Chr. 12:6, 7; [James 4:10] [c]2 Chr. 6:27, 30 **7:15** [a]2 Chr. 6:20, 40 **7:16** [a]1 Kin. 9:3; 2 Chr. 6:6 **7:17** [a]1 Kin. 9:4 **7:18** [a]2 Sam. 7:12–16; 1 Kin. 2:4; 2 Chr. 6:16 **7:19** [a]Lev. 26:14, 33; [Deut. 28:15, 36] **7:20** [a]Deut. 28:63–68; 2 Kin. 25:1–7 [b]Ps. 44:14 **7:21** [a]2 Kin. 25:9 [b]2 Chr. 29:8 [c][Deut. 29:24, 25; Jer. 22:8, 9] **8:1** [a]1 Kin. 9:10–14 [b]1 Kin. 6:38—7:1 **8:2** [1]Hebrew *Huram* (compare 2 Chronicles 2:3)

them; and he settled the children of Israel there. 3 And Solomon went to Hamath Zobah and seized it. 4 [a]He also built Tadmor in the wilderness, and all the storage cities which he built in [b]Hamath. 5 He built Upper Beth Horon and [a]Lower Beth Horon, fortified cities *with* walls, gates, and bars, 6 also Baalath and all the storage cities that Solomon had, and all the chariot cities and the cities of the cavalry, and all that Solomon [a]desired to build in Jerusalem, in Lebanon, and in all the land of his dominion.

7 [a]All the people *who were* left of the Hittites, Amorites, Perizzites, Hivites, and Jebusites, who *were* not of Israel— 8 that is, their descendants who were left in the land after them, whom the children of Israel did not destroy—from these Solomon raised forced labor, as it is to this day. 9 But Solomon did not make the children of Israel servants for his work. Some *were* men of war, captains of his officers, captains of his chariots, and his cavalry. 10 And others *were* chiefs of the officials of King Solomon: [a]two hundred and fifty, who ruled over the people.

11 Now Solomon [a]brought the daughter of Pharaoh up from the City of David to the house he had built for her, for he said, "My wife shall not dwell in the house of David king of Israel, because *the places* to which the ark of the LORD has come are holy."

12 Then Solomon offered burnt offerings to the LORD on the altar of the LORD which he had built before the vestibule, 13 according to the [a]daily rate, offering according to the commandment of Moses, for the Sabbaths, the New Moons, and the [b]three appointed yearly [c]feasts—the Feast of Unleavened Bread, the Feast of Weeks, and the Feast of Tabernacles. 14 And, according to the order of David his father, he appointed the [a]divisions of the priests for their service, [b]the Levites for their duties (to praise and serve before the priests) as the duty of each day required, and the [c]gatekeepers by their divisions at each gate; for so David the man of God had commanded. 15 They did not depart from the command of the king to the priests and Levites concerning any matter or concerning the [a]treasuries.

16 Now all the work of Solomon was well-ordered from[1] the day of the foundation of the house of the LORD until it was finished. So the house of the LORD was completed.

17 Then Solomon went to [a]Ezion Geber and Elath[1] on the seacoast, in the land of Edom. 18 [a]And Hiram sent him ships by the hand of his servants, and servants who knew the sea. They went with the servants of Solomon to [b]Ophir, and acquired four hundred and fifty talents of gold from there, and brought it to King Solomon.

### *THE QUEEN OF SHEBA'S PRAISE OF SOLOMON*

*(1 Kin. 10:1–13)*

**9** Now [a]when the queen of Sheba heard of the fame of Solomon, she came to Jerusalem to test Solomon with hard questions, *having* a very great retinue, camels that bore spices, gold in abundance, and precious stones; and when she came to Solomon, she spoke with him about all that was in her heart. 2 So Solomon answered all her questions; there was nothing so difficult for Solomon that he could not explain it to her. 3 And when the queen of Sheba had seen the wisdom of Solomon, the house that he had built, 4 the food on his table, the seating of his servants, the service of his waiters and their apparel, his [a]cupbearers and their apparel, and his entryway by which he went up to the house of the LORD, there was no more spirit in her.

5 Then she said to the king: "*It was* a true report which I heard in my own land about your words and your wisdom. 6 However I did not believe their words until I came and saw with my own eyes; and indeed the half of the greatness of your wisdom was not told me. You exceed the fame of which I heard. 7 Happy *are* your men and happy *are* these your servants, who stand continually before you and hear your wisdom! 8 Blessed be the LORD your God, who delighted in you, setting you on His throne *to be* king for the LORD your God! Because your God has [a]loved Israel, to establish them forever, therefore He made you king over them, to do justice and righteousness."

9 And she gave the king one hundred and twenty talents of gold, spices in great abundance, and precious stones; there never were any spices such as those the queen of Sheba gave to King Solomon.

10 Also, the servants of Hiram and the servants of Solomon, [a]who brought gold from Ophir, brought algum[1] wood and precious stones. 11 And the king made walkways *of* the algum[1] wood for the house of the LORD and for the king's house, also harps and stringed instruments for singers; and there were none such *as these* seen before in the land of Judah.

12 Now King Solomon gave to the queen of Sheba all she desired, whatever she asked, *much more* than she had brought to the king. So she turned and went to her own country, she and her servants.

### *SOLOMON'S GREAT WEALTH*

*(1 Kin. 10:14–29; 2 Chr. 1:14–17)*

13 [a]The weight of gold that came to Solomon yearly was six hundred and sixty-six talents of

**8:4** [a] 1 Kin. 9:17, 18 [b] 1 Chr. 18:3, 9 **8:5** [a] 1 Chr. 7:24 **8:6** [a] 2 Chr. 7:11 **8:7** [a] Gen. 15:18–21; 1 Kin. 9:20 **8:10** [a] 1 Kin. 9:23 **8:11** [a] 1 Kin. 3:1; 7:8; 9:24; 11:1 **8:13** [a] Ex. 29:38–42; Num. 28:3, 9, 11, 26; 29:1 [b] Ex. 23:14–17; 34:22, 23; Deut. 16:16 [c] Lev. 23:1–44 **8:14** [a] 1 Chr. 24:3 [b] 1 Chr. 25:1 [c] 1 Chr. 9:17; 26:1 **8:15** [a] 1 Chr. 26:20–28 **8:16** [1] Following Septuagint, Syriac, and Vulgate; Masoretic Text reads *as far as.* **8:17** [a] 1 Kin. 9:26; 2 Chr. 20:36 [1] Hebrew *Eloth* (compare 2 Kings 14:22) **8:18** [a] 1 Kin. 9:27; 2 Chr. 9:10, 13 [b] 1 Chr. 29:4 **9:1** [a] 1 Kin. 10:1; Ps. 72:10; [Matt. 12:42; Luke 11:31] **9:4** [a] Neh. 1:11 **9:8** [a] Deut. 7:8; 2 Chr. 2:11; [Ps. 44:3] **9:10** [a] 2 Chr. 8:18 [1] Or *almug* (compare 1 Kings 10:11, 12) **9:11** [1] Or *almug* (compare 1 Kings 10:11, 12) **9:13** [a] 1 Kin. 10:14–29

gold, 14 besides *what* the traveling merchants and traders brought. And all the kings of Arabia and governors of the country brought gold and silver to Solomon. 15 And King Solomon made two hundred large shields of hammered gold; six hundred *shekels* of hammered gold went into each shield. 16 *He* also *made* three hundred shields of hammered gold; three hundred *shekels*[1] of gold went into each shield. The king put them in the [a]House of the Forest of Lebanon.

17 Moreover the king made a great throne of ivory, and overlaid it with pure gold. 18 The throne *had* six steps, with a footstool of gold, *which were* fastened to the throne; there were armrests on either side of the place of the seat, and two lions stood beside the armrests. 19 Twelve lions stood there, one on each side of the six steps; nothing like *this* had been made for any *other* kingdom.

20 All King Solomon's drinking vessels *were* gold, and all the vessels of the House of the Forest of Lebanon *were* pure gold. Not *one was* silver, for this was accounted as nothing in the days of Solomon. 21 For the king's ships went to [a]Tarshish with the servants of Hiram.[1] Once every three years the merchant ships[2] came, bringing gold, silver, ivory, apes, and monkeys.[3]

22 So King Solomon surpassed all the kings of the earth in riches and wisdom. 23 And all the kings of the earth sought the presence of Solomon to hear his wisdom, which God had put in his heart. 24 Each man brought his present: articles of silver and gold, garments, [a]armor, spices, horses, and mules, at a set rate year by year.

25 Solomon [a]had four thousand stalls for horses and chariots, and twelve thousand horsemen whom he stationed in the chariot cities and with the king at Jerusalem.

26 [a]So he reigned over all the kings [b]from the River[1] to the land of the Philistines, as far as the border of Egypt. 27 [a]The king made silver *as common* in Jerusalem as stones, and he made cedar trees [b]as abundant as the sycamores which *are* in the lowland. 28 [a]And they brought horses to Solomon from Egypt and from all lands.

### *DEATH OF SOLOMON*

*(1 Kin. 11:41–43)*

29 [a]Now the rest of the acts of Solomon, first and last, *are* they not written in the book of Nathan the prophet, in the prophecy of [b]Ahijah the Shilonite, and in the visions of [c]Iddo the seer concerning Jeroboam the son of Nebat? 30 [a]Solomon reigned in Jerusalem over all Israel forty years. 31 Then Solomon rested with his fathers, and was buried in the City of David his father. And Rehoboam his son reigned in his place.

> **9:29** The **book by Nathan the prophet**, **the prophecy of Ahijah the Shilonite**, and **the visions of Iddo** have been lost for centuries. There are at least nine other books mentioned in Scripture that aren't part of the Bible either including the *Book of the Acts of Solomon* (1 Kin. 11:41), the *Book of Gad the Seer* (1 Chr. 29:29), the *Book of Shemaiah the Prophet* (2 Chr. 12:15), the *Acts of Uzziah* (2 Chr. 26:22), the *Sayings of Hozai* (2 Chr. 33:19), a third letter of Paul to the Corinthians (1 Cor. 5:9), a letter of Paul to the Laodiceans (Col. 4:16), another letter of John (3 John v. 9), and the *Book of Enoch* (Jude v. 14).

### *THE REVOLT AGAINST REHOBOAM*

*(1 Kin. 12:1–19)*

10 And [a]Rehoboam went to Shechem, for all Israel had gone to Shechem to make him king. 2 So it happened, when Jeroboam the son of Nebat heard *it* (he was in Egypt, [a]where he had fled from the presence of King Solomon), that Jeroboam returned from Egypt. 3 Then they sent for him and called him. And Jeroboam and all Israel came and spoke to Rehoboam, saying, 4 "Your father made our yoke heavy; now therefore, lighten the burdensome service of your father and his heavy yoke which he put on us, and we will serve you."

5 So he said to them, "Come back to me after three days." And the people departed.

6 Then King Rehoboam consulted the elders who stood before his father Solomon while he still lived, saying, "How do you advise *me* to answer these people?"

7 And they spoke to him, saying, "If you are kind to these people, and please them, and speak good words to them, they will be your servants forever."

8 [a]But he rejected the advice which the elders had given him, and consulted the young men who had grown up with him, who stood before him. 9 And he said to them, "What advice do you give? How should we answer this people who have spoken to me, saying, 'Lighten the yoke which your father put on us'?"

10 Then the young men who had grown up with him spoke to him, saying, "Thus you should speak to the people who have spoken to you, saying, 'Your father made our yoke heavy, but you make *it* lighter on us'—thus you shall say to them: 'My little *finger* shall be thicker than my father's waist! 11 And now, whereas my father put a heavy yoke on you, I will add to your yoke; my father chastised you with whips, but I *will chastise you* with scourges!' "[1]

**9:16** [a] 1 Kin. 7:2 [1] Or *three minas* (compare 1 Kings 10:17) **9:21** [a] 2 Chr. 20:36, 37; Ps. 72:10 [1] Hebrew *Huram* (compare 1 Kings 10:22) [2] Literally *ships of Tarshish* (deep-sea vessels) [3] Or *peacocks* **9:24** [a] 1 Kin. 20:11 **9:25** [a] Deut. 17:16; 1 Kin. 4:26; 10:26; 2 Chr. 1:14; Is. 2:7 **9:26** [a] 1 Kin. 4:21 [b] Gen. 15:18; Ps. 72:8 [1] That is, the Euphrates **9:27** [a] 1 Kin. 10:27 [b] 2 Chr. 1:15–17 **9:28** [a] 1 Kin. 10:28; 2 Chr. 1:16 **9:29** [a] 1 Kin. 11:41 [b] 1 Kin. 11:29 [c] 2 Chr. 12:15; 13:22 **9:30** [a] 1 Kin. 4:21; 11:42, 43; 1 Chr. 29:28 **10:1** [a] 1 Kin. 12:1–20 **10:2** [a] 1 Kin. 11:40 **10:8** [a] 1 Kin. 12:8–11 **10:11** [1] Literally *scorpions*

## THE KINGS OF ISRAEL AND JUDAH

**The United Kingdom**

| King | Reign | Good Aspects | Bad Aspects |
|---|---|---|---|
| Saul | 1050–1010 BC | Early in his reign, provided military victories. | Performed unlawful sacrifice; failed to obey God after victory over Amalek; became jealous of David and sought to kill him. |
| David | 1010–970 BC | Displayed great faith and courage in defeating Goliath; spared Saul's life on two occasions; loyal friend of Jonathan; provided several military victories; made Jerusalem the center of worship, bringing the ark there; desired to build a temple for God; repented of his sins. | Committed grievous sins against Bathsheba, Uriah, and God; ordered an unlawful census. |
| Solomon | 970–930 BC | Given great wisdom by God; consolidated the kingdom; built the temple. | Had multiple wives, including many who were foreign, and a large number of concubines; failed to worship only God. |

12 So [a]Jeroboam and all the people came to Rehoboam on the third day, as the king had directed, saying, "Come back to me the third day." 13 Then the king answered them roughly. King Rehoboam rejected the advice of the elders, 14 and he spoke to them according to the advice of the young men, saying, "My father[1] made your yoke heavy, but I will add to it; my father chastised you with whips, but I *will chastise you* with scourges!"[2] 15 So the king did not listen to the people; [a]for the turn *of events* was from God, that the LORD might fulfill His [b]word, which He had spoken by the hand of Ahijah the Shilonite to Jeroboam the son of Nebat.

16 Now when all Israel *saw* that the king did not listen to them, the people answered the king, saying:

"What share have we in David?
*We have* no inheritance in the son of Jesse.
Every man to your tents, O Israel!
Now see to your own house, O David!"

So all Israel departed to their tents. 17 But Rehoboam reigned over the children of Israel who dwelt in the cities of Judah.

18 Then King Rehoboam sent Hadoram, who *was* in charge of revenue; but the children of Israel stoned him with stones, and he died. Therefore King Rehoboam mounted *his* chariot in haste to flee to Jerusalem. 19 [a]So Israel has been in rebellion against the house of David to this day.

**11** Now [a]when Rehoboam came to Jerusalem, he assembled from the house of Judah and Benjamin one hundred and eighty thousand chosen *men* who were warriors, to fight against Israel, that he might restore the kingdom to Rehoboam. 2 But the word of the LORD came [a]to Shemaiah the man of God, saying, 3 "Speak to Rehoboam the son of Solomon, king of Judah, and to all Israel in Judah and Benjamin, saying, 4 'Thus says the LORD: "You shall not go up or fight against your brethren! Let every man return to his house, for this thing is from Me."'" Therefore they obeyed the words of the LORD, and turned back from attacking Jeroboam.

### REHOBOAM FORTIFIES THE CITIES

5 So Rehoboam dwelt in Jerusalem, and built cities for defense in Judah. 6 And he built Bethlehem, Etam, Tekoa, 7 Beth Zur, Sochoh, Adullam, 8 Gath, Mareshah, Ziph, 9 Adoraim, Lachish, Azekah, 10 Zorah, Aijalon, and Hebron, which are in Judah and Benjamin, fortified cities. 11 And he fortified the strongholds, and put captains in them, and stores of food, oil, and wine. 12 Also in every city *he put* shields and spears, and made them very strong, having Judah and Benjamin on his side.

### PRIESTS AND LEVITES MOVE TO JUDAH

*(1 Kin. 14:21–24)*

13 And from all their territories the priests and the Levites who *were* in all Israel took their stand with him. 14 For the Levites left [a]their common-lands and their possessions and came to Judah and Jerusalem, for [b]Jeroboam and his sons had rejected them from serving as priests to the LORD. 15 [a]Then he appointed for himself priests for the high places, for [b]the demons, and [c]the calf idols which he had made. 16 [a]And after *the* Levites *left,*[1] those from all the tribes of Israel, such as set their heart to seek the LORD God of Israel, [b]came to Jerusalem to sacrifice to the LORD God of their fathers. 17 So

**10:12** [a] 1 Kin. 12:12–14 **10:14** [1] Following many Hebrew manuscripts, Septuagint, Syriac, and Vulgate (compare verse 10 and 1 Kings 12:14); Masoretic Text reads *I*. [2] Literally *scorpions* **10:15** [a] Judg. 14:4; 1 Chr. 5:22; 2 Chr. 11:4; 22:7 [b] 1 Kin. 11:29–39 **10:19** [a] 1 Kin. 12:19 **11:1** [a] 1 Kin. 12:21–24 **11:2** [a] 1 Chr. 12:5; 2 Chr. 12:15 **11:14** [a] Num. 35:2–5 [b] 1 Kin. 12:28–33; 2 Chr. 13:9 **11:15** [a] 1 Kin. 12:31; 13:33; 14:9; [Hos. 13:2] [b] [Lev. 17:7; 1 Cor. 10:20] [c] 1 Kin. 12:28 **11:16** [a] 2 Chr. 14:7 [b] 2 Chr. 15:9, 10; 30:11, 18 [1] Literally *after them*

# THE KINGS OF ISRAEL AND JUDAH

## The Divided Kingdom

| Kings of Judah | Reign | Good or Bad King | Kings of Israel | Reign | Good or Bad King |
|---|---|---|---|---|---|
| **900s** | | | | | |
| Rehoboam | 930–913 BC | bad | Jeroboam I | 930–910 BC | bad |
| Abijah | 913–910 BC | bad | Nadab | 910–909 BC | bad |
| Asa | 910–870 BC | good | Baasha | 909–886 BC | bad |
| **800s** | | | | | |
| Jehoshaphat | 872–847 BC | good | Elah | 886–885 BC | bad |
| Jehoram | 848–841 BC | bad | Zimri | 885 BC | bad |
| Ahaziah | 841 BC | bad | Tibni | 885–880 BC | bad |
| Athaliah | 841–835 BC | bad | Omri | 885–874 BC | bad |
| Joash | 835–796 BC | mixed | Ahab | 874–853 BC | bad |
| | | | Ahaziah | 853–852 BC | bad |
| | | | Joram | 852–841 BC | bad |
| | | | Jehu | 841–814 BC | mixed |
| | | | Jehoahaz | 814–798 BC | bad |
| **700s** | | | | | |
| Amaziah | 796–767 BC | mixed | Jehoash | 798–782 BC | bad |
| Azariah (Uzziah) | 792–740 BC | good | Jeroboam II | 792–753 BC | bad |
| Jotham | 750–736 BC | good | Zechariah | 753 BC | bad |
| Ahaz | 735–715 BC | bad | Shallum | 752 BC | bad |
| Hezekiah | 715–699 BC | good | Menahem | 751–742 BC | bad |
| | | | Pekahiah | 741–740 BC | bad |
| | | | Pekah | 752–732 BC | bad |
| | | | Hoshea | 732–722 BC | bad |
| | | | Into captivity by the Assyrians (722 BC) | | |
| **600s** | | | | | |
| Manasseh | 697–642 BC | bad | | | |
| Amon | 642–640 BC | bad | | | |
| Josiah | 640–609 BC | good | | | |
| Jehoahaz | 609 BC | bad | | | |
| Jehoiakim | 609–598 BC | bad | | | |
| **500s** | | | | | |
| Jehoiachin | 598 BC | bad | | | |
| Zedekiah | 598–586 BC | bad | | | |
| Into captivity by the Babylonians (586 BC) | | | | | |

> **11:15** Jeroboam was afraid that if the people returned to Jerusalem to worship God, he would lose his control over them. To keep them away from Jerusalem, Jeroboam made two golden **idols** in the shape of calves for the people to worship in Bethel and Dan. As if that weren't enough, in direct disobedience to God, Jeroboam appointed **priests** who were not from the tribe of Levi.

they [a]strengthened the kingdom of Judah, and
made Rehoboam the son of Solomon strong for
three years, because they walked in the way of
David and Solomon for three years.

### *THE FAMILY OF REHOBOAM*

18 Then Rehoboam took for himself as wife
Mahalath the daughter of Jerimoth the son of
David, *and of* Abihail the daughter of [a]Eliah
the son of Jesse. 19 And she bore him children:
Jeush, Shamariah, and Zaham. 20 After her he
took [a]Maachah the granddaughter[1] of [b]Absalom;
and she bore him [c]Abijah, Attai, Ziza, and She-
lomith. 21 Now Rehoboam loved Maachah the
granddaughter of Absalom more than all his
[a]wives and his concubines; for he took eighteen
wives and sixty concubines, and begot twenty-
eight sons and sixty daughters. 22 And Rehobo-
am [a]appointed [b]Abijah the son of Maachah as
chief, *to be* leader among his brothers; for he
*intended* to make him king. 23 He dealt wisely,
and dispersed some of his sons throughout all
the territories of Judah and Benjamin, to every
[a]fortified city; and he gave them provisions in
abundance. He also sought many wives *for them.*

### *EGYPT ATTACKS JUDAH*
*(1 Kin. 14:25–28)*

**12** Now [a]it came to pass, when Rehoboam had
established the kingdom and had strength-
ened himself, that [b]he forsook the law of the LORD,
and all Israel along with him. 2 [a]And it happened in
the fifth year of King Rehoboam *that* Shishak king
of Egypt came up against Jerusalem, because they
had transgressed against the LORD, 3 with twelve
hundred chariots, sixty thousand horsemen, and
people without number who came with him out
of Egypt—[a]the Lubim and the Sukkiim and the
Ethiopians. 4 And he took the fortified cities of
Judah and came to Jerusalem.
5 Then [a]Shemaiah the prophet came to Reho-
boam and the leaders of Judah, who were gath-
ered together in Jerusalem because of Shishak,
and said to them, "Thus says the LORD: 'You have
forsaken Me, and therefore I also have left you
in the hand of Shishak.' "
6 So the leaders of Israel and the king [a]hum-
bled themselves; and they said, [b]"The LORD *is*
righteous."
7 Now when the LORD saw that they humbled
themselves, [a]the word of the LORD came to She-
maiah, saying, "They have humbled themselves;
*therefore* I will not destroy them, but I will grant
them some deliverance. My wrath shall not be
poured out on Jerusalem by the hand of Shi-
shak. 8 Nevertheless [a]they will be his servants,
that they may distinguish [b]My service from the
service of the kingdoms of the nations."
9 [a]So Shishak king of Egypt came up against
Jerusalem, and took away the treasures of the
house of the LORD and the treasures of the king's
house; he took everything. He also carried away
the gold shields which Solomon had [b]made.
10 Then King Rehoboam made bronze shields in
their place, and committed *them* [a]to the hands
of the captains of the guard, who guarded the
doorway of the king's house. 11 And whenever the
king entered the house of the LORD, the guard
would go and bring them out; then they would
take them back into the guardroom. 12 When he
humbled himself, the wrath of the LORD turned
from him, so as not to destroy *him* completely;
and things also went well in Judah.

### *THE END OF REHOBOAM'S REIGN*
*(1 Kin. 14:21, 22, 29–31)*

13 Thus King Rehoboam strengthened him-
self in Jerusalem and reigned. Now [a]Rehoboam
*was* forty-one years old when he became king;
and he reigned seventeen years in Jerusalem,
[b]the city which the LORD had chosen out of all
the tribes of Israel, to put His name there. His
mother's name *was* Naamah, an [c]Ammonitess.
14 And he did evil, because he did not prepare
his heart to seek the LORD.
15 The acts of Rehoboam, first and last, *are*
they not written in the book of Shemaiah the
prophet, [a]and of Iddo the seer concerning geneal-
ogies? [b]And *there were* wars between Rehoboam
and Jeroboam all their days. 16 So Rehoboam rest-
ed with his fathers, and was buried in the City of
David. Then [a]Abijah[1] his son reigned in his place.

### *ABIJAH REIGNS IN JUDAH*
*(1 Kin. 15:1–8)*

**13** In [a]the eighteenth year of King Jerobo-
am, Abijah became king over [b]Judah. 2 He
reigned three years in Jerusalem. His mother's
name *was* Michaiah[1] the daughter of Uriel of
Gibeah.

**11:17** [a] 2 Chr. 12:1, 13 **11:18** [a] 1 Sam. 16:6 **11:20** [a] 2 Chr. 13:2 [b] 1 Kin. 15:2 [c] 1 Kin. 14:31 [1] Literally *daughter,* but in the broader sense of granddaughter (compare 2 Chronicles 13:2) **11:21** [a] Deut. 17:17 **11:22** [a] Deut. 21:15–17 [b] 2 Chr. 13:1 **11:23** [a] 2 Chr. 11:5 **12:1** [a] 2 Chr. 11:17 [b] 1 Kin. 14:22–24 **12:2** [a] 1 Kin. 11:40; 14:25 **12:3** [a] 2 Chr. 16:8; Nah. 3:9 **12:5** [a] 2 Chr. 11:2 **12:6** [a] [James 4:10] [b] Ex. 9:27; [Dan. 9:14] **12:7** [a] 1 Kin. 21:28, 29 **12:8** [a] Is. 26:13 [b] [Deut. 28:47, 48] **12:9** [a] 1 Kin. 14:25, 26 [b] 1 Kin. 10:16, 17; 2 Chr. 9:15, 16 **12:10** [a] 1 Kin. 14:27 **12:13** [a] 1 Kin. 14:21 [b] 2 Chr. 6:6 [c] 1 Kin. 11:1, 5 **12:15** [a] 2 Chr. 9:29; 13:22 [b] 1 Kin. 14:30 **12:16** [a] 2 Chr. 11:20–22 [1] Spelled *Abijam* in 1 Kings 14:31 **13:1** [a] 1 Kin. 15:1 [b] 1 Kin. 12:17 **13:2** [1] Spelled *Maachah* in 11:20, 21 and 1 Kings 15:2

And there was war between Abijah and Jeroboam. 3 Abijah set the battle in order with an army of valiant warriors, four hundred thousand choice men. Jeroboam also drew up in battle formation against him with eight hundred thousand choice men, mighty men of valor.

4 Then Abijah stood on Mount [a]Zemaraim, which *is* in the mountains of Ephraim, and said, "Hear me, Jeroboam and all Israel: 5 Should you not know that the LORD God of Israel [a]gave the dominion over Israel to David forever, to him and his sons, [b]by a covenant of salt? 6 Yet Jeroboam the son of Nebat, the servant of Solomon the son of David, rose up and [a]rebelled against his lord. 7 Then [a]worthless rogues gathered to him, and strengthened themselves against Rehoboam the son of Solomon, when Rehoboam was [b]young and inexperienced and could not withstand them. 8 And now you think to withstand the kingdom of the LORD, which is in the hand of the sons of David; and you *are* a great multitude, and with you are the gold calves which Jeroboam [a]made for you as gods. 9 [a]Have you not cast out the priests of the LORD, the sons of Aaron, and the Levites, and made for yourselves priests, like the peoples of *other* lands, [b]so that whoever comes to consecrate himself with a young bull and seven rams may be a priest of [c]*things that are* not gods? 10 But as for us, the LORD *is* our [a]God, and we have not forsaken Him; and the priests who minister to the LORD *are* the sons of Aaron, and the Levites *attend* to *their* duties. 11 [a]And they burn to the LORD every morning and every evening burnt sacrifices and sweet incense; *they* also *set* the [b]showbread *in order on* the pure *gold* table, and the lampstand of gold with its lamps [c]to burn every evening; for we keep the command of the LORD our God, but you have forsaken Him. 12 Now look, God Himself is with us as *our* [a]head, [b]and His priests with sounding trumpets to sound the alarm against you. O children of Israel, do not fight against the LORD God of your fathers, for you shall not prosper!"

13 But Jeroboam caused an ambush to go around behind them; so they were in front of Judah, and the ambush *was* behind them. 14 And when Judah looked around, to their surprise the battle line *was* at both front and rear; and they [a]cried out to the LORD, and the priests sounded the trumpets. 15 Then the men of Judah gave a shout; and as the men of Judah shouted, it happened that God [a]struck Jeroboam and all Israel before Abijah and Judah. 16 And the children of Israel fled before Judah, and God delivered them into their hand. 17 Then Abijah and his people struck them with a great slaughter; so five hundred thousand choice men of Israel fell slain. 18 Thus the children of Israel were subdued at that time; and the children of Judah prevailed, [a]because they relied on the LORD God of their fathers.

19 And Abijah pursued Jeroboam and took cities from him: Bethel with its villages, Jeshanah with its villages, and [a]Ephrain[1] with its villages. 20 So Jeroboam did not recover strength again in the days of Abijah; and the LORD [a]struck him, and [b]he died.

21 But Abijah grew mighty, married fourteen wives, and begot twenty-two sons and sixteen daughters. 22 Now the rest of the acts of Abijah, his ways, and his sayings *are* written in [a]the annals of the prophet Iddo.

**14** So Abijah rested with his fathers, and they buried him in the City of David. Then [a]Asa his son reigned in his place. In his days the land was quiet for ten years.

### *ASA REIGNS IN JUDAH*

*(1 Kin. 15:9–15)*

2 Asa did *what was* good and right in the eyes of the LORD his God, 3 for he removed the altars of the foreign *gods* and [a]the high places, and [b]broke down the *sacred* pillars [c]and cut down the wooden images. 4 He commanded Judah to [a]seek the LORD God of their fathers, and to observe the law and the commandment. 5 He also removed the high places and the incense altars from all the cities of Judah, and the kingdom was quiet under him. 6 And he built fortified cities in Judah, for the land had rest; he had no war in those years, because the LORD had given him [a]rest. 7 Therefore he said to Judah, "Let us build these cities and make walls around *them,* and towers, gates, and bars, *while* the land *is* yet before us, because we have sought the LORD our God; we have sought *Him,* and He has given us rest on every side." So they built and prospered. 8 And Asa had an army of three hundred thousand from Judah who carried shields and spears, and from Benjamin two hundred and eighty thousand men who carried shields and drew [a]bows; all these *were* mighty men of [b]valor.

9 [a]Then Zerah the Ethiopian came out against them with an army of a million men and three hundred chariots, and he came to [b]Mareshah. 10 So Asa went out against him, and they set the troops in battle array in the Valley of Zephathah at Mareshah. 11 And Asa [a]cried out to the LORD his God, and said, "LORD, *it is* [b]nothing for You to help, whether with many or with those who have no power; help us, O LORD our God, for we rest on You, and [c]in Your name we go against this multitude. O LORD, You *are* our God; do not let man prevail against You!"

**13:4** [a] Josh. 18:22 **13:5** [a] 2 Sam. 7:8–16 [b] Lev. 2:13; Num. 18:19 **13:6** [a] 1 Kin. 11:28; 12:20 **13:7** [a] Judg. 9:4 [b] 2 Chr. 12:13 **13:8** [a] 1 Kin. 12:28; 14:9; 2 Chr. 11:15; [Hos. 8:4–6] **13:9** [a] 2 Chr. 11:13–15 [b] Ex. 29:29–33 [c] Jer. 2:11; 5:7 **13:10** [a] Josh. 24:15 **13:11** [a] Ex. 29:38; 2 Chr. 2:4 [b] Ex. 25:30; Lev. 24:5–9 [c] Ex. 27:20, 21; Lev. 24:2, 3 **13:12** [a] Josh. 5:13–15; [Heb. 2:10] [b] [Num. 10:8–10] **13:14** [a] Josh. 24:7; 2 Chr. 6:34, 35; 14:11 **13:15** [a] 1 Kin. 14:14; 2 Chr. 14:12 **13:18** [a] 1 Chr. 5:20; 2 Chr. 14:11; [Ps. 22:5] **13:19** [a] Josh. 15:9 [1] Or *Ephron* **13:20** [a] 1 Sam. 2:6; 25:38; Acts 12:23 [b] 1 Kin. 14:20 **13:22** [a] 2 Chr. 9:29 **14:1** [a] 1 Kin. 15:8 **14:3** [a] 1 Kin. 15:14; 2 Chr. 15:17 [b] [Ex. 34:13] [c] 1 Kin. 11:7 **14:4** [a] [2 Chr. 7:14] **14:6** [a] 2 Chr. 15:15 **14:8** [a] 1 Chr. 12:2 [b] 2 Chr. 13:3 **14:9** [a] 2 Chr. 12:2, 3; 16:8 [b] Josh. 15:44 **14:11** [a] Ex. 14:10; 2 Chr. 13:14; [Ps. 22:5] [b] [1 Sam. 14:6] [c] 1 Sam. 17:45; [Prov. 18:10]

12 So the LORD [a]struck the Ethiopians before
Asa and Judah, and the Ethiopians fled. 13 And
Asa and the people who *were* with him pursued
them to [a]Gerar. So the Ethiopians were over-
thrown, and they could not recover, for they were
broken before the LORD and His army. And they
carried away very much spoil. 14 Then they de-
feated all the cities around Gerar, for [a]the fear of
the LORD came upon them; and they plundered
all the cities, for there was exceedingly much
spoil in them. 15 They also attacked the livestock
enclosures, and carried off sheep and camels in
abundance, and returned to Jerusalem.

### *THE REFORMS OF ASA*

**15** Now [a]the Spirit of God came upon Azari-
ah the son of Oded. 2 And he went out to
meet Asa, and said to him: "Hear me, Asa, and
all Judah and Benjamin. [a]The LORD *is* with you
while you are with Him. [b]If you seek Him, He
will be found by you; but [c]if you forsake Him,
He will forsake you. 3 [a]For a long time Israel *has
been* without the true God, without a [b]teaching
priest, and without [c]law; 4 but [a]when in their
trouble they turned to the LORD God of Israel,
and sought Him, He was found by them. 5 And
in those times *there was* no peace to the one
who went out, nor to the one who came in, but
great turmoil *was* on all the inhabitants of the
lands. 6 [a]So nation was destroyed by nation,
and city by city, for God troubled them with
every adversity. 7 But you, be strong and do not
let your hands be weak, for your work shall be
rewarded!"

8 And when Asa heard these words and the
prophecy of Oded[1] the prophet, he took courage,
and removed the abominable idols from all
the land of Judah and Benjamin and from the
cities [a]which he had taken in the mountains of
Ephraim; and he restored the altar of the LORD
that *was* before the vestibule of the LORD. 9 Then
he gathered all Judah and Benjamin, and [a]those
who dwelt with them from Ephraim, Manasseh,
and Simeon, for they came over to him in great
numbers from Israel when they saw that the
LORD his God was with him.

10 So they gathered together at Jerusalem in
the third month, in the fifteenth year of the reign
of Asa. 11 [a]And they offered to the LORD at that
time seven hundred bulls and seven thousand
sheep from the spoil they had brought. 12 Then
they [a]entered into a covenant to seek the LORD
God of their fathers with all their heart and with
all their soul; 13 [a]and whoever would not seek
the LORD God of Israel [b]was to be put to death,
whether small or great, whether man or woman.
14 Then they took an oath before the LORD with
a loud voice, with shouting and trumpets and
rams' horns. 15 And all Judah rejoiced at the
oath, for they had sworn with all their heart
and [a]sought Him with all their soul; and He
was found by them, and the LORD gave them
[b]rest all around.

16 Also he removed [a]Maachah, the mother
of Asa the king, from *being* queen mother, be-
cause she had made an obscene image of Ashe-
rah;[1] and Asa cut down her obscene image, then
crushed and burned *it* by the Brook Kidron.
17 But [a]the high places were not removed from
Israel. Nevertheless the heart of Asa was loyal
all his days.

> **15:16–17** The Israelites had adopted several different Canaanite gods and goddesses as their own. Shrines to **Asherah** were scattered throughout the land, especially on hilltops and in groves of trees. The shrines were easy to spot because they were marked by carved wooden poles.

18 He also brought into the house of God
the things that his father had dedicated and
that he himself had dedicated: silver and gold
and utensils. 19 And there was no war until the
thirty-fifth year of the reign of Asa.

### *ASA'S TREATY WITH SYRIA*

*(1 Kin. 15:16–22)*

**16** In the thirty-sixth year of the reign of Asa,
[a]Baasha king of Israel came up against
Judah and built Ramah, [b]that he might let
none go out or come in to Asa king of Judah.
2 Then Asa brought silver and gold from the
treasuries of the house of the LORD and of the
king's house, and sent to Ben-Hadad king of
Syria, who dwelt in Damascus, saying, 3 "*Let
there be* a treaty between you and me, as there
was between my father and your father. See,
I have sent you silver and gold; come, break
your treaty with Baasha king of Israel, so that
he will withdraw from me."

4 So Ben-Hadad heeded King Asa, and sent
the captains of his armies against the cities of
Israel. They attacked Ijon, Dan, Abel Maim, and
all the storage cities of Naphtali. 5 Now it hap-
pened, when Baasha heard *it*, that he stopped
building Ramah and ceased his work. 6 Then
King Asa took all Judah, and they carried away
the stones and timber of Ramah, which Baasha
had used for building; and with them he built
Geba and Mizpah.

**14:12** [a] 2 Chr. 13:15 **14:13** [a] Gen. 10:19; 20:1 **14:14** [a] Gen. 35:5; Deut. 11:25; Josh. 2:9; 2 Chr. 17:10 **15:1** [a] Num. 24:2; Judg. 3:10; 2 Chr. 20:14; 24:20 **15:2** [a] [James 4:8] [b] [1 Chr. 28:9]; 2 Chr. 14:4; 33:12, 13; [Jer. 29:13; Matt. 7:7] [c] 2 Chr. 24:20 **15:3** [a] Hos. 3:4 [b] 2 Kin. 12:2 [c] Lev. 10:11; 2 Chr. 17:8, 9 **15:4** [a] [Deut. 4:29] **15:6** [a] Matt. 24:7 **15:8** [a] 2 Chr. 13:19 [1] Following Masoretic Text and Septuagint; Syriac and Vulgate read *Azariah the son of Oded* (compare verse 1). **15:9** [a] 2 Chr. 11:16 **15:11** [a] 2 Chr. 14:13–15 **15:12** [a] 2 Kin. 23:3; 2 Chr. 23:16; 34:31; Neh. 10:29 **15:13** [a] Ex. 22:20 [b] Deut. 13:5–15 **15:15** [a] 2 Chr. 15:2 [b] 2 Chr. 14:7 **15:16** [a] 1 Kin. 15:2, 10, 13 [1] A Canaanite deity **15:17** [a] 1 Kin. 15:14; 2 Chr. 14:3, 5 **16:1** [a] 1 Kin. 15:17–22 [b] 2 Chr. 15:9

### HANANI'S MESSAGE TO ASA

7 And at that time [a]Hanani the seer came to
Asa king of Judah, and said to him: [b]"Because
you have relied on the king of Syria, and have
not relied on the LORD your God, therefore the
army of the king of Syria has escaped from your
hand. 8 Were [a]the Ethiopians and [b]the Lubim
not a huge army with very many chariots and
horsemen? Yet, because you relied on the LORD,
He delivered them into your [c]hand. 9 [a]For the
eyes of the LORD run to and fro throughout the
whole earth, to show Himself strong on behalf
of *those* whose heart *is* loyal to Him. In this [b]you
have done foolishly; therefore from now on [c]you
shall have wars." 10 Then Asa was angry with the
seer, and [a]put him in prison, for *he was* enraged
at him because of this. And Asa oppressed *some*
of the people at that time.

### ILLNESS AND DEATH OF ASA

*(1 Kin. 15:23, 24)*

11 [a]Note that the acts of Asa, first and last, are
indeed written in the book of the kings of Judah
and Israel. 12 And in the thirty-ninth year of his
reign, Asa became diseased in his feet, and his
malady was severe; yet in his disease he [a]did not
seek the LORD, but the physicians.

13 [a]So Asa rested with his fathers; he died in
the forty-first year of his reign. 14 They buried
him in his own tomb, which he had made for
himself in the City of David; and they laid him in
the bed which was filled [a]with spices and various
ingredients prepared in a mixture of ointments.
They made [b]a very great burning for him.

### JEHOSHAPHAT REIGNS IN JUDAH

**17** Then [a]Jehoshaphat his son reigned in his
place, and strengthened himself against
Israel. 2 And he placed troops in all the fortified
cities of Judah, and set garrisons in the land of
[a]Judah and in the cities of Ephraim [b]which Asa
his father had taken. 3 Now the LORD was with Je-
hoshaphat, because he walked in the former ways
of his father David; he did not seek the Baals,
4 but sought the God[1] of his father, and walked in
His commandments and not according to [a]the
acts of Israel. 5 Therefore the LORD established
the kingdom in his hand; and all Judah [a]gave
presents to Jehoshaphat, [b]and he had riches and
honor in abundance. 6 And his heart took delight
in the ways of the LORD; moreover [a]he removed
the high places and wooden images from Judah.

7 Also in the third year of his reign he sent his
leaders, Ben-Hail, Obadiah, Zechariah, Nethanel,
and Michaiah, [a]to teach in the cities of Judah. 8 And
with them *he sent* Levites: Shemaiah, Nethaniah,
Zebadiah, Asahel, Shemiramoth, Jehonathan,
Adonijah, Tobijah, and Tobadonijah—the Levites;
and with them Elishama and Jehoram, the priests.
9 [a]So they taught in Judah, and *had* the Book of the
Law of the LORD with them; they went throughout
all the cities of Judah and taught the people.

10 And [a]the fear of the LORD fell on all the
kingdoms of the lands that *were* around Judah,
so that they did not make war against Jehosh-
aphat. 11 Also *some* of the Philistines [a]brought
Jehoshaphat presents and silver as tribute; and
the Arabians brought him flocks, seven thou-
sand seven hundred rams and seven thousand
seven hundred male goats.

12 So Jehoshaphat became increasingly pow-
erful, and he built fortresses and storage cities
in Judah. 13 He had much property in the cities
of Judah; and the men of war, mighty men of
valor, *were* in Jerusalem.

14 These *are* their numbers, according to
their fathers' houses. Of Judah, the captains of
thousands: Adnah the captain, and with him
three hundred thousand mighty men of valor;
15 and next to him *was* Jehohanan the captain,
and with him two hundred and eighty thousand;
16 and next to him *was* Amasiah the son of Zichri,
[a]who willingly offered himself to the LORD, and
with him two hundred thousand mighty men
of valor. 17 Of Benjamin: Eliada a mighty man
of valor, and with him two hundred thousand
men armed with bow and shield; 18 and next to
him *was* Jehozabad, and with him one hundred
and eighty thousand prepared for war. 19 These
served the king, besides [a]those the king put in
the fortified cities throughout all Judah.

### MICAIAH WARNS AHAB

*(1 Kin. 22:1–28)*

**18** Jehoshaphat [a]had riches and honor in
abundance; and by marriage he [b]allied
himself with [c]Ahab. 2 [a]After some years he went
down to *visit* Ahab in Samaria; and Ahab killed
sheep and oxen in abundance for him and the
people who were with him, and persuaded him
to go up *with him* to Ramoth Gilead. 3 So Ahab
king of Israel said to Jehoshaphat king of Judah,
"Will you go with me *against* Ramoth Gilead?"

And he answered him, "I *am* as you *are*,
and my people as your people; *we will be* with
you in the war."

4 Also Jehoshaphat said to the king of Israel,
[a]"Please inquire for the word of the LORD today."

5 Then the king of Israel gathered the proph-
ets together, four hundred men, and said to
them, "Shall we go to war against Ramoth Gilead,
or shall I refrain?"

**16:7** [a] 1 Kin. 16:1; 2 Chr. 19:2 [b] 2 Chr. 32:8–10; Ps. 118:9; [Is. 31:1; Jer. 17:5] **16:8** [a] 2 Chr. 14:9 [b] 2 Chr. 12:3 [c] 2 Chr. 13:16, 18 **16:9** [a] Job 34:21; [Prov. 5:21; 15:3; Jer. 16:17; 32:19]; Zech. 4:10 [b] 1 Sam. 13:13 [c] 1 Kin. 15:32 **16:10** [a] 2 Chr. 18:26; Jer. 20:2; Matt. 14:3 **16:11** [a] 1 Kin. 15:23, 24; 2 Chr. 14:2 **16:12** [a] [Jer. 17:5] **16:13** [a] 1 Kin. 15:24 **16:14** [a] Gen. 50:2; Mark 16:1; John 19:39, 40 [b] 2 Chr. 21:19; Jer. 34:5 **17:1** [a] 1 Kin. 15:24; 2 Chr. 20:31 **17:2** [a] 2 Chr. 11:5 [b] 2 Chr. 15:8 **17:4** [a] 1 Kin. 12:28 [1] Septuagint reads *LORD God.* **17:5** [a] 1 Sam. 10:27; 1 Kin. 10:25 [b] 2 Chr. 18:1 **17:6** [a] 1 Kin. 22:43; 2 Chr. 15:17; 19:3; 20:33 **17:7** [a] 2 Chr. 15:3; 35:3 **17:9** [a] Deut. 6:4–9; 2 Chr. 35:3; Neh. 8:3, 7 **17:10** [a] Gen. 35:5; 2 Chr. 14:14 **17:11** [a] 2 Sam. 8:2; 2 Chr. 9:14; 26:8 **17:16** [a] Judg. 5:2, 9; 1 Chr. 29:9 **17:19** [a] 2 Chr. 17:2 **18:1** [a] 2 Chr. 17:5 [b] 1 Kin. 22:44; 2 Kin. 8:18 [c] 1 Kin. 22:40 **18:2** [a] [Ex. 23:2]; 1 Kin. 22:2 **18:4** [a] 1 Sam. 23:2, 4, 9; 2 Sam. 2:1

So they said, "Go up, for God will deliver it into the king's hand."

6 But Jehoshaphat said, "*Is there* not still a prophet of the LORD here, that we may inquire of [a]Him?"[1]

7 So the king of Israel said to Jehoshaphat, "*There is* still one man by whom we may inquire of the LORD; but I hate him, because he never prophesies good concerning me, but always evil. He *is* Micaiah the son of Imla."

And Jehoshaphat said, "Let not the king say such things!"

8 Then the king of Israel called one *of his* officers and said, "Bring Micaiah the son of Imla quickly!"

9 The king of Israel and Jehoshaphat king of Judah, clothed in *their* robes, sat each on his throne; and they sat at a threshing floor at the entrance of the gate of Samaria; and all the prophets prophesied before them. 10 Now Zedekiah the son of Chenaanah had made [a]horns of iron for himself; and he said, "Thus says the LORD: 'With these you shall gore the Syrians until they are destroyed.' "

11 And all the prophets prophesied so, saying, "Go up to Ramoth Gilead and prosper, for the LORD will deliver *it* into the king's hand."

12 Then the messenger who had gone to call Micaiah spoke to him, saying, "Now listen, the words of the prophets with one accord encourage the king. Therefore please let your word be like *the word of* one of them, and speak encouragement."

13 And Micaiah said, "*As* the LORD lives, [a]whatever my God says, that I will speak."

14 Then he came to the king; and the king said to him, "Micaiah, shall we go to war against Ramoth Gilead, or shall I refrain?"

And he said, "Go and prosper, and they shall be delivered into your hand!"

15 So the king said to him, "How many times shall I make you swear that you tell me nothing but the truth in the name of the LORD?"

16 Then he said, "I saw all Israel [a]scattered on the mountains, as sheep that have no [b]shepherd. And the LORD said, 'These have no master. Let each return to his house in peace.' "

17 And the king of Israel said to Jehoshaphat, "Did I not tell you he would not prophesy good concerning me, but evil?"

18 Then *Micaiah* said, "Therefore hear the word of the LORD: I saw the LORD sitting on His [a]throne, and all the host of heaven standing on His right hand and His left. 19 And the LORD said, 'Who will persuade Ahab king of Israel to go up, that he may fall at Ramoth Gilead?' So one spoke in this manner, and another spoke in that manner. 20 Then a [a]spirit came forward and stood before the LORD, and said, 'I will persuade him.' The LORD said to him, 'In what way?' 21 So he said, 'I will go out and be a lying spirit in the mouth of all his prophets.' And *the LORD* said, 'You shall persuade *him* and also prevail; go out and do so.' 22 Therefore look! [a]The LORD has put a lying spirit in the mouth of these prophets of yours, and the LORD has declared disaster against you."

23 Then Zedekiah the son of Chenaanah went near and [a]struck Micaiah on the cheek, and said, "Which way did the spirit from the LORD go from me to speak to you?"

24 And Micaiah said, "Indeed you shall see on that day when you go into an inner chamber to hide!"

25 Then the king of Israel said, "Take Micaiah, and return him to Amon the governor of the city and to Joash the king's son; 26 and say, 'Thus says the king: [a]"Put this *fellow* in prison, and feed him with bread of affliction and water of affliction, until I return in peace." ' "

27 But Micaiah said, "If you ever return in peace, the LORD has not spoken by [a]me." And he said, "Take heed, all you people!"

### *AHAB DIES IN BATTLE*

*(1 Kin. 22:29–40)*

28 So the king of Israel and Jehoshaphat the king of Judah went up to Ramoth Gilead. 29 And the king of Israel said to Jehoshaphat, "I will [a]disguise myself and go into battle; but you put on your robes." So the king of Israel disguised himself, and they went into battle.

30 Now the king of Syria had commanded the captains of the chariots who *were* with him, saying, "Fight with no one small or great, but only with the king of Israel."

31 So it was, when the captains of the chariots saw Jehoshaphat, that they said, "It *is* the king of Israel!" Therefore they surrounded him to attack; but Jehoshaphat [a]cried out, and the LORD helped him, and God diverted them from him. 32 For so it was, when the captains of the chariots saw that it was not the king of Israel, that they turned back from pursuing him. 33 Now a certain man drew a bow at random, and struck the king of Israel between the joints of his armor. So he said to the driver of his chariot, "Turn around and take me out of the battle, for I am wounded." 34 The battle increased that day, and the king of Israel propped *himself* up in *his* chariot facing the Syrians until evening; and about the time of sunset he died.

19 Then Jehoshaphat the king of Judah returned safely to his house in Jerusalem. 2 And Jehu the son of Hanani [a]the seer went out to meet him, and said to King Jehoshaphat, "Should you help the wicked and [b]love those who hate the LORD? Therefore the [c]wrath of the LORD *is* upon you. 3 Nevertheless [a]good things are found in you, in that you have removed the wooden images from the land, and have [b]prepared your heart to seek God."

18:6 [a] 2 Kin. 3:11 [1] Or *him* 18:10 [a] Zech. 1:18–21 18:13 [a] Num. 22:18–20, 35; 23:12, 26; 1 Kin. 22:14 18:16 [a] [Jer. 23:1–8; 31:10] [b] Num. 27:17; 1 Kin. 22:17; [Ezek. 34:5–8]; Matt. 9:36; Mark 6:34 18:18 [a] Is. 6:1–5; Dan. 7:9, 10 18:20 [a] Job 1:6; 2 Thess. 2:9 18:22 [a] Job 12:16, 17; Is. 19:12–14; Ezek. 14:9 18:23 [a] Jer. 20:2; Mark 14:65; Acts 23:2 18:26 [a] 2 Chr. 16:10 18:27 [a] Deut. 18:22 18:29 [a] 2 Chr. 35:22 18:31 [a] 2 Chr. 13:14, 15 19:2 [a] 1 Sam. 9:9; 1 Kin. 16:1; 2 Chr. 20:34 [b] Ps. 139:21 [c] 2 Chr. 32:25 19:3 [a] 2 Chr. 17:4, 6 [b] 2 Chr. 30:19

### *THE REFORMS OF JEHOSHAPHAT*

4 So Jehoshaphat dwelt at Jerusalem; and he went out again among the people from Beersheba to the mountains of Ephraim, and brought them back to the LORD God of their [a]fathers. 5 Then he set [a]judges in the land throughout all the fortified cities of Judah, city by city, 6 and said to the judges, "Take heed to what you are doing, for [a]you do not judge for man but for the LORD, [b]who *is* with you in the judgment. 7 Now therefore, let the fear of the LORD be upon you; take care and do *it,* for [a]*there is* no iniquity with the LORD our God, no [b]partiality, nor taking of bribes."

8 Moreover in Jerusalem, for the judgment of the LORD and for controversies, Jehoshaphat [a]appointed some of the Levites and priests, and some of the chief fathers of Israel, when they returned to Jerusalem.[1] 9 And he commanded them, saying, "Thus you shall act [a]in the fear of the LORD, faithfully and with a loyal heart: 10 [a]Whatever case comes to you from your brethren who dwell in their cities, whether of bloodshed or offenses against law or commandment, against statutes or ordinances, you shall warn them, lest they trespass against the LORD and [b]wrath come upon [c]you and your brethren. Do this, and you will not be guilty. 11 And take notice: [a]Amariah the chief priest *is* over you [b]in all matters of the LORD; and Zebadiah the son of Ishmael, the ruler of the house of Judah, for all the king's matters; also the Levites *will be* officials before you. Behave courageously, and the LORD will be [c]with the good."

> **19:5–11 Jehoshaphat** wasn't satisfied with changing the religious life of Judah. He wanted to change the judicial system as well. He succeeded—so well, in fact, that his system became a model for Jewish society throughout the years.

### *AMMON, MOAB, AND MOUNT SEIR DEFEATED*

**20** It happened after this *that* the people of [a]Moab with the people of [b]Ammon, and *others* with them besides the [c]Ammonites,[1] came to battle against Jehoshaphat. 2 Then some came and told Jehoshaphat, saying, "A great multitude is coming against you from beyond the sea, from Syria;[1] and they are [a]in Hazazon Tamar" (which *is* [b]En Gedi). 3 And Jehoshaphat feared, and set himself to [a]seek the LORD, and [b]proclaimed a

> **20:3** A **fast**, going without food for a time, was a common practice in ancient Israel. Usually, it was done as part of a religious ceremony or to show grief or repentance. Officially, the Israelites were only required to fast on the Day of Atonement.

fast throughout all Judah. 4 So Judah gathered together to ask [a]*help* from the LORD; and from all the cities of Judah they came to seek the LORD.

5 Then Jehoshaphat stood in the assembly of Judah and Jerusalem, in the house of the LORD, before the new court, 6 and said: "O LORD God of our fathers, *are* You not [a]God in heaven, and [b]do You *not* rule over all the kingdoms of the nations, and [c]in Your hand *is there not* power and might, so that no one is able to withstand You? 7 *Are* You not [a]our God, *who* [b]drove out the inhabitants of this land before Your people Israel, and gave it to the descendants of Abraham [c]Your friend forever? 8 And they dwell in it, and have built You a sanctuary in it for Your name, saying, 9 [a]'If disaster comes upon us—sword, judgment, pestilence, or famine—we will stand before this temple and in Your presence (for Your [b]name *is* in this temple), and cry out to You in our affliction, and You will hear and save.' 10 And now, here are the people of Ammon, Moab, and Mount Seir—whom You [a]would not let Israel invade when they came out of the land of Egypt, but [b]they turned from them and did not destroy them— 11 here they are, rewarding us [a]by coming to throw us out of Your possession which You have given us to inherit. 12 O our God, will You not [a]judge them? For we have no power against this great multitude that is coming against us; nor do we know what to do, but [b]our eyes *are* upon You."

13 Now all Judah, with their little ones, their wives, and their children, stood before the LORD.

14 Then [a]the Spirit of the LORD came upon Jahaziel the son of Zechariah, the son of Benaiah, the son of Jeiel, the son of Mattaniah, a Levite of the sons of Asaph, in the midst of the assembly. 15 And he said, "Listen, all you of Judah and you inhabitants of Jerusalem, and you, King Jehoshaphat! Thus says the LORD to you: [a]'Do not be afraid nor dismayed because of this great multitude, [b]for the battle *is* not yours, but God's. 16 Tomorrow go down against them. They will surely come up by the Ascent of Ziz, and you will find them at the end of the brook

**19:4** [a] 2 Chr. 15:8–13 **19:5** [a] [Deut. 16:18–20] **19:6** [a] [Lev. 19:15; Deut. 1:17]; Ps. 58:1 [b] Ps. 82:1; [Eccl. 5:8] **19:7** [a] [Gen. 18:25; Deut. 32:4]; Rom. 9:17 [b] [Deut. 10:17, 18; Job 34:19]; Acts 10:34; Rom. 2:11; Gal. 2:6; [Eph. 6:9; Col. 3:25] **19:8** [a] Deut. 16:18; 2 Chr. 17:8 [1] Septuagint and Vulgate read *for the inhabitants of Jerusalem.* **19:9** [a] [2 Sam. 23:3] **19:10** [a] Deut. 17:8 [b] Num. 16:46 [c] [Ezek. 3:18] **19:11** [a] Ezra 7:3 [b] 1 Chr. 26:30 [c] [2 Chr. 15:2; 20:17] **20:1** [a] 1 Chr. 18:2 [b] 1 Chr. 19:15 [c] 2 Chr. 26:7 [1] Following Masoretic Text and Vulgate; Septuagint reads *Meunites* (compare 26:7). **20:2** [a] Gen. 14:7 [b] Josh. 15:62 [1] Following Masoretic Text, Septuagint, and Vulgate; some Hebrew manuscripts and Old Latin read *Edom.* **20:3** [a] 2 Chr. 19:3 [b] 1 Sam. 7:6; Ezra 8:21; Jer. 36:9; Jon. 3:5 **20:4** [a] 2 Chr. 14:11 **20:6** [a] Deut. 4:39; Josh. 2:11; [1 Kin. 8:23]; Matt. 6:9 [b] Ps. 22:28; 47:2, 8; Dan. 4:17, 25, 32 [c] 1 Chr. 29:12; 2 Chr. 25:8; Ps. 62:11; Matt. 6:13 **20:7** [a] Gen. 13:14–17; 17:7; Ex. 6:7 [b] Ps. 44:2 [c] Is. 41:8; James 2:23 **20:9** [a] 1 Kin. 8:33, 37; 2 Chr. 6:28–30 [b] 2 Chr. 6:20 **20:10** [a] Deut. 2:4, 9, 19 [b] Num. 20:21 **20:11** [a] Ps. 83:1–18 **20:12** [a] Judg. 11:27; [1 Sam. 3:13] [b] Ps. 25:15; 121:1, 2; 123:1, 2; 141:8 **20:14** [a] Num. 11:25, 26; 24:2; 2 Chr. 15:1; 24:20 **20:15** [a] Ex. 14:13, 14; [Deut. 1:29, 30; 31:6, 8]; 2 Chr. 32:7 [b] 1 Sam. 17:47; Zech. 14:3

before the Wilderness of Jeruel. 17 [a]You will not
*need* to fight in this *battle.* Position yourselves,
stand still and see the salvation of the LORD, who
is with you, O Judah and Jerusalem!' Do not fear
or be dismayed; tomorrow go out against them,
[b]for the LORD *is* with you."

18 And Jehoshaphat [a]bowed his head with *his*
face to the ground, and all Judah and the inhab-
itants of Jerusalem bowed before the LORD,
worshiping the LORD. 19 Then the Levites of the
children of the Kohathites and of the children of
the Korahites stood up to praise the LORD God
of Israel with voices loud and high.

20 So they rose early in the morning and went
out into the Wilderness of Tekoa; and as they
went out, Jehoshaphat stood and said, "Hear
me, O Judah and you inhabitants of Jerusalem:
[a]Believe in the LORD your God, and you shall be
established; believe His prophets, and you shall
prosper." 21 And when he had consulted with the
people, he appointed those who should sing to
the LORD, [a]and who should praise the beauty
of holiness, as they went out before the army
and were saying:

> [b]"Praise the LORD,
> [c]For His mercy *endures* forever."[1]

22 Now when they began to sing and to praise,
[a]the LORD set ambushes against the people of
Ammon, Moab, and Mount Seir, who had come
against Judah; and they were defeated. 23 For the
people of Ammon and Moab stood up against
the inhabitants of Mount Seir to utterly kill and
destroy *them.* And when they had made an end
of the inhabitants of Seir, [a]they helped to destroy
one another.

24 So when Judah came to a place overlook-
ing the wilderness, they looked toward the mul-
titude; and there *were* their dead bodies, fallen
on the earth. No one had escaped.

25 When Jehoshaphat and his people came
to take away their spoil, they found among them
an abundance of valuables on the dead bodies,[1]
and precious jewelry, which they stripped off
for themselves, more than they could carry
away; and they were three days gathering the
spoil because there was so much. 26 And on
the fourth day they assembled in the Valley
of Berachah, for there they blessed the LORD;
therefore the name of that place was called The
Valley of Berachah[1] until this day. 27 Then they
returned, every man of Judah and Jerusalem,
with Jehoshaphat in front of them, to go back
to Jerusalem with joy, for the LORD had [a]made
them rejoice over their enemies. 28 So they came
to Jerusalem, with stringed instruments and
harps and trumpets, to the house of the LORD.
29 And [a]the fear of God was on all the kingdoms
of *those* countries when they heard that the
LORD had fought against the enemies of Israel.
30 Then the realm of Jehoshaphat was quiet, for
his [a]God gave him rest all around.

### *THE END OF JEHOSHAPHAT'S REIGN*

*(1 Kin. 22:41–50)*

31 [a]So Jehoshaphat was king over Judah. *He*
*was* thirty-five years old when he became king,
and he reigned twenty-five years in Jerusalem.
His mother's name *was* Azubah the daughter of
Shilhi. 32 And he walked in the way of his father
[a]Asa, and did not turn aside from it, doing *what*
*was* right in the sight of the LORD. 33 Nevertheless
[a]the high places were not taken away, for as yet
the people had not [b]directed their hearts to the
God of their fathers.

34 Now the rest of the acts of Jehoshaphat,
first and last, indeed they *are* written in the book
of Jehu the son of Hanani, [a]which *is* mentioned
in the book of the kings of Israel.

35 After this [a]Jehoshaphat king of Judah al-
lied himself with Ahaziah king of Israel, [b]who
acted very [c]wickedly. 36 And he allied himself with
him [a]to make ships to go to Tarshish, and they
made the ships in Ezion Geber. 37 But Eliezer the
son of Dodavah of Mareshah prophesied against
Jehoshaphat, saying, "Because you have allied
yourself with Ahaziah, the LORD has destroyed
your works." [a]Then the ships were wrecked, so
that they were not able to go [b]to Tarshish.

### *JEHORAM REIGNS IN JUDAH*

*(1 Kin. 22:50; 2 Kin. 8:16–24)*

**21** And [a]Jehoshaphat rested with his fathers,
and was buried with his fathers in the City
of David. Then Jehoram his son reigned in his
place. 2 He had brothers, the sons of Jehosh-
aphat: Azariah, Jehiel, Zechariah, Azaryahu,
Michael, and Shephatiah; all these *were* the
sons of Jehoshaphat king of Israel. 3 Their father
gave them great gifts of silver and gold and
precious things, with fortified cities in Judah;
but he gave the kingdom to Jehoram, because
he *was* the firstborn.

4 Now when Jehoram was established over
the kingdom of his father, he strengthened him-
self and killed all his brothers with the sword,
and also *others* of the princes of Israel.

5 [a]Jehoram *was* thirty-two years old when he
became king, and he reigned eight years in Je-
rusalem. 6 And he walked in the way of the kings
of Israel, just as the house of Ahab had done, for
he had the daughter of [a]Ahab as a wife; and he
did evil in the sight of the LORD. 7 Yet the LORD

20:17 [a] Ex. 14:13, 14 [b] Num. 14:9; [2 Chr. 15:2; 32:8] 20:18 [a] Ex. 4:31; 2 Chr. 7:3; 29:28 20:20 [a] Is. 7:9 20:21 [a] 1 Chr. 16:29; Ps. 29:2; 90:17; 96:9; 110:3 [b] 1 Chr. 16:34; Ps. 106:1; 136:1 [c] 1 Chr. 16:41; 2 Chr. 5:13 [1] Compare Psalm 106:1 20:22 [a] Judg. 7:22; 1 Sam. 14:20 20:23 [a] Judg. 7:22; 1 Sam. 14:20 20:25 [1] A few Hebrew manuscripts, Old Latin, and Vulgate read *garments;* Septuagint reads *armor.* 20:26 [1] Literally *Blessing* 20:27 [a] Neh. 12:43 20:29 [a] 2 Chr. 14:14; 17:10 20:30 [a] 1 Kin. 22:41–43; 2 Chr. 14:6, 7; 15:15; Job 34:29 20:31 [a] [1 Kin. 22:41–43] 20:32 [a] 2 Chr. 14:2 20:33 [a] 2 Chr. 15:17; 17:6 [b] 2 Chr. 12:14; 19:3 20:34 [a] 1 Kin. 16:1, 7 20:35 [a] 2 Chr. 18:1 [b] 1 Kin. 22:48–53 [c] [2 Chr. 19:2] 20:36 [a] 1 Kin. 9:26; 10:22 20:37 [a] 1 Kin. 22:48 [b] 2 Chr. 9:21 21:1 [a] 1 Kin. 22:50 21:5 [a] 2 Kin. 8:17–22 21:6 [a] 2 Chr. 18:1

## SEEING JESUS IN THE SCRIPTURE

**21:7** Even when evil kings ruled God's people, God remembered His promise to save the world through them. God's covenant with David wasn't sustained by the righteousness of people, but rather by God's faithfulness to His promise to save the world through Jesus (see Heb. 9:14–15).

would not destroy the house of David, because
of the [a]covenant that He had made with David,
and since He had promised to give a lamp to
him and to his [b]sons forever.
8 [a]In his days Edom revolted against Judah's
authority, and made a king over themselves.
9 So Jehoram went out with his officers, and all
his chariots with him. And he rose by night and
attacked the Edomites who had surrounded him
and the captains of the chariots. 10 Thus Edom
has been in revolt against Judah's authority to
this day. At that time Libnah revolted against his
rule, because he had forsaken the LORD God of
his fathers. 11 Moreover he made high places in
the mountains of Judah, and caused the inhab-
itants of Jerusalem to [a]commit harlotry, and
led Judah astray.
12 And a letter came to him from Elijah the
prophet, saying,

Thus says the LORD God of your father
David:
Because you have not walked in the ways
of Jehoshaphat your father, or in the ways
of Asa king of Judah, 13 but have walked
in the way of the kings of Israel, and
have [a]made Judah and the inhabitants
of Jerusalem to [b]play the harlot like the
[c]harlotry of the house of Ahab, and also
have [d]killed your brothers, those of your
father's household, *who were* better than
yourself, 14 behold, the LORD will strike
your people with a serious affliction—
your children, your wives, and all your
possessions; 15 and you *will become* very
sick with a [a]disease of your intestines,
until your intestines come out by reason
of the sickness, day by day.

16 Moreover the [a]LORD [b]stirred up against Je-
horam the spirit of the Philistines and the [c]Ara-
bians who *were* near the Ethiopians. 17 And they
came up into Judah and invaded it, and carried
away all the possessions that were found in the
king's house, and also [a]his sons and his wives,
so that there was not a son left to him except
Jehoahaz,[1] the youngest of his sons.
18 After all this the LORD struck him [a]in his
intestines with an incurable disease. 19 Then it
happened in the course of time, after the end of
two years, that his intestines came out because
of his sickness; so he died in severe pain. And
his people made no burning for him, like [a]the
burning for his fathers.
20 He was thirty-two years old when he be-
came king. He reigned in Jerusalem eight years
and, to no one's sorrow, departed. However they
buried him in the City of David, but not in the
tombs of the kings.

### AHAZIAH REIGNS IN JUDAH
*(2 Kin. 8:25–29; 9:14–16, 27–29)*

**22** Then the inhabitants of Jerusalem made
[a]Ahaziah his youngest son king in his
place, for the raiders who came with the [b]Arabi-
ans into the camp had killed all the [c]older *sons.*
So Ahaziah the son of Jehoram, king of Judah,
reigned. 2 Ahaziah *was* forty-two[1] years old when
he became king, and he reigned one year in
Jerusalem. His mother's name *was* [a]Athaliah
the granddaughter of Omri. 3 He also walked in
the ways of the house of Ahab, for his mother
advised him to do wickedly. 4 Therefore he did
evil in the sight of the LORD, like the house of
Ahab; for they were his counselors after the
death of his father, to his destruction. 5 He also
followed their advice, and went with Jehoram[1]
the son of Ahab king of Israel to war against
Hazael king of Syria at Ramoth Gilead; and the
Syrians wounded Joram. 6 [a]Then he returned
to Jezreel to recover from the wounds which he
had received at Ramah, when he fought against
Hazael king of Syria. And Azariah[1] the son of Je-
horam, king of Judah, went down to see Jehoram
the son of Ahab in Jezreel, because he was sick.
7 His going to Joram [a]was God's occasion
for Ahaziah's downfall; for when he arrived, [b]he
went out with Jehoram against Jehu the son of
Nimshi, [c]whom the LORD had anointed to cut
off the house of Ahab. 8 And it happened, when

**22:7** The prophet Elisha had anointed **Jehu** as the eleventh king of Israel and had given him instructions to wipe out the family of **Ahab**. Ahab knew about his death sentence. Years before, the prophet Elijah had warned Ahab his family would be destroyed because of the evil things he had done.

**21:7** [a] 2 Sam. 7:8–17 [b] 1 Kin. 11:36; 2 Kin. 8:19; Ps. 132:11 **21:8** [a] 2 Kin. 8:20; 14:7, 10; 2 Chr. 25:14, 19 **21:11** [a] [Lev. 20:5] **21:13** [a] 2 Chr. 21:11 [b] [Ex. 34:15]; Deut. 31:16 [c] 1 Kin. 16:31–33; 2 Kin. 9:22 [d] 1 Kin. 2:32; 2 Chr. 21:4 **21:15** [a] 2 Chr. 21:18, 19 **21:16** [a] 2 Chr. 33:11; [Jer. 51:11] [b] 1 Kin. 11:14, 23 [c] 2 Chr. 17:11 **21:17** [a] 2 Chr. 24:7 [1] Elsewhere called *Ahaziah* (compare 2 Chronicles 22:1) **21:18** [a] 2 Chr. 13:20; 21:15; Acts 12:23 **21:19** [a] 2 Chr. 16:14 **22:1** [a] 2 Chr. 21:17; 22:6 [b] 2 Chr. 21:16 [c] 2 Chr. 21:17 **22:2** [a] 2 Chr. 21:6 [1] Or *twenty-two* (compare 2 Kings 8:26) **22:5** [1] Also spelled *Joram* (compare verses 5 and 7; 2 Kings 8:28; and elsewhere) **22:6** [a] 2 Kin. 9:15 [1] Some Hebrew manuscripts, Septuagint, Syriac, Vulgate, and 2 Kings 8:29 read *Ahaziah.* **22:7** [a] Judg. 14:4; 1 Kin. 12:15; 2 Chr. 10:15 [b] 2 Kin. 9:21–24 [c] 2 Kin. 9:6, 7

Jehu was [a]executing judgment on the house of Ahab, and [b]found the princes of Judah and the sons of Ahaziah's brothers who served Ahaziah, that he killed them. 9 [a]Then he searched for Ahaziah; and they caught him (he was hiding in Samaria), and brought him to Jehu. When they had killed him, they buried him, "because," they said, "he is the son of [b]Jehoshaphat, who [c]sought the LORD with all his heart."

So the house of Ahaziah had no one to assume power over the kingdom.

### *ATHALIAH REIGNS IN JUDAH*

*(2 Kin. 11:1–3)*

10 [a]Now when Athaliah the mother of Ahaziah saw that her son was dead, she arose and destroyed all the royal heirs of the house of Judah. 11 But Jehoshabeath,[1] the daughter of the king, took [a]Joash the son of Ahaziah, and stole him away from among the king's sons who were being murdered, and put him and his nurse in a bedroom. So Jehoshabeath, the daughter of King Jehoram, the wife of Jehoiada the priest (for she was the sister of Ahaziah), hid him from Athaliah so that she did not kill him. 12 And he was hidden with them in the house of God for six years, while Athaliah reigned over the land.

### *JOASH CROWNED KING OF JUDAH*

*(2 Kin. 11:4–12)*

**23** In [a]the seventh year [b]Jehoiada strengthened himself, *and made a* covenant with the captains of hundreds: Azariah the son of Jeroham, Ishmael the son of Jehohanan, Azariah the son of [c]Obed, Maaseiah the son of Adaiah, and Elishaphat the son of Zichri. 2 And they went throughout Judah and gathered the Levites from all the cities of Judah, and the [a]chief fathers of Israel, and they came to Jerusalem.

3 Then all the assembly made a covenant with the king in the house of God. And he said to them, "Behold, the king's son shall reign, as the LORD has [a]said of the sons of David. 4 This *is* what you shall do: One-third of you [a]entering on the Sabbath, of the priests and the Levites, *shall be* keeping watch over the doors; 5 one-third *shall be* at the king's house; and one-third at the Gate of the Foundation. All the people *shall be* in the courts of the house of the LORD. 6 But let no one come into the house of the LORD except the priests and [a]those of the Levites who serve. They may go in, for they *are* holy; but all the people shall keep the watch of the LORD. 7 And the Levites shall surround the king on all sides, every man with his weapons in his hand; and whoever comes into the house, let him be put to death. You are to be with the king when he comes in and when he goes out."

8 So the Levites and all Judah did according to all that Jehoiada the priest commanded. And each man took his men who were to be on duty on the Sabbath, with those who were going *off duty* on the Sabbath; for Jehoiada the priest had not dismissed [a]the divisions. 9 And Jehoiada the priest gave to the captains of hundreds the spears and the large and small [a]shields which *had belonged* to King David, that *were* in the temple of God. 10 Then he set all the people, every man with his weapon in his hand, from the right side of the temple to the left side of the temple, along by the altar and by the temple, all around the king. 11 And they brought out the king's son, put the crown on him, [a]*gave him* the Testimony,[1] and made him king. Then Jehoiada and his sons anointed him, and said, "*Long* live the king!"

> **23:9** Money and other valuables were often stored in the temple. David's weapons probably were considered historic relics and were stored in the temple for safekeeping.

### *DEATH OF ATHALIAH*

*(2 Kin. 11:13–20)*

12 Now when [a]Athaliah heard the noise of the people running and praising the king, she came to the people *in* the temple of the LORD. 13 *When* she looked, there was the king standing by his pillar at the entrance; and the leaders and the trumpeters *were* by the king. All the people of the land were rejoicing and blowing trumpets, also the singers with musical instruments, and [a]those who led in praise. So Athaliah tore her clothes and said, [b]"Treason! Treason!"

14 And Jehoiada the priest brought out the captains of hundreds who were set over the army, and said to them, "Take her outside under guard, and slay with the sword whoever follows her." For the priest had said, "Do not kill her in the house of the LORD."

15 So they seized her; and she went by way of the entrance [a]of the Horse Gate *into* the king's house, and they killed her there.

16 Then Jehoiada made a [a]covenant between himself, the people, and the king, that they should be the LORD's people. 17 And all the people went to the temple[1] of Baal, and tore it down. They broke in pieces its altars and images, and [a]killed Mattan the priest of Baal before the altars. 18 Also Jehoiada appointed the oversight of the house of the LORD to the hand of the priests, the Levites, whom David had [a]assigned in the house of the LORD, to offer the burnt offerings of the LORD, as *it is* written in the [b]Law of Moses, with rejoicing and with singing, *as it was established*

**22:8** [a] 2 Kin. 9:22–24 [b] 2 Kin. 10:10–14; Hos. 1:4 **22:9** [a] [2 Kin. 9:27] [b] 1 Kin. 15:24 [c] 2 Chr. 17:4; 20:3, 4 **22:10** [a] 2 Kin. 11:1–3 **22:11** [a] 2 Kin. 12:18 [1] Spelled *Jehosheba* in 2 Kings 11:2 **23:1** [a] 2 Kin. 11:4 [b] 2 Kin. 12:2 [c] 1 Chr. 2:37, 38 **23:2** [a] Ezra 1:5 **23:3** [a] 2 Sam. 7:12; 1 Kin. 2:4; 9:5; 2 Chr. 6:16; 7:18; 21:7 **23:4** [a] 1 Chr. 9:25 **23:6** [a] 1 Chr. 23:28–32 **23:8** [a] 1 Chr. 24:1–31 **23:9** [a] 2 Sam. 8:7 **23:11** [a] Deut. 17:18 [1] That is, the Law (compare Exodus 25:16, 21; 31:18) **23:12** [a] 2 Chr. 22:10 **23:13** [a] 1 Chr. 25:8 [b] 2 Kin. 9:23 **23:15** [a] Neh. 3:28; Jer. 31:40 **23:16** [a] Josh. 24:24, 25; 2 Chr. 15:12–15 **23:17** [a] Deut. 13:6–9; 1 Kin. 18:40 [1] Literally *house* **23:18** [a] 1 Chr. 23:6, 30, 31; 24:1 [b] Num. 28:2

by David. 19 And he set the [a]gatekeepers at the gates of the house of the LORD, so that no one *who was* in any way unclean should enter.

20 [a]Then he took the captains of hundreds, the nobles, the governors of the people, and all the people of the land, and brought the king down from the house of the LORD; and they went through the Upper Gate to the king's house, and set the king on the throne of the kingdom. 21 So all the people of the land rejoiced; and the city was quiet, for they had slain Athaliah with the sword.

### *JOASH REPAIRS THE TEMPLE*

*(2 Kin. 11:21—12:16)*

**24** Joash [a]*was* seven years old when he became king, and he reigned forty years in Jerusalem. His mother's name *was* Zibiah of Beersheba. 2 Joash [a]did *what was* right in the sight of the LORD all the days of Jehoiada the priest. 3 And Jehoiada took two wives for him, and he had sons and daughters.

4 Now it happened after this *that* Joash set his heart on repairing the house of the LORD. 5 Then he gathered the priests and the Levites, and said to them, "Go out to the cities of Judah, and [a]gather from all Israel money to repair the house of your God from year to year, and see that you do it quickly."

However the Levites did not do it quickly. 6 [a]So the king called Jehoiada the chief *priest,* and said to him, "Why have you not required the Levites to bring in from Judah and from Jerusalem the collection, *according to the commandment* of [b]Moses the servant of the LORD and of the assembly of Israel, for the [c]tabernacle of witness?" 7 For [a]the sons of Athaliah, that wicked woman, had broken into the house of God, and had also presented all the [b]dedicated things of the house of the LORD to the Baals.

8 Then at the king's command [a]they made a chest, and set it outside at the gate of the house of the LORD. 9 And they made a proclamation throughout Judah and Jerusalem to bring to the LORD [a]the collection *that* Moses the servant of God *had imposed* on Israel in the wilderness. 10 Then all the leaders and all the people rejoiced, brought their contributions, and put *them* into the chest until all had given. 11 So it was, at that time, when the chest was brought to the king's official by the hand of the Levites, and [a]when they saw that *there was* much money, that the king's scribe and the high priest's officer came and emptied the chest, and took it and returned it to its place. Thus they did day by day, and gathered money in abundance.

12 The king and Jehoiada gave it to those who did the work of the service of the house of the LORD; and they hired masons and carpenters to [a]repair the house of the LORD, and also those who worked in iron and bronze to restore the house of the LORD. 13 So the workmen labored, and the work was completed by them; they restored the house of God to its original condition and reinforced it. 14 When they had finished, they brought the rest of the money before the king and Jehoiada; [a]they made from it articles for the house of the LORD, articles for serving and offering, spoons and vessels of gold and silver. And they offered burnt offerings in the house of the LORD continually all the days of Jehoiada.

### *APOSTASY OF JOASH*

15 But Jehoiada grew old and was full of days, and he died; *he was* one hundred and thirty years old when he died. 16 And they buried him in the City of David among the kings, because he had done good in Israel, both toward God and His house.

17 Now after the death of Jehoiada the leaders of Judah came and bowed down to the king. And the king listened to them. 18 Therefore they left the house of the LORD God of their fathers, and served [a]wooden images and idols; and [b]wrath came upon Judah and Jerusalem because of their trespass. 19 Yet He [a]sent prophets to them, to bring them back to the LORD; and they testified against them, but they would not listen.

20 Then the Spirit of God came upon [a]Zechariah the son of Jehoiada the priest, who stood above the people, and said to them, "Thus says God: [b]'Why do you transgress the commandments of the LORD, so that you cannot prosper? [c]Because you have forsaken the LORD, He also has forsaken you.' " 21 So they conspired against him, and at the command of the king they [a]stoned him with stones in the court of the house of the LORD. 22 Thus Joash the king did not remember the kindness which Jehoiada his father had done to him, but killed his son; and as he died, he said, "The LORD look on *it,* and [a]repay!"

> **24:20–22 Zechariah** is one of the pre-Christian martyrs who gave his life for his faith in God. Some of these faithful ones are listed in Hebrews 11; some are known only to God. Jesus indicated that those killed for their faith would increase in the last days (Matt. 10:21; 24:9) and during the great tribulation, the ranks of the martyrs would swell to unprecedented size (Rev. 7:14).

**23:19** [a] 1 Chr. 26:1–19 **23:20** [a] 1 Kin. 9:22; 2 Kin. 11:19 **24:1** [a] 2 Kin. 11:21; 12:1–15 **24:2** [a] 2 Chr. 26:4, 5 **24:5** [a] 2 Kin. 12:4 **24:6** [a] 2 Kin. 12:7 [b] Ex. 30:12–16 [c] Num. 1:50; Acts 7:44 **24:7** [a] 2 Chr. 21:17 [b] 2 Kin. 12:4 **24:8** [a] 2 Kin. 12:9 **24:9** [a] 2 Chr. 24:6 **24:11** [a] 2 Kin. 12:10 **24:12** [a] 2 Chr. 30:12 **24:14** [a] 2 Kin. 12:13 **24:18** [a] 1 Kin. 14:23 [b] [Ex. 34:12–14]; Judg. 5:8; 2 Chr. 19:2; 28:13; 29:8; 32:25 **24:19** [a] 2 Kin. 17:13; 21:10–15; 2 Chr. 36:15, 16; Jer. 7:25, 26; 25:4 **24:20** [a] Judg. 6:34; Matt. 23:35 [b] Num. 14:41; [Prov. 28:13] [c] [2 Chr. 15:2] **24:21** [a] [Neh. 9:26]; Matt. 23:35; Acts 7:58, 59 **24:22** [a] [Gen. 9:5]

### *DEATH OF JOASH*

*(2 Kin. 12:19–21)*

23 So it happened in the spring of the year *that* [a]the army of Syria came up against him; and they came to Judah and Jerusalem, and destroyed all the leaders of the people from among the people, and sent all their spoil to the king of Damascus. 24 For the army of the Syrians [a]came with a small company of men; but the LORD [b]delivered a very great army into their hand, because they had forsaken the LORD God of their fathers. So they [c]executed judgment against Joash. 25 And when they had withdrawn from him (for they left him severely wounded), [a]his own servants conspired against him because of the blood of the sons[1] of Jehoiada the priest, and killed him on his bed. So he died. And they buried him in the City of David, but they did not bury him in the tombs of the kings.

26 These are the ones who conspired against him: Zabad[1] the son of Shimeath the Ammonitess, and Jehozabad the son of Shimrith[2] the Moabitess. 27 Now *concerning* his sons, and [a]the many oracles about him, and the repairing of the house of God, indeed they *are* written in the annals of the book of the kings. [b]Then Amaziah his son reigned in his place.

### *AMAZIAH REIGNS IN JUDAH*

*(2 Kin. 14:1–6)*

**25** Amaziah [a]*was* twenty-five years old *when* he became king, and he reigned twenty-nine years in Jerusalem. His mother's name *was* Jehoaddan of Jerusalem. 2 And he did *what was* right in the sight of the LORD, [a]but not with a loyal heart.

3 [a]Now it happened, as soon as the kingdom was established for him, that he executed his servants who had murdered his father the king. 4 However he did not execute their children, but *did* as *it is* written in the Law in the Book of Moses, where the LORD commanded, saying, [a]"'The fathers shall not be put to death for their children, nor shall the children be put to death for their fathers; but a person shall die for his own sin.'"[1]

### *THE WAR AGAINST EDOM*

*(2 Kin. 14:7)*

5 Moreover Amaziah gathered Judah together and set over them captains of thousands and captains of hundreds, according to *their* fathers' houses, throughout all Judah and Benjamin; and he numbered them [a]from twenty years old and above, and found them to be three hundred thousand choice *men, able* to go to war, who could handle spear and shield. 6 He also hired one hundred thousand mighty men of valor from Israel for one hundred talents of silver. 7 But a [a]man of God came to him, saying, "O king, do not let the army of Israel go with you, for the LORD *is* not with Israel—*not with* any of the children of Ephraim. 8 But if you go, be gone! Be strong in battle! *Even so,* God shall make you fall before the enemy; for God has [a]power to help and to overthrow."

9 Then Amaziah said to the man of God, "But what *shall we* do about the hundred talents which I have given to the troops of Israel?"

And the man of God answered, [a]"The LORD is able to give you much more than this." 10 So Amaziah discharged the troops that had come to him from Ephraim, to go back home. Therefore their anger was greatly aroused against Judah, and they returned home in great anger.

11 Then Amaziah strengthened himself, and leading his people, he went to [a]the Valley of Salt and killed ten thousand of the people of Seir. 12 Also the children of Judah took captive ten thousand alive, brought them to the top of the rock, and cast them down from the top of the rock, so that they all were dashed in pieces.

13 But as for the soldiers of the army which Amaziah had discharged, so that they would not go with him to battle, they raided the cities of Judah from Samaria to Beth Horon, killed three thousand in them, and took much spoil.

14 Now it was so, after Amaziah came from the slaughter of the Edomites, that [a]he brought the gods of the people of Seir, set them up *to be* [b]his gods, and bowed down before them and burned incense to them. 15 Therefore the anger of the LORD was aroused against Amaziah, and He sent him a prophet who said to him, "Why have you sought [a]the gods of the people, which [b]could not rescue their own people from your hand?"

16 So it was, as he talked with him, that *the king* said to him, "Have we made you the king's counselor? Cease! Why should you be killed?"

Then the prophet ceased, and said, "I know that God has [a]determined to destroy you, because you have done this and have not heeded my advice."

### *ISRAEL DEFEATS JUDAH*

*(2 Kin. 14:8–14)*

17 Now [a]Amaziah king of Judah asked advice and sent to Joash[1] the son of Jehoahaz, the son of Jehu, king of Israel, saying, "Come, let us face one another *in battle.*"

18 And Joash king of Israel sent to Amaziah king of Judah, saying, "The thistle that *was* in Lebanon sent to the cedar that was in Lebanon, saying, 'Give your daughter to my son as wife'; and a wild beast that *was* in Lebanon passed

**24:23** [a] 2 Kin. 12:17; Is. 7:2 **24:24** [a] Lev. 26:8; [Deut. 32:30]; Is. 30:17 [b] Lev. 26:25; [Deut. 28:25] [c] 2 Chr. 22:8; Is. 10:5 **24:25** [a] 2 Kin. 12:20, 21; 2 Chr. 25:3 [1] Septuagint and Vulgate read *son* (compare verses 20–22). **24:26** [1] Or *Jozachar* (compare 2 Kings 12:21) [2] Or *Shomer* (compare 2 Kings 12:21) **24:27** [a] 2 Kin. 12:18 [b] 2 Kin. 12:21 **25:1** [a] 2 Kin. 14:1–6 **25:2** [a] 2 Kin. 14:4; 2 Chr. 25:14 **25:3** [a] 2 Kin. 14:5; 2 Chr. 24:25 **25:4** [a] Deut. 24:16; 2 Kin. 14:6; Jer. 31:30; [Ezek. 18:20] [1] Deuteronomy 24:16 **25:5** [a] Num. 1:3 **25:7** [a] 2 Chr. 11:2 **25:8** [a] 2 Chr. 14:11; 20:6 **25:9** [a] [Deut. 8:18]; Prov. 10:22 **25:11** [a] 2 Kin. 14:7 **25:14** [a] 2 Chr. 28:23 [b] [Ex. 20:3, 5] **25:15** [a] [Ps. 96:5] [b] 2 Chr. 25:11 **25:16** [a] [1 Sam. 2:25] **25:17** [a] 2 Kin. 14:8–14 [1] Spelled *Jehoash* in 2 Kings 14:8ff

by and trampled the thistle. 19 Indeed you say
that you have defeated the Edomites, and your
heart is lifted up to [a]boast. Stay at home now;
why should you meddle with trouble, that you
should fall—you and Judah with you?"
20 But Amaziah would not heed, for [a]it *came*
from God, that He might give them into the
hand *of their enemies,* because they [b]sought the
gods of Edom. 21 So Joash king of Israel went
out; and he and Amaziah king of Judah faced
one another at [a]Beth Shemesh, which *belongs*
to Judah. 22 And Judah was defeated by Israel,
and every man fled to his tent. 23 Then Joash the
king of Israel captured Amaziah king of Judah,
the son of Joash, the son of [a]Jehoahaz, at Beth
Shemesh; and he brought him to Jerusalem, and
broke down the wall of Jerusalem from the Gate
of Ephraim to the Corner Gate—four hundred
cubits. 24 And *he took* all the gold and silver, all
the articles that were found in the house of God
with [a]Obed-Edom, the treasures of the king's
house, and hostages, and returned to Samaria.

### DEATH OF AMAZIAH
*(2 Kin. 14:17–20)*

25 [a]Amaziah the son of Joash, king of Judah,
lived fifteen years after the death of Joash the
son of Jehoahaz, king of Israel. 26 Now the rest
of the acts of Amaziah, from first to last, indeed
*are* they not written in the book of the kings of
Judah and Israel? 27 After the time that Amazi-
ah turned away from following the LORD, they
made a conspiracy against him in Jerusalem,
and he fled to Lachish; but they sent after him
to Lachish and killed him there. 28 Then they
brought him on horses and buried him with
his fathers in the City of Judah.

### UZZIAH REIGNS IN JUDAH
*(2 Kin. 14:21, 22; 15:1–3)*

26 Now all the people of Judah took Uzziah,[1]
who *was* sixteen years old, and made him
king instead of his father Amaziah. 2 He built
Elath[1] and restored it to Judah, after the king
rested with his fathers.
3 Uzziah *was* sixteen years old when he be-
came king, and he reigned fifty-two years in
Jerusalem. His mother's name was Jecholiah
of Jerusalem. 4 And he did *what was* [a]right in
the sight of the LORD, according to all that his
father Amaziah had done. 5 [a]He sought God in
the days of Zechariah, who [b]had understanding
in the visions[1] of God; and as long as he sought
the LORD, God made him [c]prosper.
6 Now he went out and [a]made war against
the Philistines, and broke down the wall of Gath,
the wall of Jabneh, and the wall of Ashdod; and
he built cities *around* Ashdod and among the
Philistines. 7 God helped him against [a]the Phi-
listines, against the Arabians who lived in Gur
Baal, and against the Meunites. 8 Also the Am-
monites [a]brought tribute to Uzziah. His fame
spread as far as the entrance of Egypt, for he
became exceedingly strong.
9 And Uzziah built towers in Jerusalem at
the [a]Corner Gate, at the Valley Gate, and at the
corner buttress of the wall; then he fortified
them. 10 Also he built towers in the desert. He
dug many wells, for he had much livestock,
both in the lowlands and in the plains; *he also
had* farmers and vinedressers in the mountains
and in Carmel, for he loved the soil.
11 Moreover Uzziah had an army of fighting
men who went out to war by companies, ac-
cording to the number on their roll as prepared
by Jeiel the scribe and Maaseiah the officer,
under the hand of Hananiah, *one* of the king's
captains. 12 The total number of chief officers[1]
of the mighty men of valor *was* two thousand
six hundred. 13 And under their authority *was* an
army of three hundred and seven thousand five
hundred, that made war with mighty power, to
help the king against the enemy. 14 Then Uzziah
prepared for them, for the entire army, shields,
spears, helmets, body armor, bows, and slings
*to cast* stones. 15 And he made devices in Jerusa-
lem, invented by [a]skillful men, to be on the tow-
ers and the corners, to shoot arrows and large
stones. So his fame spread far and wide, for he
was marvelously helped till he became strong.

> **26:15** The description of these war devices suggests they were like catapults. From about 800 BC to AD 500, catapults were among the most feared weapons of war. They were capable of firing objects between 350 and 500 yards. Bows and arrows were also dangerous weapons. An arrow fired could travel up to 300 yards.

### THE PENALTY FOR UZZIAH'S PRIDE
*(2 Kin. 15:4–7)*

16 But [a]when he was strong his heart was
[b]lifted up, to *his* destruction, for he transgressed
against the LORD his God [c]by entering the tem-
ple of the LORD to burn incense on the altar of
incense. 17 So [a]Azariah the priest went in after
him, and with him were eighty priests of the
LORD—valiant men. 18 And they withstood King
Uzziah, and said to him, "*It* [a]*is* not for you, Uz-
ziah, to burn incense to the LORD, but for the

**25:19** [a] 2 Chr. 26:16; 32:25; [Prov. 16:18] **25:20** [a] 1 Kin. 12:15; 2 Chr. 22:7 [b] 2 Chr. 25:14 **25:21** [a] Josh. 19:38 **25:23** [a] 2 Chr. 21:17; 22:1, 6 **25:24** [a] 1 Chr. 26:15 **25:25** [a] 2 Kin. 14:17–22 **26:1** [1] Called *Azariah* in 2 Kings 14:21ff **26:2** [1] Hebrew *Eloth* **26:4** [a] 2 Chr. 24:2 **26:5** [a] 2 Chr. 24:2 [b] Gen. 41:15; Dan. 1:17; 10:1 [c] [2 Chr. 15:2; 20:20; 31:21] [1] Several Hebrew manuscripts, Septuagint, Syriac, Targum, and Arabic read *fear.* **26:6** [a] Is. 14:29 **26:7** [a] 2 Chr. 21:16 **26:8** [a] 2 Sam. 8:2; 2 Chr. 17:11 **26:9** [a] 2 Kin. 14:13; 2 Chr. 25:23; Neh. 3:13, 19, 32; Zech. 14:10 **26:12** [1] Literally *chief fathers* **26:15** [a] Ex. 39:3, 8 **26:16** [a] [Deut. 32:15] [b] Deut. 8:14; 2 Chr. 25:19 [c] 1 Kin. 13:1–4; 2 Kin. 16:12, 13 **26:17** [a] 1 Chr. 6:10 **26:18** [a] [Num. 3:10; 16:39, 40; 18:7] [b] Ex. 30:7, 8; Heb. 7:14

[b]priests, the sons of Aaron, who are consecrated
to burn incense. Get out of the sanctuary, for
you have trespassed! You *shall have* no honor
from the LORD God."
19 Then Uzziah became furious; and he *had*
a censer in his hand to burn incense. And while
he was angry with the priests, [a]leprosy broke out
on his forehead, before the priests in the house
of the LORD, beside the incense altar. 20 And Aza-
riah the chief priest and all the priests looked at
him, and there, on his forehead, he *was* leprous;
so they thrust him out of that place. Indeed he
also [a]hurried to get out, because the LORD had
struck him.

**SEEING JESUS IN THE SCRIPTURE**

**26:20** God punished Uzziah for acting like a priest when he wasn't a priest; he was a king. Jesus is our perfect priest *and* king, able to offer sacrifice (Himself) and lead the people of God (see Heb. 7:27).

21 [a]King Uzziah was a leper until the day of his
death. He dwelt in an [b]isolated house, because
he was a leper; for he was cut off from the house
of the LORD. Then Jotham his son *was* over the
king's house, judging the people of the land.
22 Now the rest of the acts of Uzziah, from
first to last, the prophet [a]Isaiah the son of Amoz
wrote. 23 [a]So Uzziah rested with his fathers, and
they buried him with his fathers in the field of
burial which *belonged* to the kings, for they said,
"He is a leper." Then Jotham his son reigned in
his place.

### *JOTHAM REIGNS IN JUDAH*

*(2 Kin. 15:32–38)*

**27** Jotham [a]*was* twenty-five years old when
he became king, and he reigned sixteen
years in Jerusalem. His mother's name *was* Je-
rushah[1] the daughter of Zadok. 2 And he did *what*
*was* right in the sight of the LORD, according to
all that his father Uzziah had done (although he
did not enter the temple of the LORD). But still
[a]the people acted corruptly.
3 He built the Upper Gate of the house of the
LORD, and he built extensively on the wall of
[a]Ophel. 4 Moreover he built cities in the moun-
tains of Judah, and in the forests he built for-
tresses and towers. 5 He also fought with the king
of the [a]Ammonites and defeated them. And the
people of Ammon gave him in that year one
hundred talents of silver, ten thousand kors of
wheat, and ten thousand of barley. The people of
Ammon paid this to him in the second and third
years also. 6 So Jotham became mighty, [a]because
he prepared his ways before the LORD his God.
7 Now the rest of the acts of Jotham, and all
his wars and his ways, indeed they *are* written in
the book of the kings of Israel and Judah. 8 He
was twenty-five years old when he became king,
and he reigned sixteen years in Jerusalem. 9 [a]So
Jotham rested with his fathers, and they buried
him in the City of David. Then [b]Ahaz his son
reigned in his place.

### *AHAZ REIGNS IN JUDAH*

*(2 Kin. 16:1–4)*

**28** Ahaz [a]*was* twenty years old when he became
king, and he reigned sixteen years in Jerusa-
lem; and he did not do *what was* right in the sight
of the LORD, as his father David *had done.* 2 For
he walked in the ways of the kings of Israel, and
made [a]molded images for [b]the Baals. 3 He burned
incense in [a]the Valley of the Son of Hinnom, and
burned [b]his children in the [c]fire, according to the
abominations of the nations whom the LORD had
[d]cast out before the children of Israel. 4 And he
sacrificed and burned incense on the high places,
on the hills, and under every green tree.

**28:3** The Canaanites, like many other pagan cultures in the ancient Near East, offered human sacrifices to their gods. The required sacrifice was often a family's first-born child.

### *SYRIA AND ISRAEL DEFEAT JUDAH*

*(2 Kin. 16:5, 6; Is. 7:1)*

5 Therefore [a]the LORD his God delivered him
into the hand of the king of Syria. They [b]defeated
him, and carried away a great multitude of them
as captives, and brought *them* to Damascus. Then
he was also delivered into the hand of the king
of Israel, who defeated him with a great slaugh-
ter. 6 For [a]Pekah the son of Remaliah killed one
hundred and twenty thousand in Judah in one
day, all valiant men, [b]because they had forsaken
the LORD God of their fathers. 7 Zichri, a mighty
man of Ephraim, killed Maaseiah the king's son,
Azrikam the officer over the house, and Elkanah
*who was* second to the king. 8 And the children of
Israel carried away captive of their [a]brethren two
hundred thousand women, sons, and daughters;
and they also took away much spoil from them,
and brought the spoil to Samaria.

### *ISRAEL RETURNS THE CAPTIVES*

9 But a [a]prophet of the LORD was there, whose
name *was* Oded; and he went out before the army

**26:19** [a] Lev. 13:42; Num. 12:10; 2 Kin. 5:25–27 **26:20** [a] Esth. 6:12 **26:21** [a] 2 Kin. 15:5 [b] [Lev. 13:46; Num. 5:2] **26:22** [a] 2 Kin. 20:1; 2 Chr. 32:20, 32; Is. 1:1 **26:23** [a] 2 Kin. 15:7; 2 Chr. 21:20; 28:27; Is. 6:1 **27:1** [a] 2 Kin. 15:32–35 [1] Spelled *Jerusha* in 2 Kings 15:33 **27:2** [a] 2 Kin. 15:35; Ezek. 20:44; 30:13 **27:3** [a] 2 Chr. 33:14; Neh. 3:26 **27:5** [a] 2 Chr. 26:8 **27:6** [a] 2 Chr. 26:5 **27:9** [a] 2 Kin. 15:38 [b] Is. 1:1; Hos. 1:1; Mic. 1:1 **28:1** [a] 2 Kin. 16:2–4 **28:2** [a] Ex. 34:17; Lev. 19:4 [b] Judg. 2:11 **28:3** [a] Josh. 15:8 [b] 2 Kin. 23:10 [c] [Lev. 18:21]; 2 Kin. 16:3; 2 Chr. 33:6 [d] [Lev. 18:24–30] **28:5** [a] [Is. 10:5] [b] 2 Kin. 16:5, 6; [2 Chr. 24:24]; Is. 7:1, 17 **28:6** [a] 2 Kin. 15:27 [b] [2 Chr. 29:8] **28:8** [a] Deut. 28:25, 41; 2 Chr. 11:4 **28:9** [a] 2 Chr. 25:15

that came to Samaria, and said to them: "Look,
[b]because the LORD God of your fathers was angry
with Judah, He has delivered them into your
hand; but you have killed them in a rage *that*
[c]reaches up to heaven. 10 And now you propose
to force the children of Judah and Jerusalem to
be your [a]male and female slaves; *but are* you not
also guilty before the LORD your God? 11 Now hear
me, therefore, and return the captives, whom you
have taken captive from your brethren, [a]for the
fierce wrath of the LORD *is* upon you."

12 Then some of the heads of the children of
Ephraim, Azariah the son of Johanan, Berechiah
the son of Meshillemoth, Jehizkiah the son of
Shallum, and Amasa the son of Hadlai, stood up
against those who came from the war, 13 and said
to them, "You shall not bring the captives here, for
we *already* have offended the LORD. You intend
to add to our sins and to our guilt; for our guilt
is great, and *there is* fierce wrath against Israel."
14 So the armed men left the captives and the spoil
before the leaders and all the assembly. 15 Then
the men [a]who were designated by name rose up
and took the captives, and from the spoil they
clothed all who were naked among them, dressed
them and gave them sandals, [b]gave them food
and drink, and anointed them; and they let all
the feeble ones ride on donkeys. So they brought
them to their brethren at Jericho, [c]the city of palm
trees. Then they returned to Samaria.

### *ASSYRIA REFUSES TO HELP JUDAH*
*(2 Kin. 16:7–9)*

16 [a]At the same time King Ahaz sent to the
kings[1] of Assyria to help him. 17 For again the
[a]Edomites had come, attacked Judah, and carried
away captives. 18 [a]The Philistines also had invaded
the cities of the lowland and of the South of Judah,
and had taken Beth Shemesh, Aijalon, Gederoth,
Sochoh with its villages, Timnah with its villages,
and Gimzo with its villages; and they dwelt there.
19 For the LORD brought Judah low because of Ahaz
king of [a]Israel, for he had [b]encouraged moral de-
cline in Judah and had been continually unfaithful
to the LORD. 20 Also [a]Tiglath-Pileser[1] king of Assyria
came to him and distressed him, and did not assist
him. 21 For Ahaz took part *of the treasures* from the
house of the LORD, from the house of the king,
and from the leaders, and he gave *it* to the king
of Assyria; but he did not help him.

### *APOSTASY AND DEATH OF AHAZ*
*(2 Kin. 16:12–20)*

22 Now in the time of his distress King Ahaz
became increasingly unfaithful to the LORD.
This *is that* King Ahaz. 23 For [a]he sacrificed to
the gods of Damascus which had defeated him,
saying, "Because the gods of the kings of Syria
help them, I will sacrifice to them [b]that they may
help me." But they were the ruin of him and of
all Israel. 24 So Ahaz gathered the articles of the
house of God, cut in pieces the articles of the
house of God, [a]shut up the doors of the house of
the LORD, and made for himself altars in every
corner of Jerusalem. 25 And in every single city
of Judah he made high places to burn incense
to other gods, and provoked to anger the LORD
God of his fathers.

26 [a]Now the rest of his acts and all his ways,
from first to last, indeed they *are* written in the
book of the kings of Judah and Israel. 27 So Ahaz
rested with his fathers, and they buried him in
the city, in Jerusalem; but they [a]did not bring
him into the tombs of the kings of Israel. Then
Hezekiah his son reigned in his place.

### *HEZEKIAH REIGNS IN JUDAH*
*(2 Kin. 18:1–3)*

29 Hezekiah [a]became king *when he was*
twenty-five years old, and he reigned
twenty-nine years in Jerusalem. His mother's
name *was* Abijah[1] the daughter of Zechariah.
2 And he did *what was* right in the sight of the
LORD, according to all that his father David
had done.

### *HEZEKIAH CLEANSES THE TEMPLE*

3 In the first year of his reign, in the first
month, he [a]opened the doors of the house of the
LORD and repaired them. 4 Then he brought in
the priests and the Levites, and gathered them
in the East Square, 5 and said to them: "Hear
me, Levites! Now sanctify yourselves, [a]sanctify
the house of the LORD God of your fathers, and
carry out the rubbish from the holy *place*. 6 For
our fathers have trespassed and done evil in the
eyes of the LORD our God; they have forsaken
Him, have [a]turned their faces away from the
dwelling place of the LORD, and turned *their*
backs *on Him*. 7 [a]They have also shut up the doors
of the vestibule, put out the lamps, and have not
burned incense or offered burnt offerings in the
holy *place* to the God of Israel. 8 Therefore the
[a]wrath of the LORD fell upon Judah and Jeru-
salem, and He has [b]given them up to trouble,
to desolation, and to [c]jeering, as you see with
your [d]eyes. 9 For indeed, because of this [a]our
fathers have fallen by the sword; and our sons,
our daughters, and our wives *are* in captivity.

10 "Now *it is* in my heart to make [a]a covenant
with the LORD God of Israel, that His fierce wrath
may turn away from us. 11 My sons, do not be

**28:9** [b] Ps. 69:26; [Is. 10:5; 47:6]; Ezek. 25:12, 15; 26:2; Obad. 10; [Zech. 1:15] [c] Ezra 9:6; Rev. 18:5 **28:10** [a] [Lev. 25:39, 42, 43, 46] **28:11** [a] Ps. 78:49; James 2:13 **28:15** [a] 2 Chr. 28:12 [b] [Prov. 25:21, 22; Luke 6:27; Rom. 12:20] [c] Deut. 34:3; Judg. 1:16 **28:16** [a] 2 Kin. 16:7 [1] Septuagint, Syriac, and Vulgate read *king* (compare verse 20). **28:17** [a] 2 Chr. 21:10; Obad. 10–14 **28:18** [a] 2 Chr. 21:16, 17; Ezek. 16:27, 57 **28:19** [a] 2 Kin. 16:2; 2 Chr. 21:2 [b] Ex. 32:25 **28:20** [a] 2 Kin. 15:29; 16:7–9; 1 Chr. 5:26 [1] Hebrew *Tilgath-Pilneser* **28:23** [a] 2 Chr. 25:14 [b] Jer. 44:17, 18 **28:24** [a] 2 Chr. 29:3, 7 **28:26** [a] 2 Kin. 16:19, 20 **28:27** [a] 2 Chr. 21:20; 24:25 **29:1** [a] 2 Kin. 18:1 [1] Spelled *Abi* in 2 Kings 18:2 **29:3** [a] 2 Chr. 28:24; 29:7 **29:5** [a] 1 Chr. 15:12; 2 Chr. 29:15, 34; 35:6 **29:6** [a] [Is. 1:4]; Jer. 2:27; Ezek. 8:16 **29:7** [a] 2 Chr. 28:24 **29:8** [a] 2 Chr. 24:18 [b] 2 Chr. 28:5 [c] 1 Kin. 9:8; Jer. 18:16; 19:8; 25:9, 18; 29:18 [d] Deut. 28:32 **29:9** [a] Deut. 28:25; 2 Chr. 28:5–8, 17 **29:10** [a] 2 Chr. 15:12; 23:16

negligent now, for the LORD has [a]chosen you
to stand before Him, to serve Him, and that
you should minister to Him and burn incense."
12 Then these Levites arose: [a]Mahath the
son of Amasai and Joel the son of Azariah, of
the sons of the [b]Kohathites; of the sons of Me-
rari, Kish the son of Abdi and Azariah the son
of Jehallelel; of the Gershonites, Joah the son
of Zimmah and Eden the son of Joah; 13 of the
sons of Elizaphan, Shimri and Jeiel; of the sons
of Asaph, Zechariah and Mattaniah; 14 of the sons
of Heman, Jehiel and Shimei; and of the sons
of Jeduthun, Shemaiah and Uzziel.
15 And they gathered their brethren, [a]sanc-
tified themselves, and went according to the
commandment of the king, at the words of the
LORD, [b]to cleanse the house of the LORD. 16 Then
the priests went into the inner part of the house
of the LORD to cleanse *it,* and brought out all the
debris that they found in the temple of the LORD to
the court of the house of the LORD. And the Levites
took *it* out and carried *it* to the Brook [a]Kidron.
17 Now they began to sanctify on the first
*day* of the first month, and on the eighth day
of the month they came to the vestibule of the
LORD. So they sanctified the house of the LORD
in eight days, and on the sixteenth day of the
first month they finished.
18 Then they went in to King Hezekiah and
said, "We have cleansed all the house of the
LORD, the altar of burnt offerings with all its
articles, and the table of the showbread with
all its articles. 19 Moreover all the articles which
King Ahaz in his reign had [a]cast aside in his
transgression we have prepared and sanctified;
and there they *are,* before the altar of the LORD."

### *HEZEKIAH RESTORES TEMPLE WORSHIP*

20 Then King Hezekiah rose early, gathered
the rulers of the city, and went up to the house
of the LORD. 21 And they brought seven bulls,
seven rams, seven lambs, and seven male goats
for a [a]sin offering for the kingdom, for the sanc-
tuary, and for Judah. Then he commanded the
priests, the sons of Aaron, to offer *them* on the
altar of the LORD. 22 So they killed the bulls, and
the priests received the blood and [a]sprinkled *it*
on the altar. Likewise they killed the rams and
sprinkled the blood on the altar. They also killed
the lambs and sprinkled the blood on the altar.
23 Then they brought out the male goats *for* the
sin offering before the king and the assembly,
and they laid their [a]hands on them. 24 And the
priests killed them; and they presented their
blood on the altar as a sin offering [a]to make an
atonement for all Israel, for the king command-
ed *that* the burnt offering and the sin offering
*be made* for all Israel.

**29:23–24** Each part of the sacrifice ritual had an important meaning. Touching the sacrificial animal symbolized that the sins of the priest and the people were being transferred to the animal. The animal carrying the people's sin was then either killed or taken away. Splattering the **blood on the altar** represented the forgiveness of sins.

25 [a]And he stationed the Levites in the house
of the LORD with cymbals, with stringed in-
struments, and with harps, [b]according to the
commandment of David, of [c]Gad the king's
seer, and of Nathan the prophet; [d]for thus *was*
the commandment of the LORD by His proph-
ets. 26 The Levites stood with the instruments
[a]of David, and the priests with [b]the trumpets.
27 Then Hezekiah commanded *them* to offer
the burnt offering on the altar. And when the
burnt offering began, [a]the song of the LORD
*also* began, with the trumpets and with the in-
struments of David king of Israel. 28 So all the
assembly worshiped, the singers sang, and the
trumpeters sounded; all *this continued* until the
burnt offering was finished. 29 And when they
had finished offering, [a]the king and all who
were present with him bowed and worshiped.
30 Moreover King Hezekiah and the leaders com-
manded the Levites to sing praise to the LORD
with the words of David and of Asaph the seer.
So they sang praises with gladness, and they
bowed their heads and worshiped.
31 Then Hezekiah answered and said, "Now
*that* you have consecrated yourselves to the
LORD, come near, and bring sacrifices and [a]thank
offerings into the house of the LORD." So the
assembly brought in sacrifices and thank of-
ferings, and as many as were of a [b]willing heart
*brought* burnt offerings. 32 And the number of
the burnt offerings which the assembly brought
was seventy bulls, one hundred rams, *and* two
hundred lambs; all these *were* for a burnt of-
fering to the LORD. 33 The consecrated things
*were* six hundred bulls and three thousand
sheep. 34 But the priests were too few, so that they
could not skin all the burnt offerings; therefore
[a]their brethren the Levites helped them until
the work was ended and until the *other* priests
had sanctified themselves, [b]for the Levites were
[c]more diligent in [d]sanctifying themselves than
the priests. 35 Also the burnt offerings *were* in
abundance, with [a]the fat of the peace offerings
and *with* [b]the drink offerings for *every* burnt
offering.

**29:11** [a] Num. 3:6; 8:14; 18:2, 6; 2 Chr. 30:16, 17 **29:12** [a] 2 Chr. 31:13 [b] Num. 3:19, 20 **29:15** [a] 2 Chr. 29:5 [b] 1 Chr. 23:28 **29:16** [a] 2 Chr. 15:16; 30:14 **29:19** [a] 2 Chr. 28:24 **29:21** [a] Lev. 4:3–14 **29:22** [a] Lev. 8:14, 15, 19, 24; Heb. 9:21 **29:23** [a] Lev. 4:15, 24; 8:14 **29:24** [a] Lev. 14:20 **29:25** [a] 1 Chr. 16:4; 25:6 [b] 1 Chr. 23:5; 25:1; 2 Chr. 8:14 [c] 2 Sam. 24:11 [d] 2 Chr. 30:12 **29:26** [a] 1 Chr. 23:5; Amos 6:5 [b] Num. 10:8, 10; 1 Chr. 15:24; 16:6; 2 Chr. 5:12 **29:27** [a] 2 Chr. 23:18 **29:29** [a] 2 Chr. 20:18 **29:31** [a] Lev. 7:12 [b] Ex. 35:5, 22 **29:34** [a] 2 Chr. 35:11 [b] 2 Chr. 30:3 [c] Ps. 7:10 [d] 2 Chr. 29:5 **29:35** [a] Lev. 3:16 [b] Num. 15:5–10

So the service of the house of the LORD was set in order. 36 Then Hezekiah and all the people rejoiced that God had prepared the people, since the events took place so suddenly.

### *HEZEKIAH KEEPS THE PASSOVER*

**30** And Hezekiah sent to all Israel and Judah, and also wrote letters to Ephraim and Manasseh, that they should come to the house of the LORD at Jerusalem, to keep the Passover to the LORD God of Israel. 2 For the king and his leaders and all the assembly in Jerusalem had agreed to keep the Passover in the second [a]month. 3 For they could not keep it [a]at the regular time,[1] [b]because a sufficient number of priests had not consecrated themselves, nor had the people gathered together at Jerusalem. 4 And the matter pleased the king and all the assembly. 5 So they resolved to make a proclamation throughout all Israel, from Beersheba to Dan, that they should come to keep the Passover to the LORD God of Israel at Jerusalem, since they had not done *it* for a long *time* in the *prescribed* manner.

6 Then the [a]runners went throughout all Israel and Judah with the letters from the king and his leaders, and spoke according to the command of the king: "Children of Israel, [b]return to the LORD God of Abraham, Isaac, and Israel; then He will return to the remnant of you who have escaped from the hand of [c]the kings of [d]Assyria. 7 And do not be [a]like your fathers and your brethren, who trespassed against the LORD God of their fathers, so that He [b]gave them up to [c]desolation, as you see. 8 Now do not be [a]stiff-necked, as your fathers *were, but* yield yourselves to the LORD; and enter His sanctuary, which He has sanctified forever, and serve the LORD your God, [b]that the fierceness of His wrath may turn away from you. 9 For if you return to the LORD, your brethren and your children *will be treated* with [a]compassion by those who lead them captive, so that they may come back to this land; for the LORD your God *is* [b]gracious and merciful, and will not turn *His* face from you if you [c]return to Him."

> **30:6** The Assyrians conquered Samaria, the capital of the northern kingdom of Israel, in 722 BC. They destroyed the city and hauled the people away as captives.

10 So the runners passed from city to city through the country of Ephraim and Manasseh, as far as Zebulun; but [a]they laughed at them and mocked them. 11 Nevertheless [a]some from Asher, Manasseh, and Zebulun humbled themselves and came to Jerusalem. 12 Also [a]the hand of God was on Judah to give them singleness of heart to obey the command of the king and the leaders, [b]at the word of the LORD.

13 Now many people, a very great assembly, gathered at Jerusalem to keep the Feast of [a]Unleavened Bread in the second month. 14 They arose and took away the [a]altars that *were* in Jerusalem, and they took away all the incense altars and cast *them* into the Brook [b]Kidron. 15 Then they slaughtered the Passover *lambs* on the fourteenth *day* of the second month. The priests and the Levites were [a]ashamed, and sanctified themselves, and brought the burnt offerings to the house of the LORD. 16 They stood in their [a]place according to their custom, according to the Law of Moses the man of God; the priests sprinkled the blood *received* from the hand of the Levites. 17 For *there were* many in the assembly who had not sanctified themselves; [a]therefore the Levites had charge of the slaughter of the Passover *lambs* for everyone *who was* not clean, to sanctify *them* to the LORD. 18 For a multitude of the people, [a]many from Ephraim, Manasseh, Issachar, and Zebulun, had not cleansed themselves, [b]yet they ate the Passover contrary to what was written. But Hezekiah prayed for them, saying, "May the good LORD provide atonement for everyone 19 *who* [a]prepares his heart to seek God, the LORD God of his fathers, though *he is* not *cleansed* according to the purification of the sanctuary." 20 And the LORD listened to Hezekiah and healed the people.

> **SEEING JESUS IN THE SCRIPTURE**
>
> **30:15** The Passover lamb looked back to Egypt when God passed over the Israelites without killing their firstborn sons. It also looked ahead to Jesus, the ultimate Passover Lamb whose sacrifice took away the sin of the world (see John 1:29).

21 So the children of Israel who were present at Jerusalem kept [a]the Feast of Unleavened Bread seven days with great gladness; and the Levites and the priests praised the LORD day by day, *singing* to the LORD, accompanied by loud instruments. 22 And Hezekiah gave encouragement to all the Levites [a]who taught the good knowledge of the LORD; and they ate throughout the feast seven days, offering peace offerings and [b]making confession to the LORD God of their fathers.

**30:2** [a] Num. 9:10, 11; 2 Chr. 30:13, 15 **30:3** [a] Ex. 12:6, 18 [b] 2 Chr. 29:17, 34 [1] That is, the first month (compare Leviticus 23:5); literally *at that time* **30:6** [a] Esth. 8:14; Job 9:25; Jer. 51:31 [b] [Jer. 4:1; Joel 2:13] [c] 2 Kin. 15:19, 29 [d] 2 Chr. 28:20 **30:7** [a] Ezek. 20:18 [b] Is. 1:9 [c] 2 Chr. 29:8 **30:8** [a] Ex. 32:9; Deut. 10:16; Acts 7:51 [b] 2 Chr. 29:10 **30:9** [a] Ps. 106:46 [b] [Ex. 34:6; Mic. 7:18] [c] [Is. 55:7] **30:10** [a] 2 Chr. 36:16 **30:11** [a] 2 Chr. 11:16; 30:18, 21 **30:12** [a] [2 Cor. 3:5; Phil. 2:13; Heb. 13:20, 21] [b] 2 Chr. 29:25 **30:13** [a] Lev. 23:6; Num. 9:11 **30:14** [a] 2 Chr. 28:24 [b] 2 Chr. 29:16 **30:15** [a] 2 Chr. 29:34 **30:16** [a] 2 Chr. 35:10, 15 **30:17** [a] 2 Chr. 29:34 **30:18** [a] 2 Chr. 30:1, 11, 25 [b] Ex. 12:43–49; [Num. 9:10] **30:19** [a] 2 Chr. 19:3 **30:21** [a] Ex. 12:15; 13:6; 1 Kin. 8:65 **30:22** [a] [Deut. 33:10]; 2 Chr. 17:9; 35:3 [b] Ezra 10:11

23 Then the whole assembly agreed to keep
*the feast* [a]another seven days, and they kept it
*another* seven days with gladness. 24 For Hezekiah
king of Judah [a]gave to the assembly a thousand
bulls and seven thousand sheep, and the leaders
gave to the assembly a thousand bulls and ten
thousand sheep; and a great number of priests
[b]sanctified themselves. 25 The whole assembly
of Judah rejoiced, also the priests and Levites,
all the assembly that came from Israel, the so-
journers [a]who came from the land of Israel, and
those who dwelt in Judah. 26 So there was great
joy in Jerusalem, for since the time of [a]Solomon
the son of David, king of Israel, *there had* been
nothing like this in Jerusalem. 27 Then the priests,
the Levites, arose and [a]blessed the people, and
their voice was heard; and their prayer came *up*
to [b]His holy dwelling place, to heaven.

### *THE REFORMS OF HEZEKIAH*

*(2 Kin. 18:4)*

**31** Now when all this was finished, all Israel
who were present went out to the cities
of Judah and [a]broke the *sacred* pillars in pieces,
cut down the wooden images, and threw down
the high places and the altars—from all Judah,
Benjamin, Ephraim, and Manasseh—until they
had utterly destroyed them all. Then all the
children of Israel returned to their own cities,
every man to his possession.

2 And Hezekiah appointed [a]the divisions of
the priests and the Levites according to their
divisions, each man according to his service,
the priests and Levites [b]for burnt offerings and
peace offerings, to serve, to give thanks, and to
praise in the gates of the camp[1] of the LORD. 3 The
king also *appointed* a portion of his [a]possessions
for the burnt offerings: for the morning and
evening burnt offerings, the burnt offerings for
the Sabbaths and the New Moons and the set
feasts, as *it is* written in the [b]Law of the LORD.

4 Moreover he commanded the people who
dwelt in Jerusalem to contribute [a]support for the
priests and the Levites, that they might devote
themselves to [b]the Law of the LORD.

5 As soon as the commandment was circulat-
ed, the children of Israel brought in abundance
[a]the firstfruits of grain and wine, oil and honey, and
of all the produce of the field; and they brought in
abundantly the [b]tithe of everything. 6 And the chil-
dren of Israel and Judah, who dwelt in the cities of
Judah, brought the tithe of oxen and sheep; also
the [a]tithe of holy things which were consecrated
to the LORD their God they laid in heaps.

7 In the third month they began laying them
in heaps, and they finished in the seventh month.
8 And when Hezekiah and the leaders came and
saw the heaps, they blessed the LORD and His
people Israel. 9 Then Hezekiah questioned the
priests and the Levites concerning the heaps.
10 And Azariah the chief priest, from the [a]house of
Zadok, answered him and said, [b]"Since *the people*
began to bring the offerings into the house of
the LORD, we have had enough to eat and have
plenty left, for the LORD has blessed His people;
and what is left *is* this great [c]abundance."

11 Now Hezekiah commanded *them* to pre-
pare [a]rooms in the house of the LORD, and they
prepared them. 12 Then they faithfully brought in
the offerings, the tithes, and the dedicated things;
[a]Cononiah the Levite had charge of them, and
Shimei his brother *was* the next. 13 Jehiel, Azaziah,
Nahath, Asahel, Jerimoth, Jozabad, Eliel, Ismachi-
ah, Mahath, and Benaiah *were* overseers under the
hand of Cononiah and Shimei his brother, at the
commandment of Hezekiah the king and Azariah
the [a]ruler of the house of God. 14 Kore the son of
Imnah the Levite, the keeper of the East Gate, *was*
over the [a]freewill offerings to God, to distribute the
offerings of the LORD and the most holy things.
15 And under him *were* [a]Eden, Miniamin, Jeshua,
Shemaiah, Amariah, and Shecaniah, *his* faithful
assistants in [b]the cities of the priests, to distribute
[c]allotments to their brethren by divisions, to the
great as well as the small.

16 Besides those males from three years old and
up who were written in the genealogy, they distrib-
uted to everyone who entered the house of the
LORD his daily portion for the work of his service,
by his division, 17 and to the priests who were written
in the genealogy according to their father's house,
and to the Levites [a]from twenty years old and up
according to their work, by their divisions, 18 and to
all who were written in the genealogy—their little
ones and their wives, their sons and daughters, the
whole company of them—for in their faithfulness
they sanctified themselves in holiness.

19 Also for the sons of Aaron the priests, *who
were* in [a]the fields of the common-lands of their

> **31:5 *Tithe*** comes from a Hebrew word meaning "ten." In Genesis 14:20, Abraham gave the priest Melchizedek a tenth of his wealth. This set a pattern throughout the Old Testament for what was considered a proper portion of one's wealth to give to God. According to the law, Israelites were to set aside one tenth of their yearly produce as a tithe to support the ministry of the priests and Levites.

30:23 [a]1 Kin. 8:65; 2 Chr. 35:17, 18 30:24 [a]2 Chr. 35:7, 8 [b]2 Chr. 29:34 30:25 [a]2 Chr. 30:11, 18 30:26 [a]2 Chr. 7:8–10 30:27 [a]Num. 6:23 [b]Deut. 26:15; Ps. 68:5 31:1 [a]2 Kin. 18:4 31:2 [a]1 Chr. 23:6; 24:1 [b]1 Chr. 23:30, 31 [1]That is, the temple 31:3 [a]2 Chr. 35:7 [b]Num. 28:1—29:40 31:4 [a]Num. 18:8; 2 Kin. 12:16; Neh. 13:10; Ezek. 44:29 [b]Mal. 2:7 31:5 [a]Ex. 22:29; Neh. 13:12 [b][Lev. 27:30]; Deut. 14:28; 26:12, 13 31:6 [a][Lev. 27:30]; Deut. 14:28 31:10 [a]1 Chr. 6:8, 9 [b][Mal. 3:10] [c]Ex. 36:5 31:11 [a]1 Kin. 6:5–8 31:12 [a]2 Chr. 35:9; Neh. 13:13 31:13 [a]1 Chr. 9:11; Jer. 20:1 31:14 [a]Deut. 23:23; 2 Chr. 35:8 31:15 [a]2 Chr. 29:12 [b]Josh. 21:1–3, 9 [c]1 Chr. 9:26 31:17 [a]1 Chr. 23:24, 27 31:19 [a]Lev. 25:34; Num. 35:1–4

cities, in every single city, *there were* men who
were [b]designated by name to distribute portions
to all the males among the priests and to all who
were listed by genealogies among the Levites.
20 Thus Hezekiah did throughout all Judah,
and he [a]did what *was* good and right and true
before the LORD his God. 21 And in every work
that he began in the service of the house of God,
in the law and in the commandment, to seek his
God, he did *it* with all his heart. So he [a]prospered.

> **SEEING JESUS IN THE SCRIPTURE**
>
> **31:20** Hezekiah was one of Judah's few good kings. He did all the Lord called him to do and he redirected the people's worship people back to God. Hezekiah pictures Jesus who perfectly obeyed the Father to save us from the penalty of sin (see John 6:38).

### *SENNACHERIB BOASTS AGAINST THE LORD*

*(2 Kin. 18:13—19:34; Is. 36:1–22)*

**32** After [a]these deeds of faithfulness, Sen-
nacherib king of Assyria came and en-
tered Judah; he encamped against the fortified
cities, thinking to win them over to himself. 2 And
when Hezekiah saw that Sennacherib had come,
and that his purpose was to make war against
Jerusalem, 3 he consulted with his leaders and
commanders[1] to stop the water from the springs
which *were* outside the city; and they helped
him. 4 Thus many people gathered together who
stopped all the [a]springs and the brook that ran
through the land, saying, "Why should the kings[1]
of Assyria come and find much water?" 5 And [a]he
strengthened himself, [b]built up all the wall that
was broken, raised *it* up to the towers, and *built* an-
other wall outside; also he repaired the [c]Millo[1] *in*
the City of David, and made weapons and shields
in abundance. 6 Then he set military captains over
the people, gathered them together to him in
the open square of the city gate, and [a]gave them
encouragement, saying, 7 [a]"Be strong and coura-
geous; [b]do not be afraid nor dismayed before the
king of Assyria, nor before all the multitude that
*is* with him; for [c]*there are* more with us than with
him. 8 With him *is* an [a]arm of flesh; but [b]with us
*is* the LORD our God, to help us and to fight our
battles." And the people were strengthened by
the words of Hezekiah king of Judah.
9 [a]After this Sennacherib king of Assyria
sent his servants to Jerusalem (but he and all
the forces with him *laid siege* against Lachish),
to Hezekiah king of Judah, and to all Judah who
*were* in Jerusalem, saying, 10 [a]"Thus says Sen-
nacherib king of Assyria: 'In what do you trust,
that you remain under siege in Jerusalem? 11 Does
not Hezekiah persuade you to give yourselves
over to die by famine and by thirst, saying, [a]"The
LORD our God will deliver us from the hand of
the king of Assyria"? 12 [a]Has not the same Heze-
kiah taken away His high places and His altars,
and commanded Judah and Jerusalem, saying,
"You shall worship before one altar and burn
incense on [b]it"? 13 Do you not know what I and
my fathers have done to all the peoples of *other*
lands? [a]Were the gods of the nations of those
lands in any way able to deliver their lands out
of my hand? 14 Who *was there* among all the
gods of those nations that my fathers utterly
destroyed that could deliver his people from
my hand, that your God should be able to deliver
you from my [a]hand? 15 Now therefore, [a]do not let
Hezekiah deceive you or persuade you like this,
and do not believe him; for no god of any nation
or kingdom was able to deliver his people from
my hand or the hand of my fathers. How much
less will your God deliver you from my hand?' "
16 Furthermore, his servants spoke against
the LORD God and against His servant Hezekiah.
17 He also wrote letters to revile the LORD
God of Israel, and to speak against Him, saying,
[a]"As the gods of the nations of *other* lands have
not delivered their people from my hand, so the
God of Hezekiah will not deliver His people from
my [b]hand." 18 [a]Then they called out with a loud
voice in Hebrew[1] to the people of Jerusalem who
*were* on the wall, to frighten them and trouble
them, that they might take the city. 19 And they
spoke against the God of Jerusalem, as against
the gods of the people of the earth—[a]the work
of men's hands.

### *SENNACHERIB'S DEFEAT AND DEATH*

*(2 Kin. 19:35–37)*

20 [a]Now because of this King Hezekiah and
[b]the prophet Isaiah, the son of Amoz, prayed and
cried out to heaven. 21 [a]Then the LORD sent an
angel who cut down every mighty man of valor,
leader, and captain in the camp of the king of
Assyria. So he returned [b]shamefaced to his own
land. And when he had gone into the temple of
his god, some of his own offspring struck him
down with the sword there.
22 Thus the LORD saved Hezekiah and the
inhabitants of Jerusalem from the hand of
Sennacherib the king of Assyria, and from the
hand of all *others,* and guided them[1] on every

**31:19** [b] 2 Chr. 31:12–15 **31:20** [a] 2 Kin. 20:3; 22:2 **31:21** [a] 2 Chr. 26:5; 32:30; Ps. 1:3 **32:1** [a] 2 Kin. 18:13—19:37; Is. 36:1—37:38 **32:3** [1] Literally *mighty men* **32:4** [a] 2 Kin. 20:20 [1] Following Masoretic Text and Vulgate; Arabic, Septuagint, and Syriac read *king.* **32:5** [a] Is. 22:9, 10 [b] 2 Kin. 25:4; 2 Chr. 25:23 [c] 2 Sam. 5:9; 1 Kin. 9:15, 24; 11:27; 2 Kin. 12:20; 1 Chr. 11:8 [1] Literally *The Landfill* **32:6** [a] 2 Chr. 30:22; Is. 40:2 **32:7** [a] [Deut. 31:6] [b] 2 Chr. 20:15 [c] 2 Kin. 6:16; [Rom. 8:31] **32:8** [a] [Jer. 17:5; 1 John 4:4] [b] Ex. 14:13; [1 Sam. 17:45–47]; 2 Chr. 13:12; 20:17; [Rom. 8:31] **32:9** [a] 2 Kin. 18:17 **32:10** [a] 2 Kin. 18:19 **32:11** [a] 2 Kin. 18:30 **32:12** [a] 2 Kin. 18:22 [b] 2 Chr. 31:1, 2 **32:13** [a] 2 Kin. 18:33–35 **32:14** [a] [Is. 10:5–12] **32:15** [a] 2 Kin. 18:29 **32:17** [a] 2 Kin. 19:9; [1 Cor. 8:5, 6] [b] 2 Kin. 19:12 **32:18** [a] 2 Kin. 18:28 [1] Literally *Judean* **32:19** [a] [Ps. 96:5; 115:4–8] **32:20** [a] 2 Kin. 19:15 [b] 2 Kin. 19:2 **32:21** [a] Zech. 14:3 [b] Ps. 44:7 **32:22** [1] Septuagint reads *gave them rest;* Vulgate reads *gave them treasures.*

side. 23 And many brought gifts to the LORD at Jerusalem, and [a]presents to Hezekiah king of Judah, so that he was [b]exalted in the sight of all nations thereafter.

### *HEZEKIAH HUMBLES HIMSELF*

*(2 Kin. 20:1–11; Is. 38:1–8)*

24 [a]In those days Hezekiah was sick and near death, and he prayed to the LORD; and He spoke to him and gave him a sign. 25 But Hezekiah [a]did not repay according to the favor *shown* him, for [b]his heart was lifted up; [c]therefore wrath was looming over him and over Judah and Jerusalem. 26 [a]Then Hezekiah humbled himself for the pride of his heart, he and the inhabitants of Jerusalem, so that the wrath of the LORD did not come upon them [b]in the days of Hezekiah.

### *HEZEKIAH'S WEALTH AND HONOR*

*(2 Kin. 20:12–21; Is. 39:1–8)*

27 Hezekiah had very great riches and honor. And he made himself treasuries for silver, for gold, for precious stones, for spices, for shields, and for all kinds of desirable items; 28 storehouses for the harvest of grain, wine, and oil; and stalls for all kinds of livestock, and folds for flocks.[1] 29 Moreover he provided cities for himself, and possessions of flocks and herds in abundance; for [a]God had given him very much property. 30 [a]This same Hezekiah also stopped the water outlet of Upper Gihon, and brought the water by tunnel[1] to the west side of the City of David. Hezekiah [b]prospered in all his works.

> **32:30** To build this **tunnel**, one crew dug from the Gihon Spring, outside the city walls as another crew dug from the Pool of Siloam, inside the city walls. This 1,750-foot-long tunnel was sixty feet below the ground in some places.

31 However, *regarding* the ambassadors of the princes of Babylon, whom they [a]sent to him to inquire about the wonder that was *done* in the land, God withdrew from him, in order to [b]test him, that He might know all *that was* in his heart.

### *DEATH OF HEZEKIAH*

32 Now the rest of the acts of Hezekiah, and his goodness, indeed they *are* written in [a]the vision of Isaiah the prophet, the son of Amoz, *and* in the [b]book of the kings of Judah and Israel. 33 [a]So Hezekiah rested with his fathers, and they buried him in the upper tombs of the sons of David; and all Judah and the inhabitants of Jerusalem [b]honored him at his death. Then Manasseh his son reigned in his place.

### *MANASSEH REIGNS IN JUDAH*

*(2 Kin. 21:1–9)*

**33** Manasseh [a]*was* twelve years old when he became king, and he reigned fifty-five years in Jerusalem. 2 But he did evil in the sight of the LORD, according to the [a]abominations of the nations whom the LORD had cast out before the children of Israel. 3 For he rebuilt the high places which Hezekiah his father had [a]broken down; he raised up altars for the Baals, and [b]made wooden images; and he worshiped [c]all the host of heaven[1] and served them. 4 He also built altars in the house of the LORD, of which the LORD had said, [a]"In Jerusalem shall My name be forever." 5 And he built altars for all the host of heaven [a]in the two courts of the house of the LORD. 6 [a]Also he caused his sons to pass through the fire in the Valley of the Son of Hinnom; he practiced [b]soothsaying, used witchcraft and sorcery, and [c]consulted mediums and spiritists. He did much evil in the sight of the LORD, to provoke Him to anger. 7 [a]He even set a carved image, the idol which he had made, in the house of God, of which God had said to David and to Solomon his son, [b]"In this house and in Jerusalem, which I have chosen out of all the tribes of Israel, I will put My name forever; 8 [a]and I will not again remove the foot of Israel from the land which I have appointed for your fathers—only if they are careful to do all that I have commanded them, according to the whole law and the statutes and the ordinances by the hand of Moses." 9 So Manasseh seduced Judah and the inhabitants of Jerusalem to do more evil than the nations whom the LORD had destroyed before the children of Israel.

> **33:6–7** Human sacrifice was detested by God. **Sorcery** and **witchcraft** had been banned since the Law of Moses was handed down. Putting an **idol** in the temple was an intentional insult to the Lord.

### *MANASSEH RESTORED AFTER REPENTANCE*

10 And the LORD spoke to Manasseh and his people, but they would not listen. 11 [a]Therefore the LORD brought upon them the captains of the army of the king of Assyria, who took Manasseh with hooks,[1] [b]bound him with bronze *fetters,* and

**32:23** [a] 2 Sam. 8:10 [b] 2 Chr. 1:1 **32:24** [a] Is. 38:1–8 **32:25** [a] Ps. 116:12 [b] [Hab. 2:4] [c] 2 Chr. 24:18 **32:26** [a] Jer. 26:18, 19 [b] 2 Kin. 20:19 **32:28** [1] Following Septuagint and Vulgate; Arabic and Syriac omit *folds for flocks;* Masoretic Text reads *flocks for sheepfolds.* **32:29** [a] 1 Chr. 29:12 **32:30** [a] Is. 22:9–11 [b] 2 Chr. 31:21 [1] Literally *brought it straight* (compare 2 Kings 20:20) **32:31** [a] Is. 39:1 [b] [Deut. 8:2, 16] **32:32** [a] Is. 36—39 [b] 2 Kin. 18—20 **32:33** [a] 2 Kin. 20:21 [b] Prov. 10:7 **33:1** [a] 2 Kin. 21:1–9 **33:2** [a] 2 Chr. 28:3 **33:3** [a] 2 Kin. 18:4 [b] Deut. 16:21 [c] Deut. 17:3 [1] The gods of the Assyrians **33:4** [a] 2 Chr. 6:6; 7:16 **33:5** [a] 2 Chr. 4:9 **33:6** [a] [Lev. 18:21] [b] Deut. 18:11 [c] 2 Kin. 21:6 **33:7** [a] 2 Chr. 25:14 [b] Ps. 132:14 **33:8** [a] 2 Sam. 7:10 **33:11** [a] Deut. 28:36 [b] 2 Chr. 36:6; Job 36:8; Ps. 107:10, 11 [1] That is, nose hooks (compare 2 Kings 19:28)

carried him off to Babylon. 12 Now when he was in affliction, he implored the LORD his God, and [a]humbled himself greatly before the God of his fathers, 13 and prayed to Him; and He [a]received his entreaty, heard his supplication, and brought him back to Jerusalem into his kingdom. Then Manasseh [b]knew that the LORD *was* God.

14 After this he built a wall outside the City of David on the west side of [a]Gihon, in the valley, as far as the entrance of the Fish Gate; and *it* [b]enclosed Ophel, and he raised it to a very great height. Then he put military captains in all the fortified cities of Judah. 15 He took away [a]the foreign gods and the idol from the house of the LORD, and all the altars that he had built in the mount of the house of the LORD and in Jerusalem; and he cast *them* out of the city. 16 He also repaired the altar of the LORD, sacrificed peace offerings and [a]thank offerings on it, and commanded Judah to serve the LORD God of Israel. 17 [a]Nevertheless the people still sacrificed on the high places, *but* only to the LORD their God.

### DEATH OF MANASSEH
*(2 Kin. 21:17, 18)*

18 Now the rest of the acts of Manasseh, his prayer to his God, and the words of [a]the seers who spoke to him in the name of the LORD God of Israel, indeed they *are written* in the book[1] of the kings of Israel. 19 Also his prayer and *how God* received his entreaty, and all his sin and trespass, and the sites where he built high places and set up wooden images and carved images, before he was humbled, indeed they *are* written among the sayings of Hozai.[1] 20 [a]So Manasseh rested with his fathers, and they buried him in his own house. Then his son Amon reigned in his place.

> **33:19** Along with **the sayings of Hozai**, there are at least a dozen other books mentioned in Scripture that are not part of the Bible including the *Book of the Acts of Solomon* (1 Kin. 11:41), the *Book of Nathan the Prophet* (1 Chr. 29:29; 2 Chr. 9:29), the *Book of Gad the Seer* (1 Chr. 29:29), the *Visions of Iddo the Seer* (2 Chr. 9:29; 12:15), the *Prophecy of Abijah the Shilonite* (2 Chr. 9:29), the *Book of Shemaiah the Prophet* (2 Chr. 12:15), the *Acts of Uzziah* (2 Chr. 26:22), a third letter of Paul to the Corinthians (1 Cor. 5:9), a letter of Paul to the Laodiceans (Col. 4:16), another letter of John (3 John v. 9), and the *Book of Enoch* (Jude v. 14).

### AMON'S REIGN AND DEATH
*(2 Kin. 21:19–26)*

21 [a]Amon *was* twenty-two years old when he became king, and he reigned two years in Jerusalem. 22 But he did evil in the sight of the LORD, as his father Manasseh had done; for Amon sacrificed to all the carved images which his father Manasseh had made, and served them. 23 And he did not humble himself before the LORD, [a]as his father Manasseh had humbled himself; but Amon trespassed more and more.

24 [a]Then his servants conspired against him, and [b]killed him in his own house. 25 But the people of the land executed all those who had conspired against King Amon. Then the people of the land made his son Josiah king in his place.

### JOSIAH REIGNS IN JUDAH
*(2 Kin. 22:1, 2)*

**34** Josiah [a]*was* eight years old when he became king, and he reigned thirty-one years in Jerusalem. 2 And he did *what was* right in the sight of the LORD, and walked in the ways of his father David; *he* did *not* turn aside to the right hand or to the left.

3 For in the eighth year of his reign, while he was still [a]young, he began to [b]seek the God of his father David; and in the twelfth year he began [c]to purge Judah and Jerusalem [d]of the high places, the wooden images, the carved images, and the molded images. 4 [a]They broke down the altars of the Baals in his presence, and the incense altars which *were* above them he cut down; and the wooden images, the carved images, and the molded images he broke in pieces, and made dust of them [b]and scattered *it* on the graves of those who had sacrificed to them. 5 He also [a]burned the bones of the priests on their [b]altars, and cleansed Judah and Jerusalem. 6 And *so he did* in the cities of Manasseh, Ephraim, and Simeon, as far as Naphtali and all around, with axes.[1] 7 When he had broken down the altars and the wooden images, had [a]beaten the carved images into powder, and cut down all the incense altars throughout all the land of Israel, he returned to Jerusalem.

### HILKIAH FINDS THE BOOK OF THE LAW
*(2 Kin. 22:3–20)*

8 [a]In the eighteenth year of his reign, when he had purged the land and the temple,[1] he sent [b]Shaphan the son of Azaliah, Maaseiah the [c]governor of the city, and Joah the son of Joahaz the recorder, to repair the house of the LORD his God. 9 When they came to Hilkiah the high priest, they delivered [a]the money that was brought into the house of God, which the Levites who kept the doors had gathered from the hand of Manasseh

**33:12** [a] 2 Chr. 7:14; 32:26; [1 Pet. 5:6] **33:13** [a] 1 Chr. 5:20; Ezra 8:23 [b] 1 Kin. 20:13; Ps. 9:16; Dan. 4:25 **33:14** [a] 1 Kin. 1:33 [b] 2 Chr. 27:3 **33:15** [a] 2 Chr. 33:3, 5, 7 **33:16** [a] Lev. 7:12 **33:17** [a] 2 Chr. 32:12 **33:18** [a] 1 Sam. 9:9 [1] Literally *words* **33:19** [1] Septuagint reads *the seers.* **33:20** [a] 1 Kin. 1:21; 2 Kin. 21:18 **33:21** [a] 2 Kin. 21:19–24; 1 Chr. 3:14 **33:23** [a] 2 Chr. 33:12, 19 **33:24** [a] 2 Kin. 21:23, 24; 2 Chr. 24:25 [b] 2 Chr. 25:27 **34:1** [a] 2 Kin. 22:1, 2; Jer. 1:2; 3:6 **34:3** [a] Eccl. 12:1 [b] 2 Chr. 15:2; [Prov. 8:17] [c] 1 Kin. 13:2 [d] 2 Chr. 33:17–19, 22 **34:4** [a] Lev. 26:30; 2 Kin. 23:4 [b] 2 Kin. 23:6 **34:5** [a] 1 Kin. 13:2 [b] 2 Kin. 23:20 **34:6** [1] Literally *swords* **34:7** [a] Deut. 9:21 **34:8** [a] 2 Kin. 22:3–20 [b] 2 Kin. 25:22 [c] 2 Chr. 18:25 [1] Literally *house* **34:9** [a] 2 Kin. 12:4

and Ephraim, from all the [b]remnant of Israel,
from all Judah and Benjamin, and *which* they
had brought back to Jerusalem. 10 Then they
put *it* in the hand of the foremen who had the
oversight of the house of the LORD; and they
gave it to the workmen who worked in the house
of the LORD, to repair and restore the house.
11 They gave *it* to the craftsmen and builders to
buy hewn stone and timber for beams, and to
floor the houses which the kings of Judah had
destroyed. 12 And the men did the work faithfully.
Their overseers *were* Jahath and Obadiah the
Levites, of the sons of Merari, and Zechariah
and Meshullam, of the sons of the Kohathites,
to supervise. *Others of* the Levites, all of whom
were skillful with instruments of music, 13 *were*
[a]over the burden bearers and *were* overseers of
all who did work in any kind of service. [b]And
*some* of the Levites *were* scribes, officers, and
gatekeepers.

14 Now when they brought out the money
that was brought into the house of the LORD, Hil-
kiah the priest [a]found the Book of the Law of the
LORD *given* by Moses. 15 Then Hilkiah answered
and said to Shaphan the scribe, "I have found
the Book of the Law in the house of the LORD."
And Hilkiah gave the [a]book to Shaphan. 16 So
Shaphan carried the book to the king, bringing
the king word, saying, "All that was committed
to your servants they are doing. 17 And they have
gathered the money that was found in the house
of the LORD, and have delivered it into the hand
of the overseers and the workmen." 18 Then Sha-
phan the scribe told the king, saying, "Hilkiah
the priest has given me a book." And Shaphan
read it before the king.

> **34:15** The **book** Hilkiah found may have been Deuteronomy or it may have been the entire Pentateuch, the first five books of the Bible. The book may have been hidden when earlier kings tried to get Israel to worship idols.

19 Thus it happened, when the king heard
the words of the Law, that he tore his clothes.
20 Then the king commanded Hilkiah, [a]Ahikam
the son of Shaphan, Abdon[1] the son of Micah,
Shaphan the scribe, and Asaiah a servant of the
king, saying, 21 "Go, inquire of the LORD for me,
and for those who are left in Israel and Judah,
concerning the words of the book that is found;
for great *is* the wrath of the LORD that is poured
out on us, because our fathers have not [a]kept
the word of the LORD, to do according to all that
is written in this book."

22 So Hilkiah and those the king *had appoint-
ed* went to Huldah the prophetess, the wife of
Shallum the son of Tokhath,[1] the son of Hasrah,[2]
keeper of the wardrobe. (She dwelt in Jerusalem
in the Second Quarter.) And they spoke to her
to that *effect.*

23 Then she answered them, "Thus says the
LORD God of Israel, 'Tell the man who sent you to
Me, 24 "Thus says the LORD: 'Behold, I will [a]bring
calamity on this place and on its inhabitants, all
the curses that are written in the [b]book which
they have read before the king of Judah, 25 be-
cause they have forsaken Me and burned incense
to other gods, that they might provoke Me to
anger with all the works of their hands. There-
fore My wrath will be poured out on this place,
and not be quenched.' " ' 26 But as for the king
of Judah, who sent you to inquire of the LORD,
in this manner you shall speak to him, 'Thus
says the LORD God of Israel: "*Concerning* the
words which you have heard— 27 because your
heart was tender, and you humbled yourself
before God when you heard His words against
this place and against its inhabitants, and you
humbled yourself before Me, and you tore your
clothes and wept before Me, I also have heard
*you,*" says the [a]LORD. 28 "Surely I will gather
you to your fathers, and you shall be gathered
to your grave in peace; and your eyes shall not
see all the calamity which I will bring on this
place and its inhabitants." ' " So they brought
back word to the king.

### *JOSIAH RESTORES TRUE WORSHIP*
*(2 Kin. 23:1–20)*

29 [a]Then the king sent and gathered all the
elders of Judah and Jerusalem. 30 The king
went up to the house of the LORD, with all the
men of Judah and the inhabitants of Jerusa-
lem—the priests and the Levites, and all the
people, great and small. And he [a]read in their
hearing all the words of the Book of the Cov-
enant which had been found in the house of the
LORD. 31 Then the king [a]stood in [b]his place and
made a [c]covenant before the LORD, to follow
the LORD, and to keep His commandments
and His testimonies and His statutes with
all his heart and all his soul, to perform the
words of the covenant that were written in this
book. 32 And he made all who were present in
Jerusalem and Benjamin take a stand. So the
inhabitants of Jerusalem did according to
the covenant of God, the God of their fathers.
33 Thus Josiah removed all the [a]abominations
from all the country that *belonged* to the chil-
dren of Israel, and made all who were present
in Israel diligently serve the LORD their God.
[b]All his days they did not depart from following
the LORD God of their fathers.

**34:9** [b] 2 Chr. 30:6 **34:13** [a] 2 Chr. 8:10 [b] 1 Chr. 23:4, 5 **34:14** [a] 2 Kin. 22:8 **34:15** [a] Deut. 31:24, 26 **34:20** [a] Jer. 26:24 [1] *Achbor the son of Michaiah* in 2 Kings 22:12 **34:21** [a] 2 Kin. 17:15–19 **34:22** [1] Spelled *Tikvah* in 2 Kings 22:14 [2] Spelled *Harhas* in 2 Kings 22:14 **34:24** [a] 2 Chr. 36:14–20 [b] Deut. 28:15–68 **34:27** [a] 2 Kin. 22:19; 2 Chr. 12:7; 30:6; 33:12, 13 **34:29** [a] 2 Kin. 23:1–3 **34:30** [a] Neh. 8:1–3 **34:31** [a] 2 Chr. 6:13 [b] 2 Kin. 11:14; 23:3; 2 Chr. 30:16 [c] 2 Chr. 23:16; 29:10 **34:33** [a] 1 Kin. 11:5; 2 Chr. 33:2 [b] Jer. 3:10

### *JOSIAH KEEPS THE PASSOVER*

*(2 Kin. 23:21–23)*

**35** Now [a]Josiah kept a Passover to the LORD in Jerusalem, and they slaughtered the Passover *lambs* on the [b]fourteenth *day* of the first month. 2 And he set the priests in their [a]duties and [b]encouraged them for the service of the house of the LORD. 3 Then he said to the Levites [a]who taught all Israel, who were holy to the LORD: [b]"Put the holy ark [c]in the house which Solomon the son of David, king of Israel, built. [d]*It shall* no longer *be* a burden on *your* shoulders. Now serve the LORD your God and His people Israel. 4 Prepare *yourselves* [a]according to your fathers' houses, according to your divisions, following the [b]written instruction of David king of Israel and the [c]written instruction of Solomon his son. 5 And [a]stand in the holy *place* according to the divisions of the fathers' houses of your brethren the *lay* people, and *according to* the division of the father's house of the Levites. 6 So slaughter the Passover *offerings,* [a]consecrate yourselves, and prepare *them* for your brethren, that *they* may do according to the word of the LORD by the hand of Moses."

7 Then Josiah [a]gave the *lay* people lambs and young goats from the flock, all for Passover *offerings* for all who were present, to the number of thirty thousand, as well as three thousand cattle; these *were* from the king's [b]possessions. 8 And his [a]leaders gave willingly to the people, to the priests, and to the Levites. Hilkiah, Zechariah, and Jehiel, rulers of the house of God, gave to the priests for the Passover *offerings* two thousand six hundred *from the flock,* and three hundred cattle. 9 Also [a]Conaniah, his brothers Shemaiah and Nethanel, and Hashabiah and Jeiel and Jozabad, chief of the Levites, gave to the Levites for Passover *offerings* five thousand *from the flock* and five hundred cattle.

10 So the service was prepared, and the priests [a]stood in their places, and the [b]Levites in their divisions, according to the king's command. 11 And they slaughtered the Passover *offerings;* and the priests [a]sprinkled *the blood* with their hands, while the Levites [b]skinned *the animals.* 12 Then they removed the burnt offerings that *they* might give them to the divisions of the fathers' houses of the *lay* people, to offer to the LORD, as *it is* written [a]in the Book of Moses. And so *they did* with the cattle. 13 Also they [a]roasted the Passover *offerings* with fire according to the ordinance; but the *other* holy *offerings* they [b]boiled in pots, in caldrons, and in pans, and divided *them* quickly among all the *lay* people. 14 Then afterward they prepared portions for themselves and for the priests, because the priests, the sons of Aaron, *were busy* in offering burnt offerings and fat until night; therefore the Levites prepared portions for themselves and for the priests, the sons of Aaron. 15 And the singers, the sons of Asaph, *were* in their places, according to the [a]command of David, Asaph, Heman, and Jeduthun the king's seer. Also the gatekeepers [b]were at each gate; they did not have to leave their position, because their brethren the Levites prepared portions for them.

16 So all the service of the LORD was prepared the same day, to keep the Passover and to offer burnt offerings on the altar of the LORD, according to the command of King Josiah. 17 And the children of Israel who were present kept the Passover at that time, and the Feast of [a]Unleavened Bread for seven days. 18 [a]There had been no Passover kept in Israel like that since the days of Samuel the prophet; and none of the kings of Israel had kept such a Passover as Josiah kept, with the priests and the Levites, all Judah and Israel who were present, and the inhabitants of Jerusalem. 19 In the eighteenth year of the reign of Josiah this Passover was kept.

### *JOSIAH DIES IN BATTLE*

*(2 Kin. 23:28–30)*

20 [a]After all this, when Josiah had prepared the temple, Necho king of Egypt came up to fight against [b]Carchemish by the Euphrates; and Josiah went out against him. 21 But he sent messengers to him, saying, "What have I to do with you, king of Judah? *I have* not *come* against you this day, but against the house with which I have war; for God commanded me to make haste. Refrain *from meddling with* God, who *is* with me, lest He destroy you." 22 Nevertheless Josiah would not turn his face from him, but [a]disguised himself so that he might fight with him, and did not heed the words of Necho from the mouth of God. So he came to fight in the Valley of Megiddo.

23 And the archers shot King Josiah; and the king said to his servants, "Take me away, for I am severely wounded." 24 [a]His servants therefore took him out of that chariot and put him in the second chariot that he had, and they brought him to Jerusalem. So he died, and was buried in *one of* the tombs of his fathers. And [b]all Judah and Jerusalem mourned for Josiah.

25 Jeremiah also [a]lamented for [b]Josiah. And to this day [c]all the singing men and the singing women speak of Josiah in their lamentations. [d]They made it a custom in Israel; and indeed they *are* written in the Laments.

26 Now the rest of the acts of Josiah and his goodness, according to *what was* written in the Law of the LORD, 27 and his deeds from first to last, indeed they *are* written in the book of the kings of Israel and Judah.

**35:1** [a] 2 Kin. 23:21, 22 [b] Ex. 12:6; Num. 9:3; Ezra 6:19 **35:2** [a] 2 Chr. 23:18; Ezra 6:18 [b] 2 Chr. 29:5–15 **35:3** [a] Deut. 33:10; 2 Chr. 17:8, 9; Neh. 8:7 [b] 2 Chr. 34:14 [c] Ex. 40:21; 2 Chr. 5:7 [d] 1 Chr. 23:26 **35:4** [a] 1 Chr. 9:10–13 [b] 1 Chr. 23—26 [c] 2 Chr. 8:14 **35:5** [a] Ps. 134:1 **35:6** [a] 2 Chr. 29:5, 15 **35:7** [a] 2 Chr. 30:24 [b] 2 Chr. 31:3 **35:8** [a] Num. 7:2 **35:9** [a] 2 Chr. 31:12 **35:10** [a] Ezra 6:18; Heb. 9:6 [b] 2 Chr. 5:12; 7:6; 8:14, 15; 13:10; 29:25–34 **35:11** [a] Ex. 12:22; 2 Chr. 29:22 [b] 2 Chr. 29:34 **35:12** [a] Lev. 3:3; Ezra 6:18 **35:13** [a] Ex. 12:8, 9; Deut. 16:7 [b] 1 Sam. 2:13–15 **35:15** [a] 1 Chr. 25:1–6 [b] 1 Chr. 9:17, 18 **35:17** [a] Ex. 12:15; 13:6; 2 Chr. 30:21 **35:18** [a] 2 Kin. 23:22, 23 **35:20** [a] 2 Kin. 23:29 [b] Is. 10:9; Jer. 46:2 **35:22** [a] 1 Kin. 22:30; 2 Chr. 18:29 **35:24** [a] 2 Kin. 23:30 [b] 1 Kin. 14:18; Zech. 12:11 **35:25** [a] Lam. 4:20 [b] Jer. 22:10, 11 [c] Matt. 9:23 [d] Jer. 22:20

### *THE REIGN AND CAPTIVITY OF JEHOAHAZ*
*(2 Kin. 23:31–33)*

**36** Then [a]the people of the land took Jehoa-
haz the son of Josiah, and made him king
in his father's place in Jerusalem. 2 Jehoahaz[1]
*was* twenty-three years old when he became
king, and he reigned three months in Jerusa-
lem. 3 Now the king of Egypt deposed him at
Jerusalem; and he imposed on the land a tribute
of one hundred talents of silver and a talent of
gold. 4 Then the king of Egypt made *Jehoahaz's*[1]
brother Eliakim king over Judah and Jerusa-
lem, and changed his name to Jehoiakim. And
Necho took Jehoahaz[2] his brother and carried
him off to Egypt.

### *THE REIGN AND CAPTIVITY OF JEHOIAKIM*
*(2 Kin. 23:34—24:7)*

5 [a]Jehoiakim *was* twenty-five years old when
he became king, and he reigned eleven years in Je-
rusalem. And he did [b]evil in the sight of the LORD
his God. 6 [a]Nebuchadnezzar king of Babylon came
up against him, and bound him in bronze *fetters* to
[b]carry him off to Babylon. 7 [a]Nebuchadnezzar also
carried off *some* of the articles from the house of
the LORD to Babylon, and put them in his temple
at Babylon. 8 Now the rest of the acts of Jehoia-
kim, the abominations which he did, and what
was found against him, indeed they *are* written
in the book of the kings of Israel and Judah. Then
Jehoiachin his son reigned in his place.

### *THE REIGN AND CAPTIVITY OF JEHOIACHIN*
*(2 Kin. 24:8–17)*

9 [a]Jehoiachin *was* eight[1] years old when he
became king, and he reigned in Jerusalem three
months and ten days. And he did evil in the sight
of the LORD. 10 At the turn of the year [a]King Neb-
uchadnezzar summoned *him* and took him to
Babylon, [b]with the costly articles from the house
of the LORD, and made [c]Zedekiah, *Jehoiakim's*[1]
brother, king over Judah and Jerusalem.

### *ZEDEKIAH REIGNS IN JUDAH*
*(2 Kin. 24:18–20; Jer. 52:1–3)*

11 [a]Zedekiah *was* twenty-one years old when
he became king, and he reigned eleven years
in Jerusalem. 12 He did evil in the sight of the
LORD his God, *and* [a]did not humble himself
before Jeremiah the prophet, *who spoke* from

**36:1** [a] 2 Kin. 23:30–34 **36:2** [1] Masoretic Text reads *Joahaz.* **36:4** [1] Literally *his* [2] Masoretic Text reads *Joahaz.* **36:5** [a] 2 Kin. 23:36, 37; 1 Chr. 3:15 [b] [Jer. 22:13–19] **36:6** [a] 2 Kin. 24:1; Hab. 1:6 [b] [Deut. 29:22–29]; 2 Chr. 33:11; Jer. 36:30 **36:7** [a] 2 Kin. 24:13; Dan. 1:1, 2 **36:9** [a] 2 Kin. 24:8–17 [1] Some Hebrew manuscripts, Septuagint, Syriac, and 2 Kings 24:8 read *eighteen.* **36:10** [a] 2 Kin. 24:10–17 [b] Dan. 1:1, 2 [c] Jer. 37:1 [1] Literally *his* (compare 2 Kings 24:17) **36:11** [a] 2 Kin. 24:18–20; Jer. 52:1 **36:12** [a] Jer. 21:3–7; 44:10

2 CHRONICLES 36:11-21

STORY OF SCRIPTURE 32

## JUDAH'S FALL

### WHAT'S GOING ON?

The first fall of Jerusalem marked a pivotal moment in the history of God's people. This passage describes the reign of Zedekiah, the last king of Judah, his rebellion against Nebuchadnezzar, and the subsequent siege and destruction of Jerusalem by the Babylonians. The temple, God's dwelling place among His people, was reduced to ashes, and the people were taken into exile. While Judah survived longer than Israel because some of their kings had been good, in the end, they too followed their northern siblings into idolatry and experienced God's resulting judgment.

### WHAT DOES THIS MEAN FOR ME?

This story serves as a sobering reminder of the consequences of neglecting our relationship with God and ignoring His guidance. It challenges us to consider how we might be rebelling against God, whether through overt actions or subtle neglect. But remember, God's faithfulness is enduring even amid judgment. The exile was not the end, but a painful chapter leading to eventual restoration. No matter what bleak circumstances we fall into because of sin, God can restore us.

### DID YOU CATCH THE PATTERN?

Throughout the Bible, there's a recurring theme of rebellion, judgment, and restoration. God's people repeatedly turned away from Him and faced the consequences, but God always offered a path back to redemption. The fall of Jerusalem and exile serve as a stark example of this pattern. But it also points to the hope of restoration, as God promised to bring His people back from exile and renew His covenant with them. This promise was ultimately fulfilled in Jesus, who offers redemption and restoration to all who come to Him.

*For the next* Story of Scripture *reading and devotion, turn to Ezra 6:13–18 on page 465.*

the mouth of the LORD. 13 And he also [a]rebelled
against King Nebuchadnezzar, who had made
him swear *an oath* by God; but he [b]stiffened his
neck and hardened his heart against turning
to the LORD God of Israel. 14 Moreover all the
leaders of the priests and the people trans-
gressed more and more, *according* to all the
abominations of the nations, and defiled the
house of the LORD which He had consecrated
in Jerusalem.

### *THE FALL OF JERUSALEM*

*(2 Kin. 25:1–21; Jer. 52:4–30)*

15 [a]And the LORD God of their fathers sent
*warnings* to them by His messengers, rising
up early and sending *them,* because He had
compassion on His people and on His dwelling
place. 16 But [a]they mocked the messengers of
God, [b]despised His words, and [c]scoffed at His
prophets, until the [d]wrath of the LORD arose
against His people, till *there was* no remedy.
17 [a]Therefore He brought against them the
king of the Chaldeans, who [b]killed their young
men with the sword in the house of their sanc-
tuary, and had no compassion on young man
or virgin, on the aged or the weak; He gave *them*
all into his hand. 18 [a]And all the articles from the
house of God, great and small, the treasures
of the house of the LORD, and the treasures of
the king and of his leaders, all *these* he took to
Babylon. 19 [a]Then they burned the house of God,
broke down the wall of Jerusalem, burned all its
palaces with fire, and destroyed all its precious
possessions. 20 And [a]those who escaped from
the sword he carried away to Babylon, [b]where
they became servants to him and his sons until
the rule of the kingdom of Persia, 21 to fulfill the
word of the LORD by the mouth of [a]Jeremiah,
until the land [b]had enjoyed her Sabbaths. As
long as she lay desolate [c]she kept Sabbath, to
fulfill seventy years.

### *THE PROCLAMATION OF CYRUS*

*(Ezra 1:1–4)*

22 [a]Now in the first year of Cyrus king of Per-
sia, that the word of the LORD by the mouth of
[b]Jeremiah might be fulfilled, the LORD stirred
up the spirit of [c]Cyrus king of Persia, so that he
made a proclamation throughout all his king-
dom, and also *put it* in writing, saying,

23 [a]Thus says Cyrus king of Persia:
All the kingdoms of the earth the LORD
God of heaven has given me. And He has
commanded me to build Him a house
at Jerusalem which is in Judah. Who *is*
among you of all His people? May the LORD
his God *be* with him, and let him go up!

**36:13** [a] Jer. 52:3; Ezek. 17:15 [b] 2 Kin. 17:14; [2 Chr. 30:8] **36:15** [a] Jer. 7:13; 25:3, 4 **36:16** [a] 2 Chr. 30:10; Jer. 5:12, 13 [b] [Prov. 1:24–32] [c] Jer. 38:6; Matt. 23:34 [d] 2 Chr. 34:25; Ps. 79:5 **36:17** [a] Num. 33:56; Deut. 4:26; 28:49; 2 Kin. 25:1; Ezra 9:7; Is. 3:8 [b] Ps. 74:20 **36:18** [a] 2 Kin. 25:13–15; 2 Chr. 36:7, 10 **36:19** [a] 2 Kin. 25:9; Ps. 79:1, 7; Is. 1:7, 8; Jer. 52:13 **36:20** [a] 2 Kin. 25:11; Jer. 5:19; Mic. 4:10 [b] Jer. 17:4; 27:7 **36:21** [a] Jer. 25:9–12; 27:6–8; 29:10 [b] Lev. 26:34–43; Dan. 9:2 [c] Lev. 25:4, 5 **36:22** [a] Ezra 1:1–3 [b] Jer. 29:10 [c] Is. 44:28; 45:1 **36:23** [a] Ezra 1:2, 3

*The Book of*

# EZRA

**AUTHOR**
Ezra

**KEY VERSE**
Ezra 1:3

**READING TIME**
51 minutes

The Book of Ezra continues the Old Testament narrative of 2 Chronicles by showing how God fulfilled His word to return His people to the Land of Promise after seventy years of exile. Israel's "second exodus," this one out of Babylon, might be less impressive than the first from Egypt, with only a remnant choosing to leave Babylon, but it was no less important. Ezra relates the story of two returns from Babylon—the first led by Zerubbabel to rebuild the temple (Ezra 1–6), and the second under Ezra's leadership to rebuild the spiritual condition of the people (chs. 7–10). Sandwiched between these two returns was a gap of nearly six decades, during which Esther lived and interceded for her people as queen in Persia.

**Occasion:** The Book of Ezra records the history of the exiles' return to the land of their ancestors and the rebuilding of Jerusalem—namely, the temple.

**Main Point:** God is faithful to bring His people out of bondage and restore them in the land He had given.

**Big Ideas:** God keeps His promises. God will fix all that is broken. We are to be faithful in our work for the Lord, no matter what.

## OUTLINE:

I. The First Return Under Zerubbabel (chs. 1–2)
II. The Rebuilding of the Temple (chs. 3–6)
III. The Second Return Under Ezra (chs. 7–8)
IV. The Revival of the People (chs. 9–10)

**586 BC**
The Babylonians defeat Judah

**c. 575 BC**
Greeks use saws for cutting

**c. 560–477 BC**
Siddhartha Gautama, known as Buddha, lives in India and founds the Buddhist religion

**559–530 BC**
Cyrus reigns in Persia

**539 BC**
Cyrus conquers Babylon

**538 BC**
Jews begin returning to Judea

**536–515 BC**
The temple is rebuilt

**530–522 BC**
Cambyses of Persia builds a naval fleet with Ionians and Phoenicians

**521–486 BC**
Darius I reigns in Persia

**c. 520 BC**
Haggai and Zechariah begin to prophesy

**500 BC**
Persians begin a royal mounted messenger service

**485–465 BC**
Ahasuerus (Xerxes I) reigns in Persia

**469–399 BC**
Greek philosopher Socrates lives and teaches in Athens

**464–424 BC**
Artaxerxes Longimanus reigns in Persia

**c. 460–375 BC**
Greek physician Hippocrates maintains disease has only natural causes

**458 BC**
Ezra leads a group of returnees to Judea

**c. 457–444 BC**
**Ezra written**

**444 BC**
Nehemiah leads a group of returnees to Judea

### *END OF THE BABYLONIAN CAPTIVITY*

*(2 Chr. 36:22, 23)*

**1** Now in the first year of Cyrus king of Persia, that the word of the LORD [a]by the mouth of Jeremiah might be fulfilled, the LORD stirred up the spirit of Cyrus king of Persia, [b]so that he made a proclamation throughout all his kingdom, and also *put it* in writing, saying,

2 Thus says Cyrus king of Persia:
All the kingdoms of the earth the LORD
God of heaven has given me. And He
has [a]commanded me to build Him a
house at Jerusalem which *is* in Judah.
3 Who *is* among you of all His people?
May his God be with him, and let him
go up to Jerusalem which *is* in Judah,
and build the house of the LORD God of
Israel [a](He *is* God), which *is* in Jerusalem.
4 And whoever is left in any place where
he dwells, let the men of his place help
him with silver and gold, with goods and
livestock, besides the freewill offerings for
the house of God which *is* in Jerusalem.

> **SEEING JESUS IN THE SCRIPTURE**
>
> **1:1–4** God used Cyrus, a pagan king, to pave the way for His people to return to the land He had promised them. This is the land where Jesus came to rule over God's people—just as God had also promised (see Mark 11:9–10).

5 Then the heads of the fathers' *houses* of Judah and Benjamin, and the priests and the Levites, with all whose spirits [a]God had moved, arose to go up and build the house of the LORD which *is* in Jerusalem. 6 And all those who *were* around them encouraged them with articles of silver and gold, with goods and livestock, and with precious things, besides all *that* was [a]willingly offered.

7 [a]King Cyrus also brought out the articles of the house of the LORD, [b]which Nebuchadnezzar had taken from Jerusalem and put in the temple of his gods; 8 and Cyrus king of Persia brought them out by the hand of Mithredath the treasurer, and counted them out to [a]Sheshbazzar the prince of Judah. 9 This *is* the number of them: thirty gold platters, one thousand silver platters, twenty-nine knives, 10 thirty gold basins, four hundred and ten silver basins of a similar *kind, and* one thousand other articles. 11 All the articles of gold and silver *were* five thousand four hundred. All *these* Sheshbazzar took with the captives who were brought from Babylon to Jerusalem.

### *THE CAPTIVES WHO RETURNED TO JERUSALEM*

*(Neh. 7:6–73)*

**2** Now[1] [a]these *are* the people of the province who came back from the captivity, of those who had been carried away, [b]whom Nebuchadnezzar the king of Babylon had carried away to Babylon, and who returned to Jerusalem and Judah, everyone to his *own* city.

> **2:1** From 597 to 586 BC, **Nebuchadnezzar the king of Babylon** tormented the people of **Judah** and its capital city of **Jerusalem**. The Babylonian king led several attacks on the region, looted and burned the temple, and took thousands of Jewish people captive.

2 *Those* who came with Zerubbabel *were* Jeshua, Nehemiah, Seraiah, Reelaiah, Mordecai, Bilshan, Mispar,[1] Bigvai, Rehum,[2] *and* Baanah. The number of the men of the people of Israel: 3 the people of Parosh, two thousand one hundred and seventy-two; 4 the people of Shephatiah, three hundred and seventy-two; 5 the people of Arah, [a]seven hundred and seventy-five; 6 the people of [a]Pahath-Moab, of the people of Jeshua *and* Joab, two thousand eight hundred and twelve; 7 the people of Elam, one thousand two hundred and fifty-four; 8 the people of Zattu, nine hundred and forty-five; 9 the people of Zaccai, seven hundred and sixty; 10 the people of Bani,[1] six hundred and

**1:1** [a] 2 Chr. 36:22, 23; Jer. 25:12; 29:10 [b] Ezra 5:13, 14; Is. 44:28—45:13 **1:2** [a] Is. 44:28; 45:1, 13 **1:3** [a] 1 Kin. 8:23; 18:39; Is. 37:16; Dan. 6:26 **1:5** [a] [Phil. 2:13] **1:6** [a] Ezra 2:68 **1:7** [a] Ezra 5:14; 6:5; Dan. 1:2; 5:2, 3 [b] 2 Kin. 24:13; 2 Chr. 36:7, 18 **1:8** [a] Ezra 5:14, 16 **2:1** [a] Neh. 7:6–73; Jer. 32:15; 50:5; Ezek. 14:22 [b] 2 Kin. 24:14–16; 25:11; 2 Chr. 36:20 [1] Compare this chapter with Nehemiah 7:6–73. **2:2** [1] Spelled *Mispereth* in Nehemiah 7:7 [2] Spelled *Nehum* in Nehemiah 7:7 **2:5** [a] Neh. 7:10 **2:6** [a] Neh. 7:11 **2:10** [1] Spelled *Binnui* in Nehemiah 7:15

## RETURNS OF THE EXILES

| Return | Date | Leader | Purpose | Reference |
|---|---|---|---|---|
| **First** | 538 BC | Zerubbabel, Jeshua | Rebuild the temple | Ezra 1–6 |
| **Second** | 458 BC | Ezra | Restore the worship | Ezra 7–10 |
| **Third** | 445 BC | Nehemiah | Rebuild the walls | Nehemiah 1–13 |

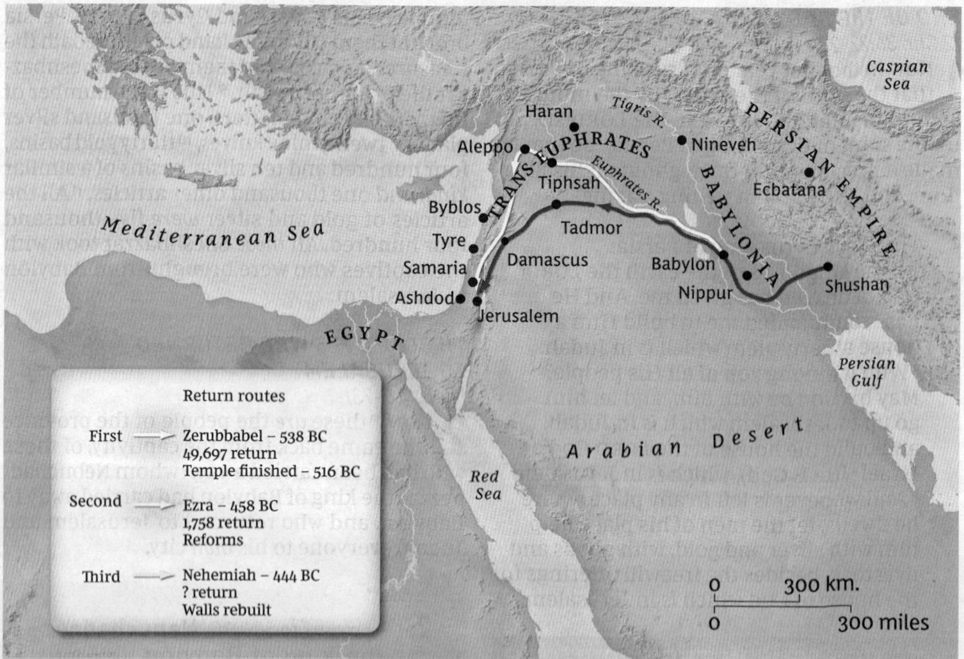


## THE RETURN FROM EXILE

Restoration of the Jewish exiles began under Cyrus (559–530 BC), who allowed them to return to Judah with the captured temple treasures. The temple was consecrated in 516 BC by official permission of Darius I (522–486).

Ezra won the approval of Artaxerxes I (465–424 BC) to return with additional exiles and to promote obedience to the law; Nehemiah, to rebuild the walls of Jerusalem.

forty-two; 11the people of Bebai, six hundred and
twenty-three; 12the people of Azgad, one thousand
two hundred and twenty-two; 13the people of Ad-
onikam, six hundred and sixty-six; 14the people of
Bigvai, two thousand and fifty-six; 15the people of
Adin, four hundred and fifty-four; 16the people
of Ater of Hezekiah, ninety-eight; 17the people
of Bezai, three hundred and twenty-three; 18the
people of Jorah,[1] one hundred and twelve; 19the
people of Hashum, two hundred and twenty-three;
20the people of Gibbar,[1] ninety-five; 21the people
of Bethlehem, one hundred and twenty-three;
22the men of Netophah, fifty-six; 23the men of
Anathoth, one hundred and twenty-eight; 24the
people of Azmaveth,[1] forty-two; 25the people of
Kirjath Arim,[1] Chephirah, and Beeroth, seven
hundred and forty-three; 26the people of Ramah
and Geba, six hundred and twenty-one; 27the men
of Michmas, one hundred and twenty-two; 28the
men of Bethel and Ai, two hundred and twenty-
three; 29the people of Nebo, fifty-two; 30the people
of Magbish, one hundred and fifty-six; 31the people
of the other [a]Elam, one thousand two hundred and
fifty-four; 32the people of Harim, three hundred
and twenty; 33the people of Lod, Hadid, and Ono,
seven hundred and twenty-five; 34the people of
Jericho, three hundred and forty-five; 35the people
of Senaah, three thousand six hundred and thirty.

36The priests: the sons of [a]Jedaiah, of the
house of Jeshua, nine hundred and seventy-
three; 37the sons of [a]Immer, one thousand and
fifty-two; 38the sons of [a]Pashhur, one thousand
two hundred and forty-seven; 39the sons of
[a]Harim, one thousand and seventeen.

40The Levites: the sons of Jeshua and Kad-
miel, of the sons of Hodaviah,[1] seventy-four.

41The singers: the sons of Asaph, one hun-
dred and twenty-eight.

42The sons of the gatekeepers: the sons of
Shallum, the sons of Ater, the sons of Talmon, the
sons of Akkub, the sons of Hatita, and the sons
of Shobai, one hundred and thirty-nine *in* all.

43[a]The Nethinim: the sons of Ziha, the sons
of Hasupha, the sons of Tabbaoth, 44the sons of
Keros, the sons of Siaha,[1] the sons of Padon, 45the
sons of Lebanah, the sons of Hagabah, the sons of

2:18 [1] Called *Hariph* in Nehemiah 7:24 2:20 [1] Called *Gibeon* in Nehemiah 7:25 2:24 [1] Called *Beth Azmaveth* in Nehemiah 7:28 2:25 [1] Called *Kirjath Jearim* in Nehemiah 7:29 2:31 [a] Ezra 2:7 2:36 [a] 1 Chr. 24:7–18 2:37 [a] 1 Chr. 24:14 2:38 [a] 1 Chr. 9:12 2:39 [a] 1 Chr. 24:8 2:40 [1] Spelled *Hodevah* in Nehemiah 7:43 2:43 [a] 1 Chr. 9:2; Ezra 7:7 2:44 [1] Spelled *Sia* in Nehemiah 7:47

Akkub, 46 the sons of Hagab, the sons of Shalmai,
the sons of Hanan, 47 the sons of Giddel, the sons of
Gahar, the sons of Reaiah, 48 the sons of Rezin, the
sons of Nekoda, the sons of Gazzam, 49 the sons of
Uzza, the sons of Paseah, the sons of Besai, 50 the
sons of Asnah, the sons of Meunim, the sons of
Nephusim,[1] 51 the sons of Bakbuk, the sons of Ha-
kupha, the sons of Harhur, 52 the sons of Bazluth,[1]
the sons of Mehida, the sons of Harsha, 53 the sons
of Barkos, the sons of Sisera, the sons of Tamah,
54 the sons of Neziah, and the sons of Hatipha.

55 The sons of [a]Solomon's servants: the sons
of Sotai, the sons of [b]Sophereth, the sons of Pe-
ruda,[1] 56 the sons of Jaala, the sons of Darkon,
the sons of Giddel, 57 the sons of Shephatiah, the
sons of Hattil, the sons of Pochereth of Zebaim,
and the sons of Ami.[1] 58 All the [a]Nethinim and
the children of [b]Solomon's servants were three
hundred and ninety-two.

59 And these *were* the ones who came up from
Tel Melah, Tel Harsha, Cherub, Addan,[1] and Immer;
but they could not identify their father's house or
their genealogy,[2] whether they *were* of Israel: 60 the
sons of Delaiah, the sons of Tobiah, and the sons
of Nekoda, six hundred and fifty-two; 61 and of the
sons of the priests: the sons of [a]Habaiah, the sons
of Koz,[1] and the sons of [b]Barzillai, who took a wife
of the daughters of Barzillai the Gileadite, and was
called by their name. 62 These sought their listing
*among* those who were registered by genealogy,
but they were not found; [a]therefore they *were
excluded* from the priesthood as defiled. 63 And the
governor[1] said to them that they [a]should not eat
of the most holy things till a priest could consult
with the [b]Urim and Thummim.

64 [a]The whole assembly together *was* forty-two
thousand three hundred *and* sixty, 65 besides their
male and female servants, of whom *there were* sev-
en thousand three hundred and thirty-seven; and
they had two hundred men and women singers.
66 Their horses *were* seven hundred and thirty-six,
their mules two hundred and forty-five, 67 their
camels four hundred and thirty-five, and *their*
donkeys six thousand seven hundred and twenty.

68 [a]*Some* of the heads of the fathers' *houses,*
when they came to the house of the LORD which *is*
in Jerusalem, offered freely for the house of God,
to erect it in its place: 69 According to their ability,
they gave to the [a]treasury for the work sixty-one
thousand gold drachmas, five thousand minas
of silver, and one hundred priestly garments.

70 [a]So the priests and the Levites, *some* of
the people, the singers, the gatekeepers, and
the Nethinim, dwelt in their cities, and all Israel
in their cities.

### WORSHIP RESTORED AT JERUSALEM

3 And when the [a]seventh month had come, and
the children of Israel *were* in the cities, the
people gathered together as one man to Jerusa-
lem. 2 Then Jeshua the son of [a]Jozadak[1] and his
brethren the priests, [b]and Zerubbabel the son of
[c]Shealtiel and his brethren, arose and built the
altar of the God of Israel, to offer burnt offerings
on it, as *it is* [d]written in the Law of Moses the
man of God. 3 Though fear *had come* upon them
because of the people of those countries, they
set the altar on its bases; and they offered [a]burnt
offerings on it to the LORD, *both* the morning
and evening burnt offerings. 4 [a]They also kept
the Feast of Tabernacles, [b]as *it is* written, and
[c]*offered* the daily burnt offerings in the number
required by ordinance for each day. 5 Afterwards
*they offered* the [a]regular burnt offering, and *those*
for New Moons and for all the appointed feasts
of the LORD that were consecrated, and *those* of
everyone who willingly offered a freewill offering
to the LORD. 6 From the first day of the seventh
month they began to offer burnt offerings to the
LORD, although the foundation of the temple
of the LORD had not been laid. 7 They also gave
money to the masons and the carpenters, and
[a]food, drink, and oil to the people of Sidon and
Tyre to bring cedar logs from Lebanon to the sea,
to [b]Joppa, [c]according to the permission which
they had from Cyrus king of Persia.

> **3:7 Lebanon** was famous for its large, beautiful **cedar** trees. The wood from these trees was used to build everything from palaces and ships to coffins and musical instruments. After being cut down, the trees probably were taken to **Tyre** and **Sidon**, two Mediterranean port cities, loaded onto rafts, and floated to **Joppa**. From there, they likely were transported across land for the remaining thirty-five miles to Jerusalem.

### RESTORATION OF THE TEMPLE BEGINS

8 Now in the second month of the second year
of their coming to the house of God at Jerusalem,
[a]Zerubbabel the son of Shealtiel, Jeshua the son
of Jozadak,[1] and the rest of their brethren the
priests and the Levites, and all those who had
come out of the captivity to Jerusalem, began
*work* [b]and appointed the Levites from twenty
years old and above to oversee the work of the

**2:50** [1] Spelled *Nephishesim* in Nehemiah 7:52 **2:52** [1] Spelled *Bazlith* in Nehemiah 7:54 **2:55** [a] 1 Kin. 9:21 [b] Neh. 7:57–60 [1] Spelled *Perida* in Nehemiah 7:57 **2:57** [1] Spelled *Amon* in Nehemiah 7:59 **2:58** [a] Josh. 9:21, 27; 1 Chr. 9:2 [b] 1 Kin. 9:21 **2:59** [1] Spelled *Addon* in Nehemiah 7:61 [2] Literally *seed* **2:61** [a] Neh. 7:63 [b] 2 Sam. 17:27; 1 Kin. 2:7 [1] Or *Hakkoz* **2:62** [a] Num. 3:10 **2:63** [a] Lev. 22:2, 10, 15, 16 [b] Ex. 28:30; Num. 27:21 [1] Hebrew *Tirshatha* **2:64** [a] Neh. 7:66; Is. 10:22 **2:68** [a] Ezra 1:6; 3:5; Neh. 7:70 **2:69** [a] 1 Chr. 26:20; Ezra 8:25–35 **2:70** [a] Ezra 6:16, 17; Neh. 7:73 **3:1** [a] Neh. 7:73; 8:1, 2 **3:2** [a] 1 Chr. 6:14, 15; Ezra 4:3; Neh. 12:1, 8; Hag. 1:1; 2:2 [b] Ezra 2:2; 4:2, 3; 5:2 [c] 1 Chr. 3:17 [d] Deut. 12:5, 6 [1] Spelled *Jehozadak* in 1 Chronicles 6:14 **3:3** [a] Num. 28:3 **3:4** [a] Lev. 23:33–43; Neh. 8:14–18; Zech. 14:16 [b] Ex. 23:16 [c] Num. 29:12, 13 **3:5** [a] Ex. 29:38; Num. 28:3, 11, 19, 26; Ezra 1:4; 2:68; 7:15, 16; 8:28 **3:7** [a] 1 Kin. 5:6, 9; 2 Chr. 2:10; Acts 12:20 [b] 2 Chr. 2:16; Acts 9:36 [c] Ezra 1:2; 6:3 **3:8** [a] Ezra 3:2; 4:3 [b] 1 Chr. 23:4, 24 [1] Spelled *Jehozadak* in 1 Chronicles 6:14

house of the LORD. 9 Then Jeshua *with* his sons
and brothers, Kadmiel *with* his sons, and the sons
of Judah,[1] arose as one to oversee those working
on the house of God: the sons of Henadad *with*
their sons and their brethren the Levites.
10 When the builders laid the foundation of
the temple of the LORD, [a]the priests stood[1] in
their apparel with trumpets, and the Levites,
the sons of Asaph, with cymbals, to praise the
LORD, according to the [b]ordinance of David king
of Israel. 11 [a]And they sang responsively, praising
and giving thanks to the LORD:

[b]"For *He is* good,
[c]For His mercy *endures* forever toward
Israel."[1]

Then all the people shouted with a great shout,
when they praised the LORD, because the foun-
dation of the house of the LORD was laid.
12 But many of the priests and Levites and
[a]heads of the fathers' *houses,* old men who had
seen the first temple, wept with a loud voice
when the foundation of this temple was laid
before their eyes. Yet many shouted aloud for joy,
13 so that the people could not discern the noise
of the shout of joy from the noise of the weeping
of the people, for the people shouted with a loud
shout, and the sound was heard afar off.

### RESISTANCE TO REBUILDING THE TEMPLE

4 Now when [a]the adversaries of Judah and
Benjamin heard that the descendants of the
captivity were building the temple of the LORD
God of Israel, 2 they came to Zerubbabel and the
heads of the fathers' *houses,* and said to them,
"Let us build with you, for we seek your God as
you *do;* and we have sacrificed to Him [a]since the
days of Esarhaddon king of Assyria, who brought
us here." 3 But Zerubbabel and Jeshua and the
rest of the heads of the fathers' *houses* of Isra-
el said to them, [a]"You may do nothing with us
to build a house for our God; but we alone will
build to the LORD God of Israel, as [b]King Cyrus
the king of Persia has commanded us." 4 Then
[a]the people of the land tried to discourage the
people of Judah. They troubled them in building,
5 and hired counselors against them to frustrate
their purpose all the days of Cyrus king of Persia,
even until the reign of [a]Darius king of Persia.

### REBUILDING OF JERUSALEM OPPOSED

6 In the reign of Ahasuerus, in the beginning
of his reign, they wrote an accusation against
the inhabitants of Judah and Jerusalem.

> **SEEING JESUS IN THE SCRIPTURE**
>
> **4:6** As they were rebuilding Jerusalem, the people of God were falsely accused of rebelling against the king in an attempt to stop them from completing their work. Jesus was falsely accused of being a criminal in an attempt to halt His work (see John 18:30).

7 In the days of [a]Artaxerxes also, Bishlam, Mith-
redath, Tabel, and the rest of their companions
wrote to Artaxerxes king of Persia; and the letter
*was* written in [b]Aramaic script, and translated into
the Aramaic language. 8 Rehum[1] the commander
and Shimshai the scribe wrote a letter against Je-
rusalem to King Artaxerxes in this fashion:

9 From[1] Rehum the commander,
Shimshai the scribe, and the rest of

3:9 [1] Or *Hodaviah* (compare 2:40) 3:10 [a] 1 Chr. 16:5, 6 [b] 1 Chr. 6:31; 16:4; 25:1 [1] Following Septuagint, Syriac, and Vulgate; Masoretic Text reads *they stationed the priests.* 3:11 [a] Ex. 15:21; 2 Chr. 7:3; Neh. 12:24 [b] 1 Chr. 16:34; Ps. 136:1 [c] 1 Chr. 16:41; Jer. 33:11 [1] Compare Psalm 136:1 3:12 [a] Ezra 2:68 4:1 [a] Ezra 4:7–9 4:2 [a] 2 Kin. 17:24; 19:37; Ezra 4:10 4:3 [a] Neh. 2:20 [b] Ezra 1:1–4 4:4 [a] Ezra 3:3 4:5 [a] Ezra 5:5; 6:1 4:7 [a] Ezra 7:1, 7, 21 [b] 2 Kin. 18:26 4:8 [1] The original language of Ezra 4:8 through 6:18 is Aramaic. 4:9 [1] Literally *Then*

> LIVE THE TRUTH
>
> ## CELEBRATING GOD
>
> **3:10** The temple was God's dwelling place on earth and where His people met Him for worship. Its destruction by the Babylonians in 586 BC was a major blow to the Israelites. After the temple lay in ruins for about fifty years, some of the Israelites who had returned from captivity rebuilt the altar, allowing worship to resume (Ezra 3:1–7). Then, they laid the foundation for the temple itself. It was going to be a much smaller temple and there was still plenty of work to do, but this important step was cause for great rejoicing. The celebration was heard from far away. There was no restraint in their celebration.
>
> Since Jesus made the way for our relationship with God to be restored, God now lives within His people, not in a temple. This is likewise cause for constant, unrestrained celebration! Because God is always with us, thanksgiving is always appropriate (see Ps. 100:4) and praise should always be on our lips (see Ps. 34:1). This isn't a legalistic action of what we *should* or *must* do; instead, it's a natural conclusion of realizing God's presence in our lives. Your Creator and loving Father is ever with you. Celebrate who He is and what He has done.

their companions—*representatives* of
[a]the Dinaites, the Apharsathchites, the
Tarpelites, the people of Persia and
Erech and Babylon and Shushan,[2] the
Dehavites, the Elamites, 10 [a]and the rest
of the nations whom the great and noble
Osnapper took captive and settled in
the cities of Samaria and the remainder
beyond the River[1]—[b]and so forth.[2]

11 (This *is* a copy of the letter that they sent him.)

To King Artaxerxes from your servants,
the men *of the region* beyond the River,
and so forth:[1]

12 Let it be known to the king that the Jews
who came up from you have come to
us at Jerusalem, and are building the
[a]rebellious and evil city, and are finishing
*its* [b]walls and repairing the foundations.
13 Let it now be known to the king that, if
this city is built and the walls completed,
they will not pay [a]tax, tribute, or custom,
and the king's treasury will be diminished.
14 Now because we receive support from
the palace, it was not proper for us to see
the king's dishonor; therefore we have
sent and informed the king, 15 that search
may be made in the book of the records
of your fathers. And you will find in the
book of the records and know that this
city *is* a rebellious city, harmful to kings
and provinces, and that they have incited
sedition within the city in former times,
for which cause this city was destroyed.

16 We inform the king that if this city is
rebuilt and its walls are completed,
the result will be that you will have no
dominion beyond the River.

17 The king sent an answer:

To Rehum the commander, *to* Shimshai
the scribe, *to* the rest of their companions
who dwell in Samaria, and *to* the
remainder beyond the River:

Peace, and so forth.[1]

18 The letter which you sent to us has been
clearly read before me. 19 And I gave the
command, and a search has been made,
and it was found that this city in former
times has revolted against kings, and
rebellion and sedition have been fostered
in it. 20 There have also been mighty kings
over Jerusalem, who have [a]ruled over
all *the region* [b]beyond the River; and tax,
tribute, and custom were paid to them.
21 Now give the command to make these
men cease, that this city may not be built
until the command is given by me.

22 Take heed now that you do not fail to do
this. Why should damage increase to the
hurt of the kings?

23 Now when the copy of King Artaxerxes'
letter *was* read before Rehum, Shimshai the
scribe, and their companions, they went up in
haste to Jerusalem against the Jews, and by force
of arms made them cease. 24 Thus the work of
the house of God which *is* at Jerusalem ceased,
and it was discontinued until the second year
of the reign of Darius king of Persia.

> **4:24** This is not the same **Darius** as the Darius of Daniel 5–6.

### *RESTORATION OF THE TEMPLE RESUMED*
*(Hab. 1:1; Zech. 1:1)*

**5** Then the prophet [a]Haggai and [b]Zechariah
the son of Iddo, prophets, prophesied to the
Jews who *were* in Judah and Jerusalem, in the
name of the God of Israel, *who was* over them.
2 So [a]Zerubbabel the son of Shealtiel and Jeshua
the son of Jozadak[1] rose up and began to build
the house of God which *is* in Jerusalem; and
[b]the prophets of God *were* with them, helping
them.
3 At the same time [a]Tattenai the governor of
*the region* beyond the River[1] and Shethar-Boznai
and their companions came to them and spoke
thus to them: [b]"Who has commanded you to
build this temple and finish this wall?" 4 [a]Then,
accordingly, we told them the names of the
men who were constructing this building. 5 But
[a]the eye of their God was upon the elders of the
Jews, so that they could not make them cease
till a report could go to Darius. Then a [b]written
answer was returned concerning this *matter.*
6 This is a copy of the letter that Tattenai sent:

The governor of *the region* beyond the
River, and Shethar-Boznai, [a]and his
companions, the Persians who *were in
the region* beyond the River, to Darius the
king.

7 (They sent a letter to him, in which was written
thus.)

**4:9** [a] 2 Kin. 17:30, 31 [2] Or *Susa* **4:10** [a] 2 Kin. 17:24; Ezra 4:1 [b] Ezra 4:11, 17; 7:12 [1] That is, the Euphrates [2] Literally *and now* **4:11** [1] Literally *and now* **4:12** [a] 2 Chr. 36:13 [b] Ezra 5:3, 9 **4:13** [a] Ezra 4:20; 7:24 **4:17** [1] Literally *and now* **4:20** [a] 1 Kin. 4:21; 1 Chr. 18:3; Ps. 72:8 [b] Gen. 15:18; Josh. 1:4 **5:1** [a] Hag. 1:1 [b] Zech. 1:1 **5:2** [a] Ezra 3:2; Hag. 1:12 [b] Ezra 6:14; Hag. 2:4 [1] Spelled *Jehozadak* in 1 Chronicles 6:14 **5:3** [a] Ezra 5:6; 6:6 [b] Ezra 1:3; 5:9 [1] That is, the Euphrates **5:4** [a] Ezra 5:10 **5:5** [a] 2 Chr. 16:9; Ezra 7:6, 28; Ps. 33:18 [b] Ezra 6:6 **5:6** [a] Ezra 4:7–10

To Darius the king:

All peace.

8 Let it be known to the king that we went
into the province of Judea, to the temple
of the great God, which is being built with
heavy stones, and timber is being laid in
the walls; and this work goes on diligently
and prospers in their hands.

9 Then we asked those elders, *and* spoke thus
to them: [a]"Who commanded you to build
this temple and to finish these walls?" 10 We
also asked them their names to inform you,
that we might write the names of the men
who *were* chief among them.

11 And thus they returned us an answer,
saying: "We are the servants of the God of
heaven and earth, and we are rebuilding
the temple that was built many years
ago, which a great king of Israel built
[a]and completed. 12 But [a]because our
fathers provoked the God of heaven to
wrath, He gave them into the hand of
[b]Nebuchadnezzar king of Babylon, the
Chaldean, *who* destroyed this temple
and [c]carried the people away to Babylon.
13 However, in the first year of [a]Cyrus king
of Babylon, King Cyrus issued a decree
to build this house of God. 14 Also, [a]the
gold and silver articles of the house of
God, which Nebuchadnezzar had taken
from the temple that *was* in Jerusalem
and carried into the temple of Babylon—
those King Cyrus took from the temple
of Babylon, and they were given to [b]one
named Sheshbazzar, whom he had made
governor. 15 And he said to him, 'Take
these articles; go, carry them to the
temple *site* that *is* in Jerusalem, and let
the house of God be rebuilt on its former
site.' 16 Then the same Sheshbazzar came
*and* [a]laid the foundation of the house of
God which *is* in Jerusalem; but from that
time even until now it has been under
construction, and [b]it is not finished."

17 Now therefore, if *it seems* good to the
king, [a]let a search be made in the king's
treasure house, which *is* there in Babylon,
whether it is *so* that a decree was issued
by King Cyrus to build this house of God
at Jerusalem, and let the king send us his
pleasure concerning this *matter.*

### THE DECREE OF DARIUS

6 Then King Darius issued a decree, [a]and a
search was made in the archives,[1] where
the treasures were stored in Babylon. 2 And at
Achmetha,[1] in the palace that *is* in the province
of [a]Media, a scroll was found, and in it a record
*was* written thus:

3 In the first year of King Cyrus, King Cyrus
issued a [a]decree *concerning* the house of
God at Jerusalem: "Let the house be rebuilt,
the place where they offered sacrifices;
and let the foundations of it be firmly
laid, its height sixty cubits *and* its width
sixty cubits, 4 [a]*with* three rows of heavy
stones and one row of new timber. Let the
[b]expenses be paid from the king's treasury.

**5:9** [a] Ezra 5:3, 4 **5:11** [a] 1 Kin. 6:1, 38 **5:12** [a] 2 Chr. 34:25; 36:16, 17 [b] 2 Kin. 24:2; 25:8–11; 2 Chr. 36:17; Jer. 52:12–15 [c] Jer. 13:19 **5:13** [a] Ezra 1:1 **5:14** [a] Ezra 1:7, 8; 6:5; Dan. 5:2 [b] Hag. 1:14; 2:2, 21 **5:16** [a] Ezra 3:8–10; Hag. 2:18 [b] Ezra 6:15 **5:17** [a] Ezra 6:1, 2 **6:1** [a] Ezra 5:17 [1] Literally *house of the scrolls* **6:2** [a] 2 Kin. 17:6 [1] Probably *Ecbatana,* the ancient capital of Media **6:3** [a] Ezra 1:1; 5:13 **6:4** [a] 1 Kin. 6:36 [b] Ezra 3:7

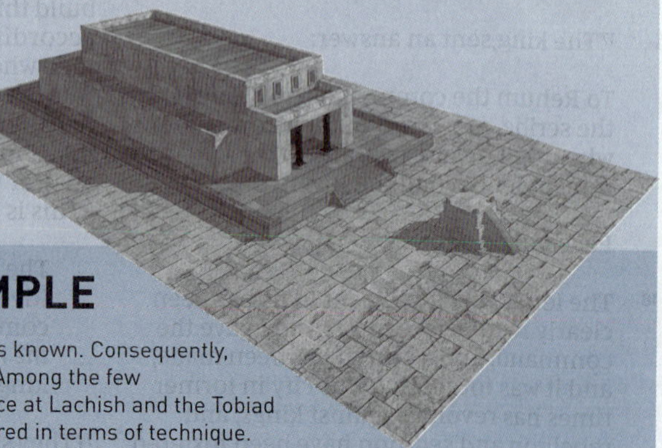

## ZERUBBABEL'S TEMPLE

Of this temple and its construction, little is known. Consequently, all art reconstructions of it are tentative. Among the few contemporary buildings, the Persian palace at Lachish and the Tobiad monument at Iraq al-Amir may be compared in terms of technique.

Unlike the more famous temple structures razed in 586 BC and AD 70, the temple begun by Zerubbabel suffered no major hostile destruction but was gradually repaired and reconstructed over a long period of time. Eventually it was replaced entirely by Herod's magnificent edifice.

Daniel Warner, PhD–Archaeologist; Derrick McKenzie–Artist; © 2011 by Zondervan

[5]Also let [a]the gold and silver articles of the
house of God, which Nebuchadnezzar took
from the temple which *is* in Jerusalem and
brought to Babylon, be restored and taken
back to the temple which *is* in Jerusalem,
*each* to its place; and deposit *them* in the
house of God"—

6 [a]Now *therefore*, Tattenai, governor
of *the region* beyond the River, and
Shethar-Boznai, and your companions
the Persians who *are* beyond the River,
keep yourselves far from there. [7]Let the
work of this house of God alone; let the
governor of the Jews and the elders of the
Jews build this house of God on its site.

8 Moreover I issue a decree *as to* what you
shall do for the elders of these Jews, for the
building of this house of God: Let the cost
be paid at the king's expense from taxes
*on the region* beyond the River; this is to be
given immediately to these men, so that
they are not hindered. [9]And whatever they
need—young bulls, rams, and lambs for the
burnt offerings of the God of heaven, wheat,
salt, wine, and oil, according to the request
of the priests who *are* in Jerusalem—let
it be given them day by day without fail,
[10][a]that they may offer sacrifices of sweet
aroma to the God of heaven, and pray for
the life of the king and his sons.

11 Also I issue a decree that whoever alters
this edict, let a timber be pulled from his
house and erected, and let him be hanged
on it; [a]and let his house be made a refuse
heap because of this. [12]And may the God
who causes His [a]name to dwell there
destroy any king or people who put their
hand to alter it, or to destroy this house of
God which is in Jerusalem. I Darius issue
a decree; let it be done diligently.

### THE TEMPLE COMPLETED AND DEDICATED

[13]Then Tattenai, governor of *the region* be-
yond the River, Shethar-Boznai, and their com-
panions diligently did according to what King
Darius had sent. [14][a]So the elders of the Jews built,
and they prospered through the prophesying of

6:5 [a] Ezra 1:7, 8; 5:14 6:6 [a] Ezra 5:3, 6 6:10 [a] Ezra 7:23; [Jer. 29:7; 1 Tim. 2:1, 2] 6:11 [a] Dan. 2:5; 3:29 6:12 [a] Deut. 12:5, 11; 1 Kin. 9:3
6:14 [a] Ezra 5:1, 2

EZRA 6:13–18

## THE TEMPLE IS REBUILT

33

STORY OF SCRIPTURE

### WHAT'S GOING ON?

The rebuilding and dedication of the Second Temple in Jerusalem after the Jews' return from exile and oppression under the boot of Babylon and Persia marked a significant moment in their history. Under Zerubbabel's leadership and with the prophets Haggai's and Zechariah's encouragement, the people overcame opposition and challenges and rebuilt the temple. Completing this work restored an important physical structure and symbolized the renewal of the people's relationship with God. It's a story of community, faith, and perseverance.

### WHAT DOES THIS MEAN FOR ME?

We're called to be builders in God's kingdom, to work toward the restoration and renewal of our lives, others' lives, and our communities. This passage encourages us to engage in this spiritual construction, relying on God's strength and guidance. It's about being active participants in God's redemptive work, committing to His will, and celebrating His faithfulness and provision. The rededication of the temple also serves as a metaphor for our spiritual lives. It's a daily call to rebuild and renew our relationship with God, commit to His purposes, and celebrate His presence.

### DID YOU CATCH THE PATTERN?

The temple's rebuilding is a powerful illustration of the biblical pattern of restoration and renewal. Throughout the Bible, we see cycles of disobedience and forgiveness, destruction and rebuilding, exile and return. This pattern is a testament to God's unfailing love and mercy and His willingness to forgive and restore us despite our failures. The rebuilding of the temple is a precursor to the ultimate act of restoration through Jesus, who rebuilt the broken relationship between people and God through His sacrifice.

*For the next* Story of Scripture *reading and devotion, turn to Esther 9:1–32 on page 494*

Haggai the prophet and Zechariah the son of Iddo. And they built and finished *it,* according to the commandment of the God of Israel, and according to the command of [b]Cyrus, [c]Darius, and [d]Artaxerxes king of Persia. 15 Now the temple was finished on the third day of the month of Adar, which was in the sixth year of the reign of King Darius. 16 Then the children of Israel, the priests and the Levites and the rest of the descendants of the captivity, celebrated [a]the dedication of this house of God with joy. 17 And they [a]offered sacrifices at the dedication of this house of God, one hundred bulls, two hundred rams, four hundred lambs, and as a sin offering for all Israel twelve male goats, according to the number of the tribes of Israel. 18 They assigned the priests to their [a]divisions and the Levites to their [b]divisions, over the service of God in Jerusalem, [c]as it is written in the Book of Moses.

### *THE PASSOVER CELEBRATED*

*(cf. Deut. 16:1–8)*

19 And the descendants of the captivity kept the Passover [a]on the fourteenth *day* of the first month. 20 For the priests and the Levites had [a]purified themselves; all of them *were ritually* clean. And they [b]slaughtered the Passover *lambs* for all the descendants of the captivity, for their brethren the priests, and for themselves. 21 Then the children of Israel who had returned from the captivity ate together with all who had separated themselves from the [a]filth of the nations of the land in order to seek the LORD God of Israel. 22 And they kept the [a]Feast of Unleavened Bread seven days with joy; for the LORD made them joyful, and [b]turned the heart [c]of the king of Assyria toward them, to strengthen their hands in the work of the house of God, the God of Israel.

**SEEING JESUS IN THE SCRIPTURE**

**6:20** Before they could lead in celebrating the Passover, the priests and the Levites had to purify themselves because of their sin. Jesus is the sinless Passover Lamb who didn't need to offer sacrifices for any sin He committed, but instead offered Himself for the sins of the world (see Heb. 7:26–28).

### *THE ARRIVAL OF EZRA*

**7** Now after these things, in the reign of [a]Artaxerxes king of Persia, Ezra the [b]son of Seraiah, [c]the son of Azariah, the son of [d]Hilkiah, 2 the son of Shallum, the son of Zadok, the son of Ahitub, 3 the son of Amariah, the son of Azariah, the son of Meraioth, 4 the son of Zerahiah, the son of Uzzi, the son of Bukki, 5 the son of Abishua, the son of Phinehas, the son of Eleazar, the son of Aaron the chief priest— 6 this Ezra came up from Babylon; and he *was* [a]a skilled scribe in the Law of Moses, which the LORD God of Israel had given. The king granted him all his request, [b]according to the hand of the LORD his God upon him. 7 [a]*Some* of the children of Israel, the priests, [b]the Levites, the singers, the gatekeepers, and [c]the Nethinim came up to Jerusalem in the seventh year of King Artaxerxes. 8 And Ezra came to Jerusalem in the fifth month, which *was* in the seventh year of the king. 9 On the first *day* of the first month he began *his* journey from Babylon, and on the first *day* of the fifth month he came to Jerusalem, [a]according to the good hand of his God upon him. 10 For Ezra had prepared his heart to [a]seek the Law of the LORD, and to do *it,* and to [b]teach statutes and ordinances in Israel.

**7:1–5** The events of chapter 6 took place during the reign of King Darius, with the temple being completed and dedicated in 515 BC. Chapter 7 jumps forward about sixty years to the reign of **Artaxerxes** (464–424 BC). The events of the Book of Esther took place during that gap of time.

### *THE LETTER OF ARTAXERXES TO EZRA*

11 This *is* a copy of the letter that King Artaxerxes gave Ezra the priest, the scribe, expert in the words of the commandments of the LORD, and of His statutes to Israel:

12 Artaxerxes,[1] [a]king of kings,

To Ezra the priest, a scribe of the Law of the God of heaven:

Perfect *peace,* [b]and so forth.[2]

13 I issue a decree that all those of the people of Israel and the priests and Levites in my realm, who volunteer to go up to Jerusalem, may go with you. 14 And whereas you are being sent by the king and his [a]seven counselors to inquire concerning Judah and Jerusalem, with regard to the Law of your God which *is* in your hand; 15 and *whereas you are* to carry the silver and gold which the king and his counselors have freely offered to the God

6:14 [b] Ezra 1:1; 5:13; 6:3 [c] Ezra 4:24; 6:12 [d] Ezra 7:1, 11; Neh. 2:1 6:16 [a] 1 Kin. 8:63; 2 Chr. 7:5 6:17 [a] Ezra 8:35 6:18 [a] 1 Chr. 24:1; 2 Chr. 35:5 [b] 1 Chr. 23:6 [c] Num. 3:6; 8:9 6:19 [a] Ex. 12:6 6:20 [a] 2 Chr. 29:34; 30:15 [b] 2 Chr. 35:11 6:21 [a] Ezra 9:11 6:22 [a] Ex. 12:15; 13:6, 7; 2 Chr. 30:21; 35:17 [b] Ezra 7:27; [Prov. 21:1] [c] 2 Kin. 23:29; 2 Chr. 33:11; Ezra 1:1; 6:1 7:1 [a] Neh. 2:1 [b] 1 Chr. 6:14 [c] Jer. 52:24 [d] 2 Chr. 35:8 7:6 [a] Ezra 7:11, 12, 21 [b] Ezra 7:9, 28; 8:22 7:7 [a] Ezra 8:1–14 [b] Ezra 8:15 [c] Ezra 2:43; 8:20 7:9 [a] Ezra 7:6; Neh. 2:8, 18 7:10 [a] Ps. 119:45 [b] Deut. 33:10; Ezra 7:6, 25; Neh. 8:1–8; [Mal. 2:7] 7:12 [a] Ezek. 26:7; Dan. 2:37 [b] Ezra 4:10 [1] The original language of Ezra 7:12–26 is Aramaic. [2] Literally *and now* 7:14 [a] Esth. 1:14

of Israel, [a]whose dwelling *is* in Jerusalem;
16 [a]and *whereas* all the silver and gold
that you may find in all the province of
Babylon, along with the freewill offering
of the people and the priests, *are to be*
[b]freely offered for the house of their God
in Jerusalem— 17 now therefore, be careful
to buy with this money bulls, rams, and
lambs, with their [a]grain offerings and
their drink offerings, and [b]offer them
on the altar of the house of your God in
Jerusalem.

18 And whatever seems good to you and
your brethren to do with the rest of the
silver and the gold, do it according to the
will of your God. 19 Also the articles that
are given to you for the service of the
house of your God, deliver in full before
the God of Jerusalem. 20 And whatever
more may be needed for the house of
your God, which you may have occasion
to provide, pay *for it* from the king's
treasury.

21 And I, *even* I, Artaxerxes the king, issue a
decree to all the treasurers who *are in the*
*region* beyond the River, that whatever
Ezra the priest, the scribe of the Law of
the God of heaven, may require of you,
let it be done diligently, 22 up to one
hundred talents of silver, one hundred
kors of wheat, one hundred baths of
wine, one hundred baths of oil, and salt
without prescribed limit. 23 Whatever is
commanded by the God of heaven, let it
diligently be done for the house of the
God of heaven. For why should there be
wrath against the realm of the king and
his sons?

24 Also we inform you that it shall not be
lawful to impose tax, tribute, or custom
on any of the priests, Levites, singers,
gatekeepers, Nethinim, or servants
of this house of God. 25 And you, Ezra,
according to your God-given wisdom,
[a]set magistrates and judges who may
judge all the people who *are in the region*
beyond the River, all such as know the
laws of your God; and [b]teach those who
do not know *them*. 26 Whoever will not
observe the law of your God and the law
of the king, let judgment be executed
speedily on him, whether *it be* death, or
banishment, or confiscation of goods, or
imprisonment.

27 [a]Blessed *be* the LORD God of our fathers,
[b]who has put *such a thing* as this in the king's
heart, to beautify the house of the LORD which *is*
in Jerusalem, 28 and [a]has extended mercy to me
before the king and his counselors, and before
all the king's mighty princes.

So I was encouraged, as [b]the hand of the
LORD my God *was* upon me; and I gathered
leading men of Israel to go up with me.

### HEADS OF FAMILIES WHO RETURNED WITH EZRA

8 These *are* the heads of their fathers' *houses*,
and *this is* the genealogy of those who went
up with me from Babylon, in the reign of King
Artaxerxes: 2 of the sons of Phinehas, Gershom;
of the sons of Ithamar, Daniel; of the sons of
David, [a]Hattush; 3 of the sons of Shecaniah, of
the sons of [a]Parosh, Zechariah; and registered
with him *were* one hundred and fifty males; 4 of
the sons of [a]Pahath-Moab, Eliehoenai the son
of Zerahiah, and with him two hundred males;
5 of the sons of Shechaniah,[1] Ben-Jahaziel, and
with him three hundred males; 6 of the sons of
Adin, Ebed the son of Jonathan, and with him
fifty males; 7 of the sons of Elam, Jeshaiah the
son of Athaliah, and with him seventy males;
8 of the sons of Shephatiah, Zebadiah the son
of Michael, and with him eighty males; 9 of the
sons of Joab, Obadiah the son of Jehiel, and with
him two hundred and eighteen males; 10 of the
sons of Shelomith,[1] Ben-Josiphiah, and with
him one hundred and sixty males; 11 of the sons
of [a]Bebai, Zechariah the son of Bebai, and with
him twenty-eight males; 12 of the sons of Azgad,
Johanan the son of Hakkatan, and with him
one hundred and ten males; 13 of the last sons
of Adonikam, whose names *are* these—Eliph-
elet, Jeiel, and Shemaiah—and with them sixty
males; 14 also of the sons of Bigvai, Uthai and
Zabbud, and with them seventy males.

### SERVANTS FOR THE TEMPLE

15 Now I gathered them by the river that flows
to Ahava, and we camped there three days. And
I looked among the people and the priests, and
found none of the [a]sons of Levi there. 16 Then I
sent for Eliezer, Ariel, Shemaiah, Elnathan, Jarib,
Elnathan, Nathan, Zechariah, and [a]Meshullam,
leaders; also for Joiarib and Elnathan, men of
understanding. 17 And I gave them a command
for Iddo the chief man at the place Casiphia,
and I told them what they should say to Iddo
*and* his brethren[1] the Nethinim at the place Ca-
siphia—that they should bring us servants for
the house of our God. 18 Then, by the good hand
of our God upon us, they [a]brought us a man of

**7:15** [a] 2 Chr. 6:2; Ezra 6:12; Ps. 135:21 **7:16** [a] Ezra 8:25 [b] 1 Chr. 29:6, 9 **7:17** [a] Num. 15:4–13 [b] Deut. 12:5–11 **7:25** [a] Ex. 18:21, 22; Deut. 16:18 [b] 2 Chr. 17:7; Ezra 7:10; [Mal. 2:7; Col. 1:28] **7:27** [a] 1 Chr. 29:10 [b] Ezra 6:22; [Prov. 21:1] **7:28** [a] Ezra 9:9 [b] Ezra 5:5; 7:6, 9; 8:18 **8:2** [a] 1 Chr. 3:22; Ezra 2:68 **8:3** [a] Ezra 2:3 **8:4** [a] Ezra 10:30 **8:5** [1] Following Masoretic Text and Vulgate; Septuagint reads *the sons of Zatho, Shechaniah.* **8:10** [1] Following Masoretic Text and Vulgate; Septuagint reads *the sons of Banni, Shelomith.* **8:11** [a] Ezra 10:28 **8:15** [a] Ezra 7:7; 8:2 **8:16** [a] Ezra 10:15 **8:17** [1] Following Vulgate; Masoretic Text reads *to Iddo his brother;* Septuagint reads *to their brethren.* **8:18** [a] 2 Chr. 30:22; Neh. 8:7

understanding, of the sons of Mahli the son of Levi, the son of Israel, namely Sherebiah, with his sons and brothers, eighteen men; 19 and [a]Hashabiah, and with him Jeshaiah of the sons of Merari, his brothers and their sons, twenty men; 20 [a]also of the Nethinim, whom David and the leaders had appointed for the service of the Levites, two hundred and twenty Nethinim. All of them were designated by name.

### *FASTING AND PRAYER FOR PROTECTION*

21 Then I [a]proclaimed a fast there at the river of Ahava, that we might [b]humble ourselves before our God, to seek from Him the [c]right way for us and our little ones and all our possessions. 22 For [a]I was ashamed to request of the king an escort of soldiers and horsemen to help us against the enemy on the road, because we had spoken to the king, saying, [b]"The hand of our God *is* upon all those for [c]good who seek Him, but His power and His wrath *are* [d]against all those who [e]forsake Him." 23 So we fasted and entreated our God for this, and He [a]answered our prayer.

### *GIFTS FOR THE TEMPLE*

24 And I separated twelve of the leaders of the priests—Sherebiah, Hashabiah, and ten of their brethren with them— 25 and weighed out to them [a]the silver, the gold, and the articles, the offering for the house of our God which the king and his counselors and his princes, and all Israel *who were* present, had offered. 26 I weighed into their hand six hundred and fifty talents of silver, silver articles *weighing* one hundred talents, one hundred talents of gold, 27 twenty gold basins *worth* a thousand drachmas, and two vessels of fine polished bronze, precious as gold. 28 And I said to them, "You *are* [a]holy to the LORD; the articles *are* [b]holy also; and the silver and the gold *are* a freewill offering to the LORD God of your fathers. 29 Watch and keep *them* until you weigh *them* before the leaders of the priests and the Levites and [a]heads of the fathers' *houses* of Israel in Jerusalem, *in* the chambers of the house of the LORD." 30 So the priests and the Levites received the silver and the gold and the articles by weight, to bring *them* to Jerusalem to the house of our God.

### *THE RETURN TO JERUSALEM*

31 Then we departed from the river of Ahava on the twelfth *day* of the first month, to go to Jerusalem. And [a]the hand of our God was upon us, and He delivered us from the hand of the enemy and from ambush along the road. 32 So we [a]came to Jerusalem, and stayed there three days.

33 Now on the fourth day the silver and the gold and the articles were [a]weighed in the house of our God by the hand of Meremoth the son of Uriah the priest, and with him *was* Eleazar the son of Phinehas; with them *were* the Levites, [b]Jozabad the son of Jeshua and Noadiah the son of Binnui, 34 with the number *and* weight of everything. All the weight was written down at that time.

35 The children of those who had been [a]carried away captive, who had come from the captivity, [b]offered burnt offerings to the God of Israel: twelve bulls for all Israel, ninety-six rams, seventy-seven lambs, and twelve male goats *as* a sin offering. All *this was* a burnt offering to the LORD.

> **8:31–35** Most of the tribes of Israel were not able to return to **Jerusalem** after the northern kingdom was conquered in 722 BC. The two tribes that were able to make the trip back were Judah and Benjamin, who offered sacrifices on behalf of the missing tribes.

36 And they delivered the king's [a]orders to the king's satraps and the governors *in the region* beyond the River. So they gave support to the people and the house of God.

### *INTERMARRIAGE WITH PAGANS*

**9** When these things were done, the leaders came to me, saying, "The people of Israel and the priests and the Levites have not [a]separated themselves from the peoples of the lands, [b]with respect to the abominations of the Canaanites, the Hittites, the Perizzites, the Jebusites, the Ammonites, the Moabites, the Egyptians, and the Amorites. 2 For they have [a]taken some of their daughters *as wives* for themselves and their sons, so that the [b]holy seed is [c]mixed with the peoples of *those* lands. Indeed, the hand of the leaders and rulers has been foremost in this trespass." 3 So when I heard this thing, [a]I tore my garment and my robe, and plucked out some of

> **9:2** Intermarrying with people who did not worship the one true God was expressly forbidden (Ex. 34:16; Deut. 7:3). While there are instances of marriages to non-Israelites being blessed (e.g., Rahab and Ruth), in these cases, these women had taken a stand as believers in God, renouncing their old religions.

**8:19** [a] Neh. 12:24 **8:20** [a] Ezra 2:43; 7:7 **8:21** [a] 1 Sam. 7:6; 2 Chr. 20:3 [b] Lev. 16:29; 23:29; Is. 58:3, 5 [c] Ps. 5:8 **8:22** [a] 1 Cor. 9:15 [b] Ezra 7:6, 9, 28 [c] [Ps. 33:18, 19; 34:15, 22; Rom. 8:28] [d] [Ps. 34:16] [e] [2 Chr. 15:2] **8:23** [a] [1 Chr. 5:20]; 2 Chr. 33:13; Is. 19:22 **8:25** [a] Ezra 7:15, 16 **8:28** [a] Lev. 21:6–9; Deut. 33:8 [b] Lev. 22:2, 3; Num. 4:4, 15, 19, 20 **8:29** [a] Ezra 4:3 **8:31** [a] Ezra 7:6, 9, 28 **8:32** [a] Neh. 2:11 **8:33** [a] Ezra 8:26, 30 [b] Neh. 11:16 **8:35** [a] Ezra 2:1 [b] Ezra 6:17 **8:36** [a] Ezra 7:21–24 **9:1** [a] Ezra 6:21; Neh. 9:2 [b] Deut. 12:30, 31 **9:2** [a] Ex. 34:16; [Deut. 7:3]; Ezra 10:2; Neh. 13:23 [b] Ex. 22:31; [Deut. 7:6] [c] [2 Cor. 6:14] **9:3** [a] Job 1:20

the hair of my head and beard, and sat down [b]astonished. 4 Then everyone who [a]trembled at the words of the God of Israel assembled to me, because of the transgression of those who had been carried away captive, and I sat astonished until the [b]evening sacrifice.

5 At the evening sacrifice I arose from my fasting; and having torn my garment and my robe, I fell on my knees and [a]spread out my hands to the LORD my God. 6 And I said: "O my God, I am too [a]ashamed and humiliated to lift up my face to You, my God; for [b]our iniquities have risen higher than *our* heads, and our guilt has [c]grown up to the heavens. 7 Since the days of our fathers to this day [a]we *have been* very guilty, and for our iniquities [b]we, our kings, *and* our priests have been delivered into the hand of the kings of the lands, to the [c]sword, to captivity, to plunder, and to [d]humiliation, as *it is* this day. 8 And now for a little while grace has been *shown* from the LORD our God, to leave us a remnant to escape, and to give us a peg in His holy place, that our God may [a]enlighten our eyes and give us a measure of revival in our bondage. 9 [a]For we *were* slaves. [b]Yet our God did not forsake us in our bondage; but [c]He extended mercy to us in the sight of the kings of Persia, to revive us, to repair the house of our God, to rebuild its ruins, and to give us [d]a wall in Judah and Jerusalem. 10 And now, O our God, what shall we say after this? For we have forsaken Your commandments, 11 which You commanded by Your servants the prophets, saying, 'The land which you are entering to possess is an unclean land, with the [a]uncleanness of the peoples of the lands, with their abominations which have filled it from one end to another with their impurity. 12 Now therefore, [a]do not give your daughters as wives for their sons, nor take their daughters to your sons; and [b]never seek their peace or prosperity, that you may be strong and eat the good of the land, and [c]leave *it* as an inheritance to your children forever.' 13 And after all that has come upon us for our evil deeds and for our great guilt, since You our God [a]have punished us less than our iniquities *deserve,* and have given us *such* deliverance as this, 14 should we [a]again break Your commandments, and [b]join in marriage with the people *committing* these abominations? Would You not be [c]angry with us until You had consumed *us,* so that *there would be* no remnant or survivor? 15 O LORD God of Israel, [a]You *are* righteous, for we are left as a remnant, as *it is* this day. [b]Here we *are* before You, [c]in our guilt, though no one can stand before You because of this!"

## CONFESSION OF IMPROPER MARRIAGES

10 Now [a]while Ezra was praying, and while he was confessing, weeping, and bowing down [b]before the house of God, a very large assembly of men, women, and children gathered to him from Israel; for the people wept very [c]bitterly. 2 And Shechaniah the son of Jehiel, *one* of the sons of Elam, spoke up and said to Ezra, "We have [a]trespassed against our God, and have taken pagan wives from the peoples of the land; yet now there is hope in Israel in spite of this. 3 Now therefore, let us make [a]a covenant with our God to put away all these wives and those who have been born to them, according to the advice of my master and of those who [b]tremble at [c]the commandment of our God; and let it be done according to the [d]law. 4 Arise, for *this* matter *is* your *responsibility.* We also *are* with you. [a]Be of good courage, and do *it.*"

5 Then Ezra arose, and made the leaders of the priests, the Levites, and all Israel [a]swear an oath that they would do according to this word. So they swore an oath. 6 Then Ezra rose up from before the house of God, and went into the chamber of Jehohanan the son of Eliashib; and *when* he came there, he [a]ate no bread and drank no water, for he mourned because of the guilt of those from the captivity.

7 And they issued a proclamation throughout Judah and Jerusalem to all the descendants of the captivity, that they must gather at Jerusalem, 8 and that whoever would not come within three days, according to the instructions of the leaders and elders, all his property would be confiscated, and he himself would be separated from the assembly of those from the captivity.

9 So all the men of Judah and Benjamin gathered at Jerusalem within three days. It *was* the ninth month, on the twentieth of the month; and [a]all the people sat in the open square of the house of God, trembling because of *this* matter and because of heavy rain. 10 Then Ezra the priest stood up and said to them, "You have transgressed and have taken pagan wives, adding to the guilt of Israel. 11 Now therefore, [a]make confession to the LORD God of your fathers,

### SEEING JESUS IN THE SCRIPTURE

**10:10–11** Ezra declared the way to be forgiven of sin is through confession and repentance. John the Baptist did the same when he called on the people to repent and believe in Jesus the Messiah (see Mark 1:15).

**9:3** [b] Ps. 143:4 **9:4** [a] Ezra 10:3; Is. 66:2 [b] Ex. 29:39 **9:5** [a] Ex. 9:29 **9:6** [a] Dan. 9:7, 8 [b] Ps. 38:4 [c] 2 Chr. 28:9; [Ezra 9:13, 15]; Rev. 18:5 **9:7** [a] 2 Chr. 36:14–17; Ps. 106:6; Dan. 9:5, 6 [b] Deut. 28:36; Neh. 9:30 [c] Deut. 32:25 [d] Dan. 9:7, 8 **9:8** [a] Ps. 34:5 **9:9** [a] Neh. 9:36; Esth. 7:4 [b] Neh. 9:17; Ps. 136:23 [c] Ezra 7:28 [d] Is. 5:2 **9:11** [a] Ezra 6:21 **9:12** [a] [Ex. 23:32; 34:15, 16; Deut. 7:3, 4]; Ezra 9:2 [b] Deut. 23:6 [c] [Prov. 13:22; 20:7] **9:13** [a] [Ps. 103:10] **9:14** [a] [John 5:14; 2 Pet. 2:20] [b] Neh. 13:23 [c] Deut. 9:8 **9:15** [a] Neh. 9:33; Dan. 9:14 [b] [Rom. 3:19] [c] 1 Cor. 15:17 **10:1** [a] Dan. 9:4, 20 [b] 2 Chr. 20:9 [c] Neh. 8:1–9 **10:2** [a] Ezra 10:10, 13, 14, 17, 18; Neh. 13:23–27 **10:3** [a] 2 Chr. 34:31 [b] Ezra 9:4 [c] Deut. 7:2, 3 [d] Deut. 24:1, 2 **10:4** [a] 1 Chr. 28:10 **10:5** [a] Ezra 10:12, 19; Neh. 5:12; 13:25 **10:6** [a] Deut. 9:18 **10:9** [a] 1 Sam. 12:18; Ezra 9:4; 10:3 **10:11** [a] [Lev. 26:40–42]; Josh. 7:19; [Prov. 28:13]

and do His will; [b]separate yourselves from the
peoples of the land, and from the pagan wives."
12 Then all the assembly answered and said
with a loud voice, "Yes! As you have said, so we
must do. 13 But *there are* many people; *it is* the
season for heavy rain, and we are not able to
stand outside. Nor *is this* the work of one or two
days, for *there are* many of us who have trans-
gressed in this matter. 14 Please, let the leaders
of our entire assembly stand; and let all those
in our cities who have taken pagan wives come
at appointed times, together with the elders and
judges of their cities, until [a]the fierce wrath of
our God is turned away from us in this matter."
15 Only Jonathan the son of Asahel and Jahaziah
the son of Tikvah opposed this, and [a]Meshullam
and Shabbethai the Levite gave them support.
16 Then the descendants of the captivity did
so. And Ezra the priest, *with* certain [a]heads of
the fathers' *households,* were set apart by the
fathers' households, each of them by name;
and they sat down on the first day of the tenth
month to examine the matter. 17 By the first day
of the first month they finished *questioning* all
the men who had taken pagan wives.

### *PAGAN WIVES PUT AWAY*

18 And among the sons of the priests who had
taken pagan wives *the following* were found of
the sons of [a]Jeshua the son of Jozadak,[1] and his
brothers: Maaseiah, Eliezer, Jarib, and Gedaliah.
19 And they [a]gave their promise that they would
put away their wives; and *being* [b]guilty, *they pre-
sented* a ram of the flock as their [c]trespass offering.
20 Also of the sons of Immer: Hanani and
Zebadiah; 21 of the sons of Harim: Maaseiah,
Elijah, Shemaiah, Jehiel, and Uzziah; 22 of the
sons of Pashhur: Elioenai, Maaseiah, Ishmael,
Nethanel, Jozabad, and Elasah.
23 Also of the Levites: Jozabad, Shimei, Ke-
laiah (the same *is* Kelita), Pethahiah, Judah,
and Eliezer.
24 Also of the singers: Eliashib; and of the
gatekeepers: Shallum, Telem, and Uri.
25 And others of Israel: of the [a]sons of Pa-
rosh: Ramiah, Jeziah, Malchiah, Mijamin, Ele-
azar, Malchijah, and Benaiah; 26 of the sons of
Elam: Mattaniah, Zechariah, Jehiel, Abdi, Jere-
moth, and Eliah; 27 of the sons of Zattu: Elioenai,
Eliashib, Mattaniah, Jeremoth, Zabad, and Aziza;
28 of the [a]sons of Bebai: Jehohanan, Hananiah,
Zabbai, *and* Athlai; 29 of the sons of Bani: Me-
shullam, Malluch, Adaiah, Jashub, Sheal, *and*
Ramoth;[1] 30 of the [a]sons of Pahath-Moab: Adna,
Chelal, Benaiah, Maaseiah, Mattaniah, Bezalel,
Binnui, and Manasseh; 31 *of* the sons of Harim:
Eliezer, Ishijah, Malchijah, Shemaiah, Shimeon,
32 Benjamin, Malluch, *and* Shemariah; 33 of the
sons of Hashum: Mattenai, Mattattah, Zabad,
Eliphelet, Jeremai, Manasseh, *and* Shimei; 34 of
the sons of Bani: Maadai, Amram, Uel, 35 Be-
naiah, Bedeiah, Cheluh,[1] 36 Vaniah, Meremoth,
Eliashib, 37 Mattaniah, Mattenai, Jaasai,[1] 38 Bani,
Binnui, Shimei, 39 Shelemiah, Nathan, Adaiah,
40 Machnadebai, Shashai, Sharai, 41 Azarel, Shel-
emiah, Shemariah, 42 Shallum, Amariah, *and*
Joseph; 43 of the sons of Nebo: Jeiel, Mattithiah,
Zabad, Zebina, Jaddai,[1] Joel, *and* Benaiah.
44 All these had taken pagan wives, and *some*
of them had wives *by whom* they had children.

10:11 [b] Ezra 10:3 10:14 [a] 2 Kin. 23:26; 2 Chr. 28:11–13; 29:10; 30:8 10:15 [a] Ezra 8:16; Neh. 3:4 10:16 [a] Ezra 4:3 10:18 [a] Ezra 5:2; Hag. 1:1, 12; 2:4; Zech. 3:1; 6:11 [1] Spelled *Jehozadak* in 1 Chronicles 6:14 10:19 [a] 2 Kin. 10:15 [b] Lev. 6:4, 6 [c] Lev. 5:6, 15 10:25 [a] Ezra 2:3; 8:3; Neh. 7:8 10:28 [a] Ezra 8:11 10:29 [1] Or *Jeremoth* 10:30 [a] Ezra 8:4 10:35 [1] Or *Cheluhi,* or *Cheluhu* 10:37 [1] Or *Jaasu* 10:43 [1] Or *Jaddu*

# *The Book of* NEHEMIAH

**AUTHOR**
Nehemiah, perhaps with Ezra

**KEY VERSES**
Nehemiah 6:15–16

**READING TIME**
1 hour 7 minutes

Nehemiah, contemporary of Ezra and cupbearer to the king in the Persian palace, led the third and final return to Jerusalem after the Babylonian exile. Nehemiah's concern for the welfare of Jerusalem and its inhabitants prompted him to take bold action and ask the Persian king for permission to rebuild Jerusalem's walls. Granted permission, Nehemiah returned to his homeland and challenged his countrymen to arise and rebuild the shattered walls of Jerusalem. Despite opposition, the task was completed in only fifty-two days, a feat even the enemies of Israel attributed to God's hand. By contrast, the task of reviving and reforming the people of God within those rebuilt walls would require years of Nehemiah's life and leadership.

**Occasion:** Nehemiah records the ambitious rebuilding project of Jerusalem's walls, which the Jews complete in astonishing time. Jerusalem no longer lies in ruins as a reproach to the God of Israel but has been rebuilt and reinhabited by God's people waiting for their true King.

**Main Point:** God's people have returned to the Land of Promise, have rebuilt its capital city, and now only lack their long-awaited true King to establish His eternal throne.

**Big Ideas:** God is a faithful provider. We should care about God's reputation in our world. We are better when we work together as one people. We should live in a good, distinct way from those around us.

## OUTLINE:

I. Preparing to Rebuild Jerusalem's Walls (chs. 1–2)
II. Rebuilding Jerusalem's Walls (chs. 3–6)
III. Renewing the Covenant with God (chs. 7–10)
IV. Obeying the Covenant with God (chs. 11–13)

**586 BC**
The Babylonians defeat Judah

**c. 575–500 BC**
Pythagoras lives in southern Italy and develops the Pythagorean Theorem

**c. 551–479 BC**
Chinese philosopher Confucius is credited with recording his teachings in the "Five Classics"

**539 BC**
Cyrus conquers Babylon

**538 BC**
Jews begin returning to Judea

**536–515 BC**
The temple is rebuilt

**464–424 BC**
Artaxerxes Longimanus reigns in Persia

**458 BC**
Ezra leads a group of returnees to Judea

**450 BC**
Overshot waterwheel used in the marketplace of Athens

**444 BC**
Nehemiah leads a group of returnees to Judea

**443 BC**
Jerusalem's wall is reconstructed

### NEHEMIAH PRAYS FOR HIS PEOPLE

**1** The words of [a]Nehemiah the son of Hachaliah. It came to pass in the month of Chislev, *in* the [b]twentieth year, as I was in [c]Shushan[1] the citadel, 2 that [a]Hanani one of my brethren came with men from Judah; and I asked them concerning the Jews who had escaped, who had survived the captivity, and concerning Jerusalem. 3 And they said to me, "The survivors who are left from the captivity in the [a]province *are* there in great distress and [b]reproach. [c]The wall of Jerusalem [d]*is* also broken down, and its gates are burned with fire."

4 So it was, when I heard these words, that I sat down and wept, and mourned *for many* days; I was fasting and praying before the God of heaven.

**SEEING JESUS IN THE SCRIPTURE**

**1:3–4** When Nehemiah heard about the broken city of Jerusalem, he wept for the city. As Jesus approached Jerusalem and anticipated His rejection on the cross, He wept for the broken people of Jerusalem (see Luke 19:41–42).

5 And I said: "I pray, [a]LORD God of heaven, O great and [b]awesome God, [c]*You* who keep *Your* covenant and mercy with those who love You[1] and observe Your[2] commandments, 6 please let Your ear be attentive and [a]Your eyes open, that You may hear the prayer of Your servant which I pray before You now, day and night, for the children of Israel Your servants, and [b]confess the sins of the children of Israel which we have sinned against You. Both my father's house and I have sinned. 7 [a]We have acted very corruptly against You, and have [b]not kept the commandments, the statutes, nor the ordinances which You commanded Your servant Moses. 8 Remember, I pray, the word that You commanded Your servant Moses, saying, [a]'*If* you are unfaithful, I will scatter you among the nations;[1] 9 [a]but *if* you return to Me, and keep My commandments and do them, [b]though some of you were cast out to the farthest part of the heavens, *yet* I will gather them from there, and bring them to the place which I have chosen as a dwelling for My name.'[1] 10 [a]Now these *are* Your servants and Your people, whom You have redeemed by Your great power, and by Your strong hand. 11 O Lord, I pray, please [a]let Your ear be attentive to the prayer of Your servant, and to the prayer of Your servants who [b]desire to fear Your name; and let Your servant prosper this day, I pray, and grant him mercy in the sight of this man."

For I was the king's [c]cupbearer.

### NEHEMIAH SENT TO JUDAH

**2** And it came to pass in the month of Nisan, in the twentieth year of [a]King Artaxerxes, *when* wine *was* before him, that [b]I took the wine and gave it to the king. Now I had never been sad in his presence before. 2 Therefore the king said to me, "Why *is* your face sad, since you *are* not sick? This *is* nothing but [a]sorrow of heart."

So I became dreadfully afraid, 3 and said to the king, [a]"May the king live forever! Why should my face not be sad, when [b]the city, the place of my fathers' tombs, *lies* waste, and its gates are burned with [c]fire?"

4 Then the king said to me, "What do you request?"

So I [a]prayed to the God of heaven. 5 And I said to the king, "If it pleases the king, and if your servant has found favor in your sight, I ask that you send me to Judah, to the city of my fathers' tombs, that I may rebuild it."

**SEEING JESUS IN THE SCRIPTURE**

**2:5** As cupbearer, Nehemiah held a high position in the king's court. His request to leave this prominent role to rebuild Jerusalem points to how Jesus left His exalted place in heaven with the Father to come to earth and provide salvation (see Phil. 2:5–8).

6 Then the king said to me (the queen also sitting beside him), "How long will your journey be? And when will you return?" So it pleased the king to send me; and I set him [a]a time.

7 Furthermore I said to the king, "If it pleases the king, let letters be given to me for the [a]governors *of the region* beyond the River,[1] that they must permit me to pass through till I come to Judah, 8 and a letter to Asaph the keeper of the king's forest, that he must give me timber to make beams for the gates of the citadel which *pertains* [a]to the temple,[1] for the city wall, and for the house that I will occupy." And the king granted *them* to me [b]according to the good hand of my God upon me.

9 Then I went to the governors *in the region* beyond the River, and gave them the king's letters. Now the king had sent captains of the army and horsemen with me. 10 When [a]Sanballat the Horonite and Tobiah the Ammonite official[1]

**1:1** [a] Neh. 10:1 [b] Neh. 2:1 [c] Esth. 1:1, 2, 5 [1] Or *Susa* **1:2** [a] Neh. 7:2 **1:3** [a] Neh. 7:6 [b] Neh. 2:17 [c] Neh. 2:17 [d] 2 Kin. 25:10 **1:5** [a] Dan. 9:4 [b] Neh. 4:14 [c] [Ex. 20:6; 34:6, 7] [1] Literally *Him* [2] Literally *His* **1:6** [a] 2 Chr. 6:40 [b] Dan. 9:20 **1:7** [a] Dan. 9:5 [b] Deut. 28:15 **1:8** [a] Lev. 26:33 [1] Leviticus 26:33 **1:9** [a] [Deut. 4:29–31; 30:2–5] [b] Deut. 30:4 [1] Deuteronomy 30:2–5 **1:10** [a] Deut. 9:29 **1:11** [a] Neh. 1:6 [b] Is. 26:8 [c] Neh. 2:1 **2:1** [a] Ezra 7:1 [b] Neh. 1:11 **2:2** [a] Prov. 15:13 **2:3** [a] Dan. 2:4; 5:10; 6:6, 21 [b] 2 Chr. 36:19 [c] Neh. 1:3 **2:4** [a] Neh. 1:4 **2:6** [a] Neh. 5:14; 13:6 **2:7** [a] Ezra 7:21; 8:36 [1] That is, the Euphrates, and so elsewhere in this book **2:8** [a] Neh. 3:7 [b] Ezra 5:5; 7:6, 9, 28; Neh. 2:18 [1] Literally *house* **2:10** [a] Neh. 2:19; 4:1 [1] Literally *servant,* and so elsewhere in this book

heard *of it,* they were deeply disturbed that a
man had come to seek the well-being of the
children of Israel.

> **2:10** When the northern kingdom of Israel was conquered by Assyria in 722 BC, many Israelites were taken captive. At the same time, foreigners from many different regions were brought to live in Israel. The Israelites who remained in the land began to mingle with their new neighbors, eventually marrying them and adopting their idol worship. As a result, they were no longer a distinct people—either physically or spiritually. The descendants of these mixed marriages would become known as Samaritans.

### *NEHEMIAH VIEWS THE WALL OF JERUSALEM*

11 So I [a]came to Jerusalem and was there three
days. 12 Then I arose in the night, I and a few men
with me; I told no one what my God had put in my
heart to do at Jerusalem; nor was there any animal
with me, except the one on which I rode. 13 And I
went out by night [a]through the Valley Gate to the
Serpent Well and the Refuse Gate, and viewed the
walls of Jerusalem which were [b]broken down and
its gates which were burned with fire. 14 Then I went
on to the [a]Fountain Gate and to the [b]King's Pool,
but *there was* no room for the animal under me to
pass. 15 So I went up in the night by the [a]valley, and
viewed the wall; then I turned back and entered by
the Valley Gate, and so returned. 16 And the officials
did not know where I had gone or what I had done;
I had not yet told the Jews, the priests, the nobles,
the officials, or the others who did the work.

17 Then I said to them, "You see the distress
that we *are* in, how Jerusalem *lies* waste, and its
gates are burned with fire. Come and let us build
the wall of Jerusalem, that we may no longer be
[a]a reproach." 18 And I told them of [a]the hand of
my God which had been good upon me, and also
of the king's words that he had spoken to me.

So they said, "Let us rise up and build." Then
they [b]set their hands to *this* good *work.*

19 But when Sanballat the Horonite, Tobiah
the Ammonite official, and Geshem the Arab
heard *of it,* they laughed at us and despised us,
and said, "What *is* this thing that you are doing?
[a]Will you rebel against the king?"

20 So I answered them, and said to them, "The
God of heaven Himself will prosper us; therefore
we His servants will arise and build, [a]but you have
no heritage or right or memorial in Jerusalem."

### *REBUILDING THE WALL*

3 Then [a]Eliashib the high priest rose up with
his brethren the priests [b]and built the Sheep
Gate; they consecrated it and hung its doors.
They built [c]as far as the Tower of the Hundred,[1]
*and* consecrated it, then as far as the Tower of
[d]Hananel. 2 Next to *Eliashib*[1] [a]the men of Jeri-
cho built. And next to them Zaccur the son of
Imri built.

3 Also the sons of Hassenaah built [a]the Fish
Gate; they laid its beams and [b]hung its doors with
its bolts and bars. 4 And next to them [a]Meremoth
the son of Urijah, the son of Koz,[1] made repairs.
Next to them [b]Meshullam the son of Berechiah,
the son of Meshezabel, made repairs. Next to
them Zadok the son of Baana made repairs.
5 Next to them the Tekoites made repairs; but
their nobles did not put their shoulders[1] to [a]the
work of their Lord.

6 Moreover Jehoiada the son of Paseah and
Meshullam the son of Besodeiah repaired [a]the
Old Gate; they laid its beams and hung its doors,
with its bolts and bars. 7 And next to them Mela-
tiah the Gibeonite, Jadon the Meronothite, the
[a]men of Gibeon and Mizpah, repaired the [b]resi-
dence[1] of the governor *of the region* beyond the
River. 8 Next to him Uzziel the son of Harhaiah,
one of the goldsmiths, made repairs. Also next
to him Hananiah, one[1] of the perfumers, made
repairs; and they fortified Jerusalem as far as
the [a]Broad Wall. 9 And next to them Rephaiah
the son of Hur, leader of half the district of Je-
rusalem, made repairs. 10 Next to them Jedaiah
the son of Harumaph made repairs in front of
his house. And next to him Hattush the son of
Hashabniah made repairs.

11 Malchijah the son of Harim and Hashub
the son of Pahath-Moab repaired another sec-
tion, [a]as well as the Tower of the Ovens. 12 And
next to him was Shallum the son of Hallohesh,
leader of half the district of Jerusalem; he and
his daughters made repairs.

13 Hanun and the inhabitants of Zanoah
repaired [a]the Valley Gate. They built it, hung
its doors with its bolts and bars, and *repaired*
a thousand cubits of the wall as far as [b]the Re-
fuse Gate.

14 Malchijah the son of Rechab, leader of
the district of [a]Beth Haccerem, repaired the
Refuse Gate; he built it and hung its doors with
its bolts and bars.

15 Shallun the son of Col-Hozeh, leader of
the district of Mizpah, repaired [a]the Fountain
Gate; he built it, covered it, hung its doors with
its bolts and bars, and repaired the wall of the
Pool of [b]Shelah by the [c]King's Garden, as far as
the stairs that go down from the City of David.

**2:11** [a] Ezra 8:32 **2:13** [a] 2 Chr. 26:9; Neh. 3:13 [b] Neh. 1:3; 2:17 **2:14** [a] Neh. 3:15 [b] 2 Kin. 20:20 **2:15** [a] 2 Sam. 15:23; Jer. 31:40 **2:17** [a] Neh. 1:3; Ps. 44:13; 79:4; Jer. 24:9; Ezek. 5:14, 15; 22:4 **2:18** [a] Neh. 2:8 [b] 2 Sam. 2:7 **2:19** [a] Neh. 6:6 **2:20** [a] Ezra 4:3; Neh. 6:16 **3:1** [a] Neh. 3:20; 12:10; 13:4, 7, 28 [b] John 5:2 [c] Neh. 12:39 [d] Jer. 31:38; Zech. 14:10 [1] Hebrew *Hammeah,* also at 12:39 **3:2** [a] Ezra 2:34; Neh. 7:36 [1] Literally *On his hand* **3:3** [a] 2 Chr. 33:14; Neh. 12:39; Zeph. 1:10 [b] Neh. 6:1; 7:1 **3:4** [a] Ezra 8:33 [b] Ezra 10:15 [1] Or *Hakkoz* **3:5** [a] [Judg. 5:23] [1] Literally *necks* **3:6** [a] Neh. 12:39 **3:7** [a] Neh. 7:25 [b] Ezra 8:36; Neh. 2:7–9 [1] Literally *throne* **3:8** [a] Neh. 12:38 [1] Literally *the son* **3:11** [a] Neh. 12:38 **3:13** [a] Neh. 2:13, 15 [b] Neh. 2:13 **3:14** [a] Jer. 6:1 **3:15** [a] Neh. 2:14 [b] Is. 8:6; John 9:7 [c] 2 Kin. 25:4

16 After him Nehemiah the son of Azbuk, leader of half the district of Beth Zur, made repairs as far as *the place* in front of the tombs[1] of David, to the [a]man-made pool, and as far as the House of the Mighty.

17 After him the Levites, *under* Rehum the son of Bani, made repairs. Next to him Hashabiah, leader of half the district of Keilah, made repairs for his district. 18 After him their brethren, *under* Bavai[1] the son of Henadad, leader of the *other* half of the district of Keilah, made repairs. 19 And next to him Ezer the son of Jeshua, the leader of Mizpah, repaired another section in front of the Ascent to the Armory at the [a]buttress. 20 After him Baruch the son of Zabbai[1] carefully repaired the other section, from the buttress to the door of the house of Eliashib the high priest. 21 After him Meremoth the son of Urijah, the son of Koz,[1] repaired another section, from the door of the house of Eliashib to the end of the house of Eliashib.

22 And after him the priests, the men of the plain, made repairs. 23 After him Benjamin and Hasshub made repairs opposite their house. After them Azariah the son of Maaseiah, the son of Ananiah, made repairs by his house. 24 After him [a]Binnui the son of Henadad repaired another section, from the house of Azariah to [b]the buttress, even as far as the corner. 25 Palal the son of Uzai *made repairs* opposite the buttress, and on the tower which projects from the king's upper house that *was* by the [a]court of the prison. After him Pedaiah the son of Parosh *made repairs.*

26 Moreover [a]the Nethinim who dwelt in [b]Ophel *made repairs* as far as *the place* in front of [c]the Water Gate toward the east, and on the projecting tower. 27 After them the Tekoites repaired another section, next to the great projecting tower, and as far as the wall of Ophel.

28 Beyond the [a]Horse Gate the priests made repairs, each in front of his *own* house. 29 After them Zadok the son of Immer made repairs in front of his *own* house. After him Shemaiah the son of Shechaniah, the keeper of the East Gate, made repairs. 30 After him Hananiah the son of Shelemiah, and Hanun, the sixth son of Zalaph, repaired another section. After him Meshullam the son of Berechiah made repairs in front of his dwelling. 31 After him Malchijah, one of the goldsmiths, made repairs as far as the house of the Nethinim and of the merchants, in front of the Miphkad[1] Gate, and as far as the upper room at the corner. 32 And between the upper room at the corner, as far as the [a]Sheep Gate, the goldsmiths and the merchants made repairs.

## THE WALL DEFENDED AGAINST ENEMIES

4 But it so happened, [a]when Sanballat heard that we were rebuilding the wall, that he was furious and very indignant, and mocked the Jews. 2 And he spoke before his brethren and the army of Samaria, and said, "What are these feeble Jews doing? Will they fortify themselves? Will they offer sacrifices? Will they complete it in a day? Will they revive the stones from the heaps of rubbish—*stones* that are burned?"

3 Now [a]Tobiah the Ammonite *was* beside him, and he said, "Whatever they build, if even a fox goes up *on it,* he will break down their stone wall."

4 [a]Hear, O our God, for we are despised; [b]turn their reproach on their own heads, and give them as plunder to a land of captivity! 5 [a]Do not cover their iniquity, and do not let their sin be blotted out from before You; for they have provoked *You* to anger before the builders.

6 So we built the wall, and the entire wall was joined together up to half its *height,* for the people had a mind to work.

7 Now it happened, [a]when Sanballat, Tobiah, [b]the Arabs, the Ammonites, and the Ashdodites heard that the walls of Jerusalem were being restored and the gaps were beginning to be closed, that they became very angry, 8 and all of them [a]conspired together to come *and* attack Jerusalem and create confusion. 9 Nevertheless [a]we made our prayer to our God, and because of them we set a watch against them day and night.

> **4:7 Jerusalem** was literally surrounded by enemies. **Sanballat** was from Samaria, which was north of Jerusalem. **Tobiah** was an Ammonite whose tribe lived east of Jerusalem. **The Ashdodites** were a Philistine tribe from west of Jerusalem. **The Arabs** were natives of the region south of Jerusalem.

10 Then Judah said, "The strength of the laborers is failing, and *there is* so much rubbish that we are not able to build the wall."

11 And our adversaries said, "They will neither know nor see anything, till we come into their midst and kill them and cause the work to cease."

12 So it was, when the Jews who dwelt near them came, that they told us ten times, "From whatever place you turn, *they will be* upon us."

13 Therefore I positioned *men* behind the lower parts of the wall, at the openings; and I set the people according to their families, with

3:16 [a] 2 Kin. 20:20; Is. 7:3; 22:11 [1] Septuagint, Syriac, and Vulgate read *tomb.* 3:18 [1] Following Masoretic Text and Vulgate; some Hebrew manuscripts, Septuagint, and Syriac read *Binnui* (compare verse 24). 3:19 [a] 2 Chr. 26:9 3:20 [1] A few Hebrew manuscripts, Syriac, and Vulgate read *Zaccai.* 3:21 [1] Or *Hakkoz* 3:24 [a] Ezra 8:33 [b] Neh. 3:19 3:25 [a] Jer. 32:2; 33:1; 37:21 3:26 [a] Ezra 2:43; Neh. 11:21 [b] 2 Chr. 27:3 [c] Neh. 8:1, 3; 12:37 3:28 [a] 2 Kin. 11:16; 2 Chr. 23:15; Jer. 31:40 3:31 [1] Literally *Inspection* or *Recruiting* 3:32 [a] Neh. 3:1; 12:39 4:1 [a] Neh. 2:10, 19 4:3 [a] Neh. 2:10, 19 4:4 [a] Ps. 123:3, 4 [b] Ps. 79:12; Prov. 3:34 4:5 [a] Ps. 69:27, 28; 109:14, 15; Jer. 18:23 4:7 [a] Neh. 4:1 [b] Neh. 2:19 4:8 [a] Ps. 83:3–5 4:9 [a] [Ps. 50:15]

their swords, their spears, and their bows. 14 And I looked, and arose and said to the nobles, to the leaders, and to the rest of the people, [a]"Do not be afraid of them. Remember the Lord, [b]great and awesome, and [c]fight for your brethren, your sons, your daughters, your wives, and your houses."

15 And it happened, when our enemies heard that it was known to us, and [a]*that* God had brought their plot to nothing, that all of us returned to the wall, everyone to his work. 16 So it was, from that time on, *that* half of my servants worked at construction, while the other half held the spears, the shields, the bows, and *wore* armor; and the leaders *were* behind all the house of Judah. 17 Those who built on the wall, and those who carried burdens, loaded themselves so that with one hand they worked at construction, and with the other held a weapon. 18 Every one of the builders had his sword girded at his side as he built. And the one who sounded the trumpet *was* beside me.

19 Then I said to the nobles, the rulers, and the rest of the people, "The work *is* great and extensive, and we are separated far from one another on the wall. 20 Wherever you hear the sound of the trumpet, rally to us there. [a]Our God will fight for us."

21 So we labored in the work, and half of *the men*[1] held the spears from daybreak until the stars appeared. 22 At the same time I also said to the people, "Let each man and his servant stay at night in Jerusalem, that they may be our guard by night and a working party by day." 23 So neither I, my brethren, my servants, nor the men of the guard who followed me took off our clothes, *except* that everyone took them off for washing.

## NEHEMIAH DEALS WITH OPPRESSION

**5** And there was a great [a]outcry of the people and their wives against their [b]Jewish brethren. 2 For there were those who said, "We, our sons, and our daughters *are* many; therefore let us get grain, that we may eat and live."

3 There were also *some* who said, "We have mortgaged our lands and vineyards and houses, that we might buy grain because of the famine."

4 There were also those who said, "We have borrowed money for the king's tax *on* our lands and vineyards. 5 Yet now [a]our flesh *is* as the flesh of our brethren, our children as their children; and indeed we [b]are forcing our sons and our daughters to be slaves, and *some* of our daughters have been brought into slavery. *It is* not in our power *to redeem them,* for other men have our lands and vineyards."

6 And I became very angry when I heard their outcry and these words. 7 After serious thought, I rebuked the nobles and rulers, and said to them, [a]"Each of you is exacting usury from his brother." So I called a great assembly against them. 8 And I said to them, "According to our ability we have [a]redeemed our Jewish brethren who were sold to the nations. Now indeed, will you even sell your brethren? Or should they be sold to us?"

Then they were silenced and found nothing *to say.* 9 Then I said, "What you are doing *is* not good. Should you not walk [a]in the fear of our God [b]because of the reproach of the nations, our enemies? 10 I also, *with* my brethren and my servants, am lending them money and grain. Please, let us stop this usury! 11 Restore now to them, even this day, their lands, their vineyards, their olive groves, and their houses, also a hundredth of the money and the grain, the new wine and the oil, that you have charged them."

12 So they said, "We will restore *it,* and will require nothing from them; we will do as you say."

Then I called the priests, [a]and required an oath from them that they would do according to this promise. 13 Then [a]I shook out the fold of my garment[1] and said, "So may God shake out each man from his house, and from his property, who does not perform this promise. Even thus may he be shaken out and emptied."

And all the assembly said, "Amen!" and praised the LORD. [b]Then the people did according to this promise.

## THE GENEROSITY OF NEHEMIAH

14 Moreover, from the time that I was appointed to be their governor in the land of Judah, from the twentieth year [a]until the thirty-second year of King Artaxerxes, twelve years, neither I nor my brothers [b]ate the governor's provisions. 15 But the former governors who *were* before me laid burdens on the people, and took from them bread and wine, besides forty shekels of silver. Yes, even their servants bore rule over the people, but [a]I did not do so, because of the [b]fear of God. 16 Indeed, I also continued the [a]work on this wall, and we[1] did not buy any land. All my servants *were* gathered there for the work.

17 And [a]at my table *were* one hundred and fifty Jews and rulers, besides those who came to us from the nations around us. 18 Now *that* [a]which was prepared daily *was* one ox *and* six choice sheep. Also fowl were prepared for me, and once every ten days an abundance of all kinds of wine. Yet in spite of this [b]I did not demand the governor's provisions, because the bondage was heavy on this people.

19 [a]Remember me, my God, for good, *according to* all that I have done for this people.

**4:14** [a] [Num. 14:9]; Deut. 1:29 [b] [Deut. 10:17] [c] 2 Sam. 10:12 **4:15** [a] Job 5:12 **4:20** [a] Ex. 14:14, 25; Deut. 1:30; 3:22; 20:4; Josh. 23:10; 2 Chr. 20:29 **4:21** [1] Literally *them* **5:1** [a] Lev. 25:35–37; Neh. 5:7, 8 [b] Deut. 15:7 **5:5** [a] Is. 58:7 [b] Ex. 21:7; [Lev. 25:39] **5:7** [a] [Ex. 22:25; Lev. 25:36; Deut. 23:19, 20]; Ezek. 22:12 **5:8** [a] Lev. 25:48 **5:9** [a] Lev. 25:36 [b] 2 Sam. 12:14; Rom. 2:24; [1 Pet. 2:12] **5:12** [a] Ezra 10:5; Jer. 34:8, 9 **5:13** [a] Matt. 10:14; Acts 13:51; 18:6 [b] 2 Kin. 23:3 [1] Literally *my lap* **5:14** [a] Neh. 2:1; 13:6 [b] [1 Cor. 9:4–15] **5:15** [a] 2 Cor. 11:9; 12:13 [b] Neh. 5:9 **5:16** [a] Neh. 4:1; 6:1 [1] Following Masoretic Text; Septuagint, Syriac, and Vulgate read *I.* **5:17** [a] 2 Sam. 9:7; 1 Kin. 18:19 **5:18** [a] 1 Kin. 4:22 [b] Neh. 5:14, 15 **5:19** [a] 2 Kin. 20:3; Neh. 13:14, 22, 31

### *CONSPIRACY AGAINST NEHEMIAH*

**6** Now it happened [a]when Sanballat, Tobiah,
Geshem the Arab, and the rest of our enemies
heard that I had rebuilt the wall, and *that* there
were no breaks left in it [b](though at that time I
had not hung the doors in the gates), 2 that San-
ballat and Geshem [a]sent to me, saying, "Come,
let us meet together among the villages in the
plain of [b]Ono." But they [c]thought to do me harm.
3 So I sent messengers to them, saying, "I
*am* doing a great work, so that I cannot come
down. Why should the work cease while I leave
it and go down to you?"
4 But they sent me this message four times,
and I answered them in the same manner.
5 Then Sanballat sent his servant to me as
before, the fifth time, with an open letter in his
hand. 6 In it *was* written:

> It is reported among the nations, and
> Geshem[1] says, *that* you and the Jews
> plan to rebel; therefore, according to
> these rumors, you are rebuilding the
> wall, [a]that you may be their king. 7 And
> you have also appointed prophets to
> proclaim concerning you at Jerusalem,
> saying, "*There is* a king in Judah!" Now
> these matters will be reported to the king.
> So come, therefore, and let us consult
> together.

8 Then I sent to him, saying, "No such things
as you say are being done, but you invent them
in your own heart."
9 For they all *were trying to* make us afraid,
saying, "Their hands will be weakened in the
work, and it will not be done."
Now therefore, *O God,* strengthen my hands.
10 Afterward I came to the house of Shema-
iah the son of Delaiah, the son of Mehetabel,
who *was* a secret informer; and he said, "Let us
meet together in the house of God, within the
temple, and let us close the doors of the temple,
for they are coming to kill you; indeed, at night
they will come to kill you."
11 And I said, "Should such a man as I flee?
And who *is there* such as I who would go into the
temple to save his life? I will not go in!" 12 Then I
perceived that God had not sent him at all, but
that [a]he pronounced *this* prophecy against me
because Tobiah and Sanballat had hired him.
13 For this reason he *was* hired, that I should
be afraid and act that way and sin, so *that* they
might have *cause* for an evil report, that they
might reproach me.
14 [a]My God, remember Tobiah and Sanballat,
according to these their works, and the [b]proph-
etess Noadiah and the rest of the prophets who
would have made me afraid.

> **6:11–13** Only priests, the descendants of the tribe of Levi, were allowed in the **temple**. Nehemiah wasn't a priest, so hiding in the temple would have been a violation of God's law. Nehemiah was trying to lead the people back to following God's ways and he refused to break the law himself.

### *THE WALL COMPLETED*

15 So the wall was finished on the twenty-fifth
*day* of Elul, in fifty-two days. 16 And it happened,
[a]when all our enemies heard *of it,* and all the na-
tions around us saw *these things,* that they were
very disheartened in their own eyes; for [b]they
perceived that this work was done by our God.
17 Also in those days the nobles of Judah
sent many letters to Tobiah, and *the letters of*
Tobiah came to them. 18 For many in Judah were
pledged to him, because he was the [a]son-in-law
of Shechaniah the son of Arah, and his son Jeho-
hanan had married the daughter of [b]Meshullam
the son of Berechiah. 19 Also they reported his
good deeds before me, and reported my words
to him. Tobiah sent letters to frighten me.

**7** Then it was, when the wall was built and I
had [a]hung the doors, when the gatekeepers,
the singers, and the Levites had been appoint-
ed, 2 that I gave the charge of Jerusalem to my
brother [a]Hanani, and Hananiah the leader [b]of
the citadel, for he *was* a faithful man and [c]feared
God more than many.
3 And I said to them, "Do not let the gates
of Jerusalem be opened until the sun is hot;
and while they stand *guard,* let them shut and
bar the doors; and appoint guards from among
the inhabitants of Jerusalem, one at his watch
station and another in front of his own house."

### *THE CAPTIVES WHO RETURNED TO JERUSALEM*

*(Ezra 2:1–70)*

4 Now the city *was* large and spacious, but
the people in it *were* [a]few, and the houses *were*
not rebuilt. 5 Then my God put it into my heart
to gather the nobles, the rulers, and the people,
that they might be registered by genealogy. And I
found a register of the genealogy of those who had
come up in the first *return,* and found written in it:

6 [a]These[1] *are* the people of the province
who came back from the captivity, of
those who had been carried away, whom
Nebuchadnezzar the king of Babylon
had carried away, and who returned to
Jerusalem and Judah, everyone to his city.

**6:1** [a] Neh. 2:10, 19; 4:1, 7; 13:28 [b] Neh. 3:1, 3 **6:2** [a] Prov. 26:24, 25 [b] 1 Chr. 8:12; Neh. 11:35 [c] Ps. 37:12, 32 **6:6** [a] Neh. 2:19 [1] Hebrew *Gashmu* **6:12** [a] Ezek. 13:22 **6:14** [a] Neh. 13:29 [b] Ezek. 13:17 **6:16** [a] Neh. 2:10, 20; 4:1, 7; 6:1 [b] Ps. 126:2 **6:18** [a] Neh. 13:4, 28 [b] Ezra 10:15; Neh. 3:4 **7:1** [a] Neh. 6:1, 15 **7:2** [a] Neh. 1:2 [b] Neh. 2:8; 10:23 [c] Ex. 18:21 **7:4** [a] Deut. 4:27 **7:6** [a] Ezra 2:1–70 [1] Compare verses 6–72 with Ezra 2:1–70

7 Those who came with [a]Zerubbabel *were* Jeshua, Nehemiah, Azariah, Raamiah, Nahamani, Mordecai, Bilshan, Mispereth,[1] Bigvai, Nehum, and Baanah.

The number of the men of the people of Israel: 8 the sons of Parosh, two thousand one hundred and seventy-two;
9 the sons of Shephatiah, three hundred and seventy-two;
10 the sons of Arah, six hundred and fifty-two;
11 the sons of Pahath-Moab, of the sons of Jeshua and Joab, two thousand eight hundred and eighteen;
12 the sons of Elam, one thousand two hundred and fifty-four;
13 the sons of Zattu, eight hundred and forty-five;
14 the sons of Zaccai, seven hundred and sixty;
15 the sons of Binnui,[1] six hundred and forty-eight;
16 the sons of Bebai, six hundred and twenty-eight;
17 the sons of Azgad, two thousand three hundred and twenty-two;
18 the sons of Adonikam, six hundred and sixty-seven;
19 the sons of Bigvai, two thousand and sixty-seven;
20 the sons of Adin, six hundred and fifty-five;
21 the sons of Ater of Hezekiah, ninety-eight;
22 the sons of Hashum, three hundred and twenty-eight;
23 the sons of Bezai, three hundred and twenty-four;
24 the sons of Hariph,[1] one hundred and twelve;
25 the sons of Gibeon,[1] ninety-five;
26 the men of Bethlehem and Netophah, one hundred and eighty-eight;
27 the men of Anathoth, one hundred and twenty-eight;
28 the men of Beth Azmaveth,[1] forty-two;
29 the men of Kirjath Jearim, Chephirah, and Beeroth, seven hundred and forty-three;
30 the men of Ramah and Geba, six hundred and twenty-one;
31 the men of Michmas, one hundred and twenty-two;
32 the men of Bethel and Ai, one hundred and twenty-three;
33 the men of the other Nebo, fifty-two;
34 the sons of the other [a]Elam, one thousand two hundred and fifty-four;
35 the sons of Harim, three hundred and twenty;
36 the sons of Jericho, three hundred and forty-five;
37 the sons of Lod, Hadid, and Ono, seven hundred and twenty-one;
38 the sons of Senaah, three thousand nine hundred and thirty.

39 The priests: the sons of [a]Jedaiah, of the house of Jeshua, nine hundred and seventy-three;
40 the sons of [a]Immer, one thousand and fifty-two;
41 the sons of [a]Pashhur, one thousand two hundred and forty-seven;
42 the sons of [a]Harim, one thousand and seventeen.

43 The Levites: the sons of Jeshua, of Kadmiel,
*and* of the sons of Hodevah,[1] seventy-four.

44 The singers: the sons of Asaph, one hundred and forty-eight.

45 The gatekeepers: the sons of Shallum,
the sons of Ater,
the sons of Talmon,
the sons of Akkub,
the sons of Hatita,
the sons of Shobai, one hundred and thirty-eight.

46 The Nethinim: the sons of Ziha,
the sons of Hasupha,
the sons of Tabbaoth,
47 the sons of Keros,
the sons of Sia,[1]
the sons of Padon,
48 the sons of Lebana,[1]
the sons of Hagaba,[2]
the sons of Salmai,[3]
49 the sons of Hanan,
the sons of Giddel,
the sons of Gahar,
50 the sons of Reaiah,
the sons of Rezin,
the sons of Nekoda,
51 the sons of Gazzam,
the sons of Uzza,
the sons of Paseah,
52 the sons of Besai,
the sons of Meunim,
the sons of Nephishesim,[1]
53 the sons of Bakbuk,
the sons of Hakupha,
the sons of Harhur,
54 the sons of Bazlith,[1]

7:7 [a] Ezra 5:2; Neh. 12:1, 47; Matt. 1:12, 13 [1] Spelled *Mispar* in Ezra 2:2 7:15 [1] Spelled *Bani* in Ezra 2:10 7:24 [1] Called *Jorah* in Ezra 2:18 7:25 [1] Called *Gibbar* in Ezra 2:20 7:28 [1] Called *Azmaveth* in Ezra 2:24 7:34 [a] Neh. 7:12 7:39 [a] 1 Chr. 24:7 7:40 [a] 1 Chr. 9:12 7:41 [a] Ezra 2:38; 10:22 7:42 [a] 1 Chr. 24:8 7:43 [1] Spelled *Hodaviah* in Ezra 2:40 7:47 [1] Spelled *Siaha* in Ezra 2:44 7:48 [1] Masoretic Text reads *Lebanah.* [2] Masoretic Text reads *Hogabah.* [3] Or *Shalmai,* or *Shamlai* 7:52 [1] Spelled *Nephusim* in Ezra 2:50 7:54 [1] Spelled *Bazluth* in Ezra 2:52

the sons of Mehida,
the sons of Harsha,
55 the sons of Barkos,
the sons of Sisera,
the sons of Tamah,
56 the sons of Neziah,
and the sons of Hatipha.

57 The sons of Solomon's servants: the sons
of Sotai,
the sons of Sophereth,
the sons of Perida,[1]
58 the sons of Jaala,
the sons of Darkon,
the sons of Giddel,
59 the sons of Shephatiah,
the sons of Hattil,
the sons of Pochereth of Zebaim,
and the sons of Amon.[1]
60 All the Nethinim, and the sons of
Solomon's servants, *were* three hundred
and ninety-two.

61 And these *were* the ones who came up
from Tel Melah, Tel Harsha, Cherub,
Addon,[1] and Immer, but they could not
identify their father's house nor their
lineage, whether they *were* of Israel: 62 the
sons of Delaiah,
the sons of Tobiah,
the sons of Nekoda, six hundred and
forty-two;
63 and of the priests: the sons of Habaiah,
the sons of Koz,[1]
the sons of Barzillai, who took a wife of
the daughters of Barzillai the Gileadite,
and was called by their name.
64 These sought their listing *among* those
who were registered by genealogy, but
it was not found; therefore they were
excluded from the priesthood as defiled.
65 And the governor[1] said to them that
they should not eat of the most holy
things till a priest could consult with the
Urim and Thummim.

66 Altogether the whole assembly *was*
forty-two thousand three hundred and
sixty, 67 besides their male and female
servants, of whom *there were* seven
thousand three hundred and thirty-seven;
and they had two hundred and forty-five
men and women singers. 68 Their horses
were seven hundred and thirty-six, their
mules two hundred and forty-five, 69 *their*
camels four hundred and thirty-five, *and*
donkeys six thousand seven hundred and
twenty.

70 And some of the heads of the fathers'
*houses* gave to the work. [a]The governor[1]
gave to the treasury one thousand gold
drachmas, fifty basins, and five hundred
and thirty priestly garments. 71 Some of
the heads of the fathers' *houses* gave to the
treasury of the work [a]twenty thousand gold
drachmas, and two thousand two hundred
silver minas. 72 And that which the rest of
the people gave *was* twenty thousand gold
drachmas, two thousand silver minas, and
sixty-seven priestly garments.

73 So the priests, the Levites, the gatekeepers,
the singers, *some* of the people, the Nethinim,
and all Israel dwelt in their cities.

### *EZRA READS THE LAW*

[a]When the seventh month came, the chil-
dren of Israel *were* in their cities.

**8** Now all [a]the people gathered together as one
man in the open square that *was* [b]in front of
the Water Gate; and they told Ezra the [c]scribe to
bring the Book of the Law of Moses, which the
LORD had commanded Israel. 2 So Ezra the priest
brought [a]the Law before the assembly of men
and women and all who *could* hear with under-
standing [b]on the first day of the seventh month.
3 Then he [a]read from it in the open square that
*was* in front of the Water Gate from morning
until midday, before the men and women and
those who could understand; and the ears of all
the people *were attentive* to the Book of the Law.
4 So Ezra the scribe stood on a platform of
wood which they had made for the purpose; and
beside him, at his right hand, stood Mattithiah,
Shema, Anaiah, Urijah, Hilkiah, and Maaseiah;
and at his left hand Pedaiah, Mishael, Malchijah,
Hashum, Hashbadana, Zechariah, *and* Meshul-
lam. 5 And Ezra opened the book in the sight of all
the people, for he was *standing* above all the peo-
ple; and when he opened it, all the people [a]stood
up. 6 And Ezra blessed the LORD, the great God.
Then all the people [a]answered, "Amen,
Amen!" while [b]lifting up their hands. And they
[c]bowed their heads and worshiped the LORD
with *their* faces to the ground.
7 Also Jeshua, Bani, Sherebiah, Jamin, Akkub,
Shabbethai, Hodijah, Maaseiah, Kelita, Azariah,
Jozabad, Hanan, Pelaiah, and the Levites, [a]helped
the people to understand the Law; and the people
[b]*stood* in their place. 8 So they read distinctly from
the book, in the Law of God; and they gave the
sense, and helped *them* to understand the reading.
9 [a]And Nehemiah, who *was* the governor,[1]
Ezra the priest *and* scribe, and the Levites who
taught the people said to all the people, [b]"This
day *is* holy to the LORD your God; [c]do not mourn

7:57 [1] Spelled *Peruda* in Ezra 2:55 7:59 [1] Spelled *Ami* in Ezra 2:57 7:61 [1] Spelled *Addan* in Ezra 2:59 7:63 [1] Or *Hakkoz*
7:65 [1] Hebrew *Tirshatha* 7:70 [a] Neh. 8:9 [1] Hebrew *Tirshatha* 7:71 [a] Ezra 2:69 7:73 [a] Ezra 3:1 8:1 [a] Ezra 3:1 [b] Neh. 3:26
[c] Ezra 7:6 8:2 [a] [Deut. 31:11, 12]; Neh. 8:9 [b] Lev. 23:24; Num. 29:1–6 8:3 [a] Deut. 31:9–11; 2 Kin. 23:2 8:5 [a] Judg. 3:20; 1 Kin. 8:12–14
8:6 [a] Neh. 5:13; [1 Cor. 14:16] [b] Ps. 28:2; Lam. 3:41; 1 Tim. 2:8 [c] Ex. 4:31; 12:27; 2 Chr. 20:18 8:7 [a] Lev. 10:11; Deut. 33:10; 2 Chr. 17:7; [Mal.
2:7] [b] Neh. 9:3 8:9 [a] Ezra 2:63; Neh. 7:65, 70; 10:1 [b] Lev. 23:24; Num. 29:1 [c] Deut. 16:14; Eccl. 3:4 [1] Hebrew *Tirshatha*

KNOW THE TRUTH

## THE DOCTRINE OF SCRIPTURE

### PART 1: OVERVIEW OF THE DOCTRINE OF SCRIPTURE

**8:7–12** Centuries of sinful living brought about by ignoring God's Word had sent Judah into seventy years of captivity in Babylon. It was among the greatest seasons of heartache in Judah's history. After returning from this captivity, Nehemiah and Ezra focused on helping God's people not make the same mistake. They, along with the Levites, diligently taught God's people God's Word. Initially, the sting of its truth caused sorrow in the people. But once they wiped their tears and got to work heeding God's Word, seven days of exceeding joy and gladness eclipsed the prior seventy years of sorrow. This illustrates the importance and power of the Scriptures.

From Genesis through Revelation, the Bible reveals who God is, what He does, and what He wants for us. Its pages describe one story of God's plan throughout history to build a family to be with Him forever.

When a person neglects its truths, wisdom, and commands, needless and constant sorrow and suffering result. When a person studies the Scriptures to know and obey the Father and the Son through the Spirit, exceeding joy, limitless blessing, satisfying purpose, and unconquerable hope follow. Studying and applying the Bible is no mere intellectual exercise; it's an endlessly fulfilling relational pursuit. Our highest honor is to mine the Word of God to forever know, love, and glorify the God of the Word.

*For* **THE DOCTRINE OF SCRIPTURE: PART 2: THE PURPOSE OF SCRIPTURE,** *turn to Deuteronomy 31:9–13 on page 208.* • • •

nor weep." For all the people wept, when they heard the words of the Law.

10 Then he said to them, "Go your way, eat the fat, drink the sweet, [a]and send portions to those for whom nothing is prepared; for *this* day *is* holy to our Lord. Do not sorrow, for the joy of the LORD is your strength."

11 So the Levites quieted all the people, saying, "Be still, for the day *is* holy; do not be grieved." 12 And all the people went their way to eat and drink, to [a]send portions and rejoice greatly, because they [b]understood the words that were declared to them.

### *THE FEAST OF TABERNACLES*

*(cf. Lev. 23:33–43)*

13 Now on the second day the heads of the fathers' *houses* of all the people, with the priests and Levites, were gathered to Ezra the scribe, in order to understand the words of the Law. 14 And they found written in the Law, which the LORD had commanded by Moses, that the children of Israel should dwell in [a]booths during the feast of the seventh month, 15 and [a]that they should announce and proclaim in all their cities and [b]in Jerusalem, saying, "Go out to the mountain, and [c]bring olive branches, branches of oil trees, myrtle branches, palm branches, and branches of leafy trees, to make booths, as *it is* written."

16 Then the people went out and brought *them* and made themselves booths, each one on the [a]roof of his house, or in their courtyards or the courts of the house of God, and in the open square of the [b]Water Gate [c]and in the open square of the Gate of Ephraim. 17 So the whole assembly of those who had returned from the captivity made booths and sat under the booths; for since the days of Joshua the son of Nun until that day the children of Israel had not done so. And there was very [a]great gladness. 18 Also [a]day by day, from the first day until the last day, he read from the Book of the Law of God. And they kept the feast [b]seven days; and on the [c]eighth day *there was* a sacred assembly, according to the *prescribed* manner.

### *THE PEOPLE CONFESS THEIR SINS*

**9** Now on the twenty-fourth day of [a]this month the children of Israel were assembled with fasting, in sackcloth, [b]and with dust on their heads.[1] 2 Then [a]those of Israelite lineage separated themselves from all foreigners; and they stood and [b]confessed their sins and the iniquities of their fathers. 3 And they stood up in their place and [a]read from the Book of the Law of the LORD their God *for one*-fourth of the day; and *for another* fourth they confessed and worshiped the LORD their God.

8:10 [a] [Deut. 26:11–13]; Esth. 9:19, 22; Rev. 11:10 8:12 [a] Neh. 8:10 [b] Neh. 8:7, 8 8:14 [a] Lev. 23:34, 40, 42; Deut. 16:13 8:15 [a] Lev. 23:4 [b] Deut. 16:16 [c] Lev. 23:40 8:16 [a] Deut. 22:8 [b] Neh. 12:37 [c] 2 Kin. 14:13; Neh. 12:39 8:17 [a] 2 Chr. 30:21 8:18 [a] Deut. 31:11 [b] Lev. 23:36 [c] Num. 29:35 9:1 [a] Neh. 8:2 [b] 1 Sam. 4:12 [1] Literally *earth on them* 9:2 [a] Neh. 13:3, 30 [b] Neh. 1:6 9:3 [a] Neh. 8:7, 8

4 Then Jeshua, Bani, Kadmiel, Shebaniah,
Bunni, Sherebiah, Bani, *and* Chenani stood on
the stairs of the Levites and cried out with a loud
voice to the LORD their God. 5 And the Levites,
Jeshua, Kadmiel, Bani, Hashabniah, Sherebiah,
Hodijah, Shebaniah, *and* Pethahiah, said:

"Stand up *and* bless the LORD your God
Forever and ever!

"Blessed be [a]Your glorious name,
Which is exalted above all blessing and praise!
6 [a]You alone *are* the LORD;
[b]You have made heaven,
[c]The heaven of heavens, with [d]all their host,
The earth and everything on it,
The seas and all that is in them,
And You [e]preserve them all.
The host of heaven worships You.

7 "You *are* the LORD God,
Who chose [a]Abram,
And brought him out of Ur of the Chaldeans,
And gave him the name [b]Abraham;
8 You found his heart [a]faithful before You,
And made a [b]covenant with him
To give the land of the Canaanites,
The Hittites, the Amorites,
The Perizzites, the Jebusites,
And the Girgashites—
To give *it* to his descendants.
You [c]have performed Your words,
For You *are* righteous.

9 "You[a] saw the affliction of our fathers in Egypt,
And [b]heard their cry by the Red Sea.
10 You [a]showed signs and wonders against Pharaoh,
Against all his servants,
And against all the people of his land.
For You knew that they [b]acted proudly against them.
So You [c]made a name for Yourself, as *it is* this day.
11 [a]And You divided the sea before them,
So that they went through the midst of the sea on the dry land;
And their persecutors You threw into the deep,
[b]As a stone into the mighty waters.
12 Moreover You [a]led them by day with a cloudy pillar,
And by night with a pillar of fire,
To give them light on the road
Which they should travel.

13 "You[a] came down also on Mount Sinai,
And spoke with them from heaven,
And gave them [b]just ordinances and true laws,
Good statutes and commandments.
14 You made known to them Your [a]holy Sabbath,
And commanded them precepts, statutes and laws,
By the hand of Moses Your servant.
15 You [a]gave them bread from heaven for their hunger,
And [b]brought them water out of the rock for their thirst,
And told them to [c]go in to possess the land
Which You had sworn to give them.

16 "But[a] they and our fathers acted proudly,
[b]Hardened their necks,
And did not heed Your commandments.
17 They refused to obey,
And [a]they were not mindful of Your wonders
That You did among them.
But they hardened their necks,
And in their rebellion[1]
They appointed [b]a leader
To return to their bondage.
But You *are* God,
Ready to pardon,
[c]Gracious and merciful,
Slow to anger,
Abundant in kindness,
And did not forsake them.

**SEEING JESUS IN THE SCRIPTURE**

**9:17** Nehemiah praised God for His readiness to forgive sin. God sent Jesus not to condemn the world but to save the world from sin (see John 3:17). Since the first sin in Genesis 3, God's mission has been salvation, not condemnation.

18 "Even [a]when they made a molded calf for themselves,
And said, 'This *is* your god
That brought you up out of Egypt,'
And worked great provocations,
19 Yet in Your [a]manifold mercies
You did not forsake them in the wilderness.
The [b]pillar of the cloud did not depart from them by day,
To lead them on the road;

**9:5** [a] 1 Chr. 29:13 **9:6** [a] 2 Kin. 19:15, 19 [b] Rev. 14:7 [c] [Deut. 10:14] [d] Gen. 2:1 [e] [Ps. 36:6] **9:7** [a] Gen. 11:31 [b] Gen. 17:5 **9:8** [a] Gen. 15:6; 22:1–3 [b] Gen. 15:18 [c] Josh. 23:14 **9:9** [a] Ex. 2:25; 3:7 [b] Ex. 14:10 **9:10** [a] Ex. 7—14 [b] Ex. 18:11 [c] Jer. 32:20 **9:11** [a] Ex. 14:20–28 [b] Ex. 15:1, 5 **9:12** [a] Ex. 13:21, 22 **9:13** [a] Ex. 20:1–18 [b] [Rom. 7:12] **9:14** [a] Gen. 2:3 **9:15** [a] Ex. 16:14–17 [b] Ex. 17:6 [c] Deut. 1:8 **9:16** [a] Ps. 106:6 [b] Deut. 1:26–33; 31:27 **9:17** [a] Ps. 78:11, 42–45 [b] Num. 14:4 [c] Joel 2:13 [1] Following Masoretic Text and Vulgate; Septuagint reads *in Egypt*. **9:18** [a] Ex. 32:4–8, 31 **9:19** [a] Ps. 106:45 [b] 1 Cor. 10:1

Nor the pillar of fire by night,
To show them light,
And the way they should go.
20 You also gave Your [a]good Spirit to instruct them,
And did not withhold Your [b]manna from their mouth,
And gave them [c]water for their thirst.
21 [a]Forty years You sustained them in the wilderness;
They lacked nothing;
Their [b]clothes did not wear out[1]
And their feet did not swell.

22 "Moreover You gave them kingdoms and nations,
And divided them into districts.[1]
So they took possession of the land of [a]Sihon,
The land of[2] the king of Heshbon,
And the land of Og king of Bashan.
23 You also multiplied [a]their children as the stars of heaven,
And brought them into the land
Which You had told their fathers
To go in and possess.
24 So [a]the people went in
And possessed the land;
[b]You subdued before them the inhabitants of the land,
The Canaanites,
And gave them into their hands,
With their kings
And the people of the land,
That they might do with them as they wished.
25 And they took strong cities and a [a]rich land,
And possessed [b]houses full of all goods,
Cisterns *already* dug, vineyards, olive groves,
And fruit trees in abundance.
So they ate and were filled and [c]grew fat,
And delighted themselves in Your great [d]goodness.

26 "Nevertheless they [a]were disobedient
And rebelled against You,
[b]Cast Your law behind their backs
And killed Your [c]prophets, who testified against them
To turn them to Yourself;
And they worked great provocations.
27 [a]Therefore You delivered them into the hand of their enemies,
Who oppressed them;
And in the time of their trouble,
When they cried to You,

## SEEING JESUS IN THE SCRIPTURE

**9:26–27** Much like the prophets in the Old Testament who were persecuted for speaking the message God sent them to speak, Jesus was persecuted and ultimately killed because His people didn't like the message He brought (see John 1:11).

You [b]heard from heaven;
And according to Your abundant mercies
[c]You gave them deliverers who saved them
From the hand of their enemies.

28 "But after they had rest,
[a]They again did evil before You.
Therefore You left them in the hand of their enemies,
So that they had dominion over them;
Yet when they returned and cried out to You,
You heard from heaven;
And [b]many times You delivered them according to Your mercies,
29 And testified against them,
That You might bring them back to Your law.
Yet they acted proudly,
And did not heed Your commandments,
But sinned against Your judgments,
[a]'Which if a man does, he shall live by them.'[1]
And they shrugged their shoulders,
Stiffened their necks,
And would not hear.
30 Yet for many years You had patience with them,
And testified [a]against them by Your Spirit [b]in Your prophets.
Yet they would not listen;
[c]Therefore You gave them into the hand of the peoples of the lands.
31 Nevertheless in Your great mercy
[a]You did not utterly consume them nor forsake them;
For You *are* God, gracious and merciful.

32 "Now therefore, our God,
The great, the [a]mighty, and awesome God,
Who keeps covenant and mercy:
Do not let all the trouble seem small before You
That has come upon us,
Our kings and our princes,
Our priests and our prophets,
Our fathers and on all Your people,
[b]From the days of the kings of Assyria until this day.

**9:20** [a] Num. 11:17 [b] Ex. 16:14–16 [c] Ex. 17:6 **9:21** [a] Deut. 2:7 [b] Deut. 8:4; 29:5 [1] Compare Deuteronomy 29:5 **9:22** [a] Num. 21:21–35 [1] Literally *corners* [2] Following Masoretic Text and Vulgate; Septuagint omits *The land of.* **9:23** [a] Gen. 15:5; 22:17; Heb. 11:12 **9:24** [a] Josh. 1:2–4 [b] Josh. 18:1; [Ps. 44:2, 3] **9:25** [a] Num. 13:27 [b] Deut. 6:11; Josh. 24:13 [c] [Deut. 32:15] [d] Hos. 3:5 **9:26** [a] Judg. 2:11 [b] 1 Kin. 14:9; Ps. 50:17 [c] 1 Kin. 18:4; 19:10; Matt. 23:37; Acts 7:52 **9:27** [a] Judg. 2:14; Ps. 106:41 [b] Ps. 106:44 [c] Judg. 2:18 **9:28** [a] Judg. 3:12 [b] Ps. 106:43 **9:29** [a] Lev. 18:5; Rom. 10:5; [Gal. 3:12] [1] Leviticus 18:5 **9:30** [a] 2 Kin. 17:13–18; 2 Chr. 36:11–20; Jer. 7:25 [b] [Acts 7:51]; 1 Pet. 1:11 [c] Is. 5:5 **9:31** [a] Jer. 4:27; [Rom. 11:2–5] **9:32** [a] [Ex. 34:6, 7] [b] 2 Kin. 15:19; 17:3–6; Ezra 4:2, 10

33 However [a]You *are* just in all that has
befallen us;
For You have dealt faithfully,
But [b]we have done wickedly.
34 Neither our kings nor our princes,
Our priests nor our fathers,
Have kept Your law,
Nor heeded Your commandments and
Your testimonies,
With which You testified against them.
35 For they have [a]not served You in their
kingdom,
Or in the many good *things* that You gave
them,
Or in the large and rich land which You
set before them;
Nor did they turn from their wicked works.

36 "Here [a]we *are,* servants today!
And the land that You gave to our fathers,
To eat its fruit and its bounty,
Here we *are,* servants in it!
37 And [a]it yields much increase to the kings
You have set over us,
Because of our sins;
Also they have [b]dominion over our bodies
and our cattle
At their pleasure;
And we *are* in great distress.

38 "And because of all this,
We [a]make a sure *covenant* and write *it;*
Our leaders, our Levites, *and* our priests
[b]seal *it.*"

### *THE PEOPLE WHO SEALED THE COVENANT*

**10** Now those who placed *their* seal on *the*
*document were:*
Nehemiah the governor, [a]the son of Hacali-
ah, and Zedekiah, 2 [a]Seraiah, Azariah, Jeremiah,
3 Pashhur, Amariah, Malchijah, 4 Hattush, Sheb-
aniah, Malluch, 5 Harim, Meremoth, Obadiah,
6 Daniel, Ginnethon, Baruch, 7 Meshullam, Abi-
jah, Mijamin, 8 Maaziah, Bilgai, *and* Shemaiah.
These *were* the priests.
9 The Levites: Jeshua the son of Azaniah,
Binnui of the sons of Henadad, *and* Kadmiel.
10 Their brethren: Shebaniah, Hodijah, Keli-
ta, Pelaiah, Hanan, 11 Micha, Rehob, Hashabiah,
12 Zaccur, Sherebiah, Shebaniah, 13 Hodijah, Bani,
*and* Beninu.
14 The leaders of the people: [a]Parosh, Pa-
hath-Moab, Elam, Zattu, Bani, 15 Bunni, Azgad,
Bebai, 16 Adonijah, Bigvai, Adin, 17 Ater, Hezekiah,
Azzur, 18 Hodijah, Hashum, Bezai, 19 Hariph, An-
athoth, Nebai, 20 Magpiash, Meshullam, Hezir,
21 Meshezabel, Zadok, Jaddua, 22 Pelatiah, Hanan,
Anaiah, 23 Hoshea, Hananiah, Hasshub, 24 Hal-
lohesh, Pilha, Shobek, 25 Rehum, Hashabnah,
Maaseiah, 26 Ahijah, Hanan, Anan, 27 Malluch,
Harim, *and* Baanah.

### *THE COVENANT THAT WAS SEALED*

28 [a]Now the rest of the people—the priests,
the Levites, the gatekeepers, the singers, the
Nethinim, [b]and all those who had separated
themselves from the peoples of the lands to
the Law of God, their wives, their sons, and their
daughters, everyone who had knowledge and
understanding— 29 these joined with their breth-
ren, their nobles, [a]and entered into a curse and
an oath [b]to walk in God's Law, which was given
by Moses the servant of God, and to observe
and do all the commandments of the LORD our
Lord, and His ordinances and His statutes: 30 We
would not give [a]our daughters as wives to the
peoples of the land, nor take their daughters for
our sons; 31 [a]*if* the peoples of the land brought
wares or any grain to sell on the Sabbath day, we
would not buy it from them on the Sabbath, or
on a holy day; and we would forego the [b]seventh
year's *produce* and the [c]exacting of every debt.
32 Also we made ordinances for ourselves, to
exact from ourselves yearly [a]one-third of a shek-
el for the service of the house of our God: 33 for
[a]the showbread, for the regular grain offering,
for the [b]regular burnt offering of the Sabbaths,
the New Moons, and the set feasts; for the holy
things, for the sin offerings to make atonement
for Israel, and all the work of the house of our
God. 34 We cast lots among the priests, the Le-
vites, and the people, [a]for bringing the wood
offering into the house of our God, according
to our fathers' houses, at the appointed times
year by year, to burn on the altar of the LORD
our God [b]as *it is* written in the Law.
35 And *we made ordinances* [a]to bring the
firstfruits of our ground and the firstfruits of
all fruit of all trees, year by year, to the house of
the LORD; 36 to bring the [a]firstborn of our sons
and our cattle, as *it is* written in the Law, and
the firstborn of our herds and our flocks, to the
house of our God, to the priests who minister in
the house of our God; 37 [a]to bring the firstfruits of
our dough, our offerings, the fruit from all kinds
of trees, *the* new wine and oil, to the priests, to
the storerooms of the house of our God; and to
bring [b]the tithes of our land to the Levites, for
the Levites should receive the tithes in all our
farming communities. 38 And the priest, the
descendant of Aaron, shall be with the Levites
[a]when the Levites receive tithes; and the Levites

9:33 [a] Ps. 119:137; [Dan. 9:14] [b] Ps. 106:6; [Dan. 9:5, 6, 8] 9:35 [a] Deut. 28:47 9:36 [a] Deut. 28:48; Ezra 9:9 9:37 [a] Deut. 28:33, 51 [b] Deut. 28:48 9:38 [a] 2 Kin. 23:3; 2 Chr. 29:10; Ezra 10:3 [b] Neh. 10:1 10:1 [a] Neh. 1:1 10:2 [a] Neh. 12:1–21 10:14 [a] Ezra 2:3 10:28 [a] Ezra 2:36–43 [b] Ezra 9:1; Neh. 13:3 10:29 [a] Deut. 29:12; Neh. 5:12; Ps. 119:106 [b] 2 Kin. 23:3; 2 Chr. 34:31 10:30 [a] Ex. 34:16; Deut. 7:3; [Ezra 9:12] 10:31 [a] Ex. 20:10; Lev. 23:3; Deut. 5:12 [b] Ex. 23:10, 11; Lev. 25:4; Jer. 34:14 [c] [Deut. 15:1, 2]; Neh. 5:12 10:32 [a] Ex. 30:11–16; 38:25, 26; 2 Chr. 24:6, 9; Matt. 17:24 10:33 [a] Lev. 24:5; 2 Chr. 2:4 [b] Num. 28; 29 10:34 [a] Neh. 13:31; [Is. 40:16] [b] Lev. 6:12 10:35 [a] Ex. 23:19; 34:26; Lev. 19:23; Num. 18:12; Deut. 26:1, 2 10:36 [a] Ex. 13:2, 12, 13; Lev. 27:26, 27; Num. 18:15, 16 10:37 [a] Lev. 23:17; Num. 15:19; 18:12; Deut. 18:4; 26:2 [b] Lev. 27:30; Num. 18:21; Mal. 3:10 10:38 [a] Num. 18:26

**10:38 The Levites** didn't have their own land or means of income. The rest of the Israelites supported them by giving them **tithes**, one-tenth of every harvest. The Levites, in turn, supported the priests by giving them one-tenth of everything they received.

shall bring up a tenth of the tithes to the house of our God, to [b]the rooms of the storehouse. 39 For the children of Israel and the children of Levi [a]shall bring the offering of the grain, of the new wine and the oil, to the storerooms where the articles of the sanctuary *are, where* the priests who minister and the gatekeepers [b]and the singers *are;* and we will not [c]neglect the house of our God.

### THE PEOPLE DWELLING IN JERUSALEM

**11** Now the leaders of the people dwelt at Jerusalem; the rest of the people cast lots to bring one out of ten to dwell in Jerusalem, [a]the holy city, and nine-tenths *were to dwell* in *other* cities. 2 And the people blessed all the men who [a]willingly offered themselves to dwell at Jerusalem.

3 [a]These *are* the heads of the province who dwelt in Jerusalem. (But in the cities of Judah everyone dwelt in his own possession in their cities—Israelites, priests, Levites, [b]Nethinim, and [c]descendants of Solomon's servants.) 4 Also [a]in Jerusalem dwelt *some* of the children of Judah and of the children of Benjamin.

The children of Judah: Athaiah the son of Uzziah, the son of Zechariah, the son of Amariah, the son of Shephatiah, the son of Mahalalel, of the children of [b]Perez; 5 and Maaseiah the son of Baruch, the son of Col-Hozeh, the son of Hazaiah, the son of Adaiah, the son of Joiarib, the son of Zechariah, the son of Shiloni. 6 All the sons of Perez who dwelt at Jerusalem *were* four hundred and sixty-eight valiant men.

7 And these are the sons of Benjamin: Sallu the son of Meshullam, the son of Joed, the son of Pedaiah, the son of Kolaiah, the son of Maaseiah, the son of Ithiel, the son of Jeshaiah; 8 and after him Gabbai *and* Sallai, nine hundred and twenty-eight. 9 Joel the son of Zichri *was* their overseer, and Judah the son of Senuah[1] *was* second over the city.

**11:4–6** Only two of the twelve tribes of Israel—**Judah** and **Benjamin**—made it back to their homeland intact following the Babylonian captivity. The Levites were not counted as a tribe, even though they were descendants of one of Israel's sons. To replace Levi in the count, Joseph was divided into two tribes, Manasseh and Ephraim.

10 [a]Of the priests: Jedaiah the son of Joiarib, and Jachin; 11 Seraiah the son of Hilkiah, the son of Meshullam, the son of Zadok, the son of Meraioth, the son of Ahitub, *was* the leader of the house of God. 12 Their brethren who did the work of the house *were* eight hundred and twenty-two; and Adaiah the son of Jeroham, the son of Pelaliah, the son of Amzi, the son of Zechariah, the son of Pashhur, the son of Malchijah, 13 and his brethren, heads of the fathers' *houses, were* two hundred and forty-two; and Amashai the son of Azarel, the son of Ahzai, the son of Meshillemoth, the son of Immer, 14 and their brethren, mighty men of valor, *were* one hundred and twenty-eight. Their overseer *was* Zabdiel the son of *one of* the great men.[1]

15 Also of the Levites: Shemaiah the son of Hasshub, the son of Azrikam, the son of Hashabiah, the son of Bunni; 16 [a]Shabbethai and [b]Jozabad, of the heads of the Levites, *had* the oversight of [c]the business outside of the house of God; 17 Mattaniah the son of Micha,[1] the son of Zabdi, the son of Asaph, the leader *who* began the thanksgiving with prayer; Bakbukiah, the second among his brethren; and Abda the son of Shammua, the son of Galal, the son of Jeduthun. 18 All the Levites in [a]the holy city *were* two hundred and eighty-four.

19 Moreover the gatekeepers, Akkub, Talmon, and their brethren who kept the gates, *were* one hundred and seventy-two.

20 And the rest of Israel, of the priests *and* Levites, *were* in all the cities of Judah, everyone in his inheritance. 21 [a]But the Nethinim dwelt in Ophel. And Ziha and Gishpa *were* over the Nethinim.

22 Also the overseer of the Levites at Jerusalem *was* Uzzi the son of Bani, the son of Hashabiah, the son of Mattaniah, the son of Micha, of the sons of Asaph, the singers in charge of the service of the house of God. 23 For [a]*it was* the king's command concerning them that a certain portion should be for the singers, a quota day by day. 24 Pethahiah the son of Meshezabel, of the children of [a]Zerah the son of Judah, *was* [b]the king's deputy[1] in all matters concerning the people.

### THE PEOPLE DWELLING OUTSIDE JERUSALEM

25 And as for the villages with their fields, *some* of the children of Judah dwelt in [a]Kirjath Arba and its villages, Dibon and its villages, Jekabzeel and its villages; 26 in Jeshua, Moladah,

**10:38** [b] 1 Chr. 9:26; 2 Chr. 31:11 **10:39** [a] Deut. 12:6, 11; 2 Chr. 31:12; Neh. 13:12 [b] Neh. 13:10, 11 [c] [Heb. 10:25] **11:1** [a] Neh. 10:18; Matt. 4:5; 5:35; 27:53 **11:2** [a] Judg. 5:9; 2 Chr. 17:16 **11:3** [a] 1 Chr. 9:2, 3 [b] Ezra 2:43 [c] Ezra 2:55 **11:4** [a] 1 Chr. 9:3 [b] Gen. 38:29 **11:9** [1] Or *Hassenuah* **11:10** [a] 1 Chr. 9:10 **11:14** [1] Or *the son of Haggedolim* **11:16** [a] Ezra 10:15 [b] Ezra 8:33 [c] 1 Chr. 26:29 **11:17** [1] Or *Michah* **11:18** [a] Neh. 11:1 **11:21** [a] 2 Chr. 27:3; Neh. 3:26 **11:23** [a] Ezra 6:8, 9; 7:20 **11:24** [a] Gen. 38:30 [b] 1 Chr. 18:17 [1] Literally *at the king's hand* **11:25** [a] Josh. 14:15

Beth Pelet, 27 Hazar Shual, and Beersheba and its villages; 28 in Ziklag and Meconah and its villages; 29 in En Rimmon, Zorah, Jarmuth, 30 Zanoah, Adullam, and their villages; in Lachish and its fields; in Azekah and its villages. They dwelt from Beersheba to the Valley of Hinnom.

31 Also the children of Benjamin from Geba *dwelt* in Michmash, Aija, and Bethel, and their villages; 32 in Anathoth, Nob, Ananiah; 33 in Hazor, Ramah, Gittaim; 34 in Hadid, Zeboim, Neballat; 35 in Lod, Ono, *and* [a]the Valley of Craftsmen. 36 Some of the Judean divisions of Levites *were* in Benjamin.

### THE PRIESTS AND LEVITES

*(cf. Ezra 2:36–40)*

**12** Now these *are* the [a]priests and the Levites who came up with [b]Zerubbabel the son of Shealtiel, and Jeshua: [c]Seraiah, Jeremiah, Ezra, 2 Amariah, Malluch, Hattush, 3 Shechaniah, Rehum, Meremoth, 4 Iddo, Ginnethoi,[1] [a]Abijah, 5 Mijamin, Maadiah, Bilgah, 6 Shemaiah, Joiarib, Jedaiah, 7 Sallu, Amok, Hilkiah, *and* Jedaiah.

These *were* the heads of the priests and their brethren in the days of [a]Jeshua.

8 Moreover the Levites *were* Jeshua, Binnui, Kadmiel, Sherebiah, Judah, *and* Mattaniah [a]*who led* the thanksgiving *psalms,* he and his brethren. 9 Also Bakbukiah and Unni, their brethren, *stood* across from them in *their* duties.

10 Jeshua begot Joiakim, Joiakim begot Eliashib, Eliashib begot Joiada, 11 Joiada begot Jonathan, and Jonathan begot Jaddua.

12 Now in the days of Joiakim, the priests, the [a]heads of the fathers' *houses were:* of Seraiah, Meraiah; of Jeremiah, Hananiah; 13 of Ezra, Meshullam; of Amariah, Jehohanan; 14 of Melichu,[1] Jonathan; of Shebaniah,[2] Joseph; 15 of Harim,[1] Adna; of Meraioth,[2] Helkai; 16 of Iddo, Zechariah; of Ginnethon, Meshullam; 17 of Abijah, Zichri; *the son* of Minjamin;[1] of Moadiah,[2] Piltai; 18 of Bilgah, Shammua; of Shemaiah, Jehonathan; 19 of Joiarib, Mattenai; of Jedaiah, Uzzi; 20 of Sallai,[1] Kallai; of Amok, Eber; 21 of Hilkiah, Hashabiah; *and* of Jedaiah, Nethanel.

22 During the reign of Darius the Persian, a record *was also kept* of the Levites and priests *who had been* [a]heads of their fathers' *houses* in the days of Eliashib, Joiada, Johanan, and Jaddua. 23 The sons of Levi, the heads of the fathers' *houses* until the days of Johanan the son of Eliashib, *were* written in the book of the [a]chronicles.

24 And the heads of the Levites *were* Hashabiah, Sherebiah, and Jeshua the son of Kadmiel, with their brothers across from them, to [a]praise *and* give thanks, [b]group alternating with group, [c]according to the command of David the man of God. 25 Mattaniah, Bakbukiah, Obadiah, Meshullam, Talmon, and Akkub *were* gatekeepers keeping the watch at the storerooms of the gates. 26 These *lived* in the days of Joiakim the son of Jeshua, the son of Jozadak,[1] and in the days of Nehemiah [a]the governor, and of Ezra the priest, [b]the scribe.

### NEHEMIAH DEDICATES THE WALL

27 Now at [a]the dedication of the wall of Jerusalem they sought out the Levites in all their places, to bring them to Jerusalem to celebrate the dedication with gladness, [b]both with thanksgivings and singing, *with* cymbals and stringed instruments and harps. 28 And the sons of the singers gathered together from the countryside around Jerusalem, from the [a]villages of the Netophathites, 29 from the house of Gilgal, and from the fields of Geba and Azmaveth; for the singers had built themselves villages all around Jerusalem. 30 Then the priests and Levites [a]purified themselves, and purified the people, the gates, and the wall.

31 So I brought the leaders of Judah up on the wall, and appointed two large thanksgiving choirs. [a]*One* went to the right hand on the wall [b]toward the Refuse Gate. 32 After them went Hoshaiah and half of the leaders of Judah, 33 and Azariah, Ezra, Meshullam, 34 Judah, Benjamin, Shemaiah, Jeremiah, 35 and some of the priests' sons [a]with trumpets—Zechariah the son of Jonathan, the son of Shemaiah, the son of Mattaniah, the son of Michaiah, the son of Zaccur, the son of Asaph, 36 and his brethren, Shemaiah, Azarel, Milalai, Gilalai, Maai, Nethanel, Judah, *and* Hanani, with [a]the musical [b]instruments of David the man of God. And Ezra the scribe *went* before them. 37 [a]By the Fountain Gate, in front of them, they went up [b]the stairs of the [c]City of David, on the stairway of the wall, beyond the house of David, as far as [d]the Water Gate eastward.

38 [a]The other thanksgiving choir went the opposite *way,* and I *was* behind them with half of the people on the wall, going past the [b]Tower of the Ovens as far as [c]the Broad Wall, 39 [a]and above the Gate of Ephraim, above [b]the Old Gate, above [c]the Fish Gate, [d]the Tower of Hananel, the Tower of the Hundred, as far as [e]the Sheep Gate; and they stopped by [f]the Gate of the Prison.

40 So the two thanksgiving choirs stood in the house of God, likewise I and the half of the rulers with me; 41 and the priests, Eliakim, Maaseiah, Minjamin,[1] Michaiah, Elioenai, Zechariah,

**11:35** [a] 1 Chr. 4:14 **12:1** [a] Ezra 2:1, 2; 7:7 [b] Neh. 7:7; Matt. 1:12, 13 [c] Neh. 10:2–8 **12:4** [a] Luke 1:5 [1] Or *Ginnethon* (compare verse 16) **12:7** [a] Ezra 3:2; Hag. 1:1; Zech. 3:1 **12:8** [a] Neh. 11:17 **12:12** [a] Neh. 7:70, 71; 8:13; 11:13 **12:14** [1] Or *Malluch* (compare verse 2) [2] Or *Shechaniah* (compare verse 3) **12:15** [1] Or *Rehum* (compare verse 3) [2] Or *Meremoth* (compare verse 3) **12:17** [1] Or *Mijamin* (compare verse 5) [2] Or *Maadiah* (compare verse 5) **12:20** [1] Or *Sallu* (compare verse 7) **12:22** [a] 1 Chr. 24:6 **12:23** [a] 1 Chr. 9:14–22 **12:24** [a] Neh. 11:17 [b] Ezra 3:11 [c] 1 Chr. 23—26 **12:26** [a] Neh. 8:9 [b] Ezra 7:6, 11 [1] Spelled *Jehozadak* in 1 Chronicles 6:14 **12:27** [a] Deut. 20:5; Neh. 7:1; Ps. 30:title [b] 1 Chr. 25:6; 2 Chr. 5:13; 7:6 **12:28** [a] 1 Chr. 9:16 **12:30** [a] Ezra 6:20; Neh. 13:22, 30 **12:31** [a] Neh. 12:38 [b] Neh. 2:13; 3:13 **12:35** [a] Num. 10:2, 8 **12:36** [a] 1 Chr. 23:5 [b] 2 Chr. 29:26, 27 **12:37** [a] Neh. 2:14; 3:15 [b] Neh. 3:15 [c] 2 Sam. 5:7–9 [d] Neh. 3:26; 8:1, 3, 16 **12:38** [a] Neh. 12:31 [b] Neh. 3:11 [c] Neh. 3:8 **12:39** [a] 2 Kin. 14:13; Neh. 8:16 [b] Neh. 3:6 [c] Neh. 3:3 [d] Neh. 3:1 [e] Neh. 3:32 [f] Jer. 32:2 **12:41** [1] Or *Mijamin* (compare verse 5)

*and* Hananiah, with trumpets; 42 also Maaseiah, Shemaiah, Eleazar, Uzzi, Jehohanan, Malchijah, Elam, and Ezer. The singers sang loudly with Jezrahiah the director.

43 Also that day they offered great sacrifices, and rejoiced, for God had made them rejoice with great joy; the women and the children also rejoiced, so that the joy of Jerusalem was heard [a]afar off.

### *TEMPLE RESPONSIBILITIES*

44 [a]And at the same time some were appointed over the rooms of the storehouse for the offerings, the firstfruits, and the [b]tithes, to gather into them from the fields of the cities the portions specified by the Law for the priests and Levites; for Judah rejoiced over the priests and Levites who ministered. 45 Both the singers and the gatekeepers kept the charge of their God and the charge of the purification, [a]according to the command of David *and* Solomon his son. 46 For in the days of David [a]and Asaph of old *there were* chiefs of the singers, and songs of praise and thanksgiving to God. 47 In the days of Zerubbabel and in the days of Nehemiah all Israel gave the portions for the singers and the gatekeepers, a portion for [a]each day. [b]They also consecrated *holy things* for the Levites, [c]and the Levites consecrated *them* for the children of Aaron.

### *PRINCIPLES OF SEPARATION*

*(Num. 22:1—24:25)*

**13** On that day [a]they read from the Book of Moses in the hearing of the people, and in it was found written [b]that no Ammonite or Moabite should ever come into the assembly of God, 2 because they had not met the children of Israel with bread and water, but [a]hired Balaam against them to curse them. [b]However, our God turned the curse into a blessing. 3 So it was, when they had heard the Law, [a]that they separated all the mixed multitude from Israel.

### *THE REFORMS OF NEHEMIAH*

4 Now before this, [a]Eliashib the priest, having authority over the storerooms of the house of our God, *was* allied with [b]Tobiah. 5 And he had prepared for him a large room, [a]where previously they had stored the grain offerings, the frankincense, the articles, the tithes of grain, the new wine and oil, [b]which were commanded *to be given* to the Levites and singers and gatekeepers, and the offerings for the priests. 6 But during all this I was not in Jerusalem, [a]for in the thirty-second year of Artaxerxes king of Babylon I had returned to the king. Then after certain days I obtained leave from the king, 7 and I came to Jerusalem and discovered the evil that Eliashib had done for Tobiah, in [a]preparing a room for him in the courts of the house of God. 8 And it grieved me bitterly; therefore I threw all the household goods of Tobiah out of the room. 9 Then I commanded them to [a]cleanse the rooms; and I brought back into them the articles of the house of God, with the grain offering and the frankincense.

> **SEEING JESUS IN THE SCRIPTURE**
>
> **13:8** When Nehemiah saw how the people were misusing the temple, he threw out everything that shouldn't have been in it. When Jesus saw how the people of His day were misusing the temple, He responded likewise (see Matt. 21:12).

10 I also realized that the portions for the Levites had [a]not been given *them;* for each of the Levites and the singers who did the work had gone back to [b]his field. 11 So [a]I contended with the rulers, and said, [b]"Why is the house of God forsaken?" And I gathered them together and set them in their place. 12 [a]Then all Judah brought the tithe of the grain and the new wine and the oil to the storehouse. 13 [a]And I appointed as treasurers over the storehouse Shelemiah the priest and Zadok the scribe, and of the Levites, Pedaiah; and next to them *was* Hanan the son of Zaccur, the son of Mattaniah; for they were considered [b]faithful, and their task *was* to distribute to their brethren.

14 [a]Remember me, O my God, concerning this, and do not wipe out my good deeds that I have done for the house of my God, and for its services!

15 In those days I saw *people* in Judah treading winepresses [a]on the Sabbath, and bringing in sheaves, and loading donkeys with wine, grapes, figs, and all *kinds of* burdens, [b]which they brought into Jerusalem on the Sabbath day. And I warned *them* about the day on which they were selling provisions. 16 Men of Tyre dwelt there also, who brought in fish and all kinds of goods, and sold *them* on the Sabbath to the children of Judah, and in Jerusalem.

17 Then I contended with the nobles of Judah, and said to them, "What evil thing *is* this that you do, by which you profane the Sabbath day? 18 [a]Did not your fathers do thus, and did not our God bring all this disaster on us and on this city? Yet you bring added wrath on Israel by profaning the Sabbath."

**12:43** [a] Ezra 3:13 **12:44** [a] 2 Chr. 31:11, 12; Neh. 13:5, 12, 13 [b] Neh. 10:37–39 **12:45** [a] 1 Chr. 25; 26 **12:46** [a] 1 Chr. 25:1; 2 Chr. 29:30 **12:47** [a] Neh. 11:23 [b] Num. 18:21, 24 [c] Num. 18:26 **13:1** [a] [Deut. 31:11, 12]; 2 Kin. 23:2; Neh. 8:3, 8; 9:3; Is. 34:16 [b] Deut. 23:3, 4 **13:2** [a] Num. 22:5; Josh. 24:9, 10 [b] Num. 23:1; 24:10; Deut. 23:5 **13:3** [a] Neh. 9:2; 10:28 **13:4** [a] Neh. 12:10 [b] Neh. 2:10; 4:3; 6:1 **13:5** [a] Neh. 12:44 [b] Num. 18:21, 24 **13:6** [a] Neh. 5:14–16 **13:7** [a] Neh. 13:1, 5 **13:9** [a] 2 Chr. 29:5, 15, 16 **13:10** [a] Neh. 10:37; Mal. 3:8 [b] Num. 35:2 **13:11** [a] Neh. 13:17, 25 [b] Neh. 10:39 **13:12** [a] Neh. 10:38; 12:44 **13:13** [a] 2 Chr. 31:12 [b] 1 Cor. 4:2 **13:14** [a] Neh. 5:19; 13:22, 31 **13:15** [a] [Ex. 20:10] [b] Neh. 10:31; [Jer. 17:21] **13:18** [a] Ezra 9:13; [Jer. 17:21]

19 So it was, at the gates of Jerusalem, as it
[a]began to be dark before the Sabbath, that I com-
manded the gates to be shut, and charged that
they must not be opened till after the Sabbath.
[b]Then I posted *some* of my servants at the gates,
*so that* no burdens would be brought in on the
Sabbath day. 20 Now the merchants and sellers
of all kinds of wares lodged outside Jerusalem
once or twice.

21 Then I warned them, and said to them,
"Why do you spend the night around the wall?
If you do *so* again, I will lay hands on you!"
From that time on they came no *more* on the
Sabbath. 22 And I commanded the Levites that
[a]they should cleanse themselves, and that they
should go and guard the gates, to sanctify the
Sabbath day.

Remember me, O my God, *concerning* this
also, and spare me according to the greatness
of Your mercy!

23 In those days I also saw Jews *who* [a]had
married women of [b]Ashdod, Ammon, *and* Moab.
24 And half of their children spoke the language
of Ashdod, and could not speak the language of
Judah, but spoke according to the language of
one or the other people.

25 So I [a]contended with them and cursed
them, struck some of them and pulled out their
hair, and made them [b]swear by God, *saying,* "You
shall not give your daughters as wives to their
sons, nor take their daughters for your sons or
yourselves. 26 [a]Did not Solomon king of Israel
sin by these things? Yet among many nations
there was no king like him, [b]who was beloved of
his God; and God made him king over all Israel.
[c]Nevertheless pagan women caused even him
to sin. 27 Should we then hear of your doing all
this great evil, [a]transgressing against our God
by marrying pagan women?"

28 And *one* of the sons [a]of Joiada, the son
of Eliashib the high priest, *was* a son-in-law of
[b]Sanballat the Horonite; therefore I drove him
from me.

29 [a]Remember them, O my God, because they
have defiled the priesthood and [b]the covenant
of the priesthood and the Levites.

30 [a]Thus I cleansed them of everything pa-
gan. I also [b]assigned duties to the priests and
the Levites, each to his service, 31 and *to bring-
ing* [a]the wood offering and the firstfruits at
appointed times.

[b]Remember me, O my God, for good!

13:19 [a] Lev. 23:32 [b] Jer. 17:21, 22 13:22 [a] Neh. 12:30 13:23 [a] Ezra 9:2 [b] Neh. 4:7 13:25 [a] Prov. 28:4 [b] Neh. 10:29, 30 13:26 [a] 1 Kin. 11:1, 2 [b] 2 Sam. 12:24, 25 [c] 1 Kin. 11:4–8 13:27 [a] [Ezra 10:2] 13:28 [a] Neh. 12:10, 12 [b] Neh. 4:1, 7; 6:1, 2 13:29 [a] Neh. 6:14 [b] Mal. 2:4, 11, 12 13:30 [a] Neh. 10:30 [b] Neh. 12:1 13:31 [a] Neh. 10:34 [b] Neh. 13:14, 22

*The Book of*

# ESTHER

| AUTHOR | KEY VERSE | READING TIME |
| --- | --- | --- |
| Unknown; perhaps Mordecai, Ezra, or Nehemiah | Esther 4:14 | 38 minutes |

God's hand of providence and protection on behalf of His people is evident throughout the Book of Esther, though His name does not appear once. When a spiteful official devised an evil plot against the Jews, he was countered by the sacrificial courage of Esther and the wise counsel of her cousin Mordecai. The Jews had been taken to the brink of extinction but were saved because of Esther and Mordecai's intervention and God's faithfulness. The Feast of Purim would become an annual reminder of the events of the Book of Esther.

**Occasion:** The events of the Book of Esther occurred during the time of the exiles' return from captivity, and the book serves as a reminder of God's providential care for His people, even when they might not be able to see it.

**Main Point:** God is always at work for His people and through His people, ensuring their protection and provision.

**Big Ideas:** God is in control of everything, even if we don't see what He's doing. God can use us wherever we are to make a big difference for His kingdom. We, too, have been saved from death because of the intercession of another.

## OUTLINE:

I. Esther Becomes Queen (chs. 1–2)
II. Haman Plots to Destroy the Jews (ch. 3)
III. Mordecai Counsels Esther to Intercede (ch. 4)
IV. Esther Saves Her People (chs. 5–7)
V. The Jews Defeat Their Enemies (chs. 8–10)

**538 BC**
Jews begin returning to Judea

**536–515 BC**
The temple is rebuilt

**521–486 BC**
Darius I reigns in Persia

**494–406 BC**
Greek tragedian Sophocles lives and works in Athens

**485–465 BC**
Ahasuerus (Xerxes I) reigns in Persia

**c. 470–424 BC**
**Esther written**

**464–424 BC**
Artaxerxes Longimanus reigns in Persia

**428–347 BC**
Greek philosopher Plato lives and teaches in Athens, Italy, Sicily, and northern Africa

**458 BC**
Ezra leads a group of returnees to Judea

**444 BC**
Nehemiah leads a group of returnees to Judea

**443 BC**
Jerusalem's wall is reconstructed

## *THE KING DETHRONES QUEEN VASHTI*

**1** Now it came to pass in the days of [a]Ahasu-
erus[1] (this *was* the Ahasuerus who reigned
[b]over one hundred and twenty-seven provinces,
[c]from India to Ethiopia), 2 in those days when
King Ahasuerus [a]sat on the throne of his king-
dom, which *was* in [b]Shushan[1] the citadel, 3 *that*
in the third year of his reign he [a]made a feast
for all his officials and servants—the powers of
Persia and Media, the nobles, and the princes
of the provinces *being* before him— 4 when he
showed the riches of his glorious kingdom and
the splendor of his excellent majesty for many
days, one hundred and eighty days *in all.*

> **1:1 Ahasuerus**, or Xerxes, became king of Persia after the death of his father, Darius. Under Darius's reign, the Jewish people, who had been held captive for over a century, were allowed to return to their homeland. But not all the Jews wanted to return to Jerusalem. Some of the ones who had been born in captivity wanted to stay in Persia, the only home they had ever known. As a result, there were thousands of Jewish people living in Persia during the reign of Ahasuerus.

5 And when these days were completed, the
king made a feast lasting seven days for all the
people who were present in Shushan the citadel,
from great to small, in the court of the garden
of the king's palace. 6 *There were* white and blue
linen *curtains* fastened with cords of fine linen
and purple on silver rods and marble pillars;
*and the* [a]couches *were* of gold and silver on a
*mosaic* pavement of alabaster, turquoise, and
white and black marble. 7 And they served drinks
in golden vessels, each vessel being different
from the other, with royal wine in abundance,
[a]according to the generosity of the king. 8 In
accordance with the law, the drinking was not
compulsory; for so the king had ordered all the
officers of his household, that they should do
according to each man's pleasure.

9 Queen Vashti also made a feast for the
women *in* the royal palace which *belonged* to
King Ahasuerus.

10 On the seventh day, when the heart of the
king was merry with wine, he commanded Mehu-
man, Biztha, [a]Harbona, Bigtha, Abagtha, Zethar,
and Carcas, seven eunuchs who served in the
presence of King Ahasuerus, 11 to bring Queen
Vashti before the king, *wearing* her royal crown,
in order to show her beauty to the people and the
officials, for she *was* beautiful to behold. 12 But
Queen Vashti refused to come at the king's com-
mand *brought* by *his* eunuchs; therefore the king
was furious, and his anger burned within him.

13 Then the king said to the [a]wise men [b]who
understood the times (for this *was* the king's
manner toward all who knew law and justice,
14 those closest to him *being* Carshena, Shethar,
Admatha, Tarshish, Meres, Marsena, and Me-
mucan, the [a]seven princes of Persia and Media,
[b]who had access to the king's presence, *and* who
ranked highest in the kingdom): 15 "What *shall*
*we* do to Queen Vashti, according to law, because
she did not obey the command of King Ahasu-
erus *brought to her* by the eunuchs?"

16 And Memucan answered before the king and
the princes: "Queen Vashti has not only wronged
the king, but also all the princes, and all the people
who *are* in all the provinces of King Ahasuerus.
17 For the queen's behavior will become known to
all women, so that they will [a]despise their hus-
bands in their eyes, when they report, 'King Ahas-
uerus commanded Queen Vashti to be brought
in before him, but she did not come.' 18 This very
day the *noble* ladies of Persia and Media will say
to all the king's officials that they have heard
of the behavior of the queen. Thus *there will be*
excessive contempt and wrath. 19 If it pleases the
king, let a royal decree go out from him, and let
it be recorded in the laws of the Persians and the
Medes, so that it will [a]not be altered, that Vashti
shall come no more before King Ahasuerus; and
let the king give her royal position to another
who is better than she. 20 When the king's decree
which he will make is proclaimed throughout all
his empire (for it is great), all wives will [a]honor
their husbands, both great and small."

21 And the reply pleased the king and the
princes, and the king did according to the word of
Memucan. 22 Then he sent letters to all the king's
provinces, [a]to each province in its own script,
and to every people in their own language, that
each man should [b]be master in his own house,
and speak in the language of his own people.

## *ESTHER BECOMES QUEEN*

**2** After these things, when the wrath of King
Ahasuerus subsided, he remembered Vashti,
[a]what she had done, and what had been decreed
against her. 2 Then the king's servants who at-
tended him said: "Let beautiful young virgins
be sought for the king; 3 and let the king appoint
officers in all the provinces of his kingdom, that
they may gather all the beautiful young virgins to
Shushan the citadel, into the women's quarters,
under the custody of Hegai[1] the king's eunuch,
custodian of the women. And let beauty prepara-
tions be given *them.* 4 Then let the young woman
who pleases the king be queen instead of Vashti."

This thing pleased the king, and he did so.

**1:1** [a] Ezra 4:6 [b] Esth. 8:9 [c] Dan. 6:1 [1] Generally identified with Xerxes I (485–464 BC) **1:2** [a] 1 Kin. 1:46 [b] Neh. 1:1 [1] Or *Susa,* and so throughout this book **1:3** [a] Gen. 40:20 **1:6** [a] Amos 2:8; 6:4 **1:7** [a] Esth. 2:18 **1:10** [a] Esth. 7:9 **1:13** [a] Jer. 10:7; Dan. 2:12; Matt. 2:1 [b] 1 Chr. 12:32 **1:14** [a] Ezra 7:14 [b] 2 Kin. 25:19; [Matt. 18:10] **1:17** [a] [Eph. 5:33] **1:19** [a] Esth. 8:8; Dan. 6:8 **1:20** [a] [Eph. 5:33; Col. 3:18; 1 Pet. 3:1] **1:22** [a] Esth. 3:12; 8:9 [b] [Eph. 5:22–24] **2:1** [a] Esth. 1:19, 20 **2:3** [1] Hebrew *Hege*

5 In Shushan the citadel there was a certain
Jew whose name *was* Mordecai the son of Jair,
the son of Shimei, the son of [a]Kish, a Benjamite.
6 [a]*Kish*[1] had been carried away from Jerusalem
with the captives who had been captured with
Jeconiah[2] king of Judah, whom Nebuchadnezzar
the king of Babylon had carried away. 7 And *Mor-*
*decai* had brought up Hadassah, that *is,* Esther,
[a]his uncle's daughter, for she had neither father
nor mother. The young woman *was* lovely and
beautiful. When her father and mother died,
Mordecai took her as his own daughter.

**2:6** The first time **Nebuchadnezzar**'s army invaded Judah, they captured the **king of Judah** and took him back to Babylon. The second and third times the Babylonian army attacked, they took all wealthy people captive and destroyed the temple.

8 So it was, when the king's command and de-
cree were heard, and when many young women
were [a]gathered at Shushan the citadel, *under* the
custody of Hegai, that Esther also was taken to
the king's palace, into the care of Hegai the cus-
todian of the women. 9 Now the young woman
pleased him, and she obtained his favor; so he
readily gave [a]beauty preparations to her, besides
her allowance. Then seven choice maidservants
were provided for her from the king's palace, and
he moved her and her maidservants to the best
*place* in the house of the women.
10 [a]Esther had not revealed her people or
family, for Mordecai had charged her not to re-
veal *it.* 11 And every day Mordecai paced in front
of the court of the women's quarters, to learn of
Esther's welfare and what was happening to her.
12 Each young woman's turn came to go in to
King Ahasuerus after she had completed twelve
months' preparation, according to the regula-
tions for the women, for thus were the days of
their preparation apportioned: six months with
oil of myrrh, and six months with perfumes and
preparations for beautifying women. 13 Thus
*prepared, each* young woman went to the king,
and she was given whatever she desired to take
with her from the women's quarters to the king's
palace. 14 In the evening she went, and in the
morning she returned to the second house of the
women, to the custody of Shaashgaz, the king's
eunuch who kept the concubines. She would not
go in to the king again unless the king delighted
in her and called for her by name.
15 Now when the turn came for Esther [a]the
daughter of Abihail the uncle of Mordecai, who
had taken her as his daughter, to go in to the king,
she requested nothing but what Hegai the king's
eunuch, the custodian of the women, advised. And
Esther [b]obtained favor in the sight of all who saw
her. 16 So Esther was taken to King Ahasuerus, into
his royal palace, in the tenth month, which *is* the
month of Tebeth, in the seventh year of his reign.
17 The king loved Esther more than all the *other*
women, and she obtained grace and favor in his
sight more than all the virgins; so he set the royal
[a]crown upon her head and made her queen instead
of Vashti. 18 Then the king [a]made a great feast, the
Feast of Esther, for all his officials and servants;
and he proclaimed a holiday in the provinces and
gave gifts according to the generosity of a king.

### *MORDECAI DISCOVERS A PLOT*

19 When virgins were gathered together a
second time, Mordecai sat within the king's gate.
20 [a]*Now* Esther had not revealed her family and
her people, just as Mordecai had charged her,
for Esther obeyed the command of Mordecai as
when she was brought up by him.
21 In those days, while Mordecai sat with-
in the king's gate, two of the king's eunuchs,
Bigthan and Teresh, doorkeepers, became furi-
ous and sought to lay hands on King Ahasuerus.
22 So the matter became known to Mordecai,
[a]who told Queen Esther, and Esther informed
the king in Mordecai's name. 23 And when an
inquiry was made into the matter, it was con-
firmed, and both were hanged on a gallows; and
it was written in [a]the book of the chronicles in
the presence of the king.

### *HAMAN'S CONSPIRACY AGAINST THE JEWS*

3 After these things King Ahasuerus promoted
Haman, the son of Hammedatha the [a]Agag-
ite, and [b]advanced him and set his seat above
all the princes who *were* with him. 2 And all the
king's servants who *were* [a]within the king's gate
bowed and paid homage to Haman, for so the
king had commanded concerning him. But
Mordecai [b]would not bow or pay homage. 3 Then
the king's servants who *were* within the king's
gate said to Mordecai, "Why do you transgress
the [a]king's command?" 4 Now it happened, when
they spoke to him daily and he would not lis-
ten to them, that they told *it* to Haman, to see
whether Mordecai's words would stand; for *Mor-*
*decai* had told them that he *was* a Jew. 5 When
Haman saw that Mordecai [a]did not bow or pay
him homage, Haman was [b]filled with wrath. 6 But
he disdained to lay hands on Mordecai alone,
for they had told him of the people of Mordecai.
Instead, Haman [a]sought to destroy all the Jews
who *were* throughout the whole kingdom of
Ahasuerus—the people of Mordecai.
7 In the first month, which is the month of
Nisan, in the twelfth year of King Ahasuerus,

**2:5** [a] 1 Sam. 9:1 **2:6** [a] 2 Kin. 24:14, 15; 2 Chr. 36:10, 20; Jer. 24:1 [1] Literally *Who* [2] Same as *Jehoiachin,* 2 Kings 24:6 and elsewhere
**2:7** [a] Esth. 2:15 **2:8** [a] Esth. 2:3 **2:9** [a] Esth. 2:3, 12 **2:10** [a] Esth. 2:20 **2:15** [a] Esth. 2:7; 9:29 [b] Esth. 5:2, 8 **2:17** [a] Esth. 1:11
**2:18** [a] Esth. 1:3 **2:20** [a] Esth. 2:10; [Prov. 22:6] **2:22** [a] Esth. 6:1, 2 **2:23** [a] Esth. 6:1 **3:1** [a] Num. 24:7; 1 Sam. 15:8 [b] Esth. 5:11
**3:2** [a] Esth. 2:19, 21; 5:9 [b] Ps. 15:4 **3:3** [a] Esth. 3:2 **3:5** [a] Esth. 3:2; 5:9 [b] Dan. 3:19 **3:6** [a] Ps. 83:4; [Rev. 12:1–17]

[a]they cast Pur (that *is*, the lot), before Haman to determine the day and the month,[1] until *it fell on the* twelfth *month*,[2] which *is* the month of Adar.

8 Then Haman said to King Ahasuerus, "There is a certain people scattered and dispersed among the people in all the provinces of your kingdom; [a]their laws *are* different from all *other* people's, and they do not keep the king's laws. Therefore it *is* not fitting for the king to let them remain. 9 If it pleases the king, let *a decree* be written that they be destroyed, and I will pay ten thousand talents of silver into the hands of those who do the work, to bring *it* into the king's treasuries."

10 So the king [a]took [b]his signet ring from his hand and gave it to Haman, the son of Hammedatha the Agagite, the [c]enemy of the Jews. 11 And the king said to Haman, "The money and the people *are* given to you, to do with them as seems good to you."

> **3:10** Authority figures in the ancient Near East each wore a unique **signet ring**. The rings were fashioned with a raised design (a name or symbol) that could make an impression in the soft clay or wax used to seal a written communication. An impression of the signet ring's design in the seal was like signing one's name today. Ahasuerus allowed **Haman** to use his ring, signifying his approval of the plan.

12 [a]Then the king's scribes were called on the thirteenth day of the first month, and *a decree* was written according to all that Haman commanded—to the king's satraps, to the governors who *were* over each province, to the officials of all people, to every province [b]according to its script, and to every people in their language. [c]In the name of King Ahasuerus it was written, and sealed with the king's signet ring. 13 And the letters were [a]sent by couriers into all the king's provinces, to destroy, to kill, and to annihilate all the Jews, both young and old, little children and women, [b]in one day, on the thirteenth *day* of the twelfth month, which *is* the month of Adar, and [c]to plunder their possessions.[1] 14 [a]A copy of the document was to be issued as law in every province, being published for all people, that they should be ready for that day. 15 The couriers went out, hastened by the king's command; and the decree was proclaimed in Shushan the citadel. So the king and Haman sat down to drink, but [a]the city of Shushan was perplexed.

### ESTHER AGREES TO HELP THE JEWS

**4** When Mordecai learned all that had happened, he [a]tore his clothes and put on sackcloth [b]and ashes, and went out into the midst of the city. He [c]cried out with a loud and bitter cry. 2 He went as far as the front of the king's gate, for no one *might* enter the king's gate clothed with sackcloth. 3 And in every province where the king's command and decree arrived, *there was* great mourning among the Jews, with fasting, weeping, and wailing; and many lay in sackcloth and ashes.

4 So Esther's maids and eunuchs came and told her, and the queen was deeply distressed. Then she sent garments to clothe Mordecai and take his sackcloth away from him, but he would not accept *them*. 5 Then Esther called Hathach, *one* of the king's eunuchs whom he had appointed to attend her, and she gave him a command concerning Mordecai, to learn what and why this *was*. 6 So Hathach went out to Mordecai in the city square that *was* in front of the king's gate. 7 And Mordecai told him all that had happened to him, and [a]the sum of money that Haman had promised to pay into the king's treasuries to destroy the Jews. 8 He also gave him [a]a copy of the written decree for their destruction, which was given at Shushan, that he might show it to Esther and explain it to her, and that he might command her to go in to the king to make supplication to him and plead before him for her people. 9 So Hathach returned and told Esther the words of Mordecai.

10 Then Esther spoke to Hathach, and gave him a command for Mordecai: 11 "All the king's servants and the people of the king's provinces know that any man or woman who goes into [a]the inner court to the king, who has not been called, [b]*he has* but one law: put *all* to death, except the one [c]to whom the king holds out the golden scepter, that he may live. Yet I myself have not been [d]called to go in to the king these thirty days." 12 So they told Mordecai Esther's words.

> **SEEING JESUS IN THE SCRIPTURE**
>
> **4:11** Esther knew going before the king to intercede on behalf of the Jews *could* mean her immediate death, but she went. Jesus knew His intercession *would* mean laying down His life on the cross, but He came (see Luke 23:34).

13 And Mordecai told *them* to answer Esther: "Do not think in your heart that you will escape in the king's palace any more than all the other Jews. 14 For if you remain completely

3:7 [a] Esth. 9:24–26 [1] Septuagint adds *to destroy the people of Mordecai in one day;* Vulgate adds *the nation of the Jews should be destroyed.* [2] Following Masoretic Text and Vulgate; Septuagint reads *and the lot fell on the fourteenth of the month.* 3:8 [a] Ezra 4:12–15; Acts 16:20, 21 3:10 [a] Gen. 41:42 [b] Esth. 8:2, 8 [c] Esth. 7:6 3:12 [a] Esth. 8:9 [b] Esth. 1:22 [c] 1 Kin. 21:8; Esth. 8:8–10 3:13 [a] Esth. 8:10, 14 [b] Esth. 8:12 [c] Esth. 8:11; 9:10 [1] Septuagint adds the text of the letter here. 3:14 [a] Esth. 8:13, 14 3:15 [a] Esth. 8:15; [Prov. 29:2] 4:1 [a] 2 Sam. 1:11; Esth. 3:8–10; Jon. 3:5, 6 [b] Josh. 7:6; Ezek. 27:30 [c] Gen. 27:34 4:7 [a] Esth. 3:9 4:8 [a] Esth. 3:14, 15 4:11 [a] Esth. 5:1; 6:4 [b] Dan. 2:9 [c] Esth. 5:2; 8:4 [d] Esth. 2:14

silent at this time, relief and deliverance will
arise for the Jews from another place, but you
and your father's house will perish. Yet who
knows whether you have come to the kingdom
for *such* a time as this?"
15 Then Esther told *them* to reply to Morde-
cai: 16 "Go, gather all the Jews who are present in
Shushan, and fast for me; neither eat nor drink
for [a]three days, night or day. My maids and I will
fast likewise. And so I will go to the king, which
*is* against the law; [b]and if I perish, I perish!"
17 So Mordecai went his way and did accord-
ing to all that Esther commanded him.[1]

### ESTHER'S BANQUET

5 Now it happened [a]on the third day that Es-
ther put on *her* royal *robes* and stood in [b]the
inner court of the king's palace, across from
the king's house, while the king sat on his royal
throne in the royal house, facing the entrance
of the house.[1] 2 So it was, when the king saw
Queen Esther standing in the court, *that* [a]she
found favor in his sight, and [b]the king held out
to Esther the golden scepter that *was* in his
hand. Then Esther went near and touched the
top of the scepter.
3 And the king said to her, "What do you
wish, Queen Esther? What *is* your request? [a]It
shall be given to you—up to half the kingdom!"
4 So Esther answered, "If it pleases the king,
let the king and Haman come today to the ban-
quet that I have prepared for him."
5 Then the king said, "Bring Haman quickly,
that he may do as Esther has said." So the king
and Haman went to the banquet that Esther
had prepared.
6 At the banquet of wine [a]the king said to Es-
ther, [b]"What *is* your petition? It shall be granted
you. What *is* your request, up to half the king-
dom? It shall be done!"
7 Then Esther answered and said, "My peti-
tion and request *is this:* 8 If I have found favor
in the sight of the king, and if it pleases the king
to grant my petition and fulfill my request, then
let the king and Haman come to the [a]banquet
which I will prepare for them, and tomorrow I
will do as the king has said."

### HAMAN'S PLOT AGAINST MORDECAI

9 So Haman went out that day [a]joyful and
with a glad heart; but when Haman saw Mor-
decai in the king's gate, and [b]that he did not
stand or tremble before him, he was filled with
indignation against Mordecai. 10 Nevertheless
Haman [a]restrained himself and went home, and
he sent and called for his friends and his wife
Zeresh. 11 Then Haman told them of his great
riches, [a]the multitude of his children, everything
in which the king had promoted him, and how
he had [b]advanced him above the officials and
servants of the king.
12 Moreover Haman said, "Besides, Queen
Esther invited no one but me to come in with the
king to the banquet that she prepared; and to-
morrow I am again invited by her, along with the
king. 13 Yet all this avails me nothing, so long as I
see Mordecai the Jew sitting at the king's gate."
14 Then his wife Zeresh and all his friends
said to him, "Let a [a]gallows be made, fifty cubits
high, and in the morning [b]suggest to the king
that Mordecai be hanged on it; then go merrily
with the king to the banquet."
And the thing pleased Haman; so he had
[c]the gallows made.

**5:14** There were no ropes involved in a Persian hanging. Instead, the person was nailed to a stake. The dead corpse remained hanging for public viewing.

### THE KING HONORS MORDECAI

6 That night the king could not sleep. So one
was commanded to bring [a]the book of the
records of the chronicles; and they were read
before the king. 2 And it was found written that
Mordecai had told of Bigthana and Teresh, two
of the king's eunuchs, the doorkeepers who had
sought to lay hands on King Ahasuerus. 3 Then
the king said, "What honor or dignity has been
bestowed on Mordecai for this?"
And the king's servants who attended him
said, "Nothing has been done for him."
4 So the king said, "Who *is* in the court?" Now
Haman had *just* entered [a]the outer court of the
king's palace [b]to suggest that the king hang Mor-
decai on the gallows that he had prepared for him.
5 The king's servants said to him, "Haman
is there, standing in the court."
And the king said, "Let him come in."
6 So Haman came in, and the king asked
him, "What shall be done for the man whom
the king delights to honor?"
Now Haman thought in his heart, "Whom
would the king delight to honor more than [a]me?"
7 And Haman answered the king, "*For* the man
whom the king delights to honor, 8 let a royal robe
be brought which the king has worn, and [a]a horse
on which the king has ridden, which has a royal
crest placed on its head. 9 Then let this robe and
horse be delivered to the hand of one of the king's
most noble princes, that he may array the man
whom the king delights to honor. Then parade
him on horseback through the city square, [a]and
proclaim before him: 'Thus shall it be done to the
man whom the king delights to honor!' "

**4:16** [a] Esth. 5:1 [b] Gen. 43:14 **4:17** [1] Septuagint adds a prayer of Mordecai here. **5:1** [a] Esth. 4:16 [b] Esth. 4:11; 6:4 [1] Septuagint adds many extra details in verses 1 and 2. **5:2** [a] [Prov. 21:1] [b] Esth. 4:11; 8:4 **5:3** [a] Esth. 7:2; Mark 6:23 **5:6** [a] Esth. 7:2 [b] Esth. 9:12 **5:8** [a] Esth. 6:14 **5:9** [a] [Job 20:5; Luke 6:25] [b] Esth. 3:5 **5:10** [a] 2 Sam. 13:22 **5:11** [a] Esth. 9:7–10 [b] Esth. 3:1 **5:14** [a] Esth. 7:9 [b] Esth. 6:4 [c] Esth. 7:10 **6:1** [a] Esth. 2:23; 10:2 **6:4** [a] Esth. 5:1 [b] Esth. 5:14 **6:6** [a] [Prov. 16:18; 18:12] **6:8** [a] 1 Kin. 1:33 **6:9** [a] Gen. 41:43

> **6:10** The term ***Jew***, derived from the word *Judah*, came into use during the exile because the people were primarily from the southern kingdom of Judah. Before this time, God's people were known as *Hebrews* or *Israelites*.

10 Then the king said to Haman, "Hurry, take
the robe and the horse, as you have suggested,
and do so for Mordecai the Jew who sits within
the king's gate! Leave nothing undone of all that
you have spoken."
11 So Haman took the robe and the horse,
arrayed Mordecai and led him on horseback
through the city square, and proclaimed before
him, "Thus shall it be done to the man whom
the king delights to honor!"

### SEEING JESUS IN THE SCRIPTURE

> **6:10–11** Because he had saved the king's life, Mordecai was paraded through the city on horseback while wearing a royal robe. This points to Jesus' triumphal entry when He rode into Jerusalem on a donkey, days ahead of laying down His life to save His people (see Matt. 21:7–9).

12 Afterward Mordecai went back to the
king's gate. But Haman [a]hurried to his house,
mourning [b]and with his head covered. 13 When
Haman told his wife Zeresh and all his friends
everything that had happened to him, his wise
men and his wife Zeresh said to him, "If Mor-
decai, before whom you have begun to fall, is
of Jewish descent, you will not prevail against
[a]him but will surely fall before him."
14 While they *were* still talking with him,
the king's eunuchs came, and hastened to
bring Haman to [a]the banquet which Esther
had prepared.

## *HAMAN HANGED INSTEAD OF MORDECAI*

**7** So the king and Haman went to dine with
Queen Esther. 2 And on the second day, [a]at
the banquet of wine, the king again said to Es-
ther, "What *is* your petition, Queen Esther? It
shall be granted you. And what *is* your request,
up to half the kingdom? It shall be done!"
3 Then Queen Esther answered and said, "If
I have found favor in your sight, O king, and
if it pleases the king, let my life be given me
at my petition, and my people at my request.
4 For we have been [a]sold, my people and I, to be
destroyed, to be killed, and to be annihilated.
Had we been sold as [b]male and female slaves, I
would have held my tongue, although the enemy
could never compensate for the king's loss."
5 So King Ahasuerus answered and said to
Queen Esther, "Who is he, and where is he, who
would dare presume in his heart to do such a
thing?"
6 And Esther said, "The adversary and [a]en-
emy *is* this wicked Haman!"
So Haman was terrified before the king
and queen.
7 Then the king arose in his wrath from the
banquet of wine *and went* into the palace gar-
den; but Haman stood before Queen Esther,
pleading for his life, for he saw that evil was
determined against him by the king. 8 When
the king returned from the palace garden to the
place of the banquet of wine, Haman had fallen
across [a]the couch where Esther *was*. Then the
king said, "Will he also assault the queen while
I *am* in the house?"
As the word left the king's mouth, they [b]cov-
ered Haman's face. 9 Now [a]Harbonah, one of the
eunuchs, said to the king, "Look! [b]The gallows,
fifty cubits high, which Haman made for Mor-
decai, who spoke [c]good on the king's behalf, is
standing at the house of Haman."
Then the king said, "Hang him on it!"
10 So [a]they [b]hanged Haman on the gallows
that he had prepared for Mordecai. Then the
king's wrath subsided.

### SEEING JESUS IN THE SCRIPTURE

> **7:10** Haman's plot backfired, and he was hung from the gallows he had prepared for Mordecai. This eventually led to the Jews' salvation. Similarly, Satan's plot to kill Jesus on the cross backfired as it led to our salvation (see Gen. 3:15).

## *ESTHER SAVES THE JEWS*

**8** On that day King Ahasuerus gave Queen
Esther the house of Haman, the [a]enemy of
the Jews. And Mordecai came before the king,
for Esther had told [b]how he *was related* to her.
2 So the king took off [a]his signet ring, which he
had taken from Haman, and gave it to Morde-
cai; and Esther appointed Mordecai over the
house of Haman.
3 Now Esther spoke again to the king, fell
down at his feet, and implored him with tears to
counteract the evil of Haman the Agagite, and
the scheme which he had devised against the
Jews. 4 And [a]the king held out the golden scepter
toward Esther. So Esther arose and stood before
the king, 5 and said, "If it pleases the king, and
if I have found favor in his sight and the thing

**6:12** [a] 2 Chr. 26:20 [b] 2 Sam. 15:30; Jer. 14:3, 4 **6:13** [a] [Gen. 12:3]; Zech. 2:8 **6:14** [a] Esth. 5:8 **7:2** [a] Esth. 5:6 **7:4** [a] Esth. 3:9; 4:7 [b] Deut. 28:68 **7:6** [a] Esth. 3:10 **7:8** [a] Esth. 1:6 [b] Job 9:24 **7:9** [a] Esth. 1:10 [b] Esth. 5:14; [Ps. 7:16; Prov. 11:5, 6] [c] Esth. 6:2 **7:10** [a] [Ps. 7:16; 94:23; Prov. 11:5, 6] [b] Ps. 37:35, 36; Dan. 6:24 **8:1** [a] Esth. 7:6 [b] Esth. 2:7, 15 **8:2** [a] Esth. 3:10 **8:4** [a] Esth. 4:11; 5:2

*seems* right to the king and I am pleasing in his eyes, let it be written to revoke the [a]letters devised by Haman, the son of Hammedatha the Agagite, which he wrote to annihilate the Jews who *are* in all the king's provinces. 6 For how can I endure to see [a]the evil that will come to my people? Or how can I endure to see the destruction of my countrymen?"

7 Then King Ahasuerus said to Queen Esther and Mordecai the Jew, "Indeed, [a]I have given Esther the house of Haman, and they have hanged him on the gallows because he *tried to* lay his hand on the Jews. 8 You yourselves write *a decree* concerning the Jews, as you please, in the king's name, and seal *it* with the king's signet ring; for whatever is written in the king's name and sealed with the king's signet ring [a]no one can revoke."

9 [a]So the king's scribes were called at that time, in the third month, which *is* the month of Sivan, on the twenty-third *day;* and it was written, according to all that Mordecai commanded, to the Jews, the satraps, the governors, and the princes of the provinces [b]from India to Ethiopia, one hundred and twenty-seven provinces *in all,* to every province [c]in its own script, to every people in their own language, and to the Jews in their own script and language. 10 [a]And he wrote in the name of King Ahasuerus, sealed *it* with the king's signet ring, and sent letters by couriers on horseback, riding on royal horses bred from swift steeds.[1]

11 By these letters the king permitted the Jews who *were* in every city to [a]gather together and protect their lives—to [b]destroy, kill, and annihilate all the forces of any people or province that would assault them, *both* little children and women, and to plunder their possessions, 12 [a]on one day in all the provinces of King Ahasuerus, on the thirteenth *day* of the twelfth month, which *is* the month of Adar.[1] 13 [a]A copy of the document was to be issued as a decree in every province and published for all people, so that the Jews would be ready on that day to avenge themselves on their enemies. 14 The couriers who rode on royal horses went out, hastened and pressed on by the king's command. And the decree was issued in Shushan the citadel.

> **8:8–12** Persian law forbade a king from revoking or changing a law once it was established. Knowing that he couldn't undo the law that called for the slaughter of the Jewish people, the quick-thinking king passed a new law that allowed Jews to defend themselves and even take revenge on their enemies.

15 So Mordecai went out from the presence of the king in royal apparel of blue and white, with a great crown of gold and a garment of fine linen and purple; and [a]the city of Shushan rejoiced and was glad. 16 The Jews had [a]light and gladness, joy and honor. 17 And in every province and city, wherever the king's command and decree came, the Jews had joy and gladness, a feast [a]and a holiday. Then many of the people of the land [b]became Jews, because [c]fear of the Jews fell upon them.

### THE JEWS DESTROY THEIR TORMENTORS

9 Now [a]in the twelfth month, that *is,* the month of Adar, on the thirteenth day, [b]*the time* came for the king's command and his decree to be executed. On the day that the enemies of the Jews had hoped to overpower them, the opposite occurred, in that the Jews themselves [c]overpowered those who hated them. 2 The Jews [a]gathered together in their cities throughout all the provinces of King Ahasuerus to lay hands on those who [b]sought their harm. And no one could withstand them, [c]because fear of them fell upon all people. 3 And all the officials of the provinces, the satraps, the governors, and all those doing the king's work, helped the Jews, because the fear of Mordecai fell upon them. 4 For Mordecai *was* great in the king's palace, and his fame spread throughout all the provinces; for this man Mordecai [a]became increasingly prominent. 5 Thus the Jews defeated all their enemies with the stroke of the sword, with slaughter and destruction, and did what they pleased with those who hated them.

6 And in [a]Shushan the citadel the Jews killed and destroyed five hundred men. 7 Also Parshandatha, Dalphon, Aspatha, 8 Poratha, Adalia, Aridatha, 9 Parmashta, Arisai, Aridai, and Vajezatha— 10 [a]the ten sons of Haman the son of Hammedatha, the enemy of the Jews—they killed; [b]but they did not lay a hand on the plunder.

11 On that day the number of those who were killed in Shushan the citadel was brought to the king. 12 And the king said to Queen Esther, "The Jews have killed and destroyed five hundred men in Shushan the citadel, and the ten sons of Haman. What have they done in the rest of the king's provinces? Now [a]what *is* your petition? It shall be granted to you. Or what *is* your further request? It shall be done."

13 Then Esther said, "If it pleases the king, let it be granted to the Jews who *are* in Shushan to do again tomorrow [a]according to today's decree, and let Haman's ten sons [b]be hanged on the gallows."

14 So the king commanded this to be done;

**8:5** [a] Esth. 3:13 **8:6** [a] Neh. 2:3 **8:7** [a] Esth. 8:1; Prov. 13:22 **8:8** [a] Esth. 1:19; Dan. 6:8, 12, 15 **8:9** [a] Esth. 3:12 [b] Esth. 1:1 [c] Esth. 1:22; 3:12 **8:10** [a] 1 Kin. 21:8; Esth. 3:12, 13 [1] Literally *sons of the swift horses* **8:11** [a] Esth. 9:2 [b] Esth. 9:10, 15, 16 **8:12** [a] Esth. 3:13; 9:1 [1] Septuagint adds the text of the letter here. **8:13** [a] Esth. 3:14, 15 **8:15** [a] Esth. 3:15; Prov. 29:2 **8:16** [a] Ps. 97:11; 112:4 **8:17** [a] 1 Sam. 25:8; Esth. 9:19 [b] Ps. 18:43 [c] Gen. 35:5; Ex. 15:16; Deut. 2:25; 11:25; 1 Chr. 14:17; Esth. 9:2 **9:1** [a] Esth. 8:12 [b] Esth. 3:13 [c] 2 Sam. 22:41 **9:2** [a] Esth. 8:11; 9:15–18 [b] Ps. 71:13, 14 [c] Esth. 8:17 **9:4** [a] 2 Sam. 3:1; 1 Chr. 11:9; [Prov. 4:18] **9:6** [a] Esth. 1:2; 3:15; 4:16 **9:10** [a] Esth. 5:11; 9:7–10; Job 18:19; 27:13–15; Ps. 21:10 [b] Esth. 8:11 **9:12** [a] Esth. 5:6; 7:2 **9:13** [a] Esth. 8:11; 9:15 [b] 2 Sam. 21:6, 9

ESTHER 9:1–32

## GOD'S SILENT HAND

34 STORY OF SCRIPTURE

### WHAT'S GOING ON?

While God isn't mentioned in the Book of Esther, His hand is evident throughout Esther's journey. Esther 9 depicts the Jews facing a decree of destruction in the Persian Empire and experiencing a miraculous reversal of fortune. Queen Esther and Mordecai had shown great courage, faith, and shrewdness against their adversary Haman to save their kinsman. This chapter culminates in the celebration of Purim, a festival commemorating their deliverance from genocide. It's a vivid picture of unexpected victory, resilience in the face of adversity, and the importance of remembrance. And it's yet another time God used unexpected people to save His chosen nation.

### WHAT DOES THIS MEAN FOR ME?

This passage encourages us to find strength and hope even in dire circumstances. We're to face challenges with courageous action, never forgetting the importance of standing up for justice and valuing human life. Purim's celebration also reminds us of the importance of remembering God's faithfulness in our lives. We're to recall times when we've seen deliverance and provision, letting these memories fuel our faith for the future.

### DID YOU CATCH THE PATTERN?

Heroic women were often called to rise up when Israel faced some form of genocide. This was true of Jochebed, Moses's mother, who saved her son when Pharaoh commanded all the Hebrew infant boys to be killed. Other nursemaids of the time also bravely defied Pharaoh. Deborah rose as judge when Sisera threatened to obliterate Israel. And Mary fled to Egypt with Jesus when Herod commanded all the male children in Bethlehem under two to be killed. This pattern shows God's protective heart for His children and reminds us even tyrants can be defeated by a strong, wise, godly woman.

*For the next* Story of Scripture *reading and devotion, turn to Jeremiah 29:1–14 on page 775.*

the decree was issued in Shushan, and they
hanged Haman's ten sons.
15 And the Jews who *were* in Shushan [a]gath-
ered together again on the fourteenth day of
the month of Adar and killed three hundred
men at Shushan; [b]but they did not lay a hand
on the plunder.
16 The remainder of the Jews in the king's
provinces [a]gathered together and protected
their lives, had rest from their enemies, and
killed seventy-five thousand of their enemies;
[b]but they did not lay a hand on the plunder.
17 *This was* on the thirteenth day of the month
of Adar. And on the fourteenth of *the month*[1]
they rested and made it a day of feasting and
gladness.

### *THE FEAST OF PURIM*

18 But the Jews who *were* at Shushan as-
sembled together [a]on the thirteenth *day,* as
well as on the fourteenth; and on the fifteenth
of *the month*[1] they rested, and made it a day of
feasting and gladness. 19 Therefore the Jews of
the villages who dwelt in the unwalled towns
celebrated the fourteenth day of the month of
Adar [a]*with* gladness and feasting, [b]as a holiday,
and for [c]sending presents to one another.
20 And Mordecai wrote these things and
sent letters to all the Jews, near and far, who
*were* in all the provinces of King Ahasuerus,
21 to establish among them that they should
celebrate yearly the fourteenth and fifteenth
days of the month of Adar, 22 as the days on
which the Jews had rest from their enemies, as
the month which was turned from sorrow to
joy for them, and from mourning to a holiday;
that they should make them days of feasting
and joy, of [a]sending presents to one another
and gifts to the [b]poor. 23 So the Jews accepted
the custom which they had begun, as Mordecai
had written to them, 24 because Haman, the son
of Hammedatha the Agagite, the enemy of all
the Jews, [a]had plotted against the Jews to anni-
hilate them, and had cast Pur (that *is,* the lot), to
consume them and destroy them; 25 but [a]when
*Esther*[1] came before the king, he commanded by

9:15 [a] Esth. 8:11; 9:2 [b] Esth. 9:10 9:16 [a] Esth. 9:2 [b] Esth. 8:11 9:17 [1] Literally *it* 9:18 [a] Esth. 9:11, 15 [1] Literally *it* 9:19 [a] Deut. 16:11, 14 [b] Esth. 8:16, 17 [c] Neh. 8:10, 12; Esth. 9:22 9:22 [a] Neh. 8:10; Esth. 9:19 [b] [Deut. 15:7–11]; Job 29:16 9:24 [a] Esth. 3:6, 7; 9:26 9:25 [a] Esth. 7:4–10; 8:3; 9:13, 14 [1] Literally *she* or *it*

letter that this[2] wicked plot which *Haman* had
devised against the Jews should [b]return on his
own head, and that he and his sons should be
hanged on the gallows.
26 So they called these days Purim, after the
name Pur. Therefore, because of all the words
of [a]this letter, what they had seen concerning
this matter, and what had happened to them,
27 the Jews established and imposed it upon
themselves and their descendants and all who
would [a]join them, that without fail they should
celebrate these two days every year, according
to the written *instructions* and according to
the *prescribed* time, 28 *that* these days *should
be* remembered and kept throughout every
generation, every family, every province, and
every city, that these days of Purim should not
fail *to be observed* among the Jews, and *that*
the memory of them should not perish among
their descendants.
29 Then Queen Esther, [a]the daughter of Ab-
ihail, with Mordecai the Jew, wrote with full
authority to confirm this [b]second letter about
Purim. 30 And *Mordecai* sent letters to all the
Jews, to [a]the one hundred and twenty-seven
provinces of the kingdom of Ahasuerus, *with*
words of peace and truth, 31 to confirm these days
of Purim at their *appointed* time, as Mordecai
the Jew and Queen Esther had prescribed for
them, and as they had decreed for themselves
and their descendants concerning matters of
their [a]fasting and lamenting. 32 So the decree of
Esther confirmed these matters of Purim, and
it was written in the book.

**9:32** Queen Esther's letter made the Festival of **Purim** an official Jewish holiday. Today Purim is observed in the month before Passover. Celebrations usually include a reading from the Book of Esther and giving gifts.

### *MORDECAI'S ADVANCEMENT*

**10** And King Ahasuerus imposed tribute on
the land and *on* [a]the islands of the sea.
2 Now all the acts of his power and his might,
and the account of the greatness of Morde-
cai, [a]to which the king advanced him, *are* they
not written in the book of the [b]chronicles of
the kings of Media and Persia? 3 For Mordecai
the Jew *was* [a]second to King Ahasuerus, and
was great among the Jews and well received
by the multitude of his brethren, [b]seeking the
good of his people and speaking peace to all
his countrymen.[1]

**9:25** [b] Esth. 7:10 [2] Literally *his* **9:26** [a] Esth. 9:20 **9:27** [a] Esth. 8:17; [Is. 56:3, 6]; Zech. 2:11 **9:29** [a] Esth. 2:15 [b] Esth. 8:10; 9:20, 21 **9:30** [a] Esth. 1:1 **9:31** [a] Esth. 4:3, 16 **10:1** [a] Is. 11:11; 24:15 **10:2** [a] Esth. 8:15; 9:4 [b] Esth. 6:1 **10:3** [a] Gen. 41:40, 43, 44 [b] Neh. 2:10
[1] Literally *seed*. Septuagint and Vulgate add a dream of Mordecai here; Vulgate adds six more chapters.

*Introduction to*

# THE BOOKS OF POETRY AND WISDOM

While these five books are called the Books of Poetry and Wisdom, these aren't the only genres in them, and poetry and wisdom do appear elsewhere. Job and the Song of Solomon each contain historical narrative elements, and prophecy runs throughout Psalms. Likewise, poetry is present in the Pentateuch, the Books of Prophecy, and the Gospels. Rather, these five books are categorized as poetry and wisdom because they center on those genres.

When reading the books of poetry and wisdom, it's helpful to remember the main purpose of each:

**Job** teaches us about suffering. It tells of a man named Job who lost almost everything and wrestled to understand why.

**Psalms** helps us to worship. It provides 150 psalms, or songs, that the Israelites used in worship. These songs trace various themes and emotions, connecting them all to the goodness of God.

**Proverbs** shows us wisdom. This book is filled with principles for godly living. While proverbs are not promises, when God's people live in line with the wisdom they express, they will probably experience full lives and blessings.

**Ecclesiastes** searches for purpose. The Preacher pursues the meaning of life in the usual places. In the end, he discovers that the purpose of life is relationship with God.

**Song of Solomon** describes love. This book records the romance of a man and his bride, using imagery from those times to depict the wonderful gift of marriage that God has given us.

While each book has much to say about other topics, considering these main ones in mind can keep you focused as you read. These books are also filled with literary devices, such as metaphors, similes, hyperbole, and anthropomorphisms. Recognizing these devices and understanding how they work will greatly aid your understanding.

# JOB • PSALMS • PROVERBS ECCLESIASTES • SONG OF SOLOMON

**THE BOOKS OF POETRY AND WISDOM**

| Book | Author | Timeframe | Theme |
|---|---|---|---|
| **Job** | Unknown | c. 2100–1900 BC | Suffering |
| **Psalms** | David, Asaph, and Others | c. 1410–430 BC | Worship |
| **Proverbs** | Solomon | c. 950–700 BC | Wisdom |
| **Ecclesiastes** | Solomon | c. 935 BC | Purpose |
| **Song of Solomon** | Solomon | c. 971–931 BC | Love |

*The Book of*

# JOB

**AUTHOR**
Unknown; perhaps Moses, Job, Solomon, Isaiah, Jeremiah, or Ezra

**KEY VERSE**
Job 42:2

**READING TIME**
2 hours 12 minutes

The events of the Book of Job are perhaps among the earliest of the Bible. Likely set in the period of the patriarchs (Abraham, Isaac, and Jacob), Job tells the story of a man who lost everything—his wealth, his children, his health—and wrestled to understand why. What had he done to deserve such affliction and suffering? Believing that he had done no wrong, the only reasonable conclusion Job could reach was that God had made a mistake. God had chastised him without cause. If only Job had a way to clear up the confusion, but he could think of none. The book begins with a pair of debates between God and Satan, moves through three cycles of debates between Job and his friends, and concludes with a dramatic confrontation between God and His struggling servant. In the end, Job acknowledged the sovereignty of God and recognized his error in assuming he knew more about his situation than God. Job was restored as God's servant and received more than he had lost.

**Occasion:** While the date of the writing of Job and its author are unknown, the reason for its writing is to address the timeless question of God's presence and goodness during times of human suffering.

**Main Point:** God is sovereign over suffering.

**Big Ideas:** God's ways are greater than our ways and can often be mysterious. When we face difficult situations, that doesn't necessarily mean we have sinned. We must trust God and believe all He does is good, even when things seem to go wrong. It's OK to question God to understand Him and His ways, but it's not OK to question God as if we know better.

**OUTLINE:**

I. Job's Suffering (chs. 1–2)
II. Job's Debate with His Friends (chs. 3–26)
III. Job's Final Defense (chs. 27–31)
IV. Job's Correction by Elihu (chs. 32–37)
V. Job's Rebuke by God (chs. 38–41)
VI. Job's Repentance and Restoration (ch. 42)

**c. 2167 BC**
Abraham is born in Ur of the Chaldeans

**c. 2100–1900 BC**
**Job written**, perhaps

**c. 2091 BC**
Abraham is called to set out for Canaan

**c. 2000 BC**
Horses are tamed and used for transport

**c. 1991 BC**
Abraham dies in Canaan

**c. 1915 BC**
Joseph is born to Jacob and Rachel

**c. 1886 BC**
Isaac dies in Canaan

**c. 1876 BC**
Jacob and his family move to Egypt

### JOB AND HIS FAMILY IN UZ

**1** There was a man [a]in the land of Uz, whose name *was* [b]Job; and that man was [c]blameless and upright, and one who [d]feared God and shunned evil. 2 And seven sons and three daughters were born to him. 3 Also, his possessions were seven thousand sheep, three thousand camels, five hundred yoke of oxen, five hundred female donkeys, and a very large household, so that this man was the greatest of all the people of the East.

4 And his sons would go and feast *in their* houses, each on his *appointed* day, and would send and invite their three sisters to eat and drink with them. 5 So it was, when the days of feasting had run their course, that Job would send and sanctify them, and he would rise early in the morning [a]and offer burnt offerings *according to* the number of them all. For Job said, "It may be that my sons have sinned and [b]cursed[1] God in their hearts." Thus Job did regularly.

### SATAN ATTACKS JOB'S CHARACTER

6 Now [a]there was a day when the sons of God came to present themselves before the LORD, and Satan[1] also came among them. 7 And the LORD said to Satan, "From where do you come?"

So Satan answered the LORD and said, "From [a]going to and fro on the earth, and from walking back and forth on it."

8 Then the LORD said to Satan, "Have you considered My servant Job, that *there is* none like him on the earth, a blameless and upright man, one who fears God and shuns evil?"

> **1:8** When the Lord said Job was **blameless and upright**, He wasn't saying Job was sinless. Rather, Job had his priorities right. Job feared the Lord and it showed in his life.

9 So Satan answered the LORD and said, "Does Job fear God for nothing? 10 [a]Have You not made a hedge around him, around his household, and around all that he has on every side? [b]You have blessed the work of his hands, and his possessions have increased in the land. 11 [a]But now, stretch out Your hand and touch all that he has, and he will surely [b]curse You to Your face!"

12 And the LORD said to Satan, "Behold, all that he has *is* in your power; only do not lay a hand on his *person*."

So Satan went out from the presence of the LORD.

### JOB LOSES HIS PROPERTY AND CHILDREN

13 Now there was a day [a]when his sons and daughters *were* eating and drinking wine in their oldest brother's house; 14 and a messenger came to Job and said, "The oxen were plowing and the donkeys feeding beside them, 15 when the Sabeans[1] raided *them* and took them away—indeed they have killed the servants with the edge of the sword; and I alone have escaped to tell you!"

16 While he *was* still speaking, another also came and said, "The fire of God fell from heaven and burned up the sheep and the servants, and consumed them; and I alone have escaped to tell you!"

17 While he *was* still speaking, another also came and said, "The Chaldeans formed three bands, raided the camels and took them away, yes, and killed the servants with the edge of the sword; and I alone have escaped to tell you!"

18 While he *was* still speaking, another also came and said, [a]"Your sons and daughters *were* eating and drinking wine in their oldest brother's house, 19 and suddenly a great wind came from across[1] the wilderness and struck the four corners of the house, and it fell on the young people, and they are dead; and I alone have escaped to tell you!"

20 Then Job arose, [a]tore his robe, and shaved his head; and he [b]fell to the ground and worshiped. 21 And he said:

[a]"Naked I came from my mother's womb,
And naked shall I return there.
The LORD [b]gave, and the LORD has [c]taken
away;
[d]Blessed be the name of the LORD."

22 [a]In all this Job did not sin nor charge God with wrong.

### SATAN ATTACKS JOB'S HEALTH

**2** Again [a]there was a day when the sons of God came to present themselves before the LORD, and Satan came also among them to present himself before the LORD. 2 And the LORD said to Satan, "From where do you come?"

[a]Satan answered the LORD and said, "From going to and fro on the earth, and from walking back and forth on it."

3 Then the LORD said to Satan, "Have you considered My servant Job, that *there is* none like him on the earth, [a]a blameless and upright man, one who fears God and shuns evil? And still he [b]holds fast to his integrity, although you incited Me against him, [c]to destroy him without cause."

4 So Satan answered the LORD and said, "Skin for skin! Yes, all that a man has he will give for his life. 5 [a]But stretch out Your hand now, and

**1:1** [a] 1 Chr. 1:17 [b] Ezek. 14:14, 20 [c] Gen. 6:9; 17:1 [d] [Prov. 16:6] **1:5** [a] [Job 42:8] [b] 1 Kin. 21:10, 13 [1] Literally *blessed,* but used here in the evil sense, and so in verse 11 and 2:5, 9 **1:6** [a] Job 2:1 [1] Literally *the Adversary,* and so throughout this book **1:7** [a] [1 Pet. 5:8] **1:10** [a] Ps. 34:7 [b] [Prov. 10:22] **1:11** [a] Job 2:5; 19:21 [b] Is. 8:21 **1:13** [a] [Eccl. 9:12] **1:15** [1] Literally *Sheba* (compare 6:19) **1:18** [a] Job 1:4, 13 **1:19** [1] Septuagint omits *across.* **1:20** [a] Gen. 37:29, 34 [b] [1 Pet. 5:6] **1:21** [a] [Eccl. 5:15] [b] [James 1:17] [c] Gen. 31:16 [d] Eph. 5:20 **1:22** [a] Job 2:10 **2:1** [a] Job 1:6–8 **2:2** [a] Job 1:7 **2:3** [a] Job 1:1, 8 [b] Job 27:5, 6 [c] Job 9:17 **2:5** [a] Job 1:11

touch his [b]bone and his flesh, and he will surely curse You to Your face!"

6 [a]And the LORD said to Satan, "Behold, he *is* in your hand, but spare his life."

7 So Satan went out from the presence of the LORD, and struck Job with painful boils [a]from the sole of his foot to the crown of his head. 8 And he took for himself a potsherd with which to scrape himself [a]while he sat in the midst of the ashes.

9 Then his wife said to him, "Do you still hold fast to your integrity? Curse God and die!"

10 But he said to her, "You speak as one of the foolish women speaks. [a]Shall we indeed accept good from God, and shall we not accept adversity?" [b]In all this Job did not [c]sin with his lips.

### JOB'S THREE FRIENDS

11 Now when Job's three friends heard of all this adversity that had come upon him, each one came from his own place—Eliphaz the [a]Temanite, Bildad the [b]Shuhite, and Zophar the Naamathite. For they had made an appointment together to come [c]and mourn with him, and to comfort him. 12 And when they raised their eyes from afar, and did not recognize him, they lifted their voices and wept; and each one tore his robe and [a]sprinkled dust on his head toward heaven. 13 So they sat down with him on the ground [a]seven days and seven nights, and no one spoke a word to him, for they saw that *his* grief was very great.

### JOB DEPLORES HIS BIRTH

3 After this Job opened his mouth and cursed the day of his *birth.* 2 And Job spoke, and said:

3 "May[a] the day perish on which I was born,
And the night *in which* it was said,
'A male child is conceived.'
4 May that day be darkness;
May God above not seek it,
Nor the light shine upon it.
5 May darkness and [a]the shadow of death claim it;
May a cloud settle on it;
May the blackness of the day terrify it.
6 *As for* that night, may darkness seize it;
May it not rejoice[1] among the days of the year,
May it not come into the number of the months.
7 Oh, may that night be barren!
May no joyful shout come into it!
8 May those curse it who curse the day,
Those [a]who are ready to arouse Leviathan.
9 May the stars of its morning be dark;
May it look for light, but *have* none,
And not see the dawning of the day;
10 Because it did not shut up the doors of my *mother's* womb,
Nor hide sorrow from my eyes.

11 "Why[a] did I not die at birth?
*Why* did I *not* perish when I came from the womb?
12 [a]Why did the knees receive me?
Or why the breasts, that I should nurse?
13 For now I would have lain still and been quiet,
I would have been asleep;
Then I would have been at rest
14 With kings and counselors of the earth,
Who [a]built ruins for themselves,
15 Or with princes who had gold,
Who filled their houses *with* silver;
16 Or *why* was I not hidden [a]like a stillborn child,
Like infants who never saw light?
17 There the wicked cease *from* troubling,
And there the weary are at [a]rest.
18 *There* the prisoners rest together;
[a]They do not hear the voice of the oppressor.

2:5 [b] Job 19:20 2:6 [a] Job 1:12 2:7 [a] Is. 1:6 2:8 [a] Ezek. 27:30 2:10 [a] Job 1:21, 22 [b] Job 1:22 [c] Ps. 39:1 2:11 [a] Gen. 36:11 [b] Gen. 25:2 [c] Rom. 12:15 2:12 [a] Neh. 9:1 2:13 [a] Gen. 50:10 3:3 [a] Jer. 20:14–18 3:5 [a] Jer. 13:16 3:6 [1] Septuagint, Syriac, Targum, and Vulgate read *be joined.* 3:8 [a] Jer. 9:17 3:11 [a] Job 10:18, 19 3:12 [a] Gen. 30:3 3:14 [a] Job 15:28; Is. 58:12 3:16 [a] Ps. 58:8 3:17 [a] Job 17:16 3:18 [a] Job 39:7

APPLY THE TRUTH

## DEPRESSION

**3:1–26** Job endured the worst of life's circumstances. He lost his family, possessions, and health, and was in conflict with his wife. Because of all the loss, he experienced deep depression. His unimaginable sorrow led him to regret his very life, refuse to be comforted, and even doubt his God. Why had all these things happened?

This is a common question people ask, especially when they feel anxious, overwhelmed, or depressed. We wish we weren't experiencing the pain, refuse to enjoy good things around us, and even become angry with God or blame Him for what's going wrong. Although Job did much of this, he's still a great example to us when we feel depressed because he got through it. How? By processing his feelings, looking to friends for encouragement, and listening to God. God's reminder to Job was that no matter how difficult life got, He was in control and would always be with Job. No matter the loss, great gain is found in God's presence. Don't turn your back on God. He cares for you. Rather, lean into His love and find comfort.

19 The small and great are there,
And the servant *is* free from his master.

20 "Why[a] is light given to him who is in misery,
And life to the [b]bitter of soul,
21 Who [a]long for death, but it does not *come*,
And search for it more than [b]hidden treasures;
22 Who rejoice exceedingly,
*And* are glad when they can find the [a]grave?
23 *Why is light given* to a man whose way is hidden,
[a]And whom God has hedged in?
24 For my sighing comes before I eat,[1]
And my groanings pour out like water.
25 For the thing I greatly [a]feared has come upon me,
And what I dreaded has happened to me.
26 I am not at ease, nor am I quiet;
I have no rest, for trouble comes."

## *ELIPHAZ: JOB HAS SINNED*

4 Then Eliphaz the Temanite answered and said:

> **4:1** Job's conversation with his friends followed a pattern of debate called "cycles." Eliphaz, Bildad, and Zophar took turns talking to Job in three different cycles. After each of their speeches, Job was given a chance to reply.

2 "*If* one attempts a word with you, will you become weary?
But who can withhold himself from speaking?
3 Surely you have instructed many,
And you [a]have strengthened weak hands.
4 Your words have upheld him who was stumbling,
And you [a]have strengthened the feeble knees;
5 But now it comes upon you, and you are weary;
It touches you, and you are troubled.
6 *Is* not [a]your reverence [b]your confidence?
And the integrity of your ways your hope?

7 "Remember now, [a]who *ever* perished being innocent?
Or where were the upright *ever* cut off?
8 Even as I have seen,
[a]Those who plow iniquity
And sow trouble reap the same.
9 By the blast of God they perish,

> **SEEING JESUS IN THE SCRIPTURE**
>
> **4:7** Though Job wasn't perfect, his affliction came because he was being tested. Jesus was also tested. Though He was innocent, He was struck down by God to forgive the sins of the world (see Matt. 4:1–2).

And by the breath of His anger they are consumed.
10 The roaring of the lion,
The voice of the fierce lion,
And [a]the teeth of the young lions are broken.
11 [a]The old lion perishes for lack of prey,
And the cubs of the lioness are scattered.

12 "Now a word was secretly brought to me,
And my ear received a whisper of it.
13 [a]In disquieting thoughts from the visions of the night,
When deep sleep falls on men,
14 Fear came upon me, and [a]trembling,
Which made all my bones shake.
15 Then a spirit passed before my face;
The hair on my body stood up.
16 It stood still,
But I could not discern its appearance.
A form *was* before my eyes;
*There was* silence;
Then I heard a voice *saying:*
17 'Can a mortal be more righteous than God?
Can a man be more pure than his Maker?
18 If He [a]puts no trust in His servants,
*If* He charges His angels with error,
19 How much more those who dwell in houses of clay,
Whose foundation is in the dust,
*Who* are crushed before a moth?
20 [a]They are broken in pieces from morning till evening;
They perish forever, with no one regarding.
21 Does not their own excellence go away?
They die, even without wisdom.'

## *ELIPHAZ: JOB IS CHASTENED BY GOD*

5 "Call out now;
Is there anyone who will answer you?
And to which of the holy ones will you turn?
2 For wrath kills a foolish man,
And envy slays a simple one.
3 [a]I have seen the foolish taking root,
But suddenly I cursed his dwelling place.
4 His sons are [a]far from safety,
They are crushed in the gate,
And [b]*there is* no deliverer.

**3:20** [a] Jer. 20:18 [b] 2 Kin. 4:27 **3:21** [a] Rev. 9:6 [b] Prov. 2:4 **3:22** [a] Job 7:15, 16 **3:23** [a] Job 19:8; Ps. 88:8; Lam. 3:7 **3:24** [1] Literally *my bread* **3:25** [a] [Job 9:28; 30:15] **4:3** [a] Is. 35:3 **4:4** [a] Is. 35:3 **4:6** [a] Job 1:1 [b] Prov. 3:26 **4:7** [a] [Job 8:20; 36:6, 7; Ps. 37:25] **4:8** [a] [Job 15:31, 35; Prov. 22:8; Hos. 10:13; Gal. 6:7] **4:10** [a] Job 5:15; Ps. 58:6 **4:11** [a] Job 29:17; Ps. 34:10 **4:13** [a] Job 33:15 **4:14** [a] Hab. 3:16 **4:18** [a] Job 15:15 **4:20** [a] Ps. 90:5, 6 **5:3** [a] [Ps. 37:35, 36]; Jer. 12:1–3 **5:4** [a] Ps. 119:155 [b] Ps. 109:12

5 Because the hungry eat up his harvest,
Taking it even from the thorns,[1]
And a snare snatches their substance.[2]
6 For affliction does not come from the
dust,
Nor does trouble spring from the ground;
7 Yet man is [a]born to trouble,
As the sparks fly upward.

8 "But as for me, I would seek God,
And to God I would commit my cause—
9 Who does great things, and unsearchable,
Marvelous things without number.
10 [a]He gives rain on the earth,
And sends waters on the fields.
11 [a]He sets on high those who are lowly,
And those who mourn are lifted to safety.
12 [a]He frustrates the devices of the crafty,
So that their hands cannot carry out their
plans.
13 He catches the [a]wise in their own craftiness,
And the counsel of the cunning comes
quickly upon them.
14 They meet with darkness in the daytime,
And grope at noontime as in the night.
15 But [a]He saves the needy from the sword,
From the mouth of the mighty,
And from their hand.
16 [a]So the poor have hope,
And injustice shuts her mouth.

17 "Behold,[a] happy *is* the man whom God
corrects;
Therefore do not despise the chastening
of the Almighty.
18 [a]For He bruises, but He binds up;
He wounds, but His hands make whole.
19 [a]He shall deliver you in six troubles,
Yes, in seven [b]no evil shall touch you.
20 [a]In famine He shall redeem you from
death,
And in war from the power of the sword.
21 [a]You shall be hidden from the scourge of
the tongue,
And you shall not be afraid of destruction
when it comes.
22 You shall laugh at destruction and
famine,
And [a]you shall not be afraid of the [b]beasts
of the earth.
23 [a]For you shall have a covenant with the
stones of the field,
And the beasts of the field shall be at
peace with you.
24 You shall know that your tent *is* in peace;
You shall visit your dwelling and find
nothing amiss.
25 You shall also know that [a]your
descendants *shall be* many,
And your offspring [b]like the grass of the
earth.
26 [a]You shall come to the grave at a full age,
As a sheaf of grain ripens in its season.
27 Behold, this we have [a]searched out;
It *is* true.
Hear it, and know for yourself."

**5:25–26** A large family and a long, healthy life were considered rewards from God for living in a way that pleased Him. Conversely, losing one's family or health was often seen as punishment for disobeying God in some way.

### *JOB: MY COMPLAINT IS JUST*

6 Then Job answered and said:

2 "Oh, that my grief were fully weighed,
And my calamity laid with it on the scales!
3 For then it would be heavier than the sand
of the sea—
Therefore my words have been rash.
4 [a]For the arrows of the Almighty *are*
within me;
My spirit drinks in their poison;
[b]The terrors of God are arrayed [c]against
me.
5 Does the [a]wild donkey bray when it has
grass,
Or does the ox low over its fodder?
6 Can flavorless food be eaten without salt?
Or is there *any* taste in the white of an egg?
7 My soul refuses to touch them;
They *are* as loathsome food to me.

8 "Oh, that I might have my request,
That God would grant *me* the thing that I
long for!
9 That it would please God to crush me,
That He would loose His hand and [a]cut
me off!
10 Then I would still have comfort;
Though in anguish I would exult,
He will not spare;
For [a]I have not concealed the words of
[b]the Holy One.

11 "What strength do I have, that I should
hope?
And what *is* my end, that I should prolong
my life?

5:5 [1] Septuagint reads *They shall not be taken from evil men;* Vulgate reads *And the armed man shall take him by violence.* [2] Septuagint reads *The might shall draw them off;* Vulgate reads *And the thirsty shall drink up their riches.* 5:7 [a] Job 14:1 5:10 [a] [Job 36:27–29; 37:6–11; 38:26] 5:11 [a] Ps. 113:7 5:12 [a] Neh. 4:15 5:13 [a] [1 Cor. 3:19] 5:15 [a] Ps. 35:10 5:16 [a] 1 Sam. 2:8 5:17 [a] Ps. 94:12 5:18 [a] [1 Sam. 2:6, 7] 5:19 [a] Ps. 34:19; 91:3 [b] Ps. 91:10 5:20 [a] Ps. 33:19, 20; 37:19 5:21 [a] Ps. 31:20 5:22 [a] Ezek. 34:25 [b] Hos. 2:18 5:23 [a] Ps. 91:12 5:25 [a] Ps. 112:2 [b] Ps. 72:16 5:26 [a] [Prov. 9:11; 10:27] 5:27 [a] Ps. 111:2 6:4 [a] Ps. 38:2 [b] Ps. 88:15, 16 [c] Job 30:15 6:5 [a] Job 39:5–8 6:9 [a] Job 7:16; 9:21; 10:1 6:10 [a] Acts 20:20 [b] [Is. 57:15]

12 *Is* my strength the strength of stones?
Or is my flesh bronze?
13 *Is* my help not within me?
And is success driven from me?

14 "To[a] him who is afflicted, kindness *should be shown* by his friend,
Even though he forsakes the fear of the Almighty.
15 [a]My brothers have dealt deceitfully like a brook,
[b]Like the streams of the brooks that pass away,
16 Which are dark because of the ice,
*And* into which the snow vanishes.
17 When it is warm, they cease to flow;
When it is hot, they vanish from their place.
18 The paths of their way turn aside,
They go nowhere and perish.
19 The caravans of [a]Tema look,
The travelers of [b]Sheba hope for them.
20 They are [a]disappointed because they were confident;
They come there and are confused.
21 For now [a]you are nothing,
You see terror and [b]are afraid.
22 Did I ever say, 'Bring *something* to me'?
Or, 'Offer a bribe for me from your wealth'?
23 Or, 'Deliver me from the enemy's hand'?
Or, 'Redeem me from the hand of oppressors'?

24 "Teach me, and I will hold my tongue;
Cause me to understand wherein I have erred.
25 How forceful are right words!
But what does your arguing prove?
26 Do you intend to rebuke *my* words,
And the speeches of a desperate one, *which are* as wind?
27 Yes, you overwhelm the fatherless,
And you [a]undermine your friend.
28 Now therefore, be pleased to look at me;
For I would never lie to your face.
29 [a]Yield now, let there be no injustice!
Yes, concede, my [b]righteousness still stands!
30 Is there injustice on my tongue?
Cannot my taste discern the unsavory?

### *JOB: MY SUFFERING IS COMFORTLESS*

**7** "*Is there* not [a]a time of hard service for man on earth?
*Are not* his days also like the days of a hired man?
2 Like a servant who earnestly desires the shade,
And like a hired man who eagerly looks for his wages,
3 So I have been allotted [a]months of futility,
And wearisome nights have been appointed to me.
4 [a]When I lie down, I say, 'When shall I arise,
And the night be ended?'
For I have had my fill of tossing till dawn.
5 My flesh is [a]caked with worms and dust,
My skin is cracked and breaks out afresh.

6 "My[a] days are swifter than a weaver's shuttle,
And are spent without hope.
7 Oh, remember that [a]my life *is* a breath!
My eye will never again see good.
8 [a]The eye of him who sees me will see me no *more;*
*While* your eyes *are* upon me, I shall no longer *be.*
9 *As* the cloud disappears and vanishes away,
So [a]he who goes down to the grave does not come up.
10 He shall never return to his house,
[a]Nor shall his place know him anymore.

11 "Therefore I will [a]not restrain my mouth;
I will speak in the anguish of my spirit;
I will [b]complain in the bitterness of my soul.
12 *Am* I a sea, or a sea serpent,
That You set a guard over me?
13 [a]When I say, 'My bed will comfort me,
My couch will ease my complaint,'
14 Then You scare me with dreams
And terrify me with visions,
15 So that my soul chooses strangling
*And* death rather than my body.[1]
16 [a]I loathe *my life;*
I would not live forever.
[b]Let me alone,
For [c]my days *are but* a breath.

17 "What[a] *is* man, that You should exalt him,
*That* You should set Your heart on him,
18 That You should visit him every morning,
*And* test him every moment?
19 How long?
Will You not look away from me,
And let me alone till I swallow my saliva?
20 Have I sinned?
What have I done to You, [a]O watcher of men?
Why [b]have You set me as Your target,
So that I am a burden to myself?[1]
21 Why then do You not pardon my transgression,
And take away my iniquity?
For now I will lie down in the dust,
And You will seek me diligently,
But I *will* no longer *be.*"

6:14 [a] [Prov. 17:17] 6:15 [a] Ps. 38:11 [b] Jer. 15:18 6:19 [a] Gen. 25:15 [b] 1 Kin. 10:1 6:20 [a] Jer. 14:3 6:21 [a] Job 13:4 [b] Ps. 38:11 6:27 [a] Ps. 57:6 6:29 [a] Job 17:10 [b] Job 27:5, 6; 34:5 7:1 [a] [Job 14:5, 13, 14] 7:3 [a] [Job 15:31] 7:4 [a] Deut. 28:67 7:5 [a] Is. 14:11 7:6 [a] Job 9:25; 16:22; 17:11 7:7 [a] Ps. 78:39; 89:47 7:8 [a] Job 8:18; 20:9 7:9 [a] 2 Sam. 12:23 7:10 [a] Ps. 103:16 7:11 [a] Ps. 39:1, 9 [b] 1 Sam. 1:10 7:13 [a] Job 9:27 7:15 [1] Literally *my bones* 7:16 [a] Job 10:1 [b] Job 14:6 [c] Ps. 62:9 7:17 [a] Ps. 8:4; 144:3 7:20 [a] Ps. 36:6 [b] Ps. 21:12
[1] Following Masoretic Text, Targum, and Vulgate; Septuagint and Jewish tradition read *to You.*

### *BILDAD: JOB SHOULD REPENT*

**8** Then Bildad the Shuhite answered and said:

2 "How long will you speak these *things,*
And the words of your mouth *be like* a
strong wind?
3 [a]Does God subvert judgment?
Or does the Almighty pervert justice?
4 If [a]your sons have sinned against Him,
He has cast them away for their
transgression.
5 [a]If you would earnestly seek God
And make your supplication to the
Almighty,
6 If you *were* pure and upright,
Surely now He would awake for you,
And prosper your rightful dwelling place.

> **8:6** God had described Job as **pure and upright** (Job 1:8; 2:3). Bildad's concept that one must "get right with God" was not inherently wrong. But his error was assuming that loss of possessions equaled loss of God's favor.

7 Though your beginning was small,
Yet your latter end would [a]increase
abundantly.

8 "For[a] inquire, please, of the former age,
And consider the things discovered by
their fathers;
9 For [a]we *were born* yesterday, and know
nothing,
Because our days on earth *are* a shadow.
10 Will they not teach you and tell you,
And utter words from their heart?

11 "Can the papyrus grow up without a
marsh?
Can the reeds flourish without water?
12 [a]While it *is* yet green *and* not cut down,
It withers before any *other* plant.
13 So *are* the paths of all who [a]forget God;
And the hope of the [b]hypocrite shall
perish,
14 Whose confidence shall be cut off,
And whose trust *is* a spider's web.
15 [a]He leans on his house, but it does not
stand.
He holds it fast, but it does not endure.
16 He grows green in the sun,
And his branches spread out in his
garden.
17 His roots wrap around the rock heap,
*And* look for a place in the stones.
18 [a]If he is destroyed from his place,
Then *it* will deny him, *saying,* 'I have not
seen you.'

19 "Behold, this is the joy of His way,
And [a]out of the earth others will grow.
20 Behold, [a]God will not cast away the
blameless,
Nor will He uphold the evildoers.
21 He will yet fill your mouth with laughing,
And your lips with rejoicing.
22 Those who hate you will be [a]clothed with
shame,
And the dwelling place of the wicked will
come to nothing."[1]

### *JOB: THERE IS NO MEDIATOR*

**9** Then Job answered and said:

2 "Truly I know *it is* so,
But how can a [a]man be [b]righteous before
God?
3 If one wished to contend with Him,
He could not answer Him one time out of
a thousand.

> **9:3** The word ***contend*** indicates a legal argument, not a quarrel. Job was seeking justice. He didn't think he had sinned—as his friends indicated—requiring God to punish him.

4 [a]*God is* wise in heart and mighty in strength.
Who has hardened *himself* against Him
and prospered?
5 He removes the mountains, and they do
not know
When He overturns them in His anger;
6 He [a]shakes the earth out of its place,
And its [b]pillars tremble;
7 He commands the sun, and it does not
rise;
He seals off the stars;
8 [a]He alone spreads out the heavens,
And treads on the waves of the sea;
9 [a]He made the Bear, Orion, and the Pleiades,
And the chambers of the south;
10 [a]He does great things past finding out,
Yes, wonders without number.
11 [a]If He goes by me, I do not see *Him;*
If He moves past, I do not perceive Him;
12 [a]If He takes away, who can hinder Him?
Who can say to Him, 'What are You doing?'
13 God will not withdraw His anger,
[a]The allies of the proud[1] lie prostrate
beneath Him.

8:3 [a] [Deut. 32:4] 8:4 [a] Job 1:5, 18, 19 8:5 [a] [Job 5:17–27; 11:13] 8:7 [a] Job 42:12 8:8 [a] Deut. 4:32; 32:7 8:9 [a] Gen. 47:9 8:12 [a] Ps. 129:6 8:13 [a] Ps. 9:17 [b] Job 11:20; 18:14; 27:8 8:15 [a] Job 8:22; 27:18 8:18 [a] Job 7:10 8:19 [a] Ps. 113:7 8:20 [a] Job 4:7 8:22 [a] Ps. 35:26; 109:29 [1] Literally *will not be* 9:2 [a] [Job 4:17; 15:14–16] [b] [Hab. 2:4] 9:4 [a] Job 36:5 9:6 [a] Heb. 12:26 [b] Job 26:11 9:8 [a] Ps. 104:2, 3 9:9 [a] Amos 5:8 9:10 [a] Job 5:9 9:11 [a] [Job 23:8, 9; 35:14] 9:12 [a] [Is. 45:9] 9:13 [a] Job 26:12 [1] Hebrew *rahab*

14 "How then can I answer Him,
*And* choose my words *to reason* with Him?
15 [a]For though I were righteous, I could not answer Him;
I would beg mercy of my Judge.
16 If I called and He answered me,
I would not believe that He was listening to my voice.
17 For He crushes me with a tempest,
And multiplies my wounds [a]without cause.
18 He will not allow me to catch my breath,
But fills me with bitterness.
19 If *it is a matter* of strength, indeed *He is* strong;
And if of justice, who will appoint my day *in court?*
20 Though I were righteous, my own mouth would condemn me;
Though I *were* blameless, it would prove me perverse.

21 "I am blameless, yet I do not know myself;
I despise my life.
22 It *is* all one *thing;*
Therefore I say, [a]'He destroys the blameless and the wicked.'
23 If the scourge slays suddenly,
He laughs at the plight of the innocent.
24 The earth is given into the hand of the wicked.
He covers the faces of its judges.
If it is not *He,* who else could it be?

25 "Now [a]my days are swifter than a runner;
They flee away, they see no good.
26 They pass by like swift ships,
[a]Like an eagle swooping on its prey.
27 [a]If I say, 'I will forget my complaint,
I will put off my sad face and wear a smile,'
28 [a]I am afraid of all my sufferings;
I know that You [b]will not hold me innocent.
29 *If* I am condemned,
Why then do I labor in vain?
30 [a]If I wash myself with snow water,
And cleanse my hands with soap,
31 Yet You will plunge me into the pit,
And my own clothes will abhor me.

32 "For [a]*He is* not a man, as I *am,*
*That* I may answer Him,
*And that* we should go to court together.
33 [a]Nor is there any mediator between us,
*Who* may lay his hand on us both.
34 [a]Let Him take His rod away from me,
And do not let dread of Him terrify me.
35 *Then* I would speak and not fear Him,
But it is not so with me.

### SEEING JESUS IN THE SCRIPTURE

**9:33** Job believed he was at an impasse with God and wished he had a mediator between them, but there was none. His hope is ultimately realized in Jesus, the perfect Mediator between people and God, bringing us together (see 1 Tim. 2:5).

## JOB: I WOULD PLEAD WITH GOD

10 "My [a]soul loathes my life;
I will give free course to my complaint,
[b]I will speak in the bitterness of my soul.
2 I will say to God, 'Do not condemn me;
Show me why You contend with me.
3 *Does it* seem good to You that You should oppress,
That You should despise the work of Your hands,
And smile on the counsel of the wicked?
4 Do You have eyes of flesh?
Or [a]do You see as man sees?
5 *Are* Your days like the days of a mortal man?
*Are* Your years like the days of a mighty man,
6 That You should seek for my iniquity
And search out my sin,
7 Although You know that I am not wicked,
And *there is* no one who can deliver from Your hand?

8 'Your[a] hands have made me and fashioned me,
An intricate unity;
Yet You would [b]destroy me.
9 Remember, I pray, [a]that You have made me like clay.
And will You turn me into dust again?
10 [a]Did You not pour me out like milk,
And curdle me like cheese,
11 Clothe me with skin and flesh,
And knit me together with bones and sinews?
12 You have granted me life and favor,
And Your care has preserved my spirit.

13 'And these *things* You have hidden in Your heart;
I know that this *was* with You:
14 If I sin, then [a]You mark me,
And will not acquit me of my iniquity.
15 If I am wicked, [a]woe to me;
[b]Even *if* I am righteous, I cannot lift up my head.
*I am* full of disgrace;
[c]See my misery!
16 If *my head* is exalted,
[a]You hunt me like a fierce lion,
And again You show Yourself awesome against me.

**9:15** [a] Job 10:15; 23:1–7 **9:17** [a] Job 2:3 **9:22** [a] Ezek. 21:3 **9:25** [a] Job 7:6, 7 **9:26** [a] Hab. 1:8 **9:27** [a] Job 7:13 **9:28** [a] Ps. 119:120 [b] Ex. 20:7 **9:30** [a] [Jer. 2:22] **9:32** [a] [Is. 45:9] **9:33** [a] [1 Sam. 2:25] **9:34** [a] Job 13:20, 21 **10:1** [a] Job 7:16 [b] Job 7:11 **10:4** [a] [1 Sam. 16:7] **10:8** [a] Ps. 119:73 [b] [Job 9:22] **10:9** [a] Gen. 2:7 **10:10** [a] [Ps. 139:14–16] **10:14** [a] Ps. 139:1 **10:15** [a] Is. 3:11 [b] [Job 9:12, 15] [c] Ps. 25:18 **10:16** [a] Is. 38:13

17 You renew Your witnesses against me,
And increase Your indignation toward me;
Changes and war are *ever* with me.

18 'Why[a] then have You brought me out of the womb?
Oh, that I had perished and no eye had seen me!
19 I would have been as though I had not been.
I would have been carried from the womb to the grave.
20 [a]Are not my days few?
Cease! [b]Leave me alone, that I may take a little comfort,
21 Before I go *to the place from which* I shall not return,
[a]To the land of darkness [b]and the shadow of death,
22 A land as dark as darkness *itself,*
As the shadow of death, without any order,
*Where* even the light *is* like darkness.' "

**10:21–22 The land of darkness and the shadow of death** refers to Sheol, the place of the dead, according to ancient Hebrew beliefs. Sheol was pictured as a dark and gloomy underground world where the souls of both good and bad people lived after death. Sheol was also the place where people were thought to receive their eternal punishment or reward, according to how they lived.

## ZOPHAR URGES JOB TO REPENT

11 Then Zophar the Naamathite answered and said:

2 "Should not the multitude of words be answered?
And should a man full of talk be vindicated?
3 Should your empty talk make men hold their peace?
And when you mock, should no one rebuke you?
4 For you have said,
[a]'My doctrine *is* pure,
And I am clean in your eyes.'
5 But oh, that God would speak,
And open His lips against you,
6 That He would show you the secrets of wisdom!
For *they would* double *your* prudence.
Know therefore that [a]God exacts from you
*Less* than your iniquity *deserves.*

### SEEING JESUS IN THE SCRIPTURE

**11:6** Zophar was right that God was gracious to Job, who deserved death like all people. God was gracious to Job because His plan was to place the penalty of Job's sins upon Jesus, who paid it in full on the cross (see Rom. 3:21–26).

7 "Can[a] you search out the deep things of God?
Can you find out the limits of the Almighty?
8 *They are* higher than heaven—what can you do?
Deeper than Sheol—what can you know?
9 Their measure *is* longer than the earth
And broader than the sea.

10 "If[a] He passes by, imprisons, and gathers *to judgment,*
Then who can hinder Him?
11 For [a]He knows deceitful men;
He sees wickedness also.
Will He not then consider *it?*
12 For an [a]empty-headed man will be wise,
When a wild donkey's colt is born a man.

13 "If you would [a]prepare your heart,
And [b]stretch out your hands toward Him;
14 If iniquity *were* in your hand, *and you* put it far away,
And [a]would not let wickedness dwell in your tents;
15 [a]Then surely you could lift up your face without spot;
Yes, you could be steadfast, and not fear;
16 Because you would [a]forget *your* misery,
And remember *it* as waters *that have* passed away,
17 And *your* life [a]would be brighter than noonday.
*Though* you were dark, you would be like the morning.
18 And you would be secure, because there is hope;
Yes, you would dig *around you, and* [a]take your rest in safety.
19 You would also lie down, and no one would make *you* afraid;
*Yes,* many would court your favor.
20 But [a]the eyes of the wicked will fail,
And they shall not escape,
And [b]their hope—loss of life!"

**10:18** [a] Job 3:11–13 **10:20** [a] Ps. 39:5 [b] Job 7:16, 19 **10:21** [a] Ps. 88:12 [b] Ps. 23:4 **11:4** [a] Job 6:30 **11:6** [a] [Ezra 9:13] **11:7** [a] [Eccl. 3:11] **11:10** [a] [Rev. 3:7] **11:11** [a] [Ps. 10:14] **11:12** [a] Rom. 1:22 **11:13** [a] [1 Sam. 7:3] [b] Ps. 88:9 **11:14** [a] Ps. 101:3 **11:15** [a] Ps. 119:6 **11:16** [a] Is. 65:16 **11:17** [a] Is. 58:8, 10 **11:18** [a] Lev. 26:5, 6 **11:20** [a] Deut. 28:65 [b] [Prov. 11:7]

## JOB ANSWERS HIS CRITICS

12 Then Job answered and said:
2 "No doubt you *are* the people,
And wisdom will die with you!
3 But I have understanding as well as you;
I *am* not [a]inferior to you.
Indeed, who does not *know* such things as these?

4 "I[a] am one mocked by his friends,
Who [b]called on God, and He answered him,
The just and blameless *who is* ridiculed.

### SEEING JESUS IN THE SCRIPTURE

**12:4** Job was a righteous but imperfect man mocked because of his affliction from God. Jesus was a righteous and perfect man mocked as He hung on the cross, bearing the world's affliction for sin (see Matt. 27:39).

5 A lamp[1] is despised in the thought of one who is at ease;
*It is* made ready for [a]those whose feet slip.
6 [a]The tents of robbers prosper,
And those who provoke God are secure—
In what God provides by His hand.

7 "But now ask the beasts, and they will teach you;
And the birds of the air, and they will tell you;
8 Or speak to the earth, and it will teach you;
And the fish of the sea will explain to you.
9 Who among all these does not know
That the hand of the LORD has done this,
10 [a]In whose hand *is* the life of every living thing,
And the [b]breath of all mankind?
11 Does not the ear test words
And the mouth taste its food?
12 Wisdom *is* with aged men,
And with length of days, understanding.

13 "With Him *are* [a]wisdom and strength,
He has counsel and understanding.
14 If [a]He breaks *a thing* down, it cannot be rebuilt;
*If* He imprisons a man, there can be no release.
15 If He [a]withholds the waters, they dry up;
*If* He [b]sends them out, they overwhelm the earth.
16 With Him *are* strength and prudence.
The deceived and the deceiver *are* His.
17 He leads counselors away plundered,
And makes fools of the judges.
18 He loosens the bonds of kings,
And binds their waist with a belt.
19 He leads princes[1] away plundered,
And overthrows the mighty.
20 [a]He deprives the trusted ones of speech,
And takes away the discernment of the elders.
21 [a]He pours contempt on princes,
And disarms the mighty.
22 He [a]uncovers deep things out of darkness,
And brings the shadow of death to light.
23 [a]He makes nations great, and destroys them;
He enlarges nations, and guides them.
24 He takes away the understanding[1] of the chiefs of the people of the earth,
And [a]makes them wander in a pathless wilderness.
25 [a]They grope in the dark without light,
And He makes them [b]stagger like a drunken *man*.

13 "Behold, my eye has seen all *this*,
My ear has heard and understood it.
2 [a]What you know, I also know;
I *am* not inferior to you.
3 [a]But I would speak to the Almighty,
And I desire to reason with God.
4 But you forgers of lies,
[a]You *are* all worthless physicians.
5 Oh, that you would be silent,
And [a]it would be your wisdom!
6 Now hear my reasoning,
And heed the pleadings of my lips.
7 [a]Will you speak wickedly for God,
And talk deceitfully for Him?
8 Will you show partiality for Him?
Will you contend for God?
9 Will it be well when He searches you out?
Or can you mock Him as one mocks a man?
10 He will surely rebuke you
If you secretly show partiality.
11 Will not His excellence make you afraid,
And the dread of Him fall upon you?
12 Your platitudes *are* proverbs of ashes,
Your defenses are defenses of clay.

13 "Hold your peace with me, and let me speak,
Then let come on me what *may*!
14 Why [a]do I take my flesh in my teeth,
And put my life in my hands?
15 [a]Though He slay me, yet will I trust Him.
[b]Even so, I will defend my own ways before Him.

**12:3** [a] Job 13:2 **12:4** [a] Job 21:3 [b] Ps. 91:15 **12:5** [a] Prov. 14:2 [1] Or *disaster* **12:6** [a] [Job 9:24; 21:6–16] **12:10** [a] [Acts 17:28] [b] Job 27:3; 33:4 **12:13** [a] Job 9:4; 36:5 **12:14** [a] Job 11:10 **12:15** [a] [1 Kin. 8:35, 36] [b] Gen. 7:11–24 **12:19** [1] Literally *priests*, but not in a technical sense **12:20** [a] Job 32:9 **12:21** [a] Ps. 107:40 **12:22** [a] [1 Cor. 4:5] **12:23** [a] Is. 9:3; 26:15 **12:24** [a] Ps. 107:4 [1] Literally *heart* **12:25** [a] Job 5:14; 15:30; 18:18 [b] Ps. 107:27 **13:2** [a] Job 12:3 **13:3** [a] Job 23:3; 31:35 **13:4** [a] Job 6:21 **13:5** [a] Prov. 17:28 **13:7** [a] Job 27:4; 36:4 **13:14** [a] Job 18:4 **13:15** [a] Ps. 23:4 [b] Job 27:5

16 He also *shall* be my salvation,
For a [a]hypocrite could not come before Him.
17 Listen carefully to my speech,
And to my declaration with your ears.
18 See now, I have prepared *my* case,
I know that I shall be [a]vindicated.
19 [a]Who *is* he *who* will contend with me?
If now I hold my tongue, I perish.

### *JOB'S DESPONDENT PRAYER*

20 "Only[a] two *things* do not do to me,
Then I will not hide myself from You:
21 [a]Withdraw Your hand far from me,
And let not the dread of You make me afraid.

**SEEING JESUS IN THE SCRIPTURE**

**13:20–21** In the midst of his sorrow, Job asked God to remove his affliction. Jesus did likewise in Gethsemane as He anticipated the cross. For our sake, Jesus wasn't spared from affliction (see Matt. 26:39).

22 Then call, and I will [a]answer;
Or let me speak, then You respond to me.
23 How many *are* my iniquities and sins?
Make me know my transgression and my sin.
24 [a]Why do You hide Your face,
And [b]regard me as Your enemy?
25 [a]Will You frighten a leaf driven to and fro?
And will You pursue dry stubble?
26 For You write bitter things against me,
And [a]make me inherit the iniquities of my youth.
27 [a]You put my feet in the stocks,
And watch closely all my paths.
You set a limit[1] for the soles of my feet.

28 "*Man*[1] decays like a rotten thing,
Like a garment that is moth-eaten.

**14** "Man *who is* born of woman
Is of few days and [a]full of trouble.
2 [a]He comes forth like a flower and fades away;
He flees like a shadow and does not continue.
3 And [a]do You open Your eyes on such a one,
And [b]bring me[1] to judgment with Yourself?
4 Who [a]can bring a clean *thing* out of an unclean?
No one!
5 [a]Since his days *are* determined,
The number of his months *is* with You;
You have appointed his limits, so that he cannot pass.
6 [a]Look away from him that he may rest,
Till [b]like a hired man he finishes his day.

7 "For there is hope for a tree,
If it is cut down, that it will sprout again,
And that its tender shoots will not cease.
8 Though its root may grow old in the earth,
And its stump may die in the ground,
9 *Yet* at the scent of water it will bud
And bring forth branches like a plant.
10 But man dies and is laid away;
Indeed he breathes his last
And where *is* [a]he?
11 *As* water disappears from the sea,
And a river becomes parched and dries up,
12 So man lies down and does not rise.
[a]Till the heavens *are* no more,
They will not awake
Nor be roused from their sleep.

13 "Oh, that You would hide me in the grave,
That You would conceal me until Your wrath is past,
That You would appoint me a set time, and remember me!
14 If a man dies, shall he live *again?*
All the days of my hard service [a]I will wait,
Till my change comes.

**SEEING JESUS IN THE SCRIPTURE**

**14:13–14** Job wished he could find shelter in the grave until God's wrath passed, and then he might live again. Jesus went to the grave, bearing God's wrath for sin, and then raised again, defeating sin and death so that we can have eternal life (see John 10:10).

15 [a]You shall call, and I will answer You;
You shall desire the work of Your hands.
16 For now [a]You number my steps,
But do not watch over my sin.
17 [a]My transgression *is* sealed up in a bag,
And You cover[1] my iniquity.

18 "But *as* a mountain falls *and* crumbles away,
And *as* a rock is moved from its place;
19 *As* water wears away stones,
*And as* torrents wash away the soil of the earth;
So You destroy the hope of man.

13:16 [a]Job 8:13 13:18 [a][Rom. 8:34] 13:19 [a]Is. 50:8 13:20 [a]Job 9:34 13:21 [a]Ps. 39:10 13:22 [a]Job 9:16; 14:15 13:24 [a][Deut. 32:20] [b]Lam. 2:5 13:25 [a]Is. 42:3 13:26 [a]Job 20:11 13:27 [a]Job 33:11 [1]Literally *inscribe a print* 13:28 [1]Literally *He* 14:1 [a]Eccl. 2:23 14:2 [a]Job 8:9 14:3 [a]Ps. 8:4; 144:3 [b][Ps. 143:2] [1]Septuagint, Syriac, and Vulgate read *him.* 14:4 [a][Ps. 51:2, 5, 10] 14:5 [a]Job 7:1; 21:21 14:6 [a]Ps. 39:13 [b]Job 7:1 14:10 [a]Job 10:21, 22 14:12 [a][Is. 51:6; 65:17; 66:22] 14:14 [a]Job 13:15 14:15 [a]Job 13:22 14:16 [a]Prov. 5:21 14:17 [a]Deut. 32:32–34 [1]Literally *plaster over*

20 You prevail forever against him, and he passes on;
You change his countenance and send him away.
21 His sons come to honor, and [a]he does not know *it;*
They are brought low, and he does not perceive *it.*
22 But his flesh will be in pain over it,
And his soul will mourn over it."

## ELIPHAZ ACCUSES JOB OF FOLLY

**15** Then [a]Eliphaz the Temanite answered and said:

2 "Should a wise man answer with empty knowledge,
And fill himself with the east wind?
3 Should he reason with unprofitable talk,
Or by speeches with which he can do no good?
4 Yes, you cast off fear,
And restrain prayer before God.
5 For your iniquity teaches your mouth,
And you choose the tongue of the crafty.
6 [a]Your own mouth condemns you, and not I;
Yes, your own lips testify against you.

7 "*Are* you the first man *who* was born?
[a]Or were you made before the hills?
8 [a]Have you heard the counsel of God?
Do you limit wisdom to yourself?
9 [a]What do you know that we do not know?
*What* do you understand that *is* not in us?
10 [a]Both the gray-haired and the aged *are* among us,
Much older than your father.
11 *Are* the consolations of God too small for you,
And the word *spoken* gently[1] with you?
12 Why does your heart carry you away,
And what do your eyes wink at,
13 That you turn your spirit against God,
And let *such* words go out of your mouth?

14 "What[a] *is* man, that he could be pure?
And *he who is* born of a woman, that he could be righteous?
15 [a]If *God* puts no trust in His saints,
And the heavens are not pure in His sight,
16 [a]How much less man, *who is* abominable and filthy,
[b]Who drinks iniquity like water!

17 "I will tell you, hear me;
What I have seen I will declare,
18 What wise men have told,
Not hiding *anything received* [a]from their fathers,
19 To whom alone the land was given,
And [a]no alien passed among them:
20 The wicked man writhes with pain all *his* days,
[a]And the number of years is hidden from the oppressor.
21 Dreadful sounds *are* in his ears;
[a]In prosperity the destroyer comes upon him.
22 He does not believe that he will [a]return from darkness,
For a sword is waiting for him.
23 He [a]wanders about for bread, *saying,* 'Where *is it?*'
He knows [b]that a day of darkness is ready at his hand.
24 Trouble and anguish make him afraid;
They overpower him, like a king ready for battle.
25 For he stretches out his hand against God,
And acts defiantly against the Almighty,
26 Running stubbornly against Him
With his strong, embossed shield.

27 "Though[a] he has covered his face with his fatness,
And made *his* waist heavy with fat,
28 He dwells in desolate cities,
In houses which no one inhabits,
Which are destined to become ruins.
29 He will not be rich,
Nor will his wealth [a]continue,
Nor will his possessions overspread the earth.
30 He will not depart from darkness;
The flame will dry out his branches,
And [a]by the breath of His mouth he will go away.
31 Let him not [a]trust in futile *things,* deceiving himself,
For futility will be his reward.
32 It will be accomplished [a]before his time,
And his branch will not be green.
33 He will shake off his unripe grape like a vine,
And cast off his blossom like an olive tree.
34 For the company of hypocrites *will be* barren,
And fire will consume the tents of bribery.
35 [a]They conceive trouble and bring forth futility;
Their womb prepares deceit."

## JOB REPROACHES HIS PITILESS FRIENDS

**16** Then Job answered and said:

2 "I have heard many such things;
[a]Miserable comforters *are* you all!

14:21 [a]Eccl. 9:5 15:1 [a]Job 4:1 15:6 [a][Luke 19:22] 15:7 [a]Prov. 8:25 15:8 [a]Rom. 11:34 15:9 [a]Job 12:3; 13:2 15:10 [a]Job 8:8–10; 12:12; 32:6, 7 15:11 [1]Septuagint reads *a secret thing.* 15:14 [a]Prov. 20:9 15:15 [a]Job 4:18; 25:5 15:16 [a]Ps. 14:3; 53:3 [b]Prov. 19:28 15:18 [a]Job 8:8; 20:4 15:19 [a]Joel 3:17 15:20 [a]Ps. 90:12 15:21 [a]1 Thess. 5:3 15:22 [a]Job 14:10–12 15:23 [a]Ps. 59:15; 109:10 [b]Job 18:12 15:27 [a]Ps. 17:10; 73:7; 119:70 15:29 [a]Job 20:28; 27:16, 17 15:30 [a]Job 4:9 15:31 [a]Is. 59:4 15:32 [a]Job 22:16 15:35 [a]Is. 59:4 16:2 [a]Job 13:4; 21:34

3 Shall words of wind have an end?
Or what provokes you that you answer?
4 I also could speak as you *do,*
If your soul were in my soul's place.
I could heap up words against you,
And [a]shake my head at you;
5 *But* I would strengthen you with my mouth,
And the comfort of my lips would relieve *your grief.*

6 "Though I speak, my grief is not relieved;
And *if* I remain silent, how am I eased?
7 But now He has [a]worn me out;
You [b]have made desolate all my company.
8 You have shriveled me up,
And it is a [a]witness *against me;*
My leanness rises up against me
*And* bears witness to my face.
9 [a]He tears *me* in His wrath, and hates me;
He gnashes at me with His teeth;
[b]My adversary sharpens His gaze on me.
10 They [a]gape at me with their mouth,
They [b]strike me reproachfully on the cheek,
They gather together against me.

**SEEING JESUS IN THE SCRIPTURE**

**16:10** When Job was at his lowest, his enemies mocked and struck him. Jesus was likewise mocked and struck by His own people (see Luke 22:63). People treated Jesus as their enemy, though He died for them as their Savior and friend.

11 God [a]has delivered me to the ungodly,
And turned me over to the hands of the wicked.
12 I was at ease, but He has [a]shattered me;
He also has taken *me* by my neck, and shaken me to pieces;
He has [b]set me up for His target,
13 His archers surround me.
He pierces my heart[1] and does not pity;
He pours out my gall on the ground.
14 He breaks me with wound upon wound;
He runs at me like a warrior.[1]

15 "I have sewn sackcloth over my skin,
And [a]laid my head[1] in the dust.
16 My face is flushed from weeping,
And on my eyelids *is* the shadow of death;
17 Although no violence *is* in my hands,
And my prayer *is* pure.

18 "O earth, do not cover my blood,
And [a]let my cry have no *resting* place!
19 Surely even now [a]my witness *is* in heaven,
And my evidence *is* on high.
20 My friends scorn me;
My eyes pour out *tears* to God.
21 [a]Oh, that one might plead for a man with God,
As a man *pleads* for his neighbor!
22 For when a few years are finished,
I shall [a]go the way of no return.

## JOB PRAYS FOR RELIEF

17 "My spirit is broken,
My days are extinguished,
[a]The grave *is ready* for me.
2 *Are* not mockers with me?
And does not my eye dwell on their [a]provocation?

3 "Now put down a pledge for me with Yourself.
Who *is* he *who* [a]will shake hands with me?
4 For You have hidden their heart from [a]understanding;
Therefore You will not exalt *them.*
5 He who speaks flattery to *his* friends,
Even the eyes of his children will [a]fail.

6 "But He has made me [a]a byword of the people,
And I have become one in whose face men spit.
7 [a]My eye has also grown dim because of sorrow,
And all my members *are* like shadows.
8 Upright *men* are astonished at this,
And the innocent stirs himself up against the hypocrite.
9 Yet the righteous will hold to his [a]way,
And he who has [b]clean hands will be stronger and stronger.

10 "But please, [a]come back again, all of you,[1]
For I shall not find *one* wise *man* among you.
11 [a]My days are past,
My purposes are broken off,
*Even* the thoughts of my heart.
12 They change the night into day;
'The light *is* near,' *they say,* in the face of darkness.
13 If I wait *for* the grave *as* my house,
If I make my bed in the darkness,
14 If I say to corruption, 'You *are* my father,'
And to the worm, 'You *are* my mother and my sister,'

**16:4** [a] Ps. 22:7; 109:25 **16:7** [a] Job 7:3 [b] Job 16:20; 19:13–15 **16:8** [a] Job 10:17 **16:9** [a] Hos. 6:1 [b] Job 13:24; 33:10 **16:10** [a] Ps. 22:13; 35:21 [b] Lam. 3:30 **16:11** [a] Job 1:15, 17 **16:12** [a] Job 9:17 [b] Job 7:20 **16:13** [1] Literally *kidneys* **16:14** [1] Vulgate reads *giant.* **16:15** [a] Ps. 7:5 [1] Literally *horn* **16:18** [a] [Ps. 66:18] **16:19** [a] Rom. 1:9 **16:21** [a] Job 31:35 **16:22** [a] Eccl. 12:5 **17:1** [a] Ps. 88:3, 4 **17:2** [a] Job 12:4; 17:6; 30:1, 9; 34:7 **17:3** [a] Prov. 6:1; 17:18; 22:26 **17:4** [a] Job 12:20; 32:9 **17:5** [a] Job 11:20 **17:6** [a] Job 30:9 **17:7** [a] Ps. 6:7; 31:9 **17:9** [a] Prov. 4:18 [b] Ps. 24:4 **17:10** [a] Job 6:29 [1] Following some Hebrew manuscripts, Septuagint, Syriac, and Vulgate; Masoretic Text and Targum read *all of them.* **17:11** [a] Job 7:6

15 Where then *is* my [a]hope?
As for my hope, who can see it?
16 *Will* they go down [a]to the gates of Sheol?
Shall *we have* [b]rest together in the dust?"

### BILDAD: THE WICKED ARE PUNISHED

18 Then [a]Bildad the Shuhite answered and said:

2 "How long *till* you put an end to words?
Gain understanding, and afterward we will speak.
3 Why are we counted [a]as beasts,
*And* regarded as stupid in your sight?
4 [a]You who tear yourself in anger,
Shall the earth be forsaken for you?
Or shall the rock be removed from its place?

5 "The[a] light of the wicked indeed goes out,
And the flame of his fire does not shine.
6 The light is dark in his tent,
[a]And his lamp beside him is put out.
7 The steps of his strength are shortened,
And [a]his own counsel casts him down.
8 For [a]he is cast into a net by his own feet,
And he walks into a snare.
9 The net takes *him* by the heel,
*And* [a]a snare lays hold of him.
10 A noose *is* hidden for him on the ground,
And a trap for him in the road.
11 [a]Terrors frighten him on every side,
And drive him to his feet.
12 His strength is starved,
And [a]destruction *is* ready at his side.
13 It devours patches of his skin;
The firstborn of death devours his limbs.
14 He is uprooted from [a]the shelter of his tent,
And they parade him before the king of terrors.
15 They dwell in his tent *who are* none of his;
Brimstone is scattered on his dwelling.
16 [a]His roots are dried out below,
And his branch withers above.
17 [a]The memory of him perishes from the earth,
And he has no name among the renowned.[1]
18 He is driven from light into darkness,
And chased out of the world.
19 [a]He has neither son nor posterity among his people,
Nor any remaining in his dwellings.
20 Those in the west are astonished [a]at his day,
As those in the east are frightened.
21 Surely such *are* the dwellings of the wicked,
And this *is* the place *of him who* [a]does not know God."

### JOB TRUSTS IN HIS REDEEMER

19 Then Job answered and said:

2 "How long will you torment my soul,
And break me in pieces with words?
3 These ten times you have reproached me;
You are not ashamed *that* you have wronged me.[1]

**19:3** Job wasn't actually counting the number of times his friends shamed him. **Ten times** was an expression meaning "often."

4 And if indeed I have erred,
My error remains with me.
5 If indeed you [a]exalt *yourselves* against me,
And plead my disgrace against me,
6 Know then that [a]God has wronged me,
And has surrounded me with His net.

7 "If I cry out concerning wrong, I am not heard.
If I cry aloud, *there is* no justice.
8 [a]He has fenced up my way, so that I cannot pass;
And He has set darkness in my paths.
9 [a]He has stripped me of my glory,
And taken the crown *from* my head.
10 He breaks me down on every side,
And I am gone;
My [a]hope He has uprooted like a tree.
11 He has also kindled His wrath against me,
And [a]He counts me as *one of* His enemies.
12 His troops come together
And build up their road against me;
They encamp all around my tent.

13 "He[a] has removed my brothers far from me,
And my acquaintances are completely estranged from me.
14 My relatives have failed,
And my close friends have forgotten me.
15 Those who dwell in my house, and my maidservants,
Count me as a stranger;
I am an alien in their sight.
16 I call my servant, but he gives no answer;

17:15 [a] Job 7:6; 13:15; 14:19; 19:10 17:16 [a] Jon. 2:6 [b] Job 3:17–19; 21:33 18:1 [a] Job 8:1 18:3 [a] Ps. 73:22 18:4 [a] Job 13:14 18:5 [a] Prov. 13:9; 20:20; 24:20 18:6 [a] Job 21:17 18:7 [a] Job 5:12, 13; 15:6 18:8 [a] Job 22:10 18:9 [a] Job 5:5 18:11 [a] Jer. 6:25 18:12 [a] Job 15:23 18:14 [a] Job 11:20 18:16 [a] Job 29:19 18:17 [a] [Ps. 34:16] [1] Literally *before the outside,* meaning distinguished, famous 18:19 [a] Is. 14:22 18:20 [a] Ps. 37:13 18:21 [a] Jer. 9:3 19:3 [1] A Jewish tradition reads *make yourselves strange to me.* 19:5 [a] Ps. 35:26; 38:16; 55:12, 13 19:6 [a] Job 16:11 19:8 [a] Job 3:23 19:9 [a] Ps. 89:44 19:10 [a] Job 17:14–16 19:11 [a] Job 13:24; 33:10 19:13 [a] Ps. 31:11; 38:11; 69:8; 88:8, 18

I beg him with my mouth.
17 My breath is offensive to my wife,
And I am repulsive to the children of my own body.
18 Even [a]young children despise me;
I arise, and they speak against me.
19 [a]All my close friends abhor me,
And those whom I love have turned against me.
20 [a]My bone clings to my skin and to my flesh,
And I have escaped by the skin of my teeth.

21 "Have pity on me, have pity on me, O you my friends,
For the hand of God has struck me!
22 Why do you [a]persecute me as God *does,*
And are not satisfied with my flesh?

23 "Oh, that my words were written!
Oh, that they were inscribed in a book!
24 That they were engraved on a rock
With an iron pen and lead, forever!
25 For I know *that* my Redeemer lives,
And He shall stand at last on the earth;
26 And after my skin is destroyed, this *I know,*
That [a]in my flesh I shall see God,
27 Whom I shall see for myself,
And my eyes shall behold, and not another.
*How* my heart yearns within me!
28 If you should say, 'How shall we persecute him?'—
Since the root of the matter is found in me,
29 Be afraid of the sword for yourselves;
For wrath *brings* the punishment of the sword,
That you may know *there is* a judgment."

### ZOPHAR'S SERMON ON THE WICKED MAN

**20** Then [a]Zophar the Naamathite answered and said:

2 "Therefore my anxious thoughts make me answer,
Because of the turmoil within me.
3 I have heard the rebuke that reproaches me,
And the spirit of my understanding causes me to answer.

4 "Do you *not* know this of [a]old,
Since man was placed on earth,
5 [a]That the triumphing of the wicked is short,
And the joy of the hypocrite is *but* for a [b]moment?
6 [a]Though his haughtiness mounts up to the heavens,
And his head reaches to the clouds,
7 *Yet* he will perish forever like his own refuse;
Those who have seen him will say, 'Where is he?'

**19:18** [a] 2 Kin. 2:23 **19:19** [a] Ps. 38:11; 55:12, 13 **19:20** [a] Ps. 102:5 **19:22** [a] Ps. 69:26 **19:26** [a] [Ps. 17:15] **20:1** [a] Job 11:1 **20:4** [a] Job 8:8; 15:10 **20:5** [a] Ps. 37:35, 36 [b] [Job 8:13; 13:16; 15:34; 27:8] **20:6** [a] Is. 14:13, 14

KNOW THE TRUTH

## THE DOCTRINE OF CREATION AND HUMANS

### PART 10: THE DEATH OF HUMANS

**19:25–26** Confident of his unavoidable demise, Job still believed he would one day see God while in his physical body. The word *resurrection* means to rise again, stemming from a word that literally means to stand back up. You can't stand back up unless you were previously standing, then laid down, and finally stood back up again. Similarly, you can't be resurrected unless you were living, died, and then raised to life again.

Due to our rebellion against God's loving and perfect rule, we are separated from Him and the result is death. Every human in history is caught in a basic cycle: live, sin, and die. One human, though, violated that cycle and established a new one. Jesus Christ lived, perfectly obeyed God, died, and then rose from the dead in His physical body. Christ now offers a new cycle to sinful people: live, sin, *receive forgiveness and eternal life by grace through faith in Christ*, die, *be spiritually and consciously immediately present with God in heaven*, and *one day physically rise from the dead and spend eternity with God*. Death is still unavoidable, but for the believer, it's no longer final. And soon, death will be destroyed, and Christ's saints will live with Him forever (Rev. 20:14).

*For* **THE DOCTRINE OF SALVATION: PART 1: OVERVIEW OF THE DOCTRINE OF SALVATION,** *turn to Hebrews 2:9–15 on page 1246.*

8 He will fly away [a]like a dream, and not be
found;
Yes, he [b]will be chased away like a vision
of the night.
9 The eye *that* saw him will *see him* no more,
Nor will his place behold him anymore.
10 His children will seek the favor of the poor,
And his hands will restore his wealth.
11 His bones are full of [a]his youthful vigor,
[b]But it will lie down with him in the dust.

12 "Though evil is sweet in his mouth,
*And* he hides it under his tongue,
13 *Though* he spares it and does not forsake it,
But still keeps it in his mouth,
14 *Yet* his food in his stomach turns sour;
It becomes cobra venom within him.
15 He swallows down riches
And vomits them up again;
God casts them out of his belly.
16 He will suck the poison of cobras;
The viper's tongue will slay him.
17 He will not see [a]the streams,
The rivers flowing with honey and cream.

**20:17 Honey and cream** inferred wealth. Cream was a staple of everyday Hebrew life, a major food source for the Israelites. Honey, on the other hand, was considered a rare delicacy.

18 He will restore that for which he labored,
And will not swallow *it* down;
From the proceeds of business
He will get no enjoyment.
19 For he has oppressed *and* forsaken the
poor,
He has violently seized a house which he
did not build.

20 "Because[a] he knows no quietness in his
heart,[1]
He will not save anything he desires.
21 Nothing is left for him to eat;
Therefore his well-being will not last.
22 In his self-sufficiency he will be in distress;
Every hand of misery will come against him.
23 *When* he is about to fill his stomach,
*God* will cast on him the fury of His wrath,
And will rain *it* on him while he is eating.
24 [a]He will flee from the iron weapon;
A bronze bow will pierce him through.
25 It is drawn, and comes out of the body;
Yes, [a]the glittering *point comes* out of his
gall.
[b]Terrors *come* upon him;
26 Total darkness *is* reserved for his treasures.
[a]An unfanned fire will consume him;
It shall go ill with him who is left in his
tent.
27 The heavens will reveal his iniquity,
And the earth will rise up against him.
28 The increase of his house will depart,
*And his goods* will flow away in the day of
His [a]wrath.
29 [a]This *is* the portion from God for a wicked
man,
The heritage appointed to him by God."

## JOB'S DISCOURSE ON THE WICKED

**21** Then Job answered and said:
2 "Listen carefully to my speech,
And let this be your consolation.
3 Bear with me that I may speak,
And after I have spoken, keep [a]mocking.

4 "As for me, *is* my complaint against man?
And if *it were,* why should I not be
impatient?
5 Look at me and be astonished;
[a]Put *your* hand over *your* mouth.
6 Even when I remember I am terrified,
And trembling takes hold of my flesh.
7 [a]Why do the wicked live *and* become old,
Yes, become mighty in power?
8 Their descendants are established with
them in their sight,
And their offspring before their eyes.
9 Their houses *are* safe from fear,
[a]Neither *is* the rod of God upon them.
10 Their bull breeds without failure;
Their cow calves [a]without miscarriage.
11 They send forth their little ones like a
flock,
And their children dance.
12 They sing to the tambourine and harp,
And rejoice to the sound of the flute.
13 They [a]spend their days in wealth,
And in a moment go down to the grave.[1]
14 [a]Yet they say to God, 'Depart from us,
For we do not desire the knowledge of
Your ways.
15 [a]Who *is* the Almighty, that we should serve
Him?
And [b]what profit do we have if we pray to
Him?'
16 Indeed their prosperity *is* not in their hand;
[a]The counsel of the wicked is far from me.

17 "How often is the lamp of the wicked put
out?
*How often* does their destruction come
upon them,
The sorrows *God* [a]distributes in His anger?

**20:8** [a] Ps. 73:20; 90:5 [b] Job 18:18; 27:21–23 **20:11** [a] Job 13:26 [b] Job 21:26 **20:17** [a] Jer. 17:8 **20:20** [a] Eccl. 5:13–15 [1] Literally *belly* **20:24** [a] Amos 5:19 **20:25** [a] Job 16:13 [b] Job 18:11, 14 **20:26** [a] Ps. 21:9 **20:28** [a] Job 20:15; 21:30 **20:29** [a] Job 27:13; 31:2, 3 **21:3** [a] Job 16:10 **21:5** [a] Judg. 18:19 **21:7** [a] [Jer. 12:1] **21:9** [a] Ps. 73:5 **21:10** [a] Ex. 23:26 **21:13** [a] Job 21:23; 36:11 [1] Or *Sheol* **21:14** [a] Job 22:17 **21:15** [a] Ex. 5:2 [b] Mal. 3:14 **21:16** [a] Prov. 1:10 **21:17** [a] [Luke 12:46]

18 [a]They are like straw before the wind,
And like chaff that a storm carries away.
19 *They say,* 'God lays up one's[1] iniquity [a]for his children';
Let Him recompense him, that he may know *it.*
20 Let his eyes see his destruction,
And [a]let him drink of the wrath of the Almighty.
21 For what does he care about his household after him,
When the number of his months is cut in half?

22 "Can[a] *anyone* teach God knowledge,
Since He judges those on high?
23 One dies in his full strength,
Being wholly at ease and secure;
24 His pails[1] are full of milk,
And the marrow of his bones is moist.
25 Another man dies in the bitterness of his soul,
Never having eaten with pleasure.
26 They [a]lie down alike in the dust,
And worms cover them.

27 "Look, I know your thoughts,
And the schemes *with which* you would wrong me.
28 For you say,
'Where *is* the house of the prince?
And where *is* the tent,[1]
The dwelling place of the wicked?'
29 Have you not asked those who travel the road?
And do you not know their signs?
30 [a]For the wicked are reserved for the day of doom;
They shall be brought out on the day of wrath.
31 Who condemns his way to his face?
And who repays him *for what* he has done?
32 Yet he shall be brought to the grave,
And a vigil kept over the tomb.
33 The clods of the valley shall be sweet to him;
[a]Everyone shall follow him,
As countless *have gone* before him.
34 How then can you comfort me with empty words,
Since falsehood remains in your answers?"

## ELIPHAZ ACCUSES JOB OF WICKEDNESS

22 Then [a]Eliphaz the Temanite answered and said:

2 "Can[a] a man be profitable to God,
Though he who is wise may be profitable to himself?
3 *Is it* any pleasure to the Almighty that you are righteous?
Or *is it* gain *to Him* that you make your ways blameless?

4 "Is it because of your fear of Him that He corrects you,
And enters into judgment with you?
5 *Is* not your wickedness great,
And your iniquity without end?
6 For you have [a]taken pledges from your brother for no reason,
And stripped the naked of their clothing.
7 You have not given the weary water to drink,
And you [a]have withheld bread from the hungry.
8 But the mighty man possessed the land,
And the honorable man dwelt in it.
9 You have sent widows away empty,
And the strength of the fatherless was crushed.

**22:6–9** In ancient times, the wealthy were expected to take care of poor people, orphans, and widows, without demanding or expecting anything in return. Homeowners were expected to welcome traveling guests and strangers alike, inviting them into their homes and treating them like family.

10 Therefore snares *are* all around you,
And sudden fear troubles you,
11 Or darkness *so that* you cannot see;
And an abundance of [a]water covers you.

12 "Is not God in the height of heaven?
And see the highest stars, how lofty they are!
13 And you say, [a]'What does God know?
Can He judge through the deep darkness?
14 [a]Thick clouds cover Him, so that He cannot see,
And He walks above the circle of heaven.'
15 Will you keep to the old way
Which wicked men have trod,
16 Who [a]were cut down before their time,
Whose foundations were swept away by a flood?
17 [a]They said to God, 'Depart from us!
What can the Almighty do to them?'[1]
18 Yet He filled their houses with good *things;*
But the counsel of the wicked is far from me.

21:18 [a] Ps. 1:4; 35:5 21:19 [a] [Ex. 20:5] [1] Literally *his* 21:20 [a] Is. 51:17 21:22 [a] [Is. 40:13; 45:9] 21:24 [1] Septuagint and Vulgate read *bowels;* Syriac reads *sides;* Targum reads *breasts.* 21:26 [a] Eccl. 9:2 21:28 [1] Vulgate omits *the tent.* 21:30 [a] [Prov. 16:4] 21:33 [a] Heb. 9:27 22:1 [a] Job 4:1; 15:1; 42:9 22:2 [a] [Luke 17:10] 22:6 [a] [Ex. 22:26, 27] 22:7 [a] Deut. 15:7 22:11 [a] Ps. 69:1, 2; 124:5 22:13 [a] Ps. 73:11 22:14 [a] Ps. 139:11, 12 22:16 [a] Job 14:19; 15:32 22:17 [a] Job 21:14, 15 [1] Septuagint and Syriac read *us.*

19 "The[a] righteous see *it* and are glad,
And the innocent laugh at them:
20 'Surely our adversaries[1] are cut down,
And the fire consumes their remnant.'

21 "Now acquaint yourself with Him, and [a]be at peace;
Thereby good will come to you.
22 Receive, please, [a]instruction from His mouth,
And [b]lay up His words in your heart.
23 If you return to the Almighty, you will be built up;
You will remove iniquity far from your tents.
24 Then you will [a]lay your gold in the dust,
And the *gold* of Ophir among the stones of the brooks.
25 Yes, the Almighty will be your gold[1]
And your precious silver;
26 For then you will have your [a]delight in the Almighty,
And lift up your face to God.
27 [a]You will make your prayer to Him,
He will hear you,
And you will pay your vows.
28 You will also declare a thing,
And it will be established for you;
So light will shine on your ways.
29 When they cast *you* down, and you say,
'Exaltation *will come!*'
Then [a]He will save the humble *person.*
30 He will *even* deliver one who is not innocent;
Yes, he will be delivered by the purity of your hands."

### JOB PROCLAIMS GOD'S RIGHTEOUS JUDGMENTS

**23** Then Job answered and said:

2 "Even today my [a]complaint is bitter;
My[1] hand is listless because of my groaning.
3 [a]Oh, that I knew where I might find Him,
*That* I might come to His seat!
4 I would present *my* case before Him,
And fill my mouth with arguments.
5 I would know the words *which* He would answer me,
And understand what He would say to me.
6 [a]Would He contend with me in His great power?
No! But He would take *note* of me.
7 There the upright could reason with Him,
And I would be delivered forever from my Judge.

8 "Look,[a] I go forward, but He is not *there,*
And backward, but I cannot perceive Him;
9 When He works on the left hand, I cannot behold *Him;*
When He turns to the right hand, I cannot see *Him.*
10 But [a]He knows the way that I take;
*When* [b]He has tested me, I shall come forth as gold.

**23:10** After **gold** is mined, it must be refined. The ore must be heated to the point that the metal separates from the rock. People who bought gold in Job's day would test it first to see if the metal had been mixed with less valuable materials. They would have an expert metalsmith (or smelter) scrape, cut, and heat the gold as part of the testing process.

11 [a]My foot has held fast to His steps;
I have kept His way and not turned aside.
12 I have not departed from the [a]commandment of His lips;
[b]I have treasured the words of His mouth
More than my necessary *food.*

13 "But He *is* unique, and who can make Him change?
And *whatever* [a]His soul desires, *that* He does.
14 For He performs *what is* [a]appointed for me,
And many such *things are* with Him.
15 Therefore I am terrified at His presence;
When I consider *this,* I am afraid of Him.
16 For God [a]made my heart weak,
And the Almighty terrifies me;
17 Because I was not [a]cut off from the presence of darkness,
And He did *not* hide deep darkness from my face.

### JOB COMPLAINS OF VIOLENCE ON THE EARTH

**24** "*Since* [a]times are not hidden from the Almighty,
Why do those who know Him see not His [b]days?

**22:19** [a] Ps. 52:6; 58:10; 107:42 **22:20** [1] Septuagint reads *substance.* **22:21** [a] Is. 27:5 **22:22** [a] Prov. 2:6 [b] [Ps. 119:11] **22:24** [a] 2 Chr. 1:15 **22:25** [1] The ancient versions suggest *defense;* Hebrew reads *gold* as in verse 24. **22:26** [a] Job 27:10; Ps. 37:4; Is. 58:14 **22:27** [a] [Is. 58:9–11] **22:29** [a] [1 Pet. 5:5] **23:2** [a] Job 7:11 [1] Following Masoretic Text, Targum, and Vulgate; Septuagint and Syriac read *His.* **23:3** [a] Job 13:3, 18; 16:21; 31:35 **23:6** [a] Is. 57:16 **23:8** [a] Job 9:11; 35:14 **23:10** [a] [Ps. 1:6; 139:1–3] [b] [James 1:12] **23:11** [a] Ps. 17:5 **23:12** [a] Job 6:10; 22:22 [b] Ps. 44:18 **23:13** [a] [Ps. 115:3] **23:14** [a] [1 Thess. 3:2–4] **23:16** [a] Ps. 22:14 **23:17** [a] Job 10:18, 19 **24:1** [a] [Acts 1:7] [b] [Is. 2:12]

2 "*Some* remove [a]landmarks;
They seize flocks violently and feed *on them;*

**24:2** In ancient times, stone **landmarks** were often used to mark the boundaries of an individual's property. Moving those stones to extend one's property was immoral and illegal.

3 They drive away the donkey of the fatherless;
They [a]take the widow's ox as a pledge.
4 They push the needy off the road;
All the [a]poor of the land are forced to hide.
5 Indeed, *like* wild donkeys in the desert,
They go out to their work, searching for food.
The wilderness *yields* food for them *and* for *their* children.
6 They gather their fodder in the field
And glean in the vineyard of the wicked.
7 They [a]spend the night naked, without clothing,
And have no covering in the cold.
8 They are wet with the showers of the mountains,
And [a]huddle around the rock for want of shelter.

9 "*Some* snatch the fatherless from the breast,
And take a pledge from the poor.
10 They cause *the poor* to go naked, without [a]clothing;
And they take away the sheaves from the hungry.
11 They press out oil within their walls,
And tread winepresses, yet suffer thirst.
12 The dying groan in the city,
And the souls of the wounded cry out;
Yet God does not charge *them* with wrong.

13 "There are those who rebel against the light;
They do not know its ways
Nor abide in its paths.
14 [a]The murderer rises with the light;
He kills the poor and needy;
And in the night he is like a thief.
15 [a]The eye of the adulterer waits for the twilight,
[b]Saying, 'No eye will see me';
And he disguises *his* face.
16 In the dark they break into houses
Which they marked for themselves in the daytime;
[a]They do not know the light.
17 For the morning is the same to them as the shadow of death;
If *someone* recognizes *them,*
*They are in* the terrors of the shadow of death.

18 "They *should be* swift on the face of the waters,
Their portion *should be* cursed in the earth,
*So that* no *one would* turn into the way of their vineyards.
19 As drought and heat consume the snow waters,
So the grave[1] *consumes those who* have sinned.
20 The womb *should* forget him,
The worm *should* feed sweetly on him;
[a]He *should* be remembered no more,
And wickedness *should* be broken like a tree.
21 For he preys on the barren *who* do not bear,
And does no good for the widow.

22 "But *God* draws the mighty away with His power;
He rises up, but no *man* is sure of life.
23 He gives them security, and they rely *on it;*
Yet [a]His eyes *are* on their ways.
24 They are exalted for a little while,
Then they are gone.
They are brought low;
They are taken out of the way like all *others;*
They dry out like the heads of grain.

25 "Now if *it is* not *so,* who will prove me a liar,
And make my speech worth nothing?"

### *BILDAD: HOW CAN MAN BE RIGHTEOUS?*

**25** Then [a]Bildad the Shuhite answered and said:

2 "Dominion and fear *belong* to Him;
He makes peace in His high places.
3 Is there any number to His armies?
Upon whom does [a]His light not rise?
4 [a]How then can man be righteous before God?
Or how can he be [b]pure *who is* born of a woman?
5 If even the moon does not shine,
And the stars are not pure in His [a]sight,
6 How much less man, *who is* [a]a maggot,
And a son of man, *who is* a worm?"

**25:6** What a contrast to the words of God when He made people in His own image and declared them "very good" (Gen. 1:26–31).

24:2 [a] [Deut. 19:14; 27:17] 24:3 [a] [Deut. 24:6, 10, 12, 17] 24:4 [a] Prov. 28:28 24:7 [a] Ex. 22:26, 27 24:8 [a] Lam. 4:5 24:10 [a] Job 31:19 24:14 [a] Ps. 10:8 24:15 [a] Prov. 7:7–10 [b] Ps. 10:11 24:16 [a] [John 3:20] 24:19 [1] Or *Sheol* 24:20 [a] Prov. 10:7 24:23 [a] [Prov. 15:3] 25:1 [a] Job 8:1; 18:1 25:3 [a] James 1:17 25:4 [a] Job 4:17; 15:14 [b] [Job 14:4] 25:5 [a] Job 15:15 25:6 [a] Ps. 22:6

### JOB: MAN'S FRAILTY AND GOD'S MAJESTY

**26** But Job answered and said:
2 "How have you helped *him who is* without power?
*How* have you saved the arm *that has* no strength?
3 How have you counseled *one who has* no wisdom?
And *how* have you declared sound advice to many?
4 To whom have you uttered words?
And whose spirit came from you?

5 "The dead tremble,
Those under the waters and those inhabiting them.
6 [a]Sheol *is* naked before Him,
And Destruction has no covering.
7 [a]He stretches out the north over empty space;
*He* hangs the earth on nothing.
8 [a]He binds up the water in His thick clouds,
Yet the clouds are not broken under it.
9 He covers the face of *His* throne,
*And* spreads His cloud over it.
10 [a]He drew a circular horizon on the face of the waters,
At the boundary of light and darkness.
11 The pillars of heaven tremble,
And are astonished at His rebuke.
12 [a]He stirs up the sea with His power,
And by His understanding He breaks up the storm.
13 [a]By His Spirit He adorned the heavens;
His hand pierced [b]the fleeing serpent.
14 Indeed these *are* the mere edges of His ways,
And how small a whisper we hear of Him!
But the thunder of His power who can understand?"

### JOB MAINTAINS HIS INTEGRITY

**27** Moreover Job continued his discourse, and said:

2 "As God lives, [a]*who* has taken away my justice,
And the Almighty, *who* has made my soul bitter,
3 As long as my breath *is* in me,
And the breath of God in my nostrils,
4 My lips will not speak wickedness,
Nor my tongue utter deceit.
5 Far be it from me
That I should say you are right;
Till I die [a]I will not put away my integrity from me.
6 My righteousness I [a]hold fast, and will not let it go;
[b]My heart shall not reproach *me* as long as I live.

7 "May my enemy be like the wicked,
And he who rises up against me like the unrighteous.
8 [a]For what is the hope of the hypocrite,
Though he may gain *much,*
If God takes away his life?
9 [a]Will God hear his cry
When trouble comes upon him?
10 [a]Will he delight himself in the Almighty?
Will he always call on God?

11 "I will teach you about the hand of God;
What *is* with the Almighty I will not conceal.
12 Surely all of you have seen *it;*
Why then do you behave with complete nonsense?

13 "This[a] is the portion of a wicked man with God,
And the heritage of oppressors, received from the Almighty:
14 [a]If his children are multiplied, *it is* for the sword;
And his offspring shall not be satisfied with bread.
15 Those who survive him shall be buried in death,
And [a]their[1] widows shall not weep,
16 Though he heaps up silver like dust,
And piles up clothing like clay—
17 He may pile *it* up, but [a]the just will wear *it,*
And the innocent will divide the silver.
18 He builds his house like a moth,[1]
[a]Like a booth *which* a watchman makes.
19 The rich man will lie down,
But not be gathered *up;*[1]
He opens his eyes,
And he *is* [a]no more.
20 [a]Terrors overtake him like a flood;
A tempest steals him away in the night.
21 The east wind carries him away, and he is gone;
It sweeps him out of his place.
22 It hurls against him and does not [a]spare;
He flees desperately from its power.
23 *Men* shall clap their hands at him,
And shall hiss him out of his place.

### JOB'S DISCOURSE ON WISDOM

**28** "Surely there is a mine for silver,
And a place *where* gold is refined.
2 Iron is taken from the earth,
And copper *is* smelted *from* ore.

**26:6** [a] Prov. 15:11 **26:7** [a] Job 9:8 **26:8** [a] Prov. 30:4 **26:10** [a] Prov. 8:29 **26:12** [a] Is. 51:15 **26:13** [a] Ps. 33:6 [b] Is. 27:1 **27:2** [a] Job 34:5 **27:5** [a] Job 2:9; 13:15 **27:6** [a] Job 2:3; 33:9 [b] Acts 24:16 **27:8** [a] Matt. 16:26 **27:9** [a] Jer. 14:12 **27:10** [a] Job 22:26, 27 **27:13** [a] Job 20:29 **27:14** [a] Deut. 28:41 **27:15** [a] Ps. 78:64 [1] Literally *his* **27:17** [a] Prov. 28:8 **27:18** [a] Is. 1:8 [1] Following Masoretic Text and Vulgate; Septuagint and Syriac read *spider* (compare 8:14); Targum reads *decay.* **27:19** [a] Job 7:8, 21; 20:7 [1] Following Masoretic Text and Targum; Septuagint and Syriac read *But shall not add* (that is, do it again); Vulgate reads *But take away nothing.* **27:20** [a] Job 18:11 **27:22** [a] Jer. 13:14

3 *Man* puts an end to darkness,
And searches every recess
For ore in the darkness and the shadow of death.
4 He breaks open a shaft away from people;
*In places* forgotten by feet
They hang far away from men;
They swing to and fro.
5 *As for* the earth, from it comes bread,
But underneath it is turned up as by fire;
6 Its stones *are* the source of sapphires,
And it contains gold dust.
7 *That* path no bird knows,
Nor has the falcon's eye seen it.
8 The proud lions[1] have not trodden it,
Nor has the fierce lion passed over it.
9 He puts his hand on the flint;
He overturns the mountains at the roots.
10 He cuts out channels in the rocks,
And his eye sees every precious thing.
11 He dams up the streams from trickling;
*What is* hidden he brings forth to light.

12 "But[a] where can wisdom be found?
And where *is* the place of understanding?
13 Man does not know its [a]value,
Nor is it found in the land of the living.
14 [a]The deep says, '*It is* not in me';
And the sea says, '*It is* not with me.'
15 It [a]cannot be purchased for gold,
Nor can silver be weighed *for* its price.
16 It cannot be valued in the gold of Ophir,
In precious onyx or sapphire.
17 Neither [a]gold nor crystal can equal it,
Nor can it be exchanged for jewelry of fine gold.
18 No mention shall be made of coral or quartz,
For the price of wisdom *is* above [a]rubies.
19 The topaz of Ethiopia cannot equal it,
Nor can it be valued in pure [a]gold.

20 "From[a] where then does wisdom come?
And where *is* the place of understanding?
21 It is hidden from the eyes of all living,
And concealed from the birds of the air.
22 [a]Destruction and Death say,
'We have heard a report about it with our ears.'
23 God understands its way,
And He knows its place.
24 For He looks to the ends of the earth,
*And* [a]sees under the whole heavens,
25 [a]To establish a weight for the wind,
And apportion the waters by measure.
26 When He [a]made a law for the rain,
And a path for the thunderbolt,
27 Then He saw *wisdom*[1] and declared it;
He prepared it, indeed, He searched it out.
28 And to man He said,
'Behold, [a]the fear of the Lord, that *is* wisdom,
And to depart from evil *is* understanding.' "

### *JOB'S SUMMARY DEFENSE*

29 Job further continued his discourse, and said:

2 "Oh, that I were as *in* months [a]past,
As *in* the days *when* God [b]watched over me;
3 [a]When His lamp shone upon my head,
*And when* by His light I walked *through* darkness;
4 Just as I was in the days of my prime,
When [a]the friendly counsel of God *was* over my tent;
5 When the Almighty *was* yet with me,
*When* my children *were* around me;
6 When [a]my steps were bathed with cream,[1]
And [b]the rock poured out rivers of oil for me!

7 "When I went out to the gate by the city,
*When* I took my seat in the open square,
8 The young men saw me and hid,
And the aged arose *and* stood;
9 The princes refrained from talking,
And [a]put *their* hand on their mouth;
10 The voice of nobles was hushed,
And their [a]tongue stuck to the roof of their mouth.
11 When the ear heard, then it blessed me,
And when the eye saw, then it approved me;
12 Because [a]I delivered the poor who cried out,
The fatherless and *the one who* had no helper.
13 The blessing of a perishing *man* came upon me,
And I caused the widow's heart to sing for joy.
14 [a]I put on righteousness, and it clothed me;
My justice *was* like a robe and a turban.
15 I *was* [a]eyes to the blind,
And I *was* feet to the lame.
16 I *was* a father to the poor,
And [a]I searched out the case *that* I did not know.
17 I broke [a]the fangs of the wicked,
And plucked the victim from his teeth.

18 "Then I said, [a]'I shall die in my nest,
And multiply *my* days as the sand.

28:8 [1] Literally *sons of pride,* figurative of the great lions 28:12 [a] Eccl. 7:24 28:13 [a] Prov. 3:15 28:14 [a] Job 28:22 28:15 [a] Prov. 3:13–15; 8:10, 11, 19 28:17 [a] Prov. 8:10; 16:16 28:18 [a] Prov. 3:15; 8:11 28:19 [a] Prov. 8:19 28:20 [a] Job 28:12 28:22 [a] Job 28:14 28:24 [a] [Prov. 15:3] 28:25 [a] Ps. 135:7 28:26 [a] Job 37:3; 38:25 28:27 [1] Literally *it* 28:28 [a] [Prov. 1:7; 9:10] 29:2 [a] Job 1:1–5 [b] Job 1:10 29:3 [a] Job 18:6 29:4 [a] [Ps. 25:14] 29:6 [a] Deut. 32:14; Job 20:17 [b] Ps. 81:16 [1] Masoretic Text reads *wrath;* ancient versions and some Hebrew manuscripts read *cream* (compare 20:17). 29:9 [a] Job 21:5 29:10 [a] Ps. 137:6 29:12 [a] [Ps. 72:12] 29:14 [a] [Is. 59:17; 61:10] 29:15 [a] Num. 10:31 29:16 [a] Prov. 29:7 29:17 [a] Prov. 30:14 29:18 [a] Ps. 30:6

19 [a]My root *is* spread out [b]to the waters,
And the dew lies all night on my branch.
20 My glory *is* fresh within me,
And my [a]bow is renewed in my hand.'

21 "*Men* listened to me and waited,
And kept silence for my counsel.
22 After my words they did not speak again,
And my speech settled on them *as dew.*
23 They waited for me *as* for the rain,
And they opened their mouth wide *as* for [a]the spring rain.
24 *If* I mocked at them, they did not believe *it,*
And the light of my countenance they did not cast down.
25 I chose the way for them, and sat as chief;
So I dwelt as a king in the army,
As one *who* comforts mourners.

# 30

"But now they mock at me, *men* younger than I,
Whose fathers I disdained to put with the dogs of my flock.
2 Indeed, what *profit* is the strength of their hands to me?
Their vigor has perished.
3 *They are* gaunt from want and famine,
Fleeing late to the wilderness, desolate and waste,
4 Who pluck mallow by the bushes,
And broom tree roots *for* their food.
5 They were driven out from among *men,*
They shouted at them as *at* a thief.
6 *They had* to live in the clefts of the valleys,
*In* caves of the earth and the rocks.
7 Among the bushes they brayed,
Under the nettles they nestled.
8 *They were* sons of fools,
Yes, sons of vile men;
They were scourged from the land.

9 "And[a] now I am their taunting song;
Yes, I am their byword.
10 They abhor me, they keep far from me;
They do not hesitate [a]to spit in my face.
11 Because [a]He has loosed my[1] bowstring and afflicted me,
They have cast off restraint before me.
12 At *my* right *hand* the rabble arises;
They push away my feet,
And [a]they raise against me their ways of destruction.
13 They break up my path,
They promote my calamity;
They have no helper.
14 They come as broad breakers;
Under the ruinous storm they roll along.
15 Terrors are turned upon me;
They pursue my honor as the wind,
And my prosperity has passed like a cloud.

16 "And[a] now my soul is [b]poured out because of my *plight;*
The days of affliction take hold of me.
17 My bones are pierced in me at night,
And my gnawing pains take no rest.
18 By great force my garment is disfigured;
It binds me about as the collar of my coat.
19 He has cast me into the mire,
And I have become like dust and ashes.

20 "I [a]cry out to You, but You do not answer me;
I stand up, and You regard me.
21 *But* You have become cruel to me;
With the strength of Your hand You [a]oppose me.
22 You lift me up to the wind and cause me to ride *on it;*
You spoil my success.
23 For I know *that* You will bring me *to* death,
And *to* the house [a]appointed for all living.

24 "Surely He would not stretch out *His* hand against a heap of ruins,
If they cry out when He destroys *it.*
25 [a]Have I not wept for him who was in trouble?
Has *not* my soul grieved for the poor?
26 [a]But when I looked for good, evil came *to me;*
And when I waited for light, then came darkness.
27 My heart is in turmoil and cannot rest;
Days of affliction confront me.
28 [a]I go about mourning, but not in the sun;
I stand up in the assembly *and* cry out for help.
29 [a]I am a brother of jackals,
And a companion of ostriches.
30 [a]My skin grows black and falls from me;
[b]My bones burn with fever.
31 My harp is *turned* to mourning,
And my flute to the voice of those who weep.

# 31

"I have made a covenant with my eyes;
Why then should I look upon a [a]young woman?
2 For what *is* the [a]allotment of God from above,
And the inheritance of the Almighty from on high?
3 *Is* it not destruction for the wicked,
And disaster for the workers of iniquity?
4 [a]Does He not see my ways,
And count all my steps?

**29:19** [a] Job 18:16 [b] Ps. 1:3 **29:20** [a] Gen. 49:24 **29:23** [a] [Zech. 10:1] **30:9** [a] Job 17:6 **30:10** [a] Is. 50:6 **30:11** [a] Job 12:18
[1] Following Masoretic Text, Syriac, and Targum; Septuagint and Vulgate read *His.* **30:12** [a] Job 19:12 **30:16** [a] Ps. 42:4 [b] Ps. 22:14
**30:20** [a] Job 19:7 **30:21** [a] Job 10:3; 16:9, 14; 19:6, 22 **30:23** [a] [Heb. 9:27] **30:25** [a] Ps. 35:13, 14 **30:26** [a] Jer. 8:15 **30:28** [a] Ps. 38:6; 42:9; 43:2 **30:29** [a] Mic. 1:8 **30:30** [a] Ps. 119:83 [b] Ps. 102:3 **31:1** [a] [Matt. 5:28] **31:2** [a] Job 20:29 **31:4** [a] [2 Chr. 16:9]

5 "If I have walked with falsehood,
Or if my foot has hastened to deceit,
6 Let me be weighed on honest scales,
That God may know my [a]integrity.
7 If my step has turned from the way,
Or [a]my heart walked after my eyes,
Or if any spot adheres to my hands,
8 *Then* [a]let me sow, and another eat;
Yes, let my harvest be rooted out.

**31:5–8** In the ancient Near East, a person accused of a crime was required to take an oath of innocence. Job went one step further and submitted himself to the toughest polygraph test imaginable. He swore he was innocent of all the accusations and called on God to punish him if he were lying.

9 "If my heart has been enticed by a woman,
Or *if* I have lurked at my neighbor's door,
10 *Then* let my wife grind for [a]another,
And let others bow down over her.
11 For that *would be* wickedness;
Yes, [a]it *would be* iniquity *deserving of* judgment.
12 For that *would be* a fire *that* consumes to destruction,
And would root out all my increase.

13 "If I have [a]despised the cause of my male or female servant
When they complained against me,
14 What then shall I do when [a]God rises up?
When He punishes, how shall I answer Him?
15 [a]Did not He who made me in the womb make them?
Did not the same One fashion us in the womb?

16 "If I have kept the poor from *their* desire,
Or caused the eyes of the widow to [a]fail,
17 Or eaten my morsel by myself,
So that the fatherless could not eat of it
18 (But from my youth I reared him as a father,
And from my mother's womb I guided *the widow*[1]);
19 If I have seen anyone perish for lack of clothing,
Or any poor *man* without covering;
20 If his heart[1] has not [a]blessed me,
And *if* he was *not* warmed with the fleece of my sheep;
21 If I have raised my hand [a]against the fatherless,
When I saw I had help in the gate;
22 *Then* let my arm fall from my shoulder,
Let my arm be torn from the socket.
23 For [a]destruction *from* God *is* a terror to me,
And because of His magnificence I cannot endure.

24 "If[a] I have made gold my hope,
Or said to fine gold, '*You are* my confidence';
25 [a]If I have rejoiced because my wealth *was* great,
And because my hand had gained much;
26 [a]If I have observed the sun[1] when it shines,
Or the moon moving *in* brightness,
27 So that my heart has been secretly enticed,
And my mouth has kissed my hand;

**31:6** [a] Job 23:10; 27:5, 6 **31:7** [a] Ezek. 6:9 **31:8** [a] Lev. 26:16 **31:10** [a] Jer. 8:10 **31:11** [a] Gen. 38:24 **31:13** [a] [Deut. 24:14, 15] **31:14** [a] [Ps. 44:21] **31:15** [a] Job 34:19 **31:16** [a] Job 29:12 **31:18** [1] Literally *her* (compare verse 16) **31:20** [a] [Deut. 24:13] [1] Literally *loins* **31:21** [a] Job 22:9 **31:23** [a] Is. 13:6 **31:24** [a] [Mark 10:23–25] **31:25** [a] Ps. 62:10 **31:26** [a] Ezek. 8:16 [1] Literally *light*

LIVE THE TRUTH

## VALUING WHO YOU ARE

**31:15** In a society obsessed with perfection, it's easy to be hyperaware of our imperfections. We envy others who seem to have it all together. They look perfect. They have their choice of dates. Everything they do turns out right. But they *aren't* perfect. No one is. Everyone has faults and struggles. Deep down, they also envy others, maybe you. When we leave it to this world to define our worth, we set ourselves up for failure. The world is a poor judge of true value.

So where do we find our value and worth? Job 31:15 reminds us we are created and designed by God. He knew exactly what He was doing when He designed you with your specific personality, traits, and gifts. When you think about yourself, you can praise God because you are "fearfully and wonderfully made" (Ps. 139:14). God knows exactly who you are, and He loves you. Not only did He design you as you are, but He also designed you with a purpose. Ephesians 2:10 reminds us we were "created in Christ Jesus for good works." That's where you find true value—in knowing you are a rare and precious creation of the God you serve. You are worthy of respect, valuable beyond measure, and infinitely lovable because of the love and creativity of Almighty God. That's who you are.

28 This also *would be* an iniquity *deserving of* judgment,
For I would have denied God *who is* above.

29 "If[a] I have rejoiced at the destruction of him who hated me,
Or lifted myself up when evil found him
30 [a](Indeed I have not allowed my mouth to sin
By asking for a curse on his soul);
31 If the men of my tent have not said,
'Who is there that has not been satisfied with his meat?'
32 [a](*But* no sojourner had to lodge in the street,
*For* I have opened my doors to the traveler[1]);
33 If I have covered my transgressions [a]as Adam,
By hiding my iniquity in my bosom,
34 Because I feared the great [a]multitude,
And dreaded the contempt of families,
So that I kept silence
*And* did not go out of the door—
35 [a]Oh, that I had one to hear me!
Here is my mark.
*Oh,* [b]*that* the Almighty would answer me,
*That* my Prosecutor had written a book!
36 Surely I would carry it on my shoulder,
*And* bind it on me *like* a crown;
37 I would declare to Him the number of my steps;
Like a prince I would approach Him.

38 "If my land cries out against me,
And its furrows weep together;
39 If [a]I have eaten its fruit[1] without money,
Or [b]caused its owners to lose their lives;
40 *Then* let [a]thistles grow instead of wheat,
And weeds instead of barley."

The words of Job are ended.

### ELIHU CONTRADICTS JOB'S FRIENDS

32 So these three men ceased answering
Job, because he *was* [a]righteous in his
own eyes. 2 Then the wrath of Elihu, the son of
Barachel the [a]Buzite, of the family of Ram, was
aroused against Job; his wrath was aroused
because he [b]justified himself rather than God.
3 Also against his three friends his wrath was
aroused, because they had found no answer,
and *yet* had condemned Job.
4 Now because they *were* years older than he,
Elihu had waited to speak to Job.[1] 5 When Elihu
saw that *there was* no answer in the mouth of
these three men, his wrath was aroused.
6 So Elihu, the son of Barachel the Buzite,
answered and said:

"I *am* [a]young in years, and you *are* very old;
Therefore I was afraid,
And dared not declare my opinion to you.
7 I said, 'Age[1] should speak,
And multitude of years should teach wisdom.'
8 But *there is* a spirit in man,
And [a]the breath of the Almighty gives him understanding.
9 [a]Great men[1] are not *always* wise,
Nor do the aged *always* understand justice.

10 "Therefore I say, 'Listen to me,
I also will declare my opinion.'
11 Indeed I waited for your words,
I listened to your reasonings, while you searched out what to say.
12 I paid close attention to you;
And surely not one of you convinced Job,
*Or* answered his words—
13 [a]Lest you say,
'We have found wisdom';
God will vanquish him, not man.
14 Now he has not directed *his* words against me;
So I will not answer him with your words.

15 "They are dismayed and answer no more;
Words escape them.
16 And I have waited, because they did not speak,
Because they stood still *and* answered no more.
17 I also will answer my part,
I too will declare my opinion.
18 For I am full of words;
The spirit within me compels me.
19 Indeed my belly *is* like wine *that* has no vent;
It is ready to burst like new wineskins.
20 I will speak, that I may find relief;
I must open my lips and answer.
21 Let me not, I pray, show partiality to anyone;
Nor let me flatter any man.
22 For I do not know how to flatter,
*Else* my Maker would soon take me [a]away.

### ELIHU CONTRADICTS JOB

33 "But please, Job, hear my speech,
And listen to all my words.
2 Now, I open my mouth;
My tongue speaks in my mouth.

31:29 [a][Prov. 17:5; 24:17] 31:30 [a][Matt. 5:44] 31:32 [a]Gen. 19:2, 3 [1]Following Septuagint, Syriac, Targum, and Vulgate; Masoretic Text reads *road.* 31:33 [a][Prov. 28:13] 31:34 [a]Ex. 23:2 31:35 [a]Job 19:7; 30:20, 24, 28 [b]Job 13:22, 24; 33:10 31:39 [a]Job 24:6, 10–12; [James 5:4] [b]1 Kin. 21:19 [1]Literally *its strength* 31:40 [a]Gen. 3:18 32:1 [a]Job 6:29; 31:6; 33:9 32:2 [a]Gen. 22:21 [b]Job 27:5, 6 32:4 [1]Vulgate reads *till Job had spoken.* 32:6 [a]Lev. 19:32 32:7 [1]Literally *Days,* that is, years 32:8 [a]1 Kin. 3:12; 4:29; [Job 35:11; 38:36; Prov. 2:6; Eccl. 2:26; Dan. 1:17; 2:21; Matt. 11:25; James 1:5] 32:9 [a][1 Cor. 1:26] [1]Or *Men of many years* 32:13 [a][Jer. 9:23; 1 Cor. 1:29] 32:22 [a]Job 27:8

3 My words *come* from my upright heart;
My lips utter pure knowledge.
4 [a]The Spirit of God has made me,
And the breath of the Almighty gives me life.
5 If you can answer me,
Set *your words* in order before me;
Take your stand.
6 [a]Truly I *am* as your spokesman[1] before God;
I also have been formed out of clay.
7 [a]Surely no fear of me will terrify you,
Nor will my hand be heavy on you.

8 "Surely you have spoken in my hearing,
And I have heard the sound of *your* words, *saying,*
9 'I[a] *am* pure, without transgression;
I *am* innocent, and *there is* no iniquity in me.
10 Yet He finds occasions against me,
[a]He counts me as His enemy;
11 [a]He puts my feet in the stocks,
He watches all my paths.'

12 "Look, *in* this you are not righteous.
I will answer you,
For God is greater than man.

> **33:12** Elihu was correct in saying God was not answerable to Job. God never has to explain Himself to us, even though He often graciously does so. Job had great respect for God and understood the fear of the Lord (Job 28:28). He was persistent in asking God for an answer; in the end, God did reply.

13 Why do you [a]contend with Him?
For He does not give an accounting of any of His words.
14 [a]For God may speak in one way, or in another,
*Yet man* does not perceive it.
15 [a]In a dream, in a vision of the night,
When deep sleep falls upon men,
While slumbering on their beds,
16 [a]Then He opens the ears of men,
And seals their instruction.
17 In order to turn man *from his* deed,
And conceal pride from man,
18 He keeps back his soul from the Pit,
And his life from perishing by the sword.

19 "*Man* is also chastened with pain on his [a]bed,
And with strong *pain* in many of his bones,
20 [a]So that his life abhors [b]bread,
And his soul succulent food.
21 His flesh wastes away from sight,
And his bones stick out *which once* were not seen.
22 Yes, his soul draws near the Pit,
And his life to the executioners.

23 "If there is a messenger for him,
A mediator, one among a thousand,
To show man His uprightness,
24 Then He is gracious to him, and says,
'Deliver him from going down to the Pit;
I have found a ransom';
25 His flesh shall be young like a child's,
He shall return to the days of his youth.
26 He shall pray to God, and He will delight in him,
He shall see His face with joy,
For He restores to man His righteousness.
27 Then he looks at men and [a]says,
'I have sinned, and perverted *what was* right,
And it [b]did not profit me.'
28 He will [a]redeem his[1] soul from going down to the Pit,
And his[2] life shall see the light.

29 "Behold, God works all these *things,*
Twice, *in fact,* three *times* with a man,
30 [a]To bring back his soul from the Pit,
That he may be enlightened with the light of life.

31 "Give ear, Job, listen to me;
Hold your peace, and I will speak.
32 If you have anything to say, answer me;
Speak, for I desire to justify you.
33 If not, [a]listen to me;
Hold your peace, and I will teach you wisdom."

## *ELIHU PROCLAIMS GOD'S JUSTICE*

**34** Elihu further answered and said:

2 "Hear my words, you wise *men;*
Give ear to me, you who have knowledge.
3 [a]For the ear tests words
As the palate tastes food.
4 Let us choose justice for ourselves;
Let us know among ourselves what *is* good.

5 "For Job has said, [a]'I am righteous,
But [b]God has taken away my justice;
6 [a]Should I lie concerning my right?
My wound *is* incurable, *though I am* without transgression.'
7 What man *is* like Job,
[a]*Who* drinks scorn like water,

33:4 [a] [Gen. 2:7]; Job 32:8 33:6 [a] Job 4:19 [1] Literally *as your mouth* 33:7 [a] Job 9:34 33:9 [a] Job 10:7 33:10 [a] Job 13:24; 16:9 33:11 [a] Job 13:27; 19:8 33:13 [a] Job 40:2; [Is. 45:9] 33:14 [a] Job 33:29; 40:5; Ps. 62:11 33:15 [a] [Num. 12:6] 33:16 [a] [Job 36:10, 15] 33:19 [a] Job 30:17 33:20 [a] Ps. 107:18 [b] Job 3:24; 6:7 33:27 [a] [Luke 15:21] [b] [Rom. 6:21] 33:28 [a] Is. 38:17 [1] Or *my* (Kethib) [2] Or *my* (Kethib) 33:30 [a] Ps. 56:13 33:33 [a] Ps. 34:11 34:3 [a] Job 6:30; 12:11 34:5 [a] Job 13:18; 33:9 [b] Job 27:2 34:6 [a] Job 6:4; 9:17 34:7 [a] Job 15:16

8 Who goes in company with the workers of
iniquity,
And walks with wicked men?
9 For [a]he has said, 'It profits a man nothing
That he should delight in God.'

10 "Therefore listen to me, you men of
understanding:
[a]Far be it from God *to do* wickedness,
And *from* the Almighty to *commit* iniquity.
11 [a]For He repays man *according to* his work,
And makes man to find a reward
according to *his* way.
12 Surely God will never do wickedly,
Nor will the Almighty [a]pervert justice.
13 Who gave Him charge over the earth?
Or who appointed *Him over* the whole
world?
14 If He should set His heart on it,
*If* He should [a]gather to Himself His Spirit
and His breath,
15 [a]All flesh would perish together,
And man would return to dust.

16 "If *you have* understanding, hear this;
Listen to the sound of my words:
17 [a]Should one who hates justice govern?
Will you [b]condemn *Him who is* most just?
18 [a]*Is it fitting* to say to a king, '*You are*
worthless,'
*And* to nobles, '*You are* wicked'?
19 Yet He [a]is not partial to princes,
Nor does He regard the rich more than
the poor;
For [b]they *are* all the work of His hands.
20 In a moment they die, [a]in the middle of
the night;
The people are shaken and pass away;
The mighty are taken away without a hand.

21 "For[a] His eyes *are* on the ways of man,
And He sees all his steps.
22 [a]There is no darkness nor shadow of death
Where the workers of iniquity may hide
themselves.
23 For He need not further consider a man,
That he should go before God in
judgment.
24 [a]He breaks in pieces mighty men without
inquiry,
And sets others in their place.
25 Therefore He knows their works;
He overthrows *them* in the night,
And they are crushed.
26 He strikes them as wicked *men*
In the open sight of others,
27 Because they [a]turned back from Him,
And [b]would not consider any of His ways,
28 So that they [a]caused the cry of the poor to
come to Him;
For He [b]hears the cry of the afflicted.
29 When He gives quietness, who then can
make trouble?
And when He hides *His* face, who then can
see Him,
Whether *it is* against a nation or a man
alone?—
30 That the hypocrite should not reign,
Lest the people be ensnared.

31 "For has *anyone* said to God,
'I have borne *chastening;*
I will offend no more;
32 Teach me *what* I do not see;
If I have done iniquity, I will do no more'?
33 Should He repay *it* according to your *terms,*
*Just* because you disavow it?
You must choose, and not I;
Therefore speak what you know.

34 "Men of understanding say to me,
Wise men who listen to me:
35 'Job[a] speaks without knowledge,
His words *are* without wisdom.'
36 Oh, that Job were tried to the utmost,
Because *his* answers *are like* those of
wicked men!
37 For he adds [a]rebellion to his sin;
He claps *his hands* among us,
And multiplies his words against God."

## ELIHU CONDEMNS SELF-RIGHTEOUSNESS

**35** Moreover Elihu answered and said:
2 "Do you think this is right?
Do you say,
'My righteousness is more than God's'?
3 For [a]you say,
'What advantage will it be to You?
What profit shall I have, more than *if* I
had sinned?'

4 "I will answer you,
And [a]your companions with you.
5 [a]Look to the heavens and see;
And behold the clouds—
They are higher than you.
6 If you sin, what do you accomplish
[a]against Him?
Or, *if* your transgressions are multiplied,
what do you do to Him?
7 [a]If you are righteous, what do you give Him?
Or what does He receive from your hand?
8 Your wickedness affects a man such as
you,
And your righteousness a son of man.

34:9 [a] Mal. 3:14 34:10 [a] Job 8:3; 36:23 34:11 [a] Ps. 62:12 34:12 [a] Job 8:3 34:14 [a] Ps. 104:29 34:15 [a] [Gen. 3:19] 34:17 [a] 2 Sam. 23:3 [b] Job 40:8 34:18 [a] Ex. 22:28 34:19 [a] [Deut. 10:17] [b] Job 31:15 34:20 [a] Ex. 12:29 34:21 [a] Job 31:4 34:22 [a] [Amos 9:2, 3] 34:24 [a] [Dan. 2:21] 34:27 [a] 1 Sam. 15:11 [b] Is. 5:12 34:28 [a] Job 35:9 [b] [Ex. 22:23] 34:35 [a] Job 35:16; 38:2 34:37 [a] Job 7:11; 10:1 35:3 [a] Job 21:15; 34:9 35:4 [a] Job 34:8 35:5 [a] [Job 22:12] 35:6 [a] [Jer. 7:19] 35:7 [a] Prov. 9:12

9 "Because[a] of the multitude of oppressions
they cry out;
They cry out for help because of the arm
of the mighty.
10 But no one says, [a]'Where *is* God my Maker,
[b]Who gives songs in the night,
11 Who [a]teaches us more than the beasts of
the earth,
And makes us wiser than the birds of
heaven?'
12 [a]There they cry out, but He does not
answer,
Because of the pride of evil men.

**35:12** Elihu accused Job of **pride** because Job had declared his own righteousness (Job 32:1). But Elihu's presumption and self-righteousness became perhaps even more excessive than Job's as he continued his speech against Job (Job 36:4). Later, Elihu would understand that God had accepted Job, while the others were condemned. Even knowledge about God and commitment to God can become a source of pride that blinds us to other things God is doing, both in ourselves and in others.

13 [a]Surely God will not listen to empty *talk,*
Nor will the Almighty regard it.
14 [a]Although you say you do not see Him,
*Yet* justice *is* before Him, and [b]you must
wait for Him.
15 And now, because He has not [a]punished
in His anger,
Nor taken much notice of folly,
16 [a]Therefore Job opens his mouth in vain;
He multiplies words without knowledge."

## ELIHU PROCLAIMS GOD'S GOODNESS

36 Elihu also proceeded and said:

2 "Bear with me a little, and I will show you
That *there are* yet words to speak on God's
behalf.
3 I will fetch my knowledge from afar;
I will ascribe righteousness to my Maker.
4 For truly my words *are* not false;
One who is perfect in knowledge *is* with
you.

5 "Behold, God *is* mighty, but despises *no
one;*
[a]*He is* mighty in strength of
understanding.
6 He does not preserve the life of the wicked,
But gives justice to the [a]oppressed.
7 [a]He does not withdraw His eyes from the
righteous;
But [b]*they are* on the throne with kings,
For He has seated them forever,
And they are exalted.
8 And [a]if *they are* bound in fetters,
Held in the cords of affliction,
9 Then He tells them their work and their
transgressions—
That they have acted defiantly.
10 [a]He also opens their ear to instruction,
And commands that they turn from
iniquity.
11 If they obey and serve *Him,*
They shall [a]spend their days in prosperity,
And their years in pleasures.
12 But if they do not obey,
They shall perish by the sword,
And they shall die without [a]knowledge.[1]

13 "But the hypocrites in heart [a]store up wrath;
They do not cry for help when He binds
them.
14 [a]They die in youth,
And their life *ends* among the perverted
persons.[1]
15 He delivers the poor in their affliction,
And opens their ears in oppression.

16 "Indeed He would have brought you out of
dire distress,
[a]*Into* a broad place where *there is* no
restraint;
And [b]what is set on your table *would be*
full of [c]richness.
17 But you are filled with the judgment due
the [a]wicked;
Judgment and justice take hold *of you.*
18 Because *there is* wrath, *beware* lest He
take you away with *one* blow;
For [a]a large ransom would not help you
avoid *it.*
19 [a]Will your riches,
Or all the mighty forces,
Keep you from distress?
20 Do not desire the night,
When people are cut off in their place.
21 Take heed, [a]do not turn to iniquity,
For [b]you have chosen this rather than
affliction.

22 "Behold, God is exalted by His power;
Who teaches like Him?
23 [a]Who has assigned Him His way,
Or who has said, 'You have done [b]wrong'?

**35:9** [a] Job 34:28 **35:10** [a] Is. 51:13 [b] Acts 16:25 **35:11** [a] Ps. 94:12 **35:12** [a] Prov. 1:28 **35:13** [a] [Is. 1:15] **35:14** [a] Job 9:11 [b] [Ps. 37:5, 6] **35:15** [a] Ps. 89:32 **35:16** [a] Job 34:35; 38:2 **36:5** [a] Job 12:13, 16; 37:23 **36:6** [a] Job 5:15 **36:7** [a] [Ps. 33:18; 34:15] [b] Ps. 113:8 **36:8** [a] Ps. 107:10 **36:10** [a] Job 33:16; 36:15 **36:11** [a] [Is. 1:19, 20] **36:12** [a] Job 4:21 [1] Masoretic Text reads *as one without knowledge.* **36:13** [a] [Rom. 2:5] **36:14** [a] Ps. 55:23 [1] Hebrew *qedeshim,* that is, those practicing sodomy and prostitution in religious rituals **36:16** [a] Ps. 18:19; 31:8; 118:5 [b] Ps. 23:5 [c] Ps. 36:8 **36:17** [a] Job 22:5, 10, 11 **36:18** [a] Ps. 49:7 **36:19** [a] [Prov. 11:4] **36:21** [a] [Ps. 31:6; 66:18] [b] [Heb. 11:25] **36:23** [a] Job 34:13; [Is. 40:13, 14] [b] Job 8:3

### *ELIHU PROCLAIMS GOD'S MAJESTY*

24 "Remember to [a]magnify His work,
Of which men have sung.
25 Everyone has seen it;
Man looks on *it* from afar.

26 "Behold, God *is* great, and we [a]do not know
*Him;*
[b]Nor can the number of His years *be*
discovered.
27 For He [a]draws up drops of water,
Which distill as rain from the mist,
28 [a]Which the clouds drop down
*And* pour abundantly on man.
29 Indeed, can *anyone* understand the
spreading of clouds,
The thunder from His canopy?
30 Look, He [a]scatters His light upon it,
And covers the depths of the sea.
31 For [a]by these He judges the peoples;
He [b]gives food in abundance.
32 [a]He covers *His* hands with lightning,
And commands it to strike.
33 [a]His thunder declares it,
The cattle also, concerning the rising
*storm.*

**37** "At this also my heart trembles,
And leaps from its place.
2 Hear attentively the thunder of His voice,
And the rumbling *that* comes from His
mouth.
3 He sends it forth under the whole heaven,
His lightning to the ends of the earth.
4 After it [a]a voice roars;
He thunders with His majestic voice,
And He does not restrain them when His
voice is heard.
5 God thunders marvelously with His voice;
[a]He does great things which we cannot
comprehend.
6 For [a]He says to the snow, 'Fall *on* the
earth';
Likewise to the gentle rain and the heavy
rain of His strength.
7 He seals the hand of every man,
[a]That [b]all men may know His work.
8 The beasts [a]go into dens,
And remain in their lairs.
9 From the chamber *of the south* comes the
whirlwind,
And cold from the scattering winds *of the*
*north.*
10 [a]By the breath of God ice is given,
And the broad waters are frozen.
11 Also with moisture He saturates the thick
clouds;
He scatters His bright clouds.
12 And they swirl about, being turned by His
guidance,
That they may [a]do whatever He
commands them
On the face of the whole earth.[1]
13 [a]He causes it to come,
Whether for correction,
Or [b]for His land,
Or [c]for mercy.

14 "Listen to this, O Job;
Stand still and [a]consider the wondrous
works of God.
15 Do you know when God dispatches
them,
And causes the light of His cloud to
shine?
16 [a]Do you know how the clouds are
balanced,
Those wondrous works of [b]Him who is
perfect in knowledge?
17 Why *are* your garments hot,
When He quiets the earth by the south
*wind?*
18 With Him, have you [a]spread out the
[b]skies,
Strong as a cast metal mirror?

19 "Teach us what we should say to Him,
*For* we can prepare nothing because of
the darkness.
20 Should He be told that I *wish to* speak?
If a man were to speak, surely he would be
swallowed up.
21 Even now *men* cannot look at the light
*when it is* bright in the skies,
When the wind has passed and cleared
them.
22 He comes from the north *as* golden
*splendor;*
With God *is* awesome majesty.
23 As *for* the Almighty, [a]we cannot find
Him;
[b]*He is* excellent in power,
*In* judgment and abundant justice;
He does not oppress.
24 Therefore men [a]fear Him;
He shows no partiality to any *who are*
[b]wise of heart."

### *THE LORD REVEALS HIS OMNIPOTENCE TO JOB*

*(Gen. 1:1–10)*

**38** Then the LORD answered Job [a]out of the
whirlwind, and said:

2 "Who[a] *is* this who darkens counsel
By [b]words without knowledge?

**36:24** [a] [Rev. 15:3] **36:26** [a] [1 Cor. 13:12] [b] Heb. 1:12 **36:27** [a] Ps. 147:8 **36:28** [a] [Prov. 3:20] **36:30** [a] Job 37:3 **36:31** [a] [Acts 14:17] [b] Ps. 104:14, 15 **36:32** [a] Ps. 147:8 **36:33** [a] 1 Kin. 18:41 **37:4** [a] Ps. 29:3 **37:5** [a] Job 5:9; 9:10; 36:26 **37:6** [a] Ps. 147:16, 17 **37:7** [a] Ps. 109:27 [b] Ps. 19:3, 4 **37:8** [a] Ps. 104:21, 22 **37:10** [a] Ps. 147:17, 18 **37:12** [a] Job 36:32 [1] Literally *the world of the earth* **37:13** [a] Ex. 9:18, 23 [b] Job 38:26, 27 [c] 1 Kin. 18:41–46 **37:14** [a] Ps. 111:2 **37:16** [a] Job 36:29 [b] Job 36:4 **37:18** [a] [Is. 44:24] [b] Ps. 104:2 **37:23** [a] [1 Tim. 6:16] [b] [Job 9:4; 36:5] **37:24** [a] [Matt. 10:28] [b] [Matt. 11:25] **38:1** [a] Ex. 19:16 **38:2** [a] Job 34:35; 42:3 [b] 1 Tim. 1:7

**38:2** The theme of the Lord's first address is given here: Job didn't know what he was talking about. There is a wide gap in understanding between God and people. God wasn't saying Job had sinned in the way his friends had accused him, but He was saying Job had been presumptuous with his superficial **knowledge** of divine things. Job, along with his friends, had to learn that suffering may serve a purpose known only to God. In that case, a follower of God is to submit even to loss and trauma, with patience and hope, for the glory of God.

3 [a]Now prepare yourself like a man;
I will question you, and you shall answer
Me.

4 "Where[a] were you when I laid the
foundations of the earth?
Tell *Me,* if you have understanding.
5 Who determined its measurements?
Surely you know!
Or who stretched the line upon it?
6 To what were its foundations fastened?
Or who laid its cornerstone,
7 When the morning stars sang together,
And all [a]the sons of God shouted for joy?

8 "Or[a] *who* shut in the sea with doors,
When it burst forth *and* issued from the
womb;
9 When I made the clouds its garment,
And thick darkness its swaddling band;
10 When [a]I fixed My limit for it,
And set bars and doors;
11 When I said,
'This far you may come, but no farther,
And here your proud waves [a]must stop!'

12 "Have you [a]commanded the morning
since your days *began,*
*And* caused the dawn to know its place,
13 That it might take hold of the ends of the
earth,
And [a]the wicked be shaken out of it?
14 It takes on form like clay *under* a seal,
And stands out like a garment.
15 From the wicked their [a]light is withheld,
And [b]the upraised arm is broken.

16 "Have you [a]entered the springs of the sea?
Or have you walked in search of the
depths?
17 Have [a]the gates of death been revealed to
you?
Or have you seen the doors of the shadow
of death?
18 Have you comprehended the breadth of
the earth?
Tell *Me,* if you know all this.

19 "Where *is* the way *to* the dwelling of light?
And darkness, where *is* its place,
20 That you may take it to its territory,
That you may know the paths *to* its home?
21 Do you know *it,* because you were born
then,
Or *because* the number of your days *is* great?

22 "Have you entered [a]the treasury of snow,
Or have you seen the treasury of hail,
23 [a]Which I have reserved for the time of
trouble,
For the day of battle and war?
24 By what way is light diffused,
*Or* the east wind scattered over the earth?

25 "Who [a]has divided a channel for the
overflowing *water,*
Or a path for the thunderbolt,
26 To cause it to rain on a land *where there is*
no one,
A wilderness in which *there is* no man;
27 [a]To satisfy the desolate waste,
And cause to spring forth the growth of
tender grass?
28 [a]Has the rain a father?
Or who has begotten the drops of dew?
29 From whose womb comes the ice?
And the [a]frost of heaven, who gives it
birth?
30 The waters harden like stone,
And the surface of the deep is [a]frozen.

31 "Can you bind the cluster of the [a]Pleiades,
Or loose the belt of Orion?
32 Can you bring out Mazzaroth[1] in its
season?
Or can you guide the Great Bear with its
cubs?
33 Do you know [a]the ordinances of the
heavens?
Can you set their dominion over the
earth?

34 "Can you lift up your voice to the clouds,
That an abundance of water may cover
you?
35 Can you send out lightnings, that they
may go,
And say to you, 'Here we *are!*'?
36 [a]Who has put wisdom in the mind?[1]
Or who has given understanding to the
heart?

38:3 [a] Job 40:7 38:4 [a] Ps. 104:5 38:7 [a] Job 1:6 38:8 [a] Gen. 1:9 38:10 [a] Job 26:10 38:11 [a] [Ps. 89:9; 93:4] 38:12 [a] [Ps. 74:16; 148:5] 38:13 [a] Ps. 104:35 38:15 [a] Job 18:5 [b] Ps. 10:15; 37:17 38:16 [a] [Ps. 77:19] 38:17 [a] Ps. 9:13 38:22 [a] Ps. 135:7 38:23 [a] Is. 30:30 38:25 [a] Job 28:26 38:27 [a] Ps. 104:13, 14; 107:35 38:28 [a] Job 36:27, 28 38:29 [a] Ps. 147:16, 17 38:30 [a] [Job 37:10] 38:31 [a] Amos 5:8 38:32 [1] Literally *Constellations* 38:33 [a] Jer. 31:35, 36 38:36 [a] [Ps. 51:6] [1] Literally *inward parts*

37 Who can number the clouds by wisdom?
Or who can pour out the bottles of heaven,
38 When the dust hardens in clumps,
And the clods cling together?

39 "Can[a] you hunt the prey for the lion,
Or satisfy the appetite of the young lions,
40 When they crouch in *their* dens,
*Or* lurk in their lairs to lie in wait?
41 [a]Who provides food for the raven,
When its young ones cry to God,
And wander about for lack of food?

**39** "Do you know the time when the wild
[a]mountain goats bear young?
*Or* can you mark when [b]the deer gives
birth?
2 Can you number the months *that* they
fulfill?
Or do you know the time when they bear
young?
3 They bow down,
They bring forth their young,
They deliver their offspring.[1]
4 Their young ones are healthy,
They grow strong with grain;
They depart and do not return to them.

5 "Who set the wild donkey free?
Who loosed the bonds of the onager,
6 [a]Whose home I have made the wilderness,
And the barren land his dwelling?
7 He scorns the tumult of the city;
He does not heed the shouts of the driver.
8 The range of the mountains *is* his pasture,
And he searches after [a]every green thing.

9 "Will the [a]wild ox be willing to serve you?
Will he bed by your manger?
10 Can you bind the wild ox in the furrow
with ropes?
Or will he plow the valleys behind you?
11 Will you trust him because his strength *is*
great?
Or will you leave your labor to him?
12 Will you trust him to bring home your
grain,
And gather it to your threshing floor?

13 "The wings of the ostrich wave proudly,
But are her wings and pinions *like the*
kindly stork's?
14 For she leaves her eggs on the ground,
And warms them in the dust;
15 She forgets that a foot may crush them,
Or that a wild beast may break them.
16 She [a]treats her young harshly, as though
*they were* not hers;
Her labor is in vain, without concern,
17 Because God deprived her of wisdom,
And did not [a]endow her with
understanding.
18 When she lifts herself on high,
She scorns the horse and its rider.

19 "Have you given the horse strength?
Have you clothed his neck with thunder?[1]
20 Can you frighten him like a locust?
His majestic snorting strikes terror.
21 He paws in the valley, and rejoices in *his*
strength;
[a]He gallops into the clash of arms.
22 He mocks at fear, and is not frightened;
Nor does he turn back from the sword.
23 The quiver rattles against him,
The glittering spear and javelin.
24 He devours the distance with fierceness
and rage;
Nor does he come to a halt because the
trumpet *has* sounded.
25 At *the blast of* the trumpet he says, 'Aha!'
He smells the battle from afar,
The thunder of captains and shouting.

26 "Does the hawk fly by your wisdom,
*And* spread its wings toward the south?
27 Does the [a]eagle mount up at your command,
And [b]make its nest on high?
28 On the rock it dwells and resides,
On the crag of the rock and the stronghold.
29 From there it spies out the prey;
Its eyes observe from afar.
30 Its young ones suck up blood;
And [a]where the slain *are*, there it *is*."

**40** Moreover the LORD [a]answered Job, and
said:

2 "Shall [a]the one who contends with the
Almighty correct *Him?*
He who [b]rebukes God, let him answer it."

### JOB'S RESPONSE TO GOD

3 Then Job answered the LORD and said:

4 "Behold,[a] I am vile;
What shall I answer You?
[b]I lay my hand over my mouth.
5 Once I have spoken, but I will not answer;
Yes, twice, but I will proceed no further."

### GOD'S CHALLENGE TO JOB

6 [a]Then the LORD answered Job out of the
whirlwind, and said:

7 "Now[a] prepare yourself like a man;
[b]I will question you, and you shall
answer Me:

**38:39** [a] Ps. 104:21 **38:41** [a] [Matt. 6:26] **39:1** [a] Ps. 104:18 [b] Ps. 29:9 **39:3** [1] Literally *pangs*, figurative of offspring **39:6** [a] Jer. 2:24 **39:8** [a] Gen. 1:29 **39:9** [a] Num. 23:22 **39:16** [a] Lam. 4:3 **39:17** [a] Job 35:11 **39:19** [1] Or *a mane* **39:21** [a] Jer. 8:6 **39:27** [a] Prov. 30:18, 19 [b] Jer. 49:16 **39:30** [a] Matt. 24:28 **40:1** [a] Job 38:1 **40:2** [a] Job 9:3; 10:2; 33:13 [b] Job 13:3; 23:4 **40:4** [a] Ezra 9:6 [b] Job 29:9 **40:6** [a] Job 38:1 **40:7** [a] Job 38:3 [b] Job 42:4

8 "Would[a] you indeed annul My judgment?
Would you condemn Me that you may be justified?
9 Have you an arm like God?
Or can you thunder with [a]a voice like His?
10 [a]Then adorn yourself *with* majesty and splendor,
And array yourself with glory and beauty.
11 Disperse the rage of your wrath;
Look on everyone *who is* proud, and humble him.
12 Look on everyone *who is* [a]proud, *and* bring him low;
Tread down the wicked in their place.
13 Hide them in the dust together,
Bind their faces in hidden *darkness.*
14 Then I will also confess to you
That your own right hand can save you.

15 "Look now at the behemoth,[1] which I made *along* with you;
He eats grass like an ox.
16 See now, his strength *is* in his hips,
And his power *is* in his stomach muscles.
17 He moves his tail like a cedar;
The sinews of his thighs are tightly knit.
18 His bones *are like* beams of bronze,
His ribs like bars of iron.
19 He *is* the first of the [a]ways of God;
Only He who made him can bring near His sword.
20 Surely the mountains [a]yield food for him,
And all the beasts of the field play there.
21 He lies under the lotus trees,
In a covert of reeds and marsh.
22 The lotus trees cover him *with* their shade;
The willows by the brook surround him.
23 Indeed the river may rage,
*Yet* he is not disturbed;
He is confident, though the Jordan gushes into his mouth,
24 *Though* he takes it in his eyes,
*Or* one pierces *his* nose with a snare.

41 "Can you draw out [a]Leviathan[1] with a hook,
Or *snare* his tongue with a line *which* you lower?
2 Can you [a]put a reed through his nose,
Or pierce his jaw with a hook?
3 Will he make many supplications to you?
Will he speak softly to you?
4 Will he make a covenant with you?
Will you take him as a servant forever?
5 Will you play with him as *with* a bird,
Or will you leash him for your maidens?
6 Will *your* companions make a banquet[1] of him?
Will they apportion him among the merchants?
7 Can you fill his skin with harpoons,
Or his head with fishing spears?
8 Lay your hand on him;
Remember the battle—
Never do it again!
9 Indeed, *any* hope of *overcoming* him is false;
Shall *one not* be overwhelmed at the sight of him?
10 No one *is so* fierce that he would dare stir him up.
Who then is able to stand against Me?
11 [a]Who has preceded Me, that I should pay *him?*
[b]Everything under heaven is Mine.

12 "I will not conceal[1] his limbs,
His mighty power, or his graceful proportions.
13 Who can remove his outer coat?
Who can approach *him* with a double bridle?
14 Who can open the doors of his face,
*With* his terrible teeth all around?
15 *His* rows of scales are *his* pride,
Shut up tightly *as with* a seal;
16 One is so near another
That no air can come between them;
17 They are joined one to another,
They stick together and cannot be parted.
18 His sneezings flash forth light,
And his eyes *are* like the eyelids of the morning.
19 Out of his mouth go burning lights;
Sparks of fire shoot out.
20 Smoke goes out of his nostrils,
As *from* a boiling pot and burning rushes.
21 His breath kindles coals,
And a flame goes out of his mouth.
22 Strength dwells in his neck,
And sorrow dances before him.
23 The folds of his flesh are joined together;
They are firm on him and cannot be moved.
24 His heart is as hard as stone,
Even as hard as the lower *millstone.*
25 When he raises himself up, the mighty are afraid;
Because of his crashings they are beside[1] themselves.
26 *Though* the sword reaches him, it cannot avail;
Nor does spear, dart, or javelin.
27 He regards iron as straw,
*And* bronze as rotten wood.
28 The arrow cannot make him flee;
Slingstones become like stubble to him.

40:8 [a] [Rom. 3:4] 40:9 [a] [Ps. 29:3, 4] 40:10 [a] Ps. 93:1; 104:1 40:12 [a] Dan. 4:37 40:15 [1] A large animal, exact identity unknown 40:19 [a] Job 26:14 40:20 [a] Ps. 104:14 41:1 [a] Is. 27:1 [1] A large sea creature, exact identity unknown 41:2 [a] 2 Kin. 19:28; Is. 37:29 41:6 [1] Or *bargain over him* 41:11 [a] [Rom. 11:35] [b] Ex. 19:5; [Deut. 10:14; Job 9:5–10; 26:6–14]; Ps. 24:1; 50:12; 1 Cor. 10:26, 28 41:12 [1] Literally *keep silent about* 41:25 [1] Or *purify themselves*

29 Darts are regarded as straw;
He laughs at the threat of javelins.
30 His undersides *are* like sharp potsherds;
He spreads pointed *marks* in the mire.
31 He makes the deep boil like a pot;
He makes the sea like a pot of ointment.
32 He leaves a shining wake behind him;
*One* would think the deep had white
hair.
33 On earth there is nothing like him,
Which is made without fear.
34 He beholds every high *thing;*
He *is* king over all the children of pride."

### *JOB'S REPENTANCE AND RESTORATION*

**42** Then Job answered the LORD and said:

2 "I know that You [a]can do everything,
And that no purpose *of Yours* can be
withheld from You.
3 *You asked,* [a]'Who *is* this who hides counsel
without knowledge?'
Therefore I have uttered what I did not
understand,
[b]Things too wonderful for me, which I did
not know.
4 Listen, please, and let me speak;
*You said,* [a]'I will question you, and you
shall answer Me.'

5 "I have [a]heard of You by the hearing of the
ear,
But now my eye sees You.
6 Therefore I [a]abhor *myself,*
And repent in dust and ashes."

7 And so it was, after the LORD had spoken
these words to Job, that the LORD said to Eliphaz
the Temanite, "My wrath is aroused against you
and your two friends, for you have not spoken
of Me *what is* right, as My servant Job *has.* 8 Now
therefore, take for yourselves [a]seven bulls and
seven rams, [b]go to My servant Job, and offer up
for yourselves a burnt offering; and My servant
Job shall [c]pray for you. For I will accept him, lest
I deal with you *according to your* folly; because
you have not spoken of Me *what is* right, as My
servant Job *has.*"
9 So Eliphaz the Temanite and Bildad the
Shuhite *and* Zophar the Naamathite went and
did as the LORD commanded them; for the LORD
had accepted Job. 10 [a]And the LORD restored Job's
losses[1] when he prayed for his friends. Indeed
the LORD gave Job [b]twice as much as he had
before. 11 Then [a]all his brothers, all his sisters,
and all those who had been his acquaintances
before, came to him and ate food with him in
his house; and they consoled him and comfort-
ed him for all the adversity that the LORD had
brought upon him. Each one gave him a piece
of silver and each a ring of gold.
12 Now the LORD blessed [a]the latter *days*
of Job more than his beginning; for he had
[b]fourteen thousand sheep, six thousand cam-
els, one thousand yoke of oxen, and one thou-
sand female donkeys. 13 [a]He also had seven
sons and three daughters. 14 And he called
the name of the first Jemimah, the name of
the second Keziah, and the name of the third
Keren-Happuch. 15 In all the land were found
no women *so* beautiful as the daughters of
Job; and their father gave them an inheritance
among their brothers.
16 After this Job [a]lived one hundred and forty
years, and saw his children and grandchildren
*for* four generations. 17 So Job died, old and [a]full
of days.

**42:4–6** Job was convicted of having too small a view of God—believing he had God all figured out. In the Bible, the revelation of the character and person of God is the criterion for proper self-evaluation (see Is. 6:5). Job repented in **dust and ashes**, a sign of mourning, because his trust in God had been so imperfect. He now understood God in a new way.

**42:2** [a] Gen. 18:14; [Matt. 19:26; Mark 10:27; 14:36; Luke 18:27] **42:3** [a] Job 38:2 [b] Ps. 40:5; 131:1; 139:6 **42:4** [a] Job 38:3; 40:7 **42:5** [a] Job 26:14; [Rom. 10:17] **42:6** [a] Ezra 9:6; Job 40:4 **42:8** [a] Num. 23:1 [b] [Matt. 5:24] [c] Gen. 20:17; [James 5:15, 16; 1 John 5:16] **42:10** [a] Deut. 30:3; Ps. 14:7; 85:1–3; 126:1 [b] Is. 40:2 [1] Literally *Job's captivity,* that is, what was captured from Job **42:11** [a] Job 19:13 **42:12** [a] Job 1:10; 8:7; James 5:11 [b] Job 1:3 **42:13** [a] Job 1:2 **42:16** [a] Job 5:26; Prov. 3:16 **42:17** [a] Gen. 15:15; 25:8; Job 5:26

# *The Book of* PSALMS

| AUTHOR | KEY VERSE | READING TIME |
|---|---|---|
| David, Asaph, the sons of Korah, Solomon, Moses, Heman, Ethan, and others | Psalm 19:14 | 5 hours 50 minutes |

The Book of Psalms is the largest and perhaps most widely read book in the Bible. The psalms were set to the accompaniment of stringed instruments and served as the temple hymnbook and devotional guide for the Jewish people. The book explores the full range of human experience in a very personal and practical way. Its one hundred and fifty songs run from creation through the patriarchal, theocratic, monarchical, exilic, and postexilic periods. The tremendous breadth of subject matter in the Book of Psalms includes jubilation, war, peace, worship, judgment, messianic prophecy, praise, and lament. At least fourteen psalms connect to events detailed in the Old Testament's books of history, most notably Psalm 51, which David wrote after his sins recorded in 2 Samuel 11–12.

**Occasion:** Individual psalms were written for many different occasions ranging from times of distress and sorrow to times of joy and celebration. Altogether, the Book of Psalms served as a worship hymnal for the Jewish people.

**Main Point:** God is good, faithful, loving, just, and deserving of worship.

**Big Ideas:** God is worthy of praise, no matter what. We can share whatever we feel with God, knowing He cares. We should worship God as a way of everyday life.

## OUTLINE:

I. Songs of Worship (Pss. 1–41)
II. Hymns of the People (Pss. 42–89)
III. Anthems of Praise (Pss. 90–150)

**c. 1445 BC**
The Law is given on Mount Sinai

**c. 1410–430 BC**
**Psalms written**

**c. 1406 BC**
Forty years of wilderness wandering end

**c. 1405–1400 BC**
The conquest of Canaan

**c. 1380–1050 BC**
Judges rule in Israel

**c. 1050 BC**
Saul becomes king of Israel

**1010 BC**
David begins to reign at Hebron

**970 BC**
Solomon becomes king of Israel

**930 BC**
The kingdom is divided

**722 BC**
The Assyrians defeat Israel

**586 BC**
The Babylonians defeat Judah

**538 BC**
Jews begin returning to Judea

**536–515 BC**
The temple is rebuilt

**443 BC**
Jerusalem's wall is reconstructed

# BOOK ONE
## PSALMS 1–41

### PSALM 1
#### THE WAY OF THE RIGHTEOUS AND THE END OF THE UNGODLY

1 Blessed [a]*is* the man
Who walks not in the counsel of the ungodly,
Nor stands in the path of sinners,
[b]Nor sits in the seat of the scornful;

**1:1** Psalm 1 sets the tone for the Book of Psalms. It contrasts the ways the **blessed** person and the wicked person live. Being blessed is not a once-for-all-time, dramatic event, but rather a lifetime of choosing to follow God and His commandments. We experience blessings when we trust in Jesus and move from grudging acceptance to enthusiastic delight in living for Him.

2 But [a]his delight *is* in the law of the LORD,
[b]And in His law he meditates day and night.
3 He shall be like a tree
[a]Planted by the rivers of water,
That brings forth its fruit in its season,
Whose leaf also shall not wither;
And whatever he does shall [b]prosper.

4 The ungodly *are* not so,
But *are* [a]like the chaff which the wind drives away.
5 Therefore the ungodly shall not stand in the judgment,
Nor sinners in the congregation of the righteous.

6 For [a]the LORD knows the way of the righteous,
But the way of the ungodly shall perish.

### PSALM 2
#### THE MESSIAH'S TRIUMPH AND KINGDOM
*(Acts 4:23–31)*

1 Why [a]do the nations rage,
And the people plot a vain thing?
2 The kings of the earth set themselves,
And the [a]rulers take counsel together,
Against the LORD and against His
[b]Anointed, *saying,*
3 "Let [a]us break Their bonds in pieces
And cast away Their cords from us."

**SEEING JESUS IN THE SCRIPTURE**

**2:1–2** This Messianic psalm anticipates how the political and religious leaders wouldn't receive Jesus but would make vain plots against Him and His followers instead (see Acts 4:25–26).

4 He who sits in the heavens [a]shall laugh;
The Lord shall hold them in derision.
5 Then He shall speak to them in His wrath,
And distress them in His deep displeasure:
6 "Yet I have set My King
On My holy hill of Zion."

**1:1** [a] Prov. 4:14 [b] Jer. 15:17 **1:2** [a] Ps. 119:14, 16, 35 [b] [Josh. 1:8] **1:3** [a] Jer. 17:8 [b] Gen. 39:2, 3, 23 **1:4** [a] Job 21:18 **1:6** [a] Ps. 37:18 **2:1** [a] Acts 4:25, 26 **2:2** [a] [Mark 3:6; 11:18] [b] [John 1:41] **2:3** [a] Luke 19:14 **2:4** [a] Ps. 37:13

**APPLY THE TRUTH**

## PEER PRESSURE

**1:1–6** Did you know God wants you to be a tree? Well, not exactly. Here, the psalmist uses the poetic imagery of a tree for what our lives should look like. They should be at peace, produce good fruit, provide blessing and shade for others, and be protected by God. This happens when we're planted in the right places by the right people. But there's also a warning about who you surround yourself with.

"Show me your friends and I'll show you your future." Who you hang out with is ultimately who you become. We even talk and dress like our friends. On one level, this isn't bad. But it is when our friends influence us away from God's plans and promises. Friends have the power to help or hurt us depending on what they do. Over time, your activities can become your identity. If you lie, you become a liar. If you steal, you become a thief. What do your friends do? That's likely who you're becoming. God, however, wants you to become a tree. Become a tree by being planted in the right place with the right people and experience positive peer pressure: where we encourage one another to grow.

> **2:6** When David conquered Jerusalem in around 1000 BC, he acquired an ancient Jebusite fortress known as **Zion**. Years later, when Solomon built the temple on Mount Moriah, the entire area in and around Jerusalem came to be known as Zion. Eventually, Zion was used to refer to the entire nation of Israel.

7 "I will declare the decree:
The LORD has said to Me,
[a]'You *are* My Son,
Today I have begotten You.
8 Ask of Me, and I will give *You*
The nations *for* Your inheritance,
And the ends of the earth *for* Your
possession.
9 [a]You shall break[1] them with a rod of
iron;
You shall dash them to pieces like a
potter's vessel.' "

10 Now therefore, be wise, O kings;
Be instructed, you judges of the
earth.
11 Serve the LORD with fear,
And rejoice with trembling.
12 Kiss the Son,[1] lest He[2] be angry,
And you perish *in* the way,
When [a]His wrath is kindled but a
little.
[b]Blessed *are* all those who put their trust in
Him.

## *PSALM 3*

### *THE LORD HELPS HIS TROUBLED PEOPLE*

*A Psalm of David [a]when he fled from Absalom his son.*

1 LORD, how they have increased who
trouble me!
Many *are* they who rise up against me.
2 Many *are* they who say of me,
"*There is* no help for him in God." *Selah*

> **3:2** The Hebrew term ***selah*** occurs in thirty-nine psalms and Habakkuk 3. What was meant by this word is unknown; it could have been a word to mark emphasis or a musical notation

3 But You, O LORD, *are* [a]a shield for me,
My glory and [b]the One who lifts up my head.
4 I cried to the LORD with my voice,
And [a]He heard me from His [b]holy hill.
*Selah*

5 [a]I lay down and slept;
I awoke, for the LORD sustained me.
6 [a]I will not be afraid of ten thousands of
people
Who have set *themselves* against me all
around.

7 Arise, O LORD;
Save me, O my God!
[a]For You have struck all my enemies on
the cheekbone;
You have broken the teeth of the ungodly.
8 [a]Salvation *belongs* to the LORD.
Your blessing *is* upon Your people. *Selah*

## *PSALM 4*

### *THE SAFETY OF THE FAITHFUL*

*To the Chief Musician. With stringed instruments. A Psalm of David.*

1 Hear me when I call, O God of my
righteousness!
You have relieved me in *my* distress;
Have mercy on me, and hear my prayer.

2 How long, O you sons of men,
*Will you turn* my glory to shame?
*How long* will you love worthlessness
*And* seek falsehood? *Selah*
3 But know that [a]the LORD has set apart[1] for
Himself him who is godly;
The LORD will hear when I call to Him.

4 [a]Be angry, and do not sin.
[b]Meditate within your heart on your bed,
and be still. *Selah*

> **4:4** The Bible speaks of the **heart** as the center of a person's character. It is the source of emotions, thoughts, and decision making. Both good and evil actions originate in the heart.

5 Offer [a]the sacrifices of righteousness,
And [b]put your trust in the LORD.

6 *There are* many who say,
"Who will show us *any* good?"

2:7 [a] [Heb. 1:5; 5:5] 2:9 [a] Ps. 89:23; 110:5, 6 [1] Following Masoretic Text and Targum; Septuagint, Syriac, and Vulgate read *rule* (compare Revelation 2:27). 2:12 [a] [Rev. 6:16, 17] [b] [Ps. 5:11; 34:22] [1] Septuagint and Vulgate read *Embrace discipline;* Targum reads *Receive instruction.* [2] Septuagint reads *the LORD.* 3:title [a] 2 Sam. 15:13–17 3:3 [a] Ps. 5:12; 28:7 [b] Ps. 9:13; 27:6 3:4 [a] Ps. 4:3; 34:4 [b] Ps. 2:6; 15:1; 43:3 3:5 [a] Lev. 26:6 3:6 [a] Ps. 23:4; 27:3 3:7 [a] Job 16:10 3:8 [a] [Is. 43:11] 4:3 [a] [2 Tim. 2:19] [1] Many Hebrew manuscripts, Septuagint, Targum, and Vulgate read *made wonderful.* 4:4 [a] [Eph. 4:26] [b] Ps. 77:6 4:5 [a] Deut. 33:19 [b] Ps. 37:3, 5; 62:8

[a]LORD, lift up the light of Your
countenance upon us.
7 You have put [a]gladness in my heart,
More than in the season that their grain
and wine increased.
8 [a]I will both lie down in peace, and sleep;
[b]For You alone, O LORD, make me dwell in
safety.

## PSALM 5

### A PRAYER FOR GUIDANCE

*To the Chief Musician. With flutes.[1]*
*A Psalm of David.*

1 Give [a]ear to my words, O LORD,
Consider my meditation.
2 Give heed to the voice of my cry,
My King and my God,
For to You I will pray.
3 My voice You shall hear in the morning,
O LORD;
[a]In the morning I will direct *it* to You,
And I will look up.

4 For You *are* not a God who takes pleasure
in wickedness,
Nor shall evil dwell with You.
5 The [a]boastful shall not [b]stand in Your
sight;
You hate all workers of iniquity.
6 You shall destroy those who speak
falsehood;
The LORD abhors the [a]bloodthirsty and
deceitful man.

7 But as for me, I will come into Your house
in the multitude of Your mercy;
In fear of You I will worship toward Your
holy temple.
8 [a]Lead me, O LORD, in Your righteousness
because of my enemies;
Make Your way straight before my face.

**4:6** [a] Num. 6:26 **4:7** [a] Is. 9:3 **4:8** [a] Ps. 3:5 [b] [Lev. 25:18] **5:title** [1] Hebrew *nehiloth* **5:1** [a] Ps. 4:1 **5:3** [a] Ps. 55:17; 88:13 **5:5** [a] [Hab. 1:13] [b] Ps. 1:5 **5:6** [a] Ps. 55:23 **5:8** [a] Ps. 25:4, 5; 27:11; 31:3

## CHRIST IN THE PSALMS

| Psalm | Portrayal | Fulfilled |
|---|---|---|
| 2:7 | The Son of God | Mathew 3:17 |
| 8:2 | Praised by children | Matthew 21:15–16 |
| 8:6 | Ruler of all | Hebrews 2:8 |
| 16:10 | Rises from death | Matthew 28:7 |
| 22:1 | Forsaken by God | Matthew 27:46 |
| 22:7–8 | Derided by enemies | Luke 23:35 |
| 22:16 | Hands and feet pierced | John 20:27 |
| 22:18 | Lots cast for clothes | Matthew 27:35–36 |
| 34:20 | Bones unbroken | John 19:32–33, 36 |
| 35:11 | Accused by false witnesses | Mark 14:57 |
| 35:19 | Hated without cause | John 15:25 |
| 40:7–8 | Delights in God's will | Hebrews 10:7 |
| 41:9 | Betrayed by a friend | Luke 22:47 |
| 45:6 | The eternal King | Hebrews 1:8 |
| 68:18 | Ascends to heaven | Acts 1:9–11 |
| 69:9 | Zealous for God's house | John 2:17 |
| 69:21 | Given vinegar and gall | Matthew 27:34 |
| 109:4 | Prays for enemies | Luke 23:34 |
| 109:8 | His betrayer replaced | Acts 1:20 |
| 110:1 | Rules over His enemies | Matthew 22:44 |
| 110:4 | A priest forever | Hebrews 5:6 |
| 118:22 | The chief stone of God's building | Matthew 21:42 |
| 118:26 | Comes in the name of the Lord | Matthew 21:9 |

9 For *there is* no faithfulness in their mouth;
Their inward part *is* destruction;
[a]Their throat *is* an open tomb;
They flatter with their tongue.
10 Pronounce them guilty, O God!
Let them fall by their own counsels;
Cast them out in the multitude of their
transgressions,
For they have rebelled against You.

11 But let all those rejoice who put their trust
in You;
Let them ever shout for joy, because You
defend them;
Let those also who love Your name
Be joyful in You.
12 For You, O LORD, will bless the righteous;
With favor You will surround him as *with*
a shield.

## PSALM 6

### A PRAYER OF FAITH IN TIME OF DISTRESS

*To the Chief Musician. With stringed instruments. [a]On an eight-stringed harp.[1] A Psalm of David.*

1 O LORD, [a]do not rebuke me in Your anger,
Nor chasten me in Your hot displeasure.
2 Have mercy on me, O LORD, for I *am*
weak;
O LORD, [a]heal me, for my bones are
troubled.
3 My soul also is greatly [a]troubled;
But You, O LORD—how long?

4 Return, O LORD, deliver me!
Oh, save me for Your mercies' sake!
5 [a]For in death *there is* no remembrance of
You;
In the grave who will give You thanks?

6 I am weary with my groaning;
All night I make my bed swim;
I drench my couch with my tears.
7 [a]My eye wastes away because of grief;
It grows old because of all my enemies.

8 [a]Depart from me, all you workers of
iniquity;
For the LORD has [b]heard the voice of my
weeping.
9 The LORD has heard my supplication;
The LORD will receive my prayer.
10 Let all my enemies be ashamed and
greatly troubled;
Let them turn back *and* be ashamed
suddenly.

## PSALM 7

### PRAYER AND PRAISE FOR DELIVERANCE FROM ENEMIES

*A [a]Meditation[1] of David, which he sang to the LORD [b]concerning the words of Cush, a Benjamite.*

1 O LORD my God, in You I put my trust;
[a]Save me from all those who persecute me;
And deliver me,
2 [a]Lest they tear me like a lion,
[b]Rending *me* in pieces, while *there is* none
to deliver.

3 O LORD my God, [a]if I have done this:
If there is [b]iniquity in my hands,
4 If I have repaid evil to him who was at
peace with me,
Or [a]have plundered my enemy without cause,
5 Let the enemy pursue me and overtake *me;*
Yes, let him trample my life to the earth,
And lay my honor in the dust. *Selah*

6 Arise, O LORD, in Your anger;
[a]Lift Yourself up because of the rage of my
enemies;
[b]Rise up for me[1] *to* the judgment You have
commanded!
7 So the congregation of the peoples shall
surround You;
For their sakes, therefore, return on high.
8 The LORD shall judge the peoples;
[a]Judge me, O LORD, [b]according to my
righteousness,
And according to my integrity within me.

9 Oh, let the wickedness of the wicked come
to an end,
But establish the just;
[a]For the righteous God tests the hearts and
minds.
10 My defense *is* of God,
Who saves the [a]upright in heart.

11 God *is* a just judge,
And God is angry *with the wicked* every day.
12 If he does not turn back,
He will [a]sharpen His sword;
He bends His bow and makes it ready.
13 He also prepares for Himself instruments
of death;
He makes His arrows into fiery shafts.

14 [a]Behold, *the wicked* brings forth iniquity;
Yes, he conceives trouble and brings forth
falsehood.
15 He made a pit and dug it out,
[a]And has fallen into the ditch *which* he
made.

5:9 [a] Rom. 3:13 6:title [a] Ps. 12:title [1] Hebrew *Sheminith* 6:1 [a] Ps. 38:1; 118:18 6:2 [a] [Hos. 6:1] 6:3 [a] Ps. 88:3 6:5 [a] [Eccl. 9:10] 6:7 [a] Job 17:7 6:8 [a] [Matt. 25:41] [b] Ps. 3:4; 28:6 7:title [a] Hab. 3:1 [b] 2 Sam. 16 [1] Hebrew *Shiggaion* 7:1 [a] Ps. 31:15 7:2 [a] Is. 38:13 [b] Ps. 50:22 7:3 [a] 2 Sam. 16:7 [b] 1 Sam. 24:11 7:4 [a] 1 Sam. 24:7; 26:9 7:6 [a] Ps. 94:2 [b] Ps. 35:23; 44:23 [1] Following Masoretic Text, Targum, and Vulgate; Septuagint reads *O LORD my God.* 7:8 [a] Ps. 26:1; 35:24; 43:1 [b] Ps. 18:20; 35:24 7:9 [a] [1 Sam. 16:7] 7:10 [a] Ps. 97:10, 11; 125:4 7:12 [a] Deut. 32:41 7:14 [a] Is. 59:4 7:15 [a] [Job 4:8]

16 [a]His trouble shall return upon his own head,
And his violent dealing shall come down on his own crown.

17 I will praise the LORD according to His righteousness,
And will sing praise to the name of the LORD Most High.

## PSALM 8

### THE GLORY OF THE LORD IN CREATION

*To the Chief Musician. On the instrument of Gath.*[1] *A Psalm of David.*

1 O LORD, our Lord,
How [a]excellent *is* Your name in all the earth,
Who have [b]set Your glory above the heavens!

2 [a]Out of the mouth of babes and nursing infants
You have ordained strength,
Because of Your enemies,
That You may silence [b]the enemy and the avenger.

> **SEEING JESUS IN THE SCRIPTURE**
>
> **8:2** Jesus used these words to show the religious leaders the praise of the children who shouted "Hosanna to the Son of David" was appropriate (see Matt. 21:16). Their praise of Jesus was ultimately prepared by the Father.

3 When I [a]consider Your heavens, the work of Your fingers,
The moon and the stars, which You have ordained,
4 [a]What is man that You are mindful of him,
And the son of man that You [b]visit him?
5 For You have made him a little lower than the angels,[1]
And You have crowned him with glory and honor.

6 [a]You have made him to have dominion over the works of Your hands;
[b]You have put all *things* under his feet,
7 All sheep and oxen—
Even the beasts of the field,
8 The birds of the air,
And the fish of the sea
That pass through the paths of the seas.

9 [a]O LORD, our Lord,
How excellent *is* Your name in all the earth!

## PSALM 9

### PRAYER AND THANKSGIVING FOR THE LORD'S RIGHTEOUS JUDGMENTS

*To the Chief Musician. To* the tune of *"Death of the Son."*[1] *A Psalm of David.*

1 I will praise *You,* O LORD, with my whole heart;
I will tell of all Your marvelous works.
2 I will be glad and [a]rejoice in You;
I will sing praise to Your name, [b]O Most High.

3 When my enemies turn back,
They shall fall and perish at Your presence.
4 For You have maintained my right and my cause;
You sat on the throne judging in righteousness.
5 You have rebuked the nations,
You have destroyed the wicked;
You have [a]blotted out their name forever and ever.

6 O enemy, destructions are finished forever!
And you have destroyed cities;
Even their memory has [a]perished.
7 [a]But the LORD shall endure forever;
He has prepared His throne for judgment.
8 [a]He shall judge the world in righteousness,
And He shall administer judgment for the peoples in uprightness.

9 The LORD also will be a [a]refuge for the oppressed,
A refuge in times of trouble.
10 And those who [a]know Your name will put their trust in You;
For You, LORD, have not forsaken those who seek You.

11 Sing praises to the LORD, who dwells in Zion!
[a]Declare His deeds among the people.

> **9:11** For the most part, the **people** who lived in the nations surrounding Israel were sinful and corrupt, enemies of God. The miracles God performed for the Israelites often caught the attention of these other nations. Those who recognized the power of Israel's God were given an opportunity to serve Him.

**7:16** [a] Esth. 9:25 **8:title** [1] Hebrew *Al Gittith* **8:1** [a] Ps. 148:13 [b] Ps. 113:4 **8:2** [a] [1 Cor. 1:27] [b] Ps. 44:16 **8:3** [a] Ps. 111:2 **8:4** [a] Job 7:17, 18 [b] [Job 10:12] **8:5** [1] Hebrew *Elohim, God;* Septuagint, Syriac, Targum, and Jewish tradition translate as *angels.* **8:6** [a] [Gen. 1:26, 28] [b] [Heb. 2:8] **8:9** [a] Ps. 8:1 **9:title** [1] Hebrew *Muth Labben* **9:2** [a] Ps. 5:11; 104:34 [b] [Ps. 83:18; 92:1] **9:5** [a] Prov. 10:7 **9:6** [a] [Ps. 34:16] **9:7** [a] Heb. 1:11 **9:8** [a] [Ps. 96:13; 98:9] **9:9** [a] Ps. 32:7; 46:1; 91:2 **9:10** [a] Ps. 91:14 **9:11** [a] Ps. 66:16; 107:22

12 [a]When He avenges blood, He remembers
them;
He does not forget the cry of the humble.

13 Have mercy on me, O LORD!
Consider my trouble from those who
hate me,
You who lift me up from the gates of
death,
14 That I may tell of all Your praise
In the gates of the daughter of Zion.
I will [a]rejoice in Your salvation.

15 [a]The nations have sunk down in the pit
*which* they made;
In the net which they hid, their own foot
is caught.
16 The LORD is [a]known *by* the judgment He
executes;
The wicked is snared in the work of his
own hands.
[b]Meditation.[1] *Selah*

17 The wicked shall be turned into hell,
*And* all the nations [a]that forget God.
18 [a]For the needy shall not always be forgotten;
[b]The expectation of the poor shall *not*
perish forever.

19 Arise, O LORD,
Do not let man prevail;
Let the nations be judged in Your sight.
20 Put them in fear, O LORD,
*That* the nations may know themselves *to
be but* men. *Selah*

## *PSALM 10*

### *A SONG OF CONFIDENCE IN GOD'S TRIUMPH OVER EVIL*

1 Why do You stand afar off, O LORD?
*Why* do You hide in times of trouble?
2 The wicked in *his* pride persecutes the
poor;
[a]Let them be caught in the plots which
they have devised.

3 For the wicked [a]boasts of his heart's
desire;
He [b]blesses the greedy *and* renounces the
LORD.
4 The wicked in his proud countenance
does not seek *God;*
God *is* in none of his [a]thoughts.

5 His ways are always prospering;
Your judgments *are* far above, out of his
sight;
*As for* all his enemies, he sneers at them.
6 [a]He has said in his heart, "I shall not be
moved;
[b]I shall never be in adversity."
7 [a]His mouth is full of cursing and [b]deceit
and oppression;
Under his tongue *is* trouble and iniquity.

8 He sits in the lurking places of the villages;
In the secret places he murders the
innocent;
His eyes are secretly fixed on the helpless.
9 He lies in wait secretly, as a lion in his den;
He lies in wait to catch the poor;
He catches the poor when he draws him
into his net.

**10:9** People in the ancient Near East continually faced the danger of **lion** attacks. The animals were known to spring from their hiding places among the thickets near the Jordan River to pounce on people passing by.

10 So he crouches, he lies low,
That the helpless may fall by his strength.
11 He has said in his heart,
"God has forgotten;
He hides His face;
He will never see."

12 Arise, O LORD!
O God, [a]lift up Your hand!
Do not forget the [b]humble.
13 Why do the wicked renounce God?
He has said in his heart,
"You will not require *an account.*"
14 But You have [a]seen, for You observe
trouble and grief,
To repay *it* by Your hand.
The helpless [b]commits himself to You;
[c]You are the helper of the fatherless.
15 Break the arm of the wicked and the evil
*man;*
Seek out his wickedness *until* You find
none.

16 [a]The LORD *is* King forever and ever;
The nations have perished out of His land.
17 LORD, You have heard the desire of the
humble;
You will prepare their heart;
You will cause Your ear to hear,
18 To do justice to the fatherless and the
oppressed,
That the man of the earth may oppress no
more.

9:12 [a] [Ps. 72:14] 9:14 [a] Ps. 13:5; 20:5; 35:9 9:15 [a] Ps. 7:15, 16 9:16 [a] Ex. 7:5 [b] Ps. 92:3 [1] Hebrew *Higgaion* 9:17 [a] Job 8:13 9:18 [a] Ps. 9:12; 12:5 [b] Prov. 23:18 10:2 [a] Ps. 7:16; 9:16 10:3 [a] Ps. 49:6; 94:3, 4 [b] Prov. 28:4 10:4 [a] Ps. 14:1; 36:1 10:6 [a] [Eccl. 8:11] [b] Rev. 18:7 10:7 [a] [Rom. 3:14] [b] Ps. 55:10, 11 10:12 [a] Mic. 5:9 [b] Ps. 9:12 10:14 [a] [Ps. 11:4] [b] [2 Tim. 1:12] [c] Ps. 68:5 10:16 [a] Ps. 29:10

## PSALM 11

### FAITH IN THE LORD'S RIGHTEOUSNESS

*To the Chief Musician. A Psalm of David.*

1 In [a]the LORD I put my trust;
How can you say to my soul,
"Flee *as* a bird to your mountain"?
2 For look! [a]The wicked bend *their* bow,
They make ready their arrow on the string,
That they may shoot secretly at the
upright in heart.
3 [a]If the foundations are destroyed,
What can the righteous do?

4 The LORD *is* in His holy temple,
The LORD's [a]throne *is* in heaven;
[b]His eyes behold,
His eyelids test the sons of men.
5 The LORD [a]tests the righteous,
But the wicked and the one who loves
violence His soul hates.
6 Upon the wicked He will rain coals;
Fire and brimstone and a burning wind
[a]*Shall be* the portion of their cup.

7 For the LORD *is* righteous,
He [a]loves righteousness;
His countenance beholds the upright.[1]

## PSALM 12

### MAN'S TREACHERY AND GOD'S CONSTANCY

*To the Chief Musician. [a]On an eight-stringed harp.[1] A Psalm of David.*

1 Help, LORD, for the godly man [a]ceases!
For the faithful disappear from among
the sons of men.
2 [a]They speak idly everyone with his neighbor;
*With* flattering lips *and* a double heart
they speak.

3 May the LORD cut off all flattering lips,
*And* the tongue that speaks proud things,
4 Who have said,
"With our tongue we will prevail;
Our lips *are* our own;
Who *is* lord over us?"

5 "For the oppression of the poor, for the
sighing of the needy,
Now I will arise," says the LORD;
"I will set *him* in the safety for which he
yearns."

6 The words of the LORD *are* [a]pure words,
*Like* silver tried in a furnace of earth,
Purified seven times.

> **12:6 Silver** is found in rocks made of lead ore. To get the silver from the rock, it is heated to extreme temperatures. Then, this intense heating process is repeated, each time making increasingly **purified** silver.

7 You shall keep them, O LORD,
You shall preserve them from this
generation forever.

8 The wicked prowl on every side,
When vileness is exalted among the sons
of men.

## PSALM 13

### TRUST IN THE SALVATION OF THE LORD

*To the Chief Musician. A Psalm of David.*

1 How long, O LORD? Will You forget me
forever?
[a]How long will You hide Your face from me?
2 How long shall I take counsel in my soul,
*Having* sorrow in my heart daily?
How long will my enemy be exalted over me?

3 Consider *and* hear me, O LORD my God;
[a]Enlighten my eyes,
[b]Lest I sleep the *sleep of* death;
4 Lest my enemy say,
"I have prevailed against him";
*Lest* those who trouble me rejoice when I
am moved.

5 But I have trusted in Your mercy;
My heart shall rejoice in Your salvation.
6 I will sing to the LORD,
Because He has dealt bountifully with me.

## PSALM 14

### FOLLY OF THE GODLESS, AND GOD'S FINAL TRIUMPH

*(Ps. 53:1–6)*
*To the Chief Musician. A Psalm of David.*

1 The [a]fool has said in his heart,
"*There is* no God."
They are corrupt,
They have done abominable works,
There is none who does good.

2 [a]The LORD looks down from heaven upon
the children of men,
To see if there are any who understand,
who seek God.

**11:1** [a]Ps. 56:11 **11:2** [a]Ps. 64:3, 4 **11:3** [a]Ps. 82:5; 87:1; 119:152 **11:4** [a][Is. 66:1] [b][Ps. 33:18; 34:15, 16] **11:5** [a]Gen. 22:1 **11:6** [a]Ps. 75:8 **11:7** [a]Ps. 33:5; 45:7 [1]Or *The upright beholds His countenance* **12:title** [a]Ps. 6:title [1]Hebrew *Sheminith* **12:1** [a][Is. 57:1] **12:2** [a]Ps. 10:7; 41:6 **12:6** [a]2 Sam. 22:31; Ps. 18:30; 119:140 **13:1** [a]Job 13:24 **13:3** [a]Ezra 9:8 [b]Jer. 51:39 **14:1** [a]Ps. 10:4; 53:1 **14:2** [a]Ps. 33:13, 14; 102:19

3 [a]They have all turned aside,
They have together become corrupt;
*There is* none who does good,
No, not one.

4 Have all the workers of iniquity no knowledge,
Who eat up my people *as* they eat bread,
And [a]do not call on the LORD?
5 There they are in great fear,
For God *is* with the generation of the righteous.
6 You shame the counsel of the poor,
But the LORD *is* his [a]refuge.
7 [a]Oh, that the salvation of Israel *would come* out of Zion!
[b]When the LORD brings back the captivity of His people,
Let Jacob rejoice *and* Israel be glad.

## PSALM 15

### THE CHARACTER OF THOSE WHO MAY DWELL WITH THE LORD

*A Psalm of David.*

1 LORD, [a]who may abide in Your tabernacle?
Who may dwell in Your holy hill?

2 He who walks uprightly,
And works righteousness,
And speaks the [a]truth in his heart;

**SEEING JESUS IN THE SCRIPTURE**

**15:1–2** The person who may come into God's presence must be righteous and pure in heart. When we trust in Jesus, we are forgiven of our sins and declared righteous by God (see 2 Cor. 5:21). Thus, we're always welcome in God's presence.

3 He *who* [a]does not backbite with his tongue,
Nor does evil to his neighbor,
[b]Nor does he take up a reproach against his friend;
4 [a]In whose eyes a vile person is despised,
But he honors those who fear the LORD;
He *who* [b]swears to his own hurt and does not change;
5 He *who* does not put out his money at usury,
Nor does he take a bribe against the innocent.

He who does these *things* [a]shall never be moved.

## PSALM 16

### THE HOPE OF THE FAITHFUL, AND THE MESSIAH'S VICTORY

*A [a]Michtam of David.*

1 Preserve me, O God, for in You I put my trust.

2 *O my soul,* you have said to the LORD,
"You *are* my Lord,
[a]My goodness is nothing apart from You."
3 As for the saints who *are* on the earth,
"They are the excellent ones, in [a]whom is all my delight."

4 Their sorrows shall be multiplied who hasten *after* another *god;*
Their drink offerings of [a]blood I will not offer,
[b]Nor take up their names on my lips.

5 O LORD, *You are* the portion of my inheritance and my cup;
You maintain my lot.
6 The lines have fallen to me in pleasant *places;*
Yes, I have a good inheritance.

7 I will bless the LORD who has given me counsel;
My heart also instructs me in the night seasons.
8 [a]I have set the LORD always before me;
Because *He is* at my right hand I shall not be moved.

9 Therefore my heart is glad, and my glory rejoices;
My flesh also will rest in hope.
10 [a]For You will not leave my soul in Sheol,
Nor will You allow Your Holy One to see corruption.

**SEEING JESUS IN THE SCRIPTURE**

**16:10** This is a Messianic prophecy about Jesus, not a description of what happened to David who indeed died and was buried in the ground. Jesus died and was buried for three days, but the grave couldn't hold Him (see Acts 2:29–32).

11 You will show me the [a]path of life;
In Your presence *is* fullness of joy;
At Your right hand *are* pleasures forevermore.

**14:3** [a] Rom. 3:12 **14:4** [a] Is. 64:7 **14:6** [a] Ps. 9:9; 40:17; 46:1; 142:5 **14:7** [a] Ps. 53:6 [b] Job 42:10 **15:1** [a] Ps. 24:3–5 **15:2** [a] [Eph. 4:25] **15:3** [a] [Lev. 19:16–18] [b] Ex. 23:1 **15:4** [a] Esth. 3:2 [b] Lev. 5:4 **15:5** [a] 2 Pet. 1:10 **16:title** [a] Ps. 56—60 **16:2** [a] Job 35:7 **16:3** [a] Ps. 119:63 **16:4** [a] Ps. 106:37, 38 [b] [Ex. 23:13] **16:8** [a] [Acts 2:25–28] **16:10** [a] Ps. 49:15; 86:13 **16:11** [a] [Matt. 7:14]

APPLY THE TRUTH

## FREEDOM

**16:1–11** What is freedom? This word conjures up many different definitions or pictures. Maybe a wild horse on the open plains? A ship at sea? Maybe you think of the ability to do whatever you want whenever you want? This is often how people think of freedom—that freedom is the absence of restraints. What we see in the Bible, though, is living without restraints leads to *bondage*, not freedom. When people do whatever is right in their own eyes, it leads to brokenness and despair.

The psalmist says real freedom is found through voluntary obedience, through submission. By living according to the boundaries God has placed, we find genuine freedom and true joy. It's like an athlete playing a sport. There's great freedom to express yourself, have fun, and do your best, but it all must be done according to the rules. The rules aren't restricting but liberating to play the game. Real freedom is found through living in the right boundaries that produce the most liberating life. When we choose to live in obedience to God and His Word, it creates a life of satisfying, lasting freedom.

## PSALM 17

### PRAYER WITH CONFIDENCE IN FINAL SALVATION

*A Prayer of David.*

1 Hear a just cause, O LORD,
Attend to my cry;
Give ear to my prayer *which is* not from deceitful lips.
2 Let my vindication come from Your presence;
Let Your eyes look on the things that are upright.

3 You have tested my heart;
You have visited *me* in the night;
[a]You have tried me and have found nothing;
I have purposed that my mouth shall not [b]transgress.
4 Concerning the works of men,
By the word of Your lips,
I have kept away from the paths of the destroyer.
5 [a]Uphold my steps in Your paths,
*That* my footsteps may not slip.

6 [a]I have called upon You, for You will hear me, O God;
Incline Your ear to me, *and* hear my speech.
7 Show Your marvelous lovingkindness by Your right hand,
O You who save those who trust *in You*
From those who rise up *against them.*
8 Keep me as the apple of Your eye;
Hide me under the shadow of Your wings,
9 From the wicked who oppress me,
*From* my deadly enemies who surround me.
10 They have closed up their [a]fat *hearts;*
With their mouths they [b]speak proudly.
11 They have now surrounded us in our steps;
They have set their eyes, crouching down to the earth,
12 As a lion is eager to tear his prey,
And like a young lion lurking in secret places.

13 Arise, O LORD,
Confront him, cast him down;
Deliver my life from the wicked with Your sword,
14 With Your hand from men, O LORD,
From men of the world *who have* their portion in *this* life,
And whose belly You fill with Your hidden treasure.
They are satisfied with children,
And leave the rest of their *possession* for their babes.

15 As for me, [a]I will see Your face in righteousness;
[b]I shall be satisfied when I [c]awake in Your likeness.

**17:8** The **eye**, one of the most sensitive and precious parts of the human body, comes equipped with its own protector, the eyelid. The eyelid instinctively closes anytime it senses danger to the eye. The eyelid "shelters" this vital organ just as a mother hen shelters her chicks beneath her **wings**.

**17:3** [a] Job 23:10 [b] Ps. 39:1 **17:5** [a] Ps. 44:18; 119:133 **17:6** [a] Ps. 86:7; 116:2 **17:10** [a] Ezek. 16:49 [b] [1 Sam. 2:3] **17:15** [a] [1 John 3:2] [b] Ps. 4:6, 7; 16:11 [c] [Is. 26:19]

## PSALM 18

### GOD THE SOVEREIGN SAVIOR

*(2 Sam. 22:1–51)*

*To the Chief Musician. A Psalm of David [a]the servant of the LORD, who spoke to the LORD the words of [b]this song on the day that the LORD delivered him from the hand of all his enemies and from the hand of Saul. And he said:*

1 I [a]will love You, O LORD, my strength.
2 The LORD is my rock and my fortress and my deliverer;
My God, my strength, [a]in whom I will trust;
My shield and the horn of my salvation, my stronghold.
3 I will call upon the LORD, [a]*who is worthy* to be praised;
So shall I be saved from my enemies.

4 [a]The pangs of death surrounded me,
And the floods of ungodliness made me afraid.
5 The sorrows of Sheol surrounded me;
The snares of death confronted me.
6 In my distress I called upon the LORD,
And cried out to my God;
He heard my voice from His temple,
And my cry came before Him, *even* to His ears.

7 [a]Then the earth shook and trembled;
The foundations of the hills also quaked and were shaken,
Because He was angry.
8 Smoke went up from His nostrils,
And devouring fire from His mouth;
Coals were kindled by it.
9 [a]He bowed the heavens also, and came down
With darkness under His feet.
10 [a]And He rode upon a cherub, and flew;
[b]He flew upon the wings of the wind.
11 He made darkness His secret place;
[a]His canopy around Him *was* dark waters
*And* thick clouds of the skies.
12 [a]From the brightness before Him,
His thick clouds passed with hailstones and coals of fire.

13 The LORD thundered from heaven,
And the Most High uttered [a]His voice,
Hailstones and coals of fire.[1]
14 [a]He sent out His arrows and scattered the foe,
Lightnings in abundance, and He vanquished them.
15 Then the channels of the sea were seen,
The foundations of the world were uncovered
At Your rebuke, O LORD,
At the blast of the breath of Your nostrils.

16 [a]He sent from above, He took me;
He drew me out of many waters.
17 He delivered me from my strong enemy,
From those who hated me,
For they were too strong for me.
18 They confronted me in the day of my calamity,
But the LORD was my support.
19 [a]He also brought me out into a broad place;
He delivered me because He delighted in me.

20 [a]The LORD rewarded me according to my righteousness;
According to the cleanness of my hands
He has recompensed me.
21 For I have kept the ways of the LORD,
And have not wickedly departed from my God.
22 For all His judgments *were* before me,
And I did not put away His statutes from me.
23 I was also blameless before Him,
And I kept myself from my iniquity.
24 [a]Therefore the LORD has recompensed me according to my righteousness,
According to the cleanness of my hands in His sight.

25 [a]With the merciful You will show Yourself merciful;
With a blameless man You will show Yourself blameless;
26 With the pure You will show Yourself pure;
And [a]with the devious You will show Yourself shrewd.
27 For You will save the humble people,
But will bring down [a]haughty looks.

28 [a]For You will light my lamp;
The LORD my God will enlighten my darkness.
29 For by You I can run against a troop,
By my God I can leap over a wall.
30 *As for* God, [a]His way *is* perfect;
[b]The word of the LORD is proven;
He *is* a shield [c]to all who trust in Him.

31 [a]For who *is* God, except the LORD?
And who *is* a rock, except our God?
32 *It is* God who [a]arms me with strength,
And makes my way perfect.

**18:title** [a] Ps. 36:title [b] 2 Sam. 22 **18:1** [a] Ps. 144:1 **18:2** [a] Heb. 2:13 **18:3** [a] Rev. 5:12 **18:4** [a] Ps. 116:3 **18:7** [a] Acts 4:31 **18:9** [a] Ps. 144:5 **18:10** [a] Ps. 80:1; 99:1 [b] [Ps. 104:3] **18:11** [a] Ps. 97:2 **18:12** [a] Ps. 97:3; 140:10 **18:13** [a] [Ps. 29:3–9; 104:7] [1] Following Masoretic Text, Targum, and Vulgate; a few Hebrew manuscripts and Septuagint omit *Hailstones and coals of fire.* **18:14** [a] Ps. 144:6 **18:16** [a] Ps. 144:7 **18:19** [a] Ps. 4:1; 31:8; 118:5 **18:20** [a] 1 Sam. 24:19 **18:24** [a] 1 Sam. 26:23 **18:25** [a] [1 Kin. 8:32] **18:26** [a] [Lev. 26:23–28] **18:27** [a] [Ps. 101:5] **18:28** [a] Job 18:6 **18:30** [a] Rev. 15:3 [b] Ps. 12:6; 119:140 [c] [Ps. 17:7] **18:31** [a] [1 Sam. 2:2] **18:32** [a] [Ps. 91:2]

KNOW THE TRUTH

# THE DOCTRINE OF GOD

## PART 16: THE PERFECTION OF GOD

**18:30** David longed for what is lovely, good, and right. Yet, he had many flaws and weaknesses. He was in constant conflict with various warriors and government officials who were often far more flawed than him. He yearned for something wholesome, yet he was filled with and surrounded by brokenness. There was one exception, though. On the day the last of his enemies fell, David wrote a long song to the only One he knew is flawless. In Psalm 18:30, David declared God's way to be *perfect*, meaning it's whole, complete, faultless, and lacking nothing.

God's way is not just perfect; He is perfect in His nature. He is completely complete. He has no flaws, weaknesses, limitations, or deficiencies. All that He is, He is entirely and eternally. God is perfect beauty. He is the standard by which all other beauty is specified and measured. God is perfect goodness. There is nothing He thinks, says, or does that isn't wholly good to its furthest possible extent. God is perfect righteousness. Every metric of right and wrong only has meaning in reference to God.

David declared God's way to be perfect because the Lord had delivered him from *all* his enemies. When God does something, including rescuing humanity, He's not done until everything undone is *fully* done.

*For* **THE DOCTRINE OF GOD: PART 17: THE IMMUTABILITY OF GOD,** *turn to Hebrews 13:8 on page 1257.* • • •

33 [a]He makes my feet like the *feet of* deer,
And [b]sets me on my high places.
34 [a]He teaches my hands to make war,
So that my arms can bend a bow of bronze.
35 You have also given me the shield of Your salvation;
Your right hand has held me up,
Your gentleness has made me great.
36 You enlarged my path under me,
[a]So my feet did not slip.

37 I have pursued my enemies and overtaken them;
Neither did I turn back again till they were destroyed.
38 I have wounded them,
So that they could not rise;
They have fallen under my feet.
39 For You have armed me with strength for the battle;
You have subdued under me those who rose up against me.
40 You have also given me the necks of my enemies,
So that I destroyed those who hated me.
41 They cried out, but *there was* none to save;
[a]*Even* to the LORD, but He did not answer them.
42 Then I beat them as fine as the dust before the wind;
I [a]cast them out like dirt in the streets.

43 You have delivered me from the strivings of the people;
[a]You have made me the head of the nations;
[b]A people I have not known shall serve me.
44 As soon as they hear of me they obey me;
The foreigners submit to me.
45 [a]The foreigners fade away,
And come frightened from their hideouts.

46 The LORD lives!
Blessed *be* my Rock!
Let the God of my salvation be exalted.
47 *It is* God who avenges me,
[a]And subdues the peoples under me;
48 He delivers me from my enemies.
[a]You also lift me up above those who rise against me;
You have delivered me from the violent man.
49 [a]Therefore I will give thanks to You, O LORD, among the Gentiles,
And sing praises to Your name.

50 [a]Great deliverance He gives to His king,
And shows mercy to His anointed,
To David and his descendants forevermore.

**18:33** [a] Hab. 3:19 [b] Deut. 32:13; 33:29 **18:34** [a] Ps. 144:1 **18:36** [a] Prov. 4:12 **18:41** [a] Job 27:9 **18:42** [a] Zech. 10:5 **18:43** [a] 2 Sam. 8 [b] Is. 52:15 **18:45** [a] Mic. 7:17 **18:47** [a] Ps. 47:3 **18:48** [a] Ps. 27:6; 59:1 **18:49** [a] Rom. 15:9 **18:50** [a] Ps. 21:1; 144:10

## PSALM 19

### THE PERFECT REVELATION OF THE LORD

*To the Chief Musician. A Psalm of David.*

1 The [a]heavens declare the glory of God;
And the [b]firmament shows His handiwork.
2 Day unto day utters speech,
And night unto night reveals knowledge.
3 *There is* no speech nor language
*Where* their voice is not heard.
4 [a]Their line[1] has gone out through all the earth,
And their words to the end of the world.

In them He has set a tabernacle for the sun,
5 Which *is* like a bridegroom coming out of his chamber,
[a]*And* rejoices like a strong man to run its race.
6 Its rising *is* from one end of heaven,
And its circuit to the other end;
And there is nothing hidden from its heat.

7 [a]The law of the LORD *is* perfect, converting the soul;
The testimony of the LORD *is* sure, making [b]wise the simple;
8 The statutes of the LORD *are* right, rejoicing the heart;
The commandment of the LORD *is* pure, enlightening the eyes;
9 The fear of the LORD *is* clean, enduring forever;
The judgments of the LORD *are* true *and* righteous altogether.
10 More to be desired *are they* than [a]gold,
Yea, than much fine gold;
Sweeter also than honey and the honeycomb.
11 Moreover by them Your servant is warned,
*And* in keeping them *there is* great reward.

12 Who can understand *his* errors?
[a]Cleanse me from secret *faults.*
13 Keep back Your servant also from [a]presumptuous *sins;*
Let them not have [b]dominion over me.
Then I shall be blameless,
And I shall be innocent of great transgression.

14 [a]Let the words of my mouth and the meditation of my heart
Be acceptable in Your sight,
O LORD, my strength and my [b]Redeemer.

## PSALM 20

### THE ASSURANCE OF GOD'S SAVING WORK

*To the Chief Musician. A Psalm of David.*

1 May the LORD answer you in the day of trouble;
May the name of the God of Jacob defend you;
2 May He send you help from the sanctuary,
And strengthen you out of Zion;
3 May He remember all your offerings,
And accept your burnt sacrifice. *Selah*

4 May He grant you according to your heart's *desire,*
And [a]fulfill all your purpose.

**19:1** [a] Is. 40:22; [Rom. 1:19, 20] [b] Gen. 1:6, 7 **19:4** [a] Rom. 10:18 [1] Septuagint, Syriac, and Vulgate read *sound;* Targum reads *business.* **19:5** [a] Eccl. 1:5 **19:7** [a] Ps. 111:7; [Rom. 7:12] [b] Ps. 119:130 **19:10** [a] Ps. 119:72, 127; Prov. 8:10, 11, 19 **19:12** [a] [Ps. 51:1, 2] **19:13** [a] Num. 15:30 [b] Ps. 119:133; [Rom. 6:12–14] **19:14** [a] Ps. 51:15 [b] Ps. 31:5; Is. 47:4 **20:4** [a] Ps. 21:2

APPLY THE TRUTH

## SCIENCE

**19:1–6** The founders of the modern scientific revolution (sixteenth–seventeenth centuries) believed God placed all things into the universe, and He created the human brain with the capacity to discover what exists. Science isn't as much about inventing things as discovering things. Math, physics, aerodynamics, and medicine are all based on laws existing in our universe. As we observe these laws and hypothesize how things work, we discover the complexity and beauty of what's possible.

Some people believe science will prove God doesn't exist. Thus, some see science as an enemy of faith. But the opposite is true. Notice what the Bible says here. The heavens declare the glory of God; the earth shows His handiwork. Science simply reveals that glory and handiwork. The more we explore our universe, the more we see God's greatness. The beauty of the world, the vastness of the universe, and the complexity of our own bodies point to a Designer. Just as a building points to a talented architect or an app points to a skilled developer, scientific discovery points to a Divine Creator. Every scientific discovery should prompt deeper awe and wonder of God's greatness.

**20:5** You could tell which side was winning a battle by the **banners**, or large flags, that were raised. Armies that were winning would be able to raise their banners, unlike those being defeated. Seeing their banner raised, then, must have been a tremendous encouragement to soldiers.

5 We will rejoice in your salvation,
And in the name of our God we will set up *our* banners!
May the LORD fulfill all your petitions.

6 Now I know that the LORD saves His anointed;
He will answer him from His holy heaven
With the saving strength of His right hand.

7 Some *trust* in chariots, and some in [a]horses;
But we will remember the name of the LORD our God.
8 They have bowed down and fallen;
But we have risen and stand upright.

9 Save, LORD!
May the King answer us when we call.

## PSALM 21

### JOY IN THE SALVATION OF THE LORD

*To the Chief Musician. A Psalm of David.*

1 The king shall have joy in Your strength, O LORD;
And in Your salvation how greatly shall he rejoice!
2 You have given him his heart's desire,
And have not withheld the [a]request of his lips. *Selah*

3 For You meet him with the blessings of goodness;
You set a crown of pure gold upon his head.
4 [a]He asked life from You, *and* You gave *it* to him—
Length of days forever and ever.
5 His glory *is* great in Your salvation;
Honor and majesty You have placed upon him.
6 For You have made him most blessed forever;
[a]You have made him exceedingly glad with Your presence.
7 For the king trusts in the LORD,
And through the mercy of the Most High he shall not be moved.

8 Your hand will find all Your enemies;
Your right hand will find those who hate You.
9 You shall make them as a fiery oven in the time of Your anger;
The LORD shall swallow them up in His wrath,
And the fire shall devour them.
10 Their offspring You shall destroy from the earth,
And their descendants from among the sons of men.
11 For they intended evil against You;
They devised a plot *which* they are not able *to* [a]*perform.*
12 Therefore You will make them turn their back;
You will make ready *Your arrows* on Your string toward their faces.

13 Be exalted, O LORD, in Your own strength!
We will sing and praise Your power.

## PSALM 22

### THE SUFFERING, PRAISE, AND POSTERITY OF THE MESSIAH

*To the Chief Musician. Set to "The Deer of the Dawn."[1] A Psalm of David.*

1 My [a]God, My God, why have You forsaken Me?
*Why are You so* far from helping Me,
*And from* the words of My groaning?
2 O My God, I cry in the daytime, but You do not hear;
And in the night season, and am not silent.

**SEEING JESUS IN THE SCRIPTURE**

**22:1** With these words, David expressed a painful sense of separation from God during great trouble. On the cross, Jesus cried out these words as He bore the weight of sin, bridging our separation from God and bringing us near Him (see Mark 15:34).

3 But You *are* holy,
Enthroned in the [a]praises of Israel.
4 Our fathers trusted in You;
They trusted, and You delivered them.
5 They cried to You, and were delivered;
[a]They trusted in You, and were not ashamed.

6 But I *am* [a]a worm, and no man;
[b]A reproach of men, and despised by the people.

**20:7** [a] Deut. 20:1; Ps. 33:16, 17; Prov. 21:31; Is. 31:1 **21:2** [a] 2 Sam. 7:26–29 **21:4** [a] Ps. 61:5, 6; 133:3 **21:6** [a] Ps. 16:11; 45:7 **21:11** [a] Ps. 2:1–4 **22:title** [1] Hebrew *Aijeleth Hashahar* **22:1** [a] [Mark 15:34] **22:3** [a] Deut. 10:21 **22:5** [a] Is. 49:23 **22:6** [a] Is. 41:14 [b] [Is. 53:3]

7 [a]All those who see Me ridicule Me;
They shoot out the lip, they shake the head, *saying,*
8 "He[a] trusted[1] in the LORD, let Him rescue Him;
[b]Let Him deliver Him, since He delights in Him!"

9 [a]But You *are* He who took Me out of the womb;
You made Me trust *while* on My mother's breasts.
10 I was cast upon You from birth.
From My mother's womb
[a]You *have been* My God.
11 Be not far from Me,
For trouble *is* near;
For *there is* none to help.

12 [a]Many bulls have surrounded Me;
Strong *bulls* of [b]Bashan have encircled Me.
13 [a]They gape at Me *with* their mouths,
*Like* a raging and roaring lion.

14 I am poured out like water,
[a]And all My bones are out of joint;
My heart is like wax;
It has melted within Me.
15 [a]My strength is dried up like a potsherd,
And [b]My tongue clings to My jaws;
You have brought Me to the dust of death.

16 For dogs have surrounded Me;
The congregation of the wicked has enclosed Me.
[a]They pierced[1] My hands and My feet;

**22:16** The **dogs** of ancient Israel were more like scavengers than house pets. Traveling in packs, these wild creatures were known for attacking and killing the weak and the helpless. They ate discarded food and anything else they could find to stay alive.

17 I can count all My bones.
[a]They look *and* stare at Me.
18 [a]They divide My garments among them,
And for My clothing they cast lots.

19 But You, O LORD, do not be far from Me;
O My Strength, hasten to help Me!
20 Deliver Me from the sword,
[a]My precious *life* from the power of the dog.
21 [a]Save Me from the lion's mouth
And from the horns of the wild oxen!

[b]You have answered Me.

22 [a]I will declare Your name to [b]My brethren;
In the midst of the assembly I will praise You.
23 [a]You who fear the LORD, praise Him!
All you descendants of Jacob, glorify Him,
And fear Him, all you offspring of Israel!
24 For He has not despised nor abhorred the affliction of the afflicted;
Nor has He hidden His face from Him;
But [a]when He cried to Him, He heard.

25 [a]My praise *shall be* of You in the great assembly;
[b]I will pay My vows before those who fear Him.
26 The poor shall eat and be satisfied;
Those who seek Him will praise the LORD.
Let your heart live forever!

27 All the ends of the world
Shall remember and turn to the LORD,
And all the families of the nations
Shall worship before You.[1]
28 [a]For the kingdom *is* the LORD's,
And He rules over the nations.

29 [a]All the prosperous of the earth
Shall eat and worship;
[b]All those who go down to the dust
Shall bow before Him,
Even he who cannot keep himself alive.

30 A posterity shall serve Him.
It will be recounted of the Lord to the *next* generation,
31 They will come and declare His righteousness to a people who will be born,
That He has done *this.*

## PSALM 23

### *THE LORD THE SHEPHERD OF HIS PEOPLE*

*A Psalm of David.*

1 The LORD *is* [a]my shepherd;
[b]I shall not want.
2 [a]He makes me to lie down in green pastures;
[b]He leads me beside the still waters.

**22:7** [a] Matt. 27:39 **22:8** [a] Matt. 27:43 [b] Ps. 91:14 [1] Septuagint, Syriac, and Vulgate read *hoped;* Targum reads *praised.* **22:9** [a] [Ps. 71:5, 6] **22:10** [a] [Is. 46:3; 49:1] **22:12** [a] Ps. 22:21; 68:30 [b] Deut. 32:14 **22:13** [a] Job 16:10 **22:14** [a] Dan. 5:6 **22:15** [a] Prov. 17:22 [b] John 19:28 **22:16** [a] Matt. 27:35 [1] Following some Hebrew manuscripts, Septuagint, Syriac, Vulgate; Masoretic Text reads *Like a lion.* **22:17** [a] Luke 23:27, 35 **22:18** [a] Matt. 27:35 **22:20** [a] Ps. 35:17 **22:21** [a] 2 Tim. 4:17 [b] Is. 34:7 **22:22** [a] Heb. 2:12 [b] [Rom. 8:29] **22:23** [a] Ps. 135:19, 20 **22:24** [a] Heb. 5:7 **22:25** [a] Ps. 35:18; 40:9, 10 [b] Eccl. 5:4 **22:27** [1] Following Masoretic Text, Septuagint, and Targum; Arabic, Syriac, and Vulgate read *Him.* **22:28** [a] Matt. 6:13 **22:29** [a] Ps. 17:10; 45:12 [b] [Is. 26:19] **23:1** [a] [Is. 40:11] [b] [Phil. 4:19] **23:2** [a] Ezek. 34:14 [b] [Rev. 7:17]

3 He restores my soul;
[a]He leads me in the paths of righteousness
For His name's sake.

4 Yea, though I walk through the valley of
[a]the shadow of death,
[b]I will fear no evil;
[c]For You *are* with me;
Your rod and Your staff, they comfort me.

**23:4** A shepherd's **rod** was a stick with a hook at the end of it. With it, a shepherd could gently nudge a stray sheep back into line or, using the hook, pull a sheep from a dangerous spot. The rod was also used as a weapon to defend the flock against wolves and other predators.

5 You [a]prepare a table before me in the
presence of my enemies;
You [b]anoint my head with oil;
My cup runs over.
6 Surely goodness and mercy shall follow me
All the days of my life;
And I will dwell[1] in the house of the LORD
Forever.

## PSALM 24

### THE KING OF GLORY AND HIS KINGDOM

*A Psalm of David.*

1 The [a]earth *is* the LORD's, and all its fullness,
The world and those who dwell therein.
2 For He has [a]founded it upon the seas,
And established it upon the waters.
3 [a]Who may ascend into the hill of the LORD?
Or who may stand in His holy place?
4 He who has [a]clean hands and [b]a pure heart,
Who has not lifted up his soul to an idol,
Nor [c]sworn deceitfully.
5 He shall receive blessing from the LORD,
And righteousness from the God of his
salvation.
6 This *is* Jacob, the generation of those who
[a]seek Him,
Who seek Your face. *Selah*

7 [a]Lift up your heads, O you gates!
And be lifted up, you everlasting doors!
[b]And the King of glory shall come in.
8 Who *is* this King of glory?
The LORD strong and mighty,
The LORD mighty in [a]battle.
9 Lift up your heads, O you gates!
Lift up, you everlasting doors!
And the King of glory shall come in.
10 Who is this King of glory?
The LORD of hosts,
He *is* the King of glory. *Selah*

## PSALM 25

### A PLEA FOR DELIVERANCE AND FORGIVENESS

*A Psalm of David.*

1 To [a]You, O LORD, I lift up my soul.
2 O my God, I [a]trust in You;
Let me not be ashamed;
[b]Let not my enemies triumph over me.
3 Indeed, let no one who waits on You be
ashamed;
Let those be ashamed who deal
treacherously without cause.

**23:3** [a] Ps. 5:8; 31:3 **23:4** [a] Job 3:5; 10:21, 22; 24:17 [b] [Ps. 3:6; 27:1] [c] [Is. 43:2] **23:5** [a] Ps. 104:15 [b] Ps. 92:10 **23:6** [1] Following Septuagint, Syriac, Targum, and Vulgate; Masoretic Text reads *return.* **24:1** [a] 1 Cor. 10:26, 28 **24:2** [a] Ps. 89:11 **24:3** [a] Ps. 15:1–5 **24:4** [a] [Job 17:9] [b] [Matt. 5:8] [c] Ps. 15:4 **24:6** [a] Ps. 27:4, 8 **24:7** [a] Is. 26:2 [b] Ps. 29:2, 9; 97:6 **24:8** [a] Rev. 19:13–16 **25:1** [a] Ps. 86:4; 143:8 **25:2** [a] Ps. 34:8 [b] Ps. 13:4; 41:11

APPLY THE TRUTH

## THE ENVIRONMENT

**24:1–10** In the Bible, *world* typically means one of three things: humanity, the universe, and human ways. The latter describes people organizing themselves apart from God in opposition to Him. This is the "world" we are warned against. God, however, loves humanity and His creation. We see this from the beginning. God created the universe, and He called it good. God created humanity, and He called us good. God placed humanity on the earth as His image bearers to steward and cultivate the earth that He loves. In other words, God cares about the environment, and He placed us on the earth as the crown of His creation to enjoy and take care of His creation.

In this psalm, David has a good grasp of this. The earth and all who dwell upon it belong to the Lord. As such, we can partner with God for the renewal of the world. This happens primarily through spreading the gospel. When people know their Creator, it gives them a desire to be good stewards of His creation. God loves the world! He loves lost humanity and wants to save them, and He loves His creation and calls us to take care of it.

4 [a]Show me Your ways, O LORD;
Teach me Your paths.
5 Lead me in Your truth and teach me,
For You *are* the God of my salvation;
On You I wait all the day.

6 Remember, O LORD, [a]Your tender mercies
and Your lovingkindnesses,
For they *are* from of old.
7 Do not remember [a]the sins of my youth,
nor my transgressions;
[b]According to Your mercy
remember me,
For Your goodness' sake, O LORD.

8 Good and upright *is* the LORD;
Therefore He teaches sinners in the
way.
9 The humble He guides in justice,
And the humble He teaches His way.
10 All the paths of the LORD *are* mercy and
truth,
To such as keep His covenant and His
testimonies.
11 [a]For Your name's sake, O LORD,
Pardon my iniquity, for it *is* great.

12 Who *is* the man that fears the LORD?
[a]Him shall He[1] teach in the way He[2]
chooses.
13 [a]He himself shall dwell in prosperity,
And [b]his descendants shall inherit the
earth.
14 [a]The secret of the LORD *is* with those who
fear Him,
And He will show them His covenant.
15 [a]My eyes *are* ever toward the LORD,
For He shall pluck my feet out of the net.

16 [a]Turn Yourself to me, and have mercy
on me,
For I *am* desolate and afflicted.
17 The troubles of my heart have enlarged;
Bring me out of my distresses!
18 [a]Look on my affliction and my pain,
And forgive all my sins.
19 Consider my enemies, for they are
many;
And they hate me with cruel hatred.
20 Keep my soul, and deliver me;
Let me not be ashamed, for I put my trust
in You.
21 Let integrity and uprightness
preserve me,
For I wait for You.

22 [a]Redeem Israel, O God,
Out of all their troubles!

## PSALM 26

### A PRAYER FOR DIVINE SCRUTINY AND REDEMPTION

A Psalm *of David.*

1 Vindicate [a]me, O LORD,
For I have [b]walked in my integrity.
[c]I have also trusted in the LORD;
I shall not slip.
2 [a]Examine me, O LORD, and prove me;
Try my mind and my heart.
3 For Your lovingkindness *is* before my eyes,
And [a]I have walked in Your truth.
4 I have not [a]sat with idolatrous mortals,
Nor will I go in with hypocrites.
5 I have [a]hated the assembly of evildoers,
And will not sit with the wicked.

6 I will wash my hands in innocence;
So I will go about Your altar, O LORD,
7 That I may proclaim with the voice of
thanksgiving,
And tell of all Your wondrous works.
8 LORD, [a]I have loved the habitation of Your
house,
And the place where Your glory dwells.

9 [a]Do not gather my soul with sinners,
Nor my life with bloodthirsty men,
10 In whose hands *is* a sinister scheme,
And whose right hand is full of [a]bribes.

11 But as for me, I will walk in my integrity;
Redeem me and be merciful to me.
12 [a]My foot stands in an even place;
In the congregations I will bless the LORD.

## PSALM 27

### AN EXUBERANT DECLARATION OF FAITH

A Psalm *of David.*

1 The LORD *is* my [a]light and my salvation;
Whom shall I fear?
The [b]LORD *is* the strength of my life;
Of whom shall I be afraid?
2 When the wicked came against me
To [a]eat up my flesh,
My enemies and foes,
They stumbled and fell.
3 [a]Though an army may encamp against me,
My heart shall not fear;
Though war may rise against me,
In this I *will be* confident.

4 [a]One *thing* I have desired of the LORD,
That will I seek:

**25:4** [a] Ex. 33:13 **25:6** [a] Ps. 103:17; 106:1 **25:7** [a] [Jer. 3:25] [b] Ps. 51:1 **25:11** [a] Ps. 31:3; 79:9; 109:21; 143:11 **25:12** [a] [Ps. 25:8; 37:23] [1] Or *he* [2] Or *he* **25:13** [a] [Prov. 19:23] [b] Matt. 5:5 **25:14** [a] [John 7:17] **25:15** [a] [Ps. 123:2; 141:8] **25:16** [a] Ps. 69:16 **25:18** [a] 2 Sam. 16:12 **25:22** [a] [Ps. 130:8] **26:1** [a] Ps. 7:8 [b] 2 Kin. 20:3 [c] [Ps. 13:5; 28:7] **26:2** [a] Ps. 17:3; 139:23 **26:3** [a] 2 Kin. 20:3 **26:4** [a] Ps. 1:1 **26:5** [a] Ps. 31:6; 139:21 **26:8** [a] Ps. 27:4; 84:1–4, 10 **26:9** [a] Ps. 28:3 **26:10** [a] 1 Sam. 8:3 **26:12** [a] Ps. 40:2 **27:1** [a] [Mic. 7:8] [b] Ps. 62:7; 118:14 **27:2** [a] Ps. 14:4 **27:3** [a] Ps. 3:6 **27:4** [a] Ps. 26:8; 65:4

That I may [b]dwell in the house of the LORD
All the days of my life,
To behold the beauty of the LORD,
And to inquire in His temple.
5 For [a]in the time of trouble
He shall hide me in His pavilion;
In the secret place of His tabernacle
He shall hide me;
He shall [b]set me high upon a rock.

6 And now [a]my head shall be lifted up
above my enemies all around me;
Therefore I will offer sacrifices of joy in
His tabernacle;
I will sing, yes, I will sing praises to the
LORD.

7 Hear, O LORD, *when* I cry with my voice!
Have mercy also upon me, and answer me.
8 *When You said,* "Seek My face,"
My heart said to You, "Your face, LORD, I
will seek."
9 [a]Do not hide Your face from me;
Do not turn Your servant away in anger;
You have been my help;
Do not leave me nor forsake me,
O God of my salvation.
10 [a]When my father and my mother forsake me,
Then the LORD will take care of me.

11 [a]Teach me Your way, O LORD,
And lead me in a smooth path, because of
my enemies.
12 Do not deliver me to the will of my
adversaries;
For [a]false witnesses have risen against me,
And such as breathe out violence.

**SEEING JESUS IN THE SCRIPTURE**

**27:12** David prayed for deliverance from his adversaries who lied and sought evil against him. Jesus eventually stood before His accusers who bore false witness against Him (see Matt. 26:60). Jesus didn't seek His own deliverance but remained silent so we could be delivered.

13 *I would have lost heart,* unless I had
believed
That I would see the goodness of the LORD
[a]In the land of the living.

14 [a]Wait on the LORD;
Be of good courage,
And He shall strengthen your heart;
Wait, I say, on the LORD!

## PSALM 28

### REJOICING IN ANSWERED PRAYER

A Psalm *of David.*

1 To You I will cry, O LORD my Rock:
[a]Do not be silent to me,
[b]Lest, if You *are* silent to me,
I become like those who go down to the
pit.
2 Hear the voice of my supplications
When I cry to You,
[a]When I lift up my hands [b]toward Your
holy sanctuary.

3 Do not take me away with the
wicked
And with the workers of iniquity,
[a]Who speak peace to their neighbors,
But evil *is* in their hearts.
4 [a]Give them according to their deeds,
And according to the wickedness of their
endeavors;
Give them according to the work of their
hands;
Render to them what they deserve.
5 Because [a]they do not regard the works of
the LORD,
Nor the operation of His hands,
He shall destroy them
And not build them up.

6 Blessed *be* the LORD,
Because He has heard the voice of my
supplications!
7 The LORD *is* [a]my strength and my
shield;
My heart [b]trusted in Him, and I am
helped;
Therefore my heart greatly rejoices,
And with my song I will praise
Him.

**28:7** Because few ancient armies wore body armor, a **shield** was the only defense a soldier had against enemy arrows and swords. These shields came in all shapes and sizes, and could be made of leather, wood, or metal.

8 The LORD *is* their strength,[1]
And He *is* the [a]saving refuge of His
anointed.
9 Save Your people,
And bless [a]Your inheritance;
Shepherd them also,
[b]And bear them up forever.

**27:4** [b] Luke 2:37 **27:5** [a] Ps. 31:20; 91:1 [b] Ps. 40:2 **27:6** [a] Ps. 3:3 **27:9** [a] Ps. 69:17; 143:7 **27:10** [a] Is. 49:15 **27:11** [a] Ps. 25:4; 86:11; 119:33 **27:12** [a] Ps. 35:11 **27:13** [a] Ezek. 26:20 **27:14** [a] Is. 25:9 **28:1** [a] Ps. 35:22; 39:12; 83:1 [b] Ps. 88:4; 143:7 **28:2** [a] Ps. 5:7 [b] Ps. 138:2 **28:3** [a] Ps. 12:2; 55:21; 62:4 **28:4** [a] [Rev. 18:6; 22:12] **28:5** [a] Is. 5:12 **28:7** [a] Ps. 18:2; 59:17 [b] Ps. 13:5; 112:7 **28:8** [a] Ps. 20:6 [1] Following Masoretic Text and Targum; Septuagint, Syriac, and Vulgate read *the strength of His people.* **28:9** [a] [Deut. 9:29; 32:9] [b] Deut. 1:31

## PSALM 29

### PRAISE TO GOD IN HIS HOLINESS AND MAJESTY

*A Psalm of David.*

1 Give [a]unto the LORD, O you mighty ones,
Give unto the LORD glory and strength.
2 Give unto the LORD the glory due to His
name;
Worship the LORD in [a]the beauty of
holiness.

3 The voice of the LORD *is* over the waters;
[a]The God of glory thunders;
The LORD *is* over many waters.
4 The voice of the LORD *is* powerful;
The voice of the LORD *is* full of majesty.

5 The voice of the LORD breaks [a]the cedars,
Yes, the LORD splinters the cedars of
Lebanon.
6 [a]He makes them also skip like a calf,
Lebanon and [b]Sirion like a young wild ox.
7 The voice of the LORD divides the flames
of fire.
8 The voice of the LORD shakes the
wilderness;
The LORD shakes the Wilderness of
[a]Kadesh.
9 The voice of the LORD makes the [a]deer
give birth,
And strips the forests bare;
And in His temple everyone says,
"Glory!"

10 The [a]LORD sat *enthroned* at the Flood,
And [b]the LORD sits as King forever.
11 [a]The LORD will give strength to His people;
The LORD will bless His people with
peace.

## PSALM 30

### THE BLESSEDNESS OF ANSWERED PRAYER

*A Psalm. A Song [a]at the dedication of the house of David.*

1 I will extol You, O LORD, for You have
[a]lifted me up,
And have not let my foes [b]rejoice over me.
2 O LORD my God, I cried out to You,
And You [a]healed me.
3 O LORD, [a]You brought my soul up from
the grave;
You have kept me alive, that I should not
go down to the pit.[1]

4 [a]Sing praise to the LORD, you saints of His,
And give thanks at the remembrance of
His holy name.[1]
5 For [a]His anger *is but for* a moment,
[b]His favor *is for* life;
Weeping may endure for a night,
But joy *comes* in the morning.

6 Now in my prosperity I said,
"I shall never be moved."
7 LORD, by Your favor You have made my
mountain stand strong;
[a]You hid Your face, *and* I was troubled.

8 I cried out to You, O LORD;
And to the LORD I made supplication:
9 "What profit *is there* in my blood,
When I go down to the pit?
[a]Will the dust praise You?
Will it declare Your truth?
10 Hear, O LORD, and have mercy on me;
LORD, be my helper!"

11 [a]You have turned for me my mourning
into dancing;
You have put off my sackcloth and
clothed me with gladness,
12 To the end that *my* glory may sing praise
to You and not be silent.
O LORD my God, I will give thanks to You
forever.

## PSALM 31

### THE LORD A FORTRESS IN ADVERSITY

*To the Chief Musician. A Psalm of David.*

1 In [a]You, O LORD, I put my trust;
Let me never be ashamed;
Deliver me in Your righteousness.
2 [a]Bow down Your ear to me,
Deliver me speedily;
Be my rock of refuge,
A fortress of defense to save me.

3 [a]For You *are* my rock and my fortress;
Therefore, [b]for Your name's sake,
Lead me and guide me.
4 Pull me out of the net which they have
secretly laid for me,
For You *are* my strength.
5 [a]Into Your hand I commit my spirit;
You have redeemed me, O LORD God of
[b]truth.

6 I have hated those [a]who regard useless
idols;
But I trust in the LORD.

29:1 [a] 1 Chr. 16:28, 29 29:2 [a] 2 Chr. 20:21 29:3 [a] [Job 37:4, 5] 29:5 [a] Is. 2:13; 14:8 29:6 [a] Ps. 114:4 [b] Deut. 3:9 29:8 [a] Num. 13:26 29:9 [a] Job 39:1 29:10 [a] Gen. 6:17 [b] Ps. 10:16 29:11 [a] Ps. 28:8; 68:35 30:title [a] Deut. 20:5 30:1 [a] Ps. 28:9 [b] Ps. 25:2 30:2 [a] Ps. 6:2; 103:3 30:3 [a] Ps. 86:13 [1] Following Qere and Targum; Kethib, Septuagint, Syriac, and Vulgate read *from those who descend to the pit.* 30:4 [a] Ps. 97:12 [1] Or *His holiness* 30:5 [a] Ps. 103:9 [b] Ps. 63:3 30:7 [a] [Ps. 104:29; 143:7] 30:9 [a] [Ps. 6:5] 30:11 [a] Jer. 31:4 31:1 [a] Ps. 22:5 31:2 [a] Ps. 17:6; 71:2; 86:1; 102:2 31:3 [a] [Ps. 18:2] [b] Ps. 23:3; 25:11 31:5 [a] Luke 23:46 [b] [Deut. 32:4] 31:6 [a] Jon. 2:8

7 I will be glad and rejoice in Your mercy,
For You have considered my trouble;
You have [a]known my soul in adversities,
8 And have not [a]shut me up into the hand
of the enemy;
[b]You have set my feet in a wide place.

9 Have mercy on me, O LORD, for I am in
trouble;
[a]My eye wastes away with grief,
*Yes,* my soul and my body!
10 For my life is spent with grief,
And my years with sighing;
My strength fails because of my iniquity,
And my bones waste away.
11 [a]I am a reproach among all my enemies,
But [b]especially among my neighbors,
And *am* repulsive to my acquaintances;
[c]Those who see me outside flee from me.
12 [a]I am forgotten like a dead man, out of
mind;
I am like a broken vessel.
13 [a]For I hear the slander of many;
[b]Fear *is* on every side;
While they [c]take counsel together
against me,
They scheme to take away my life.

14 But as for me, I trust in You, O LORD;
I say, "You *are* my God."
15 My times *are* in Your [a]hand;
Deliver me from the hand of my enemies,
And from those who persecute me.
16 [a]Make Your face shine upon Your servant;
Save me for Your mercies' sake.
17 [a]Do not let me be ashamed, O LORD, for I
have called upon You;
Let the wicked be ashamed;
[b]Let them be silent in the grave.
18 [a]Let the lying lips be put to silence,
Which [b]speak insolent things proudly and
contemptuously against the righteous.

19 [a]Oh, how great *is* Your goodness,
Which You have laid up for those who fear
You,
*Which* You have prepared for those who
trust in You
In the presence of the sons of men!
20 [a]You shall hide them in the secret place of
Your presence
From the plots of man;
[b]You shall keep them secretly in a pavilion
From the strife of tongues.

21 Blessed *be* the LORD,
For [a]He has shown me His marvelous
kindness in a strong city!
22 For I said in my haste,
"I am cut off from before Your eyes";
Nevertheless You heard the voice of my
supplications
When I cried out to You.

23 Oh, love the LORD, all you His saints!
*For* the LORD preserves the faithful,
And fully repays the proud person.
24 [a]Be of good courage,
And He shall strengthen your heart,
All you who hope in the LORD.

## PSALM 32

### THE JOY OF FORGIVENESS

A Psalm *of David. A Contemplation.*[1]

1 Blessed *is he whose* [a]transgression *is*
forgiven,
*Whose* sin *is* covered.
2 Blessed *is* the man to whom the LORD
[a]does not impute iniquity,
And [b]in whose spirit *there is* no
deceit.

3 When I kept silent, my bones grew old
Through my groaning all the day long.
4 For day and night Your [a]hand was heavy
upon me;
My vitality was turned into the drought of
summer. *Selah*
5 I acknowledged my sin to You,
And my iniquity I have not hidden.
[a]I said, "I will confess my transgressions to
the LORD,"
And You forgave the iniquity of my sin.
*Selah*

6 [a]For this cause everyone who is godly shall
[b]pray to You
In a time when You may be found;
Surely in a flood of great waters
They shall not come near him.
7 [a]You *are* my hiding place;
You shall preserve me from trouble;
You shall surround me with [b]songs of
deliverance. *Selah*

8 I will instruct you and teach you in the
way you should go;
I will guide you with My eye.
9 Do not be like the [a]horse *or* like the
mule,
*Which* have no understanding,
Which must be harnessed with bit and
bridle,
Else they will not come near you.

**31:7** [a] [John 10:27] **31:8** [a] [Deut. 32:30] [b] [Ps. 4:1; 18:19] **31:9** [a] Ps. 6:7 **31:11** [a] [Is. 53:4] [b] Job 19:13 [c] Ps. 64:8 **31:12** [a] Ps. 88:4, 5 **31:13** [a] Jer. 20:10 [b] Lam. 2:22 [c] Matt. 27:1 **31:15** [a] [Job 14:5; 24:1] **31:16** [a] Ps. 4:6; 80:3 **31:17** [a] Ps. 25:2, 20 [b] Ps. 94:17; 115:17 **31:18** [a] Ps. 109:2; 120:2 [b] Ps. 94:4 **31:19** [a] [Rom. 2:4; 11:22] **31:20** [a] [Ps. 27:5; 32:7] [b] Job 5:21 **31:21** [a] [Ps. 17:7] **31:24** [a] [Ps. 27:14] **32:title** [1] Hebrew *Maschil* **32:1** [a] [Ps. 85:2; 103:3] **32:2** [a] [2 Cor. 5:19] [b] John 1:47 **32:4** [a] 1 Sam. 5:6 **32:5** [a] [Prov. 28:13] **32:6** [a] [1 Tim. 1:16] [b] Is. 55:6 **32:7** [a] Ps. 9:9 [b] Ex. 15:1 **32:9** [a] Prov. 26:3

APPLY THE TRUTH

## GUILT AND SHAME

**32:1–11** Do you know that feeling when you've done something wrong and you're about to get caught? Someone says, "Can I talk to you about something?" Everything you've ever done wrong floods through your mind. This is guilt. Even if you don't *feel* guilt, you can still *be* guilty. Some criminals don't feel guilty when they're caught, but they're judged guilty all the same. Shame is different. Shame is a storyteller. It tells a story that not only have you made a mistake, but you *are* that mistake. Guilt tells you you've done something wrong; shame tells you there's something wrong with you.

This psalm teaches the freedom and happiness found through forgiveness. Happy ("blessed") are those who are forgiven and whose sins are covered. Jesus is the answer for guilt. He pleads your case, takes your punishment, and declares you innocent. Jesus is also the answer for shame. He gives you a new identity and, by His grace, writes a new story for you. We receive all this from Christ through confession and forgiveness. Acknowledge your sin to God, confess your failures to the Lord, and allow His grace to write a new story.

10 [a]Many sorrows *shall be* to the wicked;
But [b]he who trusts in the LORD, mercy
shall surround him.
11 [a]Be glad in the LORD and rejoice, you
righteous;
And shout for joy, all *you* upright in heart!

## *PSALM 33*

### *THE SOVEREIGNTY OF THE LORD IN CREATION AND HISTORY*

1 Rejoice [a]in the LORD, O you righteous!
*For* praise from the upright is beautiful.
2 Praise the LORD with the harp;
Make melody to Him with an instrument
of ten strings.

**33:2** Music played an important part of the Israelites' worship. Specific groups of Levites were assigned to sing in the choir or play in the orchestra that performed in or near the tabernacle. The orchestra was made up of stringed instruments, such as guitars and harps, as well as percussion instruments, such as tambourines and cymbals.

3 Sing to Him a new song;
Play skillfully with a shout of joy.

4 For the word of the LORD *is* right,
And all His work *is done* in truth.
5 He loves righteousness and justice;
The earth is full of the goodness of the
LORD.

6 [a]By the word of the LORD the heavens were
made,
And all the [b]host of them [c]by the breath of
His mouth.
7 [a]He gathers the waters of the sea together
as a heap;[1]
He lays up the deep in storehouses.

8 Let all the earth fear the LORD;
Let all the inhabitants of the world stand
in awe of Him.
9 For [a]He spoke, and it was *done;*
He commanded, and it stood fast.

10 [a]The LORD brings the counsel of the
nations to nothing;
He makes the plans of the peoples of no
effect.
11 [a]The counsel of the LORD stands forever,
The plans of His heart to all generations.
12 Blessed *is* the nation whose God *is* the
LORD,
The people He has [a]chosen as His own
inheritance.

13 [a]The LORD looks from heaven;
He sees all the sons of men.
14 From the place of His dwelling He looks
On all the inhabitants of the earth;
15 He fashions their hearts individually;
[a]He considers all their works.

16 [a]No king *is* saved by the multitude of an
army;
A mighty man is not delivered by great
strength.
17 [a]A horse *is* a vain hope for safety;
Neither shall it deliver *any* by its great
strength.

32:10 [a] [Rom. 2:9] [b] Prov. 16:20 32:11 [a] Ps. 64:10; 68:3; 97:12 33:1 [a] Ps. 32:11; 97:12 33:6 [a] [Heb. 11:3] [b] Gen. 2:1 [c] [Job 26:13] 33:7 [a] Job 26:10; 38:8 [1] Septuagint, Targum, and Vulgate read *in a vessel.* 33:9 [a] Gen. 1:3 33:10 [a] Is. 8:10; 19:3 33:11 [a] [Job 23:13] 33:12 [a] [Ex. 19:5] 33:13 [a] Job 28:24 33:15 [a] [Jer. 32:19] 33:16 [a] Ps. 44:6; 60:11 33:17 [a] [Prov. 21:31]

KNOW THE TRUTH

## THE DOCTRINE OF CREATION AND HUMANS

### PART 2: THE CREATION OF EVERYTHING

**33:6** When the psalmist wrote about the "heavens" and "hosts," he meant the expanse of the cosmos and its celestial bodies like galaxies, stars, and planets. The heavens and hosts haven't eternally existed, nor did they cause themselves. The universe is part of God's creation. God not only started it all, but He also sustains it all (see Col. 1:16–17). This means God holds together everything necessary for the life-permitting universe we live in. From nuclear fusion at the smallest scale of the universe to the near incalculable gravitational pull of red supergiants (the largest known stars) at the largest scale of the universe, God sustains every aspect of the cosmos.

Not only do the heavens and hosts reveal the handiwork of God, but the earth—its mountains, forests, oceans, creatures—declares His limitless creativity (see Ps. 19:1–6). At the pinnacle of His vast creation, God formed humans in His own image (see Gen. 1:26–28). What God creates, He rightfully owns and rules over. All that is made is created by God, owned and ruled over by God, and made for God's glory, honor, and joy.

*For* **THE DOCTRINE OF CREATION AND HUMANS: PART 3: THE CREATION OF ANGELS**, *turn to Psalm 103:20–21 on page 596.*

18 [a]Behold, the eye of the LORD *is* on those
who fear Him,
On those who hope in His mercy,
19 To deliver their soul from death,
And [a]to keep them alive in famine.

20 Our soul waits for the LORD;
He *is* our help and our shield.
21 For our heart shall rejoice in Him,
Because we have trusted in His holy
name.
22 Let Your mercy, O LORD, be upon us,
Just as we hope in You.

## PSALM 34

### *THE HAPPINESS OF THOSE WHO TRUST IN GOD*

A Psalm *of David* [a]*when he pretended madness before Abimelech, who drove him away, and he departed.*

1 I will [a]bless the LORD at all times;
His praise *shall* continually *be* in my
mouth.
2 My soul shall make its boast in the LORD;
The humble shall hear *of it* and be glad.
3 Oh, magnify the LORD with me,
And let us exalt His name together.

4 I [a]sought the LORD, and He heard me,
And delivered me from all my fears.
5 They looked to Him and were radiant,
And their faces were not ashamed.
6 This poor man cried out, and the LORD
heard *him,*
And saved him out of all his troubles.
7 [a]The angel[1] of the LORD [b]encamps all
around those who fear Him,
And delivers them.

8 Oh, [a]taste and see that the LORD *is* good;
[b]Blessed *is* the man *who* trusts in Him!
9 Oh, fear the LORD, you His saints!
*There is* no want to those who fear Him.
10 The young lions lack and suffer hunger;
[a]But those who seek the LORD shall not
lack any good *thing.*

11 Come, you children, listen to me;
[a]I will teach you the fear of the LORD.
12 [a]Who *is* the man *who* desires life,
And loves *many* days, that he may see good?
13 Keep your tongue from evil,
And your lips from speaking [a]deceit.
14 [a]Depart from evil and do good;
[b]Seek peace and pursue it.

15 [a]The eyes of the LORD *are* on the righteous,
And His ears *are open* to their cry.
16 [a]The face of the LORD *is* against those who
do evil,
[b]To cut off the remembrance of them from
the earth.

17 *The righteous* cry out, and [a]the LORD hears,
And delivers them out of all their
troubles.

33:18 [a][Job 36:7] 33:19 [a]Job 5:20 34:title [a]1 Sam. 21:10–15 34:1 [a][Eph. 5:20] 34:4 [a][Matt. 7:7] 34:7 [a]Dan. 6:22 [b]2 Kin. 6:17 [1]Or *Angel* 34:8 [a]1 Pet. 2:3 [b]Ps. 2:12 34:10 [a][Ps. 84:11] 34:11 [a]Ps. 32:8 34:12 [a][1 Pet. 3:10–12] 34:13 [a][Eph. 4:25] 34:14 [a]Ps. 37:27 [b][Rom. 14:19] 34:15 [a]Job 36:7 34:16 [a]Lev. 17:10 [b][Prov. 10:7] 34:17 [a]Ps. 34:6; 145:19

18 [a]The LORD *is* near [b]to those who have a
broken heart,
And saves such as have a contrite spirit.

19 [a]Many *are* the afflictions of the righteous,
[b]But the LORD delivers him out of them all.
20 He guards all his bones;
[a]Not one of them is broken.

### SEEING JESUS IN THE SCRIPTURE

**34:20** This prophecy has in mind the requirement for Passover lambs (see Ex. 12:46) while looking ahead to Jesus on the cross (see John 19:33). The Roman soldiers broke the legs of the crucified to speed up death, but they didn't do this to Jesus who was already dead.

21 [a]Evil shall slay the wicked,
And those who hate the righteous shall be
condemned.
22 The LORD [a]redeems the soul of His
servants,
And none of those who trust in Him shall
be condemned.

## PSALM 35

### THE LORD THE AVENGER OF HIS PEOPLE

A Psalm *of David.*

1 Plead *my cause,* O LORD, with those who
strive with me;
Fight against those who fight against me.
2 Take hold of shield and buckler,
And stand up for my help.
3 Also draw out the spear,
And stop those who pursue me.
Say to my soul,
"I *am* your salvation."

4 [a]Let those be put to shame and brought to
dishonor
Who seek after my life;
Let those be [b]turned back and brought to
confusion
Who plot my hurt.
5 [a]Let them be like chaff before the wind,
And let the angel[1] of the LORD chase *them.*
6 Let their way be [a]dark and slippery,
And let the angel of the LORD pursue them.
7 For without cause they have [a]hidden their
net for me *in* a pit,
*Which* they have dug without cause for my
life.
8 Let [a]destruction come upon him
unexpectedly,
And let his net that he has hidden catch
himself;
Into that very destruction let him fall.

9 And my soul shall be joyful in the LORD;
It shall rejoice in His salvation.
10 [a]All my bones shall say,
"LORD, [b]who *is* like You,
Delivering the poor from him who is too
strong for him,
Yes, the poor and the needy from him
who plunders him?"

11 Fierce witnesses rise up;
They ask me *things* that I do not know.
12 [a]They reward me evil for good,
*To* the sorrow of my soul.
13 But as for me, [a]when they were sick,
My clothing *was* sackcloth;
I humbled myself with fasting;
And my prayer would return to my own
heart.

**34:18** [a] [Ps. 145:18] [b] [Is. 57:15] **34:19** [a] Prov. 24:16 [b] Ps. 34:4, 6, 17 **34:20** [a] John 19:33, 36 **34:21** [a] Ps. 94:23; 140:11 **34:22** [a] 1 Kin. 1:29 **35:4** [a] Ps. 40:14, 15; 70:2, 3 [b] Ps. 129:5 **35:5** [a] Job 21:18 [1] Or *Angel* **35:6** [a] Ps. 73:18 **35:7** [a] Ps. 9:15 **35:8** [a] [1 Thess. 5:3] **35:10** [a] Ps. 51:8 [b] [Ex. 15:11] **35:12** [a] John 10:32 **35:13** [a] Job 30:25

### APPLY THE TRUTH

## CONFLICT

**35:1** Everyone wants to be right. The problem is that not everyone can be right, and when two people want to be right but they both can't be, conflict often develops. Thoughts and opinions are exchanged, tensions rise, and feelings are hurt. This happens with friends, coworkers, parents, and in dating and marriage. Sometimes these conflicts can be so intense they cause others to take sides, gossip, or end relationships. Even a small disagreement can grow like a cancer and become a devastating conflict.

How should we resolve conflicts? In the Bible, people constantly opposed David, coming against him and talking about him. In this psalm, we see how he handled those conflicts: he asked God to plead his case. David didn't seek to prove his side; he sought to be on God's side. Likewise, our goal should be to allow God to plead our case, not ourselves. Jesus echoed this when He told us to be peacemakers (see Matt. 5:9). What if instead of trying to get our way, we sought God's way? What if instead of being right, we sought to be righteous?

14 I paced about as though *he were* my
friend *or* brother;
I bowed down heavily, as one who mourns
*for his* mother.

15 But in my adversity they rejoiced
And gathered together;
Attackers gathered against me,
And I did not know *it;*
They tore *at me* and did not cease;
16 With ungodly mockers at feasts
They gnashed at me with their teeth.

17 Lord, how long will You [a]look on?
Rescue me from their destructions,
My precious *life* from the lions.
18 I will give You thanks in the great assembly;
I will praise You among many people.

19 [a]Let them not rejoice over me who are
wrongfully my enemies;
Nor let them wink with the eye who hate
me without a cause.

**SEEING JESUS IN THE SCRIPTURE**

**35:19** While David was right to lament those who hated him without cause, ultimately, this cry of despair points to Jesus. Although Jesus did no wrong, the religious leaders hated Him and ultimately rejected Him (see John 15:25).

20 For they do not speak peace,
But they devise deceitful matters
Against *the* quiet ones in the land.
21 They also opened their mouth wide
against me,
*And* said, "Aha, aha!
Our eyes have seen *it.*"

22 *This* You have seen, O LORD;
Do not keep silence.
O Lord, do not be far from me.
23 Stir up Yourself, and awake to my
vindication,
To my cause, my God and my Lord.
24 Vindicate me, O LORD my God, according
to Your righteousness;
And let them not rejoice over me.
25 Let them not say in their hearts, "Ah, so
we would have it!"
Let them not say, "We have swallowed
him up."

26 Let them be ashamed and brought to
mutual confusion
Who rejoice at my hurt;
Let them be [a]clothed with shame and
dishonor
Who exalt themselves against me.

27 [a]Let them shout for joy and be glad,
Who favor my righteous cause;
And let them say continually,
"Let the LORD be magnified,
Who has pleasure in the prosperity of His
servant."
28 And my tongue shall speak of Your
righteousness
*And* of Your praise all the day long.

## PSALM 36

### MAN'S WICKEDNESS AND GOD'S PERFECTIONS

*To the Chief Musician. A Psalm of David the servant of the LORD.*

1 An oracle within my heart concerning the
transgression of the wicked:
[a]*There is* no fear of God before his eyes.
2 For he flatters himself in his own eyes,
When he finds out his iniquity *and* when
he hates.
3 The words of his mouth *are* wickedness
and deceit;
[a]He has ceased to be wise *and* to do good.
4 [a]He devises wickedness on his bed;
He sets himself [b]in a way *that is* not good;
He does not abhor [c]evil.

5 Your mercy, O LORD, *is* in the heavens;
Your faithfulness *reaches* to the clouds.
6 Your righteousness *is* like the great
mountains;
[a]Your judgments *are* a great deep;
O LORD, You preserve man and beast.

7 How precious *is* Your lovingkindness, O God!
Therefore the children of men [a]put their
trust under the shadow of Your wings.
8 [a]They are abundantly satisfied with the
fullness of Your house,
And You give them drink from [b]the river
of Your pleasures.
9 [a]For with You *is* the fountain of life;
[b]In Your light we see light.

**36:9** Not much rain falls in the Middle East between May and September, which makes water precious. Old Testament writers often used rain (here called **the fountain of life**) as a symbol of God's blessing, and drought as a symbol of God's punishment.

35:17 [a] [Hab. 1:13] 35:19 [a] Ps. 69:4; 109:3 35:26 [a] Ps. 109:29 35:27 [a] Rom. 12:15 36:1 [a] Rom. 3:18 36:3 [a] Jer. 4:22 36:4 [a] Prov. 4:16 [b] Is. 65:2 [c] [Rom. 12:9] 36:6 [a] [Rom. 11:33] 36:7 [a] Ps. 17:8; 57:1; 91:4 36:8 [a] Ps. 63:5; 65:4 [b] Rev. 22:1 36:9 [a] [Jer. 2:13] [b] [1 Pet. 2:9]

10 Oh, continue Your lovingkindness to those who know You,
And Your righteousness to the upright in heart.
11 Let not the foot of pride come against me,
And let not the hand of the wicked drive me away.
12 There the workers of iniquity have fallen;
They have been cast down and are not able to rise.

## PSALM 37

### THE HERITAGE OF THE RIGHTEOUS AND THE CALAMITY OF THE WICKED

A Psalm *of David.*

1 Do[a] not fret because of evildoers,
Nor be envious of the workers of iniquity.
2 For they shall soon be cut down [a]like the grass,
And wither as the green herb.

3 Trust in the LORD, and do good;
Dwell in the land, and feed on His faithfulness.
4 [a]Delight yourself also in the LORD,
And He shall give you the desires of your [b]heart.

5 [a]Commit your way to the LORD,
Trust also in Him,
And He shall bring *it* to pass.
6 [a]He shall bring forth your righteousness as the light,
And your justice as the noonday.

7 Rest in the LORD, [a]and wait patiently for Him;
Do not fret because of him who [b]prospers in his way,
Because of the man who brings wicked schemes to pass.
8 [a]Cease from anger, and forsake wrath;
[b]Do not fret—*it* only *causes* harm.

9 For evildoers shall be cut off;
But those who wait on the LORD,
They shall [a]inherit the earth.
10 For [a]yet a little while and the wicked *shall be* no *more;*
Indeed, [b]you will look carefully for his place,
But it *shall be* no *more.*
11 [a]But the meek shall inherit the earth,
And shall delight themselves in the abundance of peace.

12 The wicked plots against the just,
[a]And gnashes at him with his teeth.
13 [a]The Lord laughs at him,
For He sees that [b]his day is coming.
14 The wicked have drawn the sword
And have bent their bow,
To cast down the poor and needy,
To slay those who are of upright conduct.
15 Their sword shall enter their own heart,
And their bows shall be broken.

16 [a]A little that a righteous man has
*Is* better than the riches of many wicked.
17 For the arms of the wicked shall be broken,
But the LORD upholds the righteous.

18 The LORD knows the days of the upright,
And their inheritance shall be forever.
19 They shall not be ashamed in the evil time,
And in the days of famine they shall be satisfied.
20 But the wicked shall perish;
And the enemies of the LORD,
Like the splendor of the meadows, shall vanish.
Into smoke they shall vanish away.

21 The wicked borrows and does not repay,
But [a]the righteous shows mercy and gives.
22 [a]For *those* blessed by Him shall inherit the earth,
But *those* cursed by Him shall be cut off.

23 [a]The steps of a *good* man are ordered by the LORD,
And He delights in his way.
24 [a]Though he fall, he shall not be utterly cast down;
For the LORD upholds *him with* His hand.

25 I have been young, and *now* am old;
Yet I have not seen the righteous forsaken,
Nor his descendants begging bread.
26 [a]*He is* ever merciful, and lends;
And his descendants *are* blessed.

27 Depart from evil, and do good;
And dwell forevermore.
28 For the LORD loves justice,
And does not forsake His saints;
They are preserved forever,
But the descendants of the wicked shall be cut off.
29 [a]The righteous shall inherit the land,
And dwell in it forever.

30 [a]The mouth of the righteous speaks wisdom,
And his tongue talks of justice.
31 The law of his God *is* in his heart;
None of his steps shall slide.

37:1 [a]Ps. 73:3 37:2 [a]Ps. 90:5, 6; 92:7 37:4 [a]Is. 58:14 [b]Ps. 21:2; 145:19 37:5 [a][Ps. 55:22] 37:6 [a]Job 11:17 37:7 [a][Lam. 3:26] [b][Ps. 73:3–12] 37:8 [a][Eph. 4:26] [b]Ps. 73:3 37:9 [a][Is. 57:13; 60:21] 37:10 [a][Heb. 10:37] [b]Job 7:10 37:11 [a][Matt. 5:5] 37:12 [a]Ps. 35:16 37:13 [a]Ps. 2:4; 59:8 [b]1 Sam. 26:10 37:16 [a]Prov. 15:16; 16:8 37:21 [a]Ps. 112:5, 9 37:22 [a][Prov. 3:33] 37:23 [a][1 Sam. 2:9] 37:24 [a]Prov. 24:16 37:26 [a][Deut. 15:8] 37:29 [a]Prov. 2:21 37:30 [a][Matt. 12:35]

32 The wicked [a]watches the righteous,
And seeks to slay him.
33 The LORD [a]will not leave him in his hand,
Nor condemn him when he is judged.

34 [a]Wait on the LORD,
And keep His way,
And He shall exalt you to inherit the land;
When the wicked are cut off, you shall see *it.*
35 I have seen the wicked in great power,
And spreading himself like a native green
tree.
36 Yet he passed away,[1] and behold, he *was*
no *more;*
Indeed I sought him, but he could not be
found.

37 Mark the blameless *man,* and observe the
upright;
For the future of *that* man *is* peace.
38 [a]But the transgressors shall be destroyed
together;
The future of the wicked shall be cut off.

39 But the salvation of the righteous *is* from
the LORD;
*He is* their strength [a]in the time of trouble.
40 And [a]the LORD shall help them and
deliver them;
He shall deliver them from the wicked,
And save them,
[b]Because they trust in Him.

## PSALM 38

### PRAYER IN TIME OF CHASTENING

*A Psalm of David.* [a]*To bring to remembrance.*

1 O LORD, do not [a]rebuke me in Your wrath,
Nor chasten me in Your hot displeasure!
2 For Your arrows pierce me deeply,
And Your hand presses me down.

3 *There is* no soundness in my flesh
Because of Your anger,
Nor *any* health in my bones
Because of my sin.
4 For my iniquities have gone over my head;
Like a heavy burden they are too heavy
for me.
5 My wounds are foul *and* festering
Because of my foolishness.

6 I am troubled, I am bowed down greatly;
I go mourning all the day long.
7 For my loins are full of inflammation,
And *there is* no soundness in my flesh.
8 I am feeble and severely broken;
I groan because of the turmoil of my heart.

9 Lord, all my desire *is* before You;
And my sighing is not hidden from You.
10 My heart pants, my strength fails me;
As for the light of my eyes, it also has
gone from me.

11 My loved ones and my friends [a]stand
aloof from my plague,
And my relatives stand afar off.
12 Those also who seek my life lay snares
*for me;*
Those who seek my hurt speak of
destruction,
And plan deception all the day long.

13 But I, like a deaf *man,* do not hear;
And *I am* like a mute *who* does not open
his mouth.
14 Thus I am like a man who does not hear,
And in whose mouth *is* no response.

15 For in You, O LORD, [a]I hope;
You will hear, O Lord my God.
16 For I said, "*Hear me,* lest they rejoice
over me,
Lest, when my foot slips, they exalt
*themselves* against me."

17 [a]For I *am* ready to fall,
And my sorrow *is* continually before me.
18 For I will [a]declare my iniquity;
I will be [b]in anguish over my sin.
19 But my enemies *are* vigorous, *and* they
are strong;
And those who hate me wrongfully have
multiplied.
20 Those also [a]who render evil for good,
They are my adversaries, because I follow
*what is* good.

21 Do not forsake me, O LORD;
O my God, [a]be not far from me!
22 Make haste to help me,
O Lord, my salvation!

## PSALM 39

### PRAYER FOR WISDOM AND FORGIVENESS

*To the Chief Musician. To Jeduthun. A Psalm of David.*

1 I said, "I will guard my ways,
Lest I sin with my [a]tongue;
I will restrain my mouth with a muzzle,
While the wicked are before me."
2 [a]I was mute with silence,
I held my peace *even* from good;
And my sorrow was stirred up.

**37:32** [a] Ps. 10:8; 17:11 **37:33** [a] Ps. 31:8; [2 Pet. 2:9] **37:34** [a] Ps. 27:14; 37:9 **37:36** [1] Following Masoretic Text, Septuagint, and Targum; Syriac and Vulgate read *I passed by.* **37:38** [a] [Ps. 1:4–6; 37:20, 28] **37:39** [a] Ps. 9:9; 37:19 **37:40** [a] Ps. 22:4; Is. 31:5; Dan. 3:17; 6:23 [b] 1 Chr. 5:20; Ps. 34:22 **38:title** [a] Ps. 70:title **38:1** [a] Ps. 6:1 **38:11** [a] Ps. 31:11; 88:18 **38:15** [a] [Ps. 39:7] **38:17** [a] Ps. 51:3 **38:18** [a] Ps. 32:5 [b] [2 Cor. 7:9, 10] **38:20** [a] Ps. 35:12 **38:21** [a] Ps. 22:19; 35:22 **39:1** [a] Job 2:10; Ps. 34:13; [James 3:5–12] **39:2** [a] Ps. 38:13

3 My heart was hot within me;
While I was musing, the fire burned.
*Then* I spoke with my tongue:

4 "LORD, [a]make me to know my end,
And what *is* the measure of my days,
*That* I may know how frail I *am.*
5 Indeed, You have made my days *as* handbreadths,
And my age *is* as nothing before You;
Certainly every man at his best state *is* but [a]vapor. *Selah*
6 Surely every man walks about like a shadow;
Surely they busy themselves in vain;
He heaps up *riches,*
And does not know who will gather them.

7 "And now, Lord, what do I wait for?
My [a]hope *is* in You.
8 Deliver me from all my transgressions;
Do not make me [a]the reproach of the foolish.
9 [a]I was mute, I did not open my mouth,
Because it was [b]You who did *it.*
10 [a]Remove Your plague from me;
I am consumed by the blow of Your hand.
11 When with rebukes You correct man for iniquity,
You make his beauty [a]melt away like a moth;
Surely every man *is* vapor. *Selah*

12 "Hear my prayer, O LORD,
And give ear to my cry;
Do not be silent at my tears;
For I *am* a stranger with You,
A sojourner, [a]as all my fathers *were.*
13 [a]Remove Your gaze from me, that I may regain strength,
Before I go away and [b]am no more."

## PSALM 40

### FAITH PERSEVERING IN TRIAL

*(Ps. 70:1–5)*

*To the Chief Musician. A Psalm of David.*

1 I [a]waited patiently for the LORD;
And He inclined to me,
And heard my cry.
2 He also brought me up out of a horrible pit,
Out of [a]the miry clay,
And [b]set my feet upon a rock,
*And* established my steps.
3 [a]He has put a new song in my mouth—
Praise to our God;
Many will see *it* and fear,
And will trust in the LORD.

4 [a]Blessed *is* that man who makes the LORD his trust,
And does not respect the proud, nor such as turn aside to lies.
5 [a]Many, O LORD my God, *are* Your wonderful works
*Which* You have done;
[b]And Your thoughts toward us
Cannot be recounted to You in order;
*If* I would declare and speak *of them,*
They are more than can be numbered.

6 [a]Sacrifice and offering You did not desire;
My ears You have opened.
Burnt offering and sin offering You did not require.
7 Then I said, "Behold, I come;
In the scroll of the book *it is* written of me.
8 [a]I delight to do Your will, O my God,
And Your law *is* [b]within my heart."

9 [a]I have proclaimed the good news of righteousness

**39:4** [a] Ps. 90:12; 119:84 **39:5** [a] Ps. 62:9; [Eccl. 6:12] **39:7** [a] Ps. 38:15 **39:8** [a] Ps. 44:13; 79:4; 119:22 **39:9** [a] Ps. 39:2 [b] 2 Sam. 16:10; Job 2:10 **39:10** [a] Job 9:34; 13:21 **39:11** [a] Job 13:28 **39:12** [a] Gen. 47:9 **39:13** [a] Job 7:19; 10:20, 21; 14:6 [b] [Job 14:10] **40:1** [a] Ps. 25:5; 27:14; 37:7 **40:2** [a] Ps. 69:2, 14 [b] Ps. 27:5 **40:3** [a] Ps. 32:7; 33:3 **40:4** [a] Ps. 34:8; 84:12 **40:5** [a] Job 9:10 [b] [Is. 55:8] **40:6** [a] [Heb. 10:5–9] **40:8** [a] [John 4:34; 6:38] [b] [Jer. 31:33] **40:9** [a] Ps. 22:22, 25

APPLY THE TRUTH

## EMOTIONAL HEALTH

**40:1–17** In this psalm, David described himself as being in a pit, surrounded by iniquities and evil. His heart was failing; he was poor and needy. But he also sang a new song, delighted in the Word of God, and shared God's love with the world. Clearly, he was experiencing great lows and great highs. Emotions are this way. Some days we're happy and thankful; other days we're sad and scared. Unfortunately, many people live as victims to their emotions, constantly letting their emotions guide their lives or attempting to avoid or control how they feel.

Emotions aren't bad. They're actually unavoidable. God created us with emotions. They're part of who we are. Feeling love, joy, excitement, and even fear are all good things. The danger is when we allow these emotions to drive us or cripple us. In the beginning of this psalm, David was coming *out* of the pit, but by the end he needed God to deliver him again. Yet, through all of the highs and lows, he found stability. How? By allowing the Person and promises of God to be his guide, not his situation or emotions.

In the great assembly;
Indeed, [b]I do not restrain my lips,
O LORD, You Yourself know.
10 [a]I have not hidden Your righteousness within my heart;
I have declared Your faithfulness and Your salvation;
I have not concealed Your lovingkindness and Your truth
From the great assembly.

11 Do not withhold Your tender mercies from me, O LORD;
[a]Let Your lovingkindness and Your truth continually preserve me.
12 For innumerable evils have surrounded me;
[a]My iniquities have overtaken me, so that I am not able to look up;
They are more than the hairs of my head;
Therefore my heart fails me.

13 [a]Be pleased, O LORD, to deliver me;
O LORD, make haste to help me!
14 [a]Let them be ashamed and brought to mutual confusion
Who seek to destroy my life;
Let them be driven backward and brought to dishonor
Who wish me evil.
15 Let them be [a]confounded because of their shame,
Who say to me, "Aha, aha!"

16 [a]Let all those who seek You rejoice and be glad in You;
Let such as love Your salvation [b]say continually,
"The LORD be magnified!"
17 [a]But I *am* poor and needy;
[b]*Yet* the LORD thinks upon me.
You *are* my help and my deliverer;
Do not delay, O my God.

## PSALM 41

### THE BLESSING AND SUFFERING OF THE GODLY

*To the Chief Musician. A Psalm of David.*

1 Blessed *is* he who considers the poor;
The LORD will deliver him in time of trouble.
2 The LORD will preserve him and keep him alive,
*And* he will be blessed on the earth;
[a]You will not deliver him to the will of his enemies.
3 The LORD will strengthen him on his bed of illness;
You will sustain him on his sickbed.

4 I said, "LORD, be merciful to me;
[a]Heal my soul, for I have sinned against You."
5 My enemies speak evil of me:
"When will he die, and his name perish?"
6 And if he comes to see *me,* he speaks lies;
His heart gathers iniquity to itself;
*When* he goes out, he tells *it.*

7 All who hate me whisper together against me;
Against me they devise my hurt.
8 "An evil disease," *they say,* "clings to him.
And *now* that he lies down, he will rise up no more."
9 [a]Even my own familiar friend in whom I trusted,
[b]Who ate my bread,
Has lifted up *his* heel against me.

**SEEING JESUS IN THE SCRIPTURE**

**41:9** These words describe the betrayal of a close friend. Jesus repeated them as He reclined at the table with Judas and the other disciples, knowing Judas was about to hand Him over to be delivered to the high priest (see John 13:18).

10 But You, O LORD, be merciful to me, and raise me up,
That I may repay them.
11 By this I know that You are well pleased with me,
Because my enemy does not triumph over me.
12 As for me, You uphold me in my integrity,
And [a]set me before Your face forever.

13 [a]Blessed *be* the LORD God of Israel
From everlasting to everlasting!
Amen and Amen.

# BOOK TWO

## PSALMS 42–72

## PSALM 42

### YEARNING FOR GOD IN THE MIDST OF DISTRESSES

*To the Chief Musician. A Contemplation*[1] *of the sons of Korah.*

1 As the deer pants for the water brooks,
So pants my soul for You, O God.

**40:9** [b] Ps. 119:13 **40:10** [a] Acts 20:20, 27 **40:11** [a] Ps. 61:7 **40:12** [a] Ps. 38:4; 65:3 **40:13** [a] Ps. 70:1 **40:14** [a] Ps. 35:4, 26; 70:2; 71:13 **40:15** [a] Ps. 73:19 **40:16** [a] Ps. 70:4 [b] Ps. 35:27 **40:17** [a] Ps. 70:5; 86:1; 109:22 [b] 1 Pet. 5:7 **41:2** [a] Ps. 27:12 **41:4** [a] Ps. 6:2; 103:3; 147:3 **41:9** [a] 2 Sam. 15:12 [b] John 13:18, 21–30 **41:12** [a] [Job 36:7] **41:13** [a] Ps. 72:18, 19; 89:52; 106:48; 150:6 **42:title** [1] Hebrew *Maschil*

2 [a]My soul thirsts for God, for the [b]living God.
When shall I come and appear before God?[1]
3 [a]My tears have been my food day and night,
While they continually say to me,
[b]"Where *is* your God?"

4 When I remember these *things*,
[a]I pour out my soul within me.
For I used to go with the multitude;
[b]I went with them to the house of God,
With the voice of joy and praise,
With a multitude that kept a pilgrim feast.

5 [a]Why are you cast down, O my soul?
And *why* are you disquieted within me?
[b]Hope in God, for I shall yet praise Him
*For* the help of His countenance.[1]

6 O my God,[1] my soul is cast down within me;
Therefore I will remember You from the land of the Jordan,
And from the heights of Hermon,
From the Hill Mizar.
7 Deep calls unto deep at the noise of Your waterfalls;
[a]All Your waves and billows have gone over me.
8 The LORD will [a]command His lovingkindness in the daytime,
And [b]in the night His song *shall be* with me—
A prayer to the God of my life.

9 I will say to God my Rock,
[a]"Why have You forgotten me?
Why do I go mourning because of the oppression of the enemy?"
10 *As* with a breaking of my bones,
My enemies reproach me,
[a]While they say to me all day long,
"Where *is* your God?"

11 [a]Why are you cast down, O my soul?
And why are you disquieted within me?
Hope in God;
For I shall yet praise Him,
The help of my countenance and my God.

## PSALM 43

### PRAYER TO GOD IN TIME OF TROUBLE

1 Vindicate [a]me, O God,
And [b]plead my cause against an ungodly nation;
Oh, deliver me from the deceitful and unjust man!
2 For You *are* the God of my strength;
Why do You cast me off?
[a]Why do I go mourning because of the oppression of the enemy?
3 [a]Oh, send out Your light and Your truth!
Let them lead me;
Let them bring me to [b]Your holy hill
And to Your tabernacle.
4 Then I will go to the altar of God,
To God my exceeding joy;
And on the harp I will praise You,
O God, my God.

**42:2** [a] Ps. 63:1; 84:2; 143:6 [b] 1 Thess. 1:9 [1] Following Masoretic Text and Vulgate; some Hebrew manuscripts, Septuagint, Syriac, and Targum read *I see the face of God.* **42:3** [a] Ps. 80:5; 102:9 [b] Ps. 79:10; 115:2 **42:4** [a] Job 30:16 [b] Is. 30:29 **42:5** [a] Ps. 42:11; 43:5 [b] Lam. 3:24 [1] Following Masoretic Text and Targum; a few Hebrew manuscripts, Septuagint, Syriac, and Vulgate read *The help of my countenance, my God.* **42:6** [1] Following Masoretic Text and Targum; a few Hebrew manuscripts, Septuagint, Syriac, and Vulgate put *my God* at the end of verse 5. **42:7** [a] Ps. 69:1, 2; 88:7 **42:8** [a] Deut. 28:8 [b] Job 35:10 **42:9** [a] Ps. 38:6 **42:10** [a] Joel 2:17 **42:11** [a] Ps. 43:5 **43:1** [a] [Ps. 26:1; 35:24] [b] Ps. 35:1 **43:2** [a] Ps. 42:9 **43:3** [a] [Ps. 40:11] [b] Ps. 3:4

APPLY THE TRUTH

## DISAPPOINTMENT

**42:11** Have you ever looked forward to something, only to realize it wasn't what you thought? Sometimes waiting for a package to arrive is more fun than receiving what you ordered. Or anticipation of the holiday is often better than the day itself. Even when things go exactly how you hoped they would, there often can be at least a little disappointment. What you looked forward to is gone. In these times, you might hear yourself echoing the psalmist saying, "Why are you cast down, O my soul? And why are you disquieted within me?"

When we feel this, we might look to other things in our lives that are satisfying. Or we might find something else to look forward to, hoping it will meet or exceed our wildest expectations and make us feel how we want to feel. None of this works, though. Holidays, possessions, experiences, relationships, school, and work were never meant to satisfy your soul. You're far more wonderful and complicated than that. This is where the solution this psalm provides comes in. *Hope in God!* He is where true satisfaction is found. Circumstances, feelings, people, and positions will disappoint. God never will.

5 [a]Why are you cast down, O my soul?
And why are you disquieted within me?
Hope in God;
For I shall yet praise Him,
The help of my countenance and my God.

## PSALM 44

### REDEMPTION REMEMBERED IN PRESENT DISHONOR

*To the Chief Musician. A [a]Contemplation[1] of the sons of Korah.*

1 We have heard with our ears, O God,
[a]Our fathers have told us,
The deeds You did in their days,
In days of old:

> **44:1** God wanted every generation of Israelites to know all He had done for their ancestors. Though written records of past events were kept, few people had access to them. That's why it was important for the Israelites to tell their children and grandchildren about their history.

2 [a]You drove out the nations with Your hand,
But them You planted;
You afflicted the peoples, and cast them out.
3 For [a]they did not gain possession of the land by their own sword,
Nor did their own arm save them;
But it was Your right hand, Your arm, and the light of Your countenance,
[b]Because You favored them.

4 [a]You are my King, O God;[1]
Command[2] victories for Jacob.
5 Through You [a]we will push down our enemies;
Through Your name we will trample those who rise up against us.
6 For [a]I will not trust in my bow,
Nor shall my sword save me.
7 But You have saved us from our enemies,
And have put to shame those who hated us.
8 [a]In God we boast all day long,
And praise Your name forever. *Selah*

9 But [a]You have cast *us* off and put us to shame,
And You do not go out with our armies.
10 You make us [a]turn back from the enemy,
And those who hate us have taken spoil for themselves.
11 [a]You have given us up like sheep *intended* for food,
And have [b]scattered us among the nations.
12 [a]You sell Your people for *next to* nothing,
And are not enriched by selling them.

13 [a]You make us a reproach to our neighbors,
A scorn and a derision to those all around us.
14 [a]You make us a byword among the nations,
[b]A shaking of the head among the peoples.
15 My dishonor *is* continually before me,
And the shame of my face has covered me,
16 Because of the voice of him who reproaches and reviles,
[a]Because of the enemy and the avenger.

17 [a]All this has come upon us;
But we have not forgotten You,
Nor have we dealt falsely with Your covenant.
18 Our heart has not turned back,
[a]Nor have our steps departed from Your way;
19 But You have severely broken us in [a]the place of jackals,
And covered us [b]with the shadow of death.

20 If we had forgotten the name of our God,
Or [a]stretched out our hands to a foreign god,
21 [a]Would not God search this out?
For He knows the secrets of the heart.
22 [a]Yet for Your sake we are killed all day long;
We are accounted as sheep for the slaughter.

23 [a]Awake! Why do You sleep, O Lord?
Arise! Do not cast *us* off forever.
24 [a]Why do You hide Your face,
*And* forget our affliction and our oppression?
25 For [a]our soul is bowed down to the dust;
Our body clings to the ground.
26 Arise for our help,
And redeem us for Your mercies' sake.

**43:5** [a] Ps. 42:5, 11 **44:title** [a] Ps. 42:title [1] Hebrew *Maschil* **44:1** [a] [Ex. 12:26, 27] **44:2** [a] Ex. 15:17 **44:3** [a] [Deut. 8:17, 18] [b] [Deut. 4:37; 7:7, 8] **44:4** [a] [Ps. 74:12] [1] Following Masoretic Text and Targum; Septuagint and Vulgate read *and my God.* [2] Following Masoretic Text and Targum; Septuagint, Syriac, and Vulgate read *Who commands.* **44:5** [a] [Dan. 8:4] **44:6** [a] Ps. 33:16 **44:8** [a] Ps. 34:2 **44:9** [a] Ps. 60:1 **44:10** [a] Lev. 26:17 **44:11** [a] Rom. 8:36 [b] Deut. 4:27; 28:64 **44:12** [a] Is. 52:3, 4 **44:13** [a] Jer. 24:9 **44:14** [a] Deut. 28:37 [b] Job 16:4 **44:16** [a] Ps. 8:2 **44:17** [a] Dan. 9:13 **44:18** [a] Job 23:11 **44:19** [a] Is. 34:13 [b] [Ps. 23:4] **44:20** [a] [Deut. 6:14] **44:21** [a] [Ps. 139:1, 2] **44:22** [a] Rom. 8:36 **44:23** [a] Ps. 7:6 **44:24** [a] Job 13:24 **44:25** [a] Ps. 119:25

## PSALM 45

### THE GLORIES OF THE MESSIAH AND HIS BRIDE

*To the Chief Musician. [a]Set to "The Lilies."[1]*
*A Contemplation[2] of the sons of Korah.*
*A Song of Love.*

1 My heart is overflowing with a good theme;
I recite my composition concerning the King;
My tongue *is* the pen of a ready writer.

2 You are fairer than the sons of men;
[a]Grace is poured upon Your lips;
Therefore God has blessed You forever.
3 Gird Your [a]sword upon *Your* thigh,
[b]O Mighty One,
With Your [c]glory and Your majesty.
4 [a]And in Your majesty ride prosperously
because of truth, humility, *and* righteousness;
And Your right hand shall teach You awesome things.
5 Your arrows *are* sharp in the heart of the King's enemies;
The peoples fall under You.

6 [a]Your throne, O God, *is* forever and ever;
A [b]scepter of righteousness *is* the scepter of Your kingdom.
7 You love righteousness and hate wickedness;
Therefore God, Your God, has [a]anointed You
With the oil of [b]gladness more than Your companions.
8 All Your garments *are* [a]*scented* with myrrh and aloes *and* cassia,
Out of the ivory palaces, by which they have made You glad.

> **45:8** The spices mentioned here were rare and expensive. **Myrrh** was a plant used to make perfumes, among other things. It was also one of the presents the wise men brought to the baby Jesus. The **aloes** were not the plants we know today but were trees whose fragrant wood was used for perfume and incense. **Cassia** plants smelled like cinnamon. All three spices were associated with the oil used to anoint kings.

9 [a]Kings' daughters *are* among Your honorable women;
[b]At Your right hand stands the queen in gold from Ophir.

10 Listen, O daughter,
Consider and incline your ear;
[a]Forget your own people also, and your father's house;
11 So the King will greatly desire your beauty;
[a]Because He *is* your Lord, worship Him.
12 And the daughter of Tyre *will come* with a gift;
[a]The rich among the people will seek your favor.

13 The royal daughter *is* all glorious within *the palace;*
Her clothing *is* woven with gold.
14 [a]She shall be brought to the King in robes of many colors;
The virgins, her companions who follow her, shall be brought to You.
15 With gladness and rejoicing they shall be brought;
They shall enter the King's palace.

16 Instead of Your fathers shall be Your sons,
[a]Whom You shall make princes in all the earth.
17 [a]I will make Your name to be remembered in all generations;
Therefore the people shall praise You forever and ever.

## PSALM 46

### GOD THE REFUGE OF HIS PEOPLE AND CONQUEROR OF THE NATIONS

*To the Chief Musician.* A Psalm *of the sons of Korah. A Song [a]for Alamoth.*

1 God *is* our [a]refuge and strength,
[b]A very present help in trouble.
2 Therefore we will not fear,
Even though the earth be removed,
And though the mountains be carried into the midst of the sea;
3 [a]*Though* its waters roar *and* be troubled,
*Though* the mountains shake with its swelling. *Selah*

> **46:2–4** In ancient times, oceans and seas were thought of as things to be feared, which is why they were occasionally used as a symbol of trouble in the Bible. Rivers, on the other hand, were considered good and helpful. In this passage, the **sea** represents destruction and the **river** represents God's blessings.

45:title [a] Ps. 69:title [1] Hebrew *Shoshannim* [2] Hebrew *Maschil* 45:2 [a] Luke 4:22 45:3 [a] [Heb. 4:12] [b] [Is. 9:6] [c] Jude 25 45:4 [a] Rev. 6:2 45:6 [a] [Ps. 93:2] [b] [Num. 24:17] 45:7 [a] Ps. 2:2 [b] Ps. 21:6 45:8 [a] Song 1:12, 13 45:9 [a] Song 6:8 [b] 1 Kin. 2:19 45:10 [a] Deut. 21:13 45:11 [a] [Is. 54:5] 45:12 [a] Is. 49:23 45:14 [a] Song 1:4 45:16 [a] [1 Pet. 2:9] 45:17 [a] Mal. 1:11 46:title [a] 1 Chr. 15:20 46:1 [a] Ps. 62:7, 8 [b] [Deut. 4:7] 46:3 [a] [Ps. 93:3, 4]

4 *There is* a [a]river whose streams shall make
glad the [b]city of God,
The holy *place* of the tabernacle of the
Most High.
5 God *is* [a]in the midst of her, she shall not
be moved;
God shall help her, just at the break of dawn.
6 [a]The nations raged, the kingdoms were
moved;
He uttered His voice, the earth melted.

7 The [a]LORD of hosts *is* with us;
The God of Jacob *is* our refuge. *Selah*

8 Come, behold the works of the LORD,
Who has made desolations in the earth.
9 [a]He makes wars cease to the end of the
earth;
[b]He breaks the bow and cuts the spear in
two;
[c]He burns the chariot in the fire.

10 Be still, and know that I *am* God;
[a]I will be exalted among the nations,
I will be exalted in the earth!

11 The LORD of hosts *is* with us;
The God of Jacob *is* our refuge. *Selah*

## PSALM 47

### PRAISE TO GOD, THE RULER OF THE EARTH

*To the Chief Musician. A Psalm of the sons of Korah.*

1 Oh, clap your hands, all you peoples!
Shout to God with the voice of triumph!
2 For the LORD Most High *is* awesome;
*He is* a great [a]King over all the earth.
3 [a]He will subdue the peoples under us,
And the nations under our feet.
4 He will choose our [a]inheritance for us,
The excellence of Jacob whom He
loves. *Selah*

5 [a]God has gone up with a shout,
The LORD with the sound of a trumpet.
6 Sing praises to God, sing praises!
Sing praises to our King, sing praises!
7 [a]For God *is* the King of all the earth;
[b]Sing praises with understanding.

8 [a]God reigns over the nations;
God [b]sits on His [c]holy throne.
9 The princes of the people have gathered
together,
[a]The people of the God of Abraham.
[b]For the shields of the earth *belong* to God;
He is greatly exalted.

## PSALM 48

### THE GLORY OF GOD IN ZION

*A Song. A Psalm of the sons of Korah.*

1 Great *is* the LORD, and greatly to be
praised
In the [a]city of our God,
*In* His holy mountain.
2 [a]Beautiful in elevation,
The joy of the whole earth,
*Is* Mount Zion *on* the sides of the north,
The city of the great King.
3 God *is* in her palaces;
He is known as her refuge.

**46:4** [a] [Ezek. 47:1–12] [b] Is. 60:14 **46:5** [a] [Zeph. 3:15] **46:6** [a] Ps. 2:1, 2 **46:7** [a] Num. 14:9 **46:9** [a] Is. 2:4 [b] Ps. 76:3 [c] Ezek. 39:9 **46:10** [a] [Is. 2:11, 17] **47:2** [a] Deut. 7:21; Neh. 1:5; Ps. 76:12 **47:3** [a] Ps. 18:47 **47:4** [a] [1 Pet. 1:4] **47:5** [a] Ps. 68:24, 25 **47:7** [a] Zech. 14:9 [b] 1 Cor. 14:15 **47:8** [a] 1 Chr. 16:31 [b] Ps. 97:2 [c] Ps. 48:1 **47:9** [a] [Rom. 4:11, 12] [b] [Ps. 89:18] **48:1** [a] Ps. 46:4; 87:3; Matt. 5:35 **48:2** [a] Ps. 50:2

APPLY THE TRUTH

## ENTERTAINMENT

**46:10** Life buzzes with sights, sounds, and stories vying for our attention. Streaming shows, social media, wireless headphones, and video games keep us perpetually entertained. There's always *something* to do at our fingertips. The wonderful thing is that God created life to be enjoyed. He wants us to find creative ways to flourish and enjoy His good creation. Connecting with friends, laughing, enjoying delicious food, and soaking in inspiring art can all bring glory to God.

Yet, with all this connection and entertainment, it seems increasingly difficult to connect with God. This fast-paced, update-to-the-latest-version way of life entertains for sure, but it also distracts. We can easily miss out on the things God is doing in our lives because we never set our phones down to see them. We never take off our headphones to hear them. We never pause to notice God's amazing "forest" through the "trees" of entertainment. This verse, though, tells us how to encounter our Creator: *Be still, and know*. Eliminate the distractions. Quiet the noise. Turn off notifications. Get alone with God. Slow down. Bask in God's presence. Know Him in a deeper way.

4 For behold, [a]the kings assembled,
They passed by together.
5 They saw *it, and* so they marveled;
They were troubled, they hastened away.
6 Fear [a]took hold of them there,
*And* pain, as of a woman in birth pangs,
7 As *when* You break the [a]ships of Tarshish
With an east wind.

8 As we have heard,
So we have seen
In the city of the LORD of hosts,
In the city of our God:
God will [a]establish it forever. *Selah*

9 We have thought, O God, on [a]Your lovingkindness,
In the midst of Your temple.
10 According to [a]Your name, O God,
So *is* Your praise to the ends of the earth;
Your right hand is full of righteousness.
11 Let Mount Zion rejoice,
Let the daughters of Judah be glad,
Because of Your judgments.

12 Walk about Zion,
And go all around her.
Count her towers;

**48:12** The city of Jerusalem, located on top of Mount **Zion**, was surrounded by a wall to protect its citizens from their enemies. **Towers** were built at various points on the wall so lookouts could spot coming attacks.

13 Mark well her bulwarks;
Consider her palaces;
That you may [a]tell *it* to the generation following.
14 For this *is* God,
Our God forever and ever;
[a]He will be our guide
*Even* to death.[1]

## PSALM 49

### THE CONFIDENCE OF THE FOOLISH

*To the Chief Musician. A Psalm of the sons of Korah.*

1 Hear this, all peoples;
Give ear, all inhabitants of the world,
2 Both low and high,
Rich and poor together.
3 My mouth shall speak wisdom,
And the meditation of my heart *shall give* understanding.
4 I will incline my ear to a proverb;
I will disclose my dark saying on the harp.

5 Why should I fear in the days of evil,
*When* the iniquity at my heels surrounds me?
6 Those who [a]trust in their wealth
And boast in the multitude of their riches,
7 None *of them* can by any means redeem *his* brother,
Nor [a]give to God a ransom for him—
8 For [a]the redemption of their souls *is* costly,
And it shall cease forever—
9 That he should continue to live eternally,
*And* [a]not see the Pit.

10 For he sees wise men die;
Likewise the fool and the senseless person perish,
And leave their wealth to others.
11 Their inner thought *is that* their houses *will last* forever,[1]
Their dwelling places to all generations;
They [a]call *their* lands after their own names.
12 Nevertheless man, *though* in honor, does not remain;[1]
He is like the beasts *that* perish.

13 This is the way of those who *are* [a]foolish,
And of their posterity who approve their sayings. *Selah*
14 Like sheep they are laid in the grave;
Death shall feed on them;
[a]The upright shall have dominion over them in the morning;
[b]And their beauty shall be consumed in the grave, far from their dwelling.
15 But God [a]will redeem my soul from the power of the grave,
For He shall [b]receive me. *Selah*

**SEEING JESUS IN THE SCRIPTURE**

**49:15** Like David's Messianic prophecy in Psalm 16:10, the sons of Korah also anticipated Jesus overcoming the grave (see Acts 2:31–32). Just as the grave held no power over Jesus, it holds no power over all who trust in Him.

**48:4** [a] 2 Sam. 10:6, 14 **48:6** [a] Ex. 15:15 **48:7** [a] 1 Kin. 10:22; Ezek. 27:25 **48:8** [a] [Ps. 87:5; Is. 2:2]; Mic. 4:1 **48:9** [a] Ps. 26:3 **48:10** [a] [Deut. 28:58]; Josh. 7:9; Mal. 1:11 **48:13** [a] [Ps. 78:5–7] **48:14** [a] Is. 58:11 [1] Following Masoretic Text and Syriac; Septuagint and Vulgate read *Forever*. **49:6** [a] [Mark 10:23, 24] **49:7** [a] Job 36:18, 19 **49:8** [a] [Matt. 16:26] **49:9** [a] Ps. 89:48 **49:11** [a] Gen. 4:17; Deut. 3:14 [1] Septuagint, Syriac, Targum, and Vulgate read *Their graves shall be their houses forever*. **49:12** [1] Following Masoretic Text and Targum; Septuagint, Syriac, and Vulgate read *understand* (compare verse 20). **49:13** [a] [Luke 12:20] **49:14** [a] Ps. 47:3; [Dan. 7:18; 1 Cor. 6:2; Rev. 2:26] [b] Job 4:21 **49:15** [a] [Hos. 13:4]; Mark 16:6, 7; Acts 2:31, 32 [b] Ps. 73:24

16 Do not be afraid when one becomes rich,
When the glory of his house is increased;
17 For when he dies he shall carry nothing away;
His glory shall not descend after him.
18 Though while he lives [a]he blesses himself
(For *men* will praise you when you do well for yourself),
19 He shall go to the generation of his fathers;
They shall never see [a]light.
20 A man *who is* in honor, yet does not understand,
[a]Is like the beasts *that* perish.

## PSALM 50

### GOD THE RIGHTEOUS JUDGE

*A Psalm of Asaph.*

1 The [a]Mighty One, God the LORD,
Has spoken and called the earth
From the rising of the sun to its going down.
2 Out of Zion, the perfection of beauty,
[a]God will shine forth.
3 Our God shall come, and shall not keep silent;
[a]A fire shall devour before Him,
And it shall be very tempestuous all around Him.

4 [a]He shall call to the heavens from above,
And to the earth, that He may judge His people:
5 "Gather [a]My saints together to Me,
[b]Those who have made a covenant with Me by sacrifice."
6 Let the [a]heavens declare His righteousness,
For [b]God Himself *is* Judge. *Selah*

7 "Hear, O My people, and I will speak,
O Israel, and I will testify against you;
[a]I *am* God, your God!
8 [a]I will not rebuke you [b]for your sacrifices
Or your burnt offerings,
*Which are* continually before Me.
9 [a]I will not take a bull from your house,
*Nor* goats out of your folds.
10 For every beast of the forest *is* Mine,
*And* the cattle on a thousand hills.
11 I know all the birds of the mountains,
And the wild beasts of the field *are* Mine.

12 "If I were hungry, I would not tell you;
[a]For the world *is* Mine, and all its fullness.
13 [a]Will I eat the flesh of bulls,
Or drink the blood of goats?
14 [a]Offer to God thanksgiving,
And [b]pay your vows to the Most High.
15 [a]Call upon Me in the day of trouble;
I will deliver you, and you shall glorify Me."

16 But to the wicked God says:
"What *right* have you to declare My statutes,
Or take My covenant in your mouth,
17 [a]Seeing you hate instruction
And cast My words behind you?
18 When you saw a thief, you [a]consented[1] with him,
And have been a [b]partaker with adulterers.
19 You give your mouth to evil,
And [a]your tongue frames deceit.
20 You sit *and* speak against your brother;
You slander your own mother's son.
21 These *things* you have done, and I kept silent;
[a]You thought that I was altogether like you;
*But* I will rebuke you,
And [b]set *them* in order before your eyes.

22 "Now consider this, you who [a]forget God,
Lest I tear *you* in pieces,
And *there be* none to deliver:
23 Whoever offers praise glorifies Me;
And [a]to him who orders *his* conduct *aright*
I will show the salvation of God."

## PSALM 51

### A PRAYER OF REPENTANCE

*To the Chief Musician. A Psalm of David [a]when Nathan the prophet went to him, after he had gone in to Bathsheba.*

1 Have mercy upon me, O God,
According to Your lovingkindness;
According to the multitude of Your tender mercies,
[a]Blot out my transgressions.
2 [a]Wash me thoroughly from my iniquity,
And cleanse me from my sin.
3 For I acknowledge my transgressions,
And my sin *is* always before me.

**49:18** [a] Deut. 29:19; Luke 12:19 **49:19** [a] Job 33:30 **49:20** [a] Eccl. 3:19 **50:1** [a] Is. 9:6 **50:2** [a] Deut. 33:2; Ps. 80:1 **50:3** [a] Lev. 10:2; Num. 16:35; [Ps. 97:3] **50:4** [a] Deut. 4:26; 31:28; 32:1; Is. 1:2 **50:5** [a] Deut. 33:3 [b] Ex. 24:7 **50:6** [a] [Ps. 97:6] [b] Ps. 75:7 **50:7** [a] Ex. 20:2 **50:8** [a] Jer. 7:22 [b] Is. 1:11; [Hos. 6:6] **50:9** [a] Ps. 69:31 **50:12** [a] Ex. 19:5; [Deut. 10:14; Job 41:11]; 1 Cor. 10:26 **50:13** [a] [Ps. 51:15–17] **50:14** [a] Hos. 14:2; Heb. 13:15 [b] Num. 30:2; Deut. 23:21 **50:15** [a] Job 22:27; [Zech. 13:9] **50:17** [a] Neh. 9:26; Rom. 2:21 **50:18** [a] [Rom. 1:32] [b] 1 Tim. 5:22 [1] Septuagint, Syriac, Targum, and Vulgate read *ran.* **50:19** [a] Ps. 52:2 **50:21** [a] [Rom. 2:4] [b] [Ps. 90:8] **50:22** [a] [Job 8:13] **50:23** [a] Gal. 6:16 **51:title** [a] 2 Sam. 12:1 **51:1** [a] [Is. 43:25; 44:22; Acts 3:19; Col. 2:14] **51:2** [a] Jer. 33:8; Ezek. 36:33; [Heb. 9:14; 1 John 1:7, 9]

4 [a]Against You, You only, have I sinned,
And done *this* evil [b]in Your sight—
[c]That You may be found just when You speak,[1]
*And* blameless when You judge.

**51:4** David had **sinned** against Bathsheba, Uriah, and the nation he was called to rule. But as serious as these indictments were, none was more serious than David's offense against God.

5 [a]Behold, I was brought forth in iniquity,
And in sin my mother conceived me.
6 Behold, You desire truth in the inward parts,
And in the hidden *part* You will make me to know wisdom.

7 [a]Purge me with hyssop, and I shall be clean;
Wash me, and I shall be [b]whiter than snow.
8 Make me hear joy and gladness,
*That* the bones You have broken [a]may rejoice.
9 Hide Your face from my sins,
And blot out all my iniquities.

10 [a]Create in me a clean heart, O God,
And renew a steadfast spirit within me.
11 Do not cast me away from Your presence,
And do not take Your [a]Holy Spirit from me.

12 Restore to me the joy of Your salvation,
And uphold me *by Your* [a]generous Spirit.
13 *Then* I will teach transgressors Your ways,
And sinners shall be converted to You.

14 Deliver me from the guilt of bloodshed, O God,
The God of my salvation,
*And* my tongue shall sing aloud of Your righteousness.
15 O Lord, open my lips,
And my mouth shall show forth Your praise.
16 For [a]You do not desire sacrifice, or else I would give *it;*
You do not delight in burnt offering.
17 [a]The sacrifices of God *are* a broken spirit,
A broken and a contrite heart—
These, O God, You will not despise.

18 Do good in Your good pleasure to Zion;
Build the walls of Jerusalem.
19 Then You shall be pleased with [a]the sacrifices of righteousness,
With burnt offering and whole burnt offering;
Then they shall offer bulls on Your altar.

## PSALM 52

### THE END OF THE WICKED AND THE PEACE OF THE GODLY

*To the Chief Musician. A Contemplation[1] of David [a]when Doeg the Edomite went and [b]told Saul, and said to him, "David has gone to the house of Ahimelech."*

1 Why do you boast in evil, O mighty man?
The goodness of God *endures* continually.
2 Your tongue devises destruction,
Like a sharp razor, working deceitfully.
3 You love evil more than good,
Lying rather than speaking righteousness. *Selah*
4 You love all devouring words,
*You* deceitful tongue.

5 God shall likewise destroy you forever;
He shall take you away, and pluck you out of *your* dwelling place,
And uproot you from the land of the living. *Selah*
6 The righteous also shall see and fear,
And shall laugh at him, *saying,*
7 "Here is the man *who* did not make God his strength,
But trusted in the abundance of his riches,
*And* strengthened himself in his wickedness."

8 But I *am* [a]like a green olive tree in the house of God;
I trust in the mercy of God forever and ever.
9 I will praise You forever,
Because You have done *it;*
And in the presence of Your saints
I will wait on Your name, for *it is* good.

## PSALM 53

### FOLLY OF THE GODLESS, AND THE RESTORATION OF ISRAEL

*(Ps. 14:1–7)*

*To the Chief Musician. Set to "Mahalath." A Contemplation[1] of David.*

1 The [a]fool has said in his heart,
"*There is* no God."
They are corrupt, and have done abominable iniquity;
[b]*There is* none who does good.

**51:4** [a] 2 Sam. 12:13 [b] [Luke 5:21] [c] Rom. 3:4 [1] Septuagint, Targum, and Vulgate read *in Your words.* **51:5** [a] [Job 14:4; Ps. 58:3; John 3:6; Rom. 5:12] **51:7** [a] Ex. 12:22; Lev. 14:4; Num. 19:18; Heb. 9:19 [b] [Is. 1:18] **51:8** [a] [Matt. 5:4] **51:10** [a] [Ezek. 18:31; Eph. 2:10] **51:11** [a] [Luke 11:13] **51:12** [a] [2 Cor. 3:17] **51:16** [a] [1 Sam. 15:22]; Ps. 50:8–14; [Mic. 6:6–8] **51:17** [a] Ps. 34:18; [Is. 57:15]; 66:2 **51:19** [a] Ps. 4:5 **52:title** [a] 1 Sam. 22:9 [b] Ezek. 22:9 [1] Hebrew *Maschil* **52:8** [a] Jer. 11:16 **53:title** [1] Hebrew *Maschil* **53:1** [a] Ps. 10:4 [b] Rom. 3:10–12

2 God looks down from heaven upon the
children of men,
To see if there are *any* who understand,
who [a]seek God.
3 Every one of them has turned aside;
They have together become corrupt;
*There is* none who does good,
No, not one.

4 Have the workers of iniquity [a]no
knowledge,
Who eat up my people *as* they eat
bread,
And do not call upon God?
5 [a]There they are in great fear
*Where* no fear was,
For God has scattered the bones of him
who encamps against you;
You have put *them* to shame,
Because God has despised them.

6 [a]Oh, that the salvation of Israel would
come out of Zion!
When God brings back the captivity of His
people,
Let Jacob rejoice *and* Israel be glad.

## PSALM 54

### ANSWERED PRAYER FOR DELIVERANCE FROM ADVERSARIES

*To the Chief Musician. With stringed instruments.[1] A Contemplation[2] of David [a]when the Ziphites went and said to Saul, "Is David not hiding with us?"*

1 Save me, O God, by Your name,
And vindicate me by Your strength.
2 Hear my prayer, O God;
Give ear to the words of my mouth.
3 For strangers have risen up against me,
And oppressors have sought after my
life;
They have not set God before them. *Selah*

4 Behold, God *is* my helper;
The Lord *is* with those who uphold my
life.
5 He will repay my enemies for their evil.
Cut them off in Your truth.

6 I will freely sacrifice to You;
I will praise Your name, O LORD, for *it is*
good.
7 For He has delivered me out of all
trouble;
[a]And my eye has seen *its desire* upon my
enemies.

## PSALM 55

### TRUST IN GOD CONCERNING THE TREACHERY OF FRIENDS

*To the Chief Musician. With stringed instruments.[1] A Contemplation[2] of David.*

1 Give ear to my prayer, O God,
And do not hide Yourself from my
supplication.
2 Attend to me, and hear me;
I [a]am restless in my complaint, and moan
noisily,
3 Because of the voice of the enemy,
Because of the oppression of the wicked;
[a]For they bring down trouble upon me,
And in wrath they hate me.

4 [a]My heart is severely pained within me,
And the terrors of death have fallen upon me.
5 Fearfulness and trembling have come
upon me,
And horror has overwhelmed me.
6 So I said, "Oh, that I had wings like a dove!
I would fly away and be at rest.
7 Indeed, I would wander far off,
*And* remain in the wilderness. *Selah*
8 I would hasten my escape
From the windy storm *and* tempest."

9 Destroy, O Lord, *and* divide their tongues,
For I have seen [a]violence and strife in the
city.
10 Day and night they go around it on its walls;
[a]Iniquity and trouble *are* also in the midst
of it.
11 Destruction *is* in its midst;
[a]Oppression and deceit do not depart from
its streets.

12 [a]For *it is* not an enemy *who* reproaches me;
Then I could bear *it*.
Nor *is it* one *who* hates me who has
[b]exalted *himself* against me;
Then I could hide from him.
13 But *it was* you, a man my equal,
[a]My companion and my acquaintance.
14 We took sweet counsel together,
*And* [a]walked to the house of God in the throng.

15 Let death seize them;
Let them [a]go down alive into hell,
For wickedness *is* in their dwellings *and*
among them.

16 As for me, I will call upon God,
And the LORD shall save me.
17 [a]Evening and morning and at noon
I will pray, and cry aloud,
And He shall hear my voice.

53:2 [a] [2 Chr. 15:2] 53:4 [a] Jer. 4:22 53:5 [a] Lev. 26:17, 36; Prov. 28:1 53:6 [a] Ps. 14:7 54:title [a] 1 Sam. 23:19 [1] Hebrew *neginoth* [2] Hebrew *Maschil* 54:7 [a] Ps. 59:10 55:title [1] Hebrew *neginoth* [2] Hebrew *Maschil* 55:2 [a] Is. 38:14; 59:11; Ezek. 7:16 55:3 [a] 2 Sam. 16:7, 8 55:4 [a] Ps. 116:3 55:9 [a] Jer. 6:7 55:10 [a] Ps. 10:7 55:11 [a] Ps. 10:7 55:12 [a] Ps. 41:9 [b] Ps. 35:26; 38:16 55:13 [a] 2 Sam. 15:12 55:14 [a] Ps. 42:4 55:15 [a] Num. 16:30, 33 55:17 [a] Dan. 6:10

18 He has redeemed my soul in peace from
the battle *that was* against me,
For [a]there were many against me.
19 God will hear, and afflict them,
[a]Even He who abides from of old. *Selah*
Because they do not change,
Therefore they do not fear God.

20 He has [a]put forth his hands against those
who [b]were at peace with him;
He has broken his covenant.
21 [a]*The words* of his mouth were smoother
than butter,
But war *was* in his heart;
His words were softer than oil,
Yet they *were* drawn swords.

22 [a]Cast your burden on the LORD,
And [b]He shall sustain you;
He shall never permit the righteous to be
moved.

23 But You, O God, shall bring them down to
the pit of destruction;
[a]Bloodthirsty and deceitful men [b]shall not
live out half their days;
But I will trust in You.

## PSALM 56

### PRAYER FOR RELIEF FROM TORMENTORS

*To the Chief Musician. Set to "The Silent Dove in Distant Lands."[1] A Michtam of David when the [a]Philistines captured him in Gath.*

1 Be [a]merciful to me, O God, for man would
swallow me up;
Fighting all day he oppresses me.
2 My enemies would [a]hound *me* all day,
For *there are* many who fight against me,
O Most High.

3 Whenever I am afraid,
I will trust in You.
4 In God (I will praise His word),
In God I have put my trust;
[a]I will not fear.
What can flesh do to me?

5 All day they twist my words;
All their thoughts *are* against me for evil.
6 They gather together,
They hide, they mark my steps,
When they lie in wait for my life.
7 Shall they escape by iniquity?
In anger cast down the peoples, O God!

8 You number my wanderings;
Put my tears into Your bottle;
[a]*Are they* not in Your book?
9 When I cry out *to You,*
Then my enemies will turn back;
This I know, because [a]God *is* for me.
10 In God (I will praise *His* word),
In the LORD (I will praise *His* word),
11 In God I have put my trust;
I will not be afraid.
What can man do to me?

12 Vows *made* to You *are binding* upon me,
O God;
I will render praises to You,
13 [a]For You have delivered my soul from
death.
*Have You* not *kept* my feet from falling,
That I may walk before God
In the [b]light of the living?

## PSALM 57

### PRAYER FOR SAFETY FROM ENEMIES

*(cf. Ps. 108:1–5)*

*To the Chief Musician. Set to "Do Not Destroy."[1] A Michtam of David [a]when he fled from Saul into the cave.*

1 Be merciful to me, O God, be merciful
to me!
For my soul trusts in You;
[a]And in the shadow of Your wings I will
make my refuge,
[b]Until *these* calamities have passed by.

> **57:1** Throughout the Bible, **wings** are used as symbols of protection and safety, drawing from the picture of a mother hen covering her babies with her wings. In the same way, God shelters His children from danger.

2 I will cry out to God Most High,
To God [a]who performs *all things* for me.
3 [a]He shall send from heaven and save me;
He reproaches the one who would
swallow me up. *Selah*
God [b]shall send forth His mercy and His
truth.

4 My soul *is* among lions;
I lie *among* the sons of men
Who are set on fire,
[a]Whose teeth *are* spears and arrows,
And their tongue a sharp sword.
5 [a]Be exalted, O God, above the heavens;
*Let* Your glory *be* above all the earth.

**55:18** [a] 2 Chr. 32:7, 8 **55:19** [a] [Deut. 33:27] **55:20** [a] Acts 12:1 [b] Ps. 7:4 **55:21** [a] Ps. 28:3; 57:4 **55:22** [a] [Ps. 37:5] [b] Ps. 37:24 **55:23** [a] Ps. 5:6 [b] Prov. 10:27 **56:title** [a] 1 Sam. 21:11 [1] Hebrew *Jonath Elem Rechokim* **56:1** [a] Ps. 57:1 **56:2** [a] Ps. 57:3 **56:4** [a] Ps. 118:6 **56:8** [a] [Mal. 3:16] **56:9** [a] [Rom. 8:31] **56:13** [a] Ps. 116:8, 9 [b] Job 33:30 **57:title** [a] 1 Sam. 22:1 [1] Hebrew *Al Tashcheth* **57:1** [a] Ps. 17:8; 63:7 [b] Is. 26:20 **57:2** [a] [Ps. 138:8] **57:3** [a] Ps. 144:5, 7 [b] Ps. 43:3 **57:4** [a] Prov. 30:14 **57:5** [a] Ps. 108:5

6 [a]They have prepared a net for my steps;
My soul is bowed down;
They have dug a pit before me;
Into the midst of it they *themselves* have fallen. *Selah*
7 [a]My heart is steadfast, O God, my heart is steadfast;
I will sing and give praise.
8 Awake, [a]my glory!
Awake, lute and harp!
I will awaken the dawn.

9 [a]I will praise You, O Lord, among the peoples;
I will sing to You among the nations.
10 [a]For Your mercy reaches unto the heavens,
And Your truth unto the clouds.

11 [a]Be exalted, O God, above the heavens;
*Let* Your glory *be* above all the earth.

## PSALM 58

### THE JUST JUDGMENT OF THE WICKED

*To the Chief Musician. Set to "Do Not Destroy."[1] A Michtam of David.*

1 Do you indeed speak righteousness, you silent ones?
Do you judge uprightly, you sons of men?
2 No, in heart you work wickedness;
You weigh out the violence of your hands in the earth.

3 [a]The wicked are estranged from the womb;
They go astray as soon as they are born, speaking lies.
4 [a]Their poison *is* like the poison of a serpent;
*They are* like the deaf cobra *that* stops its ear,
5 Which will not [a]heed the voice of charmers,
Charming ever so skillfully.

6 [a]Break their teeth in their mouth, O God!
Break out the fangs of the young lions, O LORD!
7 [a]Let them flow away as waters *which* run continually;
*When* he bends *his bow,*
Let his arrows be as if cut in pieces.
8 *Let them be* like a snail which melts away as it goes,
[a]*Like* a stillborn child of a woman, that they may not see the sun.
9 Before your [a]pots can feel *the burning* thorns,
He shall take them away [b]as with a whirlwind,
As in His living and burning wrath.
10 The righteous shall rejoice when he sees the [a]vengeance;
[b]He shall wash his feet in the blood of the wicked,
11 [a]So that men will say,
"Surely *there is* a reward for the righteous;
Surely He is God who [b]judges in the earth."

## PSALM 59

### THE ASSURED JUDGMENT OF THE WICKED

*To the Chief Musician. Set to "Do Not Destroy."[1] A Michtam of David [a]when Saul sent men, and they watched the house in order to kill him.*

1 Deliver me from my enemies, O my God;
Defend me from those who rise up against me.
2 Deliver me from the workers of iniquity,
And save me from bloodthirsty men.

3 For look, they lie in wait for my life;
[a]The mighty gather against me,
Not *for* my transgression nor *for* my sin, O LORD.
4 They run and prepare themselves through no fault *of mine.*

[a]Awake to help me, and behold!
5 You therefore, O LORD God of hosts, the God of Israel,
Awake to punish all the nations;
Do not be merciful to any wicked transgressors. *Selah*

6 [a]At evening they return,
They growl like a dog,
And go all around the city.
7 Indeed, they belch with their mouth;
[a]Swords *are* in their lips;
For *they say,* [b]"Who hears?"

8 But [a]You, O LORD, shall laugh at them;
You shall have all the nations in derision.
9 I will wait for You, O You his Strength;[1]
[a]For God *is* my defense.
10 My God of mercy[1] shall [a]come to meet me;
God shall let [b]me see *my desire* on my enemies.

57:6 [a] Ps. 9:15 57:7 [a] Ps. 108:1–5 57:8 [a] Ps. 16:9 57:9 [a] Ps. 108:3 57:10 [a] Ps. 103:11 57:11 [a] Ps. 57:5 58:title [1] Hebrew *Al Tashcheth* 58:3 [a] [Is. 48:8] 58:4 [a] Eccl. 10:11 58:5 [a] Jer. 8:17 58:6 [a] Job 4:10 58:7 [a] Josh. 2:11; 7:5 58:8 [a] Job 3:16 58:9 [a] Eccl. 7:6 [b] Prov. 10:25 58:10 [a] Jer. 11:20 [b] Ps. 68:23 58:11 [a] Ps. 92:15 [b] Ps. 50:6; 75:7 59:title [a] 1 Sam. 19:11 [1] Hebrew *Al Tashcheth* 59:3 [a] Ps. 56:6 59:4 [a] Ps. 35:23 59:6 [a] Ps. 59:14 59:7 [a] Prov. 12:18 [b] Ps. 10:11 59:8 [a] Prov. 1:26 59:9 [a] [Ps. 62:2] [1] Following Masoretic Text and Syriac; some Hebrew manuscripts, Septuagint, Targum, and Vulgate read *my Strength.* 59:10 [a] Ps. 21:3 [b] Ps. 54:7 [1] Following Qere; some Hebrew manuscripts, Septuagint, and Vulgate read *My God, His mercy;* Kethib, some Hebrew manuscripts and Targum read *O God, my mercy;* Syriac reads *O God, Your mercy.*

11 Do not slay them, lest my people forget;
Scatter them by Your power,
And bring them down,
O Lord our shield.
12 [a]*For* the sin of their mouth *and* the words
of their lips,
Let them even be taken in their pride,
And for the cursing and lying *which* they
speak.
13 [a]Consume *them* in wrath, consume *them*,
That they *may* not *be;*
And [b]let them know that God rules in Jacob
To the ends of the earth. *Selah*

14 And [a]at evening they return,
They growl like a dog,
And go all around the city.
15 They [a]wander up and down for food,
And howl[1] if they are not satisfied.

16 But I will sing of Your power;
Yes, I will sing aloud of Your mercy in the
morning;
For You have been my defense
And refuge in the day of my trouble.
17 To You, [a]O my Strength, I will sing praises;
For God *is* my defense,
My God of mercy.

## PSALM 60

### URGENT PRAYER FOR THE RESTORED FAVOR OF GOD

*(cf. Ps. 108:6–13)*

*To the Chief Musician. [a]Set to "Lily of the Testimony."[1] A Michtam of David. For teaching. [b]When he fought against Mesopotamia and Syria of Zobah, and Joab returned and killed twelve thousand Edomites in the Valley of Salt.*

1 O God, [a]You have cast us off;
You have broken us down;
You have been displeased;
Oh, restore us again!
2 You have made the earth tremble;
You have broken it;
[a]Heal its breaches, for it is shaking.
3 [a]You have shown Your people hard things;
[b]You have made us drink the wine of
confusion.

4 [a]You have given a banner to those who fear
You,
That it may be displayed because of the
truth. *Selah*
5 [a]That Your beloved may be delivered,
Save *with* Your right hand, and hear me.

6 God has [a]spoken in His holiness:
"I will rejoice;
I will [b]divide [c]Shechem
And measure out [d]the Valley of Succoth.
7 Gilead *is* Mine, and Manasseh *is* Mine;
[a]Ephraim also *is* the helmet for My head;
[b]Judah *is* My lawgiver.
8 [a]Moab *is* My washpot;
[b]Over Edom I will cast My shoe;
[c]Philistia, shout in triumph because of Me."

**60:6–8** When David first became leader of Israel, he was challenged not only by the nation's enemies, but also by some of the people in his own country who refused to accept him as king. Eventually, the territories mentioned in this passage recognized God had chosen David as leader of Israel and submitted to his rule.

9 Who will bring me *to* the strong city?
Who will lead me to Edom?
10 *Is it* not You, O God, [a]*who* cast us off?
And You, O God, *who* did [b]not go out with
our armies?
11 Give us help from trouble,
[a]For the help of man *is* useless.
12 Through God [a]we will do valiantly,
For *it is* He *who* shall tread down our
enemies.[1]

## PSALM 61

### ASSURANCE OF GOD'S ETERNAL PROTECTION

*To the Chief Musician. On a stringed instrument.*[1] *A Psalm of David.*

1 Hear my cry, O God;
Attend to my prayer.
2 From the end of the earth I will cry to You,
When my heart is overwhelmed;
Lead me to the rock that is higher than I.

3 For You have been a shelter for me,
[a]A strong tower from the enemy.
4 I will abide in Your tabernacle forever;
[a]I will trust in the shelter of Your
wings. *Selah*

5 For You, O God, have heard my vows;
You have given *me* the heritage of those
who fear Your name.
6 You will prolong the king's life,
His years as many generations.

**59:12** [a] Prov. 12:13 **59:13** [a] Ps. 104:35 [b] Ps. 83:18 **59:14** [a] Ps. 59:6 **59:15** [a] Job 15:23 [1] Following Septuagint and Vulgate; Masoretic Text, Syriac, and Targum read *spend the night*. **59:17** [a] Ps. 18:1 **60:title** [a] Ps. 80 [b] 2 Sam. 8:3, 13 [1] Hebrew *Shushan Eduth* **60:1** [a] Ps. 44:9 **60:2** [a] [2 Chr. 7:14] **60:3** [a] Ps. 71:20 [b] Jer. 25:15 **60:4** [a] Ps. 20:5 **60:5** [a] Ps. 108:6–13 **60:6** [a] Ps. 89:35 [b] Josh. 1:6 [c] Gen. 12:6 [d] Josh. 13:27 **60:7** [a] Deut. 33:17 [b] [Gen. 49:10] **60:8** [a] 2 Sam. 8:2 [b] 2 Sam. 8:14 [c] 2 Sam. 8:1 **60:10** [a] Ps. 108:11 [b] Josh. 7:12 **60:11** [a] Ps. 118:8; 146:3 **60:12** [a] Num. 24:18 [1] Compare verses 5–12 with 108:6–13 **61:title** [1] Hebrew *neginah* **61:3** [a] Prov. 18:10 **61:4** [a] Ps. 91:4

7 He shall abide before God forever.
Oh, prepare mercy [a]and truth, *which* may
preserve him!

8 So I will sing praise to Your name
forever,
That I may daily perform my vows.

## PSALM 62

### A CALM RESOLVE TO WAIT FOR THE SALVATION OF GOD

*To the Chief Musician. To [a]Jeduthun. A Psalm of David.*

1 Truly [a]my soul silently *waits* for God;
From Him *comes* my salvation.
2 He only *is* my rock and my salvation;
*He is* my defense;
I shall not be greatly [a]moved.

3 How long will you attack a man?
You shall be slain, all of you,
[a]Like a leaning wall and a tottering
fence.
4 They only consult to cast *him* down from
his high position;
They [a]delight in lies;
They bless with their mouth,
But they curse inwardly. *Selah*

5 My soul, wait silently for God alone,
For my expectation *is* from Him.
6 He only *is* my rock and my salvation;
*He is* my defense;
I shall not be moved.
7 [a]In God *is* my salvation and my glory;
The rock of my strength,
*And* my refuge, *is* in God.

8 Trust in Him at all times, you people;
[a]Pour out your heart before Him;
God *is* a refuge for us. *Selah*

9 [a]Surely men of low degree *are* a vapor,
Men of high degree *are* a lie;
If they are weighed on the scales,
They *are* altogether *lighter* than
vapor.
10 Do not trust in oppression,
Nor vainly hope in robbery;
[a]If riches increase,
Do not set *your* heart *on them.*

11 God has spoken once,
Twice I have heard this:
That power *belongs* to God.
12 Also to You, O Lord, *belongs* mercy;
For [a]You render to each one according to
his work.

## PSALM 63

### JOY IN THE FELLOWSHIP OF GOD

*A Psalm of David [a]when he was in the wilderness of Judah.*

1 O God, You *are* my God;
Early will I seek You;
[a]My soul thirsts for You;
My flesh longs for You
In a dry and thirsty land
Where there is no water.
2 So I have looked for You in the sanctuary,
To see [a]Your power and Your glory.

3 [a]Because Your lovingkindness *is* better
than life,
My lips shall praise You.
4 Thus I will bless You while I live;
I will [a]lift up my hands in Your name.
5 My soul shall be satisfied as with marrow
and fatness,
And my mouth shall praise *You* with
joyful lips.

6 When [a]I remember You on my bed,
I meditate on You in the *night* watches.
7 Because You have been my help,
Therefore in the shadow of Your wings I
will rejoice.
8 My soul follows close behind You;
Your right hand upholds me.

9 But those *who* seek my life, to destroy *it,*
Shall go into the lower parts of the earth.
10 They shall fall by the sword;
They shall be a portion for jackals.

11 But the king shall rejoice in God;
[a]Everyone who swears by Him shall glory;
But the mouth of those who speak lies
shall be stopped.

## PSALM 64

### OPPRESSED BY THE WICKED BUT REJOICING IN THE LORD

*To the Chief Musician. A Psalm of David.*

1 Hear my voice, O God, in my meditation;
Preserve my life from fear of the enemy.
2 Hide me from the secret plots of the wicked,
From the rebellion of the workers of
iniquity,
3 Who sharpen their tongue like a sword,
[a]And bend *their bows to shoot* their
arrows—bitter words,
4 That they may shoot in secret at the
blameless;
Suddenly they shoot at him and do not
fear.

61:7 [a] Ps. 40:11 62:title [a] 1 Chr. 25:1 62:1 [a] Ps. 33:20 62:2 [a] Ps. 55:22 62:3 [a] Is. 30:13 62:4 [a] Ps. 28:3 62:7 [a] [Jer. 3:23] 62:8 [a] 1 Sam. 1:15 62:9 [a] Is. 40:17 62:10 [a] [Luke 12:15] 62:12 [a] [Matt. 16:27] 63:title [a] 1 Sam. 22:5 63:1 [a] Ps. 42:2 63:2 [a] Ps. 27:4 63:3 [a] Ps. 138:2 63:4 [a] Ps. 28:2; 143:6 63:6 [a] Ps. 42:8 63:11 [a] Deut. 6:13; [Is. 45:23; 65:16] 64:3 [a] Ps. 58:7

5 They encourage themselves *in* an evil matter;
They talk of laying snares secretly;
[a]They say, "Who will see them?"
6 They devise iniquities:
"We have perfected a shrewd scheme."
Both the inward thought and the heart of man are deep.

7 But God shall shoot at them *with* an arrow;
Suddenly they shall be wounded.
8 So He will make them stumble over their own tongue;
[a]All who see them shall flee away.
9 All men shall fear,
And shall [a]declare the work of God;
For they shall wisely consider His doing.

10 [a]The righteous shall be glad in the LORD, and trust in Him.
And all the upright in heart shall glory.

## PSALM 65

### PRAISE TO GOD FOR HIS SALVATION AND PROVIDENCE

*To the Chief Musician. A Psalm of David. A Song.*

1 Praise is awaiting You, O God, in Zion;
And to You the vow shall be performed.
2 O You who hear prayer,
[a]To You all flesh will come.
3 Iniquities prevail against me;
*As for* our transgressions,
You will [a]provide atonement for them.

4 [a]Blessed *is the man* You [b]choose,
And cause to approach *You,*
*That* he may dwell in Your courts.
[c]We shall be satisfied with the goodness of Your house,
Of Your holy temple.

5 *By* awesome deeds in righteousness You will answer us,
O God of our salvation,
*You who are* the confidence of all the ends of the earth,
And of the far-off seas;
6 Who established the mountains by His strength,
[a]*Being* clothed with power;
7 [a]You who still the noise of the seas,
The noise of their waves,
[b]And the tumult of the peoples.
8 They also who dwell in the farthest parts are afraid of Your signs;
You make the outgoings of the morning and evening rejoice.

9 You visit the earth and [a]water it,
You greatly enrich it;
[b]The river of God is full of water;
You provide their grain,
For so You have prepared it.
10 You water its ridges abundantly,
You settle its furrows;
You make it soft with showers,
You bless its growth.

11 You crown the year with Your goodness,
And Your paths drip *with* abundance.
12 They drop *on* the pastures of the wilderness,
And the little hills rejoice on every side.
13 The pastures are clothed with flocks;
[a]The valleys also are covered with grain;
They shout for joy, they also sing.

## PSALM 66

### PRAISE TO GOD FOR HIS AWESOME WORKS

*To the Chief Musician. A Song. A Psalm.*

1 Make [a]a joyful shout to God, all the earth!
2 Sing out the honor of His name;
Make His praise glorious.
3 Say to God,
"How [a]awesome are Your works!
[b]Through the greatness of Your power
Your enemies shall submit themselves to You.
4 [a]All the earth shall worship You
And sing praises to You;
They shall sing praises *to* Your name."
*Selah*

5 Come and see the works of God;
*He is* awesome *in His* doing toward the sons of men.
6 [a]He turned the sea into dry *land;*
[b]They went through the river on foot.
There we will rejoice in Him.

**66:6** The pharaoh of Egypt, after letting the Israelites leave his country, changed his mind, and sent his army to bring them back. His plan was to trap the Israelites at the Red Sea. Just when things looked hopeless for the Israelites, God parted the waters and created a path of **dry land** through the middle of the **sea**. The Israelites were able to walk across to the other side. When the Egyptians tried to follow, the water collapsed on top of them and they drowned.

**64:5** [a] Ps. 10:11; 59:7 **64:8** [a] Ps. 31:11 **64:9** [a] Jer. 50:28; 51:10 **64:10** [a] Job 22:19; Ps. 32:11 **65:2** [a] [Is. 66:23] **65:3** [a] Ps. 51:2; 79:9; Is. 6:7; [Heb. 9:14; 1 John 1:7, 9] **65:4** [a] Ps. 33:12 [b] Ps. 4:3 [c] Ps. 36:8 **65:6** [a] Ps. 93:1 **65:7** [a] Matt. 8:26 [b] Is. 17:12, 13 **65:9** [a] [Deut. 11:12]; Jer. 5:24 [b] Ps. 46:4; 104:13; 147:8 **65:13** [a] Is. 44:23; 55:12 **66:1** [a] Ps. 100:1 **66:3** [a] Ps. 65:5 [b] Ps. 18:44 **66:4** [a] Ps. 117:1; Zech. 14:16 **66:6** [a] Ex. 14:21 [b] Josh. 3:14–16

7 He rules by His power forever;
His eyes observe the nations;
Do not let the rebellious exalt themselves. *Selah*

8 Oh, bless our God, you peoples!
And make the voice of His praise to be heard,
9 Who keeps our soul among the living,
And does not allow our feet to be moved.
10 For [a]You, O God, have tested us;
[b]You have refined us as silver is refined.
11 [a]You brought us into the net;
You laid affliction on our backs.
12 [a]You have caused men to ride over our heads;
[b]We went through fire and through water;
But You brought us out to rich *fulfillment.*

13 [a]I will go into Your house with burnt offerings;
[b]I will pay You my vows,
14 Which my lips have uttered
And my mouth has spoken when I was in trouble.
15 I will offer You burnt sacrifices of fat animals,
With the sweet aroma of rams;
I will offer bulls with goats. *Selah*

16 Come *and* hear, all you who fear God,
And I will declare what He has done for my soul.
17 I cried to Him with my mouth,
And He was extolled with my tongue.
18 [a]If I regard iniquity in my heart,
The Lord will not hear.
19 *But* certainly God [a]has heard *me;*
He has attended to the voice of my prayer.

20 Blessed *be* God,
Who has not turned away my prayer,
Nor His mercy from me!

## PSALM 67

### *AN INVOCATION AND A DOXOLOGY*

*To the Chief Musician. On stringed instruments.*[1] *A Psalm. A Song.*

1 God be merciful to us and bless us,
*And* [a]cause His face to shine upon us, *Selah*
2 That [a]Your way may be known on earth,
[b]Your salvation among all nations.

3 Let the peoples praise You, O God;
Let all the peoples praise You.
4 Oh, let the nations be glad and sing for joy!
For [a]You shall judge the people righteously,
And govern the nations on earth. *Selah*

5 Let the peoples praise You, O God;
Let all the peoples praise You.
6 [a]*Then* the earth shall yield her increase;
God, our own God, shall bless us.
7 God shall bless us,
And all the ends of the earth shall fear Him.

## PSALM 68

### *THE GLORY OF GOD IN HIS GOODNESS TO ISRAEL*

*To the Chief Musician. A Psalm of David. A Song.*

1 Let [a]God arise,
Let His enemies be scattered;
Let those also who hate Him flee before Him.
2 [a]As smoke is driven away,
So drive *them* away;
[b]As wax melts before the fire,
*So* let the wicked perish at the presence of God.
3 But [a]let the righteous be glad;
Let them rejoice before God;
Yes, let them rejoice exceedingly.

4 Sing to God, sing praises to His name;
[a]Extol Him who rides on the clouds,[1]
[b]By His name YAH,
And rejoice before Him.

5 [a]A father of the fatherless, a defender of widows,
*Is* God in His holy habitation.
6 [a]God sets the solitary in families;
[b]He brings out those who are bound into prosperity;
But [c]the rebellious dwell in a dry *land.*

7 O God, [a]when You went out before Your people,
When You marched through the wilderness, *Selah*
8 The earth shook;
The heavens also dropped *rain* at the presence of God;
Sinai itself *was moved* at the presence of God, the God of Israel.
9 [a]You, O God, sent a plentiful rain,
Whereby You confirmed Your inheritance,
When it was weary.
10 Your congregation dwelt in it;
[a]You, O God, provided from Your goodness for the poor.

**66:10** [a] Ps. 17:3 [b] [1 Pet. 1:7] **66:11** [a] Lam. 1:13 **66:12** [a] Is. 51:23 [b] Is. 43:2 **66:13** [a] Ps. 100:4; 116:14, 17–19 [b] [Eccl. 5:4] **66:18** [a] Is. 1:15 **66:19** [a] Ps. 116:1, 2 **67:title** [1] Hebrew *neginoth* **67:1** [a] Num. 6:25 **67:2** [a] Acts 18:25 [b] Titus 2:11 **67:4** [a] [Ps. 96:10, 13; 98:9] **67:6** [a] Lev. 26:4 **68:1** [a] Num. 10:35 **68:2** [a] [Is. 9:18] [b] Mic. 1:4 **68:3** [a] Ps. 32:11 **68:4** [a] Deut. 33:26 [b] [Ex. 6:3] [1] Masoretic Text reads *deserts;* Targum reads *heavens* (compare verse 34 and Isaiah 19:1). **68:5** [a] [Ps. 10:14, 18; 146:9] **68:6** [a] Ps. 107:4–7 [b] Acts 12:6–11 [c] Ps. 107:34 **68:7** [a] Ex. 13:21 **68:9** [a] Deut. 11:11 **68:10** [a] Deut. 26:5

11 The Lord gave the word;
Great *was* the company of those who
proclaimed *it*:
12 "Kings[a] of armies flee, they flee,
And she who remains at home divides the
spoil.
13 [a]Though you lie down among the
sheepfolds,
[b]*You will be* like the wings of a dove
covered with silver,
And her feathers with yellow gold."
14 [a]When the Almighty scattered kings
in it,
It was *white* as snow in Zalmon.

15 A mountain of God *is* the mountain of
Bashan;
A mountain *of many* peaks *is* the
mountain of Bashan.
16 Why do you fume with envy, you
mountains of *many* peaks?
[a]*This is* the mountain *which* God desires to
dwell in;
Yes, the LORD will dwell *in it* forever.
17 [a]The chariots of God *are* twenty
thousand,
*Even* thousands of thousands;
The Lord is among them *as in* Sinai, in the
Holy *Place*.
18 [a]You have ascended on high,
[b]You have led captivity captive;
[c]You have received gifts among men,
Even *from* [d]the rebellious,
[e]That the LORD God might dwell *there*.
19 Blessed *be* the Lord,
*Who* daily loads us *with benefits*,
The God of our salvation! *Selah*
20 Our God *is* the God of salvation;
And [a]to GOD the Lord *belong* escapes from
death.

21 But [a]God will wound the head of His
enemies,
[b]The hairy scalp of the one who still goes
on in his trespasses.
22 The Lord said, "I will bring [a]back from
Bashan,
I will bring *them* back [b]from the depths of
the sea,
23 [a]That your foot may crush *them*[1] in
blood,
[b]And the tongues of your dogs *may
have* their portion from *your*
enemies."

24 They have seen Your procession, O God,
The procession of my God, my King, into
the sanctuary.
25 [a]The singers went before, the players on
instruments *followed* after;
Among *them were* the maidens playing
timbrels.
26 Bless God in the congregations,
The Lord, from [a]the fountain of Israel.
27 [a]There *is* little Benjamin, their leader,
The princes of Judah *and* their
company,
The princes of Zebulun *and* the princes of
Naphtali.

28 Your God has [a]commanded[1] your strength;
Strengthen, O God, what You have done
for us.
29 Because of Your temple at Jerusalem,
[a]Kings will bring presents to You.
30 Rebuke the beasts of the reeds,
[a]The herd of bulls with the calves of the
peoples,
*Till everyone* [b]submits himself with pieces
of silver.
Scatter the peoples *who* delight in war.
31 [a]Envoys will come out of Egypt;
[b]Ethiopia will quickly [c]stretch out her
hands to God.

32 Sing to God, you [a]kingdoms of the earth;
Oh, sing praises to the Lord, *Selah*
33 To Him [a]who rides on the heaven of
heavens, *which were* of old!
Indeed, He sends out His voice, a [b]mighty
voice.
34 [a]Ascribe strength to God;
His excellence *is* over Israel,
And His strength *is* in the clouds.
35 O God, [a]*You are* more awesome than Your
holy places.
The God of Israel *is* He who gives strength
and power to *His* people.

Blessed *be* God!

**68:22 Bashan**, which was located east of the Jordan River, was a fertile area of land that belonged to the tribe of Manasseh. Later in Israel's history, the area became known as much for its selfish and arrogant inhabitants as for its plentiful harvests and choice livestock.

**68:12** [a]Josh. 10:16 **68:13** [a]Ps. 81:6 [b]Ps. 105:37 **68:14** [a]Josh. 10:10 **68:16** [a][Deut. 12:5] **68:17** [a]Deut. 33:2 **68:18** [a]Eph. 4:8 [b]Judg. 5:12 [c]Acts 2:4, 33; 10:44–46 [d][1 Tim. 1:13] [e]Ps. 78:60 **68:20** [a][Deut. 32:39] **68:21** [a]Hab. 3:13 [b]Ps. 55:23 **68:22** [a]Num. 21:33; Deut. 30:1–9; Amos 9:1–3 [b]Ex. 14:22 **68:23** [a]Ps. 58:10 [b]1 Kin. 21:19; Jer. 15:3 [1]Septuagint, Syriac, Targum, and Vulgate read *you may dip your foot.* **68:25** [a]1 Chr. 13:8 **68:26** [a]Deut. 33:28; Is. 48:1 **68:27** [a]Judg. 5:14; 1 Sam. 9:21 **68:28** [a]Ps. 42:8; Is. 26:12 [1]Septuagint, Syriac, Targum, and Vulgate read *Command, O God.* **68:29** [a]1 Kin. 10:10, 25; 2 Chr. 32:23; Ps. 45:12; 72:10; Is. 18:7 **68:30** [a]Ps. 22:12 [b]2 Sam. 8:2 **68:31** [a]Is. 19:19–23 [b]Is. 45:14; Zeph. 3:10 [c]Ps. 44:20 **68:32** [a][Ps. 67:3, 4] **68:33** [a]Deut. 33:26; Ps. 18:10 [b]Ps. 46:6; Is. 30:30 **68:34** [a]Ps. 29:1 **68:35** [a]Ps. 76:12

## PSALM 69

### AN URGENT PLEA FOR HELP IN TROUBLE

*To the Chief Musician. Set to "The Lilies."*[1]
A Psalm *of David.*

1 Save me, O God!
For [a]the waters have come up to *my* neck.
2 [a]I sink in deep mire,
Where *there is* no standing;
I have come into deep waters,
Where the floods overflow me.
3 [a]I am weary with my crying;
My throat is dry;
[b]My eyes fail while I wait for my God.

4 Those who [a]hate me without a cause
Are more than the hairs of my head;
They are mighty who would destroy me,
*Being* my enemies wrongfully;
Though I have stolen nothing,
I *still* must restore *it.*

5 O God, You know my foolishness;
And my sins are not hidden from You.
6 Let not those who wait for You, O Lord GOD of hosts, be ashamed because of me;
Let not those who seek You be confounded because of me, O God of Israel.
7 Because for Your sake I have borne reproach;
Shame has covered my face.
8 [a]I have become a stranger to my brothers,
And an alien to my mother's children;
9 [a]Because zeal for Your house has eaten me up,
[b]And the reproaches of those who reproach You have fallen on me.
10 When I wept *and chastened* my soul with fasting,
That became my reproach.
11 I also made sackcloth my garment;
I became a byword to them.
12 Those who sit in the gate speak against me,
And I *am* the song of the [a]drunkards.

13 But as for me, my prayer *is* to You,
O LORD, *in* the acceptable time;
O God, in the multitude of Your mercy,
Hear me in the truth of Your salvation.
14 Deliver me out of the mire,
And let me not sink;
Let me be delivered from those who hate me,
And out of the deep waters.
15 Let not the floodwater overflow me,
Nor let the deep swallow me up;
And let not the pit shut its mouth on me.

16 Hear me, O LORD, for Your lovingkindness *is* good;
Turn to me according to the multitude of Your tender mercies.
17 And do not hide Your face from Your servant,
For I am in trouble;
Hear me speedily.
18 Draw near to my soul, *and* redeem it;
Deliver me because of my enemies.

19 You know [a]my reproach, my shame, and my dishonor;
My adversaries *are* all before You.
20 Reproach has broken my heart,
And I am full of heaviness;
[a]I looked *for someone* to take pity, but *there was* none;
And for [b]comforters, but I found none.
21 They also gave me gall for my food,
[a]And for my thirst they gave me vinegar to drink.

**SEEING JESUS IN THE SCRIPTURE**

**69:21** What David spoke of figuratively, Jesus experienced literally on the cross. Jesus refused the wine offered Him to experience the full weight and agony of God's wrath (see Matt. 27:34).

22 [a]Let their table become a snare before them,
And their well-being a trap.
23 [a]Let their eyes be darkened, so that they do not see;
And make their loins shake continually.
24 [a]Pour out Your indignation upon them,
And let Your wrathful anger take hold of them.
25 [a]Let their dwelling place be desolate;
Let no one live in their tents.
26 For they persecute the *ones* [a]You have struck,
And talk of the grief of those You have wounded.
27 [a]Add iniquity to their iniquity,
[b]And let them not come into Your righteousness.
28 Let them [a]be blotted out of the book of the living,
[b]And not be written with the righteous.

29 But I *am* poor and sorrowful;
Let Your salvation, O God, set me up on high.
30 [a]I will praise the name of God with a song,
And will magnify Him with thanksgiving.

69:title [1] Hebrew *Shoshannim* 69:1 [a] Job 22:11; Jon. 2:5 69:2 [a] Ps. 40:2 69:3 [a] Ps. 6:6 [b] Deut. 28:32; Ps. 119:82, 123; Is. 38:14 69:4 [a] Ps. 35:19; John 15:25 69:8 [a] Is. 53:3; Mark 3:21; Luke 8:19; John 7:3–5 69:9 [a] John 2:17 [b] Rom. 15:3 69:12 [a] Job 30:9 69:19 [a] Ps. 22:6, 7; Heb. 12:2 69:20 [a] Is. 63:5 [b] Job 16:2 69:21 [a] Matt. 27:34, 48 69:22 [a] Rom. 11:9, 10 69:23 [a] Is. 6:9, 10 69:24 [a] [1 Thess. 2:16] 69:25 [a] Matt. 23:38 69:26 [a] [Is. 53:4] 69:27 [a] [Rom. 1:28] [b] [Is. 26:10] 69:28 [a] [Ex. 32:32] [b] Ezek. 13:9 69:30 [a] [Ps. 28:7]

31 [a]*This* also shall please the LORD better than
an ox *or* bull,
Which has horns and hooves.
32 [a]The humble shall see *this and* be glad;
And you who seek God, [b]your hearts shall
live.
33 For the LORD hears the poor,
And does not despise [a]His prisoners.

34 [a]Let heaven and earth praise Him,
The seas [b]and everything that moves in
them.
35 [a]For God will save Zion
And build the cities of Judah,
That they may dwell there and possess it.
36 Also, [a]the descendants of His servants
shall inherit it,
And those who love His name shall dwell
in it.

## PSALM 70

### PRAYER FOR RELIEF FROM ADVERSARIES

*(Ps. 40:13–17)*

*To the Chief Musician.* A Psalm *of David.* [a]*To bring to remembrance.*

1 *Make haste*, [a]O God, to deliver me!
Make haste to help me, O LORD!

2 [a]Let them be ashamed and confounded
Who seek my life;
Let them be turned back[1] and confused
Who desire my hurt.
3 [a]Let them be turned back because of their
shame,
Who say, "Aha, aha!"

4 Let all those who seek You rejoice and be
glad in You;
And let those who love Your salvation say
continually,
"Let God be magnified!"

5 [a]But I *am* poor and needy;
[b]Make haste to me, O God!
You *are* my help and my deliverer;
O LORD, do not delay.

## PSALM 71

### GOD THE ROCK OF SALVATION

1 In [a]You, O LORD, I put my trust;
Let me never be put to shame.
2 [a]Deliver me in Your righteousness, and
cause me to escape;
[b]Incline Your ear to me, and save me.
3 [a]Be my strong refuge,
To which I may resort continually;
You have given the [b]commandment to
save me,
For You *are* my rock and my fortress.

4 [a]Deliver me, O my God, out of the hand of
the wicked,
Out of the hand of the unrighteous and
cruel man.
5 For You are [a]my hope, O Lord GOD;
*You are* my trust from my youth.
6 [a]By You I have been upheld from birth;
You are He who took me out of my
mother's womb.
My praise *shall be* continually of You.

7 [a]I have become as a wonder to many,
But You *are* my strong refuge.
8 Let [a]my mouth be filled *with* Your praise
*And with* Your glory all the day.

9 Do not cast me off in the time of old age;
Do not forsake me when my strength
fails.
10 For my enemies speak against me;
And those who lie in wait for my life [a]take
counsel together,
11 Saying, "God has forsaken him;
Pursue and take him, for *there is* none to
deliver *him*."

12 [a]O God, do not be far from me;
O my God, [b]make haste to help me!
13 Let them be confounded *and* consumed
Who are adversaries of my life;
Let them be covered *with* reproach and
dishonor
Who seek my hurt.
14 But I will hope continually,
And will praise You yet more and more.
15 My mouth shall tell of Your righteousness
*And* Your salvation all the day,
For I do not know *their* limits.
16 I will go in the strength of the Lord GOD;
I will make mention of Your
righteousness, of Yours only.

17 O God, You have taught me from my
[a]youth;
And to this *day* I declare Your wondrous
works.
18 Now also [a]when *I am* old and grayheaded,
O God, do not forsake me,
Until I declare Your strength to *this*
generation,
Your power to everyone *who* is to come.

**69:31** [a] Ps. 50:13, 14, 23; 51:16 **69:32** [a] Ps. 34:2 [b] Ps. 22:26 **69:33** [a] Eph. 3:1 **69:34** [a] Ps. 96:11 [b] Is. 55:12 **69:35** [a] Is. 44:26 **69:36** [a] Ps. 102:28 **70:title** [a] Ps. 38:title **70:1** [a] Ps. 40:13–17 **70:2** [a] Ps. 35:4, 26 [1] Following Masoretic Text, Septuagint, Targum, and Vulgate; some Hebrew manuscripts and Syriac read *be appalled* (compare 40:15). **70:3** [a] Ps. 40:15 **70:5** [a] Ps. 72:12, 13 [b] Ps. 141:1 **71:1** [a] Ps. 25:2, 3 **71:2** [a] Ps. 31:1 [b] Ps. 17:6 **71:3** [a] Ps. 31:2, 3 [b] Ps. 44:4 **71:4** [a] Ps. 140:1, 3 **71:5** [a] Jer. 14:8; 17:7, 13, 17; 50:7 **71:6** [a] Ps. 22:9, 10 **71:7** [a] Is. 8:18 **71:8** [a] Ps. 35:28 **71:10** [a] 2 Sam. 17:1 **71:12** [a] Ps. 35:22 [b] Ps. 70:1 **71:17** [a] Deut. 4:5; 6:7 **71:18** [a] [Is. 46:4]

19 Also [a]Your righteousness, O God, *is* very high,
You who have done great things;
[b]O God, who *is* like You?
20 [a]*You,* who have shown me great and severe
troubles,
[b]Shall revive me again,
And bring me up again from the depths of
the earth.
21 You shall increase my greatness,
And comfort me on every side.

22 Also [a]with the lute I will praise You—
*And* Your faithfulness, O my God!
To You I will sing with the harp,
O [b]Holy One of Israel.
23 My lips shall greatly rejoice when I sing to
You,
And [a]my soul, which You have redeemed.
24 My tongue also shall talk of Your
righteousness all the day long;
For they are confounded,
For they are brought to shame
Who seek my hurt.

## PSALM 72

### GLORY AND UNIVERSALITY OF THE MESSIAH'S REIGN

A Psalm [a]*of Solomon.*

1 Give the king Your judgments, O God,
And Your righteousness to the king's Son.
2 [a]He will judge Your people with
righteousness,
And Your poor with justice.

**SEEING JESUS IN THE SCRIPTURE**

**72:1–2** Here, Solomon anticipates God fulfilling the covenant He made with David in which He promised a future Son would rule perfectly forever (see 2 Sam. 7:12–13). Jesus is that Son who rules and judges in righteousness (see Acts 17:31).

3 [a]The mountains will bring peace to the
people,
And the little hills, by righteousness.
4 [a]He will bring justice to the poor of the
people;
He will save the children of the needy,
And will break in pieces the oppressor.

5 They shall fear You[1]
[a]As long as the sun and moon endure,
Throughout all generations.
6 [a]He shall come down like rain upon the
grass before mowing,
Like showers *that* water the earth.
7 In His days the righteous shall flourish,
[a]And abundance of peace,
Until the moon is no more.

8 [a]He shall have dominion also from sea to
sea,
And from the River to the ends of the earth.
9 [a]Those who dwell in the wilderness will
bow before Him,
[b]And His enemies will lick the dust.
10 [a]The kings of Tarshish and of the isles
Will bring presents;
The kings of Sheba and Seba
Will offer gifts.
11 [a]Yes, all kings shall fall down before Him;
All nations shall serve Him.

12 For He [a]will deliver the needy when he cries,
The poor also, and *him* who has no helper.
13 He will spare the poor and needy,
And will save the souls of the needy.
14 He will redeem their life from oppression
and violence;
And [a]precious shall be their blood in His
sight.

15 And He shall live;
And the gold of [a]Sheba will be given to Him;
Prayer also will be made for Him
continually,
*And* daily He shall be praised.

16 There will be an abundance of grain in the
earth,
On the top of the mountains;
Its fruit shall wave like Lebanon;
[a]And *those* of the city shall flourish like
grass of the earth.
17 [a]His name shall endure forever;
His name shall continue as long as the sun.
And [b]*men* shall be blessed in Him;
[c]All nations shall call Him blessed.

18 [a]Blessed *be* the LORD God, the God of
Israel,
[b]Who only does wondrous things!
19 And [a]blessed *be* His glorious name
forever!
[b]And let the whole earth be filled *with* His
glory.
Amen and Amen.

20 The prayers of David the son of Jesse are
ended.

**71:19** [a] Ps. 57:10 [b] Ps. 35:10 **71:20** [a] Ps. 60:3 [b] Hos. 6:1, 2 **71:22** [a] Ps. 92:1–3 [b] 2 Kin. 19:22 **71:23** [a] Ps. 103:4 **72:title** [a] Ps. 127:title **72:2** [a] [Is. 9:7; 11:2–5; 32:1] **72:3** [a] Ps. 85:10 **72:4** [a] Is. 11:4 **72:5** [a] Ps. 72:7, 17; 89:36 [1] Following Masoretic Text and Targum; Septuagint and Vulgate read *They shall continue.* **72:6** [a] Hos. 6:3 **72:7** [a] Is. 2:4 **72:8** [a] Ex. 23:31 **72:9** [a] Is. 23:13 [b] Is. 49:23 **72:10** [a] 2 Chr. 9:21 **72:11** [a] Is. 49:23 **72:12** [a] Job 29:12 **72:14** [a] [Ps. 116:15] **72:15** [a] Is. 60:6 **72:16** [a] 1 Kin. 4:20 **72:17** [a] [Ps. 89:36] [b] [Gen. 12:3] [c] Luke 1:48 **72:18** [a] 1 Chr. 29:10 [b] Ex. 15:11 **72:19** [a] [Neh. 9:5] [b] Num. 14:21

# BOOK THREE
## *PSALMS 73–89*

### PSALM 73

**THE TRAGEDY OF THE WICKED, AND THE BLESSEDNESS OF TRUST IN GOD**

*A Psalm of* [a]*Asaph.*

1 Truly God *is* good to Israel,
To such as are pure in heart.
2 But as for me, my feet had almost stumbled;
My steps had nearly [a]slipped.
3 [a]For I *was* envious of the boastful,
When I saw the prosperity of the [b]wicked.

4 For *there are* no pangs in their death,
But their strength *is* firm.
5 [a]They *are* not in trouble *as other* men,
Nor are they plagued like *other* men.
6 Therefore pride serves as their necklace;
Violence covers them [a]*like* a garment.
7 [a]Their eyes bulge[1] with abundance;
They have more than heart could wish.
8 [a]They scoff and speak wickedly *concerning* oppression;
They [b]speak loftily.
9 They set their mouth [a]against the heavens,
And their tongue walks through the earth.

10 Therefore his people return here,
[a]And waters of a full *cup* are drained by them.
11 And they say, [a]"How does God know?
And is there knowledge in the Most High?"
12 Behold, these *are* the ungodly,
Who are always at ease;
They increase *in* riches.
13 Surely I have cleansed my heart *in* [a]vain,
And washed my hands in innocence.
14 For all day long I have been plagued,
And chastened every morning.

15 If I had said, "I will speak thus,"
Behold, I would have been untrue to the generation of Your children.
16 When I thought *how* to understand this,
It *was* too painful for me—
17 Until I went into the sanctuary of God;
*Then* I understood their [a]end.
18 Surely [a]You set them in slippery places;
You cast them down to destruction.
19 Oh, how they are *brought* to desolation, as in a moment!
They are utterly consumed with terrors.
20 As a dream when *one* awakes,
*So,* Lord, when You awake,
You shall despise their image.

21 Thus my heart was grieved,
And I was vexed in my mind.
22 [a]I *was* so foolish and ignorant;
I was *like* a beast before You.
23 Nevertheless I *am* continually with You;
You hold *me* by my right hand.
24 [a]You will guide me with Your counsel,
And afterward receive me *to* glory.

25 [a]Whom have I in heaven *but You?*
And *there is* none upon earth *that* I desire besides You.

**73:title** [a] Ps. 50:title **73:2** [a] Job 12:5 **73:3** [a] Ps. 37:1, 7 [b] Job 21:5–16 **73:5** [a] Job 21:9 **73:6** [a] Ps. 109:18 **73:7** [a] Jer. 5:28
[1] Targum reads *face bulges;* Septuagint, Syriac, and Vulgate read *iniquity bulges.* **73:8** [a] Ps. 53:1 [b] 2 Pet. 2:18 **73:9** [a] Rev. 13:6
**73:10** [a] [Ps. 75:8] **73:11** [a] Job 22:13 **73:13** [a] Job 21:15; 35:3 **73:17** [a] [Ps. 37:38; 55:23] **73:18** [a] Ps. 35:6 **73:22** [a] Ps. 92:6
**73:24** [a] Ps. 32:8; 48:14 **73:25** [a] [Phil. 3:8]

APPLY THE TRUTH

## DISCOURAGEMENT

**73:1–28** Many things in the world don't seem to make sense. People who don't work very hard are successful, while those with great talents struggle. Some people appear to have it all, yet they're miserable. Sometimes when we examine these inconsistencies it causes us to scratch our heads and feel discouraged about our lives. Why aren't things going the way we want them to go? How do our friends get everything they want, and we get so little? Why does life have to be so difficult? These observations can lead to all sorts of conclusions about ourselves, others, and even God.

The psalmist had similar observations. He saw the wicked prosper while the righteous suffered. He was discouraged and jumped to conclusions, almost slipping into despair. But then something changed. His discouragement morphed into optimism, and he even began to encourage others. What changed? He "went into the sanctuary of God" (v. 17). He got in the presence of God and found encouragement in God's love and perspective in God's plans. Feeling down? Rest in God's love and find hope in His plans.

26 [a]My flesh and my heart fail;
*But* God *is* the strength of my heart and my [b]portion forever.
27 For indeed, [a]those who are far from You shall perish;
You have destroyed all those who desert You for harlotry.
28 But *it is* good for me to [a]draw near to God;
I have put my trust in the Lord GOD,
That I may [b]declare all Your works.

## PSALM 74

### A PLEA FOR RELIEF FROM OPPRESSORS

*A Contemplation[1] of Asaph.*

1 O God, why have You cast *us* off forever?
*Why* does Your anger smoke against the sheep of Your pasture?
2 Remember Your congregation, *which* You have purchased of old,
The tribe of Your inheritance, *which* You have redeemed—
This Mount Zion where You have dwelt.
3 Lift up Your feet to the perpetual desolations.
The enemy has damaged everything in the sanctuary.
4 [a]Your enemies roar in the midst of Your meeting place;
[b]They set up their banners *for* signs.
5 They seem like men who lift up
Axes among the thick trees.
6 And now they break down its carved work, all at once,
With axes and hammers.
7 They have set fire to Your sanctuary;
They have defiled the dwelling place of Your name to the ground.
8 [a]They said in their hearts,
"Let us destroy them altogether."
They have burned up all the meeting places of God in the land.

9 We do not see our signs;
[a]*There is* no longer any prophet;
Nor *is there* any among us who knows how long.
10 O God, how long will the adversary reproach?
Will the enemy blaspheme Your name forever?
11 [a]Why do You withdraw Your hand, even Your right hand?
*Take it* out of Your bosom and destroy *them.*
12 For [a]God *is* my King from of old,
Working salvation in the midst of the earth.
13 [a]You divided the sea by Your strength;
You broke the heads of the sea serpents in the waters.
14 You broke the heads of Leviathan in pieces,
*And* gave him *as* food to the people inhabiting the wilderness.

> **74:14** The **Leviathan** was used to describe various evil forces over which God has ultimate control and victory. Eventually this creature (see Job 41:1–10) became a symbol for Satan (see Is. 27:1) who is "the dragon, that serpent of old" (Rev. 20:2).

15 [a]You broke open the fountain and the flood;
[b]You dried up mighty rivers.
16 The day *is* Yours, the night also *is* [a]Yours;
[b]You have prepared the light and the sun.
17 You have [a]set all the borders of the earth;
[b]You have made summer and winter.

18 Remember this, *that* the enemy has reproached, O LORD,
And *that* a foolish people has blasphemed Your name.
19 Oh, do not deliver the life of Your turtledove to the wild beast!
Do not forget the life of Your poor forever.
20 [a]Have respect to the covenant;
For the dark places of the earth are full of the haunts of cruelty.
21 Oh, do not let the oppressed return ashamed!
Let the poor and needy praise Your name.

22 Arise, O God, plead Your own cause;
Remember how the foolish man reproaches You daily.
23 Do not forget the voice of Your enemies;
The tumult of those who rise up against You increases continually.

## PSALM 75

### THANKSGIVING FOR GOD'S RIGHTEOUS JUDGMENT

*To the Chief Musician. Set to [a]"Do Not Destroy."[1] A Psalm of Asaph. A Song.*

1 We give thanks to You, O God, we give thanks!
For Your wondrous works declare *that* Your name is near.

2 "When I choose the proper time,
I will judge uprightly.

**73:26** [a] Ps. 84:2 [b] Ps. 16:5 **73:27** [a] [Ps. 119:155] **73:28** [a] [Heb. 10:22] [b] 2 Cor. 4:13 **74:title** [1] Hebrew *Maschil* **74:4** [a] Lam. 2:7 [b] Num. 2:2 **74:8** [a] Ps. 83:4 **74:9** [a] Amos 8:11 **74:11** [a] Lam. 2:3 **74:12** [a] Ps. 44:4 **74:13** [a] Ex. 14:21 **74:15** [a] Ex. 17:5, 6 [b] Josh. 2:10; 3:13 **74:16** [a] Job 38:12 [b] Gen. 1:14–18 **74:17** [a] Acts 17:26 [b] Gen. 8:22 **74:20** [a] Lev. 26:44, 45 **75:title** [a] Ps. 57:title [1] Hebrew *Al Tashcheth*

3 The earth and all its inhabitants are
dissolved;
I set up its pillars firmly. *Selah*

4 "I said to the boastful, 'Do not deal
boastfully,'
And to the wicked, [a]'Do not lift up the horn.
5 Do not lift up your horn on high;
Do *not* speak with a stiff neck.' "

6 For exaltation *comes* neither from the east
Nor from the west nor from the south.
7 But [a]God *is* the Judge:
[b]He puts down one,
And exalts another.
8 For [a]in the hand of the LORD *there is* a cup,
And the wine is red;
It is fully mixed, and He pours it out;
Surely its dregs shall all the wicked of the
earth
Drain *and* drink down.

9 But I will declare forever,
I will sing praises to the God of Jacob.

10 "All[a] the horns of the wicked I will also cut
off,
*But* [b]the horns of the righteous shall be
[c]exalted."

## PSALM 76

### THE MAJESTY OF GOD IN JUDGMENT

*To the Chief Musician. On stringed instruments.[1]*
*A Psalm of Asaph. A Song.*

1 In [a]Judah God *is* known;
His name *is* great in Israel.
2 In Salem[1] also is His tabernacle,
And His dwelling place in Zion.
3 There He broke the arrows of the bow,
The shield and sword of battle. *Selah*

4 You *are* more glorious and excellent
[a]*Than* the mountains of prey.
5 [a]The stouthearted were plundered;
[b]They have sunk into their sleep;
And none of the mighty men have found
the use of their hands.
6 [a]At Your rebuke, O God of Jacob,
Both the chariot and horse were cast into
a dead sleep.

7 You, Yourself, *are* to be feared;
And [a]who may stand in Your presence
When once You are angry?
8 [a]You caused judgment to be heard from
heaven;
[b]The earth feared and was still,
9 When God [a]arose to judgment,
To deliver all the oppressed of the
earth. *Selah*

10 [a]Surely the wrath of man shall praise
You;
With the remainder of wrath You shall
gird Yourself.

11 [a]Make vows to the LORD your God, and pay
*them;*
[b]Let all who are around Him bring
presents to Him who ought to be
feared.
12 He shall cut off the spirit of princes;
[a]*He is* awesome to the kings of the
earth.

## PSALM 77

### THE CONSOLING MEMORY OF GOD'S REDEMPTIVE WORKS

*To the Chief Musician. [a]To Jeduthun.*
*A Psalm of Asaph.*

1 I cried out to God with my voice—
To God with my voice;
And He gave ear to me.
2 In the day of my trouble I sought the
Lord;
My hand was stretched out in the night
without ceasing;
My soul refused to be comforted.
3 I remembered God, and was troubled;
I complained, and my spirit was
overwhelmed. *Selah*

4 You hold my eyelids *open;*
I am so troubled that I cannot speak.
5 I have considered the days of old,
The years of ancient times.
6 I call to remembrance my song in the
night;
I meditate within my heart,
And my spirit makes diligent search.

7 Will the Lord cast off forever?
And will He be favorable no more?
8 Has His mercy ceased forever?
Has *His* [a]promise failed forevermore?
9 Has God forgotten to be gracious?
Has He in anger shut up His tender
mercies? *Selah*

10 And I said, "This *is* my anguish;
*But I will remember* the years of the right
hand of the Most High."

75:4 [a] [1 Sam. 2:3] 75:7 [a] Ps. 50:6 [b] 1 Sam. 2:7; Ps. 147:6; Dan. 2:21 75:8 [a] Job 21:20; Ps. 60:3; Jer. 25:15; Rev. 14:10; 16:19
75:10 [a] Ps. 101:8; Jer. 48:25 [b] Ps. 89:17; 148:14 [c] 1 Sam. 2:1 76:title [1] Hebrew *neginoth* 76:1 [a] Ps. 48:1, 3 76:2 [1] That is, Jerusalem
76:4 [a] Ezek. 38:12 76:5 [a] Is. 10:12; 46:12 [b] Ps. 13:3 76:6 [a] Ex. 15:1–21; Ezek. 39:20; Nah. 2:13; Zech. 12:4 76:7 [a] [Ezra 9:15; Nah. 1:6; Mal. 3:2; Rev. 6:17] 76:8 [a] Ex. 19:9 [b] 1 Chr. 16:30; 2 Chr. 20:29 76:9 [a] [Ps. 9:7–9] 76:10 [a] Ex. 9:16; Rom. 9:17 76:11 [a] [Eccl. 5:4–6]
[b] 2 Chr. 32:22, 23 76:12 [a] Ps. 68:35 77:title [a] Ps. 39:title 77:8 [a] [2 Pet. 3:8, 9]

**77:10** The **right hand** is a way of describing God's strength. Specifically, the phrase is used to describe God's highly visible actions, such as the miracles He performed around the time of the Israelites' exodus from Egypt.

11 I will remember the works of the
LORD;
Surely I will remember Your wonders of
old.
12 I will also meditate on all Your work,
And talk of Your deeds.
13 Your way, O God, *is* in the [a]sanctuary;
Who *is* so great a God as *our* God?
14 You *are* the God who does wonders;
You have declared Your strength among
the peoples.
15 You have with *Your* arm redeemed Your
people,
The sons of Jacob and Joseph. *Selah*

16 The waters saw You, O God;
The waters saw You, they were [a]afraid;
The depths also trembled.
17 The clouds poured out water;
The skies sent out a sound;
Your arrows also flashed about.
18 The voice of Your thunder *was* in the
whirlwind;
The lightnings lit up the world;
The earth trembled and shook.
19 Your way *was* in the sea,
Your path in the great waters,
And Your footsteps were not
known.
20 You led Your people like a flock
By the hand of Moses and Aaron.

# PSALM 78

## *GOD'S KINDNESS TO REBELLIOUS ISRAEL*

*A [a]Contemplation[1] of Asaph.*

1 Give ear, O my people, *to* my law;
Incline your ears to the words of my
mouth.
2 I will open my mouth in a [a]parable;
I will utter dark sayings of old,

**SEEING JESUS IN THE SCRIPTURE**

**78:2** Just as Asaph taught in parables, so did Jesus (see Matt. 13:35). Asaph taught about things passed down from prior generations while Jesus revealed things not known in previous generations.

3 Which we have heard and known,
And our fathers have told us.
4 [a]We will not hide *them* from their
children,
[b]Telling to the generation to come the
praises of the LORD,
And His strength and His wonderful
works that He has done.

5 For [a]He established a testimony in
Jacob,
And appointed a law in Israel,
Which He commanded our fathers,
That [b]they should make them known to
their children;
6 [a]That the generation to come might know
*them,*
The children *who* would be born,
*That* they may arise and declare *them* to
their children,

**77:13** [a] Ps. 73:17 **77:16** [a] Ex. 14:21; Hab. 3:8, 10 **78:title** [a] Ps. 74:title [1] Hebrew *Maschil* **78:2** [a] Matt. 13:34, 35 **78:4** [a] Deut. 4:9; 6:7 [b] Ex. 13:8, 14 **78:5** [a] Ps. 147:19 [b] Deut. 4:9; 11:19 **78:6** [a] Ps. 102:18

LIVE THE TRUTH

## MEDITATING ON GOD'S WORD

**77:12** When you hear "meditate," you might picture people emptying their minds to achieve some form of inner peace. That's not biblical meditation though. Biblical meditation isn't emptying your mind to get peace; it's filling your mind with God's Word and dwelling on what He's done through Jesus that has given you peace. It's to think about the Bible and consider how it applies to your life.

As we read the Bible, we should meditate on it to ensure we understand what it says. We should pray, asking the Holy Spirit to help us see what it teaches. As we continue to meditate, we should think about how to draw out application points for our lives. That's the beauty of meditation: it continues our experience of God's Word well past our time of reading. Our meditation throughout the day—anywhere at any time—allows us to be in constant connection with God's Word. When we meditate on God's Word, we carry God's wisdom and presence into our lives. It takes Bible engagement from being a pastime or hobby to being the core of who we are and what we do.

7 That they may set their hope in God,
And not forget the works of God,
But keep His commandments;
8 And [a]may not be like their fathers,
[b]A stubborn and rebellious generation,
A generation [c]*that* did not set its heart
aright,
And whose spirit was not faithful to God.

9 The children of Ephraim, *being* armed
*and* carrying bows,
Turned back in the day of battle.
10 [a]They did not keep the covenant of God;
They refused to walk in His law,
11 And [a]forgot His works
And His wonders that He had shown them.

12 [a]Marvelous things He did in the sight of
their fathers,
In the land of Egypt, [b]*in* the field of Zoan.
13 [a]He divided the sea and caused them to
pass through;
And [b]He made the waters stand up like a
heap.
14 [a]In the daytime also He led them with the
cloud,
And all the night with a light of fire.
15 [a]He split the rocks in the wilderness,
And gave *them* drink in abundance like
the depths.
16 He also brought [a]streams out of the rock,
And caused waters to run down like rivers.

17 But they sinned even more against Him
By [a]rebelling against the Most High in the
wilderness.
18 And [a]they tested God in their heart
By asking for the food of their fancy.
19 [a]Yes, they spoke against God:
They said, "Can God prepare a table in the
wilderness?
20 [a]Behold, He struck the rock,
So that the waters gushed out,
And the streams overflowed.
Can He give bread also?
Can He provide meat for His people?"

21 Therefore the LORD heard *this* and [a]was
furious;
So a fire was kindled against Jacob,
And anger also came up against Israel,
22 Because they [a]did not believe in God,
And did not trust in His salvation.
23 Yet He had commanded the clouds above,
[a]And opened the doors of heaven,
24 [a]Had rained down manna on them to eat,
And given them of the bread of [b]heaven.
25 Men ate angels' food;
He sent them food to the full.
26 [a]He caused an east wind to blow in the
heavens;
And by His power He brought in the south
wind.
27 He also rained meat on them like the dust,
Feathered fowl like the sand of the seas;
28 And He let *them* fall in the midst of their
camp,
All around their dwellings.
29 [a]So they ate and were well filled,
For He gave them their own desire.
30 They were not deprived of their craving;
But [a]while their food *was* still in their
mouths,
31 The wrath of God came against them,
And slew the stoutest of them,
And struck down the choice *men* of Israel.

32 In spite of this [a]they still sinned,
And [b]did not believe in His wondrous works.
33 [a]Therefore their days He consumed in
futility,
And their years in fear.

34 [a]When He slew them, then they sought Him;
And they returned and sought earnestly
for God.
35 Then they remembered that [a]God *was*
their rock,
And the Most High God [b]their Redeemer.
36 Nevertheless they [a]flattered Him with
their mouth,
And they lied to Him with their tongue;
37 For their heart was not steadfast with Him,
Nor were they faithful in His covenant.
38 [a]But He, *being* full of [b]compassion, forgave
*their* iniquity,
And did not destroy *them*.
Yes, many a time [c]He turned His anger
away,
And [d]did not stir up all His wrath;
39 For [a]He remembered [b]that they *were but*
flesh,
[c]A breath that passes away and does not
come again.

40 How often they [a]provoked Him in the
wilderness,
*And* grieved Him in the desert!
41 Yes, [a]again and again they tempted God,
And limited the Holy One of Israel.
42 They did not remember His power:
The day when He redeemed them from
the enemy,

**78:8** [a] 2 Kin. 17:14 [b] Ex. 32:9 [c] Ps. 78:37 **78:10** [a] 2 Kin. 17:15 **78:11** [a] Ps. 106:13 **78:12** [a] Ex. 7—12 [b] Num. 13:22 **78:13** [a] Ex. 14:21 [b] Ex. 15:8 **78:14** [a] Ex. 13:21 **78:15** [a] Num. 20:11 **78:16** [a] Num. 20:8, 10, 11 **78:17** [a] Heb. 3:16 **78:18** [a] Ex. 16:2 **78:19** [a] Num. 11:4; 20:3; 21:5 **78:20** [a] Num. 20:11 **78:21** [a] Num. 11:1 **78:22** [a] [Heb. 3:18] **78:23** [a] [Mal. 3:10] **78:24** [a] Ex. 16:4 [b] John 6:31 **78:26** [a] Num. 11:31 **78:29** [a] Num. 11:19, 20 **78:30** [a] Num. 11:33 **78:32** [a] Num. 14:16, 17 [b] Num. 14:11 **78:33** [a] Num. 14:29, 35 **78:34** [a] [Hos. 5:15] **78:35** [a] [Deut. 32:4, 15] [b] Is. 41:14; 44:6; 63:9 **78:36** [a] Ezek. 33:31 **78:38** [a] [Num. 14:18–20] [b] Ex. 34:6 [c] [Is. 48:9] [d] 1 Kin. 21:29 **78:39** [a] Job 10:9 [b] John 3:6 [c] [Job 7:7, 16] **78:40** [a] Heb. 3:16 **78:41** [a] Num. 14:22

43 When He worked His signs in Egypt,
And His wonders in the field of Zoan;
44 [a]Turned their rivers into blood,
And their streams, that they could not drink.
45 [a]He sent swarms of flies among them, which devoured them,
And [b]frogs, which destroyed them.
46 He also gave their crops to the caterpillar,
And their labor to the [a]locust.
47 [a]He destroyed their vines with hail,
And their sycamore trees with frost.
48 He also gave up their [a]cattle to the hail,
And their flocks to fiery lightning.
49 He cast on them the fierceness of His anger,
Wrath, indignation, and trouble,
By sending angels of destruction *among them.*
50 He made a path for His anger;
He did not spare their soul from death,
But gave their life over to the plague,
51 And destroyed all the [a]firstborn in Egypt,
The first of *their* strength in the tents of Ham.
52 But He [a]made His own people go forth like sheep,
And guided them in the wilderness like a flock;
53 And He [a]led them on safely, so that they did not fear;
But the sea [b]overwhelmed their enemies.
54 And He brought them to His [a]holy border,
This mountain [b]*which* His right hand had acquired.
55 [a]He also drove out the nations before them,
[b]Allotted them an inheritance by survey,
And made the tribes of Israel dwell in their tents.

56 [a]Yet they tested and provoked the Most High God,
And did not keep His testimonies,
57 But [a]turned back and acted unfaithfully like their fathers;
They were turned aside [b]like a deceitful bow.
58 [a]For they provoked Him to anger with their [b]high places,
And moved Him to jealousy with their carved images.
59 When God heard *this,* He was furious,
And greatly abhorred Israel,
60 [a]So that He forsook the tabernacle of Shiloh,
The tent He had placed among men,
61 [a]And delivered His strength into captivity,
And His glory into the enemy's hand.
62 [a]He also gave His people over to the sword,
And was furious with His inheritance.
63 The fire consumed their young men,
And [a]their maidens were not given in marriage.
64 [a]Their priests fell by the sword,
And [b]their widows made no lamentation.

65 Then the Lord awoke as *from* sleep,
[a]Like a mighty man who shouts because of wine.
66 And [a]He beat back His enemies;
He put them to a perpetual reproach.

67 Moreover He rejected the tent of Joseph,
And did not choose the tribe of Ephraim,
68 But chose the tribe of Judah,
Mount Zion [a]which He loved.
69 And He built His [a]sanctuary like the heights,
Like the earth which He has established forever.
70 [a]He also chose David His servant,
And took him from the sheepfolds;
71 From following [a]the ewes that had young He brought him,
[b]To shepherd Jacob His people,
And Israel His inheritance.
72 So he shepherded them according to the [a]integrity of his heart,
And guided them by the skillfulness of his hands.

## PSALM 79

### A DIRGE AND A PRAYER FOR ISRAEL, DESTROYED BY ENEMIES

*A Psalm of Asaph.*

1 O God, the nations have come into [a]Your inheritance;
Your holy temple they have defiled;
[b]They have laid Jerusalem in heaps.

> **79:1** The events described in this verse took place in 597 BC, when King Nebuchadnezzar and his Babylonian army conquered **Jerusalem**. Thousands of Israelites were captured and taken to Babylon as prisoners. Others were simply killed, and their bodies left to rot.

**78:44** [a] Ex. 7:20 **78:45** [a] Ex. 8:24 [b] Ex. 8:6 **78:46** [a] Ex. 10:14 **78:47** [a] Ex. 9:23–25 **78:48** [a] Ex. 9:19 **78:51** [a] Ex. 12:29, 30 **78:52** [a] Ps. 77:20 **78:53** [a] Ex. 14:19, 20 [b] Ex. 14:27, 28 **78:54** [a] Ex. 15:17 [b] Ps. 44:3 **78:55** [a] Ps. 44:2 [b] Josh. 13:7; 19:51; 23:4 **78:56** [a] Judg. 2:11–13 **78:57** [a] Ezek. 20:27, 28 [b] Hos. 7:16 **78:58** [a] Judg. 2:12 [b] Deut. 12:2 **78:60** [a] 1 Sam. 4:11 **78:61** [a] Judg. 18:30 **78:62** [a] 1 Sam. 4:10 **78:63** [a] Jer. 7:34; 16:9; 25:10 **78:64** [a] 1 Sam. 4:17; 22:18 [b] Job 27:15; Ezek. 24:23 **78:65** [a] Is. 42:13 **78:66** [a] 1 Sam. 5:6 **78:68** [a] [Ps. 87:2] **78:69** [a] 1 Kin. 6:1–38 **78:70** [a] 1 Sam. 16:11, 12 **78:71** [a] [Is. 40:11] [b] 2 Sam. 5:2 **78:72** [a] 1 Kin. 9:4 **79:1** [a] Ps. 74:2 [b] Mic. 3:12

2 [a]The dead bodies of Your servants
They have given *as* food for the birds of the heavens,
The flesh of Your saints to the beasts of the earth.
3 Their blood they have shed like water all around Jerusalem,
And *there was* no one to bury *them.*
4 We have become a reproach to our [a]neighbors,
A scorn and derision to those who are around us.

5 [a]How long, LORD?
Will You be angry forever?
Will Your [b]jealousy burn like fire?
6 [a]Pour out Your wrath on the nations that [b]do not know You,
And on the kingdoms that [c]do not call on Your name.
7 For they have devoured Jacob,
And laid waste his dwelling place.

8 [a]Oh, do not remember former iniquities against us!
Let Your tender mercies come speedily to meet us,
For we have been brought very low.
9 Help us, O God of our salvation,
For the glory of Your name;
And deliver us, and provide atonement for our sins,
[a]For Your name's sake!
10 [a]Why should the nations say,
"Where *is* their God?"
Let there be known among the nations in our sight
The avenging of the blood of Your servants *which has been* shed.

11 Let [a]the groaning of the prisoner come before You;
According to the greatness of Your power
Preserve those who are appointed to die;
12 And return to our neighbors [a]sevenfold into their bosom
[b]Their reproach with which they have reproached You, O Lord.

13 So [a]we, Your people and sheep of Your pasture,
Will give You thanks forever;
[b]We will show forth Your praise to all generations.

## PSALM 80

### PRAYER FOR ISRAEL'S RESTORATION

*To the Chief Musician. [a]Set to "The Lilies."[1] A Testimony[2] of Asaph. A Psalm.*

1 Give ear, O Shepherd of Israel,
[a]You who lead Joseph [b]like a flock;
You who dwell *between* the cherubim, [c]shine forth!
2 Before [a]Ephraim, Benjamin, and Manasseh,
Stir up Your strength,
And come *and* save us!

3 [a]Restore us, O God;
[b]Cause Your face to shine,
And we shall be saved!

4 O LORD God of hosts,
[a]How long will You be angry
Against the prayer of Your people?
5 [a]You have fed them with the bread of tears,
And given them tears to drink in great measure.
6 You have made us a strife to our neighbors,
And our enemies laugh among themselves.

7 Restore us, O God of hosts;
Cause Your face to shine,
And we shall be saved!

8 You have brought [a]a vine out of Egypt;
[b]You have cast out the nations, and planted it.
9 You prepared *room* for it,
And caused it to take deep root,
And it filled the land.
10 The hills were covered with its shadow,
And the mighty cedars with its [a]boughs.
11 She sent out her boughs to the Sea,[1]
And her branches to the River.[2]

12 Why have You [a]broken down her hedges,
So that all who pass by the way pluck her *fruit?*
13 The boar out of the woods uproots it,
And the wild beast of the field devours it.

14 Return, we beseech You, O God of hosts;
[a]Look down from heaven and see,
And visit this vine
15 And the vineyard which Your right hand has planted,
And the branch *that* You made strong [a]for Yourself.
16 *It is* burned with fire, *it is* cut down;
[a]They perish at the rebuke of Your countenance.

79:2 [a] Jer. 7:33; 19:7; 34:20 79:4 [a] Ps. 44:13 79:5 [a] Ps. 74:1, 9 [b] [Zeph. 3:8] 79:6 [a] Jer. 10:25 [b] Is. 45:4, 5 [c] Ps. 53:4 79:8 [a] Is. 64:9 79:9 [a] Jer. 14:7, 21 79:10 [a] Ps. 42:10 79:11 [a] Ps. 102:20 79:12 [a] Gen. 4:15 [b] Ps. 74:10, 18, 22 79:13 [a] Ps. 74:1; 95:7 [b] Is. 43:21 80:title [a] Ps. 45:title [1] Hebrew *Shoshannim* [2] Hebrew *Eduth* 80:1 [a] [Ex. 25:20–22] [b] Ps. 77:20 [c] Deut. 33:2 80:2 [a] Ps. 78:9, 67 80:3 [a] Lam. 5:21 [b] Num. 6:25 80:4 [a] Ps. 79:5 80:5 [a] Is. 30:20 80:8 [a] [Is. 5:1, 7] [b] Ps. 44:2 80:10 [a] Lev. 23:40 80:11 [1] That is, the Mediterranean [2] That is, the Euphrates 80:12 [a] Is. 5:5 80:14 [a] Is. 63:15 80:15 [a] [Is. 49:5] 80:16 [a] [Ps. 39:11]

17 [a]Let Your hand be upon the man of Your
right hand,
Upon the son of man *whom* You made
strong for Yourself.
18 Then we will not turn back from You;
Revive us, and we will call upon Your name.

19 Restore us, O LORD God of hosts;
Cause Your face to shine,
And we shall be saved!

## PSALM 81

### AN APPEAL FOR ISRAEL'S REPENTANCE

*To the Chief Musician.* [a]*On an instrument of Gath.*[1]
A Psalm *of Asaph.*

1 Sing aloud to God our strength;
Make a joyful shout to the God of Jacob.
2 Raise a song and strike the timbrel,
The pleasant harp with the lute.

3 Blow the trumpet at the time of the New
Moon,
At the full moon, on our solemn feast day.
4 For [a]this *is* a statute for Israel,
A law of the God of Jacob.
5 This He established in Joseph *as* a testimony,
When He went throughout the land of
Egypt,
[a]*Where* I heard a language I did not
understand.

6 "I removed his shoulder from the burden;
His hands were freed from the baskets.

**81:6** The **burden** was the suffering the Israelites endured while they were slaves in Egypt. The **baskets** were the containers workers carried while making bricks for the Egyptians. Brick workers were often forced to carry wooden beams with a basket hanging from each end to hold materials or finished bricks.

7 [a]You called in trouble, and I delivered you;
[b]I answered you in the secret place of
thunder;
I [c]tested you at the waters of
Meribah. *Selah*

8 "Hear,[a] O My people, and I will admonish you!
O Israel, if you will listen to Me!
9 There shall be no [a]foreign god among you;
Nor shall you worship any foreign god.
10 [a]I *am* the LORD your God,
Who brought you out of the land of Egypt;
[b]Open your mouth wide, and I will fill it.

11 "But My people would not heed My voice,
And Israel would *have* [a]none of Me.
12 [a]So I gave them over to their own stubborn
heart,
To walk in their own counsels.

13 "Oh,[a] that My people would listen to Me,
That Israel would walk in My ways!
14 I would soon subdue their enemies,
And turn My hand against their adversaries.
15 [a]The haters of the LORD would pretend
submission to Him,
But their fate would endure forever.
16 He would [a]have fed them also with the
finest of wheat;
And with honey [b]from the rock I would
have satisfied you."

## PSALM 82

### A PLEA FOR JUSTICE

*A Psalm of Asaph.*

1 God [a]stands in the congregation of the
mighty;
He judges among [b]the gods.[1]
2 How long will you judge unjustly,
And [a]show partiality to the wicked? *Selah*
3 Defend the poor and fatherless;
Do justice to the afflicted and [a]needy.
4 Deliver the poor and needy;
Free *them* from the hand of the wicked.

5 They do not know, nor do they understand;
They walk about in darkness;
All the [a]foundations of the earth are
unstable.

6 I said, [a]"You *are* gods,
And all of you *are* children of the Most
High.

**82:6** Jesus quoted this verse in His exchange with the religious authorities who wanted to stone Him for declaring Himself to be the Son of God (John 10:31–35). The word translated **gods** here (*elohim*) is used and translated the same way in verse 1. This word can refer to the one true God, to false gods, to angels, or to "mighty ones" (that is, the judges).

**80:17** [a] Ps. 89:21 **81:title** [a] Ps. 8:title [1] Hebrew *Al Gittith* **81:4** [a] Num. 10:10 **81:5** [a] Ps. 114:1 **81:7** [a] Ex. 2:23; 14:10 [b] Ex. 19:19; 20:18 [c] Ex. 17:6, 7 **81:8** [a] [Ps. 50:7] **81:9** [a] [Is. 43:12] **81:10** [a] Ex. 20:2 [b] Ps. 103:5 **81:11** [a] Deut. 32:15 **81:12** [a] [Acts 7:42] **81:13** [a] [Is. 48:18] **81:15** [a] Rom. 1:30 **81:16** [a] Deut. 32:14 [b] Job 29:6 **82:1** [a] [2 Chr. 19:6] [b] Ps. 82:6 [1] Hebrew *elohim, mighty ones;* that is, the judges **82:2** [a] [Deut. 1:17] **82:3** [a] [Deut. 24:17] **82:5** [a] Ps. 11:3 **82:6** [a] John 10:34 [1] Hebrew *elohim, mighty ones;* that is, the judges

7 But you shall die like men,
And fall like one of the princes."
8 Arise, O God, judge the earth;
[a]For You shall inherit all nations.

## PSALM 83

### PRAYER TO FRUSTRATE CONSPIRACY AGAINST ISRAEL

*A Song. A Psalm of Asaph.*

1 Do[a] not keep silent, O God!
Do not hold Your peace,
And do not be still, O God!
2 For behold, [a]Your enemies make a tumult;
And those who hate You have lifted up
their head.
3 They have taken crafty counsel against
Your people,
And consulted together [a]against Your
sheltered ones.
4 They have said, "Come, and [a]let us cut
them off from *being* a nation,
That the name of Israel may be
remembered no more."

5 For they have consulted together with one
consent;
They form a confederacy against You:
6 [a]The tents of Edom and the Ishmaelites;
Moab and the Hagrites;
7 Gebal, Ammon, and Amalek;
Philistia with the inhabitants of Tyre;
8 Assyria also has joined with them;
They have helped the children of Lot.
*Selah*

9 Deal with them as *with* [a]Midian,
As *with* [b]Sisera,
As *with* Jabin at the Brook Kishon,
10 Who perished at En Dor,
[a]*Who* became *as* refuse on the earth.

> **83:9–11** These enemies had one thing in common: they had been defeated by the Israelites in an unlikely manner. **Midian** fought Israel with an enormous army, yet they were defeated by Gideon and his small band of soldiers. The army of **Jabin**, under the command of **Sisera**, lost to an Israelite army led by a woman, Deborah. Sisera escaped, but was later killed by another woman, Jael, who hammered a tent peg into his head while he slept.

11 Make their nobles like [a]Oreb and like Zeeb,
Yes, all their princes like [b]Zebah and
Zalmunna,
12 Who said, "Let us take for ourselves
The pastures of God for a possession."

13 [a]O my God, make them like the whirling
dust,
[b]Like the chaff before the wind!
14 As the fire burns the woods,
And as the flame [a]sets the mountains on
fire,
15 So pursue them with Your tempest,
And frighten them with Your storm.
16 Fill their faces with shame,
That they may seek Your name, O LORD.
17 Let them be confounded and dismayed
forever;
Yes, let them be put to shame and perish,
18 [a]That they may know that You, whose
[b]name alone *is* the LORD,
*Are* [c]the Most High over all the earth.

## PSALM 84

### THE BLESSEDNESS OF DWELLING IN THE HOUSE OF GOD

*To the Chief Musician. [a]On an instrument of Gath.[1] A Psalm of the sons of Korah.*

1 How [a]lovely *is* Your tabernacle,
O LORD of hosts!
2 [a]My soul longs, yes, even faints
For the courts of the LORD;
My heart and my flesh cry out for the
living God.

3 Even the sparrow has found a home,
And the swallow a nest for herself,
Where she may lay her young—
*Even* Your altars, O LORD of hosts,
My King and my God.
4 Blessed *are* those who dwell in Your [a]house;
They will still be praising You. *Selah*

5 Blessed *is* the man whose strength *is* in
You,
Whose heart *is* set on pilgrimage.
6 *As they* pass through the Valley [a]of Baca,
They make it a spring;
The rain also covers it with pools.
7 They go [a]from strength to strength;
*Each one* [b]appears before God in Zion.[1]

8 O LORD God of hosts, hear my prayer;
Give ear, O God of Jacob! *Selah*
9 [a]O God, behold our shield,
And look upon the face of Your anointed.

82:8 [a] [Rev. 11:15] 83:1 [a] Ps. 28:1 83:2 [a] Ps. 81:15 83:3 [a] [Ps. 27:5] 83:4 [a] Jer. 11:19; 31:36 83:6 [a] 2 Chr. 20:1, 10, 11 83:9 [a] Judg. 7:22 [b] Judg. 4:15–24; 5:20, 21 83:10 [a] Zeph. 1:17 83:11 [a] Judg. 7:25 [b] Judg. 8:12–21 83:13 [a] Is. 17:13 [b] Ps. 35:5 83:14 [a] Deut. 32:22 83:18 [a] Ps. 59:13 [b] Ex. 6:3 [c] [Ps. 92:8] 84:title [a] Ps. 8:title [1] Hebrew *Al Gittith* 84:1 [a] Ps. 27:4; 46:4, 5 84:2 [a] Ps. 42:1, 2 84:4 [a] [Ps. 65:4] 84:6 [a] 2 Sam. 5:22–25 84:7 [a] Prov. 4:18 [b] Deut. 16:16 [1] Septuagint, Syriac, and Vulgate read *The God of gods shall be seen.* 84:9 [a] Gen. 15:1

10 For a day in Your courts *is* better than a
thousand.
I would rather be a doorkeeper in the
house of my God
Than dwell in the tents of wickedness.
11 For the LORD God *is* [a]a sun and [b]shield;
The LORD will give grace and glory;
[c]No good *thing* will He withhold
From those who walk uprightly.

12 O LORD of hosts,
[a]Blessed *is* the man who trusts in You!

## PSALM 85

### PRAYER THAT THE LORD WILL RESTORE FAVOR TO THE LAND

*To the Chief Musician. A Psalm [a]of the sons of Korah.*

1 LORD, You have been favorable to Your
land;
You have [a]brought back the captivity of
Jacob.
2 You have forgiven the iniquity of Your
people;
You have covered all their sin. *Selah*
3 You have taken away all Your wrath;
You have turned from the fierceness of
Your anger.

4 [a]Restore us, O God of our salvation,
And cause Your anger toward us to cease.
5 [a]Will You be angry with us forever?
Will You prolong Your anger to all
generations?
6 Will You not [a]revive us again,
That Your people may rejoice in You?
7 Show us Your mercy, LORD,
And grant us Your salvation.

8 I will hear what God the LORD will speak,
For He will speak peace
To His people and to His saints;
But let them not turn back to folly.
9 Surely [a]His salvation *is* near to those who
fear Him,
[b]That glory may dwell in our land.

10 Mercy and truth have met together;
[a]Righteousness and peace have kissed.
11 Truth shall spring out of the earth,
And righteousness shall look down from
heaven.
12 [a]Yes, the LORD will give *what is* good;
And our land will yield its increase.
13 Righteousness will go before Him,
And shall make His footsteps *our*
pathway.

## PSALM 86

### PRAYER FOR MERCY, WITH MEDITATION ON THE EXCELLENCIES OF THE LORD

*A Prayer of David.*

1 Bow down Your ear, O LORD, hear me;
For I *am* poor and needy.
2 Preserve my life, for I *am* holy;
You are my God;
Save Your servant who trusts in You!
3 Be merciful to me, O Lord,
For I cry to You all day long.
4 Rejoice the soul of Your servant,
[a]For to You, O Lord, I lift up my soul.
5 For [a]You, Lord, *are* good, and ready to
forgive,
And abundant in mercy to all those who
call upon You.

6 Give ear, O LORD, to my prayer;
And attend to the voice of my
supplications.
7 In the day of my trouble I will call upon You,
For You will answer me.

8 [a]Among the gods *there is* none like You,
O Lord;
Nor *are there any works* like Your works.
9 All nations whom You have made
Shall come and worship before You, O Lord,
And shall glorify Your name.
10 For You *are* great, and [a]do wondrous
things;
[b]You alone *are* God.

11 [a]Teach me Your way, O LORD;
I will walk in Your truth;
Unite my heart to fear Your name.
12 I will praise You, O Lord my God, with all
my heart,
And I will glorify Your name forevermore.
13 For great *is* Your mercy toward me,
And You have delivered my soul from the
depths of Sheol.

14 O God, the proud have risen against me,
And a mob of violent *men* have sought my
life,
And have not set You before them.
15 But [a]You, O Lord, *are* a God full of
compassion, and gracious,
Longsuffering and abundant in mercy
and truth.

16 Oh, turn to me, and have mercy on me!
Give Your strength to Your servant,
And save the son of Your maidservant.
17 Show me a sign for good,

**84:11** [a] Is. 60:19, 20 [b] Gen. 15:1 [c] Ps. 34:9, 10 **84:12** [a] [Ps. 2:12; 40:4] **85:title** [a] Ps. 42:title **85:1** [a] Joel 3:1 **85:4** [a] Ps. 80:3, 7 **85:5** [a] Ps. 79:5 **85:6** [a] Hab. 3:2 **85:9** [a] Is. 46:13 [b] Hag. 2:7; Zech. 2:5; [John 1:14] **85:10** [a] Ps. 72:3; [Is. 32:17]; Luke 2:14 **85:12** [a] [Ps. 84:11; James 1:17] **86:4** [a] Ps. 25:1; 143:8 **86:5** [a] Ps. 130:7; 145:9; [Joel 2:13] **86:8** [a] [Ex. 15:11]; 2 Sam. 7:22; 1 Kin. 8:23; Ps. 89:6; Jer. 10:6 **86:10** [a] [Ex. 15:11] [b] Deut. 6:4; Is. 37:16; Mark 12:29; 1 Cor. 8:4 **86:11** [a] Ps. 27:11; 143:8 **86:15** [a] Ex. 34:6; [Ps. 86:5]

That those who hate me may see *it* and be
ashamed,
Because You, LORD, have helped me and
comforted me.

## PSALM 87

### THE GLORIES OF THE CITY OF GOD

*A Psalm of the sons of Korah. A Song.*

1 His foundation *is* in the holy mountains.
2 [a]The LORD loves the gates of Zion
More than all the dwellings of Jacob.
3 [a]Glorious things are spoken of you,
O city of God! *Selah*

4 "I will make mention of Rahab and
Babylon to those who know Me;
Behold, O Philistia and Tyre, with
Ethiopia:
'This *one* was born there.' "

5 And of Zion it will be said,
"This *one* and that *one* were born in her;
And the Most High Himself shall establish
her."
6 The LORD will record,
When He [a]registers the peoples:
"This *one* was born there." *Selah*

7 Both the singers and the players on
instruments *say,*
"All my springs *are* in you."

## PSALM 88

### A PRAYER FOR HELP IN DESPONDENCY

*A Song. A Psalm of the sons of Korah. To the Chief Musician. Set to "Mahalath Leannoth." A Contemplation*[1] *of* [a]*Heman the Ezrahite.*

1 O LORD, [a]God of my salvation,
I have cried out day and night before You.
2 Let my prayer come before You;
Incline Your ear to my cry.

3 For my soul is full of troubles,
And my life [a]draws near to the grave.
4 I am counted with those who [a]go down to
the pit;
[b]I am like a man *who has* no strength,
5 Adrift among the dead,
Like the slain who lie in the grave,
Whom You remember no more,
And who are cut off from Your hand.

6 You have laid me in the lowest pit,
In darkness, in the depths.
7 Your wrath lies heavy upon me,
And You have afflicted *me* with all [a]Your
waves. *Selah*
8 [a]You have put away my acquaintances far
from me;
You have made me an abomination to them;
[b]*I am* shut up, and I cannot get out;
9 My eye wastes away because of affliction.

[a]LORD, I have called daily upon You;
I have stretched out my hands to You.
10 Will You work wonders for the dead?
Shall the dead arise *and* praise You? *Selah*
11 Shall Your lovingkindness be declared in
the grave?
*Or* Your faithfulness in the place of
destruction?
12 Shall Your wonders be known in the dark?
And Your righteousness in the land of
forgetfulness?

13 But to You I have cried out, O LORD,
And in the morning my prayer comes
before You.
14 LORD, why do You cast off my soul?
*Why* do You hide Your face from me?
15 I *have been* afflicted and ready to die from
*my* youth;
I suffer Your terrors;
I am distraught.
16 Your fierce wrath has gone over me;
Your terrors have cut me off.
17 They came around me all day long like
water;
They engulfed me altogether.
18 [a]Loved one and friend You have put far
from me,
*And* my acquaintances into darkness.

## PSALM 89

### REMEMBERING THE COVENANT WITH DAVID, AND SORROW FOR LOST BLESSINGS

*A Contemplation*[1] *of* [a]*Ethan the Ezrahite.*

1 I will sing of the mercies of the LORD
forever;
With my mouth will I make known Your
faithfulness to all generations.
2 For I have said, "Mercy shall be built up
forever;
[a]Your faithfulness You shall establish in
the very heavens."

3 "I[a] have made a covenant with My chosen,
I have [b]sworn to My servant David:
4 'Your seed I will establish forever,
And build up your throne [a]to all
generations.' " *Selah*

87:2 [a] Ps. 78:67, 68 87:3 [a] Is. 60:1 87:6 [a] Is. 4:3 88:title [a] 1 Kin. 4:31; 1 Chr. 2:6 [1] Hebrew *Maschil* 88:1 [a] Ps. 27:9; [Luke 18:7] 88:3 [a] Ps. 107:18 88:4 [a] [Ps. 28:1] [b] Ps. 31:12 88:7 [a] Ps. 42:7 88:8 [a] Job 19:13, 19 [b] Lam. 3:7 88:9 [a] Ps. 86:3 88:18 [a] Ps. 31:11; 38:11 89:title [a] 1 Kin. 4:31 [1] Hebrew *Maschil* 89:2 [a] [Ps. 119:89, 90] 89:3 [a] 1 Kin. 8:16 [b] 2 Sam. 7:11 89:4 [a] [Luke 1:33]

5 And [a]the heavens will praise Your
wonders, O LORD;
Your faithfulness also in the assembly of
the saints.
6 [a]For who in the heavens can be compared
to the LORD?
*Who* among the sons of the mighty can be
likened to the LORD?
7 [a]God is greatly to be feared in the assembly
of the saints,
And to be held in reverence by all *those*
around Him.
8 O LORD God of hosts,
Who *is* mighty like You, O LORD?
Your faithfulness also surrounds You.
9 [a]You rule the raging of the sea;
When its waves rise, You still them.
10 [a]You have broken Rahab in pieces, as one
who is slain;
You have scattered Your enemies with
Your mighty arm.

11 [a]The heavens *are* Yours, the earth also *is*
Yours;
The world and all its fullness, You have
founded them.
12 The north and the south, You have
created them;
[a]Tabor and [b]Hermon rejoice in Your name.
13 You have a mighty arm;
Strong is Your hand, *and* high is Your
right hand.
14 Righteousness and justice *are* the
foundation of Your throne;
Mercy and truth go before Your face.
15 Blessed *are* the people who know the
[a]joyful sound!
They walk, O LORD, in the light of Your
countenance.
16 In Your name they rejoice all day long,
And in Your righteousness they are
exalted.
17 For You *are* the glory of their strength,
And in Your favor our horn is [a]exalted.
18 For our shield *belongs* to the LORD,
And our king to the Holy One of Israel.

19 Then You spoke in a vision to Your holy
one,[1]
And said: "I have given help to *one who is*
mighty;
I have exalted one [a]chosen from the people.
20 [a]I have found My servant David;
With My holy oil I have anointed him,
21 [a]With whom My hand shall be established;
Also My arm shall strengthen him.
22 The enemy shall not outwit him,
Nor the son of wickedness afflict him.

**89:5** [a] [Ps. 19:1] **89:6** [a] Ps. 86:8; 113:5 **89:7** [a] Ps. 76:7, 11 **89:9** [a] Ps. 65:7; 93:3, 4; 107:29 **89:10** [a] Ps. 87:4 **89:11** [a] [Gen. 1:1] **89:12** [a] Josh. 19:22 [b] Josh. 11:17; 12:1 **89:15** [a] Ps. 98:6 **89:17** [a] Ps. 75:10; 92:10; 132:17 **89:19** [a] 1 Kin. 11:34 [1] Following many Hebrew manuscripts; Masoretic Text, Septuagint, Targum, and Vulgate read *holy ones.* **89:20** [a] 1 Sam. 13:14; 16:1–12 **89:21** [a] Ps. 80:17

KNOW THE TRUTH

# THE DOCTRINE OF GOD

## PART 13: THE RIGHTEOUSNESS AND JUSTNESS OF GOD

**89:14** One of the most important roles an ancient king fulfilled was that of a judge. Often, he'd sit on a particular throne from which he heard civil cases and rendered judgment to seekers of justice. This throne of judgment was usually built on a foundation of rock, representing the solid justice the king and his court believed in. In Psalm 89:14, Ethan the psalmist uses this idea to create a word picture of God as Judge upon His throne. This throne of judgment isn't founded upon earthly rock, but something firmer and stronger: God's absolute "righteousness and justice."

The Hebrew word Ethan used for *righteousness* has to do with thinking, speaking, and acting in a morally and ethically right way. The word *justice* has to do with giving another what is rightfully his or her due. God always thinks, speaks, and acts morally, and consistently treats us according to His perfect morality. God is generous in His justice, always providing people what we need and giving us what we're due.

Without Christ, we are unrighteous. As a result, our righteous and just God renders the appropriate judgment upon us for our sin: eternal separation from Him. In Christ, though, we're made the righteousness of God (2 Cor. 5:21). God justly forgives our sin, accepting Christ's payment on our behalf, and renders grace and eternal life with Him upon us (Rom. 6:23).

*For* **THE DOCTRINE OF GOD: PART 14: THE GOODNESS AND BENEVOLENCE OF GOD,** *turn to Exodus 34:6–7 on page 97.*

23 I will beat down his foes before his face,
And plague those who hate him.

24 "But My faithfulness and My mercy *shall be* with him,
And in My name his horn shall be exalted.
25 Also I will [a]set his hand over the sea,
And his right hand over the rivers.
26 He shall cry to Me, 'You *are* [a]my Father,
My God, and [b]the rock of my salvation.'
27 Also I will make him [a]*My* firstborn,
[b]The highest of the kings of the earth.
28 [a]My mercy I will keep for him forever,
And My covenant shall stand firm with him.
29 His seed also I will make *to endure* forever,
[a]And his throne [b]as the days of heaven.

30 "If[a] his sons [b]forsake My law
And do not walk in My judgments,
31 If they break My statutes
And do not keep My commandments,
32 Then I will punish their transgression with the rod,
And their iniquity with stripes.
33 [a]Nevertheless My lovingkindness I will not utterly take from him,
Nor allow My faithfulness to fail.
34 My covenant I will not break,
Nor [a]alter the word that has gone out of My lips.
35 Once I have sworn [a]by My holiness;
I will not lie to David:
36 [a]His seed shall endure forever,
And his throne [b]as the sun before Me;
37 It shall be established forever like the moon,
Even *like* the faithful witness in the sky." *Selah*

38 But You have [a]cast off and [b]abhorred,
You have been furious with Your anointed.
39 You have renounced the covenant of Your servant;
[a]You have profaned his crown *by casting it* to the ground.
40 You have broken down all his hedges;
You have brought his strongholds to ruin.
41 All who pass by the way [a]plunder him;
He is a reproach to his neighbors.
42 You have exalted the right hand of his adversaries;
You have made all his enemies rejoice.
43 You have also turned back the edge of his sword,
And have not sustained him in the battle.
44 You have made his glory cease,
And cast his throne down to the ground.
45 The days of his youth You have shortened;
You have covered him with shame. *Selah*

46 How long, LORD?
Will You hide Yourself forever?
Will Your wrath burn like fire?
47 Remember how short my time [a]is;
For what [b]futility have You created all the children of men?
48 What man can live and not see [a]death?
Can he deliver his life from the power of the grave? *Selah*

49 Lord, where *are* Your former lovingkindnesses,
*Which* You [a]swore to David [b]in Your truth?
50 Remember, Lord, the reproach of Your servants—
[a]*How* I bear in my bosom *the reproach of* all the many peoples,
51 [a]With which Your enemies have reproached, O LORD,
With which they have reproached the footsteps of Your anointed.

52 [a]Blessed *be* the LORD forevermore!
Amen and Amen.

# BOOK FOUR
## *PSALMS 90–106*

## PSALM 90
### *THE ETERNITY OF GOD, AND MAN'S FRAILTY*

*A Prayer [a]of Moses the man of God.*

1 Lord, [a]You have been our dwelling place[1] in all generations.
2 [a]Before the mountains were brought forth,
Or ever You had formed the earth and the world,
Even from everlasting to everlasting, You *are* God.

**90:1** This psalm, written by Moses, is probably the oldest one in the entire collection. It was written near the end of the Israelites' forty years of wandering in the wilderness and offers a prayer for the second generation of Israelites who would enter and conquer the land God had promised them.

**89:25** [a] Ps. 72:8 **89:26** [a] [1 Chr. 22:10] [b] 2 Sam. 22:47 **89:27** [a] [Col. 1:15, 18] [b] Rev. 19:16 **89:28** [a] Is. 55:3 **89:29** [a] Jer. 33:17 [b] Deut. 11:21 **89:30** [a] [2 Sam. 7:14] [b] Ps. 119:53 **89:33** [a] 2 Sam. 7:14, 15 **89:34** [a] Jer. 33:20–22 **89:35** [a] Amos 4:2 **89:36** [a] [Luke 1:33] [b] Ps. 72:17 **89:38** [a] [1 Chr. 28:9] [b] Deut. 32:19 **89:39** [a] Lam. 5:16 **89:41** [a] Ps. 80:12 **89:47** [a] Ps. 90:9 [b] Ps. 62:9 **89:48** [a] [Eccl. 3:19] **89:49** [a] [2 Sam. 7:15] [b] Ps. 54:5 **89:50** [a] Ps. 69:9, 19 **89:51** [a] Ps. 74:10, 18, 22 **89:52** [a] Ps. 41:13 **90:title** [a] Deut. 33:1 **90:1** [a] [Ezek. 11:16] [1] Septuagint, Targum, and Vulgate read *refuge*. **90:2** [a] [Prov. 8:25, 26]

3 You turn man to destruction,
And say, [a]"Return, O children of men."
4 [a]For a thousand years in Your sight
*Are* like yesterday when it is past,
And *like* a watch in the night.
5 You carry them away *like* a flood;
[a]*They are* like a sleep.
In the morning [b]they are like grass *which*
grows up:
6 In the morning it flourishes and grows up;
In the evening it is cut down and withers.

7 For we have been consumed by Your anger,
And by Your wrath we are terrified.
8 [a]You have set our iniquities before You,
Our [b]secret *sins* in the light of Your
countenance.
9 For all our days have passed away in Your
wrath;
We finish our years like a sigh.
10 The days of our lives *are* seventy years;
And if by reason of strength *they are*
eighty years,
Yet their boast *is* only labor and sorrow;

**90:10** The point here isn't to set a maximum of **seventy** or **eighty years**, but to present a context for the brevity of human life. No matter how long people live, death is inevitable.

For it is soon cut off, and we fly away.
11 Who knows the power of Your anger?
For as the fear of You, *so is* Your wrath.
12 [a]So teach *us* to number our days,
That we may gain a heart of wisdom.

13 Return, O LORD!
How long?
And [a]have compassion on Your servants.
14 Oh, satisfy us early with Your mercy,
[a]That we may rejoice and be glad all our
days!
15 Make us glad according to the days *in
which* You have afflicted us,
The years *in which* we have seen evil.
16 Let [a]Your work appear to Your servants,
And Your glory to their children.
17 [a]And let the beauty of the LORD our God be
upon us,
And [b]establish the work of our hands for us;
Yes, establish the work of our hands.

## PSALM 91

### SAFETY OF ABIDING IN THE PRESENCE OF GOD

1 He [a]who dwells in the secret place of the
Most High
Shall abide [b]under the shadow of the
Almighty.
2 [a]I will say of the LORD, "*He is* my refuge
and my fortress;
My God, in Him I will trust."

3 Surely [a]He shall deliver you from the
snare of the fowler[1]
*And* from the perilous pestilence.
4 [a]He shall cover you with His feathers,
And under His wings you shall take
refuge;
His truth *shall be your* shield and buckler.
5 [a]You shall not be afraid of the terror by
night,
*Nor* of the arrow *that* flies by day,

**90:3** [a] Gen. 3:19 **90:4** [a] 2 Pet. 3:8 **90:5** [a] Ps. 73:20 [b] Is. 40:6 **90:8** [a] Ps. 50:21 [b] Ps. 19:12 **90:12** [a] Ps. 39:4 **90:13** [a] Deut. 32:36 **90:14** [a] Ps. 85:6 **90:16** [a] Hab. 3:2 **90:17** [a] Ps. 27:4 [b] Is. 26:12 **91:1** [a] Ps. 27:5; 31:20; 32:7 [b] Ps. 17:8 **91:2** [a] Ps. 142:5 **91:3** [a] Ps. 124:7 [1] That is, one who catches birds in a trap or snare **91:4** [a] Ps. 17:8 **91:5** [a] [Job 5:19]

LIVE THE TRUTH

## MANAGING TIME WISELY

**90:4–6** Have you ever looked at the clock and realized the day was almost over and you didn't have much to show for it? Life is full of "time thieves" that prevent us from making the most of our time. Gaming, social media, texting, sports, sleeping, and many other things compete for our attention and aren't satisfied unless they have all of it. To be clear, there's nothing wrong with these things when you enjoy them in balance, and they don't distract you from what's most important. But left unchecked, even good things can become problems.

This psalm is a prayer of Moses, a man who was surely busy. One thing Moses wanted to remember, and wants us to know, is time matters. It's a precious, God-given resource we need to manage well. We have a limited amount of time on this earth; compared to eternity that time is very short. Therefore, it matters how we use our time. We are to use it primarily to grow closer to Christ and help others know Him. We should live every day with eternity in mind, investing each minute here for an exponentially more important future there. Time is short. Do your best to make wise, God-honoring decisions with every moment.

6 *Nor* of the pestilence *that* walks in
darkness,
*Nor* of the destruction *that* lays waste at
noonday.
7 A thousand may fall at your side,
And ten thousand at your right hand;
*But* it shall not come near you.
8 Only [a]with your eyes shall you look,
And see the reward of the wicked.

9 Because you have made the LORD, *who is*
[a]my refuge,
*Even* the Most High, [b]your dwelling place,
10 [a]No evil shall befall you,
Nor shall any plague come near your
dwelling;
11 [a]For He shall give His angels charge over you,
To keep you in all your ways.

**SEEING JESUS IN THE SCRIPTURE**

**91:11–12** This is one of three Old Testament verses Satan misquoted to tempt Jesus to sin (see Matt. 4:6). Although God's angels protect the people of God, the people of God aren't to test God in this way.

12 In *their* hands they shall bear you up,
[a]Lest you dash your foot against a stone.
13 You shall tread upon the lion and the cobra,
The young lion and the serpent you shall
trample underfoot.

14 "Because he has set his love upon Me,
therefore I will deliver him;
I will set him on high, because he has
[a]known My name.
15 He shall [a]call upon Me, and I will answer
him;
I *will be* [b]with him in trouble;
I will deliver him and honor him.
16 With long life I will satisfy him,
And show him My salvation."

## PSALM 92

### PRAISE TO THE LORD FOR HIS LOVE AND FAITHFULNESS

*A Psalm. A Song for the Sabbath day.*

1 *It is* [a]good to give thanks to the LORD,
And to sing praises to Your name, O Most
High;
2 To [a]declare Your lovingkindness in the
morning,
And Your faithfulness every night,
3 [a]On an instrument of ten strings,
On the lute,
And on the harp,
With harmonious sound.
4 For You, LORD, have made me glad
through Your work;
I will triumph in the works of Your hands.

5 [a]O LORD, how great are Your works!
[b]Your thoughts are very deep.
6 [a]A senseless man does not know,
Nor does a fool understand this.
7 When [a]the wicked spring up like grass,
And when all the workers of iniquity
flourish,
*It is* that they may be destroyed forever.

8 [a]But You, LORD, *are* on high forevermore.
9 For behold, Your enemies, O LORD,
For behold, Your enemies shall perish;
All the workers of iniquity shall [a]be
scattered.

10 But [a]my horn You have exalted like a wild
ox;
I have been [b]anointed with fresh oil.
11 [a]My eye also has seen *my desire* on my
enemies;
My ears hear *my desire* on the wicked
Who rise up against me.

12 [a]The righteous shall flourish like a palm
tree,
He shall grow like a cedar in Lebanon.
13 Those who are planted in the house of the
LORD
Shall flourish in the courts of our God.
14 They shall still bear fruit in old age;
They shall be fresh and flourishing,
15 To declare that the LORD is upright;
[a]*He is* my rock, and [b]*there is* no
unrighteousness in Him.

## PSALM 93

### THE ETERNAL REIGN OF THE LORD

1 The [a]LORD reigns, He is clothed with
majesty;
The LORD is clothed,
[b]He has girded Himself with strength.
Surely the world is established, so that it
cannot be moved.
2 [a]Your throne *is* established from of old;
You *are* from everlasting.

3 The floods have lifted up, O LORD,
The floods have lifted up their voice;
The floods lift up their waves.

91:8 [a] Mal. 1:5 91:9 [a] Ps. 91:2 [b] Ps. 90:1 91:10 [a] [Prov. 12:21] 91:11 [a] [Heb. 1:14] 91:12 [a] Matt. 4:6 91:14 [a] [Ps. 9:10] 91:15 [a] Ps. 50:15 [b] Is. 43:2 92:1 [a] Ps. 147:1 92:2 [a] Ps. 89:1 92:3 [a] 1 Chr. 23:5 92:5 [a] Ps. 40:5 [b] [Is. 28:29] 92:6 [a] Ps. 73:22 92:7 [a] Job 12:6 92:8 [a] [Ps. 83:18] 92:9 [a] Ps. 68:1 92:10 [a] Ps. 89:17 [b] Ps. 23:5 92:11 [a] Ps. 54:7 92:12 [a] Ps. 52:8 92:15 [a] [Deut. 32:4] [b] [Rom. 9:14] 93:1 [a] Ps. 96:10 [b] Ps. 65:6 93:2 [a] Ps. 45:6

4 [a]The LORD on high *is* mightier
Than the noise of many waters,
*Than* the mighty waves of the sea.

5 Your testimonies are very sure;
Holiness adorns Your house,
O LORD, forever.

## PSALM 94

### GOD THE REFUGE OF THE RIGHTEOUS

1 O LORD God, [a]to whom vengeance
belongs—
O God, to whom vengeance belongs, shine
forth!
2 Rise up, O [a]Judge of the earth;
Render punishment to the proud.
3 LORD, [a]how long will the wicked,
How long will the wicked triumph?

4 They [a]utter speech, *and* speak insolent
things;
All the workers of iniquity boast in
themselves.
5 They break in pieces Your people, O LORD,
And afflict Your heritage.
6 They slay the widow and the stranger,
And murder the fatherless.
7 [a]Yet they say, "The LORD does not see,
Nor does the God of Jacob understand."

8 Understand, you senseless among the
people;
And *you* fools, when will you be wise?
9 [a]He who planted the ear, shall He not hear?
He who formed the eye, shall He not see?
10 He who instructs the nations, shall He not
correct,
He who teaches man knowledge?
11 The LORD [a]knows the thoughts of man,
That they *are* futile.

12 Blessed *is* the man whom You [a]instruct,
O LORD,
And teach out of Your law,
13 That You may give him rest from the days
of adversity,
Until the pit is dug for the wicked.
14 For the LORD will not cast off His people,
Nor will He forsake His inheritance.
15 But judgment will return to
righteousness,
And all the upright in heart will follow it.

16 Who will rise up for me against the
evildoers?
Who will stand up for me against the
workers of iniquity?
17 Unless the LORD *had been* my help,
My soul would soon have settled in silence.
18 If I say, "My foot slips,"
Your mercy, O LORD, will hold me up.
19 In the multitude of my anxieties within
me,
Your comforts delight my soul.

20 Shall [a]the throne of iniquity, which
devises evil by law,
Have fellowship with You?
21 They gather together against the life of
the righteous,
And condemn [a]innocent blood.
22 But the LORD has been my defense,
And my God the rock of my refuge.
23 He has brought on them their own
iniquity,
And shall cut them off in their own
wickedness;
The LORD our God shall cut them off.

## PSALM 95

### A CALL TO WORSHIP AND OBEDIENCE

1 Oh come, let us sing to the LORD!
Let us shout joyfully to the Rock of our
salvation.
2 Let us come before His presence with
thanksgiving;
Let us shout joyfully to Him with [a]psalms.
3 For [a]the LORD *is* the great God,
And the great King above all gods.
4 In His hand *are* the deep places of the
earth;
The heights of the hills *are* His also.
5 [a]The sea *is* His, for He made it;
And His hands formed the dry *land*.

6 Oh come, let us worship and bow down;
Let [a]us kneel before the LORD our Maker.
7 For He *is* our God,
And [a]we *are* the people of His pasture,
And the sheep of His hand.

[b]Today, if you will hear His voice:
8 "Do not harden your hearts, as in the
rebellion,[1]
[a]As *in* the day of trial[2] in the wilderness,
9 When [a]your fathers tested Me;
They tried Me, though they [b]saw My work.
10 For [a]forty years I was grieved with *that*
generation,
And said, 'It *is* a people who go astray in
their hearts,
And they do not know My ways.'
11 So [a]I swore in My wrath,
'They shall not enter My rest.' "

93:4 [a] Ps. 65:7 94:1 [a] [Nah. 1:2] 94:2 [a] [Gen. 18:25] 94:3 [a] [Job 20:5] 94:4 [a] Ps. 31:18 94:7 [a] Ps. 10:11 94:9 [a] [Ex. 4:11] 94:11 [a] 1 Cor. 3:20 94:12 [a] [Heb. 12:5, 6] 94:20 [a] Amos 6:3 94:21 [a] [Ex. 23:7] 95:2 [a] James 5:13 95:3 [a] [Ps. 96:4] 95:5 [a] Gen. 1:9, 10 95:6 [a] [Phil. 2:10] 95:7 [a] Ps. 79:13 [b] Heb. 3:7–11, 15; 4:7 95:8 [a] Ex. 17:2–7 [1] Or *Meribah* [2] Or *Massah* 95:9 [a] Ps. 78:18 [b] Num. 14:22 95:10 [a] Heb. 3:10, 17 95:11 [a] Heb. 4:3, 5

## PSALM 96

### A SONG OF PRAISE TO GOD COMING IN JUDGMENT

*(1 Chr. 16:23–33)*

1 Oh, [a]sing to the LORD a new song!
Sing to the LORD, all the earth.
2 Sing to the LORD, bless His name;
Proclaim the good news of His salvation
from day to day.
3 Declare His glory among the nations,
His wonders among all peoples.

4 For [a]the LORD *is* great and [b]greatly to be
praised;
[c]He *is* to be feared above all gods.
5 For [a]all the gods of the peoples *are* idols,
[b]But the LORD made the heavens.
6 Honor and majesty *are* before Him;
Strength and [a]beauty *are* in His
sanctuary.

7 [a]Give to the LORD, O families of the
peoples,
Give to the LORD glory and strength.
8 Give to the LORD the glory *due* His name;
Bring an offering, and come into His
courts.
9 Oh, worship the LORD [a]in the beauty of
holiness!
Tremble before Him, all the earth.

10 Say among the nations, [a]"The LORD
reigns;
The world also is firmly established,
It shall not be moved;
[b]He shall judge the peoples righteously."

11 [a]Let the heavens rejoice, and let the earth
be glad;
[b]Let the sea roar, and all its fullness;
12 Let the field be joyful, and all that *is* in it.
Then all the trees of the woods will rejoice
13 before the LORD.
For He is coming, for He is coming to
judge the earth.
[a]He shall judge the world with
righteousness,
And the peoples with His truth.

## PSALM 97

### A SONG OF PRAISE TO THE SOVEREIGN LORD

1 The LORD [a]reigns;
Let the earth rejoice;
Let the multitude of isles be glad!
2 [a]Clouds and darkness surround Him;
[b]Righteousness and justice *are* the
foundation of His throne.
3 [a]A fire goes before Him,
And burns up His enemies round about.
4 [a]His lightnings light the world;
The earth sees and trembles.
5 [a]The mountains melt like wax at the
presence of the LORD,
At the presence of the Lord of the whole
earth.
6 [a]The heavens declare His righteousness,
And all the peoples see His glory.

7 [a]Let all be put to shame who serve carved
images,
Who boast of idols.
[b]Worship Him, all *you* gods.
8 Zion hears and is glad,
And the daughters of Judah rejoice
Because of Your judgments, O LORD.
9 For You, LORD, *are* [a]most high above all
the earth;
[b]You are exalted far above all gods.

10 You who love the LORD, [a]hate evil!
[b]He preserves the souls of His saints;
[c]He delivers them out of the hand of the
wicked.
11 [a]Light is sown for the righteous,
And gladness for the upright in heart.
12 [a]Rejoice in the LORD, you righteous,
[b]And give thanks at the remembrance of
His holy name.[1]

## PSALM 98

### A SONG OF PRAISE TO THE LORD FOR HIS SALVATION AND JUDGMENT

*A Psalm.*

1 Oh, [a]sing to the LORD a new song!
For He has [b]done marvelous things;
His right hand and His holy arm have
gained Him the victory.
2 [a]The LORD has made known His salvation;
[b]His righteousness He has revealed in the
sight of the nations.
3 He has remembered His mercy and His
faithfulness to the house of Israel;
[a]All the ends of the earth have seen the
salvation of our God.

4 Shout joyfully to the LORD, all the earth;
Break forth in song, rejoice, and sing
praises.
5 Sing to the LORD with the harp,
With the harp and the sound of a psalm,

96:1 [a] 1 Chr. 16:23–33 96:4 [a] Ps. 145:3 [b] Ps. 18:3 [c] Ps. 95:3 96:5 [a] [Jer. 10:11] [b] Is. 42:5 96:6 [a] Ps. 29:2 96:7 [a] Ps. 29:1, 2 96:9 [a] Ps. 29:2 96:10 [a] Ps. 93:1; 97:1 [b] Ps. 67:4 96:11 [a] Ps. 69:34 [b] Ps. 98:7 96:13 [a] [Rev. 19:11] 97:1 [a] [Ps. 96:10] 97:2 [a] Ps. 18:11 [b] [Ps. 89:14] 97:3 [a] Ps. 18:8 97:4 [a] Ex. 19:18 97:5 [a] Mic. 1:4 97:6 [a] Ps. 19:1 97:7 [a] [Ex. 20:4] [b] [Heb. 1:6] 97:9 [a] Ps. 83:18 [b] Ex. 18:11 97:10 [a] [Ps. 34:14] [b] Prov. 2:8 [c] Ps. 37:40 97:11 [a] Job 22:28 97:12 [a] Ps. 33:1 [b] Ps. 30:4 [1] Or *His holiness* 98:1 [a] Is. 42:10 [b] Ex. 15:11 98:2 [a] Is. 52:10 [b] Is. 62:2 98:3 [a] Luke 3:6

KNOW THE TRUTH

## THE DOCTRINE OF GOD

### PART 19: THE TRANSCENDENCE OF GOD

**97:9** In the ancient world, worshipers of pagan gods often connected their deities to celestial bodies (stars, planets, etc.), geographical regions, and even specific topographies (rivers, valleys, mountains, etc.). For example, the Egyptian god Amun-Ra was viewed as the god of the sun and as the sun itself. The Syrians considered their gods mighty in valley warfare but weak in warfare fought upon hills and mountains (see 1 Kin. 20:23–28).

In Psalm 97:9, the psalmist distinguishes the one true God from all supposed deities as well as from creation. He says the Lord is both "exalted far above" and "most high above all" things. In other words, God is transcendent. This means while God is the Creator of everything and is present in His creation, He is distinct from it and has complete command and supremacy over it. All creation is *from* and *for* God, but none of creation *is* God. A car only exists because of its creator and bears the marks of its creator but it's not in any way its creator nor is its creator it.

Put more simply, *transcendence* means to be above and distinct from something. God created, sustains, and rules over the universe, but He isn't the universe. While we're called to care for creation, we solely devote our lives to worship the Creator.

*For* **THE DOCTRINE OF GOD: PART 20: THE TRIUNE NATURE OF GOD,** *turn to 2 Corinthians 13:14 on page 1192.* •••

6 With trumpets and the sound of a horn;
Shout joyfully before the LORD,
the King.

7 Let the sea roar, and all its fullness,
The world and those who dwell in it;
8 Let the rivers clap *their* hands;
Let the hills be joyful together
9 before the LORD,
[a]For He is coming to judge the earth.
With righteousness He shall judge the world,
And the peoples with equity.

### SEEING JESUS IN THE SCRIPTURE

**98:9** Jesus is the righteous Judge who one day is coming to judge the world (see John 5:22). When Jesus returns, He will judge all people based on their trust in His perfect, completed work or in their own sinful works.

## *PSALM 99*

### *PRAISE TO THE LORD FOR HIS HOLINESS*

1 The LORD reigns;
Let the peoples tremble!
[a]He dwells *between* the cherubim;
Let the earth be moved!
2 The LORD *is* great in Zion,
And He *is* high above all the peoples.
3 Let them praise Your great and awesome name—
He *is* holy.

4 The King's strength also loves justice;
You have established equity;
You have executed justice and righteousness in Jacob.
5 Exalt the LORD our God,
And worship at His footstool—
He *is* holy.

6 Moses and Aaron were among His priests,
And Samuel was among those who [a]called upon His name;
They called upon the LORD, and He answered them.
7 He spoke to them in the cloudy pillar;
They kept His testimonies and the ordinance He gave them.

8 You answered them, O LORD our God;
You were to them God-Who-Forgives,
Though You took vengeance on their deeds.
9 Exalt the LORD our God,
And worship at His holy hill;
For the LORD our God *is* holy.

**98:9** [a] [Ps. 96:10, 13] **99:1** [a] Ex. 25:22 **99:6** [a] 1 Sam. 7:9; 12:18

## PSALM 100

### *A SONG OF PRAISE FOR THE LORD'S FAITHFULNESS TO HIS PEOPLE*

[a]*A Psalm of Thanksgiving.*

1 Make [a]a joyful shout to the LORD, all you lands!
2 Serve the LORD with gladness;
Come before His presence with singing.
3 Know that the LORD, He *is* God;
[a]*It is* He *who* has made us, and not we ourselves;[1]
[b]*We are* His people and the sheep of His pasture.

4 [a]Enter into His gates with thanksgiving,
*And* into His courts with praise.
Be thankful to Him, *and* bless His name.
5 For the LORD *is* good;
[a]His mercy *is* everlasting,
And His truth *endures* to all generations.

## PSALM 101

### *PROMISED FAITHFULNESS TO THE LORD*

*A Psalm of David.*

1 I will sing of mercy and justice;
To You, O LORD, I will sing praises.

2 I will behave wisely in a perfect way.
Oh, when will You come to me?
I will [a]walk within my house with a perfect heart.

3 I will set nothing wicked before my eyes;
[a]I hate the work of those [b]who fall away;
It shall not cling to me.
4 A perverse heart shall depart from me;
I will not [a]know wickedness.

5 Whoever secretly slanders his neighbor,
Him I will destroy;
[a]The one who has a haughty look and a proud heart,
Him I will not endure.

6 My eyes *shall be* on the faithful of the land,
That they may dwell with me;
He who walks in a perfect way,
He shall serve me.
7 He who works deceit shall not dwell within my house;
He who tells lies shall not continue in my presence.
8 [a]Early I will destroy all the wicked of the land,
That I may cut off all the evildoers [b]from the city of the LORD.

## PSALM 102

### *THE LORD'S ETERNAL LOVE*

*A Prayer of the afflicted, [a]when he is overwhelmed and pours out his complaint before the LORD.*

1 Hear my prayer, O LORD,
And let my cry come to You.
2 [a]Do not hide Your face from me in the day of my trouble;
Incline Your ear to me;
In the day that I call, answer me speedily.

3 For my days are [a]consumed like smoke,
And my bones are burned like a hearth.
4 My heart is stricken and withered like grass,
So that I forget to eat my bread.

100:title [a] Ps. 145:title 100:1 [a] Ps. 95:1 100:3 [a] [Eph. 2:10] [b] Ezek. 34:30, 31 [1] Following Kethib, Septuagint, and Vulgate; Qere, many Hebrew manuscripts, and Targum read *we are His.* 100:4 [a] Ps. 66:13; 116:17–19 100:5 [a] Ps. 136:1
101:2 [a] 1 Kin. 11:4 101:3 [a] Ps. 97:10 [b] Josh. 23:6 101:4 [a] [Ps. 119:115] 101:5 [a] Prov. 6:17 101:8 [a] Jer. 21:12 [b] Ps. 48:2, 8
102:title [a] Ps. 61:2 102:2 [a] Ps. 27:9; 69:17 102:3 [a] James 4:14

LIVE THE TRUTH

## KNOWING WHO YOU ARE

**100:1–3** Every person is made in the image of God (see Gen. 1:26–27). God created us to be His representatives on earth. We are to reflect Him and His ways to everyone and everything around us. We are unique in that aspect; we alone can reflect God spiritually, intellectually, creatively, and morally. God created you to know Him and love Him, and He knows you and loves you. In short, *you* are special.

Don't miss how this psalm connects our self-image with joy. Knowing God made us and we belong to Him should elicit shouts of joy, grateful service, and singing. Because God made us in His image and gave us such a lofty purpose, we're infinitely valuable. You might not always believe that, or you might not think about it much. But it's the path to the true, lasting joy your soul longs for. It all begins with seeing yourself properly, as God sees you. Remind yourself of this truth. It can carry you through times of self-doubt and discouragement. Also, remind others of this truth. Everyone is cherished by God and should be treasured by others—because God made them.

5 Because of the sound of my groaning
My bones cling to my skin.
6 I am like a pelican of the wilderness;
I am like an owl of the desert.
7 I lie awake,
And am like a sparrow alone on the
housetop.

8 My enemies reproach me all day long;
Those who deride me swear an oath
against me.
9 For I have eaten ashes like bread,
And mingled my drink with weeping,
10 Because of Your indignation and Your wrath;
For You have lifted me up and cast me
away.
11 My days *are* like a shadow that lengthens,
And I wither away like grass.

12 But You, O LORD, shall endure forever,
And the remembrance of Your name to all
generations.
13 You will arise *and* have mercy on Zion;
For the time to favor her,
Yes, the set time, has come.
14 For Your servants take pleasure in her stones,
And show favor to her dust.
15 So the nations shall [a]fear the name of the
LORD,
And all the kings of the earth Your glory.
16 For the LORD shall build up Zion;
[a]He shall appear in His glory.
17 [a]He shall regard the prayer of the destitute,
And shall not despise their prayer.

### SEEING JESUS IN THE SCRIPTURE

**102:16** The psalmist's prayer shows our ultimate hope is in God's glorious presence. Jesus' coming to earth the first time was an answer to that prayer (see John 1:14). This prayer will be answered in full when He returns.

18 This will be [a]written for the generation to
come,
That [b]a people yet to be created may
praise the LORD.
19 For He [a]looked down from the height of
His sanctuary;
From heaven the LORD viewed the earth,
20 [a]To hear the groaning of the prisoner,
To release those appointed to death,
21 To [a]declare the name of the LORD in Zion,
And His praise in Jerusalem,
22 [a]When the peoples are gathered together,
And the kingdoms, to serve the LORD.

23 He weakened my strength in the way;
He [a]shortened my days.
24 [a]I said, "O my God,
Do not take me away in the midst of my
days;
[b]Your years *are* throughout all generations.
25 [a]Of old You laid the foundation of the
earth,
And the heavens *are* the work of Your
hands.
26 [a]They will perish, but You will endure;
Yes, they will all grow old like a garment;
Like a cloak You will change them,
And they will be changed.
27 But [a]You *are* the same,
And Your years will have no end.
28 [a]The children of Your servants will
continue,
And their descendants will be established
before You."

## PSALM 103

### PRAISE FOR THE LORD'S MERCIES

A Psalm *of David.*

1 Bless [a]the LORD, O my soul;
And all that is within me, *bless* His holy
name!
2 Bless the LORD, O my soul,
And forget not all His benefits:
3 [a]Who forgives all your iniquities,
Who [b]heals all your diseases,

**103:3** This cannot be seen as a promise that the godly will never suffer from **diseases**. Many believers have suffered and died of illnesses, despite repeated prayers for healing. Even though God doesn't always choose to heal, He is the source of all healing. This verse could also be seen as a parallel construction, coupling pardon from **iniquities** with healing from the disease of sin.

4 Who redeems your life from destruction,
[a]Who crowns you with lovingkindness and
tender mercies,
5 Who satisfies your mouth with good *things,*
*So that* [a]your youth is renewed like the
eagle's.

6 The LORD executes righteousness
And justice for all who are oppressed.
7 [a]He made known His ways to Moses,
His acts to the children of Israel.

**102:15** [a] 1 Kin. 8:43 **102:16** [a] [Is. 60:1, 2] **102:17** [a] Neh. 1:6 **102:18** [a] [Rom. 15:4] [b] Ps. 22:31 **102:19** [a] Deut. 26:15 **102:20** [a] Ps. 79:11 **102:21** [a] Ps. 22:22 **102:22** [a] [Is. 2:2, 3; 49:22, 23; 60:3] **102:23** [a] Job 21:21 **102:24** [a] Is. 38:10 [b] [Ps. 90:2] **102:25** [a] [Heb. 1:10–12] **102:26** [a] Is. 34:4; 51:6 **102:27** [a] [Mal. 3:6] **102:28** [a] Ps. 69:36 **103:1** [a] Ps. 104:1, 35 **103:3** [a] Ps. 130:8 [b] [Ex. 15:26] **103:4** [a] [Ps. 5:12] **103:5** [a] [Is. 40:31] **103:7** [a] Ps. 147:19

8 [a]The LORD *is* merciful and gracious,
Slow to anger, and abounding in mercy.
9 [a]He will not always strive *with us,*
Nor will He keep *His anger* forever.
10 [a]He has not dealt with us according to our sins,
Nor punished us according to our iniquities.

11 For as the heavens are high above the earth,
*So* great is His mercy toward those who fear Him;
12 As far as the east is from the west,
*So* far has He [a]removed our transgressions from us.
13 [a]As a father pities *his* children,
*So* the LORD pities those who fear Him.
14 For He knows our frame;
He remembers that we *are* dust.

15 *As for* man, [a]his days *are* like grass;
As a flower of the field, so he flourishes.
16 [a]For the wind passes over it, and it is gone,
And [b]its place remembers it no more.[1]
17 But the mercy of the LORD *is* from everlasting to everlasting
On those who fear Him,
And His righteousness to children's children,
18 [a]To such as keep His covenant,
And to those who remember His commandments to do them.
19 The LORD has established His throne in heaven,
And [a]His kingdom rules over all.

20 [a]Bless the LORD, you His angels,
Who excel in strength, who [b]do His word,
Heeding the voice of His word.
21 Bless the LORD, all *you* His hosts,
[a]*You* ministers of His, who do His pleasure.
22 Bless the LORD, all His works,
In all places of His dominion.

Bless the LORD, O my soul!

## PSALM 104

### PRAISE TO THE SOVEREIGN LORD FOR HIS CREATION AND PROVIDENCE

*(cf. Gen. 1:1–31)*

1 Bless [a]the LORD, O my soul!

O LORD my God, You are very great:
You are clothed with honor and majesty,
2 Who cover *Yourself* with light as *with* a garment,
Who stretch out the heavens like a curtain.

103:8 [a] [Ex. 34:6, 7] 103:9 [a] [Ps. 30:5] 103:10 [a] [Ezra 9:13] 103:12 [a] [Is. 38:17; 43:25] 103:13 [a] Mal. 3:17 103:15 [a] 1 Pet. 1:24 103:16 [a] [Is. 40:7] [b] Job 7:10 [1] Compare Job 7:10 103:18 [a] [Deut. 7:9] 103:19 [a] [Dan. 4:17, 25] 103:20 [a] Ps. 148:2 [b] [Matt. 6:10] 103:21 [a] [Heb. 1:14] 104:1 [a] Ps. 103:1

KNOW THE TRUTH

## THE DOCTRINE OF CREATION AND HUMANS

### PART 3: THE CREATION OF ANGELS

**103:20–21** Angels are a distinct creation of God in form and function. In **form**, angels don't appear to be limited by certain time-space and organic restrictions like humans. They can manifest themselves to the human eye or conceal their presence and shining glory. They appear to be generally more powerful than humans, but don't share the power or authority of God (see Luke 2:13–15; Rev. 10:1–3). Some angels appear to be human-like in form, others walk on all fours covered in eyes, and still others appear engulfed in flames in flight with six wings (see Is. 6:1–7; Matt. 28:2–6; Rev. 4:6–11). The quantity of angels is practically innumerable (see Heb. 12:22; Rev. 5:11).

In **function**, angels are worshipers of God and servants in His plans (see Ps. 104:4). The Bible shows them predominately doing two things: helping reveal and clarify God's plans to people and offering God unending worship (see Luke 1:26–28; Rev. 5:8–14). Throughout the Book of Revelation, they also help enact God's judgments on the world (see Rev. 16:1–20). Because angels are merely servants of God, believers shouldn't worship nor place undue focus on angelic beings; instead, we are to seek constant guidance from the Holy Spirit (see John 16:7–15; Rev. 19:9–10).

*For* **THE DOCTRINE OF CREATION AND HUMANS: PART 4: THE CREATION OF SATAN AND DEMONS,** *turn Mark 3:22–27 on page 1006.*

3 [a]He lays the beams of His upper chambers
in the waters,
Who makes the clouds His chariot,
Who walks on the wings of the wind,
4 Who makes His angels spirits,
His ministers a flame of fire.

5 *You who* laid the foundations of the earth,
So *that* it should not be moved forever,
6 You [a]covered it with the deep as *with* a
garment;
The waters stood above the mountains.
7 At Your rebuke they fled;
At the voice of Your thunder they
hastened away.
8 They went up over the mountains;
They went down into the valleys,
To the place which You founded for them.
9 You have [a]set a boundary that they may
not pass over,
[b]That they may not return to cover the
earth.

10 He sends the springs into the valleys;
They flow among the hills.
11 They give drink to every beast of the field;
The wild donkeys quench their thirst.
12 By them the birds of the heavens have
their home;
They sing among the branches.
13 [a]He waters the hills from His upper
chambers;
The earth is satisfied with [b]the fruit of
Your works.

14 [a]He causes the grass to grow for the cattle,
And vegetation for the service of man,
That he may bring forth [b]food from the
earth,
15 And [a]wine *that* makes glad the heart of man,
Oil to make *his* face shine,
And bread *which* strengthens man's heart.
16 The trees of the LORD are full *of sap,*
The cedars of Lebanon which He planted,
17 Where the birds make their nests;
The stork has her home in the fir trees.
18 The high hills *are* for the wild goats;
The cliffs are a refuge for the [a]rock badgers.[1]

19 [a]He appointed the moon for seasons;
The [b]sun knows its going down.
20 [a]You make darkness, and it is night,
In which all the beasts of the forest creep
about.
21 [a]The young lions roar after their prey,
And seek their food from God.
22 *When* the sun rises, they gather together
And lie down in their dens.
23 Man goes out to [a]his work
And to his labor until the evening.

24 [a]O LORD, how manifold are Your works!
In wisdom You have made them all.
The earth is full of Your [b]possessions—
25 This great and wide sea,
In which *are* innumerable teeming things,
Living things both small and great.
26 There the ships sail about;
*There is* that [a]Leviathan
Which You have made to play there.

27 [a]These all wait for You,
That You may give *them* their food in due
season.
28 *What* You give them they gather in;
You open Your hand, they are filled with
good.
29 You hide Your face, they are troubled;
[a]You take away their breath, they die and
return to their dust.
30 [a]You send forth Your Spirit, they are created;
And You renew the face of the earth.

31 May the glory of the LORD endure forever;
May the LORD [a]rejoice in His works.
32 He looks on the earth, and it [a]trembles;
[b]He touches the hills, and they smoke.

33 [a]I will sing to the LORD as long as I live;
I will sing praise to my God while I have
my being.
34 May my [a]meditation be sweet to Him;
I will be glad in the LORD.
35 May [a]sinners be consumed from the earth,
And the wicked be no more.

Bless the LORD, O my soul!
Praise the LORD!

## PSALM 105

### THE ETERNAL FAITHFULNESS OF THE LORD

*(Ex. 7:8—11:10; 1 Chr. 16:8–22)*

1 Oh, [a]give thanks to the LORD!
Call upon His name;
[b]Make known His deeds among the
peoples!
2 Sing to Him, sing psalms to Him;
[a]Talk of all His wondrous works!
3 Glory in His holy name;
Let the hearts of those rejoice who seek
the LORD!
4 Seek the LORD and His strength;
[a]Seek His face evermore!

104:3 [a] [Amos 9:6] 104:6 [a] Gen. 1:6 104:9 [a] [Jer. 5:22] [b] Gen. 9:11–15 104:13 [a] Ps. 147:8 [b] Jer. 10:13 104:14 [a] Gen. 1:29 [b] Job 28:5 104:15 [a] Judg. 9:13 104:18 [a] Lev. 11:5 [1] Or *rock hyrax* (compare Leviticus 11:5) 104:19 [a] Gen. 1:14 [b] Ps. 19:6 104:20 [a] [Is. 45:7] 104:21 [a] Job 38:39 104:23 [a] Gen. 3:19 104:24 [a] Prov. 3:19 [b] Ps. 65:9 104:26 [a] Job 41:1 104:27 [a] Ps. 136:25 104:29 [a] Job 34:15 104:30 [a] Is. 32:15 104:31 [a] Gen. 1:31 104:32 [a] Hab. 3:10 [b] Ps. 144:5 104:33 [a] Ps. 63:4 104:34 [a] Ps. 19:14 104:35 [a] Ps. 37:38 105:1 [a] Is. 12:4 [b] Ps. 145:12 105:2 [a] Ps. 119:27 105:4 [a] Ps. 27:8

5 [a]Remember His marvelous works which
He has done,
His wonders, and the judgments of His
mouth,
6 O seed of Abraham His servant,
You children of Jacob, His chosen ones!

7 He *is* the LORD our God;
[a]His judgments *are* in all the earth.
8 He [a]remembers His covenant forever,
The word *which* He commanded, for a
thousand generations,
9 [a]*The covenant* which He made with Abraham,
And His oath to Isaac,
10 And confirmed it to Jacob for a statute,
To Israel *as* an everlasting covenant,
11 Saying, [a]"To you I will give the land of
Canaan
As the allotment of your inheritance,"
12 [a]When they were few in number,
Indeed very few, [b]and strangers in it.

13 When they went from one nation to
another,
From *one* kingdom to another people,
14 [a]He permitted no one to do them wrong;
Yes, [b]He rebuked kings for their sakes,
15 *Saying,* "Do not touch My anointed ones,
And do My prophets no harm."

16 Moreover [a]He called for a famine in the
land;
He destroyed all the [b]provision of bread.
17 [a]He sent a man before them—
Joseph—*who* [b]was sold as a slave.
18 [a]They hurt his feet with fetters,
He was laid in irons.
19 Until the time that his word came to pass,
[a]The word of the LORD tested him.
20 [a]The king sent and released him,
The ruler of the people let him go free.
21 [a]He made him lord of his house,
And ruler of all his possessions,
22 To bind his princes at his pleasure,
And teach his elders wisdom.

23 [a]Israel also came into Egypt,
And Jacob dwelt [b]in the land of Ham.
24 [a]He increased His people greatly,
And made them stronger than their
enemies.
25 [a]He turned their heart to hate His people,
To deal craftily with His servants.

26 [a]He sent Moses His servant,
*And* Aaron whom He had chosen.
27 They [a]performed His signs among them,
And wonders in the land of Ham.
28 He sent darkness, and made *it* dark;
And they did not rebel against His word.
29 [a]He turned their waters into blood,
And killed their fish.
30 [a]Their land abounded with frogs,
*Even* in the chambers of their kings.
31 [a]He spoke, and there came swarms of flies,
*And* lice in all their territory.
32 [a]He gave them hail for rain,
*And* flaming fire in their land.
33 [a]He struck their vines also, and their fig trees,
And splintered the trees of their territory.
34 [a]He spoke, and locusts came,
Young locusts without number,
35 And ate up all the vegetation in their land,
And devoured the fruit of their ground.
36 [a]He also destroyed all the firstborn in their
land,
[b]The first of all their strength.

37 [a]He also brought them out with silver and
gold,
And *there was* none feeble among His
tribes.
38 [a]Egypt was glad when they departed,
For the fear of them had fallen upon them.
39 [a]He spread a cloud for a covering,
And fire to give light in the night.
40 [a]*The people* asked, and He brought quail,
And [b]satisfied them with the bread of
heaven.
41 [a]He opened the rock, and water gushed out;
It ran in the dry places *like* a river.

42 For He remembered [a]His holy promise,
*And* Abraham His servant.
43 He brought out His people with joy,
His chosen ones with gladness.
44 [a]He gave them the lands of the Gentiles,
And they inherited the labor of the
nations,
45 [a]That they might observe His statutes
And keep His laws.

Praise the LORD!

## PSALM 106

### *JOY IN FORGIVENESS OF ISRAEL'S SINS*

1 Praise the LORD!

[a]Oh, give thanks to the LORD, for *He is* good!
For His mercy *endures* forever.

105:5 [a] Ps. 77:11 105:7 [a] [Is. 26:9] 105:8 [a] Luke 1:72 105:9 [a] Gen. 17:2 105:11 [a] Gen. 13:15; 15:18 105:12 [a] [Deut. 7:7] [b] Heb. 11:9 105:14 [a] Gen. 35:5 [b] Gen. 12:17 105:16 [a] Gen. 41:54 [b] Lev. 26:26 105:17 [a] [Gen. 45:5] [b] Gen. 37:28, 36 105:18 [a] Gen. 40:15 105:19 [a] Gen. 39:11–21; 41:25, 42, 43 105:20 [a] Gen. 41:14 105:21 [a] Gen. 41:40–44 105:23 [a] Gen. 46:6 [b] Ps. 78:51 105:24 [a] Ex. 1:7, 9 105:25 [a] Ex. 1:8–10; 4:21 105:26 [a] Ex. 3:10; 4:12–15 105:27 [a] Ps. 78:43 105:29 [a] Ex. 7:20, 21 105:30 [a] Ex. 8:6 105:31 [a] Ex. 8:16, 17 105:32 [a] Ex. 9:23–25 105:33 [a] Ps. 78:47 105:34 [a] Ex. 10:4 105:36 [a] Ex. 12:29; 13:15 [b] Gen. 49:3 105:37 [a] Ex. 12:35, 36 105:38 [a] Ex. 12:33 105:39 [a] Ex. 13:21 105:40 [a] Ex. 16:12 [b] Ps. 78:24 105:41 [a] Ex. 17:6 105:42 [a] Gen. 15:13, 14 105:44 [a] Josh. 11:16–23; 13:7 105:45 [a] [Deut. 4:1, 40] 106:1 [a] 1 Chr. 16:34, 41

2 Who can utter the mighty acts of the LORD?
Who can declare all His praise?
3 Blessed *are* those who keep justice,
*And* he who [a]does[1] righteousness at [b]all
times!

4 [a]Remember me, O LORD, with the favor
*You have toward* Your people.
Oh, visit me with Your salvation,
5 That I may see the benefit of Your chosen
ones,
That I may rejoice in the gladness of Your
nation,
That I may glory with Your inheritance.

6 [a]We have sinned with our fathers,
We have committed iniquity,
We have done wickedly.
7 Our fathers in Egypt did not understand
Your wonders;
They did not remember the multitude of
Your mercies,
[a]But rebelled by the sea—the Red Sea.

8 Nevertheless He saved them for His
name's sake,
[a]That He might make His mighty power
known.
9 [a]He rebuked the Red Sea also, and it dried up;
So [b]He led them through the depths,
As through the wilderness.
10 He [a]saved them from the hand of him
who hated *them,*
And redeemed them from the hand of the
enemy.
11 [a]The waters covered their enemies;
There was not one of them left.
12 [a]Then they believed His words;
They sang His praise.

13 [a]They soon forgot His works;
They did not wait for His counsel,
14 [a]But lusted exceedingly in the wilderness,
And tested God in the desert.
15 [a]And He gave them their request,
But [b]sent leanness into their soul.

16 When [a]they envied Moses in the camp,
*And* Aaron the saint of the LORD,
17 [a]The earth opened up and swallowed
Dathan,
And covered the faction of Abiram.
18 [a]A fire was kindled in their company;
The flame burned up the wicked.

19 [a]They made a calf in Horeb,
And worshiped the molded image.
20 Thus [a]they changed their glory
Into the image of an ox that eats grass.
21 They forgot God their Savior,
Who had done great things in Egypt,
22 Wondrous works in the land of Ham,
Awesome things by the Red Sea.
23 [a]Therefore He said that He would destroy
them,
Had not Moses His chosen one [b]stood
before Him in the breach,
To turn away His wrath, lest He destroy
*them.*

24 Then they despised [a]the pleasant land;
They [b]did not believe His word,
25 [a]But complained in their tents,
*And* did not heed the voice of the LORD.
26 [a]Therefore He raised His hand *in an oath*
against them,
[b]To overthrow them in the wilderness,
27 [a]To overthrow their descendants among
the nations,
And to scatter them in the lands.

28 [a]They joined themselves also to Baal of
Peor,
And ate sacrifices made to the dead.
29 Thus they provoked *Him* to anger with
their deeds,
And the plague broke out among them.
30 [a]Then Phinehas stood up and intervened,
And the plague was stopped.
31 And that was accounted to him [a]for
righteousness
To all generations forevermore.

32 [a]They angered *Him* also at the waters of
strife,[1]
[b]So that it went ill with Moses on account
of them;

**106:17–18** As descendants of Reuben, Jacob's firstborn son, **Dathan** and **Abiram** believed they and their tribe—and not Moses—should have been the political leaders of Israel. Their punishment for challenging Moses's authority was as unusual and severe as it was unexpected. The **earth** beneath the rebels' feet **opened**, and Dathan and Abiram, along with all their belongings, disappeared into it. God took care of the other people who joined in the rebellion with **fire** from heaven (see Num. 16:1–40).

**106:3** [a] Ps. 15:2 [b] [Gal. 6:9] [1] Septuagint, Syriac, Targum, and Vulgate read *those who do.* **106:4** [a] Ps. 119:132 **106:6** [a] [Dan. 9:5] **106:7** [a] Ex. 14:11, 12 **106:8** [a] Ex. 9:16 **106:9** [a] Ex. 14:21 [b] Is. 63:11–13 **106:10** [a] Ex. 14:30 **106:11** [a] Ex. 14:27, 28; 15:5 **106:12** [a] Ex. 15:1–21 **106:13** [a] Ex. 15:24; 16:2; 17:2 **106:14** [a] 1 Cor. 10:6 **106:15** [a] Num. 11:31 [b] Is. 10:16 **106:16** [a] Num. 16:1–3 **106:17** [a] Deut. 11:6 **106:18** [a] Num. 16:35, 46 **106:19** [a] Ex. 32:1–4 **106:20** [a] Rom. 1:23 **106:23** [a] Ex. 32:10 [b] Ezek. 22:30 **106:24** [a] Deut. 8:7 [b] [Heb. 3:18, 19] **106:25** [a] Num. 14:2, 27 **106:26** [a] Ezek. 20:15, 16 [b] Num. 14:28–30 **106:27** [a] Lev. 26:33 **106:28** [a] Hos. 9:10 **106:30** [a] Num. 25:7, 8 **106:31** [a] Num. 25:11–13 **106:32** [a] Num. 20:3–13 [b] Deut. 1:37; 3:26 [1] Or *Meribah*

33 [a]Because they rebelled against His Spirit,
So that he spoke rashly with his lips.

34 [a]They did not destroy the peoples,
[b]Concerning whom the LORD had commanded them,
35 [a]But they mingled with the Gentiles
And learned their works;
36 [a]They served their idols,
[b]Which became a snare to them.
37 [a]They even sacrificed their sons
And their daughters to [b]demons,
38 And shed innocent blood,
The blood of their sons and daughters,
Whom they sacrificed to the idols of Canaan;
And [a]the land was polluted with blood.
39 Thus they were [a]defiled by their own works,
And [b]played the harlot by their own deeds.

40 Therefore [a]the wrath of the LORD was kindled against His people,
So that He abhorred [b]His own inheritance.
41 And [a]He gave them into the hand of the Gentiles,
And those who hated them ruled over them.
42 Their enemies also oppressed them,
And they were brought into subjection under their hand.
43 [a]Many times He delivered them;
But they rebelled in their counsel,
And were brought low for their iniquity.
44 Nevertheless He regarded their affliction,
When [a]He heard their cry;
45 [a]And for their sake He remembered His covenant,
And [b]relented [c]according to the multitude of His mercies.
46 [a]He also made them to be pitied
By all those who carried them away captive.

47 [a]Save us, O LORD our God,
And gather us from among the Gentiles,
To give thanks to Your holy name,
To triumph in Your praise.

48 [a]Blessed *be* the LORD God of Israel
From everlasting to everlasting!
And let all the people say, "Amen!"

Praise the LORD!

# BOOK FIVE
## *PSALMS 107–150*

## *PSALM 107*
### *THANKSGIVING TO THE LORD FOR HIS GREAT WORKS OF DELIVERANCE*

1 Oh, [a]give thanks to the LORD, for *He is* good!
For His mercy *endures* forever.
2 Let the redeemed of the LORD say *so*,
Whom He has redeemed from the hand of the enemy,
3 And [a]gathered out of the lands,
From the east and from the west,
From the north and from the south.

4 They wandered in [a]the wilderness in a desolate way;
They found no city to dwell in.
5 Hungry and thirsty,
Their soul fainted in them.
6 [a]Then they cried out to the LORD in their trouble,
*And* He delivered them out of their distresses.
7 And He led them forth by the [a]right way,
That they might go to a city for a dwelling place.
8 [a]Oh, that *men* would give thanks to the LORD *for* His goodness,
And *for* His wonderful works to the children of men!
9 For [a]He satisfies the longing soul,
And fills the hungry soul with goodness.

10 Those who [a]sat in darkness and in the shadow of death,
[b]Bound in affliction and irons—
11 Because they [a]rebelled against the words of God,
And despised [b]the counsel of the Most High,
12 Therefore He brought down their heart with labor;
They fell down, and *there was* [a]none to help.
13 Then they cried out to the LORD in their trouble,
*And* He saved them out of their distresses.
14 [a]He brought them out of darkness and the shadow of death,
And broke their chains in pieces.
15 Oh, that *men* would give thanks to the LORD *for* His goodness,

**106:33** [a] Num. 20:3, 10 **106:34** [a] Judg. 1:21 [b] [Deut. 7:2, 16] **106:35** [a] Judg. 3:5, 6 **106:36** [a] Judg. 2:12 [b] Deut. 7:16 **106:37** [a] 2 Kin. 16:3; 17:17 [b] [Lev. 17:7] **106:38** [a] [Num. 35:33] **106:39** [a] Ezek. 20:18 [b] [Lev. 17:7] **106:40** [a] Judg. 2:14 [b] [Deut. 9:29; 32:9] **106:41** [a] Judg. 2:14 **106:43** [a] Judg. 2:16 **106:44** [a] Judg. 3:9; 6:7; 10:10 **106:45** [a] [Lev. 26:41, 42] [b] Judg. 2:18 [c] Ps. 69:16 **106:46** [a] Ezra 9:9 **106:47** [a] 1 Chr. 16:35, 36 **106:48** [a] Ps. 41:13 **107:1** [a] Ps. 106:1 **107:3** [a] Is. 43:5, 6 **107:4** [a] [Deut. 2:7; 32:10] **107:6** [a] Ps. 50:15 **107:7** [a] Ezra 8:21 **107:8** [a] Ps. 107:15, 21 **107:9** [a] [Ps. 34:10] **107:10** [a] [Luke 1:79] [b] Job 36:8 **107:11** [a] Lam. 3:42 [b] [Ps. 73:24] **107:12** [a] Ps. 22:11 **107:14** [a] Ps. 68:6

And *for* His wonderful works to the
children of men!
16 For He has [a]broken the gates of bronze,
And cut the bars of iron in two.

17 Fools, [a]because of their transgression,
And because of their iniquities, were
afflicted.
18 [a]Their soul abhorred all manner of food,
And they [b]drew near to the gates of death.
19 Then they cried out to the LORD in their
trouble,
*And* He saved them out of their distresses.
20 [a]He sent His word and [b]healed them,
And [c]delivered *them* from their destructions.
21 Oh, that *men* would give thanks to the
LORD *for* His goodness,
And *for* His wonderful works to the
children of men!
22 [a]Let them sacrifice the sacrifices of
thanksgiving,
And [b]declare His works with rejoicing.

23 Those who go down to the sea in ships,
Who do business on great waters,
24 They see the works of the LORD,
And His wonders in the deep.
25 For He commands and [a]raises the stormy
wind,
Which lifts up the waves of the sea.
26 They mount up to the heavens,
They go down again to the depths;
[a]Their soul melts because of trouble.
27 They reel to and fro, and stagger like a
drunken man,
And are at their wits' end.
28 Then they cry out to the LORD in their
trouble,
And He brings them out of their distresses.
29 [a]He calms the storm,
So that its waves are still.
30 Then they are glad because they are quiet;
So He guides them to their desired haven.
31 [a]Oh, that *men* would give thanks to the
LORD *for* His goodness,
And *for* His wonderful works to the
children of men!
32 Let them exalt Him also [a]in the assembly
of the people,
And praise Him in the company of the
elders.

33 He [a]turns rivers into a wilderness,
And the watersprings into dry ground;
34 A [a]fruitful land into barrenness,
For the wickedness of those who dwell in it.
35 [a]He turns a wilderness into pools of water,
And dry land into watersprings.
36 There He makes the hungry dwell,
That they may establish a city for a
dwelling place,
37 And sow fields and plant vineyards,
That they may yield a fruitful harvest.
38 [a]He also blesses them, and they multiply
greatly;
And He does not let their cattle [b]decrease.

39 When they are [a]diminished and brought
low
Through oppression, affliction, and
sorrow,
40 [a]He pours contempt on princes,
And causes them to wander in the
wilderness *where there is* no way;
41 [a]Yet He sets the poor on high, far from
affliction,
And [b]makes *their* families like a flock.
42 [a]The righteous see *it* and rejoice,
And all [b]iniquity stops its mouth.

43 [a]Whoever *is* wise will observe these *things,*
And they will understand the
lovingkindness of the LORD.

## PSALM 108

### ASSURANCE OF GOD'S VICTORY OVER ENEMIES

*(Ps. 57:7–11; 60:5–12)*

*A Song. A Psalm of David.*

1 O [a]God, my heart is steadfast;
I will sing and give praise, even with my
glory.
2 [a]Awake, lute and harp!
I will awaken the dawn.
3 I will praise You, O LORD, among the
peoples,
And I will sing praises to You among the
nations.
4 For Your mercy *is* great above the
heavens,
And Your truth *reaches* to the clouds.

5 [a]Be exalted, O God, above the heavens,
And Your glory above all the earth;
6 [a]That Your beloved may be delivered,
Save *with* Your right hand, and hear me.

7 God has spoken in His holiness:
"I will rejoice;
I will divide Shechem
And measure out the Valley of Succoth.
8 Gilead *is* Mine; Manasseh *is* Mine;
Ephraim also *is* the helmet for My head;
[a]Judah *is* My lawgiver.

**107:16** [a] Is. 45:1, 2 **107:17** [a] Lam. 3:39 **107:18** [a] Job 33:20 [b] Job 33:22 **107:20** [a] Matt. 8:8 [b] Ps. 30:2 [c] Job 33:28, 30 **107:22** [a] Lev. 7:12 [b] Ps. 9:11 **107:25** [a] Jon. 1:4 **107:26** [a] Ps. 22:14 **107:29** [a] Ps. 89:9 **107:31** [a] Ps. 107:8, 15, 21 **107:32** [a] Ps. 22:22, 25 **107:33** [a] 1 Kin. 17:1, 7 **107:34** [a] Gen. 13:10 **107:35** [a] Ps. 114:8 **107:38** [a] Gen. 12:2; 17:16, 20 [b] [Deut. 7:14] **107:39** [a] 2 Kin. 10:32 **107:40** [a] Job 12:21, 24 **107:41** [a] 1 Sam. 2:8 [b] Ps. 78:52 **107:42** [a] Job 5:15, 16 [b] [Rom. 3:19] **107:43** [a] Jer. 9:12 **108:1** [a] Ps. 57:7–11 **108:2** [a] Ps. 57:8–11 **108:5** [a] Ps. 57:5, 11 **108:6** [a] Ps. 60:5–12 **108:8** [a] [Gen. 49:10]

9 Moab *is* My washpot;
Over Edom I will cast My shoe;
Over Philistia I will triumph."

10 [a]Who will bring me *into* the strong city?
Who will lead me to Edom?
11 *Is it* not *You,* O God, *who* cast us off?
And *You,* O God, *who* did not go out with
our armies?
12 Give us help from trouble,
For the help of man is useless.
13 [a]Through God we will do valiantly,
For *it is* He *who* shall tread down our
enemies.[1]

## PSALM 109

### PLEA FOR JUDGMENT OF FALSE ACCUSERS

*To the Chief Musician. A Psalm of David.*

1 Do[a] not keep silent,
O God of my praise!
2 For the mouth of the wicked and the
mouth of the deceitful
Have opened against me;
They have spoken against me with a
[a]lying tongue.
3 They have also surrounded me with
words of hatred,
And fought against me [a]without a cause.
4 In return for my love they are my
accusers,
But I *give myself to* prayer.
5 Thus [a]they have rewarded me evil for good,
And hatred for my love.

**SEEING JESUS IN THE SCRIPTURE**

**109:3–5** These verses anticipated Jesus' earthly ministry (see John 15:25). In return for His love, the people Jesus came to serve and save falsely accused Him and condemned Him to die. Jesus responded not with anger, but with even greater love (see Luke 23:34).

6 Set a wicked man over him,
And let [a]an accuser[1] stand at his right
hand.
7 When he is judged, let him be found guilty,
And [a]let his prayer become sin.
8 Let his days be [a]few,
*And* [b]let another take his office.
9 [a]Let his children be fatherless,
And his wife a widow.
10 Let his children continually be vagabonds,
and beg;
Let them seek *their bread*[1] also from their
desolate places.
11 [a]Let the creditor seize all that he has,
And let strangers plunder his labor.
12 Let there be none to extend mercy to him,
Nor let there be any to favor his fatherless
children.
13 [a]Let his posterity be cut off,
*And* in the generation following let their
[b]name be blotted out.

14 [a]Let the iniquity of his fathers be
remembered before the LORD,
And let not the sin of his mother [b]be
blotted out.
15 Let them be continually before the LORD,
That He may [a]cut off the memory of them
from the earth;
16 Because he did not remember to show
mercy,
But persecuted the poor and needy man,
That he might even slay the [a]broken in
heart.
17 [a]As he loved cursing, so let it come to him;
As he did not delight in blessing, so let it
be far from him.
18 As he clothed himself with cursing as with
his garment,
So let it [a]enter his body like water,
And like oil into his bones.
19 Let it be to him like the garment which
covers him,
And for a belt with which he girds himself
continually.
20 *Let* this *be* the LORD's reward to my accusers,
And to those who speak evil against my
person.

21 But You, O GOD the Lord,
Deal with me for Your name's sake;
Because Your mercy *is* good, deliver me.
22 For I *am* poor and needy,
And my heart is wounded within me.
23 I am gone [a]like a shadow when it lengthens;
I am shaken off like a locust.
24 My [a]knees are weak through fasting,
And my flesh is feeble from lack of
fatness.
25 I also have become [a]a reproach to them;
*When* they look at me, [b]they shake their
heads.

26 Help me, O LORD my God!
Oh, save me according to Your mercy,
27 [a]That they may know that this *is* Your hand—
*That* You, LORD, have done it!

**108:10** [a] Ps. 60:9 **108:13** [a] Ps. 60:12 [1] Compare verses 6–13 with 60:5–12 **109:1** [a] Ps. 83:1 **109:2** [a] Ps. 27:12 **109:3** [a] John 15:25 **109:5** [a] Ps. 35:7, 12; 38:20 **109:6** [a] Zech. 3:1 [1] Hebrew *satan* **109:7** [a] [Prov. 28:9] **109:8** [a] [Ps. 55:23] [b] Acts 1:20 **109:9** [a] Ex. 22:24 **109:10** [1] Following Masoretic Text and Targum; Septuagint and Vulgate read *be cast out.* **109:11** [a] Job 5:5; 18:9 **109:13** [a] Job 18:19 [b] Prov. 10:7 **109:14** [a] [Ex. 20:5] [b] Neh. 4:5 **109:15** [a] Job 18:17 **109:16** [a] [Ps. 34:18] **109:17** [a] Prov. 14:14 **109:18** [a] Num. 5:22 **109:23** [a] Ps. 102:11 **109:24** [a] Heb. 12:12 **109:25** [a] Ps. 22:7 [b] Matt. 27:39 **109:27** [a] Job 37:7

28 [a]Let them curse, but You bless;
When they arise, let them be ashamed,
But let [b]Your servant rejoice.
29 [a]Let my accusers be clothed with shame,
And let them cover themselves with their own disgrace as with a mantle.

30 I will greatly praise the LORD with my mouth;
Yes, [a]I will praise Him among the multitude.
31 For [a]He shall stand at the right hand of the poor,
To save *him* from those who condemn him.

## PSALM 110

### ANNOUNCEMENT OF THE MESSIAH'S REIGN

*(Matt. 22:44; Acts 2:34, 35)*

*A Psalm of David.*

1 The [a]LORD said to my Lord,
"Sit at My right hand,
Till I make Your enemies Your [b]footstool."
2 The LORD shall send the rod of Your strength [a]out of Zion.
[b]Rule in the midst of Your enemies!

> **110:1–7** This messianic psalm is quoted more often in the New Testament than any other psalm in the Bible.

3 [a]Your people *shall be* volunteers
In the day of Your power;
[b]In the beauties of holiness, from the womb of the morning,
You have the dew of Your youth.
4 The LORD has sworn
And [a]will not relent,
"You *are* a [b]priest forever
According to the order of [c]Melchizedek."

> **SEEING JESUS IN THE SCRIPTURE**
>
> **110:4** Jesus' priesthood is ordered after Melchizedek, the only other person in the Bible God appointed to be both king and priest (see Heb. 6:20). As King, Jesus reigns with all authority. As Priest, Jesus provides forgiveness of sins.

5 The Lord *is* [a]at Your right hand;
He shall execute kings [b]in the day of His wrath.
6 He shall judge among the nations,
He shall fill *the places* with dead bodies,
[a]He shall execute the heads of many countries.
7 He shall drink of the brook by the wayside;
[a]Therefore He shall lift up the head.

## PSALM 111

### PRAISE TO GOD FOR HIS FAITHFULNESS AND JUSTICE

1 Praise the LORD!

[a]I will praise the LORD with *my* whole heart,
In the assembly of the upright and *in* the congregation.

2 [a]The works of the LORD *are* great,
[b]Studied by all who have pleasure in them.
3 His work *is* [a]honorable and glorious,
And His righteousness endures forever.
4 He has made His wonderful works to be remembered;
[a]The LORD *is* gracious and full of compassion.
5 He has given food to those who fear Him;
He will ever be mindful of His covenant.
6 He has declared to His people the power of His works,
In giving them the heritage of the nations.

7 The works of His hands *are* [a]verity and justice;
All His precepts *are* sure.
8 [a]They stand fast forever and ever,
*And are* [b]done in truth and uprightness.
9 [a]He has sent redemption to His people;
He has commanded His covenant forever:
[b]Holy and awesome *is* His name.

10 [a]The fear of the LORD *is* the beginning of wisdom;
A good understanding have all those who do *His commandments*.
His praise endures forever.

## PSALM 112

### THE BLESSED STATE OF THE RIGHTEOUS

1 Praise the LORD!

Blessed *is* the man *who* fears the LORD,
*Who* [a]delights greatly in His commandments.

**109:28** [a] 2 Sam. 6:11, 12 [b] Is. 65:14 **109:29** [a] Ps. 35:26 **109:30** [a] Ps. 35:18; 111:1 **109:31** [a] [Ps. 16:8] **110:1** [a] Matt. 22:44 [b] [1 Cor. 15:25] **110:2** [a] [Rom. 11:26, 27] [b] [Dan. 7:13, 14] **110:3** [a] Judg. 5:2 [b] Ps. 96:9 **110:4** [a] [Num. 23:19] [b] [Zech. 6:13] [c] [Heb. 5:6, 10; 6:20] **110:5** [a] [Ps. 16:8] [b] Ps. 2:5, 12 **110:6** [a] Ps. 68:21 **110:7** [a] [Is. 53:12] **111:1** [a] Ps. 35:18 **111:2** [a] Ps. 92:5 [b] Ps. 143:5 **111:3** [a] Ps. 145:4, 5 **111:4** [a] [Ps. 86:5] **111:7** [a] [Rev. 15:3] **111:8** [a] Is. 40:8 [b] [Rev. 15:3] **111:9** [a] Luke 1:68 [b] Luke 1:49 **111:10** [a] Eccl. 12:13 **112:1** [a] Ps. 128:1

2 [a]His descendants will be mighty on earth;
The generation of the upright will be blessed.
3 [a]Wealth and riches *will be* in his house,
And his righteousness endures forever.
4 [a]Unto the upright there arises light in the darkness;
*He is* gracious, and full of compassion, and righteous.
5 [a]A good man deals graciously and lends;
He will guide his affairs [b]with discretion.
6 Surely he will never be shaken;
[a]The righteous will be in everlasting remembrance.
7 [a]He will not be afraid of evil tidings;
His heart is steadfast, trusting in the LORD.
8 His [a]heart *is* established;
[b]He will not be afraid,
Until he [c]sees *his desire* upon his enemies.

9 He has dispersed abroad,
He has given to the poor;
His righteousness endures forever;
His horn will be exalted with honor.
10 The wicked will see *it* and be grieved;
He will gnash his teeth and melt away;
The desire of the wicked shall perish.

## PSALM 113

### THE MAJESTY AND CONDESCENSION OF GOD

1 Praise the LORD!

[a]Praise, O servants of the LORD,
Praise the name of the LORD!
2 [a]Blessed be the name of the LORD
From this time forth and forevermore!
3 [a]From the rising of the sun to its going down
The LORD's name *is* to be praised.

4 The LORD *is* [a]high above all nations,
[b]His glory above the heavens.
5 [a]Who *is* like the LORD our God,
Who dwells on high,
6 [a]Who humbles Himself to behold
*The things that are* in the heavens and in the earth?

7 [a]He raises the poor out of the dust,
*And* lifts the [b]needy out of the ash heap,
8 That He may [a]seat *him* with princes—
With the princes of His people.
9 [a]He grants the barren woman a home,
Like a joyful mother of children.

Praise the LORD!

## PSALM 114

### THE POWER OF GOD IN HIS DELIVERANCE OF ISRAEL

*(cf. Ex. 14:1–31)*

1 When [a]Israel went out of Egypt,
The house of Jacob [b]from a people of strange language,
2 [a]Judah became His sanctuary,
*And* Israel His dominion.

3 [a]The sea saw *it* and fled;
[b]Jordan turned back.
4 [a]The mountains skipped like rams,
The little hills like lambs.
5 [a]What ails you, O sea, that you fled?
O Jordan, *that* you turned back?
6 O mountains, *that* you skipped like rams?
O little hills, like lambs?

7 Tremble, O earth, at the presence of the Lord,
At the presence of the God of Jacob,
8 [a]Who turned the rock *into* a pool of water,
The flint into a fountain of waters.

## PSALM 115

### THE FUTILITY OF IDOLS AND THE TRUSTWORTHINESS OF GOD

1 Not [a]unto us, O LORD, not unto us,
But to Your name give glory,
Because of Your mercy,
Because of Your truth.
2 Why should the Gentiles say,
[a]"So where *is* their God?"

3 [a]But our God *is* in heaven;
He does whatever He pleases.
4 [a]Their idols *are* silver and gold,
The work of men's hands.
5 They have mouths, but they do not speak;
Eyes they have, but they do not see;
6 They have ears, but they do not hear;
Noses they have, but they do not smell;
7 They have hands, but they do not handle;
Feet they have, but they do not walk;
Nor do they mutter through their throat.
8 [a]Those who make them are like them;
*So is* everyone who trusts in them.

9 [a]O Israel, trust in the LORD;
[b]He *is* their help and their shield.
10 O house of Aaron, trust in the LORD;
He *is* their help and their shield.
11 You who fear the LORD, trust in the LORD;
He *is* their help and their shield.

112:2 [a][Ps. 102:28] 112:3 [a][Matt. 6:33] 112:4 [a]Job 11:17 112:5 [a][Luke 6:35] [b][Eph. 5:15] 112:6 [a]Prov. 10:7 112:7 [a][Prov. 1:33] 112:8 [a]Heb. 13:9 [b]Prov. 1:33; 3:24 [c]Ps. 59:10 113:1 [a]Ps. 135:1 113:2 [a][Dan. 2:20] 113:3 [a]Is. 59:19 113:4 [a]Ps. 97:9; 99:2 [b][Ps. 8:1] 113:5 [a][Is. 57:15] 113:6 [a][Ps. 11:4] 113:7 [a]1 Sam. 2:8 [b]Ps. 72:12 113:8 [a][Job 36:7] 113:9 [a]1 Sam. 2:5 114:1 [a]Ex. 12:51; 13:3 [b]Ps. 81:5 114:2 [a]Ex. 6:7; 19:6; 25:8; 29:45, 46 114:3 [a]Ex. 14:21 [b]Josh. 3:13–16 114:4 [a]Ps. 29:6 114:5 [a]Hab. 3:8 114:8 [a]Ex. 17:6 115:1 [a][Is. 48:11] 115:2 [a]Ps. 42:3, 10 115:3 [a][1 Chr. 16:26] 115:4 [a]Jer. 10:3 115:8 [a]Is. 44:9–11 115:9 [a]Ps. 118:2, 3 [b]Ps. 33:20

KNOW THE TRUTH

## THE DOCTRINE OF GOD

### PART 9: THE SOVEREIGNTY OF GOD

**115:3** During the events of the Bible, the nations around Israel believed in various pantheons of pagan gods. A *pantheon* is a group of deities (gods) worshiped by a particular group. The Canaanites, Assyrians, Babylonians, Greeks, and Romans each had their own pantheon. Each pantheon had its own hierarchy, or ranking of power, of deities. Certain gods were stronger and ruled over other gods.

In Psalm 115:3, the psalmist distinguishes the one true God from all these false gods by saying the Lord "is in heaven" (above all others) and "does whatever He pleases" (rules over all). In other words, the God of the Bible is sovereign. This means He is the supreme Ruler of the universe. There is none higher, greater, or stronger than Him. God operates independent of anyone else. He's subordinate to no one. Indeed, all are subordinate to Him. No devotion to His rule strengthens Him. No rejection of His rule weakens Him. He is a self-sufficient, all-efficient, absolutely free Being.

One of God's common names in the Bible is the *Most High* (e.g., Dan. 4:32–34). This name means God is infinitely above all others in majesty and might. He is as infinitely high over an angel, as He is over a cricket, as He is over you. He's the matchless, peerless, all-powerful Ruler.

*For* **THE DOCTRINE OF GOD: PART 10: THE HOLINESS OF GOD**, *turn to Isaiah 6:1–7 on page 684.*

12 The LORD has been mindful of *us;*
He will bless us;
He will bless the house of Israel;
He will bless the house of Aaron.
13 [a]He will bless those who fear the LORD,
*Both* small and great.

14 May the LORD give you increase more and more,
You and your children.
15 *May* you *be* [a]blessed by the LORD,
[b]Who made heaven and earth.

16 The heaven, *even* the heavens, *are* the LORD's;
But the earth He has given to the children of men.
17 [a]The dead do not praise the LORD,
Nor any who go down into silence.
18 [a]But we will bless the LORD
From this time forth and forevermore.

Praise the LORD!

## PSALM 116

### THANKSGIVING FOR DELIVERANCE FROM DEATH

1 I [a]love the LORD, because He has heard
My voice *and* my supplications.
2 Because He has inclined His ear to me,
Therefore I will call *upon Him* as long as I live.

3 [a]The pains of death surrounded me,
And the pangs of Sheol laid hold of me;
I found trouble and sorrow.
4 Then I called upon the name of the LORD:
"O LORD, I implore You, deliver my soul!"

5 [a]Gracious *is* the LORD, and [b]righteous;
Yes, our God *is* merciful.
6 The LORD preserves the simple;
I was brought low, and He saved me.
7 Return to your [a]rest, O my soul,
For [b]the LORD has dealt bountifully with you.

8 [a]For You have delivered my soul from death,
My eyes from tears,
*And* my feet from falling.
9 I will walk before the LORD
[a]In the land of the living.
10 [a]I believed, therefore I spoke,
"I am greatly afflicted."
11 [a]I said in my haste,
[b]"All men *are* liars."

12 What shall I render to the LORD
*For* all His benefits toward me?

**115:13** [a] Ps. 128:1, 4 **115:15** [a] [Gen. 14:19] [b] Gen. 1:1 **115:17** [a] [Is. 38:18] **115:18** [a] Dan. 2:20 **116:1** [a] Ps. 18:1 **116:3** [a] Ps. 18:4–6 **116:5** [a] [Ps. 103:8] [b] [Ezra 9:15] **116:7** [a] [Jer. 6:16] [b] Ps. 13:6 **116:8** [a] Ps. 56:13 **116:9** [a] Ps. 27:13 **116:10** [a] 2 Cor. 4:13 **116:11** [a] Ps. 31:22 [b] Rom. 3:4

13 I will take up the cup of salvation,
And call upon the name of the LORD.
14 [a]I will pay my vows to the LORD
Now in the presence of all His people.

15 [a]Precious in the sight of the LORD
*Is* the death of His saints.

16 O LORD, truly [a]I *am* Your servant;
I *am* Your servant, [b]the son of Your maidservant;
You have loosed my bonds.
17 I will offer to You [a]the sacrifice of thanksgiving,
And will call upon the name of the LORD.

18 I will pay my vows to the LORD
Now in the presence of all His people,
19 In the [a]courts of the LORD's house,
In the midst of you, O Jerusalem.

Praise the LORD!

## PSALM 117

### LET ALL PEOPLES PRAISE THE LORD

1 Praise [a]the LORD, all you Gentiles!
Laud Him, all you peoples!
2 For His merciful kindness is great toward us,
And [a]the truth of the LORD *endures* forever.

Praise the LORD!

## PSALM 118

### PRAISE TO GOD FOR HIS EVERLASTING MERCY

1 Oh, [a]give thanks to the LORD, for *He is* good!
[b]For His mercy *endures* forever.

2 [a]Let Israel now say,
"His mercy *endures* forever."
3 Let the house of Aaron now say,
"His mercy *endures* forever."
4 Let those who fear the LORD now say,
"His mercy *endures* forever."

5 [a]I called on the LORD in distress;
The LORD answered me *and* [b]*set me* in a broad place.
6 [a]The LORD *is* on my side;
I will not fear.
What can man do to me?
7 [a]The LORD is for me among those who help me;
Therefore [b]I shall see *my desire* on those who hate me.
8 [a]*It is* better to trust in the LORD
Than to put confidence in man.
9 [a]*It is* better to trust in the LORD
Than to put confidence in princes.

10 All nations surrounded me,
But in the name of the LORD I will destroy them.
11 They [a]surrounded me,
Yes, they surrounded me;
But in the name of the LORD I will destroy them.
12 They surrounded me [a]like bees;
They were quenched [b]like a fire of thorns;
For in the name of the LORD I will destroy them.
13 You pushed me violently, that I might fall,
But the LORD helped me.
14 [a]The LORD *is* my strength and song,
And He has become my salvation.[1]

15 The voice of rejoicing and salvation
*Is* in the tents of the righteous;
The right hand of the LORD does valiantly.
16 [a]The right hand of the LORD is exalted;
The right hand of the LORD does valiantly.
17 [a]I shall not die, but live,
And [b]declare the works of the LORD.
18 The LORD has [a]chastened me severely,
But He has not given me over to death.

19 [a]Open to me the gates of righteousness;
I will go through them,
*And* I will praise the LORD.
20 [a]This is the gate of the LORD,
[b]Through which the righteous shall enter.

21 I will praise You,
For You have [a]answered me,
And have become my salvation.

22 [a]The stone *which* the builders rejected
Has become the chief cornerstone.

**SEEING JESUS IN THE SCRIPTURE**

**118:22–23** A cornerstone is the most important part of a structure. Jesus is the cornerstone of the Christian faith. Even still, many religious leaders rejected Jesus because He wasn't what they expected the Messiah to be (see Matt. 21:42).

116:14 [a]Ps. 116:18 116:15 [a]Ps. 72:14 116:16 [a]Ps. 119:125; 143:12 [b]Ps. 86:16 116:17 [a]Lev. 7:12 116:19 [a]Ps. 96:8 117:1 [a]Rom. 15:11 117:2 [a][Ps. 100:5] 118:1 [a]1 Chr. 16:8, 34 [b][Ps. 136:1–26] 118:2 [a][Ps. 115:9] 118:5 [a]Ps. 120:1 [b]Ps. 18:19 118:6 [a]Ps. 27:1; 56:9 118:7 [a]Ps. 54:4 [b]Ps. 59:10 118:8 [a]Ps. 40:4 118:9 [a]Ps. 146:3 118:11 [a]Ps. 88:17 118:12 [a]Deut. 1:44 [b]Nah. 1:10 118:14 [a]Is. 12:2 [1]Compare Exodus 15:2 118:16 [a]Ex. 15:6 118:17 [a]Hab. 1:12 [b]Ps. 73:28 118:18 [a]2 Cor. 6:9 118:19 [a]Is. 26:2 118:20 [a]Ps. 24:7 [b]Is. 35:8 118:21 [a]Ps. 116:1 118:22 [a]Matt. 21:42

23 This was the LORD's doing;
It *is* marvelous in our eyes.
24 This *is* the day the LORD has made;
We will rejoice and be glad in it.

25 Save now, I pray, O LORD;
O LORD, I pray, send now prosperity.
26 [a]Blessed *is* he who comes in the name of the LORD!
We have blessed you from the house of the LORD.

**SEEING JESUS IN THE SCRIPTURE**

**118:26** The psalmist points to Jesus' entrance into Jerusalem at the beginning of what is known as Holy Week. As Jesus entered the city, the people lined up, spread their cloaks and palm branches on the ground, and shouted these words (see Matt. 21:9).

27 God *is* the LORD,
And He has given us [a]light;
Bind the sacrifice with cords to the horns of the altar.
28 You *are* my God, and I will praise You;
[a]*You are* my God, I will exalt You.

29 Oh, give thanks to the LORD, for *He is* good!
For His mercy *endures* forever.

## PSALM 119

### MEDITATIONS ON THE EXCELLENCIES OF THE WORD OF GOD

#### א ALEPH

1 Blessed *are* the undefiled in the way,
[a]Who walk in the law of the LORD!
2 Blessed *are* those who keep His testimonies,
Who seek Him with the [a]whole heart!
3 [a]They also do no iniquity;
They walk in His ways.
4 You have commanded *us*
To keep Your precepts diligently.
5 Oh, that my ways were directed
To keep Your statutes!
6 [a]Then I would not be ashamed,
When I look into all Your commandments.
7 I will praise You with uprightness of heart,
When I learn Your righteous judgments.
8 I will keep Your statutes;
Oh, do not forsake me utterly!

#### ב BETH

9 How can a young man cleanse his way?
By taking heed according to Your word.
10 With my whole heart I have [a]sought You;
Oh, let me not wander from Your commandments!
11 [a]Your word I have hidden in my heart,
That I might not sin against You.
12 Blessed *are* You, O LORD!
Teach me Your statutes.
13 With my lips I have [a]declared
All the judgments of Your mouth.
14 I have rejoiced in the way of Your testimonies,
As *much as* in all riches.
15 I will meditate on Your precepts,
And contemplate Your ways.
16 I will [a]delight myself in Your statutes;
I will not forget Your word.

#### ג GIMEL

17 [a]Deal bountifully with Your servant,
*That* I may live and keep Your word.
18 Open my eyes, that I may see
Wondrous things from Your law.
19 [a]I *am* a stranger in the earth;
Do not hide Your commandments from me.
20 [a]My soul breaks with longing
For Your judgments at all times.
21 You rebuke the proud—the cursed,
Who stray from Your commandments.
22 [a]Remove from me reproach and contempt,
For I have kept Your testimonies.
23 Princes also sit *and* speak against me,
*But* Your servant meditates on Your statutes.
24 Your testimonies also *are* my delight
*And* my counselors.

#### ד DALETH

25 [a]My soul clings to the dust;
[b]Revive me according to Your word.
26 I have declared my ways, and You answered me;
[a]Teach me Your statutes.
27 Make me understand the way of Your precepts;
So [a]shall I meditate on Your wonderful works.
28 [a]My soul melts from heaviness;
Strengthen me according to Your word.
29 Remove from me the way of lying,
And grant me Your law graciously.
30 I have chosen the way of truth;
Your judgments I have laid *before me.*
31 I cling to Your testimonies;
O LORD, do not put me to shame!
32 I will run the course of Your commandments,
For You shall [a]enlarge my heart.

**118:26** [a]Mark 11:9 **118:27** [a][1 Pet. 2:9] **118:28** [a]Is. 25:1 **119:1** [a]Ps. 128:1 **119:2** [a]Deut. 6:5; 10:12; 11:13; 13:3 **119:3** [a][1 John 3:9; 5:18] **119:6** [a]Job 22:26 **119:10** [a]2 Chr. 15:15 **119:11** [a]Ps. 37:31; Luke 2:19 **119:13** [a]Ps. 34:11 **119:16** [a]Ps. 1:2 **119:17** [a]Ps. 116:7 **119:19** [a]Gen. 47:9; Lev. 25:23; 1 Chr. 29:15; Ps. 39:12; Heb. 11:13 **119:20** [a]Ps. 42:1, 2; 63:1; 84:2 **119:22** [a]Ps. 39:8 **119:25** [a]Ps. 44:25 [b]Ps. 143:11 **119:26** [a]Ps. 25:4; 27:11; 86:11 **119:27** [a]Ps. 145:5, 6 **119:28** [a]Ps. 107:26 **119:32** [a]1 Kin. 4:29; Is. 60:5; 2 Cor. 6:11, 13

ה *HE*

33 [a]Teach me, O LORD, the way of Your statutes,
And I shall keep it *to* the end.
34 [a]Give me understanding, and I shall keep
Your law;
Indeed, I shall observe it with *my* whole
heart.
35 Make me walk in the path of Your
commandments,
For I delight in it.
36 Incline my heart to Your testimonies,
And not to [a]covetousness.
37 [a]Turn away my eyes from [b]looking at
worthless things,
*And* revive me in Your way.[1]
38 [a]Establish Your word to Your servant,
Who *is devoted* to fearing You.
39 Turn away my reproach which I dread,
For Your judgments *are* good.
40 Behold, I long for Your precepts;
Revive me in Your righteousness.

ו *WAW*

41 Let Your mercies come also to me,
O LORD—
Your salvation according to Your word.
42 So shall I have an answer for him who
reproaches me,
For I trust in Your word.
43 And take not the word of truth utterly out
of my mouth,
For I have hoped in Your ordinances.
44 So shall I keep Your law continually,
Forever and ever.
45 And I will walk at [a]liberty,
For I seek Your precepts.
46 [a]I will speak of Your testimonies also
before kings,
And will not be ashamed.
47 And I will delight myself in Your
commandments,
Which I love.
48 My hands also I will lift up to Your
commandments,
Which I love,
And I will meditate on Your statutes.

ז *ZAYIN*

49 Remember the word to Your servant,
Upon which You have caused me to hope.
50 This *is* my [a]comfort in my affliction,
For Your word has given me life.
51 The proud have me in great derision,
*Yet* I do not turn aside from Your law.
52 I remembered Your judgments of old,
O LORD,
And have comforted myself.
53 [a]Indignation has taken hold of me
Because of the wicked, who forsake Your
law.
54 Your statutes have been my songs
In the house of my pilgrimage.
55 [a]I remember Your name in the night,
O LORD,
And I keep Your law.
56 This has become mine,
Because I kept Your precepts.

ח *HETH*

57 [a]*You are* my portion, O LORD;
I have said that I would keep Your words.
58 I entreated Your favor with *my* whole
heart;
Be merciful to me according to Your word.
59 I [a]thought about my ways,
And turned my feet to Your testimonies.
60 I made haste, and did not delay
To keep Your commandments.
61 The cords of the wicked have bound me,
*But* I have not forgotten Your law.
62 [a]At midnight I will rise to give thanks to
You,
Because of Your righteous judgments.
63 I *am* a companion of all who fear You,
And of those who keep Your precepts.
64 [a]The earth, O LORD, is full of Your mercy;
Teach me Your statutes.

ט *TETH*

65 You have dealt well with Your servant,
O LORD, according to Your word.
66 Teach me good judgment and
[a]knowledge,
For I believe Your commandments.
67 Before I was [a]afflicted I went astray,
But now I keep Your word.
68 You *are* [a]good, and do good;
Teach me Your statutes.
69 The proud have [a]forged a lie against me,
*But* I will keep Your precepts with *my*
whole heart.
70 [a]Their heart is as fat as grease,
*But* I delight in Your law.
71 *It is* good for me that I have been afflicted,
That I may learn Your statutes.
72 [a]The law of Your mouth *is* better to me
Than thousands of *coins of* gold and
silver.

י *YOD*

73 [a]Your hands have made me and fashioned
me;
Give me understanding, that I may learn
Your commandments.

119:33 [a] [Matt. 10:22; Rev. 2:26] 119:34 [a] [Prov. 2:6; James 1:5] 119:36 [a] Ezek. 33:31; [Mark 7:20–23]; Luke 12:15; [Heb. 13:5] 119:37 [a] Is. 33:15 [b] Prov. 23:5 [1] Following Masoretic Text, Septuagint, and Vulgate; Targum reads *Your words.* 119:38 [a] 2 Sam. 7:25 119:45 [a] Prov. 4:12 119:46 [a] Ps. 138:1; Matt. 10:18; Acts 26 119:50 [a] Job 6:10; [Rom. 15:4] 119:53 [a] Ex. 32:19; Ezra 9:3; Neh. 13:25 119:55 [a] Ps. 63:6 119:57 [a] Num. 18:20; Ps. 16:5; Jer. 10:16; Lam. 3:24 119:59 [a] Mark 14:72; Luke 15:17 119:62 [a] Acts 16:25 119:64 [a] Ps. 33:5 119:66 [a] Phil. 1:9 119:67 [a] Prov. 3:11; Jer. 31:18, 19; [Heb. 12:5–11] 119:68 [a] Ps. 106:1; 107:1; [Matt. 19:17] 119:69 [a] Job 13:4; Ps. 109:2 119:70 [a] Deut. 32:15; Job 15:27; Ps. 17:10; Is. 6:10; Jer. 5:28; Acts 28:27 119:72 [a] Ps. 19:10; Prov. 8:10, 11, 19 119:73 [a] Job 10:8; 31:15; [Ps. 139:15, 16]

74 [a]Those who fear You will be glad when they
see me,
Because I have hoped in Your word.
75 I know, O LORD, [a]that Your judgments *are*
right,
And *that* in faithfulness You have
afflicted me.
76 Let, I pray, Your merciful kindness be for
my comfort,
According to Your word to Your servant.
77 Let Your tender mercies come to me, that
I may live;
For Your law *is* my delight.
78 Let the proud [a]be ashamed,
For they treated me wrongfully with
falsehood;
*But* I will meditate on Your precepts.
79 Let those who fear You turn to me,
Those who know Your testimonies.
80 Let my heart be blameless regarding Your
statutes,
That I may not be ashamed.

### כ *KAPH*

81 [a]My soul faints for Your salvation,
But I hope in Your word.
82 My eyes fail *from searching* Your word,
Saying, "When will You comfort me?"
83 For [a]I have become like a wineskin in
smoke,
*Yet* I do not forget Your statutes.
84 [a]How many *are* the days of Your servant?
[b]When will You execute judgment on those
who persecute me?
85 [a]The proud have dug pits for me,
Which *is* not according to Your law.
86 All Your commandments *are* faithful;
They persecute me [a]wrongfully;
Help me!
87 They almost made an end of me on earth,
But I did not forsake Your precepts.
88 Revive me according to Your
lovingkindness,
So that I may keep the testimony of Your
mouth.

### ל *LAMED*

89 [a]Forever, O LORD,
Your word is settled in heaven.
90 Your faithfulness *endures* to all
generations;
You established the earth, and it abides.
91 They continue this day according to [a]Your
ordinances,
For all *are* Your servants.
92 Unless Your law *had been* my delight,
I would then have perished in my
affliction.
93 I will never forget Your precepts,
For by them You have given me life.
94 I *am* Yours, save me;
For I have sought Your precepts.
95 The wicked wait for me to destroy me,
*But* I will consider Your testimonies.
96 [a]I have seen the consummation of all
perfection,
*But* Your commandment *is* exceedingly
broad.

### מ *MEM*

97 Oh, how I love Your law!
[a]It *is* my meditation all the day.
98 You, through Your commandments, make
me [a]wiser than my enemies;
For they *are* ever with me.
99 I have more understanding than all my
teachers,
[a]For Your testimonies *are* my meditation.
100 [a]I understand more than the ancients,
Because I keep Your precepts.
101 I have restrained my feet from every evil
way,
That I may keep Your word.
102 I have not departed from Your judgments,
For You Yourself have taught me.
103 [a]How sweet are Your words to my taste,
*Sweeter* than honey to my mouth!
104 Through Your precepts I get understanding;
Therefore I hate every false way.

### נ *NUN*

105 [a]Your word *is* a lamp to my feet
And a light to my path.
106 [a]I have sworn and confirmed
That I will keep Your righteous
judgments.
107 I am afflicted very much;
Revive me, O LORD, according to Your
word.
108 Accept, I pray, [a]the freewill offerings of
my mouth, O LORD,
And teach me Your judgments.
109 [a]My life *is* continually in my hand,
Yet I do not forget Your law.
110 [a]The wicked have laid a snare for me,
Yet I have not strayed from Your precepts.
111 [a]Your testimonies I have taken as a
heritage forever,
For they *are* the rejoicing of my heart.
112 I have inclined my heart to perform Your
statutes
Forever, to the very end.

### ס *SAMEK*

113 I hate the double-minded,
But I love Your law.

119:74 [a] Ps. 34:2 119:75 [a] [Heb. 12:10] 119:78 [a] Ps. 25:3 119:81 [a] Ps. 73:26; 84:2 119:83 [a] Job 30:30 119:84 [a] Ps. 39:4 [b] Rev. 6:10 119:85 [a] Ps. 35:7; Prov. 16:27; Jer. 18:22 119:86 [a] Ps. 35:19 119:89 [a] Ps. 89:2; Is. 40:8; Matt. 24:35; [1 Pet. 1:25] 119:91 [a] Jer. 33:25 119:96 [a] Matt. 5:18 119:97 [a] Ps. 1:2 119:98 [a] Deut. 4:6 119:99 [a] [2 Tim. 3:15] 119:100 [a] [Job 32:7–9] 119:103 [a] Ps. 19:10; Prov. 8:11 119:105 [a] Prov. 6:23 119:106 [a] Neh. 10:29 119:108 [a] Hos. 14:2; Heb. 13:15 119:109 [a] Job 13:14 119:110 [a] Ps. 140:5 119:111 [a] Deut. 33:4

114 [a]You *are* my hiding place and my shield;
I hope in Your word.
115 [a]Depart from me, you evildoers,
For I will keep the commandments of my
God!
116 Uphold me according to Your word, that I
may live;
And do not let me [a]be ashamed of my
hope.
117 Hold me up, and I shall be safe,
And I shall observe Your statutes
continually.
118 You reject all those who stray from Your
statutes,
For their deceit *is* falsehood.
119 You put away all the wicked of the earth
[a]*like* dross;
Therefore I love Your testimonies.
120 [a]My flesh trembles for fear of You,
And I am afraid of Your judgments.

ע *AYIN*

121 I have done justice and righteousness;
Do not leave me to my oppressors.
122 Be [a]surety for Your servant for good;
Do not let the proud oppress me.
123 My eyes fail *from seeking* Your salvation
And Your righteous word.
124 Deal with Your servant according to Your
mercy,
And teach me Your statutes.
125 [a]I *am* Your servant;
Give me understanding,
That I may know Your testimonies.
126 *It is* time for *You* to act, O LORD,
*For* they have regarded Your law as void.
127 [a]Therefore I love Your commandments
More than gold, yes, than fine gold!
128 Therefore all *Your* precepts *concerning* all
*things*
I consider *to be* right;
I hate every false way.

פ *PE*

129 Your testimonies are wonderful;
Therefore my soul keeps them.
130 The entrance of Your words gives light;
[a]It gives understanding to the [b]simple.
131 I opened my mouth and [a]panted,
For I longed for Your commandments.
132 [a]Look upon me and be merciful to me,
[b]As Your custom *is* toward those who love
Your name.
133 [a]Direct my steps by Your word,
And [b]let no iniquity have dominion
over me.
134 [a]Redeem me from the oppression of man,
That I may keep Your precepts.
135 [a]Make Your face shine upon Your servant,
And teach me Your statutes.
136 [a]Rivers of water run down from my eyes,
Because *men* do not keep Your law.

צ *TSADDE*

137 [a]Righteous *are* You, O LORD,
And upright *are* Your judgments.
138 [a]Your testimonies, *which* You have
commanded,
*Are* righteous and very faithful.
139 [a]My zeal has consumed me,
Because my enemies have forgotten Your
words.
140 [a]Your word *is* very pure;
Therefore Your servant loves it.
141 I *am* small and despised,
*Yet* I do not forget Your precepts.
142 Your righteousness *is* an everlasting
righteousness,
And Your law *is* [a]truth.
143 Trouble and anguish have overtaken me,
*Yet* Your commandments *are* my delights.
144 The righteousness of Your testimonies *is*
everlasting;
Give me understanding, and I shall live.

ק *QOPH*

145 I cry out with *my* whole heart;
Hear me, O LORD!
I will keep Your statutes.
146 I cry out to You;
Save me, and I will keep Your testimonies.
147 [a]I rise before the dawning of the morning,
And cry for help;
I hope in Your word.
148 [a]My eyes are awake through the *night*
watches,
That I may meditate on Your word.
149 Hear my voice according to Your
lovingkindness;
O LORD, revive me according to Your
justice.
150 They draw near who follow after wickedness;
They are far from Your law.
151 You *are* [a]near, O LORD,
And all Your commandments *are* truth.
152 Concerning Your testimonies,
I have known of old that You have
founded them [a]forever.

ר *RESH*

153 [a]Consider my affliction and deliver me,
For I do not forget Your law.
154 [a]Plead my cause and redeem me;
Revive me according to Your word.
155 Salvation *is* far from the wicked,
For they do not seek Your statutes.

119:114 [a][Ps. 32:7] 119:115 [a]Matt. 7:23 119:116 [a][Rom. 5:5; 9:33; 10:11] 119:119 [a]Ezek. 22:18, 19 119:120 [a]Hab. 3:16 119:122 [a]Heb. 7:22 119:125 [a]Ps. 116:16 119:127 [a]Ps. 19:10 119:130 [a]Prov. 6:23 [b][Ps. 19:7] 119:131 [a]Ps. 42:1 119:132 [a]Ps. 106:4 [b][2 Thess. 1:6] 119:133 [a]Ps. 17:5 [b][Rom. 6:12] 119:134 [a]Luke 1:74 119:135 [a]Ps. 4:6 119:136 [a]Jer. 9:1, 18; 14:17 119:137 [a]Neh. 9:33 119:138 [a][Ps. 19:7–9] 119:139 [a]John 2:17 119:140 [a]Ps. 12:6 119:142 [a][John 17:17] 119:147 [a]Ps. 5:3 119:148 [a]Ps. 63:1, 6 119:151 [a][Ps. 145:18] 119:152 [a]Luke 21:33 119:153 [a]Lam. 5:1 119:154 [a]1 Sam. 24:15

156 Great *are* Your tender mercies, O LORD;
Revive me according to Your judgments.
157 Many *are* my persecutors and my enemies,
*Yet* I do not [a]turn from Your testimonies.
158 I see the treacherous, and [a]am disgusted,
Because they do not keep Your word.
159 Consider how I love Your precepts;
Revive me, O LORD, according to Your lovingkindness.
160 The entirety of Your word *is* truth,
And every one of Your righteous judgments *endures* forever.

*ש SHIN*

161 [a]Princes persecute me without a cause,
But my heart stands in awe of Your word.
162 I rejoice at Your word
As one who finds great treasure.
163 I hate and abhor lying,
*But* I love Your law.
164 Seven times a day I praise You,
Because of Your righteous judgments.
165 [a]Great peace have those who love Your law,
And nothing causes them to stumble.
166 [a] LORD, I hope for Your salvation,
And I do Your commandments.
167 My soul keeps Your testimonies,
And I love them exceedingly.
168 I keep Your precepts and Your testimonies,
[a]For all my ways *are* before You.

*ת TAU*

169 Let my cry come before You, O LORD;
[a]Give me understanding according to Your word.
170 Let my supplication come before You;
Deliver me according to Your word.
171 [a]My lips shall utter praise,
For You teach me Your statutes.
172 My tongue shall speak of Your word,
For all Your commandments *are* righteousness.
173 Let Your hand become my help,
For [a]I have chosen Your precepts.
174 [a]I long for Your salvation, O LORD,
And [b]Your law *is* my delight.
175 Let my soul live, and it shall praise You;
And let Your judgments help me.
176 [a]I have gone astray like a lost sheep;
Seek Your servant,
For I do not forget Your commandments.

## PSALM 120

### *PLEA FOR RELIEF FROM BITTER FOES*

*A Song of Ascents.*

1 In [a]my distress I cried to the LORD,
And He heard me.
2 Deliver my soul, O LORD, from lying lips
*And* from a deceitful tongue.

3 What shall be given to you,
Or what shall be done to you,
You false tongue?
4 Sharp arrows of the warrior,
With coals of the broom tree!

5 Woe is me, that I dwell in [a]Meshech,
[b]*That* I dwell among the tents of Kedar!
6 My soul has dwelt too long
With one who hates peace.
7 I *am for* peace;
But when I speak, they *are* for war.

**119:157** [a] Ps. 44:18 **119:158** [a] Ezek. 9:4 **119:161** [a] 1 Sam. 24:11; 26:18 **119:165** [a] Prov. 3:2; [Is. 26:3; 32:17] **119:166** [a] Gen. 49:18 **119:168** [a] Job 24:23; Prov. 5:21 **119:169** [a] Ps. 119:27, 144 **119:171** [a] Ps. 119:7 **119:173** [a] Josh. 24:22; Luke 10:42 **119:174** [a] Ps. 119:166 [b] Ps. 119:16, 24 **119:176** [a] [Is. 53:6]; Jer. 50:6; Matt. 18:12; Luke 15:4; [1 Pet. 2:25] **120:1** [a] Jon. 2:2 **120:5** [a] Gen. 10:2; 1 Chr. 1:5; Ezek. 27:13; 38:2, 3; 39:1 [b] Gen. 25:13; Is. 21:16; 60:7; Jer. 2:10; 49:28; Ezek. 27:21

APPLY THE TRUTH

## MORALITY AND ETHICS

**119:159–160** Every day we make countless decisions. Many are insignificant in the grand scheme of things, like having a burger or pizza for lunch. These decisions are morally neutral because there isn't a right or wrong choice. But what about decisions we make that *are* moral? The ones where there is a right thing to do? How do we choose? We're often told to "follow your heart." There's a problem with that though. Everyone's heart is flawed because of sin. As a result, our hearts—our internal compasses—lead in different directions, and not all those directions can be right. There must be a better way—a true, consistent way—to *know* what is right for us to do.

The key is finding the right standard—the one, consistent, dependable, true-for-all-people-in-all-times-and-places standard we can turn to for guidance. The Word of God is that standard. The psalmist says all of God's Word is truth. It's reliable and it endures. This allows for moral and ethical clarity in a sea of mixed feelings, thoughts, and situations. God's Word is so much better than our hearts. It gives us the true north star that guides our lives into right thinking and living.

## PSALM 121

### GOD THE HELP OF THOSE WHO SEEK HIM

*A Song of Ascents.*

1 I [a]will lift up my eyes to the hills—
From whence comes my help?
2 [a]My help *comes* from the LORD,
Who made heaven and earth.

3 [a]He will not allow your foot to be moved;
[b]He who keeps you will not slumber.
4 Behold, He who keeps Israel
Shall neither slumber nor sleep.

5 The LORD *is* your keeper;
The LORD *is* [a]your shade [b]at your right
hand.
6 [a]The sun shall not strike you by day,
Nor the moon by night.

7 The LORD shall preserve you from all evil;
He shall [a]preserve your soul.
8 The LORD shall [a]preserve your going out
and your coming in
From this time forth, and even
forevermore.

## PSALM 122

### THE JOY OF GOING TO THE HOUSE OF THE LORD

*A Song of Ascents. Of David.*

1 I was glad when they said to me,
[a]"Let us go into the house of the LORD."
2 Our feet have been standing
Within your gates, O Jerusalem!

3 Jerusalem is built
As a city that is [a]compact together,
4 [a]Where the tribes go up,
The tribes of the LORD,
To [b]the Testimony of Israel,
To give thanks to the name of the LORD.
5 [a]For thrones are set there for judgment,
The thrones of the house of David.

6 [a]Pray for the peace of Jerusalem:
"May they prosper who love you.
7 Peace be within your walls,
Prosperity within your palaces."
8 For the sake of my brethren and
companions,
I will now say, "Peace *be* within you."
9 Because of the house of the LORD our
God
I will [a]seek your good.

## PSALM 123

### PRAYER FOR RELIEF FROM CONTEMPT

*A Song of Ascents.*

1 Unto You [a]I lift up my eyes,
O You [b]who dwell in the heavens.
2 Behold, as the eyes of servants *look* to the
hand of their masters,
As the eyes of a maid to the hand of her
mistress,
[a]So our eyes *look* to the LORD our God,
Until He has mercy on us.

3 Have mercy on us, O LORD, have mercy
on us!
For we are exceedingly filled with
contempt.
4 Our soul is exceedingly filled
With the scorn of those who are at ease,
With the contempt of the proud.

## PSALM 124

### THE LORD THE DEFENSE OF HIS PEOPLE

*A Song of Ascents. Of David.*

1 "If it had not been the LORD who was on
our [a]side,"
[b]Let Israel now say—
2 "If it had not been the LORD who was on
our side,
When men rose up against us,
3 Then they would have [a]swallowed us alive,
When their wrath was kindled against us;
4 Then the waters would have
overwhelmed us,
The stream would have gone over our soul;
5 Then the swollen waters
Would have gone over our soul."

6 Blessed *be* the LORD,
Who has not given us *as* prey to their teeth.
7 [a]Our soul has escaped [b]as a bird from the
snare of the fowlers;[1]
The snare is broken, and we have escaped.
8 [a]Our help *is* in the name of the LORD,
[b]Who made heaven and earth.

## PSALM 125

### THE LORD THE STRENGTH OF HIS PEOPLE

*A Song of Ascents.*

1 Those who trust in the LORD
*Are* like Mount Zion,
*Which* cannot be moved, *but* abides
forever.

**121:1** [a] [Jer. 3:23] **121:2** [a] [Ps. 124:8] **121:3** [a] 1 Sam. 2:9; Prov. 3:23, 26 [b] [Ps. 127:1; Prov. 24:12]; Is. 27:3 **121:5** [a] Is. 25:4 [b] Ps. 16:8 **121:6** [a] Ps. 91:5; Is. 49:10; Jon. 4:8; Rev. 7:16 **121:7** [a] Ps. 41:2 **121:8** [a] Deut. 28:6; [Prov. 2:8; 3:6] **122:1** [a] [Is. 2:3; Mic. 4:2]; Zech. 8:21 **122:3** [a] 2 Sam. 5:9 **122:4** [a] Ex. 23:17; Deut. 16:16 [b] Ex. 16:34 **122:5** [a] Deut. 17:8; 2 Chr. 19:8 **122:6** [a] Ps. 51:18 **122:9** [a] Neh. 2:10 **123:1** [a] Ps. 121:1; 141:8 [b] Ps. 2:4; 11:4; 115:3 **123:2** [a] Ps. 25:15 **124:1** [a] [Rom. 8:31] [b] Ps. 129:1 **124:3** [a] Prov. 1:12 **124:7** [a] Ps. 91:3 [b] Prov. 6:5 [1] That is, persons who catch birds in a trap or snare **124:8** [a] [Ps. 121:2] [b] Gen. 1:1

2 As the mountains surround Jerusalem,
So the LORD surrounds His people
From this time forth and forever.

**125:2** Jerusalem was a fairly well-protected city. The **mountains** that **surround Jerusalem** slope into valleys on the eastern and western sides of the city and made it difficult for opposing armies to attack from those directions. The ravines that lay south of the city made it difficult for an enemy to approach from that direction as well.

3 For [a]the scepter of wickedness shall not rest
On the land allotted to the righteous,
Lest the righteous reach out their hands to iniquity.

4 Do good, O LORD, to *those who are* good,
And to *those who are* upright in their hearts.

5 As for such as turn aside to their [a]crooked ways,
The LORD shall lead them away
With the workers of iniquity.

[b]Peace *be* upon Israel!

## PSALM 126

### A JOYFUL RETURN TO ZION

*A Song of Ascents.*

1 When [a]the LORD brought back the captivity of Zion,
[b]We were like those who dream.
2 Then [a]our mouth was filled with laughter,
And our tongue with singing.
Then they said among the nations,
"The LORD has done great things for them."
3 The LORD has done great things for us,
*And* we are glad.

### SEEING JESUS IN THE SCRIPTURE

**126:1–3** When God's people returned from foreign captivity, they celebrated their salvation and restoration. Their joy mirrors the hope we have of Jesus' return, when we experience the fullness of our salvation and restoration (see Rev. 21:3–5).

4 Bring back our captivity, O LORD,
As the streams in the South.

5 [a]Those who sow in tears
Shall reap in joy.
6 He who continually goes forth weeping,
Bearing seed for sowing,
Shall doubtless come again with [a]rejoicing,
Bringing his sheaves *with him.*

## PSALM 127

### LABORING AND PROSPERING WITH THE LORD

*A Song of Ascents. Of Solomon.*

1 Unless the LORD builds the house,
They labor in vain who build it;
Unless [a]the LORD guards the city,
The watchman stays awake in vain.
2 *It is* vain for you to rise up early,
To sit up late,
To [a]eat the bread of sorrows;
*For* so He gives His beloved sleep.

3 Behold, [a]children *are* a heritage from the LORD,
[b]The fruit of the womb *is* a [c]reward.
4 Like arrows in the hand of a warrior,
So *are* the children of one's youth.
5 [a]Happy *is* the man who has his quiver full of them;
[b]They shall not be ashamed,
But shall speak with their enemies in the gate.

## PSALM 128

### BLESSINGS OF THOSE WHO FEAR THE LORD

*A Song of Ascents.*

1 Blessed [a]*is* every one who fears the LORD,
Who walks in His ways.

2 [a]When you eat the labor of your hands,
You *shall be* happy, and *it shall be* [b]well with you.
3 Your wife *shall be* [a]like a fruitful vine
In the very heart of your house,
Your [b]children [c]like olive plants
All around your table.
4 Behold, thus shall the man be blessed
Who fears the LORD.

5 [a]The LORD bless you out of Zion,
And may you see the good of Jerusalem
All the days of your life.

**125:3** [a] Prov. 22:8 **125:5** [a] Prov. 2:15 [b] [Gal. 6:16] **126:1** [a] Hos. 6:11 [b] Acts 12:9 **126:2** [a] Job 8:21 **126:5** [a] Jer. 31:9 **126:6** [a] Is. 61:3 **127:1** [a] [Ps. 121:3–5] **127:2** [a] [Gen. 3:17, 19] **127:3** [a] [Josh. 24:3, 4] [b] Deut. 7:13; 28:4 [c] [Ps. 113:9] **127:5** [a] Ps. 128:2, 3 [b] Prov. 27:11 **128:1** [a] Ps. 119:1 **128:2** [a] Is. 3:10 [b] Deut. 4:40 **128:3** [a] Ezek. 19:10 [b] Ps. 127:3–5 [c] Ps. 52:8; 144:12 **128:5** [a] Ps. 134:3

6 Yes, may you [a]see your children's
children.

[b]Peace *be* upon Israel!

## PSALM 129

### SONG OF VICTORY OVER ZION'S ENEMIES

*A Song of Ascents.*

1 "Many a time they have [a]afflicted me from
[b]my youth,"
[c]Let Israel now say—
2 "Many a time they have afflicted me from
my youth;
Yet they have not prevailed against me.
3 The plowers plowed on my back;
They made their furrows long."
4 The LORD *is* righteous;
He has cut in pieces the cords of the
wicked.

5 Let all those who hate Zion
Be put to shame and turned back.
6 Let them be as the [a]grass *on* the
housetops,
Which withers before it grows up,
7 With which the reaper does not fill his
hand,
Nor he who binds sheaves, his arms.
8 Neither let those who pass by them say,
[a]"The blessing of the LORD *be* upon you;
We bless you in the name of the LORD!"

## PSALM 130

### WAITING FOR THE REDEMPTION OF THE LORD

*A Song of Ascents.*

1 Out [a]of the depths I have cried to You,
O LORD;
2 Lord, hear my voice!
Let Your ears be attentive
To the voice of my supplications.

3 [a]If You, LORD, should mark iniquities,
O Lord, who could [b]stand?
4 But *there is* [a]forgiveness with You,
That [b]You may be feared.

5 [a]I wait for the LORD, my soul waits,
And [b]in His word I do hope.
6 [a]My soul *waits* for the Lord
More than those who watch for the
morning—
*Yes, more than* those who watch for the
morning.

7 [a]O Israel, hope in the LORD;
For [b]with the LORD *there is* mercy,
And with Him *is* abundant redemption.
8 And [a]He shall redeem Israel
From all his iniquities.

## PSALM 131

### SIMPLE TRUST IN THE LORD

*A Song of Ascents. Of David.*

1 LORD, my heart is not haughty,
Nor my eyes lofty.
[a]Neither do I concern myself with great
matters,
Nor with things too profound for me.

2 Surely I have calmed and quieted my soul,
[a]Like a weaned child with his mother;
Like a weaned child *is* my soul within me.

3 [a]O Israel, hope in the LORD
From this time forth and forever.

## PSALM 132

### THE ETERNAL DWELLING OF GOD IN ZION

*A Song of Ascents.*

1 LORD, remember David
*And* all his afflictions;
2 How he swore to the LORD,
[a]*And* vowed to [b]the Mighty One of Jacob:
3 "Surely I will not go into the chamber of
my house,
Or go up to the comfort of my bed;
4 I will [a]not give sleep to my eyes
*Or* slumber to my eyelids,
5 Until I [a]find a place for the LORD,
A dwelling place for the Mighty One of
Jacob."

6 Behold, we heard of it [a]in Ephrathah;
[b]We found it [c]in the fields of the woods.[1]
7 Let us go into His tabernacle;
[a]Let us worship at His footstool.
8 [a]Arise, O LORD, to Your resting place,
You and [b]the ark of Your strength.
9 Let Your priests [a]be clothed with
righteousness,
And let Your saints shout for joy.

**132:6 Ephrathah** is the ancient name for the town of Bethlehem.

128:6 [a] Job 42:16 [b] Ps. 125:5 129:1 [a] [Jer. 1:19; 15:20] [b] Ezek. 23:3 [c] Ps. 124:1 129:6 [a] Ps. 37:2 129:8 [a] Ruth 2:4 130:1 [a] Lam. 3:55 130:3 [a] [Ps. 143:2] [b] [Nah. 1:6] 130:4 [a] [Ex. 34:7] [b] [1 Kin. 8:39, 40] 130:5 [a] [Ps. 27:14] [b] Ps. 119:81 130:6 [a] Ps. 119:147 130:7 [a] Ps. 131:3 [b] [Is. 55:7] 130:8 [a] [Ps. 103:3, 4] 131:1 [a] [Rom. 12:16] 131:2 [a] [Matt. 18:3] 131:3 [a] [Ps. 130:7] 132:2 [a] Ps. 65:1 [b] Gen. 49:24 132:4 [a] Prov. 6:4 132:5 [a] Acts 7:46 132:6 [a] 1 Sam. 17:12 [b] 1 Sam. 7:1 [c] 1 Chr. 13:5 [1] Hebrew *Jaar* 132:7 [a] Ps. 5:7; 99:5 132:8 [a] Num. 10:35 [b] Ps. 78:61 132:9 [a] Job 29:14

10 For Your servant David's sake,
Do not turn away the face of Your
Anointed.

11 [a]The LORD has sworn *in* truth to David;
He will not turn from it:
"I will set upon your throne [b]the fruit of
your body.
12 If your sons will keep My covenant
And My testimony which I shall teach
them,
Their sons also shall sit upon your throne
forevermore."

13 [a]For the LORD has chosen Zion;
He has desired *it* for His dwelling place:
14 "This[a] *is* My resting place forever;
Here I will dwell, for I have desired it.
15 [a]I will abundantly bless her provision;
I will satisfy her poor with bread.
16 [a]I will also clothe her priests with
salvation,
[b]And her saints shall shout aloud for joy.
17 [a]There I will make the horn of David grow;
[b]I will prepare a lamp for My Anointed.
18 His enemies I will [a]clothe with shame,
But upon Himself His crown shall
flourish."

## PSALM 133

### BLESSED UNITY OF THE PEOPLE OF GOD

*A Song of Ascents. Of David.*

1 Behold, how good and how pleasant *it is*
For [a]brethren to dwell together in unity!

2 *It is* like the precious oil upon the head,
Running down on the beard,
The beard of Aaron,
Running down on the edge of his garments.
3 *It is* like the dew of [a]Hermon,
Descending upon the mountains of Zion;
For [b]there the LORD commanded the
blessing—
Life forevermore.

## PSALM 134

### PRAISING THE LORD IN HIS HOUSE AT NIGHT

*A Song of Ascents.*

1 Behold, bless the LORD,
All *you* servants of the LORD,
Who by night stand in the house of the
LORD!
2 [a]Lift up your hands *in* the sanctuary,
And bless the LORD.

3 The LORD who made heaven and earth
Bless you from Zion!

## PSALM 135

### PRAISE TO GOD IN CREATION AND REDEMPTION

1 Praise the LORD!

Praise the name of the LORD;
[a]Praise *Him,* O you servants of the LORD!
2 [a]You who stand in the house of the LORD,
In [b]the courts of the house of our God,
3 Praise the LORD, for [a]the LORD *is* good;
Sing praises to His name, [b]for *it is*
pleasant.
4 For [a]the LORD has chosen Jacob for
Himself,
Israel for His special treasure.

5 For I know that [a]the LORD *is* great,
And our Lord *is* above all gods.
6 [a]Whatever the LORD pleases He does,
In heaven and in earth,
In the seas and in all deep places.
7 [a]He causes the vapors to ascend from the
ends of the earth;
[b]He makes lightning for the rain;
He brings the wind out of His
[c]treasuries.

8 [a]He destroyed the firstborn of Egypt,
Both of man and beast.
9 [a]He sent signs and wonders into the midst
of you, O Egypt,
[b]Upon Pharaoh and all his servants.
10 [a]He defeated many nations
And slew mighty kings—
11 Sihon king of the Amorites,
Og king of Bashan,
And [a]all the kingdoms of Canaan—
12 [a]And gave their land *as* a heritage,
A heritage to Israel His people.

**135:11 Sihon** and **Og** were the first kings to try to stand in the way of the Israelites as they marched to the land God had promised them. Both kings attacked without cause when the Israelites tried to pass peacefully through their lands. Both kings were soundly defeated.

132:11 [a][Ps. 89:3, 4, 35; 110:4] [b]2 Sam. 7:12 132:13 [a][Ps. 48:1, 2] 132:14 [a]Ps. 68:16 132:15 [a]Ps. 147:14 132:16 [a]2 Chr. 6:41 [b]1 Sam. 4:5 132:17 [a]Ezek. 29:21 [b]1 Kin. 11:36; 15:4 132:18 [a]Ps. 35:26 133:1 [a]Gen. 13:8 133:3 [a]Deut. 4:48 [b]Lev. 25:21 134:2 [a][1 Tim. 2:8] 135:1 [a]Ps. 113:1 135:2 [a]Luke 2:37 [b]Ps. 116:19 135:3 [a][Ps. 119:68] [b]Ps. 147:1 135:4 [a][Ex. 19:5] 135:5 [a]Ps. 95:3; 97:9 135:6 [a]Ps. 115:3 135:7 [a]Jer. 10:13 [b]Job 28:25, 26; 38:24–28 [c]Jer. 51:16 135:8 [a]Ex. 12:12 135:9 [a]Ex. 7:10 [b]Ps. 136:15 135:10 [a]Num. 21:24 135:11 [a]Josh. 12:7–24 135:12 [a]Ps. 78:55; 136:21, 22

13 [a]Your name, O LORD, *endures* forever,
Your fame, O LORD, throughout all generations.
14 [a]For the LORD will judge His people,
And He will have compassion on His servants.

15 [a]The idols of the nations *are* silver and gold,
The work of men's hands.
16 They have mouths, but they do not speak;
Eyes they have, but they do not see;
17 They have ears, but they do not hear;
Nor is there *any* breath in their mouths.
18 Those who make them are like them;
*So is* everyone who trusts in them.

19 [a]Bless the LORD, O house of Israel!
Bless the LORD, O house of Aaron!
20 Bless the LORD, O house of Levi!
You who fear the LORD, bless the LORD!
21 Blessed be the LORD [a]out of Zion,
Who dwells in Jerusalem!

Praise the LORD!

## PSALM 136

### THANKSGIVING TO GOD FOR HIS ENDURING MERCY

1 Oh, [a]give thanks to the LORD, for *He is* good!
[b]For His mercy *endures* forever.
2 Oh, give thanks to [a]the God of gods!
For His mercy *endures* forever.
3 Oh, give thanks to the Lord of lords!
For His mercy *endures* forever:

4 To Him [a]who alone does great wonders,
For His mercy *endures* forever;
5 [a]To Him who by wisdom made the heavens,
For His mercy *endures* forever;
6 [a]To Him who laid out the earth above the waters,
For His mercy *endures* forever;
7 [a]To Him who made great lights,
For His mercy *endures* forever—
8 [a]The sun to rule by day,
For His mercy *endures* forever;
9 The moon and stars to rule by night,
For His mercy *endures* forever.

10 [a]To Him who struck Egypt in their firstborn,
For His mercy *endures* forever;
11 [a]And brought out Israel from among them,
For His mercy *endures* forever;
12 [a]With a strong hand, and with an outstretched arm,
For His mercy *endures* forever;
13 [a]To Him who divided the Red Sea in two,
For His mercy *endures* forever;
14 And made Israel pass through the midst of it,
For His mercy *endures* forever;
15 [a]But overthrew Pharaoh and his army in the Red Sea,
For His mercy *endures* forever;
16 [a]To Him who led His people through the wilderness,
For His mercy *endures* forever;
17 [a]To Him who struck down great kings,
For His mercy *endures* forever;
18 [a]And slew famous kings,
For His mercy *endures* forever—
19 [a]Sihon king of the Amorites,
For His mercy *endures* forever;
20 [a]And Og king of Bashan,
For His mercy *endures* forever—
21 [a]And gave their land as a heritage,
For His mercy *endures* forever;
22 A heritage to Israel His servant,
For His mercy *endures* forever.

23 Who [a]remembered us in our lowly state,
For His mercy *endures* forever;
24 And [a]rescued us from our enemies,
For His mercy *endures* forever;
25 [a]Who gives food to all flesh,
For His mercy *endures* forever.

26 Oh, give thanks to the God of heaven!
For His mercy *endures* forever.

## PSALM 137

### LONGING FOR ZION IN A FOREIGN LAND

1 By the rivers of Babylon,
There we sat down, yea, we wept
When we remembered Zion.
2 We hung our harps
Upon the willows in the midst of it.
3 For there those who carried us away captive asked of us a song,
And those who [a]plundered us *requested* mirth,
*Saying,* "Sing us *one* of the songs of Zion!"

4 How shall we sing the LORD's song
In a foreign land?
5 If I forget you, O Jerusalem,
Let my right hand forget *its skill!*

135:13 [a] [Ex. 3:15] 135:14 [a] Deut. 32:36 135:15 [a] [Ps. 115:4–8] 135:19 [a] [Ps. 115:9] 135:21 [a] Ps. 134:3 136:1 [a] Ps. 106:1 [b] 1 Chr. 16:34 136:2 [a] [Deut. 10:17] 136:4 [a] Ps. 72:18 136:5 [a] Jer. 51:15 136:6 [a] Jer. 10:12 136:7 [a] Gen. 1:14–18 136:8 [a] Gen. 1:16 136:10 [a] Ex. 12:29 136:11 [a] Ex. 12:51; 13:3, 16 136:12 [a] Ex. 6:6 136:13 [a] Ex. 14:21 136:15 [a] Ex. 14:27 136:16 [a] Ex. 13:18; 15:22 136:17 [a] Ps. 135:10–12 136:18 [a] Deut. 29:7 136:19 [a] Num. 21:21 136:20 [a] Num. 21:33 136:21 [a] Josh. 12:1 136:23 [a] Gen. 8:1 136:24 [a] Ps. 44:7 136:25 [a] Ps. 104:27; 145:15 137:3 [a] Ps. 79:1

6 If I do not remember you,
Let my [a]tongue cling to the roof of my mouth—
If I do not exalt Jerusalem
Above my chief joy.

7 Remember, O LORD, against [a]the sons of Edom
The day of Jerusalem,
Who said, "Raze *it,* raze *it,*
To its very foundation!"

8 O daughter of Babylon, [a]who are to be destroyed,
Happy the one [b]who repays you as you have served us!
9 Happy the one who takes and [a]dashes
Your little ones against the rock!

## PSALM 138
### THE LORD'S GOODNESS TO THE FAITHFUL

A Psalm *of David.*

1 I will praise You with my whole heart;
[a]Before the gods I will sing praises to You.
2 [a]I will worship [b]toward Your holy temple,
And praise Your name
For Your lovingkindness and Your truth;
For You have [c]magnified Your word above all Your name.
3 In the day when I cried out, You answered me,
*And* made me bold *with* strength in my soul.

4 [a]All the kings of the earth shall praise You, O LORD,
When they hear the words of Your mouth.
5 Yes, they shall sing of the ways of the LORD,
For great *is* the glory of the LORD.
6 [a]Though the LORD *is* on high,
Yet [b]He regards the lowly;
But the proud He knows from afar.

7 [a]Though I walk in the midst of trouble, You will revive me;
You will stretch out Your hand
Against the wrath of my enemies,
And Your right hand will save me.
8 [a]The LORD will perfect *that which* concerns me;
Your mercy, O LORD, *endures* forever;
[b]Do not forsake the works of Your hands.

## PSALM 139
### GOD'S PERFECT KNOWLEDGE OF MAN

For the Chief Musician. A Psalm of David.

1 O LORD, [a]You have searched me and known *me.*
2 [a]You know my sitting down and my rising up;
You [b]understand my thought afar off.
3 [a]You comprehend my path and my lying down,
And are acquainted with all my ways.
4 For *there is* not a word on my tongue,
*But* behold, O LORD, [a]You know it altogether.
5 You have hedged me behind and before,
And laid Your hand upon me.
6 [a]*Such* knowledge *is* too wonderful for me;
It is high, I cannot *attain* it.

7 [a]Where can I go from Your Spirit?
Or where can I flee from Your presence?
8 [a]If I ascend into heaven, You *are* there;
[b]If I make my bed in hell, behold, You *are there.*
9 *If* I take the wings of the morning,
*And* dwell in the uttermost parts of the sea,
10 Even there Your hand shall lead me,
And Your right hand shall hold me.
11 If I say, "Surely the darkness shall fall[1] on me,"
Even the night shall be light about me;
12 Indeed, [a]the darkness shall not hide from You,
But the night shines as the day;
The darkness and the light *are* both alike *to You.*

13 For You formed my inward parts;
You covered me in my mother's womb.
14 I will praise You, for I am fearfully *and* wonderfully made;[1]
Marvelous are Your works,
And *that* my soul knows very well.
15 [a]My frame was not hidden from You,
When I was made in secret,
*And* skillfully wrought in the lowest parts of the earth.
16 Your eyes saw my substance, being yet unformed.
And in Your book they all were written,
The days fashioned for me,
When *as yet there were* none of them.

17 [a]How precious also are Your thoughts to me, O God!
How great is the sum of them!

137:6 [a] Ezek. 3:26 137:7 [a] Jer. 49:7–22 137:8 [a] Is. 13:1–6; 47:1 [b] Jer. 50:15 137:9 [a] Is. 13:16 138:1 [a] Ps. 119:46 138:2 [a] Ps. 28:2 [b] 1 Kin. 8:29 [c] Is. 42:21 138:4 [a] Ps. 102:15 138:6 [a] [Ps. 113:4–7] [b] [James 4:6] 138:7 [a] [Ps. 23:3, 4] 138:8 [a] Ps. 57:2 [b] Job 10:3, 8 139:1 [a] Ps. 17:3 139:2 [a] 2 Kin. 19:27 [b] Matt. 9:4 139:3 [a] Job 14:16; 31:4 139:4 [a] [Heb. 4:13] 139:6 [a] Job 42:3 139:7 [a] [Jer. 23:24] 139:8 [a] [Amos 9:2–4] [b] [Job 26:6] 139:11 [1] Vulgate and Symmachus read *cover.* 139:12 [a] Job 26:6; 34:22 139:14 [1] Following Masoretic Text and Targum; Septuagint, Syriac, and Vulgate read *You are fearfully wonderful.* 139:15 [a] Job 10:8, 9 139:17 [a] [Ps. 40:5]

KNOW THE TRUTH

# THE DOCTRINE OF CREATION AND HUMANS

## PART 5: THE CREATION OF HUMANS

**139:13–18** People are a unique part of creation in how God designed us and the desires He placed deep within us. Unlike anything else in creation, each human life is made in the image of God, like Him in certain ways, but not exactly like Him (see Gen. 1:26–28). Far from being random chance, an accident, or a mistake, each human life is skillfully formed by God's Spirit in the womb with unique traits and inestimable worth.

Although at times they're unrecognized or resisted, God placed a particular set of desires within each person. First and most importantly, we **desire to know God intimately**. People, professions, or possessions can never truly satisfy the human heart because its deepest longing is for God Himself. Second, we **desire significance**; we want meaningful purpose in life. The God-given desire for significance isn't met by pursuing worldly significance. Instead, when we follow Christ, He makes our lives—our relationships, possessions, and professions—boundlessly significant in His kingdom (see Mark 1:17). Third, we **desire community**: quality relationships with others including friendship, leadership, marriage, family, and church community. Finally, we **desire to glorify God** (Eccl. 12:13–14). Bringing worship, honor, and praise to God rejoices and fulfills the heart like nothing else.

*For* **THE DOCTRINE OF CREATION AND HUMANS: PART 6: THE IMAGE OF GOD IN HUMANS**, *turn to Psalm 9:6–7 on page 15.*

18 *If* I should count them, they would be
more in number than the sand;
When I awake, I am still with You.
19 Oh, that You would [a]slay the wicked,
O God!
[b]Depart from me, therefore, you
bloodthirsty men.
20 For they [a]speak against You wickedly;
Your enemies take *Your name* in vain.[1]
21 [a]Do I not hate them, O LORD, who hate You?
And do I not loathe those who rise up
against You?
22 I hate them with perfect hatred;
I count them my enemies.
23 [a]Search me, O God, and know my heart;
Try me, and know my anxieties;
24 And see if *there is any* wicked way in me,
And [a]lead me in the way everlasting.

## *PSALM 140*

### *PRAYER FOR DELIVERANCE FROM EVIL MEN*

*To the Chief Musician. A Psalm of David.*

1 Deliver me, O LORD, from evil men;
Preserve me from violent men,
2 Who plan evil things in *their* hearts;
[a]They continually gather together *for* war.
3 They sharpen their tongues like a serpent;
The [a]poison of asps *is* under their lips.
*Selah*
4 [a]Keep me, O LORD, from the hands of the
wicked;
Preserve me from violent men,
Who have purposed to make my steps
stumble.
5 The proud have hidden a [a]snare for me,
and cords;
They have spread a net by the wayside;
They have set traps for me. *Selah*
6 I said to the LORD: "You *are* my God;
Hear the voice of my supplications,
O LORD.
7 O GOD the Lord, the strength of my
salvation,
You have covered my head in the day of
battle.
8 Do not grant, O LORD, the desires of the
wicked;
Do not further his *wicked* scheme,
[a]*Lest* they be exalted. *Selah*
9 "*As for* the head of those who surround me,
Let the evil of their lips cover them;
10 [a]Let burning coals fall upon them;
Let them be cast into the fire,
Into deep pits, that they rise not up again.

139:19 [a] [Is. 11:4] [b] Ps. 119:115 139:20 [a] Jude 15 [1] Septuagint and Vulgate read *They take Your cities in vain.* 139:21 [a] 2 Chr. 19:2 139:23 [a] Job 31:6 139:24 [a] Ps. 5:8; 143:10 140:2 [a] Ps. 56:6 140:3 [a] Ps. 58:4 140:4 [a] Ps. 71:4 140:5 [a] Jer. 18:22 140:8 [a] Deut. 32:27 140:10 [a] Ps. 11:6

11 Let not a slanderer be established in the
earth;
Let evil hunt the violent man to
overthrow *him*."

12 I know that the LORD will [a]maintain
The cause of the afflicted,
*And* justice for the poor.
13 Surely the righteous shall give thanks to
Your name;
The upright shall dwell in Your presence.

## PSALM 141

### PRAYER FOR SAFEKEEPING FROM WICKEDNESS

*A Psalm of David.*

1 LORD, I cry out to You;
Make haste to me!
Give ear to my voice when I cry out to You.
2 Let my prayer be set before You [a]*as*
incense,
[b]The lifting up of my hands *as* [c]the evening
sacrifice.

3 Set a guard, O LORD, over my [a]mouth;
Keep watch over the door of my lips.
4 Do not incline my heart to any evil thing,
To practice wicked works
With men who work iniquity;
[a]And do not let me eat of their delicacies.

5 [a]Let the righteous strike me;
*It shall be* a kindness.
And let him rebuke me;
*It shall be* as excellent oil;
Let my head not refuse it.

For still my prayer *is* against the deeds of
the wicked.
6 Their judges are overthrown by the sides
of the cliff,
And they hear my words, for they are
sweet.
7 Our bones are scattered at the mouth of
the grave,
As when one plows and breaks up the
earth.

8 But [a]my eyes *are* upon You, O GOD the
Lord;
In You I take refuge;
Do not leave my soul destitute.
9 Keep me from [a]the snares they have laid
for me,
And from the traps of the workers of
iniquity.
10 [a]Let the wicked fall into their own nets,
While I escape safely.

## PSALM 142

### A PLEA FOR RELIEF FROM PERSECUTORS

*A [a]Contemplation[1] of David. A Prayer [b]when he was in the cave.*

1 I cry out to the LORD with my voice;
With my voice to the LORD I make my
supplication.
2 I pour out my complaint before Him;
I declare before Him my trouble.

3 When my spirit was [a]overwhelmed
within me,
Then You knew my path.
In the way in which I walk
They have secretly [b]set a snare for me.
4 Look on *my* right hand and see,
For *there is* no one who acknowledges me;
Refuge has failed me;
No one cares for my soul.

5 I cried out to You, O LORD:
I said, "You *are* my refuge,
My portion in the land of the living.
6 Attend to my cry,
For I am brought very low;
Deliver me from my persecutors,
For they are stronger than I.
7 Bring my soul out of prison,
That I may [a]praise Your name;
The righteous shall surround me,
For You shall deal bountifully with me."

## PSALM 143

### AN EARNEST APPEAL FOR GUIDANCE AND DELIVERANCE

*A Psalm of David.*

1 Hear my prayer, O LORD,
Give ear to my supplications!
In Your faithfulness answer me,
*And* in Your righteousness.
2 Do not enter into judgment with Your
servant,
[a]For in Your sight no one living is
righteous.

3 For the enemy has persecuted my soul;
He has crushed my life to the ground;
He has made me dwell in darkness,
Like those who have long been dead.
4 [a]Therefore my spirit is overwhelmed
within me;
My heart within me is distressed.

5 [a]I remember the days of old;
I meditate on all Your works;
I muse on the work of Your hands.

**140:12** [a] 1 Kin. 8:45 **141:2** [a] [Rev. 5:8; 8:3, 4] [b] [1 Tim. 2:8] [c] Ex. 29:39, 41 **141:3** [a] [Prov. 13:3; 21:23] **141:4** [a] Prov. 23:6 **141:5** [a] [Prov. 9:8] **141:8** [a] Ps. 25:15 **141:9** [a] Ps. 119:110 **141:10** [a] Ps. 35:8 **142:title** [a] Ps. 32:title [b] 1 Sam. 22:1 [1] Hebrew *Maschil* **142:3** [a] Ps. 77:3 [b] Ps. 141:9 **142:7** [a] Ps. 34:1, 2 **143:2** [a] [Gal. 2:16] **143:4** [a] Ps. 77:3 **143:5** [a] Ps. 77:5, 10, 11

6 I spread out my hands to You;
[a]My soul *longs* for You like a thirsty
land. *Selah*

7 Answer me speedily, O LORD;
My spirit fails!
Do not hide Your face from me,
[a]Lest I be like those who go down into the pit.
8 Cause me to hear Your lovingkindness [a]in
the morning,
For in You do I trust;
[b]Cause me to know the way in which I
should walk,
For [c]I lift up my soul to You.

9 Deliver me, O LORD, from my enemies;
In You I take shelter.[1]
10 [a]Teach me to do Your will,
For You *are* my God;
[b]Your Spirit *is* good.
Lead me in [c]the land of uprightness.

11 [a]Revive me, O LORD, for Your name's sake!
For Your righteousness' sake bring my
soul out of trouble.
12 In Your mercy [a]cut off my enemies,
And destroy all those who afflict my soul;
For I *am* Your servant.

## PSALM 144

### A SONG TO THE LORD WHO PRESERVES AND PROSPERS HIS PEOPLE

A Psalm *of David.*

1 Blessed *be* the LORD my Rock,
[a]Who trains my hands for war,
*And* my fingers for battle—
2 My lovingkindness and my fortress,
My high tower and my deliverer,
My shield and *the One* in whom I take
refuge,
Who subdues my people[1] under me.

3 [a]LORD, what *is* man, that You take
knowledge of him?
*Or* the son of man, that You are mindful of
him?
4 [a]Man is like a breath;
[b]His days *are* like a passing shadow.

5 [a]Bow down Your heavens, O LORD, and
come down;
[b]Touch the mountains, and they shall
smoke.
6 [a]Flash forth lightning and scatter them;
Shoot out Your arrows and destroy them.
7 Stretch out Your hand from above;
Rescue me and deliver me out of great
waters,
From the hand of foreigners,
8 Whose mouth [a]speaks lying words,
And whose right hand *is* a right hand of
falsehood.

9 I will [a]sing a new song to You, O God;
On a harp of ten strings I will sing praises
to You,
10 *The One* who gives salvation to kings,
[a]Who delivers David His servant
From the deadly sword.

11 Rescue me and deliver me from the hand
of foreigners,
Whose mouth speaks lying words,
And whose right hand *is* a right hand of
falsehood—
12 That our sons *may be* [a]as plants grown up
in their youth;
*That* our daughters *may be* as pillars,
Sculptured in palace style;
13 *That* our barns *may be* full,
Supplying all kinds of produce;
*That* our sheep may bring forth thousands
And ten thousands in our fields;
14 *That* our oxen *may be* well laden;
*That there be* no breaking in or going out;
*That there be* no outcry in our streets.
15 [a]Happy *are* the people who are in such a
state;
Happy *are* the people whose God *is* the
LORD!

## PSALM 145

### A SONG OF GOD'S MAJESTY AND LOVE

[a]*A Praise of David.*

1 I will extol You, my God, O King;
And I will bless Your name forever and
ever.
2 Every day I will bless You,
And I will praise Your name forever and
ever.
3 [a]Great *is* the LORD, and greatly to be
praised;
And [b]His greatness *is* unsearchable.

4 [a]One generation shall praise Your works to
another,
And shall declare Your mighty acts.
5 I[1] will meditate on the glorious splendor
of Your majesty,
And on Your wondrous works.[2]

**143:6** [a] Ps. 63:1 **143:7** [a] Ps. 28:1 **143:8** [a] Ps. 46:5 [b] Ps. 5:8 [c] Ps. 25:1 **143:9** [1] Septuagint and Vulgate read *To You I flee.* **143:10** [a] Ps. 25:4, 5 [b] Neh. 9:20 [c] Is. 26:10 **143:11** [a] Ps. 119:25 **143:12** [a] Ps. 54:5 **144:1** [a] 2 Sam. 22:35 **144:2** [1] Following Masoretic Text, Septuagint, and Vulgate; Syriac and Targum read *the peoples* (compare 18:47). **144:3** [a] Heb. 2:6 **144:4** [a] Ps. 39:11 [b] Job 8:9; 14:2 **144:5** [a] Ps. 18:9 [b] Ps. 104:32 **144:6** [a] Ps. 18:13, 14 **144:8** [a] Ps. 12:2 **144:9** [a] Ps. 33:2, 3; 40:3 **144:10** [a] Ps. 18:50 **144:12** [a] Ps. 128:3 **144:15** [a] [Ps. 33:12] **145:title** [a] Ps. 100:title **145:3** [a] [Ps. 147:5] [b] [Rom. 11:33] **145:4** [a] Is. 38:19 **145:5** [1] Following Masoretic Text and Targum; Dead Sea Scrolls, Septuagint, Syriac, and Vulgate read *They.* [2] Literally *on the words of Your wondrous works*

**145:1–21** This psalm was written as an acrostic; each section begins with a successive letter of the Hebrew alphabet from *aleph*, the first letter, to *tav*, the last.

6 *Men* shall speak of the might of Your
awesome acts,
And I will declare Your greatness.
7 They shall utter the memory of Your great
goodness,
And shall sing of Your righteousness.

8 [a]The LORD *is* gracious and full of compassion,
Slow to anger and great in mercy.
9 [a]The LORD *is* good to all,
And His tender mercies *are* over all His
works.

10 [a]All Your works shall praise You, O LORD,
And Your saints shall bless You.
11 They shall speak of the glory of Your
kingdom,
And talk of Your power,
12 To make known to the sons of men His
mighty acts,
And the glorious majesty of His kingdom.
13 [a]Your kingdom *is* an everlasting kingdom,
And Your dominion *endures* throughout
all generations.[1]

14 The LORD upholds all who fall,
And [a]raises up all *who are* bowed down.
15 [a]The eyes of all look expectantly to You,
And [b]You give them their food in due season.
16 You open Your hand
[a]And satisfy the desire of every living thing.

17 The LORD *is* righteous in all His ways,
Gracious in all His works.
18 [a]The LORD *is* near to all who call upon Him,
To all who call upon Him [b]in truth.
19 He will fulfill the desire of those who fear
Him;
He also will hear their cry and save them.
20 [a]The LORD preserves all who love Him,
But all the wicked He will destroy.
21 My mouth shall speak the praise of the
LORD,
And all flesh shall bless His holy name
Forever and ever.

## PSALM 146

### THE HAPPINESS OF THOSE WHOSE HELP IS THE LORD

1 Praise the LORD!

[a]Praise the LORD, O my soul!
2 [a]While I live I will praise the LORD;
I will sing praises to my God while I have
my being.

3 [a]Do not put your trust in princes,
*Nor* in a son of man, in whom *there is* no
help.
4 [a]His spirit departs, he returns to his earth;
In that very day [b]his plans perish.

5 [a]Happy *is he* who *has* the God of Jacob for
his help,
Whose hope *is* in the LORD his God,
6 [a]Who made heaven and earth,
The sea, and all that *is* in them;
Who keeps truth forever,
7 [a]Who executes justice for the oppressed,

145:8 [a] [Num. 14:18] 145:9 [a] Nah. 1:7 145:10 [a] Ps. 19:1 145:13 [a] [1 Tim. 1:17] [1] Following Masoretic Text and Targum; Dead Sea Scrolls, Septuagint, Syriac, and Vulgate add *The LORD is faithful in all His words, And holy in all His works.* 145:14 [a] Ps. 146:8 145:15 [a] Ps. 104:27 [b] Ps. 136:25 145:16 [a] Ps. 104:21, 28 145:18 [a] [Deut. 4:7] [b] [John 4:24] 145:20 [a] [Ps. 31:23] 146:1 [a] Ps. 103:1 146:2 [a] Ps. 104:33 146:3 [a] [Is. 2:22] 146:4 [a] [Eccl. 12:7] [b] [1 Cor. 2:6] 146:5 [a] Jer. 17:7 146:6 [a] Rev. 14:7 146:7 [a] Ps. 103:6

LIVE THE TRUTH

## WORSHIPING GOD

**146:1–2** One of our highest callings and greatest privileges is worshiping the Lord our God. He is worthy of our worship for two primary reasons. First, because of what He has done. He created us and everything else. He gives us life and breath. He provided Jesus through whom we've been rescued from sin and death. He provides for our every need. Without God, we have nothing. Second, because of who He is. He is our Creator. He is loving, merciful, righteous, and just. Both these reasons are equally important.

You may think of worship as something that occurs through song—that is an amazing aspect of worship that should be practiced as we see here. Worship isn't *less* than that, but it's surely *more* than that. To worship is to give the sole focus of your devotion, love, and attention. It's to bow your entire being down low so that who you worship is lifted up. In this way, you can worship God through anything you do, as long as you do it for Him. No one can give God the thanksgiving and praise He truly deserves, but we can and should worship God with our lives.

[b]Who gives food to the hungry.
[c]The LORD gives freedom to the prisoners.

8 [a]The LORD opens *the eyes of* the blind;
[b]The LORD raises those who are bowed down;
The LORD loves the righteous.
9 [a]The LORD watches over the strangers;
He relieves the fatherless and widow;
[b]But the way of the wicked He turns upside down.

10 [a]The LORD shall reign forever—
Your God, O Zion, to all generations.

Praise the LORD!

## PSALM 147

### PRAISE TO GOD FOR HIS WORD AND PROVIDENCE

1 Praise the LORD!
For [a]*it is* good to sing praises to our God;
[b]For *it is* pleasant, *and* [c]praise is beautiful.

2 The LORD [a]builds up Jerusalem;
[b]He gathers together the outcasts of Israel.
3 [a]He heals the brokenhearted
And binds up their wounds.
4 [a]He counts the number of the stars;
He calls them all by name.
5 [a]Great *is* our Lord, and [b]mighty in power;
[c]His understanding *is* infinite.
6 [a]The LORD lifts up the humble;
He casts the wicked down to the ground.

7 Sing to the LORD with thanksgiving;
Sing praises on the harp to our God,
8 [a]Who covers the heavens with clouds,
Who prepares rain for the earth,
Who makes grass to grow on the mountains.
9 [a]He gives to the beast its food,
*And* [b]to the young ravens that cry.

10 [a]He does not delight in the strength of the horse;
He takes no pleasure in the legs of a man.
11 The LORD takes pleasure in those who fear Him,
In those who hope in His mercy.

12 Praise the LORD, O Jerusalem!
Praise your God, O Zion!
13 For He has strengthened the bars of your gates;
He has blessed your children within you.
14 [a]He makes peace *in* your borders,
*And* [b]fills you with the finest wheat.

15 [a]He sends out His command *to the* earth;
His word runs very swiftly.
16 [a]He gives snow like wool;
He scatters the frost like ashes;

146:7 [b] Ps. 107:9 [c] Ps. 107:10 146:8 [a] Matt. 9:30 [b] Luke 13:13 146:9 [a] Deut. 10:18 [b] Ps. 147:6 146:10 [a] Ex. 15:18 147:1 [a] Ps. 92:1 [b] Ps. 135:3 [c] Ps. 33:1 147:2 [a] Ps. 102:16 [b] Deut. 30:3 147:3 [a] [Ps. 51:17] 147:4 [a] Is. 40:26 147:5 [a] Ps. 48:1 [b] Nah. 1:3 [c] Is. 40:28 147:6 [a] Ps. 146:8, 9 147:8 [a] Job 38:26 147:9 [a] Job 38:41 [b] [Matt. 6:26] 147:10 [a] Ps. 33:16, 17 147:14 [a] Is. 54:13; 60:17, 18 [b] Ps. 132:15 147:15 [a] [Ps. 107:20] 147:16 [a] Job 37:6

KNOW THE TRUTH

## THE DOCTRINE OF GOD

### PART 7: THE OMNISCIENCE OF GOD

**147:5** To describe God's greatness, the psalmist focuses on a series of the Lord's attributes and actions. One of those attributes is described in the phrase "His understanding is infinite." *Infinite* means without number or limit. Thus, the psalmist essentially declares God has unlimited knowledge and intellect. He simply knows everything. This is what is meant when God is called omniscient. God is everlasting and unlimited. Every attribute He possesses must then be everlasting and unlimited, including His knowledge.

God instantly and effortlessly at all times knows all that is knowable. There's no corner of space, no moment in time, no secret of mind, nor mystery in all realms of creation God doesn't know. As Hebrews 4:13 says: "All things are naked and open to the eyes of Him." This attribute of God should bring us great comfort. You are known! Every hair on your head, day of your life, thought in your mind, and longing of your heart is known by our perfect, good, and loving God. His plan for you is secure and nothing will catch Him by surprise.

*For* **THE DOCTRINE OF GOD: PART 8: THE OMNIPRESENCE OF GOD**, *turn to Proverbs 15:3 on page 638*

17 He casts out His hail like morsels;
Who can stand before His cold?
18 [a]He sends out His word and melts them;
He causes His wind to blow, *and* the
waters flow.

19 [a]He declares His word to Jacob,
[b]His statutes and His judgments to Israel.
20 [a]He has not dealt thus with any nation;
And *as for His* judgments, they have not
known them.

Praise the LORD!

## PSALM 148

### PRAISE TO THE LORD FROM CREATION

1 Praise the LORD!

Praise the LORD from the heavens;
Praise Him in the heights!
2 Praise Him, all His angels;
Praise Him, all His hosts!
3 Praise Him, sun and moon;
Praise Him, all you stars of light!
4 Praise Him, [a]you heavens of heavens,
And [b]you waters above the heavens!

5 Let them praise the name of the LORD,
For [a]He commanded and they were
created.
6 [a]He also established them forever and ever;
He made a decree which shall not pass away.

7 Praise the LORD from the earth,
[a]You great sea creatures and all the depths;
8 Fire and hail, snow and clouds;
Stormy wind, fulfilling His word;
9 [a]Mountains and all hills;
Fruitful trees and all cedars;
10 Beasts and all cattle;
Creeping things and flying fowl;
11 Kings of the earth and all peoples;
Princes and all judges of the earth;
12 Both young men and maidens;
Old men and children.

13 Let them praise the name of the LORD,
For His [a]name alone is exalted;
His glory *is* above the earth and heaven.
14 And He [a]has exalted the horn of His
people,
The praise of [b]all His saints—
Of the children of Israel,
[c]A people near to Him.

Praise the LORD!

## PSALM 149

### PRAISE TO GOD FOR HIS SALVATION AND JUDGMENT

1 Praise the LORD!

[a]Sing to the LORD a new song,
*And* His praise in the assembly of saints.

2 Let Israel rejoice in their Maker;
Let the children of Zion be joyful in their
[a]King.
3 [a]Let them praise His name with the dance;
Let them sing praises to Him with the
timbrel and harp.
4 For [a]the LORD takes pleasure in His
people;
[b]He will beautify the humble with
salvation.

5 Let the saints be joyful in glory;
Let them [a]sing aloud on their beds.
6 *Let* the high praises of God *be* in their
mouth,
And [a]a two-edged sword in their hand,
7 To execute vengeance on the nations,
And punishments on the peoples;
8 To bind their kings with chains,
And their nobles with fetters of iron;
9 [a]To execute on them the written judgment—
[b]This honor have all His saints.

Praise the LORD!

## PSALM 150

### LET ALL THINGS PRAISE THE LORD

1 Praise[a] the LORD!

Praise God in His sanctuary;
Praise Him in His mighty firmament!

2 Praise Him for His mighty acts;
Praise Him according to His excellent
[a]greatness!

3 Praise Him with the sound of the trumpet;
Praise Him with the lute and harp!
4 Praise Him with the timbrel and dance;
Praise Him with stringed instruments
and flutes!
5 Praise Him with loud cymbals;
Praise Him with clashing cymbals!

6 Let everything that has breath praise the
LORD.

Praise the LORD!

147:18 [a] Job 37:10 147:19 [a] Deut. 33:4 [b] Mal. 4:4 147:20 [a] Deut. 4:32–34; [Rom. 3:1, 2] 148:4 [a] 1 Kin. 8:27 [b] Gen. 1:7 148:5 [a] Gen. 1:1, 6 148:6 [a] Ps. 89:37 148:7 [a] Is. 43:20 148:9 [a] Is. 44:23; 49:13 148:13 [a] Ps. 8:1 148:14 [a] Ps. 75:10 [b] Ps. 149:9 [c] Eph. 2:17 149:1 [a] Ps. 33:3 149:2 [a] Zech. 9:9 149:3 [a] Ps. 81:2 149:4 [a] Ps. 35:27 [b] Ps. 132:16 149:5 [a] Job 35:10 149:6 [a] Heb. 4:12 149:9 [a] Deut. 7:1, 2 [b] 1 Cor. 6:2 150:1 [a] Ps. 145:5, 6 150:2 [a] Deut. 3:24

*The Book of*

# PROVERBS

| AUTHOR | KEY VERSES | READING TIME |
|---|---|---|
| Solomon, Agur, King Lemuel, and others | Proverbs 3:5–6 | 2 hours 1 minute |

The keyword in Proverbs is *wisdom*, "the ability to live skillfully." Maintaining a godly life in an ungodly world, however, is no simple assignment. In Proverbs, God provides instructions for how His people are to deal with the practical affairs of everyday life, such as how to relate to Him, parents, children, neighbors, and government. Solomon and the other authors used a combination of poetry, parables, pithy questions, short stories, and wise maxims in a strikingly memorable form to provide the divine perspective necessary for a person to live faithfully and handle life's issues.

**Occasion:** The Book of Proverbs compiles collected wisdom from a period of more than two hundred years to help God's people live in obedience to Him and according to His ways.

**Main Point:** The key to abundant living is exercising wisdom to follow God's design.

**Big Ideas:** God is the source of true wisdom. Wise people make good, practical decisions that please God.

**OUTLINE:**

I. The Value of Wisdom (ch. 1)
II. The Proverbs of Solomon as a Father (chs. 2–9)
III. More Proverbs of Solomon (chs. 10–24)
IV. Still More Proverbs of Solomon (chs. 25–29)
V. The Proverbs of Agur (ch. 30)
VI. The Proverbs of Lemuel (ch. 31)

**c. 971–931 BC**
Song of Solomon written

**970 BC**
Solomon becomes king of Israel

**967 BC**
Solomon begins construction of the temple

**c. 950–700 BC**
**Proverbs written**

**c. 935 BC**
Ecclesiastes written

**930 BC**
The kingdom is divided

**722 BC**
The Assyrians defeat Israel

**c. 700 BC**
Proverbs compiled

### *THE BEGINNING OF KNOWLEDGE*

1 The [a]proverbs of Solomon the son of David, king of Israel:

2 To know wisdom and instruction,
To perceive the words of understanding,
3 To receive the instruction of wisdom,
Justice, judgment, and equity;
4 To give prudence to the [a]simple,
To the young man knowledge and discretion—
5 [a]A wise *man* will hear and increase learning,
And a man of understanding will attain wise counsel,
6 To understand a proverb and an enigma,
The words of the wise and their [a]riddles.

7 [a]The fear of the LORD *is* the beginning of knowledge,
*But* fools despise wisdom and instruction.

### *SHUN EVIL COUNSEL*

8 [a]My son, hear the instruction of your father,
And do not forsake the law of your mother;
9 For they *will be* a [a]graceful ornament on your head,
And chains about your neck.

10 My son, if sinners entice you,
[a]Do not consent.

> **SEEING JESUS IN THE SCRIPTURE**
>
> **1:10** When sinners entice us, it's difficult not to consent. We can resist sin, but we cannot do it perfectly. Jesus, however, was tempted by Satan and never gave in (see 2 Cor. 5:21). Jesus perfectly obeyed the Father to become our perfect sacrifice.

11 If they say, "Come with us,
Let us [a]lie in wait to *shed* blood;
Let us lurk secretly for the innocent without cause;
12 Let us swallow them alive like Sheol,[1]
And whole, [a]like those who go down to the Pit;
13 We shall find all *kinds* of precious possessions,
We shall fill our houses with spoil;
14 Cast in your lot among us,
Let us all have one purse"—
15 My son, [a]do not walk in the way with them,
[b]Keep your foot from their path;
16 [a]For their feet run to evil,
And they make haste to shed blood.
17 Surely, in vain the net is spread
In the sight of any bird;
18 But they lie in wait for their *own* blood,
They lurk secretly for their *own* lives.
19 [a]So *are* the ways of everyone who is greedy for gain;
It takes away the life of its owners.

### *THE CALL OF WISDOM*

20 [a]Wisdom calls aloud outside;
She raises her voice in the open squares.
21 She cries out in the chief concourses,[1]
At the openings of the gates in the city
She speaks her words:
22 "How long, you simple ones, will you love simplicity?
For scorners delight in their scorning,
And fools hate knowledge.
23 Turn at my rebuke;
Surely [a]I will pour out my spirit on you;
I will make my words known to you.
24 [a]Because I have called and you refused,
I have stretched out my hand and no one regarded,
25 Because you [a]disdained all my counsel,
And would have none of my rebuke,
26 [a]I also will laugh at your calamity;
I will mock when your terror comes,
27 When [a]your terror comes like a storm,
And your destruction comes like a whirlwind,
When distress and anguish come upon you.

28 "Then[a] they will call on me, but I will not answer;
They will seek me diligently, but they will not find me.
29 Because they [a]hated knowledge
And did not [b]choose the fear of the LORD,
30 [a]They would have none of my counsel
*And* despised my every rebuke.
31 Therefore [a]they shall eat the fruit of their own way,
And be filled to the full with their own fancies.
32 For the turning away of the simple will slay them,
And the complacency of fools will destroy them;
33 But whoever listens to me will dwell [a]safely,
And [b]will be secure, without fear of evil."

**1:1** [a] 1 Kin. 4:32 **1:4** [a] Prov. 9:4 **1:5** [a] Prov. 9:9 **1:6** [a] Ps. 78:2 **1:7** [a] Job 28:28 **1:8** [a] Prov. 4:1 **1:9** [a] Prov. 3:22 **1:10** [a] Gen. 39:7–10 **1:11** [a] Jer. 5:26 **1:12** [a] Ps. 28:1 [1] Or *the grave* **1:15** [a] Ps. 1:1 [b] Ps. 119:101 **1:16** [a] [Is. 59:7] **1:19** [a] [1 Tim. 6:10] **1:20** [a] [John 7:37] **1:21** [1] Septuagint, Syriac, and Targum read *top of the walls;* Vulgate reads *the head of multitudes.* **1:23** [a] Joel 2:28 **1:24** [a] Jer. 7:13 **1:25** [a] Luke 7:30 **1:26** [a] Ps. 2:4 **1:27** [a] [Prov. 10:24, 25] **1:28** [a] Is. 1:15 **1:29** [a] Job 21:14 [b] Ps. 119:173 **1:30** [a] Ps. 81:11 **1:31** [a] Job 4:8 **1:33** [a] Prov. 3:24–26 [b] Ps. 112:7

## THE VALUE OF WISDOM

**2** My son, if you receive my words,
And [a]treasure my commands within you,
2 So that you incline your ear to wisdom,
*And* apply your heart to understanding;
3 Yes, if you cry out for discernment,
*And* lift up your voice for understanding,
4 [a]If you seek her as silver,
And search for her as *for* hidden treasures;
5 [a]Then you will understand the fear of the LORD,
And find the knowledge of God.
6 [a]For the LORD gives wisdom;
From His mouth *come* knowledge and understanding;
7 He stores up sound wisdom for the upright;
[a]*He is* a shield to those who walk uprightly;
8 He guards the paths of justice,
And [a]preserves the way of His saints.
9 Then you will understand righteousness and justice,
Equity *and* every good path.

10 When wisdom enters your heart,
And knowledge is pleasant to your soul,
11 Discretion will preserve you;
[a]Understanding will keep you,
12 To deliver you from the way of evil,
From the man who speaks perverse things,
13 From those who leave the paths of uprightness
To [a]walk in the ways of darkness;
14 [a]Who rejoice in doing evil,
*And* delight in the perversity of the wicked;

### SEEING JESUS IN THE SCRIPTURE

**2:13–14** Solomon's warning of the dangers of walking in the ways of darkness points to what happened when Jesus came to earth. The people Jesus came to save preferred the darkness rather than Him, the light; as a result, they were condemned (see John 1:5; 3:19).

15 [a]Whose ways *are* crooked,
And *who are* devious in their paths;
16 To deliver you from [a]the immoral woman,
[b]From the seductress *who* flatters with her words,
17 Who forsakes the companion of her youth,
And forgets the covenant of her God.

**2:18** Ancient Israelites believed upon **death** a person's soul went to a dark underground region called Sheol. They believed the souls that existed in this world of the dead couldn't eat, drink, work, worship, or experience joy like they could when they were alive.

18 For [a]her house leads down to death,
And her paths to the dead;
19 None who go to her return,
Nor do they regain the paths of life—
20 So you may walk in the way of goodness,
And keep *to* the paths of righteousness.
21 For the upright will dwell in the [a]land,
And the blameless will remain in it;
22 But the wicked will be cut off from the earth,
And the unfaithful will be uprooted from it.

## GUIDANCE FOR THE YOUNG

**3** My son, do not forget my law,
[a]But let your heart keep my commands;
2 For length of days and long life
And [a]peace they will add to you.

3 Let not mercy and truth forsake you;
[a]Bind them around your neck,
[b]Write them on the tablet of your heart,
4 [a]*And* so find favor and high esteem
In the sight of God and man.

5 [a]Trust in the LORD with all your heart,
[b]And lean not on your own understanding;
6 [a]In all your ways acknowledge Him,
And He shall direct[1] your paths.

7 Do not be wise in your own [a]eyes;
Fear the LORD and depart from evil.
8 It will be health to your flesh,[1]
And [a]strength[2] to your bones.

9 [a]Honor the LORD with your possessions,
And with the firstfruits of all your increase;
10 [a]So your barns will be filled with plenty,
And your vats will overflow with new wine.

11 [a]My son, do not despise the chastening of the LORD,
Nor detest His correction;
12 For whom the LORD loves He corrects,
[a]Just as a father the son *in whom* he delights.

2:1 [a] [Prov. 4:21] 2:4 [a] [Prov. 3:14] 2:5 [a] [James 1:5, 6] 2:6 [a] 1 Kin. 3:9, 12 2:7 [a] [Ps. 84:11] 2:8 [a] [1 Sam. 2:9] 2:11 [a] Prov. 4:6; 6:22 2:13 [a] [John 3:19, 20] 2:14 [a] [Rom. 1:32] 2:15 [a] Ps. 125:5 2:16 [a] Prov. 5:20; 6:24; 7:5 [b] Prov. 5:3 2:18 [a] Prov. 7:27 2:21 [a] Ps. 37:3 3:1 [a] Deut. 8:1 3:2 [a] Ps. 119:165 3:3 [a] Prov. 6:21 [b] [2 Cor. 3:3] 3:4 [a] Rom. 14:18 3:5 [a] [Ps. 37:3, 5] [b] [Jer. 9:23, 24] 3:6 [a] [1 Chr. 28:9] [1] Or *make smooth* or *straight* 3:7 [a] Rom. 12:16 3:8 [a] Job 21:24 [1] Literally *navel,* figurative of the body [2] Literally *drink* or *refreshment* 3:9 [a] Ex. 22:29 3:10 [a] Deut. 28:8 3:11 [a] Job 5:17 3:12 [a] Deut. 8:5

LIVE THE TRUTH

## MAKING WISE DECISIONS

**3:5–6** God wants us to make wise decisions in every area of our lives. It's why He was pleased when Solomon asked Him for wisdom before he asked for anything else (see 1 Kin. 3). Solomon knew he needed God's guidance to live best. So do we. This is at the heart of this proverb. Our wisdom can be lacking. It can be biased. It can be wrong. God's wisdom, though, is based on His perspective, and He sees and knows all. His wisdom is flawless. It's our perfect guide.

To live in God's wisdom is to listen to Him more than you listen to friends, popular thought, or the culture. It's to turn to God through His Word and prayer, seeking to know His ways. Once you hear what God says, trust Him. It won't help your decision making if you know what God wants but don't do it. As you listen to God *and* obey where He leads (even when you don't agree or understand), you will find He's making your path straight. Seeking God before you make decisions will bring you great peace because you can be confident He is leading you exactly where He wants you to go.

13 [a]Happy *is* the man *who* finds wisdom,
And the man *who* gains understanding;
14 [a]For her proceeds *are* better than the profits of silver,
And her gain than fine gold.
15 She *is* more precious than rubies,
And [a]all the things you may desire cannot compare with her.
16 [a]Length of days *is* in her right hand,
In her left hand riches and honor.
17 [a]Her ways *are* ways of pleasantness,
And all her paths *are* peace.
18 She *is* [a]a tree of life to those who take hold of her,
And happy *are all* who retain her.

19 [a]The LORD by wisdom founded the earth;
By understanding He established the heavens;
20 By His knowledge the depths were [a]broken up,
And clouds drop down the dew.

21 My son, let them not depart from your eyes—
Keep sound wisdom and discretion;
22 So they will be life to your soul
And grace to your neck.
23 [a]Then you will walk safely in your way,
And your foot will not stumble.
24 When you lie down, you will not be afraid;
Yes, you will lie down and your sleep will be sweet.
25 [a]Do not be afraid of sudden terror,
Nor of trouble from the wicked when it comes;
26 For the LORD will be your confidence,
And will keep your foot from being caught.

27 [a]Do not withhold good from those to whom it is due,
When it is in the power of your hand to do *so*.
28 [a]Do not say to your neighbor,
"Go, and come back,
And tomorrow I will give *it*,"
When you have it with you.
29 Do not devise evil against your neighbor,
For he dwells by you for safety's sake.
30 [a]Do not strive with a man without cause,
If he has done you no harm.

31 [a]Do not envy the oppressor,
And choose none of his ways;
32 For the perverse *person is* an abomination to the LORD,
[a]But His secret counsel *is* with the upright.
33 [a]The curse of the LORD *is* on the house of the wicked,
But [b]He blesses the home of the just.
34 [a]Surely He scorns the scornful,
But gives grace to the humble.
35 The wise shall inherit glory,
But shame shall be the legacy of fools.

### SECURITY IN WISDOM

4 Hear, [a]*my* children, the instruction of a father,
And give attention to know understanding;
2 For I give you good doctrine:
Do not forsake my law.
3 When I was my father's son,
[a]Tender and the only one in the sight of my mother,
4 [a]He also taught me, and said to me:
"Let your heart retain my words;
[b]Keep my commands, and live.

**3:13** [a] Prov. 8:32, 34, 35 **3:14** [a] Job 28:13 **3:15** [a] Matt. 13:44 **3:16** [a] [1 Tim. 4:8] **3:17** [a] [Matt. 11:29] **3:18** [a] Gen. 2:9 **3:19** [a] Ps. 104:24 **3:20** [a] Gen. 7:11 **3:23** [a] Prov. 10:9 **3:25** [a] Ps. 91:5 **3:27** [a] Rom. 13:7 **3:28** [a] Lev. 19:13 **3:30** [a] [Rom. 12:18] **3:31** [a] Ps. 37:1 **3:32** [a] Ps. 25:14 **3:33** [a] Lev. 26:14, 16; Deut. 11:28; Zech. 5:3, 4; Mal. 2:2 [b] Job 8:6; Ps. 1:3 **3:34** [a] James 4:6; 1 Pet. 5:5 **4:1** [a] Ps. 34:11; Prov. 1:8 **4:3** [a] 1 Chr. 29:1 **4:4** [a] 1 Chr. 28:9; Eph. 6:4 [b] Prov. 7:2

5 [a]Get wisdom! Get understanding!
Do not forget, nor turn away from the words of my mouth.
6 Do not forsake her, and she will preserve you;
[a]Love her, and she will keep you.
7 [a]Wisdom *is* the principal thing;
*Therefore* get wisdom.
And in all your getting, get understanding.
8 [a]Exalt her, and she will promote you;
She will bring you honor, when you embrace her.
9 She will place on your head [a]an ornament of grace;
A crown of glory she will deliver to you."

10 Hear, my son, and receive my sayings,
[a]And the years of your life will be many.
11 I have [a]taught you in the way of wisdom;
I have led you in right paths.
12 When you walk, [a]your steps will not be hindered,
[b]And when you run, you will not stumble.
13 Take firm hold of instruction, do not let go;
Keep her, for she *is* your life.

14 [a]Do not enter the path of the wicked,
And do not walk in the way of evil.
15 Avoid it, do not travel on it;
Turn away from it and pass on.
16 [a]For they do not sleep unless they have done evil;
And their sleep is taken away unless they make *someone* fall.
17 For they eat the bread of wickedness,
And drink the wine of violence.

18 [a]But the path of the just [b]*is* like the shining sun,[1]
That shines ever brighter unto the perfect day.
19 [a]The way of the wicked *is* like darkness;
They do not know what makes them stumble.

20 My son, give attention to my words;
Incline your ear to my sayings.
21 Do not let them depart from your eyes;
Keep them in the midst of your heart;
22 For they *are* life to those who find them,
And health to all their flesh.
23 Keep your heart with all diligence,
For out of it *spring* the issues of [a]life.
24 Put away from you a deceitful mouth,
And put perverse lips far from you.
25 Let your eyes look straight ahead,
And your eyelids look right before you.
26 Ponder the path of your [a]feet,
And let all your ways be established.
27 Do not turn to the right or the left;
Remove your foot from evil.

## *THE PERIL OF ADULTERY*

5 My son, pay attention to my wisdom;
Lend your ear to my understanding,
2 That you may preserve discretion,
And your lips [a]may keep knowledge.
3 [a]For the lips of an immoral woman drip honey,
And her mouth *is* [b]smoother than oil;
4 But in the end she is bitter as wormwood,
Sharp as a two-edged sword.
5 Her feet go down to death,
[a]Her steps lay hold of hell.[1]
6 Lest you ponder *her* path of life—
Her ways are unstable;
You do not know *them.*

7 Therefore hear me now, *my* children,
And do not depart from the words of my mouth.
8 Remove your way far from her,
And do not go near the door of her house,
9 Lest you give your honor to others,
And your years to the cruel *one;*
10 Lest aliens be filled with your wealth,
And your labors *go* to the house of a foreigner;
11 And you mourn at last,
When your flesh and your body are consumed,
12 And say:
"How I have hated instruction,
And my heart despised correction!
13 I have not obeyed the voice of my teachers,
Nor inclined my ear to those who instructed me!
14 I was on the verge of total ruin,
In the midst of the assembly and congregation."

15 Drink water from your own cistern,
And running water from your own well.
16 Should your fountains be dispersed abroad,
Streams of water in the streets?
17 Let them be only your own,
And not for strangers with you.
18 Let your fountain be blessed,
And rejoice with [a]the wife of your youth.
19 [a]*As a* loving deer and a graceful doe,
Let her breasts satisfy you at all times;
And always be enraptured with her love.
20 For why should you, my son, be enraptured by [a]an immoral woman,
And be embraced in the arms of a seductress?

4:5 [a] Prov. 2:2, 3 4:6 [a] 2 Thess. 2:10 4:7 [a] Prov. 3:13, 14; Matt. 13:44 4:8 [a] 1 Sam. 2:30 4:9 [a] Prov. 3:22 4:10 [a] Prov. 3:2 4:11 [a] 1 Sam. 12:23 4:12 [a] Job 18:7; Ps. 18:36 [b] [Ps. 91:11]; Prov. 3:23 4:14 [a] Ps. 1:1; Prov. 1:15 4:16 [a] Ps. 36:4; Mic. 2:1 4:18 [a] Is. 26:7; Matt. 5:14, 45; Phil. 2:15 [b] 2 Sam. 23:4 [1] Literally *light* 4:19 [a] 1 Sam. 2:9; [Job 18:5, 6]; Prov. 2:13; [Is. 59:9, 10; Jer. 23:12]; John 12:35 4:23 [a] [Matt. 12:34; 15:18, 19; Mark 7:21; Luke 6:45] 4:26 [a] Prov. 5:21; Heb. 12:13 5:2 [a] Mal. 2:7 5:3 [a] Prov. 2:16 [b] Ps. 55:21 5:5 [a] Prov. 7:27 [1] Or *Sheol* 5:18 [a] Mal. 2:14 5:19 [a] Song 2:9 5:20 [a] Prov. 2:16

21 [a]For the ways of man *are* before the eyes of
the LORD,
And He ponders all his paths.
22 [a]His own iniquities entrap the wicked *man,*
And he is caught in the cords of his sin.
23 [a]He shall die for lack of instruction,
And in the greatness of his folly he shall
go astray.

### *DANGEROUS PROMISES*

**6** My son, [a]if you become surety for your
friend,
*If* you have shaken hands in pledge for a
stranger,
2 You are snared by the words of your mouth;
You are taken by the words of your mouth.
3 So do this, my son, and deliver yourself;
For you have come into the hand of your
friend:
Go and humble yourself;
Plead with your friend.
4 [a]Give no sleep to your eyes,
Nor slumber to your eyelids.
5 Deliver yourself like a gazelle from the
hand *of the hunter,*
And like a bird from the hand of the fowler.[1]

### *THE FOLLY OF INDOLENCE*

6 [a]Go to the ant, you sluggard!
Consider her ways and be wise,
7 Which, having no captain,
Overseer or ruler,
8 Provides her supplies in the summer,
*And* gathers her food in the harvest.
9 [a]How long will you slumber, O sluggard?
When will you rise from your sleep?
10 A little sleep, a little slumber,
A little folding of the hands to sleep—
11 [a]So shall your poverty come on you like a
prowler,
And your need like an armed man.

### *THE WICKED MAN*

12 A worthless person, a wicked man,
Walks with a perverse mouth;
13 [a]He winks with his eyes,
He shuffles his feet,
He points with his fingers;
14 Perversity *is* in his heart,
[a]He devises evil continually,
[b]He sows discord.
15 Therefore his calamity shall come
[a]suddenly;
Suddenly he shall [b]be broken [c]without
remedy.

16 These six *things* the LORD hates,
Yes, seven *are* an abomination to Him:

> **6:16** The use of numerical progression—**six . . . seven**—is a rhetorical device that embellishes the poetry and serves as a memory aid. It gives the impression that there is more to be said about the topic. **Abomination** is the Bible's strongest expression of hatred for wickedness.

17 [a]A proud look,
[b]A lying tongue,
[c]Hands that shed innocent blood,
18 [a]A heart that devises wicked plans,
[b]Feet that are swift in running to evil,
19 [a]A false witness *who* speaks lies,
And one who [b]sows discord among
brethren.

> **SEEING JESUS IN THE SCRIPTURE**
>
> **6:16–19** In their rejection of Jesus, the religious leaders were guilty of each of the seven abominations of the Lord. When they tried to find cause against Jesus, they couldn't, so they lied to justify His crucifixion (see Matt. 26:59).

### *BEWARE OF ADULTERY*

20 [a]My son, keep your father's command,
And do not forsake the law of your mother.
21 [a]Bind them continually upon your heart;
Tie them around your neck.
22 [a]When you roam, they[1] will lead you;
When you sleep, [b]they will keep you;
And *when* you awake, they will speak with
you.
23 [a]For the commandment *is* a lamp,
And the law a light;
Reproofs of instruction *are* the way of life,
24 [a]To keep you from the evil woman,
From the flattering tongue of a seductress.
25 [a]Do not lust after her beauty in your heart,
Nor let her allure you with her eyelids.
26 For [a]by means of a harlot
*A man is reduced* to a crust of bread;
[b]And an adulteress[1] will [c]prey upon his
precious life.
27 Can a man take fire to his bosom,
And his clothes not be burned?
28 Can one walk on hot coals,
And his feet not be seared?
29 So *is* he who goes in to his neighbor's wife;
Whoever touches her shall not be
innocent.

**5:21** [a] Hos. 7:2 **5:22** [a] Num. 32:23 **5:23** [a] Job 4:21 **6:1** [a] Prov. 11:15 **6:4** [a] Ps. 132:4 **6:5** [1] That is, one who catches birds in a trap or snare **6:6** [a] Job 12:7 **6:9** [a] Prov. 24:33, 34 **6:11** [a] Prov. 10:4 **6:13** [a] Job 15:12 **6:14** [a] Mic. 2:1 [b] Prov. 6:19 **6:15** [a] Is. 30:13 [b] Jer. 19:11 [c] 2 Chr. 36:16 **6:17** [a] Ps. 101:5 [b] Ps. 120:2 [c] Is. 1:15 **6:18** [a] Gen. 6:5 [b] Is. 59:7 **6:19** [a] Ps. 27:12 [b] Prov. 6:14 **6:20** [a] Eph. 6:1 **6:21** [a] Prov. 3:3 **6:22** [a] [Prov. 3:23] [b] Prov. 2:11 [1] Literally *it* **6:23** [a] Ps. 19:8 **6:24** [a] Prov. 2:16 **6:25** [a] Matt. 5:28 **6:26** [a] Prov. 29:3 [b] Gen. 39:14 [c] Ezek. 13:18 [1] Literally *a man's wife,* that is, of another

30 *People* do not despise a thief
If he steals to satisfy himself when he is starving.
31 Yet *when* he is found, [a]he must restore sevenfold;
He may have to give up all the substance of his house.
32 Whoever commits adultery with a woman [a]lacks understanding;
He *who* does so destroys his own soul.
33 Wounds and dishonor he will get,
And his reproach will not be wiped away.
34 For [a]jealousy *is* a husband's fury;
Therefore he will not spare in the day of vengeance.
35 He will accept no recompense,
Nor will he be appeased though you give many gifts.

7 My son, keep my words,
And [a]treasure my commands within you.
2 [a]Keep my commands and live,
[b]And my law as the apple of your eye.
3 [a]Bind them on your fingers;
Write them on the tablet of your heart.
4 Say to wisdom, "You *are* my sister,"
And call understanding *your* nearest kin,
5 [a]That they may keep you from the immoral woman,
From the seductress *who* flatters with her words.

### THE CRAFTY HARLOT

6 For at the window of my house
I looked through my lattice,
7 And saw among the simple,
I perceived among the youths,
A young man [a]devoid of understanding,
8 Passing along the street near her corner;
And he took the path to her house
9 [a]In the twilight, in the evening,
In the black and dark night.
10 And there a woman met him,
*With* the attire of a harlot, and a crafty heart.
11 [a]She *was* loud and rebellious,
[b]Her feet would not stay at home.
12 At times *she was* outside, at times in the open square,
Lurking at every corner.
13 So she caught him and kissed him;
With an impudent face she said to him:
14 "*I have* peace offerings with me;
Today I have paid my vows.
15 So I came out to meet you,
Diligently to seek your face,
And I have found you.
16 I have spread my bed with tapestry,
Colored coverings of [a]Egyptian linen.

> **7:14** According to God's law, after the priests had taken their portions of **peace offerings**, those who offered the sacrifices were given the rest of the meat to take home. The only stipulation was that it all had to be eaten within two days. Since meat wasn't served very often in ancient times, these post-sacrifice meals usually turned into festive events celebrating God's forgiveness.

17 I have perfumed my bed
With myrrh, aloes, and cinnamon.
18 Come, let us take our fill of love until morning;
Let us delight ourselves with love.
19 For my husband *is* not at home;
He has gone on a long journey;
20 He has taken a bag of money with him,
*And* will come home on the appointed day."
21 With [a]her enticing speech she caused him to yield,
[b]With her flattering lips she seduced him.
22 Immediately he went after her, as an ox goes to the slaughter,
Or as a fool to the correction of the stocks,[1]
23 Till an arrow struck his liver.
[a]As a bird hastens to the snare,
He did not know it *would cost* his life.

24 Now therefore, listen to me, *my* children;
Pay attention to the words of my mouth:
25 Do not let your heart turn aside to her ways,
Do not stray into her paths;
26 For she has cast down many wounded,
And [a]all who were slain by her were strong *men*.
27 [a]Her house *is* the way to hell,[1]
Descending to the chambers of death.

### THE EXCELLENCE OF WISDOM

8 Does not [a]wisdom cry out,
And understanding lift up her voice?
2 She takes her stand on the top of the high hill,
Beside the way, where the paths meet.
3 She cries out by the gates, at the entry of the city,
At the entrance of the doors:
4 "To you, O men, I call,
And my voice *is* to the sons of men.
5 O you simple ones, understand prudence,
And you fools, be of an understanding heart.

**6:31** [a] Ex. 22:1–4 **6:32** [a] Prov. 7:7 **6:34** [a] Song 8:6 **7:1** [a] Prov. 2:1 **7:2** [a] Lev. 18:5 [b] Deut. 32:10 **7:3** [a] Deut. 6:8 **7:5** [a] Prov. 2:16; 5:3 **7:7** [a] [Prov. 6:32; 9:4, 16] **7:9** [a] Job 24:15 **7:11** [a] Prov. 9:13 [b] Titus 2:5 **7:16** [a] Is. 19:9 **7:21** [a] Prov. 5:3 [b] Ps. 12:2 **7:22** [1] Septuagint, Syriac, and Targum read *as a dog to bonds;* Vulgate reads *as a lamb . . . to bonds.* **7:23** [a] Eccl. 9:12 **7:26** [a] Neh. 13:26 **7:27** [a] Prov. 2:18; 5:5; 9:18 [1] Or *Sheol* **8:1** [a] Prov. 1:20, 21; 9:3

6 Listen, for I will speak of [a]excellent things,
And from the opening of my lips *will come* right things;
7 For my mouth will speak truth;
Wickedness *is* an abomination to my lips.
8 All the words of my mouth *are* with righteousness;
Nothing crooked or perverse *is* in them.
9 They *are* all plain to him who understands,
And right to those who find knowledge.
10 Receive my instruction, and not silver,
And knowledge rather than choice gold;
11 [a]For wisdom *is* better than rubies,
And all the things one may desire cannot be compared with her.

12 "I, wisdom, dwell with prudence,
And find out knowledge *and* discretion.
13 [a]The fear of the LORD *is* to hate evil;
[b]Pride and arrogance and the evil way
And [c]the perverse mouth I hate.
14 Counsel *is* mine, and sound wisdom;
I *am* understanding, [a]I have strength.
15 [a]By me kings reign,
And rulers decree justice.
16 By me princes rule, and nobles,
All the judges of the earth.[1]
17 [a]I love those who love me,
And [b]those who seek me diligently will find me.
18 [a]Riches and honor *are* with me,
Enduring riches and righteousness.
19 My fruit *is* better than gold, yes, than fine gold,
And my revenue than choice silver.
20 I traverse the way of righteousness,
In the midst of the paths of justice,
21 That I may cause those who love me to inherit wealth,
That I may fill their treasuries.

22 "The[a] LORD possessed me at the beginning of His way,
Before His works of old.
23 [a]I have been established from everlasting,
From the beginning, before there was ever an earth.
24 When *there were* no depths I was brought forth,
When *there were* no fountains abounding with water.
25 [a]Before the mountains were settled,
Before the hills, I was brought forth;
26 While as yet He had not made the earth or the fields,
Or the primal dust of the world.
27 When He prepared the heavens, I *was* there,
When He drew a circle on the face of the deep,
28 When He established the clouds above,
When He strengthened the fountains of the deep,
29 [a]When He assigned to the sea its limit,
So that the waters would not transgress His command,
When [b]He marked out the foundations of the earth,
30 [a]Then I was beside Him *as* a master craftsman;[1]
[b]And I was daily *His* delight,
Rejoicing always before Him,
31 Rejoicing in His inhabited world,
And [a]my delight *was* with the sons of men.

32 "Now therefore, listen to me, *my* children,
For [a]blessed *are those who* keep my ways.
33 Hear instruction and be wise,
And do not disdain *it*.
34 [a]Blessed is the man who listens to me,
Watching daily at my gates,
Waiting at the posts of my doors.
35 For whoever finds me finds life,
And [a]obtains favor from the LORD;
36 But he who sins against me [a]wrongs his own soul;
All those who hate me love death."

### THE WAY OF WISDOM

9 Wisdom has [a]built her house,
She has hewn out her seven pillars;
2 [a]She has slaughtered her meat,
[b]She has mixed her wine,
She has also furnished her table.

**SEEING JESUS IN THE SCRIPTURE**

**8:23** In Proverbs, Solomon speaks of wisdom as a person. Ultimately, the person being portrayed is Jesus, the wisdom of God (see 1 Cor. 10:24). Just as wisdom has been established from eternity past, so has Jesus, the Son of God, existed eternally (see John 1:1).

**9:1 Seven** was an important number to the ancient Israelites, who believed the numeral represented holiness or perfection. The number's history can be traced back to creation, when God worked six days and rested on the seventh. The number seven appears throughout the Bible in dreams, visions, and rituals.

**8:6** [a] Prov. 22:20 **8:11** [a] Job 28:15 **8:13** [a] Prov. 3:7; 16:6 [b] [Prov. 16:17, 18] [c] Prov. 4:24 **8:14** [a] Eccl. 7:19; 9:16 **8:15** [a] Rom. 13:1 **8:16** [1] Masoretic Text, Syriac, Targum, and Vulgate read *righteousness;* Septuagint, Bomberg, and some manuscripts and editions read *earth.* **8:17** [a] [John 14:21] [b] James 1:5 **8:18** [a] Prov. 3:16 **8:22** [a] Prov. 3:19 **8:23** [a] [Ps. 2:6] **8:25** [a] Job 15:7, 8 **8:29** [a] Gen. 1:9, 10 [b] Job 28:4, 6 **8:30** [a] [John 1:1–3, 18] [b] [Matt. 3:17] [1] A Jewish tradition reads *one brought up.* **8:31** [a] Ps. 16:3 **8:32** [a] Luke 11:28 **8:34** [a] Prov. 3:13, 18 **8:35** [a] [John 17:3] **8:36** [a] Prov. 20:2 **9:1** [a] [Matt. 16:18] **9:2** [a] Matt. 22:4 [b] Prov. 23:30

3 She has sent out her maidens,
She cries out from the highest places of the city,
4 "Whoever[a] *is* simple, let him turn in here!"
*As for* him who lacks understanding, she says to him,
5 "Come,[a] eat of my bread
And drink of the wine I have mixed.
6 Forsake foolishness and live,
And go in the way of understanding.

7 "He who corrects a scoffer gets shame for himself,
And he who rebukes a wicked *man only* harms himself.
8 [a]Do not correct a scoffer, lest he hate you;
[b]Rebuke a wise *man,* and he will love you.
9 Give *instruction* to a wise *man,* and he will be still wiser;
Teach a just *man,* [a]and he will increase in learning.

10 "The[a] fear of the LORD *is* the beginning of wisdom,
And the knowledge of the Holy One *is* understanding.
11 [a]For by me your days will be multiplied,
And years of life will be added to you.
12 [a]If you are wise, you are wise for yourself,
And *if* you scoff, you will bear *it* alone."

### *THE WAY OF FOLLY*

13 [a]A foolish woman is clamorous;
*She is* simple, and knows nothing.
14 For she sits at the door of her house,
On a seat [a]*by* the highest places of the city,
15 To call to those who pass by,
Who go straight on their way:
16 "Whoever[a] *is* simple, let him turn in here";
And *as for* him who lacks understanding, she says to him,
17 "Stolen[a] water is sweet,
And bread *eaten* in secret is pleasant."
18 But he does not know that [a]the dead *are* there,
*That* her guests *are* in the depths of hell.[1]

### *WISE SAYINGS OF SOLOMON*

**10** The proverbs of [a]Solomon:

[b]A wise son makes a glad father,
But a foolish son *is* the grief of his mother.

2 [a]Treasures of wickedness profit nothing,
[b]But righteousness delivers from death.
3 [a]The LORD will not allow the righteous soul to famish,
But He casts away the desire of the wicked.

4 [a]He who has a slack hand becomes poor,
But [b]the hand of the diligent makes rich.
5 He who gathers in [a]summer *is* a wise son;
He who sleeps in harvest *is* [b]a son who causes shame.

6 Blessings *are* on the head of the righteous,
But violence covers the mouth of the wicked.
7 [a]The memory of the righteous *is* blessed,
But the name of the wicked will rot.

8 The wise in heart will receive commands,
[a]But a prating fool will fall.

9 [a]He who walks with integrity walks securely,
But he who perverts his ways will become known.

10 He who winks with the eye causes trouble,
But a prating fool will fall.

11 The mouth of the righteous *is* a well of life,
But violence covers the mouth of the wicked.

12 Hatred stirs up strife,
But [a]love covers all sins.
13 Wisdom is found on the lips of him who has understanding,
But [a]a rod *is* for the back of him who is devoid of understanding.

14 Wise *people* store up knowledge,
But [a]the mouth of the foolish *is* near destruction.

15 The [a]rich man's wealth *is* his strong city;
The destruction of the poor *is* their poverty.

16 The labor of the righteous *leads* to [a]life,
The wages of the wicked to sin.

17 He who keeps instruction *is in* the way of life,
But he who refuses correction goes astray.

18 Whoever [a]hides hatred *has* lying lips,
And [b]whoever spreads slander *is* a fool.

19 [a]In the multitude of words sin is not lacking,
But [b]he who restrains his lips *is* wise.
20 The tongue of the righteous *is* choice silver;
The heart of the wicked *is worth* little.

9:4 [a] Ps. 19:7 9:5 [a] Is. 55:1 9:8 [a] Matt. 7:6 [b] Ps. 141:5 9:9 [a] [Matt. 13:12] 9:10 [a] Job 28:28 9:11 [a] Prov. 3:2, 16 9:12 [a] Job 35:6, 7 9:13 [a] Prov. 7:11 9:14 [a] Prov. 9:3 9:16 [a] Prov. 7:7, 8 9:17 [a] Prov. 20:17 9:18 [a] Prov. 2:18; 7:27 [1] Or *Sheol* 10:1 [a] Prov. 1:1; 25:1 [b] Prov. 15:20; 17:21, 25; 19:13; 29:3, 15 10:2 [a] [Luke 12:19, 20] [b] Dan. 4:27 10:3 [a] Ps. 34:9, 10; 37:25 10:4 [a] Prov. 19:15 [b] Prov. 12:24; 13:4; 21:5 10:5 [a] Prov. 6:8 [b] Prov. 19:26 10:7 [a] Eccl. 8:10 10:8 [a] Prov. 10:10 10:9 [a] [Ps. 23:4] 10:12 [a] [1 Cor. 13:4–7] 10:13 [a] Prov. 26:3 10:14 [a] Prov. 18:7 10:15 [a] Job 31:24 10:16 [a] Prov. 6:23 10:18 [a] Prov. 26:24 [b] Ps. 15:3; 101:5 10:19 [a] Eccl. 5:3 [b] [James 1:19; 3:2]

21 The lips of the righteous feed many,
But fools die for lack of wisdom.[1]

22 [a]The blessing of the LORD makes *one* rich,
And He adds no sorrow with it.

23 [a]To do evil *is* like sport to a fool,
But a man of understanding has wisdom.

24 [a]The fear of the wicked will come upon him,
And [b]the desire of the righteous will be granted.

25 When the whirlwind passes by, [a]the wicked *is* no *more,*
But [b]the righteous *has* an everlasting foundation.

26 As vinegar to the teeth and smoke to the eyes,
So *is* the lazy *man* to those who send him.

27 [a]The fear of the LORD prolongs days,
But [b]the years of the wicked will be shortened.

28 The hope of the righteous *will be* gladness,
But the [a]expectation of the wicked will perish.

29 The way of the LORD *is* strength for the upright,
But [a]destruction *will come* to the workers of iniquity.

30 [a]The righteous will never be removed,
But the wicked will not inhabit the earth.

31 [a]The mouth of the righteous brings forth wisdom,
But the perverse tongue will be cut out.

32 The lips of the righteous know what is acceptable,
But the mouth of the wicked *what is* perverse.

11 [a]Dishonest scales *are* an abomination to the LORD,
But a just weight *is* His delight.

2 When pride comes, then comes [a]shame;
But with the humble *is* wisdom.

3 The integrity of the upright will guide [a]them,
But the perversity of the unfaithful will destroy them.

4 [a]Riches do not profit in the day of wrath,
But [b]righteousness delivers from death.

5 The righteousness of the blameless will direct[1] his way aright,
But the wicked will fall by his own [a]wickedness.

6 The righteousness of the upright will deliver them,
But the unfaithful will be caught by *their* lust.

7 When a wicked man dies, *his* expectation will [a]perish,
And the hope of the unjust perishes.

8 [a]The righteous is delivered from trouble,
And it comes to the wicked instead.

9 The hypocrite with *his* mouth destroys his neighbor,
But through knowledge the righteous will be delivered.

10 [a]When it goes well with the righteous, the city rejoices;
And when the wicked perish, *there is* jubilation.

11 By the blessing of the upright the city is [a]exalted,
But it is overthrown by the mouth of the wicked.

10:21 [1] Literally *heart* 10:22 [a] Gen. 24:35; 26:12 10:23 [a] Prov. 2:14; 15:21 10:24 [a] Job 15:21 [b] Ps. 145:19 10:25 [a] Ps. 37:9, 10 [b] Ps. 15:5 10:27 [a] Prov. 9:11 [b] Job 15:32 10:28 [a] Job 8:13 10:29 [a] Ps. 1:6 10:30 [a] Ps. 37:22 10:31 [a] Ps. 37:30 11:1 [a] Lev. 19:35, 36 11:2 [a] Prov. 16:18; 18:12; 29:23 11:3 [a] Prov. 13:6 11:4 [a] Ezek. 7:19 [b] Gen. 7:1 11:5 [a] Prov. 5:22 [1] Or *make smooth* or *straight* 11:7 [a] Prov. 10:28 11:8 [a] Prov. 21:18 11:10 [a] Prov. 28:12 11:11 [a] Prov. 14:34

LIVE THE TRUTH

## MAINTAINING INTEGRITY

**11:1** Integrity is consistency. It's when what's on the inside and the outside align. It's choosing to do what's right, even if you know you would get away with doing what's wrong. Here, Solomon gives an example of integrity. In his time, it was easy to use doctored scales—someone would pay more for something because it *seemed* to weigh more than it did. The scale, an instrument of fairness, became an instrument of theft when it was doctored in this way.

Integrity matters to God because it's one of His characteristics. God is always consistent in what He says and does. He never resorts to trickery. He is completely fair and righteous in all His ways. He wants us to live that way too. He wants us to reflect His integrity to the watching world and treat everyone with respect and honesty. Our right actions matter, but the right heart behind those actions matters even more. Living with integrity is an important aspect of righteousness because it's really a measure of who we are more than what we do.

12 He who is devoid of wisdom despises his
neighbor,
But a man of understanding holds his
peace.

13 [a]A talebearer reveals secrets,
But he who is of a faithful spirit [b]conceals
a matter.

14 [a]Where *there is* no counsel, the people fall;
But in the multitude of counselors *there is*
safety.

15 He who is [a]surety for a stranger will suffer,
But one who hates being surety is secure.

16 A gracious woman retains honor,
But ruthless *men* retain riches.
17 [a]The merciful man does good for his own
soul,
But *he who is* cruel troubles his own flesh.
18 The wicked *man* does deceptive work,
But [a]he who sows righteousness *will have*
a sure reward.
19 As righteousness *leads* to [a]life,
So he who pursues evil *pursues it* to his
own [b]death.
20 Those who are of a perverse heart *are* an
abomination to the LORD,
But *the* blameless in their ways *are* His
delight.
21 [a]*Though they join* forces,[1] the wicked will
not go unpunished;
But [b]the posterity of the righteous will be
delivered.

22 *As* a ring of gold in a swine's snout,
*So is* a lovely woman who lacks discretion.

**11:22** Pigs were among the least popular animals in ancient Israel. They were unclean and were unsuitable for food, according to God's law. Throughout the Bible, pigs are used to symbolize greed, filth, or shame.

23 The desire of the righteous *is* only good,
*But* the expectation of the wicked [a]*is*
wrath.

24 There is *one* who [a]scatters, yet increases
more;
And there is *one* who withholds more
than is right,
But it *leads* to poverty.

25 [a]The generous soul will be made rich,
[b]And he who waters will also be watered
himself.
26 The people will curse [a]him who withholds
grain,
But [b]blessing *will be* on the head of him
who sells *it*.

27 He who earnestly seeks good finds favor,
[a]But trouble will come to him who seeks
*evil*.

28 [a]He who trusts in his riches will fall,
But [b]the righteous will flourish like
foliage.

29 He who troubles his own house [a]will
inherit the wind,
And the fool *will be* [b]servant to the wise of
heart.

30 The fruit of the righteous *is a* tree of life,
And [a]he who wins souls *is* wise.

31 [a]If the righteous will be recompensed on
the earth,
How much more the ungodly and the
sinner.

## 12

Whoever loves instruction loves
knowledge,
But he who hates correction *is* stupid.

2 A good *man* obtains favor from the
LORD,
But a man of wicked intentions He will
condemn.

3 A man is not established by wickedness,
But the [a]root of the righteous cannot be
moved.

4 [a]An excellent[1] wife *is* the crown of her
husband,
But she who causes shame *is* [b]like
rottenness in his bones.

5 The thoughts of the righteous *are* right,
*But* the counsels of the wicked *are*
deceitful.
6 [a]The words of the wicked *are*, "Lie in wait
for blood,"
[b]But the mouth of the upright will deliver
them.

7 [a]The wicked are overthrown and *are* no
more,
But the house of the righteous will stand.

**11:13** [a] Lev. 19:16 [b] Prov. 19:11 **11:14** [a] 1 Kin. 12:1 **11:15** [a] Prov. 6:1, 2 **11:17** [a] [Matt. 5:7; 25:34–36] **11:18** [a] Hos. 10:12 **11:19** [a] Prov. 10:16; 12:28 [b] [Rom. 6:23] **11:21** [a] Prov. 16:5 [b] Ps. 112:2 [1] Literally *hand to hand* **11:23** [a] Rom. 2:8, 9 **11:24** [a] Ps. 112:9 **11:25** [a] [2 Cor. 9:6, 7] [b] [Matt. 5:7] **11:26** [a] Amos 8:5, 6 [b] Job 29:13 **11:27** [a] Esth. 7:10 **11:28** [a] Job 31:24 [b] Ps. 1:3 **11:29** [a] Eccl. 5:16 [b] Prov. 14:19 **11:30** [a] [Dan. 12:3] **11:31** [a] Jer. 25:29 **12:3** [a] [Prov. 10:25] **12:4** [a] 1 Cor. 11:7 [b] Prov. 14:30 [1] Literally *A wife of valor* **12:6** [a] Prov. 1:11, 18 [b] Prov. 14:3 **12:7** [a] Matt. 7:24–27

8 A man will be commended according to his wisdom,
[a]But he who is of a perverse heart will be despised.

9 [a]Better *is the one* who is slighted but has a servant,
Than he who honors himself but lacks bread.

10 [a]A righteous *man* regards the life of his animal,
But the tender mercies of the wicked *are* cruel.

11 [a]He who tills his land will be satisfied with [b]bread,
But he who follows frivolity [c]*is* devoid of understanding.[1]

12 The wicked covet the catch of evil *men,*
But the root of the righteous yields *fruit.*
13 [a]The wicked is ensnared by the transgression of *his* lips,
[b]But the righteous will come through trouble.
14 [a]A man will be satisfied with good by the fruit of *his* mouth,
[b]And the recompense of a man's hands will be rendered to him.

15 [a]The way of a fool *is* right in his own eyes,
But he who heeds counsel *is* wise.
16 [a]A fool's wrath is known at once,
But a prudent *man* covers shame.

17 [a]He *who* speaks truth declares righteousness,
But a false witness, deceit.
18 [a]There is one who speaks like the piercings of a sword,
But the tongue of the wise *promotes* health.
19 The truthful lip shall be established forever,
[a]But a lying tongue *is* but for a moment.
20 Deceit is in the heart of those who devise evil,
But counselors of peace have joy.
21 [a]No grave trouble will overtake the righteous,
But the wicked shall be filled with evil.
22 [a]Lying lips *are* an abomination to the LORD,
But those who deal truthfully *are* His delight.

23 [a]A prudent man conceals knowledge,
But the heart of fools proclaims foolishness.

24 [a]The hand of the diligent will rule,
But the lazy *man* will be put to forced labor.

25 [a]Anxiety in the heart of man causes depression,
But [b]a good word makes it glad.

26 The righteous should choose his friends carefully,
For the way of the wicked leads them astray.

27 The lazy *man* does not roast what he took in hunting,
But diligence *is* man's precious possession.

28 In the way of righteousness *is* life,
And in *its* pathway *there is* no death.

## 13

A wise son *heeds* his father's instruction,
[a]But a scoffer does not listen to rebuke.

2 [a]A man shall eat well by the fruit of *his* mouth,
But the soul of the unfaithful feeds on violence.
3 [a]He who guards his mouth preserves his life,
*But* he who opens wide his lips shall have destruction.

4 [a]The soul of a lazy *man* desires, and *has* nothing;
But the soul of the diligent shall be made rich.

5 A righteous *man* hates lying,
But a wicked *man* is loathsome and comes to shame.
6 [a]Righteousness guards *him whose* way is blameless,
But wickedness overthrows the sinner.

7 [a]There is one who makes himself rich, yet *has* nothing;
*And* one who makes himself poor, yet *has* great riches.

8 The ransom of a man's life *is* his riches,
But the poor does not hear rebuke.

9 The light of the righteous rejoices,
[a]But the lamp of the wicked will be put out.

10 By pride comes nothing but [a]strife,
But with the well-advised *is* wisdom.

12:8 [a] 1 Sam. 25:17 12:9 [a] Prov. 13:7 12:10 [a] Deut. 25:4 12:11 [a] Gen. 3:19 [b] Prov. 28:19 [c] Prov. 6:32 [1] Literally *heart*
12:13 [a] Prov. 18:7 [b] [2 Pet. 2:9] 12:14 [a] Prov. 13:2; 15:23; 18:20 [b] [Is. 3:10, 11] 12:15 [a] Luke 18:11 12:16 [a] Prov. 11:13; 29:11
12:17 [a] Prov. 14:5 12:18 [a] Ps. 57:4 12:19 [a] Prov. 19:9 12:21 [a] 1 Pet. 3:13 12:22 [a] Rev. 22:15 12:23 [a] Prov. 13:16 12:24 [a] Prov. 10:4 12:25 [a] Prov. 15:13 [b] Is. 50:4 13:1 [a] Is. 28:14, 15 13:2 [a] Prov. 12:14 13:3 [a] Prov. 21:23 13:4 [a] Prov. 10:4 13:6 [a] Prov. 11:3, 5, 6
13:7 [a] [Prov. 11:24; 12:9] 13:9 [a] Prov. 24:20 13:10 [a] Prov. 10:12

11 [a]Wealth *gained by* dishonesty will be
diminished,
But he who gathers by labor will increase.

12 Hope deferred makes the heart sick,
But [a]*when* the desire comes, *it is* a tree of
life.

13 He who [a]despises the word will be
destroyed,
But he who fears the commandment will
be rewarded.
14 [a]The law of the wise *is* a fountain of life,
To turn *one* away from [b]the snares of
death.

15 Good understanding gains [a]favor,
But the way of the unfaithful *is* hard.
16 [a]Every prudent *man* acts with knowledge,
But a fool lays open *his* folly.

17 A wicked messenger falls into trouble,
But [a]a faithful ambassador *brings* health.

18 Poverty and shame *will come* to him who
disdains correction,
But [a]he who regards a rebuke will be
honored.

19 A desire accomplished is sweet to the
soul,
But *it is* an abomination to fools to depart
from evil.
20 He who walks with wise *men* will be wise,
But the companion of fools will be
destroyed.

21 [a]Evil pursues sinners,
But to the righteous, good shall be repaid.

22 A good *man* leaves an inheritance to his
children's children,
But [a]the wealth of the sinner is stored up
for the righteous.

23 [a]Much food *is in* the fallow *ground* of the
poor,
And for lack of justice there is waste.[1]

24 [a]He who spares his rod hates his son,
But he who loves him disciplines him
promptly.

25 [a]The righteous eats to the satisfying of his
soul,
But the stomach of the wicked shall be in
want.

# 14

The wise woman builds her house,
But the foolish pulls it down with her
hands.

2 He who walks in his uprightness fears the
LORD,
[a]But *he who is* perverse in his ways
despises Him.

3 In the mouth of a fool *is* a rod of pride,
[a]But the lips of the wise will preserve them.

4 Where no oxen *are,* the trough *is* clean;
But much increase *comes* by the strength
of an ox.

5 A [a]faithful witness does not lie,
But a false witness will utter [b]lies.

6 A scoffer seeks wisdom and does not *find it,*
But [a]knowledge *is* easy to him who
understands.
7 Go from the presence of a foolish man,
When you do not perceive *in him* the lips
of [a]knowledge.
8 The wisdom of the prudent *is* to
understand his way,
But the folly of fools *is* deceit.

9 [a]Fools mock at sin,
But among the upright *there is* favor.

10 The heart knows its own bitterness,
And a stranger does not share its joy.

11 [a]The house of the wicked will be overthrown,
But the tent of the upright will flourish.

12 [a]There is a way *that seems* right to a man,
But [b]its end *is* the way of [c]death.

**14:12** Only when it's too late does the deluded person discover he or she is on the crowded path to **death**. It's not that this person was tricked, but rather that he or she relied too heavily on human "wisdom" rather than humbly turning to God.

13 Even in laughter the heart may sorrow,
And [a]the end of mirth *may be* grief.

14 The backslider in heart will be [a]filled with
his own ways,
But a good man *will be satisfied* from
[b]above.[1]

13:11 [a] Prov. 10:2; 20:21 13:12 [a] Prov. 13:19 13:13 [a] Num. 15:31 13:14 [a] Prov. 6:22; 10:11; 14:27 [b] 2 Sam. 22:6 13:15 [a] Prov. 3:4 13:16 [a] Prov. 12:23 13:17 [a] Prov. 25:13 13:18 [a] Prov. 15:5, 31, 32 13:21 [a] Ps. 32:10 13:22 [a] [Eccl. 2:26] 13:23 [a] Prov. 12:11 [1] Literally *what is swept away* 13:24 [a] Prov. 19:18 13:25 [a] Ps. 34:10 14:2 [a] [Rom. 2:4] 14:3 [a] Prov. 12:6 14:5 [a] Rev. 1:5; 3:14 [b] Prov. 6:19; 12:17 14:6 [a] Prov. 8:9; 17:24 14:7 [a] Prov. 23:9 14:9 [a] Prov. 10:23 14:11 [a] Job 8:15 14:12 [a] Prov. 16:25 [b] Rom. 6:21 [c] Prov. 12:15 14:13 [a] Eccl. 2:1, 2 14:14 [a] Prov. 1:31; 12:15 [b] Prov. 13:2; 18:20 [1] Literally *from above himself*

15 The simple believes every word,
But the prudent considers well his steps.
16 [a]A wise *man* fears and departs from evil,
But a fool rages and is self-confident.
17 A quick-tempered *man* acts foolishly,
And a man of wicked intentions is hated.
18 The simple inherit folly,
But the prudent are crowned with
knowledge.
19 The evil will bow before the good,
And the wicked at the gates of the
righteous.

20 [a]The poor *man* is hated even by his own
neighbor,
But the rich *has* many [b]friends.
21 He who despises his neighbor sins;
[a]But he who has mercy on the poor, happy
*is* he.

22 Do they not go astray who devise evil?
But mercy and truth *belong* to those who
devise good.

23 In all labor there is profit,
But idle chatter[1] *leads* only to poverty.

24 The crown of the wise is their riches,
*But* the foolishness of fools *is* folly.

25 A true witness delivers [a]souls,
But a deceitful *witness* speaks lies.

26 In the fear of the LORD *there is* strong
confidence,
And His children will have a place of refuge.
27 [a]The fear of the LORD *is* a fountain of life,
To turn *one* away from the snares of
death.

28 In a multitude of people *is* a king's honor,
But in the lack of people *is* the downfall of
a prince.

29 [a]*He who is* slow to wrath has great
understanding,
But *he who is* impulsive[1] exalts folly.

30 A sound heart *is* life to the body,
But [a]envy *is* [b]rottenness to the bones.

31 [a]He who oppresses the poor reproaches
[b]his Maker,
But he who honors Him has mercy on the
needy.

32 The wicked is banished in his wickedness,
But [a]the righteous has a refuge in his death.

33 Wisdom rests in the heart of him who has
understanding,
But [a]*what is* in the heart of fools is made
known.

34 Righteousness exalts a [a]nation,
But sin *is* a reproach to *any* people.

35 [a]The king's favor *is* toward a wise servant,
But his wrath *is against* him who causes
shame.

15 A [a]soft answer turns away wrath,
But [b]a harsh word stirs up anger.
2 The tongue of the wise uses knowledge
rightly,
[a]But the mouth of fools pours forth
foolishness.

3 [a]The eyes of the LORD *are* in every place,
Keeping watch on the evil and the good.

4 A wholesome tongue *is* a tree of life,
But perverseness in it breaks the spirit.

5 [a]A fool despises his father's instruction,
[b]But he who receives correction is
prudent.

6 *In* the house of the righteous *there is*
much treasure,
But in the revenue of the wicked is
trouble.

7 The lips of the wise disperse knowledge,
But the heart of the fool *does* not *do* so.

8 [a]The sacrifice of the wicked *is* an
abomination to the LORD,
But the prayer of the upright *is* His
delight.
9 The way of the wicked *is* an abomination
to the LORD,
But He loves him who [a]follows
righteousness.

10 [a]Harsh discipline *is* for him who forsakes
the way,
*And* [b]he who hates correction will die.

11 [a]Hell[1] and Destruction[2] *are* before the
LORD;
So how much more [b]the hearts of the
sons of men.

12 [a]A scoffer does not love one who corrects
him,
Nor will he go to the wise.

**14:16** [a] Prov. 22:3 **14:20** [a] Prov. 19:7 [b] Prov. 19:4 **14:21** [a] Ps. 112:9 **14:23** [1] Literally *talk of the lips* **14:25** [a] [Ezek. 3:18–21] **14:27** [a] Prov. 13:14 **14:29** [a] James 1:19 [1] Literally *short of spirit* **14:30** [a] Ps. 112:10 [b] Prov. 12:4 **14:31** [a] Matt. 25:40 [b] [Prov. 22:2] **14:32** [a] Job 13:15 **14:33** [a] Prov. 12:16 **14:34** [a] Prov. 11:11 **14:35** [a] Matt. 24:45–47 **15:1** [a] Prov. 25:15 [b] 1 Sam. 25:10 **15:2** [a] Prov. 12:23 **15:3** [a] Job 34:21 **15:5** [a] Prov. 10:1 [b] Prov. 13:18 **15:8** [a] Is. 1:11 **15:9** [a] Prov. 21:21 **15:10** [a] 1 Kin. 22:8 [b] Prov. 5:12 **15:11** [a] Job 26:6 [b] 2 Chr. 6:30 [1] Or *Sheol* [2] Hebrew *Abaddon* **15:12** [a] Amos 5:10

KNOW THE TRUTH

# THE DOCTRINE OF GOD

## PART 8: THE OMNIPRESENCE OF GOD

**15:3** God is Spirit. This means He's not in physical form bound by physical space. Often, we refer to God's limitless presence as His omnipresence, meaning to be present everywhere. While we are limited to one location at one point in time, God isn't. Indeed, God made physical space so He cannot be limited by what He made. Instead, God is present in every location of His creation. It's not as if God is so big *part* of Him is everywhere. Rather, He is fully and completely present everywhere at once.

This is why Proverbs 15:3 asserts God's ability to see all activity in any and all spaces of His creation. There's no action hidden from His sight nor any location too remote for His presence (see Jer. 23:24). This truth should bring us tremendous comfort and encouragement. God is with us anywhere at any time (see John 14:15–23). He is with us in any location we're in, in any situation we face, on any given day. Simply stated: God is always with us! To encounter certain pagan gods, one had to ascend a specific mountain or journey to a specific temple. Not so with the one true omnipresent God. He can be worshiped and experienced by anyone, anywhere, anytime (see John 4:23–24).

*For* **THE DOCTRINE OF GOD: PART 9: THE SOVEREIGNTY OF GOD,** *turn to Psalm 115:3 on page 684.*

13 [a]A merry heart makes a cheerful
countenance,
But [b]by sorrow of the heart the spirit is
broken.

14 The heart of him who has understanding
seeks knowledge,
But the mouth of fools feeds on
foolishness.

15 All the days of the afflicted *are* evil,
[a]But he who is of a merry heart *has* a
continual feast.

16 [a]Better *is* a little with the fear of the
LORD,
Than great treasure with trouble.

17 [a]Better *is* a dinner of herbs[1] where love is,
Than a fatted calf with hatred.

18 [a]A wrathful man stirs up strife,
But *he who is* slow to anger allays
contention.

19 [a]The way of the lazy *man is* like a hedge of
thorns,
But the way of the upright *is* a
highway.

20 [a]A wise son makes a father glad,
But a foolish man despises his
mother.

21 [a]Folly *is* joy *to him who is* destitute of
discernment,
[b]But a man of understanding walks uprightly.

22 [a]Without counsel, plans go awry,
But in the multitude of counselors they
are established.

23 A man has joy by the answer of his mouth,
And [a]a word *spoken* in due season, how
good *it is!*

24 [a]The way of life *winds* upward for the wise,
That he may [b]turn away from hell[1] below.

25 [a]The LORD will destroy the house of the
proud,
But [b]He will establish the boundary of the
widow.

26 [a]The thoughts of the wicked *are* an
abomination to the LORD,
[b]But the words of the pure *are* pleasant.

27 [a]He who is greedy for gain troubles his
own house,
But he who hates bribes will live.

28 The heart of the righteous [a]studies how to
answer,
But the mouth of the wicked pours forth
evil.

15:13 [a] Prov. 12:25 [b] Prov. 17:22 15:15 [a] Prov. 17:22 15:16 [a] Ps. 37:16 15:17 [a] Prov. 17:1 [1] Or *vegetables* 15:18 [a] Prov. 26:21 15:19 [a] Prov. 22:5 15:20 [a] Prov. 10:1 15:21 [a] Prov. 10:23 [b] Eph. 5:15 15:22 [a] Prov. 11:14 15:23 [a] Prov. 25:11 15:24 [a] Phil. 3:20 [b] Prov. 14:16 [1] Or *Sheol* 15:25 [a] Prov. 12:7 [b] Ps. 68:5, 6 15:26 [a] Prov. 6:16, 18 [b] Ps. 37:30 15:27 [a] Is. 5:8 15:28 [a] 1 Pet. 3:15

29 [a]The LORD *is* far from the wicked,
But [b]He hears the prayer of the righteous.

30 The light of the eyes rejoices the heart,
*And* a good report makes the bones healthy.[1]

31 The ear that hears the rebukes of life
Will abide among the wise.
32 He who disdains instruction despises his own soul,
But he who heeds rebuke gets understanding.
33 [a]The fear of the LORD *is* the instruction of wisdom,
And [b]before honor *is* humility.

16 The [a]preparations of the heart *belong* to man,
[b]But the answer of the tongue *is* from the LORD.

2 All the ways of a man *are* pure in his own [a]eyes,
But the LORD weighs the spirits.

3 [a]Commit your works to the LORD,
And your thoughts will be established.

4 The [a]LORD has made all for Himself,
[b]Yes, even the wicked for the day of doom.

5 [a]Everyone proud in heart *is* an abomination to the LORD;
*Though they join* forces,[1] none will go unpunished.

6 [a]In mercy and truth
Atonement is provided for iniquity;
And [b]by the fear of the LORD *one* departs from evil.

7 When a man's ways please the LORD,
He makes even his enemies to be at peace with him.

8 [a]Better *is* a little with righteousness,
Than vast revenues without justice.

9 [a]A man's heart plans his way,
[b]But the LORD directs his steps.

10 Divination *is* on the lips of the king;
His mouth must not transgress in judgment.
11 [a]Honest weights and scales *are* the LORD's;
All the weights in the bag *are* His work.
12 *It is* an abomination for kings to commit wickedness,
For [a]a throne is established by righteousness.
13 [a]Righteous lips *are* the delight of kings,
And they love him who speaks *what is* right.
14 As messengers of death *is* the king's wrath,
But a wise man will [a]appease it.
15 In the light of the king's face *is* life,
And his favor *is* like a [a]cloud of the latter rain.

**16:15** Located in a desert region, the land of Israel experiences frequent droughts. Because the ancient Israelites relied on farming for so many of their basic needs, they considered **rain** a precious gift from God. Long droughts were thought by many to be God's judgment on the sins of the people.

16 [a]How much better to get wisdom than gold!
And to get understanding is to be chosen rather than silver.

17 The highway of the upright *is* to depart from evil;
He who keeps his way preserves his soul.

18 Pride *goes* before destruction,
And a haughty spirit before a fall.
19 Better *to be* of a humble spirit with the lowly,
Than to divide the spoil with the proud.

20 He who heeds the word wisely will find good,
And whoever [a]trusts in the LORD, happy *is* he.

21 The wise in heart will be called prudent,
And sweetness of the lips increases learning.

22 Understanding *is* a wellspring of life to him who has it.
But the correction of fools *is* folly.

23 The heart of the wise teaches his mouth,
And adds learning to his lips.

24 Pleasant words *are like* a honeycomb,
Sweetness to the soul and health to the bones.

25 There is a way *that seems* right to a man,
But its end *is* the way of [a]death.

**15:29** [a] Ps. 10:1; 34:16 [b] Ps. 145:18 **15:30** [1] Literally *fat* **15:33** [a] Prov. 1:7 [b] Prov. 18:12 **16:1** [a] Jer. 10:23 [b] Matt. 10:19 **16:2** [a] Prov. 21:2 **16:3** [a] Ps. 37:5 **16:4** [a] Is. 43:7 [b] [Rom. 9:22] **16:5** [a] Prov. 6:17; 8:13 [1] Literally *hand to hand* **16:6** [a] Dan. 4:27 [b] Prov. 8:13; 14:16 **16:8** [a] Ps. 37:16 **16:9** [a] Prov. 19:21 [b] Jer. 10:23 **16:11** [a] Lev. 19:36 **16:12** [a] Prov. 25:5 **16:13** [a] Prov. 14:35 **16:14** [a] Prov. 25:15 **16:15** [a] Zech. 10:1 **16:16** [a] Prov. 8:10, 11, 19 **16:20** [a] Ps. 34:8 **16:25** [a] Prov. 14:12

26 The person who labors, labors for himself,
For his *hungry* mouth drives [a]him *on.*

27 An ungodly man digs up evil,
And *it is* on his lips like a burning [a]fire.

28 A perverse man sows strife,
And [a]a whisperer separates the best of friends.

29 A violent man entices his neighbor,
And leads him in a way *that is* not good.

30 He winks his eye to devise perverse things;
He purses his lips *and* brings about evil.

31 [a]The silver-haired head *is* a crown of glory,
*If* it is found in the way of righteousness.

32 [a]*He who is* slow to anger *is* better than the mighty,
And he who rules his spirit than he who takes a city.

33 The lot is cast into the lap,
But its every decision *is* from the LORD.

17 Better *is* [a]a dry morsel with quietness,
Than a house full of feasting[1] *with* strife.

2 A wise servant will rule over [a]a son who causes shame,
And will share an inheritance among the brothers.

3 The refining pot *is* for silver and the furnace for gold,
[a]But the LORD tests the hearts.

4 An evildoer gives heed to false lips;
A liar listens eagerly to a spiteful tongue.

5 [a]He who mocks the poor reproaches his Maker;
[b]He who is glad at calamity will not go unpunished.

6 [a]Children's children *are* the crown of old men,
And the glory of children *is* their father.

7 Excellent speech is not becoming to a fool,
Much less lying lips to a prince.

8 A present *is* a precious stone in the eyes of its possessor;
Wherever he turns, he prospers.

9 [a]He who covers a transgression seeks love,
But [b]he who repeats a matter separates friends.

10 [a]Rebuke is more effective for a wise *man*
Than a hundred blows on a fool.

11 An evil *man* seeks only rebellion;
Therefore a cruel messenger will be sent against him.

12 Let a man meet [a]a bear robbed of her cubs,
Rather than a fool in his folly.

13 Whoever [a]rewards evil for good,
Evil will not depart from his house.

14 The beginning of strife *is like* releasing water;
Therefore [a]stop contention before a quarrel starts.

16:26 [a] [Eccl. 6:7] 16:27 [a] [James 3:6] 16:28 [a] Prov. 17:9 16:31 [a] Prov. 20:29 16:32 [a] Prov. 14:29; 19:11 17:1 [a] Prov. 15:17 [1] Or *sacrificial meals* 17:2 [a] Prov. 10:5 17:3 [a] Jer. 17:10 17:5 [a] Prov. 14:31 [b] Job 31:29 17:6 [a] [Ps. 127:3; 128:3] 17:9 [a] [Prov. 10:12] [b] Prov. 16:28 17:10 [a] [Mic. 7:9] 17:12 [a] Hos. 13:8 17:13 [a] Ps. 109:4, 5 17:14 [a] [Prov. 20:3]

LIVE THE TRUTH

## VALUING SIBLINGS

**17:17** Siblings can be challenging. The relationship of the first two brothers in history was characterized by jealousy and ended in tragedy (see Gen. 4:1–8). Proximity and natural competition can make "sibling rivalries" very real inside of the home. But the Bible also shows us how good it is to have a sibling. Those who are the closest to us have the power to hurt us the deepest, but they also have the power to build us up the highest. In a difficult time, there's no one better to walk next to you than a faithful brother or sister. No one can provide support when you lean on them like a sibling. Close friends are a wonderful gift from God, but a sibling can be closer than the closest of friends.

Not everyone has biological or adoptive siblings, but as followers of Jesus, we have countless spiritual brother and sisters and the same is true of them. When you are in need, turn to your brothers and sisters in Christ. Lean on them. Walk with them. And be there to support them in their time of need too. Siblings—in the home and in the church—are an amazing blessing from God our Father.

15 [a]He who justifies the wicked, and he who
condemns the just,
Both of them alike *are* an abomination to
the LORD.

16 Why *is there* in the hand of a fool the
purchase price of wisdom,
Since *he has* no heart *for it?*

17 [a]A friend loves at all times,
And a brother is born for adversity.

18 [a]A man devoid of understanding shakes
hands in a pledge,
*And* becomes surety for his friend.

19 He who loves transgression loves strife,
And [a]he who exalts his gate seeks
destruction.

20 He who has a deceitful heart finds no
good,
And he who has [a]a perverse tongue falls
into evil.

21 He who begets a scoffer *does so* to his
sorrow,
And the father of a fool has no joy.

22 A [a]merry heart does good, *like* medicine,[1]
But a broken spirit dries the bones.

23 A wicked *man* accepts a bribe behind the
back[1]
To pervert the ways of justice.

24 [a]Wisdom *is* in the sight of him who has
understanding,
But the eyes of a fool *are* on the ends of
the earth.

25 A [a]foolish son *is* a grief to his father,
And bitterness to her who bore him.

26 Also, to punish the righteous *is* not good,
*Nor* to strike princes for *their*
uprightness.

27 [a]He who has knowledge spares his words,
*And* a man of understanding is of a calm
spirit.

28 [a]Even a fool is counted wise when he holds
his peace;
*When* he shuts his lips, *he is considered*
perceptive.

**18** A man who isolates himself seeks his
own desire;
He rages against all wise judgment.

2 A fool has no delight in understanding,
But in expressing his [a]own heart.

3 When the wicked comes, contempt comes
also;
And with dishonor *comes* reproach.

4 [a]The words of a man's mouth *are* deep
waters;
[b]The wellspring of wisdom *is* a flowing
brook.

5 *It is* not good to show partiality to the
wicked,
*Or* to overthrow the righteous in
[a]judgment.

6 A fool's lips enter into contention,
And his mouth calls for blows.

7 [a]A fool's mouth *is* his destruction,
And his lips *are* the snare of his [b]soul.

8 [a]The words of a talebearer *are* like tasty
trifles,[1]
And they go down into the inmost
body.

9 He who is slothful in his work
Is a brother to him who is a great
destroyer.

10 The name of the LORD *is* a strong
[a]tower;
The righteous run to it and are safe.

11 The rich man's wealth *is* his strong city,
And like a high wall in his own esteem.

12 [a]Before destruction the heart of a man is
haughty,
And before honor *is* humility.

13 He who answers a matter before he hears
*it*,
It *is* folly and shame to him.

14 The spirit of a man will sustain him in
sickness,
But who can bear a broken spirit?

15 The heart of the prudent acquires
knowledge,
And the ear of the wise seeks knowledge.

16 [a]A man's gift makes room for him,
And brings him before great men.

17 The first *one* to plead his cause *seems*
right,
Until his neighbor comes and examines
him.

**17:15** [a] Ex. 23:7 **17:17** [a] Ruth 1:16 **17:18** [a] Prov. 6:1 **17:19** [a] Prov. 16:18 **17:20** [a] James 3:8 **17:22** [a] Prov. 12:25; 15:13, 15 [1] Or *makes medicine even better* **17:23** [1] Literally *from the bosom* **17:24** [a] Eccl. 2:14 **17:25** [a] Prov. 10:1; 15:20; 19:13 **17:27** [a] James 1:19 **17:28** [a] Job 13:5 **18:2** [a] Eccl. 10:3 **18:4** [a] Prov. 10:11 [b] [James 3:17] **18:5** [a] Prov. 17:15 **18:7** [a] Prov. 10:14 [b] Eccl. 10:12 **18:8** [a] Prov. 12:18 [1] A Jewish tradition reads *wounds.* **18:10** [a] 2 Sam. 22:2, 3, 33 **18:12** [a] Prov. 15:33; 16:18 **18:16** [a] Gen. 32:20, 21

18 Casting [a]lots causes contentions to cease,
And keeps the mighty apart.

**18:18 Casting lots** was an ancient way of selecting, much like flipping a coin or drawing a straw today. The difference was the Israelites believed God influenced the outcome of the lots. Therefore, it was His will, and not blind luck, that determined the results. Lots were often used to make important decisions, including choosing the scapegoat (Lev. 16:8–10), dividing the land (Num. 26:55–56; Josh. 14:2), dividing Jesus' garments (Matt. 27:35), and choosing Judas's replacement (Acts 1:24–26).

19 A brother offended *is harder to win* than a strong city,
And contentions *are* like the bars of a castle.

20 [a]A man's stomach shall be satisfied from the fruit of his mouth;
*From* the produce of his lips he shall be filled.

21 [a]Death and life *are* in the power of the tongue,
And those who love it will eat its fruit.

22 [a]*He who* finds a wife finds a good *thing,*
And obtains favor from the LORD.

23 The poor *man* uses entreaties,
But the rich answers [a]roughly.

24 A man *who has* friends must himself be friendly,[1]
[a]But there is a friend *who* sticks closer than a brother.

19 Better [a]*is* the poor who walks in his integrity
Than *one who is* perverse in his lips, and is a fool.

2 Also it is not good *for* a soul *to be* without knowledge,
And he sins who hastens with *his* feet.

3 The foolishness of a man twists his way,
And his heart frets against the LORD.

4 [a]Wealth makes many friends,
But the poor is separated from his friend.

5 A [a]false witness will not go unpunished,
And *he who* speaks lies will not escape.

6 Many entreat the favor of the nobility,
And every man *is* a friend to one who gives gifts.

7 [a]All the brothers of the poor hate him;
How much more do his friends go [b]far from him!
He may pursue *them with* words, *yet* they abandon *him.*

8 He who gets wisdom loves his own soul;
He who keeps understanding [a]will find good.

9 A false witness will not go unpunished,
And *he who* speaks lies shall perish.

10 Luxury is not fitting for a fool,
Much less [a]for a servant to rule over princes.

**18:18** [a][Prov. 16:33] **18:20** [a]Prov. 12:14; 14:14 **18:21** [a]Matt. 12:37 **18:22** [a][Prov. 12:4; 19:14] **18:23** [a]James 2:3, 6 **18:24** [a]Prov. 17:17 [1]Following Greek manuscripts, Syriac, Targum, and Vulgate; Masoretic Text reads *may come to ruin.* **19:1** [a]Prov. 28:6 **19:4** [a]Prov. 14:20 **19:5** [a]Ex. 23:1 **19:7** [a]Prov. 14:20 [b]Ps. 38:11 **19:8** [a]Prov. 16:20 **19:10** [a]Prov. 30:21, 22

LIVE THE TRUTH

## VALUING YOUR WORDS

**18:20** It might seem like it at times, but words don't just float away, never to be heard again. Words bear fruit—they have consequences, for better or worse. They have weight. People can be burdened or empowered by them. Because words matter, God wants you to choose them carefully. This is what the Bible means when it talks about the power of the tongue (e.g., James 3). As followers of Jesus, we should place great emphasis on the words we speak because Jesus said our words reveal the condition of the heart (Matt. 12:34).

Solomon reminds us we will always experience the effects of our words. For instance, if you use your words to encourage others, it's likely they will be blessed and others will be more likely to encourage you. However, if you use your words to tear others down, they will probably do the same to you. Cursing and blessing. Foolish talk and biblical guidance. Each bears fruit, rancid or sweet. However you choose to use your words, know they have value. It would be best for you to use them wisely.

11 [a]The discretion of a man makes him slow to anger,
[b]And his glory *is* to overlook a transgression.

12 [a]The king's wrath *is* like the roaring of a lion,
But his favor *is* [b]like dew on the grass.

13 [a]A foolish son *is* the ruin of his father,
[b]And the contentions of a wife *are* a continual dripping.

14 [a]Houses and riches *are* an inheritance from fathers,
But [b]a prudent wife *is* from the LORD.

15 [a]Laziness casts *one* into a deep sleep,
And an idle person will [b]suffer hunger.

16 [a]He who keeps the commandment keeps his soul,
*But* he who is careless[1] of his ways will die.

17 [a]He who has pity on the poor lends to the LORD,
And He will pay back what he has given.

18 [a]Chasten your son while there is hope,
And do not set your heart on his destruction.[1]

19 *A man of* great wrath will suffer punishment;
For if you rescue *him,* you will have to do it again.

20 Listen to counsel and receive instruction,
That you may be wise [a]in your latter days.

21 There are many plans in a man's heart,
[a]Nevertheless the LORD's counsel—that will stand.

22 What is desired in a man is kindness,
And a poor man is better than a liar.

23 [a]The fear of the LORD *leads* to life,
And *he who has it* will abide in satisfaction;
He will not be visited with evil.

24 [a]A lazy *man* buries his hand in the bowl,[1]
And will not so much as bring it to his mouth again.

25 Strike a scoffer, and the simple [a]will become wary;
[b]Rebuke one who has understanding, *and* he will discern knowledge.

26 He who mistreats *his* father *and* chases away *his* mother
*Is* [a]a son who causes shame and brings reproach.

27 Cease listening to instruction, my son,
And you will stray from the words of knowledge.

28 A disreputable witness scorns justice,
And [a]the mouth of the wicked devours iniquity.

29 Judgments are prepared for scoffers,
[a]And beatings for the backs of fools.

## 20

Wine [a]*is* a mocker,
Strong drink *is* a brawler,
And whoever is led astray by it is not wise.

2 The wrath[1] of a king *is* like the roaring of a lion;
*Whoever* provokes him to anger sins *against* his own life.

3 [a]*It is* honorable for a man to stop striving,
Since any fool can start a quarrel.

4 [a]The lazy *man* will not plow because of winter;
[b]He will beg during harvest and *have* nothing.

5 Counsel in the heart of man *is like* deep water,
But a man of understanding will draw it out.

6 Most men will proclaim each his own goodness,
But who can find a faithful man?

7 [a]The righteous *man* walks in his integrity;
[b]His children *are* blessed after him.

8 A king who sits on the throne of judgment
Scatters all evil with his eyes.

9 [a]Who can say, "I have made my heart clean,
I am pure from my sin"?

10 [a]Diverse weights *and* diverse measures,
They *are* both alike, an abomination to the LORD.

**19:11** [a] James 1:19 [b] Eph. 4:32 **19:12** [a] Prov. 16:14 [b] Hos. 14:5 **19:13** [a] Prov. 10:1 [b] Prov. 21:9, 19 **19:14** [a] 2 Cor. 12:14 [b] Prov. 18:22 **19:15** [a] Prov. 6:9 [b] Prov. 10:4 **19:16** [a] Luke 10:28; 11:28 [1] Literally *despises,* figurative of recklessness or carelessness **19:17** [a] [2 Cor. 9:6–8] **19:18** [a] Prov. 13:24 [1] Literally *to put him to death;* a Jewish tradition reads *on his crying.* **19:20** [a] Ps. 37:37 **19:21** [a] Heb. 6:17 **19:23** [a] [1 Tim. 4:8] **19:24** [a] Prov. 15:19 [1] Septuagint and Syriac read *bosom;* Targum and Vulgate read *armpit.* **19:25** [a] Deut. 13:11 [b] Prov. 9:8 **19:26** [a] Prov. 17:2 **19:28** [a] Job 15:16 **19:29** [a] Prov. 26:3 **20:1** [a] Gen. 9:21 **20:2** [1] Literally *fear* or *terror* which is produced by the king's wrath **20:3** [a] Prov. 17:14 **20:4** [a] Prov. 10:4 [b] Prov. 19:15 **20:7** [a] 2 Cor. 1:12 [b] Ps. 37:26 **20:9** [a] [1 Kin. 8:46] **20:10** [a] Deut. 25:13

11 Even a child is [a]known by his deeds,
Whether what he does *is* pure and right.

12 [a]The hearing ear and the seeing eye,
The LORD has made them both.

13 [a]Do not love sleep, lest you come to poverty;
Open your eyes, *and* you will be satisfied
with bread.

14 "*It is* good for nothing,"[1] cries the buyer;
But when he has gone his way, then he
boasts.

15 There is gold and a multitude of rubies,
But [a]the lips of knowledge *are* a precious
jewel.

16 [a]Take the garment of one who is surety *for*
a stranger,
And hold it as a pledge *when it* is for a
seductress.

17 [a]Bread gained by deceit *is* sweet to a man,
But afterward his mouth will be filled with
gravel.

18 [a]Plans are established by counsel;
[b]By wise counsel wage war.

19 [a]He who goes about *as* a talebearer reveals
secrets;
Therefore do not associate with one [b]who
flatters with his lips.

20 [a]Whoever curses his father or his mother,
[b]His lamp will be put out in deep darkness.

21 [a]An inheritance gained hastily at the
beginning
[b]Will not be blessed at the end.

22 [a]Do not say, "I will recompense evil";
[b]Wait for the LORD, and He will save you.

23 Diverse weights *are* an abomination to
the LORD,
And dishonest scales *are* not good.

24 A man's steps *are* of the LORD;
How then can a man understand his own
way?

25 *It is* a snare for a man to devote rashly
*something as* holy,
And afterward to reconsider *his* vows.

26 [a]A wise king sifts out the wicked,
And brings the threshing wheel over
them.

27 [a]The spirit of a man *is* the lamp of the LORD,
Searching all the inner depths of his heart.[1]

28 [a]Mercy and truth preserve the king,
And by lovingkindness he upholds his
throne.

29 The glory of young men *is* their strength,
And [a]the splendor of old men *is* their gray
head.

30 Blows that hurt cleanse away evil,
As *do* stripes the inner depths of the
heart.[1]

21 The king's heart *is* in the hand of the
LORD,
*Like* the rivers of water;
He turns it wherever He wishes.

2 [a]Every way of a man *is* right in his own eyes,
[b]But the LORD weighs the hearts.

3 [a]To do righteousness and justice
*Is* more acceptable to the LORD than
sacrifice.

4 [a]A haughty look, a proud heart,
*And* the plowing[1] of the wicked *are* sin.

5 [a]The plans of the diligent *lead* surely to
plenty,
But *those of* everyone *who is* hasty, surely
to poverty.

6 [a]Getting treasures by a lying tongue
*Is* the fleeting fantasy of those who seek
death.[1]

7 The violence of the wicked will destroy
them,[1]
Because they refuse to do justice.

8 The way of a guilty man *is* perverse;[1]
But *as for* the pure, his work *is* right.

9 Better to dwell in a corner of a housetop,
Than in a house shared with [a]a
contentious woman.

10 [a]The soul of the wicked desires evil;
His neighbor finds no favor in his eyes.

20:11 [a] Matt. 7:16 20:12 [a] Ex. 4:11 20:13 [a] Rom. 12:11 20:14 [1] Literally *evil, evil* 20:15 [a] [Prov. 3:13–15] 20:16 [a] Prov. 22:26 20:17 [a] Prov. 9:17 20:18 [a] Prov. 24:6 [b] Luke 14:31 20:19 [a] Prov. 11:13 [b] Rom. 16:18 20:20 [a] Matt. 15:4 [b] Job 18:5, 6 20:21 [a] Prov. 28:20 [b] Hab. 2:6 20:22 [a] [Rom. 12:17–19] [b] 2 Sam. 16:12 20:26 [a] Ps. 101:8 20:27 [a] 1 Cor. 2:11 [1] Literally *the rooms of the belly* 20:28 [a] Prov. 21:21 20:29 [a] Prov. 16:31 20:30 [1] Literally *the rooms of the belly* 21:2 [a] Prov. 16:2 [b] Prov. 24:12 21:3 [a] 1 Sam. 15:22 21:4 [a] Prov. 6:17 [1] Or *lamp* 21:5 [a] Prov. 10:4 21:6 [a] 2 Pet. 2:3 [1] Septuagint reads *Pursue vanity on the snares of death;* Vulgate reads *Is vain and foolish, and shall stumble on the snares of death;* Targum reads *They shall be destroyed, and they shall fall who seek death.* 21:7 [1] Literally *drag them away* 21:8 [1] Or *The way of a man is perverse and strange* 21:9 [a] Prov. 19:13 21:10 [a] James 4:5

11 When the scoffer is punished, the simple
is made wise;
But when the [a]wise is instructed, he
receives knowledge.

12 The righteous *God* wisely considers the
house of the wicked,
Overthrowing the wicked for *their*
wickedness.

13 [a]Whoever shuts his ears to the cry of the
poor
Will also cry himself and not be heard.

14 A gift in secret pacifies anger,
And a bribe behind the back,[1] strong
wrath.

15 *It is* a joy for the just to do justice,
But destruction *will come* to the workers
of iniquity.

16 A man who wanders from the way of
understanding
Will rest in the assembly of the [a]dead.

17 He who loves pleasure *will be* a poor man;
He who loves wine and oil will not be rich.

18 The wicked *shall be* a ransom for the
righteous,
And the unfaithful for the upright.

19 Better to dwell in the wilderness,
Than with a contentious and angry
woman.

20 [a]*There is* desirable treasure,
And oil in the dwelling of the wise,
But a foolish man squanders it.

21 [a]He who follows righteousness and mercy
Finds life, righteousness, and honor.

22 A [a]wise *man* scales the city of the mighty,
And brings down the trusted stronghold.

23 [a]Whoever guards his mouth and tongue
Keeps his soul from troubles.

24 A proud *and* haughty *man*—"Scoffer" *is*
his name;
He acts with arrogant pride.

25 The [a]desire of the lazy *man* kills him,
For his hands refuse to labor.

26 He covets greedily all day long,
But the righteous [a]gives and does not
spare.

27 [a]The sacrifice of the wicked *is* an
abomination;
How much more *when* he brings it with
wicked intent!

28 A false witness shall perish,
But the man who hears *him* will speak
endlessly.

29 A wicked man hardens his face,
But *as for* the upright, he establishes[1] his
way.

30 [a]*There is* no wisdom or understanding
Or counsel against the LORD.

31 The horse *is* prepared for the day of battle,
But [a]deliverance *is* of the LORD.

**22** A [a]*good* name is to be chosen rather
than great riches,
Loving favor rather than silver and gold.

2 The [a]rich and the poor have this in common,
The [b]LORD *is* the maker of them all.

3 A prudent *man* foresees evil and hides
himself,
But the simple pass on and are [a]punished.

4 By humility *and* the fear of the LORD
*Are* riches and honor and life.

5 Thorns *and* snares *are* in the way of the
perverse;
He who guards his soul will be far from
them.

6 [a]Train up a child in the way he should go,
And when he is old he will not depart
from it.

**22:6** This verse, like the other proverbs, contains a wise statement that is usually true. Parents are to **train up**, or teach, their children **in the way** of the Lord. Not only are they to teach it purposefully, but they are to do it constantly—when they talk and sit and walk and lie down and get up (see Deut. 6:7–8). The most important training a child receives is the continual teaching and daily example of their parents' dependence on the Lord. This training doesn't guarantee a child will come to trust in Christ, but God will often use it to that end.

**21:11** [a] Prov. 19:25 **21:13** [a] [Matt. 7:2; 18:30–34] **21:14** [1] Literally *in the bosom* **21:16** [a] Ps. 49:14 **21:20** [a] Ps. 112:3 **21:21** [a] Matt. 5:6 **21:22** [a] Prov. 24:5 **21:23** [a] [James 3:2] **21:25** [a] Prov. 13:4 **21:26** [a] [Prov. 22:9] **21:27** [a] Jer. 6:20 **21:29** [1] Qere and Septuagint read *understands.* **21:30** [a] [Jer. 9:23, 24] **21:31** [a] Ps. 3:8 **22:1** [a] Eccl. 7:1 **22:2** [a] Prov. 29:13 [b] Job 31:15 **22:3** [a] Prov. 27:12 **22:6** [a] Eph. 6:4

7 The [a]rich rules over the poor,
And the borrower *is* servant to the lender.

8 He who sows iniquity will reap [a]sorrow,
And the rod of his anger will fail.

9 [a]He who has a generous eye will be [b]blessed,
For he gives of his bread to the poor.

10 [a]Cast out the scoffer, and contention will leave;
Yes, strife and reproach will cease.

11 [a]He who loves purity of heart
*And has* grace on his lips,
The king *will be* his friend.

12 The eyes of the LORD preserve knowledge,
But He overthrows the words of the faithless.

13 [a]The lazy *man* says, "*There is* a lion outside!
I shall be slain in the streets!"

14 [a]The mouth of an immoral woman *is* a deep pit;
[b]He who is abhorred by the LORD will fall there.

15 Foolishness *is* bound up in the heart of a child;
[a]The rod of correction will drive it far from him.

16 He who oppresses the poor to increase his *riches,*
*And* he who gives to the rich, *will* surely *come* to poverty.

*SAYINGS OF THE WISE*

17 Incline your ear and hear the words of the wise,
And apply your heart to my knowledge;
18 For *it is* a pleasant thing if you keep them within you;
Let them all be fixed upon your lips,
19 So that your trust may be in the LORD;
I have instructed you today, even you.
20 Have I not written to you excellent things
Of counsels and knowledge,
21 [a]That I may make you know the certainty of the words of truth,
[b]That you may answer words of truth
To those who send to you?

22 Do not rob the [a]poor because he *is* poor,
Nor oppress the afflicted at the gate;
23 [a]For the LORD will plead their cause,
And plunder the soul of those who plunder them.

24 Make no friendship with an angry man,
And with a [a]furious man do not go,
25 Lest you learn his ways
And set a snare for your soul.

26 [a]Do not be one of those who shakes hands in a pledge,
One of those who is surety for debts;
27 If you have nothing *with which* to pay,
Why should he take away your bed from under you?

28 [a]Do not remove the ancient landmark
Which your fathers have set.

22:7 [a] James 2:6 22:8 [a] Job 4:8 22:9 [a] 2 Cor. 9:6 [b] [Prov. 19:17] 22:10 [a] Ps. 101:5 22:11 [a] Ps. 101:6 22:13 [a] Prov. 26:13 22:14 [a] Prov. 2:16; 5:3; 7:5 [b] Eccl. 7:26 22:15 [a] Prov. 13:24; 23:13, 14 22:21 [a] Luke 1:3, 4 [b] 1 Pet. 3:15 22:22 [a] Ex. 23:6 22:23 [a] 1 Sam. 24:12 22:24 [a] Prov. 29:22 22:26 [a] Prov. 11:15 22:28 [a] Deut. 19:14; 27:17

LIVE THE TRUTH

## HAVING CHARACTER

**22:1** How do you have a good name—a good reputation? You might try always being on your best behavior when others are watching. That might work for a time, but eventually you'll slip up, let your guard down, or not realize people are watching. Instead, the Bible talks about the importance of having good character. Character is a deep, moral integrity that begins in the heart and overflows into our actions. Having good character means we aren't concerned about our behavior only when people are watching, but always, as we strive to stay true to God's calling and commands.

When we focus on being people of quality character, we realize it isn't about how we *seem* to others. Having character is about who we *truly* are. When we focus on ourselves and not on how others perceive us, we'll find people have thought well of us all along. That isn't our main goal, of course, pleasing God is, but it's a positive by-product. Having good character pleases God because it exemplifies a heart focused on what God says. When our character is solid, people will think well of us—and even if they don't, God will be glorified by our obedience.

29 Do you see a man *who* excels in his work?
He will stand before kings;
He will not stand before unknown *men.*

23 When you sit down to eat with a ruler,
Consider carefully what *is* before you;
2 And put a knife to your throat
If you *are* a man given to appetite.
3 Do not desire his delicacies,
For they *are* deceptive food.

4 [a]Do not overwork to be rich;
[b]Because of your own understanding, cease!
5 Will you set your eyes on that which is not?
For *riches* certainly make themselves wings;
They fly away like an eagle *toward* heaven.

6 Do not eat the bread of [a]a miser,[1]
Nor desire his delicacies;
7 For as he thinks in his heart, so *is* he.
"Eat and drink!" [a]he says to you,
But his heart is not with you.
8 The morsel you have eaten, you will vomit up,
And waste your pleasant words.

9 [a]Do not speak in the hearing of a fool,
For he will despise the wisdom of your words.

10 Do not remove the ancient landmark,
Nor enter the fields of the fatherless;
11 [a]For their Redeemer *is* mighty;
He will plead their cause against you.

**23:10** In ancient times, property lines were marked by stones. Moving a stone **landmark** was a way to steal land from someone else.

12 Apply your heart to instruction,
And your ears to words of knowledge.

13 [a]Do not withhold correction from a child,
For *if* you beat him with a rod, he will not die.
14 You shall beat him with a rod,
And deliver his soul from hell.[1]

15 My son, if your heart is wise,
My heart will rejoice—indeed, I myself;
16 Yes, my inmost being will rejoice
When your lips speak right things.

17 [a]Do not let your heart envy sinners,
But [b]*be zealous* for the fear of the LORD all the day;
18 [a]For surely there is a hereafter,
And your hope will not be cut off.

19 Hear, my son, and be wise;
And guide your heart in the way.
20 [a]Do not mix with winebibbers,
*Or* with gluttonous eaters of meat;
21 For the drunkard and the glutton will come to poverty,
And drowsiness will clothe *a man* with rags.

22 [a]Listen to your father who begot you,
And do not despise your mother when she is old.

23 [a]Buy the truth, and do not sell *it,*
*Also* wisdom and instruction and understanding.

24 [a]The father of the righteous will greatly rejoice,
And he who begets a wise *child* will delight in him.
25 Let your father and your mother be glad,
And let her who bore you rejoice.

26 My son, give me your heart,
And let your eyes observe my ways.
27 [a]For a harlot *is* a deep pit,
And a seductress *is* a narrow well.
28 [a]She also lies in wait as *for* a victim,
And increases the unfaithful among men.

29 [a]Who has woe?
Who has sorrow?
Who has contentions?
Who has complaints?
Who has wounds without cause?
Who [b]has redness of eyes?
30 [a]Those who linger long at the wine,
Those who go in search of [b]mixed wine.
31 Do not look on the wine when it is red,
When it sparkles in the cup,
*When* it swirls around smoothly;
32 At the last it bites like a serpent,
And stings like a viper.
33 Your eyes will see strange things,
And your heart will utter perverse things.
34 Yes, you will be like one who lies down in the midst of the sea,
Or like one who lies at the top of the mast, *saying:*
35 "They[a] have struck me, *but* I was not hurt;
They have beaten me, but I did not feel *it.*
When shall [b]I awake, that I may seek another *drink?*"

23:4 [a][1 Tim. 6:9, 10] [b]Rom. 12:16 23:6 [a]Deut. 15:9 [1]Literally *one who has an evil eye* 23:7 [a]Prov. 12:2 23:9 [a]Matt. 7:6 23:11 [a]Prov. 22:23 23:13 [a]Prov. 13:24 23:14 [1]Or *Sheol* 23:17 [a]Ps. 37:1 [b]Prov. 28:14 23:18 [a][Ps. 37:37] 23:20 [a]Is. 5:22 23:22 [a]Prov. 1:8 23:23 [a][Matt. 13:44] 23:24 [a]Prov. 10:1 23:27 [a]Prov. 22:14 23:28 [a]Prov. 7:12 23:29 [a]Is. 5:11, 22 [b]Gen. 49:12 23:30 [a][Eph. 5:18] [b]Ps. 75:8 23:35 [a]Jer. 5:3 [b]Eph. 4:19

24 Do not be [a]envious of evil men,
Nor desire to be with them;
2 For their heart devises violence,
And their lips talk of troublemaking.

3 Through wisdom a house is built,
And by understanding it is established;
4 By knowledge the rooms are filled
With all precious and pleasant riches.

5 [a]A wise man *is* strong,
Yes, a man of knowledge increases strength;
6 [a]For by wise counsel you will wage your own war,
And in a multitude of counselors *there is* safety.

7 [a]Wisdom *is* too lofty for a fool;
He does not open his mouth in the gate.

8 He who [a]plots to do evil
Will be called a schemer.
9 The devising of foolishness *is* sin,
And the scoffer *is* an abomination to men.

10 *If* you [a]faint in the day of adversity,
Your strength *is* small.

11 [a]Deliver *those who* are drawn toward death,
And hold back *those* stumbling to the slaughter.
12 If you say, "Surely we did not know this,"
Does not [a]He who weighs the hearts consider *it?*
He who keeps your soul, does He *not* know *it?*
And will He *not* render to *each* man
[b]according to his deeds?

13 My son, [a]eat honey because *it is* good,
And the honeycomb *which is* sweet to your taste;
14 [a]So *shall* the knowledge of wisdom *be* to your soul;
If you have found *it,* there is a prospect,
And your hope will not be cut off.

15 Do not lie in wait, O wicked *man,* against the dwelling of the righteous;
Do not plunder his resting place;
16 [a]For a righteous *man* may fall seven times
And rise again,
[b]But the wicked shall fall by calamity.

17 [a]Do not rejoice when your enemy falls,
And do not let your heart be glad when he stumbles;
18 Lest the LORD see *it,* and it displease Him,
And He turn away His wrath from him.

19 [a]Do not fret because of evildoers,
Nor be envious of the wicked;
20 For there will be no prospect for the evil *man;*
The lamp of the wicked will be put out.

21 My son, [a]fear the LORD and the king;
Do not associate with those given to change;

**24:21** The first three kings of Israel were all anointed by a prophet before they were officially crowned. Anointing involved pouring olive oil on the head of the king-to-be. The ritual was important because it indicated the king had been chosen by God. Questioning the king's authority was like questioning God's authority. When Saul was trying to kill him, David refused to retaliate because King Saul had been anointed by God.

24:1 [a]Ps. 1:1; 37:1 24:5 [a]Prov. 21:22 24:6 [a]Luke 14:31 24:7 [a]Ps. 10:5 24:8 [a]Rom. 1:30 24:10 [a]Heb. 12:3 24:11 [a]Ps. 82:4 24:12 [a]Prov. 21:2 [b]Ps. 62:12 24:13 [a]Song 5:1 24:14 [a]Ps. 19:10; 58:11 24:16 [a][Mic. 7:8] [b]Esth. 7:10 24:17 [a]Obad. 12 24:19 [a]Ps. 37:1 24:21 [a][1 Pet. 2:17]

APPLY THE TRUTH

## FAILURE

**24:16** What does failing look like? For many, it's a change of one letter to *falling*, like learning to ride a bike. Seeing failure this way can keep us from trying things. We don't want to fall. We don't want to look foolish, especially when it comes to something important, like our relationship with God. We want to do what is right, but so often we trip and fall. We sin. We don't prioritize God. We do our own thing. And as a result, we feel shame because of our "failure" when we go into God's presence.

This proverb doesn't define *failing* as falling though. Notice what it says: "A righteous man may fall seven times." How can someone be righteous *and* fall? More than that, in the Bible, the number seven often speaks of completion. So, a righteous person can *completely* fall! How can we fall like this and still be righteous? By getting back up. Failure is not falling; failure is not rising back up when you fall. The next time you fall—and you will—don't turn that fall into a failure. Get back up with God's help. Rest in His love and forgiveness. Keep moving toward what He has called you to do.

22 For their calamity will rise suddenly,
And who knows the ruin those two can bring?

## FURTHER SAYINGS OF THE WISE

23 These *things* also *belong* to the wise:

[a]*It is* not good to show partiality in judgment.
24 [a]He who says to the wicked, "You *are* righteous,"
Him the people will curse;
Nations will abhor him.
25 But those who rebuke *the wicked* will have [a]delight,
And a good blessing will come upon them.

26 He who gives a right answer kisses the lips.

27 [a]Prepare your outside work,
Make it fit for yourself in the field;
And afterward build your house.

28 [a]Do not be a witness against your neighbor without cause,
For would you deceive[1] with your lips?
29 [a]Do not say, "I will do to him just as he has done to me;
I will render to the man according to his work."

30 I went by the field of the lazy *man*,
And by the vineyard of the man devoid of understanding;
31 And there it was, [a]all overgrown with thorns;
Its surface was covered with nettles;
Its stone wall was broken down.
32 When I saw *it*, I considered *it* well;
I looked on *it and* received instruction:
33 [a]A little sleep, a little slumber,
A little folding of the hands to rest;
34 [a]So shall your poverty come *like* a prowler,
And your need like an armed man.

## FURTHER WISE SAYINGS OF SOLOMON

**25** These[a] also *are* proverbs of Solomon which the men of Hezekiah king of Judah copied:

2 [a]*It is* the glory of God to conceal a matter,
But the glory of kings *is* to search out a matter.

3 *As* the heavens for height and the earth for depth,
So the heart of kings *is* unsearchable.

4 [a]Take away the dross from silver,
And it will go to the silversmith *for* jewelry.
5 Take away the wicked from before the king,
And his throne will be established in [a]righteousness.

6 Do not exalt yourself in the presence of the king,
And do not stand in the place of the great;
7 [a]For *it is* better that he say to you,
"Come up here,"
Than that you should be put lower in the presence of the prince,
Whom your eyes have seen.

8 [a]Do not go hastily to court;
For what will you do in the end,
When your neighbor has put you to shame?
9 [a]Debate your case with your neighbor,
And do not disclose the secret to another;
10 Lest he who hears *it* expose your shame,
And your reputation be ruined.

11 A word fitly [a]spoken *is like* apples of gold
In settings of silver.
12 *Like* an earring of gold and an ornament of fine gold
*Is* a wise rebuker to an obedient ear.

13 [a]Like the cold of snow in time of harvest
*Is* a faithful messenger to those who send him,
For he refreshes the soul of his masters.

14 [a]Whoever falsely boasts of giving
*Is like* [b]clouds and wind without rain.

15 [a]By long forbearance a ruler is persuaded,
And a gentle tongue breaks a bone.

16 Have you found honey?
Eat only as much as you need,
Lest you be filled with it and vomit.

17 Seldom set foot in your neighbor's house,
Lest he become weary of you and hate you.

18 [a]A man who bears false witness against his neighbor
*Is like* a club, a sword, and a sharp arrow.

19 Confidence in an unfaithful *man* in time of trouble
*Is like* a bad tooth and a foot out of joint.

20 *Like* one who takes away a garment in cold weather,
*And like* vinegar on soda,
*Is* one who [a]sings songs to a heavy heart.

**24:23** [a] Lev. 19:15 **24:24** [a] Is. 5:23 **24:25** [a] Prov. 28:23 **24:27** [a] Prov. 27:23–27 **24:28** [a] Eph. 4:25 [1] Septuagint and Vulgate read *Do not deceive.* **24:29** [a] [Prov. 20:22] **24:31** [a] Gen. 3:18 **24:33** [a] Prov. 6:9, 10 **24:34** [a] Prov. 6:9–11 **25:1** [a] 1 Kin. 4:32 **25:2** [a] Deut. 29:29 **25:4** [a] 2 Tim. 2:21 **25:5** [a] Prov. 16:12; 20:8 **25:7** [a] Luke 14:7–11 **25:8** [a] Matt. 5:25 **25:9** [a] [Matt. 18:15] **25:11** [a] Prov. 15:23 **25:13** [a] Prov. 13:17 **25:14** [a] Prov. 20:6 [b] Jude 12 **25:15** [a] Prov. 15:1 **25:18** [a] Ps. 57:4 **25:20** [a] Dan. 6:18

21 [a]If your enemy is hungry, give him bread
to eat;
And if he is thirsty, give him water to
drink;
22 For *so* you will heap coals of fire on his
head,
[a]And the LORD will reward you.

## SEEING JESUS IN THE SCRIPTURE

**25:21–22** By loving our enemies, we live in the way of Jesus, who loved His enemies to the point of dying for us (see Rom. 5:8–10). Jesus taught that loving others in practical ways is how we'll be known as His followers (see Matt. 25:33–36).

23 The north wind brings forth rain,
And [a]a backbiting tongue an angry
countenance.

24 [a]*It is* better to dwell in a corner of a housetop,
Than in a house shared with a
contentious woman.

25 *As* cold water to a weary soul,
So *is* [a]good news from a far country.

26 A righteous *man* who falters before the
wicked
*Is like* a murky spring and a polluted well.

27 *It is* not good to eat much honey;
So [a]to seek one's own glory *is not* glory.

28 [a]Whoever *has* no rule over his own spirit
*Is like* a city broken down, without walls.

**26** As snow in summer [a]and rain in harvest,
So honor is not fitting for a fool.

2 Like a flitting sparrow, like a flying swallow,
So [a]a curse without cause shall not alight.

3 [a]A whip for the horse,
A bridle for the donkey,
And a rod for the fool's back.
4 Do not answer a fool according to his
folly,
Lest you also be like him.
5 [a]Answer a fool according to his folly,
Lest he be wise in his own eyes.
6 He who sends a message by the hand of a
fool
Cuts off *his own* feet *and* drinks violence.
7 *Like* the legs of the lame that hang limp
*Is* a proverb in the mouth of fools.
8 Like one who binds a stone in a sling
*Is* he who gives honor to a fool.
9 *Like* a thorn *that* goes into the hand of a
drunkard
*Is* a proverb in the mouth of fools.
10 The great *God* who formed everything
Gives the fool *his* hire and the
transgressor *his* wages.[1]
11 [a]As a dog returns to his own vomit,
[b]*So* a fool repeats his folly.
12 [a]Do you see a man wise in his own eyes?
*There is* more hope for a fool than for him.

13 The lazy *man* says, "*There is* a lion in the
road!
A fierce lion *is* in the streets!"
14 As a door turns on its hinges,
So *does* the lazy *man* on his bed.
15 The [a]lazy *man* buries his hand in the
bowl;[1]
It wearies him to bring it back to his
mouth.
16 The lazy *man is* wiser in his own eyes
Than seven men who can answer sensibly.

17 He who passes by *and* meddles in a
quarrel not his own
*Is like* one who takes a dog by the ears.

18 Like a madman who throws firebrands,
arrows, and death,
19 *Is* the man *who* deceives his neighbor,
And says, [a]"I was only joking!"

20 Where *there is* no wood, the fire goes out;
And where *there is* no talebearer, strife
ceases.
21 [a]*As* charcoal *is* to burning coals, and wood
to fire,
So *is* a contentious man to kindle strife.
22 The words of a talebearer *are* like tasty
trifles,
And they go down into the inmost body.

**26:4–5** Some people see these two proverbs here contradictory, but that isn't necessarily true. The phrase appears twice as a play on words with two shades of meaning. On the one hand, it means avoid the temptation to stoop to his level; that is, do not use his methods, **lest you also be like him**. On the other hand, it means avoid the temptation to ignore him altogether; that is, respond in some way, or else he will become **wise in his own eyes** and his folly will get worse.

**25:21** [a]Rom. 12:20 **25:22** [a]2 Sam. 16:12 **25:23** [a]Ps. 101:5 **25:24** [a]Prov. 19:13 **25:25** [a]Prov. 15:30 **25:27** [a]Prov. 27:2 **25:28** [a]Prov. 16:32 **26:1** [a]1 Sam. 12:17 **26:2** [a]Deut. 23:5 **26:3** [a]Ps. 32:9 **26:5** [a]Matt. 16:1–4 **26:10** [1]The Hebrew is difficult; ancient and modern translators differ greatly. **26:11** [a]2 Pet. 2:22 [b]Ex. 8:15 **26:12** [a][Rev. 3:17] **26:15** [a]Prov. 19:24 [1]Compare 19:24 **26:19** [a]Eph. 5:4 **26:21** [a]Prov. 15:18

23 Fervent lips with a wicked heart
*Are like* earthenware covered with silver
dross.

24 He who hates, disguises *it* with his lips,
And lays up deceit within himself;
25 [a]When he speaks kindly, do not believe
him,
For *there are* seven abominations in his
heart;
26 *Though his* hatred is covered by deceit,
His wickedness will be revealed before the
assembly.

27 [a]Whoever digs a pit will fall into it,
And he who rolls a stone will have it roll
back on him.

28 A lying tongue hates *those who are*
crushed by it,
And a flattering mouth works [a]ruin.

27 Do[a] not boast about tomorrow,
For you do not know what a day may
bring forth.

2 [a]Let another man praise you, and not your
own mouth;
A stranger, and not your own lips.

3 A stone *is* heavy and sand *is* weighty,
But a fool's wrath *is* heavier than both of
them.

4 Wrath *is* cruel and anger a torrent,
But [a]who *is* able to stand before jealousy?

5 [a]Open rebuke *is* better
Than love carefully concealed.

6 Faithful *are* the wounds of a friend,
But the kisses of an enemy *are* [a]deceitful.

7 A satisfied soul loathes the honeycomb,
But to a hungry soul every bitter thing *is*
sweet.

8 Like a bird that wanders from its nest
*Is* a man who wanders from his place.

9 Ointment and perfume delight the heart,
And the sweetness of a man's friend *gives*
*delight* by hearty counsel.

10 Do not forsake your own friend or your
father's friend,
Nor go to your brother's house in the day
of your calamity;
[a]Better *is* a neighbor nearby than a brother
far away.

11 My son, be wise, and make my heart glad,
[a]That I may answer him who reproaches me.

12 A prudent *man* foresees evil *and* hides
himself;
The simple pass on *and* are [a]punished.

13 Take the garment of him who is surety for
a stranger,
And hold it in pledge *when* he is surety for
a seductress.

14 He who blesses his friend with a loud
voice, rising early in the morning,
It will be counted a curse to him.

15 A [a]continual dripping on a very rainy day
And a contentious woman are alike;
16 Whoever restrains her restrains the wind,
And grasps oil with his right hand.

17 *As* iron sharpens iron,
So a man sharpens the countenance of
his friend.

26:25 [a] Ps. 28:3 26:27 [a] Ps. 7:15 26:28 [a] Prov. 29:5 27:1 [a] James 4:13–16 27:2 [a] Prov. 25:27 27:4 [a] 1 John 3:12 27:5 [a] [Prov. 28:23] 27:6 [a] Matt. 26:49 27:10 [a] Prov. 17:17; 18:24 27:11 [a] Prov. 10:1; 23:15–26 27:12 [a] Prov. 22:3 27:15 [a] Prov. 19:13

APPLY THE TRUTH

## RELATIONSHIPS

**27:17** God cares about your friends. In fact, He cares about every detail of your life. From the hairs on your head to the friends who make you laugh. Part of the reason God cares about those details is because He is shaping your life. He wants to form you into an active member of His good family. And one of the ways we're formed the most is through the people we hang out with. As this proverb says, our friends can sharpen us.

We each need two types of friends: friends who invest in us and shape us, and friends we invest in and shape. We need people in our lives who encourage us to grow in our relationship with God, be the people God wants us to be, and walk in God's good ways. We also need people we encourage to do those same things. When we don't have people investing in us, we can too easily get dragged away from God's calling on our lives. When we aren't investing in others, we can turn inward. But when we have the right relationships, we'll be like iron—strong, useful, and resilient.

18 [a]Whoever keeps the fig tree will eat its fruit;
So he who waits on his master will be honored.

19 As in water face *reflects* face,
So a man's heart *reveals* the man.

20 [a]Hell[1] and Destruction[2] are never full;
So [b]the eyes of man are never satisfied.

21 [a]The refining pot *is* for silver and the furnace for gold,
And a man *is valued* by what others say of him.

22 [a]Though you grind a fool in a mortar with a pestle along with crushed grain,
*Yet* his foolishness will not depart from him.

23 Be diligent to know the state of your [a]flocks,
*And* attend to your herds;
24 For riches *are* not forever,
Nor does a crown *endure* to all generations.
25 [a]*When* the hay is removed, and the tender grass shows itself,
And the herbs of the mountains are gathered in,
26 The lambs *will provide* your clothing,
And the goats the price of a field;
27 *You shall have* enough goats' milk for your food,
For the food of your household,
And the nourishment of your maidservants.

**28** The [a]wicked flee when no one pursues,
But the righteous are bold as a lion.

2 Because of the transgression of a land, many *are* its princes;
But by a man of understanding *and* knowledge
Right will be prolonged.

3 [a]A poor man who oppresses the poor
*Is like* a driving rain which leaves no food.

4 [a]Those who forsake the law praise the wicked,
[b]But such as keep the law contend with them.

5 [a]Evil men do not understand justice,
But [b]those who seek the LORD understand all.

6 Better *is* the poor who walks in his integrity
Than one perverse *in his* ways, though he *be* rich.

7 Whoever keeps the law *is* a discerning son,
But a companion of gluttons shames his father.

8 One who increases his possessions by usury and extortion
Gathers it for him who will pity the poor.

9 One who turns away his ear from hearing the law,
[a]Even his prayer *is* an abomination.

**28:8** God's law prohibited people from charging **usury**, or interest, on loans made to **poor** people. Borrowers couldn't be forced to give up their coats as collateral for loans. Lenders weren't allowed to use force to collect payment. Instead, every person in the community was responsible for taking care of the poor, the widowed, the orphaned, and the disabled members of society.

10 [a]Whoever causes the upright to go astray in an evil way,
He himself will fall into his own pit;
[b]But the blameless will inherit good.

11 The rich man *is* wise in his own eyes,
But the poor who has understanding searches him out.

12 When the righteous rejoice, *there is* great [a]glory;
But when the wicked arise, men hide themselves.

13 [a]He who covers his sins will not prosper,
But whoever confesses and forsakes *them* will have mercy.

14 Happy *is* the man who is always reverent,
But he who hardens his heart will fall into calamity.

15 [a]*Like* a roaring lion and a charging bear
[b]*Is* a wicked ruler over poor people.

16 A ruler who lacks understanding *is* a great [a]oppressor,
*But* he who hates covetousness will prolong *his* days.

17 [a]A man burdened with bloodshed will flee into a pit;
Let no one help him.

27:18 [a][1 Cor. 3:8; 9:7–13] 27:20 [a]Hab. 2:5 [b]Eccl. 1:8; 4:8 [1]Or *Sheol* [2]Hebrew *Abaddon* 27:21 [a]Prov. 17:3 27:22 [a]Jer. 5:3 27:23 [a]Prov. 24:27 27:25 [a]Ps. 104:14 28:1 [a]Ps. 53:5 28:3 [a]Matt. 18:28 28:4 [a]Ps. 49:18 [b]1 Kin. 18:18 28:5 [a]Ps. 92:6 [b]John 17:17 28:9 [a]Prov. 15:8 28:10 [a]Prov. 26:27 [b][Matt. 6:33] 28:12 [a]Prov. 11:10; 29:2 28:13 [a]Ps. 32:3–5 28:15 [a]1 Pet. 5:8 [b]Matt. 2:16 28:16 [a]Eccl. 10:16 28:17 [a]Gen. 9:6

18 Whoever walks blamelessly will be saved,
But *he who is* perverse *in his* ways will
suddenly fall.

19 [a]He who tills his land will have plenty of
bread,
But he who follows frivolity will have
poverty enough!

20 A faithful man will abound with blessings,
[a]But he who hastens to be rich will not go
unpunished.

21 [a]To show partiality *is* not good,
[b]Because for a piece of bread a man will
transgress.

22 A man with an evil eye hastens after riches,
And does not consider that [a]poverty will
come upon him.

23 [a]He who rebukes a man will find more
favor afterward
Than he who flatters with the tongue.

24 Whoever robs his father or his mother,
And says, "*It is* no transgression,"
The same [a]*is* companion to a destroyer.

25 [a]He who is of a proud heart stirs up strife,
[b]But he who trusts in the LORD will be
prospered.

26 He who [a]trusts in his own heart is a fool,
But whoever walks wisely will be delivered.

27 [a]He who gives to the poor will not lack,
But he who hides his eyes will have many
curses.

28 When the wicked arise, [a]men hide
themselves;
But when they perish, the righteous increase.

**29** He[a] who is often rebuked, *and* hardens
*his* neck,
Will suddenly be destroyed, and that
without remedy.

2 When the righteous are in authority, the
[a]people rejoice;
But when a wicked *man* rules, [b]the people
groan.

3 Whoever loves wisdom makes his father
rejoice,
But a companion of harlots wastes *his*
wealth.

4 The king establishes the land by justice,
But he who receives bribes overthrows it.

5 A man who [a]flatters his neighbor
Spreads a net for his feet.

6 By transgression an evil man is snared,
But the righteous sings and rejoices.

7 The righteous [a]considers the cause of the
poor,
*But* the wicked does not understand *such*
knowledge.

8 Scoffers [a]set a city aflame,
But wise *men* turn away wrath.

9 *If* a wise man contends with a foolish
man,
[a]Whether *the fool* rages or laughs, *there is*
no peace.

10 [a]The bloodthirsty hate the blameless,
But the upright seek his well-being.[1]

11 A fool vents all his [a]feelings,[1]
But a wise *man* holds them back.

12 If a ruler pays attention to lies,
All his servants *become* wicked.

13 The poor *man* and the oppressor have this
in common:
[a]The LORD gives light to the eyes of both.

14 The king who judges the [a]poor with truth,
His throne will be established forever.

15 The rod and rebuke give [a]wisdom,
But a child left *to himself* brings shame to
his mother.

16 When the wicked are multiplied,
transgression increases;
But the righteous will see their [a]fall.

17 Correct your son, and he will give you
rest;
Yes, he will give delight to your soul.

18 [a]Where *there is* no revelation,[1] the people
cast off restraint;
But [b]happy *is* he who keeps the law.

19 A servant will not be corrected by mere
words;
For though he understands, he will not
respond.

**28:19** [a]Prov. 12:11; 20:13 **28:20** [a]1 Tim. 6:9 **28:21** [a]Prov. 18:5 [b]Ezek. 13:19 **28:22** [a]Prov. 21:5 **28:23** [a]Prov. 27:5, 6 **28:24** [a]Prov. 18:9 **28:25** [a]Prov. 13:10 [b]1 Tim. 6:6 **28:26** [a]Prov. 3:5 **28:27** [a]Deut. 15:7 **28:28** [a]Job 24:4 **29:1** [a]2 Chr. 36:16 **29:2** [a]Prov. 28:12 [b]Esth. 4:3 **29:5** [a]Prov. 26:28 **29:7** [a]Job 29:16 **29:8** [a]Prov. 11:11 **29:9** [a]Matt. 11:17 **29:10** [a]1 John 3:12 [1]Literally *soul* **29:11** [a]Prov. 14:33 [1]Literally *spirit* **29:13** [a][Matt. 5:45] **29:14** [a]Is. 11:4 **29:15** [a]Prov. 22:15 **29:16** [a]Ps. 37:34 **29:18** [a]1 Sam. 3:1 [b]John 13:17 [1]Or *prophetic vision*

20 Do you see a man hasty in his words?
[a] *There is* more hope for a fool than for him.

21 He who pampers his servant from childhood
Will have him as a son in the end.

22 [a] An angry man stirs up strife,
And a furious man abounds in transgression.

23 [a] A man's pride will bring him low,
But the humble in spirit will retain honor.

24 Whoever is a partner with a thief hates his own life;
[a] He swears to tell the truth,[1] but reveals nothing.

25 [a] The fear of man brings a snare,
But whoever trusts in the LORD shall be safe.

26 [a] Many seek the ruler's favor,
But justice for man *comes* from the LORD.

27 An unjust man *is* an abomination to the righteous,
And *he who is* upright in the way *is* an abomination to the wicked.

### THE WISDOM OF AGUR

30 The words of Agur the son of Jakeh, *his* utterance. This man declared to Ithiel—to Ithiel and Ucal:

2 [a] Surely I *am* more stupid than *any* man,
And do not have the understanding of a man.
3 I neither learned wisdom
Nor have [a] knowledge of the Holy One.

4 [a] Who has ascended into heaven, or descended?
[b] Who has gathered the wind in His fists?
Who has bound the waters in a garment?
Who has established all the ends of the earth?
What *is* His name, and what *is* His Son's name,
If you know?

5 [a] Every word of God *is* pure;
[b] He *is* a shield to those who put their trust in Him.
6 [a] Do not add to His words,
Lest He rebuke you, and you be found a liar.

7 Two *things* I request of You
(Deprive me not before I die):
8 Remove falsehood and lies far from me;
Give me neither poverty nor riches—
[a] Feed me with the food allotted to me;
9 [a] Lest I be full and deny *You*,
And say, "Who *is* the LORD?"
Or lest I be poor and steal,
And profane the name of my God.

10 Do not malign a servant to his master,
Lest he curse you, and you be found guilty.

11 *There is* a generation *that* curses its [a] father,
And does not bless its mother.
12 *There is* a generation [a] *that is* pure in its own eyes,
*Yet* is not washed from its filthiness.
13 *There is* a generation—oh, how [a] lofty are their eyes!
And their eyelids are lifted up.
14 [a] *There is* a generation whose teeth *are like* swords,
And whose fangs *are like* knives,
[b] To devour the poor from off the earth,
And the needy from *among* men.

15 The leech has two daughters—
Give *and* Give!

There are three *things that* are never satisfied,
Four never say, "Enough!":
16 [a] The grave,[1]
The barren womb,
The earth *that* is not satisfied with water—
And the fire never says, "Enough!"

17 [a] The eye *that* mocks *his* father,
And scorns obedience to *his* mother,
The ravens of the valley will pick it out,
And the young eagles will eat it.

18 There are three *things which* are too wonderful for me,
Yes, four *which* I do not understand:
19 The way of an eagle in the air,
The way of a serpent on a rock,
The way of a ship in the midst of the sea,
And the way of a man with a virgin.

20 This *is* the way of an adulterous woman:
She eats and wipes her mouth,
And says, "I have done no wickedness."

21 For three *things* the earth is perturbed,
Yes, for four it cannot bear up:
22 [a] For a servant when he reigns,
A fool when he is filled with food,

29:20 [a] Prov. 26:12 29:22 [a] Prov. 26:21 29:23 [a] Is. 66:2 29:24 [a] Lev. 5:1 [1] Literally *hears the adjuration* 29:25 [a] Gen. 12:12; 20:2 29:26 [a] Ps. 20:9 30:2 [a] Ps. 73:22 30:3 [a] [Prov. 9:10] 30:4 [a] [John 3:13] [b] Job 38:4 30:5 [a] Ps. 12:6; 19:8; 119:140 [b] Ps. 18:30; 84:11; 115:9–11 30:6 [a] Deut. 4:2; 12:32 30:8 [a] Matt. 6:11 30:9 [a] Deut. 8:12–14 30:11 [a] Ex. 21:17 30:12 [a] Luke 18:11 30:13 [a] Prov. 6:17 30:14 [a] Job 29:17 [b] Amos 8:4 30:16 [a] Prov. 27:20 [1] Or *Sheol* 30:17 [a] Gen. 9:22 30:22 [a] Prov. 19:10

23 A hateful *woman* when she is married,
And a maidservant who succeeds her mistress.

24 There are four *things which* are little on the earth,
But they *are* exceedingly wise:
25 [a]The ants *are* a people not strong,
Yet they prepare their food in the summer;
26 [a]The rock badgers[1] are a feeble folk,
Yet they make their homes in the crags;
27 The locusts have no king,
Yet they all advance in ranks;
28 The spider[1] skillfully grasps with its hands,
And it is in kings' palaces.

29 There are three *things which* are majestic in pace,
Yes, four *which* are stately in walk:
30 A lion, *which is* mighty among beasts
And does not turn away from any;
31 A greyhound,[1]
A male goat also,
And a king *whose* troops *are* with him.[2]

32 If you have been foolish in exalting yourself,
Or if you have devised evil, [a]*put your* hand on *your* mouth.
33 For *as* the churning of milk produces butter,
And wringing the nose produces blood,
So the forcing of wrath produces strife.

## THE WORDS OF KING LEMUEL'S MOTHER

31 The words of King Lemuel, the utterance which his mother taught him:

2 What, my son?
And what, son of my womb?
And what, [a]son of my vows?
3 [a]Do not give your strength to women,
Nor your ways [b]to that which destroys kings.

4 [a]*It is* not for kings, O Lemuel,
*It is* not for kings to drink wine,
Nor for princes intoxicating drink;
5 [a]Lest they drink and forget the law,
And pervert the justice of all the afflicted.
6 [a]Give strong drink to him who is perishing,
And wine to those who are bitter of heart.
7 Let him drink and forget his poverty,
And remember his misery no more.
8 [a]Open your mouth for the speechless,
In the cause of all *who are* appointed to die.[1]
9 Open your mouth, [a]judge righteously,
And [b]plead the cause of the poor and needy.

## THE VIRTUOUS WIFE

10 [a]Who[1] can find a virtuous[2] wife?
For her worth *is* far above rubies.

**31:10** Proverbs 31:10–31 is an acrostic poem; each verse begins with a successive letter of the Hebrew alphabet from *aleph*, the first letter, to *tav*, the last. As the Book of Proverbs begins with a Prologue (Prov. 1:1–7), which gives the goals of wisdom in general terms, so now it concludes with this Epilogue, which presents them in a case study.

11 The heart of her husband safely trusts her;
So he will have no lack of gain.
12 She does him good and not evil
All the days of her life.
13 She seeks wool and flax,
And willingly works with her hands.
14 She is like the merchant ships,
She brings her food from afar.
15 [a]She also rises while it is yet night,
And [b]provides food for her household,
And a portion for her maidservants.
16 She considers a field and buys it;
From her profits she plants a vineyard.
17 She girds herself with strength,
And strengthens her arms.
18 She perceives that her merchandise *is* good,
And her lamp does not go out by night.
19 She stretches out her hands to the distaff,
And her hand holds the spindle.
20 [a]She extends her hand to the poor,
Yes, she reaches out her hands to the needy.
21 She is not afraid of snow for her household,
For all her household *is* clothed with scarlet.
22 She makes tapestry for herself;
Her clothing *is* fine linen and purple.
23 [a]Her husband is known in the gates,
When he sits among the elders of the land.

**30:25** [a] Prov. 6:6 **30:26** [a] Ps. 104:18 [1] Or *hyraxes* **30:28** [1] Or *lizard* **30:31** [1] Exact identity unknown [2] A Jewish tradition reads *a king against whom there is no uprising.* **30:32** [a] Mic. 7:16 **31:2** [a] Is. 49:15 **31:3** [a] Prov. 5:9 [b] Deut. 17:17; 1 Kin. 11:1; Neh. 13:26; Prov. 7:26; Hos. 4:11 **31:4** [a] Eccl. 10:17 **31:5** [a] Hos. 4:11 **31:6** [a] Ps. 104:15 **31:8** [a] Job 29:15, 16; Ps. 82 [1] Literally *sons of passing away* **31:9** [a] Lev. 19:15; Deut. 1:16 [b] Job 29:12; Is. 1:17; Jer. 22:16 **31:10** [a] Ruth 3:11; Prov. 12:4; 19:14 [1] Verses 10 through 31 are an alphabetic acrostic in Hebrew (compare Psalm 119). [2] Literally *a wife of valor,* in the sense of all forms of excellence **31:15** [a] Prov. 20:13; Rom. 12:11 [b] Luke 12:42 **31:20** [a] Deut. 15:11; Job 31:16–20; Prov. 22:9; Rom. 12:13; Eph. 4:28; Heb. 13:16 **31:23** [a] Prov. 12:4

24 She makes linen garments and sells *them,*
And supplies sashes for the merchants.
25 Strength and honor *are* her clothing;
She shall rejoice in time to come.
26 She opens her mouth with wisdom,
And on her tongue *is* the law of
kindness.
27 She watches over the ways of her
household,
And does not eat the bread of idleness.
28 Her children rise up and call her blessed;
Her husband *also,* and he praises her:
29 "Many daughters have done well,
But you excel them all."
30 Charm *is* deceitful and beauty *is* passing,
But a woman *who* fears the LORD, she
shall be praised.
31 Give her of the fruit of her hands,
And let her own works praise her in the
gates.

# *The Book of* ECCLESIASTES

**AUTHOR**
Solomon

**KEY VERSE**
Ecclesiastes 12:13

**READING TIME**
41 minutes

The keyword in Ecclesiastes is *vanity*, "the futile emptiness of trying to be happy apart from God." Solomon, referring to himself as "the Preacher" (Eccl. 1:1, 12), the wisest and richest king in Israel's history, looked at life "under the sun" (1:9). From a human perspective, he declared it was all vanity. Power, popularity, prestige, pleasure—none of these can fill the God-shaped void in a person's life. Only God Himself can fill that emptiness. However, once seen from God's perspective, life takes on great meaning and purpose, which caused Solomon to exclaim, "Eat . . . drink . . . rejoice . . . do good . . . live joyfully . . . fear God . . . keep His commandments!" Skepticism and despair melt away when one sees life as a daily gift from God to be used for God.

**Occasion:** Solomon wrote Ecclesiastes to warn the people of his kingdom of their need to walk by the wisdom God gave to them (Eccl. 12:9–14).

**Main Point:** Life is meaningless apart from God.

**Big Ideas:** God is the greatest treasure in the world. Pursuing anything in life apart from God will lead only to disappointment and emptiness. Your life has purpose, and that purpose is found in knowing, loving, and serving God.

## OUTLINE:

I. The Search for Meaning in Life (chs. 1–2)
II. The Injustice and Disappointment of Life (chs. 3–6)
III. The Value of Practical Wisdom (chs. 7–8)
IV. The Uncertainty of the Future (chs. 9–10)
V. The Solution of Seeking God (chs. 11–12)

**c. 971–931 BC**
Song of Solomon written

**970 BC**
Solomon becomes king of Israel

**967 BC**
Solomon begins construction of the temple

**c. 950–700 BC**
Proverbs written

**c. 935 BC**
**Ecclesiastes written**

**930 BC**
The kingdom is divided

**722 BC**
The Assyrians defeat Israel

**c. 700 BC**
Proverbs compiled

### *THE VANITY OF LIFE*

1 The words of the Preacher, the son of David,
[a]king in Jerusalem.

2 "Vanity[a][1] of vanities," says the Preacher;
"Vanity of vanities, [b]all *is* vanity."

> **1:2** This phrase translates the Hebrew superlative, familiar from such phrases as "Song of Songs" and "holy of holies." Here it might express "the ultimate absurdity" or "utter emptiness." **Vanity** means "breath" or "vapor" and thus speaks of life as "quickly passing." Life is like a vapor; indeed, it's like the thinnest of vapors. Wherever we read the word *vanity* in Ecclesiastes, we should think not of what is "meaningless," but of what is "quickly passing" (Eccl. 1:14; 6:12). This key term is found thirty-eight times in the Book of Ecclesiastes, but only thirty-four times throughout the rest of the Old Testament. The teaching of the **Preacher** is for others to realize life is fleeting and needs to be savored and enjoyed as a gift from God.

3 [a]What profit has a man from all his labor
In which he toils under the sun?
4 *One* generation passes away, and *another*
generation comes;
[a]But the earth abides forever.
5 [a]The sun also rises, and the sun goes down,
And hastens to the place where it arose.
6 [a]The wind goes toward the south,
And turns around to the north;
The wind whirls about continually,
And comes again on its circuit.
7 [a]All the rivers run into the sea,
Yet the sea *is* not full;
To the place from which the rivers come,
There they return again.
8 All things *are* full of labor;
Man cannot express *it*.
[a]The eye is not satisfied with seeing,
Nor the ear filled with hearing.

9 [a]That which has been *is* what will be,
That which *is* done is what will be done,
And *there is* nothing new under the sun.
10 Is there anything of which it may be said,
"See, this *is* new"?
It has already been in ancient times
before us.
11 *There is* [a]no remembrance of former
*things*,
Nor will there be any remembrance of
*things* that are to come
By *those* who will come after.

### *THE GRIEF OF WISDOM*

12 I, the Preacher, was king over Israel in
Jerusalem. 13 And I set my heart to seek and
[a]search out by wisdom concerning all that is
done under heaven; [b]this burdensome task God
has given to the sons of man, by which they may
be exercised. 14 I have seen all the works that are
done under the sun; and indeed, all *is* vanity and
grasping for the wind.

15 [a]*What is* crooked cannot be made straight,
And what is lacking cannot be numbered.

16 I communed with my heart, saying, "Look,
I have attained greatness, and have gained
[a]more wisdom than all who were before me
in Jerusalem. My heart has understood great
wisdom and knowledge." 17 [a]And I set my heart
to know wisdom and to know madness and folly.
I perceived that this also is grasping for the
wind.

18 For [a]in much wisdom *is* much grief,
And he who increases knowledge
increases sorrow.

### *THE VANITY OF PLEASURE*

*(cf. 1 Kin. 4:20–28)*

2 I said [a]in my heart, "Come now, I will test you
with [b]mirth; therefore enjoy pleasure"; but
surely, [c]this also *was* vanity. 2 I said of laughter—
"Madness!"; and of mirth, "What does it accom-
plish?" 3 [a]I searched in my heart *how* to gratify
my flesh with wine, while guiding my heart with
wisdom, and how to lay hold on folly, till I might
see what *was* [b]good for the sons of men to do
under heaven all the days of their lives.
4 I made my works great, I built myself
[a]houses, and planted myself vineyards. 5 I made
myself gardens and orchards, and I planted
all *kinds* of fruit trees in them. 6 I made myself
water pools from which to water the growing
trees of the grove. 7 I acquired male and female
servants, and had servants born in my house.
Yes, I had greater possessions of herds and flocks
than all who were in Jerusalem before me. 8 [a]I
also gathered for myself silver and gold and the
special treasures of kings and of the provinces.
I acquired male and female singers, the delights
of the sons of men, *and* musical instruments[1]
of all kinds.
9 [a]So I became great and excelled [b]more than
all who were before me in Jerusalem. Also my
wisdom remained with me.

**1:1** [a] Prov. 1:1 **1:2** [a] Ps. 39:5, 6; 62:9; 144:4 [b] [Rom. 8:20, 21] [1] Or *Absurdity, Frustration, Futility, Nonsense;* and so throughout this book **1:3** [a] Eccl. 2:22; 3:9 **1:4** [a] Ps. 104:5; 119:90 **1:5** [a] Ps. 19:4–6 **1:6** [a] John 3:8 **1:7** [a] [Jer. 5:22] **1:8** [a] Prov. 27:20 **1:9** [a] Eccl. 3:15 **1:11** [a] Eccl. 2:16 **1:13** [a] [Eccl. 7:25; 8:16, 17] [b] Eccl. 3:10 **1:15** [a] Eccl. 7:13 **1:16** [a] 1 Kin. 3:12, 13 **1:17** [a] Eccl. 2:3, 12; 7:23, 25 **1:18** [a] Eccl. 12:12 **2:1** [a] Luke 12:19 [b] [Eccl. 7:4; 8:15] [c] Eccl. 1:2 **2:3** [a] Eccl. 1:17 [b] [Eccl. 3:12, 13; 5:18; 6:12] **2:4** [a] 1 Kin. 7:1–12 **2:8** [a] 1 Kin. 9:28; 10:10, 14, 21 [1] Exact meaning unknown **2:9** [a] Eccl. 1:16 [b] 2 Chr. 9:22

10 Whatever my eyes desired I did not keep
from them.
I did not withhold my heart from any
pleasure,
For my heart rejoiced in all my labor;
And [a]this was my reward from all my
labor.
11 Then I looked on all the works that my
hands had done
And on the labor in which I had toiled;
And indeed all *was* [a]vanity and grasping
for the wind.
*There was* no profit under the sun.

## SEEING JESUS IN THE SCRIPTURE

**2:11** This is the central message of Ecclesiastes: anything done apart from living for God is meaningless. Jesus told this to the crowds who only followed Him for His miracles (see John 6:27). Meaning and contentment aren't found in gifts, but in knowing their Giver and living for Him.

### *THE END OF THE WISE AND THE FOOL*

12 Then I turned myself to consider wisdom
[a]and madness and folly;
For what *can* the man *do* who succeeds
the king?—
*Only* what he has already [b]done.
13 Then I saw that wisdom [a]excels folly
As light excels darkness.
14 [a]The wise man's eyes *are* in his head,
But the fool walks in darkness.
Yet I myself perceived
That [b]the same event happens to them all.

15 So I said in my heart,
"As it happens to the fool,
It also happens to me,
And why was I then more wise?"
Then I said in my heart,
"This also *is* vanity."
16 For *there is* [a]no more remembrance of the
wise than of the fool forever,
Since all that now *is* will be forgotten in
the days to come.
And how does a wise *man* die?
As the fool!

17 Therefore I hated life because the work that
was done under the sun *was* distressing to me,
for all *is* vanity and grasping for the wind.
18 Then I hated all my labor in which I had
toiled under the sun, because [a]I must leave it
to the man who will come after me. 19 And who
knows whether he will be wise or a fool? Yet he
will rule over all my labor in which I toiled and
in which I have shown myself wise under the
sun. This also *is* vanity. 20 Therefore I turned my
heart and despaired of all the labor in which I
had toiled under the sun. 21 For there is a man
whose labor *is* with wisdom, knowledge, and
skill; yet he must leave his heritage to a man
who has not labored for it. This also *is* vanity
and a great evil. 22 [a]For what has man for all
his labor, and for the striving of his heart with
which he has toiled under the sun? 23 For all his
days *are* [a]sorrowful, and his work burdensome;
even in the night his heart takes no rest. This
also is vanity.
24 [a]Nothing *is* better for a man *than* that he
should eat and drink, and *that* his soul should
enjoy good in his labor. This also, I saw, was from
the hand of God. 25 For who can eat, or who can
have enjoyment, more than I?[1] 26 For *God* gives
[a]wisdom and knowledge and joy to a man who
*is* good in His sight; but to the sinner He gives
the work of gathering and collecting, that [b]he
may give to *him who is* good before God. This
also *is* vanity and grasping for the wind.

### *EVERYTHING HAS ITS TIME*

3 To everything *there is* a season,
A [a]time for every purpose under heaven:

2 A time to be born,
And [a]a time to die;
A time to plant,
And a time to pluck *what is* planted;
3 A time to kill,
And a time to heal;
A time to break down,
And a time to build up;
4 A time to [a]weep,
And a time to laugh;
A time to mourn,
And a time to dance;
5 A time to cast away stones,
And a time to gather stones;
[a]A time to embrace,
And a time to refrain from embracing;
6 A time to gain,
And a time to lose;
A time to keep,
And a time to throw away;
7 A time to tear,
And a time to sew;
[a]A time to keep silence,
And a time to [b]speak;
8 A time to love,
And a time to [a]hate;
A time of war,
And a time of peace.

2:10 [a] Eccl. 3:22; 5:18; 9:9 2:11 [a] Eccl. 1:3, 14 2:12 [a] Eccl. 1:17; 7:25 [b] Eccl. 1:9 2:13 [a] Eccl. 7:11, 12, 19; 9:18; 10:10 2:14 [a] Prov. 17:24 [b] Ps. 49:10 2:16 [a] Eccl. 1:11; 4:16 2:18 [a] Ps. 49:10 2:22 [a] Eccl. 1:3; 3:9 2:23 [a] Job 5:7; 14:1 2:24 [a] Eccl. 3:12, 13, 22 2:25 [1] Following Masoretic Text, Targum, and Vulgate; some Hebrew manuscripts, Septuagint, and Syriac read *without Him*. 2:26 [a] Prov. 2:6 [b] Prov. 28:8 3:1 [a] Eccl. 3:17; 8:6 3:2 [a] Heb. 9:27 3:4 [a] Rom. 12:15 3:5 [a] Joel 2:16 3:7 [a] Amos 5:13 [b] Prov. 25:11 3:8 [a] Luke 14:26

LIVE THE TRUTH

## USING SILENCE WISELY

**3:6–7** The words you use matter. The Bible says life and death are in the power of the tongue, so what we say has tremendous weight. You can kill a relationship just through words. You can bring life and hope to a downcast friend with an encouraging conversation. Words can build up and tear down, and once they're out of your mouth, you cannot reel them back in. How we communicate to others and about others can really shape their lives.

In Ecclesiastes 3, Solomon tells us when we aren't sure what to say or feel tempted to spew negativity, it's okay to be quiet. In fact, sometimes it's best. For instance, in the Book of Job, when Job's friends came to visit him, they did well to sit and mourn with him as he wrestled with incredible heartache (see Job 2:11–13). It all went downhill when they opened their mouths and ended up arguing with Job about theology rather than loving him in his moment of grief. Our words are powerful. Therefore, as followers of Jesus, we must be careful how we wield them. When we feel we're about to use our words to destroy, it's wise to be silent instead.

### *THE GOD-GIVEN TASK*

9 [a]What profit has the worker from that in
which he labors? 10 [a]I have seen the God-given
task with which the sons of men are to be occu-
pied. 11 He has made everything beautiful in its
time. Also He has put eternity in their hearts,
except that [a]no one can find out the work that
God does from beginning to end.

### SEEING JESUS IN THE SCRIPTURE

**3:11** God has placed a longing for eternity within our hearts. The life, death, and resurrection of Jesus made eternity with God possible (see John 3:16). When we trust in Jesus, we have what our hearts long for, thus we can rest in Him (see John 14:1).

12 I know that nothing *is* [a]better for them than
to rejoice, and to do good in their lives, 13 and also
that [a]every man should eat and drink and enjoy
the good of all his labor—it *is* the gift of God.

14 I know that whatever God does,
It shall be forever.
[a]Nothing can be added to it,
And nothing taken from it.
God does *it,* that men should fear before
Him.
15 [a]That which is has already been,
And what is to be has already been;
And God requires an account of what is past.

### *INJUSTICE SEEMS TO PREVAIL*

16 Moreover [a]I saw under the sun:

*In* the place of judgment,
Wickedness *was* there;
And *in* the place of righteousness,
Iniquity *was* there.

17 I said in my heart,

[a]"God shall judge the righteous and the
wicked,
For *there is* a time there for every purpose
and for every work."

18 I said in my heart, "Concerning the condition
of the sons of men, God tests them, that they may
see that they themselves are *like* animals." 19 [a]For
what happens to the sons of men also happens
to animals; one thing befalls them: as one dies,
so dies the other. Surely, they all have one breath;
man has no advantage over animals, for all *is*
vanity. 20 All go to one place: [a]all are from the
dust, and all return to dust. 21 [a]Who knows the
spirit of the sons of men, which goes upward,
and the spirit of the animal, which goes down
to the earth?[1] 22 [a]So I perceived that nothing *is*
better than that a man should rejoice in his own
works, for [b]that *is* his heritage. [c]For who can
bring him to see what will happen after him?

4 Then I returned and considered all the [a]op-
pression that is done under the sun:

And look! The tears of the oppressed,
But they have no comforter—
On the side of their oppressors *there is*
power,
But they have no comforter.
2 [a]Therefore I praised the dead who were
already dead,
More than the living who are still alive.
3 [a]Yet, better than both *is he* who has never
existed,
Who has not seen the evil work that is
done under the sun.

**3:9** [a] Eccl. 1:3 **3:10** [a] Eccl. 1:13 **3:11** [a] Rom. 11:33 **3:12** [a] Eccl. 2:3, 24 **3:13** [a] Eccl. 2:24 **3:14** [a] James 1:17 **3:15** [a] Eccl. 1:9 **3:16** [a] Eccl. 5:8 **3:17** [a] [Rom. 2:6–10] **3:19** [a] [Eccl. 2:16] **3:20** [a] Gen. 3:19 **3:21** [a] Eccl. 12:7 [1] Septuagint, Syriac, Targum, and Vulgate read *Who knows whether the spirit . . . goes upward, and whether . . . goes downward to the earth?* **3:22** [a] Eccl. 2:24; 5:18 [b] Eccl. 2:10 [c] Eccl. 6:12; 8:7 **4:1** [a] Eccl. 3:16; 5:8 **4:2** [a] Job 3:17, 18 **4:3** [a] Job 3:11–22

### *THE VANITY OF SELFISH TOIL*

4 Again, I saw that for all toil and every skill-
ful work a man is envied by his neighbor. This
also *is* vanity and grasping for the wind.

5 [a]The fool folds his hands
And consumes his own flesh.
6 [a]Better a handful *with* quietness
Than both hands full, *together with* toil
and grasping for the wind.

7 Then I returned, and I saw vanity under
the sun:

8 There is one alone, without companion:
He has neither son nor brother.
Yet *there is* no end to all his labors,
Nor is his [a]eye satisfied with riches.
*But* [b]*he never asks,*
"For whom do I toil and deprive myself of
[c]good?"
This also *is* vanity and a grave misfortune.

> **4:8** In ancient times, success was measured by the size of a person's family. The more children a person had, the more successful—and favored by God—he was thought to be. Women who were unable to bear children were thought to be cursed by God.

### *THE VALUE OF A FRIEND*

9 Two *are* better than one,
Because they have a good reward for their
labor.
10 For if they fall, one will lift up his
companion.
But woe to him *who is* alone when he falls,
For *he has* no one to help him up.
11 Again, if two lie down together, they will
keep warm;
But how can one be warm *alone?*
12 Though one may be overpowered by
another, two can withstand him.
And a threefold cord is not quickly broken.

### *POPULARITY PASSES AWAY*

13 Better a poor and wise youth
Than an old and foolish king who will be
admonished no more.
14 For he comes out of prison to be king,
Although he was born poor in his
kingdom.
15 I saw all the living who walk under the
sun;
They were with the second youth who
stands in his place.
16 *There was* no end of all the people over
whom he was made king;
Yet those who come afterward will not
rejoice in him.
Surely this also *is* vanity and grasping for
the wind.

### *FEAR GOD, KEEP YOUR VOWS*

5 Walk [a]prudently when you go to the house of
God; and draw near to hear rather [b]than to
give the sacrifice of fools, for they do not know
that they do evil.

2 Do not be [a]rash with your mouth,
And let not your heart utter anything
hastily before God.
For God *is* in heaven, and you on earth;
Therefore let your words [b]be few.
3 For a dream comes through much
activity,
And [a]a fool's voice *is known* by *his* many
words.

4 [a]When you make a vow to God, do not
delay to [b]pay it;
For *He has* no pleasure in fools.
Pay what you have vowed—
5 [a]Better not to vow than to vow and not pay.

6 Do not let your [a]mouth cause your flesh to
sin, [b]nor say before the messenger *of God* that it
*was* an error. Why should God be angry at your
excuse[1] and destroy the work of your hands?
7 For in the multitude of dreams and many words
*there is* also vanity. But [a]fear God.

### *THE VANITY OF GAIN AND HONOR*

8 If you [a]see the oppression of the poor, and
the violent perversion of justice and righteous-
ness in a province, do not marvel at the matter;
for [b]high official watches over high official, and
higher officials are over them.
9 Moreover the profit of the land is for all;
*even* the king is served from the field.

10 He who loves silver will not be satisfied
with silver;
Nor he who loves abundance, with
increase.
This also *is* vanity.

11 When goods increase,
They increase who eat them;
So what profit have the owners
Except to see *them* with their eyes?

12 The sleep of a laboring man *is* sweet,
Whether he eats little or much;
But the abundance of the rich will not
permit him to sleep.

**4:5** [a] Prov. 6:10; 24:33 **4:6** [a] Prov. 15:16, 17; 16:8 **4:8** [a] [1 John 2:16] [b] Ps. 39:6 [c] Eccl. 2:18–21 **5:1** [a] Ex. 3:5 [b] [1 Sam. 15:22] **5:2** [a] Prov. 20:25 [b] Matt. 6:7 **5:3** [a] Prov. 10:19 **5:4** [a] Num. 30:2 [b] Ps. 66:13, 14 **5:5** [a] Acts 5:4 **5:6** [a] Prov. 6:2 [b] 1 Cor. 11:10 [1] Literally *voice* **5:7** [a] [Eccl. 12:13] **5:8** [a] Eccl. 3:16 [b] [Ps. 12:5; 58:11; 82:1]

APPLY THE TRUTH

## MATERIALISM

**5:10** There are over 58,000 storage unit facilities in the United States. Not individual units. *Facilities*. That's over ten times more than the total number of storage *units* in all of Europe. There are more storage facilities in the U.S. than several of the largest franchises *combined* (Starbucks®, 7-Eleven®, Walmart®, CVS®, Walgreens®, McDonalds®). All of this to say, people love stuff. Not only do they pay for homes for themselves, but they pay for homes for their stuff. This is because our culture tells us if we had more stuff, we'd be happy. But what we get still isn't enough. It never is.

The Bible tells us if we aren't content with what we have, we won't be content with more. If we love silver, we won't be satisfied with silver. But if we love God, we'll see all we have is a blessing from God to use for His glory. Godliness, not gain, is our goal. When God is our goal, all these other things can be added to us. But when we aim only for the other things, we miss God *and* those things we strive for.

13 [a]There is a severe evil *which* I have seen
under the sun:
Riches kept for their owner to his hurt.
14 But those riches perish through
misfortune;
When he begets a son, *there is* nothing in
his hand.
15 [a]As he came from his mother's womb,
naked shall he return,
To go as he came;
And he shall take nothing from his labor
Which he may carry away in his hand.
16 And this also *is* a severe evil—
Just exactly as he came, so shall he go.
And [a]what profit has he [b]who has labored
for the wind?
17 All his days [a]he also eats in darkness,
And *he has* much sorrow and sickness and
anger.

18 Here is what I have seen: [a]*It is* good and fit-
ting *for one* to eat and drink, and to enjoy the good
of all his labor in which he toils under the sun all
the days of his life which God gives him; [b]for it *is*
his heritage. 19 As for [a]every man to whom God has
given riches and wealth, and given him power to
eat of it, to receive his heritage and rejoice in his
labor—this *is* the [b]gift of God. 20 For he will not
dwell unduly on the days of his life, because God
keeps *him* busy with the joy of his heart.

6 There[a] is an evil which I have seen under the
sun, and it *is* common among men: 2 A man
to whom God has given riches and wealth and
honor, [a]so that he lacks nothing for himself of
all he desires; [b]yet God does not give him power
to eat of it, but a foreigner consumes it. This *is*
vanity, and it *is* an evil affliction.

3 If a man begets a hundred *children* and lives
many years, so that the days of his years are many,
but his soul is not satisfied with goodness, or
[a]indeed he has no burial, I say *that* [b]a stillborn
child *is* better than he— 4 for it comes in vanity
and departs in darkness, and its name is covered
with darkness. 5 Though it has not seen the sun or
known *anything*, this has more rest than that man,
6 even if he lives a thousand years twice—but has
not seen goodness. Do not all go to one [a]place?

7 [a]All the labor of man *is* for his mouth,
And yet the soul is not satisfied.
8 For what more has the wise *man* than the
fool?
What does the poor man have,
Who knows *how* to walk before the living?
9 Better *is* the [a]sight of the eyes than the
wandering of desire.
This also *is* vanity and grasping for the wind.

10 Whatever one is, he has been named
[a]already,
For it is known that he *is* man;
[b]And he cannot contend with Him who is
mightier than he.
11 Since there are many things that increase
vanity,
How *is* man the better?

12 For who knows what *is* good for man in
life, all the days of his vain life which he passes
like [a]a shadow? [b]Who can tell a man what will
happen after him under the sun?

### *THE VALUE OF PRACTICAL WISDOM*

7 A [a]good name *is* better than precious
ointment,
And the day of death than the day of one's
[b]birth;
2 Better to go to the house of mourning
Than to go to the house of feasting,
For that *is* the end of all men;
And the living will take *it* to [a]heart.

**5:13** [a] Eccl. 6:1, 2 **5:15** [a] 1 Tim. 6:7 **5:16** [a] Eccl. 1:3 [b] Prov. 11:29 **5:17** [a] Ps. 127:2 **5:18** [a] [1 Tim. 6:17] [b] Eccl. 2:10; 3:22
**5:19** [a] [Eccl. 6:2] [b] Eccl. 2:24; 3:13 **6:1** [a] Eccl. 5:13 **6:2** [a] Job 21:10 [b] Luke 12:20 **6:3** [a] Is. 14:19, 20 [b] Job 3:16 **6:6** [a] Eccl. 2:14, 15
**6:7** [a] Prov. 16:26 **6:9** [a] Eccl. 11:9 **6:10** [a] Eccl. 1:9; 3:15 [b] Job 9:32 **6:12** [a] James 4:14 [b] Eccl. 3:22 **7:1** [a] Prov. 22:1 [b] Eccl. 4:2
**7:2** [a] [Ps. 90:12]

3 Sorrow *is* better than laughter,
[a]For by a sad countenance the heart is
made better.
4 The heart of the wise *is* in the house of
mourning,
But the heart of fools *is* in the house of mirth.
5 [a]*It is* better to hear the rebuke of the wise
Than for a man to hear the song of fools.
6 [a]For like the crackling of thorns under a pot,
So *is* the laughter of the fool.
This also is vanity.
7 Surely oppression destroys a wise *man's*
reason,
[a]And a bribe debases the heart.
8 The end of a thing *is* better than its
beginning;
[a]The patient in spirit *is* better than the
proud in spirit.
9 [a]Do not hasten in your spirit to be angry,
For anger rests in the bosom of fools.
10 Do not say,
"Why were the former days better than
these?"
For you do not inquire wisely concerning
this.

11 Wisdom *is* good with an inheritance,
And profitable [a]to those who see the sun.
12 For wisdom *is* a [a]defense *as* money *is* a
defense,
But the excellence of knowledge *is that*
wisdom gives [b]life to those who have it.

13 Consider the work of God;
For [a]who can make straight what He has
made crooked?
14 [a]In the day of prosperity be joyful,
But in the day of adversity consider:
Surely God has appointed the one as well
as the other,
So that man can find out nothing *that will*
*come* after him.

15 I have seen everything in my days of vanity:

[a]There is a just *man* who perishes in his
righteousness,
And there is a wicked *man* who prolongs
*life* in his wickedness.

16 [a]Do not be overly righteous,
[b]Nor be overly wise:
Why should you destroy yourself?
17 Do not be overly wicked,
Nor be foolish:
[a]Why should you die before your time?
18 *It is* good that you grasp this,
And also not remove your hand from the
other;
For he who [a]fears God will escape them all.

19 [a]Wisdom strengthens the wise
More than ten rulers of the city.

20 [a]For *there is* not a just man on earth who
does good
And does not sin.

21 Also do not take to heart everything
people say,
Lest you hear your servant cursing you.
22 For many times, also, your own heart has
known
That even you have cursed others.

23 All this I have proved by wisdom.
[a]I said, "I will be wise";
But it *was* far from me.
24 [a]As for that which is far off and
[b]exceedingly deep,
Who can find it out?
25 [a]I applied my heart to know,
To search and seek out wisdom and the
reason *of things,*
To know the wickedness of folly,
Even of foolishness *and* madness.
26 [a]And I find more bitter than death
The woman whose heart *is* snares and nets,
Whose hands *are* fetters.
He who pleases God shall escape from her,
But the sinner shall be trapped by her.

27 "Here is what I have found," says [a]the Preacher,
"*Adding* one thing to the other to find out
the reason,
28 Which my soul still seeks but I cannot find:
[a]One man among a thousand I have found,
But a woman among all these I have not
found.

**7:28** Most women received very little respect in ancient times and were often treated more like possessions than people. Some women were even given as gifts. For example, when two countries signed a treaty, it was customary for the less powerful nation to present women to the leader of the more powerful nation. That's how Solomon, the leader of the very powerful Israelite nation, came to have hundreds of wives and concubines. Many of Solomon's wives came from foreign countries and worshiped foreign gods.

7:3 [a][2 Cor. 7:10] 7:5 [a]Ps. 141:5 7:6 [a]Eccl. 2:2 7:7 [a]Ex. 23:8 7:8 [a]Prov. 14:29 7:9 [a]James 1:19 7:11 [a]Eccl. 11:7 7:12 [a]Eccl. 9:18 [b]Prov. 3:18 7:13 [a]Job 12:14 7:14 [a]Deut. 28:47 7:15 [a]Eccl. 8:12–14 7:16 [a]Prov. 25:16 [b]Rom. 12:3 7:17 [a]Job 15:32 7:18 [a]Eccl. 3:14; 5:7; 8:12, 13 7:19 [a]Prov. 21:22 7:20 [a]1 John 1:8 7:23 [a]Rom. 1:22 7:24 [a]1 Tim. 6:16 [b]Rom. 11:33 7:25 [a]Eccl. 1:17 7:26 [a]Prov. 5:3, 4 7:27 [a]Eccl. 1:1, 2 7:28 [a]Job 33:23

29 Truly, this only I have found:
[a]That God made man upright,
But [b]they have sought out many schemes."

8 Who *is* like a wise *man?*
And who knows the interpretation of a thing?
[a]A man's wisdom makes his face shine,
And [b]the sternness of his face is changed.

### OBEY AUTHORITIES FOR GOD'S SAKE

2 I *say,* "Keep the king's commandment [a]for
the sake of your oath to God. 3 [a]Do not be hasty to
go from his presence. Do not take your stand for
an evil thing, for he does whatever pleases him."

4 Where the word of a king *is, there is* power;
And [a]who may say to him, "What are you doing?"
5 He who keeps his command will experience nothing harmful;
And a wise man's heart discerns both time and judgment,
6 Because [a]for every matter there is a time and judgment,
Though the misery of man increases greatly.
7 [a]For he does not know what will happen;
So who can tell him when it will occur?
8 [a]No one has power over the spirit to retain the spirit,
And no one has power in the day of death.
*There is* [b]no release from that war,
And wickedness will not deliver those who are given to it.

9 All this I have seen, and applied my heart
to every work that is done under the sun: *There
is* a time in which one man rules over another
to his own hurt.

### DEATH COMES TO ALL

10 Then I saw the wicked buried, who had
come and gone from the place of holiness, and
they were [a]forgotten[1] in the city where they
had so done. This also *is* vanity. 11 [a]Because the
sentence against an evil work is not executed
speedily, therefore the heart of the sons of men
is fully set in them to do evil. 12 [a]Though a sin-
ner does evil a hundred *times,* and his *days* are
prolonged, yet I surely know that [b]it will be well
with those who fear God, who fear before Him.
13 But it will not be well with the wicked; nor
will he prolong *his* days, *which are* as a shadow,
because he does not fear before God.
14 There is a vanity which occurs on earth,
that there are just *men* to whom it [a]happens
according to the work of the wicked; again, there
are wicked *men* to whom it happens according
to the work of the [b]righteous. I said that this
also *is* vanity.
15 [a]So I commended enjoyment, because a
man has nothing better under the sun than to
eat, drink, and be merry; for this will remain
with him in his labor *all* the days of his life which
God gives him under the sun.
16 When I applied my heart to know wisdom
and to see the business that is done on earth,
even though one sees no sleep day or night,
17 then I saw all the work of God, that [a]a man
cannot find out the work that is done under the
sun. For though a man labors to discover *it,* yet
he will not find *it;* moreover, though a wise *man*
attempts to know *it,* he will not be able to find *it.*

9 For I considered all this in my heart, so that
I could declare it all: [a]that the righteous and
the wise and their works *are* in the hand of God.
People know neither love nor hatred *by* anything
*they see* before them. 2 [a]All things *come* alike to all:

One event *happens* to the righteous and the wicked;
To the good,[1] the clean, and the unclean;
To him who sacrifices and him who does not sacrifice.
As is the good, so *is* the sinner;
He who takes an oath as *he* who fears an oath.

3 This *is* an evil in all that is done under the sun:
that one thing *happens* to all. Truly the hearts
of the sons of men are full of evil; madness *is* in
their hearts while they live, and after that *they
go* to the dead. 4 But for him who is joined to all
the living there is hope, for a living dog is better
than a dead lion.

> **9:4** In ancient Israel, dogs were wild creatures that traveled in packs, preyed on the weak, ate garbage, and stole food from the villages. Lions, on the other hand, were respected for their size and strength. Although they were a very real danger to the Israelites, they also served as symbols of majesty and courage. Calling someone a **dog** in ancient Israel was an extremely offensive insult. Calling someone a **lion** was an extremely high compliment.

5 For the living know that they will die;
But [a]the dead know nothing,
And they have no more reward,
For [b]the memory of them is forgotten.

**7:29** [a] Gen. 1:27 [b] Gen. 3:6, 7 **8:1** [a] Acts 6:15 [b] Deut. 28:50 **8:2** [a] 1 Chr. 29:24 **8:3** [a] Eccl. 10:4 **8:4** [a] Job 34:18 **8:6** [a] Eccl. 3:1, 17 **8:7** [a] Eccl. 6:12 **8:8** [a] Ps. 49:6, 7 [b] Deut. 20:5–8 **8:10** [a] Eccl. 2:16; 9:5 [1] Some Hebrew manuscripts, Septuagint, and Vulgate read *praised.* **8:11** [a] Is. 26:10 **8:12** [a] Is. 65:20 [b] [Is. 3:10] **8:14** [a] Ps. 73:14 [b] Eccl. 2:14; 7:15; 9:1–3 **8:15** [a] Eccl. 2:24 **8:17** [a] Job 5:9; Ps. 73:16; Eccl. 3:11; Rom. 11:33 **9:1** [a] Deut. 33:3; Job 12:10; Eccl. 8:14 **9:2** [a] Gen. 3:17–19; Job 21:7; Ps. 73:3, 12, 13; Mal. 3:15 [1] Septuagint, Syriac, and Vulgate read *good and bad.* **9:5** [a] Job 14:21; Is. 63:16 [b] Job 7:8–10; Eccl. 1:11; 2:16; 8:10; Is. 26:14

6 Also their love, their hatred, and their
envy have now perished;
Nevermore will they have a share
In anything done under the sun.

7 Go, [a]eat your bread with joy,
And drink your wine with a merry heart;
For God has already accepted your works.
8 Let your garments always be white,
And let your head lack no oil.

9 Live joyfully with the wife whom you love
all the days of your vain life which He has given
you under the sun, all your days of vanity; [a]for
that *is* your portion in life, and in the labor which
you perform under the sun.

**SEEING JESUS IN THE SCRIPTURE**

**9:7–9** The instruction to live with joy is only possible in Jesus. Jesus came to provide forgiveness of sin *and* to give abundant life (see John 10:10). Apart from Jesus, any happiness we find is fleeting. In Jesus, though, we can experience joy without measure.

10 [a]Whatever your hand finds to do, do *it* with
your [b]might; for *there is* no work or device or knowl-
edge or wisdom in the grave where you are going.
11 I returned [a]and saw under the sun that—

The race *is* not to the swift,
Nor the battle to the strong,
Nor bread to the wise,
Nor riches to men of understanding,
Nor favor to men of skill;
But time and [b]chance happen to them all.
12 For [a]man also does not know his time:
Like fish taken in a cruel net,
Like birds caught in a snare,
So the sons of men *are* [b]snared in an evil time,
When it falls suddenly upon them.

### *WISDOM SUPERIOR TO FOLLY*

13 This wisdom I have also seen under the
sun, and it *seemed* great to me: 14 [a]*There was* a lit-
tle city with few men in it; and a great king came
against it, besieged it, and built great snares[1]
around it. 15 Now there was found in it a poor wise
man, and he by his wisdom delivered the city.
Yet no one remembered that same poor man.
16 Then I said:

"Wisdom *is* better than [a]strength.
Nevertheless [b]the poor man's wisdom *is*
despised,
And his words are not heard.
17 Words of the wise, *spoken* quietly, *should*
*be* heard
Rather than the shout of a ruler of fools.
18 Wisdom *is* better than weapons of war;
But [a]one sinner destroys much good."

10 Dead flies putrefy[1] the perfumer's
ointment,
And cause it to give off a foul odor;
*So does* a little folly to one respected for
wisdom *and* honor.
2 A wise man's heart *is* at his right hand,
But a fool's heart at his left.
3 Even when a fool walks along the way,
He lacks wisdom,
[a]And he shows everyone *that* he *is* a fool.
4 If the spirit of the ruler rises against you,
[a]Do not leave your post;
For [b]conciliation pacifies great offenses.

5 There is an evil I have seen under the
sun,
As an error proceeding from the ruler:
6 [a]Folly is set in great dignity,
While the rich sit in a lowly place.
7 I have seen servants [a]on horses,
While princes walk on the ground like
servants.

8 [a]He who digs a pit will fall into it,
And whoever breaks through a wall will be
bitten by a serpent.
9 He who quarries stones may be hurt by
them,
*And* he who splits wood may be
endangered by it.
10 If the ax is dull,
And one does not sharpen the edge,
Then he must use more strength;
But wisdom brings success.

11 A serpent may bite [a]when *it is* not
charmed;
The babbler is no different.
12 [a]The words of a wise man's mouth *are*
gracious,
But [b]the lips of a fool shall swallow him
up;
13 The words of his mouth begin with
foolishness,
And the end of his talk *is* raving madness.
14 [a]A fool also multiplies words.
No man knows what is to be;
Who can tell him [b]what will be after him?
15 The labor of fools wearies them,
For they do not even know how to go to
the city!

**9:7** [a] Eccl. 8:15 **9:9** [a] Eccl. 2:10 **9:10** [a] [Col. 3:17] [b] Rom. 12:11; Col. 3:23 **9:11** [a] Jer. 9:23; Amos 2:14, 15 [b] 1 Sam. 6:9 **9:12** [a] Eccl. 8:7 [b] Prov. 29:6; Luke 12:20, 39; 17:26; 1 Thess. 5:3 **9:14** [a] 2 Sam. 20:16–22 [1] Septuagint, Syriac, and Vulgate read *bulwarks.* **9:16** [a] Eccl. 7:12, 19 [b] Mark 6:2, 3 **9:18** [a] Josh. 7:1–26; 2 Kin. 21:2–17 **10:1** [1] Targum and Vulgate omit *putrefy.* **10:3** [a] Prov. 13:16; 18:2 **10:4** [a] Eccl. 8:3 [b] 1 Sam. 25:24–33; Prov. 25:15 **10:6** [a] Esth. 3:1 **10:7** [a] Prov. 19:10; 30:22 **10:8** [a] Prov. 26:27 **10:11** [a] Jer. 8:17 **10:12** [a] Prov. 10:32 [b] Prov. 10:14 **10:14** [a] [Prov. 15:2] [b] Eccl. 3:22; 8:7

16 [a]Woe to you, O land, when your king *is* a
child,
And your princes feast in the morning!
17 Blessed *are* you, O land, when your king *is*
the son of nobles,
And your [a]princes feast at the proper
time—
For strength and not for drunkenness!
18 Because of laziness the building decays,
And [a]through idleness of hands the house
leaks.
19 A feast is made for laughter,
And [a]wine makes merry;
But money answers everything.

20 [a]Do not curse the king, even in your thought;
Do not curse the rich, even in your
bedroom;
For a bird of the air may carry your voice,
And a bird in flight may tell the matter.

## THE VALUE OF DILIGENCE

11 Cast your bread [a]upon the waters,
[b]For you will find it after many days.
2 [a]Give a serving [b]to seven, and also to eight,
[c]For you do not know what evil will be on
the earth.

3 If the clouds are full of rain,
They empty *themselves* upon the earth;
And if a tree falls to the south or the
north,
In the place where the tree falls, there it
shall lie.
4 He who observes the wind will not sow,
And he who regards the clouds will not
reap.

5 As [a]you do not know what *is* the way of
the wind,[1]
[b]*Or* how the bones *grow* in the womb of her
who is with child,
So you do not know the works of God who
makes everything.
6 In the morning sow your seed,
And in the evening do not withhold your
hand;
For you do not know which will prosper,
Either this or that,
Or whether both alike *will be* good.

7 Truly the light is sweet,
And *it is* pleasant for the eyes [a]to behold
the sun;
8 But if a man lives many years
*And* [a]rejoices in them all,
Yet let him [b]remember the days of
darkness,
For they will be many.
All that is coming *is* vanity.

## SEEK GOD IN EARLY LIFE

9 Rejoice, O young man, in your youth,
And let your heart cheer you in the days
of your youth;
[a]Walk in the ways of your heart,
And in the sight of your eyes;
But know that for all these
[b]God will bring you into judgment.
10 Therefore remove sorrow from your
heart,
And [a]put away evil from your flesh,
[b]For childhood and youth *are* vanity.

12 Remember[a] now your Creator in the
days of your youth,
Before the difficult days come,
And the years draw near [b]when you say,
"I have no pleasure in them":
2 While the sun and the light,
The moon and the stars,
Are not darkened,
And the clouds do not return after the
rain;
3 In the day when the keepers of the house
tremble,
And the strong men bow down;
When the grinders cease because they are
few,
And those that look through the windows
grow dim;
4 When the doors are shut in the streets,
And the sound of grinding is low;
When one rises up at the sound of a bird,
And all [a]the daughters of music are
brought low.
5 Also they are afraid of height,
And of terrors in the way;
When the almond tree blossoms,
The grasshopper is a burden,
And desire fails.
For man goes to [a]his eternal home,
And [b]the mourners go about the streets.

6 *Remember your Creator* before the silver
cord is loosed,[1]
Or the golden bowl is broken,
Or the pitcher shattered at the fountain,
Or the wheel broken at the well.
7 [a]Then the dust will return to the earth as it
was,
[b]And the spirit will return to God [c]who
gave it.

8 "Vanity[a] of vanities," says the Preacher,
"All *is* vanity."

10:16 [a] Is. 3:4, 5; 5:11 10:17 [a] Prov. 31:4 10:18 [a] Prov. 24:30–34 10:19 [a] Ps. 104:15 10:20 [a] Acts 23:5 11:1 [a] Is. 32:20 [b] [Deut. 15:10] 11:2 [a] [1 Tim. 6:18, 19] [b] Mic. 5:5 [c] Eph. 5:16 11:5 [a] John 3:8 [b] Ps. 139:14 [1] Or *spirit* 11:7 [a] Eccl. 7:11 11:8 [a] Eccl. 9:7 [b] Eccl. 12:1 11:9 [a] Num. 15:39 [b] Eccl. 3:17; 12:14 11:10 [a] 2 Cor. 7:1 [b] Ps. 39:5 12:1 [a] Lam. 3:27 [b] 2 Sam. 19:35 12:4 [a] 2 Sam. 19:35 12:5 [a] Job 17:13 [b] Jer. 9:17 12:6 [1] Following Qere and Targum; Kethib reads *removed;* Septuagint and Vulgate read *broken.* 12:7 [a] Gen. 3:19 [b] Eccl. 3:21 [c] Job 34:14 12:8 [a] Ps. 62:9

### *THE WHOLE DUTY OF MAN*

9 And moreover, because the Preacher was
wise, he still taught the people knowledge; yes,
he pondered and sought out *and* [a]set in order
many proverbs. 10 The Preacher sought to find
acceptable words; and *what was* written *was*
upright—words of truth. 11 The words of the wise
are like goads, and the words of scholars[1] are like
well-driven nails, given by one Shepherd. 12 And
further, my son, be admonished by these. Of
making many books *there is* no end, and [a]much
study *is* wearisome to the flesh.
13 Let us hear the conclusion of the whole
matter:

[a]Fear God and keep His commandments,
For this is man's all.

14 For [a]God will bring every work into
judgment,
Including every secret thing,
Whether good or evil.

**SEEING JESUS IN THE SCRIPTURE**

**12:13** The conclusion of Ecclesiastes is our need to fear the Lord and obey His commands. This points to Jesus, the only one who perfectly feared and obeyed the Father, even to the point of dying on the cross (see Phil. 2:8).

12:9 [a] 1 Kin. 4:32 12:11 [1] Literally *masters of the assemblies* 12:12 [a] Eccl. 1:18 12:13 [a] [Deut. 6:2; 10:12]; Mic. 6:8 12:14 [a] Eccl. 11:9; Matt. 12:36; [Acts 17:30, 31; Rom. 2:16; 1 Cor. 4:5; 2 Cor. 5:10]

# *The* SONG OF SOLOMON

| AUTHOR | KEY VERSE | READING TIME |
|---|---|---|
| Solomon | Song of Solomon 7:10 | 24 minutes |

The Song of Solomon is a love song celebrating God's gift of marriage. Using metaphors and Near Eastern imagery, Solomon described his wooing of an unnamed shepherdess, their wedding, and the joys and heartaches of their early marriage. As such, the song reads much like a drama, with the action occurring in three main scenes and dialogue provided by three main speakers: the bride (Shulamite), the king (Solomon), and a chorus (daughters of Jerusalem). A relative (Song 8:5) and the bride's brothers (8:8–9) also have speaking roles.

**Occasion:** Solomon wrote Song of Solomon at some point during his reign as Israel's third king to celebrate God's gift of marriage.

**Main Point:** Marriage is a good gift from God.

**Big Ideas:** God created love, marriage, and sex for our good. Marriage is not always easy, but it's always better with God in the middle of it.

## OUTLINE:

I. The Couple Fall in Love (chs. 1–2)
II. The Couple Marry (chs. 3–4)
III. The Couple Face Difficulty (chs. 5–6)
IV. The Couple Renew Their Love (chs. 7–8)

**c. 971–931 BC**
**Song of Solomon written**

**970 BC**
Solomon becomes king of Israel

**967 BC**
Solomon begins construction of the temple

**c. 950–700 BC**
Proverbs written

**c. 935 BC**
Ecclesiastes written

**930 BC**
The kingdom is divided

**722 BC**
The Assyrians defeat Israel

**c. 700 BC**
Proverbs compiled

1 The [a]song of songs, which *is* Solomon's.

### THE BANQUET

*The Shulamite*[1]

2 Let him kiss me with the kisses of his mouth—
[a]For your[2] love *is* better than wine.
3 Because of the fragrance of your good ointments,
Your name *is* ointment poured forth;
Therefore the virgins love you.
4 [a]Draw me away!

*The Daughters of Jerusalem*

[b]We will run after you.[1]

*The Shulamite*

The king [c]has brought me into his chambers.

*The Daughters of Jerusalem*

We will be glad and rejoice in you.[2]

We will remember your[3] love more than wine.

*The Shulamite*

Rightly do they love you.[4]

5 I *am* dark, but lovely,
O daughters of Jerusalem,
Like the tents of Kedar,
Like the curtains of Solomon.
6 Do not look upon me, because I *am* dark,
Because the sun has tanned me.
My mother's sons were angry with me;
They made me the keeper of the vineyards,
*But* my own [a]vineyard I have not kept.

**1:5–6** The Shulamite contrasted her **dark** coloring acquired from long hours working in the **vineyards** with the lighter complexion of the city maidens. The point here is her class and station in life. Unlike the young women of the court in Jerusalem who had been raised in comfort and conditions of ease, this woman had worked as a field hand in the **sun**.

*(To Her Beloved)*

7 Tell me, O you whom I love,
Where you feed *your flock,*
Where you make *it* rest at noon.
For why should I be as one who veils herself[1]
By the flocks of your companions?

*The Beloved*

8 If you do not know, [a]O fairest among women,
Follow in the footsteps of the flock,
And feed your little goats
Beside the shepherds' tents.
9 I have compared you, [a]my love,
[b]To my filly among Pharaoh's chariots.
10 [a]Your cheeks are lovely with ornaments,
Your neck with chains *of gold.*

*The Daughters of Jerusalem*

11 We will make you[1] ornaments of gold
With studs of silver.

*The Shulamite*

12 While the king *is* at his table,
My spikenard sends forth its fragrance.
13 A bundle of myrrh *is* my beloved to me,
That lies all night between my breasts.
14 My beloved *is* to me a cluster of henna *blooms*
In the vineyards of En Gedi.

*The Beloved*

15 [a]Behold, you *are* fair, my love!
Behold, you *are* fair!
You *have* dove's eyes.

*The Shulamite*

16 Behold, you *are* [a]handsome, my beloved!
Yes, pleasant!
Also our bed *is* green.
17 The beams of our houses *are* cedar,
*And* our rafters of fir.

2 I *am* the rose of Sharon,
*And* the lily of the valleys.

*The Beloved*

2 Like a lily among thorns,
So is my love among the daughters.

**2:1 Sharon** refers to a fertile coastal region in Israel known for its beautiful flowers. The **rose** mentioned in this verse probably wasn't what we know as a rose. Instead, it may have been a mountain tulip, anemone, or saffron. Since those flowers grew in abundance in Sharon, the woman was implying she was nothing special.

**1:1** [a] 1 Kin. 4:32 **1:2** [a] Song 4:10 [1] A young woman from the town of Shulam or Shunem (compare 6:13). The speaker and audience are identified according to the number, gender, and person of the Hebrew words. Occasionally the identity is not certain. [2] Masculine singular, that is, the Beloved **1:4** [a] Hos. 11:4 [b] Phil. 3:12–14 [c] Ps. 45:14, 15 [1] Masculine singular, that is, the Beloved [2] Feminine singular, that is, the Shulamite [3] Masculine singular, that is, the Beloved [4] Masculine singular, that is, the Beloved **1:6** [a] Song 8:11, 12 **1:7** [1] Septuagint, Syriac, and Vulgate read *wanders.* **1:8** [a] Song 5:9 **1:9** [a] Song 2:2, 10, 13; 4:1, 7 [b] 2 Chr. 1:16 **1:10** [a] Ezek. 16:11 **1:11** [1] Feminine singular, that is, the Shulamite **1:15** [a] Song 4:1; 5:12 **1:16** [a] Song 5:10–16

*The Shulamite*

3 Like an apple tree among the trees of the woods,
So *is* my beloved among the sons.
I sat down in his shade with great delight,
And [a]his fruit *was* sweet to my taste.

*The Shulamite to the Daughters of Jerusalem*

4 He brought me to the banqueting house,
And his banner over me *was* love.
5 Sustain me with cakes of raisins,
Refresh me with apples,
For I *am* lovesick.

6 [a]His left hand *is* under my head,
And his right hand embraces me.
7 [a]I charge you, O daughters of Jerusalem,
By the gazelles or by the does of the field,
Do not stir up nor awaken love
Until it pleases.

## THE BELOVED'S REQUEST

*The Shulamite*

8 The voice of my beloved!
Behold, he comes
Leaping upon the mountains,
Skipping upon the hills.
9 [a]My beloved is like a gazelle or a young stag.
Behold, he stands behind our wall;
He is looking through the windows,
Gazing through the lattice.

10 My beloved spoke, and said to me:
"Rise up, my love, my fair one,
And come away.
11 For lo, the winter is past,
The rain is over *and* gone.
12 The flowers appear on the earth;
The time of singing has come,
And the voice of the turtledove
Is heard in our land.
13 The fig tree puts forth her green figs,
And the vines *with* the tender grapes
Give a *good* smell.
Rise up, my love, my fair one,
And come away!

14 "O my [a]dove, in the clefts of the rock,
In the secret *places* of the cliff,
Let me see your face,
[b]Let me hear your voice;
For your voice *is* sweet,
And your face *is* lovely."

*Her Brothers*

15 Catch us [a]the foxes,
The little foxes that spoil the vines,
For our vines *have* tender grapes.

**2:15** The Shulamite's brothers called on Solomon to **catch . . . the foxes**. Foxes could creep into vineyards and destroy the roots by gnawing on them. Thus, these foxes symbolized threats.

*The Shulamite*

16 [a]My beloved *is* mine, and I *am* his.
He feeds *his flock* among the lilies.

*(To Her Beloved)*

17 [a]Until the day breaks
And the shadows flee away,
Turn, my beloved,
And be [b]like a gazelle
Or a young stag
Upon the mountains of Bether.[1]

## A TROUBLED NIGHT

*The Shulamite*

3 By [a]night on my bed I sought the one I love;
I sought him, but I did not find him.
2 "I will rise now," *I said,*
"And go about the city;
In the streets and in the squares
I will seek the one I love."
I sought him, but I did not find him.
3 [a]The watchmen who go about the city found me;
*I said,*
"Have you seen the one I love?"

4 Scarcely had I passed by them,
When I found the one I love.
I held him and would not let him go,
Until I had brought him to the [a]house of my mother,
And into the chamber of her who conceived me.

5 [a]I charge you, O daughters of Jerusalem,
By the gazelles or by the does of the field,
Do not stir up nor awaken love
Until it pleases.

## THE COMING OF SOLOMON

*The Shulamite*

6 [a]Who *is* this coming out of the wilderness
Like pillars of smoke,
Perfumed with myrrh and frankincense,
With all the merchant's fragrant powders?
7 Behold, it *is* Solomon's couch,
*With* sixty valiant men around it,
Of the valiant of Israel.
8 They all hold swords,
*Being* expert in war.
Every man *has* his sword on his thigh
Because of fear in the night.

**2:3** [a]Rev. 22:1, 2 **2:6** [a]Song 8:3 **2:7** [a]Song 3:5; 8:4 **2:9** [a]Song 2:17 **2:14** [a]Song 5:2 [b]Song 8:13 **2:15** [a]Ezek. 13:4 **2:16** [a]Song 6:3 **2:17** [a]Song 4:6 [b]Song 8:14 [1]Literally *Separation* **3:1** [a]Is. 26:9 **3:3** [a]Song 5:7 **3:4** [a]Song 8:2 **3:5** [a]Song 2:7; 8:4 **3:6** [a]Song 8:5

9 Of the wood of Lebanon
Solomon the King
Made himself a palanquin:[1]
10 He made its pillars *of* silver,
Its support *of* gold,
Its seat *of* purple,
Its interior paved *with* love
By the daughters of Jerusalem.
11 Go forth, O daughters of Zion,
And see King Solomon with the crown
With which his mother crowned him
On the day of his wedding,
The day of the gladness of his heart.

## THE BRIDEGROOM PRAISES THE BRIDE

### The Beloved

4 Behold, [a]you *are* fair, my love!
Behold, you *are* fair!
You *have* dove's eyes behind your veil.
Your hair *is* like a [b]flock of goats,
Going down from Mount Gilead.
2 [a]Your teeth *are* like a flock of shorn
*sheep*
Which have come up from the washing,
Every one of which bears twins,
And none *is* barren among them.
3 Your lips *are* like a strand of scarlet,
And your mouth is lovely.
[a]Your temples behind your veil
*Are* like a piece of pomegranate.
4 [a]Your neck *is* like the tower of David,
Built [b]for an armory,
On which hang a thousand bucklers,
All shields of mighty men.
5 [a]Your two breasts *are* like two fawns,
Twins of a gazelle,
Which feed among the lilies.

6 [a]Until the day breaks
And the shadows flee away,
I will go my way to the mountain of
myrrh
And to the hill of frankincense.

7 [a]You *are* all fair, my love,
And *there is* no spot in you.
8 Come with me from Lebanon, *my*
spouse,
With me from Lebanon.
Look from the top of Amana,
From the top of Senir [a]and Hermon,
From the lions' dens,
From the mountains of the leopards.

9 You have ravished my heart,
My sister, *my* spouse;
You have ravished my heart
With one *look* of your eyes,
With one link of your necklace.
10 How fair is your love,
My sister, *my* spouse!
[a]How much better than wine is your love,
And the scent of your perfumes
Than all spices!
11 Your lips, O *my* spouse,
Drip as the honeycomb;
[a]Honey and milk *are* under your
tongue;
And the fragrance of your garments
*Is* [b]like the fragrance of Lebanon.

12 A garden enclosed
*Is* my sister, *my* spouse,
A spring shut up,
A fountain sealed.

> **4:12** Some people in the ancient Near East **enclosed** a **garden** to visitors to protect their privacy and preserve their water supply. Because of the frequent droughts in the area, water in Israel was tough to come by.

13 Your plants *are* an orchard of
pomegranates
With pleasant fruits,
Fragrant henna with spikenard,
14 Spikenard and saffron,
Calamus and cinnamon,
With all trees of frankincense,
Myrrh and aloes,
With all the chief spices—
15 A fountain of gardens,
A well of [a]living waters,
And streams from Lebanon.

### The Shulamite

16 Awake, O north *wind*,
And come, O south!
Blow upon my garden,
*That* its spices may flow out.
[a]Let my beloved come to his garden
And eat its pleasant [b]fruits.

### The Beloved

5 I [a]have come to my garden, my [b]sister, *my*
spouse;
I have gathered my myrrh with my spice;
[c]I have eaten my honeycomb with my
honey;
I have drunk my wine with my milk.

### (To His Friends)

Eat, O [d]friends!
Drink, yes, drink deeply,
O beloved ones!

3:9 [1] A portable enclosed chair **4:1** [a] Song 1:15; 5:12 [b] Song 6:5 **4:2** [a] Song 6:6 **4:3** [a] Song 6:7 **4:4** [a] Song 7:4 [b] Neh. 3:19 **4:5** [a] Song 7:3 **4:6** [a] Song 2:17 **4:7** [a] Song 1:15; Eph. 5:27 **4:8** [a] Deut. 3:9; 1 Chr. 5:23; Ezek. 27:5 **4:10** [a] Song 1:2, 4 **4:11** [a] Prov. 24:13, 14; Song 5:1 [b] Gen. 27:27; Hos. 14:6, 7 **4:15** [a] Zech. 14:8; John 4:10; 7:38 **4:16** [a] Song 5:1 [b] Song 7:13 **5:1** [a] Song 4:16 [b] Song 4:9 [c] Song 4:11 [d] Luke 15:7, 10; John 3:29

## *THE SHULAMITE'S TROUBLED EVENING*

### *The Shulamite*

2 I sleep, but my heart is awake;
*It is* the voice of my beloved!
[a]He knocks, *saying,*
"Open for me, my sister, my love,
My dove, my perfect one;
For my head is covered with dew,
My locks with the drops of the night."

3 I have taken off my robe;
How can I put it on *again?*
I have washed my feet;
How can I defile them?
4 My beloved put his hand
By the latch *of the door,*
And my heart yearned for him.
5 I arose to open for my beloved,
And my hands dripped *with* myrrh,
My fingers with liquid myrrh,
On the handles of the lock.

6 I opened for my beloved,
But my beloved had turned away *and* was gone.
My heart leaped up when he spoke.
[a]I sought him, but I could not find him;
I called him, but he gave me no answer.
7 [a]The watchmen who went about the city found me.
They struck me, they wounded me;
The keepers of the walls
Took my veil away from me.
8 I charge you, O daughters of Jerusalem,
If you find my beloved,
That you tell him I *am* lovesick!

### *The Daughters of Jerusalem*

9 What *is* your beloved
More than *another* beloved,
[a]O fairest among women?
What *is* your beloved
More than *another* beloved,
That you so charge us?

### *The Shulamite*

10 My beloved *is* white and ruddy,
Chief among ten thousand.
11 His head *is like* the finest gold;
His locks *are* wavy,
*And* black as a raven.
12 [a]His eyes *are* like doves
By the rivers of waters,
Washed with milk,
*And* fitly set.
13 His cheeks *are* like a bed of spices,
Banks of scented herbs.
His lips *are* lilies,
Dripping liquid myrrh.
14 His hands *are* rods of gold
Set with beryl.
His body *is* carved ivory
Inlaid *with* sapphires.
15 His legs *are* pillars of marble
Set on bases of fine gold.
His countenance *is* like Lebanon,
Excellent as the cedars.
16 His mouth *is* most sweet,
Yes, he *is* altogether lovely.
This *is* my beloved,
And this *is* my friend,
O daughters of Jerusalem!

### *The Daughters of Jerusalem*

6 Where has your beloved gone,
[a]O fairest among women?
Where has your beloved turned aside,
That we may seek him with you?

### *The Shulamite*

2 My beloved has gone to his [a]garden,
To the beds of spices,
To feed *his flock* in the gardens,
And to gather lilies.
3 [a]I *am* my beloved's,
And my beloved *is* mine.
He feeds *his flock* among the lilies.

## *PRAISE OF THE SHULAMITE'S BEAUTY*

### *The Beloved*

4 O my love, you *are as* beautiful as Tirzah,
Lovely as Jerusalem,
Awesome as *an army* with banners!
5 Turn your eyes away from me,
For they have overcome me.
Your hair *is* [a]like a flock of goats
Going down from Gilead.
6 [a]Your teeth *are* like a flock of sheep
Which have come up from the washing;
Every one bears twins,
And none *is* barren among them.
7 [a]Like a piece of pomegranate
*Are* your temples behind your veil.

8 There are sixty queens
And eighty concubines,
And [a]virgins without number.

> **6:8** If this references Solomon's **queens** and **concubines**, it dates the book to an earlier period of his reign. Eventually, Solomon would have 700 wives and 300 concubines (see 1 Kin. 11:3).

9 My dove, my [a]perfect one,
Is the only one,
The only one of her mother,

**5:2** [a] Rev. 3:20 **5:6** [a] Song 3:1 **5:7** [a] Song 3:3 **5:9** [a] Song 1:8; 6:1 **5:12** [a] Song 1:15; 4:1 **6:1** [a] Song 1:8; 5:9 **6:2** [a] Song 4:16; 5:1 **6:3** [a] Song 2:16; 7:10 **6:5** [a] Song 4:1 **6:6** [a] Song 4:2 **6:7** [a] Song 4:3 **6:8** [a] Song 1:3 **6:9** [a] Song 2:14; 5:2

The favorite of the one who bore her.
The daughters saw her
And called her blessed,
The queens and the concubines,
And they praised her.

10 Who is she who looks forth as the morning,
Fair as the moon,
Clear as the sun,
[a] Awesome as *an army* with banners?

### The Shulamite

11 I went down to the garden of nuts
To see the verdure of the valley,
[a] To see whether the vine had budded
*And* the pomegranates had bloomed.
12 Before I was even aware,
My soul had made me
*As* the chariots of my noble people.[1]

### The Beloved and His Friends

13 Return, return, O Shulamite;
Return, return, that we may look upon you!

### The Shulamite

What would you see in the Shulamite—
As it were, the dance of the two camps?[1]

## EXPRESSIONS OF PRAISE

### The Beloved

7 How beautiful are your feet in sandals,
[a] O prince's daughter!
The curves of your thighs *are* like jewels,
The work of the hands of a skillful workman.
2 Your navel *is* a rounded goblet;
It lacks no blended beverage.
Your waist *is* a heap of wheat
Set about with lilies.
3 [a] Your two breasts *are* like two fawns,
Twins of a gazelle.
4 [a] Your neck *is* like an ivory tower,
Your eyes *like* the pools in Heshbon
By the gate of Bath Rabbim.
Your nose *is* like the tower of Lebanon
Which looks toward Damascus.
5 Your head *crowns* you like *Mount* Carmel,
And the hair of your head *is* like purple;
A king *is* held captive by *your* tresses.

6 How fair and how pleasant you are,
O love, with your delights!
7 This stature of yours is like a palm tree,
And your breasts *like* its clusters.
8 I said, "I will go up to the palm tree,
I will take hold of its branches."
Let now your breasts be like clusters of the vine,
The fragrance of your breath like apples,
9 And the roof of your mouth like the best wine.

### The Shulamite

*The wine* goes *down* smoothly for my beloved,
Moving gently the lips of sleepers.[1]
10 [a] I *am* my beloved's,
And [b] his desire *is* toward me.

11 Come, my beloved,
Let us go forth to the field;
Let us lodge in the villages.
12 Let us get up early to the vineyards;
Let us [a] see if the vine has budded,
*Whether* the grape blossoms are open,
*And* the pomegranates are in bloom.
There I will give you my love.
13 The [a] mandrakes give off a fragrance,
And at our gates [b] *are* pleasant *fruits,*
All manner, new and old,
Which I have laid up for you, my beloved.

8 Oh, that you were like my brother,
Who nursed at my mother's breasts!
*If* I should find you outside,
I would kiss you;
I would not be despised.
2 I would lead you *and* bring you
Into the [a] house of my mother,
She *who* used to instruct me.
I would cause you to drink of [b] spiced wine,
Of the juice of my pomegranate.

### (To the Daughters of Jerusalem)

3 [a] His left hand *is* under my head,
And his right hand embraces me.
4 [a] I charge you, O daughters of Jerusalem,
Do not stir up nor awaken love
Until it pleases.

## LOVE RENEWED IN LEBANON

### A Relative

5 [a] Who *is* this coming up from the wilderness,
Leaning upon her beloved?

I awakened you under the apple tree.
There your mother brought you forth;
There she *who* bore you brought *you* forth.

**6:10** [a] Song 6:4 **6:11** [a] Song 7:12 **6:12** [1] Hebrew *Ammi Nadib* **6:13** [1] Hebrew *Mahanaim* **7:1** [a] Ps. 45:13 **7:3** [a] Song 4:5 **7:4** [a] Song 4:4 **7:9** [1] Septuagint, Syriac, and Vulgate read *lips and teeth.* **7:10** [a] Song 2:16; 6:3 [b] Ps. 45:11 **7:12** [a] Song 6:11 **7:13** [a] Gen. 30:14 [b] Song 2:3; 4:13, 16; Matt. 13:52 **8:2** [a] Song 3:4 [b] Prov. 9:2 **8:3** [a] Song 2:6 **8:4** [a] Song 2:7; 3:5 **8:5** [a] Song 3:6

*The Shulamite to Her Beloved*

6 [a]Set me as a seal upon your heart,
As a seal upon your arm;
For love *is as* strong as death,
[b]Jealousy *as* cruel as the grave;[1]
Its flames *are* flames of fire,
A most vehement flame.[2]

**SEEING JESUS IN THE SCRIPTURE**

**8:6** The picture of love's power points to the love Jesus displayed to save humanity. Jesus' love for us compelled Him to die so that we might be sealed together with Him forever (see John 15:13).

7 Many waters cannot quench love,
Nor can the floods drown it.
[a]If a man would give for love
All the wealth of his house,
It would be utterly despised.

*The Shulamite's Brothers*

8 [a]We have a little sister,
And she has no breasts.
What shall we do for our sister
In the day when she is spoken for?
9 If she *is* a wall,
We will build upon her
A battlement of silver;
And if she *is* a door,
We will enclose her
With boards of cedar.

*The Shulamite*

10 I *am* a wall,
And my breasts like towers;
Then I became in his eyes
As one who found peace.

**8:10** The woman explained that she has been virtuous in youth and that she would remain faithful in her adulthood.

11 Solomon had a vineyard at Baal Hamon;
[a]He leased the vineyard to keepers;
Everyone was to bring for its fruit
A thousand silver *coins.*

*(To Solomon)*

12 My own vineyard *is* before me.
You, O Solomon, *may have* a thousand,
And those who tend its fruit two hundred.

*The Beloved*

13 You who dwell in the gardens,
The companions listen for your voice—
[a]Let me hear it!

*The Shulamite*

14 [a]Make haste, my beloved,
And [b]be like a gazelle
Or a young stag
On the mountains of spices.

**8:6** [a] Is. 49:16; Jer. 22:24; Hag. 2:23 [b] Prov. 6:34, 35 [1] Or *Sheol* [2] Literally *A flame of YAH* (a poetic form of *YHWH, the LORD*) **8:7** [a] Prov. 6:35 **8:8** [a] Ezek. 23:33 **8:11** [a] Matt. 21:33 **8:13** [a] Song 2:14 **8:14** [a] Rev. 22:17, 20 [b] Song 2:7, 9, 17

*Introduction to*

# THE BOOKS OF PROPHECY

These books contain the stories, visions, dreams, and declarations of God's spokespersons, the prophets. God called these prophets to declare to His people the messages He gave. These prophetic messages often included calling the people to repent of their sins—most notably idolatry and mistreating one another—and to return to God, warning of God's coming judgment, and reminding the people of God's standing promises. These books are often divided into the Major Prophets (Isaiah through Daniel) and the Minor Prophets (Hosea through Malachi). These designations don't indicate the books' importance but rather their size. The Major Prophets' books are simply longer.

When reading the Books of Prophecy, it's important to understand the historical context of each, namely when they were written and whom was being addressed. For example, knowing that Nineveh was the capital of the Assyrians, a people known for their cruelty and a major threat to Israel in that day, explains why Jonah was reluctant to go there and why he wasn't happy they were spared from God's judgment. Furthermore, while it's true every promise in Scripture needs to be read in context (not all promises are for everyone), it's even more important to read them carefully in the Books of Prophecy. Related to this, these books contain Messianic prophecies about Jesus, many of which were fulfilled in His first coming, some of which will not be fulfilled until His return. Identifying which is which is key. Finally, while most of these books are written in poetic form and include different literary devices needing to be read properly, they also contain portions of history and narrative that need to be read accordingly. For example, returning to Jonah, the book describes an account of a real person and a real event; it is not a fable.

*Introduction to*

# THE BOOKS OF PROPHECY

These books contain the stories, visions, dreams, and declarations of God's spokespersons, the prophets. God called these prophets to declare to His people the messages He gave. These prophetic messages often included calling the people to repent of their sins—most notably idolatry and mistreating one another—and to return to God, warning of God's coming judgment and reminding the people of God's standing promises. These books are often divided into the Major Prophets (**Isaiah** through **Daniel**) and the Minor Prophets (**Hosea** through **Malachi**). These designations don't indicate the books' importance but rather their size. The Major Prophets' books are simply longer.

When reading the Books of Prophecy, it's important to understand the historical context of each, namely when they were written and whom was being addressed. For example, knowing that Nineveh was the capital of the Assyrians, a people known for their cruelty and a major threat to Israel in that day, explains why Jonah was reluctant to go there and why he wasn't happy they were spared from God's judgment. Furthermore, while it's true every promise in Scripture needs to be read in context (not all promises are for everyone), it's even more important to read them carefully in the Books of Prophecy. Related to this, these books contain Messianic prophecies about Jesus, many of which were fulfilled in His first coming, some of which will not be fulfilled until His return. Identifying which is which is key. Finally, while most of these books are written in poetic form and include different literary devices needing to be read properly, they also contain portions of history and narrative that need to be read accordingly. For example, returning to Jonah, the book describes an account of a real person and a real event; it is not a fable.

# ISAIAH • JEREMIAH • LAMENTATIONS • EZEKIEL DANIEL • HOSEA • JOEL • AMOS • OBADIAH JONAH • MICAH • NAHUM • HABAKKUK ZEPHANIAH • HAGGAI • ZECHARIAH • MALACHI

## THE BOOKS OF PROPHECY (IN CHRONOLOGICAL ORDER)

| Book | Author | Prophet To | Timeframe | Period | Theme |
|---|---|---|---|---|---|
| **Obadiah** | Obadiah | Edom | c. 848–840 BC | Before the Exile | Vindication |
| **Joel** | Joel | Judah | c. 835–796 BC | Before the Exile | Judgment |
| **Jonah** | Jonah | Nineveh | c. 760 BC | Before the Exile | Grace |
| **Amos** | Amos | Israel | c. 760–755 BC | Before the Exile | Justice |
| **Hosea** | Hosea | Judah | c. 755–710 BC | Before the Exile | Love |
| **Isaiah** | Isaiah | Judah | c. 739–680 BC | Before the Exile | Salvation |
| **Micah** | Micah | Judah | c. 735–710 BC | Before the Exile | Righteousness |
| **Nahum** | Nahum | Nineveh | c. 660–650 BC | Before the Exile | Judgment |
| **Zephaniah** | Zephaniah | Judah | c. 635–625 BC | Before the Exile | Blessing |
| **Jeremiah** | Jeremiah | Judah | c. 627–580 BC | Before the Exile | Judgment |
| **Habakkuk** | Habakkuk | Judah | c. 607–604 BC | Before the Exile | Faith |
| **Daniel** | Daniel | Babylon | c. 605–536 BC | Exile | Sovereignty |
| **Ezekiel** | Ezekiel | Babylon | c. 592–570 BC | Exile | Hope |
| **Lamentations** | Jeremiah | Judah | 586 BC | Exile | Mercy |
| **Haggai** | Haggai | Judah | c. 520 BC | After the Exile | Priority |
| **Zechariah** | Zechariah | Judah | c. 520–518 BC / c. 480–470 BC | After the Exile | Obedience |
| **Malachi** | Malachi | Judah | c. 450–420 BC | After the Exile | Devotion |

*The Book of the Prophet*

# ISAIAH

| AUTHOR | KEY VERSE | READING TIME |
| --- | --- | --- |
| Isaiah | Isaiah 53:6 | 4 hours 37 minutes |

Isaiah's prophetic ministry spanned at least forty years and the reigns of four kings of Judah. His writings include some of the most well-known messianic prophecies in Scripture. The Book of Isaiah is much like a Bible in miniature. The first thirty-nine chapters are filled with God's judgment poured out upon immoral and idolatrous people, much like the thirty-nine books of the Old Testament. Judah had sinned; the surrounding nations had sinned; the whole earth had sinned. Judgment must come. God would not allow such blatant and unrepentant sin to go unpunished forever. But the final twenty-seven chapters declare a message of hope and forgiveness, much like the twenty-seven books of the New Testament. The Messiah was coming. He is a Savior who would bear a cross and a Sovereign who would wear a crown.

**Occasion:** Isaiah's prophetic ministry began during the period of the divided monarchy and continued into Israel's captivity, all along warning God's people of their idolatry and empty religiosity.

**Main Point:** God's people must turn from their sins to avoid the coming judgment, a judgment that will be experienced in its fullest form by the Messiah who is to come.

**Big Ideas:** God keeps His promises; all the promises He has made have come true or will come true. God's greatest promise is to send the Messiah, a promise that was fulfilled in Jesus. We cannot say we believe God and live in disobedience and without faith.

## OUTLINE:

I. The Judgment of Judah (chs. 1–12)
II. The Judgment of the Nations (chs. 13–23)
III. The Hope of the Day of the Lord (chs. 24–27)
IV. The Judgments and Blessings (chs. 28–35)
V. The Reign of King Hezekiah (chs. 36–39)
VI. The Future Deliverance of Israel (chs. 40–48)
VII. The Future Redeemer of Israel (chs. 49–57)
VIII. The Future Glory of Israel (chs. 58–66)

**930 BC**
The kingdom is divided

**792 BC**
Azariah (Uzziah) becomes king in Judah

**780 BC**
The first solar eclipse is recorded in China

**755 BC**
Isaiah begins to prophesy in Judah

**752 BC**
Jotham becomes king in Judah

**736 BC**
Ahaz becomes king in Judah

**734 BC**
Israel and Syria war against Judah

**732 BC**
The Assyrians defeat Damascus

**729 BC**
Hezekiah becomes king in Judah

**722 BC**
The Assyrians defeat Israel

1 The [a]vision of Isaiah the son of Amoz, which he saw concerning Judah and Jerusalem in the [b]days of Uzziah, Jotham, Ahaz, *and* Hezekiah, kings of Judah.

**1:1** Solomon's reign marked the end of Israel as a united country. After Solomon died in 931 BC, the nation split into two kingdoms, Israel and **Judah**. The prophet **Isaiah** was alive when Israel, the northern kingdom, was conquered by the Assyrians in 722 BC.

### *THE WICKEDNESS OF JUDAH*

2 [a]Hear, O heavens, and give ear, O earth!
For the LORD has spoken:
"I have nourished and brought up children,
And they have rebelled against Me;
3 [a]The ox knows its owner
And the donkey its master's crib;
*But* Israel [b]does not know,
My people do not consider."

4 Alas, sinful nation,
A people laden with iniquity,
[a]A brood of evildoers,
Children who are corrupters!
They have forsaken the LORD,
They have provoked to anger
The Holy One of Israel,
They have turned away backward.

5 [a]Why should you be stricken again?
You will revolt more and more.
The whole head is sick,
And the whole heart faints.
6 From the sole of the foot even to the head,
*There is* no soundness in it,
*But* wounds and bruises and putrefying sores;
They have not been closed or bound up,
Or soothed with ointment.

7 [a]Your country *is* desolate,
Your cities *are* burned with fire;
Strangers devour your land in your presence;
And *it is* desolate, as overthrown by strangers.
8 So the daughter of Zion is left [a]as a booth in a vineyard,
As a hut in a garden of cucumbers,
[b]As a besieged city.
9 [a]Unless the LORD of hosts
Had left to us a very small remnant,
We would have become like [b]Sodom,
We would have been made like Gomorrah.

10 Hear the word of the LORD,
You rulers [a]of Sodom;
Give ear to the law of our God,
You people of Gomorrah:
11 "To what purpose *is* the multitude of your [a]sacrifices to Me?"
Says the LORD.
"I have had enough of burnt offerings of rams
And the fat of fed cattle.
I do not delight in the blood of bulls,
Or of lambs or goats.

12 "When you come [a]to appear before Me,
Who has required this from your hand,
To trample My courts?
13 Bring no more [a]futile sacrifices;
Incense is an abomination to Me.
The New Moons, the Sabbaths, and [b]the calling of assemblies—
I cannot endure iniquity and the sacred meeting.
14 Your [a]New Moons and your [b]appointed feasts
My soul hates;
They are a trouble to Me,
I am weary of bearing *them.*
15 [a]When you spread out your hands,
I will hide My eyes from you;
[b]Even though you make many prayers,
I will not hear.
Your hands are full of blood.

16 "Wash[a] yourselves, make yourselves clean;
Put away the evil of your doings from before My eyes.
[b]Cease to do evil,
17 Learn to do good;
Seek justice,
Rebuke the oppressor;[1]
Defend the fatherless,
Plead for the widow.

18 "Come now, and let us [a]reason together,"
Says the LORD,
"Though your sins are like scarlet,
[b]They shall be as white as snow;
Though they are red like crimson,
They shall be as wool.
19 If you are willing and obedient,
You shall eat the good of the land;
20 But if you refuse and rebel,
You shall be devoured by the sword";
[a]For the mouth of the LORD has spoken.

**1:1** [a] Num. 12:6 [b] 2 Chr. 26—32 **1:2** [a] Jer. 2:12 **1:3** [a] Jer. 8:7 [b] Jer. 9:3, 6 **1:4** [a] Matt. 3:7 **1:5** [a] Jer. 5:3 **1:7** [a] Deut. 28:51, 52 **1:8** [a] Job 27:18 [b] Jer. 4:17 **1:9** [a] Lam. 3:22 [b] Gen. 19:24 **1:10** [a] Deut. 32:32 **1:11** [a] [1 Sam. 15:22] **1:12** [a] Ex. 23:17 **1:13** [a] Matt. 15:9 [b] Joel 1:14 **1:14** [a] Num. 28:11 [b] Lam. 2:6 **1:15** [a] Prov. 1:28 [b] Mic. 3:4 **1:16** [a] Jer. 4:14 [b] Rom. 12:9 **1:17** [1] Some ancient versions read *the oppressed.* **1:18** [a] Is. 43:26 [b] Ps. 51:7 **1:20** [a] [Titus 1:2]

### THE DEGENERATE CITY

21 [a]How the faithful city has become a harlot!
It was full of justice;
Righteousness lodged in it,
But now [b]murderers.
22 [a]Your silver has become dross,
Your wine mixed with water.
23 [a]Your princes *are* rebellious,
And [b]companions of thieves;
[c]Everyone loves bribes,
And follows after rewards.
They [d]do not defend the fatherless,
Nor does the cause of the widow come
before them.

24 Therefore the Lord says,
The LORD of hosts, the Mighty One of Israel,
"Ah, [a]I will rid Myself of My adversaries,
And take vengeance on My enemies.
25 I will turn My hand against you,
And [a]thoroughly purge away your dross,
And take away all your alloy.
26 I will restore your judges [a]as at the first,
And your counselors as at the beginning.
Afterward [b]you shall be called the city of
righteousness, the faithful city."

27 Zion shall be redeemed with justice,
And her penitents with righteousness.
28 The [a]destruction of transgressors and of
sinners *shall be* together,
And those who forsake the LORD shall be
consumed.
29 For they[1] shall be ashamed of the
terebinth trees
Which you have desired;
And you shall be embarrassed because of
the gardens
Which you have chosen.
30 For you shall be as a terebinth whose leaf
fades,
And as a garden that has no water.
31 [a]The strong shall be as tinder,
And the work of it as a spark;
Both will burn together,
And no one shall [b]quench *them.*

### THE FUTURE HOUSE OF GOD
*(Mic. 4:1–5)*

**2** The word that Isaiah the son of Amoz saw
concerning Judah and Jerusalem.

2 Now [a]it shall come to pass [b]in the latter
days
[c]*That* the mountain of the LORD's house
Shall be established on the top of the
mountains,
And shall be exalted above the hills;
And all nations shall flow to it.
3 Many people shall come and say,
[a]"Come, and let us go up to the mountain of
the LORD,
To the house of the God of Jacob;
He will teach us His ways,
And we shall walk in His paths."
[b]For out of Zion shall go forth the law,
And the word of the LORD from Jerusalem.

**SEEING JESUS IN THE SCRIPTURE**

**2:3** Isaiah's vision points to when God would teach His people directly from Jerusalem. Jesus fulfilled this prophecy when He came to earth and spent much of His three-year ministry teaching from this city and its surrounding regions (see Luke 21:37).

4 He shall judge between the nations,
And rebuke many people;
They shall beat their swords into
plowshares,
And their spears into pruning hooks;
Nation shall not lift up sword against
nation,
Neither shall they learn war anymore.

### THE DAY OF THE LORD

5 O house of Jacob, come and let us [a]walk
In the light of the LORD.

6 For You have forsaken Your people, the
house of Jacob,
Because they are filled [a]with eastern ways;
They *are* [b]soothsayers like the Philistines,
[c]And they are pleased with the children of
foreigners.
7 [a]Their land is also full of silver and gold,
And there is no end to their treasures;
Their land is also full of horses,
And there is no end to their chariots.
8 [a]Their land is also full of idols;
They worship the work of their own hands,
That which their own fingers have made.
9 People bow down,
And each man humbles himself;
Therefore do not forgive them.

10 [a]Enter into the rock, and hide in the dust,
From the terror of the LORD
And the glory of His majesty.
11 The lofty looks of man shall be [a]humbled,
The haughtiness of men shall be bowed
down,
And the LORD alone shall be exalted [b]in
that day.

1:21 [a]Jer. 2:20 [b]Mic. 3:1–3 1:22 [a]Jer. 6:28 1:23 [a]Hos. 9:15 [b]Prov. 29:24 [c]Jer. 22:17 [d]Jer. 5:28 1:24 [a]Deut. 28:63 1:25 [a]Mal. 3:3 1:26 [a]Jer. 33:7–11 [b]Zech. 8:3 1:28 [a][2 Thess. 1:8, 9] 1:29 [1]Following Masoretic Text, Septuagint, and Vulgate; some Hebrew manuscripts and Targum read *you.* 1:31 [a]Ezek. 32:21 [b]Mark 9:43 2:2 [a]Mic. 4:1 [b]Gen. 49:1 [c]Ps. 68:15 2:3 [a]Jer. 50:5 [b]Luke 24:47 2:5 [a]Eph. 5:8 2:6 [a]Num. 23:7 [b]Deut. 18:14 [c]Ps. 106:35 2:7 [a]Deut. 17:16 2:8 [a]Jer. 2:28 2:10 [a]Rev. 6:15, 16 2:11 [a]Prov. 16:5 [b]Hos. 2:16

12 For the day of the LORD of hosts
*Shall come* upon everything proud and lofty,
Upon everything lifted up—
And it shall be brought low—
13 Upon all [a]the cedars of Lebanon *that are* high and lifted up,
And upon all the oaks of Bashan;
14 [a]Upon all the high mountains,
And upon all the hills *that are* lifted up;
15 Upon every high tower,
And upon every fortified wall;
16 [a]Upon all the ships of Tarshish,
And upon all the beautiful sloops.
17 The loftiness of man shall be bowed down,
And the haughtiness of men shall be brought low;
The LORD alone will be exalted in that day,
18 But the idols He shall utterly abolish.

19 They shall go into the [a]holes of the rocks,
And into the caves of the earth,
[b]From the terror of the LORD
And the glory of His majesty,
When He arises [c]to shake the earth mightily.

20 In that day a man will cast away his idols of silver
And his idols of gold,
Which they made, *each* for himself to worship,
To the moles and bats,
21 To go into the clefts of the rocks,
And into the crags of the rugged rocks,
From the terror of the LORD
And the glory of His majesty,
When He arises to shake the earth mightily.

22 [a]Sever yourselves from such a man,
Whose [b]breath *is* in his nostrils;
For of what account is he?

### JUDGMENT ON JUDAH AND JERUSALEM

3 For behold, the Lord, the LORD of hosts,
[a]Takes away from Jerusalem and from Judah
[b]The stock and the store,
The whole supply of bread and the whole supply of water;
2 [a]The mighty man and the man of war,
The judge and the prophet,
And the diviner and the elder;
3 The captain of fifty and the honorable man,
The counselor and the skillful artisan,
And the expert enchanter.

4 "I will give [a]children *to be* their princes,
And babes shall rule over them.
5 The people will be oppressed,
Every one by another and every one by his neighbor;
The child will be insolent toward the elder,
And the base toward the honorable."

6 When a man takes hold of his brother
In the house of his father, *saying,*
"You have clothing;
You be our ruler,
And *let* these ruins *be* under your power,"[1]
7 In that day he will protest, saying,
"I cannot cure *your* ills,
For in my house *is* neither food nor clothing;
Do not make me a ruler of the people."

8 For [a]Jerusalem stumbled,
And Judah is fallen,
Because their tongue and their doings
*Are* against the LORD,
To provoke the eyes of His glory.
9 The look on their countenance witnesses against them,
And they declare their sin as [a]Sodom;
They do not hide *it.*
Woe to their soul!
For they have brought evil upon themselves.

10 "Say to the righteous [a]that *it shall be* well *with them,*
[b]For they shall eat the fruit of their doings.
11 Woe to the wicked! [a]*It shall be* ill *with him,*
For the reward of his hands shall be given him.
12 *As for* My people, children *are* their oppressors,
And women rule over them.
O My people! [a]Those who lead you cause *you* to err,
And destroy the way of your paths."

### OPPRESSION AND LUXURY CONDEMNED

13 The LORD stands up [a]to plead,
And stands to judge the people.
14 The LORD will enter into judgment
With the elders of His people
And His princes:
"For you have eaten up [a]the vineyard;
The plunder of the poor *is* in your houses.
15 What do you mean by [a]crushing My people
And grinding the faces of the poor?"
Says the Lord GOD of hosts.

2:13 [a] Zech. 11:1, 2 2:14 [a] Is. 30:25 2:16 [a] 1 Kin. 10:22 2:19 [a] Hos. 10:8 [b] [2 Thess. 1:9] [c] Hag. 2:6, 7 2:22 [a] Jer. 17:5 [b] Job 27:3 3:1 [a] Jer. 37:21 [b] Lev. 26:26 3:2 [a] 2 Kin. 24:14 3:4 [a] Eccl. 10:16 3:6 [1] Literally *hand* 3:8 [a] Mic. 3:12 3:9 [a] Gen. 13:13 3:10 [a] [Eccl. 8:12] [b] Ps. 128:2 3:11 [a] [Ps. 11:6] 3:12 [a] Is. 9:16 3:13 [a] Mic. 6:2 3:14 [a] Matt. 21:33 3:15 [a] Mic. 3:2, 3

16 Moreover the LORD says:

"Because the daughters of Zion are haughty,
And walk with outstretched necks
And wanton eyes,
Walking and mincing *as* they go,
Making a jingling with their feet,
17 Therefore the Lord will strike with [a]a scab
The crown of the head of the daughters of
Zion,
And the LORD will [b]uncover their secret
parts."

18 In that day the Lord will take away the
finery:
The jingling anklets, the scarves, and the
[a]crescents;
19 The pendants, the bracelets, and the veils;
20 The headdresses, the leg ornaments, and
the headbands;
The perfume boxes, the charms,
21 and the rings;
The nose jewels,
22 the festal apparel, and the mantles;
The outer garments, the purses,
23 and the mirrors;
The fine linen, the turbans, and the robes.

24 And so it shall be:

Instead of a sweet smell there will be a
stench;
Instead of a sash, a rope;
Instead of well-set hair, [a]baldness;
Instead of a rich robe, a girding of
sackcloth;
And branding instead of beauty.
25 Your men shall fall by the sword,
And your mighty in the war.
26 [a]Her gates shall lament and mourn,
And she *being* desolate [b]shall sit on the
ground.

**4** And [a]in that day seven women shall take
hold of one man, saying,
"We will [b]eat our own food and wear our
own apparel;
Only let us be called by your name,
To take away [c]our reproach."

## THE RENEWAL OF ZION

2 In that day [a]the Branch of the LORD shall
be beautiful and glorious;
And the fruit of the earth *shall be*
excellent and appealing
For those of Israel who have escaped.

3 And it shall come to pass that *he who is*
left in Zion and remains in Jerusalem [a]will be
called holy—everyone who is [b]recorded among
the living in Jerusalem. 4 When [a]the Lord has
washed away the filth of the daughters of Zion,
and purged the blood of Jerusalem from her
midst, by the spirit of judgment and by the spirit
of burning, 5 then the LORD will create above
every dwelling place of Mount Zion, and above
her assemblies, [a]a cloud and smoke by day and
[b]the shining of a flaming fire by night. For over
all the glory there *will be* a covering. 6 And there
will be a tabernacle for shade in the daytime
from the heat, [a]for a place of refuge, and for a
shelter from storm and rain.

## GOD'S DISAPPOINTING VINEYARD

**5** Now let me sing to my Well-beloved
A song of my Beloved [a]regarding His
vineyard:

My Well-beloved has a vineyard
On a very fruitful hill.
2 He dug it up and cleared out its stones,
And planted it with the choicest vine.
He built a tower in its midst,
And also made a winepress in it;
[a]So He expected *it* to bring forth *good*
grapes,
But it brought forth wild grapes.

**5:2** Towers were often built in the middle of vineyards to prevent people from stealing **grapes**. From the **tower**, a guard could spot thieves and defend the vineyard with a bow and arrow or slingshot.

3 "And now, O inhabitants of Jerusalem and
men of Judah,
[a]Judge, please, between Me and My
vineyard.
4 What more could have been done to My
vineyard
That I have not done in [a]it?
Why then, when I expected *it* to bring
forth *good* grapes,
Did it bring forth wild grapes?
5 And now, please let Me tell you what I will
do to My vineyard:
[a]I will take away its hedge, and it shall be
burned;
*And* break down its wall, and it shall be
trampled down.
6 I will lay it [a]waste;
It shall not be pruned or dug,
But there shall come up briers and
[b]thorns.
I will also command the clouds
That they rain no rain on it."

3:17 [a] Deut. 28:27 [b] Jer. 13:22 3:18 [a] Judg. 8:21, 26 3:24 [a] Is. 22:12 3:26 [a] Jer. 14:2 [b] Lam. 2:10 4:1 [a] Is. 2:11, 17 [b] 2 Thess. 3:12 [c] Luke 1:25 4:2 [a] [Jer. 23:5] 4:3 [a] Is. 60:21 [b] Phil. 4:3 4:4 [a] Mal. 3:2, 3 4:5 [a] Ex. 13:21, 22 [b] Zech. 2:5 4:6 [a] Is. 25:4 5:1 [a] Matt. 21:33 5:2 [a] Deut. 32:6 5:3 [a] [Rom. 3:4] 5:4 [a] 2 Chr. 36:15, 16 5:5 [a] Ps. 80:12; 89:40, 41 5:6 [a] 2 Chr. 36:19–21 [b] Is. 7:19–25

7 For the vineyard of the LORD of hosts *is*
the house of Israel,
And the men of Judah are His pleasant
plant.
He looked for justice, but behold,
oppression;
For righteousness, but behold, a cry *for help.*

### IMPENDING JUDGMENT ON EXCESSES

8 Woe to those who join [a]house to house;
They add field to field,
Till *there is* no place
Where they may dwell alone in the midst
of the land!
9 [a]In my hearing the LORD of hosts *said,*
"Truly, many houses shall be desolate,
Great and beautiful ones, without
inhabitant.
10 For ten acres of vineyard shall yield one
[a]bath,
And a homer of seed shall yield one ephah."

11 [a]Woe to those who rise early in the
morning,
*That* they may follow intoxicating drink;
Who continue until night, *till* wine
inflames them!
12 [a]The harp and the strings,
The tambourine and flute,
And wine are in their feasts;
But [b]they do not regard the work of the
LORD,
Nor consider the operation of His hands.

13 [a]Therefore my people have gone into
captivity,
Because *they have* no [b]knowledge;
Their honorable men *are* famished,
And their multitude dried up with thirst.
14 Therefore Sheol has enlarged itself
And opened its mouth beyond measure;
Their glory and their multitude and their
pomp,
And he who is jubilant, shall descend into it.
15 People shall be brought down,
[a]Each man shall be humbled,
And the eyes of the lofty shall be
humbled.
16 But the LORD of hosts shall be [a]exalted in
judgment,
And God who is holy shall be hallowed in
righteousness.
17 Then the lambs shall feed in their pasture,
And in the waste places of [a]the fat ones
strangers shall eat.

18 Woe to those who draw iniquity with
cords of vanity,
And sin as if with a cart rope;
19 [a]That say, "Let Him make speed *and* hasten
His work,
That we may see *it;*
And let the counsel of the Holy One of
Israel draw near and come,
That we may know *it.*"

20 Woe to those who call evil good, and good
evil;
Who put darkness for light, and light for
darkness;
Who put bitter for sweet, and sweet for bitter!

21 Woe to *those who are* [a]wise in their own eyes,
And prudent in their own sight!

22 Woe to men mighty at drinking wine,
Woe to men valiant for mixing
intoxicating drink,

**5:8** [a] Mic. 2:2 **5:9** [a] Is. 22:14 **5:10** [a] Ezek. 45:11 **5:11** [a] Prov. 23:29, 30 **5:12** [a] Amos 6:5 [b] Job 34:27 **5:13** [a] 2 Kin. 24:14–16 [b] Hos. 4:6 **5:15** [a] Is. 2:9, 11 **5:16** [a] Is. 2:11 **5:17** [a] Is. 10:16 **5:19** [a] Jer. 17:15 **5:21** [a] Rom. 1:22; 12:16

APPLY THE TRUTH

## SUBSTANCE ABUSE

**5:11** Substance abuse, the harmful or hazardous use of alcohol, drugs, or other dangerous items, is far too common today. Some abused substances are illegal and known to be dangerous. Others are legal but become dangerous without moderation. Too much of a good thing can become a bad thing; too much of a bad thing becomes a dangerous thing. This is what we are warned of in Isaiah. What controls us and drives us? If it's anything but God, such as here where intoxicating drink controls a person's thoughts and actions, then we're in a dangerous place. We don't want to be controlled by anything other than the Holy Spirit (Eph. 5:18).

Giving away control often stems from a desire to distract ourselves or mask things going on within us. People often do this with alcohol and drugs, but it can be done with social media, entertainment, hobbies, or relationships. We distract ourselves from something, rather than deal with it. The call of Christ is to yield to the Holy Spirit and allow Him to confront our weaknesses and bring us into strength. Live in freedom by yielding to the power of the Holy Spirit—and only His power—in your life.

23 Who [a]justify the wicked for a bribe,
And take away justice from the righteous man!

24 Therefore, [a]as the fire devours the stubble,
And the flame consumes the chaff,
*So* [b]their root will be as rottenness,
And their blossom will ascend like dust;
Because they have rejected the law of the LORD of hosts,
And despised the word of the Holy One of Israel.

25 [a]Therefore the anger of the LORD is aroused against His people;
He has stretched out His hand against them
And stricken them,
And [b]the hills trembled.
Their carcasses *were* as refuse in the midst of the streets.

[c]For all this His anger is not turned away,
But His hand *is* stretched out still.

26 [a]He will lift up a banner to the nations from afar,
And will [b]whistle to them from [c]the end of the earth;
Surely [d]they shall come with speed, swiftly.

27 No one will be weary or stumble among them,
No one will slumber or sleep;
Nor [a]will the belt on their loins be loosed,
Nor the strap of their sandals be broken;

28 [a]Whose arrows *are* sharp,
And all their bows bent;
Their horses' hooves will seem like flint,
And their wheels like a whirlwind.

29 Their roaring *will be* like a lion,
They will roar like young lions;
Yes, they will roar
And lay hold of the prey;
They will carry *it* away safely,
And no one will deliver.

30 In that day they will roar against them
Like the roaring of the sea.
And if *one* [a]looks to the land,
Behold, darkness *and* sorrow;
And the light is darkened by the clouds.

### *ISAIAH CALLED TO BE A PROPHET*
*(cf. Ezek. 1:4–28)*

6 In the year that [a]King Uzziah died, I [b]saw
the Lord sitting on a throne, high and lifted
up, and the train of His *robe* filled the temple.
2 Above it stood seraphim; each one had six
wings: with two he covered his face, [a]with two

5:23 [a] Prov. 17:15 5:24 [a] Ex. 15:7 [b] Job 18:16 5:25 [a] 2 Kin. 22:13, 17 [b] Jer. 4:24 [c] Is. 9:12, 17 5:26 [a] Is. 11:10, 12 [b] Is. 7:18 [c] Mal. 1:11 [d] Joel 2:7 5:27 [a] Dan. 5:6 5:28 [a] Jer. 5:16 5:30 [a] Is. 8:22 6:1 [a] 2 Kin. 15:7 [b] John 12:41 6:2 [a] Ezek. 1:11

KNOW THE TRUTH

## THE DOCTRINE OF GOD
### PART 10: THE HOLINESS OF GOD

**6:1–7** When someone wants to emphasize a detail in writing, it's common to use an exclamation mark at the end of a sentence or spell a word in all capital letters. For example: "That was the coldest Christmas morning of my lifetime!" Or: "One word to describe that Christmas: COLD." The writers of Scripture had a different way of emphasizing something: repetition. Repeating something twice was a way to make it stand out. Repeating something three times was the highest form of emphasis in Hebrew writing.

When Isaiah was given a vision of the Lord, fiery flying angelic beings described God by crying out, "Holy, holy, holy is the LORD of hosts." That emphasis is so strong, one could scream "holy" as long and loud as his or her lungs could permit, and it wouldn't overstate the angels' expression. God is holy! To be *holy* is to be set apart, pure, sacred, or distinct. God is utterly unique. He's matchless, peerless, perfect, and in a category of His own. He's separate from all that is sinful, evil, and corrupt. He's absolutely righteous, just, loving, and good. He is perfect purity.

Our sin separates us from God's holy presence. In His mercy, though, God declares us holy when we trust in the Holy One sent for us, Jesus Christ (see Eph. 1:3–6).

*For* **THE DOCTRINE OF GOD: PART 11: THE LOVE OF GOD**, *turn to 1 John 4:8 on page 1280.*

he covered his feet, and with two he flew. [3]And
one cried to another and said:

[a]"Holy, holy, holy *is* the LORD of hosts;
[b]The whole earth *is* full of His glory!"

[4]And the posts of the door were shaken by the
voice of him who cried out, and the house was
filled with smoke.
[5]So I said:

"Woe *is* me, for I am undone!
Because I *am* a man of [a]unclean lips,
And I dwell in the midst of a people of
unclean lips;
For my eyes have seen the King,
The LORD of hosts."

[6]Then one of the seraphim flew to me, hav-
ing in his hand a live coal *which* he had taken
with the tongs from [a]the altar. [7]And he [a]touched
my mouth *with it,* and said:

"Behold, this has touched your lips;
Your iniquity is taken away,
And your sin purged."

[8]Also I heard the voice of the Lord, saying:

"Whom shall I send,
And who will go for [a]Us?"

Then I said, "Here *am* I! Send me."
[9]And He said, "Go, and [a]tell this people:

'Keep on hearing, but do not
understand;
Keep on seeing, but do not perceive.'

10 "Make [a]the heart of this people dull,
And their ears heavy,
And shut their eyes;
[b]Lest they see with their eyes,
And hear with their ears,
And understand with their heart,
And return and be healed."

[11]Then I said, "Lord, how long?"

SEEING JESUS IN THE SCRIPTURE

**6:9–10** Isaiah revealed Israel's hardened hearts. Jesus also encountered the hardened hearts of the Israelites during His earthly ministry. Ultimately, Jesus using parables and some people not understanding them fulfilled this prophecy (see Matt. 13:14).

And He answered:

[a]"Until the cities are laid waste and without
inhabitant,
The houses are without a man,
The land is utterly desolate,
12 [a]The LORD has removed men far away,
And the forsaken places *are* many in the
midst of the land.
13 But yet a tenth *will be* in it,
And will return and be for consuming,
As a terebinth tree or as an oak,
Whose stump *remains* when it is cut
down.
So [a]the holy seed *shall be* its stump."

## *ISAIAH SENT TO KING AHAZ*

*(2 Kin. 16:5; 2 Chr. 28:5–15)*

7 Now it came to pass in the days of [a]Ahaz the
son of Jotham, the son of Uzziah, king of
Judah, *that* Rezin king of Syria and Pekah the
son of Remaliah, king of Israel, went up to Je-
rusalem to *make* war against [b]it, but could not
prevail against it. [2]And it was told to the house
of David, saying, "Syria's forces are deployed
in Ephraim." So his heart and the heart of his
people were moved as the trees of the woods
are moved with the wind.
[3]Then the LORD said to Isaiah, "Go out now
to meet Ahaz, you and Shear-Jashub[1] your son,
at the end of the aqueduct from the upper pool,
on the highway to the Fuller's Field, [4]and say to
him: 'Take heed, and be [a]quiet; do not fear or
be fainthearted for these two stubs of smoking
firebrands, for the fierce anger of Rezin and
Syria, and the son of Remaliah. [5]Because Syria,
Ephraim, and the son of Remaliah have plotted
evil against you, saying, [6]"Let us go up against
Judah and trouble it, and let us make a gap in
its wall for ourselves, and set a king over them,
the son of Tabel"— [7]thus says the Lord GOD:

[a]"It shall not stand,
Nor shall it come to pass.
8 [a]For the head of Syria *is* Damascus,
And the head of Damascus *is* Rezin.
Within sixty-five years Ephraim will be
broken,
*So that it will* not *be* a people.
9 The head of Ephraim *is* Samaria,
And the head of Samaria *is* Remaliah's
son.
[a]If you will not believe,
Surely you shall not be established." ' "

## *THE IMMANUEL PROPHECY*

[10]Moreover the LORD spoke again to Ahaz,
saying, [11a]"Ask a sign for yourself from the LORD
your God; ask it either in the depth or in the
height above."

**6:3** [a] Rev. 4:8 [b] Num. 14:21 **6:5** [a] Ex. 6:12, 30 **6:6** [a] Rev. 8:3 **6:7** [a] Jer. 1:9 **6:8** [a] Gen. 1:26 **6:9** [a] Matt. 13:14 **6:10** [a] Ps. 119:70 [b] Jer. 5:21 **6:11** [a] Mic. 3:12 **6:12** [a] 2 Kin. 25:21 **6:13** [a] Ezra 9:2 **7:1** [a] 2 Chr. 28 [b] 2 Kin. 16:5, 9 **7:3** [1] Literally *A Remnant Shall Return* **7:4** [a] Is. 30:15 **7:7** [a] Is. 8:10 **7:8** [a] 2 Sam. 8:6 **7:9** [a] 2 Chr. 20:20 **7:11** [a] Matt. 12:38

12 But Ahaz said, "I will not ask, nor will I
test the LORD!"
13 Then he said, "Hear now, O house of David!
*Is it* a small thing for you to weary men, but will
you weary my God also? 14 Therefore the Lord
Himself will give you a sign: [a]Behold, the virgin
shall conceive and bear [b]a Son, and shall call
His name [c]Immanuel.[1] 15 Curds and honey He
shall eat, that He may know to refuse the evil
and choose the good. 16 [a]For before the Child
shall know to refuse the evil and choose the
good, the land that you dread will be forsaken by
[b]both her kings. 17 [a]The LORD will bring the king
of Assyria upon you and your people and your
father's house—days that have not come since
the day that [b]Ephraim departed from Judah."

> **SEEING JESUS IN THE SCRIPTURE**
>
> **7:14** *Immanuel* means "God with us." The Son of God took on the flesh and was born of a virgin to fulfill this sign (see Luke 1:31). Through Jesus' life, death, and resurrection, we are forgiven, and God is with us forevermore.

18 And it shall come to pass in that day
*That* the LORD [a]will whistle for the fly
That *is* in the farthest part of the rivers of Egypt,
And for the bee that *is* in the land of Assyria.
19 They will come, and all of them will rest
In the desolate valleys and in [a]the clefts of the rocks,
And on all thorns and in all pastures.

20 In the same day the Lord will shave with a [a]hired [b]razor,
With those from beyond the River,[1] with the king of Assyria,
The head and the hair of the legs,
And will also remove the beard.

21 It shall be in that day
*That* a man will keep alive a young cow and two sheep;
22 So it shall be, from the abundance of milk they give,
That he will eat curds;
For curds and honey everyone will eat who is left in the land.

23 It shall happen in that day,
*That* wherever there could be a thousand vines
*Worth* a thousand *shekels* of silver,
[a]It will be for briers and thorns.
24 With arrows and bows *men* will come there,
Because all the land will become briers and thorns.

25 And to any hill which could be dug with the hoe,
You will not go there for fear of briers and thorns;
But it will become a range for oxen
And a place for sheep to roam.

### ASSYRIA WILL INVADE THE LAND

8 Moreover the LORD said to me, "Take a large
scroll, and [a]write on it with a man's pen con-
cerning Maher-Shalal-Hash-Baz.[1] 2 And I will take
for Myself faithful witnesses to record, [a]Uriah
the priest and Zechariah the son of Jeberechiah."
3 Then I went to the prophetess, and she
conceived and bore a son. Then the LORD said
to me, "Call his name Maher-Shalal-Hash-Baz;
4 [a]for before the child shall have knowledge to
cry 'My father' and 'My mother,' [b]the riches of
Damascus and the spoil of Samaria will be taken
away before the king of Assyria."
5 The LORD also spoke to me again, saying:

6 "Inasmuch as these people refused
The waters of [a]Shiloah that flow softly,
And rejoice [b]in Rezin and in Remaliah's son;
7 Now therefore, behold, the Lord brings up over them
The waters of the River,[1] strong and mighty—
The king of Assyria and all his glory;
He will go up over all his channels
And go over all his banks.
8 He will pass through Judah,
He will overflow and pass over,
[a]He will reach up to the neck;
And the stretching out of his wings
Will fill the breadth of Your land,
O [b]Immanuel.[1]

9 "Be[a] shattered, O you peoples, and be broken in pieces!
Give ear, all you from far countries.
Gird yourselves, but be broken in pieces;
Gird yourselves, but be broken in pieces.
10 [a]Take counsel together, but it will come to nothing;
Speak the word, [b]but it will not stand,
[c]For God *is* with us."[1]

### FEAR GOD, HEED HIS WORD

11 For the LORD spoke thus to me with a
strong hand, and instructed me that I should
not walk in the way of this people, saying:

**7:14** [a] Matt. 1:23 [b] [Is. 9:6] [c] Is. 8:8, 10 [1] Literally *God-With-Us* **7:16** [a] Is. 8:4 [b] 2 Kin. 15:30 **7:17** [a] 2 Chr. 28:19, 20 [b] 1 Kin. 12:16 **7:18** [a] Is. 5:26 **7:19** [a] Jer. 16:16 **7:20** [a] Is. 10:5, 15 [b] 2 Kin. 16:7 [1] That is, the Euphrates **7:23** [a] Is. 5:6 **8:1** [a] Hab. 2:2 [1] Literally *Speed the Spoil, Hasten the Booty* **8:2** [a] 2 Kin. 16:10 **8:4** [a] 2 Kin. 17:6; Is. 7:16 [b] 2 Kin. 15:29 **8:6** [a] John 9:7 [b] Is. 7:1, 2 **8:7** [1] That is, the Euphrates **8:8** [a] Is. 30:28 [b] Is. 7:14 [1] Literally *God-With-Us* **8:9** [a] Joel 3:9 **8:10** [a] Is. 7:7 [b] Is. 7:14 [c] Rom. 8:31 [1] Hebrew *Immanuel*

12 "Do not say, 'A conspiracy,'
Concerning all that this people call a
conspiracy,
Nor be afraid of their threats, nor be
troubled.
13 The LORD of hosts, Him you shall
hallow;
*Let* Him *be* your fear,
And *let* Him *be* your dread.
14 [a]He will be as a sanctuary,
But [b]a stone of stumbling and a rock of
offense
To both the houses of Israel,
As a trap and a snare to the inhabitants of
Jerusalem.

### SEEING JESUS IN THE SCRIPTURE

**8:14** Jesus came to be our sanctuary, but the religious leaders and most of the people saw Him as a stumbling block and rejected Him (see Luke 20:17–19). As a result of their hardness of heart and unbelief, Jesus became a snare for them instead.

15 And many among them shall [a]stumble;
They shall fall and be broken,
Be snared and taken."

16 Bind up the testimony,
Seal the law among my disciples.
17 And I will wait on the LORD,
Who [a]hides His face from the house of
Jacob;
And I [b]will hope in Him.
18 [a]Here am I and the children whom the
LORD has given me!
*We* [b]are for signs and wonders in
Israel
From the LORD of hosts,
Who dwells in Mount Zion.

19 And when they say to you, [a]"Seek those
who are mediums and wizards, [b]who whisper
and mutter," should not a people seek their
God? *Should they* [c]*seek* the dead on behalf of
the living? 20 [a]To the law and to the testimony!
If they do not speak according to this word, *it*
*is* because [b]*there is* no light in them.
21 They will pass through it hard-pressed
and hungry; and it shall happen, when they are
hungry, that they will be enraged and [a]curse their
king and their God, and look upward. 22 Then
they will look to the earth, and see trouble and
darkness, gloom of anguish; and *they will be*
driven into darkness.

## *THE GOVERNMENT OF THE PROMISED SON*

*(Is. 11:1–9)*

9 Nevertheless [a]the gloom *will* not *be* upon
her who *is* distressed,
As when at [b]first He lightly esteemed
The land of Zebulun and the land of
Naphtali,
And [c]afterward more heavily oppressed *her*,
*By* the way of the sea, beyond the Jordan,
In Galilee of the Gentiles.
2 [a]The people who walked in darkness
Have seen a great light;
Those who dwelt in the land of the
shadow of death,
Upon them a light has shined.

3 You have multiplied the nation
*And* increased its joy;[1]
They rejoice before You
According to the joy of harvest,
As *men* rejoice [a]when they divide the spoil.
4 For You have broken the yoke of his burden
And the staff of his shoulder,
The rod of his oppressor,
As in the day of [a]Midian.
5 For every warrior's sandal from the noisy
battle,
And garments rolled in blood,
[a]Will be used for burning *and* fuel of fire.

6 [a]For unto us a Child is born,
Unto us a [b]Son is given;
And [c]the government will be upon His
shoulder.
And His name will be called
[d]Wonderful, Counselor, [e]Mighty God,
Everlasting Father, [f]Prince of Peace.
7 Of the increase of *His* government and
peace
[a]*There will be* no end,
Upon the throne of David and over His
kingdom,
To order it and establish it with judgment
and justice
From that time forward, even forever.
The [b]zeal of the LORD of hosts will
perform this.

### SEEING JESUS IN THE SCRIPTURE

**9:6–7** This is one of the most well-known Messianic prophecies, often quoted and sung at Christmas. Jesus is the Son of God who came to rule over His people with justice and bring everlasting peace (see Luke 1:32–33; 2:11).

**8:14** [a] Ezek. 11:16 [b] Luke 2:34; 20:17 **8:15** [a] Matt. 21:44 **8:17** [a] Is. 54:8 [b] Hab. 2:3 **8:18** [a] Heb. 2:13 [b] Ps. 71:7 **8:19** [a] 1 Sam. 28:8 [b] Is. 29:4 [c] Ps. 106:28 **8:20** [a] Luke 16:29 [b] Mic. 3:6 **8:21** [a] Rev. 16:11 **9:1** [a] Is. 8:22 [b] 2 Kin. 15:29 [c] Matt. 4:13–16 **9:2** [a] Matt. 4:16 **9:3** [a] Judg. 5:30 [1] Following Qere and Targum; Kethib and Vulgate read *not increased joy;* Septuagint reads *Most of the people You brought down in Your joy.* **9:4** [a] Judg. 7:22 **9:5** [a] Is. 66:15 **9:6** [a] [Luke 2:11] [b] [John 3:16] [c] [Matt. 28:18] [d] Judg. 13:18 [e] Titus 2:13 [f] Eph. 2:14 **9:7** [a] Dan. 2:44 [b] Is. 37:32

### *THE PUNISHMENT OF SAMARIA*

8 The Lord sent a word against [a]Jacob,
And it has fallen on Israel.
9 All the people will know—
Ephraim and the inhabitant of Samaria—
Who say in pride and arrogance of heart:
10 "The bricks have fallen down,
But we will rebuild with hewn stones;
The sycamores are cut down,
But we will replace *them* with cedars."
11 Therefore the LORD shall set up
The adversaries of Rezin against him,
And spur his enemies on,
12 The Syrians before and the Philistines behind;
And they shall devour Israel with an open mouth.

For all this His anger is not turned away,
But His hand *is* stretched out still.

13 For the people do not turn to Him who strikes them,
Nor do they seek the LORD of hosts.
14 Therefore the LORD will cut off head and tail from Israel,
Palm branch and bulrush [a]in one day.
15 The elder and honorable, he *is* the head;
The prophet who teaches lies, he *is* the tail.
16 For [a]the leaders of this people cause *them* to err,
And *those who are* led by them are destroyed.
17 Therefore the Lord [a]will have no joy in their young men,
Nor have mercy on their fatherless and widows;
For everyone *is* a hypocrite and an evildoer,
And every mouth speaks folly.

[b]For all this His anger is not turned away,
But His hand *is* stretched out still.

18 For wickedness [a]burns as the fire;
It shall devour the briers and thorns,
And kindle in the thickets of the forest;
They shall mount up *like* rising smoke.
19 Through the wrath of the LORD of hosts
[a]The land is burned up,
And the people shall be as fuel for the fire;
[b]No man shall spare his brother.
20 And he shall snatch on the right hand
And be hungry;
He shall devour on the left hand
[a]And not be satisfied;
[b]Every man shall eat the flesh of his own arm.
21 Manasseh *shall devour* Ephraim, and Ephraim Manasseh;
Together they *shall be* [a]against Judah.

[b]For all this His anger is not turned away,
But His hand *is* stretched out still.

10 "Woe to those who [a]decree unrighteous decrees,
Who write misfortune,
*Which* they have prescribed
2 To rob the needy of justice,
And to take what is right from the poor of My people,
That widows may be their prey,
And *that* they may rob the fatherless.
3 [a]What will you do in [b]the day of punishment,
And in the desolation *which* will come from [c]afar?
To whom will you flee for help?
And where will you leave your glory?
4 Without Me they shall bow down among the [a]prisoners,
And they shall fall among the slain."

[b]For all this His anger is not turned away,
But His hand *is* stretched out still.

### *ARROGANT ASSYRIA ALSO JUDGED*

5 "Woe to Assyria, [a]the rod of My anger
And the staff in whose hand is My indignation.
6 I will send him against [a]an ungodly nation,
And against the people of My wrath
I will [b]give him charge,
To seize the spoil, to take the prey,
And to tread them down like the mire of the streets.
7 [a]Yet he does not mean so,
Nor does his heart think so;
But *it is* in his heart to destroy,
And cut off not a few nations.
8 [a]For he says,
'*Are* not my princes altogether kings?
9 *Is* not [a]Calno [b]like Carchemish?
*Is* not Hamath like Arpad?
*Is* not Samaria [c]like Damascus?
10 As my hand has found the kingdoms of the idols,
Whose carved images excelled those of Jerusalem and Samaria,
11 As I have done to Samaria and her idols,
Shall I not do also to Jerusalem and her idols?' "

9:8 [a]Gen. 32:28 9:14 [a]Rev. 18:8 9:16 [a]Is. 3:12 9:17 [a]Ps. 147:10 [b]Is. 5:25 9:18 [a]Mal. 4:1 9:19 [a]Is. 8:22 [b]Mic. 7:2, 6 9:20 [a]Lev. 26:26 [b]Jer. 19:9 9:21 [a]2 Chr. 28:6, 8 [b]Is. 9:12, 17 10:1 [a]Ps. 58:2 10:3 [a]Job 31:14 [b]Hos. 9:7 [c]Is. 5:26 10:4 [a]Is. 24:22 [b]Is. 5:25 10:5 [a]Jer. 51:20 10:6 [a]Is. 9:17 [b]Jer. 34:22 10:7 [a]Gen. 50:20 10:8 [a]2 Kin. 19:10 10:9 [a]Amos 6:2 [b]2 Chr. 35:20 [c]2 Kin. 16:9

12 Therefore it shall come to pass, when the
Lord has performed all His work [a]on Mount
Zion and on Jerusalem, *that He will say,* [b]"I will
punish the fruit of the arrogant heart of the king
of Assyria, and the glory of his haughty looks."
13 [a]For he says:

"By the strength of my hand I have done *it,*
And by my wisdom, for I am prudent;
Also I have removed the boundaries of the people,
And have robbed their treasuries;
So I have put down the inhabitants like a valiant *man.*
14 [a]My hand has found like a nest the riches of the people,
And as one gathers eggs *that are* left,
I have gathered all the earth;
And there was no one who moved *his* wing,
Nor opened *his* mouth with even a peep."

15 Shall [a]the ax boast itself against him who chops with it?
*Or* shall the saw exalt itself against him who saws with it?
As if a rod could wield *itself* against those who lift it up,
*Or* as if a staff could lift up, *as if it were* not wood!
16 Therefore the Lord, the Lord[1] of hosts,
Will send leanness among his fat ones;
And under his glory
He will kindle a burning
Like the burning of a fire.
17 So the Light of Israel will be for a fire,
And his Holy One for a flame;
[a]It will burn and devour
His thorns and his briers in one day.
18 And it will consume the glory of his forest and of [a]his fruitful field,
Both soul and body;
And they will be as when a sick man wastes away.
19 Then the rest of the trees of his forest
Will be so few in number
That a child may write them.

### *THE RETURNING REMNANT OF ISRAEL*

20 And it shall come to pass in that day
*That* the remnant of Israel,
And such as have escaped of the house of Jacob,
[a]Will never again depend on him who defeated them,
But will depend on the LORD, the Holy One of Israel, in truth.
21 The remnant will return, the remnant of Jacob,
To the [a]Mighty God.
22 [a]For though your people, O Israel, be as the sand of the sea,
[b]A remnant of them will return;
The destruction decreed shall overflow with righteousness.
23 [a]For the Lord GOD of hosts
Will make a determined end
In the midst of all the land.

24 Therefore thus says the Lord GOD of hosts:
"O My people, who dwell in Zion, [a]do not be afraid
of the Assyrian. He shall strike you with a rod
and lift up his staff against you, in the manner
of [b]Egypt. 25 For yet a very little while [a]and the
indignation will cease, as will My anger in their
destruction." 26 And the LORD of hosts will stir up
[a]a scourge for him like the slaughter of [b]Midian
at the rock of Oreb; [c]*as* His rod was on the sea, so
will He lift it up in the manner of Egypt.

27 It shall come to pass in that day
*That* his burden will be taken away from your shoulder,
And his yoke from your neck,
And the yoke will be destroyed because of [a]the anointing oil.

28 He has come to Aiath,
He has passed Migron;
At Michmash he has attended to his equipment.
29 They have gone along [a]the ridge,
They have taken up lodging at Geba.
Ramah is afraid,
[b]Gibeah of Saul has fled.
30 Lift up your voice,
O daughter [a]of Gallim!
Cause it to be heard as far as [b]Laish—
O poor Anathoth![1]
31 [a]Madmenah has fled,
The inhabitants of Gebim seek refuge.
32 As yet he will remain [a]at Nob that day;
He will [b]shake his fist at the mount of [c]the daughter of Zion,
The hill of Jerusalem.

33 Behold, the Lord,
The LORD of hosts,
Will lop off the bough with terror;
[a]Those of high stature *will be* hewn down,
And the haughty will be humbled.
34 He will cut down the thickets of the forest with iron,
And Lebanon will fall by the Mighty One.

10:12 [a]2 Kin. 19:31 [b]Jer. 50:18 10:13 [a]Is. 37:24–27 10:14 [a]Job 31:25 10:15 [a]Jer. 51:20 10:16 [1]Following Bomberg; Masoretic Text and Dead Sea Scrolls read *YHWH (the LORD).* 10:17 [a]Is. 9:18 10:18 [a]2 Kin. 19:23 10:20 [a]2 Kin. 16:7 10:21 [a][Is. 9:6] 10:22 [a]Rom. 9:27, 28 [b]Is. 6:13 10:23 [a]Dan. 9:27 10:24 [a]Is. 7:4; 12:2 [b]Ex. 14 10:25 [a]Dan. 11:36 10:26 [a]2 Kin. 19:35 [b]Is. 9:4 [c]Ex. 14:26, 27 10:27 [a]Ps. 105:15 10:29 [a]1 Sam. 13:23 [b]1 Sam. 11:4 10:30 [a]1 Sam. 25:44 [b]Judg. 18:7 [1]Following Masoretic Text, Targum, and Vulgate; Septuagint and Syriac read *Listen to her, O Anathoth.* 10:31 [a]Josh. 15:31 10:32 [a]1 Sam. 21:1 [b]Is. 13:2 [c]Is. 37:22 10:33 [a]Amos 2:9

### THE REIGN OF JESSE'S OFFSPRING
*(Is. 9:1–7)*

11 There [a]shall come forth a Rod from the stem of [b]Jesse,
And [c]a Branch shall grow out of his roots.
2 [a]The Spirit of the LORD shall rest upon Him,
The Spirit of wisdom and understanding,
The Spirit of counsel and might,
The Spirit of knowledge and of the fear of the LORD.

**SEEING JESUS IN THE SCRIPTURE**

**11:2** Isaiah's prophecy that the Spirit of the Lord would rest upon the Messiah was fulfilled at Jesus' baptism (see John 1:32). The Father's statement and Spirit's descending like a dove symbolizing that the Father, Son, and Spirit worked in harmony during Jesus' earthly ministry.

3 His delight *is* in the fear of the LORD,
And He shall not judge by the sight of His eyes,
Nor decide by the hearing of His ears;
4 But [a]with righteousness He shall judge the poor,
And decide with equity for the meek of the earth;
He shall [b]strike the earth with the rod of His mouth,
And with the breath of His lips He shall slay the wicked.
5 Righteousness shall be the belt of His loins,
And faithfulness the belt of His waist.

6 "The[a] wolf also shall dwell with the lamb,
The leopard shall lie down with the young goat,
The calf and the young lion and the fatling together;
And a little child shall lead them.
7 The cow and the bear shall graze;
Their young ones shall lie down together;
And the lion shall eat straw like the ox.
8 The nursing child shall play by the cobra's hole,
And the weaned child shall put his hand in the viper's den.
9 [a]They shall not hurt nor destroy in all My holy mountain,
For [b]the earth shall be full of the knowledge of the LORD
As the waters cover the sea.

10 "And[a] in that day [b]there shall be a Root of Jesse,
Who shall stand as a [c]banner to the people;
For the [d]Gentiles shall seek Him,
And His resting place shall be glorious."

**11:1** [a] [Zech. 6:12] [b] [Acts 13:23] [c] Is. 4:2 **11:2** [a] [John 1:32] **11:4** [a] Rev. 19:11 [b] Job 4:9 **11:6** [a] Hos. 2:18 **11:9** [a] Job 5:23 [b] Hab. 2:14 **11:10** [a] Is. 2:11 [b] Rom. 15:12 [c] Is. 27:12, 13 [d] Rom. 15:10

**KNOW THE TRUTH**

## THE DOCTRINE OF THE HOLY SPIRIT
### PART 3: THE HOLY SPIRIT'S WORK IN CHRIST'S LIFE

**11:1–5** Jesus lived the Spirit-filled, Spirit-empowered life. After the Holy Spirit came upon Jesus, He led Jesus into the wilderness to be tempted by the devil (see Luke 4:1–2). Jesus then returned to Galilee to begin His ministry in the power of the Holy Spirit (see Luke 4:14–15). The gospel Jesus preached, the blind eyes He opened, and the liberty He brought the oppressed came through the anointing of the Holy Spirit (see Luke 4:18–19). As Isaiah foretold, Jesus the Messiah displayed supernatural wisdom, understanding, and power because the Spirit of the Lord remained upon Him.

Jesus wasn't just anointed with the Holy Spirit; He baptizes with the Holy Spirit (see John 1:33–34). This means Jesus clothes His followers with the Holy Spirit's power to be His witnesses in the world (see Luke 24:46–49; Acts 1:8). Jesus modeled a life of Spirit-empowered wisdom and might and His disciples followed His example (see Acts 4:23–33). After spending about three years with His disciples, Jesus prepared them for continuing His mission without His physical presence. He assured them the Holy Spirit would be the Helper, Teacher, and Guide they needed (see John 14:16–18, 26; 15:26; 16:12–13). The same Spirit who anointed Christ and His early followers will anoint you as a willing witness of Jesus.

*For* **THE DOCTRINE OF THE HOLY SPIRIT: PART 4: THE HOLY SPIRIT'S WORK IN REVELATION,** *turn to John 14:26 on page 1092.*

11 It shall come to pass in that day
*That* the Lord shall set His hand again the second time
To recover the remnant of His people who are left,
[a]From Assyria and Egypt,
From Pathros and Cush,
From Elam and Shinar,
From Hamath and the islands of the sea.

12 He will set up a banner for the nations,
And will assemble the outcasts of Israel,
And gather together [a]the dispersed of Judah
From the four corners of the earth.
13 Also [a]the envy of Ephraim shall depart,
And the adversaries of Judah shall be cut off;
Ephraim shall not envy Judah,
And Judah shall not harass Ephraim.
14 But they shall fly down upon the shoulder of the Philistines toward the west;
Together they shall plunder the people of the East;
[a]They shall lay their hand on Edom and Moab;
And the people of Ammon shall obey them.
15 The LORD [a]will utterly destroy[1] the tongue of the Sea of Egypt;
With His mighty wind He will shake His fist over the River,[2]
And strike it in the seven streams,
And make *men* cross over dry-shod.
16 [a]There will be a highway for the remnant of His people
Who will be left from Assyria,
[b]As it was for Israel
In the day that he came up from the land of Egypt.

### A HYMN OF PRAISE

12 And [a]in that day you will say:

"O LORD, I will praise You;
Though You were angry with me,
Your anger is turned away, and You comfort me.
2 Behold, God *is* my salvation,
I will trust and not be afraid;
[a]'For [b]YAH, the LORD, *is* my strength and song;
He also has become my salvation.'[1]"

3 Therefore with joy you will draw [a]water
From the wells of salvation.

4 And in that day you will say:

[a]"Praise the LORD, call upon His name;
[b]Declare His deeds among the peoples,
Make mention that His [c]name is exalted.
5 [a]Sing to the LORD,
For He has done excellent things;
This *is* known in all the earth.
6 [a]Cry out and shout, O inhabitant of Zion,
For great *is* [b]the Holy One of Israel in your midst!"

### PROCLAMATION AGAINST BABYLON

13 The [a]burden against Babylon which Isaiah the son of Amoz saw.

2 "Lift[a] up a banner [b]on the high mountain,
Raise your voice to them;
[c]Wave your hand, that they may enter the gates of the nobles.
3 I have commanded My sanctified ones;
I have also called [a]My mighty ones for My anger—
Those who [b]rejoice in My exaltation."

4 The [a]noise of a multitude in the mountains,
Like that of many people!
A tumultuous noise of the kingdoms of nations gathered together!
The LORD of hosts musters
The army for battle.
5 They come from a far country,
From the end of heaven—
The [a]LORD and His weapons of indignation,
To destroy the whole [b]land.

6 Wail, [a]for the day of the LORD *is* at hand!
[b]It will come as destruction from the Almighty.
7 Therefore all hands will be limp,
Every man's heart will melt,
8 And they will be afraid.
[a]Pangs and sorrows will take hold of *them;*
They will be in pain as a woman in childbirth;
They will be amazed at one another;
Their faces *will be like* flames.

9 Behold, [a]the day of the LORD comes,
Cruel, with both wrath and fierce anger,
To lay the land desolate;
And He will destroy [b]its sinners from it.
10 For the stars of heaven and their constellations
Will not give their light;
The sun will be [a]darkened in its going forth,
And the moon will not cause its light to shine.

**11:11** [a] Zech. 10:10 **11:12** [a] John 7:35 **11:13** [a] Jer. 3:18 **11:14** [a] Dan. 11:41 **11:15** [a] Zech. 10:10, 11 [1] Following Masoretic Text and Vulgate; Septuagint, Syriac, and Targum read *dry up.* [2] That is, the Euphrates **11:16** [a] Is. 19:23 [b] Ex. 14:29 **12:1** [a] Is. 2:11 **12:2** [a] Ps. 83:18 [b] Ex. 15:2 [1] Exodus 15:2 **12:3** [a] [John 4:10, 14; 7:37, 38] **12:4** [a] 1 Chr. 16:8 [b] Ps. 145:4–6 [c] Ps. 34:3 **12:5** [a] Ex. 15:1 **12:6** [a] Zeph. 3:14, 15 [b] Ps. 89:18 **13:1** [a] Jer. 50; 51 **13:2** [a] Is. 18:3 [b] Jer. 51:25 [c] Is. 10:32 **13:3** [a] Joel 3:11 [b] Ps. 149:2 **13:4** [a] Is. 17:12 **13:5** [a] Is. 42:13 [b] Is. 24:1; 34:2 **13:6** [a] Zeph. 1:7 [b] Joel 1:15 **13:8** [a] Ps. 48:6 **13:9** [a] Mal. 4:1 [b] Prov. 2:22 **13:10** [a] Joel 2:31

11 "I will [a]punish the world for *its* evil,
And the wicked for their iniquity;
[b]I will halt the arrogance of the proud,
And will lay low the haughtiness of the terrible.
12 I will make a mortal more rare than fine gold,
A man more than the golden wedge of Ophir.
13 [a]Therefore I will shake the heavens,
And the earth will move out of her place,
In the wrath of the LORD of hosts
And in [b]the day of His fierce anger.
14 It shall be as the hunted gazelle,
And as a sheep that no man takes up;
[a]Every man will turn to his own people,
And everyone will flee to his own land.
15 Everyone who is found will be thrust through,
And everyone who is captured will fall by the sword.
16 Their children also will be [a]dashed to pieces before their eyes;
Their houses will be plundered
And their wives [b]ravished.

17 "Behold,[a] I will stir up the Medes against them,
Who will not regard silver;
And *as for* gold, they will not delight in it.
18 Also *their* bows will dash the young men to pieces,
And they will have no pity on the fruit of the womb;
Their eye will not spare children.
19 [a]And Babylon, the glory of kingdoms,
The beauty of the Chaldeans' pride,
Will be as when God overthrew [b]Sodom and Gomorrah.

**13:19** The city of **Babylon** was spread over six square miles and was protected by walls eighty-five feet thick. Eight major gates led to the city, each one named for a Babylonian god. The main temple, which was dedicated to Marduk, the god of war, featured a seven-story tower built with nearly sixty million bricks. To top it all off, the royal palace contained the hanging gardens of Babylon, one of the seven wonders of the ancient world.

20 [a]It will never be inhabited,
Nor will it be settled from generation to generation;
Nor will the Arabian pitch tents there,
Nor will the shepherds make their sheepfolds there.
21 [a]But wild beasts of the desert will lie there,
And their houses will be full of owls;
Ostriches will dwell there,
And wild goats will caper there.
22 The hyenas will howl in their citadels,
And jackals in their pleasant palaces.
[a]Her time *is* near to come,
And her days will not be prolonged."

### *MERCY ON JACOB*

14 For the LORD [a]will have mercy on Jacob, and
[b]will still choose Israel, and settle them in
their own land. [c]The strangers will be joined with
them, and they will cling to the house of Jacob.
2 Then people will take them [a]and bring them to
their place, and the house of Israel will possess
them for servants and maids in the land of the
LORD; they will take them captive whose captives
they were, [b]and rule over their oppressors.

### *FALL OF THE KING OF BABYLON*

3 It shall come to pass in the day the LORD
gives you rest from your sorrow, and from your
fear and the hard bondage in which you were
made to serve, 4 that you [a]will take up this prov-
erb against the king of Babylon, and say:

"How the oppressor has ceased,
The [b]golden[1] city ceased!
5 The LORD has broken [a]the staff of the wicked,
The scepter of the rulers;
6 He who struck the people in wrath with a continual stroke,
He who ruled the nations in anger,
Is persecuted *and* no one hinders.
7 The whole earth is at rest *and* quiet;
They break forth into singing.
8 [a]Indeed the cypress trees rejoice over you,
*And* the cedars of Lebanon,
*Saying,* 'Since you were cut down,
No woodsman has come up against us.'

9 "Hell[a] from beneath is excited about you,
To meet *you* at your coming;
It stirs up the dead for you,
All the chief ones of the earth;
It has raised up from their thrones
All the kings of the nations.
10 They all shall [a]speak and say to you:
'Have you also become as weak as we?
Have you become like us?
11 Your pomp is brought down to Sheol,
*And* the sound of your stringed instruments;
The maggot is spread under you,
And worms cover you.'

13:11 [a] Is. 26:21 [b] [Is. 2:17] 13:13 [a] Hag. 2:6 [b] Lam. 1:12 13:14 [a] Jer. 50:16; 51:9 13:16 [a] Nah. 3:10 [b] Zech. 14:2 13:17 [a] Dan. 5:28, 31 13:19 [a] Is. 14:4 [b] Gen. 19:24 13:20 [a] Jer. 50:3 13:21 [a] Is. 34:11–15 13:22 [a] Jer. 51:33 14:1 [a] Ps. 102:13 [b] Zech. 1:17; 2:12 [c] Is. 60:4, 5, 10 14:2 [a] Is. 49:22; 60:9; 66:20 [b] Is. 60:14 14:4 [a] Hab. 2:6 [b] Rev. 18:16 [1] Or *insolent* 14:5 [a] Ps. 125:3 14:8 [a] Ezek. 31:16 14:9 [a] Ezek. 32:21 14:10 [a] Ezek. 32:21

### *THE FALL OF LUCIFER*

12 "How[a] you are fallen from heaven,
O Lucifer,[1] son of the morning!
*How* you are cut down to the ground,
You who weakened the nations!
13 For you have said in your heart:
[a]'I will ascend into heaven,
[b]I will exalt my throne above the stars of God;
I will also sit on the [c]mount of the congregation
[d]On the farthest sides of the north;
14 I will ascend above the heights of the clouds,
[a]I will be like the Most High.'
15 Yet you [a]shall be brought down to Sheol,
To the lowest depths of the Pit.

16 "Those who see you will gaze at you,
*And* consider you, *saying:*
'*Is* this the man who made the earth tremble,
Who shook kingdoms,
17 Who made the world as a wilderness
And destroyed its cities,
*Who* did not open the house of his prisoners?'

18 "All the kings of the nations,
All of them, sleep in glory,
Everyone in his own house;
19 But you are cast out of your grave
Like an abominable branch,
*Like* the garment of those who are slain,
Thrust through with a sword,
Who go down to the stones of the pit,
Like a corpse trodden underfoot.
20 You will not be joined with them in burial,
Because you have destroyed your land
*And* slain your people.
[a]The brood of evildoers shall never be named.
21 Prepare slaughter for his children
[a]Because of the iniquity of their fathers,
Lest they rise up and possess the land,
And fill the face of the world with cities."

### *BABYLON DESTROYED*

22 "For I will rise up against them," says the LORD of hosts,
"And cut off from Babylon [a]the name and [b]remnant,
[c]And offspring and posterity," says the LORD.
23 "I will also make it a possession for the [a]porcupine,
And marshes of muddy water;
I will sweep it with the broom of destruction," says the LORD of hosts.

### *ASSYRIA DESTROYED*

24 The LORD of hosts has sworn, saying,
"Surely, as I have thought, so it shall come to pass,
And as I have purposed, *so* it shall [a]stand:
25 That I will break the [a]Assyrian in My land,
And on My mountains tread him underfoot.
Then [b]his yoke shall be removed from them,
And his burden removed from their shoulders.
26 This *is* the [a]purpose that is purposed against the whole earth,
And this *is* the hand that is stretched out over all the nations.
27 For the LORD of hosts has [a]purposed,
And who will annul *it?*
His hand *is* stretched out,
And who will turn it back?"

**14:12** [a] Is. 34:4 [1] Literally *Day Star* **14:13** [a] Ezek. 28:2 [b] Dan. 8:10 [c] Ezek. 28:14 [d] Ps. 48:2 **14:14** [a] 2 Thess. 2:4 **14:15** [a] Matt. 11:23 **14:20** [a] Ps. 21:10; 109:13 **14:21** [a] Ex. 20:5 **14:22** [a] Prov. 10:7 [b] 1 Kin. 14:10 [c] Job 18:19 **14:23** [a] Zeph. 2:14 **14:24** [a] Is. 43:13 **14:25** [a] Mic. 5:5, 6 [b] Is. 10:27 **14:26** [a] Is. 23:9 **14:27** [a] Dan. 4:31, 35

APPLY THE TRUTH

## REBELLION

**14:12–15** "In the beginning God created the heavens and the earth" (Gen. 1:1). This includes every creature on the earth and in the heavens—even those we cannot see. The Bible gives us a detailed cast of these heavenly characters: cherubim, seraphim, angels, demons, and most notably, Satan. We are introduced to Satan as the serpent within the first few pages of the Bible, but his origins are from before that. This passage in Isaiah describes how Satan was once named Lucifer and was one of God's angelic beings. But he rebelled against God, believing he could be like God. Pride caused him to think he didn't need to obey God. Rather, he could do his own thing and be like God. This is the lie Satan perpetuates toward others.

We rebel when we believe the lie we don't need God and we can do things our own way. This lie only leads to ruin. The antidote to rebellion is obedience and dependence upon God. And the key to obedience and dependence is humility, the antidote to pride. Recognize you need God every single day. You are not better without Him, and you can never replace Him. Love God, obey God, and flourish.

### PHILISTIA DESTROYED

28 This is the burden which came in the year that [a]King Ahaz died.

29 "Do not rejoice, all you of Philistia,
[a]Because the rod that struck you is broken;
For out of the serpent's roots will come forth a viper,
[b]And its offspring *will be* a fiery flying serpent.
30 The firstborn of the poor will feed,
And the needy will lie down in safety;
I will kill your roots with famine,
And it will slay your remnant.
31 Wail, O gate! Cry, O city!
All you of Philistia *are* dissolved;
For smoke will come from the north,
And no one *will be* alone in his appointed times."

32 What will they answer the messengers of the nation?
That [a]the LORD has founded Zion,
And [b]the poor of His people shall take refuge in it.

### PROCLAMATION AGAINST MOAB

15 The [a]burden against Moab.

Because in the night [b]Ar of [c]Moab is laid waste
*And* destroyed,
Because in the night Kir of Moab is laid waste
*And* destroyed,
2 He has gone up to the temple[1] and Dibon,
To the high places to weep.
Moab will wail over Nebo and over Medeba;
[a]On all their heads *will be* baldness,
*And* every beard cut off.
3 In their streets they will clothe themselves with sackcloth;
On the tops of their houses
And in their streets
Everyone will wail, [a]weeping bitterly.
4 Heshbon and Elealeh will cry out,
Their voice shall be heard as far as [a]Jahaz;
Therefore the armed soldiers[1] of Moab will cry out;
His life will be burdensome to him.

5 "My[a] heart will cry out for Moab;
His fugitives *shall flee* to Zoar,
*Like* a three-year-old heifer.[1]
For [b]by the Ascent of Luhith
They will go up with weeping;
For in the way of Horonaim
They will raise up a cry of destruction,
6 For the waters [a]of Nimrim will be desolate,
For the green grass has withered away;
The grass fails, there is nothing green.
7 Therefore the abundance they have gained,
And what they have laid up,
They will carry away to the Brook of the Willows.
8 For the cry has gone all around the borders of Moab,
Its wailing to Eglaim
And its wailing to Beer Elim.
9 For the waters of Dimon[1] will be full of blood;
Because I will bring more upon Dimon,[2]
[a]Lions upon him who escapes from Moab,
And on the remnant of the land."

### MOAB DESTROYED

16 Send [a]the lamb to the ruler of the land,
[b]From Sela to the wilderness,
To the mount of the daughter of Zion.
2 For it shall be as a [a]wandering bird thrown out of the nest;
*So* shall be the daughters of Moab at the fords of the [b]Arnon.

3 "Take counsel, execute judgment;
Make your shadow like the night in the middle of the day;
Hide the outcasts,
Do not betray him who escapes.
4 Let My outcasts dwell with you, O Moab;
Be a shelter to them from the face of the spoiler.
For the extortioner is at an end,
Devastation ceases,
The oppressors are consumed out of the land.
5 In mercy [a]the throne will be established;
And One will sit on it in truth, in the tabernacle of David,
[b]Judging and seeking justice and hastening [c]righteousness."

6 We have heard of the [a]pride of Moab—
*He is* very proud—
Of his haughtiness and his pride and his wrath;
[b]*But* his lies *shall* not *be* so.
7 Therefore Moab shall [a]wail for Moab;
Everyone shall wail.
For the foundations [b]of Kir Hareseth you shall mourn;
Surely *they are* stricken.

14:28 [a]2 Kin. 16:20 14:29 [a]2 Chr. 26:6 [b]2 Kin. 18:8 14:32 [a]Ps. 87:1, 5 [b]Zech. 11:11 15:1 [a]2 Kin. 3:4 [b]Deut. 2:9 [c]Amos 2:1–3 15:2 [a]Lev. 21:5 [1]Hebrew *bayith,* literally *house* 15:3 [a]Jer. 48:38 15:4 [a]Jer. 48:34 [1]Following Masoretic Text, Targum, and Vulgate; Septuagint and Syriac read *loins.* 15:5 [a]Jer. 48:31 [b]Jer. 48:5 [1]Or *The Third Eglath,* an unknown city (compare Jeremiah 48:34) 15:6 [a]Num. 32:36 15:9 [a]2 Kin. 17:25 [1]Following Masoretic Text and Targum; Dead Sea Scrolls and Vulgate read *Dibon;* Septuagint reads *Rimon.* [2]Following Masoretic Text and Targum; Dead Sea Scrolls and Vulgate read *Dibon;* Septuagint reads *Rimon.* 16:1 [a]2 Kin. 3:4 [b]2 Kin. 14:7 16:2 [a]Prov. 27:8 [b]Num. 21:13 16:5 [a][Dan. 7:14] [b]Ps. 72:2 [c]Is. 9:7 16:6 [a]Jer. 48:29 [b]Is. 28:15 16:7 [a]Jer. 48:20 [b]2 Kin. 3:25

8 For [a]the fields of Heshbon languish,
*And* [b]the vine of Sibmah;
The lords of the nations have broken
down its choice plants,
Which have reached to Jazer
And wandered through the wilderness.
Her branches are stretched out,
They are gone over the [c]sea.
9 Therefore I will bewail the vine of Sibmah,
With the weeping of Jazer;
I will drench you with my tears,
[a]O Heshbon and Elealeh;
For battle cries have fallen
Over your summer fruits and your
harvest.

10 [a]Gladness is taken away,
And joy from the plentiful field;
In the vineyards there will be no singing,
Nor will there be shouting;
No treaders will tread out wine in the
presses;
I have made their shouting cease.
11 Therefore [a]my heart shall resound like a
harp for Moab,
And my inner being for Kir Heres.

12 And it shall come to pass,
When it is seen that Moab is weary on [a]the
high place,
That he will come to his sanctuary to pray;
But he will not prevail.

13 This *is* the word which the LORD has spoken
concerning Moab since that time. 14 But now the
LORD has spoken, saying, "Within three years,
[a]as the years of a hired man, the glory of Moab
will be despised with all that great multitude,
and the remnant *will be* very small *and* feeble."

## PROCLAMATION AGAINST SYRIA AND ISRAEL

**17** The [a]burden against Damascus.

"Behold, Damascus will cease from *being* a
city,
And it will be a ruinous heap.
2 The cities of [a]Aroer *are* forsaken;[1]
They will be for flocks
Which lie down, and [b]no one will make
*them* afraid.
3 [a]The fortress also will cease from Ephraim,
The kingdom from Damascus,
And the remnant of Syria;
They will be as the glory of the children of
Israel,"
Says the LORD of hosts.

4 "In that day it shall come to pass
*That* the glory of Jacob will wane,
And [a]the fatness of his flesh grow lean.
5 [a]It shall be as when the harvester gathers
the grain,
And reaps the heads with his arm;
It shall be as he who gathers heads of grain
In the Valley of Rephaim.
6 [a]Yet gleaning grapes will be left in it,
Like the shaking of an olive tree,
Two *or* three olives at the top of the
uppermost bough,
Four *or* five in its most fruitful branches,"
Says the LORD God of Israel.

7 In that day a man will [a]look to his Maker,
And his eyes will have respect for the Holy
One of Israel.
8 He will not look to the altars,
The work of his hands;
He will not respect what his [a]fingers have
made,
Nor the wooden images[1] nor the incense
altars.

> **17:8** The **altars** described here were probably used in the worship of Asherah, a Canaanite goddess who had been adopted by the Israelites. Wooden poles, possibly carved into statues of some kind, marked the spots where Asherah was worshiped.

9 In that day his strong cities will be as a
forsaken bough[1]
And an uppermost branch,[2]
Which they left because of the children of
Israel;
And there will be desolation.

10 Because you have forgotten [a]the God of
your salvation,
And have not been mindful of the Rock of
your stronghold,
Therefore you will plant pleasant plants
And set out foreign seedlings;
11 In the day you will make your plant to grow,
And in the morning you will make your
seed to flourish;
*But* the harvest *will be* a heap of ruins
In the day of grief and desperate sorrow.

12 Woe to the multitude of many people
*Who* make a noise [a]like the roar of the seas,
And to the rushing of nations

16:8 [a] Is. 24:7 [b] Is. 16:9 [c] Jer. 48:32 16:9 [a] Is. 15:4 16:10 [a] Is. 24:8 16:11 [a] Jer. 48:36 16:12 [a] Is. 15:2 16:14 [a] Is. 21:16
17:1 [a] Zech. 9:1 17:2 [a] Num. 32:34 [b] Jer. 7:33 [1] Following Masoretic Text and Vulgate; Septuagint reads *It shall be forsaken forever;* Targum reads *Its cities shall be forsaken and desolate.* 17:3 [a] Is. 7:16; 8:4 17:4 [a] Is. 10:16 17:5 [a] Jer. 51:33 17:6 [a] Is. 24:13
17:7 [a] Mic. 7:7 17:8 [a] Is. 2:8; 31:7 [1] Hebrew *Asherim,* Canaanite deities 17:9 [1] Septuagint reads *Hivites;* Targum reads *laid waste;* Vulgate reads *as the plows.* [2] Septuagint reads *Amorites;* Targum reads *in ruins;* Vulgate reads *corn.* 17:10 [a] Ps. 68:19
17:12 [a] Jer. 6:23

*That* make a rushing like the rushing of
mighty waters!
13 The nations will rush like the rushing of
many waters;
But *God* will [a]rebuke them and they will
flee far away,
And [b]be chased like the chaff of the
mountains before the wind,
Like a rolling thing before the whirlwind.
14 Then behold, at eventide, trouble!
*And* before the morning, he *is* no more.
This *is* the portion of those who plunder us,
And the lot of those who rob us.

## PROCLAMATION AGAINST ETHIOPIA

18 Woe [a]to the land shadowed with buzzing
wings,
Which *is* beyond the rivers of Ethiopia,
2 Which sends ambassadors by sea,
Even in vessels of reed on the waters, *saying,*
"Go, swift messengers, to a nation tall and
smooth *of skin,*
To a people terrible from their beginning
onward,
A nation powerful and treading down,
Whose land the rivers divide."

3 All inhabitants of the world and dwellers
on the earth:
[a]When he lifts up a banner on the
mountains, you see *it;*
And when he blows a trumpet, you hear *it.*
4 For so the LORD said to me,
"I will take My rest,
And I will look from My dwelling place
Like clear heat in sunshine,
Like a cloud of dew in the heat of harvest."
5 For before the harvest, when the bud is
perfect
And the sour grape is ripening in the flower,
He will both cut off the sprigs with
pruning hooks
And take away *and* cut down the branches.
6 They will be left together for the
mountain birds of prey
And for the beasts of the earth;
The birds of prey will summer on them,
And all the beasts of the earth will winter
on them.

7 In that time [a]a present will be brought to
the LORD of hosts
From[1] a people tall and smooth *of skin,*
And from a people terrible from their
beginning onward,
A nation powerful and treading down,
Whose land the rivers divide—
To the place of the name of the LORD of
hosts,
To Mount Zion.

## PROCLAMATION AGAINST EGYPT

19 The [a]burden against Egypt.

Behold, the LORD [b]rides on a swift cloud,
And will come into Egypt;
[c]The idols of Egypt will totter at His
presence,
And the heart of Egypt will melt in its midst.

2 "I will [a]set Egyptians against Egyptians;
Everyone will fight against his brother,
And everyone against his neighbor,
City against city, kingdom against kingdom.
3 The spirit of Egypt will fail in its midst;
I will destroy their counsel,
And they will [a]consult the idols and the
charmers,
The mediums and the sorcerers.
4 And the Egyptians I will give
[a]Into the hand of a cruel master,
And a fierce king will rule over them,"
Says the Lord, the LORD of hosts.

5 [a]The waters will fail from the sea,
And the river will be wasted and dried up.

> **19:5** Because Egypt received very little rainfall, ancient inhabitants relied heavily on the Nile for their water. This **river** flooded its banks nearly every year, watering the soil and creating a fertile farmland in a desert region. When the Nile didn't flood, the Egyptians experienced drought and famine. Today the Aswan Dam and the High Dam allow Egyptian officials to control the flooding and preserve water.

6 The rivers will turn foul;
The brooks [a]of defense will be emptied
and dried up;
The reeds and rushes will wither.
7 The papyrus reeds by the River,[1] by the
mouth of the River,
And everything sown by the River,
Will wither, be driven away, and be no
more.
8 The fishermen also will mourn;
All those will lament who cast hooks into
the River,
And they will languish who spread nets
on the waters.
9 Moreover those who work in [a]fine flax
And those who weave fine fabric will be
ashamed;
10 And its foundations will be broken.
All who make wages *will be* troubled of
soul.

**17:13** [a] Ps. 9:5 [b] Hos. 13:3 **18:1** [a] Zeph. 2:12; 3:10 **18:3** [a] Is. 5:26 **18:7** [a] Zeph. 3:10 [1] Following Dead Sea Scrolls, Septuagint, and Vulgate; Masoretic Text omits *From;* Targum reads *To.* **19:1** [a] Joel 3:19 [b] Ps. 18:10; 104:3 [c] Jer. 43:12 **19:2** [a] Judg. 7:22 **19:3** [a] Is. 8:19; 47:12 **19:4** [a] Ezek. 29:19 **19:5** [a] Jer. 51:36 **19:6** [a] 2 Kin. 19:24 **19:7** [1] That is, the Nile **19:9** [a] Prov. 7:16

11 Surely the princes of [a]Zoan *are* fools;
Pharaoh's wise counselors give foolish counsel.
[b]How do you say to Pharaoh, "I *am* the son of the wise,
The son of ancient kings?"
12 [a]Where *are* they?
Where are your wise men?
Let them tell you now,
And let them know what the LORD of hosts has [b]purposed against Egypt.
13 The princes of Zoan have become fools;
[a]The princes of Noph[1] are deceived;
They have also deluded Egypt,
*Those who are* the mainstay of its tribes.
14 The LORD has mingled [a]a perverse spirit in her midst;
And they have caused Egypt to err in all her work,
As a drunken man staggers in his vomit.
15 Neither will there be *any* work for Egypt,
Which [a]the head or tail,
Palm branch or bulrush, may do.[1]

16 In that day Egypt will [a]be like women, and
will be afraid and fear because of the waving of the
hand of the LORD of hosts, [b]which He waves over
it. 17 And the land of Judah will be a terror to Egypt;
everyone who makes mention of it will be afraid
in himself, because of the counsel of the LORD of
hosts which He has [a]determined against it.

### EGYPT, ASSYRIA, AND ISRAEL BLESSED

18 In that day five cities in the land of Egypt
will [a]speak the language of Canaan and [b]swear
by the LORD of hosts; one will be called the City
of Destruction.[1]
19 In that day [a]there will be an altar to the
LORD in the midst of the land of Egypt, and a
pillar to the [b]LORD at its border. 20 And [a]it will be
for a sign and for a witness to the LORD of hosts
in the land of Egypt; for they will cry to the LORD
because of the oppressors, and He will send them
a [b]Savior and a Mighty One, and He will deliver
them. 21 Then the LORD will be known to Egypt,
and the Egyptians will [a]know the LORD in that
day, and [b]will make sacrifice and offering; yes,
they will make a vow to the LORD and perform *it.*
22 And the LORD will strike Egypt, He will strike
and [a]heal *it;* they will return to the LORD, and He
will be entreated by them and heal them.
23 In that day [a]there will be a highway from
Egypt to Assyria, and the Assyrian will come
into Egypt and the Egyptian into Assyria, and
the Egyptians will [b]serve with the Assyrians.
24 In that day Israel will be one of three with
Egypt and Assyria—a blessing in the midst of the
land, 25 whom the LORD of hosts shall bless, say-
ing, "Blessed *is* Egypt My people, and Assyria [a]the
work of My hands, and Israel My inheritance."

### THE SIGN AGAINST EGYPT AND ETHIOPIA

20 In the year that [a]Tartan[1] came to Ashdod,
when Sargon the king of Assyria sent him,
and he fought against Ashdod and took it, 2 at
the same time the LORD spoke by Isaiah the son
of Amoz, saying, "Go, and remove [a]the sackcloth
from your body, and take your sandals off your
feet." And he did so, [b]walking naked and barefoot.
3 Then the LORD said, "Just as My servant
Isaiah has walked naked and barefoot three
years [a]*for* a sign and a wonder against Egypt and
Ethiopia, 4 so shall the [a]king of Assyria lead away
the Egyptians as prisoners and the Ethiopians
as captives, young and old, naked and barefoot,
[b]with their buttocks uncovered, to the shame of
Egypt. 5 [a]Then they shall be afraid and ashamed
of Ethiopia their expectation and Egypt their
glory. 6 And the inhabitant of this territory will
say in that day, 'Surely such *is* our expectation,
wherever we flee for [a]help to be delivered from
the king of Assyria; and how shall we escape?' "

**20:3–4 Assyria** was brutal with the people it conquered. Some were taken captive, stripped naked, and deported to other regions in the Assyrian Empire. Those who were left behind faced such torture as having their arms and legs cut off, having their skin peeled off, and being decapitated.

### THE FALL OF BABYLON PROCLAIMED

21 The burden against the Wilderness of
the Sea.

As [a]whirlwinds in the South pass through,
*So* it comes from the desert, from a terrible land.
2 A distressing vision is declared to me;
[a]The treacherous dealer deals treacherously,
And the plunderer plunders.
[b]Go up, O Elam!
Besiege, O Media!
All its sighing I have made to cease.
3 Therefore [a]my loins are filled with pain;
[b]Pangs have taken hold of me, like the pangs of a woman in labor.

**19:11** [a] Num. 13:22 [b] 1 Kin. 4:29, 30 **19:12** [a] 1 Cor. 1:20 [b] Ps. 33:11 **19:13** [a] Jer. 2:16 [1] That is, ancient Memphis **19:14** [a] Is. 29:10 **19:15** [a] Is. 9:14–16 [1] Compare Isaiah 9:14–16 **19:16** [a] Nah. 3:13 [b] Is. 11:15 **19:17** [a] Dan. 4:35 **19:18** [a] Zeph. 3:9 [b] Is. 45:23 [1] Some Hebrew manuscripts, Arabic, Dead Sea Scrolls, Targum, and Vulgate read *Sun;* Septuagint reads *Asedek* (literally *Righteousness*). **19:19** [a] Ex. 24:4 [b] Ps. 68:31 **19:20** [a] Josh. 4:20; 22:27 [b] Is. 43:11 **19:21** [a] [Is. 2:3, 4; 11:9] [b] Mal. 1:11 **19:22** [a] Deut. 32:39 **19:23** [a] Is. 11:16; 35:8; 49:11; 62:10 [b] Is. 27:13 **19:25** [a] Is. 29:23 **20:1** [a] 2 Kin. 18:17 [1] Or *the Commander in Chief* **20:2** [a] Zech. 13:4 [b] 1 Sam. 19:24 **20:3** [a] Is. 8:18 **20:4** [a] Is. 19:4 [b] Jer. 13:22 **20:5** [a] 2 Kin. 18:21 **20:6** [a] Is. 30:5, 7 **21:1** [a] Zech. 9:14 **21:2** [a] Is. 33:1 [b] Jer. 49:34 **21:3** [a] Is. 15:5; 16:11 [b] Is. 13:8

I was distressed when *I* heard *it;*
I was dismayed when *I* saw *it.*
4 My heart wavered, fearfulness
frightened me;
[a]The night for which I longed He turned
into fear for me.

5 [a]Prepare the table,
Set a watchman in the tower,
Eat and drink.
Arise, you princes,
Anoint the shield!

6 For thus has the Lord said to me:
"Go, set a watchman,
Let him declare what he sees."
7 And he saw a chariot *with* a pair of
horsemen,
A chariot of donkeys, *and* a chariot of
camels,
And he listened earnestly with great care.
8 Then he cried, "A lion,[1] my Lord!
I stand continually on the [a]watchtower in
the daytime;
I have sat at my post every night.
9 And look, here comes a chariot of men
*with* a pair of horsemen!"
Then he answered and said,
[a]"Babylon is fallen, is fallen!
And [b]all the carved images of her gods
He has broken to the ground."

10 [a]Oh, my threshing and the grain of my
floor!
That which I have heard from the LORD of
hosts,
The God of Israel,
I have declared to you.

### PROCLAMATION AGAINST EDOM

11 [a]The burden against Dumah.

He calls to me out of [b]Seir,
"Watchman, what of the night?
Watchman, what of the night?"
12 The watchman said,
"The morning comes, and also the
night.
If you will inquire, inquire;
Return! Come back!"

> **21:11** The **watchman** was the **night** patrol who kept watch on the city. The metaphor refers to the prophet Isaiah, who, as a guard on the walls, could see the dawn—the light of salvation—in the east before the others.

### PROCLAMATION AGAINST ARABIA

13 [a]The burden against Arabia.

In the forest in Arabia you will lodge,
O you traveling companies [b]of Dedanites.
14 O inhabitants of the land of Tema,
Bring water to him who is thirsty;
With their bread they met him who fled.
15 For they fled from the swords, from the
drawn sword,
From the bent bow, and from the distress
of war.

16 For thus the LORD has said to me: "Within
a year, [a]according to the year of a hired man, all
the glory of [b]Kedar will fail; 17 and the remainder
of the number of archers, the mighty men of
the people of Kedar, will be diminished; for the
LORD God of Israel has spoken *it.*"

### PROCLAMATION AGAINST JERUSALEM

22 The burden against the Valley of Vision.

What ails you now, that you have all gone
up to the housetops,
2 You who are full of noise,
A tumultuous city, [a]a joyous city?
Your slain *men are* not slain with the
sword,
Nor dead in battle.
3 All your rulers have fled together;
They are captured by the archers.
All who are found in you are bound
together;
They have fled from afar.
4 Therefore I said, "Look away from me,
[a]I will weep bitterly;
Do not labor to comfort me
Because of the plundering of the daughter
of my people."

5 [a]For *it is* a day of trouble and treading
down and perplexity
[b]By the Lord GOD of hosts
In the Valley of Vision—
Breaking down the walls
And of crying to the mountain.
6 [a]Elam bore the quiver
With chariots of men *and* horsemen,
And [b]Kir uncovered the shield.
7 It shall come to pass *that* your choicest
valleys
Shall be full of chariots,
And the horsemen shall set themselves in
array at the gate.

8 [a]He removed the protection of Judah.
You looked in that day to the armor [b]of
the House of the Forest;

21:4 [a]Deut. 28:67 21:5 [a]Dan. 5:5 21:8 [a]Hab. 2:1 [1]Dead Sea Scrolls read *Then the observer cried.* 21:9 [a]Jer. 51:8 [b]Is. 46:1 21:10 [a]Jer. 51:33 21:11 [a]Gen. 25:14 [b]Gen. 32:3 21:13 [a]Jer. 25:24; 49:28 [b]1 Chr. 1:9, 32 21:16 [a]Is. 16:14 [b]Ps. 120:5 22:2 [a]Is. 32:13 22:4 [a]Jer. 4:19 22:5 [a]Is. 37:3 [b]Lam. 1:5; 2:2 22:6 [a]Jer. 49:35 [b]Is. 15:1 22:8 [a]2 Kin. 18:15, 16 [b]1 Kin. 7:2; 10:17

9 [a]You also saw the damage to the city of David,
That it was great;
And you gathered together the waters of the lower pool.
10 You numbered the houses of Jerusalem,
And the houses you broke down
To fortify the wall.
11 [a]You also made a reservoir between the two walls
For the water of the old [b]pool.
But you did not look to its Maker,
Nor did you have respect for Him who fashioned it long ago.

12 And in that day the Lord GOD of hosts
[a]Called for weeping and for mourning,
[b]For baldness and for girding with sackcloth.
13 But instead, joy and gladness,
Slaying oxen and killing sheep,
Eating meat and [a]drinking wine:
[b]"Let us eat and drink, for tomorrow we die!"

14 [a]Then it was revealed in my hearing by the LORD of hosts,
"Surely for this iniquity there [b]will be no atonement for you,
Even to your death," says the Lord GOD of hosts.

### THE JUDGMENT ON SHEBNA

15 Thus says the Lord GOD of hosts:

"Go, proceed to this steward,
To [a]Shebna, who *is* over the house, *and say:*
16 'What have you here, and whom have you here,
That you have hewn a sepulcher here,
*As* he [a]who hews himself a sepulcher on high,
Who carves a tomb for himself in a rock?
17 Indeed, the LORD will throw you away violently,
O mighty man,
[a]And will surely seize you.
18 He will surely turn violently and toss you like a ball
Into a large country;
There you shall die, and there [a]your glorious chariots
*Shall be* the shame of your master's house.
19 So I will drive you out of your office,
And from your position he will pull you down.[1]

20 'Then it shall be in that day,
That I will call My servant [a]Eliakim the son of Hilkiah;

**22:15–19** When ordinary people died in the ancient Near East, they were buried in shallow graves covered with stone slabs. The wealthy and powerful, on the other hand, often built elaborate tombs for themselves. These tombs were either created from natural caves or carved out of stone. The person's possessions were usually buried in the **tomb** along with the body, in case they were needed in the afterlife.

21 I will clothe him with your robe
And strengthen him with your belt;
I will commit your responsibility into his hand.
He shall be a father to the inhabitants of Jerusalem
And to the house of Judah.
22 The key of the house of David
I will lay on his [a]shoulder;
So he shall [b]open, and no one shall shut;
And he shall shut, and no one shall open.
23 I will fasten him *as* [a]a peg in a secure place,
And he will become a glorious throne to his father's house.

24 'They will hang on him all the glory of his
father's house, the offspring and the posterity,
all vessels of small quantity, from the cups to
all the pitchers. 25 In that day,' says the LORD
of hosts, 'the peg that is fastened in the secure
place will be removed and be cut down and fall,
and the burden that *was* on it will be cut off; for
the LORD has spoken.' "

### PROCLAMATION AGAINST TYRE

23 The [a]burden against Tyre.

Wail, you ships of Tarshish!
For it is laid waste,
So that there is no house, no harbor;
From the land of Cyprus[1] it is revealed to them.

2 Be still, you inhabitants of the coastland,
You merchants of Sidon,
Whom those who cross the sea have filled.[1]
3 And on great waters the grain of Shihor,
The harvest of the River,[1] *is* her revenue;
And [a]she is a marketplace for the nations.

4 Be ashamed, O Sidon;
For the sea has spoken,
The strength of the sea, saying,
"I do not labor, nor bring forth children;

**22:9** [a] 2 Kin. 20:20 **22:11** [a] Neh. 3:16 [b] 2 Chr. 32:3, 4 **22:12** [a] Joel 1:13; 2:17 [b] Mic. 1:16 **22:13** [a] Luke 17:26–29 [b] 1 Cor. 15:32 **22:14** [a] Is. 5:9 [b] Ezek. 24:13 **22:15** [a] Is. 36:3 **22:16** [a] Matt. 27:60 **22:17** [a] Esth. 7:8 **22:18** [a] Is. 2:7 **22:19** [1] Septuagint omits *he will pull you down;* Syriac, Targum, and Vulgate read *I will pull you down.* **22:20** [a] 2 Kin. 18:18 **22:22** [a] Is. 9:6 [b] Job 12:14; Rev. 3:7 **22:23** [a] Ezra 9:8 **23:1** [a] Zech. 9:2, 4 [1] Hebrew *Kittim,* western lands, especially Cyprus **23:2** [1] Following Masoretic Text and Vulgate; Septuagint and Targum read *Passing over the water;* Dead Sea Scrolls read *Your messengers passing over the sea.* **23:3** [a] Ezek. 27:3–23 [1] That is, the Nile

Neither do I rear young men,
*Nor* bring up virgins."
5 [a]When the report *reaches* Egypt,
They also will be in agony at the report of Tyre.

6 Cross over to Tarshish;
Wail, you inhabitants of the coastland!
7 *Is* this your [a]joyous *city*,
Whose antiquity *is* from ancient days,
Whose feet carried her far off to dwell?
8 Who has taken this counsel against Tyre,
[a]the crowning *city*,
Whose merchants *are* princes,
Whose traders *are* the honorable of the earth?
9 The LORD of hosts has [a]purposed it,
To bring to dishonor the [b]pride of all glory,
To bring into contempt all the honorable of the earth.

10 Overflow through your land like the River,[1]
O daughter of Tarshish;
*There is* no more strength.
11 He stretched out His hand over the sea,
He shook the kingdoms;
The LORD has given a commandment [a]against Canaan
To destroy its strongholds.
12 And He said, "You will rejoice no more,
O you oppressed virgin daughter of Sidon.
Arise, [a]cross over to Cyprus;
There also you will have no rest."
13 Behold, the land of the [a]Chaldeans,
This people *which* was not;
Assyria founded it for [b]wild beasts of the desert.
They set up its towers,
They raised up its palaces,
*And* brought it to ruin.

14 [a]Wail, you ships of Tarshish!
For your strength is laid waste.

15 Now it shall come to pass in that day that
Tyre will be forgotten seventy years, according
to the days of one king. At the end of seventy
years it will happen to Tyre as *in* the song of
the harlot:

16 "Take a harp, go about the city,
You forgotten harlot;
Make sweet melody, sing many songs,
That you may be remembered."

17 And it shall be, at the end of seventy years,
that the LORD will deal with Tyre. She will return
to her hire, and [a]commit fornication with all the
kingdoms of the world on the face of the earth.
18 Her gain and her pay [a]will be set apart for the
LORD; it will not be treasured nor laid up, for
her gain will be for those who dwell before the
LORD, to eat sufficiently, and for fine clothing.

### *IMPENDING JUDGMENT ON THE EARTH*

24 Behold, the LORD makes the earth empty and makes it waste,
Distorts its surface
And scatters abroad its inhabitants.
2 And it shall be:
As with the people, so with the [a]priest;
As with the servant, so with his master;
As with the maid, so with her mistress;
[b]As with the buyer, so with the seller;
As with the lender, so with the borrower;
As with the creditor, so with the debtor.
3 The land shall be entirely emptied and utterly plundered,
For the LORD has spoken this word.

4 The earth mourns *and* fades away,
The world languishes *and* fades away;
The [a]haughty people of the earth languish.
5 [a]The earth is also defiled under its inhabitants,
Because they have [b]transgressed the laws,
Changed the ordinance,
Broken the [c]everlasting covenant.
6 Therefore [a]the curse has devoured the earth,
And those who dwell in it are desolate.
Therefore the inhabitants of the earth are [b]burned,
And few men *are* left.
7 [a]The new wine fails, the vine languishes,
All the merry-hearted sigh.
8 The mirth [a]of the tambourine ceases,
The noise of the jubilant ends,
The joy of the harp ceases.
9 They shall not drink wine with a song;
Strong drink is bitter to those who drink it.
10 The city of confusion is broken down;
Every house is shut up, so that none may go in.
11 *There is* a cry for wine in the streets,
All joy is darkened,
The mirth of the land is gone.
12 In the city desolation is left,
And the gate is stricken with destruction.
13 When it shall be thus in the midst of the land among the people,
[a]*It shall be* like the shaking of an olive tree,
Like the gleaning of grapes when the vintage is done.

23:5 [a] Is. 19:16 23:7 [a] Is. 22:2; 32:13 23:8 [a] Ezek. 28:2, 12 23:9 [a] Is. 14:26 [b] Dan. 4:37 23:10 [1] That is, the Nile 23:11 [a] Zech. 9:2–4 23:12 [a] Rev. 18:22 23:13 [a] Is. 47:1 [b] Ps. 72:9 23:14 [a] Ezek. 27:25–30 23:17 [a] Rev. 17:2 23:18 [a] Zech. 14:20, 21 24:2 [a] Hos. 4:9 [b] Ezek. 7:12, 13 24:4 [a] Is. 25:11 24:5 [a] Num. 35:33 [b] Is. 59:12 [c] 1 Chr. 16:14–19 24:6 [a] Mal. 4:6 [b] Is. 9:19 24:7 [a] Joel 1:10, 12 24:8 [a] Ezek. 26:13 24:13 [a] [Is. 17:5, 6; 27:12]

14 They shall lift up their voice, they shall sing;
For the majesty of the LORD
They shall cry aloud from the sea.
15 Therefore [a]glorify the LORD in the dawning light,
[b]The name of the LORD God of Israel in the coastlands of the sea.
16 From the ends of the earth we have heard songs:
"Glory to the righteous!"
But I said, "I am ruined, ruined!
Woe to me!
[a]The treacherous dealers have dealt treacherously,
Indeed, the treacherous dealers have dealt very treacherously."

17 [a]Fear and the pit and the snare
*Are* upon you, O inhabitant of the earth.
18 And it shall be
*That* he who flees from the noise of the fear
Shall fall into the pit,
And he who comes up from the midst of the pit
Shall be caught in the snare;
For [a]the windows from on high are open,
And [b]the foundations of the earth are shaken.

19 [a]The earth is violently broken,
The earth is split open,
The earth is shaken exceedingly.
20 The earth shall [a]reel to and fro like a drunkard,
And shall totter like a hut;
Its transgression shall be heavy upon it,
And it will fall, and not rise again.

21 It shall come to pass in that day
*That* the LORD will punish on high the host of exalted ones,
And on the earth [a]the kings of the earth.
22 They will be gathered together,
*As* prisoners are gathered in the pit,
And will be shut up in the prison;
After many days they will be punished.
23 Then the [a]moon will be disgraced
And the sun ashamed;
For the LORD of hosts will [b]reign
On [c]Mount Zion and in Jerusalem
And before His elders, gloriously.

### *PRAISE TO GOD*

**25** O LORD, You *are* my God.
[a]I will exalt You,
I will praise Your name,
[b]For You have done wonderful *things;*
[c]*Your* counsels of old *are* faithfulness *and* truth.
2 For You have made [a]a city a ruin,
A fortified city a ruin,
A palace of foreigners to be a city no more;
It will never be rebuilt.
3 Therefore the strong people will [a]glorify You;
The city of the terrible nations will fear You.
4 For You have been a strength to the poor,
A strength to the needy in his distress,
[a]A refuge from the storm,
A shade from the heat;
For the blast of the terrible ones *is* as a storm *against* the wall.
5 You will reduce the noise of aliens,
As heat in a dry place;
*As* heat in the shadow of a cloud,
The song of the terrible ones will be diminished.

6 And in [a]this mountain
[b]The LORD of hosts will make for [c]all people
A feast of choice pieces,
A feast of wines on the lees,
Of fat things full of marrow,
Of well-refined wines on the lees.
7 And He will destroy on this mountain
The surface of the covering cast over all people,
And [a]the veil that is spread over all nations.
8 He will [a]swallow up death forever,
And the Lord GOD will [b]wipe away tears from all faces;
The rebuke of His people
He will take away from all the earth;
For the LORD has spoken.

**SEEING JESUS IN THE SCRIPTURE**

**25:8** God's promise to swallow up death and wipe away every tear finds its fulfillment in Jesus Christ. Jesus lived, died, and rose from the grave to defeat death. When He returns, all that is broken will be restored and tears will be no more (see Rev. 21:4).

9 And it will be said in that day:
"Behold, this *is* our God;
[a]We have waited for Him, and He will save us.
This *is* the LORD;
We have waited for Him;
[b]We will be glad and rejoice in His salvation."

10 For on this mountain the hand of the LORD will rest,
And [a]Moab shall be trampled down under Him,

**24:15** [a] Is. 25:3 [b] Mal. 1:11 **24:16** [a] Jer. 3:20; 5:11 **24:17** [a] Jer. 48:43 **24:18** [a] Gen. 7:11 [b] Ps. 18:7; 46:2 **24:19** [a] Jer. 4:23 **24:20** [a] Is. 19:14; 24:1; 28:7 **24:21** [a] Ps. 76:12 **24:23** [a] Is. 13:10; 60:19 [b] Rev. 19:4, 6 [c] [Heb. 12:22] **25:1** [a] Ex. 15:2 [b] Ps. 98:1 [c] Num. 23:19 **25:2** [a] Jer. 51:37 **25:3** [a] Is. 24:15 **25:4** [a] Is. 4:6 **25:6** [a] [Is. 2:2–4; 56:7] [b] Prov. 9:2 [c] [Dan. 7:14] **25:7** [a] [Eph. 4:18] **25:8** [a] [Hos. 13:14] [b] Rev. 7:17; 21:4 **25:9** [a] Gen. 49:18 [b] Ps. 20:5 **25:10** [a] Amos 2:1–3

As straw is trampled down for the refuse
heap.
11 And He will spread out His hands in their
midst
As a swimmer reaches out to swim,
And He will bring down their [a]pride
Together with the trickery of their hands.
12 The [a]fortress of the high fort of your walls
He will bring down, lay low,
*And* bring to the ground, down to the dust.

### A SONG OF SALVATION

26 In [a]that day this song will be sung in the
land of Judah:

"We have a strong city;
[b]*God* will appoint salvation *for* walls and
bulwarks.
2 [a]Open the gates,
That the righteous nation which keeps the
truth may enter in.
3 You will keep *him* in perfect [a]peace,
*Whose* mind *is* stayed *on You,*
Because he trusts in You.
4 Trust in the LORD forever,
[a]For in YAH, the LORD, *is* everlasting
strength.[1]
5 For He brings down those who dwell on
high,
[a]The lofty city;
He lays it low,
He lays it low to the ground,
He brings it down to the dust.
6 The foot shall tread it down—
The feet of the poor
*And* the steps of the needy."

7 The way of the just *is* uprightness;
[a]O Most Upright,
You weigh the path of the just.
8 Yes, [a]in the way of Your judgments,
O LORD, we have [b]waited for You;
The desire of *our* soul *is* for Your name
And for the remembrance of You.
9 [a]With my soul I have desired You in the
night,
Yes, by my spirit within me I will seek You
early;
For when Your judgments *are* in the earth,
The inhabitants of the world will learn
righteousness.

10 [a]Let grace be shown to the wicked,
*Yet* he will not learn righteousness;
In [b]the land of uprightness he will deal
unjustly,
And will not behold the majesty of the
LORD.

11 LORD, *when* Your hand is lifted up, [a]they
will not see.
But they will see and be ashamed
For *their* envy of people;
Yes, the fire of Your enemies shall devour
them.

12 LORD, You will establish peace for us,
For You have also done all our works
in us.
13 O LORD our God, [a]masters besides You
Have had dominion over us;
*But* by You only we make mention of Your
name.
14 *They are* dead, they will not live;
*They are* deceased, they will not rise.
Therefore You have punished and
destroyed them,
And made all their memory to [a]perish.
15 You have increased the nation, O LORD,
You have [a]increased the nation;
You are glorified;
You have expanded all the borders of the
land.

16 LORD, [a]in trouble they have visited You,
They poured out a prayer *when* Your
chastening *was* upon them.
17 As [a]a woman with child
Is in pain and cries out in her pangs,
*When* she draws near the time of her
delivery,
So have we been in Your sight, O LORD.
18 We have been with child, we have been in
pain;
We have, as it were, brought forth wind;
We have not accomplished any
deliverance in the earth,
Nor have [a]the inhabitants of the world
fallen.

19 [a]Your dead shall live;
*Together with* my dead body[1] they shall
arise.
[b]Awake and sing, you who dwell in dust;
For your dew *is like* the dew of herbs,
And the earth shall cast out the dead.

**SEEING JESUS IN THE SCRIPTURE**

**26:19** This Messianic prophecy was partially fulfilled in Jesus' day and will be completely fulfilled one day. When Jesus died on the cross, some of the saints were raised, foreshadowing what Jesus' death accomplishes for all who believe (see Matt. 27:52).

**25:11** [a] Is. 24:4; 26:5 **25:12** [a] Is. 26:5 **26:1** [a] Is. 2:11; 12:1 [b] Is. 60:18 **26:2** [a] Ps. 118:19, 20 **26:3** [a] Is. 57:19 **26:4** [a] Is. 12:2; 45:17 [1] Or *Rock of Ages* **26:5** [a] Is. 25:11, 12 **26:7** [a] Ps. 37:23 **26:8** [a] Is. 64:5 [b] Is. 25:9; 33:2 **26:9** [a] Ps. 63:6 **26:10** [a] [Rom. 2:4] [b] Ps. 143:10 **26:11** [a] Is. 5:12 **26:13** [a] 2 Chr. 12:8 **26:14** [a] Eccl. 9:5 **26:15** [a] Is. 9:3 **26:16** [a] Hos. 5:15 **26:17** [a] [John 16:21] **26:18** [a] Ps. 17:14 **26:19** [a] [Ezek. 37:1–14] [b] [Dan. 12:2] [1] Following Masoretic Text and Vulgate; Syriac and Targum read *their dead bodies;* Septuagint reads *those in the tombs.*

### *TAKE REFUGE FROM THE COMING JUDGMENT*

20 Come, my people, [a]enter your chambers,
And shut your doors behind you;
Hide yourself, as it were, [b]for a little moment,
Until the indignation is past.
21 For behold, the LORD [a]comes out of His place
To punish the inhabitants of the earth for their iniquity;
The earth will also disclose her blood,
And will no more cover her slain.

**27** In that day the LORD with His severe sword, great and strong,
Will punish Leviathan the fleeing serpent,
[a]Leviathan that twisted serpent;
And He will slay [b]the reptile that *is* in the sea.

### *THE RESTORATION OF ISRAEL*

2 In that day [a]sing to her,
[b]"A vineyard of red wine![1]
3 [a]I, the LORD, keep it,
I water it every moment;
Lest any hurt it,
I keep it night and day.
4 Fury *is* not in Me.
Who would set [a]briers *and* thorns
Against Me in battle?
I would go through them,
I would burn them together.
5 Or let him take hold [a]of My strength,
*That* he may [b]make peace with Me;
*And* he shall make peace with Me."

6 Those who come He shall cause [a]to take root in Jacob;
Israel shall blossom and bud,
And fill the face of the world with fruit.

7 [a]Has He struck Israel as He struck those who struck him?
Or has He been slain according to the slaughter of those who were slain by Him?
8 [a]In measure, by sending it away,
You contended with it.
[b]He removes *it* by His rough wind
In the day of the east wind.
9 Therefore by this the iniquity of Jacob will be covered;
And this *is* all the fruit of taking away his sin:
When he makes all the stones of the altar
Like chalkstones that are beaten to dust,
Wooden images[1] and incense altars shall not stand.
10 Yet the fortified city *will be* [a]desolate,
The habitation forsaken and left like a wilderness;
There the calf will feed, and there it will lie down
And consume its branches.
11 When its boughs are withered, they will be broken off;
The women come *and* set them on fire.
For [a]it *is* a people of no understanding;
Therefore He who made them will [b]not have mercy on them,
And [c]He who formed them will show them no favor.

12 And it shall come to pass in that day
*That* the LORD will thresh,
From the channel of the River[1] to the Brook of Egypt;
And you will be [a]gathered one by one,
O you children of Israel.

> **27:12** God's intended boundaries for Israel were the Euphrates **River** on the east and **Egypt** on the west. The Lord had promised to give all the land in between to the descendants of Abraham, Isaac, and Jacob. The **children of Israel**, though, never claimed all of what was rightfully theirs. They allowed other nations to live in the land God had given them.

13 [a]So it shall be in that day:
[b]The great trumpet will be blown;
They will come, who are about to perish in the land of Assyria,
And they who are outcasts in the land of [c]Egypt,
And shall [d]worship the LORD in the holy mount at Jerusalem.

### *WOE TO EPHRAIM AND JERUSALEM*

**28** Woe to the crown of pride, to the drunkards of Ephraim,
Whose glorious beauty *is* a fading flower
Which *is* at the head of the verdant valleys,
To those who are overcome with wine!
2 Behold, the Lord has a mighty and strong one,
[a]Like a tempest of hail and a destroying storm,
Like a flood of mighty waters overflowing,
Who will bring *them* down to the earth with *His* hand.

**26:20** [a] Ex. 12:22, 23 [b] [Ps. 30:5] **26:21** [a] Mic. 1:3 **27:1** [a] Ps. 74:13, 14 [b] Is. 51:9 **27:2** [a] Is. 5:1 [b] Is. 5:7 [1] Following Masoretic Text (Kittel's *Biblia Hebraica*), Bomberg, and Vulgate; Masoretic Text (*Biblia Hebraica Stuttgartensia*), some Hebrew manuscripts, and Septuagint read *delight;* Targum reads *choice vineyard.* **27:3** [a] Is. 31:5 **27:4** [a] 2 Sam. 23:6 **27:5** [a] Is. 25:4 [b] Job 22:21 **27:6** [a] Is. 37:31 **27:7** [a] Is. 10:12, 17; 30:30–33 **27:8** [a] Job 23:6 [b] [Ps. 78:38] **27:9** [1] Hebrew *Asherim,* Canaanite deities **27:10** [a] Is. 5:6, 17; 32:14 **27:11** [a] Deut. 32:28 [b] Is. 9:17 [c] Deut. 32:18 **27:12** [a] [Is. 11:11; 56:8] [1] That is, the Euphrates **27:13** [a] Is. 2:11 [b] Rev. 11:15 [c] Is. 19:21, 22 [d] Zech. 14:16 **28:2** [a] Ezek. 13:11

3 The crown of pride, the drunkards of
Ephraim,
Will be trampled underfoot;
4 And the glorious beauty is a fading flower
Which *is* at the head of the verdant valley,
Like the first fruit before the summer,
Which an observer sees;
He eats it up while it is still in his hand.

5 In that day the LORD of hosts will be
For a crown of glory and a diadem of beauty
To the remnant of His people,
6 For a spirit of justice to him who sits in
judgment,
And for strength to those who turn back
the battle at the gate.

7 But they also [a]have erred through wine,
And through intoxicating drink are out of
the way;
[b]The priest and the prophet have erred
through intoxicating drink,
They are swallowed up by wine,
They are out of the way through
intoxicating drink;
They err in vision, they stumble *in*
judgment.
8 For all tables are full of vomit *and* filth;
No place *is clean*.

9 "Whom[a] will he teach knowledge?
And whom will he make to understand
the message?
Those *just* weaned from milk?
Those *just* drawn from the breasts?
10 [a]For precept *must be* upon precept, precept
upon precept,
Line upon line, line upon line,
Here a little, there a little."
11 For with [a]stammering lips and another
tongue
He will speak to this people,
12 To whom He said, "This *is* the [a]rest *with
which*
You may cause the weary to rest,"
And, "This *is* the refreshing";
Yet they would not hear.
13 But the word of the LORD was to them,
"Precept upon precept, precept upon
precept,
Line upon line, line upon line,
Here a little, there a little,"
That they might go and fall backward, and
be broken
And snared and caught.

14 Therefore hear the word of the LORD, you
scornful men,
Who rule this people who *are* in
Jerusalem,
15 Because you have said, "We have made a
covenant with death,
And with Sheol we are in agreement.
When the overflowing scourge passes
through,
It will not come to us,
[a]For we have made lies our refuge,
And under falsehood we have hidden
ourselves."

### A CORNERSTONE IN ZION

16 Therefore thus says the Lord GOD:

"Behold, I lay in Zion [a]a stone for a
foundation,
A tried stone, a precious cornerstone, a
sure foundation;
Whoever believes will not act hastily.

> **SEEING JESUS IN THE SCRIPTURE**
>
> **28:16** The cornerstone is the most important part of a foundation, ensuring it's built properly and able to support whatever is placed upon it. Jesus is our sure foundation, giving our lives stability, meaning, and strength (see 1 Pet. 2:6–8).

17 Also I will make justice the measuring line,
And righteousness the plummet;
The hail will sweep away the refuge of lies,
And the waters will overflow the hiding
place.
18 Your covenant with death will be annulled,
And your agreement with Sheol will not
stand;
When the overflowing scourge passes
through,
Then you will be trampled down by it.
19 As often as it goes out it will take you;
For morning by morning it will pass over,
And by day and by night;
It will be a terror just to understand the
report."

20 For the bed is too short to stretch out *on*,
And the covering so narrow that one
cannot wrap himself *in it*.
21 For the LORD will rise up as *at* Mount
[a]Perazim,
He will be angry as in the Valley of [b]Gibeon—
That He may do His work, [c]His awesome
work,
And bring to pass His act, His unusual act.
22 Now therefore, do not be mockers,
Lest your bonds be made strong;
For I have heard from the Lord GOD of hosts,
[a]A destruction determined even upon the
whole earth.

**28:7** [a] Hos. 4:11 [b] Is. 56:10, 12 **28:9** [a] Jer. 6:10 **28:10** [a] [2 Chr. 36:15] **28:11** [a] 1 Cor. 14:21 **28:12** [a] Is. 30:15 **28:15** [a] Is. 9:15 **28:16** [a] Matt. 21:42 **28:21** [a] 2 Sam. 5:20 [b] Josh. 10:10, 12 [c] [Lam. 3:33] **28:22** [a] Is. 10:22

### LISTEN TO THE TEACHING OF GOD

23 Give ear and hear my voice,
Listen and hear my speech.
24 Does the plowman keep plowing all day to sow?
Does he keep turning his soil and breaking the clods?
25 When he has leveled its surface,
Does he not sow the black cummin
And scatter the cummin,
Plant the wheat in rows,
The barley in the appointed place,
And the spelt in its place?
26 For He instructs him in right judgment,
His God teaches him.

27 For the black cummin is not threshed with a threshing sledge,
Nor is a cartwheel rolled over the cummin;
But the black cummin is beaten out with a stick,
And the cummin with a rod.
28 Bread *flour* must be ground;
Therefore he does not thresh it forever,
Break *it with* his cartwheel,
Or crush it *with* his horsemen.
29 This also comes from the LORD of hosts,
[a]*Who* is wonderful in counsel *and* excellent in guidance.

### WOE TO JERUSALEM

**29** "Woe [a]to Ariel,[1] to Ariel, the city [b]*where* David dwelt!
Add year to year;
Let feasts come around.
2 Yet I will distress Ariel;
There shall be heaviness and sorrow,
And it shall be to Me as Ariel.
3 I will encamp against you all around,
I will lay siege against you with a mound,
And I will raise siegeworks against you.
4 You shall be brought down,
You shall speak out of the ground;
Your speech shall be low, out of the dust;
Your voice shall be like a medium's, [a]out of the ground;
And your speech shall whisper out of the dust.

5 "Moreover the multitude of your [a]foes
Shall be like fine dust,
And the multitude of the terrible ones
Like [b]chaff that passes away;
Yes, it shall be [c]in an instant, suddenly.
6 [a]You will be punished by the LORD of hosts
With thunder and [b]earthquake and great noise,
*With* storm and tempest
And the flame of devouring fire.
7 [a]The multitude of all the nations who fight against Ariel,
Even all who fight against her and her fortress,
And distress her,
Shall be [b]as a dream of a night vision.
8 [a]It shall even be as when a hungry man dreams,
And look—he eats;
But he awakes, and his soul is still empty;
Or as when a thirsty man dreams,
And look—he drinks;
But he awakes, and indeed *he is* faint,
And his soul still craves:
So the multitude of all the nations shall be,
Who fight against Mount Zion."

### THE BLINDNESS OF DISOBEDIENCE

9 Pause and wonder!
Blind yourselves and be blind!
[a]They are drunk, [b]but not with wine;
They stagger, but not with intoxicating drink.
10 For [a]the LORD has poured out on you
The spirit of deep sleep,
And has [b]closed your eyes, namely, the prophets;
And He has covered your heads, *namely,*
[c]the seers.

11 The whole vision has become to you like the
words of a book [a]that is sealed, which *men* deliver
to one who is literate, saying, "Read this, please."
[b]And he says, "I cannot, for it *is* sealed."
12 Then the book is delivered to one who is
illiterate, saying, "Read this, please."
And he says, "I am not literate."
13 Therefore the Lord said:

[a]"Inasmuch as these people draw near with their mouths
And honor Me [b]with their lips,
But have removed their hearts far from Me,
And their fear toward Me is taught by the commandment of men,
14 [a]Therefore, behold, I will again do a marvelous work
Among this people,
A marvelous work and a wonder;
[b]For the wisdom of their wise *men* shall perish,
And the understanding of their prudent *men* shall be hidden."
15 [a]Woe to those who seek deep to hide their counsel far from the LORD,
And their works are in the dark;
[b]They say, "Who sees us?" and, "Who knows us?"

**28:29** [a] Ps. 92:5 **29:1** [a] Ezek. 24:6, 9 [b] 2 Sam. 5:9 [1] That is, Jerusalem **29:4** [a] Is. 8:19 **29:5** [a] Is. 25:5 [b] Job 21:18 [c] Is. 30:13; 47:11 **29:6** [a] Is. 28:2; 30:30 [b] Rev. 16:18, 19 **29:7** [a] Mic. 4:11, 12 [b] Job 20:8 **29:8** [a] Ps. 73:20 **29:9** [a] Is. 28:7, 8 [b] Is. 51:21 **29:10** [a] Rom. 11:8 [b] Ps. 69:23 [c] Is. 44:18 **29:11** [a] Is. 8:16 [b] Dan. 12:4, 9 **29:13** [a] Ezek. 33:31 [b] Col. 2:22 **29:14** [a] Hab. 1:5 [b] Jer. 49:7 **29:15** [a] Is. 30:1 [b] Ps. 10:11; 94:7

16 Surely you have things turned around!
Shall the potter be esteemed as the clay;
For shall the [a]thing made say of him who made it,
"He did not make me"?
Or shall the thing formed say of him who formed it,
"He has no understanding"?

### FUTURE RECOVERY OF WISDOM

17 *Is* it not yet a very little while
Till [a]Lebanon shall be turned into a fruitful field,
And the fruitful field be esteemed as a forest?
18 [a]In that day the deaf shall hear the words of the book,
And the eyes of the blind shall see out of obscurity and out of darkness.
19 [a]The humble also shall increase *their* joy in the LORD,
And [b]the poor among men shall rejoice
In the Holy One of Israel.
20 For the terrible one is brought to nothing,
[a]The scornful one is consumed,
And all who [b]watch for iniquity are cut off—
21 Who make a man an offender by a word,
And [a]lay a snare for him who reproves in the gate,
And turn aside the just [b]by empty words.

22 Therefore thus says the LORD, [a]who re-
deemed Abraham, concerning the house of
Jacob:

"Jacob shall not now be [b]ashamed,
Nor shall his face now grow pale;
23 But when he sees his children,
[a]The work of My hands, in his midst,
They will hallow My name,
And hallow the Holy One of Jacob,
And fear the God of Israel.
24 These also [a]who erred in spirit will come to understanding,
And those who complained will learn doctrine."

### FUTILE CONFIDENCE IN EGYPT

30 "Woe to the rebellious children," says the LORD,
[a]"Who take counsel, but not of Me,
And who devise plans, but not of My Spirit,
[b]That they may add sin to sin;
2 [a]Who walk to go down to Egypt,
And [b]have not asked My advice,
To strengthen themselves in the strength of Pharaoh,
And to trust in the shadow of Egypt!
3 [a]Therefore the strength of Pharaoh
Shall be your shame,
And trust in the shadow of Egypt
Shall be *your* humiliation.
4 For his princes were at [a]Zoan,
And his ambassadors came to Hanes.
5 [a]They were all ashamed of a people *who* could not benefit them,
Or be help or benefit,
But a shame and also a reproach."

6 [a]The burden against the beasts of the
South.

Through a land of trouble and anguish,
From which *came* the lioness and lion,
[b]The viper and fiery flying serpent,
They will carry their riches on the backs of young donkeys,
And their treasures on the humps of camels,
To a people *who* shall not profit;
7 [a]For the Egyptians shall help in vain and to no purpose.
Therefore I have called her
Rahab-Hem-Shebeth.[1]

### A REBELLIOUS PEOPLE

8 Now go, [a]write it before them on a tablet,
And note it on a scroll,
That it may be for time to come,
Forever and ever:
9 That [a]this *is* a rebellious people,
Lying children,
Children *who* will not hear the law of the LORD;
10 [a]Who say to the seers, "Do not see,"
And to the prophets, "Do not prophesy to us right things;
[b]Speak to us smooth things, prophesy deceits.
11 Get out of the way,
Turn aside from the path,
Cause the Holy One of Israel
To cease from before us."

12 Therefore thus says the Holy One of Israel:

"Because you [a]despise this word,
And trust in oppression and perversity,
And rely on them,
13 Therefore this iniquity shall be to you
[a]Like a breach ready to fall,
A bulge in a high wall,
Whose breaking [b]comes suddenly, in an instant.

29:16 [a] Is. 45:9 29:17 [a] Is. 32:15 29:18 [a] Is. 35:5 29:19 [a] [Is. 11:4; 61:1] [b] [James 2:5] 29:20 [a] Is. 28:14 [b] Mic. 2:1 29:21 [a] Amos 5:10, 12 [b] Prov. 28:21 29:22 [a] Josh. 24:3 [b] Is. 45:17 29:23 [a] [Is. 45:11; 49:20–26] 29:24 [a] Is. 28:7 30:1 [a] Is. 29:15 [b] Deut. 29:19 30:2 [a] Is. 31:1 [b] Josh. 9:14 30:3 [a] Is. 20:5 30:4 [a] Is. 19:11 30:5 [a] Jer. 2:36 30:6 [a] Is. 57:9 [b] Deut. 8:15 30:7 [a] Jer. 37:7 [1] Literally *Rahab Sits Idle* 30:8 [a] Hab. 2:2 30:9 [a] Is. 1:2, 4; 65:2 30:10 [a] Jer. 11:21 [b] 1 Kin. 22:8, 13 30:12 [a] Is. 5:24 30:13 [a] Ps. 62:3, 4 [b] Is. 29:5

14 And [a]He shall break it like the breaking of
the potter's vessel,
Which is broken in pieces;
He shall not spare.
So there shall not be found among its
fragments
A shard to take fire from the hearth,
Or to take water from the cistern."

15 For thus says the Lord GOD, the Holy One
of Israel:

[a]"In returning and rest you shall be saved;
In quietness and confidence shall be your
strength."
[b]But you would not,
16 And you said, "No, for we will flee on
horses"—
Therefore you shall flee!
And, "We will ride on swift *horses*"—
Therefore those who pursue you shall be
swift!

17 [a]One thousand *shall flee* at the threat of
one,
At the threat of five you shall flee,
Till you are left as a pole on top of a
mountain
And as a banner on a hill.

### GOD WILL BE GRACIOUS

18 Therefore the LORD will wait, that He may
be [a]gracious to you;
And therefore He will be exalted, that He
may have mercy on you.
For the LORD *is* a God of justice;
[b]Blessed *are* all those who [c]wait for Him.

19 For the people [a]shall dwell in Zion at
Jerusalem;
You shall [b]weep no more.
He will be very gracious to you at the
sound of your cry;
When He hears it, He will [c]answer you.
20 And *though* the Lord gives you
[a]The bread of adversity and the water of
affliction,
Yet [b]your teachers will not be moved into
a corner anymore,
But your eyes shall see your teachers.
21 Your ears shall hear a word behind you,
saying,
"This *is* the way, walk in it,"
Whenever you [a]turn to the right hand
Or whenever you turn to the left.
22 [a]You will also defile the covering of your
images of silver,
And the ornament of your molded images
of gold.
You will throw them away as an unclean
thing;
[b]You will say to them, "Get away!"

23 [a]Then He will give the rain for your seed
With which you sow the ground,
And bread of the increase of the earth;
It will be fat and plentiful.
In that day your cattle will feed
In large pastures.
24 Likewise the oxen and the young donkeys
that work the ground
Will eat cured fodder,
Which has been winnowed with the
shovel and fan.
25 There will be [a]on every high mountain
And on every high hill
Rivers *and* streams of waters,
In the day of the [b]great slaughter,
When the towers fall.
26 Moreover [a]the light of the moon will be as
the light of the sun,
And the light of the sun will be sevenfold,
As the light of seven days,
In the day that the LORD binds up the
bruise of His people
And heals the stroke of their wound.

### JUDGMENT ON ASSYRIA

27 Behold, the name of the LORD comes
from afar,
Burning *with* His anger,
And *His* burden *is* heavy;
His lips are full of indignation,
And His tongue like a devouring fire.
28 [a]His breath is like an overflowing stream,
[b]Which reaches up to the neck,
To sift the nations with the sieve of
futility;
And *there shall be* [c]a bridle in the jaws of
the people,
Causing *them* to err.

29 You shall have a song
As in the night *when* a holy festival is
kept,
And gladness of heart as when one goes
with a flute,
To come into [a]the mountain of the LORD,
To the Mighty One of Israel.
30 [a]The LORD will cause His glorious voice to
be heard,
And show the descent of His arm,
With the indignation of *His* anger
And the flame of a devouring fire,
*With* scattering, tempest, [b]and hailstones.
31 For [a]through the voice of the LORD
Assyria will be beaten down,
*As* He strikes with the [b]rod.

30:14 [a] Jer. 19:11 30:15 [a] Is. 7:4; 28:12 [b] Matt. 23:37 30:17 [a] Josh. 23:10 30:18 [a] Is. 33:2 [b] Jer. 17:7 [c] Is. 26:8 30:19 [a] Is. 65:9 [b] Is. 25:8 [c] Is. 65:24 30:20 [a] 1 Kin. 22:27 [b] Amos 8:11 30:21 [a] Josh. 1:7 30:22 [a] Is. 2:20; 31:7 [b] Hos. 14:8 30:23 [a] [Matt. 6:33]; 1 Tim. 6:8 30:25 [a] Is. 2:14, 15 [b] Is. 2:10–21; 34:2 30:26 [a] [Is. 60:19, 20; Rev. 21:23; 22:5] 30:28 [a] Is. 11:4; 2 Thess. 2:8 [b] Is. 8:8 [c] 2 Kin. 19:28; Is. 37:29 30:29 [a] [Is. 2:3] 30:30 [a] Is. 29:6 [b] Is. 28:2 30:31 [a] Is. 14:25; 37:36 [b] Is. 10:5, 24

32 And *in* every place where the staff of
punishment passes,
Which the LORD lays on him,
*It* will be with tambourines and harps;
And in battles of [a]brandishing He will
fight with it.
33 [a]For Tophet *was* established of old,
Yes, for the king it is prepared.
He has made *it* deep and large;
Its pyre *is* fire with much wood;
The breath of the LORD, like a stream of
brimstone,
Kindles it.

### *THE FOLLY OF NOT TRUSTING GOD*

**31** Woe to those [a]who go down to Egypt for
help,
*And* [b]rely on horses,
Who trust in chariots because *they are*
many,
And in horsemen because they are very
strong,
But who do not look to the Holy One of
Israel,
[c]Nor seek the LORD!
2 Yet He also *is* wise and will bring disaster,
And [a]will not call back His words,
But will arise against the house of
evildoers,
And against the help of those who work
iniquity.
3 Now the Egyptians *are* men, and not God;
And their horses are flesh, and not spirit.
When the LORD stretches out His hand,
Both he who helps will fall,
And he who is helped will fall down;
They all will perish [a]together.

### *GOD WILL DELIVER JERUSALEM*

4 For thus the LORD has spoken to me:

[a]"As a lion roars,
And a young lion over his prey
(When a multitude of shepherds is
summoned against him,
*He* will not be afraid of their voice
Nor be disturbed by their noise),
So the LORD of hosts will come down
To fight for Mount Zion and for its hill.
5 [a]Like birds flying about,
So will the LORD of hosts defend Jerusalem.
Defending, He will also deliver *it;*
Passing over, He will preserve *it.*"

6 Return *to Him* against whom the children
of Israel have [a]deeply revolted. 7 For in that day
every man shall [a]throw away his idols of silver
and his idols of gold—[b]sin, which your own
hands have made for yourselves.

8 "Then Assyria shall [a]fall by a sword not of
man,
And a sword not of mankind shall
[b]devour him.
But he shall flee from the sword,
And his young men shall become forced
labor.
9 [a]He shall cross over to his stronghold for fear,
And his princes shall be afraid of the
banner,"
Says the LORD,
Whose fire *is* in Zion
And whose furnace *is* in Jerusalem.

### *A REIGN OF RIGHTEOUSNESS*

**32** Behold, [a]a king will reign in
righteousness,
And princes will rule with justice.
2 A man will be as a hiding place from the
wind,
And [a]a cover from the tempest,
As rivers of water in a dry place,
As the shadow of a great rock in a weary
land.
3 [a]The eyes of those who see will not be dim,
And the ears of those who hear will listen.
4 Also the heart of the rash will [a]understand
knowledge,
And the tongue of the stammerers will be
ready to speak plainly.

5 The foolish person will no longer be
called generous,
Nor the miser said *to be* bountiful;
6 For the foolish person will speak foolishness,
And his heart will work [a]iniquity:
To practice ungodliness,
To utter error against the LORD,
To keep the hungry unsatisfied,
And he will cause the drink of the thirsty
to fail.
7 Also the schemes of the schemer *are* evil;
He devises wicked plans
To destroy the poor with [a]lying words,
Even when the needy speaks justice.
8 But a generous man devises generous
things,
And by generosity he shall stand.

### *CONSEQUENCES OF COMPLACENCY*

9 Rise up, you women [a]who are at ease,
Hear my voice;
You complacent daughters,
Give ear to my speech.
10 In a year and *some* days
You will be troubled, you complacent
women;
For the vintage will fail,
The gathering will not come.

30:32 [a] Is. 11:15 30:33 [a] 2 Kin. 23:10; Jer. 7:31 31:1 [a] Is. 30:1, 2 [b] Deut. 17:16; Ps. 20:7; Is. 2:7; 30:16 [c] Is. 9:13; Dan. 9:13; Amos 5:4–8 31:2 [a] Num. 23:19; Jer. 44:29 31:3 [a] Is. 20:6 31:4 [a] Num. 24:9; Hos. 11:10; Amos 3:8 31:5 [a] Deut. 32:11; Ps. 91:4 31:6 [a] Hos. 9:9 31:7 [a] Is. 2:20; 30:22 [b] 1 Kin. 12:30 31:8 [a] 2 Kin. 19:35, 36 [b] Is. 37:36 31:9 [a] Is. 37:37 32:1 [a] Ps. 45:1 32:2 [a] Is. 4:6 32:3 [a] Is. 29:18; 35:5 32:4 [a] Is. 29:24 32:6 [a] Prov. 24:7–9 32:7 [a] Jer. 5:26–28 32:9 [a] Amos 6:1

11 Tremble, you *women* who are at ease;
Be troubled, you complacent ones;
Strip yourselves, make yourselves bare,
And gird *sackcloth* on *your* waists.

12 People shall mourn upon their breasts
For the pleasant fields, for the fruitful vine.
13 [a]On the land of my people will come up
thorns *and* briers,
Yes, on all the happy homes *in* [b]the joyous
city;
14 [a]Because the palaces will be forsaken,
The bustling city will be deserted.
The forts and towers will become lairs
forever,
A joy of wild donkeys, a pasture of
flocks—
15 Until [a]the Spirit is poured upon us from
on high,
And [b]the wilderness becomes a fruitful
field,
And the fruitful field is counted as a forest.

### THE PEACE OF GOD'S REIGN

16 Then justice will dwell in the wilderness,
And righteousness remain in the fruitful
field.
17 [a]The work of righteousness will be peace,
And the effect of righteousness, quietness
and assurance forever.
18 My people will dwell in a peaceful
habitation,
In secure dwellings, and in quiet [a]resting
places,
19 [a]Though hail comes down [b]on the forest,
And the city is brought low in
humiliation.

20 Blessed *are* you who sow beside all waters,
Who send out freely the feet of [a]the ox
and the donkey.

### A PRAYER IN DEEP DISTRESS

**33** Woe to you [a]who plunder, though you
*have* not *been* plundered;
And you who deal treacherously, though
they have not dealt treacherously with
you!
[b]When you cease plundering,
You will be [c]plundered;
When you make an end of dealing
treacherously,
They will deal treacherously with you.

2 O LORD, be gracious to us;
[a]We have waited for You.
Be their[1] arm every morning,
Our salvation also in the time of trouble.

3 At the noise of the tumult the people
[a]shall flee;
When You lift Yourself up, the nations
shall be scattered;
4 And Your plunder shall be gathered
*Like* the gathering of the caterpillar;
As the running to and fro of locusts,
He shall run upon them.

5 [a]The LORD is exalted, for He dwells on high;
He has filled Zion with justice and
righteousness.
6 Wisdom and knowledge will be the
stability of your times,
*And* the strength of salvation;
The fear of the LORD *is* His treasure.

7 Surely their valiant ones shall cry outside,
[a]The ambassadors of peace shall weep
bitterly.
8 [a]The highways lie waste,
The traveling man ceases.
[b]He has broken the covenant,
He has despised the cities,[1]
He regards no man.
9 [a]The earth mourns *and* languishes,
Lebanon is shamed *and* shriveled;
Sharon is like a wilderness,
And Bashan and Carmel shake off *their fruits.*

> **33:9** Mount **Lebanon** towers over the region and produces majestic cedar trees. The fertile **Sharon** Valley was known for its breathtaking variety of flowers and plant life. **Bashan** was famous for its abundant wheat fields and vast herds of livestock. Mount **Carmel** is a beautiful, wooded mountain overlooking the Mediterranean Sea.

### IMPENDING JUDGMENT ON ZION

10 "Now[a] I will rise," says the LORD;
"Now I will be exalted,
Now I will lift Myself up.
11 [a]You shall conceive chaff,
You shall bring forth stubble;
Your breath, *as* fire, shall devour you.
12 And the people shall be *like* the burnings
of lime;
[a]*Like* thorns cut up they shall be burned in
the fire.
13 Hear, [a]you *who are* afar off, what I have
done;
And you *who are* near, acknowledge My
might."

**32:13** [a] Hos. 9:6 [b] Is. 22:2 **32:14** [a] Is. 27:10 **32:15** [a] [Joel 2:28] [b] Is. 29:17 **32:17** [a] James 3:18 **32:18** [a] [Zech. 2:5; 3:10] **32:19** [a] Is. 30:30 [b] Zech. 11:2 **32:20** [a] Is. 30:23, 24 **33:1** [a] Hab. 2:8 [b] Rev. 13:10 [c] Is. 10:12; 14:25; 31:8 **33:2** [a] Is. 25:9; 26:8 [1] Septuagint omits *their;* Syriac, Targum, and Vulgate read *our.* **33:3** [a] Is. 17:13 **33:5** [a] Ps. 97:9 **33:7** [a] 2 Kin. 18:18, 37 **33:8** [a] Judg. 5:6 [b] 2 Kin. 18:13–17 [1] Following Masoretic Text and Vulgate; Dead Sea Scrolls read *witnesses;* Septuagint omits *cities;* Targum reads *They have been removed from their cities.* **33:9** [a] Is. 24:4 **33:10** [a] Ps. 12:5 **33:11** [a] [Ps. 7:14] **33:12** [a] Is. 9:18 **33:13** [a] Is. 49:1

14 The sinners in Zion are afraid;
Fearfulness has seized the hypocrites:
"Who among us shall dwell with the
devouring [a]fire?
Who among us shall dwell with
everlasting burnings?"
15 He who [a]walks righteously and speaks
uprightly,
He who despises the gain of oppressions,
Who gestures with his hands, refusing
bribes,
Who stops his ears from hearing of
bloodshed,
And [b]shuts his eyes from seeing evil:
16 He will dwell on high;
His place of defense *will be* the fortress of
rocks;
Bread will be given him,
His water *will be* sure.

## THE LAND OF THE MAJESTIC KING

17 Your eyes will see the King in His [a]beauty;
They will see the land that is very far off.
18 Your heart will meditate on terror:
[a]"Where *is* the scribe?
Where *is* he who weighs?
Where *is* he who counts the towers?"
19 [a]You will not see a fierce people,
[b]A people of obscure speech, beyond
perception,
Of a stammering tongue *that you* cannot
understand.

20 [a]Look upon Zion, the city of our appointed
feasts;
Your eyes will see [b]Jerusalem, a quiet
home,
A tabernacle *that* will not be taken down;
[c]Not one of [d]its stakes will ever be
removed,
Nor will any of its cords be broken.
21 But there the majestic LORD *will be* for us
A place of broad rivers *and* streams,
In which no galley with oars will sail,
Nor majestic ships pass by
22 (For the LORD *is* our [a]Judge,
The LORD *is* our [b]Lawgiver,
[c]The LORD *is* our King;
He will save us);
23 Your tackle is loosed,
They could not strengthen their mast,
They could not spread the sail.

Then the prey of great plunder is divided;
The lame take the prey.
24 And the inhabitant will not say, "I am
sick";
[a]The people who dwell in it *will be* forgiven
*their* iniquity.

## JUDGMENT ON THE NATIONS

34 Come [a]near, you nations, to hear;
And heed, you people!
[b]Let the earth hear, and all that is in it,
The world and all things that come forth
from it.
2 For the indignation of the LORD *is* against
all nations,
And *His* fury against all their armies;
He has utterly destroyed them,
He has given them over to the [a]slaughter.
3 Also their slain shall be thrown out;
[a]Their stench shall rise from their corpses,
And the mountains shall be melted with
their blood.
4 [a]All the host of heaven shall be dissolved,
And the heavens shall be rolled up like a
scroll;
[b]All their host shall fall down
As the leaf falls from the vine,
And as [c]*fruit* falling from a fig tree.

5 "For [a]My sword shall be bathed in heaven;
Indeed it [b]shall come down on Edom,
And on the people of My curse, for
judgment.
6 The [a]sword of the LORD is filled with blood,
It is made overflowing with fatness,
With the blood of lambs and goats,
With the fat of the kidneys of rams.
For [b]the LORD has a sacrifice in Bozrah,
And a great slaughter in the land of Edom.
7 The wild oxen shall come down with them,
And the young bulls with the mighty
bulls;
Their land shall be soaked with blood,
And their dust saturated with fatness."

8 For *it is* the day of the LORD's [a]vengeance,
The year of recompense for the cause of
Zion.
9 [a]Its streams shall be turned into pitch,
And its dust into brimstone;
Its land shall become burning pitch.
10 It shall not be quenched night or day;
[a]Its smoke shall ascend forever.
[b]From generation to generation it shall lie
waste;
No one shall pass through it forever and
ever.
11 [a]But the pelican and the porcupine shall
possess it,
Also the owl and the raven shall dwell in it.
And [b]He shall stretch out over it
The line of confusion and the stones of
emptiness.
12 They shall call its nobles to the kingdom,
But none *shall be* there, and all its princes
shall be nothing.

**33:14** [a] Heb. 12:29 **33:15** [a] Ps. 15:2; 24:3, 4 [b] Ps. 119:37 **33:17** [a] Ps. 27:4 **33:18** [a] 1 Cor. 1:20 **33:19** [a] 2 Kin. 19:32 [b] Jer. 5:15 **33:20** [a] Ps. 48:12 [b] Ps. 46:5; 125:1 [c] Is. 37:33 [d] Is. 54:2 **33:22** [a] [Acts 10:42] [b] James 4:12 [c] Ps. 89:18 **33:24** [a] Is. 40:2 **34:1** [a] Ps. 49:1 [b] Deut. 32:1 **34:2** [a] Is. 13:5 **34:3** [a] Joel 2:20 **34:4** [a] Is. 13:13 [b] Is. 14:12 [c] Rev. 6:12–14 **34:5** [a] Jer. 46:10 [b] Mal. 1:4 **34:6** [a] Is. 66:16 [b] Zeph. 1:7 **34:8** [a] Is. 63:4 **34:9** [a] Deut. 29:23 **34:10** [a] Rev. 14:11; 18:18; 19:3 [b] Mal. 1:3, 4 **34:11** [a] Zeph. 2:14 [b] Lam. 2:8

13 And [a]thorns shall come up in its palaces,
Nettles and brambles in its fortresses;
[b]It shall be a habitation of jackals,
A courtyard for ostriches.
14 The wild beasts of the desert shall also
meet with the jackals,
And the wild goat shall bleat to its
companion;
Also the night creature shall rest there,
And find for herself a place of rest.
15 There the arrow snake shall make her nest
and lay *eggs*
And hatch, and gather *them* under her
shadow;
There also shall the hawks be gathered,
Every one with her mate.

16 "Search from [a]the book of the LORD, and
read:
Not one of these shall fail;
Not one shall lack her mate.
For My mouth has commanded it, and His
Spirit has gathered them.
17 He has cast the lot for them,
And His hand has divided it among them
with a measuring line.
They shall possess it forever;
From generation to generation they shall
dwell in it."

### *THE FUTURE GLORY OF ZION*

**35** The [a]wilderness and the wasteland
shall be glad for them,
And the [b]desert shall rejoice and blossom
as the rose;
2 [a]It shall blossom abundantly and rejoice,
Even with joy and singing.
The glory of Lebanon shall be given to it,
The excellence of Carmel and Sharon.
They shall see the [b]glory of the LORD,
The excellency of our God.

3 [a]Strengthen the weak hands,
And make firm the feeble knees.
4 Say to those *who are* fearful-hearted,
"Be strong, do not fear!
Behold, your God will come *with* [a]vengeance,
*With* the recompense of God;
He will come and [b]save you."

5 Then the [a]eyes of the blind shall be opened,
And [b]the ears of the deaf shall be
unstopped.
6 Then the [a]lame shall leap like a deer,
And the [b]tongue of the dumb sing.
For [c]waters shall burst forth in the
wilderness,
And streams in the desert.

**SEEING JESUS IN THE SCRIPTURE**

**35:5–6** Jesus fulfilled this prophecy over the course of His three-year earthly ministry, showing He cares about us holistically (see Matt. 15:30). Each miraculous healing was to prove Jesus' identity as the Son of God and was based on His love for people.

7 The parched ground shall become a pool,
And the thirsty land springs of water;
In [a]the habitation of jackals, where each
lay,
*There shall be* grass with reeds and rushes.

8 A [a]highway shall be there, and a road,
And it shall be called the Highway of
Holiness.
[b]The unclean shall not pass over it,
But it *shall be* for others.
Whoever walks the road, although a fool,
Shall not go astray.
9 [a]No lion shall be there,
Nor shall *any* ravenous beast go up on it;
It shall not be found there.
But the redeemed shall walk *there*,
10 And the [a]ransomed of the LORD shall
return,
And come to Zion with singing,
With everlasting joy on their heads.
They shall obtain joy and gladness,
And [b]sorrow and sighing shall flee away.

### *SENNACHERIB BOASTS AGAINST THE LORD*

*(2 Kin. 18:13–37; 2 Chr. 32:1–19)*

**36** Now [a]it came to pass in the fourteenth
year of King Hezekiah *that* Sennacherib
king of Assyria came up against all the fortified
cities of Judah and took them. 2 Then the king of
Assyria sent *the* Rabshakeh[1] with a great army
from Lachish to King Hezekiah at Jerusalem.
And he stood by the aqueduct from the upper
pool, on the highway to the Fuller's Field. 3 And
[a]Eliakim the son of Hilkiah, who was over the
household, [b]Shebna the scribe, and Joah the
son of Asaph, the recorder, came out to him.
4 [a]Then *the* Rabshakeh said to them, "Say
now to Hezekiah, 'Thus says the great king,
the king of Assyria: "What confidence is this
in which you trust? 5 I say you speak of having
plans and power for war; but *they are* mere
words. Now in whom do you trust, that you rebel
against me? 6 Look! You are trusting in the [a]staff
of this broken reed, Egypt, on which if a man
leans, it will go into his hand and pierce it. So *is*
Pharaoh king of Egypt to all who [b]trust in him.

**34:13** [a] Is. 32:13 [b] Is. 13:21 **34:16** [a] [Mal. 3:16] **35:1** [a] Is. 32:15; 55:12 [b] Is. 41:19; 51:3 **35:2** [a] Is. 32:15 [b] Is. 40:5 **35:3** [a] Heb. 12:12 **35:4** [a] Is. 34:8 [b] Is. 33:22 **35:5** [a] Is. 29:18 [b] [Matt. 11:5] **35:6** [a] Acts 8:7 [b] Is. 32:4 [c] [John 7:38] **35:7** [a] Is. 34:13 **35:8** [a] Is. 19:23 [b] Is. 52:1; Joel 3:17; [Matt. 7:13, 14]; 1 Pet. 1:15, 16; Rev. 21:27 **35:9** [a] Lev. 26:6; [Is. 11:7, 9]; Ezek. 34:25 **35:10** [a] Is. 51:11 [b] Is. 25:8; 30:19; 65:19; [Rev. 7:17; 21:4] **36:1** [a] 2 Kin. 18:13, 17; 2 Chr. 32:1 **36:2** [1] A title, probably *Chief of Staff* or *Governor* **36:3** [a] Is. 22:20 [b] Is. 22:15 **36:4** [a] 2 Kin. 18:19 **36:6** [a] Ezek. 29:6 [b] Ps. 146:3; Is. 30:3, 5, 7

7"But if you say to me, 'We trust in the LORD
our God,' *is it* not He whose high places and whose
altars Hezekiah has taken away, and said to Judah
and Jerusalem, 'You shall worship before this
altar'?"' 8Now therefore, I urge you, give a pledge
to my master the king of Assyria, and I will give
you two thousand horses—if you are able on
your part to put riders on them! 9How then will
you repel one captain of the least of my master's
servants, and put your trust in Egypt for chariots
and horsemen? 10Have I now come up without the
LORD against this land to destroy it? The LORD said
to me, 'Go up against this land, and destroy it.'"

11Then Eliakim, Shebna, and Joah said to
*the* Rabshakeh, "Please speak to your servants
in Aramaic, for we understand *it;* and do not
speak to us in Hebrew[1] in the hearing of the
people who *are* on the wall."

> **36:11** The average Israelite of Isaiah's day spoke and understood only **Hebrew**. Some, especially those who did business with people from other countries, also spoke **Aramaic**, the language of the Persians, Syrians, and Babylonians.

12But *the* Rabshakeh said, "Has my master
sent me to your master and to you to speak these
words, and not to the men who sit on the wall,
who will eat and drink their own waste with you?"

13Then *the* Rabshakeh stood and called out
with a loud voice in Hebrew, and said, "Hear
the words of the great king, the king of Assyr-
ia! 14Thus says the king: 'Do not let Hezekiah
deceive you, for he will not be able to deliver
you; 15nor let Hezekiah make you trust in the
LORD, saying, "The LORD will surely deliver us;
this city will not be given into the hand of the
king of Assyria."' 16Do not listen to Hezekiah; for
thus says the king of Assyria: 'Make *peace* with
me *by a* present and come out to me; [a]and every
one of you eat from his own vine and every one
from his own fig tree, and every one of you drink
the waters of his own cistern; 17until I come and
take you away to a land like your own land, a
land of grain and new wine, a land of bread and
vineyards. 18*Beware* lest Hezekiah persuade you,
saying, "The LORD will deliver us." Has any one
of the [a]gods of the nations delivered its land
from the hand of the king of Assyria? 19Where
*are* the gods of Hamath and Arpad? Where *are*
the gods of Sepharvaim? Indeed, have they de-
livered [a]Samaria from my hand? 20Who among
all the gods of these lands have delivered their
countries from my hand, that the LORD should
deliver Jerusalem from my hand?'"

21But they held their peace and answered
him not a word; for the king's commandment
was, "Do not answer him." 22Then Eliakim the
son of Hilkiah, who *was* over the household,
Shebna the scribe, and Joah the son of Asaph,
the recorder, came to Hezekiah with *their* clothes
torn, and told him the words of *the* Rabshakeh.

### *ISAIAH ASSURES DELIVERANCE*

*(2 Kin. 19:1–7)*

**37** And [a]so it was, when King Hezekiah heard
*it,* that he tore his clothes, covered himself
with sackcloth, and went into the house of the
LORD. 2Then he sent Eliakim, who *was* over the
household, Shebna the scribe, and the elders of
the priests, covered with sackcloth, to Isaiah the
prophet, the son of Amoz. 3And they said to him,
"Thus says Hezekiah: 'This day *is* a day of [a]trouble
and rebuke and blasphemy; for the children have
come to birth, but *there is* no strength to bring
them forth. 4It may be that the LORD your God
will hear the words of *the* Rabshakeh, whom his
master the king of Assyria has sent to [a]reproach
the living God, and will rebuke the words which
the LORD your God has heard. Therefore lift up
*your* prayer for the remnant that is left.'"

5So the servants of King Hezekiah came
to Isaiah. 6And Isaiah said to them, "Thus you
shall say to your master, 'Thus says the LORD:
"Do not be afraid of the words which you have
heard, with which the servants of the king of As-
syria have blasphemed Me. 7Surely I will send a
spirit upon him, and he shall hear a rumor and
return to his own land; and I will cause him to
fall by the sword in his own land."'"

### *SENNACHERIB'S THREAT AND HEZEKIAH'S PRAYER*

*(2 Kin. 19:8–19)*

8Then *the* Rabshakeh returned, and found
the king of Assyria warring against Libnah, for
he heard that he had departed from Lachish.
9And the king heard concerning Tirhakah king
of Ethiopia, "He has come out to make war with
you." So when he heard *it,* he sent messengers
to Hezekiah, saying, 10"Thus you shall speak to
Hezekiah king of Judah, saying: 'Do not let your
God in whom you trust deceive you, saying, "Je-
rusalem shall not be given into the hand of the
king of Assyria." 11Look! You have heard what
the kings of Assyria have done to all lands by
utterly destroying them; and shall you be deliv-
ered? 12Have the [a]gods of the nations delivered
those whom my fathers have destroyed, Gozan
and Haran and Rezeph, and the people of Eden
who *were* in Telassar? 13Where *is* the king of
[a]Hamath, the king of Arpad, and the king of the
city of Sepharvaim, Hena, and Ivah?'"

14And Hezekiah received the letter from the
hand of the messengers, and read it; and Hezeki-
ah went up to the house of the LORD, and spread
it before the LORD. 15Then Hezekiah prayed to the
LORD, saying: 16"O LORD of hosts, God of Israel,

36:11 [1] Literally *Judean* 36:16 [a] 1 Kin. 4:25; Mic. 4:4; Zech. 3:10 36:18 [a] 2 Kin. 19:12; Is. 37:12 36:19 [a] 2 Kin. 17:6 37:1 [a] 2 Kin. 19:1–37; Is. 37:1–38 37:3 [a] Is. 22:5; 26:16; 33:2 37:4 [a] Is. 36:15, 18, 20 37:12 [a] Is. 36:18, 19 37:13 [a] Is. 49:23

*the One* who dwells *between* the cherubim, You *are*
God, You [a]alone, of all the kingdoms of the earth.
You have made heaven and earth. 17 [a]Incline Your
ear, O LORD, and hear; open Your eyes, O LORD,
and see; and [b]hear all the words of Sennacherib,
which he has sent to reproach the living God.
18 Truly, LORD, the kings of Assyria have laid waste
all the nations and their [a]lands, 19 and have cast
their gods into the fire; for they *were* [a]not gods,
but the work of men's hands—wood and stone.
Therefore they destroyed them. 20 Now therefore,
O LORD our God, [a]save us from his hand, that all
the kingdoms of the earth may [b]know that You
*are* the LORD, You alone."

### *THE WORD OF THE LORD CONCERNING SENNACHERIB*

*(2 Kin. 19:20–34)*

21 Then Isaiah the son of Amoz sent to Hez-
ekiah, saying, "Thus says the LORD God of Is-
rael, 'Because you have prayed to Me against
Sennacherib king of Assyria, 22 this *is* the word
which the LORD has spoken concerning him:

"The virgin, the daughter of Zion,
Has despised you, laughed you to scorn;
The daughter of Jerusalem
Has shaken *her* head behind your back!

23 "Whom have you reproached and
blasphemed?
Against whom have you raised *your* voice,
And lifted up your eyes on high?
Against the Holy One of Israel.
24 By your servants you have reproached the
Lord,
And said, 'By the multitude of my chariots
I have come up to the height of the
mountains,
To the limits of Lebanon;
I will cut down its tall cedars
*And* its choice cypress trees;
I will enter its farthest height,
To its fruitful forest.
25 I have dug and drunk water,
And with the soles of my feet I have dried up
All the brooks of defense.'

26 "Did you not hear [a]long ago
*How* I made it,
From ancient times that I formed it?
Now I have brought it to pass,
That you should be
For crushing fortified cities *into* heaps of
ruins.
27 Therefore their inhabitants *had* little power;
They were dismayed and confounded;
They were *as* the grass of the field
And the green herb,
*As* the grass on the housetops
And *grain* blighted before it is grown.

28 "But I know your dwelling place,
Your going out and your coming in,
And your rage against Me.
29 Because your rage against Me and your
tumult
Have come up to My ears,
Therefore [a]I will put My hook in your nose
And My bridle in your lips,
And I will [b]turn you back
By the way which you came."'

30 "This *shall be* a sign to you:

You shall eat this year such as grows of
itself,
And the second year what springs from
the same;
Also in the third year sow and reap,
Plant vineyards and eat the fruit of them.
31 And the remnant who have escaped of the
house of Judah
Shall again take root downward,
And bear fruit upward.
32 For out of Jerusalem shall go a remnant,
And those who escape from Mount Zion.
The [a]zeal of the LORD of hosts will do this.

33 "Therefore thus says the LORD concerning
the king of Assyria:

'He shall not come into this city,
Nor shoot an arrow there,
Nor come before it with shield,
Nor build a siege mound against it.
34 By the way that he came,
By the same shall he return;
And he shall not come into this city,'
Says the LORD.
35 'For I will [a]defend this city, to save it
For My own sake and for My servant
[b]David's sake.'"

### *SENNACHERIB'S DEFEAT AND DEATH*

*(2 Kin. 19:35–37)*

36 Then the [a]angel[1] of the LORD went out,
and killed in the camp of the Assyrians one
hundred and eighty-five thousand; and when
*people* arose early in the morning, there were
the corpses—all dead. 37 So Sennacherib king
of Assyria departed and went away, returned
*home,* and remained at Nineveh. 38 Now it came
to pass, as he was worshiping in the house of
Nisroch his god, that his sons Adrammelech
and Sharezer struck him down with the sword;
and they escaped into the land of Ararat. Then
[a]Esarhaddon his son reigned in his place.

37:16 [a] Is. 43:10, 11 37:17 [a] 2 Chr. 6:40; Ps. 17:6; Dan. 9:18 [b] Ps. 74:22 37:18 [a] 2 Kin. 15:29; 16:9; 17:6, 24; 1 Chr. 5:26 37:19 [a] Is. 40:19, 20
37:20 [a] Is. 33:22 [b] Ps. 83:18 37:26 [a] Is. 25:1; 40:21; 45:21 37:29 [a] 2 Kin. 19:35–37; 2 Chr. 32:21; Is. 30:28; Ezek. 38:4 [b] Ezek. 38:4; 39:2
37:32 [a] 2 Kin. 19:31; Is. 9:7; 59:17; Joel 2:18; Zech. 1:14 37:35 [a] 2 Kin. 20:6; Is. 31:5; 38:6 [b] 1 Kin. 11:13 37:36 [a] 2 Kin. 19:35; Is. 10:12, 33, 34
[1] Or *Angel* 37:38 [a] Ezra 4:2

### *HEZEKIAH'S LIFE EXTENDED*

*(2 Kin. 20:1–11; 2 Chr. 32:24–26)*

**38** In [a]those days Hezekiah was sick and near
death. And Isaiah the prophet, the son of
Amoz, went to him and said to him, "Thus says
the LORD: [b]'Set your house in order, for you shall
die and not live.' "
2 Then Hezekiah turned his face toward the
wall, and prayed to the LORD, 3 and said, [a]"Re-
member now, O LORD, I pray, how I have walked
before You in truth and with a loyal heart, and
have done *what is* good in Your [b]sight." And
Hezekiah wept bitterly.
4 And the word of the LORD came to Isaiah,
saying, 5 "Go and tell Hezekiah, 'Thus says the
LORD, the God of David your father: "I have heard
your prayer, I have seen your tears; surely I will
add to your days fifteen years. 6 I will deliver you
and this city from the hand of the king of Assyr-
ia, and [a]I will defend this city." ' 7 And this *is* [a]the
sign to you from the LORD, that the LORD will
do this thing which He has spoken: 8 Behold, I
will bring the shadow on the sundial, which has
gone down with the sun on the sundial of Ahaz,
ten degrees backward." So the sun returned ten
degrees on the dial by which it had gone down.
9 This is the writing of Hezekiah king of
Judah, when he had been sick and had recov-
ered from his sickness:

10 I said,
"In the prime of my life
I shall go to the gates of Sheol;
I am deprived of the remainder of my years."
11 I said,
"I shall not see YAH,
The LORD[1] [a]in the land of the living;
I shall observe man no more among the
inhabitants of the world.[2]
12 [a]My life span is gone,
Taken from me like a shepherd's tent;
I have cut off my life like a weaver.
He cuts me off from the loom;
From day until night You make an end of me.
13 I have considered until morning—
Like a lion,
So He breaks all my bones;
From day until night You make an end of me.
14 Like a crane *or* a swallow, so I chattered;
[a]I mourned like a dove;
My eyes fail *from looking* upward.
O LORD,[1] I am oppressed;
Undertake for me!
15 "What shall I say?
He has both spoken to me,[1]
And He Himself has done *it*.
I shall walk carefully all my years
[a]In the bitterness of my soul.
16 O Lord, by these *things men* live;
And in all these *things is* the life of my spirit;
So You will restore me and make me live.
17 Indeed *it was* for *my own* peace
*That* I had great bitterness;
But You have lovingly *delivered* my soul
from the pit of corruption,
For You have cast all my sins behind Your
back.
18 For [a]Sheol cannot thank You,
Death cannot praise You;
Those who go down to the pit cannot
hope for Your truth.
19 The living, the living man, he shall praise
You,
As I *do* this day;
[a]The father shall make known Your truth
to the children.
20 "The LORD *was ready* to save me;
Therefore we will sing my songs with
stringed instruments
All the days of our life, in the house of the
LORD."

21 Now [a]Isaiah had said, "Let them take a
lump of figs, and apply *it* as a poultice on the
boil, and he shall recover."
22 And [a]Hezekiah had said, "What *is* the sign
that I shall go up to the house of the LORD?"

### *THE BABYLONIAN ENVOYS*

*(2 Kin. 20:12–19)*

**39** At [a]that time Merodach-Baladan[1] the son
of Baladan, king of Babylon, sent letters
and a present to Hezekiah, for he heard that he
had been sick and had recovered. 2 [a]And Heze-
kiah was pleased with them, and showed them
the house of his treasures—the silver and gold,
the spices and precious ointment, and all his
armory—all that was found among his trea-
sures. There was nothing in his house or in all
his dominion that Hezekiah did not show them.
3 Then Isaiah the prophet went to King Hez-
ekiah, and said to him, "What did these men say,
and from where did they come to you?"
So Hezekiah said, "They came to me from
a [a]far country, from Babylon."
4 And he said, "What have they seen in your
house?"
So Hezekiah answered, "They have seen all
that *is* in my house; there is nothing among my
treasures that I have not shown them."

38:1 [a] 2 Kin. 20:1–6, 9–11; 2 Chr. 32:24; Is. 38:1–8 [b] 2 Sam. 17:23 38:3 [a] Neh. 13:14 [b] 2 Kin. 18:5, 6; Ps. 26:3 38:6 [a] 2 Kin. 19:35–37; 2 Chr. 32:21; Is. 31:5; 37:35 38:7 [a] Judg. 6:17, 21, 36–40; 2 Kin. 20:8; Is. 7:11 38:11 [a] Ps. 27:13; 116:9 [1] Hebrew *YAH, YAH* [2] Following some Hebrew manuscripts; Masoretic Text and Vulgate read *rest;* Septuagint omits *among the inhabitants of the world;* Targum reads *land.* 38:12 [a] Job 7:6 38:14 [a] Is. 59:11; Ezek. 7:16; Nah. 2:7 [1] Following Bomberg; Masoretic Text and Dead Sea Scrolls read *Lord.* 38:15 [a] Job 7:11; 10:1; Is. 38:17 [1] Following Masoretic Text and Vulgate; Dead Sea Scrolls and Targum read *And shall I say to Him;* Septuagint omits first half of this verse. 38:18 [a] Ps. 6:5; 30:9; 88:11; 115:17; [Eccl. 9:10] 38:19 [a] Deut. 4:9; 6:7; Ps. 78:3, 4 38:21 [a] 2 Kin. 20:7 38:22 [a] 2 Kin. 20:8 39:1 [a] 2 Kin. 20:12–19 [1] Spelled *Berodach-Baladan* in 2 Kings 20:12 39:2 [a] 2 Chr. 32:25, 31 39:3 [a] Deut. 28:49

5 Then Isaiah said to Hezekiah, "Hear the
word of the LORD of hosts: 6 'Behold, the days
are coming [a]when all that *is* in your house, and
what your fathers have accumulated until this
day, shall be carried to Babylon; nothing shall
be left,' says the LORD. 7 'And they shall take away
*some* of your [a]sons who will descend from you,
whom you will beget; and they shall be eunuchs
in the palace of the king of Babylon.'"
8 So Hezekiah said to Isaiah, [a]"The word of the
LORD which you have spoken *is* good!" For he said,
"At least there will be peace and truth in my days."

### GOD'S PEOPLE ARE COMFORTED

*(cf. Luke 3:4–6)*

**40** "Comfort, yes, comfort My people!"
Says your God.
2 "Speak comfort to Jerusalem, and cry out
to her,
That her warfare is ended,
That her iniquity is pardoned;
[a]For she has received from the LORD's hand
Double for all her sins."

3 [a]The voice of one crying in the wilderness:
[b]"Prepare the way of the LORD;
[c]Make straight in the desert[1]
A highway for our God.

> **SEEING JESUS IN THE SCRIPTURE**
>
> **40:3** Just as Isaiah's message prepared the way for God to return His people to the Promised Land, John the Baptist's message prepared the way for Jesus' coming. The Israelites' salvation pictures what was to come with Jesus (see Matt. 3:3).

4 Every valley shall be exalted
And every mountain and hill brought low;
[a]The crooked places shall be made straight
And the rough places smooth;
5 The [a]glory of the LORD shall be revealed,
And all flesh shall see *it* together;
For the mouth of the LORD has spoken."

6 The voice said, "Cry out!"
And he[1] said, "What shall I cry?"

[a]"All flesh *is* grass,
And all its loveliness *is* like the flower of
the field.
7 The grass withers, the flower fades,
Because the breath of the LORD blows
upon it;
Surely the people *are* grass.
8 The grass withers, the flower fades,
But [a]the word of our God stands forever."

9 O Zion,
You who bring good tidings,
Get up into the high mountain;
O Jerusalem,
You who bring good tidings,
Lift up your voice with strength,
Lift *it* up, be not afraid;
Say to the cities of Judah, "Behold your
God!"
10 Behold, the Lord GOD shall come with a
strong *hand*,
And [a]His arm shall rule for Him;
Behold, [b]His reward *is* with Him,
And His work before Him.
11 He will [a]feed His flock like a shepherd;
He will gather the lambs with His arm,
And carry *them* in His bosom,
*And* gently lead those who are with young.

12 [a]Who has measured the waters[1] in the
hollow of His hand,
Measured heaven with a span
And calculated the dust of the earth in a
measure?
Weighed the mountains in scales
And the hills in a balance?
13 [a]Who has directed the Spirit of the LORD,
Or *as* His counselor has taught Him?
14 With whom did He take counsel, and *who*
instructed Him,
And [a]taught Him in the path of justice?
Who taught Him knowledge,
And showed Him the way of understanding?

15 Behold, the nations *are* as a drop in a
bucket,
And are counted as the small dust on the
scales;
Look, He lifts up the isles as a very little
thing.
16 And Lebanon *is* not sufficient to burn,
Nor its beasts sufficient for a burnt
offering.
17 All nations before Him *are* as [a]nothing,
And [b]they are counted by Him less than
nothing and worthless.

18 To whom then will you [a]liken God?
Or what likeness will you compare to Him?
19 [a]The workman molds an image,
The goldsmith overspreads it with gold,
And the silversmith casts silver chains.

**39:6** [a] Jer. 20:5 **39:7** [a] Dan. 1:1–7 **39:8** [a] 1 Sam. 3:18 **40:2** [a] Is. 61:7 **40:3** [a] Matt. 3:3 [b] [Mal. 3:1; 4:5, 6] [c] Ps. 68:4 [1] Following Masoretic Text, Targum, and Vulgate; Septuagint omits *in the desert.* **40:4** [a] Is. 45:2 **40:5** [a] Is. 35:2 **40:6** [a] Job 14:2 [1] Following Masoretic Text and Targum; Dead Sea Scrolls, Septuagint, and Vulgate read *I.* **40:8** [a] [John 12:34] **40:10** [a] Is. 59:16, 18 [b] Is. 62:11 **40:11** [a] [John 10:11, 14–16] **40:12** [a] Prov. 30:4 [1] Following Masoretic Text, Septuagint, and Vulgate; Dead Sea Scrolls read *waters of the sea;* Targum reads *waters of the world.* **40:13** [a] [1 Cor. 2:16] **40:14** [a] Job 36:22, 23 **40:17** [a] Dan. 4:35 [b] Ps. 62:9 **40:18** [a] Is. 46:5 **40:19** [a] Is. 41:7; 44:10

20 Whoever *is* too impoverished for *such* a
contribution
Chooses a tree *that* will not rot;
He seeks for himself a skillful workman
[a]To prepare a carved image *that* will not
totter.

21 [a]Have you not known?
Have you not heard?
Has it not been told you from the
beginning?
Have you not understood from the
foundations of the earth?
22 *It is* He who sits above the circle of the
earth,
And its inhabitants *are* like grasshoppers,
Who [a]stretches out the heavens like a
curtain,
And spreads them out like a [b]tent to
dwell in.
23 He brings the [a]princes to nothing;
He makes the judges of the earth
useless.

24 Scarcely shall they be planted,
Scarcely shall they be sown,
Scarcely shall their stock take root in the
earth,
When He will also blow on them,
And they will wither,
And the whirlwind will take them away
like stubble.

25 "To[a] whom then will you liken Me,
Or *to whom* shall I be equal?" says the
Holy One.
26 Lift up your eyes on high,
And see who has created these *things,*
Who brings out their host by number;
[a]He calls them all by name,
By the greatness of His might
And the strength of *His* power;
Not one is missing.

27 [a]Why do you say, O Jacob,
And speak, O Israel:
"My way is hidden from the LORD,
And my just claim is passed over by my
God"?
28 Have you not known?
Have you not heard?
The everlasting God, the LORD,
The Creator of the ends of the earth,
Neither faints nor is weary.
[a]His understanding is unsearchable.
29 He gives power to the weak,
And to *those who have* no might He
increases strength.
30 Even the youths shall faint and be weary,
And the young men shall utterly fall,
31 But those who [a]wait on the LORD
[b]Shall renew *their* strength;
They shall mount up with wings like eagles,
They shall run and not be weary,
They shall walk and not faint.

40:20 [a] Is. 41:7; 46:7 40:21 [a] Rom. 1:19 40:22 [a] Jer. 10:12 [b] Ps. 19:4 40:23 [a] Ps. 107:40 40:25 [a] Is. 40:18 40:26 [a] Ps. 147:4 40:27 [a] Is. 54:7, 8 40:28 [a] Rom. 11:33 40:31 [a] Is. 30:15; 49:23 [b] Ps. 103:5

KNOW THE TRUTH

## THE DOCTRINE OF GOD

### PART 4: THE ETERNALITY OF GOD

**40:28** The Hebrew word for *everlasting* most often describes what is perpetual, constant, eternal, unending, permanent, timeless, and enduring. In this verse, it's used to describe the nature of God. He's without beginning and without end. He's timeless, ageless, deathless, and changeless. It's difficult for us to grasp an everlasting Being. We have a definite beginning, are always changing, and are moving toward an unavoidable physical death. On the contrary, God has no starting part, no ending point, and is immutable (unchanging). He's unaffected by time. He created time; thus, He's not bound by it any more than a car maker is bound by a car he or she made.

The eternality of God should bring us great comfort. People come and go, but God remains. Nations rise and fall, but God remains. Trial and tragedy are here and gone, but God remains. Jesus Christ rules an unending kingdom (see Is. 9:7; Dan. 7:13–14). Those who trust in Christ are given an everlasting, unchanging position as God's forever sons and daughters (see John 14:1–3). While God has neither beginning nor end, in Christ we had a beginning, but have no end.

*For* **THE DOCTRINE OF GOD: PART 5: THE INFINITY OF GOD**, *turn to Luke 1:37 on page 1031.*

### ISRAEL ASSURED OF GOD'S HELP

41 "Keep [a]silence before Me, O coastlands,
And let the people renew *their* strength!
Let them come near, then let them speak;
Let us [b]come near together for judgment.

2 "Who raised up one [a]from the east?
Who in righteousness called him to His feet?
Who [b]gave the nations before him,
And made *him* rule over kings?
Who gave *them* as the dust *to* his sword,
As driven stubble to his bow?
3 Who pursued them, *and* passed safely
By the way *that* he had not gone with his feet?
4 [a]Who has performed and done *it,*
Calling the generations from the beginning?
'I, the LORD, am [b]the first;
And with the last I *am* [c]He.' "

5 The coastlands saw *it* and feared,
The ends of the earth were afraid;
They drew near and came.
6 [a]Everyone helped his neighbor,
And said to his brother,
"Be of good courage!"
7 [a]So the craftsman encouraged the [b]goldsmith;
He who smooths *with* the hammer
*inspired* him who strikes the anvil,
Saying, "It *is* ready for the soldering";
Then he fastened it with pegs,
[c]*That* it might not totter.

8 "But you, Israel, *are* My servant,
Jacob whom I have [a]chosen,
The descendants of Abraham My [b]friend.
9 *You* whom I have taken from the ends of the earth,
And called from its farthest regions,
And said to you,
'You *are* My servant,
I have chosen you and have not cast you away:
10 [a]Fear not, [b]for I *am* with you;
Be not dismayed, for I *am* your God.
I will strengthen you,
Yes, I will help you,
I will uphold you with My righteous right hand.'

11 "Behold, all those who were incensed against you
Shall be [a]ashamed and disgraced;
They shall be as nothing,
And those who strive with you shall perish.
12 You shall seek them and not find them—
Those who contended with you.
Those who war against you
Shall be as nothing,
As a nonexistent thing.
13 For I, the LORD your God, will hold your right hand,
Saying to you, 'Fear not, I will help you.'

14 "Fear not, you [a]worm Jacob,
You men of Israel!
I will help you," says the LORD
And your Redeemer, the Holy One of Israel.
15 "Behold, [a]I will make you into a new threshing sledge with sharp teeth;
You shall thresh the mountains and beat *them* small,
And make the hills like chaff.
16 You shall [a]winnow them, the wind shall carry them away,
And the whirlwind shall scatter them;
You shall rejoice in the LORD,
*And* [b]glory in the Holy One of Israel.

17 "The poor and needy seek water, but *there is* none,
Their tongues fail for thirst.
I, the LORD, will hear them;
*I,* the God of Israel, will not [a]forsake them.
18 I will open [a]rivers in desolate heights,
And fountains in the midst of the valleys;
I will make the [b]wilderness a pool of water,
And the dry land springs of water.
19 I will plant in the wilderness the cedar and the acacia tree,
The myrtle and the oil tree;
I will set in the [a]desert the cypress tree *and* the pine
And the box tree together,
20 [a]That they may see and know,
And consider and understand together,
That the hand of the LORD has done this,
And the Holy One of Israel has created it.

### THE FUTILITY OF IDOLS

21 "Present your case," says the LORD.
"Bring forth your strong *reasons,*" says the [a]King of Jacob.
22 "Let[a] them bring forth and show us what will happen;
Let them show the [b]former things, what they *were,*
That we may consider them,
And know the latter end of them;
Or declare to us things to come.
23 [a]Show the things that are to come hereafter,
That we may know that you *are* gods;
Yes, [b]do good or do evil,
That we may be dismayed and see *it* together.

41:1 [a]Zech. 2:13 [b]Is. 1:18 41:2 [a]Is. 46:11 [b]Is. 45:1, 13 41:4 [a]Is. 41:26 [b]Rev. 1:8, 17; 22:13 [c]Is. 43:10; 44:6 41:6 [a]Is. 40:19 41:7 [a]Is. 44:13 [b]Is. 40:19 [c]Is. 40:20 41:8 [a]Deut. 7:6; 10:15 [b]James 2:23 41:10 [a]Is. 41:13, 14; 43:5 [b][Deut. 31:6] 41:11 [a]Zech. 12:3 41:14 [a]Job 25:6 41:15 [a]Mic. 4:13 41:16 [a]Jer. 51:2 [b]Is. 45:25 41:17 [a]Rom. 11:2 41:18 [a]Is. 35:6, 7; 43:19; 44:3 [b]Ps. 107:35 41:19 [a]Is. 35:1 41:20 [a]Job 12:9 41:21 [a]Is. 43:15 41:22 [a]Is. 45:21 [b]Is. 43:9 41:23 [a][John 13:19] [b]Jer. 10:5

24 Indeed [a]you *are* nothing,
And your work *is* nothing;
*He who* chooses you *is* an abomination.

25 "I have raised up one from the north,
And he shall come;
From the rising of the sun [a]he shall call
on My name;
[b]And he shall come against princes as
*though* mortar,
As the potter treads clay.
26 [a]Who has declared from the beginning,
that we may know?
And former times, that we may say, '*He is*
righteous'?
Surely *there is* no one who shows,
Surely *there is* no one who declares,
Surely *there is* no one who hears your words.
27 [a]The first time [b]*I said* to Zion,
'Look, there they are!'
And I will give to Jerusalem one who
brings good tidings.
28 [a]For I looked, and *there was* no man;
I looked among them, but *there was* no
counselor,
Who, when I asked of them, could answer
a word.
29 [a]Indeed they *are* all worthless;[1]
Their works *are* nothing;
Their molded images *are* wind and
confusion.

### THE SERVANT OF THE LORD

42 "Behold! [a]My Servant whom I uphold,
My Elect One *in whom* My soul
[b]delights!
[c]I have put My Spirit upon Him;
He will bring forth justice to the Gentiles.
2 He will not cry out, nor raise *His voice,*
Nor cause His voice to be heard in the
street.
3 A bruised reed He will not break,
And smoking flax He will not quench;
He will bring forth justice for truth.
4 He will not fail nor be discouraged,
Till He has established justice in the
earth;
[a]And the coastlands shall wait for His law."

**SEEING JESUS IN THE SCRIPTURE**

**42:1–4** The Servant that Isaiah spoke of was Jesus, who perfectly fulfilled His role as God's Servant (see Matt. 12:18–21). Jesus was just to all, gentle but bold, and unwavering in His mission to proclaim God's kingdom and be the sacrifice for sin.

5 Thus says God the LORD,
[a]Who created the heavens and stretched
them out,
Who spread forth the earth and that
which comes from it,
[b]Who gives breath to the people on it,
And spirit to those who walk on it:
6 "I,[a] the LORD, have called You in
righteousness,
And will hold Your hand;
I will keep You [b]and give You as a
covenant to the people,
As [c]a light to the Gentiles,
7 [a]To open blind eyes,
To [b]bring out prisoners from the prison,
Those who sit in [c]darkness from the
prison house.
8 I *am* the LORD, that *is* My name;
And My [a]glory I will not give to another,
Nor My praise to carved images.
9 Behold, the former things have come to
pass,
And new things I declare;
Before they spring forth I tell you of them."

### PRAISE TO THE LORD

10 [a]Sing to the LORD a new song,
*And* His praise from the ends of the earth,
[b]You who go down to the sea, and all that is
in it,
You coastlands and you inhabitants of
them!
11 Let the wilderness and its cities lift up
*their voice,*
The villages *that* Kedar inhabits.
Let the inhabitants of Sela sing,
Let them shout from the top of the
mountains.
12 Let them give glory to the LORD,
And declare His praise in the coastlands.
13 The LORD shall go forth like a mighty
man;
He shall stir up *His* zeal like a man of war.
He shall cry out, [a]yes, shout aloud;
He shall prevail against His enemies.

### PROMISE OF THE LORD'S HELP

14 "I have held My peace a long time,
I have been still and restrained Myself.
*Now* I will cry like a woman in labor,
I will pant and gasp at once.
15 I will lay waste the mountains and hills,
And dry up all their vegetation;
I will make the rivers coastlands,
And I will dry up the pools.
16 I will bring the blind by a way they did not
know;
I will lead them in paths they have not
known.

**41:24** [a] [1 Cor. 8:4] **41:25** [a] Ezra 1:2 [b] Is. 41:2 **41:26** [a] Is. 43:9 **41:27** [a] Is. 41:4 [b] Is. 40:9 **41:28** [a] Is. 63:5 **41:29** [a] Is. 41:24
[1] Following Masoretic Text and Vulgate; Dead Sea Scrolls, Syriac, and Targum read *nothing;* Septuagint omits the first line. **42:1** [a] [Phil. 2:7] [b] Matt. 3:17; 17:5 [c] [Is. 11:2] **42:4** [a] [Gen. 49:10] **42:5** [a] Zech. 12:1 [b] Acts 17:25 **42:6** [a] Is. 43:1 [b] Is. 49:8 [c] Luke 2:32 **42:7** [a] Is. 35:5 [b] Luke 4:18 [c] Is. 9:2 **42:8** [a] Is. 48:11 **42:10** [a] Ps. 33:3; 40:3; 98:1 [b] Ps. 107:23 **42:13** [a] Is. 31:4

I will make darkness light before them,
And crooked places straight.
These things I will do for them,
And not forsake them.
17 They shall be [a]turned back,
They shall be greatly ashamed,
Who trust in carved images,
Who say to the molded images,
'You *are* our gods.'

18 "Hear, you deaf;
And look, you blind, that you may see.
19 [a]Who *is* blind but My servant,
Or deaf as My messenger *whom* I send?
Who *is* blind as *he who is* perfect,
And blind as the LORD's servant?
20 Seeing many things, [a]but you do not observe;
Opening the ears, but he does not hear."

### ISRAEL'S OBSTINATE DISOBEDIENCE

21 The LORD is well pleased for His righteousness' sake;
He will exalt the law and make *it* honorable.
22 But this *is* a people robbed and plundered;
All of them are snared in holes,
And they are hidden in prison houses;
They are for prey, and no one delivers;
For plunder, and no one says, "Restore!"

23 Who among you will give ear to this?
*Who* will listen and hear for the time to come?
24 Who gave Jacob for plunder, and Israel to the robbers?
Was it not the LORD,
He against whom we have sinned?
[a]For they would not walk in His ways,
Nor were they obedient to His law.
25 Therefore He has poured on him the fury of His anger
And the strength of battle;
[a]It has set him on fire all around,
[b]Yet he did not know;
And it burned him,
Yet he did not take *it* to [c]heart.

### THE REDEEMER OF ISRAEL

43 But now, thus says the LORD, who created you, O Jacob,
And He who formed you, O Israel:
"Fear not, [a]for I have redeemed you;
[b]I have called *you* by your name;
You *are* Mine.
2 [a]When you pass through the waters, [b]I *will be* with you;
And through the rivers, they shall not overflow you.
When you [c]walk through the fire, you shall not be burned,
Nor shall the flame scorch you.
3 For I *am* the LORD your God,
The Holy One of Israel, your Savior;
[a]I gave Egypt for your ransom,
Ethiopia and Seba in your place.
4 Since you were precious in My sight,
You have been honored,
And I have [a]loved you;
Therefore I will give men for you,
And people for your life.
5 [a]Fear not, for I *am* with you;
I will bring your descendants from the east,
And [b]gather you from the west;
6 I will say to the [a]north, 'Give them up!'
And to the south, 'Do not keep them back!'
Bring My sons from afar,
And My daughters from the ends of the earth—
7 Everyone who is [a]called by My name,
Whom [b]I have created for My glory;
I have formed him, yes, I have made him."

8 [a]Bring out the blind people who have eyes,
And the [b]deaf who have ears.
9 Let all the nations be gathered together,
And let the people be assembled.
[a]Who among them can declare this,
And show us former things?
Let them bring out their witnesses, that they may be justified;
Or let them hear and say, "*It is* truth."
10 "You[a] *are* My witnesses," says the LORD,
[b]"And My servant whom I have chosen,
That you may know and [c]believe Me,
And understand that I *am* He.
Before Me there was no God formed,
Nor shall there be after Me.
11 I, *even* I, [a]*am* the LORD,
And besides Me *there is* no savior.
12 I have declared and saved,
I have proclaimed,
And *there was* no [a]foreign *god* among you;
[b]Therefore you *are* My witnesses,"
Says the LORD, "that I *am* God.
13 [a]Indeed before the day *was*, I *am* He;
And *there is* no one who can deliver out of My hand;
I work, and who will [b]reverse it?"

14 Thus says the LORD, your Redeemer,
The Holy One of Israel:
"For your sake I will send to Babylon,
And bring them all down as fugitives—
The Chaldeans, who rejoice in their ships.
15 I *am* the LORD, your Holy One,
The Creator of Israel, your [a]King."

**42:17** [a] Ps. 97:7 **42:19** [a] [John 9:39, 41] **42:20** [a] Rom. 2:21 **42:24** [a] Is. 65:2 **42:25** [a] 2 Kin. 25:9 [b] Hos. 7:9 [c] Is. 29:13 **43:1** [a] Is. 43:5; 44:6 [b] Is. 42:6; 45:4 **43:2** [a] [Ps. 66:12; 91:3] [b] [Deut. 31:6] [c] Dan. 3:25 **43:3** [a] [Prov. 11:8; 21:18] **43:4** [a] Is. 63:9 **43:5** [a] Is. 41:10; 44:2 [b] Is. 54:7 **43:6** [a] Is. 49:12 **43:7** [a] James 2:7 [b] [2 Cor. 5:17] **43:8** [a] Ezek. 12:2 [b] Is. 29:18 **43:9** [a] Is. 41:21, 22, 26 **43:10** [a] Is. 44:8 [b] Is. 55:4 [c] Is. 41:4; 44:6 **43:11** [a] Hos. 13:4 **43:12** [a] Deut. 32:16 [b] Is. 44:8 **43:13** [a] Ps. 90:2 [b] Job 9:12 **43:15** [a] Is. 41:20, 21

16 Thus says the LORD, who [a]makes a way in
the sea
And a [b]path through the mighty waters,

> **43:16** The pharaoh of Egypt, after letting the Israelites leave his country, changed his mind, and sent his army to bring them back. His plan was to trap the Israelites at the Red Sea. Just when things looked hopeless for the Israelites, God parted the waters and created a **path** of dry land **through** the middle of the **sea**. The Israelites were able to walk across to the other side. When the Egyptians tried to follow, the water collapsed on top of them, and they drowned.

17 Who [a]brings forth the chariot and horse,
The army and the power
(They shall lie down together, they shall
not rise;
They are extinguished, they are quenched
like a wick):
18 "Do[a] not remember the former things,
Nor consider the things of old.
19 Behold, I will do a [a]new thing,
Now it shall spring forth;
Shall you not know it?
[b]I will even make a road in the wilderness
*And* rivers in the desert.
20 The beast of the field will honor Me,
The jackals and the ostriches,
Because [a]I give waters in the wilderness
*And* rivers in the desert,
To give drink to My people, My chosen.
21 [a]This people I have formed for Myself;
They shall declare My [b]praise.

### PLEADING WITH UNFAITHFUL ISRAEL

22 "But you have not called upon Me, O Jacob;
And you [a]have been weary of Me, O Israel.
23 [a]You have not brought Me the sheep for
your burnt offerings,
Nor have you honored Me with your
sacrifices.
I have not caused you to serve with grain
offerings,
Nor wearied you with incense.
24 You have bought Me no sweet cane with
money,
Nor have you satisfied Me with the fat of
your sacrifices;
But you have burdened Me with your sins,
You have [a]wearied Me with your iniquities.

25 "I, *even* I, *am* He who [a]blots out your
transgressions [b]for My own sake;
[c]And I will not remember your sins.
26 Put Me in remembrance;
Let us contend together;
State your *case,* that you may be acquitted.
27 Your first father sinned,
And your mediators have transgressed
against Me.
28 Therefore I will profane the princes of the
sanctuary;
[a]I will give Jacob to the curse,
And Israel to reproaches.

### GOD'S BLESSING ON ISRAEL

44 "Yet hear now, O Jacob My servant,
And Israel whom I have chosen.
2 Thus says the LORD who made you
And formed you from the womb, *who* will
help you:
'Fear not, O Jacob My servant;
And you, Jeshurun, whom I have chosen.
3 For I will pour water on him who is
thirsty,
And floods on the dry ground;
I will pour My Spirit on your descendants,
And My blessing on your offspring;
4 They will spring up among the grass
Like willows by the watercourses.'
5 One will say, 'I *am* the LORD's';
Another will call *himself* by the name of
Jacob;
Another will write *with* his hand, 'The
LORD's,'
And name *himself* by the name of Israel.

### THERE IS NO OTHER GOD

6 "Thus says the LORD, the King of Israel,
And his Redeemer, the LORD of hosts:
[a]'I *am* the First and I *am* the Last;
Besides Me *there is* no God.
7 And [a]who can proclaim as I do?
Then let him declare it and set it in order
for Me,
Since I appointed the ancient people.
And the things that are coming and shall
come,
Let them show these to them.
8 Do not fear, nor be afraid;
[a]Have I not told you from that time, and
declared *it?*
[b]You *are* My witnesses.
Is there a God besides Me?
Indeed [c]*there is* no other Rock;
I know not *one.*' "

### IDOLATRY IS FOOLISHNESS

9 [a]Those who make an image, all of them *are*
useless,
And their precious things shall not profit;
They *are* their own witnesses;
[b]They neither see nor know, that they may
be ashamed.

**43:16** [a] Ex. 14:16, 21, 22 [b] Josh. 3:13 **43:17** [a] Ex. 14:4–9, 25 **43:18** [a] Jer. 16:14 **43:19** [a] [2 Cor. 5:17] [b] Ex. 17:6 **43:20** [a] Is. 48:21 **43:21** [a] Ps. 102:18 [b] Jer. 13:11 **43:22** [a] Mal. 1:13; 3:14 **43:23** [a] Amos 5:25 **43:24** [a] Is. 1:14; 7:13 **43:25** [a] Jer. 50:20 [b] Ezek. 36:22 [c] Is. 1:18 **43:28** [a] Dan. 9:11 **44:6** [a] Is. 41:4 **44:7** [a] Is. 41:4, 22, 26 **44:8** [a] Is. 41:22 [b] Is. 43:10, 12 [c] 1 Sam. 2:2 **44:9** [a] Is. 41:24 [b] Ps. 115:4

10 Who would form a god or mold an image
[a]*That* profits him nothing?
11 Surely all his companions would be
[a]ashamed;
And the workmen, they *are* mere men.
Let them all be gathered together,
Let them stand up;
Yet they shall fear,
They shall be ashamed together.

12 [a]The blacksmith with the tongs works one
in the coals,
Fashions it with hammers,
And works it with the strength of his arms.
Even so, he is hungry, and his strength fails;
He drinks no water and is faint.

13 The craftsman stretches out *his* rule,
He marks one out with chalk;
He fashions it with a plane,
He marks it out with the compass,
And makes it like the figure of a man,
According to the beauty of a man, that it
may remain in the house.
14 He cuts down cedars for himself,
And takes the cypress and the oak;
He secures *it* for himself among the trees
of the forest.
He plants a pine, and the rain nourishes *it.*

15 Then it shall be for a man to burn,
For he will take some of it and warm
himself;
Yes, he kindles *it* and bakes bread;
Indeed he makes a god and worships *it;*
He makes it a carved image, and falls
down to it.
16 He burns half of it in the fire;
With this half he eats meat;
He roasts a roast, and is satisfied.
He even warms *himself* and says,
"Ah! I am warm,
I have seen the fire."
17 And the rest of it he makes into a god,
His carved image.
He falls down before it and worships *it,*
Prays to it and says,
"Deliver me, for you *are* my god!"

18 [a]They do not know nor understand;
For [b]He has shut their eyes, so that they
cannot see,
*And* their hearts, so that they cannot
[c]understand.
19 And no one [a]considers in his heart,
Nor *is there* knowledge nor understanding
to say,
"I have burned half of it in the fire,
Yes, I have also baked bread on its coals;
I have roasted meat and eaten *it;*
And shall I make the rest of it an
abomination?
Shall I fall down before a block of wood?"
20 He feeds on ashes;
[a]A deceived heart has turned him aside;
And he cannot deliver his soul,
Nor say, "*Is there* not a [b]lie in my right hand?"

### *ISRAEL IS NOT FORGOTTEN*

21 "Remember these, O Jacob,
And Israel, for you *are* My servant;
I have formed you, you *are* My servant;
O Israel, you will not be [a]forgotten by Me!
22 [a]I have blotted out, like a thick cloud, your
transgressions,
And like a cloud, your sins.
Return to Me, for [b]I have redeemed you."

23 [a]Sing, O heavens, for the LORD has done *it!*
Shout, you lower parts of the earth;
Break forth into singing, you mountains,
O forest, and every tree in it!
For the LORD has redeemed Jacob,
And [b]glorified Himself in Israel.

### *JUDAH WILL BE RESTORED*

24 Thus says the LORD, [a]your Redeemer,
And [b]He who formed you from the womb:
"I *am* the LORD, who makes all *things,*
[c]Who stretches out the heavens all alone,
Who spreads abroad the earth by Myself;
25 Who [a]frustrates the signs [b]of the babblers,
And drives diviners mad;
Who turns wise men backward,
[c]And makes their knowledge foolishness;
26 [a]Who confirms the word of His servant,
And performs the counsel of His
messengers;
Who says to Jerusalem, 'You shall be
inhabited,'
To the cities of Judah, 'You shall be built,'
And I will raise up her waste places;
27 [a]Who says to the deep, 'Be dry!
And I will dry up your rivers';
28 Who says of [a]Cyrus, '*He is* My shepherd,
And he shall perform all My pleasure,
Saying to Jerusalem, [b]"You shall be built,"
And to the temple, "Your foundation shall
be laid." '

### *CYRUS, GOD'S INSTRUMENT*

45 "Thus says the LORD to His anointed,
To [a]Cyrus, whose [b]right hand I have
held—
[c]To subdue nations before him
And [d]loose the armor of kings,
To open before him the double doors,
So that the gates will not be shut:

**44:10** [a]Hab. 2:18 **44:11** [a]Ps. 97:7 **44:12** [a]Jer. 10:3–5 **44:18** [a]Is. 45:20 [b]Is. 6:9, 10; 29:10 [c]Jer. 10:14 **44:19** [a]Is. 46:8 **44:20** [a]2 Thess. 2:11 [b]Rom. 1:25 **44:21** [a]Is. 49:15 **44:22** [a]Is. 43:25 [b]1 Cor. 6:20 **44:23** [a]Ps. 69:34 [b]Is. 49:3; 60:21 **44:24** [a]Is. 43:14 [b]Is. 43:1 [c]Job 9:8 **44:25** [a]Is. 47:13 [b]Jer. 50:36 [c]1 Cor. 1:20, 27 **44:26** [a]Zech. 1:6 **44:27** [a]Jer. 50:38; 51:36 **44:28** [a]Ezra 1:1 [b]Ezra 6:7 **45:1** [a]Is. 44:28 [b]Is. 41:13 [c]Dan. 5:30 [d]Job 12:21

2 'I will go before you
[a]And make the crooked places[1] straight;
[b]I will break in pieces the gates of bronze
And cut the bars of iron.
3 I will give you the treasures of darkness
And hidden riches of secret places,
[a]That you may know that I, the LORD,
Who [b]call *you* by your name,
*Am* the God of Israel.
4 For [a]Jacob My servant's sake,
And Israel My elect,
I have even called you by your name;
I have named you, though you have not
known Me.
5 I [a]*am* the LORD, and [b]*there is* no other;
*There is* no God besides Me.
[c]I will gird you, though you have not
known Me,
6 [a]That they may [b]know from the rising of
the sun to its setting
That *there is* none besides Me.
I *am* the LORD, and *there is* no other;
7 I form the light and create darkness,
I make peace and [a]create calamity;
I, the LORD, do all these *things*.'

8 "Rain[a] down, you heavens, from above,
And let the skies pour down righteousness;
Let the earth open, let them bring forth
salvation,
And let righteousness spring up together.
I, the LORD, have created it.

9 "Woe to him who strives with [a]his Maker!
*Let* the potsherd *strive* with the potsherds
of the earth!
[b]Shall the clay say to him who forms it,
'What are you making?'
Or shall your handiwork *say*, 'He has no
hands'?
10 Woe to him who says to *his* father, 'What
are you begetting?'
Or to the woman, 'What have you brought
forth?' "

11 Thus says the LORD,
The Holy One of Israel, and his Maker:
[a]"Ask Me of things to come concerning [b]My
sons;
And concerning [c]the work of My hands,
you command Me.
12 [a]I have made the earth,
And [b]created man on it.
I—My hands—stretched out the heavens,
And [c]all their host I have commanded.
13 [a]I have raised him up in righteousness,
And I will direct all his ways;
He shall [b]build My city
And let My exiles go free,
[c]Not for price nor reward,"
Says the LORD of hosts.

### THE LORD, THE ONLY SAVIOR

14 Thus says the LORD:

[a]"The labor of Egypt and merchandise of
Cush
And of the Sabeans, men of stature,
Shall come over to you, and they shall be
yours;
They shall walk behind you,
They shall come over [b]in chains;
And they shall bow down to you.
They will make supplication to you,
*saying*, [c]'Surely God *is* in you,
And *there is* no other;
[d]*There is* no other God.' "

15 Truly You *are* God, [a]who hide Yourself,
O God of Israel, the Savior!
16 They shall be [a]ashamed
And also disgraced, all of them;
They shall go in confusion together,
*Who are* makers of idols.
17 [a]*But* Israel shall be saved by the LORD
With an [b]everlasting salvation;
You shall not be ashamed or [c]disgraced
Forever and ever.

18 For thus says the LORD,
[a]Who created the heavens,
Who is God,
Who formed the earth and made it,
Who has established it,
Who did not create it in vain,
Who formed it to be [b]inhabited:
[c]"I *am* the LORD, and *there is* no other.
19 I have not spoken in [a]secret,
In a dark place of the earth;
I did not say to the seed of Jacob,
'Seek Me in vain';
[b]I, the LORD, speak righteousness,
I declare things that are right.

20 "Assemble yourselves and come;
Draw near together,
You *who have* escaped from the nations.
[a]They have no knowledge,
Who carry the wood of their carved
image,
And pray to a god *that* cannot save.
21 Tell and bring forth *your case*;
Yes, let them take counsel together.
[a]Who has declared this from ancient time?

45:2 [a] Is. 40:4 [b] Ps. 107:16 [1] Dead Sea Scrolls and Septuagint read *mountains;* Targum reads *I will trample down the walls;* Vulgate reads *I will humble the great ones of the earth.* 45:3 [a] Is. 41:23 [b] Ex. 33:12 45:4 [a] Is. 44:1 45:5 [a] Deut. 4:35; 32:39 [b] Is. 45:14, 18 [c] Ps. 18:32 45:6 [a] Mal. 1:11 [b] [Is. 11:9; 52:10] 45:7 [a] Amos 3:6 45:8 [a] Ps. 85:11 45:9 [a] Is. 64:8 [b] Jer. 18:6 45:11 [a] Is. 8:19 [b] Jer. 31:9 [c] Is. 29:23; 60:21; 64:8 45:12 [a] Is. 42:5 [b] Gen. 1:26 [c] Gen. 2:1 45:13 [a] Is. 41:2 [b] 2 Chr. 36:22 [c] [Rom. 3:24] 45:14 [a] Zech. 8:22, 23 [b] Ps. 149:8 [c] 1 Cor. 14:25 [d] Is. 45:5 45:15 [a] Ps. 44:24 45:16 [a] Is. 44:11 45:17 [a] Is. 26:4 [b] Is. 51:6 [c] Is. 29:22 45:18 [a] Is. 42:5 [b] Ps. 115:16 [c] Is. 45:5 45:19 [a] Deut. 30:11 [b] Ps. 19:8 45:20 [a] Is. 44:9; 46:7 45:21 [a] Is. 41:22; 43:9

*Who* has told it from that time?
*Have* not I, the LORD?
[b]And *there is* no other God besides Me,
A just God and a Savior;
*There is* none besides Me.

22 "Look to Me, and be saved,
[a]All you ends of the earth!
For I *am* God, and *there is* no other.
23 [a]I have sworn by Myself;
The word has gone out of My mouth *in* righteousness,
And shall not return,
That to Me every [b]knee shall bow,
[c]Every tongue shall take an oath.
24 He shall say,
'Surely in the LORD I have [a]righteousness and strength.
To Him *men* shall come,
And [b]all shall be ashamed
Who are incensed against Him.
25 [a]In the LORD all the descendants of Israel
Shall be justified, and [b]shall glory.' "

### *DEAD IDOLS AND THE LIVING GOD*

**46** Bel [a]bows down, Nebo stoops;
Their idols were on the beasts and on the cattle.
Your carriages *were* heavily loaded,
[b]A burden to the weary *beast*.

> **46:1 Bel**, also called Marduk, was the god of war and main deity of Babylon. **Nebo**, the god of education and wisdom, was thought to be Bel's son. The first part of King Nebuchadnezzar's name derives from Nebo.

2 They stoop, they bow down together;
They could not deliver the burden,
[a]But have themselves gone into captivity.

3 "Listen to Me, O house of Jacob,
And all the remnant of the house of Israel,
[a]Who have been upheld *by Me* from birth,
Who have been carried from the womb:
4 Even to *your* old age, [a]I *am* He,
And *even* to gray hairs [b]I will carry *you!*
I have made, and I will bear;
Even I will carry, and will deliver *you.*

5 "To[a] whom will you liken Me, and make *Me* equal
And compare Me, that we should be alike?
6 [a]They lavish gold out of the bag,
And weigh silver on the scales;
They hire a [b]goldsmith, and he makes it a god;
They prostrate themselves, yes, they worship.
7 [a]They bear it on the shoulder, they carry it
And set it in its place, and it stands;
From its place it shall not move.
Though [b]*one* cries out to it, yet it cannot answer
Nor save him out of his trouble.

8 "Remember this, and show yourselves men;
[a]Recall to mind, O you transgressors.
9 [a]Remember the former things of old,
For I *am* God, and [b]*there is* no other;
*I am* God, and *there is* none like Me,
10 [a]Declaring the end from the beginning,
And from ancient times *things* that are not *yet* done,
Saying, [b]'My counsel shall stand,
And I will do all My pleasure,'
11 Calling a bird of prey [a]from the east,
The man [b]who executes My counsel, from a far country.
Indeed [c]I have spoken *it;*
I will also bring it to pass.
I have purposed *it;*
I will also do it.

12 "Listen to Me, you [a]stubborn-hearted,
[b]Who *are* far from righteousness:
13 [a]I bring My righteousness near, it shall not be far off;
My salvation [b]shall not linger.
And I will place [c]salvation in Zion,
For Israel My glory.

### *THE HUMILIATION OF BABYLON*

**47** "Come [a]down and [b]sit in the dust,
O virgin daughter of [c]Babylon;
Sit on the ground without a throne,
O daughter of the Chaldeans!
For you shall no more be called
Tender and delicate.
2 [a]Take the millstones and grind meal.
Remove your veil,
Take off the skirt,
Uncover the thigh,
Pass through the rivers.
3 [a]Your nakedness shall be uncovered,
Yes, your shame will be seen;
[b]I will take vengeance,
And I will not arbitrate with a man."

4 *As for* [a]our Redeemer, the LORD of hosts *is* His name,
The Holy One of Israel.

**45:21** [b] Is. 44:8 **45:22** [a] Ps. 22:27; 65:5 **45:23** [a] [Heb. 6:13] [b] Rom. 14:11 [c] Deut. 6:13 **45:24** [a] [1 Cor. 1:30] [b] Is. 41:11 **45:25** [a] Is. 45:17 [b] 1 Cor. 1:31 **46:1** [a] Jer. 50:2 [b] Jer. 10:5 **46:2** [a] Jer. 48:7 **46:3** [a] Ps. 71:6 **46:4** [a] Mal. 3:6 [b] Ps. 48:14 **46:5** [a] Is. 40:18, 25 **46:6** [a] Is. 40:19; 41:6 [b] Is. 44:12 **46:7** [a] Jer. 10:5 [b] Is. 45:20 **46:8** [a] Is. 44:19 **46:9** [a] Deut. 32:7 [b] Is. 45:5, 21 **46:10** [a] Is. 45:21; 48:3 [b] Ps. 33:11 **46:11** [a] Is. 41:2, 25 [b] Is. 44:28 [c] Num. 23:19 **46:12** [a] Ps. 76:5 [b] [Rom. 10:3] **46:13** [a] [Rom. 1:17] [b] Hab. 2:3 [c] Is. 62:11 **47:1** [a] Jer. 48:18 [b] Is. 3:26 [c] Jer. 25:12; 50:1—51:64 **47:2** [a] Ex. 11:5 **47:3** [a] Is. 3:17; 20:4 [b] [Rom. 12:19] **47:4** [a] Jer. 50:34

5 "Sit in [a]silence, and go into darkness,
O daughter of the Chaldeans;
[b]For you shall no longer be called
The Lady of Kingdoms.
6 [a]I was angry with My people;
[b]I have profaned My inheritance,
And given them into your hand.
You showed them no mercy;
[c]On the elderly you laid your yoke very
heavily.
7 And you said, 'I shall be [a]a lady forever,'
*So* that you did not [b]take these *things* to
heart,
[c]Nor remember the latter end of them.

8 "Therefore hear this now, *you who are*
given to pleasures,
Who dwell securely,
Who say in your heart, 'I *am,* and *there is*
no one else besides me;
I shall not sit *as* a widow,
Nor shall I know the loss of children';
9 But these two *things* shall come to you
[a]In a moment, in one day:
The loss of children, and widowhood.
They shall come upon you in their fullness
Because of the multitude of your sorceries,
For the great abundance of your
enchantments.

10 "For you have trusted in your wickedness;
You have said, 'No one [a]sees me';
Your wisdom and your knowledge have
warped you;
And you have said in your heart,
'I *am,* and *there is* no one else besides me.'
11 Therefore evil shall come upon you;
You shall not know from where it arises.
And trouble shall fall upon you;
You will not be able to put it off.
And [a]desolation shall come upon you
[b]suddenly,
*Which* you shall not know.

12 "Stand now with your enchantments
And the multitude of your sorceries,
In which you have labored from your
youth—
Perhaps you will be able to profit,
Perhaps you will prevail.
13 [a]You are wearied in the multitude of your
counsels;
Let now [b]the astrologers, the stargazers,
*And* the monthly prognosticators
Stand up and save you
From what shall come upon you.
14 Behold, they shall be [a]as stubble,
The fire shall [b]burn them;
They shall not deliver themselves
From the power of the flame;
*It shall* not *be* a coal to be warmed by,
*Nor* a fire to sit before!
15 Thus shall they be to you
With whom you have labored,
[a]Your merchants from your youth;
They shall wander each one to his quarter.
No one shall save you.

## ISRAEL REFINED FOR GOD'S GLORY

48 "Hear this, O house of Jacob,
Who are called by the name of Israel,
And have come forth from the
wellsprings of Judah;
Who swear by the name of the LORD,
And make mention of the God of Israel,
*But* [a]not in truth or in righteousness;
2 For they call themselves [a]after the holy
city,
And [b]lean on the God of Israel;
The LORD of hosts *is* His name:

3 "I have [a]declared the former things from
the beginning;
They went forth from My mouth, and I
caused them to hear it.
Suddenly I did *them,* [b]and they came to
pass.
4 Because I knew that you *were* obstinate,
And [a]your neck *was* an iron sinew,
And your brow bronze,
5 Even from the beginning I have declared
*it* to you;
Before it came to pass I proclaimed *it* to
you,
Lest you should say, 'My idol has done them,
And my carved image and my molded
image
Have commanded them.'

6 "You have heard;
See all this.
And will you not declare *it?*
I have made you hear new things from
this time,
Even hidden things, and you did not know
them.
7 They are created now and not from the
beginning;
And before this day you have not heard
them,
Lest you should say, 'Of course I knew
them.'
8 Surely you did not hear,
Surely you did not know;
Surely from long ago your ear was not
opened.
For I knew that you would deal very
treacherously,
And were called [a]a transgressor from the
womb.

**47:5** [a] 1 Sam. 2:9 [b] [Dan. 2:37] **47:6** [a] 2 Sam. 24:14 [b] Is. 43:28 [c] Deut. 28:49, 50 **47:7** [a] Rev. 18:7 [b] Is. 42:25; 46:8 [c] Deut. 32:29 **47:9** [a] 1 Thess. 5:3 **47:10** [a] Is. 29:15 **47:11** [a] 1 Thess. 5:3 [b] Is. 29:5 **47:13** [a] Is. 57:10 [b] Dan. 2:2, 10 **47:14** [a] Nah. 1:10 [b] Jer. 51:58 **47:15** [a] Rev. 18:11 **48:1** [a] Jer. 4:2; 5:2 **48:2** [a] Is. 52:1; 64:10 [b] Mic. 3:11 **48:3** [a] Is. 44:7, 8; 46:10 [b] Josh. 21:45 **48:4** [a] Deut. 31:27 **48:8** [a] Ps. 58:3

9 "For[a] My name's sake [b]I will defer My anger,
And *for* My praise I will restrain it from you,
So that I do not cut you off.
10 Behold, [a]I have refined you, but not as silver;
I have tested you in the [b]furnace of affliction.
11 For My own sake, for My own sake, I will do *it;*
For [a]how should *My name* be profaned?
And [b]I will not give My glory to another.

### GOD'S ANCIENT PLAN TO REDEEM ISRAEL

12 "Listen to Me, O Jacob,
And Israel, My called:
I *am* He, [a]I *am* the [b]First,
I *am* also the Last.
13 Indeed [a]My hand has laid the foundation of the earth,
And My right hand has stretched out the heavens;
*When* [b]I call to them,
They stand up together.

14 "All of you, assemble yourselves, and hear!
Who among them has declared these *things?*
[a]The LORD loves him;
[b]He shall do His pleasure on Babylon,
And His arm *shall be against* the Chaldeans.
15 I, *even* I, have spoken;
Yes, [a]I have called him,
I have brought him, and his way will prosper.

16 "Come near to Me, hear this:
[a]I have not spoken in secret from the beginning;
From the time that it was, I *was* there.
And now [b]the Lord GOD and His Spirit
Have[1] sent Me."

17 Thus says [a]the LORD, your Redeemer,
The Holy One of Israel:
"I *am* the LORD your God,
Who teaches you to profit,
[b]Who leads you by the way you should go.
18 [a]Oh, that you had heeded My commandments!
[b]Then your peace would have been like a river,
And your righteousness like the waves of the sea.
19 [a]Your descendants also would have been like the sand,
And the offspring of your body like the grains of sand;
His name would not have been cut off
Nor destroyed from before Me."

20 [a]Go forth from Babylon!
Flee from the Chaldeans!
With a voice of singing,
Declare, proclaim this,
Utter it to the end of the earth;
Say, "The LORD has [b]redeemed
His servant Jacob!"
21 And they [a]did not thirst
When He led them through the deserts;
He [b]caused the waters to flow from the rock for them;
He also split the rock, and the waters gushed out.

22 "*There*[a] *is* no peace," says the LORD, "for the wicked."

> **48:21** God took care of the thirsty Israelites in the desert by giving them water to drink from an ordinary **rock**. The Israelites remembered that period—just after their ancestors' release from Egypt—as a time when God was especially close to them.

### THE SERVANT, THE LIGHT TO THE GENTILES

**49** "Listen, [a]O coastlands, to Me,
And take heed, you peoples from afar!
[b]The LORD has called Me from the womb;
From the matrix of My mother He has made mention of My name.
2 And He has made [a]My mouth like a sharp sword;
[b]In the shadow of His hand He has hidden Me,
And made Me [c]a polished shaft;
In His quiver He has hidden Me."

3 "And He said to me,
[a]'You *are* My servant, O Israel,
[b]In whom I will be glorified.'
4 [a]Then I said, 'I have labored in vain,
I have spent my strength for nothing and in vain;
Yet surely my just reward *is* with the LORD,
And my work with my God.' "

5 "And now the LORD says,
Who formed Me from the womb *to be* His Servant,
To bring Jacob back to Him,
So that Israel [a]is gathered to Him[1]
(For I shall be glorious in the eyes of the LORD,
And My God shall be My strength),

**48:9** [a] Ezek. 20:9, 14, 22, 44 [b] Ps. 78:38 **48:10** [a] Ps. 66:10 [b] Deut. 4:20 **48:11** [a] Ezek. 20:9 [b] Is. 42:8 **48:12** [a] Deut. 32:39 [b] [Rev. 22:13] **48:13** [a] Ps. 102:25 [b] Is. 40:26 **48:14** [a] Is. 45:1 [b] Is. 44:28; 47:1–15 **48:15** [a] Is. 45:1, 2 **48:16** [a] Is. 45:19 [b] Zech. 2:8, 9, 11 [1] The Hebrew verb is singular. **48:17** [a] Is. 43:14 [b] Ps. 32:8 **48:18** [a] Ps. 81:13 [b] Ps. 119:165 **48:19** [a] Gen. 22:17 **48:20** [a] Zech. 2:6, 7 [b] [Ex. 19:4–6] **48:21** [a] [Is. 41:17, 18] [b] Ex. 17:6 **48:22** [a] [Is. 57:21] **49:1** [a] Is. 41:1 [b] Jer. 1:5 **49:2** [a] Rev. 1:16; 2:12 [b] Is. 51:16 [c] Ps. 45:5 **49:3** [a] [Zech. 3:8] [b] Is. 44:23 **49:4** [a] [Ezek. 3:19] **49:5** [a] Matt. 23:37 [1] Qere, Dead Sea Scrolls, and Septuagint read *is gathered to Him;* Kethib reads *is not gathered.*

6 Indeed He says,
'It is too small a thing that You should be
My Servant
To raise up the tribes of Jacob,
And to restore the preserved ones of Israel;
I will also give You as a [a]light to the Gentiles,
That You should be My salvation to the
ends of the earth.' "

**SEEING JESUS IN THE SCRIPTURE**

**49:6** Many Jews believed God would send the Messiah only for them. But all along, God's plan was to deliver *all* people from sin (see Gen. 12:3). Simeon quoted this passage when he blessed Jesus as a child, making clear the Savior's worldwide mission (see Luke 2:32).

7 Thus says the LORD,
The Redeemer of Israel, their Holy One,
[a]To Him whom man despises,
To Him whom the nation abhors,
To the Servant of rulers:
[b]"Kings shall see and arise,
Princes also shall worship,
Because of the LORD who is faithful,
The Holy One of Israel;
And He has chosen You."

8 Thus says the LORD:

"In an [a]acceptable time I have heard You,
And in the day of salvation I have helped
You;
I will preserve You [b]and give You
As a covenant to the people,
To restore the earth,
To cause them to inherit the desolate
heritages;
9 That You may say [a]to the prisoners, 'Go
forth,'
To those who *are* in darkness, 'Show
yourselves.'

"They shall feed along the roads,
And their pastures *shall be* on all desolate
heights.
10 They shall neither [a]hunger nor thirst,
[b]Neither heat nor sun shall strike them;
For He who has mercy on them [c]will lead
them,
Even by the springs of water He will guide
them.
11 [a]I will make each of My mountains a road,
And My highways shall be elevated.
12 Surely [a]these shall come from afar;
Look! Those from the north and the west,
And these from the land of Sinim."

13 [a]Sing, O heavens!
Be joyful, O earth!
And break out in singing, O mountains!
For the LORD has comforted His people,
And will have mercy on His afflicted.

### GOD WILL REMEMBER ZION

14 [a]But Zion said, "The LORD has forsaken me,
And my Lord has forgotten me."

15 "Can[a] a woman forget her nursing child,
And not have compassion on the son of
her womb?
Surely they may forget,
[b]Yet I will not forget you.
16 See, [a]I have inscribed you on the palms *of
My hands;*
Your walls *are* continually before Me.
17 Your sons[1] shall make haste;
Your destroyers and those who laid you
waste
Shall go away from you.
18 [a]Lift up your eyes, look around and see;
All these gather together *and* come to you.
*As* I live," says the LORD,
"You shall surely clothe yourselves with
them all [b]as an ornament,
And bind them *on you* as a bride *does.*

19 "For your waste and desolate places,
And the land of your destruction,
[a]Will even now be too small for the
inhabitants;
And those who swallowed you up will be
far away.
20 [a]The children you will have,
[b]After you have lost the others,
Will say again in your ears,
'The place *is* too small for me;
Give me a place where I may dwell.'
21 Then you will say in your heart,
'Who has begotten these for me,
Since I have lost my children and am
desolate,
A captive, and wandering to and fro?
And who has brought these up?
There I was, left alone;
But these, where *were* they?' "

22 [a]Thus says the Lord GOD:

"Behold, I will lift My hand in an oath to
the nations,
And set up My standard for the peoples;

49:6 [a] [Luke 2:32] 49:7 [a] [Ps. 22:6; Is. 53:3; Matt. 26:67; 27:41]; Mark 15:29; Luke 23:35 [b] [Is. 52:15] 49:8 [a] Ps. 69:13; 2 Cor. 6:2 [b] Is. 42:6 49:9 [a] Is. 61:1; Zech. 9:12; Luke 4:18 49:10 [a] Is. 33:16; 48:21; Rev. 7:16 [b] Ps. 121:6 [c] Ps. 23:2; Is. 40:11; 48:17 49:11 [a] Is. 40:4 49:12 [a] Is. 43:5, 6 49:13 [a] Is. 44:23 49:14 [a] Is. 40:27 49:15 [a] Ps. 103:13; Mal. 3:17 [b] Rom. 11:29 49:16 [a] Ex. 13:9; Song 8:6; Hag. 2:23 49:17 [1] Dead Sea Scrolls, Septuagint, Targum, and Vulgate read *builders*. 49:18 [a] Is. 60:4; John 4:35 [b] Prov. 17:6 49:19 [a] Is. 54:1, 2; Zech. 10:10 49:20 [a] Is. 60:4 [b] [Matt. 3:9; Rom. 11:11] 49:22 [a] Is. 60:4

They shall bring your sons in *their* arms,
And your daughters shall be carried on *their* shoulders;
23 [a]Kings shall be your foster fathers,
And their queens your nursing mothers;
They shall bow down to you with *their* faces to the earth,
And [b]lick up the dust of your feet.
Then you will know that I *am* the LORD,
[c]For they shall not be ashamed who wait for Me."

24 [a]Shall the prey be taken from the mighty,
Or the captives of the righteous[1] be delivered?

25 But thus says the LORD:

"Even the captives of the mighty shall be taken away,
And the prey of the terrible be delivered;
For I will contend with him who contends with you,
And I will save your children.
26 I will [a]feed those who oppress you with their own flesh,
And they shall be drunk with their own [b]blood as with sweet wine.
All flesh [c]shall know
That I, the LORD, *am* your Savior,
And your Redeemer, the Mighty One of Jacob."

## *THE SERVANT, ISRAEL'S HOPE*

50 Thus says the LORD:

"Where *is* [a]the certificate of your mother's divorce,
Whom I have put away?
Or which of My [b]creditors *is it* to whom I have sold you?
For your iniquities [c]you have sold yourselves,
And for your transgressions your mother has been put away.
2 Why, when I came, *was there* no man?
*Why,* when I called, *was there* none to answer?
Is My hand shortened at all that it cannot redeem?
Or have I no power to deliver?
Indeed with My [a]rebuke I dry up the sea,
I make the rivers a wilderness;
Their fish stink because *there is* no water,
And die of thirst.
3 [a]I clothe the heavens with blackness,
[b]And I make sackcloth their covering."

4 "The[a] Lord GOD has given Me
The tongue of the learned,
That I should know how to speak
A word in season to *him who is* [b]weary.
He awakens Me morning by morning,
He awakens My ear
To hear as the learned.
5 The Lord GOD [a]has opened My ear;
And I was not [b]rebellious,
Nor did I turn away.
6 [a]I gave My back to those who struck *Me,*
And [b]My cheeks to those who plucked out the beard;
I did not hide My face from shame and [c]spitting.

**SEEING JESUS IN THE SCRIPTURE**

**50:6** Much of Jesus' birth, life, and death was prophesied, including the details of His suffering leading up to the cross. Jesus endured the humiliation of being struck and spit upon for God's glory and our good (see Matt. 27:30).

7 "For the Lord GOD will help Me;
Therefore I will not be disgraced;
Therefore [a]I have set My face like a flint,
And I know that I will not be ashamed.
8 [a]*He is* near who justifies Me;
Who will contend with Me?
Let us stand together.
Who *is* My adversary?
Let him come near Me.
9 Surely the Lord GOD will help Me;
Who *is* he *who* will condemn Me?
[a]Indeed they will all grow old like a garment;
[b]The moth will eat them up.

10 "Who among you fears the LORD?
Who obeys the voice of His Servant?
Who [a]walks in darkness
And has no light?
[b]Let him trust in the name of the LORD
And rely upon his God.
11 Look, all you who kindle a fire,
Who encircle *yourselves* with sparks:
Walk in the light of your fire and in the sparks you have kindled—
[a]This you shall have from My hand:
You shall lie down [b]in torment.

**49:23** [a] Ps. 72:11; Is. 52:15 [b] Ps. 72:9; Mic. 7:17 [c] Ps. 34:22; [Rom. 5:5] **49:24** [a] Matt. 12:29; Luke 11:21, 22 [1] Following Masoretic Text and Targum; Dead Sea Scrolls, Syriac, and Vulgate read *the mighty;* Septuagint reads *unjustly.* **49:26** [a] Is. 9:20 [b] Rev. 14:20 [c] Ps. 9:16; Is. 60:16 **50:1** [a] Deut. 24:1; Jer. 3:8 [b] Deut. 32:30; 2 Kin. 4:1; Neh. 5:5 [c] Is. 52:3 **50:2** [a] Ps. 106:9; Nah. 1:4 **50:3** [a] Ex. 10:21 [b] Is. 13:10; Rev. 6:12 **50:4** [a] Ex. 4:11 [b] Matt. 11:28 **50:5** [a] Ps. 40:6 [b] Matt. 26:39 **50:6** [a] Matt. 27:26 [b] Matt. 26:67; 27:30 [c] Lam. 3:30 **50:7** [a] Ezek. 3:8, 9 **50:8** [a] [Rom. 8:32–34] **50:9** [a] Job 13:28 [b] Is. 51:6, 8 **50:10** [a] Ps. 23:4 [b] 2 Chr. 20:20 **50:11** [a] [John 9:39] [b] Ps. 16:4

### *THE LORD COMFORTS ZION*
*(cf. Gen. 12:1–3)*

51 "Listen to Me, [a]you who follow after
righteousness,
You who seek the LORD:
Look to the rock *from which* you were hewn,
And to the hole of the pit *from which* you
were dug.
2 [a]Look to Abraham your father,
And to Sarah *who* bore you;
[b]For I called him alone,
And [c]blessed him and increased him."
3 For the LORD will [a]comfort Zion,
He will comfort all her waste places;
He will make her wilderness like Eden,
And her desert [b]like the garden of the
LORD;
Joy and gladness will be found in it,
Thanksgiving and the voice of melody.

4 "Listen to Me, My people;
And give ear to Me, O My nation:
[a]For law will proceed from Me,
And I will make My justice rest
[b]As a light of the peoples.
5 [a]My righteousness *is* near,
My salvation has gone forth,
[b]And My arms will judge the peoples;
[c]The coastlands will wait upon Me,
And [d]on My arm they will trust.
6 [a]Lift up your eyes to the heavens,
And look on the earth beneath.
For [b]the heavens will vanish away like
smoke,
[c]The earth will grow old like a garment,
And those who dwell in it will die in like
manner;
But My salvation will be [d]forever,
And My righteousness will not be abolished.

7 "Listen to Me, you who know righteousness,
You people [a]in whose heart *is* My law:
[b]Do not fear the reproach of men,
Nor be afraid of their insults.
8 For [a]the moth will eat them up like a
garment,
And the worm will eat them like wool;
But My righteousness will be forever,
And My salvation from generation to
generation."

9 [a]Awake, awake, [b]put on strength,
O arm of the LORD!
Awake [c]as in the ancient days,
In the generations of old.
[d]*Are* You not *the arm* that cut [e]Rahab apart,
*And* wounded the [f]serpent?

> **51:9 Rahab** in this passage is not a woman, but a sea monster. According to a popular ancient myth, a dragon-like creature named Rahab tried to prevent God from creating the world. Later, the name Rahab came to symbolize Egypt and the years the Israelites spent there.

10 *Are* You not *the One* who [a]dried up the sea,
The waters of the great deep;
That made the depths of the sea a road
For the redeemed to cross over?
11 So [a]the ransomed of the LORD shall
return,
And come to Zion with singing,
With everlasting joy on their heads.
They shall obtain joy and gladness;
Sorrow and sighing shall flee away.

12 "I, *even* I, *am* He [a]who comforts you.
Who *are* you that you should be afraid
[b]Of a man *who* will die,
And of the son of a man *who* will be made
[c]like grass?
13 And [a]you forget the LORD your Maker,
[b]Who stretched out the heavens
And laid the foundations of the earth;
You have feared continually every day
Because of the fury of the oppressor,
When *he has* prepared to destroy.
[c]And where *is* the fury of the oppressor?
14 The captive exile hastens, that he may be
loosed,
[a]That he should not die in the pit,
And that his bread should not fail.
15 But I *am* the LORD your God,
Who [a]divided the sea whose waves
roared—
The LORD of hosts *is* His name.
16 And [a]I have put My words in your mouth;
[b]I have covered you with the shadow of My
hand,
[c]That I may plant the heavens,
Lay the foundations of the earth,
And say to Zion, 'You *are* My people.' "

### *GOD'S FURY REMOVED*

17 [a]Awake, awake!
Stand up, O Jerusalem,
You who [b]have drunk at the hand of the
LORD
The cup of His fury;
You have drunk the dregs of the cup of
trembling,
*And* drained *it* out.

51:1 [a] [Rom. 9:30–32] 51:2 [a] Heb. 11:11 [b] Gen. 12:1 [c] Gen. 24:35 51:3 [a] Is. 40:1; 52:9 [b] Gen. 13:10 51:4 [a] Is. 2:3 [b] Is. 42:6 51:5 [a] Is. 46:13 [b] Ps. 67:4 [c] Is. 60:9 [d] [Rom. 1:16] 51:6 [a] Is. 40:26 [b] Matt. 24:35 [c] Is. 24:19, 20; 50:9 [d] Is. 45:17 51:7 [a] Ps. 37:31 [b] [Matt. 5:11, 12; 10:28] 51:8 [a] Is. 50:9 51:9 [a] Ps. 44:23 [b] Ps. 93:1 [c] Ps. 44:1 [d] Job 26:12 [e] Ps. 87:4 [f] Ps. 74:13 51:10 [a] Ex. 14:21 51:11 [a] Is. 35:10 51:12 [a] 2 Cor. 1:3 [b] Ps. 118:6 [c] Is. 40:6, 7 51:13 [a] Is. 17:10 [b] Ps. 104:2 [c] Job 20:7 51:14 [a] Zech. 9:11 51:15 [a] Job 26:12 51:16 [a] Deut. 18:18 [b] Is. 49:2 [c] Is. 65:17 51:17 [a] Is. 52:1 [b] Job 21:20

18 *There is* no one to guide her
Among all the sons she has brought forth;
Nor *is there any* who takes her by the hand
Among all the sons she has brought up.
19 [a]These two *things* have come to you;
Who will be sorry for you?—
Desolation and destruction, famine and sword—
[b]By whom will I comfort you?
20 [a]Your sons have fainted,
They lie at the head of all the streets,
Like an antelope in a net;
They are full of the fury of the LORD,
The rebuke of your God.

21 Therefore please hear this, you afflicted,
And drunk [a]but not with wine.
22 Thus says your Lord,
The LORD and your God,
*Who* [a]pleads the cause of His people:
"See, I have taken out of your hand
The cup of trembling,
The dregs of the cup of My fury;
You shall no longer drink it.
23 [a]But I will put it into the hand of those who afflict you,
Who have said to you,[1]
'Lie down, that we may walk over you.'
And you have laid your body like the ground,
And as the street, for those who walk over."

### GOD REDEEMS JERUSALEM

**52** Awake, awake!
Put on your strength, O Zion;
Put on your beautiful garments,
O Jerusalem, the holy city!
For the uncircumcised [a]and the unclean
Shall no longer come to you.
2 [a]Shake yourself from the dust, arise;
Sit down, O Jerusalem!
[b]Loose yourself from the bonds of your neck,
O captive daughter of Zion!

3 For thus says the LORD:

[a]"You have sold yourselves for nothing,
And you shall be redeemed [b]without money."

4 For thus says the Lord GOD:

"My people went down at first
Into [a]Egypt to dwell there;
Then the Assyrian oppressed them without cause.
5 Now therefore, what have I here," says the LORD,
"That My people are taken away for nothing?
Those who rule over them
Make them wail,"[1] says the LORD,
"And My name *is* [a]blasphemed continually every day.
6 Therefore My people shall know My name;
Therefore *they shall know* in that day
That I *am* He who speaks:
'Behold, *it is* I.' "

7 [a]How beautiful upon the mountains
Are the feet of him who brings good news,
Who proclaims peace,
Who brings glad tidings of good *things*,
Who proclaims salvation,
Who says to Zion,
[b]"Your God reigns!"

51:19 [a]Is. 47:9 [b]Amos 7:2 51:20 [a]Lam. 2:11 51:21 [a]Lam. 3:15 51:22 [a]Jer. 50:34 51:23 [a]Zech. 12:2 [1]Literally *your soul* 52:1 [a][Rev. 21:2–27] 52:2 [a]Is. 3:26 [b]Zech. 2:7 52:3 [a]Ps. 44:12 [b]Is. 45:13 52:4 [a]Gen. 46:6 52:5 [a]Ezek. 36:20, 23 [1]Dead Sea Scrolls read *Mock;* Septuagint reads *Marvel and wail;* Targum reads *Boast themselves;* Vulgate reads *Treat them unjustly.* 52:7 [a]Rom. 10:15 [b]Ps. 93:1

APPLY THE TRUTH

## EVANGELISM

**52:7** We love good news. Hearing good news is great, but sharing it is even better. Whether it's a movie you saw, a restaurant you tried, a workout routine that transformed your life, a great accomplishment at school or on the ball field, or something else, it's always fun to share good news with others. In fact, good news cannot be contained or else it wouldn't be news at all.

The word *gospel* means "good news." The Bible speaks of specific good news, the message of Jesus Christ. This verse gives a great summary as to why this gospel is such good news. It's news about peace and good things. And it alone is the way to salvation. Like any good news, this message of the gospel is too wonderful not to share. If you don't know quite how to do that, start with what's in this verse. Simply tell others how your relationship with Jesus has brought you salvation, joy, and peace. If the message of Jesus has transformed your life, then you can share with others how He can transform their lives as well.

8 Your watchmen shall lift up *their* voices,
With their voices they shall sing together;
For they shall see eye to eye
When the LORD brings back Zion.
9 Break forth into joy, sing together,
You waste places of Jerusalem!
For the LORD has comforted His people,
He has redeemed Jerusalem.
10 [a]The LORD has made bare His holy arm
In the eyes of [b]all the nations;
And all the ends of the earth shall see
The salvation of our God.

11 [a]Depart! Depart! Go out from there,
Touch no unclean *thing;*
Go out from the midst of her,
[b]Be clean,
You who bear the vessels of the LORD.
12 For [a]you shall not go out with haste,
Nor go by flight;
[b]For the LORD will go before you,
[c]And the God of Israel *will be* your rear guard.

### *THE SIN-BEARING SERVANT*

13 Behold, [a]My Servant shall deal prudently;
[b]He shall be exalted and extolled and be very high.

#### SEEING JESUS IN THE SCRIPTURE

**52:13** Isaiah's prophecy points to Jesus' post-resurrection exaltation. Forty days after Jesus was raised from the dead, He ascended to return to the right hand of the Father (see Phil. 2:9–10). One day, every knee will bow, and tongue will confess Jesus is Lord.

14 Just as many were astonished at you,
So His [a]visage was marred more than any man,
And His form more than the sons of men;
15 [a]So shall He sprinkle[1] many nations.
Kings shall shut their mouths at Him;
For [b]what had not been told them they shall see,
And what they had not heard they shall consider.

**53** Who [a]has believed our report?
And to whom has the arm of the LORD been revealed?
2 For He shall grow up before Him as a tender plant,
And as a root out of dry ground.
He has no form or comeliness;
And when we see Him,

#### SEEING JESUS IN THE SCRIPTURE

**53:1–12** Jesus is the ultimate sacrifice given for the sins of the world (see Rom. 4:25). Jesus never sinned, yet He suffered like a sinner to take our judgment. Our sins are forgiven, and we become righteous through Christ's work on the cross.

*There is* no beauty that we should desire Him.
3 [a]He is despised and rejected by men,
A Man of sorrows and [b]acquainted with grief.
And we hid, as it were, *our* faces from Him;
He was despised, and [c]we did not esteem Him.

4 Surely [a]He has borne our griefs
And carried our sorrows;
Yet we esteemed Him stricken,
Smitten by God, and afflicted.
5 But He *was* [a]wounded for our transgressions,
*He was* bruised for our iniquities;
The chastisement for our peace *was* upon Him,
And by His [b]stripes we are healed.
6 All we like sheep have gone astray;
We have turned, every one, to his own way;
And the LORD has laid on Him the iniquity of us all.

7 He was oppressed and He was afflicted,
Yet [a]He opened not His mouth;
[b]He was led as a lamb to the slaughter,
And as a sheep before its shearers is silent,
So He opened not His mouth.
8 He was [a]taken from prison and from judgment,
And who will declare His generation?
For [b]He was cut off from the land of the living;
For the transgressions of My people He was stricken.
9 [a]And they[1] made His grave with the wicked—
But with the rich at His death,
Because He had done no violence,
Nor *was any* [b]deceit in His mouth.

10 Yet it pleased the LORD to bruise Him;
He has put *Him* to grief.
When You make His soul [a]an offering for sin,
He shall see *His* seed, He shall prolong *His* days,

**52:10** [a]Ps. 98:1–3 [b]Luke 3:6 **52:11** [a]Is. 48:20 [b]Lev. 22:2 **52:12** [a]Ex. 12:11, 33 [b]Mic. 2:13 [c]Ex. 14:19, 20 **52:13** [a]Is. 42:1 [b]Phil. 2:9 **52:14** [a]Ps. 22:6, 7 **52:15** [a]Ezek. 36:25 [b]Rom. 15:21 [1]Or *startle* **53:1** [a]John 12:38 **53:3** [a]Ps. 22:6 [b][Heb. 4:15] [c][John 1:10, 11] **53:4** [a][Matt. 8:17] **53:5** [a][Rom. 4:25] [b][1 Pet. 2:24, 25] **53:7** [a]Matt. 26:63; 27:12–14 [b]Acts 8:32, 33 **53:8** [a]Luke 23:1–25 [b][Dan. 9:26] **53:9** [a]Matt. 27:57–60 [b]1 Pet. 2:22 [1]Literally *he* or *He* **53:10** [a][2 Cor. 5:21]

KNOW THE TRUTH

## THE DOCTRINE OF JESUS

### PART 7: THE SACRIFICE OF JESUS

**53:4–12** The gruesome suffering and death of Jesus teaches us several important truths. First, Christ's suffering and death reveal **God's righteous response to sin**. This response is often called wrath. God the Father poured out His righteous, holy wrath for sin on the sinless one, Jesus Christ. Second, Christ's suffering and death reveal **God's endless and glorious mercy and grace**. God's plan to destroy sin without destroying sinful people is enacted through Christ's perfect life being offered as the sacrifice for our sinful lives. Christ took on our sin. Through trust in Him, we take on His righteousness. God's mercy doesn't give us what we deserve (death and eternal separation from Him), and His grace gives us what we don't deserve (eternal life in God's forever family). God wants people to experience His mercy and grace in Christ instead of His wrath. Third, Christ's suffering and death reveal **Christ's perfection**. Not one bit of the suffering Christ endured was for His own sin. Not one drop of blood was for His own failure. Every ounce of pain He endured was to pay for our sin. Finally, Christ's suffering and death reveal **Christ's determination to have us forever**. At no point in His suffering did He try to stop it. He endured the pain to pay for those who trust in Him to be His forever.

*For* **THE DOCTRINE OF JESUS: PART 8: THE RESURRECTION OF JESUS,** *turn to 1 Peter 1:3–5 on page 1266.*

And the pleasure of the LORD shall
prosper in His hand.
11 He shall see the labor of His soul,[1] *and* be
satisfied.
By His knowledge [a]My righteous [b]Servant
shall [c]justify many,
For He shall bear their iniquities.
12 [a]Therefore I will divide Him a portion with
the great,
[b]And He shall divide the spoil with the strong,
Because He [c]poured out His soul unto death,
And He was [d]numbered with the
transgressors,
And He bore the sin of many,
And [e]made intercession for the
transgressors.

### A PERPETUAL COVENANT OF PEACE

54 "Sing, O [a]barren,
You *who* have not borne!
Break forth into singing, and cry aloud,
You *who* have not labored with child!
For more *are* the children of the desolate
Than the children of the married woman,"
says the LORD.
2 "Enlarge[a] the place of your tent,
And let them stretch out the curtains of
your dwellings;
Do not spare;
Lengthen your cords,
And strengthen your stakes.
3 For you shall expand to the right and to
the left,
And your descendants will [a]inherit the
nations,
And make the desolate cities inhabited.
4 "Do[a] not fear, for you will not be ashamed;
Neither be disgraced, for you will not be
put to shame;
For you will forget the shame of your
youth,
And will not remember the reproach of
your widowhood anymore.
5 [a]For your Maker *is* your husband,
The LORD of hosts *is* His name;
And your Redeemer *is* the Holy One of
Israel;
He is called [b]the God of the whole earth.
6 For the LORD [a]has called you
Like a woman forsaken and grieved in
spirit,
Like a youthful wife when you were
refused,"
Says your God.
7 "For[a] a mere moment I have forsaken you,
But with great mercies [b]I will gather you.
8 With a little wrath I hid My face from you
for a moment;
[a]But with everlasting kindness I will have
mercy on you,"
Says the LORD, your Redeemer.

**53:11** [a] [1 John 2:1] [b] Is. 42:1 [c] [Rom. 5:15–18] [1] Following Masoretic Text, Targum, and Vulgate; Dead Sea Scrolls and Septuagint read *From the labor of His soul He shall see light.* **53:12** [a] Ps. 2:8 [b] Col. 2:15 [c] Is. 50:6 [d] Matt. 27:38 [e] Luke 23:34 **54:1** [a] Gal. 4:27 **54:2** [a] Is. 49:19, 20 **54:3** [a] Is. 14:2; 49:22, 23; 60:9 **54:4** [a] Is. 41:10 **54:5** [a] Jer. 3:14 [b] Zech. 14:9 **54:6** [a] Is. 62:4 **54:7** [a] Is. 26:20; 60:10 [b] [Is. 43:5; 56:8] **54:8** [a] Jer. 31:3

9 "For this *is* like the waters of [a]Noah to Me;
For as I have sworn
That the waters of Noah would no longer
cover the earth,
So have I sworn
That I would not be angry with [b]you, nor
rebuke you.
10 For [a]the mountains shall depart
And the hills be removed,
[b]But My kindness shall not depart from you,
Nor shall My covenant of peace be removed,"
Says the LORD, who has mercy on you.

11 "O you afflicted one,
Tossed with tempest, *and* not comforted,
Behold, I will lay your stones with
[a]colorful gems,
And lay your foundations with sapphires.
12 I will make your pinnacles of rubies,
Your gates of crystal,
And all your walls of precious stones.
13 All your children *shall be* [a]taught by the
LORD,
And [b]great *shall be* the peace of your
children.
14 In righteousness you shall be established;
You shall be far from oppression, for you
shall not fear;
And from terror, for it shall not come near
you.
15 Indeed they shall surely assemble, *but* not
because of Me.
Whoever assembles against you shall [a]fall
for your sake.

16 "Behold, I have created the blacksmith
Who blows the coals in the fire,
Who brings forth an instrument for his work;
And I have created the spoiler to destroy.
17 No weapon formed against you shall
[a]prosper,
And every tongue *which* rises against you
in judgment
You shall condemn.
This *is* the heritage of the servants of the
LORD,
[b]And their righteousness *is* from Me,"
Says the LORD.

## *AN INVITATION TO ABUNDANT LIFE*

55 "Ho! [a]Everyone who thirsts,
Come to the waters;
And you who have no money,
[b]Come, buy and eat.
Yes, come, buy wine and milk
Without money and without price.
2 Why do you spend money for *what is* not
bread,
And your wages for *what* does not satisfy?
Listen carefully to Me, and eat *what is* good,
And let your soul delight itself in abundance.
3 Incline your ear, and [a]come to Me.
Hear, and your soul shall live;
[b]And I will make an everlasting covenant
with you—
The [c]sure mercies of David.
4 Indeed I have given him *as* [a]a witness to
the people,
[b]A leader and commander for the people.
5 [a]Surely you shall call a nation you do not
know,
[b]And nations *who* do not know you shall
run to you,
Because of the LORD your God,
And the Holy One of Israel;
[c]For He has glorified you."

**SEEING JESUS IN THE SCRIPTURE**

**55:5** The promise of salvation was never intended only for the Jews. Here, Isaiah pointed to the day when Gentiles would be gathered to Jesus. Paul affirmed Jesus fulfilled this prophecy when he reminded the Gentile believers in Ephesus how Jesus had saved them (see Eph. 2:11–13).

6 [a]Seek the LORD while He may be [b]found,
Call upon Him while He is near.
7 [a]Let the wicked forsake his way,
And the unrighteous man [b]his thoughts;
Let him return to the LORD,
[c]And He will have mercy on him;
And to our God,
For He will abundantly pardon.

8 "For[a] My thoughts *are* not your thoughts,
Nor *are* your ways My ways," says the LORD.
9 "For[a] *as* the heavens are higher than the earth,
So are My ways higher than your ways,
And My thoughts than your thoughts.

10 "For [a]as the rain comes down, and the
snow from heaven,
And do not return there,
But water the earth,
And make it bring forth and bud,
That it may give seed to the sower
And bread to the eater,
11 [a]So shall My word be that goes forth from
My mouth;
It shall not return to Me void,
But it shall accomplish what I please,
And it shall [b]prosper *in the thing* for which
I sent it.

54:9 [a] Gen. 8:21; 9:11 [b] Ezek. 39:29 54:10 [a] Is. 51:6 [b] Ps. 89:33, 34 54:11 [a] Rev. 21:18, 19 54:13 [a] [John 6:45] [b] Ps. 119:165 54:15 [a] Is. 41:11–16 54:17 [a] Is. 17:12–14; 29:8 [b] Is. 45:24, 25; 54:14 55:1 [a] [John 4:14; 7:37] [b] [Rev. 3:18] 55:3 [a] Matt. 11:28 [b] Jer. 32:40 [c] 2 Sam. 7:8 55:4 [a] [Rev. 1:5] [b] [Dan. 9:25] 55:5 [a] Eph. 2:11, 12 [b] Is. 60:5 [c] Is. 60:9 55:6 [a] [Heb. 3:13] [b] Ps. 32:6 55:7 [a] Is. 1:16 [b] Zech. 8:17 [c] Jer. 3:12 55:8 [a] 2 Sam. 7:19 55:9 [a] Ps. 103:11 55:10 [a] Deut. 32:2 55:11 [a] Is. 45:23 [b] Is. 46:9–11

12 "For[a] you shall go out with joy,
And be led out with peace;
The mountains and the hills
Shall [b]break forth into singing before you,
And [c]all the trees of the field shall clap
*their* hands.
13 [a]Instead of [b]the thorn shall come up the
cypress tree,
And instead of the brier shall come up the
myrtle tree;
And it shall be to the LORD [c]for a name,
For an everlasting sign *that* shall not be
cut off."

## SALVATION FOR THE GENTILES

56 Thus says the LORD:
"Keep justice, and do righteousness,
[a]For My salvation *is* about to come,
And My righteousness to be revealed.
2 Blessed *is* the man *who* does this,
And the son of man *who* lays hold on it;
[a]Who keeps from defiling the Sabbath,
And keeps his hand from doing any evil."

3 Do not let [a]the son of the foreigner
Who has joined himself to the LORD
Speak, saying,
"The LORD has utterly separated me from
His people";
Nor let the [b]eunuch say,
"Here I am, a dry tree."
4 For thus says the LORD:
"To the eunuchs who keep My Sabbaths,
And choose what pleases Me,
And hold fast My covenant,

**56:4** The Old Testament Sabbath is the seventh day of the week—Saturday. God instructed His people to set aside the seventh day of each week for Him. All forms of normal work were forbidden on the Sabbath. Only acts of kindness, worship, and emergency were allowed. Most Christians worship on Sunday instead, because it was the day of the week Jesus rose from death.

5 Even to them I will give in [a]My house
And within My walls a place [b]and a name
Better than that of sons and daughters;
I will give them[1] an everlasting name
That shall not be cut off.

6 "Also the sons of the foreigner
Who join themselves to the LORD, to serve
Him,
And to love the name of the LORD, to be
His servants—
Everyone who keeps from defiling the
Sabbath,
And holds fast My covenant—
7 Even them I will [a]bring to My holy
mountain,
And make them joyful in My [b]house of
prayer.
[c]Their burnt offerings and their sacrifices
*Will be* [d]accepted on My altar;
For [e]My house shall be called a house of
prayer [f]for all nations."
8 The Lord GOD, [a]who gathers the outcasts
of Israel, says,
[b]"Yet I will gather to him
*Others* besides those who are gathered to
him."

## ISRAEL'S IRRESPONSIBLE LEADERS

9 [a]All you beasts of the field, come to devour,
All you beasts in the forest.
10 His watchmen *are* [a]blind,
They are all ignorant;
[b]They *are* all dumb dogs,
They cannot bark;
Sleeping, lying down, loving to slumber.
11 Yes, *they are* [a]greedy dogs
*Which* [b]never have enough.
And they *are* shepherds
Who cannot understand;
They all look to their own way,
Every one for his own gain,
From his *own* territory.
12 "Come," *one says,* "I will bring wine,
And we will fill ourselves with
intoxicating [a]drink;
[b]Tomorrow will be [c]as today,
*And* much more abundant."

## ISRAEL'S FUTILE IDOLATRY

57 The righteous perishes,
And no man takes *it* to heart;
[a]Merciful men *are* taken away,
[b]While no one considers
That the righteous is taken away from evil.
2 He shall enter into peace;
They shall rest in [a]their beds,
*Each one* walking *in* his uprightness.

3 "But come here,
[a]You sons of the sorceress,
You offspring of the adulterer and the
harlot!
4 Whom do you ridicule?
Against whom do you make a wide mouth
*And* stick out the tongue?
*Are* you not children of transgression,
Offspring of falsehood,

**55:12** [a] Is. 35:10 [b] Ps. 98:8 [c] 1 Chr. 16:33 **55:13** [a] Is. 41:19 [b] Mic. 7:4 [c] Jer. 13:11 **56:1** [a] Matt. 3:2; 4:17 **56:2** [a] Is. 58:13 **56:3** [a] [Eph. 2:12–19] [b] Acts 8:27 **56:5** [a] 1 Tim. 3:15 [b] [1 John 3:1, 2] [1] Literally *him* **56:7** [a] [Is. 2:2, 3; 60:11] [b] Mark 11:17 [c] [Rom. 12:1] [d] Is. 60:7 [e] Matt. 21:13 [f] [Mal. 1:11] **56:8** [a] Is. 11:12; 27:12; 54:7 [b] [John 10:16] **56:9** [a] Jer. 12:9 **56:10** [a] Matt. 15:14 [b] Phil. 3:2 **56:11** [a] [Mic. 3:5, 11] [b] Ezek. 34:2–10 **56:12** [a] Is. 28:7 [b] Luke 12:19 [c] 2 Pet. 3:4 **57:1** [a] Ps. 12:1 [b] 1 Kin. 14:13 **57:2** [a] 2 Chr. 16:14 **57:3** [a] Matt. 16:4

**57:5** Pagan religions in and around Israel built their temples of idol worship on hilltops or in groves of trees. They practiced all kinds of sexual perversion during their worship ceremonies. Some rituals called for children to be sacrificed. God despised such pagan rituals and specifically told the Israelites not to get involved in them.

5 Inflaming yourselves with gods [a]under
every green tree,
[b]Slaying the children in the valleys,
Under the clefts of the rocks?
6 Among the smooth [a]*stones* of the stream
*Is* your portion;
They, they, *are* your lot!
Even to them you have poured a drink
offering,
You have offered a grain offering.
Should I receive comfort in [b]these?

7 "On[a] a lofty and high mountain
You have set [b]your bed;
Even there you went up
To offer sacrifice.
8 Also behind the doors and their posts
You have set up your remembrance;
For you have uncovered yourself *to those
other* than Me,
And have gone up to them;
You have enlarged your bed
And made *a covenant* with them;
[a]You have loved their bed,
Where you saw *their* nudity.[1]
9 [a]You went to the king with ointment,
And increased your perfumes;
You sent your [b]messengers far off,
And *even* descended to Sheol.
10 You are wearied in the length of your way;
[a]*Yet* you did not say, 'There is no hope.'
You have found the life of your hand;
Therefore you were not grieved.

11 "And [a]of whom have you been afraid, or
feared,
That you have lied
And not remembered Me,
Nor taken *it* to your heart?
Is it not because [b]I have held My peace
from of old
That you do not fear Me?
12 I will declare your righteousness
And your works,
For they will not profit you.
13 When you cry out,
Let your collection *of idols* deliver you.
But the wind will carry them all away,
A breath will take *them.*
But he who puts his trust in Me shall
possess the land,
And shall inherit My holy mountain."

### HEALING FOR THE BACKSLIDER

14 And one shall say,
[a]"Heap it up! Heap it up!
Prepare the way,
Take the stumbling block out of the way
of My people."

15 For thus says the High and Lofty One
Who inhabits eternity, [a]whose name *is*
Holy:
[b]"I dwell in the high and holy *place,*
[c]With him *who* has a contrite and humble
spirit,
[d]To revive the spirit of the humble,
And to revive the heart of the contrite ones.
16 [a]For I will not contend forever,
Nor will I always be angry;
For the spirit would fail before Me,
And the souls [b]*which* I have made.
17 For the iniquity of [a]his covetousness
I was angry and struck him;
[b]I hid and was angry,
[c]And he went on backsliding in the way of
his heart.
18 I have seen his ways, and [a]will heal him;
I will also lead him,
And restore comforts to him
And to [b]his mourners.

19 "I create [a]the fruit of the lips:
Peace, peace [b]to *him who is* far off and to
*him who is* near,"
Says the LORD,
"And I will heal him."
20 [a]But the wicked *are* like the troubled sea,
When it cannot rest,
Whose waters cast up mire and dirt.

21 "*There*[a] *is* no peace,"
Says my God, "for the wicked."

### FASTING THAT PLEASES GOD

58 "Cry aloud, spare not;
Lift up your voice like a trumpet;
[a]Tell My people their transgression,
And the house of Jacob their sins.
2 Yet they seek Me daily,
And delight to know My ways,
As a nation that did righteousness,
And did not forsake the ordinance of their
God.
They ask of Me the ordinances of justice;
They take delight in approaching God.

**57:5** [a] 2 Kin. 16:4 [b] Jer. 7:31 **57:6** [a] Jer. 3:9 [b] Jer. 5:9, 29; 9:9 **57:7** [a] Ezek. 16:16 [b] Ezek. 23:41 **57:8** [a] Ezek. 16:26 [1] Literally *hand,* a euphemism **57:9** [a] Hos. 7:11 [b] Ezek. 23:16, 40 **57:10** [a] Jer. 2:25; 18:12 **57:11** [a] Is. 51:12, 13 [b] Ps. 50:21 **57:14** [a] Is. 40:3; 62:10 **57:15** [a] Job 6:10 [b] Zech. 2:13 [c] Ps. 34:18; 51:17 [d] Is. 61:1–3 **57:16** [a] [Mic. 7:18] [b] Num. 16:22 **57:17** [a] Jer. 6:13 [b] Is. 8:17; 45:15; 59:2 [c] Is. 9:13 **57:18** [a] Jer. 3:22 [b] Is. 61:2 **57:19** [a] Heb. 13:15 [b] Eph. 2:17 **57:20** [a] Job 15:20 **57:21** [a] Is. 48:22 **58:1** [a] Mic. 3:8

3 'Why[a] have we fasted,' *they say,* 'and You
have not seen?
*Why* have we [b]afflicted our souls, and You
take no notice?'

"In fact, in the day of your fast you find
pleasure,
And exploit all your laborers.
4 [a]Indeed you fast for strife and debate,
And to strike with the fist of wickedness.
You will not fast as *you do* this day,
To make your voice heard on high.
5 Is [a]it a fast that I have chosen,
[b]A day for a man to afflict his soul?
*Is it* to bow down his head like a bulrush,
And [c]to spread out sackcloth and ashes?
Would you call this a fast,
And an acceptable day to the LORD?

6 "*Is* this not the fast that I have chosen:
To [a]loose the bonds of wickedness,
[b]To undo the heavy burdens,
[c]To let the oppressed go free,
And that you break every yoke?
7 *Is it* not [a]to share your bread with the
hungry,
And that you bring to your house the poor
who are cast out;
[b]When you see the naked, that you cover
him,
And not hide yourself from [c]your own flesh?
8 [a]Then your light shall break forth like the
morning,
Your healing shall spring forth speedily,
And your righteousness shall go before
you;
[b]The glory of the LORD shall be your rear
guard.
9 Then you shall call, and the LORD will
answer;
You shall cry, and He will say, 'Here I *am.*'

"If you take away the yoke from your midst,
The pointing of the finger, and [a]speaking
wickedness,
10 *If* you extend your soul to the hungry
And satisfy the afflicted soul,
Then your light shall dawn in the
darkness,
And your darkness shall *be* as the
noonday.
11 The LORD will guide you continually,
And satisfy your soul in drought,
And strengthen your bones;
You shall be like a watered garden,
And like a spring of water, whose waters
do not fail.
12 Those from among you
[a]Shall build the old waste places;
You shall raise up the foundations of
many generations;
And you shall be called the Repairer of
the Breach,
The Restorer of Streets to Dwell In.

13 "If [a]you turn away your foot from the
Sabbath,
*From* doing your pleasure on My holy day,
And call the Sabbath a delight,
The holy *day* of the LORD honorable,
And shall honor Him, not doing your own
ways,
Nor finding your own pleasure,
Nor speaking *your own* words,
14 [a]Then you shall delight yourself in the LORD;
And I will cause you to [b]ride on the high
hills of the earth,
And feed you with the heritage of Jacob
your father.
[c]The mouth of the LORD has spoken."

### SEPARATED FROM GOD

59 Behold, the LORD's hand is not
[a]shortened,
That it cannot save;
Nor His ear heavy,
That it cannot hear.
2 But your iniquities have separated you
from your God;
And your sins have hidden *His* face from
you,
So that He will [a]not hear.
3 For [a]your hands are defiled with blood,
And your fingers with iniquity;
Your lips have spoken lies,
Your tongue has muttered perversity.

4 No one calls for justice,
Nor does *any* plead for truth.
They trust in [a]empty words and speak lies;
[b]They conceive evil and bring forth
iniquity.
5 They hatch vipers' eggs and weave the
spider's web;
He who eats of their eggs dies,
And *from* that which is crushed a viper
breaks out.

6 [a]Their webs will not become garments,
Nor will they cover themselves with their
works;
Their works *are* works of iniquity,
And the act of violence *is* in their hands.
7 [a]Their feet run to evil,
And they make haste to shed [b]innocent
blood;
[c]Their thoughts *are* thoughts of iniquity;
Wasting and [d]destruction *are* in their paths.

**58:3** [a] Mal. 3:13–18 [b] Lev. 16:29; 23:27 **58:4** [a] 1 Kin. 21:9 **58:5** [a] Zech. 7:5 [b] Lev. 16:29 [c] Esth. 4:3 **58:6** [a] Luke 4:18, 19 [b] Neh. 5:10–12 [c] Jer. 34:9 **58:7** [a] Ezek. 18:7 [b] Job 31:19–22 [c] Neh. 5:5 **58:8** [a] Job 11:17 [b] Ex. 14:19 **58:9** [a] Ps. 12:2 **58:12** [a] Is. 61:4 **58:13** [a] Is. 56:2, 4, 6 **58:14** [a] Job 22:26 [b] Deut. 32:13; 33:29 [c] Is. 1:20; 40:5 **59:1** [a] Num. 11:23 **59:2** [a] Is. 1:15 **59:3** [a] Ezek. 7:23 **59:4** [a] Is. 30:12; Jer. 7:4 [b] Job 15:35; Ps. 7:14; Is. 33:11 **59:6** [a] Job 8:14 **59:7** [a] Prov. 1:16; Rom. 3:15 [b] Prov. 6:17 [c] Is. 55:7 [d] Rom. 3:16, 17

8 The way of [a]peace they have not known,
And *there is* no justice in their ways;
[b]They have made themselves crooked paths;
Whoever takes that way shall not know
peace.

### SIN CONFESSED

9 Therefore justice is far from us,
Nor does righteousness overtake us;
[a]We look for light, but there is darkness!
For brightness, *but* we walk in blackness!
10 [a]We grope for the wall like the blind,
And we grope as if *we had* no eyes;
We stumble at noonday as at twilight;
*We are* as dead *men* in desolate places.
11 We all growl like bears,
And [a]moan sadly like doves;
We look for justice, but *there is* none;
For salvation, *but* it is far from us.
12 For our [a]transgressions are multiplied
before You,
And our sins testify against us;
For our transgressions *are* with us,
And *as for* our iniquities, we know them:
13 In transgressing and lying against the
LORD,
And departing from our God,
Speaking oppression and revolt,
Conceiving and uttering [a]from the heart
words of falsehood.
14 Justice is turned back,
And righteousness stands afar off;
For truth is fallen in the street,
And equity cannot enter.
15 So truth fails,
And he *who* departs from evil makes
himself a [a]prey.

### THE REDEEMER OF ZION

Then the LORD saw *it,* and it displeased Him
That *there was* no justice.
16 [a]He saw that *there was* no man,
And [b]wondered that *there was* no
intercessor;
[c]Therefore His own arm brought salvation
for Him;
And His own righteousness, it sustained
Him.
17 [a]For He put on righteousness as a
breastplate,
And a helmet of salvation on His head;
He put on the garments of vengeance for
clothing,
And was clad with zeal as a cloak.
18 [a]According to *their* deeds, accordingly He
will repay,
Fury to His adversaries,
Recompense to His enemies;
The coastlands He will fully repay.
19 [a]So shall they fear
The name of the LORD from the west,
And His glory from the rising of the sun;
When the enemy comes in [b]like a flood,
The Spirit of the LORD will lift up a
standard against him.

20 "The[a] Redeemer will come to Zion,
And to those who turn from transgression
in Jacob,"
Says the LORD.

**SEEING JESUS IN THE SCRIPTURE**

**59:20** Isaiah's prophecy finds its fulfillment in the person and work of Jesus, the ultimate Redeemer (see Rom. 11:26). Just as we await Jesus' salvation at His second coming, those in the Old Testament awaited His salvation at His first coming.

21 "As[a] for Me," says the LORD, "this *is* My
covenant with them: My Spirit who *is* upon you,
and My words which I have put in your mouth,
shall not depart from your mouth, nor from
the mouth of your descendants, nor from the
mouth of your descendants' descendants," says
the LORD, "from this time and forevermore."

### THE GENTILES BLESS ZION

60 Arise, [a]shine;
For your light has come!
And [b]the glory of the LORD is risen upon
you.
2 For behold, the darkness shall cover the
earth,
And deep darkness the people;
But the LORD will arise over you,
And His glory will be seen upon you.
3 The [a]Gentiles shall come to your light,
And kings to the brightness of your rising.

**SEEING JESUS IN THE SCRIPTURE**

**60:3** Because of Jesus' first coming, salvation extended beyond the Jews to the Gentiles. But this prophecy finds its ultimate fulfillment at His second coming. When Jesus returns, all the nations will be gathered as one eternal kingdom (see Rev. 21:24).

4 "Lift[a] up your eyes all around, and see:
They all gather together, [b]they come to you;
Your sons shall come from afar,

**59:8** [a] Is. 57:20, 21 [b] Ps. 125:5; Prov. 2:15 **59:9** [a] Jer. 8:15 **59:10** [a] Deut. 28:29; Job 5:14; Amos 8:9 **59:11** [a] Is. 38:14; Ezek. 7:16 **59:12** [a] Is. 24:5; 58:1 **59:13** [a] Matt. 12:34 **59:15** [a] Is. 5:23; 10:2; 29:21; 32:7 **59:16** [a] Is. 41:28; 63:5; 64:7; Ezek. 22:30 [b] Mark 6:6 [c] Ps. 98:1; Is. 63:5 **59:17** [a] Eph. 6:14, 17; 1 Thess. 5:8 **59:18** [a] Is. 63:6; Rom. 2:6 **59:19** [a] Ps. 113:3; Mal. 1:11 [b] Rev. 12:15 **59:20** [a] Rom. 11:26 **59:21** [a] [Heb. 8:10; 10:16] **60:1** [a] Eph. 5:14 [b] Mal. 4:2 **60:3** [a] Is. 49:6, 23; Rev. 21:24 **60:4** [a] Is. 49:18 [b] Is. 49:20–22

And your daughters shall be nursed at
*your* side.
5 Then you shall see and become radiant,
And your heart shall swell with joy;
Because [a]the abundance of the sea shall
be turned to you,
The wealth of the Gentiles shall come to you.
6 The multitude of camels shall cover your
*land,*
The dromedaries of Midian and [a]Ephah;
All those from [b]Sheba shall come;
They shall bring [c]gold and incense,
And they shall proclaim the praises of the
LORD.
7 All the flocks of [a]Kedar shall be gathered
together to you,
The rams of Nebaioth shall minister to you;
They shall ascend with [b]acceptance on My
altar,
And [c]I will glorify the house of My glory.

8 "Who *are* these *who* fly like a cloud,
And like doves to their roosts?
9 [a]Surely the coastlands shall wait for Me;
And the ships of Tarshish *will come* first,
[b]To bring your sons from afar,
[c]Their silver and their gold with them,
To the name of the LORD your God,
And to the Holy One of Israel,
[d]Because He has glorified you.

10 "The[a] sons of foreigners shall build up
your walls,
[b]And their kings shall minister to you;
For [c]in My wrath I struck you,
[d]But in My favor I have had mercy on you.
11 Therefore your gates [a]shall be open
continually;
They shall not be shut day or night,
That *men* may bring to you the wealth of
the Gentiles,
And their kings in procession.
12 [a]For the nation and kingdom which will
not serve you shall perish,
And *those* nations shall be utterly ruined.

13 "The[a] glory of Lebanon shall come to you,
The cypress, the pine, and the box tree
together,
To beautify the place of My sanctuary;
And I will make [b]the place of My feet
glorious.
14 Also the sons of those who afflicted you
Shall come [a]bowing to you,
And all those who despised you shall [b]fall
prostrate at the soles of your feet;
And they shall call you The City of the LORD,
[c]Zion of the Holy One of Israel.

15 "Whereas you have been forsaken and
hated,
So that no one went through *you,*
I will make you an eternal excellence,
A joy of many generations.
16 You shall drink the milk of the Gentiles,
[a]And milk the breast of kings;
You shall know that [b]I, the LORD, *am* your
Savior
And your Redeemer, the Mighty One of
Jacob.

17 "Instead of bronze I will bring gold,
Instead of iron I will bring silver,
Instead of wood, bronze,
And instead of stones, iron.
I will also make your officers peace,
And your magistrates righteousness.
18 Violence shall no longer be heard in your
land,
Neither wasting nor destruction within
your borders;
But you shall call [a]your walls Salvation,
And your gates Praise.

### GOD THE GLORY OF HIS PEOPLE

19 "The [a]sun shall no longer be your light by
day,
Nor for brightness shall the moon give
light to you;
But the LORD will be to you an everlasting
light,
And [b]your God your glory.
20 [a]Your sun shall no longer go down,
Nor shall your moon withdraw itself;
For the LORD will be your everlasting
light,
And the days of your mourning shall be
ended.
21 [a]Also your people *shall* all *be* righteous;
[b]They shall inherit the land forever,
[c]The branch of My planting,
[d]The work of My hands,
That I may be glorified.
22 [a]A little one shall become a thousand,
And a small one a strong nation.
I, the LORD, will hasten it in its
time."

### THE GOOD NEWS OF SALVATION

61 "The [a]Spirit of the Lord GOD *is* upon Me,
Because the LORD [b]has anointed Me
To preach good tidings to the poor;
He has sent Me [c]to heal the
brokenhearted,
To proclaim [d]liberty to the captives,
And the opening of the prison to *those*
*who are* bound;

60:5 [a] [Rom. 11:25–27] 60:6 [a] Gen. 25:4 [b] Gen. 25:3; Ps. 72:10 [c] Is. 61:6; Matt. 2:11 60:7 [a] Gen. 25:13 [b] Is. 56:7 [c] Is. 60:13; Hag. 2:7, 9 60:9 [a] Ps. 72:10 [b] [Gal. 4:26] [c] Jer. 3:17 [d] Is. 55:5 60:10 [a] Zech. 6:15 [b] Rev. 21:24 [c] Is. 57:17 [d] Is. 54:7, 8 60:11 [a] Rev. 21:25, 26 60:12 [a] Zech. 14:17 60:13 [a] Is. 35:2 [b] 1 Chr. 28:2 60:14 [a] Is. 45:14 [b] Rev. 3:9 [c] [Heb. 12:22] 60:16 [a] Is. 49:23 [b] Is. 43:3 60:18 [a] Is. 26:1 60:19 [a] Rev. 21:23; 22:5 [b] Zech. 2:5 60:20 [a] Amos 8:9 60:21 [a] Rev. 21:27 [b] Ps. 37:11 [c] Is. 61:3 [d] [Eph. 2:10] 60:22 [a] Matt. 13:31, 32 61:1 [a] Luke 4:18, 19 [b] Luke 7:22 [c] Ps. 147:3 [d] Is. 42:7

### SEEING JESUS IN THE SCRIPTURE

**61:1** When Jesus entered the synagogue in Nazareth, He read this portion of Isaiah (see Luke 4:16–19). In doing so, Jesus pointed to how He fulfilled this prophecy. His earthly ministry was marked by these actions.

2 [a]To proclaim the acceptable year of the LORD,
And [b]the day of vengeance of our God;
[c]To comfort all who mourn,
3 To console those who mourn in Zion,
[a]To give them beauty for ashes,
The oil of joy for mourning,
The garment of praise for the spirit of heaviness;
That they may be called trees of righteousness,
[b]The planting of the LORD, [c]that He may be glorified."

4 And they shall [a]rebuild the old ruins,
They shall raise up the former desolations,
And they shall repair the ruined cities,
The desolations of many generations.
5 [a]Strangers shall stand and feed your flocks,
And the sons of the foreigner
*Shall be* your plowmen and your vinedressers.
6 [a]But you shall be named the priests of the LORD,
They shall call you the servants of our God.
[b]You shall eat the riches of the Gentiles,
And in their glory you shall boast.
7 [a]Instead of your shame *you shall have* double *honor,*
And *instead of* confusion they shall rejoice in their portion.
Therefore in their land they shall possess double;
Everlasting joy shall be theirs.

8 "For [a]I, the LORD, love justice;
[b]I hate robbery for burnt offering;
I will direct their work in truth,
[c]And will make with them an everlasting covenant.
9 Their descendants shall be known among the Gentiles,
And their offspring among the people.
All who see them shall acknowledge them,
[a]That they *are* the posterity *whom* the LORD has blessed."

10 [a]I will greatly rejoice in the LORD,
My soul shall be joyful in my God;
For [b]He has clothed me with the garments of salvation,
He has covered me with the robe of righteousness,
[c]As a bridegroom decks *himself* with ornaments,
And as a bride adorns *herself* with her jewels.
11 For as the earth brings forth its bud,
As the garden causes the things that are sown in it to spring forth,
So the Lord GOD will cause [a]righteousness and [b]praise to spring forth before all the nations.

### ASSURANCE OF ZION'S SALVATION

62 For Zion's sake I will not hold My peace,
And for Jerusalem's sake I will not rest,
Until her righteousness goes forth as brightness,
And her salvation as a lamp *that* burns.
2 [a]The Gentiles shall see your righteousness,
And all [b]kings your glory.
[c]You shall be called by a new name,
Which the mouth of the LORD will name.
3 You shall also be [a]a crown of glory
In the hand of the LORD,
And a royal diadem
In the hand of your God.
4 [a]You shall no longer be termed [b]Forsaken,
Nor shall your land any more be termed [c]Desolate;
But you shall be called Hephzibah,[1] and your land Beulah;[2]
For the LORD delights in you,
And your land shall be married.
5 For *as* a young man marries a virgin,
*So* shall your sons marry you;
And *as* the bridegroom rejoices over the bride,
[a]*So* shall your God rejoice over you.

6 [a]I have set watchmen on your walls, O Jerusalem;
They shall never hold their peace day or night.
You who make mention of the LORD, do not keep silent,
7 And give Him no rest till He establishes
And till He makes Jerusalem [a]a praise in the earth.

8 The LORD has sworn by His right hand
And by the arm of His strength:
"Surely I will no longer [a]give your grain
*As* food for your enemies;
And the sons of the foreigner shall not drink your new wine,
For which you have labored.

**61:2** [a] Lev. 25:9 [b] Is. 34:8 [c] Matt. 5:4 **61:3** [a] Ps. 30:11 [b] Is. 60:21 [c] [John 15:8] **61:4** [a] Ezek. 36:33 **61:5** [a] [Eph. 2:12] **61:6** [a] Ex. 19:6 [b] Is. 60:5, 11 **61:7** [a] Zech. 9:12 **61:8** [a] Ps. 11:7 [b] Is. 1:11, 13 [c] Is. 55:3 **61:9** [a] Is. 65:23 **61:10** [a] Hab. 3:18 [b] Ps. 132:9, 16 [c] Is. 49:18 **61:11** [a] Ps. 72:3; 85:11 [b] Is. 60:18; 62:7 **62:2** [a] Is. 60:3 [b] Ps. 102:15, 16; 138:4, 5; 148:11, 13 [c] Is. 62:4, 12; 65:15 **62:3** [a] Zech. 9:16 **62:4** [a] Hos. 1:10 [b] Is. 49:14; 54:6, 7 [c] Is. 54:1 [1] Literally *My Delight Is in Her* [2] Literally *Married* **62:5** [a] Is. 65:19 **62:6** [a] Ezek. 3:17; 33:7 **62:7** [a] Zeph. 3:19, 20 **62:8** [a] Deut. 28:31, 33

9 But those who have gathered it shall eat it,
And praise the LORD;
Those who have brought it together shall
drink it [a]in My holy courts."

10 Go through,
Go through the gates!
[a]Prepare the way for the people;
Build up,
Build up the highway!
Take out the stones,
[b]Lift up a banner for the peoples!

11 Indeed the LORD has proclaimed
To the end of the world:
[a]"Say to the daughter of Zion,
'Surely your salvation is coming;
Behold, His [b]reward *is* with Him,
And His work before Him.'"
12 And they shall call them The Holy
People,
The Redeemed of the LORD;
And you shall be called Sought Out,
A City Not Forsaken.

### THE LORD IN JUDGMENT AND SALVATION

63 Who *is* this who comes from Edom,
With dyed garments from Bozrah,
This *One who is* glorious in His apparel,
Traveling in the greatness of His
strength?—

"I who speak in righteousness, mighty to
save."

2 Why [a]*is* Your apparel red,
And Your garments like one who treads in
the winepress?

**63:2** People who pressed grapes for a living literally stomped on the grapes with their bare feet to make juice. As a result, these **winepress** workers developed permanent **red** stains on their legs and clothes.

3 "I have [a]trodden the winepress alone,
And from the peoples no one *was* with Me.
For I have trodden them in My anger,
And trampled them in My fury;
Their blood is sprinkled upon My
garments,
And I have stained all My robes.
4 For the [a]day of vengeance *is* in My heart,
And the year of My redeemed has come.
5 [a]I looked, but [b]*there was* no one to help,
And I wondered

### SEEING JESUS IN THE SCRIPTURE

**63:2–3** Isaiah envisioned Jesus with red garments like someone walking in a winepress. Jesus fulfilled this prophecy in part when He shed His blood on the cross. He will fulfill it in full at His return (see Rev. 19:13, 15).

That *there was* no one to uphold;
Therefore My own [c]arm brought salvation
for Me;
And My own fury, it sustained Me.
6 I have trodden down the peoples in My
anger,
Made them drunk in My fury,
And brought down their strength to the
earth."

### GOD'S MERCY REMEMBERED

7 I will mention the lovingkindnesses of the
LORD
*And* the praises of the LORD,
According to all that the LORD has
bestowed on us,
And the great goodness toward the house
of Israel,
Which He has bestowed on them
according to His mercies,
According to the multitude of His
lovingkindnesses.
8 For He said, "Surely they *are* My people,
Children *who* will not lie."
So He became their Savior.
9 [a]In all their affliction He was afflicted,
[b]And the Angel of His Presence saved
them;
[c]In His love and in His pity He redeemed
them;
And [d]He bore them and carried them
All the days of old.
10 But they [a]rebelled and [b]grieved His Holy
Spirit;
[c]So He turned Himself against them as an
enemy,
*And* He fought against them.

11 Then he [a]remembered the days of old,
Moses *and* his people, *saying:*
"Where *is* He who [b]brought them up out of
the sea
With the shepherd of His flock?
[c]Where *is* He who put His Holy Spirit
within them,
12 Who led *them* by the right hand of Moses,
[a]With His glorious arm,
[b]Dividing the water before them
To make for Himself an everlasting name,

**62:9** [a] Deut. 12:12; 14:23, 26 **62:10** [a] Is. 40:3; 57:14 [b] Is. 11:12 **62:11** [a] Zech. 9:9 [b] [Rev. 22:12] **63:2** [a] [Rev. 19:13, 15] **63:3** [a] Rev. 14:19, 20; 19:15 **63:4** [a] Is. 34:8; 35:4; 61:2 **63:5** [a] Is. 41:28; 59:16 [b] [John 16:32] [c] Ps. 98:1 **63:9** [a] Judg. 10:16 [b] Ex. 14:19 [c] Deut. 7:7 [d] Ex. 19:4 **63:10** [a] Ex. 15:24 [b] Ps. 78:40 [c] Ex. 23:21 **63:11** [a] Ps. 106:44, 45 [b] Ex. 14:30 [c] Num. 11:17, 25, 29 **63:12** [a] Ex. 15:6 [b] Ex. 14:21, 22

13 [a]Who led them through the deep,
As a horse in the wilderness,
*That* they might not stumble?"

14 As a beast goes down into the valley,
*And* the Spirit of the LORD causes him to rest,
So You lead Your people,
[a]To make Yourself a glorious name.

### *A PRAYER OF PENITENCE*

15 [a]Look down from heaven,
And see [b]from Your habitation, holy and glorious.
Where *are* Your zeal and Your strength,
The yearning [c]of Your heart and Your mercies toward me?
Are they restrained?
16 [a]Doubtless You *are* our Father,
Though Abraham [b]was ignorant of us,
And Israel does not acknowledge us.
You, O LORD, *are* our Father;
Our Redeemer from Everlasting *is* Your name.
17 O LORD, why have You [a]made us stray from Your ways,
*And* hardened our heart from Your fear?
Return for Your servants' sake,
The tribes of Your inheritance.
18 [a]Your holy people have possessed *it* but a little while;
[b]Our adversaries have trodden down Your sanctuary.
19 We have become *like* those of old, over whom You never ruled,
Those who were never called by Your name.

**64** Oh, that You would rend the heavens!
That You would come down!
That the mountains might shake at Your [a]presence—
2 As fire burns brushwood,
As fire causes water to boil—
To make Your name known to Your adversaries,
*That* the nations may tremble at Your presence!
3 When [a]You did awesome things *for which* we did not look,
You came down,
The mountains shook at Your presence.
4 For since the beginning of the world
[a]*Men* have not heard nor perceived by the ear,
Nor has the eye seen any God besides You,
Who acts for the one who waits for Him.
5 You meet him who rejoices and does righteousness,
*Who* remembers You in Your ways.
You are indeed angry, for we have sinned—
[a]In these ways we continue;
And we need to be saved.
6 But we are all like an unclean *thing,*
And all [a]our righteousnesses *are* like filthy rags;
We all [b]fade as a leaf,
And our iniquities, like the wind,
Have taken us away.
7 And *there is* no one who calls on Your name,
Who stirs himself up to take hold of You;
For You have hidden Your face from us,
And have consumed us because of our iniquities.
8 But now, O LORD,
You *are* our Father;
We *are* the clay, and You our [a]potter;
And all we *are* the work of Your hand.
9 Do not be furious, O LORD,
Nor remember iniquity forever;
Indeed, please look—we all *are* Your people!
10 Your holy cities are a wilderness,
Zion is a wilderness,
Jerusalem a desolation.
11 Our holy and beautiful temple,
Where our fathers praised You,
Is burned up with fire;
And all [a]our pleasant things are laid waste.
12 [a]Will You restrain Yourself because of these *things,* O LORD?
[b]Will You hold Your peace, and afflict us very severely?

### *THE RIGHTEOUSNESS OF GOD'S JUDGMENT*

**65** "I was [a]sought by *those who* did not ask *for Me;*
I was found by *those who* did not seek Me.
I said, 'Here I am, here I am,'
To a nation *that* [b]was not called by My name.
2 [a]I have stretched out My hands all day long to a [b]rebellious people,
Who [c]walk in a way *that is* not good,
According to their own thoughts;

**SEEING JESUS IN THE SCRIPTURE**

**65:2** Throughout the Old Testament, God's people chose rebellion over obedience. The same was true when Jesus came into the world (see John 1:11). Just as Isaiah prophesied, those who rejected Jesus ended up choosing judgment over grace and mercy (see Rom. 10:21).

63:13 [a]Ps. 106:9 63:14 [a]2 Sam. 7:23 63:15 [a]Deut. 26:15 [b]Ps. 33:14 [c]Jer. 31:20 63:16 [a]Deut. 32:6 [b]Job 14:21 63:17 [a]John 12:40 63:18 [a]Deut. 7:6 [b]Ps. 74:3–7 64:1 [a]Mic. 1:3, 4 64:3 [a]Ex. 34:10 64:4 [a]Ps. 31:19 64:5 [a]Mal. 3:6 64:6 [a][Phil. 3:9] [b]Ps. 90:5, 6 64:8 [a]Is. 29:16; 45:9 64:11 [a]Ezek. 24:21 64:12 [a]Is. 42:14 [b]Ps. 83:1 65:1 [a]Rom. 9:24; 10:20 [b]Is. 63:19 65:2 [a]Rom. 10:21 [b]Is. 1:2, 23 [c]Is. 42:24

3 A people [a]who provoke Me to anger
continually to My face;
[b]Who sacrifice in gardens,
And burn incense on altars of brick;
4 [a]Who sit among the graves,
And spend the night in the tombs;
[b]Who eat swine's flesh,
And the broth of abominable things is *in*
their vessels;
5 [a]Who say, 'Keep to yourself,
Do not come near me,
For I am holier than you!'
These *are* smoke in My nostrils,
A fire that burns all the day.

6 "Behold, [a]*it is* written before Me:
[b]I will not keep silence, [c]but will repay—
Even repay into their bosom—
7 Your iniquities and [a]the iniquities of your
fathers together,"
Says the LORD,
[b]"Who have burned incense on the
mountains
[c]And blasphemed Me on the hills;
Therefore I will measure their former
work into their bosom."

8 Thus says the LORD:

"As the new wine is found in the cluster,
And *one* says, 'Do not destroy it,
For [a]a blessing *is* in it,'
So will I do for My servants' sake,
That I may not destroy them [b]all.
9 I will bring forth descendants from Jacob,
And from Judah an heir of My mountains;
My [a]elect shall inherit it,
And My servants shall dwell there.
10 [a]Sharon shall be a fold of flocks,
And [b]the Valley of Achor a place for herds
to lie down,
For My people who have [c]sought Me.

11 "But you *are* those who forsake the LORD,
Who forget [a]My holy mountain,
Who prepare [b]a table for Gad,[1]
And who furnish a drink offering for
Meni.[2]
12 Therefore I will number you for the
sword,
And you shall all bow down to the
slaughter;
[a]Because, when I called, you did not
answer;
When I spoke, you did not hear,
But did evil before My eyes,
And chose *that* in which I do not
delight."

13 Therefore thus says the Lord GOD:

"Behold, My servants shall eat,
But you shall be hungry;
Behold, My servants shall drink,
But you shall be thirsty;
Behold, My servants shall rejoice,
But you shall be ashamed;
14 Behold, My servants shall sing for joy of
heart,
But you shall cry for sorrow of heart,
And [a]wail for grief of spirit.
15 You shall leave your name [a]as a curse to
[b]My chosen;
For the Lord GOD will slay you,
And [c]call His servants by another name;
16 [a]So that he who blesses himself in the
earth
Shall bless himself in the God of truth;
And [b]he who swears in the earth
Shall swear by the God of truth;
Because the former troubles are
forgotten,
And because they are hidden from My
eyes.

### *THE GLORIOUS NEW CREATION*

17 "For behold, I create [a]new heavens and a
new earth;
And the former shall not be remembered
or come to mind.
18 But be glad and rejoice forever in what I
create;
For behold, I create Jerusalem *as* a rejoicing,
And her people a joy.
19 [a]I will rejoice in Jerusalem,
And joy in My people;
The [b]voice of weeping shall no longer be
heard in her,
Nor the voice of crying.

20 "No more shall an infant from there *live
but a few* days,
Nor an old man who has not fulfilled his
days;
For the child shall die one hundred years
old,
[a]But the sinner *being* one hundred years
old shall be accursed.
21 [a]They shall build houses and inhabit *them;*
They shall plant vineyards and eat their
fruit.
22 They shall not build and another inhabit;
They shall not plant and [a]another eat;
For [b]as the days of a tree, *so shall be* the
days of My people,
And [c]My elect shall long enjoy the work of
their hands.

**65:3** [a] Deut. 32:21 [b] Is. 1:29 **65:4** [a] Deut. 18:11 [b] Is. 66:17 **65:5** [a] Matt. 9:11 **65:6** [a] Deut. 32:34 [b] Ps. 50:3 [c] Ps. 79:12 **65:7** [a] Ex. 20:5 [b] Ezek. 18:6 [c] Ezek. 20:27, 28 **65:8** [a] Joel 2:14 [b] Is. 1:9 **65:9** [a] Matt. 24:22 **65:10** [a] Is. 33:9 [b] Josh. 7:24 [c] Is. 55:6 **65:11** [a] Is. 56:7 [b] Ezek. 23:41 [1] Literally *Troop* or *Fortune,* a pagan deity [2] Literally *Number* or *Destiny,* a pagan deity **65:12** [a] Prov. 1:24 **65:14** [a] Matt. 8:12 **65:15** [a] Jer. 29:22 [b] Is. 65:9, 22 [c] [Acts 11:26] **65:16** [a] Jer. 4:2 [b] Zeph. 1:5 **65:17** [a] Rev. 21:1 **65:19** [a] Is. 62:4, 5 [b] Rev. 7:17; 21:4 **65:20** [a] Eccl. 8:12, 13 **65:21** [a] Amos 9:14 **65:22** [a] Is. 62:8, 9 [b] Ps. 92:12 [c] Is. 65:9, 15

APPLY THE TRUTH

## HEARTACHE

**65:17–25** Have you ever had your heart broken? Have you felt the pain of loss, betrayal, or disappointment? Heartache often comes from unfulfilled desire. You thought something was going to work out a certain way and perhaps even depended on it, but it never came to pass. The loved one never got better. The relationship didn't work out. Your best friend suddenly moved away. When things don't go according to plan, it can be devastating.

Is there a cure for a broken heart? When we're left empty because of unfulfilled desires, is there a way to move forward? There is! These verses can be a balm for a wounded heart. Isaiah prophesied about a day when God will make all wrongs right and make all things new. No more crying. No more loss. No more unfairness. No more pain. This is the new creation God is in the process of bringing about. But unlike our unfulfilled desires, God's plans always work out. This means we can have hope in heartbreak even now because we trust that God always does what He says. We can live with expectation of good things to come because God has made a promise. Find comfort and joy in that today.

23 They shall not labor in vain,
[a]Nor bring forth children for trouble;
For [b]they *shall be* the descendants of the
blessed of the LORD,
And their offspring with them.

24 "It shall come to pass
That [a]before they call, I will answer;
And while they are still speaking, I will
[b]hear.
25 The [a]wolf and the lamb shall feed
together,
The lion shall eat straw like the ox,
[b]And dust *shall be* the serpent's food.
They shall not hurt nor destroy in all My
holy mountain,"
Says the LORD.

### TRUE WORSHIP AND FALSE

66 Thus says the LORD:
[a]"Heaven *is* My throne,
And earth *is* My footstool.
Where *is* the house that you will build Me?
And where *is* the place of My rest?
2 For all those *things* My hand has made,
And all those *things* exist,"
Says the LORD.
[a]"But on this *one* will I look:
[b]On *him who is* poor and of a contrite
spirit,
And who trembles at My word.

3 "He[a] who kills a bull *is as if* he slays a man;
He who sacrifices a lamb, *as if* he [b]breaks
a dog's neck;
He who offers a grain offering, *as if he
offers* swine's blood;
He who burns incense, *as if* he blesses an
idol.
Just as they have chosen their own ways,
And their soul delights in their
abominations,
4 So will I choose their delusions,
And bring their fears on them;
[a]Because, when I called, no one answered,
When I spoke they did not hear;
But they did evil before My eyes,
And chose *that* in which I do not delight."

### THE LORD VINDICATES ZION

5 Hear the word of the LORD,
You who tremble at His word:
"Your brethren who [a]hated you,
Who cast you out for My name's sake, said,
[b]'Let the LORD be glorified,
That [c]we may see your joy.'
But they shall be ashamed."

6 The sound of noise from the city!
A voice from the temple!
The voice of the LORD,
Who fully repays His enemies!

7 "Before she was in labor, she gave birth;
Before her pain came,
She delivered a male child.
8 Who has heard such a thing?
Who has seen such things?
Shall the earth be made to give birth in
one day?
*Or* shall a nation be born at once?
For as soon as Zion was in labor,
She gave birth to her children.
9 Shall I bring to the time of birth, and not
cause delivery?" says the LORD.

**65:23** [a] Hos. 9:12 [b] Is. 61:9 **65:24** [a] Is. 58:9 [b] Dan. 9:20–23 **65:25** [a] Is. 11:6–9 [b] Gen. 3:14 **66:1** [a] 1 Kin. 8:27 **66:2** [a] [Is. 57:15; 61:1] [b] Ps. 34:18; 51:17 **66:3** [a] [Is. 1:10–17; 58:1–7] [b] Deut. 23:18 **66:4** [a] Is. 65:12 **66:5** [a] Is. 60:15 [b] Is. 5:19 [c] [Titus 2:13]

"Shall I who cause delivery shut up *the*
womb?" says your God.
10 "Rejoice with Jerusalem,
And be glad with her, all you who love her;
Rejoice for joy with her, all you who
mourn for her;
11 That you may feed and be satisfied
With the consolation of her bosom,
That you may drink deeply and be
delighted
With the abundance of her glory."

12 For thus says the LORD:

"Behold, [a]I will extend peace to her like a
river,
And the glory of the Gentiles like a
flowing stream.
Then you shall [b]feed;
On *her* sides shall you be [c]carried,
And be dandled on *her* knees.
13 As one whom his mother comforts,
So I will [a]comfort you;
And you shall be comforted in
Jerusalem."

### *THE REIGN AND INDIGNATION OF GOD*

14 When you see *this*, your heart shall
rejoice,
And [a]your bones shall flourish like grass;
The hand of the LORD shall be known to
His servants,
And *His* indignation to His enemies.
15 [a]For behold, the LORD will come with fire
And with His chariots, like a whirlwind,
To render His anger with fury,
And His rebuke with flames of fire.
16 For by fire and by [a]His sword
The LORD will judge all flesh;
And the slain of the LORD shall be [b]many.

17 "Those[a] who sanctify themselves and
purify themselves,
*To go* to the gardens
After an *idol* in the midst,
Eating swine's flesh and the abomination
and the mouse,
Shall be consumed together," says the
LORD.

18 "For I *know* their works and their [a]thoughts.
It shall be that I will [b]gather all nations and
tongues; and they shall come and see My glory.
19 [a]I will set a sign among them; and those among
them who escape I will send to the nations: *to*
Tarshish and Pul[1] and Lud, who draw the bow,
and Tubal and Javan, *to* the coastlands afar
off who have not heard My fame nor seen My
glory. [b]And they shall declare My glory among
the Gentiles. 20 Then they shall [a]bring all your
brethren [b]for an offering to the LORD out of all
nations, on horses and in chariots and in litters,
on mules and on camels, to My holy mountain
Jerusalem," says the LORD, "as the children of
Israel bring an offering in a clean vessel into the
house of the LORD. 21 And I will also take some
of them for [a]priests *and* Levites," says the LORD.

22 "For as [a]the new heavens and the new
earth
Which I will make shall remain before
Me," says the LORD,
"So shall your descendants and your name
remain.
23 And [a]it shall come to pass
*That* from one New Moon to another,
And from one Sabbath to another,
[b]All flesh shall come to worship before
Me," says the LORD.

24 "And they shall go forth and look
Upon the corpses of the men
Who have transgressed against Me.
For their [a]worm does not die,
And their fire is not quenched.
They shall be an abhorrence to all flesh."

**66:12** [a] Is. 48:18; 60:5 [b] Is. 60:16 [c] Is. 49:22; 60:4 **66:13** [a] Is. 51:3 **66:14** [a] Ezek. 37:1 **66:15** [a] Is. 9:5 **66:16** [a] Is. 27:1 [b] Is. 34:6 **66:17** [a] Is. 65:3–8 **66:18** [a] Is. 59:7 [b] Is. 45:22–25; Jer. 3:17 **66:19** [a] Luke 2:34 [b] Mal. 1:11 [1] Following Masoretic Text and Targum; Septuagint reads *Put* (compare Jeremiah 46:9). **66:20** [a] Is. 49:22 [b] Is. 18:7; [Rom. 15:16] **66:21** [a] Ex. 19:6; Is. 61:6; 1 Pet. 2:9; Rev. 1:6 **66:22** [a] Is. 65:17; Heb. 12:26, 27; 2 Pet. 3:13; Rev. 21:1 **66:23** [a] Zech. 14:16 [b] Zech. 14:17–21 **66:24** [a] Is. 14:11; Mark 9:44, 46, 48

*The Book of the Prophet*

# JEREMIAH

| AUTHOR | KEY VERSES | READING TIME |
|---|---|---|
| Jeremiah, with a portion by Baruch | Jeremiah 7:23–24 | 4 hours 42 minutes |

The Book of Jeremiah depicts Jeremiah as a youth being called by God to be a prophet, followed by the painful ministry that followed. Known as the weeping prophet, Jeremiah was given a heartbreaking message of judgment to share with God's people. Jeremiah labored for more than forty years proclaiming a message of doom to the stiff-necked people of Judah. Despised and persecuted by his own people, Jeremiah bathed his harsh prophecies in tears of compassion. Through his sermons and signs, Jeremiah faithfully declared that surrendering to God's will was the only way to escape the coming calamity.

**Occasion:** Jeremiah wrote his dire warnings to the people of Judah before Jerusalem's fall and then continued during the early days of their Babylonian exile.

**Main Point:** Because of sin, God's judgment is coming unless His people repent.

**Big Ideas:** God never gives up on His people. Even when we sin, God never stops loving us. God has a great plan for our lives.

## OUTLINE:

I. Jeremiah Is Called by God (ch. 1)
II. Jeremiah Warns of God's Punishment (chs. 2–26)
III. Jeremiah Faces the Lying Prophets (chs. 27–29)
IV. Jeremiah Tells of God's Restoration (chs. 30–33)
V. The Fall of Jerusalem (chs. 34–45)
VI. Jeremiah Warns the Nations (chs. 46–51)
VII. The Fall of Jerusalem Retold (ch. 52)

**722 BC**
The Assyrians defeat Israel

**640 BC**
Josiah becomes king in Judah

**626 BC**
Jeremiah is called to prophesy

**612 BC**
The Babylonians and Medes defeat Assyria

**609 BC**
Jehoahaz becomes king in Judah

**608 BC**
Jehoiakim becomes king in Judah

**605 BC**
Nebuchadnezzar rules in Babylon

**598 BC**
Jehoiachin becomes king in Judah

**598 BC**
Zedekiah becomes king in Judah

**586 BC**
The Babylonians conquer Jerusalem

**585 BC**
Jeremiah is taken to Egypt

1 The words of Jeremiah the son of Hilkiah, of the priests who *were* [a]in Anathoth in the land of Benjamin, 2 to whom the word of the LORD came in the days of [a]Josiah the son of Amon, king of Judah, [b]in the thirteenth year of his reign. 3 It came also in the days of [a]Jehoiakim the son of Josiah, king of Judah, [b]until the end of the eleventh year of Zedekiah the son of Josiah, king of Judah, [c]until the carrying away of Jerusalem captive [d]in the fifth month.

### *THE PROPHET IS CALLED*

4 Then the word of the LORD came to me, saying:

5 "Before I [a]formed you in the womb [b]I knew
you;
Before you were born I [c]sanctified you;
I ordained you a prophet to the nations."

6 Then said I:

[a]"Ah, Lord GOD!
Behold, I cannot speak, for I *am* a youth."

7 But the LORD said to me:

"Do not say, 'I *am* a youth,'
For you shall go to all to whom I send you,
And [a]whatever I command you, you shall
speak.
8 [a]Do not be afraid of their faces,
For [b]I *am* with you to deliver you," says
the LORD.

9 Then the LORD put forth His hand and [a]touched my mouth, and the LORD said to me:

"Behold, I have [b]put My words in your
mouth.
10 [a]See, I have this day set you over the
nations and over the kingdoms,
To [b]root out and to pull down,
To destroy and to throw down,
To build and to plant."

11 Moreover the word of the LORD came to me, saying, "Jeremiah, what do you see?"

And I said, "I see a branch of an almond tree."

12 Then the LORD said to me, "You have seen well, for I am ready to perform My word."

13 And the word of the LORD came to me the second time, saying, "What do you see?"

And I said, "I see [a]a boiling pot, and it is facing away from the north."

14 Then the LORD said to me:

"Out of the [a]north calamity shall break forth
On all the inhabitants of the land.
15 For behold, I am [a]calling
All the families of the kingdoms of the
north," says the LORD;
"They shall come and [b]each one set his
throne
At the entrance of the gates of Jerusalem,
Against all its walls all around,
And against all the cities of Judah.
16 I will utter My judgments
Against them concerning all their
wickedness,
Because [a]they have forsaken Me,
Burned [b]incense to other gods,
And worshiped the works of their own
[c]hands.

1:1 [a]Josh. 21:18 1:2 [a]2 Kin. 21:24 [b]Jer. 25:3 1:3 [a]2 Kin. 23:34 [b]Jer. 39:2 [c]Jer. 52:12 [d]2 Kin. 25:8 1:5 [a]Is. 49:1, 5 [b]Ex. 33:12 [c][Luke 1:15] 1:6 [a]Ex. 4:10; 6:12, 30 1:7 [a]Num. 22:20, 38 1:8 [a]Ezek. 2:6; 3:9 [b]Ex. 3:12 1:9 [a]Is. 6:7 [b]Is. 51:16 1:10 [a]1 Kin. 19:17 [b][2 Cor. 10:4, 5] 1:13 [a]Ezek. 11:3; 24:3 1:14 [a]Jer. 6:1 1:15 [a]Jer. 6:22; 25:9 [b]Jer. 39:3 1:16 [a]Deut. 28:20 [b]Jer. 7:9 [c]Is. 37:19

APPLY THE TRUTH

## ACCEPTANCE AND BELONGING

**1:5** Not everyone who applies for a job is hired. Some applicants don't make it past the first round of cuts because they lack the experience, education, connections, or skills needed for the job. Sometimes, we think God works this way. We think we need certain qualifications to be in God's presence or to be used by Him. It seems to make sense. God is perfect, just, holy, and good. We are not. Furthermore, in many ways, we're inexperienced and unskilled, and we're young. How can *we* be in God's presence or be used by Him?

Jeremiah was young when God called him to be a prophet and he felt unworthy to be used by God. What did God do? He reminded Jeremiah that before Jeremiah even took his first breath, God already had a plan for him. God chose Jeremiah not because of his experience or abilities, but because of God's own desire. Jeremiah didn't have to be acceptable and useful for God to choose him. God chose him and, in doing so, made him acceptable and useful. He does the same for us. As the adage goes: "God doesn't call the qualified; He qualifies the called." In Christ, you are acceptable to God and belong to Him no matter what.

17 "Therefore [a]prepare yourself and arise,
And speak to them all that I command you.
[b]Do not be dismayed before their faces,
Lest I dismay you before them.
18 For behold, I have made you this day
[a]A fortified city and an iron pillar,
And bronze walls against the whole land—
Against the kings of Judah,
Against its princes,
Against its priests,
And against the people of the land.
19 They will fight against you,
But they shall not prevail against you.
For I *am* with you," says the LORD, "to
deliver you."

### *GOD'S CASE AGAINST ISRAEL*

2 Moreover the word of the LORD came to me,
saying, 2 "Go and cry in the hearing of Jeru-
salem, saying, 'Thus says the LORD:

"I remember you,
The kindness of your [a]youth,
The love of your betrothal,
[b]When you went after Me in the wilderness,
In a land not sown.
3 [a]Israel *was* holiness to the LORD,
[b]The firstfruits of His increase.
[c]All that devour him will offend;
Disaster will [d]come upon them," says the
LORD.' "

4 Hear the word of the LORD, O house of Ja-
cob and all the families of the house of Israel.
5 Thus says the LORD:

[a]"What injustice have your fathers found
in Me,
That they have gone far from Me,
[b]Have followed idols,
And have become idolaters?
6 Neither did they say, 'Where *is* the LORD,
Who [a]brought us up out of the land of
Egypt,
Who led us through [b]the wilderness,
Through a land of deserts and pits,
Through a land of drought and the
shadow of death,
Through a land that no one crossed
And where no one dwelt?'
7 I brought you into [a]a bountiful country,
To eat its fruit and its goodness.
But when you entered, you [b]defiled My
land
And made My heritage an abomination.
8 The priests did not say, 'Where *is* the LORD?'
And those who handle the [a]law did not
know Me;
The rulers also transgressed against Me;
[b]The prophets prophesied by Baal,
And walked after *things that* do not profit.

9 "Therefore [a]I will yet bring charges against
you," says the LORD,
"And against your children's children I will
bring charges.
10 For pass beyond the coasts of Cyprus[1] and
see,
Send to Kedar[2] and consider diligently,
And see if there has been such *a* [a]*thing.*
11 [a]Has a nation changed *its* gods,
Which *are* [b]not gods?
[c]But My people have changed their Glory
For *what* does not profit.
12 Be astonished, O heavens, at this,
And be horribly afraid;
Be very desolate," says the LORD.
13 "For My people have committed two evils:
They have forsaken Me, the [a]fountain of
living waters,
*And* hewn themselves cisterns—broken
cisterns that can hold no water.

> **2:13** The people could have chosen a **fountain of living waters**. Instead, they chose **broken cisterns** that leaked **water**, making them useless for sustaining life.

14 "*Is* Israel [a]a servant?
*Is* he a homeborn *slave?*
Why is he plundered?
15 [a]The young lions roared at him, *and*
growled;
They made his land waste;
His cities are burned, without inhabitant.
16 Also the people of Noph[1] and [a]Tahpanhes
Have broken the crown of your head.
17 [a]Have you not brought this on yourself,
In that you have forsaken the LORD your
God
When [b]He led you in the way?
18 And now why take [a]the road to Egypt,
To drink the waters of [b]Sihor?
Or why take the road to [c]Assyria,
To drink the waters of the River?[1]
19 Your own wickedness will [a]correct you,
And your backslidings will rebuke you.
Know therefore and see that *it is* an evil
and bitter *thing*
That you have forsaken the LORD your God,
And the fear of Me *is* not in you,"
Says the Lord GOD of hosts.

1:17 [a]Job 38:3 [b]Ezek. 2:6 1:18 [a]Is. 50:7 2:2 [a]Ezek. 16:8 [b]Deut. 2:7 2:3 [a][Ex. 19:5, 6] [b]Rev. 14:4 [c]Jer. 12:14 [d]Is. 41:11 2:5 [a]Is. 5:4 [b]2 Kin. 17:15 2:6 [a]Is. 63:11 [b]Deut. 8:15; 32:10 2:7 [a]Num. 13:27 [b]Num. 35:33 2:8 [a]Rom. 2:20 [b]Jer. 23:13 2:9 [a]Mic. 6:2 2:10 [a]Jer. 18:13 [1]Hebrew *Kittim,* western lands, especially Cyprus [2]In the northern Arabian desert, representative of the eastern cultures 2:11 [a]Mic. 4:5 [b]Is. 37:19 [c]Rom. 1:23 2:13 [a]Ps. 36:9 2:14 [a][Ex. 4:22] 2:15 [a]Is. 1:7 2:16 [a]Jer. 43:7–9 [1]That is, Memphis in ancient Egypt 2:17 [a]Jer. 4:18 [b]Deut. 32:10 2:18 [a]Is. 30:1–3 [b]Josh. 13:3 [c]Hos. 5:13 [1]That is, the Euphrates 2:19 [a]Jer. 4:18

20 "For of old I have [a]broken your yoke *and*
burst your bonds;
And [b]you said, 'I will not transgress,'
When [c]on every high hill and under every
green tree
You lay down, [d]playing the harlot.
21 Yet I had [a]planted you a noble vine, a seed
of highest quality.
How then have you turned before Me
Into [b]the degenerate plant of an alien vine?
22 For though you wash yourself with lye,
and use much soap,
*Yet* your iniquity is [a]marked before Me,"
says the Lord GOD.

23 "How[a] can you say, 'I am not polluted,
I have not gone after the Baals'?
See your way in the valley;
Know what you have done:
*You are* a swift dromedary breaking loose
in her ways,
24 A wild donkey used to the wilderness,
*That* sniffs at the wind in her desire;
In her time of mating, who can turn her
away?
All those who seek her will not weary
themselves;
In her month they will find her.
25 Withhold your foot from being unshod,
and your throat from thirst.
But you said, [a]'There is no hope.
No! For I have loved [b]aliens, and after
them I will go.'

26 "As the thief is ashamed when he is found
out,
So is the house of Israel ashamed;
They and their kings and their princes,
and their priests and their [a]prophets,
27 Saying to a tree, 'You *are* my father,'
And to a [a]stone, 'You gave birth to me.'
For they have turned *their* back to Me, and
not *their* face.
But in the time of their [b]trouble
They will say, 'Arise and save us.'
28 But [a]where *are* your gods that you have
made for yourselves?
Let them arise,
If they [b]can save you in the time of your
trouble;
For [c]*according to* the number of your cities
Are your gods, O Judah.

29 "Why will you plead with Me?
You all have transgressed against Me,"
says the LORD.
30 "In vain I have [a]chastened your children;
They [b]received no correction.
Your sword has [c]devoured your prophets
Like a destroying lion.

31 "O generation, see the word of the LORD!
Have I been a wilderness to Israel,
Or a land of darkness?
Why do My people say, 'We are lords;
[a]We will come no more to You'?
32 Can a virgin forget her ornaments,
*Or* a bride her attire?
Yet My people [a]have forgotten Me days
without number.

33 "Why do you beautify your way to seek
love?
Therefore you have also taught
The wicked women your ways.
34 Also on your skirts is found
[a]The blood of the lives of the poor
innocents.
I have not found it by secret search,
But plainly on all these things.
35 [a]Yet you say, 'Because I am innocent,
Surely His anger shall turn from me.'
Behold, [b]I will plead My case against you,
[c]Because you say, 'I have not sinned.'
36 [a]Why do you gad about so much to change
your way?
Also [b]you shall be ashamed of Egypt [c]as
you were ashamed of Assyria.
37 Indeed you will go forth from him
With your hands on [a]your head;
For the LORD has rejected your trusted
allies,
And you will [b]not prosper by them.

## ISRAEL IS SHAMELESS

3 "They say, 'If a man divorces his wife,
And she goes from him
And becomes another man's,
[a]May he return to her again?'
Would not that [b]land be greatly polluted?
But you have [c]played the harlot with
many lovers;
[d]Yet return to Me," says the LORD.

2 "Lift up your eyes to [a]the desolate heights
and see:
Where have you not lain *with men*?
[b]By the road you have sat for them
Like an Arabian in the wilderness;
[c]And you have polluted the land
With your harlotries and your wickedness.
3 Therefore the [a]showers have been
withheld,
And there has been no latter rain.
You have had a [b]harlot's forehead;
You refuse to be ashamed.

**2:20** [a]Lev. 26:13 [b]Judg. 10:16 [c]Deut. 12:2 [d]Ex. 34:15 **2:21** [a]Ex. 15:17 [b]Is. 5:4 **2:22** [a]Job 14:16, 17 **2:23** [a]Prov. 30:12 **2:25** [a]Jer. 18:12 [b]Jer. 3:13 **2:26** [a]Is. 28:7 **2:27** [a]Jer. 3:9 [b]Is. 26:16 **2:28** [a]Judg. 10:14 [b]Is. 45:20 [c]Jer. 11:13 **2:30** [a]Is. 9:13 [b]Jer. 5:3; 7:28 [c]Neh. 9:26 **2:31** [a]Deut. 32:15 **2:32** [a]Ps. 106:21 **2:34** [a]Ps. 106:38 **2:35** [a]Jer. 2:23, 29 [b]Jer. 2:9 [c][Prov. 28:13] **2:36** [a]Hos. 5:13; 12:1 [b]Is. 30:3 [c]2 Chr. 28:16 **2:37** [a]2 Sam. 13:19 [b]Jer. 37:7–10 **3:1** [a]Deut. 24:1–4 [b]Jer. 2:7 [c]Ezek. 16:26 [d][Zech. 1:3] **3:2** [a]Deut. 12:2 [b]Prov. 23:28 [c]Jer. 2:7 **3:3** [a]Lev. 26:19 [b]Zeph. 3:5

4 Will you not from this time cry to Me,
'My Father, You *are* [a]the guide of [b]my
youth?
5 [a]Will He remain angry forever?
Will He keep it to the end?'
Behold, you have spoken and done evil
things,
As you were able."

## *A CALL TO REPENTANCE*

6 The LORD said also to me in the days of Josiah the king: "Have you seen what [a]backsliding Israel has done? She has [b]gone up on every high mountain and under every green tree, and there played the harlot. 7 [a]And I said, after she had done all these *things,* 'Return to Me.' But she did not return. And her treacherous [b]sister Judah saw it. 8 Then I saw that [a]for all the causes for which backsliding Israel had committed adultery, I had [b]put her away and given her a certificate of divorce; [c]yet her treacherous sister Judah did not fear, but went and played the harlot also. 9 So it came to pass, through her casual harlotry, that she [a]defiled the land and committed adultery with [b]stones and trees. 10 And yet for all this her treacherous sister Judah has not turned to Me [a]with her whole heart, but in pretense," says the LORD.

11 Then the LORD said to me, [a]"Backsliding Israel has shown herself more righteous than treacherous Judah. 12 Go and proclaim these words toward [a]the north, and say:

'Return, backsliding Israel,' says the LORD;
'I will not cause My anger to fall on you.
For I *am* [b]merciful,' says the LORD;
'I will not remain angry forever.
13 [a]Only acknowledge your iniquity,
That you have transgressed against the
LORD your God,
And have [b]scattered your charms
To [c]alien deities [d]under every green tree,
And you have not obeyed My voice,' says
the LORD.

14 "Return, O backsliding children," says the LORD; [a]"for I am married to you. I will take you, [b]one from a city and two from a family, and I will bring you to [c]Zion. 15 And I will give you [a]shepherds according to My heart, who will [b]feed you with knowledge and understanding.

16 "Then it shall come to pass, when you are multiplied and [a]increased in the land in those days," says the LORD, "that they will say no more, 'The ark of the covenant of the LORD.' [b]It shall not come to mind, nor shall they remember it, nor shall they visit *it,* nor shall it be made anymore.

17 "At that time Jerusalem shall be called The Throne of the LORD, and all the nations shall be gathered to it, [a]to the name of the LORD, to Jerusalem. No more shall they [b]follow the dictates of their evil hearts.

18 "In those days [a]the house of Judah shall walk with the house of Israel, and they shall come together out of the land of [b]the north to [c]the land that I have given as an inheritance to your fathers.

19 "But I said:

'How can I put you among the children
And give you [a]a pleasant land,
A beautiful heritage of the hosts of nations?'

"And I said:

'You shall call Me, [b]"My Father,"
And not turn away from Me.'
20 Surely, *as* a wife treacherously departs
from her husband,
So [a]have you dealt treacherously with Me,
O house of Israel," says the LORD.

21 A voice was heard on [a]the desolate
heights,
Weeping *and* supplications of the
children of Israel.
For they have perverted their way;
They have forgotten the LORD their God.

22 "Return, you backsliding children,
*And* I will [a]heal your backslidings."

"Indeed we do come to You,
For You are the LORD our God.
23 [a]Truly, in vain *is salvation hoped for* from
the hills,
*And from* the multitude of mountains;
[b]Truly, in the LORD our God
*Is* the salvation of Israel.
24 [a]For shame has devoured
The labor of our fathers from our youth—
Their flocks and their herds,
Their sons and their daughters.
25 We lie down in our shame,
And our reproach covers us.
[a]For we have sinned against the LORD
our God,
We and our fathers,
From our youth even to this day,
And [b]have not obeyed the voice of the
LORD our God."

4 "If you will return, O Israel," says the
LORD,
[a]"Return to Me;
And if you will put away your
abominations out of My sight,
Then you shall not be moved.

3:4 [a] Prov. 2:17 [b] Jer. 2:2 3:5 [a] [Is. 57:16] 3:6 [a] Jer. 7:24 [b] Jer. 2:20 3:7 [a] 2 Kin. 17:13 [b] Ezek. 16:47, 48 3:8 [a] Ezek. 23:9 [b] 2 Kin. 17:6 [c] Ezek. 23:11 3:9 [a] Jer. 2:7 [b] Jer. 2:27 3:10 [a] Jer. 12:2 3:11 [a] Ezek. 16:51, 52 3:12 [a] 2 Kin. 17:6 [b] Ps. 86:15 3:13 [a] Deut. 30:1, 2 [b] Ezek. 16:15 [c] Jer. 2:25 [d] Deut. 12:2 3:14 [a] Hos. 2:19, 20 [b] Jer. 31:6 [c] [Rom. 11:5] 3:15 [a] Eph. 4:11 [b] Acts 20:28 3:16 [a] Is. 49:19 [b] Is. 65:17 3:17 [a] Is. 60:9 [b] Deut. 29:19; Jer. 7:24 3:18 [a] Is. 11:13 [b] Jer. 31:8 [c] Amos 9:15 3:19 [a] Ps. 106:24 [b] Is. 63:16 3:20 [a] Is. 48:8 3:21 [a] Is. 15:2 3:22 [a] Hos. 6:1; 14:4 3:23 [a] Ps. 121:1, 2 [b] Ps. 3:8 3:24 [a] Hos. 9:10 3:25 [a] Ezra 9:6, 7 [b] Jer. 22:21 4:1 [a] Joel 2:12

2 [a]And you shall swear, 'The LORD lives,'
[b]In truth, in judgment, and in
righteousness;
[c]The nations shall bless themselves in Him,
And in Him they shall [d]glory."

3 For thus says the LORD to the men of Judah
and Jerusalem:

[a]"Break up your fallow ground,
And [b]do not sow among thorns.
4 [a]Circumcise yourselves to the LORD,
And take away the foreskins of your hearts,
You men of Judah and inhabitants of
Jerusalem,
Lest My fury come forth like fire,
And burn so that no one can quench *it*,
Because of the evil of your doings."

### AN IMMINENT INVASION

5 Declare in Judah and proclaim in Jerusa-
lem, and say:

[a]"Blow the trumpet in the land;
Cry, 'Gather together,'
And say, [b]'Assemble yourselves,
And let us go into the fortified cities.'
6 Set up the standard toward Zion.
Take refuge! Do not delay!
For I will bring disaster from the [a]north,
And great destruction."

7 [a]The lion has come up from his thicket,
And [b]the destroyer of nations is on his way.
He has gone forth from his place
[c]To make your land desolate.
Your cities will be laid waste,
Without inhabitant.
8 For this, [a]clothe yourself with sackcloth,
Lament and wail.
For the fierce anger of the LORD
Has not turned back from us.

9 "And it shall come to pass in that day," says
the LORD,
"*That* the heart of the king shall perish,
And the heart of the princes;
The priests shall be astonished,
And the prophets shall wonder."

10 Then I said, "Ah, Lord GOD!
[a]Surely You have greatly deceived this
people and Jerusalem,
[b]Saying, 'You shall have peace,'
Whereas the sword reaches to the heart."

11 At that time it will be said
To this people and to Jerusalem,
[a]"A dry wind of the desolate heights *blows*
in the wilderness
Toward the daughter of My people—
Not to fan or to cleanse—
12 A wind too strong for these will come for
Me;
Now [a]I will also speak judgment against
them."

13 "Behold, he shall come up like clouds,
And [a]his chariots like a whirlwind.
[b]His horses are swifter than eagles.
Woe to us, for we are plundered!"

14 O Jerusalem, [a]wash your heart from
wickedness,
That you may be saved.
How long shall your evil thoughts lodge
within you?
15 For a voice declares [a]from Dan
And proclaims affliction from Mount
Ephraim:
16 "Make mention to the nations,
Yes, proclaim against Jerusalem,
*That* watchers come from a [a]far country
And raise their voice against the cities of
Judah.
17 [a]Like keepers of a field they are against her
all around,
Because she has been rebellious against
Me," says the LORD.
18 "Your[a] ways and your doings
Have procured these *things* for you.
This *is* your wickedness,
Because it is bitter,
Because it reaches to your heart."

### SORROW FOR THE DOOMED NATION

19 O my [a]soul, my soul!
I am pained in my very heart!
My heart makes a noise in me;
I cannot hold my peace,
Because you have heard, O my soul,
The sound of the trumpet,
The alarm of war.
20 [a]Destruction upon destruction is cried,
For the whole land is plundered.
Suddenly [b]my tents are plundered,
*And* my curtains in a moment.
21 How long will I see the standard,
*And* hear the sound of the trumpet?

22 "For My people *are* foolish,
They have not known Me.
They *are* silly children,
And they have no understanding.
[a]They *are* wise to do evil,
But to do good they have no knowledge."

**4:2** [a] Deut. 10:20 [b] Zech. 8:8 [c] [Gen. 22:18] [d] 1 Cor. 1:31 **4:3** [a] Hos. 10:12 [b] Matt. 13:7 **4:4** [a] Deut. 10:16; 30:6 **4:5** [a] Hos. 8:1 [b] Jer. 8:14 **4:6** [a] Jer. 1:13–15; 6:1, 22; 50:17 **4:7** [a] Dan. 7:4 [b] Jer. 25:9 [c] Is. 1:7; 6:11 **4:8** [a] Is. 22:12 **4:10** [a] Ezek. 14:9 [b] Jer. 5:12; 14:13 **4:11** [a] Hos. 13:15 **4:12** [a] Jer. 1:16 **4:13** [a] Is. 5:28 [b] Deut. 28:49 **4:14** [a] James 4:8 **4:15** [a] Jer. 8:16; 50:17 **4:16** [a] Is. 39:3 **4:17** [a] 2 Kin. 25:1, 4 **4:18** [a] Is. 50:1 **4:19** [a] Is. 15:5; 16:11; 21:3; 22:4 **4:20** [a] Ezek. 7:26 [b] Jer. 10:20 **4:22** [a] Rom. 16:19

23 [a]I beheld the earth, and indeed *it was*
[b]without form, and void;
And the heavens, they *had* no light.
24 [a]I beheld the mountains, and indeed they
trembled,
And all the hills moved back and forth.
25 I beheld, and indeed *there was* no man,
And [a]all the birds of the heavens had fled.
26 I beheld, and indeed the fruitful land *was*
a [a]wilderness,
And all its cities were broken down
At the presence of the LORD,
By His fierce anger.

27 For thus says the LORD:

"The whole land shall be desolate;
[a]Yet I will not make a full end.
28 For this [a]shall the earth mourn,
And [b]the heavens above be black,
Because I have spoken.
I have [c]purposed and [d]will not relent,
Nor will I turn back from it.
29 The whole city shall flee from the noise of
the horsemen and bowmen.
They shall go into thickets and climb up
on the rocks.
Every city *shall be* forsaken,
And not a man shall dwell in it.

30 "And *when* you *are* plundered,
What will you do?
Though you clothe yourself with crimson,
Though you adorn *yourself* with
ornaments of gold,
[a]Though you enlarge your eyes with paint,
In vain you will make yourself fair;
[b]*Your* lovers will despise you;
They will seek your life.

31 "For I have heard a voice as of a woman in
labor,
The anguish as of her who brings forth
her first child,
The voice of the daughter of Zion
bewailing herself;
She [a]spreads her hands, *saying,*
'Woe *is* me now, for my soul is weary
Because of murderers!'

### *THE JUSTICE OF GOD'S JUDGMENT*

5 "Run to and fro through the streets of
Jerusalem;
See now and know;
And seek in her open places
[a]If you can find a man,
[b]If there is *anyone* who executes judgment,
Who seeks the truth,
[c]And I will pardon her.
2 [a]Though they say, '*As* [b]the LORD lives,'
Surely they [c]swear falsely."
3 O LORD, *are* not [a]Your eyes on the truth?
You have [b]stricken them,
But they have not grieved;
You have consumed them,
But [c]they have refused to receive
correction.
They have made their faces harder than
rock;
They have refused to return.

4 Therefore I said, "Surely these *are* poor.
They are foolish;
For [a]they do not know the way of the
LORD,
The judgment of their God.
5 I will go to the great men and speak to
them,
For [a]they have known the way of the
LORD,
The judgment of their God."

But these have altogether [b]broken the
yoke
*And* burst the bonds.
6 Therefore [a]a lion from the forest shall slay
them,
[b]A wolf of the deserts shall destroy them;
[c]A leopard will watch over their cities.
Everyone who goes out from there shall
be torn in pieces,
Because their transgressions are many;
Their backslidings have increased.

7 "How shall I pardon you for this?
Your children have forsaken Me
And [a]sworn by *those* [b]*that are* not gods.
[c]When I had fed them to the full,
Then they committed adultery
And assembled themselves by troops in
the harlots' houses.
8 [a]They were *like* well-fed lusty stallions;
Every one neighed after his neighbor's
wife.
9 Shall I not punish *them* for these *things?*"
says the LORD.
"And shall I not [a]avenge Myself on such a
nation as this?

10 "Go up on her walls and destroy,
But do not make a [a]complete end.
Take away her branches,
For they *are* not the LORD's.
11 For [a]the house of Israel and the house of
Judah
Have dealt very treacherously with Me,"
says the LORD.

**4:23** [a] Is. 24:19 [b] Gen. 1:2 **4:24** [a] Ezek. 38:20 **4:25** [a] Zeph. 1:3 **4:26** [a] Jer. 9:10 **4:27** [a] Jer. 5:10, 18; 30:11; 46:28 **4:28** [a] Hos. 4:3 [b] Is. 5:30; 50:3 [c] [Dan. 4:35] [d] [Num. 23:19] **4:30** [a] 2 Kin. 9:30 [b] Jer. 22:20, 22 **4:31** [a] Lam. 1:17 **5:1** [a] Ezek. 22:30 [b] Gen. 18:23–32 [c] Gen. 18:26 **5:2** [a] Titus 1:16 [b] Jer. 4:2 [c] Jer. 7:9 **5:3** [a] [2 Chr. 16:9] [b] Is. 1:5; 9:13 [c] Zeph. 3:2 **5:4** [a] Jer. 8:7 **5:5** [a] Mic. 3:1 [b] Ps. 2:3 **5:6** [a] Jer. 4:7 [b] Zeph. 3:3 [c] Hos. 13:7 **5:7** [a] Zeph. 1:5 [b] Deut. 32:21 [c] Deut. 32:15 **5:8** [a] Ezek. 22:11 **5:9** [a] Jer. 9:9 **5:10** [a] Jer. 4:27 **5:11** [a] Jer. 3:6, 7, 20

12 [a]They have lied about the LORD,
And said, [b]"*It is* not He.
[c]Neither will evil come upon us,
Nor shall we see sword or famine.
13 And the prophets become wind,
For the word *is* not in them.
Thus shall it be done to them."

14 Therefore thus says the LORD God of hosts:

"Because you speak this word,
[a]Behold, I will make My words in your mouth fire,
And this people wood,
And it shall devour them.
15 Behold, I will bring a [a]nation against you [b]from afar,
O house of Israel," says the LORD.
"It *is* a mighty nation,
It *is* an ancient nation,
A nation whose language you do not know,
Nor can you understand what they say.
16 Their quiver *is* like an open tomb;
They *are* all mighty men.
17 And they shall eat up your [a]harvest and your bread,
*Which* your sons and daughters should eat.
They shall eat up your flocks and your herds;
They shall eat up your vines and your fig trees;
They shall destroy your fortified cities,
In which you trust, with the sword.

18 "Nevertheless in those days," says the
LORD, "I [a]will not make a complete end of you.
19 And it will be when you say, [a]'Why does the
LORD our God do all these *things* to us?' then you
shall answer them, 'Just as you have [b]forsaken
Me and served foreign gods in your land, so [c]you
shall serve aliens in a land *that is* not yours.'

20 "Declare this in the house of Jacob
And proclaim it in Judah, saying,
21 'Hear this now, O [a]foolish people,
Without understanding,
Who have eyes and see not,
And who have ears and hear not:
22 [a]Do you not fear Me?' says the LORD.
'Will you not tremble at My presence,
Who have placed the sand as the [b]bound of the sea,
By a perpetual decree, that it cannot pass beyond it?
And though its waves toss to and fro,
Yet they cannot prevail;
Though they roar, yet they cannot pass over it.
23 But this people has a defiant and rebellious heart;
They have revolted and departed.
24 They do not say in their heart,
"Let us now fear the LORD our God,
[a]Who gives rain, both the [b]former and the latter, in its season.
[c]He reserves for us the appointed weeks of the harvest."
25 [a]Your iniquities have turned these *things* away,
And your sins have withheld good from you.

26 'For among My people are found wicked *men;*
They [a]lie in wait as one who sets snares;
They set a trap;
They catch men.
27 As a cage is full of birds,
So their houses *are* full of deceit.
Therefore they have become great and grown rich.
28 They have grown [a]fat, they are sleek;
Yes, they surpass the deeds of the wicked;
They do not plead [b]the cause,
The cause of the fatherless;
[c]Yet they prosper,
And the right of the needy they do not defend.
29 [a]Shall I not punish *them* for these *things?'*
says the LORD.
'Shall I not avenge Myself on such a nation as this?'

30 "An astonishing and [a]horrible thing
Has been committed in the land:
31 The prophets prophesy [a]falsely,
And the priests rule by their *own* power;
And My people [b]love *to have it* so.
But what will you do in the end?

### IMPENDING DESTRUCTION FROM THE NORTH

6 "O you children of Benjamin,
Gather yourselves to flee from the midst of Jerusalem!
Blow the trumpet in Tekoa,
And set up a signal-fire in [a]Beth Haccerem;
[b]For disaster appears out of the north,
And great destruction.
2 I have likened the daughter of Zion
To a lovely and delicate woman.
3 The [a]shepherds with their flocks shall come to her.
They shall pitch *their* tents against her all around.
Each one shall pasture in his own place."

5:12 [a] 2 Chr. 36:16 [b] Jer. 23:17 [c] Jer. 14:13 5:14 [a] Jer. 1:9; 23:29 5:15 [a] Deut. 28:49 [b] Jer. 4:16 5:17 [a] Lev. 26:16 5:18 [a] Jer. 30:11 5:19 [a] Deut. 29:24–29 [b] Jer. 1:16; 2:13 [c] Deut. 28:48 5:21 [a] Matt. 13:14 5:22 [a] [Rev. 15:4] [b] Job 26:10 5:24 [a] Acts 14:17 [b] Joel 2:23 [c] [Gen. 8:22] 5:25 [a] Jer. 3:3 5:26 [a] Hab. 1:15 5:28 [a] Deut. 32:15 [b] Zech. 7:10 [c] Job 12:6 5:29 [a] Mal. 3:5 5:30 [a] Hos. 6:10 5:31 [a] Ezek. 13:6 [b] Mic. 2:11 6:1 [a] Neh. 3:14 [b] Jer. 4:6 6:3 [a] 2 Kin. 25:1–4

4 "Prepare[a] war against her;
Arise, and let us go up [b]at noon.
Woe to us, for the day goes away,
For the shadows of the evening are lengthening.
5 Arise, and let us go by night,
And let us destroy her palaces."

6 For thus has the LORD of hosts said:

"Cut down trees,
And build a mound against Jerusalem.
This *is* the city to be punished.
She *is* full of oppression in her midst.
7 [a]As a fountain wells up with water,
So she wells up with her wickedness.
[b]Violence and plundering are heard in her.
Before Me continually *are* grief and wounds.
8 Be instructed, O Jerusalem,
Lest [a]My soul depart from you;
Lest I make you desolate,
A land not inhabited."

9 Thus says the LORD of hosts:

"They shall thoroughly glean as a vine the remnant of Israel;
As a grape-gatherer, put your hand back into the branches."

10 To whom shall I speak and give warning,
That they may hear?
Indeed their [a]ear *is* uncircumcised,
And they cannot give heed.
Behold, [b]the word of the LORD is a reproach to them;
They have no delight in it.
11 Therefore I am full of the fury of the LORD.
[a]I am weary of holding *it* in.
"I will pour it out [b]on the children outside,
And on the assembly of young men together;
For even the husband shall be taken with the wife,
The aged with *him who is* full of days.
12 And [a]their houses shall be turned over to others,
Fields and wives together;
For I will stretch out My hand
Against the inhabitants of the land," says the LORD.
13 "Because from the least of them even to the greatest of them,
Everyone *is* given to [a]covetousness;
And from the prophet even to the [b]priest,
Everyone deals falsely.
14 They have also [a]healed the hurt of My people slightly,
[b]Saying, 'Peace, peace!'
When *there is* no peace.
15 Were they [a]ashamed when they had committed abomination?
No! They were not at all ashamed;
Nor did they know how to blush.
Therefore they shall fall among those who fall;
At the time I punish them,
They shall be cast down," says the LORD.

16 Thus says the LORD:

"Stand in the ways and see,
And ask for the [a]old paths, where the good way *is*,
And walk in it;
Then you will find [b]rest for your souls.
But they said, 'We will not walk *in it*.'
17 Also, I set [a]watchmen over you, *saying*,
[b]'Listen to the sound of the trumpet!'
But they said, 'We will not listen.'
18 Therefore hear, you nations,
And know, O congregation, what *is* among them.
19 [a]Hear, O earth!
Behold, I will certainly bring [b]calamity on this people—
[c]The fruit of their thoughts,
Because they have not heeded My words
Nor My law, but rejected it.
20 [a]For what purpose to Me
Comes frankincense [b]from Sheba,
And [c]sweet cane from a far country?
[d]Your burnt offerings *are* not acceptable,
Nor your sacrifices sweet to Me."

21 Therefore thus says the LORD:

"Behold, I will lay stumbling blocks before this people,
And the fathers and the sons together shall fall on them.
The neighbor and his friend shall perish."

22 Thus says the LORD:

"Behold, a people comes from the [a]north country,
And a great nation will be raised from the farthest parts of the earth.
23 They will lay hold on bow and spear;
They *are* cruel and have no mercy;
Their voice [a]roars like the sea;
And they ride on horses,
As men of war set in array against you,
O daughter of Zion."

24 We have heard the report of it;
Our hands grow feeble.

6:4 [a] Joel 3:9 [b] Jer. 15:8 6:7 [a] Is. 57:20 [b] Ps. 55:9 6:8 [a] Hos. 9:12 6:10 [a] [Acts 7:51] [b] Jer. 8:9; 20:8 6:11 [a] Jer. 20:9 [b] Jer. 9:21 6:12 [a] Deut. 28:30 6:13 [a] Is. 56:11; Jer. 8:10; 22:17 [b] Jer. 5:31; 23:11 6:14 [a] Jer. 8:11–15 [b] Jer. 4:10; 23:17 6:15 [a] Jer. 3:3; 8:12 6:16 [a] Jer. 18:15 [b] Matt. 11:29 6:17 [a] Hab. 2:1 [b] Deut. 4:1 6:19 [a] Is. 1:2 [b] Jer. 19:3, 15 [c] Prov. 1:31 6:20 [a] Mic. 6:6, 7 [b] Is. 60:6 [c] Is. 43:24 [d] Jer. 7:21–23 6:22 [a] Jer. 1:15; 10:22; 50:41–43 6:23 [a] Is. 5:30

[a]Anguish has taken hold of us,
Pain as of a woman in labor.
25 Do not go out into the field,
Nor walk by the way.
Because of the sword of the enemy,
Fear *is* on every side.
26 O daughter of my people,
[a]Dress in sackcloth
[b]And roll about in ashes!
[c]Make mourning *as for* an only son, most bitter lamentation;
For the plunderer will suddenly come upon us.

27 "I have set you *as* an assayer *and* [a]a fortress among My people,
That you may know and test their way.
28 [a]They *are* all stubborn rebels, [b]walking as slanderers.
*They are* [c]bronze and iron,
They *are* all corrupters;
29 The bellows blow fiercely,
The lead is consumed by the fire;
The smelter refines in vain,
For the wicked are not drawn off.
30 *People* will call them [a]rejected silver,
Because the LORD has rejected them."

### TRUSTING IN LYING WORDS

*(cf. Jer. 26:4–6)*

7 The word that came to Jeremiah from the
LORD, saying, 2 [a]"Stand in the gate of the
LORD's house, and proclaim there this word,
and say, 'Hear the word of the LORD, all *you of*
Judah who enter in at these gates to worship the
LORD!'" 3 Thus says the LORD of hosts, the God of
Israel: [a]"Amend your ways and your doings, and
I will cause you to dwell in this place. 4 [a]Do not
trust in these lying words, saying, 'The temple
of the LORD, the temple of the LORD, the temple
of the LORD *are* these.'

5 "For if you thoroughly amend your ways
and your doings, if you thoroughly [a]execute
judgment between a man and his neighbor, 6 *if*
you do not oppress the stranger, the fatherless,
and the widow, and do not shed innocent blood
in this place, [a]or walk after other gods to your
hurt, 7 [a]then I will cause you to dwell in this
place, in [b]the land that I gave to your fathers
forever and ever.

8 "Behold, you trust in [a]lying words that
cannot profit. 9 [a]Will you steal, murder, commit
adultery, swear falsely, burn incense to Baal, and
[b]walk after other gods whom you do not know,
10 [a]and *then* come and stand before Me in this
house [b]which is called by My name, and say,
'We are delivered to do all these abominations'?
11 Has [a]this house, which is called by My name,
become a [b]den of thieves in your eyes? Behold,
I, even I, have seen *it*," says the LORD.

### SEEING JESUS IN THE SCRIPTURE

**7:11** When Jesus entered the temple grounds and saw His Father's house of prayer turned into a place where merchants and money changers were exploiting the people, He quoted this verse (see Matt. 21:13).

12 "But go now to [a]My place which *was* in
Shiloh, [b]where I set My name at the first, and
see [c]what I did to it because of the wickedness
of My people Israel. 13 And now, because you
have done all these works," says the LORD, "and I
spoke to you, [a]rising up early and speaking, but
you did not hear, and I [b]called you, but you did
not answer, 14 therefore I will do to the house
which is called by My name, in which you trust,
and to this place which I gave to you and your fa-
thers, as I have done to [a]Shiloh. 15 And I will cast
you out of My sight, [a]as I have cast out all your
brethren—[b]the whole posterity of Ephraim.

16 "Therefore [a]do not pray for this people,
nor lift up a cry or prayer for them, nor make
intercession to Me; [b]for I will not hear you. 17 Do
you not see what they do in the cities of Judah
and in the streets of Jerusalem? 18 [a]The children
gather wood, the fathers kindle the fire, and
the women knead dough, to make cakes for
the queen of heaven; and *they* [b]pour out drink
offerings to other gods, that they may provoke
Me to anger. 19 [a]Do they provoke Me to anger?"
says the LORD. "*Do they* not *provoke* themselves,
to the shame of their own faces?"

**7:18** The **queen of heaven** refers to the goddess Ishtar, which was worshiped throughout the eastern Mediterranean region and Mesopotamia. Worship of Ishtar involved the preparation of special **cakes** that bore the goddess's image, as well as **drink offerings** (see Jer. 44:19). A family cooperating in the idolatrous worship of Ishtar stood in direct opposition to the covenant demands that a father instruct his children in the ways of the Lord (Deut. 6:4–9).

20 Therefore thus says the Lord GOD: "Be-
hold, My anger and My fury will be poured out

**6:24** [a] Jer. 4:31; 13:21; 49:24 **6:26** [a] Jer. 4:8 [b] Mic. 1:10 [c] [Zech. 12:10] **6:27** [a] Jer. 1:18 **6:28** [a] Jer. 5:23 [b] Jer. 9:4 [c] Ezek. 22:18 **6:30** [a] Is. 1:22 **7:2** [a] Jer. 17:19; 26:2 **7:3** [a] Jer. 4:1; 18:11; 26:13 **7:4** [a] Mic. 3:11 **7:5** [a] Jer. 21:12; 22:3 **7:6** [a] Deut. 6:14, 15 **7:7** [a] Deut. 4:40 [b] Jer. 3:18 **7:8** [a] Jer. 5:31; 14:13, 14 **7:9** [a] 1 Kin. 18:21 [b] Ex. 20:3 **7:10** [a] Ezek. 23:39 [b] Jer. 7:11, 14; 32:34; 34:15 **7:11** [a] Is. 56:7 [b] Matt. 21:13 **7:12** [a] Josh. 18:1 [b] Deut. 12:11 [c] 1 Sam. 4:10 **7:13** [a] 2 Chr. 36:15 [b] Prov. 1:24 **7:14** [a] 1 Sam. 4:10, 11 **7:15** [a] 2 Kin. 17:23 [b] Ps. 78:67 **7:16** [a] Ex. 32:10; Jer. 11:14 [b] Jer. 15:1 **7:18** [a] Jer. 44:17 [b] Jer. 19:13 **7:19** [a] Deut. 32:16, 21

on this place—on man and on beast, on the trees of the field and on the fruit of the ground. And it will burn and not be quenched."

21 Thus says the LORD of hosts, the God of Israel: [a]"Add your burnt offerings to your sacrifices and eat meat. 22 [a]For I did not speak to your fathers, or command them in the day that I brought them out of the land of Egypt, concerning burnt offerings or sacrifices. 23 But this is what I commanded them, saying, [a]'Obey My voice, and [b]I will be your God, and you shall be My people. And walk in all the ways that I have commanded you, that it may be well with you.' 24 [a]Yet they did not obey or incline their ear, but [b]followed the counsels *and* the dictates of their evil hearts, and [c]went backward and not forward. 25 Since the day that your fathers came out of the land of Egypt until this day, I have even [a]sent to you all My servants the prophets, daily rising up early and sending *them.* 26 [a]Yet they did not obey Me or incline their ear, but [b]stiffened their neck. [c]They did worse than their fathers.

27 "Therefore [a]you shall speak all these words to them, but they will not obey you. You shall also call to them, but they will not answer you.

### *JUDGMENT ON OBSCENE RELIGION*

28 "So you shall say to them, 'This *is* a nation that does not obey the voice of the LORD their God [a]nor receive correction. [b]Truth has perished and has been cut off from their mouth. 29 [a]Cut off your hair and cast *it* away, and take up a lamentation on the desolate heights; for the LORD has rejected and forsaken the generation of His wrath.' 30 For the children of Judah have done evil in My sight," says the LORD. [a]"They have set their abominations in the house which is called by My name, to pollute it. 31 And they have built the [a]high places of Tophet, which *is* in the Valley of the Son of Hinnom, to [b]burn their sons and their daughters in the fire, [c]which I did not command, nor did it come into My heart.

32 "Therefore behold, [a]the days are coming," says the LORD, "when it will no more be called Tophet, or the Valley of the Son of Hinnom, but the Valley of Slaughter; [b]for they will bury in Tophet until there is no room. 33 The [a]corpses of this people will be food for the birds of the heaven and for the beasts of the earth. And no one will frighten *them away.* 34 Then I will cause to [a]cease from the cities of Judah and from the streets of Jerusalem the voice of mirth and the voice of gladness, the voice of the bridegroom and the voice of the bride. For [b]the land shall be desolate.

**8** "At that time," says the LORD, "they shall bring out the bones of the kings of Judah, and the bones of its princes, and the bones of the priests, and the bones of the prophets, and the bones of the inhabitants of Jerusalem, out of their graves. 2 They shall spread them before the sun and the moon and all the host of heaven, which they have loved and which they have served and after which they have walked, which they have sought and [a]which they have worshiped. They shall not be gathered [b]nor buried; they shall be like refuse on the face of the earth. 3 Then [a]death shall be chosen rather than life by all the residue of those who remain of this evil family, who remain in all the places where I have driven them," says the LORD of hosts.

### *THE PERIL OF FALSE TEACHING*

4 "Moreover you shall say to them, 'Thus says the LORD:

"Will they fall and not rise?
Will one turn away and not return?
5 Why has this people [a]slidden back,
Jerusalem, in a perpetual backsliding?
[b]They hold fast to deceit,
[c]They refuse to return.
6 [a]I listened and heard,
*But* they do not speak aright.
[b]No man repented of his wickedness,
Saying, 'What have I done?'
Everyone turned to his own course,
As the horse rushes into the battle.

7 "Even [a]the stork in the heavens
Knows her appointed times;
And the turtledove, the swift, and the swallow
Observe the time of their coming.
But [b]My people do not know the judgment of the LORD.

8 "How can you say, 'We *are* wise,
[a]And the law of the LORD *is* with us'?
Look, the false pen of the scribe certainly works falsehood.
9 [a]The wise men are ashamed,
They are dismayed and taken.
Behold, they have rejected the word of the LORD;
So [b]what wisdom do they have?
10 Therefore [a]I will give their wives to others,
*And* their fields to those who will inherit *them;*
Because from the least even to the greatest
Everyone is given to [b]covetousness;
From the prophet even to the priest
Everyone deals falsely.
11 For they have [a]healed the hurt of the daughter of My people slightly,
Saying, [b]'Peace, peace!'
When *there is* no peace.

**7:21** [a]Jer. 6:20 **7:22** [a][Hos. 6:6] **7:23** [a]Deut. 6:3 [b][Ex. 19:5, 6] **7:24** [a]Ps. 81:11 [b]Deut. 29:19 [c]Jer. 32:33 **7:25** [a]2 Chr. 36:15 **7:26** [a]Jer. 11:8 [b]Neh. 9:17 [c]Jer. 16:12 **7:27** [a]Ezek. 2:7 **7:28** [a]Jer. 5:3 [b]Jer. 9:3 **7:29** [a]Mic. 1:16 **7:30** [a]Dan. 9:27; 11:31 **7:31** [a]2 Kin. 23:10 [b]Ps. 106:38 [c]Deut. 17:3 **7:32** [a]Jer. 19:6 [b]2 Kin. 23:10 **7:33** [a]Jer. 9:22; 19:11 **7:34** [a]Is. 24:7, 8 [b]Lev. 26:33 **8:2** [a]2 Kin. 23:5 [b]Jer. 22:19 **8:3** [a]Rev. 9:6 **8:5** [a]Jer. 7:24 [b]Jer. 9:6 [c]Jer. 5:3 **8:6** [a]Ps. 14:2 [b]Mic. 7:2 **8:7** [a]Song 2:12 [b]Jer. 5:4; 9:3 **8:8** [a]Rom. 2:17 **8:9** [a]Jer. 6:15 [b]Jer. 4:22 **8:10** [a]Deut. 28:30 [b]Is. 56:11; 57:17 **8:11** [a]Jer. 6:14 [b]Ezek. 13:10

12 Were they [a]ashamed when they had
committed abomination?
No! They were not at all ashamed,
Nor did they know how to blush.
Therefore they shall fall among those who
fall;
In the time of their punishment
They shall be cast down," says the LORD.

13 "I will surely consume them," says the LORD.
"No grapes *shall be* [a]on the vine,
Nor figs on the [b]fig tree,
And the leaf shall fade;
And *the things* I have given them shall
[c]pass away from them." ' "

14 "Why do we sit still?
[a]Assemble yourselves,
And let us enter the fortified cities,
And let us be silent there.
For the LORD our God has put us to silence
And given us [b]water of gall to drink,
Because we have sinned against the LORD.

15 "*We* [a]looked for peace, but no good *came;*
And for a time of health, and there was
trouble!
16 The snorting of His horses was heard
from [a]Dan.
The whole land trembled at the sound of
the neighing of His [b]strong ones;
For they have come and devoured the
land and all that is in it,
The city and those who dwell in it."

17 "For behold, I will send serpents among
you,
Vipers which cannot be [a]charmed,
And they shall bite you," says the LORD.

### *THE PROPHET MOURNS FOR THE PEOPLE*

18 I would comfort myself in sorrow;
My heart *is* faint in me.
19 Listen! The voice,
The cry of the daughter of my people
From [a]a far country:
"*Is* not the LORD in Zion?
*Is* not her King in her?"

"Why have they provoked Me to anger
With their carved images—
With foreign idols?"

20 "The harvest is past,
The summer is ended,
And we are not saved!"

21 [a]For the hurt of the daughter of my people
I am hurt.
I am [b]mourning;
Astonishment has taken hold of me.
22 *Is there* no [a]balm in Gilead,
*Is there* no physician there?
Why then is there no recovery
For the health of the daughter of my people?

9 Oh, [a]that my head were waters,
And my eyes a fountain of tears,
That I might weep day and night
For the slain of the daughter of my people!
2 Oh, that I had in the wilderness
A lodging place for travelers;
That I might leave my people,
And go from them!
For [a]they *are* all adulterers,
An assembly of treacherous men.

3 "And *like* their bow [a]they have bent their
tongues *for* lies.
They are not valiant for the truth on the
earth.
For they proceed from [b]evil to evil,
And they [c]do not know Me," says the LORD.
4 "Everyone[a] take heed to his neighbor,
And do not trust any brother;
For every brother will utterly supplant,
And every neighbor will [b]walk with
slanderers.
5 Everyone will [a]deceive his neighbor,
And will not speak the truth;
They have taught their tongue to speak lies;
They weary themselves to commit iniquity.
6 Your dwelling place *is* in the midst of deceit;
Through deceit they refuse to know Me,"
says the LORD.

7 Therefore thus says the LORD of hosts:

"Behold, [a]I will refine them and try them;
[b]For how shall I deal with the daughter of
My people?
8 Their tongue *is* an arrow shot out;
It speaks [a]deceit;
*One* speaks [b]peaceably to his neighbor
with his mouth,
But in his heart he lies in wait.
9 [a]Shall I not punish them for these *things?*"
says the LORD.
"Shall I not avenge Myself on such a nation
as this?"

10 I will take up a weeping and wailing for
the mountains,
And [a]for the dwelling places of the
wilderness a lamentation,
Because they are burned up,
So that no one can pass through;
Nor can *men* hear the voice of the cattle.

**8:12** [a] Jer. 3:3; 6:15 **8:13** [a] Joel 1:17 [b] Matt. 21:19 [c] Deut. 28:39, 40 **8:14** [a] Jer. 4:5 [b] Jer. 9:15 **8:15** [a] Jer. 14:19 **8:16** [a] Jer. 4:15 [b] Jer. 47:3 **8:17** [a] Ps. 58:4, 5 **8:19** [a] Is. 39:3 **8:21** [a] Jer. 9:1 [b] Joel 2:6 **8:22** [a] Jer. 46:11 **9:1** [a] Is. 22:4 **9:2** [a] Jer. 5:7, 8; 23:10 **9:3** [a] Ps. 64:3 [b] Jer. 4:22; 13:23 [c] 1 Sam. 2:12 **9:4** [a] Mic. 7:5, 6 [b] Jer. 6:28 **9:5** [a] Is. 59:4 **9:7** [a] Is. 1:25 [b] Hos. 11:8 **9:8** [a] Ps. 12:2 [b] Ps. 55:21 **9:9** [a] Jer. 5:9, 29 **9:10** [a] Hos. 4:3

[b]Both the birds of the heavens and the
beasts have fled;
They are gone.

11 "I will make Jerusalem [a]a heap of ruins, [b]a
den of jackals.
I will make the cities of Judah desolate,
without an inhabitant."

12 [a]Who *is* the wise man who may under-
stand this? And *who is he* to whom the mouth
of the LORD has spoken, that he may declare
it? Why does the land perish *and* burn up like
a wilderness, so that no one can pass through?
13 And the LORD said, "Because they have
forsaken My law which I set before them, and
have [a]not obeyed My voice, nor walked according
to it, 14 but they have [a]walked according to the
dictates of their own hearts and after the Baals,
[b]which their fathers taught them," 15 therefore
thus says the LORD of hosts, the God of Israel:
"Behold, I will [a]feed them, this people, [b]with
wormwood, and give them water of gall to drink.
16 I will [a]scatter them also among the Gentiles,
whom neither they nor their fathers have known.
[b]And I will send a sword after them until I have
consumed them."

### THE PEOPLE MOURN IN JUDGMENT

17 Thus says the LORD of hosts:

"Consider and call for [a]the mourning
women,
That they may come;
And send for skillful *wailing* women,
That they may come.
18 Let them make haste
And take up a wailing for us,
That [a]our eyes may run with tears,
And our eyelids gush with water.
19 For a voice of wailing is heard from Zion:
'How we are plundered!
We are greatly ashamed,
Because we have forsaken the land,
Because we have been cast out of [a]our
dwellings.' "

20 Yet hear the word of the LORD, O women,
And let your ear receive the word of His
mouth;
Teach your daughters wailing,
And everyone her neighbor a
lamentation.
21 For death has come through our windows,
Has entered our palaces,
To kill off [a]the children—*no longer to be*
outside!
*And* the young men—*no longer* on the
streets!

22 Speak, "Thus says the LORD:
'Even the carcasses of men shall fall [a]as
refuse on the open field,
Like cuttings after the harvester,
And no one shall gather *them.*' "

23 Thus says the LORD:

[a]"Let not the wise *man* glory in his wisdom,
Let not the mighty *man* glory in his [b]might,
Nor let the rich *man* glory in his riches;
24 But [a]let him who glories glory in this,
That he understands and knows Me,
That I *am* the LORD, exercising
lovingkindness, judgment, and
righteousness in the earth.
[b]For in these I delight," says the LORD.

25 "Behold, the days are coming," says the
LORD, "that [a]I will punish all *who are* circumcised
with the uncircumcised— 26 Egypt, Judah, Edom,
the people of Ammon, Moab, and all *who are* in
the [a]farthest corners, who dwell in the wilderness.
For all *these* nations *are* uncircumcised, and all the
house of Israel *are* [b]uncircumcised in the heart."

### IDOLS AND THE TRUE GOD

10 Hear the word which the LORD speaks to
you, O house of Israel.
2 Thus says the LORD:

[a]"Do not learn the way of the Gentiles;
Do not be dismayed at the signs of heaven,
For the Gentiles are dismayed at them.
3 For the customs of the peoples *are* futile;
For [a]*one* cuts a tree from the forest,
The work of the hands of the workman,
with the ax.
4 They decorate it with silver and gold;
They [a]fasten it with nails and hammers
So that it will not topple.
5 They *are* upright, like a palm tree,
And [a]they cannot speak;
They must be [b]carried,
Because they cannot go *by themselves.*
Do not be afraid of them,
For [c]they cannot do evil,
Nor can they do any good."

6 Inasmuch as *there is* none [a]like You, O LORD
(You *are* great, and Your name *is* great in
might),
7 [a]Who would not fear You, O King of the
nations?
For this is Your rightful due.
For [b]among all the wise *men* of the nations,
And in all their kingdoms,
*There is* none like You.

9:10 [b]Jer. 4:25 9:11 [a]Is. 25:2 [b]Is. 13:22; 34:13 9:12 [a]Hos. 14:9 9:13 [a]Jer. 3:25; 7:24 9:14 [a]Jer. 7:24; 11:8 [b]Gal. 1:14 9:15 [a]Ps. 80:5 [b]Lam. 3:15 9:16 [a]Lev. 26:33 [b]Ezek. 5:2 9:17 [a]2 Chr. 35:25 9:18 [a]Jer. 9:1; 14:17 9:19 [a]Lev. 18:28 9:21 [a]Jer. 6:11; 18:21 9:22 [a]Jer. 8:1, 2 9:23 [a][Eccl. 9:11] [b]Ps. 33:16–18 9:24 [a]1 Cor. 1:31 [b]Mic. 7:18 9:25 [a][Rom. 2:28, 29] 9:26 [a]Jer. 25:23 [b][Rom. 2:28] 10:2 [a][Lev. 18:3; 20:23] 10:3 [a]Is. 40:19; 45:20 10:4 [a]Is. 41:7 10:5 [a]Ps. 115:5 [b]Ps. 115:7 [c]Is. 41:23, 24 10:6 [a]Ex. 15:11 10:7 [a]Rev. 15:4 [b]Ps. 89:6

8 But they are altogether [a]dull-hearted and
foolish;
A wooden idol *is* a worthless doctrine.
9 Silver is beaten into plates;
It is brought from Tarshish,
And [a]gold from Uphaz,
The work of the craftsman
And of the hands of the metalsmith;
Blue and purple *are* their clothing;
They *are* all [b]the work of skillful *men*.
10 But the LORD *is* the true God;
He *is* [a]the living God and the [b]everlasting
King.
At His wrath the earth will tremble,
And the nations will not be able to endure
His indignation.

11 Thus you shall say to them: [a]"The gods
that have not made the heavens and the earth
[b]shall perish from the earth and from under
these heavens."

12 He [a]has made the earth by His power,
He has [b]established the world by His
wisdom,
And [c]has stretched out the heavens at His
discretion.
13 [a]When He utters His voice,
*There is* a multitude of waters in the heavens:
[b]"And He causes the vapors to ascend from
the ends of the earth.
He makes lightning for the rain,
He brings the wind out of His treasuries."[1]
14 [a]Everyone is [b]dull-hearted, without
knowledge;
[c]Every metalsmith is put to shame by an
image;
[d]For his molded image *is* falsehood,
And *there is* no breath in them.
15 They *are* futile, a work of errors;
In the time of their punishment they shall
perish.
16 [a]The Portion of Jacob *is* not like them,
For He *is* the Maker of all *things*,
And [b]Israel *is* the tribe of His inheritance;
[c]The LORD of hosts *is* His name.

### THE COMING CAPTIVITY OF JUDAH

17 [a]Gather up your wares from the land,
O inhabitant of the fortress!
18 For thus says the LORD:

"Behold, I will [a]throw out at this time
The inhabitants of the land,
And will distress them,
[b]That they may find *it so*."

19 [a]Woe is me for my hurt!
My wound is severe.
But I say, [b]"Truly this *is* an infirmity,
And [c]I must bear it."
20 [a]My tent is plundered,
And all my cords are broken;
My children have gone from me,
And they *are* [b]no more.
*There is* no one to pitch my tent anymore,
Or set up my curtains.

21 For the shepherds have become
dull-hearted,
And have not sought the LORD;
Therefore they shall not prosper,
And all their flocks shall be [a]scattered.
22 Behold, the noise of the report has come,
And a great commotion out of the [a]north
country,
To make the cities of Judah desolate, a
[b]den of jackals.

**10:22 Jackals** were dog-like desert creatures that fed on garbage. They were especially unpopular with the Israelites not only because they destroyed crops, but also because they were filthy scavengers.

23 O LORD, I know the [a]way of man *is* not in
himself;
*It is* not in man who walks to direct his
own steps.
24 O LORD, [a]correct me, but with justice;
Not in Your anger, lest You bring me to
nothing.
25 [a]Pour out Your fury on the Gentiles, [b]who
do not know You,
And on the families who do not call on
Your name;
For they have eaten up Jacob,
[c]Devoured him and consumed him,
And made his dwelling place desolate.

### THE BROKEN COVENANT

11 The word that came to Jeremiah from the
LORD, saying, 2 "Hear the words of this cov-
enant, and speak to the men of Judah and to
the inhabitants of Jerusalem; 3 and say to them,
'Thus says the LORD God of Israel: [a]"Cursed *is*
the man who does not obey the words of this
covenant 4 which I commanded your fathers in
the day I brought them out of the land of Egypt,
[a]from the iron furnace, saying, [b]'Obey My voice,
and do according to all that I command you; so
shall you be My people, and I will be your God,'

**10:8** [a] Hab. 2:18 **10:9** [a] Dan. 10:5 [b] Ps. 115:4 **10:10** [a] 1 Tim. 6:17 [b] Ps. 10:16 **10:11** [a] Ps. 96:5 [b] Zeph. 2:11 **10:12** [a] Jer. 51:15 [b] Ps. 93:1 [c] Job 9:8 **10:13** [a] Job 38:34 [b] Ps. 135:7 [1] Psalm 135:7 **10:14** [a] Jer. 51:17 [b] Prov. 30:2 [c] Is. 42:17; 44:11 [d] Hab. 2:18 **10:16** [a] Lam. 3:24 [b] Deut. 32:9 [c] Is. 47:4 **10:17** [a] Jer. 6:1 **10:18** [a] 1 Sam. 25:29 [b] Ezek. 6:10 **10:19** [a] Jer. 8:21 [b] Ps. 77:10 [c] Mic. 7:9 **10:20** [a] Jer. 4:20 [b] Jer. 31:15 **10:21** [a] Jer. 23:2 **10:22** [a] Jer. 5:15 [b] Jer. 9:11 **10:23** [a] Prov. 16:1; 20:24 **10:24** [a] Jer. 30:11 **10:25** [a] Ps. 79:6, 7 [b] Job 18:21 [c] Jer. 8:16 **11:3** [a] Deut. 27:26 **11:4** [a] Deut. 4:20 [b] Lev. 26:3

LIVE THE TRUTH

## FULFILLING YOUR PURPOSE

**11:1–5** Few things are more energizing than having a purpose in life. When we have a goal beyond ourselves, it can focus us, enliven us, and bring us joy. What, then, should be our purpose? The Bible consistently teaches our purpose is to bring glory to God. Whatever we do, we should ultimately do it for God and not ourselves. As followers of Jesus, we should submit to God each day, and delight in living for our Maker who loves us.

Sometimes, fulfilling our purpose in glorifying God isn't easy. Here, God commanded Jeremiah to deliver a harsh message to His people: God was going to discipline the Israelites. When Jeremiah brought God words to the people, they plotted to kill him. No matter, Jeremiah continued obeying God even when it was difficult. His obedience brought God glory, and his words to the people brought hope, even if they weren't what they wanted to hear. Our calling is the same—we are to listen to God's words and follow them, even when it's difficult. Our obedience and trust in God can bring great hope to others, even when we don't realize it. It starts when we live for God's purpose and not our own.

5 that I may establish the [a]oath which I have sworn to your fathers, to give them [b]'a land flowing with milk and honey,'[1] as *it is* this day." ' "

And I answered and said, "So be it, LORD."

6 Then the LORD said to me, "Proclaim all these words in the cities of Judah and in the streets of Jerusalem, saying: 'Hear the words of this covenant [a]and do them. 7 For I earnestly exhorted your fathers in the day I brought them up out of the land of Egypt, until this day, [a]rising early and exhorting, saying, "Obey My voice." 8 [a]Yet they did not obey or incline their ear, but [b]everyone followed the dictates of his evil heart; therefore I will bring upon them all the words of this covenant, which I commanded *them* to do, but *which* they have not done.' "

9 And the LORD said to me, [a]"A conspiracy has been found among the men of Judah and among the inhabitants of Jerusalem. 10 They have turned back to [a]the iniquities of their forefathers who refused to hear My words, and they have gone after other gods to serve them; the house of Israel and the house of Judah have broken My covenant which I made with their fathers."

11 Therefore thus says the LORD: "Behold, I will surely bring calamity on them which they will not be able to escape; and [a]though they cry out to Me, I will not listen to them. 12 Then the cities of Judah and the inhabitants of Jerusalem will go and [a]cry out to the gods to whom they offer incense, but they will not save them at all in the time of their trouble. 13 For *according to* the number of your [a]cities were your gods, O Judah; and *according to* the number of the streets of Jerusalem you have set up altars to *that* shameful thing, altars to burn incense to Baal.

14 "So [a]do not pray for this people, or lift up a cry or prayer for them; for I will not hear *them* in the time that they cry out to Me because of their trouble.

15 "What[a] has My beloved to do in My house,
Having [b]done lewd deeds with many?
And [c]the holy flesh has passed from you.
When you do evil, then you [d]rejoice.
16 The LORD called your name,
[a]Green Olive Tree, Lovely *and* of Good Fruit.
With the noise of a great tumult
He has kindled fire on it,
And its branches are broken.

17 "For the LORD of hosts, [a]who planted you, has pronounced doom against you for the evil of the house of Israel and of the house of Judah, which they have done against themselves to provoke Me to anger in offering incense to Baal."

### *JEREMIAH'S LIFE THREATENED*

18 Now the LORD gave me knowledge *of it,* and I know *it;* for You showed me their doings. 19 But I *was* like a docile lamb brought to the slaughter; and I did not know that they had devised schemes against me, *saying,* "Let us destroy the tree with its fruit, [a]and let us cut him off from [b]the land of the living, that his name may be remembered no more."

20 But, O LORD of hosts,
You who judge righteously,
[a]Testing the mind and the heart,
Let me see Your [b]vengeance on them,
For to You I have revealed my cause.

21 "Therefore thus says the LORD concerning the men of [a]Anathoth who seek your life, saying, [b]'Do not prophesy in the name of the LORD, lest you die by our hand'— 22 therefore thus says the LORD of hosts: 'Behold, I will punish them.

**11:5** [a] Ps. 105:9 [b] Ex. 3:8 [1] Exodus 3:8 **11:6** [a] [Rom. 2:13] **11:7** [a] Jer. 35:15 **11:8** [a] Jer. 7:26 [b] Jer. 13:10 **11:9** [a] Ezek. 22:25 **11:10** [a] Ezek. 20:18 **11:11** [a] Prov. 1:28 **11:12** [a] Deut. 32:37 **11:13** [a] Jer. 2:28 **11:14** [a] Ex. 32:10 **11:15** [a] Ps. 50:16 [b] Ezek. 16:25 [c] [Titus 1:15] [d] Prov. 2:14 **11:16** [a] Ps. 52:8 **11:17** [a] Is. 5:2 **11:19** [a] Ps. 83:4 [b] Ps. 27:13 **11:20** [a] Ps. 7:9 [b] Jer. 15:15 **11:21** [a] Jer. 1:1; 12:5, 6 [b] Mic. 2:6

The young men shall die by the sword, their sons and their daughters shall [a]die by famine;
23 and there shall be no remnant of them, for I will bring catastrophe on the men of Anathoth, *even* [a]the year of their punishment.' "

### JEREMIAH'S QUESTION

12 Righteous [a]*are* You, O LORD, when I plead with You;
Yet let me talk with You about *Your* judgments.
[b]Why does the way of the wicked prosper?
*Why* are those happy who deal so treacherously?
2 You have planted them, yes, they have taken root;
They grow, yes, they bear fruit.
[a]You *are* near in their mouth
But far from their mind.

3 But You, O LORD, [a]know me;
You have seen me,
And You have [b]tested my heart toward You.
Pull them out like sheep for the slaughter,
And prepare them for [c]the day of slaughter.
4 How long will [a]the land mourn,
And the herbs of every field wither?
[b]The beasts and birds are consumed,
[c]For the wickedness of those who dwell there,
Because they said, "He will not see our final end."

### THE LORD ANSWERS JEREMIAH

5 "If you have run with the footmen, and they have wearied you,
Then how can you contend with horses?
And *if* in the land of peace,
*In which* you trusted, *they wearied you,*
Then how will you do in [a]the floodplain[1] of the Jordan?

> **12:5** Traveling the **floodplain of the Jordan** River would have been extremely difficult. It was overgrown with shrubs, brush, trees, and vines, and wild animals attacking was a constant threat.

6 For even [a]your brothers, the house of your father,
Even they have dealt treacherously with you;
Yes, they have called a multitude after you.
[b]Do not believe them,
Even though they speak smooth words to you.

7 "I have forsaken My house, I have left My heritage;
I have given the dearly beloved of My soul into the hand of her enemies.
8 My heritage is to Me like a lion in the forest;
It cries out against Me;
Therefore I have [a]hated it.
9 My heritage *is* to Me *like* a speckled vulture;
The vultures all around *are* against her.
Come, assemble all the beasts of the field,
[a]Bring them to devour!

10 "Many [a]rulers[1] have destroyed [b]My vineyard,
They have [c]trodden My portion underfoot;
They have made My pleasant portion a desolate wilderness.
11 They have made it [a]desolate;
Desolate, it mourns to Me;
The whole land is made desolate,
Because [b]no one takes *it* to heart.
12 The plunderers have come
On all the desolate heights in the wilderness,
For the sword of the LORD shall devour
From *one* end of the land to the *other* end of the land;
No flesh shall have peace.
13 [a]They have sown wheat but reaped thorns;
They have put themselves to pain *but* do not profit.
But be ashamed of your harvest
Because of the fierce anger of the LORD."

14 Thus says the LORD: "Against all My evil
neighbors who [a]touch the inheritance which
I have caused My people Israel to inherit—
behold, I will [b]pluck them out of their land and
pluck out the house of Judah from among them.
15 [a]Then it shall be, after I have plucked them out,
that I will return and have compassion on them
[b]and bring them back, everyone to his heritage
and everyone to his land. 16 And it shall be, if they
will learn carefully the ways of My people, [a]to
swear by My name, 'As the LORD lives,' as they
taught My people to swear by Baal, then they
shall be [b]established in the midst of My people.
17 But if they do not [a]obey, I will utterly pluck up
and destroy that nation," says the LORD.

### SYMBOL OF THE LINEN SASH

13 Thus the LORD said to me: "Go and get
yourself a linen sash, and put it around
your waist, but do not put it in water." 2 So I got
a sash according to the word of the LORD, and
put *it* around my waist.
3 And the word of the LORD came to me the
second time, saying, 4 "Take the sash that you

**11:22** [a]Jer. 9:21 **11:23** [a]Jer. 23:12 **12:1** [a]Ps. 51:4 [b]Mal. 3:15 **12:2** [a]Matt. 15:8 **12:3** [a]Ps. 17:3 [b]Jer. 11:20 [c]James 5:5 **12:4** [a]Hos. 4:3 [b]Jer. 9:10 [c]Ps. 107:34 **12:5** [a]Josh. 3:15 [1]Or *thicket* **12:6** [a]Jer. 9:4, 5 [b]Prov. 26:25 **12:8** [a]Hos. 9:15 **12:9** [a]Lev. 26:22 **12:10** [a]Jer. 6:3; 23:1 [b]Is. 5:1–7 [c]Is. 63:18 [1]Literally *shepherds* or *pastors* **12:11** [a]Jer. 10:22; 22:6 [b]Is. 42:25 **12:13** [a]Hag. 1:6 **12:14** [a]Zech. 2:8 [b]Deut. 30:3 **12:15** [a]Ezek. 28:25 [b]Amos 9:14 **12:16** [a][Jer. 4:2] [b][1 Pet. 2:5] **12:17** [a]Is. 60:12

acquired, which *is* around your waist, and arise,
go to the Euphrates,[1] and hide it there in a hole in
the rock." 5 So I went and hid it by the Euphrates,
as the LORD commanded me.
6 Now it came to pass after many days that
the LORD said to me, "Arise, go to the Euphra-
tes, and take from there the sash which I com-
manded you to hide there." 7 Then I went to the
Euphrates and dug, and I took the sash from
the place where I had hidden it; and there was
the sash, ruined. It was profitable for nothing.
8 Then the word of the LORD came to me,
saying, 9 "Thus says the LORD: 'In this manner [a]I
will ruin the pride of Judah and the great [b]pride
of Jerusalem. 10 This evil people, who [a]refuse to
hear My words, who [b]follow the dictates of their
hearts, and walk after other gods to serve them
and worship them, shall be just like this sash
which is profitable for nothing. 11 For as the sash
clings to the waist of a man, so I have caused
the whole house of Israel and the whole house
of Judah to cling to Me,' says the LORD, 'that
[a]they may become My people, [b]for renown, for
praise, and for [c]glory; but they would [d]not hear.'

### *SYMBOL OF THE WINE BOTTLES*

12 "Therefore you shall speak to them this
word: 'Thus says the LORD God of Israel: "Every
bottle shall be filled with wine." '

"And they will say to you, 'Do we not certainly
know that every bottle will be filled with wine?'
13 "Then you shall say to them, 'Thus says
the LORD: "Behold, I will fill all the inhabitants
of this land—even the kings who sit on David's
throne, the priests, the prophets, and all the
inhabitants of Jerusalem—[a]with drunkenness!
14 And [a]I will dash them one against another,
even the fathers and the sons together," says the
LORD. "I will not pity nor spare nor have mercy,
but will destroy them." ' "

### *PRIDE PRECEDES CAPTIVITY*

15 Hear and give ear:
Do not be proud,
For the LORD has spoken.
16 [a]Give glory to the LORD your God
Before He causes [b]darkness,
And before your feet stumble
On the dark mountains,
And while you are [c]looking for light,
He turns it into [d]the shadow of death
*And* makes *it* dense darkness.
17 But if you will not hear it,
My soul will [a]weep in secret for *your*
pride;
My eyes will weep bitterly
And run down with tears,
Because the LORD's flock has been taken
captive.

18 Say to [a]the king and to the queen mother,
"Humble yourselves;
Sit down,
For your rule shall collapse, the crown of
your glory."
19 The cities of the South shall be shut up,
And no one shall open *them;*
Judah shall be carried away captive, all of it;
It shall be wholly carried away captive.

20 Lift up your eyes and see
Those who come from the [a]north.
Where *is* the flock *that* was given to you,
Your beautiful sheep?
21 What will you say when He punishes you?
For you have taught them
*To be* chieftains, to be head over you.
Will not [a]pangs seize you,
Like a woman in labor?
22 And if you say in your heart,
[a]"Why have these things come upon me?"
For the greatness of your iniquity
[b]Your skirts have been uncovered,
Your heels made bare.
23 Can the Ethiopian change his skin or the
leopard its spots?
*Then* may you also do good who are
accustomed to do evil.

24 "Therefore I will [a]scatter them [b]like stubble
That passes away by the wind of the
wilderness.
25 [a]This is your lot,
The portion of your measures from Me,"
says the LORD,
"Because you have forgotten Me
And trusted in [b]falsehood.
26 Therefore [a]I will uncover your skirts over
your face,
That your shame may appear.
27 I have seen your adulteries
And your *lustful* [a]neighings,
The lewdness of your harlotry,
Your abominations [b]on the hills in the
fields.
Woe to you, O Jerusalem!
Will you still not be made clean?"

### *SWORD, FAMINE, AND PESTILENCE*

**14** The word of the LORD that came to Jere-
miah concerning the droughts.

2 "Judah mourns,
And [a]her gates languish;
They [b]mourn for the land,
And [c]the cry of Jerusalem has gone up.
3 Their nobles have sent their lads for water;
They went to the cisterns *and* found no
water.

13:4 [1] Hebrew *Perath* 13:9 [a] Lev. 26:19 [b] Zeph. 3:11 13:10 [a] Jer. 16:12 [b] Jer. 7:24; 16:12 13:11 [a] [Ex. 19:5, 6] [b] Jer. 33:9 [c] Is. 43:21 [d] Jer. 7:13, 24, 26 13:13 [a] Is. 51:17; 63:6 13:14 [a] Jer. 19:9–11 13:16 [a] Josh. 7:19 [b] Amos 8:9 [c] Is. 59:9 [d] Ps. 44:19 13:17 [a] Jer. 9:1; 14:17 13:18 [a] Jer. 22:26 13:20 [a] Jer. 10:22; 46:20 13:21 [a] Jer. 6:24 13:22 [a] Jer. 16:10 [b] Is. 47:2 13:24 [a] Jer. 9:16 [b] Hos. 13:3 13:25 [a] Job 20:29 [b] Jer. 10:14 13:26 [a] Lam. 1:8 13:27 [a] Jer. 5:7, 8 [b] Is. 65:7; Ezek. 6:13 14:2 [a] Is. 3:26 [b] Jer. 8:21 [c] 1 Sam. 5:12

They returned with their vessels empty;
They were [a]ashamed and confounded
[b]And covered their heads.
4 Because the ground is parched,
For there was [a]no rain in the land,
The plowmen were ashamed;
They covered their heads.
5 Yes, the deer also gave birth in the field,
But left because there was no grass.
6 And [a]the wild donkeys stood in the desolate heights;
They sniffed at the wind like jackals;
Their eyes failed because *there was* no grass."

7 O LORD, though our iniquities testify against us,
Do it [a]for Your name's sake;
For our backslidings are many,
We have sinned against You.
8 [a]O the Hope of Israel, his Savior in time of trouble,
Why should You be like a stranger in the land,
And like a traveler *who* turns aside to tarry for a night?
9 Why should You be like a man astonished,
Like a mighty one [a]*who* cannot save?
Yet You, O LORD, [b]*are* in our midst,
And we are called by Your name;
Do not leave us!

10 Thus says the LORD to this people:

[a]"Thus they have loved to wander;
They have not restrained their feet.
Therefore the LORD does not accept them;
[b]He will remember their iniquity now,
And punish their sins."

11 Then the LORD said to me, [a]"Do not pray
for this people, for *their* good. 12 [a]When they
fast, I will not hear their cry; and [b]when they
offer burnt offering and grain offering, I will
not accept them. But [c]I will consume them by
the sword, by the famine, and by the pestilence."
13 [a]Then I said, "Ah, Lord GOD! Behold, the
prophets say to them, 'You shall not see the
sword, nor shall you have famine, but I will give
you assured [b]peace in this place.' "
14 And the LORD said to me, [a]"The prophets
prophesy lies in My name. [b]I have not sent them,
commanded them, nor spoken to them; they
prophesy to you a false vision, divination, a worth-
less thing, and the [c]deceit of their heart. 15 There-
fore thus says the LORD concerning the prophets
who prophesy in My name, whom I did not send,
[a]and who say, 'Sword and famine shall not be in
this land'—'By sword and famine those prophets
shall be consumed! 16 And the people to whom
they prophesy shall be cast out in the streets of
Jerusalem because of the famine and the sword;
[a]they will have no one to bury them—them nor
their wives, their sons nor their daughters—for
I will pour their wickedness on them.'
17 "Therefore you shall say this word to them:

[a]'Let my eyes flow with tears night and day,
And let them not cease;
[b]For the virgin daughter of my people
Has been broken with a mighty stroke, with a very severe blow.
18 If I go out to [a]the field,
Then behold, those slain with the sword!
And if I enter the city,
Then behold, those sick from famine!
Yes, both prophet and [b]priest go about in a land they do not know.' "

### THE PEOPLE PLEAD FOR MERCY

19 [a]Have You utterly rejected Judah?
Has Your soul loathed Zion?
Why have You stricken us so that [b]*there is* no healing for us?
[c]We looked for peace, but *there was* no good;
And for the time of healing, and there was trouble.
20 We acknowledge, O LORD, our wickedness
*And* the iniquity of our [a]fathers,
For [b]we have sinned against You.
21 Do not abhor *us*, for Your name's sake;
Do not disgrace the throne of Your glory.
[a]Remember, do not break Your covenant with us.
22 [a]Are there any among [b]the idols of the nations that can cause [c]rain?
Or can the heavens give showers?
[d]*Are* You not He, O LORD our God?
Therefore we will wait for You,
Since You have made all these.

### THE LORD WILL NOT RELENT

15 Then the LORD said to me, [a]"*Even* if [b]Moses
and [c]Samuel stood before Me, My mind
*would* not *be* favorable toward this people. Cast
*them* out of My sight, and let them go forth. 2 And
it shall be, if they say to you, 'Where should we
go?' then you shall tell them, 'Thus says the
LORD:

[a]"Such as *are* for death, to death;
And such as *are* for the sword, to the sword;
And such as *are* for the famine, to the famine;
And such as *are* for the [b]captivity, to the captivity." '

14:3 [a]Ps. 40:14 [b]2 Sam. 15:30 14:4 [a]Jer. 3:3 14:6 [a]Jer. 2:24 14:7 [a]Ps. 25:11 14:8 [a]Jer. 17:13 14:9 [a]Is. 59:1 [b]Ex. 29:45 14:10 [a]Jer. 2:23–25 [b]Hos. 8:13 14:11 [a]Ex. 32:10 14:12 [a]Ezek. 8:18 [b]Jer. 6:20 [c]Jer. 9:16 14:13 [a]Jer. 4:10 [b]Jer. 8:11; 23:17 14:14 [a]Jer. 27:10 [b]Jer. 29:8, 9 [c]Jer. 23:16 14:15 [a]Ezek. 14:10 14:16 [a]Ps. 79:2, 3 14:17 [a]Jer. 9:1; 13:17 [b]Jer. 8:21 14:18 [a]Ezek. 7:15 [b]Jer. 23:11 14:19 [a]Lam. 5:22 [b]Jer. 15:18 [c]Jer. 8:15 14:20 [a]Jer. 3:25 [b]Dan. 9:8 14:21 [a]Ps. 106:45 14:22 [a]Zech. 10:1 [b]Deut. 32:21 [c]Jer. 5:24 [d]Ps. 135:7 15:1 [a]Ezek. 14:14 [b]Ex. 32:11–14 [c]1 Sam. 7:9 15:2 [a]Zech. 11:9 [b]Jer. 9:16; 16:13

3 "And I will [a]appoint over them four forms
*of destruction,"* says the LORD: "the sword to slay,
the dogs to drag, [b]the birds of the heavens and the
beasts of the earth to devour and destroy. 4 I will
hand them over to [a]trouble, to all kingdoms of
the earth, because of [b]Manasseh the son of Heze-
kiah, king of Judah, for what he did in Jerusalem.

> **15:4** Of all the kings of Judah, **Manasseh** was the most evil. He was unbelievably wicked, even sacrificing his own son to the pagan god Molech.

5 "For who will have pity on you, O Jerusalem?
Or who will bemoan you?
Or who will turn aside to ask how you are
doing?
6 [a]You have forsaken Me," says the LORD,
"You have [b]gone backward.
Therefore I will stretch out My hand
against you and destroy you;
[c]I am weary of relenting!
7 And I will winnow them with a winnowing
fan in the gates of the land;
I will [a]bereave *them* of children;
I will destroy My people,
*Since* they [b]do not return from their ways.
8 Their widows will be increased to Me
more than the sand of the seas;
I will bring against them,
Against the mother of the young men,
A plunderer at noonday;
I will cause anguish and terror to fall on
them [a]suddenly.

9 "She[a] languishes who has borne seven;
She has breathed her last;
[b]Her sun has gone down
While *it was* yet day;
She has been ashamed and confounded.
And the remnant of them I will deliver to
the sword
Before their enemies," says the LORD.

### JEREMIAH'S DEJECTION

10 [a]Woe is me, my mother,
That you have borne me,
A man of strife and a man of contention
to the whole earth!
I have neither lent for interest,
Nor have men lent to me for interest.
Every one of them curses me.

11 The LORD said:

"Surely it will be well with your remnant;
Surely I will cause [a]the enemy to
intercede with you
In the time of adversity and in the time of
affliction.
12 Can anyone break iron,
The northern iron and the bronze?
13 Your wealth and your treasures
I will give as [a]plunder without price,
Because of all your sins,
Throughout your territories.
14 And I will make *you* cross over with[1] your
enemies
[a]Into a land *which* you do not know;
For a [b]fire is kindled in My anger,
*Which* shall burn upon you."

15 O LORD, [a]You know;
Remember me and visit me,
And [b]take vengeance for me on my
persecutors.
In Your enduring patience, do not take
me away.
Know that [c]for Your sake I have suffered
rebuke.
16 Your words were found, and I [a]ate them,
And [b]Your word was to me the joy and
rejoicing of my heart;
For I am called by Your name,
O LORD God of hosts.

> **15:16** "Eating" the Lord's **words** meant to internalize them and allow their meaning to become a reality in one's life.

17 [a]I did not sit in the assembly of the
mockers,
Nor did I rejoice;
I sat alone because of Your hand,
For You have filled me with indignation.
18 Why is my [a]pain perpetual
And my wound incurable,
*Which* refuses to be healed?
Will You surely be to me [b]like an
unreliable stream,
*As* waters *that* fail?

### THE LORD REASSURES JEREMIAH

19 Therefore thus says the LORD:

[a]"If you return,
Then I will bring you back;
You shall [b]stand before Me;
If you [c]take out the precious from the vile,
You shall be as My mouth.
Let them return to you,
But you must not return to them.

15:3 [a] Ezek. 14:21 [b] Jer. 7:33 15:4 [a] Deut. 28:25 [b] 2 Kin. 24:3, 4 15:6 [a] Jer. 2:13 [b] Jer. 7:24 [c] Jer. 20:16 15:7 [a] Jer. 18:21 [b] Is. 9:13 15:8 [a] Is. 29:5 15:9 [a] 1 Sam. 2:5 [b] Amos 8:9 15:10 [a] Job 3:1 15:11 [a] Jer. 40:4, 5 15:13 [a] Ps. 44:12 15:14 [a] Jer. 16:13 [b] Deut. 32:22 [1] Following Masoretic Text and Vulgate; Septuagint, Syriac, and Targum read *cause you to serve* (compare 17:4). 15:15 [a] Jer. 12:3 [b] Jer. 20:12 [c] Ps. 69:7–9 15:16 [a] Ezek. 3:1, 3 [b] [Job 23:12] 15:17 [a] Ps. 26:4, 5 15:18 [a] Jer. 10:19; 30:15 [b] Job 6:15 15:19 [a] Zech. 3:7 [b] Jer. 15:1 [c] Ezek. 22:26; 44:23

20 And I will make you to this people a
fortified bronze [a]wall;
And they will fight against you,
But [b]they shall not prevail against you;
For I *am* with you to save you
And deliver you," says the LORD.
21 "I will deliver you from the hand of the
wicked,
And I will redeem you from the grip of
the terrible."

### JEREMIAH'S LIFESTYLE AND MESSAGE

16 The word of the LORD also came to me,
saying, 2 "You shall not take a wife, nor
shall you have sons or daughters in this place."
3 For thus says the LORD concerning the sons
and daughters who are born in this place, and
concerning their mothers who bore them and
their fathers who begot them in this land: 4 "They
shall die [a]gruesome deaths; they shall not be
[b]lamented nor shall they be [c]buried, *but* they
shall be [d]like refuse on the face of the earth.
They shall be consumed by the sword and by
famine, and their [e]corpses shall be meat for the
birds of heaven and for the beasts of the earth."
5 For thus says the LORD: [a]"Do not enter the
house of mourning, nor go to lament or bemoan
them; for I have taken away My peace from this
people," says the LORD, "lovingkindness and
mercies. 6 Both the great and the small shall die in
this land. They shall not be buried; [a]neither shall
men lament for them, [b]cut themselves, nor [c]make
themselves bald for them. 7 Nor shall *men* break
*bread* in mourning for them, to comfort them
for the dead; nor shall *men* give them the cup
of consolation to [a]drink for their father or their
mother. 8 Also you shall not go into the house
of feasting to sit with them, to eat and drink."
9 For thus says the LORD of hosts, the God of
Israel: "Behold, [a]I will cause to cease from this
place, before your eyes and in your days, the
voice of mirth and the voice of gladness, the voice
of the bridegroom and the voice of the bride.
10 "And it shall be, when you show this people
all these words, and they say to you, [a]'Why has
the LORD pronounced all this great disaster
against us? Or what *is* our iniquity? Or what *is*
our sin that we have committed against the LORD
our God?' 11 then you shall say to them, [a]'Because
your fathers have forsaken Me,' says the LORD;
'they have walked after other gods and have
served them and worshiped them, and have
forsaken Me and not kept My law. 12 And you have
done [a]worse than your fathers, for behold, [b]each
one follows the dictates of his own evil heart,
so that no one listens to Me. 13 [a]Therefore I will
cast you out of this land [b]into a land that you
do not know, neither you nor your fathers; and

> **16:13** When Jerusalem was conquered by Babylon in 586 BC, the Jewish people who were taken captive were taught a whole new way of life, including new religions and new customs. The Jews were held captive for seventy years.

there you shall serve other gods day and night,
where I will not show you favor.'

### GOD WILL RESTORE ISRAEL

*(cf. Jer. 23:7, 8)*

14 "Therefore behold, the [a]days are coming,"
says the LORD, "that it shall no more be said, 'The
LORD lives who brought up the children of Israel
from the land of Egypt,' 15 but, 'The LORD lives
who brought up the children of Israel from the
land of the [a]north and from all the lands where
He had driven them.' For [b]I will bring them back
into their land which I gave to their fathers.
16 "Behold, I will send for many [a]fishermen,"
says the LORD, "and they shall fish them; and after-
ward I will send for many hunters, and they shall
hunt them from every mountain and every hill,
and out of the holes of the rocks. 17 For My [a]eyes
*are* on all their ways; they are not hidden from My
face, nor is their iniquity hidden from My eyes.
18 And first I will repay [a]double for their iniquity
and their sin, because [b]they have defiled My land;
they have filled My inheritance with the carcasses
of their detestable and abominable idols."

19 O LORD, [a]my strength and my fortress,
[b]My refuge in the day of affliction,
The Gentiles shall come to You
From the ends of the earth and say,
"Surely our fathers have inherited lies,
Worthlessness and [c]unprofitable *things*."
20 Will a man make gods for himself,
[a]Which *are* not gods?
21 "Therefore behold, I will this once cause
them to know,
I will cause them to know
My hand and My might;
And they shall know that [a]My name *is* the
LORD.

### JUDAH'S SIN AND PUNISHMENT

17 "The sin of Judah *is* [a]written with a [b]pen
of iron;
With the point of a diamond *it is*
[c]engraved
On the tablet of their heart,
And on the horns of your altars,

**15:20** [a] Ezek. 3:9 [b] Jer. 1:8, 19; 20:11; 37:21; 38:13; 39:11, 12 **16:4** [a] Jer. 15:2 [b] Jer. 22:18; 25:33 [c] Jer. 14:16; 19:11 [d] Ps. 83:10 [e] Ps. 79:2 **16:5** [a] Ezek. 24:17, 22, 23 **16:6** [a] Jer. 22:18 [b] Deut. 14:1 [c] Is. 22:12 **16:7** [a] Prov. 31:6 **16:9** [a] Rev. 18:23 **16:10** [a] Deut. 29:24 **16:11** [a] Jer. 22:9 **16:12** [a] Jer. 7:26 [b] Jer. 3:17; 18:12 **16:13** [a] Deut. 4:26; 28:36, 63 [b] Jer. 15:14 **16:14** [a] Jer. 23:7, 8 **16:15** [a] Jer. 3:18 [b] Jer. 24:6; 30:3; 32:37 **16:16** [a] Amos 4:2 **16:17** [a] Heb. 4:13 **16:18** [a] Jer. 17:18 [b] [Ezek. 43:7] **16:19** [a] Ps. 18:1, 2 [b] Jer. 17:17 [c] Is. 44:10 **16:20** [a] Gal. 4:8 **16:21** [a] Amos 5:8 **17:1** [a] Jer. 2:22 [b] Job 19:24 [c] 2 Cor. 3:3

**17:1 A pen of iron** was used to carve permanent public records, announcements, and calendars in stone. The stones were then displayed in places where people could see them. Often the same announcement was posted in more than one place.

2 While their children remember
Their altars and their [a]wooden images[1]
By the green trees on the high hills.
3 O My mountain in the field,
I will give as plunder your wealth, all your
treasures,
*And* your high places of sin within all your
borders.
4 And you, even yourself,
Shall let go of your heritage which I gave
you;
And I will cause you to serve your
enemies
In [a]the land which you do not know;
For [b]you have kindled a fire in My anger
*which* shall burn forever."

5 Thus says the LORD:

[a]"Cursed *is* the man who trusts in man
And makes [b]flesh his strength,
Whose heart departs from the LORD.
6 For he shall be [a]like a shrub in the desert,
And [b]shall not see when good comes,
But shall inhabit the parched places in the
wilderness,
[c]*In* a salt land *which is* not inhabited.

7 "Blessed[a] *is* the man who trusts in the
LORD,
And whose hope is the LORD.
8 For he shall be [a]like a tree planted by the
waters,
Which spreads out its roots by the river,
And will not fear[1] when heat comes;
But its leaf will be green,
And will not be anxious in the year of
drought,
Nor will cease from yielding fruit.

9 "The [a]heart *is* deceitful above all *things,*
And desperately wicked;
Who can know it?
10 I, the LORD, [a]search the heart,
*I* test the mind,
[b]Even to give every man according to his
ways,
According to the fruit of his doings.

11 "*As* a partridge that broods but does not
hatch,
*So is* he who gets riches, but not by right;
It [a]will leave him in the midst of his days,
And at his end he will be [b]a fool."

12 A glorious high throne from the beginning
*Is* the place of our sanctuary.
13 O LORD, [a]the hope of Israel,
[b]All who forsake You shall be ashamed.

"Those who depart from Me
Shall be [c]written in the earth,
Because they have forsaken the LORD,
The [d]fountain of living waters."

### *JEREMIAH PRAYS FOR DELIVERANCE*

14 Heal me, O LORD, and I shall be healed;
Save me, and I shall be saved,
For [a]You *are* my praise.
15 Indeed they say to me,
[a]"Where *is* the word of the LORD?
Let it come now!"
16 As for me, [a]I have not hurried away from
*being* a shepherd *who* follows You,
Nor have I desired the woeful day;
You know what came out of my lips;
It was right there before You.
17 Do not be a terror to me;
[a]You *are* my hope in the day of doom.
18 [a]Let them be ashamed who persecute me,
But [b]do not let me be put to shame;
Let them be dismayed,
But do not let me be dismayed.
Bring on them the day of doom,
And [c]destroy them with double destruction!

### *HALLOW THE SABBATH DAY*

19 Thus the LORD said to me: "Go and stand in
the gate of the children of the people, by which
the kings of Judah come in and by which they go
out, and in all the gates of Jerusalem; 20 and say
to them, [a]'Hear the word of the LORD, you kings
of Judah, and all Judah, and all the inhabitants
of Jerusalem, who enter by these gates. 21 Thus
says the LORD: [a]"Take heed to yourselves, and
bear no burden on the Sabbath day, nor bring *it*
in by the gates of Jerusalem; 22 nor carry a burden
out of your houses on the Sabbath day, nor do
any work, but hallow the Sabbath day, as I [a]com-
manded your fathers. 23 [a]But they did not obey
nor incline their ear, but made their neck stiff,
that they might not hear nor receive instruction.
24 "And it shall be, [a]if you heed Me carefully,"
says the LORD, "to bring no burden through the
gates of this city on the [b]Sabbath day, but hallow
the Sabbath day, to do no work in it, 25 [a]then shall
enter the gates of this city kings and princes sitting

17:2 [a] Judg. 3:7 [1] Hebrew *Asherim,* Canaanite deities 17:4 [a] Jer. 16:13 [b] Jer. 15:14 17:5 [a] Is. 30:1, 2; 31:1 [b] Is. 31:3 17:6 [a] Jer. 48:6 [b] Job 20:17 [c] Deut. 29:23 17:7 [a] [Is. 30:18] 17:8 [a] [Ps. 1:3] [1] Qere and Targum read *see.* 17:9 [a] [Eccl. 9:3] 17:10 [a] Rev. 2:23 [b] Rom. 2:6 17:11 [a] Ps. 55:23 [b] Luke 12:20 17:13 [a] Jer. 14:8 [b] [Is. 1:28] [c] Luke 10:20 [d] Jer. 2:13 17:14 [a] Deut. 10:21 17:15 [a] Is. 5:19 17:16 [a] Jer. 1:4–12 17:17 [a] Jer. 16:19 17:18 [a] Ps. 35:4; 70:2 [b] Ps. 25:2 [c] Jer. 11:20 17:20 [a] Jer. 19:3, 4 17:21 [a] Neh. 13:19 17:22 [a] Ex. 20:8; 31:13 17:23 [a] Jer. 7:24, 26 17:24 [a] Jer. 11:4; 26:3 [b] Ex. 16:23–30; 20:8–10 17:25 [a] Jer. 22:4

on the throne of David, riding in chariots and on
horses, they and their princes, accompanied by the
men of Judah and the inhabitants of Jerusalem;
and this city shall remain forever. 26 And they shall
come from the cities of Judah and from [a]the places
around Jerusalem, from the land of Benjamin and
from [b]the lowland, from the mountains and from
[c]the South, bringing burnt offerings and sacrifices,
grain offerings and incense, bringing [d]sacrifices
of praise to the house of the LORD.

27 "But if you will not heed Me to hallow the
Sabbath day, such as not carrying a burden when
entering the gates of Jerusalem on the Sabbath
day, then [a]I will kindle a fire in its gates, [b]and
it shall devour the palaces of Jerusalem, and it
shall not be [c]quenched." ' "

### THE POTTER AND THE CLAY

18 The word which came to Jeremiah from
the LORD, saying: 2 "Arise and go down to
the potter's house, and there I will cause you to
hear My words." 3 Then I went down to the pot-
ter's house, and there he was, making something
at the wheel. 4 And the vessel that he made of
clay was marred in the hand of the potter; so he
made it again into another vessel, as it seemed
good to the potter to make.

5 Then the word of the LORD came to me, say-
ing: 6 "O house of Israel, [a]can I not do with you as
this potter?" says the LORD. "Look, [b]as the clay *is* in
the potter's hand, so *are* you in My hand, O house
of Israel! 7 The instant I speak concerning a nation
and concerning a kingdom, to [a]pluck up, to pull
down, and to destroy *it*, 8 [a]if that nation against
whom I have spoken turns from its evil, [b]I will
relent of the disaster that I thought to bring upon
it. 9 And the instant I speak concerning a nation
and concerning a kingdom, to build and to plant
*it*, 10 if it does evil in My sight so that it does not
obey My voice, then I will relent concerning the
good with which I said I would benefit it.

11 "Now therefore, speak to the men of Judah
and to the inhabitants of Jerusalem, saying,
'Thus says the LORD: "Behold, I am fashioning a
disaster and devising a plan against you. [a]Return
now every one from his evil way, and make your
ways and your doings [b]good." ' "

### GOD'S WARNING REJECTED

12 And they said, [a]"That is hopeless! So we
will walk according to our own plans, and we will
every one obey the [b]dictates of his evil heart."

13 Therefore thus says the LORD:

[a]"Ask now among the Gentiles,
Who has heard such things?
The virgin of Israel has done [b]a very
horrible thing.

14 Will *a man* leave the snow water of Lebanon,
*Which comes* from the rock of the field?
Will the cold flowing waters be forsaken
for strange waters?

15 "Because My people have forgotten [a]Me,
They have burned incense to worthless
idols.
And they have caused themselves to
stumble in their ways,
*From* the [b]ancient paths,
To walk in pathways and not on a highway,
16 To make their land [a]desolate *and* a
perpetual [b]hissing;
Everyone who passes by it will be astonished
And shake his head.
17 [a]I will scatter them [b]as with an east wind
before the enemy;
[c]I will show them[1] the back and not the face
In the day of their calamity."

### JEREMIAH PERSECUTED

18 Then they said, [a]"Come and let us devise
plans against Jeremiah; [b]for the law shall not
perish from the priest, nor counsel from the
wise, nor the word from the prophet. Come and
let us attack him with the tongue, and let us not
give heed to any of his words."

19 Give heed to me, O LORD,
And listen to the voice of those who
contend with me!
20 [a]Shall evil be repaid for good?
For they have [b]dug a pit for my life.
Remember that I [c]stood before You
To speak good for them,
To turn away Your wrath from them.
21 Therefore [a]deliver up their children to the
famine,
And pour out their *blood*
By the force of the sword;
Let their wives *become* widows
And [b]bereaved of their children.
Let their men be put to death,
Their young men *be* slain
By the sword in battle.
22 Let a cry be heard from their houses,
When You bring a troop suddenly upon
them;
For they have dug a pit to take me,
And hidden snares for my feet.
23 Yet, LORD, You know all their counsel
Which is against me, to slay *me*.
[a]Provide no atonement for their iniquity,
Nor blot out their sin from Your sight;
But let them be overthrown before You.
Deal *thus* with them
In the time of Your [b]anger.

**17:26** [a]Jer. 33:13 [b]Zech. 7:7 [c]Judg. 1:9 [d]Ps. 107:22; 116:17 **17:27** [a]Lam. 4:11 [b]2 Kin. 25:9 [c]Jer. 7:20 **18:6** [a]Rom. 9:20, 21 [b]Is. 64:8 **18:7** [a]Jer. 1:10 **18:8** [a][Ezek. 18:21; 33:11] [b]Jer. 26:3 **18:11** [a]2 Kin. 17:13 [b]Jer. 7:3–7 **18:12** [a]Jer. 2:25 [b]Jer. 3:17; 23:17 **18:13** [a]Jer. 2:10, 11 [b]Jer. 5:30 **18:15** [a]Jer. 2:13, 32 [b]Jer. 6:16 **18:16** [a]Jer. 19:8 [b]1 Kin. 9:8 **18:17** [a]Jer. 13:24 [b]Ps. 48:7 [c]Jer. 2:27 [1]Following Septuagint, Syriac, Targum, and Vulgate; Masoretic Text reads *look them in.* **18:18** [a]Jer. 11:19 [b]Lev. 10:11 **18:20** [a]Ps. 109:4 [b]Jer. 5:26 [c]Jer. 14:7—15:1 **18:21** [a]Ps. 109:9–20 [b]Jer. 15:7, 8 **18:23** [a]Ps. 35:14; 109:14 [b]Jer. 7:20

### *THE SIGN OF THE BROKEN FLASK*

**19** Thus says the LORD: "Go and get a potter's
earthen flask, and *take* some of the elders of
the people and some of the elders of the priests.
2 And go out to [a]the Valley of the Son of Hinnom,
which *is* by the entry of the Potsherd Gate; and
proclaim there the words that I will tell you,
3 [a]and say, 'Hear the word of the LORD, O kings of
Judah and inhabitants of Jerusalem. Thus says
the LORD of hosts, the God of Israel: "Behold, I
will bring such a catastrophe on this place, that
whoever hears of it, his ears will [b]tingle.

4 "Because they [a]have forsaken Me and made
this an alien place, because they have burned
incense in it to other gods whom neither they,
their fathers, nor the kings of Judah have known,
and have filled this place with [b]the blood of the
innocents 5 [a](they have also built the high places
of Baal, to burn their sons with fire *for* burnt offer-
ings to Baal, [b]which I did not command or speak,
nor did it come into My mind), 6 therefore behold,
the days are coming," says the LORD, "that this
place shall no more be called Tophet or [a]the Valley
of the Son of Hinnom, but the Valley of Slaughter.
7 And I will make void the counsel of Judah and
Jerusalem in this place, [a]and I will cause them to
fall by the sword before their enemies and by the
hands of those who seek their lives; their [b]corpses
I will give as meat for the birds of the heaven and
for the beasts of the earth. 8 I will make this city
[a]desolate and a hissing; everyone who passes by
it will be astonished and hiss because of all its
plagues. 9 And I will cause them to eat the [a]flesh
of their sons and the flesh of their daughters,
and everyone shall eat the flesh of his friend in
the siege and in the desperation with which their
enemies and those who seek their lives shall drive
them to despair." '

10 [a]"Then you shall break the flask in the
sight of the men who go with you, 11 and say to
them, 'Thus says the LORD of hosts: [a]"Even so I
will break this people and this city, as *one* breaks
a potter's vessel, which cannot be made whole
again; and they shall [b]bury *them* in Tophet till
*there is* no place to bury. 12 Thus I will do to this
place," says the LORD, "and to its inhabitants, and
make this city like Tophet. 13 And the houses of
Jerusalem and the houses of the kings of Judah
shall be defiled [a]like the place of Tophet, because
of all the houses on whose [b]roofs they have
burned incense to all the host of heaven, and
[c]poured out drink offerings to other gods." ' "

14 Then Jeremiah came from Tophet, where
the LORD had sent him to prophesy; and he stood
in [a]the court of the LORD's house and said to all the
people, 15 "Thus says the LORD of hosts, the God of
Israel: 'Behold, I will bring on this city and on all
her towns all the doom that I have pronounced
against it, because [a]they have stiffened their necks
that they might not hear My words.' "

### *THE WORD OF GOD TO PASHHUR*

**20** Now [a]Pashhur the son of [b]Immer, the
priest who *was* also chief governor in
the house of the LORD, heard that Jeremiah
prophesied these things. 2 Then Pashhur struck
Jeremiah the prophet, and put him in the stocks
that *were* in the high [a]gate of Benjamin, which
*was* by the house of the LORD.

3 And it happened on the next day that Pash-
hur brought Jeremiah out of the stocks. Then
Jeremiah said to him, "The LORD has not called
your name Pashhur, but Magor-Missabib.[1] 4 For
thus says the LORD: 'Behold, I will make you a
terror to yourself and to all your friends; and
they shall fall by the sword of their enemies,
and your eyes shall see *it*. I will [a]give all Judah
into the hand of the king of Babylon, and he
shall carry them captive to Babylon and slay
them with the sword. 5 Moreover I [a]will deliver
all the wealth of this city, all its produce, and
all its precious things; all the treasures of the
kings of Judah I will give into the hand of their
enemies, who will plunder them, seize them,
and [b]carry them to Babylon. 6 And you, Pashhur,
and all who dwell in your house, shall go into
captivity. You shall go to Babylon, and there you
shall die, and be buried there, you and all your
friends, to whom you have [a]prophesied lies.' "

### *JEREMIAH'S UNPOPULAR MINISTRY*

7 O LORD, You induced me, and I was
  persuaded;
[a]You are stronger than I, and have prevailed.
[b]I am in derision daily;
Everyone mocks me.
8 For when I spoke, I cried out;
[a]I shouted, "Violence and plunder!"
Because the word of the LORD was made
  to me
A reproach and a derision daily.
9 Then I said, "I will not make mention of Him,
Nor speak anymore in His name."
But *His word* was in my heart like a
  [a]burning fire
Shut up in my bones;
I was weary of holding *it* back,
And [b]I could not.
10 [a]For I heard many mocking:
"Fear on every side!"
"Report," *they say,* "and we will report it!"
[b]All my acquaintances watched for my
  stumbling, *saying,*
"Perhaps he can be induced;
Then we will prevail against him,
And we will take our revenge on him."

**19:2** [a] Josh. 15:8 **19:3** [a] Jer. 17:20 [b] 1 Sam. 3:11 **19:4** [a] Is. 65:11 [b] 2 Kin. 21:12 **19:5** [a] Jer. 7:31; 32:35 [b] Lev. 18:21 **19:6** [a] Josh. 15:8 **19:7** [a] Lev. 26:17 [b] Ps. 79:2 **19:8** [a] Jer. 18:16; 49:13; 50:13 **19:9** [a] Lev. 26:29 **19:10** [a] Jer. 51:63, 64 **19:11** [a] Is. 30:14 [b] Jer. 7:32 **19:13** [a] 2 Kin. 23:10 [b] Zeph. 1:5 [c] Jer. 7:18 **19:14** [a] 2 Chr. 20:5 **19:15** [a] Neh. 9:17, 29 **20:1** [a] Ezra 2:37, 38 [b] 1 Chr. 24:14 **20:2** [a] Jer. 37:13 **20:3** [1] Literally *Fear on Every Side* **20:4** [a] Jer. 21:4–10 **20:5** [a] 2 Kin. 20:17 [b] Is. 39:6 **20:6** [a] Jer. 14:13–15 **20:7** [a] Jer. 1:6, 7 [b] Lam. 3:14 **20:8** [a] Jer. 6:7 **20:9** [a] Ps. 39:3 [b] Job 32:18 **20:10** [a] Ps. 31:13 [b] Ps. 41:9; 55:13, 14

11 But the LORD *is* [a]with me as a mighty, awesome One.
Therefore my persecutors will stumble, and will not [b]prevail.
They will be greatly ashamed, for they will not prosper.
*Their* [c]everlasting confusion will never be forgotten.
12 But, O LORD of hosts,
You who [a]test the righteous,
*And* see the mind and heart,
[b]Let me see Your vengeance on them;
For I have pleaded my cause before You.

13 Sing to the LORD! Praise the LORD!
For [a]He has delivered the life of the poor
From the hand of evildoers.

14 [a]Cursed *be* the day in which I was born!
Let the day not be blessed in which my mother bore me!
15 Let the man *be* cursed
Who brought news to my father, saying,
"A male child has been born to you!"
Making him very glad.
16 And let that man be like the cities
Which the LORD [a]overthrew, and did not relent;
Let him [b]hear the cry in the morning
And the shouting at noon,
17 [a]Because he did not kill me from the womb,
That my mother might have been my grave,
And her womb always enlarged *with me.*
18 [a]Why did I come forth from the womb to [b]see labor and sorrow,
That my days should be consumed with shame?

## *JERUSALEM'S DOOM IS SEALED*

21 The word which came to Jeremiah from
the LORD when [a]King Zedekiah sent to him
[b]Pashhur the son of Melchiah, and [c]Zephaniah
the son of Maaseiah, the priest, saying, 2 [a]"Please
inquire of the LORD for us, for Nebuchadnezzar[1]

> **21:2** During **Nebuchadnezzar**'s forty-year reign as **king of Babylon**, he demanded heavy taxes from the people of Judah. When King Hezekiah of Judah refused to pay taxes, Nebuchadnezzar and his forces attacked Jerusalem and held the city in siege until 586 BC, when the people of Judah finally surrendered. Nebuchadnezzar then destroyed the temple and took many Jews back to Babylon as prisoners.

king of Babylon makes war against us. Perhaps
the LORD will deal with us according to all His
wonderful works, that *the king* may go away
from us."
3 Then Jeremiah said to them, "Thus you
shall say to Zedekiah, 4 'Thus says the LORD God
of Israel: "Behold, I will turn back the weapons of
war that *are* in your hands, with which you fight
against the king of Babylon and the Chaldeans[1]
who besiege you outside the walls; and [a]I will
assemble them in the midst of this city. 5 I [a]Myself
will fight against you with an [b]outstretched hand
and with a strong arm, even in anger and fury
and great wrath. 6 I will strike the inhabitants of
this city, both man and beast; they shall die of a
great pestilence. 7 And afterward," says the LORD,
[a]"I will deliver Zedekiah king of Judah, his servants
and the people, and such as are left in this
city from the pestilence and the sword and the
famine, into the hand of Nebuchadnezzar king
of Babylon, into the hand of their enemies, and
into the hand of those who seek their life; and
he shall strike them with the edge of the sword.
[b]He shall not spare them, or have pity or mercy." '
8 "Now you shall say to this people, 'Thus says
the LORD: "Behold, [a]I set before you the way of
life and the way of death. 9 He who [a]remains in
this city shall die by the sword, by famine, and
by pestilence; but he who goes out and defects
to the Chaldeans who besiege you, he shall [b]live,
and his life shall be as a prize to him. 10 For I
have [a]set My face against this city for adversity
and not for good," says the LORD. [b]"It shall be
given into the hand of the king of Babylon, and
he shall [c]burn it with fire." '

## *MESSAGE TO THE HOUSE OF DAVID*

11 "And concerning the house of the king of
Judah, *say,* 'Hear the word of the LORD, 12 O house
of David! Thus says the LORD:

[a]"Execute judgment [b]in the morning;
And deliver *him who is* plundered
Out of the hand of the oppressor,
Lest My fury go forth like fire
And burn so that no one can quench *it,*
Because of the evil of your doings.

13 "Behold, [a]I *am* against you, O inhabitant of the valley,
*And* rock of the plain," says the LORD,
"Who say, [b]'Who shall come down against us?
Or who shall enter our dwellings?'
14 But I will punish you according to the [a]fruit of your doings," says the LORD;
"I will kindle a fire in its forest,
And [b]it shall devour all things around it." ' "

**20:11** [a] Jer. 1:18, 19 [b] Jer. 15:20; 17:18 [c] Jer. 23:40 **20:12** [a] [Jer. 11:20; 17:10] [b] Ps. 54:7; 59:10 **20:13** [a] Ps. 35:9, 10; 109:30, 31 **20:14** [a] Job 3:3 **20:16** [a] Gen. 19:25 [b] Jer. 18:22 **20:17** [a] Job 3:10, 11 **20:18** [a] Job 3:20 [b] Lam. 3:1 **21:1** [a] 2 Kin. 24:17, 18 [b] Jer. 38:1 [c] 2 Kin. 25:18 **21:2** [a] Jer. 37:3, 7 [1] Hebrew *Nebuchadrezzar,* and so elsewhere **21:4** [a] Is. 13:4 [1] Or *Babylonians* **21:5** [a] Is. 63:10 [b] Ex. 6:6 **21:7** [a] Jer. 37:17; 39:5; 52:9 [b] 2 Chr. 36:17 **21:8** [a] Deut. 30:15, 19 **21:9** [a] Jer. 38:2 [b] Jer. 39:18 **21:10** [a] Amos 9:4 [b] Jer. 38:3 [c] Jer. 34:2, 22; 37:10 **21:12** [a] Zech. 7:9 [b] Ps. 101:8 **21:13** [a] [Ezek. 13:8] [b] Jer. 49:4 **21:14** [a] Is. 3:10, 11 [b] 2 Chr. 36:19

**22** Thus says the LORD: "Go down to the
house of the king of Judah, and there
speak this word, 2 and say, [a]'Hear the word of
the LORD, O king of Judah, you who sit on the
throne of David, you and your servants and your
people who enter these gates! 3 Thus says the
LORD: [a]"Execute judgment and righteousness,
and deliver the plundered out of the hand of
the oppressor. Do no wrong and do no violence
to the stranger, the [b]fatherless, or the widow,
nor shed innocent blood in this place. 4 For if
you indeed do this thing, [a]then shall enter the
gates of this house, riding on horses and in
chariots, accompanied by servants and people,
kings who sit on the throne of David. 5 But if you
will not hear these words, [a]I swear by Myself,"
says the LORD, "that this house shall become a
desolation." ' "

6 For thus says the LORD to the house of the
king of Judah:

"You *are* [a]Gilead to Me,
The head of Lebanon;
*Yet* I surely will make you a wilderness,
Cities *which* are not inhabited.
7 I will prepare destroyers against you,
Everyone with his weapons;
They shall cut down [a]your choice cedars
[b]And cast *them* into the fire.

8 And many nations will pass by this city; and
everyone will say to his neighbor, [a]'Why has the
LORD done so to this great city?' 9 Then they
will answer, [a]'Because they have forsaken the
covenant of the LORD their God, and worshiped
other gods and served them.' "

10 Weep not for [a]the dead, nor bemoan
him;
Weep bitterly for him [b]who goes away,
For he shall return no more,
Nor see his native country.

### *MESSAGE TO THE SONS OF JOSIAH*

11 For thus says the LORD concerning [a]Shal-
lum[1] the son of Josiah, king of Judah, who
reigned instead of Josiah his father, [b]who went
from this place: "He shall not return here any-
more, 12 but he shall die in the place where they
have led him captive, and shall see this land
no more.

13 "Woe[a] to him who builds his house by
unrighteousness
And his chambers by injustice,
[b]*Who* uses his neighbor's service without
wages
And gives him nothing for his work,
14 Who says, 'I will build myself a wide
house with spacious chambers,
And cut out windows for it,
Paneling *it* with cedar
And painting *it* with vermilion.'

15 "Shall you reign because you enclose
*yourself* in cedar?
Did not your father eat and drink,
And do justice and righteousness?
Then [a]*it was* well with him.
16 He judged the cause of the poor and
needy;
Then *it was* well.
*Was* not this knowing Me?" says the LORD.
17 "Yet[a] your eyes and your heart *are* for
nothing but your covetousness,
For shedding innocent blood,
And practicing oppression and violence."

18 Therefore thus says the LORD concerning
Jehoiakim the son of Josiah, king of Judah:

[a]"They shall not lament for him,
*Saying,* [b]'Alas, my brother!' or 'Alas, my
sister!'
"They shall not lament for him,
*Saying,* 'Alas, master!' or 'Alas, his glory!'
19 [a]He shall be buried with the burial of a
donkey,
Dragged and cast out beyond the gates of
Jerusalem.

20 "Go up to Lebanon, and cry out,
And lift up your voice in Bashan;
Cry from Abarim,
For all your lovers are destroyed.
21 I spoke to you in your prosperity,
*But* you said, 'I will not hear.'
[a]This *has been* your manner from your
youth,
That you did not obey My voice.
22 The wind shall eat up all [a]your rulers,
And your lovers shall go into captivity;
Surely then you will be ashamed and
humiliated
For all your wickedness.
23 O inhabitant of Lebanon,
Making your nest in the cedars,
How gracious will you be when pangs
come upon you,
Like [a]the pain of a woman in labor?

### *MESSAGE TO CONIAH*

24 "*As* I live," says the LORD, [a]"though Coni-
ah[1] the son of Jehoiakim, king of Judah, [b]were
the signet on My right hand, yet I would pluck

**22:2** [a] Jer. 17:20 **22:3** [a] Jer. 21:12 [b] Jer. 7:6 **22:4** [a] Jer. 17:25 **22:5** [a] Heb. 6:13, 17 **22:6** [a] Song 4:1 **22:7** [a] Is. 37:24 [b] Jer. 21:14 **22:8** [a] Deut. 29:24–26 **22:9** [a] 2 Chr. 34:25 **22:10** [a] 2 Kin. 22:20 [b] Jer. 14:17; 22:11 **22:11** [a] 1 Chr. 3:15 [b] 2 Kin. 23:34 [1] Also called *Jehoahaz* **22:13** [a] 2 Kin. 23:35 [b] James 5:4 **22:15** [a] Ps. 128:2 **22:17** [a] Ezek. 19:6 **22:18** [a] Jer. 16:4, 6 [b] 1 Kin. 13:30 **22:19** [a] Jer. 36:30 **22:21** [a] Jer. 3:24, 25; 32:30 **22:22** [a] Jer. 23:1 **22:23** [a] Jer. 6:24 **22:24** [a] 2 Kin. 24:6, 8 [b] Hag. 2:23 [1] Also called *Jeconiah* and *Jehoiachin*

you off; 25 [a]and I will give you into the hand of
those who seek your life, and into the hand *of*
*those* whose face you fear—the hand of Nebu-
chadnezzar king of Babylon and the hand of the
Chaldeans. 26 [a]So I will cast you out, and your
mother who bore you, into another country
where you were not born; and there you shall
die. 27 But to the land to which they desire to
return, there they shall not return.

28 "Is this man Coniah a despised, broken
idol—
[a]A vessel in which *is* no pleasure?
Why are they cast out, he and his
descendants,
And cast into a land which they do not
know?
29 [a]O earth, earth, earth,
Hear the word of the LORD!
30 Thus says the LORD:
'Write this man down as [a]childless,
A man *who* shall not prosper in his days;
For [b]none of his descendants shall
prosper,
Sitting on the throne of David,
And ruling anymore in Judah.' "

### *THE BRANCH OF RIGHTEOUSNESS*

23 "Woe [a]to the shepherds who destroy and
scatter the sheep of My pasture!" says the
LORD. 2 Therefore thus says the LORD God of Is-
rael against the shepherds who feed My people:
"You have scattered My flock, driven them away,
and not attended to them. [a]Behold, I will attend
to you for the evil of your doings," says the LORD.
3 "But [a]I will gather the remnant of My flock out
of all countries where I have driven them, and
bring them back to their folds; and they shall be
fruitful and increase. 4 I will set up [a]shepherds
over them who will feed them; and they shall
fear no more, nor be dismayed, nor shall they
be lacking," says the LORD.

5 "Behold, [a]*the* days are coming," says the
LORD,
"That I will raise to David a Branch of
righteousness;
A King shall reign and prosper,
[b]And execute judgment and righteousness
in the earth.
6 [a]In His days Judah will be saved,
And Israel [b]will dwell safely;
Now [c]this *is* His name by which He will be
called:

THE LORD OUR RIGHTEOUSNESS.[1]

7 "Therefore, behold, [a]*the* days are coming,"
says the LORD, "that they shall no longer say, 'As
the LORD lives who brought up the children of
Israel from the land of Egypt,' 8 but, 'As the LORD
lives who brought up and led the descendants
of the house of Israel from the north country
[a]and from all the countries where I had driven
them.' And they shall dwell in their own [b]land."

**SEEING JESUS IN THE SCRIPTURE**

**23:5–8** Jesus is the prophesied Branch of righteousness raised from David (see Matt. 1:1). On the cross, Jesus brought righteousness upon the people of Israel and the world by taking God's judgment of sin upon Himself.

### *FALSE PROPHETS AND EMPTY ORACLES*

9 My heart within me is broken
Because of the prophets;
[a]All my bones shake.
I am like a drunken man,
And like a man whom wine has
overcome,
Because of the LORD,
And because of His holy words.
10 For [a]the land is full of adulterers;
For [b]because of a curse the land
mourns.
[c]The pleasant places of the wilderness are
dried up.
Their course of life is evil,
And their might *is* not right.

11 "For [a]both prophet and priest are
profane;
Yes, [b]in My house I have found their
wickedness," says the LORD.
12 "Therefore[a] their way shall be to them
Like slippery *ways*;
In the darkness they shall be driven on
And fall in them;
For I [b]will bring disaster on them,
The year of their punishment," says the
LORD.
13 "And I have seen folly in the prophets of
Samaria:
[a]They prophesied by Baal
And [b]caused My people Israel to err.
14 Also I have seen a horrible thing in the
prophets of Jerusalem:
[a]They commit adultery and walk in lies;
They also [b]strengthen the hands of
evildoers,
So that no one turns back from his
wickedness.
All of them are like [c]Sodom to Me,
And her inhabitants like Gomorrah.

**22:25** [a] Jer. 34:20 **22:26** [a] 2 Kin. 24:15 **22:28** [a] Hos. 8:8 **22:29** [a] Deut. 32:1 **22:30** [a] Matt. 1:12 [b] Jer. 36:30 **23:1** [a] Jer. 10:21 **23:2** [a] Ex. 32:34 **23:3** [a] Jer. 32:37 **23:4** [a] Jer. 3:15 **23:5** [a] Jer. 33:14 [b] Ps. 72:2 **23:6** [a] Zech. 14:11 [b] Jer. 32:37 [c] [1 Cor. 1:30] [1] Hebrew *YHWH Tsidkenu* **23:7** [a] Jer. 16:14 **23:8** [a] Is. 43:5, 6 [b] Gen. 12:7 **23:9** [a] Hab. 3:16 **23:10** [a] Jer. 9:2 [b] Hos. 4:2 [c] Jer. 9:10 **23:11** [a] Zeph. 3:4 [b] Jer. 7:30; 32:34 **23:12** [a] [Prov. 4:19] [b] Jer. 11:23 **23:13** [a] Jer. 2:8 [b] Is. 9:16 **23:14** [a] Jer. 29:23 [b] Ezek. 13:22, 23 [c] Is. 1:9, 10

15 "Therefore thus says the LORD of hosts
concerning the prophets:

'Behold, I will feed them with [a]wormwood,
And make them drink the water of gall;
For from the prophets of Jerusalem
Profaneness has gone out into all the
land.' "

16 Thus says the LORD of hosts:

"Do not listen to the words of the prophets
who prophesy to you.
They make you worthless;
[a]They speak a vision of their own heart,
Not from the mouth of the LORD.
17 They continually say to those who
despise Me,
'The LORD has said, [a]"You shall have
peace" ';
And *to* everyone who [b]walks according to
the dictates of his own heart, they say,
[c]'No evil shall come upon you.' "

18 For [a]who has stood in the counsel of the
LORD,
And has perceived and heard His word?
Who has marked His word and heard *it?*
19 Behold, a [a]whirlwind of the LORD has
gone forth in fury—
A violent whirlwind!
It will fall violently on the head of the
wicked.
20 The [a]anger of the LORD will not turn
back
Until He has executed and performed the
thoughts of His heart.
[b]In the latter days you will understand it
perfectly.

21 "I[a] have not sent these prophets, yet they
ran.
I have not spoken to them, yet they
prophesied.
22 But if they had stood in My counsel,
And had caused My people to hear My
words,
Then they would have [a]turned them from
their evil way
And from the evil of their doings.

23 "*Am* I a God near at hand," says the LORD,
"And not a God afar off?
24 Can anyone [a]hide himself in secret places,
So I shall not see him?" says the LORD;
[b]"Do I not fill heaven and earth?" says the
LORD.

25 "I have heard what the prophets have said
who prophesy lies in My name, saying, 'I have
dreamed, I have dreamed!' 26 How long will *this*
be in the heart of the prophets who prophesy
lies? Indeed *they are* prophets of the deceit of
their own heart, 27 who try to make My people
forget My name by their dreams which every-
one tells his neighbor, [a]as their fathers forgot
My name for Baal.

28 "The prophet who has a dream, let him tell
a dream;
And he who has My word, let him speak
My word faithfully.
What *is* the chaff to the wheat?" says the
LORD.
29 "*Is* not My word like a [a]fire?" says the LORD,
"And like a hammer *that* breaks the rock in
pieces?

30 "Therefore behold, [a]I *am* against the
prophets," says the LORD, "who steal My words
every one from his neighbor. 31 Behold, I *am*
[a]against the prophets," says the LORD, "who use
their tongues and say, 'He says.' 32 Behold, I *am*
against those who prophesy false dreams," says
the LORD, "and tell them, and cause My people
to err by their [a]lies and by [b]their recklessness.
Yet I did not send them or command them;
therefore they shall not [c]profit this people at
all," says the LORD.
33 "So when these people or the prophet or
the priest ask you, saying, 'What is [a]the oracle
of the LORD?' you shall then say to them, 'What
oracle?'[1] I will even forsake you," says the LORD.
34 "And *as for* the prophet and the priest and the
people who say, 'The oracle of the LORD!' I will
even punish that man and his house. 35 Thus
every one of you shall say to his neighbor, and
every one to his brother, 'What has the LORD
answered?' and, 'What has the LORD spoken?'
36 And the oracle of the LORD you shall mention
no more. For every man's word will be his oracle,
for you have [a]perverted the words of the living
God, the LORD of hosts, our God. 37 Thus you
shall say to the prophet, 'What has the LORD an-
swered you?' and, 'What has the LORD spoken?'
38 But since you say, 'The oracle of the LORD!'
therefore thus says the LORD: 'Because you say
this word, "The oracle of the LORD!" and I have
sent to you, saying, "Do not say, 'The oracle of
the LORD!' " 39 therefore behold, I, even I, [a]will
utterly forget you and forsake you, and the city
that I gave you and your fathers, and *will cast
you* out of My presence. 40 And I will bring [a]an
everlasting reproach upon you, and a perpetual
[b]shame, which shall not be forgotten.' "

**23:15** [a] Jer. 9:15 **23:16** [a] Jer. 14:14; Ezek. 13:3, 6 **23:17** [a] Jer. 8:11; Ezek. 13:10; Zech. 10:2 [b] Deut. 29:19; Jer. 3:17 [c] Jer. 5:12; Amos 9:10; Mic. 3:11 **23:18** [a] Job 15:8, 9; [Jer. 23:22; 1 Cor. 2:16] **23:19** [a] Jer. 25:32; 30:23; Amos 1:14 **23:20** [a] 2 Kin. 23:26, 27; Jer. 30:24 [b] Gen. 49:1 **23:21** [a] Jer. 14:14; 23:32; 27:15 **23:22** [a] Jer. 25:5 **23:24** [a] [Ps. 139:7]; Amos 9:2, 3 [b] [1 Kin. 8:27]; Ps. 139:7 **23:27** [a] Judg. 3:7 **23:29** [a] Jer. 5:14 **23:30** [a] Deut. 18:20; Ps. 34:16; Jer. 14:14, 15; Ezek. 13:8, 9 **23:31** [a] Ezek. 13:9 **23:32** [a] Jer. 20:6; 27:10; Lam. 2:14; 3:37 [b] Zeph. 3:4 [c] Jer. 7:8; Lam. 2:14 **23:33** [a] Is. 13:1; Nah. 1:1; Hab. 1:1; Zech. 9:1; Mal. 1:1 [1] Septuagint, Targum, and Vulgate read '*You are the burden.*' **23:36** [a] Deut. 4:2 **23:39** [a] Hos. 4:6 **23:40** [a] Jer. 20:11; Ezek. 5:14, 15 [b] Mic. 3:5–7

### *THE SIGN OF TWO BASKETS OF FIGS*

**24** The [a]LORD showed me, and there were two baskets of figs set before the temple of the LORD, after Nebuchadnezzar [b]king of Babylon had carried away captive [c]Jeconiah the son of Jehoiakim, king of Judah, and the princes of Judah with the craftsmen and smiths, from Jerusalem, and had brought them to Babylon. 2 One basket *had* very good figs, like the figs *that are* first ripe; and the other basket *had* very bad figs which could not be eaten, they were so [a]bad. 3 Then the LORD said to me, "What do you see, Jeremiah?"

And I said, "Figs, the good figs, very good; and the bad, very bad, which cannot be eaten, they are so bad."

4 Again the word of the LORD came to me, saying, 5 "Thus says the LORD, the God of Israel: 'Like these good figs, so will I acknowledge those who are carried away captive from Judah, whom I have sent out of this place for *their own* good, into the land of the Chaldeans. 6 For I will set My eyes on them for good, and [a]I will bring them back to this land; [b]I will build them and not pull *them* down, and I will plant them and not pluck *them* up. 7 Then I will give them [a]a heart to know Me, that I *am* the LORD; and they shall be [b]My people, and I will be their God, for they shall return to Me [c]with their whole heart.

8 'And as the bad [a]figs which cannot be eaten, they are so bad'—surely thus says the LORD—'so will I give up Zedekiah the king of Judah, his princes, the [b]residue of Jerusalem who remain in this land, and [c]those who dwell in the land of Egypt. 9 I will deliver them to [a]trouble into all the kingdoms of the earth, for *their* harm, [b]*to be* a reproach and a byword, a taunt and a curse, in all places where I shall drive them. 10 And I will send the sword, the famine, and the pestilence among them, till they are consumed from the land that I gave to them and their fathers.' "

### *SEVENTY YEARS OF DESOLATION*

**25** The word that came to Jeremiah concerning all the people of Judah, [a]in the fourth year of [b]Jehoiakim the son of Josiah, king of Judah (which *was* the first year of Nebuchadnezzar king of Babylon), 2 which Jeremiah the prophet spoke to all the people of Judah and to all the inhabitants of Jerusalem, saying: 3 [a]"From the thirteenth year of Josiah the son of Amon, king of Judah, even to this day, this *is* the twenty-third year in which the word of the LORD has come to me; and I have spoken to you, rising early and speaking, [b]but you have not listened. 4 And the LORD has sent to you all His servants the prophets, [a]rising early and sending *them,* but you have not listened nor inclined your ear to hear. 5 They said, [a]'Repent now everyone of his evil way and his evil doings, and dwell in the land that the LORD has given to you and your fathers forever and ever. 6 Do not go after other gods to serve them and worship them, and do not provoke Me to anger with the works of your hands; and I will not harm you.' 7 Yet you have not listened to Me," says the LORD, "that you might [a]provoke Me to anger with the works of your hands to your own hurt.

8 "Therefore thus says the LORD of hosts: 'Because you have not heard My words, 9 behold, I will send and take [a]all the families of the north,' says the LORD, 'and Nebuchadnezzar the king of Babylon, [b]My servant, and will bring them against this land, against its inhabitants, and against these nations all around, and will utterly destroy them, and [c]make them an astonishment, a hissing, and perpetual desolations. 10 Moreover I will take from them the [a]voice of mirth and the voice of gladness, the voice of the bridegroom and the voice of the bride, [b]the sound of the millstones and the light of the lamp. 11 And this whole land shall be a desolation *and* an astonishment, and these nations shall serve the king of Babylon seventy [a]years.

12 'Then it will come to pass, [a]when seventy years are completed, *that* I will punish the king of Babylon and that nation, the land of the Chaldeans, for their iniquity,' says the LORD; [b]'and I will make it a perpetual desolation. 13 So I will bring on that land all My words which I have pronounced against it, all that is written in this book, which Jeremiah has prophesied concerning all the nations. 14 [a](For many nations [b]and great kings shall [c]be served by them also; [d]and I will repay them according to their deeds and according to the works of their own hands.)' "

### *JUDGMENT ON THE NATIONS*

15 For thus says the LORD God of Israel to me: "Take this [a]wine cup of fury from My hand, and cause all the nations, to whom I send you, to drink it. 16 And [a]they will drink and stagger and go mad because of the sword that I will send among them."

17 Then I took the cup from the LORD's hand, and made all the nations drink, to whom the LORD had sent me: 18 Jerusalem and the cities of Judah, its kings and its princes, to make them [a]a desolation, an astonishment, a hissing, and [b]a curse, as *it is* this day; 19 Pharaoh king of Egypt, his servants, his princes, and all his people; 20 all the mixed multitude, all the kings of [a]the land of Uz, all the kings of the land of the [b]Philistines (namely, Ashkelon, Gaza, Ekron, and [c]the remnant of Ashdod); 21 [a]Edom, Moab, and the people of Ammon; 22 all the kings of [a]Tyre, all the kings

**24:1** [a] Amos 7:1, 4; 8:1 [b] 2 Kin. 24:12–16; 2 Chr. 36:10 [c] Jer. 22:24–28; 29:2 **24:2** [a] Is. 5:4, 7; Jer. 29:17 **24:6** [a] Jer. 12:15; 29:10 [b] Jer. 32:41; 33:7; 42:10 **24:7** [a] [Deut. 30:6] [b] Jer. 30:22; 31:33; 32:38 [c] Jer. 29:13 **24:8** [a] Jer. 29:17 [b] Jer. 39:9 [c] Jer. 44:1, 26–30 **24:9** [a] Deut. 28:25, 37 [b] Ps. 44:13, 14 **25:1** [a] Jer. 36:1 [b] 2 Kin. 24:1, 2 **25:3** [a] Jer. 1:2 [b] Jer. 7:13; 11:7, 8, 10 **25:4** [a] Jer. 7:13, 25 **25:5** [a] Jer. 18:11 **25:7** [a] Deut. 32:21 **25:9** [a] Jer. 1:15 [b] Is. 45:1 [c] Jer. 18:16 **25:10** [a] Rev. 18:23 [b] Eccl. 12:4 **25:11** [a] Jer. 29:10 **25:12** [a] Ezra 1:1 [b] Is. 13:20 **25:14** [a] Jer. 50:9; 51:27, 28 [b] Jer. 51:27 [c] Jer. 27:7 [d] Jer. 50:29; 51:6, 24 **25:15** [a] Rev. 14:10 **25:16** [a] Nah. 3:11 **25:18** [a] Jer. 25:9, 11 [b] Jer. 24:9 **25:20** [a] Job 1:1 [b] Jer. 47:1–7 [c] Is. 20:1 **25:21** [a] Jer. 49:7 **25:22** [a] Jer. 47:4

of Sidon, and the kings of the coastlands which
*are* across the [b]sea; 23 [a]Dedan, Tema, Buz, and all
*who are* in the farthest corners; 24 all the kings of
Arabia and all the kings of the [a]mixed multitude
who dwell in the desert; 25 all the kings of Zimri,
all the kings of [a]Elam, and all the kings of the
[b]Medes; 26 [a]all the kings of the north, far and
near, one with another; and all the kingdoms
of the world which *are* on the face of the earth.
Also the king of Sheshach[1] shall drink after them.
27 "Therefore you shall say to them, 'Thus says
the LORD of hosts, the God of Israel: [a]"Drink, [b]be
drunk, and vomit! Fall and rise no more, because
of the sword which I will send among you." ' 28 And
it shall be, if they refuse to take the cup from your
hand to drink, then you shall say to them, 'Thus
says the LORD of hosts: "You shall certainly drink!
29 For behold, [a]I begin to bring calamity on the city
[b]which is called by My name, and should you be
utterly unpunished? You shall not be unpunished,
for [c]I will call for a sword on all the inhabitants
of the earth," says the LORD of hosts.'
30 "Therefore prophesy against them all
these words, and say to them:

'The LORD will [a]roar from on high,
And utter His voice from [b]His holy
habitation;
He will roar mightily against [c]His fold.
He will give [d]a shout, as those who tread
*the grapes,*
Against all the inhabitants of the earth.
31 A noise will come to the ends of the earth—
For the LORD has [a]a controversy with the
nations;
[b]He will plead His case with all flesh.
He will give those *who are* wicked to the
sword,' says the LORD."

32 Thus says the LORD of hosts:

"Behold, disaster shall go forth
From nation to nation,
And [a]a great whirlwind shall be raised up
From the farthest parts of the earth.

33 [a]And at that day the slain of the LORD shall be
from *one* end of the earth even to the *other* end
of the earth. They shall not be [b]lamented, [c]or
gathered, or buried; they shall become refuse
on the ground.

34 "Wail,[a] shepherds, and cry!
Roll about *in the ashes,*
You leaders of the flock!
For the days of your slaughter and your
dispersions are fulfilled;
You shall fall like a precious vessel.
35 And the shepherds will have no way to
flee,
Nor the leaders of the flock to escape.
36 A voice of the cry of the shepherds,
And a wailing of the leaders to the flock
*will be heard.*
For the LORD has plundered their pasture,
37 And the peaceful dwellings are cut down
Because of the fierce anger of the LORD.
38 He has left His lair like the lion;
For their land is desolate
Because of the fierceness of the
Oppressor,
And because of His fierce anger."

### *JEREMIAH SAVED FROM DEATH*
*(cf. Jer. 7:1–15)*

26 In the beginning of the reign of Jehoia-
kim the son of Josiah, king of Judah, this
word came from the LORD, saying, 2 "Thus says
the LORD: 'Stand in [a]the court of the LORD's
house, and speak to all the cities of Judah, which
come to worship *in* the LORD's house, [b]all the
words that I command you to speak to them.
[c]Do not diminish a word. 3 [a]Perhaps everyone
will listen and turn from his evil way, that I
may [b]relent concerning the calamity which I
purpose to bring on them because of the evil of
their doings.' 4 And you shall say to them, 'Thus
says the LORD: [a]"If you will not listen to Me, to
walk in My law which I have set before you, 5 to
heed the words of My servants the prophets
[a]whom I sent to you, both rising up early and
sending *them* (but you have not heeded), 6 then
I will make this house like [a]Shiloh, and will
make this city [b]a curse to all the nations of the
earth." ' "
7 So the priests and the prophets and all the
people heard Jeremiah speaking these words in
the house of the LORD. 8 Now it happened, when
Jeremiah had made an end of speaking all that
the LORD had commanded *him* to speak to all the
people, that the priests and the prophets and all
the people seized him, saying, "You will surely
die! 9 Why have you prophesied in the name of
the LORD, saying, 'This house shall be like Shi-
loh, and this city shall be [a]desolate, without an
inhabitant'?" And all the people were gathered
against Jeremiah in the house of the LORD.
10 When the princes of Judah heard these
things, they came up from the king's house to
the house of the LORD and sat down in the entry
of the New Gate of the LORD's *house.* 11 And the
priests and the prophets spoke to the princes
and all the people, saying, "This man deserves
to [a]die! For he has prophesied against this city,
as you have heard with your ears."
12 Then Jeremiah spoke to all the princes

25:22 [b] Jer. 49:23 25:23 [a] Jer. 49:7, 8 25:24 [a] Ezek. 30:5 25:25 [a] Jer. 49:34 [b] Jer. 51:11, 28 25:26 [a] Jer. 50:9 [1] A code word for Babylon (compare 51:41) 25:27 [a] Hab. 2:16 [b] Is. 63:6 25:29 [a] Ezek. 9:6 [b] Dan. 9:18 [c] Ezek. 38:21 25:30 [a] Amos 1:2 [b] Ps. 11:4 [c] 1 Kin. 9:3 [d] Is. 16:9 25:31 [a] Mic. 6:2 [b] Is. 66:16 25:32 [a] Jer. 23:19; 30:23 25:33 [a] Is. 34:2, 3; 66:16 [b] Jer. 16:4, 6 [c] Ps. 79:3 25:34 [a] Jer. 4:8; 6:26 26:2 [a] Jer. 19:14 [b] Matt. 28:20 [c] Acts 20:27 26:3 [a] Jer. 36:3–7 [b] Jer. 18:8 26:4 [a] Lev. 26:14, 15 26:5 [a] Jer. 25:4; 29:19 26:6 [a] 1 Sam. 4:10, 11 [b] Is. 65:15 26:9 [a] Jer. 9:11 26:11 [a] Jer. 38:4

and all the people, saying: "The LORD sent me
to prophesy against this house and against this
city with all the words that you have heard. 13 Now
therefore, [a]amend your ways and your doings,
and obey the voice of the LORD your God; then
the LORD will relent concerning the doom that
He has pronounced against you. 14 As for me,
here [a]I am, in your hand; do with me as seems
good and proper to you. 15 But know for cer-
tain that if you put me to death, you will surely
bring innocent blood on yourselves, on this city,
and on its inhabitants; for truly the LORD has
sent me to you to speak all these words in your
hearing."
16 So the princes and all the people said to
the priests and the prophets, "This man does
not deserve to die. For he has spoken to us in
the name of the LORD our God."
17 [a]Then certain of the elders of the land rose
up and spoke to all the assembly of the people,
saying: 18 [a]"Micah of Moresheth prophesied in
the days of Hezekiah king of Judah, and spoke
to all the people of Judah, saying, 'Thus says
the LORD of hosts:

[b]"Zion shall be plowed *like* a field,
Jerusalem shall become [c]heaps of ruins,
And the mountain of the temple[1]
Like the bare hills of the forest." '[2]

19 Did Hezekiah king of Judah and all Judah ever
put him to death? [a]Did he not fear the LORD and
[b]seek the LORD's favor? And the LORD [c]relent-
ed concerning the doom which He had pro-
nounced against them. [d]But we are doing great
evil against ourselves."
20 Now there was also a man who prophesied
in the name of the LORD, Urijah the son of She-
maiah of Kirjath Jearim, who prophesied against
this city and against this land according to all
the words of Jeremiah. 21 And when Jehoiakim
the king, with all his mighty men and all the
princes, heard his words, the king sought to
put him to death; but when Urijah heard *it*, he
was afraid and fled, and went to Egypt. 22 Then
Jehoiakim the king sent men to Egypt: Elnathan
the son of Achbor, and *other* men *who went* with
him to Egypt. 23 And they brought Urijah from
Egypt and brought him to Jehoiakim the king,
who killed him with the sword and cast his dead
body into the graves of the common people.
24 Nevertheless [a]the hand of Ahikam the
son of Shaphan was with Jeremiah, so that they
should not give him into the hand of the people
to put him to death.

### *SYMBOL OF THE BONDS AND YOKES*

27 In the beginning of the reign of Jehoia-
kim[1] the son of Josiah, [a]king of Judah, this
word came to Jeremiah from the LORD, saying,[2]
2 "Thus says the LORD to me: 'Make for yourselves
bonds and yokes, [a]and put them on your neck,
3 and send them to the king of Edom, the king
of Moab, the king of the Ammonites, the king of
Tyre, and the king of Sidon, by the hand of the
messengers who come to Jerusalem to Zedekiah
king of Judah. 4 And command them to say to
their masters, "Thus says the LORD of hosts, the
God of Israel—thus you shall say to your mas-
ters: 5 [a]'I have made the earth, the man and the
beast that *are* on the ground, by My great power
and by My outstretched arm, and [b]have given it
to whom it seemed proper to Me. 6 [a]And now I
have given all these lands into the hand of Neb-
uchadnezzar the king of Babylon, [b]My servant;
and [c]the beasts of the field I have also given him
to serve him. 7 [a]So all nations shall serve him and
his son and his son's son, [b]until the time of his
land comes; [c]and then many nations and great
kings shall make him serve them. 8 And it shall
be, *that* the nation and kingdom which will not
serve Nebuchadnezzar the king of Babylon, and
which will not put its neck under the yoke of the
king of Babylon, that nation I will punish,' says
the LORD, 'with the sword, the famine, and the
pestilence, until I have consumed them by his
hand. 9 Therefore do not listen to your prophets,
your diviners, your dreamers, your soothsayers,
or your sorcerers, who speak to you, saying, "You
shall not serve the king of Babylon." 10 For they
prophesy a [a]lie to you, to remove you far from
your land; and I will drive you out, and you will
perish. 11 But the nations that bring their necks
under the yoke of the king of Babylon and serve
him, I will let them remain in their own land,' says
the LORD, 'and they shall till it and dwell in it.' " ' "
12 I also spoke to [a]Zedekiah king of Judah
according to all these words, saying, "Bring your
necks under the yoke of the king of Babylon, and
serve him and his people, and live! 13 [a]Why will
you die, you and your people, by the sword, by
the famine, and by the pestilence, as the LORD
has spoken against the nation that will not serve
the king of Babylon? 14 Therefore [a]do not listen
to the words of the prophets who speak to you,
saying, 'You shall not serve the king of Babylon,'
for they prophesy [b]a lie to you; 15 for I have [a]not
sent them," says the LORD, "yet they prophesy
a lie in My name, that I may drive you out, and
that you may perish, you and the prophets who
prophesy to you."

**26:13** [a] Jer. 7:3; [Joel 2:13]; Jon. 3:8 **26:14** [a] Jer. 38:5 **26:17** [a] Acts 5:34 **26:18** [a] Mic. 1:1 [b] Mic. 3:12 [c] Jer. 9:11 [1] Literally *house* [2] Compare Micah 3:12 **26:19** [a] 2 Chr. 32:26; Is. 37:1, 4, 15–20 [b] 2 Kin. 20:1–19 [c] Ex. 32:14; 2 Sam. 24:16; Jer. 18:8 [d] [Acts 5:39] **26:24** [a] 2 Kin. 22:12–14; Jer. 39:14; 40:5–7 **27:1** [a] Jer. 27:3, 12, 20; 28:1 [1] Following Masoretic Text, Targum, and Vulgate; some Hebrew manuscripts, Arabic, and Syriac read *Zedekiah* (compare 27:3, 12; 28:1). [2] Septuagint omits verse 1. **27:2** [a] Jer. 28:10, 12; Ezek. 4:1; 12:3; 24:3 **27:5** [a] Ps. 115:15; 146:6; Is. 45:12 [b] Deut. 9:29; Ps. 115:16; Jer. 32:17; Dan. 4:17, 25, 32 **27:6** [a] Jer. 28:14 [b] Jer. 25:9; 43:10; Ezek. 29:18, 20 [c] Jer. 28:14; Dan. 2:38 **27:7** [a] 2 Chr. 36:20 [b] Jer. 25:12; 50:27; [Dan. 5:26]; Zech. 2:8, 9 [c] Jer. 25:14 **27:10** [a] Jer. 23:16, 32; 28:15 **27:12** [a] Jer. 28:1; 38:17 **27:13** [a] [Prov. 8:36]; Jer. 27:8; 38:23; [Ezek. 18:31] **27:14** [a] Jer. 23:16 [b] Jer. 14:14; 23:21; 29:8, 9; Ezek. 13:22 **27:15** [a] Jer. 23:21; 29:9

16 Also I spoke to the priests and to all this
people, saying, "Thus says the LORD: 'Do not lis-
ten to the words of your prophets who prophesy
to you, saying, "Behold, [a]the vessels of the LORD's
house will now shortly be brought back from
Babylon"; for they prophesy a lie to you. 17 Do not
listen to them; serve the king of Babylon, and
live! Why should this city be laid waste? 18 But if
they *are* prophets, and if the word of the LORD
is with them, let them now make intercession to
the LORD of hosts, that the vessels which are left
in the house of the LORD, *in* the house of the king
of Judah, and at Jerusalem, do not go to Babylon.'
19 "For thus says the LORD of hosts [a]concern-
ing the pillars, concerning the Sea, concerning
the carts, and concerning the remainder of the
vessels that remain in this city, 20 which Nebu-
chadnezzar king of Babylon did not take, when
he carried away [a]captive Jeconiah the son of
Jehoiakim, king of Judah, from Jerusalem to
Babylon, and all the nobles of Judah and Je-
rusalem— 21 yes, thus says the LORD of hosts,
the God of Israel, concerning the [a]vessels that
remain in the house of the LORD, and in the
house of the king of Judah and of Jerusalem:
22 'They shall be [a]carried to Babylon, and there
they shall be until the day that I [b]visit them,'
says the LORD. 'Then [c]I will bring them up and
restore them to this place.' "

**27:19–21** The bronze **Sea** was almost fifteen feet in diameter, more than seven feet deep, and three inches thick. It weighed more than ten tons and could hold about ten thousand gallons of water. The Sea, positioned in front of the temple, was used by the priest for ceremonial cleansing. The basin was supported by metal statues of twelve bulls. **Nebuchadnezzar**'s forces broke the bowl when they destroyed the temple in 586 BC.

### *HANANIAH'S FALSEHOOD AND DOOM*

**28** And [a]it happened in the same year, at the
beginning of the reign of Zedekiah king of
Judah, in the [b]fourth year *and* in the fifth month,
*that* Hananiah the son of [c]Azur the prophet, who
*was* from Gibeon, spoke to me in the house of
the LORD in the presence of the priests and of
all the people, saying, 2 "Thus speaks the LORD
of hosts, the God of Israel, saying: 'I have broken
[a]the yoke of the king of Babylon. 3 [a]Within two
full years I will bring back to this place all the
vessels of the LORD's house, that Nebuchadnez-
zar king of Babylon [b]took away from this place
and carried to Babylon. 4 And I will bring back to
this place Jeconiah the son of Jehoiakim, king of
Judah, with all the captives of Judah who went
to Babylon,' says the LORD, 'for I will break the
yoke of the king of Babylon.' "
5 Then the prophet Jeremiah spoke to the
prophet Hananiah in the presence of the priests
and in the presence of all the people who stood
in the house of the LORD, 6 and the prophet Jer-
emiah said, [a]"Amen! The LORD do so; the LORD
perform your words which you have prophesied,
to bring back the vessels of the LORD's house and
all who were carried away captive, from Babylon
to this place. 7 Nevertheless hear now this word
that I speak in your hearing and in the hearing
of all the people: 8 The prophets who have been
before me and before you of old prophesied
against many countries and great kingdoms—
of war and disaster and pestilence. 9 As for [a]the
prophet who prophesies of [b]peace, when the word
of the prophet comes to pass, the prophet will be
known *as* one whom the LORD has truly sent."
10 Then Hananiah the prophet took the [a]yoke
off the prophet Jeremiah's neck and broke it.
11 And Hananiah spoke in the presence of all the
people, saying, "Thus says the LORD: 'Even so I
will break the yoke of Nebuchadnezzar king of
Babylon [a]from the neck of all nations within
the space of two full years.' " And the prophet
Jeremiah went his way.
12 Now the word of the LORD came to Jere-
miah, after Hananiah the prophet had broken
the yoke from the neck of the prophet Jeremiah,
saying, 13 "Go and tell Hananiah, saying, 'Thus
says the LORD: "You have broken the yokes of
wood, but you have made in their place yokes
of iron." 14 For thus says the LORD of hosts, the
God of Israel: [a]"I have put a yoke of iron on the
neck of all these nations, that they may serve
Nebuchadnezzar king of Babylon; and they shall
serve him. [b]I have given him the beasts of the
field also." ' "

**28:13–14** A **yoke** was a bar that rested on the **neck** of a work animal, such as an ox, horse, or cow. The wagon or plow that the animal pulled was then attached to the yoke. Most yokes were made of **wood** and could be fashioned for one animal or to link two together for a task.

15 Then the prophet Jeremiah said to Hanani-
ah the prophet, "Hear now, Hananiah, the LORD
has not sent you, but [a]you make this people trust
in a [b]lie. 16 Therefore thus says the LORD: 'Behold,

**27:16** [a] 2 Kin. 24:13; 2 Chr. 36:7, 10; Jer. 28:3; Dan. 1:2 **27:19** [a] 1 Kin. 7:15; 2 Kin. 25:13–17; Jer. 52:17, 20, 21 **27:20** [a] 2 Kin. 24:14, 15; 2 Chr. 36:10, 18; Jer. 24:1 **27:21** [a] Jer. 20:5 **27:22** [a] 2 Kin. 25:13; 2 Chr. 36:18 [b] 2 Chr. 36:21; Jer. 29:10; 32:5 [c] Ezra 1:7; 7:19 **28:1** [a] Jer. 27:1 [b] Jer. 51:59 [c] Ezek. 11:1 **28:2** [a] Jer. 27:12 **28:3** [a] Jer. 27:16 [b] 2 Kin. 24:13; Dan. 1:2 **28:6** [a] 1 Kin. 1:36; Ps. 41:13; Jer. 11:5 **28:9** [a] Deut. 18:22 [b] Jer. 23:17; Ezek. 13:10, 16 **28:10** [a] Jer. 27:2 **28:11** [a] Jer. 27:7 **28:14** [a] Deut. 28:48; Jer. 27:7, 8 [b] Jer. 27:6 **28:15** [a] Jer. 20:6; 29:31; Lam. 2:14; Ezek. 13:22; Zech. 13:3 [b] Jer. 27:10; 29:9

I will cast you from the face of the earth. This
year you shall [a]die, because you have taught
[b]rebellion against the LORD.' "
17 So Hananiah the prophet died the same
year in the seventh month.

### *JEREMIAH'S LETTER TO THE CAPTIVES*

29 Now these *are* the words of the letter
that Jeremiah the prophet sent from
Jerusalem to the remainder of the elders who
were [a]carried away captive—to the priests,
the prophets, and all the people whom Neb-
uchadnezzar had carried away captive from
Jerusalem to Babylon. 2 (This happened after
[a]Jeconiah the king, the [b]queen mother, the eu-
nuchs, the princes of Judah and Jerusalem, the
craftsmen, and the smiths had departed from
Jerusalem.) 3 *The letter was sent* by the hand of
Elasah the son of [a]Shaphan, and Gemariah the
son of Hilkiah, whom Zedekiah king of Judah
sent to Babylon, to Nebuchadnezzar king of
Babylon, saying,

4 Thus says the LORD of hosts, the God
of Israel, to all who were carried away
captive, whom I have caused to be carried
away from Jerusalem to Babylon:
5 Build houses and dwell *in them;* plant
gardens and eat their fruit. 6 Take wives and
beget sons and daughters; and take wives
for your sons and give your daughters to
husbands, so that they may bear sons and
daughters—that you may be increased
there, and not diminished. 7 And seek the
peace of the city where I have caused you
to be carried away captive, [a]and pray to the
LORD for it; for in its peace you will have
peace. 8 For thus says the LORD of hosts,
the God of Israel: Do not let your prophets
and your diviners who are in your midst
[a]deceive you, nor listen to your dreams
which you cause to be dreamed. 9 For they
prophesy [a]falsely to you in My name; I have
not sent them, says the LORD.

10 For thus says the LORD: After [a]seventy
years are completed at Babylon, I will
visit you and perform My good word
toward you, and cause you to [b]return to
this place. 11 For I know the thoughts that I
think toward you, says the LORD, thoughts
of peace and not of evil, to give you a
future and a hope. 12 Then you will [a]call
upon Me and go and pray to Me, and I will

**28:16** [a] Jer. 20:6 [b] Deut. 13:5; Jer. 29:32 **29:1** [a] Jer. 27:20 **29:2** [a] 2 Kin. 24:12–16; 2 Chr. 36:9, 10; Jer. 22:24–28 [b] 2 Kin. 24:12, 15; Jer. 13:18 **29:3** [a] 2 Chr. 34:8 **29:7** [a] Ezra 6:10; Neh. 1:4–11; Dan. 9:16; 1 Tim. 2:2 **29:8** [a] Jer. 14:14; 23:21; 27:14, 15; Eph. 5:6 **29:9** [a] Jer. 28:15; 37:19 **29:10** [a] 2 Chr. 36:21–23; Ezra 1:1–4; Jer. 25:12; 27:22; Dan. 9:2; Zech. 7:5 [b] [Jer. 24:6, 7]; Zeph. 2:7 **29:12** [a] Ps. 50:15; Jer. 33:3; Dan. 9:3

JEREMIAH 29:1–14

## GOD PROMISES HOPE

35

STORY OF SCRIPTURE

### WHAT'S GOING ON?

Jeremiah 29:11 is often quoted as a promise of hope and declaration of trust that everything will be okay because God has good plans for us. This is true, but the context is crucial here: the Israelites were in exile. In a time of confusion and despair, Jeremiah's letter was a message from God to a disheartened people, assuring them their current situation wasn't the end of their story. God spoke of a plan for their welfare, not for harm, to give them a future filled with hope. The backdrop of Jeremiah 29:11 reminds us that hardship often precedes flourishing.

### WHAT DOES THIS MEAN FOR ME?

This passage speaks profoundly to anyone going through challenging times. It's a reminder that God hasn't forgotten us, even in our darkest hours. The promise of plans for welfare, hope, and a future is as applicable today as it was to the Israelites. Verses 1–6 remind us amid hardship, it's important to be outward-focused, seeking the welfare of others and our communities. We must not allow trials to make us bitter and keep us from doing what's right.

### DID YOU CATCH THE PATTERN?

Throughout the Bible, there's a recurring theme of God's faithfulness in difficult times. Time and again, God showed up for His people in their distress and led them into a season of restoration and blessing. This pattern is seen in the stories of Joseph, Moses, the judges, David, the exiles, Daniel, and, of course, in the ultimate act of deliverance through Jesus.

*For the next* Story of Scripture *reading and devotion, turn to Ezekiel 37:1–14 on page 849.*

[b]listen to you. 13 And [a]you will seek Me and
find *Me,* when you search for Me [b]with all
your heart. 14 [a]I will be found by you, says
the LORD, and I will bring you back from
your captivity; [b]I will gather you from all
the nations and from all the places where
I have driven you, says the LORD, and I
will bring you to the place from which I
cause you to be carried away captive.

15 Because you have said, "The LORD has
raised up prophets for us in Babylon"—
16 [a]therefore thus says the LORD
concerning the king who sits on the
throne of David, concerning all the people
who dwell in this city, and concerning
your brethren who have not gone out with
you into captivity— 17 thus says the LORD
of hosts: Behold, I will send on them the
sword, the famine, and the pestilence,
and will make them like [a]rotten figs that
cannot be eaten, they are so bad. 18 And
I will pursue them with the sword, with
famine, and with pestilence; and I [a]will
deliver them to trouble among all the
kingdoms of the earth—to be [b]a curse, an
astonishment, a hissing, and a reproach
among all the nations where I have driven
them, 19 because they have not heeded
My words, says the LORD, which [a]I sent to
them by My servants the prophets, rising
up early and sending *them;* neither would
you heed, says the LORD. 20 Therefore
hear the word of the LORD, all you of
the captivity, whom I have sent from
Jerusalem to Babylon.

21 Thus says the LORD of hosts, the God
of Israel, concerning Ahab the son
of Kolaiah, and Zedekiah the son of
Maaseiah, who prophesy a [a]lie to you
in My name: Behold, I will deliver them
into the hand of Nebuchadnezzar king of
Babylon, and he shall slay them before
your eyes. 22 [a]And because of them a
curse shall be taken up by all the captivity
of Judah who *are* in Babylon, saying,
"The LORD make you like Zedekiah
and Ahab, [b]whom the king of Babylon
roasted in the fire"; 23 because [a]they have
done disgraceful things in Israel, have
committed adultery with their neighbors'
wives, and have spoken lying words in
My name, which I have not commanded
them. Indeed I [b]know, and *am* a witness,
says the LORD.

24 You shall also speak to Shemaiah the
Nehelamite, saying, 25 Thus speaks the
LORD of hosts, the God of Israel, saying:
You have sent letters in your name to
all the people who *are* at Jerusalem, [a]to
Zephaniah the son of Maaseiah the priest,
and to all the priests, saying, 26 "The LORD
has made you priest instead of Jehoiada
the priest, so that there should be [a]officers
*in* the house of the LORD over every man
*who* is [b]demented and considers himself
a prophet, that you should [c]put him in
prison and in the stocks. 27 Now therefore,
why have you not rebuked Jeremiah of
Anathoth who makes himself a prophet
to you? 28 For he has sent to us *in* Babylon,
saying, 'This *captivity is* long; build houses
and dwell *in them,* and plant gardens and
eat their fruit.' "

29 Now Zephaniah the priest read this letter
in the hearing of Jeremiah the prophet. 30 Then
the word of the LORD came to Jeremiah, saying:
31 Send to all those in captivity, saying, Thus says
the LORD concerning Shemaiah the Nehelamite:
Because Shemaiah has prophesied to you, [a]and
I have not sent him, and he has caused you to
trust in a [b]lie— 32 therefore thus says the LORD:
Behold, I will punish Shemaiah the Nehelamite
and his family: he shall not have anyone to dwell
among this people, nor shall he see the good that
I will do for My people, says the LORD, [a]because
he has taught rebellion against the LORD.

## *RESTORATION OF ISRAEL AND JUDAH*

**30** The word that came to Jeremiah from the
LORD, saying, 2 "Thus speaks the LORD
God of Israel, saying: 'Write in a book for your-
self all the words that I have spoken to you. 3 For
behold, the days are coming,' says the LORD, 'that
[a]I will bring back from captivity My people Isra-
el and Judah,' says the LORD. [b]'And I will cause
them to return to the land that I gave to their
fathers, and they shall possess it.' "

4 Now these *are* the words that the LORD
spoke concerning Israel and Judah.

5 "For thus says the LORD:

'We have heard a voice of trembling,
Of fear, and not of peace.
6 Ask now, and see,
Whether a man is ever in labor with child?
So why do I see every man *with* his hands
on his loins
[a]Like a woman in labor,
And all faces turned pale?

**29:12** [b] Ps. 145:19 **29:13** [a] Lev. 26:39–42; Deut. 30:1–3 [b] 1 Chr. 22:19; 2 Chr. 22:9; Jer. 24:7 **29:14** [a] [Deut. 4:7]; Ps. 32:6; 46:1; [Is. 55:6, 7]; Jer. 24:7 [b] Is. 43:5, 6; Jer. 23:8; 32:37 **29:16** [a] Jer. 38:2, 3, 17–23 **29:17** [a] Jer. 24:3, 8–10 **29:18** [a] Deut. 28:25; 2 Chr. 29:8; Jer. 15:4; 24:9; 34:17; Ezek. 12:15 [b] Jer. 26:6; 42:18 **29:19** [a] Jer. 25:4; 26:5; 35:15 **29:21** [a] Jer. 14:14, 15; Lam. 2:14; 2 Pet. 2:1 **29:22** [a] Gen. 48:20; Is. 65:15 [b] Dan. 3:6, 21 **29:23** [a] Jer. 23:14 [b] [Prov. 5:21; Jer. 16:17]; Mal. 3:5; [Heb. 4:13] **29:25** [a] 2 Kin. 25:18; Jer. 21:1 **29:26** [a] Jer. 20:1 [b] 2 Kin. 9:11; Hos. 9:7; Mark 3:21; John 10:20; Acts 26:24; [2 Cor. 5:13] [c] Jer. 20:1, 2; Acts 16:24 **29:31** [a] Jer. 28:15 [b] Ezek. 13:8–16, 22, 23 **29:32** [a] Jer. 28:16 **30:3** [a] Ps. 53:6; Jer. 29:14; 30:18; 32:44; Ezek. 39:25; Amos 9:14; Zeph. 3:20 [b] Jer. 16:15; Ezek. 20:42; 36:24 **30:6** [a] Jer. 4:31; 6:24

7 [a]Alas! For that day *is* great,
[b]So that none *is* like it;
And it *is* the time of Jacob's trouble,
But he shall be saved out of it.

8 'For it shall come to pass in that day,'
Says the LORD of hosts,
'*That* I will break his yoke from your neck,
And will burst your bonds;
Foreigners shall no more enslave them.
9 But they shall serve the LORD their God,
And [a]David their king,
Whom I will [b]raise up for them.

### SEEING JESUS IN THE SCRIPTURE

**30:9** Ultimately, Jesus is the King who Jeremiah spoke of. Zacharias quoted this verse when he prophesied how his son John would serve as the messenger of Jesus, the Messiah (see Luke 1:69).

10 'Therefore [a]do not fear, O My servant Jacob,' says the LORD,
'Nor be dismayed, O Israel;
For behold, I will save you from afar,
And your seed [b]from the land of their captivity.
Jacob shall return, have rest and be quiet,
And no one shall make *him* afraid.
11 For I *am* with [a]you,' says the LORD, 'to save you;
[b]Though I make a full end of all nations
Where I have scattered you,
[c]Yet I will not make a complete end of you.
But I will correct you [d]in justice,
And will not let you go altogether unpunished.'

12 "For thus says the LORD:

[a]'Your affliction *is* incurable,
Your wound *is* severe.
13 *There is* no one to plead your cause,
That you may be bound up;
[a]You have no healing medicines.
14 [a]All your lovers have forgotten you;
They do not seek you;
For I have wounded you with the wound
[b]of an enemy,
With the chastisement [c]of a cruel one,
For the multitude of your iniquities,
[d]*Because* your sins have increased.
15 Why [a]do you cry about your affliction?
Your sorrow *is* incurable.
Because of the multitude of your iniquities,
*Because* your sins have increased,
I have done these things to you.

16 'Therefore all those who devour you [a]shall be devoured;
And all your adversaries, every one of them, shall go into [b]captivity;
Those who plunder you shall become [c]plunder,
And all who prey upon you I will make a [d]prey.
17 [a]For I will restore health to you
And heal you of your wounds,' says the LORD,
'Because they called you an outcast *saying*:
"This *is* Zion;
No one seeks her." '

18 "Thus says the LORD:

'Behold, I will bring back the captivity of Jacob's tents,
And [a]have mercy on his dwelling places;
The city shall be built upon its own mound,
And the palace shall remain according to its own plan.

**30:18** The people of Judah were held captive by the Babylonians for seventy years. Their **captivity** ended when Babylon was conquered by Persia. Cyrus, the king of Persia, allowed the Jewish people to return to their homeland and rebuild their temple.

19 Then [a]out of them shall proceed thanksgiving
And the voice of those who make merry;
[b]I will multiply them, and they shall not diminish;
I will also glorify them, and they shall not be small.
20 Their children also shall be [a]as before,
And their congregation shall be established before Me;
And I will punish all who oppress them.
21 Their nobles shall be from among them,
[a]And their governor shall come from their midst;
Then I will [b]cause him to draw near,
And he shall approach Me;
For who *is* this who pledged his heart to approach Me?' says the LORD.

**30:7** [a] [Is. 2:12]; Hos. 1:11; Joel 2:11; Amos 5:18; Zeph. 1:14 [b] Lam. 1:12; Dan. 9:12; 12:1 **30:9** [a] Is. 55:3; Ezek. 34:23; 37:24; Hos. 3:5 [b] [Luke 1:69; Acts 2:30; 13:23] **30:10** [a] Is. 41:13; 43:5; 44:2; Jer. 46:27, 28 [b] Jer. 3:18 **30:11** [a] [Is. 43:2–5] [b] Amos 9:8 [c] Jer. 4:27; 46:27, 28 [d] Ps. 6:1; Is. 27:8; Jer. 10:24; 46:28 **30:12** [a] 2 Chr. 36:16; Jer. 15:18 **30:13** [a] Jer. 8:22 **30:14** [a] Jer. 22:20, 22; Lam. 1:2 [b] Job 13:24; 16:9; 19:11 [c] Job 30:21 [d] Jer. 5:6 **30:15** [a] Jer. 15:18 **30:16** [a] Ex. 23:22; Is. 41:11; Jer. 10:25 [b] Is. 14:2; Joel 3:8 [c] Is. 33:1; Ezek. 39:10 [d] Jer. 2:3 **30:17** [a] Ex. 15:26; Ps. 107:20; Is. 30:26; Jer. 33:6 **30:18** [a] Ps. 102:13 **30:19** [a] Is. 51:11 [b] Zech. 10:8 **30:20** [a] Is. 1:26 **30:21** [a] Gen. 49:10 [b] Num. 16:5

22 'You shall be [a]My people,
And I will be your God.' "

23 Behold, the [a]whirlwind of the LORD
Goes forth with fury,
A continuing whirlwind;
It will fall violently on the head of the wicked.
24 The fierce anger of the LORD will not return until He has done it,
And until He has performed the intents of His heart.

[a]In the latter days you will consider it.

### *THE REMNANT OF ISRAEL SAVED*

31 "At [a]the same time," says the LORD, [b]"I will
be the God of all the families of Israel, and
they shall be My people."
2 Thus says the LORD:

"The people who survived the sword
Found grace in the wilderness—
Israel, when [a]I went to give him rest."

3 The LORD has appeared of old to me, *saying:*
"Yes, [a]I have loved you with [b]an everlasting love;
Therefore with lovingkindness I have [c]drawn you.
4 Again [a]I will build you, and you shall be rebuilt,
O virgin of Israel!
You shall again be adorned with your [b]tambourines,
And shall go forth in the dances of those who rejoice.
5 [a]You shall yet plant vines on the mountains of Samaria;
The planters shall plant and eat *them* as ordinary food.
6 For there shall be a day
*When* the watchmen will cry on Mount Ephraim,
[a]'Arise, and let us go up *to* Zion,
To the LORD our God.' "

7 For thus says the LORD:

[a]"Sing with gladness for Jacob,
And shout among the chief of the nations;
Proclaim, give praise, and say,
'O LORD, save Your people,
The remnant of Israel!'
8 Behold, I will bring them [a]from the north country,
And [b]gather them from the ends of the earth,
*Among* them the blind and the lame,
The woman with child
And the one who labors with child, together;
A great throng shall return there.
9 [a]They shall come with weeping,
And with supplications I will lead them.
I will cause them to walk [b]by the rivers of waters,
In a straight way in which they shall not stumble;
For I am a Father to Israel,
And Ephraim *is* My [c]firstborn.

10 "Hear the word of the LORD, O nations,
And declare *it* in the isles afar off, and say,
'He who scattered Israel [a]will gather him,
And keep him as a shepherd *does* his flock.'
11 For [a]the LORD has redeemed Jacob,
And ransomed him [b]from the hand of one stronger than he.
12 Therefore they shall come and sing in [a]the height of Zion,
Streaming to [b]the goodness of the LORD—
For wheat and new wine and oil,
For the young of the flock and the herd;
Their souls shall be like a [c]well-watered garden,
[d]And they shall sorrow no more at all.

13 "Then shall the virgin rejoice in the dance,
And the young men and the old, together;
For I will turn their mourning to joy,
Will comfort them,
And make them rejoice rather than sorrow.
14 I will satiate the soul of the priests with abundance,
And My people shall be satisfied with My goodness, says the LORD."

### *MERCY ON EPHRAIM*

15 Thus says the LORD:

[a]"A voice was heard in [b]Ramah,
Lamentation *and* bitter [c]weeping,
Rachel weeping for her children,
Refusing to be comforted for her children,
Because [d]they *are* no more."

**SEEING JESUS IN THE SCRIPTURE**

**31:15** This prophecy points to Herod, who ordered the killing of boys two-years old and younger in Bethlehem and the surrounding region in search of Jesus (see Matt. 2:16–18). Rachel's weeping and mourning represent the weeping and mourning of all these mothers who lost their sons.

30:22 [a]Ezek. 36:28 30:23 [a]Jer. 23:19, 20; 25:32 30:24 [a]Gen. 49:1 31:1 [a]Jer. 30:24 [b]Jer. 30:22 31:2 [a]Num. 10:33 31:3 [a]Mal. 1:2 [b]Rom. 11:28 [c]Hos. 11:4 31:4 [a]Jer. 33:7 [b]Judg. 11:34 31:5 [a]Amos 9:14 31:6 [a][Mic. 4:2] 31:7 [a]Is. 12:5, 6 31:8 [a]Jer. 3:12, 18; 23:8 [b]Ezek. 20:34, 41; 34:13 31:9 [a][Jer. 50:4] [b]Is. 35:8; 43:19; 49:10, 11 [c]Ex. 4:22 31:10 [a]Is. 40:11 31:11 [a]Is. 44:23; 48:20 [b]Is. 49:24 31:12 [a]Ezek. 17:23 [b]Hos. 3:5 [c]Is. 58:11 [d]Is. 35:10; 65:19 31:15 [a]Matt. 2:17, 18 [b]Josh. 18:25 [c]Gen. 37:35 [d]Jer. 10:20

16 Thus says the LORD:

"Refrain your voice from [a]weeping,
And your eyes from tears;
For your work shall be rewarded, says the LORD,
And they shall come back from the land of the enemy.
17 There is [a]hope in your future, says the LORD,
That *your* children shall come back to their own border.

18 "I have surely heard Ephraim bemoaning himself:
'You have [a]chastised me, and I was chastised,
Like an untrained bull;
[b]Restore me, and I will return,
For You *are* the LORD my God.
19 Surely, [a]after my turning, I repented;
And after I was instructed, I struck myself on the thigh;
I was [b]ashamed, yes, even humiliated,
Because I bore the reproach of my youth.'
20 *Is* Ephraim My dear son?
*Is he* a pleasant child?
For though I spoke against him,
I earnestly remember him still;
[a]Therefore My heart yearns for him;
[b]I will surely have mercy on him, says the LORD.

21 "Set up signposts,
Make landmarks;
[a]Set your heart toward the highway,
The way in *which* you went.
Turn back, O virgin of Israel,
Turn back to these your cities.
22 How long will you [a]gad about,
O you [b]backsliding daughter?
For the LORD has created a new thing in the earth—
A woman shall encompass a man."

## FUTURE PROSPERITY OF JUDAH

23 Thus says the LORD of hosts, the God of
Israel: "They shall again use this speech in the
land of Judah and in its cities, when I bring back
their captivity: [a]'The LORD bless you, O home
of justice, *and* [b]mountain of holiness!' 24 And
there shall dwell in Judah itself, and [a]in all its
cities together, farmers and those going out
with flocks. 25 For I have satiated the weary soul,
and I have replenished every sorrowful soul."
26 After this I awoke and looked around, and
my sleep was [a]sweet to me.
27 "Behold, the days are coming, says the
LORD, that [a]I will sow the house of Israel and the
house of Judah with the seed of man and the seed
of beast. 28 And it shall come to pass, *that* as I have
[a]watched over them [b]to pluck up, to break down,
to throw down, to destroy, and to afflict, so I will
watch over them [c]to build and to plant, says the
LORD. 29 [a]In those days they shall say no more:

'The fathers have eaten sour grapes,
And the children's teeth are set on edge.'

30 [a]But every one shall die for his own iniquity;
every man who eats the sour grapes, his teeth
shall be set on edge.

## A NEW COVENANT

31 "Behold, the [a]days are coming, says the
LORD, when I will make a new covenant with the
house of Israel and with the house of Judah—
32 not according to the covenant that I made
with their fathers in the day *that* [a]I took them by
the hand to lead them out of the land of Egypt,
My covenant which they broke, though I was a
husband to them,[1] says the LORD. 33 [a]But this *is*
the covenant that I will make with the house
of Israel after those days, says the LORD: [b]I will
put My law in their minds, and write it on their
hearts; [c]and I will be their God, and they shall
be My people. 34 No more shall every man teach
his neighbor, and every man his brother, saying,
'Know the LORD,' for [a]they all shall know Me,
from the least of them to the greatest of them,
says the LORD. For [b]I will forgive their iniquity,
and their sin I will remember no more."

> **31:31–34** The **new covenant** described here is called "new" in contrast to the covenant with Moses which is called "old" (see Heb. 8:6–13) because it accomplishes what the Mosaic covenant could only point to, that is, the child of God living in a manner consistent with the character of God. The new covenant is made sure by the blood that Jesus shed on Calvary's cross.

35 Thus says the LORD,
[a]Who gives the sun for a light by day,
The ordinances of the moon and the stars for a light by night,
Who disturbs [b]the sea,
And its waves roar
[c](The LORD of hosts *is* His name):

36 "If [a]those ordinances depart
From before Me, says the LORD,
*Then* the seed of Israel shall also cease
From being a nation before Me forever."

**31:16** [a] [Is. 25:8; 30:19] **31:17** [a] Jer. 29:11 **31:18** [a] Ps. 94:12 [b] Lam. 5:21 **31:19** [a] Deut. 30:2 [b] Ezek. 36:31 **31:20** [a] Is. 63:15 [b] [Hos. 14:4] **31:21** [a] Jer. 50:5 **31:22** [a] Jer. 2:18, 23, 36 [b] Jer. 3:6, 8, 11, 12, 14, 22 **31:23** [a] Is. 1:26 [b] [Zech. 8:3] **31:24** [a] Jer. 33:12 **31:26** [a] Prov. 3:24 **31:27** [a] Ezek. 36:9–11 **31:28** [a] Jer. 44:27 [b] Jer. 1:10; 18:7 [c] Jer. 24:6 **31:29** [a] Ezek. 18:2, 3 **31:30** [a] [Gal. 6:5, 7] **31:31** [a] Heb. 8:8–12; 10:16, 17 **31:32** [a] Deut. 1:31 [1] Following Masoretic Text, Targum, and Vulgate; Septuagint and Syriac read *and I turned away from them.* **31:33** [a] Jer. 32:40 [b] Ps. 40:8 [c] Jer. 24:7; 30:22; 32:38 **31:34** [a] [John 6:45] [b] [Rom. 11:27] **31:35** [a] Gen. 1:14–18 [b] Is. 51:15 [c] Jer. 10:16 **31:36** [a] Ps. 148:6

37 Thus says the LORD:
[a]"If heaven above can be measured,
And the foundations of the earth
searched out beneath,
I will also [b]cast off all the seed of Israel
For all that they have done, says the LORD.

38 "Behold, the days are coming, says the LORD,
that the city shall be built for the LORD [a]from the
Tower of Hananel to the Corner Gate. 39 [a]The sur-
veyor's line shall again extend straight forward
over the hill Gareb; then it shall turn toward Goath.
40 And the whole valley of the dead bodies and of
the ashes, and all the fields as far as the Brook
Kidron, [a]to the corner of the Horse Gate toward
the east, [b]*shall be* holy to the LORD. It shall not be
plucked up or thrown down anymore forever."

### *JEREMIAH BUYS A FIELD*

**32** The word that came to Jeremiah from the
LORD [a]in the tenth year of Zedekiah king
of Judah, which was the eighteenth year of Nebu-
chadnezzar. 2 For then the king of Babylon's army
besieged Jerusalem, and Jeremiah the prophet
was shut up [a]in the court of the prison, which
*was in* the king of Judah's house. 3 For Zedekiah
king of Judah had shut him up, saying, "Why
do you [a]prophesy and say, 'Thus says the LORD:
[b]"Behold, I will give this city into the hand of
the king of Babylon, and he shall take it; 4 and
Zedekiah king of Judah [a]shall not escape from
the hand of the Chaldeans, but shall surely be
delivered into the hand of the king of Babylon,
and shall speak with him face to face,[1] and see
him [b]eye to eye; 5 then he shall [a]lead Zedekiah
to Babylon, and there he shall be [b]until I visit
him," says the LORD; [c]"though you fight with the
Chaldeans, you shall not succeed" '?"
6 And Jeremiah said, "The word of the LORD
came to me, saying, 7 'Behold, Hanamel the son
of Shallum your uncle will come to you, saying,
"Buy my field which *is* in Anathoth, for the [a]right
of redemption *is* yours to buy *it*." ' 8 Then Hana-
mel my uncle's son came to me in the court of
the prison according to the word of the LORD,
and said to me, 'Please buy my field that *is* in
Anathoth, which *is* in the country of Benjamin;
for the right of inheritance *is* yours, and the
redemption yours; buy *it* for yourself.' Then I
knew that this was the word of the LORD. 9 So I
bought the field from Hanamel, the son of my
uncle who *was* in Anathoth, and [a]weighed *out
to* him the money—seventeen shekels of silver.
10 And I signed the deed and sealed *it*, took wit-
nesses, and weighed the money on the scales.
11 So I took the purchase deed, *both* that which
was sealed *according* to the law and custom, and
that which was open; 12 and I gave the purchase
deed to [a]Baruch the son of Neriah, son of Mah-
seiah, in the presence of Hanamel my uncle's
*son*, and in the presence of the [b]witnesses who
signed the purchase deed, before all the Jews
who sat in the court of the prison.
13 "Then I charged [a]Baruch before them,
saying, 14 'Thus says the LORD of hosts, the God
of Israel: "Take these deeds, both this purchase
deed which is sealed and this deed which is
open, and put them in an earthen vessel, that
they may last many days." 15 For thus says the
LORD of hosts, the God of Israel: "Houses and
fields and vineyards shall be [a]possessed again
in this land." '

### *JEREMIAH PRAYS FOR UNDERSTANDING*

16 "Now when I had delivered the purchase
deed to Baruch the son of Neriah, I prayed to
the LORD, saying: 17 'Ah, Lord GOD! Behold, [a]You
have made the heavens and the earth by Your
great power and outstretched arm. [b]There is
nothing too hard for You. 18 *You* show [a]loving-
kindness to thousands, and repay the iniquity
of the fathers into the bosom of their children
after them—the Great, [b]the Mighty God, whose
name *is* [c]the LORD of hosts. 19 *You are* [a]great in
counsel and mighty in work, for Your [b]eyes *are*
open to all the ways of the sons of men, [c]to give
everyone according to his ways and according to
the fruit of his doings. 20 You have set signs and
wonders in the land of Egypt, to this day, and
in Israel and among *other* men; and You have
made Yourself [a]a name, as it is this day. 21 You
[a]have brought Your people Israel out of the land
of Egypt with signs and wonders, with a strong
hand and an outstretched arm, and with great
terror; 22 You have given them this land, of which
You swore to their fathers to give them—[a]"a land
flowing with milk and honey."[1] 23 And they came
in and took possession of it, but [a]they have not
obeyed Your voice or walked in Your law. They
have done nothing of all that You commanded
them to do; therefore You have caused all this
calamity to come upon them.
24 'Look, the siege mounds! They have come
to the city to take it; and the city has been given
into the hand of the Chaldeans who fight against
it, because of [a]the sword and famine and pes-
tilence. What You have spoken has happened;
there You see *it*! 25 And You have said to me,
O Lord GOD, "Buy the field for money, and take
witnesses"!—yet the city has been given into
the hand of the Chaldeans.' "

**31:37** [a] Jer. 33:22 [b] [Rom. 11:2–5, 26, 27] **31:38** [a] Zech. 14:10 **31:39** [a] Zech. 2:1, 2 **31:40** [a] Neh. 3:28 [b] [Joel 3:17] **32:1** [a] Jer. 39:1, 2 **32:2** [a] Jer. 33:1; 37:21; 39:14 **32:3** [a] Jer. 26:8, 9 [b] Jer. 21:3–7; 34:2 **32:4** [a] Jer. 34:3; 38:18, 23; 39:5; 52:9 [b] Jer. 39:5 [1] Literally *mouth to mouth* **32:5** [a] Ezek. 12:12, 13 [b] Jer. 27:22 [c] Jer. 21:4; 33:5 **32:7** [a] Lev. 25:24, 25, 32; Ruth 4:4 **32:9** [a] Gen. 23:16; Zech. 11:12 **32:12** [a] Jer. 36:4 [b] Is. 8:2 **32:13** [a] Jer. 36:4 **32:15** [a] Ezra 2:1; [Jer. 31:5, 12, 14]; Amos 9:14, 15; Zech. 3:10 **32:17** [a] 2 Kin. 19:15; Ps. 102:25; Is. 40:26–29; Jer. 27:5 [b] Gen. 18:14; Jer. 32:27; Zech. 8:6; Matt. 19:26; Mark 10:27; Luke 18:27 **32:18** [a] Ex. 20:6; 34:7; Deut. 5:9, 10 [b] Ps. 50:1; [Is. 9:6]; Jer. 20:11 [c] Jer. 10:16 **32:19** [a] Is. 28:29 [b] Job 34:21; Ps. 33:13; Prov. 5:21; Jer. 16:17 [c] Ps. 62:12; Jer. 17:10; [Matt. 16:27; John 5:29] **32:20** [a] Ex. 9:16; 1 Chr. 17:21; Is. 63:12; Jer. 13:11; Dan. 9:15 **32:21** [a] Ex. 6:6; 2 Sam. 7:23; 1 Chr. 17:21; Ps. 136:11, 12 **32:22** [a] Ex. 3:8, 17; Deut. 1:8; Ps. 105:9–11; Jer. 11:5 [1] Exodus 3:8 **32:23** [a] [Neh. 9:26]; Jer. 11:8; [Dan. 9:10–14] **32:24** [a] Jer. 14:12; Ezek. 14:21

### *GOD'S ASSURANCE OF THE PEOPLE'S RETURN*

26 Then the word of the LORD came to Jere-
miah, saying, 27 "Behold, I *am* the LORD, the [a]God
of all flesh. Is there anything too hard for Me?
28 Therefore thus says the LORD: 'Behold, I will
give this city into the hand of the Chaldeans, into
the hand of Nebuchadnezzar king of Babylon, and
he shall take it. 29 And the Chaldeans who fight
against this city shall come and [a]set fire to this
city and burn it, with the houses [b]on whose roofs
they have offered incense to Baal and poured out
drink offerings to other gods, to provoke Me to
anger; 30 because the children of Israel and the
children of Judah [a]have done only evil before Me
from their youth. For the children of Israel have
provoked Me only to anger with the work of their
hands,' says the LORD. 31 'For this city has been to
Me *a provocation of* My anger and My fury from
the day that they built it, even to this day; [a]so I will
remove it from before My face 32 because of all
the evil of the children of Israel and the children
of Judah, which they have done to provoke Me
to anger—[a]they, their kings, their princes, their
priests, [b]their prophets, the men of Judah, and
the inhabitants of Jerusalem. 33 And they have
turned to Me the [a]back, and not the face; though I
taught them, [b]rising up early and teaching *them*,
yet they have not listened to receive instruction.
34 But they [a]set their abominations in the house
which is called by My name, to defile it. 35 And
they built the high places of Baal which *are* in
the Valley of the Son of Hinnom, to [a]cause their
sons and their daughters to pass through *the fire*
to [b]Molech, [c]which I did not command them, nor
did it come into My mind that they should do this
abomination, to cause Judah to sin.'

36 "Now therefore, thus says the LORD, the
God of Israel, concerning this city of which you
say, 'It shall be delivered into the hand of the
king of Babylon by the sword, by the famine, and
by the pestilence: 37 Behold, I will [a]gather them
out of all countries where I have driven them in
My anger, in My fury, and in great wrath; I will
bring them back to this place, and I will cause
them [b]to dwell safely. 38 They shall be [a]My people,
and I will be their God; 39 then I will [a]give them
one heart and one way, that they may fear Me
forever, for the good of them and their children
after them. 40 And [a]I will make an everlasting
covenant with them, that I will not turn away
from doing them good; but [b]I will put My fear
in their hearts so that they will not depart from
Me. 41 Yes, [a]I will rejoice over them to do them
good, and [b]I will assuredly plant them in this
land, with all My heart and with all My soul.'

32:27 [a] [Num. 16:22] 32:29 [a] 2 Chr. 36:19; Jer. 21:10; 37:8, 10; 52:13 [b] Jer. 19:13 32:30 [a] Deut. 9:7–12; Is. 63:10; Jer. 2:7; 3:25; 7:22–26; Ezek. 20:28 32:31 [a] 2 Kin. 23:27; 24:3; Jer. 27:10 32:32 [a] Dan. 9:8 [b] Jer. 23:14 32:33 [a] Jer. 2:27; 7:24 [b] Jer. 7:13 32:34 [a] Jer. 7:10–12, 30; 23:11 32:35 [a] Jer. 7:31; 19:5 [b] Lev. 18:21 [c] Jer. 7:31 32:37 [a] Deut. 30:3 [b] Jer. 33:16 32:38 [a] [Jer. 24:7; 30:22; 31:33] 32:39 [a] [Ezek. 11:19] 32:40 [a] Is. 55:3 [b] [Jer. 31:33] 32:41 [a] Deut. 30:9 [b] Amos 9:15

KNOW THE TRUTH

## THE DOCTRINE OF GOD

### PART 6: THE OMNIPOTENCE OF GOD

**32:27** God's claims must have sounded ridiculous to Jeremiah. Babylon was a destroyer of nations. God claimed Babylon would conquer the nation of Judah, destroy the city of Jerusalem, and deport thousands of captives, *yet* those captives would eventually return to Judah, rebuild the temple, and resettle Jerusalem. It sounded preposterous! There was no way a decimated Judah could do those things. In response to the skeptics, God asked a rhetorical question: "Is there anything too hard for Me?" Within the exact timeframe God laid out, all He promised of Judah came true, and the Babylonian empire ceased to exist. This showed that God is omnipotent.

*Omnipotent* means God possesses all power to do as He desires. His power and ability are limitless. There's nothing He can't do, beyond violate His own character or revealed will. In other words, God cannot sin, stop being God, or destroy the world by flood. But all that is according to His character and will, He can most surely do.

One of God's names emphasizing His omnipotence is *Almighty*. In Genesis 17:1, He told Abraham, "I am Almighty God." Abraham needed to hear that because God promised the old man a near innumerable family. The Almighty used an old man and his aging, barren wife to create one of the largest family units in human history. God is truly all-powerful!

*For* **THE DOCTRINE OF GOD: PART 7: THE OMNISCIENCE OF GOD**, *turn to Psalm 147:5 on page 622.*

42 "For thus says the LORD: [a]'Just as I have
brought all this great calamity on this people,
so I will bring on them all the good that I have
promised them. 43 And fields will be bought
in this land [a]of which you say, "*It is* desolate,
without man or beast; it has been given into the
hand of the Chaldeans." 44 Men will buy fields
for money, sign deeds and seal *them,* and take
witnesses, in [a]the land of Benjamin, in the plac-
es around Jerusalem, in the cities of Judah, in
the cities of the mountains, in the cities of the
lowland, and in the cities of the South; for [b]I will
cause their captives to return,' says the LORD."

## *EXCELLENCE OF THE RESTORED NATION*

**33** Moreover the word of the LORD came to
Jeremiah a second time, while he was still
[a]shut up in the court of the prison, saying, 2 "Thus
says the LORD [a]who made it, the LORD who formed
it to establish it [b](the LORD *is* His name): 3 [a]'Call to
Me, and I will answer you, and show you great and
mighty things, which you do not know.'

4 "For thus says the LORD, the God of Israel,
concerning the houses of this city and the houses
of the kings of Judah, which have been pulled
down *to fortify*[1] against [a]the siege mounds and the
sword: 5 'They come to fight with the Chaldeans,
but *only* to [a]fill their places[1] with the dead bodies
of men whom I will slay in My anger and My fury,
all for whose wickedness I have hidden My face
from this city. 6 Behold, [a]I will bring it health and
healing; I will heal them and reveal to them the
abundance of peace and truth. 7 And [a]I will cause
the captives of Judah and the captives of Israel
to return, and will rebuild those places [b]as at the
first. 8 I will [a]cleanse them from all their iniquity
by which they have sinned against Me, and I will
pardon all their iniquities by which they have
sinned and by which they have transgressed
against Me. 9 [a]Then it shall be to Me a name of joy,
a praise, and an honor before all nations of the
earth, who shall hear all the good that I do to them;
they shall [b]fear and tremble for all the goodness
and all the prosperity that I provide for it.'

10 "Thus says the LORD: 'Again there shall
be heard in this place—[a]of which you say, "It *is*
desolate, without man and without beast"—in
the cities of Judah, in the streets of Jerusalem
that are desolate, without man and without
inhabitant and without beast, 11 the [a]voice of
joy and the voice of gladness, the voice of the
bridegroom and the voice of the bride, the voice
of those who will say:

[b]"Praise the LORD of hosts,
For the LORD *is* good,
For His mercy *endures* forever"—

*and* of those *who will* bring [c]the sacrifice of
praise into the house of the LORD. For I will
cause the captives of the land to return as at
the first,' says the LORD.

12 "Thus says the LORD of hosts: [a]'In this place
which is desolate, without man and without
beast, and in all its cities, there shall again be a
dwelling place of shepherds causing *their* flocks
to lie down. 13 [a]In the cities of the mountains,
in the cities of the lowland, in the cities of the
South, in the land of Benjamin, in the places
around Jerusalem, and in the cities of Judah,
the flocks shall again [b]pass under the hands of
him who counts *them,*' says the LORD.

14 [a]'Behold, the days are coming,' says the
LORD, 'that [b]I will perform that good thing which
I have promised to the house of Israel and to
the house of Judah:

15 'In those days and at that time
I will cause to grow up to David
A [a]Branch of righteousness;
He shall execute judgment and
righteousness in the earth.
16 In those days Judah will be saved,
And Jerusalem will dwell safely.
And this *is the name* by which she will be
called:

THE LORD OUR RIGHTEOUSNESS.'[1]

17 "For thus says the LORD: 'David shall never
[a]lack a man to sit on the throne of the house of
Israel; 18 nor shall the [a]priests, the Levites, lack a
man to [b]offer burnt offerings before Me, to kin-
dle grain offerings, and to sacrifice continually.' "

## *THE PERMANENCE OF GOD'S COVENANT*

19 And the word of the LORD came to Jere-
miah, saying, 20 "Thus says the LORD: 'If you can
break My covenant with the day and My covenant
with the night, so that there will not be day and
night in their season, 21 then [a]My covenant may
also be broken with David My servant, so that he
shall not have a son to reign on his throne, and
with the Levites, the priests, My ministers. 22 As
[a]the host of heaven cannot be numbered, nor
the sand of the sea measured, so will I [b]multiply
the descendants of David My servant and the
[c]Levites who minister to Me.' "

23 Moreover the word of the LORD came to
Jeremiah, saying, 24 "Have you not considered
what these people have spoken, saying, 'The
two families which the LORD has chosen, He has
also cast them off'? Thus they have [a]despised My
people, as if they should no more be a nation
before them.

32:42 [a] Jer. 31:28 32:43 [a] Jer. 33:10 32:44 [a] Jer. 17:26 [b] Jer. 33:7, 11 33:1 [a] Jer. 32:2, 3 33:2 [a] Is. 37:26 [b] Ex. 15:3 33:3 [a] Jer. 29:12 33:4 [a] Is. 22:10 [1] Compare Isaiah 22:10 33:5 [a] 2 Kin. 23:14 [1] Compare 2 Kings 23:14 33:6 [a] Jer. 30:17 33:7 [a] Jer. 30:3; 32:44 [b] Is. 1:26 33:8 [a] Zech. 13:1 33:9 [a] Is. 62:7 [b] Is. 60:5 33:10 [a] Jer. 32:43 33:11 [a] Rev. 18:23 [b] Is. 12:4 [c] Lev. 7:12 33:12 [a] Is. 65:10 33:13 [a] Jer. 17:26; 32:44 [b] Lev. 27:32 33:14 [a] Jer. 23:5; 31:27, 31 [b] Jer. 29:10; 32:42 33:15 [a] Jer. 23:5 33:16 [1] Compare 23:5, 6 33:17 [a] 2 Sam. 7:16 33:18 [a] Ezek. 44:15 [b] [1 Pet. 2:5, 9] 33:21 [a] 2 Sam. 23:5; Ps. 89:34 33:22 [a] Gen. 15:5; 22:17 [b] Jer. 30:19 [c] Is. 66:21 33:24 [a] Esth. 3:6–8

25 "Thus says the LORD: 'If [a]My covenant *is* not
with day and night, *and if* I have not [b]appointed
the ordinances of heaven and earth, 26 [a]then I
will [b]cast away the descendants of Jacob and
David My servant, *so* that I will not take *any* of his
descendants *to be* rulers over the descendants of
Abraham, Isaac, and Jacob. For I will cause their
captives to return, and will have mercy on them.' "

### *ZEDEKIAH WARNED BY GOD*

**34** The word which came to Jeremiah from
the LORD, [a]when Nebuchadnezzar king
of Babylon and all his army, [b]all the kingdoms of
the earth under his dominion, and all the people,
fought against Jerusalem and all its cities, saying,
2 "Thus says the LORD, the God of Israel: 'Go and
[a]speak to Zedekiah king of Judah and tell him,
"Thus says the LORD: 'Behold, [b]I will give this city
into the hand of the king of Babylon, and he shall
burn it with fire. 3 And [a]you shall not escape from
his hand, but shall surely be taken and delivered
into his hand; your eyes shall see the eyes of the
king of Babylon, he shall speak with you [b]face to
face,[1] and you shall go to Babylon.' " ' 4 Yet hear
the word of the LORD, O Zedekiah king of Judah!
Thus says the LORD concerning you: 'You shall
not die by the sword. 5 You shall die in peace; as in
[a]the ceremonies of your fathers, the former kings
who were before you, [b]so they shall burn *incense*
for you and [c]lament for you, *saying,* "Alas, lord!"
For I have pronounced the word, says the LORD.' "

6 Then Jeremiah the prophet spoke all these
words to Zedekiah king of Judah in Jerusalem,
7 when the king of Babylon's army fought against
Jerusalem and all the cities of Judah that were
left, against Lachish and Azekah; for *only* [a]these
fortified cities remained of the cities of Judah.

### *TREACHEROUS TREATMENT OF SLAVES*

8 *This is* the word that came to Jeremiah from
the LORD, after King Zedekiah had made a cov-
enant with all the people who *were* at Jerusalem
to proclaim [a]liberty to them: 9 [a]that every man
should set free his male and female slave—a He-
brew man or woman—[b]that no one should keep
a Jewish brother in bondage. 10 Now when all the
princes and all the people, who had entered into
the covenant, heard that everyone should set free
his male and female slaves, that no one should
keep them in bondage anymore, they obeyed and
let *them* go. 11 But afterward they changed their
minds and made the male and female slaves
return, whom they had set free, and brought
them into subjection as male and female slaves.

12 Therefore the word of the LORD came to Jere-
miah from the LORD, saying, 13 "Thus says the LORD,
the God of Israel: 'I made a [a]covenant with your
fathers in the day that I brought them out of the
land of Egypt, out of the house of bondage, saying,
14 "At the end of [a]seven years let every man set free
his Hebrew brother, who has been sold to him;
and when he has served you six years, you shall
let him go free from you." But your fathers did not
obey Me nor incline their ear. 15 Then you recently
turned and did what was right in My sight—every
man proclaiming liberty to his neighbor; and you
[a]made a covenant before Me [b]in the house which is
called by My name. 16 Then you turned around and
[a]profaned My name, and every one of you brought
back his male and female slaves, whom you had set
at liberty, at their pleasure, and brought them back
into subjection, to be your male and female slaves.'

17 "Therefore thus says the LORD: 'You have not
obeyed Me in proclaiming liberty, every one to his
brother and every one to his neighbor. [a]Behold, I
proclaim liberty to you,' says the LORD—[b]'to the
sword, to pestilence, and to famine! And I will
deliver you to [c]trouble among all the kingdoms
of the earth. 18 And I will give the men who have
transgressed My covenant, who have not per-
formed the words of the covenant which they
made before Me, when [a]they cut the calf in two and
passed between the parts of it— 19 the princes of
Judah, the princes of Jerusalem, the eunuchs, the
priests, and all the people of the land who passed
between the parts of the calf— 20 I will [a]give them
into the hand of their enemies and into the hand
of those who seek their life. Their [b]dead bodies
shall be for meat for the birds of the heaven and
the beasts of the earth. 21 And I will give Zedekiah
king of Judah and his princes into the hand of
their enemies, into the hand of those who seek
their life, and into the hand of the king of Babylon's
army [a]which has gone back from you. 22 [a]Behold,
I will command,' says the LORD, 'and cause them
to return to this city. They will fight against it [b]and
take it and burn it with fire; and [c]I will make the
cities of Judah a desolation without inhabitant.' "

### *THE OBEDIENT RECHABITES*

**35** The word which came to Jeremiah from
the LORD in the days of Jehoiakim the
son of Josiah, king of Judah, saying, 2 "Go to the
house of the [a]Rechabites, speak to them, and
bring them into the house of the LORD, into one
of [b]the chambers, and give them wine to drink."

> **35:2** The **Rechabites** were nomads who refused to drink **wine** or participate in the corrupt lifestyle of the people around them.

**33:25** [a] Gen. 8:22 [b] Ps. 74:16; 104:19 **33:26** [a] Jer. 31:37 [b] Rom. 11:1, 2 **34:1** [a] 2 Kin. 25:1 [b] Jer. 1:15; 25:9 **34:2** [a] 2 Chr. 36:11, 12 [b] Jer. 21:10; 32:3, 28 **34:3** [a] 2 Kin. 25:4, 5 [b] Jer. 32:4; 39:5, 6 [1] Literally *mouth to mouth* **34:5** [a] 2 Chr. 16:14; 21:19 [b] Dan. 2:46 [c] Jer. 22:18 **34:7** [a] 2 Kin. 18:13; 19:8 **34:8** [a] Ex. 21:2 **34:9** [a] Neh. 5:11 [b] Lev. 25:39–46 **34:13** [a] Ex. 24:3, 7, 8; Deut. 5:2, 3, 27; Jer. 31:32 **34:14** [a] Ex. 21:2; 23:10; Deut. 15:12; 1 Kin. 9:22 **34:15** [a] 2 Kin. 23:3; Neh. 10:29 [b] Jer. 7:10 **34:16** [a] Ex. 20:7; Lev. 19:12 **34:17** [a] Lev. 26:34, 35; Esth. 7:10; Dan. 6:24; [Matt. 7:2; Gal. 6:7]; James 2:13 [b] Jer. 32:24, 36 [c] Deut. 28:25, 64; Jer. 29:18 **34:18** [a] Gen. 15:10, 17 **34:20** [a] 2 Kin. 25:19–21; Jer. 22:25 [b] Deut. 28:26; 1 Sam. 17:44, 46; 1 Kin. 14:11; 16:4; Ps. 79:2; Jer. 7:33; 16:4; 19:7 **34:21** [a] Jer. 37:5–11; 39:4–7 **34:22** [a] Jer. 37:8, 10 [b] Jer. 38:3; 39:1, 2, 8; 52:7, 13 [c] Jer. 9:11; 44:2, 6 **35:2** [a] 2 Sam. 4:2; 2 Kin. 10:15; 1 Chr. 2:55 [b] 1 Kin. 6:5, 8; 1 Chr. 9:26, 33

3 Then I took Jaazaniah the son of Jeremiah,
the son of Habazziniah, his brothers and all his
sons, and the whole house of the Rechabites,
4 and I brought them into the house of the LORD,
into the chamber of the sons of Hanan the son
of Igdaliah, a man of God, which *was* by the
chamber of the princes, above the chamber of
Maaseiah the son of Shallum, [a]the keeper of the
door. 5 Then I set before the sons of the house
of the Rechabites bowls full of wine, and cups;
and I said to them, "Drink wine."
6 But they said, "We will drink no wine, for
[a]Jonadab the son of Rechab, our father, com-
manded us, saying, 'You shall drink [b]no wine,
you nor your sons, forever. 7 You shall not build
a house, sow seed, plant a vineyard, nor have *any
of these;* but all your days you shall dwell in tents,
[a]that you may live many days in the land where
you are sojourners.' 8 Thus we have [a]obeyed the
voice of Jonadab the son of Rechab, our father,
in all that he charged us, to drink no wine all our
days, we, our wives, our sons, or our daughters,
9 nor to build ourselves houses to dwell in; nor
do we have vineyard, field, or seed. 10 But we have
dwelt in tents, and have obeyed and done accord-
ing to all that Jonadab our father commanded
us. 11 But it came to pass, when Nebuchadnezzar
king of Babylon came up into the land, that we
said, 'Come, let us [a]go to Jerusalem for fear of
the army of the Chaldeans and for fear of the
army of the Syrians.' So we dwell at Jerusalem."
12 Then came the word of the LORD to Jeremi-
ah, saying, 13 "Thus says the LORD of hosts, the God
of Israel: 'Go and tell the men of Judah and the
inhabitants of Jerusalem, "Will you not [a]receive
instruction to obey My words?" says the LORD.
14 "The words of Jonadab the son of Rechab, which
he commanded his sons, not to drink wine, are
performed; for to this day they drink none, and
obey their father's commandment. [a]But although
I have spoken to you, [b]rising early and speaking,
you did not obey Me. 15 I have also sent to you all
My [a]servants the prophets, rising up early and
sending *them,* saying, [b]'Turn now everyone from
his evil way, amend your doings, and do not go
after other gods to serve them; then you will
[c]dwell in the land which I have given you and your
fathers.' But you have not inclined your ear, nor
obeyed Me. 16 Surely the sons of Jonadab the son
of Rechab have performed the commandment
of their [a]father, which he commanded them, but
this people has not obeyed Me." '
17 "Therefore thus says the LORD God of
hosts, the God of Israel: 'Behold, I will bring on
Judah and on all the inhabitants of Jerusalem
all the doom that I have pronounced against
them; [a]because I have spoken to them but they
have not heard, and I have called to them but
they have not answered.' "
18 And Jeremiah said to the house of the
Rechabites, "Thus says the LORD of hosts, the
God of Israel: 'Because you have obeyed the
commandment of Jonadab your father, and
kept all his precepts and done according to all
that he commanded you, 19 therefore thus says
the LORD of hosts, the God of Israel: "Jonadab
the son of Rechab shall not lack a man to [a]stand
before Me forever." ' "

### *THE SCROLL READ IN THE TEMPLE*

36 Now it came to pass in the [a]fourth year
of Jehoiakim the son of Josiah, king of
Judah, *that* this word came to Jeremiah from
the LORD, saying: 2 "Take a [a]scroll of a book and
[b]write on it all the words that I have spoken to
you against Israel, against Judah, and against
[c]all the nations, from the day I spoke to you,
from the days of [d]Josiah even to this day. 3 It
[a]may be that the house of Judah will hear all
the adversities which I purpose to bring upon
them, that everyone may [b]turn from his evil way,
that I may forgive their iniquity and their sin."
4 Then Jeremiah [a]called Baruch the son of
Neriah; and [b]Baruch wrote on a scroll of a book,
at the instruction of Jeremiah,[1] all the words of
the LORD which He had spoken to him. 5 And
Jeremiah commanded Baruch, saying, "I *am*
confined, I cannot go into the house of the LORD.
6 You go, therefore, and read from the scroll which
you have written at my instruction,[1] the words
of the LORD, in the hearing of the people in the
LORD's house on [a]the day of fasting. And you shall
also read them in the hearing of all Judah who
come from their cities. 7 It may be that they will
present their supplication before the LORD, and
everyone will turn from his evil way. For great *is*
the anger and the fury that the LORD has pro-
nounced against this people." 8 And Baruch the
son of Neriah did according to all that Jeremiah
the prophet commanded him, reading from the
book the words of the LORD in the LORD's house.
9 Now it came to pass in the fifth year of Je-
hoiakim the son of Josiah, king of Judah, in the
ninth month, *that* they proclaimed a fast before
the LORD to all the people in Jerusalem, and
to all the people who came from the cities of
Judah to Jerusalem. 10 Then Baruch read from
the book the words of Jeremiah in the house of
the LORD, in the chamber of Gemariah the son
of Shaphan the scribe, in the upper court at the
[a]entry of the New Gate of the LORD's house, in
the hearing of all the people.

35:4 [a] 2 Kin. 12:9; 25:18; 1 Chr. 9:18, 19 35:6 [a] 2 Kin. 10:15, 23 [b] Lev. 10:9; Num. 6:2–4; Judg. 13:7, 14; Prov. 31:4; Ezek. 44:21; Luke 1:15 35:7 [a] Ex. 20:12; Eph. 6:2, 3 35:8 [a] [Prov. 1:8, 9; 4:1, 2, 10; 6:20; Eph. 6:1; Col. 3:20] 35:11 [a] Jer. 4:5–7; 8:14 35:13 [a] [Is. 28:9–12]; Jer. 6:10; 17:23; 32:33 35:14 [a] 2 Chr. 36:15 [b] Jer. 7:13; 25:3 35:15 [a] Jer. 26:4, 5; 29:19 [b] [Is. 1:16, 17]; Jer. 18:11; 25:5, 6; [Ezek. 18:30–32]; Acts 26:20 [c] Jer. 7:7; 25:5, 6 35:16 [a] [Heb. 12:9] 35:17 [a] Prov. 1:24; Is. 65:12; 66:4; Jer. 7:13 35:19 [a] [Ex. 20:12]; Jer. 15:19; [Luke 21:36; Eph. 6:2, 3] 36:1 [a] 2 Kin. 24:1; 2 Chr. 36:5–7; Jer. 25:1, 3; 45:1; Dan. 1:1 36:2 [a] Is. 8:1; Ezek. 2:9; Zech. 5:1 [b] Jer. 30:2; Hab. 2:2 [c] Jer. 25:15 [d] Jer. 25:3 36:3 [a] Jer. 26:3; Ezek. 12:3 [b] [Deut. 30:2, 8; 1 Sam. 7:3]; Is. 55:7; Jer. 18:8; Jon. 3:8 36:4 [a] Jer. 32:12 [b] Jer. 45:1 [1] Literally *from Jeremiah's mouth* 36:6 [a] Lev. 16:29; 23:27–32; Acts 27:9 [1] Literally *from my mouth* 36:10 [a] Jer. 26:10

### THE SCROLL READ IN THE PALACE

11 When Michaiah the son of Gemariah, the son of Shaphan, heard all the words of the LORD from the book, 12 he then went down to the king's house, into the scribe's chamber; and there all the princes were sitting—[a]Elishama the scribe, Delaiah the son of Shemaiah, [b]Elnathan the son of Achbor, Gemariah the son of Shaphan, Zedekiah the son of Hananiah, and all the princes. 13 Then Michaiah declared to them all the words that he had heard when Baruch read the book in the hearing of the people. 14 Therefore all the princes sent Jehudi the son of Nethaniah, the son of Shelemiah, the son of Cushi, to Baruch, saying, "Take in your hand the scroll from which you have read in the hearing of the people, and come." So Baruch the son of Neriah took the scroll in his hand and came to them. 15 And they said to him, "Sit down now, and read it in our hearing." So Baruch read *it* in their hearing.

16 Now it happened, when they had heard all the words, that they looked in fear from one to another, and said to Baruch, "We will surely tell the king of all these words." 17 And they asked Baruch, saying, "Tell us now, how did you write all these words—at his instruction?"[1]

18 So Baruch answered them, "He proclaimed with his mouth all these words to me, and I wrote *them* with ink in the book."

19 Then the princes said to Baruch, "Go and hide, you and Jeremiah; and let no one know where you are."

### THE KING DESTROYS JEREMIAH'S SCROLL

20 And they went to the king, into the court; but they stored the scroll in the chamber of Elishama the scribe, and told all the words in the hearing of the king. 21 So the king sent Jehudi to bring the scroll, and he took it from Elishama the scribe's chamber. And Jehudi read it in the hearing of the king and in the hearing of all the princes who stood beside the king. 22 Now the king was sitting in [a]the winter house in the ninth month, with *a fire* burning on the hearth before him. 23 And it happened, when Jehudi had read three or four columns, *that the king* cut it with the scribe's knife and cast *it* into the fire that *was* on the hearth, until all the scroll was consumed in the fire that *was* on the hearth. 24 Yet they were [a]not afraid, nor did they [b]tear their garments, the king nor any of his servants who heard all these words. 25 Nevertheless Elnathan, Delaiah, and Gemariah implored the king not to burn the scroll; but he would not listen to them. 26 And the king commanded Jerahmeel the king's[1] son, Seraiah the son of Azriel, and Shelemiah the son of Abdeel, to seize Baruch the scribe and Jeremiah the prophet, but the LORD hid them.

### JEREMIAH REWRITES THE SCROLL

27 Now after the king had burned the scroll with the words which Baruch had written at the instruction of Jeremiah,[1] the word of the LORD came to Jeremiah, saying: 28 "Take yet another scroll, and write on it all the former words that were in the first scroll which Jehoiakim the king of Judah has burned. 29 And you shall say to Jehoiakim king of Judah, 'Thus says the LORD: "You have burned this scroll, saying, [a]'Why have you written in it that the king of Babylon will certainly come and destroy this land, and cause man and beast to [b]cease from here?' " 30 Therefore thus says the LORD concerning Jehoiakim king of Judah: [a]"He shall have no one to sit on the throne of David, and his dead body shall be [b]cast out to the heat of the day and the frost of the night. 31 I will punish him, his family, and his servants for their iniquity; and I will bring on them, on the inhabitants of Jerusalem, and on the men of Judah all the doom that I have pronounced against them; but they did not heed." ' "

32 Then Jeremiah took another scroll and gave it to Baruch the scribe, the son of Neriah, who wrote on it at the instruction of Jeremiah[1] all the words of the book which Jehoiakim king of Judah had burned in the fire. And besides, there were added to them many similar words.

### ZEDEKIAH'S VAIN HOPE

*(2 Kin. 24:17; 2 Chr. 36:10)*

**37** Now King [a]Zedekiah the son of Josiah reigned instead of Coniah the son of Jehoiakim, whom Nebuchadnezzar king of Babylon made king in the land of Judah. 2 [a]But neither he nor his servants nor the people of the land gave heed to the words of the LORD which He spoke by the prophet Jeremiah.

3 And Zedekiah the king sent Jehucal the son of Shelemiah, and [a]Zephaniah the son of Maaseiah, the priest, to the prophet Jeremiah, saying, [b]"Pray now to the LORD our God for us." 4 Now Jeremiah was coming and going among the people, for they had not *yet* put him in prison. 5 Then [a]Pharaoh's army came up from Egypt; and when the Chaldeans who were besieging Jerusalem heard news of them, they departed from Jerusalem.

6 Then the word of the LORD came to the prophet Jeremiah, saying, 7 "Thus says the LORD, the God of Israel, 'Thus you shall say to the king of Judah, [a]who sent you to Me to inquire of Me: "Behold, Pharaoh's army which has come up to help you will return to Egypt, to their own land. 8 [a]And the Chaldeans shall come back and fight against this city, and take it and burn it with fire." ' 9 Thus says the LORD: 'Do not deceive

**36:12** [a] Jer. 41:1 [b] Jer. 26:22 **36:17** [1] Literally *with his mouth* **36:22** [a] Judg. 3:20; Amos 3:15 **36:24** [a] [Ps. 36:1]; Jer. 36:16 [b] Gen. 37:29, 34; 2 Sam. 1:11; 1 Kin. 21:27; 2 Kin. 19:1, 2; 22:11; Is. 36:22; 37:1; Jon. 3:6 **36:26** [1] Hebrew *Hammelech* **36:27** [1] Literally *from Jeremiah's mouth* **36:29** [a] Jer. 32:3 [b] Jer. 25:9–11; 26:9 **36:30** [a] Jer. 22:30 [b] Jer. 22:19 **36:32** [1] Literally *from Jeremiah's mouth* **37:1** [a] 2 Kin. 24:17; 1 Chr. 3:15; 2 Chr. 36:10; Jer. 22:24 **37:2** [a] 2 Kin. 24:19, 20; 2 Chr. 36:12–16; [Prov. 29:12] **37:3** [a] Jer. 21:1, 2; 29:25; 52:24 [b] 1 Kin. 13:6; Jer. 42:2; Acts 8:24 **37:5** [a] 2 Kin. 24:7; Jer. 37:7; Ezek. 17:15 **37:7** [a] Is. 36:6; Jer. 21:2; Ezek. 17:17 **37:8** [a] 2 Chr. 36:19; Jer. 34:22

KNOW THE TRUTH

# THE DOCTRINE OF SCRIPTURE

## PART 8: THE TRANSMISSION OF SCRIPTURE

**36:32** When Baruch wrote God's words dictated to him by Jeremiah, he created what's called an autograph. When it comes to the Bible, an *autograph* is an original writing of Scripture, such as Jeremiah here, Moses's recording of Genesis, and John's writing of Revelation. Because the autographs were written on materials that degraded and, because of several orders to destroy the sacred writings of Scripture throughout history, no autograph of Scripture exists today. Instead, we have manuscripts, faithful copies of those autographs, through the process of transmission.

If you've ever copied something by hand, you know how easy it can be to make errors. To prevent this from happening, meticulous safeguards were put in place by those who copied the Old Testament. Manuscripts were vigorously tested for accuracy. The middle letter of the book being copied, the number of occurrences of certain letters, the total number of words, and other tests were run. If any test failed, the manuscript was disposed of, and work started over. Similar care was taken in the transmission of the New Testament.

The result is we have thousands of manuscripts of Scripture from all across Africa, Asia, and Europe, with some manuscripts dating to within decades of their autographs. As such, we can have great confidence in the reliability of the Bible. Under God's sovereign hand, the Bible has been accurately transmitted to us today.

*For* **THE DOCTRINE OF SCRIPTURE: PART 9: THE CANONIZATION OF SCRIPTURE**, *turn to Acts 18:27–28 on page 1131.*

yourselves, saying, "The Chaldeans will surely
depart from us," for they will not depart. 10 [a]For
though you had defeated the whole army of
the Chaldeans who fight against you, and there
remained *only* wounded men among them, they
would rise up, every man in his tent, and burn
the city with fire.'"

### *JEREMIAH IMPRISONED*

11 And it happened, when the army of the
Chaldeans left *the siege* of Jerusalem for fear
of Pharaoh's army, 12 that Jeremiah went out
of Jerusalem to go into the land of Benjamin
to claim his property there among the people.
13 And when he was in the Gate of Benjamin, a
captain of the guard *was* there whose name *was*
Irijah the son of Shelemiah, the son of Hananiah; and he seized Jeremiah the prophet, saying,
"You are defecting to the Chaldeans!"
14 Then Jeremiah said, "False! I am not defecting to the Chaldeans." But he did not listen
to him.

So Irijah seized Jeremiah and brought him
to the princes. 15 Therefore the princes were
angry with Jeremiah, and they struck him [a]and
put him in prison in the [b]house of Jonathan
the scribe. For they had made that the prison.

16 When Jeremiah entered [a]the dungeon
and the cells, and Jeremiah had remained there
many days, 17 then Zedekiah the king sent and
took him *out.* The king asked him secretly in
his house, and said, "Is there *any* word from
the LORD?"

And Jeremiah said, "There is." Then he said,
"You shall be [a]delivered into the hand of the
king of Babylon!"
18 Moreover Jeremiah said to King Zedekiah,
"What offense have I committed against you,
against your servants, or against this people,
that you have put me in prison? 19 Where now *are*
your prophets who prophesied to you, saying,
'The king of Babylon will not come against you
or against this land'? 20 Therefore please hear
now, O my lord the king. Please, let my petition
be accepted before you, and do not make me
return to the house of Jonathan the scribe, lest
I die there."
21 Then Zedekiah the king commanded
that they should commit Jeremiah [a]to the
court of the prison, and that they should give
him daily a piece of bread from the bakers'
street, [b]until all the bread in the city was gone.
Thus Jeremiah remained in the court of the
prison.

**37:10** [a] Lev. 26:36–38; Is. 30:17; Jer. 21:4, 5 **37:15** [a] Jer. 20:2; [Matt. 21:35] [b] Gen. 39:20; 2 Chr. 16:10; 18:26; Jer. 38:26; Acts 5:18 **37:16** [a] Jer. 38:6 **37:17** [a] 2 Kin. 25:4–7; Jer. 21:7; Ezek. 12:12, 13; 17:19–21 **37:21** [a] Jer. 32:2; 38:13, 28 [b] 2 Kin. 25:3; Jer. 38:9; 52:6

### *JEREMIAH IN THE DUNGEON*

**38** Now Shephatiah the son of Mattan, Geda-
liah the son of Pashhur, [a]Jucal[1] the son of
Shelemiah, and [b]Pashhur the son of Malchiah
[c]heard the words that Jeremiah had spoken to
all the people, saying, 2"Thus says the LORD: [a]'He
who remains in this city shall die by the sword, by
famine, and by pestilence; but he who goes over to
the Chaldeans shall live; his life shall be as a prize
to him, and he shall live.' 3Thus says the LORD:
[a]'This city shall surely be [b]given into the hand of
the king of Babylon's army, which shall take it.' "
4Therefore the princes said to the king,
"Please, [a]let this man be put to death, for thus
he weakens the hands of the men of war who
remain in this city, and the hands of all the peo-
ple, by speaking such words to them. For this
man does not seek the welfare of this people,
but their harm."
5Then Zedekiah the king said, "Look, he
*is* in your hand. For the king can *do* nothing
against you." 6[a]So they took Jeremiah and cast
him into the dungeon of Malchiah the king's[1]
son, which *was* in the court of the prison, and
they let Jeremiah down with ropes. And in the
dungeon *there was* no water, but mire. So Jere-
miah sank in the mire.
7[a]Now Ebed-Melech the Ethiopian, one of the
eunuchs, who was in the king's house, heard that
they had put Jeremiah in the dungeon. When the
king was sitting at the Gate of Benjamin, 8Ebed-
Melech went out of the king's house and spoke
to the king, saying: 9"My lord the king, these
men have done evil in all that they have done to
Jeremiah the prophet, whom they have cast into
the dungeon, and he is likely to die from hunger
in the place where he is. For *there is* [a]no more
bread in the city." 10Then the king commanded
Ebed-Melech the Ethiopian, saying, "Take from
here thirty men with you, and lift Jeremiah the
prophet out of the dungeon before he dies." 11So
Ebed-Melech took the men with him and went
into the house of the king under the treasury, and
took from there old clothes and old rags, and let
them down by ropes into the dungeon to Jere-
miah. 12Then Ebed-Melech the Ethiopian said to
Jeremiah, "Please put these old clothes and rags
under your armpits, under the ropes." And Jere-
miah did so. 13So they pulled Jeremiah up with
ropes and lifted him out of the dungeon. And
Jeremiah remained [a]in the court of the prison.

### *ZEDEKIAH'S FEARS AND JEREMIAH'S ADVICE*

14Then Zedekiah the king sent and had Jer-
emiah the prophet brought to him at the third
entrance of the house of the LORD. And the king
said to Jeremiah, "I will [a]ask you something.
Hide nothing from me."
15Jeremiah said to Zedekiah, "If I declare *it*
to you, will you not surely put me to death? And
if I give you advice, you will not listen to me."
16So Zedekiah the king swore secretly to Jere-
miah, saying, "*As* the LORD lives, [a]who made our
very souls, I will not put you to death, nor will I give
you into the hand of these men who seek your life."
17Then Jeremiah said to Zedekiah, "Thus says
the LORD, the God of hosts, the God of Israel: 'If
you surely [a]surrender [b]to the king of Babylon's
princes, then your soul shall live; this city shall not
be burned with fire, and you and your house shall
live. 18But if you do not surrender to the king of
Babylon's princes, then this city shall be given into
the hand of the Chaldeans; they shall burn it with
fire, and [a]you shall not escape from their hand.' "
19And Zedekiah the king said to Jeremiah,
"I am afraid of the Jews who have [a]defected to
the Chaldeans, lest they deliver me into their
hand, and they [b]abuse me."
20But Jeremiah said, "They shall not deliver
*you*. Please, obey the voice of the LORD which
I speak to you. So it shall be [a]well with you,
and your soul shall live. 21But if you refuse to
surrender, this *is* the word that the LORD has
shown me: 22'Now behold, all the [a]women who
are left in the king of Judah's house *shall be*
surrendered to the king of Babylon's princes,
and those *women* shall say:

"Your close friends have set upon you
And prevailed against you;
Your feet have sunk in the mire,
*And* they have turned away again."

23'So they shall surrender all your wives
and [a]children to the Chaldeans. [b]You shall not
escape from their hand, but shall be taken by
the hand of the king of Babylon. And you shall
cause this city to be burned with fire.' "
24Then Zedekiah said to Jeremiah, "Let no
one know of these words, and you shall not
die. 25But if the princes hear that I have talked
with you, and they come to you and say to you,
'Declare to us now what you have said to the
king, and also what the king said to you; do not
hide *it* from us, and we will not put you to death,'
26then you shall say to them, [a]'I presented my
request before the king, that he would not make
me return [b]to Jonathan's house to die there.' "
27Then all the princes came to Jeremiah
and asked him. And he told them according to
all these words that the king had commanded.
So they stopped speaking with him, for the con-
versation had not been heard. 28Now [a]Jeremiah
remained in the court of the prison until the
day that Jerusalem was taken. And he was *there*
when Jerusalem was taken.

**38:1** [a] Jer. 37:3 [b] Jer. 21:1 [c] Jer. 21:8 [1] Same as *Jehucal* (compare 37:3) **38:2** [a] Jer. 21:9 [1] Compare 21:9 **38:3** [a] Jer. 21:10; 32:3 [b] Jer. 34:2 **38:4** [a] Jer. 26:11 **38:6** [a] Jer. 37:21; Lam. 3:55 [1] Hebrew *Hammelech* **38:7** [a] Jer. 39:16 **38:9** [a] Jer. 37:21 **38:13** [a] Neh. 3:25; Jer. 37:21; Acts 23:35; 24:27; 28:16, 30 **38:14** [a] Jer. 21:1, 2; 37:17 **38:16** [a] Num. 16:22; Is. 57:16; Zech. 12:1; [Acts 17:25, 28] **38:17** [a] 2 Kin. 24:12 [b] Jer. 39:3 **38:18** [a] Jer. 32:4; 34:3 **38:19** [a] Jer. 39:9 [b] 1 Sam. 31:4 **38:20** [a] Jer. 40:9 **38:22** [a] Jer. 8:10 **38:23** [a] Jer. 39:6; 41:10 [b] Jer. 39:5 **38:26** [a] Jer. 37:20 [b] Jer. 37:15 **38:28** [a] [Ps. 23:4]; Jer. 37:21; 39:14

### *THE FALL OF JERUSALEM*
*(2 Kin. 25:1–12; Jer. 52:4–16)*

**39** In the [a]ninth year of Zedekiah king of Judah, in the tenth month, Nebuchadnezzar king of Babylon and all his army came against Jerusalem, and besieged it. 2 In the [a]eleventh year of Zedekiah, in the fourth month, on the ninth *day* of the month, the city was penetrated.

3 [a]Then all the princes of the king of Babylon came in and sat in the Middle Gate: Nergal-Sharezer, Samgar-Nebo, Sarsechim, Rabsaris,[1] Nergal-Sarezer, Rabmag,[2] with the rest of the princes of the king of Babylon.

4 [a]So it was, when Zedekiah the king of Judah and all the men of war saw them, that they fled and went out of the city by night, by way of the king's garden, by the gate between the two walls. And he went out by way of the plain.[1] 5 But the Chaldean army pursued them and [a]overtook Zedekiah in the plains of Jericho. And when they had captured him, they brought him up to Nebuchadnezzar king of Babylon, to [b]Riblah in the land of Hamath, where he pronounced judgment on him. 6 Then the king of Babylon killed the sons of Zedekiah before his [a]eyes in Riblah; the king of Babylon also killed all the [b]nobles of Judah. 7 Moreover [a]he put out Zedekiah's eyes, and bound him with bronze fetters to carry him off to Babylon. 8 [a]And the Chaldeans burned the king's house and the houses of the people with [b]fire, and broke down the [c]walls of Jerusalem. 9 [a]Then Nebuzaradan the captain of the guard carried away captive to Babylon the remnant of the people who remained in the city and those who [b]defected to him, with the rest of the people who remained. 10 But Nebuzaradan the captain of the guard left in the land of Judah the [a]poor people, who had nothing, and gave them vineyards and fields at the same time.

### *JEREMIAH GOES FREE*

11 Now Nebuchadnezzar king of Babylon gave charge concerning Jeremiah to Nebuzaradan the captain of the guard, saying, 12 "Take him and look after him, and do him no [a]harm; but do to him just as he says to you." 13 So Nebuzaradan the captain of the guard sent Nebushasban, Rabsaris, Nergal-Sharezer, Rabmag, and all the king of Babylon's chief officers; 14 then they sent *someone* [a]to take Jeremiah from the court of the prison, and committed him [b]to Gedaliah the son of [c]Ahikam, the son of Shaphan, that he should take him home. So he dwelt among the people.

15 Meanwhile the word of the LORD had come to Jeremiah while he was shut up in the court of the prison, saying, 16 "Go and speak to [a]Ebed-Melech the Ethiopian, saying, 'Thus says the LORD of hosts, the God of Israel: "Behold, [b]I will bring My words upon this city for adversity and not for good, and they shall be *performed* in that day before you. 17 But I will deliver you in that day," says the LORD, "and you shall not be given into the hand of the men of whom you *are* afraid. 18 For I will surely deliver you, and you shall not fall by the sword; but [a]your life shall be as a prize to you, [b]because you have put your trust in Me," says the LORD.' "

### *JEREMIAH WITH GEDALIAH THE GOVERNOR*
*(2 Kin. 25:22–26)*

**40** The word that came to Jeremiah from the LORD [a]after Nebuzaradan the captain of the guard had let him go from Ramah, when he had taken him bound in chains among all who were carried away captive from Jerusalem and Judah, who were carried away captive to Babylon.

2 And the captain of the guard took Jeremiah and [a]said to him: "The LORD your God has pronounced this doom on this place. 3 Now the LORD has brought *it,* and has done just as He said. [a]Because you *people* have sinned against the LORD, and not obeyed His voice, therefore this thing has come upon you. 4 And now look, I free you this day from the chains that *were* on your hand. [a]If it seems good to you to come with me to Babylon, come, and I will look after you. But if it seems wrong for you to come with me to Babylon, remain here. See, [b]all the land *is* before you; wherever it seems good and convenient for you to go, go there."

5 Now while Jeremiah had not yet gone back, *Nebuzaradan said,* "Go back to [a]Gedaliah the son of Ahikam, the son of Shaphan, [b]whom the king of Babylon has made governor over the cities of Judah, and dwell with him among the people. Or go wherever it seems convenient for you to go." So the captain of the guard gave him rations and a gift and let him go. 6 [a]Then Jeremiah went to Gedaliah the son of Ahikam, to [b]Mizpah, and dwelt with him among the people who were left in the land.

7 [a]And when all the captains of the armies who *were* in the fields, they and their men, heard that the king of Babylon had made Gedaliah the son of Ahikam governor in the land, and had committed to him men, women, children, and [b]the poorest of the land who had not been carried away captive to Babylon, 8 then they came to Gedaliah at Mizpah—[a]Ishmael the son of Nethaniah, [b]Johanan and Jonathan the sons of Kareah, Seraiah the son of Tanhumeth, the sons of Ephai the Netophathite, and [c]Jezaniah[1] the son of a [d]Maachathite, they and their

39:1 [a] 2 Kin. 25:1–12; Jer. 52:4; Ezek. 24:1, 2 39:2 [a] Jer. 1:3 39:3 [a] Jer. 1:15; 38:17 [1] A title, probably *Chief Officer;* also verse 13 [2] A title, probably *Troop Commander;* also verse 13 39:4 [a] 2 Kin. 25:4; Is. 30:16; Jer. 52:7; Amos 2:14 [1] Or *the Arabah,* that is, the Jordan Valley 39:5 [a] Jer. 21:7; 32:4; 38:18, 23 [b] 2 Kin. 23:33; Jer. 52:9, 26, 27 39:6 [a] Deut. 28:34 [b] Jer. 34:19–21 39:7 [a] 2 Kin. 25:7; Jer. 52:11; Ezek. 12:13 39:8 [a] 2 Kin. 25:9; Jer. 38:18; 52:13 [b] Jer. 21:10 [c] 2 Kin. 25:10; Neh. 1:3; Jer. 52:14 39:9 [a] 2 Kin. 25:8, 11, 12, 20 [b] Jer. 38:19 39:10 [a] Jer. 40:7 39:12 [a] Jer. 1:18, 19; 15:20, 21 39:14 [a] Jer. 38:28 [b] Jer. 40:5 [c] 2 Kin. 22:12, 14; 2 Chr. 34:20; Jer. 26:24 39:16 [a] Jer. 38:7, 12 [b] Jer. 21:10; [Dan. 9:12; Zech. 1:6] 39:18 [a] Jer. 21:9; 45:5 [b] 1 Chr. 5:20; Ps. 37:40; [Jer. 17:7, 8] 40:1 [a] Jer. 39:9, 11 40:2 [a] Jer. 50:7 40:3 [a] Deut. 29:24, 25; Jer. 50:7; Dan. 9:11; [Rom. 2:5] 40:4 [a] Jer. 39:12 [b] Gen. 20:15 40:5 [a] Jer. 39:14 [b] 2 Kin. 25:22; Jer. 41:10 40:6 [a] Jer. 39:14 [b] Judg. 20:1; 1 Sam. 7:5; 2 Chr. 16:6 40:7 [a] 2 Kin. 25:23, 24 [b] Jer. 39:10 40:8 [a] Jer. 41:1–10 [b] Jer. 41:11; 43:2 [c] Jer. 42:1 [d] Deut. 3:14; Josh. 12:5; 2 Sam. 10:6 [1] Spelled *Jaazaniah* in 2 Kings 25:23

men. 9 And Gedaliah the son of Ahikam, the son of Shaphan, took an oath before them and their men, saying, "Do not be afraid to serve the Chaldeans. Dwell in the land and serve the king of Babylon, and it shall be [a]well with you. 10 As for me, I will indeed dwell at Mizpah and serve the Chaldeans who come to us. But you, gather wine and summer fruit and oil, put *them* in your vessels, and dwell in your cities that you have taken." 11 Likewise, when all the Jews who *were* in Moab, among the Ammonites, in Edom, and who *were* in all the countries, heard that the king of Babylon had left a remnant of Judah, and that he had set over them Gedaliah the son of Ahikam, the son of Shaphan, 12 then all the Jews [a]returned out of all places where they had been driven, and came to the land of Judah, to Gedaliah at Mizpah, and gathered wine and summer fruit in abundance.

13 Moreover Johanan the son of Kareah and all the captains of the forces that *were* in the fields came to Gedaliah at Mizpah, 14 and said to him, "Do you certainly know that [a]Baalis the king of the Ammonites has sent Ishmael the son of Nethaniah to murder you?" But Gedaliah the son of Ahikam did not believe them.

15 Then Johanan the son of Kareah spoke secretly to Gedaliah in Mizpah, saying, "Let me go, please, and I will kill Ishmael the son of Nethaniah, and no one will know *it*. Why should he murder you, so that all the Jews who are gathered to you would be scattered, and the [a]remnant in Judah perish?"

16 But Gedaliah the son of Ahikam said to Johanan the son of Kareah, "You shall not do this thing, for you speak falsely concerning Ishmael."

### *INSURRECTION AGAINST GEDALIAH*

**41** Now it came to pass in the seventh month [a]*that* Ishmael the son of Nethaniah, the son of Elishama, of the royal family and of the officers of the king, came with ten men to Gedaliah the son of Ahikam, at [b]Mizpah. And there they ate bread together in Mizpah. 2 Then Ishmael the son of Nethaniah, and the ten men who were with him, arose and [a]struck Gedaliah the son of [b]Ahikam, the son of Shaphan, with the sword, and killed him whom the king of Babylon had made [c]governor over the land. 3 Ishmael also struck down all the Jews who were with him, *that is,* with Gedaliah at Mizpah, and the Chaldeans who were found there, the men of war.

4 And it happened, on the second day after he had killed Gedaliah, when as yet no one knew *it,* 5 that certain men came from Shechem, from Shiloh, and from Samaria, eighty men [a]with their beards shaved and their clothes torn, having cut themselves, with offerings and incense in their hand, to bring *them* to [b]the house of the LORD. 6 Now Ishmael the son of Nethaniah went out from Mizpah to meet them, weeping as he went along; and it happened as he met them that he said to them, "Come to Gedaliah the son of Ahikam!" 7 So it was, when they came into the midst of the city, that Ishmael the son of Nethaniah [a]killed them *and cast them* into the midst of a pit, he and the men who were with him. 8 But ten men were found among them who said to Ishmael, "Do not kill us, for we have treasures of wheat, barley, oil, and honey in the field." So he desisted and did not kill them among their brethren. 9 Now the pit into which Ishmael had cast all the dead bodies of the men whom he had slain, because of Gedaliah, *was* [a]the same one Asa the king had made for fear of Baasha king of Israel. Ishmael the son of Nethaniah filled it with *the* slain. 10 Then Ishmael carried away captive all the [a]rest of the people who *were* in Mizpah, [b]the king's daughters and all the people who remained in Mizpah, [c]whom Nebuzaradan the captain of the guard had committed to Gedaliah the son of Ahikam. And Ishmael the son of Nethaniah carried them away captive and departed to go over to [d]the Ammonites.

11 But when [a]Johanan the son of Kareah and all the captains of the forces that *were* with him heard of all the evil that Ishmael the son of Nethaniah had done, 12 they took all the men and went to fight with Ishmael the son of Nethaniah; and they found him by [a]the great pool that *is* in Gibeon. 13 So it was, when all the people who *were* with Ishmael saw Johanan the son of Kareah, and all the captains of the forces who *were* with him, that they were glad. 14 Then all the people whom Ishmael had carried away captive from Mizpah turned around and came back, and went to Johanan the son of Kareah. 15 But Ishmael the son of Nethaniah escaped from Johanan with eight men and went to the Ammonites.

16 Then Johanan the son of Kareah, and all the captains of the forces that were with him, took from Mizpah all the [a]rest of the people whom he had recovered from Ishmael the son of Nethaniah after he had murdered Gedaliah the son of Ahikam—the mighty men of war and the women and the children and the eunuchs, whom he had brought back from Gibeon. 17 And they departed and dwelt in the habitation of [a]Chimham, which is near Bethlehem, as they went on their way to [b]Egypt, 18 because of the Chaldeans; for they were afraid of them, because Ishmael the son of Nethaniah had murdered Gedaliah the son of Ahikam, [a]whom the king of Babylon had made governor in the land.

**40:9** [a] Jer. 27:11; 38:17–20 **40:12** [a] Jer. 43:5 **40:14** [a] Jer. 41:10 **40:15** [a] Jer. 42:2 **41:1** [a] 2 Kin. 25:25 [b] Jer. 40:6, 10 **41:2** [a] 2 Sam. 3:27; 20:9, 10; 2 Kin. 25:25; Ps. 41:9; 109:5; John 13:18 [b] Jer. 26:24 [c] Jer. 40:5 **41:5** [a] Lev. 19:27, 28; Deut. 14:1; Is. 15:2 [b] 1 Sam. 1:7; 2 Kin. 25:9; Neh. 10:34, 35 **41:7** [a] Ps. 55:23; Is. 59:7; Ezek. 22:27; 33:24, 26 **41:9** [a] 1 Kin. 15:22; 2 Chr. 16:6 **41:10** [a] Jer. 40:11, 12 [b] Jer. 43:6 [c] Jer. 40:7 [d] Jer. 40:14 **41:11** [a] Jer. 40:7, 8, 13–16 **41:12** [a] 2 Sam. 2:13 **41:16** [a] Jer. 40:11, 12; 43:4–7 **41:17** [a] 2 Sam. 19:37, 38 [b] Jer. 43:7 **41:18** [a] Jer. 40:5

### *THE FLIGHT TO EGYPT FORBIDDEN*

**42** Now all the captains of the forces, [a]Johanan the son of Kareah, Jezaniah the son of Hoshaiah, and all the people, from the least to the greatest, came near 2 and said to Jeremiah the prophet, [a]"Please, let our petition be acceptable to you, and [b]pray for us to the LORD your God, for all this remnant (since we are left *but* [c]a few of many, as you can see), 3 that the LORD your God may show us [a]the way in which we should walk and the thing we should do."

4 Then Jeremiah the prophet said to them, "I have heard. Indeed, I will pray to the LORD your God according to your words, and it shall be, *that* [a]whatever the LORD answers you, I will declare *it* to you. I will [b]keep nothing back from you."

5 So they said to Jeremiah, [a]"Let the LORD be a true and faithful witness between us, if we do not do according to everything which the LORD your God sends us by you. 6 Whether *it is* pleasing or displeasing, we will [a]obey the voice of the LORD our God to whom we send you, [b]that it may be well with us when we obey the voice of the LORD our God."

7 And it happened after ten days that the word of the LORD came to Jeremiah. 8 Then he called Johanan the son of Kareah, all the captains of the forces which *were* with him, and all the people from the least even to the greatest, 9 and said to them, "Thus says the LORD, the God of Israel, to whom you sent me to present your petition before Him: 10 'If you will still remain in this land, then [a]I will build you and not pull *you* down, and I will plant you and not pluck *you* up. For I [b]relent concerning the disaster that I have brought upon you. 11 Do not be afraid of the king of Babylon, of whom you are afraid; do not be afraid of him,' says the LORD, [a]'for I *am* with you, to save you and deliver you from his hand. 12 And [a]I will show you mercy, that he may have mercy on you and cause you to return to your own land.'

13 "But if [a]you say, 'We will not dwell in this land,' disobeying the voice of the LORD your God, 14 saying, 'No, but we will go to the land of [a]Egypt where we shall see no war, nor hear the sound of the trumpet, nor be hungry for bread, and there we will dwell'— 15 Then hear now the word of the LORD, O remnant of Judah! Thus says the LORD of hosts, the God of Israel: 'If you [a]wholly set [b]your faces to enter Egypt, and go to dwell there, 16 then it shall be *that* the [a]sword which you feared shall overtake you there in the land of Egypt; the famine of which you were afraid shall follow close after you there *in* Egypt; and there you shall die. 17 So shall it be with all the men who set their faces to go to Egypt to dwell there. They shall die by the sword, by famine, and by pestilence. And [a]none of them shall remain or escape from the disaster that I will bring upon them.'

18 "For thus says the LORD of hosts, the God of Israel: 'As My anger and My fury have been [a]poured out on the inhabitants of Jerusalem, so will My fury be poured out on you when you enter Egypt. And [b]you shall be an oath, an astonishment, a curse, and a reproach; and you shall see this place no more.'

19 "The LORD has said concerning you, O remnant of Judah, [a]'Do not go to Egypt!' Know certainly that I have admonished you this day. 20 For you were hypocrites in your hearts when you sent me to the LORD your God, saying, 'Pray for us to the LORD our God, and according to all that the LORD your God says, so declare to us and we will do *it*.' 21 And I have this day declared *it* to you, but you have [a]not obeyed the voice of the LORD your God, or anything which He has sent you by me. 22 Now therefore, know certainly that you [a]shall die by the sword, by famine, and by pestilence in the place where you desire to go to dwell."

### *JEREMIAH TAKEN TO EGYPT*

**43** Now it happened, when Jeremiah had stopped speaking to all the people all the [a]words of the LORD their God, for which the LORD their God had sent him to them, all these words, 2 [a]that Azariah the son of Hoshaiah, Johanan the son of Kareah, and all the proud men spoke, saying to Jeremiah, "You speak falsely! The LORD our God has not sent you to say, 'Do not go to Egypt to dwell there.' 3 But [a]Baruch the son of Neriah has set you against us, to deliver us into the hand of the Chaldeans, that they may put us to death or carry us away captive to Babylon." 4 So Johanan the son of Kareah, all the captains of the forces, and all the people would [a]not obey the voice of the LORD, to remain in the land of Judah. 5 But Johanan the son of Kareah and all the captains of the forces took [a]all the remnant of Judah who had returned to dwell in the land of Judah, from all nations where they had been driven— 6 men, women, children, [a]the king's daughters, [b]and every person whom Nebuzaradan the captain of the guard had left with Gedaliah the son of Ahikam, the son of Shaphan, and Jeremiah the prophet and Baruch the son of Neriah. 7 [a]So they went to the land of Egypt, for they did not obey the voice of the LORD. And they went as far as [b]Tahpanhes.

8 Then the [a]word of the LORD came to Jeremiah in Tahpanhes, saying, 9 "Take large stones in your hand, and hide them in the sight of the men of Judah, in the clay in the brick courtyard which *is* at the entrance to Pharaoh's house in Tahpanhes; 10 and say to them, 'Thus says the LORD of hosts, the God of Israel: "Behold, I will send

**42:1** [a] Jer. 40:8, 13; 41:11 **42:2** [a] Jer. 15:11 [b] Is. 37:4 [c] Lev. 26:22 **42:3** [a] Ezra 8:21 **42:4** [a] 1 Kin. 22:14 [b] 1 Sam. 3:17, 18 **42:5** [a] Gen. 31:50 **42:6** [a] Ex. 24:7 [b] Jer. 7:23 **42:10** [a] Jer. 24:6; 31:28; 33:7 [b] [Jer. 18:8] **42:11** [a] Rom. 8:31 **42:12** [a] Ps. 106:46 **42:13** [a] Jer. 44:16 **42:14** [a] Jer. 41:17; 43:7 **42:15** [a] Deut. 17:16 [b] Luke 9:51 **42:16** [a] Ezek. 11:8 **42:17** [a] Jer. 44:14, 28 **42:18** [a] Jer. 7:20 [b] Is. 65:15 **42:19** [a] Deut. 17:16 **42:21** [a] Is. 30:1–7 **42:22** [a] Ezek. 6:11 **43:1** [a] Jer. 42:9–18 **43:2** [a] Jer. 42:1 **43:3** [a] Jer. 36:4; 45:1 **43:4** [a] 2 Kin. 25:26 **43:5** [a] Jer. 40:11, 12 **43:6** [a] Jer. 41:10 [b] Jer. 39:10; 40:7 **43:7** [a] Jer. 42:19 [b] Jer. 2:16; 44:1 **43:8** [a] Jer. 44:1–30

and bring Nebuchadnezzar the king of Babylon,
[a]My servant, and will set his throne above these
stones that I have hidden. And he will spread his
royal pavilion over them. 11 [a]When he comes, he
shall strike the land of Egypt *and deliver* to death
[b]*those appointed* for death, and to captivity *those*
*appointed* for captivity, and to the sword *those*
*appointed* for the sword. 12 I[1] will kindle a fire in
the houses of [a]the gods of Egypt, and he shall
burn them and carry them away captive. And he
shall array himself with the land of Egypt, as a
shepherd puts on his garment, and he shall go
out from there in peace. 13 He shall also break the
*sacred* pillars of Beth Shemesh[1] that *are* in the
land of Egypt; and the houses of the gods of the
Egyptians he shall burn with fire." ' "

### *ISRAELITES WILL BE PUNISHED IN EGYPT*

**44** The word that came to Jeremiah concern-
ing all the Jews who dwell in the land of
Egypt, who dwell at [a]Migdol, at [b]Tahpanhes, at
[c]Noph,[1] and in the country of [d]Pathros, saying,
2 "Thus says the LORD of hosts, the God of Isra-
el: 'You have seen all the calamity that I have
brought on Jerusalem and on all the cities of
Judah; and behold, this day they *are* [a]a deso-
lation, and no one dwells in them, 3 because of
their wickedness which they have committed to
provoke Me to anger, in that they went [a]to burn
incense *and* to [b]serve other gods whom they
did not know, they nor you nor your fathers.
4 However [a]I have sent to you all My servants
the prophets, rising early and sending *them,*
saying, "Oh, do not do this abominable thing
that I hate!" 5 But they did not listen or incline
their ear to turn from their wickedness, to burn
no incense to other gods. 6 So My fury and My
anger were poured out and kindled in the cities
of Judah and in the streets of Jerusalem; and
they are wasted *and* desolate, as it is this day.'

7 "Now therefore, thus says the LORD, the
God of hosts, the God of Israel: 'Why do you
commit *this* great evil [a]against yourselves, to
cut off from you man and woman, child and
infant, out of Judah, leaving none to remain, 8 in
that you [a]provoke Me to wrath with the works
of your hands, burning incense to other gods
in the land of Egypt where you have gone to
dwell, that you may cut yourselves off and be [b]a
curse and a reproach among all the nations of
the earth? 9 Have you forgotten the wickedness
of your fathers, the wickedness of the kings of
Judah, the wickedness of their wives, your own
wickedness, and the wickedness of your wives,
which they committed in the land of Judah
and in the streets of Jerusalem? 10 They have
not been [a]humbled, to this day, nor have they
[b]feared; they have not walked in My law or in My
statutes that I set before you and your fathers.'

11 "Therefore thus says the LORD of hosts, the
God of Israel: 'Behold, [a]I will set My face against
you for catastrophe and for cutting off all Judah.
12 And I will take the remnant of Judah who
have set their faces to go into the land of Egypt
to dwell there, and [a]they shall all be consumed
*and* fall in the land of Egypt. They shall be con-
sumed by the sword *and* by famine. They shall
die, from the least to the greatest, by the sword
and by famine; and [b]they shall be an oath, an
astonishment, a curse and a reproach! 13 [a]For I
will punish those who dwell in the land of Egypt,
as I have punished Jerusalem, by the sword, by
famine, and by pestilence, 14 so that none of the
remnant of Judah who have gone into the land
of Egypt to dwell there shall escape or survive,
lest they return to the land of Judah, to which
they [a]desire to return and dwell. For [b]none shall
return except those who escape.' "

15 Then all the men who knew that their wives
had burned incense to other gods, with all the
women who stood by, a great multitude, and all
the people who dwelt in the land of Egypt, in
Pathros, answered Jeremiah, saying: 16 "*As for*
the word that you have spoken to us in the name
of the LORD, [a]we will not listen to you! 17 But we
will certainly do [a]whatever has gone out of our
own mouth, to burn incense to the [b]queen of
heaven and pour out drink offerings to her, as
we have done, we and our fathers, our kings
and our princes, in the cities of Judah and in
the streets of Jerusalem. For *then* we had plenty
of food, were well-off, and saw no trouble. 18 But
since we stopped burning incense to the queen
of heaven and pouring out drink offerings to
her, we have lacked everything and have been
consumed by the sword and by famine."

> **44:17 Queen of heaven** refers to the goddess Astarte, the companion of the Canaanite god, Baal. Also known as Ishtar or Ashtoreth, Astarte was similar to Venus, the Roman goddess of love.

19 *The women also said,* [a]"And when we
burned incense to the queen of heaven and
poured out drink offerings to her, did we make
cakes for her, to worship her, and pour out
drink offerings to her without our husbands'
*permission?*"

**43:10** [a] Jer. 25:9; 27:6; Ezek. 29:18, 20 **43:11** [a] Is. 19:1–25; Jer. 25:15–19; 44:13; 46:1, 2, 13–26; Ezek. 29:19, 20 [b] Jer. 15:2; Zech. 11:9 **43:12** [a] Ex. 12:12; Is. 19:1; Jer. 46:25; Ezek. 30:13 [1] Following Masoretic Text and Targum; Septuagint, Syriac, and Vulgate read *He.* **43:13** [1] Literally *House of the Sun,* ancient On; later called Heliopolis **44:1** [a] Ex. 14:2; Jer. 46:14 [b] Jer. 43:7; Ezek. 30:18 [c] Is. 19:13; Jer. 2:16; 46:14; Ezek. 30:13, 16; Hos. 9:6 [d] Is. 11:11; Ezek. 29:14; 30:14 [1] That is, ancient Memphis **44:2** [a] Is. 6:11; Jer. 4:7; 9:11; 34:22; Mic. 3:12 **44:3** [a] Jer. 19:4 [b] Deut. 13:6; 32:17 **44:4** [a] 2 Chr. 36:15; Jer. 7:25; 25:4; 26:5; 29:19; Zech. 7:7 **44:7** [a] Num. 16:38; Jer. 7:19; [Ezek. 33:11]; Hab. 2:10 **44:8** [a] 2 Kin. 17:15–17; Jer. 25:6, 7; 44:3; 1 Cor. 10:21, 22 [b] 1 Kin. 9:7, 8; 2 Chr. 7:20; Jer. 42:18 **44:10** [a] 2 Chr. 36:12; Jer. 6:15; 8:12; Dan. 5:22 [b] [Prov. 28:14] **44:11** [a] Lev. 17:10; 20:5, 6; Jer. 21:10; Amos 9:4 **44:12** [a] Jer. 42:15–17, 22 [b] Is. 65:15; Jer. 42:18 **44:13** [a] Jer. 43:11 **44:14** [a] Jer. 22:26, 27 [b] [Is. 4:2; 10:20]; Jer. 44:28; [Rom. 9:27] **44:16** [a] Jer. 6:16 **44:17** [a] Num. 30:12; Deut. 23:23; Judg. 11:36 [b] 2 Kin. 17:16; Jer. 7:18 **44:19** [a] Jer. 7:18

20 Then Jeremiah spoke to all the people—
the men, the women, and all the people who had
given him *that* answer—saying: 21 "The incense
that you burned in the cities of Judah and in
the streets of Jerusalem, you and your fathers,
your kings and your princes, and the people of
the land, did not the LORD remember them, and
did it *not* come into His mind? 22 So the LORD
could no longer bear *it,* because of the evil of
your doings *and* because of the abominations
which you committed. Therefore your land is a
desolation, an astonishment, a curse, and with-
out an inhabitant, [a]as *it is* this day. 23 Because
you have burned incense and because you have
sinned against the LORD, and have not obeyed
the voice of the LORD or walked in His law, in
His statutes or in His testimonies, [a]therefore this
calamity has happened to you, as *at* this day."

24 Moreover Jeremiah said to all the people
and to all the women, "Hear the word of the LORD,
all Judah who *are* in the land of Egypt! 25 Thus says
the LORD of hosts, the God of Israel, saying: 'You
and your wives have spoken with your mouths and
fulfilled with your hands, saying, "We will surely
keep our vows that we have made, to burn incense
to the queen of heaven and pour out drink offer-
ings to her." You will surely keep your vows and
perform your vows!' 26 Therefore hear the word of
the LORD, all Judah who dwell in the land of Egypt:
'Behold, [a]I have sworn by My [b]great name,' says
the LORD, 'that [c]My name shall no more be named
in the mouth of any man of Judah in all the land
of Egypt, saying, "The Lord GOD lives." 27 Behold,
I will watch over them for adversity and not for
good. And all the men of Judah who *are* in the land
of Egypt [a]shall be consumed by the sword and by
famine, until there is an end to them. 28 Yet [a]a small
number who escape the sword shall return from
the land of Egypt to the land of Judah; and all the
remnant of Judah, who have gone to the land of
Egypt to dwell there, shall know whose words will
stand, Mine or theirs. 29 And this *shall be* a sign to
you,' says the LORD, 'that I will punish you in this
place, that you may know that My words will surely
[a]stand against you for adversity.'

30 "Thus says the LORD: 'Behold, [a]I will give
Pharaoh Hophra king of Egypt into the hand of
his enemies and into the hand of those who seek
his life, as I gave [b]Zedekiah king of Judah into
the hand of Nebuchadnezzar king of Babylon,
his enemy who sought his life.' "

## ASSURANCE TO BARUCH

45 The [a]word that Jeremiah the prophet
spoke to [b]Baruch the son of Neriah, when
he had written these words in a book at the
instruction of Jeremiah,[1] in the [c]fourth year
of Jehoiakim the son of Josiah, king of Judah,
saying, 2 "Thus says the LORD, the God of Israel,
to you, O Baruch: 3 'You said, "Woe is me now!
For the LORD has added grief to my sorrow. I
[a]fainted in my sighing, and I find no rest." '

4 "Thus you shall say to him, 'Thus says the
LORD: "Behold, [a]what I have built I will break
down, and what I have planted I will pluck up,
that is, this whole land. 5 And do you seek great
things for yourself? Do not seek *them;* for behold,
[a]I will bring adversity on all flesh," says the LORD.
"But I will give your [b]life to you as a prize in all
places, wherever you go." ' "

**45:1 Baruch** was Jeremiah's scribe or secretary.

## JUDGMENT ON EGYPT

46 The word of the LORD which came to Jer-
emiah the prophet against [a]the nations.
2 Against [a]Egypt.

[b]Concerning the army of Pharaoh Necho,
king of Egypt, which was by the River Euphra-
tes in Carchemish, and which Nebuchadnezzar
king of Babylon [c]defeated in the [d]fourth year
of Jehoiakim the son of Josiah, king of Judah:

3 "Order the buckler and shield,
And draw near to battle!
4 Harness the horses,
And mount up, you horsemen!
Stand forth with *your* helmets,
Polish the spears,
[a]Put on the armor!
5 Why have I seen them dismayed *and*
turned back?
Their mighty ones are beaten down;
They have speedily fled,
And did not look back,
*For* [a]fear *was* all around," says the LORD.
6 "Do not let the swift flee away,
Nor the mighty man escape;
They will [a]stumble and fall
Toward the north, by the River Euphrates.
7 "Who *is* this coming up [a]like a flood,
Whose waters move like the rivers?
8 Egypt rises up like a flood,
And *its* waters move like the rivers;
And he says, 'I will go up *and* cover the
earth,
I will destroy the city and its inhabitants.'
9 Come up, O horses, and rage, O chariots!
And let the mighty men come forth:

44:22 [a]Jer. 25:11, 18, 38 44:23 [a]1 Kin. 9:9; Neh. 13:18; Jer. 44:2; Dan. 9:11, 12 44:26 [a]Gen. 22:16; Deut. 32:40, 41; Jer. 22:5; Amos 6:8; Heb. 6:13 [b]Jer. 10:6 [c]Neh. 9:5; Ps. 50:16; Ezek. 20:39 44:27 [a]Jer. 1:10; 31:28; Ezek. 7:6 44:28 [a]Is. 10:19; 27:12, 13 44:29 [a][Ps. 33:11] 44:30 [a]Jer. 46:25, 26; Ezek. 29:3; 30:21 [b]2 Kin. 25:4–7; Jer. 39:5 45:1 [a]Jer. 36:1, 4, 32 [b]Jer. 32:12, 16; 43:3 [c]Jer. 25:1; 36:1; 46:2 [1]Literally *from Jeremiah's mouth* 45:3 [a]Ps. 6:6; 69:3; [2 Cor. 4:1, 16; Gal. 6:9] 45:4 [a]Is. 5:5; Jer. 1:10; 11:17; 18:7–10; 31:28 45:5 [a]Jer. 25:26 [b]Jer. 21:9; 38:2; 39:18 46:1 [a]Jer. 25:15 46:2 [a]Jer. 25:17–19 [b]2 Kin. 23:33–35 [c]2 Chr. 35:20 [d]Jer. 45:1 46:4 [a]Jer. 51:11, 12 46:5 [a]Jer. 49:29 46:6 [a]Dan. 11:19 46:7 [a]Jer. 47:2

The Ethiopians and the Libyans who
handle the shield,
And the Lydians [a]who handle *and* bend
the bow.

10 For this *is* [a]the day of the Lord GOD of
hosts,
A day of vengeance,
That He may avenge Himself on His
adversaries.
[b]The sword shall devour;
It shall be satiated and made drunk with
their blood;
For the Lord GOD of hosts [c]has a sacrifice
In the north country by the River
Euphrates.

11 "Go[a] up to Gilead and take balm,
[b]O virgin, the daughter of Egypt;
In vain you will use many medicines;
[c]You shall not be cured.

12 The nations have heard of your [a]shame,
And your cry has filled the land;
For the mighty man has stumbled against
the mighty;
They both have fallen together."

### BABYLONIA WILL STRIKE EGYPT

13 The word that the LORD spoke to Jeremiah
the prophet, how Nebuchadnezzar king of Babylon would come *and* [a]strike the land of Egypt.

14 "Declare in Egypt, and proclaim in
[a]Migdol;
Proclaim in Noph[1] and in [b]Tahpanhes;
Say, 'Stand fast and prepare yourselves,
For the sword devours all around you.'

15 Why are your valiant *men* swept away?
They did not stand
Because the LORD drove them away.

16 He made many fall;
Yes, [a]one fell upon another.
And they said, 'Arise!
[b]Let us go back to our own people
And to the land of our nativity
From the oppressing sword.'

17 They cried there,
'Pharaoh, king of Egypt, *is but* a noise.
He has passed by the appointed time!'

18 "*As* I live," says the King,
[a]Whose name *is* the LORD of hosts,
"Surely as Tabor *is* among the mountains
And as Carmel by the sea, *so* he shall
come.

19 O [a]you daughter dwelling in Egypt,
Prepare yourself [b]to go into captivity!
For Noph[1] shall be waste and desolate,
without inhabitant.

20 "Egypt *is* a very pretty [a]heifer,
*But* destruction comes, it comes [b]from
the north.

21 Also her mercenaries are in her midst like
fat bulls,
For they also are turned back,
They have fled away together.
They did not stand,
For [a]the day of their calamity had come
upon them,
The time of their punishment.

22 [a]Her noise shall go like a serpent,
For they shall march with an army
And come against her with axes,
Like those who chop wood.

23 "They shall [a]cut down her forest," says the
LORD,
"Though it cannot be searched,
Because they *are* innumerable,
And more numerous than
[b]grasshoppers.

24 The daughter of Egypt shall be
ashamed;
She shall be delivered into the hand
Of [a]the people of the north."

25 The LORD of hosts, the God of Israel, says:
"Behold, I will bring punishment on Amon[1] of
[a]No,[2] and Pharaoh and Egypt, [b]with their gods
and their kings—Pharaoh and those who [c]trust
in him. 26 [a]And I will deliver them into the hand
of those who seek their lives, into the hand of
Nebuchadnezzar king of Babylon and the hand
of his servants. [b]Afterward it shall be inhabited
as in the days of old," says the LORD.

### GOD WILL PRESERVE ISRAEL

*(cf. Jer. 30:10, 11)*

27 "But[a] do not fear, O My servant Jacob,
And do not be dismayed, O Israel!
For behold, I will [b]save you from afar,
And your offspring from the land of their
captivity;
Jacob shall return, have rest and be at
ease;
No one shall make *him* afraid.

28 Do not fear, O Jacob My servant," says the
LORD,
"For I *am* with you;
For I will make a complete end of all the
nations
To which I have driven you,
But I will not make [a]a complete end of
you.
I will rightly [b]correct you,
For I will not leave you wholly
unpunished."

46:9 [a] Is. 66:19 46:10 [a] Joel 1:15 [b] Deut. 32:42 [c] Is. 34:6 46:11 [a] Jer. 8:22 [b] Is. 47:1 [c] Ezek. 30:21 46:12 [a] Jer. 2:36 46:13 [a] Is. 19:1 46:14 [a] Jer. 44:1 [b] Ezek. 30:18 [1] That is, ancient Memphis 46:16 [a] Lev. 26:36, 37 [b] Jer. 51:9 46:18 [a] Jer. 48:15 46:19 [a] Jer. 48:18 [b] Is. 20:4 [1] That is, ancient Memphis 46:20 [a] Hos. 10:11 [b] Jer. 1:14 46:21 [a] [Ps. 37:13] 46:22 [a] [Is. 29:4] 46:23 [a] Is. 10:34 [b] Judg. 6:5; 7:12 46:24 [a] Jer. 1:15 46:25 [a] Ezek. 30:14–16 [b] Jer. 43:12, 13 [c] Is. 30:1–5; 31:1–3 [1] A sun god [2] That is, ancient Thebes 46:26 [a] Ezek. 32:11 [b] Ezek. 29:8–14 46:27 [a] Is. 41:13, 14; 43:5; 44:2 [b] Is. 11:11 46:28 [a] Amos 9:8, 9 [b] Jer. 30:11

### *JUDGMENT ON PHILISTIA*

**47** The word of the LORD that came to Jeremiah the prophet [a]against the Philistines, [b]before Pharaoh attacked Gaza.

2 Thus says the LORD:

"Behold, [a]waters rise [b]out of the north,
And shall be an overflowing flood;
They shall overflow the land and all that is in it,
The city and those who dwell within;
Then the men shall cry,
And all the inhabitants of the land shall wail.
3 At the [a]noise of the stamping hooves of his strong horses,
At the rushing of his chariots,
*At* the rumbling of his wheels,
The fathers will not look back for *their* children,
Lacking courage,
4 Because of the day that comes to plunder all the [a]Philistines,
To cut off from [b]Tyre and Sidon every helper who remains;
For the LORD shall plunder the Philistines,
[c]The remnant of the country of [d]Caphtor.
5 [a]Baldness has come upon Gaza,
[b]Ashkelon is cut off
*With* the remnant of their valley.
How long will you cut yourself?
6 "O you [a]sword of the LORD,
How long until you are quiet?
Put yourself up into your scabbard,
Rest and be still!
7 How can it be quiet,
Seeing the LORD has [a]given it a charge
Against Ashkelon and against the seashore?
There He has [b]appointed it."

### *JUDGMENT ON MOAB*

**48** Against [a]Moab.
Thus says the LORD of hosts, the God of Israel:

"Woe to [b]Nebo!
For it is plundered,
[c]Kirjathaim is shamed *and* taken;
The high stronghold[1] is shamed and dismayed—
2 [a]No more praise of Moab.
In [b]Heshbon they have devised evil against her:
'Come, and let us cut her off as a nation.'
You also shall be cut down, O [c]Madmen![1]
The sword shall pursue you;
3 A voice of crying *shall be* from [a]Horonaim:
'Plundering and great destruction!'
4 "Moab is destroyed;
Her little ones have caused a cry to be heard;[1]
5 [a]For in the Ascent of Luhith they ascend with continual weeping;
For in the descent of Horonaim the enemies have heard a cry of destruction.

6 "Flee, save your lives!
And be like the [a]juniper[1] in the wilderness.
7 For because you have trusted in your works and your [a]treasures,
You also shall be taken.
And [b]Chemosh shall go forth into captivity,
His [c]priests and his princes together.
8 And [a]the plunderer shall come against every city;
No one shall escape.
The valley also shall perish,
And the plain shall be destroyed,
As the LORD has spoken.

9 "Give[a] wings to Moab,
That she may flee and get away;
For her cities shall be desolate,
Without any to dwell in them.
10 [a]Cursed *is* he who does the work of the LORD deceitfully,
And cursed *is* he who keeps back his sword from blood.

11 "Moab has been at ease from his[1] youth;
He [a]has settled on his dregs,
And has not been emptied from vessel to vessel,
Nor has he gone into captivity.
Therefore his taste remained in him,
And his scent has not changed.

> **48:11** In the ancient Near East, newly bottled wine was left untouched until the grape juice had time to ferment and the sediment had **settled** to the bottom of the container. The wine was not considered fit for drinking until it had been poured through a strainer to remove the sediment.

12 "Therefore behold, the days are coming,"
says the LORD,
"That I shall send him wine-workers
Who will tip him over

47:1 [a] Zeph. 2:4, 5 [b] Amos 1:6 47:2 [a] Is. 8:7, 8 [b] Jer. 1:14 47:3 [a] Jer. 8:16 47:4 [a] Is. 14:29–31 [b] Jer. 25:22 [c] Ezek. 25:16 [d] Gen. 10:14 47:5 [a] Mic. 1:16 [b] Jer. 25:20 47:6 [a] Ezek. 21:3–5 47:7 [a] Ezek. 14:17 [b] Mic. 6:9 48:1 [a] Is. 15:1—16:14; 25:10 [b] Is. 15:2 [c] Num. 32:37 [1] Hebrew *Misgab* 48:2 [a] Is. 16:14 [b] Jer. 49:3 [c] Is. 10:31 [1] A city of Moab 48:3 [a] Is. 15:5 48:4 [1] Following Masoretic Text, Targum, and Vulgate; Septuagint reads *Proclaim it in Zoar*. 48:5 [a] Is. 15:5 48:6 [a] Jer. 17:6 [1] Or *Aroer,* a city of Moab 48:7 [a] Jer. 9:23 [b] Jer. 48:13 [c] Jer. 49:3 48:8 [a] Jer. 6:26 48:9 [a] Ps. 55:6 48:10 [a] 1 Sam. 15:3 48:11 [a] Zeph. 1:12 [1] The Hebrew uses masculine and feminine pronouns interchangeably in this chapter.

And empty his vessels
And break the bottles.
13 Moab shall be ashamed of [a]Chemosh,
As the house of Israel [b]was ashamed of
[c]Bethel, their confidence.

14 "How can you say, [a]'We *are* mighty
And strong men for the war'?
15 Moab is plundered and gone up *from* her
cities;
Her chosen young men have [a]gone down
to the slaughter," says [b]the King,
Whose name *is* the LORD of hosts.

16 "The calamity of Moab *is* near at hand,
And his affliction comes quickly.
17 Bemoan him, all you who are around him;
And all you who know his name,
Say, [a]'How the strong staff is broken,
The beautiful rod!'

18 "O [a]daughter inhabiting [b]Dibon,
Come down from *your* glory,
And sit in thirst;
For the plunderer of Moab has come
against you,
He has destroyed your strongholds.
19 O inhabitant of [a]Aroer,
[b]Stand by the way and watch;
Ask him who flees
And her who escapes;
Say, 'What has happened?'
20 Moab is shamed, for he is broken down.
[a]Wail and cry!
Tell it in [b]Arnon, that Moab is plundered.

21 "And judgment has come on the plain
country:
On Holon and Jahzah and Mephaath,
22 On Dibon and Nebo and Beth Diblathaim,
23 On Kirjathaim and Beth Gamul and Beth
Meon,
24 On [a]Kerioth and Bozrah,
On all the cities of the land of Moab,
Far or near.
25 [a]The horn of Moab is cut off,
And his [b]arm is broken," says the LORD.

26 "Make[a] him drunk,
Because he exalted *himself* against the
LORD.
Moab shall wallow in his vomit,
And he shall also be in derision.
27 For [a]was not Israel a derision to you?
[b]Was he found among thieves?
For whenever you speak of him,
You shake *your head* in [c]*scorn.*

28 You who dwell in Moab,
Leave the cities and [a]dwell in the rock,
And be like [b]the dove *which* makes her nest
In the sides of the cave's mouth.

29 "We have heard the [a]pride of Moab
(He *is* exceedingly proud),
Of his loftiness and arrogance and [b]pride,
And of the haughtiness of his heart."

30 "I know his wrath," says the LORD,
"But it *is* not right;
[a]His lies have made nothing right.
31 Therefore [a]I will wail for Moab,
And I will cry out for all Moab;
I[1] will mourn for the men of Kir Heres.
32 [a]O vine of Sibmah! I will weep for you with
the weeping of [b]Jazer.
Your plants have gone over the sea,
They reach to the sea of Jazer.
The plunderer has fallen on your summer
fruit and your vintage.
33 [a]Joy and gladness are taken
From the plentiful field
And from the land of Moab;
I have caused wine to fail from the
winepresses;
No one will tread with joyous shouting—
Not joyous shouting!

34 "From[a] the cry of Heshbon to [b]Elealeh and
to Jahaz
They have uttered their voice,
[c]From Zoar to Horonaim,
*Like* a three-year-old heifer;[1]
For the waters of Nimrim also shall be
desolate.

35 "Moreover," says the LORD,
"I will cause to cease in Moab
[a]The one who offers *sacrifices* in the high
places
And burns incense to his gods.
36 Therefore [a]My heart shall wail like flutes
for Moab,
And like flutes My heart shall wail
For the men of Kir Heres.
Therefore [b]the riches they have acquired
have perished.

37 "For [a]every head *shall be* bald, and every
beard clipped;
On all the hands *shall be* cuts, and [b]on the
loins sackcloth—
38 A general lamentation
On all the [a]housetops of Moab,
And in its streets;

48:13 [a] 1 Kin. 11:7 [b] Hos. 10:6 [c] 1 Kin. 12:29; 13:32–34 48:14 [a] Is. 16:6 48:15 [a] Jer. 50:27 [b] Jer. 46:18; 51:57 48:17 [a] Is. 9:4; 14:4, 5 48:18 [a] Is. 47:1 [b] Is. 15:2 48:19 [a] Deut. 2:36 [b] 1 Sam. 4:13, 14, 16 48:20 [a] Is. 16:7 [b] Num. 21:13 48:24 [a] Amos 2:2 48:25 [a] Ps. 75:10 [b] Ezek. 30:21 48:26 [a] Jer. 25:15 48:27 [a] Zeph. 2:8 [b] Jer. 2:26 [c] Lam. 2:15 48:28 [a] Ps. 55:6, 7 [b] Song 2:14 48:29 [a] Is. 16:6 [b] Jer. 49:16 48:30 [a] Jer. 50:36 48:31 [a] Is. 15:5; 16:7, 11 [1] Following Dead Sea Scrolls, Septuagint, and Vulgate; Masoretic Text reads *He.* 48:32 [a] Is. 16:8, 9 [b] Num. 21:32 48:33 [a] Joel 1:12 48:34 [a] Is. 15:4–6 [b] Num. 32:3, 37 [c] Is. 15:5, 6 [1] Or *The Third Eglath,* an unknown city (compare Isaiah 15:5) 48:35 [a] Is. 15:2; 16:12 48:36 [a] Is. 15:5; 16:11 [b] Is. 15:7 48:37 [a] Is. 15:2, 3 [b] Gen. 37:34 48:38 [a] Is. 15:3

For I have [b]broken Moab like a vessel in
which *is* no pleasure," says the LORD.
39 "They shall wail:
'How she is broken down!
How Moab has turned her back with
shame!'
So Moab shall be a derision
And a dismay to all those about her."

40 For thus says the LORD:

"Behold, [a]one shall fly like an eagle,
And [b]spread his wings over Moab.
41 Kerioth is taken,
And the strongholds are surprised;
[a]The mighty men's hearts in Moab on that
day shall be
Like the heart of a woman in birth pangs.
42 And Moab shall be destroyed [a]as a people,
Because he exalted *himself* against the
LORD.
43 [a]Fear and the pit and the snare *shall be*
upon you,
O inhabitant of Moab," says the LORD.
44 "He who flees from the fear shall fall into
the pit,
And he who gets out of the pit shall be
caught in the [a]snare.
For upon Moab, upon it [b]I will bring
The year of their punishment," says the
LORD.

45 "Those who fled stood under the shadow of
Heshbon
Because of exhaustion.
But [a]a fire shall come out of Heshbon,
A flame from the midst of [b]Sihon,
And [c]shall devour the brow of Moab,
The crown of the head of the sons of
tumult.
46 [a]Woe to you, O Moab!
The people of Chemosh perish;
For your sons have been taken captive,
And your daughters captive.

47 "Yet I will bring back the captives of Moab
[a]In the latter days," says the LORD.

Thus far *is* the judgment of Moab.

## JUDGMENT ON AMMON

49 Against the [a]Ammonites.
Thus says the LORD:

"Has Israel no sons?
Has he no heir?
Why *then* does Milcom[1] inherit [b]Gad,
And his people dwell in its cities?
2 [a]Therefore behold, the days are coming,"
says the LORD,
"That I will cause to be heard an alarm of
war
In [b]Rabbah of the Ammonites;
It shall be a desolate mound,
And her villages shall be burned with fire.
Then Israel shall take possession of his
inheritance," says the LORD.

3 "Wail, O [a]Heshbon, for Ai is plundered!
Cry, you daughters of Rabbah,
[b]Gird yourselves with sackcloth!
Lament and run to and fro by the walls;
For Milcom shall go into captivity
With his [c]priests and his princes together.
4 Why [a]do you boast in the valleys,
Your flowing valley, O [b]backsliding
daughter?
Who trusted in her [c]treasures, [d]*saying,*
'Who will come against me?'
5 Behold, I will bring fear upon you,"
Says the Lord GOD of hosts,
"From all those who are around you;
You shall be driven out, everyone
headlong,
And no one will gather those who wander
off.
6 But [a]afterward I will bring back
The captives of the people of Ammon,"
says the LORD.

## JUDGMENT ON EDOM

7 [a]Against Edom.
Thus says the LORD of hosts:

[b]"*Is* wisdom no more in Teman?
[c]Has counsel perished from the prudent?
Has their wisdom [d]vanished?
8 Flee, turn back, dwell in the depths,
O inhabitants of [a]Dedan!
For I will bring the calamity of Esau upon
him,
The time *that* I will punish him.
9 [a]If grape-gatherers came to you,
Would they not leave *some* gleaning grapes?
If thieves by night,
Would they not destroy until they have
enough?
10 [a]But I have made Esau bare;
I have uncovered his secret places,[1]
And he shall not be able to hide himself.
His descendants are plundered,
His brethren and his neighbors,
And [b]he *is* no more.
11 Leave your fatherless children,
I will preserve *them* alive;
And let your widows trust in Me."

48:38 [b] Jer. 22:28 48:40 [a] Deut. 28:49 [b] Is. 8:8 48:41 [a] Is. 13:8; 21:3 48:42 [a] Ps. 83:4 48:43 [a] Is. 24:17, 18 48:44 [a] Is. 24:18 [b] Jer. 11:23 48:45 [a] Num. 21:28, 29 [b] Ps. 135:11 [c] Num. 24:17 48:46 [a] Num. 21:29 48:47 [a] Jer. 49:6, 39 49:1 [a] Ezek. 21:28–32; 25:1–7 [b] Amos 1:13–15 [1] Hebrew *Malcam,* literally *their king,* a god of the Ammonites; also called *Molech* (compare verse 3) 49:2 [a] Amos 1:13–15 [b] Ezek. 25:5 49:3 [a] Jer. 48:2 [b] Is. 32:11 [c] Jer. 48:7 49:4 [a] Jer. 9:23 [b] Jer. 3:14 [c] Jer. 48:7 [d] Jer. 21:13 49:6 [a] Jer. 48:47 49:7 [a] Ezek. 25:12–14; 35:1–15 [b] Gen. 36:11 [c] Is. 19:11 [d] Jer. 8:9 49:8 [a] Jer. 25:23 49:9 [a] Obad. 5, 6 49:10 [a] Mal. 1:3 [b] Is. 17:14 [1] Compare Obadiah 5, 6

12 For thus says the LORD: "Behold, [a]those
whose judgment *was* not to drink of the cup have
assuredly drunk. And *are* you the one who will
altogether go unpunished? You shall not go un-
punished, but you shall surely drink *of it.* 13 For [a]I
have sworn by Myself," says the LORD, "that [b]Bozrah
shall become a desolation, a reproach, a waste, and
a curse. And all its cities shall be perpetual wastes."

14 [a]I have heard a message from the LORD,
And an ambassador has been sent to the nations:
"Gather together, come against her,
And rise up to battle!

15 "For indeed, I will make you small among nations,
Despised among men.
16 Your fierceness has deceived you,
The [a]pride of your heart,
O you who dwell in the clefts of the rock,
Who hold the height of the hill!
[b]Though you make your [c]nest as high as the eagle,
[d]I will bring you down from there," says the LORD.[1]

17 "Edom also shall be an astonishment;
[a]Everyone who goes by it will be astonished
And will hiss at all its plagues.
18 [a]As in the overthrow of Sodom and Gomorrah
And their neighbors," says the LORD,
"No one shall remain there,
Nor shall a son of man dwell in it.

19 "Behold,[a] he shall come up like a lion from
[b]the floodplain[1] of the Jordan
Against the dwelling place of the strong;
But I will suddenly make him run away from her.
And who *is* a chosen *man that* I may appoint over her?
For [c]who *is* like Me?
Who will arraign Me?
And [d]who *is* that shepherd
Who will withstand Me?"

20 [a]Therefore hear the counsel of the LORD
that He has taken against Edom,
And His purposes that He has proposed
against the inhabitants of Teman:
Surely the least of the flock shall draw them out;
Surely He shall make their dwelling places
desolate with them.
21 [a]The earth shakes at the noise of their fall;
At the cry its noise is heard at the Red Sea.
22 Behold, [a]He shall come up and fly like the eagle,
And spread His wings over Bozrah;
The heart of the mighty men of Edom in
that day shall be
Like the heart of a woman in birth pangs.

## *JUDGMENT ON DAMASCUS*

23 [a]Against Damascus.

[b]"Hamath and Arpad are shamed,
For they have heard bad news.
They are fainthearted;
[c]*There is* trouble on the sea;
It cannot be quiet.
24 Damascus has grown feeble;
She turns to flee,
And fear has seized *her.*
[a]Anguish and sorrows have taken her like a woman in labor.
25 Why is [a]the city of praise not deserted, the city of My joy?
26 [a]Therefore her young men shall fall in her streets,
And all the men of war shall be cut off in
that day," says the LORD of hosts.
27 "I[a] will kindle a fire in the wall of Damascus,
And it shall consume the palaces of Ben-Hadad."[1]

## *JUDGMENT ON KEDAR AND HAZOR*

28 [a]Against Kedar and against the kingdoms
of Hazor, which Nebuchadnezzar king of Bab-
ylon shall strike.
Thus says the LORD:

"Arise, go up to Kedar,
And devastate [b]the men of the East!
29 Their [a]tents and their flocks they shall take away.
They shall take for themselves their curtains,
All their vessels and their camels;
And they shall cry out to them,
[b]'Fear *is* on every side!'

30 "Flee, get far away! Dwell in the depths,
O inhabitants of Hazor!" says the LORD.
"For Nebuchadnezzar king of Babylon has
taken counsel against you,
And has conceived a plan against you.

31 "Arise, go up to [a]the wealthy nation that
dwells securely," says the LORD,
"Which has neither gates nor bars,
[b]Dwelling alone.
32 Their camels shall be for booty,
And the multitude of their cattle for plunder.

49:12 [a]Jer. 25:29 49:13 [a]Amos 6:8 [b]Is. 34:6; 63:1 49:14 [a]Obad. 1–4 49:16 [a]Jer. 48:29 [b]Obad. 3, 4 [c]Job 39:27 [d]Amos 9:2 [1]Compare Obadiah 3, 4 49:17 [a]Jer. 18:16; 49:13; 50:13 49:18 [a]Deut. 29:23 49:19 [a]Jer. 50:44 [b]Jer. 12:5 [c]Ex. 15:11 [d]Job 41:10 [1]Or *thicket* 49:20 [a]Jer. 50:45 49:21 [a]Jer. 50:46 49:22 [a]Jer. 48:40, 41 49:23 [a]Amos 1:3, 5 [b]Jer. 39:5 [c][Is. 57:20] 49:24 [a]Is. 13:8 49:25 [a]Jer. 33:9 49:26 [a]Jer. 50:30 49:27 [a]Amos 1:4 [1]Compare Amos 1:4 49:28 [a]Ezek. 27:21 [b]Judg. 6:3 49:29 [a]Ps. 120:5 [b]Jer. 46:5 49:31 [a]Ezek. 38:11 [b]Num. 23:9

I will [a]scatter to all winds those in the
farthest corners,
And I will bring their calamity from all its
sides," says the LORD.
33 "Hazor [a]shall be a dwelling for jackals, a
desolation forever;
No one shall reside there,
Nor son of man dwell in it."

### *JUDGMENT ON ELAM*

34 The word of the LORD that came to Jeremi-
ah the prophet against [a]Elam, in the [b]beginning
of the reign of Zedekiah king of Judah, saying,
35 "Thus says the LORD of hosts:

'Behold, I will break [a]the bow of Elam,
The foremost of their might.
36 Against Elam I will bring the four winds
From the four quarters of heaven,
And scatter them toward all those winds;
There shall be no nations where the
outcasts of Elam will not go.
37 For I will cause Elam to be dismayed
before their enemies
And before those who seek their life.
[a]I will bring disaster upon them,
My fierce anger,' says the LORD;
'And I will send the sword after them
Until I have consumed them.
38 I will [a]set My throne in Elam,
And will destroy from there the king and
the princes,' says the LORD.

39 'But it shall come to pass [a]in the latter days:
I will bring back the captives of Elam,'
says the LORD."

### *JUDGMENT ON BABYLON AND BABYLONIA*

**50** The word that the LORD spoke [a]against
Babylon *and* against the land of the Chal-
deans by Jeremiah the prophet.

2 "Declare among the nations,
Proclaim, and set up a standard;
Proclaim—do not conceal *it*—
Say, 'Babylon is [a]taken, [b]Bel is shamed.
Merodach[1] is broken in pieces;
[c]Her idols are humiliated,
Her images are broken in pieces.'
3 [a]For out of the north [b]a nation comes up
against her,
Which shall make her land desolate,
And no one shall dwell therein.
They shall move, they shall depart,
Both man and beast.

4 "In those days and in that time," says the
LORD,
"The children of Israel shall come,
[a]They and the children of Judah together;
[b]With continual weeping they shall come,
[c]And seek the LORD their God.
5 They shall ask the way to Zion,
With their faces toward it, *saying,*
'Come and let us join ourselves to the LORD
*In* [a]a perpetual covenant
*That* will not be forgotten.'

6 "My people have been [a]lost sheep.
Their shepherds have led them [b]astray;
They have turned them away *on* [c]the
mountains.
They have gone from mountain to hill;
They have forgotten their resting place.
7 All who found them have [a]devoured them;
And [b]their adversaries said, [c]'We have not
offended,
Because they have sinned against the
LORD, [d]the habitation of justice,
The LORD, [e]the hope of their fathers.'

8 "Move[a] from the midst of Babylon,
Go out of the land of the Chaldeans;
And be like the rams before the flocks.
9 [a]For behold, I will raise and cause to come
up against Babylon
An assembly of great nations from the
north country,
And they shall array themselves against her;
From there she shall be captured.
Their arrows *shall be* like *those* of an
expert warrior;[1]
[b]None shall return in vain.
10 And Chaldea shall become plunder;
[a]All who plunder her shall be satisfied,"
says the LORD.

11 "Because[a] you were glad, because you
rejoiced,
You destroyers of My heritage,
Because you have grown fat [b]like a heifer
threshing grain,
And you bellow like bulls,
12 Your mother shall be deeply ashamed;
She who bore you shall be ashamed.

**50:2 Merodach** was another name for Marduk, the chief god of the Babylonians. The people of **Babylon** believed that Marduk created the world and they looked to it to protect their kingdom.

49:32 [a] Ezek. 5:10 49:33 [a] Mal. 1:3 49:34 [a] Jer. 25:25 [b] 2 Kin. 24:17, 18 49:35 [a] Is. 22:6 49:37 [a] Jer. 9:16 49:38 [a] Jer. 43:10 49:39 [a] Jer. 48:47 50:1 [a] Is. 13:1; 47:1 50:2 [a] Is. 21:9 [b] Is. 46:1 [c] Jer. 43:12, 13 [1] A Babylonian god; sometimes spelled *Marduk* 50:3 [a] Jer. 51:48 [b] Is. 13:17, 18, 20 50:4 [a] Hos. 1:11 [b] Ezra 3:12, 13 [c] Hos. 3:5 50:5 [a] Jer. 31:31 50:6 [a] Is. 53:6 [b] Jer. 23:1 [c] [Jer. 2:20; 3:6, 23] 50:7 [a] Ps. 79:7 [b] Zech. 11:5 [c] Jer. 2:3 [d] [Ps. 90:1; 91:1] [e] Ps. 22:4 50:8 [a] Is. 48:20 50:9 [a] Jer. 15:14; 51:27 [b] 2 Sam. 1:22

[1] Following some Hebrew manuscripts, Septuagint, and Syriac; Masoretic Text, Targum, and Vulgate read *a warrior who makes childless.*

50:10 [a] [Rev. 17:16] 50:11 [a] Is. 47:6 [b] Hos. 10:11

Behold, the least of the nations *shall be* a
[a]wilderness,
A dry land and a desert.
13 Because of the wrath of the LORD
She shall not be inhabited,
[a]But she shall be wholly desolate.
[b]Everyone who goes by Babylon shall be
horrified
And hiss at all her plagues.

14 "Put[a] yourselves in array against Babylon
all around,
All you who bend the bow;
Shoot at her, spare no arrows,
For she has sinned against the LORD.
15 Shout against her all around;
She has [a]given her hand,
Her foundations have fallen,
[b]Her walls are thrown down;
For [c]it *is* the vengeance of the LORD.
Take vengeance on her.
As she has done, so do to her.
16 Cut off the sower from Babylon,
And him who handles the sickle at
harvest time.
For fear of the oppressing sword
[a]Everyone shall turn to his own people,
And everyone shall flee to his own land.

17 "Israel *is* like [a]scattered sheep;
[b]The lions have driven *him* away.
First [c]the king of Assyria devoured him;
Now at last this [d]Nebuchadnezzar king of
Babylon has broken his bones."

18 Therefore thus says the LORD of hosts,
the God of Israel:

"Behold, I will punish the king of Babylon
and his land,
As I have punished the king of [a]Assyria.
19 [a]But I will bring back Israel to his home,
And he shall feed on Carmel and Bashan;
His soul shall be satisfied on Mount
Ephraim and Gilead.
20 In those days and in that time," says the LORD,
[a]"The iniquity of Israel shall be sought, but
*there shall be* none;
And the sins of Judah, but they shall not
be found;
For I will pardon those [b]whom I preserve.

21 "Go up against the land of Merathaim,
against it,
And against the inhabitants of [a]Pekod.
Waste and utterly destroy them," says the
LORD,
"And do [b]according to all that I have
commanded you.
22 [a]A sound of battle *is* in the land,
And of great destruction.
23 How [a]the hammer of the whole earth has
been cut apart and broken!
How Babylon has become a desolation
among the nations!
24 I have laid a snare for you;
You have indeed been [a]trapped, O Babylon,
And you were not aware;
You have been found and also caught,
Because you have [b]contended against the
LORD.
25 The LORD has opened His armory,
And has brought out [a]the weapons of His
indignation;
For this *is* the work of the Lord GOD of
hosts
In the land of the Chaldeans.
26 Come against her from the farthest border;
Open her storehouses;
Cast her up as heaps of ruins,
And destroy her utterly;
Let nothing of her be left.
27 Slay all her [a]bulls,
Let them go down to the slaughter.
Woe to them!
For their day has come, the time of [b]their
punishment.
28 The voice of those who flee and escape
from the land of Babylon
[a]Declares in Zion the vengeance of the
LORD our God,
The vengeance of His temple.

29 "Call together the archers against Babylon.
All you who bend the bow, encamp
against it all around;
Let none of them escape.[1]
[a]Repay her according to her work;
According to all she has done, do to her;
[b]For she has been proud against the LORD,
Against the Holy One of Israel.
30 [a]Therefore her young men shall fall in the
streets,
And all her men of war shall be cut off in
that day," says the LORD.
31 "Behold, I *am* against you,
O most haughty one!" says the Lord GOD
of hosts;
"For your day has come,
The time *that* I will punish you.[1]
32 The most [a]proud shall stumble and fall,
And no one will raise him up;
[b]I will kindle a fire in his cities,
And it will devour all around him."

50:12 [a] Jer. 51:43 50:13 [a] Jer. 25:12 [b] Jer. 49:17 50:14 [a] Jer. 51:2 50:15 [a] Lam. 5:6 [b] Jer. 51:58 [c] Jer. 51:6, 11 50:16 [a] Is. 13:14 50:17 [a] 2 Kin. 24:10, 14 [b] Jer. 2:15 [c] 2 Kin. 15:29; 17:6; 18:9–13 [d] 2 Kin. 24:10–14; 25:1–7 50:18 [a] Ezek. 31:3, 11, 12 50:19 [a] Is. 65:10 50:20 [a] [Jer. 31:34] [b] Is. 1:9 50:21 [a] Ezek. 23:23 [b] 2 Sam. 16:11 50:22 [a] Jer. 51:54 50:23 [a] Jer. 51:20–24 50:24 [a] Dan. 5:30 [b] [Is. 45:9] 50:25 [a] Is. 13:5 50:27 [a] Is. 34:7 [b] Jer. 48:44 50:28 [a] Jer. 51:10 50:29 [a] Jer. 51:56 [b] [Is. 47:10] [1] Qere, some Hebrew manuscripts, Septuagint, and Targum add *to her*. 50:30 [a] Jer. 49:26; 51:4 50:31 [1] Following Masoretic Text and Targum; Septuagint and Vulgate read *The time of your punishment*. 50:32 [a] Mal. 4:1 [b] Jer. 21:14

33 Thus says the LORD of hosts:

"The children of Israel *were* oppressed,
Along with the children of Judah;
All who took them captive have held them
fast;
They have refused to let them go.
34 [a]Their Redeemer *is* strong;
[b]The LORD of hosts *is* His name.
He will thoroughly plead their [c]case,
That He may give rest to the land,
And disquiet the inhabitants of Babylon.

35 "A sword *is* against the Chaldeans," says
the LORD,
"Against the inhabitants of Babylon,
And [a]against her princes and [b]her wise
men.
36 A sword *is* [a]against the soothsayers, and
they will be fools.
A sword *is* against her mighty men, and
they will be dismayed.
37 A sword *is* against their horses,
Against their chariots,
And against all [a]the mixed peoples who
*are* in her midst;
And [b]they will become like women.
A sword *is* against her treasures, and they
will be robbed.
38 [a]A drought[1] *is* against her waters, and they
will be dried up.
For it *is* the land of carved images,
And they are insane with *their* idols.

39 "Therefore[a] the wild desert beasts shall
dwell *there* with the jackals,
And the ostriches shall dwell in it.
[b]It shall be inhabited no more forever,
Nor shall it be dwelt in from generation to
generation.
40 [a]As God overthrew Sodom and Gomorrah
And their neighbors," says the LORD,
"*So* no one shall reside there,
Nor son of man [b]dwell in it.

41 "Behold,[a] a people shall come from the
north,
And a great nation and many kings
Shall be raised up from the ends of the
earth.
42 [a]They shall hold the bow and the lance;
[b]They *are* cruel and shall not show mercy.
[c]Their voice shall roar like the sea;
They shall ride on horses,
Set in array, like a man for the battle,
Against you, O daughter of Babylon.

43 "The king of Babylon has [a]heard the report
about them,
And his hands grow feeble;
Anguish has taken hold of him,
Pangs as of a woman in [b]childbirth.

44 "Behold,[a] he shall come up like a lion from
the floodplain[1] of the Jordan
Against the dwelling place of the strong;
But I will make them suddenly run away
from her.
And who *is* a chosen *man that* I may
appoint over her?
For who *is* like Me?
Who will arraign Me?
And [b]who *is* that shepherd
Who will withstand Me?"

45 Therefore hear [a]the counsel of the LORD
that He has taken against Babylon,
And His [b]purposes that He has proposed
against the land of the Chaldeans:
[c]Surely the least of the flock shall draw
them out;
Surely He will make their dwelling place
desolate with them.
46 [a]At the noise of the taking of Babylon
The earth trembles,
And the cry is heard among the nations.

## *THE UTTER DESTRUCTION OF BABYLON*

51 Thus says the LORD:

"Behold, I will raise up against [a]Babylon,
Against those who dwell in Leb Kamai,[1]
[b]A destroying wind.
2 And I will send [a]winnowers to Babylon,
Who shall winnow her and empty her land.
[b]For in the day of doom
They shall be against her all around.
3 Against *her* [a]let the archer bend his bow,
And lift himself up against *her* in his
armor.
Do not spare her young men;
[b]Utterly destroy all her army.
4 Thus the slain shall fall in the land of the
Chaldeans,
[a]And *those* thrust through in her streets.
5 For Israel is [a]not forsaken, nor Judah,
By his God, the LORD of hosts,
Though their land was filled with sin
against the Holy One of Israel."

6 [a]Flee from the midst of Babylon,
And every one save his life!
Do not be cut off in her iniquity,

50:34 [a] Rev. 18:8 [b] Is. 47:4 [c] Jer. 51:36; Mic. 7:9 50:35 [a] Dan. 5:30 [b] Is. 47:13 50:36 [a] Is. 44:25 50:37 [a] Jer. 25:20 [b] Jer. 51:30 50:38 [a] Rev. 16:12 [1] Following Masoretic Text, Targum, and Vulgate; Syriac reads *sword;* Septuagint omits *A drought is.* 50:39 [a] Rev. 18:2 [b] Is. 13:20 50:40 [a] Is. 13:19 [b] Is. 13:20 50:41 [a] Jer. 6:22; 25:14; 51:27 50:42 [a] Jer. 6:23 [b] Is. 13:18 [c] Is. 5:30 50:43 [a] Jer. 51:31 [b] Jer. 6:24 50:44 [a] Jer. 49:19–21 [b] Job 41:10 [1] Or *thicket* 50:45 [a] Jer. 51:10, 11 [b] Jer. 51:29 [c] Jer. 49:19, 20 50:46 [a] Rev. 18:9 51:1 [a] Is. 47:1 [b] Jer. 4:11 [1] A code word for Chaldea (Babylonia); may be translated *The Midst of Those Who Rise Up Against Me* 51:2 [a] Jer. 15:7 [b] Jer. 50:14 51:3 [a] Jer. 50:14, 29 [b] Jer. 50:21 51:4 [a] Jer. 49:26; 50:30, 37 51:5 [a] [Jer. 33:24–26; 46:28] 51:6 [a] Rev. 18:4

For [b]this *is* the time of the LORD's
vengeance;
[c]He shall recompense her.
7 [a]Babylon *was* a golden cup in the LORD's
hand,
That made all the earth drunk.
[b]The nations drank her wine;
Therefore the nations [c]are deranged.
8 Babylon has suddenly [a]fallen and been
destroyed.
[b]Wail for her!
[c]Take balm for her pain;
Perhaps she may be healed.

9 We would have healed Babylon,
But she is not healed.
Forsake her, and [a]let us go everyone to his
own country;
[b]For her judgment reaches to heaven and
is lifted up to the skies.
10 The LORD has [a]revealed our
righteousness.
Come and let us [b]declare in Zion the work
of the LORD our God.

11 [a]Make the arrows bright!
Gather the shields!
[b]The LORD has raised up the spirit of the
kings of the Medes.
[c]For His plan *is* against Babylon to destroy
it,
Because it *is* [d]the vengeance of the LORD,
The vengeance for His temple.
12 [a]Set up the standard on the walls of
Babylon;
Make the guard strong,
Set up the watchmen,
Prepare the ambushes.
For the LORD has both devised and done
What He spoke against the inhabitants of
Babylon.
13 [a]O you who dwell by many waters,
Abundant in treasures,
Your end has come,
The measure of your covetousness.
14 [a]The LORD of hosts has sworn by Himself:
"Surely I will fill you with men, [b]as with
locusts,
And they shall lift [c]up a shout against
you."

15 [a]He has made the earth by His power;
He has established the world by His
wisdom,
And [b]stretched out the heaven by His
understanding.
16 When He utters *His* voice—
*There is* a multitude of waters in the
heavens:
[a]"He causes the vapors to ascend from the
ends of the earth;
He makes lightnings for the rain;
He brings the wind out of His treasuries."[1]

17 [a]Everyone is dull-hearted, without
knowledge;
Every metalsmith is put to shame by the
carved image;
[b]For his molded image *is* falsehood,
And *there is* no breath in them.
18 They *are* futile, a work of errors;
In the time of their punishment they shall
perish.
19 The Portion of Jacob *is* not like them,
For He *is* the Maker of all things;
And *Israel is* the tribe of His
inheritance.
The LORD of hosts *is* His name.

20 "You[a] *are* My battle-ax *and* weapons of war:
For with you I will break the nation in
pieces;
With you I will destroy kingdoms;
21 With you I will break in pieces the horse
and its rider;
With you I will break in pieces the chariot
and its rider;
22 With you also I will break in pieces man
and woman;
With you I will break in pieces [a]old and
young;
With you I will break in pieces the young
man and the maiden;
23 With you also I will break in pieces the
shepherd and his flock;
With you I will break in pieces the farmer
and his yoke of oxen;
And with you I will break in pieces
governors and rulers.

24 "And[a] I will repay Babylon
And all the inhabitants of Chaldea
For all the evil they have done
In Zion in your sight," says the LORD.

25 "Behold, I *am* against you, [a]O destroying
mountain,
Who destroys all the earth," says the
LORD.
"And I will stretch out My hand against
you,
Roll you down from the rocks,
[b]And make you a burnt mountain.
26 They shall not take from you a stone for a
corner
Nor a stone for a foundation,
[a]But you shall be desolate forever," says
the LORD.

51:6 [b]Jer. 50:15 [c]Jer. 25:14 51:7 [a]Rev. 17:4 [b]Rev. 14:8 [c]Jer. 25:16 51:8 [a]Is. 21:9 [b]Rev. 18:9, 11, 19 [c]Jer. 46:11 51:9 [a]Is. 13:14 [b]Rev. 18:5 51:10 [a]Ps. 37:6 [b]Jer. 50:28 51:11 [a]Jer. 46:4, 9 [b]Is. 13:17 [c]Jer. 50:45 [d]Jer. 50:28 51:12 [a]Nah. 2:1; 3:14 51:13 [a]Rev. 17:1, 15 51:14 [a]Jer. 49:13 [b]Nah. 3:15 [c]Jer. 50:15 51:15 [a]Gen. 1:1, 6 [b]Job 9:8 51:16 [a]Ps. 135:7 [1]Psalm 135:7 51:17 [a]Jer. 10:14 [b]Jer. 50:2 51:20 [a]Is. 10:5, 15 51:22 [a]2 Chr. 36:17 51:24 [a]Jer. 50:15, 29 51:25 [a]Zech. 4:7 [b]Rev. 8:8 51:26 [a]Jer. 50:26, 40

27 [a]Set up a banner in the land,
Blow the trumpet among the nations!
[b]Prepare the nations against her,
Call [c]the kingdoms together against her:
Ararat, Minni, and Ashkenaz.
Appoint a general against her;
Cause the horses to come up like the
bristling locusts.
28 Prepare against her the nations,
With the kings of the Medes,
Its governors and all its rulers,
All the land of his dominion.
29 And the land will tremble and sorrow;
For every [a]purpose of the LORD shall be
performed against Babylon,
[b]To make the land of Babylon a desolation
without inhabitant.
30 The mighty men of Babylon have ceased
fighting,
They have remained in their
strongholds;
Their might has failed,
[a]They became *like* women;
They have burned her dwelling places,
[b]The bars of her *gate* are broken.
31 [a]One runner will run to meet another,
And one messenger to meet another,
To show the king of Babylon that his city
is taken on *all* sides;
32 [a]The passages are blocked,
The reeds they have burned with fire,
And the men of war are terrified.

33 For thus says the LORD of hosts, the God
of Israel:

"The daughter of Babylon *is* [a]like a
threshing floor
*When* [b]*it is* time to thresh her;
Yet a little while
[c]And the time of her harvest will come."

34 "Nebuchadnezzar the king of Babylon
Has [a]devoured me, he has crushed me;
He has made me an [b]empty vessel,
He has swallowed me up like a
monster;
He has filled his stomach with my
delicacies,
He has spit me out.
35 Let the violence *done* to me and my flesh
*be* upon Babylon,"
The inhabitant of Zion will say;
"And my blood be upon the inhabitants of
Chaldea!"
Jerusalem will say.

36 Therefore thus says the LORD:

"Behold, [a]I will plead your case and take
vengeance for you.
[b]I will dry up her sea and make her springs
dry.
37 [a]Babylon shall become a heap,
A dwelling place for jackals,
[b]An astonishment and a hissing,
Without an inhabitant.
38 They shall roar together like lions,
They shall growl like lions' whelps.
39 In their excitement I will prepare their
feasts;
[a]I will make them drunk,
That they may rejoice,
And sleep a perpetual sleep
And not awake," says the LORD.
40 "I will bring them down
Like lambs to the slaughter,
Like rams with male goats.

41 "Oh, how [a]Sheshach[1] is taken!
Oh, how [b]the praise of the whole earth is
seized!
How Babylon has become desolate among
the nations!
42 [a]The sea has come up over Babylon;
She is covered with the multitude of its
waves.
43 [a]Her cities are a desolation,
A dry land and a wilderness,
A land where [b]no one dwells,
Through which no son of man passes.
44 I will punish [a]Bel in Babylon,
And I will bring out of his mouth what he
has swallowed;
And the nations shall not stream to him
anymore.
Yes, [b]the wall of Babylon shall fall.
45 "My[a] people, go out of the midst of her!
And let everyone deliver himself from the
fierce anger of the LORD.
46 And lest your heart faint,
And you fear [a]for the rumor that *will be*
heard in the land
(A rumor will come *one* year,
And after that, in *another* year
A rumor *will come,*
And violence in the land,
Ruler against ruler),
47 Therefore behold, the days are coming
That I will bring judgment on the carved
images of Babylon;
Her whole land shall be ashamed,
And all her slain shall fall in her midst.
48 Then [a]the heavens and the earth and all
that *is* in them
Shall sing joyously over Babylon;

51:27 [a] Is. 13:2 [b] Jer. 25:14 [c] Jer. 50:41, 42 51:29 [a] Jer. 50:45 [b] Jer. 50:13; 51:26, 43 51:30 [a] Is. 19:16 [b] Lam. 2:9 51:31 [a] Jer. 50:24 51:32 [a] Jer. 50:38 51:33 [a] Is. 21:10 [b] Hab. 3:12 [c] Rev. 14:15 51:34 [a] Jer. 50:17 [b] Is. 24:1–3 51:36 [a] Jer. 50:34 [b] Jer. 50:38 51:37 [a] Is. 13:22 [b] Jer. 25:9, 11 51:39 [a] Jer. 51:57 51:41 [a] Jer. 25:26 [b] Is. 13:19 [1] A code word for Babylon (compare Jeremiah 25:26) 51:42 [a] Is. 8:7, 8 51:43 [a] Jer. 50:39, 40 [b] Is. 13:20 51:44 [a] Jer. 50:2 [b] Jer. 50:15 51:45 [a] [Rev. 18:4] 51:46 [a] 2 Kin. 19:7 51:48 [a] Is. 44:23; 48:20; 49:13

[b]For the plunderers shall come to her from
the north," says the LORD.

49 As Babylon *has caused* the slain of Israel
to fall,
So at Babylon the slain of all the earth
shall fall.

50 [a]You who have escaped the sword,
Get away! Do not stand still!
[b]Remember the LORD afar off,
And let Jerusalem come to your mind.

51 [a]We are ashamed because we have heard
reproach.
Shame has covered our faces,
For strangers [b]have come into the
sanctuaries of the LORD's house.

52 "Therefore behold, the days are coming,"
says the LORD,
"That I will bring judgment on her carved
images,
And throughout all her land the wounded
shall groan.

53 [a]Though Babylon were to mount up to
heaven,
And though she were to fortify the height
of her strength,
*Yet* from Me plunderers would come to
her," says the LORD.

54 [a]The sound of a cry *comes* from Babylon,
And great destruction from the land of
the Chaldeans,

55 Because the LORD is plundering Babylon
And silencing her loud voice,
Though her waves roar like great waters,
And the noise of their voice is uttered,

56 Because the plunderer comes against her,
against Babylon,
And her mighty men are taken.
Every one of their bows is broken;
[a]For the LORD *is* the God of recompense,
He will surely repay.

57 "And I will make drunk
Her princes and [a]wise men,
Her governors, her deputies, and her
mighty men.
And they shall sleep a perpetual sleep
And not awake," says [b]the King,
Whose name *is* the LORD of hosts.

58 Thus says the LORD of hosts:

"The broad walls of Babylon shall be
utterly [a]broken,
And her high gates shall be burned with fire;
[b]The people will labor in vain,
And the nations, because of the fire;
And they shall be weary."

## *JEREMIAH'S COMMAND TO SERAIAH*

59 The word which Jeremiah the prophet
commanded Seraiah the son of [a]Neriah, the son
of Mahseiah, when he went with Zedekiah the
king of Judah to Babylon in the fourth year of
his reign. And Seraiah *was* the quartermaster.
60 So Jeremiah [a]wrote in a book all the evil that
would come upon Babylon, all these words that
are written against Babylon. 61 And Jeremiah
said to Seraiah, "When you arrive in Babylon
and see it, and read all these words, 62 then you
shall say, 'O LORD, You have spoken against this
place to cut it off, so that [a]none shall remain in
it, neither man nor beast, but it shall be deso-
late forever.' 63 Now it shall be, when you have
finished reading this book, [a]*that* you shall tie a
stone to it and throw it out into the Euphrates.
64 Then you shall say, 'Thus Babylon shall sink
and not rise from the catastrophe that I will
bring upon her. And they shall be weary.' "

Thus far *are* the words of Jeremiah.

## *THE FALL OF JERUSALEM REVIEWED*

*(2 Kin. 24:18—25:26; 2 Chr. 36:11–20; Jer. 39:1–10)*

**52** Zedekiah *was* [a]twenty-one years old when
he became king, and he reigned eleven
years in Jerusalem. His mother's name *was* Ha-
mutal the daughter of Jeremiah of [b]Libnah. 2 He
also did evil in the sight of the LORD, according
to all that Jehoiakim had done. 3 For because of
the anger of the LORD *this* happened in Jerusa-
lem and Judah, till He finally cast them out from
His presence. Then Zedekiah [a]rebelled against
the king of Babylon.

4 Now it came to pass in the [a]ninth year of his
reign, in the tenth month, on the tenth *day* of the
month, *that* Nebuchadnezzar king of Babylon
and all his army came against Jerusalem and
encamped against it; and *they* built a siege wall
against it all around. 5 So the city was besieged
until the eleventh year of King Zedekiah. 6 By the
fourth month, on the ninth day of the month,
the famine had become so severe in the city that
there was no food for the people of the land.
7 Then the city *wall* was broken through, and all
the men of war fled and went out of the city at
night by way of the gate between the two walls,
which *was* by the king's garden, even though
the Chaldeans *were* near the city all around.
And they went by way of the plain.[1]

8 But the army of the Chaldeans pursued the
king, and they overtook Zedekiah in the plains
of Jericho. All his army was scattered from him.
9 [a]So they took the king and brought him up

**51:48** [b] Jer. 50:3, 41 **51:50** [a] Jer. 44:28 [b] [Deut. 4:29–31] **51:51** [a] Ps. 44:15; 79:4 [b] Lam. 1:10 **51:53** [a] Amos 9:2 **51:54** [a] Jer. 50:22
**51:56** [a] Jer. 50:29 **51:57** [a] Jer. 50:35 [b] Jer. 46:18; 48:15 **51:58** [a] Jer. 50:15 [b] Hab. 2:13 **51:59** [a] Jer. 32:12 **51:60** [a] Is. 30:8; Jer. 36:2
**51:62** [a] Is. 13:20; 14:22, 23; Jer. 50:3, 39 **51:63** [a] Jer. 19:10, 11; Rev. 18:21 **52:1** [a] 2 Kin. 24:18; 2 Chr. 36:11 [b] Josh. 10:29; 2 Kin. 8:22; Is. 37:8
**52:3** [a] 2 Chr. 36:13 **52:4** [a] 2 Kin. 25:1; Jer. 39:1; Ezek. 24:1, 2; Zech. 8:19 **52:7** [1] Or *the Arabah,* that is, the Jordan Valley **52:9** [a] 2 Kin.
25:6; Jer. 32:4; 39:5

to the king of Babylon at Riblah in the land of Hamath, and he pronounced judgment on him. 10 [a]Then the king of Babylon killed the sons of Zedekiah before his eyes. And he killed all the princes of Judah in Riblah. 11 He also [a]put out the eyes of Zedekiah; and the king of Babylon bound him in bronze fetters, took him to Babylon, and put him in prison till the day of his death.

### *THE TEMPLE AND CITY PLUNDERED AND BURNED*

12 [a]Now in the fifth month, on the tenth *day* of the month ([b]which *was* the nineteenth year of King Nebuchadnezzar king of Babylon), [c]Nebuzaradan, the captain of the guard, *who* served the king of Babylon, came to Jerusalem. 13 He burned the house of the LORD and the king's house; all the houses of Jerusalem, that is, all the houses of the great, he burned with fire. 14 And all the army of the Chaldeans who *were* with the captain of the guard broke down all the walls of Jerusalem all around. 15 [a]Then Nebuzaradan the captain of the guard carried away captive *some* of the poor people, the rest of the people who remained in the city, the defectors who had deserted to the king of Babylon, and the rest of the craftsmen. 16 But Nebuzaradan the captain of the guard left *some* of the poor of the land as vinedressers and farmers.

17 [a]The [b]bronze pillars that *were* in the house of the LORD, and the carts and the bronze Sea that *were* in the house of the LORD, the Chaldeans broke in pieces, and carried all their bronze to Babylon. 18 They also took away [a]the pots, the shovels, the trimmers, the bowls, the spoons, and all the bronze utensils with which the *priests* ministered. 19 The basins, the firepans, the bowls, the pots, the lampstands, the spoons, and the cups, whatever *was* solid gold and whatever *was* solid silver, the captain of the guard took away. 20 The two pillars, one Sea, the twelve bronze bulls which *were* under *it, and* the carts, which King Solomon had made for the house of the LORD—[a]the bronze of all these articles was beyond measure. 21 Now *concerning* the [a]pillars: the height of one pillar *was* eighteen cubits, a measuring line of twelve cubits could measure its circumference, and its thickness *was* four fingers; *it was* hollow. 22 A capital of bronze *was* on it; and the height of one capital *was* five cubits, with a network and pomegranates all around the capital, all of bronze. The second pillar, with pomegranates was the same. 23 There were ninety-six pomegranates on the sides; [a]all the pomegranates, all around on the network, *were* one hundred.

### *THE PEOPLE TAKEN CAPTIVE TO BABYLONIA*

24 [a]The captain of the guard took Seraiah the chief priest, [b]Zephaniah the second priest, and the three doorkeepers. 25 He also took out of the city an officer who had charge of the men of war, seven men of the king's close associates who were found in the city, the principal scribe of the army who mustered the people of the land, and sixty men of the people of the land who were found in the midst of the city. 26 And Nebuzaradan the captain of the guard took these and brought them to the king of Babylon at Riblah. 27 Then the king of Babylon struck them and put them to death at Riblah in the land of Hamath. Thus Judah was carried away captive from its own land.

28 [a]These *are* the people whom Nebuchadnezzar carried away captive: [b]in the seventh year, [c]three thousand and twenty-three Jews; 29 [a]in the eighteenth year of Nebuchadnezzar he carried away captive from Jerusalem eight hundred and thirty-two persons; 30 in the twenty-third year of Nebuchadnezzar, Nebuzaradan the captain of the guard carried away captive of the Jews seven hundred and forty-five persons. All the persons *were* four thousand six hundred.

### *JEHOIACHIN RELEASED FROM PRISON*

*(2 Kin. 25:27–30)*

31 [a]Now it came to pass in the thirty-seventh year of the captivity of Jehoiachin king of Judah, in the twelfth month, on the twenty-fifth *day* of the month, *that* Evil-Merodach[1] king of Babylon, in the *first* year of his reign, [b]lifted up the head of Jehoiachin king of Judah and brought him out of prison. 32 And he spoke kindly to him and gave him a more prominent seat than those of the kings who *were* with him in Babylon. 33 So Jehoiachin changed from his prison garments, [a]and he ate bread regularly before the *king* all the days of his life. 34 And as for his provisions, there was a regular ration given him by the king of Babylon, a portion for each day until the day of his death, all the days of his life.

52:10 [a] Ezek. 12:13 52:11 [a] Ezek. 12:13 52:12 [a] 2 Kin. 25:8–21 [b] Jer. 52:29 [c] Jer. 39:9 52:15 [a] Jer. 39:9 52:17 [a] Jer. 27:19 [b] 1 Kin. 7:15, 23, 27, 50 52:18 [a] Ex. 27:3; 1 Kin. 7:40, 45; 2 Kin. 25:14 52:20 [a] 1 Kin. 7:47; 2 Kin. 25:16 52:21 [a] 1 Kin. 7:15; 2 Kin. 25:17; 2 Chr. 3:15 52:23 [a] 1 Kin. 7:20 52:24 [a] 2 Kin. 25:18; 1 Chr. 6:14; Ezra 7:1 [b] Jer. 21:1; 29:25 52:28 [a] 2 Kin. 24:2 [b] 2 Kin. 24:12 [c] 2 Kin. 24:14 52:29 [a] 2 Kin. 25:11; Jer. 39:9 52:31 [a] 2 Kin. 25:27–30 [b] Gen. 40:13, 20; Ps. 3:3; 27:6 [1] Or *Awil-Marduk* 52:33 [a] 2 Sam. 9:7, 13; 1 Kin. 2:7

# *The* LAMENTATIONS *of the Prophet Jeremiah*

| AUTHOR | KEY VERSES | READING TIME |
|---|---|---|
| Jeremiah | Lamentations 3:22–23 | 25 minutes |

Lamentations describes the funeral of a city. The book is a tear-stained portrait of the once-proud Jerusalem, a city reduced to rubble by the invading Babylonian army. In a five-poem dirge, Jeremiah responded emotionally to what had taken place. A death had occurred. Jerusalem was barren. But even amid this terrible calamity, Jeremiah could cry out, "Great is Your faithfulness" (Lam. 3:23). In the face of death and destruction, with life seemingly coming apart, Jeremiah turned tragedy into a triumph of faith. God had never failed in the past. God had promised to remain faithful in the future. In the light of the God he knew and loved, Jeremiah found hope and comfort even in the shadow of death and destruction.

**Occasion:** Jeremiah was an eyewitness to the destruction of Jerusalem and wrote Lamentations as a reminder of the horrors of that event.

**Main Point:** God's judgment of sin is harsh, but His mercy is greater.

**Big Ideas:** God is just but He is also merciful. Sin causes great sorrow and pain, but even in those times, we can find hope and comfort in the Lord.

**OUTLINE:**

I. The City's Destruction (ch. 1)
II. The Lord's Punishment (ch. 2)
III. The Prophet's Grief (ch. 3)
IV. The Lord's Wrath (ch. 4)
V. The Remnant's Hope (ch. 5)

**722 BC** The Assyrians defeat Israel

**640 BC** Josiah becomes king in Judah

**626 BC** Jeremiah is called to prophesy

**612 BC** The Babylonians and Medes defeat Assyria

**609 BC** Jehoahaz becomes king in Judah

**608 BC** Jehoiakim becomes king in Judah

**605 BC** Nebuchadnezzar rules in Babylon

**598 BC** Jehoiachin becomes king in Judah

**598 BC** Zedekiah becomes king in Judah

**586 BC** The Babylonians destroy Jerusalem

**585 BC** Jeremiah is taken to Egypt

### *JERUSALEM IN AFFLICTION*

1 How lonely sits the city
*That was* full of people!
[a]*How* like a widow is she,
Who *was* great among the nations!
The [b]princess among the provinces
Has become a slave!

2 She [a]weeps bitterly in the [b]night,
Her tears *are* on her cheeks;
Among all her lovers
She has none to comfort *her.*
All her friends have dealt treacherously with her;
They have become her enemies.

3 [a]Judah has gone into captivity,
Under affliction and hard servitude;
[b]She dwells among the nations,
She finds no [c]rest;
All her persecutors overtake her in dire straits.

4 The roads to Zion mourn
Because no one comes to the set feasts.
All her gates are [a]desolate;
Her priests sigh,
Her virgins are afflicted,
And she *is* in bitterness.

**1:4** The **gates** of ancient cities were normally crowded with people. In addition to being the entrance for a constant flow of traffic in and out of the city, the gates were where most business and legal transactions took place.

5 Her adversaries [a]have become the master,
Her enemies prosper;
For the LORD has afflicted her
[b]Because of the multitude of her transgressions.
Her [c]children have gone into captivity before the enemy.

6 And from the daughter of Zion
All her splendor has departed.
Her princes have become like deer
*That* find no pasture,
That flee without strength
Before the pursuer.

7 In the days of her affliction and roaming,
Jerusalem [a]remembers all her pleasant things
That she had in the days of old.
When her people fell into the hand of the enemy,
With no one to help her,
The adversaries saw her
*And* mocked at her downfall.[1]

8 [a]Jerusalem has sinned gravely,
Therefore she has become vile.[1]
All who honored her despise her
Because [b]they have seen her nakedness;
Yes, she sighs and turns away.

9 Her uncleanness *is* in her skirts;
She [a]did not consider her destiny;
Therefore her collapse was awesome;
She had no comforter.
"O LORD, behold my affliction,
For *the* enemy is exalted!"

10 The adversary has spread his hand
Over all her pleasant things;
For she has seen [a]the nations enter her sanctuary,
Those whom You commanded
[b]Not to enter Your assembly.

11 All her people sigh,
[a]They seek bread;
They have given their valuables for food to restore life.
"See, O LORD, and consider,
For I am scorned."

12 "*Is it* nothing to you, all you who pass by?
Behold and see
[a]If there is any sorrow like my sorrow,
Which has been brought on me,
Which the LORD has inflicted
In the day of His fierce anger.

13 "From above He has sent fire into my bones,
And it overpowered them;
He has [a]spread a net for my feet
And turned me back;
He has made me desolate
*And* faint all the day.

14 "The[a] yoke of my transgressions was bound;[1]
They were woven together by His hands,
*And* thrust upon my neck.
He made my strength fail;
The Lord delivered me into the hands of *those whom* I am not able to withstand.

15 "The Lord has trampled underfoot all my mighty *men* in my midst;
He has called an assembly against me
To crush my young men;

1:1 [a] Is. 47:7–9 [b] Ezra 4:20 1:2 [a] Jer. 13:17 [b] Job 7:3 1:3 [a] Jer. 52:27 [b] Lam. 2:9 [c] Deut. 28:65 1:4 [a] Is. 27:10 1:5 [a] Deut. 28:43 [b] Dan. 9:7, 16 [c] Jer. 52:28 1:7 [a] Ps. 137:1 [1] Vulgate reads *her Sabbaths.* 1:8 [a] [1 Kin. 8:46] [b] Ezek. 16:37 [1] Septuagint and Vulgate read *moved* or *removed.* 1:9 [a] Is. 47:7 1:10 [a] Jer. 51:51 [b] Deut. 23:3 1:11 [a] Jer. 38:9; 52:6 1:12 [a] Dan. 9:12 1:13 [a] Ezek. 12:13; 17:20 1:14 [a] Deut. 28:48 [1] Following Masoretic Text and Targum; Septuagint, Syriac, and Vulgate read *watched over.*

[a]The Lord trampled *as* in a winepress
The virgin daughter of Judah.

16 "For these *things* I weep;
My eye, [a]my eye overflows with water;
Because the comforter, who should
restore my life,
Is far from me.
My children are desolate
Because the enemy prevailed."

17 [a]Zion spreads out her hands,
*But* no one comforts her;
The LORD has commanded concerning
Jacob
*That* those [b]around him *become* his
adversaries;
Jerusalem has become an unclean thing
among them.

18 "The LORD is [a]righteous,
For I [b]rebelled against His commandment.
Hear now, all peoples,
And behold my sorrow;
My virgins and my young men
Have gone into captivity.

19 "I called for my lovers,
*But* they deceived me;
My priests and my elders
Breathed their last in the city,
While they sought food
To restore their life.

20 "See, O LORD, that I *am* in distress;
My [a]soul is troubled;
My heart is overturned within me,
For I have been very rebellious.
[b]Outside the sword bereaves,
At home *it is* like death.

21 "They have heard that I sigh,
*But* no one comforts me.
All my enemies have heard of my trouble;
They are [a]glad that You have done *it*.
Bring on [b]the day You have announced,
That they may become like me.

22 "Let[a] all their wickedness come before You,
And do to them as You have done to me
For all my transgressions;
For my sighs *are* many,
And my heart *is* faint."

## *GOD'S ANGER WITH JERUSALEM*

2 How the Lord has covered the daughter of
Zion
With a [a]cloud in His anger!
[b]He cast down from heaven to the earth
[c]The beauty of Israel,
And did not remember [d]His footstool
In the day of His anger.

2 The Lord has swallowed up and has [a]not
pitied
All the dwelling places of Jacob.
He has thrown down in His wrath
The strongholds of the daughter of Judah;
He has brought *them* down to the ground;
[b]He has profaned the kingdom and its
princes.

3 He has cut off in fierce anger
Every horn of Israel;
[a]He has drawn back His right hand
From before the enemy.
[b]He has blazed against Jacob like a flaming
fire
Devouring all around.

4 [a]Standing like an enemy, He has bent His
bow;
With His right hand, like an adversary,
He has slain [b]all *who were* pleasing to His
eye;
On the tent of the daughter of Zion,
He has poured out His fury like fire.

5 [a]The Lord was like an enemy.
He has swallowed up Israel,
He has swallowed up all her palaces;
[b]He has destroyed her strongholds,
And has increased mourning and
lamentation
In the daughter of Judah.

6 He has done violence [a]to His tabernacle,
[b]*As if it were* a garden;
He has destroyed His place of assembly;
The LORD has caused
The appointed feasts and Sabbaths to be
forgotten in Zion.
In His burning indignation He has
[c]spurned the king and the priest.

7 The Lord has spurned His altar,
He has [a]abandoned His sanctuary;
He has given up the walls of her palaces
Into the hand of the enemy.
[b]They have made a noise in the house of
the LORD
As on the day of a set feast.

8 The LORD has purposed to destroy
The [a]wall of the daughter of Zion.
[b]He has stretched out a line;
He has not withdrawn His hand from
destroying;

1:15 [a][Rev. 14:19] 1:16 [a]Eccl. 4:1 1:17 [a]Jer. 4:31 [b]2 Kin. 24:2–4 1:18 [a]Dan. 9:7, 14 [b]1 Sam. 12:14, 15 1:20 [a]Is. 16:11 [b]Ezek. 7:15 1:21 [a]Ps. 35:15 [b][Jer. 46] 1:22 [a]Ps. 109:15; 137:7, 8 2:1 [a][Lam. 3:44] [b]Matt. 11:23 [c]2 Sam. 1:19 [d]Ps. 99:5 2:2 [a]Lam. 3:43 [b]Ps. 89:39, 40 2:3 [a]Ps. 74:11 [b]Ps. 89:46 2:4 [a]Is. 63:10 [b]Ezek. 24:25 2:5 [a]Jer. 30:14 [b]Jer. 52:13 2:6 [a]Ps. 80:12; 89:40 [b]Is. 1:8 [c]Is. 43:28 2:7 [a]Ezek. 24:21 [b]Ps. 74:3–8 2:8 [a]Jer. 52:14 [b][Is. 34:11]

Therefore He has caused the rampart and wall to lament;
They languished together.

9 Her gates have sunk into the ground;
He has destroyed and [a]broken her bars.
[b]Her king and her princes *are* among the nations;
[c]The Law *is* no *more,*
And her [d]prophets find no vision from the LORD.

10 The elders of the daughter of Zion
[a]Sit on the ground *and* keep silence;
They [b]throw dust on their heads
And [c]gird themselves with sackcloth.
The virgins of Jerusalem
Bow their heads to the ground.

11 [a]My eyes fail with tears,
My heart is troubled;
[b]My bile is poured on the ground
Because of the destruction of the daughter of my people,
Because [c]the children and the infants
Faint in the streets of the city.

12 They say to their mothers,
"Where *is* grain and wine?"
As they swoon like the wounded
In the streets of the city,
As their life is poured out
In their mothers' bosom.

13 How shall I [a]console you?
To what shall I liken you,
O daughter of Jerusalem?
What shall I compare with you, that I may comfort you,
O virgin daughter of Zion?
For your ruin *is* spread wide as the sea;
Who can heal you?

14 Your [a]prophets have seen for you
False and deceptive visions;
They have not [b]uncovered your iniquity,
To bring back your captives,
But have envisioned for you false [c]prophecies and delusions.

15 All who pass by [a]clap *their* hands at you;
They hiss [b]and shake their heads
At the daughter of Jerusalem:
"*Is* this the city that is called
[c]'The perfection of beauty,
The joy of the whole earth'?"

16 [a]All your enemies have opened their mouth against you;
They hiss and gnash *their* teeth.
They say, [b]"We have swallowed *her* up!
Surely this *is* the [c]day we have waited for;
We have found *it,* [d]we have seen *it!*"

17 The LORD has done what He [a]purposed;
He has fulfilled His word
Which He commanded in days of old.
He has thrown down and has not pitied,
And He has caused an enemy to [b]rejoice over you;
He has exalted the horn of your adversaries.

18 Their heart cried out to the Lord,
"O wall of the daughter of Zion,
[a]Let tears run down like a river day and night;
Give yourself no relief;
Give your eyes no rest.

19 "Arise, [a]cry out in the night,
At the beginning of the watches;
[b]Pour out your heart like water before the face of the Lord.
Lift your hands toward Him
For the life of your young children,
Who faint from hunger [c]at the head of every street."

20 "See, O LORD, and consider!
To whom have You done this?
[a]Should the women eat their offspring,
The children they have cuddled?[1]
Should the priest and prophet be slain
In the sanctuary of the Lord?

21 "Young[a] and old lie
On the ground in the streets;
My virgins and my young men
Have fallen by the [b]sword;
You have slain *them* in the day of Your anger,
You have slaughtered *and* not pitied.

22 "You have invited as to a feast day
[a]The terrors that surround me.
In the day of the LORD's anger
There was no refugee or survivor.
[b]Those whom I have borne and brought up
My enemies have [c]destroyed."

## *THE PROPHET'S ANGUISH AND HOPE*

3 I *am* the man *who* has seen affliction by the rod of His wrath.
2 He has led me and made *me* walk
*In* darkness and not *in* light.
3 Surely He has turned His hand against me
Time and time again throughout the day.

2:9 [a]Jer. 51:30 [b]Deut. 28:36 [c]2 Chr. 15:3 [d]Ps. 74:9 2:10 [a]Is. 3:26 [b]Job 2:12 [c]Is. 15:3 2:11 [a]Lam. 3:48 [b]Job 16:13 [c]Lam. 4:4 2:13 [a]Lam. 1:12 2:14 [a]Jer. 2:8; 23:25–29; 29:8, 9; 37:19 [b]Is. 58:1 [c]Jer. 23:33–36 2:15 [a]Ezek. 25:6 [b]Ps. 44:14 [c][Ps. 48:2; 50:2] 2:16 [a]Job 16:9, 10 [b]Ps. 56:2; 124:3 [c]Lam. 1:21 [d]Ps. 35:21 2:17 [a]Lev. 26:16 [b]Ps. 38:16 2:18 [a]Jer. 14:17 2:19 [a]Ps. 119:147 [b]Ps. 42:4; 62:8 [c]Is. 51:20 2:20 [a]Lev. 26:29 [1]Vulgate reads *a span long.* 2:21 [a]2 Chr. 36:17 [b]Jer. 18:21 2:22 [a]Ps. 31:13 [b]Hos. 9:12 [c]Jer. 16:2–4; 44:7

4 He has aged [a]my flesh and my skin,
And [b]broken my bones.
5 He has besieged me
And surrounded *me* with bitterness and woe.
6 [a]He has set me in dark places
Like the dead of long ago.

7 [a]He has hedged me in so that I cannot get out;
He has made my chain heavy.
8 Even [a]when I cry and shout,
He shuts out my prayer.
9 He has blocked my ways with hewn stone;
He has made my paths crooked.

10 [a]He *has been* to me a bear lying in wait,
*Like* a lion in ambush.
11 He has turned aside my ways and [a]torn me in pieces;
He has made me desolate.
12 He has bent His bow
And [a]set me up as a target for the arrow.

13 He has caused [a]the arrows of His quiver
To pierce my loins.[1]
14 I have become the [a]ridicule of all my people—
[b]Their taunting song all the day.
15 [a]He has filled me with bitterness,
He has made me drink wormwood.

16 He has also broken my teeth [a]with gravel,
And covered me with ashes.

**3:16** Some tribes in the ancient Near East mixed sand, **gravel**, and other solid substances in the food they gave to prisoners. The hard objects wore down and broke the prisoners' **teeth** and caused horrible intestinal problems; both resulted in tremendous pain.

17 You have moved my soul far from peace;
I have forgotten prosperity.
18 [a]And I said, "My strength and my hope
Have perished from the LORD."

19 Remember my affliction and roaming,
[a]The wormwood and the gall.
20 My soul still remembers
And sinks within me.
21 This I recall to my mind,
Therefore I have [a]hope.

22 [a]*Through* the LORD's mercies we are not consumed,
Because His compassions [b]fail not.
23 *They are* new [a]every morning;
Great *is* Your faithfulness.
24 "The LORD *is* my [a]portion," says my soul,
"Therefore I [b]hope in Him!"

25 The LORD *is* good to those who [a]wait for Him,
To the soul *who* seeks Him.
26 *It is* good that *one* should [a]hope [b]and wait quietly
For the salvation of the LORD.
27 [a]*It is* good for a man to bear
The yoke in his youth.

28 [a]Let him sit alone and keep silent,
Because *God* has laid *it* on him;
29 [a]Let him put his mouth in the dust—
There may yet be hope.
30 [a]Let him give *his* cheek to the one who strikes him,
*And* be full of reproach.

### SEEING JESUS IN THE SCRIPTURE

**3:28–30** This lament shows the people of God how to suffer patiently. It also points to Jesus who remained silent before His accusers, was struck repeatedly, and suffered to the point of death on our behalf (see Mark 14:61, 65).

31 [a]For the Lord will not cast off forever.
32 Though He causes grief,
Yet He will show compassion
According to the multitude of His mercies.
33 For [a]He does not afflict willingly,
Nor grieve the children of men.

34 To crush under one's feet
All the prisoners of the earth,
35 To turn aside the justice *due* a man
Before the face of the Most High,
36 Or subvert a man in his cause—
[a]The Lord does not approve.

37 Who *is* he [a]*who* speaks and it comes to pass,
*When* the Lord has not commanded *it?*
38 *Is it* not from the mouth of the Most High
That [a]woe and well-being proceed?
39 [a]Why should a living man complain,
[b]A man for the punishment of his sins?

3:4 [a]Job 16:8 [b]Ps. 51:8 3:6 [a][Ps. 88:5, 6; 143:3] 3:7 [a]Hos. 2:6 3:8 [a]Job 30:20 3:10 [a]Is. 38:13 3:11 [a]Hos. 6:1 3:12 [a]Job 7:20; 16:12 3:13 [a]Job 6:4 [1]Literally *kidneys* 3:14 [a]Jer. 20:7 [b]Job 30:9 3:15 [a]Jer. 9:15 3:16 [a][Prov. 20:17] 3:18 [a]Ps. 31:22 3:19 [a]Jer. 9:15 3:21 [a]Ps. 130:7 3:22 [a][Mal. 3:6] [b]Ps. 78:38 3:23 [a]Is. 33:2 3:24 [a]Ps. 16:5; 73:26; 119:57 [b]Mic. 7:7 3:25 [a]Is. 30:18 3:26 [a][Rom. 4:16–18] [b]Ps. 37:7 3:27 [a]Ps. 94:12 3:28 [a]Jer. 15:17 3:29 [a]Job 42:6 3:30 [a]Is. 50:6 3:31 [a]Ps. 77:7; 94:14 3:33 [a][Ezek. 33:11] 3:36 [a][Hab. 1:13] 3:37 [a][Ps. 33:9–11] 3:38 [a]Job 2:10 3:39 [a]Prov. 19:3 [b]Mic. 7:9

40 Let us search out and examine our ways,
And turn back to the LORD;
41 [a]Let us lift our hearts and hands
To God in heaven.
42 [a]We have transgressed and rebelled;
You have not pardoned.

43 You have covered *Yourself* with anger
And pursued us;
You have slain *and* not pitied.
44 You have covered Yourself with a cloud,
That prayer should not pass through.
45 You have made us an [a]offscouring and refuse
In the midst of the peoples.

46 [a]All our enemies
Have opened their mouths against us.
47 [a]Fear and a snare have come upon us,
[b]Desolation and destruction.
48 [a]My eyes overflow with rivers of water
For the destruction of the daughter of my people.

49 [a]My eyes flow and do not cease,
Without interruption,
50 Till the LORD from heaven
[a]Looks down and sees.
51 My eyes bring suffering to my soul
Because of all the daughters of my city.

52 My enemies [a]without cause
Hunted me down like a bird.
53 They silenced[1] my life [a]in the pit
And [b]threw stones at me.
54 [a]The waters flowed over my head;
[b]I said, "I am cut off!"

55 [a]I called on Your name, O LORD,
From the lowest [b]pit.
56 [a]You have heard my voice:
"Do not hide Your ear
From my sighing, from my cry for help."
57 You [a]drew near on the day I called on You,
And said, [b]"Do not fear!"

58 O Lord, You have [a]pleaded the case for my soul;
[b]You have redeemed my life.
59 O LORD, You have seen *how* I am wronged;
[a]Judge my case.
60 You have seen all their vengeance,
All their [a]schemes against me.

61 You have heard their reproach, O LORD,
All their schemes against me,
62 The lips of my enemies
And their whispering against me all the day.
63 Look at their [a]sitting down and their rising up;
I *am* their taunting song.

64 [a]Repay them, O LORD,
According to the work of their hands.
65 Give them a veiled[1] heart;
Your curse *be* upon them!
66 In Your anger,
Pursue and destroy them
[a]From under the heavens of the [b]LORD.

### THE DEGRADATION OF ZION

4 How the gold has become dim!
*How* changed the fine gold!
The stones of the sanctuary are scattered
At the head of every street.

2 The precious sons of Zion,
Valuable as fine gold,
How they are regarded [a]as clay pots,
The work of the hands of the potter!

3 Even the jackals present their breasts
To nurse their young;
*But* the daughter of my people *is* cruel,
[a]Like ostriches in the wilderness.

**4:3** A mother ostrich drops her eggs in the sand and then leaves, letting the heat of the sun warm them. Even after the eggs have hatched, if she feels threatened, she won't hesitate to abandon her young ones to save herself.

4 The tongue of the infant clings
To the roof of its mouth for thirst;
[a]The young children ask for bread,
*But* no one breaks *it* for them.

5 Those who ate delicacies
Are desolate in the streets;
Those who were brought up in scarlet
[a]Embrace ash heaps.

6 The punishment of the iniquity of the daughter of my people
Is greater than the punishment of the [a]sin of Sodom,
Which was [b]overthrown in a moment,
With no hand to help her!

3:41 [a] Ps. 86:4 3:42 [a] Dan. 9:5 3:45 [a] 1 Cor. 4:13 3:46 [a] Lam. 2:16 3:47 [a] Is. 24:17, 18 [b] Is. 51:19 3:48 [a] Jer. 4:19; 14:17 3:49 [a] Jer. 14:17 3:50 [a] Is. 63:15 3:52 [a] Ps. 35:7, 19 3:53 [a] Jer. 37:16 [b] Dan. 6:17 [1] Septuagint reads *put to death.* 3:54 [a] Ps. 69:2 [b] Is. 38:10 3:55 [a] Ps. 130:1 [b] Jer. 38:6–13 3:56 [a] Ps. 3:4 3:57 [a] James 4:8 [b] Is. 41:10, 14 3:58 [a] Jer. 51:36 [b] Ps. 71:23 3:59 [a] Ps. 9:4 3:60 [a] Jer. 11:19 3:63 [a] Ps. 139:2 3:64 [a] Ps. 28:4 3:65 [1] A Jewish tradition reads *sorrow of.* 3:66 [a] Deut. 25:19 [b] Ps. 8:3 4:2 [a] Is. 30:14 4:3 [a] Job 39:14–17 4:4 [a] Ps. 22:15 4:5 [a] Job 24:8 4:6 [a] Ezek. 16:48 [b] Gen. 19:25

7 Her Nazirites[1] were brighter than snow
And whiter than milk;
They were more ruddy in body than
rubies,
*Like* sapphire in their appearance.

8 *Now* their appearance is blacker than
soot;
They go unrecognized in the streets;
[a]Their skin clings to their bones,
It has become as dry as wood.

9 *Those* slain by the sword are better off
Than *those* who die of hunger;
For these [a]pine away,
Stricken *for lack* of the fruits of the [b]field.

10 The hands of the [a]compassionate
women
Have cooked their [b]own children;
They became [c]food for them
In the destruction of the daughter of my
people.

11 The LORD has fulfilled His fury,
[a]He has poured out His fierce anger.
[b]He kindled a fire in Zion,
And it has devoured its foundations.

12 The kings of the earth,
And all inhabitants of the world,
Would not have believed
That the adversary and the enemy
Could [a]enter the gates of Jerusalem—

13 [a]Because of the sins of her prophets
*And* the iniquities of her priests,
[b]Who shed in her midst
The blood of the just.

14 They wandered blind in the streets;
[a]They have defiled themselves with
blood,
[b]So that no one would touch their
garments.

15 They cried out to them,
"Go away, [a]unclean!
Go away, go away,
Do not touch us!"
When they fled and wandered,
*Those* among the nations said,
"They shall no longer dwell *here*."

16 The face[1] of the LORD scattered them;
He no longer regards them.
[a]*The people* do not respect the priests
Nor show favor to the elders.

17 Still [a]our eyes failed us,
*Watching* vainly for our help;
In our watching we watched
For a nation *that* could not save *us*.

18 [a]They tracked our steps
So that we could not walk in our streets.
[b]Our end was near;
Our days were over,
For our end had come.

19 Our pursuers were [a]swifter
Than the eagles of the heavens.
They pursued us on the mountains
And lay in wait for us in the wilderness.

20 The [a]breath of our nostrils, the anointed
of the LORD,
[b]Was caught in their pits,
Of whom we said, "Under his shadow
We shall live among the nations."

21 Rejoice and be glad, O daughter of [a]Edom,
*You* who dwell in the land of Uz!
[b]The cup shall also pass over to you
And you shall become drunk and make
yourself naked.

22 [a]*The punishment of* your iniquity is
accomplished,
O daughter of Zion;
He will no longer send you into captivity.
[b]He will punish your iniquity,
O daughter of Edom;
He will uncover your sins!

## PRAYER FOR RESTORATION

5 Remember, [a]O LORD, what has come
upon us;
Look, and behold [b]our reproach!
2 [a]Our inheritance has been turned over to
aliens,
And our houses to foreigners.
3 We have become orphans and waifs,
Our mothers *are* like [a]widows.

4 We pay for the water we drink,
And our wood comes at a price.
5 [a]*They* pursue at our heels;[1]
We labor *and* have no rest.
6 [a]We have given our hand [b]*to* the Egyptians
*And* the [c]Assyrians, to be satisfied with
bread.

7 [a]Our fathers sinned *and are* no more,
But we bear their iniquities.
8 Servants rule over us;
*There is* none to deliver *us* from their hand.

4:7 [1] Or *nobles* 4:8 [a] Ps. 102:5 4:9 [a] Lev. 26:39 [b] Jer. 16:4 4:10 [a] Lam. 2:20 [b] Is. 49:15 [c] Deut. 28:57 4:11 [a] Jer. 7:20 [b] Deut. 32:22 4:12 [a] Jer. 21:13 4:13 [a] Jer. 5:31 [b] Matt. 23:31 4:14 [a] Jer. 2:34 [b] Num. 19:16 4:15 [a] Lev. 13:45, 46 4:16 [a] Lam. 5:12 [1] Targum reads *anger.* 4:17 [a] 2 Kin. 24:7 4:18 [a] 2 Kin. 25:4 [b] Ezek. 7:2, 3, 6 4:19 [a] Deut. 28:49 4:20 [a] Gen. 2:7 [b] Jer. 52:9 4:21 [a] Ps. 83:3–6 [b] Jer. 25:15 4:22 [a] [Is. 40:2] [b] Ps. 137:7 5:1 [a] Ps. 89:50 [b] Lam. 2:15 5:2 [a] Ps. 79:1 5:3 [a] Jer. 15:8; 18:21 5:5 [a] Jer. 28:14 [1] Literally *necks* 5:6 [a] Gen. 24:2 [b] Hos. 9:3; 12:1 [c] Hos. 5:13 5:7 [a] Jer. 31:29

9 We get our bread *at the risk* of our lives,
Because of the sword in the wilderness.

10 Our skin is hot as an oven,
Because of the fever of famine.
11 They [a]ravished the women in Zion,
The maidens in the cities of Judah.
12 Princes were hung up by their hands,
And elders were not respected.
13 Young men [a]ground at the millstones;
Boys staggered under *loads of* wood.
14 The elders have ceased *gathering at* the gate,
And the young men from their [a]music.

15 The joy of our heart has ceased;
Our dance has turned into [a]mourning.
16 [a]The crown has fallen *from* our head.
Woe to us, for we have sinned!
17 Because of this our heart is faint;
[a]Because of these *things* our eyes grow dim;
18 Because of Mount Zion which is [a]desolate,
With foxes walking about on it.

19 You, O LORD, [a]remain forever;
[b]Your throne from generation to generation.
20 [a]Why do You forget us forever,
*And* forsake us for so long a time?
21 [a]Turn us back to You, O LORD, and we will be restored;
Renew our days as of old,
22 Unless You have utterly rejected us,
*And* are very angry with us!

5:11 [a] Zech. 14:2 5:13 [a] Judg. 16:21 5:14 [a] Jer. 7:34 5:15 [a] Amos 8:10 5:16 [a] Ps. 89:39 5:17 [a] Ps. 6:7 5:18 [a] Is. 27:10 5:19 [a] Ps. 9:7 [b] Ps. 45:6 5:20 [a] Ps. 13:1; 44:24 5:21 [a] Jer. 31:18

# *The Book of the Prophet* EZEKIEL

| AUTHOR | KEY VERSE | READING TIME |
|---|---|---|
| Ezekiel | Ezekiel 36:26 | 4 hours 21 minutes |

The people of Israel, once prosperous in their homeland, were decimated and in foreign captivity. During those darkest of days, Ezekiel, a priest and a prophet in exile himself, ministered to God's people with a message defending God's justice. But Ezekiel's message was also one of hope. Though God's people were like dry bones in the sun, God would reassemble the nation, breathe life into it, and bring it blessings once again. The people's present judgment would be followed by future glory so that they would "know that I am the LORD" (Ezek. 6:7).

**Occasion:** Ezekiel's prophetic ministry began during the period of Judah's fall and took place in Babylonian exile.

**Main Point:** God was just in His judgment of His people, but His promise of future blessings stands.

**Big Ideas:** God is righteous and just in all He does. When we disobey God, we will experience God's loving correction. When we obey God, we will be blessed.

## OUTLINE:

I. Ezekiel's Visions (ch. 1)
II. Ezekiel's Calling (chs. 2–3)
III. Ezekiel's Message: Judgment on Judah (chs. 4–24)
IV. Ezekiel's Message: Judgment on the Nations (chs. 25–32)
V. Ezekiel's Message: The Return of Israel (chs. 33–39)
VI. Ezekiel's Message: The Restoration of Israel (chs. 40–48)

**640 BC** Josiah becomes king in Judah

**609 BC** Jehoahaz becomes king in Judah

**608 BC** Jehoiakim becomes king in Judah

**605 BC** Daniel and others exiled in Babylon

**598 BC** Jehoiachin becomes king in Judah

**598 BC** Zedekiah becomes king in Judah

**597 BC** Ezekiel and others exiled in Babylon

**c. 593–571 BC** Ezekiel prophesies

**586 BC** The Babylonians destroy Jerusalem

**586 BC** Much of Judah exiled in Babylon

## *EZEKIEL'S VISION OF GOD*

**1** Now it came to pass in the thirtieth year, in the fourth *month,* on the fifth *day* of the month, as I *was* among the captives by [a]the River Chebar, *that* [b]the heavens were opened and I saw [c]visions[1] of God. 2 On the fifth *day* of the month, which *was* in the fifth year of King Jehoiachin's captivity, 3 the word of the LORD came expressly to Ezekiel the priest, the son of Buzi, in the land of the Chaldeans[1] by the River Chebar; and [a]the hand of the LORD was upon him there.

4 Then I looked, and behold, [a]a whirlwind was coming [b]out of the north, a great cloud with raging fire engulfing itself; and brightness *was* all around it and radiating out of its midst like the color of amber, out of the midst of the fire. 5 [a]Also from within it *came* the likeness of four living creatures. And [b]this *was* their appearance: they had [c]the likeness of a man. 6 Each one had four faces, and each one had four wings. 7 Their legs *were* straight, and the soles of their feet *were* like the soles of calves' feet. They sparkled [a]like the color of burnished bronze. 8 [a]The hands of a man *were* under their wings on their four sides; and each of the four had faces and wings. 9 Their wings touched one another. *The creatures* did not turn when they went, but each one went straight [a]forward.

> **1:5** These **living creatures** are related to the cherubim—celestial beings associated with God's holiness and glory, and sometimes poetically with storm winds upon which God travels (see Ps. 18:10). There are two basic approaches to understanding them here: as a symbolic representation of deity, or as symbolic representations of angelic beings who serve in God's presence. Probably they are angels because God Himself is not revealed until the end of the section (Ezek. 1:26).

10 As for [a]the likeness of their faces, *each* [b]had the face of a man; each of the four had [c]the face of a lion on the right side, [d]each of the four had the face of an ox on the left side, [e]and each of the four had the face of an eagle. 11 Thus *were* their faces. Their wings stretched upward; two *wings* of each one touched one another, and [a]two covered their bodies. 12 And [a]each one went straight forward; they went wherever the spirit wanted to go, and they did not turn when they went.

13 As for the likeness of the living creatures, their appearance *was* like burning coals of fire, [a]like the appearance of torches going back and forth among the living creatures. The fire was bright, and out of the fire went lightning. 14 And the living creatures ran back and forth, [a]in appearance like a flash of lightning.

15 Now as I looked at the living creatures, behold, [a]a wheel *was* on the earth beside each living creature with its four faces. 16 [a]The appearance of the wheels and their workings *was* [b]like the color of beryl, and all four had the same likeness. The appearance of their workings *was,* as it were, a wheel in the middle of a wheel. 17 When they moved, they went toward any one of four directions; they did not turn aside when they went. 18 As for their rims, they were so high they were awesome; and their rims *were* [a]full of eyes, all around the four of them. 19 [a]When the living creatures went, the wheels went beside them; and when the living creatures were lifted up from the earth, the wheels were lifted up. 20 Wherever the spirit wanted to go, they went, *because* there the spirit went; and the wheels were lifted together with them, [a]for the spirit of the living creatures[1] *was* in the wheels. 21 When those went, *these* went; when those stood, *these* stood; and when those were lifted up from the earth, the wheels were lifted up together with them, for the spirit of the living creatures[1] *was* in the wheels.

22 [a]The likeness of the firmament above the heads of the living creatures[1] *was* like the color of an awesome [b]crystal, stretched out [c]over their heads. 23 And under the firmament their wings *spread out* straight, one toward another. Each one had two which covered one side, and each one had two which covered the other side of the body. 24 [a]When they went, I heard the noise of their wings, [b]like the noise of many waters, like [c]the voice of the Almighty, a tumult like the noise of an army; and when they stood still, they let down their wings. 25 A voice came from above the firmament that *was* over their heads; whenever they stood, they let down their wings.

26 [a]And above the firmament over their heads *was* the likeness of a throne, [b]in appearance like a sapphire stone; on the likeness of the throne *was* a likeness with the appearance of a man high above [c]it. 27 Also from the appearance of His waist and upward [a]I saw, as it were, the color of amber with the appearance of fire all around within it; and from the appearance of His waist and downward I saw, as it were, the appearance of fire with brightness all around. 28 [a]Like the appearance of a rainbow in a cloud

1:1 [a] Ezek. 3:15, 23; 10:15 [b] Rev. 4:1; 19:11 [c] Ezek. 8:3 [1] Following Masoretic Text, Septuagint, and Vulgate; Syriac and Targum read *a vision.* 1:3 [a] Ezek. 3:14, 22 [1] Or *Babylonians,* and so elsewhere in this book 1:4 [a] Jer. 23:19; 25:32 [b] Jer. 1:14 1:5 [a] Rev. 4:6–8 [b] Ezek. 10:8 [c] Ezek. 10:14 1:7 [a] Dan. 10:6 1:8 [a] Ezek. 10:8, 21 1:9 [a] Ezek. 1:12; 10:20–22 1:10 [a] Rev. 4:7 [b] Num. 2:10 [c] Num. 2:3 [d] Num. 2:18 [e] Num. 2:25 1:11 [a] Is. 6:2 1:12 [a] Ezek. 10:11, 22 1:13 [a] Rev. 4:5 1:14 [a] [Matt. 24:27] 1:15 [a] Ezek. 10:9 1:16 [a] Ezek. 10:9, 10 [b] Dan. 10:6 1:18 [a] Ezek. 10:12 1:19 [a] Ezek. 10:16, 17 1:20 [a] Ezek. 10:17 [1] Literally *living creature;* Septuagint and Vulgate read *spirit of life;* Targum reads *creatures.* 1:21 [1] Literally *living creature;* Septuagint and Vulgate read *spirit of life;* Targum reads *creatures.* 1:22 [a] Ezek. 10:1 [b] Rev. 4:6 [c] Ezek. 10:1 [1] Following Septuagint, Targum, and Vulgate; Masoretic Text reads *living creature.* 1:24 [a] Ezek. 3:13; 10:5 [b] Rev. 1:15 [c] Job 37:4, 5 1:26 [a] Ezek. 10:1 [b] Ex. 24:10, 16 [c] Ezek. 8:2 1:27 [a] Ezek. 8:2 1:28 [a] Rev. 4:3; 10:1

on a rainy day, so *was* the appearance of the brightness all around it. [b]This *was* the appearance of the likeness of the glory of the LORD.

### *EZEKIEL SENT TO REBELLIOUS ISRAEL*

So when I saw *it,* [c]I fell on my face, and I heard a voice of One speaking.

**2** And He said to me, "Son of man, [a]stand on your feet, and I will speak to you." 2 Then [a]the Spirit entered me when He spoke to me, and set me on my feet; and I heard Him who spoke to me. 3 And He said to me: "Son of man, I am sending you to the children of Israel, to a rebellious nation that has [a]rebelled against Me; [b]they and their fathers have transgressed against Me to this very day. 4 [a]For *they are* impudent and stubborn children. I am sending you to them, and you shall say to them, 'Thus says the Lord GOD.' 5 [a]As for them, whether they hear or whether they refuse—for they *are* a [b]rebellious house—yet they [c]will know that a prophet has been among them.

6 "And you, son of man, [a]do not be afraid of them nor be afraid of their words, though [b]briers and thorns *are* with you and you dwell among scorpions; [c]do not be afraid of their words or dismayed by their looks, [d]though they *are* a rebellious house. 7 [a]You shall speak My words to them, whether they hear or whether they refuse, for they *are* rebellious. 8 But you, son of man, hear what I say to you. Do not be rebellious like that rebellious house; open your mouth and [a]eat what I give you."

9 Now when I looked, there was [a]a hand stretched out to me; and behold, [b]a scroll of a book *was* in it. 10 Then He spread it before me; and *there was* writing on the inside and on the outside, and written on it *were* lamentations and mourning and woe.

> **2:9** Ancient documents were written on long pieces of paper or leather scrolls. Since a **scroll** could be thirty-five feet or more, the best way to store it was to roll it up on a short rod.

**3** Moreover He said to me, "Son of man, eat what you find; [a]eat this scroll, and go, speak to the house of Israel." 2 So I opened my mouth, and He caused me to eat that scroll.

3 And He said to me, "Son of man, feed your belly, and fill your stomach with this scroll that I give you." So I [a]ate, and it was in my mouth [b]like honey in sweetness.

4 Then He said to me: "Son of man, go to the house of Israel and speak with My words to them. 5 For you *are* not sent to a people of unfamiliar

> **3:1–3** The symbolic act of eating the scroll demonstrated Ezekiel internalized the message in preparation for speaking to the people.

speech and of hard language, *but* to the house of Israel, 6 not to many people of unfamiliar speech and of hard language, whose words you cannot understand. Surely, [a]had I sent you to them, they would have listened to you. 7 But the house of Israel will not listen to you, [a]because they will not listen to Me; [b]for all the house of Israel *are* impudent and hard-hearted. 8 Behold, I have made your face strong against their faces, and your forehead strong against their foreheads. 9 [a]Like adamant stone, harder than flint, I have made your forehead; [b]do not be afraid of them, nor be dismayed at their looks, though they *are* a rebellious house."

10 Moreover He said to me: "Son of man, receive into your heart all My words that I speak to you, and hear with your ears. 11 And go, get to the captives, to the children of your people, and speak to them and tell them, [a]'Thus says the Lord GOD,' whether they hear, or whether they refuse."

12 Then [a]the Spirit lifted me up, and I heard behind me a great thunderous voice: "Blessed *is* the [b]glory of the LORD from His place!" 13 *I also heard* the [a]noise of the wings of the living creatures that touched one another, and the noise of the wheels beside them, and a great thunderous noise. 14 So the Spirit lifted me up and took me away, and I went in bitterness, in the heat of my spirit; but [a]the hand of the LORD was strong upon me. 15 Then I came to the captives at Tel Abib, who dwelt by the River Chebar; and [a]I sat where they sat, and remained there astonished among them seven days.

### *EZEKIEL IS A WATCHMAN*

16 Now it [a]came to pass at the end of seven days that the word of the LORD came to me, saying, 17 [a]"Son of man, I have made you [b]a watchman for the house of Israel; therefore hear a word from My mouth, and give them [c]warning

> **3:17** A city **watchman** was a security guard who kept a lookout from city walls for any danger. Watchmen were responsible for the safety of the citizens and were held personally responsible if their failure to do their job resulted in lost lives or damaged property. God made Ezekiel a spiritual watchman over His people.

**1:28** [b] Ezek. 3:23; 8:4 [c] Dan. 8:17 **2:1** [a] Dan. 10:11 **2:2** [a] Ezek. 3:24 **2:3** [a] Ezek. 5:6; 20:8, 13, 18 [b] Jer. 3:25 **2:4** [a] Ezek. 3:7 **2:5** [a] Ezek. 3:11, 26, 27 [b] Ezek. 3:26 [c] Ezek. 33:33 **2:6** [a] Jer. 1:8, 17 [b] Mic. 7:4 [c] [1 Pet. 3:14] [d] Ezek. 3:9, 26, 27 **2:7** [a] Jer. 1:7, 17 **2:8** [a] Rev. 10:9 **2:9** [a] [Ezek. 8:3] [b] Ezek. 3:1 **3:1** [a] Ezek. 2:8, 9 **3:3** [a] Rev. 10:9 [b] Ps. 19:10; 119:103 **3:6** [a] Matt. 11:21 **3:7** [a] John 15:20, 21 [b] Ezek. 2:4 **3:9** [a] Mic. 3:8 [b] Jer. 1:8, 17 **3:11** [a] Ezek. 2:5, 7 **3:12** [a] Acts 8:39 [b] Ezek. 1:28; 8:4 **3:13** [a] Ezek. 1:24; 10:5 **3:14** [a] 2 Kin. 3:15; Ezek. 1:3; 8:1 **3:15** [a] Job 2:13; Ps. 137:1 **3:16** [a] Jer. 42:7 **3:17** [a] Ezek. 33:7–9 [b] Is. 52:8; 56:10; Jer. 6:17 [c] [Lev. 19:17; Prov. 14:25]; Is. 58:1

from Me: 18 When I say to the wicked, 'You shall surely die,' and you give him no warning, nor speak to warn the wicked from his wicked way, to save his life, that same wicked *man* [a]shall die in his iniquity; but his blood I will require at your hand. 19 Yet, if you warn the wicked, and he does not turn from his wickedness, nor from his wicked way, he shall die in his iniquity; [a]but you have delivered your soul.

20 "Again, when a [a]righteous *man* turns from his righteousness and commits iniquity, and I lay a stumbling block before him, he shall die; because you did not give him warning, he shall die in his sin, and his righteousness which he has done shall not be remembered; but his blood I will require at your hand. 21 Nevertheless if you warn the righteous *man* that the righteous should not sin, and he does not sin, he shall surely live because he took warning; also you will have delivered your soul."

22 [a]Then the hand of the LORD was upon me there, and He said to me, "Arise, go out [b]into the plain, and there I shall talk with you."

23 So I arose and went out into the plain, and behold, [a]the glory of the LORD stood there, like the glory which I [b]saw by the River Chebar; [c]and I fell on my face. 24 Then [a]the Spirit entered me and set me on my feet, and spoke with me and said to me: "Go, shut yourself inside your house. 25 And you, O son of man, surely [a]they will put ropes on you and bind you with them, so that you cannot go out among them. 26 [a]I will make your tongue cling to the roof of your mouth, so that you shall be mute and [b]not be one to rebuke them, [c]for they *are* a rebellious house. 27 [a]But when I speak with you, I will open your mouth, and you shall say to them, [b]'Thus says the Lord GOD.' He who hears, let him hear; and he who refuses, let him refuse; for they *are* a rebellious house.

### *THE SIEGE OF JERUSALEM PORTRAYED*

**4** "You also, son of man, take a clay tablet and lay it before you, and portray on it a city, Jerusalem. 2 [a]Lay siege against it, build a [b]siege wall against it, and heap up a mound against it; set camps against it also, and place battering rams against it all around. 3 Moreover take for yourself an iron plate, and set it *as* an iron wall between you and the city. Set your face against it, and it shall be [a]besieged, and you shall lay siege against it. [b]This *will be* a sign to the house of Israel.

4 "Lie also on your left side, and lay the iniquity of the house of Israel upon it. *According* to the number of the days that you lie on it, you shall bear their iniquity. 5 For I have laid on you the years of their iniquity, according to the number of the days, three hundred and ninety days; [a]so you shall bear the iniquity of the house of Israel. 6 And when you have completed them, lie again on your right side; then you shall bear the iniquity of the house of Judah forty days. I have laid on you a day for each year.

7 "Therefore you shall set your face toward the siege of Jerusalem; your arm *shall be* uncovered, and you shall prophesy against it. 8 [a]And surely I will restrain you so that you cannot turn from one side to another till you have ended the days of your siege.

9 "Also take for yourself wheat, barley, beans, lentils, millet, and spelt; put them into one vessel, and make bread of them for yourself. *During* the number of days that you lie on your side, three hundred and ninety days, you shall eat it. 10 And your food which you eat *shall be* by weight, twenty shekels a day; from time to time you shall eat it. 11 You shall also drink water by measure, one-sixth of a hin; from time to time you shall drink. 12 And you shall eat it *as* barley cakes; and bake it using fuel of human waste in their sight."

13 Then the LORD said, "So [a]shall the children of Israel eat their defiled bread among the Gentiles, where I will drive them."

14 So I said, [a]"Ah, Lord GOD! Indeed I have never defiled myself from my youth till now; I have never eaten [b]what died of itself or was torn by beasts, nor has [c]abominable flesh ever come into my mouth."

15 Then He said to me, "See, I am giving you cow dung instead of human waste, and you shall prepare your bread over it."

16 Moreover He said to me, "Son of man, surely I will cut off the [a]supply of bread in Jerusalem; they shall [b]eat bread by weight and with anxiety, and shall [c]drink water by measure and with dread, 17 that they may lack bread and water, and be dismayed with one another, and [a]waste away because of their iniquity.

### *A SWORD AGAINST JERUSALEM*

**5** "And you, son of man, take a sharp sword, take it as a barber's razor, [a]and pass *it* over your head and your beard; then take scales to weigh and divide the *hair*. 2 [a]You shall burn with fire one-third in the midst of [b]the city, when [c]the days of the siege are finished; then you shall take one-third and strike around *it* with the sword, and one-third you shall scatter in the wind: I will draw out a sword after [d]them. 3 [a]You shall also take a small number of them and bind them in the edge of your *garment*. 4 Then take some of them again and [a]throw them into the midst of the fire, and burn them in the fire. From there a fire will go out into all the house of Israel.

5 "Thus says the Lord GOD: 'This *is* Jerusalem;

**3:18** [a] Ezek. 33:6; [John 8:21, 24] **3:19** [a] Is. 49:4, 5; Ezek. 14:14, 20; Acts 18:6; 20:26; 1 Tim. 4:16 **3:20** [a] Ps. 125:5; Ezek. 18:24; 33:18; Zeph. 1:6 **3:22** [a] Ezek. 1:3 [b] Ezek. 8:4 **3:23** [a] Ezek. 1:28; Acts 7:55 [b] Ezek. 1:1 [c] Ezek. 1:28 **3:24** [a] Ezek. 2:2 **3:25** [a] Ezek. 4:8 **3:26** [a] Ezek. 24:27; Luke 1:20, 22 [b] Hos. 4:17; Amos 8:11 [c] Ezek. 2:5–7 **3:27** [a] Ex. 4:11, 12; Ezek. 24:27; 33:22 [b] Ezek. 3:11 **4:2** [a] Jer. 6:6; Ezek. 21:22 [b] 2 Kin. 25:1 **4:3** [a] Jer. 39:1, 2; Ezek. 5:2 [b] Ezek. 12:6, 11; 24:24, 27 **4:5** [a] Num. 14:34 **4:8** [a] Ezek. 3:25 **4:13** [a] Hos. 9:3 **4:14** [a] Acts 10:14 [b] Lev. 17:15; 22:8 [c] Deut. 14:3 **4:16** [a] Is. 3:1 [b] Ezek. 4:10, 11; 12:19 [c] Ezek. 4:11 **4:17** [a] Lev. 26:39 **5:1** [a] Is. 7:20 **5:2** [a] Ezek. 5:12 [b] Ezek. 4:1 [c] Ezek. 4:8, 9 [d] Lev. 26:25 **5:3** [a] Jer. 40:6; 52:16 **5:4** [a] Jer. 41:1, 2; 44:14

> **5:1** Shaving the **head** was an act showing shame or disgrace in Hebrew culture (see Ezek. 7:18). It also represented a type of pagan mourning forbidden by the law (see Ezek. 27:31). Shaving the head was a mark of defilement, making a priest like Ezekiel ritually unclean, and so unable to perform his duties in the temple (see Lev. 21:5). This message warned the people they were about to be humiliated and defiled.

I have set her in the midst of the nations and
the countries all around her. 6 She has rebelled
against My judgments by doing wickedness
more than the nations, and against My statutes
more than the countries that *are* all around her;
for they have refused My judgments, and they
have not walked in My statutes.' 7 Therefore thus
says the Lord GOD: 'Because you have multiplied
*disobedience* more than the nations that *are* all
around you, have not walked in My statutes [a]nor
kept My judgments, nor even done[1] according
to the judgments of the nations that *are* all
around you'— 8 therefore thus says the Lord
GOD: 'Indeed I, even I, *am* against you and will
execute judgments in your midst in the sight
of the nations. 9 [a]And I will do among you what
I have never done, and the like of which I will
never do again, because of all your abomina-
tions. 10 Therefore fathers [a]shall eat *their* sons in
your midst, and sons shall eat their fathers; and
I will execute judgments among you, and all of
you who remain I will [b]scatter to all the winds.
11 'Therefore, *as* I live,' says the Lord GOD,
'surely, because you have [a]defiled My sanctuary
with all your [b]detestable things and with all your
abominations, therefore I will also diminish *you;*
[c]My eye will not spare, nor will I have any pity.
12 [a]One-third of you shall die of the pestilence,
and be consumed with famine in your midst;
and one-third shall fall by the sword all around
you; and [b]I will scatter another third to all the
winds, and I will draw out a sword after [c]them.
13 'Thus shall My anger [a]be spent, and I will
[b]cause My fury to rest upon them, [c]and I will be
avenged; [d]and they shall know that I, the LORD,
have spoken *it* in My zeal, when I have spent My
fury upon them. 14 Moreover [a]I will make you a
waste and a reproach among the nations that
*are* all around you, in the sight of all who pass by.
15 'So it[1] shall be a [a]reproach, a taunt, a [b]les-
son, and an astonishment to the nations that
*are* all around you, when I execute judgments
among you in anger and in fury and in [c]furious
rebukes. I, the LORD, have spoken. 16 When I
[a]send against them the terrible arrows of famine
which shall be for destruction, which I will send
to destroy you, I will increase the famine upon
you and cut off your [b]supply of bread. 17 So I will
send against you famine and [a]wild beasts, and
they will bereave you. [b]Pestilence and blood
shall pass through you, and I will bring the
sword against you. I, the LORD, have spoken.' "

## *JUDGMENT ON IDOLATROUS ISRAEL*

6 Now the word of the LORD came to me, saying:
2 "Son of man, [a]set your face toward the [b]moun-
tains of Israel, and prophesy against them, 3 and
say, 'O mountains of Israel, hear the word of the
Lord GOD! Thus says the Lord GOD to the moun-
tains, to the hills, to the ravines, and to the valleys:
"Indeed I, *even* I, will bring a sword against you,
and [a]I will destroy your high places. 4 Then your
altars shall be desolate, your incense altars shall
be broken, and [a]I will cast down your slain *men*
before your idols. 5 And I will lay the corpses of the
children of Israel before their idols, and I will scat-
ter your bones all around your altars. 6 In all your
dwelling places the cities shall be laid waste, and
the high places shall be desolate, so that your altars
may be laid waste and made desolate, your idols
may be broken and made to cease, your incense
altars may be cut down, and your works may be
abolished. 7 The slain shall fall in your midst, and
[a]you shall know that I *am* the LORD.

> **6:5** Touching a dead body was enough to disqualify a person from taking part in a religious ceremony. A ritual or sacrifice was required before the person who touched a **corpse** was considered clean again.

8 [a]"Yet I will leave a remnant, so that you
may have *some* who escape the sword among
the nations, when you are [b]scattered through the
countries. 9 Then those of you who escape will
[a]remember Me among the nations where they are
carried captive, because [b]I was crushed by their
adulterous heart which has departed from Me, and
[c]by their eyes which play the harlot after their idols;
[d]they will loathe themselves for the evils which they
committed in all their abominations. 10 And they
shall know that I *am* the LORD; I have not said in
vain that I would bring this calamity upon them."
11 'Thus says the Lord GOD: [a]"Pound your
fists and stamp your feet, and say, 'Alas, for all
the evil abominations of the house of Israel!
[b]For they shall fall by the sword, by famine, and

**5:7** [a] Jer. 2:10, 11 [1] Following Masoretic Text, Septuagint, Targum, and Vulgate; many Hebrew manuscripts and Syriac read *but have done* (compare 11:12). **5:9** [a] [Amos 3:2] **5:10** [a] Jer. 19:9 [b] Zech. 2:6; 7:14 **5:11** [a] [Jer. 7:9–11] [b] Ezek. 11:21 [c] Ezek. 7:4, 9; 8:18; 9:10 **5:12** [a] Ezek. 6:12 [b] Jer. 9:16 [c] Jer. 43:10, 11; 44:27 **5:13** [a] Lam. 4:11 [b] Ezek. 21:17 [c] Is. 1:24 [d] Ezek. 36:6; 38:19 **5:14** [a] Lev. 26:31 **5:15** [a] Jer. 24:9 [b] [Is. 26:9] [c] Ezek. 5:8; 25:17 [1] Septuagint, Syriac, Targum, and Vulgate read *you.* **5:16** [a] Deut. 32:23 [b] Lev. 26:26 **5:17** [a] Lev. 26:22 [b] Ezek. 38:22 **6:2** [a] Ezek. 20:46; 21:2; 25:2 [b] Ezek. 36:1 **6:3** [a] Lev. 26:30 **6:4** [a] Lev. 26:30 **6:7** [a] Ezek. 7:4, 9 **6:8** [a] Jer. 44:28 [b] Ezek. 5:12 **6:9** [a] [Deut. 4:29] [b] Ps. 78:40 [c] Ezek. 20:7, 24 [d] Ezek. 20:43; 36:31 **6:11** [a] Ezek. 21:14 [b] Ezek. 5:12

by pestilence. 12 He who is far off shall die by
the pestilence, he who is near shall fall by the
sword, and he who remains and is besieged shall
die by the famine. [a]Thus will I spend My fury
upon them. 13 Then you shall know that I *am* the
LORD, when their slain are among their idols all
around their altars, [a]on every high hill, [b]on all
the mountaintops, [c]under every green tree, and
under every thick oak, wherever they offered
sweet incense to all their idols. 14 So I will [a]stretch
out My hand against them and make the land
desolate, yes, more desolate than the wilderness
toward [b]Diblah, in all their dwelling places. Then
they shall know that I *am* the LORD.' " ' "

## *JUDGMENT ON ISRAEL IS NEAR*

7 Moreover the word of the LORD came to me,
saying, 2 "And you, son of man, thus says the
Lord GOD to the land of Israel:

[a]'An end! The end has come upon the four
corners of the land.
3 Now the end *has come* upon you,
And I will send My anger against you;
I will judge you [a]according to your ways,
And I will repay you for all your
abominations.
4 [a]My eye will not spare you,
Nor will I have pity;
But I will repay your ways,
And your abominations will be in your
midst;
[b]Then you shall know that I *am* the LORD!'

5 "Thus says the Lord GOD:

'A disaster, a singular [a]disaster;
Behold, it has come!
6 An end has come,
The end has come;
It has dawned for you;
Behold, it has come!
7 [a]Doom has come to you, you who dwell in
the land;
[b]The time has come,
A day of trouble *is* near,
And not of rejoicing in the mountains.
8 Now upon you I will soon [a]pour out My fury,
And spend My anger upon you;
I will judge you according to your ways,
And I will repay you for all your
abominations.
9 'My eye will not spare,
Nor will I have pity;
I will repay you according to your ways,
And your abominations will be in your
midst.
Then you shall know that I *am* the LORD
who strikes.

10 'Behold, the day!
Behold, it has come!
[a]Doom has gone out;
The rod has blossomed,
Pride has budded.
11 [a]Violence has risen up into a rod of
wickedness;
None of them *shall remain,*
None of their multitude,
None of them;
[b]Nor *shall there be* wailing for them.
12 The time has come,
The day draws near.

'Let not the buyer [a]rejoice,
Nor the seller [b]mourn,
For wrath *is* on their whole multitude.
13 For the seller shall not return to what has
been sold,
Though he may still be alive;
For the vision concerns the whole
multitude,
And it shall not turn back;
No one will strengthen himself
Who lives in iniquity.
14 'They have blown the trumpet and made
everyone ready,
But no one goes to battle;
For My wrath *is* on all their multitude.
15 [a]The sword *is* outside,
And the pestilence and famine within.
Whoever *is* in the field
Will die by the sword;
And whoever *is* in the city,
Famine and pestilence will devour him.
16 'Those who [a]survive will escape and be on
the mountains
Like doves of the valleys,
All of them mourning,
Each for his iniquity.
17 Every [a]hand will be feeble,
And every knee will be *as* weak *as*
water.
18 They will also [a]be girded with sackcloth;
Horror will cover them;
Shame *will be* on every face,
Baldness on all their heads.
19 'They will throw their silver into the
streets,
And their gold will be like refuse;
Their [a]silver and their gold will not be
able to deliver them
In the day of the wrath of the LORD;
They will not satisfy their souls,
Nor fill their stomachs,
Because it became their stumbling block
of iniquity.

6:12 [a]Ezek. 5:13 6:13 [a]Jer. 2:20; 3:6 [b]Hos. 4:13 [c]Is. 57:5 6:14 [a]Is. 5:25 [b]Num. 33:46 7:2 [a]Amos 8:2, 10 7:3 [a][Rom. 2:6] 7:4 [a]Ezek. 5:11 [b]Ezek. 12:20 7:5 [a]2 Kin. 21:12, 13 7:7 [a]Ezek. 7:10 [b]Zeph. 1:14, 15 7:8 [a]Ezek. 20:8, 21 7:10 [a]Ezek. 7:7 7:11 [a]Jer. 6:7 [b]Jer. 16:5, 6 7:12 [a]Prov. 20:14 [b]Is. 24:2 7:15 [a]Jer. 14:18 7:16 [a]Ezek. 6:8; 14:22 7:17 [a]Is. 13:7 7:18 [a]Amos 8:10 7:19 [a]Zeph. 1:18

20 'As for the beauty of his ornaments,
He set it in majesty;
[a]But they made from it
The images of their abominations—
Their detestable things;
Therefore I have made it
Like refuse to them.
21 I will give it as [a]plunder
Into the hands of strangers,
And to the wicked of the earth as spoil;
And they shall defile it.
22 I will turn My face from them,
And they will defile My secret place;
For robbers shall enter it and defile it.

23 'Make a chain,
For [a]the land is filled with crimes of
blood,
And the city is full of violence.
24 Therefore I will bring the [a]worst of the
Gentiles,
And they will possess their houses;
I will cause the pomp of the strong to
cease,
And their holy places shall be [b]defiled.
25 Destruction comes;
They will seek peace, but *there shall be*
none.
26 [a]Disaster will come upon disaster,
And rumor will be upon rumor.
[b]Then they will seek a vision from a
prophet;
But the law will perish from the priest,
And counsel from the elders.

27 'The king will mourn,
The prince will be clothed with
desolation,
And the hands of the common people will
tremble.
I will do to them according to their way,
And according to what they deserve I will
judge them;
Then they shall know that I *am* the
LORD!' "

## *ABOMINATIONS IN THE TEMPLE*

8 And it came to pass in the sixth year, in the
sixth *month,* on the fifth *day* of the month,
as I sat in my house with [a]the elders of Judah
sitting before me, that [b]the hand of the Lord GOD
fell upon me there. 2 [a]Then I looked, and there
was a likeness, like the appearance of fire—from
the appearance of His waist and downward, fire;
and from His waist and upward, like the appear-
ance of brightness, [b]like the color of amber. 3 He
[a]stretched out the form of a hand, and took me
by a lock of my hair; and [b]the Spirit lifted me up
between earth and heaven, and [c]brought me in
visions of God to Jerusalem, to the door of the
north gate of the inner *court,* [d]where the seat of
the image of jealousy *was,* which [e]provokes to jeal-
ousy. 4 And behold, the [a]glory of the God of Israel
*was* there, like the vision that I [b]saw in the plain.
5 Then He said to me, "Son of man, lift your
eyes now toward the north." So I lifted my eyes
toward the north, and there, north of the altar
gate, was this image of jealousy in the entrance.
6 Furthermore He said to me, "Son of man,
do you see what they are doing, the great [a]abom-
inations that the house of Israel commits here,
to make Me go far away from My sanctuary? Now
turn again, you will see greater abominations."
7 So He brought me to the door of the court; and
when I looked, there was a hole in the wall. 8 Then
He said to me, "Son of man, dig into the wall";
and when I dug into the wall, there was a door.
9 And He said to me, "Go in, and see the wick-
ed abominations which they are doing there."
10 So I went in and saw, and there—every [a]sort
of [b]creeping thing, abominable beasts, and all
the idols of the house of Israel, portrayed all
around on the walls. 11 And there stood before
them [a]seventy men of the elders of the house
of Israel, and in their midst stood Jaazaniah
the son of Shaphan. Each man had a censer in
his hand, and a thick cloud of incense went up.
12 Then He said to me, "Son of man, have you
seen what the elders of the house of Israel do
in the dark, every man in the room of his idols?
For they say, [a]'The LORD does not see us, the
LORD has forsaken the land.' "

> **8:10** The Lord identified certain animals as clean and others as unclean. Clean animals included cattle, goats, sheep, fish with scales, and many kinds of birds. Animals considered unclean included snails, pigs, vultures, shellfish, and dogs.

13 And He said to me, "Turn again, *and* you
will see greater abominations that they are do-
ing." 14 So He brought me to the door of the north
gate of the LORD's house; and to my dismay,
women were sitting there weeping for Tammuz.
15 Then He said to me, "Have you seen *this,*
O son of man? Turn again, you will see greater
abominations than these." 16 So He brought me
into the inner court of the LORD's house; and
there, at the door of the temple of the LORD,
[a]between the porch and the altar, [b]*were* about
twenty-five men [c]with their backs toward the
temple of the LORD and their faces toward the
east, and they were worshiping [d]the sun toward
the east.

**7:20** [a] Jer. 7:30 **7:21** [a] 2 Kin. 24:13 **7:23** [a] 2 Kin. 21:16 **7:24** [a] Ezek. 21:31; 28:7 [b] Ezek. 24:21 **7:26** [a] Jer. 4:20 [b] Ps. 74:9 **8:1** [a] Ezek. 14:1; 20:1; 33:31 [b] Ezek. 1:3; 3:22 **8:2** [a] Ezek. 1:26, 27 [b] Ezek. 1:4, 27 **8:3** [a] Dan. 5:5 [b] Ezek. 3:14 [c] Ezek. 11:1, 24; 40:2 [d] Ezek. 5:11 [e] Deut. 32:16, 21 **8:4** [a] Ezek. 3:12; 9:3 [b] Ezek. 1:28; 3:22, 23 **8:6** [a] 2 Kin. 23:4, 5 **8:10** [a] Ex. 20:4 [b] Rom. 1:23 **8:11** [a] Num. 11:16, 25 **8:12** [a] Ezek. 9:9 **8:16** [a] Joel 2:17 [b] Ezek. 11:1 [c] Jer. 2:27; 32:33 [d] Deut. 4:19

17 And He said to me, "Have you seen *this,* O son of man? Is it a trivial thing to the house of Judah to commit the abominations which they commit here? For they have [a]filled the land with violence; then they have returned to provoke Me to anger. Indeed they put the branch to their nose. 18 [a]Therefore I also will act in fury. My [b]eye will not spare nor will I have pity; and though they [c]cry in My ears with a loud voice, I will not hear them."

### THE WICKED ARE SLAIN

**9** Then He called out in my hearing with a loud voice, saying, "Let those who have charge over the city draw near, each *with* a deadly weapon in his hand." 2 And suddenly six men came from the direction of the upper gate, which faces north, each with his battle-ax in his hand. [a]One man among them *was* clothed with linen and had a writer's inkhorn at his side. They went in and stood beside the bronze altar.

> **9:2 Linen** was a fabric hand-woven from the fibers of the hemp plant. Considered to be the highest-quality fabric in the ancient world, it was worn mostly by people of great wealth or power. Yet priests and temple workers wore linen robes designed according to God's instructions in the Law of Moses.

3 Now [a]the glory of the God of Israel had gone up from the cherub, where it had been, to the threshold of the temple.[1] And He called to the man clothed with linen, who *had* the writer's inkhorn at his side; 4 and the LORD said to him, "Go through the midst of the city, through the midst of Jerusalem, and put [a]a mark on the foreheads of the men [b]who sigh and cry over all the abominations that are done within it."

5 To the others He said in my hearing, "Go after him through the city and [a]kill; [b]do not let your eye spare, nor have any pity. 6 [a]Utterly slay old *and* young men, maidens and little children and women; but [b]do not come near anyone on whom *is* the mark; and [c]begin at My sanctuary." [d]So they began with the elders who *were* before the temple. 7 Then He said to them, "Defile the temple, and fill the courts with the slain. Go out!" And they went out and killed in the city.

8 So it was, that while they were killing them, I was left *alone;* and I [a]fell on my face and cried out, and said, [b]"Ah, Lord GOD! Will You destroy all the remnant of Israel in pouring out Your fury on Jerusalem?"

9 Then He said to me, "The iniquity of the house of Israel and Judah *is* exceedingly great, and [a]the land is full of bloodshed, and the city full of perversity; for they say, [b]'The LORD has forsaken the land, and [c]the LORD does not see!' 10 And as for Me also, My [a]eye will neither spare, nor will I have pity, *but* [b]I will recompense their deeds on their own head."

11 Just then, the man clothed with linen, who *had* the inkhorn at his side, reported back and said, "I have done as You commanded me."

### THE GLORY DEPARTS FROM THE TEMPLE

**10** And I looked, and there in the [a]firmament that was above the head of the cherubim, there appeared something like a sapphire stone, having the appearance of the likeness of a throne. 2 [a]Then He spoke to the man clothed with linen, and said, "Go in among the wheels, under the cherub, fill your hands with [b]coals of fire from among the cherubim, and [c]scatter *them* over the city." And he went in as I watched.

3 Now the cherubim were standing on the south side of the temple[1] when the man went in, and the [a]cloud filled the inner court. 4 [a]Then the glory of the LORD went up from the cherub, *and paused* over the threshold of the temple; and [b]the house was filled with the cloud, and the court was full of the brightness of the LORD's [c]glory. 5 And the [a]sound of the wings of the cherubim was heard *even* in the outer court, like [b]the voice of Almighty God when He speaks.

6 Then it happened, when He commanded the man clothed in linen, saying, "Take fire from among the wheels, from among the cherubim," that he went in and stood beside the wheels. 7 And the cherub stretched out his hand from among the cherubim to the fire that *was* among the cherubim, and took *some of it* and put *it* into the hands of the *man* clothed with linen, who took *it* and went out. 8 [a]The cherubim appeared to have the form of a man's hand under their wings.

9 [a]And when I looked, there were four wheels by the cherubim, one wheel by one cherub and another wheel by each other cherub; the wheels appeared *to have* the color of a [b]beryl stone. 10 *As for* their appearance, all four looked alike—as it were, a wheel in the middle of a wheel. 11 [a]When they went, they went toward *any of* their four directions; they did not turn aside when they went, but followed in the direction the head was facing. They did not turn aside when they went. 12 And their whole body, with their back, their hands, their wings, and the wheels that the four had, *were* [a]full of eyes all around. 13 As for the wheels, they were called in my hearing, "Wheel."

14 [a]Each one had four faces: the first face *was* the face of a cherub, the second face the face of

**8:17** [a] Ezek. 9:9 **8:18** [a] Ezek. 5:13; 16:42; 24:13 [b] Ezek. 5:11; 7:4, 9; 9:5, 10 [c] Mic. 3:4 **9:2** [a] Lev. 16:4 **9:3** [a] Ezek. 3:23; 8:4; 10:4, 18; 11:22, 23 [1] Literally *house* **9:4** [a] Rev. 7:2, 3; 9:4; 14:1 [b] Jer. 13:17 **9:5** [a] Ezek. 7:9 [b] Ezek. 5:11 **9:6** [a] 2 Chr. 36:17 [b] Rev. 9:4 [c] Jer. 25:29 [d] Ezek. 8:11, 12, 16 **9:8** [a] Josh. 7:6 [b] Ezek. 11:13 **9:9** [a] 2 Kin. 21:16 [b] Ezek. 8:12 [c] Is. 29:15 **9:10** [a] Ezek. 5:11; 7:4; 8:18 [b] Ezek. 11:21 **10:1** [a] Ezek. 1:22, 26 **10:2** [a] Dan. 10:5 [b] Ezek. 1:13 [c] Rev. 8:5 **10:3** [a] 1 Kin. 8:10, 11 [1] Literally *house,* also in verses 4 and 18 **10:4** [a] Ezek. 1:28 [b] 1 Kin. 8:10; Ezek. 43:5 [c] Ezek. 11:22, 23 **10:5** [a] [Job 40:9]; Ezek. 1:24; [Rev. 10:3] [b] [Ps. 29:3] **10:8** [a] Ezek. 1:8; 10:21 **10:9** [a] Ezek. 1:15 [b] Ezek. 1:16 **10:11** [a] Ezek. 1:17 **10:12** [a] Rev. 4:6, 8 **10:14** [a] 1 Kin. 7:29, 36; Ezek. 1:6, 10, 11; Rev. 4:7

a man, the third the face of a lion, and the fourth the face of an eagle. 15 And the cherubim were lifted up. This *was* [a]the living creature I saw by the River Chebar. 16 [a]When the cherubim went, the wheels went beside them; and when the cherubim lifted their wings to mount up from the earth, the same wheels also did not turn from beside them. 17 [a]When *the cherubim*[1] stood still, *the wheels* stood still, and when *one*[2] was lifted up, *the other*[3] lifted itself up, for the spirit of the living creature *was* in them.

> **10:9–17** While one of the four faces in Ezekiel 1:10 is an ox, here it is a **cherub**. These are ancient sculptures with animal bodies and wings but human faces. It's possible that the images that Ezekiel saw were changing.

18 Then [a]the glory of the LORD [b]departed from the threshold of the temple and stood over the cherubim. 19 And [a]the cherubim lifted their wings and mounted up from the earth in my sight. When they went out, the wheels *were* beside them; and they stood at the door of the [b]east gate of the LORD's house, and the glory of the God of Israel *was* above them.

20 [a]This *is* the living creature I saw under the God of Israel [b]by the River Chebar, and I knew they *were* cherubim. 21 [a]Each one had four faces and each one four wings, and the likeness of the hands of a man *was* under their wings. 22 And [a]the likeness of their faces *was* the same *as* the faces which I had seen by the River Chebar, their appearance and their persons. [b]They each went straight forward.

### *JUDGMENT ON WICKED COUNSELORS*

**11** Then [a]the Spirit lifted me up and brought me to [b]the East Gate of the LORD's house, which faces eastward; and there [c]at the door of the gate were twenty-five men, among whom I saw Jaazaniah the son of Azzur, and Pelatiah the son of Benaiah, princes of the people. 2 And He said to me: "Son of man, these *are* the men who devise iniquity and give wicked counsel in this city, 3 who say, '*The time is* not [a]near to build houses; [b]this *city is* the caldron, and we *are* the meat.' 4 Therefore prophesy against them, prophesy, O son of man!"

5 Then [a]the Spirit of the LORD fell upon me, and said to me, "Speak! 'Thus says the LORD: "Thus you have said, O house of Israel; for [b]I know the things that come into your mind. 6 [a]You have multiplied your slain in this city, and you have filled its streets with the slain." 7 Therefore thus says the Lord GOD: [a]"Your slain whom you have laid in its midst, they *are* the meat, and this *city is* the caldron; [b]but I shall bring you out of the midst of it. 8 You have [a]feared the sword; and I will bring a sword upon you," says the Lord GOD. 9 "And I will bring you out of its midst, and deliver you into the hands of strangers, and [a]execute judgments on you. 10 [a]You shall fall by the sword. I will judge you at [b]the border of Israel. [c]Then you shall know that I *am* the LORD. 11 [a]This *city* shall not be your caldron, nor shall you be the meat in its midst. I will judge you at the border of Israel. 12 And you shall know that I *am* the LORD; for you have not walked in My statutes nor executed My judgments, but [a]have done according to the customs of the Gentiles which *are* all around you." ' "

13 Now it happened, while I was prophesying, that [a]Pelatiah the son of Benaiah died. Then [b]I fell on my face and cried with a loud voice, and said, "Ah, Lord GOD! Will You make a complete end of the remnant of Israel?"

### *GOD WILL RESTORE ISRAEL*

14 Again the word of the LORD came to me, saying, 15 "Son of man, your brethren, your relatives, your countrymen, and all the house of Israel in its entirety, *are* those about whom the inhabitants of Jerusalem have said, 'Get far away from the LORD; this land has been given to us as a possession.' 16 Therefore say, 'Thus says the Lord GOD: "Although I have cast them far off among the Gentiles, and although I have scattered them among the countries, [a]yet I shall be a little sanctuary for them in the countries where they have gone." ' 17 Therefore say, 'Thus says the Lord GOD: [a]"I will gather you from the peoples, assemble you from the countries where you have been scattered, and I will give you the land of Israel." ' 18 And they will go there, and they will take away all its [a]detestable things and all its abominations from there. 19 Then [a]I will give them one heart, and I will put [b]a new spirit within them,[1] and take [c]the stony heart out of their flesh, and give them a heart of flesh, 20 [a]that they may walk in My statutes and keep My judgments and do them; [b]and they shall be My people, and I will be their God. 21 But *as for those* whose hearts follow the desire for their detestable things and their abominations, [a]I will recompense their deeds on their own heads," says the Lord GOD.

22 So the cherubim [a]lifted up their wings, with the wheels beside them, and the glory of the God of Israel *was* high above them. 23 And [a]the glory of the LORD went up from the midst

**10:15** [a] Ezek. 1:3, 5 **10:16** [a] Ezek. 1:19 **10:17** [a] Ezek. 1:12, 20, 21 [1] Literally *they* [2] Literally *they* [3] Literally *they* **10:18** [a] Ezek. 10:4 [b] Hos. 9:12 **10:19** [a] Ezek. 11:22 [b] Ezek. 11:1 **10:20** [a] Ezek. 1:22 [b] Ezek. 1:1 **10:21** [a] Ezek. 1:6, 8; 10:14; 41:18, 19 **10:22** [a] Ezek. 1:10 [b] Ezek. 1:9, 12 **11:1** [a] Ezek. 3:12, 14 [b] Ezek. 10:19 [c] Ezek. 8:16 **11:3** [a] Ezek. 12:22, 27; 2 Pet. 3:4 [b] Jer. 1:13; Ezek. 11:7, 11; 24:3, 6 **11:5** [a] Ezek. 2:2; 3:24 [b] [Jer. 16:17; 17:10] **11:6** [a] Is. 1:15; Ezek. 7:23; 22:2–6, 9, 12, 27 **11:7** [a] Ezek. 24:3, 6; Mic. 3:2, 3 [b] 2 Kin. 25:18–22; Jer. 52:24–27; Ezek. 11:9 **11:8** [a] Jer. 42:16 **11:9** [a] Ezek. 5:8 **11:10** [a] Jer. 39:6; 52:10 [b] 2 Kin. 14:25 [c] Ps. 9:16 **11:11** [a] Ezek. 11:3, 7 **11:12** [a] Deut. 12:30, 31 **11:13** [a] Acts 5:5 [b] Ezek. 9:8 **11:16** [a] Is. 8:14 **11:17** [a] Jer. 3:12, 18; 24:5 **11:18** [a] Ezek. 37:23 **11:19** [a] Jer. 32:39 [b] Ezek. 18:31 [c] Zech. 7:12 [1] Literally *you* **11:20** [a] Ps. 105:45 [b] Jer. 24:7 **11:21** [a] Ezek. 9:10 **11:22** [a] Ezek. 1:19 **11:23** [a] Ezek. 8:4; 9:3

KNOW THE TRUTH

# THE DOCTRINE OF SCRIPTURE

## PART 6: THE INERRANCY OF SCRIPTURE

**11:19–20** For centuries, God's Word was not received and obeyed by His people. What needed to change wasn't God's Word, but God's people. So that His statutes and judgments would be done, God promised to change human hearts, not His Word. The reason God's Word needs no changes is because it's inerrant. *Inerrant* means being without error and incapable of being wrong. God is eternally and entirely perfect; He is without error. Thus, God's Word is perfect because it is God-breathed. Every word in the Bible comes from God's mind, not human minds (see 2 Tim. 3:14–17).

The original autographs of each book of Scripture contained no errors or mistakes. This is because the writers faithfully wrote what the Holy Spirit guided them to write (see 2 Pet. 1:20–21). The Holy Spirit then protected His inspired Word through generations of faithful scribes copying the original autographs and resulting manuscripts. Through extensive historical, archeological, and textual evidence, we can be extremely confident the Bible is a faithful, essential transmission of the original, God-breathed autographs. God's Word has not, and does not, change (see Ps. 19:7–8). However, human hearts are indeed changed by it through repenting and trusting in Jesus. A truly changed heart can receive and obey God's true and unchanged Word.

*For* **THE DOCTRINE OF SCRIPTURE: PART 7: THE ILLUMINATION OF SCRIPTURE**, *turn to Matthew 23:8–10 on page 991.*

of the city and stood [b]on the mountain, [c]which *is* on the east side of the city.

24 Then [a]the Spirit took me up and brought me in a vision by the Spirit of God into Chaldea,[1] to those in captivity. And the vision that I had seen went up from me. 25 So I spoke to those in captivity of all the things the LORD had shown me.

### *JUDAH'S CAPTIVITY PORTRAYED*

**12** Now the word of the LORD came to me, saying: 2 "Son of man, you dwell in the midst of [a]a rebellious house, which [b]has eyes to see but does not see, and ears to hear but does not hear; [c]for they *are* a rebellious house.

3 "Therefore, son of man, prepare your belongings for captivity, and go into captivity by day in their sight. You shall go from your place into captivity to another place in their sight. It may be that they will consider, though they *are* a rebellious house. 4 By day you shall bring out your belongings in their sight, as though going into captivity; and at evening you shall go in their sight, like those who go into captivity. 5 Dig through the wall in their sight, and carry *your belongings* out through it. 6 In their sight you shall bear *them* on *your* shoulders *and* carry *them* out at twilight; you shall cover your face, so that you cannot see the ground, [a]for I have made you a sign to the house of Israel."

7 So I did as I was commanded. I brought out my belongings by day, as though going into captivity, and at evening I dug through the wall with my hand. I brought *them* out at twilight, *and* I bore *them* on *my* shoulder in their sight.

8 And in the morning the word of the LORD came to me, saying, 9 "Son of man, has not the house of Israel, [a]the rebellious house, said to you, [b]'What are you doing?' 10 Say to them, 'Thus says the Lord GOD: "This [a]burden *concerns* the prince in Jerusalem and all the house of Israel who are among them." ' 11 Say, [a]'I *am* a sign to you. As I have done, so shall it be done to them; [b]they shall be carried away into captivity.' 12 And [a]the prince who *is* among them shall bear *his belongings* on *his* shoulder at twilight and go out. They shall dig through the wall to carry *them* out through it. He shall cover his face, so that he cannot see the ground with *his* eyes. 13 I will also spread My [a]net over him, and he shall be caught in My snare. [b]I will bring him to Babylon, *to* the land of the Chaldeans; yet he shall not see it, though he shall die there. 14 [a]I will scatter to every wind all who *are* around him to help him, and all his troops; and [b]I will draw out the sword after them.

**12:13** Zedekiah was forced to watch while his sons were put to death. It would be the last thing he ever saw. His eyes were then poked out, and he was led away to Babylon as a blind captive.

**11:23** [b]Zech. 14:4 [c]Ezek. 43:2 **11:24** [a]Ezek. 8:3 [1]Or *Babylon,* and so elsewhere in this book **12:2** [a]Ezek. 2:3, 6–8 [b]Jer. 5:21 [c]Ezek. 2:5 **12:6** [a]Ezek. 4:3; 24:24 **12:9** [a]Ezek. 2:5 [b]Ezek. 17:12; 24:19 **12:10** [a]Mal. 1:1 **12:11** [a]Ezek. 12:6 [b]2 Kin. 25:4, 5, 7 **12:12** [a]Jer. 39:4; 52:7 **12:13** [a]Jer. 52:9 [b]Jer. 52:11 **12:14** [a]Ezek. 5:10 [b]Ezek. 5:2, 12

15 [a]“Then they shall know that I *am* the LORD,
when I scatter them among the nations and
disperse them throughout the countries. 16 [a]But
I will spare a few of their men from the sword,
from famine, and from pestilence, that they
may declare all their abominations among the
Gentiles wherever they go. Then they shall know
that I *am* the LORD.”

### JUDGMENT NOT POSTPONED

17 Moreover the word of the LORD came to
me, saying, 18 “Son of man, [a]eat your bread with
quaking, and drink your water with trembling and
anxiety. 19 And say to the people of the land, ‘Thus
says the Lord GOD to the inhabitants of Jerusalem
*and* to the land of Israel: “They shall eat their bread
with anxiety, and drink their water with dread, so
that her land may [a]be emptied of all who are in it,
[b]because of the violence of all those who dwell in
it. 20 Then the cities that are inhabited shall be laid
waste, and the land shall become desolate; and
you shall know that I *am* the LORD.” ’ ”

21 And the word of the LORD came to me,
saying, 22 “Son of man, what *is* this proverb *that*
you *people* have about the land of Israel, which
says, [a]‘The days are prolonged, and every vision
fails’? 23 Tell them therefore, ‘Thus says the Lord
GOD: “I will lay this proverb to rest, and they
shall no more use it as a proverb in Israel.” ’ But
say to them, ‘ [a]“The days are at hand, and the
fulfillment of every vision. 24 For [a]no more shall
there be any [b]false vision or flattering divination
within the house of Israel. 25 For I *am* the LORD.
I speak, and [a]the word which I speak will come
to pass; it will no more be postponed; for in your
days, O rebellious house, I will say the word and
[b]perform it,” says the Lord GOD.’ ”

26 Again the word of the LORD came to me,
saying, 27 [a]“Son of man, look, the house of Israel
is saying, ‘The vision that he sees *is* [b]for many
days *from now,* and he prophesies of times far
off.’ 28 [a]Therefore say to them, ‘Thus says the
Lord GOD: “None of My words will be postponed
any more, but the word which I speak [b]will be
done,” says the Lord GOD.’ ”

### WOE TO FOOLISH PROPHETS

13 And the word of the LORD came to me,
saying, 2 “Son of man, prophesy [a]against
the prophets of Israel who prophesy, and say to
[b]those who prophesy out of their own [c]heart,
‘Hear the word of the LORD!’ ”

3 Thus says the Lord GOD: “Woe to the foolish
prophets, who follow their own spirit and have
seen nothing! 4 O Israel, your prophets are [a]like
foxes in the deserts. 5 You [a]have not gone up into
the gaps to build a wall for the house of Israel to
stand in battle on the day of the LORD. 6 [a]They
have envisioned futility and false divination,
saying, ‘Thus says the LORD!’ But the LORD has
[b]not sent them; yet they hope that the word may
be confirmed. 7 Have you not seen a futile vision,
and have you not spoken false divination? You
say, ‘The LORD says,’ but I have not spoken.”

8 Therefore thus says the Lord GOD: “Because
you have spoken nonsense and envisioned lies,
therefore I *am* indeed against you,” says the Lord
GOD. 9 “My hand will be [a]against the prophets
who envision futility and who [b]divine lies; they
shall not be in the assembly of My people, [c]nor
be written in the record of the house of Israel,
[d]nor shall they enter into the land of Israel.
[e]Then you shall know that I *am* the Lord GOD.

10 “Because, indeed, because they have se-
duced My people, saying, [a]‘Peace!’ when *there*
*is* no peace—and one builds a wall, and they
[b]plaster it with untempered *mortar*— 11 say to
those who plaster *it* with untempered *mortar,*
that it will fall. [a]There will be flooding rain, and
you, O great hailstones, shall fall; and a stormy
wind shall tear *it* down. 12 Surely, when the wall
has fallen, will it not be said to you, ‘Where *is* the
mortar with which you plastered *it?*’ ”

13 Therefore thus says the Lord GOD: “I will
cause a stormy wind to break forth in My fury;
and there shall be a flooding rain in My anger,
and great hailstones in fury to consume *it.* 14 So I
will break down the wall you have plastered with
untempered *mortar,* and bring it down to the
ground, so that its foundation will be uncovered;
it will fall, and you shall be consumed in the midst
of it. [a]Then you shall know that I *am* the LORD.

15 “Thus will I accomplish My wrath on the
wall and on those who have plastered it with un-
tempered *mortar;* and I will say to you, ‘The wall
*is* no *more,* nor those who plastered it, 16 *that is,*
the prophets of Israel who prophesy concerning
Jerusalem, and who [a]see visions of peace for
her when *there is* no peace,’ ” says the Lord GOD.

17 “Likewise, son of man, [a]set your face
against the daughters of your people, [b]who
prophesy out of their own heart; prophesy
against them, 18 and say, ‘Thus says the Lord
GOD: “Woe to the *women* who sew *magic* charms

**13:18** These so-called **magic charms** were pieces of jewelry that had spells and chants written on them. Some people believed these charms protected them from sickness, evil spirits, and other dangers. Today, such charms, often called amulets, are still very popular in some parts of the world.

12:15 [a] Ezek. 6:7, 14; 12:16, 20 12:16 [a] Ezek. 6:8–10 12:18 [a] Ezek. 4:16 12:19 [a] Zech. 7:14 [b] Ps. 107:34 12:22 [a] Ezek. 11:3; 12:27 12:23 [a] Zeph. 1:14 12:24 [a] Ezek. 13:6 [b] Lam. 2:14 12:25 [a] [Luke 21:33] [b] [Is. 14:24] 12:27 [a] Ezek. 12:22 [b] Dan. 10:14 12:28 [a] Ezek. 12:23, 25 [b] Jer. 4:7 13:2 [a] Ezek. 22:25–28 [b] Ezek. 13:17 [c] Jer. 14:14; 23:16, 26 13:4 [a] Song 2:15 13:5 [a] Ps. 106:23 13:6 [a] Ezek. 22:28 [b] Jer. 27:8–15 13:9 [a] Jer. 23:30 [b] Jer. 20:3–6 [c] Ezra 2:59, 62 [d] Jer. 20:3–6 [e] Ezek. 11:10, 12 13:10 [a] Jer. 6:14; 8:11 [b] Ezek. 22:28 13:11 [a] Ezek. 38:22 13:14 [a] Ezek. 13:9, 21, 23; 14:8 13:16 [a] Jer. 6:14; 8:11; 28:9 13:17 [a] Ezek. 20:46; 21:2 [b] Ezek. 13:2

on their sleeves[1] and make veils for the heads of people of every height to hunt souls! Will you [a]hunt the souls of My people, and keep yourselves alive? 19 And will you profane Me among My people [a]for handfuls of barley and for pieces of bread, killing people who should not die, and keeping people alive who should not live, by your lying to My people who listen to lies?"

20 'Therefore thus says the Lord GOD: "Behold, I *am* against your *magic* charms by which you hunt souls there like birds. I will tear them from your arms, and let the souls go, the souls you hunt like birds. 21 I will also tear off your veils and deliver My people out of your hand, and they shall no longer be as prey in your hand. [a]Then you shall know that I *am* the LORD.

22 "Because with [a]lies you have made the heart of the righteous sad, whom I have not made sad; and you have [b]strengthened the hands of the wicked, so that he does not turn from his wicked way to save his life. 23 Therefore [a]you shall no longer envision futility nor practice divination; for I will deliver My people out of your hand, and you shall know that I *am* the LORD." ' "

### *IDOLATRY WILL BE PUNISHED*

**14** Now [a]some of the elders of Israel came to me and sat before me. 2 And the word of the LORD came to me, saying, 3 "Son of man, these men have set up their idols in their hearts, and put before them [a]that which causes them to stumble into iniquity. [b]Should I let Myself be inquired of at all by them?

4 "Therefore speak to them, and say to them, 'Thus says the Lord GOD: "Everyone of the house of Israel who sets up his idols in his heart, and puts before him what causes him to stumble into iniquity, and then comes to the prophet, I the LORD will answer him who comes, according to the multitude of his idols, 5 that I may seize the house of Israel by their heart, because they are all estranged from Me by their idols." '

6 "Therefore say to the house of Israel, 'Thus says the Lord GOD: "Repent, turn away from your idols, and [a]turn your faces away from all your abominations. 7 For anyone of the house of Israel, or of the strangers who dwell in Israel, who separates himself from Me and sets up his idols in his heart and puts before him what causes him to stumble into iniquity, then comes to a prophet to inquire of him concerning Me, I the LORD will answer him by Myself. 8 [a]I will set My face against that man and make him a [b]sign and a proverb, and I will cut him off from the midst of My people. [c]Then you shall know that I *am* the LORD.

9 "And if the prophet is induced to speak anything, I the LORD [a]have induced that prophet, and I will stretch out My hand against him and destroy him from among My people Israel. 10 And they shall bear their iniquity; the punishment of the prophet shall be the same as the punishment of the one who inquired, 11 that the house of Israel may [a]no longer stray from Me, nor be profaned anymore with all their transgressions, [b]but that they may be My people and I may be their God," says the Lord GOD.' "

### *JUDGMENT ON PERSISTENT UNFAITHFULNESS*

12 The word of the LORD came again to me, saying: 13 "Son of man, when a land sins against Me by persistent unfaithfulness, I will stretch out My hand against it; I will cut off its [a]supply of bread, send famine on it, and cut off man and beast from it. 14 [a]Even *if* these three men, Noah, Daniel, and Job, were in it, they would deliver *only* themselves [b]by their righteousness," says the Lord GOD.

15 "If I cause [a]wild beasts to pass through the land, and they empty it, and make it so desolate that no man may pass through because of the beasts, 16 *even* [a]*though* these three men *were* in it, *as* I live," says the Lord GOD, "they would deliver neither sons nor daughters; only they would be delivered, and the land would be [b]desolate.

17 "Or *if* [a]I bring a sword on that land, and say, 'Sword, go through the land,' and I [b]cut off man and beast from it, 18 even [a]*though* these three men *were* in it, *as* I live," says the Lord GOD, "they would deliver neither sons nor daughters, but only they themselves would be delivered.

19 "Or *if* I send [a]a pestilence into that land and [b]pour out My fury on it in blood, and cut off from it man and beast, 20 even [a]*though* Noah, Daniel, and Job *were* in it, *as* I live," says the Lord GOD, "they would deliver neither son nor daughter; they would deliver *only* themselves by their righteousness."

21 For thus says the Lord GOD: "How much more it shall be when [a]I send My four severe judgments on Jerusalem—the sword and famine and wild beasts and pestilence—to cut off man and beast from it? 22 [a]Yet behold, there shall be left in it a remnant who will be [b]brought out, *both* sons and daughters; surely they will come out to you, and [c]you will see their ways and their doings. Then you will be comforted concerning the disaster that I have brought upon Jerusalem, all that I have brought upon it. 23 And they will comfort you, when you see their ways and their doings; and you shall know that I have done nothing [a]without cause that I have done in it," says the Lord GOD.

13:18 [a] [2 Pet. 2:14] [1] Literally *over all the joints of My hands;* Vulgate reads *under every elbow;* Septuagint and Targum read *on all elbows of the hands.* 13:19 [a] Mic. 3:5 13:21 [a] Ezek. 13:9 13:22 [a] Jer. 28:15 [b] Jer. 23:14 13:23 [a] Mic. 3:5, 6 14:1 [a] Ezek. 8:1; 20:1; 33:31 14:3 [a] Ezek. 7:19 [b] Ezek. 20:3, 31 14:6 [a] Is. 2:20; 30:22; 55:6, 7 14:8 [a] Jer. 44:11 [b] Num. 26:10 [c] Ezek. 6:7; 13:14 14:9 [a] 2 Thess. 2:11 14:11 [a] 2 Pet. 2:15 [b] Ezek. 11:20; 37:27 14:13 [a] Is. 3:1 14:14 [a] Jer. 15:1 [b] [Prov. 11:4] 14:15 [a] Lev. 26:22 14:16 [a] Ezek. 14:14, 18, 20 [b] Ezek. 15:8; 33:28, 29 14:17 [a] Lev. 26:25 [b] Zeph. 1:3 14:18 [a] Ezek. 14:14 14:19 [a] 2 Sam. 24:15 [b] Ezek. 7:8 14:20 [a] Ezek. 14:14 14:21 [a] Ezek. 5:17; 33:27 14:22 [a] Ezek. 12:16; 36:20 [b] Ezek. 6:8 [c] Ezek. 20:43 14:23 [a] Jer. 22:8, 9

### *THE OUTCAST VINE*

**15** Then the word of the LORD came to me, saying: 2 "Son of man, how is the wood of the vine *better* than any other wood, the vine branch which is among the trees of the forest? 3 Is wood taken from it to make any object? Or can *men* make a peg from it to hang any vessel on? 4 Instead, [a]it is thrown into the fire for fuel; the fire devours both ends of it, and its middle is burned. Is it useful for *any* work? 5 Indeed, when it was whole, no object could be made from it. How much less will it be useful for *any* work when the fire has devoured it, and it is burned?

6 "Therefore thus says the Lord GOD: 'Like the wood of the vine among the trees of the forest, which I have given to the fire for fuel, so I will give up the inhabitants of Jerusalem; 7 and [a]I will set My face against them. [b]They will go out from *one* fire, but *another* fire shall devour them. [c]Then you shall know that I *am* the LORD, when I set My face against them. 8 Thus I will make the land desolate, because they have persisted in unfaithfulness,' says the Lord GOD."

### *GOD'S LOVE FOR JERUSALEM*

**16** Again the word of the LORD came to me, saying, 2 "Son of man, [a]cause Jerusalem to know her abominations, 3 and say, 'Thus says the Lord GOD to Jerusalem: "Your birth [a]and your nativity *are* from the land of Canaan; [b]your father *was* an Amorite and your mother a Hittite. 4 *As for* your nativity, [a]on the day you were born your navel cord was not cut, nor were you washed in water to cleanse *you;* you were not rubbed with salt nor wrapped in swaddling cloths. 5 No eye pitied you, to do any of these things for you, to have compassion on you; but you were thrown out into the open field, when you yourself were loathed on the day you were born.

6 "And when I passed by you and saw you struggling in your own blood, I said to you in your blood, 'Live!' Yes, I said to you in your blood, 'Live!' 7 [a]I made you thrive like a plant in the field; and you grew, matured, and became very beautiful. *Your* breasts were formed, your hair grew, but you *were* naked and bare.

8 "When I passed by you again and looked upon you, indeed your time *was* the time of love; [a]so I spread My wing over you and covered your nakedness. Yes, I [b]swore an oath to you and entered into a [c]covenant with you, and [d]you became Mine," says the Lord GOD.

9 "Then I washed you in water; yes, I thoroughly washed off your blood, and I anointed you with oil. 10 I clothed you in embroidered cloth and gave you sandals of badger skin; I clothed you with fine linen and covered you with silk. 11 I adorned you with ornaments, [a]put bracelets on your wrists, [b]and a chain on your neck. 12 And I put a jewel in your nose, earrings in your ears, and a beautiful crown on your head. 13 Thus you were adorned with gold and silver, and your clothing *was of* fine linen, silk, and embroidered cloth. [a]You ate *pastry of* fine flour, honey, and oil. You were exceedingly [b]beautiful, and succeeded to royalty. 14 [a]Your fame went out among the nations because of your beauty, for it *was* perfect through My splendor which I had bestowed on you," says the Lord GOD.

### *JERUSALEM'S HARLOTRY*

15 [a]"But you trusted in your own beauty, [b]played the harlot because of your fame, and poured out your harlotry on everyone passing by who *would have* it. 16 [a]You took some of your garments and adorned multicolored high places for yourself, and played the harlot on them. *Such* things should not happen, nor be. 17 You have also taken your beautiful jewelry from My gold and My silver, which I had given you, and made for yourself male images and played the harlot with them. 18 You took your embroidered garments and covered them, and you set My oil and My incense before them. 19 Also [a]My food which I gave you—the pastry of fine flour, oil, and honey *which* I fed you—you set it before them as sweet incense; and *so* it was," says the Lord GOD.

20 [a]"Moreover you took your sons and your daughters, whom you bore to Me, and these you sacrificed to them to be devoured. *Were* your *acts* of harlotry a small matter, 21 that you have slain My children and offered them up to them by causing them to pass through *the* [a]*fire?* 22 And in all your abominations and acts of harlotry you did not remember the days of your [a]youth, [b]when you were naked and bare, struggling in your blood.

23 "Then it was so, after all your wickedness—'Woe, woe to you!' says the Lord GOD— 24 *that* [a]you also built for yourself a shrine, and [b]made a high place for yourself in every street. 25 You built your high places [a]at the head of every road, and made your beauty to be abhorred. You offered yourself to everyone who passed by, and multiplied your acts of harlotry. 26 You also committed harlotry with [a]the Egyptians, your very fleshly neighbors, and increased your acts of harlotry to [b]provoke Me to anger.

27 "Behold, therefore, I stretched out My hand against you, diminished your allotment, and gave you up to the will of those who hate you, [a]the daughters of the Philistines, who were ashamed of your lewd behavior. 28 You also played the harlot with the [a]Assyrians, because you were insatiable; indeed you played the harlot with them and still were not satisfied. 29 Moreover you multiplied your acts of harlotry

**15:4** [a] [John 15:6] **15:7** [a] Ezek. 14:8 [b] Is. 24:18 [c] Ezek. 7:4 **16:2** [a] Ezek. 20:4; 22:2 **16:3** [a] Ezek. 21:30 [b] Ezek. 16:45 **16:4** [a] Hos. 2:3 **16:7** [a] Ex. 1:7 **16:8** [a] Ruth 3:9 [b] Gen. 22:16–18 [c] Ex. 24:6–8 [d] [Ex. 19:5] **16:11** [a] Gen. 24:22, 47 [b] Prov. 1:9 **16:13** [a] Deut. 32:13, 14 [b] Ps. 48:2 **16:14** [a] Lam. 2:15 **16:15** [a] Mic. 3:11 [b] Is. 1:21; 57:8 **16:16** [a] Ezek. 7:20 **16:19** [a] Hos. 2:8 **16:20** [a] Jer. 7:31 **16:21** [a] Jer. 19:5 **16:22** [a] Jer. 2:2 [b] Ezek. 16:4–6 **16:24** [a] Jer. 11:13 [b] Jer. 2:20; 3:2 **16:25** [a] Prov. 9:14 **16:26** [a] Ezek. 16:26; 20:7, 8 [b] Deut. 31:20 **16:27** [a] Ezek. 16:57 **16:28** [a] Jer. 2:18, 36

as far as the land of the trader, [a]Chaldea; and even then you were not satisfied.

30 "How degenerate is your heart!" says the Lord GOD, "seeing you do all these *things,* the deeds of a brazen harlot.

### *JERUSALEM'S ADULTERY*

31 [a]"You erected your shrine at the head of every road, and built your high place in every street. Yet you were not like a harlot, because you scorned [b]payment. 32 *You are* an adulterous wife, *who* takes strangers instead of her husband. 33 Men make payment to all harlots, but [a]you made your payments to all your lovers, and hired them to come to you from all around for your harlotry. 34 You are the opposite of *other* women in your harlotry, because no one solicited you to be a harlot. In that you gave payment but no payment was given you, therefore you are the opposite."

### *JERUSALEM'S LOVERS WILL ABUSE HER*

35 'Now then, O harlot, hear the word of the LORD! 36 Thus says the Lord GOD: "Because your filthiness was poured out and your nakedness uncovered in your harlotry with your lovers, and with all your abominable idols, and because of [a]the blood of your children which you gave to them, 37 surely, therefore, [a]I will gather all your lovers with whom you took pleasure, all those you loved, *and* all those you hated; I will gather them from all around against you and will uncover your nakedness to them, that they may see all your nakedness. 38 And I will judge you as [a]women who break wedlock or [b]shed blood are judged; I will bring blood upon you in fury and jealousy. 39 I will also give you into their hand, and they shall throw down your shrines and break down [a]your high places. [b]They shall also strip you of your clothes, take your beautiful jewelry, and leave you naked and bare.

40 [a]"They shall also bring up an assembly against you, [b]and they shall stone you with stones and thrust you through with their swords. 41 They shall [a]burn your houses with fire, and [b]execute judgments on you in the sight of many women; and I will make you [c]cease playing the harlot, and you shall no longer hire lovers. 42 So [a]I will lay to rest My fury toward you, and My jealousy shall depart from you. I will be quiet, and be angry no more. 43 Because [a]you did not remember the days of your youth, but agitated Me[1] with all these *things,* surely [b]I will also recompense your deeds on *your own* head," says the Lord GOD. "And you shall not commit lewdness in addition to all your abominations.

### *MORE WICKED THAN SAMARIA AND SODOM*

44 "Indeed everyone who quotes proverbs will use *this* proverb against you: 'Like mother, like daughter!' 45 You *are* your mother's daughter, loathing husband and children; and you *are* the [a]sister of your sisters, who loathed their husbands and children; [b]your mother *was* a Hittite and your father an Amorite.

46 "Your elder sister *is* Samaria, who dwells with her daughters to the north of you; and [a]your younger sister, who dwells to the south of you, *is* Sodom and her daughters. 47 You did not walk in their ways nor act according to their abominations; but, as *if that were* too little, [a]you became more corrupt than they in all your ways.

48 "*As* I live," says the Lord GOD, "neither [a]your sister Sodom nor her daughters have done as you and your daughters have done. 49 Look, this was the iniquity of your sister Sodom: She and her daughter had pride, [a]fullness of food, and abundance of idleness; neither did she strengthen the hand of the poor and needy. 50 And they were haughty and [a]committed abomination before Me; therefore [b]I took them away as I saw *fit.*[1]

51 "Samaria did not commit [a]half of your sins; but you have multiplied your abominations more than they, and [b]have justified your sisters by all the abominations which you have done. 52 You who judged your sisters, bear your own shame also, because the sins which you committed were more abominable than theirs; they are more righteous than you. Yes, be disgraced also, and bear your own shame, because you justified your sisters.

53 [a]"When I bring back their captives, the captives of Sodom and her daughters, and the captives of Samaria and her daughters, then *I will also bring back* [b]the captives of your captivity among them, 54 that you may bear your own shame and be disgraced by all that you did when [a]you comforted them. 55 When your sisters, Sodom and her daughters, return to their former state, and Samaria and her daughters return to their former state, then you and your daughters will return to your former state. 56 For your sister Sodom was not a byword in your mouth in the days of your pride, 57 before your wickedness was uncovered. It was like the time of the [a]reproach of the daughters of Syria[1] and all *those* around her, and of [b]the daughters of the Philistines, who despise you everywhere. 58 [a]You have paid for your lewdness and your abominations," says the LORD. 59 For thus says the Lord GOD: "I will deal with you as you have done, who [a]despised [b]the oath by breaking the covenant.

16:29 [a] Ezek. 23:14–17 16:31 [a] Ezek. 16:24, 39 [b] Is. 52:3 16:33 [a] Hos. 8:9, 10 16:36 [a] Jer. 2:34 16:37 [a] Lam. 1:8 16:38 [a] Lev. 20:10 [b] Gen. 9:6 16:39 [a] Ezek. 16:24, 31 [b] Hos. 2:3 16:40 [a] Ezek. 23:45–47 [b] John 8:5, 7 16:41 [a] Deut. 13:16 [b] Ezek. 5:8; 23:10, 48 [c] Ezek. 23:27 16:42 [a] Ezek. 5:13; 21:17 16:43 [a] Ps. 78:42 [b] Ezek. 9:10; 11:21; 22:31 [1] Following Septuagint, Syriac, Targum, and Vulgate; Masoretic Text reads *were agitated with Me.* 16:45 [a] Ezek. 23:2–4 [b] Ezek. 16:3 16:46 [a] Is. 1:10 16:47 [a] Ezek. 5:6, 7 16:48 [a] Matt. 10:15; 11:24 16:49 [a] Gen. 13:10 16:50 [a] Gen. 13:13; 18:20; 19:5 [b] Gen. 19:24 [1] Vulgate reads *you saw;* Septuagint reads *he saw;* Targum reads *as was revealed to Me.* 16:51 [a] Ezek. 23:11 [b] Jer. 3:8–11 16:53 [a] Is. 1:9 [b] Jer. 20:16 16:54 [a] Ezek. 14:22 16:57 [a] 2 Kin. 16:5 [b] Ezek. 16:27 [1] Following Masoretic Text, Septuagint, Targum, and Vulgate; many Hebrew manuscripts and Syriac read *Edom.* 16:58 [a] Ezek. 23:49 16:59 [a] Ezek. 17:13 [b] Deut. 29:12

### *AN EVERLASTING COVENANT*

60 "Nevertheless I will [a]remember My cov-
enant with you in the days of your youth, and I
will establish [b]an everlasting covenant with you.
61 Then [a]you will remember your ways and be
ashamed, when you receive your older and your
younger sisters; for I will give them to you for
[b]daughters, [c]but not because of My covenant with
you. 62 [a]And I will establish My covenant with
you. Then you shall know that I *am* the LORD,
63 that you may [a]remember and be ashamed, [b]and
never open your mouth anymore because of your
shame, when I provide you an atonement for all
you have done," says the Lord GOD.' "

**SEEING JESUS IN THE SCRIPTURE**

**16:60** Although God's people broke their promise to obey God, God didn't break His promise to forgive them. This promise was fulfilled through Jesus, who perfectly satisfied the righteous demands of the law (see Rom. 3:21–22).

### *THE EAGLES AND THE VINE*

**17** And the word of the LORD came to me,
saying, 2 "Son of man, pose a riddle, and
speak a [a]parable to the house of Israel, 3 and say,
'Thus says the Lord GOD:

[a]"A great eagle with large wings and long
 pinions,
Full of feathers of various colors,
Came to Lebanon
And [b]took from the cedar the highest
 branch.
4 He cropped off its topmost young twig
And carried it to a land of trade;
He set it in a city of merchants.
5 Then he took some of the seed of the land
And planted it in [a]a fertile field;
He placed *it* by abundant waters
*And* set it [b]like a willow tree.
6 And it grew and became a spreading vine
 [a]of low stature;
Its branches turned toward him,
But its roots were under it.
So it became a vine,
Brought forth branches,
And put forth shoots.

7 "But there was another[1] great eagle with
 large wings and many feathers;
And behold, [a]this vine bent its roots
 toward him,
And stretched its branches toward him,
From the garden terrace where it had
 been planted,
That he might water it.
8 It was planted in good soil by many
 waters,
To bring forth branches, bear fruit,
*And* become a majestic vine." '

9 "Say, 'Thus says the Lord GOD:

"Will it thrive?
[a]Will he not pull up its roots,
Cut off its fruit,
And leave it to wither?
All of its spring leaves will wither,
And no great power or many people
Will be needed to pluck it up by its roots.
10 Behold, *it is* planted,
Will it thrive?
[a]Will it not utterly wither when the east
 wind touches it?
It will wither in the garden terrace where
 it grew." ' "

11 Moreover the word of the LORD came to
me, saying, 12 "Say now to [a]the rebellious house:
'Do you not know what these *things mean?*' Tell
*them,* 'Indeed [b]the king of Babylon went to Je-
rusalem and took its king and princes, and led
them with him to Babylon. 13 [a]And he took the
king's offspring, made a covenant with him,
[b]and put him under oath. He also took away the
mighty of the land, 14 that the kingdom might
be [a]brought low and not lift itself up, *but* that
by keeping his covenant it might stand. 15 But
[a]he rebelled against him by sending his am-
bassadors to Egypt, [b]that they might give him
horses and many people. [c]Will he prosper? Will
he who does such *things* escape? Can he break
a covenant and still be delivered?
16 '*As* I live,' says the Lord GOD, 'surely [a]in the
place *where* the king *dwells* who made him king,
whose oath he despised and whose covenant
he broke—with him in the midst of Babylon
he shall die. 17 [a]Nor will Pharaoh with *his* mighty
army and great company do anything in the war,
[b]when they heap up a siege mound and build a
wall to cut off many persons. 18 Since he despised
the oath by breaking the covenant, and in fact
[a]gave his hand and still did all these *things,* he
shall not escape.' "
19 Therefore thus says the Lord GOD: "*As* I
live, surely My oath which he despised, and My
covenant which he broke, I will recompense
on his own head. 20 I will [a]spread My net over
him, and he shall be taken in My snare. I will
bring him to Babylon and [b]try him there for
the treason which he committed against Me.

**16:60** [a] Ps. 106:45 [b] Is. 55:3 **16:61** [a] Ezek. 20:43; 36:31 [b] [Gal. 4:26] [c] Jer. 31:31 **16:62** [a] Hos. 2:19, 20 **16:63** [a] Ezek. 36:31, 32 [b] [Rom. 3:19] **17:2** [a] Ezek. 20:49; 24:3 **17:3** [a] Ezek. 17:12 [b] 2 Kin. 24:12 **17:5** [a] Deut. 8:7–9 [b] Is. 44:4 **17:6** [a] Ezek. 17:14 **17:7** [a] Ezek. 17:15 [1] Following Septuagint, Syriac, and Vulgate; Masoretic Text and Targum read *one.* **17:9** [a] 2 Kin. 25:7 **17:10** [a] Hos. 13:15 **17:12** [a] Ezek. 2:3–5; 12:9 [b] 2 Kin. 24:11–16 **17:13** [a] 2 Kin. 24:17 [b] 2 Chr. 36:13 **17:14** [a] Ezek. 29:14 **17:15** [a] 2 Kin. 24:20 [b] Deut. 17:16 [c] Ezek. 17:9 **17:16** [a] Ezek. 12:13 **17:17** [a] Jer. 37:7 [b] Jer. 52:4 **17:18** [a] 1 Chr. 29:24 **17:20** [a] Ezek. 12:13 [b] Ezek. 20:36

21 [a]All his fugitives[1] with all his troops shall fall
by the sword, and those who remain shall be
[b]scattered to every wind; and you shall know
that I, the LORD, have spoken."

> **17:22** A **cedar** tree can grow as high as one hundred feet and as wide as fifty feet.

### *ISRAEL EXALTED AT LAST*
*(cf. Ezek. 31:1–9)*

22 Thus says the Lord GOD: "I will take also
*one* of the highest [a]branches of the high cedar
and set *it* out. I will crop off from the topmost
of its young twigs [b]a tender one, and will [c]plant
*it* on a high and prominent mountain. 23 [a]On the
mountain height of Israel I will plant it; and it
will bring forth boughs, and bear fruit, and be
a majestic cedar. [b]Under it will dwell birds of
every sort; in the shadow of its branches they
will dwell. 24 And all the trees of the field shall
know that I, the LORD, [a]have brought down the
high tree and exalted the low tree, dried up the
green tree and made the dry tree flourish; [b]I, the
LORD, have spoken and have done *it*."

### *A FALSE PROVERB REFUTED*

**18** The word of the LORD came to me again,
saying, 2 "What do you mean when you
use this proverb concerning the land of Israel,
saying:

'The [a]fathers have eaten sour grapes,
And the children's teeth are set on edge'?

3 "*As* I live," says the Lord GOD, "you shall no
longer use this proverb in Israel.

4 "Behold, all souls are [a]Mine;
The soul of the father
As well as the soul of the son is Mine;
[b]The soul who sins shall die.
5 But if a man is just
And does what is lawful and right;
6 [a]If he has not eaten on the mountains,
Nor lifted up his eyes to the idols of the
house of Israel,
Nor [b]defiled his neighbor's wife,
Nor approached [c]a woman during her
impurity;
7 If he has not [a]oppressed anyone,
*But* has restored to the debtor his [b]pledge;
Has robbed no one by violence,
*But* has [c]given his bread to the hungry
And covered the naked with [d]clothing;
8 If he has not exacted [a]usury
Nor taken any increase,
*But* has withdrawn his hand from iniquity
*And* [b]executed true judgment between
man and man;
9 *If* he has walked in My statutes
And kept My judgments faithfully—
He *is* just;
He shall surely [a]live!"
Says the Lord GOD.

10 "If he begets a son *who is* a robber
Or [a]a shedder of blood,
*Who* does any of these *things*
11 And does none of those *duties*,
But has eaten on the mountains
Or defiled his neighbor's wife;
12 If he has oppressed the poor and needy,
Robbed by violence,
Not restored the pledge,
Lifted his eyes to the idols,
*Or* [a]committed abomination;
13 If he has exacted usury
Or taken increase—
Shall he then live?
He shall not live!
If he has done any of these abominations,
He shall surely die;
[a]His blood shall be upon him.

14 "*If*, however, he begets a son
Who sees all the sins which his father has
done,
And considers but does not do likewise;
15 [a]*Who* has not eaten on the mountains,
Nor lifted his eyes to the idols of the
house of Israel,
Nor defiled his neighbor's wife;
16 Has not oppressed anyone,
Nor withheld a pledge,
Nor robbed by violence,
*But* has given his bread to the hungry
And covered the naked with clothing;
17 *Who* has withdrawn his hand from the
poor[1]
*And* not received usury or increase,
But has executed My judgments
And walked in My statutes—
He shall not die for the iniquity of his
father;
He shall surely live!

18 "*As for* his father,
Because he cruelly oppressed,
Robbed his brother by violence,
And did what *is* not good among his people,
Behold, [a]he shall die for his iniquity.

**17:21** [a] Ezek. 12:14 [b] Ezek. 12:15; 22:15 [1] Following Masoretic Text and Vulgate; many Hebrew manuscripts and Syriac read *choice men;* Targum reads *mighty men;* Septuagint omits *All his fugitives.* **17:22** [a] [Zech. 3:8] [b] Is. 53:2 [c] [Ps. 2:6] **17:23** [a] [Is. 2:2, 3] [b] Dan. 4:12 **17:24** [a] Amos 9:11 [b] Ezek. 22:14 **18:2** [a] Lam. 5:7 **18:4** [a] Num. 16:22; 27:16 [b] [Rom. 6:23] **18:6** [a] Ezek. 22:9 [b] Lev. 18:20; 20:10 [c] Lev. 18:19; 20:18 **18:7** [a] Ex. 22:21 [b] Deut. 24:12 [c] Deut. 15:7, 11 [d] Is. 58:7 **18:8** [a] Ex. 22:25 [b] Zech. 8:16 **18:9** [a] Amos 5:4 **18:10** [a] Num. 35:31 **18:12** [a] Ezek. 8:6, 17 **18:13** [a] Lev. 20:9, 11–13, 16, 27 **18:15** [a] Ezek. 18:6 **18:17** [1] Following Masoretic Text, Targum, and Vulgate; Septuagint reads *iniquity* (compare verse 8). **18:18** [a] Ezek. 3:18

### *TURN AND LIVE*

19 "Yet you say, 'Why [a]should the son not bear the guilt of the father?' Because the son has done what is lawful and right, and has kept all My statutes and observed them, he shall surely live. 20 [a]The soul who sins shall die. [b]The son shall not bear the guilt of the father, nor the father bear the guilt of the son. [c]The righteousness of the righteous shall be upon himself, [d]and the wickedness of the wicked shall be upon himself.

21 "But [a]if a wicked man turns from all his sins which he has committed, keeps all My statutes, and does what is lawful and right, he shall surely live; he shall not die. 22 [a]None of the transgressions which he has committed shall be remembered against him; because of the righteousness which he has done, he shall [b]live. 23 [a]Do I have any pleasure at all that the wicked should die?" says the Lord GOD, "*and* not that he should turn from his ways and live?

24 "But [a]when a righteous man turns away from his righteousness and commits iniquity, and does according to all the abominations that the wicked *man* does, shall he live? [b]All the righteousness which he has done shall not be remembered; because of the unfaithfulness of which he is guilty and the sin which he has committed, because of them he shall die.

25 "Yet you say, [a]'The way of the Lord is not fair.' Hear now, O house of Israel, is it not My way which is fair, and your ways which are not fair? 26 [a]When a righteous *man* turns away from his righteousness, commits iniquity, and dies in it, it is because of the iniquity which he has done that he dies. 27 Again, [a]when a wicked *man* turns away from the wickedness which he committed, and does what is lawful and right, he preserves himself alive. 28 Because he [a]considers and turns away from all the transgressions which he committed, he shall surely live; he shall not die. 29 [a]Yet the house of Israel says, 'The way of the Lord is not fair.' O house of Israel, is it not My ways which are fair, and your ways which are not fair?

30 [a]"Therefore I will judge you, O house of Israel, every one according to his ways," says the Lord GOD. [b]"Repent, and turn from all your transgressions, so that iniquity will not be your ruin. 31 [a]Cast away from you all the transgressions which you have committed, and get yourselves a [b]new heart and a new spirit. For why should you die, O house of Israel? 32 For [a]I have no pleasure in the death of one who dies," says the Lord GOD. "Therefore turn and [b]live!"

### *ISRAEL DEGRADED*

**19** "Moreover [a]take up a lamentation for the princes of Israel, 2 and say:

'What *is* your mother? A lioness:
She lay down among the lions;
Among the young lions she nourished her cubs.
3 She brought up one of her cubs,
And [a]he became a young lion;
He learned to catch prey,
And he devoured men.
4 The nations also heard of him;
He was trapped in their pit,
And they brought him with chains to the land of [a]Egypt.
5 'When she saw that she waited, *that* her hope was lost,
She took [a]another of her cubs *and* made him a young lion.
6 [a]He roved among the lions,
And [b]became a young lion;
He learned to catch prey;
He devoured men.
7 He knew their desolate places,[1]
And laid waste their cities;
The land with its fullness was desolated
By the noise of his roaring.
8 [a]Then the nations set against him from the provinces on every side,
And spread their net over him;
[b]He was trapped in their pit.
9 [a]They put him in a cage with chains,
And brought him to the king of Babylon;
They brought him in nets,
That his voice should no longer be heard on [b]the mountains of Israel.

10 'Your mother *was* [a]like a vine in your bloodline,[1]
Planted by the waters,
[b]Fruitful and full of branches
Because of many waters.
11 She had strong branches for scepters of rulers.
[a]She towered in stature above the thick branches,
And was seen in her height amid the dense foliage.
12 But she was [a]plucked up in fury,
She was cast down to the ground,
And the [b]east wind dried her fruit.
Her strong branches were broken and withered;
The fire consumed them.

**18:19** [a] Ex. 20:5 **18:20** [a] Ezek. 18:4 [b] Deut. 24:16 [c] Is. 3:10, 11 [d] Rom. 2:6–9 **18:21** [a] Ezek. 18:27; 33:12, 19 **18:22** [a] Ezek. 18:24; 33:16 [b] [Ps. 18:20–24] **18:23** [a] [Ezek. 18:32; 33:11] **18:24** [a] Ezek. 3:20; 18:26; 33:18 [b] [2 Pet. 2:20] **18:25** [a] Ezek. 18:29; 33:17, 20 **18:26** [a] Ezek. 18:24 **18:27** [a] Ezek. 18:21 **18:28** [a] Ezek. 18:14 **18:29** [a] Ezek. 18:25 **18:30** [a] Ezek. 7:3; 33:20 [b] Matt. 3:2 **18:31** [a] Eph. 4:22, 23 [b] Jer. 32:39 **18:32** [a] Lam. 3:33 [b] [Prov. 4:2, 5, 6] **19:1** [a] Ezek. 26:17; 27:2 **19:3** [a] 2 Kin. 23:31, 32 **19:4** [a] 2 Kin. 23:33, 34 **19:5** [a] 2 Kin. 23:34 **19:6** [a] 2 Kin. 24:8, 9 [b] Ezek. 19:3 **19:7** [1] Septuagint reads *He stood in insolence;* Targum reads *He destroyed its palaces;* Vulgate reads *He learned to make widows.* **19:8** [a] 2 Kin. 24:2, 11 [b] Ezek. 19:4 **19:9** [a] 2 Chr. 36:6 [b] Ezek. 6:2 **19:10** [a] Ezek. 17:6 [b] Deut. 8:7–9 [1] Literally *blood,* following Masoretic Text, Syriac, and Vulgate; Septuagint reads *like a flower on a pomegranate tree;* Targum reads *in your likeness.* **19:11** [a] Dan. 4:11 **19:12** [a] Jer. 31:27, 28 [b] Hos. 13:5

13 And now she *is* planted in the wilderness,
In a dry and thirsty land.
14 [a]Fire has come out from a rod of her branches
*And* devoured her fruit,
So that she has no strong branch—a
scepter for ruling.' "

[b]This *is* a lamentation, and has become a
lamentation.

## *THE REBELLIONS OF ISRAEL*

**20** It came to pass in the seventh year, in the
fifth *month,* on the tenth *day* of the month,
*that* [a]certain of the elders of Israel came to inquire
of the LORD, and sat before me. 2 Then the word
of the LORD came to me, saying, 3 "Son of man,
speak to the elders of Israel, and say to them, 'Thus
says the Lord GOD: "Have you come to inquire of
Me? *As* I live," says the Lord GOD, [a]"I will not be
inquired of by you." ' 4 Will you judge them, son of
man, will you judge *them?* Then [a]make known to
them the abominations of their fathers.

5 "Say to them, 'Thus says the Lord GOD: "On
the day when [a]I chose Israel and raised My hand in
an oath to the descendants of the house of Jacob,
and made Myself [b]known to them in the land of
Egypt, I raised My hand in an oath to them, saying,
[c]'I *am* the LORD your God.' 6 On that day I raised
My hand in an oath to them, [a]to bring them out of
the land of Egypt into a land that I had searched
out for them, [b]'flowing with milk and honey,'[1] [c]the
glory of all lands. 7 Then I said to them, 'Each of
you, [a]throw away [b]the abominations which are
before his eyes, and do not defile yourselves with
[c]the idols of Egypt. I *am* the LORD your God.' 8 But
they rebelled against Me and would not obey Me.
They did not all cast away the abominations which
were before their eyes, nor did they forsake the
idols of Egypt. Then I said, 'I will [a]pour out My
fury on them and fulfill My anger against them
in the midst of the land of Egypt.' 9 [a]But I acted for
My name's sake, that it should not be profaned
before the Gentiles among whom they *were,* in
whose sight I had made Myself [b]known to them,
to bring them out of the land of Egypt.

10 "Therefore I [a]made them go out of the land
of Egypt and brought them into the wilderness.
11 [a]And I gave them My statutes and showed them
My judgments, [b]'which, *if* a man does, he shall live
by them.'[1] 12 Moreover I also gave them My [a]Sab-
baths, to be a sign between them and Me, that they
might know that I *am* the LORD who sanctifies
them. 13 Yet the house of Israel [a]rebelled against
Me in the wilderness; they did not walk in My
statutes; they [b]despised My judgments, [c]'which,
*if* a man does, he shall live by them';[1] and they
greatly [d]defiled My Sabbaths. Then I said I would
pour out My fury on them in the [e]wilderness,
to consume them. 14 [a]But I acted for My name's
sake, that it should not be profaned before the
Gentiles, in whose sight I had brought them out.
15 So [a]I also raised My hand in an oath to them in
the wilderness, that I would not bring them into
the land which I had given *them,* [b]'flowing with
milk and honey,'[1] [c]the glory of all lands, 16 [a]because
they despised My judgments and did not walk in
My statutes, but profaned My Sabbaths; for [b]their
heart went after their idols. 17 [a]Nevertheless My
eye spared them from destruction. I did not make
an end of them in the wilderness.

18 "But I said to their children in the wil-
derness, 'Do not walk in the statutes of your
fathers, nor observe their judgments, nor defile
yourselves with their idols. 19 I *am* the LORD your
God: [a]Walk in My statutes, keep My judgments,
and do them; 20 [a]hallow My Sabbaths, and they
will be a sign between Me and you, that you may
know that I *am* the LORD your God.'

21 "Notwithstanding, [a]the children rebelled
against Me; they did not walk in My statutes, and
were not careful to observe My judgments, [b]'which,
*if* a man does, he shall live by them';[1] but they pro-
faned My Sabbaths. Then I said I would pour out My
fury on them and fulfill My anger against them in
the wilderness. 22 Nevertheless I withdrew My hand
and acted for My name's sake, that it should not
be profaned in the sight of the Gentiles, in whose
sight I had brought them out. 23 Also I raised My
hand in an oath to those in the wilderness, that
[a]I would scatter them among the Gentiles and
disperse them throughout the countries, 24 [a]be-
cause they had not executed My judgments, but
had despised My statutes, profaned My Sabbaths,
and [b]their eyes were fixed on their fathers' idols.

25 "Therefore [a]I also gave them up to statutes
*that were* not good, and judgments by which
they could not live; 26 and I pronounced them
unclean because of their ritual gifts, in that they
caused all their firstborn to pass [a]through *the
fire,* that I might make them desolate and that
they [b]might know that I am the LORD." '

27 "Therefore, son of man, speak to the house
of Israel, and say to them, 'Thus says the Lord
GOD: "In this too your fathers have [a]blasphemed
Me, by being unfaithful to Me. 28 When I brought
them into the land *concerning* which I had raised
My hand in an oath to give them, and [a]they saw
all the high hills and all the thick trees, there they
offered their sacrifices and provoked Me with their
offerings. There they also sent up their [b]sweet aro-
ma and poured out their drink offerings. 29 Then
I said to them, 'What *is* this high place to which

**19:14** [a] Judg. 9:15 [b] Lam. 2:5 **20:1** [a] Ezek. 8:1, 11, 12; 14:1 **20:3** [a] Ezek. 7:26; 14:3 **20:4** [a] Ezek. 16:2; 22:2 **20:5** [a] Ex. 6:6–8 [b] Deut. 4:34 [c] Ex. 20:2 **20:6** [a] Jer. 32:22 [b] Ex. 3:8 [c] Jer. 11:5; 32:22 [1] Exodus 3:8 **20:7** [a] Ezek. 18:31 [b] 2 Chr. 15:8 [c] Lev. 18:3 **20:8** [a] Ezek. 7:8 **20:9** [a] Num. 14:13 [b] Josh. 2:10; 9:9, 10 **20:10** [a] Ex. 13:18 **20:11** [a] Neh. 9:13 [b] Lev. 18:5 [1] Leviticus 18:5 **20:12** [a] Deut. 5:12 **20:13** [a] Num. 14:22 [b] Prov. 1:25 [c] Lev. 18:5 [d] Ex. 16:27 [e] Num. 14:29 [1] Leviticus 18:5 **20:14** [a] Ezek. 20:9, 20 **20:15** [a] Num. 14:28 [b] Ex. 3:8 [c] Ezek. 20:6 [1] Exodus 3:8 **20:16** [a] Ezek. 20:13, 24 [b] Amos 5:25 **20:17** [a] [Ps. 78:38] **20:19** [a] Deut. 5:32 **20:20** [a] Jer. 17:22 **20:21** [a] Num. 25:1 [b] Lev. 18:5 [1] Leviticus 18:5 **20:23** [a] Lev. 26:33 **20:24** [a] Ezek. 20:13, 16 [b] Ezek. 6:9 **20:25** [a] Rom. 1:24 **20:26** [a] Jer. 32:35 [b] Ezek. 6:7; 20:12, 20 **20:27** [a] Rom. 2:24 **20:28** [a] Ezek. 6:13 [b] Ezek. 16:19

you go?' So its name is called Bamah[1] to this day." '
30 Therefore say to the house of Israel, 'Thus says
the Lord GOD: "Are you defiling yourselves in the
manner of your [a]fathers, and committing harlotry
according to their [b]abominations? 31 For when you
offer [a]your gifts and make your sons pass through
the fire, you defile yourselves with all your idols,
even to this day. So shall I be inquired of by you,
O house of Israel? *As* I live," says the Lord GOD, "I
will [b]not be inquired of by you. 32 [a]What you have
in your mind shall never be, when you say, 'We
will be like the Gentiles, like the families in other
countries, serving wood and stone.'

### GOD WILL RESTORE ISRAEL

33 "*As* I live," says the Lord GOD, "surely with
a mighty hand, [a]with an outstretched arm, and
with fury poured out, I will rule over you. 34 I will
bring you out from the peoples and gather you
out of the countries where you are scattered,
with a mighty hand, with an outstretched arm,
and with fury poured out. 35 And I will bring you
into the wilderness of the peoples, and there [a]I
will plead My case with you face to face. 36 [a]Just
as I pleaded My case with your fathers in the
wilderness of the land of Egypt, so I will plead
My case with you," says the Lord GOD.

37 "I will make you [a]pass under the rod, and
I will bring you into the bond of the [b]covenant;
38 [a]I will purge the rebels from among you, and
those who transgress against Me; I will bring
them out of the country where they dwell, but
[b]they shall not enter the land of Israel. Then you
will know that I *am* the LORD.

39 "As for you, O house of Israel," thus says
the Lord GOD: [a]"Go, serve every one of you his
idols—and hereafter—if you will not obey Me;
[b]but profane My holy name no more with your
gifts and your idols. 40 For [a]on My holy mountain,
on the mountain height of Israel," says the Lord
GOD, "there [b]all the house of Israel, all of them
in the land, shall serve Me; there [c]I will accept
them, and there I will require your offerings and
the firstfruits of your sacrifices, together with all
your holy things. 41 I will accept you as a [a]sweet
aroma when I bring you out from the peoples
and gather you out of the countries where you
have been scattered; and I will be hallowed in
you before the Gentiles. 42 [a]Then you shall know
that I *am* the LORD, [b]when I bring you into the
land of Israel, into the country *for* which I raised
My hand in an oath to give to your fathers. 43 And
[a]there you shall remember your ways and all your
doings with which you were defiled; and [b]you shall
loathe yourselves in your own sight because of all
the evils that you have committed. 44 [a]Then you
shall know that I *am* the LORD, when I have dealt
with you [b]for My name's sake, not according to
your wicked ways nor according to your corrupt
doings, O house of Israel," says the Lord GOD.' "

### FIRE IN THE FOREST

45 Furthermore the word of the LORD came to
me, saying, 46 [a]"Son of man, set your face toward
the south; preach against the south and proph-
esy against the forest land, the South,[1] 47 and say
to the forest of the South, 'Hear the word of the
LORD! Thus says the Lord GOD: "Behold, [a]I will
kindle a fire in you, and it shall devour [b]every
green tree and every dry tree in you; the blaz-
ing flame shall not be quenched, and all faces
[c]from the south to the north shall be scorched
by it. 48 All flesh shall see that I, the LORD, have
kindled it; it shall not be quenched." ' "

49 Then I said, "Ah, Lord GOD! They say of
me, 'Does he not speak [a]parables?' "

### BABYLON, THE SWORD OF GOD

21 And the word of the LORD came to me,
saying, 2 [a]"Son of man, set your face toward
Jerusalem, [b]preach against the holy places, and
prophesy against the land of Israel; 3 and say to
the land of Israel, 'Thus says the LORD: "Behold,
I *am* [a]against you, and I will draw My sword out
of its sheath and cut off both [b]righteous and
wicked from you. 4 Because I will cut off both
righteous and wicked from you, therefore My
sword shall go out of its sheath against all flesh
[a]from south *to* north, 5 that all flesh may know
that I, the LORD, have drawn My sword out of its
sheath; it [a]shall not return anymore." ' 6 [a]Sigh
therefore, son of man, with a breaking heart,
and sigh with bitterness before their eyes. 7 And
it shall be when they say to you, 'Why are you
sighing?' that you shall answer, 'Because of the
news; when it comes, every heart will melt, [a]all
hands will be feeble, every spirit will faint, and all
knees will be weak *as* water. Behold, it is coming
and shall be brought to pass,' says the Lord GOD."
8 Again the word of the LORD came to me,
saying, 9 "Son of man, prophesy and say, 'Thus
says the LORD!' Say:

[a]'A sword, a sword is sharpened
And also polished!
10 Sharpened to make a dreadful slaughter,
Polished to flash like lightning!
Should we then make mirth?
It despises the scepter of My son,
*As it does* all wood.
11 And He has given it to be polished,
That it may be handled;
This sword is sharpened, and it is polished
To be given into the hand of [a]the slayer.'

20:29 [1] Literally *High Place* 20:30 [a] Judg. 2:19 [b] Jer. 7:26; 16:12 20:31 [a] Ezek. 16:20; 20:26 [b] Ezek. 20:3 20:32 [a] Ezek. 11:5 20:33 [a] Jer. 21:5 20:35 [a] Jer. 2:9, 35; Ezek. 17:20 20:36 [a] Num. 14:21–23, 28 20:37 [a] Lev. 27:32 [b] Ps. 89:30–34 20:38 [a] Ezek. 34:17 [b] Jer. 44:14 20:39 [a] Amos 4:4 [b] Is. 1:13–15 20:40 [a] Is. 2:2, 3 [b] Ezek. 37:22 [c] Zech. 8:20–22 20:41 [a] Phil. 4:18 20:42 [a] Ezek. 36:23; 38:23 [b] Ezek. 11:17; 34:13; 36:24 20:43 [a] Ezek. 16:61 [b] Lev. 26:39 20:44 [a] Ezek. 24:24 [b] Ezek. 36:22 20:46 [a] Ezek. 21:2 [1] Hebrew *Negev* 20:47 [a] Jer. 21:14 [b] Luke 23:31 [c] Ezek. 21:4 20:49 [a] Ezek. 12:9; 17:2 21:2 [a] Ezek. 20:46 [b] Amos 7:16 21:3 [a] Ezek. 5:8 [b] Job 9:22 21:4 [a] Ezek. 20:47 21:5 [a] [Is. 45:23; 55:11] 21:6 [a] Is. 22:4 21:7 [a] Ezek. 7:17 21:9 [a] Deut. 32:41 21:11 [a] Ezek. 21:19

12 "Cry and wail, son of man;
For it will be against My people,
Against all the princes of Israel.
Terrors including the sword will be
against My people;
Therefore [a]strike *your* thigh.

13 "Because *it is* [a]a testing,
And what if *the sword* despises even the
scepter?
[b]*The scepter* shall be no *more*,"
says the Lord GOD.

14 "You therefore, son of man, prophesy,
And [a]strike *your* hands together.
The third time let the sword do double
*damage*.
It *is* the sword *that* slays,
The sword that slays the great *men*,
That enters their [b]private chambers.
15 I have set the point of the sword against
all their gates,
That the heart may melt and many may
stumble.
Ah! [a]*It is* made bright;
*It is* grasped for slaughter:

16 "Swords[a] at the ready!
Thrust right!
Set your blade!
Thrust left—
Wherever your edge is ordered!

17 "I also will [a]beat My fists together,
And [b]I will cause My fury to rest;
I, the LORD, have spoken."

18 The word of the LORD came to me again,
saying: 19 "And son of man, appoint for yourself
two ways for the sword of the king of Babylon to
go; both of them shall go from the same land.
Make a sign; put *it* at the head of the road to
the city. 20 Appoint a road for the sword to go to
[a]Rabbah of the Ammonites, and to Judah, into
fortified Jerusalem. 21 For the king of Babylon
stands at the parting of the road, at the fork of
the two roads, to use divination: he shakes the
arrows, he consults the images, he looks at the
liver. 22 In his right hand is the divination for
Jerusalem: to set up battering rams, to call for
a slaughter, to [a]lift the voice with shouting, [b]to
set battering rams against the gates, to heap up
a *siege* mound, and to build a wall. 23 And it will
be to them like a false divination in the eyes of
those who [a]have sworn oaths with them; but he
will bring their iniquity to remembrance, that
they may be taken.

24 "Therefore thus says the Lord GOD: 'Because you have made your iniquity to be remembered, in that your transgressions are uncovered, so that in all your doings your sins appear—because you have come to remembrance, you shall be taken in hand.

25 'Now to you, O [a]profane, wicked prince
of Israel, [b]whose day has come, whose iniquity
*shall* end, 26 thus says the Lord GOD:

"Remove the turban, and take off the
crown;
Nothing *shall remain* the same.
[a]Exalt the humble, and humble the exalted.
27 Overthrown, overthrown,
I will make it overthrown!
[a]It shall be no *longer*,
Until He comes whose right it is,
And I will give it *to* [b]*Him*." '

**21:21** The Babylonians used all sorts of rituals to determine their strategies. They planned military strategy based on the way **arrows** landed when dropped; they tried to consult the dead using idols; they cut open a sheep and predicted the future based on the shape and condition of its **liver**.

## *A SWORD AGAINST THE AMMONITES*

28 "And you, son of man, prophesy and say,
'Thus says the Lord GOD [a]concerning the Ammonites and concerning their reproach,' and say:

'A sword, a sword *is* drawn,
Polished for slaughter,
For consuming, for flashing—
29 While they [a]see false visions for you,
While they divine a lie to you,
To bring you on the necks of the wicked,
the slain
[b]Whose day has come,
Whose iniquity *shall* end.

30 'Return[a] *it* to its sheath.
[b]I will judge you
In the place where you were created,
[c]In the land of your nativity.
31 I will [a]pour out My indignation on you;
I will [b]blow against you with the fire of My
wrath,
And deliver you into the hands of brutal
men *who are* skillful to [c]destroy.
32 You shall be fuel for the fire;
Your blood shall be in the midst of the
land.
[a]You shall not be remembered,
For I the LORD have spoken.' "

21:12 [a]Jer. 31:19 21:13 [a]Job 9:23 [b]Ezek. 21:27 21:14 [a]Num. 24:10 [b]1 Kin. 20:30 21:15 [a]Ezek. 21:10, 28 21:16 [a]Ezek. 14:17 21:17 [a]Ezek. 22:13 [b]Ezek. 5:13; 16:42; 24:13 21:20 [a]Jer. 49:2 21:22 [a]Jer. 51:14 [b]Ezek. 4:2 21:23 [a]Ezek. 17:16, 18 21:25 [a]Jer. 52:2 [b]Ezek. 21:29 21:26 [a]Luke 1:52 21:27 [a][Luke 1:32, 33] [b][Jer. 23:5, 6] 21:28 [a]Ezek. 25:1–7 21:29 [a]Ezek. 12:24; 13:6–9; 22:28 [b]Job 18:20 21:30 [a]Jer. 47:6, 7 [b]Gen. 15:14 [c]Ezek. 16:3 21:31 [a]Ezek. 7:8 [b]Ezek. 22:20, 21 [c]Hab. 1:6–10 21:32 [a]Ezek. 25:10

### SINS OF JERUSALEM

22 Moreover the word of the LORD came to
me, saying, 2 "Now, son of man, [a]will you
judge, will you judge [b]the bloody city? Yes, show
her all her abominations! 3 Then say, 'Thus says
the Lord GOD: "The city sheds [a]blood in her
own midst, that her time may come; and she
makes idols within herself to defile herself.
4 You have become guilty by the blood which
you have [a]shed, and have defiled yourself with
the idols which you have made. You have caused
your days to draw near, and have come to *the
end of* your years; [b]therefore I have made you
a reproach to the nations, and a mockery to all
countries. 5 *Those* near and *those* far from you
will mock you as infamous *and* full of tumult.

6 "Look, [a]the princes of Israel: each one has
used his power to shed blood in you. 7 In you they
have [a]made light of father and mother; in your
midst they have [b]oppressed the stranger; in you
they have mistreated the fatherless and the widow.
8 You have despised My holy things and [a]profaned
My Sabbaths. 9 In you are [a]men who slander to
cause bloodshed; [b]in you are those who eat on the
mountains; in your midst they commit lewdness.
10 In you men [a]uncover their fathers' nakedness; in
you they violate women who are [b]set apart during
their impurity. 11 One commits abomination [a]with
his neighbor's wife; [b]another lewdly defiles his
daughter-in-law; and another in you violates his
sister, his father's [c]daughter. 12 In you [a]they take
bribes to shed blood; [b]you take usury and increase;
you have made profit from your neighbors by ex-
tortion, and [c]have forgotten Me," says the Lord GOD.

13 "Behold, therefore, I [a]beat My fists at the
dishonest profit which you have made, and at
the bloodshed which has been in your midst.
14 [a]Can your heart endure, or can your hands
remain strong, in the days when I shall deal with
you? [b]I, the LORD, have spoken, and will do *it.*
15 [a]I will scatter you among the nations, disperse
you throughout the countries, and [b]remove your
filthiness completely from you. 16 You shall defile
yourself in the sight of the nations; then [a]you
shall know that I *am* the LORD." ' "

### ISRAEL IN THE FURNACE

17 The word of the LORD came to me, saying,
18 "Son of man, [a]the house of Israel has become
dross to Me; they *are* all bronze, tin, iron, and
lead, in the midst of a [b]furnace; they have be-
come dross from silver. 19 Therefore thus says
the Lord GOD: 'Because you have all become
dross, therefore behold, I will gather you into
the midst of Jerusalem. 20 *As men* gather silver,
bronze, iron, lead, and tin into the midst of a
furnace, to blow fire on it, to [a]melt *it;* so I will
gather *you* in My anger and in My fury, and I will
leave *you there* and melt you. 21 Yes, I will gather
you and blow on you with the fire of My wrath,
and you shall be melted in its midst. 22 As silver
is melted in the midst of a furnace, so shall you
be melted in its midst; then you shall know that
I, the LORD, have [a]poured out My fury on you.' "

### ISRAEL'S WICKED LEADERS

23 And the word of the LORD came to me, say-
ing, 24 "Son of man, say to her: 'You *are* a land
that is [a]not cleansed[1] or rained on in the day of
indignation.' 25 [a]The conspiracy of her prophets[1]
in her midst is like a roaring lion tearing the prey;
they [b]have devoured people; [c]they have taken trea-
sure and precious things; they have made many
widows in her midst. 26 [a]Her priests have violated
My law and [b]profaned My holy things; they have
not [c]distinguished between the holy and unholy,
nor have they made known *the difference* between
the unclean and the clean; and they have hidden
their eyes from My Sabbaths, so that I am profaned
among them. 27 Her [a]princes in her midst *are* like
wolves tearing the prey, to shed blood, to destroy
people, and to get dishonest gain. 28 [a]Her prophets
plastered them with untempered *mortar,* [b]seeing
false visions, and divining [c]lies for them, saying,
'Thus says the Lord GOD,' when the LORD had
not spoken. 29 The people of the land have used
oppressions, committed robbery, and mistreated
the poor and needy; and they wrongfully [a]oppress
the stranger. 30 [a]So I sought for a man among
them who would [b]make a wall, and [c]stand in the
gap before Me on behalf of the land, that I should
not destroy it; but I found no one. 31 Therefore I
have [a]poured out My indignation on them; I have
consumed them with the fire of My wrath; and
I have recompensed [b]their deeds on their own
heads," says the Lord GOD.

### TWO HARLOT SISTERS

23 The word of the LORD came again to me,
saying:

2 "Son of man, there were [a]two women,
The daughters of one mother.
3 [a]They committed harlotry in Egypt,
They committed harlotry in [b]their youth;
Their breasts were there embraced,
Their virgin bosom was there pressed.
4 Their names: Oholah[1] the elder and
Oholibah[2] [a]her sister;
[b]They were Mine,

22:2 [a] Ezek. 20:4 [b] Nah. 3:1 22:3 [a] Ezek. 24:6, 7 22:4 [a] 2 Kin. 21:16 [b] Deut. 28:37 22:6 [a] Is. 1:23 22:7 [a] Lev. 20:9 [b] Ex. 22:22 22:8 [a] Lev. 19:30 22:9 [a] Lev. 19:16 [b] Ezek. 18:6, 11 22:10 [a] Lev. 18:7, 8 [b] Lev. 18:19; 20:18 22:11 [a] Ezek. 18:11 [b] Lev. 18:15 [c] Lev. 18:9 22:12 [a] Ex. 23:8 [b] Ex. 22:25 [c] Ezek. 23:35 22:13 [a] Ezek. 21:17 22:14 [a] Ezek. 21:7 [b] Ezek. 17:24 22:15 [a] Deut. 4:27 [b] Ezek. 23:27, 48 22:16 [a] Ps. 9:16 22:18 [a] Is. 1:22 [b] Prov. 17:3 22:20 [a] Is. 1:25 22:22 [a] Ezek. 20:8, 33 22:24 [a] Ezek. 24:13 [1] Following Masoretic Text, Syriac, and Vulgate; Septuagint reads *showered upon.* 22:25 [a] Hos. 6:9 [b] Matt. 23:14 [c] Mic. 3:11 [1] Following Masoretic Text and Vulgate; Septuagint reads *princes;* Targum reads *scribes.* 22:26 [a] Mal. 2:8 [b] 1 Sam. 2:29 [c] Lev. 10:10 22:27 [a] Is. 1:23 22:28 [a] Ezek. 13:10 [b] Ezek. 13:6, 7 [c] Jer. 23:25–32 22:29 [a] Ex. 23:9 22:30 [a] Jer. 5:1 [b] Ezek. 13:5 [c] Ps. 106:23 22:31 [a] Ezek. 22:22 [b] Ezek. 9:10 23:2 [a] Ezek. 16:44–46 23:3 [a] Lev. 17:7 [b] Ezek. 16:22 23:4 [a] Jer. 3:6, 7 [b] Ezek. 16:8, 20 [1] Literally *Her Own Tabernacle* [2] Literally *My Tabernacle Is in Her*

And they bore sons and daughters.
*As for* their names,
Samaria *is* Oholah, and Jerusalem *is*
Oholibah.

### *THE OLDER SISTER, SAMARIA*

5 "Oholah played the harlot even though she
was Mine;
And she lusted for her lovers, the
neighboring [a]Assyrians,
6 *Who were* clothed in purple,
Captains and rulers,
All of them desirable young men,
Horsemen riding on horses.
7 Thus she committed her harlotry with them,
All of them choice men of Assyria;
And with all for whom she lusted,
With all their idols, she defiled herself.
8 She has never given up her harlotry
*brought* [a]from Egypt,
For in her youth they had lain with her,
Pressed her virgin bosom,
And poured out their immorality upon her.

9 "Therefore I have delivered her
Into the hand of her lovers,
Into the hand of the [a]Assyrians,
For whom she lusted.
10 They uncovered her nakedness,
Took away her sons and daughters,
And slew her with the sword;
She became a byword among women,
For they had executed judgment on her.

### *THE YOUNGER SISTER, JERUSALEM*

11 "Now [a]although her sister Oholibah saw
*this,* [b]she became more corrupt in her lust than
she, and in her harlotry more corrupt than her
sister's harlotry.

12 "She lusted for the neighboring [a]Assyrians,
[b]Captains and rulers,
Clothed most gorgeously,
Horsemen riding on horses,
All of them desirable young men.
13 Then I saw that she was defiled;
Both *took* the same way.
14 But she increased her harlotry;
She looked at men portrayed on the wall,
Images of [a]Chaldeans portrayed in
vermilion,
15 Girded with belts around their waists,
Flowing turbans on their heads,
All of them looking like captains,
In the manner of the Babylonians of
Chaldea,
The land of their nativity.
16 [a]As soon as her eyes saw them,
She lusted for them
And sent [b]messengers to them in Chaldea.
17 "Then the Babylonians came to her, into
the bed of love,
And they defiled her with their
immorality;
So she was defiled by them, [a]and
alienated herself from them.
18 She revealed her harlotry and uncovered
her nakedness.
Then [a]I [b]alienated Myself from her,
As I had alienated Myself from her sister.

19 "Yet she multiplied her harlotry
In calling to remembrance the days of her
youth,
[a]When she had played the harlot in the
land of Egypt.
20 For she lusted for her paramours,
Whose flesh *is like* the flesh of donkeys,
And whose issue *is like* the issue of horses.
21 Thus you called to remembrance the
lewdness of your youth,
When the [a]Egyptians pressed your bosom
Because of your youthful breasts.

### *JUDGMENT ON JERUSALEM*

22 "Therefore, Oholibah, thus says the Lord
GOD:

[a]'Behold, I will stir up your lovers against
you,
From whom you have alienated yourself,
And I will bring them against you from
every side:
23 The Babylonians,
All the Chaldeans,
[a]Pekod, Shoa, Koa,
[b]All the Assyrians with them,
All of them desirable young men,
Governors and rulers,
Captains and men of renown,
All of them riding on horses.
24 And they shall come against you
With chariots, wagons, and war-horses,
With a horde of people.
They shall array against you
Buckler, shield, and helmet all around.

'I will delegate judgment to them,
And they shall judge you according to
their judgments.
25 I will set My [a]jealousy against you,
And they shall deal furiously with you;
They shall remove your nose and your ears,
And your remnant shall fall by the sword;
They shall take your sons and your
daughters,
And your remnant shall be devoured by
fire.
26 [a]They shall also strip you of your clothes
And take away your beautiful jewelry.

23:5 [a] Hos. 5:13; 8:9, 10 23:8 [a] Ezek. 23:3, 19 23:9 [a] 2 Kin. 17:3 23:11 [a] Jer. 3:8 [b] Jer. 3:8–11 23:12 [a] 2 Kin. 16:7, 8 [b] Ezek. 23:6, 23 23:14 [a] Ezek. 8:10; 16:29 23:16 [a] 2 Kin. 24:1 [b] Is. 57:9 23:17 [a] Ezek. 23:22, 28 23:18 [a] Jer. 6:8 [b] Jer. 12:8 23:19 [a] Ezek. 23:2 23:21 [a] Ezek. 16:26 23:22 [a] Ezek. 16:37–41; 23:28 23:23 [a] Jer. 50:21 [b] Ezek. 23:12 23:25 [a] Ex. 34:14 23:26 [a] Is. 3:18–23

27 'Thus [a]I will make you cease your lewdness
and your [b]harlotry
*Brought* from the land of Egypt,
So that you will not lift your eyes to them,
Nor remember Egypt anymore.'

28 "For thus says the Lord GOD: 'Surely I will
deliver you into the hand of [a]those you hate,
into the hand *of those* [b]from whom you alienated
yourself. 29 [a]They will deal hatefully with you,
take away all you have worked for, and [b]leave
you naked and bare. The nakedness of your
harlotry shall be uncovered, both your lewdness
and your harlotry. 30 I will do these *things* to you
because you have [a]gone as a harlot after the
Gentiles, because you have become defiled by
their idols. 31 You have walked in the way of your
sister; therefore I will put her [a]cup in your hand.'
32 "Thus says the Lord GOD:

'You shall drink of your sister's cup,
The deep and wide one;
[a]You shall be laughed to scorn
And held in derision;
It contains much.
33 You will be filled with drunkenness and
sorrow,
The cup of horror and desolation,
The cup of your sister Samaria.
34 You shall [a]drink and drain it,
You shall break its shards,
And tear at your own breasts;
For I have spoken,'
Says the Lord GOD.

35 "Therefore thus says the Lord GOD:

'Because you [a]have forgotten Me and [b]cast
Me behind your back,
Therefore you shall bear the *penalty*
*Of* your lewdness and your harlotry.' "

### *BOTH SISTERS JUDGED*

36 The LORD also said to me: "Son of man, will
you [a]judge Oholah and Oholibah? Then [b]declare
to them their abominations. 37 For they have
committed adultery, and [a]blood *is* on their hands.
They have committed adultery with their idols,
and even *sacrificed* their sons [b]whom they bore
to Me, passing them through *the fire,* to devour
*them.* 38 Moreover they have done this to Me: They
have [a]defiled My sanctuary on the same day and
[b]profaned My Sabbaths. 39 For after they had slain
their children for their idols, on the same day they
came into My sanctuary to profane it; and indeed
[a]thus they have done in the midst of My house.
40 "Furthermore you sent for men to come
from afar, [a]to whom a messenger *was* sent; and
there they came. And you [b]washed yourself for
them, [c]painted your eyes, and adorned yourself
with ornaments. 41 You sat on a stately [a]couch,
with a table prepared before it, [b]on which you had
set My incense and My oil. 42 The sound of a care-
free multitude *was* with her, and Sabeans *were*
brought from the wilderness with men of the
common sort, who put bracelets on their wrists
and beautiful crowns on their heads. 43 Then I
said concerning *her who had grown* old in adul-
teries, 'Will they commit harlotry with her now,
and she *with them?*' 44 Yet they went in to her, as
men go in to a woman who plays the harlot; thus
they went in to Oholah and Oholibah, the lewd
women. 45 But righteous men will [a]judge them
after the manner of adulteresses, and after the
manner of women who shed blood, because they
*are* adulteresses, and [b]blood *is* on their hands.
46 "For thus says the Lord GOD: [a]'Bring up an
assembly against them, give them up to trouble
and plunder. 47 [a]The assembly shall stone them
with stones and execute them with their swords;
[b]they shall slay their sons and their daughters,
and burn their houses with fire. 48 Thus [a]I will
cause lewdness to cease from the land, [b]that
all women may be taught not to practice your
lewdness. 49 They shall repay you for your lewd-
ness, and you shall [a]pay for your idolatrous sins.
[b]Then you shall know that I *am* the Lord GOD.' "

### *SYMBOL OF THE COOKING POT*
*(cf. Jer. 1:13–19)*

**24** Again, in the ninth year, in the tenth
month, on the tenth *day* of the month,
the word of the LORD came to me, saying, 2 "Son
of man, write down the name of the day, this
very day—the king of Babylon started his siege
against Jerusalem [a]this very day. 3 [a]And utter a
parable to the rebellious house, and say to them,
'Thus says the Lord GOD:

[b]"Put on a pot, set *it* on,
And also pour water into it.
4 Gather pieces *of meat* in it,
Every good piece,
The thigh and the shoulder.
Fill *it* with choice cuts;
5 Take the choice of the flock.
Also pile *fuel* bones under it,
Make it boil well,
And let the cuts simmer in it."

6 'Therefore thus says the Lord GOD:

"Woe to [a]the bloody city,
To the pot whose scum *is* in it,

23:27 [a] Ezek. 16:41; 22:15 [b] Ezek. 23:3, 19 23:28 [a] Ezek. 16:37–41 [b] Ezek. 23:17 23:29 [a] Deut. 28:48 [b] Ezek. 16:39 23:30 [a] Ezek. 6:9 23:31 [a] Jer. 7:14, 15; 25:15 23:32 [a] Ezek. 22:4, 5 23:34 [a] Is. 51:17 23:35 [a] Jer. 3:21 [b] 1 Kin. 14:9 23:36 [a] Ezek. 20:4; 22:2 [b] Is. 58:1 23:37 [a] Ezek. 16:38 [b] Ezek. 16:20, 21, 36, 45; 20:26, 31 23:38 [a] 2 Kin. 21:4, 7 [b] Ezek. 22:8 23:39 [a] 2 Kin. 21:2–8 23:40 [a] Is. 57:9 [b] Ruth 3:3 [c] Jer. 4:30 23:41 [a] Is. 57:7 [b] Prov. 7:17 23:45 [a] Ezek. 16:38 [b] Ezek. 23:37 23:46 [a] Ezek. 16:40 23:47 [a] Ezek. 16:40 [b] Ezek. 24:21 23:48 [a] Ezek. 22:15 [b] Deut. 13:11 23:49 [a] Ezek. 23:35 [b] Ezek. 20:38, 42, 44; 25:5 24:2 [a] 2 Kin. 25:1 24:3 [a] Ezek. 17:12 [b] Jer. 1:13 24:6 [a] Ezek. 22:2, 3, 27

And whose scum is not gone from it!
Bring it out piece by piece,
On which no [b]lot has fallen.
7 For her blood is in her midst;
She set it on top of a rock;
[a]She did not pour it on the ground,
To cover it with dust.
8 That it may raise up fury and take
vengeance,
[a]I have set her blood on top of a rock,
That it may not be covered."

9 'Therefore thus says the Lord GOD:

[a]"Woe to the bloody city!
I too will make the pyre great.
10 Heap on the wood,
Kindle the fire;
Cook the meat well,
Mix in the spices,
And let the cuts be burned up.

11 "Then set the pot empty on the coals,
That it may become hot and its bronze
may burn,
*That* [a]its filthiness may be melted in it,
*That* its scum may be consumed.
12 She has grown weary with lies,
And her great scum has not gone from
her.
*Let* her scum *be* in the fire!
13 In your [a]filthiness *is* lewdness.
Because I have cleansed you, and you
were not cleansed,
You will [b]not be cleansed of your
filthiness anymore,
[c]Till I have caused My fury to rest upon you.
14 [a]I, the LORD, have spoken *it;*
[b]It shall come to pass, and I will do *it;*
I will not hold back,
[c]Nor will I spare,
Nor will I relent;
According to your ways
And according to your deeds
They[1] will judge you,"
Says the Lord GOD.' "

### *THE PROPHET'S WIFE DIES*

15 Also the word of the LORD came to me, say-
ing, 16 "Son of man, behold, I take away from you
the desire of your eyes with one stroke; yet you
shall [a]neither mourn nor weep, nor shall your tears
run down. 17 Sigh in silence, [a]make no mourning
for the dead; [b]bind your turban on your head, and
[c]put your sandals on your feet; [d]do not cover *your*
lips, and do not eat man's bread *of sorrow.*"
18 So I spoke to the people in the morning,
and at evening my wife died; and the next morn-
ing I did as I was commanded.
19 And the people said to me, [a]"Will you not
tell us what these *things signify* to us, that you
behave so?"
20 Then I answered them, "The word of the
LORD came to me, saying, 21 'Speak to the house
of Israel, "Thus says the Lord GOD: 'Behold, [a]I will
profane My sanctuary, your arrogant boast, the
desire of your eyes, the delight of your soul; [b]and
your sons and daughters whom you left behind
shall fall by the sword. 22 And you shall do as I have
done; [a]you shall not cover *your* lips nor eat man's
bread *of sorrow.* 23 Your turbans shall be on your
heads and your sandals on your feet; [a]you shall
neither mourn nor weep, but [b]you shall pine away
in your iniquities and mourn with one another.
24 Thus [a]Ezekiel is a sign to you; according to all
that he has done you shall do; [b]and when this
comes, [c]you shall know that I *am* the Lord GOD.' "
25 'And you, son of man—*will it* not *be* in the
day when I take from them [a]their stronghold,
their joy and their glory, the desire of their eyes,
and that on which they set their minds, their sons
and their daughters: 26 *that* on that day [a]one who
escapes will come to you to let *you* hear *it* with
*your* ears? 27 [a]On that day your mouth will be
opened to him who has escaped; you shall speak
and no longer be mute. Thus you will be a sign to
them, and they shall know that I *am* the LORD.' "

### *PROCLAMATION AGAINST AMMON*

25 The word of the LORD came to me, saying,
2 "Son of man, [a]set your face [b]against the
Ammonites, and prophesy against them. 3 Say
to the Ammonites, 'Hear the word of the Lord
GOD! Thus says the Lord GOD: [a]"Because you
said, 'Aha!' against My sanctuary when it was
profaned, and against the land of Israel when
it was desolate, and against the house of Judah
when they went into captivity, 4 indeed, there-
fore, I will deliver you as a possession to the men
of the East, and they shall set their encampments
among you and make their dwellings among
you; they shall eat your fruit, and they shall
drink your milk. 5 And I will make [a]Rabbah [b]a
stable for camels and Ammon a resting place for
flocks. [c]Then you shall know that I *am* the LORD."
6 'For thus says the Lord GOD: "Because you
[a]clapped *your* hands, stamped your feet, and
[b]rejoiced in heart with all your disdain for the
land of Israel, 7 indeed, therefore, I will [a]stretch
out My hand against you, and give you as plun-
der to the nations; I will cut you off from the
peoples, and I will cause you to perish from
the countries; I will destroy you, and you shall
know that I *am* the LORD."

24:6 [b] Nah. 3:10 24:7 [a] Lev. 17:13 24:8 [a] [Matt. 7:2] 24:9 [a] Hab. 2:12 24:11 [a] Ezek. 22:15 24:13 [a] Ezek. 23:36–48 [b] Jer. 6:28–30 [c] Ezek. 5:13; 8:18; 16:42 24:14 [a] [1 Sam. 15:29] [b] Is. 55:11 [c] Ezek. 5:11 [1] Septuagint, Syriac, Targum, and Vulgate read *I*. 24:16 [a] Jer. 16:5 24:17 [a] Jer. 16:5 [b] Lev. 10:6; 21:10 [c] 2 Sam. 15:30 [d] Mic. 3:7 24:19 [a] Ezek. 12:9; 37:18 24:21 [a] Jer. 7:14 [b] Ezek. 23:25, 47 24:22 [a] Jer. 16:6, 7 24:23 [a] Job 27:15 [b] Lev. 26:39 24:24 [a] Is. 20:3 [b] Jer. 17:15 [c] Ezek. 6:7; 25:5 24:25 [a] Ezek. 24:21 24:26 [a] Ezek. 33:21 24:27 [a] Ezek. 3:26; 33:22 25:2 [a] Ezek. 35:2 [b] Jer. 49:1 25:3 [a] Ezek. 26:2 25:5 [a] Ezek. 21:20 [b] Is. 17:2 [c] Ezek. 24:24 25:6 [a] Job 27:23 [b] Ezek. 36:5 25:7 [a] Ezek. 35:3

### PROCLAMATION AGAINST MOAB

8 'Thus says the Lord GOD: "Because [a]Moab and [b]Seir say, 'Look! The house of Judah *is* like all the nations,' 9 therefore, behold, I will clear the territory of Moab of cities, of the cities on its frontier, the glory of the country, Beth Jeshimoth, Baal Meon, and [a]Kirjathaim. 10 [a]To the men of the East I will give it as a possession, together with the Ammonites, that the Ammonites [b]may not be remembered among the nations. 11 And I will execute judgments upon Moab, and they shall know that I *am* the LORD."

### PROCLAMATION AGAINST EDOM

12 'Thus says the Lord GOD: [a]"Because of what Edom did against the house of Judah by taking vengeance, and has greatly offended by avenging itself on them," 13 therefore thus says the Lord GOD: "I will also stretch out My hand against Edom, cut off man and beast from it, and make it desolate from Teman; Dedan shall fall by the sword. 14 [a]I will lay My vengeance on Edom by the hand of My people Israel, that they may do in Edom according to My anger and according to My fury; and they shall know My vengeance," says the Lord GOD.

### PROCLAMATION AGAINST PHILISTIA

15 'Thus says the Lord GOD: [a]"Because [b]the Philistines dealt vengefully and took vengeance with a spiteful heart, to destroy because of the old hatred," 16 therefore thus says the Lord GOD: [a]"I will stretch out My hand against the Philistines, and I will cut off the [b]Cherethites [c]and destroy the remnant of the seacoast. 17 I will [a]execute great vengeance on them with furious rebukes; [b]and they shall know that I *am* the LORD, when I lay My vengeance upon them." ' "

### PROCLAMATION AGAINST TYRE

**26** And it came to pass in the eleventh year, on the first *day* of the month, *that* the word of the LORD came to me, saying, 2 "Son of man, [a]because Tyre has said against Jerusalem, [b]'Aha! She is broken *who was* the gateway of the peoples; now she is turned over to me; I shall be filled; she is laid waste.'

> **26:2** With Israel out of the way, **Tyre** was free to expand its control over the caravans that passed through the area and boost its already successful trade business.

3 "Therefore thus says the Lord GOD: 'Behold, I *am* against you, O Tyre, and will cause many nations to come up against you, as the sea causes its waves to come up. 4 And they shall destroy the walls of Tyre and break down her towers; I will also scrape her dust from her, and [a]make her like the top of a rock. 5 It shall be *a place for* spreading nets [a]in the midst of the sea, for I have spoken,' says the Lord GOD; 'it shall become plunder for the nations. 6 Also her daughter *villages* which *are* in the fields shall be slain by the sword. [a]Then they shall know that I *am* the LORD.'

7 "For thus says the Lord GOD: 'Behold, I will bring against Tyre from the north [a]Nebuchadnezzar[1] king of Babylon, [b]king of kings, with horses, with chariots, and with horsemen, and an army with many people. 8 He will slay with the sword your daughter *villages* in the fields; he will [a]heap up a siege mound against you, build a wall against you, and raise a defense against you. 9 He will direct his battering rams against your walls, and with his axes he will break down your towers. 10 Because of the abundance of his horses, their dust will cover you; your walls will shake at the noise of the horsemen, the wagons, and the chariots, when he enters your gates, as men enter a city that has been breached. 11 With the hooves of his [a]horses he will trample all your streets; he will slay your people by the sword, and your strong pillars will fall to the ground. 12 They will plunder your riches and pillage your merchandise; they will break down your walls and destroy your pleasant houses; they will lay your stones, your timber, and your soil in the [a]midst of the water. 13 [a]I will put an end to the sound of [b]your songs, and the sound of your harps shall be heard no more. 14 [a]I will make you like the top of a rock; you shall be *a place for* spreading nets, and you shall never be rebuilt, for I the LORD have spoken,' says the Lord GOD.

15 "Thus says the Lord GOD to Tyre: 'Will the coastlands not [a]shake at the sound of your fall, when the wounded cry, when slaughter is made in the midst of you? 16 Then all the [a]princes of the sea will [b]come down from their thrones, lay aside their robes, and take off their embroidered garments; they will clothe themselves with trembling; [c]they will sit on the ground, [d]tremble *every* moment, and [e]be astonished at you. 17 And they will take up a [a]lamentation for you, and say to you:

"How you have perished,
O one inhabited by seafaring men,
O renowned city,
Who was [b]strong at sea,
She and her inhabitants,
Who caused their terror *to be* on all her
inhabitants!
18 Now [a]the coastlands tremble on the day of
your fall;
Yes, the coastlands by the sea are troubled
at your departure." '

**25:8** [a] Amos 2:1, 2 [b] Ezek. 35:2, 5 **25:9** [a] Jer. 48:23 **25:10** [a] Ezek. 25:4 [b] Ezek. 21:32 **25:12** [a] Obad. 10–14 **25:14** [a] Is. 11:14 **25:15** [a] Jer. 25:20 [b] 2 Chr. 28:18 **25:16** [a] Zeph. 2:4 [b] 1 Sam. 30:14 [c] Jer. 47:4 **25:17** [a] Ezek. 5:15 [b] Ps. 9:16 **26:2** [a] Jer. 25:22 [b] Ezek. 25:3 **26:4** [a] Ezek. 26:14 **26:5** [a] Ezek. 27:32 **26:6** [a] Ezek. 25:5 **26:7** [a] Jer. 27:3–6 [b] Dan. 2:37, 47 [1] Hebrew *Nebuchadrezzar,* and so elsewhere in this book **26:8** [a] Ezek. 21:22 **26:11** [a] Hab. 1:8 **26:12** [a] Ezek. 27:27, 32 **26:13** [a] Is. 14:11; 24:8 [b] Rev. 18:22 **26:14** [a] Ezek. 26:4, 5 **26:15** [a] Jer. 49:21 **26:16** [a] Is. 23:8 [b] Jon. 3:6 [c] Job 2:13 [d] Ezek. 32:10 [e] Ezek. 27:35 **26:17** [a] Ezek. 27:2–36 [b] Is. 23:4 **26:18** [a] Ezek. 26:15

19 "For thus says the Lord GOD: 'When I make
you a desolate city, like cities that are not in-
habited, when I bring the deep upon you, and
great waters cover you, 20 then I will bring you
down [a]with those who descend into the Pit, to
the people of old, and I will make you dwell in
the lowest part of the earth, in places desolate
from antiquity, with those who go down to the
Pit, so that you may never be inhabited; and I
shall establish glory [b]in the land of the living.
21 [a]I will make you a terror, and you *shall be* no
*more;* [b]though you are sought for, you will never
be found again,' says the Lord GOD."

### *LAMENTATION FOR TYRE*

**27** The word of the LORD came again to me,
saying, 2 "Now, son of man, [a]take up a
lamentation for Tyre, 3 and say to Tyre, [a]'You
who are situated at the entrance of the sea,
[b]merchant of the peoples on many coastlands,
thus says the Lord GOD:

"O Tyre, you have said,
[c]'I *am* perfect in beauty.'
4 Your borders *are* in the midst of the seas.
Your builders have perfected your beauty.
5 They made all *your* planks of fir trees
from [a]Senir;
They took a cedar from Lebanon to make
you a mast.
6 *Of* [a]oaks from Bashan they made your
oars;
The company of Ashurites have inlaid
your planks
*With* ivory from [b]the coasts of Cyprus.[1]
7 Fine embroidered linen from Egypt was
what you spread for your sail;
Blue and purple from the coasts of
Elishah was what covered you.

8 "Inhabitants of Sidon and Arvad were your
oarsmen;
Your wise men, O Tyre, were in you;
They became your pilots.
9 Elders of [a]Gebal and its wise men
Were in you to caulk your seams;
All the ships of the sea
And their oarsmen were in you
To market your merchandise.

10 "Those from Persia, Lydia,[1] and Libya[2]
Were in your army as men of war;
They hung shield and helmet in you;
They gave splendor to you.
11 Men of Arvad with your army *were* on
your walls *all* around,
And the men of Gammad were in your
towers;
They hung their shields on your walls *all*
around;
They made [a]your beauty perfect.

12 [a]"Tarshish *was* your merchant because
of your many luxury goods. They gave you sil-
ver, iron, tin, and lead for your goods. 13 [a]Javan,
Tubal, and Meshech *were* your traders. They
bartered [b]human lives and vessels of bronze for
your merchandise. 14 Those from the house of
[a]Togarmah traded for your wares with horses,
steeds, and mules. 15 The men of [a]Dedan *were*
your traders; many isles *were* the market of your
hand. They brought you ivory tusks and ebony
as payment. 16 Syria *was* your merchant because
of the abundance of goods you made. They gave
you for your wares emeralds, purple, embroi-
dery, fine linen, corals, and rubies. 17 Judah and
the land of Israel *were* your traders. They traded
for your merchandise wheat of [a]Minnith, millet,
honey, oil, and [b]balm. 18 Damascus *was* your mer-
chant because of the abundance of goods you
made, because of your many luxury items, with
the wine of Helbon and with white wool. 19 Dan
and Javan paid for your wares, traversing back
and forth. Wrought iron, cassia, and cane were
among your merchandise. 20 [a]Dedan *was* your
merchant in saddlecloths for riding. 21 Arabia
and all the princes of [a]Kedar *were* your regu-
lar merchants. They traded with you in lambs,
rams, and goats. 22 The merchants of [a]Sheba
and Raamah *were* your merchants. They traded
for your wares the choicest spices, all kinds of
precious stones, and gold. 23 [a]Haran, Canneh,
Eden, the merchants of [b]Sheba, Assyria, *and*
Chilmad *were* your merchants. 24 These *were*
your merchants in choice items—in purple
clothes, in embroidered garments, in chests of
multicolored apparel, in sturdy woven cords,
which were in your marketplace.

25 "The [a]ships of Tarshish were carriers of
your merchandise.
You were filled and very glorious [b]in the
midst of the seas.
26 Your oarsmen brought you into many
waters,
But [a]the east wind broke you in the midst
of the seas.

27 "Your [a]riches, wares, and merchandise,
Your mariners and pilots,
Your caulkers and merchandisers,
All your men of war who *are* in you,
And the entire company which *is* in your
midst,
Will fall into the midst of the seas on the
day of your ruin.

**26:20** [a] Ezek. 32:18 [b] Ezek. 32:23 **26:21** [a] Ezek. 27:36; 28:19 [b] Ps. 37:10, 36 **27:2** [a] Ezek. 26:17 **27:3** [a] Ezek. 26:17; 28:2 [b] Is. 23:3 [c] Ezek. 28:12 **27:5** [a] Deut. 3:9 **27:6** [a] Is. 2:12, 13 [b] Jer. 2:10 [1] Hebrew *Kittim,* western lands, especially Cyprus **27:9** [a] 1 Kin. 5:18 **27:10** [1] Hebrew *Lud* [2] Hebrew *Put* **27:11** [a] Ezek. 27:3 **27:12** [a] Gen. 10:4 **27:13** [a] Gen. 10:2 [b] Rev. 18:13 **27:14** [a] Gen. 10:3 **27:15** [a] Gen. 10:7 **27:17** [a] Judg. 11:33 [b] Jer. 8:22 **27:20** [a] Gen. 25:3 **27:21** [a] Is. 60:7 **27:22** [a] Gen. 10:7 **27:23** [a] 2 Kin. 19:12 [b] Gen. 25:3 **27:25** [a] Is. 2:16 [b] Ezek. 27:4 **27:26** [a] Ps. 48:7 **27:27** [a] [Prov. 11:4]

28 The [a]common-land will shake at the
sound of the cry of your pilots.

29 "All [a]who handle the oar,
The mariners,
All the pilots of the sea
Will come down from their ships *and*
stand on the shore.
30 They will make their voice heard because
of you;
They will cry bitterly and [a]cast dust on
their heads;
They [b]will roll about in ashes;
31 They will [a]shave themselves completely
bald because of you,
Gird themselves with sackcloth,
And weep for you
With bitterness of heart *and* bitter
wailing.
32 In their wailing for you
They will [a]take up a lamentation,
And lament for you:
[b]'What *city is* like Tyre,
Destroyed in the midst of the sea?

33 'When[a] your wares went out by sea,
You satisfied many people;
You enriched the kings of the earth
With your many luxury goods and your
merchandise.
34 But [a]you are broken by the seas in the
depths of the waters;
[b]Your merchandise and the entire
company will fall in your midst.
35 [a]All the inhabitants of the isles will be
astonished at you;
Their kings will be greatly afraid,
And *their* countenance will be
troubled.
36 The merchants among the peoples [a]will
hiss at you;
[b]You will become a horror, and *be* no
[c]more forever.' " ' "

### PROCLAMATION AGAINST THE KING OF TYRE

**28** The word of the LORD came to me again,
saying, 2 "Son of man, say to the prince of
Tyre, 'Thus says the Lord GOD:

"Because your heart *is* [a]lifted up,
And [b]you say, 'I *am* a god,
I sit *in* the seat of gods,
[c]In the midst of the seas,'
[d]Yet you *are* a man, and not a god,
Though you set your heart as the heart of
a god
3 (Behold, [a]you *are* wiser than Daniel!

> **28:3 Daniel**, a captive Jew in Babylon, had the God-given ability to explain dreams (often without even hearing them described first) and, in some cases, to predict the future based on those dreams. Because of his ability, he was made an advisor to the king of Babylon.

There is no secret that can be hidden
from you!
4 With your wisdom and your understanding
You have gained [a]riches for yourself,
And gathered gold and silver into your
treasuries;
5 [a]By your great wisdom in trade you have
increased your riches,
And your heart is lifted up because of
your riches),"

6 'Therefore thus says the Lord GOD:

"Because you have set your heart as the
heart of a god,
7 Behold, therefore, I will bring [a]strangers
against you,
[b]The most terrible of the nations;
And they shall draw their swords against
the beauty of your wisdom,
And defile your splendor.
8 They shall throw you down into the [a]Pit,
And you shall die the death of the slain
In the midst of the seas.

9 "Will you still [a]say before him who slays you,
'I *am* a god'?
But you *shall be* a man, and not a god,
In the hand of him who slays you.
10 You shall die the death of [a]the
uncircumcised
By the hand of aliens;
For I have spoken," says the Lord GOD.' "

### LAMENTATION FOR THE KING OF TYRE

11 Moreover the word of the LORD came to
me, saying, 12 "Son of man, [a]take up a lamenta-
tion for the king of Tyre, and say to him, 'Thus
says the Lord GOD:

[b]"You *were* the seal of perfection,
Full of wisdom and perfect in beauty.
13 You were in [a]Eden, the garden of God;
Every precious stone *was* your covering:
The sardius, topaz, and diamond,
Beryl, onyx, and jasper,
Sapphire, turquoise, and emerald with gold.

**27:28** [a] Ezek. 26:15 **27:29** [a] Rev. 18:17 **27:30** [a] Rev. 18:19 [b] Jer. 6:26 **27:31** [a] Ezek. 29:18 **27:32** [a] Ezek. 26:17 [b] Rev. 18:18 **27:33** [a] Rev. 18:19 **27:34** [a] Ezek. 26:19 [b] Ezek. 27:27 **27:35** [a] Ezek. 26:15, 16 **27:36** [a] Jer. 18:16 [b] Ezek. 26:2 [c] Ps. 37:10, 36 **28:2** [a] Jer. 49:16 [b] Ezek. 28:9 [c] Ezek. 27:3, 4 [d] Is. 31:3 **28:3** [a] Dan. 1:20; 2:20–23, 28; 5:11, 12 **28:4** [a] Zech. 9:1–3 **28:5** [a] Ps. 62:10 **28:7** [a] Ezek. 26:7 [b] Ezek. 7:24; 21:31; 30:11 **28:8** [a] Is. 14:15 **28:9** [a] Ezek. 28:2 **28:10** [a] Ezek. 31:18; 32:19, 21, 25, 27 **28:12** [a] Ezek. 27:2 [b] Ezek. 27:3; 28:3 **28:13** [a] Ezek. 31:8, 9; 36:35

The workmanship of [b]your timbrels and pipes
Was prepared for you on the day you were
created.

14 "You *were* the anointed [a]cherub who covers;
I established you;
You were on [b]the holy mountain of God;
You walked back and forth in the midst of
fiery stones.
15 You *were* perfect in your ways from the
day you were created,
Till [a]iniquity was found in you.

16 "By the abundance of your trading
You became filled with violence within,
And you sinned;
Therefore I cast you as a profane thing
Out of the mountain of God;
And I destroyed you, [a]O covering cherub,
From the midst of the fiery stones.

17 "Your [a]heart was lifted up because of your
beauty;
You corrupted your wisdom for the sake
of your splendor;
I cast you to the ground,
I laid you before kings,
That they might gaze at you.

18 "You defiled your sanctuaries
By the multitude of your iniquities,
By the iniquity of your trading;
Therefore I brought fire from your midst;
It devoured you,
And I turned you to ashes upon the earth
In the sight of all who saw you.
19 All who knew you among the peoples are
astonished at you;
[a]You have become a horror,
And *shall be* no [b]more forever." ' "

### PROCLAMATION AGAINST SIDON

20 Then the word of the LORD came to me,
saying, 21 "Son of man, [a]set your face [b]toward
Sidon, and prophesy against her, 22 and say,
'Thus says the Lord GOD:

[a]"Behold, I *am* against you, O Sidon;
I will be glorified in your midst;
And [b]they shall know that I *am* the LORD,
When I execute judgments in her and am
[c]hallowed in her.
23 [a]For I will send pestilence upon her,
And blood in her streets;
The wounded shall be judged in her midst
By the sword against her on every side;
Then they shall know that I *am* the LORD.

24 "And there shall no longer be a pricking
brier or [a]a painful thorn for the house of Isra-
el from among all *who are* around them, who
[b]despise them. Then they shall know that I *am*
the Lord GOD."

### ISRAEL'S FUTURE BLESSING

25 'Thus says the Lord GOD: "When I have
[a]gathered the house of Israel from the peoples
among whom they are scattered, and am [b]hal-
lowed in them in the sight of the Gentiles, then
they will dwell in their own land which I gave to
My servant Jacob. 26 And they will [a]dwell safely
there, [b]build houses, and [c]plant vineyards; yes,
they will dwell securely, when I execute judgments
on all those around them who despise them. Then
they shall know that I *am* the LORD their God." ' "

### PROCLAMATION AGAINST EGYPT

29 In the tenth year, in the tenth *month,* on
the twelfth *day* of the month, the word of
the LORD came to me, saying, 2 "Son of man, [a]set
your face against Pharaoh king of Egypt, and
prophesy against him, and [b]against all Egypt.
3 Speak, and say, 'Thus says the Lord GOD:

[a]"Behold, I *am* against you,
O Pharaoh king of Egypt,
O great [b]monster who lies in the midst of
his rivers,
[c]Who has said, 'My River[1] *is* my own;
I have made *it* for myself.'
4 But [a]I will put hooks in your jaws,
And cause the fish of your rivers to stick
to your scales;
I will bring you up out of the midst of
your rivers,
And all the fish in your rivers will stick to
your scales.
5 I will leave you in the wilderness,
You and all the fish of your rivers;
You shall fall on the open [a]field;
[b]You shall not be picked up or gathered.[1]
[c]I have given you as food
To the beasts of the field
And to the birds of the heavens.

6 "Then all the inhabitants of Egypt
Shall know that I *am* the LORD,
Because they have been a [a]staff of reed to
the house of Israel.
7 [a]When they took hold of you with the
hand,
You broke and tore all their shoulders;[1]
When they leaned on you,
You broke and made all their backs
quiver."

**28:13** [b] Ezek. 26:13 **28:14** [a] Ex. 25:20 [b] Ezek. 20:40 **28:15** [a] [Is. 14:12] **28:16** [a] Ezek. 28:14 **28:17** [a] Ezek. 28:2, 5 **28:19** [a] Ezek. 26:21 [b] Ezek. 27:36 **28:21** [a] Ezek. 6:2; 25:2; 29:2 [b] Is. 23:2, 4, 12 **28:22** [a] Ex. 14:4, 17 [b] Ps. 9:16 [c] Ezek. 28:25 **28:23** [a] Ezek. 38:22 **28:24** [a] Josh. 23:13 [b] Ezek. 16:57; 25:6, 7 **28:25** [a] Is. 11:12, 13 [b] Ezek. 28:22 **28:26** [a] Jer. 23:6 [b] Amos 9:13, 14 [c] Jer. 31:5 **29:2** [a] Ezek. 28:21 [b] Is. 19:1 **29:3** [a] Jer. 44:30 [b] Ps. 74:13, 14 [c] Ezek. 28:2 [1] That is, the Nile **29:4** [a] Ezek. 38:4 **29:5** [a] Ezek. 32:4–6 [b] Jer. 8:2; 16:4; 25:33 [c] Jer. 7:33; 34:20 [1] Following Masoretic Text, Septuagint, and Vulgate; some Hebrew manuscripts and Targum read *buried.* **29:6** [a] Is. 36:6 **29:7** [a] Ezek. 17:17 [1] Following Masoretic Text and Vulgate; Septuagint and Syriac read *hand.*

8 ‘Therefore thus says the Lord GOD: “Surely
I will bring [a]a sword upon you and cut off from
you man and beast. 9 And the land of Egypt shall
become [a]desolate and waste; then they will know
that I *am* the LORD, because he said, ‘The River *is*
mine, and I have made *it*.’ 10 Indeed, therefore, I
*am* against you and against your rivers, [a]and I will
make the land of Egypt utterly waste and desolate,
[b]from Migdol[1] *to* Syene, as far as the border of
Ethiopia. 11 [a]Neither foot of man shall pass through
it nor foot of beast pass through it, and it shall be
uninhabited forty years. 12 [a]I will make the land of
Egypt desolate in the midst of the countries *that*
*are* desolate; and among the cities *that are* laid
waste, her cities shall be desolate forty years; and
I will [b]scatter the Egyptians among the nations
and disperse them throughout the countries.”
13 ‘Yet, thus says the Lord GOD: “At the [a]end
of forty years I will gather the Egyptians from
the peoples among whom they were scattered.
14 I will bring back the captives of Egypt and
cause them to return to the land of Pathros, to
the land of their origin, and there they shall be
a [a]lowly kingdom. 15 It shall be the lowliest of
kingdoms; it shall never again exalt itself above
the nations, for I will diminish them so that they
will not rule over the nations anymore. 16 No
longer shall it be [a]the confidence of the house
of Israel, but will remind them of *their* iniquity
when they turned to follow them. Then they
shall know that I *am* the Lord GOD.” ’ ”

### *BABYLONIA WILL PLUNDER EGYPT*

17 And it came to pass in the twenty-seventh
year, in the first *month,* on the first *day* of the
month, *that* the word of the LORD came to me,
saying, 18 “Son of man, [a]Nebuchadnezzar king of
Babylon caused his army to labor strenuously
against Tyre; every head *was* made [b]bald, and
every shoulder rubbed raw; yet neither he nor
his army received wages from Tyre, for the labor
which they expended on it. 19 Therefore thus
says the Lord GOD: ‘Surely I will give the land of
Egypt to [a]Nebuchadnezzar king of Babylon; he
shall take away her wealth, carry off her spoil,
and remove her pillage; and that will be the
wages for his army. 20 I have given him the land
of Egypt *for* his labor, because they [a]worked for
Me,’ says the Lord GOD.
21 ‘In that day [a]I will cause the horn of the
house of Israel to spring forth, and I will [b]open
your mouth to speak in their midst. Then they
shall know that I *am* the LORD.’ ”

### *EGYPT AND HER ALLIES WILL FALL*

**30** The word of the LORD came to me again,
saying, 2 “Son of man, prophesy and say,
‘Thus says the Lord GOD:

[a]“Wail, ‘Woe to the day!’
3 For [a]the day *is* near,
Even the day of the LORD *is* near;
It will be a day of clouds, the time of the
Gentiles.
4 The sword shall come upon Egypt,
And great anguish shall be in Ethiopia,
When the slain fall in Egypt,
And they [a]take away her wealth,
And [b]her foundations are broken
down.

5 “Ethiopia, Libya,[1] Lydia,[2] [a]all the mingled
people, Chub, and the men of the lands who are
allied, shall fall with them by the sword.”
6 ‘Thus says the LORD:

“Those who uphold Egypt shall fall,
And the pride of her power shall come
down.
[a]From Migdol *to* Syene
Those within her shall fall by the sword,”
Says the Lord GOD.

7 “They[a] shall be desolate in the midst of the
desolate countries,
And her cities shall be in the midst of the
cities *that are* laid waste.
8 Then they will know that I *am* the LORD,
When I have set a fire in Egypt
And all her helpers are destroyed.
9 On that day [a]messengers shall go forth
from Me in ships
To make the careless Ethiopians afraid,
And great anguish shall come upon
them,
As on the day of Egypt;
For indeed it is coming!”

10 ‘Thus says the Lord GOD:

[a]“I will also make a multitude of Egypt to
cease
By the hand of Nebuchadnezzar king of
Babylon.
11 He and his people with him, [a]the most
terrible of the nations,
Shall be brought to destroy the land;
They shall draw their swords against
Egypt,
And fill the land with the slain.
12 [a]I will make the rivers dry,
And [b]sell the land into the hand of the
wicked;
I will make the land waste, and all that is
in it,
By the hand of aliens.
I, the LORD, have spoken.”

**29:8** [a] Ezek. 14:17; 32:11–13 **29:9** [a] Ezek. 30:7, 8 **29:10** [a] Ezek. 30:12 [b] Ezek. 30:6 [1] Or *tower* **29:11** [a] Ezek. 32:13 **29:12** [a] Ezek. 30:7, 26 [b] Ezek. 30:23, 26 **29:13** [a] Jer. 46:26 **29:14** [a] Ezek. 17:6, 14 **29:16** [a] Is. 30:2, 3; 36:4, 6 **29:18** [a] Jer. 25:9; 27:6 [b] Ezek. 27:31 **29:19** [a] Jer. 43:10–13 **29:20** [a] Jer. 25:9 **29:21** [a] Ps. 92:10; 132:17 [b] Ezek. 24:27 **30:2** [a] Is. 13:6; 15:2 **30:3** [a] Joel 2:1 **30:4** [a] Ezek. 29:19 [b] Jer. 50:15 **30:5** [a] Jer. 25:20, 24 [1] Hebrew *Put* [2] Hebrew *Lud* **30:6** [a] Ezek. 29:10 **30:7** [a] Ezek. 29:12 **30:9** [a] Is. 18:1, 2 **30:10** [a] Ezek. 29:19 **30:11** [a] Ezek. 28:7; 31:12 **30:12** [a] Is. 19:5, 6 [b] Is. 19:4

13 'Thus says the Lord GOD:

"I will also [a]destroy the idols,
And cause the images to cease from Noph;[1]
[b]There shall no longer be princes from the
land of Egypt;
[c]I will put fear in the land of Egypt.
14 I will make [a]Pathros desolate,
Set fire to [b]Zoan,
[c]And execute judgments in No.[1]
15 I will pour My fury on Sin,[1] the strength of
Egypt;
[a]I will cut off the multitude of No,
16 And [a]set a fire in Egypt;
Sin shall have great pain,
No shall be split open,
And Noph *shall be in* distress daily.
17 The young men of Aven[1] and Pi Beseth
shall fall by the sword,
And these *cities* shall go into captivity.
18 [a]At Tehaphnehes[1] the day shall also be
darkened,[2]
When I break the yokes of Egypt there.
And her arrogant strength shall cease in
her;
As for her, a cloud shall cover her,
And her daughters shall go into captivity.
19 Thus I will [a]execute judgments on Egypt,
Then they shall know that I *am* the LORD." ' "

## PROCLAMATION AGAINST PHARAOH

20 And it came to pass in the eleventh year, in
the first *month,* on the seventh *day* of the month,
*that* the word of the LORD came to me, saying,
21 "Son of man, I have [a]broken the arm of Pharaoh
king of Egypt; and see, [b]it has not been bandaged
for healing, nor a splint put on to bind it, to make
it strong enough to hold a sword. 22 Therefore
thus says the Lord GOD: 'Surely I *am* [a]against
Pharaoh king of Egypt, and will [b]break his arms,
both the strong one and the one that was broken;
and I will make the sword fall out of his hand. 23 [a]I
will scatter the Egyptians among the nations, and
disperse them throughout the countries. 24 I will
strengthen the arms of the king of Babylon and
put My sword in his hand; but I will break Phar-
aoh's arms, and he will groan before him with the
groanings of a mortally wounded *man.* 25 Thus I
will strengthen the arms of the king of Babylon,
but the arms of Pharaoh shall fall down; [a]they
shall know that I *am* the LORD, when I put My
sword into the hand of the king of Babylon and
he stretches it out against the land of Egypt. 26 [a]I
will scatter the Egyptians among the nations and
disperse them throughout the countries. Then
they shall know that I *am* the LORD.' "

## EGYPT CUT DOWN LIKE A GREAT TREE

*(cf. Ezek. 17:22–24)*

31 Now it came to pass in the [a]eleventh year,
in the third *month,* on the first *day* of the
month, *that* the word of the LORD came to me,
saying, 2 "Son of man, say to Pharaoh king of
Egypt and to his multitude:

[a]'Whom are you like in your greatness?
3 [a]Indeed Assyria *was* a cedar in Lebanon,
With fine branches that shaded the forest,
And of high stature;
And its top was among the thick boughs.
4 [a]The waters made it grow;
Underground waters gave it height,
With their rivers running around the
place where it was planted,
And sent out rivulets to all the trees of the
field.
5 'Therefore [a]its height was exalted above all
the trees of the field;
Its boughs were multiplied,
And its branches became long because of
the abundance of water,
As it sent them out.
6 All the [a]birds of the heavens made their
nests in its boughs;
Under its branches all the beasts of the
field brought forth their young;
And in its shadow all great nations made
their home.

7 'Thus it was beautiful in greatness and in
the length of its branches,
Because its roots reached to abundant
waters.
8 The cedars in the [a]garden of God could
not hide it;
The fir trees were not like its boughs,
And the chestnut[1] trees were not like its
branches;
No tree in the garden of God was like it in
beauty.
9 I made it beautiful with a multitude of
branches,
So that all the trees of Eden envied it,
That *were* in the garden of God.'

10 "Therefore thus says the Lord GOD: 'Be-
cause you have increased in height, and it sets its
top among the thick boughs, and [a]its heart was
lifted up in its height, 11 therefore I will deliver it
into the hand of the [a]mighty one of the nations,
and he shall surely deal with it; I have driven it
out for its wickedness. 12 And aliens, [a]the most

30:13 [a] Is. 19:1 [b] Zech. 10:11 [c] Is. 19:16 [1] That is, ancient Memphis 30:14 [a] Ezek. 29:14 [b] Ps. 78:12, 43 [c] Nah. 3:8–10 [1] That is, ancient Thebes 30:15 [a] Jer. 46:25 [1] That is, ancient Pelusium 30:16 [a] Ezek. 30:8 30:17 [1] That is, ancient On (Heliopolis) 30:18 [a] Jer. 2:16 [1] Spelled *Tahpanhes* in Jeremiah 43:7 and elsewhere [2] Following many Hebrew manuscripts, Bomberg, Septuagint, Syriac, Targum, and Vulgate; Masoretic Text reads *refrained.* 30:19 [a] [Ps. 9:16] 30:21 [a] Jer. 48:25 [b] Jer. 46:11 30:22 [a] Jer. 46:25 [b] Ps. 37:17 30:23 [a] Ezek. 29:12; 30:17, 18, 26 30:25 [a] Ps. 9:16 30:26 [a] Ezek. 29:12 31:1 [a] Ezek. 30:20; 32:1 31:2 [a] Ezek. 31:18 31:3 [a] Dan. 4:10, 20–23 31:4 [a] Jer. 51:36 31:5 [a] Dan. 4:11 31:6 [a] Dan. 4:12, 21 31:8 [a] Gen. 2:8, 9; 13:10 [1] Hebrew *armon* 31:10 [a] Dan. 5:20 31:11 [a] Ezek. 30:10 31:12 [a] Ezek. 28:7; 30:11; 32:12

terrible of the nations, have cut it down and left
it; its branches have fallen [b]on the mountains
and in all the valleys; its boughs lie [c]broken by
all the rivers of the land; and all the peoples
of the earth have gone from under its shadow
and left it.

13 'On [a]its ruin will remain all the birds of the heavens,
And all the beasts of the field will come to its branches—

14 So that no trees by the waters may ever again
exalt themselves for their height, nor set their
tops among the thick boughs, that no tree which
drinks water may ever be high enough to reach
up to them.

'For [a]they have all been delivered to death,
[b]To the depths of the earth,
Among the children of men who go down to the Pit.'

15 "Thus says the Lord GOD: 'In the day when
it [a]went down to hell, I caused mourning. I cov-
ered the deep because of it. I restrained its rivers,
and the great waters were held back. I caused
Lebanon to mourn for it, and all the trees of the
field wilted because of it. 16 I made the nations
[a]shake at the sound of its fall, when I [b]cast it
down to hell together with those who descend
into the Pit; and [c]all the trees of Eden, the choice
and best of Lebanon, all that drink water, [d]were
comforted in the depths of the earth. 17 They also
went down to hell with it, with those slain by the
sword; and *those who were* its *strong* arm [a]dwelt
in its shadows among the nations.

18 [a]'To which of the trees in Eden will you
then be likened in glory and greatness? Yet you
shall be brought down with the trees of Eden
to the depths of the earth; [b]you shall lie in the
midst of the uncircumcised, with *those* slain by
the sword. This *is* Pharaoh and all his multitude,'
says the Lord GOD."

### *LAMENTATION FOR PHARAOH AND EGYPT*

**32** And it came to pass in the twelfth year,
in the [a]twelfth *month,* on the first *day* of
the month, *that* the word of the LORD came to
me, saying, 2 "Son of man, [a]take up a lamenta-
tion for Pharaoh king of Egypt, and say to him:

[b]'You are like a young lion among the nations,
And [c]you *are* like a monster in the seas,
[d]Bursting forth in your rivers,
Troubling the waters with your feet,
And [e]fouling their rivers.

3 'Thus says the Lord GOD:

"I will therefore [a]spread My net over you with a company of many people,
And they will draw you up in My net.
4 Then [a]I will leave you on the land;
I will cast you out on the open fields,
[b]And cause to settle on you all the birds of the heavens.
And with you I will fill the beasts of the whole earth.
5 I will lay your flesh [a]on the mountains,
And fill the valleys with your carcass.

6 "I will also water the land with the flow of your blood,
*Even* to the mountains;
And the riverbeds will be full of you.
7 When *I* put out your light,
[a]I will cover the heavens, and make its stars dark;
I will cover the sun with a cloud,
And the moon shall not give her light.
8 All the bright lights of the heavens I will make dark over you,
And bring darkness upon your land,"
Says the Lord GOD.

9 'I will also trouble the hearts of many peo-
ples, when I bring your destruction among the
nations, into the countries which you have not
known. 10 Yes, I will make many peoples aston-
ished at you, and their kings shall be horribly
afraid of you when I brandish My sword before
them; and [a]they shall tremble *every* moment,
every man for his own life, in the day of your fall.

11 [a]"For thus says the Lord GOD: 'The sword of
the king of Babylon shall come upon you. 12 By
the swords of the mighty warriors, all of them
[a]the most terrible of the nations, I will cause
your multitude to fall.

[b]'They shall plunder the pomp of Egypt,
And all its multitude shall be destroyed.
13 Also I will destroy all its animals
From beside its great waters;
[a]The foot of man shall muddy them no more,
Nor shall the hooves of animals muddy them.
14 Then I will make their waters clear,
And make their rivers run like oil,'
Says the Lord GOD.

15 'When I make the land of Egypt desolate,
And the country is destitute of all that once filled it,
When I strike all who dwell in it,
[a]Then they shall know that I *am* the LORD.

**31:12** [b] Ezek. 32:5; 35:8 [c] Ezek. 30:24, 25 **31:13** [a] Is. 18:6 **31:14** [a] Ps. 82:7 [b] Ezek. 32:18 **31:15** [a] Ezek. 32:22, 23 **31:16** [a] Ezek. 26:15 [b] Is. 14:15 [c] Is. 14:8 [d] Ezek. 32:31 **31:17** [a] Lam. 4:20 **31:18** [a] Ezek. 32:19 [b] Ezek. 28:10; 32:19, 21 **32:1** [a] Ezek. 31:1; 33:21 **32:2** [a] Ezek. 27:2 [b] Ezek. 19:2–6 [c] Ezek. 29:3 [d] Jer. 46:7, 8 [e] Ezek. 34:18 **32:3** [a] Ezek. 12:13; 17:20 **32:4** [a] Ezek. 29:5 [b] Is. 18:6; Ezek. 31:13 **32:5** [a] Ezek. 31:12 **32:7** [a] Rev. 6:12, 13; 8:12 **32:10** [a] Ezek. 26:16 **32:11** [a] Jer. 46:26 **32:12** [a] Ezek. 28:7; 30:11; 31:12 [b] Ezek. 29:19 **32:13** [a] Ezek. 29:11 **32:15** [a] Ps. 9:16

16 'This *is* the [a]lamentation
With which they shall lament her;
The daughters of the nations shall lament her;
They shall lament for her, for Egypt,
And for all her multitude,'
Says the Lord GOD."

### EGYPT AND OTHERS CONSIGNED TO THE PIT

17 It came to pass also in the twelfth year, on
the fifteenth *day* of the month, [a]*that* the word
of the LORD came to me, saying:

18 "Son of man, wail over the multitude of Egypt,
And [a]cast them down to the depths of the earth,
Her and the daughters of the famous nations,
With those who go down to the Pit:
19 'Whom [a]do you surpass in beauty?
[b]Go down, be placed with the uncircumcised.'

20 "They shall fall in the midst of *those* slain by the sword;
She is delivered to the sword,
[a]Drawing her and all her multitudes.
21 [a]The strong among the mighty
Shall speak to him out of the midst of hell
With those who help him:
'They have [b]gone down,
They lie with the uncircumcised, slain by the sword.'

22 "Assyria[a] *is* there, and all her company,
With their graves all around her,
All of them slain, fallen by the sword.
23 [a]Her graves are set in the recesses of the Pit,
And her company is all around her grave,
All of them slain, fallen by the sword,
Who [b]caused terror in the land of the living.

24 "There *is* [a]Elam and all her multitude,
All around her grave,
All of them slain, fallen by the sword,
Who have [b]gone down uncircumcised to the lower parts of the earth,
[c]Who caused their terror in the land of the living;
Now they bear their shame with those who go down to the Pit.
25 They have set her [a]bed in the midst of the slain,
With all her multitude,
With her graves all around it,
All of them uncircumcised, slain by the sword;
Though their terror was caused
In the land of the living,
Yet they bear their shame
With those who go down to the Pit;
It was put in the midst of the slain.

26 "There *are* [a]Meshech and Tubal and all their multitudes,
With all their graves around it,
All of them [b]uncircumcised, slain by the sword,
Though they caused their terror in the land of the living.
27 [a]They do not lie with the mighty
*Who are* fallen of the uncircumcised,
Who have gone down to hell with their weapons of war;
They have laid their swords under their heads,
But their iniquities will be on their bones,
Because of the terror of the mighty in the land of the living.
28 Yes, you shall be broken in the midst of the uncircumcised,
And lie with *those* slain by the sword.

29 "There *is* [a]Edom,
Her kings and all her princes,
Who despite their might
Are laid beside *those* slain by the sword;
They shall lie with the uncircumcised,
And with those who go down to the Pit.
30 [a]There *are* the princes of the north,
All of them, and all the [b]Sidonians,
Who have gone down with the slain
In shame at the terror which they caused by their might;
They lie uncircumcised with *those* slain by the sword,
And bear their shame with those who go down to the Pit.

31 "Pharaoh will see them
And be [a]comforted over all his multitude,
Pharaoh and all his army,
Slain by the sword,"
Says the Lord GOD.
32 "For I have caused My terror in the land of the living;
And he shall be placed in the midst of the uncircumcised
With *those* slain by the sword,
Pharaoh and all his multitude,"
Says the Lord GOD.

**32:16** [a] Ezek. 26:17 **32:17** [a] Ezek. 32:1; 33:21 **32:18** [a] Ezek. 26:20; 31:14 **32:19** [a] Ezek. 31:2, 18 [b] Ezek. 28:10 **32:20** [a] Ps. 28:3 **32:21** [a] Is. 1:31; 14:9, 10 [b] Ezek. 32:19, 25 **32:22** [a] Ezek. 31:3, 16 **32:23** [a] Is. 14:15 [b] Ezek. 32:24–27, 32 **32:24** [a] Gen. 10:22; 14:1; Is. 11:11; Jer. 25:25; 49:34–39 [b] Ezek. 32:21 [c] Ezek. 32:23 **32:25** [a] Ps. 139:8 **32:26** [a] Gen. 10:2; Ezek. 27:13; 38:2, 3; 39:1 [b] Ezek. 32:19 **32:27** [a] Is. 14:18, 19 **32:29** [a] Ezek. 25:12–14 **32:30** [a] Jer. 1:15; 25:26; Ezek. 38:6, 15; 39:2 [b] Jer. 25:22; Ezek. 28:21–23 **32:31** [a] Ezek. 14:22; 31:16

### THE WATCHMAN AND HIS MESSAGE

**33** Again the word of the LORD came to me, saying, [2] "Son of man, speak to [a]the children of your people, and say to them: [b]'When I bring the sword upon a land, and the people of the land take a man from their territory and make him their [c]watchman, [3] when he sees the sword coming upon the land, if he blows the trumpet and warns the people, [4] then whoever hears the sound of the trumpet and does [a]not take warning, if the sword comes and takes him away, [b]his blood shall be on his *own* head. [5] He heard the sound of the trumpet, but did not take warning; his blood shall be upon himself. But he who takes warning will save his life. [6] But if the watchman sees the sword coming and does not blow the trumpet, and the people are not warned, and the sword comes and takes *any* person from among them, [a]he is taken away in his iniquity; but his blood I will require at the watchman's hand.'

[7] [a]"So you, son of man: I have made you a watchman for the house of Israel; therefore you shall hear a word from My mouth and warn them for Me. [8] When I say to the wicked, 'O wicked *man,* you shall surely die!' and you do not speak to warn the wicked from his way, that wicked *man* shall die in his iniquity; but his blood I will require at your hand. [9] Nevertheless if you warn the wicked to turn from his way, and he does not turn from his way, he shall die in his iniquity; but you have delivered your soul.

[10] "Therefore you, O son of man, say to the house of Israel: 'Thus you say, "If our transgressions and our sins *lie* upon us, and we [a]pine away in them, [b]how can we then live?"' [11] Say to them: *'As* I live,' says the Lord GOD, [a]'I have no pleasure in the death of the wicked, but that the wicked [b]turn from his way and live. Turn, turn from your evil ways! For [c]why should you die, O house of Israel?'

### THE FAIRNESS OF GOD'S JUDGMENT

[12] "Therefore you, O son of man, say to the children of your people: 'The [a]righteousness of the righteous man shall not deliver him in the day of his transgression; as for the wickedness of the wicked, [b]he shall not fall because of it in the day that he turns from his wickedness; nor shall the righteous be able to live because of *his righteousness* in the day that he sins.' [13] When I say to the righteous *that* he shall surely live, [a]but he trusts in his own righteousness and commits iniquity, none of his righteous works shall be remembered; but because of the iniquity that he has committed, he shall die. [14] Again, [a]when I say to the wicked, 'You shall surely die,' if he turns from his sin and does what is lawful and right, [15] *if* the wicked [a]restores the pledge, [b]gives back what he has stolen, and walks in [c]the statutes of life without committing iniquity, he shall surely live; he shall not die. [16] [a]None of his sins which he has committed shall be remembered against him; he has done what is lawful and right; he shall surely live.

[17] [a]"Yet the children of your people say, 'The way of the Lord is not fair.' But it is their way which is not fair! [18] [a]When the righteous turns from his righteousness and commits iniquity, he shall die because of it. [19] But when the wicked turns from his wickedness and does what is lawful and right, he shall live because of it. [20] Yet you say, [a]'The way of the Lord is not fair.' O house of Israel, I will judge every one of you according to his own ways."

### THE FALL OF JERUSALEM

[21] And it came to pass in the twelfth year [a]of our captivity, in the tenth *month,* on the fifth *day* of the month, [b]*that* one who had escaped from Jerusalem came to me and said, [c]"The city has been captured!"

[22] Now [a]the hand of the LORD had been upon me the evening before the man came who had escaped. And He had [b]opened my mouth; so when he came to me in the morning, my mouth was opened, and I was no longer mute.

### THE CAUSE OF JUDAH'S RUIN

[23] Then the word of the LORD came to me, saying: [24] "Son of man, [a]they who inhabit those [b]ruins in the land of Israel are saying, [c]'Abraham was only one, and he inherited the land. [d]But we *are* many; the land has been given to us as a [e]possession.'

[25] "Therefore say to them, 'Thus says the Lord GOD: [a]"You eat *meat* with blood, you [b]lift up your eyes toward your idols, and [c]shed blood. Should you then possess the [d]land? [26] You rely on your sword, you commit abominations, and you [a]defile one another's wives. Should you then possess the land?"'

**33:25** God's law specifically prohibited the ancient Israelites from eating or drinking **blood** in any form. All **meat** had to be drained and thoroughly cooked before it was served. In part, this was because Israel's idol-worshiping neighbors included blood-drinking rituals in their religious ceremonies.

**33:2** [a] Ezek. 3:11 [b] Ezek. 14:17 [c] 2 Sam. 18:24, 25; 2 Kin. 9:17; Hos. 9:8 **33:4** [a] 2 Chr. 25:16; Jer. 6:17; Zech. 1:4 [b] Ezek. 18:13; 35:9; [Acts 18:6] **33:6** [a] Ezek. 33:8 **33:7** [a] Is. 62:6; Ezek. 3:17–21 **33:10** [a] Lev. 26:39; Ezek. 24:23 [b] Is. 49:14; Ezek. 37:11 **33:11** [a] [2 Sam. 14:14; Lam. 3:33]; Ezek. 18:23, 32; Hos. 11:8; [2 Pet. 3:9] [b] Ezek. 18:21, 30; [Hos. 14:1, 4; Acts 3:19] [c] [Is. 55:6, 7]; Jer. 3:22; Ezek. 18:30, 31; Hos. 14:1; [Acts 3:19] **33:12** [a] Ezek. 3:20; 18:24, 26 [b] [2 Chr. 7:14]; Ezek. 18:21; 33:19 **33:13** [a] Ezek. 3:20; 18:24 **33:14** [a] Ezek. 3:18, 19; 18:27 **33:15** [a] Ezek. 18:7 [b] Lev. 6:2, 4, 5 [c] Ezek. 20:11, 13, 21 **33:16** [a] [Is. 1:18; 43:25] **33:17** [a] Ezek. 18:25, 29 **33:18** [a] Ezek. 18:26 **33:20** [a] Ezek. 18:25, 29 **33:21** [a] Ezek. 1:2 [b] Ezek. 24:26 [c] 2 Kin. 25:4 **33:22** [a] Ezek. 1:3; 8:1; 37:1 [b] Ezek. 24:27 **33:24** [a] Ezek. 34:2 [b] Ezek. 36:4 [c] Is. 51:2 [d] [Matt. 3:9] [e] Ezek. 11:15 **33:25** [a] Lev. 3:17; 7:26; 17:10–14; 19:26 [b] Ezek. 18:6 [c] Ezek. 22:6, 9 [d] Deut. 29:28 **33:26** [a] Ezek. 18:6; 22:11

27 "Say thus to them, 'Thus says the Lord GOD:
"*As* I live, surely [a]those who *are* in the ruins shall
fall by the sword, and the one who *is* in the open
field [b]I will give to the beasts to be devoured,
and those who *are* in the strongholds and [c]caves
shall die of the pestilence. 28 [a]For I will make the
land most desolate, her [b]arrogant strength shall
cease, and [c]the mountains of Israel shall be so
desolate that no one will pass through. 29 Then
they shall know that I *am* the LORD, when I have
made the land most desolate because of all their
abominations which they have committed." '

### *HEARING AND NOT DOING*

30 "As for you, son of man, the children of
your people are talking about you beside the
walls and in the doors of the houses; and they
[a]speak to one another, everyone saying to his
brother, 'Please come and hear what the word
is that comes from the LORD.' 31 So [a]they come
to you as people do, they [b]sit before you *as* My
people, and they [c]hear your words, but they do
not do them; [d]for with their mouth they show
much love, *but* [e]their hearts pursue their *own*
gain. 32 Indeed you *are* to them as a very lovely
song of one who has a pleasant voice and can
play well on an instrument; for they hear your
words, but they do [a]not do them. 33 [a]And when this
comes to pass—surely it will come—then [b]they
will know that a prophet has been among them."

### *IRRESPONSIBLE SHEPHERDS*

**34** And the word of the LORD came to me,
saying, 2 "Son of man, prophesy against
the shepherds of Israel, prophesy and say to
them, 'Thus says the Lord GOD to the shepherds:
[a]"Woe to the shepherds of Israel who feed them-
selves! Should not the shepherds feed the flocks?

> **34:2** Sheep are mentioned in the Bible more often than any other animal and are an especially important part of Israel's history. They provided the Israelites with wool for clothes and meat for food and sacrifices. Sheep are nearly helpless by themselves and need **shepherds** to guide and protect them. A good shepherd faithfully cares for his **flock** and is willing to risk his life for the animals.

3 [a]You eat the fat and clothe yourselves with
the wool; you [b]slaughter the fatlings, *but* you
do not feed the flock. 4 [a]The weak you have not
strengthened, nor have you healed those who
were sick, nor bound up the broken, nor brought
back what was driven away, nor [b]sought what
was lost; but with [c]force and cruelty you have
ruled them. 5 [a]So they were [b]scattered because
*there was* no shepherd; [c]and they became food
for all the beasts of the field when they were
scattered. 6 My sheep [a]wandered through all the
mountains, and on every high hill; yes, My flock
was scattered over the whole face of the earth,
and no one was seeking or searching *for them.*"

7 'Therefore, you shepherds, hear the word
of the LORD: 8 "*As* I live," says the Lord GOD,
"surely because My flock became a prey, and My
flock [a]became food for every beast of the field,
because *there was* no shepherd, nor did My shep-
herds search for My flock, [b]but the shepherds
fed themselves and did not feed My flock"—
9 therefore, O shepherds, hear the word of the
LORD! 10 Thus says the Lord GOD: "Behold, I *am*
[a]against the shepherds, and [b]I will require My
flock at their hand; I will cause them to cease
feeding the sheep, and the shepherds shall [c]feed
themselves no more; for I will [d]deliver My flock
from their mouths, that they may no longer be
food for them."

### *GOD, THE TRUE SHEPHERD*

11 'For thus says the Lord GOD: "Indeed I My-
self will search for My sheep and seek them out.
12 As a [a]shepherd seeks out his flock on the day
he is among his scattered sheep, so will I seek out
My sheep and deliver them from all the places
where they were scattered on [b]a cloudy and dark
day. 13 And [a]I will bring them out from the peoples
and gather them from the countries, and will
bring them to their own land; I will feed them on
the mountains of Israel, in the valleys and in all
the inhabited places of the country. 14 [a]I will feed
them in good pasture, and their fold shall be on
the high mountains of Israel. [b]There they shall
lie down in a good fold and feed in rich pasture
on the mountains of Israel. 15 I will feed My flock,
and I will make them lie down," says the Lord
GOD. 16 [a]"I will seek what was lost and bring back
what was driven away, bind up the broken and
strengthen what was sick; but I will destroy [b]the
fat and the strong, and feed them [c]in judgment."

17 'And *as for* you, O My flock, thus says the
Lord GOD: [a]"Behold, I shall judge between sheep
and sheep, between rams and goats. 18 *Is it* too
little for you to have eaten up the good pasture,
that you must tread down with your feet the
residue of your pasture—and to have drunk of
the clear waters, that you must foul the residue
with your feet? 19 And *as for* My flock, they eat
what you have trampled with your feet, and
they drink what you have fouled with your feet."

33:27 [a] Ezek. 33:24 [b] Ezek. 39:4 [c] 1 Sam. 13:6 33:28 [a] Jer. 44:2, 6, 22 [b] Ezek. 7:24; 24:21 [c] Ezek. 6:2, 3, 6 33:30 [a] Is. 29:13 33:31 [a] Ezek. 14:1 [b] Ezek. 8:1 [c] Is. 58:2 [d] Ps. 78:36, 37 [e] [Matt. 13:22] 33:32 [a] [Matt. 7:21–28] 33:33 [a] 1 Sam. 3:20 [b] Ezek. 2:5 34:2 [a] Zech. 11:17 34:3 [a] Zech. 11:16 [b] Ezek. 33:25, 26 34:4 [a] Zech. 11:16 [b] Luke 15:4 [c] [1 Pet. 5:3] 34:5 [a] Ezek. 33:21 [b] Matt. 9:36 [c] Is. 56:9 34:6 [a] 1 Pet. 2:25 34:8 [a] Ezek. 34:5, 6 [b] Ezek. 34:2, 10 34:10 [a] Jer. 21:13; 52:24–27 [b] Heb. 13:17 [c] Ezek. 34:2, 8 [d] Ezek. 13:23 34:12 [a] Jer. 31:10 [b] Ezek. 30:3 34:13 [a] Jer. 23:3 34:14 [a] [John 10:9] [b] Jer. 33:12 34:16 [a] Mic. 4:6 [b] Is. 10:16 [c] Jer. 10:24 34:17 [a] [Matt. 25:32]

20 'Therefore thus says the Lord GOD to them:
[a]"Behold, I Myself will judge between the fat and
the lean sheep. 21 Because you have pushed with
side and shoulder, butted all the weak ones with
your horns, and scattered them abroad, 22 there-
fore I will save My flock, and they shall no longer
be a prey; and I will judge between sheep and
sheep. 23 I will establish one [a]shepherd over them,
and he shall feed them—[b]My servant David. He
shall feed them and be their shepherd. 24 And [a]I,
the LORD, will be their God, and My servant David
[b]a prince among them; I, the LORD, have spoken.

**SEEING JESUS IN THE SCRIPTURE**

**34:23** Jesus is the shepherd God promised to place over His people. He is the Good Shepherd who fed God's sheep with the Word while on earth, and then laid down His life to save them (see John 10:11).

25 [a]"I will make a covenant of peace with
them, and [b]cause wild beasts to cease from the
land; and they [c]will dwell safely in the wilderness
and sleep in the woods. 26 I will make them and
the places all around [a]My hill [b]a blessing; and I
will [c]cause showers to come down in their sea-
son; there shall be [d]showers of blessing. 27 Then
[a]the trees of the field shall yield their fruit, and
the earth shall yield her increase. They shall be
safe in their land; and they shall know that I *am*
the LORD, when I have [b]broken the bands of their
yoke and delivered them from the hand of those
who [c]enslaved them. 28 And they shall no longer
be a prey for the nations, nor shall beasts of the
land devour them; but [a]they shall dwell safely,
and no one shall make *them* afraid. 29 I will raise
up for them a [a]garden of renown, and they shall
[b]no longer be consumed with hunger in the land,
[c]nor bear the shame of the Gentiles anymore.
30 Thus they shall know that [a]I, the LORD their
God, *am* with them, and they, the house of Israel,
*are* [b]My people," says the Lord GOD.'

31 "You are My [a]flock, the flock of My pasture;
you *are* men, *and* I *am* your God," says the Lord GOD.

### *JUDGMENT ON MOUNT SEIR*

**35** Moreover the word of the LORD came to
me, saying, 2 "Son of man, set your face
against [a]Mount Seir and [b]prophesy against it,
3 and say to it, 'Thus says the Lord GOD:

"Behold, O Mount Seir, I *am* against you;
[a]I will stretch out My hand against you,
And make you most desolate;
4 I shall lay your cities waste,
And you shall be desolate.
Then you shall know that I *am* the LORD.

5 [a]"Because you have had an ancient hatred,
and have shed *the blood of* the children of Israel
by the power of the sword at the time of their
calamity, [b]when their iniquity *came to an* end,
6 therefore, *as* I live," says the Lord GOD, "I will
prepare you for [a]blood, and blood shall pursue
you; [b]since you have not hated blood, therefore
blood shall pursue you. 7 Thus I will make Mount
Seir most desolate, and cut off from it the [a]one
who leaves and the one who returns. 8 And I will
fill its mountains with the slain; on your hills and
in your valleys and in all your ravines those who
are slain by the sword shall fall. 9 [a]I will make you
perpetually desolate, and your cities shall be unin-
habited; [b]then you shall know that I *am* the LORD.

10 "Because you have said, 'These two nations
and these two countries shall be mine, and we
will [a]possess them,' although [b]the LORD was there,
11 therefore, *as* I live," says the Lord GOD, "I will
do [a]according to your anger and according to the
envy which you showed in your hatred against
them; and I will make Myself known among them
when I judge you. 12 [a]Then you shall know that I
*am* the LORD. I have [b]heard all your [c]blasphemies
which you have spoken against the mountains of
Israel, saying, 'They are desolate; they are given
to us to consume.' 13 Thus [a]with your mouth you
have boasted against Me and multiplied your
[b]words against Me; I have heard *them*."

14 'Thus says the Lord GOD: [a]"The whole earth
will rejoice when I make you desolate. 15 [a]As you
rejoiced because the inheritance of the house
of Israel was desolate, [b]so I will do to you; you
shall be desolate, O Mount Seir, as well as all
of Edom—all of it! Then they shall know that I
*am* the LORD." '

### *BLESSING ON ISRAEL*

**36** "And you, son of man, prophesy to the
[a]mountains of Israel, and say, 'O moun-
tains of Israel, hear the word of the LORD! 2 Thus
says the Lord GOD: "Because [a]the enemy has
said of you, 'Aha! [b]The ancient heights [c]have
become our possession,' " ' 3 therefore prophesy,
and say, 'Thus says the Lord GOD: "Because they
made *you* desolate and swallowed you up on
every side, so that you became the possession
of the rest of the nations, [a]and you are taken
up by the lips of [b]talkers and slandered by the
people"— 4 therefore, O mountains of Israel,
hear the word of the Lord GOD! Thus says the

**34:20** [a] Ezek. 34:17 **34:23** [a] [Is. 40:11] [b] Jer. 30:9 **34:24** [a] Ex. 29:45 [b] Ezek. 37:24, 25 **34:25** [a] Ezek. 37:26 [b] Is. 11:6–9 [c] Jer. 23:6 **34:26** [a] Is. 56:7 [b] Zech. 8:13 [c] Lev. 26:4 [d] Ps. 68:9 **34:27** [a] Is. 4:2 [b] Jer. 2:20 [c] Jer. 25:14 **34:28** [a] Jer. 30:10 **34:29** [a] [Is. 11:1] [b] Ezek. 36:29 [c] Ezek. 36:3, 6, 15 **34:30** [a] Ezek. 34:24 [b] Ezek. 14:11; 36:28 **34:31** [a] Ps. 100:3 **35:2** [a] Ezek. 25:12–14 [b] Amos 1:11 **35:3** [a] Ezek. 6:14 **35:5** [a] Ezek. 25:12 [b] Ps. 137:7 **35:6** [a] Is. 63:1–6 [b] Ps. 109:17 **35:7** [a] Judg. 5:6 **35:9** [a] Jer. 49:13 [b] Ezek. 36:11 **35:10** [a] Ps. 83:4–12 [b] [Ps. 48:1–3; 132:13, 14] **35:11** [a] [James 2:13] **35:12** [a] Ps. 9:16 [b] Zeph. 2:8 [c] Is. 52:5 **35:13** [a] [1 Sam. 2:3] [b] Ezek. 36:3 **35:14** [a] Is. 65:13, 14 **35:15** [a] Obad. 12, 15 [b] Lam. 4:21 **36:1** [a] Ezek. 6:2, 3 **36:2** [a] Ezek. 25:3; 26:2 [b] Deut. 32:13 [c] Ezek. 35:10 **36:3** [a] Deut. 28:37 [b] Ezek. 35:13

Lord GOD to the mountains, the hills, the rivers, the valleys, the desolate wastes, and the cities that have been forsaken, which [a]became plunder and [b]mockery to the rest of the nations all around— 5 therefore thus says the Lord GOD: [a]"Surely I have spoken in My burning jealousy against the rest of the nations and against all Edom, [b]who gave My land to themselves as a possession, with wholehearted joy *and* spiteful minds, in order to plunder its open country." '

6 "Therefore prophesy concerning the land of Israel, and say to the mountains, the hills, the rivers, and the valleys, 'Thus says the Lord GOD: "Behold, I have spoken in My jealousy and My fury, because you have [a]borne the shame of the nations." 7 Therefore thus says the Lord GOD: "I have [a]raised My hand in an oath that surely the nations that *are* around you shall [b]bear their own shame. 8 But you, O mountains of Israel, you shall shoot forth your branches and yield your fruit to My people Israel, for they are about to come. 9 For indeed I *am* for you, and I will turn to you, and you shall be tilled and sown. 10 I will multiply men upon you, all the house of Israel, all of it; and the cities shall be inhabited and [a]the ruins rebuilt. 11 [a]I will multiply upon you man and beast; and they shall increase and bear young; I will make you inhabited as in former times, and do [b]better *for you* than at your beginnings. [c]Then you shall know that I *am* the LORD. 12 Yes, I will cause men to walk on you, My people Israel; [a]they shall take possession of you, and you shall be their inheritance; no more shall you [b]bereave them *of children.*"

13 'Thus says the Lord GOD: "Because they say to you, [a]'You devour men and bereave your nation *of children,*' 14 therefore you shall devour men no more, nor bereave your nation anymore," says the Lord GOD. 15 [a]"Nor will I let you hear the taunts of the nations anymore, nor bear the reproach of the peoples anymore, nor shall you cause your nation to stumble anymore," says the Lord GOD.' "

### *THE RENEWAL OF ISRAEL*

16 Moreover the word of the LORD came to me, saying: 17 "Son of man, when the house of Israel dwelt in their own land, [a]they defiled it by their own ways and deeds; to Me their way was like [b]the uncleanness of a woman in her customary impurity. 18 Therefore I poured out My fury on them [a]for the blood they had shed on the land, and for their idols *with which* they had defiled it. 19 So I [a]scattered them among the nations, and they were dispersed throughout the countries; I judged them [b]according to their ways and their deeds. 20 When they came to the nations, wherever they went, they [a]profaned My holy name—when they said of them, 'These *are* the people of the LORD, *and* yet they have gone out of His land.' 21 But I had concern [a]for My holy name, which the house of Israel had profaned among the nations wherever they went.

22 "Therefore say to the house of Israel, 'Thus says the Lord GOD: "I do not do *this* for your sake, O house of Israel, [a]but for My holy name's sake, which you have profaned among the nations wherever you went. 23 And I will sanctify My great name, which has been profaned among the nations, which you have profaned in their midst; and the nations shall know that I *am* the LORD," says the Lord GOD, "when I am [a]hallowed in you before their eyes. 24 For [a]I will take you from among the nations, gather you out of all countries, and bring you into your own land. 25 [a]Then I will sprinkle clean water on you, and you shall be clean; I will cleanse you [b]from all your filthiness and from all your idols. 26 I will give you a [a]new heart and put a new spirit within you; I will take the heart of stone out of your flesh and give you a heart of flesh. 27 I will put My [a]Spirit within you and cause you to walk in My statutes, and you will keep My judgments and do *them.* 28 [a]Then you shall dwell in the land that I gave to your fathers; [b]you shall be My people, and I will be your God. 29 I will [a]deliver you from all your uncleannesses. [b]I will call for the grain and multiply it, and [c]bring no famine upon you. 30 [a]And I will multiply the fruit of your trees and the increase of your fields, so that you need never again bear the reproach of famine among the nations. 31 Then [a]you will remember your evil ways and your deeds that *were* not good; and you [b]will loathe yourselves in your own sight, for your iniquities and your abominations. 32 [a]Not for your sake do I do *this,*" says the Lord GOD, "let it be known to you. Be ashamed and confounded for your own ways, O house of Israel!"

33 'Thus says the Lord GOD: "On the day that I cleanse you from all your iniquities, I will also

> **36:27–30** The regenerating and empowering work of the Holy **Spirit** on individuals not only would restore the people physically to the **land** but would restore them spiritually, by giving them a new heart and new spirit to help them follow Him and do His will (Ezek. 11:19–20; 18:31; 37:14; Jer. 31:31–34; Joel 2:28–29; Rom. 7:7—8:11). The purpose of the Mosaic covenant would finally be realized (Deut. 26:16–19; 29:13; 30:8). The Israelites would become a people dedicated to God's ways.

36:4 [a] Ezek. 34:8, 28 [b] Ps. 79:4 36:5 [a] Deut. 4:24 [b] Ezek. 35:10, 12 36:6 [a] Ps. 74:10; 123:3, 4 36:7 [a] Ezek. 20:5 [b] Jer. 25:9, 15, 29 36:10 [a] Amos 9:14 36:11 [a] Jer. 31:27; 33:12 [b] Is. 51:3 [c] Ezek. 35:9; 37:6, 13 36:12 [a] Obad. 17 [b] Jer. 15:7 36:13 [a] Num. 13:32 36:15 [a] Ezek. 34:29 36:17 [a] Jer. 2:7 [b] Lev. 15:19 36:18 [a] Ezek. 16:36, 38; 23:37 36:19 [a] Deut. 28:64 [b] [Rom. 2:6] 36:20 [a] Rom. 2:24 36:21 [a] Ezek. 20:9, 14 36:22 [a] Ps. 106:8 36:23 [a] Ezek. 20:41; 28:22 36:24 [a] Ezek. 34:13; 37:21 36:25 [a] Heb. 9:13, 19; 10:22 [b] Jer. 33:8 36:26 [a] Ezek. 11:19 36:27 [a] Ezek. 11:19; 37:14 36:28 [a] Ezek. 28:25; 37:25 [b] Jer. 30:22 36:29 [a] [Rom. 11:26] [b] Ps. 105:16 [c] Ezek. 34:27, 29 36:30 [a] Ezek. 34:27 36:31 [a] Ezek. 16:61, 63 [b] Ezek. 6:9; 20:43 36:32 [a] Deut. 9:5

enable *you* to dwell in the cities, [a]and the ruins shall be rebuilt. 34 The desolate land shall be tilled instead of lying desolate in the sight of all who pass by. 35 So they will say, 'This land that was desolate has become like the garden of [a]Eden; and the wasted, desolate, and ruined cities *are now* fortified *and* inhabited.' 36 Then the nations which are left all around you shall know that I, the LORD, have rebuilt the ruined places *and* planted what was desolate. [a]I, the LORD, have spoken *it*, and I will do *it*."

37 "Thus says the Lord GOD: [a]"I will also let the house of Israel inquire of Me to do this for them: I will [b]increase their men like a flock. 38 Like a flock *offered as* holy *sacrifices*, like the flock at Jerusalem on its feast days, so shall the ruined cities be filled with flocks of men. Then they shall know that I *am* the LORD."'"

### *THE DRY BONES LIVE*

**37** The [a]hand of the LORD came upon me and brought me out [b]in the Spirit of the LORD, and set me down in the midst of the valley; and it *was* full of bones. 2 Then He caused me to pass by them all around, and behold, *there were* very many in the open valley; and indeed *they were* very dry. 3 And He said to me, "Son of man, can these bones live?"

So I answered, "O Lord GOD, [a]You know."

4 Again He said to me, "Prophesy to these bones, and say to them, 'O dry bones, hear the word of the LORD! 5 Thus says the Lord GOD to these bones: "Surely I will [a]cause breath to enter into you, and you shall live. 6 I will put sinews on you and bring flesh upon you, cover you with skin and put breath in you; and you shall live. [a]Then you shall know that I *am* the LORD."'"

7 So I prophesied as I was commanded; and as I prophesied, there was a noise, and suddenly a rattling; and the bones came together, bone to bone. 8 Indeed, as I looked, the sinews and the flesh came upon them, and the skin covered them over; but *there was* no breath in them.

9 Also He said to me, "Prophesy to the breath, prophesy, son of man, and say to the breath, 'Thus says the Lord GOD: [a]"Come from the four winds, O breath, and breathe on these slain, that they may live."'" 10 So I prophesied as He commanded me, [a]and breath came into them, and they lived, and stood upon their feet, an exceedingly great army.

**36:33** [a] Ezek. 36:10 **36:35** [a] Joel 2:3 **36:36** [a] Ezek. 17:24; 22:14; 37:14 **36:37** [a] Ezek. 14:3; 20:3, 31 [b] Ezek. 36:10 **37:1** [a] Ezek. 1:3 [b] Ezek. 3:14; 8:3; 11:24 **37:3** [a] [1 Sam. 2:6] **37:5** [a] Ps. 104:29, 30 **37:6** [a] Joel 2:27; 3:17 **37:9** [a] [Ps. 104:30] **37:10** [a] Rev. 11:11

EZEKIEL 37:1–14

## THE BREATH OF GOD

36

STORY OF SCRIPTURE

### WHAT'S GOING ON?

This passage describes an epic, haunting vision of a valley filled with dry bones, lifeless and desolate, given to the prophet Ezekiel. God commanded Ezekiel to prophesy to those bones and as he did, they came together, grew flesh, and were covered with skin. Yet, they remained lifeless until God commanded Ezekiel to prophesy to the breath (or wind), and the breath of life entered them. This powerful vision symbolizes the restoration of Israel, promising rejuvenation and revival even from a state of hopelessness. But it also speaks to a more ancient and metaphysical truth: God's Spirit is called *ruach* in Hebrew, meaning "breath" or "wind." God's Spirit is the giver of life.

### WHAT DOES THIS MEAN FOR ME?

We were once dead in our trespasses but have been made alive in Christ (see Eph. 2:1). We were once like that valley of dry bones, lifeless and devoid of purpose. But when we receive God's Spirit, we become alive and effective for God's Kingdom. God's Spirit is meant to give you life and purpose!

### DID YOU CATCH THE PATTERN?

The Spirit of God is often compared to wind or breath. We see God's Spirit in Genesis when life was breathed into all living things, including humanity (see Gen. 2:7). After Jesus rose from the grave, He breathed on His disciples and said, "Receive the Holy Spirit" (John 20:22), and the Spirit descending at Pentecost was accompanied by a "rushing mighty wind" (Acts 2:2). The Bible also shows God's Spirit as the restorer and giver of life, from the creation story, where God brought order and life to a formless void (see Gen. 1:2) to the resurrection of Jesus Christ (see Rom. 8:11), which signifies ultimate victory over death.

*For the next* Story of Scripture *reading and devotion, turn to Daniel 6:1–28 on page 871.*

[11]Then He said to me, "Son of man, these bones are the [a]whole house of Israel. They indeed say, [b]'Our bones are dry, our hope is lost, and we ourselves are cut off!' [12]Therefore prophesy and say to them, 'Thus says the Lord GOD: "Behold, [a]O My people, I will open your graves and cause you to come up from your graves, and [b]bring you into the land of Israel. [13]Then you shall know that I *am* the LORD, when I have opened your graves, O My people, and brought you up from your graves. [14]I [a]will put My Spirit in you, and you shall live, and I will place you in your own land. Then you shall know that I, the LORD, have spoken *it* and performed *it*," says the LORD.' "

### *ONE KINGDOM, ONE KING*

[15]Again the word of the LORD came to me, saying, [16]"As for you, son of man, [a]take a stick for yourself and write on it: 'For Judah and for [b]the children of Israel, his companions.' Then take another stick and write on it, 'For Joseph, the stick of Ephraim, and *for* all the house of Israel, his companions.' [17]Then [a]join them one to another for yourself into one stick, and they will become one in your hand.

[18]"And when the children of your people speak to you, saying, [a]'Will you not show us what you *mean* by these?'— [19][a]say to them, 'Thus says the Lord GOD: "Surely I will take [b]the stick of Joseph, which *is* in the hand of Ephraim, and the tribes of Israel, his companions; and I will join them with it, with the stick of Judah, and make them one stick, and they will be one in My hand." ' [20]And the sticks on which you write will be in your hand [a]before their eyes.

[21]"Then say to them, 'Thus says the Lord GOD: "Surely [a]I will take the children of Israel from among the nations, wherever they have gone, and will gather them from every side and bring them into their own land; [22]and [a]I will make them one nation in the land, on the mountains of Israel; and [b]one king shall be king over them all; they shall no longer be two nations, nor shall they ever be divided into two kingdoms again. [23][a]They shall not defile themselves anymore with their idols, nor with their detestable things, nor with any of their transgressions; but [b]I will deliver them from all their dwelling places in which they have sinned, and will cleanse them. Then they shall be My people, and I will be their God.

[24][a]"David My servant *shall be* king over them, and [b]they shall all have one shepherd; [c]they shall also walk in My judgments and observe My statutes, and do them. [25][a]Then they shall dwell in the land that I have given to Jacob My servant, where your fathers dwelt; and they shall dwell there, they,

> **SEEING JESUS IN THE SCRIPTURE**
>
> **37:25** Jesus is the Prince God promised would reign over His people forever. This prophecy confused the people when Jesus claimed to be the Son of Man and that the Son of Man would be crucified (see John 12:34).

their children, and their children's children, [b]forever; and [c]My servant David *shall be* their prince forever. [26]Moreover I will make [a]a covenant of peace with them, and it shall be an everlasting covenant with them; I will establish them and [b]multiply them, and I will set My [c]sanctuary in their midst forevermore. [27][a]My tabernacle also shall be with them; indeed I will be [b]their God, and they shall be My people. [28][a]The nations also will know that I, the LORD, [b]sanctify Israel, when My sanctuary is in their midst forevermore." ' "

### *GOG AND ALLIES ATTACK ISRAEL*

**38** Now the word of the LORD came to me, saying, [2][a]"Son of man, [b]set your face against [c]Gog, of the land of [d]Magog, the prince of Rosh,[1] [e]Meshech, and Tubal, and prophesy against him, [3]and say, 'Thus says the Lord GOD: "Behold, I *am* against you, O Gog, the prince of Rosh, Meshech, and Tubal. [4][a]I will turn you around, put hooks into your jaws, and [b]lead you out, with all your army, horses, and horsemen, [c]all splendidly clothed, a great company *with* bucklers and shields, all of them handling swords. [5]Persia, Ethiopia,[1] and Libya[2] are with them, all of them *with* shield and helmet; [6][a]Gomer and all its troops; the house of [b]Togarmah *from* the far north and all its troops—many people *are* with you.

[7][a]"Prepare yourself and be ready, you and all your companies that are gathered about you; and be a guard for them. [8][a]After many days [b]you will be visited. In the latter years you will come into the land of those brought back from the sword [c]*and* gathered from many people on [d]the mountains of Israel, which had long been desolate; they were brought out of the nations, and now all of them [e]dwell safely. [9]You will ascend, coming [a]like a storm, covering the [b]land like a cloud, you and all your troops and many peoples with you."

[10]'Thus says the Lord GOD: "On that day it shall come to pass *that* thoughts will arise in your mind, and you will make an evil plan: [11]You will say, 'I will go up against a land of [a]unwalled villages; I will [b]go to a peaceful people, [c]who dwell safely, all of them dwelling without walls, and

**37:11** [a] Ezek. 36:10 [b] Ps. 141:7 **37:12** [a] Is. 26:19; 66:14 [b] Ezek. 36:24 **37:14** [a] Ezek. 36:27 **37:16** [a] Num. 17:2, 3 [b] 2 Chr. 11:12, 13, 16; 15:9; 30:11, 18 **37:17** [a] Hos. 1:11 **37:18** [a] Ezek. 12:9; 24:19 **37:19** [a] Zech. 10:6 [b] Ezek. 37:16, 17 **37:20** [a] Ezek. 12:3 **37:21** [a] Ezek. 36:24 **37:22** [a] Jer. 3:18 [b] Ezek. 34:23 **37:23** [a] Ezek. 36:25 [b] Ezek. 36:28, 29 **37:24** [a] Is. 40:11 [b] [John 10:16] [c] Ezek. 36:27 **37:25** [a] Ezek. 36:28 [b] Is. 60:21 [c] John 12:34 **37:26** [a] Is. 55:3 [b] Ezek. 36:10 [c] [2 Cor. 6:16] **37:27** [a] [John 1:14] [b] Ezek. 11:20 **37:28** [a] Ezek. 36:23 [b] Ezek. 20:12 **38:2** [a] Ezek. 39:1 [b] Ezek. 35:2, 3 [c] Rev. 20:8 [d] Gen. 10:2 [e] Ezek. 32:26 [1] Targum, Vulgate, and Aquila read *chief prince of* (also verse 3). **38:4** [a] 2 Kin. 19:28 [b] Is. 43:17 [c] Ezek. 23:12 **38:5** [1] Hebrew *Cush* [2] Hebrew *Put* **38:6** [a] Gen. 10:2 [b] Ezek. 27:14 **38:7** [a] Is. 8:9, 10 **38:8** [a] Is. 24:22 [b] Is. 29:6 [c] Ezek. 34:13 [d] Ezek. 36:1, 4 [e] Ezek. 34:25; 39:26 **38:9** [a] Is. 28:2 [b] Jer. 4:13 **38:11** [a] Zech. 2:4 [b] Jer. 49:31 [c] Ezek. 38:8

having neither bars nor gates'— 12 to take plunder and to take booty, to stretch out your hand against the waste places *that are again* inhabited, [a]and against a people gathered from the nations, who have acquired livestock and goods, who dwell in the midst of the land. 13 [a]Sheba, [b]Dedan, the merchants [c]of Tarshish, and all [d]their young lions will say to you, 'Have you come to take plunder? Have you gathered your army to take booty, to carry away silver and gold, to take away livestock and goods, to take great plunder?' " '

14 "Therefore, son of man, prophesy and say to Gog, 'Thus says the Lord GOD: [a]"On that day when My people Israel [b]dwell safely, will you not know *it?* 15 [a]Then you will come from your place out of the far north, you and many peoples with you, all of them riding on horses, a great company and a mighty army. 16 You will come up against My people Israel like a cloud, to cover the land. It will be in the latter days that I will bring you against My land, so that the nations may [a]know Me, when I am [b]hallowed in you, O Gog, before their eyes." 17 Thus says the Lord GOD: "Are *you* he of whom I have spoken in former days by My servants the prophets of Israel, who prophesied for years in those days that I would bring you against them?

### JUDGMENT ON GOG

18 "And it will come to pass at the same time, when Gog comes against the land of Israel," says the Lord GOD, "*that* My fury will show in My face. 19 For [a]in My jealousy [b]*and* in the fire of My wrath I have spoken: [c]'Surely in that day there shall be a great earthquake in the land of Israel, 20 so that [a]the fish of the sea, the birds of the heavens, the beasts of the field, all creeping things that creep on the earth, and all men who *are* on the face of the earth shall shake at My presence. [b]The mountains shall be thrown down, the steep places shall fall, and every wall shall fall to the ground.' 21 I will [a]call for [b]a sword against Gog throughout all My mountains," says the Lord GOD. [c]"Every man's sword will be against his brother. 22 And I will [a]bring him to judgment with [b]pestilence and bloodshed; [c]I will rain down on him, on his troops, and on the many peoples who *are* with him, flooding rain, [d]great hailstones, fire, and brimstone. 23 Thus I will magnify Myself and [a]sanctify Myself, [b]and I will be known in the eyes of many nations. Then they shall know that I *am* the LORD." '

### GOG'S ARMIES DESTROYED

39 "And [a]you, son of man, prophesy against Gog, and say, 'Thus says the Lord GOD: "Behold, I *am* against you, O Gog, the prince of Rosh,[1] Meshech, and Tubal; 2 and I will [a]turn you around and lead you on, [b]bringing you up from the far north, and bring you against the mountains of Israel. 3 Then I will knock the bow out of your left hand, and cause the arrows to fall out of your right hand. 4 [a]You shall fall upon the mountains of Israel, you and all your troops and the peoples who *are* with you; [b]I will give you to birds of prey of every sort and *to* the beasts of the field to be devoured. 5 You shall fall on the open field; for I have spoken," says the Lord GOD. 6 [a]"And I will send fire on Magog and on those who live in security in [b]the coastlands. Then they shall know that I *am* the LORD. 7 [a]So I will make My holy name known in the midst of My people Israel, and I will not *let them* [b]profane My holy name anymore. [c]Then the nations shall know that *I am* the LORD, the Holy One in Israel. 8 [a]Surely it is coming, and it shall be done," says the Lord GOD. "This *is* the day [b]of which I have spoken.

9 "Then those who dwell in the cities of Israel will go out and set on fire and burn the weapons, both the shields and bucklers, the bows and arrows, the javelins and spears; and they will make fires with them for seven years. 10 They will not take wood from the field nor cut down *any* from the forests, because they will make fires with the weapons; [a]and they will plunder those who plundered them, and pillage those who pillaged them," says the Lord GOD.

### THE BURIAL OF GOG

11 "It will come to pass in that day *that* I will give Gog a burial place there in Israel, the valley of those who pass by east of the sea; and it will obstruct travelers, because there they will bury Gog and all his multitude. Therefore they will call *it* the Valley of Hamon Gog.[1] 12 For seven months the house of Israel will be burying them, [a]in order to cleanse the land. 13 Indeed all the people of the land will be burying, and they will gain [a]renown for it on the day that [b]I am glorified," says the Lord GOD. 14 "They will set apart men regularly employed, with the help of a search party,[1] to pass through the land and bury those bodies remaining on the ground, in order [a]to cleanse it. At the end of seven months they will make a search. 15 The search party will pass through the land; and *when anyone* sees a man's bone, he shall set up a marker by it, till the buriers have buried it in the Valley of Hamon Gog. 16 *The* name of *the* city *will* also *be* Hamonah. Thus they shall [a]cleanse the land." '

**38:12** [a] Ezek. 38:8 **38:13** [a] Ezek. 27:22 [b] Ezek. 27:15, 20 [c] Ezek. 27:12 [d] Ezek. 19:3, 5 **38:14** [a] Is. 4:1 [b] Ezek. 38:8, 11 **38:15** [a] Ezek. 39:2 **38:16** [a] Ezek. 35:11 [b] Ezek. 28:22 **38:19** [a] Ezek. 36:5, 6 [b] Ps. 89:46 [c] Rev. 16:18 **38:20** [a] Hos. 4:3 [b] Jer. 4:24 **38:21** [a] Ps. 105:16 [b] Ezek. 14:17 [c] 1 Sam. 14:20 **38:22** [a] Is. 66:16 [b] Ezek. 5:17 [c] Ps. 11:6 [d] Rev. 16:21 **38:23** [a] Ezek. 36:23 [b] Ezek. 37:28; 38:16 **39:1** [a] Ezek. 38:2, 3 [1] Targum, Vulgate and Aquila read *chief prince of.* **39:2** [a] Ezek. 38:8 [b] Ezek. 38:15 **39:4** [a] Ezek. 38:4, 21 [b] Ezek. 33:27 **39:6** [a] Amos 1:4, 7, 10 [b] Ps. 72:10 **39:7** [a] Ezek. 39:25 [b] Lev. 18:21 [c] Ezek. 38:16 **39:8** [a] Rev. 16:17; 21:6 [b] Ezek. 38:17 **39:10** [a] Is. 14:2; 33:1 **39:11** [1] Literally *The Multitude of Gog* **39:12** [a] Deut. 21:23 **39:13** [a] Zeph. 3:19, 20 [b] Ezek. 28:22 **39:14** [a] Ezek. 39:12 [1] Literally *those who pass through* **39:16** [a] Ezek. 39:12

### *A TRIUMPHANT FESTIVAL*

17 "And as for you, son of man, thus says the
Lord GOD, [a]'Speak to every sort of bird and to
every beast of the field:

[b]"Assemble yourselves and come;
Gather together from all sides to My
[c]sacrificial meal
Which I am sacrificing for you,
A great sacrificial meal [d]on the mountains
of Israel,
That you may eat flesh and drink blood.
18 [a]You shall eat the flesh of the mighty,
Drink the blood of the princes of the
earth,
Of rams and lambs,
Of goats and bulls,
All of them [b]fatlings of Bashan.
19 You shall eat fat till you are full,
And drink blood till you are drunk,
At My sacrificial meal
Which I am sacrificing for you.
20 [a]You shall be filled at My table
With horses and riders,
[b]With mighty men
And with all the men of war," says the
Lord GOD.

### *ISRAEL RESTORED TO THE LAND*

21 [a]"I will set My glory among the nations;
all the nations shall see My judgment which I
have executed, and [b]My hand which I have laid
on them. 22 [a]So the house of Israel shall know
that I *am* the LORD their God from that day for-
ward. 23 [a]The Gentiles shall know that the house
of Israel went into captivity for their iniquity;
because they were unfaithful to Me, therefore
[b]I hid My face from them. I [c]gave them into the
hand of their enemies, and they all fell by the
sword. 24 [a]According to their uncleanness and
according to their transgressions I have dealt
with them, and hidden My face from them." '
25 "Therefore thus says the Lord GOD: [a]'Now
I will bring back the captives of Jacob, and have
mercy on the [b]whole house of Israel; and I will
be jealous for My holy name— 26 [a]after they have
borne their shame, and all their unfaithfulness in
which they were unfaithful to Me, when they [b]dwelt
safely in their *own* land and no one made *them*
afraid. 27 [a]When I have brought them back from the
peoples and gathered them out of their enemies'
lands, and I [b]am hallowed in them in the sight of
many nations, 28 [a]then they shall know that I *am*
the LORD their God, who sent them into captivity
among the nations, but also brought them back
to their land, and left none of them captive any
longer. 29 [a]And I will not hide My face from them
anymore; for I shall have [b]poured out My Spirit
on the house of Israel,' says the Lord GOD."

### *A NEW CITY, A NEW TEMPLE*

40 In the twenty-fifth year of our captivity,
at the beginning of the year, on the tenth
*day* of the month, in the fourteenth year after
[a]the city was captured, on the very same day
[b]the hand of the LORD was upon me; and He
took me there. 2 [a]In the visions of God He took
me into the land of Israel and [b]set me on a very
high mountain; on it toward the south *was*
something like the structure of a city. 3 He took
me there, and behold, *there was* a man whose
appearance *was* [a]like the appearance of bronze.
[b]He had a line of flax [c]and a measuring rod in
his hand, and he stood in the gateway.
4 And the man said to me, [a]"Son of man, look
with your eyes and hear with your ears, and fix
your mind on everything I show you; for you *were*
brought here so that I might show *them* to you.
[b]Declare to the house of Israel everything you
see." 5 Now there was [a]a wall all around the outside
of the temple.[1] In the man's hand was a measur-
ing rod six cubits *long, each being a* cubit and a
handbreadth; and he measured the width of the
wall structure, one rod; and the height, one rod.

### *THE EASTERN GATEWAY OF THE TEMPLE*

6 Then he went to the gateway which faced
[a]east; and he went up its stairs and measured
the threshold of the gateway, *which was* one rod
wide, and the other threshold *was* one rod wide.
7 Each gate chamber *was* one rod long and one
rod wide; between the gate chambers *was a space*
*of* five cubits; and the threshold of the gateway
by the vestibule of the inside gate *was* one rod.
8 He also measured the vestibule of the inside
gate, one rod. 9 Then he measured the vestibule
of the gateway, eight cubits; and the gateposts,
two cubits. The vestibule of the gate *was* on the
inside. 10 In the eastern gateway *were* three gate
chambers on one side and three on the other; the
three *were* all the same size; also the gateposts
were of the same size on this side and that side.
11 He measured the width of the entrance to
the gateway, ten cubits; *and* the length of the
gate, thirteen cubits. 12 *There was* a space in front
of the gate chambers, one cubit *on this side* and
one cubit on that side; the gate chambers *were*
six cubits on this side and six cubits on that side.
13 Then he measured the gateway from the roof
of *one* gate chamber to the roof of the other; the
width *was* twenty-five cubits, as door faces door.
14 He measured the gateposts, sixty cubits high,
and the court all around the gateway *extended*
to the gatepost. 15 *From* the front of the entrance

**39:17** [a] Rev. 19:17, 18 [b] Is. 18:6 [c] Zeph. 1:7 [d] Ezek. 39:4 **39:18** [a] Rev. 19:18 [b] Deut. 32:14 **39:20** [a] Ps. 76:5, 6 [b] Rev. 19:18 **39:21** [a] Ezek. 36:23; 38:23 [b] Ex. 7:4 **39:22** [a] Ex. 39:7, 28 **39:23** [a] Ezek. 36:18–20, 23 [b] Is. 1:15; 59:2 [c] Lev. 26:25 **39:24** [a] Ezek. 36:19 **39:25** [a] Ezek. 34:13; 36:24 [b] Hos. 1:11 **39:26** [a] Dan. 9:16 [b] Lev. 26:5, 6 **39:27** [a] Ezek. 28:25, 26 [b] Ezek. 36:23, 24; 38:16 **39:28** [a] Ezek. 34:30 **39:29** [a] Is. 54:8, 9 [b] [Joel 2:28] **40:1** [a] Ezek. 33:21 [b] Ezek. 1:3; 3:14, 22; 37:1 **40:2** [a] Ezek. 1:1; 3:14; 8:3; 37:1 [b] [Is. 2:2, 3]; Ezek. 17:23; 20:40; 37:22; [Mic. 4:1]; Rev. 21:10 **40:3** [a] Ezek. 1:7; Dan. 10:6; Rev. 1:15 [b] Ezek. 47:3; Zech. 2:1, 2 [c] Rev. 11:1; 21:15 **40:4** [a] Ezek. 44:5 [b] Ezek. 43:10 **40:5** [a] [Is. 26:1]; Ezek. 42:20 [1] Literally *house,* and so elsewhere in this book **40:6** [a] Ezek. 43:1

gate to the front of the vestibule of the inner gate *was* fifty cubits. 16 *There were* [a]beveled window *frames* in the gate chambers and in their intervening archways on the inside of the gateway all around, and likewise in the vestibules. *There were* windows all around on the inside. And on each gatepost *were* [b]palm trees.

### THE OUTER COURT

17 Then he brought me into [a]the outer court; and *there were* [b]chambers and a pavement made all around the court; [c]thirty chambers faced the pavement. 18 The pavement was by the side of the gateways, corresponding to the length of the gateways; *this was* the lower pavement. 19 Then he measured the width from the front of the lower gateway to the front of the inner court exterior, one hundred cubits toward the east and the north.

### THE NORTHERN GATEWAY

20 On the outer court was also a gateway facing north, and he measured its length and its width. 21 Its gate chambers, three on this side and three on that side, its gateposts and its archways, had the same measurements as the first gate; its length *was* fifty cubits and its width twenty-five cubits. 22 Its windows and those of its archways, and also its palm trees, *had* the same measurements as the gateway facing east; it was ascended by seven steps, and its archway *was* in front of it. 23 A gate of the inner court was opposite the northern gateway, just as the eastern *gateway;* and he measured from gateway to gateway, one hundred cubits.

### THE SOUTHERN GATEWAY

24 After that he brought me toward the south, and there a gateway was facing south; and he measured its gateposts and archways according to these same measurements. 25 *There were* windows in it and in its archways all around like those windows; its length *was* fifty cubits and its width twenty-five cubits. 26 Seven steps led up to it, and its archway *was* in front of them; and it had palm trees on its gateposts, one on this side and one on that side. 27 *There was* also a gateway on the inner court, facing south; and he measured from gateway to gateway toward the south, one hundred cubits.

### GATEWAYS OF THE INNER COURT

28 Then he brought me to the inner court through the southern gateway; he measured the southern gateway according to these same measurements. 29 Also its gate chambers, its gateposts, and its archways *were* according to these same measurements; *there were* windows in it and in its archways all around; *it was* fifty cubits long and twenty-five cubits wide. 30 *There were* archways all around, [a]twenty-five cubits long and five cubits wide. 31 Its archways faced the outer court, palm trees *were* on its gateposts, and going up to it *were* eight steps.

32 And he brought me into the inner court facing east; he measured the gateway according to these same measurements. 33 Also its gate chambers, its gateposts, and its archways *were* according to these same measurements; and *there were* windows in it and in its archways all around; *it was* fifty cubits long and twenty-five cubits wide. 34 Its archways faced the outer court, and palm trees *were* on its gateposts on this side and on that side; and going up to it *were* eight steps.

35 Then he brought me to the north gateway and measured *it* according to these same measurements— 36 also its gate chambers, its gateposts, and its archways. It had windows all around; its length *was* fifty cubits and its width twenty-five cubits. 37 Its gateposts faced the outer court, palm trees *were* on its gateposts on this side and on that side, and going up to it *were* eight steps.

### WHERE SACRIFICES WERE PREPARED

38 *There was* a chamber and its entrance by the gateposts of the gateway, where they [a]washed the burnt offering. 39 In the vestibule of the gateway *were* two tables on this side and two tables on that side, on which to slay the burnt offering, [a]the sin offering, and [b]the trespass offering. 40 At the outer side of the *vestibule,* as one goes up to the entrance of the northern gateway, *were* two tables; and on the other side of the vestibule of the gateway *were* two tables. 41 Four tables *were* on this side and four tables on that side, by the side of the gateway, eight tables on which they slaughtered *the sacrifices.* 42 *There were* also four tables of hewn stone for the burnt offering, one cubit and a half long, one cubit and a half wide, and one cubit high; on these they laid the instruments with which they slaughtered the burnt offering and the sacrifice. 43 Inside *were* hooks, a handbreadth wide, fastened all around; and the flesh of the sacrifices *was* on the tables.

### CHAMBERS FOR SINGERS AND PRIESTS

44 Outside the inner gate *were* the chambers for [a]the singers in the inner court, one facing south at the side of the northern gateway, and the other facing north at the side of the southern[1] gateway. 45 Then he said to me, "This chamber which faces south *is* for [a]the priests who have charge of the temple. 46 The chamber which faces north *is* for the priests [a]who have charge of the altar; these *are* the sons of [b]Zadok, from the sons of Levi, who come near the LORD to minister to Him."

**40:16** [a] 1 Kin. 6:4; Ezek. 41:16, 26 [b] 1 Kin. 6:29, 32, 35; 2 Chr. 3:5; Ezek. 40:22, 26, 31, 34, 37; 41:18–20, 25, 26 **40:17** [a] Ezek. 10:5; 42:1; 46:21; Rev. 11:2 [b] 1 Kin. 6:5; 2 Chr. 31:11; Ezek. 40:38 [c] Ezek. 45:5 **40:30** [a] Ezek. 40:21, 25, 33, 36 **40:38** [a] 2 Chr. 4:6 **40:39** [a] Lev. 4:2, 3 [b] Lev. 5:6; 6:6; 7:1 **40:44** [a] 1 Chr. 6:31, 32; 16:41–43; 25:1–7 [1] Following Septuagint; Masoretic Text and Vulgate read *eastern.* **40:45** [a] Lev. 8:35; Num. 3:27, 28, 32, 38; 18:5; 1 Chr. 9:23; 2 Chr. 13:11; Ps. 134:1 **40:46** [a] Lev. 6:12, 13; Num. 18:5; Ezek. 44:15 [b] 1 Kin. 2:35; Ezek. 43:19; 44:15, 16

### *DIMENSIONS OF THE INNER COURT AND VESTIBULE*
*(cf. 1 Kin. 7:14–22)*

47 And he measured the court, one hundred
cubits long and one hundred cubits wide, four-
square. The altar *was* in front of the temple.
48 Then he brought me to the [a]vestibule of the
temple and measured the doorposts of the ves-
tibule, five cubits on this side and five cubits on
that side; and the width of the gateway was three
cubits on this side and three cubits on that side.
49 [a]The length of the vestibule *was* twenty cubits,
and the width eleven cubits; and by the steps
which led up to it *there were* [b]pillars by the door-
posts, one on this side and another on that side.

### *DIMENSIONS OF THE SANCTUARY*

**41** Then he [a]brought me into the sanctuary[1]
and measured the doorposts, six cubits
wide on one side and six cubits wide on the other
side—the width of the tabernacle. 2 The width of
the entryway *was* ten cubits, and the side walls
of the entrance *were* five cubits on this side and
five cubits on the other side; and he measured its
length, forty cubits, and its width, twenty cubits.
3 Also he went inside and measured the
doorposts, two cubits; and the entrance, six
cubits *high;* and the width of the entrance, sev-
en cubits. 4 [a]He measured the length, twenty
cubits; and the width, twenty cubits, beyond
the sanctuary; and he said to me, "This *is* the
Most Holy *Place.*"

> **41:3–4** The floor plan of the temple Ezekiel saw is similar to the one Solomon used when he built the original temple and is much like the layout of the tabernacle. The temple in Ezekiel's vision has not been built.

### *THE SIDE CHAMBERS ON THE WALL*

5 Next, he measured the wall of the temple,
six cubits. The width of each side chamber all
around the temple *was* four cubits on every side.
6 [a]The side chambers *were* in three stories, one
above the other, thirty chambers in each story;
they rested on ledges which *were* for the side
chambers all around, that they might be support-
ed, but [b]not fastened to the wall of the temple.
7 As one went up from story to story, the side
chambers [a]became wider all around, because
their supporting ledges in the wall of the temple
ascended like steps; therefore the width of the
structure increased as one went up *from* the low-
est *story* to the highest by way of the middle one.
8 I also saw an elevation all around the temple;
it was the foundation of the side chambers, [a]a
full rod, *that is,* six cubits *high.* 9 The thickness
of the outer wall of the side chambers *was* five
cubits, and so also the remaining terrace by the
place of the side chambers of the temple. 10 And
between *it and* the *wall* chambers was a width
of twenty cubits all around the temple on every
side. 11 The doors of the side chambers opened
on the terrace, one door toward the north and
another toward the south; and the width of the
terrace *was* five cubits all around.

### *THE BUILDING AT THE WESTERN END*

12 The building that faced the separating
courtyard at its western end *was* seventy cubits
wide; the wall of the building *was* five cubits
thick all around, and its length ninety cubits.

### *DIMENSIONS AND DESIGN OF THE TEMPLE AREA*

13 So he measured the temple, one [a]hundred
cubits long; and the separating courtyard with
the building and its walls *was* one hundred cubits
long; 14 also the width of the eastern face of the
temple, including the separating courtyard, *was*
one hundred cubits. 15 He measured the length of
the building behind it, facing the separating court-
yard, with its [a]galleries on the one side and on
the other side, one hundred cubits, as well as the
inner temple and the porches of the court, 16 their
doorposts and [a]the beveled window frames. And
the galleries all around their three stories opposite
the threshold were paneled with [b]wood from the
ground to the windows—the windows were cov-
ered— 17 from the space above the door, even to
the inner room,[1] as well as outside, and on every
wall all around, inside and outside, by measure.
18 And *it was* made [a]with cherubim and [b]palm
trees, a palm tree between cherub and cherub.
*Each* cherub had two faces, 19 [a]so that the face of
a man *was* toward a palm tree on one side, and
the face of a young lion toward a palm tree on
the other side; thus *it was* made throughout the
temple all around. 20 From the floor to the space
above the door, and on the wall of the sanctuary,
cherubim and palm trees *were* carved.
21 The [a]doorposts of the temple *were* square,
*as was* the front of the sanctuary; their appear-
ance was similar. 22 [a]The altar *was* of wood, three
cubits high, and its length two cubits. Its corners,
its length, and its sides *were* of wood; and he said
to me, "This *is* [b]the table that *is* [c]before the LORD."
23 [a]The temple and the sanctuary had two
doors. 24 The doors had two [a]panels *apiece,* two
folding panels: two *panels* for one door and two
panels for the other *door.* 25 Cherubim and palm
trees *were* carved on the doors of the temple
just as they *were* carved on the walls. A wooden

**40:48** [a] 1 Kin. 6:3; 2 Chr. 3:4 **40:49** [a] 1 Kin. 6:3 [b] 1 Kin. 7:15–22; 2 Chr. 3:17; Jer. 52:17–23; [Rev. 3:12] **41:1** [a] Ezek. 40:2, 3, 17 [1] Hebrew *heykal,* here the main room of the temple, sometimes called the *holy place* (compare Exodus 26:33) **41:4** [a] 1 Kin. 6:20; 2 Chr. 3:8 **41:6** [a] 1 Kin. 6:5–10 [b] 1 Kin. 6:6, 10 **41:7** [a] 1 Kin. 6:8 **41:8** [a] Ezek. 40:5 **41:13** [a] Ezek. 40:47 **41:15** [a] Ezek. 42:3, 5 **41:16** [a] Ezek. 40:16, 25 [b] 1 Kin. 6:15 **41:17** [1] Literally *house,* here *the Most Holy Place* **41:18** [a] 1 Kin. 6:29 [b] Ezek. 40:16 **41:19** [a] Ezek. 1:10; 10:14 **41:21** [a] 1 Kin. 6:33 **41:22** [a] Ex. 30:1–3 [b] Ex. 25:23, 30 [c] Ex. 30:8 **41:23** [a] 1 Kin. 6:31–35 **41:24** [a] 1 Kin. 6:34

canopy *was* on the front of the vestibule outside.
26 *There were* [a]beveled window *frames* and palm
trees on one side and on the other, on the sides
of the vestibule—also on the side chambers of
the temple and on the canopies.

### THE CHAMBERS FOR THE PRIESTS

**42** Then he [a]brought me out into the outer
court, by the way toward the [b]north; and he
brought me into [c]the chamber which *was* opposite
the separating courtyard, and which *was* opposite
the building toward the north. 2 Facing the length,
*which was* one hundred cubits (the width was
fifty cubits), was the north door. 3 Opposite the
inner court of twenty *cubits,* and opposite the
[a]pavement of the outer court, *was* [b]gallery against
gallery in three *stories.* 4 In front of the chambers,
toward the inside, *was* a walk ten cubits wide, at
a distance of one cubit; and their doors faced
north. 5 Now the upper chambers *were* shorter,
because the galleries took away *space* from them
more than from the lower and middle stories of
the building. 6 For they *were* in three *stories* and
did not have pillars like the pillars of the courts;
therefore *the upper level* was shortened more than
the lower and middle levels from the ground up.
7 And a wall which *was* outside ran parallel to the
chambers, at the front of the chambers, toward
the outer court; its length *was* fifty cubits. 8 The
length of the chambers toward the outer court
*was* fifty cubits, whereas that facing the temple
*was* one [a]hundred cubits. 9 At the lower chambers
*was* the entrance on the east side, as one goes into
them from the outer court.
10 Also *there were* chambers in the thickness
of the wall of the court toward the east, oppo-
site the separating courtyard and opposite the
building. 11 [a]*There was* a walk in front of them
also, and their appearance *was* like the cham-
bers which *were* toward the north; they *were* as
long and as wide as the others, and all their exits
and entrances *were* according to plan. 12 And
corresponding to the doors of the chambers
that *were* facing south, as one enters them, *there
was* a door in front of the walk, the way directly
in front of the wall toward the east.
13 Then he said to me, "The north chambers
*and* the south chambers, which *are* opposite the
separating courtyard, *are* the holy chambers
where the priests who approach the LORD [a]shall
eat the most holy offerings. There they shall lay
the most holy offerings—[b]the grain offering, the
sin offering, and the trespass offering—for the
place *is* holy. 14 [a]When the priests enter them,
they shall not go out of the holy *chamber* into
the outer court; but there they shall leave their
garments in which they minister, for they *are*
holy. They shall put on other garments; then
they may approach *that* which *is* for the people."

### OUTER DIMENSIONS OF THE TEMPLE

15 Now when he had finished measuring the
inner temple, he brought me out through the
gateway that faces toward the [a]east, and mea-
sured it all around. 16 He measured the east side
with the measuring rod,[1] five hundred rods by
the measuring rod all around. 17 He measured the
north side, five hundred rods by the measuring
rod all around. 18 He measured the south side, five
hundred rods by the measuring rod. 19 He came
around to the west side *and* measured five hun-
dred rods by the measuring rod. 20 He measured
it on the four sides; [a]it had a wall all around, [b]five
hundred *cubits* long and five hundred wide, to
separate the holy areas from the common.

### THE TEMPLE, THE LORD'S DWELLING PLACE

**43** Afterward he brought me to the gate, the
gate [a]that faces toward the east. 2 [a]And
behold, the glory of the God of Israel came from
the way of the east. [b]His voice *was* like the sound
of many waters; [c]and the earth shone with His
glory. 3 *It was* [a]like the appearance of the vision
which I saw—like the vision which I saw when I[1]
came [b]to destroy the city. The visions *were* like
the vision which I saw [c]by the River Chebar; and
I fell on my face. 4 [a]And the glory of the LORD
came into the temple by way of the gate which
faces toward the east. 5 [a]The Spirit lifted me up
and brought me into the inner court; and behold,
[b]the glory of the LORD filled the temple.
6 Then I heard *Him* speaking to me from the
temple, while [a]a man stood beside me. 7 And He
said to me, "Son of man, *this is* [a]the place of My
throne and [b]the place of the soles of My feet,
[c]where I will dwell in the midst of the children
of Israel forever. [d]No more shall the house of
Israel defile My holy name, they nor their kings,
by their harlotry or with [e]the carcasses of their
kings on their high places. 8 [a]When they set their
threshold by My threshold, and their doorpost by
My doorpost, with a wall between them and Me,
they defiled My holy name by the abominations
which they committed; therefore I have con-
sumed them in My anger. 9 Now let them put their
harlotry and the carcasses of their kings far away
from Me, and I will dwell in their midst forever.
10 "Son of man, [a]describe the temple to the
house of Israel, that they may be ashamed of
their iniquities; and let them measure the pat-
tern. 11 And if they are ashamed of all that they
have done, make known to them the design
of the temple and its arrangement, its exits
and its entrances, its entire design and all its

**41:26** [a] Ezek. 40:16 **42:1** [a] Ezek. 41:1 [b] Ezek. 40:20 [c] Ezek. 41:12, 15 **42:3** [a] Ezek. 40:17 [b] Ezek. 41:15, 16; 42:5 **42:8** [a] Ezek. 41:13, 14 **42:11** [a] Ezek. 42:4 **42:13** [a] Lev. 6:16, 26; 24:9 [b] Lev. 2:3, 10; 6:14, 17, 25 **42:14** [a] Ezek. 44:19 **42:15** [a] Ezek. 40:6; 43:1 **42:16** [1] Compare 40:5 **42:20** [a] Ezek. 40:5 [b] Ezek. 45:2 **43:1** [a] Ezek. 10:19; 46:1 **43:2** [a] Ezek. 11:23 [b] Rev. 1:15; 14:2 [c] Rev. 18:1 **43:3** [a] Ezek. 1:4–28 [b] Jer. 1:10 [c] Ezek. 1:28; 3:23 [1] Some Hebrew manuscripts and Vulgate read *He.* **43:4** [a] Ezek. 10:19; 11:23 **43:5** [a] Ezek. 3:12, 14; 8:3 [b] 1 Kin. 8:10, 11 **43:6** [a] Ezek. 1:26; 40:3 **43:7** [a] Ps. 99:1 [b] 1 Chr. 28:2 [c] Joel 3:17 [d] Ezek. 39:7 [e] Lev. 26:30 **43:8** [a] Ezek. 8:3; 23:39; 44:7 **43:10** [a] Ezek. 40:4

[a]ordinances, all its forms and all its laws. Write *it* down in their sight, so that they may keep its whole design and all its ordinances, and [b]perform them. 12 This *is* the law of the temple: The whole area surrounding [a]the mountaintop *is* most holy. Behold, this *is* the law of the temple.

### DIMENSIONS OF THE ALTAR

13 "These are the measurements of the [a]altar in cubits [b](the cubit *is* one cubit and a handbreadth): the base one cubit high and one cubit wide, with a rim all around its edge of one span. This *is* the height of the altar: 14 from the base on the ground to the lower ledge, two cubits; the width of the ledge, one cubit; from the smaller ledge to the larger ledge, four cubits; and the width of the ledge, *one* cubit. 15 The altar hearth *is* four cubits high, with four [a]horns extending upward from the hearth. 16 The altar hearth *is* twelve *cubits* long, twelve wide, [a]square at its four corners; 17 the ledge, fourteen *cubits* long and fourteen wide on its four sides, with a rim of half a cubit around it; its base, one cubit all around; and [a]its steps face toward the east."

### CONSECRATING THE ALTAR

18 And He said to me, "Son of man, thus says the Lord GOD: 'These *are* the ordinances for the altar on the day when it is made, for sacrificing [a]burnt offerings on it, and for [b]sprinkling blood on it. 19 You shall give [a]a young bull for a sin offering to [b]the priests, the Levites, who are of the seed of [c]Zadok, who approach Me to minister to Me,' says the Lord GOD. 20 'You shall take some of its blood and put *it* on the four horns of the altar, on the four corners of the ledge, and on the rim around it; thus you shall cleanse it and make atonement for it. 21 Then you shall also take the bull of the sin offering, and [a]burn it in the appointed place of the temple, [b]outside the sanctuary. 22 On the second day you shall offer a kid of the goats without blemish for a sin offering; and they shall cleanse the altar, as they cleansed *it* with the bull. 23 When you have finished cleansing *it,* you shall offer a young bull without blemish, and a ram from the flock without blemish. 24 When you offer them before the LORD, [a]the priests shall throw salt on them, and they will offer them up *as* a burnt offering to the LORD. 25 Every day for [a]seven days you shall prepare a goat *for* a sin offering; they shall also prepare a young bull and a ram from the flock, both without blemish. 26 Seven days they shall make atonement for the altar and purify it, and so consecrate *it.* 27 [a]When these days are over it shall be, on the eighth day and thereafter, that the priests shall offer your burnt offerings and your peace offerings on the altar; and I will [b]accept you,' says the Lord GOD."

### THE EAST GATE AND THE PRINCE

**44** Then He brought me back to the outer gate of the sanctuary [a]which faces toward the east, but it *was* shut. 2 And the LORD said to me, "This gate shall be shut; it shall not be opened, and no man shall enter by it, [a]because the LORD God of Israel has entered by it; therefore it shall be shut. 3 *As for* the [a]prince, *because* he *is* the prince, he may sit in it to [b]eat bread before the LORD; he shall enter by way of the vestibule of the gateway, and go out the same way."

### THOSE ADMITTED TO THE TEMPLE

4 Also He brought me by way of the north gate to the front of the temple; so I looked, and [a]behold, the glory of the LORD filled the house of the LORD; [b]and I fell on my face. 5 And the LORD said to me, [a]"Son of man, mark well, see with your eyes and hear with your ears, all that I say to you concerning all the [b]ordinances of the house of the LORD and all its laws. Mark well who may enter the house and all who go out from the sanctuary.

6 "Now say to the [a]rebellious, to the house of Israel, 'Thus says the Lord GOD: "O house of Israel, [b]let Us have no more of all your abominations. 7 [a]When you brought in [b]foreigners, [c]uncircumcised in heart and uncircumcised in flesh, to be in My sanctuary to defile it—My house—and when you offered [d]My food, [e]the fat and the blood, then they broke My covenant because of all your abominations. 8 And you have not [a]kept charge of My holy things, but you have set *others* to keep charge of My sanctuary for you." 9 Thus says the Lord GOD: [a]"No foreigner, uncircumcised in heart or uncircumcised in flesh, shall enter My sanctuary, including any foreigner who *is* among the children of Israel.

### LAWS GOVERNING PRIESTS

10 [a]"And the Levites who went far from Me, when Israel went astray, who strayed away from Me after their idols, they shall bear their iniquity. 11 Yet they shall be ministers in My sanctuary, [a]*as* gatekeepers of the house and ministers of the house; [b]they shall slay the burnt offering and the sacrifice for the people, and [c]they shall stand before them to minister to them. 12 Because they ministered to them before their idols and [a]caused the house of Israel to fall into iniquity, therefore I have [b]raised My hand in an oath against them," says the Lord GOD, "that they shall bear their iniquity. 13 [a]And they shall not come near Me to minister to Me as priest, nor come near any of My holy things, nor into the Most Holy *Place;* but they

43:11 [a] Ezek. 44:5 [b] Ezek. 11:20 43:12 [a] Ezek. 40:2 43:13 [a] Ex. 27:1–8 [b] Ezek. 41:8 43:15 [a] Ex. 27:2 43:16 [a] Ex. 27:1 43:17 [a] Ex. 20:26 43:18 [a] Ex. 40:29 [b] Lev. 1:5, 11 43:19 [a] Lev. 8:14 [b] Ezek. 44:15, 16 [c] Ezek. 40:46 43:21 [a] Ex. 29:14 [b] Heb. 13:11 43:24 [a] Lev. 2:13 43:25 [a] Ex. 29:35 43:27 [a] Lev. 9:1–4 [b] Ezek. 20:40, 41 44:1 [a] Ezek. 43:1 44:2 [a] Ezek. 43:2–4 44:3 [a] Gen. 31:54 [b] Ezek. 46:2, 8 44:4 [a] Ezek. 3:23; 43:5 [b] Ezek. 1:28; 43:3 44:5 [a] Ezek. 40:4 [b] Ezek. 43:10, 11 44:6 [a] Ezek. 2:5 [b] 1 Pet. 4:3 44:7 [a] Acts 21:28 [b] Lev. 22:25 [c] Lev. 26:41 [d] Lev. 21:17 [e] Lev. 3:16 44:8 [a] Lev. 22:2 44:9 [a] Ezek. 44:7 44:10 [a] 2 Kin. 23:8 44:11 [a] 1 Chr. 26:1–19 [b] 2 Chr. 29:34; 30:17 [c] Num. 16:9 44:12 [a] Is. 9:16 [b] Ps. 106:26 44:13 [a] 2 Kin. 23:9

shall [b]bear their shame and their abominations
which they have committed. 14 Nevertheless I
will make them [a]keep charge of the temple, for
all its work, and for all that has to be done in it.
15 [a]"But the priests, the Levites, [b]the sons of
Zadok, who kept charge of My sanctuary [c]when
the children of Israel went astray from Me, they
shall come near Me to minister to Me; and they
[d]shall stand before Me to offer to Me the [e]fat
and the blood," says the Lord GOD. 16 "They shall
[a]enter My sanctuary, and they shall come near
[b]My table to minister to Me, and they shall keep
My charge. 17 And it shall be, whenever they enter
the gates of the inner court, that [a]they shall put
on linen garments; no wool shall come upon
them while they minister within the gates of the
inner court or within the house. 18 [a]They shall
have linen turbans on their heads and linen
trousers on their bodies; they shall not clothe
themselves with *anything that causes* sweat.
19 When they go out to the outer court, to the
outer court to the people, [a]they shall take off
their garments in which they have ministered,
leave them in the holy chambers, and put on
other garments; and in their holy garments
they shall [b]not sanctify the people.

> **44:17 Linen** cloth was hand-woven from the fibers of the flax plant and bleached snow-white to symbolize innocence and purity. Every part of the priest's uniform, from his headwear to his underwear, was made of white linen.

20 [a]"They shall neither shave their heads nor
let their hair grow [b]long, but they shall keep their
hair well trimmed. 21 [a]No priest shall drink wine
when he enters the inner court. 22 They shall not
take as wife a [a]widow or a divorced woman, but
take virgins of the descendants of the house of
Israel, or widows of priests.
23 "And [a]they shall teach My people *the differ-
ence* between the holy and the unholy, and cause
them to [b]discern between the unclean and the
clean. 24 [a]In controversy they shall stand as judges,
*and* judge it according to My judgments. They shall
keep My laws and My statutes in all My appointed
meetings, [b]and they shall hallow My Sabbaths.
25 "They shall not defile *themselves* by coming
near a dead person. Only for father or mother,
for son or daughter, for brother or unmarried
sister may they defile themselves. 26 [a]After he is
cleansed, they shall count seven days for him.
27 And on the day that he goes to the sanctuary to
minister in the sanctuary, [a]he must offer his sin
offering [b]in the inner court," says the Lord GOD.
28 "It shall be, in regard to their inheritance,
*that* I [a]*am* their inheritance. You shall give them
no [b]possession in Israel, for I *am* their posses-
sion. 29 [a]They shall eat the grain offering, the
sin offering, and the trespass offering; [b]every
dedicated thing in Israel shall be theirs. 30 The
[a]best of all firstfruits of any kind, and every
sacrifice of any kind from all your sacrifices,
shall be the priest's; also you [b]shall give to the
priest the first of your ground meal, [c]to cause
a blessing to rest on your house. 31 The priests
shall not eat anything, bird or beast, that [a]died
naturally or was torn *by wild beasts.*

### THE HOLY DISTRICT

**45** "Moreover, when you [a]divide the land by
lot into inheritance, you shall [b]set apart
a district for the LORD, a holy section of the
land; its length *shall be* twenty-five thousand
*cubits,* and the width ten thousand. It *shall be*
holy throughout its territory all around. 2 Of this
there shall be a square plot for the sanctuary,
[a]five hundred by five hundred *rods,* with fifty
cubits around it for an open space. 3 So this is
the district you shall measure: twenty-five thou-
sand *cubits* long and ten thousand wide; [a]in it
shall be the sanctuary, the Most Holy *Place.* 4 It
shall be [a]a holy *section* of the land, belonging
to the priests, the ministers of the sanctuary,
who come near to minister to the LORD; it shall
be a place for their houses and a holy place for
the sanctuary. 5 [a]*An area* twenty-five thousand
*cubits* long and ten thousand wide shall belong
to the Levites, the ministers of the temple; they
shall have [b]twenty chambers as a possession.[1]

### PROPERTIES OF THE CITY AND THE PRINCE

6 [a]"You shall appoint as the property of
the city *an area* five thousand *cubits* wide and
twenty-five thousand long, adjacent to the dis-
trict of the holy *section;* it shall belong to the
whole house of Israel.
7 [a]"The prince shall have *a section* on one side
and the other of the holy district and the city's
property; and bordering on the holy district
and the city's property, extending westward
on the west side and eastward on the east side,
the length *shall be* side by side with one of the
*tribal* portions, from the west border to the east
border. 8 The land shall be his possession in Is-
rael; and [a]My princes shall no more oppress My
people, but they shall give *the rest of* the land to
the house of Israel, according to their tribes."

**44:13** [b] Ezek. 32:30 **44:14** [a] Num. 18:4 **44:15** [a] Ezek. 40:46 [b] [1 Sam. 2:35] [c] Ezek. 44:10 [d] Deut. 10:8 [e] Ezek. 44:7 **44:16** [a] Num. 18:5, 7, 8 [b] Ezek. 41:22 **44:17** [a] Ex. 28:39–43; 39:27–29 **44:18** [a] Ex. 28:40; 39:28 **44:19** [a] Ezek. 42:14 [b] Lev. 6:27 **44:20** [a] Lev. 21:5 [b] Num. 6:5 **44:21** [a] Lev. 10:9 **44:22** [a] Lev. 21:7, 13, 14 **44:23** [a] Mal. 2:6–8 [b] Lev. 20:25 **44:24** [a] Deut. 17:8, 9 [b] Ezek. 22:26 **44:26** [a] Num. 6:10; 19:11, 13–19 **44:27** [a] Lev. 5:3, 6 [b] Ezek. 44:17 **44:28** [a] Num. 18:20 [b] Ezek. 45:4 **44:29** [a] Lev. 7:6 [b] Lev. 27:21, 28 **44:30** [a] Num. 3:13; 18:12 [b] Neh. 10:37 [c] [Mal. 3:10] **44:31** [a] Lev. 22:8 **45:1** [a] Ezek. 47:22 [b] Ezek. 48:8, 9 **45:2** [a] Ezek. 42:20 **45:3** [a] Ezek. 48:10 **45:4** [a] Ezek. 48:10, 11 **45:5** [a] Ezek. 48:13 [b] Ezek. 40:17 [1] Following Masoretic Text, Targum, and Vulgate; Septuagint reads *a possession, cities of dwelling.* **45:6** [a] Ezek. 48:15 **45:7** [a] Ezek. 48:21 **45:8** [a] [Is. 11:3–5]; Jer. 22:17; Ezek. 22:27

### *LAWS GOVERNING THE PRINCE*

9 'Thus says the Lord GOD: [a]"Enough, O princ-
es of Israel! [b]Remove violence and plundering,
execute justice and righteousness, and stop dis-
possessing My people," says the Lord GOD. 10 "You
shall have [a]honest scales, an honest ephah, and
an honest bath. 11 The ephah and the bath shall be
of the same measure, so that the bath contains
one-tenth of a homer, and the ephah one-tenth
of a homer; their measure shall be according to
the homer. 12 The [a]shekel *shall be* twenty gerahs;
twenty shekels, twenty-five shekels, *and* fifteen
shekels shall be your mina.

13 "This *is* the offering which you shall offer:
you shall give one-sixth of an ephah from a homer
of wheat, and one-sixth of an ephah from a homer
of barley. 14 The ordinance concerning oil, the bath
of oil, *is* one-tenth of a bath from a kor. *A kor is*
a homer or ten baths, for ten baths *are* a homer.
15 And one lamb shall be given from a flock of two
hundred, from the rich pastures of Israel. These
shall be for grain offerings, burnt offerings, and
peace offerings, [a]to make atonement for them,"
says the Lord GOD. 16 "All the people of the land
shall give this offering for the prince in Israel.
17 Then it shall be the [a]prince's part *to give* burnt
offerings, grain offerings, and drink offerings, at
the feasts, the New Moons, the Sabbaths, and at all
the appointed seasons of the house of Israel. He
shall prepare the sin offering, the grain offering,
the burnt offering, and the peace offerings to
make atonement for the house of Israel."

### *KEEPING THE FEASTS*

*(Ex. 12:1–20; Lev. 23:33–43)*

18 'Thus says the Lord GOD: "In the first
*month,* on the first *day* of the month, you shall
take a young bull without blemish and [a]cleanse
the sanctuary. 19 [a]The priest shall take some of
the blood of the sin offering and put *it* on the
doorposts of the temple, on the four corners of
the ledge of the altar, and on the gateposts of the
gate of the inner court. 20 And so you shall do
on the seventh *day* of the month [a]for everyone
who has sinned unintentionally or in ignorance.
Thus you shall make atonement for the temple.

21 [a]"In the first *month,* on the fourteenth day
of the month, you shall observe the Passover, a
feast of seven days; unleavened bread shall be
eaten. 22 And on that day the prince shall prepare
for himself and for all the people of the land [a]a
bull *for* a sin offering. 23 On the [a]seven days of
the feast he shall prepare a burnt offering to
the LORD, seven bulls and seven rams without
blemish, daily for seven days, [b]and a kid of the
goats daily *for* a sin offering. 24 [a]And he shall
prepare a grain offering of one ephah for each
bull and one ephah for each ram, together with
a hin of oil for each ephah.

25 "In the seventh *month,* on the fifteenth day
of the month, at the [a]feast, he shall do likewise
for seven days, according to the sin offering, the
burnt offering, the grain offering, and the oil."

### *THE MANNER OF WORSHIP*

46 "Thus says the Lord GOD: "The gateway of
the inner court that faces toward the east
shall be shut the six [a]working days; but on the
Sabbath it shall be opened, and on the day of
the New Moon it shall be opened. 2 [a]The prince
shall enter by way of the vestibule of the gateway
from the outside, and stand by the gatepost. The
priests shall prepare his burnt offering and his
peace offerings. He shall worship at the threshold
of the gate. Then he shall go out, but the gate shall
not be shut until evening. 3 Likewise the people
of the land shall worship at the entrance to this
gateway before the LORD on the Sabbaths and
the New Moons. 4 The burnt offering that [a]the
prince offers to the LORD on the [b]Sabbath day
*shall be* six lambs without blemish, and a ram
without blemish; 5 [a]and the grain offering *shall
be one* ephah for a ram, and the grain offering
for the lambs, as much as he wants to give, as
well as a hin of oil with every ephah. 6 On the day
of the New Moon *it shall be* a young bull without
blemish, six lambs, and a ram; they shall be with-
out blemish. 7 He shall prepare a grain offering
of an ephah for a bull, an ephah for a ram, as
much as he wants to give for the lambs, and a
hin of oil with every ephah. 8 [a]When the prince
enters, he shall go in by way of the vestibule of
the gateway, and go out the same way.

9 "But when the people of the land [a]come
before the LORD on the appointed feast days,
whoever enters by way of the north [b]gate to wor-
ship shall go out by way of the south gate; and
whoever enters by way of the south gate shall go
out by way of the north gate. He shall not return
by way of the gate through which he came, but
shall go out through the opposite gate. 10 The
prince shall then be in their midst. When they go

**45:21** On the day of the first **Passover**, God passed through the streets of Egypt, killing the firstborn in every house that was not marked with blood. Because God had warned the Israelites, directing them to smear blood on their doorposts, God "passed over" their homes and their firstborn were spared.

**45:9** [a] Ezek. 44:6 [b] Jer. 22:3; Zech. 8:16 **45:10** [a] Lev. 19:36; Deut. 25:15; Prov. 16:11; Amos 8:4–6; Mic. 6:10, 11 **45:12** [a] Ex. 30:13; Lev. 27:25; Num. 3:47 **45:15** [a] Lev. 1:4; 6:30 **45:17** [a] Ezek. 46:4–12 **45:18** [a] Lev. 16:16, 33; Ezek. 43:22, 26 **45:19** [a] Lev. 16:18–20; Ezek. 43:20 **45:20** [a] Lev. 4:27; Ps. 19:12 **45:21** [a] Ex. 12:18; Lev. 23:5, 6; Num. 9:2, 3; 28:16, 17; Deut. 16:1 **45:22** [a] Lev. 4:14 **45:23** [a] Lev. 23:8 [b] Num. 28:15, 22, 30; 29:5, 11, 16, 19 **45:24** [a] Num. 28:12–15; Ezek. 46:5, 7 **45:25** [a] Lev. 23:34; Num. 29:12; Deut. 16:13; 2 Chr. 5:3; 7:8, 10 **46:1** [a] Ex. 20:9 **46:2** [a] Ezek. 44:3 **46:4** [a] Ezek. 45:17 [b] Num. 28:9, 10 **46:5** [a] Num. 28:12; Ezek. 45:24; 46:7, 11 **46:8** [a] Ezek. 44:3; 46:2 **46:9** [a] Ex. 23:14–17; 34:23; Deut. 16:16, 17; Ps. 84:7; Mic. 6:6 [b] Ezek. 48:31, 33

in, he shall go in; and when they go out, he shall go out. 11 At the festivals and the appointed feast days [a]the grain offering shall be an ephah for a bull, an ephah for a ram, as much as he wants to give for the lambs, and a hin of oil with every ephah.

12 "Now when the prince makes a voluntary burnt offering or voluntary peace offering to the LORD, the gate that faces toward the east [a]shall then be opened for him; and he shall prepare his burnt offering and his peace offerings as he did on the Sabbath day. Then he shall go out, and after he goes out the gate shall be shut.

13 [a]"You shall daily make a burnt offering to the LORD *of* a lamb of the first year without blemish; you shall prepare it every morning. 14 And you shall prepare a grain offering with it every morning, a sixth of an ephah, and a third of a hin of oil to moisten the fine flour. This grain offering is a perpetual ordinance, to be made regularly to the LORD. 15 Thus they shall prepare the lamb, the grain offering, and the oil, *as* a [a]regular burnt offering every morning."

### THE PRINCE AND INHERITANCE LAWS

16 'Thus says the Lord GOD: "If the prince gives a gift *of some* of his inheritance to any of his sons, it shall belong to his sons; it is their possession by inheritance. 17 But if he gives a gift of some of his inheritance to one of his servants, it shall be his until [a]the year of liberty, after which it shall return to the prince. But his inheritance shall belong to his sons; it shall become theirs. 18 Moreover [a]the prince shall not take any of the people's inheritance by evicting them from their property; he shall provide an inheritance for his sons from his own property, so that none of My people may be scattered from his property." ' "

### HOW THE OFFERINGS WERE PREPARED

19 Now he brought me through the entrance, which *was* at the side of the gate, into the holy [a]chambers of the priests which face toward the north; and there a place *was* situated at their extreme western end. 20 And he said to me, "This *is* the place where the priests shall [a]boil the trespass offering and the sin offering, *and* where they shall [b]bake the grain offering, so that they do not bring *them* out into the outer court [c]to sanctify the people."

21 Then he brought me out into the outer court and caused me to pass by the four corners of the court; and in fact, in every corner of the court *there was another* court. 22 In the four corners of the court *were* enclosed courts, forty *cubits* long and thirty wide; all four corners *were* the same size. 23 *There was* a row *of building stones* all around in them, all around the four of them; and cooking hearths were made under the rows of stones all around. 24 And he said to me, "These *are* the kitchens where the ministers of the temple shall [a]boil the sacrifices of the people."

### THE HEALING WATERS AND TREES

47 Then he brought me back to the door of the temple; and there was [a]water, flowing from under the threshold of the temple toward the east, for the front of the temple faced east; the water was flowing from under the right side of the temple, south of the altar. 2 He brought me out by way of the north gate, and led me around on the outside to the outer gateway that faces [a]east; and there was water, running out on the right side.

3 And when [a]the man went out to the east with the line in his hand, he measured one thousand cubits, and he brought me through the waters; the water *came up to my* ankles. 4 Again he measured one thousand and brought me through the waters; the water *came up to my* knees. Again he measured one thousand and brought me through; the water *came up to my* waist. 5 Again he measured one thousand, *and it was* a river that I could not cross; for the water was too deep, water in which one must swim, a river that could not be crossed. 6 He said to me, "Son of man, have you seen *this?*" Then he brought me and returned me to the bank of the river.

7 When I returned, there, along the bank of the river, *were* very many [a]trees on one side and the other. 8 Then he said to me: "This water flows toward the eastern region, goes down into the valley, and enters the sea. *When it* reaches the sea, *its* waters are healed. 9 And it shall be *that* every living thing that moves, wherever the rivers go, will live. There will be a very great multitude of fish, because these waters go there; for they will be healed, and everything will live wherever the river goes. 10 It shall be *that* fishermen will stand by it from En Gedi to En Eglaim; they will be *places* for spreading their nets. Their fish will be of the same kinds as the fish [a]of the Great Sea, exceedingly many. 11 But its swamps and marshes will not be healed; they will be given over to salt. 12 [a]Along the bank of the river, on this side and that, will grow all *kinds of* trees used for food; [b]their leaves will not wither, and their fruit will not fail. They will bear fruit every month, because their water flows from the sanctuary. Their fruit will be for food, and their leaves for [c]medicine."

**47:8** The Dead **Sea** is unable to support fish or plant life. Its **water** is ten times saltier than ocean water. The idea of the Dead Sea one day supporting life is an incredible notion.

**46:11** [a] Ezek. 46:5, 7 **46:12** [a] Ezek. 44:3; 46:1, 2, 8 **46:13** [a] Ex. 29:38; Num. 28:3–5 **46:15** [a] Ex. 29:42; Num. 28:6 **46:17** [a] Lev. 25:10 **46:18** [a] Ezek. 45:8 **46:19** [a] Ezek. 42:13 **46:20** [a] 2 Chr. 35:13 [b] Lev. 2:4, 5, 7 [c] Ezek. 44:19 **46:24** [a] Ezek. 46:20 **47:1** [a] Ps. 46:4; Is. 30:25; 55:1; [Jer. 2:13]; Joel 3:18; Zech. 13:1; 14:8; [Rev. 22:1, 17] **47:2** [a] Ezek. 44:1, 2 **47:3** [a] Ezek. 40:3 **47:7** [a] [Is. 60:13, 21; 61:3; Ezek. 47:12; Rev. 22:2] **47:10** [a] Num. 34:3; Josh. 23:4; Ezek. 48:28 **47:12** [a] Ezek. 47:7; [Rev. 22:2] [b] Job 18:16; [Ps. 1:3; Jer. 17:8] [c] [Rev. 22:2]

### *BORDERS OF THE LAND*

*(cf. Num. 34:1–12)*

13 Thus says the Lord GOD: "These *are* the
[a]borders by which you shall divide the land as
an inheritance among the twelve tribes of Isra-
el. [b]Joseph *shall have two* portions. 14 You shall
inherit it equally with one another; for I [a]raised
My hand in an oath to give it to your fathers, and
this land shall [b]fall to you as your inheritance.

15 "This *shall be* the border of the land on
the north: from the Great Sea, *by* [a]the road to
Hethlon, as one goes to [b]Zedad, 16 [a]Hamath, [b]Be-
rothah, Sibraim (which *is* between the border of
Damascus and the border of Hamath), to Hazar
Hatticon (which *is* on the border of Hauran).
17 Thus the boundary shall be from the Sea to
[a]Hazar Enan, the border of Damascus; and as
for the north, northward, it is the border of Ha-
math. *This is* the north side.

18 "On the east side you shall mark out the
border from between Hauran and Damascus,
and between Gilead and the land of Israel, along
the Jordan, and along the eastern side of the
sea. *This is* the east side.

19 "The south side, toward the South,[1] *shall
be* from Tamar to [a]the waters of Meribah by
Kadesh, along the brook to the Great Sea. *This
is* the south side, toward the South.

20 "The west side *shall be* the Great Sea, from
the *southern* boundary until one comes to a
point opposite Hamath. This *is* the west side.

21 "Thus you shall [a]divide this land among
yourselves according to the tribes of Israel. 22 It
shall be that you will divide it by [a]lot as an in-
heritance for yourselves, [b]and for the strangers
who dwell among you and who bear children
among you. [c]They shall be to you as native-born
among the children of Israel; they shall have
an inheritance with you among the tribes of
Israel. 23 And it shall be *that* in whatever tribe
the stranger dwells, there you shall give *him* his
inheritance," says the Lord GOD.

### *DIVISION OF THE LAND*

**48** "Now these *are* the names of the tribes:
[a]From the northern border along the
road to Hethlon at the entrance of Hamath, to
Hazar Enan, the border of Damascus northward,
in the direction of Hamath, *there shall be* one
*section for* [b]Dan from its east to its west side; 2 by
the border of Dan, from the east side to the west,
one *section for* [a]Asher; 3 by the border of Asher,
from the east side to the west, one *section for*
[a]Naphtali; 4 by the border of Naphtali, from the
east side to the west, one *section for* [a]Manasseh;
5 by the border of Manasseh, from the east side
to the west, one *section for* [a]Ephraim; 6 by the
border of Ephraim, from the east side to the
west, one *section for* [a]Reuben; 7 by the border
of Reuben, from the east side to the west, one
*section for* [a]Judah; 8 by the border of Judah, from
the east side to the west, shall be [a]the district
which you shall set apart, twenty-five thousand
*cubits* in width, and *in* length the same as one
of the *other* portions, from the east side to the
west, with the [b]sanctuary in the center.

9 "The district that you shall set apart for
the LORD *shall be* twenty-five thousand *cubits* in
length and ten thousand in width. 10 To these—to
the priests—the holy district shall belong: on
the north twenty-five thousand *cubits in length,*
on the west ten thousand in width, on the east
ten thousand in width, and on the south twenty-
five thousand in length. The sanctuary of the
LORD shall be in the center. 11 [a]*It shall be* for the
priests of the sons of Zadok, who are sanctified,
who have kept My charge, who did not go astray
when the children of Israel went astray, [b]as the
Levites went astray. 12 And *this* district of land
that is set apart shall be to them a thing most
[a]holy by the border of the Levites.

13 "Opposite the border of the priests, the
[a]Levites *shall have an area* twenty-five thousand
*cubits* in length and ten thousand in width; its
entire length *shall be* twenty-five thousand and
its width ten thousand. 14 [a]And they shall not sell
or exchange any of it; they may not alienate this
best *part* of the land, for *it is* holy to the LORD.

15 [a]"The five thousand *cubits* in width that
remain, along the edge of the twenty-five
thousand, shall be [b]for general use by the city,
for dwellings and common-land; and the city
shall be in the center. 16 These *shall be* its mea-
surements: the north side four thousand five
hundred *cubits,* the south side four thousand
five hundred, the east side four thousand five
hundred, and the west side four thousand five
hundred. 17 The common-land of the city shall
be: to the north two hundred and fifty *cubits,* to
the south two hundred and fifty, to the east two
hundred and fifty, and to the west two hundred
and fifty. 18 The rest of the length, alongside the
district of the holy *section, shall be* ten thou-
sand *cubits* to the east and ten thousand to the
west. It shall be adjacent to the district of the
holy *section,* and its produce shall be food for
the workers of the city. 19 [a]The workers of the
city, from all the tribes of Israel, shall culti-
vate it. 20 The entire district *shall be* twenty-five
thousand *cubits* by twenty-five thousand *cubits,*
foursquare. You shall set apart the holy district
with the property of the city.

**47:13** [a] Num. 34:1–29 [b] Gen. 48:5; 1 Chr. 5:1; Ezek. 48:4, 5 **47:14** [a] Gen. 12:7; 13:15; 15:7; 17:8; 26:3; 28:13; Deut. 1:8; Ezek. 20:5, 6, 28, 42 [b] Ezek. 48:29 **47:15** [a] Ezek. 48:1 [b] Num. 34:7, 8 **47:16** [a] Num. 34:8 [b] 2 Sam. 8:8 **47:17** [a] Num. 34:9; Ezek. 48:1 **47:19** [a] Num. 20:13; Deut. 32:51; Ps. 81:7; Ezek. 48:28 [1] Hebrew *Negev* **47:21** [a] Ezek. 45:1 **47:22** [a] Num. 26:55, 56 [b] [Eph. 3:6; Rev. 7:9, 10] [c] [Acts 11:18; 15:9; Gal. 3:28; Eph. 2:12–14; Col. 3:11] **48:1** [a] Ezek. 47:15 [b] Josh. 19:40–48 **48:2** [a] Josh. 19:24–31 **48:3** [a] Josh. 19:32–39 **48:4** [a] Josh. 13:29–31; 17:1–11, 17, 18 **48:5** [a] Josh. 16:5–10; 17:8–10, 14–18 **48:6** [a] Josh. 13:15–23 **48:7** [a] Josh. 15:1–63; 19:9 **48:8** [a] Ezek. 45:1–6 [b] [Is. 12:6; 33:20–22]; Ezek. 45:3, 4 **48:11** [a] Ezek. 40:46; 44:15 [b] Ezek. 44:10, 12 **48:12** [a] Ezek. 45:4 **48:13** [a] Ezek. 45:5 **48:14** [a] Ex. 22:29; Lev. 27:10, 28, 33; Ezek. 44:30 **48:15** [a] Ezek. 45:6 [b] Ezek. 42:20 **48:19** [a] Ezek. 45:6

21 [a]"The rest *shall belong* to the prince, on
one side and on the other of the holy district
and of the city's property, next to the twenty-
five thousand *cubits* of the *holy* district as far
as the eastern border, and westward next to
the twenty-five thousand as far as the western
border, adjacent to the *tribal* portions; *it shall*
*belong* to the prince. It shall be the holy district,
[b]and the sanctuary of the temple *shall be* in the
center. 22 Moreover, apart from the possession of
the Levites and the possession of the city *which*
*are* in the midst of what *belongs* to the prince,
*the area* between the border of Judah and the
border of [a]Benjamin shall belong to the prince.
23 "As for the rest of the tribes, from the east
side to the west, Benjamin *shall have* one *section;*
24 by the border of Benjamin, from the east side
to the west, [a]Simeon *shall have* one *section;* 25 by
the border of Simeon, from the east side to the
west, [a]Issachar *shall have* one *section;* 26 by the
border of Issachar, from the east side to the west,
[a]Zebulun *shall have* one *section;* 27 by the border
of Zebulun, from the east side to the west, [a]Gad
*shall have* one *section;* 28 by the border of Gad,
on the south side, toward the South,[1] the border
shall be from Tamar *to* [a]the waters of Meribah
*by* Kadesh, along the brook to the [b]Great Sea.
29 [a]This *is* the land which you shall divide by lot
as an inheritance among the tribes of Israel,
and these *are* their portions," says the Lord GOD.

### *THE GATES OF THE CITY AND ITS NAME*

30 "These *are* the exits of the city. On the
north side, measuring four thousand five hun-
dred *cubits* 31 [a](the gates of the city *shall be* named
after the tribes of Israel), the three gates north-
ward: one gate for Reuben, one gate for Judah,
and one gate for Levi; 32 on the east side, four
thousand five hundred *cubits,* three gates: one
gate for Joseph, one gate for Benjamin, and one
gate for Dan; 33 on the south side, measuring
four thousand five hundred *cubits,* three gates:
one gate for Simeon, one gate for Issachar, and
one gate for Zebulun; 34 on the west side, four
thousand five hundred *cubits* with their three
gates: one gate for Gad, one gate for Asher, and
one gate for Naphtali. 35 All the way around *shall*
*be* eighteen thousand *cubits;* [a]and the name of
the city from *that* day *shall be:* [b]THE LORD *IS*
THERE."[1]

**48:21** [a] Ezek. 34:24; 45:7; 48:22 [b] Ezek. 48:8, 10 **48:22** [a] Josh. 18:21–28 **48:24** [a] Josh. 19:1–9 **48:25** [a] Josh. 19:17–23 **48:26** [a] Josh. 19:10–16 **48:27** [a] Josh. 13:24–28 **48:28** [a] Gen. 14:7; 2 Chr. 20:2; Ezek. 47:19 [b] Ezek. 47:10, 15, 19, 20 [1] Hebrew *Negev* **48:29** [a] Ezek. 47:14, 21, 22 **48:31** [a] [Rev. 21:10–14] **48:35** [a] Jer. 23:6; 33:16 [b] Is. 12:6; 14:32; 24:23; Jer. 3:17; 8:19; 14:9; Ezek. 35:10; Joel 3:21; Zech. 2:10; Rev. 21:3; 22:3 [1] Hebrew *YHWH Shammah*

*The Book of the Prophet*

# DANIEL

**AUTHOR**
Daniel

**KEY VERSE**
Daniel 9:7

**READING TIME**
1 hour 19 minutes

Daniel was deported to Babylon as a sixteen-year-old and handpicked for government service. He became God's prophetic mouthpiece to the Gentile and Jewish world, declaring God's present and eternal purposes. Nine of the twelve chapters in this book revolve around dreams, including God-given visions of trees, animals, and beasts. In both his personal experiences and prophetic visions, Daniel showed God's guidance, intervention, and power in the affairs of humanity.

**Occasion:** The Book of Daniel in part describes life during exile in Babylon and in part advances the prophecies of Israel's future.

**Main Point:** Daniel wrote to encourage the Israelites that God is sovereign over the nations, a message intended to bring comfort and hope to a people exiled in a foreign land.

**Big Ideas:** God controls the present and the future of every nation. We can trust that God has a plan and is working out that plan no matter what we face. We must obey God above any king or ruler. We are to take bold stands for God when we are able, no matter the cost.

## OUTLINE:

I. The Faith of Daniel and His Three Friends (ch. 1)
II. King Nebuchadnezzar's Dream (ch. 2)
III. Shadrach, Meshach, and Abed-Nego in the Furnace (ch. 3)
IV. Nebuchadnezzar's Humiliation (ch. 4)
V. The Writing on the Wall (ch. 5)
VI. Daniel in the Den of Lions (ch. 6)
VII. The Vision of the Four Beasts (ch. 7)
VIII. The Vision of the Ram and Goat (ch. 8)
IX. Daniel Prays for His People (ch. 9)
X. The Vision Beside the Tigris River (chs. 10–12)

**612 BC**
The Babylonians and Medes defeat Assyria

**605 BC**
Nebuchadnezzar rules in Babylon

**603 BC**
Daniel interprets the king's dream

**586 BC**
The Babylonians destroy Jerusalem

**c. 580 BC**
Shadrach, Meshach, and Abed-Nego survive the fiery furnace

**c. 550 BC**
Belshazzar assumes the throne

**539 BC**
Cyrus conquers Babylon

**538 BC**
The Jews are allowed to return to Jerusalem

**c. 537 BC**
Daniel thrown into the lions' den

### *DANIEL AND HIS FRIENDS OBEY GOD*

*(cf. 2 Kin. 24:10–17)*

**1** In the third year of the reign of [a]Jehoiakim king of Judah, Nebuchadnezzar king of Babylon came to Jerusalem and besieged it. 2 And the Lord gave Jehoiakim king of Judah into his hand, with [a]some of the articles of the house of God, which he carried [b]into the land of Shinar to the house of his god; [c]and he brought the articles into the treasure house of his god.

3 Then the king instructed Ashpenaz, the master of his eunuchs, to bring [a]some of the children of Israel and some of the king's descendants and some of the nobles, 4 young men [a]in whom *there was* no blemish, but good-looking, gifted in all wisdom, possessing knowledge and quick to understand, who *had* ability to serve in the king's palace, and [b]whom they might teach the language and literature of the Chaldeans. 5 And the king appointed for them a daily provision of the king's delicacies and of the wine which he drank, and three years of training for them, so that at the end of *that time* they might [a]serve before the king. 6 Now from among those of the sons of Judah were Daniel, Hananiah, Mishael, and Azariah. 7 [a]To them the chief of the eunuchs gave names: [b]he gave Daniel *the name* Belteshazzar; to Hananiah, Shadrach; to Mishael, Meshach; and to Azariah, Abed-Nego.

> **1:7 Daniel** means "God is my judge." **Belteshazzar** means "lady protect the king," referring to the goddess Sarpanitu, wife of the god Marduk. **Hananiah** means "the Lord is gracious." **Shadrach** means "I am fearful of the God." **Mishael** means "who is what God is?" **Meshach** means "I am of little account." **Azariah** means "the Lord has helped me." **Abed-Nego** means "servant of [the god] Nebo."

8 But Daniel purposed in his heart that he would not defile himself [a]with the portion of the king's delicacies, nor with the wine which he drank; therefore he requested of the chief of the eunuchs that he might not defile himself. 9 Now [a]God had brought Daniel into the favor and goodwill of the chief of the eunuchs. 10 And the chief of the eunuchs said to Daniel, "I fear my lord the king, who has appointed your food and drink. For why should he see your faces looking worse than the young men who *are* your age? Then you would endanger my head before the king."

11 So Daniel said to the steward[1] whom the chief of the eunuchs had set over Daniel, Hananiah, Mishael, and Azariah, 12 "Please test your servants for ten days, and let them give us vegetables to eat and water to drink. 13 Then let our appearance be examined before you, and the appearance of the young men who eat the portion of the king's delicacies; and as you see fit, *so* deal with your servants." 14 So he consented with them in this matter, and tested them ten days.

15 And at the end of ten days their features appeared better and fatter in flesh than all the young men who ate the portion of the king's delicacies. 16 Thus the steward took away their portion of delicacies and the wine that they were to drink, and gave them vegetables.

17 As for these four young men, [a]God gave them [b]knowledge and skill in all literature and wisdom; and Daniel had [c]understanding in all visions and dreams.

18 Now at the end of the days, when the king had said that they should be brought in, the chief of the eunuchs brought them in before Nebuchadnezzar. 19 Then the king interviewed[1] them, and among them all none was found like Daniel, Hananiah, Mishael, and Azariah; therefore [a]they served before the king. 20 [a]And in all matters of wisdom *and* understanding about which the king examined them, he found them ten times better than all the magicians *and* astrologers who *were* in all his realm. 21 [a]Thus Daniel continued until the first year of King Cyrus.

### *NEBUCHADNEZZAR'S DREAM*

**2** Now in the second year of Nebuchadnezzar's reign, Nebuchadnezzar had dreams; [a]and his spirit was *so* troubled that [b]his sleep left him. 2 [a]Then the king gave the command to call the magicians, the astrologers, the sorcerers, and the Chaldeans to tell the king his dreams. So they came and stood before the king. 3 And the king said to them, "I have had a dream, and my spirit is anxious to know the dream."

4 Then the Chaldeans spoke to the king in Aramaic,[1] [a]"O king, live forever! Tell your servants the dream, and we will give the interpretation."

5 The king answered and said to the Chaldeans, "My decision is firm: if you do not make known the dream to me, and its interpretation, you shall be [a]cut in pieces, and your houses shall be made an ash heap. 6 [a]However, if you tell the dream and its interpretation, you shall receive from me gifts, rewards, and great honor. Therefore tell me the dream and its interpretation."

7 They answered again and said, "Let the king tell his servants the dream, and we will give its interpretation."

**1:1** [a] 2 Kin. 24:1, 2 **1:2** [a] Jer. 27:19, 20 [b] Zech. 5:11 [c] 2 Chr. 36:7 **1:3** [a] Is. 39:7 **1:4** [a] Lev. 24:19, 20 [b] Acts 7:22 **1:5** [a] Dan. 1:19 **1:7** [a] 2 Kin. 24:17 [b] Dan. 2:26; 4:8; 5:12 **1:8** [a] Hos. 9:3 **1:9** [a] Gen. 39:21 **1:11** [1] Hebrew *Melzar,* also in verse 16 **1:17** [a] 1 Kin. 3:12, 28; 2 Chr. 1:10–12; [Luke 21:15; James 1:5–7] [b] Acts 7:22 [c] Num. 12:6; 2 Chr. 26:5; Dan. 5:11, 12, 14; 10:1 **1:19** [a] Gen. 41:46; [Prov. 22:29]; Dan. 1:5 [1] Literally *talked with them* **1:20** [a] 1 Kin. 10:1 **1:21** [a] Dan. 6:28; 10:1 **2:1** [a] Gen. 40:5–8; 41:1, 8; Job 33:15–17; Dan. 2:3; 4:5 [b] Esth. 6:1; Dan. 6:18 **2:2** [a] Gen. 41:8; Ex. 7:11; Is. 47:12, 13; Dan. 1:20; 2:10, 27; 4:6; 5:7 **2:4** [a] 1 Kin. 1:31; Dan. 3:9; 5:10; 6:6, 21 [1] The original language of Daniel 2:4b through 7:28 is Aramaic. **2:5** [a] 2 Kin. 10:27; Ezra 6:11; Dan. 3:29 **2:6** [a] Dan. 5:16

8 The king answered and said, "I know for
certain that you would gain time, because you
see that my decision is firm: 9 if you do not make
known the dream to me, *there is only* one decree
for you! For you have agreed to speak lying
and corrupt words before me till the time has
changed. Therefore tell me the dream, and I shall
know that you can give me its interpretation."
10 The Chaldeans answered the king, and
said, "There is not a man on earth who can tell
the king's matter; therefore no king, lord, or
ruler has *ever* asked such things of any magician,
astrologer, or Chaldean. 11 *It is* a difficult thing
that the king requests, and there is no other who
can tell it to the king [a]except the gods, whose
dwelling is not with flesh."
12 For this reason the king was angry and very
furious, and gave the command to destroy all the
wise *men* of Babylon. 13 So the decree went out,
and they began killing the wise *men;* and they
sought [a]Daniel and his companions, to kill *them.*

### GOD REVEALS NEBUCHADNEZZAR'S DREAM

14 Then with counsel and wisdom Daniel
answered Arioch, the captain of the king's guard,
who had gone out to kill the wise *men* of Babylon;
15 he answered and said to Arioch the king's cap-
tain, "Why is the decree from the king so urgent?"
Then Arioch made the decision known to Daniel.
16 So Daniel went in and asked the king to
give him time, that he might tell the king the
interpretation. 17 Then Daniel went to his house,
and made the decision known to Hananiah,
Mishael, and Azariah, his companions, 18 [a]that
they might seek mercies from the God of heaven
concerning this secret, so that Daniel and his
companions might not perish with the rest of
the wise *men* of Babylon. 19 Then the secret was
revealed to Daniel [a]in a night vision. So Daniel
blessed the God of heaven.
20 Daniel answered and said:

[a]"Blessed be the name of God forever and
ever,
[b]For wisdom and might are His.
21 And He changes [a]the times and the
seasons;
[b]He removes kings and raises up kings;
[c]He gives wisdom to the wise
And knowledge to those who have
understanding.
22 [a]He reveals deep and secret things;
[b]He knows what *is* in the darkness,
And [c]light dwells with Him.

23 "I thank You and praise You,
O God of my fathers;
You have given me wisdom and might,
And have now made known to me what
we [a]asked of You,
For You have made known to us the king's
demand."

### DANIEL EXPLAINS THE DREAM

24 Therefore Daniel went to Arioch, whom the
king had appointed to destroy the wise *men* of
Babylon. He went and said thus to him: "Do not
destroy the wise *men* of Babylon; take me before
the king, and I will tell the king the interpretation."
25 Then Arioch quickly brought Daniel be-
fore the king, and said thus to him, "I have found
a man of the captives[1] of Judah, who will make
known to the king the interpretation."
26 The king answered and said to Daniel,
whose name *was* Belteshazzar, "Are you able
to make known to me the dream which I have
seen, and its interpretation?"
27 Daniel answered in the presence of the king,
and said, "The secret which the king has demanded,
the wise *men,* the astrologers, the magicians, and
the soothsayers cannot declare to the king. 28 [a]But
there is a God in heaven who reveals secrets, and
He has made known to King Nebuchadnezzar
[b]what will be in the latter days. Your dream, and
the visions of your head upon your bed, were these:
29 As for you, O king, thoughts came *to* your *mind*
*while* on your bed, *about* what would come to pass
after this; [a]and He who reveals secrets has made
known to you what will be. 30 [a]But as for me, this
secret has not been revealed to me because I have
more wisdom than anyone living, but for *our* sakes
who make known the interpretation to the king,
[b]and that you may know the thoughts of your heart.
31 "You, O king, were watching; and behold, a
great image! This great image, whose splendor
*was* excellent, stood before you; and its form *was*
awesome. 32 [a]This image's head *was* of fine gold,
its chest and arms of silver, its belly and thighs[1] of
bronze, 33 its legs of iron, its feet partly of iron and
partly of clay.[1] 34 You watched while a stone was cut
out [a]without hands, which struck the image on its
feet of iron and clay, and broke them in pieces.
35 [a]Then the iron, the clay, the bronze, the silver,
and the gold were crushed together, and became
[b]like chaff from the summer threshing floors; the
wind carried them away so that [c]no trace of them
was found. And the stone that struck the image [d]be-
came a great mountain [e]and filled the whole earth.
36 "This *is* the dream. Now we will tell the in-
terpretation of it before the king. 37 [a]You, O king,
*are* a king of kings. [b]For the God of heaven has
given you a kingdom, power, strength, and glo-
ry; 38 [a]and wherever the children of men dwell,
or the beasts of the field and the birds of the
heaven, He has given *them* into your hand, and
has made you ruler over them all—[b]you *are* this

2:11 [a] Gen. 41:39; Dan. 5:11 2:13 [a] Dan. 1:19, 20 2:18 [a] [Matt. 18:19] 2:19 [a] Job 33:15 2:20 [a] Ps. 113:2 [b] [Jer. 32:19] 2:21 [a] Esth. 1:13 [b] [Ps. 75:6, 7] [c] [James 1:5] 2:22 [a] Ps. 25:14 [b] [Heb. 4:13] [c] Dan. 5:11, 14 2:23 [a] Dan. 2:18, 29, 30 2:25 [1] Literally *of the sons of the captivity* 2:28 [a] Gen. 40:8 [b] Gen. 49:1 2:29 [a] [Dan. 2:22, 28] 2:30 [a] Acts 3:12 [b] Dan. 2:47 2:32 [a] Dan. 2:38, 45 [1] Or *sides* 2:33 [1] Or *baked clay,* and so in verses 34, 35, and 42 2:34 [a] [Zech. 4:6] 2:35 [a] [Rev. 16:14] [b] Hos. 13:3 [c] Ps. 37:10, 36 [d] [Is. 2:2, 3] [e] Ps. 80:9 2:37 [a] Jer. 27:6, 7 [b] Ezra 1:2 2:38 [a] Dan. 4:21, 22 [b] Dan. 2:32

**2:31–45** The first worldwide empire, the **head of gold**, was Babylon. The second empire, the **chest and arms of silver**, was Medo-Persia. Just as silver is inferior to gold, Medo-Persia was inferior to Babylon, not in size but in its effectiveness in governing its people. The third kingdom of a **belly and thighs of bronze** would be the Greek Empire. The fourth kingdom, the **legs of iron**, is the only one not specifically identified within the Book of Daniel. Rome is the most likely choice, for it succeeded Greece, and was certainly a very strong empire. This kingdom being divided likely refers to the Roman Empire's decline when the kingdom was split in two in the early centuries after Christ. The **kingdom which shall never be destroyed**, obviously the kingdom of God, is a spiritual kingdom introduced by Christ at His first coming, and the **mountain** that grew from the rock would be a reference to the spread of Christianity, which eventually was named the state religion of the Roman Empire.

head of gold. 39 But after you shall arise [a]another
kingdom [b]inferior to yours; then another, a
third kingdom of bronze, which shall rule over
all the earth. 40 And [a]the fourth kingdom shall
be as strong as iron, inasmuch as iron breaks
in pieces and shatters everything; and like iron
that crushes, *that kingdom* will break in pieces
and crush all the others. 41 Whereas you saw the
feet and toes, partly of potter's clay and partly
of iron, the kingdom shall be divided; yet the
strength of the iron shall be in it, just as you saw
the iron mixed with ceramic clay. 42 And *as* the
toes of the feet *were* partly of iron and partly
of clay, [a]*so* the kingdom shall be partly strong
and partly fragile. 43 As you saw iron mixed with
ceramic clay, they will mingle with the seed of
men; but they will not adhere to one another,
just as iron does not mix with clay. 44 And in the
days of these kings [a]the God of heaven will set up

### SEEING JESUS IN THE SCRIPTURE

**2:44** All earthly kingdoms come and go, but God's kingdom is eternal. Jesus is the King of kings who presently rules over His people. One day when Jesus returns, His kingdom will be complete (see 1 Cor. 15:24).

a kingdom [b]which shall never be destroyed; and
the kingdom shall not be left to other people;
[c]it shall break in pieces and consume all these
kingdoms, and it shall stand forever. 45 [a]Inasmuch
as you saw that the stone was cut out of
the mountain without hands, and that it broke
in pieces the iron, the bronze, the clay, the silver,
and the gold—the great God has made known
to the king what will come to pass after this. The
dream is certain, and its interpretation is sure."

### DANIEL AND HIS FRIENDS PROMOTED

46 [a]Then King Nebuchadnezzar fell on his
face, prostrate before Daniel, and commanded
that they should present an offering [b]and incense
to him. 47 The king answered Daniel, and
said, "Truly [a]your God *is* the God of [b]gods, the
Lord of kings, and a revealer of secrets, since
you could reveal this secret." 48 [a]Then the king
promoted Daniel [b]and gave him many great gifts;
and he made him ruler over the whole province
of Babylon, and [c]chief administrator over all the
wise *men* of Babylon. 49 Also Daniel petitioned
the king, [a]and he set Shadrach, Meshach, and
Abed-Nego over the affairs of the province of
Babylon; but Daniel [b]*sat* in the gate[1] of the king.

### THE IMAGE OF GOLD

3 Nebuchadnezzar the king made an image
of gold, whose height *was* sixty cubits *and*
its width six cubits. He set it up in the plain of
Dura, in the province of Babylon. 2 And King
Nebuchadnezzar sent *word* to gather together
the satraps, the administrators, the governors,
the counselors, the treasurers, the judges, the
magistrates, and all the officials of the provinces,
to come to the dedication of the image
which King Nebuchadnezzar had set up. 3 So
the satraps, the administrators, the governors,
the counselors, the treasurers, the judges, the
magistrates, and all the officials of the provinces
gathered together for the dedication of the image
that King Nebuchadnezzar had set up; and they
stood before the image that Nebuchadnezzar had
set up. 4 Then a herald cried aloud: "To you it is
commanded, [a]O peoples, nations, and languages,
5 *that* at the time you hear the sound of the horn,
flute, harp, lyre, *and* psaltery, in symphony with
all kinds of music, you shall fall down and worship
the gold image that King Nebuchadnezzar
has set up; 6 and whoever does not fall down
and worship shall [a]be cast immediately into the
midst of a burning fiery furnace."
7 So at that time, when all the people heard the
sound of the horn, flute, harp, *and* lyre, in symphony
with all kinds of music, all the people, nations,
and languages fell down *and* worshiped the gold
image which King Nebuchadnezzar had set up.

**2:39** [a] Dan. 5:28, 31 [b] Dan. 2:32 **2:40** [a] Dan. 7:7, 23 **2:42** [a] Dan. 7:24 **2:44** [a] Dan. 2:28, 37 [b] Is. 9:6, 7; Ezek. 37:25; Dan. 4:3, 34; 6:26; 7:14, 27; Mic. 4:7; [Luke 1:32, 33] [c] Ps. 2:9; Is. 60:12; Dan. 2:34, 35; [1 Cor. 15:24] **2:45** [a] Dan. 2:35; Is. 28:16 **2:46** [a] Dan. 3:5, 7; Acts 10:25; 14:13; Rev. 19:10; 22:8 [b] Lev. 26:31; Ezra 6:10 **2:47** [a] Dan. 3:28, 29; 4:34–37 [b] [Deut. 10:17] **2:48** [a] [Prov. 14:35; 21:1] [b] Dan. 2:6 [c] Dan. 4:9; 5:11 **2:49** [a] Dan. 1:7; 3:12 [b] Esth. 2:19, 21; 3:2 [1] That is, the king's court **3:4** [a] Dan. 4:1; 6:25 **3:6** [a] Jer. 29:22; Ezek. 22:18–22; Matt. 13:42, 50; Rev. 9:2; 13:15; 14:11

### *DANIEL'S FRIENDS DISOBEY THE KING*

8 Therefore at that time certain Chaldeans [a]came forward and accused the Jews. 9 They spoke and said to King Nebuchadnezzar, [a]"O king, live forever! 10 You, O king, have made a decree that everyone who hears the sound of the horn, flute, harp, lyre, *and* psaltery, in symphony with all kinds of music, shall fall down and worship the gold image; 11 and whoever does not fall down and worship shall be cast into the midst of a burning fiery furnace. 12 [a]There are certain Jews whom you have set over the affairs of the province of Babylon: Shadrach, Meshach, and Abed-Nego; these men, O king, have [b]not paid due regard to you. They do not serve your gods or worship the gold image which you have set up."

13 Then Nebuchadnezzar, in [a]rage and fury, gave the command to bring Shadrach, Meshach, and Abed-Nego. So they brought these men before the king. 14 Nebuchadnezzar spoke, saying to them, "*Is it* true, Shadrach, Meshach, and Abed-Nego, *that* you do not serve my gods or worship the gold image which I have set up? 15 Now if you are ready at the time you hear the sound of the horn, flute, harp, lyre, *and* psaltery, in symphony with all kinds of music, and you fall down and worship the image which I have made, [a]*good!* But if you do not worship, you shall be cast immediately into the midst of a burning fiery furnace. [b]And who *is* the god who will deliver you from my hands?"

16 Shadrach, Meshach, and Abed-Nego answered and said to the king, "O Nebuchadnezzar, [a]we have no need to answer you in this matter. 17 If that *is the case,* our [a]God whom we serve is able to [b]deliver us from the burning fiery furnace, and He will deliver *us* from your hand, O king. 18 But if not, let it be known to you, O king, that we do not serve your gods, nor will we [a]worship the gold image which you have set up."

### *SAVED IN FIERY TRIAL*

19 Then Nebuchadnezzar was full of fury, and the expression on his face changed toward Shadrach, Meshach, and Abed-Nego. He spoke and commanded that they heat the furnace seven times more than it was usually heated. 20 And he commanded certain mighty men of valor who *were* in his army to bind Shadrach, Meshach, and Abed-Nego, *and* cast *them* into the burning fiery furnace. 21 Then these men were bound in their coats, their trousers, their turbans, and their *other* garments, and were cast into the midst of the burning fiery furnace. 22 Therefore, because the king's command was urgent, and the furnace exceedingly hot, the flame of the fire killed those men who took up Shadrach, Meshach, and Abed-Nego. 23 And these three men, Shadrach, Meshach, and Abed-Nego, fell down bound into the midst of the burning fiery furnace.

24 Then King Nebuchadnezzar was astonished; and he rose in haste *and* spoke, saying to his counselors, "Did we not cast three men bound into the midst of the fire?"

They answered and said to the king, "True, O king."

25 "Look!" he answered, "I see four men loose, [a]walking in the midst of the fire; and they are not hurt, and the form of the fourth is like [b]the Son of God."[1]

**SEEING JESUS IN THE SCRIPTURE**

**3:25** The fourth person in the fire may have been Jesus, making an earthly appearance before the Incarnation. Jesus walking in the fire of King Nebuchadnezzar's judgment points to what He did on the cross: walking through God's judgment on our behalf (see John 13:36).

### *NEBUCHADNEZZAR PRAISES GOD*

26 Then Nebuchadnezzar went near the mouth of the burning fiery furnace *and* spoke, saying, "Shadrach, Meshach, and Abed-Nego, servants of the [a]Most High God, come out, and come *here.*" Then Shadrach, Meshach, and Abed-Nego came from the midst of the fire. 27 And the satraps, administrators, governors, and the king's counselors gathered together, and they saw these men [a]on whose bodies the fire had no power; the hair of their head was not singed nor were their garments affected, and the smell of fire was not on them.

28 Nebuchadnezzar spoke, saying, "Blessed be the God of Shadrach, Meshach, and Abed-Nego, who sent His [a]Angel[1] and delivered His servants who trusted in Him, and they have frustrated the king's word, and yielded their bodies, that they should not serve nor worship any god except their own God! 29 [a]Therefore I make a decree that any people, nation, or language which speaks anything amiss against the [b]God of Shadrach, Meshach, and Abed-Nego shall be [c]cut in pieces, and their houses shall be made an ash heap; [d]because there is no other God who can deliver like this."

30 Then the king promoted Shadrach, Meshach, and Abed-Nego in the province of Babylon.

**3:8** [a] Ezra 4:12–16; Esth. 3:8, 9; Dan. 6:12, 13 **3:9** [a] Dan. 2:4; 5:10; 6:6, 21 **3:12** [a] Dan. 2:49 [b] Dan. 1:8; 6:12, 13 **3:13** [a] Dan. 2:12; 3:19 **3:15** [a] Ex. 32:32; Luke 13:9 [b] Ex. 5:2; 2 Kin. 18:35; Is. 36:18–20; Dan. 2:47 **3:16** [a] [Matt. 10:19] **3:17** [a] Job 5:19; [Ps. 27:1, 2; Is. 26:3, 4]; Jer. 1:8; 15:20, 21; Dan. 6:19–22 [b] 1 Sam. 17:37; Jer. 1:8; 15:20, 21; 42:11; Dan. 6:16, 19–22; Mic. 7:7; 2 Cor. 1:10 **3:18** [a] Job 13:15 **3:25** [a] [Ps. 91:3–9]; Is. 43:2 [b] Job 1:6; 38:7; [Ps. 34:7]; Dan. 3:28 [1] Or *a son of the gods* **3:26** [a] [Dan. 4:2, 3, 17, 34, 35] **3:27** [a] [Is. 43:2]; Heb. 11:34 **3:28** [a] [Ps. 34:7, 8]; Is. 37:36; [Jer. 17:7]; Dan. 6:22, 23; Acts 5:19; 12:7 [1] Or *angel* **3:29** [a] Dan. 6:26 [b] Dan. 2:46, 47; 4:34–37 [c] Ezra 6:11; Dan. 2:5 [d] Dan. 6:27

### *NEBUCHADNEZZAR'S SECOND DREAM*

4 Nebuchadnezzar the king,

[a]To all peoples, nations, and languages
that dwell in all the earth:

Peace be multiplied to you.

2 I thought it good to declare the signs and
wonders [a]that the Most High God has
worked for me.

3 [a]How great *are* His signs,
And how mighty His wonders!
His kingdom *is* [b]an everlasting kingdom,
And His dominion *is* from generation to
generation.

4 I, Nebuchadnezzar, was at rest in my
house, and flourishing in my palace. 5 I
saw a dream which made me afraid, [a]and
the thoughts on my bed and the visions
of my head [b]troubled me. 6 Therefore I
issued a decree to bring in all the wise *men*
of Babylon before me, that they might
make known to me the interpretation
of the dream. 7 [a]Then the magicians,
the astrologers, the Chaldeans, and the
soothsayers came in, and I told them the
dream; but they did not make known
to me its interpretation. 8 But at last
Daniel came before me [a](his name *is*
Belteshazzar, according to the name of my
god; [b]in him *is* the Spirit of the Holy God),
and I told the dream before him, *saying:*
9 "Belteshazzar, [a]chief of the magicians,
because I know that the Spirit of the Holy
God *is* in you, and no secret troubles you,
explain to me the visions of my dream
that I have seen, and its interpretation.

10 "These *were* the visions of my head *while*
on my bed:

I was looking, and behold,
[a]A tree in the midst of the earth,
And its height was great.
11 The tree grew and became strong;
Its height reached to the heavens,
And it could be seen to the ends of all the
earth.
12 Its leaves *were* lovely,
Its fruit abundant,
And in it *was* food for all.
[a]The beasts of the field found shade under it,
The birds of the heavens dwelt in its
branches,
And all flesh was fed from it.

13 "I saw in the visions of my head *while* on
my bed, and there was [a]a watcher, [b]a holy
one, coming down from heaven. 14 He
cried aloud and said thus:

[a]'Chop down the tree and cut off its
branches,
Strip off its leaves and scatter its fruit.
[b]Let the beasts get out from under it,
And the birds from its branches.
15 Nevertheless leave the stump and roots in
the earth,
*Bound* with a band of iron and bronze,
In the tender grass of the field.
Let it be wet with the dew of heaven,
And *let* him graze with the beasts
On the grass of the earth.
16 Let his heart be changed from *that of* a man,
Let him be given the heart of a beast,
And let seven [a]times[1] pass over him.

17 'This decision *is* by the decree of the
watchers,
And the sentence by the word of the holy
ones,
In order [a]that the living may know
[b]That the Most High rules in the kingdom
of men,
[c]Gives it to whomever He will,
And sets over it the [d]lowest of men.'

18 "This dream I, King Nebuchadnezzar, have
seen. Now you, Belteshazzar, declare its
interpretation, [a]since all the wise *men* of
my kingdom are not able to make known
to me the interpretation; but you *are* able,
[b]for the Spirit of the Holy God *is* in you."

### *DANIEL EXPLAINS THE SECOND DREAM*

19 Then Daniel, [a]whose name *was*
Belteshazzar, was astonished for a time,
and his thoughts [b]troubled him. *So* the
king spoke, and said, "Belteshazzar, do
not let the dream or its interpretation
trouble you."

Belteshazzar answered and said, "My lord,
*may* [c]the dream concern those who hate
you, and its interpretation concern your
enemies!

20 [a]"The tree that you saw, which grew and
became strong, whose height reached to
the heavens and which *could be* seen by
all the earth, 21 whose leaves *were* lovely
and its fruit abundant, in which *was* food
for all, under which the beasts of the field
dwelt, and in whose branches the birds

**4:1** [a] Ezra 4:17; Dan. 3:4; 6:25 **4:2** [a] Dan. 3:26 **4:3** [a] 2 Sam. 7:16; Ps. 89:35–37; Dan. 6:27; 7:13, 14; [Luke 1:31–33] [b] [Dan. 2:44; 4:34; 6:26] **4:5** [a] Dan. 2:28, 29 [b] Dan. 2:1 **4:7** [a] Dan. 2:2 **4:8** [a] Dan. 1:7 [b] Is. 63:11; Dan. 2:11; 4:18; 5:11, 14 **4:9** [a] Dan. 2:48; 5:11 **4:10** [a] Ezek. 31:3; Dan. 4:20 **4:12** [a] Lam. 4:20 **4:13** [a] [Dan. 4:17, 23] [b] Deut. 33:2 **4:14** [a] Ezek. 31:10–14 [b] Ezek. 31:12, 13 **4:16** [a] Dan. 11:13; 12:7 [1] Possibly *seven years,* and so in verses 23, 25, and 32 **4:17** [a] Ps. 9:16; 83:18 [b] Dan. 2:21; 4:25, 32; 5:21 [c] Jer. 27:5–7 [d] 1 Sam. 2:8 **4:18** [a] Gen. 41:8, 15 [b] Dan. 4:8, 9; 5:11, 14 **4:19** [a] Dan. 4:8 [b] Dan. 7:15, 28; 8:27 [c] 2 Sam. 18:32 **4:20** [a] Dan. 4:10–12

of the heaven had their home— [22][a]it *is*
you, O king, who have grown and become
strong; for your greatness has grown
and reaches to the heavens, [b]and your
dominion to the end of the earth.
23 [a]"And inasmuch as the king saw a
watcher, a holy one, coming down from
heaven and saying, 'Chop down the tree
and destroy it, but leave its stump and
roots in the earth, *bound* with a band
of iron and bronze in the tender grass
of the field; let it be wet with the dew of
heaven, [b]and let him graze with the beasts
of the field, till seven times pass over
him'; [24]this is the interpretation, O king,
and this is the decree of the Most High,
which has come upon my lord the king:
[25]They shall [a]drive you from men, your
dwelling shall be with the beasts of the
field, and they shall make you [b]eat grass
like oxen. They shall wet you with the dew
of heaven, and seven times shall pass over
you, [c]till you know that the Most High
rules in the kingdom of men, and [d]gives it
to whomever He chooses.
26 "And inasmuch as they gave the command
to leave the stump *and* roots of the tree,
your kingdom shall be assured to you,
after you come to know that [a]Heaven
rules. [27]Therefore, O king, let my advice
be acceptable to you; [a]break off your sins
by *being* righteous, and your iniquities by
showing mercy to *the* poor. [b]Perhaps there
may be [c]a lengthening of your prosperity."

### NEBUCHADNEZZAR'S HUMILIATION

28 All *this* came upon King Nebuchadnezzar.
[29]At the end of the twelve months he
was walking about the royal palace of
Babylon. [30]The king [a]spoke, saying, "Is
not this great Babylon, that I have built
for a royal dwelling by my mighty power
and for the honor of my majesty?"
31 [a]While the word *was still* in the king's
mouth, [b]a voice fell from heaven: "King
Nebuchadnezzar, to you it is spoken: the
kingdom has departed from you! [32]And
[a]they shall drive you from men, and your
dwelling *shall be* with the beasts of the
field. They shall make you eat grass like
oxen; and seven times shall pass over you,
until you know that the Most High rules
in the kingdom of men, and gives it to
whomever He chooses."
33 That very hour the word was fulfilled
concerning Nebuchadnezzar; he was
driven from men and ate grass like oxen;
his body was wet with the dew of heaven
till his hair had grown like eagles' *feathers*
and his nails like birds' *claws*.

### NEBUCHADNEZZAR PRAISES GOD

34 And [a]at the end of the time[1] I,
Nebuchadnezzar, lifted my eyes to heaven,
and my understanding returned to me;
and I blessed the Most High and praised
and honored Him [b]who lives forever:

For His dominion *is* [c]an everlasting
dominion,
And His kingdom *is* from generation to
generation.
35 [a]All the inhabitants of the earth *are*
reputed as nothing;
[b]He does according to His will in the army
of heaven

**4:22** [a] Dan. 2:37, 38 [b] Jer. 27:6–8 **4:23** [a] Dan. 4:13–15 [b] Dan. 5:21 **4:25** [a] Dan. 4:32; 5:21 [b] Ps. 106:20 [c] Dan. 4:2, 17, 32 [d] Jer. 27:5 **4:26** [a] Matt. 21:25 **4:27** [a] [1 Pet. 4:8] [b] [Ps. 41:1–3] [c] 1 Kin. 21:29 **4:30** [a] Prov. 16:18 **4:31** [a] Luke 12:20 [b] Dan. 4:24 **4:32** [a] [Dan. 4:25] **4:34** [a] Dan. 4:26 [b] Ps. 102:24–27; Dan. 6:26; 12:7; [Rev. 4:10] [c] [Ps. 10:16]; Dan. 2:44; 7:14; Mic. 4:7; [Luke 1:33] [1] Literally *days* **4:35** [a] Ps. 39:5; Is. 40:15, 17 [b] Ps. 115:3; 135:6; Dan. 6:27

APPLY THE TRUTH

## PRIDE

**4:28–34** Pride takes different forms. We can be proud of something we accomplish, or of something a parent or sibling accomplishes. Is this wrong? Is it sinful? The Bible differentiates being "well pleased" (e.g., Ps. 41:11; Is. 42:21; Matt. 3:17; 2 Cor. 5:8) and being prideful (e.g., Job 35:12; Prov. 8:13; 16:18; 1 Tim. 3:6). To be well pleased is to delight in God's goodness and provision. It's a posture of gratitude. To be prideful, though, is to delight in yourself. It's a posture of arrogance. This is why it's sinful and dangerous. It fuels self-righteousness, self-sufficiency, and self-worship. Pride leads us to believe we're the best things in the universe—the center of it even—and we don't need God.

Nebuchadnezzar gives a picture of how warped pride is and the danger it puts us in. When he boasted of his accomplishments, God went to extreme measures to humble him. Nebuchadnezzar was forced to bow down to the ground and eat grass like a wild animal. God will go to great lengths to destroy pride in our lives too. He will break even the hardest heart of pride and replace it with a tender heart of humility.

And *among* the inhabitants of the earth.
[c]No one can restrain His hand
Or say to Him, [d]"What have You done?"

36 At the same time my reason returned to
me, [a]and for the glory of my kingdom,
my honor and splendor returned to me.
My counselors and nobles resorted to
me, I was [b]restored to my kingdom, and
excellent majesty was [c]added to me.
37 Now I, Nebuchadnezzar, [a]praise and
extol and honor the King of heaven, [b]all
of whose works *are* truth, and His ways
justice. [c]And those who walk in pride He
is able to put down.

## BELSHAZZAR'S FEAST

**5** Belshazzar the king [a]made a great feast for a thousand of his lords, and drank wine in the presence of the thousand. 2 While he tasted the wine, Belshazzar gave the command to bring the gold and silver vessels [a]which his father Nebuchadnezzar had taken from the temple which *had been* in Jerusalem, that the king and his lords, his wives, and his concubines might drink from them. 3 Then they brought the gold [a]vessels that had been taken from the temple of the house of God which *had been* in Jerusalem; and the king and his lords, his wives, and his concubines drank from them. 4 They drank wine, [a]and praised the gods of gold and silver, bronze and iron, wood and stone.

5 [a]In the same hour the fingers of a man's hand appeared and wrote opposite the lampstand on the plaster of the wall of the king's palace; and the king saw the part of the hand that wrote. 6 Then the king's countenance changed, and his thoughts troubled him, so that the joints of his hips were loosened and his [a]knees knocked against each other. 7 [a]The king cried aloud to bring in [b]the astrologers, the Chaldeans, and the soothsayers. The king spoke, saying to the wise *men* of Babylon, "Whoever reads this writing, and tells me its interpretation, shall be clothed with purple and *have* a chain of gold around his neck; [c]and he shall be the third ruler in the kingdom." 8 Now all the king's wise *men* came, [a]but they could not read the writing, or make known to the king its interpretation. 9 Then King Belshazzar was greatly [a]troubled, his countenance was changed, and his lords were astonished.

10 The queen, because of the words of the king and his lords, came to the banquet hall. The queen spoke, saying, "O king, live forever! Do not let your thoughts trouble you, nor let your countenance change. 11 [a]There is a man in your kingdom in whom *is* the Spirit of the Holy God. And in the days of your father, light and understanding and wisdom, like the wisdom of the gods, were found in him; and King Nebuchadnezzar your father—your father the king—made him chief of the magicians, astrologers, Chaldeans, *and* soothsayers. 12 Inasmuch as an excellent spirit, knowledge, understanding, interpreting dreams, solving riddles, and explaining enigmas[1] were found in this Daniel, [a]whom the king named Belteshazzar, now let Daniel be called, and he will give the interpretation."

## THE WRITING ON THE WALL EXPLAINED

13 Then Daniel was brought in before the king. The king spoke, and said to Daniel, "*Are* you that Daniel who is one of the captives[1] from Judah, whom my father the king brought from Judah? 14 I have heard of you, that [a]the Spirit of God *is* in you, and *that* light and understanding and excellent wisdom are found in you. 15 Now [a]the wise *men,* the astrologers, have been brought in before me, that they should read this writing and make known to me its interpretation, but they could not give the interpretation of the thing. 16 And I have heard of you, that you can give interpretations and explain enigmas. [a]Now if you can read the writing and make known to me its interpretation, you shall be clothed with purple and *have* a chain of gold around your neck, and shall be the third ruler in the kingdom."

17 Then Daniel answered, and said before the king, "Let your gifts be for yourself, and give your rewards to another; yet I will read the writing to the king, and make known to him the interpretation. 18 O king, [a]the Most High God gave Nebuchadnezzar your father a kingdom and majesty, glory and honor. 19 And because of the majesty that He gave him, [a]all peoples, nations, and languages trembled and feared before him. Whomever he wished, he [b]executed; whomever he wished, he kept alive; whomever he wished, he set up; and whomever he wished, he put down. 20 [a]But when his heart was lifted up, and his spirit was hardened in pride, he was deposed from his kingly throne, and they took his glory from him. 21 Then he was [a]driven from the sons of men, his heart was made like the beasts, and his dwelling *was* with the wild donkeys. They fed him with grass like oxen, and his body was wet with the dew of heaven, [b]till he knew that the Most High God rules in the kingdom of men, and appoints over it whomever He chooses.

22 "But you his son, Belshazzar, [a]have not humbled your heart, although you knew all this.

4:35 [c] Job 34:29; Is. 43:13 [d] Job 9:12; Is. 45:9; Jer. 18:6; Rom. 9:20; [1 Cor. 2:16] 4:36 [a] Dan. 4:26 [b] 2 Chr. 20:20 [c] Job 42:12; [Prov. 22:4; Matt. 6:33] 4:37 [a] Dan. 2:46, 47; 3:28, 29 [b] Deut. 32:4; [Ps. 33:4]; Is. 5:16; [Rev. 15:3] [c] Ex. 18:11; Job 40:11, 12; Dan. 5:20 5:1 [a] Esth. 1:3; Is. 22:12–14 5:2 [a] 2 Kin. 24:13; 25:15; Ezra 1:7–11; Jer. 52:19; Dan. 1:2 5:3 [a] 2 Chr. 36:10 5:4 [a] Is. 42:8; Dan. 5:23; Rev. 9:20 5:5 [a] Dan. 4:31 5:6 [a] Ezek. 7:17; 21:7 5:7 [a] Dan. 4:6, 7; 5:11, 15 [b] Is. 47:13 [c] Dan. 6:2, 3 5:8 [a] Gen. 41:8; Dan. 2:27; 4:7; 5:15 5:9 [a] Job 18:11; Is. 21:2–4; Jer. 6:24; Dan. 2:1; 5:6 5:11 [a] Dan. 2:48; 4:8, 9, 18 5:12 [a] Dan. 1:7; 4:8 [1] Literally *untying knots,* and so in verse 16 5:13 [1] Literally *of the sons of the captivity* 5:14 [a] Dan. 4:8, 9, 18; 5:11, 12 5:15 [a] Dan. 5:7, 8 5:16 [a] Dan. 5:7, 29 5:18 [a] Dan. 2:37, 38; 4:17, 22, 25 5:19 [a] Jer. 27:7 [b] Dan. 2:12, 13; 3:6 5:20 [a] Dan. 4:30, 37 5:21 [a] Dan. 4:32, 33 [b] Ezek. 17:24 5:22 [a] 2 Chr. 33:23; 36:12

23[a] And you have lifted yourself up against the
Lord of heaven. They have brought the [b]ves-
sels of His house before you, and you and your
lords, your wives and your concubines, have
drunk wine from them. And you have praised the
gods of silver and gold, bronze and iron, wood
and stone, [c]which do not see or hear or know;
and the God who *holds* your breath in His hand
[d]and owns all your ways, you have not glorified.
24 Then the fingers[1] of the hand were sent from
Him, and this writing was written.

25 "And this is the inscription that was written:

MENE,[1] MENE, TEKEL,[2] UPHARSIN.[3]

26 This *is* the interpretation of *each* word. MENE:
God has numbered your kingdom, and finished
it; 27 TEKEL: [a]You have been weighed in the
balances, and found wanting; 28 PERES: Your
kingdom has been divided, and given to the
[a]Medes and [b]Persians."[1] 29 Then Belshazzar gave
the command, and they clothed Daniel with
purple and *put* a chain of gold around his neck,
and made a proclamation concerning him [a]that
he should be the third ruler in the kingdom.

> **5:25–28 MENE** means "numbered." The repetition is for emphasis. God had numbered the days of Belshazzar's **kingdom**, and the time was up. **TEKEL** means "weighed." God had weighed Belshazzar's character, and he did not measure up. **UPHARSIN** (the plural of **PERES**) means "divided." That very night Babylon would be divided and defeated by the **Medes and Persians**.

### *BELSHAZZAR'S FALL*

30[a] That very night Belshazzar, king of the
Chaldeans, was slain. 31[a] And Darius the Mede
received the kingdom, *being* about sixty-two
years old.

### *THE PLOT AGAINST DANIEL*

6 It pleased Darius to set over the kingdom one
hundred and twenty satraps, to be over the
whole kingdom; 2 and over these, three governors,
of whom Daniel *was* one, that the satraps might
give account to them, so that the king would suffer
no loss. 3 Then this Daniel distinguished himself
above the governors and satraps, [a]because an
excellent spirit *was* in him; and the king gave
thought to setting him over the whole realm. 4[a] So
the governors and satraps sought to find *some*
charge against Daniel concerning the kingdom;
but they could find no charge or fault, because
he *was* faithful; nor was there any error or fault
found in him. 5 Then these men said, "We shall
not find any charge against this Daniel unless we
find *it* against him concerning the law of his God."

6 So these governors and satraps thronged
before the king, and said thus to him: [a]"King
Darius, live forever! 7 All the governors of the
kingdom, the administrators and satraps, the
counselors and advisors, have [a]consulted to-
gether to establish a royal statute and to make
a firm decree, that whoever petitions any god or
man for thirty days, except you, O king, shall be
cast into the den of lions. 8 Now, O king, establish
the decree and sign the writing, so that it cannot
be changed, according to the [a]law of the Medes
and Persians, which does not alter." 9 Therefore
King Darius signed the written decree.

### *DANIEL IN THE LIONS' DEN*

10 Now when Daniel knew that the writing
was signed, he went home. And in his upper
room, with his windows open [a]toward Jerusa-
lem, he knelt down on his knees [b]three times
that day, and prayed and gave thanks before his
God, as was his custom since early days.

11 Then these men assembled and found
Daniel praying and making supplication before
his God. 12[a] And they went before the king, and
spoke concerning the king's decree: "Have you
not signed a decree that every man who peti-
tions any god or man within thirty days, except
you, O king, shall be cast into the den of lions?"

The king answered and said, "The thing *is*
true, [b]according to the law of the Medes and
Persians, which does not alter."

13 So they answered and said before the
king, "That Daniel, [a]who is one of the captives[1]
from Judah, [b]does not show due regard for you,
O king, or for the decree that you have signed,
but makes his petition three times a day."

14 And the king, when he heard *these* words,
[a]was greatly displeased with himself, and set *his*
heart on Daniel to deliver him; and he labored
till the going down of the sun to deliver him.
15 Then these men approached the king, and said
to the king, "Know, O king, that *it is* [a]the law of
the Medes and Persians that no decree or statute
which the king establishes may be changed."

16 So the king gave the command, and they
brought Daniel and cast *him* into the den of
lions. *But* the king spoke, saying to Daniel, "Your
God, whom you serve continually, He will deliver
you." 17[a] Then a stone was brought and laid on
the mouth of the den, [b]and the king sealed it
with his own signet ring and with the signets of

5:23 [a] Dan. 5:3, 4 [b] Ex. 40:9 [c] Ps. 115:5, 6 [d] [Jer. 10:23] 5:24 [1] Literally *palm* 5:25 [1] Literally *a mina* (50 shekels) from the verb "to number" [2] Literally *a shekel* from the verb "to weigh" [3] Literally *and half-shekels* from the verb "to divide" 5:27 [a] Ps. 62:9 5:28 [a] Dan. 5:31; 9:1 [b] Dan. 6:28 [1] Aramaic *Paras,* consonant with *Peres* 5:29 [a] Dan. 5:7, 16 5:30 [a] Jer. 51:31, 39, 57 5:31 [a] Dan. 2:39; 9:1 6:3 [a] Dan. 5:12 6:4 [a] Eccl. 4:4 6:6 [a] Neh. 2:3 6:7 [a] Ps. 59:3; 62:4; 64:2–6 6:8 [a] Esth. 1:19; 8:8 6:10 [a] Jon. 2:4 [b] Ps. 55:17 6:12 [a] Dan. 3:8–12 [b] Dan. 6:8, 15 6:13 [a] Dan. 1:6; 5:13 [b] Dan. 3:12 [1] Literally *of the sons of the captivity* 6:14 [a] Mark 6:26 6:15 [a] Dan. 6:8, 12 6:17 [a] Lam. 3:53 [b] Matt. 27:66

DANIEL 6:1–28

# THE LESSON OF THE LIONS

37

STORY OF SCRIPTURE

## WHAT'S GOING ON?

Despite being taken captive in Babylon, Daniel thrived. He became a governor in the empire, even when Babylon was taken over by Persia. Jealous of his success, the other governors conspired against him and prompted a decree that anyone who prayed to any god or human besides King Darius would be thrown into a lions' den. Yet, Daniel continued to pray openly to God and was cast into the den. However, God protected Daniel, shutting the lions' jaws. Daniel emerged unscathed the next morning. This miraculous event led King Darius to decree that people in every part of his kingdom should fear and revere Daniel's God.

## WHAT DOES THIS MEAN FOR ME?

Dare to be a Daniel. His story is a powerful testament to the strength of faith and the importance of staying true to your beliefs, even in the face of persecution. No matter what challenges came his way, Daniel never wavered. His example challenges us to examine our own resolve in the face of a culture that seeks to thwart our faith.

## DID YOU CATCH THE PATTERN?

Daniel was innocent, persecuted for his righteousness, and spent the night in a pit to die. Death growled at him, but Daniel emerged alive and victorious. Does this sound familiar? Jesus was innocent, persecuted for His righteousness, and sent to the grave, dead. Death tried to keep Him down, but Jesus emerged from the tomb victorious. The story of Daniel in the lions' den is another foreshadowing of Jesus.

*For the next* Story of Scripture *reading and devotion, turn to Jonah 2:1–10 on page 911.*

his lords, that the purpose concerning Daniel
might not be changed.

### *DANIEL SAVED FROM THE LIONS*

18 Now the king went to his palace and
spent the night fasting; and no musicians[1] were
brought before him. [a]Also his sleep went from
him. 19 Then the [a]king arose very early in the
morning and went in haste to the den of lions.
20 And when he came to the den, he cried out
with a lamenting voice to Daniel. The king spoke,
saying to Daniel, "Daniel, servant of the living
God, [a]has your God, whom you serve continually,
been able to deliver you from the lions?"
21 Then Daniel said to the king, [a]"O king, live
forever! 22 [a]My God sent His angel and [b]shut the
lions' mouths, so that they have not hurt me,
because I was found innocent before Him; and
also, O king, I have done no wrong before you."
23 Now the king was exceedingly glad for
him, and commanded that they should take
Daniel up out of the den. So Daniel was taken
up out of the den, and no injury whatever was
found on him, [a]because he believed in his God.

### *DARIUS HONORS GOD*

24 And the king gave the command, [a]and they
brought those men who had accused Daniel, and
they cast *them* into the den of lions—them, [b]their
children, and their wives; and the lions over-
powered them, and broke all their bones in pieces
before they ever came to the bottom of the den.
25 [a]Then King Darius wrote:

To all peoples, nations, and languages
that dwell in all the earth:

Peace be multiplied to you.

26 [a]I make a decree that in every dominion
of my kingdom *men must* [b]tremble and
fear before the God of Daniel.

[c]For He *is* the living God,
And steadfast forever;
His kingdom *is the one* which shall not be
[d]destroyed,
And His dominion *shall endure* to the end.
27 He delivers and rescues,
[a]And He works signs and wonders
In heaven and on earth,
Who has delivered Daniel from the power
of the lions.

28 So this Daniel prospered in the reign of
Darius [a]and in the reign of [b]Cyrus the Persian.

**6:18** [a] Dan. 2:1 [1] Exact meaning unknown **6:19** [a] Dan. 3:24 **6:20** [a] Dan. 3:17 **6:21** [a] Dan. 2:4; 6:6 **6:22** [a] Dan. 3:28 [b] Heb. 11:33 **6:23** [a] Heb. 11:33 **6:24** [a] Deut. 19:18, 19 [b] Deut. 24:16 **6:25** [a] Dan. 4:1 **6:26** [a] Dan. 3:29 [b] Ps. 99:1 [c] Dan. 4:34; 6:20 [d] Dan. 2:44; 4:3; 7:14, 27 **6:27** [a] Dan. 4:2, 3 **6:28** [a] Dan. 1:21 [b] Ezra 1:1, 2

### *VISION OF THE FOUR BEASTS*

**7** In the first year of Belshazzar king of Bab-
ylon, [a]Daniel had a dream and [b]visions of
his head *while* on his bed. Then he wrote down
the dream, telling the main facts.[1]
2 Daniel spoke, saying, "I saw in my vision
by night, and behold, the four winds of heav-
en were stirring up the Great Sea. 3 And four
great beasts [a]came up from the sea, each dif-
ferent from the other. 4 The first *was* [a]like a
lion, and had eagle's wings. I watched till its
wings were plucked off; and it was lifted up
from the earth and made to stand on two
feet like a man, and a [b]man's heart was given
to it.
5 [a]"And suddenly another beast, a second,
like a bear. It was raised up on one side, and *had*
three ribs in its mouth between its teeth. And
they said thus to it: 'Arise, devour much flesh!'
6 "After this I looked, and there was another,
like a leopard, which had on its back four wings
of a bird. The beast also had [a]four heads, and
dominion was given to it.
7 "After this I saw in the night visions, and
behold, [a]a fourth beast, dreadful and terrible,
exceedingly strong. It had huge iron teeth; it
was devouring, breaking in pieces, and tram-
pling the residue with its feet. It *was* different
from all the beasts that *were* before it, [b]and it
had ten horns. 8 I was considering the horns,
and [a]there was another horn, a little one, com-
ing up among them, before whom three of
the first horns were plucked out by the roots.
And there, in this horn, *were* eyes like the eyes
[b]of a man, [c]and a mouth speaking pompous
words.

> **7:3–7** These **four great beasts** represent kings or kingdoms, like the four metals of the statue in chapter 2. There has been almost universal agreement that the **lion** with **eagle's wings** represents Babylon. The **bear** seems to represent Babylon's successor, the Medo-Persian Empire. The **three ribs** may represent the three kingdoms that Medo-Persia devoured—Babylon, Libya, and Egypt. The **leopard** is believed to represent Greece. The Greeks, under the leadership of Alexander the Great, rapidly conquered the known world. After Alexander's death, his empire was divided into four different parts—Macedonia, Egypt, Syria, and Thracia. The **fourth beast** may represent Rome.

### *VISION OF THE ANCIENT OF DAYS*

9 "I[a] watched till thrones were put in place,
And [b]the Ancient of Days was seated;
[c]His garment *was* white as snow,
And the hair of His head *was* like pure wool.
His throne *was* a fiery flame,
[d]Its wheels a burning fire;
10 [a]A fiery stream issued
And came forth from before Him.
[b]A thousand thousands ministered to Him;
Ten thousand times ten thousand stood
before Him.
[c]The court[1] was seated,
And the books were opened.

11 "I watched then because of the sound of the
pompous words which the horn was speaking;
[a]I watched till the beast was slain, and its body
destroyed and given to the burning flame. 12 As
for the rest of the beasts, they had their domin-
ion taken away, yet their lives were prolonged
for a season and a time.

13 "I was watching in the night visions,
And behold, [a]*One* like the Son of Man,
Coming with the clouds of heaven!
He came to the Ancient of Days,
And they brought Him near before Him.
14 [a]Then to Him was given dominion and
glory and a kingdom,
That all [b]peoples, nations, and languages
should serve Him.
His dominion *is* [c]an everlasting dominion,
Which shall not pass away,
And His kingdom *the one*
Which shall not be destroyed.

> **SEEING JESUS IN THE SCRIPTURE**
>
> **7:14** The kingdom of all peoples, nations, and languages Daniel described is Jesus' kingdom. While earthly kingdoms are limited to certain peoples, nations, languages, and times, Jesus' kingdom is for all people and has no end (see Luke 1:33).

### *DANIEL'S VISIONS INTERPRETED*

15 "I, Daniel, was grieved in my spirit within *my*
body, and the visions of my head troubled me. 16 I
came near to one of those who stood by, and asked
him the truth of all this. So he told me and made
known to me the interpretation of these things:
17 'Those great beasts, which are four, *are* four kings[1]
*which* arise out of the earth. 18 But [a]the saints of the
Most High shall receive the kingdom, and possess
the kingdom forever, even forever and ever.'

**7:1** [a] [Amos 3:7] [b] [Dan. 2:28] [1] Literally *the head* (or *chief*) *of the words* **7:3** [a] Rev. 13:1; 17:8 **7:4** [a] Deut. 28:49 [b] Dan. 4:16, 34 **7:5** [a] Dan. 2:39 **7:6** [a] Dan. 8:8, 22 **7:7** [a] Dan. 2:40 [b] Rev. 12:3; 13:1 **7:8** [a] Dan. 8:9 [b] Rev. 9:7 [c] Rev. 13:5, 6 **7:9** [a] [Rev. 20:4] [b] Ps. 90:2 [c] Rev. 1:14 [d] Ezek. 1:15 **7:10** [a] Is. 30:33; 66:15 [b] Rev. 5:11 [c] [Rev. 20:11–15] [1] Or *judgment* **7:11** [a] [Rev. 19:20; 20:10] **7:13** [a] [Matt. 24:30; 26:64] **7:14** [a] [John 3:35, 36] [b] Dan. 3:4 [c] Mic. 4:7 **7:17** [1] Representing their kingdoms (compare verse 23) **7:18** [a] Is. 60:12–14

19 "Then I wished to know the truth about
the fourth beast, which was different from all
the others, exceedingly dreadful, *with* its teeth
of iron and its nails of bronze, *which* devoured,
broke in pieces, and trampled the residue with
its feet; 20 and the ten horns that *were* on its
head, and the other *horn* which came up, before
which three fell, namely, that horn which had
eyes and a mouth which spoke pompous words,
whose appearance *was* greater than his fellows.
21 "I was watching; [a]and the same horn was
making war against the saints, and prevailing
against them, 22 until the Ancient of Days came,
[a]and a judgment was made *in favor* of the saints
of the Most High, and the time came for the
saints to possess the kingdom.
23 "Thus he said:

'The fourth beast shall be
[a]A fourth kingdom on earth,
Which shall be different from all *other*
kingdoms,
And shall devour the whole earth,
Trample it and break it in pieces.
24 [a]The ten horns *are* ten kings
*Who* shall arise from this kingdom.
And another shall rise after them;
He shall be different from the first *ones,*
And shall subdue three kings.
25 [a]He shall speak *pompous* words against the
Most High,
Shall [b]persecute[1] the saints of the Most High,
And shall [c]intend to change times and law.
Then [d]*the saints* shall be given into his hand
[e]For a time and times and half a time.

26 'But[a] the court shall be seated,
And they shall [b]take away his dominion,
To consume and destroy *it* forever.
27 Then the [a]kingdom and dominion,
And the greatness of the kingdoms under
the whole heaven,
Shall be given to the people, the saints of
the Most High.
[b]His kingdom *is* an everlasting kingdom,
[c]And all dominions shall serve and obey
Him.'

28 "This *is* the end of the account.[1] As for
me, Daniel, [a]my thoughts greatly troubled me,
and my countenance changed; but I [b]kept the
matter in my heart."

### *VISION OF A RAM AND A GOAT*

**8** In the third year of the reign of King Belshaz-
zar a vision appeared *to* me—to me, Daniel—
after the one that appeared to me [a]the first time. 2 I
saw in the vision, and it so happened while I was
looking, that I *was* in [a]Shushan, the citadel, which
*is* in the province of Elam; and I saw in the vision
that I was by the River Ulai. 3 Then I lifted my eyes
and saw, and there, standing beside the river, was
a ram which had two horns, and the two horns
*were* high; but one *was* [a]higher than the other,
and the higher *one* came up last. 4 I saw the ram
pushing westward, northward, and southward,
so that no animal could withstand him; nor *was
there any* that could deliver from his hand, [a]but
he did according to his will and became great.
5 And as I was considering, suddenly a male
goat came from the west, across the surface of
the whole earth, without touching the ground;
and the goat *had* a notable [a]horn between his
eyes. 6 Then he came to the ram that had two
horns, which I had seen standing beside the
river, and ran at him with furious power. 7 And
I saw him confronting the ram; he was moved
with rage against him, attacked the ram, and
broke his two horns. There was no power in the
ram to withstand him, but he cast him down to
the ground and trampled him; and there was no
one that could deliver the ram from his hand.
8 Therefore the male goat grew very great;
but when he became strong, the large horn was
broken, and in place of it [a]four notable ones
came up toward the four winds of heaven. 9 [a]And
out of one of them came a little horn which grew
exceedingly great toward the south, [b]toward the
east, and toward the [c]Glorious *Land.* 10 [a]And it
grew up to [b]the host of heaven; and [c]it cast down
*some* of the host and *some* of the stars to the
ground, and trampled them. 11 [a]He even exalted
*himself* as high as [b]the Prince of the host; [c]and
by him [d]the daily *sacrifices* were taken away,
and the place of His sanctuary was cast down.
12 Because of transgression, [a]an army was given
over *to the horn* to oppose the daily *sacrifices;*
and he cast [b]truth down to the ground. He [c]did
*all this* and prospered.

**8:9–12** The **little horn** described in these verses may refer to a Syrian king named Antiochus Epiphanes. After the Medes and Persians conquered Babylon, Antiochus Epiphanes took control of the temple in Jerusalem. In an act of blasphemy, he built an altar to the Greek god Zeus directly over what had been the Jewish altar of burnt offering. He then sacrificed a pig—an unclean animal—on the altar. In response, the Jews revolted and overthrew the Syrian leaders. Today, the Jewish people celebrate this revolution at Hanukkah.

**7:21** [a] Rev. 11:7; 13:7; 17:14 **7:22** [a] [Rev. 1:6] **7:23** [a] Dan. 2:40 **7:24** [a] Rev. 13:1; 17:12 **7:25** [a] Rev. 13:1–6 [b] Rev. 17:6 [c] Dan. 2:21 [d] Rev. 13:7; 18:24 [e] Rev. 12:14 [1] Literally *wear out* **7:26** [a] [Dan. 2:35; 7:10, 22] [b] Rev. 19:20 **7:27** [a] Dan. 7:14, 18, 22 [b] [Luke 1:32, 33] [c] Is. 60:12 **7:28** [a] Dan. 8:27 [b] Luke 2:19, 51 [1] Literally *the word* **8:1** [a] Dan. 7:1 **8:2** [a] Esth. 1:2; 2:8 **8:3** [a] Dan. 7:5 **8:4** [a] Dan. 5:19 **8:5** [a] Dan. 8:8, 21; 11:3 **8:8** [a] Dan. 7:6; 8:22; 11:4 **8:9** [a] Dan. 11:21 [b] Dan. 11:25 [c] Ps. 48:2 **8:10** [a] Dan. 11:28 [b] Is. 14:13 [c] Rev. 12:4 **8:11** [a] Dan. 8:25; 11:36, 37 [b] Josh. 5:14 [c] Dan. 11:31; 12:11 [d] Ex. 29:38 **8:12** [a] Dan. 11:31 [b] Is. 59:14 [c] Dan. 8:4; 11:36

13 Then I heard [a]a holy one speaking; and *another* holy one said to that certain *one* who was speaking, "How long *will* the vision *be, concerning* the daily *sacrifices* and the transgression of desolation, the giving of both the sanctuary and the host to be trampled underfoot?"

14 And he said to me, "For two thousand three hundred days;[1] then the sanctuary shall be cleansed."

## GABRIEL INTERPRETS THE VISION

15 Then it happened, when I, Daniel, had seen the vision and [a]was seeking the meaning, that suddenly there stood before me [b]one having the appearance of a man. 16 And I heard a man's voice [a]between *the banks of* the Ulai, who called, and said, [b]"Gabriel, make this *man* understand the vision." 17 So he came near where I stood, and when he came I was afraid and [a]fell on my face; but he said to me, "Understand, son of man, that the vision *refers* to the time of the end."

18 [a]Now, as he was speaking with me, I was in a deep sleep with my face to the ground; [b]but he touched me, and stood me upright. 19 And he said, "Look, I am making known to you what shall happen in the latter time of the indignation; [a]for at the appointed time the end *shall be.* 20 The ram which you saw, having the two horns—*they are* the kings of Media and Persia. 21 And the male goat *is* the kingdom[1] of Greece. The large horn that *is* between its eyes [a]*is* the first king. 22 [a]As for the broken *horn* and the four that stood up in its place, four kingdoms shall arise out of that nation, but not with its power.

23 "And in the latter time of their kingdom,
When the transgressors have reached
their fullness,
A king shall arise,
[a]Having fierce features,
Who understands sinister schemes.
24 His power shall be mighty, [a]but not by his
own power;
He shall destroy fearfully,
[b]And shall prosper and thrive;
[c]He shall destroy the mighty, and *also* the
holy people.

25 "Through[a] his cunning
He shall cause deceit to prosper under his
rule;[1]
[b]And he shall exalt *himself* in his heart.
He shall destroy many in *their* prosperity.
[c]He shall even rise against the Prince of
princes;
But he shall be [d]broken without *human*
means.[2]

26 "And the vision of the evenings and mornings
Which was told is true;
[a]Therefore seal up the vision,
For *it refers* to many days *in the future.*"

27 [a]And I, Daniel, fainted and was sick for days; afterward I arose and went about the king's business. I was astonished by the vision, but no one understood it.

## DANIEL'S PRAYER FOR THE PEOPLE

9 In the first year [a]of Darius the son of Ahasuerus, of the lineage of the Medes, who was made king over the realm of the Chaldeans— 2 in the first year of his reign I, Daniel, understood by the books the number of the years *specified* by the word of the LORD through [a]Jeremiah the prophet, that He would accomplish seventy years in the desolations of Jerusalem.

3 [a]Then I set my face toward the Lord God to make request by prayer and supplications, with fasting, sackcloth, and ashes. 4 And I prayed to the LORD my God, and made confession, and said, "O [a]Lord, great and awesome God, who keeps His covenant and mercy with those who love Him, and with those who keep His commandments, 5 [a]we have sinned and committed iniquity, we have done wickedly and rebelled, even by departing from Your precepts and Your judgments. 6 [a]Neither have we heeded Your servants the prophets, who spoke in Your name to our kings and our princes, to our fathers and all the people of the land. 7 O Lord, [a]righteousness *belongs* to You, but to us shame of face, as *it is* this day—to the men of Judah, to the inhabitants of Jerusalem and all Israel, those near and those far off in all the countries to which You have driven them, because of the unfaithfulness which they have committed against You.

8 "O Lord, to us *belongs* shame of face, to our kings, our princes, and our fathers, because we have sinned against You. 9 [a]To the Lord our God *belong* mercy and forgiveness, though we have rebelled against Him. 10 We have not obeyed the voice of the LORD our God, to walk in His laws, which He set before us by His servants the prophets. 11 Yes, [a]all Israel has transgressed Your law, and has departed so as not to obey Your voice; therefore the curse and the oath written in the [b]Law of Moses the servant of God have been poured out on us, because we have sinned against Him. 12 And He has [a]confirmed His words, which He spoke against us and against our judges who judged us, by bringing upon us a great disaster; [b]for under the whole heaven such has never been done as what has been done to Jerusalem.

8:13 [a] Dan. 4:13, 23 8:14 [1] Literally *evening-mornings* 8:15 [a] 1 Pet. 1:10 [b] Ezek. 1:26 8:16 [a] Dan. 12:6, 7 [b] Luke 1:19, 26 8:17 [a] Rev. 1:17 8:18 [a] Luke 9:32 [b] Ezek. 2:2 8:19 [a] Hab. 2:3 8:21 [a] Dan. 11:3 [1] Literally *king,* representing his kingdom (compare 7:17, 23) 8:22 [a] Dan. 11:4 8:23 [a] Deut. 28:50 8:24 [a] Rev. 17:13 [b] Dan. 11:36 [c] Dan. 7:25 8:25 [a] Dan. 11:21 [b] Dan. 8:11–13; 11:36; 12:7 [c] Rev. 19:19, 20 [d] Job 34:20 [1] Literally *hand* [2] Literally *hand* 8:26 [a] Ezek. 12:27 8:27 [a] Dan. 7:28; 8:17 9:1 [a] Dan. 1:21 9:2 [a] 2 Chr. 36:21 9:3 [a] Neh. 1:4 9:4 [a] Ex. 20:6 9:5 [a] 1 Kin. 8:47, 48 9:6 [a] 2 Chr. 36:15 9:7 [a] Neh. 9:33 9:9 [a] [Ps. 130:4, 7] 9:11 [a] Is. 1:3–6 [b] Lev. 26:14 9:12 [a] Zech. 1:6 [b] Lam. 1:12; 2:13

13 [a]"As *it is* written in the Law of Moses, all
this disaster has come upon us; [b]yet we have not
made our prayer before the LORD our God, that
we might turn from our iniquities and under-
stand Your truth. 14 Therefore the LORD has
[a]kept the disaster in mind, and brought it upon
us; for [b]the LORD our God *is* righteous in all
the works which He does, though we have not
obeyed His voice. 15 And now, O Lord our God,
[a]who brought Your people out of the land of
Egypt with a mighty hand, and made Yourself
[b]a name, as *it is* this day—we have sinned, we
have done wickedly!

16 "O Lord, [a]according to all Your righteous-
ness, I pray, let Your anger and Your fury be
turned away from Your city Jerusalem, [b]Your
holy mountain; because for our sins, [c]and for
the iniquities of our fathers, [d]Jerusalem and
Your people [e]*are* a reproach to all *those* around
us. 17 Now therefore, our God, hear the prayer of
Your servant, and his supplications, [a]and [b]for the
Lord's sake cause Your face to shine on Your sanc-
tuary, [c]which is desolate. 18 [a]O my God, incline
Your ear and hear; open Your eyes [b]and see our
desolations, and the city [c]which is called by Your
name; for we do not present our supplications
before You because of our righteous deeds, but
because of Your great mercies. 19 O Lord, hear!
O Lord, forgive! O Lord, listen and act! Do not
delay for Your own sake, my God, for Your city
and Your people are called by Your name."

### THE SEVENTY-WEEKS PROPHECY

20 Now while I *was* speaking, praying, and
confessing my sin and the sin of my people Israel,
and presenting my supplication before the LORD
my God for the holy mountain of my God, 21 yes,
while I *was* speaking in prayer, the man [a]Gabriel,
whom I had seen in the vision at the beginning,
being caused to fly swiftly, reached me about the
time of the evening offering. 22 And he informed
*me,* and talked with me, and said, "O Daniel, I have
now come forth to give you skill to understand.
23 At the beginning of your supplications the
command went out, and I have come to tell *you,*
for you *are* greatly [a]beloved; therefore [b]consider
the matter, and understand the vision:

24 "Seventy weeks[1] are determined
For your people and for your holy city,
To finish the transgression,
To make an end of[2] sins,
[a]To make reconciliation for iniquity,
[b]To bring in everlasting righteousness,
To seal up vision and prophecy,
[c]And to anoint the Most Holy.

25 "Know therefore and understand,
*That* from the going forth of the command
To restore and build Jerusalem
Until [a]Messiah [b]the Prince,
*There shall be* seven weeks and sixty-two weeks;
The street[1] shall be built again, and the wall,[2]
Even in troublesome times.

## SEEING JESUS IN THE SCRIPTURE

**9:25** Daniel's hope and declaration was that one day the Messiah would come. Daniel's hope was realized in Jesus. Jesus is the Messiah who revealed what had been hidden in the Old Testament (see John 4:25).

26 "And after the sixty-two weeks
[a]Messiah shall be cut off, [b]but not for Himself;
And [c]the people of the prince who is to come
[d]Shall destroy the city and the sanctuary.
The end of it *shall be* with a flood,
And till the end of the war desolations are determined.

27 Then he shall confirm [a]a covenant with [b]many for one week;
But in the middle of the week
He shall bring an end to sacrifice and offering.
And on the wing of abominations shall be one who makes desolate,
[c]Even until the consummation, which is determined,
Is poured out on the desolate."

### VISION OF THE GLORIOUS MAN

10 In the third year of Cyrus king of Persia a mes-
sage was revealed to Daniel, whose [a]name
was called Belteshazzar. The message *was* true, but
the appointed time *was* long;[1] and he understood
the message, and had understanding of the vision.
2 In those days I, Daniel, was mourning three full
weeks. 3 I ate no pleasant food, no meat or wine
came into my mouth, nor did I anoint myself at
all, till three whole weeks were fulfilled.

4 Now on the twenty-fourth day of the first
month, as I was by the side of the great river,
that *is,* the Tigris,[1] 5 I lifted my eyes and looked,
and behold, a certain man clothed in [a]linen,
whose waist *was* [b]girded with gold of Uphaz!

**9:13** [a] Deut. 28:15–68 [b] Is. 9:13 **9:14** [a] Jer. 31:28; 44:27 [b] Neh. 9:33 **9:15** [a] Neh. 1:10 [b] Neh. 9:10 **9:16** [a] 1 Sam. 12:7 [b] Zech. 8:3 [c] Ex. 20:5 [d] Lam. 2:16 [e] Ps. 79:4 **9:17** [a] Num. 6:24–26 [b] Lam. 5:18 [c] [John 16:24] **9:18** [a] Is. 37:17 [b] Ex. 3:7 [c] Jer. 25:29 **9:21** [a] Dan. 8:16 **9:23** [a] Dan. 10:11, 19 [b] Matt. 24:15 **9:24** [a] [Is. 53:10] [b] Rev. 14:6 [c] Ps. 45:7 [1] Literally *sevens,* and so throughout the chapter [2] Following Qere, Septuagint, Syriac, and Vulgate; Kethib and Theodotion read *To seal up.* **9:25** [a] Luke 2:1, 2; John 1:41; 4:25 [b] Is. 55:4 [1] Or *open square* [2] Or *moat* **9:26** [a] [Is. 53:8]; Matt. 27:50; Mark 9:12; 15:37; [Luke 23:46; 24:26]; John 19:30; Acts 8:32 [b] [1 Pet. 2:21] [c] Matt. 22:7 [d] Matt. 24:2; Mark 13:2; Luke 19:43, 44 **9:27** [a] Is. 42:6 [b] [Matt. 26:28] [c] Dan. 11:36 **10:1** [a] Dan. 1:7 [1] Or *and of great conflict* **10:4** [1] Hebrew *Hiddekel* **10:5** [a] Ezek. 9:2; 10:2 [b] Rev. 1:13; 15:6

6 His body *was* like beryl, his face like the appearance of lightning, his eyes like torches of fire, his arms and feet like burnished bronze in color, [a]and the sound of his words like the voice of a multitude.

7 And I, Daniel, alone saw the vision, for the men who were with me did not see the vision; but a great terror fell upon them, so that they fled to hide themselves. 8 Therefore I was left alone when I saw this great vision, and no strength remained in me; for my vigor was turned to frailty in me, and I retained no strength. 9 Yet I heard the sound of his words; and while I heard the sound of his words I was in a deep sleep on my face, with my face to the ground.

### *PROPHECIES CONCERNING PERSIA AND GREECE*

10 [a]Suddenly, a hand touched me, which made me tremble on my knees and *on* the palms of my hands. 11 And he said to me, "O Daniel, [a]man greatly beloved, understand the words that I speak to you, and stand upright, for I have now been sent to you." While he was speaking this word to me, I stood trembling.

12 Then he said to me, [a]"Do not fear, Daniel, for from the first day that you set your heart to understand, and to humble yourself before your God, [b]your words were heard; and I have come because of your words. 13 [a]But the prince of the kingdom of Persia withstood me twenty-one days; and behold, [b]Michael, one of the chief princes, came to help me, for I had been left alone there with the kings of Persia. 14 Now I have come to make you understand what will happen to your people [a]in the latter days, [b]for the vision *refers* to *many* days yet *to come*."

> **10:13 Michael** seems to be one of the most powerful angels. He is mentioned three times in the Old Testament, all in the Book of Daniel (v. 21; 12:1), and twice in the New Testament (Jude v. 9; Rev. 12:7).

15 When he had spoken such words to me, [a]I turned my face toward the ground and became speechless. 16 And suddenly, [a]*one* having the likeness of the sons[1] of men [b]touched my lips; then I opened my mouth and spoke, saying to him who stood before me, "My lord, because of the vision [c]my sorrows have overwhelmed me, and I have retained no strength. 17 For how can this servant of my lord talk with you, my lord? As for me, no strength remains in me now, nor is any breath left in me."

18 Then again, *the one* having the likeness of a man touched me and strengthened me. 19 [a]And he said, "O man greatly beloved, [b]fear not! Peace *be* to you; be strong, yes, be strong!"

So when he spoke to me I was strengthened, and said, "Let my lord speak, for you have strengthened me."

20 Then he said, "Do you know why I have come to you? And now I must return to fight [a]with the prince of Persia; and when I have gone forth, indeed the prince of Greece will come. 21 But I will tell you what is noted in the Scripture of Truth. (No one upholds me against these, [a]except Michael your prince.

11 "Also [a]in the first year of [b]Darius the Mede, I, *even* I, stood up to confirm and strengthen him.) 2 And now I will tell you the truth: Behold, three more kings will arise in Persia, and the fourth shall be far richer than *them* all; by his strength, through his riches, he shall stir up all against the realm of Greece. 3 Then [a]a mighty king shall arise, who shall rule with great dominion, and [b]do according to his will. 4 And when he has arisen, [a]his kingdom shall be broken up and divided toward the four winds of heaven, but not among his posterity [b]nor according to his dominion with which he ruled; for his kingdom shall be uprooted, even for others besides these.

### *WARRING KINGS OF NORTH AND SOUTH*

5 "Also the king of the South shall become strong, as well as *one* of his princes; and he shall gain power over him and have dominion. His dominion *shall be* a great dominion. 6 And at the end of *some* years they shall join forces, for the daughter of the king of the South shall go to the king of the North to make an agreement; but she shall not retain the power of her authority,[1] and neither he nor his authority[2] shall stand; but she shall be given up, with those who brought her, and with him who begot her, and with him who strengthened her in *those* times. 7 But from a branch of her roots *one* shall arise in his place, who shall come with an army, enter the fortress of the king of the North, and deal with them and prevail. 8 And he shall also carry their gods captive to Egypt, with their princes[1] *and* their precious articles of silver and gold; and he shall continue *more* years than the king of the North.

9 "Also *the king of the North* shall come to the kingdom of the king of the South, but shall return to his own land. 10 However his sons shall stir up strife, and assemble a multitude of great forces; and *one* shall certainly come [a]and overwhelm and pass through; then he shall return [b]to his fortress and stir up strife.

**10:6** [a] [Rev. 1:15] **10:10** [a] Dan. 9:21 **10:11** [a] Dan. 9:23 **10:12** [a] Rev. 1:17 [b] Dan. 9:3, 4, 22, 23; Acts 10:4 **10:13** [a] Dan. 10:20 [b] Dan. 10:21; 12:1; Jude 9; [Rev. 12:7] **10:14** [a] Gen. 49:1; Deut. 31:29; Dan. 2:28 [b] Dan. 8:26; 10:1 **10:15** [a] Dan. 8:18; 10:9 **10:16** [a] Dan. 8:15 [b] Jer. 1:9; Dan. 10:10 [c] Dan. 10:8, 9 [1] Theodotion and Vulgate read *the son;* Septuagint reads *a hand.* **10:19** [a] Dan. 10:11 [b] Judg. 6:23; Is. 43:1; Dan. 10:12 **10:20** [a] Dan. 10:13 **10:21** [a] [Rev. 12:7] **11:1** [a] Dan. 9:1 [b] Dan. 5:31 **11:3** [a] Dan. 7:6; 8:5 [b] Dan. 8:4; 11:16, 36 **11:4** [a] Zech. 2:6 [b] Dan. 8:22 **11:6** [1] Literally *arm* [2] Literally *arm* **11:8** [1] Or *molded images* **11:10** [a] Is. 8:8 [b] Dan. 11:7

LIVE THE TRUTH

## DOING WHAT IS RIGHT

**11:1** Daniel was in a difficult situation. He had committed his life to following God, but he lived among the Babylonians after they had destroyed and plundered Jerusalem. He faced unimaginable pressure to join the Babylonians around him in their ungodly lifestyle. Yet, he didn't. Instead, Daniel obeyed God at every turn. Even more than that, he lived civilly toward the Babylonians and served them faithfully, just as God had commanded (see Jer. 29:4–7). Daniel perfectly balanced obedience to God and respect toward ungodly authority. He did what was right by God, even when it was difficult.

Every day we have choices to make. The right thing to do, in every circumstance, is to obey God, even if that requires personal sacrifice. Daniel did the right things, and he did them the right way, even when he was the only one. It worked out amazingly well for Daniel, but we may not see the same sort of results in our lives. Even if we don't, we must believe God's way is the right way. To do what is right, we listen, and obey the One who is always right—God Himself.

11 "And the king of the South shall be [a]moved with rage, and go out and fight with him, with the king of the North, who shall muster a great multitude; but the [b]multitude shall be given into the hand of his *enemy.* 12 When he has taken away the multitude, his heart will be lifted up; and he will cast down tens of thousands, but he will not prevail. 13 For the king of the North will return and muster a multitude greater than the former, and shall certainly come at the end of some years with a great army and much equipment.

14 "Now in those times many shall rise up against the king of the South. Also, violent men[1] of your people shall exalt themselves in fulfillment of the vision, but they shall [a]fall. 15 So the king of the North shall come and [a]build a siege mound, and take a fortified city; and the forces[1] of the South shall not withstand *him.* Even his choice troops *shall have* no strength to resist. 16 But he who comes against him [a]shall do according to his own will, and [b]no one shall stand against him. He shall stand in the Glorious Land with destruction in his power.[1]

17 "He shall also [a]set his face to enter with the strength of his whole kingdom, and upright ones[1] with him; thus shall he do. And he shall give him the daughter of women to destroy it; but she shall not stand *with him,* [b]or be for him. 18 After this he shall turn his face to the coastlands, and shall take many. But a ruler shall bring the reproach against them to an end; and with the reproach removed, he shall turn back on him. 19 Then he shall turn his face toward the fortress of his own land; but he shall [a]stumble and fall, [b]and not be found.

20 "There shall arise in his place one who imposes taxes *on* the glorious kingdom; but within a few days he shall be destroyed, but not in anger or in battle. 21 And in his place [a]shall arise a vile person, to whom they will not give the honor of royalty; but he shall come in peaceably, and seize the kingdom by intrigue. 22 With the force[1] of a [a]flood they shall be swept away from before him and be broken, [b]and also the prince of the covenant. 23 And after the league *is made* with him [a]he shall act deceitfully, for he shall come up and become strong with a small *number of* people. 24 He shall enter peaceably, even into the richest places of the province; and he shall do *what* his fathers have not done, nor his forefathers: he shall disperse among them the plunder, spoil, and riches; and he shall devise his plans against the strongholds, but *only* for a time.

25 "He shall stir up his power and his courage against the king of the South with a great army. And the king of the South shall be stirred up to battle with a very great and mighty army; but he shall not stand, for they shall devise plans against him. 26 Yes, those who eat of the portion of his delicacies shall destroy him; his army shall be swept away, and many shall fall down slain. 27 Both these kings' hearts *shall be* bent on evil, and they shall speak lies at the same table; but it shall not prosper, for the end *will* still *be* at the [a]appointed time. 28 While returning to his land with great riches, his heart shall be *moved* against the holy covenant; so he shall do *damage* and return to his own land.

### THE NORTHERN KING'S BLASPHEMIES

29 "At the appointed time he shall return and go toward the south; but it shall not be like the former or the latter. 30 [a]For ships from Cyprus[1] shall come against him; therefore he shall be grieved, and return in rage against the holy covenant, and do *damage.*

"So he shall return and show regard for those who forsake the holy covenant. 31 And

**11:11** [a] Prov. 16:14 [b] [Ps. 33:10, 16] **11:14** [a] Job 9:13 [1] Or *robbers,* literally *sons of breakage* **11:15** [a] Ezek. 4:2; 17:17 [1] Literally *arms* **11:16** [a] Dan. 8:4, 7 [b] Josh. 1:5 [1] Literally *hand* **11:17** [a] 2 Chr. 20:3 [b] Dan. 9:26 [1] Or *bring equitable terms* **11:19** [a] Jer. 46:6 [b] Ps. 37:36 **11:21** [a] Dan. 7:8 **11:22** [a] Dan. 9:26 [b] Dan. 8:10, 11 [1] Literally *arms* **11:23** [a] Dan. 8:25 **11:27** [a] Hab. 2:3 **11:30** [a] Jer. 2:10 [1] Hebrew *Kittim,* western lands, especially Cyprus

> **11:31** Antiochus would **defile the sanctuary** by sacrificing a pig on the altar. He put a stop to the daily sacrifices, and he set up an image of Zeus in the holy place. Jesus said that a similar thing would happen just prior to His return (Matt. 24:15).

forces[1] shall be mustered by him, [a]and they
shall defile the sanctuary fortress; then they
shall take away the daily *sacrifices,* and place
*there* the abomination of desolation. 32 Those
who do wickedly against the covenant he shall
corrupt with flattery; but the people who know
their God shall be strong, and carry out *great
exploits.* 33 And those of the people who under-
stand shall instruct many; yet *for many* days
they shall fall by sword and flame, by captivity
and plundering. 34 Now when they fall, they
shall be aided with a little help; but many shall
join with them by intrigue. 35 And *some* of those
of understanding shall fall, [a]to refine them,
purify *them,* and make *them* white, *until* the
time of the end; because *it is* still for the ap-
pointed time.
36 "Then the king shall do according to his
own will: he shall [a]exalt and magnify himself
above every god, shall speak blasphemies
against the God of gods, and shall prosper till
the wrath has been accomplished; for what has
been determined shall be done. 37 He shall regard
neither the God[1] of his fathers nor the desire of
women, [a]nor regard any god; for he shall exalt
himself above *them* all. 38 But in their place
he shall honor a god of fortresses; and a god
which his fathers did not know he shall honor
with gold and silver, with precious stones and
pleasant things. 39 Thus he shall act against the
strongest fortresses with a foreign god, which
he shall acknowledge, *and* advance *its* glory;
and he shall cause them to rule over many, and
divide the land for gain.

### *THE NORTHERN KING'S CONQUESTS*

40 "At the [a]time of the end the king of the
South shall attack him; and the king of the
North shall come against him [b]like a whirl-
wind, with chariots, [c]horsemen, and with many
ships; and he shall enter the countries, over-
whelm *them,* and pass through. 41 He shall also
enter the Glorious Land, and many *countries*
shall be overthrown; but these shall escape
from his hand: [a]Edom, Moab, and the promi-
nent people of Ammon. 42 He shall stretch out
his hand against the countries, and the land
of [a]Egypt shall not escape. 43 He shall have
power over the treasures of gold and silver,
and over all the precious things of Egypt; also
the Libyans and Ethiopians *shall follow* [a]at
his heels. 44 But news from the east and the
north shall trouble him; therefore he shall go
out with great fury to destroy and annihilate
many. 45 And he shall plant the tents of his
palace between the seas and [a]the glorious holy
mountain; [b]yet he shall come to his end, and
no one will help him.

### *PROPHECY OF THE END TIME*

12 "At that time Michael shall stand up,
The great prince who stands *watch* over
the sons of your people;
[a]And there shall be a time of trouble,
Such as never was since there was a
nation,
*Even* to that time.
And at that time your people [b]shall be
delivered,
Every one who is found [c]written in the
book.
2 And many of those who sleep in the dust
of the earth shall awake,
[a]Some to everlasting life,
Some to shame [b]*and* everlasting
contempt.
3 Those who are wise shall [a]shine
Like the brightness of the firmament,
[b]And those who turn many to
righteousness
[c]Like the stars forever and ever.

4 "But you, Daniel, [a]shut up the words, and
seal the book until the time of the end; many
shall [b]run to and fro, and knowledge shall
increase."
5 Then I, Daniel, looked; and there stood
two others, one on this riverbank and the other
on that [a]riverbank. 6 And *one* said to the man
clothed in [a]linen, who *was* above the waters of
the river, [b]"How long shall the fulfillment of
these wonders *be?*"
7 Then I heard the man clothed in linen, who
*was* above the waters of the river, when he [a]held
up his right hand and his left hand to heaven,
and swore by Him [b]who lives forever, [c]that *it
shall be* for a time, times, and half *a time;* [d]and
when the power of [e]the holy people has been
completely shattered, all these *things* shall be
finished.
8 Although I heard, I did not understand.
Then I said, "My lord, what *shall be* the end of
these *things?*"
9 And he said, "Go *your way,* Daniel, for the
words *are* closed up and sealed till the time of
the end. 10 [a]Many shall be purified, made white,

**11:31** [a] Dan. 8:11–13; 12:11 [1] Literally *arms* **11:35** [a] Dan. 12:10 **11:36** [a] Dan. 7:8, 25 **11:37** [a] Is. 14:13 [1] Or *gods* **11:40** [a] Dan. 11:27, 35; 12:4, 9 [b] Is. 21:1 [c] Rev. 9:16 **11:41** [a] Is. 11:14 **11:42** [a] Joel 3:19 **11:43** [a] Ex. 11:8 **11:45** [a] Ps. 48:2 [b] Rev. 19:20 **12:1** [a] Jer. 30:7 [b] Rom. 11:26 [c] Ex. 32:32 **12:2** [a] [John 5:28, 29] [b] [Is. 66:24] **12:3** [a] Matt. 13:43 [b] [James 5:19, 20] [c] 1 Cor. 15:41 **12:4** [a] Rev. 22:10 [b] Amos 8:12 **12:5** [a] Dan. 10:4 **12:6** [a] Ezek. 9:2 [b] Dan. 8:13; 12:8 **12:7** [a] Deut. 32:40 [b] Dan. 4:34 [c] Dan. 7:25 [d] Luke 21:24 [e] Dan. 8:24 **12:10** [a] Zech. 13:9

KNOW THE TRUTH

# THE DOCTRINE OF THE FUTURE

## PART 1: OVERVIEW OF THE DOCTRINE OF THE FUTURE

**12:1–3** The Bible is the reliable record of God's dealings with people in the past, the only authoritative source of truth and practice for our present, and the sole trustworthy glance into the future. The Bible contains two main forms of prophecy: forthtelling and foretelling. **Forthtelling** is a word from God concerning present needs, wisdom, rebuke, instruction, and so forth. An example of forthtelling is Haggai exhorting God's people to prioritize rebuilding the temple and cease competing occupations (see Hag. 1:1–8). Haggai gave a "now" word for a "now" need.

**Foretelling** is a message from God about a future event. Foretelling prophecies in the Bible split into two main categories. First, numerous biblical prophecies concerning the future were *fulfilled* during the biblical period of history. For example, Israel's deliverance from Egypt, David's ascension to the throne, Judah's exile and return, and a multitude of fulfilled prophecies in the life of Jesus. Second, some prophecies concern the future and have *not yet come to pass* but certainly will. These prophecies include the return of Jesus, the resurrection of the righteous to eternal life, the resurrection of the unrighteous to eternal destruction, and the creation of a new heaven and earth in which God will dwell with His people.

*For* **THE DOCTRINE OF THE FUTURE: PART 2: THE RETURN OF JESUS,** *turn to 1 Thessalonians 5:23 on page 1222.*

and refined, [b]but the wicked shall do wickedly;
and none of the wicked shall understand, but
[c]the wise shall understand.
11"And from the time *that* the daily *sacrifice* is
taken away, and the abomination of desolation is
set up, *there shall be* one thousand two hundred
and ninety days. 12 Blessed *is* he who waits, and
comes to the one thousand three hundred and
thirty-five days.
13"But you, go *your way* till the end; [a]for you
shall rest, [b]and will arise to your inheritance at
the end of the days."

**12:10** [b] Is. 32:6, 7 [c] John 7:17; 8:47 **12:13** [a] Rev. 14:13 [b] Ps. 1:5

# *The Book of the Prophet*
# HOSEA

| AUTHOR | KEY VERSES | READING TIME |
|---|---|---|
| Hosea | Hosea 3:4–5 | 39 minutes |

The prophet Hosea ministered to the northern kingdom of Israel (also called Ephraim, after its largest tribe) with a message fit for the southern kingdom of Judah as well. The nation enjoyed prosperity and growth, but moral corruption and spiritual adultery permeated the people. God instructed Hosea to take a wife named Gomer, but the prophet would find his troubled marriage to be an accurate and tragic dramatization of the unfaithfulness of God's people. During his half-century of prophetic ministry, Hosea repeatedly echoed his threefold message: God abhors sin. Judgment is certain. God's love stands.

**Occasion:** Hosea offers the possibility of salvation to both the northern and southern kingdoms if only they will turn back to God from idolatry.

**Main Point:** God cannot tolerate His people's sin and judgment must come, but His love for them endures.

**Big Ideas:** God is faithful to us even when we are unfaithful to Him. God's judgment is for our good, pushing us back toward obedience. We are to be faithful to God because He is faithful to us.

## OUTLINE:

I. The Unfaithfulness and Restoration in Hosea's Family (chs. 1–3)
II. The Unfaithfulness of Israel (chs. 4–8)
III. The Judgment upon Israel (chs. 9–10)
IV. The Restoration of Israel (chs. 11–14)

**792 BC**
Azariah (Uzziah) becomes king in Judah

**792 BC**
Jeroboam II becomes king in Israel

**c. 785 BC**
Hosea begins to prophesy in Israel

**755 BC**
Isaiah begins to prophesy in Judah

**752 BC**
Jotham becomes king in Judah

**c. 745 BC**
The Assyrian Empire begins under Tiglath-Pileser

**736 BC**
Ahaz becomes king in Judah

**732 BC**
The Assyrians defeat Damascus

**729 BC**
Hezekiah becomes king in Judah

**725 BC**
Hosea's ministry ends

**722 BC**
The Assyrians defeat Israel

1 The word of the LORD that came to Hosea the son of Beeri, in the days of [a]Uzziah, [b]Jotham, [c]Ahaz, *and* [d]Hezekiah, kings of Judah, and in the days of [e]Jeroboam the son of Joash, king of Israel.

### THE FAMILY OF HOSEA

[2]When the LORD began to speak by Hosea, the LORD said to Hosea:

[a]"Go, take yourself a wife of harlotry
And children of harlotry,
For [b]the land has committed great harlotry
*By departing* from the LORD."

[3]So he went and took Gomer the daughter of Diblaim, and she conceived and bore him a son.

> **1:2–3 Gomer** may have been a prostitute at the time **Hosea** married her, or perhaps she had participated in a ritual sexual act as part of a Baal cult. Or, that descriptive phrase anticipates what Gomer would become following her marriage to Hosea.

[4]Then the LORD said to him:

"Call his name Jezreel,
For in a little *while*
[a]I will avenge the bloodshed of Jezreel on the house of Jehu,
[b]And bring an end to the kingdom of the house of Israel.
5 [a]It shall come to pass in that day
That I will break the bow of Israel in the Valley of Jezreel."

[6]And she conceived again and bore a daughter. Then *God* said to him:

"Call her name Lo-Ruhamah,[1]
[a]For I will no longer have mercy on the house of Israel,
But I will utterly take them away.[2]
7 [a]Yet I will have mercy on the house of Judah,
Will save them by the LORD their God,
And [b]will not save them by bow,
Nor by sword or battle,
By horses or horsemen."

[8]Now when she had weaned Lo-Ruhamah, she conceived and bore a son. [9]Then *God* said:

"Call his name Lo-Ammi,[1]
For you *are* not My people,
And I will not be your *God.*

> **1:6–9 Lo-Ruhamah** means "no mercy" or "not loved," foreshadowing the Lord's rejection of Israel. **Lo-Ammi** means "not my people," threatening the termination of the Lord's covenant relationship with His people (see Lev. 26:12).

### THE RESTORATION OF ISRAEL

10 "Yet [a]the number of the children of Israel
Shall be as the sand of the sea,
Which cannot be measured or numbered.
[b]And it shall come to pass
In the place where it was said to them,
'You *are* not My [c]people,'[1]
*There* it shall be said to them,
'*You are* [d]sons of the living God.'

**1:1** [a] Amos 1:1 [b] 2 Chr. 27 [c] 2 Chr. 28 [d] 2 Chr. 29:1—32:33 [e] 2 Kin. 13:13; 14:23–29 **1:2** [a] Hos. 3:1 [b] Jer. 2:13 **1:4** [a] 2 Kin. 10:11 [b] 2 Kin. 15:8–10; 17:6, 23; 18:11 **1:5** [a] 2 Kin. 15:29 **1:6** [a] 2 Kin. 17:6 [1] Literally *No-Mercy* [2] Or *That I may forgive them at all* **1:7** [a] 2 Kin. 19:29–35 [b] [Zech. 4:6] **1:9** [1] Literally *Not-My-People* **1:10** [a] Gen. 22:17; 32:12 [b] 1 Pet. 2:10 [c] Rom. 9:26 [d] [John 1:12] [1] Hebrew *lo-ammi* (compare verse 9)

APPLY THE TRUTH

## BETRAYAL

**1:2** Hosea's story is heartbreaking. God instructed him to marry a woman who would be unfaithful to him. Over and over, Hosea dealt with the devastation of betrayal. Yet, he chose to love, forgive, and care for his wife. God had Hosea go through this to illustrate how He felt about the Israelites. Though they had been unfaithful to Him, He would not stop loving them and being faithful to them. God had every reason to give up on His people, but He didn't because they were *His* people. Instead, He continued to love them, forgive them, and do what it took to restore them to Himself.

No one wants to experience betrayal, whether it's by a friend, sibling, parent, or significant other. But if we do, God can sympathize with us. He knows how we feel, and He sets an example for how to forgive and move forward. Just as He had Hosea move toward his wife to restore their relationship, God has moved toward us to restore our relationship through Jesus. It's now our turn. The next time you feel betrayed, treat that person how God has treated you. Love. Forgive. Move toward that person to reconcile.

11 [a]Then the children of Judah and the
children of Israel
Shall be gathered together,
And appoint for themselves one head;
And they shall come up out of the land,
For great *will be* the day of Jezreel!

2 Say to your brethren, 'My people,'[1]
And to your sisters, 'Mercy[2] *is shown.*'

## GOD'S UNFAITHFUL PEOPLE

2 "Bring charges against your mother, bring
charges;
For [a]she *is* not My wife, nor *am* I her
Husband!
Let her put away her [b]harlotries from her
sight,
And her adulteries from between her breasts;
3 Lest [a]I strip her naked
And expose her, as in the day she was
[b]born,
And make her like a wilderness,
And set her like a dry land,
And slay her with [c]thirst.

4 "I will not have mercy on her children,
For they *are* the [a]children of harlotry.
5 For their mother has played the harlot;
She who conceived them has behaved
shamefully.
For she said, 'I will go after my lovers,
[a]Who give *me* my bread and my water,
My wool and my linen,
My oil and my drink.'

6 "Therefore, behold,
[a]I will hedge up your way with thorns,
And wall her in,
So that she cannot find her paths.
7 She will chase her lovers,
But not overtake them;
Yes, she will seek them, but not find *them*.
Then she will say,
[a]'I will go and return to my [b]first husband,
For then *it was* better for me than now.'
8 For she did not [a]know
That I gave her grain, new wine, and oil,
And multiplied her silver and gold—
*Which* they prepared for Baal.

9 "Therefore I will return and take away
My grain in its time
And My new wine in its season,
And will take back My wool and My linen,
*Given* to cover her nakedness.
10 Now [a]I will uncover her lewdness in the
sight of her lovers,
And no one shall deliver her from My hand.
11 [a]I will also cause all her mirth to cease,
Her feast days,
Her New Moons,
Her Sabbaths—
All her appointed feasts.

12 "And I will destroy her vines and her fig
trees,
Of which she has said,
'These *are* my wages that my lovers have
given me.'
So I will make them a forest,
And the beasts of the field shall eat them.
13 I will punish her
For the days of the Baals to which she
burned incense.
She decked herself with her earrings and
jewelry,
And went after her lovers;
But Me she forgot," says the LORD.

## GOD'S MERCY ON HIS PEOPLE

14 "Therefore, behold, I will allure her,
Will bring her into the wilderness,
And speak comfort to her.
15 I will give her her vineyards from there,
And [a]the Valley of Achor as a door of hope;
She shall sing there,
As in [b]the days of her youth,
[c]As in the day when she came up from the
land of Egypt.

16 "And it shall be, in that day,"
Says the LORD,
"*That* you will call Me 'My Husband,'[1]
And no longer call Me 'My Master,'[2]
17 For [a]I will take from her mouth the names
of the Baals,
And they shall be remembered by their
name no more.
18 In that day I will make a [a]covenant for
them
With the beasts of the field,
With the birds of the air,
And *with* the creeping things of the
ground.
Bow and sword of battle [b]I will shatter
from the earth,
To make them [c]lie down safely.

19 "I will betroth you to Me forever;
Yes, I will betroth you to Me
In righteousness and justice,
In lovingkindness and mercy;
20 I will betroth you to Me in faithfulness,
And [a]you shall know the LORD.

21 "It shall come to pass in that day
*That* [a]I will answer," says the LORD;
"I will answer the heavens,
And they shall answer the earth.

1:11 [a] Is. 11:11–13 2:1 [1] Hebrew *Ammi* (compare 1:9, 10) [2] Hebrew *Ruhamah* (compare 1:6) 2:2 [a] Is. 50:1 [b] Ezek. 16:25 2:3 [a] Jer. 13:22, 26 [b] Ezek. 16:4–7, 22 [c] Amos 8:11–13 2:4 [a] John 8:41 2:5 [a] Hos. 2:8, 12 2:6 [a] Lam. 3:7, 9 2:7 [a] Luke 15:17, 18 [b] Ezek. 16:8; 23:4 2:8 [a] Is. 1:3 2:10 [a] Ezek. 16:37 2:11 [a] Amos 5:21; 8:10 2:15 [a] Josh. 7:26 [b] Ezek. 16:8–14 [c] Ex. 15:1 2:16 [1] Hebrew *Ishi* [2] Hebrew *Baali* 2:17 [a] Ex. 23:13 2:18 [a] Job 5:23 [b] Is. 2:4 [c] Lev. 26:5 2:20 [a] [Jer. 31:33, 34] 2:21 [a] Zech. 8:12

22 The earth shall answer
With grain,
With new wine,
And with oil;
They shall answer Jezreel.[1]
23 Then [a]I will sow her for Myself in the earth,
[b]And I will have mercy on *her who had* not
obtained mercy;[1]
Then [c]I will say to *those who were* not My
people,[2]
'You *are* My people!'
And they shall say, '*You are* my God!' "

### *ISRAEL WILL RETURN TO GOD*

**3** Then the LORD said to me, "Go again, love a
woman *who is* loved by a [a]lover[1] and is com-
mitting adultery, just like the love of the LORD
for the children of Israel, who look to other gods
and love *the* raisin cakes *of the pagans.*"
2 So I bought her for myself for fifteen *shekels*
of silver, and one and one-half homers of barley.
3 And I said to her, "You shall [a]stay with me many
days; you shall not play the harlot, nor shall
you have a man—so, too, *will* I *be* toward you."
4 For the children of Israel shall abide many
days [a]without king or prince, without sacrifice
or *sacred* pillar, without [b]ephod or [c]teraphim.
5 Afterward the children of Israel shall return
and [a]seek the LORD their God and [b]David their
king. They shall fear the LORD and His goodness
in the [c]latter days.

**SEEING JESUS IN THE SCRIPTURE**

**3:2–3** Hosea bought back Gomer with silver and barley so they could be reunited as husband and wife. This looks to how Judas betrayed Jesus for silver coins, an act that led to Jesus being crucified to reunite sinful people with God (see Matt. 26:15).

### *GOD'S CHARGE AGAINST ISRAEL*

**4** Hear the word of the LORD,
You children of Israel,
For the LORD *brings* a [a]charge against the
inhabitants of the land:

"There is no truth or mercy
Or [b]knowledge of God in the land.
2 *By* swearing and lying,
Killing and stealing and committing
adultery,
They break all restraint,
With bloodshed upon bloodshed.
3 Therefore [a]the land will mourn;
And [b]everyone who dwells there will
waste away
With the beasts of the field
And the birds of the air;
Even the fish of the sea will be taken away.

4 "Now let no man contend, or rebuke another;
For your people *are* like those [a]who
contend with the priest.
5 Therefore you shall stumble [a]in the day;
The prophet also shall stumble with you
in the night;
And I will destroy your mother.
6 [a]My people are destroyed for lack of
knowledge.
Because you have rejected knowledge,
I also will reject you from being priest
for Me;
[b]Because you have forgotten the law of
your God,
I also will forget your children.

7 "The more they increased,
The more they sinned against Me;
[a]I will change[1] their glory[2] into shame.
8 They eat up the sin of My people;
They set their heart on their iniquity.
9 And it shall be: [a]like people, like priest.
So I will punish them for their ways,
And reward them for their deeds.
10 For [a]they shall eat, but not have enough;
They shall commit harlotry, but not increase;
Because they have ceased obeying the
LORD.

### *THE IDOLATRY OF ISRAEL*

11 "Harlotry, wine, and new wine [a]enslave the
heart.
12 My people ask counsel from their
[a]wooden *idols,*
And their staff informs them.
For [b]the spirit of harlotry has caused *them*
to stray,
And they have played the harlot against
their God.
13 [a]They offer sacrifices on the
mountaintops,
And burn incense on the hills,
Under oaks, poplars, and terebinths,
Because their shade *is* good.
[b]Therefore your daughters commit harlotry,
And your brides commit adultery.

14 "I will not punish your daughters when
they commit harlotry,
Nor your brides when they commit
adultery;

2:22 [1] Literally *God Will Sow* 2:23 [a] Jer. 31:27 [b] Hos. 1:6 [c] Hos. 1:10 [1] Hebrew *lo-ruhamah* [2] Hebrew *lo-ammi* 3:1 [a] Jer. 3:20 [1] Literally *friend* or *husband* 3:3 [a] Deut. 21:13 3:4 [a] Hos. 10:3 [b] Ex. 28:4–12 [c] Judg. 17:5; 18:14, 17 3:5 [a] Jer. 50:4 [b] Jer. 30:9 [c] [Is. 2:2, 3] 4:1 [a] Is. 1:18 [b] Jer. 4:22 4:3 [a] Amos 5:16; 8:8 [b] Zeph. 1:3 4:4 [a] Deut. 17:12 4:5 [a] Jer. 15:8 4:6 [a] Is. 5:13 [b] Ezek. 22:26 4:7 [a] 1 Sam. 2:30 [1] Following Masoretic Text, Septuagint, and Vulgate; scribal tradition, Syriac, and Targum read *They will change.* [2] Following Masoretic Text, Septuagint, Syriac, Targum, and Vulgate; scribal tradition reads *My glory.* 4:9 [a] Is. 24:2 4:10 [a] Lev. 26:26 4:11 [a] Is. 5:12; 28:7 4:12 [a] Jer. 2:27 [b] Is. 44:19, 20 4:13 [a] Is. 1:29; 57:5, 7 [b] Amos 7:17

For *the men* themselves go apart with
harlots,
And offer sacrifices with a [a]ritual harlot.[1]
Therefore people *who* do not understand
will be trampled.

15 "Though you, Israel, play the harlot,
Let not Judah offend.
[a]Do not come up to Gilgal,
Nor go up to [b]Beth Aven,
[c]Nor swear an oath, *saying,* 'As the LORD
lives'—

16 "For Israel [a]is stubborn
Like a stubborn calf;
Now the LORD will let them forage
Like a lamb in open country.

17 "Ephraim *is* joined to idols,
[a]Let him alone.
18 Their drink is rebellion,
They commit harlotry continually.
[a]Her rulers dearly[1] love dishonor.
19 [a]The wind has wrapped her up in its wings,
And [b]they shall be ashamed because of
their sacrifices.

## IMPENDING JUDGMENT ON ISRAEL AND JUDAH

5 "Hear this, O priests!
Take heed, O house of Israel!
Give ear, O house of the king!
For yours *is* the judgment,
Because [a]you have been a snare to Mizpah
And a net spread on Tabor.
2 The revolters are [a]deeply involved in
slaughter,
Though I rebuke them all.
3 [a]I know Ephraim,
And Israel is not hidden from Me;
For now, O Ephraim, [b]you commit harlotry;
Israel is defiled.

4 "They do not direct their deeds
Toward turning to their God,
For [a]the spirit of harlotry is in their midst,
And they do not know the LORD.
5 The [a]pride of Israel testifies to his face;
Therefore Israel and Ephraim stumble in
their iniquity;
Judah also stumbles with them.

6 "With their flocks and herds
[a]They shall go to seek the LORD,
But they will not find *Him;*
He has withdrawn Himself from them.
7 They have [a]dealt treacherously with the
LORD,
For they have begotten pagan children.
Now a New Moon shall devour them and
their heritage.

8 "Blow[a] the ram's horn in Gibeah,
The trumpet in Ramah!
[b]Cry aloud *at* [c]Beth Aven,
'*Look* behind you, O Benjamin!'
9 Ephraim shall be desolate in the day of
rebuke;
Among the tribes of Israel I make known
what is sure.

10 "The princes of Judah are like those who
[a]remove a landmark;
I will pour out My wrath on them like water.
11 Ephraim is [a]oppressed *and* broken in
judgment,
Because he willingly walked by [b]*human*
precept.
12 Therefore I *will be* to Ephraim like a moth,
And to the house of Judah [a]like
rottenness.

13 "When Ephraim saw his sickness,
And Judah *saw* his [a]wound,
Then Ephraim went [b]to Assyria
And sent to King Jareb;
Yet he cannot cure you,
Nor heal you of your wound.
14 For [a]I *will be* like a lion to Ephraim,
And like a young lion to the house of
Judah.
[b]I, *even* I, will tear *them* and go away;
I will take *them* away, and no one shall
rescue.
15 I will return again to My place
Till they acknowledge their offense.
Then they will seek My face;
In their affliction they will earnestly seek Me."

## A CALL TO REPENTANCE

6 Come,[a] and let us return to the LORD;
For [b]He has torn, but [c]He will heal us;
He has stricken, but He will bind us up.
2 [a]After two days He will revive us;
On the third day He will raise us up,
That we may live in His sight.

**SEEING JESUS IN THE SCRIPTURE**

**6:2** This is a prophecy of Jesus' resurrection. On the third day, Jesus rose from the dead, defeating sin and death (see 1 Cor. 15:4). All who believe in Jesus will live with Him forevermore.

**4:14** [a] Deut. 23:18 [1] Compare Deuteronomy 23:18 **4:15** [a] Hos. 9:15; 12:11 [b] 1 Kin. 12:29 [c] Amos 8:14 **4:16** [a] Jer. 3:6; 7:24; 8:5 **4:17** [a] Matt. 15:14 **4:18** [a] Mic. 3:11 [1] Hebrew is difficult; a Jewish tradition reads *Her rulers shamefully love, 'Give!'* **4:19** [a] Jer. 51:1 [b] Is. 1:29 **5:1** [a] Hos. 6:9 **5:2** [a] Is. 29:15 **5:3** [a] Amos 3:2; 5:12 [b] Hos. 4:17 **5:4** [a] Hos. 4:12 **5:5** [a] Hos. 7:10 **5:6** [a] Prov. 1:28 **5:7** [a] Jer. 3:20 **5:8** [a] Joel 2:1 [b] Is. 10:30 [c] Josh. 7:2 **5:10** [a] Deut. 19:14; 27:17 **5:11** [a] Deut. 28:33 [b] Mic. 6:16 **5:12** [a] Prov. 12:4 **5:13** [a] Jer. 30:12–15 [b] 2 Kin. 15:19 **5:14** [a] Lam. 3:10 [b] Ps. 50:22 **6:1** [a] Is. 1:18 [b] Deut. 32:39 [c] Jer. 30:17 **6:2** [a] [1 Cor. 15:4]

3 [a]Let us know,
Let us pursue the knowledge of the LORD.
His going forth is established [b]as the morning;
[c]He will come to us [d]like the rain,
Like the latter *and* former rain to the earth.

## *IMPENITENCE OF ISRAEL AND JUDAH*

4 "O Ephraim, what shall I do to you?
O Judah, what shall I do to you?
For your faithfulness is like a morning cloud,
And like the early dew it goes away.
5 Therefore I have hewn *them* by the prophets,
I have slain them by [a]the words of My mouth;
And your judgments *are like* light *that* goes forth.
6 For I desire [a]mercy and [b]not sacrifice,
And the [c]knowledge of God more than burnt offerings.

7 "But like men[1] they transgressed the covenant;
There they dealt treacherously with Me.
8 [a]Gilead *is* a city of evildoers
*And* defiled with blood.
9 As bands of robbers lie in wait for a man,
*So* the company of [a]priests [b]murder on the way to Shechem;
Surely they commit [c]lewdness.
10 I have seen a horrible thing in the house of Israel:
There *is* the harlotry of Ephraim;
Israel is defiled.
11 Also, O Judah, a harvest is appointed for you,
When I return the captives of My people.

7 "When I would have healed Israel,
Then the iniquity of Ephraim was uncovered,
And the wickedness of Samaria.
For [a]they have committed fraud;
A thief comes in;
A band of robbers takes spoil outside.
2 They do not consider in their hearts
*That* [a]I remember all their wickedness;
Now their own deeds have surrounded them;
They are before My face.
3 They make a [a]king glad with their wickedness,
And princes [b]with their lies.

4 "They[a] *are* all adulterers.
Like an oven heated by a baker—
He ceases stirring *the fire* after kneading the dough,
Until it is leavened.
5 In the day of our king
Princes have made *him* sick, inflamed with [a]wine;
He stretched out his hand with scoffers.
6 They prepare their heart like an oven,
While they lie in wait;
Their baker[1] sleeps all night;
In the morning it burns like a flaming fire.
7 They are all hot, like an oven,
And have devoured their judges;
All their kings have fallen.
[a]None among them calls upon Me.

8 "Ephraim [a]has mixed himself among the peoples;
Ephraim is a cake unturned.
9 [a]Aliens have devoured his strength,
But he does not know *it;*
Yes, gray hairs are here and there on him,
Yet he does not know *it.*
10 And the [a]pride of Israel testifies to his face,
But [b]they do not return to the LORD their God,
Nor seek Him for all this.

## *FUTILE RELIANCE ON THE NATIONS*

11 "Ephraim[a] also is like a silly dove, without sense—
[b]They call to Egypt,
They go to [c]Assyria.

> **7:11** For a while, Israel paid "protection money" in the form of taxes to **Assyria** to keep them from attacking. When the Israelites got tired of sending money to a foreign king, they decided to join with **Egypt** and fight Assyria. In 722 BC, the Assyrians responded by attacking Samaria, the capital of the northern kingdom, and taking many people captive. The northern kingdom never recovered from the devastation.

12 Wherever they go, I will [a]spread My net on them;
I will bring them down like birds of the air;
I will chastise them
[b]According to what their congregation has heard.

13 "Woe to them, for they have fled from Me!
Destruction to them,
Because they have transgressed against Me!
Though [a]I redeemed them,
Yet they have spoken lies against Me.

**6:3** [a] Is. 54:13 [b] 2 Sam. 23:4 [c] Ps. 72:6 [d] Job 29:23 **6:5** [a] [Jer. 23:29] **6:6** [a] Matt. 9:13; 12:7 [b] [Mic. 6:6–8] [c] [John 17:3] **6:7** [1] Or *like Adam* **6:8** [a] Hos. 12:11 **6:9** [a] Hos. 5:1 [b] Jer. 7:9, 10 [c] Ezek. 22:9; 23:27 **7:1** [a] Hos. 5:1 **7:2** [a] Jer. 14:10; 17:1 **7:3** [a] Hos. 1:1 [b] [Rom. 1:32] **7:4** [a] Jer. 9:2; 23:10 **7:5** [a] Is. 28:1, 7 **7:6** [1] Following Masoretic Text and Vulgate; Syriac and Targum read *Their anger;* Septuagint reads *Ephraim.* **7:7** [a] Is. 64:7 **7:8** [a] Ps. 106:35 **7:9** [a] Hos. 8:7 **7:10** [a] Hos. 5:5 [b] Is. 9:13 **7:11** [a] Hos. 11:11 [b] Is. 30:3 [c] Hos. 5:13; 8:9 **7:12** [a] Ezek. 12:13 [b] Lev. 26:14 **7:13** [a] Mic. 6:4

14 [a]They did not cry out to Me with their heart
When they wailed upon their beds.

"They assemble together for[1] grain and
new [b]wine,
They rebel against Me;[2]
15 Though I disciplined *and* strengthened
their arms,
Yet they devise evil against Me;
16 They return, *but* not to the Most High;[1]
[a]They are like a treacherous bow.
Their princes shall fall by the sword
For the [b]cursings of their tongue.
This *shall be* their derision [c]in the land of
Egypt.

## THE APOSTASY OF ISRAEL

8 "*Set* the trumpet[1] to your mouth!
*He shall come* [a]like an eagle against the
house of the LORD,
Because they have transgressed My covenant
And rebelled against My law.
2 [a]Israel will cry to Me,
'My God, [b]we know You!'
3 Israel has rejected the good;
The enemy will pursue him.

4 "They[a] set up kings, but not by Me;
They made princes, but I did not
acknowledge *them.*
From their silver and gold
They made idols for themselves—
That they might be cut off.
5 Your calf is rejected, O Samaria!
My anger is aroused against them—
[a]How long until they attain to innocence?
6 For from Israel *is* even this:
A [a]workman made it, and it *is* not God;
But the calf of Samaria shall be broken to
pieces.

**8:5** The **calf** in this verse was probably an idol that people worshiped in **Samaria**. Calves and bulls were especially popular idols in ancient times. People believed the animals symbolized fertility.

7 "They[a] sow the wind,
And reap the whirlwind.
The stalk has no bud;
It shall never produce meal.
If it should produce,
[b]Aliens would swallow it up.
8 [a]Israel is swallowed up;
Now they are among the Gentiles
[b]Like a vessel in which *is* no pleasure.
9 For they have gone up to Assyria,
*Like* [a]a wild donkey alone by itself;
Ephraim [b]has hired lovers.
10 Yes, though they have hired among the
nations,
Now [a]I will gather them;
And they shall sorrow a little,[1]
Because of the burden[2] of [b]the king of
princes.

11 "Because Ephraim has made many altars
for sin,
They have become for him altars for
sinning.
12 I have written for him [a]the great things of
My law,
*But* they were considered a strange thing.
13 *For* the sacrifices of My offerings [a]they
sacrifice flesh and eat *it,*
[b]*But* the LORD does not accept them.
[c]Now He will remember their iniquity and
punish their sins.
They shall return to Egypt.

14 "For[a] Israel has forgotten [b]his Maker,
And has built temples;[1]
Judah also has multiplied [c]fortified cities;
But [d]I will send fire upon his cities,
And it shall devour his palaces."

## JUDGMENT OF ISRAEL'S SIN

9 Do[a] not rejoice, O Israel, with joy like
*other* peoples,
For you have played the harlot against
your God.
You have made love *for* [b]hire on every
threshing floor.
2 The threshing floor and the winepress
Shall not feed them,
And the new wine shall fail in her.
3 They shall not dwell in [a]the LORD's land,
[b]But Ephraim shall return to Egypt,
And [c]shall eat unclean *things* in Assyria.
4 They shall not offer wine *offerings* to the
LORD,
Nor [a]shall their [b]sacrifices be pleasing to
Him.
*It shall be* like bread of mourners to them;
All who eat it shall be defiled.
For their bread *shall be* for their *own* life;
It shall not come into the house of the
LORD.

**7:14** [a] Job 35:9, 10 [b] Amos 2:8 [1] Following Masoretic Text and Targum; Vulgate reads *thought upon;* Septuagint reads *slashed themselves for* (compare 1 Kings 18:28). [2] Following Masoretic Text, Syriac, and Targum; Septuagint omits *They rebel against Me;* Vulgate reads *They departed from Me.* **7:16** [a] Ps. 78:57 [b] Ps. 73:9 [c] Hos. 8:13; 9:3 [1] Or *upward* **8:1** [a] Deut. 28:49 [1] Hebrew *shophar,* ram's horn **8:2** [a] Ps. 78:34 [b] Titus 1:16 **8:4** [a] 2 Kin. 15:23, 25 **8:5** [a] Jer. 13:27 **8:6** [a] Is. 40:19 **8:7** [a] Prov. 22:8 [b] Hos. 7:9 **8:8** [a] 2 Kin. 17:6 [b] Jer. 22:28; 25:34 **8:9** [a] Jer. 2:24 [b] Ezek. 16:33, 34 **8:10** [a] Ezek. 16:37; 22:20 [b] Is. 10:8 [1] Or *begin to diminish* [2] Or *oracle* **8:12** [a] [Deut. 4:6–8] **8:13** [a] Zech. 7:6 [b] Jer. 14:10 [c] Amos 8:7 **8:14** [a] Deut. 32:18 [b] Is. 29:23 [c] Num. 32:17 [d] Jer. 17:27 [1] Or *palaces* **9:1** [a] Is. 22:12, 13 [b] Jer. 44:17 **9:3** [a] [Lev. 25:23] [b] Hos. 7:16; 8:13 [c] Ezek. 4:13 **9:4** [a] Jer. 6:20 [b] Hos. 8:13

5 What will you do in the appointed day,
And in the day of the feast of the LORD?
6 For indeed they are gone because of
destruction.
Egypt shall gather them up;
Memphis shall bury them.
[a]Nettles shall possess their valuables of
silver;
Thorns *shall be* in their tents.

7 The [a]days of punishment have come;
The days of recompense have come.
Israel knows!
The prophet *is* a [b]fool,
[c]The spiritual man *is* insane,
Because of the greatness of your iniquity
and great enmity.
8 The [a]watchman of Ephraim *is* with my God;
But the prophet *is* a fowler's[1] snare in all
his ways—
Enmity in the house of his God.
9 [a]They are deeply corrupted,
As in the days of [b]Gibeah.
He will remember their iniquity;
He will punish their sins.

10 "I found Israel
Like grapes in the [a]wilderness;
I saw your fathers
As the [b]firstfruits on the fig tree in its first
season.
*But* they went to [c]Baal Peor,
And separated themselves *to that* shame;
[d]They became an abomination like the
thing they loved.
11 *As for* Ephraim, their glory shall fly away
like a bird—
No birth, no pregnancy, and no
conception!
12 Though they bring up their children,
Yet I will bereave them to the last man.
Yes, [a]woe to them when I depart from
them!
13 Just [a]as I saw Ephraim like Tyre, planted
in a pleasant place,
So Ephraim will bring out his children to
the murderer."

14 Give them, O LORD—
What will You give?
Give them [a]a miscarrying womb
And dry breasts!

15 "All their wickedness *is* in [a]Gilgal,
For there I hated them.
Because of the evil of their deeds
I will drive them from My house;
I will love them no more.
[b]All their princes *are* rebellious.
16 Ephraim is [a]stricken,
Their root is dried up;
They shall bear no fruit.
Yes, were they to bear children,
I would kill the darlings of their womb."

17 My God will [a]cast them away,
Because they did not obey Him;
And they shall be [b]wanderers among the
nations.

### ISRAEL'S SIN AND CAPTIVITY

10 Israel [a]empties *his* vine;
He brings forth fruit for himself.
According to the multitude of his fruit
[b]He has increased the altars;
According to the bounty of his land
They have embellished *his sacred* pillars.
2 Their heart is [a]divided;
Now they are held guilty.
He will break down their altars;
He will ruin their *sacred* pillars.

3 For now they say,
"We have no king,
Because we did not fear the LORD.
And as for a king, what would he do for us?"
4 They have spoken words,
Swearing falsely in making a covenant.
Thus judgment springs up [a]like hemlock
in the furrows of the field.

5 The inhabitants of Samaria fear
Because of the [a]calf[1] of Beth Aven.
For its people mourn for it,
And its priests shriek for it—
Because its [b]glory has departed from it.
6 *The idol* also shall be carried to Assyria
As a present for King [a]Jareb.
Ephraim shall receive shame,
And Israel shall be ashamed of his own
counsel.

**10:5** Jeroboam, Solomon's son, had two golden calves made and placed in Bethel and Dan to make them convenient for worshipers in the northern kingdom. Aaron had committed the same sin centuries earlier while Moses was on Mount Sinai talking to God.

7 *As for* Samaria, her king is cut off
Like a twig on the water.
8 Also the [a]high places of Aven, [b]the sin of
Israel,
Shall be destroyed.

9:6 [a]Is. 5:6; 7:23 9:7 [a]Is. 10:3 [b]Lam. 2:14 [c]Mic. 2:11 9:8 [a]Ezek. 3:17; 33:7 [1]That is, one who catches birds in a trap or snare 9:9 [a]Hos. 10:9 [b]Judg. 19:22 9:10 [a]Jer. 2:2 [b]Is. 28:4 [c]Num. 25:3 [d]Ps. 81:12 9:12 [a]Deut. 31:17 9:13 [a]Ezek. 26—28 9:14 [a]Luke 23:29 9:15 [a]Hos. 4:15; 12:11 [b]Is. 1:23 9:16 [a]Hos. 5:11 9:17 [a][Zech. 10:6] [b]Lev. 26:33 10:1 [a]Nah. 2:2 [b]Jer. 2:28 10:2 [a]1 Kin. 18:21 10:4 [a]Amos 5:7 10:5 [a]Hos. 8:5, 6; 13:2 [b]Hos. 9:11 [1]Literally *calves* 10:6 [a]Hos. 5:13 10:8 [a]Hos. 4:15 [b]1 Kin. 13:34

The thorn and thistle shall grow on their altars;
[c]They shall say to the mountains, "Cover us!"
And to the hills, "Fall on us!"

9 "O Israel, you have sinned from the days of [a]Gibeah;
There they stood.
The [b]battle in Gibeah against the children of iniquity[1]
Did not overtake them.
10 When *it is* My desire, I will chasten them.
[a]Peoples shall be gathered against them
When I bind them for their two transgressions.[1]
11 Ephraim *is* [a]a trained heifer
That loves to thresh *grain;*
But I harnessed her fair neck,
I will make Ephraim pull *a plow.*
Judah shall plow;
Jacob shall break his clods."

12 Sow for yourselves righteousness;
Reap in mercy;
[a]Break up your fallow ground,
For *it is* time to seek the LORD,
Till He [b]comes and rains righteousness on you.

13 [a]You have plowed wickedness;
You have reaped iniquity.
You have eaten the fruit of lies,
Because you trusted in your own way,
In the multitude of your mighty men.
14 Therefore tumult shall arise among your people,
And all your fortresses shall be plundered
As Shalman plundered Beth Arbel in the day of battle—
A mother dashed in pieces upon *her* children.
15 Thus it shall be done to you, O Bethel,
Because of your great wickedness.
At dawn the king of Israel
Shall be cut off utterly.

## GOD'S CONTINUING LOVE FOR ISRAEL

11 "When Israel *was* a child, I loved him,
And out of Egypt [a]I called My [b]son.
2 As they called them,[1]
So they [a]went from them;[2]
They sacrificed to the Baals,
And burned incense to carved images.

### SEEING JESUS IN THE SCRIPTURE

**11:1–2** God called His people out of Egypt by His mighty hand. They responded in disobedience, worshiping and serving idols. Later, Jesus was called out of Egypt (see Matt. 2:13–15). In perfect obedience, Jesus came forth from Egypt to deliver the world from sin.

3 "I[a] taught Ephraim to walk,
Taking them by their arms;[1]
But they did not know that [b]I healed them.
4 I drew them with gentle cords,[1]
With bands of love,
And [a]I was to them as those who take the yoke from their neck.[2]
[b]I stooped *and* fed them.

5 "He shall not return to the land of Egypt;
But the Assyrian shall be his king,
Because they refused to repent.
6 And the sword shall slash in his cities,
Devour his districts,
And consume *them,*
Because of their own counsels.
7 My people are bent on [a]backsliding from Me.
Though they call to the Most High,[1]
None at all exalt *Him.*

8 "How[a] can I give you up, Ephraim?
*How* can I hand you over, Israel?
How can I make you like [b]Admah?
*How* can I set you like Zeboiim?
My heart churns within Me;
My sympathy is stirred.
9 I will not execute the fierceness of My anger;
I will not again destroy Ephraim.
[a]For I *am* God, and not man,
The Holy One in your midst;
And I will not come with terror.[1]

10 "They shall walk after the LORD.
[a]He will roar like a lion.
When He roars,
Then *His* sons shall come trembling from the west;
11 They shall come trembling like a bird from Egypt,
[a]Like a dove from the land of Assyria.
[b]And I will let them dwell in their houses,"
Says the LORD.

**10:8** [c] Luke 23:30 **10:9** [a] Hos. 9:9 [b] Judg. 20 [1] So read many Hebrew manuscripts, Septuagint, and Vulgate; Masoretic Text reads *unruliness.* **10:10** [a] Jer. 16:16 [1] Or *in their two habitations* **10:11** [a] [Mic. 4:13] **10:12** [a] Jer. 4:3 [b] Hos. 6:3 **10:13** [a] [Prov. 22:8] **11:1** [a] Matt. 2:15 [b] Ex. 4:22, 23 **11:2** [a] 2 Kin. 17:13–15 [1] Following Masoretic Text and Vulgate; Septuagint reads *Just as I called them;* Targum interprets as *I sent prophets to a thousand of them.* [2] Following Masoretic Text, Targum, and Vulgate; Septuagint reads *from My face.* **11:3** [a] Deut. 1:31; 32:10, 11 [b] Ex. 15:26 [1] Some Hebrew manuscripts, Septuagint, Syriac, and Vulgate read *My arms.* **11:4** [a] Lev. 26:13 [b] Ps. 78:25 [1] Literally *cords of a man* [2] Literally *jaws* **11:7** [a] Jer. 3:6, 7; 8:5 [1] Or *upward* **11:8** [a] Jer. 9:7 [b] Gen. 14:8; 19:24, 25 **11:9** [a] Num. 23:19 [1] Or *I will not enter a city* **11:10** [a] [Joel 3:16] **11:11** [a] Is. 11:11; 60:8 [b] Ezek. 28:25, 26; 34:27, 28

### *GOD'S CHARGE AGAINST EPHRAIM*

12 "Ephraim has encircled Me with lies,
And the house of Israel with deceit;
But Judah still walks with God,
Even with the Holy One[1] *who is* faithful.

12 "Ephraim [a]feeds on the wind,
And pursues the east wind;
He daily increases lies and desolation.
[b]Also they make a covenant with the
Assyrians,
And [c]oil is carried to Egypt.

2 "The[a] LORD also *brings* a charge against
Judah,
And will punish Jacob according to his
ways;
According to his deeds He will
recompense him.
3 He took his brother [a]by the heel in the
womb,
And in his strength he [b]struggled with God.[1]
4 Yes, he struggled with the Angel and
prevailed;
He wept, and sought favor from Him.
He found Him *in* [a]Bethel,
And there He spoke to us—
5 That is, the LORD God of hosts.
The LORD *is* His [a]memorable name.
6 [a]So you, by *the help of* your God, return;
Observe mercy and justice,
And wait on your God continually.

7 "A cunning Canaanite!
[a]Deceitful scales *are* in his hand;
He loves to oppress.
8 And Ephraim said,
[a]'Surely I have become rich,
I have found wealth for myself;
*In* all my labors
They shall find in me no iniquity that *is*
sin.'

9 "But I *am* the LORD your God,
Ever since the land of Egypt;
[a]I will again make you dwell in tents,
As in the days of the appointed feast.
10 [a]I have also spoken by the prophets,
And have multiplied visions;
I have given symbols through the witness
of the prophets."

11 Though [a]Gilead *has* idols—
Surely they are vanity—
Though they sacrifice bulls in [b]Gilgal,
Indeed their altars *shall be* heaps in the
furrows of the field.
12 Jacob [a]fled to the country of Syria;
[b]Israel served for a spouse,
And for a wife he tended *sheep.*
13 [a]By a prophet the LORD brought Israel out
of Egypt,
And by a prophet he was preserved.
14 Ephraim [a]provoked *Him* to anger most
bitterly;
Therefore his Lord will leave the guilt of
his bloodshed upon him,
[b]And return his reproach upon him.

### *RELENTLESS JUDGMENT ON ISRAEL*

13 When Ephraim spoke, trembling,
He exalted *himself* in Israel;
But when he offended through Baal
*worship,* he died.
2 Now they sin more and more,
And have made for themselves molded
images,
Idols of their silver, according to their skill;
All of it *is* the work of craftsmen.
They say of them,
"Let the men who sacrifice[1] kiss the
calves!"
3 Therefore they shall be like the morning
cloud
And like the early dew that passes away,
[a]Like chaff blown off from a threshing floor
And like smoke from a chimney.

4 "Yet [a]I *am* the LORD your God
Ever since the land of Egypt,
And you shall know no God but Me;
For [b]*there is* no savior besides Me.
5 [a]I knew you in the wilderness,
[b]In the land of great drought.
6 [a]When they had pasture, they were filled;
They were filled and their heart was
exalted;
Therefore they forgot Me.

7 "So [a]I will be to them like a lion;
Like [b]a leopard by the road I will lurk;
8 I will meet them [a]like a bear deprived *of
her cubs;*
I will tear open their rib cage,
And there I will devour them like a lion.
The wild beast shall tear them.

9 "O Israel, you are destroyed,[1]
But your help[2] *is* from Me.
10 I will be your King;[1]
[a]Where *is any other,*
That he may save you in all your cities?
And your judges to whom [b]you said,
'Give me a king and princes'?

11:12 [1] Or *holy ones* 12:1 [a] Job 15:2, 3 [b] 2 Kin. 17:4 [c] Is. 30:6 12:2 [a] Mic. 6:2 12:3 [a] Gen. 25:26 [b] Gen. 32:24–28 [1] Compare Genesis 32:28 12:4 [a] [Gen. 28:12–19; 35:9–15] 12:5 [a] Ex. 3:15 12:6 [a] Mic. 6:8 12:7 [a] Amos 8:5 12:8 [a] Rev. 3:17 12:9 [a] Lev. 23:42 12:10 [a] 2 Kin. 17:13 12:11 [a] Hos. 6:8 [b] Hos. 9:15 12:12 [a] Gen. 28:5 [b] Gen. 29:20, 28 12:13 [a] Ex. 12:50, 51; 13:3 12:14 [a] Ezek. 18:10–13 [b] Dan. 11:18 13:2 [1] Or *those who offer human sacrifice* 13:3 [a] Dan. 2:35 13:4 [a] Is. 43:11 [b] Is. 43:11; 45:21, 22 13:5 [a] Deut. 2:7; 32:10 [b] Deut. 8:15 13:6 [a] Deut. 8:12, 14; 32:13–15 13:7 [a] Lam. 3:10 [b] Jer. 5:6 13:8 [a] 2 Sam. 17:8 13:9 [1] Literally *it* or *he destroyed you* [2] Literally *in your help* 13:10 [a] Deut. 32:38 [b] 1 Sam. 8:5, 6 [1] Septuagint, Syriac, Targum, and Vulgate read *Where is your king?*

11 [a]I gave you a king in My anger,
And took *him* away in My wrath.

12 "The[a] iniquity of Ephraim *is* bound up;
His sin *is* stored up.
13 [a]The sorrows of a woman in childbirth
shall come upon him.
He *is* an unwise son,
For he should not stay long where
children are born.

14 "I will ransom them from the power of the
grave;[1]
I will redeem them from death.
[a]O Death, I will be your plagues![2]
O Grave,[3] I will be your destruction![4]
[b]Pity is hidden from My eyes."

15 Though he is fruitful among *his*
brethren,
[a]An east wind shall come;
The wind of the LORD shall come up from
the wilderness.
Then his spring shall become dry,
And his fountain shall be dried up.
He shall plunder the treasury of every
desirable prize.
16 Samaria is held guilty,[1]
For she has [a]rebelled against her God.
They shall fall by the sword,
Their infants shall be dashed in pieces,
And their women with child [b]ripped open.

## *ISRAEL RESTORED AT LAST*

**14** O Israel, [a]return to the LORD your God,
For you have stumbled because of your
iniquity;
2 Take words with you,
And return to the LORD.
Say to Him,
"Take away all iniquity;
Receive *us* graciously,
For we will offer the [a]sacrifices[1] of our lips.
3 Assyria shall [a]not save us,
[b]We will not ride on horses,
Nor will we say anymore to the work of
our hands, '*You are* our gods.'
[c]For in You the fatherless finds mercy."

4 "I will heal their [a]backsliding,
I will [b]love them freely,
For My anger has turned away from him.
5 I will be like the [a]dew to Israel;
He shall grow like the lily,
And lengthen his roots like Lebanon.
6 His branches shall spread;
[a]His beauty shall be like an olive tree,
And [b]his fragrance like Lebanon.
7 [a]Those who dwell under his shadow shall
return;
They shall be revived *like* grain,
And grow like a vine.
Their scent[1] *shall be* like the wine of
Lebanon.

8 "Ephraim *shall say,* 'What have I to do
anymore with idols?'
I have heard and observed him.
I *am* like a green cypress tree;
[a]Your fruit is found in Me."

9 Who *is* wise?
Let him understand these things.
*Who is* prudent?
Let him know them.
For [a]the ways of the LORD *are* right;
The righteous walk in them,
But transgressors stumble in them.

13:11 [a] 1 Sam. 8:7; 10:17–24 13:12 [a] Deut. 32:34, 35 13:13 [a] Is. 13:8 13:14 [a] [1 Cor. 15:54, 55] [b] Jer. 15:6 [1] Or *Sheol* [2] Septuagint reads *where is your punishment?* [3] Or *Sheol* [4] Septuagint reads *where is your sting?* 13:15 [a] Jer. 4:11, 12 13:16 [a] 2 Kin. 18:12 [b] 2 Kin. 15:16 [1] Septuagint reads *shall be disfigured* 14:1 [a] [Joel 2:13] 14:2 [a] [Heb. 13:15] [1] Literally *bull calves;* Septuagint reads *fruit.* 14:3 [a] Hos. 7:11; 10:13; 12:1 [b] [Ps. 33:17] [c] Ps. 10:14; 68:5 14:4 [a] Jer. 14:7 [b] [Eph. 1:6] 14:5 [a] Prov. 19:12 14:6 [a] Ps. 52:8; 128:3 [b] Gen. 27:27 14:7 [a] Dan. 4:12 [1] Literally *remembrance* 14:8 [a] [John 15:4] 14:9 [a] [Prov. 10:29]

*The Book of the Prophet*

# JOEL

| AUTHOR | KEY VERSE | READING TIME |
|---|---|---|
| Joel | Joel 2:1 | 14 minutes |

**835 BC**
Joash becomes king in Judah

**c. 830 BC**
Joel begins to prophesy to Judah

**722 BC**
The Assyrians defeat Israel

**c. 600 BC**
Alternate dating option for Joel's ministry

**586 BC**
The Babylonians destroy Jerusalem

The Book of Joel describes a disaster striking the southern kingdom of Judah without warning. An ominous black cloud of dreaded locusts would descend upon the land and leave every living green thing stripped bare in a matter of hours. Although the locust plague (whether a literal plague or a symbol of invading armies) would be a terrible judgment of sin, God's future judgments during the day of the Lord would make this plague pale by comparison. In that day, God will destroy His enemies but bring unparalleled blessing to those who obey Him.

**Occasion:** Joel wrote to explain God's judgment on His people but also to give them hope that God will not withhold judgment from the surrounding nations either.

**Main Point:** The day of the Lord will bring judgment on all those who have not turned to the Lord.

**Big Ideas:** God is a righteous judge, and His judgment is coming.

## OUTLINE:

I. Present Judgment (ch. 1)
II. Future Judgment (ch. 2)
III. Future Reward (ch. 3)

1 The word of the LORD that came to [a]Joel the son of Pethuel.

### *THE LAND LAID WASTE*

*(Ex. 10:1–20)*

2 Hear this, you elders,
And give ear, all you inhabitants of the land!
[a]Has *anything like* this happened in your days,
Or even in the days of your fathers?
3 [a]Tell your children about it,
*Let* your children *tell* their children,
And their children another generation.

4 [a]What the chewing locust[1] left, the [b]swarming locust has eaten;
What the swarming locust left, the crawling locust has eaten;
And what the crawling locust left, the consuming locust has eaten.

**1:4** The **locust** travels in swarms that can number in the millions. The swarm can be large enough to blot out the sun in the sky and strip a field completely bare—down to its last leaf—within minutes. Many interpreters have viewed these locusts as foreign armies that attacked Judah in successive waves—Assyria, Babylon, Greece, and Rome. Yet literal locust plagues were one of the judgments promised if the people disobeyed God and broke their covenant with Him (Deut. 28:38–42). Further, Joel's description of the damage done by the locusts compares with eyewitness reports. The impression given is one of overwhelming devastation.

5 Awake, you [a]drunkards, and weep;
And wail, all you drinkers of wine,
Because of the new wine,
[b]For it has been cut off from your mouth.
6 For [a]a nation has come up against My land,
Strong, and without number;
[b]His teeth *are* the teeth of a lion,
And he has the fangs of a fierce lion.
7 He has [a]laid waste My vine,
And ruined My fig tree;
He has stripped it bare and thrown *it* away;
Its branches are made white.

8 [a]Lament like a virgin girded with sackcloth
For [b]the husband of her youth.
9 [a]The grain offering and the drink offering
Have been cut off from the house of the LORD;
The priests [b]mourn, who minister to the LORD.
10 The field is wasted,
[a]The land mourns;
For the grain is ruined,
[b]The new wine is dried up,
The oil fails.

11 [a]Be ashamed, you farmers,
Wail, you vinedressers,
For the wheat and the barley;
Because the harvest of the field has perished.
12 [a]The vine has dried up,
And the fig tree has withered;
The pomegranate tree,
The palm tree also,
And the apple tree—
All the trees of the field are withered;
Surely [b]joy has withered away from the sons of men.

### *MOURNING FOR THE LAND*

13 [a]Gird yourselves and lament, you priests;
Wail, you who minister before the altar;
Come, lie all night in sackcloth,
You who minister to my God;
For the grain offering and the drink offering
Are withheld from the house of your God.
14 [a]Consecrate a fast,
Call [b]a sacred assembly;
Gather the elders
*And* [c]all the inhabitants of the land
*Into* the house of the LORD your God,
And cry out to the LORD.

15 [a]Alas for the day!
For [b]the day of the LORD *is* at hand;
It shall come as destruction from the Almighty.

**1:15** The **day of the LORD** is a major theme of Old Testament prophecy. Thirteen of the sixteen prophets wrote about this subject that represents different periods of time or events in Israel's history. Both the birth of Jesus and His return to earth are called "the day of the Lord" in Scripture. It is used to speak of the time when God will bring wrath and judgment on the wicked and salvation on the righteous.

**1:1** [a]Acts 2:16 **1:2** [a]Joel 2:2 **1:3** [a]Ps. 78:4 **1:4** [a]Deut. 28:38 [b]Is. 33:4 [1]Exact identity of these locusts is unknown. **1:5** [a]Is. 5:11; 28:1 [b]Is. 32:10 **1:6** [a]Joel 2:2, 11, 25 [b]Rev. 9:8 **1:7** [a]Is. 5:6 **1:8** [a]Is. 22:12 [b]Jer. 3:4 **1:9** [a]Joel 1:13; 2:14 [b]Joel 2:17 **1:10** [a]Jer. 12:11 [b]Is. 24:7 **1:11** [a]Jer. 14:3, 4 **1:12** [a]Joel 1:10 [b]Jer. 48:33 **1:13** [a]Jer. 4:8 **1:14** [a]Joel 2:15, 16 [b]Lev. 23:36 [c]2 Chr. 20:13 **1:15** [a][Jer. 30:7] [b]Is. 13:6

16 Is not the food [a]cut off before our eyes,
[b]Joy and gladness from the house of our God?
17 The seed shrivels under the clods,
Storehouses are in shambles;
Barns are broken down,
For the grain has withered.
18 How [a]the animals groan!
The herds of cattle are restless,
Because they have no pasture;
Even the flocks of sheep suffer punishment.[1]

19 O LORD, [a]to You I cry out;
For [b]fire has devoured the open pastures,
And a flame has burned all the trees of the field.
20 The beasts of the field also [a]cry out to You,
For [b]the water brooks are dried up,
And fire has devoured the open pastures.

### *THE DAY OF THE LORD*

2 Blow [a]the trumpet in Zion,
And [b]sound an alarm in My holy mountain!
Let all the inhabitants of the land tremble;
For [c]the day of the LORD is coming,
For it is at hand:
2 [a]A day of darkness and gloominess,
A day of clouds and thick darkness,
Like the morning *clouds* spread over the mountains.
[b]A people *come,* great and strong,
[c]The like of whom has never been;
Nor will there ever be any *such* after them,
Even for many successive generations.

3 A fire devours before them,
And behind them a flame burns;
The land *is* like [a]the Garden of Eden before them,
[b]And behind them a desolate wilderness;
Surely nothing shall escape them.
4 [a]Their appearance is like the appearance of horses;
And like swift steeds, so they run.
5 [a]With a noise like chariots
Over mountaintops they leap,
Like the noise of a flaming fire that devours the stubble,
Like a strong people set in battle array.

6 Before them the people writhe in pain;
[a]All faces are drained of color.[1]
7 They run like mighty men,
They climb the wall like men of war;
Every one marches in formation,
And they do not break [a]ranks.
8 They do not push one another;
Every one marches in his own column.[1]
Though they lunge between the weapons,
They are not cut down.[2]
9 They run to and fro in the city,
They run on the wall;
They climb into the houses,
They [a]enter at the windows [b]like a thief.

10 [a]The earth quakes before them,
The heavens tremble;
[b]The sun and moon grow dark,
And the stars diminish their brightness.
11 [a]The LORD gives voice before His army,
For His camp is very great;
[b]For strong *is the One* who executes His word.
For the [c]day of the LORD *is* great and very terrible;
[d]Who can endure it?

### *A CALL TO REPENTANCE*

12 "Now, therefore," says the LORD,
[a]"Turn to Me with all your heart,
With fasting, with weeping, and with mourning."
13 So [a]rend your heart, and not [b]your garments;
Return to the LORD your God,
For He *is* [c]gracious and merciful,
Slow to anger, and of great kindness;
And He relents from doing harm.
14 [a]Who knows *if* He will turn and relent,
And leave [b]a blessing behind Him—
[c]A grain offering and a drink offering
For the LORD your God?

15 [a]Blow the trumpet in Zion,
[b]Consecrate a fast,
Call a sacred assembly;
16 Gather the people,
[a]Sanctify the congregation,
Assemble the elders,
Gather the children and nursing babes;
[b]Let the bridegroom go out from his chamber,
And the bride from her dressing room.
17 Let the priests, who minister to the LORD,
Weep [a]between the porch and the altar;
Let them say, [b]"Spare Your people, O LORD,
And do not give Your heritage to reproach,
That the nations should rule over them.
[c]Why should they say among the peoples,
'Where *is* their God?' "

1:16 [a] Is. 3:1 [b] Deut. 12:7 1:18 [a] Hos. 4:3 [1] Septuagint and Vulgate read *are made desolate.* 1:19 [a] [Ps. 50:15] [b] Jer. 9:10 1:20 [a] Ps. 104:21; 147:9 [b] 1 Kin. 17:7; 18:5 2:1 [a] Jer. 4:5 [b] Num. 10:5 [c] [Obad. 15] 2:2 [a] Amos 5:18 [b] Joel 1:6; 2:11, 25 [c] Dan. 9:12; 12:1 2:3 [a] Is. 51:3 [b] Zech. 7:14 2:4 [a] Rev. 9:7 2:5 [a] Rev. 9:9 2:6 [a] Nah. 2:10 [1] Septuagint, Targum, and Vulgate read *gather blackness.* 2:7 [a] Prov. 30:27 2:8 [1] Literally *his own highway* [2] That is, they are not halted by losses 2:9 [a] Jer. 9:21 [b] John 10:1 2:10 [a] Ps. 18:7 [b] Is. 13:10; 34:4 2:11 [a] Jer. 25:30 [b] Rev. 18:8 [c] Amos 5:18 [d] [Mal. 3:2] 2:12 [a] Jer. 4:1 2:13 [a] [Ps. 34:18; 51:17] [b] Gen. 37:34 [c] [Ex. 34:6] 2:14 [a] Jer. 26:3 [b] Hag. 2:19 [c] Joel 1:9, 13 2:15 [a] Num. 10:3 [b] Joel 1:14 2:16 [a] Ex. 19:10 [b] Ps. 19:5 2:17 [a] Matt. 23:35 [b] Ex. 32:11, 12 [c] Ps. 42:10

LIVE THE TRUTH

## FASTING

**2:12** When the Israelites strayed from God, they experienced a national disaster—either a literal plague of locusts or a symbolic plague of invading armies (see Joel 1). God used this plague to get His people's attention. He wanted them to experience the sting of discipline so they would seek Him. This is why He commanded them to return to Him with fasting, weeping, and mourning.

You're likely familiar with weeping and mourning but fasting might be new for you. Fasting is forgoing something in our lives—usually food—for a time so we depend more fully upon God. In the Old Testament especially, fasting was often part of repentance but it doesn't always have to be. As followers of Jesus, we need His presence more than anything else, but in the busyness of everyday life, we can forget that. Fasting can be a way we slow down, refocus, and reprioritize on what matters most: God. The hunger we feel for food or the desire we have for whatever else we might fast reminds us there's a greater hunger and greater need in our lives. When we fast and turn to God through prayer and meditation, we will find we're satisfied in a different and more complete way.

### *THE LAND REFRESHED*

*(Acts 2:17)*

18 Then the LORD will [a]be zealous for His land,
And pity His people.
19 The LORD will answer and say to His people,
"Behold, I will send you [a]grain and new wine and oil,
And you will be satisfied by them;
I will no longer make you a reproach among the nations.

20 "But [a]I will remove far from you [b]the northern *army,*
And will drive him away into a barren and desolate land,
With his face toward the eastern sea
And his back [c]toward the western sea;
His stench will come up,
And his foul odor will rise,
Because he has done monstrous things."

21 Fear not, O land;
Be glad and rejoice,
For the LORD has done marvelous things!
22 Do not be afraid, you beasts of the field;
For [a]the open pastures are springing up,
And the tree bears its fruit;
The fig tree and the vine yield their strength.
23 Be glad then, you children of Zion,
And [a]rejoice in the LORD your God;
For He has given you the former rain faithfully,[1]
And He [b]will cause the rain to come down for you—
The former rain,
And the latter rain in the first *month.*
24 The threshing floors shall be full of wheat,
And the vats shall overflow with new wine and oil.

25 "So I will restore to you the years [a]that the swarming locust has eaten,
The crawling locust,
The consuming locust,
And the chewing locust,[1]
My great army which I sent among you.
26 You shall [a]eat in plenty and be satisfied,
And praise the name of the LORD your God,
Who has dealt wondrously with you;
And My people shall never be put to [b]shame.
27 Then you shall know that I *am* [a]in the midst of Israel:
[b]I *am* the LORD your God
And there is no other.
My people shall never be put to shame.

### *GOD'S SPIRIT POURED OUT*

28 "And[a] it shall come to pass afterward
That [b]I will pour out My Spirit on all flesh;
[c]Your sons and your [d]daughters shall prophesy,
Your old men shall dream dreams,
Your young men shall see visions.

**SEEING JESUS IN THE SCRIPTURE**

**2:28** Jesus promised that after His departure He would send the Holy Spirit to help His disciples and bear witness of Him (see John 15:26–27). That promise and this prophecy were fulfilled at Pentecost when the Holy Spirit came upon those who believed (see Acts 2:4).

**2:18** [a] [Is. 60:10; 63:9, 15] **2:19** [a] [Mal. 3:10] **2:20** [a] Ex. 10:19 [b] Jer. 1:14, 15 [c] Deut. 11:24 **2:22** [a] Joel 1:19 **2:23** [a] Is. 41:16 [b] Lev. 26:4
[1] Or *the teacher of righteousness* **2:25** [a] Joel 1:4–7; 2:2–11 [1] Compare 1:4 **2:26** [a] Lev. 26:5 [b] Is. 45:17 **2:27** [a] Lev. 26:11, 12 [b] [Is. 45:5, 6]
**2:28** [a] Ezek. 39:29 [b] Zech. 12:10 [c] Is. 54:13 [d] Acts 21:9

29 And also on *My* [a]menservants and on *My* maidservants
I will pour out My Spirit in those days.

30 "And [a]I will show wonders in the heavens and in the earth:
Blood and fire and pillars of smoke.
31 [a]The sun shall be turned into darkness,
And the moon into blood,
[b]Before the coming of the great and awesome day of the LORD.
32 And it shall come to pass
*That* [a]whoever calls on the name of the LORD
Shall be saved.
For [b]in Mount Zion and in Jerusalem there shall be deliverance,
As the LORD has said,
Among [c]the remnant whom the LORD calls.

### GOD JUDGES THE NATIONS

3 "For behold, [a]in those days and at that time,
When I bring back the captives of Judah and Jerusalem,
2 [a]I will also gather all nations,
And bring them down to the Valley of Jehoshaphat;
And I [b]will enter into judgment with them there
On account of My people, My heritage Israel,
Whom they have scattered among the nations;
They have also divided up My land.
3 They have [a]cast lots for My people,
Have given a boy *as payment* for a harlot,
And sold a girl for wine, that they may drink.

4 "Indeed, what have you to do with Me,
[a]O Tyre and Sidon, and all the coasts of Philistia?
Will you retaliate against Me?
But if you retaliate against Me,
Swiftly and speedily I will return your retaliation upon your own head;
5 Because you have taken My silver and My gold,
And have carried into your temples My prized possessions.
6 Also the people of Judah and the people of Jerusalem
You have sold to the Greeks,
That you may remove them far from their borders.

7 "Behold, [a]I will raise them
Out of the place to which you have sold them,
And will return your retaliation upon your own head.
8 I will sell your sons and your daughters
Into the hand of the people of Judah,
And they will sell them to the [a]Sabeans,[1]
To a people [b]far off;
For the LORD has spoken."

9 [a]Proclaim this among the nations:
"Prepare for war!
Wake up the mighty men,
Let all the men of war draw near,
Let them come up.
10 [a]Beat your plowshares into swords
And your pruning hooks into spears;
[b]Let the weak say, 'I *am* strong.' "
11 Assemble and come, all you nations,
And gather together all around.
Cause [a]Your mighty ones to go down there, O LORD.

12 "Let the nations be wakened, and come up to the Valley of Jehoshaphat;
For there I will sit to [a]judge all the surrounding nations.
13 [a]Put in the sickle, for [b]the harvest is ripe.
Come, go down;
For the [c]winepress is full,
The vats overflow—
For their wickedness *is* great."

**3:13** At **harvest** time, grapes were gathered in baskets and carried to large **vats**. Barefoot workers would then stomp on the grapes in a **winepress**, squeezing out the juice that flowed down a slope into another container. There it was collected in clay jars or wineskins and stored until it fermented and became wine. The days of harvesting and squashing the grapes were times of celebration and joy for the people of Judah and Israel.

14 Multitudes, multitudes in the valley of decision!
For [a]the day of the LORD *is* near in the valley of decision.
15 The sun and moon will grow dark,
And the stars will diminish their brightness.

2:29 [a][Gal. 3:28] 2:30 [a]Matt. 24:29 2:31 [a]Is. 13:9, 10; 34:4 [b][Mal. 4:1, 5, 6] 2:32 [a]Rom. 10:13 [b]Is. 46:13 [c][Mic. 4:7] 3:1 [a]Jer. 30:3 3:2 [a]Zech. 14:2 [b]Is. 66:16 3:3 [a]Nah. 3:10 3:4 [a]Amos 1:6–8 3:7 [a]Jer. 23:8 3:8 [a]Ezek. 23:42 [b]Jer. 6:20 [1]Literally *Shebaites* (compare Isaiah 60:6 and Ezekiel 27:22) 3:9 [a]Ezek. 38:7 3:10 [a][Is. 2:4] [b]Zech. 12:8 3:11 [a]Is. 13:3 3:12 [a]Is. 2:4 3:13 [a]Rev. 14:15 [b]Jer. 51:33 [c][Is. 63:3] 3:14 [a]Joel 2:1

16 The LORD also will roar from Zion,
And utter His voice from Jerusalem;
The heavens and earth will shake;
[a]But the LORD will be a shelter for His people,
And the strength of the children of Israel.

17 "So you shall know that I *am* the LORD your God,
Dwelling in Zion My [a]holy mountain.
Then Jerusalem shall be holy,
And no aliens shall ever pass through her again."

## GOD BLESSES HIS PEOPLE

18 And it will come to pass in that day
*That* the mountains shall drip with new wine,
The hills shall flow with milk,
And all the brooks of Judah shall be flooded with water;
A [a]fountain shall flow from the house of the LORD
And water the Valley of Acacias.

19 "Egypt shall be a desolation,
And Edom a desolate wilderness,
Because of violence *against* the people of Judah,
For they have shed innocent blood in their land.
20 But Judah shall abide forever,
And Jerusalem from generation to generation.
21 For I will [a]acquit them of the guilt of bloodshed, whom I had not acquitted;
For the LORD dwells in Zion."

3:16 [a] [Is. 51:5, 6] 3:17 [a] Zech. 8:3 3:18 [a] Ezek. 47:1 3:21 [a] Is. 4:4

# *The Book of the Prophet*
# AMOS

| AUTHOR | KEY VERSES | READING TIME |
|---|---|---|
| Amos | Amos 5:23–24 | 30 minutes |

**792 BC**
Azariah (Uzziah) becomes king in Judah

**792 BC**
Jeroboam II becomes king in Israel

**c. 785 BC**
Hosea begins to prophesy in Israel

**c. 755 BC**
Amos prophesies in Israel

**755 BC**
Isaiah begins to prophesy in Judah

**753 BC**
Jeroboam's reign ends

**752 BC**
Jotham becomes king in Judah

**722 BC**
The Assyrians defeat Israel

During King Jeroboam II's reign, Israel experienced impressive financial and political success. Israel's businesses boomed and its boundaries bulged. National optimism was the feeling of the day. Below the surface, however, greed and injustice festered. Hypocritical religious acts had replaced true worship, creating a false sense of security and a growing callousness to God's disciplining hand. Famine, drought, plagues, death, destruction—nothing could force the people to their knees. Amos stepped forward onto this stage to be God's instrument to bring His people to their senses. Amos lashed out at sin unflinchingly, declaring the nearness of God's judgment to draw the nation to repentance. The nation, like a basket of rotting fruit, stood ripe for judgment because of its hypocrisy and spiritual indifference.

**Occasion:** Amos warns Israel that their prosperity is superficial and that God's promised judgment of their sin is still coming.

**Main Point:** God does not tolerate spiritual indifference and hypocrisy; rather, He requires His people to be faithful to Him and live justly with one another.

**Big Ideas:** God will judge people for their obedience to Him and how they treat others. Money, comfort, and safety often provide a false sense of security. Because God is just and merciful to us, we should live the same way with others.

## OUTLINE:

I. The Judgment of the Nations (chs. 1–2)
II. The Sins of Israel (chs. 3–6)
III. The Judgment and Restoration of Israel (chs. 7–9)

1 The words of Amos, who was among the
[a]sheepbreeders[1] of [b]Tekoa, which he saw
concerning Israel in the days of [c]Uzziah king
of Judah, and in the days of [d]Jeroboam the
son of Joash, king of Israel, two years before
the [e]earthquake.
2 And he said:

"The LORD [a]roars from Zion,
And utters His voice from Jerusalem;
The pastures of the shepherds mourn,
And the top of [b]Carmel withers."

### *JUDGMENT ON THE NATIONS*

3 Thus says the LORD:

"For three transgressions of [a]Damascus,
and for four,
I will not turn away its *punishment*,
Because they have [b]threshed Gilead with
implements of iron.

**1:3 For three . . . and for four** is a stylistic device indicating the exhaustion of God's patience—the Syrians had continued to sin, again and again. This device is repeated as Amos spoke God's words against nation after sinful nation surrounding Israel, until he addressed that nation too (Amos 2:6–16).

4 [a]But I will send a fire into the house of
Hazael,
Which shall devour the palaces of [b]Ben-
Hadad.
5 I will also break the *gate* [a]bar of
Damascus,
And cut off the inhabitant from the Valley
of Aven,
And the one who holds the scepter from
Beth Eden.
The people of Syria shall go captive to
Kir,"
Says the LORD.

6 Thus says the LORD:

"For three transgressions of [a]Gaza, and for
four,
I will not turn away its *punishment*,
Because they took captive the whole
captivity
To deliver *them* up to Edom.
7 [a]But I will send a fire upon the wall of
Gaza,
Which shall devour its palaces.
8 I will cut off the inhabitant [a]from Ashdod,
And the one who holds the scepter from
Ashkelon;
I will [b]turn My hand against Ekron,
And [c]the remnant of the Philistines shall
perish,"
Says the Lord GOD.

9 Thus says the LORD:

"For three transgressions of [a]Tyre, and for
four,
I will not turn away its *punishment*,
Because they delivered up the whole
captivity to Edom,
And did not remember the covenant of
brotherhood.
10 But I will send a fire upon the wall of Tyre,
Which shall devour its palaces."

11 Thus says the LORD:

"For three transgressions of [a]Edom, and
for four,
I will not turn away its *punishment*,
Because he pursued his [b]brother with the
sword,
And cast off all pity;
His anger tore perpetually,
And he kept his wrath forever.
12 But [a]I will send a fire upon Teman,
Which shall devour the palaces of
Bozrah."

13 Thus says the LORD:

"For three transgressions of [a]the people of
Ammon, and for four,
I will not turn away its *punishment*,
Because they ripped open the women
with child in Gilead,
That they might enlarge their territory.
14 But I will kindle a fire in the wall of
[a]Rabbah,
And it shall devour its palaces,
[b]Amid shouting in the day of battle,
And a tempest in the day of the
whirlwind.
15 [a]Their king shall go into captivity,
He and his princes together,"
Says the LORD.

2 Thus says the LORD:

[a]"For three transgressions of Moab, and for
four,
I will not turn away its *punishment*,
Because he [b]burned the bones of the king
of Edom to lime.

1:1 [a] 2 Kin. 3:4; Amos 7:14 [b] 2 Sam. 14:2 [c] 2 Chr. 26:1–23 [d] Amos 7:10 [e] Zech. 14:5 [1] Compare 2 Kings 3:4 1:2 [a] Joel 3:16 [b] 1 Sam. 25:2 1:3 [a] Is. 8:4; 17:1–3 [b] 2 Kin. 10:32, 33 1:4 [a] Jer. 49:27; 51:30 [b] 2 Kin. 6:24 1:5 [a] Jer. 51:30 1:6 [a] Jer. 47:1, 5 1:7 [a] Jer. 47:1 1:8 [a] Zeph. 2:4 [b] Ps. 81:14 [c] Ezek. 25:16 1:9 [a] Is. 23:1–18 1:11 [a] Is. 21:11 [b] Obad. 10–12 1:12 [a] Obad. 9, 10 1:13 [a] Ezek. 25:2 1:14 [a] Deut. 3:11 [b] Amos 2:2 1:15 [a] Jer. 49:3 2:1 [a] Zeph. 2:8–11 [b] 2 Kin. 3:26, 27

2 But I will send a fire upon Moab,
And it shall devour the palaces of [a]Kerioth;
Moab shall die with tumult,
With shouting *and* trumpet sound.
3 And I will cut off [a]the judge from its midst,
And slay all its princes with him,"
Says the LORD.

### JUDGMENT ON JUDAH

4 Thus says the LORD:

"For three transgressions of [a]Judah, and for four,
I will not turn away its *punishment*,
[b]Because they have despised the law of the LORD,
And have not kept His commandments.
[c]Their lies lead them astray,
*Lies* [d]which their fathers followed.
5 [a]But I will send a fire upon Judah,
And it shall devour the palaces of Jerusalem."

### JUDGMENT ON ISRAEL

6 Thus says the LORD:

"For three transgressions of [a]Israel, and for four,
I will not turn away its *punishment*,
Because [b]they sell the righteous for silver,
And the [c]poor for a pair of sandals.
7 They pant after[1] the dust of the earth
*which is* on the head of the poor,
And [a]pervert the way of the humble.
[b]A man and his father go in to the *same* girl,
[c]To defile My holy name.
8 They lie down [a]by every altar on clothes [b]taken in pledge,
And drink the wine of the condemned *in* the house of their god.

9 "Yet *it was* I *who* destroyed the [a]Amorite before them,
Whose height *was* like the [b]height of the cedars,
And he *was as* strong as the oaks;
Yet I [c]destroyed his fruit above
And his roots beneath.
10 Also *it was* [a]I *who* brought you up from the land of Egypt,
And [b]led you forty years through the wilderness,
To possess the land of the Amorite.
11 I raised up some of your sons as [a]prophets,
And some of your young men as [b]Nazirites.
*Is it* not so, O you children of Israel?"
Says the LORD.

12 "But you gave the Nazirites wine to drink,
And commanded the prophets [a]saying,
'Do not prophesy!'

13 "Behold,[a] I am weighed down by you,
As a cart full of sheaves is weighed down.
14 [a]Therefore flight shall perish from the swift,
The strong shall not strengthen his power,
[b]Nor shall the mighty deliver himself;
15 He shall not stand who handles the bow,
The swift of foot shall not escape,
Nor shall he who rides a horse deliver himself.
16 The most courageous men of might
Shall flee naked in that day,"
Says the LORD.

### AUTHORITY OF THE PROPHET'S MESSAGE

3 Hear this word that the LORD has spoken
against you, O children of Israel, against the
whole family which I brought up from the land
of Egypt, saying:

2 "You[a] only have I known of all the families of the earth;
[b]Therefore I will punish you for all your iniquities."

3 Can two walk together, unless they are agreed?
4 Will a lion roar in the forest, when he has no prey?
Will a young lion cry out of his den, if he has caught nothing?
5 Will a bird fall into a snare on the earth, where there is no trap for it?
Will a snare spring up from the earth, if it has caught nothing at all?
6 If a trumpet is blown in a city, will not the people be afraid?
[a]If there is calamity in a city, will not the LORD have done *it*?
7 Surely the Lord GOD does nothing,
Unless [a]He reveals His secret to His servants the prophets.
8 A lion has roared!
Who will not fear?
The Lord GOD has spoken!
[a]Who can but prophesy?

### PUNISHMENT OF ISRAEL'S SINS

9 "Proclaim in the palaces at Ashdod,[1]
And in the palaces in the land of Egypt, and say:
'Assemble on the mountains of Samaria;
See great tumults in her midst,
And the oppressed within her.

**2:2** [a]Jer. 48:24, 41 **2:3** [a]Num. 24:17 **2:4** [a]Hos. 12:2 [b]Lev. 26:14 [c]Jer. 16:19 [d]Ezek. 20:13, 16, 18 **2:5** [a]Hos. 8:14 **2:6** [a]2 Kin. 17:7–18; 18:12 [b]Is. 29:21 [c]Amos 4:1; 5:11; 8:6 **2:7** [a]Amos 5:12 [b]Ezek. 22:11 [c]Lev. 20:3 [1]Or *trample on* **2:8** [a]1 Cor. 8:10 [b]Ex. 22:26 **2:9** [a]Num. 21:25 [b]Ezek. 31:3 [c][Mal. 4:1] **2:10** [a]Ex. 12:51 [b]Deut. 2:7 **2:11** [a]Num. 12:6 [b]Num. 6:2, 3 **2:12** [a]Is. 30:10 **2:13** [a]Is. 1:14 **2:14** [a]Jer. 46:6 [b]Ps. 33:16 **3:2** [a][Deut. 7:6] [b][Rom. 2:9] **3:6** [a]Is. 45:7 **3:7** [a][John 15:15] **3:8** [a]Acts 4:20 **3:9** [1]Following Masoretic Text; Septuagint reads *Assyria*.

10 For they [a]do not know to do right,'
Says the LORD,
'Who store up violence and robbery in
their palaces.' "

11 Therefore thus says the Lord GOD:

"An adversary *shall be* all around the
land;
He shall sap your strength from you,
And your palaces shall be plundered."

12 Thus says the LORD:

"As a shepherd takes from the mouth of a
lion
Two legs or a piece of an ear,
So shall the children of Israel be taken out
Who dwell in Samaria—
In the corner of a bed and on the edge[1] of
a couch!

**3:12** When the northern kingdom of Israel was conquered by Assyria in 722 BC, many of **the children of Israel** were **taken** captive. At the same time, foreigners from many different regions were brought to live in Israel. The Israelites who remained in the land began to mingle with their new neighbors, eventually marrying them and adopting their idol worship. As a result, they were no longer a distinct people—either physically or spiritually. The descendants of these mixed marriages would become known as Samaritans.

13 Hear and testify against the house of
Jacob,"
Says the Lord GOD, the God of hosts,
14 "That in the day I punish Israel for their
transgressions,
I will also visit *destruction* on the altars of
[a]Bethel;
And the horns of the altar shall be cut off
And fall to the ground.
15 I will destroy [a]the winter house along with
[b]the summer house;
The [c]houses of ivory shall perish,
And the great houses shall have an end,"
Says the LORD.

4 Hear this word, you [a]cows of Bashan, who
*are* on the mountain of Samaria,
Who oppress the [b]poor,
Who crush the needy,
Who say to your husbands,[1] "Bring *wine*,
let us [c]drink!"
2 [a]The Lord GOD has sworn by His holiness:
"Behold, the days shall come upon you
When He will take you away [b]with
fishhooks,
And your posterity with fishhooks.
3 [a]You will go out *through* broken *walls*,
Each one straight ahead of her,
And you will be cast into Harmon,"
Says the LORD.

4 "Come[a] to Bethel and transgress,
At [b]Gilgal multiply transgression;
[c]Bring your sacrifices every morning,
[d]Your tithes every three days.[1]

**4:4 Bethel** and **Gilgal** were both important cities in Israel's history. Bethel was the place where Jacob had his life-changing dream of a stairway to heaven. Gilgal was the site of a memorial to God for His protection of the Israelites when they crossed the Jordan River. The people of Israel proved their lack of respect for their history by making both places centers for pagan worship.

5 [a]Offer a sacrifice of thanksgiving with leaven,
Proclaim *and* announce [b]the freewill
offerings;
For this you love,
*You* children of Israel!"
Says the Lord GOD.

### *ISRAEL DID NOT ACCEPT CORRECTION*

6 "Also I gave you cleanness of teeth in all
your cities,
And lack of bread in all your places;
[a]Yet you have not returned to Me,"
Says the LORD.

7 "I also withheld rain from you,
When *there were* still three months to the
harvest.
I made it rain on one city,
I withheld rain from another city.
One part was rained upon,
And where it did not rain the part withered.
8 So two *or* three cities wandered to another
city to drink water,
But they were not satisfied;
Yet you have not returned to Me,"
Says the LORD.

9 "I[a] blasted you with blight and mildew.
When your gardens increased,
Your vineyards,
Your fig trees,

3:10 [a] Jer. 4:22 3:12 [1] The Hebrew is uncertain. 3:14 [a] Amos 4:4 3:15 [a] Jer. 36:22 [b] Judg. 3:20 [c] 1 Kin. 22:39 4:1 [a] Ps. 22:12 [b] Amos 2:6 [c] Prov. 23:20 [1] Literally *their lords* or *their masters* 4:2 [a] Ps. 89:35 [b] Jer. 16:16 4:3 [a] Ezek. 12:5 4:4 [a] Ezek. 20:39 [b] Hos. 4:15 [c] Num. 28:3 [d] Deut. 14:28 [1] Or *years* (compare Deuteronomy 14:28) 4:5 [a] Lev. 7:13 [b] Lev. 22:18 4:6 [a] Jer. 5:3 4:9 [a] Hag. 2:17

And your olive trees,
[b]The locust devoured *them;*
Yet you have not returned to Me,"
Says the LORD.

10 "I sent among you a plague [a]after the manner of Egypt;
Your young men I killed with a sword,
Along with your captive horses;
I made the stench of your camps come up into your nostrils;
Yet you have not returned to Me,"
Says the LORD.

11 "I overthrew *some* of you,
As God overthrew [a]Sodom and Gomorrah,
And you were like a firebrand plucked from the burning;
Yet you have not returned to Me,"
Says the LORD.

12 "Therefore thus will I do to you, O Israel;
Because I will do this to you,
[a]Prepare to meet your God, O Israel!"

13 For behold,
He who forms mountains,
And creates the wind,
[a]Who declares to man what his[1] thought *is,*
And makes the morning darkness,
[b]Who treads the high places of the earth—
[c]The LORD God of hosts *is* His name.

## A LAMENT FOR ISRAEL

5 Hear this word which I [a]take up against you, a lamentation, O house of Israel:

2 The virgin of Israel has fallen;
She will rise no more.
She lies forsaken on her land;
*There is* no one to raise her up.

3 For thus says the Lord GOD:

"The city that goes out by a thousand
Shall have a hundred left,
And that which goes out by a hundred
Shall have ten left to the house of Israel."

## A CALL TO REPENTANCE

4 For thus says the LORD to the house of Israel:

[a]"Seek Me [b]and live;
5 But do not seek [a]Bethel,
Nor enter Gilgal,
Nor pass over to [b]Beersheba;
For Gilgal shall surely go into captivity,
And [c]Bethel shall come to nothing.
6 [a]Seek the LORD and live,
Lest He break out like fire *in* the house of Joseph,
And devour *it,*
With no one to quench *it* in Bethel—
7 You who [a]turn justice to wormwood,
And lay righteousness to rest in the earth!"

8 He made the [a]Pleiades and Orion;
He turns the shadow of death into morning
[b]And makes the day dark as night;
He [c]calls for the waters of the sea
And pours them out on the face of the earth;
[d]The LORD *is* His name.
9 He rains ruin upon the strong,
So that fury comes upon the fortress.

10 [a]They hate the one who rebukes in the gate,
And they [b]abhor the one who speaks uprightly.
11 [a]Therefore, because you tread down the poor
And take grain taxes from him,
Though [b]you have built houses of hewn stone,
Yet you shall not dwell in them;
You have planted pleasant vineyards,
But you shall not drink wine from them.
12 For I [a]know your manifold transgressions
And your mighty sins:
[b]Afflicting the just *and* taking bribes;
[c]Diverting the poor *from justice* at the gate.
13 Therefore [a]the prudent keep silent at that time,
For it *is* an evil time.

14 Seek good and not evil,
That you may live;
So the LORD God of hosts will be with you,
[a]As you have spoken.
15 [a]Hate evil, love good;
Establish justice in the gate.
[b]It may be that the LORD God of hosts
Will be gracious to the remnant of Joseph.

## THE DAY OF THE LORD

16 Therefore the LORD God of hosts, the Lord, says this:

"*There shall be* wailing in all streets,
And they shall say in all the highways,
'Alas! Alas!'
They shall call the farmer to mourning,
[a]And skillful lamenters to wailing.
17 In all vineyards *there shall be* wailing,
For [a]I will pass through you,"
Says the LORD.

4:9 [b]Joel 1:4, 7 4:10 [a]Ps. 78:50 4:11 [a]Is. 13:19 4:12 [a]Jer. 5:22 4:13 [a]Ps. 139:2 [b]Mic. 1:3 [c]Is. 47:4 [1]Or *His* 5:1 [a]Jer. 7:29; 9:10, 17 5:4 [a][Jer. 29:13] [b][Is. 55:3] 5:5 [a]Amos 4:4 [b]Amos 8:14 [c]Hos. 4:15 5:6 [a][Is. 55:3, 6, 7] 5:7 [a]Amos 6:12 5:8 [a]Job 9:9; 38:31 [b]Ps. 104:20 [c]Job 38:34 [d][Amos 4:13] 5:10 [a]Is. 29:21; 66:5 [b]1 Kin. 22:8 5:11 [a]Amos 2:6 [b]Mic. 6:15 5:12 [a]Hos. 5:3 [b]Amos 2:6 [c]Is. 29:21 5:13 [a]Amos 6:10 5:14 [a]Mic. 3:11 5:15 [a]Rom. 12:9 [b]Joel 2:14 5:16 [a]Jer. 9:17 5:17 [a]Ex. 12:12

18 [a]Woe to you who desire the day of the
LORD!
For what good *is* [b]the day of the LORD to
you?
It *will be* darkness, and not light.
19 It *will be* [a]as though a man fled from a lion,
And a bear met him!
Or *as though* he went into the house,
Leaned his hand on the wall,
And a serpent bit him!
20 *Is* not the day of the LORD darkness, and
not light?
*Is it not* very dark, with no brightness in it?

21 "I[a] hate, I despise your feast days,
And [b]I do not savor your sacred assemblies.
22 [a]Though you offer Me burnt offerings and
your grain offerings,
I will not accept *them,*
Nor will I regard your fattened peace
offerings.
23 Take away from Me the noise of your
songs,
For I will not hear the melody of your
stringed instruments.
24 [a]But let justice run down like water,
And righteousness like a mighty stream.

> **5:21–23** By stating He would no longer accept Israel's sacrifices or listen to their music, God was rejecting Israel's worship as hypocritical, dishonest, and meaningless. In this, we see we cannot claim to love God while failing to love others (see Matt. 22:36–40).

25 "Did[a] you offer Me sacrifices and offerings
In the wilderness forty years, O house of
Israel?
26 You also carried Sikkuth[1] [a]your king[2]
And Chiun,[3] your idols,
The star of your gods,
Which you made for yourselves.
27 Therefore I will send you into captivity
[a]beyond Damascus,"
Says the LORD, [b]whose name *is* the God of
hosts.

## *WARNINGS TO ZION AND SAMARIA*

6 Woe [a]to you *who are* at [b]ease in Zion,
And [c]trust in Mount Samaria,
Notable persons in the [d]chief nation,
To whom the house of Israel comes!
2 [a]Go over to [b]Calneh and see;
And from there go to [c]Hamath the great;
Then go down to Gath of the Philistines.
[d]*Are you* better than these kingdoms?
Or is their territory greater than your
territory?

3 *Woe to* you who [a]put far off the day of [b]doom,
[c]Who cause [d]the seat of violence to come
near;
4 Who lie on beds of ivory,
Stretch out on your couches,
Eat lambs from the flock
And calves from the midst of the stall;
5 [a]Who sing idly to the sound of stringed
instruments,
*And* invent for yourselves [b]musical
instruments [c]like David;
6 Who [a]drink wine from bowls,
And anoint yourselves with the best
ointments,
[b]But are not grieved for the affliction of
Joseph.
7 Therefore they shall now go [a]captive as
the first of the captives,
And those who recline at banquets shall
be removed.

8 [a]The Lord GOD has sworn by Himself,
The LORD God of hosts says:
"I abhor [b]the pride of Jacob,
And hate his palaces;
Therefore I will deliver up *the* city
And all that is in it."

9 Then it shall come to pass, that if ten men
remain in one house, they shall die. 10 And when
a relative *of the dead,* with one who will burn *the*
*bodies,* picks up the bodies[1] to take them out of
the house, he will say to one inside the house,
"*Are there* any more with you?"
Then someone will say, "None."
And he will say, [a]"Hold your tongue! [b]For
we dare not mention the name of the LORD."

11 For behold, [a]the LORD gives a command:
[b]He will break the great house into bits,
And the little house into pieces.

12 Do horses run on rocks?
Does *one* plow *there* with oxen?
Yet [a]you have turned justice into gall,
And the fruit of righteousness into
wormwood,
13 You who rejoice over Lo Debar,[1]
Who say, "Have we not taken Karnaim[2] for
ourselves
By our own strength?"

5:18 [a] Is. 5:19 [b] Joel 2:2 5:19 [a] Jer. 48:44 5:21 [a] Is. 1:11–16 [b] Lev. 26:31 5:22 [a] Mic. 6:6, 7 5:24 [a] Mic. 6:8 5:25 [a] Deut. 32:17 5:26 [a] 1 Kin. 11:33 [1] A pagan deity [2] Septuagint and Vulgate read *tabernacle of Moloch.* [3] A pagan deity 5:27 [a] 2 Kin. 17:6 [b] Amos 4:13 6:1 [a] Luke 6:24 [b] Zeph. 1:12 [c] Is. 31:1 [d] Ex. 19:5 6:2 [a] Jer. 2:10 [b] Is. 10:9 [c] 2 Kin. 18:34 [d] Nah. 3:8 6:3 [a] Is. 56:12 [b] Amos 5:18 [c] Amos 5:12 [d] Ps. 94:20 6:5 [a] Is. 5:12; Amos 5:23 [b] 1 Chr. 15:16; 16:42 [c] 1 Chr. 23:5 6:6 [a] Amos 2:8; 4:1 [b] Gen. 37:25 6:7 [a] Amos 5:27 6:8 [a] Jer. 51:14 [b] Amos 8:7 6:10 [a] Amos 5:13 [b] Amos 8:3 [1] Literally *bones* 6:11 [a] Is. 55:11 [b] Amos 3:15 6:12 [a] Hos. 10:4 6:13 [1] Literally *Nothing* [2] Literally *Horns,* symbol of strength

14 "But, behold, [a]I will raise up a nation
against you,
O house of Israel,"
Says the LORD God of hosts;
"And they will afflict you from the
[b]entrance of Hamath
To the Valley of the Arabah."

## VISION OF THE LOCUSTS

7 Thus the Lord GOD showed me: Behold, He
formed locust swarms at the beginning of
the late crop; indeed *it was* the late crop after the
king's mowings. 2 And so it was, when they had
finished eating the grass of the land, that I said:

"O Lord GOD, forgive, I pray!
[a]Oh, that Jacob may stand,
For he *is* small!"
3 *So* [a]the LORD relented concerning this.
"It shall not be," said the LORD.

## VISION OF THE FIRE

4 Thus the Lord GOD showed me: Behold,
the Lord GOD called for conflict by fire, and it
consumed the great deep and devoured the
territory. 5 Then I said:

"O Lord GOD, cease, I pray!
[a]Oh, that Jacob may stand,
For he *is* small!"
6 *So* the LORD relented concerning this.
"This also shall not be," said the Lord GOD.

## VISION OF THE PLUMB LINE

7 Thus He showed me: Behold, the Lord stood
on a wall *made* with a plumb line, with a plumb
line in His hand. 8 And the LORD said to me,
"Amos, what do you see?"
And I said, "A plumb line."
Then the Lord said:

"Behold, [a]I am setting a plumb line
In the midst of My people Israel;
[b]I will not pass by them anymore.
9 [a]The high places of Isaac shall be desolate,
And the sanctuaries of Israel shall be laid
waste.
[b]I will rise with the sword against the
house of Jeroboam."

## AMAZIAH'S COMPLAINT

10 Then Amaziah the [a]priest of [b]Bethel sent
to [c]Jeroboam king of Israel, saying, "Amos has
conspired against you in the midst of the house
of Israel. The land is not able to bear all his
words. 11 For thus Amos has said:

'Jeroboam shall die by the sword,
And Israel shall surely be led away [a]captive
From their own land.'"

**7:7–9** A **plumb line** is a string with a weight tied to one end, used to establish a vertical line so that a wall can be built straight. Unlike the first two visions of natural disasters, the visions of the plumb line and the basket of summer fruit were not self-explanatory. God asked Amos what he saw, then explained the visions' meaning. Also, unlike the first two visions, God did not give Amos opportunity to intercede, nor did He relent. These judgments would be executed.

12 Then Amaziah said to Amos:

"Go, you seer!
Flee to the land of Judah.
There eat bread,
And there prophesy.
13 But [a]never again prophesy at Bethel,
[b]For it *is* the king's sanctuary,
And it *is* the royal residence."

14 Then Amos answered, and said to Amaziah:

"I *was* no prophet,
Nor *was* I [a]a son of a prophet,
But I *was* a [b]sheepbreeder[1]
And a tender of sycamore fruit.
15 Then the LORD took me as I followed the
flock,
And the LORD said to me,
'Go, [a]prophesy to My people Israel.'
16 Now therefore, hear the word of the LORD:
You say, 'Do not prophesy against Israel,
And [a]do not spout against the house of
Isaac.'

17 "Therefore[a] thus says the LORD:

[b]'Your wife shall be a harlot in the city;
Your sons and daughters shall fall by the
sword;
Your land shall be divided by *survey* line;
You shall die in a [c]defiled land;
And Israel shall surely be led away captive
From his own land.'"

## VISION OF THE SUMMER FRUIT

8 Thus the Lord GOD showed me: Behold,
a basket of summer fruit. 2 And He said,
"Amos, what do you see?"
So I said, "A basket of summer fruit."
Then the LORD said to me:

[a]"The end has come upon My people Israel;
[b]I will not pass by them anymore.

**6:14** [a] Jer. 5:15 [b] 1 Kin. 8:65 **7:2** [a] Is. 51:19 **7:3** [a] Jon. 3:10 **7:5** [a] Amos 7:2, 3 **7:8** [a] 2 Kin. 21:13 [b] Mic. 7:18 **7:9** [a] Gen. 46:1 [b] 2 Kin. 15:8–10 **7:10** [a] 1 Kin. 12:31, 32; 13:33 [b] Amos 4:4 [c] 2 Kin. 14:23 **7:11** [a] Amos 5:27; 6:7 **7:13** [a] Amos 2:12 [b] 1 Kin. 12:29, 32 **7:14** [a] 1 Kin. 20:35 [b] Zech. 13:5 [1] Compare 2 Kings 3:4 **7:15** [a] Amos 3:8 **7:16** [a] Ezek. 21:2 **7:17** [a] Jer. 28:12; 29:21, 32 [b] Zech. 14:2 [c] Hos. 9:3 **8:2** [a] Ezek. 7:2 [b] Amos 7:8

**8:1–3** The **summer fruit** that came at the end of the harvest in late summer included grapes, pomegranates, and figs. Israel's wickedness was about to result in a harvest of judgment.

3 And [a]the songs of the temple
Shall be wailing in that day,"
Says the Lord GOD—
"Many dead bodies everywhere,
[b]They shall be thrown out in silence."

4 Hear this, you who swallow up[1] the needy,
And make the poor of the land fail,

5 Saying:

"When will the New Moon be past,
That we may sell grain?
And [a]the Sabbath,
That we may trade wheat?
[b]Making the ephah small and the shekel large,
Falsifying the scales by [c]deceit,
6 That we may buy the poor for [a]silver,
And the needy for a pair of sandals—
Even sell the bad wheat?"

7 The LORD has sworn by [a]the pride of Jacob:
"Surely [b]I will never forget any of their works.
8 [a]Shall the land not tremble for this,
And everyone mourn who dwells in it?
All of it shall swell like the River,[1]
Heave and subside
[b]Like the River of Egypt.

9 "And it shall come to pass in that day," says the Lord GOD,
[a]"That I will make the sun go down at noon,
And I will darken the earth in broad daylight;

## SEEING JESUS IN THE SCRIPTURE

**8:9** Darkness is often a symbol of sin, distress, and judgment. Here, Amos warned his people their sins would lead to God's judgment, marked by darkness instead of light across the land. This sign also occurred at the cross when the earth became dark at noon (see Luke 23:44).

10 I will turn your feasts into [a]mourning,
[b]And all your songs into lamentation;
[c]I will bring sackcloth on every waist,
And baldness on every head;
I will make it like mourning for an only *son*,
And its end like a bitter day.

11 "Behold, the days are coming," says the Lord GOD,
"That I will send a famine on the land,
Not a famine of bread,
Nor a thirst for water,
But [a]of hearing the words of the LORD.
12 They shall wander from sea to sea,
And from north to east;
They shall run to and fro, seeking the word of the LORD,
But shall [a]not find *it*.

13 "In that day the fair virgins
And strong young men
Shall faint from thirst.
14 Those who [a]swear by [b]the sin[1] of Samaria,
Who say,
'As your god lives, O Dan!'
And, 'As the way of [c]Beersheba lives!'
They shall fall and never rise again."

### THE DESTRUCTION OF ISRAEL

9 I saw the Lord standing by the altar, and He said:

"Strike the doorposts, that the thresholds may shake,
And [a]break them on the heads of them all.
I will slay the last of them with the sword.
[b]He who flees from them shall not get away,
And he who escapes from them shall not be delivered.

2 "Though[a] they dig into hell,[1]
From there My hand shall take them;
[b]Though they climb up to heaven,
From there I will bring them down;
3 And though they [a]hide themselves on top of Carmel,
From there I will search and take them;
Though they hide from My sight at the bottom of the sea,
From there I will command the serpent, and it shall bite them;
4 Though they go into captivity before their enemies,
From there [a]I will command the sword,
And it shall slay them.
[b]I will set My eyes on them for harm and not for good."

**8:3** [a] Amos 5:23 [b] Amos 6:9, 10 **8:4** [1] Or *trample on* (compare 2:7) **8:5** [a] Neh. 13:15 [b] Mic. 6:10, 11 [c] Lev. 19:35, 36 **8:6** [a] Amos 2:6 **8:7** [a] Amos 6:8 [b] Hos. 7:2; 8:13 **8:8** [a] Hos. 4:3 [b] Amos 9:5 [1] That is, the Nile; some Hebrew manuscripts, Septuagint, Syriac, Targum, and Vulgate read *River;* Masoretic Text reads *the light.* **8:9** [a] Job 5:14 **8:10** [a] Ezek. 7:18 [b] Ezek. 27:31 [c] [Zech. 12:10] **8:11** [a] Ezek. 7:26 **8:12** [a] Hos. 5:6 **8:14** [a] Hos. 4:15 [b] Deut. 9:21 [c] Amos 5:5 [1] Or *Ashima,* a Syrian goddess **9:1** [a] Hab. 3:13 [b] Amos 2:14 **9:2** [a] Ps. 139:8 [b] Jer. 51:53 [1] Or *Sheol* **9:3** [a] Jer. 23:24 **9:4** [a] Lev. 26:33 [b] Jer. 21:10; 39:16; 44:11

5 The Lord GOD of hosts,
He who touches the earth and it [a]melts,
[b]And all who dwell there mourn;
All of it shall swell like the River,[1]
And subside like the River of Egypt.
6 He who builds His [a]layers in the sky,
And has founded His strata in the earth;
Who [b]calls for the waters of the sea,
And pours them out on the face of the earth—
[c]The LORD *is* His name.

7 "*Are* you not like the people of Ethiopia to Me,
O children of Israel?" says the LORD.
"Did I not bring up Israel from the land of Egypt,
The [a]Philistines from [b]Caphtor,
And the Syrians from [c]Kir?

8 "Behold, [a]the eyes of the Lord GOD *are* on the sinful kingdom,
And I [b]will destroy it from the face of the earth;
Yet I will not utterly destroy the house of Jacob,"
Says the LORD.

9 "For surely I will command,
And will sift the house of Israel among all nations,
As *grain* is sifted in a sieve;
[a]Yet not the smallest grain shall fall to the ground.
10 All the sinners of My people shall die by the sword,
[a]Who say, 'The calamity shall not overtake nor confront us.'

### ISRAEL WILL BE RESTORED

11 "On[a] that day I will raise up
The tabernacle[1] of David, which has fallen down,
And repair its damages;
I will raise up its ruins,
And rebuild it as in the days of old;
12 [a]That they may possess the remnant of [b]Edom,[1]
And all the Gentiles who are called by My name,"
Says the LORD who does this thing.

13 "Behold, [a]the days are coming," says the LORD,
"When the plowman shall overtake the reaper,
And the treader of grapes him who sows seed;
[b]The mountains shall drip with sweet wine,
And all the hills shall flow *with it.*
14 [a]I will bring back the captives of My people Israel;
[b]They shall build the waste cities and inhabit *them;*
They shall plant vineyards and drink wine from them;
They shall also make gardens and eat fruit from them.
15 I will plant them in their land,
[a]And no longer shall they be pulled up
From the land I have given them,"
Says the LORD your God.

> **SEEING JESUS IN THE SCRIPTURE**
>
> **9:11–12** The tabernacle ultimately points to the coming Messiah, Jesus, and the salvation He brought. God raised up Jesus to be the way all people can experience forgiveness of sin and eternal life with God (see John 1:14).

9:5 [a] Mic. 1:4 [b] Amos 8:8 [1] That is, the Nile 9:6 [a] Ps. 104:3, 13 [b] Amos 5:8 [c] Amos 4:13; 5:27 9:7 [a] Jer. 47:4 [b] Deut. 2:23 [c] Amos 1:5 9:8 [a] Amos 9:4 [b] Jer. 5:10; 30:11 9:9 [a] [Is. 65:8–16] 9:10 [a] Amos 6:3 9:11 [a] Acts 15:16–18 [1] Literally *booth*, figure of a deposed dynasty 9:12 [a] Obad. 19 [b] Num. 24:18 [1] Septuagint reads *mankind*. 9:13 [a] Lev. 26:5 [b] Joel 3:18 9:14 [a] Jer. 30:3, 18 [b] Is. 61:4 9:15 [a] Ezek. 34:28; 37:25

# *The Book of the Prophet*
# OBADIAH

| AUTHOR | KEY VERSE | READING TIME |
|---|---|---|
| Obadiah | Obadiah v. 10 | 5 minutes |

**848 BC**
Jehoram becomes king in Judah

**c. 845 BC**
Edom revolts; Obadiah prophesies

**722 BC**
The Assyrians defeat Israel

**660 BC**
Traditional founding date of Japan by Emperor Jimmu

**586 BC**
The Babylonians destroy Jerusalem

**586 BC**
Alternate dating option for Obadiah's ministry

A struggle between twin brothers, Esau and Jacob, that began in the womb (see Gen. 25:22–26) eventually turned into a struggle between their respective descendants, the Edomites and the Israelites. For the Edomites' stubborn refusal to aid Israel, first during the time of wilderness wandering (see Num. 20:14–21) and later during a time of invasion (see Ps. 137:7), they are roundly condemned by Obadiah. God's prophet described the Edomites' crimes, tried their case, and pronounced judgment: total destruction.

**Occasion:** Unlike most of the prophets who focused on the transgressions of God's people, Obadiah declares a message of God's judgment on those who rejoiced in Israel's struggles.

**Main Point:** The nation of Edom will be judged by God for its treatment of His people.

**Big Ideas:** God is the protector and vindicator of His people. God will judge proud and arrogant nations and people. We should live in humility, always being ready to help those in need.

## OUTLINE:

I. Edom's Coming Judgment (vv. 1–9)
II. Edom's Cruelty Toward Israel (vv. 10–16)
III. Israel's Future Triumph (vv. 17–21)

### *THE COMING JUDGMENT ON EDOM*

The vision of Obadiah.

Thus says the Lord GOD [a]concerning
Edom
[b](We have heard a report from the LORD,
And a messenger has been sent among
the nations, *saying,*
"Arise, and let us rise up against her for
battle"):

> **V. 1** The Edomites were the descendants of Esau, and the Israelites descended from Jacob. The rivalry that existed between the two brothers was passed on to their descendants. **Edom** refused to let Israel cross through their land as the Israelites' traveled to the Promised Land. The Israelites were forced to travel through the desert. The tension between the two countries continued for centuries.

2 "Behold, I will make you small among the
nations;
You shall be greatly despised.
3 The [a]pride of your heart has deceived you,
*You* who dwell in the clefts of the rock,
Whose habitation is high;
[b]*You* who say in your heart, 'Who will bring
me down to the ground?'
4 [a]Though you ascend *as* high as the eagle,
And though you [b]set your nest among the
stars,
From there I will bring you down," says
the LORD.

5 "If [a]thieves had come to you,
If robbers by night—
Oh, how you will be cut off!—
Would they not have stolen till they had
enough?
If grape-gatherers had come to you,
[b]Would they not have left *some* gleanings?

6 "Oh, how Esau shall be searched out!
*How* his hidden treasures shall be sought
after!
7 All the men in your confederacy
Shall force you to the border;
[a]The men at peace with you
Shall deceive you *and* prevail against you.
*Those who eat* your bread shall lay a trap[1]
for you.
[b]No one is aware of it.

8 "Will[a] I not in that day," says the LORD,
"Even destroy the wise *men* from Edom,
And understanding from the mountains
of Esau?
9 Then your [a]mighty men, O [b]Teman, shall
be dismayed,
To the end that everyone from the
mountains of Esau
May be cut off by slaughter.

### *EDOM MISTREATED HIS BROTHER*

10 "For [a]violence against your brother Jacob,
Shame shall cover you,
And [b]you shall be cut off forever.
11 In the day that you [a]stood on the other
side—
In the day that strangers carried captive
his forces,
When foreigners entered his gates
And [b]cast lots for Jerusalem—
Even you *were* as one of them.

12 "But you should not have [a]gazed on the
day of your brother
In the day of his captivity;[1]
Nor should you have [b]rejoiced over the
children of Judah
In the day of their destruction;
Nor should you have spoken proudly
In the day of distress.
13 You should not have entered the gate of
My people
In the day of their calamity.
Indeed, you should not have gazed on
their affliction
In the day of their calamity,
Nor laid *hands* on their substance
In the day of their calamity.
14 You should not have stood at the
crossroads
To cut off those among them who escaped;
Nor should you have delivered up those
among them who remained
In the day of distress.

15 "For[a] the day of the LORD upon all the
nations *is* near;
[b]As you have done, it shall be done to you;
Your reprisal shall return upon your own
head.
16 [a]For as you drank on My holy mountain,
*So* shall all the nations drink continually;
Yes, they shall drink, and swallow,
And they shall be as though they had
never been.

### *ISRAEL'S FINAL TRIUMPH*

17 "But on Mount Zion there [a]shall be
deliverance,
And there shall be holiness;
The house of Jacob shall possess their
possessions.

**1** [a] Is. 21:11 [b] Jer. 49:14–16 **3** [a] Jer. 49:16 [b] Rev. 18:7 **4** [a] Job 20:6 [b] Hab. 2:9 **5** [a] Jer. 49:9 [b] Deut. 24:21 **7** [a] Jer. 38:22 [b] Is. 19:11 [1] Or *wound,* or *plot* **8** [a] [Job 5:12–14] **9** [a] Ps. 76:5 [b] Jer. 49:7 **10** [a] Gen. 27:41 [b] Ezek. 35:9 **11** [a] Ps. 83:5–8 [b] Nah. 3:10 **12** [a] Mic. 4:11; 7:10 [b] [Prov. 17:5] [1] Literally *On the day he became a foreigner* **15** [a] Ezek. 30:3 [b] Hab. 2:8 **16** [a] Joel 3:17 **17** [a] Amos 9:8

18 The house of Jacob shall be a fire,
And the house of Joseph [a]a flame;
But the house of Esau *shall be* stubble;
They shall kindle them and devour them,
And no survivor shall *remain* of the house
of Esau,"
For the LORD has spoken.

19 The South[1] [a]shall possess the mountains
of Esau,
[b]And the Lowland shall possess Philistia.
They shall possess the fields of Ephraim
And the fields of Samaria.
Benjamin *shall possess* Gilead.
20 And the captives of this host of the
children of Israel
*Shall possess the land* of the Canaanites
As [a]far as Zarephath.
The captives of Jerusalem who are in
Sepharad
[b]Shall possess the cities of the South.[1]
21 Then [a]saviors[1] shall come to Mount Zion
To judge the mountains of Esau,
And the [b]kingdom shall be the LORD's.

18 [a] Zech. 12:6 19 [a] Is. 11:14 [b] Zeph. 2:7 [1] Hebrew *Negev* 20 [a] 1 Kin. 17:9 [b] Jer. 32:44 [1] Hebrew *Negev* 21 [a] [James 5:20] [b] [Rev. 11:15] [1] Or *deliverers*

# *The Book of the Prophet*
# JONAH

**AUTHOR**
Jonah

**KEY VERSE**
Jonah 4:11

**READING TIME**
10 minutes

In a time of peace and prosperity, one of Israel's major foes, Assyria, was in a posture of relative weakness. Many Israelites likely saw this time as evidence of God's righteousness: God was blessing His people while their enemies languished. One can understand the shock, then, when God commissioned the prophet Jonah to go to Assyria's capital and call on Israel's enemy to repent of their sins. If they repented, God would spare judgment. Why would God offer mercy and grace to the wicked Assyrians? Jonah's response was to board a ship bound for Tarshish, west of Israel. Nineveh was to its northeast. But God would not allow His wayward prophet to run far. He would get his attention in a startling way, and the prophet would preach repentance in Nineveh after all. Although Jonah's preaching was a success, he came away angry and discouraged. God would need to teach His prophet that He had compassion for all sinful people.

**Occasion:** The Book of Jonah is one of the few Old Testament books of prophecy focused on foreign nations instead of God's people, but it includes the same message: repent of your sin to experience God's forgiveness.

**Main Point:** God is ready to extend grace and mercy to anyone who repents of sin.

**Big Ideas:** God cares for all people, everywhere. God gives everyone the opportunity to repent. Because God is compassionate to us, we should be compassionate to others.

**OUTLINE:**

I. Jonah's Disobedience (ch. 1)
II. Jonah's Prayer (ch. 2)
III. Jonah's Obedience (ch. 3)
IV. Jonah's Anger (ch. 4)

**792 BC**
Jeroboam II becomes king in Israel

**c. 770 BC**
Jonah prophesies to Nineveh

**c. 755 BC**
Amos prophesies in Israel

**c. 745 BC**
Assyrian Empire pushes westward under Tiglath-Pilesar

**722 BC**
The Assyrians defeat Israel

**c. 667 BC**
City of Byzantium is founded

**612 BC**
The Babylonians and Medes defeat Assyria

### *JONAH'S DISOBEDIENCE*

**1** Now the word of the LORD came to [a]Jonah the son of Amittai, saying, 2 "Arise, go to [a]Nineveh, that [b]great city, and cry out against it; for [c]their wickedness has come up before Me." 3 But Jonah arose to flee to Tarshish from the presence of the LORD. He went down to [a]Joppa, and found a ship going to Tarshish; so he paid the fare, and went down into it, to go with them to [b]Tarshish [c]from the presence of the LORD.

> **1:1–3** The city of **Nineveh** was about 500 miles northeast of Jonah's home and the largest city in the ancient world. The wall around Nineveh stretched for almost eight miles. Each of its fifteen gates was "guarded" by a statue of a bull. **Joppa** was about 50 miles southwest of Jonah's hometown in the opposite direction from Nineveh. The location of **Tarshish** is uncertain, but it could be Tartessus on the southeast coast of Spain. The city represents the most distant place known to the Israelites and was about as far away from Nineveh as Jonah could go.

### *THE STORM AT SEA*

4 But [a]the LORD sent out a great wind on the sea, and there was a mighty tempest on the sea, so that the ship was about to be broken up.

5 Then the mariners were afraid; and every man cried out to his god, and threw the cargo that *was* in the ship into the sea, to lighten the load.[1] But Jonah had gone down [a]into the lowest parts of the ship, had lain down, and was fast asleep.

6 So the captain came to him, and said to him, "What do you mean, sleeper? Arise, [a]call on your God; [b]perhaps your God will consider us, so that we may not perish."

7 And they said to one another, "Come, let us [a]cast lots, that we may know for whose cause this trouble *has come* upon us." So they cast lots, and the lot fell on Jonah. 8 Then they said to him, [a]"Please tell us! For whose cause *is* this trouble upon us? What is your occupation? And where do you come from? What is your country? And of what people are you?"

9 So he said to them, "I *am* a Hebrew; and I fear the LORD, the God of heaven, [a]who made the sea and the dry *land*."

### *JONAH THROWN INTO THE SEA*

10 Then the men were exceedingly afraid, and said to him, "Why have you done this?" For the men knew that he fled from the presence of the LORD, because he had told them. 11 Then they said to him, "What shall we do to you that the sea may be calm for us?"—for the sea was growing more tempestuous.

12 And he said to them, [a]"Pick me up and throw me into the sea; then the sea will become calm for you. For I know that this great tempest *is* because of me."

13 Nevertheless the men rowed hard to return to land, [a]but they could not, for the sea continued to grow more tempestuous against them. 14 Therefore they cried out to the LORD and said, "We pray, O LORD, please do not let us perish for this man's life, and [a]do not charge us with innocent blood; for You, O LORD, [b]have done as it pleased You." 15 So they picked up Jonah and threw him into the sea, [a]and the sea ceased from its raging. 16 Then the men [a]feared the LORD exceedingly, and offered a sacrifice to the LORD and took vows.

1:1 [a] 2 Kin. 14:25 1:2 [a] Is. 37:37 [b] Gen. 10:11, 12 [c] Gen. 18:20 1:3 [a] Josh. 19:46 [b] Is. 23:1 [c] Gen. 4:16 1:4 [a] Ps. 107:25 1:5 [a] 1 Sam. 24:3 [1] Literally *from upon them* 1:6 [a] Ps. 107:28 [b] Joel 2:14 1:7 [a] Josh. 7:14 1:8 [a] Josh. 7:19 1:9 [a] [Neh. 9:6] 1:12 [a] John 11:50 1:13 [a] [Prov. 21:30] 1:14 [a] Deut. 21:8 [b] Ps. 115:3 1:15 [a] [Ps. 89:9; 107:29] 1:16 [a] Acts 5:11

LIVE THE TRUTH

## DOING WHAT IS BEST

**1:10–16** Some decisions are straightforward: we either do what's right or what's wrong. We either obey or disobey God. Many decisions, however, are more complicated than that. They aren't a matter of right or wrong as much as a matter of doing what's best. But how do we know what's best? The key is focusing on the heart: our heart and God's heart.

Jonah is an interesting book because it depicts the Gentiles around Jonah as godlier than God's prophet. Here, we see even though the sailors' lives were at risk and Jonah told them they would be spared by tossing him into the sea, they did all they could besides that. They didn't want to be responsible for sending a man to his death, even if he were a stranger. This shows these sailors shared more of God's heart for others than Jonah did. And that heart compelled them to pursue what was best, not just what may have been right. Likewise, as you make complicated decisions, pursue whatever delights God's heart the most. Always choose the most loving, most kind, most humble, most compassionate, most God-glorifying path before you. Its destination is always what's best.

**SEEING JESUS IN THE SCRIPTURE**

**1:17** Jonah's time in the fish's belly and miraculous deliverance after three days foreshadows the resurrection of Jesus on the third day (see Matt. 12:40). Both events illustrate God's mercy and redemption, and the message of salvation for all people.

***JONAH'S PRAYER AND DELIVERANCE***

17 Now the LORD had prepared a great fish to swallow Jonah. And [a]Jonah was in the belly of the fish three days and three nights.

2 Then Jonah prayed to the LORD his God from the fish's belly. 2 And he said:

"I [a]cried out to the LORD because of my
affliction,
[b]And He answered me.

"Out of the belly of Sheol I cried,
*And* You heard my voice.
3 [a]For You cast me into the deep,
Into the heart of the seas,
And the floods surrounded me;
[b]All Your billows and Your waves passed
over me.
4 [a]Then I said, 'I have been cast out of Your
sight;
Yet I will look again [b]toward Your holy
temple.'
5 The [a]waters surrounded me, *even* to my
soul;
The deep closed around me;
Weeds were wrapped around my head.
6 I went down to the moorings of the
mountains;
The earth with its bars *closed* behind me
forever;
Yet You have brought up my [a]life from the
pit,
O LORD, my God.

7 "When my soul fainted within me,
I remembered the LORD;
[a]And my prayer went *up* to You,
Into Your holy temple.

8 "Those who regard [a]worthless idols
Forsake their own Mercy.

1:17 [a] [Matt. 12:40] 2:2 [a] Ps. 120:1 [b] Ps. 65:2 2:3 [a] Ps. 88:6 [b] Ps. 42:7 2:4 [a] Ps. 31:22 [b] 1 Kin. 8:38 2:5 [a] Lam. 3:54 2:6 [a] [Ps. 16:10] 2:7 [a] Ps. 18:6 2:8 [a] Jer. 10:8

**STORY OF SCRIPTURE** 38

JONAH 2:1–10

## THE PROPHECY OF JONAH

### WHAT'S GOING ON?

Jonah, having fled from God's command to go to Nineveh, found himself in the belly of a giant fish for three days and nights. In this moment of despair, Jonah turned to God in prayer, acknowledging his distress and God's salvation. He recognized despite his own disobedience, salvation comes from the Lord. His anthem of hope crescendos into a moment of salvation when the fish spits him out and he swims to shore. Jonah finally obeys and preaches salvation to the Assyrians in Nineveh, an enemy of God's people. In this, we see God wants *all* to be saved.

### WHAT DOES THIS MEAN FOR ME?

Jonah's experience in the belly of the fish is a powerful metaphor for when we feel engulfed by life's challenges and trials—especially those we bring upon ourselves. In our darkest moments, when we feel swallowed up by our circumstances, we can turn to God in prayer. Jonah's prayer is an act of surrender and recognition of God's sovereignty. This passage also encourages us to examine how we respond to God's call, especially when it leads us out of our comfort zones. It challenges us to trust God's plan, even when it's difficult to understand or follow.

### DID YOU CATCH THE PATTERN?

Jonah refers to the belly of the fish as Sheol, or "the grave." Jonah was in this grave for three days, then emerged to preach salvation to the people of Ninevah. Once again, we have a foreshadowing of Jesus' death, burial, and resurrection. Like Joseph going from the prison to the palace, Jonah's story foreshadows the gospel. Jesus said His death and resurrection would be like Jonah's emergence from the belly of the fish (see Matt. 12:38–42).

*For the next* Story of Scripture *reading and devotion, turn to Malachi 3:1–7 on page 950.*

9 But I will [a]sacrifice to You
With the voice of thanksgiving;
I will pay what I have [b]vowed.
[c]Salvation *is* of the [d]LORD."

10 So the LORD spoke to the fish, and it vomited Jonah onto dry *land.*

### JONAH PREACHES AT NINEVEH

**3** Now the word of the LORD came to Jonah the second time, saying, 2 "Arise, go to Nineveh, that great city, and preach to it the message that I tell you." 3 So Jonah arose and went to Nineveh, according to the word of the LORD. Now Nineveh was an exceedingly great city, a three-day journey[1] *in extent.* 4 And Jonah began to enter the city on the first day's walk. Then [a]he cried out and said, "Yet forty days, and Nineveh shall be overthrown!"

### THE PEOPLE OF NINEVEH BELIEVE

5 So the [a]people of Nineveh believed God, proclaimed a fast, and put on sackcloth, from the greatest to the least of them. 6 Then word came to the king of Nineveh; and he arose from his throne and laid aside his robe, covered *himself* with sackcloth [a]and sat in ashes. 7 [a]And he caused *it* to be proclaimed and published throughout Nineveh by the decree of the king and his nobles, saying,

> **3:5** The term used for ***God*** here is the general term for deity. In contrast, the sailors in chapter 1 proclaimed faith in "the LORD," using the personal, covenant name for God (Jonah 1:16). This may suggest that the Ninevites had a short-lived, or imperfect, understanding of God's message. History bears this out. We have no historical record of a lasting period of belief in Nineveh. Eventually the city was destroyed in 612 BC.

Let neither man nor beast, herd nor flock, taste anything; do not let them eat, or drink water. 8 But let man and beast be covered with sackcloth, and cry mightily to God; yes, [a]let every one turn from his evil way and from [b]the violence that is in his hands. 9 [a]Who can tell *if* God will turn and relent, and turn away from His fierce anger, so that we may not perish?

10 [a]Then God saw their works, that they turned from their evil way; and God relented from the disaster that He had said He would bring upon them, and He did not do it.

### JONAH'S ANGER AND GOD'S KINDNESS

**4** But it displeased Jonah exceedingly, and he became angry. 2 So he prayed to the LORD, and said, "Ah, LORD, was not this what I said when I was still in my country? Therefore I [a]fled previously to Tarshish; for I know that You *are* a [b]gracious and merciful God, slow to anger and abundant in lovingkindness, One who relents from doing harm. 3 [a]Therefore now, O LORD, please take my life from me, for [b]*it is* better for me to die than to live!"

4 Then the LORD said, "*Is it* right for you to be angry?"

5 So Jonah went out of the city and sat on the east side of the city. There he made himself a shelter and sat under it in the shade, till he might see what would become of the city. 6 And the LORD God prepared a plant[1] and made it come up over Jonah, that it might be shade for his head to deliver him from his misery. So Jonah was very grateful for the plant. 7 But as morning dawned the next day God prepared a worm, and it *so* damaged the plant that it withered. 8 And it happened, when the sun arose, that God prepared a vehement east wind; and the sun beat on Jonah's head, so that he grew faint. Then he wished death for himself, and said, [a]"*It is* better for me to die than to live."

9 Then God said to Jonah, "*Is it* right for you to be angry about the plant?"

And he said, "*It is* right for me to be angry, even to death!"

10 But the LORD said, "You have had pity on the plant for which you have not labored, nor made it grow, which came up in a night and perished in a night. 11 And should I not pity Nineveh, [a]that great city, in which are more than one hundred and twenty thousand persons [b]who cannot discern between their right hand and their left—and much livestock?"

> **4:11** The same word used to describe Jonah's feeling toward the plant in verse 10, **pity**, is used for God's feeling toward the people of Nineveh. People are of more value than animals and animals of more value than plants, but the Lord has a concern that extends to all His creation. The Lord's compassion comes from His character (see Jon. 4:2; Joel 2:13–14).

2:9 [a] Hos. 14:2 [b] [Eccl. 5:4, 5] [c] Ps. 3:8 [d] [Jer. 3:23] 3:3 [1] Exact meaning unknown 3:4 [a] [Deut. 18:22] 3:5 [a] [Matt. 12:41] 3:6 [a] Job 2:8 3:7 [a] 2 Chr. 20:3 3:8 [a] Is. 58:6 [b] Is. 59:6 3:9 [a] Joel 2:14 3:10 [a] Jer. 18:8 4:2 [a] Jon. 1:3 [b] Joel 2:13 4:3 [a] 1 Kin. 19:4 [b] Jon. 4:8 4:6 [1] Hebrew *kikayon,* exact identity unknown 4:8 [a] Jon. 4:3 4:11 [a] Jon. 1:2; 3:2, 3 [b] Deut. 1:39

# *The Book of the Prophet*
# MICAH

**AUTHOR**
Micah

**KEY VERSE**
Micah 6:8

**READING TIME**
22 minutes

**752 BC**
Jotham becomes king in Judah

**c. 740–710 BC**
Micah prophesies in Judah

**736 BC**
Ahaz becomes king in Judah

**729 BC**
Hezekiah becomes king in Judah

**722 BC**
The Assyrians defeat Israel

**701 BC**
Assyria lays siege against Jerusalem

Micah, called from his rustic home to be a prophet, left his familiar surroundings to deliver a stern message of judgment to the princes and people of Jerusalem. Burdened by the wealthy and affluential's abusive treatment of the poor, the prophet rebuked all who used their social or political power for personal gain. Through it all, God's righteous demands upon His people were clear: "To do justly, to love mercy, and to walk humbly with your God" (Mic. 6:8).

**Occasion:** Micah shares a stern warning primarily to the southern kingdom of Judah, calling on them to cease their unjust practices.

**Main Point:** God will not tolerate the injustices of His people and one day will rule over them in perfect justice.

**Big Ideas:** God is righteous and just and demands that His people live likewise. We are to look for ways to show God's mercy and justice to others.

## OUTLINE:

I. God's Judgment on the People (chs. 1–2)
II. God's Judgment on the Leaders (ch. 3)
III. God's Promise of Restoration (chs. 4–5)
IV. God's Call for Repentance (chs. 6–7)

**1** The word of the LORD that came to [a]Micah
of Moresheth in the days of [b]Jotham, Ahaz,
*and* Hezekiah, kings of Judah, which he saw
concerning Samaria and Jerusalem.

### *THE COMING JUDGMENT ON ISRAEL*

2 Hear, all you peoples!
Listen, O earth, and all that is in it!
Let the Lord GOD be a witness against you,
The Lord from [a]His holy temple.

3 For behold, the LORD is coming out of His place;
He will come down
And tread on the high places of the earth.
4 [a]The mountains will melt under Him,
And the valleys will split
Like wax before the fire,
Like waters poured down a steep place.
5 All this is for the transgression of Jacob
And for the sins of the house of Israel.
What *is* the transgression of Jacob?
*Is it* not Samaria?
And what *are* the [a]high places of Judah?
*Are they* not Jerusalem?

**SEEING JESUS IN THE SCRIPTURE**

**1:3–4** This prophecy points to God's judgment of Israel for breaking the covenant. Just as God came down to judge their sin, Jesus is the promised Savior who came to earth to take the judgment due because of our sin (1 John 2:1–2).

6 "Therefore I will make Samaria [a]a heap of ruins in the field,
Places for planting a vineyard;
I will pour down her stones into the valley,
And I will [b]uncover her foundations.
7 All her carved images shall be beaten to pieces,
And all her [a]pay as a harlot shall be burned with the fire;
All her idols I will lay desolate,
For she gathered *it* from the pay of a harlot,
And they shall return to the [b]pay of a harlot."

### *MOURNING FOR ISRAEL AND JUDAH*

8 Therefore I will wail and howl,
I will go stripped and naked;
[a]I will make a wailing like the jackals
And a mourning like the ostriches,
9 For her wounds *are* incurable.
For [a]it has come to Judah;
It has come to the gate of My people—
To Jerusalem.

10 [a]Tell *it* not in Gath,
Weep not at all;
In Beth Aphrah[1]
Roll yourself in the dust.
11 Pass by in naked shame, you inhabitant of Shaphir;
The inhabitant of Zaanan[1] does not go out.
Beth Ezel mourns;
Its place to stand is taken away from you.

12 For the inhabitant of Maroth pined[1] for good,
But [a]disaster came down from the LORD
To the gate of Jerusalem.
13 O inhabitant of [a]Lachish,
Harness the chariot to the swift steeds
(She *was* the beginning of sin to the daughter of Zion),
For the transgressions of Israel were [b]found in you.

14 Therefore you shall [a]give presents to Moresheth Gath;[1]
The houses of [b]Achzib[2] *shall be* a lie to the kings of Israel.
15 I will yet bring an heir to you, O inhabitant of [a]Mareshah;[1]
The glory of Israel shall come to [b]Adullam.
16 Make yourself [a]bald and cut off your hair,
Because of your [b]precious children;
Enlarge your baldness like an eagle,
For they shall go from you into [c]captivity.

**1:16** The Israelites considered a clean-shaven head shameful. Aside from priests and Levites, the only Israelite man who would have considered shaving his head was one who was going through a time of extreme sadness or mourning.

### *WOE TO EVILDOERS*

**2** Woe to those who devise iniquity,
And work out evil on their beds!
At [a]morning light they practice it,
Because it is in the power of their hand.
2 They [a]covet fields and take *them* by violence,
Also houses, and seize *them.*
So they oppress a man and his house,
A man and his inheritance.

3 Therefore thus says the LORD:

"Behold, against this [a]family I am devising [b]disaster,
From which you cannot remove your necks;

**1:1** [a] Jer. 26:18 [b] Is. 1:1 **1:2** [a] [Ps. 11:4] **1:4** [a] Amos 9:5 **1:5** [a] Deut. 32:13; 33:29 **1:6** [a] 2 Kin. 19:25 [b] Ezek. 13:14 **1:7** [a] Hos. 2:5 [b] Deut. 23:18 **1:8** [a] Ps. 102:6 **1:9** [a] 2 Kin. 18:13 **1:10** [a] 2 Sam. 1:20 [1] Literally *House of Dust* **1:11** [1] Literally *Going Out* **1:12** [a] Is. 59:9–11 [1] Literally *was sick* **1:13** [a] Is. 36:2 [b] Ezek. 23:11 **1:14** [a] 2 Sam. 8:2 [b] Josh. 15:44 [1] Literally *Possession of Gath* [2] Literally *Lie* **1:15** [a] Josh. 15:44 [b] 2 Chr. 11:7 [1] Literally *Inheritance* **1:16** [a] Job 1:20 [b] Lam. 4:5 [c] Amos 7:11, 17 **2:1** [a] Hos. 7:6, 7 **2:2** [a] Is. 5:8 **2:3** [a] Jer. 8:3 [b] Amos 5:13

Nor shall you walk haughtily,
For this *is* an evil time.
4 In that day *one* shall take up a proverb
against you,
And [a]lament with a bitter lamentation,
saying:
'We are utterly destroyed!
He has changed the heritage of my people;
How He has removed *it* from me!
To a turncoat He has divided our fields.' "

5 Therefore you will have no one to
determine boundaries[1] by lot
In the assembly of the LORD.

### LYING PROPHETS

6 "Do not prattle," *you say to those* who
prophesy.
So they shall not prophesy to you;[1]
They shall not return insult for insult.[2]
7 *You who are* named the house of Jacob:
"Is the Spirit of the LORD restricted?
*Are* these His doings?
Do not My words do good
To him who walks uprightly?

8 "Lately My people have risen up as an
enemy—
You pull off the robe with the garment
From those who trust *you,* as they pass by,
Like men returned from war.
9 The women of My people you cast out
From their pleasant houses;
From their children
You have taken away My glory forever.

10 "Arise and depart,
For this *is* not *your* [a]rest;
Because it is [b]defiled, it shall destroy,
Yes, with utter destruction.
11 If a man should walk in a false spirit
And speak a lie, *saying,*
'I will prophesy to you of wine and drink,'
Even he would be the [a]prattler of this people.

### ISRAEL RESTORED

12 "I[a] will surely assemble all of you, O Jacob,
I will surely gather the remnant of Israel;
I will put them together [b]like sheep of the
fold,[1]
Like a flock in the midst of their pasture;
[c]They shall make a loud noise because of
*so many* people.
13 The one who breaks open will come up
before them;
They will break out,
Pass through the gate,
And go out by it;
[a]Their king will pass before them,
[b]With the LORD at their head."

### WICKED RULERS AND PROPHETS

3 And I said:
"Hear now, O heads of Jacob,
And you [a]rulers of the house of Israel:
[b]*Is it* not for you to know justice?
2 You who hate good and love evil;
Who strip the skin from My people,[1]
And the flesh from their bones;
3 Who also [a]eat the flesh of My people,
Flay their skin from them,
Break their bones,
And chop *them* in pieces
Like *meat* for the pot,
[b]Like flesh in the caldron."
4 Then [a]they will cry to the LORD,
But He will not hear them;
He will even hide His face from them at
that time,
Because they have been evil in their deeds.

5 Thus says the LORD [a]concerning the
prophets
Who make my people stray;
Who chant "Peace"
While they [b]chew with their teeth,
But who prepare war against him
[c]Who puts nothing into their mouths:
6 "Therefore[a] you shall have night without
vision,
And you shall have darkness without
divination;
The sun shall go down on the prophets,
And the day shall be dark for [b]them.
7 So the seers shall be ashamed,
And the diviners abashed;
Indeed they shall all cover their lips;
[a]For *there is* no answer from God."
8 But truly I am full of power by the Spirit
of the LORD,
And of justice and might,
[a]To declare to Jacob his transgression
And to Israel his sin.
9 Now hear this,
You heads of the house of Jacob
And rulers of the house of Israel,
Who abhor justice
And pervert all equity,
10 [a]Who build up Zion with [b]bloodshed
And Jerusalem with iniquity:
11 [a]Her heads judge for a bribe,
[b]Her priests teach for pay,
And her prophets divine for money.

2:4 [a] 2 Sam. 1:17 2:5 [1] Literally *one casting a surveyor's line* 2:6 [1] Literally *to these* [2] Vulgate reads *He shall not take shame.*
2:10 [a] Deut. 12:9 [b] Lev. 18:25 2:11 [a] Is. 30:10 2:12 [a] [Mic. 4:6, 7] [b] Jer. 31:10 [c] Ezek. 33:22; 36:37 [1] Hebrew *Bozrah* 2:13 [a] [Hos. 3:5] [b] Is. 52:12 3:1 [a] Ezek. 22:27 [b] Jer. 5:4, 5 3:2 [1] Literally *them* 3:3 [a] Ps. 14:4; 27:2 [b] Ezek. 11:3, 6, 7 3:4 [a] Jer. 11:11 3:5 [a] Ezek. 13:10, 19 [b] Matt. 7:15 [c] Ezek. 13:18 3:6 [a] Is. 8:20–22; 29:10–12 [b] Is. 29:10 3:7 [a] Amos 8:11 3:8 [a] Is. 58:1 3:10 [a] Jer. 22:13, 17 [b] Hab. 2:12 3:11 [a] Is. 1:23 [b] Jer. 6:13

[c]Yet they lean on the LORD, and say,
"Is not the LORD among us?
No harm can come upon us."
12 Therefore because of you
Zion shall be [a]plowed *like* a field,
[b]Jerusalem shall become heaps of ruins,
And [c]the mountain of the temple[1]
Like the bare hills of the forest.

### THE LORD'S REIGN IN ZION

*(cf. Is. 2:2–4)*

**4** Now [a]it shall come to pass in the latter days
*That* the mountain of the LORD's house
Shall be established on the top of the mountains,
And shall be exalted above the hills;
And peoples shall flow to it.
2 Many nations shall come and say,
"Come, and let us go up to the mountain of the LORD,
To the house of the God of Jacob;
He will teach us His ways,
And we shall walk in His paths."
For out of Zion the law shall go forth,
And the word of the LORD from Jerusalem.
3 He shall judge between many peoples,
And rebuke strong nations afar off;
They shall beat their swords into [a]plowshares,
And their spears into pruning hooks;
Nation shall not lift up sword against nation,
[b]Neither shall they learn war anymore.[1]
4 [a]But everyone shall sit under his vine and under his fig tree,
And no one shall make *them* afraid;
For the mouth of the LORD of hosts has spoken.
5 For all people walk each in the name of his god,
But [a]we will walk in the name of the LORD our God
Forever and ever.

### ZION'S FUTURE TRIUMPH

6 "In that day," says the LORD,
[a]"I will assemble the lame,
[b]I will gather the outcast
And those whom I have afflicted;
7 I will make the lame [a]a remnant,
And the outcast a strong nation;
So the LORD [b]will reign over them in Mount Zion
From now on, even forever.
8 And you, O tower of the flock,
The stronghold of the daughter of Zion,
To you shall it come,
Even the former dominion shall come,
The kingdom of the daughter of Jerusalem."
9 Now why do you cry aloud?
[a]*Is there* no king in your midst?
Has your counselor perished?
For [b]pangs have seized you like a woman in labor.
10 Be in pain, and labor to bring forth,
O daughter of Zion,
Like a woman in birth pangs.
For now you shall go forth from the city,
You shall dwell in the field,
And to [a]Babylon you shall go.
There you shall be delivered;
There the [b]LORD will [c]redeem you
From the hand of your enemies.

> **4:10** Nebuchadnezzar, the king of **Babylon**, led three different attacks against Judah. He took thousands of Jews back to Babylon as prisoners. In 586 BC, the Babylonian army burned down the temple in Jerusalem.

11 [a]Now also many nations have gathered against you,
Who say, "Let her be defiled,
And let our eye [b]look upon Zion."
12 But they do not know [a]the thoughts of the LORD,
Nor do they understand His counsel;
For He will gather them [b]like sheaves to the threshing floor.

13 "Arise[a] and [b]thresh, O daughter of Zion;
For I will make your horn iron,
And I will make your hooves bronze;
You shall [c]beat in pieces many peoples;
[d]I will consecrate their gain to the LORD,
And their substance to [e]the Lord of the whole earth."

**5** Now gather yourself in troops,
O daughter of troops;
He has laid siege against us;
They will [a]strike the judge of Israel with a rod on the cheek.

### THE COMING MESSIAH

2 "But you, [a]Bethlehem [b]Ephrathah,
*Though* you are little [c]among the [d]thousands of Judah,
*Yet* out of you shall come forth to Me
The One to be [e]Ruler in Israel,
[f]Whose goings forth *are* from of old,
From everlasting."

**3:11** [c] Is. 48:2 **3:12** [a] Jer. 26:18 [b] Ps. 79:1 [c] Mic. 4:1, 2 [1] Literally *house* **4:1** [a] Is. 2:2–4 **4:3** [a] Is. 2:4 [b] Ps. 72:7 [1] Compare Isaiah 2:2–4 **4:4** [a] Zech. 3:10 **4:5** [a] Zech. 10:12 **4:6** [a] Ezek. 34:16 [b] Ps. 147:2 **4:7** [a] Mic. 2:12 [b] [Is. 9:6; 24:23] **4:9** [a] Jer. 8:19 [b] Is. 13:8 **4:10** [a] Amos 5:27 [b] [Is. 45:13] [c] Ps. 18:17 **4:11** [a] Lam. 2:16 [b] Obad. 12 **4:12** [a] [Is. 55:8, 9] [b] Is. 21:10 **4:13** [a] Jer. 51:33 [b] Is. 41:15 [c] Dan. 2:44 [d] Is. 18:7 [e] Zech. 4:14 **5:1** [a] Lam. 3:30; Matt. 27:30; Mark 15:19 **5:2** [a] John 7:42 [b] Gen. 35:19; 48:7 [c] 1 Sam. 23:23 [d] Ex. 18:25 [e] [Is. 9:6] [f] Ps. 90:2

**SEEING JESUS IN THE SCRIPTURE**

**5:2** *Bethlehem* means "house of bread." In this small, inconsequential town Jesus was born in fulfillment of this prophecy (see Luke 2:4, 11). Jesus is the bread of life who completely satisfies all who come to Him in faith (see John 6:35).

3 Therefore He shall give them up,
Until the time *that* [a]she who is in labor has given birth;
Then [b]the remnant of His brethren
Shall return to the children of Israel.
4 And He shall stand and [a]feed *His flock*
In the strength of the LORD,
In the majesty of the name of the LORD His God;
And they shall abide,
For now He [b]shall be great
To the ends of the earth;
5 And this *One* [a]shall be peace.

### *JUDGMENT ON ISRAEL'S ENEMIES*

When the Assyrian comes into our land,
And when he treads in our palaces,
Then we will raise against him
Seven shepherds and eight princely men.
6 They shall waste with the sword the land of Assyria,
And the land of [a]Nimrod at its entrances;
Thus He shall [b]deliver *us* from the Assyrian,
When he comes into our land
And when he treads within our borders.
7 Then [a]the remnant of Jacob
Shall be in the midst of many peoples,
[b]Like dew from the LORD,
Like showers on the grass,
That tarry for no man
Nor wait for the sons of men.
8 And the remnant of Jacob
Shall be among the Gentiles,
In the midst of many peoples,
Like a [a]lion among the beasts of the forest,
Like a young lion among flocks of sheep,
Who, if he passes through,
Both treads down and tears in pieces,
And none can deliver.
9 Your hand shall be lifted against your adversaries,
And all your enemies shall be cut off.

10 "And it shall be in that day," says the LORD,
"That I will [a]cut off your [b]horses from your midst
And destroy your [c]chariots.
11 I will cut off the cities of your land
And throw down all your strongholds.
12 I will cut off sorceries from your hand,
And you shall have no [a]soothsayers.
13 [a]Your carved images I will also cut off,
And your *sacred* pillars from your midst;
You shall [b]no more worship the work of your hands;
14 I will pluck your wooden images[1] from your midst;
Thus I will destroy your cities.
15 And I will [a]execute vengeance in anger and fury
On the nations that have not heard."[1]

### *GOD PLEADS WITH ISRAEL*

6 Hear now what the LORD says:
"Arise, plead your case before the mountains,
And let the hills hear your voice.
2 [a]Hear, O you mountains, [b]the LORD's complaint,
And you strong foundations of the earth;
For [c]the LORD has a complaint against His people,
And He will contend with Israel.

3 "O My people, what [a]have I done to you?
And how have I [b]wearied you?
Testify against Me.
4 [a]For I brought you up from the land of Egypt,
I redeemed you from the house of bondage;
And I sent before you Moses, Aaron, and Miriam.
5 O My people, remember now
What [a]Balak king of Moab counseled,
And what Balaam the son of Beor answered him,
From Acacia Grove[1] to Gilgal,
That you may know [b]the righteousness of the LORD."

6 With what shall I come before the LORD,
*And* bow myself before the High God?
Shall I come before Him with burnt offerings,
With calves a year old?
7 [a]Will the LORD be pleased with thousands of rams,
Ten thousand [b]rivers of oil?
[c]Shall I give my firstborn *for* my transgression,
The fruit of my body *for* the sin of my soul?

**5:3** [a] Mic. 4:10 [b] Mic. 4:7; 7:18 **5:4** [a] [Is. 40:11; 49:9] [b] Ps. 72:8 **5:5** [a] [Is. 9:6] **5:6** [a] Gen. 10:8–11 [b] Is. 14:25 **5:7** [a] Mic. 5:3 [b] Deut. 32:2 **5:8** [a] Num. 24:9 **5:10** [a] Zech. 9:10 [b] Deut. 17:16 [c] Is. 2:7; 22:18 **5:12** [a] Is. 2:6 **5:13** [a] Zech. 13:2 [b] Is. 2:8 **5:14** [1] Hebrew *Asherim,* Canaanite deities **5:15** [a] [2 Thess. 1:8] [1] Or *obeyed* **6:2** [a] Ps. 50:1, 4 [b] Hos. 12:2 [c] [Is. 1:18] **6:3** [a] Jer. 2:5, 31 [b] Is. 43:22, 23 **6:4** [a] [Deut. 4:20] **6:5** [a] Num. 22:5, 6 [b] Judg. 5:11 [1] Hebrew *Shittim* (compare Numbers 25:1; Joshua 2:1; 3:1) **6:7** [a] Is. 1:11 [b] Job 29:6 [c] 2 Kin. 16:3

LIVE THE TRUTH

## HELPING OTHERS

**6:8** Servanthood was at the heart of Jesus' earthly ministry, so helping others should be a big part of who we are as His followers. Each day, we should look for people we can help. Often, they aren't hard to find. People all around us have various physical needs: the homeless person who needs food, the retired person who needs lawncare, the child with a broken bicycle. Helping others surely means we do whatever we can to meet these needs, but it's more than that. The best way we can help others is by showing them God's love of God and helping them see what Jesus has done for us.

In Micah 6:8, God describes three key ingredients to helping others. First, we are to "do justly," meaning we live with fairness toward others. God wants us to do what's right, and He wants us to do our best to make sure all people are treated in a right manner. Second, we are to "love mercy," meaning we should have compassion for others and extend loving, undeserved forgiveness. Compassion is the fuel of helping others. And forgiveness is often needed when others take advantage of our desire to help. Third, we are to "walk humbly," meaning we see others as more important than ourselves. When we do, we cannot *not* serve others with lovingkindness.

8 He has [a]shown you, O man, what *is* good;
And what does the LORD require of you
But [b]to do justly,
To love mercy,
And to walk humbly with your God?

### PUNISHMENT OF ISRAEL'S INJUSTICE

9 The LORD's voice cries to the city—
Wisdom shall see Your name:

"Hear the rod!
Who has appointed it?
10 Are there yet the treasures of wickedness
In the house of the wicked,
And the short measure *that is* an abomination?
11 Shall I count pure *those* with [a]the wicked scales,
And with the bag of deceitful weights?
12 For her rich men are full of [a]violence,
Her inhabitants have spoken lies,
And [b]their tongue is deceitful in their mouth.

13 "Therefore I will also [a]make *you* sick by striking you,
By making *you* desolate because of your sins.
14 [a]You shall eat, but not be satisfied;
Hunger[1] *shall be* in your midst.
You may carry *some* away,[2] but shall not save *them;*
And what you do rescue I will give over to the sword.

15 "You shall [a]sow, but not reap;
You shall tread the olives, but not anoint yourselves with oil;
And *make* sweet wine, but not drink wine.
16 For the statutes of [a]Omri are [b]kept;
All the works of Ahab's house *are done;*
And you walk in their counsels,
That I may make you a desolation,
And your inhabitants a hissing.
Therefore you shall bear the [c]reproach of My people."[1]

### SORROW FOR ISRAEL'S SINS

7 Woe is me!
For I am like those who gather summer fruits,
Like those who [a]glean vintage grapes;
*There is no* cluster to eat
Of the first-ripe fruit *which* [b]my soul desires.
2 The [a]faithful *man* has perished from the earth,
And *there is* no one upright among men.
They all lie in wait for blood;
[b]Every man hunts his brother with a net.

3 That they may successfully do evil with both hands—
The prince asks *for gifts,*
The judge *seeks* a [a]bribe,
And the great *man* utters his evil desire;
So they scheme together.
4 The best of them *is* [a]like a brier;
The most upright *is sharper* than a thorn hedge;
The day of your watchman and your punishment comes;
Now shall be their perplexity.

6:8 [a] [Deut. 10:12] [b] Gen. 18:19 6:11 [a] Hos. 12:7 6:12 [a] Mic. 2:1, 2 [b] Jer. 9:2–6, 8 6:13 [a] Lev. 26:16 6:14 [a] Lev. 26:26 [1] Or *Emptiness* or *Humiliation* [2] Targum and Vulgate read *You shall take hold.* 6:15 [a] Amos 5:11 6:16 [a] 1 Kin. 16:25, 26 [b] Hos. 5:11 [c] Is. 25:8 [1] Following Masoretic Text, Targum, and Vulgate; Septuagint reads *of nations.* 7:1 [a] Is. 17:6 [b] Is. 28:4 7:2 [a] Is. 57:1 [b] Hab. 1:15 7:3 [a] Mic. 3:11 7:4 [a] Ezek. 2:6

5 [a]Do not trust in a friend;
Do not put your confidence in a companion;
Guard the doors of your mouth
From her who lies in your [b]bosom.
6 For [a]son dishonors father,
Daughter rises against her mother,
Daughter-in-law against her mother-in-law;
A man's enemies *are* the men of his own household.
7 Therefore I will look to the LORD;
I will [a]wait for the God of my salvation;
My God will hear me.

**SEEING JESUS IN THE SCRIPTURE**

**7:6** The decline of Israel's faithfulness to God led to a breakdown within the family. Jesus repeated these words, pointing to how there will be a separation between those who have and who don't have faith in Him (see Matt. 10:35).

### *ISRAEL'S CONFESSION AND COMFORT*

8 [a]Do not rejoice over me, my enemy;
[b]When I fall, I will arise;
When I sit in darkness,
The LORD *will be* a light to me.
9 [a]I will bear the indignation of the LORD,
Because I have sinned against Him,
Until He pleads my [b]case
And executes justice for me.
He will bring me forth to the light;
I will see His righteousness.
10 Then *she who is* my enemy will see,
And [a]shame will cover her who said to me,
[b]"Where is the LORD your God?"
My eyes will see her;
Now she will be trampled down
Like mud in the streets.

11 *In* the day when your [a]walls are to be built,
*In* that day the decree shall go far and wide.[1]
12 *In* that day [a]they[1] shall come to you
From Assyria and the fortified cities,[2]
From the fortress[3] to the River,[4]
From sea to sea,
And mountain *to* mountain.
13 Yet the land shall be desolate
Because of those who dwell in it,
And [a]for the fruit of their deeds.

### *GOD WILL FORGIVE ISRAEL*

14 Shepherd Your people with Your staff,
The flock of Your heritage,
Who dwell solitarily *in* a [a]woodland,
In the midst of Carmel;
Let them feed *in* Bashan and Gilead,
As in days of old.

15 "As[a] in the days when you came out of the land of Egypt,
I will show them[1] [b]wonders."

16 The nations [a]shall see and be ashamed of all their might;
[b]They shall put *their* hand over *their* mouth;
Their ears shall be deaf.
17 They shall lick the [a]dust like a serpent;
[b]They shall crawl from their holes like snakes of the earth.
[c]They shall be afraid of the LORD our God,
And shall fear because of You.
18 [a]Who *is* a God like You,
[b]Pardoning iniquity
And passing over the transgression of
[c]the remnant of His heritage?

[d]He does not retain His anger forever,
Because He delights *in* [e]mercy.
19 He will again have compassion on us,
And will subdue our iniquities.

You will cast all our[1] sins
Into the depths of the sea.
20 [a]You will give truth to Jacob
*And* mercy to Abraham,
[b]Which You have sworn to our fathers
From days of old.

**SEEING JESUS IN THE SCRIPTURE**

**7:20** The Book of Micah ends with a declaration of God's covenant faithfulness, which is most evident in His provision of Jesus. When Zacharias prophesied how his son John would prepare the way for the Jesus, he quoted this passage (see Luke 1:72–73).

**7:5** [a]Jer. 9:4 [b]Deut. 28:56 **7:6** [a]Matt. 10:36 **7:7** [a]Is. 25:9 **7:8** [a]Prov. 24:17 [b][Prov. 24:16] **7:9** [a]Lam. 3:39, 40 [b]Jer. 50:34 **7:10** [a]Ps. 35:26 [b]Ps. 42:3 **7:11** [a][Amos 9:11] [1]Or *the boundary shall be extended* **7:12** [a][Is. 11:16; 19:23–25] [1]Literally *he,* collective of the captives [2]Hebrew *arey mazor,* possibly *cities of Egypt* [3]Hebrew *mazor,* possibly *Egypt* [4]That is, the Euphrates **7:13** [a]Jer. 21:14 **7:14** [a]Is. 37:24 **7:15** [a]Ps. 68:22; 78:12 [b]Ex. 34:10 [1]Literally *him,* collective for the captives **7:16** [a]Is. 26:11 [b]Job 21:5 **7:17** [a][Is. 49:23] [b]Ps. 18:45 [c]Jer. 33:9 **7:18** [a]Ex. 15:11 [b]Ex. 34:6, 7, 9 [c]Mic. 4:7 [d]Ps. 103:8, 9, 13 [e][Ezek. 33:11] **7:19** [1]Literally *their* **7:20** [a]Luke 1:72, 73 [b]Ps. 105:9

# *The Book of the Prophet*
# NAHUM

| AUTHOR | KEY VERSES | READING TIME |
|---|---|---|
| Nahum | Nahum 1:7–8 | 10 minutes |

**722 BC**
The Assyrians defeat Israel

**669 BC**
Ashurbanipal's rules in Assyria

**663–654 BC**
Assyria occupies Egypt's capital Thebes

**622 BC**
Revival in Jerusalem under Josiah

**612 BC**
The Babylonians and Medes defeat Assyria

**605 BC**
Nebuchadnezzar rules in Babylon

Under Jonah's preaching, Nineveh had been given the privilege of knowing the one true God. This large Gentile city had repented, and God had graciously withheld His judgment. However, a hundred years later, Nahum proclaimed the downfall of this same city. The Assyrians had abandoned their revival and had returned to their habits of idolatry, violence, and arrogance. Nahum's message was clear: Babylon would so destroy the city that no trace of it would remain—a prophecy fulfilled in painful detail. While Nahum's prophecy was one of despair for its recipients, the destruction of Nineveh was a message of comfort and consolation to Judah and all who lived in fear of the cruelty of the Assyrians.

**Occasion:** Nahum wrote to pronounce God's judgment on the Assyrians but also to offer hope to God's people who were among those oppressed by this mighty nation.

**Main Point:** God will judge all who rebel against Him.

**Big Ideas:** God is just and will judge every person and nation for their sins.

## OUTLINE:

I. God's Wrath Against Nineveh (ch. 1)
II. God's Judgment Against Nineveh (ch. 2)
III. God's Charges Against Nineveh (ch. 3)

**1** The burden[1] [a]against Nineveh. The book of the vision of Nahum the Elkoshite.

> **1:1 Nineveh** was the capital of Assyria. The Assyrians destroyed Samaria, the capital of the northern kingdom of Israel, in 722 BC. They also tried to conquer Judah, the southern kingdom, by surrounding Jerusalem and not allowing any food, water, or supplies to enter the city. Ultimately, they failed in their attempt, but not before causing the people of Jerusalem to suffer terribly.

### *GOD'S WRATH ON HIS ENEMIES*

2 God *is* [a]jealous, and the LORD avenges;
The LORD avenges and *is* furious.
The LORD will take vengeance on His adversaries,
And He reserves *wrath* for His enemies;
3 The LORD *is* [a]slow to anger and [b]great in power,
And will not at all acquit *the wicked.*

[c]The LORD has His way
In the whirlwind and in the storm,
And the clouds *are* the dust of His feet.
4 [a]He rebukes the sea and makes it dry,
And dries up all the rivers.
[b]Bashan and Carmel wither,
And the flower of Lebanon wilts.
5 The mountains quake before Him,
The hills melt,
And the earth heaves[1] at His presence,
Yes, the world and all who dwell in it.

6 Who can stand before His indignation?
And [a]who can endure the fierceness of His anger?
His fury is poured out like fire,
And the rocks are thrown down by Him.

7 [a]The LORD *is* good,
A stronghold in the day of trouble;
And [b]He knows those who trust in Him.
8 But with an overflowing flood
He will make an utter end of its place,
And darkness will pursue His enemies.

9 [a]What do you conspire against the LORD?
[b]He will make an utter end *of it.*
Affliction will not rise up a second time.
10 For while tangled [a]*like* thorns,
[b]And while drunken *like* drunkards,
[c]They shall be devoured like stubble fully dried.
11 From you comes forth *one*
Who plots evil against the LORD,
A wicked counselor.

12 Thus says the LORD:

"Though *they are* safe, and likewise many,
Yet in this manner they will be [a]cut down
When he passes through.
Though I have afflicted you,
I will afflict you no more;
13 For now I will break off his yoke from you,
And burst your bonds apart."

14 The LORD has given a command concerning you:
"Your name shall be perpetuated no longer.
Out of the house of your gods
I will cut off the carved image and the molded image.
I will dig your [a]grave,
For you are [b]vile."

15 Behold, on the mountains
The [a]feet of him who brings good tidings,
Who proclaims peace!
O Judah, keep your appointed feasts,
Perform your vows.
For the wicked one shall no more pass through you;
He is [b]utterly cut off.

### *THE DESTRUCTION OF NINEVEH*

**2** He who scatters[1] has come up before your face.
Man the fort!
Watch the road!
Strengthen *your* flanks!
Fortify *your* power mightily.
2 For the LORD will restore the excellence of Jacob
Like the excellence of Israel,
For the emptiers have emptied them out
And ruined their vine branches.

3 The shields of his mighty men *are* made red,
The valiant men *are* in scarlet.
The chariots *come* with flaming torches
In the day of his preparation,
And the spears are brandished.[1]
4 The chariots rage in the streets,
They jostle one another in the broad roads;
They seem like torches,
They run like lightning.

**1:1** [a]Zeph. 2:13 [1]Or *oracle* **1:2** [a]Ex. 20:5 **1:3** [a]Ex. 34:6, 7 [b][Job 9:4] [c]Ps. 18:17 **1:4** [a]Matt. 8:26 [b]Is. 33:9 **1:5** [1]Targum reads *burns.* **1:6** [a][Mal. 3:2] **1:7** [a][Jer. 33:11] [b]2 Tim. 2:19 **1:9** [a]Ps. 2:1 [b]1 Sam. 3:12 **1:10** [a]2 Sam. 23:6 [b]Nah. 3:11 [c]Mal. 4:1 **1:12** [a][Is. 10:16–19, 33, 34] **1:14** [a]Ezek. 32:22, 23 [b]Nah. 3:6 **1:15** [a]Rom. 10:15 [b]Is. 29:7, 8 **2:1** [1]Vulgate reads *He who destroys.* **2:3** [1]Literally *the cypresses are shaken;* Septuagint and Syriac read *the horses rush about;* Vulgate reads *the drivers are stupefied.*

5 He remembers his nobles;
They stumble in their walk;
They make haste to her walls,
And the defense is prepared.
6 The gates of the rivers are opened,
And the palace is dissolved.
7 It is decreed:[1]
She shall be led away captive,
She shall be brought up;
And her maidservants shall lead *her* as
with the voice of doves,
Beating their breasts.

8 Though Nineveh of old *was* like a pool of
water,
Now they flee away.
"Halt! Halt!" *they cry;*
But no one turns back.
9 Take spoil of silver!
Take spoil of [a]gold!
*There is* no end of treasure,
Or wealth of every desirable prize.
10 She is empty, desolate, and waste!
The heart melts, and the knees shake;
Much pain *is* in every side,
And all their faces are drained of color.[1]

11 Where *is* the dwelling of the [a]lions,
And the feeding place of the young lions,
Where the lion walked, the lioness *and*
lion's cub,
And no one made *them* afraid?
12 The lion tore in pieces enough for his
cubs,
Killed for his lionesses,
[a]Filled his caves with prey,
And his dens with flesh.

13 "Behold, [a]I *am* against you," says the LORD
of hosts, "I will burn your[1] chariots in smoke, and
the sword shall devour your young lions; I will
cut off your prey from the earth, and the voice
of your [b]messengers shall be heard no more."

### THE WOE OF NINEVEH

3 Woe to the [a]bloody city!
It *is* all full of lies *and* robbery.
*Its* victim never departs.
2 The noise of a whip
And the noise of rattling wheels,
Of galloping horses,
Of clattering chariots!
3 Horsemen charge with bright sword and
glittering spear.
*There is* a multitude of slain,
A great number of bodies,
Countless corpses—
They stumble over the corpses—

4 Because of the multitude of harlotries of
the seductive harlot,
[a]The mistress of sorceries,
Who sells nations through her harlotries,
And families through her sorceries.

5 "Behold, I *am* [a]against you," says the LORD
of hosts;
[b]"I will lift your skirts over your face,
I will show the nations your nakedness,
And the kingdoms your shame.
6 I will cast abominable filth upon you,
Make you [a]vile,
And make you [b]a spectacle.
7 It shall come to pass *that* all who look
upon you
[a]Will flee from you, and say,
[b]'Nineveh is laid waste!
[c]Who will bemoan her?'
Where shall I seek comforters for you?"

**SEEING JESUS IN THE SCRIPTURE**

**3:6** Nahum's prophecy of public humiliation and shame for Nineveh because of its sins reflects the righteous judgment it deserved. While we deserve the same for our sins, Jesus bore the public humiliation for us, offering salvation in its place (see 2 Cor. 5:21).

8 [a]Are you better than [b]No Amon[1]
*That was* situated by the River,[2]
That had the waters around her,
Whose rampart *was* the sea,
Whose wall *was* the sea?
9 Ethiopia and Egypt *were* her strength,
And *it was* boundless;
[a]Put and Lubim were your[1] helpers.
10 Yet she *was* carried away,
She went into captivity;
[a]Her young children also were dashed to
pieces
[b]At the head of every street;
They [c]cast lots for her honorable men,
And all her great men were bound in
chains.
11 You also will be [a]drunk;
You will be hidden;
You also will seek refuge from the
enemy.

12 All your strongholds *are* [a]fig trees with
ripened figs:
If they are shaken,
They fall into the mouth of the eater.

**2:7** [1] Hebrew *Huzzab* **2:9** [a] Zeph. 1:18 **2:10** [1] Compare Joel 2:6 **2:11** [a] Job 4:10, 11 **2:12** [a] Jer. 51:34 **2:13** [a] Nah. 3:5 [b] 2 Kin. 18:17–25; 19:9–13, 23 [1] Literally *her* **3:1** [a] Hab. 2:12 **3:4** [a] Is. 47:9–12 **3:5** [a] Nah. 2:13 [b] Is. 47:2, 3 **3:6** [a] Nah. 1:14 [b] Heb. 10:33 **3:7** [a] Rev. 18:10 [b] Jon. 3:3; 4:11 [c] Jer. 15:5 **3:8** [a] Amos 6:2 [b] Jer. 46:25 [1] That is, ancient Thebes; Targum and Vulgate read *populous Alexandria.* [2] Literally *rivers,* that is, the Nile and the surrounding canals **3:9** [a] Ezek. 27:10 [1] Septuagint reads *her.* **3:10** [a] Hos. 13:16 [b] Lam. 2:19 [c] Joel 3:3 **3:11** [a] Nah. 1:10 **3:12** [a] Rev. 6:12, 13

13 Surely, [a]your people in your midst *are*
women!
The gates of your land are wide open for
your enemies;
Fire shall devour the [b]bars of your *gates*.

14 Draw your water for the siege!
[a]Fortify your strongholds!
Go into the clay and tread the mortar!
Make strong the brick kiln!
15 There the fire will devour you,
The sword will cut you off;
It will eat you up like a [a]locust.

Make yourself many—like the locust!
Make yourself many—like the *swarming*
locusts!
16 You have multiplied your [a]merchants
more than the stars of heaven.
The locust plunders and flies away.

17 [a]Your commanders *are* like *swarming*
locusts,
And your generals like great grasshoppers,
Which camp in the hedges on a cold day;
When the sun rises they flee away,
And the place where they *are* is not
known.

18 [a]Your shepherds slumber, O [b]king of
Assyria;
Your nobles rest *in the dust*.
Your people are [c]scattered on the
mountains,
And no one gathers them.
19 Your injury *has* no healing,
[a]Your wound is severe.
[b]All who hear news of you
Will clap *their* hands over you,
For upon whom has not your wickedness
passed continually?

**3:13** [a] Is. 19:16 [b] Jer. 51:30 **3:14** [a] Nah. 2:1 **3:15** [a] Joel 1:4 **3:16** [a] Rev. 18:3, 11–19 **3:17** [a] Rev. 9:7 **3:18** [a] Ps. 76:5, 6 [b] Jer. 50:18 [c] 1 Kin. 22:17 **3:19** [a] Mic. 1:9 [b] Lam. 2:15

*The Book of the Prophet*

# HABAKKUK

| **AUTHOR** | **KEY VERSE** | **READING TIME** |
|---|---|---|
| Habakkuk | Habakkuk 2:4 | 11 minutes |

**612 BC**
The Babylonians and Medes defeat Assyria

**609 BC**
Josiah dies

**605 BC**
Daniel and others exiled in Babylon

**586 BC**
The Babylonians destroy Jerusalem

Habakkuk ministered during the death throes of the nation of Judah. Although repeatedly called to repentance, the nation stubbornly refused to change its sinful ways, even after witnessing what had come of their siblings to the north. God had chastened the northern kingdom of Israel for its idolatry, but Judah stubbornly repeated the same transgression. Habakkuk did what few other prophets dared to do and questioned God. The prophet asked God how long He would allow wickedness to reign in Judah and how long He would permit an evil foreign power like Babylon to prevail. God replied that the Babylonians would be His chastening rod upon the nation, but that He would also hold them accountable. Habakkuk, like the righteous of any generation, had to live by faith (see Hab. 2:4), not by sight. At the end of his book, Habakkuk chose to cling firmly to God regardless of what might happen to his nation (see 3:16–19).

**Occasion:** Habakkuk writes just before the fall of Jerusalem to share God's warning of judgment once more but also to remind the people of God's righteousness.

**Main Point:** God is patient, allowing people time to repent, but He is also just and will hold sinners accountable.

**Big Ideas:** God is in control of all things and will not let sin go unpunished. When things in life get tough, trust that God will never fail you. We are to live by faith.

## OUTLINE:

I. Habakkuk Questions God (chs. 1–2)
II. Habakkuk Praises God (ch. 3)

1 The burden[1] which the prophet Habakkuk saw.

### THE PROPHET'S QUESTION

2 O LORD, how long shall I cry,
[a]And You will not hear?
Even cry out to You, [b]"Violence!"
And You will [c]not save.
3 Why do You show me iniquity,
And cause *me* to see trouble?
For plundering and violence *are* before me;
There is strife, and contention arises.
4 Therefore the law is powerless,
And justice never goes forth.
For the [a]wicked surround the righteous;
Therefore perverse judgment proceeds.

### THE LORD'S REPLY

5 "Look[a] among the nations and watch—
Be utterly astounded!
For *I will* work a work in your days
*Which* you would not believe, though it were told *you.*
6 For indeed I am [a]raising up the Chaldeans,
A bitter and hasty [b]nation
Which marches through the breadth of the earth,
To possess dwelling places *that are* not theirs.
7 They are terrible and dreadful;
Their judgment and their dignity proceed from themselves.
8 Their horses also are [a]swifter than leopards,
And more fierce than evening wolves.
Their chargers charge ahead;
Their cavalry comes from afar;
They fly as the [b]eagle *that* hastens to eat.
9 "They all come for violence;
Their faces are set *like* the east wind.
They gather captives like sand.
10 They scoff at kings,
And princes are scorned by them.
They deride every stronghold,
For they heap up earthen *mounds* and seize it.
11 Then *his* mind[1] changes, and he transgresses;
He commits offense,
[a]*Ascribing* this power to his god."

### THE PROPHET'S SECOND QUESTION

12 Are You not [a]from everlasting,
O LORD my God, my Holy One?
We shall not die.
O LORD, [b]You have appointed them for judgment;
O Rock, You have marked them for [c]correction.
13 *You are* of purer eyes than to behold evil,
And cannot look on wickedness.
Why do You look on those who deal treacherously,
*And* hold Your tongue when the wicked devours
A *person* more righteous than he?
14 *Why* do You make men like fish of the sea,
Like creeping things *that have* no ruler over them?
15 They take up all of them with a hook,
They catch them in their net,
And gather them in their dragnet.
Therefore they rejoice and are glad.
16 Therefore [a]they sacrifice to their net,
And burn incense to their dragnet;
Because by them their share *is* sumptuous
And their food plentiful.
17 Shall they therefore empty their net,
And continue to slay nations without pity?

2 I will [a]stand my watch
And set myself on the rampart,
And watch to see what He will say to me,
And what I will answer when I am corrected.

### THE JUST LIVE BY FAITH

2 Then the LORD answered me and said:

[a]"Write the vision
And make *it* plain on tablets,
That he may run who reads it.
3 For [a]the vision *is* yet for an appointed time;
But at the end it will speak, and it will [b]not lie.
Though it tarries, [c]wait for it;
Because it will [d]surely come,
It will not tarry.

4 "Behold the proud,
His soul is not upright in him;
But the [a]just shall live by his faith.

**SEEING JESUS IN THE SCRIPTURE**

**2:4** As Habakkuk wrestled to understand God's ways and plans, God explained those who are just will live by faith. Trusting in Jesus is how we receive eternal life and how we experience abundant living today (see Gal. 2:16).

**1:1** [1] Or *oracle* **1:2** [a] Lam. 3:8 [b] Mic. 2:1, 2; 3:1–3 [c] [Job 21:5–16] **1:4** [a] Jer. 12:1 **1:5** [a] Is. 29:14 **1:6** [a] 2 Kin. 24:2 [b] Ezek. 7:24; 21:31 **1:8** [a] Jer. 4:13 [b] Hos. 8:1 **1:11** [a] Dan. 5:4 [1] Literally *spirit* or *wind* **1:12** [a] Ps. 90:2; 93:2 [b] Is. 10:5–7 [c] Jer. 25:9 **1:16** [a] Deut. 8:17 **2:1** [a] Is. 21:8, 11 **2:2** [a] Is. 8:1 **2:3** [a] Dan. 8:17, 19; 10:14 [b] Ezek. 12:24, 25 [c] [Heb. 10:37, 38] [d] [2 Pet. 3:9] **2:4** [a] [John 3:36]

LIVE THE TRUTH

## GROWING IN FAITH

**2:4** Our relationship with God is based on faith (see Eph. 2:8–9). We can only have true and eternal life through faith in Jesus. We must believe in who Jesus is and what He did in His life, death, and resurrection, and rely on Him to save us from our sin. That's the core of what the Bible means by saving faith. Faith doesn't end with our salvation, though. Rather, that's just when it begins.

Here we see the just (or righteous) person will live by his or her faith. That doesn't just speak to eternal life in the future, it also concerns how we live each day. Saving faith is active faith; that was James's primary message in the book of the Bible he wrote. True faith in Jesus is not just believing what is true about Him; it's basing your life on that truth too. We let Him lead our lives instead of trying to control things ourselves. This is hard and it feels risky, but as we depend on God, we'll see His faithfulness and that, in turn, will grow our faith. Faith—even a very little amount—is a seed that takes root and grows into increased, larger, sturdier faith.

### *WOE TO THE WICKED*

5 "Indeed, because he transgresses by wine,
*He is* a proud man,
And he does not stay at home.
Because he [a]enlarges his desire as hell,[1]
And he *is* like death, and cannot be satisfied,
He gathers to himself all nations
And heaps up for himself all peoples.

6 "Will not all these [a]take up a proverb against him,
And a taunting riddle against him, and say,
'Woe to him who increases
*What* is not his—how long?
And to him who loads himself with many pledges'?[1]
7 Will not your creditors[1] rise up suddenly?
Will they not awaken who oppress you?
And you will become their booty.
8 [a]Because you have plundered many nations,
All the remnant of the people shall plunder you,
Because of men's blood
And the violence of the land *and* the city,
And of all who dwell in it.

9 "Woe to him who covets evil gain for his house,
That he may [a]set his nest on high,
That he may be delivered from the power of disaster!
10 You give shameful counsel to your house,
Cutting off many peoples,
And sin *against* your soul.
11 For the stone will cry out from the wall,
And the beam from the timbers will answer it.

12 "Woe to him who builds a town with bloodshed,
Who establishes a city by iniquity!
13 Behold, *is it* not of the LORD of hosts
That the peoples labor to feed the fire,[1]
And nations weary themselves in vain?
14 For the earth will be filled
With the knowledge of the glory of the LORD,
As the waters cover the sea.

15 "Woe to him who gives drink to his neighbor,
Pressing[1] *him to* your [a]bottle,
Even to make *him* drunk,
That you may look on his nakedness!
16 You are filled with shame instead of glory.
You also—drink!
And be exposed as uncircumcised![1]
The cup of the LORD's right hand *will be* turned against you,
And utter shame will be on your glory.
17 For the violence *done to* Lebanon will cover you,
And the plunder of beasts *which* made them afraid,
Because of men's blood
And the violence of the land *and* the city,
And of all who dwell in it.

18 "What profit is the image, that its maker should carve it,
The molded image, a teacher of lies,
That the maker of its mold should trust in it,
To make mute idols?
19 Woe to him who says to wood, 'Awake!'
To silent stone, 'Arise! It shall teach!'
Behold, it is overlaid with gold and silver,
Yet in it there is no breath at all.

2:5 [a] Is. 5:11–15 [1] Or *Sheol* 2:6 [a] Mic. 2:4 [1] Syriac and Vulgate read *thick clay.* 2:7 [1] Literally *those who bite you* 2:8 [a] Is. 33:1 2:9 [a] Obad. 4 2:13 [1] Literally *for what satisfies fire,* that is, for what is of no lasting value 2:15 [a] Hos. 7:5 [1] Literally *Attaching* or *Joining* 2:16 [1] Dead Sea Scrolls and Septuagint read *And reel!;* Syriac and Vulgate read *And fall fast asleep!*

20 "But[a] the LORD is in His holy temple.
Let all the earth keep silence before Him."

### THE PROPHET'S PRAYER

3 A prayer of Habakkuk the prophet, on Shigionoth.[1]

2 O LORD, I have heard Your speech *and* was afraid;
O LORD, revive Your work in the midst of the years!
In the midst of the years make *it* known;
In wrath remember mercy.

3 God came from Teman,
The Holy One from Mount Paran. *Selah*

His glory covered the heavens,
And the earth was full of His praise.
4 *His* brightness was like the light;
He had rays *flashing* from His hand,
And there His power *was* hidden.
5 Before Him went pestilence,
And fever followed at His feet.

6 He stood and measured the earth;
He looked and startled the nations.
[a]And the everlasting mountains were scattered,
The perpetual hills bowed.
His ways *are* everlasting.
7 I saw the tents of Cushan in affliction;
The curtains of the land of Midian trembled.

**3:3–6** Because **Paran** is near Mount Sinai, these verses likely refer to God's appearance to Moses at Sinai when He gave the Ten Commandments. The light, noise, and earthquake were all signs of God's presence.

8 O LORD, were *You* displeased with the rivers,
*Was* Your anger against the rivers,
*Was* Your wrath against the sea,
That You rode on Your horses,
Your chariots of salvation?
9 Your bow was made quite ready;
Oaths were sworn over *Your* arrows.[1] *Selah*

You divided the earth with rivers.
10 The mountains saw You *and* trembled;
The overflowing of the water passed by.
The deep uttered its voice,
*And* [a]lifted its hands on high.
11 The [a]sun and moon stood still in their habitation;
At the light of Your arrows they went,
At the shining of Your glittering spear.

12 You marched through the land in indignation;
You trampled the nations in anger.
13 You went forth for the salvation of Your people,
For salvation with Your Anointed.
You struck the head from the house of the wicked,
By laying bare from foundation to neck. *Selah*

14 You thrust through with his own arrows
The head of his villages.
They came out like a whirlwind to scatter me;
Their rejoicing was like feasting on the poor in secret.
15 [a]You walked through the sea with Your horses,
Through the heap of great waters.

16 When I heard, [a]my body trembled;
My lips quivered at *the* voice;
Rottenness entered my bones;
And I trembled in myself,
That I might rest in the day of trouble.
When he comes up to the people,
He will invade them with his troops.

### A HYMN OF FAITH

17 Though the fig tree may not blossom,
Nor fruit be on the vines;
Though the labor of the olive may fail,
And the fields yield no food;
Though the flock may be cut off from the fold,
And there be no herd in the stalls—
18 Yet I will [a]rejoice in the LORD,
I will joy in the God of my salvation.

19 The LORD God[1] is my strength;
He will make my feet like [a]deer's *feet*,
And He will make me [b]walk on my high hills.

To the Chief Musician. With my stringed instruments.

2:20 [a] Zeph. 1:7; Zech. 2:13 3:1 [1] Exact meaning unknown 3:6 [a] Nah. 1:5 3:9 [1] Literally *rods* or *tribes* (compare verse 14) 3:10 [a] Ex. 14:22 3:11 [a] Josh. 10:12–14 3:15 [a] Ps. 77:19; Hab. 3:8 3:16 [a] Ps. 119:120 3:18 [a] Is. 41:16; 61:10 3:19 [a] 2 Sam. 22:34; Ps. 18:33 [b] Deut. 32:13; 33:29 [1] Hebrew *YHWH Adonai*

*The Book of the Prophet*

# ZEPHANIAH

| AUTHOR | KEY VERSE | READING TIME |
|---|---|---|
| Zephaniah | Zephaniah 1:14 | 12 minutes |

**640–609 BC**
Josiah reigns in Jerusalem

**c. 631 BC**
Cyrene, a Greek colony in Libya, founded

**627 BC**
Zephaniah prophesies in Judah

**612 BC**
The Babylonians and Medes defeat Assyria

**605 BC**
Nebuchadnezzar rules in Babylon

**586 BC**
The Babylonians destroy Jerusalem

Unlike the northern kingdom of Israel, which was led by only evil kings, the southern kingdom of Judah was led by good kings at times. King Josiah's reign (640–609 BC) began with continuing spiritual and moral decay, but when the Book of the Law was found in the temple in 622 BC, that changed. Josiah began a series of reforms, no doubt strengthened by Zephaniah's prophetic ministry. But the "revival" only produced outward change without removing the inward heart of corruption that characterized the nation. Zephaniah repeatedly hammered home his message that the day of the Lord—judgment day—was coming. On this day, God would deal with the malignancy of sin. The people of God and their neighbors would soon experience the crushing hand of God's wrath. But after the chastening process was complete, blessing would come in the Person of the Messiah, who would be cause for praise and singing.

**Occasion:** Zephaniah writes during a time of relative peace to warn God's people of the coming day of the Lord and to remind them of the hope they can have in God's promises.

**Main Point:** God judges all who rebel against Him, but He gives refreshment to all who are faithful.

**Big Ideas:** God will punish sin. If we have a relationship with God, we will have a purposeful and fulfilling life.

## OUTLINE:

I. A Day of Future Judgment (chs. 1–2)
II. A Day of Future Blessing (ch. 3)

1 The word of the LORD which came to Zephaniah the son of Cushi, the son of Gedaliah, the son of Amariah, the son of Hezekiah, in the days of [a]Josiah the son of Amon, king of Judah.

### *THE GREAT DAY OF THE LORD*

2 "I will utterly consume everything
From the face of the land,"
Says the LORD;
3 "I[a] will consume man and beast;
I will consume the birds of the heavens,
The fish of the sea,
And the stumbling blocks[1] along with the wicked.
I will cut off man from the face of the land,"
Says the LORD.

4 "I will stretch out My hand against Judah,
And against all the inhabitants of Jerusalem.
I will cut off every trace of Baal from this place,
The names of the [a]idolatrous priests[1] with the *pagan* priests—
5 Those [a]who worship the host of heaven on the housetops;
Those who worship and swear *oaths* by the LORD,
But who *also* swear [b]by Milcom;[1]
6 [a]Those who have turned back from *following* the LORD,
And [b]have not sought the LORD, nor inquired of Him."

> **1:4–5 Baal** was the chief god of the Canaanites, but the Israelites adopted it as their own. Although God had specifically forbidden human sacrifice, they joined the followers of **Milcom** (or Molech) in sacrificing children as part of their worship rituals. The Israelites embraced astrology and the worship of the sun, moon, and stars. As part of their idol worship, they poured out drink offerings and burnt incense on their rooftops.

7 [a]Be silent in the presence of the Lord GOD;
[b]For the day of the LORD *is* at hand,
For [c]the LORD has prepared a sacrifice;
He has invited[1] His guests.

8 "And it shall be,
In the day of the LORD's sacrifice,
That I will punish [a]the princes and the king's children,
And all such as are clothed with foreign apparel.
9 In the same day I will punish
All those who [a]leap over the threshold,[1]
Who fill their masters' houses with violence and deceit.

10 "And there shall be on that day," says the LORD,
"The sound of a mournful cry from [a]the Fish Gate,
A wailing from the Second Quarter,
And a loud crashing from the hills.
11 [a]Wail, you inhabitants of Maktesh![1]
For all the merchant people are cut down;
All those who handle money are cut off.

12 "And it shall come to pass at that time
*That* I will search Jerusalem with lamps,
And punish the men
Who are [a]settled in complacency,[1]
[b]Who say in their heart,
'The LORD will not do good,
Nor will He do evil.'
13 Therefore their goods shall become booty,
And their houses a desolation;
They shall build houses, but not inhabit *them;*
They shall plant vineyards, but [a]not drink their wine."

14 [a]The great day of the LORD *is* near;
*It is* near and hastens quickly.
The noise of the day of the LORD is bitter;
There the mighty men shall cry out.
15 [a]That day *is* a day of wrath,
A day of trouble and distress,
A day of devastation and desolation,
A day of darkness and gloominess,
A day of clouds and thick darkness,
16 A day of [a]trumpet and alarm
Against the fortified cities
And against the high towers.

17 "I will bring distress upon men,
And they shall [a]walk like blind men,
Because they have sinned against the LORD;
Their blood shall be poured out like dust,
And their flesh like refuse."

18 [a]Neither their silver nor their gold
Shall be able to deliver them
In the day of the LORD's wrath;
But the whole land shall be devoured
By the fire of His jealousy,
For He will make speedy riddance
Of all those who dwell in the land.

**1:1** [a] 2 Kin. 22:1, 2 **1:3** [a] Hos. 4:3 [1] Figurative of idols **1:4** [a] Hos. 10:5 [1] Hebrew *chemarim* **1:5** [a] 2 Kin. 23:12 [b] Josh. 23:7 [1] Or *Malcam,* an Ammonite god, also called *Molech* (compare Leviticus 18:21) **1:6** [a] Is. 1:4 [b] Hos. 7:7 **1:7** [a] Zech. 2:13 [b] Is. 13:6 [c] Jer. 46:10 [1] Literally *set apart, consecrated* **1:8** [a] Jer. 39:6 **1:9** [a] 1 Sam. 5:5 [1] Compare 1 Samuel 5:5 **1:10** [a] 2 Chr. 33:14 **1:11** [a] James 5:1 [1] Literally *Mortar,* a market district of Jerusalem **1:12** [a] Jer. 48:11 [b] Ps. 94:7 [1] Literally *on their lees,* that is, settled like the dregs of wine **1:13** [a] Deut. 28:39 **1:14** [a] Joel 2:1, 11 **1:15** [a] Is. 22:5 **1:16** [a] Jer. 4:19 **1:17** [a] Deut. 28:29 **1:18** [a] Ezek. 7:19

### *A CALL TO REPENTANCE*

**2** Gather[a] yourselves together, yes, gather
together,
O undesirable[1] nation,
2 Before the decree is issued,
*Or* the day passes like chaff,
Before the LORD's fierce anger comes
upon you,
Before the day of the LORD's anger comes
upon you!
3 [a]Seek the LORD, [b]all you meek of the earth,
Who have upheld His justice.
Seek righteousness, seek humility.
[c]It may be that you will be hidden
In the day of the LORD's anger.

### *JUDGMENT ON NATIONS*

4 For [a]Gaza shall be forsaken,
And Ashkelon desolate;
They shall drive out Ashdod [b]at
noonday,
And Ekron shall be uprooted.
5 Woe to the inhabitants of [a]the seacoast,
The nation of the Cherethites!
The word of the LORD *is* against you,
O [b]Canaan, land of the Philistines:
"I will destroy you;
So there shall be no inhabitant."

6 The seacoast shall be pastures,
With shelters[1] for shepherds [a]and folds
for flocks.
7 The coast shall be for [a]the remnant of the
house of Judah;
They shall feed *their* flocks there;
In the houses of Ashkelon they shall lie
down at evening.
For the LORD their God will [b]intervene for
them,
And [c]return their captives.

8 "I[a] have heard the reproach of Moab,
And [b]the insults of the people of Ammon,
With which they have reproached My
people,
And [c]made arrogant threats against their
borders.
9 Therefore, as I live,"
Says the LORD of hosts, the God of Israel,
"Surely [a]Moab shall be like Sodom,
And [b]the people of Ammon like
Gomorrah—
[c]Overrun with weeds and saltpits,
And a perpetual desolation.
The residue of My people shall plunder
them,
And the remnant of My people shall
possess them."

> **2:8–9** The people of **Moab** and **Ammon** were distant relatives of the Israelites. The Moabites and Ammonites were descendants of Lot, Abraham's nephew, while the Israelites were descendants of Abraham. Even though they were relatives, the people of Moab and Ammon were enemies of Israel.

10 This they shall have [a]for their pride,
Because they have reproached and made
arrogant threats
Against the people of the LORD of hosts.
11 The LORD *will be* awesome to them,
For He will reduce to nothing all the gods
of the earth;
[a]*People* shall worship Him,
Each one from his place,
Indeed all [b]the shores of the nations.

12 "You[a] Ethiopians also,
You shall be slain by [b]My sword."

13 And He will stretch out His hand against
the north,
[a]Destroy Assyria,
And make Nineveh a desolation,
As dry as the wilderness.
14 The herds shall lie down in her midst,
[a]Every beast of the nation.
Both the [b]pelican and the bittern
Shall lodge on the capitals *of* her *pillars;*
Their voice shall sing in the windows;
Desolation *shall be* at the threshold;
For He will lay bare the [c]cedar work.
15 This is the rejoicing city
[a]That dwelt securely,
[b]That said in her heart,
"I *am it,* and *there is* none besides me."
How has she become a desolation,
A place for beasts to lie down!
Everyone who passes by her
[c]Shall hiss and [d]shake his fist.

### *THE WICKEDNESS OF JERUSALEM*

**3** Woe to her who is rebellious and polluted,
To the oppressing city!
2 She has not obeyed *His* voice,
She has not received correction;
She has not trusted in the LORD,
She has not drawn near to her God.

3 [a]Her princes in her midst *are* roaring lions;
Her judges *are* [b]evening wolves
That leave not a bone till morning.

**2:1** [a] Joel 1:14; 2:16 [1] Or *shameless* **2:3** [a] Amos 5:6 [b] Ps. 76:9 [c] Amos 5:14, 15 **2:4** [a] Zech. 9:5 [b] Jer. 6:4 **2:5** [a] Ezek. 25:15–17 [b] Josh. 13:3 **2:6** [a] Is. 17:2 [1] Literally *excavations,* either underground huts or cisterns **2:7** [a] [Mic. 5:7, 8] [b] Luke 1:68 [c] Jer. 29:14 **2:8** [a] Jer. 48:27 [b] Ezek. 25:3 [c] Jer. 49:1 **2:9** [a] Is. 15:1–9 [b] Amos 1:13 [c] Deut. 29:23 **2:10** [a] Is. 16:6 **2:11** [a] Mal. 1:11 [b] Gen. 10:5 **2:12** [a] Is. 18:1–7 [b] Ps. 17:13 **2:13** [a] Is. 10:5–27; 14:24–27 **2:14** [a] Is. 13:21 [b] Is. 14:23; 34:11 [c] Jer. 22:14 **2:15** [a] Is. 47:8 [b] Rev. 18:7 [c] Lam. 2:15 [d] Nah. 3:19 **3:3** [a] Ezek. 22:27 [b] Hab. 1:8

4 Her [a]prophets are insolent, treacherous
people;
Her priests have polluted the sanctuary,
They have done [b]violence to the law.
5 The LORD *is* righteous in her midst,
He will do no unrighteousness.
Every morning He brings His justice to
light;
He never fails,
But [a]the unjust knows no shame.

6 "I have cut off nations,
Their fortresses are devastated;
I have made their streets desolate,
With none passing by.
Their cities are destroyed;
*There is* no one, no inhabitant.
7 [a]I said, 'Surely you will fear Me,
You will receive instruction'—
So that her dwelling would not be
cut off,
*Despite* everything for which I punished
her.
But they rose early and [b]corrupted all
their deeds.

### *A FAITHFUL REMNANT*
*(cf. Gen. 11:1–9; Acts 2:1–11)*

8 "Therefore [a]wait for Me," says the LORD,
"Until the day I rise up for plunder;[1]
My determination *is* to [b]gather the
nations
To My assembly of kingdoms,
To pour on them My indignation,
All My fierce anger;
All the earth [c]shall be devoured
With the fire of My jealousy.

9 "For then I will restore to the peoples [a]a
pure language,
That they all may call on the name of the
LORD,
To serve Him with one accord.
10 [a]From beyond the rivers of Ethiopia
My worshipers,
The daughter of My dispersed ones,
Shall bring My offering.
11 In that day you shall not be shamed for
any of your deeds
In which you transgress against Me;
For then I will take away from your midst
Those who [a]rejoice in your pride,
And you shall no longer be haughty
In My holy mountain.
12 I will leave in your midst
[a]A meek and humble people,
And they shall trust in the name of the
LORD.
13 [a]The remnant of Israel [b]shall do no
unrighteousness
[c]And speak no lies,
Nor shall a deceitful tongue be found in
their mouth;
For [d]they shall feed *their* flocks and lie
down,
And no one shall make *them* afraid."

### *JOY IN GOD'S FAITHFULNESS*

14 [a]Sing, O daughter of Zion!
Shout, O Israel!
Be glad and rejoice with all *your* heart,
O daughter of Jerusalem!
15 The LORD has taken away your judgments,
He has cast out your enemy.
[a]The King of Israel, the LORD, [b]*is* in your
midst;
You shall see[1] disaster no more.

#### SEEING JESUS IN THE SCRIPTURE

**3:15** God promised faithful Israel that one day He would take away judgment, cast out their enemy, and be in their midst. This was ultimately fulfilled in Jesus, who came to earth, took God's judgment upon Himself, and cast out our enemies of sin and death (see 1 Cor. 15:54–57).

16 In that day [a]it shall be said to Jerusalem:
"Do not fear;
Zion, [b]let not your hands be weak.
17 The LORD your God [a]in your midst,
The Mighty One, will save;
[b]He will rejoice over you with gladness,
He will quiet *you* with His love,
He will rejoice over you with singing."

18 "I will gather those who [a]sorrow over the
appointed assembly,
Who are among you,
*To whom* its reproach *is* a burden.
19 Behold, at that time
I will deal with all who afflict you;
I will save the [a]lame,
And gather those who were driven out;
I will appoint them for praise and fame
In every land where they were put to shame.
20 At that time [a]I will bring you back,
Even at the time I gather you;
For I will give you fame and praise
Among all the peoples of the earth,
When I return your captives before your
eyes,"
Says the LORD.

**3:4** [a] Hos. 9:7 [b] Ezek. 22:26 **3:5** [a] Jer. 3:3 **3:7** [a] Jer. 8:6 [b] Gen. 6:12 **3:8** [a] Hab. 2:3 [b] Joel 3:2 [c] Zeph. 1:18 [1] Septuagint and Syriac read *for witness;* Targum reads *for the day of My revelation for judgment;* Vulgate reads *for the day of My resurrection that is to come.* **3:9** [a] Is. 19:18; 57:19 **3:10** [a] Ps. 68:31 **3:11** [a] Is. 2:12; 5:15 **3:12** [a] Is. 14:32 **3:13** [a] [Mic. 4:7] [b] Is. 60:21 [c] Rev. 14:5 [d] Ezek. 34:13–15, 28 **3:14** [a] Is. 12:6 **3:15** [a] [John 1:49] [b] Ezek. 48:35 [1] Some Hebrew manuscripts, Septuagint, and Bomberg read *see;* Masoretic Text and Vulgate read *fear.* **3:16** [a] Is. 35:3, 4 [b] Heb. 12:12 **3:17** [a] Zeph. 3:5, 15 [b] Is. 62:5; 65:19 **3:18** [a] Lam. 2:6 **3:19** [a] [Mic. 4:6, 7] **3:20** [a] Is. 11:12

*The Book of the Prophet*

# HAGGAI

| AUTHOR | KEY VERSES | READING TIME |
|---|---|---|
| Haggai | Haggai 1:7–8 | 8 minutes |

With the Babylonian exile in the past and a newly returned group of Jews back in the land, the work of rebuilding the temple could begin. However, sixteen years after the process began, the people had yet to finish the project. The people had allowed their personal affairs to interfere with God's work. Haggai preached a series of fiery sermons designed to stir up the nation so that they might finish the temple. He called the builders to renewed courage in the Lord, renewed holiness of life, and renewed faith in the God who controls the future.

**Occasion:** With the temple only partially rebuilt, Haggai issues a series of prophetic messages admonishing the people to finish the work so that true worship might occur.

**Main Point:** God's people are to be faithful to complete the task He has given them.

**Big Ideas:** God is most important. We are to keep our priorities straight, keeping God first in everything we do.

## OUTLINE:

I. The Command to Rebuild the Temple of God (ch. 1)
II. The Coming Glory of God (ch. 2)

**586 BC**
The Babylonians destroy Jerusalem

**539 BC**
Cyrus conquers Babylon

**538 BC**
Jews begin returning to Judea

**536–534 BC**
The temple rebuilding begins and stops

**c. 525 BC**
Coins started to have an image on two sides

**520 BC**
Haggai preaches; the temple rebuilding resumes

**515 BC**
The temple is completed

**508 BC**
Office of *pontifex maximus* created in Rome

## THE COMMAND TO BUILD GOD'S HOUSE

*(Ezra 5:1)*

1 In [a]the second year of King Darius, in the
sixth month, on the first day of the month, the
word of the LORD came by [b]Haggai the prophet
to [c]Zerubbabel the son of Shealtiel, governor of
Judah, and to [d]Joshua the son of [e]Jehozadak,
the high priest, saying, 2“Thus speaks the LORD
of hosts, saying: ‘This people says, “The time
has not come, the time that the LORD's house
should be built.” ’ ”

> **1:1 King Darius** allowed his captives to practice their own religion. He also allowed the Jews who returned to Jerusalem to continue rebuilding the temple, even sending money to help with the construction and livestock to be used as sacrifices.

3Then the word of the LORD [a]came by Hag-
gai the prophet, saying, 4“*Is it* [a]time for you
yourselves to dwell in your paneled houses, and
this temple[1] *to lie* in ruins?” 5Now therefore, thus
says the LORD of hosts: [a]“Consider your ways!

6 “You have [a]sown much, and bring in little;
You eat, but do not have enough;
You drink, but you are not filled with
drink;
You clothe yourselves, but no one is
warm;
And [b]he who earns wages,
Earns wages *to put* into a bag with holes.”

7Thus says the LORD of hosts: “Consider your
ways! 8Go up to the [a]mountains and bring wood
and build the temple, that I may take pleasure
in it and be glorified,” says the LORD. 9[a]“You
looked for much, but indeed *it came to* little;
and when you brought it home, [b]I blew it away.
Why?” says the LORD of hosts. “Because of My
house that *is in* ruins, while every one of you
runs to his own house. 10Therefore [a]the heav-
ens above you withhold the dew, and the earth
withholds its fruit. 11For I [a]called for a drought
on the land and the mountains, on the grain
and the new wine and the oil, on whatever the
ground brings forth, on men and livestock, and
on [b]all the labor of *your* hands.”

## THE PEOPLE'S OBEDIENCE

12[a]Then Zerubbabel the son of Shealtiel, and
Joshua the son of Jehozadak, the high priest,
with all the remnant of the people, obeyed the

> **1:12 Zerubbabel** was the grandson of Jehoiakim, one of the last kings to reign in Judah before the Babylonian invasion. King Cyrus of Persia allowed Zerubbabel to lead a group of Jews back to Jerusalem to begin rebuilding the temple. Cyrus also appointed Zerubbabel governor of Judah. **Joshua** was **the son of Jehozadak**, who was **high priest** when the Jewish people were deported to Babylon. Zerubbabel served as the political leader of the returning Jews; Joshua served as the spiritual leader.

voice of the LORD their God, and the words of
Haggai the prophet, as the LORD their God had
sent him; and the people feared the presence of
the LORD. 13Then Haggai, the LORD's messenger,
spoke the LORD's message to the people, saying,
[a]“I *am* with you, says the LORD.” 14So [a]the LORD
stirred up the spirit of Zerubbabel the son of
Shealtiel, [b]governor of Judah, and the spirit of
Joshua the son of Jehozadak, the high priest,
and the spirit of all the remnant of the people;
[c]and they came and worked on the house of the
LORD of hosts, their God, 15on the twenty-fourth
day of the sixth month, in the second year of
King Darius.

## THE COMING GLORY OF GOD'S HOUSE

2 In the seventh *month,* on the twenty-first
of the month, the word of the LORD came
by Haggai the prophet, saying: 2“Speak now
to Zerubbabel the son of Shealtiel, governor of
Judah, and to Joshua the son of Jehozadak, the
high priest, and to the remnant of the people,
saying: 3[a]‘Who is left among you who saw this
temple[1] in its former glory? And how do you see
it now? In comparison with it, [b]*is this* not in your
eyes as nothing? 4Yet now [a]be strong, Zerubba-
bel,’ says the LORD; ‘and be strong, Joshua, son
of Jehozadak, the high priest; and be strong,
all you people of the land,’ says the LORD, ‘and
work; for I *am* with you,’ says the LORD of hosts.
5[a]‘*According to* the word that I covenanted with
you when you came out of Egypt, so [b]My Spirit
remains among you; do not fear!’

6“For thus says the LORD of hosts: [a]‘Once
more (it *is* a little while) [b]I will shake heaven and
earth, the sea and dry land; 7and I will shake all
nations, and they shall come to [a]the Desire of All
Nations,[1] and I will fill this temple with [b]glory,’
says the LORD of hosts. 8‘The silver *is* Mine, and
the gold *is* Mine,’ says the LORD of hosts. 9[a]‘The
glory of this latter temple shall be greater than

**1:1** [a] Ezra 4:24 [b] Ezra 5:1; 6:14 [c] Ezra 2:2 [d] Ezra 5:2, 3 [e] 1 Chr. 6:15 **1:3** [a] Ezra 5:1 **1:4** [a] 2 Sam. 7:2 [1] Literally *house,* and so in verse 8 **1:5** [a] Lam. 3:40 **1:6** [a] Deut. 28:38–40; Hos. 8:7; Hag. 1:9, 10; 2:16, 17 [b] Zech. 8:10 **1:8** [a] Ezra 3:7 **1:9** [a] Hag. 2:16 [b] Hag. 2:17 **1:10** [a] Lev. 26:19; Deut. 28:23; 1 Kin. 8:35; Joel 1:18–20 **1:11** [a] 1 Kin. 17:1; 2 Kin. 8:1 [b] Hag. 2:17 **1:12** [a] Ezra 5:2 **1:13** [a] [Matt. 28:20; Rom. 8:31] **1:14** [a] 2 Chr. 36:22; Ezra 1:1 [b] Hag. 2:21 [c] Ezra 5:2, 8; Neh. 4:6 **2:3** [a] Ezra 3:12, 13 [b] Zech. 4:10 [1] Literally *house,* and so in verses 7 and 9 **2:4** [a] Deut. 31:23; 1 Chr. 22:13; 28:20; Zech. 8:9; Eph. 6:10 **2:5** [a] Ex. 29:45, 46 [b] [Neh. 9:20]; Is. 63:11, 14 **2:6** [a] Heb. 12:26 [b] [Joel 3:16] **2:7** [a] Gen. 49:10; Mal. 3:1 [b] 1 Kin. 8:11; Is. 60:7; Zech. 2:5 [1] Or *the desire of all nations* **2:9** [a] [John 1:14]

**SEEING JESUS IN THE SCRIPTURE**

**2:9** The temple the people built after returning from captivity wasn't as glorious as Solomon's. But no physical temple could come close to the glory of Jesus, the Son of God who came to dwell among His people (see John 1:14).

the former,' says the LORD of hosts. 'And in this
place I will give [b]peace,' says the LORD of hosts."

### *THE PEOPLE ARE DEFILED*

10 On the twenty-fourth *day* of the ninth
*month,* in the second year of Darius, the word
of the LORD came by Haggai the prophet, say-
ing, 11 "Thus says the LORD of hosts: 'Now, [a]ask
the priests *concerning the* law, saying, 12 "If one
carries holy meat in the fold of his garment, and
with the edge he touches bread or stew, wine or
oil, or any food, will it become holy?" ' "

Then the priests answered and said, "No."

13 And Haggai said, "If *one who is* [a]unclean
*because* of a dead body touches any of these,
will it be unclean?"

So the priests answered and said, "It shall
be unclean."

14 Then Haggai answered and said, [a]" 'So is
this people, and so is this nation before Me,' says
the LORD, 'and so is every work of their hands;
and what they offer there is unclean.

### *PROMISED BLESSING*

15 'And now, carefully [a]consider from this
day forward: from before stone was laid upon
stone in the temple of the LORD— 16 since
those *days,* [a]when *one* came to a heap of twenty
ephahs, there were *but* ten; when *one* came to
the wine vat to draw out fifty baths from the
press, there were *but* twenty. 17 [a]I struck you with
blight and mildew and hail [b]in all the labors of
your hands; [c]yet you did not *turn* to Me,' says
the LORD. 18 'Consider now from this day for-
ward, from the twenty-fourth day of the ninth
month, from [a]the day that the foundation of
the LORD's temple was laid—consider it: 19 [a]Is
the seed still in the barn? As yet the vine, the
fig tree, the pomegranate, and the olive tree
have not yielded *fruit. But* from this day I will
[b]bless *you.*' "

### *ZERUBBABEL CHOSEN AS A SIGNET*

20 And again the word of the LORD came to
Haggai on the twenty-fourth day of the month,
saying, 21 "Speak to Zerubbabel, [a]governor of
Judah, saying:

[b]'I will shake heaven and earth.
22 [a]I will overthrow the throne of kingdoms;
I will destroy the strength of the Gentile
kingdoms.
[b]I will overthrow the chariots
And those who ride in them;
The horses and their riders shall come
down,
Every one by the sword of his brother.

23 'In that day,' says the LORD of hosts, 'I
will take you, Zerubbabel My servant, the son
of Shealtiel,' says the LORD, [a]'and will make you
like a signet *ring;* for [b]I have chosen you,' says
the LORD of hosts."

**2:9** [b] Ps. 85:8, 9; Luke 2:14; [Eph. 2:14] **2:11** [a] Lev. 10:10, 11; Deut. 33:10; Mal. 2:7 **2:13** [a] Lev. 22:4–6; Num. 19:11, 22 **2:14** [a] [Titus 1:15] **2:15** [a] Hag. 1:5, 7; 2:18 **2:16** [a] Hag. 1:6, 9; Zech. 8:10 **2:17** [a] Deut. 28:22; 1 Kin. 8:37; Amos 4:9 [b] Hag. 1:11 [c] Jer. 5:3; Amos 4:6–11 **2:18** [a] Ezra 5:1, 2, 16; Zech. 8:9 **2:19** [a] Zech. 8:12 [b] Ps. 128:1–6; Jer. 31:12, 14; [Mal. 3:10] **2:21** [a] Ezra 5:2; Hag. 1:1, 14; Zech. 4:6–10 [b] Hag. 2:6, 7; [Heb. 12:26, 27] **2:22** [a] [Dan. 2:44; Rev. 19:11–21] [b] Ps. 46:9; Ezek. 39:20; Mic. 5:10; Zech. 9:10 **2:23** [a] Song 8:6; Jer. 22:24 [b] Is. 42:1; 43:10

# *The Book of the Prophet*
# ZECHARIAH

**AUTHOR**
Zechariah

**KEY VERSE**
Zechariah 1:3

**READING TIME**
44 minutes

For a dozen years or more, the task of rebuilding the temple had been half completed. God commissioned Zechariah to call the people to fulfill their unfinished responsibility. Rather than exhorting them to action with strong words of rebuke, Zechariah sought to encourage his people by reminding them of the importance of the temple. They must build the temple, for one day the Messiah's glory would inhabit it. That future blessing was contingent upon their present obedience. Motivated accordingly, they could resume the building project with wholehearted zeal, for their Messiah was coming.

**Occasion:** Zechariah writes to encourage God's people to be faithful and to provide a final push for the completion of the temple.

**Main Point:** God's people must turn from their sins to experience His blessings.

**Big Ideas:** God is faithful and will make good on all He has promised. God's promise to dwell on earth came to pass in the life and ministry of Jesus.

## OUTLINE:

I. Zechariah's Eight Visions (chs. 1–6)
II. Zechariah's Four Messages (chs. 7–8)
III. Zechariah's Two Prophecies (chs. 9–14)

**605 BC**
Nebuchadnezzar rules in Babylon

**605 BC**
Daniel and others exiled in Babylon

**586 BC**
The Babylonians destroy Jerusalem

**539 BC**
Cyrus conquers Babylon

**538 BC**
Jews begin returning to Judea

**536–534 BC**
The temple rebuilding begins and stops

**520 BC**
Haggai preaches; the temple rebuilding resumes

**515 BC**
The temple is completed

**505 BC**
First pair of Roman consuls elected

### A CALL TO REPENTANCE

*(Ezra 5:1)*

**1** In the eighth month [a]of the second year of Darius, the word of the LORD came [b]to Zechariah the son of Berechiah, the son of [c]Iddo the prophet, saying, 2 "The LORD has been very angry with your fathers. 3 Therefore say to them, 'Thus says the LORD of hosts: "Return [a]to Me," says the LORD of hosts, "and I will return to you," says the LORD of hosts. 4 "Do not be like your fathers, [a]to whom the former prophets preached, saying, 'Thus says the LORD of hosts: [b]"Turn now from your evil ways and your evil deeds." ' But they did not hear nor heed Me," says the LORD.

5 "Your fathers, where *are* they?
And the prophets, do they live forever?
6 Yet surely [a]My words and My statutes,
Which I commanded My servants the prophets,
Did they not overtake your fathers?

"So they returned and said:

[b]'Just as the LORD of hosts determined to do to us,
According to our ways and according to our deeds,
So He has dealt with us.' " ' "

### VISION OF THE HORSES

7 On the twenty-fourth day of the eleventh month, which is the month Shebat, in the second year of Darius, the word of the LORD came to Zechariah the son of Berechiah, the son of Iddo the prophet: 8 I saw by night, and behold, [a]a man riding on a red horse, and it stood among the myrtle trees in the hollow; and behind him *were* [b]horses: red, sorrel, and white. 9 Then I said, [a]"My lord, what *are* these?" So the angel who talked with me said to me, "I will show you what they *are*."

10 And the man who stood among the myrtle trees answered and said, [a]"These *are the ones* whom the LORD has sent to walk to and fro throughout the earth."

11 [a]So they answered the Angel of the LORD, who stood among the myrtle trees, and said, "We have walked to and fro throughout the earth, and behold, all the earth is resting quietly."

### THE LORD WILL COMFORT ZION

12 Then the Angel of the LORD answered and said, "O LORD of hosts, [a]how long will You not have mercy on Jerusalem and on the cities of Judah, against which You were angry [b]these seventy years?"

13 And the LORD answered the angel who talked to me, *with* [a]good *and* comforting words.

> **1:12** About **seventy years** passed between the time Nebuchadnezzar's forces burned down the temple in Jerusalem and the time King Cyrus of Persia allowed a group of Jews to return to **Jerusalem** to begin rebuilding the temple. The construction was still going on when Zechariah wrote this book.

14 So the angel who spoke with me said to me, "Proclaim, saying, 'Thus says the LORD of hosts:

"I am [a]zealous for Jerusalem
And for Zion with great zeal.
15 I am exceedingly angry with the nations at ease;
For [a]I was a little angry,
And they helped—*but* with evil *intent*."

16 'Therefore thus says the LORD:

[a]"I am returning to Jerusalem with mercy;
My [b]house [c]shall be built in it," says the LORD of hosts,
"And [d]a *surveyor's* line shall be stretched out over Jerusalem." '

17 "Again proclaim, saying, 'Thus says the LORD of hosts:

"My cities shall again spread out through prosperity;
[a]The LORD will again comfort Zion,
And [b]will again choose Jerusalem." ' "

### VISION OF THE HORNS

18 Then I raised my eyes and looked, and there *were* four [a]horns. 19 And I said to the angel who talked with me, "What *are* these?"

So he answered me, [a]"These *are* the horns that have scattered Judah, Israel, and Jerusalem."

20 Then the LORD showed me four craftsmen. 21 And I said, "What are these coming to do?"

So he said, "These *are* the [a]horns that scattered Judah, so that no one could lift up his head; but the craftsmen[1] are coming to terrify them, to cast out the horns of the nations that [b]lifted up *their* horn against the land of Judah to scatter it."

### VISION OF THE MEASURING LINE

**2** Then I raised my eyes and looked, and behold, [a]a man with a measuring line in his hand. 2 So I said, "Where are you going?"

And he said to me, [a]"To measure Jerusalem, to see what *is* its width and what *is* its length."

**1:1** [a]Zech. 7:1 [b]Matt. 23:35 [c]Neh. 12:4, 16 **1:3** [a][Mal. 3:7–10] **1:4** [a]2 Chr. 36:15, 16 [b]Is. 31:6 **1:6** [a][Is. 55:11] [b]Lam. 1:18; 2:17 **1:8** [a][Rev. 6:4] [b][Zech. 6:2–7] **1:9** [a]Zech. 4:4, 5, 13; 6:4 **1:10** [a][Heb. 1:14] **1:11** [a][Ps. 103:20, 21] **1:12** [a]Ps. 74:10 [b]Jer. 25:11, 12; 29:10 **1:13** [a]Jer. 29:10 **1:14** [a]Zech. 8:2 **1:15** [a]Is. 47:6 **1:16** [a][Zech. 2:10; 8:3] [b]Ezra 6:14, 15 [c]Is. 44:28 [d]Zech. 2:1–3 **1:17** [a][Is. 40:1, 2; 51:3] [b]Zech. 2:12 **1:18** [a][Lam. 2:17] **1:19** [a]Ezra 4:1, 4, 7 **1:21** [a][Ps. 75:10] [b]Ps. 75:4, 5 [1]Literally *these* **2:1** [a]Jer. 31:39 **2:2** [a]Rev. 11:1

3 And there *was* the angel who talked with me, going out; and another angel was coming out to meet him, 4 who said to him, "Run, speak to this young man, saying: [a]'Jerusalem shall be inhabited *as* towns without walls, because of the multitude of men and livestock in it. 5 For I,' says the LORD, 'will be [a]a wall of fire all around her, [b]and I will be the glory in her midst.' "

### FUTURE JOY OF ZION AND MANY NATIONS

6 "Up, up! Flee [a]from the land of the north," says the LORD; "for I have [b]spread you abroad like the four winds of heaven," says the LORD. 7 "Up, Zion! [a]Escape, you who dwell with the daughter of Babylon."

8 For thus says the LORD of hosts: "He sent Me after glory, to the nations which plunder you; for he who [a]touches you touches the apple of His eye. 9 For surely I will [a]shake My hand against them, and they shall become spoil for their servants. Then [b]you will know that the LORD of hosts has sent Me.

10 [a]"Sing and rejoice, O daughter of Zion! For behold, I am coming and I [b]will dwell in your midst," says the LORD. 11 [a]"Many nations shall be joined to the LORD [b]in that day, and they shall become [c]My people. And I will dwell in your midst. Then [d]you will know that the LORD of hosts has sent Me to you. 12 And the LORD will [a]take possession of Judah as His inheritance in the Holy Land, and will again choose Jerusalem. 13 [a]Be silent, all flesh, before the LORD, for He is aroused [b]from His holy habitation!"

### VISION OF THE HIGH PRIEST

**3** Then he showed me [a]Joshua the high priest standing before the Angel of the LORD, and [b]Satan standing at his right hand to oppose him. 2 And the LORD said to Satan, [a]"The LORD rebuke you, Satan! The LORD who [b]has chosen Jerusalem rebuke you! [c]*Is* this not a brand plucked from the fire?"

3 Now Joshua was clothed with [a]filthy garments, and was standing before the Angel.

4 Then He answered and spoke to those who stood before Him, saying, "Take away the filthy garments from him." And to him He said, "See, I have removed your iniquity from you, [a]and I will clothe you with rich robes."

5 And I said, "Let them put a clean [a]turban on his head."

So they put a clean turban on his head, and they put the clothes on him. And the Angel of the LORD stood by.

### THE COMING BRANCH

6 Then the Angel of the LORD admonished Joshua, saying, 7 "Thus says the LORD of hosts:

> **3:5** The high priests of Israel wore a **turban**—a long piece of white linen cloth wrapped around the **head** and fastened in the back. Attached to the front of the turban was a gold sign engraved with the words "Holiness to the Lord."

'If you will walk in My ways,
And if you will [a]keep My command,
Then you shall also [b]judge My house,
And likewise have charge of My courts;
I will give you places to walk
Among these who [c]stand here.

8 'Hear, O Joshua, the high priest,
You and your companions who sit before you,
For they are [a]a wondrous sign;
For behold, I am bringing forth [b]My Servant the [c]BRANCH.
9 For behold, the stone
That I have laid before Joshua:
[a]Upon the stone *are* [b]seven eyes.
Behold, I will engrave its inscription,'
Says the LORD of hosts,
'And [c]I will remove the iniquity of that land in one day.
10 [a]In that day,' says the LORD of hosts,
'Everyone will invite his neighbor
[b]Under his vine and under his fig tree.' "

## SEEING JESUS IN THE SCRIPTURE

> **3:8** Jesus is the Servant Zechariah spoke of. Jesus is the Branch of David who came the first time not to reign as king, but to empty Himself as a Servant in service to the Father (see Phil. 2:7). One day He will return as conquering King.

### VISION OF THE LAMPSTAND AND OLIVE TREES

**4** Now [a]the angel who talked with me came back and wakened me, [b]as a man who is wakened out of his sleep. 2 And he said to me, "What do you see?"

So I said, "I am looking, and there *is* [a]a lampstand of solid gold with a bowl on top of it, [b]and on the *stand* seven lamps with seven pipes to the seven lamps. 3 [a]Two olive trees *are* by it, one at the right of the bowl and the other at its left." 4 So I answered and spoke to the angel who talked with me, saying, "What *are* these, my lord?"

**2:4** [a] Jer. 31:27 **2:5** [a] [Is. 26:1] [b] [Is. 60:19] **2:6** [a] Is. 48:20 [b] Deut. 28:64 **2:7** [a] Is. 48:20 **2:8** [a] Deut. 32:10 **2:9** [a] Is. 19:16 [b] Zech. 4:9 **2:10** [a] Is. 12:6 [b] [Lev. 26:12] **2:11** [a] [Is. 2:2, 3] [b] Zech. 3:10 [c] Ex. 12:49 [d] Ezek. 33:33 **2:12** [a] [Deut. 32:9] **2:13** [a] Hab. 2:20 [b] Ps. 68:5 **3:1** [a] Hag. 1:1 [b] Ps. 109:6 **3:2** [a] [Jude 9] [b] [Rom. 8:33] [c] Amos 4:11 **3:3** [a] Is. 64:6 **3:4** [a] Is. 61:10 **3:5** [a] Ex. 29:6 **3:7** [a] Lev. 8:35 [b] Deut. 17:9, 12 [c] Zech. 3:4 **3:8** [a] Ps. 71:7 [b] Is. 42:1 [c] Is. 11:1; 53:2 **3:9** [a] [Zech. 4:10] [b] Ps. 118:22 [c] Jer. 31:34; 50:20 **3:10** [a] Zech. 2:11 [b] Is. 36:16 **4:1** [a] Zech. 1:9; 2:3 [b] Dan. 8:18 **4:2** [a] Rev. 1:12 [b] [Rev. 4:5] **4:3** [a] Rev. 11:3, 4

5 Then the angel who talked with me an-
swered and said to me, "Do you not know what
these are?"

And I said, "No, my lord."

6 So he answered and said to me:

"This *is* the word of the LORD to [a]Zerubbabel:
[b]'Not by might nor by power, but by My
Spirit,'
Says the LORD of hosts.
7 'Who *are* you, [a]O great mountain?
Before Zerubbabel *you shall become* a
plain!
And he shall bring forth [b]the capstone
[c]With shouts of "Grace, grace to it!" ' "

8 Moreover the word of the LORD came to
me, saying:

9 "The hands of Zerubbabel
[a]Have laid the foundation of this temple;[1]
His hands [b]shall also finish *it.*
Then [c]you will know
That the [d]LORD of hosts has sent Me to
you.
10 For who has despised the day of [a]small
things?
For these seven rejoice to see
The plumb line in the hand of Zerubbabel.
[b]They are the eyes of the LORD,
Which scan to and fro throughout the
whole earth."

11 Then I answered and said to him, "What
*are* these [a]two olive trees—at the right of the
lampstand and at its left?" 12 And I further an-
swered and said to him, "What *are these* two olive
branches that *drip* into the receptacles[1] of the two
gold pipes from which the golden *oil* drains?"
13 Then he answered me and said, "Do you
not know what these *are?*"

And I said, "No, my lord."

14 So he said, [a]"These *are* the two anointed ones,
[b]who stand beside the Lord of the whole earth."

### VISION OF THE FLYING SCROLL

**5** Then I turned and raised my eyes, and saw
there a flying [a]scroll.

2 And he said to me, "What do you see?"

So I answered, "I see a flying scroll. Its length
*is* twenty cubits and its width ten cubits."

3 Then he said to me, "This *is* the [a]curse that
goes out over the face of the whole earth: 'Every
thief shall be expelled,' according *to* this side of
*the scroll;* and, 'Every perjurer shall be expelled,'
according *to* that side of it."

4 "I will send out *the curse,*" says the LORD of
hosts;
"It shall enter the house of the [a]thief
And the house of [b]the one who swears
falsely by My name.
It shall remain in the midst of his house
And consume [c]it, with its timber and
stones."

4:6 [a] Hag. 1:1 [b] Hos. 1:7 4:7 [a] Jer. 51:25 [b] Ps. 118:22 [c] Ezra 3:10, 11, 13 4:9 [a] Ezra 3:8–10; 5:16 [b] Ezra 6:14, 15 [c] Zech. 2:9, 11; 6:15 [d] [Is. 43:16] [1] Literally *house* 4:10 [a] Hag. 2:3 [b] 2 Chr. 16:9 4:11 [a] Zech. 4:3 4:12 [1] Literally *into the hands of* 4:14 [a] Rev. 11:4 [b] Zech. 3:1–7 5:1 [a] Ezek. 2:9 5:3 [a] Mal. 4:6 5:4 [a] Ex. 20:15 [b] Lev. 19:12 [c] Lev. 14:34, 35

KNOW THE TRUTH

## THE DOCTRINE OF THE HOLY SPIRIT

### PART 2: THE DEITY OF THE HOLY SPIRIT

**4:6–9** God the Father, God the Son, and God the Holy Spirit are distinct Persons who share one nature, essence, and substance. As such, the Holy Spirit is God, coequal with the Father and the Son. The Holy Spirit is a distinct Person, not to be confused with any other spirit (angelic, demonic, or human). This is why Zechariah 4:6 doesn't say, "by *a* spirit" but rather, "by My Spirit." Further evidence of the Spirit's deity is that He's eternal and uncreated. Hebrews 9:14 calls Him the "eternal Spirit.

The Holy Spirit accomplishes divine work throughout the Bible including creating the physical universe, making human beings animate and conscious, empowering prophets, judges, and kings for God's purposes, conceiving Jesus in Mary's virgin womb, empowering Jesus to fulfill His mission, regenerating sinful people into born again sons and daughters of God, sanctifying believers to become more like Christ, empowering believers to be witnesses for Christ, and inspiring the writers of Scripture. When we think of the Spirit, we must remember we're thinking of a Person; and not just any person, but rather one of the three Persons of God.

*For* **THE DOCTRINE OF THE HOLY SPIRIT: PART 3: THE HOLY SPIRIT'S WORK IN CHRIST'S LIFE,** *turn to Isaiah 11:1–5 on page 690.*

### *VISION OF THE WOMAN IN A BASKET*

5 Then the angel who talked with me came out and said to me, "Lift your eyes now, and see what this *is* that goes forth."

6 So I asked, "What *is* it?" And he said, "It *is* a basket[1] that is going forth."

He also said, "This *is* their resemblance throughout the earth: 7 Here *is* a lead disc lifted up, and this *is* a woman sitting inside the basket"; 8 then he said, "This *is* Wickedness!" And he thrust her down into the basket, and threw the lead cover[1] over its mouth. 9 Then I raised my eyes and looked, and there *were* two women, coming with the wind in their wings; for they had wings like the wings of a [a]stork, and they lifted up the basket between earth and heaven.

10 So I said to the [a]angel who talked with me, "Where are they carrying the basket?"

11 And he said to me, "To [a]build a house for it in [b]the land of Shinar;[1] when it is ready, *the basket* will be set there on its base."

### *VISION OF THE FOUR CHARIOTS*

**6** Then I turned and raised my eyes and looked, and behold, four chariots *were* coming from between two mountains, and the mountains *were* mountains of bronze. 2 With the first chariot *were* [a]red horses, with the second chariot [b]black horses, 3 with the third chariot white horses, and with the fourth chariot dappled horses—strong *steeds.* 4 Then I answered [a]and said to the angel who talked with me, "What *are* these, my lord?"

5 And the angel answered and said to me, [a]"These *are* four spirits of heaven, who go out from *their* [b]station before the Lord of all the earth. 6 The one with the black horses is going to [a]the north country, the white are going after them, and the dappled are going toward the south country." 7 Then the strong *steeds* went out, eager to go, that they might [a]walk to and fro throughout the earth. And He said, "Go, walk to and fro throughout the earth." So they walked to and fro throughout the earth. 8 And He called to me, and spoke to me, saying, "See, those who go toward the north country have given rest to My [a]Spirit in the north country."

### *THE COMMAND TO CROWN JOSHUA*

9 Then the word of the LORD came to me, saying: 10 "Receive *the gift* from the captives—from Heldai, Tobijah, and Jedaiah, who have come from Babylon—and go the same day and enter the house of Josiah the son of Zephaniah. 11 Take the silver and gold, make [a]an elaborate crown, and set *it* on the head of [b]Joshua the son of Jehozadak, the high priest. 12 Then speak to him, saying, 'Thus says the LORD of hosts, saying:

"Behold, [a]the Man whose name *is* the
[b]BRANCH!
From His place He shall branch out,
[c]And He shall build the temple of the
LORD;
13 Yes, He shall build the temple of the
LORD.
He [a]shall bear the glory,
And shall sit and rule on His throne;
So [b]He shall be a priest on His throne,
And the counsel of peace shall be between
them both." '

**SEEING JESUS IN THE SCRIPTURE**

**6:12** Though this prophecy spoke of Zerubbabel, it also foreshadows the coming of Christ. Jesus was the temple broken down and rebuilt on the third day (see John 2:19).

14 "Now the elaborate crown shall be [a]for a memorial in the temple of the LORD for Helem,[1] Tobijah, Jedaiah, and Hen the son of Zephaniah. 15 Even [a]those from afar shall come and build the temple of the LORD. Then you shall know that the LORD of hosts has sent Me to you. And *this* shall come to pass if you diligently obey the voice of the LORD your God."

### *OBEDIENCE BETTER THAN FASTING*

**7** Now in the fourth year of King Darius it came to pass *that* the word of the LORD came to Zechariah, on the fourth *day* of the ninth month, Chislev, 2 when *the people*[1] sent Sherezer,[2] with Regem-Melech and his men, *to* the house of God,[3] to pray before the LORD, 3 *and* to [a]ask the priests who *were* in the house of the LORD of hosts, and the prophets, saying, "Should I weep in [b]the fifth month and fast as I have done for so many years?"

4 Then the word of the LORD of hosts came to me, saying, 5 "Say to all the people of the land, and to the priests: 'When you [a]fasted and mourned in the fifth [b]and seventh *months* [c]during those seventy years, did you really fast [d]for Me—for Me? 6 [a]When you eat and when you drink, do you not eat and drink *for yourselves?* 7 *Should you* not *have obeyed* the words which the LORD proclaimed through the [a]former prophets when Jerusalem and the cities around it were inhabited and prosperous, and [b]the South[1] and the Lowland were inhabited?' "

**5:6** [1] Hebrew *ephah,* a measuring container, and so elsewhere **5:8** [1] Literally *stone* **5:9** [a] Lev. 11:13, 19 **5:10** [a] Zech. 5:5 **5:11** [a] Jer. 29:5, 28 [b] Gen. 10:10 [1] That is, Babylon **6:2** [a] Zech. 1:8 [b] Rev. 6:5 **6:4** [a] Zech. 5:10 **6:5** [a] [Heb. 1:7, 14] [b] Dan. 7:10 **6:6** [a] Jer. 1:14 **6:7** [a] Zech. 1:10 **6:8** [a] Eccl. 10:4 **6:11** [a] Ex. 29:6 [b] Hag. 1:1 **6:12** [a] John 1:45 [b] Zech. 3:8 [c] [Eph. 2:20] **6:13** [a] Is. 22:24 [b] Ps. 110:4 **6:14** [a] Ex. 12:14 [1] Following Masoretic Text, Targum, and Vulgate; Syriac reads *for Heldai* (compare verse 10); Septuagint reads *for the patient ones.* **6:15** [a] Is. 57:19 **7:2** [1] Literally *they* (compare verse 5) [2] Or *Sar-Ezer* [3] Hebrew *Bethel* **7:3** [a] Mal. 2:7 [b] Zech. 8:19 **7:5** [a] [Is. 58:1–9] [b] Jer. 41:1 [c] Zech. 1:12 [d] [Rom. 14:6] **7:6** [a] 1 Chr. 29:22 **7:7** [a] Zech. 1:4 [b] Jer. 17:26 [1] Hebrew *Negev*

### DISOBEDIENCE RESULTED IN CAPTIVITY

8 Then the word of the LORD came to Zech-
ariah, saying, 9 "Thus says the LORD of hosts:

[a]'Execute true justice,
Show mercy and compassion
Everyone to his brother.
10 [a]Do not oppress the widow or the fatherless,
The alien or the poor.
[b]Let none of you plan evil in his heart
Against his brother.'

11 "But they refused to heed, [a]shrugged their
shoulders, and [b]stopped their ears so that they
could not hear. 12 Yes, they made their [a]hearts like
flint, [b]refusing to hear the law and the words which
the LORD of hosts had sent by His Spirit through
the former prophets. [c]Thus great wrath came
from the LORD of hosts. 13 Therefore it happened,
*that* just as He proclaimed and they would not
hear, so [a]they called out and I would not listen,"
says the LORD of hosts. 14 "But [a]I scattered them
with a whirlwind among all the nations which they
had not known. Thus the land became desolate
after them, so that no one passed through or re-
turned; for they made the pleasant land desolate."

### JERUSALEM, HOLY CITY OF THE FUTURE

8 Again the word of the LORD of hosts came,
saying, 2 "Thus says the LORD of hosts:

[a]'I am zealous for Zion with great zeal;
With great fervor I am zealous for her.'

3 "Thus says the LORD:

[a]'I will return to Zion,
And [b]dwell in the midst of Jerusalem.
Jerusalem [c]shall be called the City of Truth,
[d]The Mountain of the LORD of hosts,
[e]The Holy Mountain.'

4 "Thus says the LORD of hosts:

[a]'Old men and old women shall again sit
In the streets of Jerusalem,
Each one with his staff in his hand
Because of great age.
5 The streets of the city
Shall be [a]full of boys and girls
Playing in its streets.'

6 "Thus says the LORD of hosts:

'If it is marvelous in the eyes of the
remnant of this people in these
days,
[a]Will it also be marvelous in My eyes?'
Says the LORD of hosts.

7 "Thus says the LORD of hosts:

'Behold, [a]I will save My people from the
land of the east
And from the land of the west;
8 I will [a]bring them *back*,

**SEEING JESUS IN THE SCRIPTURE**

**8:7–8** God's promise to regather His people from captivity partially pointed toward what happened at Pentecost when Jews gathered in Jerusalem to hear the gospel (see Acts 2:5). It's ultimate fulfillment will be when God gathers believers from every nation (see Rev. 7:9–10).

**7:9** [a] Jer. 7:28 **7:10** [a] Ex. 22:22 [b] Mic. 2:1 **7:11** [a] Neh. 9:29 [b] Jer. 17:23 **7:12** [a] Ezek. 11:19 [b] Neh. 9:29, 30 [c] Dan. 9:11, 12 **7:13** [a] Prov. 1:24–28 **7:14** [a] Deut. 4:27; 28:64 **8:2** [a] Zech. 1:14 **8:3** [a] Zech. 1:16 [b] Zech. 2:10, 11 [c] Is. 1:21 [d] [Is. 2:2, 3] [e] Jer. 31:23 **8:4** [a] Is. 65:20 **8:5** [a] Jer. 30:19, 20 **8:6** [a] [Luke 1:37] **8:7** [a] Is. 11:11 **8:8** [a] Zeph. 3:20

**LIVE THE TRUTH**

## CARING FOR OTHERS

**7:9–10** To care for others is to look at them with great interest, not eyeing their potential value to yourself, but rather seeing their unwavering infinite value. Every human is made in the image of God, created with dignity and worth (see Gen. 1:26–27). That means we are to care for others in ways that are best for *them*, not us. This becomes easier—and even desirable—when we see others as close friends and loved ones. Caring for others isn't a chore when we have a deep sense of compassion for them.

In the Old Testament, God spoke through the prophet Zechariah to remind His people of His commands. They had been mistreating each other for years and had misrepresented God's heart to the surrounding nations. Justice, compassion, and mercy saturate God's character. Instead of displaying that beautiful picture, God's people had shown the opposite: evil. Cherishing human lives is a must for the Christian, and caring for others is the active, outward response to that critical heart posture. Refusing to care for others is a symptom of a hard heart, like God's people in Zechariah 7. Ask God to help you show His love by first developing a compassionate heart and then by living that compassion out each day.

And they shall dwell in the midst of
Jerusalem.
[b]They shall be My people
And I will be their God,
[c]In truth and righteousness.'

9 "Thus says the LORD of hosts:

[a]'Let your hands be strong,
You who have been hearing in these
days
These words by the mouth of [b]the
prophets,
Who *spoke* in [c]the day the foundation was
laid
For the house of the LORD of hosts,
That the temple might be built.
10 For before these days
There were no [a]wages for man nor any
hire for beast;
*There was* no peace from the enemy for
whoever went out or came in;
For I set all men, everyone, against his
neighbor.

11 [a]But now I *will* not *treat* the remnant of this
people as in the former days,' says the LORD
of hosts.

12 'For[a] the seed *shall be* prosperous,
The vine shall give its fruit,
[b]The ground shall give her increase,
And [c]the heavens shall give their dew—
I will cause the remnant of this people
To possess all these.
13 And it shall come to pass
*That* just as you were [a]a curse among the
nations,
O house of Judah and house of Israel,
So I will save you, and [b]you shall be a
blessing.
Do not fear,
Let your hands be strong.'

14 "For thus says the LORD of hosts:

[a]'Just as I determined to punish you
When your fathers provoked Me to wrath,'
Says the LORD of hosts,
[b]'And I would not relent,
15 So again in these days
I am determined to do good
To Jerusalem and to the house of Judah.
Do not fear.
16 These *are* the things you shall [a]do:
[b]Speak each man the truth to his neighbor;
Give judgment in your gates for truth,
justice, and peace;
17 [a]Let none of you think evil in your[1] heart
against your neighbor;
And do not love a false oath.
For all these *are things* that I hate,'
Says the LORD."

18 Then the word of the LORD of hosts came
to me, saying, 19 "Thus says the LORD of hosts:

[a]'The fast of the fourth *month,*
[b]The fast of the fifth,
[c]The fast of the seventh,
[d]And the fast of the tenth,
Shall be [e]joy and gladness and cheerful
feasts
For the house of Judah.
[f]Therefore love truth and peace.'

20 "Thus says the LORD of hosts:

'Peoples shall yet come,
Inhabitants of many cities;
21 The inhabitants of one *city* shall go to
another, saying,
[a]"Let us continue to go and pray before the
LORD,
And seek the LORD of hosts.
I myself will go also."
22 Yes, [a]many peoples and strong
nations
Shall come to seek the LORD of hosts in
Jerusalem,
And to pray before the LORD.'

23 "Thus says the LORD of hosts: 'In those
days ten men [a]from every language of the na-
tions shall [b]grasp the sleeve of a Jewish man,
saying, "Let us go with you, for we have heard
[c]*that* God *is* with you." ' "

## *ISRAEL DEFENDED AGAINST ENEMIES*

9 The burden[1] of the word of the LORD
Against the land of Hadrach,
And [a]Damascus its resting place
(For [b]the eyes of men
And all the tribes of Israel
Are on the LORD);
2 Also *against* [a]Hamath, *which* borders on it,
And *against* [b]Tyre and [c]Sidon, though
they are very [d]wise.

3 For Tyre built herself a tower,
Heaped up silver like the dust,
And gold like the mire of the streets.
4 Behold, [a]the Lord will cast her out;
He will destroy [b]her power in the
sea,
And she will be devoured by fire.

8:8 [b] [Jer. 30:22; 31:1, 33] [c] Jer. 4:2 8:9 [a] Hag. 2:4 [b] Ezra 5:1, 2; 6:14 [c] Hag. 2:18 8:10 [a] Hag. 1:6, 9 8:11 [a] Hag. 2:15–19 8:12 [a] Joel 2:22 [b] Ps. 67:6 [c] Hag. 1:10 8:13 [a] Jer. 42:18 [b] Gen. 12:2 8:14 [a] Jer. 31:28 [b] [2 Chr. 36:16] 8:16 [a] Zech. 7:9, 10 [b] [Eph. 4:25] 8:17 [a] Prov. 3:29 [1] Literally *his* 8:19 [a] Jer. 52:6 [b] Jer. 52:12 [c] 2 Kin. 25:25 [d] Jer. 52:4 [e] Esth. 8:17 [f] Zech. 8:16 8:21 [a] [Is. 2:2, 3] 8:22 [a] Is. 60:3; 66:23 8:23 [a] Is. 3:6 [b] [Is. 45:14] [c] 1 Cor. 14:25 9:1 [a] Is. 17:1 [b] Amos 1:3–5 [1] Or *oracle* 9:2 [a] Jer. 49:23 [b] Is. 23 [c] 1 Kin. 17:9 [d] Ezek. 28:3 9:4 [a] Is. 23:1 [b] Ezek. 26:17

5 Ashkelon shall see *it* and fear;
Gaza also shall be very sorrowful;
And [a]Ekron, for He dried up her
expectation.
The king shall perish from Gaza,
And Ashkelon shall not be inhabited.

6 "A mixed race shall settle [a]in Ashdod,
And I will cut off the pride of the
[b]Philistines.
7 I will take away the blood from his mouth,
And the abominations from between his
teeth.
But he who remains, even he *shall be* for
our God,
And shall be like a leader in Judah,
And Ekron like a Jebusite.
8 [a]I will camp around My house
Because of the army,
Because of him who passes by and him
who returns.
No more shall an oppressor pass through
them,
For now I have seen with My eyes.

### *THE COMING KING*
*(Matt. 21:5; John 12:14, 15)*

9 "Rejoice [a]greatly, O daughter of Zion!
Shout, O daughter of Jerusalem!
Behold, [b]your King is coming to you;
He *is* just and having salvation,
Lowly and riding on a donkey,
A colt, the foal of a donkey.
10 I [a]will cut off the chariot from Ephraim
And the horse from Jerusalem;
The [b]battle bow shall be cut off.
He shall speak peace to the nations;
His dominion *shall be* [c]'from sea to sea,
And from the River to the ends of the earth.'[1]

**SEEING JESUS IN THE SCRIPTURE**

**9:9** Zechariah foretold of the coming of Israel's long-awaited King. Humble and mounted on a donkey, Jesus entered Jerusalem to complete the mission of His first coming: dying on the cross for the salvation of the world (see Matt. 21:5).

### *GOD WILL SAVE HIS PEOPLE*

11 "As for you also,
Because of the blood of your covenant,
I will set your [a]prisoners free from the
waterless pit.
12 Return to the stronghold,
[a]You prisoners of hope.
Even today I declare
*That* I will restore [b]double to you.
13 For I have bent Judah, My *bow*,
Fitted the bow with Ephraim,
And raised up your sons, O Zion,
Against your sons, O Greece,
And made you like the sword of a mighty
man."

14 Then the LORD will be seen over them,
And [a]His arrow will go forth like
lightning.
The Lord GOD will blow the trumpet,
And go [b]with whirlwinds from the south.
15 The LORD of hosts will [a]defend them;
They shall devour and subdue with
slingstones.
They shall drink *and* roar as if with wine;
They shall be filled *with blood* like basins,
Like the corners of the altar.
16 The LORD their God will [a]save them in
that day,
As the flock of His people.
For [b]they *shall be like* the jewels of a
crown,
[c]Lifted like a banner over His land—
17 For [a]how great is its[1] goodness
And how great its[2] [b]beauty!
[c]Grain shall make the young men thrive,
And new wine the young women.

### *RESTORATION OF JUDAH AND ISRAEL*

**10** Ask [a]the LORD for [b]rain
In [c]the time of the latter rain.[1]
The LORD will make flashing clouds;
He will give them showers of rain,
Grass in the field for everyone.

2 For the [a]idols[1] speak delusion;
The diviners envision [b]lies,
And tell false dreams;
They [c]comfort in vain.
Therefore *the people* wend their way like
[d]sheep;
They are in trouble [e]because *there is* no
shepherd.

3 "My anger is kindled against the
[a]shepherds,
[b]And I will punish the goatherds.
For the LORD of hosts [c]will visit His flock,
The house of Judah,
And [d]will make them as His royal horse in
the battle.
4 From him comes [a]the cornerstone,
From him [b]the tent peg,
From him the battle bow,
From him every ruler[1] together.

**9:5** [a] Zeph. 2:4, 5 **9:6** [a] Amos 1:8 [b] Ezek. 25:15–17 **9:8** [a] [Ps. 34:7] **9:9** [a] Zech. 2:10 [b] [Jer. 23:5, 6] **9:10** [a] Hos. 1:7 [b] Hos. 2:18 [c] Ps. 72:8 [1] Psalm 72:8 **9:11** [a] Is. 42:7 **9:12** [a] Is. 49:9 [b] Is. 61:7 **9:14** [a] Ps. 18:14 [b] Is. 21:1 **9:15** [a] Zech. 12:8 **9:16** [a] Jer. 31:10, 11 [b] Is. 62:3 [c] Is. 11:12 **9:17** [a] [Ps. 31:19] [b] [Ps. 45:1–16] [c] Joel 3:18 [1] Or *His* [2] Or *His* **10:1** [a] [Jer. 14:22] [b] [Deut. 11:13, 14] [c] [Joel 2:23] [1] That is, spring rain **10:2** [a] Jer. 10:8 [b] Jer. 27:9 [c] Job 13:4 [d] Jer. 50:6, 17 [e] Ezek. 34:5–8 [1] Hebrew *teraphim* **10:3** [a] Jer. 25:34–36 [b] Ezek. 34:17 [c] Luke 1:68 [d] Song 1:9 **10:4** [a] Is. 28:16 [b] Is. 22:23 [1] Or *despot*

5 They shall be like mighty men,
Who [a]tread down *their enemies*
In the mire of the streets in the battle.
They shall fight because the LORD is with them,
And the riders on horses shall be put to shame.

6 "I will strengthen the house of Judah,
And I will save the house of Joseph.
[a]I will bring them back,
Because I [b]have mercy on them.
They shall be as though I had not cast them aside;
For I *am* the LORD their God,
And I [c]will hear them.
7 *Those of* Ephraim shall be like a mighty man,
And their [a]heart shall rejoice as if with wine.
Yes, their children shall see *it* and be glad;
Their heart shall rejoice in the LORD.
8 I will [a]whistle for them and gather them,
For I will redeem them;
[b]And they shall increase as they once increased.

9 "I[a] will sow them among the peoples,
And they shall [b]remember Me in far countries;
They shall live, together with their children,
And they shall return.
10 [a]I will also bring them back from the land of Egypt,
And gather them from Assyria.
I will bring them into the land of Gilead and Lebanon,
[b]Until no *more room* is found for them.

**10:10 Gilead and Lebanon** refer to the regions on each side of the Jordan River. Together they form the land that God originally gave to the Israelites.

11 [a]He shall pass through the sea with affliction,
And strike the waves of the sea:
All the depths of the River[1] shall dry up.
Then [b]the pride of Assyria shall be brought down,
And [c]the scepter of Egypt shall depart.

12 "So I will strengthen them in the LORD,
And [a]they shall walk up and down in His name,"
Says the LORD.

## *DESOLATION OF ISRAEL*

11 Open [a]your doors, O Lebanon,
That fire may devour your cedars.
2 Wail, O cypress, for the [a]cedar has fallen,
Because the mighty *trees* are ruined.
Wail, O oaks of Bashan,
[b]For the thick forest has come down.
3 *There is* the sound of wailing [a]shepherds!
For their glory is in ruins.
*There is* the sound of roaring lions!
For the pride[1] of the Jordan is in ruins.

## *PROPHECY OF THE SHEPHERDS*

4 Thus says the LORD my God, "Feed the
flock for slaughter, 5 whose owners slaughter
them and [a]feel no guilt; those who sell them
[b]say, 'Blessed be the LORD, for I am rich'; and
their shepherds do [c]not pity them. 6 For I will no
longer pity the inhabitants of the land," says the
LORD. "But indeed I will give everyone into his
neighbor's hand and into the hand of his king.
They shall attack the land, and I will not deliver
*them* from their hand."
7 So I fed the flock for slaughter, in particu-
lar [a]the poor of the flock.[1] I took for myself two
staffs: the one I called Beauty,[2] and the other I
called Bonds;[3] and I fed the flock. 8 I dismissed
the three shepherds [a]in one month. My soul
loathed them, and their soul also abhorred me.
9 Then I said, "I will not feed you. [a]Let what is
dying die, and what is perishing perish. Let those
that are left eat each other's flesh." 10 And I took
my staff, Beauty, and cut it in two, that I might
break the covenant which I had made with all
the peoples. 11 So it was broken on that day. Thus
[a]the poor[1] of the flock, who were watching me,
knew that it *was* the word of the LORD. 12 Then
I said to them, "If it is agreeable to you, give *me*
my wages; and if not, refrain." So they [a]weighed
out for my wages thirty *pieces* of silver.
13 And the LORD said to me, "Throw it to the
[a]potter"—that princely price they set on me. So
I took the thirty *pieces* of silver and threw them
into the house of the LORD for the potter. 14 Then
I cut in two my other staff, Bonds, that I might
break the brotherhood between Judah and Israel.

**SEEING JESUS IN THE SCRIPTURE**

**11:12–13** The thirty pieces of silver paid to Zechariah was an insult; it was the price of a slave. This was the same amount Judas accepted from the religious leaders to betray Jesus and the same amount he threw down in anguish (see Matt. 27:3–10).

**10:5** [a] Ps. 18:42 **10:6** [a] Jer. 3:18 [b] Hos. 1:7 [c] Zech. 13:9 **10:7** [a] Ps. 104:15 **10:8** [a] Is. 5:26 [b] Ezek. 36:37 **10:9** [a] Hos. 2:23 [b] Deut. 30:1 **10:10** [a] Is. 11:11 [b] Is. 49:19, 20 **10:11** [a] Is. 11:15 [b] Zeph. 2:13 [c] Ezek. 30:13 [1] That is, the Nile **10:12** [a] Mic. 4:5 **11:1** [a] Zech. 10:10 **11:2** [a] Ezek. 31:3 [b] Is. 32:19 **11:3** [a] Jer. 25:34–36 [1] Or *floodplain, thicket* **11:5** [a] [Jer. 2:3]; 50:7 [b] Hos. 12:8 [c] Ezek. 34:2, 3 **11:7** [a] Zeph. 3:12 [1] Following Masoretic Text, Targum, and Vulgate; Septuagint reads *for the Canaanites.* [2] Or *Grace,* and so in verse 10 [3] Or *Unity,* and so in verse 14 **11:8** [a] Hos. 5:7 **11:9** [a] Jer. 15:2 **11:11** [a] Zeph. 3:12 [1] Following Masoretic Text, Targum, and Vulgate; Septuagint reads *the Canaanites.* **11:12** [a] Ex. 21:32 **11:13** [a] Matt. 27:3–10

15 And the LORD said to me, [a]"Next, take for yourself the implements of a foolish shepherd. 16 For indeed I will raise up a shepherd in the land *who* will not care for those who are cut off, nor seek the young, nor heal those that are broken, nor feed those that still stand. But he will eat the flesh of the fat and tear their hooves in [a]pieces.

17 "Woe[a] to the worthless shepherd,
Who leaves the flock!
A sword *shall be* against his arm
And against his right eye;
His arm shall completely wither,
And his right eye shall be totally blinded."

## THE COMING DELIVERANCE OF JUDAH

**12** The burden[1] of the word of the LORD against Israel. Thus says the LORD, [a]who stretches out the heavens, lays the foundation of the earth, and [b]forms the spirit of man within him: 2 "Behold, I will make Jerusalem [a]a cup of drunkenness to all the surrounding peoples, when they lay siege against Judah and Jerusalem. 3 [a]And it shall happen in that day that I will make Jerusalem [b]a very heavy stone for all peoples; all who would heave it away will surely be cut in pieces, though all nations of the earth are gathered against it. 4 In that day," says the LORD, [a]"I will strike every horse with confusion, and its rider with madness; I will open My eyes on the house of Judah, and will strike every horse of the peoples with blindness. 5 And the governors of Judah shall say in their heart, 'The inhabitants of Jerusalem *are* my strength in the LORD of hosts, their God.' 6 In that day I will make the governors of Judah [a]like a firepan in the woodpile, and like a fiery torch in the sheaves; they shall devour all the surrounding peoples on the right hand and on the left, but Jerusalem shall be inhabited again in her own place—Jerusalem.

> **12:2** A **cup** that came from God's hand was a common symbol in ancient times for a person's, or a nation's, destiny. A cup of His anger symbolized punishment for a sin. A cup of His blessing symbolized a bright future.

7 "The LORD will save the tents of Judah first, so that the glory of the house of David and the glory of the inhabitants of Jerusalem shall not become greater than that of Judah. 8 In that day the LORD will defend the inhabitants of Jerusalem; the one who is feeble among them in that day shall be like David, and the house of David *shall be* like God, like the Angel of the LORD before them. 9 It shall be in that day *that* I will seek to [a]destroy all the nations that come against Jerusalem.

## MOURNING FOR THE PIERCED ONE

10 [a]"And I will pour on the house of David and on the inhabitants of Jerusalem the Spirit of grace and supplication; then they will [b]look on Me whom they pierced. Yes, they will mourn for Him [c]as one mourns for *his* only *son,* and grieve for Him as one grieves for a firstborn. 11 In that day there shall be a great [a]mourning in Jerusalem, [b]like the mourning at Hadad Rimmon in the plain of Megiddo.[1] 12 [a]And the land shall mourn, every family by itself: the family of the house of David by itself, and their wives by themselves; the family of the house of [b]Nathan by itself, and their wives by themselves; 13 the family of the house of Levi by itself, and their wives by themselves; the family of Shimei by itself, and their wives by themselves; 14 all the families that remain, every family by itself, and their wives by themselves.

> **SEEING JESUS IN THE SCRIPTURE**
>
> **12:10** This prophecy finds its fulfillment at the cross. Jesus was pierced, suffered, and died for our transgressions (see John 20:27). While that day was filled with mourning, when we look upon the cross in faith, we experience the joy of salvation.

## IDOLATRY CUT OFF

**13** "In that [a]day [b]a fountain shall be opened for the house of David and for the inhabitants of Jerusalem, for sin and for [c]uncleanness.

2 "It shall be in that day," says the LORD of hosts, "*that* I will [a]cut off the names of the idols from the land, and they shall no longer be remembered. I will also cause [b]the prophets and the unclean spirit to depart from the land. 3 It shall come to pass *that* if anyone still prophesies, then his father and mother who begot him will say to him, 'You shall [a]not live, because you have spoken lies in the name of the LORD.' And his father and mother who begot him [b]shall thrust him through when he prophesies.

4 "And it shall be in that day *that* [a]every prophet will be ashamed of his vision when he prophesies; they will not wear [b]a robe of coarse hair to deceive. 5 [a]But he will say, 'I *am* no prophet, I *am* a farmer; for a man taught me to keep cattle from my youth.' 6 And *one* will say to him, 'What are these wounds between your arms?'[1] Then he will answer, '*Those* with which I was wounded in the house of my friends.'

**11:15** [a] Is. 56:11 **11:16** [a] Ezek. 34:1–10 **11:17** [a] Jer. 23:1 **12:1** [a] Is. 42:5; 44:24 [b] [Is. 57:16] [1] Or *oracle* **12:2** [a] Is. 51:17 **12:3** [a] Zech. 12:4, 6, 8; 13:1 [b] Matt. 21:44 **12:4** [a] Ezek. 38:4 **12:6** [a] Obad. 18 **12:9** [a] Hag. 2:22 **12:10** [a] [Joel 2:28, 29] [b] John 19:34, 37; 20:27 [c] Jer. 6:26 **12:11** [a] [Rev. 1:7] [b] 2 Kin. 23:29 [1] Hebrew *Megiddon* **12:12** [a] [Matt. 24:30] [b] Luke 3:31 **13:1** [a] [Rev. 21:6, 7] [b] [Heb. 9:14] [c] Ezek. 36:25 **13:2** [a] Ex. 23:13 [b] Jer. 23:14, 15 **13:3** [a] Deut. 18:20 [b] Deut. 13:6–11 **13:4** [a] [Mic. 3:6, 7] [b] 2 Kin. 1:8 **13:5** [a] Amos 7:14 **13:6** [1] Or *hands*

### *THE SHEPHERD SAVIOR*

7 "Awake, O sword, against [a]My Shepherd,
Against the Man [b]who is My Companion,"
Says the LORD of hosts.
[c]"Strike the Shepherd,
And the sheep will be scattered;
Then I will turn My hand against [d]the little ones.

> **SEEING JESUS IN THE SCRIPTURE**
>
> **13:7** The arrest of Jesus was confusing for His disciples because they didn't understand the Father's plan of salvation, so they fled. Jesus would indeed be struck by the Father, who used human agents to kill His Son for our salvation (see Matt. 26:31).

8 And it shall come to pass in all the land,"
Says the LORD,
"*That* [a]two-thirds in it shall be cut off *and* die,
[b]But *one*-third shall be left in it:
9 I will bring the *one*-third [a]through the fire,
Will [b]refine them as silver is refined,
And test them as gold is tested.
[c]They will call on My name,
And I will answer them.
[d]I will say, 'This *is* My people';
And each one will say, 'The LORD *is* my God.' "

### *THE DAY OF THE LORD*

*(cf. Ezek. 38; 39; Mark 13; Rev. 20—22)*

**14** Behold, [a]the day of the LORD is coming,
And your spoil will be divided in your midst.
2 For [a]I will gather all the nations to battle against Jerusalem;
The city shall be taken,
The houses rifled,
And the women ravished.
Half of the city shall go into captivity,
But the remnant of the people shall not be cut off from the city.

3 Then the LORD will go forth
And fight against those nations,
As He fights in the day of battle.
4 And in that day His feet will stand [a]on the Mount of Olives,
Which faces Jerusalem on the east.
And the Mount of Olives shall be split in two,
From east to west,
[b]*Making* a very large valley;
Half of the mountain shall move toward the north
And half of it toward the south.
5 Then you shall flee *through* My mountain valley,
For the mountain valley shall reach to Azal.
Yes, you shall flee
As you fled from the [a]earthquake
In the days of Uzziah king of Judah.
[b]Thus the LORD my God will come,
*And* [c]all the saints with You.[1]

6 It shall come to pass in that day
*That* there will be no light;
The lights will diminish.
7 It shall be one day
[a]Which is known to the LORD—
Neither day nor night.
But at [b]evening time it shall happen
*That* it will be light.

8 And in that day it shall be
*That* living [a]waters shall flow from Jerusalem,
Half of them toward the eastern sea
And half of them toward the western sea;
In both summer and winter it shall occur.
9 And the LORD shall be [a]King over all the earth.
In that day it shall be—
[b]"The LORD *is* one,"[1]
And His name one.

10 All the land shall be turned into a plain from Geba to Rimmon south of Jerusalem. *Jerusalem*[1] shall be raised up and [a]inhabited in her place from Benjamin's Gate to the place of the First Gate and the Corner Gate, [b]and *from* the Tower of Hananel to the king's winepresses.

11 *The people* shall dwell in it;
And [a]no longer shall there be utter destruction,
[b]But Jerusalem shall be safely inhabited.

12 And this shall be the plague with which the LORD will strike all the people who fought against Jerusalem:

Their flesh shall dissolve while they stand on their feet,
Their eyes shall dissolve in their sockets,
And their tongues shall dissolve in their mouths.

13 It shall come to pass in that day
*That* [a]a great panic from the LORD will be among them.
Everyone will seize the hand of his neighbor,

**13:7** [a] Is. 40:11 [b] [John 10:30] [c] Matt. 26:31, 56, 67 [d] Luke 12:32 **13:8** [a] Ezek. 5:2, 4, 12 [b] [Rom. 11:5] **13:9** [a] Is. 48:10 [b] 1 Pet. 1:6, 7 [c] Ps. 50:15 [d] Hos. 2:23 **14:1** [a] [Is. 13:6, 9] **14:2** [a] Zech. 12:2, 3 **14:4** [a] Ezek. 11:23 [b] Joel 3:12 **14:5** [a] Amos 1:1 [b] Matt. 24:30, 31; 25:31 [c] Joel 3:11 [1] Or *you;* Septuagint, Targum, and Vulgate read *Him.* **14:7** [a] Matt. 24:36 [b] Is. 30:26 **14:8** [a] Ezek. 47:1–12 **14:9** [a] [Rev. 11:15] [b] Deut. 6:4 [1] Compare Deuteronomy 6:4 **14:10** [a] Zech. 12:6 [b] Jer. 31:38 [1] Literally *She* **14:11** [a] Jer. 31:40 [b] Jer. 23:6 **14:13** [a] 1 Sam. 14:15, 20

And raise [b]his hand against his neighbor's
hand;
14 Judah also will fight at Jerusalem.
[a]And the wealth of all the surrounding
nations
Shall be gathered together:
Gold, silver, and apparel in great
abundance.

15 [a]Such also shall be the plague
On the horse *and* the mule,
On the camel and the donkey,
And on all the cattle that will be in those
camps.
So *shall* this plague *be.*

### *THE NATIONS WORSHIP THE KING*

16 And it shall come to pass *that* everyone
who is left of all the nations which came against
Jerusalem shall [a]go up from year to year to
[b]worship the King, the LORD of hosts, and to
keep [c]the Feast of Tabernacles.
17 [a]And it shall
be *that* whichever of the families of the earth
do not come up to Jerusalem to worship the
King, the LORD of hosts, on them there will be
no rain.
18 If the family of [a]Egypt will not come
up and enter in, [b]they *shall have* no *rain;* they
shall receive the plague with which the LORD
strikes the nations who do not come up to keep
the Feast of Tabernacles.
19 This shall be the
punishment of Egypt and the punishment of
all the nations that do not come up to keep the
Feast of Tabernacles.

20 In that day [a]"HOLINESS TO THE LORD"
shall be *engraved* on the bells of the horses. The
[b]pots in the LORD's house shall be like the bowls
before the altar.
21 Yes, every pot in Jerusalem
and Judah shall be holiness to the LORD of hosts.[1]
Everyone who sacrifices shall come and take
them and cook in them. In that day there shall
no longer be a [a]Canaanite [b]in the house of the
LORD of hosts.

14:13 [b]Judg. 7:22 14:14 [a]Ezek. 39:10, 17 14:15 [a]Zech. 14:12 14:16 [a][Is. 2:2, 3; 60:6–9; 66:18–21] [b]Is. 27:13 [c]Lev. 23:34–44 14:17 [a]Is. 60:12 14:18 [a]Is. 19:21 [b]Deut. 11:10 14:20 [a]Is. 23:18 [b]Ezek. 46:20 14:21 [a]Is. 35:8 [b][Eph. 2:19–22] [1]Or *on every pot . . . shall be (engraved) "HOLINESS TO THE LORD OF HOSTS"*

# *The Book of the Prophet*
# MALACHI

| AUTHOR | KEY VERSE | READING TIME |
|---|---|---|
| Malachi | Malachi 1:9 | 14 minutes |

Malachi, a prophet in the days of Nehemiah, directed his message of judgment to a people plagued with corrupt priests, wicked practices, and a false sense of security in their privileged relationship with God. Using a question-and-answer method, Malachi probed their problems of hypocrisy, infidelity, mixed marriages, divorce, false worship, and arrogance. So sinful had the nation become that God's words to the people no longer had any effect. After Malachi's ringing condemnations, God remained silent over the next four hundred years. No more prophetic messages were given. Only with the coming of John the Baptist (prophesied in Malachi 3:1) would God again communicate with His people through a prophet's voice.

**Occasion:** Malachi writes to warn the people who had once more lapsed into spiritual depravity, calling on them not to forget their love for God.

**Main Point:** God's people are not to forget their love for God.

**Big Ideas:** God deserves true worship and our fullest devotion. We must love and honor God even when life is difficult.

## OUTLINE:

I. The Problems of the Nation (chs. 1–3)
II. The Promise to the Nation (ch. 4)

**536–534 BC**
The temple rebuilding begins and stops

**520 BC**
Haggai preaches; the temple rebuilding resumes

**515 BC**
The temple is completed

**464–424 BC**
Artaxerxes Longimanus reigns in Persia

**458 BC**
Ezra leads a group of returnees to Judea

**c. 450 BC**
The Samaritan temple built on Mount Gerizim

**449 BC**
The Twelve Tables, the first public laws of the Roman Republic, are given to the people

**444 BC**
Nehemiah leads a group of returnees to Judea

**443 BC**
Jerusalem's wall is reconstructed

**c. 420 BC**
Malachi prophesies in Judah

1 The burden[1] of the word of the LORD to Israel by Malachi.

## ISRAEL BELOVED OF GOD

2 "I[a] have loved you," says the LORD.
"Yet you say, 'In what way have You loved us?'
*Was* not Esau Jacob's brother?"
Says the LORD.
"Yet [b]Jacob I have loved;
3 But Esau I have hated,
And [a]laid waste his mountains and his heritage
For the jackals of the wilderness."

> **1:2–3 Jacob** and **Esau** were sons of Isaac. As the older brother, Esau was legally entitled to the larger inheritance from his father. Yet, God chose to bless Jacob and he became Isaac's primary heir. God gave Jacob the name Israel. His twelve sons are the twelve tribes that made up the nation of Israel. The contrast between the words **loved** and **hated** here seems strong. But on many occasions in the Old Testament, the verb *hate* has the basic meaning of "not to choose." God's love for Jacob was expressed in His electing grace in extending His covenant to Jacob and to his descendants (see Gen. 25:21–26; Is. 44:1–5). In His sovereign purpose, God set His love on the one and not the other. The term *hate* may carry the idea of indifference as well.

4 Even though Edom has said,
"We have been impoverished,
But we will return and build the desolate places,"
Thus says the LORD of hosts:

"They may build, but I will [a]throw down;
They shall be called the Territory of Wickedness,
And the people against whom the LORD will have indignation forever.
5 Your eyes shall see,
And you shall say,
[a]'The LORD is magnified beyond the border of Israel.'

## POLLUTED OFFERINGS

6 "A son [a]honors *his* father,
And a servant *his* master.
[b]If then I am the Father,
Where *is* My honor?
And if I *am* a Master,
Where *is* My reverence?
Says the LORD of hosts
To you priests who despise My name.
[c]Yet you say, 'In what way have we despised Your name?'

7 "You offer [a]defiled food on My altar,
But say,
'In what way have we defiled You?'
By saying,
[b]'The table of the LORD is contemptible.'
8 And [a]when you offer the blind as a sacrifice,
*Is it* not evil?
And when you offer the lame and sick,
*Is it* not evil?
Offer it then to your governor!
Would he be pleased with you?
Would he [b]accept you favorably?"
Says the LORD of hosts.

9 "But now entreat God's favor,
That He may be gracious to us.
[a]*While* this is being *done* by your hands,
Will He accept you favorably?"
Says the LORD of hosts.
10 "Who *is there* even among you who would shut the doors,
[a]So that you would not kindle fire *on* My altar in vain?
I have no pleasure in you,"
Says the LORD of hosts,
[b]"Nor will I accept an offering from your hands.
11 For [a]from the rising of the sun, even to its going down,
My name *shall be* great [b]among the Gentiles;
[c]In every place [d]incense *shall be* offered to My name,
And a pure offering;
[e]For My name shall be great among the nations,"
Says the LORD of hosts.

12 "But you profane it,
In that you say,
[a]'The table of the LORD[1] is defiled;
And its fruit, its food, *is* contemptible.'
13 You also say,
'Oh, what a [a]weariness!'
And you sneer at it,"
Says the LORD of hosts.
"And you bring the stolen, the lame, and the sick;
Thus you bring an offering!
[b]Should I accept this from your hand?"
Says the LORD.

**1:1** [1] Or *oracle* **1:2** [a] Deut. 4:37; 7:8; 23:5 [b] Rom. 9:13 **1:3** [a] Jer. 49:18 **1:4** [a] Jer. 49:16–18 **1:5** [a] Ps. 35:27 **1:6** [a] [Ex. 20:12] [b] Luke 6:46 [c] Mal. 2:14 **1:7** [a] Deut. 15:21 [b] Ezek. 41:22 **1:8** [a] Lev. 22:22 [b] [Job 42:8] **1:9** [a] Hos. 13:9 **1:10** [a] 1 Cor. 9:13 [b] Is. 1:11 **1:11** [a] Is. 59:19 [b] Is. 60:3, 5 [c] 1 Tim. 2:8 [d] Rev. 8:3 [e] Is. 66:18, 19 **1:12** [a] Mal. 1:7 [1] Following Bomberg; Masoretic Text reads *Lord.* **1:13** [a] Is. 43:22 [b] Lev. 22:20

14 "But cursed *be* [a]the deceiver
Who has in his flock a male,
And takes a vow,
But sacrifices to the Lord [b]what is blemished—
For [c]I *am* a great King,"
Says the LORD of hosts,
"And My name *is to be* feared among the nations.

### CORRUPT PRIESTS

2 "And now, O [a]priests, this commandment is for you.
2 [a]If you will not hear,
And if you will not take *it* to heart,
To give glory to My name,"
Says the LORD of hosts,
"I will send a curse upon you,
And I will curse your blessings.
Yes, I have cursed them [b]already,
Because you do not take *it* to heart.

3 "Behold, I will rebuke your descendants
And spread [a]refuse on your faces,
The refuse of your solemn feasts;
And *one* will [b]take you away with it.
4 Then you shall know that I have sent this commandment to you,
That My covenant with Levi may continue,"
Says the LORD of hosts.
5 "My[a] covenant was with him, *one* of life and peace,
And I gave them to him [b]*that he might* fear *Me;*
So he feared Me
And was reverent before My name.
6 [a]The law of truth[1] was in his mouth,
And injustice was not found on his lips.
He walked with Me in peace and equity,
And [b]turned many away from iniquity.

7 "For[a] the lips of a priest should keep knowledge,
And *people* should seek the law from his mouth;
[b]For he is the messenger of the LORD of hosts.
8 But you have departed from the way;
You [a]have caused many to stumble at the law.
[b]You have corrupted the covenant of Levi,"
Says the LORD of hosts.
9 "Therefore [a]I also have made you contemptible and base
Before all the people,
Because you have not kept My ways
But have shown [b]partiality in the law."

### TREACHERY OF INFIDELITY

10 [a]Have we not all one Father?
[b]Has not one God created us?
Why do we deal treacherously with one another
By profaning the covenant of the fathers?
11 Judah has dealt treacherously,
And an abomination has been committed in Israel and in Jerusalem,
For Judah has [a]profaned
The LORD's holy *institution* which He loves:
He has married the daughter of a foreign god.
12 May the LORD cut off from the tents of Jacob
The man who does this, being awake and aware,[1]
Yet [a]who brings an offering to the LORD of hosts!

13 And this is the second thing you do:
You cover the altar of the LORD with tears,
With weeping and crying;
So He does not regard the offering anymore,
Nor receive *it* with goodwill from your hands.
14 Yet you say, "For what reason?"
Because the LORD has been witness
Between you and [a]the wife of your youth,
With whom you have dealt treacherously;
[b]Yet she is your companion
And your wife by covenant.
15 But [a]did He not make *them* one,
Having a remnant of the Spirit?
And why one?
He seeks [b]godly offspring.
Therefore take heed to your spirit,
And let none deal treacherously with the wife of his youth.

16 "For [a]the LORD God of Israel says
That He hates divorce,
For it covers one's garment with violence,"
Says the LORD of hosts.
"Therefore take heed to your spirit,
That you do not deal treacherously."

17 [a]You have wearied the LORD with your words;
Yet you say,
"In what way have we wearied *Him?*"
In that you say,
[b]"Everyone who does evil
*Is* good in the sight of the LORD,
And He delights in them,"
Or, "Where *is* the God of justice?"

**1:14** [a] Mal. 1:8 [b] Lev. 22:18–20 [c] Ps. 47:2 **2:1** [a] Mal. 1:6 **2:2** [a] [Deut. 28:15] [b] Mal. 3:9 **2:3** [a] Ex. 29:14 [b] 1 Kin. 14:10 **2:5** [a] Num. 25:12 [b] Deut. 33:9 **2:6** [a] Deut. 33:10 [b] Jer. 23:22 [1] Or *true instruction* **2:7** [a] Deut. 17:8–11 [b] [Gal. 4:14] **2:8** [a] Jer. 18:15 [b] Neh. 13:29 **2:9** [a] 1 Sam. 2:30 [b] Deut. 1:17 **2:10** [a] 1 Cor. 8:6 [b] Job 31:15 **2:11** [a] Ezra 9:1, 2 **2:12** [a] Neh. 13:29 [1] Talmud and Vulgate read *teacher and student.* **2:14** [a] Mal. 3:5 [b] Prov. 2:17 **2:15** [a] Matt. 19:4, 5 [b] [1 Cor. 7:14] **2:16** [a] [Matt. 5:31; 19:6–8] **2:17** [a] Is. 43:22, 24 [b] Is. 5:20

### THE COMING MESSENGER

3 "Behold, [a]I send My messenger,
And he will [b]prepare the way before Me.
And the Lord, whom you seek,
Will suddenly come to His temple,
[c]Even the Messenger of the covenant,
In whom you delight.
Behold, [d]He is coming,"
Says the LORD of hosts.

**SEEING JESUS IN THE SCRIPTURE**

**3:1** The messenger Malachi referred to was John the Baptist (see Matt. 11:10). John the Baptist prepared the way for Jesus by calling God's people to repent and believe.

2 "But who can endure [a]the day of His coming?
And [b]who can stand when He appears?
For [c]He *is* like a refiner's fire
And like launderers' soap.
3 [a]He will sit as a refiner and a purifier of silver;
He will purify the sons of Levi,
And purge them as gold and silver,
That they may [b]offer to the LORD
An offering in righteousness.

4 "Then [a]the offering of Judah and Jerusalem
Will be pleasant to the LORD,
As in the days of old,
As in former years.
5 And I will come near you for judgment;
I will be a swift witness
Against sorcerers,
Against adulterers,
[a]Against perjurers,
Against those who [b]exploit wage earners and [c]widows and orphans,
And against those who turn away an alien—
Because they do not fear Me,"
Says the LORD of hosts.

6 "For I *am* the LORD, [a]I do not change;
[b]Therefore you are not consumed, O sons of Jacob.

**3:1** [a] Matt. 11:10 [b] [Is. 40:3] [c] Is. 63:9 [d] Hab. 2:7 **3:2** [a] [Mal. 4:1] [b] Rev. 6:17 [c] [Matt. 3:10–12] **3:3** [a] Is. 1:25 [b] [1 Pet. 2:5] **3:4** [a] Mal. 1:11 **3:5** [a] Zech. 5:4 [b] James 5:4 [c] Ex. 22:22 **3:6** [a] [Rom. 11:29] [b] [Lam. 3:22]

MALACHI 3:1–7

## REFINER'S FIRE

39

STORY OF SCRIPTURE

### WHAT'S GOING ON?

Malachi 3 speaks of a messenger preparing the way for the Lord and the subsequent coming of the Lord to His temple. The Lord's arrival wouldn't be a gentle visitation, but a purifying and refining process. He is likened to a refiner's fire and launderers' soap, indicating cleansing will occur. This is among the final Old Testament prophecies about the promised Messiah. Four hundred years of silence followed. Then John the Baptist broke that silence by drawing the people's attention to Jesus.

### WHAT DOES THIS MEAN FOR ME?

This chapter invites us to reflect on the nature of spiritual refinement. The imagery of a refiner's fire implies heat, melting, and the removal of impurities to maximize purity and value. This process can be uncomfortable and painful, as it involves confronting and letting go of deeply ingrained sins and flaws. Consider your life as precious metal in the hands of God, the master refiner. Are there areas where impurities—attitudes, actions, or habits not in line with God's will—have settled in? Embrace the refining process. While it may be challenging, it's intended for your purification and growth. Remember, the goal isn't harm but bringing out the best in you, to be a vessel for honor, sanctified, and useful for the Master's work.

### DID YOU CATCH THE PATTERN?

Throughout the Bible, we see the theme of God as a purifier of His people. From the trials of Israel in the wilderness to the challenges faced by various people like Job, God used difficult circumstances and periods of testing to refine and strengthen faith. Some other passages referencing the "refiner's fire" include Job 23:10; Psalm 12:6; 66:10–12; Proverbs 17:3; Isaiah 48:10; Zechariah 13:9; and 1 Peter 1:7.

*For the next* Story of Scripture *reading and devotion, turn to John 1:1–5 on page 1069.*

7 Yet from the days of [a]your fathers
You have gone away from My ordinances
And have not kept *them*.
[b]Return to Me, and I will return to you,"
Says the LORD of hosts.
[c]"But you said,
'In what way shall we return?'

### DO NOT ROB GOD

8 "Will a man rob God?
Yet you have robbed Me!
But you say,
'In what way have we robbed You?'
[a]In tithes and offerings.
9 You are cursed with a curse,
For you have robbed Me,
*Even* this whole nation.
10 [a]Bring all the tithes into the [b]storehouse,
That there may be food in My house,
And try Me now in this,"
Says the LORD of hosts,
"If I will not open for you the [c]windows of heaven
And [d]pour out for you *such* blessing
That *there will* not *be room* enough *to receive it.*

**3:10** The Israelites were commanded to give **tithes** (10 percent) of everything they had—including crops, livestock, and money—to God. The Israelites gave their tithes to the Levites, the people who worked in the temple. The Levites, in turn, gave 10 percent of everything they received to the priests. The priests offered a sacrifice to the Lord for their tithe. The third-year tithe was given to help support the poor and needy.

11 "And I will rebuke [a]the devourer for your sakes,
So that he will not destroy the fruit of your ground,
Nor shall the vine fail to bear fruit for you in the field,"
Says the LORD of hosts;
12 "And all nations will call you blessed,
For you will be [a]a delightful land,"
Says the LORD of hosts.

### THE PEOPLE COMPLAIN HARSHLY

13 "Your[a] words have been harsh against Me,"
Says the LORD,
"Yet you say,
'What have we spoken against You?'
14 [a]You have said,
'It is useless to serve God;
What profit *is it* that we have kept His ordinance,
And that we have walked as mourners
Before the LORD of hosts?
15 So now [a]we call the proud blessed,
For those who do wickedness are raised up;
They even [b]tempt God and go free.' "

### A BOOK OF REMEMBRANCE

16 Then those [a]who feared the LORD [b]spoke to one another,
And the LORD listened and heard *them;*
So [c]a book of remembrance was written before Him
For those who fear the LORD
And who meditate on His name.

17 "They[a] shall be Mine," says the LORD of hosts,
"On the day that I make them My [b]jewels.[1]
And [c]I will spare them
As a man spares his own son who serves him."
18 [a]Then you shall again discern
Between the righteous and the wicked,
Between one who serves God
And one who does not serve Him.

### THE GREAT DAY OF GOD

4 "For behold, [a]the day is coming,
Burning like an oven,
And all [b]the proud, yes, all who do wickedly will be [c]stubble.
And the day which is coming shall burn them up,"
Says the LORD of hosts,
"That will [d]leave them neither root nor branch.
2 But to you who [a]fear My name
The [b]Sun of Righteousness shall arise
With healing in His wings;
And you shall go out
And grow fat like stall-fed calves.
3 [a]You shall trample the wicked,
For they shall be ashes under the soles of your feet
On the day that I do *this,*"
Says the LORD of hosts.

4 "Remember the [a]Law of Moses, My servant,
Which I commanded him in Horeb for all Israel,
*With* [b]*the* statutes and judgments.

**3:7** [a]Acts 7:51 [b]Zech. 1:3 [c]Mal. 1:6 **3:8** [a]Neh. 13:10–12 **3:10** [a]Prov. 3:9, 10 [b]1 Chr. 26:20 [c]Gen. 7:11 [d]2 Chr. 31:10 **3:11** [a]Amos 4:9 **3:12** [a]Dan. 8:9 **3:13** [a]Mal. 2:17 **3:14** [a]Job 21:14 **3:15** [a]Ps. 73:12 [b]Ps. 95:9 **3:16** [a]Ps. 66:16 [b]Heb. 3:13 [c]Ps. 56:8 **3:17** [a]Ex. 19:5 [b]Is. 62:3 [c]Ps. 103:13 [1]Literally *special treasure* **3:18** [a][Ps. 58:11] **4:1** [a][2 Pet. 3:7] [b]Mal. 3:18 [c]Obad. 18 [d]Amos 2:9 **4:2** [a]Mal. 3:16 [b]Luke 1:78 **4:3** [a]Mic. 7:10 **4:4** [a]Ex. 20:3 [b]Deut. 4:10

5 Behold, I will send you [a]Elijah the prophet
[b]Before the coming of the great and dreadful day of the LORD.
6 And [a]he will turn
The hearts of the fathers to the children,
And the hearts of the children to their fathers,
Lest I come and [b]strike the earth with [c]a curse."

## SEEING JESUS IN THE SCRIPTURE

**4:6** This message of repentance would be the last word the people heard from God until John the Baptist came preaching the same message (see Matt. 3:2). The call for repentance prepared the way for the work of the Messiah, Jesus.

**4:5** [a] [Matt. 11:14; 17:10–13] [b] Joel 2:31 **4:6** [a] Luke 1:17 [b] Zech. 14:12 [c] Zech. 5:3

# BETWEEN THE TESTAMENTS

The 400 years between the prophecy of Malachi and the advent of Christ are frequently described as "silent," but they were, in fact, crowded with activity. Although no inspired prophet arose in Israel during these centuries and the Old Testament was regarded as complete, providential events took place that gave later Judaism its distinctive ideology and prepared the way for the coming of Christ and the proclamation of His gospel (Gal. 4:4; Eph. 1:10). This time between the testaments consisted of four periods, based on who governed Palestine: Persian Rule (539–336 BC), Greek Rule (336–167 BC), Jewish Independence (165–63 BC), and Roman Rule (63 BC–NT Period).

## THE PERIOD OF PERSIAN RULE (539–336 BC)

From the tail-end of the Old Testament until about 100 years after Nehemiah's time, the Jewish people are subjects of the Persian Empire. While the Jews are not free, they fare better under Persian rule than they had during the Assyrian and Babylonian rule and captivity.

- The temple, which had been destroyed by Babylonians, is rebuilt between 536–516 BC. This temple, often called the second temple or Zerubbabel's Temple, was not as grand as Solomon's had been.
- A Samaritan temple is built on Mount Gerizim around 450 BC. John Hyrcanus (134–104 BC) would later destroy this temple.
- Nehemiah leads the rebuilding of Jerusalem's walls in 444 BC.
- A contemporary of Nehemiah, Ezra encourages the Jewish community to live faithfully according to the law.
- The high priesthood rises to greater prominence than before and becomes not only a religious office, but a ruling one as well.
- Malachi is written in about 420 BC, bringing the Old Testament period to its end.

## THE PERIOD OF GREEK RULE (336–167 BC)

Around 350 BC, Philip of Macedonia conquers all of Greece, prompting what would become the fall of the Persian Empire. Philip is assassinated in 336 BC, giving way for his son, Alexander the Great, to rule. Within two years, Alexander extends the Greek territories considerably, including assuming control of Palestine.

- Hellenism brings the Greek language, philosophy, and way of life to Palestine. Many in Israel are glad to accept this veneer of Greek culture, but others resist what they consider a compromise to their culture and faith. A lasting wedge is formed between those Jews who welcome outside influences, those who want to ignore them, and those who want to resist them.
- After Alexander's death, one of his generals, Ptolemy Soter seizes Jerusalem. The Ptolemies rule Palestine from 320 BC until 198 BC. During this time, Jews in Alexandria, Egypt, translate the Old Testament from Hebrew into Greek, what would become known as the Septuagint.
- Antiochus the Great defeats Egypt and gains control of Palestine in 198 BC, beginning roughly thirty years of rule by the Seleucids of Syria. While the Ptolemies had been tolerant of Judaism and Jewish culture, the Seleucids return to a posture of strict Hellenization.
- Tension between the Jews who favor Hellenization and those who resist it flare, resulting in Antiochus Epiphanes attacking Jerusalem in 168 BC. Antiochus attempts to remove all traces of orthodox Jewish faith. Israel's God is identified with Jupiter, a bearded image of the pagan deity is erected, Sabbath observance and circumcision are forbidden, copies of the law are to be burned, and, perhaps most grievous of all, a pig is slaughtered on the altar.

## THE PERIOD OF JEWISH INDEPENDENCE

The actions that Antiochus takes to shut down Judaism have the opposite effect. His zeal, along with that of his Hellenistic supporters, prove to be his undoing. The orthodox are willing to die for their faith, but at this point, many determine that they do not have to die passively. Instead of going away quietly, they revolt, leading to a brief time of Jewish independence.

- Triggered by the resistance of an aged priest named Mattathias, a guerrilla war against the Seleucids and the Hellenistic Jews takes place from 167–160 BC, under the leadership of Mattathias's son, Judas "the Maccabee." The Maccabees, as his followers are known, take back Jerusalem, remove all signs of paganism installed there, and erect a new, pure altar. Beginning with the twenty-fifth of Kislev (December), they celebrate an eight-day Feast of Dedication, known as Hanukkah, the Festival of Lights, to mark the end of the three-year period during which the temple had been desecrated.
- The Maccabees are defeated, agree to terms of peace, but are then betrayed. Civil war erupts again, and Judas is killed in battle. His brother Jonathan assumes leadership and negotiates his way to

peace and becoming the high priest and governor. His brother, Simon, becomes priest after him and likewise negotiates continued independence for the Jews. His rule would begin what is known as the Hasmonean Dynasty.

- The Hasmoneans are well-received by the nationalistic element in Judea and extend the nation's borders on every side. This time of prosperity, however, does not end the rivalries increasing among the people. The older Hellenists are discredited, but their ideas are grafted into the party of the Sadducees. Meanwhile, the orthodox become part of the Pharisees. These two groups continue to oppose one another, with the Pharisees, in time, developing an advantage among the people.

## THE PERIOD OF ROMAN RULE (63 BC–NT PERIOD)

While the Sadducees and Pharisees quarrel, a new threat to Jewish independence arises in Rome. In 63 BC, Pompey besieges Jerusalem. After three months, he breaches the fortifications, enters the city, and reportedly murders 12,000 Jews. Pompey and his officers enter the Holy of Holies, but do not touch its costly furnishings. Pompey allows temple worship to continue, but the last vestige of Jewish independence ends. Jerusalem is made a tributary to the Romans, and Judea is incorporated into the Roman province of Syria.

- In the crisis that follows the murder of Julius Caesar in 44 BC, the Idumaean governor, Antipater, and his sons prove their loyalty to the new regime of Cassius by zealously collecting tribute taxes. One of those sons, Herod the Great, is given the title Procurator of Judea and promised that he will be named king one day.
- The Parthians, from the eastern part of the old Persian Empire, attack Jerusalem in 41 BC. Herod flees to Rome where he is officially named "King of the Jews." Herod returns to Judea with a Roman force and purges the Parthians.
- Herod rules from 37–4 BC. A ruthless ruler, he seeks the people's favor by building and rebuilding cities. In 19 BC, he begins rebuilding the temple. This temple would not be completed until AD 62–64. Soon after, it would be destroyed by the Romans under Titus in AD 70.
- Two additional political parties develop during this time. The Herodians are those devoted to Herod and Hellenism. The Zealots are those who refuse to submit to Rome and advocate for armed rebellion.
- Around 5–4 BC, when Herod learns of a rival "King of the Jews" being born in Bethlehem, he decrees the murder of all infants in that town.

# THE JEWISH SECTS

| SECT | ORIGIN | DESCRIPTION | CORE BELIEFS | ATTITUDE TOWARD ROME |
|---|---|---|---|---|
| **Herodians** | Supporters of Herod the Great and his dynasty | • Political party<br>• Probably had representation from varied religious perspectives<br>• Wealthy and politically influential Jews | • Supported the Hellenization of culture and incorporation of Graeco-Roman policies<br>• Accepted foreign rule<br>• Favored autonomy on local level<br>• Resisted challenge to the status quo | Accept |
| **Sadducees** | Claimed to be descendants of Zadok, the high priest under David and Solomon (see 2 Sam. 8:17; 1 Kin. 1:34–35) and boasted of a possible link to Aaron | • Political/religious party<br>• Possibly from Hasmonaean priesthood but definitely from aristocracy<br>• Sect from which most high priests came during the days of Jesus (Acts 5:17–18)<br>• In charge of the temple and its services (Ezek. 40:44–46) | • Accepted only the Torah as authoritative<br>• Held to literal interpretation of the written law and rejected the oral law<br>• Believed in absolute freedom of human will<br>• Denied life after death, resurrection of the body, divine providence, and existence of demons and angels (Mark 12:18–27; Luke 20:27–40) | Use |
| **Pharisees** | Probably descendants of the Hasidim, freedom fighters during the Maccabean period, later the most strict and orthodox Jews | • Religious party<br>• Largest of the Jewish sects<br>• Mostly middle class, especially merchants and tradesmen (John 3:1–21)<br>• Developers of the oral tradition and interpreters of the law (Talmud and Mishnah)<br>• Legalistic, self-righteous, and haughty (Matt. 5:20; 9:14; Luke 7:36–39; 18:9–14) | • Monotheistic<br>• Concerned with Sabbath observance, tithing, and purification rituals (Matt. 23:2–36; Luke 11:37–44)<br>• Believed in resurrection of the body, life after death, and the reality of demons and angels (Acts 23:6–10) | Tolerate |
| **Essenes** | Could have evolved from Hasidim or Zealots because of their reaction to a corrupt priesthood | • Religious party<br>• Ascetics who withdrew to settle in monastic, communal communities like Qumran on the Dead Sea | • Held property and possessions in common<br>• Most were celibate (adopted male children to perpetuate the communities)<br>• Pacifists<br>• Exclusive, caring for their own needs within the sect<br>• Simple in dress and lifestyle<br>• Rigidly kept the Law and observed ritual self-baptism | Escape |
| **Zealots** | Possibly came from those involved in the Jewish revolt against Rome | • Religious/political party<br>• Extremists<br>• Noted for zeal and nationalism | • Saw patriotism and religion as inseparable<br>• Fanatical in their Jewish faith and devotion to the Law<br>• Opposed Roman rule in the Holy Land<br>• Refused to pay taxes<br>• Engaged in insurrection against Rome<br>• Opposed the Herodians and Sadducees | Resist |

# THE NEW TESTAMENT

*WORDS OF CHRIST IN RED*

*Introduction to*

# THE GOSPELS AND THE BOOK OF HISTORY

The word *gospel* comes from the Greek *euangelion*, meaning "good news." This term can mean the good news preached *by* Jesus or the good news preached *about* Jesus. That certainly makes sense because we have been called to share with others what Jesus shared. But *Gospel* can also mean the four books in Scripture that contain the true story of Jesus' life and ministry. Gospels, however, are not biographies. The writers' goal isn't to present all the information about Jesus or even to present the events of His life in chronological order. Instead, they desired to put together true details in a way that makes a point: Jesus is the Son of God, the Savior of the world.

It's helpful to understand why there are four Gospels. Each writer wanted to say something specific about who Jesus is, as he examined His life from a different perspective and wrote to a different audience. This, then, determined the material each writer included and how he structured his account. **Matthew**, **Mark**, and **Luke** are called the Synoptic Gospels because they can be "seen together," the meaning of *synoptic*. While each of these Gospels still has unique material (Luke about 60 percent, Matthew about 40 percent, and Mark about 10 percent), they share quite a bit more with each other than with **John**, which is about 90 percent unique. Matthew wrote his Gospel to the Jews to show them Jesus is the Messiah. This is why his Gospel contains the most Old Testament quotations. Mark wrote his Gospel to the Romans to show Jesus is the Suffering Servant. This is why his Gospel shows Jesus always on the move. Luke wrote his Gospel to the Greeks to show Jesus is the Son of Man, the perfect human. This is why his Gospel traces Jesus' lineage back to Adam and emphasizes His being the Savior of all people. Finally, John wrote his Gospel to everyone to show Jesus is the Son of God. This is why his Gospel includes more theological teachings of Jesus.

The Book of **Acts** is not a Gospel; rather it's a book of history detailing the start of the church. Acts was written by Luke, probably as a follow-up to his Gospel and possibly to be used in Paul's defense in Rome. When reading Acts, consider two longer names often given to the book: The Acts of the Apostles and The Acts of the Holy Spirit. The first name emphasizes the people God worked through to begin

# MATTHEW • MARK • LUKE • JOHN • ACTS

the church, namely Peter, Stephen, Philip, and Paul. The second name reminds us that ultimately the Holy Spirit worked through these leaders just as He works in and through all believers today.

## THE GOSPELS

| Book | Author | Primary Audience | Date | Theme |
|---|---|---|---|---|
| **Matthew** | Matthew | Jews | c. AD 50–60 | Messiah |
| **Mark** | Mark | Romans | c. AD 50–60 | Servant |
| **Luke** | Luke | Greeks | c. AD 60–61 | Son of Man |
| **John** | John | World | c. AD 80–90 | Son of God |

## THE BOOK OF HISTORY

| Book | Author | Date | Timeframe | Theme |
|---|---|---|---|---|
| **Acts** | Luke | c. AD 62 | c. AD 33–62 | Church |

*The Gospel According to*

# MATTHEW

**AUTHOR**
Matthew

**KEY VERSE**
Matthew 16:16

**READING TIME**
2 hours 49 minutes

God's promise to provide the Messiah—the One who would rescue people from sin—runs throughout the Old Testament. Every generation of Abraham's descendants provided another opportunity for the prophecies to be fulfilled, but each was left with dashed hopes. The waiting would go on. But it would not continue for good. Matthew's message is one of relief and joy: The long-awaited Messiah had come! Through a carefully selected series of Old Testament quotations, Matthew documents compelling evidence supporting Jesus' claim to be the Messiah. Jesus' genealogy, baptism, message, and miracles all pointed to the same inescapable conclusion: Jesus is King. Even in Christ's death, seeming defeat was turned into victory by the resurrection, and the message again echoed forth: The King of the Jews lives!

**Occasion:** Matthew wrote his Gospel to a primarily Jewish audience to show Jesus as the Messiah.

**Main Point:** Jesus is the Messiah, the King of the Jews and fulfillment of the Old Testament prophecies.

**Big Ideas:** Jesus is the long-awaited Messiah. What Jesus said and what He did prove He is the Son of God. All who place faith in Jesus are saved. Jesus shows us how we are to live as His followers.

**OUTLINE:**

I. The Presentation of Jesus the Messiah (chs. 1–4)
II. The Teachings of Jesus the Messiah (chs. 5–7)
III. The Power of Jesus the Messiah (chs. 8–10)
IV. The Ministry of Jesus the Messiah (chs. 11–18)
V. The Discipleship of Jesus the Messiah (chs. 19–20)
VI. The Rejection of Jesus the Messiah (chs. 21–27)
VII. The Resurrection of Jesus the Messiah (ch. 28)

**c. 420 BC**
Malachi prophesies in Judah

**c. 400 BC**
Invention of the screw

**356–323 BC**
Alexander the Great lives in Macedonia

**246 BC**
Great Wall of China is built

**164 BC**
Judas Maccabaeus restores the temple in Jerusalem, celebrated yearly by the festival of Hanukkah

**37 BC**
Julius Caesar is murdered

**37–4 BC**
Herod the Great is king in Jerusalem

**31 BC–AD 14**
Augustus Caesar is Roman emperor

**c. 5–4 BC**
Jesus is born in Bethlehem

**4 BC–AD 39**
Herod Antipas rules in Galilee and Perea

**AD 1**
Lions become extinct in Western Europe

**AD 14–37**
Tiberius is Roman emperor

**AD 25–27**
John the Baptist ministers

**AD 26–36**
Pontius Pilate is procurator of Judea

**c. AD 27**
Jesus' first Judean ministry

**c. AD 27–29**
Jesus' Galilean ministry

**c. AD 30**
Jesus' second Judean ministry; crucifixion and resurrection

**c. AD 50–60**
**Matthew written**

## THE GENEALOGY OF JESUS CHRIST

*(Ruth 4:18–22; 1 Chr. 2:1–15; Luke 3:23–38)*

1 The book of the [a]genealogy of Jesus Christ,
[b]the Son of David, [c]the Son of Abraham:

### SEEING JESUS IN THE SCRIPTURE

**1:1, 6** Jesus was a descendent of Abraham and David, fulfilling prophecy and God's covenant promises (see Gen. 17:7; 1 Kin. 2:33).

2 [a]Abraham begot Isaac, [b]Isaac begot Ja-
cob, and Jacob begot [c]Judah and his brothers.
3 [a]Judah begot Perez and Zerah by Tamar, [b]Perez
begot Hezron, and Hezron begot Ram. 4 Ram
begot Amminadab, Amminadab begot Nahshon,
and Nahshon begot Salmon. 5 Salmon begot
[a]Boaz by Rahab, Boaz begot Obed by Ruth, Obed
begot Jesse, 6 and [a]Jesse begot David the king.

**1:3** The mention of women in a Jewish genealogy is unusual. But in addition to Mary, four women are listed in this catalogue of names: **Tamar**, who was involved in a scandal with **Judah** (Gen. 38); Rahab, the Canaanite harlot of Jericho (Josh. 2:1–21); Ruth, who was not an Israelite, but a Moabite (Ruth 1:4); and Bathsheba, the wife of Uriah, who David sinned against (2 Sam. 11:1–5). At the beginning of his Gospel, Matthew shows how God's grace forgives the darkest of sins and reaches beyond the nation of Israel to the world. He also points out that God can lift the lowest and place them in royal lineage.

[b]David the king begot Solomon by her *who
had been the wife*[1] of Uriah. 7 [a]Solomon begot Re-
hoboam, Rehoboam begot [b]Abijah, and Abijah
begot Asa.[1] 8 Asa begot [a]Jehoshaphat, Jehoshaphat
begot Joram, and Joram begot [b]Uzziah. 9 Uzziah be-
got Jotham, Jotham begot [a]Ahaz, and Ahaz begot
Hezekiah. 10 [a]Hezekiah begot Manasseh, Manasseh
begot Amon,[1] and Amon begot [b]Josiah. 11 [a]Josiah
begot Jeconiah and his brothers about the time
they were [b]carried away to Babylon.
12 And after they were brought to Babylon,
[a]Jeconiah begot Shealtiel, and Shealtiel begot
[b]Zerubbabel. 13 Zerubbabel begot Abiud, Abiud
begot Eliakim, and Eliakim begot Azor. 14 Azor
begot Zadok, Zadok begot Achim, and Achim
begot Eliud. 15 Eliud begot Eleazar, Eleazar begot
Matthan, and Matthan begot Jacob. 16 And Jacob
begot Joseph the husband of [a]Mary, of whom
was born Jesus who is called Christ.
17 So all the generations from Abraham to
David *are* fourteen generations, from David
until the captivity in Babylon *are* fourteen gen-
erations, and from the captivity in Babylon until
the Christ *are* fourteen generations.

## CHRIST BORN OF MARY

*(Luke 2:1–7)*

18 Now the [a]birth of Jesus Christ was as fol-
lows: After His mother Mary was betrothed to
Joseph, before they came together, she was
found with child [b]of the Holy Spirit. 19 Then
Joseph her husband, being a just *man,* and not
wanting [a]to make her a public example, was
minded to put her away secretly. 20 But while he
thought about these things, behold, an angel of
the Lord appeared to him in a dream, saying,
"Joseph, son of David, do not be afraid to take to
you Mary your wife, [a]for that which is conceived
in her is of the Holy Spirit. 21 [a]And she will bring
forth a Son, and you shall call His name JESUS,
[b]for He will save His people from their sins."

### SEEING JESUS IN THE SCRIPTURE

**1:18** Jesus was born of the virgin Mary, fulfilling prophecy (see Is. 7:14).

22 So all this was done that it might be ful-
filled which was spoken by the Lord through
the prophet, saying: 23 [a]"Behold, the virgin shall
be with child, and bear a Son, and they shall
call His name Immanuel,"[1] which is translated,
"God with us."
24 Then Joseph, being aroused from sleep,
did as the angel of the Lord commanded him
and took to him his wife, 25 and did not know her
till she had brought forth [a]her firstborn Son.[1]
And he called His name JESUS.

## WISE MEN FROM THE EAST

2 Now after [a]Jesus was born in Bethlehem of
Judea in the days of Herod the king, behold,
wise men [b]from the East came to Jerusalem,
2 saying, [a]"Where is He who has been born King
of the Jews? For we have seen [b]His star in the
East and have come to worship Him."
3 When Herod the king heard *this,* he was
troubled, and all Jerusalem with him. 4 And
when he had gathered all [a]the chief priests and
[b]scribes of the people together, [c]he inquired of
them where the Christ was to be born.

**1:1** [a] Luke 3:23 [b] John 7:42 [c] Gen. 12:3; 22:18 **1:2** [a] Gen. 21:2, 12 [b] Gen. 25:26; 28:14 [c] Gen. 29:35 **1:3** [a] Gen. 38:27; 49:10 [b] Ruth 4:18–22 **1:5** [a] Ruth 2:1; 4:1–13 **1:6** [a] 1 Sam. 16:1 [b] 2 Sam. 7:12; 12:24 [1] Words in italic type have been added for clarity. They are not found in the original Greek. **1:7** [a] 1 Chr. 3:10 [b] 2 Chr. 11:20 [1] NU-Text reads *Asaph.* **1:8** [a] 1 Chr. 3:10 [b] 2 Kin. 15:13 **1:9** [a] 2 Kin. 15:38 **1:10** [a] 2 Kin. 20:21 [b] 1 Kin. 13:2 [1] NU-Text reads *Amos.* **1:11** [a] 1 Chr. 3:15, 16 [b] 2 Kin. 24:14–16 **1:12** [a] 1 Chr. 3:17 [b] Ezra 3:2 **1:16** [a] Matt. 13:55 **1:18** [a] Luke 1:27 [b] Luke 1:35 **1:19** [a] Deut. 24:1 **1:20** [a] Luke 1:35 **1:21** [a] Luke 1:31; 2:21 [b] John 1:29 **1:23** [a] Is. 7:14 [1] Isaiah 7:14 **1:25** [a] Luke 2:7, 21 [1] NU-Text reads *a Son.* **2:1** [a] Luke 2:4 [b] Gen. 25:6 **2:2** [a] Luke 2:11 [b] [Num. 24:17; Is. 60:3] **2:4** [a] 2 Chr. 36:14 [b] 2 Chr. 34:13 [c] Mal. 2:7

MATTHEW 1:18–24

# JESUS, GOD WITH US

41

STORY OF SCRIPTURE

## WHAT'S GOING ON?

This passage describes the divine and miraculous circumstances surrounding Jesus' birth. Joseph, betrothed to Mary, discovered she was pregnant before they came together. He planned to divorce her quietly to save her from public disgrace. However, an angel of the Lord appeared to him in a dream, revealing the child conceived in her was from the Holy Spirit. The angel instructed Joseph to name the child *Jesus*, for He would save His people from their sins. This event fulfills the prophecy of Isaiah 7:14, showcasing Jesus as the long-awaited Messiah. The name for Jesus in Isaiah is *Immanuel*, meaning "God with us." This wasn't only because the birth of Christ was God coming to earth, but also because the relationship lost in Eden because of sin was about to be restored.

## WHAT DOES THIS MEAN FOR ME?

The birth of Christ is a glorious reminder that God isn't distant; God is near, present, and active in your life. The Son of God humbled Himself by being born into lowly and messy circumstances. He does likewise in our lives. He enters our mess and brings new life with Him.

## DID YOU CATCH THE PATTERN?

The pattern of God's presence was first seen with Adam and Eve in the garden of Eden. Then, He was present in Abraham's family. He later traveled with the people of Israel in the ark of the covenant and tabernacle. After that, He dwelled among His people in the temple built by Solomon. Christ's birth is another link in the chain of God's presence among people.

*For the next* Story of Scripture *reading and devotion, turn to Matthew 3:1–17 on page 964.*

**2:1** These **wise men** would have been of the same class as the "wise men" of Babylon over whom Daniel was made ruler (see Dan. 2:48). Contrary to popular belief, the events of this chapter probably took place some months **after Jesus was born**. Herod murdered all the male children age two and under, going by the time the wise men said the star had appeared (and probably leaving a significant margin for error). In addition, it would have been strange for Mary and Joseph to offer the sacrifice of the poor (see Lev. 12:8; Luke 2:24) if the wise men had just given them such lavish gifts.

5 So they said to him, "In Bethlehem of
Judea, for thus it is written by the prophet:

6 'But[a] you, Bethlehem, *in* the land of
Judah,
Are not the least among the rulers of
Judah;
For out of you shall come a Ruler
[b]Who will shepherd My people Israel.' "[1]

7 Then Herod, when he had secretly called
the wise men, determined from them what
time the [a]star appeared. 8 And he sent them to
Bethlehem and said, "Go and search carefully
for the young Child, and when you have found
*Him,* bring back word to me, that I may come
and worship Him also."
9 When they heard the king, they departed;
and behold, the star which they had seen in the
East went before them, till it came and stood
over where the young Child was. 10 When they
saw the star, they rejoiced with exceedingly great
joy. 11 And when they had come into the house,
they saw the young Child with Mary His mother,
and fell down and worshiped Him. And when
they had opened their treasures, [a]they presented
gifts to Him: gold, frankincense, and myrrh.
12 Then, being divinely warned [a]in a dream
that they should not return to Herod, they de-
parted for their own country another way.

### SEEING JESUS IN THE SCRIPTURE

**2:5–6** Jesus came from the small village of Bethlehem, fulfilling prophecy (see Mic. 5:2–4).

**2:6** [a] Mic. 5:2; John 7:42 [b] Gen. 49:10; [Rev. 2:27] [1] Micah 5:2 **2:7** [a] Num. 24:17 **2:11** [a] Ps. 72:10; Is. 60:6 **2:12** [a] [Job 33:15, 16]; Matt. 1:20

### *THE FLIGHT INTO EGYPT*

13 Now when they had departed, behold, an
angel of the Lord appeared to Joseph in a dream,
saying, "Arise, take the young Child and His
mother, flee to Egypt, and stay there until I
bring you word; for Herod will seek the young
Child to destroy Him."
14 When he arose, he took the young Child
and His mother by night and departed for Egypt,
15 and was there until the death of Herod, that it
might be fulfilled which was spoken by the Lord
through the prophet, saying, [a]"Out of Egypt I
called My Son."[1]

### *MASSACRE OF THE INNOCENTS*

16 Then Herod, when he saw that he was de-
ceived by the wise men, was exceedingly angry;
and he sent forth and put to death all the male
children who were in Bethlehem and in all its
districts, from two years old and under, accord-
ing to the time which he had determined from
the wise men. 17 Then was fulfilled what was
spoken by Jeremiah the prophet, saying:

18 "A [a]voice was heard in Ramah,
Lamentation, weeping, and great
mourning,
Rachel weeping *for* her children,
Refusing to be comforted,
Because they are no more."[1]

### *THE HOME IN NAZARETH*

*(Luke 2:39)*

19 Now when Herod was dead, behold, an
angel of the Lord appeared in a dream to Joseph
in Egypt, 20 [a]saying, "Arise, take the young Child
and His mother, and go to the land of Israel, for
those who [b]sought the young Child's life are
dead." 21 Then he arose, took the young Child and
His mother, and came into the land of Israel.
22 But when he heard that Archelaus was
reigning over Judea instead of his father Herod,
he was afraid to go there. And being warned
by God in a [a]dream, he turned aside [b]into the
region of Galilee. 23 And he came and dwelt in
a city called [a]Nazareth, that it might be fulfilled
[b]which was spoken by the prophets, "He shall
be called a Nazarene."

### *JOHN THE BAPTIST PREPARES THE WAY*

*(Mark 1:2–8; Luke 3:1–20)*

**3** In those days [a]John the Baptist came preach-
ing [b]in the wilderness of Judea, 2 and saying,
"Repent, for [a]the kingdom of heaven is at hand!"
3 For this is he who was spoken of by the prophet
Isaiah, saying:

[a]"The voice of one crying in the wilderness:
[b]'Prepare the way of the LORD;
Make His paths straight.' "[1]

**SEEING JESUS IN THE SCRIPTURE**

**3:2–3** John is the prophet who prepared the way for Jesus by calling sinners to repent, fulfilling prophecy (see Mal. 4:5–6).

4 Now [a]John himself was clothed in camel's
hair, with a leather belt around his waist; and
his food was [b]locusts and [c]wild honey. 5 [a]Then
Jerusalem, all Judea, and all the region around
the Jordan went out to him 6 [a]and were baptized
by him in the Jordan, confessing their sins.
7 But when he saw many of the Pharisees
and Sadducees coming to his baptism, he said
to them, [a]"Brood of vipers! Who warned you
to flee from [b]the wrath to come? 8 Therefore
bear fruits worthy of repentance, 9 and do not
think to say to yourselves, [a]'We have Abraham
as *our* father.' For I say to you that God is able
to raise up children to Abraham from these
stones. 10 And even now the ax is laid to the root
of the trees. [a]Therefore every tree which does
not bear good fruit is cut down and thrown
into the fire. 11 [a]I indeed baptize you with water
unto repentance, but He who is coming after
me is mightier than I, whose sandals I am not
worthy to carry. [b]He will baptize you with the
Holy Spirit and fire.[1] 12 [a]His winnowing fan *is*
in His hand, and He will thoroughly clean out
His threshing floor, and gather His wheat into
the barn; but He will [b]burn up the chaff with
unquenchable fire."

### *JOHN BAPTIZES JESUS*

*(Mark 1:9–11; Luke 3:21, 22; John 1:29–34)*

13 [a]Then Jesus came [b]from Galilee to John at
the Jordan to be baptized by him. 14 And John
*tried to* prevent Him, saying, "I need to be bap-
tized by You, and are You coming to me?"
15 But Jesus answered and said to him, "Per-
mit *it to be so* now, for thus it is fitting for us
to fulfill all righteousness." Then he allowed
Him.
16 [a]When He had been baptized, Jesus came
up immediately from the water; and behold,
the heavens were opened to Him, and He[1] saw
[b]the Spirit of God descending like a dove and
alighting upon Him. 17 [a]And suddenly a voice
*came* from heaven, saying, [b]"This is My beloved
Son, in whom I am well pleased."

**2:15** [a] Num. 24:8; Hos. 11:1 [1] Hosea 11:1 **2:18** [a] Jer. 31:15 [1] Jeremiah 31:15 **2:20** [a] Luke 2:39 [b] Matt. 2:16 **2:22** [a] Matt. 2:12, 13, 19 [b] Matt. 3:13; Luke 2:39 **2:23** [a] Luke 1:26; 2:39; John 1:45, 46 [b] Judg. 13:5 **3:1** [a] Matt. 3:1–12; Mark 1:3–8; Luke 3:2–17; John 1:6–8, 19–28 [b] Josh. 14:10 **3:2** [a] Dan. 2:44; Mal. 4:6; Matt. 4:17; Mark 1:15; Luke 1:17; 10:9; 11:20; 21:31 **3:3** [a] Is. 40:3; Luke 3:4; John 1:23 [b] Luke 1:76 [1] Isaiah 40:3 **3:4** [a] 2 Kin. 1:8; Zech. 13:4; Matt. 11:8; Mark 1:6 [b] Lev. 11:22 [c] 1 Sam. 14:25, 26 **3:5** [a] Mark 1:5 **3:6** [a] Acts 19:4, 18 **3:7** [a] Matt. 12:34; Luke 3:7–9 [b] [Rom. 5:9; 1 Thess. 1:10] **3:9** [a] John 8:33 **3:10** [a] Matt. 7:19 **3:11** [a] Luke 3:16 [b] [Acts 2:3, 4] [1] M-Text omits *and fire.* **3:12** [a] Mal. 3:3 [b] Matt. 13:30 **3:13** [a] Mark 1:9–11 [b] Matt. 2:22 **3:16** [a] Mark 1:10 [b] John 1:32 [1] Or *he* **3:17** [a] John 12:28 [b] Ps. 2:7

MATTHEW 3:1–17

# JESUS, THE BELOVED SON

42

STORY OF SCRIPTURE

## WHAT'S GOING ON?

John the Baptist was an eccentric relative of Jesus and a fiery preacher who called the Jews to repent of their sins and turn from a corrupt religious system. His ministry was the fulfillment of the prophecy of a forerunner preparing the way for the Messiah's arrival (see Mal. 3:1–7). One of the central marks of John's ministry was baptism, immersing people in the Jordan River as a sign of their repentance. Then one day, John was shocked by Jesus coming to be baptized. John was hesitant; Jesus had no sin to repent of and John's ministry was designed to point toward Jesus, not the other way around. But Jesus insisted and John relented. As Jesus emerged from the waters, the heavens opened, the Spirit of God descended like a dove, and a voice from heaven proclaimed Jesus as God's beloved Son. This baptism marks the beginning of Jesus' public ministry.

## WHAT DOES THIS MEAN FOR ME?

The Father declared He is pleased with Jesus and the same is true of you. If you've trusted in Christ, God is pleased with you because He is pleased with Jesus. Even when you sin, mess up, and fail, God loves you and remains pleased with you because He sees you through the lens of complete forgiveness and acceptance in Christ.

## DID YOU CATCH THE PATTERN?

The Jordan River, referenced over 185 times in the Bible, represents both a barrier and a pathway. After the exodus, God stopped the waters of the Jordan so His people could cross into the Promised Land. This miraculous act demonstrated God's power and guidance and hinted how He would turn all barriers into pathways for the Israelites. Jesus' baptism marks a new pathway He was forging, transitioning God's people from the Old Covenant to the New Covenant.

*For the next* Story of Scripture *reading and devotion, turn to Mark 4:35—5:20 on page 1009.*

### *SATAN TEMPTS JESUS*

*(Mark 1:12, 13; Luke 4:1–13)*

**4** Then [a]Jesus was led up by [b]the Spirit into
the wilderness to be tempted by the devil.
2 And when He had fasted forty days and forty
nights, afterward He was hungry. 3 Now when
the tempter came to Him, he said, "If You are
the Son of God, command that these stones
become bread."
4 But He answered and said, "It is written,
[a]'Man shall not live by bread alone, but by every
word that proceeds from the mouth of God.' "[1]
5 Then the devil took Him up [a]into the holy
city, set Him on the pinnacle of the temple, 6 and
said to Him, "If You are the Son of God, throw
Yourself down. For it is written:

[a]'He shall give His angels charge over you,'

and,

[b]'In *their* hands they shall bear you up,
Lest you dash your foot against a stone.' "[1]

7 Jesus said to him, "It is written again, [a]'You
shall not tempt the LORD your God.' "[1]
8 Again, the devil took Him up on an exceed-
ingly high mountain, and [a]showed Him all the
kingdoms of the world and their glory. 9 And he
said to Him, "All these things I will give You if
You will fall down and worship me."
10 Then Jesus said to him, "Away with you,[1]
Satan! For it is written, [a]'You shall worship
the LORD your God, and Him only you shall
serve.' "[2]
11 Then the devil [a]left Him, and behold, [b]an-
gels came and ministered to Him.

### *JESUS BEGINS HIS GALILEAN MINISTRY*

*(Mark 1:14, 15; Luke 4:14, 15)*

12 [a]Now when Jesus heard that John had been
put in prison, He departed to Galilee. 13 And leav-
ing Nazareth, He came and dwelt in Capernaum,
which is by the sea, in the regions of Zebulun
and Naphtali, 14 that it might be fulfilled which
was spoken by Isaiah the prophet, saying:

**4:1** [a] Mark 1:12 [b] Ezek. 3:14 **4:4** [a] Deut. 8:3 [1] Deuteronomy 8:3 **4:5** [a] Neh. 11:1, 18 **4:6** [a] Ps. 91:11 [b] Ps. 91:12 [1] Psalm 91:11, 12 **4:7** [a] Deut. 6:16 [1] Deuteronomy 6:16 **4:8** [a] [1 John 2:15–17] **4:10** [a] Deut. 6:13; 10:20 [1] M-Text reads *Get behind Me.* [2] Deuteronomy 6:13 **4:11** [a] [James 4:7] [b] [Heb. 1:14] **4:12** [a] John 4:43

15 "The[a] land of Zebulun and the land of
Naphtali,
*By* the way of the sea, beyond the Jordan,
Galilee of the Gentiles:
16 [a]The people who sat in darkness have seen
a great light,
And upon those who sat in the region and
shadow of death
Light has dawned."[1]

17[a]From that time Jesus began to preach
and to say, [b]"Repent, for the kingdom of heaven
is at hand."

### *FOUR FISHERMEN CALLED AS DISCIPLES*
*(Mark 1:16–20; Luke 5:1–11)*

18[a]And Jesus, walking by the Sea of Gal-
ilee, saw two brothers, Simon [b]called Peter,
and Andrew his brother, casting a net into the
sea; for they were fishermen. 19Then He said to
them, "Follow Me, and [a]I will make you fishers
of men." 20[a]They immediately left *their* nets
and followed Him.
21[a]Going on from there, He saw two other
brothers, James *the son* of Zebedee, and John
his brother, in the boat with Zebedee their fa-
ther, mending their nets. He called them, 22and
immediately they left the boat and their father,
and followed Him.

### *JESUS HEALS A GREAT MULTITUDE*
*(Mark 1:35–39; Luke 4:44; 6:17–19)*

23And Jesus went about all Galilee, [a]teaching
in their synagogues, preaching [b]the gospel of the
kingdom, [c]and healing all kinds of sickness and
all kinds of disease among the people. 24Then
His fame went throughout all Syria; and they
[a]brought to Him all sick people who were afflicted
with various diseases and torments, and those
who were demon-possessed, epileptics, and par-
alytics; and He healed them. 25[a]Great multitudes
followed Him—from Galilee, and *from* Decapolis,
Jerusalem, Judea, and beyond the Jordan.

### *THE BEATITUDES*
*(Luke 6:20–26)*

**5** And seeing the multitudes, [a]He went up on
a mountain, and when He was seated His
disciples came to Him. 2Then He opened His
mouth and [a]taught them, saying:

3 "Blessed[a] *are* the poor in spirit,
For theirs is the kingdom of heaven.
4 [a]Blessed *are* those who mourn,
For they shall be comforted.
5 [a]Blessed *are* the meek,
For [b]they shall inherit the earth.
6 Blessed *are* those who [a]hunger and thirst
for righteousness,
[b]For they shall be filled.
7 Blessed *are* the merciful,
[a]For they shall obtain mercy.
8 [a]Blessed *are* the pure in heart,
For [b]they shall see God.
9 Blessed *are* the peacemakers,
For they shall be called sons of God.
10 [a]Blessed *are* those who are persecuted for
righteousness' sake,
For theirs is the kingdom of heaven.

**SEEING JESUS IN THE SCRIPTURE**

**5:8** The pure in heart are those who are spiritually righteous. One day, they will see God in all His glory (see Rev. 22:4).

11[a]Blessed are you when they revile and perse-
cute you, and say all kinds of [b]evil against you
falsely for My sake. 12[a]Rejoice and be exceed-
ingly glad, for great *is* your reward in heaven,
for [b]so they persecuted the prophets who were
before you.

### *BELIEVERS ARE SALT AND LIGHT*
*(Mark 9:50; Luke 14:34, 35)*

13"You are the salt of the earth; [a]but if the
salt loses its flavor, how shall it be seasoned? It
is then good for nothing but to be thrown out
and trampled underfoot by men.
14[a]"You are the light of the world. A city that
is set on a hill cannot be hidden. 15Nor do they
[a]light a lamp and put it under a basket, but on
a lampstand, and it gives light to all *who are* in
the house. 16Let your light so shine before men,
[a]that they may see your good works and [b]glorify
your Father in heaven.

### *CHRIST FULFILLS THE LAW*

17[a]"Do not think that I came to destroy the
Law or the Prophets. I did not come to destroy
but to fulfill. 18For assuredly, I say to you, [a]till
heaven and earth pass away, one jot or one
tittle will by no means pass from the law till all
is fulfilled. 19[a]Whoever therefore breaks one of
the least of these commandments, and teaches
men so, shall be called least in the kingdom of
heaven; but whoever does and teaches *them,* he
shall be called great in the kingdom of heaven.
20For I say to you, that unless your righteous-
ness exceeds [a]*the righteousness* of the scribes
and Pharisees, you will by no means enter the
kingdom of heaven.

**4:15** [a] Is. 9:1, 2 **4:16** [a] Luke 2:32 [1] Isaiah 9:1, 2 **4:17** [a] Mark 1:14, 15 [b] Matt. 3:2; 10:7 **4:18** [a] Mark 1:16–20 [b] John 1:40–42 **4:19** [a] Luke 5:10 **4:20** [a] Mark 10:28 **4:21** [a] Mark 1:19 **4:23** [a] Matt. 9:35 [b] [Matt. 24:14] [c] Mark 1:34 **4:24** [a] Luke 4:40 **4:25** [a] Mark 3:7, 8 **5:1** [a] Mark 3:13 **5:2** [a] [Matt. 7:29] **5:3** [a] Luke 6:20–23 **5:4** [a] Rev. 21:4 **5:5** [a] Ps. 37:11 [b] [Rom. 4:13] **5:6** [a] Luke 1:53 [b] [Is. 55:1; 65:13] **5:7** [a] Ps. 41:1 **5:8** [a] Ps. 15:2; 24:4 [b] 1 Cor. 13:12 **5:10** [a] 1 Pet. 3:14 **5:11** [a] Luke 6:22 [b] 1 Pet. 4:14 **5:12** [a] 1 Pet. 4:13, 14 [b] Acts 7:52 **5:13** [a] Luke 14:34 **5:14** [a] [John 8:12] **5:15** [a] Luke 8:16 **5:16** [a] 1 Pet. 2:12 [b] [John 15:8] **5:17** [a] Rom. 10:4 **5:18** [a] Luke 16:17 **5:19** [a] [James 2:10] **5:20** [a] [Rom. 10:3]

KNOW THE TRUTH

## THE DOCTRINE OF SCRIPTURE

### PART 4: THE AUTHORITY OF SCRIPTURE

**5:17–18** If ever there were someone who could go "off script" and make it work, it would seem to be the God-Man, Jesus Christ. On the contrary, Jesus not only refused to go off script, but He was "by-the-book"—the Scriptures—more than anyone else. Jesus came to "fulfill" Scripture by applying the truth of God's Word in every situation of His life. Scripture was the authoritative basis for His every word and deed. When tempted by the devil, Jesus didn't reply, "In my opinion." Instead, He authoritatively replied, "It is written." (Matt. 4:4) The authority of His messianic ministry was based on His obedience to Scripture (see Luke 4:17–21). His suffering, death, and resurrection were in obedience to Scripture (see Luke 24:44–47).

The Bible has divine authority because its origin is God, not human imagination. All Scripture is God-breathed, coming from God's mind alone (2 Tim. 3:15–17). When we study, apply, and teach the Bible, we do so with divine authority because the Bible isn't our word but God's Word. Like Jesus, our authority to declare what is true comes from one source: Scripture.

*For* **THE DOCTRINE OF SCRIPTURE: PART 5: THE INSPIRATION OF SCRIPTURE**, *turn to 2 Timothy 3:14–17 on page 1236.* •••

### *MURDER BEGINS IN THE HEART*
*(Luke 12:57–59)*

21"You have heard that it was said to those of
old, [a]'You shall not murder,'[1] and whoever mur-
ders will be in danger of the judgment.' 22But I
say to you that [a]whoever is angry with his brother
without a cause[1] shall be in danger of the judg-
ment. And whoever says to his brother, [b]'Raca!'
shall be in danger of the council. But whoever
says, 'You fool!' shall be in danger of hell fire.
23Therefore [a]if you bring your gift to the altar,
and there remember that your brother has some-
thing against you, 24[a]leave your gift there before
the altar, and go your way. First be reconciled
to your brother, and then come and offer your
gift. 25[a]Agree with your adversary quickly, [b]while
you are on the way with him, lest your adversary
deliver you to the judge, the judge hand you over
to the officer, and you be thrown into prison.
26Assuredly, I say to you, you will by no means
get out of there till you have paid the last penny.

### *ADULTERY IN THE HEART*

27"You have heard that it was said to those of
old,[1] [a]'You shall not commit adultery.'[2] 28But I say
to you that whoever [a]looks at a woman to lust for
her has already committed adultery with her in
his heart. 29[a]If your right eye causes you to sin,
[b]pluck it out and cast *it* from you; for it is more
profitable for you that one of your members per-
ish, than for your whole body to be cast into hell.
30And if your right hand causes you to sin, cut it
off and cast *it* from you; for it is more profitable
for you that one of your members perish, than
for your whole body to be cast into hell.

### *MARRIAGE IS SACRED AND BINDING*
*(Matt. 19:9; Mark 10:11, 12; Luke 16:18)*

31"Furthermore it has been said, [a]'Whoever
divorces his wife, let him give her a certificate of
divorce.' 32But I say to you that [a]whoever divorces
his wife for any reason except sexual immorality[1]
causes her to commit adultery; and whoever mar-
ries a woman who is divorced commits adultery.

### *JESUS FORBIDS OATHS*

33"Again you have heard that [a]it was said to
those of old, [b]'You shall not swear falsely, but
[c]shall perform your oaths to the Lord.' 34But I say
to you, [a]do not swear at all: neither by heaven, for
it is [b]God's throne; 35nor by the earth, for it is His
footstool; nor by Jerusalem, for it is the city of [a]the
great King. 36Nor shall you swear by your head,
because you cannot make one hair white or black.
37[a]But let your 'Yes' be 'Yes,' and your 'No,' 'No.' For
whatever is more than these is from the evil one.

### *GO THE SECOND MILE*
*(Luke 6:29–31)*

38"You have heard that it was said, [a]'An eye for
an eye and a tooth for a tooth.'[1] 39[a]But I tell you
not to resist an evil person. [b]But whoever slaps

**5:21** [a] Ex. 20:13; Deut. 5:17 [1] Exodus 20:13; Deuteronomy 5:17 **5:22** [a] [1 John 3:15] [b] [James 2:20; 3:6] [1] NU-Text omits *without a cause.* **5:23** [a] Matt. 8:4 **5:24** [a] [Job 42:8] **5:25** [a] Luke 12:58, 59 [b] [Is. 55:6] **5:27** [a] Ex. 20:14; Deut. 5:18 [1] NU-Text and M-Text omit *to those of old.* [2] Exodus 20:14; Deuteronomy 5:18 **5:28** [a] Prov. 6:25 **5:29** [a] Mark 9:43 [b] [Col. 3:5] **5:31** [a] Deut. 24:1 **5:32** [a] [Luke 16:18] [1] Or *fornication* **5:33** [a] Matt. 23:16 [b] Lev. 19:12 [c] Deut. 23:23 **5:34** [a] James 5:12 [b] Is. 66:1 **5:35** [a] Ps. 48:2 **5:37** [a] [Col. 4:6] **5:38** [a] Ex. 21:24; Lev. 24:20; Deut. 19:21 [1] Exodus 21:24; Leviticus 24:20; Deuteronomy 19:21 **5:39** [a] Luke 6:29 [b] Is. 50:6

you on your right cheek, turn the other to him also. 40 If anyone wants to sue you and take away your tunic, let him have *your* cloak also. 41 And whoever [a]compels you to go one mile, go with him two. 42 Give to him who asks you, and [a]from him who wants to borrow from you do not turn away.

### LOVE YOUR ENEMIES

*(Luke 6:27, 28, 32–36)*

43 "You have heard that it was said, [a]'You shall love your neighbor[1] [b]and hate your enemy.' 44 But I say to you, [a]love your enemies, bless those who curse you, [b]do good to those who hate you, and pray [c]for those who spitefully use you and persecute you,[1] 45 that you may be sons of your Father in heaven; for [a]He makes His sun rise on the evil and on the good, and sends rain on the just and on the unjust. 46 [a]For if you love those who love you, what reward have you? Do not even the tax collectors do the same? 47 And if you greet your brethren[1] only, what do you do more *than others?* Do not even the tax collectors[2] do so? 48 [a]Therefore you shall be perfect, just [b]as your Father in heaven is perfect.

### DO GOOD TO PLEASE GOD

**6** "Take heed that you do not do your charitable deeds before men, to be seen by them. Otherwise you have no reward from your Father in heaven. 2 Therefore, [a]when you do a charitable deed, do not sound a trumpet before you as the hypocrites do in the synagogues and in the streets, that they may have glory from men. Assuredly, I say to you, they have their reward. 3 But when you do a charitable deed, do not let your left hand know what your right hand is doing, 4 that your charitable deed may be in secret; and your Father who sees in secret [a]will Himself reward you openly.[1]

> **6:2** The **reward** the **hypocrites** will receive is to be honored by people, but not by God.

### THE MODEL PRAYER

*(Luke 11:2–4)*

5 "And when you pray, you shall not be like the hypocrites. For they love to pray standing in the synagogues and on the corners of the streets, that they may be seen by men. Assuredly, I say to you, they have their reward. 6 But you, when you pray, [a]go into your room, and when you have shut your door, pray to your Father who *is* in the secret *place;* and your Father who sees in secret will reward you openly.[1] 7 And when you pray, [a]do not use vain repetitions as the heathen *do.* [b]For they think that they will be heard for their many words.

8 "Therefore do not be like them. For your Father [a]knows the things you have need of before you ask Him. 9 In this [a]manner, therefore, pray:

[b]Our Father in heaven,
Hallowed be Your [c]name.
10 Your kingdom come.
[a]Your will be done
On earth [b]as *it is* in heaven.
11 Give us this day our [a]daily bread.
12 And [a]forgive us our debts,
As we forgive our debtors.
13 [a]And do not lead us into temptation,
But [b]deliver us from the evil one.
For Yours is the kingdom and the power
and the glory forever. Amen.[1]

14 [a]"For if you forgive men their trespasses, your heavenly Father will also forgive you. 15 But [a]if you do not forgive men their trespasses, neither will your Father forgive your trespasses.

### FASTING TO BE SEEN ONLY BY GOD

16 "Moreover, [a]when you fast, do not be like the hypocrites, with a sad countenance. For they disfigure their faces that they may appear to men to be fasting. Assuredly, I say to you, they have their reward. 17 But you, when you fast, [a]anoint your head and wash your face, 18 so that you do not appear to men to be fasting, but to your Father who *is* in the secret *place;* and your Father who sees in secret will reward you openly.[1]

### LAY UP TREASURES IN HEAVEN

*(Luke 12:33, 34)*

19 [a]"Do not lay up for yourselves treasures on earth, where moth and rust destroy and where thieves break in and steal; 20 [a]but lay up for yourselves treasures in heaven, where neither moth nor rust destroys and where thieves do not break in and steal. 21 For where your treasure is, there your heart will be also.

### THE LAMP OF THE BODY

*(Luke 11:34–36)*

22 [a]"The lamp of the body is the eye. If therefore your eye is good, your whole body will be full of light. 23 But if your eye is bad, your whole body will be full of darkness. If therefore the light that is in you is darkness, how great *is* that darkness!

### YOU CANNOT SERVE GOD AND RICHES

24 [a]"No one can serve two masters; for either he will hate the one and love the other, or else

**5:41** [a] Matt. 27:32 **5:42** [a] Luke 6:30–34 **5:43** [a] Lev. 19:18 [b] Deut. 23:3–6 [1] Compare Leviticus 19:18 **5:44** [a] Luke 6:27 [b] [Rom. 12:20] [c] Acts 7:60 [1] NU-Text omits three clauses from this verse, leaving, *"But I say to you, love your enemies and pray for those who persecute you."* **5:45** [a] Job 25:3 **5:46** [a] Luke 6:32 **5:47** [1] M-Text reads *friends.* [2] NU-Text reads *Gentiles.* **5:48** [a] [Col. 1:28; 4:12] [b] Eph. 5:1 **6:2** [a] Rom. 12:8 **6:4** [a] Luke 14:12–14 [1] NU-Text omits *openly.* **6:6** [a] 2 Kin. 4:33 [1] NU-Text omits *openly.* **6:7** [a] Eccl. 5:2 [b] 1 Kin. 18:26 **6:8** [a] [Rom. 8:26, 27] **6:9** [a] Luke 11:2–4 [b] [Matt. 5:9, 16] [c] Mal. 1:11 **6:10** [a] Matt. 26:42 [b] Ps. 103:20 **6:11** [a] Prov. 30:8 **6:12** [a] [Matt. 18:21, 22] **6:13** [a] [2 Pet. 2:9] [b] John 17:15 [1] NU-Text omits *For Yours* through *Amen.* **6:14** [a] Mark 11:25 **6:15** [a] Matt. 18:35 **6:16** [a] Is. 58:3–7 **6:17** [a] Ruth 3:3 **6:18** [1] NU-Text and M-Text omit *openly.* **6:19** [a] Prov. 23:4 **6:20** [a] Matt. 19:21 **6:22** [a] Luke 11:34, 35 **6:24** [a] Luke 16:9, 11, 13

he will be loyal to the one and despise the other.
[b]You cannot serve God and mammon.

### *DO NOT WORRY*
*(Luke 12:22–31)*

25 “Therefore I say to you, [a]do not worry
about your life, what you will eat or what you
will drink; nor about your body, what you will
put on. Is not life more than food and the body
more than clothing? 26 [a]Look at the birds of the
air, for they neither sow nor reap nor gather into
barns; yet your heavenly Father feeds them. Are
you not of more value than they? 27 Which of you
by worrying can add one cubit to his stature?
28 “So why do you worry about clothing? Con-
sider the lilies of the field, how they grow: they
neither toil nor spin; 29 and yet I say to you that
even Solomon in all his glory was not arrayed
like one of these. 30 Now if God so clothes the
grass of the field, which today is, and tomorrow
is thrown into the oven, *will He* not much more
*clothe* you, O you of little faith?
31 “Therefore do not worry, saying, ‘What
shall we eat?’ or ‘What shall we drink?’ or ‘What
shall we wear?’ 32 For after all these things the
Gentiles seek. For your heavenly Father knows
that you need all these things. 33 But [a]seek first
the kingdom of God and His righteousness, and
all these things shall be added to you. 34 There-
fore do not worry about tomorrow, for tomorrow
will worry about its own things. Sufficient for
the day *is* its own trouble.

### *DO NOT JUDGE*
*(Luke 6:37–42)*

7 “Judge [a]not, that you be not judged. 2 For
with what judgment you judge, you will be
judged; [a]and with the measure you use, it will be
measured back to you. 3 [a]And why do you look
at the speck in your brother’s eye, but do not
consider the plank in your own eye? 4 Or how
can you say to your brother, ‘Let me remove
the speck from your eye’; and look, a plank *is*
in your own eye? 5 Hypocrite! First remove the
plank from your own eye, and then you will see
clearly to remove the speck from your brother’s
eye.
6 [a]“Do not give what is holy to the dogs; nor
cast your pearls before swine, lest they trample
them under their feet, and turn and tear you
in pieces.

> **7:1–2** The point of these verses is that we must not **judge** or criticize in a way that we would not want to be **judged** or criticized. Every judgment a person makes becomes a basis for his or her own judgment (see James 3:1–2).

### *KEEP ASKING, SEEKING, KNOCKING*
*(Luke 11:9–13)*

7 [a]“Ask, and it will be given to you; seek, and
you will find; knock, and it will be opened to
you. 8 For [a]everyone who asks receives, and he
who seeks finds, and to him who knocks it will
be opened. 9 [a]Or what man is there among you
who, if his son asks for bread, will give him a
stone? 10 Or if he asks for a fish, will he give him
a serpent? 11 If you then, [a]being evil, know how
to give good gifts to your children, how much
more will your Father who is in heaven give
good things to those who ask Him! 12 There-
fore, [a]whatever you want men to do to you,
do also to them, for [b]this is the Law and the
Prophets.

**6:24** [b] [Gal. 1:10] **6:25** [a] Luke 12:22 **6:26** [a] Luke 12:24 **6:33** [a] [1 Tim. 4:8] **7:1** [a] Rom. 14:3 **7:2** [a] Luke 6:38 **7:3** [a] Luke 6:41 **7:6** [a] Prov. 9:7, 8 **7:7** [a] [Mark 11:24] **7:8** [a] Prov. 8:17 **7:9** [a] Luke 11:11 **7:11** [a] Gen. 6:5; 8:21 **7:12** [a] Luke 6:31 [b] Gal. 5:14

APPLY THE TRUTH

## WORRY

**6:25–34** When you’re worrying, one of the worst things someone can say is “don’t worry.” That doesn’t seem to help much, does it? If you could just *not* worry, then you wouldn’t be worrying! But that’s exactly what Jesus tells us here. Are you worrying? Well, then don’t. But what Jesus says after this is what makes it possible. He brings life into perspective. The birds don’t have grocery stores or jobs, yet they eat every day. How? Because God feeds them. Likewise, flowers don’t make any clothing, but they are stunning in their appearance because God dresses them.

God feeds the birds and clothes the flowers because He cares for them. How much more does He care for us? Is it reasonable that He wouldn’t take even greater care of us? Jesus is telling us that when we worry about things like how we look, provision, and protection, we need to think more about God’s care for us and His resources. He knows our needs; He wants to provide for them, and He can do that. Take comfort in this. It won’t automatically turn your worry off, but it will give you perspective. God knows. God cares. God provides.

APPLY THE TRUTH

## PLURALISM

**7:13–14** The next time you go somewhere, head in any direction you want and make whatever turns you feel like making. Do you think you'll reach your destination? Hardly, right? We know this is nonsense. To get to the right destination, we must head in the right direction. But this is how many people see life. They believe all beliefs and lifestyles are the same, a philosophy called pluralism. No belief is more right or wrong than any other. They're all the same.

Pluralism may be popular, but it isn't compatible with the Christian faith. All religions and beliefs aren't the same. They don't all reach God. It's only through faith *in* Jesus that we can be saved and made righteous *by* Jesus. There's no other way. Some think that this message of Jesus is too exclusive, arrogant, and unfair. If God is so loving, how could He turn sincere people away just because they're on a different path? But the gospel isn't exclusive; it's *specific*. It would be unloving for Jesus to invite us to His house but not give us directions to get there. He has in the Bible. There's only one path to God, but Jesus has made that path, and He invites *all* to travel it.

### *THE NARROW WAY*

*(Luke 13:24)*

13 [a]"Enter by the narrow gate; for wide *is* the gate and broad *is* the way that leads to destruction, and there are many who go in by it. 14 Because[1] narrow *is* the gate and difficult *is* the way which leads to life, and there are few who find it.

### *YOU WILL KNOW THEM BY THEIR FRUITS*

*(Matt. 12:33; Luke 6:43–45)*

15 [a]"Beware of false prophets, [b]who come to you in sheep's clothing, but inwardly they are ravenous wolves. 16 [a]You will know them by their fruits. [b]Do men gather grapes from thornbushes or figs from thistles? 17 Even so, [a]every good tree bears good fruit, but a bad tree bears bad fruit. 18 A good tree cannot bear bad fruit, nor *can* a bad tree bear good fruit. 19 [a]Every tree that does not bear good fruit is cut down and thrown into the fire. 20 Therefore by their fruits you will know them.

### *I NEVER KNEW YOU*

*(Luke 6:46; 13:26, 27)*

21 "Not everyone who says to Me, [a]'Lord, Lord,' shall enter the kingdom of heaven, but he who [b]does the will of My Father in heaven. 22 Many will say to Me in that day, 'Lord, Lord, have we [a]not prophesied in Your name, cast out demons in Your name, and done many wonders in Your name?' 23 And [a]then I will declare to them, 'I never knew you; [b]depart from Me, you who practice lawlessness!'

**SEEING JESUS IN THE SCRIPTURE**

**7:23** When Jesus returns for the final judgment of the lost, they will hear these tragic, final words (see Rev. 20:11–15).

### *BUILD ON THE ROCK*

*(Luke 6:47–49)*

24 "Therefore [a]whoever hears these sayings of Mine, and does them, I will liken him to a wise man who built his house on the rock: 25 and the rain descended, the floods came, and the winds blew and beat on that house; and it did not fall, for it was founded on the rock.

26 "But everyone who hears these sayings of Mine, and does not do them, will be like a foolish man who built his house on the sand: 27 and the rain descended, the floods came, and the winds blew and beat on that house; and it fell. And great was its fall."

28 And so it was, when Jesus had ended these sayings, that [a]the people were astonished at His teaching, 29 [a]for He taught them as one having authority, and not as the scribes.

### *JESUS CLEANSES A LEPER*

*(Mark 1:40–45; Luke 5:12–16)*

**8** When He had come down from the mountain, great multitudes followed Him. 2 [a]And behold, a leper came and [b]worshiped Him, saying, "Lord, if You are willing, You can make me clean."

3 Then Jesus put out *His* hand and touched him, saying, "I am willing; be cleansed." Immediately his leprosy [a]was cleansed.

4 And Jesus said to him, [a]"See that you tell no one; but go your way, show yourself to the priest,

**7:13** [a] Luke 13:24 **7:14** [1] NU-Text and M-Text read *How . . . !* **7:15** [a] Jer. 23:16 [b] Mic. 3:5 **7:16** [a] Matt. 7:20; 12:33 [b] Luke 6:43 **7:17** [a] Jer. 11:19; Matt. 12:33 **7:19** [a] Matt. 3:10; Luke 3:9; [John 15:2, 6] **7:21** [a] Hos. 8:2; Matt. 25:11; Luke 6:46; Acts 19:13 [b] Rom. 2:13; James 1:22 **7:22** [a] Num. 24:4 **7:23** [a] Matt. 25:12; Luke 13:25; [2 Tim. 2:19] [b] Ps. 5:5; 6:8; [Matt. 25:41]; Luke 13:27 **7:24** [a] Matt. 7:24–27; Luke 6:47–49 **7:28** [a] Matt. 13:54; Mark 1:22; 6:2; Luke 4:32; John 7:46 **7:29** [a] [John 7:46] **8:2** [a] Matt. 8:2–4; Mark 1:40–45; Luke 5:12–14 [b] Matt. 2:11; 9:18; 15:25; John 9:38; Acts 10:25 **8:3** [a] Matt. 11:5; Luke 4:27 **8:4** [a] Matt. 9:30; Mark 5:43; Luke 4:41; 8:56; 9:21

and offer the gift that [b]Moses [c]commanded, as a testimony to them."

### *JESUS HEALS A CENTURION'S SERVANT*
*(Luke 7:1–10)*

5 [a]Now when Jesus had entered Capernaum, a [b]centurion came to Him, pleading with Him, 6 saying, "Lord, my servant is lying at home paralyzed, dreadfully tormented."

7 And Jesus said to him, "I will come and heal him."

8 The centurion answered and said, "Lord, [a]I am not worthy that You should come under my roof. But only [b]speak a word, and my servant will be healed. 9 For I also am a man under authority, having soldiers under me. And I say to this *one,* 'Go,' and he goes; and to another, 'Come,' and he comes; and to my servant, 'Do this,' and he does *it.*"

10 When Jesus heard *it,* He marveled, and said to those who followed, "Assuredly, I say to you, I have not found such great faith, not even in Israel! 11 And I say to you that [a]many will come from east and west, and sit down with Abraham, Isaac, and Jacob in the kingdom of heaven. 12 But [a]the sons of the kingdom [b]will be cast out into outer darkness. There will be weeping and gnashing of teeth." 13 Then Jesus said to the centurion, "Go your way; and as you have believed, *so* let it be done for you." And his servant was healed that same hour.

> **SEEING JESUS IN THE SCRIPTURE**
>
> **8:11** Though the promise of salvation came through Israel, salvation through faith in Christ is for everyone (see Mal. 1:11).

### *PETER'S MOTHER-IN-LAW HEALED*
*(Mark 1:29–31; Luke 4:38, 39)*

14 [a]Now when Jesus had come into Peter's house, He saw [b]his wife's mother lying sick with a fever. 15 So He touched her hand, and the fever left her. And she arose and served them.[1]

### *MANY HEALED IN THE EVENING*
*(Mark 1:32–34; Luke 4:40, 41)*

16 [a]When evening had come, they brought to Him many who were demon-possessed. And He cast out the spirits with a word, and healed all who were sick, 17 that it might be fulfilled which was spoken by Isaiah the prophet, saying:

[a]"He Himself took our infirmities
And bore *our* sicknesses."[1]

> **SEEING JESUS IN THE SCRIPTURE**
>
> **8:16–17** Jesus healed sicknesses and took our greatest infirmity, sin, on Himself, fulfilling prophecy (see Is. 53:4).

### *THE COST OF DISCIPLESHIP*
*(Luke 9:57–62)*

18 And when Jesus saw great multitudes about Him, He gave a command to depart to the other side. 19 [a]Then a certain scribe came and said to Him, "Teacher, I will follow You wherever You go."

20 And Jesus said to him, "Foxes have holes and birds of the air *have* nests, but the Son of Man has nowhere to lay *His* head."

21 [a]Then another of His disciples said to Him, "Lord, [b]let me first go and bury my father."

22 But Jesus said to him, "Follow Me, and let the dead bury their own dead."

### *WIND AND WAVE OBEY JESUS*
*(Mark 4:35–41; Luke 8:22–25)*

23 Now when He got into a boat, His disciples followed Him. 24 [a]And suddenly a great tempest arose on the sea, so that the boat was covered with the waves. But He was asleep. 25 Then His disciples came to *Him* and awoke Him, saying, "Lord, save us! We are perishing!"

26 But He said to them, "Why are you fearful, O you of little faith?" Then [a]He arose and rebuked the winds and the sea, and there was a great calm. 27 So the men marveled, saying, "Who can this be, that even the winds and the sea obey Him?"

### *TWO DEMON-POSSESSED MEN HEALED*
*(Mark 5:1–20; Luke 8:26–39)*

28 [a]When He had come to the other side, to the country of the Gergesenes,[1] there met Him two demon-possessed *men,* coming out of the tombs, exceedingly fierce, so that no one could pass that way. 29 And suddenly they cried out, saying, "What have we to do with You, Jesus, You Son of God? Have You come here to torment us before the time?"

30 Now a good way off from them there was a herd of many swine feeding. 31 So the demons begged Him, saying, "If You cast us out, permit us to go away[1] into the herd of swine."

32 And He said to them, "Go." So when they had come out, they went into the herd of swine. And suddenly the whole herd of swine ran violently down the steep place into the sea, and perished in the water.

33 Then those who kept *them* fled; and they went away into the city and told everything,

8:4 [b] Lev. 14:3, 4, 10; Mark 1:44; Luke 5:14 [c] Lev. 14:4–32; Deut. 24:8 8:5 [a] Luke 7:1–3 [b] Matt. 27:54; Acts 10:1 8:8 [a] Luke 15:19, 21 [b] Ps. 107:20 8:11 [a] Is. 2:2, 3; Mal. 1:11 8:12 [a] [Matt. 21:43] [b] Matt. 13:42, 50; 22:13; 24:51; 25:30; Luke 13:28; 2 Pet. 2:17; Jude 13 8:14 [a] Matt. 8:14–16; Mark 1:29–31; Luke 4:38, 39 [b] 1 Cor. 9:5 8:15 [1] NU-Text and M-Text read *Him.* 8:16 [a] Mark 1:32–34; Luke 4:40, 41 8:17 [a] Is. 53:4; 1 Pet. 2:24 [1] Isaiah 53:4 8:19 [a] Matt. 8:19–22; Luke 9:57, 58 8:21 [a] Luke 9:59, 60 [b] 1 Kin. 19:20 8:24 [a] Mark 4:37; Luke 8:23–25 8:26 [a] Ps. 65:7; 89:9; 107:29 8:28 [a] Mark 5:1–4; Luke 8:26–33 [1] NU-Text reads *Gadarenes.* 8:31 [1] NU-Text reads *send us.*

including what *had happened* to the demon-
possessed *men.* 34 And behold, the whole city
came out to meet Jesus. And when they saw Him,
[a]they begged *Him* to depart from their region.

### *JESUS FORGIVES AND HEALS A PARALYTIC*

*(Mark 2:1–12; Luke 5:17–26)*

9 So He got into a boat, crossed over, [a]and came
to His own city. 2 [a]Then behold, they brought
to Him a paralytic lying on a bed. [b]When Jesus
saw their faith, He said to the paralytic, "Son,
be of good cheer; your sins are forgiven you."
3 And at once some of the scribes said within
themselves, "This Man blasphemes!"
4 But Jesus, [a]knowing their thoughts, said,
"Why do you think evil in your hearts? 5 For
which is easier, to say, '*Your* sins are forgiven
you,' or to say, 'Arise and walk'? 6 But that you
may know that the Son of Man has power on
earth to forgive sins"—then He said to the par-
alytic, "Arise, take up your bed, and go to your
house." 7 And he arose and departed to his house.
8 Now when the multitudes saw *it,* they [a]mar-
veled[1] and glorified God, who had given such
power to men.

### *MATTHEW THE TAX COLLECTOR*

*(Mark 2:13–17; Luke 5:27–32)*

9 [a]As Jesus passed on from there, He saw a
man named Matthew sitting at the tax office.
And He said to him, "Follow Me." So he arose
and followed Him.

> **9:9** The Romans taxed everything from property to imported goods to fishing rights. They even collected taxes from the Jews for worshiping at the temple, claiming that the money was used to pay for the upkeep of the building. Tax collectors were often despised not only because they were seen as traitors, working for the hated Roman government, but also because they generally collected more than necessary and pocketed the difference. The average Jewish household may have been taxed as much as 40 percent of their income.

10 [a]Now it happened, as Jesus sat at the table
in the house, *that* behold, many tax collectors
and sinners came and sat down with Him and
His disciples. 11 And when the Pharisees saw
*it,* they said to His disciples, "Why does your
Teacher eat with [a]tax collectors and [b]sinners?"
12 When Jesus heard *that,* He said to them,
"Those who are well have no need of a physician,
but those who are sick. 13 But go and learn what
*this* means: [a]'I desire mercy and not sacrifice.'[1]
For I did not come to call the righteous, [b]but
sinners, to repentance."[2]

### *JESUS IS QUESTIONED ABOUT FASTING*

*(Mark 2:18–22; Luke 5:33–39)*

14 Then the disciples of John came to Him,
saying, [a]"Why do we and the Pharisees fast often,[1]
but Your disciples do not fast?"
15 And Jesus said to them, "Can [a]the friends
of the bridegroom mourn as long as the bride-
groom is with them? But the days will come
when the bridegroom will be taken away from
them, and [b]then they will fast. 16 No one puts a
piece of unshrunk cloth on an old garment; for
the patch pulls away from the garment, and the
tear is made worse. 17 Nor do they put new wine
into old wineskins, or else the wineskins break,
the wine is spilled, and the wineskins are ruined.
But they put new wine into new wineskins, and
both are preserved."

> **9:17** A wineskin was a bag used for storing liquids in the days before bottles. It was like a canteen made of the hide (or skin) of a goat or another animal. When grape juice was stored in **new wineskins**, the fermentation process made these wineskins stretch and swell. The more a wineskin aged, the more stiff and brittle it became. When grape juice was poured into **old wineskins**, often they would **break**.

### *A GIRL RESTORED TO LIFE AND A WOMAN HEALED*

*(Mark 5:21–43; Luke 8:40–56)*

18 [a]While He spoke these things to them,
behold, a ruler came and worshiped Him, say-
ing, "My daughter has just died, but come and
lay Your hand on her and she will live." 19 So
Jesus arose and followed him, and so *did* His
[a]disciples.
20 [a]And suddenly, a woman who had a flow
of blood for twelve years came from behind and
[b]touched the hem of His garment. 21 For she said
to herself, "If only I may touch His garment, I
shall be made well." 22 But Jesus turned around,
and when He saw her He said, "Be of good cheer,
daughter; [a]your faith has made you well." And
the woman was made well from that hour.
23 [a]When Jesus came into the ruler's house,
and saw [b]the flute players and the noisy crowd

**8:34** [a] Deut. 5:25; 1 Kin. 17:18; Amos 7:12; Luke 5:8; Acts 16:39 **9:1** [a] Matt. 4:13; 11:23; Mark 5:21 **9:2** [a] Mark 2:3–12; Luke 5:18–26 [b] Matt. 8:10 **9:4** [a] Ps. 139:2; Matt. 12:25; Mark 12:15; Luke 5:22; 6:8; 9:47; 11:17 **9:8** [a] Matt. 8:27; John 7:15 [1] NU-Text reads *were afraid.* **9:9** [a] Mark 2:14; Luke 5:27 **9:10** [a] Mark 2:15; Luke 5:29 **9:11** [a] Matt. 11:19; Mark 2:16; Luke 5:30; 15:2 [b] [Gal. 2:15] **9:13** [a] Hos. 6:6; [Mic. 6:6–8]; Matt. 12:7 [b] Mark 2:17; Luke 5:32; 1 Tim. 1:15 [1] Hosea 6:6 [2] NU-Text omits *to repentance.* **9:14** [a] Mark 2:18; Luke 5:33–35; 18:12 [1] NU-Text brackets *often* as disputed. **9:15** [a] John 3:29 [b] Acts 13:2, 3; 14:23 **9:18** [a] Luke 8:41–56 **9:19** [a] Matt. 10:2–4 **9:20** [a] Luke 8:43 [b] Matt. 14:36; 23:5 **9:22** [a] Luke 7:50; 8:48; 17:19; 18:42 **9:23** [a] Mark 5:38 [b] 2 Chr. 35:25

wailing, 24 He said to them, [a]"Make room, for the girl is not dead, but sleeping." And they ridiculed Him. 25 But when the crowd was put outside, He went in and [a]took her by the hand, and the girl arose. 26 And the [a]report of this went out into all that land.

### TWO BLIND MEN HEALED

27 When Jesus departed from there, [a]two blind men followed Him, crying out and saying, [b]"Son of David, have mercy on us!"

28 And when He had come into the house, the blind men came to Him. And Jesus said to them, "Do you believe that I am able to do this?"

They said to Him, "Yes, Lord."

29 Then He touched their eyes, saying, "According to your faith let it be to you." 30 And their eyes were opened. And Jesus sternly warned them, saying, [a]"See *that* no one knows *it.*" 31 [a]But when they had departed, they spread the news about Him in all that country.

### A MUTE MAN SPEAKS

32 [a]As they went out, behold, they brought to Him a man, mute and demon-possessed. 33 And when the demon was cast out, the mute spoke. And the multitudes marveled, saying, "It was never seen like this in Israel!"

34 But the Pharisees said, [a]"He casts out demons by the ruler of the demons."

### THE COMPASSION OF JESUS
*(Luke 10:2, 3)*

35 Then Jesus went about all the cities and villages, [a]teaching in their synagogues, preaching the gospel of the kingdom, and healing every sickness and every disease among the people.[1] 36 [a]But when He saw the multitudes, He was moved with compassion for them, because they were weary[1] and scattered, [b]like sheep having no shepherd. 37 Then He said to His disciples, [a]"The harvest truly *is* plentiful, but the laborers *are* few. 38 [a]Therefore pray the Lord of the harvest to send out laborers into His harvest."

### THE TWELVE APOSTLES
*(Mark 3:13–19; Luke 6:12–16)*

**10** And [a]when He had called His twelve disciples to *Him,* He gave them power *over* unclean spirits, to cast them out, and to heal all kinds of sickness and all kinds of disease. 2 Now the names of the twelve apostles are these: first, Simon, [a]who is called Peter, and Andrew his brother; James the *son* of Zebedee, and John his brother; 3 Philip and Bartholomew; Thomas and Matthew the tax collector; James the *son* of Alphaeus, and Lebbaeus, whose surname was[1] Thaddaeus; 4 [a]Simon the Cananite,[1] and Judas [b]Iscariot, who also betrayed Him.

### SENDING OUT THE TWELVE
*(Mark 6:7–13; Luke 9:1–6)*

5 These twelve Jesus sent out and commanded them, saying: [a]"Do not go into the way of the Gentiles, and do not enter a city of [b]the Samaritans. 6 [a]But go rather to the [b]lost sheep of the house of Israel. 7 [a]And as you go, preach, saying, [b]'The kingdom of heaven is at hand.' 8 Heal the sick, cleanse the lepers, raise the dead,[1] cast out demons. [a]Freely you have received, freely give. 9 [a]Provide neither gold nor silver nor [b]copper in your money belts, 10 nor bag for *your* journey, nor two tunics, nor sandals, nor staffs; [a]for a worker is worthy of his food.

11 [a]"Now whatever city or town you enter, inquire who in it is worthy, and stay there till you go out. 12 And when you go into a household, greet it. 13 [a]If the household is worthy, let your peace come upon it. [b]But if it is not worthy, let your peace return to you. 14 [a]And whoever will not receive you nor hear your words, when you depart from that house or city, [b]shake off the dust from your feet. 15 Assuredly, I say to you, [a]it will be more tolerable for the land of Sodom and Gomorrah in the day of judgment than for that city!

### PERSECUTIONS ARE COMING
*(Mark 13:9–13; Luke 21:12–17)*

16 [a]"Behold, I send you out as sheep in the midst of wolves. [b]Therefore be wise as serpents and [c]harmless as doves. 17 But beware of men, for [a]they will deliver you up to councils and [b]scourge you in their synagogues. 18 [a]You will be brought before governors and kings for My sake, as a testimony to them and to the Gentiles. 19 [a]But when they deliver you up, do not worry about how or what you should speak. For [b]it will be given to you in that hour what you should speak; 20 [a]for it is not you who speak, but the Spirit of your Father who speaks in you.

21 [a]"Now brother will deliver up brother to death, and a father *his* child; and children will rise up against parents and cause them to be put to death. 22 And [a]you will be hated by all for My name's sake. [b]But he who endures to the end will be saved. 23 [a]When they persecute you in this city, flee to another. For assuredly, I say to you, you will not have [b]gone through the cities of Israel [c]before the Son of Man comes.

**9:24** [a] Acts 20:10 **9:25** [a] Mark 1:31 **9:26** [a] Matt. 4:24 **9:27** [a] Matt. 20:29–34 [b] Luke 18:38, 39 **9:30** [a] Matt. 8:4 **9:31** [a] Mark 7:36 **9:32** [a] Matt. 12:22, 24 **9:34** [a] Luke 11:15 **9:35** [a] Matt. 4:23 [1] NU-Text omits *among the people.* **9:36** [a] Mark 6:34 [b] Num. 27:17 [1] NU-Text and M-Text read *harassed.* **9:37** [a] Luke 10:2 **9:38** [a] 2 Thess. 3:1 **10:1** [a] Luke 6:13 **10:2** [a] John 1:42 **10:3** [1] NU-Text omits *Lebbaeus, whose surname was.* **10:4** [a] Acts 1:13 [b] John 13:2, 26 [1] NU-Text reads *Cananaean.* **10:5** [a] Matt. 4:15 [b] John 4:9 **10:6** [a] Matt. 15:24 [b] Jer. 50:6 **10:7** [a] Luke 9:2 [b] Matt. 3:2 **10:8** [a] [Acts 8:18] [1] NU-Text reads *raise the dead, cleanse the lepers;* M-Text omits *raise the dead.* **10:9** [a] 1 Sam. 9:7 [b] Mark 6:8 **10:10** [a] 1 Tim. 5:18 **10:11** [a] Luke 10:8 **10:13** [a] Luke 10:5 [b] Ps. 35:13 **10:14** [a] Mark 6:11 [b] Acts 13:51 **10:15** [a] Matt. 11:22, 24 **10:16** [a] Luke 10:3 [b] Eph. 5:15 [c] [Phil. 2:14–16] **10:17** [a] Mark 13:9 [b] Acts 5:40; 22:19; 26:11 **10:18** [a] 2 Tim. 4:16 **10:19** [a] Luke 12:11, 12; 21:14, 15 [b] Ex. 4:12 **10:20** [a] 2 Sam. 23:2 **10:21** [a] Mic. 7:6 **10:22** [a] Luke 21:17 [b] Mark 13:13 **10:23** [a] Acts 8:1 [b] [Mark 13:10] [c] Matt. 16:28

24 [a]“A disciple is not above *his* teacher, nor
a servant above his master. 25 It is enough for a
disciple that he be like his teacher, and a servant
like his master. If [a]they have called the master
of the house Beelzebub,[1] how much more *will*
*they call* those of his household! 26 Therefore
do not fear them. [a]For there is nothing covered
that will not be revealed, and hidden that will
not be known.

### *JESUS TEACHES THE FEAR OF GOD*
*(Luke 12:3–7)*

27 “Whatever I tell you in the dark, [a]speak in
the light; and what you hear in the ear, preach
on the housetops. 28 [a]And do not fear those who
kill the body but cannot kill the soul. But rather
[b]fear Him who is able to destroy both soul and
body in hell. 29 Are not two [a]sparrows sold for
a copper coin? And not one of them falls to the
ground apart from your Father's will. 30 [a]But the
very hairs of your head are all numbered. 31 Do
not fear therefore; you are of more value than
many sparrows.

### *CONFESS CHRIST BEFORE MEN*
*(Luke 12:8, 9)*

32 [a]“Therefore whoever confesses Me before
men, [b]him I will also confess before My Father
who is in heaven. 33 [a]But whoever denies Me
before men, him I will also deny before My
Father who is in heaven.

### *CHRIST BRINGS DIVISION*
*(Luke 12:51–53; 14:26, 27)*

34 [a]“Do not think that I came to bring peace
on earth. I did not come to bring peace but a
sword. 35 For I have come to [a]‘set a man against
his father, a daughter against her mother, and
a daughter-in-law against her mother-in-law';
36 and [a]‘a man's enemies *will be* those of his *own*
household.'[1] 37 [a]He who loves father or mother
more than Me is not worthy of Me. And he who
loves son or daughter more than Me is not wor-
thy of Me. 38 [a]And he who does not take his cross
and follow after Me is not worthy of Me. 39 [a]He
who finds his life will lose it, and he who loses
his life for My sake will find it.

> **10:38** To **take a cross** means to be committed to the extent of being willing to die for something.

### *A CUP OF COLD WATER*
*(Mark 9:41)*

40 [a]“He who receives you receives Me, and
he who receives Me receives Him who sent Me.
41 [a]He who receives a prophet in the name of a
prophet shall receive a prophet's reward. And
he who receives a righteous man in the name of
a righteous man shall receive a righteous man's
reward. 42 [a]And whoever gives one of these little
ones only a cup of cold *water* in the name of a
disciple, assuredly, I say to you, he shall by no
means lose his reward.”

### *JOHN THE BAPTIST SENDS MESSENGERS TO JESUS*
*(Luke 7:18–35)*

11 Now it came to pass, when Jesus finished
commanding His twelve disciples, that He
departed from there to [a]teach and to preach in
their cities.
2 [a]And when John had heard [b]in prison about
the works of Christ, he sent two of[1] his disciples

**10:24** [a] John 15:20 **10:25** [a] John 8:48, 52 [1] NU-Text and M-Text read *Beelzebul.* **10:26** [a] Mark 4:22 **10:27** [a] Acts 5:20 **10:28** [a] Luke 12:4 [b] Luke 12:5 **10:29** [a] Luke 12:6, 7 **10:30** [a] Luke 21:18 **10:32** [a] Luke 12:8 [b] [Rev. 3:5] **10:33** [a] 2 Tim. 2:12 **10:34** [a] [Luke 12:49] **10:35** [a] Mic. 7:6 **10:36** [a] John 13:18 [1] Micah 7:6 **10:37** [a] Luke 14:26 **10:38** [a] [Mark 8:34] **10:39** [a] John 12:25 **10:40** [a] Luke 9:48 **10:41** [a] 1 Kin. 17:10 **10:42** [a] Mark 9:41 **11:1** [a] Luke 23:5 **11:2** [a] Luke 7:18–35 [b] Matt. 4:12; 14:3 [1] NU-Text reads *by* for *two of.*

APPLY THE TRUTH

## FAME

**10:40–41** Have you ever heard the phrase, “They had their fifteen seconds of fame”? It's the idea that someone will burst into the spotlight because of a viral video, catchy song, or part in a show, but just as quickly as they became famous, they disappear. This is the problem with fame. You're celebrated one day and forgotten the next. People's interests and opinions can change as quickly as the tides of the ocean. When we live for the approval of people, we subject ourselves to something evasive and fleeting.

Instead, we should live for an audience of one—God. His opinion doesn't change. He is the same yesterday, today, and forever. Living for God as our sole audience allows us to use whatever fame we might get as an opportunity to point others to Him. The goal isn't for people to accept us and become famous, but for them to accept Christ and add to His fame. Our fame isn't necessarily bad. But if you live for the applause of people, you'll die from their criticism. Rather, if you get famous, give glory to God and live for His glory so others may come to experience it too.

LIVE THE TRUTH

## HOLDING ON TO HOPE

**11:2–6** We all need hope, the belief the best is yet to come. As Christians, we hope differently. The world hopes with uncertainty; believers hope with confidence. The reason is our hope is based on Jesus and the truth of God's Word. When Jesus is at work, and He always is, there's hope. He's at work changing, guiding, and restoring. It might not happen in the timing and manner we want, but God's plan is perfect. Even when we don't see or understand, we can have confidence that our hope is in the right place. If we hope in Christ, we will never be disappointed.

When John the Baptist was imprisoned, doubts crept into his mind and heart about Jesus. John had committed his life to preparing the way for Jesus' ministry, one he expected to change the world. But John became the victim of the same old corrupt systems. His confidence was shaken because his circumstances weren't what he expected. Jesus' answer is instructive. He told John to see differently; He was indeed changing the world. The effects of sin were being reversed. The victory wasn't yet in full, but it was in progress. This is what we must remember also. Each day can be better than yesterday because Jesus is at work. But no matter what, a perfect tomorrow is coming.

3 and said to Him, "Are You [a]the Coming One, or
do we look for another?"
4 Jesus answered and said to them, "Go and
tell John the things which you hear and see:
5 [a]*The* blind see and *the* lame walk; *the* lepers are
cleansed and *the* deaf hear; *the* dead are raised
up and [b]*the* poor have the gospel preached to
them. 6 And blessed is he who is not [a]offended
because of Me."
7 [a]As they departed, Jesus began to say to the
multitudes concerning John: "What did you go
out into the wilderness to see? [b]A reed shaken
by the wind? 8 But what did you go out to see?
A man clothed in soft garments? Indeed, those
who wear soft *clothing* are in kings' houses. 9 But
what did you go out to see? A prophet? Yes, I say
to you, [a]and more than a prophet. 10 For this is
*he* of whom it is written:

[a]'Behold, I send My messenger before Your
face,
Who will prepare Your way before You.'[1]

### SEEING JESUS IN THE SCRIPTURE

**11:10** Jesus affirmed John's identity as Malachi's promised forerunner of the Messiah, and in doing so, affirmed His own identity as the Messiah (see Mal. 3:1).

11 "Assuredly, I say to you, among those born
of women there has not risen one greater than
John the Baptist; but he who is least in the
kingdom of heaven is greater than he. 12 [a]And
from the days of John the Baptist until now the
kingdom of heaven suffers violence, and the
violent take it by force. 13 [a]For all the prophets
and the law prophesied until John. 14 And if you
are willing to receive *it,* he is [a]Elijah who is to
come. 15 [a]He who has ears to hear, let him hear!
16 [a]"But to what shall I liken this generation?
It is like children sitting in the marketplaces
and calling to their companions, 17 and saying:

'We played the flute for you,
And you did not dance;
We mourned to you,
And you did not lament.'

18 For John came neither eating nor drinking,
and they say, 'He has a demon.' 19 The Son of
Man came eating and drinking, and they say,
'Look, a glutton and a winebibber, [a]a friend
of tax collectors and sinners!' [b]But wisdom is
justified by her children."[1]

### *WOE TO THE IMPENITENT CITIES*
*(Gen. 19:12–14; Luke 10:13–15)*

20 [a]Then He began to rebuke the cities in
which most of His mighty works had been
done, because they did not repent: 21 "Woe to
you, Chorazin! Woe to you, Bethsaida! For if
the mighty works which were done in you had
been done in Tyre and Sidon, they would have
repented long ago [a]in sackcloth and ashes. 22 But
I say to you, [a]it will be more tolerable for Tyre
and Sidon in the day of judgment than for you.
23 And you, Capernaum, [a]who are exalted to
heaven, will be[1] brought down to Hades; for if
the mighty works which were done in you had

**11:3** [a] John 6:14 **11:5** [a] Is. 29:18; 35:4–6 [b] Is. 61:1 **11:6** [a] [Rom. 9:32] **11:7** [a] Luke 7:24 [b] [Eph. 4:14] **11:9** [a] Luke 1:76; 20:6 **11:10** [a] Mal. 3:1 [1] Malachi 3:1 **11:12** [a] Luke 16:16 **11:13** [a] Mal. 4:4–6 **11:14** [a] Luke 1:17 **11:15** [a] Luke 8:8 **11:16** [a] Luke 7:31 **11:19** [a] Matt. 9:10 [b] Luke 7:35 [1] NU-Text reads *works.* **11:20** [a] Luke 10:13–15, 18 **11:21** [a] Jon. 3:6–8 **11:22** [a] Matt. 10:15; 11:24 **11:23** [a] Is. 14:13 [1] NU-Text reads *will you be exalted to heaven? No, you will be.*

been done in Sodom, it would have remained until this day. 24 But I say to you [a]that it shall be more tolerable for the land of Sodom in the day of judgment than for you."

### *JESUS GIVES TRUE REST*

*(Luke 10:21, 22)*

25 [a]At that time Jesus answered and said, "I thank You, Father, Lord of heaven and earth, that [b]You have hidden these things from *the* wise and prudent [c]and have revealed them to babes. 26 Even so, Father, for so it seemed good in Your sight. 27 [a]All things have been delivered to Me by My Father, and no one knows the Son except the Father. [b]Nor does anyone know the Father except the Son, and *the one* to whom the Son wills to reveal *Him.* 28 Come to [a]Me, all *you* who labor and are heavy laden, and I will give you rest. 29 Take My yoke upon you [a]and learn from Me, for I am gentle and [b]lowly in heart, [c]and you will find rest for your souls. 30 [a]For My yoke *is* easy and My burden is light."

### *JESUS IS LORD OF THE SABBATH*

*(Mark 2:23–28; Luke 6:1–5)*

12 At that time [a]Jesus went through the grainfields on the Sabbath. And His disciples were hungry, and began to [b]pluck heads of grain and to eat. 2 And when the Pharisees saw *it,* they said to Him, "Look, Your disciples are doing what is not lawful to do on the Sabbath!"

3 But He said to them, "Have you not read [a]what David did when he was hungry, he and those who were with him: 4 how he entered the house of God and ate [a]the showbread which was not lawful for him to eat, nor for those who were with him, [b]but only for the priests? 5 Or have you not read in the [a]law that on the Sabbath the priests in the temple profane the Sabbath, and are blameless? 6 Yet I say to you that in this place there is [a]*One* greater than the temple. 7 But if you had known what *this* means, [a]'I desire mercy and not sacrifice,'[1] you would not have condemned the guiltless. 8 For the Son of Man is Lord even[1] of the Sabbath."

### *HEALING ON THE SABBATH*

*(Mark 3:1–6; Luke 6:6–11)*

9 [a]Now when He had departed from there, He went into their synagogue. 10 And behold, there was a man who had a withered hand. And they asked Him, saying, [a]"Is it lawful to heal on the Sabbath?"—that they might accuse Him.

11 Then He said to them, "What man is there among you who has one sheep, and if it falls into a pit on the Sabbath, will not lay hold of it and lift *it* out? 12 Of how much more value then is a man than a sheep? Therefore it is lawful to do good on the Sabbath." 13 Then He said to the man, "Stretch out your hand." And he stretched *it* out, and it was restored as whole as the other. 14 Then [a]the Pharisees went out and plotted against Him, how they might destroy Him.

### *BEHOLD, MY SERVANT*

15 But when Jesus knew *it,* [a]He withdrew from there. [b]And great multitudes[1] followed Him, and He healed them all. 16 Yet He [a]warned them not to make Him known, 17 that it might be fulfilled which was spoken by Isaiah the prophet, saying:

18 "Behold![a] My Servant whom I have chosen,
My Beloved [b]in whom My soul is well
pleased!
I will put My Spirit upon Him,
And He will declare justice to the Gentiles.
19 He will not quarrel nor cry out,
Nor will anyone hear His voice in the
streets.
20 A bruised reed He will not break,
And smoking flax He will not quench,
Till He sends forth justice to victory;
21 And in His name Gentiles will trust."[1]

### *A HOUSE DIVIDED CANNOT STAND*

*(Mark 3:22–27; Luke 11:14–23)*

22 [a]Then one was brought to Him who was demon-possessed, blind and mute; and He healed him, so that the blind and[1] mute man both spoke and saw. 23 And all the multitudes were amazed and said, "Could this be the [a]Son of David?"

24 [a]Now when the Pharisees heard *it* they said, "This *fellow* does not cast out demons except by Beelzebub,[1] the ruler of the demons."

25 But Jesus [a]knew their thoughts, and said to them: "Every kingdom divided against itself is brought to desolation, and every city or house divided against itself will not stand. 26 If Satan casts out Satan, he is divided against himself. How then will his kingdom stand? 27 And if I cast out demons by Beelzebub, by whom do your sons cast *them* out? Therefore they shall be your judges. 28 But if I cast out demons by the Spirit of God, [a]surely the kingdom of God has come upon you. 29 [a]Or how can one enter a strong man's house and plunder his goods, unless he first binds the strong man? And then he will plunder his house. 30 He who is not with Me is against Me, and he who does not gather with Me scatters abroad.

**11:24** [a]Matt. 10:15 **11:25** [a]Luke 10:21, 22 [b]Ps. 8:2 [c]Matt. 16:17 **11:27** [a]Matt. 28:18 [b]John 1:18; 6:46; 10:15 **11:28** [a][John 6:35–37] **11:29** [a][Phil. 2:5] [b]Zech. 9:9 [c]Jer. 6:16 **11:30** [a][1 John 5:3] **12:1** [a]Luke 6:1–5 [b]Deut. 23:25 **12:3** [a]1 Sam. 21:6 **12:4** [a]Lev. 24:5 [b]Ex. 29:32 **12:5** [a]Num. 28:9 **12:6** [a][Is. 66:1, 2] **12:7** [a][Hos. 6:6] [1]Hosea 6:6 **12:8** [1]NU-Text and M-Text omit *even.* **12:9** [a]Mark 3:1–6 **12:10** [a]John 9:16 **12:14** [a]Mark 3:6 **12:15** [a]Mark 3:7 [b]Matt. 19:2 [1]NU-Text brackets *multitudes* as disputed. **12:16** [a]Matt. 8:4; 9:30; 17:9 **12:18** [a]Is. 42:1–4; 49:3 [b]Matt. 3:17; 17:5 **12:21** [1]Isaiah 42:1–4 **12:22** [a]Luke 11:14, 15 [1]NU-Text omits *blind and.* **12:23** [a]Matt. 9:27; 21:9 **12:24** [a]Matt. 9:34 [1]NU-Text and M-Text read *Beelzebul.* **12:25** [a]Matt. 9:4 **12:28** [a][Dan. 2:44; 7:14] **12:29** [a]Is. 49:24

**12:31–32** The person who commits **blasphemy against the Spirit** places himself or herself outside the redeeming grace of God. The words and works of Christ were spoken and performed by the power of the Holy Spirit. To attribute them to Satan is to call the work of heaven a work of hell (see Matt. 12:24). For such perverse belief there is no remedy. This is apparently not a single act of defiant behavior, but a continued state of opposition entered into willingly. How someone can commit this sin today is a difficult question to answer, but those who persist in denigrating Christ by insulting His work or by attributing it to Satan may drive themselves past a point of no return (see Mark 3:28–30).

### *THE UNPARDONABLE SIN*

*(Mark 3:28–30)*

31 “Therefore I say to you, [a]every sin and blas-
phemy will be forgiven men, [b]but the blasphe-
my *against* the Spirit will not be forgiven men.
32 Anyone who [a]speaks a word against the Son of
Man, [b]it will be forgiven him; but whoever speaks
against the Holy Spirit, it will not be forgiven him,
either in this age or in the *age* to come.

### *A TREE KNOWN BY ITS FRUIT*

*(Matt. 7:15–20)*

33 “Either make the tree good and [a]its fruit
good, or else make the tree bad and its fruit
bad; for a tree is known by *its* fruit. 34 [a]Brood
of vipers! How can you, being evil, speak good
things? [b]For out of the abundance of the heart
the mouth speaks. 35 A good man out of the
good treasure of his heart[1] brings forth good
things, and an evil man out of the evil treasure
brings forth evil things. 36 But I say to you that
for every idle word men may speak, they will
give account of it in the day of judgment. 37 For
by your words you will be justified, and by your
words you will be condemned.”

### *THE SCRIBES AND PHARISEES ASK FOR A SIGN*

*(Luke 11:29–32)*

38 [a]Then some of the scribes and Pharisees
answered, saying, “Teacher, we want to see a
sign from You.”
39 But He answered and said to them, “An
evil and [a]adulterous generation seeks after a
sign, and no sign will be given to it except the
sign of the prophet Jonah. 40 [a]For as Jonah was
three days and three nights in the belly of the
great fish, so will the Son of Man be three days
and three nights in the heart of the earth. 41 [a]The
men of Nineveh will rise up in the judgment with
this generation and [b]condemn it, [c]because they
repented at the preaching of Jonah; and indeed
a greater than Jonah *is* here. 42 [a]The queen of the
South will rise up in the judgment with this gen-
eration and condemn it, for she came from the
ends of the earth to hear the wisdom of Solomon;
and indeed a greater than Solomon *is* here.

**SEEING JESUS IN THE SCRIPTURE**

**12:40** Jonah was buried in the waters and figuratively came back to life; Jesus was buried in the grave and literally came back to life (see Jon. 1:17).

**12:31** [a] Mark 3:28–30 [b] Acts 7:51 **12:32** [a] John 7:12, 52 [b] 1 Tim. 1:13 **12:33** [a] Matt. 7:16–18 **12:34** [a] Matt. 3:7; 23:33 [b] Luke 6:45 **12:35** [1] NU-Text and M-Text omit *of his heart.* **12:38** [a] Mark 8:11 **12:39** [a] Matt. 16:4 **12:40** [a] Jon. 1:17 **12:41** [a] Luke 11:32 [b] Jer. 3:11 [c] Jon. 3:5 **12:42** [a] 1 Kin. 10:1–13

**APPLY THE TRUTH**

## THE BIBLE'S RELIABILITY

**12:40** Have you ever wondered if you can trust that the Bible *you* read is the same as it was originally written? The Bible was written by over forty authors, on three continents, in three languages, from about 1400 BC to AD 100. We don't have to trust in this book by blind faith though. There are legitimate proofs that the Bible is reliable: historical evidence, eyewitness accounts, and even personal testimony. The Bible's historical events can be confirmed by extrabiblical sources, and none have ever been refuted. There were over five hundred eyewitnesses of Jesus' resurrection. Plus, we have millions of people who have been changed by the power of the Word of God.

In this verse, Jesus validated one of the Bible's stories that many find hardest to believe—Jonah's life being preserved in the belly of a fish. Jesus taught this event not as myth, but as historical. This is important because He connected Jonah's account to His resurrection. If Jonah was made up, what does that say about the resurrection? Jesus believed in the Bible, and we can too. Despite all its critics and scrutiny, the Bible has remained trustworthy. You can trust God's Word with your life!

### AN UNCLEAN SPIRIT RETURNS
*(Luke 11:24–26)*

43 [a]"When an unclean spirit goes out of a
man, [b]he goes through dry places, seeking rest,
and finds none. 44 Then he says, 'I will return
to my house from which I came.' And when he
comes, he finds *it* empty, swept, and put in order.
45 Then he goes and takes with him seven other
spirits more wicked than himself, and they enter
and dwell there; [a]and the last *state* of that man
is worse than the first. So shall it also be with
this wicked generation."

### JESUS' MOTHER AND BROTHERS SEND FOR HIM
*(Mark 3:31–35; Luke 8:19–21)*

46 While He was still talking to the multitudes,
[a]behold, His mother and [b]brothers stood outside,
seeking to speak with Him. 47 Then one said to
Him, "Look, [a]Your mother and Your brothers are
standing outside, seeking to speak with You."

48 But He answered and said to the one who
told Him, "Who is My mother and who are My
brothers?" 49 And He stretched out His hand
toward His disciples and said, "Here are My
mother and My [a]brothers! 50 For [a]whoever does
the will of My Father in heaven is My brother
and sister and mother."

### THE PARABLE OF THE SOWER
*(Mark 4:1–9; Luke 8:4–8)*

13 On the same day Jesus went out of the
house [a]and sat by the sea. 2 [a]And great
multitudes were gathered together to Him, so
that [b]He got into a boat and sat; and the whole
multitude stood on the shore.

3 Then He spoke many things to them in par-
ables, saying: [a]"Behold, a sower went out to sow.
4 And as he sowed, some *seed* fell by the wayside;
and the birds came and devoured them. 5 Some
fell on stony places, where they did not have much
earth; and they immediately sprang up because
they had no depth of earth. 6 But when the sun was
up they were scorched, and because they had no
root they withered away. 7 And some fell among
thorns, and the thorns sprang up and choked
them. 8 But others fell on good ground and yielded
a crop: some [a]a hundredfold, some sixty, some
thirty. 9 [a]He who has ears to hear, let him hear!"

### THE PURPOSE OF PARABLES
*(Mark 4:10–12; Luke 8:9, 10)*

10 And the disciples came and said to Him,
"Why do You speak to them in parables?"

11 He answered and said to them, "Because [a]it
has been given to you to know the mysteries of
the kingdom of heaven, but to them it has not
been given. 12 [a]For whoever has, to him more

> **SEEING JESUS IN THE SCRIPTURE**
>
> **13:14** Jesus spoke to the multitudes in parables, fulfilling prophecy (see Is. 6:9–10).

will be given, and he will have abundance; but
whoever does not have, even what he has will
be taken away from him. 13 Therefore I speak to
them in parables, because seeing they do not
see, and hearing they do not hear, nor do they
understand. 14 And in them the prophecy of
Isaiah is fulfilled, which says:

[a]'Hearing you will hear and shall not
understand,
And seeing you will see and not [b]perceive;
15 For the hearts of this people have grown
dull.
*Their* ears [a]are hard of hearing,
And their eyes they have [b]closed,
Lest they should see with *their* eyes and
hear with *their* ears,
Lest they should understand with *their*
hearts and turn,
So that I should[1] [c]heal them.'[2]

16 But [a]blessed *are* your eyes for they see, and
your ears for they hear; 17 for assuredly, I say to
you [a]that many prophets and righteous *men*
desired to see what you see, and did not see *it*,
and to hear what you hear, and did not hear *it*.

### THE PARABLE OF THE SOWER EXPLAINED
*(Mark 4:13–20; Luke 8:11–15)*

18 [a]"Therefore hear the parable of the sower:
19 When anyone hears the word [a]of the kingdom,
and does not understand *it*, then the wicked *one*
comes and snatches away what was sown in his
heart. This is he who received seed by the wayside.
20 But he who received the seed on stony places,
this is he who hears the word and immediately
[a]receives it with joy; 21 yet he has no root in himself,
but endures only for a while. For when [a]tribulation
or persecution arises because of the word, imme-
diately [b]he stumbles. 22 Now [a]he who received seed
[b]among the thorns is he who hears the word, and
the cares of this world and the deceitfulness of
riches choke the word, and he becomes unfruitful.
23 But he who received seed on the good ground
is he who hears the word and understands *it*,
who indeed bears [a]fruit and produces: some a
hundredfold, some sixty, some thirty."

### THE PARABLE OF THE WHEAT AND THE TARES

24 Another parable He put forth to them, say-
ing: "The kingdom of heaven is like a man who

**12:43** [a] Luke 11:24–26 [b] [1 Pet. 5:8] **12:45** [a] [2 Pet. 2:20–22] **12:46** [a] Luke 8:19–21 [b] John 2:12; 7:3, 5 **12:47** [a] Matt. 13:55, 56 **12:49** [a] John 20:17 **12:50** [a] John 15:14 **13:1** [a] Mark 4:1–12 **13:2** [a] Luke 8:4 [b] Luke 5:3 **13:3** [a] Luke 8:5 **13:8** [a] Gen. 26:12 **13:9** [a] Matt. 11:15 **13:11** [a] Mark 4:10, 11 **13:12** [a] Matt. 25:29 **13:14** [a] Is. 6:9, 10 [b] [John 3:36] **13:15** [a] Heb. 5:11 [b] Luke 19:42 [c] Acts 28:26, 27 [1] NU-Text and M-Text read *would*. [2] Isaiah 6:9, 10 **13:16** [a] Luke 10:23, 24 **13:17** [a] Heb. 11:13 **13:18** [a] Mark 4:13–20 **13:19** [a] Matt. 4:23 **13:20** [a] Is. 58:2 **13:21** [a] [Acts 14:22] [b] Matt. 11:6 **13:22** [a] 1 Tim. 6:9 [b] Jer. 4:3 **13:23** [a] Col. 1:6

sowed good seed in his field; 25 but while men slept, his enemy came and sowed tares among the wheat and went his way. 26 But when the grain had sprouted and produced a crop, then the tares also appeared. 27 So the servants of the owner came and said to him, 'Sir, did you not sow good seed in your field? How then does it have tares?' 28 He said to them, 'An enemy has done this.' The servants said to him, 'Do you want us then to go and gather them up?' 29 But he said, 'No, lest while you gather up the tares you also uproot the wheat with them. 30 Let both grow together until the harvest, and at the time of harvest I will say to the reapers, "First gather together the tares and bind them in bundles to burn them, but [a]gather the wheat into my barn." ' "

### *THE PARABLE OF THE MUSTARD SEED*

*(Mark 4:30–32; Luke 13:18, 19)*

31 Another parable He put forth to them, saying: [a]"The kingdom of heaven is like a mustard seed, which a man took and sowed in his field, 32 which indeed is the least of all the seeds; but when it is grown it is greater than the herbs and becomes a [a]tree, so that the birds of the air come and nest in its branches."

### *THE PARABLE OF THE LEAVEN*

*(Luke 13:20, 21)*

33 [a]Another parable He spoke to them: "The kingdom of heaven is like leaven, which a woman took and hid in three measures[1] of meal till [b]it was all leavened."

### *PROPHECY AND THE PARABLES*

34 [a]All these things Jesus spoke to the multitude in parables; and without a parable He did not speak to them, 35 that it might be fulfilled which was spoken by the prophet, saying:

[a]"I will open My mouth in parables;
[b]I will utter things kept secret from the
foundation of the world."[1]

### *THE PARABLE OF THE TARES EXPLAINED*

36 Then Jesus sent the multitude away and went into the house. And His disciples came to Him, saying, "Explain to us the parable of the tares of the field."

37 He answered and said to them: "He who sows the good seed is the Son of Man. 38 [a]The field is the world, the good seeds are the sons of the kingdom, but the tares are [b]the sons of the wicked *one.* 39 The enemy who sowed them is the devil, [a]the harvest is the end of the age, and the reapers are the angels. 40 Therefore as the tares are gathered and burned in the fire, so it will be at the end of this age. 41 The Son of Man will send out His angels, [a]and they will gather out of His kingdom all things that offend, and those who practice lawlessness, 42 [a]and will cast them into the furnace of fire. [b]There will be wailing and gnashing of teeth. 43 [a]Then the righteous will shine forth as the sun in the kingdom of their Father. [b]He who has ears to hear, let him hear!

### *THE PARABLE OF THE HIDDEN TREASURE*

44 "Again, the kingdom of heaven is like treasure hidden in a field, which a man found and hid; and for joy over it he goes and [a]sells all that he has and [b]buys that field.

### *THE PARABLE OF THE PEARL OF GREAT PRICE*

45 "Again, the kingdom of heaven is like a merchant seeking beautiful pearls, 46 who, when he had found [a]one pearl of great price, went and sold all that he had and bought it.

### *THE PARABLE OF THE DRAGNET*

47 "Again, the kingdom of heaven is like a dragnet that was cast into the sea and [a]gathered some of every kind, 48 which, when it was full, they drew to shore; and they sat down and gathered the good into vessels, but threw the bad away. 49 So it will be at the end of the age. The angels will come forth, [a]separate the wicked from among the just, 50 and cast them into the furnace of fire. There will be wailing and gnashing of teeth."

51 Jesus said to them,[1] "Have you understood all these things?"

They said to Him, "Yes, Lord."[2]

52 Then He said to them, "Therefore every scribe instructed concerning[1] the kingdom of heaven is like a householder who brings out of his treasure [a]*things* new and old."

**13:54** The **synagogue** was a local gathering place for Jews to pray and study. A synagogue could be founded in any town with at least ten men who wanted to gather. Sacrifices were not offered at synagogues; they could only be made at the temple. Synagogue buildings were usually rectangular with a large sitting area. The congregation sat on stone benches along the walls or on the floor. The main piece of furniture in the synagogue was where the scrolls of Scripture were kept.

**13:30** [a] Matt. 3:12 **13:31** [a] [Is. 2:2, 3; Mic. 4:1]; Mark 4:30; Luke 13:18, 19 **13:32** [a] Ps. 104:12; Ezek. 17:22–24; 31:3–9; Dan. 4:12 **13:33** [a] Luke 13:20, 21 [b] [1 Cor. 5:6; Gal. 5:9] [1] Greek *sata,* approximately two pecks in all **13:34** [a] Ps. 78:2; Mark 4:33, 34 **13:35** [a] Ps. 78:2 [b] Rom. 16:25, 26; 1 Cor. 2:7; Eph. 3:9; Col. 1:26 [1] Psalm 78:2 **13:38** [a] Matt. 24:14; 28:19; Mark 16:15; Luke 24:47; Rom. 10:18; Col. 1:6 [b] Gen. 3:15; John 8:44; Acts 13:10 **13:39** [a] Joel 3:13; Rev. 14:15 **13:41** [a] Matt. 18:7; 2 Pet. 2:1, 2 **13:42** [a] Matt. 3:12; Rev. 19:20; 20:10 [b] Matt. 8:12; 13:50 **13:43** [a] [Dan. 12:3; 1 Cor. 15:42, 43, 58] [b] Matt. 13:9 **13:44** [a] Phil. 3:7, 8 [b] [Is. 55:1; Rev. 3:18] **13:46** [a] Prov. 2:4; 3:14, 15; 8:10, 19 **13:47** [a] Matt. 22:9, 10 **13:49** [a] Matt. 25:32 **13:51** [1] NU-Text omits *Jesus said to them.* [2] NU-Text omits *Lord.* **13:52** [a] Song 7:13 [1] Or *for*

### *JESUS REJECTED AT NAZARETH*
*(Mark 6:1–6; Luke 4:16–30)*

53 Now it came to pass, when Jesus had fin-
ished these parables, that He departed from
there. 54 [a]When He had come to His own country,
He taught them in their synagogue, so that they
were astonished and said, "Where did this *Man*
get this wisdom and *these* mighty works? 55 [a]Is
this not the carpenter's son? Is not His mother
called Mary? And [b]His brothers [c]James, Joses,[1]
Simon, and Judas? 56 And His sisters, are they
not all with us? Where then did this *Man* get all
these things?" 57 So they [a]were offended at Him.
But Jesus said to them, [b]"A prophet is not
without honor except in his own country and
in his own house." 58 Now [a]He did not do many
mighty works there because of their unbelief.

### *JOHN THE BAPTIST BEHEADED*
*(Mark 6:14–29; Luke 9:7–9)*

**14** At that time [a]Herod the tetrarch heard
the report about Jesus 2 and said to his
servants, "This is John the Baptist; he is risen
from the dead, and therefore these powers are
at work in him." 3 [a]For Herod had laid hold of
John and bound him, and put *him* in prison for

> **14:1** Herod the Great, the ruler of Judea, died when Jesus was very young. His kingdom was divided among his three sons. Antipas was the name of the son who inherited the region of Galilee, the place where both Jesus and John the Baptist lived most of their adult lives. Whenever **Herod** is mentioned in the Bible, it usually refers to Antipas. Not only was Antipas the one who had John the Baptist murdered, he also played a part in **Jesus**' trial and death.

the sake of Herodias, his brother Philip's wife.
4 Because John had said to him, [a]"It is not lawful
for you to have her." 5 And although he wanted
to put him to death, he feared the multitude,
[a]because they counted him as a prophet.
6 But when Herod's birthday was celebrated,
the daughter of Herodias danced before them
and pleased Herod. 7 Therefore he promised
with an oath to give her whatever she might ask.
8 So she, having been prompted by her
mother, said, "Give me John the Baptist's head
here on a platter."
9 And the king was sorry; nevertheless, be-
cause of the oaths and because of those who
sat with him, he commanded *it* to be given to
*her.* 10 So he sent and had John beheaded in
prison. 11 And his head was brought on a platter
and given to the girl, and she brought *it* to her
mother. 12 Then his disciples came and took away
the body and buried it, and went and told Jesus.

### *FEEDING THE FIVE THOUSAND*
*(Mark 6:30–44; Luke 9:10–17; John 6:1–14)*

13 [a]When Jesus heard *it,* He departed from
there by boat to a deserted place by Himself. But
when the multitudes heard it, they followed Him
on foot from the cities. 14 And when Jesus went
out He saw a great multitude; and He [a]was moved
with compassion for them, and healed their sick.
15 [a]When it was evening, His disciples came to Him,
saying, "This is a deserted place, and the hour is
already late. Send the multitudes away, that they
may go into the villages and buy themselves food."
16 But Jesus said to them, "They do not need
to go away. You give them something to eat."
17 And they said to Him, "We have here only
five loaves and two fish."
18 He said, "Bring them here to Me." 19 Then He
commanded the multitudes to sit down on the
grass. And He took the five loaves and the two
fish, and looking up to heaven, [a]He blessed and
broke and gave the loaves to the disciples; and
the disciples gave to the multitudes. 20 So they all
ate and were filled, and they took up twelve bas-
kets full of the fragments that remained. 21 Now
those who had eaten were about five thousand
men, besides women and children.

### *JESUS WALKS ON THE SEA*
*(Mark 6:45–52; John 6:15–21)*

22 Immediately Jesus made His disciples get
into the boat and go before Him to the other
side, while He sent the multitudes away. 23 [a]And
when He had sent the multitudes away, He went
up on the mountain by Himself to pray. [b]Now
when evening came, He was alone there. 24 But
the boat was now in the middle of the sea,[1] tossed
by the waves, for the wind was contrary.
25 Now in the fourth watch of the night Jesus went
to them, walking on the sea. 26 And when the disciples
saw Him [a]walking on the sea, they were troubled,
saying, "It is a ghost!" And they cried out for fear.
27 But immediately Jesus spoke to them, say-
ing, "Be of good [a]cheer! It is I; do not be afraid."

> **SEEING JESUS IN THE SCRIPTURE**
>
> **14:27** Jesus' words are the Greek equivalent of the words the Father spoke to Moses when He revealed His name, I AM (see Ex. 3:14).

**13:54** [a] Ps. 22:22; Matt. 2:23; Mark 6:1; Luke 4:16; John 7:15 **13:55** [a] Is. 49:7; Mark 6:3; [Luke 3:23]; John 6:42 [b] Matt. 12:46 [c] Mark 15:40 [1] NU-Text reads *Joseph.* **13:57** [a] Matt. 11:6; Mark 6:3, 4 [b] Luke 4:24; John 4:44 **13:58** [a] Mark 6:5, 6; John 5:44, 46, 47 **14:1** [a] Mark 6:14–29; Luke 9:7–9 **14:3** [a] Matt. 4:12; Mark 6:17; Luke 3:19, 20 **14:4** [a] Lev. 18:16; 20:21 **14:5** [a] Matt. 21:26; Luke 20:6 **14:13** [a] Matt. 10:23; 12:15; Mark 6:32–44; Luke 9:10–17; John 6:1, 2 **14:14** [a] Matt. 9:36; Mark 6:34 **14:15** [a] Mark 6:35; Luke 9:12 **14:19** [a] 1 Sam. 9:13; Matt. 15:36; 26:26; Mark 6:41; 8:7; 14:22; Luke 24:30; Acts 27:35; [Rom. 14:6] **14:23** [a] Mark 6:46; Luke 9:28; John 6:15 [b] John 6:16 **14:24** [1] NU-Text reads *many furlongs away from the land.* **14:26** [a] Job 9:8 **14:27** [a] Acts 23:11; 27:22, 25, 36

APPLY THE TRUTH

## DOUBT

**14:25–31** Doubt isn't disbelief. To disbelieve is to reject. Those who disbelieve in Jesus reject Him as the Son of God and Savior. Consequently, they remain dead in their sins unless they repent. Doubting is different. It requires some level of belief to begin with, only that belief wavers. It's possible, then, to have genuine, saving faith in Jesus and doubt at times. This is what we see with Peter.

In this passage, Jesus came to the disciples by walking on water. We tend to focus on what happened at the end of the account—when Peter began to doubt Jesus and began to sink. We wonder how Peter could have done this. After all, he had seen Jesus do countless miracles before this and Jesus *was* walking on water right in front of him. But this moment of doubt wouldn't have happened without Peter's faith. No one else got out of the boat! Notice also that Peter turned to his faith—as small as it may have been in the moment—remembering that Jesus could save him. In the times you doubt, do likewise. Turn your attention back to the faith undergirding that doubt and most importantly, to the One that faith is in: Jesus.

28 And Peter answered Him and said, "Lord, if it
is You, command me to come to You on the water."
29 So He said, "Come." And when Peter had
come down out of the boat, he walked on the
water to go to Jesus. 30 But when he saw that the
wind *was* boisterous,[1] he was afraid; and begin-
ning to sink he cried out, saying, "Lord, save me!"
31 And immediately Jesus stretched out *His*
hand and caught him, and said to him, "O you
of [a]little faith, why did you doubt?" 32 And when
they got into the boat, the wind ceased.
33 Then those who were in the boat came
and[1] worshiped Him, saying, "Truly [a]You are
the Son of God."

### *MANY TOUCH HIM AND ARE MADE WELL*
*(Mark 6:53–56)*

34 [a]When they had crossed over, they came
to the land of[1] Gennesaret. 35 And when the men
of that place recognized Him, they sent out into
all that surrounding region, brought to Him
all who were sick, 36 and begged Him that they
might only [a]touch the hem of His garment. And
[b]as many as touched *it* were made perfectly well.

### *DEFILEMENT COMES FROM WITHIN*
*(Mark 7:1–23)*

15 Then [a]the scribes and Pharisees who were
from Jerusalem came to Jesus, saying,
2 [a]"Why do Your disciples transgress the tradition
of the elders? For they do not wash their hands
when they eat bread."
3 He answered and said to them, "Why do
you also transgress the commandment of God
because of your tradition? 4 For God commanded,
saying, [a]'Honor your father and your mother';[1]
and, [b]'He who curses father or mother, let him be
put to death.'[2] 5 But you say, 'Whoever says to his
father or mother, [a]"Whatever profit you might
have received from me *is* a gift *to God*"— 6 then
he need not honor his father or mother.'[1] Thus
you have made the commandment[2] of God of
no effect by your tradition. 7 [a]Hypocrites! Well
did Isaiah prophesy about you, saying:

8 'These[a] people draw near to Me with their
mouth,
And[1] honor Me with *their* lips,
But their heart is far from Me.
9 And in vain they worship Me,
[a]Teaching *as* doctrines the
commandments of men.' "[1]

10 [a]When He had called the multitude to *Him-
self,* He said to them, "Hear and understand: 11 [a]Not
what goes into the mouth defiles a man; but what
comes out of the mouth, this defiles a man."
12 Then His disciples came and said to Him,
"Do You know that the Pharisees were offended
when they heard this saying?"
13 But He answered and said, [a]"Every plant
which My heavenly Father has not planted will
be uprooted. 14 Let them alone. [a]They are blind
leaders of the blind. And if the blind leads the
blind, both will fall into a ditch."
15 [a]Then Peter answered and said to Him,
"Explain this parable to us."
16 So Jesus said, [a]"Are you also still without
understanding? 17 Do you not yet understand
that [a]whatever enters the mouth goes into the
stomach and is eliminated? 18 But [a]those things
which proceed out of the mouth come from the

**14:30** [1] NU-Text brackets *that* and *boisterous* as disputed. **14:31** [a] Matt. 6:30; 8:26 **14:33** [a] Ps. 2:7; Matt. 16:16; 26:63; Mark 1:1; Luke 4:41; John 1:49; 6:69; 11:27; Acts 8:37; Rom. 1:4 [1] NU-Text omits *came and.* **14:34** [a] Mark 6:53 [1] NU-Text reads *came to land at.* **14:36** [a] [Mark 5:24–34] [b] [Luke 6:19] **15:1** [a] Mark 7:1 **15:2** [a] Mark 7:5 **15:4** [a] [Deut. 5:16] [b] Ex. 21:17 [1] Exodus 20:12; Deuteronomy 5:16 [2] Exodus 21:17 **15:5** [a] Mark 7:11, 12 **15:6** [1] NU-Text omits *or mother.* [2] NU-Text reads *word.* **15:7** [a] Mark 7:6 **15:8** [a] Is. 29:13 [1] NU-Text omits *draw near to Me with their mouth, And.* **15:9** [a] [Col. 2:18–22] [1] Isaiah 29:13 **15:10** [a] Mark 7:14 **15:11** [a] [Acts 10:15] **15:13** [a] [John 15:2] **15:14** [a] Luke 6:39 **15:15** [a] Mark 7:17 **15:16** [a] Matt. 16:9 **15:17** [a] [1 Cor. 6:13] **15:18** [a] [James 3:6]

heart, and they defile a man. 19[a]For out of the
heart proceed evil thoughts, murders, adulteries,
fornications, thefts, false witness, blasphemies.
20These are *the things* which defile a man, but to
eat with unwashed hands does not defile a man."

### *A GENTILE SHOWS HER FAITH*
*(Mark 7:24–30)*

21[a]Then Jesus went out from there and de-
parted to the region of Tyre and Sidon. 22And
behold, a woman of Canaan came from that re-
gion and cried out to Him, saying, "Have mercy
on me, O Lord, [a]Son of David! My daughter is
severely demon-possessed."
23But He answered her not a word.
And His disciples came and urged Him,
saying, "Send her away, for she cries out after us."
24But He answered and said, [a]"I was not sent
except to the lost sheep of the house of Israel."
25Then she came and worshiped Him, say-
ing, "Lord, help me!"
26But He answered and said, "It is not good
to take the children's bread and throw *it* to the
little [a]dogs."
27And she said, "Yes, Lord, yet even the lit-
tle dogs eat the crumbs which fall from their
masters' table."
28Then Jesus answered and said to her,
"O woman, [a]great *is* your faith! Let it be to you
as you desire." And her daughter was healed
from that very hour.

### *JESUS HEALS GREAT MULTITUDES*
*(Mark 7:31–37)*

29[a]Jesus departed from there, [b]skirted the
Sea of Galilee, and went up on the mountain
and sat down there. 30[a]Then great multitudes
came to Him, having with them *the* lame, blind,
mute, maimed, and many others; and they laid
them down at Jesus' [b]feet, and He healed them.
31So the multitude marveled when they saw *the*
mute speaking, *the* maimed made whole, *the*
lame walking, and *the* blind seeing; and they
[a]glorified the God of Israel.

### *FEEDING THE FOUR THOUSAND*
*(Mark 8:1–10)*

32[a]Now Jesus called His disciples to *Himself*
and said, "I have compassion on the multitude,
because they have now continued with Me three
days and have nothing to eat. And I do not want to
send them away hungry, lest they faint on the way."
33[a]Then His disciples said to Him, "Where
could we get enough bread in the wilderness to
fill such a great multitude?"
34Jesus said to them, "How many loaves
do you have?"
And they said, "Seven, and a few little fish."
35So He commanded the multitude to sit
down on the ground. 36And [a]He took the seven
loaves and the fish and [b]gave thanks, broke *them*
and gave *them* to His disciples; and the disciples
*gave* to the multitude. 37So they all ate and were
filled, and they took up seven large baskets full
of the fragments that were left. 38Now those who
ate were four thousand men, besides women and
children. 39[a]And He sent away the multitude, got
into the boat, and came to the region of Magdala.[1]

### *THE PHARISEES AND SADDUCEES SEEK A SIGN*
*(Mark 8:11–13; Luke 12:54–56)*

16 Then the [a]Pharisees and Sadducees came,
and testing Him asked that He would show
them a sign from heaven. 2He answered and
said to them, "When it is evening you say, '*It
will be* fair weather, for the sky is red'; 3and in
the morning, '*It will be* foul weather today, for

**15:19** [a] Prov. 6:14 **15:21** [a] Mark 7:24–30 **15:22** [a] Matt. 1:1; 22:41, 42 **15:24** [a] Matt. 10:5, 6 **15:26** [a] Matt. 7:6 **15:28** [a] Luke 7:9 **15:29** [a] Mark 7:31–37 [b] Matt. 4:18 **15:30** [a] Is. 35:5, 6 [b] Luke 7:38; 8:41; 10:39 **15:31** [a] Luke 5:25, 26; 19:37, 38 **15:32** [a] Mark 8:1–10 **15:33** [a] 2 Kin. 4:43 **15:36** [a] Matt. 14:19; 26:27 [b] Luke 22:19 **15:39** [a] Mark 8:10 [1] NU-Text reads *Magadan.* **16:1** [a] Mark 8:11

APPLY THE TRUTH

## HUNGER

**15:32–39** This isn't the only time Jesus fed a multitude. Another time, He fed over five thousand people. Including women and children, He likely fed around thirty thousand people. If God has the capacity to multiply food like this, why doesn't He end world hunger in one simple act?

The answer is not in what God *could* do, but rather in what He *did* do. In these two miracles, Jesus showed an amazing heart of compassion for people and helped them from His capacity. Like Jesus, we must have a heart of compassion toward people's needs, and we should step in and help based on our capacity. We may not be able to multiply food miraculously, but we can use our resources, passions, and abilities to meet other people's needs. Christ working through us, His people, could end world hunger.

But even more than this, Jesus wants to solve a bigger problem: satisfaction. Food comes and goes. A relationship with Jesus lasts and satisfies our every need. Turn to Jesus as the bread of life and point others to Him (see John 6:35).

the sky is red and threatening.' Hypocrites![1] You
know how to discern the face of the sky, but you
cannot *discern* the signs of the times. 4 [a]A wicked
and adulterous generation seeks after a sign, and
no sign shall be given to it except the sign of the
prophet[1] Jonah." And He left them and departed.

### *THE LEAVEN OF THE PHARISEES AND SADDUCEES*

*(Mark 8:14–21)*

5 Now [a]when His disciples had come to the
other side, they had forgotten to take bread.
6 Then Jesus said to them, [a]"Take heed and beware
of the leaven of the Pharisees and the Sadducees."
7 And they reasoned among themselves,
saying, "*It is* because we have taken no bread."
8 But Jesus, being aware of *it*, said to them,
"O you of little faith, why do you reason among
yourselves because you have brought no bread?[1]
9 [a]Do you not yet understand, or remember the
five loaves of the five thousand and how many
baskets you took up? 10 [a]Nor the seven loaves of
the four thousand and how many large baskets
you took up? 11 How is it you do not understand
that I did not speak to you concerning bread?—
*but* to beware of the leaven of the Pharisees and
Sadducees." 12 Then they understood that He did
not tell *them* to beware of the leaven of bread, but
of the doctrine of the Pharisees and Sadducees.

### *PETER CONFESSES JESUS AS THE CHRIST*

*(Mark 8:27–30; Luke 9:18–20)*

13 When Jesus came into the region of Caes-
area Philippi, He asked His disciples, saying,
[a]"Who do men say that I, the Son of Man, am?"
14 So they said, [a]"Some *say* John the Baptist,
some Elijah, and others Jeremiah or [b]one of
the prophets."
15 He said to them, "But who do [a]you say
that I am?"

**16:3** [1] NU-Text omits *Hypocrites.* **16:4** [a] Matt. 12:39 [1] NU-Text omits *the prophet.* **16:5** [a] Mark 8:14 **16:6** [a] Luke 12:1 **16:8** [1] NU-Text reads *you have no bread.* **16:9** [a] Matt. 14:15–21 **16:10** [a] Matt. 15:32–38 **16:13** [a] Luke 9:18 **16:14** [a] Matt. 14:2 [b] Matt. 21:11 **16:15** [a] John 6:67

MATTHEW 16:13–23

## JESUS, THE CHRIST

45

STORY OF SCRIPTURE

### WHAT'S GOING ON?

When Jesus asked His disciples who people said He was, He asked a profound question. We may think the answer is obvious, but that's because we have the full picture. When Jesus asked this question midway through His earthly ministry, His identity was still coming into focus. The disciples offered various answers—Elijah or Jeremiah (a prophet) or John the Baptist (a provocative figure). However, Jesus wasn't *just* a prophet. He was more than that.

When Peter answered, "You are the Christ, the Son of the living God," he was absolutely correct. This answer came from the Spirit of God and saw Jesus as the divine Redeemer. However, the story quickly turns when Jesus explained His impending suffering and death. Peter, unable to fathom the Messiah dying, rebuked Jesus. Jesus' response was intense: "Get behind Me, Satan!" This jarring response reveals the centrality of Jesus' mission to die on the cross for people's sins. If Jesus didn't suffer, there could be no salvation.

### WHAT DOES THIS MEAN FOR ME?

It can be difficult to accept that sometimes God's blessings must come through suffering. At least it was for Peter. Peter recognized Jesus's identity as the Christ but failed to understand His mission as the Christ. He tried to fit Jesus within a mold he had created. Sometimes, our expectations of God can blind us to His true nature and plans too. This passage invites us to recognize our faith may require suffering and God's plans don't necessarily work out in comfortable ways.

### DID YOU CATCH THE PATTERN?

The title *Christ* means "anointed one," and is the Greek equivalent of *Messiah* in the Old Testament. The Christ was first promised in Genesis 3:15 and dozens of prophecies concerning the One God would send to bring salvation to the world follow. As you read God's promises of the Promised One given to Moses, David, the prophets, and others, remember they all point to Jesus.

*For the next* Story of Scripture *reading and devotion, turn to John 11:38–44 on page 1088.*

16 Simon Peter answered and said, [a]"You are the Christ, the Son of the living God."

17 Jesus answered and said to him, "Blessed are you, Simon Bar-Jonah, [a]for flesh and blood has not revealed *this* to you, but [b]My Father who is in heaven. 18 And I also say to you that [a]you are Peter, and [b]on this rock I will build My church, and [c]the gates of Hades shall not prevail against it. 19 [a]And I will give you the keys of the kingdom of heaven, and whatever you bind on earth will be bound in heaven, and whatever you loose on earth will be loosed[1] in heaven."

## SEEING JESUS IN THE SCRIPTURE

**16:18** The growth of Jesus' church was never in doubt. Just as Jesus promised, it grew from the very first day (see Acts 2:41).

20 [a]Then He commanded His disciples that they should tell no one that He was Jesus the Christ.

### *JESUS PREDICTS HIS DEATH AND RESURRECTION*

*(Mark 8:31–33; Luke 9:21, 22)*

21 From that time Jesus began [a]to show to His disciples that He must go to Jerusalem, and suffer many things from the elders and chief priests and scribes, and be killed, and be raised the third day.

22 Then Peter took Him aside and began to rebuke Him, saying, "Far be it from You, Lord; this shall not happen to You!"

23 But He turned and said to Peter, "Get behind Me, [a]Satan! [b]You are an offense to Me, for you are not mindful of the things of God, but the things of men."

### *TAKE UP THE CROSS AND FOLLOW HIM*

*(Mark 8:34–38; Luke 9:23–26)*

24 [a]Then Jesus said to His disciples, "If anyone desires to come after Me, let him deny himself, and take up his cross, and [b]follow Me. 25 For [a]whoever desires to save his life will lose it, but whoever loses his life for My sake will find it. 26 For what [a]profit is it to a man if he gains the whole world, and loses his own soul? Or [b]what will a man give in exchange for his soul? 27 For [a]the Son of Man will come in the glory of His Father [b]with His angels, [c]and then He will reward each according to his works. 28 Assuredly, I say to you, [a]there are some standing here who shall not taste death till they see the Son of Man coming in His kingdom."

**16:28** In the transfiguration, Peter, James, and John saw a preview of the **kingdom**. Jesus was explaining that very soon those three disciples would see Him glorified as He will be in the kingdom.

### *JESUS TRANSFIGURED ON THE MOUNT*

*(Mark 9:1–13; Luke 9:27–36; 2 Pet. 1:16–18)*

**17** Now [a]after six days Jesus took Peter, James, and John his brother, led them up on a high mountain by themselves; 2 and He was transfigured before them. His face shone like the sun, and His clothes became as white as the light. 3 And behold, Moses and Elijah appeared to them, talking with Him. 4 Then Peter answered and said to Jesus, "Lord, it is good for us to be here; if You wish, let us[1] make here three tabernacles: one for You, one for Moses, and one for Elijah."

5 [a]While he was still speaking, behold, a bright cloud overshadowed them; and suddenly a voice came out of the cloud, saying, [b]"This is My beloved Son, [c]in whom I am well pleased. [d]Hear Him!" 6 [a]And when the disciples heard *it,* they fell on their faces and were greatly afraid. 7 But Jesus came and [a]touched them and said, "Arise, and do not be afraid." 8 When they had lifted up their eyes, they saw no one but Jesus only.

9 Now as they came down from the mountain, Jesus commanded them, saying, "Tell the vision to no one until the Son of Man is risen from the dead."

10 And His disciples asked Him, saying, [a]"Why then do the scribes say that Elijah must come first?"

11 Jesus answered and said to them, "Indeed, Elijah is coming first[1] and will [a]restore all things. 12 [a]But I say to you that Elijah has come already, and they [b]did not know him but did to him whatever they wished. Likewise [c]the Son of Man is also about to suffer at their hands." 13 [a]Then the disciples understood that He spoke to them of John the Baptist.

### *A BOY IS HEALED*

*(Mark 9:14–29; Luke 9:37–42)*

14 [a]And when they had come to the multitude, a man came to Him, kneeling down to Him and saying, 15 "Lord, have mercy on my son, for he is an epileptic[1] and suffers severely; for he often falls into the fire and often into the water. 16 So I brought him to Your disciples, but they could not cure him."

17 Then Jesus answered and said, "O faithless and [a]perverse generation, how long shall I be

**16:16** [a] Acts 8:37; 9:20 **16:17** [a] [Eph. 2:8] [b] Gal. 1:16 **16:18** [a] John 1:42 [b] [Eph. 2:20] [c] Is. 38:10 **16:19** [a] Matt. 18:18 [1] Or *will have been bound . . . will have been loosed* **16:20** [a] Luke 9:21 **16:21** [a] Luke 9:22; 18:31; 24:46 **16:23** [a] Matt. 4:10 [b] [Rom. 8:7] **16:24** [a] [2 Tim. 3:12] [b] [1 Pet. 2:21] **16:25** [a] John 12:25 **16:26** [a] Luke 12:20, 21 [b] Ps. 49:7, 8 **16:27** [a] Mark 8:38 [b] [Dan. 7:10] [c] Rom. 2:6 **16:28** [a] Luke 9:27 **17:1** [a] Mark 9:2–8 **17:4** [1] NU-Text reads *I will.* **17:5** [a] 2 Pet. 1:17 [b] Mark 1:11 [c] Matt. 3:17; 12:18 [d] [Deut. 18:15, 19] **17:6** [a] 2 Pet. 1:18 **17:7** [a] Dan. 8:18 **17:10** [a] Mal. 4:5 **17:11** [a] [Mal. 4:6] [1] NU-Text omits *first.* **17:12** [a] Mark 9:12, 13 [b] Matt. 14:3, 10 [c] Matt. 16:21 **17:13** [a] Matt. 11:14 **17:14** [a] Mark 9:14–28 **17:15** [1] Literally *moonstruck* **17:17** [a] Phil. 2:15

with you? How long shall I bear with you? Bring him here to Me." 18 And Jesus [a]rebuked the demon, and it came out of him; and the child was cured from that very hour.

19 Then the disciples came to Jesus privately and said, "Why could we not cast it out?"

20 So Jesus said to them, "Because of your unbelief;[1] for assuredly, I say to you, [a]if you have faith as a mustard seed, you will say to this mountain, 'Move from here to there,' and it will move; and nothing will be impossible for you. 21 However, this kind does not go out except by prayer and fasting."[1]

### *JESUS AGAIN PREDICTS HIS DEATH AND RESURRECTION*

*(Mark 9:30–32; Luke 9:43–45)*

22 [a]Now while they were staying[1] in Galilee, Jesus said to them, "The Son of Man is about to be betrayed into the hands of men, 23 and they will kill Him, and the third day He will be raised up." And they were exceedingly [a]sorrowful.

> **SEEING JESUS IN THE SCRIPTURE**
>
> **17:23** Jesus spoke of the crucifixion and resurrection beforehand to prove His identity as the Messiah. His followers spoke of it afterward for the same reason (see Acts 10:40).

### *PETER AND HIS MASTER PAY THEIR TAXES*

24 [a]When they had come to Capernaum,[1] those who received the *temple* tax came to Peter and said, "Does your Teacher not pay the *temple* tax?"

25 He said, "Yes."

And when he had come into the house, Jesus anticipated him, saying, "What do you think, Simon? From whom do the kings of the earth take customs or taxes, from their sons or from [a]strangers?"

26 Peter said to Him, "From strangers."

Jesus said to him, "Then the sons are free. 27 Nevertheless, lest we offend them, go to the sea, cast in a hook, and take the fish that comes up first. And when you have opened its mouth, you will find a piece of money;[1] take that and give it to them for Me and you."

### *WHO IS THE GREATEST?*

*(Mark 9:33–37; Luke 9:46–48)*

**18** At [a]that time the disciples came to Jesus, saying, "Who then is greatest in the kingdom of heaven?"

2 Then Jesus called a little [a]child to Him, set him in the midst of them, 3 and said, "Assuredly, I say to you, [a]unless you are converted and become as little children, you will by no means enter the kingdom of heaven. 4 [a]Therefore whoever humbles himself as this little child is the greatest in the kingdom of heaven. 5 [a]Whoever receives one little child like this in My name receives Me.

### *JESUS WARNS OF OFFENSES*

*(Mark 9:42–48; Luke 17:1, 2)*

6 [a]"But whoever causes one of these little ones who believe in Me to sin, it would be better for him if a millstone were hung around his neck, and he were drowned in the depth of the sea. 7 Woe to the world because of offenses! For [a]offenses must come, but [b]woe to that man by whom the offense comes!

8 [a]"If your hand or foot causes you to sin, cut it off and cast *it* from you. It is better for you to enter into life lame or maimed, rather than having two hands or two feet, to be cast into the everlasting fire. 9 And if your eye causes you to sin, pluck it out and cast *it* from you. It is better for you to enter into life with one eye, rather than having two eyes, to be cast into hell fire.

### *THE PARABLE OF THE LOST SHEEP*

*(Luke 15:1–7)*

10 "Take heed that you do not despise one of these little ones, for I say to you that in heaven [a]their angels always [b]see the face of My Father who is in heaven. 11 [a]For the Son of Man has come to save that which was lost.[1]

12 [a]"What do you think? If a man has a hundred sheep, and one of them goes astray, does he not leave the ninety-nine and go to the mountains to seek the one that is straying? 13 And if he should find it, assuredly, I say to you, he rejoices more over that *sheep* than over the ninety-nine that did not go astray. 14 Even so it is not the [a]will of your Father who is in heaven that one of these little ones should perish.

### *DEALING WITH A SINNING BROTHER*

15 "Moreover [a]if your brother sins against you, go and tell him his fault between you and him alone. If he hears you, [b]you have gained your brother. 16 But if he will not hear, take with you one or two more, that [a]'by the mouth of two or three witnesses every word may be established.'[1] 17 And if he refuses to hear them, tell *it* to the church. But if he refuses even to hear the church, let him be to you like a [a]heathen and a tax collector.

18 "Assuredly, I say to you, [a]whatever you bind on earth will be bound in heaven, and whatever you loose on earth will be loosed in heaven.

**17:18** [a] Luke 4:41 **17:20** [a] Luke 17:6 [1] NU-Text reads *little faith.* **17:21** [1] NU-Text omits this verse. **17:22** [a] Mark 8:31 [1] NU-Text reads *gathering together.* **17:23** [a] John 16:6; 19:30 **17:24** [a] Mark 9:33 [1] NU-Text reads *Capharnaum* (here and elsewhere). **17:25** [a] [Is. 60:10–17] **17:27** [1] Greek *stater,* the exact amount to pay the temple tax (didrachma) for two **18:1** [a] Luke 9:46–48; 22:24–27 **18:2** [a] Matt. 19:14 **18:3** [a] Luke 18:16 **18:4** [a] [Matt. 20:27; 23:11] **18:5** [a] [Matt. 10:42] **18:6** [a] Mark 9:42 **18:7** [a] [1 Cor. 11:19] [b] Matt. 26:24; 27:4, 5 **18:8** [a] Matt. 5:29, 30 **18:10** [a] [Heb. 1:14] [b] Luke 1:19 **18:11** [a] Luke 9:56 [1] NU-Text omits this verse. **18:12** [a] Luke 15:4–7 **18:14** [a] [1 Tim. 2:4] **18:15** [a] Lev. 19:17 [b] [James 5:20] **18:16** [a] Deut. 17:6; 19:15 [1] Deuteronomy 19:15 **18:17** [a] [2 Thess. 3:6, 14] **18:18** [a] [John 20:22, 23]

19 [a]"Again I say[1] to you that if two of you agree
on earth concerning anything that they ask, [b]it
will be done for them by My Father in heaven.
20 For where two or three are gathered [a]together
in My name, I am there in the midst of them."

### THE PARABLE OF THE UNFORGIVING SERVANT

21 Then Peter came to Him and said, "Lord,
how often shall my brother sin against me, and
I forgive him? [a]Up to seven times?"
22 Jesus said to him, "I do not say to you, [a]up
to seven times, but up to seventy times seven.
23 Therefore the kingdom of heaven is like a cer-
tain king who wanted to settle accounts with his
servants. 24 And when he had begun to settle
accounts, one was brought to him who owed him
ten thousand talents. 25 But as he was not able to
pay, his master commanded [a]that he be sold, with
his wife and children and all that he had, and that
payment be made. 26 The servant therefore fell
down before him, saying, 'Master, have patience
with me, and I will pay you all.' 27 Then the mas-
ter of that servant was moved with compassion,
released him, and forgave him the debt.
28 "But that servant went out and found one
of his fellow servants who owed him a hundred
denarii; and he laid hands on him and took *him*
by the throat, saying, 'Pay me what you owe!'
29 So his fellow servant fell down at his feet[1] and
begged him, saying, 'Have patience with me, and
I will pay you all.'[2] 30 And he would not, but went
and threw him into prison till he should pay the
debt. 31 So when his fellow servants saw what had
been done, they were very grieved, and came and
told their master all that had been done. 32 Then
his master, after he had called him, said to him,
'You wicked servant! I forgave you [a]all that debt
because you begged me. 33 Should you not also
have had compassion on your fellow servant,
just as I had pity on you?' 34 And his master was
angry, and delivered him to the torturers until
he should pay all that was due to him.
35 [a]"So My heavenly Father also will do to you
if each of you, from his heart, does not forgive
his brother his trespasses."[1]

### MARRIAGE AND DIVORCE

*(Mark 10:1–12)*

19 Now it came to pass, [a]when Jesus had fin-
ished these sayings, *that* He departed from
Galilee and came to the region of Judea beyond
the Jordan. 2 [a]And great multitudes followed
Him, and He healed them there.
3 The Pharisees also came to Him, testing
Him, and saying to Him, "Is it lawful for a man
to divorce his wife for *just* any reason?"
4 And He answered and said to them, "Have
you not read that He who made[1] *them* at the
beginning [a]'made them male and female,'[2] 5 and
said, [a]'For this reason a man shall leave his father
and mother and be joined to his wife, and [b]the
two shall become one flesh'?[1] 6 So then, they are
no longer two but one flesh. Therefore what
God has joined together, let not man separate."
7 They said to Him, [a]"Why then did Moses
command to give a certificate of divorce, and
to put her away?"
8 He said to them, "Moses, because of the
[a]hardness of your hearts, permitted you to di-
vorce your [b]wives, but from the beginning it was
not so. 9 [a]And I say to you, whoever divorces his
wife, except for sexual immorality,[1] and mar-
ries another, commits adultery; and whoever
marries her who is divorced commits adultery."
10 His disciples said to Him, [a]"If such is the
case of the man with *his* wife, it is better not
to marry."

**18:19** [a] [1 Cor. 1:10] [b] [1 John 3:22; 5:14] [1] NU-Text and M-Text read *Again, assuredly, I say.* **18:20** [a] Acts 20:7 **18:21** [a] Luke 17:4 **18:22** [a] Col. 3:13 **18:25** [a] 2 Kin. 4:1 **18:29** [1] NU-Text omits *at his feet.* [2] NU-Text and M-Text omit *all.* **18:32** [a] Luke 7:41–43 **18:35** [a] James 2:13 [1] NU-Text omits *his trespasses.* **19:1** [a] Mark 10:1–12 **19:2** [a] Matt. 12:15 **19:4** [a] Gen. 1:27; 5:2 [1] NU-Text reads *created.* [2] Genesis 1:27; 5:2 **19:5** [a] Gen. 2:24 [b] [1 Cor. 6:16; 7:2] [1] Genesis 2:24 **19:7** [a] Deut. 24:1–4 **19:8** [a] Heb. 3:15 [b] Mal. 2:16 **19:9** [a] [Matt. 5:32] [1] Or *fornication* **19:10** [a] [Prov. 21:19]

LIVE THE TRUTH

## FORGIVING OTHERS

**18:21–35** No relationship is easy in a world broken by sin. We have sinned against others, and others have sinned against us. But we can be part of reversing the effects of sin by seeking forgiveness from those we wrong and offering forgiveness to those who have wronged us. It isn't always easy, but forgiveness is powerful because it can break the cycle of hurt and give both parties a chance to heal. Offering forgiveness instead of seeking retribution is how Jesus commands us to live.

Forgiveness is key to the believer's life because it's key to the gospel. Jesus reminds us if we're not quick to forgive others, it may be because we haven't truly accepted the forgiveness He has for us. Jesus has forgiven us of a debt we could never pay on our own. We were His enemy and yet He died for us even though He did nothing wrong. It makes any sin committed against us pale in comparison, even if the offense is painful and the hurt is deep. Because of what Jesus has done for us, we can and must forgive others.

APPLY THE TRUTH

## GENDER AND SEXUALITY

**19:1–6** Gender and sexuality are common topics today, and they're more controversial than ever. We live in a world where gender and sexuality are *discovered* rather than *defined*, and many people fuse them to their identity more deeply than perhaps anything else. Part of life is certainly discovering who we are—our interests, our joys and pleasures, our hopes and dreams—but not all of life is this way. Some things are defined *for* us, not *by* us. They are objective, not subjective. Gender and sexuality are among them. But the world has flipped this script. Now, individuals discover their gender and sexuality, even creating their own should nothing they try on "fit."

We can learn much from where Jesus turned to define marriage. He didn't look at societal norms. He didn't tell the questioners to search their own hearts. Rather, He turned to the Word of God (Gen. 1–2) for the definitive answer. And in doing so, He reinforced the biblical definitions of both gender and sexuality. Marriage is between a male and a female and where God designed sexuality to blossom and flourish. While the world sees God's definitions of gender and sexuality as restrictive, they are far from it. God's design is born out of His desire for human fruitfulness and flourishing. We need to allow the Word of God to define us and the ways of God to direct us.

### *JESUS TEACHES ON CELIBACY*

11 But He said to them, [a]"All cannot accept
this saying, but only *those* to whom it has been
given: 12 For there are eunuchs who were born
thus from *their* mother's womb, and [a]there are
eunuchs who were made eunuchs by men, and
there are eunuchs who have made themselves
eunuchs for the kingdom of heaven's sake. He
who is able to accept *it,* let him accept *it.*"

### *JESUS BLESSES LITTLE CHILDREN*

*(Mark 10:13–16; Luke 18:15–17)*

13 [a]Then little children were brought to Him
that He might put *His* hands on them and pray,
but the disciples rebuked them. 14 But Jesus
said, "Let the little children come to Me, and do
not forbid them; for [a]of such is the kingdom of
heaven." 15 And He laid *His* hands on them and
departed from there.

### *JESUS COUNSELS THE RICH YOUNG RULER*

*(Mark 10:17–22; Luke 18:18–23)*

16 [a]Now behold, one came and said to Him,
[b]"Good[1] Teacher, what good thing shall I do that
I may have eternal life?"
17 So He said to him, "Why do you call Me
good?[1] No one *is* [a]good but One, *that is,* God.[2]
But if you want to enter into life, [b]keep the
commandments."
18 He said to Him, "Which ones?"
Jesus said, [a]" 'You shall not murder,' 'You
shall not commit adultery,' 'You shall not steal,'
'You shall not bear false witness,' 19 [a]'Honor your
father and *your* mother,'[1] and, [b]'You shall love
your neighbor as yourself.' "[2]
20 The young man said to Him, "All these
things I have [a]kept from my youth.[1] What do
I still lack?"
21 Jesus said to him, "If you want to be per-
fect, [a]go, sell what you have and give to the poor,
and you will have treasure in heaven; and come,
follow Me."

**19:21** This verse does not teach salvation by works (see Rom. 3:23–24; Eph. 2:8–9). Rather, Jesus was proving that the rich young man could not have truly fulfilled all the law of Moses. If he really loved his neighbor as the law required (Lev. 19:18), he would not have had any difficulty in giving away his wealth to the poor.

22 But when the young man heard that say-
ing, he went away sorrowful, for he had great
possessions.

### *WITH GOD ALL THINGS ARE POSSIBLE*

*(Mark 10:23–31; Luke 18:24–30)*

23 Then Jesus said to His disciples, "Assured-
ly, I say to you that [a]it is hard for a rich man to
enter the kingdom of heaven. 24 And again I say
to you, it is easier for a camel to go through the
eye of a needle than for a rich man to enter the
kingdom of God."
25 When His disciples heard *it,* they were
greatly astonished, saying, "Who then can be
saved?"
26 But Jesus looked at *them* and said to them,

**19:11** [a] [1 Cor. 7:2, 7, 9, 17] **19:12** [a] [1 Cor. 7:32] **19:13** [a] Luke 18:15 **19:14** [a] Matt. 18:3, 4 **19:16** [a] Mark 10:17–30 [b] Luke 10:25 [1] NU-Text omits *Good.* **19:17** [a] Nah. 1:7 [b] Lev. 18:5 [1] NU-Text reads *Why do you ask Me about what is good?* [2] NU-Text reads *There is One who is good.* **19:18** [a] Ex. 20:13–16 **19:19** [a] Ex. 20:12–16; Deut. 5:16–20 [b] Lev. 19:18 [1] Exodus 20:12–16; Deuteronomy 5:16–20 [2] Leviticus 19:18 **19:20** [a] [Phil. 3:6, 7] [1] NU-Text omits *from my youth.* **19:21** [a] Acts 2:45; 4:34, 35 **19:23** [a] [1 Tim. 6:9]

"With men this is impossible, but [a]with God all things are possible."

27 Then Peter answered and said to Him, "See, [a]we have left all and followed You. Therefore what shall we have?"

28 So Jesus said to them, "Assuredly I say to you, that in the regeneration, when the Son of Man sits on the throne of His glory, [a]you who have followed Me will also sit on twelve thrones, judging the twelve tribes of Israel. 29 [a]And everyone who has left houses or brothers or sisters or father or mother or wife[1] or children or lands, for My name's sake, shall receive a hundredfold, and inherit eternal life. 30 [a]But many *who are* first will be last, and the last first.

### THE PARABLE OF THE WORKERS IN THE VINEYARD

**20** "For the kingdom of heaven is like a landowner who went out early in the morning to hire laborers for his vineyard. 2 Now when he had agreed with the laborers for a denarius a day, he sent them into his vineyard. 3 And he went out about the third hour and saw others standing idle in the marketplace, 4 and said to them, 'You also go into the vineyard, and whatever is right I will give you.' So they went. 5 Again he went out about the sixth and the ninth hour, and did likewise. 6 And about the eleventh hour he went out and found others standing idle,[1] and said to them, 'Why have you been standing here idle all day?' 7 They said to him, 'Because no one hired us.' He said to them, 'You also go into the vineyard, and whatever is right you will receive.'[1]

8 "So when evening had come, the owner of the vineyard said to his steward, 'Call the laborers and give them *their* wages, beginning with the last to the first.' 9 And when those came who *were hired* about the eleventh hour, they each received a denarius. 10 But when the first came, they supposed that they would receive more; and they likewise received each a denarius. 11 And when they had received *it,* they complained against the landowner, 12 saying, 'These last *men* have worked *only* one hour, and you made them equal to us who have borne the burden and the heat of the day.' 13 But he answered one of them and said, 'Friend, I am doing you no wrong. Did you not agree with me for a denarius? 14 Take *what is* yours and go your way. I wish to give to this last man *the same* as to you. 15 [a]Is it not lawful for me to do what I wish with my own things? Or [b]is your eye evil because I am good?' 16 [a]So the last will be first, and the first last. [b]For many are called, but few chosen."[1]

### JESUS A THIRD TIME PREDICTS HIS DEATH AND RESURRECTION

*(Mark 10:32–34; Luke 18:31–34)*

17 [a]Now Jesus, going up to Jerusalem, took the twelve disciples aside on the road and said to them, 18 [a]"Behold, we are going up to Jerusalem, and the Son of Man will be betrayed to the chief priests and to the scribes; and they will condemn Him to death, 19 [a]and deliver Him to the Gentiles to [b]mock and to [c]scourge and to [d]crucify. And the third day He will [e]rise again."

### GREATNESS IS SERVING

*(Mark 10:35–45)*

20 [a]Then the mother of [b]Zebedee's sons came to Him with her sons, kneeling down and asking something from Him.

21 And He said to her, "What do you wish?"

She said to Him, "Grant that these two sons of mine [a]may sit, one on Your right hand and the other on the left, in Your kingdom."

22 But Jesus answered and said, "You do not know what you ask. Are you able to drink [a]the cup that I am about to drink, and be baptized with [b]the baptism that I am baptized with?"[1]

They said to Him, "We are able."

23 So He said to them, [a]"You will indeed drink My cup, and be baptized with the baptism that I am baptized with;[1] but to sit on My right hand and on My left is not Mine to give, but *it is for those* for whom it is prepared by My Father."

24 [a]And when the ten heard *it,* they were greatly displeased with the two brothers. 25 But Jesus called them to *Himself* and said, "You know that the rulers of the Gentiles lord it over them, and those who are great exercise authority over them. 26 Yet [a]it shall not be so among you; but [b]whoever desires to become great among you, let him be your servant. 27 [a]And whoever desires to be first among you, let him be your slave— 28 [a]just as the [b]Son of Man did not come to be served, [c]but to serve, and [d]to give His life a ransom [e]for many."

> **SEEING JESUS IN THE SCRIPTURE**
>
> **20:28** Jesus came to serve the Father by completing the work of our salvation. His death in our place was the Father's plan from the beginning (see Is. 53:10–11).

### TWO BLIND MEN RECEIVE THEIR SIGHT

*(Mark 10:46–52; Luke 18:35–43)*

29 [a]Now as they went out of Jericho, a great multitude followed Him. 30 And behold, [a]two

**19:26** [a] Jer. 32:17 **19:27** [a] Deut. 33:9 **19:28** [a] Luke 22:28–30 **19:29** [a] Mark 10:29, 30 [1] NU-Text omits *or wife.* **19:30** [a] Luke 13:30 **20:6** [1] NU-Text omits *idle.* **20:7** [1] NU-Text omits the last clause of this verse. **20:15** [a] [Rom. 9:20, 21] [b] Deut. 15:9 **20:16** [a] Matt. 19:30 [b] Matt. 22:14 [1] NU-Text omits the last sentence of this verse. **20:17** [a] Mark 10:32–34 **20:18** [a] Matt. 16:21; 26:47–57 **20:19** [a] Matt. 27:2 [b] Matt. 26:67, 68; 27:29, 41 [c] Matt. 27:26 [d] Acts 3:13–15 [e] Matt. 28:5, 6 **20:20** [a] Mark 10:35–45 [b] Matt. 4:21; 10:2 **20:21** [a] [Matt. 19:28] **20:22** [a] Luke 22:42 [b] Luke 12:50 [1] NU-Text omits *and be baptized with the baptism that I am baptized with.* **20:23** [a] [Acts 12:2] [1] NU-Text omits *and be baptized with the baptism that I am baptized with.* **20:24** [a] Mark 10:41 **20:26** [a] [1 Pet. 5:3] [b] Matt. 23:11 **20:27** [a] [Matt. 18:4] **20:28** [a] John 13:4 [b] [Phil. 2:6, 7] [c] Luke 22:27 [d] [Is. 53:10, 11] [e] [Rom. 5:15, 19] **20:29** [a] Mark 10:46–52 **20:30** [a] Matt. 9:27

blind men sitting by the road, when they heard that Jesus was passing by, cried out, saying, "Have mercy on us, O Lord, [b]Son of David!"

31 Then the multitude [a]warned them that they should be quiet; but they cried out all the more, saying, "Have mercy on us, O Lord, Son of David!"

32 So Jesus stood still and called them, and said, "What do you want Me to do for you?"

33 They said to Him, "Lord, that our eyes may be opened." 34 So Jesus had [a]compassion and touched their eyes. And immediately their eyes received sight, and they followed Him.

### *THE TRIUMPHAL ENTRY*

*(Mark 11:1–10; Luke 19:28–40; John 12:12–19)*

**21** Now [a]when they drew near Jerusalem, and came to Bethphage,[1] at [b]the Mount of Olives, then Jesus sent two disciples, 2 saying to them, "Go into the village opposite you, and immediately you will find a donkey tied, and a colt with her. Loose *them* and bring *them* to Me. 3 And if anyone says anything to you, you shall say, 'The Lord has need of them,' and immediately he will send them."

4 All[1] this was done that it might be fulfilled which was spoken by the prophet, saying:

5 "Tell[a] the daughter of Zion,
'Behold, your King is coming to you,
Lowly, and sitting on a donkey,
A colt, the foal of a donkey.' "[1]

> **SEEING JESUS IN THE SCRIPTURE**
>
> **21:5** Instead of entering Jerusalem on a horse as king, Jesus rode humbly on a donkey as servant, fulfilling prophecy (see Zech. 9:9).

6 [a]So the disciples went and did as Jesus commanded them. 7 They brought the donkey and the colt, [a]laid their clothes on them, and set *Him*[1] on them. 8 And a very great multitude spread their clothes on the road; [a]others cut down branches from the trees and spread *them* on the road. 9 Then the multitudes who went before and those who followed cried out, saying:

"Hosanna to the Son of David!
[a]'Blessed *is* He who comes in the name of the LORD!'[1]
Hosanna in the highest!"

10 [a]And when He had come into Jerusalem, all the city was moved, saying, "Who is this?"

11 So the multitudes said, "This is Jesus, [a]the prophet from Nazareth of Galilee."

### *JESUS CLEANSES THE TEMPLE*

*(Mark 11:15–19; Luke 19:45–48; John 2:13–22)*

12 [a]Then Jesus went into the temple of God[1] and drove out all those who bought and sold in the temple, and overturned the tables of the [b]money changers and the seats of those who sold doves. 13 And He said to them, "It is written, [a]'My house shall be called a house of prayer,'[1] but you have made it a [b]'den of thieves.' "[2]

> **21:12** Coins with pagan symbols on them could not be used in the **temple**. They had to be exchanged for acceptable coins. Likewise, only certain animals could be offered as sacrifices. People who were too poor to own a goat or a sheep could offer **doves** as sacrifices. Some saw these restrictions as an opportunity to make money. They set up **tables** in the temple courtyard and sold approved coins and doves for outrageous prices.

14 Then *the* blind and *the* lame came to Him in the temple, and He healed them. 15 But when the chief priests and scribes saw the wonderful things that He did, and the children crying out in the temple and saying, "Hosanna to the [a]Son of David!" they were indignant 16 and said to Him, "Do You hear what these are saying?"

And Jesus said to them, "Yes. Have you never read,

[a]'Out of the mouth of babes and nursing infants
You have perfected praise'?"[1]

17 Then He left them and [a]went out of the city to Bethany, and He lodged there.

### *THE FIG TREE WITHERED*

*(Mark 11:12–14)*

18 [a]Now in the morning, as He returned to the city, He was hungry. 19 [a]And seeing a fig tree by the road, He came to it and found nothing on it but leaves, and said to it, "Let no fruit grow on you ever again." Immediately the fig tree withered away.

### *THE LESSON OF THE WITHERED FIG TREE*

*(Mark 11:20–24)*

20 [a]And when the disciples saw *it*, they marveled, saying, "How did the fig tree wither away so soon?"

21 So Jesus answered and said to them, "Assuredly, I say to you, [a]if you have faith and [b]do not doubt, you will not only do what was done to

**20:30** [b] [Ezek. 37:21–25] **20:31** [a] Matt. 19:13 **20:34** [a] Matt. 9:36; 14:14; 15:32; 18:27 **21:1** [a] Luke 19:29–38 [b] [Zech. 14:4] [1] M-Text reads *Bethsphage.* **21:4** [1] NU-Text omits *All.* **21:5** [a] Zech. 9:9 [1] Zechariah 9:9 **21:6** [a] Mark 11:4 **21:7** [a] 2 Kin. 9:13 [1] NU-Text reads *and He sat.* **21:8** [a] Lev. 23:40 **21:9** [a] Ps. 118:26; Matt. 23:39 [1] Psalm 118:26 **21:10** [a] John 2:13, 15 **21:11** [a] John 6:14; 7:40; 9:17 **21:12** [a] Mark 11:15–18 [b] Deut. 14:25 [1] NU-Text omits *of God.* **21:13** [a] Is. 56:7 [b] Jer. 7:11 [1] Isaiah 56:7 [2] Jeremiah 7:11 **21:15** [a] John 7:42 **21:16** [a] Ps. 8:2 [1] Psalm 8:2 **21:17** [a] John 11:1, 18; 12:1 **21:18** [a] Mark 11:12–14, 20–24 **21:19** [a] Mark 11:13 **21:20** [a] Mark 11:20 **21:21** [a] Matt. 17:20 [b] James 1:6

the fig tree, [c]but also if you say to this mountain, 'Be removed and be cast into the sea,' it will be done. 22 And [a]whatever things you ask in prayer, believing, you will receive."

### *JESUS' AUTHORITY QUESTIONED*
*(Mark 11:27–33; Luke 20:1–8)*

23 [a]Now when He came into the temple, the chief priests and the elders of the people confronted Him as He was teaching, and [b]said, "By what authority are You doing these things? And who gave You this authority?"

24 But Jesus answered and said to them, "I also will ask you one thing, which if you tell Me, I likewise will tell you by what authority I do these things: 25 The [a]baptism of [b]John—where was it from? From heaven or from men?"

And they reasoned among themselves, saying, "If we say, 'From heaven,' He will say to us, 'Why then did you not believe him?' 26 But if we say, 'From men,' we [a]fear the multitude, [b]for all count John as a prophet." 27 So they answered Jesus and said, "We do not know."

And He said to them, "Neither will I tell you by what authority I do these things.

### *THE PARABLE OF THE TWO SONS*

28 "But what do you think? A man had two sons, and he came to the first and said, 'Son, go, work today in my [a]vineyard.' 29 He answered and said, 'I will not,' but afterward he regretted it and went. 30 Then he came to the second and said likewise. And he answered and said, 'I *go,* sir,' but he did not go. 31 Which of the two did the will of *his* father?"

They said to Him, "The first."

Jesus said to them, [a]"Assuredly, I say to you that tax collectors and harlots enter the kingdom of God before you. 32 For [a]John came to you in the way of righteousness, and you did not believe him; [b]but tax collectors and harlots believed him; and when you saw *it,* you did not afterward relent and believe him.

### *THE PARABLE OF THE WICKED VINEDRESSERS*
*(Mark 12:1–12; Luke 20:9–19)*

33 "Hear another parable: There was a certain landowner [a]who planted a vineyard and set a hedge around it, dug a winepress in it and built a tower. And he leased it to vinedressers and [b]went into a far country. 34 Now when vintage-time drew near, he sent his servants to the vinedressers, that they might receive its fruit. 35 [a]And the vinedressers took his servants, beat one, killed one, and stoned another. 36 Again he sent other servants, more than the first, and they did likewise to them. 37 Then last of all he sent his [a]son to them, saying, 'They will respect my son.' 38 But when the vinedressers saw the son, they said among themselves, [a]'This is the heir. [b]Come, let us kill him and seize his inheritance.' 39 [a]So they took him and cast *him* out of the vineyard and killed *him.*

40 "Therefore, when the owner of the vineyard comes, what will he do to those vinedressers?"

41 [a]They said to Him, [b]"He will destroy those wicked men miserably, [c]and lease *his* vineyard to other vinedressers who will render to him the fruits in their seasons."

42 Jesus said to them, "Have you never read in the Scriptures:

[a]'The stone which the builders rejected
Has become the chief cornerstone.
This was the LORD's doing,
And it is marvelous in our eyes'?[1]

43 "Therefore I say to you, [a]the kingdom of God will be taken from you and given to a nation bearing the fruits of it. 44 And [a]whoever falls on this stone will be broken; but on whomever it falls, [b]it will grind him to powder."

45 Now when the chief priests and Pharisees heard His parables, they perceived that He was speaking of them. 46 But when they sought to lay hands on Him, they [a]feared the multitudes, because [b]they took Him for a prophet.

### *THE PARABLE OF THE WEDDING FEAST*
*(Luke 14:15–24)*

**22** And Jesus answered [a]and spoke to them again by parables and said: 2 "The kingdom of heaven is like a certain king who arranged a marriage for his son, 3 and sent out his servants to call those who were invited to the wedding; and they were not willing to come. 4 Again, he sent out other servants, saying, 'Tell those who are invited, "See, I have prepared my dinner; [a]my oxen and fatted cattle *are* killed, and all things *are* ready. Come to the wedding."' 5 But they made light of it and went their ways, one to his own farm, another to his business. 6 And the rest seized his servants, treated *them* spitefully, and killed *them.* 7 But when the king heard *about it,* he was furious. And he sent out [a]his armies, destroyed those murderers, and burned up their city. 8 Then he said to his servants, 'The wedding is ready, but those who were invited were not [a]worthy. 9 Therefore go into the highways, and as many as you find, invite to the wedding.' 10 So those servants went out into the highways and [a]gathered together all whom they found, both bad and good. And the wedding *hall* was filled with guests.

11 "But when the king came in to see the guests, he saw a man there [a]who did not have on a wedding garment. 12 So he said to him,

**21:21** [c] 1 Cor. 13:2 **21:22** [a] Matt. 7:7–11 **21:23** [a] Luke 20:1–8 [b] Ex. 2:14 **21:25** [a] [John 1:29–34] [b] John 1:15–28 **21:26** [a] Matt. 14:5; 21:46 [b] Mark 6:20 **21:28** [a] Matt. 20:1; 21:33 **21:31** [a] Luke 7:29, 37–50 **21:32** [a] Luke 3:1–12; 7:29 [b] Luke 3:12, 13 **21:33** [a] Luke 20:9–19 [b] Matt. 25:14 **21:35** [a] [1 Thess. 2:15] **21:37** [a] [John 3:16] **21:38** [a] [Heb. 1:2] [b] John 11:53 **21:39** [a] [Acts 2:23] **21:41** [a] Luke 20:16 [b] [Luke 21:24] [c] [Acts 13:46] **21:42** [a] Ps. 118:22, 23 [1] Psalm 118:22, 23 **21:43** [a] [Matt. 8:12] **21:44** [a] Is. 8:14, 15 [b] [Dan. 2:44] **21:46** [a] Matt. 21:26 [b] Matt. 21:11 **22:1** [a] [Rev. 19:7–9] **22:4** [a] Prov. 9:2 **22:7** [a] [Dan. 9:26] **22:8** [a] Matt. 10:11 **22:10** [a] Matt. 13:38, 47, 48 **22:11** [a] [Col. 3:10, 12]

'Friend, how did you come in here without a
wedding garment?' And he was [a]speechless.
13 Then the king said to the servants, 'Bind him
hand and foot, take him away, and[1] cast *him*
[a]into outer darkness; there will be weeping and
gnashing of teeth.'
14 [a]"For many are called, but few *are* chosen."

### THE PHARISEES: IS IT LAWFUL TO PAY TAXES TO CAESAR?

*(Mark 12:13–17; Luke 20:20–26)*

15 [a]Then the Pharisees went and plotted how
they might entangle Him in *His* talk. 16 And they
sent to Him their disciples with the [a]Herodians,
saying, "Teacher, we know that You are true, and
teach the way of God in truth; nor do You care
about anyone, for You do not regard the person
of men. 17 Tell us, therefore, what do You think?
Is it lawful to pay taxes to Caesar, or not?"
18 But Jesus perceived their wickedness,
and said, "Why do you test Me, *you* hypocrites?
19 Show Me the tax money."
So they brought Him a denarius.
20 And He said to them, "Whose image and
inscription *is* this?"
21 They said to Him, "Caesar's."
And He said to them, [a]"Render therefore
to Caesar the things that are [b]Caesar's, and to
God the things that are [c]God's." 22 When they
had heard *these words,* they marveled, and left
Him and went their way.

### THE SADDUCEES: WHAT ABOUT THE RESURRECTION?

*(Mark 12:18–27; Luke 20:27–40)*

23 [a]The same day the Sadducees, [b]who say
there is no resurrection, came to Him and asked
Him, 24 saying: "Teacher, [a]Moses said that if
a man dies, having no children, his brother
shall marry his wife and raise up offspring for
his brother. 25 Now there were with us seven
brothers. The first died after he had married, and
having no offspring, left his wife to his brother.
26 Likewise the second also, and the third, even
to the seventh. 27 Last of all the woman died also.
28 Therefore, in the resurrection, whose wife
of the seven will she be? For they all had her."
29 Jesus answered and said to them, "You
are mistaken, [a]not knowing the Scriptures nor
the power of God. 30 For in the resurrection
they neither marry nor are given in marriage,
but [a]are like angels of God[1] in heaven. 31 But
concerning the resurrection of the dead, have
you not read what was spoken to you by God,
saying, 32 [a]'I am the God of Abraham, the God
of Isaac, and the God of Jacob'?[1] God is not the
God of the dead, but of the living." 33 And when
the multitudes heard *this,* [a]they were astonished
at His teaching.

### THE SCRIBES: WHICH IS THE FIRST COMMANDMENT OF ALL?

*(Mark 12:28–34; Luke 10:25–28)*

34 [a]But when the Pharisees heard that He had
silenced the Sadducees, they gathered together.
35 Then one of them, [a]a lawyer, asked *Him a
question,* testing Him, and saying, 36 "Teach-
er, which *is* the great commandment in the
law?"
37 Jesus said to him, [a]" 'You shall love the
LORD your God with all your heart, with all your
soul, and with all your mind.'[1] 38 This is *the* first
and great commandment. 39 And *the* second *is*
like it: [a]'You shall love your neighbor as your-
self.'[1] 40 [a]On these two commandments hang all
the Law and the Prophets."

### JESUS: HOW CAN DAVID CALL HIS DESCENDANT "LORD"?

*(Mark 12:35–37; Luke 20:41–44)*

41 [a]While the Pharisees were gathered to-
gether, Jesus asked them, 42 saying, "What do
you think about the Christ? Whose Son is He?"
They said to Him, "*The* [a]*Son* of David."
43 He said to them, "How then does David in
the Spirit call Him 'Lord,' saying:
44 'The[a] LORD said to my Lord,
"Sit at My right hand,
Till I make Your enemies Your footstool" '?[1]
45 If David then calls Him 'Lord,' how is He his
Son?" 46 [a]And no one was able to answer Him a
word, [b]nor from that day on did anyone dare
question Him anymore.

> **22:42–45** The Old Testament foretold that **the Christ** would come from David's royal line (see 2 Sam. 7:12–16; Ps. 89:3–4, 34–36; Is. 9:7; 16:5; 55:3–4). The Hebrew text of Psalm 110:1 quoted here uses two different Hebrew words for Lord. The first, translated **LORD**, is the name *Yahweh*, the proper name of Israel's God. The second **Lord** means "master." David, the great king of Israel, called one of his offspring "Lord" or "master." Generally, respect would have gone the other way—a descendant would have called his ancestor "Lord." The implication is that Jesus, the **Son of David**, is not "normal," but rather is divine.

**22:12** [a] [Rom. 3:19] **22:13** [a] Matt. 8:12; 25:30 [1] NU-Text omits *take him away, and.* **22:14** [a] Matt. 20:16 **22:15** [a] Mark 12:13–17 **22:16** [a] Mark 3:6; 8:15; 12:13 **22:21** [a] Matt. 17:25 [b] [Rom. 13:1–7] [c] [1 Cor. 3:23; 6:19, 20; 12:27] **22:23** [a] Luke 20:27–40 [b] Acts 23:8 **22:24** [a] Deut. 25:5 **22:29** [a] John 20:9 **22:30** [a] [1 John 3:2] [1] NU-Text omits *of God.* **22:32** [a] Ex. 3:6, 15 [1] Exodus 3:6, 15 **22:33** [a] Matt. 7:28 **22:34** [a] Mark 12:28–31 **22:35** [a] Luke 7:30; 10:25; 11:45, 46, 52; 14:3 **22:37** [a] Deut. 6:5; 10:12; 30:6 [1] Deuteronomy 6:5 **22:39** [a] Lev. 19:18 [1] Leviticus 19:18 **22:40** [a] [Matt. 7:12] **22:41** [a] Luke 20:41–44 **22:42** [a] Matt. 1:1; 21:9 **22:44** [a] Ps. 110:1 [1] Psalm 110:1 **22:46** [a] Luke 14:6 [b] Mark 12:34

### WOE TO THE SCRIBES AND PHARISEES
*(Mark 12:38–40; Luke 20:45–47)*

**23** Then Jesus spoke to the multitudes and to His disciples, 2 saying: [a]"The scribes and the Pharisees sit in Moses' seat. 3 Therefore whatever they tell you to observe,[1] *that* observe and do, but do not do according to their works; for [a]they say, and do not do. 4 [a]For they bind heavy burdens, hard to bear, and lay *them* on men's shoulders; but they *themselves* will not move them with one of their fingers. 5 But all their works they do to [a]be seen by men. They make their phylacteries broad and enlarge the borders of their garments. 6 [a]They love the best places at feasts, the best seats in the synagogues, 7 greetings in the marketplaces, and to be called by men, 'Rabbi, Rabbi.' 8 [a]But you, do not be called 'Rabbi'; for One is your Teacher, the Christ,[1] and you are all brethren. 9 Do not call anyone on earth your father; [a]for One is your Father, He who is in heaven. 10 And do not be called teachers; for One is your Teacher, the Christ. 11 But [a]he who is greatest among you shall be your servant. 12 [a]And whoever exalts himself will be humbled, and he who humbles himself will be exalted.

13 "But [a]woe to you, scribes and Pharisees, hypocrites! For you shut up the kingdom of heaven against men; for you neither go in *yourselves,* nor do you allow those who are entering to go in. 14 Woe to you, scribes and Pharisees, hypocrites! [a]For you devour widows' houses, and for a pretense make long prayers. Therefore you will receive greater condemnation.[1]

15 "Woe to you, scribes and Pharisees, hypocrites! For you travel land and sea to win one proselyte, and when he is won, you make him twice as much a son of hell as yourselves.

16 "Woe to you, [a]blind guides, who say, [b]'Whoever swears by the temple, it is nothing; but whoever swears by the gold of the temple, he is obliged *to perform it.*' 17 Fools and blind! For which is greater, the gold [a]or the temple that sanctifies[1] the gold? 18 And, 'Whoever swears by the altar, it is nothing; but whoever swears by the gift that is on it, he is obliged *to perform it.*' 19 Fools and blind! For which is greater, the gift [a]or the altar that sanctifies the gift? 20 Therefore he who swears by the altar, swears by it and by all things on it. 21 He who swears by the temple, swears by it and by [a]Him who dwells[1] in it. 22 And he who swears by heaven, swears by [a]the throne of God and by Him who sits on it.

23 "Woe to you, scribes and Pharisees, hypocrites! [a]For you pay tithe of mint and anise and cummin, and [b]have neglected the weightier *matters* of the law: justice and mercy and faith.

**23:2** [a] Neh. 8:4, 8 **23:3** [a] [Rom. 2:19] [1] NU-Text omits *to observe.* **23:4** [a] Luke 11:46 **23:5** [a] [Matt. 6:1–6, 16–18] **23:6** [a] Luke 11:43; 20:46 **23:8** [a] [James 3:1] [1] NU-Text omits *the Christ.* **23:9** [a] [Mal. 1:6] **23:11** [a] Matt. 20:26, 27 **23:12** [a] Luke 14:11; 18:14 **23:13** [a] Luke 11:52 **23:14** [a] Mark 12:40 [1] NU-Text omits this verse. **23:16** [a] Matt. 15:14; 23:24 [b] [Matt. 5:33, 34] **23:17** [a] Ex. 30:29 [1] NU-Text reads *sanctified.* **23:19** [a] Ex. 29:37 **23:21** [a] 1 Kin. 8:13 [1] M-Text reads *dwelt.* **23:22** [a] Matt. 5:34 **23:23** [a] Luke 11:42; 18:12 [b] [Hos. 6:6]

KNOW THE TRUTH

## THE DOCTRINE OF SCRIPTURE
### PART 7: THE ILLUMINATION OF SCRIPTURE

**23:8–10** *Rabbi* in verse 8 is a Hebrew word meaning a teacher, instructor, master, or guide. The scribes and Pharisees wanted to be the people's primary rabbis, their scriptural guides. In turn, some of the people wanted to become rabbis just like the religious experts. Jesus corrected this. He said the Christ is *the* Teacher—the primary scriptural guide—each person needs. Only Jesus Christ can bring illumination to His truth, the Bible. *Illumination* describes how the Lord reveals, clarifies, and teaches us the Bible. The Scriptures were written by the Holy Spirit giving God's truth to faithful scribes, and thus the Bible can only be properly understood by the Holy Spirit revealing God's truth to faithful students.

Following Jesus' death, His disciples were devastated because they didn't understand the Scriptures. In Luke 24:27, after rising from the dead, Jesus "expounded" the Scriptures to His disciples. *Expounded* means clarifying something to make it understandable. Then, in Luke 24:45, Jesus opened His disciples' understanding to "comprehend" the Scriptures. *Comprehend* means Jesus gave them the ability to mentally grasp what the Bible teaches. While we need Bible teachers to help us with methods of interpretation, only Jesus can bring illumination. Jesus is the primary scriptural guide we need to grasp and understand the Bible's truth.

*For* **THE DOCTRINE OF SCRIPTURE: PART 8: THE TRANSMISSION OF SCRIPTURE,** *turn to Jeremiah 36:32 on page 786.*

These you ought to have done, without leaving
the others undone. 24 Blind guides, who strain
out a gnat and swallow a camel!
25 "Woe to you, scribes and Pharisees, hyp-
ocrites! [a]For you cleanse the outside of the cup
and dish, but inside they are full of extortion and
self-indulgence.[1] 26 Blind Pharisee, first cleanse
the inside of the cup and dish, that the outside
of them may be clean also.
27 "Woe to you, scribes and Pharisees, hyp-
ocrites! [a]For you are like whitewashed tombs
which indeed appear beautiful outwardly, but
inside are full of dead *men's* bones and all un-
cleanness. 28 Even so you also outwardly appear
righteous to men, but inside you are full of
hypocrisy and lawlessness.
29 [a]"Woe to you, scribes and Pharisees, hyp-
ocrites! Because you build the tombs of the
prophets and adorn the monuments of the righ-
teous, 30 and say, 'If we had lived in the days of
our fathers, we would not have been partakers
with them in the blood of the prophets.'
31 "Therefore you are witnesses against
yourselves that [a]you are sons of those who
murdered the prophets. 32 [a]Fill up, then, the
measure of your fathers' *guilt.* 33 Serpents,
[a]brood of vipers! How can you escape the con-
demnation of hell? 34 [a]Therefore, indeed, I send
you prophets, wise men, and scribes: [b]*some*
of them you will kill and crucify, and [c]*some*
of them you will scourge in your synagogues
and persecute from city to city, 35 [a]that on you
may come all the righteous blood shed on the
earth, [b]from the blood of righteous Abel to [c]the
blood of Zechariah, son of Berechiah, whom
you murdered between the temple and the
altar. 36 Assuredly, I say to you, all these things
will come upon this generation.

### JESUS LAMENTS OVER JERUSALEM

*(Luke 13:34, 35)*

37 [a]"O Jerusalem, Jerusalem, the one who
kills the prophets [b]and stones those who are sent
to her! How often [c]I wanted to gather your chil-
dren together, as a hen gathers her chicks [d]under
*her* wings, but you were not willing! 38 See! Your
house is left to you desolate; 39 for I say to you,
you shall see Me no more till you say, [a]'Blessed
*is* He who comes in the name of the LORD!' "[1]

### JESUS PREDICTS THE DESTRUCTION OF THE TEMPLE

*(Mark 13:1, 2; Luke 21:5, 6)*

24 Then [a]Jesus went out and departed from
the temple, and His disciples came up
to show Him the buildings of the temple. 2 And
Jesus said to them, "Do you not see all these
things? Assuredly, I say to you, [a]not *one* stone
shall be left here upon another, that shall not
be thrown down."

### THE SIGNS OF THE TIMES AND THE END OF THE AGE

*(Mark 13:3–13; Luke 21:7–19)*

3 Now as He sat on the Mount of Olives, [a]the
disciples came to Him privately, saying, [b]"Tell us,
when will these things be? And what *will be* the
sign of Your coming, and of the end of the age?"
4 And Jesus answered and said to them:
[a]"Take heed that no one deceives you. 5 For
[a]many will come in My name, saying, 'I am the
Christ,' [b]and will deceive many. 6 And you will

**23:25** [a] Luke 11:39 [1] M-Text reads *unrighteousness.* **23:27** [a] Acts 23:3 **23:29** [a] Luke 11:47, 48 **23:31** [a] [Acts 7:51, 52] **23:32** [a] [1 Thess. 2:16] **23:33** [a] Matt. 3:7; 12:34 **23:34** [a] Luke 11:49 [b] Acts 7:54–60; 22:19 [c] 2 Cor. 11:24, 25 **23:35** [a] Rev. 18:24 [b] Gen. 4:8 [c] 2 Chr. 24:20, 21 **23:37** [a] Luke 13:34, 35 [b] 2 Chr. 24:20, 21; 36:15, 16 [c] Deut. 32:11, 12 [d] Ps. 17:8; 91:4 **23:39** [a] Ps. 118:26 [1] Psalm 118:26 **24:1** [a] Mark 13:1 **24:2** [a] Luke 19:44 **24:3** [a] Mark 13:3 [b] [1 Thess. 5:1–3] **24:4** [a] [Col. 2:8, 18] **24:5** [a] John 5:43 [b] Matt. 24:11

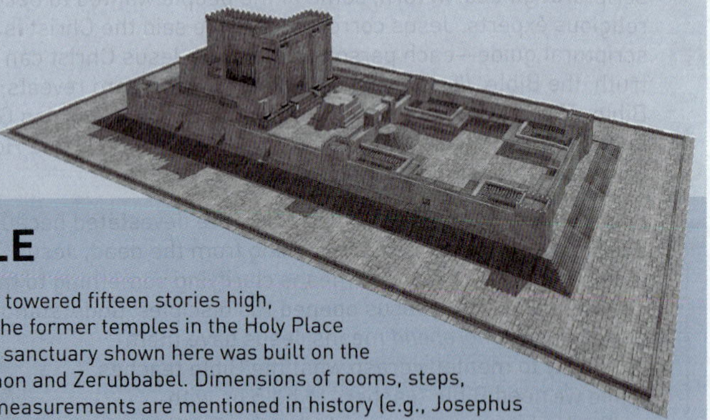

## HEROD'S TEMPLE

Begun in 20 BC, Herod's structure towered fifteen stories high, following the floor dimensions of the former temples in the Holy Place and the Most Holy Place. The high sanctuary shown here was built on the site of the former temples of Solmon and Zerubbabel. Dimensions of rooms, steps, doorways, cornices, and exterior measurements are mentioned in history (e.g., Josephus and the Mishnah) but are subject to interpretation.

The outer courts surrounding the temple mount were not completed until AD 64. The entire structure was demolished by the Romans in AD 70.

hear of [a]wars and rumors of wars. See that you are not troubled; for all[1] *these things* must come to pass, but the end is not yet. 7 For [a]nation will rise against nation, and kingdom against kingdom. And there will be [b]famines, pestilences,[1] and earthquakes in various places. 8 All these *are* the beginning of sorrows.

9 [a]"Then they will deliver you up to tribulation and kill you, and you will be hated by all nations for My name's sake. 10 And then many will be offended, will betray one another, and will hate one another. 11 Then [a]many false prophets will rise up and [b]deceive many. 12 And because lawlessness will abound, the love of many will grow [a]cold. 13 [a]But he who endures to the end shall be saved. 14 And this [a]gospel of the kingdom [b]will be preached in all the world as a witness to all the nations, and then the end will come.

### THE GREAT TRIBULATION

*(Mark 13:14–23; Luke 17:23, 24, 37; 21:20–24)*

15 [a]"Therefore when you see the [b]'abomination of desolation,'[1] spoken of by Daniel the prophet, standing in the holy place" [c](whoever reads, let him understand), 16 "then let those who are in Judea flee to the mountains. 17 Let him who is on the housetop not go down to take anything out of his house. 18 And let him who is in the field not go back to get his clothes. 19 But [a]woe to those who are pregnant and to those who are nursing babies in those days! 20 And pray that your flight may not be in winter or on the Sabbath. 21 For [a]then there will be great tribulation, such as has not been since the beginning of the world until this time, no, nor ever shall be. 22 And unless those days were shortened, no flesh would be saved; [a]but for the elect's sake those days will be shortened.

23 [a]"Then if anyone says to you, 'Look, here *is* the Christ!' or 'There!' do not believe *it.* 24 For [a]false christs and false prophets will rise and show great signs and wonders to deceive, [b]if possible, even the elect. 25 See, I have told you beforehand.

26 "Therefore if they say to you, 'Look, He is in the desert!' do not go out; *or* 'Look, *He is* in the inner rooms!' do not believe *it.* 27 [a]For as the lightning comes from the east and flashes to the west, so also will the coming of the Son of Man be. 28 [a]For wherever the carcass is, there the eagles will be gathered together.

### THE COMING OF THE SON OF MAN

*(Mark 13:24–27; Luke 21:25–28)*

29 [a]"Immediately after the tribulation of those days [b]the sun will be darkened, and the moon will not give its light; the stars will fall from heaven, and the powers of the heavens will be shaken. 30 [a]Then the sign of the Son of Man will appear in heaven, [b]and then all the tribes of the earth will mourn, and they will see the Son of Man coming on the clouds of heaven with power and great glory. 31 [a]And He will send His angels with a great sound of a trumpet, and they will gather together His elect from the four winds, from one end of heaven to the other.

### THE PARABLE OF THE FIG TREE

*(Mark 13:28–31; Luke 21:29–33)*

32 "Now learn [a]this parable from the fig tree: When its branch has already become tender and puts forth leaves, you know that summer *is* near. 33 So you also, when you see all these things, know [a]that it[1] is near—at the doors! 34 Assuredly, I say to you, [a]this generation will by no means pass away till all these things take place. 35 [a]Heaven and earth will pass away, but My words will by no means pass away.

### NO ONE KNOWS THE DAY OR HOUR

*(Mark 13:32–37; Luke 17:26, 27, 34, 35; 21:34–36)*

36 [a]"But of that day and hour no one knows, not even the angels of heaven,[1] [b]but My Father only. 37 But as the days of Noah *were,* so also will the coming of the Son of Man be. 38 [a]For as in the days before the flood, they were eating and drinking, marrying and giving in marriage, until the day that Noah entered the ark, 39 and did not know until the flood came and took them all away, so also will the coming of the Son of Man be. 40 [a]Then two *men* will be in the field: one will be taken and the other left. 41 Two *women will be* grinding at the mill: one will be taken and the other left. 42 [a]Watch therefore, for you do not know what hour[1] your Lord is coming. 43 [a]But know this, that if the master of the house had known what hour the thief would come, he would have watched and not allowed his house to be broken into. 44 [a]Therefore you also be ready, for the Son of Man is coming at an hour you do not expect.

### THE FAITHFUL SERVANT AND THE EVIL SERVANT

*(Luke 12:41–48)*

45 [a]"Who then is a faithful and wise servant, whom his master made ruler over his household, to give them food in due season? 46 [a]Blessed *is* that servant whom his master, when he comes, will find so doing. 47 Assuredly, I say to you that [a]he will make him ruler over all his goods. 48 But if that evil servant says in his heart, 'My master [a]is delaying his coming,'[1] 49 and begins to beat *his* fellow

24:6 [a] [Rev. 6:2–4] [1] NU-Text omits *all.* 24:7 [a] Hag. 2:22 [b] Rev. 6:5, 6 [1] NU-Text omits *pestilences.* 24:9 [a] Matt. 10:17 24:11 [a] 2 Pet. 2:1 [b] [1 Tim. 4:1] 24:12 [a] [2 Thess. 2:3] 24:13 [a] Matt. 10:22 24:14 [a] Matt. 4:23 [b] Rom. 10:18 24:15 [a] Mark 13:14 [b] Dan. 9:27; 11:31; 12:11 [c] Dan. 9:23 [1] Daniel 11:31; 12:11 24:19 [a] Luke 23:29 24:21 [a] Dan. 9:26 24:22 [a] Is. 65:8, 9 24:23 [a] Luke 17:23 24:24 [a] [2 Thess. 2:9] [b] [2 Tim. 2:19] 24:27 [a] Luke 17:24 24:28 [a] Luke 17:37 24:29 [a] [Dan. 7:11] [b] Ezek. 32:7 24:30 [a] [Dan. 7:13, 14] [b] Zech. 12:12 24:31 [a] [1 Cor. 15:52] 24:32 [a] Luke 21:29 24:33 [a] [James 5:9] [1] Or *He* 24:34 [a] [Matt. 10:23; 16:28; 23:36] 24:35 [a] Luke 21:33 24:36 [a] Acts 1:7 [b] Zech. 14:7 [1] NU-Text adds *nor the Son.* 24:38 [a] [Gen. 6:3–5] 24:40 [a] Luke 17:34 24:42 [a] Matt. 25:13; Luke 21:36; 1 Thess. 5:6 [1] NU-Text reads *day.* 24:43 [a] Luke 12:39; 1 Thess. 5:2; Rev. 3:3 24:44 [a] Luke 12:35–40; [1 Thess. 5:6] 24:45 [a] Luke 12:42–46; [Acts 20:28] 24:46 [a] Rev. 16:15 24:47 [a] Matt. 25:21, 23; Luke 22:29 24:48 [a] [2 Pet. 3:4–9] [1] NU-Text omits *his coming.*

servants, and to eat and drink with the drunkards, 50 the master of that servant will come on a day when he is not looking for *him* and at an hour that he is [a]not aware of, 51 and will cut him in two and appoint *him* his portion with the hypocrites. [a]There shall be weeping and gnashing of teeth.

### THE PARABLE OF THE WISE AND FOOLISH VIRGINS

**25** "Then the kingdom of heaven shall be likened to ten virgins who took their lamps and went out to meet [a]the bridegroom. 2 [a]Now five of them were wise, and five *were* foolish. 3 Those who *were* foolish took their lamps and took no oil with them, 4 but the wise took oil in their vessels with their lamps. 5 But while the bridegroom was delayed, [a]they all slumbered and slept.

> **25:1** The **lamps** of New Testament times looked like miniature teapots. A wick was placed in the spout and olive oil was poured through a hole in the top. A lamp with one wick and a full load of oil could burn for about four hours.

6 "And at midnight [a]a cry was *heard:* 'Behold, the bridegroom is coming;[1] go out to meet him!' 7 Then all those virgins arose and [a]trimmed their lamps. 8 And the foolish said to the wise, 'Give us *some* of your oil, for our lamps are going out.' 9 But the wise answered, saying, '*No,* lest there should not be enough for us and you; but go rather to those who sell, and buy for yourselves.' 10 And while they went to buy, the bridegroom came, and those who were ready went in with him to the wedding; and [a]the door was shut.

11 "Afterward the other virgins came also, saying, [a]'Lord, Lord, open to us!' 12 But he answered and said, 'Assuredly, I say to you, [a]I do not know you.'

13 [a]"Watch therefore, for you [b]know neither the day nor the hour[1] in which the Son of Man is coming.

### THE PARABLE OF THE TALENTS

*(Luke 19:11–27)*

14 [a]"For *the kingdom of heaven is* [b]like a man traveling to a far country, *who* called his own servants and delivered his goods to them. 15 And to one he gave five talents, to another two, and to another one, [a]to each according to his own ability; and immediately he went on a journey. 16 Then he who had received the five talents went and traded with them, and made another five talents. 17 And likewise he who *had received* two gained two more also. 18 But he who had received one went and dug in the ground, and hid his lord's money. 19 After a long time the lord of those servants came and settled accounts with them.

20 "So he who had received five talents came and brought five other talents, saying, 'Lord, you delivered to me five talents; look, I have gained five more talents besides them.' 21 His lord said to him, 'Well *done,* good and faithful servant; you were [a]faithful over a few things, [b]I will make you ruler over many things. Enter into [c]the joy of your lord.' 22 He also who had received two talents came and said, 'Lord, you delivered to me two talents; look, I have gained two more talents besides them.' 23 His lord said to him, [a]'Well *done,* good and faithful servant; you have been faithful over a few things, I will make you ruler over many things. Enter into [b]the joy of your lord.'

24 "Then he who had received the one talent came and said, 'Lord, I knew you to be a hard man, reaping where you have not sown, and gathering where you have not scattered seed. 25 And I was afraid, and went and hid your talent in the ground. Look, *there* you have *what is* yours.'

26 "But his lord answered and said to him, 'You [a]wicked and lazy servant, you knew that I reap where I have not sown, and gather where I have not scattered seed. 27 So you ought to have deposited my money with the bankers, and at my coming I would have received back my own with interest. 28 So take the talent from him, and give *it* to him who has ten talents.

29 [a]'For to everyone who has, more will be given, and he will have abundance; but from him who does not have, even what he has will be taken away. 30 And cast the unprofitable servant [a]into the outer darkness. [b]There will be weeping and [c]gnashing of teeth.'

### THE SON OF MAN WILL JUDGE THE NATIONS

31 [a]"When the Son of Man comes in His glory, and all the holy[1] angels with Him, then He will sit on the throne of His glory. 32 [a]All the nations will be gathered before Him, and [b]He will separate them one from another, as a shepherd divides *his* sheep from the goats. 33 And He will set the [a]sheep on His right hand, but the goats on the left. 34 Then the King will say to those on His right hand, 'Come, you blessed of My Father, [a]inherit the kingdom [b]prepared for you from the foundation of the world: 35 [a]for I was hungry and you gave Me food; I was thirsty and you gave Me drink; [b]I was a stranger and you took Me in; 36 I *was*

**24:50** [a] Mark 13:32 **24:51** [a] Matt. 8:12; 25:30 **25:1** [a] [Eph. 5:29, 30; Rev. 19:7; 21:2, 9] **25:2** [a] Matt. 13:47; 22:10 **25:5** [a] 1 Thess. 5:6 **25:6** [a] [Matt. 24:31; 1 Thess. 4:16] [1] NU-Text omits *is coming.* **25:7** [a] Luke 12:35 **25:10** [a] [Matt. 7:21]; Luke 13:25 **25:11** [a] [Matt. 7:21–23; Luke 13:25–30] **25:12** [a] [Ps. 5:5; Hab. 1:13; John 9:31] **25:13** [a] Mark 13:35; [Luke 21:36]; 1 Thess. 5:6 [b] Matt. 24:36, 42 [1] NU-Text omits the rest of this verse. **25:14** [a] Luke 19:12–27 [b] Matt. 21:33 **25:15** [a] [Rom. 12:6; 1 Cor. 12:7, 11, 29; Eph. 4:11] **25:21** [a] [Luke 16:10; 1 Cor. 4:2; 2 Tim. 4:7, 8] [b] [Matt. 24:47; 25:34, 46; Luke 12:44; 22:29, 30; Rev. 3:21; 21:7] [c] [2 Tim. 2:12; Heb. 12:2; 1 Pet. 1:8] **25:23** [a] Matt. 24:45, 47; 25:21 [b] [Ps. 16:11; John 15:10, 11] **25:26** [a] Matt. 18:32; Luke 19:22 **25:29** [a] Matt. 13:12 **25:30** [a] Matt. 8:12; 22:13 [b] Matt. 7:23; 8:12; 24:51 [c] Ps. 112:10 **25:31** [a] [1 Thess. 4:16] [1] NU-Text omits *holy.* **25:32** [a] [2 Cor. 5:10] [b] Ezek. 20:38 **25:33** [a] [John 10:11, 27, 28] **25:34** [a] [Rom. 8:17] [b] Mark 10:40 **25:35** [a] Is. 58:7 [b] [Heb. 13:2]

LIVE THE TRUTH

## SERVING YOUR COMMUNITY

**25:35–40** Jesus' three-year earthly ministry was about showing people the kingdom of God and reversing sin's effects on their lives. Hunger, illness, infirmity, emotional distress, rejection, and more are all the results of sin—sometimes directly but often indirectly. Jesus proclaimed God's kingdom and showed how it was meant to function, apart from sin and its ugly consequences. In other words, Jesus cared about saving *and* serving His community. When we give our time and resources to those in need, we tangibly show the love of Jesus. Through community service, we can have a healing effect on this broken world.

In this passage, Jesus explained serving the "least of these"—those who are often overlooked and forgotten—is extremely important to Him. When we serve the hungry, the homeless, the stranger, the prisoner, the widow, and the orphan with the love of God in mind, we work for Jesus and follow His perfect example. That's why Jesus said if we don't make serving others a priority, it brings to question if we have a relationship with Him. Jesus made community service a priority; if we're following Him, we will do the same.

[a]naked and you clothed Me; I was sick and you visited Me; [b]I was in prison and you came to Me.'

37 "Then the righteous will answer Him, saying, 'Lord, when did we see You hungry and feed *You,* or thirsty and give *You* drink? 38 When did we see You a stranger and take *You* in, or naked and clothe *You?* 39 Or when did we see You sick, or in prison, and come to You?' 40 And the King will answer and say to them, 'Assuredly, I say to you, [a]inasmuch as you did *it* to one of the least of these My brethren, you did *it* to Me.'

41 "Then He will also say to those on the left hand, [a]'Depart from Me, you cursed, [b]into the everlasting fire prepared for [c]the devil and his angels: 42 for I was hungry and you gave Me no food; I was thirsty and you gave Me no drink; 43 I was a stranger and you did not take Me in, naked and you did not clothe Me, sick and in prison and you did not visit Me.'

44 "Then they also will answer Him,[1] saying, 'Lord, when did we see You hungry or thirsty or a stranger or naked or sick or in prison, and did not minister to You?' 45 Then He will answer them, saying, 'Assuredly, I say to you, [a]inasmuch as you did not do *it* to one of the least of these, you did not do *it* to Me.' 46 And [a]these will go away into everlasting punishment, but the righteous into eternal life."

### *THE PLOT TO KILL JESUS*

*(Mark 14:1, 2; Luke 22:1, 2; John 11:45–53)*

**26** Now it came to pass, when Jesus had finished all these sayings, *that* He said to His disciples, 2 [a]"You know that after two days is the Passover, and the Son of Man will be delivered up to be crucified."

3 [a]Then the chief priests, the scribes,[1] and the elders of the people assembled at the palace of the high priest, who was called Caiaphas, 4 and [a]plotted to take Jesus by trickery and kill *Him.* 5 But they said, "Not during the feast, lest there be an uproar among the [a]people."

### *THE ANOINTING AT BETHANY*

*(Mark 14:3–9; John 12:1–8)*

6 And when Jesus was in [a]Bethany at the house of Simon the leper, 7 a woman came to Him having an alabaster flask of very costly fragrant oil, and she poured *it* on His head as He sat *at the table.* 8 [a]But when His disciples saw *it,* they were indignant, saying, "Why this waste? 9 For this fragrant oil might have been sold for much and given to *the* poor."

10 But when Jesus was aware of *it,* He said to them, "Why do you trouble the woman? For she has done a good work for Me. 11 [a]For you have the poor with you always, but [b]Me you do not have always. 12 For in pouring this fragrant oil on My body, she did *it* for My [a]burial. 13 Assuredly, I say to you, wherever this gospel is preached in the whole world, what this woman has done will also be told as a memorial to her."

### *JUDAS AGREES TO BETRAY JESUS*

*(Mark 14:10, 11; Luke 22:3–6)*

14 [a]Then one of the twelve, called [b]Judas Iscariot, went to the chief priests 15 and said, [a]"What are you willing to give me if I deliver Him to you?" And they counted out to him thirty

**SEEING JESUS IN THE SCRIPTURE**

**26:15** Thirty pieces of silver was the price of a slave (Ex. 21:32). Zechariah prophesied this sum (see Zech. 11:12–13).

**25:36** [a] [James 2:15, 16] [b] 2 Tim. 1:16 **25:40** [a] Mark 9:41 **25:41** [a] Matt. 7:23 [b] Matt. 13:40, 42 [c] [2 Pet. 2:4] **25:44** [1] NU-Text and M-Text omit *Him.* **25:45** [a] Prov. 14:31 **25:46** [a] [Dan. 12:2] **26:2** [a] Luke 22:1, 2 **26:3** [a] John 11:47 [1] NU-Text omits *the scribes.* **26:4** [a] Acts 4:25–28 **26:5** [a] Matt. 21:26 **26:6** [a] Mark 14:3–9 **26:8** [a] John 12:4 **26:11** [a] [Deut. 15:11] [b] [John 13:33; 14:19; 16:5, 28; 17:11] **26:12** [a] John 19:38–42 **26:14** [a] Mark 14:10, 11; Luke 22:3–6 [b] Matt. 10:4 **26:15** [a] Zech. 11:12

pieces of silver. 16 So from that time he sought opportunity to betray Him.

### *JESUS CELEBRATES PASSOVER WITH HIS DISCIPLES*

*(Mark 14:12–21; Luke 22:7–13)*

17 [a]Now on the first *day of the Feast* of the Unleavened Bread the disciples came to Jesus, saying to Him, "Where do You want us to prepare for You to eat the Passover?"

18 And He said, "Go into the city to a certain man, and say to him, 'The Teacher says, [a]"My time is at hand; I will keep the Passover at your house with My disciples." ' "

19 So the disciples did as Jesus had directed them; and they prepared the Passover.

20 [a]When evening had come, He sat down with the twelve. 21 Now as they were eating, He said, "Assuredly, I say to you, one of you will [a]betray Me."

22 And they were exceedingly sorrowful, and each of them began to say to Him, "Lord, is it I?"

23 He answered and said, [a]"He who dipped *his* hand with Me in the dish will betray Me. 24 The Son of Man indeed goes just [a]as it is written of Him, but [b]woe to that man by whom the Son of Man is betrayed! [c]It would have been good for that man if he had not been born."

25 Then Judas, who was betraying Him, answered and said, "Rabbi, is it I?"

He said to him, "You have said it."

### *JESUS INSTITUTES THE LORD'S SUPPER*

*(Mark 14:22–26; Luke 22:14–23; 1 Cor. 11:23–26)*

26 [a]And as they were eating, [b]Jesus took bread, blessed[1] and broke *it,* and gave *it* to the disciples and said, "Take, eat; [c]this is My body."

27 Then He took the cup, and gave thanks, and gave *it* to them, saying, [a]"Drink from it, all of you. 28 For [a]this is My blood [b]of the new[1] covenant, which is shed [c]for many for the remission of sins. 29 But [a]I say to you, I will not drink of this fruit of the vine from now on [b]until that day when I drink it new with you in My Father's kingdom."

30 [a]And when they had sung a hymn, they went out to the Mount of Olives.

### *JESUS PREDICTS PETER'S DENIAL*

*(Mark 14:27–31; Luke 22:31–34; John 13:36–38)*

31 Then Jesus said to them, [a]"All of you will [b]be made to stumble because of Me this night, for it is written:

> [c]'I will strike the Shepherd,
> And the sheep of the flock will be
> scattered.'[1]

32 But after I have been raised, [a]I will go before you to Galilee."

33 Peter answered and said to Him, "Even if all are made to stumble because of You, I will never be made to stumble."

34 Jesus said to him, [a]"Assuredly, I say to you that this night, before the rooster crows, you will deny Me three times."

35 Peter said to Him, "Even if I have to die with You, I will not deny You!"

And so said all the disciples.

### *THE PRAYER IN THE GARDEN*

*(Mark 14:32–42; Luke 22:39–46)*

36 [a]Then Jesus came with them to a place called Gethsemane, and said to the disciples, "Sit here while I go and pray over there." 37 And He took with Him Peter and [a]the two sons of Zebedee, and He began to be sorrowful and deeply distressed. 38 Then He said to them, [a]"My soul is exceedingly sorrowful, even to death. Stay here and watch with Me."

39 He went a little farther and fell on His face, and [a]prayed, saying, [b]"O My Father, if it is possible, [c]let this cup pass from Me; nevertheless, [d]not as I will, but as You *will*."

40 Then He came to the disciples and found them sleeping, and said to Peter, "What! Could you not watch with Me one hour? 41 [a]Watch and pray, lest you enter into temptation. [b]The spirit indeed *is* willing, but the flesh *is* weak."

42 Again, a second time, He went away and prayed, saying, "O My Father, if this cup cannot pass away from Me unless[1] I drink it, Your will be done." 43 And He came and found them asleep again, for their eyes were heavy.

44 So He left them, went away again, and prayed the third time, saying the same words. 45 Then He came to His disciples and said to them, "Are *you* still sleeping and resting? Behold, the hour is at hand, and the Son of Man is being [a]betrayed into the hands of sinners. 46 Rise, let us be going. See, My betrayer is at hand."

### *BETRAYAL AND ARREST IN GETHSEMANE*

*(Mark 14:43–52; Luke 22:47–53; John 18:1–11)*

47 And [a]while He was still speaking, behold, Judas, one of the twelve, with a great multitude with swords and clubs, came from the chief priests and elders of the people.

48 Now His betrayer had given them a sign, saying, "Whomever I kiss, He is the One; seize Him." 49 Immediately he went up to Jesus and said, "Greetings, Rabbi!" [a]and kissed Him.

50 But Jesus said to him, [a]"Friend, why have you come?"

**26:17** [a] Ex. 12:6, 18–20 **26:18** [a] Luke 9:51 **26:20** [a] Mark 14:17–21 **26:21** [a] John 6:70, 71; 13:21 **26:23** [a] Ps. 41:9 **26:24** [a] 1 Cor. 15:3 [b] Luke 17:1 [c] John 17:12 **26:26** [a] Mark 14:22–25 [b] 1 Cor. 11:23–25 [c] [1 Pet. 2:24] [1] M-Text reads *gave thanks for.* **26:27** [a] Mark 14:23 **26:28** [a] [Ex. 24:8] [b] Jer. 31:31 [c] Matt. 20:28 [1] NU-Text omits *new.* **26:29** [a] Mark 14:25 [b] Acts 10:41 **26:30** [a] Mark 14:26–31 **26:31** [a] John 16:32 [b] [Matt. 11:6] [c] Zech. 13:7 [1] Zechariah 13:7 **26:32** [a] Matt. 28:7, 10, 16 **26:34** [a] John 13:38 **26:36** [a] Mark 14:32–35 **26:37** [a] Matt. 4:21; 17:1 **26:38** [a] John 12:27 **26:39** [a] [Heb. 5:7–9] [b] John 12:27 [c] Matt. 20:22 [d] John 5:30; 6:38 **26:41** [a] Luke 22:40, 46 [b] [Gal. 5:17] **26:42** [1] NU-Text reads *if this may not pass away unless.* **26:45** [a] Matt. 17:22, 23; 20:18, 19 **26:47** [a] Acts 1:16 **26:49** [a] 2 Sam. 20:9 **26:50** [a] Ps. 41:9; 55:13

### SEEING JESUS IN THE SCRIPTURE

**26:47–57** Jesus wasn't surprised when Judas showed up with a multitude of soldiers; He said it would happen (see Matt. 20:18).

Then they came and laid hands on Jesus
and took Him. 51 And suddenly, [a]one of those
*who were* with Jesus stretched out *his* hand and
drew his sword, struck the servant of the high
priest, and cut off his ear.
52 But Jesus said to him, "Put your sword in
its place, [a]for all who take the sword will perish[1]
by the sword. 53 Or do you think that I cannot
now pray to My Father, and He will provide Me
with [a]more than twelve legions of angels? 54 How
then could the Scriptures be fulfilled, [a]that it
must happen thus?"
55 In that hour Jesus said to the multitudes,
"Have you come out, as against a robber, with
swords and clubs to take Me? I sat daily with you,
teaching in the temple, and you did not seize
Me. 56 But all this was done that the [a]Scriptures
of the prophets might be fulfilled."
Then [b]all the disciples forsook Him and fled.

### *JESUS FACES THE SANHEDRIN*

*(Mark 14:53–65; Luke 22:66–71; John 18:12–14, 19–24)*

57 [a]And those who had laid hold of Jesus led
*Him* away to Caiaphas the high priest, where the
scribes and the elders were assembled. 58 But
[a]Peter followed Him at a distance to the high
priest's courtyard. And he went in and sat with
the servants to see the end.
59 Now the chief priests, the elders,[1] and all
the council sought [a]false testimony against Jesus
to put Him to death, 60 but found none. Even
though [a]many false witnesses came forward,
they found none.[1] But at last [b]two false witness-
es[2] came forward 61 and said, "This *fellow* said,
[a]'I am able to destroy the temple of God and to
build it in three days.'"
62 [a]And the high priest arose and said to Him,
"Do You answer nothing? What *is it* these men
testify against You?" 63 But [a]Jesus kept silent.
And the high priest answered and said to Him,
[b]"I put You under oath by the living God: Tell us
if You are the Christ, the Son of God!"
64 Jesus said to him, "*It is as* you said. Nev-
ertheless, I say to you, [a]hereafter you will see
the Son of Man [b]sitting at the right hand of the
Power, and coming on the clouds of heaven."
65 [a]Then the high priest tore his clothes, say-
ing, "He has spoken blasphemy! What further
need do we have of witnesses? Look, now you have
heard His [b]blasphemy! 66 What do you think?"
They answered and said, [a]"He is deserving
of death."
67 [a]Then they spat in His face and beat Him;
and [b]others struck *Him* with the palms of their
hands, 68 saying, [a]"Prophesy to us, Christ! Who
is the one who struck You?"

### *PETER DENIES JESUS, AND WEEPS BITTERLY*

*(Mark 14:66–72; Luke 22:54–62; John 18:15–18, 25–27)*

69 [a]Now Peter sat outside in the courtyard.
And a servant girl came to him, saying, "You
also were with Jesus of Galilee."
70 But he denied it before *them* all, saying,
"I do not know what you are saying."
71 And when he had gone out to the gateway,
another *girl* saw him and said to those *who were*
there, "This *fellow* also was with Jesus of Nazareth."
72 But again he denied with an oath, "I do
not know the Man!"
73 And a little later those who stood by came
up and said to Peter, "Surely you also are *one* of
them, for your [a]speech betrays you."
74 Then [a]he began to curse and swear, *saying,*
"I do not know the Man!"
Immediately a rooster crowed. 75 And Peter
remembered the word of Jesus who had said to
him, [a]"Before the rooster crows, you will deny Me
three times." So he went out and wept bitterly.

### SEEING JESUS IN THE SCRIPTURE

**26:74–75** Just as Jesus foretold, Peter denied Him three times (see Matt. 26:34). Peter remembered Jesus' words and wept because of his denial.

### *JESUS HANDED OVER TO PONTIUS PILATE*

*(Mark 15:1; Luke 23:1; John 18:28)*

27 When morning came, [a]all the chief priests
and elders of the people plotted against
Jesus to put Him to death. 2 And when they had
bound Him, they led Him away and [a]delivered
Him to Pontius[1] Pilate the governor.

### *JUDAS HANGS HIMSELF*

*(Acts 1:18, 19)*

3 [a]Then Judas, His betrayer, seeing that He
had been condemned, was remorseful and
brought back the thirty [b]pieces of silver to the

**26:51** [a] John 18:10 **26:52** [a] Rev. 13:10 [1] M-Text reads *die.* **26:53** [a] Dan. 7:10 **26:54** [a] Is. 50:6; 53:2–11 **26:56** [a] Lam. 4:20 [b] John 18:15 **26:57** [a] John 18:12, 19–24 **26:58** [a] John 18:15, 16 **26:59** [a] Ps. 35:11 [1] NU-Text omits *the elders.* **26:60** [a] Mark 14:55 [b] Deut. 19:15 [1] NU-Text puts a comma after *but found none,* does not capitalize *Even,* and omits *they found none.* [2] NU-Text omits *false witnesses.* **26:61** [a] John 2:19 **26:62** [a] Mark 14:60 **26:63** [a] Is. 53:7 [b] Lev. 5:1 **26:64** [a] Dan. 7:13 [b] [Acts 7:55] **26:65** [a] 2 Kin. 18:37 [b] John 10:30–36 **26:66** [a] Lev. 24:16 **26:67** [a] Is. 50:6; 53:3 [b] Luke 22:63–65 **26:68** [a] Mark 14:65 **26:69** [a] John 18:16–18, 25–27 **26:73** [a] Luke 22:59 **26:74** [a] Mark 14:71 **26:75** [a] Matt. 26:34 **27:1** [a] John 18:28 **27:2** [a] Acts 3:13 [1] NU-Text omits *Pontius.* **27:3** [a] Matt. 26:14 [b] Matt. 26:15

chief priests and elders, 4 saying, "I have sinned
by betraying innocent blood."
And they said, "What *is that* to us? You see *to it!*"
5 Then he threw down the pieces of silver in
the temple and [a]departed, and went and hanged
himself.
6 But the chief priests took the silver pieces
and said, "It is not lawful to put them into the trea-
sury, because they are the price of blood." 7 And
they consulted together and bought with them the
potter's field, to bury strangers in. 8 Therefore that
field has been called [a]the Field of Blood to this day.
9 Then was fulfilled what was spoken by
Jeremiah the prophet, saying, [a]"And they took
the thirty pieces of silver, the value of Him who
was priced, whom they of the children of Israel
priced, 10 and [a]gave them for the potter's field,
as the LORD directed me."[1]

### JESUS FACES PILATE

*(Mark 15:2–5; Luke 23:2–5; John 18:29–38)*

11 Now Jesus stood before the governor. [a]And
the governor asked Him, saying, "Are You the
King of the Jews?"
Jesus said to him, [b]"*It is as* you say." 12 And
while He was being accused by the chief priests
and elders, [a]He answered nothing.
13 Then Pilate said to Him, [a]"Do You not hear
how many things they testify against You?"
14 But He answered him not one word, so that
the governor marveled greatly.

### TAKING THE PLACE OF BARABBAS

*(Mark 15:6–15; Luke 23:13–25; John 18:39, 40)*

15 [a]Now at the feast the governor was accus-
tomed to releasing to the multitude one prisoner
whom they wished. 16 And at that time they had a
notorious prisoner called Barabbas.[1] 17 Therefore,
when they had gathered together, Pilate said to
them, "Whom do you want me to release to you?
Barabbas, or Jesus who is called Christ?" 18 For he
knew that they had handed Him over because
of [a]envy.
19 While he was sitting on the judgment seat,
his wife sent to him, saying, "Have nothing to
do with that just Man, for I have suffered many
things today in a dream because of Him."
20 [a]But the chief priests and elders persuad-
ed the multitudes that they should ask for Barab-
bas and destroy Jesus. 21 The governor answered
and said to them, "Which of the two do you want
me to release to you?"
They said, [a]"Barabbas!"
22 Pilate said to them, "What then shall I do
with Jesus who is called Christ?"
*They* all said to him, "Let Him be crucified!"
23 Then the governor said, [a]"Why, what evil
has He done?"
But they cried out all the more, saying, "Let
Him be crucified!"
24 When Pilate saw that he could not prevail
at all, but rather *that* a tumult was rising, he
[a]took water and washed *his* hands before the
multitude, saying, "I am innocent of the blood
of this just Person.[1] You see *to it.*"
25 And all the people answered and said,
[a]"His blood *be* on us and on our children."
26 Then he released Barabbas to them; and
when [a]he had scourged Jesus, he delivered *Him*
to be crucified.

### THE SOLDIERS MOCK JESUS

*(Mark 15:16–20)*

27 [a]Then the soldiers of the governor took
Jesus into the Praetorium and gathered the whole
garrison around Him. 28 And they [a]stripped Him

**27:5** [a] Acts 1:18 **27:8** [a] Acts 1:19 **27:9** [a] Zech. 11:12 **27:10** [a] Jer. 32:6–9; Zech. 11:12, 13 [1] Jeremiah 32:6–9 **27:11** [a] Mark 15:2–5 [b] John 18:37 **27:12** [a] John 19:9 **27:13** [a] Matt. 26:62 **27:15** [a] Luke 23:17–25 **27:16** [1] NU-Text reads *Jesus Barabbas.* **27:18** [a] Matt. 21:38 **27:20** [a] Acts 3:14 **27:21** [a] Acts 3:14 **27:23** [a] Acts 3:13 **27:24** [a] Deut. 21:6–8 [1] NU-Text omits *just.* **27:25** [a] Josh. 2:19 **27:26** [a] [Is. 50:6; 53:5] **27:27** [a] Mark 15:16–20 **27:28** [a] John 19:2

APPLY THE TRUTH

## ARCHEOLOGICAL FINDS

**27:11–26** While the Bible isn't a history textbook, it is a book of history. It tells the real story of real people in real places doing real things. While not everything in the Bible has been proven by archaeological finds, much of it has been. Critics, though, often try to point to certain things in the Bible that haven't been proven true to claim the Bible is false—like Pontius Pilate.

Pilate was the governor who condemned Jesus to death to please the crowds and avoid a riot. The problem was that no evidence of Pilate's existence could be found outside of the Bible. It seems unlikely such an important official who made such an important decision wouldn't be mentioned *anywhere* else, or so the critics argued. That is, until 1961. That year, a stone sign dating to the time of Jesus was found in Caesarea Maritime with the name Pontius Pilate on it. You can go to Israel today and see King David's palace, an upper room like the one Jesus had His last supper in, and even an empty tomb that dates to the time of Jesus. Because we can trust the Bible for history, we can trust it for our future.

and [b]put a scarlet robe on Him. 29 [a]When they had twisted a crown of thorns, they put *it* on His head, and a reed in His right hand. And they bowed the knee before Him and mocked Him, saying, "Hail, King of the Jews!" 30 Then [a]they spat on Him, and took the reed and struck Him on the head. 31 And when they had mocked Him, they took the robe off Him, put His *own* clothes on Him, [a]and led Him away to be crucified.

> **27:31** Crucifixion, a practice probably adopted from Persia, was considered by the Romans to be the cruelest form of execution. This punishment was reserved for the worst criminals. The offender usually died after two or three days of agonizing suffering, enduring not only incomprehensible pain, but also hunger, thirst, and exposure. The offender's arms were tied or nailed to a beam that was hoisted up and fixed to a post, to which his feet were nailed.

### *THE KING ON A CROSS*

*(Mark 15:21–32; Luke 23:26–43; John 19:17–27)*

32 [a]Now as they came out, [b]they found a man of Cyrene, Simon by name. Him they compelled to bear His cross. 33 [a]And when they had come to a place called Golgotha, that is to say, Place of a Skull, 34 [a]they gave Him sour[1] wine mingled with gall to drink. But when He had tasted *it,* He would not drink.

35 [a]Then they crucified Him, and divided His garments, casting lots,[1] that it might be fulfilled which was spoken by the prophet:

[b]"They divided My garments among them,
And for My clothing they cast lots."[2]

36 [a]Sitting down, they kept watch over Him there. 37 And they [a]put up over His head the accusation written against Him:

THIS IS JESUS THE KING OF THE JEWS.

38 [a]Then two robbers were crucified with Him, one on the right and another on the left.

39 And [a]those who passed by blasphemed Him, wagging their heads 40 and saying, [a]"You who destroy the temple and build *it* in three days, save Yourself! [b]If You are the Son of God, come down from the cross."

41 Likewise the chief priests also, mocking with the scribes and elders,[1] said, 42 "He [a]saved others; Himself He cannot save. If He is the King of Israel,[1] let Him now come down from the cross, and we will believe Him.[2] 43 [a]He trusted in God; let Him deliver Him now if He will have Him; for He said, 'I am the Son of God.' "

44 [a]Even the robbers who were crucified with Him reviled Him with the same thing.

### *JESUS DIES ON THE CROSS*

*(Mark 15:33–41; Luke 23:44–49; John 19:28–30)*

45 [a]Now from the sixth hour until the ninth hour there was darkness over all the land. 46 And about the ninth hour [a]Jesus cried out with a loud voice, saying, "Eli, Eli, lama sabachthani?" that is, [b]"My God, My God, why have You forsaken Me?"[1]

47 Some of those who stood there, when they heard *that,* said, "This Man is calling for Elijah!" 48 Immediately one of them ran and took a sponge, [a]filled *it* with sour wine and put *it* on a reed, and offered it to Him to drink.

49 The rest said, "Let Him alone; let us see if Elijah will come to save Him."

50 And Jesus [a]cried out again with a loud voice, and [b]yielded up His spirit.

51 Then, behold, [a]the veil of the temple was torn in two from top to bottom; and the earth quaked, and the rocks were split, 52 and the graves were opened; and many bodies of the saints who had fallen asleep were raised; 53 and coming out of the graves after His resurrection, they went into the holy city and appeared to many.

> **27:51** The **temple** had two veils or curtains, one in front of the holy place and the other separating the holy place from the Most Holy Place. These curtains were heavy and very strong and thick. It was the second **veil** that was likely **torn**, demonstrating that through the death of Jesus, there was now open access to God. Jesus' blood covered our sins from God's sight.

54 [a]So when the centurion and those with him, who were guarding Jesus, saw the earthquake and the things that had happened, they feared greatly, saying, [b]"Truly this was the Son of God!"

55 And many women [a]who followed Jesus from Galilee, ministering to Him, were there looking on from afar, 56 [a]among whom were Mary Magdalene, Mary the mother of James and Joses,[1] and the mother of Zebedee's sons.

**27:28** [b] Luke 23:11 **27:29** [a] Is. 53:3 **27:30** [a] Matt. 26:67 **27:31** [a] Is. 53:7 **27:32** [a] Heb. 13:12 [b] Mark 15:21 **27:33** [a] John 19:17 **27:34** [a] Ps. 69:21 [1] NU-Text omits *sour.* **27:35** [a] Luke 23:34 [b] Ps. 22:18 [1] NU-Text and M-Text omit the rest of this verse. [2] Psalm 22:18 **27:36** [a] Matt. 27:54 **27:37** [a] John 19:19 **27:38** [a] Is. 53:9, 12 **27:39** [a] Mark 15:29 **27:40** [a] John 2:19 [b] Matt. 26:63 **27:41** [1] M-Text reads *with the scribes, the Pharisees, and the elders.* **27:42** [a] [John 3:14, 15] [1] NU-Text reads *He is the King of Israel!* [2] NU-Text and M-Text read *we will believe in Him.* **27:43** [a] Ps. 22:8 **27:44** [a] Luke 23:39–43 **27:45** [a] Mark 15:33–41 **27:46** [a] [Heb. 5:7] [b] Ps. 22:1 [1] Psalm 22:1 **27:48** [a] Ps. 69:21 **27:50** [a] Luke 23:46 [b] [John 10:18] **27:51** [a] Ex. 26:31 **27:54** [a] Mark 15:39 [b] Matt. 14:33 **27:55** [a] Luke 8:2, 3 **27:56** [a] Mark 15:40, 47; 16:9 [1] NU-Text reads *Joseph.*

### *JESUS BURIED IN JOSEPH'S TOMB*

*(Mark 15:42–47; Luke 23:50–56; John 19:38–42)*

57 Now [a]when evening had come, there came
a rich man from Arimathea, named Joseph, who
himself had also become a disciple of Jesus.
58 This man went to Pilate and asked for the body
of Jesus. Then Pilate commanded the body to
be given to him. 59 When Joseph had taken the
body, he wrapped it in a clean linen cloth, 60 and
[a]laid it in his new tomb which he had hewn out
of the rock; and he rolled a large stone against
the door of the tomb, and departed. 61 And Mary
Magdalene was there, and the other Mary, sitting
opposite the tomb.

> **SEEING JESUS IN THE SCRIPTURE**
>
> **27:57–60** Jesus' body was laid in the tomb of a rich man, Joseph, fulfilling prophecy (see Is. 53:9).

### *PILATE SETS A GUARD*

62 On the next day, which followed the Day
of Preparation, the chief priests and Pharisees
gathered together to Pilate, 63 saying, "Sir, we
remember, while He was still alive, how that
deceiver said, [a]'After three days I will rise.'
64 Therefore command that the tomb be made
secure until the third day, lest His disciples
come by night[1] and steal Him *away,* and say
to the people, 'He has risen from the dead.' So
the last deception will be worse than the first."
65 Pilate said to them, "You have a guard; go
your way, make *it* as secure as you know how."
66 So they went and made the tomb secure, [a]seal-
ing the stone and setting the guard.

### *HE IS RISEN*

*(Mark 16:1–8; Luke 24:1–12; John 20:1–10)*

**28** Now [a]after the Sabbath, as the first *day* of
the week began to dawn, Mary Magdalene
[b]and the other Mary came to see the tomb. 2 And
behold, there was a great earthquake; for [a]an
angel of the Lord descended from heaven, and

**27:57** [a] John 19:38–42 **27:60** [a] Is. 53:9 **27:63** [a] Mark 8:31; 10:34 **27:64** [1] NU-Text omits *by night.* **27:66** [a] Dan. 6:17
**28:1** [a] Luke 24:1–10 [b] Matt. 27:56, 61 **28:2** [a] Mark 16:5

MATTHEW 28:16–20

## THE GREAT COMMISSION

49

STORY OF SCRIPTURE

### WHAT'S GOING ON?

After His resurrection, Jesus appeared on earth for forty days, verifying He was alive and preparing the disciples to continue the mission He began. One of His final acts was to give the Great Commission—a summary of their assignment. They were to make disciples of all nations, baptizing and teaching these new followers about Him and His ways.

This task must have seemed impossible to the disciples until Jesus assured them of His presence, saying, "I am with you always, even to the end of the age." This moment is pivotal in the story of Scripture because it reminds us the church's ministry has always been and still is Jesus' ministry. He is with His people to the end of the age, working through us to accomplish great things.

### WHAT DOES THIS MEAN FOR ME?

The Great Commission isn't just a historical event; it's a continuous call to all believers. This passage challenges us to share the gospel and make disciples wherever we are. It's an invitation to step out of our comfort zones and engage with the world, empowered by Jesus' presence. With Jesus empowering and directing us, we can do far more than we might imagine.

### DID YOU CATCH THE PATTERN?

God has always appointed messengers and representatives to carry out His will. It began with Him creating people as His image-bearers to represent Him in the world. Then, God called Abraham to be the father of a great nation. He assigned Moses to lead the Israelites out of bondage. He chose prophets to be His mouthpieces, calling Israel back to Him. This pattern of divine calling and human service is everywhere. The Great Commission continues this pattern, calling us to participate in God's redemptive plan for humanity.

*For the next* Story of Scripture *reading and devotion, turn to Acts 1:1—2:4 on page 1105.*

came and rolled back the stone from the door,[1] and sat on it. 3 [a]His countenance was like lightning, and his clothing as white as snow. 4 And the guards shook for fear of him, and became like [a]dead *men.*

5 But the angel answered and said to the women, "Do not be afraid, for I know that you seek Jesus who was crucified. 6 He is not here; for He is risen, [a]as He said. Come, see the place where the Lord lay. 7 And go quickly and tell His disciples that He is risen from the dead, and indeed [a]He is going before you into Galilee; there you will see Him. Behold, I have told you."

8 So they went out quickly from the tomb with fear and great joy, and ran to bring His disciples word.

### THE WOMEN WORSHIP THE RISEN LORD

9 And as they went to tell His disciples,[1] behold, [a]Jesus met them, saying, "Rejoice!" So they came and held Him by the feet and worshiped Him. 10 Then Jesus said to them, "Do not be afraid. Go *and* tell [a]My brethren to go to Galilee, and there they will see Me."

### THE SOLDIERS ARE BRIBED

11 Now while they were going, behold, some of the guard came into the city and reported to the chief priests all the things that had happened. 12 When they had assembled with the elders and consulted together, they gave a large sum of money to the soldiers, 13 saying, "Tell them, 'His disciples came at night and stole Him *away* while we slept.' 14 And if this comes to the governor's ears, we will appease him and make you secure." 15 So they took the money and did as they were instructed; and this saying is commonly reported among the Jews until this day.

### SEEING JESUS IN THE SCRIPTURE

**28:16–17** Just as Jesus had foretold, He met His disciples in Galilee after His resurrection (see Matt. 26:32). Seeing their resurrected Savior led the disciples to worship.

### THE GREAT COMMISSION

*(Mark 16:14–18; Luke 24:36–49; John 20:19–23; Acts 1:6–8)*

16 Then the eleven disciples went away into Galilee, to the mountain [a]which Jesus had appointed for them. 17 When they saw Him, they worshiped Him; but some [a]doubted.

18 And Jesus came and spoke to them, saying, [a]"All authority has been given to Me in heaven and on earth. 19 [a]Go therefore[1] and [b]make disciples of all the nations, baptizing them in the name of the Father and of the Son and of the Holy Spirit, 20 [a]teaching them to observe all things that I have commanded you; and lo, I am [b]with you always, *even* to the end of the age." Amen.[1]

**28:2** [1] NU-Text omits *from the door.* **28:3** [a] Dan. 7:9; 10:6 **28:4** [a] Rev. 1:17 **28:6** [a] Matt. 12:40; 16:21; 17:23; 20:19 **28:7** [a] Mark 16:7 **28:9** [a] John 20:14 [1] NU-Text omits the first clause of this verse. **28:10** [a] John 20:17 **28:16** [a] Matt. 26:32; 28:7, 10 **28:17** [a] John 20:24–29 **28:18** [a] [Dan. 7:13, 14] **28:19** [a] Mark 16:15 [b] Luke 24:47 [1] M-Text omits *therefore.* **28:20** [a] [Acts 2:42] [b] [Acts 4:31; 18:10; 23:11] [1] NU-Text omits *Amen.*

*The Gospel According to*

# MARK

| AUTHOR | KEY VERSE | READING TIME |
|---|---|---|
| Mark | Mark 10:45 | 1 hour 45 minutes |

Mark's Gospel has a sense of immediacy to it. Unlike Matthew and Luke, Mark did not provide details of the birth or childhood of Jesus. Instead, Mark began with Jesus' ministry itself. The shortest of the four Gospels, Mark then traces Jesus' earthly life through concise accounts, with Jesus always seeming to be on the move. Such a pace fit Mark's core message: Jesus is the servant sent by God to make payment for sin. This sense of service and sacrifice dominates the Gospel. Through Jesus' preaching, teaching, and healing, He ministered to the needs of others, even to the point of laying down His life. After the resurrection, Jesus commissioned His followers to continue His work in His power—they were to be faithful servants following in the steps of the perfect Servant.

**Occasion:** Mark wrote his Gospel to a primarily Roman audience to show Jesus as the Servant of God.

**Main Point:** Jesus is the Suffering Servant who came to give His life as payment for sin.

**Big Ideas:** Jesus is the Suffering Servant. What Jesus said and what He did prove He is the Son of God. All who place faith in Jesus are saved. Like Jesus, we must be servants who love, care for, and are kind to others.

## OUTLINE:

I. The Presentation of the Servant (chs. 1–2)
II. The Opposition to the Servant (chs. 3–8)
III. The Teachings by the Servant (chs. 9–10)
IV. The Rejection of the Servant (chs. 11–15)
V. The Resurrection of the Servant (ch. 16)

**c. 420 BC**
Malachi prophesies in Judah

**356–323 BC**
Alexander the Great lives in Macedonia

**246 BC**
Great Wall of China is built

**164 BC**
Judas Maccabaeus restores the temple in Jerusalem, celebrated yearly by the festival of Hanukkah

**37 BC**
Julius Caesar is murdered

**37–4 BC**
Herod the Great is king in Jerusalem

**31 BC–AD 14**
Augustus Caesar is Roman emperor

**c. 5–4 BC**
Jesus is born in Bethlehem

**4 BC–AD 39**
Herod Antipas rules in Galilee and Perea

**AD 1**
Lions become extinct in Western Europe

**c. AD 7**
Jesus questions teachers at the temple

**AD 14–37**
Tiberius is Roman emperor

**AD 25–27**
John the Baptist ministers

**AD 26–36**
Pontius Pilate is procurator of Judea

**c. AD 27**
Jesus' first Judean ministry

**c. AD 27–29**
Jesus' Galilean ministry

**c. AD 30**
Jesus' second Judean ministry; crucifixion and resurrection

**c. AD 50–60**
**Mark written**

### *JOHN THE BAPTIST PREPARES THE WAY*
*(Matt. 3:1–12; Luke 3:1–20; John 1:19–28)*

1 The [a]beginning of the gospel of Jesus Christ,
[b]the Son of God. 2 As it is written in the
Prophets:[1]

> [a]"Behold, I send My messenger before Your
> face,
> Who will prepare Your way before You."[2]
> 3 "The[a] voice of one crying in the wilderness:
> 'Prepare the way of the LORD;
> Make His paths straight.' "[1]

**SEEING JESUS IN THE SCRIPTURE**

**1:2** God sent John the Baptist ahead of Jesus as a messenger to prepare the way for Jesus, fulfilling prophecy (see Mal. 3:1).

4 [a]John came baptizing in the wilderness
and preaching a baptism of repentance for the
remission of sins. 5 [a]Then all the land of Judea,
and those from Jerusalem, went out to him and
were all baptized by him in the Jordan River,
confessing their sins.
6 Now John was [a]clothed with camel's hair
and with a leather belt around his waist, and he
ate locusts and wild honey. 7 And he preached,
saying, [a]"There comes One after me who is
mightier than I, whose sandal strap I am not
worthy to stoop down and loose. 8 [a]I indeed
baptized you with water, but He will baptize you
[b]with the Holy Spirit."

### *JOHN BAPTIZES JESUS*
*(Matt. 3:13–17; Luke 3:21, 22; John 1:29–34)*

9 [a]It came to pass in those days *that* Jesus
came from Nazareth of Galilee, and was bap-
tized by John in the Jordan. 10 [a]And immediately,
coming up from[1] the water, He saw the heavens
parting and the Spirit [b]descending upon Him like
a dove. 11 Then a voice came from heaven, [a]"You
are My beloved Son, in whom I am well pleased."

### *SATAN TEMPTS JESUS*
*(Matt. 4:1–11; Luke 4:1–13)*

12 [a]Immediately the Spirit drove Him into the
wilderness. 13 And He was there in the wilderness
forty days, tempted by Satan, and was with the
wild beasts; [a]and the angels ministered to Him.

### *JESUS BEGINS HIS GALILEAN MINISTRY*
*(Matt. 4:12–17; Luke 4:14, 15)*

14 [a]Now after John was put in prison, Jesus
came to Galilee, [b]preaching the gospel of the
kingdom[1] of God, 15 and saying, [a]"The time is
fulfilled, and [b]the kingdom of God is at hand.
Repent, and believe in the gospel."

### *FOUR FISHERMEN CALLED AS DISCIPLES*
*(Matt. 4:18–22; Luke 5:1–11)*

16 [a]And as He walked by the Sea of Galilee,
He saw Simon and Andrew his brother casting
a net into the sea; for they were fishermen.

**1:1** [a] Luke 3:22 [b] Matt. 14:33 **1:2** [a] Mal. 3:1 [1] NU-Text reads *Isaiah the prophet.* [2] Malachi 3:1 **1:3** [a] Is. 40:3 [1] Isaiah 40:3 **1:4** [a] Matt. 3:1 **1:5** [a] Matt. 3:5 **1:6** [a] Matt. 3:4 **1:7** [a] John 1:27 **1:8** [a] Acts 1:5; 11:16 [b] Is. 44:3 **1:9** [a] Matt. 3:13–17 **1:10** [a] Matt. 3:16 [b] Acts 10:38 [1] NU-Text reads *out of.* **1:11** [a] Matt. 3:17; 12:18 **1:12** [a] Matt. 4:1–11 **1:13** [a] Matt. 4:10, 11 **1:14** [a] Matt. 4:12 [b] Matt. 4:23 [1] NU-Text omits *of the kingdom.* **1:15** [a] [Gal. 4:4] [b] Matt. 3:2; 4:17 **1:16** [a] Luke 5:2–11

KNOW THE TRUTH

## THE DOCTRINE OF JESUS

### PART 1: OVERVIEW OF THE DOCTRINE OF JESUS

**1:1** Mark says much about Jesus in very few words. First, Jesus is the "Son of God." This means Jesus is fully divine like His heavenly Father. Second, Jesus is the "Christ": God's anointed heir of King David. This means Jesus is fully human like His ancestor David. *Christ* isn't Jesus' last name; it's a title classifying Jesus of Nazareth as the one who would suffer and die for the sins of His people, rise from the dead, and rule the nations (see Luke 24:44–48). Finally, Mark says the gospel centers on Jesus, the Son of God. Every good promise, noble ruler, bloody sacrifice, and holy commandment of the Old Testament anticipates Jesus. Every sinful person made God's son or daughter, every demon defeated, all freedom, joy, and eternal peace in the New Testament are possible because of Jesus. He's the star of the story, the Savior of the world, the healer of all that is broken, and the ruler every heart longs for. He's the consummation of all perfection: the most gentle, loving, righteous, just, kind, strong, humble, holy, and wonderfully worthy person for all time past, present, and future. He's the matchless focal point of the Bible.

*For* **THE DOCTRINE OF JESUS: PART 2: THE DEITY OF JESUS**, *turn to Mark 14:61–62 on page 1025.*

17 Then Jesus said to them, "Follow Me, and I
will make you become [a]fishers of men." 18 [a]They
immediately left their nets and followed Him.
19 When He had gone a little farther from
there, He saw James the *son* of Zebedee, and John
his brother, who also *were* in the boat mending
their nets. 20 And immediately He called them,
and they left their father Zebedee in the boat with
the hired servants, and went after Him.

### JESUS CASTS OUT AN UNCLEAN SPIRIT

*(Luke 4:31–37)*

21 [a]Then they went into Capernaum, and
immediately on the Sabbath He entered the
[b]synagogue and taught. 22 [a]And they were as-
tonished at His teaching, for He taught them
as one having authority, and not as the scribes.
23 Now there was a man in their synagogue
with an [a]unclean spirit. And he cried out, 24 say-
ing, "Let *us* alone! [a]What have we to do with You,
Jesus of Nazareth? Did You come to destroy us?
I [b]know who You are—the [c]Holy One of God!"
25 But Jesus [a]rebuked him, saying, "Be quiet,
and come out of him!" 26 And when the unclean
spirit [a]had convulsed him and cried out with
a loud voice, he came out of him. 27 Then they
were all amazed, so that they questioned among
themselves, saying, "What is this? What new doc-
trine *is* this? For with authority[1] He commands
even the unclean spirits, and they obey Him."
28 And immediately His [a]fame spread through-
out all the region around Galilee.

### PETER'S MOTHER-IN-LAW HEALED

*(Matt. 8:14, 15; Luke 4:38, 39)*

29 [a]Now as soon as they had come out of the
synagogue, they entered the house of Simon and
Andrew, with James and John. 30 But Simon's
wife's mother lay sick with a fever, and they told
Him about her at once. 31 So He came and took
her by the hand and lifted her up, and imme-
diately the fever left her. And she served them.

### MANY HEALED AFTER SABBATH SUNSET

*(Matt. 8:16, 17; Luke 4:40, 41)*

32 [a]At evening, when the sun had set, they
brought to Him all who were sick and those who
were demon-possessed. 33 And the whole city was
gathered together at the door. 34 Then He healed
many who were sick with various diseases, and
[a]cast out many demons; and He [b]did not allow
the demons to speak, because they knew Him.

### PREACHING IN GALILEE

*(Matt. 4:23–25; Luke 4:42–44)*

35 Now [a]in the morning, having risen a
long while before daylight, He went out and
departed to a solitary place; and there He
[b]prayed. 36 And Simon and those *who were* with
Him searched for Him. 37 When they found Him,
they said to Him, [a]"Everyone [b]is looking for
You."
38 But He said to them, [a]"Let us go into the
next towns, that I may preach there also, because
[b]for this purpose I have come forth."
39 [a]And He was preaching in their syna-
gogues throughout all Galilee, and [b]casting
out demons.

### JESUS CLEANSES A LEPER

*(Matt. 8:1–4; Luke 5:12–16)*

40 [a]Now a leper came to Him, imploring Him,
kneeling down to Him and saying to Him, "If
You are willing, You can make me clean."
41 Then Jesus, moved with [a]compassion,
stretched out *His* hand and touched him, and
said to him, "I am willing; be cleansed." 42 As
soon as He had spoken, [a]immediately the lep-
rosy left him, and he was cleansed. 43 And He
strictly warned him and sent him away at once,
44 and said to him, "See that you say nothing to
anyone; but go your way, show yourself to the
priest, and offer for your cleansing those things
[a]which Moses commanded, as a testimony to
them."
45 [a]However, he went out and began to pro-
claim *it* freely, and to spread the matter, so that
Jesus could no longer openly enter the city, but
was outside in deserted places; [b]and they came
to Him from every direction.

### JESUS FORGIVES AND HEALS A PARALYTIC

*(Matt. 9:2–8; Luke 5:17–26)*

2 And again [a]He entered Capernaum after
*some* days, and it was heard that He was
in the house. 2 Immediately[1] many gathered
together, so that there was no longer room to
receive *them,* not even near the door. And He
preached the word to them. 3 Then they came to
Him, bringing a [a]paralytic who was carried by
four *men.* 4 And when they could not come near
Him because of the crowd, they uncovered the
roof where He was. So when they had broken
through, they let down the bed on which the
paralytic was lying.
5 When Jesus saw their faith, He said to the
paralytic, "Son, your sins are forgiven you."
6 And some of the scribes were sitting there
and reasoning in their hearts, 7 "Why does this
*Man* speak blasphemies like this? [a]Who can
forgive sins but God alone?"
8 But immediately, when Jesus perceived in
His spirit that they reasoned thus within them-
selves, He said to them, "Why do you reason about

**1:17** [a] Matt. 13:47, 48 **1:18** [a] [Luke 14:26] **1:21** [a] Luke 4:31–37 [b] Matt. 4:23 **1:22** [a] Matt. 7:28, 29; 13:54 **1:23** [a] [Matt. 12:43] **1:24** [a] Matt. 8:28, 29 [b] James 2:19 [c] Ps. 16:10 **1:25** [a] [Luke 4:39] **1:26** [a] Mark 9:20 **1:27** [1] NU-Text reads *What is this? A new doctrine with authority.* **1:28** [a] Matt. 4:24; 9:31 **1:29** [a] Luke 4:38, 39 **1:32** [a] Matt. 8:16, 17 **1:34** [a] Luke 13:32 [b] Acts 16:17, 18 **1:35** [a] Luke 4:42, 43 [b] Luke 5:16; 6:12; 9:28, 29 **1:37** [a] John 3:26; 12:19 [b] [Heb. 11:6] **1:38** [a] Luke 4:43 [b] [Is. 61:1, 2] **1:39** [a] Matt. 4:23; 9:35 [b] Mark 5:8, 13; 7:29, 30 **1:40** [a] Luke 5:12–14 **1:41** [a] Luke 7:13 **1:42** [a] Matt. 15:28 **1:44** [a] Lev. 14:1–32 **1:45** [a] Matt. 28:15; Luke 5:15 [b] Mark 2:2, 13; 3:7; Luke 5:17; John 6:2 **2:1** [a] Matt. 9:1 **2:2** [1] NU-Text omits *Immediately.* **2:3** [a] Matt. 4:24; 8:6; Acts 8:7; 9:33 **2:7** [a] Job 14:4; Is. 43:25; Dan. 9:9

these things in your hearts? 9 [a]Which is easier, to say to the paralytic, '*Your* sins are forgiven you,' or to say, 'Arise, take up your bed and walk'? 10 But that you may know that the Son of Man has power on earth to forgive sins"—He said to the paralytic, 11 "I say to you, arise, take up your bed, and go to your house." 12 Immediately he arose, took up the bed, and went out in the presence of them all, so that all were amazed and [a]glorified God, saying, "We never saw *anything* like this!"

> **2:11** By healing the paralytic, Jesus made His pronouncement of forgiveness far more credible.

### MATTHEW THE TAX COLLECTOR
*(Matt. 9:9–13; Luke 5:27–32)*

13 [a]Then He went out again by the sea; and all the multitude came to Him, and He taught them. 14 [a]As He passed by, He saw Levi the *son* of Alphaeus sitting at the tax office. And He said to him, [b]"Follow Me." So he arose and [c]followed Him.

15 [a]Now it happened, as He was dining in *Levi's* house, that many tax collectors and sinners also sat together with Jesus and His disciples; for there were many, and they followed Him. 16 And when the scribes and[1] Pharisees saw Him eating with the tax collectors and sinners, they said to His disciples, "How *is it* that He eats and drinks with tax collectors and sinners?"

17 When Jesus heard *it,* He said to them, [a]"Those who are well have no need of a physician, but those who are sick. I did not come to call *the* righteous, but sinners, to repentance."[1]

### JESUS IS QUESTIONED ABOUT FASTING
*(Matt. 9:14–17; Luke 5:33–39)*

18 [a]The disciples of John and of the Pharisees were fasting. Then they came and said to Him, "Why do the disciples of John and of the Pharisees fast, but Your disciples do not fast?"

19 And Jesus said to them, "Can the friends of the bridegroom fast while the bridegroom is with them? As long as they have the bridegroom with them they cannot fast. 20 But the days will come when the bridegroom will be [a]taken away from them, and then they will fast in those days. 21 No one sews a piece of unshrunk cloth on an old garment; or else the new piece pulls away from the old, and the tear is made worse. 22 And no one puts new wine into old wineskins; or else the new wine bursts the wineskins, the wine is spilled, and the wineskins are ruined. But new wine must be put into new wineskins."

### JESUS IS LORD OF THE SABBATH
*(Matt. 12:1–8; Luke 6:1–5)*

23 [a]Now it happened that He went through the grainfields on the Sabbath; and as they went His disciples began [b]to pluck the heads of grain. 24 And the Pharisees said to Him, "Look, why do they do what is [a]not lawful on the Sabbath?"

25 But He said to them, "Have you never read [a]what David did when he was in need and hungry, he and those with him: 26 how he went into the house of God *in the days* of Abiathar the high priest, and ate the showbread, [a]which is not lawful to eat except for the priests, and also gave some to those who were with him?"

27 And He said to them, "The Sabbath was made for man, and not man for the [a]Sabbath. 28 Therefore [a]the Son of Man is also Lord of the Sabbath."

### HEALING ON THE SABBATH
*(Matt. 12:9–14; Luke 6:6–11)*

3 And [a]He entered the synagogue again, and a man was there who had a withered hand. 2 So they [a]watched Him closely, whether He would [b]heal him on the Sabbath, so that they might accuse Him. 3 And He said to the man who had the withered hand, "Step forward." 4 Then He said to them, "Is it lawful on the Sabbath to do good or to do evil, to save life or to kill?" But they kept silent. 5 And when He had looked around at them with anger, being grieved by the [a]hardness of their hearts, He said to the man, "Stretch out your hand." And he stretched *it* out, and his hand was restored as whole as the other.[1] 6 [a]Then the Pharisees went out and immediately plotted with [b]the Herodians against Him, how they might destroy Him.

> **SEEING JESUS IN THE SCRIPTURE**
>
> **3:6** The Pharisees counseled together to plan a way to kill Jesus, fulfilling prophecy (see Ps. 2:2).

### A GREAT MULTITUDE FOLLOWS JESUS
*(Matt. 12:15–21)*

7 But Jesus withdrew with His disciples to the sea. And a great multitude from Galilee followed Him, [a]and from Judea 8 and Jerusalem and Idumea and beyond the Jordan; and those from Tyre and Sidon, a great multitude, when they heard how [a]many things He was doing, came to Him. 9 So He told His disciples that a small boat should be kept ready for Him because of the multitude, lest they should crush Him. 10 For He healed [a]many, so that as many as had afflictions

**2:9** [a] Matt. 9:5 **2:12** [a] Matt. 15:31; [Phil. 2:11] **2:13** [a] Matt. 9:9 **2:14** [a] Matt. 9:9–13; Luke 5:27–32 [b] Matt. 4:19; 8:22; 19:21; John 1:43; 12:26; 21:22 [c] Luke 18:28 **2:15** [a] Matt. 9:10 **2:16** [1] NU-Text reads *of the.* **2:17** [a] Matt. 9:12, 13; 18:11; Luke 5:31, 32; 19:10 [1] NU-Text omits *to repentance.* **2:18** [a] Matt. 9:14–17; Luke 5:33–38 **2:20** [a] Acts 1:9; 13:2, 3; 14:23 **2:23** [a] Matt. 12:1–8; Luke 6:1–5 [b] Deut. 23:25 **2:24** [a] Ex. 20:10; 31:15 **2:25** [a] 1 Sam. 21:1–6 **2:26** [a] Lev. 24:5–9 **2:27** [a] Deut. 5:14 **2:28** [a] Matt. 12:8 **3:1** [a] Luke 6:6–11 **3:2** [a] Luke 14:1; 20:20 [b] Luke 13:14 **3:5** [a] Zech. 7:12 [1] NU-Text omits *as whole as the other.* **3:6** [a] Mark 12:13 [b] Matt. 22:16 **3:7** [a] Luke 6:17 **3:8** [a] Mark 5:19 **3:10** [a] Luke 7:21

pressed about Him to [b]touch Him. 11 [a]And the unclean spirits, whenever they saw Him, fell down before Him and cried out, saying, [b]"You are the Son of God." 12 But [a]He sternly warned them that they should not make Him known.

### *THE TWELVE APOSTLES*
*(Matt. 10:1–4; Luke 6:12–16)*

13 [a]And He went up on the mountain and called to *Him* those He Himself wanted. And they came to Him. 14 Then He appointed twelve,[1] that they might be with Him and that He might send them out to preach, 15 and to have power to heal sicknesses and[1] to cast out demons: 16 Simon,[1] [a]to whom He gave the name Peter; 17 James the *son* of Zebedee and John the brother of James, to whom He gave the name Boanerges, that is, "Sons of Thunder"; 18 Andrew, Philip, Bartholomew, Matthew, Thomas, James the *son* of Alphaeus, Thaddaeus, Simon the Cananite; 19 and Judas Iscariot, who also betrayed Him. And they went into a house.

### *A HOUSE DIVIDED CANNOT STAND*
*(Matt. 12:22–30; Luke 11:14–23)*

20 Then the multitude came together again, [a]so that they could not so much as eat bread. 21 But when His [a]own people heard *about this,* they went out to lay hold of Him, [b]for they said, "He is out of His mind."

22 And the scribes who came down from Jerusalem said, [a]"He has Beelzebub," and, "By the [b]ruler of the demons He casts out demons."

23 [a]So He called them to *Himself* and said to them in parables: "How can Satan cast out Satan? 24 If a kingdom is divided against itself, that kingdom cannot stand. 25 And if a house is divided against itself, that house cannot stand. 26 And if Satan has risen up against himself, and is divided, he cannot stand, but has an end. 27 [a]No one can enter a strong man's house and plunder his goods, unless he first binds the strong man. And then he will plunder his house.

### *THE UNPARDONABLE SIN*
*(Matt. 12:31, 32; Luke 12:10)*

28 [a]"Assuredly, I say to you, all sins will be forgiven the sons of men, and whatever blasphemies they may utter; 29 but he who blasphemes against the Holy Spirit never has forgiveness, but is subject to eternal condemnation"— 30 because they [a]said, "He has an unclean spirit."

### *JESUS' MOTHER AND BROTHERS SEND FOR HIM*
*(Matt. 12:46–50; Luke 8:19–21)*

31 [a]Then His brothers and His mother came, and standing outside they sent to Him, calling Him. 32 And a multitude was sitting around Him; and they said to Him, "Look, Your mother and Your brothers[1] are outside seeking You."

**3:10** [b] Matt. 9:21; 14:36 **3:11** [a] Luke 4:41 [b] Matt. 8:29; 14:33 **3:12** [a] Mark 1:25, 34 **3:13** [a] Luke 9:1 **3:14** [1] NU-Text adds *whom He also named apostles.* **3:15** [1] NU-Text omits *to heal sicknesses and.* **3:16** [a] John 1:42 [1] NU-Text reads *and He appointed the twelve: Simon....* **3:20** [a] Mark 6:31 **3:21** [a] Mark 6:3 [b] John 7:5; 10:20 **3:22** [a] Matt. 9:34; 10:25 [b] [John 12:31; 14:30; 16:11] **3:23** [a] Matt. 12:25–29 **3:27** [a] [Is. 49:24, 25] **3:28** [a] Luke 12:10 **3:30** [a] Matt. 9:34 **3:31** [a] Matt. 12:46–50 **3:32** [1] NU-Text and M-Text add *and Your sisters.*

KNOW THE TRUTH

## THE DOCTRINE OF CREATION AND HUMANS
### PART 4: THE CREATION OF SATAN AND DEMONS

**3:22–27** The spiritual being who leads rebellion against God's rule and plans has many names and titles in the Bible including "Satan" (adversary, accuser), "the devil" (slanderer, liar), "Beelzebul"/"Beelzebub" (master of flies, decay, death), and "the serpent of old who deceives the whole earth." This being's followers are called "demons," "unclean spirits," "cast out angels," and more.

Only God—Father, Son, and Spirit—is unmade. Everything else was made by God and was made good because God is good. Therefore, Satan and his demons are created beings, originally good. Possessing freewill, they chose rebellion against God's rule (see Rev. 12:7–10). While angels ceaselessly worship God and assist in His work, including revealing and clarifying God's plans to humans, in contrast, demons seek to hinder worship of God and oppose His plans by oppressing, possessing, and deceiving people.

Jesus came to destroy the works of the devil and heal all oppressed by him (see Acts 10:38; 1 John 3:8). Christ's followers have authority from Him to resist the devil, overcome his lies and schemes, and live victoriously for Jesus (see Luke 10:17–20). Jesus will soon judge demons with eternal destruction (see Rev. 20:10).

*For* **THE DOCTRINE OF CREATION AND HUMANS: PART 5: THE CREATION OF HUMANS**, *turn to Psalm 139:13–18 on page 618.*

**3:28–30** The person **who blasphemes against the Holy Spirit** places himself or herself outside the redeeming grace of God. The words and works of Christ were spoken and performed by the power of the Holy Spirit. To attribute them to Satan is to call the work of heaven a work of hell. For such perverse belief there is no remedy. The tense of **they said** indicates a continued action, not a one-time event. Thus, it is apparently not a single act of defiant behavior, but a continued state of opposition entered into willingly. How someone can commit this sin today is a difficult question to answer, but those who persist in denigrating Christ by insulting His work or by attributing it to Satan may drive themselves past a point of no return (see Matt. 12:31–32).

33 But He answered them, saying, "Who is My mother, or My brothers?" 34 And He looked around in a circle at those who sat about Him, and said, "Here are My mother and My brothers! 35 For whoever does the [a]will of God is My brother and My sister and mother."

### THE PARABLE OF THE SOWER
*(Matt. 13:1–9; Luke 8:4–8)*

**4** And [a]again He began to teach by the sea. And a great multitude was gathered to Him, so that He got into a boat and sat *in it* on the sea; and the whole multitude was on the land facing the sea. 2 Then He taught them many things by parables, [a]and said to them in His teaching:

3 "Listen! Behold, a sower went out to sow. 4 And it happened, as he sowed, *that* some *seed* fell by the wayside; and the birds of the air[1] came and devoured it. 5 Some fell on stony ground, where it did not have much earth; and immediately it sprang up because it had no depth of earth. 6 But when the sun was up it was scorched, and because it had no root it withered away. 7 And some *seed* fell among thorns; and the thorns grew up and choked it, and it yielded no crop. 8 But other *seed* fell on good ground and yielded a crop that sprang up, increased and produced: some thirtyfold, some sixty, and some a hundred."

9 And He said to them,[1] "He who has ears to hear, let him hear!"

### THE PURPOSE OF PARABLES
*(Matt. 13:10–17; Luke 8:9, 10)*

10 [a]But when He was alone, those around Him with the twelve asked Him about the parable. 11 And He said to them, "To you it has been given to [a]know the mystery of the kingdom of God; but to [b]those who are outside, all things come in parables, 12 so that

[a]'Seeing they may see and not perceive,
And hearing they may hear and not understand;
Lest they should turn,
And *their* sins be forgiven them.' "[1]

### THE PARABLE OF THE SOWER EXPLAINED
*(Matt. 13:18–23; Luke 8:11–15)*

13 And He said to them, "Do you not understand this parable? How then will you understand all the parables? 14 [a]The sower sows the word. 15 And these are the ones by the wayside where the word is sown. When they hear, Satan comes immediately and takes away the word that was sown in their hearts. 16 These likewise are the ones sown on stony ground who, when they hear the word, immediately receive it with gladness; 17 and they have no root in themselves, and so endure only for a time. Afterward, when tribulation or persecution arises for the word's sake, immediately they stumble. 18 Now these are the ones sown among thorns; *they are* the ones who hear the word, 19 and the [a]cares of this world, [b]the deceitfulness of riches, and the desires for other things entering in choke the word, and it becomes unfruitful. 20 But these are the ones sown on good ground, those who hear the word, accept *it,* and bear [a]fruit: some thirtyfold, some sixty, and some a hundred."

### LIGHT UNDER A BASKET
*(Luke 8:16–18)*

21 [a]Also He said to them, "Is a lamp brought to be put under a basket or under a bed? Is it not to be set on a lampstand? 22 [a]For there is nothing hidden which will not be revealed, nor has anything been kept secret but that it should come to light. 23 [a]If anyone has ears to hear, let him hear."

24 Then He said to them, "Take heed what you hear. [a]With the same measure you use, it will be measured to you; and to you who hear, more will be given. 25 [a]For whoever has, to him more will be given; but whoever does not have, even what he has will be taken away from him."

### THE PARABLE OF THE GROWING SEED

26 And He said, [a]"The kingdom of God is as if a man should scatter seed on the ground, 27 and should sleep by night and rise by day, and the seed should sprout and [a]grow, he himself does not know how. 28 For the earth [a]yields crops by itself: first the blade, then the head, after that the full grain in the head. 29 But when the grain ripens, immediately [a]he puts in the sickle, because the harvest has come."

**3:35** [a] Eph. 6:6 **4:1** [a] Luke 8:4–10 **4:2** [a] Mark 12:38 **4:4** [1] NU-Text and M-Text omit *of the air.* **4:9** [1] NU-Text and M-Text omit *to them.* **4:10** [a] Luke 8:9 **4:11** [a] [1 Cor. 2:10–16] [b] [Col. 4:5] **4:12** [a] Is. 6:9, 10; 43:8 [1] Isaiah 6:9, 10 **4:14** [a] Matt. 13:18–23 **4:19** [a] Luke 21:34 [b] 1 Tim. 6:9, 10, 17 **4:20** [a] [Rom. 7:4] **4:21** [a] Matt. 5:15 **4:22** [a] Matt. 10:26, 27 **4:23** [a] Matt. 11:15; 13:9, 43 **4:24** [a] Matt. 7:2 **4:25** [a] Luke 8:18; 19:26 **4:26** [a] [Matt. 13:24–30, 36–43] **4:27** [a] [2 Pet. 3:18] **4:28** [a] [John 12:24] **4:29** [a] Rev. 14:15

### THE PARABLE OF THE MUSTARD SEED

*(Matt. 13:31, 32; Luke 13:18, 19)*

30 Then He said, [a]"To what shall we liken the kingdom of God? Or with what parable shall we picture it? 31 *It is* like a mustard seed which, when it is sown on the ground, is smaller than all the seeds on earth; 32 but when it is sown, it grows up and becomes greater than all herbs, and shoots out large branches, so that the birds of the air may nest under its shade."

> **4:31** One tiny **mustard seed**—a seed much smaller than a kernel of corn—is capable of producing a plant up to fifteen feet high.

### JESUS' USE OF PARABLES

33 [a]And with many such parables He spoke the word to them as they were able to hear *it.* 34 But without a parable He did not speak to them. And when they were alone, [a]He explained all things to His disciples.

### WIND AND WAVE OBEY JESUS

*(Matt. 8:23–27; Luke 8:22–25)*

35 [a]On the same day, when evening had come, He said to them, "Let us cross over to the other side." 36 Now when they had left the multitude, they took Him along in the boat as He was. And other little boats were also with Him. 37 And a great windstorm arose, and the waves beat into the boat, so that it was already filling. 38 But He was in the stern, asleep on a pillow. And they awoke Him and said to Him, [a]"Teacher, [b]do You not care that we are perishing?"

39 Then He arose and [a]rebuked the wind, and said to the sea, [b]"Peace, be still!" And the wind ceased and there was a great calm. 40 But He said to them, "Why are you so fearful? [a]How *is it* that you have no faith?"[1] 41 And they feared exceedingly, and said to one another, "Who can this be, that even the wind and the sea obey Him!"

### A DEMON-POSSESSED MAN HEALED

*(Matt. 8:28—9:1; Luke 8:26–39)*

**5** Then [a]they came to the other side of the sea, to the country of the Gadarenes.[1] 2 And when He had come out of the boat, immediately there met Him out of the tombs a man with an [a]unclean spirit, 3 who had *his* dwelling among the tombs; and no one could bind him,[1] not even with chains, 4 because he had often been bound with shackles and chains. And the chains had been pulled apart by him, and the shackles broken in pieces; neither could anyone tame him. 5 And always, night and day, he was in the mountains and in the tombs, crying out and cutting himself with stones.

6 When he saw Jesus from afar, he ran and worshiped Him. 7 And he cried out with a loud voice and said, "What have I to do with You, Jesus, Son of the Most High God? I [a]implore You by God that You do not torment me."

8 For He said to him, [a]"Come out of the man, unclean spirit!" 9 Then He asked him, "What *is* your name?"

And he answered, saying, "My name *is* Legion; for we are many." 10 Also he begged Him earnestly that He would not send them out of the country.

11 Now a large herd of [a]swine was feeding there near the mountains. 12 So all the demons begged Him, saying, "Send us to the swine, that we may enter them." 13 And at once Jesus[1] gave them permission. Then the unclean spirits went out and entered the swine (there were about two thousand); and the herd ran violently down the steep place into the sea, and drowned in the sea.

14 So those who fed the swine fled, and they told *it* in the city and in the country. And they went out to see what it was that had happened. 15 Then they came to Jesus, and saw the one *who had been* [a]demon-possessed and had the legion, [b]sitting and [c]clothed and in his right mind. And they were afraid. 16 And those who saw it told them how it happened to him *who had been* demon-possessed, and about the swine. 17 Then [a]they began to plead with Him to depart from their region.

18 And when He got into the boat, [a]he who had been demon-possessed begged Him that he might be with Him. 19 However, Jesus did not permit him, but said to him, "Go home to your friends, and tell them what great things the Lord has done for you, and how He has had compassion on you." 20 And he departed and began to [a]proclaim in Decapolis all that Jesus had done for him; and all [b]marveled.

### A GIRL RESTORED TO LIFE AND A WOMAN HEALED

*(Matt. 9:18–26; Luke 8:40–56)*

21 [a]Now when Jesus had crossed over again by boat to the other side, a great multitude gathered to Him; and He was by the sea. 22 [a]And behold, one of the rulers of the synagogue came, Jairus by name. And when he saw Him, he fell at His feet 23 and begged Him earnestly, saying, "My little daughter lies at the point of death. Come and [a]lay Your hands on her, that she may be healed, and she will live." 24 So *Jesus* went with him, and a great multitude followed Him and thronged Him.

25 Now a certain woman [a]had a flow of blood for twelve years, 26 and had suffered many things from many physicians. She had spent all that she

**4:30** [a] Matt. 13:31, 32 **4:33** [a] Matt. 13:34, 35 **4:34** [a] Luke 24:27, 45 **4:35** [a] Luke 8:22, 25 **4:38** [a] [Matt. 23:8–10] [b] Ps. 44:23 **4:39** [a] Luke 4:39 [b] Ps. 65:7; 89:9; 93:4; 104:6, 7 **4:40** [a] Matt. 14:31, 32 [1] NU-Text reads *Have you still no faith?* **5:1** [a] Matt. 8:28–34 [1] NU-Text reads *Gerasenes.* **5:2** [a] Mark 1:23; 7:25 **5:3** [1] NU-Text adds *anymore.* **5:7** [a] Acts 19:13 **5:8** [a] Mark 1:25; 9:25 **5:11** [a] Deut. 14:8 **5:13** [1] NU-Text reads *And He gave.* **5:15** [a] Matt. 4:24; 8:16 [b] Luke 10:39 [c] [Is. 61:10] **5:17** [a] Acts 16:39 **5:18** [a] Luke 8:38, 39 **5:20** [a] Ps. 66:16 [b] Matt. 9:8, 33 **5:21** [a] Luke 8:40 **5:22** [a] Matt. 9:18–26 **5:23** [a] Acts 9:17; 28:8 **5:25** [a] Lev. 15:19, 25

MARK 4:35—5:20

## JESUS, THE STORM CALMER

43

STORY OF SCRIPTURE

### WHAT'S GOING ON?

This passage takes us on an emotional roller coaster across the Sea of Galilee and into the region of Gadarenes. As Jesus and His disciples crossed the sea, a fierce storm arose, terrifying the disciples. Jesus, asleep in the boat, awakened and rebuked the wind and waves, bringing immediate calm. Then on shore, Jesus encountered a man possessed by a legion of demons. This man lived among the tombs and was uncontrollable. Jesus, though, miraculously healed him, casting the demons from him into a herd of pigs, which then rushed into the sea and drowned.

These back-to-back events are linked. Jesus has the power to speak peace both to the storm raging around the disciples and to the storm raging within the demon-possessed man. In both instances, Jesus used His words. And in both cases, the chaotic and dangerous forces obeyed His commands.

### WHAT DOES THIS MEAN FOR ME?

Whether you're facing an intense storm raging all around you or you're struggling with something deep within you, Jesus offers peace. He is here with you; He is here for you. His word can bring you back from despair. He is the captain of every and any raging storm you might face.

### DID YOU CATCH THE PATTERN?

This story might sound vaguely familiar. In Genesis 1, God spoke, and the waters were tamed for land to emerge. In Exodus 14, God parted the dangerous seas for His people to pass through. Through every storm and choppy sea, God creates a path to salvation.

*For the next* Story of Scripture *reading and devotion, turn to Luke 4:16–30 on page 1036.*

had and was no better, but rather grew worse.
27 When she heard about Jesus, she came behind
*Him* in the crowd and [a]touched His garment.
28 For she said, "If only I may touch His clothes,
I shall be made well."
29 Immediately the fountain of her blood
was dried up, and she felt in *her* body that she
was healed of the affliction. 30 And Jesus, im-
mediately knowing in Himself that [a]power had
gone out of Him, turned around in the crowd
and said, "Who touched My clothes?"
31 But His disciples said to Him, "You see the
multitude thronging You, and You say, 'Who
touched Me?' "
32 And He looked around to see her who had
done this thing. 33 But the woman, [a]fearing and
trembling, knowing what had happened to her,
came and fell down before Him and told Him
the whole truth. 34 And He said to her, "Daughter,
[a]your faith has made you well. [b]Go in peace, and
be healed of your affliction."
35 [a]While He was still speaking, *some* came
from the ruler of the synagogue's *house* who
said, "Your daughter is dead. Why trouble the
Teacher any further?"
36 As soon as Jesus heard the word that was
spoken, He said to the ruler of the synagogue,
"Do not be afraid; only [a]believe." 37 And He per-
mitted no one to follow Him except Peter, James,
and John the brother of James. 38 Then He came
to the house of the ruler of the synagogue, and
saw a tumult and those who [a]wept and wailed
loudly. 39 When He came in, He said to them,
"Why make this commotion and weep? The
child is not dead, but [a]sleeping."
40 And they ridiculed Him. [a]But when He
had put them all outside, He took the father
and the mother of the child, and those *who
were* with Him, and entered where the child was
lying. 41 Then He took the child by the hand, and
said to her, "Talitha, cumi," which is translated,
"Little girl, I say to you, arise." 42 Immediately
the girl arose and walked, for she was twelve
years *of age*. And they were [a]overcome with
great amazement. 43 But [a]He commanded them
strictly that no one should know it, and said that
*something* should be given her to eat.

### *JESUS REJECTED AT NAZARETH*

*(Matt. 13:53–58; Luke 4:16–30)*

**6** Then [a]He went out from there and came to
His own country, and His disciples followed
Him. 2 And when the Sabbath had come, He be-
gan to teach in the synagogue. And many hearing

5:27 [a] Matt. 14:35, 36 5:30 [a] Luke 6:19; 8:46 5:33 [a] [Ps. 89:7] 5:34 [a] Matt. 9:22 [b] Luke 7:50; 8:48 5:35 [a] Luke 8:49 5:36 [a] [John 11:40] 5:38 [a] Acts 9:39 5:39 [a] John 11:4, 11 5:40 [a] Acts 9:40 5:42 [a] Mark 1:27; 7:37 5:43 [a] [Matt. 8:4; 12:16–19; 17:9] 6:1 [a] Matt. 13:54

> **6:2** The **synagogue** was a local gathering place for Jews to pray and study. A synagogue could be founded in any town with at least ten men who wanted to gather. Sacrifices were not offered at synagogues; they could only be made at the temple. Synagogue buildings were usually rectangular with a large sitting area. The congregation sat on stone benches along the walls or on the floor. The main piece of furniture in the synagogue was where the scrolls of Scripture were kept.

*Him* were [a]astonished, saying, [b]"Where *did* this Man *get* these things? And what wisdom *is* this which is given to Him, that such mighty works are performed by His hands! 3 Is this not the carpenter, the Son of Mary, and [a]brother of James, Joses, Judas, and Simon? And are not His sisters here with us?" So they [b]were offended at Him.

4 But Jesus said to them, [a]"A prophet is not without honor except in his own country, among his own relatives, and in his own house." 5 [a]Now He could do no mighty work there, except that He laid His hands on a few sick people and healed *them.* 6 And [a]He marveled because of their unbelief. [b]Then He went about the villages in a circuit, teaching.

### *SENDING OUT THE TWELVE*
*(Matt. 10:1, 5–15; Luke 9:1–6)*

7 [a]And He called the twelve to *Himself,* and began to send them out [b]two *by* two, and gave them power over unclean spirits. 8 He commanded them to take nothing for the journey except a staff—no bag, no bread, no copper in *their* money belts— 9 but [a]to wear sandals, and not to put on two tunics.

10 [a]Also He said to them, "In whatever place you enter a house, stay there till you depart from that place. 11 [a]And whoever[1] will not receive you nor hear you, when you depart from there, [b]shake off the dust under your feet as a testimony against them.[2] Assuredly, I say to you, it will be more tolerable for Sodom and Gomorrah in the day of judgment than for that city!"

12 So they went out and preached that *people* should repent. 13 And they cast out many demons, [a]and anointed with oil many who were sick, and healed *them.*

### *JOHN THE BAPTIST BEHEADED*
*(Matt. 14:1–12; Luke 9:7–9)*

14 [a]Now King Herod heard *of Him,* for His name had become well known. And he said, "John the Baptist is risen from the dead, and therefore [b]these powers are at work in him."

15 [a]Others said, "It is Elijah."

And others said, "It is the Prophet, [b]or[1] like one of the prophets."

> **6:15** The prophet **Elijah** prophesied more than 850 years before Jesus. Why would anyone confuse him with John the Baptist? Perhaps it was because of the way Elijah's time on earth ended. Elijah didn't die; he was taken directly to heaven. Some Old Testament writers predicted that the living, breathing Elijah would return to earth one day. Many of the Jewish people expected him to return just before the Messiah came to set them free from Rome's control.

16 [a]But when Herod heard, he said, "This is John, whom I beheaded; he has been raised from the dead!" 17 For Herod himself had sent and laid hold of John, and bound him in prison for the sake of Herodias, his brother Philip's wife; for he had married her. 18 Because John had said to Herod, [a]"It is not lawful for you to have your brother's wife."

19 Therefore Herodias held it against him and wanted to kill him, but she could not; 20 for Herod [a]feared John, knowing that he *was* a just and holy man, and he protected him. And when he heard him, he did many things, and heard him gladly.

21 [a]Then an opportune day came when Herod [b]on his birthday gave a feast for his nobles, the high officers, and the chief *men* of Galilee. 22 And when Herodias' daughter herself came in and danced, and pleased Herod and those who sat with him, the king said to the girl, "Ask me whatever you want, and I will give *it* to you." 23 He also swore to her, [a]"Whatever you ask me, I will give you, up to half my kingdom."

24 So she went out and said to her mother, "What shall I ask?"

And she said, "The head of John the Baptist!"

25 Immediately she came in with haste to the king and asked, saying, "I want you to give me at once the head of John the Baptist on a platter."

26 [a]And the king was exceedingly sorry; *yet,* because of the oaths and because of those who sat with him, he did not want to refuse her. 27 Immediately the king sent an executioner and commanded his head to be brought. And he went and beheaded him in prison, 28 brought his head on a platter, and gave it to the girl; and the girl gave it to her mother. 29 When his disciples heard *of it,* they came and [a]took away his corpse and laid it in a tomb.

**6:2** [a] Matt. 7:28 [b] John 6:42 **6:3** [a] Matt. 12:46 [b] [Matt. 11:6] **6:4** [a] John 4:44 **6:5** [a] Gen. 19:22; 32:25 **6:6** [a] Is. 59:16 [b] Matt. 9:35 **6:7** [a] Mark 3:13, 14 [b] [Eccl. 4:9, 10] **6:9** [a] [Eph. 6:15] **6:10** [a] Matt. 10:11 **6:11** [a] Matt. 10:14 [b] Acts 13:51; 18:6 [1] NU-Text reads *whatever place.* [2] NU-Text omits the rest of this verse. **6:13** [a] [James 5:14] **6:14** [a] Luke 9:7–9 [b] Luke 19:37 **6:15** [a] Matt. 16:14; Mark 8:28; Luke 9:19 [b] Matt. 21:11 [1] NU-Text and M-Text omit *or.* **6:16** [a] Matt. 14:2; Luke 3:19 **6:18** [a] Lev. 18:16; 20:21 **6:20** [a] Matt. 14:5; 21:26 **6:21** [a] Matt. 14:6 [b] Gen. 40:20 **6:23** [a] Esth. 5:3, 6; 7:2 **6:26** [a] Matt. 14:9 **6:29** [a] 1 Kin. 13:29, 30; Matt. 27:58–61; Acts 8:2

### *FEEDING THE FIVE THOUSAND*

*(Matt. 14:13–21; Luke 9:10–17; John 6:1–14)*

30 [a]Then the apostles gathered to Jesus and
told Him all things, both what they had done and
what they had taught. 31 [a]And He said to them,
"Come aside by yourselves to a deserted place
and rest a while." For [b]there were many coming
and going, and they did not even have time to
eat. 32 [a]So they departed to a deserted place in
the boat by themselves.

33 But the multitudes[1] saw them departing,
and many [a]knew Him and ran there on foot from
all the cities. They arrived before them and came
together to Him. 34 [a]And Jesus, when He came
out, saw a great multitude and was moved with
compassion for them, because they were like
[b]sheep not having a shepherd. So [c]He began to
teach them many things. 35 [a]When the day was
now far spent, His disciples came to Him and said,
"This is a deserted place, and already the hour
*is* late. 36 Send them away, that they may go into
the surrounding country and villages and buy
themselves bread;[1] for they have nothing to eat."

37 But He answered and said to them, "You
give them something to eat."

And they said to Him, [a]"Shall we go and buy
two hundred denarii worth of bread and give
them *something* to eat?"

38 But He said to them, "How many loaves
do you have? Go and see."

And when they found out they said, [a]"Five,
and two fish."

39 Then He [a]commanded them to make
them all sit down in groups on the green grass.
40 So they sat down in ranks, in hundreds and
in fifties. 41 And when He had taken the five
loaves and the two fish, He [a]looked up to heaven,
[b]blessed and broke the loaves, and gave *them* to
His disciples to set before them; and the two
fish He divided among *them* all. 42 So they all
ate and were filled. 43 And they took up twelve
baskets full of fragments and of the fish. 44 Now
those who had eaten the loaves were about[1] five
thousand men.

### *JESUS WALKS ON THE SEA*

*(Matt. 14:22–33; John 6:15–21)*

45 [a]Immediately He made His disciples get
into the boat and go before Him to the other
side, to Bethsaida, while He sent the multitude
away. 46 And when He had sent them away, He
[a]departed to the mountain to pray. 47 Now when
evening came, the boat was in the middle of the
sea; and He *was* alone on the land. 48 Then He
saw them straining at rowing, for the wind was
against them. Now about the fourth watch of the
night He came to them, walking on the sea, and
[a]would have passed them by. 49 And when they
saw Him walking on the sea, they supposed it
was a [a]ghost, and cried out; 50 for they all saw
Him and were troubled. But immediately He
talked with them and said to them, [a]"Be of good
cheer! It is I; do not be [b]afraid." 51 Then He went
up into the boat to them, and the wind [a]ceased.
And they were greatly [b]amazed in themselves
beyond measure, and marveled. 52 For [a]they had
not understood about the loaves, because their
[b]heart was hardened.

**6:30** [a] Luke 9:10 **6:31** [a] Matt. 14:13 [b] Mark 3:20 **6:32** [a] Matt. 14:13–21; Luke 9:10–17; John 6:5–13 **6:33** [a] [Col. 1:6] [1] NU-Text and M-Text read *they.* **6:34** [a] Matt. 9:36; 14:14; [Heb. 5:2] [b] Num. 27:17; 1 Kin. 22:17; 2 Chr. 18:16; Zech. 10:2 [c] [Is. 48:17; 61:1–3]; Luke 9:11 **6:35** [a] Matt. 14:15; Luke 9:12 **6:36** [1] NU-Text reads *something to eat* and omits the rest of this verse. **6:37** [a] Num. 11:13, 22; 2 Kin. 4:43 **6:38** [a] Matt. 14:17; Luke 9:13; John 6:9 **6:39** [a] Matt. 15:35; Mark 8:6 **6:41** [a] John 11:41, 42 [b] 1 Sam. 9:13; Matt. 15:36; 26:26; Mark 8:7; Luke 24:30 **6:44** [1] NU-Text and M-Text omit *about.* **6:45** [a] Matt. 14:22–32; John 6:15–21 **6:46** [a] Mark 1:35; Luke 5:16 **6:48** [a] Luke 24:28 **6:49** [a] Matt. 14:26 **6:50** [a] Matt. 9:2 [b] Is. 41:10 **6:51** [a] Ps. 107:29 [b] Mark 1:27; 2:12; 5:42; 7:37 **6:52** [a] Mark 8:17, 18 [b] Mark 3:5; 16:14

LIVE THE TRUTH

## PERSEVERING

**6:48–52** How can you continue to strive for what's right in the world today? How can you continue in your relationship with Jesus when life gets difficult? The answer is found in Jesus Christ. In Jesus, we have a Savior who defeated death—He is alive today. He is a Savior who defeated sin—He took on the sin of the world and won. He is a Savior who defeated Satan—He was victorious over the devil's temptations and schemes. And here it is: Because Jesus is victorious over these things, if you have trusted in Him, you have victory over them too. Jesus fought all those battles in your place and *won*. Because you trust in Jesus, you can keep going, no matter what comes up against you. It's nothing Jesus hasn't given you victory over.

In Mark 6, the disciples were struggling to row their boat against high winds. As Jesus approached them, they were shocked because He was walking on water; they believed He was a ghost! Jesus immediately told them not to be afraid, but for a specific reason: It was the Son of God who approached them. We can persevere, without fear, because of who is with us. Because Jesus has power and victory over all, we can keep going, knowing our victory is secured.

### *MANY TOUCH HIM AND ARE MADE WELL*
*(Matt. 14:34–36)*

53 [a]When they had crossed over, they came
to the land of Gennesaret and anchored there.
54 And when they came out of the boat, immedi-
ately the people recognized Him, 55 ran through
that whole surrounding region, and began to
carry about on beds those who were sick to wher-
ever they heard He was. 56 Wherever He entered,
into villages, cities, or the country, they laid the
sick in the marketplaces, and begged Him that
[a]they might just touch the [b]hem of His garment.
And as many as touched Him were made well.

### *DEFILEMENT COMES FROM WITHIN*
*(Matt. 15:1–20)*

7 Then [a]the Pharisees and some of the scribes
came together to Him, having come from
Jerusalem. 2 Now when[1] they saw some of His
disciples eat bread with defiled, that is, with
[a]unwashed hands, they found fault. 3 For the
Pharisees and all the Jews do not eat unless they
wash *their* hands in a special way, holding the
[a]tradition of the elders. 4 *When they come* from
the marketplace, they do not eat unless they
wash. And there are many other things which
they have received and hold, *like* the washing
of cups, pitchers, copper vessels, and couches.
5 [a]Then the Pharisees and scribes asked Him,
"Why do Your disciples not walk according to
the tradition of the elders, but eat bread with
unwashed hands?"

> **7:5 The tradition of the elders** refers to a series of rules meant to protect or bolster the ceremonial law of the Jews. Its authority was not supported by Scripture. The question indirectly challenged Jesus, for as the disciples' teacher He was judged responsible for their actions.

6 He answered and said to them, "Well did Isa-
iah prophesy of you [a]hypocrites, as it is written:

[b]'This people honors Me with *their* lips,
But their heart is far from Me.
7 And in vain they worship Me,
Teaching *as* doctrines the
commandments of men.'[1]

8 For laying aside the commandment of God, you
hold the tradition of men[1]—the washing of pitch-
ers and cups, and many other such things you do."

9 He said to them, "*All too* well [a]you reject
the commandment of God, that you may keep
your tradition. 10 For Moses said, [a]'Honor your
father and your mother';[1] and, [b]'He who curses
father or mother, let him be put to death.'[2] 11 But
you say, 'If a man says to his father or mother,
[a]"Whatever profit you might have received
from me *is* Corban"—' (that is, a gift *to God*),
12 then you no longer let him do anything for
his father or his mother, 13 making the word
of God of no effect through your tradition
which you have handed down. And many such
things you do."

> **7:11–13 Corban** was a way of declaring something to be dedicated to the temple, thus these goods could not be used to support one's parents. This, then, was a pious-sounding evasion of the requirement of honoring one's parents by supporting them financially.

14 [a]When He had called all the multitude to
*Himself,* He said to them, "Hear Me, everyone,
and [b]understand: 15 There is nothing that enters
a man from outside which can defile him; but
the things which come out of him, those are the
things that [a]defile a man. 16 [a]If anyone has ears
to hear, let him hear!"[1]
17 [a]When He had entered a house away from
the crowd, His disciples asked Him concerning
the parable. 18 So He said to them, [a]"Are you thus
without understanding also? Do you not per-
ceive that whatever enters a man from outside
cannot defile him, 19 because it does not enter
his heart but his stomach, and is eliminated,
*thus* purifying all foods?"[1] 20 And He said, [a]"What
comes out of a man, that defiles a man. 21 [a]For
from within, out of the heart of men, [b]proceed
evil thoughts, [c]adulteries, [d]fornications, mur-
ders, 22 thefts, [a]covetousness, wickedness, [b]de-
ceit, [c]lewdness, an evil eye, [d]blasphemy, [e]pride,
foolishness. 23 All these evil things come from
within and defile a man."

> **SEEING JESUS IN THE SCRIPTURE**
>
> **7:6–7** Jesus agreed with the prophet Isaiah that the Pharisees and the scribes were hypocrites who worshiped God in vain (see Is. 29:13).

**6:53** [a] Matt. 14:34–36 **6:56** [a] Matt. 9:20 [b] Num. 15:38, 39 **7:1** [a] Matt. 15:1–20 **7:2** [a] Matt. 15:20 [1] NU-Text omits *when* and *they found fault.* **7:3** [a] Gal. 1:14 **7:5** [a] Matt. 15:2 **7:6** [a] Matt. 23:13–29 [b] Is. 29:13 **7:7** [1] Isaiah 29:13 **7:8** [1] NU-Text omits the rest of this verse. **7:9** [a] Prov. 1:25 **7:10** [a] Ex. 20:12; Deut. 5:16 [b] Ex. 21:17 [1] Exodus 20:12; Deuteronomy 5:16 [2] Exodus 21:17 **7:11** [a] Matt. 15:5; 23:18 **7:14** [a] Matt. 15:10 [b] Matt. 16:9, 11, 12 **7:15** [a] Is. 59:3 **7:16** [a] Matt. 11:15 [1] NU-Text omits this verse. **7:17** [a] Matt. 15:15 **7:18** [a] [Heb. 5:11–14] **7:19** [1] NU-Text ends quotation with *eliminated,* setting off the final clause as Mark's comment that Jesus has declared all foods clean. **7:20** [a] Ps. 39:1 **7:21** [a] Gen. 6:5; 8:21 [b] [Gal. 5:19–21] [c] 2 Pet. 2:14 [d] 1 Thess. 4:3 **7:22** [a] Luke 12:15 [b] Rom. 1:28, 29 [c] 1 Pet. 4:3 [d] Rev. 2:9 [e] 1 John 2:16

### A GENTILE SHOWS HER FAITH

(Matt. 15:21–28)

24 [a]From there He arose and went to the re-
gion of Tyre and Sidon.[1] And He entered a house
and wanted no one to know *it,* but He could
not be [b]hidden. 25 For a woman whose young
daughter had an unclean spirit heard about Him,
and she came and [a]fell at His feet. 26 The woman
was a Greek, a Syro-Phoenician by birth, and she
kept asking Him to cast the demon out of her
daughter. 27 But Jesus said to her, "Let the chil-
dren be filled first, for it is not good to take the
children's bread and throw *it* to the little dogs."
28 And she answered and said to Him, "Yes,
Lord, yet even the little dogs under the table eat
from the children's crumbs."
29 Then He said to her, "For this saying go
your way; the demon has gone out of your
daughter."
30 And when she had come to her house, she
found the demon gone out, and her daughter
lying on the bed.

### JESUS HEALS A DEAF-MUTE

(Matt. 15:29–31)

31 [a]Again, departing from the region of Tyre
and Sidon, He came through the midst of the
region of Decapolis to the Sea of Galilee. 32 Then
[a]they brought to Him one who was deaf and had
an impediment in his speech, and they begged
Him to put His hand on him. 33 And He took him
aside from the multitude, and put His fingers in
his ears, and [a]He spat and touched his tongue.
34 Then, [a]looking up to heaven, [b]He sighed, and
said to him, "Ephphatha," that is, "Be opened."
35 [a]Immediately his ears were opened, and
the impediment of his tongue was loosed, and he
spoke plainly. 36 Then [a]He commanded them that
they should tell no one; but the more He com-
manded them, the more widely they proclaimed
*it.* 37 And they were [a]astonished beyond measure,
saying, "He has done all things well. He [b]makes
both the deaf to hear and the mute to speak."

### FEEDING THE FOUR THOUSAND

(Matt. 15:32–39)

**8** In those days, [a]the multitude being very
great and having nothing to eat, Jesus called
His disciples *to Him* and said to them, 2 "I have
[a]compassion on the multitude, because they
have now continued with Me three days and
have nothing to eat. 3 And if I send them away
hungry to their own houses, they will faint on
the way; for some of them have come from afar."
4 Then His disciples answered Him, "How
can one satisfy these people with bread here
in the wilderness?"
5 [a]He asked them, "How many loaves do
you have?"
And they said, "Seven."
6 So He commanded the multitude to sit
down on the ground. And He took the seven
loaves and gave thanks, broke *them* and gave *them*
to His disciples to set before *them;* and they set
*them* before the multitude. 7 They also had a few
small fish; and [a]having blessed them, He said to
set them also before *them.* 8 So they ate and were
filled, and they took up seven large baskets of
leftover fragments. 9 Now those who had eaten
were about four thousand. And He sent them
away, 10 [a]immediately got into the boat with His
disciples, and came to the region of Dalmanutha.

### THE PHARISEES SEEK A SIGN

(Matt. 16:1–4)

11 [a]Then the Pharisees came out and began to
dispute with Him, seeking from Him a sign from
heaven, testing Him. 12 But He [a]sighed deeply in
His spirit, and said, "Why does this generation
seek a sign? Assuredly, I say to you, [b]no sign
shall be given to this generation."

### BEWARE OF THE LEAVEN OF THE PHARISEES AND HEROD

(Matt. 16:5–12)

13 And He left them, and getting into the
boat again, departed to the other side. 14 [a]Now
the disciples[1] had forgotten to take bread, and
they did not have more than one loaf with them
in the boat. 15 [a]Then He charged them, saying,
"Take heed, beware of the leaven of the Pharisees
and the leaven of Herod."

> **8:15** As **leaven,** or yeast, ferments, it makes dough bubble and then rise. Before long, the entire loaf is affected. The fast-acting and wide-reaching effects of leaven may explain why the Bible often uses it to symbolize sin or evil.

16 And they reasoned among themselves,
saying, "*It is* because we have no bread."
17 But Jesus, being aware of *it,* said to them,
"Why do you reason because you have no bread?
[a]Do you not yet perceive nor understand? Is your
heart still[1] hardened? 18 Having eyes, do you not
see? And having ears, do you not hear? And do
you not remember? 19 [a]When I broke the five
loaves for the five thousand, how many baskets
full of fragments did you take up?"
They said to Him, "Twelve."

**7:24** [a] Matt. 15:21 [b] Mark 2:1, 2 [1] NU-Text omits *and Sidon.* **7:25** [a] Mark 5:22; John 11:32; Rev. 1:17 **7:31** [a] Matt. 15:29; Mark 15:37; Luke 23:46; 24:46; Acts 10:40; 1 Cor. 15:4 **7:32** [a] Matt. 9:32; Luke 11:14 **7:33** [a] Mark 8:23; John 9:6 **7:34** [a] Mark 6:41; John 11:41; 17:1 [b] John 11:33, 38 **7:35** [a] Is. 35:5, 6 **7:36** [a] Mark 5:43 **7:37** [a] Mark 6:51; 10:26 [b] Matt. 12:22 **8:1** [a] Matt. 15:32–39; Mark 6:34–44; Luke 9:12 **8:2** [a] Matt. 9:36; 14:14; Mark 1:41; 6:34 **8:5** [a] Matt. 15:34; Mark 6:38; John 6:9 **8:7** [a] Matt. 14:19; Mark 6:41 **8:10** [a] Matt. 15:39 **8:11** [a] Matt. 12:38; 16:1; Luke 11:16; John 2:18; 6:30; 1 Cor. 1:22 **8:12** [a] Mark 7:34 [b] Matt. 12:39 **8:14** [a] Matt. 16:5 [1] NU-Text and M-Text read *they.* **8:15** [a] Matt. 16:6; Luke 12:1 **8:17** [a] Mark 6:52; 16:14 [1] NU-Text omits *still.* **8:19** [a] Matt. 14:20; Mark 6:43; Luke 9:17; John 6:13

20 "Also, [a]when I broke the seven for the four thousand, how many large baskets full of fragments did you take up?"

And they said, "Seven."

21 So He said to them, "How *is it* [a]you do not understand?"

### A BLIND MAN HEALED AT BETHSAIDA

22 Then He came to Bethsaida; and they brought a [a]blind man to Him, and begged Him to [b]touch him. 23 So He took the blind man by the hand and led him out of the town. And when [a]He had spit on his eyes and put His hands on him, He asked him if he saw anything.

24 And he looked up and said, "I see men like trees, walking."

25 Then He put *His* hands on his eyes again and made him look up. And he was restored and saw everyone clearly. 26 Then He sent him away to his house, saying, "Neither go into the town, [1]nor tell anyone in the town."

### PETER CONFESSES JESUS AS THE CHRIST

*(Matt. 16:13–20; Luke 9:18–20)*

27 [a]Now Jesus and His disciples went out to the towns of Caesarea Philippi; and on the road He asked His disciples, saying to them, "Who do men say that I am?"

28 So they answered, [a]"John the Baptist; but some *say,* [b]Elijah; and others, one of the prophets."

29 He said to them, "But who do you say that I am?"

Peter answered and said to Him, [a]"You are the Christ."

30 [a]Then He strictly warned them that they should tell no one about Him.

### JESUS PREDICTS HIS DEATH AND RESURRECTION

*(Matt. 16:21–23; Luke 9:21, 22)*

31 And [a]He began to teach them that the Son of Man must suffer many things, and be [b]rejected by the elders and chief priests and scribes, and be [c]killed, and after three days rise again. 32 He spoke this word openly. Then Peter took Him aside and began to rebuke Him. 33 But when He had turned around and looked at His disciples, He [a]rebuked Peter, saying, "Get behind Me, Satan! For you are not mindful of the things of God, but the things of men."

### TAKE UP THE CROSS AND FOLLOW HIM

*(Matt. 16:24–27; Luke 9:23–26)*

34 When He had called the people to *Himself,* with His disciples also, He said to them, [a]"Whoever desires to come after Me, let him deny himself, and take up his cross, and follow Me. 35 For [a]whoever desires to save his life will lose it, but whoever loses his life for My sake and the gospel's will save it. 36 For what will it profit a man if he gains the whole world, and loses his own soul? 37 Or what will a man give in exchange for his soul? 38 [a]For whoever [b]is ashamed of Me and My words in this adulterous and sinful generation, of him the Son of Man also will be ashamed when He comes in the glory of His Father with the holy angels."

9 And He said to them, [a]"Assuredly, I say to you that there are some standing here who will not taste death till they see [b]the kingdom of God present with power."

### JESUS TRANSFIGURED ON THE MOUNT

*(Matt. 16:28—17:13; Luke 9:27–36; 2 Pet. 1:16–18)*

2 [a]Now after six days Jesus took Peter, James, and John, and led them up on a high mountain

**8:20** [a] Matt. 15:37 **8:21** [a] [Mark 6:52] **8:22** [a] John 9:1 [b] Luke 18:15 **8:23** [a] Mark 7:33 **8:26** [a] Mark 5:43; 7:36 [1] NU-Text reads *"Do not even go into the town."* **8:27** [a] Luke 9:18–20 **8:28** [a] Matt. 14:2 [b] Luke 9:7, 8 **8:29** [a] John 1:41; 4:42; 6:69; 11:27 **8:30** [a] Matt. 8:4; 16:20 **8:31** [a] Matt. 16:21; 20:19 [b] Mark 10:33 [c] Mark 9:31; 10:34 **8:33** [a] [Rev. 3:19] **8:34** [a] Luke 14:27 **8:35** [a] John 12:25 **8:38** [a] Matt. 10:33 [b] 2 Tim. 1:8, 9; 2:12 **9:1** [a] Luke 9:27 [b] [Matt. 24:30] **9:2** [a] Matt. 17:1–8

LIVE THE TRUTH

## SETTING GOALS

**8:36** There's nothing wrong with goals. It's good to have a plan for what you want to achieve. Goals can help us stay on track, measure progress, and improve many parts of our lives. However, we never want to lose sight of what's most important as we accomplish our goals. To be a Christian means to be a follower of Jesus; to follow Jesus faithfully means He must be our ultimate goal. All other goals should lead us toward Him, directly or indirectly. As followers of Jesus, we must make our relationship with Jesus our number one priority.

In this verse, Jesus reminds us of a sobering truth—all the achievements in the world mean nothing without a relationship with Him. When we make Jesus our main goal, we may stumble into some incredible blessings along the way. But if our life's focus is our own gain and our own name, we'll end up realizing all we have is slipping through our fingers and won't last. The greatest goal—what will last through eternity—is living fully for Jesus Christ. When this is our pursuit, we will find it's really the only goal worth having.

apart by themselves; and He was transfigured
before them. 3 His clothes became shining, ex-
ceedingly [a]white, like snow, such as no launderer
on earth can whiten them. 4 And Elijah appeared
to them with Moses, and they were talking with
Jesus. 5 Then Peter answered and said to Jesus,
"Rabbi, it is good for us to be here; and let us
make three tabernacles: one for You, one for
Moses, and one for Elijah"— 6 because he did not
know what to say, for they were greatly afraid.
7 And a [a]cloud came and overshadowed
them; and a voice came out of the cloud, saying,
"This is [b]My beloved Son. [c]Hear Him!" 8 Sudden-
ly, when they had looked around, they saw no
one anymore, but only Jesus with themselves.

**SEEING JESUS IN THE SCRIPTURE**

**9:7** At Jesus' transfiguration, like His baptism, Isaiah's words were fulfilled as the Father declared His pleasure in the Son (see Is. 42:1).

9 [a]Now as they came down from the moun-
tain, He commanded them that they should tell
no one the things they had seen, till the Son of
Man had risen from the dead. 10 So they kept
this word to themselves, questioning [a]what the
rising from the dead meant.
11 And they asked Him, saying, "Why do the
scribes say [a]that Elijah must come first?"
12 Then He answered and told them, "Indeed,
Elijah is coming first and restores all things. And
[a]how is it written concerning the Son of Man,
that He must suffer many things and [b]be treated
with contempt? 13 But I say to you that [a]Elijah
has also come, and they did to him whatever
they wished, as it is written of him."

### *A BOY IS HEALED*

*(Matt. 17:14–21; Luke 9:37–42)*

14 [a]And when He came to the disciples, He
saw a great multitude around them, and scribes
disputing with them. 15 Immediately, when they
saw Him, all the people were greatly amazed, and
running to *Him,* greeted Him. 16 And He asked the
scribes, "What are you discussing with them?"
17 Then [a]one of the crowd answered and said,
"Teacher, I brought You my son, who has a mute
spirit. 18 And wherever it seizes him, it throws him
down; he foams at the mouth, gnashes his teeth,
and becomes rigid. So I spoke to Your disciples,
that they should cast it out, but they could not."
19 He answered him and said, "O [a]faithless gen-
eration, how long shall I be with you? How long
shall I bear with you? Bring him to Me." 20 Then they
brought him to Him. And [a]when he saw Him, im-
mediately the spirit convulsed him, and he fell on
the ground and wallowed, foaming at the mouth.
21 So He asked his father, "How long has this
been happening to him?"
And he said, "From childhood. 22 And often
he has thrown him both into the fire and into the
water to destroy him. But if You can do anything,
have compassion on us and help us."
23 Jesus said to him, [a]"If you can believe,[1] all
things *are* possible to him who believes."
24 Immediately the father of the child cried
out and said with tears, "Lord, I believe; [a]help
my unbelief!"

**9:24** The **father of the child** expressed the dilemma that even those who **believe** can be nagged by doubt and hopelessness. This man took the correct course by appealing to Jesus for help.

**9:3** [a] Dan. 7:9 **9:7** [a] Ex. 40:34 [b] Mark 1:11 [c] Acts 3:22 **9:9** [a] Matt. 17:9–13 **9:10** [a] John 2:19–22 **9:11** [a] Mal. 4:5 **9:12** [a] Is. 53:3 [b] Phil. 2:7 **9:13** [a] Luke 1:17 **9:14** [a] Matt. 17:14–19 **9:17** [a] Luke 9:38 **9:19** [a] John 4:48 **9:20** [a] Mark 1:26 **9:23** [a] John 11:40 [1] NU-Text reads *"'If You can!' All things . . . ."* **9:24** [a] Luke 17:5

**LIVE THE TRUTH**

## KNOWING YOUR IDENTITY

**9:7** How would you respond if someone asked, "Who are you?" Often, we respond with something we do, like, or are involved in. "I'm a student," "I'm an athlete," "I'm a musician," and so forth. Those surely can be *part* of who we are, but they aren't the *entirety* of who we are. Indeed, they aren't even *mainly* who we are. They're only partial descriptions of our identity. As believers, we have an ultimate, unchanging answer to this question: "We are children of God."

Jesus could have answered this question in different ways, too. He was a son, brother, Israelite, carpenter, and more. But here we see the Father's defining statement of Jesus: He is His beloved Son. That's what is most important about Jesus. And our relationship to God is most important about us, too. If we trust in Jesus, God accepts us into His family as His sons and daughters. To all who have received Jesus, God has given the right to become children of God (John 1:12). God is pleased with you and accepts you always because when He looks upon you, He sees the perfection of Jesus. That's your identity.

25 When Jesus saw that the people came
running together, He [a]rebuked the unclean
spirit, saying to it, "Deaf and dumb spirit, I com-
mand you, come out of him and enter him no
more!" 26 Then *the spirit* cried out, convulsed him
greatly, and came out of him. And he became as
one dead, so that many said, "He is dead." 27 But
Jesus took him by the hand and lifted him up,
and he arose.

28 [a]And when He had come into the house,
His disciples asked Him privately, "Why could
we not cast it out?"

29 So He said to them, "This kind can come
out by nothing but [a]prayer and fasting."[1]

### JESUS AGAIN PREDICTS HIS DEATH AND RESURRECTION

30 Then they departed from there and passed
through Galilee, and He did not want anyone to
know *it.* 31 [a]For He taught His disciples and said
to them, "The Son of Man is being betrayed into
the hands of men, and they will [b]kill Him. And
after He is killed, He will [c]rise the third day."
32 But they [a]did not understand this saying, and
were afraid to ask Him.

### WHO IS THE GREATEST?

*(Matt. 18:1–5; Luke 9:46–48)*

33 [a]Then He came to Capernaum. And when
He was in the house He asked them, "What was
it you disputed among yourselves on the road?"
34 But they kept silent, for on the road they had
[a]disputed among themselves who *would be the*
[b]greatest. 35 And He sat down, called the twelve,
and said to them, [a]"If anyone desires to be first,
he shall be last of all and servant of all." 36 Then
[a]He took a little child and set him in the midst
of them. And when He had taken him in His
arms, He said to them, 37 "Whoever receives one
of these little children in My name receives Me;
and [a]whoever receives Me, receives not Me but
Him who sent Me."

### JESUS FORBIDS SECTARIANISM

*(Matt. 10:40–42; Luke 9:49, 50)*

38 [a]Now John answered Him, saying, "Teach-
er, we saw someone who does not follow us cast-
ing out demons in Your name, and we forbade
him because he does not follow us."

39 But Jesus said, "Do not forbid him, [a]for no
one who works a miracle in My name can soon
afterward speak evil of Me. 40 For [a]he who is not
against us is on our[1] side. 41 [a]For whoever gives
you a cup of water to drink in My name, because
you belong to Christ, assuredly, I say to you, he
will by no means lose his reward.

### JESUS WARNS OF OFFENSES

*(Matt. 18:6–9; Luke 17:1, 2)*

42 [a]"But whoever causes one of these little
ones who believe in Me to stumble, it would be
better for him if a millstone were hung around
his neck, and he were thrown into the sea. 43 [a]If
your hand causes you to sin, cut it off. It is better
for you to enter into life maimed, rather than
having two hands, to go to hell, into the fire that
shall never be quenched— 44 where

[a]'Their worm does not die,
And the fire is not quenched.'[1]

45 And if your foot causes you to sin, cut it off. It
is better for you to enter life lame, rather than
having two feet, to be cast into hell, into the fire
that shall never be quenched— 46 where

[a]'Their worm does not die,
And the fire is not quenched.'[1]

47 And if your eye causes you to sin, pluck it out.
It is better for you to enter the kingdom of God
with one eye, rather than having two eyes, to be
cast into hell fire— 48 where

[a]'Their worm does not die,
And the [b]fire is not quenched.'[1]

### TASTELESS SALT IS WORTHLESS

49 "For everyone will be [a]seasoned with fire,[1]
[b]and every sacrifice will be seasoned with salt.
50 [a]Salt *is* good, but if the salt loses its flavor, how
will you season it? [b]Have salt in yourselves, and
[c]have peace with one another."

### MARRIAGE AND DIVORCE

*(Matt. 19:1–9)*

10 Then [a]He arose from there and came to the
region of Judea by the other side of the Jor-
dan. And multitudes gathered to Him again, and
as He was accustomed, He taught them again.

2 [a]The Pharisees came and asked Him, "Is it
lawful for a man to divorce *his* wife?" testing Him.

3 And He answered and said to them, "What
did Moses command you?"

4 They said, [a]"Moses permitted *a man* to
write a certificate of divorce, and to dismiss *her.*"

5 And Jesus answered and said to them, "Be-
cause of the hardness of your heart he wrote you
this precept. 6 But from the beginning of the
creation, God [a]'made them male and female.'[1]
7 [a]'For this reason a man shall leave his father
and mother and be joined to his wife, 8 and the
two shall become one flesh';[1] so then they are

**9:25** [a] Mark 1:25 **9:28** [a] Matt. 17:19 **9:29** [a] [James 5:16] [1] NU-Text omits *and fasting.* **9:31** [a] Luke 9:44 [b] Matt. 16:21; 27:50 [c] 1 Cor. 15:4 **9:32** [a] Luke 2:50; 18:34 **9:33** [a] Matt. 18:1–5 **9:34** [a] [Prov. 13:10] [b] Luke 22:24; 23:46; 24:46 **9:35** [a] Luke 22:26, 27 **9:36** [a] Mark 10:13–16 **9:37** [a] Matt. 10:40 **9:38** [a] Num. 11:27–29 **9:39** [a] 1 Cor. 12:3 **9:40** [a] [Matt. 12:30] [1] M-Text reads *against you is on your side.* **9:41** [a] Matt. 10:42 **9:42** [a] Luke 17:1, 2 **9:43** [a] Matt. 5:29, 30; 18:8, 9 **9:44** [a] Is. 66:24 [1] NU-Text omits this verse. **9:46** [a] Is. 66:24 [1] NU-Text omits the last clause of verse 45 and all of verse 46. **9:48** [a] Is. 66:24 [b] Jer. 7:20 [1] Isaiah 66:24 **9:49** [a] [Matt. 3:11] [b] Lev. 2:13 [1] NU-Text omits the rest of this verse. **9:50** [a] Matt. 5:13 [b] Col. 4:6 [c] Rom. 12:18; 14:19 **10:1** [a] Matt. 19:1–9 **10:2** [a] Matt. 19:3 **10:4** [a] Deut. 24:1–4 **10:6** [a] Gen. 1:27; 5:2 [1] Genesis 1:27; 5:2 **10:7** [a] Gen. 2:24 **10:8** [1] Genesis 2:24

no longer two, but one flesh. 9 Therefore what
God has joined together, let not man separate."
10 In the house His disciples also asked Him
again about the same *matter*. 11 So He said to
them, [a]"Whoever divorces his wife and marries
another commits adultery against her. 12 And
if a woman divorces her husband and marries
another, she commits adultery."

### *JESUS BLESSES LITTLE CHILDREN*

*(Matt. 19:13–15; Luke 18:15–17)*

13 [a]Then they brought little children to Him,
that He might touch them; but the disciples re-
buked those who brought *them*. 14 But when Jesus
saw *it*, He was greatly displeased and said to them,
"Let the little children come to Me, and do not
forbid them; for [a]of such is the kingdom of God.
15 Assuredly, I say to you, [a]whoever does not re-
ceive the kingdom of God as a little child will [b]by
no means enter it." 16 And He took them up in His
arms, laid *His* hands on them, and blessed them.

### *JESUS COUNSELS THE RICH YOUNG RULER*

*(Matt. 19:16–22; Luke 18:18–23)*

17 [a]Now as He was going out on the road, one
came running, knelt before Him, and asked
Him, "Good Teacher, what shall I [b]do that I may
inherit eternal life?"

18 So Jesus said to him, "Why do you call Me
good? No one *is* good but One, *that is*, [a]God. 19 You
know the commandments: [a]'Do not commit
adultery,' 'Do not murder,' 'Do not steal,' 'Do
not bear false witness,' 'Do not defraud,' 'Honor
your father and your mother.'"[1]

20 And he answered and said to Him, "Teach-
er, all these things I have [a]kept from my youth."

21 Then Jesus, looking at him, loved him, and
said to him, "One thing you lack: Go your way,

> **10:18** Jesus' question might sound argumentative at first, but it isn't. Rather, it's *the* answer to the young ruler's question. The ruler was right to call Jesus **good** because He is **God**. If the young ruler would have recognized this, he would have found the answer to inheriting eternal life.

[a]sell whatever you have and give to the poor, and
you will have [b]treasure in heaven; and come,
[c]take up the cross, and follow Me."

22 But he was sad at this word, and went away
sorrowful, for he had great possessions.

### *WITH GOD ALL THINGS ARE POSSIBLE*

*(Matt. 19:23–30; Luke 18:24–30)*

23 [a]Then Jesus looked around and said to
His disciples, "How hard it is for those who have
riches to enter the kingdom of God!" 24 And the
disciples were astonished at His words. But Jesus
answered again and said to them, "Children, how
hard it is for those [a]who trust in riches[1] to enter
the kingdom of God! 25 It is easier for a camel to
go through the eye of a needle than for a [a]rich
man to enter the kingdom of God."

26 And they were greatly astonished, saying
among themselves, "Who then can be saved?"

27 But Jesus looked at them and said, "With
men *it is* impossible, but not [a]with God; for with
God all things are possible."

28 [a]Then Peter began to say to Him, "See, we
have left all and followed You."

29 So Jesus answered and said, "Assuredly,
I say to you, there is no one who has left house
or brothers or sisters or father or mother or

**10:11** [a] [Matt. 5:32; 19:9] **10:13** [a] Luke 18:15–17 **10:14** [a] [1 Pet. 2:2] **10:15** [a] Matt. 18:3, 4; 19:14 [b] Luke 13:28 **10:17** [a] Matt. 19:16–30 [b] John 6:28 **10:18** [a] 1 Sam. 2:2 **10:19** [a] Ex. 20:12–16; Deut. 5:16–20 [1] Exodus 20:12–16; Deuteronomy 5:16–20 **10:20** [a] Phil. 3:6 **10:21** [a] [Luke 12:33; 16:9] [b] Matt. 6:19, 20; 19:21 [c] [Mark 8:34] **10:23** [a] Matt. 19:23 **10:24** [a] [1 Tim. 6:17] [1] NU-Text omits *for those who trust in riches.* **10:25** [a] [Matt. 13:22; 19:24] **10:27** [a] Jer. 32:17 **10:28** [a] Luke 18:28

LIVE THE TRUTH

## BEING CONTENT

**10:17–30** Contentment is countercultural. The way of the world is always to chase more, whether to make a name for yourself or to find happiness, meaning, and security. Contentment is quite the opposite. It's choosing to be happy and at peace with whatever you have. For the believer, the key to contentment is realizing possessions aren't the goal of life. Jesus is. Therefore, followers of Jesus should hold Him as our most prized possession. After Jesus, all else is a bonus.

In Mark 10, a young man came to see Jesus, wanting to know the key to having a relationship with God. The answer was right in front of Him—he needed to make Jesus the Lord of his life. But Jesus saw something stood in the way: the young man was very rich. When Jesus told him to sell his possessions and follow Him, the young man couldn't do it. This is the danger with possessions: they can possess us. They can take our attention, our love, and even our lives. As followers of Jesus, we must choose Jesus over everything else and chase after Jesus more than anything else. When we believe Jesus is enough, we can be truly content.

wife[1] or children or lands, for My sake and the
gospel's, 30 [a]who shall not receive a hundredfold
now in this time—houses and brothers and
sisters and mothers and children and lands,
with [b]persecutions—and in the age to come,
eternal life. 31 [a]But many *who are* first will be
last, and the last first."

### JESUS A THIRD TIME PREDICTS HIS DEATH AND RESURRECTION
*(Matt. 20:17–19; Luke 18:31–34)*

32 [a]Now they were on the road, going up to
Jerusalem, and Jesus was going before them;
and they were amazed. And as they followed they
were afraid. [b]Then He took the twelve aside again
and began to tell them the things that would
happen to Him: 33 "Behold, we are going up to
Jerusalem, and the Son of Man will be betrayed
to the chief priests and to the scribes; and they
will condemn Him to death and deliver Him
to the Gentiles; 34 and they will mock Him, and
scourge Him, and spit on Him, and kill Him.
And the third day He will rise again."

### GREATNESS IS SERVING
*(Matt. 20:20–28)*

35 [a]Then James and John, the sons of Zeb-
edee, came to Him, saying, "Teacher, we want
You to do for us whatever we ask."

36 And He said to them, "What do you want
Me to do for you?"

37 They said to Him, "Grant us that we may
sit, one on Your right hand and the other on
Your left, in Your glory."

38 But Jesus said to them, "You do not know
what you ask. Are you able to drink the [a]cup that
I drink, and be baptized with the [b]baptism that
I am baptized with?"

39 They said to Him, "We are able."

So Jesus said to them, [a]"You will indeed
drink the cup that I drink, and with the baptism
I am baptized with you will be baptized; 40 but to
sit on My right hand and on My left is not Mine to
give, but *it is for those* [a]for whom it is prepared."

41 [a]And when the ten heard *it,* they began
to be greatly displeased with James and John.
42 But Jesus called them to *Himself* and said to
them, [a]"You know that those who are considered
rulers over the Gentiles lord it over them, and
their great ones exercise authority over them.
43 [a]Yet it shall not be so among you; but whoever
desires to become great among you shall be your
servant. 44 And whoever of you desires to be first
shall be slave of all. 45 For even [a]the Son of Man
did not come to be served, but to serve, and [b]to
give His life a ransom for many."

### JESUS HEALS BLIND BARTIMAEUS
*(Matt. 20:29–34; Luke 18:35–43)*

46 [a]Now they came to Jericho. As He went out
of Jericho with His disciples and a great multi-
tude, blind Bartimaeus, the son of Timaeus, sat
by the road begging. 47 And when he heard that
it was Jesus of Nazareth, he began to cry out and
say, "Jesus, [a]Son of David, [b]have mercy on me!"

48 Then many warned him to be quiet; but
he cried out all the more, "Son of David, have
mercy on me!"

49 So Jesus stood still and commanded him
to be called.

Then they called the blind man, saying to
him, "Be of good cheer. Rise, He is calling you."
50 And throwing aside his garment, he rose
and came to Jesus.

51 So Jesus answered and said to him, "What
do you want Me to do for you?"

The blind man said to Him, "Rabboni, that
I may receive my sight."

52 Then Jesus said to him, "Go your way;
[a]your faith has made you well." And immedi-
ately he received his sight and followed Jesus
on the road.

### THE TRIUMPHAL ENTRY
*(Matt. 21:1–11; Luke 19:28–40; John 12:12–19)*

11 Now [a]when they drew near Jerusalem, to
Bethphage[1] and Bethany, at the Mount of
Olives, He sent two of His disciples; 2 and He
said to them, "Go into the village opposite you;
and as soon as you have entered it you will find
a colt tied, on which no one has sat. Loose it and
bring *it.* 3 And if anyone says to you, 'Why are
you doing this?' say, 'The Lord has need of it,'
and immediately he will send it here."

4 So they went their way, and found the[1] colt
tied by the door outside on the street, and they
loosed it. 5 But some of those who stood there said
to them, "What are you doing, loosing the colt?"

6 And they spoke to them just as Jesus had
commanded. So they let them go. 7 Then they
brought the colt to Jesus and threw their clothes
on it, and He sat on it. 8 [a]And many spread their
clothes on the road, and others cut down leafy
branches from the trees and spread *them* on the
road. 9 Then those who went before and those
who followed cried out, saying:

"Hosanna!
[a]'Blessed *is* He who comes in the name of
the LORD!'[1]
10 Blessed *is* the kingdom of our father David
That comes in the name of the Lord![1]
[a]Hosanna in the highest!"

**10:29** [1] NU-Text omits *or wife.* **10:30** [a] Luke 18:29, 30 [b] [1 Pet. 4:12, 13] **10:31** [a] Luke 13:30 **10:32** [a] Matt. 20:17–19 [b] Mark 8:31; 9:31; Luke 9:22; 18:31 **10:35** [a] [James 4:3] **10:38** [a] Matt. 26:39, 42; Mark 14:36; Luke 22:42; John 18:11 [b] Luke 12:50 **10:39** [a] Matt. 10:17, 18, 21, 22; 24:9; John 16:33; Acts 12:2; Rev. 1:9 **10:40** [a] [Matt. 25:34; John 17:2, 6, 24; Rom. 8:30; Heb. 11:16] **10:41** [a] Matt. 20:24 **10:42** [a] Luke 22:25 **10:43** [a] Matt. 20:26, 28; Mark 9:35; Luke 9:48 **10:45** [a] Luke 22:27; John 13:14; [Phil. 2:7, 8] [b] Matt. 20:28; [2 Cor. 5:21; 1 Tim. 2:5, 6; Titus 2:14] **10:46** [a] Matt. 20:29–34; Luke 18:35–43 **10:47** [a] Jer. 23:5; Matt. 22:42; Rom. 1:3, 4; Rev. 22:16 [b] Matt. 15:22; Luke 17:13 **10:52** [a] Matt. 9:22; Mark 5:34 **11:1** [a] Matt. 21:1–9; Luke 19:29; John 2:13 [1] M-Text reads *Bethsphage.* **11:4** [1] NU-Text and M-Text read *a.* **11:8** [a] Matt. 21:8 **11:9** [a] Ps. 118:25, 26; Matt. 21:9 [1] Psalm 118:26 **11:10** [a] Ps. 148:1 [1] NU-Text omits *in the name of the Lord.*

### SEEING JESUS IN THE SCRIPTURE

**11:9** As Jesus entered Jerusalem, the Jews shouted the words of Psalm 118, a Messianic Psalm, revealing their hope that He was its fulfillment (see Ps. 118:25–26).

11[a]And Jesus went into Jerusalem and into the
temple. So when He had looked around at all
things, as the hour was already late, He went
out to Bethany with the twelve.

### *THE FIG TREE WITHERED*

*(Matt. 21:18, 19)*

12[a]Now the next day, when they had come
out from Bethany, He was hungry. 13[a]And see-
ing from afar a fig tree having leaves, He went
to see if perhaps He would find something on
it. When He came to it, He found nothing but
leaves, for it was not the season for figs. 14In
response Jesus said to it, "Let no one eat fruit
from you ever again."

And His disciples heard *it*.

### *JESUS CLEANSES THE TEMPLE*

*(Matt. 21:12–17; Luke 19:45–48; John 2:13–22)*

15[a]So they came to Jerusalem. Then Jesus
went into the temple and began to drive
out those who bought and sold in the tem-
ple, and overturned the tables of the mon-
ey changers and the seats of those who sold
[b]doves. 16And He would not allow anyone to
carry wares through the temple. 17Then He
taught, saying to them, "Is it not written, [a]'My
house shall be called a house of prayer for
all nations'?[1] But you have made it a [b]'den of
thieves.' "[2]

18And [a]the scribes and chief priests heard
it and sought how they might destroy Him; for
they feared Him, because [b]all the people were
astonished at His teaching. 19When evening had
come, He went out of the city.

**11:11** [a] Matt. 21:12 **11:12** [a] Matt. 21:18–22 **11:13** [a] Matt. 21:19 **11:15** [a] Mal. 3:1; Matt. 21:12–16; Luke 19:45–47; John 2:13–16 [b] Lev. 14:22 **11:17** [a] Is. 56:7 [b] Jer. 7:11 [1] Isaiah 56:7 [2] Jeremiah 7:11 **11:18** [a] Ps. 2:2; Matt. 21:45, 46; Luke 19:47 [b] Matt. 7:28; Mark 1:22; 6:2; Luke 4:32

## EVENTS OF JESUS' FINAL WEEK

| Day | Event | Reference |
|---|---|---|
| **Sunday** | The triumphal entry into Jerusalem | Mark 11:1–11 |
| **Monday** | Cleanses the temple in Jerusalem | Mark 11:15–19 |
| **Tuesday** | The Sanhedrin challenges Jesus' authority | Luke 20:1–8 |
| | Jesus foretells the destruction of Jerusalem and His Second Coming | Matthew 24–25 |
| | Mary anoints Jesus at Bethany | John 12:2–8 |
| | Judas bargains with the Jewish rulers to betray Jesus | Luke 22:3–6 |
| **Thursday** | Jesus eats the Passover meal with His disciples and institutes the Lord's Supper | Mark 14:22–26; John 13:1–30 |
| | Prays in Gethsemane | John 17 |
| **Friday** | His betrayal and arrest in the Garden of Gethsemane | Mark 14:43–50 |
| | Jesus questioned by Annas, the former high priest | John 18:12–24 |
| | Condemned by Caiaphas and the Sanhedrin | Mark 14:53–65 |
| | Peter denies Jesus three times | John 18:15–27 |
| | Jesus is formally condemned by the Sanhedrin | Luke 22:66–71 |
| | Judas commits suicide | Matthew 27:3–10 |
| | The trial of Jesus before Pilate | Luke 23:1–5 |
| | Jesus' appearance before Herod Antipas | Luke 23:6–12 |
| | Formally sentenced to death by Pilate | Luke 23:13–25 |
| | Jesus is mocked and crucified between two thieves | Mark 15:16–27 |
| | The veil of the temple is torn as Jesus dies | Matthew 27:51–56 |
| | His burial in the tomb of Joseph of Arimathea | John 19:31–42 |
| **Sunday** | Jesus is raised from the dead | Luke 24:1–9 |

### THE LESSON OF THE WITHERED FIG TREE
*(Matt. 21:20–22)*

20 [a]Now in the morning, as they passed by, they
saw the fig tree dried up from the roots. 21 And
Peter, remembering, said to Him, "Rabbi, look!
The fig tree which You cursed has withered away."
22 So Jesus answered and said to them, "Have
faith in God. 23 For [a]assuredly, I say to you, who-
ever says to this mountain, 'Be removed and
be cast into the sea,' and does not doubt in his
heart, but believes that those things he says
will be done, he will have whatever he says.
24 Therefore I say to you, [a]whatever things you
ask when you pray, believe that you receive *them,*
and you will have *them.*

### FORGIVENESS AND PRAYER
*(Matt. 6:14, 15)*

25 "And whenever you stand praying, [a]if you
have anything against anyone, forgive him, that
your Father in heaven may also forgive you
your trespasses. 26 But [a]if you do not forgive,
neither will your Father in heaven forgive your
trespasses."[1]

### JESUS' AUTHORITY QUESTIONED
*(Matt. 21:23–27; Luke 20:1–8)*

27 Then they came again to Jerusalem.
[a]And as He was walking in the temple, the chief
priests, the scribes, and the elders came to Him.
28 And they said to Him, "By what [a]authority are
You doing these things? And who gave You this
authority to do these things?"
29 But Jesus answered and said to them, "I
also will ask you one question; then answer Me,
and I will tell you by what authority I do these
things: 30 The [a]baptism of John—was it from
heaven or from men? Answer Me."
31 And they reasoned among themselves, say-
ing, "If we say, 'From heaven,' He will say, 'Why then
did you not believe him?' 32 But if we say, 'From
men' "—they feared the people, for [a]all counted
John to have been a prophet indeed. 33 So they
answered and said to Jesus, "We do not know."
And Jesus answered and said to them, "Nei-
ther will I tell you by what authority I do these
things."

### THE PARABLE OF THE WICKED VINEDRESSERS
*(Matt. 21:33–46; Luke 20:9–19)*

12 Then [a]He began to speak to them in para-
bles: "A man planted a vineyard and set a
hedge around *it,* dug *a place for* the wine vat and
built a tower. And he leased it to vinedressers and
went into a far country. 2 Now at vintage-time he
sent a servant to the vinedressers, that he might
receive some of the fruit of the vineyard from
the vinedressers. 3 And they took *him* and beat
him and sent *him* away empty-handed. 4 Again
he sent them another servant, and at him they
threw stones,[1] wounded *him* in the head, and sent
*him* away shamefully treated. 5 And again he sent
another, and him they killed; and many others,
[a]beating some and killing some. 6 Therefore still
having one son, his beloved, he also sent him
to them last, saying, 'They will respect my son.'
7 But those vinedressers said among themselves,
'This is the heir. Come, let us kill him, and the
inheritance will be ours.' 8 So they took him and
[a]killed *him* and cast *him* out of the vineyard.
9 "Therefore what will the owner of the vine-
yard do? He will come and destroy the vine-
dressers, and give the vineyard to others. 10 Have
you not even read this Scripture:

10 [a]'The stone which the builders rejected
Has become the chief cornerstone.
11 This was the LORD's doing,
And it is marvelous in our eyes'?"[1]

**SEEING JESUS IN THE SCRIPTURE**

**12:10** Israel's rejection of Jesus was part of God's plan for Him being the chief cornerstone upon which the church is built (see Ps. 118:22–23).

12 [a]And they sought to lay hands on Him, but
feared the multitude, for they knew He had
spoken the parable against them. So they left
Him and went away.

### THE PHARISEES: IS IT LAWFUL TO PAY TAXES TO CAESAR?
*(Matt. 22:15–22; Luke 20:20–26)*

13 [a]Then they sent to Him some of the Phari-
sees and the Herodians, to catch Him in *His* words.
14 When they had come, they said to Him, "Teacher,
we know that You are true, and care about no one;
for You do not regard the person of men, but teach
the [a]way of God in truth. Is it lawful to pay taxes to
Caesar, or not? 15 Shall we pay, or shall we not pay?"
But He, knowing their [a]hypocrisy, said to
them, "Why do you test Me? Bring Me a denarius
that I may see *it.*" 16 So they brought *it.*
And He said to them, "Whose image and
inscription *is* this?" They said to Him, "Caesar's."
17 And Jesus answered and said to them,
"Render to Caesar the things that are Caesar's,
and to [a]God the things that are God's."
And they marveled at Him.

**11:20** [a] Matt. 21:19–22 **11:23** [a] Matt. 17:20; 21:21; Luke 17:6 **11:24** [a] Matt. 7:7; Luke 11:9; [John 14:13; 15:7; 16:24; James 1:5, 6] **11:25** [a] Matt. 6:14; 18:23–35; Eph. 4:32; [Col. 3:13] **11:26** [a] Matt. 6:15; 18:35 [1] NU-Text omits this verse. **11:27** [a] Matt. 21:23–27; Luke 20:1–8 **11:28** [a] John 5:27 **11:30** [a] [Mark 1:4, 5, 8]; Luke 7:29, 30 **11:32** [a] Matt. 3:5; 14:5; Mark 6:20 **12:1** [a] Matt. 21:33–46; Luke 20:9–19 **12:4** [1] NU-Text omits *and at him they threw stones.* **12:5** [a] 2 Chr. 36:16 **12:8** [a] [Acts 2:23] **12:10** [a] Ps. 118:22, 23 **12:11** [1] Psalm 118:22, 23 **12:12** [a] Matt. 21:45, 46; Mark 11:18; John 7:25, 30, 44 **12:13** [a] Matt. 22:15–22; Luke 20:20–26 **12:14** [a] Acts 18:26 **12:15** [a] Matt. 23:28; Luke 12:1 **12:17** [a] [Eccl. 5:4, 5]

### *THE SADDUCEES: WHAT ABOUT THE RESURRECTION?*
*(Matt. 22:23–33; Luke 20:27–40)*

18 [a]Then *some* Sadducees, [b]who say there is
no resurrection, came to Him; and they asked
Him, saying: 19 "Teacher, [a]Moses wrote to us
that if a man's brother dies, and leaves *his* wife
behind, and leaves no children, his brother
should take his wife and raise up offspring for his
brother. 20 Now there were seven brothers. The
first took a wife; and dying, he left no offspring.
21 And the second took her, and he died; nor did
he leave any offspring. And the third likewise.
22 So the seven had her and left no offspring.
Last of all the woman died also. 23 Therefore, in
the resurrection, when they rise, whose wife will
she be? For all seven had her as wife."
24 Jesus answered and said to them, "Are
you not therefore mistaken, because you do
not know the Scriptures nor the power of God?
25 For when they rise from the dead, they neither
marry nor are given in marriage, but [a]are like
angels in heaven. 26 But concerning the dead,
that they [a]rise, have you not read in the book
of Moses, in the *burning* bush *passage,* how God
spoke to him, saying, [b]'I *am* the God of Abra-
ham, the God of Isaac, and the God of Jacob'?[1]
27 He is not the God of the dead, but the God of
the living. You are therefore greatly mistaken."

> **12:26–27** Jesus quoted from the Law—the Book of Exodus—to make His point. God had said **I am the God of** the three patriarchs mentioned, not "I *was* their God, but now they are dead." He still is their God because they are still alive. Their souls not only live after death, but their bodies will be raised anew as well.

### *THE SCRIBES: WHICH IS THE FIRST COMMANDMENT OF ALL?*
*(Matt. 22:34–40; Luke 10:25–28)*

28 [a]Then one of the scribes came, and having
heard them reasoning together, perceiving[1] that
He had answered them well, asked Him, "Which
is the first commandment of all?"
29 Jesus answered him, "The first of all the
commandments *is:* [a]'Hear, O Israel, the LORD
our God, the LORD is one. 30 And you shall [a]love
the LORD your God with all your heart, with all
your soul, with all your mind, and with all your
strength.'[1] This *is* the first commandment.[2] 31 And
the second, like *it, is* this: [a]'You shall love your
neighbor as yourself.'[1] There is no other com-
mandment greater than [b]these."
32 So the scribe said to Him, "Well *said,* Teach-
er. You have spoken the truth, for there is one
God, [a]and there is no other but He. 33 And to love
Him with all the heart, with all the understand-
ing, with all the soul,[1] and with all the strength,
and to love one's neighbor as oneself, [a]is more
than all the whole burnt offerings and sacrifices."
34 Now when Jesus saw that he answered
wisely, He said to him, "You are not far from
the kingdom of God."
[a]But after that no one dared question Him.

### *JESUS: HOW CAN DAVID CALL HIS DESCENDANT "LORD"?*
*(Matt. 22:41–46; Luke 20:41–44)*

35 [a]Then Jesus answered and said, while He
taught in the temple, "How *is it* that the scribes
say that the Christ is the Son of David? 36 For
David himself said [a]by the Holy Spirit:

[b]'The LORD said to my Lord,
"Sit at My right hand,
Till I make Your enemies Your
footstool." '[1]

37 Therefore David himself calls Him 'Lord'; how
is He *then* his [a]Son?"
And the common people heard Him gladly.

### *BEWARE OF THE SCRIBES*
*(Matt. 23:1–7; Luke 20:45–47)*

38 Then [a]He said to them in His teaching,
[b]"Beware of the scribes, who desire to go around
in long robes, [c]*love* greetings in the marketplac-
es, 39 the [a]best seats in the synagogues, and the
best places at feasts, 40 [a]who devour widows'
houses, and for a pretense make long prayers.
These will receive greater condemnation."

### *THE WIDOW'S TWO MITES*
*(Luke 21:1–4)*

41 [a]Now Jesus sat opposite the treasury and
saw how the people put money [b]into the trea-
sury. And many *who were* rich put in much.
42 Then one poor widow came and threw in two
mites,[1] which make a quadrans. 43 So He called
His disciples to *Himself* and said to them, "As-
suredly, I say to you that [a]this poor widow has
put in more than all those who have given to
the treasury; 44 for they all put in out of their
abundance, but she out of her poverty put in all
that she had, [a]her whole livelihood."

**12:18** [a] Matt. 22:23–33; Luke 20:27–38 [b] Acts 23:8 **12:19** [a] Deut. 25:5 **12:25** [a] [1 Cor. 15:42, 49, 52] **12:26** [a] [John 5:25, 28, 29]; Acts 26:8; Rom. 4:17; [Rev. 20:12, 13] [b] Ex. 3:6, 15 [1] Exodus 3:6, 15 **12:28** [a] Matt. 22:34–40; Luke 10:25–28; 20:39 [1] NU-Text reads *seeing.* **12:29** [a] Deut. 6:4, 5; Is. 44:8; 45:22; 46:9; 1 Cor. 8:6 **12:30** [a] [Deut. 10:12; 30:6]; Luke 10:27 [1] Deuteronomy 6:4, 5 [2] NU-Text omits this sentence. **12:31** [a] Lev. 19:18; Matt. 22:39; Gal. 5:14; James 2:8 [b] [Rom. 13:9] [1] Leviticus 19:18 **12:32** [a] Deut. 4:39; Is. 45:6, 14; 46:9; [John 1:14, 17; 14:6] **12:33** [a] [1 Sam. 15:22; Hos. 6:6; Mic. 6:6–8; Matt. 9:13; 12:7] [1] NU-Text omits *with all the soul.* **12:34** [a] Matt. 22:46 **12:35** [a] Matt. 22:41–46; Luke 20:41–44 **12:36** [a] 2 Sam. 23:2 [b] Ps. 110:1 [1] Psalm 110:1 **12:37** [a] [Acts 2:29–31] **12:38** [a] Mark 4:2 [b] Matt. 23:1–7; Luke 20:45–47 [c] Matt. 23:7; Luke 11:43 **12:39** [a] Luke 14:7 **12:40** [a] Matt. 23:14 **12:41** [a] Luke 21:1–4 [b] 2 Kin. 12:9 **12:42** [1] Greek *lepta,* very small copper coins worth a fraction of a penny **12:43** [a] [2 Cor. 8:12] **12:44** [a] Deut. 24:6

### *JESUS PREDICTS THE DESTRUCTION OF THE TEMPLE*
*(Matt. 24:1, 2; Luke 21:5, 6)*

**13** Then [a]as He went out of the temple, one
of His disciples said to Him, "Teacher,
see what manner of stones and what buildings
*are here!*"

> **13:1** The **temple** was a work of art, renovated over a thirty-year period on the orders of Herod the Great. The front columns stood forty feet high. Some of the marble **stones** used for the walls of the building were almost forty feet long.

2 And Jesus answered and said to him, "Do
you see these great buildings? [a]Not *one* stone
shall be left upon another, that shall not be
thrown down."

### *THE SIGNS OF THE TIMES AND THE END OF THE AGE*
*(Matt. 24:3–14; Luke 21:7–19)*

3 Now as He sat on the Mount of Olives opposite the temple, [a]Peter, [b]James, [c]John, and
[d]Andrew asked Him privately, 4 [a]"Tell us, when
will these things be? And what *will be* the sign
when all these things will be fulfilled?"
5 And Jesus, answering them, began to say:
[a]"Take heed that no one deceives you. 6 For many
will come in My name, saying, 'I am *He*,' and will
deceive many. 7 But when you hear of wars and
rumors of wars, do not be troubled; for *such*
*things* must happen, but the end *is* not yet. 8 For
nation will rise against nation, and [a]kingdom
against kingdom. And there will be earthquakes
in various places, and there will be famines and
troubles.[1] [b]These *are* the beginnings of sorrows.
9 "But [a]watch out for yourselves, for they
will deliver you up to councils, and you will be
beaten in the synagogues. You will be brought[1]
before rulers and kings for My sake, for a testimony to them. 10 And [a]the gospel must first be
preached to all the nations. 11 [a]But when they
arrest *you* and deliver you up, do not worry beforehand, or premeditate[1] what you will speak.
But whatever is given you in that hour, speak
that; for it is not you who speak, [b]but the Holy
Spirit. 12 Now [a]brother will betray brother to
death, and a father *his* child; and children will
rise up against parents and cause them to be
put to death. 13 [a]And you will be hated by all for
My name's sake. But [b]he who endures to the end
shall be saved.

### *THE GREAT TRIBULATION*
*(Matt. 24:15–28; Luke 21:20–24)*

14 [a]"So when you see the [b]'abomination of
desolation,'[1] spoken of by Daniel the prophet,[2]
standing where it ought not" (let the reader
understand), "then [c]let those who are in Judea
flee to the mountains. 15 Let him who is on the
housetop not go down into the house, nor enter to take anything out of his house. 16 And let
him who is in the field not go back to get his
clothes. 17 [a]But woe to those who are pregnant
and to those who are nursing babies in those
days! 18 And pray that your flight may not be in
winter. 19 [a]For *in* those days there will be tribulation, such as has not been since the beginning
of the creation which God created until this
time, nor ever shall be. 20 And unless the Lord
had shortened those days, no flesh would be
saved; but for the elect's sake, whom He chose,
He shortened the days.
21 [a]"Then if anyone says to you, 'Look, here *is*
the Christ!' or, 'Look, *He is* there!' do not believe
it. 22 For false christs and false prophets will
rise and show signs and [a]wonders to deceive, if
possible, even the elect. 23 But [a]take heed; see, I
have told you all things beforehand.

### *THE COMING OF THE SON OF MAN*
*(Matt. 24:29–31; Luke 21:25–28)*

24 [a]"But in those days, after that tribulation,
the sun will be darkened, and the moon will
not give its light; 25 the stars of heaven will fall,
and the powers in the heavens will be [a]shaken.
26 [a]Then they will see the Son of Man coming in
the clouds with great power and glory. 27 And
then He will send His angels, and gather together
His elect from the four winds, from the farthest
part of earth to the farthest part of heaven.

> **SEEING JESUS IN THE SCRIPTURE**
>
> **13:26** Jesus first came to earth as the Suffering Servant; He will return as the Conquering King, accompanied by an army (see Rev. 19:11–16).

### *THE PARABLE OF THE FIG TREE*
*(Matt. 24:32–35; Luke 21:29–33)*

28 [a]"Now learn this parable from the fig tree:
When its branch has already become tender,
and puts forth leaves, you know that summer is
near. 29 So you also, when you see these things
happening, know that it[1] is near—at the doors!
30 Assuredly, I say to you, this generation will
by no means pass away till all these things take

**13:1** [a] Luke 21:5–36 **13:2** [a] Luke 19:44 **13:3** [a] Matt. 16:18 [b] Mark 1:19 [c] Mark 1:19 [d] John 1:40 **13:4** [a] Matt. 24:3 **13:5** [a] Eph. 5:6 **13:8** [a] Hag. 2:22 [b] Matt. 24:8 [1] NU-Text omits *and troubles.* **13:9** [a] Matt. 10:17, 18; 24:9 [1] NU-Text and M-Text read *will stand.* **13:10** [a] Matt. 24:14 **13:11** [a] Luke 12:11; 21:12–17 [b] Acts 2:4; 4:8, 31 [1] NU-Text omits *or premeditate.* **13:12** [a] Mic. 7:6 **13:13** [a] Luke 21:17 [b] Matt. 10:22; 24:13 **13:14** [a] Matt. 24:15 [b] Dan. 9:27; 11:31; 12:11 [c] Luke 21:21 [1] Daniel 11:31; 12:11 [2] NU-Text omits *spoken of by Daniel the prophet.* **13:17** [a] Luke 21:23 **13:19** [a] Dan. 9:26; 12:1 **13:21** [a] Luke 17:23; 21:8 **13:22** [a] Rev. 13:13, 14 **13:23** [a] [2 Pet. 3:17] **13:24** [a] Zeph. 1:15 **13:25** [a] Is. 13:10; 34:4 **13:26** [a] [Dan. 7:13, 14] **13:28** [a] Matt. 24:32; Luke 21:29 **13:29** [1] Or *He*

place. 31 Heaven and earth will pass away, but [a]My
words will by no means pass away.

### NO ONE KNOWS THE DAY OR HOUR

(Matt. 24:36–44; Luke 21:34–36)

32 "But of that day and hour [a]no one knows,
not even the angels in heaven, nor the Son, but
only the [b]Father. 33 [a]Take heed, watch and pray;
for you do not know when the time is. 34 [a]*It is* like
a man going to a far country, who left his house
and gave [b]authority to his servants, and to each
his work, and commanded the doorkeeper to
watch. 35 [a]Watch therefore, for you do not know
when the master of the house is coming—in
the evening, at midnight, at the crowing of the
rooster, or in the morning— 36 lest, coming
suddenly, he find you sleeping. 37 And what I
say to you, I say to all: Watch!"

### THE PLOT TO KILL JESUS

(Matt. 26:1–5; Luke 22:1, 2; John 11:45–53)

**14** After [a]two days it was the Passover and [b]*the*
*Feast* of Unleavened Bread. And the chief
priests and the scribes sought how they might
take Him by trickery and put *Him* to death. 2 But
they said, "Not during the feast, lest there be an
uproar of the people."

### THE ANOINTING AT BETHANY

(Matt. 26:6–13; John 12:1–8)

3 [a]And being in Bethany at the house of Simon
the leper, as He sat at the table, a woman came
having an alabaster flask of very costly oil of
spikenard. Then she broke the flask and poured
*it* on His head. 4 But there were some who were
indignant among themselves, and said, "Why was
this fragrant oil wasted? 5 For it might have been
sold for more than three hundred [a]denarii and
given to the poor." And they [b]criticized her sharply.
6 But Jesus said, "Let her alone. Why do you
trouble her? She has done a good work for Me. 7 [a]For
you have the poor with you always, and whenever
you wish you may do them good; [b]but Me you do
not have always. 8 She has done what she could. She
has come beforehand to anoint My body for burial.
9 Assuredly, I say to you, wherever this gospel is
[a]preached in the whole world, what this woman
has done will also be told as a memorial to her."

### JUDAS AGREES TO BETRAY JESUS

(Matt. 26:14–16; Luke 22:3–6)

10 [a]Then Judas Iscariot, one of the twelve,
went to the chief priests to betray Him to them.
11 And when they heard *it,* they were glad, and
promised to give him money. So he sought how
he might conveniently betray Him.

### JESUS CELEBRATES THE PASSOVER WITH HIS DISCIPLES

(Matt. 26:17–25; Luke 22:7–13; John 13:21–30)

12 [a]Now on the first day of Unleavened Bread,
when they killed the Passover *lamb,* His disciples
said to Him, "Where do You want us to go and
prepare, that You may eat the Passover?"
13 And He sent out two of His disciples and
said to them, "Go into the city, and a man will
meet you carrying a pitcher of water; follow
him. 14 Wherever he goes in, say to the master
of the house, 'The Teacher says, "Where is the
guest room in which I may eat the Passover
with My disciples?"' 15 Then he will show you
a large upper room, furnished *and* prepared;
there make ready for us."
16 So His disciples went out, and came into
the city, and found it just as He had said to them;
and they prepared the Passover.
17 [a]In the evening He came with the twelve.
18 Now as they sat and ate, Jesus said, "Assuredly,
I say to you, [a]one of you who eats with Me will
betray Me."

> **SEEING JESUS IN THE SCRIPTURE**
>
> **14:18** Jesus, the Son of David, was betrayed by a friend just as His ancestor had been (see Ps. 41:9).

19 And they began to be sorrowful, and to
say to Him one by one, "*Is* it I?" And another
*said,* "*Is* it I?"[1]
20 He answered and said to them, "*It is* one of
the twelve, who dips with Me in the dish. 21 [a]The
Son of Man indeed goes just as it is written of
Him, but woe to that man by whom the Son of
Man is betrayed! It would have been good for
that man if he had never been born."

### JESUS INSTITUTES THE LORD'S SUPPER

(Matt. 26:26–29; Luke 22:14–23; 1 Cor. 11:23–26)

22 [a]And as they were eating, Jesus took bread,
blessed and broke *it,* and gave *it* to them and
said, "Take, eat;[1] this is My [b]body."
23 Then He took the cup, and when He had
given thanks He gave *it* to them, and they all
drank from it. 24 And He said to them, "This is
My blood of the new[1] covenant, which is shed for
many. 25 Assuredly, I say to you, I will no longer
drink of the fruit of the vine until that day when
I drink it new in the kingdom of God."
26 [a]And when they had sung a hymn, they
went out to the Mount of Olives.

**13:31** [a] Is. 40:8; [2 Pet. 3:7, 10, 12] **13:32** [a] Matt. 25:13 [b] Matt. 24:36; Acts 1:7 **13:33** [a] Matt. 24:42; 25:13; Luke 12:40; 21:34; [Rom. 13:11]; 1 Thess. 5:6; 1 Pet. 4:7 **13:34** [a] Matt. 24:45; 25:14 [b] [Matt. 16:19] **13:35** [a] Matt. 24:42, 44 **14:1** [a] Matt. 26:2–5; Luke 22:1, 2; John 11:55; 13:1 [b] Ex. 12:1–27; Mark 14:12 **14:3** [a] Matt. 26:6; Luke 7:37; John 12:1, 3 **14:5** [a] Matt. 18:28; Mark 12:15 [b] Matt. 20:11; John 6:61 **14:7** [a] Deut. 15:11; Matt. 26:11; John 12:8 [b] [John 7:33; 8:21; 14:2, 12; 16:10, 17, 28] **14:9** [a] Matt. 28:19, 20; Mark 16:15; Luke 24:47 **14:10** [a] Ps. 41:9; 55:12–14; Matt. 10:2–4 **14:12** [a] Ex. 12:8; Matt. 26:17–19; Luke 22:7–13 **14:17** [a] Matt. 26:20–24; Luke 22:14, 21–23 **14:18** [a] Ps. 41:9; Matt. 26:46; Mark 14:42; John 6:70, 71; 13:18 **14:19** [1] NU-Text omits this sentence. **14:21** [a] Matt. 26:24; Luke 22:22; Acts 1:16–20 **14:22** [a] Matt. 26:26–29; Luke 22:17–20; 1 Cor. 11:23–25 [b] [1 Pet. 2:24] [1] NU-Text omits *eat.* **14:24** [1] NU-Text omits *new.* **14:26** [a] Matt. 26:30

### JESUS PREDICTS PETER'S DENIAL

*(Matt. 26:31–35; Luke 22:31–34; John 13:36–38)*

27 [a]Then Jesus said to them, "All of you will be made to stumble because of Me this night,[1] for it is written:

[b]'I will strike the Shepherd,
And the sheep will be scattered.'[2]

28 "But [a]after I have been raised, I will go before you to Galilee."

29 [a]Peter said to Him, "Even if all are made to stumble, yet I *will* not *be*."

30 Jesus said to him, "Assuredly, I say to you that today, *even* this night, before the rooster crows twice, you will deny Me three times."

31 But he spoke more vehemently, "If I have to die with You, I will not deny You!"

And they all said likewise.

### THE PRAYER IN THE GARDEN

*(Matt. 26:36–46; Luke 22:39–46)*

32 [a]Then they came to a place which was named Gethsemane; and He said to His disciples, "Sit here while I pray." 33 And He [a]took Peter, James, and John with Him, and He began to be troubled and deeply distressed. 34 Then He said to them, [a]"My soul is exceedingly sorrowful, *even* to death. Stay here and watch."

35 He went a little farther, and fell on the ground, and prayed that if it were possible, the hour might pass from Him. 36 And He said, [a]"Abba, Father, [b]all things *are* possible for You. Take this cup away from Me; [c]nevertheless, not what I will, but what You *will*."

37 Then He came and found them sleeping, and said to Peter, "Simon, are you sleeping? Could you not watch one hour? 38 [a]Watch and pray, lest you enter into temptation. [b]The spirit indeed *is* willing, but the flesh *is* weak."

39 Again He went away and prayed, and spoke the same words. 40 And when He returned, He found them asleep again, for their eyes were heavy; and they did not know what to answer Him.

41 Then He came the third time and said to them, "Are you still sleeping and resting? It is enough! [a]The hour has come; behold, the Son of Man is being betrayed into the hands of sinners. 42 [a]Rise, let us be going. See, My betrayer is at hand."

### BETRAYAL AND ARREST IN GETHSEMANE

*(Matt. 26:47–56; Luke 22:47–53; John 18:1–11)*

43 [a]And immediately, while He was still speaking, Judas, one of the twelve, with a great multitude with swords and clubs, came from the chief priests and the scribes and the elders. 44 Now His betrayer had given them a signal, saying, "Whomever I [a]kiss, He is the One; seize Him and lead *Him* away safely."

45 As soon as he had come, immediately he went up to Him and said to Him, "Rabbi, Rabbi!" and kissed Him.

46 Then they laid their hands on Him and took Him. 47 And one of those who stood by drew his sword and struck the servant of the high priest, and cut off his ear.

48 [a]Then Jesus answered and said to them, "Have you come out, as against a robber, with swords and clubs to take Me? 49 I was daily with you in the temple [a]teaching, and you did not seize Me. But [b]the Scriptures must be fulfilled."

50 [a]Then they all forsook Him and fled.

### A YOUNG MAN FLEES NAKED

51 Now a certain young man followed Him, having a linen cloth thrown around *his* naked *body*. And the young men laid hold of him, 52 and he left the linen cloth and fled from them naked.

### JESUS FACES THE SANHEDRIN

*(Matt. 26:57–68; Luke 22:66–71; John 18:12–14, 19–24)*

53 [a]And they led Jesus away to the high priest; and with him were [b]assembled all the [c]chief priests, the elders, and the scribes. 54 But [a]Peter followed Him at a distance, right into the courtyard of the high priest. And he sat with the servants and warmed himself at the fire.

55 [a]Now the chief priests and all the council sought testimony against Jesus to put Him to death, but found none. 56 For many bore [a]false witness against Him, but their testimonies did not agree.

57 Then some rose up and bore false witness against Him, saying, 58 "We heard Him say, [a]'I will destroy this temple made with hands, and within three days I will build another made without hands.' " 59 But not even then did their testimony agree.

60 [a]And the high priest stood up in the midst and asked Jesus, saying, "Do You answer nothing? What *is it* these men testify against You?" 61 But [a]He kept silent and answered nothing.

[b]Again the high priest asked Him, saying to Him, "Are You the Christ, the Son of the Blessed?"

62 Jesus said, "I am. [a]And you will see the Son of Man sitting at the right hand of the Power, and coming with the clouds of heaven."

63 Then the high priest tore his clothes and said, "What further need do we have of witnesses? 64 You have heard the [a]blasphemy! What do you think?"

And they all condemned Him to be deserving of [b]death.

**14:27** [a] Matt. 26:31–35 [b] Zech. 13:7 [1] NU-Text omits *because of Me this night.* [2] Zechariah 13:7 **14:28** [a] Mark 16:7 **14:29** [a] John 13:37, 38 **14:32** [a] Luke 22:40–46 **14:33** [a] Mark 5:37; 9:2; 13:3 **14:34** [a] John 12:27 **14:36** [a] Gal. 4:6 [b] [Heb. 5:7] [c] John 5:30; 6:38 **14:38** [a] Luke 21:36 [b] [Rom. 7:18, 21–24] **14:41** [a] John 13:1; 17:1 **14:42** [a] John 13:21; 18:1, 2 **14:43** [a] Luke 22:47–53 **14:44** [a] [Prov. 27:6] **14:48** [a] Matt. 26:55 **14:49** [a] Matt. 21:23 [b] Is. 53:7 **14:50** [a] Ps. 88:8 **14:53** [a] Matt. 26:57–68 [b] Mark 15:1 [c] John 7:32; 18:3; 19:6 **14:54** [a] John 18:15 **14:55** [a] Matt. 26:59 **14:56** [a] Ex. 20:16 **14:58** [a] John 2:19 **14:60** [a] Matt. 26:62 **14:61** [a] Is. 53:7 [b] Luke 22:67–71 **14:62** [a] Luke 22:69 **14:64** [a] John 10:33, 36 [b] John 19:7

65 Then some began to [a]spit on Him, and to
blindfold Him, and to beat Him, and to say to
Him, "Prophesy!" And the officers struck Him
with the palms of their hands.[1]

### PETER DENIES JESUS, AND WEEPS

*(Matt. 26:69–75; Luke 22:54–62; John 18:15–18, 25–27)*

66 [a]Now as Peter was below in the courtyard,
one of the servant girls of the high priest came.
67 And when she saw Peter warming himself,
she looked at him and said, "You also were with
[a]Jesus of Nazareth."
68 But he denied it, saying, "I neither know
nor understand what you are saying." And he
went out on the porch, and a rooster crowed.
69 [a]And the servant girl saw him again, and
began to say to those who stood by, "This is *one*
of them." 70 But he denied it again.
[a]And a little later those who stood by said
to Peter again, "Surely you are *one* of them; [b]for
you are a Galilean, and your speech shows *it*."[1]
71 Then he began to curse and swear, "I do
not know this Man of whom you speak!"
72 [a]A second time *the* rooster crowed. Then
Peter called to mind the word that Jesus had
said to him, "Before the rooster crows twice,
you will deny Me three times." And when he
thought about it, he wept.

### JESUS FACES PILATE

*(Matthew 27:1, 2, 11–14; Luke 23:1–5; John 18:28–38)*

15 Immediately, [a]in the morning, the chief
priests held a consultation with the elders
and scribes and the whole council; and they
bound Jesus, led *Him* away, and [b]delivered *Him*
to Pilate. 2 [a]Then Pilate asked Him, "Are You the
King of the Jews?"
He answered and said to him, "*It is as you say.*"
3 And the chief priests accused Him of many
things, but He [a]answered nothing. 4 [a]Then Pilate
asked Him again, saying, "Do You answer nothing? See how many things they testify against
You!"[1] 5 [a]But Jesus still answered nothing, so
that Pilate marveled.

**SEEING JESUS IN THE SCRIPTURE**

**15:5** As the religious leaders sought to kill Jesus, He stood silent, not defending Himself, fulfilling prophecy (see Ps. 38:12–13).

### TAKING THE PLACE OF BARABBAS

*(Matt. 27:15–26; Luke 23:17–25; John 18:39—19:16)*

6 Now [a]at the feast he was accustomed to releasing one prisoner to them, whomever they
requested. 7 And there was one named Barabbas,
*who was* chained with his fellow rebels; they had

**14:65** [a] Is. 50:6; 52:14 [1] NU-Text reads *received Him with slaps.* **14:66** [a] John 18:16–18, 25–27 **14:67** [a] John 1:45 **14:69** [a] Matt. 26:71 **14:70** [a] Luke 22:59 [b] Acts 2:7 [1] NU-Text omits *and your speech shows it.* **14:72** [a] Matt. 26:75 **15:1** [a] Ps. 2:2 [b] Acts 3:13 **15:2** [a] Matt. 27:11–14 **15:3** [a] John 19:9 **15:4** [a] Matt. 27:13 [1] NU-Text reads *of which they accuse You.* **15:5** [a] Is. 53:7 **15:6** [a] Matt. 27:15–26

KNOW THE TRUTH

## THE DOCTRINE OF JESUS

### PART 2: THE DEITY OF JESUS

**14:61–62** All fair-minded students of history, regardless of religious belief, acknowledges Jesus of Nazareth was a real person in the Roman provinces of Galilee and Judea in the early first century. Simply put, there are hardly any modern challenges to Jesus being a real person of history. However, Jesus and His early followers claimed He was far more than that.

Here, under threat of torture and death and asked bluntly if He was God's Son (and thus God), Jesus replied, "I am." There's an abundance of evidence supporting Jesus of Nazareth not only being fully human, but fully divine. He was conceived of God's Spirit (see Matt. 1:18). God the Father attested to Jesus being His beloved Son (see Matt. 3:17). Jesus performed naturally impossible miracles (see Luke 7:11–15). He taught with unparalleled authority (see Matt. 7:28–29). He supernaturally knew information about people's lives (see John 4:16–19). He suffered, died, and rose from the dead in the exact methods and timeline He foretold (see Luke 18:31–33). He transforms the lives of men and women, young and old, from every culture, background, and ethnicity, across time. Jesus is fully human and indeed a real person of history. But He's more than that. Jesus is the fully divine Son of God, our Savior and Lord.

*For* **THE DOCTRINE OF JESUS: PART 3: THE HUMANITY OF JESUS**, *turn to Hebrews 4:14–16 on page 1248.*

committed murder in the rebellion. 8 Then the
multitude, crying aloud,[1] began to ask *him to do*
just as he had always done for them. 9 But Pilate
answered them, saying, "Do you want me to release
to you the King of the Jews?" 10 For he knew that the
chief priests had handed Him over because of envy.
11 But [a]the chief priests stirred up the crowd,
so that he should rather release Barabbas to
them. 12 Pilate answered and said to them again,
"What then do you want me to do *with Him*
whom you call the [a]King of the Jews?"
13 So they cried out again, "Crucify Him!"
14 Then Pilate said to them, "Why, [a]what evil
has He done?"

But they cried out all the more, "Crucify Him!"
15 [a]So Pilate, wanting to gratify the crowd, re-
leased Barabbas to them; and he delivered Jesus,
after he had scourged *Him,* to be [b]crucified.

### *THE SOLDIERS MOCK JESUS*

*(Matt. 27:27–31)*

16 [a]Then the soldiers led Him away into the
hall called Praetorium, and they called together
the whole garrison. 17 And they clothed Him with
purple; and they twisted a crown of thorns, put
it on His *head,* 18 and began to salute Him, "Hail,
King of the Jews!" 19 Then they [a]struck Him on
the head with a reed and spat on Him; and bow-
ing the knee, they worshiped Him. 20 And when
they had [a]mocked Him, they took the purple off
Him, put His own clothes on Him, and led Him
out to crucify Him.

### *THE KING ON A CROSS*

*(Matt. 27:32–44; Luke 23:26–43; John 19:17–27)*

21 [a]Then they compelled a certain man,
Simon a Cyrenian, the father of Alexander and
Rufus, as he was coming out of the country
and passing by, to bear His cross. 22 [a]And they
brought Him to the place Golgotha, which is
translated, Place of a Skull. 23 [a]Then they gave
Him wine mingled with myrrh to drink, but He
did not take *it.* 24 And when they crucified Him,
[a]they divided His garments, casting lots for
them *to determine* what every man should take.
25 Now [a]it was the third hour, and they cru-
cified Him. 26 And [a]the inscription of His accu-
sation was written above:

THE KING OF THE JEWS.

**15:8** [1] NU-Text reads *going up.* **15:11** [a] Acts 3:14 **15:12** [a] Mic. 5:2 **15:14** [a] 1 Pet. 2:21–23 **15:15** [a] Matt. 27:26 [b] [Is. 53:8] **15:16** [a] Matt. 27:27–31 **15:19** [a] [Is. 50:6; 52:14; 53:5] **15:20** [a] Luke 22:63; 23:11 **15:21** [a] Matt. 27:32 **15:22** [a] John 19:17–24 **15:23** [a] Matt. 27:34 **15:24** [a] Ps. 22:18 **15:25** [a] John 19:14 **15:26** [a] Matt. 27:37

**MARK 15:6–39**

## THE CRUCIFIXION

47

STORY OF SCRIPTURE

### WHAT'S GOING ON?

This is the dramatic climax of Jesus' earthly ministry. Pilate, faced with the choice of releasing Jesus or Barabbas, a known criminal, succumbed to the crowd's demand to free Barabbas and crucify Jesus. Mocked, beaten, and burdened with a cross, Jesus was led to Golgotha. There, He was crucified between two thieves. In His final moments, Jesus cried out, "My God, My God, why have You forsaken Me?" before taking His last breath. The curtain of the temple tore in two, symbolizing the end of the old covenant and the establishment of a new way to God through Jesus' sacrifice. A Roman centurion, witnessing Jesus' death, proclaimed, "Truly this Man was the Son of God!"

This weighty, emotional passage showcases Jesus' compassion for us. He didn't endure only the physical torment of the cross but also the separation from God we deserved because of our sins.

### WHAT DOES THIS MEAN FOR ME?

Jesus' crucifixion is a powerful reminder of the depth of God's love for you. Christ's sacrifice on the cross is the ultimate act of love and redemption. Let this truth sink in: God loves *you* so much He gave Jesus to die to save *you.*

### DID YOU CATCH THE PATTERN?

Remember the curse God gave the serpent in Genesis? "And I will put enmity between you and the woman, and between your seed and her Seed; He shall bruise your head, and you shall bruise His heel" (Gen. 3:15). That Seed is Jesus. Jesus crushed the serpent's head and conquered sin, but He was bruised in the process. The cross has been foreshadowed since the very beginning, making Mark 15 the fulfillment of dozens of Old Testament prophecies.

*For the next* Story of Scripture *reading and devotion, turn to Luke 24:1–25 on page 1066.*

27 [a]With Him they also crucified two robbers,
one on His right and the other on His left. 28 So
the Scripture was fulfilled[1] which says, [a]"And He
was numbered with the transgressors."[2]
29 And [a]those who passed by blasphemed
Him, [b]wagging their heads and saying, "Aha! [c]*You*
who destroy the temple and build *it* in three days,
30 save Yourself, and come down from the cross!"
31 Likewise the chief priests also, [a]mocking
among themselves with the scribes, said, "He
saved [b]others; Himself He cannot save. 32 Let the
Christ, the King of Israel, descend now from the
cross, that we may see and believe."[1]
Even [a]those who were crucified with Him
reviled Him.

### *JESUS DIES ON THE CROSS*

*(Matt. 27:45–56; Luke 23:44–49; John 19:28–30)*

33 Now [a]when the sixth hour had come, there
was darkness over the whole land until the ninth
hour. 34 And at the ninth hour Jesus cried out
with a loud voice, saying, "Eloi, Eloi, lama sa-
bachthani?" which is translated, [a]"My God, My
God, why have You forsaken Me?"[1]
35 Some of those who stood by, when they
heard *that,* said, "Look, He is calling for Elijah!"
36 Then [a]someone ran and filled a sponge full
of sour wine, put *it* on a reed, and [b]offered *it* to
Him to drink, saying, "Let Him alone; let us see
if Elijah will come to take Him down."
37 [a]And Jesus cried out with a loud voice,
and breathed His last.
38 Then [a]the veil of the temple was torn in
two from top to bottom. 39 So [a]when the cen-
turion, who stood opposite Him, saw that He
cried out like this and breathed His last,[1] he said,
"Truly this Man was the Son of God!"

**SEEING JESUS IN THE SCRIPTURE**

**15:38** The veil that separated God's people from God's presence tore open, demonstrating Jesus has provided entrance for all (see Ex. 26:33).

40 [a]There were also women looking on [b]from
afar, among whom were Mary Magdalene, Mary
the mother of James the Less and of Joses, and
Salome, 41 who also [a]followed Him and ministered
to Him when He was in Galilee, and many other
women who came up with Him to Jerusalem.

### *JESUS BURIED IN JOSEPH'S TOMB*

*(Matt. 27:57–61; Luke 23:50–56; John 19:38–42)*

42 [a]Now when evening had come, because it
was the Preparation Day, that is, the day before
the Sabbath, 43 Joseph of Arimathea, a promi-
nent council member, who [a]was himself waiting
for the kingdom of God, coming and taking
courage, went in to Pilate and asked for the
body of Jesus. 44 Pilate marveled that He was
already dead; and summoning the centurion, he
asked him if He had been dead for some time.
45 So when he found out from the centurion, he
granted the body to Joseph. 46 [a]Then he bought
fine linen, took Him down, and wrapped Him in
the linen. And he laid Him in a tomb which had
been hewn out of the rock, and rolled a stone
against the door of the tomb. 47 And Mary Mag-
dalene and Mary *the mother* of Joses observed
where He was laid.

**15:44** Crucifixion was usually not a quick way to die. Unless the crucified person had been severely beaten before being crucified, he could survive several days on a cross. One of the most common causes of death among those who were crucified was suffocation. Because of the outstretched position, the person became too exhausted to raise himself up to breathe and suffocated.

### *HE IS RISEN*

*(Matt. 28:1–8; Luke 24:1–12; John 20:1–10)*

16 Now [a]when the Sabbath was past, Mary
Magdalene, Mary *the mother* of James, and
Salome [b]bought spices, that they might come and
anoint Him. 2 [a]Very early in the morning, on the
first *day* of the week, they came to the tomb when
the sun had risen. 3 And they said among them-
selves, "Who will roll away the stone from the door
of the tomb for us?" 4 But when they looked up,
they saw that the stone had been rolled away—for
it was very large. 5 [a]And entering the tomb, they
saw a young man clothed in a long white robe
sitting on the right side; and they were alarmed.
6 [a]But he said to them, "Do not be alarmed.
You seek Jesus of Nazareth, who was crucified.
He is risen! He is not here. See the place where
they laid Him. 7 But go, tell His disciples—and
Peter—that He is going before you into Galilee;
there you will see Him, [a]as He said to you."

**SEEING JESUS IN THE SCRIPTURE**

**16:6** The resurrection of Jesus on the third day was prophesied by Hosea and points to the future resurrection of all believers (see Hos. 6:2).

**15:27** [a] Luke 22:37 **15:28** [a] Is. 53:12 [1] Isaiah 53:12 [2] NU-Text omits this verse. **15:29** [a] Ps. 22:6, 7; 69:7 [b] Ps. 109:25 [c] John 2:19–21 **15:31** [a] Luke 18:32 [b] John 11:43, 44 **15:32** [a] Matt. 27:44 [1] M-Text reads *believe Him.* **15:33** [a] Luke 23:44–49 **15:34** [a] Ps. 22:1 [1] Psalm 22:1 **15:36** [a] John 19:29 [b] Ps. 69:21 **15:37** [a] Matt. 27:50 **15:38** [a] Ex. 26:31–33 **15:39** [a] Luke 23:47 [1] NU-Text reads *that He thus breathed His last.* **15:40** [a] Matt. 27:55 [b] Ps. 38:11 **15:41** [a] Luke 8:2, 3 **15:42** [a] John 19:38–42 **15:43** [a] Luke 2:25, 38; 23:51 **15:46** [a] Matt. 27:59, 60 **16:1** [a] John 20:1–8 [b] Luke 23:56 **16:2** [a] Luke 24:1 **16:5** [a] John 20:11, 12 **16:6** [a] Matt. 28:6 **16:7** [a] Matt. 26:32; 28:16, 17

LIVE THE TRUTH

## BEING ON MISSION

**16:15** Christians are to share the gospel wherever we go. We are to live as Christ each day. When God gives us an opportunity, we share what Jesus has done in our lives. This can, and should, happen in our local communities, but we're also to spread the Good News to the entire world. That doesn't mean we have to do it on our own. It might not be possible for you to leave your community to share the gospel but you can still support individuals, churches, and organizations who are sharing God's Word in each corner of the world.

Before Jesus ascended into heaven, He gave the disciples a clear command: to spread the gospel to the entire world. Each of them made that mission his life's work and because of them, we know about Jesus today. The gospel has reached almost everyone, but there are unreached people groups in the world. Thus, we are still under Christ's mandate. As individuals and local churches, we have people we must reach for Jesus. We can do this directly or indirectly through praying and supporting others around the world. We can do one or both, but we can't do neither.

8 So they went out quickly[1] and fled from the
tomb, for they trembled and were amazed. [a]And
they said nothing to anyone, for they were afraid.

### *MARY MAGDALENE SEES THE RISEN LORD*

*(Matt. 28:9, 10; John 20:11–18)*

9 Now when *He* rose early on the first *day*
of the week, He appeared first to Mary Magda-
lene, [a]out of whom He had cast seven demons.
10 [a]She went and told those who had been with
Him, as they mourned and wept. 11 [a]And when
they heard that He was alive and had been seen
by her, they did not believe.

### *JESUS APPEARS TO TWO DISCIPLES*

*(Luke 24:13–35)*

12 After that, He appeared in another form
[a]to two of them as they walked and went into the
country. 13 And they went and told *it* to the rest,
*but* they did not believe them either.

### *THE GREAT COMMISSION*

*(Matt. 28:16–20; Luke 24:44–49; Acts 1:6–8)*

14 [a]Later He appeared to the eleven as they
sat at the table; and He rebuked their unbelief
and hardness of heart, because they did not
believe those who had seen Him after He had
risen. 15 [a]And He said to them, "Go into all the
world [b]and preach the gospel to every crea-
ture. 16 [a]He who believes and is baptized will
be saved; [b]but he who does not believe will
be condemned. 17 And these [a]signs will follow
those who believe: [b]In My name they will cast
out demons; [c]they will speak with new tongues;
18 [a]they[1] will take up serpents; and if they drink
anything deadly, it will by no means hurt them;
[b]they will lay hands on the sick, and they will
recover."

### *CHRIST ASCENDS TO GOD'S RIGHT HAND*

*(Luke 24:50–53)*

19 So then, [a]after the Lord had spoken to
them, He was [b]received up into heaven, and
[c]sat down at the right hand of God. 20 And
they went out and preached everywhere, the
Lord working with *them* [a]and confirming
the word through the accompanying signs.
Amen.[1]

**16:8** [a] Matt. 28:8 [1] NU-Text and M-Text omit *quickly.* **16:9** [a] Luke 8:2 **16:10** [a] Luke 24:10 **16:11** [a] Luke 24:11, 41 **16:12** [a] Luke 24:13–35 **16:14** [a] 1 Cor. 15:5 **16:15** [a] Matt. 28:19 [b] [Col. 1:23] **16:16** [a] [John 3:18, 36] [b] [John 12:48] **16:17** [a] Acts 5:12 [b] Luke 10:17 [c] [Acts 2:4] **16:18** [a] Acts 28:3–6 [b] James 5:14 [1] NU-Text reads *and in their hands they will.* **16:19** [a] Acts 1:2, 3 [b] Luke 9:51; 24:51 [c] [Ps. 110:1] **16:20** [a] [Heb. 2:4] [1] Verses 9–20 are bracketed in NU-Text as not original. They are lacking in Codex Sinaiticus and Codex Vaticanus, although nearly all other manuscripts of Mark contain them.

# *The Gospel According to* LUKE

| AUTHOR | KEY VERSE | READING TIME |
|---|---|---|
| Luke | Luke 19:10 | 3 hours |

Luke, a physician, wrote with the precision, compassion, and warmth of a family doctor. In his Gospel, Luke carefully documented the perfect humanity of the Son of Man, Jesus Christ. Writing primarily to the Greeks, Luke emphasized Jesus' ancestry, birth, and early life before moving purposefully and mostly chronologically through His earthly ministry. Growing belief in Jesus and growing opposition to Jesus developed side by side. Those who believed in Jesus were challenged to count the cost of discipleship. Those who opposed Him would not be satisfied until the Son of Man hung lifeless on a cross. But the resurrection ensured that Jesus' purpose "to seek and to save that which was lost" (Luke 19:10) would be fulfilled.

**Occasion:** Luke wrote his Gospel to a primarily Greek audience to show Jesus as the Son of Man.

**Main Point:** Jesus is the Son of Man who has come to seek and save all who are lost.

**Big Ideas:** Jesus is the Son of Man, the Messiah. What Jesus said and what He did prove He is the Son of God. All who place faith in Jesus are saved. Jesus, the perfect human, provides us with a model for how we are to live.

**OUTLINE:**

I. The Introduction to the Son of Man (chs. 1–3)
II. The Ministry of the Son of Man (chs. 4–9)
III. The Rejection of the Son of Man (chs. 10–19)
IV. The Crucifixion of the Son of Man (chs. 20–23)
V. The Resurrection of the Son of Man (ch. 24)

**c. 420 BC**
Malachi prophesies in Judah

**356–323 BC**
Alexander the Great lives in Macedonia

**246 BC**
Great Wall of China is built

**164 BC**
Judas Maccabaeus restores the temple in Jerusalem, celebrated yearly by the festival of Hanukkah

**37 BC**
Julius Caesar is murdered

**37–4 BC**
Herod the Great is king in Jerusalem

**31 BC–AD 14**
Augustus Caesar is Roman emperor

**c. 5–4 BC**
Jesus is born in Bethlehem

**4 BC–AD 39**
Herod Antipas rules in Galilee and Perea

**AD 1**
Lions become extinct in Western Europe

**c. AD 7**
Jesus questions teachers at the temple

**AD 14–37**
Tiberius is Roman emperor

**AD 25–27**
John the Baptist ministers

**AD 26–36**
Pontius Pilate is procurator of Judea

**c. AD 27**
Jesus' first Judean ministry

**c. AD 27–29**
Jesus' Galilean ministry

**c. AD 30**
Jesus' second Judean ministry; crucifixion and resurrection

**c. AD 60–61**
**Luke written**

### DEDICATION TO THEOPHILUS

1 Inasmuch as many have taken in hand to set in order a narrative of those [a]things which have been fulfilled[1] among us, 2 just as those who [a]from the beginning were [b]eyewitnesses and ministers of the word [c]delivered them to us, 3 it seemed good to me also, having had perfect understanding of all things from the very first, to write to you an orderly account, [a]most excellent Theophilus, 4 [a]that you may know the certainty of those things in which you were instructed.

### JOHN'S BIRTH ANNOUNCED TO ZACHARIAS

5 There was [a]in the days of Herod, the king of Judea, a certain priest named Zacharias, [b]of the division of [c]Abijah. His [d]wife *was* of the daughters of Aaron, and her name *was* Elizabeth. 6 And they were both righteous before God, walking in all the commandments and ordinances of the Lord blameless. 7 But they had no child, because Elizabeth was barren, and they were both well advanced in years.

8 So it was, that while he was serving as priest before God in the order of his division, 9 according to the custom of the priesthood, his lot fell [a]to burn incense when he went into the temple of the Lord. 10 [a]And the whole multitude of the people was praying outside at the hour of incense. 11 Then an angel of the Lord appeared to him, standing on the right side of [a]the altar of incense. 12 And when Zacharias saw *him,* [a]he was troubled, and fear fell upon him.

13 But the angel said to him, "Do not be afraid, Zacharias, for your prayer is heard; and your wife Elizabeth will bear you a son, and [a]you shall call his name John. 14 And you will have joy and gladness, and [a]many will rejoice at his birth. 15 For he will be [a]great in the sight of the Lord, and [b]shall drink neither wine nor strong drink. He will also be filled with the Holy Spirit, [c]even from his mother's womb. 16 And he will turn many of the children of Israel to the Lord their God. 17 [a]He will also go before Him in the spirit and power of Elijah, 'to turn the hearts of the fathers to the children,'[1] and the disobedient to the wisdom of the just, to make ready a people prepared for the Lord."

18 And Zacharias said to the angel, [a]"How shall I know this? For I am an old man, and my wife is well advanced in years."

19 And the angel answered and said to him, "I am [a]Gabriel, who stands in the presence of God, and was sent to speak to you and bring you these glad [b]tidings. 20 But behold, [a]you will be mute and not able to speak until the day these things take place, because you did not believe my words which will be fulfilled in their own time."

21 And the people waited for Zacharias, and marveled that he lingered so long in the temple. 22 But when he came out, he could not speak to them; and they perceived that he had seen a vision in the temple, for he beckoned to them and remained speechless.

23 So it was, as soon as [a]the days of his service were completed, that he departed to his own house. 24 Now after those days his wife Elizabeth conceived; and she hid herself five months, saying, 25 "Thus the Lord has dealt with me, in the days when He looked on *me,* to [a]take away my reproach among people."

### CHRIST'S BIRTH ANNOUNCED TO MARY

26 Now in the sixth month the angel Gabriel was sent by God to a city of Galilee named Nazareth, 27 to a virgin [a]betrothed to a man whose name was Joseph, of the house of David. The virgin's name *was* Mary. 28 And having come in, the angel said to her, [a]"Rejoice, highly favored *one,* [b]the Lord *is* with you; blessed *are* you among women!"[1]

29 But when she saw *him,*[1] [a]she was troubled at his saying, and considered what manner of greeting this was. 30 Then the angel said to her, "Do not be afraid, Mary, for you have found [a]favor with God. 31 [a]And behold, you will conceive in your womb and bring forth a Son, and [b]shall call His name JESUS. 32 He will be great, [a]and will be called the Son of the Highest; and [b]the Lord God will give Him the [c]throne of His [d]father David. 33 [a]And He will reign over the house of Jacob forever, and of His kingdom there will be no end."

> **SEEING JESUS IN THE SCRIPTURE**
>
> **1:31** Jesus being born of a virgin was proof that He is unique and fulfilled prophecy (see Is. 7:14).

34 Then Mary said to the angel, "How can this be, since I do not know a man?"

35 And the angel answered and said to her, [a]"*The* Holy Spirit will come upon you, and the power of the Highest will overshadow you; therefore, also, that Holy One who is to be born will be called [b]the Son of God. 36 Now indeed, Elizabeth your relative has also conceived a son in her old age; and this is now the sixth month for her who was called barren. 37 For [a]with God nothing will be impossible."

38 Then Mary said, "Behold the maidservant of the Lord! Let it be to me according to your word." And the angel departed from her.

**1:1** [a] John 20:31 [1] Or *are most surely believed* **1:2** [a] Acts 1:21, 22 [b] Acts 1:2 [c] Heb. 2:3 **1:3** [a] Acts 1:1 **1:4** [a] [John 20:31] **1:5** [a] Matt. 2:1 [b] 1 Chr. 24:1, 10 [c] Neh. 12:4 [d] Lev. 21:13, 14 **1:9** [a] Ex. 30:7, 8 **1:10** [a] Lev. 16:17 **1:11** [a] Ex. 30:1 **1:12** [a] Luke 2:9 **1:13** [a] Luke 1:57, 60, 63 **1:14** [a] Luke 1:58 **1:15** [a] [Luke 7:24–28] [b] Num. 6:3 [c] Jer. 1:5 **1:17** [a] Mal. 4:5, 6; Matt. 3:2; 11:14 [1] Malachi 4:5, 6 **1:18** [a] Gen. 17:17 **1:19** [a] Dan. 8:16 [b] Luke 2:10 **1:20** [a] Ezek. 3:26; 24:27 **1:23** [a] 2 Kin. 11:5 **1:25** [a] Gen. 30:23 **1:27** [a] Matt. 1:18 **1:28** [a] Dan. 9:23 [b] Judg. 6:12 [1] NU-Text omits *blessed are you among women.* **1:29** [a] Luke 1:12 [1] NU-Text omits *when she saw him.* **1:30** [a] Luke 2:52 **1:31** [a] Is. 7:14 [b] Luke 2:21 **1:32** [a] Mark 5:7 [b] 2 Sam. 7:12, 13, 16 [c] 2 Sam. 7:14–17 [d] Matt. 1:1 **1:33** [a] [Dan. 2:44] **1:35** [a] Matt. 1:20 [b] [Heb. 1:2, 8] **1:37** [a] Jer. 32:17

KNOW THE TRUTH

## THE DOCTRINE OF GOD

### PART 5: THE INFINITY OF GOD

**1:37** We have limited capacities. We can think, speak, and produce only so much. When it came to conceiving a child, Mary knew her limitations. She knew conception requires a woman *and* a man. She also knew her relative Elizabeth's limitations. Elizabeth had been barren her entire life and was beyond the age of conception. Yet, Mary conceived by the Holy Spirit and bore the Son of God, and Elizabeth and her husband Zacharias—also too old to have children—conceived and bore John the Baptist. At a human level, these conceptions were impossibilities. But Luke 1:37 asserts, "For with God nothing will be impossible."

God is infinite, meaning limitless. Humans have limits; God doesn't. Every attribute of God is without limit. This is why we call Him omnipotent (all-powerful), omnipresent (all-present), and omniscient (all-knowing). His capacity to create, love, save, redeem, and restore is limitless. His power, goodness, righteousness, justice, compassion, holiness, humility, and kindness are limitless. Most things are impossible for finite (limited) creatures like us. But nothing is impossible for the infinite God. All God is, He is limitlessly. All God does, He does limitlessly. In eternity, God's people will never tire of beholding Him because limitless facets of His glory will endlessly shine.

*For* **THE DOCTRINE OF GOD: PART 6: THE OMNIPOTENCE OF GOD,** *turn to Jeremiah 32:27 on page 781.* • • •

### *MARY VISITS ELIZABETH*

39 Now Mary arose in those days and went into
the hill country with haste, [a]to a city of Judah,
40 and entered the house of Zacharias and greeted
Elizabeth. 41 And it happened, when Elizabeth
heard the greeting of Mary, that the babe leaped
in her womb; and Elizabeth was [a]filled with the
Holy Spirit. 42 Then she spoke out with a loud
voice and said, [a]"Blessed *are* you among women,
and blessed *is* the fruit of your womb! 43 But why
*is* this *granted* to me, that the mother of my Lord
should come to me? 44 For indeed, as soon as the
voice of your greeting sounded in my ears, the
babe leaped in my womb for joy. 45 [a]Blessed *is* she
who believed, for there will be a fulfillment of
those things which were told her from the Lord."

### *THE SONG OF MARY*

46 And Mary said:

[a]"My soul magnifies the Lord,
47 And my spirit has [a]rejoiced in [b]God my
Savior.
48 For [a]He has regarded the lowly state of
His maidservant;
For behold, henceforth [b]all generations
will call me blessed.
49 For He who is mighty [a]has done great
things for me,
And [b]holy *is* His name.
50 And [a]His mercy *is* on those who fear Him
From generation to generation.
51 [a]He has shown strength with His arm;
[b]He has scattered *the* proud in the
imagination of their hearts.
52 [a]He has put down the mighty from *their*
thrones,
And exalted *the* lowly.
53 He has [a]filled *the* hungry with good things,
And *the* rich He has sent away empty.
54 He has helped His [a]servant Israel,
[b]In remembrance of *His* mercy,
55 [a]As He spoke to our [b]fathers,
To Abraham and to his [c]seed forever."

56 And Mary remained with her about three
months, and returned to her house.

### *BIRTH OF JOHN THE BAPTIST*

57 Now Elizabeth's full time came for her to be
delivered, and she brought forth a son. 58 When her
neighbors and relatives heard how the Lord had
shown great mercy to her, they [a]rejoiced with her.

### *CIRCUMCISION OF JOHN THE BAPTIST*

59 So it was, [a]on the eighth day, that they
came to circumcise the child; and they would
have called him by the name of his father, Zach-
arias. 60 His mother answered and said, [a]"No; he
shall be called John."

**1:39** [a] Josh. 21:9 **1:41** [a] Acts 6:3 **1:42** [a] Judg. 5:24 **1:45** [a] John 20:29 **1:46** [a] 1 Sam. 2:1–10 **1:47** [a] Hab. 3:18 [b] 1 Tim. 1:1; 2:3 **1:48** [a] Ps. 138:6 [b] Luke 11:27 **1:49** [a] Ps. 71:19; 126:2, 3 [b] Ps. 111:9 **1:50** [a] Ps. 103:17 **1:51** [a] Ps. 98:1; 118:15 [b] [1 Pet. 5:5] **1:52** [a] 1 Sam. 2:7, 8 **1:53** [a] [Matt. 5:6] **1:54** [a] Is. 41:8 [b] [Jer. 31:3] **1:55** [a] Gen. 17:19 [b] [Rom. 11:28] [c] Gen. 17:7 **1:58** [a] [Rom. 12:15] **1:59** [a] Gen. 17:12 **1:60** [a] Luke 1:13, 63

61 But they said to her, "There is no one
among your relatives who is called by this name."
62 So they made signs to his father—what he
would have him called.

63 And he asked for a writing tablet, and
wrote, saying, "His name is John." So they all
marveled. 64 Immediately his mouth was opened
and his tongue *loosed,* and he spoke, praising
God. 65 Then fear came on all who dwelt around
them; and all these sayings were discussed
throughout all the hill country of Judea. 66 And
all those who heard *them* [a]kept *them* in their
hearts, saying, "What kind of child will this be?"
And [b]the hand of the Lord was with him.

### *ZACHARIAS' PROPHECY*

67 Now his father Zacharias [a]was filled with
the Holy Spirit, and prophesied, saying:

68 "Blessed[a] *is* the Lord God of Israel,
For [b]He has visited and redeemed His
people,
69 [a]And has raised up a horn of salvation for us
In the house of His servant David,
70 [a]As He spoke by the mouth of His holy
prophets,
Who *have been* [b]since the world began,
71 That we should be saved from our enemies
And from the hand of all who hate us,
72 [a]To perform the mercy *promised* to our
fathers
And to remember His holy covenant,
73 [a]The oath which He swore to our father
Abraham:
74 To grant us that we,
Being delivered from the hand of our
enemies,
Might [a]serve Him without fear,
75 [a]In holiness and righteousness before Him
all the days of our life.

76 "And you, child, will be called the [a]prophet
of the Highest;
For [b]you will go before the face of the
Lord to prepare His ways,
77 To give [a]knowledge of salvation to His people
By the remission of their sins,
78 Through the tender mercy of our God,
With which the Dayspring from on high
has visited[1] us;
79 [a]To give light to those who sit in darkness
and the shadow of death,
To [b]guide our feet into the way of peace."

80 So [a]the child grew and became strong in
spirit, and [b]was in the deserts till the day of his
manifestation to Israel.

### *CHRIST BORN OF MARY*

*(Matt. 1:18–25)*

2 And it came to pass in those days *that* a
decree went out from Caesar Augustus that
all the world should be registered. 2 [a]This census
first took place while Quirinius was governing
Syria. 3 So all went to be registered, everyone
to his own city.

4 Joseph also went up from Galilee, out of
the city of Nazareth, into Judea, to [a]the city of
David, which is called Bethlehem, [b]because he
was of the house and lineage of David, 5 to be
registered with Mary, [a]his betrothed wife,[1] who
was with child. 6 So it was, that while they were
there, the days were completed for her to be
delivered. 7 And [a]she brought forth her firstborn
Son, and wrapped Him in swaddling cloths, and
laid Him in a manger, because there was no
room for them in the inn.

### *GLORY IN THE HIGHEST*

8 Now there were in the same country shep-
herds living out in the fields, keeping watch over
their flock by night. 9 And behold,[1] an angel of
the Lord stood before them, and the glory of
the Lord shone around them, [a]and they were
greatly afraid. 10 Then the angel said to them,
[a]"Do not be afraid, for behold, I bring you good
tidings of great joy [b]which will be to all people.
11 [a]For there is born to you this day in the city of
David [b]a Savior, [c]who is Christ the Lord. 12 And
this *will be* the sign to you: You will find a Babe
wrapped in swaddling cloths, lying in a manger."

13 [a]And suddenly there was with the angel
a multitude of the heavenly host praising God
and saying:

14 "Glory[a] to God in the highest,
And on earth [b]peace, [c]goodwill toward
men!"[1]

15 So it was, when the angels had gone away
from them into heaven, that the shepherds said
to one another, "Let us now go to Bethlehem and
see this thing that has come to pass, which the
Lord has made known to us." 16 And they came
with haste and found Mary and Joseph, and
the Babe lying in a manger. 17 Now when they
had seen *Him,* they made widely[1] known the
saying which was told them concerning this
Child. 18 And all those who heard *it* marveled
at those things which were told them by the
shepherds. 19 [a]But Mary kept all these things
and pondered *them* in her heart. 20 Then the
shepherds returned, glorifying and [a]praising
God for all the things that they had heard and
seen, as it was told them.

1:66 [a] Luke 2:19 [b] Acts 11:21 1:67 [a] Joel 2:28 1:68 [a] 1 Kin. 1:48 [b] Ex. 3:16 1:69 [a] Ps. 132:17 1:70 [a] Rom. 1:2 [b] Acts 3:21 1:72 [a] Lev. 26:42 1:73 [a] Gen. 12:3; 22:16–18 1:74 [a] [Heb. 9:14] 1:75 [a] [Eph. 4:24] 1:76 [a] Matt. 3:3; 11:9 [b] Is. 40:3 1:77 [a] [Mark 1:4] 1:78 [1] NU-Text reads *shall visit.* 1:79 [a] Is. 9:2 [b] [John 10:4; 14:27; 16:33] 1:80 [a] Luke 2:40 [b] Matt. 3:1 2:2 [a] Acts 5:37 2:4 [a] 1 Sam. 16:1 [b] Matt. 1:16 2:5 [a] [Matt. 1:18] [1] NU-Text omits *wife.* 2:7 [a] Matt. 1:25 2:9 [a] Luke 1:12 [1] NU-Text omits *behold.* 2:10 [a] Luke 1:13, 30 [b] Gen. 12:3 2:11 [a] Is. 9:6 [b] Matt. 1:21 [c] Acts 2:36 2:13 [a] Dan. 7:10 2:14 [a] Luke 19:38 [b] Is. 57:19 [c] [Eph. 2:4, 7] [1] NU-Text reads *toward men of goodwill.* 2:17 [1] NU-Text omits *widely.* 2:19 [a] Gen. 37:11 2:20 [a] Luke 19:37

### CIRCUMCISION OF JESUS

21 [a]And when eight days were completed
for the circumcision of the Child,[1] His name
was called [b]JESUS, the name given by the angel
[c]before He was conceived in the womb.

### JESUS PRESENTED IN THE TEMPLE

22 Now when [a]the days of her purification
according to the law of Moses were completed,
they brought Him to Jerusalem to present *Him*
to the Lord 23 [a](as it is written in the law of the
Lord, [b]"Every male who opens the womb shall
be called holy to the LORD"),[1] 24 and to offer a
sacrifice according to what is said in the law of
the Lord, [a]"A pair of turtledoves or two young
pigeons."[1]

> **SEEING JESUS IN THE SCRIPTURE**
>
> **2:22–24** Joseph and Mary offered a sacrifice to redeem their firstborn Son, the One who would become the sacrifice to redeem people (see Ex. 13:11–16).

### SIMEON SEES GOD'S SALVATION

25 And behold, there was a man in Jerusalem
whose name *was* Simeon, and this man *was* just
and devout, [a]waiting for the Consolation of Is-
rael, and the Holy Spirit was upon him. 26 And it
had been revealed to him by the Holy Spirit that
he would not [a]see death before he had seen the
Lord's Christ. 27 So he came [a]by the Spirit into
the temple. And when the parents brought in
the Child Jesus, to do for Him according to the
custom of the law, 28 he took Him up in his arms
and blessed God and said:

29 "Lord, [a]now You are letting Your servant
depart in peace,
According to Your word;
30 For my eyes [a]have seen Your salvation
31 Which You have prepared before the face
of all peoples,
32 [a]A light to *bring* revelation to the Gentiles,
And the glory of Your people Israel."

33 And Joseph and His mother[1] marveled at
those things which were spoken of Him. 34 Then
Simeon blessed them, and said to Mary His
mother, "Behold, this *Child* is destined for the
[a]fall and rising of many in Israel, and for [b]a sign
which will be spoken against 35 (yes, [a]a sword
will pierce through your own soul also), that
the thoughts of many hearts may be revealed."

### ANNA BEARS WITNESS TO THE REDEEMER

36 Now there was one, Anna, a prophetess,
the daughter of Phanuel, of the tribe of [a]Asher.
She was of a great age, and had lived with a hus-
band seven years from her virginity; 37 and this
woman *was* a widow of about eighty-four years,[1]
who did not depart from the temple, but served
*God* with fastings and prayers [a]night and day.
38 And coming in that instant she gave thanks
to the Lord,[1] and spoke of Him to all those who
[a]looked for redemption in Jerusalem.

### THE FAMILY RETURNS TO NAZARETH

39 So when they had performed all things
according to the law of the Lord, they returned
to Galilee, to their *own* city, Nazareth. 40 [a]And
the Child grew and became strong in spirit,[1]
filled with wisdom; and the grace of God was
upon Him.

### THE BOY JESUS AMAZES THE SCHOLARS

41 His parents went to [a]Jerusalem [b]every year
at the Feast of the Passover. 42 And when He was
twelve years old, they went up to Jerusalem
according to the [a]custom of the feast. 43 When
they had finished the [a]days, as they returned,
the Boy Jesus lingered behind in Jerusalem. And
Joseph and His mother[1] did not know *it;* 44 but
supposing Him to have been in the company,
they went a day's journey, and sought Him
among *their* relatives and acquaintances. 45 So
when they did not find Him, they returned to
Jerusalem, seeking Him. 46 Now so it was *that*
after three days they found Him in the tem-
ple, sitting in the midst of the teachers, both
listening to them and asking them questions.
47 And [a]all who heard Him were astonished at
His understanding and answers. 48 So when they
saw Him, they were amazed; and His mother
said to Him, "Son, why have You done this to
us? Look, Your father and I have sought You
anxiously."
49 And He said to them, "Why did you seek
Me? Did you not know that I must be [a]about
[b]My Father's business?" 50 But [a]they did not
understand the statement which He spoke to
them.

### JESUS ADVANCES IN WISDOM AND FAVOR

51 Then He went down with them and came
to Nazareth, and was subject to them, but His
mother [a]kept all these things in her heart. 52 And
Jesus [a]increased in wisdom and stature, [b]and
in favor with God and men.

**2:21** [a] Lev. 12:3 [b] [Matt. 1:21] [c] Luke 1:31 [1] NU-Text reads *for His circumcision.* **2:22** [a] Lev. 12:2–8 **2:23** [a] Deut. 18:4 [b] Ex. 13:2, 12, 15 [1] Exodus 13:2, 12, 15 **2:24** [a] Lev. 12:2, 8 [1] Leviticus 12:8 **2:25** [a] Mark 15:43 **2:26** [a] [Heb. 11:5] **2:27** [a] Matt. 4:1 **2:29** [a] Gen. 46:30 **2:30** [a] [Is. 52:10] **2:32** [a] Acts 10:45; 13:47; 28:28 **2:33** [1] NU-Text reads *And His father and mother.* **2:34** [a] [1 Pet. 2:7, 8] [b] Acts 4:2; 17:32; 28:22 **2:35** [a] Ps. 42:10 **2:36** [a] Josh. 19:24 **2:37** [a] 1 Tim. 5:5 [1] NU-Text reads *a widow until she was eighty-four.* **2:38** [a] Mark 15:43 [1] NU-Text reads *to God.* **2:40** [a] Luke 1:80; 2:52 [1] NU-Text omits *in spirit.* **2:41** [a] John 4:20 [b] Deut. 16:1, 16 **2:42** [a] Ex. 23:14, 15 **2:43** [a] Ex. 12:15 [1] NU-Text reads *And His parents.* **2:47** [a] Matt. 7:28; 13:54; 22:33 **2:49** [a] John 9:4 [b] [Luke 4:22, 32] **2:50** [a] John 7:15, 46 **2:51** [a] Dan. 7:28 **2:52** [a] [Col. 2:2, 3] [b] 1 Sam. 2:26

### *JOHN THE BAPTIST PREPARES THE WAY*
*(Matt. 3:1–6; Mark 1:2–6; John 1:19–23)*

**3** Now in the fifteenth year of the reign of
Tiberius Caesar, [a]Pontius Pilate being gov-
ernor of Judea, Herod being tetrarch of Galilee,
his brother Philip tetrarch of Iturea and the
region of Trachonitis, and Lysanias tetrarch of
Abilene, 2 while [a]Annas and Caiaphas were high
priests,[1] the word of God came to [b]John the son
of Zacharias in the wilderness. 3 [a]And he went
into all the region around the Jordan, preaching
a baptism of repentance [b]for the remission of
sins, 4 as it is written in the book of the words
of Isaiah the prophet, saying:

> [a]"The voice of one crying in the wilderness:
> 'Prepare the way of the LORD;
> Make His paths straight.
> 5 Every valley shall be filled
> And every mountain and hill brought low;
> The crooked places shall be made straight
> And the rough ways smooth;
> 6 And [a]all flesh shall see the salvation of
> God.' "[1]

### *JOHN PREACHES TO THE PEOPLE*
*(Matt. 3:7–12; Mark 1:7, 8; John 1:24–28)*

7 Then he said to the multitudes that came
out to be baptized by him, [a]"Brood of vipers!
Who warned you to flee from the wrath to come?
8 Therefore bear fruits [a]worthy of repentance,
and do not begin to say to yourselves, 'We have
Abraham as *our* father.' For I say to you that
God is able to raise up children to Abraham
from these stones. 9 And even now the ax is laid
to the root of the trees. Therefore [a]every tree
which does not bear good fruit is cut down and
thrown into the fire."

10 So the people asked him, saying, [a]"What
shall we do then?"

11 He answered and said to them, [a]"He who
has two tunics, let him give to him who has
none; and he who has food, [b]let him do likewise."

12 Then [a]tax collectors also came to be bap-
tized, and said to him, "Teacher, what shall we do?"

13 And he said to them, [a]"Collect no more
than what is appointed for you."

14 Likewise the soldiers asked him, saying,
"And what shall we do?"

So he said to them, "Do not intimidate anyone
[a]or accuse falsely, and be content with your wages."

15 Now as the people were in expectation, and
all reasoned in their hearts about John, whether
he was the Christ *or* not, 16 John answered, saying
to all, [a]"I indeed baptize you with water; but One
mightier than I is coming, whose sandal strap I am
not worthy to loose. He will [b]baptize you with the
Holy Spirit and fire. 17 His winnowing fan *is* in His
hand, and He will thoroughly clean out His thresh-
ing floor, and [a]gather the wheat into His barn; but
the chaff He will burn with unquenchable fire."

18 And with many other exhortations he
preached to the people. 19 [a]But Herod the te-
trarch, being rebuked by him concerning He-
rodias, his brother Philip's wife,[1] and for all the
evils which Herod had done, 20 also added this,
above all, that he shut John up in prison.

### *JOHN BAPTIZES JESUS*
*(Matt. 3:13–17; Mark 1:9–11; John 1:29–34)*

21 When all the people were baptized, [a]it
came to pass that Jesus also was baptized; and
while He prayed, the heaven was opened. 22 And
the Holy Spirit descended in bodily form like a
dove upon Him, and a voice came from heaven
which said, "You are My beloved Son; in You I
am [a]well pleased."

### *THE GENEALOGY OF JESUS CHRIST*
*(Gen. 5:1–32; 11:10–26; Ruth 4:18–22; 1 Chr. 1:1–4, 24–27, 34; 2:1–15; Matt. 1:2–16)*

23 Now Jesus Himself began *His ministry at*
[a]about thirty years of age, being (as was supposed)
[b]*the* son of Joseph, *the son* of Heli, 24 *the son* of
Matthat,[1] *the son* of Levi, *the son* of Melchi, *the son*
of Janna, *the son* of Joseph, 25 *the son* of Mattathi-
ah, *the son* of Amos, *the son* of Nahum, *the son* of
Esli, *the son* of Naggai, 26 *the son* of Maath, *the son*
of Mattathiah, *the son* of Semei, *the son* of Joseph,
*the son* of Judah, 27 *the son* of Joannas, *the son* of
Rhesa, *the son* of [a]Zerubbabel, *the son* of Shealti-
el, *the son* of Neri, 28 *the son* of Melchi, *the son* of
Addi, *the son* of Cosam, *the son* of Elmodam, *the
son* of Er, 29 *the son* of Jose, *the son* of Eliezer, *the
son* of Jorim, *the son* of Matthat, *the son* of Levi,
30 *the son* of Simeon, *the son* of Judah, *the son*
of Joseph, *the son* of Jonan, *the son* of Eliakim,
31 *the son* of Melea, *the son* of Menan, *the son* of
Mattathah, *the son* of [a]Nathan, [b]*the son* of David,
32 [a]*the son* of Jesse, *the son* of Obed, *the son* of Boaz,
*the son* of Salmon, *the son* of Nahshon, 33 *the son*

**SEEING JESUS IN THE SCRIPTURE**

**3:31** God's promise to establish David's throne forever was fulfilled through Jesus, the descendant who rules eternally (see Is. 9:7).

**3:1** [a] Matt. 27:2 **3:2** [a] Acts 4:6 [b] Luke 1:13 [1] NU-Text and M-Text read *in the high priesthood of Annas and Caiaphas.* **3:3** [a] Mark 1:4 [b] Luke 1:77 **3:4** [a] Is. 40:3–5 **3:6** [a] Is. 52:10 [1] Isaiah 40:3–5 **3:7** [a] Matt. 3:7; 12:34; 23:33 **3:8** [a] [2 Cor. 7:9–11] **3:9** [a] Matt. 7:19 **3:10** [a] [Acts 2:37, 38; 16:30, 31] **3:11** [a] 2 Cor. 8:14 [b] Is. 58:7 **3:12** [a] Luke 7:29 **3:13** [a] Luke 19:8 **3:14** [a] Ex. 20:16; 23:1 **3:16** [a] Matt. 3:11, 12 [b] John 7:39; 20:22 **3:17** [a] Matt. 13:24–30 **3:19** [a] Matt. 14:3; Mark 6:17 [1] NU-Text reads *his brother's wife.* **3:21** [a] Matt. 3:13–17; John 1:32 **3:22** [a] Ps. 2:7; [Is. 42:1]; Matt. 3:17; 17:5; Mark 1:11; Luke 1:35; 9:35; 2 Pet. 1:17 **3:23** [a] [Num. 4:3, 35, 39, 43, 47] [b] Matt. 13:55; John 6:42 **3:24** [1] This and several other names in the genealogy are spelled somewhat differently in the NU-Text. Since the New King James Version uses the Old Testament spelling for persons mentioned in the New Testament, these variations, which come from the Greek, have not been footnoted. **3:27** [a] Ezra 2:2; 3:8 **3:31** [a] Zech. 12:12 [b] 2 Sam. 5:14; 7:12; 1 Chr. 3:5; 17:11; Is. 9:7; Jer. 23:5 **3:32** [a] Ruth 4:18–22; 1 Chr. 2:10–12; Is. 11:1, 10

of Amminadab, *the son* of Ram, *the son* of Hez-
ron, *the son* of Perez, *the son* of Judah, 34 *the son*
of Jacob, *the son* of Isaac, *the son* of Abraham, [a]*the*
*son* of Terah, *the son* of Nahor, 35 *the son* of Serug,
*the son* of Reu, *the son* of Peleg, *the son* of Eber,
*the son* of Shelah, 36 [a]*the son* of Cainan, *the son* of
[b]Arphaxad, [c]*the son* of Shem, *the son* of Noah, *the*
*son* of Lamech, 37 *the son* of Methuselah, *the son*
of Enoch, *the son* of Jared, *the son* of Mahalalel,
*the son* of Cainan, 38 *the son* of Enosh, *the son* of
Seth, *the son* of Adam, [a]*the son* of God.

### SATAN TEMPTS JESUS

*(Matt. 4:1–11; Mark 1:12, 13)*

4 Then [a]Jesus, being filled with the Holy Spirit,
returned from the Jordan and [b]was led by
the Spirit into[1] the wilderness, 2 being tempted
for forty days by the devil. And [a]in those days
He ate nothing, and afterward, when they had
ended, He was hungry.
3 And the devil said to Him, "If You are [a]the
Son of God, command this stone to become
bread."
4 But Jesus answered him, saying,[1] "It is writ-
ten, [a]'Man shall not live by bread alone, but by
every word of God.' "[2]
5 Then the devil, taking Him up on a high
mountain, showed Him[1] all the kingdoms of the
world in a moment of time. 6 And the devil said
to Him, "All this authority I will give You, and
their glory; for [a]*this* has been delivered to me,
and I give it to whomever I wish. 7 Therefore, if
You will worship before me, all will be Yours."
8 And Jesus answered and said to him, "Get
behind Me, Satan![1] For[2] it is written, [a]'You shall
worship the LORD your God, and Him only you
shall serve.' "[3]
9 [a]Then he brought Him to Jerusalem, set
Him on the pinnacle of the temple, and said to
Him, "If You are the Son of God, throw Yourself
down from here. 10 For it is written:

[a]'He shall give His angels charge over you,
To keep you,'

11 and,

[a]'In *their* hands they shall bear you up,
Lest you dash your foot against a stone.' "[1]

12 And Jesus answered and said to him, "It
has been said, [a]'You shall not tempt the LORD
your God.' "[1]
13 Now when the devil had ended every
temptation, he departed from Him [a]until an
opportune time.

**4:12** In response to Satan's third temptation, Jesus cited Deuteronomy 6:16. God is to be trusted, not tested. The Deuteronomy passage refers to Israel's attempt to test God at Meribah (Ex. 17:1–7). Jesus would not repeat the nation's error of unfaithfulness to God.

### JESUS BEGINS HIS GALILEAN MINISTRY

*(Matt. 4:12–17; Mark 1:14, 15)*

14 [a]Then Jesus returned [b]in the power of the
Spirit to [c]Galilee, and [d]news of Him went out
through all the surrounding region. 15 And He
[a]taught in their synagogues, [b]being glorified by all.

**SEEING JESUS IN THE SCRIPTURE**

**4:15** Jesus taught in the temple to the Jews' amazement, fulfilling prophecy (see Is. 52:13).

### JESUS REJECTED AT NAZARETH

*(Matt. 13:54–58; Mark 6:1–6)*

16 So He came to [a]Nazareth, where He had
been brought up. And as His custom was, [b]He
went into the synagogue on the Sabbath day, and
stood up to read. 17 And He was handed the book
of the prophet Isaiah. And when He had opened
the book, He found the place where it was written:

18 "The[a] Spirit of the LORD *is* upon Me,
Because He has anointed Me
To preach the gospel to *the* poor;
He has sent Me to heal the brokenhearted,[1]
To proclaim liberty to *the* captives
And recovery of sight to *the* blind,
*To* [b]set at liberty those who are oppressed;
19 To proclaim the acceptable year of the
LORD."[1]

20 Then He closed the book, and gave *it* back to
the attendant and sat down. And the eyes of all

**4:17–20** Jesus closed the book in the middle of the sentence. He did not continue because the next phrase—"The day of vengeance of our God" (Is. 61:2)—was not being fulfilled then.

**3:34** [a]Gen. 11:24, 26–30; 12:3; Num. 24:17; 1 Chr. 1:24–27 **3:36** [a]Gen. 11:12 [b]Gen. 10:22, 24; 11:10–13; 1 Chr. 1:17, 18 [c]Gen. 5:6–32; 9:27; 11:10 **3:38** [a]Gen. 5:1, 2 **4:1** [a][Is. 11:2; 61:1]; Matt. 4:1–11; Mark 1:12, 13 [b]Ezek. 3:12; Luke 2:27 [1]NU-Text reads *in.* **4:2** [a]Ex. 34:28; 1 Kin. 19:8 **4:3** [a]Mark 3:11; John 20:31 **4:4** [a]Deut. 8:3 [1]Deuteronomy 8:3 [2]NU-Text omits *but by every word of God.* **4:5** [1]NU-Text reads *And taking Him up, he showed Him.* **4:6** [a][John 12:31; 14:30; Rev. 13:2, 7] **4:8** [a]Deut. 6:13; 10:20; Matt. 4:10 [1]NU-Text omits *Get behind Me, Satan.* [2]NU-Text and M-Text omit *For.* [3]Deuteronomy 6:13 **4:9** [a]Matt. 4:5–7 **4:10** [a]Ps. 91:11 **4:11** [a]Ps. 91:12 [1]Psalm 91:11, 12 **4:12** [a]Deut. 6:16 [1]Deuteronomy 6:16 **4:13** [a][Heb. 4:15] **4:14** [a]Matt. 4:12 [b]John 4:43 [c]Acts 10:37 [d]Matt. 4:24 **4:15** [a]Matt. 4:23 [b]Is. 52:13 **4:16** [a]Mark 6:1 [b]Acts 13:14–16; 17:2 **4:18** [a]Is. 49:8, 9; 61:1, 2 [b][Dan. 9:24] [1]NU-Text omits *to heal the brokenhearted.* **4:19** [1]Isaiah 61:1, 2

LUKE 4:16–30

## JESUS, THE SAVIOR OF ALL

44 STORY OF SCRIPTURE

### WHAT'S GOING ON?

In this passage, Jesus returned to Nazareth, where He grew up. On the Sabbath, He went to the synagogue and read a well-known Messianic prophecy from the Book of Isaiah. The Christ would preach to the poor, heal the brokenhearted, proclaim liberty to captives, give sight to the blind, and more. After reading, He proclaimed this passage was fulfilled in their hearing of it read, essentially saying He is the Christ.

The people were open but skeptical of this claim at first. They knew Jesus as Joseph's son and a carpenter. Their mood quickly changed to hostility though when Jesus continued to explain the Gentiles have been and would be the recipients of God's grace and mercy too. This crossed the line for the Jews and they tried to throw Jesus off a cliff, but He escaped.

### WHAT DOES THIS MEAN FOR ME?

Sometimes, it's hardest to share Jesus with those closest to us. People who knew us before God began working in us can find it challenging to treat us differently. Sometimes, a healthy and respectful distance is necessary while God continues to work in us. But never grow calloused or harsh toward those who don't understand what God is doing in and through you.

### DID YOU CATCH THE PATTERN?

What set the people in the synagogue over the edge that day wasn't the potential of Jesus being divine, but rather God loving the Gentiles. They thought the Christ would be just for them. God's plan always has been to provide salvation to the world though. God promised Abram *all* the families of the earth would be blessed (Gen. 12:3), and as Jesus showed, God has always cared for Jews and Gentiles alike.

*For the next* Story of Scripture *reading and devotion, turn to Matthew 16:13–23 on page 982.*

who were in the synagogue were fixed on Him.
21 And He began to say to them, "Today this Scrip-
ture is [a]fulfilled in your hearing." 22 So all bore
witness to Him, and [a]marveled at the gracious
words which proceeded out of His mouth. And
they said, [b]"Is this not Joseph's son?"
23 He said to them, "You will surely say this
proverb to Me, 'Physician, heal yourself! Whatever
we have heard done in [a]Capernaum,[1] do also here
in [b]Your country.' " 24 Then He said, "Assuredly,
I say to you, no [a]prophet is accepted in his own
country. 25 But I tell you truly, [a]many widows were
in Israel in the days of Elijah, when the heaven
was shut up three years and six months, and
there was a great famine throughout all the land;
26 but to none of them was Elijah sent except to
Zarephath,[1] *in the region* of Sidon, to a woman *who
was* a widow. 27 [a]And many lepers were in Israel
in the time of Elisha the prophet, and none of
them was cleansed except Naaman the Syrian."
28 So all those in the synagogue, when they
heard these things, were [a]filled with wrath,
29 [a]and rose up and thrust Him out of the city;
and they led Him to the brow of the hill on which
their city was built, that they might throw Him
down over the cliff. 30 Then [a]passing through
the midst of them, He went His way.

### *JESUS CASTS OUT AN UNCLEAN SPIRIT*
*(Mark 1:21–28)*

31 Then [a]He went down to Capernaum, a city of
Galilee, and was teaching them on the Sabbaths.
32 And they were [a]astonished at His teaching, [b]for
His word was with authority. 33 [a]Now in the syn-
agogue there was a man who had a spirit of an
unclean demon. And he cried out with a loud voice,
34 saying, "Let *us* alone! What have we to do with
You, Jesus of Nazareth? Did You come to destroy
us? [a]I know who You are—[b]the Holy One of God!"
35 But Jesus rebuked him, saying, "Be quiet,
and come out of him!" And when the demon had
thrown him in *their* midst, it came out of him and
did not hurt him. 36 Then they were all amazed
and spoke among themselves, saying, "What a
word this *is!* For with authority and power He
commands the unclean spirits, and they come
out." 37 And the report about Him went out into
every place in the surrounding region.

4:21 [a] Acts 13:29 4:22 [a] [Ps. 45:2] [b] John 6:42 4:23 [a] Matt. 4:13; 11:23 [b] Matt. 13:54 [1] Here and elsewhere the NU-Text spelling is *Capharnaum.* 4:24 [a] John 4:44 4:25 [a] 1 Kin. 17:9 4:26 [1] Greek *Sarepta* 4:27 [a] 2 Kin. 5:1–14 4:28 [a] Luke 6:11 4:29 [a] John 8:37; 10:31 4:30 [a] John 8:59; 10:39 4:31 [a] Matt. 4:13 4:32 [a] Matt. 7:28, 29 [b] [John 6:63; 7:46; 8:26, 28, 38, 47; 12:49, 50] 4:33 [a] Mark 1:23 4:34 [a] Luke 4:41 [b] Ps. 16:10

### PETER'S MOTHER-IN-LAW HEALED
*(Matt. 8:14, 15; Mark 1:29–31)*

38 [a]Now He arose from the synagogue and en-
tered Simon's house. But Simon's wife's mother
was sick with a high fever, and they [b]made re-
quest of Him concerning her. 39 So He stood over
her and [a]rebuked the fever, and it left her. And
immediately she arose and served them.

### MANY HEALED AFTER SABBATH SUNSET
*(Matt. 8:16, 17; Mark 1:32–34)*

40 [a]When the sun was setting, all those who
had any that were sick with various diseases
brought them to Him; and He laid His hands
on every one of them and healed them. 41 [a]And
demons also came out of many, crying out and
saying, [b]"You are the Christ,[1] the Son of God!"
And He, [c]rebuking *them,* did not allow them
to speak, for they knew that He was the Christ.

### JESUS PREACHES IN GALILEE
*(Matt. 4:23–25; Mark 1:35–39)*

42 [a]Now when it was day, He departed and
went into a deserted place. And the crowd sought
Him and came to Him, and tried to keep Him
from leaving them; 43 but He said to them, "I
must [a]preach the kingdom of God to the other
cities also, because for this purpose I have been
sent." 44 [a]And He was preaching in the syna-
gogues of Galilee.[1]

### FOUR FISHERMEN CALLED AS DISCIPLES
*(Matt. 4:18–22; Mark 1:16–20)*

5 So [a]it was, as the multitude pressed about Him
to [b]hear the word of God, that He stood by the
Lake of Gennesaret, 2 and saw two boats standing
by the lake; but the fishermen had gone from them
and were washing *their* nets. 3 Then He got into
one of the boats, which was Simon's, and asked
him to put out a little from the land. And He [a]sat
down and taught the multitudes from the boat.
4 When He had stopped speaking, He said
to Simon, [a]"Launch out into the deep and let
down your nets for a catch."
5 But Simon answered and said to Him,
"Master, we have toiled all night and caught
[a]nothing; nevertheless [b]at Your word I will let
down the net." 6 And when they had done this,
they caught a great number of fish, and their net
was breaking. 7 So they signaled to *their* partners
in the other boat to come and help them. And
they came and filled both the boats, so that they
began to sink. 8 When Simon Peter saw *it,* he fell
down at Jesus' knees, saying, [a]"Depart from me,
for I am a sinful man, O Lord!"
9 For he and all who were with him were
[a]astonished at the catch of fish which they had
taken; 10 and so also *were* James and John, the
sons of Zebedee, who were partners with Simon.
And Jesus said to Simon, "Do not be afraid.
[a]From now on you will catch men." 11 So when
they had brought their boats to land, [a]they for-
sook all and followed Him.

### JESUS CLEANSES A LEPER
*(Matt. 8:1–4; Mark 1:40–45)*

12 [a]And it happened when He was in a certain
city, that behold, a man who was full of [b]leprosy
saw Jesus; and he fell on *his* face and implored
Him, saying, "Lord, if You are willing, You can
make me clean."
13 Then He put out *His* hand and touched
him, saying, "I am willing; be cleansed." [a]Imme-
diately the leprosy left him. 14 [a]And He charged
him to tell no one, "But go and show yourself
to the priest, and make an offering for your
cleansing, as a testimony to them, [b]just as Moses
commanded."
15 However, [a]the report went around con-
cerning Him all the more; and [b]great multitudes
came together to hear, and to be healed by Him
of their infirmities. 16 [a]So He Himself *often* with-
drew into the wilderness and [b]prayed.

### JESUS FORGIVES AND HEALS A PARALYTIC
*(Matt. 9:2–8; Mark 2:1–12)*

17 Now it happened on a certain day, as He
was teaching, that there were Pharisees and
teachers of the law sitting by, who had come out
of every town of Galilee, Judea, and Jerusalem.
And the power of the Lord was *present* to heal
them.[1] 18 [a]Then behold, men brought on a bed
a man who was paralyzed, whom they sought
to bring in and lay before Him. 19 And when
they could not find how they might bring him
in, because of the crowd, they went up on the
housetop and let him down with *his* bed through
the tiling into the midst [a]before Jesus.

> **5:17** The **Pharisees** were obsessive about following the Law of Moses. They lived by a strict code of conduct, going out of their way to make sure they honored the Sabbath and maintained their purity. They had elaborate rules concerning what they could and couldn't do—rules that ultimately didn't have much to do with the Spirit of God's Word. The Pharisees also had a tendency to look down on people who seemed to be less strict in following the Law of Moses.

**4:38** [a] Mark 1:29–31 [b] Mark 5:23 **4:39** [a] Luke 8:24 **4:40** [a] Matt. 8:16, 17 **4:41** [a] Mark 1:34; 3:11 [b] Mark 8:29 [c] Mark 1:25, 34; 3:11 [1] NU-Text omits *the Christ.* **4:42** [a] Mark 1:35–38 **4:43** [a] [John 9:4] **4:44** [a] Matt. 4:23; 9:35 [1] NU-Text reads *Judea.* **5:1** [a] Mark 1:16–20 [b] Acts 13:44 **5:3** [a] John 8:2 **5:4** [a] John 21:6 **5:5** [a] John 21:3 [b] Ps. 33:9 **5:8** [a] 1 Kin. 17:18 **5:9** [a] Mark 5:42; 10:24, 26 **5:10** [a] Matt. 4:19 **5:11** [a] Matt. 4:20; 19:27 **5:12** [a] Mark 1:40–44 [b] Lev. 13:14 **5:13** [a] John 5:9 **5:14** [a] Matt. 8:4 [b] Lev. 13:1–3; 14:2–32 **5:15** [a] Mark 1:45 [b] John 6:2 **5:16** [a] Luke 9:10 [b] Matt. 14:23 **5:17** [1] NU-Text reads *present with Him to heal.* **5:18** [a] Mark 2:3–12 **5:19** [a] Matt. 15:30

LIVE THE TRUTH

## BEING ALONE

**5:16** Few of us enjoy being alone. But in the busyness of life, there's value in spending intentional time in solitude. Often, we need to get away from it all so we can have space to talk with God and hear from Him. Distractions are everywhere, and the enemy will accept any invitation to interrupt our communion with God. That's why it's important to be deliberate in setting aside time each day to clear our minds and hearts and invite God to be at the center of it all.

In the Gospels, Jesus often went away from the crowds to spend time in prayer. His ministry was filled with powerful miracles and life-changing teachings for the people, but Jesus knew the importance of solitude. The people mattered, of course, but Jesus knew His relationship with the Father was more important. He knew He had to recharge His spiritual "batteries" to be ready for the ups and downs of human life. We need to do the same. Take time to rest. Make time to pray. Get away from the distractions and uproars of life. You'll find when it's time to step back into the noise, you'll hear and see God more clearly.

20 When He saw their faith, He said to him, "Man, your sins are forgiven you."

21 [a]And the scribes and the Pharisees began to reason, saying, "Who is this who speaks blasphemies? [b]Who can forgive sins but God alone?"

22 But when Jesus [a]perceived their thoughts, He answered and said to them, "Why are you reasoning in your hearts? 23 Which is easier, to say, 'Your sins are forgiven you,' or to say, 'Rise up and walk'? 24 But that you may know that the Son of Man has power on earth to forgive sins"—He said to the man who was paralyzed, [a]"I say to you, arise, take up your bed, and go to your house."

**5:23** Jesus posed a riddle to His audience. From an external point of view, it would seem easier to declare **sins are forgiven** than to heal a person, because the latter is falsifiable—it can be disproven. In reality, however, one has to possess more authority to forgive sin. Jesus linked the healing to what it represented, the forgiveness of sin. Jesus forgave the man's sins and healed him at the same time.

25 Immediately he rose up before them, took up what he had been lying on, and departed to his own house, [a]glorifying God. 26 And they were all amazed, and they [a]glorified God and were filled with fear, saying, "We have seen strange things today!"

### *MATTHEW THE TAX COLLECTOR*

*(Matt. 9:9–13; Mark 2:13–17)*

27 [a]After these things He went out and saw a tax collector named Levi, sitting at the tax office. And He said to him, [b]"Follow Me." 28 So he left all, rose up, and [a]followed Him.

29 [a]Then Levi gave Him a great feast in his own house. And [b]there were a great number of tax collectors and others who sat down with them. 30 And their scribes and the Pharisees[1] complained against His disciples, saying, [a]"Why do You eat and drink with tax collectors and sinners?"

31 Jesus answered and said to them, "Those who are well have no need of a physician, but those who are sick. 32 [a]I have not come to call *the* righteous, but sinners, to repentance."

### *JESUS IS QUESTIONED ABOUT FASTING*

*(Matt. 9:14–17; Mark 2:18–22)*

33 Then they said to Him, [a]"Why do[1] the disciples of John fast often and make prayers, and likewise those of the Pharisees, but Yours eat and drink?"

34 And He said to them, "Can you make the friends of the bridegroom fast while the [a]bridegroom is with them? 35 But the days will come when the bridegroom will be taken away from them; then they will fast in those days."

36 [a]Then He spoke a parable to them: "No one puts a piece from a new garment on an old one;[1] otherwise the new makes a tear, and also the piece that was *taken* out of the new does not match the old. 37 And no one puts new wine into old wineskins; or else the new wine will burst the wineskins and be spilled, and the wineskins will be ruined. 38 But new wine must be put into new wineskins, and both are preserved.[1] 39 And no one, having drunk old *wine,* immediately[1] desires new; for he says, 'The old is better.' "[2]

**5:21** [a] Mark 2:6, 7 [b] Is. 43:25 **5:22** [a] John 2:25 **5:24** [a] Luke 7:14 **5:25** [a] Acts 3:8 **5:26** [a] Luke 1:65; 7:16 **5:27** [a] Matt. 9:9–17 [b] John 12:26; 21:19, 22 **5:28** [a] Mark 10:28 **5:29** [a] Matt. 9:9, 10; Mark 2:15 [b] Luke 15:1 **5:30** [a] Matt. 11:19; Luke 15:2; Acts 23:9 [1] NU-Text reads *But the Pharisees and their scribes.* **5:32** [a] Matt. 9:13; 1 Tim. 1:15 **5:33** [a] Matt. 9:14; Mark 2:18; Luke 7:33 [1] NU-Text omits *Why do,* making the verse a statement. **5:34** [a] John 3:29 **5:36** [a] Matt. 9:16, 17; Mark 2:21, 22 [1] NU-Text reads *No one tears a piece from a new garment and puts it on an old one.* **5:38** [1] NU-Text omits *and both are preserved.* **5:39** [1] NU-Text omits *immediately.* [2] NU-Text reads *good.*

### *JESUS IS LORD OF THE SABBATH*
*(Matt. 12:1–8; Mark 2:23–28)*

**6** Now [a]it happened on the second Sabbath after the first[1] that He went through the grainfields. And His disciples plucked the heads of grain and ate *them,* rubbing *them* in *their* hands. 2 And some of the Pharisees said to them, "Why are you doing [a]what is not lawful to do on the Sabbath?"

3 But Jesus answering them said, "Have you not even read this, [a]what David did when he was hungry, he and those who were with him: 4 how he went into the house of God, took and ate the showbread, and also gave some to those with him, [a]which is not lawful for any but the priests to eat?" 5 And He said to them, "The Son of Man is also Lord of the Sabbath."

### *HEALING ON THE SABBATH*
*(Matt. 12:9–14; Mark 3:1–6)*

6 [a]Now it happened on another Sabbath, also, that He entered the synagogue and taught. And a man was there whose right hand was withered. 7 So the scribes and Pharisees watched Him closely, whether He would [a]heal on the Sabbath, that they might find an [b]accusation against Him. 8 But He [a]knew their thoughts, and said to the man who had the withered hand, "Arise and stand here." And he arose and stood. 9 Then Jesus said to them, "I will ask you one thing: [a]Is it lawful on the Sabbath to do good or to do evil, to save life or to destroy?"[1] 10 And when He had looked around at them all, He said to the man,[1] "Stretch out your hand." And he did so, and his hand was restored as whole as the other.[2] 11 But they were filled with rage, and discussed with one another what they might do to Jesus.

### *THE TWELVE APOSTLES*
*(Matt. 10:1–4; Mark 3:13–19)*

12 Now it came to pass in those days that He went out to the mountain to pray, and continued all night in [a]prayer to God. 13 And when it was day, He called His disciples to *Himself;* [a]and from them He chose [b]twelve whom He also named apostles: 14 Simon, [a]whom He also named Peter, and Andrew his brother; James and John; Philip and Bartholomew; 15 Matthew and Thomas; James the *son* of Alphaeus, and Simon called the Zealot; 16 Judas [a]*the son* of James, and [b]Judas Iscariot who also became a traitor.

### *JESUS HEALS A GREAT MULTITUDE*
*(cf. Matt. 4:24, 25; Mark 3:7–12)*

17 And He came down with them and stood on a level place with a crowd of His disciples [a]and a great multitude of people from all Judea and Jerusalem, and from the seacoast of Tyre and Sidon, who came to hear Him and be healed of their diseases, 18 as well as those who were tormented with unclean spirits. And they were healed. 19 And the whole multitude [a]sought to [b]touch Him, for [c]power went out from Him and healed *them* all.

### *THE BEATITUDES*
*(Matt. 5:1–12)*

20 Then He lifted up His eyes toward His disciples, and said:

[a]"Blessed *are you* poor,  
For yours is the kingdom of God.  
21 [a]Blessed *are you* who hunger now,  
For you shall be [b]filled.  
[c]Blessed *are you* who weep now,  
For you shall [d]laugh.  
22 [a]Blessed are you when men hate you,  
And when they [b]exclude you,  
And revile *you,* and cast out your name as evil,  
For the Son of Man's sake.  
23 [a]Rejoice in that day and leap for joy!  
For indeed your reward *is* great in heaven,  
For [b]in like manner their fathers did to the prophets.

### *JESUS PRONOUNCES WOES*

24 "But[a] woe to you [b]who are rich,  
For [c]you have received your consolation.  
25 [a]Woe to you who are full,  
For you shall hunger.  
[b]Woe to you who laugh now,  
For you shall mourn and [c]weep.  
26 [a]Woe to you[1] when all[2] men speak well of you,  
For so did their fathers to the false prophets.

### *LOVE YOUR ENEMIES*
*(Matt. 5:38–48)*

27 [a]"But I say to you who hear: Love your enemies, do good to those who hate you, 28 [a]bless those who curse you, and [b]pray for those who spitefully use you. 29 [a]To him who strikes you on the *one* cheek, offer the other also. [b]And from him who takes away your cloak, do not withhold *your* tunic either. 30 [a]Give to everyone who asks of you. And from him who takes away your goods do not ask *them* back. 31 [a]And just as you want men to do to you, you also do to them likewise.

32 [a]"But if you love those who love you, what credit is that to you? For even sinners love those who love them. 33 And if you do good to those

**6:1** [a] Matt. 12:1–8; Mark 2:23–28 [1] NU-Text reads *on a Sabbath.* **6:2** [a] Ex. 20:10 **6:3** [a] 1 Sam. 21:6 **6:4** [a] Lev. 24:9 **6:6** [a] Matt. 12:9–14; Mark 3:1–6; Luke 13:14; 14:3; John 9:16 **6:7** [a] Luke 13:14; 14:1–6 [b] Luke 20:20 **6:8** [a] Matt. 9:4; John 2:24, 25 **6:9** [a] John 7:23 [1] M-Text reads *to kill.* **6:10** [1] NU-Text and M-Text read *to him.* [2] NU-Text omits *as whole as the other.* **6:12** [a] Matt. 14:23; Mark 1:35; Luke 5:16; 9:18; 11:1 **6:13** [a] John 6:70 [b] Matt. 10:1 **6:14** [a] John 1:42 **6:16** [a] Jude 1 [b] Luke 22:3–6 **6:17** [a] Matt. 4:25; Mark 3:7, 8 **6:19** [a] Matt. 9:21; 14:36; Mark 3:10 [b] Mark 5:27, 28; Luke 8:44–47 [c] Mark 5:30; Luke 8:46 **6:20** [a] Matt. 5:3–12; [11:5] **6:21** [a] Is. 55:1; 65:13 [b] [Rev. 7:16] [c] [Is. 61:3] [d] Ps. 126:5 **6:22** [a] 1 Pet. 2:19; 3:14; 4:14 [b] [John 16:2] **6:23** [a] James 1:2 [b] Acts 7:51 **6:24** [a] James 5:1–6 [b] Luke 12:21 [c] Luke 16:25 **6:25** [a] [Is. 65:13] [b] [Prov. 14:13] [c] James 4:9 **6:26** [a] [John 15:19] [1] NU-Text and M-Text omit *to you.* [2] M-Text omits *all.* **6:27** [a] Rom. 12:20 **6:28** [a] Rom. 12:14 [b] Acts 7:60 **6:29** [a] Matt. 5:39–42 [b] [1 Cor. 6:7] **6:30** [a] Deut. 15:7, 8 **6:31** [a] Matt. 7:12 **6:32** [a] Matt. 5:46

who do good to you, what credit is that to you?
For even sinners do the same. 34 [a]And if you lend
*to those* from whom you hope to receive back,
what credit is that to you? For even sinners lend
to sinners to receive as much back. 35 But [a]love
your enemies, [b]do good, and [c]lend, hoping for
nothing in return; and your reward will be great,
and [d]you will be sons of the Most High. For He
is kind to the unthankful and evil. 36 [a]Therefore
be merciful, just as your Father also is merciful.

### DO NOT JUDGE

*(Matt. 7:1–5)*

37 [a]"Judge not, and you shall not be judged.
Condemn not, and you shall not be condemned.
[b]Forgive, and you will be forgiven. 38 [a]Give, and it
will be given to you: good measure, pressed down,
shaken together, and running over will be put
into your [b]bosom. For [c]with the same measure
that you use, it will be measured back to you."

39 And He spoke a parable to them: [a]"Can
the blind lead the blind? Will they not both fall
into the ditch? 40 [a]A disciple is not above his
teacher, but everyone who is perfectly trained
will be like his teacher. 41 [a]And why do you look
at the speck in your brother's eye, but do not
perceive the plank in your own eye? 42 Or how
can you say to your brother, 'Brother, let me
remove the speck that *is* in your eye,' when you
yourself do not see the plank that *is* in your own
eye? Hypocrite! First remove the plank from
your own eye, and then you will see clearly to
remove the speck that is in your brother's eye.

### A TREE IS KNOWN BY ITS FRUIT

*(Matt. 7:15–20)*

43 [a]"For a good tree does not bear bad fruit,
nor does a bad tree bear good fruit. 44 For [a]every
tree is known by its own fruit. For *men* do not
gather figs from thorns, nor do they gather
grapes from a bramble bush. 45 [a]A good man out
of the good treasure of his heart brings forth
good; and an evil man out of the evil treasure
of his heart[1] brings forth evil. For out [b]of the
abundance of the heart his mouth speaks.

### BUILD ON THE ROCK

*(Matt. 7:21–27)*

46 [a]"But why do you call Me 'Lord, Lord,' and
not do the things which I say? 47 [a]Whoever comes
to Me, and hears My sayings and does them, I
will show you whom he is like: 48 He is like a
man building a house, who dug deep and laid
the foundation on the rock. And when the flood
arose, the stream beat vehemently against that
house, and could not shake it, for it was founded
on the rock.[1] 49 But he who heard and did noth-
ing is like a man who built a house on the earth
without a foundation, against which the stream
beat vehemently; and immediately it fell.[1] And
the ruin of that house was great."

### JESUS HEALS A CENTURION'S SERVANT

*(Matt. 8:5–13)*

7 Now when He concluded all His sayings in the
hearing of the people, He [a]entered Caperna-
um. 2 And a certain centurion's servant, who was
dear to him, was sick and ready to die. 3 So when
he heard about Jesus, he sent elders of the Jews
to Him, pleading with Him to come and heal his
servant. 4 And when they came to Jesus, they
begged Him earnestly, saying that the one for
whom He should do this was deserving, 5 "for he
loves our nation, and has built us a synagogue."

6 Then Jesus went with them. And when He
was already not far from the house, the centurion
sent friends to Him, saying to Him, "Lord, do not
trouble Yourself, for I am not worthy that You
should enter under my roof. 7 Therefore I did not
even think myself worthy to come to You. But
[a]say the word, and my servant will be healed. 8 For
I also am a man placed under [a]authority, having
soldiers under me. And I say to one, 'Go,' and he
goes; and to another, 'Come,' and he comes; and
to my servant, 'Do this,' and he does *it.*"

9 When Jesus heard these things, He mar-
veled at him, and turned around and said to the
crowd that followed Him, "I say to you, I have
not found such great faith, not even in Israel!"
10 And those who were sent, returning to the
house, found the servant well who had been sick.[1]

### JESUS RAISES THE SON OF THE WIDOW OF NAIN

11 Now it happened, the day after, *that* He went
into a city called Nain; and many of His disciples
went with Him, and a large crowd. 12 And when
He came near the gate of the city, behold, a dead
man was being carried out, the only son of his
mother; and she was a widow. And a large crowd
from the city was with her. 13 When the Lord saw
her, He had [a]compassion on her and said to her,
[b]"Do not weep." 14 Then He came and touched the
open coffin, and those who carried *him* stood still.
And He said, "Young man, I say to you, [a]arise."
15 So he who was dead [a]sat up and began to speak.
And He [b]presented him to his mother.

16 [a]Then fear came upon all, and they [b]glori-
fied God, saying, [c]"A great prophet has risen up
among us"; and, [d]"God has visited His people."
17 And this report about Him went throughout
all Judea and all the surrounding region.

**6:34** [a] Matt. 5:42 **6:35** [a] [Rom. 13:10] [b] Heb. 13:16 [c] Ps. 37:26 [d] Matt. 5:46 **6:36** [a] Matt. 5:48 **6:37** [a] Matt. 7:1–5 [b] Matt. 18:21–35 **6:38** [a] [Prov. 19:17; 28:27] [b] Ps. 79:12 [c] James 2:13 **6:39** [a] Matt. 15:14; 23:16 **6:40** [a] [John 13:16; 15:20] **6:41** [a] Matt. 7:3 **6:43** [a] Matt. 7:16–18, 20 **6:44** [a] Matt. 12:33 **6:45** [a] Matt. 12:35 [b] Matt. 12:34 [1] NU-Text omits *treasure of his heart.* **6:46** [a] Mal. 1:6 **6:47** [a] James 1:22–25 **6:48** [1] NU-Text reads *for it was well built.* **6:49** [1] NU-Text reads *collapsed.* **7:1** [a] Matt. 8:5–13 **7:7** [a] Ps. 33:9; 107:20 **7:8** [a] [Mark 13:34] **7:10** [1] NU-Text omits *who had been sick.* **7:13** [a] Lam. 3:32; John 11:35; [Heb. 4:15] [b] Luke 8:52 **7:14** [a] Mark 5:41; Luke 8:54; John 11:43; Acts 9:40; [Rom. 4:17] **7:15** [a] Matt. 11:5; Luke 8:55; John 11:44 [b] 1 Kin. 17:23; 2 Kin. 4:36 **7:16** [a] Luke 1:65 [b] Luke 5:26 [c] Luke 24:19; John 4:19; 6:14; 9:17 [d] Luke 1:68

### *JOHN THE BAPTIST SENDS MESSENGERS TO JESUS*

*(Matt. 11:2–19)*

18[a]Then the disciples of John reported to
him concerning all these things. 19And John,
calling two of his disciples to *him,* sent *them* to
Jesus,[1] saying, "Are You [a]the Coming One, or do
we look for another?"

20When the men had come to Him, they
said, "John the Baptist has sent us to You, say-
ing, 'Are You the Coming One, or do we look for
another?' " 21And that very hour He cured many
of infirmities, afflictions, and evil spirits; and
to many blind He gave sight.

22[a]Jesus answered and said to them, "Go and
tell John the things you have seen and heard:
[b]that *the* blind [c]see, *the* lame [d]walk, *the* lepers are
[e]cleansed, *the* deaf [f]hear, *the* dead are raised, [g]*the*
poor have the gospel preached to them. 23And
blessed is *he* who is not offended because of Me."

**SEEING JESUS IN THE SCRIPTURE**

**7:22** Jesus confirmed His identity as the Messiah by pointing to Isaiah's prophesies He fulfilled (see Is. 35:5).

24[a]When the messengers of John had depart-
ed, He began to speak to the multitudes concerning
John: "What did you go out into the wilderness to
see? A reed shaken by the wind? 25But what did you
go out to see? A man clothed in soft garments? In-
deed those who are gorgeously appareled and live
in luxury are in kings' courts. 26But what did you go
out to see? A prophet? Yes, I say to you, and more
than a prophet. 27This is *he* of whom it is written:

[a]'Behold, I send My messenger before Your face,
Who will prepare Your way before You.'[1]

28For I say to you, among those born of women
there is not a [a]greater prophet than John the
Baptist;[1] but he who is least in the kingdom of
God is greater than he."

29And when all the people heard *Him,* even
the tax collectors justified God, [a]having been
baptized with the baptism of John. 30But the
Pharisees and lawyers rejected [a]the will of God
for themselves, not having been baptized by him.

31And the Lord said,[1] [a]"To what then shall I
liken the men of this generation, and what are
they like? 32They are like children sitting in the
marketplace and calling to one another, saying:

'We played the flute for you,
And you did not dance;
We mourned to you,
And you did not weep.'

33For [a]John the Baptist came [b]neither eating
bread nor drinking wine, and you say, 'He has
a demon.' 34The Son of Man has come [a]eating
and drinking, and you say, 'Look, a glutton and a
winebibber, a friend of tax collectors and sinners!'
35[a]But wisdom is justified by all her children."

### *A SINFUL WOMAN FORGIVEN*

36[a]Then one of the Pharisees asked Him to eat
with him. And He went to the Pharisee's house, and
sat down to eat. 37And behold, a woman in the city
who was a sinner, when she knew that *Jesus* sat at
the table in the Pharisee's house, brought an ala-
baster flask of fragrant oil, 38and stood at His feet
behind *Him* weeping; and she began to wash His
feet with her tears, and wiped *them* with the hair
of her head; and she kissed His feet and anointed
*them* with the fragrant oil. 39Now when the Phar-
isee who had invited Him saw *this,* he spoke to
himself, saying, [a]"This Man, if He were a prophet,
would know who and what manner of woman *this*
*is* who is touching Him, for she is a sinner."

40And Jesus answered and said to him,
"Simon, I have something to say to you."

So he said, "Teacher, say it."

41"There was a certain creditor who had two
debtors. One owed five hundred [a]denarii, and the
other fifty. 42And when they had nothing with
which to repay, he freely forgave them both. Tell
Me, therefore, which of them will love him more?"

43Simon answered and said, "I suppose the
*one* whom he forgave more."

And He said to him, "You have rightly
judged." 44Then He turned to the woman and
said to Simon, "Do you see this woman? I en-
tered your house; you gave Me no [a]water for
My feet, but she has washed My feet with her
tears and wiped *them* with the hair of her head.
45You gave Me no [a]kiss, but this woman has not
ceased to kiss My feet since the time I came in.
46[a]You did not anoint My head with oil, but this
woman has anointed My feet with fragrant oil.
47[a]Therefore I say to you, her sins, which *are*
many, are forgiven, for she loved much. But to
whom little is forgiven, *the same* loves little."

48Then He said to her, [a]"Your sins are forgiven."

49And those who sat at the table with Him
began to say to themselves, [a]"Who is this who
even forgives sins?"

50Then He said to the woman, [a]"Your faith
has saved you. Go in peace."

**7:18** [a] Matt. 11:2–19 **7:19** [a] [Mic. 5:2; Zech. 9:9; Mal. 3:1–3] [1] NU-Text reads *the Lord.* **7:22** [a] Matt. 11:4 [b] Is. 35:5 [c] John 9:7 [d] Matt. 15:31 [e] Luke 17:12–14 [f] Mark 7:37 [g] [Is. 61:1–3; Luke 4:18] **7:24** [a] Matt. 11:7 **7:27** [a] Is. 40:3; Mal. 3:1; Matt. 11:10; Mark 1:2 [1] Malachi 3:1 **7:28** [a] [Luke 1:15] [1] NU-Text reads *there is none greater than John.* **7:29** [a] Matt. 3:5; Luke 3:12 **7:30** [a] Acts 20:27 **7:31** [a] Matt. 11:16 [1] NU-Text and M-Text omit *And the Lord said.* **7:33** [a] Matt. 3:1 [b] [Matt. 3:4]; Luke 1:15 **7:34** [a] Luke 15:2 **7:35** [a] Matt. 11:19 **7:36** [a] Matt. 26:6; Mark 14:3; John 11:2 **7:39** [a] Luke 15:2 **7:41** [a] Matt. 18:28; Mark 6:37 **7:44** [a] Gen. 18:4; 19:2; 43:24; Judg. 19:21; 1 Tim. 5:10 **7:45** [a] Rom. 16:16 **7:46** [a] 2 Sam. 12:20; Ps. 23:5; Eccl. 9:8; Dan. 10:3 **7:47** [a] [1 Tim. 1:14] **7:48** [a] Matt. 9:2; Mark 2:5 **7:49** [a] Matt. 9:3; [Mark 2:7]; Luke 5:21 **7:50** [a] Matt. 9:22; Mark 5:34; 10:52; Luke 8:48; 18:42

### *MANY WOMEN MINISTER TO JESUS*

**8** Now it came to pass, afterward, that He went through every city and village, preaching and bringing the glad tidings of the kingdom of God. And the twelve *were* with Him, 2 and [a]certain women who had been healed of evil spirits and infirmities—Mary called Magdalene, [b]out of whom had come seven demons, 3 and Joanna the wife of Chuza, Herod's steward, and Susanna, and many others who provided for Him[1] from their substance.

### *THE PARABLE OF THE SOWER*

*(Matt. 13:1–9; Mark 4:1–9)*

4 [a]And when a great multitude had gathered, and they had come to Him from every city, He spoke by a parable: 5 "A sower went out to sow his seed. And as he sowed, some fell by the wayside; and it was trampled down, and the birds of the air devoured it. 6 Some fell on rock; and as soon as it sprang up, it withered away because it lacked moisture. 7 And some fell among thorns, and the thorns sprang up with it and choked it. 8 But others fell on good ground, sprang up, and yielded a crop a hundredfold." When He had said these things He cried, [a]"He who has ears to hear, let him hear!"

### *THE PURPOSE OF PARABLES*

*(Matt. 13:10–17; Mark 4:10–12)*

9 [a]Then His disciples asked Him, saying, "What does this parable mean?"

10 And He said, "To you it has been given to know the mysteries of the kingdom of God, but to the rest *it is given* in parables, that

[a]'Seeing they may not see,
And hearing they may not understand.'[1]

> **SEEING JESUS IN THE SCRIPTURE**
>
> **8:10** Jesus taught in parables that not everyone could understand, fulfilling prophecy (see Is. 6:9).

### *THE PARABLE OF THE SOWER EXPLAINED*

*(Matt. 13:18–23; Mark 4:13–20)*

11 [a]"Now the parable is this: The seed is the [b]word of God. 12 Those by the wayside are the ones who hear; then the devil comes and takes away the word out of their hearts, lest they should believe and be saved. 13 But the ones on the rock *are those* who, when they hear, receive the word with joy; and these have no root, who believe for a while and in time of temptation fall away. 14 Now the ones *that* fell among thorns are those who, when they have heard, go out and are choked with cares, [a]riches, and pleasures of life, and bring no fruit to maturity. 15 But the ones *that* fell on the good ground are those who, having heard the word with a noble and good heart, keep *it* and bear fruit with [a]patience.

### *THE PARABLE OF THE REVEALED LIGHT*

*(Mark 4:21–25)*

16 [a]"No one, when he has lit a lamp, covers it with a vessel or puts *it* under a bed, but sets *it* on a lampstand, that those who enter may see the [b]light. 17 [a]For nothing is secret that will not be [b]revealed, nor *anything* hidden that will not be known and come to light. 18 Therefore take heed how you hear. [a]For whoever has, to him *more* will be given; and whoever does not have, even what he seems to [b]have will be taken from him."

### *JESUS' MOTHER AND BROTHERS COME TO HIM*

*(Matt. 12:46–50, Mark 3:31–35)*

19 [a]Then His mother and brothers came to Him, and could not approach Him because of the crowd. 20 And it was told Him *by some,* who said, "Your mother and Your brothers are standing outside, desiring to see You."

21 But He answered and said to them, "My mother and My brothers are these who hear the word of God and do it."

### *WIND AND WAVE OBEY JESUS*

*(Matt. 8:23–27; Mark 4:35–41)*

22 [a]Now it happened, on a certain day, that He got into a boat with His disciples. And He said to them, "Let us cross over to the other side of the lake." And they launched out. 23 But as they sailed He fell asleep. And a windstorm came down on the lake, and they were filling *with water,* and were in jeopardy. 24 And they came to Him and awoke Him, saying, "Master, Master, we are perishing!"

> **8:23** The Sea of Galilee is surrounded on three sides by cliffs and mountains. The winds rushing down from those mountains can suddenly kick up a storm without notice.

Then He arose and rebuked the wind and the raging of the water. And they ceased, and there was a calm. 25 But He said to them, [a]"Where is your faith?"

And they were afraid, and marveled, saying to one another, [b]"Who can this be? For He commands even the winds and water, and they obey Him!"

**8:2** [a] Matt. 27:55; Mark 15:40, 41; Luke 23:49, 55 [b] Matt. 27:56; Mark 16:9 **8:3** [1] NU-Text and M-Text read *them.* **8:4** [a] Matt. 13:2–9; Mark 4:1–9 **8:8** [a] Matt. 11:15; Mark 7:16; Luke 14:35; Rev. 2:7, 11, 17, 29; 3:6, 13, 22; 13:9 **8:9** [a] Matt. 13:10–23; Mark 4:10–20 **8:10** [a] Is. 6:9; Matt. 13:14; Acts 28:26 [1] Isaiah 6:9 **8:11** [a] Matt. 13:18; Mark 4:14; [1 Pet. 1:23] [b] Luke 5:1; 11:28 **8:14** [a] Matt. 19:23; 1 Tim. 6:9, 10 **8:15** [a] [Rom. 2:7; Heb. 10:36–39; James 5:7, 8] **8:16** [a] Matt. 5:15; Mark 4:21; Luke 11:33 [b] Matt. 5:14 **8:17** [a] Matt. 10:26; Luke 12:2; [1 Cor. 4:5] [b] [Eccl. 12:14; 2 Cor. 5:10] **8:18** [a] Matt. 25:29 [b] Matt. 13:12 **8:19** [a] Ps. 69:8; Matt. 12:46–50; Mark 3:31–35 **8:22** [a] Matt. 8:23–27; Mark 4:36–41 **8:25** [a] Luke 9:41 [b] Luke 4:36; 5:26

### *A DEMON-POSSESSED MAN HEALED*
*(Matt. 8:28—9:1; Mark 5:1-20)*

26[a]Then they sailed to the country of the Gad-
arenes,[1] which is opposite Galilee. 27And when He
stepped out on the land, there met Him a certain
man from the city who had demons for a long time.
And he wore no clothes,[1] nor did he live in a house
but in the tombs. 28When he saw Jesus, he [a]cried
out, fell down before Him, and with a loud voice
said, [b]"What have I to do with [c]You, Jesus, Son of
the Most High God? I beg You, do not torment me!"
29For He had commanded the unclean spirit to
come out of the man. For it had often seized him,
and he was kept under guard, bound with chains
and shackles; and he broke the bonds and was
driven by the demon into the wilderness.
30Jesus asked him, saying, "What is your
name?"

And he said, "Legion," because many de-
mons had entered him. 31And they begged Him
that He would not command them to go out
[a]into the abyss.
32Now a herd of many [a]swine was feeding
there on the mountain. So they begged Him
that He would permit them to enter them. And
He permitted them. 33Then the demons went
out of the man and entered the swine, and the
herd ran violently down the steep place into the
lake and drowned.
34When those who fed *them* saw what had
happened, they fled and told *it* in the city and in
the country. 35Then they went out to see what had
happened, and came to Jesus, and found the man
from whom the demons had departed, [a]sitting at
the [b]feet of Jesus, clothed and in his [c]right mind.
And they were afraid. 36They also who had seen *it*
told them by what means he who had been demon-
possessed was healed. 37[a]Then the whole multitude
of the surrounding region of the Gadarenes[1] [b]asked
Him to [c]depart from them, for they were seized with
great [d]fear. And He got into the boat and returned.
38Now [a]the man from whom the demons
had departed begged Him that he might be with
Him. But Jesus sent him away, saying, 39"Return
to your own house, and tell what great things
God has done for you." And he went his way and
proclaimed throughout the whole city what
great things Jesus had done for him.

### *A GIRL RESTORED TO LIFE AND A WOMAN HEALED*

40So it was, when Jesus returned, that the
multitude welcomed Him, for they were all waiting
for Him. 41[a]And behold, there came a man named
Jairus, and he was a ruler of the synagogue. And he
fell down at Jesus' feet and begged Him to come
to his house, 42for he had an only daughter about
twelve years of age, and she [a]was dying.

But as He went, the multitudes thronged Him.
43[a]Now a woman, having a [b]flow of blood for twelve
years, who had spent all her livelihood on physi-
cians and could not be healed by any, 44came from
behind and [a]touched the border of His garment.
And immediately her flow of blood stopped.
45And Jesus said, "Who touched Me?"

When all denied it, Peter and those with
him[1] said, "Master, the multitudes throng and
press You, and You say, 'Who touched Me?' "[2]
46But Jesus said, "Somebody touched Me, for
I perceived [a]power going out from Me." 47Now
when the woman saw that she was not hidden,
she came trembling; and falling down before
Him, she declared to Him in the presence of
all the people the reason she had touched Him
and how she was healed immediately.
48And He said to her, "Daughter, be of good
cheer;[1] [a]your faith has made you well. [b]Go in peace."
49[a]While He was still speaking, someone
came from the ruler of the synagogue's *house,*
saying to him, "Your daughter is dead. Do not
trouble the Teacher."[1]
50But when Jesus heard *it,* He answered him,
saying, "Do not be afraid; [a]only believe, and she will
be made well." 51When He came into the house, He
permitted no one to go in[1] except Peter, James, and
John,[2] and the father and mother of the girl. 52Now
all wept and mourned for her; but He said, [a]"Do
not weep; she is not dead, [b]but sleeping." 53And
they ridiculed Him, knowing that she was dead.
54But He put them all outside,[1] took her by
the hand and called, saying, "Little girl, [a]arise."
55Then her spirit returned, and she arose im-
mediately. And He commanded that she be
given *something* to eat. 56And her parents were
astonished, but [a]He charged them to tell no one
what had happened.

### *SENDING OUT THE TWELVE*
*(Matt. 10:5-15)*

9 Then [a]He called His twelve disciples together
and [b]gave them power and authority over all
demons, and to cure diseases. 2[a]He sent them
to preach the kingdom of God and to heal the
sick. 3[a]And He said to them, "Take nothing for
the journey, neither staffs nor bag nor bread
nor money; and do not have two tunics apiece.
4[a]"Whatever house you enter, stay there,
and from there depart. 5[a]And whoever will not

8:26 [a] Matt. 8:28–34; Mark 5:1–17 [1] NU-Text reads *Gerasenes.* 8:27 [1] NU-Text reads *who had demons and for a long time wore no clothes.* 8:28 [a] Mark 1:26; 9:26 [b] Mark 1:23, 24 [c] Luke 4:41 8:31 [a] Rom. 10:7; [Rev. 20:1, 3] 8:32 [a] Lev. 11:7; Deut. 14:8 8:35 [a] [Matt. 11:28] [b] Matt. 28:9; Mark 7:25; Luke 10:39; 17:16; John 11:32 [c] [2 Tim. 1:7] 8:37 [a] Matt. 8:34 [b] Mark 1:24; Luke 4:34 [c] Job 21:14; Acts 16:39 [d] Luke 5:26 [1] NU-Text reads *Gerasenes.* 8:38 [a] Mark 5:18–20 8:41 [a] Matt. 9:18–26; Mark 5:22–43 8:42 [a] Luke 7:2 8:43 [a] Matt. 9:20 [b] Luke 15:19–22 8:44 [a] Mark 6:56; Luke 5:13 8:45 [1] NU-Text omits *and those with him.* [2] NU-Text omits *and You say, 'Who touched Me?'* 8:46 [a] Mark 5:30; Luke 6:19 8:48 [a] Mark 5:34; Luke 7:50 [b] John 8:11 [1] NU-Text omits *be of good cheer.* 8:49 [a] Mark 5:35 [1] NU-Text adds *anymore.* 8:50 [a] [Mark 11:22–24] 8:51 [1] NU-Text adds *with Him.* [2] NU-Text and M-Text read *Peter, John, and James.* 8:52 [a] Luke 7:13 [b] [John 11:11, 13] 8:54 [a] Luke 7:14; John 11:43 [1] NU-Text omits *put them all outside.* 8:56 [a] Matt. 8:4; 9:30; Mark 5:43 9:1 [a] Matt. 10:1, 2; Mark 3:13; 6:7 [b] Mark 16:17, 18; [John 14:12] 9:2 [a] Matt. 10:7, 8; Mark 6:12; Luke 10:1, 9 9:3 [a] Matt. 10:9–15; Mark 6:8–11; Luke 10:4–12; 22:35 9:4 [a] Matt. 10:11; Mark 6:10 9:5 [a] Matt. 10:14

receive you, when you go out of that city, [b]shake off the very dust from your feet as a testimony against them."

6 [a]So they departed and went through the towns, preaching the gospel and healing everywhere.

### HEROD SEEKS TO SEE JESUS

*(Matt. 14:1–12; Mark 6:14–29)*

7 [a]Now Herod the tetrarch heard of all that was done by Him; and he was perplexed, because it was said by some that John had risen from the dead, 8 and by some that Elijah had appeared, and by others that one of the old prophets had risen again. 9 Herod said, "John I have beheaded, but who is this of whom I hear such things?" [a]So he sought to see Him.

### FEEDING THE FIVE THOUSAND

*(Matt. 14:13–21; Mark 6:30–44; John 6:1–15)*

10 [a]And the apostles, when they had returned, told Him all that they had done. [b]Then He took them and went aside privately into a deserted place belonging to the city called Bethsaida. 11 But when the multitudes knew *it,* they followed Him; and He received them and spoke to them about the kingdom of God, and healed those who had need of healing. 12 [a]When the day began to wear away, the twelve came and said to Him, "Send the multitude away, that they may go into the surrounding towns and country, and lodge and get provisions; for we are in a deserted place here."

13 But He said to them, "You give them something to eat."

And they said, "We have no more than five loaves and two fish, unless we go and buy food for all these people." 14 For there were about five thousand men.

Then He said to His disciples, "Make them sit down in groups of fifty." 15 And they did so, and made them all sit down.

16 Then He took the five loaves and the two fish, and looking up to heaven, He [a]blessed and broke them, and gave *them* to the disciples to set before the multitude. 17 So they all ate and were filled, and twelve baskets of the leftover fragments were taken up by them.

### PETER CONFESSES JESUS AS THE CHRIST

*(Matt. 16:13–20; Mark 8:27–30)*

18 [a]And it happened, as He was alone praying, *that* His disciples joined Him, and He asked them, saying, "Who do the crowds say that I am?"

19 So they answered and said, [a]"John the Baptist, but some *say* Elijah; and others *say* that one of the old prophets has risen again."

20 He said to them, "But who do you say that I am?"

[a]Peter answered and said, "The Christ of God."

### JESUS PREDICTS HIS DEATH AND RESURRECTION

*(Matt. 16:20–23; Mark 8:30–33)*

21 [a]And He strictly warned and commanded them to tell this to no one, 22 saying, [a]"The Son of Man must suffer many things, and be rejected by the elders and chief priests and scribes, and be killed, and be raised the third day."

### TAKE UP THE CROSS AND FOLLOW HIM

*(Matt. 16:24–27; Mark 8:34–38)*

23 [a]Then He said to *them* all, "If anyone desires to come after Me, let him deny himself, and take up his cross daily,[1] and follow Me. 24 [a]For whoever desires to save his life will lose it, but whoever loses his life for My sake will save it. 25 [a]For what profit is it to a man if he gains the whole world, and is himself destroyed or lost? 26 [a]For whoever is ashamed of Me and My words, of him the Son of Man will be [b]ashamed when He comes in His *own* glory, and *in His* Father's, and of the holy angels. 27 [a]But I tell you truly, there are some standing here who shall not taste death till they see the kingdom of God."

### JESUS TRANSFIGURED ON THE MOUNT

*(Matt. 16:28—17:9; Mark 9:2–10; 2 Pet. 1:16–18)*

28 [a]Now it came to pass, about eight days after these sayings, that He took Peter, John, and James and went up on the mountain to pray. 29 As He prayed, the appearance of His face was altered, and His robe *became* white *and* glistening. 30 And behold, two men talked with Him, who were [a]Moses and [b]Elijah, 31 who appeared in glory and spoke of His decease which He was about to accomplish at Jerusalem. 32 But Peter and those with him [a]were heavy with sleep; and when they were fully awake, they saw His glory and the two men who stood with Him. 33 Then it happened, as they were parting from Him, *that* Peter said to Jesus, "Master, it is good for us to be here; and let us make three tabernacles: one for You, one for Moses, and one for Elijah"—not knowing what he said.

34 While he was saying this, a cloud came and overshadowed them; and they were fearful as they entered the [a]cloud. 35 And a voice came out of the cloud, saying, [a]"This is My beloved Son.[1] [b]Hear Him!" 36 When the voice had ceased, Jesus was found alone. [a]But they kept quiet, and told no one in those days any of the things they had seen.

### A BOY IS HEALED

*(Matt. 17:14–21; Mark 9:14–29)*

37 [a]Now it happened on the next day, when they had come down from the mountain, that a great multitude met Him. 38 Suddenly a man

**9:5** [b] Luke 10:11; Acts 13:51 **9:6** [a] Mark 6:12; Luke 8:1 **9:7** [a] Matt. 14:1, 2; Mark 6:14 **9:9** [a] Luke 23:8 **9:10** [a] Mark 6:30 [b] Matt. 14:13 **9:12** [a] Matt. 14:15; Mark 6:35; John 6:1, 5 **9:16** [a] Luke 22:19; 24:30 **9:18** [a] Matt. 16:13–16 **9:19** [a] Matt. 14:2 **9:20** [a] John 6:68, 69 **9:21** [a] Matt. 8:4; 16:20 **9:22** [a] Matt. 16:21; 17:22 **9:23** [a] Matt. 10:38; 16:24 [1] M-Text omits *daily.* **9:24** [a] [John 12:25] **9:25** [a] Mark 8:36 **9:26** [a] [Rom. 1:16] [b] Matt. 10:33 **9:27** [a] Matt. 16:28 **9:28** [a] Mark 9:2–8 **9:30** [a] Heb. 11:23–29 [b] 2 Kin. 2:1–11 **9:32** [a] Dan. 8:18; 10:9 **9:34** [a] Ex. 13:21 **9:35** [a] [Matt. 3:17; 12:18] [b] Acts 3:22 [1] NU-Text reads *This is My Son, the Chosen One.* **9:36** [a] Matt. 17:9 **9:37** [a] Mark 9:14–27

from the multitude cried out, saying, "Teacher, I implore You, look on my son, for he is my only child. 39 And behold, a spirit seizes him, and he suddenly cries out; it convulses him so that he foams *at the mouth;* and it departs from him with great difficulty, bruising him. 40 So I implored Your disciples to cast it out, but they could not."

41 Then Jesus answered and said, "O faithless and perverse generation, how long shall I be with you and bear with you? Bring your son here." 42 And as he was still coming, the demon threw him down and convulsed *him.* Then Jesus rebuked the unclean spirit, healed the child, and gave him back to his father.

### JESUS AGAIN PREDICTS HIS DEATH

*(Matt. 17:22, 23; Mark 9:30–32)*

43 And they were all amazed at the majesty of God.

But while everyone marveled at all the things which Jesus did, He said to His disciples, 44 [a]"Let these words sink down into your ears, for the Son of Man is about to be betrayed into the hands of men." 45 [a]But they did not understand this saying, and it was hidden from them so that they did not perceive it; and they were afraid to ask Him about this saying.

### WHO IS THE GREATEST?

*(Matt. 18:1–5; Mark 9:33–37)*

46 [a]Then a dispute arose among them as to which of them would be greatest. 47 And Jesus, [a]perceiving the thought of their heart, took a [b]little child and set him by Him, 48 and said to them, [a]"Whoever receives this little child in My name receives Me; and [b]whoever receives Me [c]receives Him who sent Me. [d]For he who is least among you all will be great."

### JESUS FORBIDS SECTARIANISM

*(Mark 9:38–41)*

49 [a]Now John answered and said, "Master, we saw someone casting out demons in Your name, and we forbade him because he does not follow with us."

50 But Jesus said to him, "Do not forbid *him,* for [a]he who is not against us[1] is on our[2] side."

### A SAMARITAN VILLAGE REJECTS THE SAVIOR

51 Now it came to pass, when the time had come for [a]Him to be received up, that He steadfastly set His face to go to Jerusalem, 52 and sent messengers before His face. And as they went, they entered a village of the Samaritans, to prepare for Him. 53 But [a]they did not receive Him, because His face was *set* for the journey to Jerusalem. 54 And when His disciples [a]James

**9:52** To get from Judea to Galilee in New Testament times, you had to pass through Samaria or take the very long way around the place. The **Samaritans** weren't popular with "pure-blooded" Jews because they were the descendants of mixed marriages between Jews and Gentiles. The Jews disliked the Samaritans not only for their mixed bloodlines, but also for their compromised worship.

and John saw *this,* they said, "Lord, do You want us to command fire to come down from heaven and consume them, just as [b]Elijah did?"[1]

55 But He turned and rebuked them,[1] and said, "You do not know what manner of [a]spirit you are of. 56 For [a]the Son of Man did not come to destroy men's lives but to save *them.*"[1] And they went to another village.

### THE COST OF DISCIPLESHIP

*(Matt. 8:18–22)*

57 [a]Now it happened as they journeyed on the road, *that* someone said to Him, "Lord, I will follow You wherever You go."

58 And Jesus said to him, "Foxes have holes and birds of the air *have* nests, but the Son of Man [a]has nowhere to lay *His* head."

59 [a]Then He said to another, "Follow Me."

But he said, "Lord, let me first go and bury my father."

**9:59** This aspiring disciple placed family responsibilities ahead of following Jesus. The concerns of home were this man's stumbling block.

60 Jesus said to him, "Let the dead bury their own dead, but you go and preach the kingdom of God."

61 And another also said, "Lord, [a]I will follow You, but let me first go *and* bid them farewell who are at my house."

**SEEING JESUS IN THE SCRIPTURE**

**9:61–62** Unlike Elisha, Jesus' followers are required to give Him their undivided attention, forsaking all to follow Him (see 1 Kin. 19:19–21).

**9:44** [a] Matt. 17:22 **9:45** [a] Mark 9:32 **9:46** [a] Matt. 18:1–5 **9:47** [a] Matt. 9:4 [b] Luke 18:17 **9:48** [a] Matt. 18:5 [b] John 12:44 [c] John 13:20 [d] Eph. 3:8 **9:49** [a] Mark 9:38–40 **9:50** [a] Luke 11:23 [1] NU-Text reads *you.* [2] NU-Text reads *your.* **9:51** [a] Mark 16:19 **9:53** [a] John 4:4, 9 **9:54** [a] Mark 3:17 [b] 2 Kin. 1:10, 12 [1] NU-Text omits *just as Elijah did.* **9:55** [a] [2 Tim. 1:7] [1] NU-Text omits the rest of this verse. **9:56** [a] John 3:17; 12:47 [1] NU-Text omits the first sentence of this verse. **9:57** [a] Matt. 8:19–22 **9:58** [a] Luke 2:7; 8:23 **9:59** [a] Matt. 8:21, 22 **9:61** [a] 1 Kin. 19:20

[62]But Jesus said to him, "No one, having put his hand to the plow, and looking back, is [a]fit for the kingdom of God."

### THE SEVENTY SENT OUT

**10** After these things the Lord appointed seventy others also,[1] and [a]sent them two by two before His face into every city and place where He Himself was about to go. [2]Then He said to them, [a]"The harvest truly *is* great, but the laborers *are* few; therefore [b]pray the Lord of the harvest to send out laborers into His harvest. [3]Go your way; [a]behold, I send you out as lambs among wolves. [4][a]Carry neither money bag, knapsack, nor sandals; and [b]greet no one along the road. [5][a]But whatever house you enter, first say, 'Peace to this house.' [6]And if a son of peace is there, your peace will rest on it; if not, it will return to you. [7][a]And remain in the same house, [b]eating and drinking such things as they give, for [c]the laborer is worthy of his wages. Do not go from house to house. [8]Whatever city you enter, and they receive you, eat such things as are set before you. [9][a]And heal the sick there, and say to them, [b]'The kingdom of God has come near to you.' [10]But whatever city you enter, and they do not receive you, go out into its streets and say, [11][a]'The very dust of your city which clings to us[1] we wipe off against you. Nevertheless know this, that the kingdom of God has come near you.' [12]But[1] I say to you that [a]it will be more tolerable in that Day for Sodom than for that city.

### WOE TO THE IMPENITENT CITIES

*(Matt. 11:20–24)*

[13][a]"Woe to you, Chorazin! Woe to you, Bethsaida! [b]For if the mighty works which were done in you had been done in Tyre and Sidon, they would have repented long ago, sitting in sackcloth and ashes. [14]But it will be more tolerable for Tyre and Sidon at the judgment than for you. [15][a]And you, Capernaum, who are [b]exalted to heaven, [c]will be brought down to Hades.[1] [16][a]He who hears you hears Me, [b]he who rejects you rejects Me, and [c]he who rejects Me rejects Him who sent Me."

### THE SEVENTY RETURN WITH JOY

[17]Then [a]the seventy[1] returned with joy, saying, "Lord, even the demons are subject to us in Your name."

[18]And He said to them, [a]"I saw Satan fall like lightning from heaven. [19]Behold, [a]I give you the authority to trample on serpents and scorpions, and over all the power of the enemy, and nothing shall by any means hurt you. [20]Nevertheless do not rejoice in this, that the spirits are subject to you, but rather[1] rejoice because [a]your names are written in heaven."

### JESUS REJOICES IN THE SPIRIT

*(Matt. 11:25–27)*

[21][a]In that hour Jesus rejoiced in the Spirit and said, "I thank You, Father, Lord of heaven and earth, that You have hidden these things from *the* wise and prudent and revealed them to babes. Even so, Father, for so it seemed good in Your sight. [22][a]All[1] things have been delivered to Me by My Father, and [b]no one knows who the Son is except the Father, and who the Father is except the Son, and *the one* to whom the Son wills to reveal *Him*."

[23]Then He turned to *His* disciples and said privately, [a]"Blessed *are* the eyes which see the things you see; [24]for I tell you [a]that many prophets and kings have desired to see what you see, and have not seen *it*, and to hear what you hear, and have not heard *it*."

### THE PARABLE OF THE GOOD SAMARITAN

*(Matt. 22:34–40; Mark 12:28–34)*

[25]And behold, a certain lawyer stood up and tested Him, saying, [a]"Teacher, what shall I do to inherit eternal life?"

[26]He said to him, "What is written in the law? What is your reading *of it*?"

[27]So he answered and said, [a]" 'You shall love the LORD your God with all your heart, with all your soul, with all your strength, and with all your mind,'[1] and [b]'your neighbor as yourself.' "[2]

[28]And He said to him, "You have answered rightly; do this and [a]you will live."

[29]But he, wanting to [a]justify himself, said to Jesus, "And who is my neighbor?"

[30]Then Jesus answered and said: "A certain *man* went down from Jerusalem to Jericho, and fell among thieves, who stripped him of his clothing, wounded *him*, and departed, leaving *him* half dead. [31]Now by chance a certain priest came down that road. And when he saw him, [a]he passed by on the other side. [32]Likewise a Levite, when he arrived at the place, came and looked, and passed by on the other side. [33]But a certain [a]Samaritan, as he journeyed, came where he was. And when he saw him, he had [b]compassion. [34]So he went to *him* and bandaged his wounds, pouring on oil and wine; and he set him on his own animal, brought him to an inn, and took care of him. [35]On the next day, when he departed,[1] he took out two [a]denarii, gave *them* to the innkeeper, and said to him, 'Take care

**9:62** [a] 2 Tim. 4:10 **10:1** [a] Mark 6:7 [1] NU-Text reads *seventy-two others.* **10:2** [a] John 4:35 [b] 2 Thess. 3:1 **10:3** [a] Matt. 10:16 **10:4** [a] Luke 9:3–5 [b] 2 Kin. 4:29 **10:5** [a] Matt. 10:12 **10:7** [a] Matt. 10:11 [b] 1 Cor. 10:27 [c] 1 Tim. 5:18 **10:9** [a] Mark 3:15 [b] Matt. 3:2; 10:7 **10:11** [a] Acts 13:51 [1] NU-Text reads *our feet.* **10:12** [a] Matt. 10:15; 11:24 [1] NU-Text and M-Text omit *But.* **10:13** [a] Matt. 11:21–23 [b] Ezek. 3:6 **10:15** [a] Matt. 11:23 [b] Is. 14:13–15 [c] Ezek. 26:20 [1] NU-Text reads *will you be exalted to heaven? You will be thrust down to Hades!* **10:16** [a] John 13:20 [b] 1 Thess. 4:8 [c] John 5:23 **10:17** [a] Luke 10:1 [1] NU-Text reads *seventy-two.* **10:18** [a] John 12:31 **10:19** [a] Mark 16:18 **10:20** [a] [Ex. 32:32, 33]; Ps. 69:28; Is. 4:3; Dan. 12:1; Phil. 4:3; Heb. 12:23; Rev. 13:8 [1] NU-Text and M-Text omit *rather.* **10:21** [a] Matt. 11:25–27 **10:22** [a] Matt. 28:18; John 3:35; 5:27; 17:2 [b] [John 1:18; 6:44, 46] [1] M-Text reads *And turning to the disciples He said, "All . . .* **10:23** [a] Matt. 13:16, 17 **10:24** [a] 1 Pet. 1:10, 11 **10:25** [a] Matt. 19:16–19; 22:35 **10:27** [a] Deut. 6:5 [b] Lev. 19:18; Matt. 19:19 [1] Deuteronomy 6:5 [2] Leviticus 19:18 **10:28** [a] Lev. 18:5; Neh. 9:29; Ezek. 20:11, 13, 21; Matt. 19:17; Rom. 10:5 **10:29** [a] Luke 16:15 **10:31** [a] Ps. 38:11 **10:33** [a] John 4:9 [b] Luke 15:20 **10:35** [a] Matt. 20:2 [1] NU-Text omits *when he departed.*

LIVE THE TRUTH

## RESPECTING OTHERS

**10:25–37** As believers, we're ambassadors, or representatives, of Christ. Therefore, we should carry ourselves in a way that reflects His love to others. That doesn't mean we will always agree with everyone else, but it does mean we should always respect them. We especially have a chance to stand out when we respect those who live and believe differently than we do. The world expects us to love our own, but few expect us to respect those who are against us. That's how Jesus lived, though. The perfect Son of God spent time with sinners because He valued and loved them. We should live the same way.

This is the core message of the parable of the good Samaritan. Samaritans and Jews were at odds socially, religiously, and politically. They didn't get along in any area of life. However, when the Samaritan in Jesus' story saw a Jewish man in distress, he came to his aide. He respected him as a person created by God. He didn't agree with him religiously. He came from a different culture. But the Samaritan went out of his way to care for him anyway. That's what it means to respect others. As Jesus said, we should "go and do likewise."

of him; and whatever more you spend, when
I come again, I will repay you.' 36 So which of
these three do you think was neighbor to him
who fell among the thieves?"

37 And he said, "He who showed mercy on
him."

Then Jesus said to him, [a]"Go and do likewise."

### *MARY AND MARTHA WORSHIP AND SERVE*

38 Now it happened as they went that He
entered a certain village; and a certain woman
named [a]Martha welcomed Him into her house.
39 And she had a sister called Mary, [a]who also
[b]sat at Jesus'[1] feet and heard His word. 40 But
Martha was distracted with much serving, and
she approached Him and said, "Lord, do You not
care that my sister has left me to serve alone?
Therefore tell her to help me."

41 And Jesus[1] answered and said to her, "Martha, Martha, you are worried and troubled about
many things. 42 But [a]one thing is needed, and
Mary has chosen that good part, which will not
be taken away from her."

### *THE MODEL PRAYER*

*(Matt. 6:9–15)*

11 Now it came to pass, as He was praying in a certain place, when He ceased, *that* one of His disciples said to Him, "Lord, teach us to pray, as John also taught his disciples."

2 So He said to them, "When you pray, say:

[a]Our Father in heaven,[1]
Hallowed be Your name.
Your kingdom come.[2]
Your will be done
On earth as *it is* in heaven.
3 Give us day by day our daily bread.
4 And [a]forgive us our sins,
For we also forgive everyone who is indebted to us.
And do not lead us into temptation,
But deliver us from the evil one."[1]

### *A FRIEND COMES AT MIDNIGHT*

5 And He said to them, "Which of you shall
have a friend, and go to him at midnight and
say to him, 'Friend, lend me three loaves; 6 for a
friend of mine has come to me on his journey,
and I have nothing to set before him'; 7 and he
will answer from within and say, 'Do not trouble
me; the door is now shut, and my children are
with me in bed; I cannot rise and give to you'?
8 I say to you, [a]though he will not rise and give
to him because he is his friend, yet because
of his persistence he will rise and give him as
many as he needs.

### *KEEP ASKING, SEEKING, KNOCKING*

*(Matt. 7:7–11)*

9 [a]"So I say to you, ask, and it will be given to
you; [b]seek, and you will find; knock, and it will be
opened to you. 10 For everyone who asks receives,
and he who seeks finds, and to him who knocks
it will be opened. 11 [a]If a son asks for bread[1] from
any father among you, will he give him a stone?
Or if *he asks* for a fish, will he give him a serpent
instead of a fish? 12 Or if he asks for an egg, will
he offer him a scorpion? 13 If you then, being evil,
know how to give [a]good gifts to your children,
how much more will *your* heavenly Father give
the Holy Spirit to those who ask Him!"

**10:37** [a] Prov. 14:21; [Matt. 9:13; 12:7] **10:38** [a] John 11:1; 12:2, 3 **10:39** [a] [1 Cor. 7:32–40] [b] Luke 8:35; Acts 22:3 [1] NU-Text reads *the Lord's.* **10:41** [1] NU-Text reads *the Lord.* **10:42** [a] [Ps. 27:4; John 6:27] **11:2** [a] Matt. 6:9–13 [1] NU-Text omits *Our* and *in heaven.* [2] NU-Text omits the rest of this verse. **11:4** [a] [Eph. 4:32] [1] NU-Text omits *But deliver us from the evil one.* **11:8** [a] [Luke 18:1–5] **11:9** [a] [John 15:7] [b] Is. 55:6 **11:11** [a] Matt. 7:9 [1] NU-Text omits the words from *bread* through *for* in the next sentence. **11:13** [a] James 1:17

### A HOUSE DIVIDED CANNOT STAND
*(Matt. 12:22–30; Mark 3:22–27)*

14 [a]And He was casting out a demon, and it
was mute. So it was, when the demon had gone
out, that the mute spoke; and the multitudes
marveled. 15 But some of them said, [a]"He casts out
demons by Beelzebub,[1] the ruler of the demons."
16 Others, testing *Him,* [a]sought from Him
a sign from heaven. 17 [a]But [b]He, knowing their
thoughts, said to them: "Every kingdom divided
against itself is brought to desolation, and a
house *divided* against a house falls. 18 If Satan
also is divided against himself, how will his
kingdom stand? Because you say I cast out de-
mons by Beelzebub. 19 And if I cast out demons
by Beelzebub, by whom do your sons cast *them*
out? Therefore they will be your judges. 20 But
if I cast out demons [a]with the finger of God,
surely the kingdom of God has come upon you.
21 [a]When a strong man, fully armed, guards his
own palace, his goods are in peace. 22 But [a]when
a stronger than he comes upon him and over-
comes him, he takes from him all his armor in
which he trusted, and divides his spoils. 23 [a]He
who is not with Me is against Me, and he who
does not gather with Me scatters.

### AN UNCLEAN SPIRIT RETURNS
*(Matt. 12:43–45)*

24 [a]"When an unclean spirit goes out of
a man, he goes through dry places, seeking
rest; and finding none, he says, 'I will return to
my house from which I came.' 25 And when he
comes, he finds *it* swept and put in order. 26 Then
he goes and takes with *him* seven other spirits
more wicked than himself, and they enter and
dwell there; and [a]the last *state* of that man is
worse than the first."

### KEEPING THE WORD

27 And it happened, as He spoke these things,
that a certain woman from the crowd raised her
voice and said to Him, [a]"Blessed *is* the womb that
bore You, and *the* breasts which nursed You!"
28 But He said, [a]"More than that, blessed *are*
those who hear the word of God and keep it!"

### SEEKING A SIGN
*(Matt. 12:38–42)*

29 [a]And while the crowds were thickly gath-
ered together, He began to say, "This is an evil
generation. It seeks a [b]sign, and no sign will be
given to it except the sign of Jonah the prophet.[1]
30 For as [a]Jonah became a sign to the Ninevites,
so also the Son of Man will be to this generation.
31 [a]The queen of the South will rise up in the

**SEEING JESUS IN THE SCRIPTURE**

**11:30** Jesus fulfilled the sign of Jonah when He rose from the grave on the third day, providing salvation to all who repent (see 1 Cor. 15:4).

judgment with the men of this generation and
condemn them, for she came from the ends of
the earth to hear the wisdom of Solomon; and
indeed a [b]greater than Solomon *is* here. 32 The
men of Nineveh will rise up in the judgment
with this generation and condemn it, for [a]they
repented at the preaching of Jonah; and indeed
a greater than Jonah *is* here.

### THE LAMP OF THE BODY
*(Matt. 6:22, 23)*

33 [a]"No one, when he has lit a lamp, puts *it*
in a secret place or under a [b]basket, but on a
lampstand, that those who come in may see
the light. 34 [a]The lamp of the body is the eye.
Therefore, when your eye is good, your whole
body also is full of light. But when *your eye* is bad,
your body also *is* full of darkness. 35 Therefore
take heed that the light which is in you is not
darkness. 36 If then your whole body *is* full of
light, having no part dark, *the* whole *body* will
be full of light, as when the bright shining of a
lamp gives you light."

### WOE TO THE PHARISEES AND LAWYERS

37 And as He spoke, a certain Pharisee asked
Him to dine with him. So He went in and sat
down to eat. 38 [a]When the Pharisee saw *it,* he
marveled that He had not first washed before
dinner.
39 [a]Then the Lord said to him, "Now you
Pharisees make the outside of the cup and dish
clean, but [b]your inward part is full of greed and
wickedness. 40 Foolish ones! Did not [a]He who
made the outside make the inside also? 41 [a]But
rather give alms of such things as you have; then
indeed all things are clean to you.
42 [a]"But woe to you Pharisees! For you tithe
mint and rue and all manner of herbs, and [b]pass
by justice and the [c]love of God. These you ought
to have done, without leaving the others un-
done. 43 [a]Woe to you Pharisees! For you love
the best seats in the synagogues and greetings
in the marketplaces. 44 [a]Woe to you, scribes and
Pharisees, hypocrites![1] [b]For you are like graves
which are not seen, and the men who walk over
*them* are not aware *of them.*"

**11:14** [a] Matt. 9:32–34; 12:22, 24 **11:15** [a] Matt. 9:34; 12:24 [1] NU-Text and M-Text read *Beelzebul.* **11:16** [a] Matt. 12:38; 16:1 **11:17** [a] Matt. 12:25–29 [b] John 2:25 **11:20** [a] Ex. 8:19 **11:21** [a] Mark 3:27 **11:22** [a] [Is. 53:12] **11:23** [a] Matt. 12:30 **11:24** [a] Matt. 12:43–45 **11:26** [a] [2 Pet. 2:20] **11:27** [a] Luke 1:28, 48 **11:28** [a] [Luke 8:21] **11:29** [a] Matt. 12:38–42 [b] 1 Cor. 1:22 [1] NU-Text omits *the prophet.* **11:30** [a] Jon. 1:17; 2:10; 3:3–10 **11:31** [a] 1 Kin. 10:1–9 [b] [Rom. 9:5] **11:32** [a] Jon. 3:5 **11:33** [a] Mark 4:21 [b] Matt. 5:15 **11:34** [a] Matt. 6:22, 23 **11:38** [a] Mark 7:2, 3 **11:39** [a] Matt. 23:25 [b] Titus 1:15 **11:40** [a] Gen. 1:26, 27 **11:41** [a] [Luke 12:33; 16:9] **11:42** [a] Matt. 23:23 [b] [Mic. 6:7, 8] [c] John 5:42 **11:43** [a] Mark 12:38, 39 **11:44** [a] Matt. 23:27 [b] Ps. 5:9 [1] NU-Text omits *scribes and Pharisees, hypocrites.*

45 Then one of the lawyers answered and said to Him, "Teacher, by saying these things You reproach us also."

46 And He said, "Woe to you also, lawyers! [a]For you load men with burdens hard to bear, and you yourselves do not touch the burdens with one of your fingers. 47 [a]Woe to you! For you build the tombs of the prophets, and your fathers killed them. 48 In fact, you bear witness that you approve the deeds of your fathers; for they indeed killed them, and you build their tombs. 49 Therefore the wisdom of God also said, [a]'I will send them prophets and apostles, and *some* of them they will kill and persecute,' 50 that the blood of all the prophets which was shed from the foundation of the world may be required of this generation, 51 [a]from the blood of Abel to [b]the blood of Zechariah who perished between the altar and the temple. Yes, I say to you, it shall be required of this generation.

52 [a]"Woe to you lawyers! For you have taken away the key of knowledge. You did not enter in yourselves, and those who were entering in you hindered."

53 And as He said these things to them,[1] the scribes and the Pharisees began to assail *Him* vehemently, and to cross-examine Him about many things, 54 lying in wait for Him, and [a]seeking to catch Him in something He might say, that they might accuse Him.[1]

### BEWARE OF HYPOCRISY

*(Matt. 10:26, 27)*

**12** In [a]the meantime, when an innumerable multitude of people had gathered together, so that they trampled one another, He began to say to His disciples first *of all,* [b]"Beware of the leaven of the Pharisees, which is hypocrisy. 2 [a]For there is nothing covered that will not be revealed, nor hidden that will not be known. 3 Therefore whatever you have spoken in the dark will be heard in the light, and what you have spoken in the ear in inner rooms will be proclaimed on the housetops.

### JESUS TEACHES THE FEAR OF GOD

*(Matt. 10:8–31)*

4 [a]"And I say to you, [b]My friends, do not be afraid of those who kill the body, and after that have no more that they can do. 5 But I will show you whom you should fear: Fear Him who, after He has killed, has power to cast into hell; yes, I say to you, [a]fear Him!

6 "Are not five sparrows sold for two copper coins?[1] And [a]not one of them is forgotten before God. 7 But the very hairs of your head are all numbered. Do not fear therefore; you are of more value than many sparrows.

### CONFESS CHRIST BEFORE MEN

*(Matt. 10:32, 33)*

8 [a]"Also I say to you, whoever confesses Me [b]before men, him the Son of Man also will confess before the angels of God. 9 But he who [a]denies Me before men will be denied before the angels of God.

10 "And [a]anyone who speaks a word against the Son of Man, it will be forgiven him; but to him who blasphemes against the Holy Spirit, it will not be forgiven.

11 [a]"Now when they bring you to the synagogues and magistrates and authorities, do not worry about how or what you should answer, or what you should say. 12 For the Holy Spirit will [a]teach you in that very hour what you ought to say."

### THE PARABLE OF THE RICH FOOL

13 Then one from the crowd said to Him, "Teacher, tell my brother to divide the inheritance with me."

14 But He said to him, [a]"Man, who made Me a judge or an arbitrator over you?" 15 And He said to them, [a]"Take heed and beware of covetousness,[1] for one's life does not consist in the abundance of the things he possesses."

16 Then He spoke a parable to them, saying: "The ground of a certain rich man yielded plentifully. 17 And he thought within himself, saying, 'What shall I do, since I have no room to store my crops?' 18 So he said, 'I will do this: I will pull down my barns and build greater, and there I will store all my crops and my goods. 19 And I will say to my soul, [a]"Soul, you have many goods laid up for many years; take your ease; [b]eat, drink, *and* be merry." ' 20 But God said to him, 'Fool! This night [a]your soul will be required of you; [b]then whose will those things be which you have provided?'

21 "So *is* he who lays up treasure for himself, [a]and is not rich toward God."

### DO NOT WORRY

*(Matt. 6:19–21, 25–34)*

22 Then He said to His disciples, "Therefore I say to you, [a]do not worry about your life, what you will eat; nor about the body, what you will put on. 23 Life is more than food, and the body *is more* than clothing. 24 Consider the ravens, for they neither sow nor reap, which have neither storehouse nor barn; and [a]God feeds them. Of how much more value are you than the birds? 25 And which of you by worrying can add one cubit to his stature? 26 If you then are not able to do *the* least, why are you anxious for the rest? 27 Consider the lilies, how they grow: they neither toil nor spin; and yet I say to you, even

**11:46** [a] Matt. 23:4 **11:47** [a] Matt. 23:29 **11:49** [a] Matt. 23:34 **11:51** [a] Gen. 4:8 [b] 2 Chr. 24:20, 21 **11:52** [a] Matt. 23:13 **11:53** [1] NU-Text reads *And when He left there.* **11:54** [a] Mark 12:13 [1] NU-Text omits *and seeking* and *that they might accuse Him.* **12:1** [a] Mark 8:15 [b] Matt. 16:12 **12:2** [a] Matt. 10:26; [1 Cor. 4:5] **12:4** [a] Is. 51:7, 8, 12, 13 [b] [John 15:13–15] **12:5** [a] Ps. 119:120 **12:6** [a] Matt. 6:26 [1] Greek *assarion,* a coin of very small value **12:8** [a] Matt. 10:32 [b] Ps. 119:46 **12:9** [a] Matt. 10:33 **12:10** [a] [Matt. 12:31, 32] **12:11** [a] Mark 13:11 **12:12** [a] [John 14:26] **12:14** [a] [John 18:36] **12:15** [a] [1 Tim. 6:6–10] [1] NU-Text reads *all covetousness.* **12:19** [a] Eccl. 11:9 [b] [Eccl. 2:24; 3:13; 5:18; 8:15] **12:20** [a] Ps. 52:7 [b] Ps. 39:6 **12:21** [a] [James 2:5; 5:1–5] **12:22** [a] Matt. 6:25–33 **12:24** [a] Job 38:41

LIVE THE TRUTH

## BEING FRUGAL

**12:13–21** Spending your money as soon as you receive it or deciding what you should immediately buy for yourself once you get enough is tempting. There's nothing wrong with having possessions, of course. And it's not even inherently wrong to want them. However, the Bible warns us not to go too far and treasure or be greedy with our possessions. Instead, we're to be open-handed, frugal, and generous. Jesus spoke directly to the issue of frugality in Luke 12. A man had a large amount of savings through his crops. Instead of giving it away or using it to benefit others, he built a bigger storehouse to hold it. Unfortunately, he died that night; all his possessions were of no use to him.

Possessions and wealth are great things, but we cannot take them with us when we leave this earth. Therefore, they can never be ultimate in our lives. Rather, we are to steward our money and possessions well, not overindulging in what we might think gives us happiness and worth, but rather living with gratitude for God's faithful provision and goodness to us. It's better to live modestly, be wise with the resources God has given us for a time, and have the means to use God's gifts to benefit what lasts: others.

[a]Solomon in all his glory was not arrayed like
one of these. 28 If then God so clothes the grass,
which today is in the field and tomorrow is
thrown into the oven, how much more *will He
clothe* you, O *you* of [a]little faith?
29 "And do not seek what you should eat or
what you should drink, nor have an anxious
mind. 30 For all these things the nations of the
world seek after, and your Father [a]knows that you
need these things. 31 [a]But seek the kingdom of
God, and all these things[1] shall be added to you.
32 "Do not fear, little flock, for [a]it is your Fa-
ther's good pleasure to give you the kingdom.
33 [a]Sell what you have and give [b]alms; [c]provide
yourselves money bags which do not grow old, a
treasure in the heavens that does not fail, where no
thief approaches nor moth destroys. 34 For where
your treasure is, there your heart will be also.

### SEEING JESUS IN THE SCRIPTURE

**12:32** Jesus is the Good Shepherd who cared for and protected His flock, even when they were scattered and distressed (see Zech. 13:7).

### *THE FAITHFUL SERVANT AND THE EVIL SERVANT*

*(Matt. 24:42–51)*

35 [a]"Let your waist be girded and [b]*your* lamps
burning; 36 and you yourselves be like men who
wait for their master, when he will return from
the wedding, that when he comes and knocks
they may open to him immediately. 37 [a]Blessed
*are* those servants whom the master, when he
comes, will find watching. Assuredly, I say to you
that he will gird himself and have them sit down
*to eat*, and will come and serve them. 38 And if he
should come in the second watch, or come in the
third watch, and find *them* so, blessed are those
servants. 39 [a]But know this, that if the master of
the house had known what hour the thief would
come, he would have watched and[1] not allowed
his house to be broken into. 40 [a]Therefore you
also be ready, for the Son of Man is coming at
an hour you do not expect."

**41 Then Peter said to Him, "Lord, do You
speak this parable *only* to us, or to all *people*?"**

42 And the Lord said, [a]"Who then is that
faithful and wise steward, whom *his* master will
make ruler over his household, to give *them their*
portion of food in due season? 43 Blessed *is* that
servant whom his master will find so doing when
he comes. 44 [a]Truly, I say to you that he will make
him ruler over all that he has. 45 [a]But if that ser-
vant says in his heart, 'My master is delaying his
coming,' and begins to beat the male and female
servants, and to eat and drink and be drunk, 46 the
master of that servant will come on a [a]day when
he is not looking for *him*, and at an hour when he
is not aware, and will cut him in two and appoint
*him* his portion with the unbelievers. 47 And [a]that
servant who [b]knew his master's will, and did not
prepare *himself* or do according to his will, shall
be beaten with many *stripes*. 48 [a]But he who did not
know, yet committed things deserving of stripes,
shall be beaten with few. For everyone to whom
much is given, from him much will be required;
and to whom much has been committed, of him
they will ask the more.

**12:27** [a] 1 Kin. 10:4–7 **12:28** [a] Matt. 6:30; 8:26; 14:31; 16:8 **12:30** [a] Matt. 6:31, 32 **12:31** [a] Matt. 6:33 [1] NU-Text reads *His kingdom, and these things.* **12:32** [a] [Matt. 11:25, 26] **12:33** [a] Matt. 19:21 [b] Luke 11:41 [c] Matt. 6:20 **12:35** [a] [1 Pet. 1:13] [b] [Matt. 25:1–13] **12:37** [a] Matt. 24:46 **12:39** [a] Rev. 3:3; 16:15 [1] NU-Text reads *he would not have allowed.* **12:40** [a] Mark 13:33 **12:42** [a] Matt. 24:45, 46; 25:21 **12:44** [a] Matt. 24:47; 25:21 **12:45** [a] 2 Pet. 3:3, 4 **12:46** [a] 1 Thess. 5:3 **12:47** [a] Deut. 25:2 [b] [James 4:17] **12:48** [a] [Lev. 5:17]

### *CHRIST BRINGS DIVISION*
*(Matt. 10:34–39)*

49 [a]"I came to send fire on the earth, and how
I wish it were already kindled! 50 But [a]I have a
baptism to be baptized with, and how distressed
I am till it is [b]accomplished! 51 [a]Do *you* suppose
that I came to give peace on earth? I tell you, not
at all, [b]but rather division. 52 [a]For from now on
five in one house will be divided: three against
two, and two against three. 53 [a]Father will be di-
vided against son and son against father, mother
against daughter and daughter against mother,
mother-in-law against her daughter-in-law and
daughter-in-law against her mother-in-law."

### *DISCERN THE TIME*
*(Matt. 16:1–4)*

54 Then He also said to the multitudes,
[a]"Whenever you see a cloud rising out of the
west, immediately you say, 'A shower is coming';
and so it is. 55 And when *you see* the [a]south wind
blow, you say, 'There will be hot weather'; and
there is. 56 Hypocrites! You can discern the face
of the sky and of the earth, but how *is it* you do
not discern [a]this time?

### *MAKE PEACE WITH YOUR ADVERSARY*

57 "Yes, and why, even of yourselves, do you
not judge what is right? 58 [a]When you go with
your adversary to the magistrate, make every
effort [b]along the way to settle with him, lest he
drag you to the judge, the judge deliver you to
the officer, and the officer throw you into prison.
59 I tell you, you shall not depart from there till
you have paid the very last mite."

### *REPENT OR PERISH*

13 There were present at that season some
who told Him about the Galileans whose
blood Pilate had mingled with their sacrifices.
2 And Jesus answered and said to them, "Do
you suppose that these Galileans were worse
sinners than all *other* Galileans, because they
suffered such things? 3 I tell you, no; but unless
you repent you will all likewise perish. 4 Or those
eighteen on whom the tower in Siloam fell and
killed them, do you think that they were worse
sinners than all *other* men who dwelt in Jerusa-
lem? 5 I tell you, no; but unless you repent you
will all likewise perish."

### *THE PARABLE OF THE BARREN FIG TREE*

6 He also spoke this parable: [a]"A certain *man*
had a fig tree planted in his vineyard, and he
came seeking fruit on it and found none. 7 Then
he said to the keeper of his vineyard, 'Look, for
three years I have come seeking fruit on this
fig tree and find none. Cut it down; why does it
use up the ground?' 8 But he answered and said
to him, 'Sir, let it alone this year also, until I dig
around it and fertilize *it*. 9 And if it bears fruit,
*well*. But if not, after that[1] you can [a]cut it down.' "

### *A SPIRIT OF INFIRMITY*

10 Now He was teaching in one of the syna-
gogues on the Sabbath. 11 And behold, there was
a woman who had a spirit of infirmity eighteen
years, and was bent over and could in no way
raise *herself* up. 12 But when Jesus saw her, He
called *her* to *Him* and said to her, "Woman, you
are loosed from your [a]infirmity." 13 [a]And He laid
*His* hands on her, and immediately she was
made straight, and glorified God.

14 But the ruler of the synagogue answered
with indignation, because Jesus had [a]healed on
the Sabbath; and he said to the crowd, [b]"There
are six days on which men ought to work; there-
fore come and be healed on them, and [c]not on
the Sabbath day."

15 The Lord then answered him and said,
"Hypocrite![1] [a]Does not each one of you on the
Sabbath loose his ox or donkey from the stall,
and lead *it* away to water it? 16 So ought not this
woman, [a]being a daughter of Abraham, whom
Satan has bound—think of it—for eighteen
years, be loosed from this bond on the Sabbath?"
17 And when He said these things, all His adver-
saries were put to shame; and all the multitude
rejoiced for all the glorious things that were
[a]done by Him.

### *THE PARABLE OF THE MUSTARD SEED*
*(Matt. 13:31, 32; Mark 4:30–32)*

18 [a]Then He said, "What is the kingdom of
God like? And to what shall I compare it? 19 It is
like a mustard seed, which a man took and put in
his garden; and it grew and became a large[1] tree,
and the birds of the air nested in its branches."

### *THE PARABLE OF THE LEAVEN*
*(Matt. 13:33)*

20 And again He said, "To what shall I liken
the kingdom of God? 21 It is like leaven, which
a woman took and hid in three [a]measures[1] of
meal till it was all leavened."

### *THE NARROW WAY*
*(Matt. 7:13, 14)*

22 [a]And He went through the cities and villag-
es, teaching, and journeying toward Jerusalem.
23 Then one said to Him, "Lord, are there [a]few
who are saved?"

12:49 [a] Luke 12:51 12:50 [a] Mark 10:38 [b] John 12:27; 19:30 12:51 [a] Matt. 10:34–36 [b] John 7:43; 9:16; 10:19 12:52 [a] Mark 13:12 12:53 [a] Matt. 10:21, 36 12:54 [a] Matt. 16:2, 3 12:55 [a] Job 37:17 12:56 [a] Luke 19:41–44 12:58 [a] Prov. 25:8; Matt. 5:25, 26 [b] [Ps. 32:6; Is. 55:6] 13:6 [a] Is. 5:2; Matt. 21:19 13:9 [a] [John 15:2] [1] NU-Text reads *And if it bears fruit after that, well. But if not, you can cut it down.* 13:12 [a] Luke 7:21; 8:2 13:13 [a] Mark 16:18; Acts 9:17 13:14 [a] [Luke 6:6–11; 14:1–6]; John 5:16 [b] Ex. 20:9; 23:12 [c] Matt. 12:10; Mark 3:2; Luke 6:7; 14:3 13:15 [a] [Matt. 7:5; 23:13]; Luke 14:5 [1] NU-Text and M-Text read *Hypocrites.* 13:16 [a] Luke 19:9 13:17 [a] Mark 5:19, 20 13:18 [a] Matt. 13:31, 32; Mark 4:30–32 13:19 [1] NU-Text omits *large.* 13:21 [a] Matt. 13:33 [1] Greek *sata,* approximately two pecks in all 13:22 [a] Matt. 9:35; Mark 6:6 13:23 [a] [Matt. 7:14; 20:16]

And He said to them, 24 [a]"Strive to enter through the narrow gate, for [b]many, I say to you, will seek to enter and will not be able. 25 [a]When once the Master of the house has risen up and [b]shut the door, and you begin to stand outside and knock at the door, saying, [c]'Lord, Lord, open for us,' and He will answer and say to you, [d]'I do not know you, where you are from,' 26 then you will begin to say, 'We ate and drank in Your presence, and You taught in our streets.' 27 [a]But He will say, 'I tell you I do not know you, where you are from. [b]Depart from Me, all you workers of iniquity.' 28 [a]There will be weeping and gnashing of teeth, [b]when you see Abraham and Isaac and Jacob and all the prophets in the kingdom of God, and yourselves thrust out. 29 They will come from the east and the west, from the north and the south, and sit down in the kingdom of God. 30 [a]And indeed there are last who will be first, and there are first who will be last."

31 On that very day[1] some Pharisees came, saying to Him, "Get out and depart from here, for Herod wants to kill You."

32 And He said to them, "Go, tell that fox, 'Behold, I cast out demons and perform cures today and tomorrow, and the third *day* [a]I shall be perfected.' 33 Nevertheless I must journey today, tomorrow, and the *day* following; for it cannot be that a prophet should perish outside of Jerusalem.

### *JESUS LAMENTS OVER JERUSALEM*
*(Matt. 23:37–39)*

34 [a]"O Jerusalem, Jerusalem, the one who kills the prophets and stones those who are sent to her! How often I wanted to gather your children together, as a hen *gathers* her brood under *her* wings, but you were not willing! 35 See! [a]Your house is left to you desolate; and assuredly,[1] I say to you, you shall not see Me until *the time* comes when you say, [b]'Blessed is He who comes in the name of the LORD!'"[2]

**SEEING JESUS IN THE SCRIPTURE**

**13:35** The Pharisees' rejection of Jesus left their house desolate, fulfilling prophecy (see Jer. 22:5).

### *A MAN WITH DROPSY HEALED ON THE SABBATH*

**14** Now it happened, as He went into the house of one of the rulers of the Pharisees to eat bread on the Sabbath, that they watched Him closely. 2 And behold, there was a certain man before Him who had dropsy. 3 And Jesus, answering, spoke to the lawyers and Pharisees, saying, [a]"Is it lawful to heal on the Sabbath?"[1]

4 But they kept silent. And He took *him* and healed him, and let him go. 5 Then He answered them, saying, [a]"Which of you, having a donkey[1] or an ox that has fallen into a pit, will not immediately pull him out on the Sabbath day?" 6 And they could not answer Him regarding these things.

### *TAKE THE LOWLY PLACE*

7 So He told a parable to those who were invited, when He noted how they chose the best places, saying to them: 8 "When you are invited by anyone to a wedding feast, do not sit down in the best place, lest one more honorable than you be invited by him; 9 and he who invited you and him come and say to you, 'Give place to this man,' and then you begin with shame to take the lowest place. 10 [a]But when you are invited, go and sit down in the lowest place, so that when he who invited you comes he may say to you, 'Friend, go up higher.' Then you will have glory in the presence of those who sit at the table with you. 11 [a]For whoever exalts himself will be humbled, and he who humbles himself will be exalted."

12 Then He also said to him who invited Him, "When you give a dinner or a supper, do not ask your friends, your brothers, your relatives, nor rich neighbors, lest they also invite you back, and you be repaid. 13 But when you give a feast, invite [a]*the* poor, *the* maimed, *the* lame, *the* blind. 14 And you will be [a]blessed, because they cannot repay you; for you shall be repaid at the resurrection of the just."

### *THE PARABLE OF THE GREAT SUPPER*
*(Matt. 22:1–14)*

15 Now when one of those who sat at the table with Him heard these things, he said to Him, [a]"Blessed *is* he who shall eat bread[1] in the kingdom of God!"

16 [a]Then He said to him, "A certain man gave a great supper and invited many, 17 and [a]sent his servant at supper time to say to those who were invited, 'Come, for all things are now ready.' 18 But they all with one *accord* began to make excuses. The first said to him, 'I have bought a piece of ground, and I must go and see it. I ask you to have me excused.' 19 And another said, 'I have bought five yoke of oxen, and I am going to test them. I ask you to have me excused.' 20 Still another said, 'I have married a wife, and therefore I cannot come.' 21 So that servant came and reported these things to his master. Then the master of the house, being angry, said to his servant, 'Go out quickly into

**13:24** [a] [Matt. 7:13] [b] [John 7:34; 8:21; 13:33; Rom. 9:31] **13:25** [a] Is. 55:6 [b] Matt. 25:10 [c] Luke 6:46 [d] Matt. 7:23; 25:12 **13:27** [a] [Matt. 7:23; 25:41] [b] Ps. 6:8 **13:28** [a] Matt. 8:12; 13:42; 24:51 [b] Matt. 8:11 **13:30** [a] [Matt. 19:30; 20:16] **13:31** [1] NU-Text reads *In that very hour.* **13:32** [a] [Heb. 2:10; 5:9; 7:28] **13:34** [a] Matt. 23:37–39 **13:35** [a] Lev. 26:31, 32 [b] Ps. 118:26; Matt. 21:9 [1] NU-Text and M-Text omit *assuredly.* [2] Psalm 118:26 **14:3** [a] Matt. 12:10 [1] NU-Text adds *or not.* **14:5** [a] [Ex. 23:5] [1] NU-Text and M-Text read *son.* **14:10** [a] Prov. 25:6, 7 **14:11** [a] Matt. 23:12 **14:13** [a] Neh. 8:10, 12 **14:14** [a] [Matt. 25:34–40] **14:15** [a] Rev. 19:9 [1] M-Text reads *dinner.* **14:16** [a] Matt. 22:2–14 **14:17** [a] Prov. 9:2, 5

the streets and lanes of the city, and bring in here *the* poor and *the* maimed and *the* lame and *the* blind.' 22 And the servant said, 'Master, it is done as you commanded, and still there is room.' 23 Then the master said to the servant, 'Go out into the highways and hedges, and compel *them* to come in, that my house may be filled. 24 For I say to you [a]that none of those men who were invited shall taste my supper.' "

### LEAVING ALL TO FOLLOW CHRIST

*(Matt. 10:34–39)*

25 Now great multitudes went with Him. And He turned and said to them, 26 [a]"If anyone comes to Me [b]and does not hate his father and mother, wife and children, brothers and sisters, [c]yes, and his own life also, he cannot be My disciple. 27 And [a]whoever does not bear his cross and come after Me cannot be My disciple. 28 For [a]which of you, intending to build a tower, does not sit down first and count the cost, whether he has *enough* to finish *it*— 29 lest, after he has laid the foundation, and is not able to finish, all who see *it* begin to mock him, 30 saying, 'This man began to build and was not able to finish'? 31 Or what king, going to make war against another king, does not sit down first and consider whether he is able with ten thousand to meet him who comes against him with twenty thousand? 32 Or else, while the other is still a great way off, he sends a delegation and asks conditions of peace. 33 So likewise, whoever of you [a]does not forsake all that he has cannot be My disciple.

### TASTELESS SALT IS WORTHLESS

*(Matt. 5:13; Mark 9:50)*

34 [a]"Salt *is* good; but if the salt has lost its flavor, how shall it be seasoned? 35 It is neither fit for the land nor for the dunghill, *but* men throw it out. He who has ears to hear, let him hear!"

### THE PARABLE OF THE LOST SHEEP

*(Matt. 18:10–14)*

15 Then [a]all the tax collectors and the sinners drew near to Him to hear Him. 2 And the Pharisees and scribes complained, saying, "This Man receives sinners [a]and eats with them." 3 So He spoke this parable to them, saying:

4 [a]"What man of you, having a hundred sheep, if he loses one of them, does not leave the ninety-nine in the wilderness, and go after the one which is lost until he finds it? 5 And when he has found *it*, he lays *it* on his shoulders, rejoicing. 6 And when he comes home, he calls together *his* friends and neighbors, saying to them, [a]'Rejoice with me, for I have found my sheep [b]which was lost!' 7 I say to you that likewise there will be more joy in heaven over one sinner who repents [a]than over ninety-nine just persons who [b]need no repentance.

### THE PARABLE OF THE LOST COIN

8 "Or what woman, having ten silver coins,[1] if she loses one coin, does not light a lamp, sweep the house, and search carefully until she finds *it?* 9 And when she has found *it*, she calls *her* friends and neighbors together, saying, 'Rejoice with me, for I have found the piece which I lost!' 10 Likewise, I say to you, there is joy in the presence of the angels of God over one sinner who repents."

### THE PARABLE OF THE LOST SON

11 Then He said: "A certain man had two sons. 12 And the younger of them said to *his* father, 'Father, give me the portion of goods that falls *to me*.' So he divided to them [a]*his* livelihood. 13 And not many days after, the younger son gathered all together, journeyed to a far country, and there wasted his possessions with prodigal living. 14 But when he had spent all, there arose a severe famine in that land, and he began to be in want. 15 Then he went and joined himself to a citizen of that country, and he sent him into his fields to feed swine. 16 And he would gladly have filled his stomach with the pods that the swine ate, and no one gave him *anything*.

> **15:15** According to the law God gave Moses, certain animals, such as pigs and shellfish, were "unclean," unacceptable as either food or sacrifices. Not only were Jewish people not allowed to eat pork, but they also weren't even allowed to touch pigs.

17 "But when he came to himself, he said, 'How many of my father's hired servants have bread enough and to spare, and I perish with hunger! 18 I will arise and go to my father, and will say to him, "Father, [a]I have sinned against heaven and before you, 19 and I am no longer worthy to be called your son. Make me like one of your hired servants." '

20 "And he arose and came to his father. But [a]when he was still a great way off, his father saw him and had compassion, and ran and fell on his neck and kissed him. 21 And the son said to him, 'Father, I have sinned against heaven [a]and in your sight, and am no longer worthy to be called your son.'

22 "But the father said to his servants, 'Bring[1] out the best robe and put *it* on him, and put a ring on his hand and sandals on *his* feet. 23 And

**14:24** [a] [Matt. 21:43; 22:8; Acts 13:46] **14:26** [a] Deut. 13:6; 33:9; Matt. 10:37 [b] Rom. 9:13 [c] Rev. 12:11 **14:27** [a] Matt. 16:24; Mark 8:34; Luke 9:23; [2 Tim. 3:12] **14:28** [a] Prov. 24:27 **14:33** [a] Matt. 19:27 **14:34** [a] Matt. 5:13; [Mark 9:50] **15:1** [a] [Matt. 9:10–13] **15:2** [a] Acts 11:3; Gal. 2:12 **15:4** [a] Matt. 18:12–14; 1 Pet. 2:25 **15:6** [a] [Rom. 12:15] [b] [Luke 19:10; 1 Pet. 2:10, 25] **15:7** [a] [Luke 5:32] [b] [Mark 2:17] **15:8** [1] Greek *drachma,* a valuable coin often worn in a ten-piece garland by married women **15:12** [a] Mark 12:44 **15:18** [a] Ex. 9:27; 10:16; Num. 22:34; Josh. 7:20; 1 Sam. 15:24, 30; 26:21; 2 Sam. 12:13; 24:10, 17; Ps. 51:4; Matt. 27:4 **15:20** [a] [Jer. 3:12]; Matt. 9:36; [Acts 2:39; Eph. 2:13, 17] **15:21** [a] Ps. 51:4 **15:22** [1] NU-Text reads *Quickly bring.*

bring the fatted calf here and kill *it,* and let us
eat and be merry; 24 [a]for this my son was dead
and is alive again; he was lost and is found.' And
they began to be merry.

25 "Now his older son was in the field. And as
he came and drew near to the house, he heard
music and dancing. 26 So he called one of the
servants and asked what these things meant.
27 And he said to him, 'Your brother has come,
and because he has received him safe and sound,
your father has killed the fatted calf.'

28 "But he was angry and would not go in.
Therefore his father came out and pleaded with
him. 29 So he answered and said to *his* father,
'Lo, these many years I have been serving you;
I never transgressed your commandment at
any time; and yet you never gave me a young
goat, that I might make merry with my friends.
30 But as soon as this son of yours came, who
has devoured your livelihood with harlots, you
killed the fatted calf for him.'

31 "And he said to him, 'Son, you are always
with me, and all that I have is yours. 32 It was
right that we should make merry and be glad,
[a]for your brother was dead and is alive again,
and was lost and is found.' "

### THE PARABLE OF THE UNJUST STEWARD

**16** He also said to His disciples: "There was a
certain rich man who had a steward, and
an accusation was brought to him that this man
was wasting his goods. 2 So he called him and
said to him, 'What is this I hear about you? Give
an [a]account of your stewardship, for you can no
longer be steward.'

3 "Then the steward said within himself,
'What shall I do? For my master is taking the
stewardship away from me. I cannot dig; I am
ashamed to beg. 4 I have resolved what to do,
that when I am put out of the stewardship, they
may receive me into their houses.'

5 "So he called every one of his master's debt-
ors to *him,* and said to the first, 'How much do
you owe my master?' 6 And he said, 'A hundred
measures[1] of oil.' So he said to him, 'Take your
bill, and sit down quickly and write fifty.' 7 Then
he said to another, 'And how much do you owe?'
So he said, 'A hundred measures[1] of wheat.' And
he said to him, 'Take your bill, and write eighty.'
8 So the master commended the unjust steward
because he had dealt shrewdly. For the sons of
this world are more shrewd in their generation
than [a]the sons of light.

9 "And I say to you, [a]make friends for your-
selves by unrighteous mammon, that when you
fail,[1] they may receive you into an everlasting
home. 10 [a]He who *is* faithful in *what is* least is faith-
ful also in much; and he who is unjust in *what is*
least is unjust also in much. 11 Therefore if you have
not been faithful in the unrighteous mammon,
who will commit to your trust the true *riches?*
12 And if you have not been faithful in what is an-
other man's, who will give you what is your [a]own?

13 [a]"No servant can serve two masters; for
either he will hate the one and love the other,
or else he will be loyal to the one and despise
the other. You cannot serve God and mammon."

### THE LAW, THE PROPHETS, AND THE KINGDOM

14 Now the Pharisees, [a]who were lovers of
money, also heard all these things, and they
derided Him. 15 And He said to them, "You are
those who [a]justify yourselves [b]before men, but
[c]God knows your hearts. For [d]what is highly
esteemed among men is an abomination in
the sight of God.

16 [a]"The law and the prophets *were* until
John. Since that time the kingdom of God has
been preached, and everyone is pressing into it.
17 [a]And it is easier for heaven and earth to pass
away than for one tittle of the law to fail.

18 [a]"Whoever divorces his wife and marries
another commits adultery; and whoever marries
her who is divorced from *her* husband commits
adultery.

### THE RICH MAN AND LAZARUS

19 "There was a certain rich man who was
clothed in purple and fine linen and fared sump-
tuously every day. 20 But there was a certain
beggar named Lazarus, full of sores, who was
laid at his gate, 21 desiring to be fed with the
crumbs which fell[1] from the rich man's table.
Moreover the dogs came and licked his sores.
22 So it was that the beggar died, and was carried
by the angels to [a]Abraham's bosom. The rich
man also died and was buried. 23 And being in
torments in Hades, he lifted up his eyes and saw
Abraham afar off, and Lazarus in his bosom.

> **16:22 Abraham's bosom** was the blessed place of the dead. Angelic escorts for the dead were also believed in Judaism. This verse indicates that the dead know their fate immediately.

24 "Then he cried and said, 'Father Abraham,
have mercy on me, and send Lazarus that he

**15:24** [a] Matt. 8:22; Luke 9:60; 15:32; Rom. 11:15; [Eph. 2:1, 5; 5:14; Col. 2:13; 1 Tim. 5:6] **15:32** [a] Luke 15:24 **16:2** [a] [Rom. 14:12; 2 Cor. 5:10; 1 Pet. 4:5, 6] **16:6** [1] Greek *batos,* eight or nine gallons each (Old Testament *bath*) **16:7** [1] Greek *koros,* ten or twelve bushels each (Old Testament *kor*) **16:8** [a] [John 12:36; Eph. 5:8]; 1 Thess. 5:5 **16:9** [a] Dan. 4:27; [Matt. 6:19; 19:21]; Luke 11:41; [1 Tim. 6:17–19] [1] NU-Text reads *it fails.* **16:10** [a] Matt. 25:21; Luke 19:17 **16:12** [a] [1 Pet. 1:3, 4] **16:13** [a] Matt. 6:24; Gal. 1:10 **16:14** [a] Matt. 23:14 **16:15** [a] Luke 10:29 [b] [Matt. 6:2, 5, 16] [c] 1 Chr. 28:9; 2 Chr. 6:30; Ps. 7:9; Prov. 15:11; Jer. 17:10 [d] 1 Sam. 16:7; Ps. 10:3; Prov. 6:16–19; 16:5 **16:16** [a] Matt. 3:1–12; 4:17; 11:12, 13; Luke 7:29 **16:17** [a] Ps. 102:26, 27; Is. 40:8; 51:6; Matt. 5:18; 1 Pet. 1:25 **16:18** [a] Matt. 5:32; 19:9; Mark 10:11; 1 Cor. 7:10, 11 **16:21** [1] NU-Text reads *with what fell.* **16:22** [a] Matt. 8:11

may dip the tip of his finger in water and [a]cool my tongue; for I [b]am tormented in this flame.' 25 But Abraham said, 'Son, [a]remember that in your lifetime you received your good things, and likewise Lazarus evil things; but now he is comforted and you are tormented. 26 And besides all this, between us and you there is a great gulf fixed, so that those who want to pass from here to you cannot, nor can those from there pass to us.'

27 "Then he said, 'I beg you therefore, father, that you would send him to my father's house, 28 for I have five brothers, that he may testify to them, lest they also come to this place of torment.' 29 Abraham said to him, [a]'They have Moses and the prophets; let them hear them.' 30 And he said, 'No, father Abraham; but if one goes to them from the dead, they will repent.' 31 But he said to him, [a]'If they do not hear Moses and the prophets, [b]neither will they be persuaded though one rise from the dead.' "

### *JESUS WARNS OF OFFENSES*

*(Matt. 18:6, 7; Mark 9:42)*

**17** Then He said to the disciples, [a]"It is impossible that no offenses should come, but [b]woe *to him* through whom they do come! 2 It would be better for him if a millstone were hung around his neck, and he were thrown into the sea, than that he should offend one of these little ones. 3 Take heed to yourselves. [a]If your brother sins against you,[1] [b]rebuke him; and if he repents, forgive him. 4 And if he sins against you seven times in a day, and seven times in a day returns to you,[1] saying, 'I repent,' you shall forgive him."

### *FAITH AND DUTY*

*(Matt. 17:19–21; Mark 9:28, 29)*

5 And the apostles said to the Lord, "Increase our faith."

6 [a]So the Lord said, "If you have faith as a mustard seed, you can say to this mulberry tree, 'Be pulled up by the roots and be planted in the sea,' and it would obey you. 7 And which of you, having a servant plowing or tending sheep, will say to him when he has come in from the field, 'Come at once and sit down to eat'? 8 But will he not rather say to him, 'Prepare something for my supper, and gird yourself [a]and serve me till I have eaten and drunk, and afterward you will eat and drink'? 9 Does he thank that servant because he did the things that were commanded him? I think not.[1] 10 So likewise you, when you have done all those things which you are commanded, say, 'We are [a]unprofitable servants. We have done what was our duty to do.' "

### *TEN LEPERS CLEANSED*

11 Now it happened [a]as He went to Jerusalem that He passed through the midst of Samaria and Galilee. 12 Then as He entered a certain village, there met Him ten men who were lepers, [a]who stood afar off. 13 And they lifted up *their* voices and said, "Jesus, Master, have mercy on us!"

14 So when He saw *them,* He said to them, [a]"Go, show yourselves to the priests." And so it was that as they went, they were cleansed.

15 And one of them, when he saw that he was healed, returned, and with a loud voice [a]glorified God, 16 and fell down on *his* face at His feet, giving Him thanks. And he was a [a]Samaritan.

17 So Jesus answered and said, "Were there

**16:24** [a] Zech. 14:12 [b] [Is. 66:24; Mark 9:42–48] **16:25** [a] Job 21:13; Luke 6:24; James 5:5 **16:29** [a] Is. 8:20; 34:16; [John 5:39, 45]; Acts 15:21; 17:11; [2 Tim. 3:15] **16:31** [a] [John 5:46] [b] John 12:10, 11 **17:1** [a] [1 Cor. 11:19] [b] [2 Thess. 1:6] **17:3** [a] [Matt. 18:15, 21] [b] Lev. 19:17; [Prov. 17:10; Gal. 6:1; James 5:19, 20] [1] NU-Text omits *against you.* **17:4** [1] M-Text omits *to you.* **17:6** [a] Matt. 17:20; 21:21; [Mark 9:23; 11:23]; Luke 13:19 **17:8** [a] [Luke 12:37] **17:9** [1] NU-Text ends verse with *commanded;* M-Text omits *him.* **17:10** [a] Job 22:3; 35:7; Ps. 16:2; Matt. 25:30; Rom. 3:12; 11:35; [1 Cor. 9:16, 17]; Philem. 11 **17:11** [a] Luke 9:51, 52; John 4:4 **17:12** [a] Lev. 13:46; Num. 5:2 **17:14** [a] Lev. 13:1–59; 14:1–32; Matt. 8:4; Luke 5:14 **17:15** [a] Luke 5:25; 18:43 **17:16** [a] 2 Kin. 17:24; Luke 9:52, 53; John 4:9

LIVE THE TRUTH

## BEING GRATEFUL

**17:11–19** To be grateful is to recognize God's faithfulness to you and have a deep desire to express thankfulness back to Him. Every gift we have comes from God (see James 1:17). Our resources, skills, abilities, and relationships—everything—are given to us by God. Even each moment of life is a gift we shouldn't take for granted. Not everyone has what you have; some people have more, some people have less. But gratitude isn't based on the quantity of God's gifts, but rather on His kindness and love in giving them—whatever they might be.

In Luke 17, ten lepers cried out to Jesus for healing. Jesus healed them, but of the ten, only one expressed his gratitude toward Jesus. The others, perhaps in excitement, went on to other things. The one who was grateful, however, returned and fell on his face in worship. We have much to learn from this. Often, we live more like the nine than the one. We take God's good gifts for granted or we aren't satisfied because we still want more. To be grateful begins by counting your blessings. It is to recognize everything you have—great or small—is evidence of God's grace and kindness to you. When we remember that, we can never thank God enough.

not ten cleansed? But where *are* the nine? 18 Were there not any found who returned to give glory to God except this foreigner?" 19 [a]And He said to him, "Arise, go your way. Your faith has made you well."

### *THE COMING OF THE KINGDOM*

*(Gen. 6:5—8:22; 19:12–14)*

20 Now when He was asked by the Pharisees when the kingdom of God would come, He answered them and said, "The kingdom of God does not come with observation; 21 [a]nor will they say, 'See here!' or 'See there!'[1] For indeed, [b]the kingdom of God is within you."

22 Then He said to the disciples, [a]"The days will come when you will desire to see one of the days of the Son of Man, and you will not see *it.* 23 [a]And they will say to you, 'Look here!' or 'Look there!'[1] Do not go after *them* or follow *them.* 24 [a]For as the lightning that flashes out of one *part* under heaven shines to the other *part* under heaven, so also the Son of Man will be in His day. 25 [a]But first He must suffer many things and be [b]rejected by this generation. 26 [a]And as it [b]was in the [c]days of [d]Noah, so it will be also in the days of the Son of Man: 27 They ate, they drank, they married wives, they were given in marriage, until the [a]day that Noah entered the ark, and the flood came and [b]destroyed them all. 28 [a]Likewise as it was also in the days of Lot: They ate, they drank, they bought, they sold, they planted, they built; 29 but on [a]the day that Lot went out of Sodom it rained fire and brimstone from heaven and destroyed *them* all. 30 Even so will it be in the day when the Son of Man [a]is revealed.

31 "In that day, he [a]who is on the housetop, and his goods *are* in the house, let him not come down to take them away. And likewise the one who is in the field, let him not turn back. 32 [a]Remember Lot's wife. 33 [a]Whoever seeks to save his life will lose it, and whoever loses his life will preserve it. 34 [a]I tell you, in that night there will be two *men* in one bed: the one will be taken and the other will be left. 35 [a]Two *women* will be grinding together: the one will be taken and the other left. 36 Two *men* will be in the field: the one will be taken and the other left."[1]

37 And they answered and said to Him, [a]"Where, Lord?"

So He said to them, "Wherever the body is, there the eagles will be gathered together."

### *THE PARABLE OF THE PERSISTENT WIDOW*

**18** Then He spoke a parable to them, that men [a]always ought to pray and not lose heart, 2 saying: "There was in a certain city a judge who did not fear God nor regard man. 3 Now there was a widow in that city; and she came to him, saying, 'Get justice for me from my adversary.' 4 And he would not for a while; but afterward he said within himself, 'Though I do not fear God nor regard man, 5 [a]yet because this widow troubles me I will avenge her, lest by her continual coming she weary me.'"

6 Then the Lord said, "Hear what the unjust judge said. 7 And [a]shall God not avenge His own elect who cry out day and night to Him, though He bears long with them? 8 I tell you [a]that He will avenge them speedily. Nevertheless, when the Son of Man comes, will He really find faith on the earth?"

### *THE PARABLE OF THE PHARISEE AND THE TAX COLLECTOR*

9 Also He spoke this parable to some [a]who trusted in themselves that they were righteous, and despised others: 10 "Two men went up to the temple to pray, one a Pharisee and the other a tax collector. 11 The Pharisee [a]stood and prayed thus with himself, [b]'God, I thank You that I am not like other men—extortioners, unjust, adulterers, or even as this tax collector. 12 I fast twice a week; I give tithes of all that I possess.' 13 And the tax collector, standing afar off, would not so much as raise *his* eyes to heaven, but beat his breast, saying, 'God, be merciful to me a sinner!' 14 I tell you, this man went down to his house justified *rather* than the other; [a]for everyone who exalts himself will be humbled, and he who humbles himself will be exalted."

### *JESUS BLESSES LITTLE CHILDREN*

*(Matt. 19:13–15; Mark 10:13–16)*

15 [a]Then they also brought infants to Him that He might touch them; but when the disciples saw *it,* they rebuked them. 16 But Jesus called them to *Him* and said, "Let the little children come to Me, and do not forbid them; for [a]of such is the kingdom of God. 17 [a]Assuredly, I say to you, whoever does not receive the kingdom of God as a little child will by no means enter it."

### *JESUS COUNSELS THE RICH YOUNG RULER*

*(Matt. 19:16–22; Mark 10:17–22)*

18 [a]Now a certain ruler asked Him, saying, "Good Teacher, what shall I do to inherit eternal life?"

19 So Jesus said to him, "Why do you call Me good? No one *is* good but [a]One, *that is,* God. 20 You know the commandments: [a]'Do not commit adultery,' 'Do not murder,' 'Do not steal,' 'Do not bear false witness,' [b]'Honor your father and your mother.'"[1]

**17:19** [a] Matt. 9:22; Mark 5:34; 10:52; Luke 7:50; 8:48; 18:42 **17:21** [a] Luke 17:23 [b] [Rom. 14:17] [1] NU-Text reverses *here* and *there.* **17:22** [a] Matt. 9:15; Mark 2:20; Luke 5:35; [John 17:12] **17:23** [a] Matt. 24:23; Mark 13:21; [Luke 21:8] [1] NU-Text reverses *here* and *there.* **17:24** [a] Matt. 24:27 **17:25** [a] Mark 8:31; 9:31; 10:33 [b] Luke 9:22 **17:26** [a] Matt. 24:37–39 [b] [Gen. 6:5–7] [c] [Gen. 6:8–13] [d] 1 Pet. 3:20 **17:27** [a] Gen. 7:1–16 [b] Gen. 7:19–23 **17:28** [a] Gen. 19 **17:29** [a] Gen. 19:16, 24, 29 **17:30** [a] [2 Thess. 1:7] **17:31** [a] Mark 13:15 **17:32** [a] Gen. 19:26 **17:33** [a] Matt. 10:39; 16:25 **17:34** [a] [1 Thess. 4:17] **17:35** [a] Matt. 24:40, 41 **17:36** [1] NU-Text and M-Text omit verse 36. **17:37** [a] Matt. 24:28 **18:1** [a] Luke 11:5–10 **18:5** [a] Luke 11:8 **18:7** [a] Rev. 6:10 **18:8** [a] Heb. 10:37 **18:9** [a] Luke 10:29; 16:15 **18:11** [a] Ps. 135:2 [b] Is. 1:15; 58:2 **18:14** [a] Luke 14:11 **18:15** [a] Mark 10:13–16 **18:16** [a] 1 Pet. 2:2 **18:17** [a] Mark 10:15 **18:18** [a] Matt. 19:16–29 **18:19** [a] Ps. 86:5; 119:68 **18:20** [a] Ex. 20:12–16; Deut. 5:16–20 [b] Eph. 6:2; Col. 3:20 [1] Exodus 20:12–16; Deuteronomy 5:16–20

21 And he said, "All [a]these things I have kept
from my youth."
22 So when Jesus heard these things, He said
to him, "You still lack one thing. [a]Sell all that you
have and distribute to the poor, and you will
have treasure in heaven; and come, follow Me."
23 But when he heard this, he became very
sorrowful, for he was very rich.

### *WITH GOD ALL THINGS ARE POSSIBLE*

*(Matt. 19:23–30; Mark 10:23–31)*

24 And when Jesus saw that he became very
sorrowful, He said, [a]"How hard it is for those who
have riches to enter the kingdom of God! 25 For it is
easier for a camel to go through the eye of a needle
than for a rich man to enter the kingdom of God."
26 And those who heard it said, "Who then
can be saved?"
27 But He said, [a]"The things which are impos-
sible with men are possible with God."
28 [a]Then Peter said, "See, we have left all[1]
and followed You."
29 So He said to them, "Assuredly, I say to you,
[a]there is no one who has left house or parents
or brothers or wife or children, for the sake of
the kingdom of God, 30 [a]who shall not receive
many times more in this present time, and in
the age to come eternal life."

### *JESUS A THIRD TIME PREDICTS HIS DEATH AND RESURRECTION*

*(Matt. 20:17–19; Mark 10:32–34)*

31 [a]Then He took the twelve aside and said
to them, "Behold, we are going up to Jerusalem,
and all things [b]that are written by the prophets
concerning the Son of Man will be accomplished.
32 For [a]He will be delivered to the Gentiles and
will be mocked and insulted and spit upon.
33 They will scourge *Him* and kill Him. And the
third day He will rise again."
34 [a]But they understood none of these things;
this saying was hidden from them, and they did
not know the things which were spoken.

### *A BLIND MAN RECEIVES HIS SIGHT*

*(Matt. 20:29–34; Mark 10:46–52)*

35 [a]Then it happened, as He was coming near
Jericho, that a certain blind man sat by the road
begging. 36 And hearing a multitude passing by, he
asked what it meant. 37 So they told him that Jesus
of Nazareth was passing by. 38 And he cried out,
saying, "Jesus, [a]Son of David, have mercy on me!"
39 Then those who went before warned him
that he should be quiet; but he cried out all the
more, "Son of David, have mercy on me!"
40 So Jesus stood still and commanded him
to be brought to Him. And when he had come
near, He asked him, 41 saying, "What do you want
Me to do for you?"
He said, "Lord, that I may receive my sight."
42 Then Jesus said to him, "Receive your
sight; [a]your faith has made you well." 43 And
immediately he received his sight, and followed
Him, [a]glorifying God. And all the people, when
they saw *it,* gave praise to God.

### *JESUS COMES TO ZACCHAEUS' HOUSE*

19 Then *Jesus* entered and passed through
[a]Jericho. 2 Now behold, *there was* a man
named Zacchaeus who was a chief tax collector,
and he was rich. 3 And he sought to [a]see who
Jesus was, but could not because of the crowd,
for he was of short stature. 4 So he ran ahead
and climbed up into a sycamore tree to see Him,
for He was going to pass that *way.* 5 And when
Jesus came to the place, He looked up and saw

**18:21** [a] Phil. 3:6 **18:22** [a] Matt. 6:19, 20; 19:21 **18:24** [a] Prov. 11:28; Matt. 19:23; Mark 10:23 **18:27** [a] Job 42:2; Jer. 32:17; Zech. 8:6; Matt. 19:26; Luke 1:37 **18:28** [a] Matt. 19:27 [1] NU-Text reads *our own.* **18:29** [a] Deut. 33:9 **18:30** [a] Job 42:10 **18:31** [a] Matt. 16:21; 17:22; 20:17; Mark 10:32; Luke 9:51 [b] Ps. 22; [Is. 53] **18:32** [a] Matt. 26:67; 27:2, 29, 41; Mark 14:65; 15:1, 19, 20, 31; Luke 23:1; John 18:28; Acts 3:13 **18:34** [a] Mark 9:32; Luke 2:50; 9:45; [John 10:6; 12:16] **18:35** [a] Matt. 20:29–34; Mark 10:46–52 **18:38** [a] Matt. 9:27 **18:42** [a] Luke 17:19 **18:43** [a] Luke 5:26; Acts 4:21; 11:18 **19:1** [a] Josh. 6:26; 1 Kin. 16:34 **19:3** [a] John 12:21

LIVE THE TRUTH

## SEEKING TRUE SUCCESS

**19:1–10** God defines success much differently than the world does. Worldly success is about building your name, gaining popularity, or accruing possessions. People often name those with the most fame or riches as successes. That's not how God sees success, though. There's nothing inherently wrong with fame and possessions, but they aren't lasting, and they'll never lead to peace, joy, and purpose.

Zacchaeus offers an illustration of true success. From the world's perspective, he was quite successful. He was wealthy and prominent. However, all that fell by the wayside when he met Jesus. In that moment, nothing mattered more than Jesus, which is why he joyfully gave away most of his possessions. Zacchaeus understood in that moment that God's kingdom mattered far more than any personal kingdom he could build. Building God's kingdom and living for Him is the only way to have everlasting success. Everything in this world will pass away, but God's kingdom lasts forever. It's only when you serve God and love others that you will experience real success.

him,[1] and said to him, "Zacchaeus, make haste and come down, for today I must stay at your house." 6 So he made haste and came down, and received Him joyfully. 7 But when they saw *it,* they all complained, saying, [a]"He has gone to be a guest with a man who is a sinner."

8 Then Zacchaeus stood and said to the Lord, "Look, Lord, I give half of my goods to the [a]poor; and if I have taken anything from anyone by [b]false accusation, [c]I restore fourfold."

9 And Jesus said to him, "Today salvation has come to this house, because [a]he also is [b]a son of Abraham; 10 [a]for the Son of Man has come to seek and to save that which was lost."

### THE PARABLE OF THE MINAS

*(Matt. 25:14–30)*

11 Now as they heard these things, He spoke another parable, because He was near Jerusalem and because [a]they thought the kingdom of God would appear immediately. 12 [a]Therefore He said: "A certain nobleman went into a far country to receive for himself a kingdom and to return. 13 So he called ten of his servants, delivered to them ten minas,[1] and said to them, 'Do business till I come.' 14 [a]But his citizens hated him, and sent a delegation after him, saying, 'We will not have this *man* to reign over us.'

> **SEEING JESUS IN THE SCRIPTURE**
>
> **19:14** Jesus knew His people would reject Him, but it still caused Him sorrow. He knew what they didn't know (see Is. 53:3).

15 "And so it was that when he returned, having received the kingdom, he then commanded these servants, to whom he had given the money, to be called to him, that he might know how much every man had gained by trading. 16 Then came the first, saying, 'Master, your mina has earned ten minas.' 17 And he said to him, [a]'Well *done,* good servant; because you were [b]faithful in a very little, have authority over ten cities.' 18 And the second came, saying, 'Master, your mina has earned five minas.' 19 Likewise he said to him, 'You also be over five cities.'

20 "Then another came, saying, 'Master, here is your mina, which I have kept put away in a handkerchief. 21 [a]For I feared you, because you are an austere man. You collect what you did not deposit, and reap what you did not sow.' 22 And he said to him, [a]'Out of your own mouth I will judge you, *you* wicked servant. [b]You knew that I was an austere man, collecting what I did not deposit and reaping what I did not sow. 23 Why then did you not put my money in the bank, that at my coming I might have collected it with interest?'

24 "And he said to those who stood by, 'Take the mina from him, and give *it* to him who has ten minas.' 25 (But they said to him, 'Master, he has ten minas.') 26 'For I say to you, [a]that to everyone who has will be given; and from him who does not have, even what he has will be taken away from him. 27 But bring here those enemies of mine, who did not want me to reign over them, and slay *them* before me.' "

### THE TRIUMPHAL ENTRY

*(Matt. 21:1–11; Mark 11:1–11; John 12:12–19)*

28 When He had said this, [a]He went on ahead, going up to Jerusalem. 29 [a]And it came to pass, when He drew near to Bethphage[1] and [b]Bethany, at the mountain called [c]Olivet, *that* He sent two of His disciples, 30 saying, "Go into the village opposite *you,* where as you enter you will find a colt tied, on which no one has ever sat. Loose it and bring *it here.* 31 And if anyone asks you, 'Why are you loosing *it?*' thus you shall say to him, 'Because the Lord has need of it.' "

32 So those who were sent went their way and found *it* just [a]as He had said to them. 33 But as they were loosing the colt, the owners of it said to them, "Why are you loosing the colt?"

34 And they said, "The Lord has need of him." 35 Then they brought him to Jesus. [a]And they threw their own clothes on the colt, and they set Jesus on him. 36 And as He went, *many* spread their clothes on the road.

37 Then, as He was now drawing near the descent of the Mount of Olives, the whole multitude of the disciples began to [a]rejoice and praise God with a loud voice for all the mighty works they had seen, 38 saying:

[a]" 'Blessed *is* the King who comes in the
name of the LORD!'[1]
[b]Peace in heaven and glory in the highest!"

39 And some of the Pharisees called to Him from the crowd, "Teacher, rebuke Your disciples."

40 But He answered and said to them, "I tell you that if these should keep silent, [a]the stones would immediately cry out."

### JESUS WEEPS OVER JERUSALEM

41 Now as He drew near, He saw the city and [a]wept over it, 42 saying, "If you had known, even you, especially in this [a]your day, the things *that* [b]*make* for your [c]peace! But now they are hidden

**19:5** [1] NU-Text omits *and saw him.* **19:7** [a] Matt. 9:11; Luke 5:30; 15:2 **19:8** [a] [Ps. 41:1] [b] Luke 3:14 [c] Ex. 22:1; Lev. 6:5; Num. 5:7; 1 Sam. 12:3; 2 Sam. 12:6 **19:9** [a] Luke 3:8; 13:16; [Rom. 4:16; Gal. 3:7] [b] [Luke 13:16] **19:10** [a] Matt. 18:11; [Luke 5:32; Rom. 5:8] **19:11** [a] Acts 1:6 **19:12** [a] Matt. 25:14–30; Mark 13:34 **19:13** [1] The *mina* (Greek *mna,* Hebrew *minah*) was worth about three months' salary. **19:14** [a] [John 1:11] **19:17** [a] Matt. 25:21, 23 [b] Luke 16:10 **19:21** [a] Matt. 25:24 **19:22** [a] 2 Sam. 1:16; Job 15:6; [Matt. 12:37] [b] Matt. 25:26 **19:26** [a] Matt. 13:12; 25:29; Mark 4:25; Luke 8:18 **19:28** [a] Mark 10:32 **19:29** [a] Matt. 21:1; Mark 11:1 [b] Matt. 26:6; John 12:1 [c] John 8:1; Acts 1:12 [1] M-Text reads *Bethsphage.* **19:32** [a] Luke 22:13 **19:35** [a] 2 Kin. 9:13; Matt. 21:7; Mark 11:7 **19:37** [a] Luke 13:17; 18:43 **19:38** [a] Ps. 118:26; Luke 13:35 [b] Luke 2:14; [Eph. 2:14] [1] Psalm 118:26 **19:40** [a] Hab. 2:11 **19:41** [a] Is. 53:3; John 11:35 **19:42** [a] Ps. 95:7, 8; Heb. 3:13 [b] [Luke 1:77–79; Acts 10:36] [c] [Rom. 5:1]

from your eyes. 43 For days will come upon you
when your enemies will [a]build an embankment
around you, surround you and close you in on
every side, 44 [a]and level you, and your children
within you, to the ground; and [b]they will not
leave in you one stone upon another, [c]because
you did not know the time of your visitation."

> **19:43** This passage predicts the total destruction of Jerusalem—the kind of destruction that occurred in AD 70. After the Jews tried to rebel against Rome, the empire retaliated by sending its army, led by a general named Titus, to attack Jerusalem. When the Roman army was done, the temple had been burned to the ground, its sacred furnishings had been taken back to Rome, and the city of Jerusalem had been reduced to rubble. The Jews were no longer permitted any kind of self-rule.

### JESUS CLEANSES THE TEMPLE
*(Matt. 21:12–17; Mark 11:15–19; John 2:12–25)*

45 [a]Then He went into the temple and began
to drive out those who bought and sold in it,[1]
46 saying to them, "It is written, [a]'My house is[1] a
house of prayer,'[2] but you have made it a [b]'den
of thieves.'"[3]
47 And He [a]was teaching daily in the temple.
But [b]the chief priests, the scribes, and the leaders
of the people sought to destroy Him, 48 and were
unable to do anything; for all the people were
very attentive to [a]hear Him.

### JESUS' AUTHORITY QUESTIONED
*(Matt. 21:23–27; Mark 11:27–33)*

**20** Now [a]it happened on one of those days,
as He taught the people in the temple and
preached the gospel, *that* the chief priests and
the scribes, together with the elders, confronted
*Him* 2 and spoke to Him, saying, "Tell us, [a]by what
authority are You doing these things? Or who is
he who gave You this authority?"
3 But He answered and said to them, "I also
will ask you one thing, and answer Me: 4 The
[a]baptism of John—was it from heaven or from
men?"
5 And they reasoned among themselves,
saying, "If we say, 'From heaven,' He will say,
'Why then[1] did you not believe him?' 6 But if we
say, 'From men,' all the people will stone us, [a]for
they are persuaded that John was a prophet."
7 So they answered that they did not know where
*it was* from.
8 And Jesus said to them, "Neither will I tell
you by what authority I do these things."

### THE PARABLE OF THE WICKED VINEDRESSERS
*(Matt. 21:33–46; Mark 12:1–12)*

9 Then He began to tell the people this para-
ble: [a]"A certain man planted a vineyard, leased
it to vinedressers, and went into a far country
for a long time. 10 Now at vintage-time he [a]sent
a servant to the vinedressers, that they might
give him some of the fruit of the vineyard. But
the vinedressers beat him and sent *him* away
empty-handed. 11 Again he sent another servant;
and they beat him also, treated *him* shamefully,
and sent *him* away empty-handed. 12 And again
he sent a third; and they wounded him also and
cast *him* out.
13 "Then the owner of the vineyard said,
'What shall I do? I will send my beloved son.
Probably they will respect *him* when they see
him.' 14 But when the vinedressers saw him, they
reasoned among themselves, saying, 'This is the
[a]heir. Come, [b]let us kill him, that the inheritance
may be [c]ours.' 15 So they cast him out of the
vineyard and [a]killed *him*. Therefore what will
the owner of the vineyard do to them? 16 He will
come and destroy those vinedressers and give
the vineyard to [a]others."
And when they heard *it* they said, "Certainly
not!"
17 Then He looked at them and said, "What
then is this that is written:

> [a]'The stone which the builders rejected
> Has become the chief cornerstone'?[1]

> **SEEING JESUS IN THE SCRIPTURE**
>
> **20:17** Israel's rejection of Jesus was part of God's plan for Him being the chief cornerstone upon which the church is built (see Ps. 118:22-23).

18 Whoever falls on that stone will be [a]broken;
but [b]on whomever it falls, it will grind him to
powder."
19 And the chief priests and the scribes that
very hour sought to lay hands on Him, but they
feared the people[1]—for they knew He had spo-
ken this parable against them.

**19:43** [a] Is. 29:3, 4; Jer. 6:3, 6; Luke 21:20 **19:44** [a] 1 Kin. 9:7, 8; Mic. 3:12 [b] Matt. 24:2; Mark 13:2; Luke 21:6 [c] [Dan. 9:24; Luke 1:68, 78; 1 Pet. 2:12] **19:45** [a] Mal. 3:1; Matt. 21:12, 13; Mark 11:11, 15–17; John 2:13–16 [1] NU-Text reads *those who were selling.* **19:46** [a] Is. 56:7 [b] Jer. 7:11 [1] NU-Text reads *shall be.* [2] Isaiah 56:7 [3] Jeremiah 7:11 **19:47** [a] Luke 21:37; 22:53 [b] Mark 11:18; Luke 20:19; John 7:19; 8:37 **19:48** [a] Luke 21:38 **20:1** [a] Matt. 21:23–27; Mark 11:27–33 **20:2** [a] Acts 4:7; 7:27 **20:4** [a] John 1:26, 31 **20:5** [1] NU-Text and M-Text omit *then.* **20:6** [a] Matt. 14:5; 21:26; Mark 6:20; Luke 7:24–30 **20:9** [a] Ps. 80:8; Matt. 21:33–46; Mark 12:1–12 **20:10** [a] 2 Kin. 17:13, 14; 2 Chr. 36:15, 16; [Acts 7:52; 1 Thess. 2:15] **20:14** [a] [Heb. 1:1–3] [b] Matt. 27:21–23 [c] John 11:47, 48 **20:15** [a] Luke 23:33; Acts 2:22, 23; 3:15 **20:16** [a] [John 1:11–13]; Rom. 11:1, 11; 1 Cor. 6:15; Gal. 2:17; 3:21; 6:14 **20:17** [a] Ps. 118:22; Matt. 21:42; 1 Pet. 2:7, 8 [1] Psalm 118:22 **20:18** [a] Is. 8:14, 15 [b] [Dan. 2:34, 35, 44, 45]; Matt. 21:44 **20:19** [1] M-Text reads *but they were afraid.*

### *THE PHARISEES: IS IT LAWFUL TO PAY TAXES TO CAESAR?*

*(Matt. 22:15–22; Mark 12:13–17)*

20 [a]So they watched *Him,* and sent spies who pretended to be righteous, that they might seize on His words, in order to deliver Him to the power and the authority of the governor.

21 Then they asked Him, saying, [a]"Teacher, we know that You say and teach rightly, and You do not show personal favoritism, but teach the way of God in truth: 22 Is it lawful for us to pay taxes to Caesar or not?"

23 But He perceived their craftiness, and said to them, "Why do you test Me?[1] 24 Show Me a denarius. Whose image and inscription does it have?"

They answered and said, "Caesar's."

25 And He said to them, [a]"Render therefore to Caesar the things that are Caesar's, and to God the things that are God's."

26 But they could not catch Him in His words in the presence of the people. And they marveled at His answer and kept silent.

### *THE SADDUCEES: WHAT ABOUT THE RESURRECTION?*

*(Matt. 22:23–33; Mark 12:18–27)*

27 [a]Then some of the Sadducees, [b]who deny that there is a resurrection, came to *Him* and asked Him, 28 saying: "Teacher, Moses wrote to us *that* if a man's brother dies, having a wife, and he dies without children, his brother should take his wife and raise up offspring for his brother. 29 Now there were seven brothers. And the first took a wife, and died without children. 30 And the second[1] took her as wife, and he died childless. 31 Then the third took her, and in like manner the seven also; and they left no children,[1] and died. 32 Last of all the woman died also. 33 Therefore, in the resurrection, whose wife does she become? For all seven had her as wife."

34 Jesus answered and said to them, "The sons of this age marry and are given in marriage. 35 But those who are [a]counted worthy to attain that age, and the resurrection from the dead, neither marry nor are given in marriage; 36 nor can they die anymore, for [a]they are equal to the angels and are sons of God, [b]being sons of the resurrection. 37 But even Moses showed in the *burning* bush *passage* that the dead are raised, when he called the Lord [a]'the God of Abraham, the God of Isaac, and the God of Jacob.'[1] 38 For He is not the God of the dead but of the living, for [a]all live to Him."

39 Then some of the scribes answered and said, "Teacher, You have spoken well." 40 But after that they dared not question Him anymore.

### *JESUS: HOW CAN DAVID CALL HIS DESCENDANT "LORD"?*

*(Matt. 22:41–46; Mark 12:35–37)*

41 And He said to them, [a]"How can they say that the Christ is the Son of David? 42 Now David himself said in the Book of Psalms:

[a]'The LORD said to my Lord,
"Sit at My right hand,
43 Till I make Your enemies Your footstool." '[1]

44 Therefore David calls Him 'Lord'; [a]how is He then his Son?"

### *BEWARE OF THE SCRIBES*

*(Matt. 23:1–7; Mark 12:38–40)*

45 [a]Then, in the hearing of all the people, He said to His disciples, 46 [a]"Beware of the scribes, who desire to go around in long robes, [b]love greetings in the marketplaces, the best seats in the synagogues, and the best places at feasts, 47 [a]who devour widows' houses, and for a [b]pretense make long prayers. These will receive greater condemnation."

### *THE WIDOW'S TWO MITES*

*(Mark 12:41–44)*

**21** And He looked up [a]and saw the rich putting their gifts into the treasury, 2 and He saw also a certain [a]poor widow putting in two [b]mites. 3 So He said, "Truly I say to you [a]that this poor widow has put in more than all; 4 for all these out of their abundance have put in offerings for God,[1] but she out of her poverty put in [a]all the livelihood that she had."

### *JESUS PREDICTS THE DESTRUCTION OF THE TEMPLE*

*(Matt. 24:1, 2; Mark 13:1, 2)*

5 [a]Then, as some spoke of the temple, how it was adorned with beautiful stones and donations, He said, 6 "These things which you see—the days will come in which [a]not *one* stone shall be left upon another that shall not be thrown down."

### *THE SIGNS OF THE TIMES AND THE END OF THE AGE*

*(Matt. 24:3–14; Mark 13:3–13)*

7 So they asked Him, saying, "Teacher, but when will these things be? And what sign *will there be* when these things are about to take place?"

8 And He said: [a]"Take heed that you not be deceived. For many will come in My name, saying, 'I am *He,*' and, 'The time has drawn near.' Therefore[1] do not go after them. 9 But when

**20:20** [a] Matt. 22:15 **20:21** [a] Matt. 22:16; Mark 12:14 **20:23** [1] NU-Text omits *Why do you test Me?* **20:25** [a] Matt. 17:24–27; Rom. 13:7; [1 Pet. 2:13–17] **20:27** [a] Matt. 22:23–33; Mark 12:18–27 [b] Acts 23:6, 8 **20:30** [1] NU-Text ends verse 30 here. **20:31** [1] NU-Text and M-Text read *the seven also left no children.* **20:35** [a] Phil. 3:11 **20:36** [a] [1 Cor. 15:42, 49, 52; 1 John 3:2] [b] Rom. 8:23 **20:37** [a] Ex. 3:1–6, 15 [1] Exodus 3:6, 15 **20:38** [a] [Rom. 6:10, 11; 14:8, 9] **20:41** [a] Matt. 22:41–46 **20:42** [a] Ps. 110:1 **20:43** [1] Psalm 110:1 **20:44** [a] Rom. 1:3; 9:4, 5 **20:45** [a] Matt. 23:1–7 **20:46** [a] Matt. 23:5 [b] Luke 11:43; 14:7 **20:47** [a] Matt. 23:14 [b] [Matt. 6:5, 6] **21:1** [a] Mark 12:41–44 **21:2** [a] [2 Cor. 6:10] [b] Mark 12:42 **21:3** [a] [2 Cor. 8:12] **21:4** [a] [2 Cor. 8:12] [1] NU-Text omits *for God.* **21:5** [a] Mark 13:1 **21:6** [a] Luke 19:41–44 **21:8** [a] Eph. 5:6 [1] NU-Text omits *Therefore.*

you hear of [a]wars and commotions, do not be terrified; for these things must come to pass first, but the end *will* not *come* immediately."

10 [a]Then He said to them, "Nation will rise against nation, and kingdom against kingdom. 11 And there will be great [a]earthquakes in various places, and famines and pestilences; and there will be fearful sights and great signs from heaven. 12 [a]But before all these things, they will lay their hands on you and persecute *you,* delivering *you* up to the synagogues and [b]prisons. [c]You will be brought before kings and rulers [d]for My name's sake. 13 But [a]it will turn out for you as an occasion for testimony. 14 [a]Therefore settle *it* in your hearts not to meditate beforehand on what you will answer; 15 for I will give you a mouth and wisdom [a]which all your adversaries will not be able to contradict or resist. 16 [a]You will be betrayed even by parents and brothers, relatives and friends; and they will put [b]*some* of you to death. 17 And [a]you will be hated by all for My name's sake. 18 [a]But not a hair of your head shall be lost. 19 By your patience possess your souls.

### THE DESTRUCTION OF JERUSALEM

*(Matt. 24:15–28; Mark 13:14–23)*

20 [a]"But when you see Jerusalem surrounded by armies, then know that its desolation is near. 21 Then let those who are in Judea flee to the mountains, let those who are in the midst of her depart, and let not those who are in the country enter her. 22 For these are the days of vengeance, that [a]all things which are written may be fulfilled. 23 [a]But woe to those who are pregnant and to those who are nursing babies in those days! For there will be great distress in the land and wrath upon this people. 24 And they will fall by the edge of the sword, and be led away captive into all nations. And Jerusalem will be trampled by Gentiles [a]until the times of the Gentiles are fulfilled.

### THE COMING OF THE SON OF MAN

*(Matt. 24:29–31; Mark 13:24–27)*

25 [a]"And there will be signs in the sun, in the moon, and in the stars; and on the earth distress of nations, with perplexity, the sea and the waves roaring; 26 men's hearts failing them from fear and the expectation of those things which are coming on the earth, [a]for the powers of the heavens will be shaken. 27 Then they will see the Son of Man [a]coming in a cloud with power and great glory. 28 Now when these things begin to happen, look up and lift up your heads, because [a]your redemption draws near."

### THE PARABLE OF THE FIG TREE

*(Matt. 24:32–35; Mark 13:28–31)*

29 [a]Then He spoke to them a parable: "Look at the fig tree, and all the trees. 30 When they are already budding, you see and know for yourselves that summer is now near. 31 So you also, when you see these things happening, know that the kingdom of God is near. 32 Assuredly, I say to you, this generation will by no means pass away till all things take place. 33 [a]Heaven and earth will pass away, but My [b]words will by no means pass away.

### THE IMPORTANCE OF WATCHING

*(Matt. 24:36–44; Mark 13:32–37)*

34 "But [a]take heed to yourselves, lest your hearts be weighed down with carousing, drunkenness, and [b]cares of this life, and that Day come on you unexpectedly. 35 For [a]it will come as a snare on all those who dwell on the face of the whole earth. 36 [a]Watch therefore, and [b]pray always that you may be counted [c]worthy[1] to escape all these things that will come to pass, and [d]to stand before the Son of Man."

37 [a]And in the daytime He was teaching in the temple, but [b]at night He went out and stayed on the mountain called Olivet. 38 Then early in the morning all the people came to Him in the temple to hear Him.

### THE PLOT TO KILL JESUS

*(Matt. 26:1–5, 14–16; Mark 14:1, 2, 10, 11; John 11:45–53)*

22 Now [a]the Feast of Unleavened Bread drew near, which is called Passover. 2 And [a]the chief priests and the scribes sought how they might kill Him, for they feared the people.

> **22:1 Passover** was one of the most important holidays on the Jewish calendar. It was set aside as a time for recalling how God had rescued the Israelites from slavery in Egypt. To celebrate, the Jewish people ate a meal like the one their ancestors had eaten when they prepared to leave Egypt.

3 [a]Then Satan entered Judas, surnamed Iscariot, who was numbered among the [b]twelve. 4 So he went his way and conferred with the chief priests and captains, how he might betray Him to them. 5 And they were glad, and [a]agreed to give him money. 6 So he promised and sought opportunity to [a]betray Him to them in the absence of the multitude.

**21:9** [a] Rev. 6:4 **21:10** [a] Matt. 24:7 **21:11** [a] Rev. 6:12 **21:12** [a] [Rev. 2:10] [b] Acts 4:3; 5:18; 12:4; 16:24 [c] Acts 25:23 [d] 1 Pet. 2:13 **21:13** [a] [Phil. 1:12–14, 28] **21:14** [a] Luke 12:11 **21:15** [a] Acts 6:10 **21:16** [a] Mic. 7:6 [b] Acts 7:59; 12:2 **21:17** [a] Matt. 10:22 **21:18** [a] Matt. 10:30 **21:20** [a] Mark 13:14 **21:22** [a] [Dan. 9:24–27] **21:23** [a] Matt. 24:19 **21:24** [a] [Dan. 9:27; 12:7] **21:25** [a] [2 Pet. 3:10–12] **21:26** [a] Matt. 24:29 **21:27** [a] Rev. 1:7; 14:14 **21:28** [a] [Rom. 8:19, 23] **21:29** [a] Mark 13:28 **21:33** [a] Matt. 24:35 [b] Is. 40:8 **21:34** [a] 1 Thess. 5:6 [b] Luke 8:14 **21:35** [a] Rev. 3:3; 16:15 **21:36** [a] Matt. 24:42; 25:13 [b] Luke 18:1 [c] Luke 20:35 [d] [Eph. 6:13] [1] NU-Text reads *may have strength.* **21:37** [a] John 8:1, 2 [b] Luke 22:39 **22:1** [a] Matt. 26:2–5 **22:2** [a] John 11:47 **22:3** [a] Mark 14:10, 11 [b] Matt. 10:2–4 **22:5** [a] Zech. 11:12 **22:6** [a] Ps. 41:9

### *JESUS AND HIS DISCIPLES PREPARE THE PASSOVER*

7 [a]Then came the Day of Unleavened Bread, when the Passover must be killed. 8 And He sent Peter and John, saying, "Go and prepare the Passover for us, that we may eat."

9 So they said to Him, "Where do You want us to prepare?"

10 And He said to them, "Behold, when you have entered the city, a man will meet you carrying a pitcher of water; follow him into the house which he enters. 11 Then you shall say to the master of the house, 'The Teacher says to you, "Where is the guest room where I may eat the Passover with My disciples?"' 12 Then he will show you a large, furnished upper room; there make ready."

13 So they went and [a]found it just as He had said to them, and they prepared the Passover.

### *JESUS INSTITUTES THE LORD'S SUPPER*

14 [a]When the hour had come, He sat down, and the twelve[1] apostles with Him. 15 Then He said to them, "With *fervent* desire I have desired to eat this Passover with you before I suffer; 16 for I say to you, I will no longer eat of it [a]until it is fulfilled in the kingdom of God."

17 Then He took the cup, and gave thanks, and said, "Take this and divide *it* among yourselves; 18 for [a]I say to you,[1] I will not drink of the fruit of the vine until the kingdom of God comes."

19 [a]And He took bread, gave thanks and broke *it,* and gave *it* to them, saying, "This is My [b]body which is given for you; [c]do this in remembrance of Me."

20 Likewise He also *took* the cup after supper, saying, [a]"This cup *is* the new covenant in My blood, which is shed for you. 21 [a]But behold, the hand of My betrayer *is* with Me on the table. 22 [a]And truly the Son of Man goes [b]as it has been determined, but woe to that man by whom He is betrayed!"

23 [a]Then they began to question among themselves, which of them it was who would do this thing.

### *THE DISCIPLES ARGUE ABOUT GREATNESS*

24 [a]Now there was also a dispute among them, as to which of them should be considered the greatest. 25 [a]And He said to them, "The kings of the Gentiles exercise lordship over them, and those who exercise authority over them are called 'benefactors.' 26 [a]But not so *among* you; on the contrary, [b]he who is greatest among you, let him be as the younger, and he who governs as he who serves. 27 [a]For who *is* greater, he who sits at the table, or he who serves? *Is* it not he who sits at the table? Yet [b]I am among you as the One who serves.

28 "But you are those who have continued with Me in [a]My trials. 29 And [a]I bestow upon you a kingdom, just as My Father bestowed *one* upon Me, 30 that [a]you may eat and drink at My table in My kingdom, [b]and sit on thrones judging the twelve tribes of Israel."

### *JESUS PREDICTS PETER'S DENIAL*

*(Matt. 26:31–35; Mark 14:27–31; John 13:36–38)*

31 And the Lord said,[1] "Simon, Simon! Indeed, [a]Satan has asked for you, that he may [b]sift *you* as wheat. 32 But [a]I have prayed for you, that your faith should not fail; and when you have returned to *Me,* [b]strengthen your brethren."

33 But he said to Him, "Lord, I am ready to go with You, both to prison and to death."

34 [a]Then He said, "I tell you, Peter, the rooster shall not crow this day before you will deny three times that you know Me."

### *SUPPLIES FOR THE ROAD*

35 [a]And He said to them, "When I sent you without money bag, knapsack, and sandals, did you lack anything?"

So they said, "Nothing."

36 Then He said to them, "But now, he who has a money bag, let him take *it,* and likewise a knapsack; and he who has no sword, let him sell his garment and buy one. 37 For I say to you that this which is written must still be accomplished in Me: [a]'And He was numbered with the transgressors.'[1] For the things concerning Me have an end."

> **SEEING JESUS IN THE SCRIPTURE**
>
> **22:37** Jesus was identified as a sinner on the cross. This identification with us made our salvation possible (see Is. 53:12).

38 So they said, "Lord, look, here *are* two swords."

And He said to them, "It is enough."

### *THE PRAYER IN THE GARDEN*

*(Matt. 26:36–46; Mark 14:32–42; John 18:1)*

39 [a]Coming out, [b]He went to the Mount of Olives, as He was accustomed, and His disciples also followed Him. 40 [a]When He came to the place, He said to them, "Pray that you may not enter into temptation."

41 [a]And He was withdrawn from them about a stone's throw, and He knelt down and prayed, 42 saying, "Father, if it is Your will, take this cup away from Me; nevertheless [a]not My will, but

**22:7** [a] Matt. 26:17–19 **22:13** [a] Luke 19:32 **22:14** [a] Mark 14:17 [1] NU-Text omits *twelve.* **22:16** [a] [Rev. 19:9] **22:18** [a] Mark 14:25 [1] NU-Text adds *from now on.* **22:19** [a] Matt. 26:26 [b] [1 Pet. 2:24] [c] 1 Cor. 11:23–26 **22:20** [a] 1 Cor. 10:16 **22:21** [a] John 13:21, 26, 27 **22:22** [a] Matt. 26:24 [b] Acts 2:23 **22:23** [a] John 13:22, 25 **22:24** [a] Mark 9:34 **22:25** [a] Mark 10:42–45 **22:26** [a] [1 Pet. 5:3] [b] Luke 9:48 **22:27** [a] [Luke 12:37] [b] Phil. 2:7 **22:28** [a] [Heb. 2:18; 4:15] **22:29** [a] Matt. 24:47 **22:30** [a] [Matt. 8:11] [b] [Rev. 3:21] **22:31** [a] 1 Pet. 5:8 [b] Amos 9:9 [1] NU-Text omits *And the Lord said.* **22:32** [a] [John 17:9, 11, 15] [b] John 21:15–17 **22:34** [a] John 13:37, 38 **22:35** [a] Matt. 10:9 **22:37** [a] Is. 53:12 [1] Isaiah 53:12 **22:39** [a] John 18:1 [b] Luke 21:37 **22:40** [a] Mark 14:32–42 **22:41** [a] Matt. 26:39 **22:42** [a] John 4:34; 5:30; 6:38; 8:29

Yours, be done." 43 Then [a]an angel appeared to
Him from heaven, strengthening Him. 44 [a]And
being in agony, He prayed more earnestly. Then
His sweat became like great drops of blood
falling down to the ground.[1]
45 When He rose up from prayer, and had
come to His disciples, He found them sleeping
from sorrow. 46 Then He said to them, "Why [a]do
you sleep? Rise and [b]pray, lest you enter into
temptation."

### *BETRAYAL AND ARREST IN GETHSEMANE*

*(Matt. 26:47–56; Mark 14:43–52; John 18:1–11)*

47 And while He was still speaking, [a]behold, a
multitude; and he who was called [b]Judas, one of
the twelve, went before them and drew near to
Jesus to kiss Him. 48 But Jesus said to him, "Judas,
are you betraying the Son of Man with a [a]kiss?"
49 When those around Him saw what was
going to happen, they said to Him, "Lord, shall
we strike with the sword?" 50 And [a]one of them
struck the servant of the high priest and cut off
his right ear.
51 But Jesus answered and said, "Permit even
this." And He touched his ear and healed him.
52 [a]Then Jesus said to the chief priests, cap-
tains of the temple, and the elders who had come
to Him, "Have you come out, as against a [b]robber,
with swords and clubs? 53 When I was with you
daily in the [a]temple, you did not try to seize Me.
But this is your [b]hour, and the power of darkness."

### *PETER DENIES JESUS, AND WEEPS BITTERLY*

*(Matt. 26:69–75; Mark 14:66–72; John 18:13–18, 25–27)*

54 [a]Having arrested Him, they led *Him* and
brought Him into the high priest's house. [b]But
Peter followed at a distance. 55 [a]Now when they
had kindled a fire in the midst of the courtyard
and sat down together, Peter sat among them.
56 And a certain servant girl, seeing him as he
sat by the fire, looked intently at him and said,
"This man was also with Him."
57 But he denied Him,[1] saying, "Woman, I do
not know Him."
58 [a]And after a little while another saw him
and said, "You also are of them."
But Peter said, "Man, I am not!"
59 [a]Then after about an hour had passed, an-
other confidently affirmed, saying, "Surely this
*fellow* also was with Him, for he is a [b]Galilean."
60 But Peter said, "Man, I do not know what
you are saying!"
Immediately, while he was still speaking,
the rooster[1] crowed. 61 And the Lord turned and
looked at Peter. Then [a]Peter remembered the
word of the Lord, how He had said to him, [b]"Be-
fore the rooster crows,[1] you will deny Me three
times." 62 So Peter went out and wept bitterly.

### *JESUS MOCKED AND BEATEN*

*(Matt. 26:67, 68; Mark 14:65)*

63 [a]Now the men who held Jesus mocked
Him and [b]beat Him. 64 And having blindfolded
Him, they [a]struck Him on the face and asked
Him,[1] saying, "Prophesy! Who is the one who
struck You?" 65 And many other things they
blasphemously spoke against Him.

### *JESUS FACES THE SANHEDRIN*

*(Matt. 26:57–68; Mark 14:61–64; John 18:12–14, 19–24)*

66 [a]As soon as it was day, [b]the elders of the
people, both chief priests and scribes, came
together and led Him into their council, saying,
67 [a]"If You are the Christ, tell us."
But He said to them, "If I tell you, you will
[b]by no means believe. 68 And if I also ask *you*,
you will by no means answer Me or let *Me* go.[1]
69 [a]Hereafter the Son of Man will sit on the right
hand of the power of God."
70 Then they all said, "Are You then the Son
of God?"
So He said to them, [a]"You *rightly* say that
I am."
71 [a]And they said, "What further testimony
do we need? For we have heard it ourselves from
His own mouth."

### *JESUS HANDED OVER TO PONTIUS PILATE*

*(Matt. 27:1, 2, 11–14; Mark 15:1–5; John 18:28–38)*

23 Then [a]the whole multitude of them arose
and led Him to [b]Pilate. 2 And they began to
[a]accuse Him, saying, "We found this *fellow* [b]per-
verting the[1] nation, and [c]forbidding to pay taxes to
Caesar, saying [d]that He Himself is Christ, a King."
3 [a]Then Pilate asked Him, saying, "Are You
the King of the Jews?"
He answered him and said, "*It is as* you say."

> **SEEING JESUS IN THE SCRIPTURE**
>
> **23:2–3** The people of God rejected God as their king in the Old Testament and did the same with Jesus in the New Testament (see 1 Sam. 8:7).

4 So Pilate said to the chief priests and the
crowd, [a]"I find no fault in this Man."

**22:43** [a] Matt. 4:11 **22:44** [a] [Heb. 5:7] [1] NU-Text brackets verses 43 and 44 as not in the original text. **22:46** [a] Luke 9:32 [b] Luke 22:40 **22:47** [a] John 18:3–11 [b] Acts 1:16, 17 **22:48** [a] [Prov. 27:6] **22:50** [a] Matt. 26:51 **22:52** [a] Matt. 26:55 [b] Luke 23:32 **22:53** [a] Luke 19:47, 48 [b] [John 12:27] **22:54** [a] Matt. 26:57 [b] John 18:15 **22:55** [a] Mark 14:66–72 **22:57** [1] NU-Text reads *denied it.* **22:58** [a] John 18:25 **22:59** [a] Mark 14:70 [b] Acts 1:11; 2:7 **22:60** [1] NU-Text and M-Text read *a rooster.* **22:61** [a] Matt. 26:75 [b] John 13:38 [1] NU-Text adds *today.* **22:63** [a] Ps. 69:1, 4, 7–9 [b] Is. 50:6 **22:64** [a] Zech. 13:7 [1] NU-Text reads *And having blindfolded Him, they asked Him.* **22:66** [a] Matt. 27:1 [b] Acts 4:26 **22:67** [a] Matt. 26:63–66 [b] Luke 20:5–7 **22:68** [1] NU-Text omits *also* and *Me or let Me go.* **22:69** [a] Heb. 1:3; 8:1 **22:70** [a] Matt. 26:64; 27:11 **22:71** [a] Mark 14:63 **23:1** [a] John 18:28 [b] Luke 3:1; 13:1 **23:2** [a] Acts 24:2 [b] Acts 17:7 [c] Matt. 17:27 [d] John 19:12 [1] NU-Text reads *our.* **23:3** [a] 1 Tim. 6:13 **23:4** [a] [1 Pet. 2:22]

5 But they were the more fierce, saying, "He stirs up the people, teaching throughout all Judea, beginning from [a]Galilee to this place."

## JESUS FACES HEROD

6 When Pilate heard of Galilee,[1] he asked if the Man were a Galilean. 7 And as soon as he knew that He belonged to [a]Herod's jurisdiction, he sent Him to Herod, who was also in Jerusalem at that time. 8 Now when Herod saw Jesus, [a]he was exceedingly glad; for he had desired for a long *time* to see Him, because [b]he had heard many things about Him, and he hoped to see some miracle done by Him. 9 Then he questioned Him with many words, but He answered him [a]nothing. 10 And the chief priests and scribes stood and vehemently accused Him. 11 [a]Then Herod, with his men of war, treated Him with contempt and mocked *Him,* arrayed Him in a gorgeous robe, and sent Him back to Pilate. 12 That very day [a]Pilate and Herod became friends with each other, for previously they had been at enmity with each other.

## TAKING THE PLACE OF BARABBAS

*(Matt. 27:15–26; Mark 15:6–15; John 18:38—19:16)*

13 [a]Then Pilate, when he had called together the chief priests, the rulers, and the people, 14 said to them, [a]"You have brought this Man to me, as one who misleads the people. And indeed, [b]having examined *Him* in your presence, I have found no fault in this Man concerning those things of which you accuse Him; 15 no, neither did Herod, for I sent you back to him;[1] and indeed nothing deserving of death has been done by Him. 16 [a]I will therefore chastise Him and release *Him*" 17 [a](for it was necessary for him to release one to them at the feast).[1]

18 And [a]they all cried out at once, saying, "Away with this *Man,* and release to us Barabbas"— 19 who had been thrown into prison for a certain rebellion made in the city, and for murder.

20 Pilate, therefore, wishing to release Jesus, again called out to them. 21 But they shouted, saying, "Crucify *Him,* crucify Him!"

22 Then he said to them the third time, "Why, what evil has He done? I have found no reason for death in Him. I will therefore chastise Him and let *Him* go."

23 But they were insistent, demanding with loud voices that He be crucified. And the voices of these men and of the chief priests prevailed.[1] 24 So [a]Pilate gave sentence that it should be as they requested. 25 [a]And he released to them[1] the one they requested, who for rebellion and murder had been thrown into prison; but he delivered Jesus to their will.

## THE KING ON A CROSS

*(Matt. 27:32–44; Mark 15:21–32; John 19:17–24)*

26 [a]Now as they led Him away, they laid hold of a certain man, Simon a Cyrenian, who was coming from the country, and on him they laid the cross that he might bear *it* after Jesus.

27 And a great multitude of the people followed Him, and women who also mourned and lamented Him. 28 But Jesus, turning to them, said, "Daughters of Jerusalem, do not weep for Me, but weep for yourselves and for your children. 29 [a]For indeed the days are coming in which they will say, 'Blessed *are* the barren, wombs that never bore, and breasts which never nursed!' 30 Then they will begin [a]'to say to the mountains, "Fall on us!" and to the hills, "Cover us!"'[1] 31 [a]For if they do these things in the green wood, what will be done in the dry?"

32 [a]There were also two others, criminals, led with Him to be put to death. 33 And [a]when they had come to the place called Calvary, there they crucified Him, and the criminals, one on the right hand and the other on the left. 34 Then Jesus said, "Father, [a]forgive them, for [b]they do not know what they do."[1]

And [c]they divided His garments and cast lots. 35 And [a]the people stood looking on. But even the [b]rulers with them sneered, saying, "He saved others; let Him save Himself if He is the Christ, the chosen of God."

36 The soldiers also mocked Him, coming and offering Him [a]sour wine, 37 and saying, "If You are the King of the Jews, save Yourself."

38 [a]And an inscription also was written over Him in letters of Greek, Latin, and Hebrew:[1]

THIS IS THE KING OF THE JEWS.

39 [a]Then one of the criminals who were hanged blasphemed Him, saying, "If You are the Christ,[1] save Yourself and us."

40 But the other, answering, rebuked him, saying, "Do you not even fear God, seeing you are under the same condemnation? 41 And we indeed justly, for we receive the due reward of our deeds; but this Man has done [a]nothing wrong." 42 Then he said to Jesus, "Lord,[1] remember me when You come into Your kingdom."

43 And Jesus said to him, "Assuredly, I say to you, today you will be with Me in [a]Paradise."

23:5 [a] John 7:41 23:6 [1] NU-Text omits *of Galilee.* 23:7 [a] Luke 3:1; 9:7; 13:31 23:8 [a] Luke 9:9 [b] Matt. 14:1 23:9 [a] John 19:9 23:11 [a] Is. 53:3 23:12 [a] Acts 4:26, 27 23:13 [a] Mark 15:14 23:14 [a] Luke 23:1, 2 [b] Luke 23:4 23:15 [1] NU-Text reads *for he sent Him back to us.* 23:16 [a] John 19:1 23:17 [a] John 18:39 [1] NU-Text omits verse 17. 23:18 [a] Acts 3:13–15 23:23 [1] NU-Text omits *and of the chief priests.* 23:24 [a] Mark 15:15 23:25 [a] Is. 53:8 [1] NU-Text and M-Text omit *to them.* 23:26 [a] Matt. 27:32 23:29 [a] Matt. 24:19 23:30 [a] Hos. 10:8; Rev. 6:16, 17; 9:6 [1] Hosea 10:8 23:31 [a] [Jer. 25:29] 23:32 [a] Is. 53:9, 12 23:33 [a] John 19:17–24 23:34 [a] 1 Cor. 4:12 [b] Acts 3:17 [c] Matt. 27:35 [1] NU-Text brackets the first sentence as a later addition. 23:35 [a] Ps. 22:17 [b] Matt. 27:39 23:36 [a] Ps. 69:21 23:38 [a] John 19:19 [1] NU-Text omits *written* and *in letters of Greek, Latin, and Hebrew.* 23:39 [a] Mark 15:32 [1] NU-Text reads *Are You not the Christ?* 23:41 [a] [Heb. 7:26] 23:42 [1] NU-Text reads *And he said, "Jesus, remember me.* 23:43 [a] [Rev. 2:7]

### *JESUS DIES ON THE CROSS*

*(Matt. 27:45–56; Mark 15:33–41; John 19:25–30)*

44 [a]Now it was[1] about the sixth hour, and
there was darkness over all the earth until the
ninth hour. 45 Then the sun was darkened,[1] and
[a]the veil of the temple was torn in two. 46 And
when Jesus had cried out with a loud voice, He
said, "Father, [a]'into Your hands I commit My
spirit.'"[1] [b]Having said this, He breathed His last.

47 [a]So when the centurion saw what had hap-
pened, he glorified God, saying, "Certainly this
was a righteous Man!"

48 And the whole crowd who came togeth-
er to that sight, seeing what had been done,
beat their breasts and returned. 49 [a]But all His
acquaintances, and the women who followed
Him from Galilee, stood at a distance, watching
these things.

### *JESUS BURIED IN JOSEPH'S TOMB*

*(Matt. 27:57–61; Mark 15:42–47; John 19:38–42)*

50 [a]Now behold, *there was* a man named Jo-
seph, a council member, a good and just man.
51 He had not consented to their decision and
deed. *He was* from Arimathea, a city of the Jews,
[a]who himself was also waiting[1] for the kingdom
of God. 52 This man went to Pilate and asked
for the body of Jesus. 53 [a]Then he took it down,
wrapped it in linen, and laid it in a tomb *that
was* hewn out of the rock, where no one had ever
lain before. 54 That day was [a]the Preparation, and
the Sabbath drew near.

**23:53** Jesus' **tomb** was a small room carved into a large **rock**. The heavy stone that was placed in front of the tomb was intended to keep animals from getting in.

55 And the women [a]who had come with Him
from Galilee followed after, and [b]they observed
the tomb and how His body was laid. 56 Then they
returned and [a]prepared spices and fragrant oils.
And they rested on the Sabbath [b]according to
the commandment.

### *HE IS RISEN*

*(Matt. 28:1–10; Mark 16:1–8; John 20:1–10)*

**24** Now [a]on the first *day* of the week, very
early in the morning, they, and certain
*other women* with them,[1] came to the tomb
[b]bringing the spices which they had prepared.
2 [a]But they found the stone rolled away from
the tomb. 3 [a]Then they went in and did not find
the body of the Lord Jesus. 4 And it happened,
as they were greatly[1] perplexed about this, that
[a]behold, two men stood by them in shining
garments. 5 Then, as they were afraid and bowed
*their* faces to the earth, they said to them, "Why
do you seek the living among the dead? 6 He is
not here, but is risen! [a]Remember how He spoke
to you when He was still in Galilee, 7 saying, 'The
Son of Man must be [a]delivered into the hands
of sinful men, and be crucified, and the third
day rise again.'"

8 And [a]they remembered His words. 9 [a]Then
they returned from the tomb and told all these
things to the eleven and to all the rest. 10 It was
Mary Magdalene, [a]Joanna, Mary *the mother* of
James, and the other *women* with them, who
told these things to the apostles. 11 [a]And their
words seemed to them like idle tales, and they
did not believe them. 12 [a]But Peter arose and
ran to the tomb; and stooping down, he saw
the linen cloths lying[1] by themselves; and he
departed, marveling to himself at what had
happened.

### *THE ROAD TO EMMAUS*

*(Mark 16:12, 13)*

13 [a]Now behold, two of them were traveling
that same day to a village called Emmaus, which
was seven miles[1] from Jerusalem. 14 And they
talked together of all these things which had
happened. 15 So it was, while they conversed
and reasoned, that [a]Jesus Himself drew near
and went with them. 16 But [a]their eyes were re-
strained, so that they did not know Him.

17 And He said to them, "What kind of con-
versation *is* this that you have with one another
as you walk and are sad?"[1]

18 Then the one [a]whose name was Cleopas
answered and said to Him, "Are You the only
stranger in Jerusalem, and have You not known
the things which happened there in these days?"

19 And He said to them, "What things?"

So they said to Him, "The things concerning
Jesus of Nazareth, [a]who was a Prophet [b]mighty
in deed and word before God and all the people,
20 [a]and how the chief priests and our rulers
delivered Him to be condemned to death, and
crucified Him. 21 But we were hoping [a]that it was
He who was going to redeem Israel. Indeed,
besides all this, today is the third day since these
things happened. 22 Yes, and [a]certain women
of our company, who arrived at the tomb early,
astonished us. 23 When they did not find His
body, they came saying that they had also seen

**23:44** [a] Matt. 27:45–56 [1] NU-Text adds *already.* **23:45** [a] Matt. 27:51 [1] NU-Text reads *obscured.* **23:46** [a] Ps. 31:5 [b] John 19:30 [1] Psalm 31:5 **23:47** [a] Mark 15:39 **23:49** [a] Ps. 38:11 **23:50** [a] Matt. 27:57–61 **23:51** [a] Luke 2:25, 38 [1] NU-Text reads *who was waiting.* **23:53** [a] Mark 15:46 **23:54** [a] Matt. 27:62 **23:55** [a] Luke 8:2 [b] Mark 15:47 **23:56** [a] Mark 16:1; Luke 24:1 [b] Ex. 20:10; Deut. 5:14 **24:1** [a] Matt. 28:1–8; Mark 16:1–8; John 20:1–8 [b] Luke 23:56 [1] NU-Text omits *and certain other women with them.* **24:2** [a] Matt. 28:2; Mark 16:4 **24:3** [a] Mark 16:5 **24:4** [a] John 20:12; Acts 1:10 [1] NU-Text omits *greatly.* **24:6** [a] Matt. 16:21; Mark 8:31; Luke 9:22 **24:7** [a] Hos. 6:1, 2; Luke 9:44; 11:29, 30; 18:31–33 **24:8** [a] Luke 9:22, 44; John 2:19–22 **24:9** [a] Matt. 28:8; Mark 16:10 **24:10** [a] Luke 8:3 **24:11** [a] Luke 24:25 **24:12** [a] John 20:3–6 [1] NU-Text omits *lying.* **24:13** [a] Mark 16:12 [1] Literally *sixty stadia* **24:15** [a] [Matt. 18:20] **24:16** [a] John 20:14; 21:4 **24:17** [1] NU-Text reads *as you walk? And they stood still, looking sad.* **24:18** [a] John 19:25 **24:19** [a] Matt. 21:11; Luke 7:16; John 3:2; Acts 2:22 [b] Acts 7:22 **24:20** [a] Luke 23:1; Acts 13:27, 28 **24:21** [a] Luke 1:68; 2:38; [Acts 1:6] **24:22** [a] Matt. 28:8; Mark 16:10; Luke 24:9, 10

STORY OF SCRIPTURE 48

LUKE 24:1–35

## THE RESURRECTION

### WHAT'S GOING ON?

If the cross is history's darkest day, the empty tomb is its brightest. We're taken from the greatest of lows to the greatest of highs: Jesus, the One who died to pay our sin penalty lives! In the resurrection, we find proof that Jesus has defeated sin and death forevermore.

On that Sunday morning, Jesus began appearing to His followers—Mary Magdalene, Joana, the other Mary, Peter and John (see John 20:1–10), and later two disciples on the road to Emmaus. Jesus joined these travelers as they discussed the events of the week, but His identity was hidden from them. In response to their confusion, He told them how the Christ would suffer and enter His glory. He then walked through the Old Testament, explaining how it all points toward what happened. It's only when Jesus broke bread with them that their eyes were opened, and they recognized Him. He then disappeared, and the pair rushed back to Jerusalem to share the news.

### WHAT DOES THIS MEAN FOR ME?

Jesus' resurrection is powerful enough to stand on its own, but here, we also find a beautiful illustration of how Jesus meets us on our faith journey. Often, we're like the two disciples, confused by God's works and unaware of Jesus' presence in our lives, especially during times of confusion and despair. This passage reminds us Jesus walks with us always, even when we don't recognize Him.

### DID YOU CATCH THE PATTERN?

Notice the pattern of breaking bread. When Jesus broke the bread, the disciples' eyes were opened. Earlier, Jesus, had broken bread with His disciples and said, "This is My body which is given for you; do this in remembrance of Me" (Luke 22:19), pointing to what would happen on the cross. Jesus is the bread of life (see John 6:35), who, like manna from heaven (see Ex. 16), gives people life. This is what we remember when we take the Lord's Supper at church.

*For the next* Story of Scripture *reading and devotion, turn to Matthew 28:16–20 on page 1000.*

a vision of angels who said He was alive. 24 And
[a]certain of those *who were* with us went to the
tomb and found *it* just as the women had said;
but Him they did not see."
25 Then He said to them, "O foolish ones, and
slow of heart to believe in all that the prophets
have spoken! 26 [a]Ought not the Christ to have suf-
fered these things and to enter into His [b]glory?"
27 And beginning at [a]Moses and [b]all the Prophets,
He expounded to them in all the Scriptures the
things concerning Himself.

**24:27** Going from the books of **Moses** to **the Prophets**, Jesus provided an overview of God's plan in the **Scriptures** of how He would provide salvation. This plan is present throughout the entire Old Testament (see Acts 3:22–26; 10:43).

### *THE DISCIPLES' EYES OPENED*

28 Then they drew near to the village where they
were going, and [a]He indicated that He would have
gone farther. 29 But [a]they constrained Him, saying,
[b]"Abide with us, for it is toward evening, and the
day is far spent." And He went in to stay with them.
30 Now it came to pass, as [a]He sat at the table
with them, that He took bread, blessed and broke
*it*, and gave it to them. 31 Then their eyes were
opened and they knew Him; and He vanished
from their sight.
32 And they said to one another, "Did not our
heart burn within us while He talked with us on
the road, and while He opened the Scriptures
to us?" 33 So they rose up that very hour and re-
turned to Jerusalem, and found the eleven and
those *who were* with them gathered together,
34 saying, "The Lord is risen indeed, and [a]has
appeared to Simon!" 35 And they told about the
things *that had happened* on the road, and how
He was known to them in the breaking of bread.

**24:24** [a] Luke 24:12 **24:26** [a] Acts 17:2, 3; [Heb. 2:9, 10] [b] [1 Pet. 1:10–12] **24:27** [a] [Gen. 3:15; 12:3; Num. 21:9; Deut. 18:15]; John 5:46 [b] [Ps. 16:9, 10; 22; 132:11; Is. 7:14; 9:6; Jer. 23:5; 33:14, 15; Ezek. 34:23; 37:25; Dan. 9:24]; Mic. 7:20; [Mal. 3:1; 4:2]; John 1:45; 5:39; [Rom. 1:1–6] **24:28** [a] Gen. 32:26; 42:7; Mark 6:48 **24:29** [a] Gen. 19:2, 3; Acts 16:15 [b] [John 14:23] **24:30** [a] Matt. 14:19; Mark 8:6; Luke 9:16 **24:34** [a] 1 Cor. 15:5

### *JESUS APPEARS TO HIS DISCIPLES*
*(John 20:19–23; Acts 1:3–5; 1 Cor. 15:5)*

36[a] Now as they said these things, Jesus Him-
self stood in the midst of them, and said to them,
"Peace to you." 37 But they were terrified and
frightened, and supposed they had seen [a]a spirit.
38 And He said to them, "Why are you troubled?
And why do doubts arise in your hearts? 39 Be-
hold My hands and My feet, that it is I Myself.
[a]Handle Me and see, for a [b]spirit does not have
flesh and bones as you see I have."
40 When He had said this, He showed them
His hands and His feet.[1] 41 But while they still did
not believe [a]for joy, and marveled, He said to
them, [b]"Have you any food here?" 42 So they gave
Him a piece of a broiled fish and some honey-
comb.[1] 43[a] And He took *it* and ate in their presence.

### *THE SCRIPTURES OPENED*

44 Then He said to them, [a]"These *are* the
words which I spoke to you while I was still with
you, that all things must be fulfilled which were
written in the Law of Moses and *the* Prophets and
*the* Psalms concerning Me." 45 And [a]He opened
their understanding, that they might compre-
hend the Scriptures.
46 Then He said to them, [a]"Thus it is written,
and thus it was necessary for the Christ to suffer
and to rise[1] from the dead the third day, 47 and
that repentance and [a]remission of sins should
be preached in His name [b]to all nations, begin-
ning at Jerusalem. 48 And [a]you are witnesses
of these things. 49[a] Behold, I send the Promise
of My Father upon you; but tarry in the city of
Jerusalem[1] until you are endued with power
from on high."

### SEEING JESUS IN THE SCRIPTURE

**24:51** After His work on earth was fulfilled, Jesus returned to the Father's side where He awaits His return in final judgment (see Ps. 110:1).

### *THE ASCENSION*
*(Mark 16:19, 20; Acts 1:9)*

50 And He led them out [a]as far as Bethany,
and He lifted up His hands and blessed them.
51[a] Now it came to pass, while He blessed them,
that He was parted from them and carried up
into heaven. 52[a] And they worshiped Him, and
returned to Jerusalem with great joy, 53 and
were continually [a]in the temple praising and[1]
blessing God. Amen.[2]

**24:36** [a] Mark 16:14 **24:37** [a] Mark 6:49 **24:39** [a] John 20:20, 27 [b] [1 Cor. 15:50] **24:40** [1] Some printed New Testaments omit this verse. It is found in nearly all Greek manuscripts. **24:41** [a] Gen. 45:26 [b] John 21:5 **24:42** [1] NU-Text omits *and some honeycomb.* **24:43** [a] Acts 10:39–41 **24:44** [a] Matt. 16:21; 17:22; 20:18 **24:45** [a] Acts 16:14 **24:46** [a] Acts 17:3 [1] NU-Text reads *written, that the Christ should suffer and rise.* **24:47** [a] Acts 5:31; 10:43; 13:38; 26:18 [b] [Jer. 31:34] **24:48** [a] [Acts 1:8] **24:49** [a] Joel 2:28 [1] NU-Text omits *of Jerusalem.* **24:50** [a] Acts 1:12 **24:51** [a] Mark 16:19 **24:52** [a] Matt. 28:9 **24:53** [a] Acts 2:46 [1] NU-Text omits *praising and.* [2] NU-Text omits *Amen.*

*The Gospel According to*

# JOHN

| AUTHOR | KEY VERSES | READING TIME |
|---|---|---|
| John | John 20:30–31 | 2 hours 23 minutes |

Just as a coin has two sides, Jesus has two natures: deity and humanity. From the very beginning of his Gospel, John portrays Jesus as the divine Son of God who came to earth as God incarnate. John's purpose is crystal clear: to present Christ in His deity so that his readers, the entire world, might "believe that Jesus is the Christ, the Son of God" (John 20:31). John's Gospel is topical as well as chronological and revolves around seven miracles and seven "I am" statements of Christ. Following an extended eyewitness description of the upper room meal and discourse, John records events leading through the crucifixion and resurrection, the final climactic proof that Jesus is who He claimed to be—the Son of God.

**Occasion:** John wrote his Gospel to all people to show Jesus is the divine Son of God.

**Main Point:** Jesus is the Son of God who has come in the flesh to save the world.

**Big Ideas:** Jesus is the long-awaited Savior. What Jesus said and what He did prove He is the Son of God. All who place faith in Jesus are saved. Jesus shows us how we are to live as His followers.

## OUTLINE:

I. The Presentation of the Son of God (chs. 1–4)
II. The Opposition to the Son of God (chs. 5–12)
III. The Teaching of the Son of God (chs. 13–16)
IV. The Prayer of the Son of God (ch. 17)
V. The Crucifixion of the Son of God (chs. 18–19)
VI. The Resurrection of the Son of God (chs. 20–21)

**c. 420 BC**
Malachi prophesies in Judah

**356–323 BC**
Alexander the Great lives in Macedonia

**246 BC**
Great Wall of China is built

**164 BC**
Judas Maccabaeus restores the temple in Jerusalem, celebrated yearly by the festival of Hanukkah

**37 BC**
Julius Caesar is murdered

**37–4 BC**
Herod the Great is king in Jerusalem

**31 BC–AD 14**
Augustus Caesar is Roman emperor

**c. 5–4 BC**
Jesus is born in Bethlehem

**4 BC–AD 39**
Herod Antipas rules in Galilee and Perea

**AD 1**
Lions become extinct in Western Europe

**c. AD 7**
Jesus questions teachers at the temple

**AD 14–37**
Tiberius is Roman emperor

**AD 25–27**
John the Baptist ministers

**AD 26–36**
Pontius Pilate is procurator of Judea

**c. AD 27**
Jesus' first Judean ministry

**c. AD 27–29**
Jesus' Galilean ministry

**c. AD 30**
Jesus' second Judean ministry; crucifixion and resurrection

**c. AD 80–90**
**John written**

### *THE ETERNAL WORD*

*(Gen. 1:1–2:3)*

**1** In the beginning [a]was the Word, and the
[b]Word was [c]with God, and the Word was [d]God.
2 [a]He was in the beginning with God. 3 [a]All things
were made through Him, and without Him
nothing was made that was made. 4 [a]In Him was
life, and [b]the life was the light of men. 5 And [a]the
light shines in the darkness, and the darkness
did not comprehend[1] it.

### *JOHN'S WITNESS: THE TRUE LIGHT*

6 There was a [a]man sent from God, whose
name *was* John. 7 This man came for a [a]witness,
to bear witness of the Light, that all through him
might [b]believe. 8 He was not that Light, but *was*
*sent* to bear witness of that [a]Light. 9 [a]That was
the true Light which gives light to every man
coming into the world.[1]
10 He was in the world, and the world was
made through Him, and [a]the world did not know
Him. 11 [a]He came to His own,[1] and His own[2] did
not receive Him. 12 But [a]as many as received Him,
to them He gave the right to become children of
God, to those who believe in His name: 13 [a]who
were born, not of blood, nor of the will of the
flesh, nor of the will of man, but of God.

### *THE WORD BECOMES FLESH*

14 [a]And the Word [b]became [c]flesh and dwelt
among us, and [d]we beheld His glory, the glory
as of the only begotten of the Father, [e]full of
grace and truth.
15 [a]John bore witness of Him and cried out,
saying, "This was He of whom I said, [b]'He who
comes after me is preferred before me, [c]for He
was before me.' "
16 And[1] of His [a]fullness we have all received,
and grace for grace. 17 For [a]the law was given
through Moses, *but* [b]grace and [c]truth came

**1:1** [a]1 John 1:1 [b]Rev. 19:13 [c][John 17:5] [d][1 John 5:20] **1:2** [a]Gen. 1:1 **1:3** [a][Col. 1:16, 17] **1:4** [a][1 John 5:11] [b]John 8:12; 9:5; 12:46 **1:5** [a][John 3:19] [1]Or *overcome* **1:6** [a]Matt. 3:1–17 **1:7** [a]John 3:25–36; 5:33–35 [b][John 3:16] **1:8** [a]Is. 9:2; 49:6 **1:9** [a]Is. 49:6 [1]Or *That was the true Light which, coming into the world, gives light to every man.* **1:10** [a]Heb. 1:2 **1:11** [a][Luke 19:14] [1]That is, His own things or domain [2]That is, His own people **1:12** [a]Gal. 3:26 **1:13** [a][1 Pet. 1:23] **1:14** [a]Rev. 19:13 [b]Gal. 4:4 [c]Heb. 2:11 [d]Is. 40:5 [e][John 8:32; 14:6; 18:37] **1:15** [a]John 3:32 [b][Matt. 3:11] [c][Col. 1:17] **1:16** [a][Col. 1:19; 2:9] [1]NU-Text reads *For.* **1:17** [a][Ex. 20:1] [b][Rom. 5:21; 6:14] [c][John 8:32; 14:6; 18:37]

STORY OF SCRIPTURE 40

JOHN 1:1–5

## JESUS, THE WORD AND THE LIGHT

### WHAT'S GOING ON?

John's Gospel stands apart from the Gospels of Matthew, Mark, and Luke. While each depicts the one true story of Jesus without contradiction, they do so from distinct perspectives. John's perspective was most different; he took a more philosophical and abstract approach. For example, John doesn't begin with Jesus' genealogy like Matthew, Jesus' birth like Luke, or Jesus' ministry beginning like Mark. Instead, John start at the *very* beginning, retelling the creation story of Genesis 1 and describing Jesus as the "Word" who holds the universe together and the "light" penetrating the darkness.

When John called Jesus the "Word," he was drawing from Jewish and Greek thinking of the time. This "Word" was the ultimate truth that binds the universe together. Jesus that ultimate truth of the universe. John also described Jesus as the "light of men," shining in the darkness. Just as God brought light to the dark and chaotic world in Genesis, Jesus shines a light on our dark and chaotic hearts.

### WHAT DOES THIS MEAN FOR ME?

Because Jesus is the Word, He is the truth we can rely on. The world may have loose and flighty definitions of right and wrong, but we have a firm and eternal guide in Jesus. He is also the light. Just as the sun defeats the darkness and brings life to the world, Jesus has defeated the darkness of sin and death, bringing us eternal life.

### DID YOU CATCH THE PATTERN?

John constructed the beginning of his Gospel account to mirror the cadence and flow of Genesis 1. Go back and read that chapter, paying close attention to how God created by the spoken word and where you see "light" mentioned. John wanted to show us that just as God acted to bring all creation into existence, He acted again by sending Jesus to usher in a new creative work—the salvation of people and formation of the church.

*For the next* Story of Scripture *reading and devotion, turn to Matthew 1:18–24 on page 962.*

through Jesus Christ. 18 [a]No one has seen God at any time. [b]The only begotten Son,[1] who is in the bosom of the Father, He has declared *Him.*

### A VOICE IN THE WILDERNESS

*(Matt. 3:1–12; Mark 1:1–8; Luke 3:1–20)*

19 Now this is [a]the testimony of John, when the Jews sent priests and Levites from Jerusalem to ask him, "Who are you?"

20 [a]He confessed, and did not deny, but confessed, "I am not the Christ."

21 And they asked him, "What then? Are you Elijah?"

He said, "I am not."

"Are you [a]the Prophet?"

And he answered, "No."

22 Then they said to him, "Who are you, that we may give an answer to those who sent us? What do you say about yourself?"

23 He said: [a]"I *am*

> [b]'The voice of one crying in the wilderness:
> "Make straight the way of the LORD," '[1]

as the prophet Isaiah said."

> **SEEING JESUS IN THE SCRIPTURE**
>
> **1:23** John was the voice in the wilderness who prepared the way for Jesus' ministry, fulfilling prophecy (see Is. 40:3).

24 Now those who were sent were from the Pharisees. 25 And they asked him, saying, "Why then do you baptize if you are not the Christ, nor Elijah, nor the Prophet?"

26 John answered them, saying, [a]"I baptize with water, [b]but there stands One among you whom you do not know. 27 [a]It is He who, coming after me, is preferred before me, whose sandal strap I am not worthy to loose."

28 These things were done [a]in Bethabara[1] beyond the Jordan, where John was baptizing.

### THE LAMB OF GOD

*(Matt. 3:13–17; Mark 1:9–11; Luke 3:21, 22)*

29 The next day John saw Jesus coming toward him, and said, "Behold! [a]The Lamb of God [b]who takes away the sin of the world! 30 This is He of whom I said, 'After me comes a Man who is preferred before me, for He was before me.' 31 I did not know Him; but that He should be revealed to Israel, [a]therefore I came baptizing with water."

32 [a]And John bore witness, saying, "I saw the Spirit descending from heaven like a dove, and He remained upon Him. 33 I did not know Him, but He who sent me to baptize with water said to me, 'Upon whom you see the Spirit descending, and remaining on Him, [a]this is He who baptizes with the Holy Spirit.' 34 And I have seen and testified that this is the [a]Son of God."

### THE FIRST DISCIPLES

35 Again, the next day, John stood with two of his disciples. 36 And looking at Jesus as He walked, he said, [a]"Behold the Lamb of God!"

37 The two disciples heard him speak, and they [a]followed Jesus. 38 Then Jesus turned, and seeing them following, said to them, "What do you seek?"

They said to Him, "Rabbi" (which is to say, when translated, Teacher), "where are You staying?"

39 He said to them, "Come and see." They came and saw where He was staying, and remained with Him that day (now it was about the tenth hour).

40 One of the two who heard John *speak,* and followed Him, was [a]Andrew, Simon Peter's brother. 41 He first found his own brother Simon, and said to him, "We have found the Messiah" (which is translated, the Christ). 42 And he brought him to Jesus.

Now when Jesus looked at him, He said, "You are Simon the son of Jonah.[1] [a]You shall be called Cephas" (which is translated, A Stone).

### PHILIP AND NATHANAEL

43 The following day Jesus wanted to go to Galilee, and He found [a]Philip and said to him, "Follow Me." 44 Now [a]Philip was from Bethsaida, the city of Andrew and Peter. 45 Philip found [a]Nathanael and said to him, "We have found Him of whom [b]Moses in the law, and also the [c]prophets, wrote—Jesus [d]of Nazareth, the [e]son of Joseph."

46 And Nathanael said to him, [a]"Can anything good come out of Nazareth?"

Philip said to him, "Come and see."

47 Jesus saw Nathanael coming toward Him, and said of him, "Behold, [a]an Israelite indeed, in whom is no deceit!"

48 Nathanael said to Him, "How do You know me?"

Jesus answered and said to him, "Before Philip called you, when you were under the fig tree, I saw you."

49 Nathanael answered and said to Him, "Rabbi, [a]You are the Son of God! You are [b]the King of Israel!"

50 Jesus answered and said to him, "Because I said to you, 'I saw you under the fig tree,' do you believe? You will see greater things than these." 51 And He said to him, "Most assuredly, I say to you, [a]hereafter[1] you shall see heaven open, and the angels of God ascending and descending upon the Son of Man."

**1:18** [a] Ex. 33:20 [b] 1 John 4:9 [1] NU-Text reads *only begotten God.* **1:19** [a] John 5:33 **1:20** [a] Luke 3:15 **1:21** [a] Deut. 18:15, 18 **1:23** [a] Matt. 3:3 [b] Is. 40:3 [1] Isaiah 40:3 **1:26** [a] Matt. 3:11 [b] Mal. 3:1 **1:27** [a] Acts 19:4 **1:28** [a] Judg. 7:24 [1] NU-Text and M-Text read *Bethany.* **1:29** [a] Rev. 5:6–14 [b] [1 Pet. 2:24] **1:31** [a] Matt. 3:6 **1:32** [a] Mark 1:10 **1:33** [a] Matt. 3:11 **1:34** [a] John 11:27 **1:36** [a] John 1:29 **1:37** [a] Matt. 4:20, 22 **1:40** [a] Matt. 4:18 **1:42** [a] Matt. 16:18 [1] NU-Text reads *John.* **1:43** [a] John 6:5; 12:21, 22; 14:8, 9 **1:44** [a] John 12:21 **1:45** [a] John 21:2 [b] Luke 24:27 [c] [Zech. 6:12] [d] [Matt. 2:23] [e] Luke 3:23 **1:46** [a] John 7:41, 42, 52 **1:47** [a] Ps. 32:2; 73:1 **1:49** [a] Matt. 14:33 [b] Matt. 21:5 **1:51** [a] Gen. 28:12 [1] NU-Text omits *hereafter.*

### *WATER TURNED TO WINE*

**2** On the third day there was a [a]wedding in
[b]Cana of Galilee, and the [c]mother of Jesus
was there. 2 Now both Jesus and His disciples
were invited to the wedding. 3 And when they
ran out of wine, the mother of Jesus said to Him,
"They have no wine."
4 Jesus said to her, [a]"Woman, [b]what does
your concern have to do with Me? [c]My hour has
not yet come."
5 His mother said to the servants, "Whatever
He says to you, do *it*."
6 Now there were set there six waterpots of
stone, [a]according to the manner of purification
of the Jews, containing twenty or thirty gallons
apiece. 7 Jesus said to them, "Fill the waterpots
with water." And they filled them up to the brim.
8 And He said to them, "Draw *some* out now, and
take *it* to the master of the feast." And they took
*it*. 9 When the master of the feast had tasted [a]the
water that was made wine, and did not know
where it came from (but the servants who had
drawn the water knew), the master of the feast
called the bridegroom. 10 And he said to him, "Ev-
ery man at the beginning sets out the good wine,
and when the *guests* have well drunk, then the
inferior. You have kept the good wine until now!"
11 This [a]beginning of signs Jesus did in Cana
of Galilee, [b]and manifested His glory; and His
disciples believed in Him.

> **2:11** In the Gospel of John, the miracles of Jesus are called **signs**, indicating they pointed to His messiahship. This sign signified Christ's **glory**—that is, His deity. When Jesus transformed water into wine, He demonstrated His power.

12 After this He went down to [a]Capernaum,
He, His mother, [b]His brothers, and His disciples;
and they did not stay there many days.

### *JESUS CLEANSES THE TEMPLE*

*(Matt. 21:12–17; Mark 11:15–19; Luke 19:45–48)*

13 [a]Now the Passover of the Jews was at hand,
and Jesus went up to Jerusalem. 14 [a]And He found
in the temple those who sold oxen and sheep and
doves, and the money changers doing business.
15 When He had made a whip of cords, He drove
them all out of the temple, with the sheep and the
oxen, and poured out the changers' money and
overturned the tables. 16 And He said to those who
sold doves, "Take these things away! Do not make
[a]My Father's house a house of merchandise!"
17 Then His disciples remembered that it was
written, [a]"Zeal for Your house has eaten[1] Me up."[2]

> **SEEING JESUS IN THE SCRIPTURE**
>
> **2:17** When Jesus cleansed the temple of the money changers, His disciples recognized that it fulfilled prophecy (see Ps. 69:9).

18 So the Jews answered and said to Him,
[a]"What sign do You show to us, since You do
these things?"
19 Jesus answered and said to them, [a]"Destroy
this temple, and in three days I will raise it up."
20 Then the Jews said, "It has taken forty-six
years to build this temple, and will You raise it
up in three days?"
21 But He was speaking [a]of the temple of
His body. 22 Therefore, when He had risen from
the dead, [a]His disciples remembered that He
had said this to them;[1] and they believed the
Scripture and the word which Jesus had said.

**2:1** [a] [Heb. 13:4] [b] John 4:46 [c] John 19:25 **2:4** [a] John 19:26 [b] 2 Sam. 16:10 [c] John 7:6, 8, 30; 8:20 **2:6** [a] [Mark 7:3] **2:9** [a] John 4:46 **2:11** [a] John 4:54 [b] [John 1:14] **2:12** [a] Matt. 4:13 [b] Matt. 12:46; 13:55 **2:13** [a] Deut. 16:1–6 **2:14** [a] Mark 11:15, 17 **2:16** [a] Luke 2:49 **2:17** [a] Ps. 69:9 [1] NU-Text and M-Text read *will eat.* [2] Psalm 69:9 **2:18** [a] Matt. 12:38 **2:19** [a] Matt. 26:61; 27:40 **2:21** [a] [1 Cor. 3:16; 6:19] **2:22** [a] Luke 24:8 [1] NU-Text and M-Text omit *to them.*

## THE SEVEN SIGNS IN JOHN

| Sign | Meaning | Reference |
|---|---|---|
| **Turning water into wine** | The ritual of law is replaced by the reality of grace | John 2:1–11 |
| **Healing the nobleman's son** | The gospel brings spiritual restoration | John 4:46–54 |
| **Healing the paralytic** | Weakness is replaced by strength | John 5:1–16 |
| **Feeding the multitude** | Christ satisfies spiritual hunger | John 6:1–13 |
| **Walking on water** | The Lord transforms fear to faith | John 6:16–21 |
| **Giving sight to the man born blind** | Jesus overcomes darkness and brings in light | John 9:1–7 |
| **Raising Lazarus** | The gospel brings people from death to life | John 11:1–44 |

### *THE DISCERNER OF HEARTS*

23 Now when He was in Jerusalem at the
Passover, during the feast, many believed in His
name when they saw the [a]signs which He did.
24 But Jesus did not commit Himself to them,
because He [a]knew all *men*, 25 and had no need
that anyone should testify of man, for [a]He knew
what was in man.

### *THE NEW BIRTH*

3 There was a man of the Pharisees named
Nicodemus, a ruler of the Jews. 2 [a]This man
came to Jesus by night and said to Him, "Rabbi,
we know that You are a teacher come from God;
for [b]no one can do these signs that You do unless
[c]God is with him."

3 Jesus answered and said to him, "Most as-
suredly, I say to you, [a]unless one is born again,
he cannot see the kingdom of God."

4 Nicodemus said to Him, "How can a man
be born when he is old? Can he enter a second
time into his mother's womb and be born?"

5 Jesus answered, "Most assuredly, I say to
you, [a]unless one is born of water and the Spirit,
he cannot enter the kingdom of God. 6 That
which is born of the flesh is [a]flesh, and that
which is born of the Spirit is spirit. 7 Do not
marvel that I said to you, 'You must be born
again.' 8 [a]The wind blows where it wishes, and
you hear the sound of it, but cannot tell where
it comes from and where it goes. So is everyone
who is born of the Spirit."

**3:3–6** Jesus was explaining to Nicodemus there is more to having a right relationship with God than being physically **born** a Jew. There are several interpretations of being **born of water**. (1) Jesus was referring to water baptism (see Acts 10:43–47). (2) Water is to be understood as a symbol for the Holy Spirit. (3) Water is to be understood as a symbol of the Word of God. (4) Jesus used the phrase "born of water" to refer to physical birth. He then used the contrasting phrase **born of the Spirit** to refer to spiritual birth. (5) Jesus used the phrase "born of water" to refer to John the Baptist's baptism. (6) Jesus used the Old Testament imagery of "water" and "wind" to refer to the work of God from above (see Is. 44:3–5). Ultimately, the new birth is not physical; rather, it is spiritual (John 3:6). It must come by the Spirit of God if it is a spiritual birth (3:5).

9 Nicodemus answered and said to Him,
[a]"How can these things be?"

10 Jesus answered and said to him, "Are you the
teacher of Israel, and do not know these things?
11 [a]Most assuredly, I say to you, We speak what We
know and testify what We have seen, and [b]you
do not receive Our witness. 12 If I have told you
earthly things and you do not believe, how will
you believe if I tell you heavenly things? 13 [a]No one
has ascended to heaven but He who came down
from heaven, *that is*, the Son of Man who is in
heaven.[1] 14 [a]And as Moses lifted up the serpent in
the wilderness, even so [b]must the Son of Man be
lifted up, 15 that whoever [a]believes in Him should
not perish but[1] [b]have eternal life. 16 [a]For God so
loved the world that He gave His only begotten
[b]Son, that whoever believes in Him should not
perish but have everlasting life. 17 [a]For God did not
send His Son into the world to condemn the world,
but that the world through Him might be saved.

**SEEING JESUS IN THE SCRIPTURE**

**3:14–17** Just as the Israelites found life by looking upon a bronze serpent high on a pole, all who look upon Jesus lifted high on a cross find eternal life (see Num. 21:9).

18 [a]"He who believes in Him is not con-
demned; but he who does not believe is con-
demned already, because he has not believed in
the name of the only begotten Son of God. 19 And
this is the condemnation, [a]that the light has
come into the world, and men loved darkness
rather than light, because their deeds were evil.
20 For [a]everyone practicing evil hates the light
and does not come to the light, lest his deeds
should be exposed. 21 But he who does the truth
comes to the light, that his deeds may be clearly
seen, that they have been [a]done in God."

**3:16, 18 Only begotten Son** emphasizes Jesus' uniqueness. Although the Father has begotten many children through the new birth, none of these are exactly like Jesus Christ, the **Son of God**. We become children, but Jesus has always been the Son of God. Our sonship begins at salvation; His Sonship is from eternity.

### *JOHN THE BAPTIST EXALTS CHRIST*

22 After these things Jesus and His disci-
ples came into the land of Judea, and there

**2:23** [a] [Acts 2:22] **2:24** [a] Rev. 2:23 **2:25** [a] Matt. 9:4 **3:2** [a] John 7:50; 19:39 [b] John 9:16, 33 [c] [Acts 10:38] **3:3** [a] [1 Pet. 1:23] **3:5** [a] [Acts 2:38] **3:6** [a] 1 Cor. 15:50 **3:8** [a] Eccl. 11:5 **3:9** [a] John 6:52, 60 **3:11** [a] [Matt. 11:27] [b] John 3:32; 8:14 **3:13** [a] Eph. 4:9 [1] NU-Text omits *who is in heaven.* **3:14** [a] Num. 21:9 [b] John 8:28; 12:34; 19:18 **3:15** [a] John 6:47 [b] John 3:36 [1] NU-Text omits *not perish but.* **3:16** [a] Rom. 5:8 [b] [Is. 9:6] **3:17** [a] Luke 9:56 **3:18** [a] John 5:24; 6:40, 47; 20:31 **3:19** [a] [John 1:4, 9–11] **3:20** [a] Eph. 5:11, 13 **3:21** [a] 1 Cor. 15:10

KNOW THE TRUTH

## THE DOCTRINE OF THE CHURCH

### PART 2: THE KINGDOM OF GOD

**3:3–5** In the New Testament, the "kingdom," "the kingdom of God," "the kingdom of heaven," "the kingdom of Christ and God," "the kingdom of the Son of His love," and "His kingdom" refer to the same thing: God's rule and reign over His creation. This kingdom isn't experienced in full in the present physical realm; sinful people continue to rebel against the King and things aren't as they are supposed to be. The kingdom is, though, experienced in full in the spiritual realm. In whomever Christ the King reigns as Lord, the kingdom is present. Wherever that servant goes, the kingdom and its resources and power go.

Like a mustard seed that grows hundreds of times its original size, the kingdom begins humbly in an individual's life yet grows exponentially in that person as it also grows numerically throughout the world (see Matt. 13:31–32). Like yeast in dough, the kingdom spreads through every fiber of a person's life and spreads from person to person throughout the world, one life surrendered to Christ at a time. Christ's kingdom will never end, and its global advance is unstoppable (see Is. 9:7; Dan. 2:44–45; 7:13–14; Matt. 13:33). Soon, Christ will return in glory to setup a physical kingdom with His people, without rival, and without end (see Rev. 11:15; 19:11–21:8).

*For* **THE DOCTRINE OF THE CHURCH: PART 3: THE NATURE OF THE CHURCH**, *turn to Philemon v. 2 on page 1242.*

He remained with them [a]and baptized. 23 Now
John also was baptizing in Aenon near [a]Salim,
because there was much water there. [b]And they
came and were baptized. 24 For [a]John had not
yet been thrown into prison.
25 Then there arose a dispute between *some*
of John's disciples and the Jews about purifi-
cation. 26 And they came to John and said to
him, "Rabbi, He who was with you beyond the
Jordan, [a]to whom you have testified—behold,
He is baptizing, and all [b]are coming to Him!"
27 John answered and said, [a]"A man can re-
ceive nothing unless it has been given to him
from heaven. 28 You yourselves bear me witness,
that I said, [a]'I am not the Christ,' but, [b]'I have been
sent before Him.' 29 [a]He who has the bride is the
bridegroom; but [b]the friend of the bridegroom,
who stands and hears him, rejoices greatly be-
cause of the bridegroom's voice. Therefore this
joy of mine is fulfilled. 30 [a]He must increase, but
I *must* decrease. 31 [a]He who comes from above [b]is
above all; [c]he who is of the earth is earthly and
speaks of the earth. [d]He who comes from heaven
is above all. 32 And [a]what He has seen and heard,
that He testifies; and no one receives His testi-
mony. 33 He who has received His testimony [a]has
certified that God is true. 34 [a]For He whom God has
sent speaks the words of God, for God does not
give the Spirit [b]by measure. 35 [a]The Father loves
the Son, and has given all things into His hand.
36 [a]He who believes in the Son has everlasting
life; and he who does not believe the Son shall
not see life, but the [b]wrath of God abides on him."

### A SAMARITAN WOMAN MEETS HER MESSIAH

4 Therefore, when the Lord knew that the
Pharisees had heard that Jesus made and
[a]baptized more disciples than John 2 (though
Jesus Himself did not baptize, but His disciples),
3 He left Judea and departed again to Galilee.
4 But He needed to go through Samaria.
5 So He came to a city of Samaria which is
called Sychar, near the plot of ground that [a]Ja-
cob [b]gave to his son Joseph. 6 Now Jacob's well
was there. Jesus therefore, being wearied from
*His* journey, sat thus by the well. It was about
the sixth hour.
7 A woman of Samaria came to draw water.
Jesus said to her, "Give Me a drink." 8 For His
disciples had gone away into the city to buy food.
9 Then the woman of Samaria said to Him,
"How is it that You, being a Jew, ask a drink from
me, a Samaritan woman?" For [a]Jews have no
dealings with [b]Samaritans.
10 Jesus answered and said to her, "If you
knew the [a]gift of God, and who it is who says
to you, 'Give Me a drink,' you would have asked
Him, and He would have given you [b]living water."

**3:22** [a] John 4:1, 2 **3:23** [a] 1 Sam. 9:4 [b] Matt. 3:5, 6 **3:24** [a] Matt. 4:12; 14:3 **3:26** [a] John 1:7, 15, 27, 34 [b] Mark 2:2; 3:10; 5:24 **3:27** [a] 1 Cor. 3:5, 6; 4:7 **3:28** [a] John 1:19–27 [b] Mal. 3:1 **3:29** [a] [2 Cor. 11:2] [b] Song 5:1 **3:30** [a] [Is. 9:7] **3:31** [a] John 3:13; 8:23 [b] Matt. 28:18 [c] 1 Cor. 15:47 [d] John 6:33 **3:32** [a] John 3:11; 15:15 **3:33** [a] 1 John 5:10 **3:34** [a] John 7:16 [b] John 1:16 **3:35** [a] [Heb. 2:8] **3:36** [a] John 3:16, 17; 6:47 [b] Rom. 1:18; Eph. 5:6; 1 Thess. 1:10 **4:1** [a] John 3:22, 26; 1 Cor. 1:17 **4:5** [a] Gen. 33:19; Josh. 24:32 [b] Gen. 48:22; Josh. 4:12 **4:9** [a] Acts 10:28 [b] 2 Kin. 17:24; Matt. 10:5, 6; Luke 9:52; 10:33; 17:16; John 8:48 **4:10** [a] [Rom. 5:15] [b] Is. 12:3; 44:3; Jer. 2:13; Zech. 13:1; 14:8; John 7:38

**4:4 Samaria** was the region between Judea in the south and Galilee in the north. However, the Jews hated the Samaritans so much that they often avoided going through Samaria by going around it along the Jordan River instead. This hatred went back to the days of the exile. When the northern kingdom was exiled to Assyria in 722 BC, some Jews were left in the land. King Sargon then repopulated the area with captives from other lands. The intermarriage of these foreigners and the Jews who had been left formed a new people that became known as the Samaritans. The Jews hated the Samaritans because they were no longer "pure" Jews and had also compromised their faith.

11 The woman said to Him, "Sir, You have
nothing to draw with, and the well is deep. Where
then do You get that living water? 12 Are You
greater than our father Jacob, who gave us the
well, and drank from it himself, as well as his
sons and his livestock?"
13 Jesus answered and said to her, "Whoever
drinks of this water will thirst again, 14 but [a]who-
ever drinks of the water that I shall give him
will never thirst. But the water that I shall give
him [b]will become in him a fountain of water
springing up into everlasting life."
15 [a]The woman said to Him, "Sir, give me
this water, that I may not thirst, nor come here
to draw."
16 Jesus said to her, "Go, call your husband,
and come here."
17 The woman answered and said, "I have
no husband."
Jesus said to her, "You have well said, 'I have
no husband,' 18 for you have had five husbands,
and the one whom you now have is not your
husband; in that you spoke truly."
19 The woman said to Him, "Sir, [a]I perceive
that You are a prophet. 20 Our fathers worshiped
on [a]this mountain, and you *Jews* say that in
[b]Jerusalem is the place where one ought to
worship."
21 Jesus said to her, "Woman, believe Me,
the hour is coming [a]when you will neither on
this mountain, nor in Jerusalem, worship the
Father. 22 You worship [a]what you do not know;
we know what we worship, for [b]salvation is of
the Jews. 23 But the hour is coming, and now
is, when the true worshipers will [a]worship the
Father in [b]spirit [c]and truth; for the Father is
seeking such to worship Him. 24 [a]God *is* Spirit,
and those who worship Him must worship in
spirit and truth."
25 The woman said to Him, "I know that Mes-
siah [a]is coming" (who is called Christ). "When
He comes, [b]He will tell us all things."
26 Jesus said to her, [a]"I who speak to you
am *He.*"

## SEEING JESUS IN THE SCRIPTURE

**4:25** The woman at the well placed her hope in the promised Messiah who would come and reveal all things (see Deut. 18:18). Jesus is that Messiah.

### *THE WHITENED HARVEST*

27 And at this *point* His disciples came, and
they marveled that He talked with a woman; yet
no one said, "What do You seek?" or, "Why are
You talking with her?"
28 The woman then left her waterpot, went
her way into the city, and said to the men,
29 "Come, see a Man [a]who told me all things that
I ever did. Could this be the Christ?" 30 Then they
went out of the city and came to Him.
31 In the meantime His disciples urged Him,
saying, "Rabbi, eat."
32 But He said to them, "I have food to eat
of which you do not know."
33 Therefore the disciples said to one anoth-
er, "Has anyone brought Him *anything* to eat?"
34 Jesus said to them, [a]"My food is to do the
will of Him who sent Me, and to [b]finish His work.
35 Do you not say, 'There are still four months
and *then* comes [a]the harvest'? Behold, I say
to you, lift up your eyes and look at the fields,
[b]for they are already white for harvest! 36 [a]And
he who reaps receives wages, and gathers fruit
for eternal life, that [b]both he who sows and he
who reaps may rejoice together. 37 For in this the
saying is true: [a]'One sows and another reaps.'
38 I sent you to reap that for which you have not
labored; [a]others have labored, and you have
entered into their labors."

### *THE SAVIOR OF THE WORLD*

39 And many of the Samaritans of that city
believed in Him [a]because of the word of the
woman who testified, "He told me all that I
*ever* did." 40 So when the Samaritans had come
to Him, they urged Him to stay with them; and
He stayed there two days. 41 And many more
believed because of His own [a]word.
42 Then they said to the woman, "Now we

**4:14** [a] [John 6:35, 58] [b] John 7:37, 38 **4:15** [a] John 6:34, 35; 17:2, 3; [Rom. 6:23; 1 John 5:20] **4:19** [a] Matt. 21:11; Luke 7:16, 39; 24:19; John 6:14; 7:40; 9:17 **4:20** [a] Gen. 12:6–8; 33:18, 20; Judg. 9:7 [b] Deut. 12:5, 11; 1 Kin. 9:3; 2 Chr. 7:12; Ps. 122:1–9 **4:21** [a] [Mal. 1:11]; 1 Tim. 2:8 **4:22** [a] [2 Kin. 17:28–41] [b] [Is. 2:3; Luke 24:47; Rom. 3:1; 9:4, 5] **4:23** [a] Matt. 18:20; [Heb. 13:10–14] [b] Phil. 3:3 [c] [John 1:17] **4:24** [a] 2 Cor. 3:17 **4:25** [a] Deut. 18:15 [b] John 4:29, 39 **4:26** [a] Dan. 9:25; Matt. 26:63, 64; Mark 14:61, 62 **4:29** [a] John 4:25 **4:34** [a] Ps. 40:7, 8; Heb. 10:9 [b] Job 23:12; [John 6:38; 17:4; 19:30] **4:35** [a] Gen. 8:22 [b] Matt. 9:37; Luke 10:2 **4:36** [a] Dan. 12:3; Rom. 6:22 [b] 1 Thess. 2:19 **4:37** [a] 1 Cor. 3:5–9 **4:38** [a] Jer. 44:4; [1 Pet. 1:12] **4:39** [a] John 4:29 **4:41** [a] Luke 4:32; [John 6:63]

KNOW THE TRUTH

## THE DOCTRINE OF GOD

### PART 3: GOD THE SPIRIT

**4:24** To bow down to a human king, one would have to go to that king's physical location. You cannot bow before what's not there. Yet, when the Samaritan woman asked about the physical location of worship, Jesus explained God the Father isn't bound to a physical location. Thus, a person can genuinely worship God anywhere.

God is Spirit. This means His essence is not in any way composed of the matter He created in the physical universe. God the Son, Jesus Christ, became fully human with a physical body while remaining fully divine, but God the Father has no physical form. This is, in part, why His people were strictly prohibited from making any physical image to represent Him (see Ex. 20:4–5).

Some writers of Scripture (e.g., Moses, Isaiah, Ezekiel) and prophets were given visions of God's glory without specific descriptions of His form. In John's vision of God, the Father is described as "Him who sits on the throne" whose glory exudes brilliant reds, radiant greens, crashing thunder, blazing lightning, and more (Rev. 4:3–5; 5:13). Whatever form God has, He is Spirit and is no way a physical being. One day, redeemed and resurrected people will eternally behold His divine form and His exceedingly bright glory (see Rev. 21:22–27).

*For* **THE DOCTRINE OF GOD: PART 4: THE ETERNALITY OF GOD**, *turn to Isaiah 40:28 on page 716.*

believe, not because of what you said, for [a]we
ourselves have heard *Him* and we know that this
is indeed the Christ,[1] the Savior of the world."

### *WELCOME AT GALILEE*

43 Now after the two days He departed from
there and went to Galilee. 44 For [a]Jesus Himself
testified that a prophet has no honor in his own
country. 45 So when He came to Galilee, the Gal-
ileans received Him, [a]having seen all the things
He did in Jerusalem at the feast; [b]for they also
had gone to the feast.

### *A NOBLEMAN'S SON HEALED*

46 So Jesus came again to Cana of Galilee
[a]where He had made the water wine. And there
was a certain nobleman whose son was sick at
Capernaum. 47 When he heard that Jesus had
come out of Judea into Galilee, he went to Him
and implored Him to come down and heal his
son, for he was at the point of death. 48 Then
Jesus said to him, [a]"Unless you *people* see signs
and wonders, you will by no means believe."
49 The nobleman said to Him, "Sir, come
down before my child dies!"
50 Jesus said to him, "Go your way; your son
lives." So the man believed the word that Jesus
spoke to him, and he went his way. 51 And as he
was now going down, his servants met him and
told *him,* saying, "Your son lives!"
52 Then he inquired of them the hour when
he got better. And they said to him, "Yesterday
at the seventh hour the fever left him." 53 So
the father knew that *it was* at the same hour in
which Jesus said to him, "Your son lives." And
he himself believed, and his whole household.
54 This again *is* the second sign Jesus did
when He had come out of Judea into Galilee.

### *A MAN HEALED AT THE POOL OF BETHESDA*

5 After [a]this there was a feast of the Jews, and
Jesus [b]went up to Jerusalem. 2 Now there is
in Jerusalem [a]by the Sheep *Gate* a pool, which is
called in Hebrew, Bethesda,[1] having five porches.
3 In these lay a great multitude of sick people,
blind, lame, paralyzed, waiting for the moving of
the water. 4 For an angel went down at a certain
time into the pool and stirred up the water; then
whoever stepped in first, after the stirring of
the water, was made well of whatever disease
he had.[1] 5 Now a certain man was there who had
an infirmity thirty-eight years. 6 When Jesus saw
him lying there, and knew that he already had
been *in that condition* a long time, He said to
him, "Do you want to be made well?"
7 The sick man answered Him, "Sir, I have
no man to put me into the pool when the water
is stirred up; but while I am coming, another
steps down before me."
8 Jesus said to him, [a]"Rise, take up your bed

**4:42** [a] John 17:8; 1 John 4:14 [1] NU-Text omits *the Christ.* **4:44** [a] Matt. 13:57; Mark 6:4; Luke 4:24 **4:45** [a] John 2:13, 23; 3:2 [b] Deut. 16:16 **4:46** [a] John 2:1, 11 **4:48** [a] John 6:30; Rom. 15:19; 1 Cor. 1:22; 2 Cor. 12:12; [2 Thess. 2:9]; Heb. 2:4 **5:1** [a] Lev. 23:2; Deut. 16:16 [b] John 2:13 **5:2** [a] Neh. 3:1, 32; 12:39 [1] NU-Text reads *Bethzatha.* **5:4** [1] NU-Text omits *waiting for the moving of the water* at the end of verse 3, and all of verse 4. **5:8** [a] Matt. 9:6; Mark 2:11; Luke 5:24

and walk." 9 And immediately the man was made well, took up his bed, and walked.

And [a]that day was the Sabbath. 10 The Jews therefore said to him who was cured, "It is the Sabbath; [a]it is not lawful for you to carry your bed."

11 He answered them, "He who made me well said to me, 'Take up your bed and walk.' "

12 Then they asked him, "Who is the Man who said to you, 'Take up your bed and walk'?" 13 But the one who was [a]healed did not know who it was, for Jesus had withdrawn, a multitude being in *that* place. 14 Afterward Jesus found him in the temple, and said to him, "See, you have been made well. [a]Sin no more, lest a worse thing come upon you."

15 The man departed and told the Jews that it was Jesus who had made him well.

### HONOR THE FATHER AND THE SON

16 For this reason the Jews [a]persecuted Jesus, and sought to kill Him,[1] because He had done these things on the Sabbath. 17 But Jesus answered them, [a]"My Father has been working until now, and I have been working."

18 Therefore the Jews [a]sought all the more to kill Him, because He not only broke the Sabbath, but also said that God was His Father, [b]making Himself equal with God. 19 Then Jesus answered and said to them, "Most assuredly, I say to you, [a]the Son can do nothing of Himself, but what He sees the Father do; for whatever He does, the Son also does in like manner. 20 For [a]the Father loves the Son, and [b]shows Him all things that He Himself does; and He will show Him greater works than these, that you may marvel. 21 For as the Father raises the dead and gives life to *them,* [a]even so the Son gives life to whom He will. 22 For the Father judges no one, but [a]has committed all judgment to the Son, 23 that all should honor the Son just as they honor the Father. [a]He who does not honor the Son does not honor the Father who sent Him.

### LIFE AND JUDGMENT ARE THROUGH THE SON

24 "Most assuredly, I say to you, [a]he who hears My word and believes in Him who sent Me has everlasting life, and shall not come into judgment, [b]but has passed from death into life. 25 Most assuredly, I say to you, the hour is coming, and now is, when [a]the dead will hear the voice of the Son of God; and those who hear will live. 26 For [a]as the Father has life in Himself, so He has granted the Son to have [b]life in Himself, 27 and [a]has given Him authority to execute judgment also, [b]because He is the Son of Man. 28 Do not marvel at this; for the hour is coming in which all who are in the graves will [a]hear His voice 29 [a]and come forth—[b]those who have done good, to the resurrection of life, and those who have done evil, to the resurrection of condemnation. 30 [a]I can of Myself do nothing. As I hear, I judge; and My judgment is righteous, because [b]I do not seek My own will but the will of the Father who sent Me.

### THE FOURFOLD WITNESS

31 [a]"If I bear witness of Myself, My witness is not true. 32 [a]There is another who bears witness of Me, and I know that the witness which He witnesses of Me is true. 33 You have sent to John, [a]and he has borne witness to the truth. 34 Yet I do not receive testimony from man, but I say these things that you may be saved. 35 He was the burning and [a]shining lamp, and [b]you were willing for a time to rejoice in his light. 36 But [a]I have a greater witness than John's; for [b]the works which the Father has given Me to finish—the very [c]works that I do—bear witness of Me, that the Father has sent Me. 37 And the Father Himself, who sent Me, [a]has testified of Me. You have neither heard His voice at any time, [b]nor seen His form. 38 But you do not have His word abiding in you, because whom He sent, Him you do not believe. 39 [a]You search the Scriptures, for in them you think you have eternal life; and [b]these are they which testify of Me. 40 [a]But you are not willing to come to Me that you may have life.

41 [a]"I do not receive honor from men. 42 But I know you, that you do not have the love of God in you. 43 I have come in My Father's name, and you do not receive Me; if another comes in his own name, him you will receive. 44 [a]How can you believe, who receive honor from one another, and do not seek [b]the honor that *comes* from the only God? 45 Do not think that I shall accuse you to the Father; [a]there is *one* who accuses you—Moses, in whom you trust. 46 For if you believed Moses, you would believe Me; [a]for he wrote about Me. 47 But if you [a]do not believe his writings, how will you believe My words?"

### FEEDING THE FIVE THOUSAND

*(Matt. 14:13–21; Mark 6:30–44; Luke 9:10–17)*

6 After [a]these things Jesus went over the Sea of Galilee, which is *the Sea* of [b]Tiberias. 2 Then a great multitude followed Him, because they saw His signs which He performed on those who were [a]diseased. 3 And Jesus went up on the mountain, and there He sat with His disciples.

4 [a]Now the Passover, a feast of the Jews, was near. 5 [a]Then Jesus lifted up *His* eyes, and seeing

5:9 [a] John 9:14 5:10 [a] Ex. 20:10; Neh. 13:19; Jer. 17:21, 22; Matt. 12:2; Mark 2:24; Luke 6:2 5:13 [a] Luke 13:14; 22:51 5:14 [a] Matt. 12:45; [Mark 2:5]; John 8:11 5:16 [a] Luke 4:29; John 8:37; 10:39 [1] NU-Text omits *and sought to kill Him.* 5:17 [a] [John 9:4; 17:4] 5:18 [a] John 7:1, 19 [b] John 10:30; Phil. 2:6 5:19 [a] Matt. 26:39; John 5:30; 6:38; 8:28; 12:49; 14:10 5:20 [a] Matt. 3:17 [b] [Matt. 11:27] 5:21 [a] [John 11:25] 5:22 [a] [Acts 17:31] 5:23 [a] 1 John 2:23 5:24 [a] John 3:16, 18; 6:47 [b] [1 John 3:14] 5:25 [a] [Col. 2:13] 5:26 [a] Ps. 36:9 [b] 1 Cor. 15:45 5:27 [a] [Acts 10:42; 17:31] [b] Dan. 7:13 5:28 [a] [1 Thess. 4:15–17] 5:29 [a] Is. 26:19 [b] Dan. 12:2 5:30 [a] John 5:19 [b] Matt. 26:39 5:31 [a] John 8:14 5:32 [a] [Matt. 3:17] 5:33 [a] [John 1:15, 19, 27, 32] 5:35 [a] 2 Pet. 1:19 [b] Mark 6:20 5:36 [a] 1 John 5:9 [b] John 3:2; 10:25; 17:4 [c] John 9:16; 10:38 5:37 [a] Matt. 3:17 [b] 1 John 4:12 5:39 [a] Is. 8:20; 34:16 [b] Luke 24:27 5:40 [a] [John 1:11; 3:19] 5:41 [a] 1 Thess. 2:6 5:44 [a] John 12:43 [b] [Rom. 2:29] 5:45 [a] Rom. 2:12 5:46 [a] Deut. 18:15, 18 5:47 [a] Luke 16:29, 31 6:1 [a] Mark 6:32 [b] John 6:23; 21:1 6:2 [a] Matt. 4:23; 8:16; 9:35; 14:36; 15:30; 19:2 6:4 [a] Deut. 16:1 6:5 [a] Matt. 14:14

KNOW THE TRUTH

## THE DOCTRINE OF SCRIPTURE

### PART 3: THE CONTENT OF SCRIPTURE

**5:39** Jesus threatened the religious leaders' understanding of Scripture and their religious practices. They read and applied Scripture to fit their agenda. Jesus corrected this error by proclaiming the one true story of Scripture centers on Him.

Though the Bible is a collection of sixty-six books written by around forty authors over around a 1,500-year period, it tells one unified story: the story of God building His forever family. In the beginning, God created the heavens and earth where He and people could walk together under His perfect rule. People, however, chose self-rule resulting in physical death and spiritual separation from God. Through the family of Abram, God set in motion a global rescue and restoration mission. Then through a holy law given to Moses, God revealed His perfect, righteous nature while revealing humanity's sinful nature and its need for a Savior. A series of patriarchs, judges, kings, and prophets foreshadowed the need of a Ruler who would honor God's rule, release the blessings promised to Abraham, lead like a perfect David, and suffer as a servant for sinful people. That Ruler is God-become-human: Jesus Christ. Through faith in Jesus, rebels become eternal sons and daughters of God the Father. The story ends with God and His forever family, restored completely, in a new heavens and new earth.

*For* **THE DOCTRINE OF SCRIPTURE: PART 4: THE AUTHORITY OF SCRIPTURE**, *turn to Matthew 5:17–18 on page 966.*

a great multitude coming toward Him, He said
to [b]Philip, "Where shall we buy bread, that these
may eat?" [6]But this He said to test him, for He
Himself knew what He would do.

**SEEING JESUS IN THE SCRIPTURE**

**6:4–5** God miraculously gave Israel manna from heaven (see Ex. 16:15). Likewise, Jesus miraculously multiplied two fish and five loaves of bread to feed a multitude.

[7]Philip answered Him, [a]"Two hundred de-
narii worth of bread is not sufficient for them,
that every one of them may have a little."
[8]One of His disciples, [a]Andrew, Simon Pe-
ter's brother, said to Him, [9]"There is a lad here
who has five barley loaves and two small fish,
[a]but what are they among so many?"
[10]Then Jesus said, "Make the people sit
down." Now there was much grass in the place.
So the men sat down, in number about five thou-
sand. [11]And Jesus took the loaves, and when He
had given thanks He distributed *them* to the disci-
ples, and the disciples[1] to those sitting down; and
likewise of the fish, as much as they wanted. [12]So
when they were filled, He said to His disciples,
"Gather up the fragments that remain, so that
nothing is lost." [13]Therefore they gathered *them*
up, and filled twelve baskets with the fragments
of the five barley loaves which were left over by
those who had eaten. [14]Then those men, when
they had seen the sign that Jesus did, said, "This is
truly [a]the Prophet who is to come into the world."

### JESUS WALKS ON THE SEA

*(Matt. 14:22–33; Mark 6:45–52)*

[15]Therefore when Jesus perceived that they
were about to come and take Him by force to
make Him [a]king, He departed again to the
mountain by Himself alone.
[16][a]Now when evening came, His disciples
went down to the sea, [17]got into the boat, and
went over the sea toward Capernaum. And it was
already dark, and Jesus had not come to them.
[18]Then the sea arose because a great wind was
blowing. [19]So when they had rowed about three
or four miles,[1] they saw Jesus walking on the
sea and drawing near the boat; and they were
[a]afraid. [20]But He said to them, [a]"It is I; do not
be afraid." [21]Then they willingly received Him
into the boat, and immediately the boat was at
the land where they were going.

### THE BREAD FROM HEAVEN

[22]On the following day, when the people
who were standing on the other side of the sea
saw that there was no other boat there, except
that one which His disciples had entered,[1] and
that Jesus had not entered the boat with His

**6:5** [b] John 1:43 **6:7** [a] Num. 11:21, 22 **6:8** [a] John 1:40 **6:9** [a] 2 Kin. 4:43 **6:11** [1] NU-Text omits *to the disciples, and the disciples.* **6:14** [a] Gen. 49:10; Deut. 18:15, 18; John 1:21; 7:40; Acts 3:22; 7:37 **6:15** [a] [John 18:36] **6:16** [a] Matt. 14:23; Mark 6:47 **6:19** [a] Matt. 17:6 [1] Literally *twenty-five or thirty stadia* **6:20** [a] Is. 43:1, 2 **6:22** [1] NU-Text omits *that* and *which His disciples had entered.*

disciples, but His disciples had gone away
alone— 23 however, other boats came from Ti-
berias, near the place where they ate bread after
the Lord had given thanks— 24 when the people
therefore saw that Jesus was not there, nor His
disciples, they also got into boats and came to
Capernaum, [a]seeking Jesus. 25 And when they
found Him on the other side of the sea, they
said to Him, "Rabbi, when did You come here?"
26 Jesus answered them and said, "Most as-
suredly, I say to you, you seek Me, not because
you saw the signs, but because you ate of the
loaves and were filled. 27 [a]Do not labor for the
food which perishes, but [b]for the food which
endures to everlasting life, which the Son of
Man will give you, [c]because God the Father has
set His seal on Him."
28 Then they said to Him, "What shall we do,
that we may work the works of God?"
29 Jesus answered and said to them, [a]"This is
the work of God, that you believe in Him whom
He sent."
30 Therefore they said to Him, [a]"What sign
will You perform then, that we may see it and
believe You? What work will You do? 31 [a]Our fa-
thers ate the manna in the desert; as it is written,
[b]'He gave them bread from heaven to eat.' "[1]
32 Then Jesus said to them, "Most assuredly,
I say to you, Moses did not give you the bread
from heaven, but [a]My Father gives you the true
bread from heaven. 33 For the bread of God is
He who comes down from heaven and gives
life to the world."
34 [a]Then they said to Him, "Lord, give us this
bread always."
35 And Jesus said to them, [a]"I am the bread
of life. [b]He who comes to Me shall never hunger,
and he who believes in Me shall never [c]thirst.
36 [a]But I said to you that you have seen Me and
yet [b]do not believe. 37 [a]All that the Father gives
Me will come to Me, and [b]the one who comes to
Me I will by no means cast out. 38 For I have come
down from heaven, [a]not to do My own will, [b]but
the will of Him who sent Me. 39 This is the will of
the Father who sent Me, [a]that of all He has given
Me I should lose nothing, but should raise it up
at the last day. 40 And this is the will of Him who
sent Me, [a]that everyone who sees the Son and
believes in Him may have everlasting life; and
I will raise him up at the last day."

### *REJECTED BY HIS OWN*

41 The Jews then complained about Him,
because He said, "I am the bread which came
down from heaven." 42 And they said, [a]"Is not
this Jesus, the son of Joseph, whose father and
mother we know? How is it then that He says,
'I have come down from heaven'?"
43 Jesus therefore answered and said to
them, "Do not murmur among yourselves. 44 [a]No

**6:24** [a] Mark 1:37; Luke 4:42 **6:27** [a] Matt. 6:19 [b] John 4:14; [Eph. 2:8, 9] [c] Ps. 2:7; Is. 42:1; Matt. 3:17; 17:5; Mark 1:11; 9:7; Luke 3:22; 9:35; John 5:37; Acts 2:22; 2 Pet. 1:17 **6:29** [a] 1 Thess. 1:3; James 2:22; [1 John 3:23]; Rev. 2:26 **6:30** [a] Matt. 12:38; 16:1; Mark 8:11; 1 Cor. 1:22 **6:31** [a] Ex. 16:15; Num. 11:7; 1 Cor. 10:3 [b] Ex. 16:4, 15; Neh. 9:15; Ps. 78:24 [1] Exodus 16:4; Nehemiah 9:15; Psalm 78:24 **6:32** [a] John 3:13, 16 **6:34** [a] John 4:15 **6:35** [a] John 6:48, 58 [b] John 4:14; 7:37; Rev. 7:16 [c] Is. 55:1, 2 **6:36** [a] John 6:26, 64; 15:24 [b] John 10:26 **6:37** [a] John 6:45 [b] [Matt. 24:24; John 10:28, 29]; 2 Tim. 2:19; 1 John 2:19 **6:38** [a] Matt. 26:39; John 5:30 [b] John 4:34 **6:39** [a] John 10:28; 17:12; 18:9 **6:40** [a] John 3:15, 16; 4:14; 6:27, 47, 54 **6:42** [a] Matt. 13:55; Mark 6:3; Luke 4:22 **6:44** [a] Song 1:4

KNOW THE TRUTH

## THE DOCTRINE OF THE FUTURE

### PART 3: THE RESURRECTION OF THE DEAD

**6:39–40** Humans were created to live with God forever. Death, however, is a consequence of sin. The Bible highlights three kinds of death. The first is **physical death**. The second is **spiritual death**, meaning that one's spirit and mind are dead in sin and unable to perceive or relate to the living God (see Eph. 2:1–3). The final and most serious kind of death is **eternal separation** from God and unending destruction (see Mark 9:42–48).

Jesus suffered and died to pay the price a just and holy God required for our sins, and in doing so, He defeated all three forms of death. Those who trust in Jesus as Savior are rescued from spiritual death and made spiritually alive with Christ (see Eph. 2:4–7). Although believers may physically die, all His followers will be raised like He has been raised and will be given a glorified body like He has (see 1 Cor. 15:20–58; 1 Thess. 4:14–18). Believers will live forevermore in these new, resurrected physical bodies. Those not made spiritually alive with Christ will also be raised, yet not to eternal life with Him, but to eternal separation (see Rev. 20:11–15).

*For* **THE DOCTRINE OF THE FUTURE: PART 4: THE FINAL JUDGMENT**, *turn to Revelation 20:11–15 on page 1308.*

### SEEING JESUS IN THE SCRIPTURE

**6:45** Jesus teaching the crowds fulfilled prophecy that God would teach His people directly (see Is. 54:13).

one can come to Me unless the Father who sent Me [b]draws him; and I will raise him up at the last day. 45 It is written in the prophets, [a]'And they shall all be taught by God.'[1] [b]Therefore everyone who has heard and learned[2] from the Father comes to Me. 46 [a]Not that anyone has seen the Father, [b]except He who is from God; He has seen the Father. 47 Most assuredly, I say to you, [a]he who believes in Me[1] has everlasting life. 48 [a]I am the bread of life. 49 [a]Your fathers ate the manna in the wilderness, and are dead. 50 [a]This is the bread which comes down from heaven, that one may eat of it and not die. 51 I am the living bread [a]which came down from heaven. If anyone eats of this bread, he will live forever; and [b]the bread that I shall give is My flesh, which I shall give for the life of the world."

52 The Jews therefore [a]quarreled among themselves, saying, "How can this Man give us *His* flesh to eat?"

53 Then Jesus said to them, "Most assuredly, I say to you, unless [a]you eat the flesh of the Son of Man and drink His blood, you have no life in you. 54 [a]Whoever eats My flesh and drinks My blood has eternal life, and I will raise him up at the last day. 55 For My flesh is food indeed,[1] and My blood is drink indeed. 56 He who eats My flesh and drinks My blood [a]abides in Me, and I in him. 57 As the living Father sent Me, and I live because of the Father, so he who feeds on Me will live because of Me. 58 [a]This is the bread which came down from heaven—not [b]as your fathers ate the manna, and are dead. He who eats this bread will live forever."

**6:53–58** Jesus had made it abundantly clear in this context that eternal life is gained by believing (see John 6:29, 35, 40, 47). These verses teach the benefits of Jesus' death must be appropriated, by faith, by each individual.

59 These things He said in the synagogue as He taught in Capernaum.

### *MANY DISCIPLES TURN AWAY*

60 [a]Therefore many of His disciples, when they heard *this,* said, "This is a hard saying; who can understand it?"

61 When Jesus knew in Himself that His disciples complained about this, He said to them, "Does this offend you? 62 [a]*What* then if you should see the Son of Man ascend where He was before? 63 [a]It is the Spirit who gives life; the [b]flesh profits nothing. The [c]words that I speak to you are spirit, and *they* are life. 64 But [a]there are some of you who do not believe." For [b]Jesus knew from the beginning who they were who did not believe, and who would betray Him. 65 And He said, "Therefore [a]I have said to you that no one can come to Me unless it has been granted to him by My Father."

66 [a]From that *time* many of His disciples went back and walked with Him no more. 67 Then Jesus said to the twelve, "Do you also want to go away?"

68 But Simon Peter answered Him, "Lord, to whom shall we go? You have [a]the words of eternal life. 69 [a]Also we have come to believe and know that You are the Christ, the Son of the living God."[1]

70 Jesus answered them, [a]"Did I not choose you, the twelve, [b]and one of you is a devil?" 71 He spoke of [a]Judas Iscariot, *the son* of Simon, for it was he who would [b]betray Him, being one of the twelve.

### *JESUS' BROTHERS DISBELIEVE*

**7** After these things Jesus walked in Galilee; for He did not want to walk in Judea, [a]because the Jews[1] sought to kill Him. 2 [a]Now the Jews' Feast of Tabernacles was at hand. 3 [a]His brothers therefore said to Him, "Depart from here and go into Judea, that Your disciples also may see the works that You are doing. 4 For no one does anything in secret while he himself seeks to be known openly. If You do these things, show Yourself to the world." 5 For [a]even His [b]brothers did not believe in Him.

6 Then Jesus said to them, [a]"My time has not yet come, but your time is always ready. 7 [a]The world cannot hate you, but it hates Me [b]because I testify of it that its works are evil. 8 You go up to this feast. I am not yet[1] going up to this feast, [a]for My time has not yet fully come." 9 When He had said these things to them, He remained in Galilee.

### *THE HEAVENLY SCHOLAR*

10 But when His brothers had gone up, then He also went up to the feast, not openly, but as it were in secret. 11 Then [a]the Jews sought Him

**6:44** [b] [Phil. 1:29; 2:12, 13] **6:45** [a] Is. 54:13 [b] John 6:37 [1] Isaiah 54:13 [2] M-Text reads *hears and has learned.* **6:46** [a] John 1:18 [b] Matt. 11:27 **6:47** [a] [John 3:16, 18] [1] NU-Text omits *in Me.* **6:48** [a] John 6:33, 35 **6:49** [a] John 6:31, 58 **6:50** [a] John 6:51, 58 **6:51** [a] John 3:13 [b] Heb. 10:5 **6:52** [a] John 7:43; 9:16; 10:19 **6:53** [a] Matt. 26:26 **6:54** [a] John 4:14; 6:27, 40 **6:55** [1] NU-Text reads *true food* and *true drink.* **6:56** [a] [1 John 3:24; 4:15, 16] **6:58** [a] John 6:49–51 [b] Ex. 16:14–35 **6:60** [a] John 6:66 **6:62** [a] Acts 1:9; 2:32, 33 **6:63** [a] 2 Cor. 3:6 [b] John 3:6 [c] [John 6:68; 14:24] **6:64** [a] John 6:36 [b] John 2:24, 25; 13:11 **6:65** [a] John 6:37, 44, 45 **6:66** [a] Luke 9:62 **6:68** [a] Acts 5:20 **6:69** [a] Luke 9:20 [1] NU-Text reads *You are the Holy One of God.* **6:70** [a] Luke 6:13 [b] [John 13:27] **6:71** [a] John 12:4; 13:2, 26 [b] Matt. 26:14–16 **7:1** [a] John 5:18; 7:19, 25; 8:37, 40 [1] That is, the ruling authorities **7:2** [a] Lev. 23:34 **7:3** [a] Matt. 12:46 **7:5** [a] Ps. 69:8 [b] Mark 3:21 **7:6** [a] John 2:4; 8:20 **7:7** [a] [John 15:19] [b] John 3:19 **7:8** [a] John 8:20 [1] NU-Text omits *yet.* **7:11** [a] John 11:56

at the feast, and said, "Where is He?" 12 And
[a]there was much complaining among the peo-
ple concerning Him. [b]Some said, "He is good";
others said, "No, on the contrary, He deceives
the people." 13 However, no one spoke openly of
Him [a]for fear of the Jews.
14 Now about the middle of the feast Jesus
went up into the temple and [a]taught. 15 [a]And
the Jews marveled, saying, "How does this Man
know letters, having never studied?"

**SEEING JESUS IN THE SCRIPTURE**

**7:14** Jesus teaching in the temple fulfilled prophecy that God would teach His people in the assembly (see Ps. 22:22).

16 Jesus[1] answered them and said, [a]"My doc-
trine is not Mine, but His who sent Me. 17 [a]If
anyone wills to do His will, he shall know con-
cerning the doctrine, whether it is from God
or *whether* I speak on My own *authority.* 18 [a]He
who speaks from himself seeks his own glory;
but He who [b]seeks the glory of the One who
sent Him is true, and [c]no unrighteousness is
in Him. 19 [a]Did not Moses give you the law, yet
none of you keeps the law? [b]Why do you seek
to kill Me?"
20 The people answered and said, [a]"You have
a demon. Who is seeking to kill You?"
21 Jesus answered and said to them, "I did
one work, and you all marvel. 22 [a]Moses therefore
gave you circumcision (not that it is from Moses,
[b]but from the fathers), and you circumcise a man
on the Sabbath. 23 If a man receives circumcision
on the Sabbath, so that the law of Moses should
not be broken, are you angry with Me because
[a]I made a man completely well on the Sabbath?
24 [a]Do not judge according to appearance, but
judge with righteous judgment."

### COULD THIS BE THE CHRIST?

25 Now some of them from Jerusalem said,
"Is this not He whom they seek to [a]kill? 26 But
look! He speaks boldly, and they say nothing
to Him. [a]Do the rulers know indeed that this is
truly[1] the Christ? 27 [a]However, we know where
this Man is from; but when the Christ comes,
no one knows where He is from."
28 Then Jesus cried out, as He taught in the
temple, saying, [a]"You both know Me, and you
know where I am from; and [b]I have not come
of Myself, but He who sent Me [c]is true, [d]whom
you do not know. 29 But[1] [a]I know Him, for I am
from Him, and He sent Me."
30 Therefore [a]they sought to take Him; but
[b]no one laid a hand on Him, because His hour
had not yet come. 31 And [a]many of the people
believed in Him, and said, "When the Christ
comes, will He do more signs than these which
this *Man* has done?"

### JESUS AND THE RELIGIOUS LEADERS

32 The Pharisees heard the crowd murmur-
ing these things concerning Him, and the Phar-
isees and the chief priests sent officers to take
Him. 33 Then Jesus said to them,[1] [a]"I shall be with
you a little while longer, and *then* I [b]go to Him
who sent Me. 34 You [a]will seek Me and not find
*Me,* and where I am you [b]cannot come."
35 Then the Jews said among themselves,
"Where does He intend to go that we shall not
find Him? Does He intend to go to [a]the Disper-
sion among the Greeks and teach the Greeks?
36 What is this thing that He said, 'You will seek
Me and not find Me, and where I am you cannot
come'?"

### THE PROMISE OF THE HOLY SPIRIT

37 [a]On the last day, that great *day* of the feast,
Jesus stood and cried out, saying, [b]"If anyone
thirsts, let him come to Me and drink. 38 [a]He who
believes in Me, as the Scripture has said, [b]out of
his heart will flow rivers of living water." 39 [a]But
this He spoke concerning the Spirit, whom those
believing[1] in Him would receive; for the Holy[2]
Spirit was not yet *given,* because Jesus was not
yet [b]glorified.

### WHO IS HE?

40 Therefore many[1] from the crowd, when
they heard this saying, said, "Truly this is [a]the
Prophet." 41 Others said, "This is [a]the Christ."
But some said, "Will the Christ come out of
Galilee? 42 [a]Has not the Scripture said that the
Christ comes from the seed of David and from
the town of Bethlehem, [b]where David was?" 43 So
[a]there was a division among the people because
of Him. 44 Now [a]some of them wanted to take
Him, but no one laid hands on Him.

### REJECTED BY THE AUTHORITIES

45 Then the officers came to the chief priests
and Pharisees, who said to them, "Why have you
not brought Him?"
46 The officers answered, [a]"No man ever
spoke like this Man!"

**7:12** [a] John 9:16; 10:19 [b] Luke 7:16 **7:13** [a] [John 9:22; 12:42; 19:38] **7:14** [a] Mark 6:34 **7:15** [a] Matt. 13:54 **7:16** [a] John 3:11 [1] NU-Text and M-Text read *So Jesus.* **7:17** [a] John 3:21; 8:43 **7:18** [a] John 5:41 [b] John 8:50 [c] [2 Cor. 5:21] **7:19** [a] Deut. 33:4 [b] Matt. 12:14 **7:20** [a] John 8:48, 52 **7:22** [a] Lev. 12:3 [b] Gen. 17:9–14 **7:23** [a] John 5:8, 9, 16 **7:24** [a] Prov. 24:23 **7:25** [a] Matt. 21:38; 26:4 **7:26** [a] John 7:48 [1] NU-Text omits *truly.* **7:27** [a] Luke 4:22 **7:28** [a] John 8:14 [b] John 5:43 [c] Rom. 3:4 [d] John 1:18; 8:55 **7:29** [a] Matt. 11:27 [1] NU-Text and M-Text omit *But.* **7:30** [a] Mark 11:18 [b] John 7:32, 44; 8:20; 10:39 **7:31** [a] Matt. 12:23 **7:33** [a] John 13:33 [b] [1 Pet. 3:22] [1] NU-Text and M-Text omit *to them.* **7:34** [a] Hos. 5:6 [b] [Matt. 5:20] **7:35** [a] James 1:1 **7:37** [a] Lev. 23:36 [b] [Is. 55:1] **7:38** [a] Deut. 18:15 [b] Is. 12:3; 43:20; 44:3; 55:1 **7:39** [a] Is. 44:3 [b] John 12:16; 13:31; 17:5 [1] NU-Text reads *who believed.* [2] NU-Text omits *Holy.* **7:40** [a] Deut. 18:15, 18 [1] NU-Text reads *some.* **7:41** [a] John 4:42; 6:69 **7:42** [a] Mic. 5:2 [b] 1 Sam. 16:1, 4 **7:43** [a] John 7:12 **7:44** [a] John 7:30 **7:46** [a] Luke 4:22

KNOW THE TRUTH

## THE DOCTRINE OF JESUS

### PART 6: THE TEACHINGS OF JESUS

**7:37–46** Jesus' teachings accomplish at least four important functions: clarification, instruction, division, and revelation. Jesus' earthly ministry came at a time of extreme religious confusion. The Pharisees, Sadducees, scribes, and lawyers (Torah scholars) were widely taking the precepts of the Torah (Genesis–Deuteronomy) out of context and to various extremes. First, Jesus' teachings brought unprecedented **clarification** concerning the true intent of the Torah's commands (see Matt. 5:27–32). He made clear what others made confusing and exhausting. Second, Jesus' teachings gave **instruction** on how to live in His kingdom. He helped people understand what to do and how to do it from the right heart motivation (see Matt. 6:5–15). Third, Jesus' teachings brought **division** between those who wanted to live for God and those living only for their own interests (see John 7:40–52). His teachings usually separated His hearers into no less than three groups: devoted disciples, curious crowds, and resistant religious leaders. Finally, His teaching brought **revelation** to His hearers concerning who He is, who they are, and how they must respond to Him (see John 3:17–20). Jesus' teachings reveal He is the Christ, His hearers are sinful people in need of forgiveness and eternal life, and the only way to be saved is through faith in Him (see John 8:31–36).

*For* **THE DOCTRINE OF JESUS: PART 7: THE SACRIFICE OF JESUS,** *turn to Isaiah 53:4–12 on page 731.*

47 Then the Pharisees answered them,
"Are you also deceived? 48 Have any of the rul-
ers or the Pharisees believed in Him? 49 But
this crowd that does not know the law is
accursed."
50 Nicodemus [a](he who came to Jesus by
night,[1] being one of them) said to them, 51 [a]"Does
our law judge a man before it hears him and
knows what he is doing?"
52 They answered and said to him, "Are you
also from Galilee? Search and look, for [a]no
prophet has arisen[1] out of Galilee."

**7:47–48** Even though the Romans controlled the land of Israel, they gave the Jews some say in the way things were run. The Sanhedrin, or Jewish council, was a group of seventy-one community leaders who served as a type of "supreme court." They made decisions and rulings on legal matters and other special concerns. The council could not impose the death penalty, and its rulings could always be overturned by the Roman rulers.

#### *AN ADULTERESS FACES THE LIGHT OF THE WORLD*

53 And everyone went to his *own* house.[1]
8 But Jesus went to the Mount of Olives.
2 Now early[1] in the morning He came again
into the temple, and all the people came to Him;
and He sat down and [a]taught them. 3 Then the
scribes and Pharisees brought to Him a woman
caught in adultery. And when they had set her
in the midst, 4 they said to Him, "Teacher, this
woman was caught[1] in [a]adultery, in the very act.
5 [a]Now Moses, in the law, commanded[1] us that
such should be stoned.[2] But what do You say?"[3]
6 This they said, testing Him, that they [a]might
have *something* of which to accuse Him. But
Jesus stooped down and wrote on the ground
with *His* finger, as though He did not hear.[1]
7 So when they continued asking Him, He raised
Himself up[1] and said to them, [a]"He who is without
sin among you, let him throw a stone at her first."
8 And again He stooped down and wrote on the
ground. 9 Then those who heard *it,* [a]being convicted
by *their* conscience,[1] went out one by one, beginning
with the oldest *even* to the last. And Jesus was left
alone, and the woman standing in the midst. 10 When
Jesus had raised Himself up and saw no one but the
woman, He said to her,[1] "Woman, where are those
accusers of yours?[2] Has no one condemned you?"

**7:50** [a] John 3:1, 2; 19:39 [1] NU-Text reads *before.* **7:51** [a] Deut. 1:16, 17; 19:15 **7:52** [a] [Is. 9:1, 2] [1] NU-Text reads *is to rise.* **7:53** [1] The words *And everyone* through *sin no more* (8:11) are bracketed by NU-Text as not original. They are present in over 900 manuscripts. **8:2** [a] John 8:20; 18:20 [1] M-Text reads *very early.* **8:4** [a] Ex. 20:14 [1] M-Text reads *we found this woman.* **8:5** [a] Lev. 20:10 [1] M-Text reads *in our law Moses commanded.* [2] NU-Text and M-Text read *to stone such.* [3] M-Text adds *about her.* **8:6** [a] Matt. 22:15 [1] NU-Text and M-Text omit *as though He did not hear.* **8:7** [a] Deut. 17:7 [1] M-Text reads *He looked up.* **8:9** [a] Rom. 2:22 [1] NU-Text and M-Text omit *being convicted by their conscience.* **8:10** [1] NU-Text omits *and saw no one but the woman;* M-Text reads *He saw her and said.* [2] NU-Text and M-Text omit *of yours.*

11 She said, "No one, Lord."
And Jesus said to her, [a]"Neither do I condemn you; go and[1] [b]sin no more."
12 Then Jesus spoke to them again, saying,
[a]"I am the light of the world. He who [b]follows Me shall not walk in darkness, but have the light of life."

### JESUS DEFENDS HIS SELF-WITNESS

13 The Pharisees therefore said to Him, [a]"You bear witness of Yourself; Your witness is not true."
14 Jesus answered and said to them, "Even if I bear witness of Myself, My witness is true, for I know where I came from and where I am going; but [a]you do not know where I come from
and where I am going. 15 [a]You judge according
to the flesh; [b]I judge no one. 16 And yet if I do
judge, My judgment is true; for [a]I am not alone,
but I *am* with the Father who sent Me. 17 [a]It is
also written in your law that the testimony of
two men is true. 18 I am One who bears witness
of Myself, and [a]the Father who sent Me bears witness of Me."
19 Then they said to Him, "Where is Your Father?"
Jesus answered, [a]"You know neither Me nor My Father. [b]If you had known Me, you would have known My Father also."

8:11 [a] [John 3:17] [b] [John 5:14] [1] NU-Text and M-Text add *from now on.* 8:12 [a] John 1:4; 9:5; 12:35 [b] 1 Thess. 5:5 8:13 [a] John 5:31 8:14 [a] John 7:28; 9:29 8:15 [a] John 7:24 [b] [John 3:17; 12:47; 18:36] 8:16 [a] John 16:32 8:17 [a] Deut. 17:6; 19:15 8:18 [a] John 5:37 8:19 [a] John 16:3 [b] John 14:7

## THE SEVEN "I AM" STATEMENTS IN JOHN

Jesus' "I am" statements would have particular significance to the first-century Jewish listener. God had revealed Himself to Moses with a resounding "I AM" (Exodus 3:14). Now Jesus was using the same words to describe Himself (John 4:26; 6:20; 13:19).

| Use | Meaning | Reference |
|---|---|---|
| **"I am the bread of life"** | As bread sustains physical life, so Christ offers and sustains spiritual life. The nourishment and satisfaction He offers are permanent. | John 6:35, 41, 48, 51 |
| **"I am the light of the world"** | To a world stumbling about in the darkness of sin, Christ offers Himself as a constant guide. Light is also symbolic of holiness. | John 8:12 |
| **"I am the door of the sheep"** | Shepherds guided their flocks into stone enclosures each night to protect them. These structures had no doors. The shepherd would sit or lie in the opening to prevent predators from attacking. Thus Jesus was describing His care and constant devotion to those who are His. | John 10:7, 9 |
| **"I am the good shepherd"** | Unlike hirelings who might run away and leave the flock unprotected, Jesus is committed to caring for and keeping watch over His people. | John 10:11, 14 |
| **"I am the resurrection and the life"** | Jesus is the Lord of all life and possesses the power to raise the dead. Death is not the final word, for all who are in Christ will live forever. | John 11:25 |
| **"I am the way, the truth, and the life"** | Jesus is the one and only way to the Father. He is the source of all truth and the source for all knowledge about God. He offers to spiritually dead people the very life of God. | John 14:6 |
| **"I am the true vine"** | The Old Testament contains many references to Israel as God's vine (Ps. 80:8; Is. 5:1–7; Ezek. 15; Hos. 10:1). But because of the nation's unfruitfulness, Jesus came to fulfill God's plan. By attaching ourselves to Christ, we enable His life to flow in and through us. Then we cannot help but bear fruit that will honor the Father. In this metaphor, He is the Gardener. | John 15:1, 5 |

20 These words Jesus spoke in [a]the treasury,
as He taught in the temple; and [b]no one laid
hands on Him, for [c]His hour had not yet come.

> **8:20** The **treasury** was a room in the **temple** set aside specifically for collecting and storing the taxes and tithes collected from the people of Jerusalem.

### JESUS PREDICTS HIS DEPARTURE

21 Then Jesus said to them again, "I am going
away, and [a]you will seek Me, and [b]will die in your
sin. Where I go you cannot come."
22 So the Jews said, "Will He kill Himself,
because He says, 'Where I go you cannot come'?"
23 And He said to them, [a]"You are from be-
neath; I am from above. [b]You are of this world;
I am not of this world. 24 [a]Therefore I said to you
that you will die in your sins; [b]for if you do not
believe that I am *He,* you will die in your sins."
25 Then they said to Him, "Who are You?"
And Jesus said to them, "Just what I [a]have
been saying to you from the beginning. 26 I have
many things to say and to judge concerning you,
but [a]He who sent Me is true; and [b]I speak to the
world those things which I heard from Him."
27 They did not understand that He spoke to
them of the Father.
28 Then Jesus said to them, "When you [a]lift
up the Son of Man, [b]then you will know that I am
*He,* and [c]*that* I do nothing of Myself; but [d]as My
Father taught Me, I speak these things. 29 And
[a]He who sent Me is with Me. [b]The Father has
not left Me alone, [c]for I always do those things
that please Him." 30 As He spoke these words,
[a]many believed in Him.

### THE TRUTH SHALL MAKE YOU FREE

31 Then Jesus said to those Jews who believed
Him, "If you [a]abide in My word, you are My dis-
ciples indeed. 32 And you shall know the [a]truth,
and [b]the truth shall make you free."
33 They answered Him, [a]"We are Abraham's
descendants, and have never been in bondage
to anyone. How *can* You say, 'You will be made
free'?"
34 Jesus answered them, "Most assuredly, I
say to you, [a]whoever commits sin is a slave of
sin. 35 And [a]a slave does not abide in the house
forever, *but* a son abides forever. 36 [a]Therefore
if the Son makes you free, you shall be free
indeed.

### ABRAHAM'S SEED AND SATAN'S

37 "I know that you are Abraham's descen-
dants, but [a]you seek to kill Me, because My word
has no place in you. 38 [a]I speak what I have seen
with My Father, and you do what you have seen
with[1] your father."
39 They answered and said to Him, [a]"Abra-
ham is our father."
Jesus said to them, [b]"If you were Abraham's
children, you would do the works of Abraham.
40 [a]But now you seek to kill Me, a Man who has told
you the truth [b]which I heard from God. Abraham
did not do this. 41 You do the deeds of your father."
Then they said to Him, "We were not born of
fornication; [a]we have one Father—God."
42 Jesus said to them, [a]"If God were your Fa-
ther, you would love Me, for [b]I proceeded forth
and came from God; [c]nor have I come of Myself,
but He sent Me. 43 [a]Why do you not understand
My speech? Because you are not able to listen to
My word. 44 [a]You are of *your* father the devil, and
the [b]desires of your father you want to [c]do. He
was a murderer from the beginning, and [d]does
not stand in the truth, because there is no truth
in him. When he speaks a lie, he speaks from
his own *resources,* for he is a liar and the father
of it. 45 But because I tell the truth, you do not
believe Me. 46 Which of you convicts Me of sin?
And if I tell the truth, why do you not believe Me?
47 [a]He who is of God hears God's words; therefore
you do not hear, because you are not of God."

### BEFORE ABRAHAM WAS, I AM

48 Then the Jews answered and said to Him,
"Do we not say rightly that You are a Samaritan
and [a]have a demon?"
49 Jesus answered, "I do not have a demon;
but I honor My Father, and [a]you dishonor Me.
50 And [a]I do not seek My *own* glory; there is
One who seeks and judges. 51 Most assuredly, I
say to you, [a]if anyone keeps My word he shall
never see death."
52 Then the Jews said to Him, "Now we know
that You [a]have a demon! [b]Abraham is dead, and
the prophets; and You say, 'If anyone keeps
My word he shall never taste death.' 53 Are You
greater than our father Abraham, who is dead?
And the prophets are dead. [a]Who do You make
Yourself out to be?"
54 Jesus answered, [a]"If I honor Myself, My
honor is nothing. [b]It is My Father who honors
Me, of whom you say that He is your[1] God. 55 Yet
[a]you have not known Him, but I know Him. And
if I say, 'I do not know Him,' I shall be a liar like
you; but I do know Him and [b]keep His word.

**8:20** [a] Mark 12:41, 43 [b] John 2:4; 7:30 [c] John 7:8 **8:21** [a] John 7:34; 13:33 [b] John 8:24 **8:23** [a] John 3:31 [b] 1 John 4:5 **8:24** [a] John 8:21 [b] [Mark 16:16] **8:25** [a] John 4:26 **8:26** [a] John 7:28 [b] John 3:32; 15:15 **8:28** [a] John 3:14; 12:32; 19:18 [b] [Rom. 1:4] [c] John 5:19, 30 [d] John 3:11 **8:29** [a] John 14:10 [b] John 8:16; 16:32 [c] John 4:34; 5:30; 6:38 **8:30** [a] John 7:31; 10:42; 11:45 **8:31** [a] [John 14:15, 23] **8:32** [a] [John 1:14, 17; 14:6] [b] [Rom. 6:14, 18, 22] **8:33** [a] [Matt. 3:9] **8:34** [a] 2 Pet. 2:19 **8:35** [a] Gal. 4:30 **8:36** [a] Gal. 5:1 **8:37** [a] John 7:19 **8:38** [a] [John 3:32; 5:19, 30; 14:10, 24] [1] NU-Text reads *heard from.* **8:39** [a] Matt. 3:9 [b] [Rom. 2:28] **8:40** [a] John 8:37 [b] John 8:26 **8:41** [a] Is. 63:16 **8:42** [a] 1 John 5:1 [b] John 16:27; 17:8, 25 [c] Gal. 4:4 **8:43** [a] [John 7:17] **8:44** [a] Matt. 13:38 [b] 1 John 2:16, 17 [c] [1 John 3:8–10, 15] [d] [Jude 6] **8:47** [a] 1 John 4:6 **8:48** [a] John 7:20; 10:20 **8:49** [a] John 5:41 **8:50** [a] John 5:41; 7:18 **8:51** [a] John 5:24; 11:26 **8:52** [a] John 7:20; 10:20 [b] Zech. 1:5 **8:53** [a] John 10:33; 19:7 **8:54** [a] John 5:31, 32 [b] Acts 3:13 [1] NU-Text and M-Text read *our.* **8:55** [a] John 7:28, 29 [b] [John 15:10]

56 Your father Abraham [a]rejoiced to see My day,
[b]and he saw *it* and was glad."
57 Then the Jews said to Him, "You are not
yet fifty years old, and have You seen Abraham?"
58 Jesus said to them, "Most assuredly, I say
to you, [a]before Abraham was, [b]I AM."
59 Then [a]they took up stones to throw at Him;
but Jesus hid Himself and went out of the temple,[1]
[b]going through the midst of them, and so passed by.

**SEEING JESUS IN THE SCRIPTURE**

**8:58–59** "I AM" was a declaration of divinity. They are the same words God spoke to Moses at the burning bush (see Ex. 3:14).

### *A MAN BORN BLIND RECEIVES SIGHT*

9 Now as *Jesus* passed by, He saw a man who
was blind from birth. 2 And His disciples
asked Him, saying, "Rabbi, [a]who sinned, this
man or his parents, that he was born blind?"

**9:2** It was commonly believed that sickness was a result of sin. It would follow, then, that someone **born blind** must have either sinned in the womb or was paying for the sins of his or her parents. Jesus rejected both suggestions (v. 3). Neither is right because the premise is wrong: while sickness and infirmity *can* result from sin, it doesn't always have to.

3 Jesus answered, "Neither this man nor
his parents sinned, [a]but that the works of God
should be revealed in him. 4 [a]I[1] must work the
works of Him who sent Me while it is [b]day; *the*
night is coming when no one can work. 5 As long
as I am in the world, [a]I am the light of the world."
6 When He had said these things, [a]He spat
on the ground and made clay with the saliva;
and He anointed the eyes of the blind man with
the clay. 7 And He said to him, "Go, wash [a]in the
pool of Siloam" (which is translated, Sent). So
[b]he went and washed, and came back seeing.
8 Therefore the neighbors and those who
previously had seen that he was blind[1] said, "Is
not this he who sat and begged?"
9 Some said, "This is he." Others *said,* "He
is like him."[1]
He said, "I am *he.*"
10 Therefore they said to him, "How were
your eyes opened?"
11 He answered and said, [a]"A Man called Jesus
made clay and anointed my eyes and said to me,
'Go to the pool of[1] Siloam and wash.' So I went
and washed, and I received sight."
12 Then they said to him, "Where is He?"
He said, "I do not know."

### *THE PHARISEES EXCOMMUNICATE THE HEALED MAN*

13 They brought him who formerly was blind
to the Pharisees. 14 Now it was a Sabbath when
Jesus made the clay and opened his eyes. 15 Then
the Pharisees also asked him again how he had
received his sight. He said to them, "He put clay
on my eyes, and I washed, and I see."
16 Therefore some of the Pharisees said, "This
Man is not from God, because He does not keep
the Sabbath."
Others said, [a]"How can a man who is a sinner do such signs?" And [b]there was a division
among them.
17 They said to the blind man again, "What do
you say about Him because He opened your eyes?"
He said, [a]"He is a prophet."
18 But the Jews did not believe concerning
him, that he had been blind and received his
sight, until they called the parents of him who
had received his sight. 19 And they asked them,
saying, "Is this your son, who you say was born
blind? How then does he now see?"
20 His parents answered them and said, "We
know that this is our son, and that he was born
blind; 21 but by what means he now sees we do not
know, or who opened his eyes we do not know.
He is of age; ask him. He will speak for himself."
22 His parents said these *things* because [a]they
feared the Jews, for the Jews had agreed already
that if anyone confessed *that* He *was* Christ, he
[b]would be put out of the synagogue. 23 Therefore
his parents said, "He is of age; ask him."
24 So they again called the man who was
blind, and said to him, [a]"Give God the glory!
[b]We know that this Man is a sinner."
25 He answered and said, "Whether He is a
sinner *or not* I do not know. One thing I know:
that though I was blind, now I see."
26 Then they said to him again, "What did He
do to you? How did He open your eyes?"
27 He answered them, "I told you already, and
you did not listen. Why do you want to hear *it*
again? Do you also want to become His disciples?"
28 Then they reviled him and said, "You are
His disciple, but we are Moses' disciples. 29 We
know that God [a]spoke to [b]Moses; *as for* this *fellow,* [c]we do not know where He is from."
30 The man answered and said to them,
[a]"Why, this is a marvelous thing, that you do

**8:56** [a] Luke 10:24 [b] Heb. 11:13 **8:58** [a] Mic. 5:2 [b] Rev. 1:8 **8:59** [a] John 10:31; 11:8 [b] Luke 4:30 [1] NU-Text omits the rest of this verse. **9:2** [a] John 9:34 **9:3** [a] John 11:4 **9:4** [a] [John 4:34; 5:19, 36; 17:4] [b] John 11:9, 10; 12:35 [1] NU-Text reads *We.* **9:5** [a] [John 1:5, 9; 3:19; 8:12; 12:35, 46] **9:6** [a] Mark 7:33; 8:23 **9:7** [a] Neh. 3:15 [b] 2 Kin. 5:14 **9:8** [1] NU-Text reads *a beggar.* **9:9** [1] NU-Text reads *"No, but he is like him."* **9:11** [a] John 9:6, 7 [1] NU-Text omits *the pool of.* **9:16** [a] John 3:2; 9:33 [b] John 7:12, 43; 10:19 **9:17** [a] [John 4:19; 6:14] **9:22** [a] John 7:13; 12:42; 19:38; Acts 5:13 [b] John 16:2 **9:24** [a] Josh. 7:19; 1 Sam. 6:5; Ezra 10:11; Rev. 11:13 [b] John 9:16 **9:29** [a] Ex. 19:19, 20; 33:11; 34:29; Num. 12:6–8 [b] [John 5:45–47] [c] John 7:27, 28; 8:14 **9:30** [a] John 3:10

not know where He is from; yet He has opened my eyes! 31 Now we know that [a]God does not hear sinners; but if anyone is a worshiper of God and does His will, He hears him. 32 Since the world began it has been unheard of that anyone opened the eyes of one who was born blind. 33 [a]If this Man were not from God, He could do nothing."

34 They answered and said to him, [a]"You were completely born in sins, and are you teaching us?" And they cast him out.

### *TRUE VISION AND TRUE BLINDNESS*

35 Jesus heard that they had cast him out; and when He had [a]found him, He said to him, "Do you [b]believe in [c]the Son of God?"[1]

36 He answered and said, "Who is He, Lord, that I may believe in Him?"

37 And Jesus said to him, "You have both seen Him and [a]it is He who is talking with you."

38 Then he said, "Lord, I believe!" And he [a]worshiped Him.

39 And Jesus said, [a]"For judgment I have come into this world, [b]that those who do not see may see, and that those who see may be made blind."

40 Then *some* of the Pharisees who were with Him heard these words, [a]and said to Him, "Are we blind also?"

41 Jesus said to them, [a]"If you were blind, you would have no sin; but now you say, 'We see.' Therefore your sin remains.

### *JESUS THE TRUE SHEPHERD*

**10** "Most assuredly, I say to you, he who does not enter the sheepfold by the door, but climbs up some other way, the same is a thief and a robber. 2 But he who enters by the door is the shepherd of the sheep. 3 To him the doorkeeper opens, and the sheep hear his voice; and he calls his own sheep by [a]name and leads them out. 4 And when he brings out his own sheep, he goes before them; and the sheep follow him, for they know his voice. 5 Yet they will by no means follow a [a]stranger, but will flee from him, for they do not know the voice of strangers." 6 Jesus used this illustration, but they did not understand the things which He spoke to them.

### *JESUS THE GOOD SHEPHERD*

7 Then Jesus said to them again, "Most assuredly, I say to you, I am the door of the sheep. 8 All who *ever* came before Me[1] are thieves and robbers, but the sheep did not hear them. 9 [a]I am the door. If anyone enters by Me, he will be saved, and will go in and out and find pasture. 10 The thief does not come except to steal, and to kill, and to destroy. I have come that they may have life, and that they may have *it* more abundantly.

11 [a]"I am the good shepherd. The good shepherd gives His life for the sheep. 12 But a hireling, *he who is* not the shepherd, one who does not own the sheep, sees the wolf coming and [a]leaves the sheep and flees; and the wolf catches the sheep and scatters them. 13 The hireling flees because he is a hireling and does not care about the sheep. 14 I am the good shepherd; and [a]I know My *sheep,* and [b]am known by My own. 15 [a]As the Father knows Me, even so I know the Father; [b]and I lay down My life for the sheep. 16 And [a]other sheep I have which are not of this fold; them also I must bring, and they will hear My voice; [b]and there will be one flock *and* one shepherd.

> **SEEING JESUS IN THE SCRIPTURE**
>
> **10:11** Jesus is God's promised shepherd who cares for the sheep by laying down His life for them (see Is. 40:10–11).

17 "Therefore My Father [a]loves Me, [b]because I lay down My life that I may take it again. 18 No one takes it from Me, but I lay it down of Myself. I [a]have power to lay it down, and I have power to take it again. [b]This command I have received from My Father."

19 Therefore [a]there was a division again among the Jews because of these sayings. 20 And many of them said, [a]"He has a demon and is mad. Why do you listen to Him?"

21 Others said, "These are not the words of one who has a demon. [a]Can a demon [b]open the eyes of the blind?"

### *THE SHEPHERD KNOWS HIS SHEEP*

22 Now it was the Feast of Dedication in Jerusalem, and it was winter. 23 And Jesus walked in the temple, [a]in Solomon's porch. 24 Then the Jews surrounded Him and said to Him, "How long do You keep us in doubt? If You are the Christ, tell us plainly."

25 Jesus answered them, "I told you, and you do not believe. [a]The works that I do in My Father's name, they [b]bear witness of Me. 26 But [a]you do not believe, because you are not of My sheep, as I said to you.[1] 27 [a]My sheep hear My

**9:31** [a] Job 27:9; 35:12; Ps. 18:41; Prov. 1:28; 15:29; 28:9; Is. 1:15; Jer. 11:11; 14:12; Ezek. 8:18; Mic. 3:4; Zech. 7:13; [James 5:16] **9:33** [a] John 3:2; 9:16 **9:34** [a] Ps. 51:5; John 9:2 **9:35** [a] John 5:14 [b] John 1:7; 16:31 [c] Matt. 14:33; 16:16; Mark 1:1; John 10:36; 1 John 5:13 [1] NU-Text reads *Son of Man.* **9:37** [a] John 4:26 **9:38** [a] Matt. 8:2 **9:39** [a] [John 3:17; 5:22, 27; 12:47] [b] Matt. 13:13; 15:14 **9:40** [a] [Rom. 2:19] **9:41** [a] John 15:22, 24 **10:3** [a] John 20:16 **10:5** [a] [2 Cor. 11:13–15] **10:8** [1] M-Text omits *before Me.* **10:9** [a] [John 14:6; Eph. 2:18] **10:11** [a] Gen. 49:24; Is. 40:11; Ezek. 34:23; [Heb. 13:20]; 1 Pet. 2:25; 5:4; Rev. 7:17 **10:12** [a] Zech. 11:16, 17 **10:14** [a] 2 Tim. 2:19 [b] 2 Tim. 1:12 **10:15** [a] Matt. 11:27 [b] [John 15:13; 19:30] **10:16** [a] Is. 42:6; 56:8 [b] Eph. 2:13–18 **10:17** [a] John 5:20 [b] [Heb. 2:9] **10:18** [a] [John 2:19; 5:26] [b] [John 6:38; 14:31; 17:4; Acts 2:24, 32] **10:19** [a] John 7:43; 9:16 **10:20** [a] John 7:20 **10:21** [a] [Ex. 4:11] [b] John 9:6, 7, 32, 33 **10:23** [a] Acts 3:11; 5:12 **10:25** [a] John 5:36; 10:38 [b] Matt. 11:4 **10:26** [a] [John 8:47] [1] NU-Text omits *as I said to you.* **10:27** [a] John 10:4, 14

> **10:22** After the Medes and Persians conquered Babylon, the Syrian king Antiochus Epiphanes took control of the temple in Jerusalem. In a vile act of blasphemy, he built an altar to the Greek god Zeus directly over what had been the Jewish altar of burnt offering. As if that weren't bad enough, he then sacrificed a pig, an unclean animal, on the altar. The Jews became so enraged that they revolted and overthrew the Syrians. In 165 BC, a group of Jews led by Judas Maccabeus cleansed the temple of its desecration. The eight-day **Feast of Dedication**, or Hanukkah, celebrated that cleansing.

voice, and I know them, and they follow Me. 28 And I give them eternal life, and they shall never perish; neither shall anyone snatch them out of My hand. 29 [a]My Father, [b]who has given *them* to Me, is greater than all; and no one is able to snatch *them* out of My Father's hand. 30 [a]I and *My* Father are one."

### *RENEWED EFFORTS TO STONE JESUS*

31 Then [a]the Jews took up stones again to stone Him. 32 Jesus answered them, "Many good works I have shown you from My Father. For which of those works do you stone Me?"

33 The Jews answered Him, saying, "For a good work we do not stone You, but for [a]blasphemy, and because You, being a Man, [b]make Yourself God."

34 Jesus answered them, "Is it not written in your law, [a]'I said, "You are gods"'?[1] 35 If He called them gods, [a]to whom the word of God came (and the Scripture [b]cannot be broken), 36 do you say of Him [a]whom the Father sanctified and [b]sent into the world, 'You are blaspheming,' [c]because I said, 'I am [d]the Son of God'? 37 [a]If I do not do the works of My Father, do not believe Me; 38 but if I do, though you do not believe Me, [a]believe the works, that you may know and believe[1] [b]that the Father *is* in Me, and I in Him." 39 [a]Therefore they sought again to seize Him, but He escaped out of their hand.

### *THE BELIEVERS BEYOND JORDAN*

40 And He went away again beyond the Jordan to the place [a]where John was baptizing at first, and there He stayed. 41 Then many came to Him and said, "John performed no sign, [a]but all the things that John spoke about this Man were true." 42 And many believed in Him there.

### *THE DEATH OF LAZARUS*

**11** Now a certain *man* was sick, Lazarus of Bethany, the town of [a]Mary and her sister Martha. 2 [a]It was *that* Mary who anointed the Lord with fragrant oil and wiped His feet with her hair, whose brother Lazarus was sick. 3 Therefore the sisters sent to Him, saying, "Lord, behold, he whom You love is sick."

4 When Jesus heard *that,* He said, "This sickness is not unto death, but for the glory of God, that the Son of God may be glorified through it."

5 Now Jesus loved Martha and her sister and Lazarus. 6 So, when He heard that he was sick, [a]He stayed two more days in the place where He was. 7 Then after this He said to *the* disciples, "Let us go to Judea again."

8 *The* disciples said to Him, "Rabbi, lately the Jews sought to [a]stone You, and are You going there again?"

9 Jesus answered, "Are there not twelve hours in the day? [a]If anyone walks in the day, he does not stumble, because he sees the [b]light of this world. 10 But [a]if one walks in the night, he stumbles, because the light is not in him." 11 These things He said, and after that He said to them, "Our friend Lazarus [a]sleeps, but I go that I may wake him up."

> **11:9** In New Testament Israel, the Jewish workday lasted **twelve hours**, from sunrise to sunset.

12 Then His disciples said, "Lord, if he sleeps he will get well." 13 However, Jesus spoke of his death, but they thought that He was speaking about taking rest in sleep.

14 Then Jesus said to them plainly, "Lazarus is dead. 15 And I am glad for your sakes that I was not there, that you may believe. Nevertheless let us go to him."

16 Then [a]Thomas, who is called the Twin, said to his fellow disciples, "Let us also go, that we may die with Him."

### *I AM THE RESURRECTION AND THE LIFE*

17 So when Jesus came, He found that he had already been in the tomb four days. 18 Now Bethany was near Jerusalem, about two miles[1] away. 19 And many of the Jews had joined the women around Martha and Mary, to comfort them concerning their brother.

20 Then Martha, as soon as she heard that Jesus was coming, went and met Him, but Mary was sitting in the house. 21 Now Martha said to Jesus, "Lord, if You had been here, my brother

**10:29** [a]John 14:28 [b][John 17:2, 6, 12, 24] **10:30** [a]John 17:11, 21–24 **10:31** [a]John 8:59 **10:33** [a]Matt. 9:3 [b]John 5:18 **10:34** [a]Ps. 82:6 [1]Psalm 82:6 **10:35** [a]Matt. 5:17, 18 [b]1 Pet. 1:25 **10:36** [a]John 6:27 [b]John 3:17 [c]John 5:17, 18 [d]Luke 1:35 **10:37** [a]John 10:25; 15:24 **10:38** [a]John 5:36 [b]John 14:10, 11 [1]NU-Text reads *understand.* **10:39** [a]John 7:30, 44 **10:40** [a]John 1:28 **10:41** [a][John 1:29, 36; 3:28–36; 5:33] **11:1** [a]Luke 10:38, 39 **11:2** [a]Matt. 26:7 **11:6** [a]John 10:40 **11:8** [a]John 8:59; 10:31 **11:9** [a]John 9:4; 12:35 [b]Is. 9:2 **11:10** [a]John 12:35 **11:11** [a]Deut. 31:16; [Dan. 12:2]; Matt. 9:24; Acts 7:60; [1 Cor. 15:18, 51] **11:16** [a]Matt. 10:3; Mark 3:18; Luke 6:15; John 14:5; 20:26–28; Acts 1:13 **11:18** [1]Literally *fifteen stadia*

would not have died. 22 But even now I know that
[a]whatever You ask of God, God will give You."

23 Jesus said to her, "Your brother will rise
again."

24 Martha said to Him, [a]"I know that he will
rise again in the resurrection at the last day."

25 Jesus said to her, "I am [a]the resurrection
and the life. [b]He who believes in Me, though he
may [c]die, he shall live. 26 And whoever lives and
believes in Me shall never die. Do you believe
this?"

27 She said to Him, "Yes, Lord, [a]I believe
that You are the Christ, the Son of God, who is
to come into the world."

### *JESUS AND DEATH, THE LAST ENEMY*

28 And when she had said these things, she
went her way and secretly called Mary her sister,
saying, "The Teacher has come and is calling
for you." 29 As soon as she heard *that,* she arose
quickly and came to Him. 30 Now Jesus had not
yet come into the town, but was[1] in the place
where Martha met Him. 31 [a]Then the Jews who
were with her in the house, and comforting her,
when they saw that Mary rose up quickly and
went out, followed her, saying, "She is going to
the tomb to weep there."[1]

32 Then, when Mary came where Jesus was,
and saw Him, she [a]fell down at His feet, saying
to Him, [b]"Lord, if You had been here, my brother
would not have died."

33 Therefore, when Jesus saw her weeping,
and the Jews who came with her weeping, He
groaned in the spirit and was troubled. 34 And
He said, "Where have you laid him?"

They said to Him, "Lord, come and see."

35 [a]Jesus wept. 36 Then the Jews said, "See
how He loved him!"

37 And some of them said, "Could not this
Man, [a]who opened the eyes of the blind, also
have kept this man from dying?"

### *LAZARUS RAISED FROM THE DEAD*

38 Then Jesus, again groaning in Himself,
came to the tomb. It was a cave, and a [a]stone lay
against it. 39 Jesus said, "Take away the stone."

Martha, the sister of him who was dead, said
to Him, "Lord, by this time there is a stench, for
he has been *dead* four days."

40 Jesus said to her, "Did I not say to you that
if you would believe you would [a]see the glory of
God?" 41 Then they took away the stone *from the
place* where the dead man was lying.[1] And Jesus
lifted up *His* eyes and said, "Father, I thank You
that You have heard Me. 42 And I know that You
always hear Me, but [a]because of the people who
are standing by I said *this,* that they may believe
that You sent Me." 43 Now when He had said these
things, He cried with a loud voice, "Lazarus,
come forth!" 44 And he who had died came out
bound hand and foot with [a]graveclothes, and
[b]his face was wrapped with a cloth. Jesus said
to them, "Loose him, and let him go."

### *THE PLOT TO KILL JESUS*

*(Matt. 26:1–5; Mark 14:1, 2; Luke 22:1, 2)*

45 Then many of the Jews who had come to
Mary, [a]and had seen the things Jesus did, believed
in Him. 46 But some of them went away to the Phar-
isees and [a]told them the things Jesus did. 47 [a]Then
the chief priests and the Pharisees gathered a
council and said, [b]"What shall we do? For this Man
works many signs. 48 If we let Him alone like this,
everyone will believe in Him, and the Romans will
come and take away both our place and nation."

49 And one of them, [a]Caiaphas, being high
priest that year, said to them, "You know nothing
at all, 50 [a]nor do you consider that it is expedient for
us[1] that one man should die for the people, and not
that the whole nation should perish." 51 Now this he
did not say on his own *authority;* but being high
priest that year he prophesied that Jesus would
die for the nation, 52 and [a]not for that nation only,
but [b]also that He would gather together in one
the children of God who were scattered abroad.

53 Then, from that day on, they plotted to [a]put
Him to death. 54 [a]Therefore Jesus no longer walked
openly among the Jews, but went from there into
the country near the wilderness, to a city called
[b]Ephraim, and there remained with His disciples.

55 [a]And the Passover of the Jews was near,
and many went from the country up to Jerusa-
lem before the Passover, to [b]purify themselves.
56 [a]Then they sought Jesus, and spoke among
themselves as they stood in the temple, "What do
you think—that He will not come to the feast?"
57 Now both the chief priests and the Pharisees
had given a command, that if anyone knew
where He was, he should report *it,* that they
might [a]seize Him.

### *THE ANOINTING AT BETHANY*

*(Matt. 26:6–13; Mark 14:3–9)*

12 Then, six days before the Passover, Jesus
came to Bethany, [a]where Lazarus was who
had been dead,[1] whom He had raised from the
dead. 2 [a]There they made Him a supper; and Mar-
tha served, but Lazarus was one of those who sat
at the table with Him. 3 Then [a]Mary took a pound
of very costly oil of [b]spikenard, anointed the feet

**11:22** [a] [John 9:31; 11:41] **11:24** [a] [Luke 14:14; John 5:29] **11:25** [a] John 5:21; 6:39, 40, 44; [Rev. 1:18] [b] John 3:16, 36; 1 John 5:10 [c] 1 Cor. 15:22; [Heb. 9:27] **11:27** [a] Matt. 16:16; Luke 2:11; John 4:42; 6:14, 69 **11:30** [1] NU-Text adds *still.* **11:31** [a] John 11:19, 33 [1] NU-Text reads *supposing that she was going to the tomb to weep there.* **11:32** [a] Mark 5:22; 7:25; Rev. 1:17 [b] John 11:21 **11:35** [a] Luke 19:41 **11:37** [a] John 9:6, 7 **11:38** [a] Matt. 27:60, 66; Mark 15:46; Luke 24:2; John 20:1 **11:40** [a] [John 11:4, 23] **11:41** [1] NU-Text omits *from the place where the dead man was lying.* **11:42** [a] John 12:30; 17:21 **11:44** [a] John 19:40 [b] John 20:7 **11:45** [a] John 2:23; 10:42; 12:11, 18 **11:46** [a] John 5:15 **11:47** [a] Ps. 2:2; Matt. 26:3; Mark 14:1; Luke 22:2 [b] John 12:19; Acts 4:16 **11:49** [a] Matt. 26:3; Luke 3:2; John 18:14; Acts 4:6 **11:50** [a] John 18:14 [1] NU-Text reads *you.* **11:52** [a] Is. 49:6 [b] [Eph. 2:14–17] **11:53** [a] Matt. 26:4 **11:54** [a] John 4:1, 3; 7:1 [b] 2 Chr. 13:19 **11:55** [a] John 2:13; 5:1; 6:4 [b] Num. 9:10, 13; 31:19, 20 **11:56** [a] John 7:11 **11:57** [a] Matt. 26:14–16 **12:1** [a] John 11:1, 43 [1] NU-Text omits *who had been dead.* **12:2** [a] Mark 14:3; Luke 10:38–41 **12:3** [a] John 11:2 [b] Song 1:12

JOHN 11:38–44

# JESUS, THE LIFE GIVER

46

STORY OF SCRIPTURE

## WHAT'S GOING ON?

This passage recounts Jesus' miraculous raising of Lazarus from the dead. Lazarus had been dead four days when Jesus arrived. Despite people's concern about the stench of a decaying body, Jesus insisted they remove the stone from the tomb's entrance. Jesus then prayed to the Father and called Lazarus out of the tomb. Lazarus emerged, still wrapped in burial cloths, alive.

This was a pivotal event in Jesus' ministry in two ways. First, it further cemented the religious leaders rejecting Jesus. Their initial interest in Jesus had given way to dislike, resentment, and hatred. They had begun to consider how to rid themselves of Jesus and Lazarus's resurrection was a "line in the sand" moment that caused them to seek a way to kill Jesus (see Luke 11:53). Second, Lazarus's resurrection was a foreshadowing of Jesus' resurrection that would soon take place.

## WHAT DOES THIS MEAN FOR ME?

Jesus told everyone to remove Lazarus's grave clothes because he was no longer dead. Living people shouldn't dress like the dead. This is a metaphor for how you've been saved. Since trusting in Jesus, you're no longer spiritually dead, so don't act like it. This is what Paul had in mind when he told us to put off the old and put on the new (see Eph. 4:22–24).

## DID YOU CATCH THE PATTERN?

Resurrection is surprisingly common in Scripture. In the Old Testament, the widow's son in Zarephath (1 Kin. 17:17–22), the Shunammite's son (2 Kin. 4:18–37), and the man thrown into Elisha's grave (2 Kin. 13:20–21) were raised. In the New Testament, along with Lazarus, Jairus' daughter (Mark 5:41–42), the young man at Nain (Luke 7:14–15), Tabitha (Acts 9:36–42) and Eutychus (Acts 20:7–12) were raised. These all point to Jesus' resurrection with the difference being they all eventually died again. Jesus, however, ascended to heaven and lives at the right hand of God.

*For the next* Story of Scripture *reading and devotion, turn to Mark 15:6–39 on page 1026.*

of Jesus, and wiped His feet with her hair. And
the house was filled with the fragrance of the oil.
4 But one of His disciples, [a]Judas Iscariot,
Simon's *son,* who would betray Him, said, 5 "Why
was this fragrant oil not sold for three hundred
denarii[1] and given to the poor?" 6 This he said,
not that he cared for the poor, but because he
was a thief, and [a]had the money box; and he
used to take what was put in it.
7 But Jesus said, "Let her alone; she has kept[1] this
for the day of My burial. 8 For [a]the poor you have
with you always, but Me you do not have always."

### SEEING JESUS IN THE SCRIPTURE

**12:3, 7** Jesus was anointed with oil in preparation for saving God's people, just as Old Testament kings were anointed for service (see 1 Sam. 16:12).

### *THE PLOT TO KILL LAZARUS*

9 Now a great many of the Jews knew that
He was there; and they came, not for Jesus'
sake only, but that they might also see Lazarus,
[a]whom He had raised from the dead. 10 [a]But the
chief priests plotted to put Lazarus to death also,
11 [a]because on account of him many of the Jews
went away and believed in Jesus.

### *THE TRIUMPHAL ENTRY*

*(Matt. 21:1–11; Mark 11:1–11; Luke 19:28–40)*

12 [a]The next day a great multitude that had
come to the feast, when they heard that Jesus
was coming to Jerusalem, 13 took branches of
palm trees and went out to meet Him, and cried
out:

"Hosanna!
[a]'Blessed *is* He who comes in the name of
the LORD!'[1]
The King of Israel!"

**12:4** [a] John 13:26 **12:5** [1] About one year's wages for a worker **12:6** [a] John 13:29 **12:7** [1] NU-Text reads *that she may keep.* **12:8** [a] Mark 14:7 **12:9** [a] John 11:43, 44 **12:10** [a] Luke 16:31 **12:11** [a] John 11:45; 12:18 **12:12** [a] Matt. 21:4–9 **12:13** [a] Ps. 118:25, 26 [1] Psalm 118:26

14[a]Then Jesus, when He had found a young
donkey, sat on it; as it is written:

15 "Fear[a] not, daughter of Zion;
Behold, your King is coming,
Sitting on a donkey's colt."[1]

16[a]His disciples did not understand these
things at first; [b]but when Jesus was glorified,
[c]then they remembered that these things were
written about Him and *that* they had done these
things to Him.
17Therefore the people, who were with Him
when He called Lazarus out of his tomb and
raised him from the dead, bore witness. 18[a]For
this reason the people also met Him, because
they heard that He had done this sign. 19The
Pharisees therefore said among themselves,
[a]"You see that you are accomplishing nothing.
Look, the world has gone after Him!"

### THE FRUITFUL GRAIN OF WHEAT

20Now there [a]were certain Greeks among
those [b]who came up to worship at the feast.
21Then they came to Philip, [a]who was from Beth-
saida of Galilee, and asked him, saying, "Sir, we
wish to see Jesus."
22Philip came and told Andrew, and in turn
Andrew and Philip told Jesus.
23But Jesus answered them, saying, [a]"The
hour has come that the Son of Man should be
glorified. 24Most assuredly, I say to you, [a]unless
a grain of wheat falls into the ground and dies,
it remains alone; but if it dies, it produces much
grain. 25[a]He who loves his life will lose it, and he
who hates his life in this world will keep it for
eternal life. 26If anyone serves Me, let him [a]follow
Me; and [b]where I am, there My servant will be also.
If anyone serves Me, him *My* Father will honor.

### JESUS PREDICTS HIS DEATH ON THE CROSS

27[a]"Now My soul is troubled, and what shall
I say? 'Father, save Me from this hour'? [b]But
for this purpose I came to this hour. 28Father,
glorify Your name."
[a]Then a voice came from heaven, *saying,* "I
have both glorified *it* and will glorify *it* again."
29Therefore the people who stood by and
heard *it* said that it had thundered. Others said,
"An angel has spoken to Him."
30Jesus answered and said, [a]"This voice
did not come because of Me, but for your sake.
31Now is the judgment of this world; now [a]the
ruler of this world will be cast out. 32And I, [a]if I
am lifted up from the earth, will draw [b]all *peoples*
to Myself." 33[a]This He said, signifying by what
death He would die.
34The people answered Him, [a]"We have
heard from the law that the Christ remains for-
ever; and how *can* You say, 'The Son of Man must
be lifted up'? Who is this Son of Man?"
35Then Jesus said to them, "A little while lon-
ger [a]the light is with you. [b]Walk while you have the
light, lest darkness overtake you; [c]he who walks in
darkness does not know where he is going. 36While
you have the light, believe in the light, that you
may become [a]sons of light." These things Jesus
spoke, and departed, and [b]was hidden from them.

### WHO HAS BELIEVED OUR REPORT?

37But although He had done so many [a]signs
before them, they did not believe in Him, 38that
the word of Isaiah the prophet might be fulfilled,
which he spoke:

[a]"Lord, who has believed our report?
And to whom has the arm of the LORD
been revealed?"[1]

39Therefore they could not believe, because
Isaiah said again:

40 "He[a] has blinded their eyes and hardened
their hearts,
[b]Lest they should see with *their* eyes,
Lest they should understand with *their*
hearts and turn,
So that I should heal them."[1]

41[a]These things Isaiah said when[1] he saw His
glory and spoke of Him.

### WALK IN THE LIGHT

42Nevertheless even among the rulers many
believed in Him, but [a]because of the Pharisees
they did not confess *Him,* lest they should be
put out of the synagogue; 43[a]for they loved the
praise of men more than the praise of God.
44Then Jesus cried out and said, [a]"He who
believes in Me, [b]believes not in Me [c]but in Him
who sent Me. 45And [a]he who sees Me sees Him
who sent Me. 46[a]I have come *as* a light into the
world, that whoever believes in Me should not
abide in darkness. 47And if anyone hears My
words and does not believe,[1] [a]I do not judge
him; for [b]I did not come to judge the world but
to save the world. 48[a]He who rejects Me, and does
not receive My words, has that which judges
him—[b]the word that I have spoken will judge
him in the last day. 49For [a]I have not spoken on

**12:14** [a] Matt. 21:7 **12:15** [a] Zech. 9:9 [1] Zechariah 9:9 **12:16** [a] Luke 18:34 [b] John 7:39; 12:23 [c] [John 14:26] **12:18** [a] John 12:11 **12:19** [a] John 11:47, 48 **12:20** [a] Acts 17:4 [b] 1 Kin. 8:41, 42 **12:21** [a] John 1:43, 44; 14:8–11 **12:23** [a] John 13:32 **12:24** [a] 1 Cor. 15:36 **12:25** [a] Mark 8:35 **12:26** [a] [Matt. 16:24] [b] John 14:3; 17:24 **12:27** [a] [Matt. 26:38, 39] [b] Luke 22:53 **12:28** [a] Matt. 3:17; 17:5 **12:30** [a] John 11:42 **12:31** [a] [2 Cor. 4:4] **12:32** [a] John 3:14; 8:28 [b] [Rom. 5:18] **12:33** [a] John 18:32; 21:19 **12:34** [a] Mic. 4:7 **12:35** [a] [John 1:9; 7:33; 8:12] [b] Eph. 5:8 [c] [1 John 2:9–11] **12:36** [a] Luke 16:8 [b] John 8:59 **12:37** [a] John 11:47 **12:38** [a] Is. 53:1 [1] Isaiah 53:1 **12:40** [a] Is. 6:9, 10 [b] Matt. 13:14 [1] Isaiah 6:10 **12:41** [a] Is. 6:1 [1] NU-Text reads *because.* **12:42** [a] John 7:13; 9:22 **12:43** [a] John 5:41, 44 **12:44** [a] Mark 9:37 [b] [John 3:16, 18, 36; 11:25, 26] [c] [John 5:24] **12:45** [a] [John 14:9] **12:46** [a] John 1:4, 5; 8:12; 12:35, 36 **12:47** [a] John 5:45 [b] John 3:17 [1] NU-Text reads *keep them.* **12:48** [a] [Luke 10:16] [b] Deut. 18:18, 19 **12:49** [a] John 8:38

LIVE THE TRUTH

## SUBMITTING TO AUTHORITY

**12:49** Everyone wants to make their own choices in life. That's basically at the root of how we've gotten to where we are today. In the garden of Eden, Adam and Eve believed they knew better than God and decided not to submit to His instructions and go their own way (see Gen. 3). Submission is one of the hardest choices to make, but it's the best decision we can make. God wants us to submit to Him in all things and it's best for us when we let Him lead. Really, that's what it means when we make Him Lord of our lives. We submit our entire lives—our goals, choices, authority, and resources—to Him.

While on earth, Jesus submitted to the Father in all things; that is, He obeyed the Father's will even when it was extremely difficult. This caliber of submission came from love and trust. Jesus changed the world through His submission and perfect obedience. As followers of Jesus, we too can change the world. We have been called to live out the truth of the gospel and share the message of the gospel all around us. That's not easy at times. But if we remember God loves us and is trustworthy, we can find the ability to submit and watch God work in us and through us.

My own *authority;* but the Father who sent Me gave Me a command, [b]what I should say and what I should speak. 50 And I know that His command is everlasting life. Therefore, whatever I speak, just as the Father has told Me, so I [a]speak."

### *JESUS WASHES THE DISCIPLES' FEET*

**13** Now [a]before the Feast of the Passover, when Jesus knew that [b]His hour had come that He should depart from this world to the Father, having loved His own who were in the world, He [c]loved them to the end.

2 And supper being ended,[1] [a]the devil having already put it into the heart of Judas Iscariot, Simon's *son,* to betray Him, 3 Jesus, knowing [a]that the Father had given all things into His hands, and that He [b]had come from God and [c]was going to God, 4 [a]rose from supper and laid aside His garments, took a towel and girded Himself. 5 After that, He poured water into a basin and began to wash the disciples' feet, and to wipe *them* with the towel with which He was girded. 6 Then He came to Simon Peter. And *Peter* said to Him, [a]"Lord, are You washing my feet?"

7 Jesus answered and said to him, "What I am doing you [a]do not understand now, [b]but you will know after this."

8 Peter said to Him, "You shall never wash my feet!"

Jesus answered him, [a]"If I do not wash you, you have no part with Me."

9 Simon Peter said to Him, "Lord, not my feet only, but also *my* hands and *my* head!"

10 Jesus said to him, "He who is bathed needs only to wash *his* feet, but is completely clean; and [a]you are clean, but not all of you." 11 For [a]He knew who would betray Him; therefore He said, "You are not all clean."

12 So when He had washed their feet, taken His garments, and sat down again, He said to them, "Do you know what I have done to you? 13 [a]You call Me Teacher and Lord, and you say well, for *so* I am. 14 [a]If I then, *your* Lord and Teacher, have washed your feet, [b]you also ought to wash one another's feet. 15 For [a]I have given you an example, that you should do as I have done to you. 16 [a]Most assuredly, I say to you, a servant is not greater than his master; nor is he who is sent greater than he who sent him. 17 [a]If you know these things, blessed are you if you do them.

### *JESUS IDENTIFIES HIS BETRAYER*

*(Matt. 26:21–25; Mark 14:18, 19; Luke 22:21–23)*

18 "I do not speak concerning all of you. I know whom I have chosen; but that the [a]Scripture may be fulfilled, [b]'He who eats bread with Me[1] has lifted up his heel against Me.'[2] 19 [a]Now I tell you before it comes, that when it does come to pass, you may believe that I am *He.* 20 [a]Most assuredly, I say to you, he who receives whomever I send receives Me; and he who receives Me receives Him who sent Me."

21 [a]When Jesus had said these things, [b]He was troubled in spirit, and testified and said, "Most assuredly, I say to you, [c]one of you will betray

**SEEING JESUS IN THE SCRIPTURE**

**13:18** Judas betrayed Jesus right after sharing a meal, fulfilling prophecy (see Ps. 41:9).

**12:49** [b] Deut. 18:18 **12:50** [a] John 5:19; 8:28 **13:1** [a] Matt. 26:2 [b] John 12:23; 17:1 [c] John 15:9 **13:2** [a] Luke 22:3 [1] NU-Text reads *And during supper.* **13:3** [a] Acts 2:36 [b] John 8:42; 16:28 [c] John 17:11; 20:17 **13:4** [a] [Luke 22:27] **13:6** [a] Matt. 3:14 **13:7** [a] John 12:16; 16:12 [b] John 13:19 **13:8** [a] [1 Cor. 6:11] **13:10** [a] [John 15:3] **13:11** [a] John 6:64; 18:4 **13:13** [a] Matt. 23:8, 10 **13:14** [a] Luke 22:27 [b] [Rom. 12:10] **13:15** [a] [1 Pet. 2:21–24] **13:16** [a] Matt. 10:24 **13:17** [a] [James 1:25] **13:18** [a] John 15:25; 17:12 [b] Ps. 41:9 [1] NU-Text reads *My bread.* [2] Psalm 41:9 **13:19** [a] John 14:29; 16:4 **13:20** [a] Matt. 10:40 **13:21** [a] Luke 22:21 [b] John 12:27 [c] 1 John 2:19

LIVE THE TRUTH

## BEING HUMBLE

**13:2–5** Humility is putting others first. It isn't counting yourself as less important but deferring to others' needs before your own. There's no better example of humility than Jesus Christ. Jesus is fully God, yet He became fully human also for the sole purpose of living and dying for us. He deserved to be esteemed above everyone; instead, He chose to become the greatest example of a servant. To follow that example—to be Christlike in our lives—we must love other people to the point of finding greater joy in serving them than being served by them.

The night before He was betrayed, Jesus served His disciples (including Judas, His betrayer) in an amazing way. It was the lowliest servant's job to wash feet. It was a dirty job. Yet Jesus lowered Himself and took that responsibility upon Himself. The disciples were shocked, but Jesus wanted them to know humility is of utmost importance. Valuing and serving others is the way of our King and His kingdom. Humility is part of God's nature. Jesus put others first, serving us even through death. Because Jesus served us to give us life, our lives should be filled with humble, joyful service to all.

Me." 22 Then the disciples looked at one another,
perplexed about whom He spoke.
23 Now [a]there was leaning on Jesus' bosom
one of His disciples, whom Jesus loved. 24 Simon
Peter therefore motioned to him to ask who it
was of whom He spoke.
25 Then, leaning back[1] on Jesus' breast, he
said to Him, "Lord, who is it?"

**13:23** At this time, people did not generally sit at a table to eat. They reclined on the left side of a low platform, resting on the left elbow and eating with the right hand, their feet extended outward. Reclining in such a way, a person's head was near the chest of the person on his or her left. The disciple **whom Jesus loved** is never named in Scripture, but many believe it was John, the author of this Gospel.

26 Jesus answered, "It is he to whom I shall
give a piece of bread when I have dipped *it*." And
having dipped the bread, He gave *it* to [a]Judas
Iscariot, *the son* of Simon. 27 [a]Now after the piece
of bread, Satan entered him. Then Jesus said to
him, "What you do, do quickly." 28 But no one at
the table knew for what reason He said this to
him. 29 For some thought, because [a]Judas had
the money box, that Jesus had said to him, "Buy
*those things* we need for the feast," or that he
should give something to the poor.
30 Having received the piece of bread, he
then went out immediately. And it was night.

### *THE NEW COMMANDMENT*

31 So, when he had gone out, Jesus said,
[a]"Now the Son of Man is glorified, and [b]God is
glorified in Him. 32 If God is glorified in Him,
God will also glorify Him in Himself, and [a]glorify
Him immediately. 33 Little children, I shall be
with you a [a]little while longer. You will seek Me;
[b]and as I said to the Jews, 'Where I am going,
you cannot come,' so now I say to you. 34 [a]A new
commandment I give to you, that you love one
another; as I have loved you, that you also love
one another. 35 [a]By this all will know that you are
My disciples, if you have love for one another."

### *JESUS PREDICTS PETER'S DENIAL*

36 Simon Peter said to Him, "Lord, where
are You going?"
Jesus answered him, "Where I [a]am going
you cannot follow Me now, but [b]you shall follow
Me afterward."
37 Peter said to Him, "Lord, why can I not follow
You now? I will [a]lay down my life for Your sake."
38 Jesus answered him, "Will you lay down
your life for My sake? Most assuredly, I say to
you, the rooster shall not [a]crow till you have
denied Me three times.

### *THE WAY, THE TRUTH, AND THE LIFE*

14 "Let [a]not your heart be troubled; you be-
lieve in God, believe also in Me. 2 In My
Father's house are many mansions;[1] if *it were* not
*so*, I would have told you. [a]I go to prepare a place
for you.[2] 3 And if I go and prepare a place for you,
[a]I will come again and receive you to Myself;
that [b]where I am, *there* you may be also. 4 And
where I go you know, and the way you know."

**13:23** [a] John 19:26; 20:2; 21:7, 20 **13:25** [1] NU-Text and M-Text add *thus.* **13:26** [a] John 6:70, 71; 12:4 **13:27** [a] Luke 22:3 **13:29** [a] John 12:6 **13:31** [a] John 12:23 [b] [1 Pet. 4:11] **13:32** [a] John 12:23 **13:33** [a] John 12:35; 14:19; 16:16–19 [b] [John 7:34; 8:21] **13:34** [a] 1 Thess. 4:9 **13:35** [a] 1 John 2:5 **13:36** [a] John 13:33; 14:2; 16:5 [b] 2 Pet. 1:14 **13:37** [a] Mark 14:29–31 **13:38** [a] John 18:25–27 **14:1** [a] [John 14:27; 16:22, 24] **14:2** [a] John 13:33, 36 [1] Literally *dwellings* [2] NU-Text adds a word which would cause the text to read either *if it were not so, would I have told you that I go to prepare a place for you?* or *if it were not so I would have told you; for I go to prepare a place for you.* **14:3** [a] [Acts 1:11] [b] [John 12:26]

5 [a]Thomas said to Him, "Lord, we do not
know where You are going, and how can we
know the way?"
6 Jesus said to him, "I am [a]the way, [b]the truth,
and [c]the life. [d]No one comes to the Father [e]ex-
cept through Me.

### THE FATHER REVEALED

7 [a]"If you had known Me, you would have
known My Father also; and from now on you
know Him and have seen Him."
8 Philip said to Him, "Lord, show us the Fa-
ther, and it is sufficient for us."
9 Jesus said to him, "Have I been with you
so long, and yet you have not known Me, Philip?
[a]He who has seen Me has seen the Father; so how
can you say, 'Show us the Father'? 10 Do you not
believe that [a]I am in the Father, and the Father
in Me? The words that I speak to you [b]I do not
speak on My own *authority;* but the Father who
dwells in Me does the works. 11 Believe Me that I
*am* in the Father and the Father in Me, [a]or else
believe Me for the sake of the works themselves.

### THE ANSWERED PRAYER

12 [a]"Most assuredly, I say to you, he who be-
lieves in Me, the works that I do he will do also;
and greater *works* than these he will do, because
I go to My Father. 13 [a]And whatever you ask in
My name, that I will do, that the Father may be
[b]glorified in the Son. 14 If you ask[1] anything in
My name, I will do *it.*

### JESUS PROMISES ANOTHER HELPER

15 [a]"If you love Me, keep[1] My commandments.
16 And I will pray the Father, and [a]He will give
you another Helper, that He may abide with you
forever— 17 [a]the Spirit of truth, [b]whom the world
cannot receive, because it neither sees Him nor
knows Him; but you know Him, for He dwells
with you [c]and will be in you. 18 [a]I will not leave
you orphans; [b]I will come to you.

> **SEEING JESUS IN THE SCRIPTURE**
>
> **14:16** Jesus' promise that He would send the disciples a Helper who would abide in them forever was fulfilled at Pentecost (see Acts 2:4, 33).

### INDWELLING OF THE FATHER AND THE SON

19 "A little while longer and the world will see
Me no more, but [a]you will see Me. [b]Because I live,
you will live also. 20 At that day you will know
that [a]I *am* in My Father, and you in Me, and I
in you. 21 [a]He who has My commandments and
keeps them, it is he who loves Me. And he who
loves Me will be loved by My Father, and I will
love him and manifest Myself to him."
22 [a]Judas (not Iscariot) said to Him, "Lord,
how is it that You will manifest Yourself to us,
and not to the world?"
23 Jesus answered and said to him, "If anyone

14:5 [a] Matt. 10:3 14:6 [a] [Heb. 9:8; 10:19, 20] [b] [John 1:14, 17; 8:32; 18:37] [c] [John 11:25] [d] 1 Tim. 2:5 [e] [John 10:7–9] 14:7 [a] John 8:19 14:9 [a] Col. 1:15 14:10 [a] John 10:38; 14:11, 20 [b] John 5:19; 14:24 14:11 [a] John 5:36; 10:38 14:12 [a] Luke 10:17 14:13 [a] Matt. 7:7 [b] John 13:31 14:14 [1] NU-Text adds *Me.* 14:15 [a] 1 John 5:3 [1] NU-Text reads *you will keep.* 14:16 [a] Rom. 8:15 14:17 [a] [1 John 4:6; 5:7] [b] [1 Cor. 2:14] [c] [1 John 2:27] 14:18 [a] [Matt. 28:20] [b] [John 14:3, 28] 14:19 [a] John 16:16, 22 [b] [1 Cor. 15:20] 14:20 [a] John 10:38; 14:11 14:21 [a] 1 John 2:5 14:22 [a] Luke 6:16

KNOW THE TRUTH

## THE DOCTRINE OF THE HOLY SPIRIT

### PART 4: THE HOLY SPIRIT'S WORK IN REVELATION

**14:26** The Holy Spirit makes clear to believers what we could never be clear about on our own. There are at least four ways we need the Spirit's revelation. First, before we can become believers in Jesus, we need the Holy Spirit to reveal **our sinfulness, Christ's righteousness, and the eternal judgment** based on whether we trust in or reject Jesus (see John 16:8). Second, we need the Spirit to reveal **the Bible's truth**. The Scriptures were inspired by the Holy Spirit through faithful scribes and thus can only be understood by faithful students with the Holy Spirit's help (see 2 Tim. 3:14–17). As Jesus told His disciples in John 14:26, the Spirit teaches us in all things—including the Word of God. Third, the Spirit reveals **our inheritance in Christ** (see 1 Cor. 2:6–16). We receive numerous privileges and responsibilities when we trust in Jesus. Only the Holy Spirit can reveal all these things freely given to us by God. Finally, the Holy Spirit reveals **the will and plans of the Father and Son** (see John 16:12–15). He speaks what the Father and Son want us to know so we can walk away from sin and error and into truth.

*For* **THE DOCTRINE OF THE HOLY SPIRIT: PART 5: THE HOLY SPIRIT'S WORK IN SALVATION**, *turn to John 16:7–15 on page 1094.*

loves Me, he will keep My word; and My Father
will love him, [a]and We will come to him and
make Our home with him. 24 He who does not
love Me does not keep My words; and [a]the word
which you hear is not Mine but the Father's
who sent Me.

### *THE GIFT OF HIS PEACE*

25 "These things I have spoken to you while
being present with you. 26 But [a]the Helper, the
Holy Spirit, whom the Father will [b]send in My
name, [c]He will teach you all things, and bring to
your [d]remembrance all things that I said to you.
27 [a]Peace I leave with you, My peace I give to you;
not as the world gives do I give to you. Let not
your heart be troubled, neither let it be afraid.
28 You have heard Me [a]say to you, 'I am going
away and coming *back* to you.' If you loved Me,
you would rejoice because I said,[1] [b]'I am going
to the Father,' for [c]My Father is greater than I.
29 "And [a]now I have told you before it comes,
that when it does come to pass, you may be-
lieve. 30 I will no longer talk much with you,
[a]for the ruler of this world is coming, and he
has [b]nothing in Me. 31 But that the world may
know that I love the Father, and [a]as the Father
gave Me commandment, so I do. Arise, let us
go from here.

### *THE TRUE VINE*

15 "I am the true vine, and My Father is the
vinedresser. 2 [a]Every branch in Me that
does not bear fruit He takes away;[1] and every
*branch* that bears fruit He prunes, that it may
bear [b]more fruit. 3 [a]You are already clean because
of the word which I have spoken to you. 4 [a]Abide
in Me, and I in you. As the branch cannot bear
fruit of itself, unless it abides in the vine, neither
can you, unless you abide in Me.
5 "I am the vine, you *are* the branches. He who
abides in Me, and I in him, bears much [a]fruit;
for without Me you can do [b]nothing. 6 If anyone
does not abide in Me, [a]he is cast out as a branch
and is withered; and they gather them and throw
*them* into the fire, and they are burned. 7 If you
abide in Me, and My words [a]abide in you, [b]you
will[1] ask what you desire, and it shall be done
for you. 8 [a]By this My Father is glorified, that you
bear much fruit; [b]so you will be My disciples.

### *LOVE AND JOY PERFECTED*

9 "As the Father [a]loved Me, I also have loved
you; abide in My love. 10 [a]If you keep My com-
mandments, you will abide in My love, just as
I have kept My Father's commandments and
abide in His love.
11 "These things I have spoken to you, that My
joy may remain in you, and [a]*that* your joy may be
full. 12 [a]This is My [b]commandment, that you love
one another as I have loved you. 13 [a]Greater love
has no one than this, than to lay down one's life
for his friends. 14 [a]You are My friends if you do
whatever I command you. 15 No longer do I call
you servants, for a servant does not know what
his master is doing; but I have called you friends,
[a]for all things that I heard from My Father I have
made known to you. 16 [a]You did not choose Me,
but I chose you and [b]appointed you that you
should go and bear fruit, and *that* your fruit
should remain, that whatever you ask the Father
[c]in My name He may give you. 17 These things I
command you, that you love one another.

14:23 [a] Rev. 3:20; 21:3 14:24 [a] John 5:19 14:26 [a] Luke 24:49 [b] John 15:26 [c] 1 Cor. 2:13 [d] John 2:22; 12:16 14:27 [a] [Phil. 4:7] 14:28 [a] John 14:3, 18 [b] John 16:16 [c] [Phil. 2:6] [1] NU-Text omits *I said.* 14:29 [a] John 13:19 14:30 [a] [John 12:31] [b] [Heb. 4:15] 14:31 [a] John 10:18 15:2 [a] Matt. 15:13 [b] [Matt. 13:12] [1] Or *lifts up* 15:3 [a] [John 13:10; 17:17] 15:4 [a] [Col. 1:23] 15:5 [a] Hos. 14:8 [b] 2 Cor. 3:5 15:6 [a] Matt. 3:10 15:7 [a] 1 John 2:14 [b] John 14:13; 16:23 [1] NU-Text omits *you will.* 15:8 [a] [Matt. 5:16] [b] John 8:31 15:9 [a] John 5:20; 17:26 15:10 [a] John 14:15 15:11 [a] 1 John 1:4 15:12 [a] 1 John 3:11 [b] Rom. 12:9 15:13 [a] 1 John 3:16 15:14 [a] [Matt. 12:50; 28:20] 15:15 [a] Gen. 18:17 15:16 [a] John 6:70; 13:18; 15:19 [b] [Col. 1:6] [c] John 14:13; 16:23, 24

LIVE THE TRUTH

## BEING JOYFUL

**15:11** Joy and happiness often overlap, but they aren't the same. Happiness tends to be dependent upon circumstances. We're happy when things go the way we want. But joy goes beyond that. Joy isn't based on life's circumstances and can be experienced with happiness or even sadness. The reason is joy is based on understanding the power and presence of God in our lives. Even when a situation looks cloudy or disheartening, we can have joy knowing God has everything under control and there's purpose in whatever we face. Joy remembers Jesus is with us and for us—even when He is the only one.

Jesus reminded the disciples they would face difficult times. The world would hate them because they followed Jesus. They weren't to focus on that though. They were to remember the Creator of the universe loved them and cared for them. Knowing that, they could withstand anything the world threw at them. The same is true for you. Even when people hate and reject you, choose joy. The most important relationship you have can never be broken. Jesus is with you. He sees you. He is for you. He proved that when He died in your place. You can have joy because Jesus is greater than anything else.

### *THE WORLD'S HATRED*

18 [a]“If the world hates you, you know that
it hated Me before *it hated* you. 19 [a]If you were
of the world, the world would love its own. Yet
[b]because you are not of the world, but I chose
you out of the world, therefore the world hates
you. 20 Remember the word that I said to you,
[a]‘A servant is not greater than his master.’ If they
persecuted Me, they will also persecute you. [b]If
they kept My word, they will keep yours also.
21 But [a]all these things they will do to you for
My name's sake, because they do not know Him
who sent Me. 22 [a]If I had not come and spoken
to them, they would have no sin, [b]but now they
have no excuse for their sin. 23 [a]He who hates
Me hates My Father also. 24 If I had not done
among them [a]the works which no one else did,
they would have no sin; but now they have [b]seen
and also hated both Me and My Father. 25 But
*this happened* that the word might be fulfilled
which is written in their law, [a]‘They hated Me
without a cause.’[1]

### *THE COMING REJECTION*

26 [a]“But when the Helper comes, whom I
shall send to you from the Father, the Spirit
of truth who proceeds from the Father, [b]He
will testify of Me. 27 And [a]you also will bear wit-
ness, because [b]you have been with Me from
the beginning.

16 “These things I have spoken to you, that
you [a]should not be made to stumble.
2 [a]They will put you out of the synagogues; yes,
the time is coming [b]that whoever kills you will
think that he offers God service. 3 And [a]these
things they will do to you[1] because they have
not known the Father nor Me. 4 But these things
I have told you, that when the[1] time comes, you
may remember that I told you of them.
“And these things I did not say to you at the
beginning, because I was with you.

### *THE WORK OF THE HOLY SPIRIT*

5 “But now I [a]go away to Him who sent Me,
and none of you asks Me, ‘Where are You going?’
6 But because I have said these things to you,
[a]sorrow has filled your heart. 7 Nevertheless I tell
you the truth. It is to your advantage that I go
away; for if I do not go away, the Helper will not
come to you; but [a]if I depart, I will send Him to
you. 8 And when He has [a]come, He will convict
the world of sin, and of righteousness, and of
judgment: 9 [a]of sin, because they do not believe
in Me; 10 [a]of righteousness, [b]because I go to My
Father and you see Me no more; 11 [a]of judgment,
because [b]the ruler of this world is judged.
12 “I still have many things to say to you, [a]but
you cannot bear *them* now. 13 However, when He,
[a]the Spirit of truth, has come, [b]He will guide you
into all truth; for He will not speak on His own

**15:18** [a] 1 John 3:13 **15:19** [a] 1 John 4:5 [b] John 17:14 **15:20** [a] John 13:16 [b] Ezek. 3:7 **15:21** [a] Matt. 10:22; 24:9 **15:22** [a] John 9:41; 15:24 [b] [James 4:17] **15:23** [a] 1 John 2:23 **15:24** [a] John 3:2 [b] John 14:9 **15:25** [a] Ps. 35:19; 69:4; 109:3–5 [1] Psalm 69:4 **15:26** [a] Luke 24:49 [b] 1 John 5:6 **15:27** [a] Luke 24:48 [b] Luke 1:2 **16:1** [a] Matt. 11:6 **16:2** [a] John 9:22 [b] Acts 8:1 **16:3** [a] John 8:19; 15:21 [1] NU-Text and M-Text omit *to you.* **16:4** [1] NU-Text reads *their.* **16:5** [a] John 7:33; 13:33; 14:28; 17:11 **16:6** [a] [John 16:20, 22] **16:7** [a] Acts 2:33 **16:8** [a] Acts 1:8; 2:1–4, 37 **16:9** [a] Acts 2:22 **16:10** [a] Acts 2:32 [b] John 5:32 **16:11** [a] Acts 26:18 [b] [Luke 10:18] **16:12** [a] Mark 4:33 **16:13** [a] [John 14:17] [b] John 14:26

KNOW THE TRUTH

## THE DOCTRINE OF THE HOLY SPIRIT

### PART 5: THE HOLY SPIRIT'S WORK IN SALVATION

**16:7–15** The Holy Spirit carries out at least five key actions in the work of salvation—a person trusting in Jesus as Savior, being saved from God's wrath against sin, and being born again into God's eternal family. First, the Holy Spirit **convicts** people of our sins following the proclamation of the good news. He shows our sinful condition and need for forgiveness and salvation from God's coming judgment. Second, He **clarifies** who Jesus is, the Son of God and Savior we need. Third, He **convinces** people of the gospel's truth (see 1 Cor. 1:18). The gospel sounds foolish to the world, but the Spirit reveals it as wisdom. Fourth, the Spirit **converts** lost people into sons and daughters of God (see John 1:12–13; Titus 3:4–7). He cleanses our sin-soaked, desperately wicked hearts and writes God's good commands on our new hearts through His indwelling presence (see Jer. 17:9; Ezek. 36:26–28). Fifth, He **comforts** and **confirms** born again believers as eternal sons and daughters of God (see John 14:15–18). Throughout life's trials and triumphs, the Spirit reinforces the exhilarating truth that we are blood-bought, saved sons and daughters who belong to God and are destined for eternity with Him.

*For* **THE DOCTRINE OF THE HOLY SPIRIT: PART 6: THE HOLY SPIRIT'S WORK IN SANCTIFICATION,** *turn to 2 Corinthians 3:17–18 on page 1185.*

*authority,* but whatever He hears He will speak;
and He will tell you things to come. 14 [a]He will
glorify Me, for He will take of what is Mine and
declare *it* to you. 15 [a]All things that the Father
has are Mine. Therefore I said that He will take
of Mine and declare *it* to you.[1]

### SEEING JESUS IN THE SCRIPTURE

**16:13** Jesus' promise to reveal what was to come was fulfilled in John's writing of the Book of Revelation (see Rev. 1:19).

### *SORROW WILL TURN TO JOY*

16 "A [a]little while, and you will not see Me;
and again a little while, and you will see Me,
[b]because I go to the Father."
17 Then *some* of His disciples said among
themselves, "What is this that He says to us, 'A
little while, and you will not see Me; and again a
little while, and you will see Me'; and, 'because I
go to the Father'?" 18 They said therefore, "What
is this that He says, 'A little while'? We do not
know what He is saying."
19 Now Jesus knew that they desired to ask
Him, and He said to them, "Are you inquiring
among yourselves about what I said, 'A little
while, and you will not see Me; and again a little
while, and you will see Me'? 20 Most assuredly, I
say to you that you will weep and [a]lament, but the
world will rejoice; and you will be sorrowful, but
your sorrow will be turned into [b]joy. 21 [a]A woman,
when she is in labor, has sorrow because her hour
has come; but as soon as she has given birth to
the child, she no longer remembers the anguish,
for joy that a human being has been born into
the world. 22 Therefore you now have sorrow; but
I will see you again and [a]your heart will rejoice,
and your joy no one will take from you.
23 "And in that day you will ask Me nothing.
[a]Most assuredly, I say to you, whatever you ask
the Father in My name He will give you. 24 Until
now you have asked nothing in My name. Ask,
and you will receive, [a]that your joy may be [b]full.

### *JESUS CHRIST HAS OVERCOME THE WORLD*

25 "These things I have spoken to you in
figurative language; but the time is coming
when I will no longer speak to you in figurative
language, but I will tell you [a]plainly about the
Father. 26 In that day you will ask in My name,
and I do not say to you that I shall pray the Fa-
ther for you; 27 [a]for the Father Himself loves you,
because you have loved Me, and [b]have believed
that I came forth from God. 28 [a]I came forth from
the Father and have come into the world. Again,
I leave the world and go to the Father."
29 His disciples said to Him, "See, now You are
speaking plainly, and using no figure of speech!
30 Now we are sure that [a]You know all things, and
have no need that anyone should question You.
By this [b]we believe that You came forth from God."
31 Jesus answered them, "Do you now be-
lieve? 32 [a]Indeed the hour is coming, yes, has
now come, that you will be scattered, [b]each
to his own, and will leave Me alone. And [c]yet
I am not alone, because the Father is with Me.
33 These things I have spoken to you, that [a]in
Me you may have peace. [b]In the world you will[1]
have tribulation; but be of good cheer, [c]I have
overcome the world."

### *JESUS PRAYS FOR HIMSELF*

**17** Jesus spoke these words, lifted up His eyes
to heaven, and said: "Father, [a]the hour has
come. Glorify Your Son, that Your Son also may
glorify You, 2 [a]as You have given Him authority
over all flesh, that He should[1] give eternal life to
as many [b]as You have given Him. 3 And [a]this is
eternal life, that they may know You, [b]the only
true God, and Jesus Christ [c]whom You have
sent. 4 [a]I have glorified You on the earth. [b]I have
finished the work [c]which You have given Me to
do. 5 And now, O Father, glorify Me together with
Yourself, with the glory [a]which I had with You
before the world was.

### *JESUS PRAYS FOR HIS DISCIPLES*

6 [a]"I have manifested Your name to the men
[b]whom You have given Me out of the world.
[c]They were Yours, You gave them to Me, and they
have kept Your word. 7 Now they have known that
all things which You have given Me are from You.
8 For I have given to them the words [a]which You
have given Me; and they have received *them,*
[b]and have known surely that I came forth from
You; and they have believed that [c]You sent Me.

### SEEING JESUS IN THE SCRIPTURE

**17:8** Jesus is the great Prophet of God who spoke all the words the Father gave Him and is the subject of them all (see Deut. 18:15, 18).

9 "I pray for them. [a]I do not pray for the world
but for those whom You have given Me, for they
are Yours. 10 And all Mine are Yours, and [a]Yours are

**16:14** [a] John 15:26 **16:15** [a] Matt. 11:27 [1] NU-Text and M-Text read *He takes of Mine and will declare it to you.* **16:16** [a] John 7:33; 12:35; 13:33; 14:19; 19:40–42; 20:19 [b] John 13:3 **16:20** [a] Mark 16:10 [b] Luke 24:32, 41 **16:21** [a] Is. 13:8; 26:17; 42:14 **16:22** [a] 1 Pet. 1:8 **16:23** [a] Matt. 7:7 **16:24** [a] John 17:13 [b] John 15:11 **16:25** [a] John 7:13 **16:27** [a] [John 14:21, 23] [b] John 3:13 **16:28** [a] John 13:1, 3; 16:5, 10, 17 **16:30** [a] John 21:17 [b] John 17:8 **16:32** [a] Matt. 26:31, 56 [b] John 20:10 [c] John 8:29 **16:33** [a] [Eph. 2:14] [b] 2 Tim. 3:12 [c] Rom. 8:37 [1] NU-Text and M-Text omit *will.* **17:1** [a] John 12:23 **17:2** [a] John 3:35 [b] John 6:37, 39; 17:6, 9, 24 [1] M-Text reads *shall.* **17:3** [a] Jer. 9:23, 24 [b] 1 Cor. 8:4 [c] John 3:34 **17:4** [a] John 13:31 [b] John 4:34; 19:30 [c] John 14:31 **17:5** [a] Phil. 2:6 **17:6** [a] Ps. 22:22 [b] John 6:37 [c] Ezek. 18:4 **17:8** [a] John 8:28 [b] John 8:42; 16:27, 30 [c] Deut. 18:15, 18 **17:9** [a] [1 John 5:19] **17:10** [a] John 16:15

Mine, and I am glorified in them. [11][a]Now I am no
longer in the world, but these are in the world, and
I come to You. Holy Father, [b]keep through Your
name those whom You have given Me,[1] that they
may be one [c]as We *are.* [12]While I was with them in
the world,[1] [a]I kept them in Your name. Those whom
You gave Me I have kept;[2] and [b]none of them is lost
[c]except the son of perdition, [d]that the Scripture
might be fulfilled. [13]But now I come to You, and
these things I speak in the world, that they may
have My joy fulfilled in themselves. [14]I have given
them Your word; [a]and the world has hated them
because they are not of the world, [b]just as I am
not of the world. [15]I do not pray that You should
take them out of the world, but [a]that You should
keep them from the evil one. [16]They are not of
the world, just as I am not of the world. [17][a]Sanctify
them by Your truth. [b]Your word is truth. [18][a]As You
sent Me into the world, I also have sent them into
the world. [19]And [a]for their sakes I sanctify Myself,
that they also may be sanctified by the truth.

### *JESUS PRAYS FOR ALL BELIEVERS*

[20]"I do not pray for these alone, but also for
those who will[1] believe in Me through their word;
[21][a]that they all may be one, as [b]You, Father, *are*
in Me, and I in You; that they also may be one
in Us, that the world may believe that You sent
Me. [22]And the [a]glory which You gave Me I have
given them, [b]that they may be one just as We
are one: [23]I in them, and You in Me; [a]that they
may be made perfect in one, and that the world
may know that You have sent Me, and have loved
them as You have loved Me.

[24][a]"Father, I desire that they also whom You
gave Me may be with Me where I am, that they
may behold My glory which You have given Me;
[b]for You loved Me before the foundation of the
world. [25]O righteous Father! [a]The world has not
known You, but [b]I have known You; and [c]these
have known that You sent Me. [26][a]And I have
declared to them Your name, and will declare
*it,* that the love [b]with which You loved Me may
be in them, and I in them."

**17:20–21** Here, Jesus prayed that His followers would be united so much so, that they reflected the perfect unity of the Triune God. The result, in part, would be the world coming to faith upon seeing such amazing unity. Jesus didn't just pray this for His followers in that day, though. He also prayed this for us—**those who will believe in Me through their word**.

### *BETRAYAL AND ARREST IN GETHSEMANE*

*(Matt. 26:47–56; Mark 14:43–52; Luke 22:47–53)*

**18** When Jesus had spoken these words, [a]He
went out with His disciples over [b]the Brook
Kidron, where there was a garden, which He
and His disciples entered. [2]And Judas, who
betrayed Him, also knew the place; [a]for Jesus
often met there with His disciples. [3][a]Then Judas,
having received a detachment *of troops,* and
officers from the chief priests and Pharisees,
came there with lanterns, torches, and weapons.
[4]Jesus therefore, [a]knowing all things that would
come upon Him, went forward and said to them,
"Whom are you seeking?"

**17:11** [a] John 13:1 [b] [1 Pet. 1:5] [c] John 10:30 [1] NU-Text and M-Text read *keep them through Your name which You have given Me.* **17:12** [a] Heb. 2:13 [b] 1 John 2:19 [c] John 6:70 [d] Ps. 41:9; 109:8 [1] NU-Text omits *in the world.* [2] NU-Text reads *in Your name which You gave Me. And I guarded them;* (or it;). **17:14** [a] John 15:19 [b] John 8:23 **17:15** [a] 1 John 5:18 **17:17** [a] [Eph. 5:26] [b] Ps. 119:9, 142, 151 **17:18** [a] John 4:38; 20:21 **17:19** [a] [Heb. 10:10] **17:20** [1] NU-Text and M-Text omit *will.* **17:21** [a] [Gal. 3:28] [b] John 10:38; 17:11, 23 **17:22** [a] 1 John 1:3 [b] [2 Cor. 3:18] **17:23** [a] [Col. 3:14] **17:24** [a] [1 Thess. 4:17] [b] John 17:5 **17:25** [a] John 15:21 [b] John 7:29; 8:55; 10:15 [c] John 3:17; 17:3, 8, 18, 21, 23 **17:26** [a] John 17:6 [b] John 15:9 **18:1** [a] Mark 14:26, 32 [b] 2 Sam. 15:23 **18:2** [a] Luke 21:37; 22:39 **18:3** [a] Luke 22:47–53 **18:4** [a] John 6:64; 13:1, 3; 19:28

APPLY THE TRUTH

## TRUTH

**17:17** Water is wet. The sky is blue. Grass is green. One plus one equals two. Many things seem easy for everyone to agree on but sometimes even what seems obvious can be disputed. In John 18:38, Pilate asked a question that is still being asked today, "What is truth?" Or perhaps more specifically, can we *know* something is truth? There's an entire field of philosophy dedicated to this question: epistemology. Is there a way we can know for certain what we think we know?

Here, Jesus gives us a definite answer. Yes, there is truth, and its source is God. Truth—what is real and dependable always, everywhere, and for everyone—comes from God. One of the best ways to know this truth is by reading the Word of God. Notice what Jesus says will happen when we do: it will sanctify us, or make us more like Jesus. It's the very Word of God that transforms us into the people God desires us to be. Truth is not relative or subjective. It comes from God and produces God's perfect plans. All we experience and learn must be filtered through the lens of God's Word.

5 They answered Him, [a]"Jesus of Nazareth."
Jesus said to them, "I am *He.*" And Judas,
who [b]betrayed Him, also stood with them. 6 Now
when He said to them, "I am *He,*" they drew back
and fell to the ground.
7 Then He asked them again, "Whom are
you seeking?"
And they said, "Jesus of Nazareth."
8 Jesus answered, "I have told you that I am
*He.* Therefore, if you seek Me, let these go their
way," 9 that the saying might be fulfilled which
He spoke, [a]"Of those whom You gave Me I have
lost none."
10 [a]Then Simon Peter, having a sword, drew it
and struck the high priest's servant, and cut off
his right ear. The servant's name was Malchus.
11 So Jesus said to Peter, "Put your sword into
the sheath. Shall I not drink [a]the cup which My
Father has given Me?"

### BEFORE THE HIGH PRIEST

12 Then the detachment *of troops* and the
captain and the officers of the Jews arrested
Jesus and bound Him. 13 And [a]they led Him
away to [b]Annas first, for he was the father-in-
law of [c]Caiaphas who was high priest that year.
14 [a]Now it was Caiaphas who advised the Jews
that it was expedient that one man should die
for the people.

### PETER DENIES JESUS

*(Matt. 26:69–75; Mark 14:66–72; Luke 22:54–62)*

15 [a]And Simon Peter followed Jesus, and so
*did* [b]another[1] disciple. Now that disciple was
known to the high priest, and went with Jesus
into the courtyard of the high priest. 16 [a]But
Peter stood at the door outside. Then the other
disciple, who was known to the high priest, went
out and spoke to her who kept the door, and
brought Peter in. 17 Then the servant girl who
kept the door said to Peter, "You are not also
*one* of this Man's disciples, are you?"
He said, "I am [a]not."
18 Now the servants and officers who had
made a fire of coals stood there, for it was cold,
and they warmed themselves. And Peter stood
with them and warmed himself.

### JESUS QUESTIONED BY THE HIGH PRIEST

19 The high priest then asked Jesus about
His disciples and His doctrine.
20 Jesus answered him, [a]"I spoke openly to
the world. I always taught [b]in synagogues and
[c]in the temple, where the Jews always meet,[1] and
in secret I have said nothing. 21 Why do you ask
Me? Ask [a]those who have heard Me what I said
to them. Indeed they know what I said."
22 And when He had said these things, one
of the officers who stood by [a]struck Jesus with
the palm of his hand, saying, "Do You answer
the high priest like that?"
23 Jesus answered him, "If I have spoken
evil, bear witness of the evil; but if well, why do
you strike Me?"
24 [a]Then Annas sent Him bound to [b]Caiaphas
the high priest.

> **SEEING JESUS IN THE SCRIPTURE**
>
> **18:22** Jesus was struck on the cheek, fulfilling prophecy (see Lam. 3:30).

### PETER DENIES TWICE MORE

25 Now Simon Peter stood and warmed him-
self. [a]Therefore they said to him, "You are not
also *one* of His disciples, are you?"
He denied *it* and said, "I am not!"
26 One of the servants of the high priest,
a relative *of him* whose ear Peter cut off, said,
"Did I not see you in the garden with Him?"
27 Peter then denied again; and [a]immediately
a rooster crowed.

### IN PILATE'S COURT

*(Matt. 27:1, 2, 11–14; Mark 15:1–5; Luke 23:1–5)*

28 [a]Then they led Jesus from Caiaphas to the
Praetorium, and it was early morning. [b]But they
themselves did not go into the Praetorium, lest
they should be defiled, but that they might eat
the Passover. 29 [a]Pilate then went out to them
and said, "What accusation do you bring against
this Man?"
30 They answered and said to him, "If He
were not an evildoer, we would not have deliv-
ered Him up to you."
31 Then Pilate said to them, "You take Him
and judge Him according to your law."
Therefore the Jews said to him, "It is not
lawful for us to put anyone to death," 32 [a]that
the saying of Jesus might be fulfilled which He
spoke, [b]signifying by what death He would die.
33 [a]Then Pilate entered the Praetorium again,
called Jesus, and said to Him, "Are You the King
of the Jews?"
34 Jesus answered him, "Are you speaking
for yourself about this, or did others tell you
this concerning Me?"
35 Pilate answered, "Am I a Jew? Your own
nation and the chief priests have delivered You
to me. What have You done?"
36 [a]Jesus answered, [b]"My kingdom is not of
this world. If My kingdom were of this world,
My servants would fight, so that I should not

**18:5** [a]Matt. 21:11 [b]Ps. 41:9 **18:9** [a][John 6:39; 17:12] **18:10** [a]Matt. 26:51 **18:11** [a]Matt. 20:22; 26:39 **18:13** [a]Matt. 26:57 [b]Luke 3:2 [c]Matt. 26:3 **18:14** [a]John 11:50 **18:15** [a]Mark 14:54 [b]John 20:2–5 [1]M-Text reads *the other.* **18:16** [a]Matt. 26:69 **18:17** [a]Matt. 26:34 **18:20** [a]Luke 4:15 [b]John 6:59 [c]Mark 14:49 [1]NU-Text reads *where all the Jews meet.* **18:21** [a]Mark 12:37 **18:22** [a]Jer. 20:2 **18:24** [a]Matt. 26:57 [b]John 11:49 **18:25** [a]Luke 22:58–62 **18:27** [a]John 13:38 **18:28** [a]Mark 15:1 [b]Acts 10:28; 11:3 **18:29** [a]Matt. 27:11–14 **18:32** [a]Matt. 20:17–19; 26:2 [b]John 3:14; 8:28; 12:32, 33 **18:33** [a]Matt. 27:11 **18:36** [a]1 Tim. 6:13 [b][Dan. 2:44; 7:14]

be delivered to the Jews; but now My kingdom
is not from here."
37 Pilate therefore said to Him, "Are You a
king then?"
Jesus answered, "You say *rightly* that I am
a king. For this cause I was born, and for this
cause I have come into the world, [a]that I should
bear [b]witness to the truth. Everyone who [c]is of
the truth [d]hears My voice."
38 Pilate said to Him, "What is truth?" And when
he had said this, he went out again to the Jews,
and said to them, [a]"I find no fault in Him at all.

### TAKING THE PLACE OF BARABBAS

*(Matt. 27:15–23; Mark 15:6–14; Luke 23:13–23)*

39 [a]"But you have a custom that I should
release someone to you at the Passover. Do you
therefore want me to release to you the King
of the Jews?"
40 [a]Then they all cried again, saying, "Not
this Man, but Barabbas!" [b]Now Barabbas was
a robber.

### THE SOLDIERS MOCK JESUS

*(Matt. 27:27–31; Mark 15:16–20)*

**19** So then [a]Pilate took Jesus and scourged
*Him.* 2 And the soldiers twisted a crown
of thorns and put *it* on His head, and they put
on Him a purple robe. 3 Then they said,[1] "Hail,
King of the Jews!" And they [a]struck Him with
their hands.

> **19:2** In ancient times, the color **purple** was a symbol of royalty. Purple dye, which came from a special type of shellfish in the Mediterranean Sea, was extremely expensive. Only royalty and other wealthy and important people could afford it.

4 Pilate then went out again, and said to
them, "Behold, I am bringing Him out to you,
[a]that you may know that I find no fault in Him."

### PILATE'S DECISION

5 Then Jesus came out, wearing the crown
of thorns and the purple robe. And *Pilate* said
to them, "Behold the Man!"
6 [a]Therefore, when the chief priests and of-
ficers saw Him, they cried out, saying, "Crucify
*Him,* crucify *Him!*"
Pilate said to them, "You take Him and cru-
cify *Him,* for I find no fault in Him."
7 The Jews answered him, [a]"We have a law,
and according to our[1] law He ought to die, be-
cause [b]He made Himself the Son of God."
8 Therefore, when Pilate heard that saying,
he was the more afraid, 9 and went again into the
Praetorium, and said to Jesus, "Where are You
from?" [a]But Jesus gave him no answer.
10 Then Pilate said to Him, "Are You not
speaking to me? Do You not know that I have
power to crucify You, and power to release You?"
11 Jesus answered, [a]"You could have no power
at all against Me unless it had been given you
from above. Therefore [b]the one who delivered
Me to you has the greater sin."
12 From then on Pilate sought to release Him,
but the Jews cried out, saying, "If you let this
Man go, you are not Caesar's friend. [a]Whoever
makes himself a king speaks against Caesar."
13 [a]When Pilate therefore heard that say-
ing, he brought Jesus out and sat down in the
judgment seat in a place that is called *The* Pave-
ment, but in Hebrew, Gabbatha. 14 Now [a]it was
the Preparation Day of the Passover, and about
the sixth hour. And he said to the Jews, "Behold
your King!"
15 But they cried out, "Away with *Him,* away
with *Him!* Crucify Him!"
Pilate said to them, "Shall I crucify your
King?"
The chief priests answered, [a]"We have no
king but Caesar!"
16 [a]Then he delivered Him to them to be cru-
cified. Then they took Jesus and led *Him* away.[1]

### THE KING ON A CROSS

*(Matt. 27:32–56; Mark 15:21–41; Luke 23:26–49)*

17 [a]And He, bearing His cross, [b]went out to a
place called *the Place* of a Skull, which is called in
Hebrew, Golgotha, 18 where they crucified Him,
and [a]two others with Him, one on either side,
and Jesus in the center. 19 [a]Now Pilate wrote a
title and put *it* on the cross. And the writing was:

JESUS OF NAZARETH, THE KING
OF THE JEWS.

20 Then many of the Jews read this title, for
the place where Jesus was crucified was near
the city; and it was written in Hebrew, Greek,
*and* Latin.
21 Therefore the chief priests of the Jews said
to Pilate, "Do not write, 'The King of the Jews,'
but, 'He said, "I am the King of the Jews." ' "
22 Pilate answered, "What I have written, I
have written."
23 [a]Then the soldiers, when they had cruci-
fied Jesus, took His garments and made four
parts, to each soldier a part, and also the tunic.
Now the tunic was without seam, woven from the
top in one piece. 24 They said therefore among
themselves, "Let us not tear it, but cast lots for

**18:37** [a] [Matt. 5:17; 20:28] [b] Is. 55:4 [c] [John 14:6] [d] John 8:47; 10:27 **18:38** [a] John 19:4, 6 **18:39** [a] Luke 23:17–25 **18:40** [a] Acts 3:14 [b] Luke 23:19 **19:1** [a] Matt. 20:19; 27:26 **19:3** [a] Is. 50:6 [1] NU-Text reads *And they came up to Him and said.* **19:4** [a] John 18:33, 38 **19:6** [a] Acts 3:13 **19:7** [a] Lev. 24:16 [b] Matt. 26:63–66 [1] NU-Text reads *the law.* **19:9** [a] Is. 53:7 **19:11** [a] [Luke 22:53] [b] Rom. 13:1 **19:12** [a] Luke 23:2 **19:13** [a] 1 Sam. 15:24 **19:14** [a] Matt. 27:62 **19:15** [a] [Gen. 49:10] **19:16** [a] Luke 23:24 [1] NU-Text omits *and led Him away.* **19:17** [a] Mark 15:21, 22 [b] Num. 15:36 **19:18** [a] Is. 53:12 **19:19** [a] Matt. 27:37 **19:23** [a] Luke 23:34

it, whose it shall be," that the Scripture might be fulfilled which says:

> [a]"They divided My garments among them,
> And for My clothing they cast lots."[1]

Therefore the soldiers did these things.

**SEEING JESUS IN THE SCRIPTURE**

**19:23–24** The soldiers divided Jesus' garments and cast lots for them, fulfilling prophecy (see Ps. 22:18).

### *BEHOLD YOUR MOTHER*

25 [a]Now there stood by the cross of Jesus His mother, and His mother's sister, Mary the *wife* of [b]Clopas, and Mary Magdalene. 26 When Jesus therefore saw His mother, and [a]the disciple whom He loved standing by, He said to His mother, [b]"Woman, behold your son!" 27 Then He said to the disciple, "Behold your mother!" And from that hour that disciple took her [a]to his own *home.*

### *IT IS FINISHED*

28 After this, Jesus, knowing[1] that all things were now accomplished, [a]that the Scripture might be fulfilled, said, "I thirst!" 29 Now a vessel full of sour wine was sitting there; and [a]they filled a sponge with sour wine, put *it* on hyssop, and put *it* to His mouth. 30 So when Jesus had received the sour wine, He said, [a]"It is finished!" And bowing His head, He gave up His spirit.

### *JESUS' SIDE IS PIERCED*

31 [a]Therefore, because it was the Preparation *Day,* [b]that the bodies should not remain on the cross on the Sabbath (for that Sabbath was a [c]high day), the Jews asked Pilate that their legs might be broken, and *that* they might be taken away. 32 Then the soldiers came and broke the legs of the first and of the other who was crucified with Him. 33 But when they came to Jesus and saw that He was already dead, they did not break His legs. 34 But one of the soldiers pierced His side with a spear, and immediately [a]blood and water

**19:34** After the soldier **pierced** Jesus' **side, blood and water came out,** indicating that Jesus was already dead. Only blood, not water, would have flowed from a living body.

**SEEING JESUS IN THE SCRIPTURE**

**19:36** Jesus' legs being left unbroken was another sign that God ordained His death to fulfill Scripture (see Num. 9:12).

came out. 35 And he who has seen has testified, and his testimony is [a]true; and he knows that he is telling the truth, so that you may [b]believe. 36 For these things were done that the Scripture should be fulfilled, [a]"Not *one* of His bones shall be broken."[1] 37 And again another Scripture says, [a]"They shall look on Him whom they pierced."[1]

### *JESUS BURIED IN JOSEPH'S TOMB*

*(Matt. 27:57–61; Mark 15:42–47; Luke 23:50–56)*

38 [a]After this, Joseph of Arimathea, being a disciple of Jesus, but secretly, [b]for fear of the Jews, asked Pilate that he might take away the body of Jesus; and Pilate gave *him* permission. So he came and took the body of Jesus. 39 And [a]Nicodemus, who at first came to Jesus by night, also came, bringing a mixture of [b]myrrh and aloes, about a hundred pounds. 40 Then they took the body of Jesus, and [a]bound it in strips of linen with the spices, as the custom of the Jews is to bury. 41 Now in the place where He was crucified there was a garden, and in the garden a new tomb in which no one had yet been laid. 42 So [a]there they laid Jesus, [b]because of the Jews' Preparation *Day,* for the tomb was nearby.

### *THE EMPTY TOMB*

*(Matt. 28:1–10; Mark 16:1–8; Luke 24:1–12)*

**20** Now the [a]first *day* of the week Mary Magdalene went to the tomb early, while it was still dark, and saw *that* the [b]stone had been taken away from the tomb. 2 Then she ran and came to Simon Peter, and to the [a]other disciple, [b]whom Jesus loved, and said to them, "They have taken away the Lord out of the tomb, and we do not know where they have laid Him."

3 [a]Peter therefore went out, and the other disciple, and were going to the tomb. 4 So they both ran together, and the other disciple outran Peter and came to the tomb first. 5 And he, stooping down and looking in, saw [a]the linen cloths lying *there;* yet he did not go in. 6 Then Simon Peter came, following him, and went into the tomb; and he saw the linen cloths lying *there,* 7 and [a]the handkerchief that had been around His head, not lying with the linen cloths, but folded together in a place by itself. 8 Then the [a]other disciple, who came to the tomb first, went in also; and he saw and believed. 9 For as yet they

**19:24** [a] Ps. 22:18 [1] Psalm 22:18 **19:25** [a] Mark 15:40 [b] Luke 24:18 **19:26** [a] John 13:23; 20:2; 21:7, 20, 24 [b] John 2:4 **19:27** [a] John 1:11; 16:32 **19:28** [a] Ps. 22:15 [1] M-Text reads *seeing.* **19:29** [a] Matt. 27:48, 50 **19:30** [a] John 17:4 **19:31** [a] Mark 15:42 [b] Deut. 21:23 [c] Ex. 12:16 **19:34** [a] [1 John 5:6, 8] **19:35** [a] John 21:24 [b] [John 20:31] **19:36** [a] [Ex. 12:46; Num. 9:12]; Ps. 34:20 [1] Exodus 12:46; Numbers 9:12; Psalm 34:20 **19:37** [a] Zech. 12:10; 13:6 [1] Zechariah 12:10 **19:38** [a] Luke 23:50–56 [b] [John 7:13; 9:22; 12:42] **19:39** [a] John 3:1, 2; 7:50 [b] Matt. 2:11 **19:40** [a] John 20:5, 7 **19:42** [a] Is. 53:9 [b] John 19:14, 31 **20:1** [a] Matt. 28:1–8 [b] Matt. 27:60, 66; 28:2 **20:2** [a] John 21:23, 24 [b] John 13:23; 19:26; 21:7, 20, 24 **20:3** [a] Luke 24:12 **20:5** [a] John 19:40 **20:7** [a] John 11:44 **20:8** [a] John 21:23, 24

did not know the [a]Scripture, that He must rise
again from the dead. 10 Then the disciples went
away again to their own homes.

### *MARY MAGDALENE SEES THE RISEN LORD*

11 [a]But Mary stood outside by the tomb weep-
ing, and as she wept she stooped down *and*
*looked* into the tomb. 12 And she saw two angels
in white sitting, one at the head and the other at
the feet, where the body of Jesus had lain. 13 Then
they said to her, "Woman, why are you weeping?"
She said to them, "Because they have taken
away my Lord, and I do not know where they
have laid Him."
14 [a]Now when she had said this, she turned
around and saw Jesus standing *there,* and [b]did not
know that it was Jesus. 15 Jesus said to her, "Woman,
why are you weeping? Whom are you seeking?"
She, supposing Him to be the gardener, said
to Him, "Sir, if You have carried Him away, tell me
where You have laid Him, and I will take Him away."
16 Jesus said to her, [a]"Mary!"
She turned and said to Him,[1] "Rabboni!"
(which is to say, Teacher).
17 Jesus said to her, "Do not cling to Me, for I
have not yet [a]ascended to My Father; but go to
[b]My brethren and say to them, [c]'I am ascending
to My Father and your Father, and *to* [d]My God
and your God.' "
18 [a]Mary Magdalene came and told the dis-
ciples that she had seen the Lord,[1] and *that* He
had spoken these things to her.

## SEEING JESUS IN THE SCRIPTURE

**20:17** Jesus spent forty days on earth after His resurrection, and then ascended to the Father, just as He told Mary (see Acts 1:9).

### *THE APOSTLES COMMISSIONED*

*(Luke 24:36–43; 1 Cor. 15:5)*

19 [a]Then, the same day at evening, being the
first *day* of the week, when the doors were shut
where the disciples were assembled,[1] for [b]fear
of the Jews, Jesus came and stood in the midst,
and said to them, [c]"Peace *be* with you." 20 When
He had said this, He [a]showed them *His* hands
and His side. [b]Then the disciples were glad when
they saw the Lord.
21 So Jesus said to them again, "Peace to you!
[a]As the Father has sent Me, I also send you." 22 And
when He had said this, He breathed on *them,* and
said to them, "Receive the Holy Spirit. 23 [a]If you
forgive the sins of any, they are forgiven them;
if you retain the *sins* of any, they are retained."

### *SEEING AND BELIEVING*

24 Now Thomas, [a]called the Twin, one of the
twelve, was not with them when Jesus came.
25 The other disciples therefore said to him, "We
have seen the Lord."
So he said to them, "Unless I see in His hands
the print of the nails, and put my finger into the

**20:9** [a] Ps. 16:10 **20:11** [a] Mark 16:5 **20:14** [a] Matt. 28:9; Mark 16:9 [b] [Luke 24:16, 31]; John 21:4 **20:16** [a] John 10:3 [1] NU-Text adds *in Hebrew.* **20:17** [a] Mark 16:19; Luke 24:5; Acts 1:9; 2:34–36; Eph. 4:8–10; Heb. 4:14 [b] Ps. 22:22; Matt. 18:10; Rom. 8:29; Heb. 2:11 [c] John 16:28; 17:11 [d] Eph. 1:17 **20:18** [a] Matt. 28:10; Luke 24:10, 23 [1] NU-Text reads *disciples, "I have seen the Lord,"* . . . . **20:19** [a] Luke 24:36 [b] John 9:22; 19:38 [c] John 14:27; 16:33 [1] NU-Text omits *assembled.* **20:20** [a] Acts 1:3 [b] John 16:20, 22 **20:21** [a] [Matt. 28:18–20]; John 17:18, 19; [2 Tim. 2:2]; Heb. 3:1 **20:23** [a] Matt. 16:19; 18:18 **20:24** [a] John 11:16

## THE APPEARANCES OF THE RISEN CHRIST

In chronological order

| To | Location | Reference |
|---|---|---|
| **Mary Magdalene** | Golgotha and Jerusalem | John 20:11–18 |
| **The Other Women** | Jerusalem | Matthew 28:8–10 |
| **Cleopas and Another Disciple** | On the Road to Emmaus | Luke 24:13–32 |
| **Peter** | Jerusalem | Luke 24:34 |
| **Ten Disciples** | Jerusalem | Luke 24:36–43; John 20:19–25 |
| **Eleven Disciples** | Jerusalem | John 20:26–29 |
| **Seven Disciples** | Sea of Galilee | John 21:1–24 |
| **Eleven Disciples** | Galilee | Matthew 28:16–20 |
| **Five-hundred People** | Unknown | 1 Corinthians 15:6 |
| **James** | Unknown | 1 Corinthians 15:7 |
| **The Disciples** | Jerusalem | Luke 24:44–53; Acts 1:3–12 |
| **Paul** | On the Road to Damascus | Acts 9:1–6 |

KNOW THE TRUTH

## THE DOCTRINE OF JESUS

### PART 5: THE MIRACLES OF JESUS

**20:30–31** Jesus is the Creator of the universe and the laws of nature governing it. He has the authority and power to operate within or beyond those laws as He wills. Natural laws that bind us don't bind their Creator. A father, for example, isn't bound by the crib he constructs for his infant. The father can place toys and blankets in the crib or remove them. He can remove the infant from the crib or climb into it. What seems impossible to the infant in the crib is quite possible for the constructor of the crib.

John called Jesus' miracles "signs" because they pointed to something about Jesus: His miracles clarified He is the Christ, the anointed Son of God. Jesus is fully human *and* fully God. Everything He did and said during His earthly ministry was overflowing with divine power. His displays of power demonstrated His divine nature. No blind eye, lame body, infectious skin disease, hemorrhaging, or corpse was beyond His miraculous power. Perhaps His greatest miracle is making hopeless sinful people eternal sons and daughters of God (see John 1:11–13). Diseases, demons, and death are no match for the miraculous One. Jesus is no mere teacher nor a smoke-and-mirrors miracle man. He is the Creator and miracle-working Savior.

*For* **THE DOCTRINE OF JESUS: PART 6: THE TEACHINGS OF JESUS,** *turn to John 7:37–46 on page 1081.*

print of the nails, and put my hand into His side,
I will not believe."
26 And after eight days His disciples were
again inside, and Thomas with them. Jesus
came, the doors being shut, and stood in the
midst, and said, "Peace to you!" 27 Then He said
to Thomas, "Reach your finger here, and look
at My hands; and [a]reach your hand *here,* and
put *it* into My side. Do not be [b]unbelieving, but
believing."
28 And Thomas answered and said to Him,
"My Lord and my God!"
29 Jesus said to him, "Thomas,[1] because you
have seen Me, you have believed. [a]Blessed *are*
those who have not seen and *yet* have believed."

### *THAT YOU MAY BELIEVE*

30 And [a]truly Jesus did many other signs
in the presence of His disciples, which are not
written in this book; 31 [a]but these are written that
[b]you may believe that Jesus [c]is the Christ, the
Son of God, [d]and that believing you may have
life in His name.

### *BREAKFAST BY THE SEA*

**21** After these things Jesus showed Himself
again to the disciples at the [a]Sea of Tiberi-
as, and in this way He showed *Himself:* 2 Simon
Peter, [a]Thomas called the Twin, [b]Nathanael of
[c]Cana in Galilee, [d]the *sons* of Zebedee, and two
others of His disciples were together. 3 Simon
Peter said to them, "I am going fishing."
They said to him, "We are going with you
also." They went out and immediately[1] got into
the boat, and that night they caught nothing.
4 But when the morning had now come, Jesus
stood on the shore; yet the disciples [a]did not
know that it was Jesus. 5 Then [a]Jesus said to
them, "Children, have you any food?"
They answered Him, "No."
6 And He said to them, [a]"Cast the net on the
right side of the boat, and you will find *some.*" So
they cast, and now they were not able to draw it
in because of the multitude of fish.
7 Therefore [a]that disciple whom Jesus loved
said to Peter, "It is the Lord!" Now when Simon
Peter heard that it was the Lord, he put on *his*
outer garment (for he had removed it), and
plunged into the sea. 8 But the other disciples
came in the little boat (for they were not far from
land, but about two hundred cubits), dragging
the net with fish. 9 Then, as soon as they had
come to land, they saw a fire of coals there,
and fish laid on it, and bread. 10 Jesus said to
them, "Bring some of the fish which you have
just caught."
11 Simon Peter went up and dragged the net
to land, full of large fish, one hundred and fifty-
three; and although there were so many, the net
was not broken. 12 Jesus said to them, [a]"Come
*and* eat breakfast." Yet none of the disciples
dared ask Him, "Who are You?"—knowing that
it was the Lord. 13 Jesus then came and took the
bread and gave it to them, and likewise the fish.

**20:27** [a] Ps. 22:16; Zech. 12:10; 13:6; 1 John 1:1 [b] Mark 16:14 **20:29** [a] 2 Cor. 5:7; 1 Pet. 1:8 [1] NU-Text and M-Text omit *Thomas.* **20:30** [a] John 21:25 **20:31** [a] Luke 1:4 [b] John 19:35; 1 John 5:13 [c] Luke 2:11; 1 John 5:1 [d] John 3:15, 16; 5:24; [1 Pet. 1:8, 9] **21:1** [a] Matt. 26:32; Mark 14:28; John 6:1 **21:2** [a] John 20:24 [b] John 1:45–51 [c] John 2:1 [d] Matt. 4:21; Mark 1:19; Luke 5:10 **21:3** [1] NU-Text omits *immediately.* **21:4** [a] Luke 24:16; John 20:14 **21:5** [a] Luke 24:41 **21:6** [a] Luke 5:4, 6, 7 **21:7** [a] John 13:23; 20:2 **21:12** [a] Acts 10:41

14 This *is* now [a]the third time Jesus showed
Himself to His disciples after He was raised
from the dead.

### *JESUS RESTORES PETER*

15 So when they had eaten breakfast, Jesus
said to Simon Peter, "Simon, *son* of Jonah,[1] do
you love Me more than these?"

He said to Him, "Yes, Lord; You know that
I love You."

He said to him, [a]"Feed My lambs."

16 He said to him again a second time,
"Simon, *son* of Jonah,[1] do you love Me?"

He said to Him, "Yes, Lord; You know that
I love You."

[a]He said to him, "Tend My [b]sheep."

17 He said to him the third time, "Simon, *son*
of Jonah,[1] do you love Me?" Peter was grieved
because He said to him the third time, "Do you
love Me?"

And he said to Him, "Lord, [a]You know all
things; You know that I love You."

Jesus said to him, "Feed My sheep. 18 [a]Most
assuredly, I say to you, when you were younger,
you girded yourself and walked where you
wished; but when you are old, you will stretch
out your hands, and another will gird you and
carry *you* where you do not wish." 19 This He
spoke, signifying [a]by what death he would glorify
God. And when He had spoken this, He said to
him, [b]"Follow Me."

### *THE BELOVED DISCIPLE AND HIS BOOK*

20 Then Peter, turning around, saw the dis-
ciple [a]whom Jesus loved following, [b]who also
had leaned on His breast at the supper, and
said, "Lord, who is the one who betrays You?"
21 Peter, seeing him, said to Jesus, "But Lord,
what *about* this man?"

22 Jesus said to him, "If I will that he remain
[a]till I come, what *is that* to you? You follow Me."

23 Then this saying went out among the
brethren that this disciple would not die. Yet
Jesus did not say to him that he would not die,
but, "If I will that he remain till I come, what *is*
*that* to you?"

24 This is the disciple who [a]testifies of these
things, and wrote these things; and we know
that his testimony is true.

25 [a]And there are also many other things
that Jesus did, which if they were written one by
one, [b]I suppose that even the world itself could
not contain the books that would be written.
Amen.

> **21:17** Peter had denied the Lord three times. Here, Jesus gave him the opportunity to affirm his **love** for Him three times.

**21:14** [a] John 20:19, 26 **21:15** [a] Acts 20:28; 1 Tim. 4:6; 1 Pet. 5:2 [1] NU-Text reads *John.* **21:16** [a] Matt. 2:6; Acts 20:28; Heb. 13:20; 1 Pet. 2:25; 5:2, 4 [b] Ps. 79:13; Matt. 10:16; 15:24; 25:33; 26:31 [1] NU-Text reads *John.* **21:17** [a] John 2:24, 25; 16:30 [1] NU-Text reads *John.* **21:18** [a] John 13:36; Acts 12:3, 4 **21:19** [a] 2 Pet. 1:13, 14 [b] [Matt. 4:19; 16:24]; John 21:22 **21:20** [a] John 13:23; 20:2 [b] John 13:25 **21:22** [a] [Matt. 16:27, 28; 25:31; 1 Cor. 4:5; 11:26; Rev. 2:25; 3:11; 22:7, 20] **21:24** [a] John 19:35; 3 John 12 **21:25** [a] John 20:30 [b] Amos 7:10

# *The* ACTS *of the Apostles*

| AUTHOR | KEY VERSE | READING TIME |
|---|---|---|
| Luke | Acts 1:8 | 2 hours 51 minutes |

The time frame of Jesus' earthly ministry was rather brief—only about three years—but His impact would carry over throughout the generations and into eternity. Jesus would no longer be present on earth physically, but His ministry to save the world would continue through His followers. The Book of Acts is the story of the Holy Spirit's work through what was at first a small group of men and women. These first followers took Christ's commission seriously and began to spread the news of a risen Savior toward the most remote corners of the world. The spread of the gospel message began in Jerusalem, carried over into the surrounding region of Judea, and then crossed political, religious, and ethnic boundaries as it made its way into Samaria and beyond.

**Occasion:** Luke traces the early days of Christ's church to record how the gospel began to spread throughout the world.

**Main Point:** The church continues Jesus' mission to share the message of salvation to the world.

**Big Ideas:** Jesus' church began through the power of the Holy Spirit and the faithfulness of His followers. The Holy Spirit is a gift given to all who believe. We are to continue the mission Jesus gave to spread the gospel throughout the world.

## OUTLINE:

I. The Preaching of Peter (chs. 1–5)
II. The Martyrdom of Stephen (chs. 6–7)
III. The Evangelism of Philip (ch. 8)
IV. The Salvation of Paul (ch. 9)
V. The Witness of Peter (chs. 10–12)
VI. The Missions of Paul (chs. 13–21)
VII. The Imprisonment of Paul (chs. 22–28)

**AD 14–37**
Tiberius Caesar is Roman emperor

**c. AD 30**
Jesus' crucifixion and resurrection

**c. AD 30–35**
Pentecost; the early church in Jerusalem

**c. AD 34**
Paul is converted

**c. AD 35–37**
The church grows in Judea and Samaria

**c. AD 37**
Jewish historian Josephus is born

**AD 37–41**
Caligula is Roman emperor

**AD 37–44**
Herod Agrippa I rules in Judea

**AD 41–54**
Claudius is Roman emperor

**c. AD 44**
James the son of Zebedee is martyred

**c. AD 47–49**
Paul's first missionary journey

**c. AD 50**
The Jerusalem Council

**c. AD 50–53**
Paul's second missionary journey

**AD 52–60**
Felix is procurator of Judea

**c. AD 53–57**
Paul's third missionary journey

**AD 54–68**
Nero is Roman emperor

**c. AD 58**
Paul is arrested in Jerusalem

**AD 60–62**
Festus is procurator of Judea

**c. AD 60–62**
Paul is imprisoned in Rome

**c. AD 62**
**Acts written**

### PROLOGUE

**1** The former account I made, O [a]Theophilus, of all that Jesus began both to do and teach, 2 [a]until the day in which He was taken up, after He through the Holy Spirit [b]had given commandments to the apostles whom He had chosen, 3 [a]to whom He also presented Himself alive after His suffering by many infallible proofs, being seen by them during forty days and speaking of the things pertaining to the kingdom of God.

### THE HOLY SPIRIT PROMISED

4 [a]And being assembled together with *them,* He commanded them not to depart from Jerusalem, but to wait for the Promise of the Father, "which," *He said,* "you have [b]heard from Me; 5 [a]for John truly baptized with water, [b]but you shall be baptized with the Holy Spirit not many days from now." 6 Therefore, when they had come together, they asked Him, saying, "Lord, will You at this time restore the kingdom to Israel?" 7 And He said to them, [a]"It is not for you to [b]know times or seasons which the Father has put in His own authority. 8 [a]But you shall receive power [b]when the Holy Spirit has come upon you; and [c]you shall be witnesses to Me[1] in Jerusalem, and in all Judea and [d]Samaria, and to the [e]end of the earth."

> **1:6** Even some of Jesus' followers had expected Him to wrestle control of Israel from the Roman Empire, which had been in charge of the land since 63 BC.

### JESUS ASCENDS TO HEAVEN

*(Mark 16:19, 20; Luke 24:50–53)*

9 [a]Now when He had spoken these things, while they watched, [b]He was taken up, and a cloud received Him out of their sight. 10 And while they looked steadfastly toward heaven as He went up, behold, two men stood by them [a]in white apparel, 11 who also said, "Men of Galilee, why do you stand gazing up into heaven? This *same* Jesus, who was taken up from you into heaven, [a]will so come in like manner as you saw Him go into heaven."

> **SEEING JESUS IN THE SCRIPTURE**
>
> **1:11** Jesus came to earth the first time as the Suffering Servant; He will return as the Conquering King (see Rev. 19:11–16).

### THE UPPER ROOM PRAYER MEETING

12 [a]Then they returned to Jerusalem from the mount called Olivet, which is near Jerusalem, a Sabbath day's journey. 13 And when they had entered, they went up [a]into the upper room where they were staying: [b]Peter, James, John, and Andrew; Philip and Thomas; Bartholomew and Matthew; James *the son* of Alphaeus and [c]Simon the Zealot; and [d]Judas *the son* of James. 14 [a]These all continued with one accord in prayer and supplication,[1] with [b]the women and Mary the mother of Jesus, and with [c]His brothers.

### MATTHIAS CHOSEN

*(cf. Ps. 109:8; Matt. 27:7, 8)*

15 And in those days Peter stood up in the midst of the disciples[1] (altogether the number [a]of names was about a hundred and twenty), and said, 16 "Men *and* brethren, this Scripture had to be fulfilled, [a]which the Holy Spirit spoke before by the mouth of David concerning Judas, [b]who became a guide to those who arrested Jesus; 17 for [a]he was numbered with us and obtained a part in [b]this ministry."

18 [a](Now this man purchased a field with [b]the wages of iniquity; and falling headlong, he burst open in the middle and all his entrails gushed out. 19 And it became known to all those dwelling in Jerusalem; so that field is called in their own language, Akel Dama, that is, Field of Blood.)

20 "For it is written in the Book of Psalms:

[a]'Let his dwelling place be desolate,
And let no one live in it';[1]

and,

[b]'Let[2] another take his office.'[3]

21 "Therefore, of these men who have accompanied us all the time that the Lord Jesus went in and out among us, 22 beginning from the baptism of John to that day when [a]He was taken up from us, one of these must [b]become a witness with us of His resurrection."

23 And they proposed two: Joseph called [a]Barsabas, who was surnamed Justus, and Matthias. 24 And they prayed and said, "You, O Lord, [a]who know the hearts of all, show which of these two You have chosen 25 [a]to take part in this ministry and apostleship from which Judas by transgression fell, that he might go to his own place." 26 And they cast their lots, and the lot fell on Matthias. And he was numbered with the eleven apostles.

**1:1** [a] Luke 1:3 **1:2** [a] Mark 16:19 [b] Matt. 28:19 **1:3** [a] Mark 16:12, 14 **1:4** [a] Luke 24:49 [b] [John 14:16, 17, 26; 15:26] **1:5** [a] Matt. 3:11 [b] [Joel 2:28] **1:7** [a] 1 Thess. 5:1 [b] Matt. 24:36 **1:8** [a] [Acts 2:1, 4] [b] Luke 24:49 [c] Luke 24:48 [d] Acts 8:1, 5, 14 [e] Col. 1:23 [1] NU-Text reads *My witnesses.* **1:9** [a] Luke 24:50, 51 [b] Acts 1:2 **1:10** [a] John 20:12 **1:11** [a] Dan. 7:13 **1:12** [a] Luke 24:52 **1:13** [a] Acts 9:37, 39; 20:8 [b] Matt. 10:2–4 [c] Luke 6:15 [d] Jude 1 **1:14** [a] Acts 2:1, 46 [b] Luke 23:49, 55 [c] Matt. 13:55 [1] NU-Text omits *and supplication.* **1:15** [a] Rev. 3:4 [1] NU-Text reads *brethren.* **1:16** [a] Ps. 41:9 [b] Luke 22:47 **1:17** [a] Matt. 10:4 [b] Acts 1:25 **1:18** [a] Matt. 27:3–10 [b] Mark 14:21 **1:20** [a] Ps. 69:25 [b] Ps. 109:8 [1] Psalm 69:25 [2] Psalm 109:8 [3] Greek *episkopen,* position of overseer **1:22** [a] Acts 1:9 [b] Acts 1:8; 2:32 **1:23** [a] Acts 15:22 **1:24** [a] 1 Sam. 16:7 **1:25** [a] Acts 1:17

ACTS 1:1—2:4

## THE CHURCH IS BORN

50

STORY OF SCRIPTURE

### WHAT'S GOING ON?

The Book of Acts recounts the beginning of Christ's church. Before ascending to heaven, Jesus promised the disciples they would receive power when the Holy Spirit came upon them (see Acts 1:8). The disciples waited, prayed, and earnestly sought God during this time. Then, on the day of Pentecost, Jesus' promise was fulfilled when the Holy Spirit descended upon the disciples in dramatic fashion. The disciples began speaking in various tongues, empowered by the Spirit to proclaim the gospel to people of different nations gathered in Jerusalem. People were saved and gathered under the name of Jesus, and a movement began that echoes into eternity.

### WHAT DOES THIS MEAN FOR ME?

What fuels your church and keeps it living and active? Preaching? Music? Leaders? Yes and no. Those are all important, but the one thing the church desperately needs—the one thing that empowers those other things—is the Holy Spirit's empowerment. The Holy Spirit lives and moves within each person in the church, including you.

### DID YOU CATCH THE PATTERN?

The Holy Spirit is not exclusive to the Book of Acts. He has been moving among God's people since the very beginning. The very breath given to Adam and Eve was given by the Spirit. He came upon heroes like Samson and David in times of need. He has guided, convicted, moved, and worked in the margins of the Bible. The difference now is the Spirit is available to everyone who calls upon the name of Jesus.

*For the next* Story of Scripture *reading and devotion, turn to Acts 9:1–31 on page 1116.*

### *COMING OF THE HOLY SPIRIT*

**2** When [a]the Day of Pentecost had fully come,
[b]they were all with one accord[1] in one place.
2 And suddenly there came a sound from heaven,
as of a rushing mighty wind, and [a]it filled the
whole house where they were sitting. 3 Then
there appeared to them divided tongues, as of
fire, and *one* sat upon each of them. 4 And [a]they
were all filled with the Holy Spirit and began
[b]to speak with other tongues, as the Spirit gave
them utterance.

**SEEING JESUS IN THE SCRIPTURE**

**2:3–4** Just as John the Baptist prophesied, those who placed their faith in Jesus were baptized with the Holy Spirit (see Matt. 3:11).

### *THE CROWD'S RESPONSE*

5 And there were dwelling in Jerusalem Jews,
[a]devout men, from every nation under heaven.
6 And when this sound occurred, the [a]multitude
came together, and were confused, because
everyone heard them speak in his own language.
7 Then they were all amazed and marveled, say-
ing to one another, "Look, are not all these who
speak [a]Galileans? 8 And how *is it that* we hear,
each in our own language in which we were
born? 9 Parthians and Medes and Elamites, those
dwelling in Mesopotamia, Judea and [a]Cappado-
cia, Pontus and Asia, 10 Phrygia and Pamphylia,
Egypt and the parts of Libya adjoining Cyrene,
visitors from Rome, both Jews and proselytes,
11 Cretans and Arabs—we hear them speaking in
our own tongues the wonderful works of God."
12 So they were all amazed and perplexed, saying
to one another, "Whatever could this mean?"
13 Others mocking said, "They are full of
new wine."

### *PETER'S SERMON*

*(Joel 2:28–32)*

14 But Peter, standing up with the eleven,
raised his voice and said to them, "Men of Judea
and all who dwell in Jerusalem, let this be known
to you, and heed my words. 15 For these are not
drunk, as you suppose, [a]since it is *only* the third
hour of the day. 16 But this is what was spoken
by the prophet Joel:

17 'And[a] it shall come to pass in the last days, says God,
[b]That I will pour out of My Spirit on all flesh;

**2:1** [a] Lev. 23:15 [b] Acts 1:14 [1] NU-Text reads *together.* **2:2** [a] Acts 4:31 **2:4** [a] Acts 1:5 [b] Mark 16:17 **2:5** [a] Acts 8:2 **2:6** [a] Acts 4:32 **2:7** [a] Acts 1:11 **2:9** [a] 1 Pet. 1:1 **2:15** [a] 1 Thess. 5:7 **2:17** [a] Joel 2:28–32 [b] Acts 10:45

Your sons and [c]your daughters shall
prophesy,
Your young men shall see visions,
Your old men shall dream dreams.
18 And on My menservants and on My
maidservants
I will pour out My Spirit in those days;
[a]And they shall prophesy.
19 [a]I will show wonders in heaven above
And signs in the earth beneath:
Blood and fire and vapor of smoke.
20 [a]The sun shall be turned into darkness,
And the moon into blood,
Before the coming of the great and
awesome day of the LORD.
21 And it shall come to pass
*That* [a]whoever calls on the name of the
LORD
Shall be saved.'[1]

22 "Men of Israel, hear these words: Jesus
of Nazareth, a Man attested by God to you [a]by
miracles, wonders, and signs which God did
through Him in your midst, as you yourselves
also know— 23 Him, [a]being delivered by the
determined purpose and foreknowledge of
God, [b]you have taken[1] by lawless hands, have
crucified, and put to death; 24 [a]whom God raised
up, having loosed the pains of death, because
it was not possible that He should be held by it.
25 For David says concerning Him:

[a]'I foresaw the LORD always before my face,
For He is at my right hand, that I may not
be shaken.
26 Therefore my heart rejoiced, and my
tongue was glad;
Moreover my flesh also will rest in hope.
27 For You will not leave my soul in Hades,
Nor will You allow Your Holy One to see
[a]corruption.
28 You have made known to me the ways of
life;
You will make me full of joy in Your
presence.'[1]

29 "Men *and* brethren, let *me* speak freely to
you [a]of the patriarch David, that he is both dead
and buried, and his tomb is with us to this day.
30 Therefore, being a prophet, [a]and knowing
that God had sworn with an oath to him that of
the fruit of his body, according to the flesh, He
would raise up the Christ to sit on his throne,[1]
31 he, foreseeing this, spoke concerning the res-
urrection of the Christ, [a]that His soul was not
left in Hades, nor did His flesh see corruption.
32 [a]This Jesus God has raised up, [b]of which we
are all witnesses. 33 Therefore [a]being exalted to
[b]the right hand of God, and [c]having received
from the Father the promise of the Holy Spirit,
He [d]poured out this which you now see and hear.
34 "For David did not ascend into the heav-
ens, but he says himself:

[a]'The LORD said to my Lord,
"Sit at My right hand,
35 Till I make Your enemies Your footstool." '[1]

36 "Therefore let all the house of Israel know
assuredly that God has made this Jesus, whom
you crucified, both Lord and Christ."
37 Now when they heard *this,* [a]they were cut
to the heart, and said to Peter and the rest of the
apostles, "Men *and* brethren, what shall we do?"
38 Then Peter said to them, [a]"Repent, and let
every one of you be baptized in the name of Jesus
Christ for the remission of sins; and you shall re-
ceive the gift of the Holy Spirit. 39 For the promise
is to you and [a]to your children, and [b]to all who are
afar off, as many as the Lord our God will call."

### A VITAL CHURCH GROWS

40 And with many other words he testified
and exhorted them, saying, "Be saved from this
perverse generation." 41 Then those who gladly[1]
received his word were baptized; and that day
about three thousand souls were added *to them.*
42 [a]And they continued steadfastly in the apostles'
doctrine and fellowship, in the breaking of bread,
and in prayers. 43 Then fear came upon every
soul, and [a]many wonders and signs were done
through the apostles. 44 Now all who believed were
together, and [a]had all things in common, 45 and
sold their possessions and goods, and [a]divided
them among all, as anyone had need.
46 [a]So continuing daily with one accord [b]in
the temple, and [c]breaking bread from house
to house, they ate their food with gladness and
simplicity of heart, 47 praising God and having
favor with all the people. And [a]the Lord added
to the church[1] daily those who were being saved.

### A LAME MAN HEALED

3 Now Peter and John went up together [a]to the
temple at the hour of prayer, [b]the ninth *hour.*
2 And [a]a certain man lame from his mother's
womb was carried, whom they laid daily at the
gate of the temple which is called Beautiful, [b]to
ask alms from those who entered the temple;
3 who, seeing Peter and John about to go into the
temple, asked for alms. 4 And fixing his eyes on
him, with John, Peter said, "Look at us." 5 So he

2:17 [c] Acts 21:9 2:18 [a] 1 Cor. 12:10 2:19 [a] Joel 2:30 2:20 [a] Matt. 24:29 2:21 [a] Rom. 10:13 [1] Joel 2:28–32 2:22 [a] John 3:2; 5:6 2:23 [a] Luke 22:22 [b] Acts 5:30 [1] NU-Text omits *have taken.* 2:24 [a] [Rom. 8:11] 2:25 [a] Ps. 16:8–11 2:27 [a] Acts 13:30–37 2:28 [1] Psalm 16:8–11 2:29 [a] Acts 13:36 2:30 [a] Ps. 132:11 [1] NU-Text omits *according to the flesh, He would raise up the Christ* and completes the verse with *He would seat one on his throne.* 2:31 [a] Ps. 16:10 2:32 [a] Acts 2:24 [b] Acts 1:8; 3:15 2:33 [a] [Acts 5:31] [b] [Heb. 10:12] [c] [John 14:26] [d] Acts 2:1–11, 17; 10:45 2:34 [a] Ps. 68:18; 110:1 2:35 [1] Psalm 110:1 2:37 [a] Luke 3:10, 12, 14 2:38 [a] Luke 24:47 2:39 [a] Joel 2:28, 32 [b] Eph. 2:13 2:41 [1] NU-Text omits *gladly.* 2:42 [a] Acts 1:14 2:43 [a] Acts 2:22 2:44 [a] Acts 4:32, 34, 37; 5:2 2:45 [a] Is. 58:7 2:46 [a] Acts 1:14 [b] Luke 24:53 [c] Acts 2:42; 20:7 2:47 [a] Acts 5:14 [1] NU-Text omits *to the church.* 3:1 [a] Acts 2:46 [b] Ps. 55:17 3:2 [a] Acts 14:8 [b] John 9:8

KNOW THE TRUTH

## THE DOCTRINE OF THE CHURCH

### PART 4: THE UNIVERSAL AND LOCAL CHURCH

**2:47** It's proper to think of the church as a local gathering of believers, but it's also far more than that. The church is all believers from all places throughout all time. This grand and complete assembly of those Christ has saved is often referred to as the universal church. The church Jesus is building and shall one day complete is made up of people from everywhere in the world (see Matt. 24:14; 28:18–20). People of every ethnicity, language, geographical region, and time will be gathered and eternally cared for by God (see Rev. 21:24–27).

The church is also made up of local assemblies often referred to as the local church. During Jesus' earthly ministry, He called individuals to follow Him within a local community (see Luke 10:1–20). Immediately after Jesus' ascension to heaven, His early followers served Him in a community located in Jerusalem while starting new communities in cities around the Roman Empire (see Acts 2:43–47; 5:42; 19:17–28). Scripture prescribes the local church to gather as often as possible, particularly on the first day of the week, and to be led by qualified leaders who preach and teach God's Word, equip the saints for ministry, serve one another, and share the gospel with the world (see Acts 4:31–32; 20:7; Rom. 12:13; Eph. 4:11–16; Titus 1:5–9; Heb. 10:19–25).

*For* **THE DOCTRINE OF THE CHURCH: PART 5: THE PURPOSE OF THE CHURCH,** *turn to Acts 11:19–26 on page 1119.*

gave them his attention, expecting to receive
something from them. 6 Then Peter said, "Silver
and gold I do not have, but what I do have I give
you: [a]In the name of Jesus Christ of Nazareth,
rise up and walk." 7 And he took him by the right
hand and lifted *him* up, and immediately his
feet and ankle bones received strength. 8 So he,
[a]leaping up, stood and walked and entered the
temple with them—walking, leaping, and prais-
ing God. 9 [a]And all the people saw him walking
and praising God. 10 Then they knew that it was
he who [a]sat begging alms at the Beautiful Gate
of the temple; and they were filled with wonder
and amazement at what had happened to him.

### PREACHING IN SOLOMON'S PORTICO

11 Now as the lame man who was healed
held on to Peter and John, all the people ran
together to them in the porch [a]which is called
Solomon's, greatly amazed. 12 So when Peter
saw *it,* he responded to the people: "Men of Is-
rael, why do you marvel at this? Or why look so
intently at us, as though by our own power or
godliness we had made this man walk? 13 [a]The
God of Abraham, Isaac, and Jacob, the God of
our fathers, [b]glorified His Servant Jesus, whom
you [c]delivered up and [d]denied in the presence
of Pilate, when he was determined to let *Him*
go. 14 But you denied [a]the Holy One [b]and the
Just, and [c]asked for a murderer to be granted
to you, 15 and killed the Prince of life, [a]whom
God raised from the dead, [b]of which we are
witnesses. 16 [a]And His name, through faith in His
name, has made this man strong, whom you see
and know. Yes, the faith which *comes* through
Him has given him this perfect soundness in
the presence of you all.

17 "Yet now, brethren, I know that [a]you did *it*
in ignorance, as *did* also your rulers. 18 But [a]those
things which God foretold [b]by the mouth of all
His prophets, that the Christ would suffer, He
has thus fulfilled. 19 [a]Repent therefore and be
converted, that your sins may be blotted out,
so that times of refreshing may come from the
presence of the Lord, 20 and that He may send
Jesus Christ, who was preached to you before,[1]
21 [a]whom heaven must receive until the times
of [b]restoration of all things, [c]which God has
spoken by the mouth of all His holy prophets
since the world began. 22 For Moses truly said to
the fathers, [a]'The LORD your God will raise up for
you a Prophet like me from your brethren. Him
you shall hear in all things, whatever He says to
you. 23 And it shall be *that* every soul who will
not hear that Prophet shall be utterly destroyed
from among the people.'[1] 24 Yes, and [a]all the
prophets, from Samuel and those who follow, as
many as have spoken, have also foretold[1] these

**3:6** [a] Acts 4:10 **3:8** [a] Is. 35:6 **3:9** [a] Acts 4:16, 21 **3:10** [a] John 9:8 **3:11** [a] John 10:23 **3:13** [a] John 5:30 [b] John 7:39; 12:23; 13:31 [c] Matt. 27:2 [d] Matt. 27:20 **3:14** [a] Mark 1:24 [b] Acts 7:52 [c] John 18:40 **3:15** [a] Acts 2:24 [b] Acts 2:32 **3:16** [a] Matt. 9:22 **3:17** [a] Luke 23:34 **3:18** [a] Acts 26:22 [b] 1 Pet. 1:10 **3:19** [a] [Acts 2:38; 26:20] **3:20** [1] NU-Text and M-Text read *Christ Jesus, who was ordained for you before.* **3:21** [a] Acts 1:11 [b] Matt. 17:11 [c] Luke 1:70 **3:22** [a] Deut. 18:15, 18, 19 **3:23** [1] Deuteronomy 18:15, 18, 19 **3:24** [a] Luke 24:25 [1] NU-Text and M-Text read *proclaimed.*

days. 25 [a]You are sons of the prophets, and of the covenant which God made with our fathers, saying to Abraham, [b]'And in your seed all the families of the earth shall be blessed.'[1] 26 To you [a]first, God, having raised up His Servant Jesus, sent Him to bless you, [b]in turning away every one *of you* from your iniquities."

### PETER AND JOHN ARRESTED

4 Now as they spoke to the people, the priests, the captain of the temple, and the [a]Sadducees came upon them, 2 being greatly disturbed that they taught the people and preached in Jesus the resurrection from the dead. 3 And they laid hands on them, and put *them* in custody until the next day, for it was already evening. 4 However, many of those who heard the word believed; and the number of the men came to be about five thousand.

### ADDRESSING THE SANHEDRIN

5 And it came to pass, on the next day, that their rulers, elders, and scribes, 6 as well as [a]Annas the high priest, Caiaphas, John, and Alexander, and as many as were of the family of the high priest, were gathered together at Jerusalem. 7 And when they had set them in the midst, they asked, [a]"By what power or by what name have you done this?"

> **4:6** The Sanhedrin, a council made up of seventy men plus the **high priest**, was the highest Jewish court in the land. The council met regularly to settle disputes among the Jewish people. **Caiaphas** had been selected by the Romans to replace his father-in-law, **Annas**, as high priest. Annas, though, was high priest emeritus and was the highest-ranking member of the Sanhedrin.

8 [a]Then Peter, filled with the Holy Spirit, said to them, "Rulers of the people and elders of Israel: 9 If we this day are judged for a good deed *done* to a helpless man, by what means he has been made well, 10 let it be known to you all, and to all the people of Israel, [a]that by the name of Jesus Christ of Nazareth, whom you crucified, [b]whom God raised from the dead, by Him this man stands here before you whole. 11 This is the [a]'stone which was rejected by you builders, which has become the chief cornerstone.'[1] 12 [a]Nor is there salvation in any other, for there is no other name under heaven given among men by which we must be saved."

> **SEEING JESUS IN THE SCRIPTURE**
>
> **4:11** Peter declared to the Sanhedrin that Jesus, the stone they rejected, was the one the prophet Isaiah spoke about (see Is. 28:16).

### THE NAME OF JESUS FORBIDDEN

13 Now when they saw the boldness of Peter and John, [a]and perceived that they were uneducated and untrained men, they marveled. And they realized that they had been with Jesus. 14 And seeing the man who had been healed [a]standing with them, they could say nothing against it. 15 But when they had commanded them to go aside out of the council, they conferred among themselves, 16 saying, [a]"What shall we do to these men? For, indeed, that a notable miracle has been done through them *is* [b]evident to all who dwell in Jerusalem, and we cannot deny *it.* 17 But so that it spreads no further among the people, let us severely threaten them, that from now on they speak to no man in this name."

18 [a]So they called them and commanded them not to speak at all nor teach in the name of Jesus. 19 But Peter and John answered and said to them, [a]"Whether it is right in the sight of God to listen to you more than to God, you judge. 20 [a]For we cannot but speak the things which [b]we have seen and heard." 21 So when they had further threatened them, they let them go, finding no way of punishing them, [a]because of the people, since they all [b]glorified God for [c]what had been done. 22 For the man was over forty years old on whom this miracle of healing had been performed.

### PRAYER FOR BOLDNESS

*(cf. Ps. 2:1, 2)*

23 And being let go, [a]they went to their own *companions* and reported all that the chief priests and elders had said to them. 24 So when they heard that, they raised their voice to God with one accord and said: "Lord, [a]You *are* God, who made heaven and earth and the sea, and all that is in them, 25 who by the mouth of Your servant David[1] have said:

[a]'Why did the nations rage,
And the people plot vain things?
26 The kings of the earth took their stand,
And the rulers were gathered together
Against the LORD and against His Christ.'[1]

27 "For [a]truly against [b]Your holy Servant Jesus, [c]whom You anointed, both Herod and Pontius Pilate, with the Gentiles and the people

**3:25** [a] [Rom. 9:4, 8] [b] Gen. 12:3; 18:18; 22:18; 26:4; 28:14 [1] Genesis 22:18; 26:4; 28:14 **3:26** [a] [Rom. 1:16; 2:9] [b] Matt. 1:21 **4:1** [a] Matt. 22:23 **4:6** [a] Luke 3:2 **4:7** [a] Matt. 21:23 **4:8** [a] Luke 12:11, 12 **4:10** [a] Acts 2:22; 3:6, 16 [b] Acts 2:24 **4:11** [a] Ps. 118:22 [1] Psalm 118:22 **4:12** [a] [1 Tim. 2:5, 6] **4:13** [a] [1 Cor. 1:27] **4:14** [a] Acts 3:11 **4:16** [a] John 11:47 [b] Acts 3:7–10 **4:18** [a] Acts 5:28, 40 **4:19** [a] Acts 5:29 **4:20** [a] Acts 1:8; 2:32 [b] [1 John 1:1, 3] **4:21** [a] Acts 5:26 [b] Matt. 15:31 [c] Acts 3:7, 8 **4:23** [a] Acts 2:44–46; 12:12 **4:24** [a] Ex. 20:11 **4:25** [a] Ps. 2:1, 2 [1] NU-Text reads *who through the Holy Spirit, by the mouth of our father, Your servant David.* **4:26** [1] Psalm 2:1, 2 **4:27** [a] Luke 22:2; 23:1, 8 [b] [Luke 1:35] [c] John 10:36

of Israel, were gathered together 28 [a]to do what-
ever Your hand and Your purpose determined
before to be done. 29 Now, Lord, look on their
threats, and grant to Your servants [a]that with
all boldness they may speak Your word, 30 by
stretching out Your hand to heal, [a]and that signs
and wonders may be done [b]through the name
of [c]Your holy Servant Jesus."
31 And when they had prayed, [a]the place
where they were assembled together was shak-
en; and they were all filled with the Holy Spirit,
[b]and they spoke the word of God with boldness.

### *SHARING IN ALL THINGS*

32 Now the multitude of those who believed
[a]were of one heart and one soul; [b]neither did
anyone say that any of the things he possessed
was his own, but they had all things in common.
33 And with [a]great power the apostles gave [b]wit-
ness to the resurrection of the Lord Jesus. And
[c]great grace was upon them all. 34 Nor was there
anyone among them who lacked; [a]for all who
were possessors of lands or houses sold them,
and brought the proceeds of the things that were
sold, 35 [a]and laid *them* at the apostles' feet; [b]and
they distributed to each as anyone had need.
36 And Joses,[1] who was also named Barna-
bas by the apostles (which is translated Son
of Encouragement), a Levite of the country of
Cyprus, 37 [a]having land, sold *it,* and brought the
money and laid *it* at the apostles' feet.

### *LYING TO THE HOLY SPIRIT*

5 But a certain man named Ananias, with Sap-
phira his wife, sold a possession. 2 And he kept
back *part* of the proceeds, his wife also being
aware *of it,* and brought a certain part and laid
*it* at the apostles' feet. 3 [a]But Peter said, "Ananias,
why has [b]Satan filled your heart to lie to the Holy
Spirit and keep back *part* of the price of the land
for yourself? 4 While it remained, was it not your
own? And after it was sold, was it not in your own
control? Why have you conceived this thing in
your heart? You have not lied to men but to God."
5 Then Ananias, hearing these words, [a]fell
down and breathed his last. So great fear came
upon all those who heard these things. 6 And the
young men arose and [a]wrapped him up, carried
*him* out, and buried *him.*
7 Now it was about three hours later when his
wife came in, not knowing what had happened.
8 And Peter answered her, "Tell me whether you
sold the land for so much?"
She said, "Yes, for so much."
9 Then Peter said to her, "How is it that you
have agreed together [a]to test the Spirit of the

**4:28** [a] Acts 2:23; 3:18 **4:29** [a] Acts 4:13, 31; 9:27; 13:46; 14:3; 19:8; 26:26 **4:30** [a] Acts 2:43; 5:12 [b] Acts 3:6, 16 [c] Acts 4:27 **4:31** [a] Acts 2:2, 4; 16:26 [b] Acts 4:29 **4:32** [a] Acts 5:12; Rom. 15:5, 6; 2 Cor. 13:11; Phil. 1:27; 2:2; 1 Pet. 3:8 [b] Acts 2:44 **4:33** [a] [Acts 1:8] [b] Acts 1:22 [c] Rom. 6:15 **4:34** [a] [Matt. 19:21]; Acts 2:45 **4:35** [a] Acts 4:37; 5:2 [b] Acts 2:45; 6:1 **4:36** [1] NU-Text reads *Joseph.* **4:37** [a] Acts 4:34, 35; 5:1, 2 **5:3** [a] Num. 30:2; Deut. 23:21; Eccl. 5:4 [b] Matt. 4:10; Luke 22:3; John 13:2, 27 **5:5** [a] Ezek. 11:13; Acts 5:10, 11 **5:6** [a] John 19:40 **5:9** [a] Matt. 4:7; Acts 5:3, 4

KNOW THE TRUTH

## THE DOCTRINE OF THE CHURCH

### PART 1: OVERVIEW OF THE DOCTRINE OF THE CHURCH

**4:21–37** When we hear *church*, we normally think of a building. But as you read the Book of Acts—Luke's written history of the early church—it's hard not to notice he gave little detail of where the church gathered. That's because in the New Testament era, the Greek term translated into English as "church" had almost nothing to do with *where* a people gathered and almost everything to do with *who* was gathered. In other words, *church* described the *people* assembled, not the *place* of assembly. Because *church* means an assembly of people called together, our best definition centers on it being the people Jesus Christ has saved and called together to serve Him, one another, and the world in His name.

Jesus was the first to use the term *church* in the New Testament (see Matt. 16:18). There, we see the church doesn't build itself; it's built by Jesus. This is why Luke didn't credit Peter, John, Paul, or any other leader with the numerical growth and cultural effect of the church. Credit goes to Christ working in and through His people, namely through the ministry of the Holy Spirit (see Acts 2:47).

Throughout the Book of Acts, the power of the Holy Spirit at work, the doctrine of the apostles, and the changed lives of the church are all credited to Jesus Christ (see Acts 1:8; 2:32–33; 4:9–13; 5:27–42).

*For* **THE DOCTRINE OF THE CHURCH: PART 2: THE KINGDOM OF GOD,** *turn to John 3:3–5 on page 1073.*

Lord? Look, the feet of those who have buried your
husband *are* at the door, and they will carry you
out." 10 [a]Then immediately she fell down at his feet
and breathed her last. And the young men came in
and found her dead, and carrying *her* out, buried
*her* by her husband. 11 [a]So great fear came upon all
the church and upon all who heard these things.

### CONTINUING POWER IN THE CHURCH

12 And [a]through the hands of the apostles
many signs and wonders were done among the
people. [b]And they were all with one accord in
Solomon's Porch. 13 Yet [a]none of the rest dared
join them, [b]but the people esteemed them high-
ly. 14 And believers were increasingly added to the
Lord, multitudes of both men and women, 15 so
that they brought the sick out into the streets
and laid *them* on beds and couches, [a]that at least
the shadow of Peter passing by might fall on
some of them. 16 Also a multitude gathered from
the surrounding cities to Jerusalem, bringing
[a]sick people and those who were tormented by
unclean spirits, and they were all healed.

### IMPRISONED APOSTLES FREED

17 [a]Then the high priest rose up, and all those
who *were* with him (which is the sect of the Saddu-
cees), and they were filled with indignation, 18 [a]and
laid their hands on the apostles and put them in
the common prison. 19 But at night [a]an angel of
the Lord opened the prison doors and brought
them out, and said, 20 "Go, stand in the temple
and speak to the people [a]all the words of this life."
21 And when they heard *that,* they entered the
temple early in the morning and taught. [a]But
the high priest and those with him came and
called the council together, with all the elders
of the children of Israel, and sent to the prison
to have them brought.

### APOSTLES ON TRIAL AGAIN

22 But when the officers came and did not find
them in the prison, they returned and reported,
23 saying, "Indeed we found the prison shut se-
curely, and the guards standing outside[1] before the
doors; but when we opened them, we found no one
inside!" 24 Now when the high priest,[1] [a]the captain
of the temple, and the chief priests heard these
things, they wondered what the outcome would
be. 25 So one came and told them, saying,[1] "Look,
the men whom you put in prison are standing in
the temple and teaching the people!"
26 Then the captain went with the officers
and brought them without violence, [a]for they
feared the people, lest they should be stoned.
27 And when they had brought them, they set
*them* before the council. And the high priest
asked them, 28 saying, [a]"Did we not strictly com-
mand you not to teach in this name? And look,
you have filled Jerusalem with your doctrine,
[b]and intend to bring this Man's [c]blood on us!"
29 But Peter and the *other* apostles answered
and said: [a]"We ought to obey God rather than men.
30 [a]The God of our fathers raised up Jesus whom
you murdered by [b]hanging on a tree. 31 [a]Him God
has exalted to His right hand *to be* [b]Prince and
[c]Savior, [d]to give repentance to Israel and forgive-
ness of sins. 32 And [a]we are His witnesses to these
things, and *so* also *is* the Holy Spirit [b]whom God
has given to those who obey Him."

**5:10** [a] Ezek. 11:13; Acts 5:5 **5:11** [a] Acts 2:43; 5:5; 19:17 **5:12** [a] Acts 2:43; 4:30; 6:8; 14:3; 15:12; [Rom. 15:19]; 2 Cor. 12:12; Heb. 2:4 [b] Acts 3:11; 4:32 **5:13** [a] John 9:22 [b] Acts 2:47; 4:21 **5:15** [a] Matt. 9:21; 14:36; Acts 19:12 **5:16** [a] Mark 16:17, 18; [John 14:12] **5:17** [a] Matt. 3:7; Acts 4:1, 2, 6 **5:18** [a] Luke 21:12; Acts 4:3; 16:37 **5:19** [a] Matt. 1:20, 24; 2:13, 19; 28:2; Luke 1:11; 2:9; Acts 12:7; 16:26 **5:20** [a] [John 6:63, 68; 17:3; 1 John 5:11] **5:21** [a] Acts 4:5, 6 **5:23** [1] NU-Text and M-Text omit *outside.* **5:24** [a] Luke 22:4; Acts 4:1; 5:26 [1] NU-Text omits *the high priest.* **5:25** [1] NU-Text and M-Text omit *saying.* **5:26** [a] Matt. 21:26 **5:28** [a] Acts 4:17, 18 [b] Acts 2:23, 36 [c] Matt. 23:35 **5:29** [a] Acts 4:19 **5:30** [a] Acts 3:13, 15 [b] [1 Pet. 2:24] **5:31** [a] [Acts 2:33, 36] [b] Acts 3:15 [c] Matt. 1:21 [d] Luke 24:47 **5:32** [a] John 15:26, 27 [b] Acts 2:4; 10:44

LIVE THE TRUTH

## HAVING THE RIGHT ATTITUDE

**5:1–11** We cannot focus solely on our actions as believers; our attitude is important also. God commands us to have an attitude of thankfulness (1 Thess. 5:18), a spirit of humility (Phil. 2), a posture of loving others (John 13:34), and more. Even when it's difficult, we must reject hard-heartedness and cold dispositions. A negative attitude inevitably leads to negative actions.

In Acts 5, God shows His heart against sinful and selfish attitudes. On the surface, Ananias and Sapphira's act of donating money to the church seemed quite good. But their attitude was wrong. Instead of giving in a way that glorified God, they sought to glorify themselves. They wanted it to look like they had given more than they did—like they were more generous than they really were—to make themselves look good to others. You can probably imagine how smug and self-righteous they felt as they brought their offering to Peter. But this reminds us we too can let our attitudes slip even when our actions seem correct. We can live with our hearts in the wrong place even if nothing seems wrong externally. As a follower of Jesus, always be aware of your attitude; God is concerned with your heart and attitude even more than what you do.

### GAMALIEL'S ADVICE

33 When they heard *this,* they were [a]furious and plotted to kill them. 34 Then one in the council stood up, a Pharisee named [a]Gamaliel, a teacher of the law held in respect by all the people, and commanded them to put the apostles outside for a little while. 35 And he said to them: "Men of Israel, take heed to yourselves what you intend to do regarding these men. 36 For some time ago Theudas rose up, claiming to be somebody. A number of men, about four hundred, joined him. He was slain, and all who obeyed him were scattered and came to nothing. 37 After this man, Judas of Galilee rose up in the days of the census, and drew away many people after him. He also perished, and all who obeyed him were dispersed. 38 And now I say to you, keep away from these men and let them alone; for if this plan or this work is of men, it will come to nothing; 39 [a]but if it is of God, you cannot overthrow it—lest you even be found [b]to fight against God."

> **5:34** Though **Gamaliel** was a highly respected member of the Jewish **council** and an extremely well-educated **Pharisee**, he is perhaps best known as the teacher of the apostle Paul.

40 And they agreed with him, and when they had [a]called for the apostles [b]and beaten *them,* they commanded that they should not speak in the name of Jesus, and let them go. 41 So they departed from the presence of the council, [a]rejoicing that they were counted worthy to suffer shame for His[1] name. 42 And daily [a]in the temple, and in every house, [b]they did not cease teaching and preaching Jesus *as* the Christ.

### SEVEN CHOSEN TO SERVE

**6** Now in those days, [a]when *the number of* the disciples was multiplying, there arose a complaint against the Hebrews by the [b]Hellenists,[1] because their widows were neglected [c]in the daily distribution. 2 Then the twelve summoned the multitude of the disciples and said, [a]"It is not desirable that we should leave the word of God and serve tables. 3 Therefore, brethren, [a]seek out from among you seven men of *good* reputation, full of the Holy Spirit and wisdom, whom we may appoint over this [b]business; 4 but we [a]will give ourselves continually to prayer and to the ministry of the word."

5 And the saying pleased the whole multitude. And they chose Stephen, [a]a man full of faith and the Holy Spirit, and [b]Philip, Prochorus, Nicanor, Timon, Parmenas, and [c]Nicolas, a proselyte from Antioch, 6 whom they set before the apostles; and [a]when they had prayed, [b]they laid hands on them.

7 Then [a]the word of God spread, and the number of the disciples multiplied greatly in Jerusalem, and a great many [b]of the priests were obedient to the faith.

### STEPHEN ACCUSED OF BLASPHEMY

8 And Stephen, full of faith[1] and power, did great [a]wonders and signs among the people. 9 Then there arose some from what is called the Synagogue of the Freedmen (Cyrenians, Alexandrians, and those from Cilicia and Asia), disputing with Stephen. 10 And [a]they were not able to resist the wisdom and the Spirit by which he spoke. 11 [a]Then they secretly induced men to say, "We have heard him speak blasphemous words against Moses and God." 12 And they stirred up the people, the elders, and the scribes; and they came upon *him,* seized him, and brought *him* to the council. 13 They also set up false witnesses who said, "This man does not cease to speak blasphemous[1] words against this holy place and the law; 14 [a]for we have heard him say that this Jesus of Nazareth will destroy this place and change the customs which Moses delivered to us." 15 And all who sat in the council, looking steadfastly at him, saw his face as the face of an angel.

### STEPHEN'S ADDRESS: THE CALL OF ABRAHAM

**7** Then the high priest said, "Are these things so?"

2 And he said, [a]"Brethren and fathers, listen: The [b]God of glory appeared to our father Abraham when he was in Mesopotamia, before he dwelt in [c]Haran, 3 and said to him, [a]'Get out of your country and from your relatives, and come to a land that I will show you.'[1] 4 Then [a]he came out of the land of the Chaldeans and dwelt in Haran. And from there, when his father was [b]dead, He moved him to this land in which you now dwell. 5 And *God* gave him no inheritance in it, not even *enough* to set his foot on. But even when *Abraham* had no child, [a]He promised to give it to him for a possession, and to his descendants after him. 6 But God spoke in this way: [a]that his descendants would dwell in a foreign land, and that they would bring them into [b]bondage and oppress *them* four hundred years. 7 [a]'And the nation to whom they will be in bondage I will [b]judge,'[1] said God, [c]'and after that they shall come out and serve Me in this place.'[2] 8 [a]Then He gave him the covenant of circumcision; [b]and

**5:33** [a] Acts 2:37; 7:54 **5:34** [a] Acts 22:3 **5:39** [a] 1 Cor. 1:25 [b] Acts 7:51; 9:5 **5:40** [a] Acts 4:18 [b] Matt. 10:17 **5:41** [a] [1 Pet. 4:13–16] [1] NU-Text reads *the name;* M-Text reads *the name of Jesus.* **5:42** [a] Acts 2:46 [b] Acts 4:20, 29 **6:1** [a] Acts 2:41; 4:4 [b] Acts 9:29; 11:20 [c] Acts 4:35; 11:29 [1] That is, Greek-speaking Jews **6:2** [a] Ex. 18:17 **6:3** [a] 1 Tim. 3:7 [b] 1 Tim. 3:8–13 **6:4** [a] Acts 2:42 **6:5** [a] Acts 6:3; 11:24 [b] Acts 8:5, 26; 21:8 [c] Rev. 2:6, 15 **6:6** [a] Acts 1:24 [b] [2 Tim. 1:6] **6:7** [a] Acts 12:24 [b] John 12:42 **6:8** [a] Acts 2:43; 5:12; 8:15; 14:3 [1] NU-Text reads *grace.* **6:10** [a] Luke 21:15 **6:11** [a] 1 Kin. 21:10, 13 **6:13** [1] NU-Text omits *blasphemous.* **6:14** [a] Acts 10:38; 25:8 **7:2** [a] Acts 22:1 [b] Ps. 29:3 [c] Gen. 11:31, 32 **7:3** [a] Gen. 12:1 [1] Genesis 12:1 **7:4** [a] Gen. 11:31; 15:7 [b] Gen. 11:32 **7:5** [a] Gen. 12:7; 13:15; 15:3, 18; 17:8; 26:3 **7:6** [a] Gen. 15:13, 14, 16; 47:11, 12 [b] Ex. 1:8–14; 12:40, 41 **7:7** [a] Gen. 15:14 [b] Ex. 14:13–31 [c] Ex. 3:12 [1] Genesis 15:14 [2] Exodus 3:12 **7:8** [a] Gen. 17:9–14 [b] Gen. 21:1–5

so *Abraham* begot Isaac and circumcised him
on the eighth day; [c]and Isaac *begot* Jacob, and
[d]Jacob *begot* the twelve patriarchs.

### THE PATRIARCHS IN EGYPT

9 [a]"And the patriarchs, becoming envious,
[b]sold Joseph into Egypt. [c]But God was with him
10 and delivered him out of all his troubles, [a]and
gave him favor and wisdom in the presence of
Pharaoh, king of Egypt; and he made him gover-
nor over Egypt and all his house. 11 [a]Now a famine
and great trouble came over all the land of Egypt
and Canaan, and our fathers found no suste-
nance. 12 [a]But when Jacob heard that there was
grain in Egypt, he sent out our fathers first. 13 And
the [a]second *time* Joseph was made known to his
brothers, and Joseph's family became known to
the Pharaoh. 14 [a]Then Joseph sent and called his
father Jacob and [b]all his relatives to *him,* seventy-
five[1] people. 15 [a]So Jacob went down to Egypt;
[b]and he died, he and our fathers. 16 And [a]they
were carried back to Shechem and laid in [b]the
tomb that Abraham bought for a sum of money
from the sons of Hamor, *the father* of Shechem.

### GOD DELIVERS ISRAEL BY MOSES

17 "But when [a]the time of the promise drew
near which God had sworn to Abraham, [b]the
people grew and multiplied in Egypt 18 till an-
other king [a]arose who did not know Joseph.
19 This man dealt treacherously with our people,
and oppressed our forefathers, [a]making them
expose their babies, so that they might not live.
20 [a]At this time Moses was born, and [b]was well
pleasing to God; and he was brought up in his
father's house for three months. 21 But [a]when
he was set out, [b]Pharaoh's daughter took him
away and brought him up as her own son. 22 And
Moses was learned in all the wisdom of the
Egyptians, and was [a]mighty in words and deeds.
23 [a]"Now when he was forty years old, it came
into his heart to visit his brethren, the children of
Israel. 24 And seeing one of *them* suffer wrong, he
defended and avenged him who was oppressed,
and struck down the Egyptian. 25 For he supposed
that his brethren would have understood that God
would deliver them by his hand, but they did not
understand. 26 And the next day he appeared to *two
of* them as they were fighting, and *tried to* reconcile
them, saying, 'Men, you are brethren; why do you
wrong one another?' 27 But he who did his neighbor
wrong pushed him away, saying, [a]'Who made you
a ruler and a judge over us? 28 Do you want to kill
me as you did the Egyptian yesterday?'[1] 29 [a]Then,
at this saying, Moses fled and became a dweller
in the land of Midian, where he [b]had two sons.

30 [a]"And when forty years had passed, an Angel
of the Lord[1] appeared to him in a flame of fire in
a bush, in the wilderness of Mount Sinai. 31 When
Moses saw *it,* he marveled at the sight; and as he
drew near to observe, the voice of the Lord came to
him, 32 *saying,* [a]'I *am* the God of your fathers—the
God of Abraham, the God of Isaac, and the God of
Jacob.'[1] And Moses trembled and dared not look.
33 [a]"Then the LORD said to him, "Take your sandals
off your feet, for the place where you stand is holy
ground. 34 I have surely [a]seen the oppression of
My people who are in Egypt; I have heard their
groaning and have come down to deliver them.
And now come, I will [b]send you to Egypt." '[1]
35 "This Moses whom they rejected, saying,
[a]'Who made you a ruler and a judge?'[1] is the one
God sent *to be* a ruler and a deliverer [b]by the hand
of the Angel who appeared to him in the bush.
36 [a]He brought them out, after he had [b]shown
wonders and signs in the land of Egypt, [c]and in
the Red Sea, [d]and in the wilderness forty years.

### ISRAEL REBELS AGAINST GOD

37 "This is that Moses who said to the children
of Israel,[1] [a]'The LORD your God will raise up for
you a Prophet like me from your brethren. [b]Him
you shall hear.'[2]

**SEEING JESUS IN THE SCRIPTURE**

**7:37** Stephen made it clear that Jesus is the ultimate fulfillment of God's promise to raise up a Prophet from Israel (see Deut. 18:15, 18–19).

38 [a]"This is he who was in the congregation
in the wilderness with [b]the Angel who spoke to
him on Mount Sinai, and *with* our fathers, [c]the
one who received the living [d]oracles to give to us,
39 whom our fathers [a]would not obey, but rejected.
And in their hearts they turned back to Egypt,
40 [a]saying to Aaron, 'Make us gods to go before
us; *as for* this Moses who brought us out of the
land of Egypt, we do not know what has become
of him.'[1] 41 [a]And they made a calf in those days,
offered sacrifices to the idol, and [b]rejoiced in the
works of their own hands. 42 Then [a]God turned
and gave them up to worship [b]the host of heaven,
as it is written in the book of the Prophets:

[c]'Did you offer Me slaughtered animals
and sacrifices *during* forty years in the
wilderness,
O house of Israel?

**7:8** [c] Gen. 25:21–26 [d] Gen. 29:31—30:24; 35:18, 22–26 **7:9** [a] Gen. 37:4, 11, 28 [b] Gen. 37:28 [c] Gen. 39:2, 21, 23 **7:10** [a] Gen. 41:38–44 **7:11** [a] Gen. 41:54; 42:5 **7:12** [a] Gen. 42:1, 2 **7:13** [a] Gen. 45:4, 16 **7:14** [a] Gen. 45:9, 27 [b] Deut. 10:22 [1] Or *seventy* (compare Exodus 1:5) **7:15** [a] Gen. 46:1–7 [b] Gen. 49:33 **7:16** [a] Josh. 24:32 [b] Gen. 23:16 **7:17** [a] Gen. 15:13 [b] Ex. 1:7–9 **7:18** [a] Ex. 1:8 **7:19** [a] Ex. 1:22 **7:20** [a] Ex. 2:1, 2 [b] Heb. 11:23 **7:21** [a] Ex. 2:3, 4 [b] Ex. 2:5–10 **7:22** [a] Luke 24:19 **7:23** [a] Ex. 2:11, 12 **7:27** [a] Ex. 2:14 **7:28** [1] Exodus 2:14 **7:29** [a] Heb. 11:27 [b] Ex. 2:15, 21, 22; 4:20; 18:3 **7:30** [a] Ex. 3:1–10 [1] NU-Text omits *of the Lord.* **7:32** [a] Ex. 3:6, 15 [1] Exodus 3:6, 15 **7:33** [a] Ex. 3:5, 7, 8, 10 **7:34** [a] Ex. 2:24, 25 [b] Ps. 105:26 [1] Exodus 3:5, 7, 8, 10 **7:35** [a] Ex. 2:14 [b] Ex. 14:21 [1] Exodus 2:14 **7:36** [a] Ex. 12:41; 33:1 [b] Ps. 105:27 [c] Ex. 14:21 [d] Ex. 16:1, 35 **7:37** [a] Deut. 18:15, 18, 19 [b] Matt. 17:5 [1] Deuteronomy 18:15 [2] NU-Text and M-Text omit *Him you shall hear.* **7:38** [a] Ex. 19:3 [b] Gal. 3:19 [c] Deut. 5:27 [d] Heb. 5:12 **7:39** [a] Ps. 95:8–11 **7:40** [a] Ex. 32:1, 23 [1] Exodus 32:1, 23 **7:41** [a] Deut. 9:16 [b] Ex. 32:6, 18, 19 **7:42** [a] [2 Thess. 2:11] [b] 2 Kin. 21:3 [c] Amos 5:25–27

43 You also took up the tabernacle of
Moloch,
And the star of your god Remphan,
Images which you made to worship;
And [a]I will carry you away beyond
Babylon.'[1]

### GOD'S TRUE TABERNACLE

44 "Our fathers had the tabernacle of witness in the wilderness, as He appointed, instructing Moses [a]to make it according to the pattern that he had seen, 45 [a]which our fathers, having received it in turn, also brought with Joshua into the land possessed by the Gentiles, [b]whom God drove out before the face of our fathers until the [c]days of David, 46 [a]who found favor before God and [b]asked to find a dwelling for the God of Jacob. 47 [a]But Solomon built Him a house.

48 "However, [a]the Most High does not dwell in temples made with hands, as the prophet says:

49 'Heaven[a] *is* My throne,
And earth *is* My footstool.
What house will you build for Me? says
the LORD,
Or what *is* the place of My rest?
50 Has My hand not [a]made all these things?'[1]

### ISRAEL RESISTS THE HOLY SPIRIT

51 "*You* [a]stiff-necked and [b]uncircumcised in heart and ears! You always resist the Holy Spirit; as your fathers *did,* so *do* you. 52 [a]Which of the prophets did your fathers not persecute? And they killed those who foretold the coming of [b]the Just One, of whom you now have become the betrayers and murderers, 53 [a]who have received the law by the direction of angels and have not kept *it.*"

### STEPHEN THE MARTYR

54 [a]When they heard these things they were cut to the heart, and they gnashed at him with *their* teeth. 55 But he, [a]being full of the Holy Spirit, gazed into heaven and saw the [b]glory of God, and Jesus standing at the right hand of God, 56 and said, "Look! [a]I see the heavens opened and the [b]Son of Man standing at the right hand of God!"

57 Then they cried out with a loud voice, stopped their ears, and ran at him with one accord; 58 and they cast *him* out of the city and stoned *him.* And [a]the witnesses laid down their clothes at the feet of a young man named Saul. 59 And they stoned Stephen as he was calling on *God* and saying, "Lord Jesus, [a]receive my spirit." 60 Then he knelt down and cried out with a loud voice, [a]"Lord, do not charge them with this sin." And when he had said this, he fell asleep.

### SAUL PERSECUTES THE CHURCH

8 Now Saul was consenting to his death. At that time a great persecution arose against the church which was at Jerusalem; and [a]they were all scattered throughout the regions of Judea and Samaria, except the apostles. 2 And devout men carried Stephen *to his burial,* and [a]made great lamentation over him.

3 As for Saul, [a]he made havoc of the church, entering every house, and dragging off men and women, committing *them* to prison.

### CHRIST IS PREACHED IN SAMARIA

4 Therefore [a]those who were scattered went everywhere preaching the word. 5 Then [a]Philip went down to the[1] city of Samaria and preached Christ to them. 6 And the multitudes with one accord heeded the things spoken by Philip, hearing and seeing the miracles which he did. 7 For [a]unclean spirits, crying with a loud voice, came out of many who were possessed; and many who were paralyzed and lame were healed. 8 And there was great joy in that city.

### THE SORCERER'S PROFESSION OF FAITH

9 But there was a certain man called Simon, who previously [a]practiced sorcery in the city and [b]astonished the people of Samaria, claiming that he was someone great, 10 to whom they all gave heed, from the least to the greatest, saying, "This man is the great power of God." 11 And they heeded him because he had astonished them with his sorceries for a long time. 12 But when they believed Philip as he preached the things [a]concerning the kingdom of God and the name of Jesus Christ, both men and women were baptized. 13 Then Simon himself also believed; and when he was baptized he continued with Philip, and was amazed, seeing the miracles and signs which were done.

### THE SORCERER'S SIN

14 Now when the [a]apostles who were at Jerusalem heard that Samaria had received the word of God, they sent Peter and John to them, 15 who, when they had come down, prayed for them [a]that they might receive the Holy Spirit. 16 For [a]as yet He had fallen upon none of them. [b]They had only been baptized in [c]the name of the Lord Jesus. 17 Then [a]they laid hands on them, and they received the Holy Spirit.

18 And when Simon saw that through the laying on of the apostles' hands the Holy Spirit was given, he offered them money, 19 saying, "Give me this power also, that anyone on whom I lay hands may receive the Holy Spirit."

20 But Peter said to him, "Your money perish

**7:43** [a] Jer. 25:9–12 [1] Amos 5:25–27 **7:44** [a] [Heb. 8:5] **7:45** [a] Josh. 3:14; 18:1; 23:9 [b] Ps. 44:2 [c] 2 Sam. 6:2–15 **7:46** [a] 2 Sam. 7:1–13 [b] 1 Chr. 22:7 **7:47** [a] 1 Kin. 6:1–38; 8:20, 21 **7:48** [a] 1 Kin. 8:27 **7:49** [a] Is. 66:1, 2 **7:50** [a] Ps. 102:25 [1] Isaiah 66:1, 2 **7:51** [a] Ex. 32:9 [b] Lev. 26:41 **7:52** [a] 2 Chr. 36:16 [b] Acts 3:14; 22:14 **7:53** [a] Ex. 20:1 **7:54** [a] Acts 5:33 **7:55** [a] Acts 6:5 [b] [Ex. 24:17] **7:56** [a] Matt. 3:16 [b] Dan. 7:13 **7:58** [a] Acts 22:20 **7:59** [a] Ps. 31:5 **7:60** [a] Matt. 5:44 **8:1** [a] Acts 8:4; 11:19 **8:2** [a] Gen. 23:2 **8:3** [a] Phil. 3:6 **8:4** [a] Matt. 10:23 **8:5** [a] Acts 6:5; 8:26, 30 [1] Or *a* **8:7** [a] Mark 16:17 **8:9** [a] Acts 8:11; 13:6 [b] Acts 5:36 **8:12** [a] Acts 1:3; 8:4 **8:14** [a] Acts 5:12, 29, 40 **8:15** [a] Acts 2:38; 19:2 **8:16** [a] Acts 19:2 [b] Matt. 28:19; Acts 2:38 [c] Acts 10:48; 19:5 **8:17** [a] Acts 6:6; 19:6; Heb. 6:2

with you, because [a]you thought that [b]the gift of God could be purchased with money! 21 You have neither part nor portion in this matter, for your [a]heart is not right in the sight of God. 22 Repent therefore of this your wickedness, and pray God [a]if perhaps the thought of your heart may be forgiven you. 23 For I see that you are [a]poisoned by bitterness and bound by iniquity."

24 Then Simon answered and said, [a]"Pray to the Lord for me, that none of the things which you have spoken may come upon me."

25 So when they had testified and preached the word of the Lord, they returned to Jerusalem, preaching the gospel in many villages of the Samaritans.

### *CHRIST IS PREACHED TO AN ETHIOPIAN*

*(cf. Is. 53:7, 8)*

26 Now an angel of the Lord spoke to [a]Philip, saying, "Arise and go toward the south along the road which goes down from Jerusalem to Gaza." This is desert. 27 So he arose and went. And behold, [a]a man of Ethiopia, a eunuch of great authority under Candace the queen of the Ethiopians, who had charge of all her treasury, and [b]had come to Jerusalem to worship, 28 was returning. And sitting in his chariot, he was reading Isaiah the prophet. 29 Then the Spirit said to Philip, "Go near and overtake this chariot."

> **8:26** Angels are often seen serving as God's messengers in the New Testament. Angels also guided and protected God's people, and even ministered to Jesus. Some of the other occurrences of angels include: giving news to Elizabeth (Luke 1:11–20), giving news to Mary (Luke 1:26–38), announcing Jesus' birth to shepherds (Luke 2:8–15), warning Joseph to flee from Herod (Matt. 2:13, 19–20), caring for Jesus in the wilderness (Matt. 4:11), rolling the tombstone away (Matt. 28:2–6), instructing Cornelius to send for Peter (Acts 10:3–8), releasing Peter from prison (Acts 12:7), making Herod ill (Acts 12:23), and reassuring Paul in a storm (Acts 27:23–24).

30 So Philip ran to him, and heard him reading the prophet Isaiah, and said, "Do you understand what you are reading?"

31 And he said, "How can I, unless someone guides me?" And he asked Philip to come up and sit with him. 32 The place in the Scripture which he read was this:

[a]"He was led as a sheep to the slaughter;
And as a lamb before its shearer *is* silent,
[b]So He opened not His mouth.
33 In His humiliation His [a]justice was taken away,
And who will declare His generation?
For His life is [b]taken from the earth."[1]

> **SEEING JESUS IN THE SCRIPTURE**
>
> **8:32–33** The Ethiopian man was saved after reading Isaiah's prophecy, 700 years before it happened, that Jesus would be led to slaughter (see Is. 53:7–8).

34 So the eunuch answered Philip and said, "I ask you, of whom does the prophet say this, of himself or of some other man?" 35 Then Philip opened his mouth, [a]and beginning at this Scripture, preached Jesus to him. 36 Now as they went down the road, they came to some water. And the eunuch said, "See, *here is* water. [a]What hinders me from being baptized?"

37 Then Philip said, [a]"If you believe with all your heart, you may."

And he answered and said, [b]"I believe that Jesus Christ is the Son of God."[1]

38 So he commanded the chariot to stand still. And both Philip and the eunuch went down into the water, and he baptized him. 39 Now when they came up out of the water, [a]the Spirit of the Lord caught Philip away, so that the eunuch saw him no more; and he went on his way rejoicing. 40 But Philip was found at Azotus. And passing through, he preached in all the cities till he came to [a]Caesarea.

### *THE DAMASCUS ROAD: SAUL CONVERTED*

*(Acts 22:6–16; 26:12–18)*

**9** Then [a]Saul, still breathing threats and murder against the disciples of the Lord, went to the high priest 2 and asked [a]letters from him to the synagogues of Damascus, so that if he found any who were of the Way, whether men or women, he might bring them bound to Jerusalem.

3 [a]As he journeyed he came near Damascus, and suddenly a light shone around him from heaven. 4 Then he fell to the ground, and heard a voice saying to him, "Saul, Saul, [a]why are you persecuting Me?"

5 And he said, "Who are You, Lord?"

Then the Lord said, "I am Jesus, whom you are persecuting.[1] It *is* hard for you to kick against the goads."

**8:20** [a] 2 Kin. 5:16; Is. 55:1; Dan. 5:17; [Matt. 10:8] [b] [Acts 2:38; 10:45; 11:17] **8:21** [a] Jer. 17:9 **8:22** [a] Dan. 4:27; 2 Tim. 2:25 **8:23** [a] Heb. 12:15 **8:24** [a] Gen. 20:7, 17; Ex. 8:8; Num. 21:7; 1 Kin. 13:6; Job 42:8; James 5:16 **8:26** [a] Acts 6:5 **8:27** [a] Ps. 68:31; 87:4; Is. 56:3; Zeph. 3:10 [b] 1 Kin. 8:41, 42; John 12:20 **8:32** [a] Is. 53:7, 8 [b] Matt. 26:62, 63; 27:12, 14; John 19:9 **8:33** [a] Luke 23:1–25 [b] Luke 23:33–46 [1] Isaiah 53:7, 8 **8:35** [a] Luke 24:27; Acts 17:2; 18:28; 28:23 **8:36** [a] Acts 10:47; 16:33 **8:37** [a] Matt. 28:19; [Mark 16:16; Rom. 10:9, 10] [b] Matt. 16:16; John 6:69; 9:35, 38; 11:27 [1] NU-Text and M-Text omit this verse. It is found in Western texts, including the Latin tradition. **8:39** [a] Ezek. 3:12, 14 **8:40** [a] Acts 21:8 **9:1** [a] Acts 7:57; 8:1, 3; 26:10, 11 **9:2** [a] Acts 22:5 **9:3** [a] 1 Cor. 15:8 **9:4** [a] [Matt. 25:40] **9:5** [1] NU-Text and M-Text omit the last sentence of verse 5 and begin verse 6 with *But arise and go.*

6 So he, trembling and astonished, said,
"Lord, what do You want me to do?"
Then the Lord *said* to him, "Arise and go into
the city, and you will be told what you must do."
7 And [a]the men who journeyed with him
stood speechless, hearing a voice but seeing
no one. 8 Then Saul arose from the ground, and
when his eyes were opened he saw no one. But
they led him by the hand and brought *him* into
Damascus. 9 And he was three days without
sight, and neither ate nor drank.

### ANANIAS BAPTIZES SAUL

10 Now there was a certain disciple at Da-
mascus [a]named Ananias; and to him the Lord
said in a vision, "Ananias."
And he said, "Here I am, Lord."
11 So the Lord *said* to him, "Arise and go to the
street called Straight, and inquire at the house of
Judas for *one* called Saul [a]of Tarsus, for behold,
he is praying. 12 And in a vision he has seen a
man named Ananias coming in and putting *his*
hand on him, so that he might receive his sight."
13 Then Ananias answered, "Lord, I have
heard from many about this man, [a]how much
harm he has done to Your saints in Jerusalem.
14 And here he has authority from the chief
priests to bind all [a]who call on Your name."
15 But the Lord said to him, "Go, for [a]he is a
chosen vessel of Mine to bear My name before
[b]Gentiles, [c]kings, and the [d]children of Israel.
16 For [a]I will show him how many things he must
suffer for My [b]name's sake."
17 [a]And Ananias went his way and entered
the house; and [b]laying his hands on him he said,
"Brother Saul, the Lord Jesus,[1] who appeared to
you on the road as you came, has sent me that
you may receive your sight and [c]be filled with
the Holy Spirit." 18 Immediately there fell from
his eyes *something* like scales, and he received
his sight at once; and he arose and was baptized.
19 So when he had received food, he was
strengthened. [a]Then Saul spent some days with
the disciples at Damascus.

### SAUL PREACHES CHRIST

20 Immediately he preached the Christ[1] in
the synagogues, that He is the Son of God.
21 Then all who heard were amazed, and said,
[a]"Is this not he who destroyed those who called
on this name in Jerusalem, and has come here
for that purpose, so that he might bring them
bound to the chief priests?"
22 But Saul increased all the more in strength,
[a]and confounded the Jews who dwelt in Damas-
cus, proving that this *Jesus* is the Christ.

### SAUL ESCAPES DEATH

23 Now after many days were past, [a]the Jews
plotted to kill him. 24 [a]But their plot became
known to Saul. And they watched the gates day
and night, to kill him. 25 Then the disciples took
him by night and [a]let *him* down through the wall
in a large basket.

### SAUL AT JERUSALEM

26 And [a]when Saul had come to Jerusalem,
he tried to join the disciples; but they were all
afraid of him, and did not believe that he was a
disciple. 27 [a]But Barnabas took him and brought
*him* to the apostles. And he declared to them how
he had seen the Lord on the road, and that He
had spoken to him, [b]and how he had preached
boldly at Damascus in the name of Jesus. 28 So
[a]he was with them at Jerusalem, coming in and
going out. 29 And he spoke boldly in the name of
the Lord Jesus and disputed against the [a]Helle-
nists, [b]but they attempted to kill him. 30 When
the brethren found out, they brought him down
to Caesarea and sent him out to Tarsus.

### THE CHURCH PROSPERS

31 [a]Then the churches[1] throughout all Judea,
Galilee, and Samaria had peace and were [b]edified.
And walking in the [c]fear of the Lord and in the
[d]comfort of the Holy Spirit, they were [e]multiplied.

### AENEAS HEALED

32 Now it came to pass, as Peter went [a]through
all *parts of the country,* that he also came down to
the saints who dwelt in Lydda. 33 There he found
a certain man named Aeneas, who had been
bedridden eight years and was paralyzed. 34 And
Peter said to him, "Aeneas, [a]Jesus the Christ
heals you. Arise and make your bed." Then he
arose immediately. 35 So all who dwelt at Lydda
and [a]Sharon saw him and [b]turned to the Lord.

### DORCAS RESTORED TO LIFE

36 At Joppa there was a certain disciple named
Tabitha, which is translated Dorcas. This woman
was full [a]of good works and charitable deeds
which she did. 37 But it happened in those days
that she became sick and died. When they had
washed her, they laid *her* in [a]an upper room. 38 And
since Lydda was near Joppa, and the disciples had
heard that Peter was there, they sent two men
to him, imploring *him* not to delay in coming to
them. 39 Then Peter arose and went with them.
When he had come, they brought *him* to the upper
room. And all the widows stood by him weeping,
showing the tunics and garments which Dorcas
had made while she was with them. 40 But Peter

**9:7** [a] [Acts 22:9; 26:13] **9:10** [a] Acts 22:12 **9:11** [a] Acts 21:39; 22:3 **9:13** [a] Acts 9:1 **9:14** [a] Acts 7:59; 9:2, 21 **9:15** [a] Eph. 3:7, 8 [b] Rom. 1:5; 11:13 [c] Acts 25:22, 23; 26:1 [d] Rom. 1:16; 9:1–5 **9:16** [a] Acts 20:23 [b] 2 Cor. 4:11 **9:17** [a] Acts 22:12, 13 [b] Acts 8:17 [c] Acts 2:4; 4:31; 8:17; 13:52 [1] M-Text omits *Jesus.* **9:19** [a] Acts 26:20 **9:20** [1] NU-Text reads *Jesus.* **9:21** [a] Gal. 1:13, 23 **9:22** [a] Acts 18:28 **9:23** [a] 2 Cor. 11:26 **9:24** [a] 2 Cor. 11:32 **9:25** [a] Josh. 2:15 **9:26** [a] Acts 22:17–20; 26:20 **9:27** [a] Acts 4:36; 13:2 [b] Acts 9:20, 22 **9:28** [a] Gal. 1:18 **9:29** [a] Acts 6:1; 11:20 [b] 2 Cor. 11:26 **9:31** [a] Acts 5:11; 8:1; 16:5 [b] [Eph. 4:16, 29] [c] Ps. 34:9 [d] John 14:16 [e] Acts 16:5 [1] NU-Text reads *church . . . was edified.* **9:32** [a] Acts 8:14 **9:34** [a] [Acts 3:6, 16; 4:10] **9:35** [a] 1 Chr. 5:16; 27:29; Is. 33:9; 35:2; 65:10 [b] Acts 11:21; 15:19 **9:36** [a] 1 Tim. 2:10; Titus 3:8 **9:37** [a] Acts 1:13; 9:39

ACTS 9:1–31

# SAUL'S CONVERSION

51 STORY OF SCRIPTURE

## WHAT'S GOING ON?

Saul, a zealous Pharisee, fervently persecuted Christians, seeing them as a threat to the Jewish faith. On his way to Damascus to arrest more followers of Jesus, Saul encountered Jesus in a blinding light instead. This dramatic event led to Saul's conversion. This was the pivotal moment when a chief opponent of Jesus and the gospel became perhaps one of the greatest advocates of Jesus and the gospel ever. Saul, also known as Paul, traveled on at least three major missionary journeys, spreading the gospel and starting new churches, and wrote much of the New Testament. All the while, the one who had brought great suffering upon the church endured great suffering on behalf of the church.

## WHAT DOES THIS MEAN FOR ME?

Paul's transformation is a powerful testament to the life-changing power of an encounter with Christ. It shows no one is beyond the reach of God's grace. Just as Paul went from being a persecutor of the church to become a pillar of the church, our lives can be likewise transformed by God's grace, regardless of our past.

The story of Paul also demonstrates the ripple effect of a changed life. His conversion had a profound effect on the spread of Christianity. Our testimony can have far-reaching consequences beyond our personal experience, influencing the lives of others and advancing God's kingdom.

## DID YOU CATCH THE PATTERN?

Paul was a Pharisee and a prominent member of the Sanhedrin, the very group that conspired to kill Jesus. In many ways, he represented the Old Covenant with God—the covenant of law, sacrifices, and tradition. Paul's life was a picture of God's transition from the Old Covenant of the law and bondage to the New Covenant of grace and freedom.

*For the next* Story of Scripture *reading and devotion, turn to Acts 13:4–52 on page 1122.*

[a]put them all out, and [b]knelt down and prayed.
And turning to the body he [c]said, "Tabitha, arise."
And she opened her eyes, and when she saw Peter
she sat up. 41 Then he gave her *his* hand and lifted
her up; and when he had called the saints and
widows, he presented her alive. 42 And it became
known throughout all Joppa, [a]and many believed
on the Lord. 43 So it was that he stayed many days
in Joppa with [a]Simon, a tanner.

### CORNELIUS SENDS A DELEGATION

10 There was a certain man in [a]Caesarea
called Cornelius, a centurion of what was
called the Italian Regiment, 2 [a]a devout *man* and
one who [b]feared God with all his household,
who gave alms generously to the people, and
prayed to God always. 3 About the ninth hour of
the day [a]he saw clearly in a vision an angel of
God coming in and saying to him, "Cornelius!"
4 And when he observed him, he was afraid,
and said, "What is it, lord?"
So he said to him, "Your prayers and your
alms have come up for a memorial before
God. 5 Now [a]send men to Joppa, and send for
Simon whose surname is Peter. 6 He is lodging
with [a]Simon, a tanner, whose house is by the
sea.[1] [b]He will tell you what you must do." 7 And
when the angel who spoke to him had departed,
Cornelius called two of his household servants
and a devout soldier from among those who
waited on him continually. 8 So when he had
explained all *these* things to them, he sent
them to Joppa.

### PETER'S VISION

9 The next day, as they went on their journey
and drew near the city, [a]Peter went up on the
housetop to pray, about the sixth hour. 10 Then he
became very hungry and wanted to eat; but while
they made ready, he fell into a trance 11 and [a]saw
heaven opened and an object like a great sheet
bound at the four corners, descending to him
and let down to the earth. 12 In it were all kinds
of four-footed animals of the earth, wild beasts,
creeping things, and birds of the air. 13 And a
voice came to him, "Rise, Peter; kill and eat."

**9:40** [a] Matt. 9:25 [b] Luke 22:41; Acts 7:60 [c] Mark 5:41, 42; John 11:43 **9:42** [a] John 11:45 **9:43** [a] Acts 10:6 **10:1** [a] Acts 8:40; 23:23 **10:2** [a] Acts 8:2; 9:22; 22:12 [b] [Acts 10:22, 35; 13:16, 26] **10:3** [a] Acts 10:30; 11:13 **10:5** [a] Acts 11:13, 14 **10:6** [a] Acts 9:43 [b] Acts 11:14
[1] NU-Text and M-Text omit the last sentence of this verse. **10:9** [a] Acts 10:9–32; 11:5–14 **10:11** [a] Ezek. 1:1; Matt. 3:16; Acts 7:56; Rev. 4:1; 19:11

14 But Peter said, "Not so, Lord! [a]For I have
never eaten anything common or unclean."
15 And a voice *spoke* to him again the second
time, [a]"What God has cleansed you must not call
common." 16 This was done three times. And the
object was taken up into heaven again.

**10:15** Food may have been his first consideration, but Peter would soon understand the greater message. The vision was a sign from heaven that Jews were no longer to call Gentiles unclean.

### *SUMMONED TO CAESAREA*

17 Now while Peter wondered within himself
what this vision which he had seen meant, be-
hold, the men who had been sent from Cornelius
had made inquiry for Simon's house, and stood
before the gate. 18 And they called and asked
whether Simon, whose surname was Peter, was
lodging there.
19 While Peter thought about the vision, [a]the
Spirit said to him, "Behold, three men are seek-
ing you. 20 [a]Arise therefore, go down and go with
them, doubting nothing; for I have sent them."
21 Then Peter went down to the men who
had been sent to him from Cornelius,[1] and said,
"Yes, I am he whom you seek. For what reason
have you come?"
22 And they said, "Cornelius *the* centurion,
a just man, one who fears God and [a]has a good
reputation among all the nation of the Jews, was
divinely instructed by a holy angel to summon
you to his house, and to hear words from you."
23 Then he invited them in and lodged *them.*
On the next day Peter went away with them,
[a]and some brethren from Joppa accompanied
him.

### *PETER MEETS CORNELIUS*

24 And the following day they entered Caesa-
rea. Now Cornelius was waiting for them, and had
called together his relatives and close friends.
25 As Peter was coming in, Cornelius met him
and fell down at his feet and worshiped *him.*
26 But Peter lifted him up, saying, [a]"Stand up; I
myself am also a man." 27 And as he talked with
him, he went in and found many who had come
together. 28 Then he said to them, "You know how
[a]unlawful it is for a Jewish man to keep company
with or go to one of another nation. But [b]God
has shown me that I should not call any man
common or unclean. 29 Therefore I came without
objection as soon as I was sent for. I ask, then,
for what reason have you sent for me?"
30 So Cornelius said, "Four days ago I was
fasting until this hour; and at the ninth hour[1] I
prayed in my house, and behold, [a]a man stood
before me [b]in bright clothing, 31 and said, 'Cor-
nelius, [a]your prayer has been heard, and [b]your
alms are remembered in the sight of God. 32 Send
therefore to Joppa and call Simon here, whose
surname is Peter. He is lodging in the house of
Simon, a tanner, by the sea.[1] When he comes, he
will speak to you.' 33 So I sent to you immediately,
and you have done well to come. Now therefore,
we are all present before God, to hear all the
things commanded you by God."

### *PREACHING TO CORNELIUS' HOUSEHOLD*

34 Then Peter opened *his* mouth and said:
[a]"In truth I perceive that God shows no partiality.
35 But [a]in every nation whoever fears Him and
works righteousness is [b]accepted by Him. 36 The
word which *God* sent to the children of Israel,
[a]preaching peace through Jesus Christ— [b]He
is Lord of all— 37 that word you know, which
was proclaimed throughout all Judea, and
[a]began from Galilee after the baptism which
John preached: 38 how [a]God anointed Jesus of
Nazareth with the Holy Spirit and with power,
who [b]went about doing good and healing all
who were oppressed by the devil, [c]for God was
with Him. 39 And we are [a]witnesses of all things
which He did both in the land of the Jews and
in Jerusalem, whom they[1] [b]killed by hanging on
a tree. 40 Him [a]God raised up on the third day,
and showed Him openly, 41 [a]not to all the people,
but to witnesses chosen before by God, *even* to
us [b]who ate and drank with Him after He arose
from the dead. 42 And [a]He commanded us to
preach to the people, and to testify [b]that it is
He who was ordained by God *to be* Judge [c]of the
living and the dead. 43 [a]To Him all the prophets
witness that, through His name, [b]whoever be-
lieves in Him will receive [c]remission of sins."

**SEEING JESUS IN THE SCRIPTURE**

**10:40–41** Peter's testimony about the resurrection was true. He heard Jesus foretell His resurrection (see Matt. 17:23) and saw Jesus resurrected (see John 20:3–10).

### *THE HOLY SPIRIT FALLS ON THE GENTILES*

44 While Peter was still speaking these words,
[a]the Holy Spirit fell upon all those who heard

**10:14** [a] Lev. 11:4; 20:25; Deut. 14:3, 7; Ezek. 4:14 **10:15** [a] [Matt. 15:11; Mark 7:19]; Acts 10:28; [Rom. 14:14]; 1 Cor. 10:25; [1 Tim. 4:4; Titus 1:15] **10:19** [a] Acts 11:12 **10:20** [a] Acts 15:7–9 **10:21** [1] NU-Text and M-Text omit *who had been sent to him from Cornelius.* **10:22** [a] Acts 22:12 **10:23** [a] Acts 10:45; 11:12 **10:26** [a] Acts 14:14, 15 **10:28** [a] John 4:9; 18:28 [b] [Acts 10:14, 35; 15:8, 9] **10:30** [a] Acts 1:10 [b] Matt. 28:3 [1] NU-Text reads *Four days ago to this hour, at the ninth hour.* **10:31** [a] Dan. 10:12 [b] Heb. 6:10 **10:32** [1] NU-Text omits the last sentence of this verse. **10:34** [a] Deut. 10:17 **10:35** [a] [Eph. 2:13] [b] Ps. 15:1, 2 **10:36** [a] Is. 57:19 [b] Rom. 10:12 **10:37** [a] Luke 4:14 **10:38** [a] Luke 4:18 [b] Matt. 4:23 [c] John 3:2; 8:29 **10:39** [a] Acts 1:8 [b] Acts 2:23 [1] NU-Text and M-Text add *also.* **10:40** [a] Acts 2:24 **10:41** [a] [John 14:17, 19, 22; 15:27] [b] Luke 24:30, 41–43 **10:42** [a] Matt. 28:19 [b] John 5:22, 27 [c] 1 Pet. 4:5 **10:43** [a] Zech. 13:1 [b] Gal. 3:22 [c] Acts 13:38, 39 **10:44** [a] Acts 4:31

KNOW THE TRUTH

# THE DOCTRINE OF SALVATION

## PART 2: THE NEED OF SALVATION

**10:42–43** Jesus is the only name by which we are saved (see Acts 4:12). This raises a question: *Why* must we be saved? The reason, as Peter said in Acts 10:43, is we need "remission of sins." *Sin* has to do with missing the mark of God's will. All humans have been born into sin and have freely chosen to sin and rebel against God's laws. Each of us sins by missing the mark of God's good and perfect laws. We know how we ought to live (e.g., serve others, tell the truth, be just and merciful) and we hold others accountable for the ways they fail to live up to this standard, but we excuse ourselves from this same standard.

Just because we all sin, that doesn't make it right. Sin separates us from a holy God and requires a righteous response. This righteous response to rejecting God's rule and ultimately Him is eternal separation from His holy presence. Eternal separation from a good, loving, joyous God means unending conscious suffering (see 2 Thess. 1:9). Saving people from this eternal misery is why Jesus came. He alone paid the price for our sins and, when we trust in Him, gives us the gift of His righteousness and eternal life in the presence of God.

*For* **THE DOCTRINE OF SALVATION: PART 3: THE MANNER OF SALVATION,** *turn to 2 Corinthians 5:21 on page 1187.* •••

the word. 45 [a]And those of the circumcision who
believed were astonished, as many as came with
Peter, [b]because the gift of the Holy Spirit had
been poured out on the Gentiles also. 46 For they
heard them speak with tongues and magnify God.
Then Peter answered, 47 "Can anyone forbid
water, that these should not be baptized who
have received the Holy Spirit [a]just as we *have?*"
48 [a]And he commanded them to be baptized [b]in
the name of the Lord. Then they asked him to
stay a few days.

### PETER DEFENDS GOD'S GRACE

11 Now the apostles and brethren who were
in Judea heard that the Gentiles had also
received the word of God. 2 And when Peter came
up to Jerusalem, [a]those of the circumcision
contended with him, 3 saying, [a]"You went in to
uncircumcised men [b]and ate with them!"
4 But Peter explained *it* to them [a]in order
from the beginning, saying: 5 [a]"I was in the city
of Joppa praying; and in a trance I saw a vision,
an object descending like a great sheet, let down
from heaven by four corners; and it came to me.
6 When I observed it intently and considered, I
saw four-footed animals of the earth, wild beasts,
creeping things, and birds of the air. 7 And I
heard a voice saying to me, 'Rise, Peter; kill
and eat.' 8 But I said, 'Not so, Lord! For nothing
common or unclean has at any time entered
my mouth.' 9 But the voice answered me again
from heaven, 'What God has cleansed you must
not call common.' 10 Now this was done three
times, and all were drawn up again into heaven.
11 At that very moment, three men stood before
the house where I was, having been sent to me
from Caesarea. 12 Then [a]the Spirit told me to go
with them, doubting nothing. Moreover [b]these
six brethren accompanied me, and we entered
the man's house. 13 [a]And he told us how he had
seen an angel standing in his house, who said
to him, 'Send men to Joppa, and call for Simon
whose surname is Peter, 14 who will tell you words
by which you and all your household will be
saved.' 15 And as I began to speak, the Holy Spirit
fell upon them, [a]as upon us at the beginning.
16 Then I remembered the word of the Lord,
how He said, [a]'John indeed baptized with water,
but [b]you shall be baptized with the Holy Spirit.'
17 [a]If therefore God gave them the same gift as
*He gave* us when we believed on the Lord Jesus
Christ, [b]who was I that I could withstand God?"
18 When they heard these things they be-
came silent; and they glorified God, saying,
[a]"Then God has also granted to the Gentiles
repentance to life."

### BARNABAS AND SAUL AT ANTIOCH

19 [a]Now those who were scattered after the
persecution that arose over Stephen traveled as
far as Phoenicia, Cyprus, and Antioch, preaching
the word to no one but the Jews only. 20 But some
of them were men from Cyprus and Cyrene,
who, when they had come to Antioch, spoke to

**10:45** [a] Acts 10:23 [b] Acts 11:18 **10:47** [a] Acts 2:4; 10:44; 11:17; 15:8 **10:48** [a] 1 Cor. 1:14–17 [b] Acts 2:38; 8:16; 19:5 **11:2** [a] Acts 10:45 **11:3** [a] Acts 10:28 [b] Gal. 2:12 **11:4** [a] Luke 1:3 **11:5** [a] Acts 10:9 **11:12** [a] [John 16:13]; Acts 10:19; 15:7 [b] Acts 10:23 **11:13** [a] Acts 10:30 **11:15** [a] Acts 2:1–4; 15:7–9 **11:16** [a] Matt. 3:11; Mark 1:8; John 1:26, 33; Acts 1:5; 19:4 [b] Is. 44:3 **11:17** [a] [Acts 15:8, 9] [b] Acts 10:47 **11:18** [a] Is. 42:1, 6; 49:6; Luke 2:32; John 11:52; Rom. 10:12, 13; 15:9, 16 **11:19** [a] Acts 8:1, 4

[a]the Hellenists, preaching the Lord Jesus. 21 And
[a]the hand of the Lord was with them, and a great
number believed and [b]turned to the Lord.
22 Then news of these things came to the ears
of the church in Jerusalem, and they sent out
[a]Barnabas to go as far as Antioch. 23 When he came
and had seen the grace of God, he was glad, and
[a]encouraged them all that with purpose of heart
they should continue with the Lord. 24 For he was
a good man, [a]full of the Holy Spirit and of faith.
[b]And a great many people were added to the Lord.
25 Then Barnabas departed for [a]Tarsus to
seek Saul. 26 And when he had found him, he
brought him to Antioch. So it was that for a
whole year they assembled with the church and
taught a great many people. And the disciples
were first called Christians in Antioch.

### *RELIEF TO JUDEA*

27 And in these days [a]prophets came from
Jerusalem to Antioch. 28 Then one of them,
named [a]Agabus, stood up and showed by the
Spirit that there was going to be a great famine
throughout all the world, which also happened
in the days of [b]Claudius Caesar. 29 Then the dis-
ciples, each according to his ability, determined
to send [a]relief to the brethren dwelling in Judea.
30 [a]This they also did, and sent it to the elders
by the hands of Barnabas and Saul.

### *HEROD'S VIOLENCE TO THE CHURCH*

**12** Now about that time Herod the king
stretched out *his* hand to harass some from
the church. 2 Then he killed James [a]the brother
of John with the sword. 3 And because he saw
that it pleased the Jews, he proceeded further to
seize Peter also. Now it was *during* [a]the Days of
Unleavened Bread. 4 So [a]when he had arrested
him, he put *him* in prison, and delivered *him* to
four squads of soldiers to keep him, intending
to bring him before the people after Passover.

### *PETER FREED FROM PRISON*

5 Peter was therefore kept in prison, but con-
stant[1] prayer was offered to God for him by the
church. 6 And when Herod was about to bring
him out, that night Peter was sleeping, bound
with two chains between two soldiers; and the
guards before the door were keeping the prison.
7 Now behold, [a]an angel of the Lord stood by *him,*
and a light shone in the prison; and he struck
Peter on the side and raised him up, saying,
"Arise quickly!" And his chains fell off *his* hands.
8 Then the angel said to him, "Gird yourself and
tie on your sandals"; and so he did. And he said
to him, "Put on your garment and follow me."
9 So he went out and followed him, and [a]did not
know that what was done by the angel was real,
but thought [b]he was seeing a vision. 10 When they

**11:20** [a] Acts 6:1; 9:29 **11:21** [a] Luke 1:66; Acts 2:47 [b] Acts 9:35; 14:1 **11:22** [a] Acts 4:36; 9:27 **11:23** [a] Acts 13:43; 14:22 **11:24** [a] Acts 6:5 [b] Acts 5:14; 11:21 **11:25** [a] Acts 9:11, 30 **11:27** [a] Acts 2:17; 13:1; 15:32; 21:9; 1 Cor. 12:28; Eph. 4:11 **11:28** [a] John 16:13; Acts 21:10 [b] Acts 18:2 **11:29** [a] Rom. 15:26; 1 Cor. 16:1; 2 Cor. 9:1 **11:30** [a] Acts 12:25 **12:2** [a] Matt. 4:21; 20:23 **12:3** [a] Ex. 12:15; 23:15; Acts 20:6 **12:4** [a] John 21:18 **12:5** [1] NU-Text reads *constantly* (or *earnestly*). **12:7** [a] Acts 5:19 **12:9** [a] Ps. 126:1 [b] Acts 10:3, 17; 11:5

KNOW THE TRUTH

## THE DOCTRINE OF THE CHURCH

### PART 5: THE PURPOSE OF THE CHURCH

**11:19–26** While the church waits for Christ's return and the consummation of His kingdom, it has two primary purposes: lost people saved and disciples made (see Matt. 28:18–20). The believers' work in the city of Antioch is an excellent example of the church fulfilling both purposes.

First, the Antioch church **preached** Jesus. Christ commanded His followers to preach a message of repentance for the remission, or forgiveness, of sins in His name to all nations (see Luke 24:44–49; Acts 1:8). As the early church obeyed, many people believed the message, repented, trusted in Jesus as Savior, and were saved (see Acts 2:40–47). We are to do likewise. We are to proclaim Jesus in our local communities, our nations, and our world through conduct that reflects the character of Jesus and words that explain the gospel message by which they can be saved.

Second, the Antioch church **made disciples** by teaching those who believed in Jesus. A disciple is taught and equipped to be a lifelong learner, doer, and preacher of the words and ways of Jesus. These disciples then make further disciples and on and on. This commission of lost people saved and disciples made remains until Christ returns (see Matt. 24:14).

*For* **THE DOCTRINE OF THE CHURCH: PART 6: THE FUNCTIONS OF THE CHURCH,** *turn to Hebrews 10:19–25 on page 1253.*

were past the first and the second guard posts,
they came to the iron gate that leads to the city,
[a]which opened to them of its own accord; and
they went out and went down one street, and
immediately the angel departed from him.
11 And when Peter had come to himself, he
said, "Now I know for certain that [a]the Lord has
sent His angel, and [b]has delivered me from the
hand of Herod and *from* all the expectation of
the Jewish people."
12 So, when he had considered *this*, [a]he came
to the house of Mary, the mother of [b]John whose
surname was Mark, where many were gathered
together [c]praying. 13 And as Peter knocked at the
door of the gate, a girl named Rhoda came to
answer. 14 When she recognized Peter's voice,
because of *her* gladness she did not open the
gate, but ran in and announced that Peter stood
before the gate. 15 But they said to her, "You are
beside yourself!" Yet she kept insisting that it
was so. So they said, [a]"It is his angel."
16 Now Peter continued knocking; and when
they opened *the door* and saw him, they were
astonished. 17 But [a]motioning to them with his
hand to keep silent, he declared to them how
the Lord had brought him out of the prison.
And he said, "Go, tell these things to James and
to the brethren." And he departed and went to
another place.
18 Then, as soon as it was day, there was no
small stir among the soldiers about what had be-
come of Peter. 19 But when Herod had searched for
him and not found him, he examined the guards
and commanded that *they* should be put to death.

And he went down from Judea to Caesarea,
and stayed *there*.

### HEROD'S VIOLENT DEATH

20 Now Herod had been very angry with the
people of [a]Tyre and Sidon; but they came to him
with one accord, and having made Blastus the
king's personal aide their friend, they asked for
peace, because [b]their country was supplied with
food by the king's *country*.
21 So on a set day Herod, arrayed in royal
apparel, sat on his throne and gave an oration
to them. 22 And the people kept shouting, "The
voice of a god and not of a man!" 23 Then imme-
diately an angel of the Lord [a]struck him, because
[b]he did not give glory to God. And he was eaten
by worms and died.
24 But [a]the word of God grew and multiplied.

### BARNABAS AND SAUL APPOINTED

25 And [a]Barnabas and Saul returned from[1]
Jerusalem when they had [b]fulfilled *their* minis-
try, and they also [c]took with them [d]John whose
surname was Mark.

**13** Now [a]in the church that was at Antioch
there were certain prophets and teachers:
[b]Barnabas, Simeon who was called Niger, [c]Lu-
cius of Cyrene, Manaen who had been brought
up with Herod the tetrarch, and Saul. 2 As they
ministered to the Lord and fasted, the Holy Spirit
said, [a]"Now separate to Me Barnabas and Saul for
the work [b]to which I have called them." 3 Then,
[a]having fasted and prayed, and laid hands on
them, they sent *them* away.

### PREACHING IN CYPRUS

4 So, being sent out by the Holy Spirit, they
went down to Seleucia, and from there they sailed
to [a]Cyprus. 5 And when they arrived in Salamis,
[a]they preached the word of God in the synagogues
of the Jews. They also had [b]John as *their* assistant.
6 Now when they had gone through the island[1]
to Paphos, they found [a]a certain sorcerer, a false
prophet, a Jew whose name *was* Bar-Jesus, 7 who
was with the proconsul, Sergius Paulus, an intelli-
gent man. This man called for Barnabas and Saul
and sought to hear the word of God. 8 But [a]Ely-
mas the sorcerer (for so his name is translated)
withstood them, seeking to turn the proconsul
away from the faith. 9 Then Saul, who also *is called*
Paul, [a]filled with the Holy Spirit, looked intently at
him 10 and said, "O full of all deceit and all fraud,
[a]*you* son of the devil, *you* enemy of all righteous-
ness, will you not cease perverting the straight
ways of the Lord? 11 And now, indeed, [a]the hand
of the Lord *is* upon you, and you shall be blind,
not seeing the sun for a time."

> **13:9 Saul** was his Jewish name, and **Paul** was the Greek translation of it. When he was in his Jewish surroundings, he used the name Saul. When he was ministering to the Gentiles, he used the name Paul. Using the Greek version of his name would have helped Paul identify with the people he was teaching about Jesus.

And immediately a dark mist fell on him,
and he went around seeking someone to lead
him by the hand. 12 Then the proconsul believed,
when he saw what had been done, being aston-
ished at the teaching of the Lord.

### AT ANTIOCH IN PISIDIA

13 Now when Paul and his party set sail from
Paphos, they came to Perga in Pamphylia; and
[a]John, departing from them, returned to Jerusa-
lem. 14 But when they departed from Perga, they
came to Antioch in Pisidia, and [a]went into the

**12:10** [a]Acts 5:19; 16:26 **12:11** [a][Ps. 34:7] [b]Job 5:19 **12:12** [a]Acts 4:23 [b]Acts 13:5, 13; 15:37 [c]Acts 12:5 **12:15** [a][Matt. 18:10] **12:17** [a]Acts 13:16; 19:33; 21:40 **12:20** [a]Matt. 11:21 [b]Ezek. 27:17 **12:23** [a]2 Sam. 24:16, 17 [b]Ps. 115:1 **12:24** [a]Acts 6:7; 19:20 **12:25** [a]Acts 11:30 [b]Acts 11:30 [c]Acts 13:5, 13 [d]Acts 12:12; 15:37 [1]NU-Text and M-Text read *to*. **13:1** [a]Acts 14:26 [b]Acts 11:22 [c]Rom. 16:21 **13:2** [a]Gal. 1:15; 2:9 [b]Heb. 5:4 **13:3** [a]Acts 6:6 **13:4** [a]Acts 4:36 **13:5** [a][Acts 13:46] [b]Acts 12:25; 15:37 **13:6** [a]Acts 8:9 [1]NU-Text reads *the whole island*. **13:8** [a]Ex. 7:11 **13:9** [a]Acts 2:4; 4:8 **13:10** [a]Matt. 13:38 **13:11** [a]1 Sam. 5:6 **13:13** [a]Acts 15:38 **13:14** [a]Acts 16:13

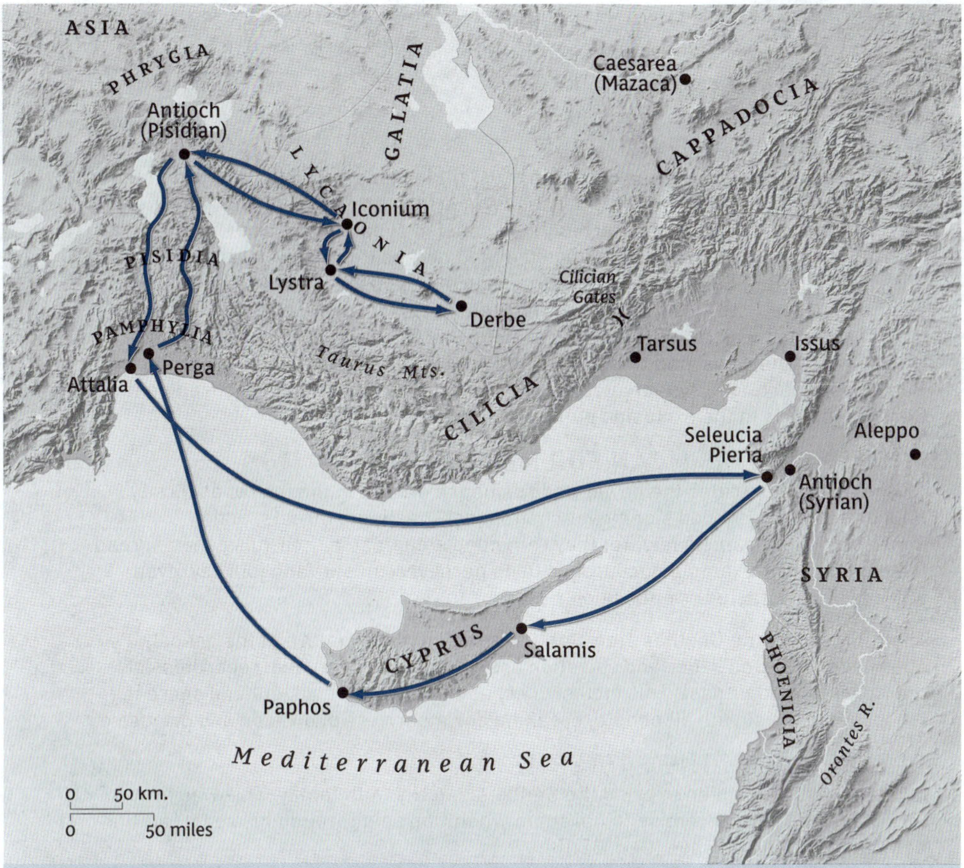


## PAUL'S FIRST MISSIONARY JOURNEY
ACTS 13:4–14:28 (C. AD 46–48)

synagogue on the Sabbath day and sat down.
15 And [a]after the reading of the Law and the
Prophets, the rulers of the synagogue sent to
them, saying, "Men *and* brethren, if you have
[b]any word of exhortation for the people, say on."
16 Then Paul stood up, and motioning with
*his* hand said, "Men of Israel, and [a]you who fear
God, listen: 17 The God of this people Israel[1] [a]chose
our fathers, and exalted the people [b]when they
dwelt as strangers in the land of Egypt, and with
an uplifted arm He [c]brought them out of it. 18 Now
[a]for a time of about forty years He put up with
their ways in the wilderness. 19 And when He had
destroyed [a]seven nations in the land of Canaan,
[b]He distributed their land to them by allotment.
20 "After that [a]He gave *them* judges for about
four hundred and fifty years, [b]until Samuel the
prophet. 21 [a]And afterward they asked for a king;
so God gave them [b]Saul the son of Kish, a man
of the tribe of Benjamin, for forty years. 22 And
[a]when He had removed him, [b]He raised up for
them David as king, to whom also He gave testi-
mony and said, [c]'I have found David[1] the *son* of
Jesse, [d]a man after My *own* heart, who will do all
My will.'[2] 23 [a]From this man's seed, according [b]to
*the* promise, God raised up for Israel [c]a Savior—
Jesus—[1] 24 [a]after John had first preached, before
His coming, the baptism of repentance to all the
people of Israel. 25 And as John was finishing his
course, he said, [a]'Who do you think I am? I am not
*He.* But behold, [b]there comes One after me, the
sandals of whose feet I am not worthy to loose.'

### SEEING JESUS IN THE SCRIPTURE

**13:22–23** Paul preached that Jesus is the promised descendant of David God raised up to save Israel (see Is. 11:1).

**13:15** [a] Luke 4:16 [b] Heb. 13:22 **13:16** [a] Acts 10:35 **13:17** [a] Deut. 7:6–8 [b] Acts 7:17 [c] Ex. 14:8 [1] M-Text omits *Israel.* **13:18** [a] Num. 14:34 **13:19** [a] Deut. 7:1 [b] Josh. 14:1, 2; 19:51 **13:20** [a] Judg. 2:16 [b] 1 Sam. 3:20 **13:21** [a] 1 Sam. 8:5 [b] 1 Sam. 10:20–24 **13:22** [a] 1 Sam. 15:23, 26, 28 [b] 1 Sam. 16:1, 12, 13 [c] Ps. 89:20 [d] 1 Sam. 13:14 [1] Psalm 89:20 [2] 1 Samuel 13:14 **13:23** [a] Is. 11:1 [b] Ps. 132:11 [c] [Matt. 1:21] [1] M-Text reads *for Israel salvation.* **13:24** [a] [Luke 3:3] **13:25** [a] Mark 1:7 [b] John 1:20, 27

ACTS 13:4–52

# PAUL'S MISSION

52

STORY OF SCRIPTURE

## WHAT'S GOING ON?

Paul, called by God to take the gospel to the Gentiles (see Acts 9:15) and prompted by the Holy Spirit, embarked with Barnabas on his first missionary journey. They traveled to various regions, preaching the gospel in synagogues, and engaging both Jews and Gentiles. Despite opposition and persecution, they persisted in their mission. Their journey solidifies the expansion of the gospel beyond the Jewish community (see Acts 8:4–40), affirming the gospel is for all people. Just as God's plan of salvation was never for the Jews alone, neither had it become one just for the Gentiles. The Jews' had rejected Jesus, but He had not rejected them. Paul and Barnabas's starting in synagogues shows their mission might have focused on the Gentiles, but not to the exclusion of the Jews.

## WHAT DOES THIS MEAN FOR ME?

This passage illustrates the power and resilience of faith in the face of adversity. Paul and Barnabas faced significant challenges—beatings, threats, and imprisonment to name a few. Yet they remained steadfast in their mission to spread the gospel. Their example encourages us to persevere in our faith journey, even when facing obstacles or opposition.

Their mission to the Gentiles also highlights the inclusive nature of the gospel. It's a reminder that God's love and salvation are available to everyone, regardless of their background or past. This inclusivity challenges us to reach out and share the message of Christ with all people, breaking down barriers of division and prejudice.

## DID YOU CATCH THE PATTERN?

It was always God's plan to bring the Gentiles into His faith family. This was first foreshadowed in His promise to Abraham when God said through his seed, "all the nations" would be blessed (Gen. 22:18).

*For the next* Story of Scripture *reading and devotion, turn to Acts 15:1–21 on page 1125.*

26 "Men *and* brethren, sons of the family of
Abraham, and [a]those among you who fear God,
[b]to you the word of this salvation has been sent.
27 For those who dwell in Jerusalem, and their
rulers, [a]because they did not know Him, nor even
the voices of the Prophets which are read every
Sabbath, have fulfilled *them* in condemning
*Him.* 28 [a]And though they found no cause for
death *in Him,* they asked Pilate that He should
be put to death. 29 [a]Now when they had fulfilled
all that was written concerning Him, [b]they took
*Him* down from the tree and laid *Him* in a tomb.
30 [a]But God raised Him from the dead. 31 [a]He was
seen for many days by those who came up with
Him from Galilee to Jerusalem, who are His
witnesses to the people. 32 And we declare to you
glad tidings—[a]that promise which was made to
the fathers. 33 God has fulfilled this for us their
children, in that He has raised up Jesus. As it is
also written in the second Psalm:

> [a]'You are My Son,
> Today I have begotten You.'[1]

34 And that He raised Him from the dead, no
more to return to corruption, He has spoken
thus:

> [a]'I will give you the sure mercies
> of David.'[1]

35 Therefore He also says in another *Psalm:*

> [a]'You will not allow Your Holy One to see
> corruption.'[1]

36 "For David, after he had served his own
generation by the will of God, [a]fell asleep, was
buried with his fathers, and saw corruption;
37 but He whom God raised up saw no corruption.
38 Therefore let it be known to you, brethren,
that [a]through this Man is preached to you the
forgiveness of sins; 39 and [a]by Him everyone who
believes is justified from all things from which
you could not be justified by the law of Moses.
40 Beware therefore, lest what has been spoken
in the prophets come upon you:

13:26 [a] Ps. 66:16 [b] Matt. 10:6 13:27 [a] Luke 23:34 13:28 [a] Matt. 27:22, 23 13:29 [a] Luke 18:31 [b] Matt. 27:57–61 13:30 [a] Matt. 12:39, 40; 28:6 13:31 [a] Acts 1:3, 11 13:32 [a] [Gen. 3:15] 13:33 [a] Ps. 2:7 [1] Psalm 2:7 13:34 [a] Is. 55:3 [1] Isaiah 55:3 13:35 [a] Ps. 16:10 [1] Psalm 16:10 13:36 [a] Acts 2:29 13:38 [a] Jer. 31:34 13:39 [a] [Is. 53:11]

41 'Behold,[a] you despisers,
Marvel and perish!
For I work a work in your days,
A work which you will by no means
believe,
Though one were to declare it to you.' "[1]

### *BLESSING AND CONFLICT AT ANTIOCH*

42 So when the Jews went out of the syna-
gogue,[1] the Gentiles begged that these words
might be preached to them the next Sabbath.
43 Now when the congregation had broken up,
many of the Jews and devout proselytes followed
Paul and Barnabas, who, speaking to them, [a]per-
suaded them to continue in [b]the grace of God.
44 On the next Sabbath almost the whole
city came together to hear the word of God.
45 But when the Jews saw the multitudes, they
were filled with envy; and contradicting and
blaspheming, they [a]opposed the things spoken
by Paul. 46 Then Paul and Barnabas grew bold
and said, [a]"It was necessary that the word of
God should be spoken to you first; but [b]since
you reject it, and judge yourselves unworthy of
everlasting life, behold, [c]we turn to the Gentiles.
47 For so the Lord has commanded us:

[a]'I have set you as a light to the Gentiles,
That you should be for salvation to the
ends of the earth.' "[1]

48 Now when the Gentiles heard this, they
were glad and glorified the word of the Lord.
[a]And as many as had been appointed to eternal
life believed.
49 And the word of the Lord was being spread
throughout all the region. 50 But the Jews stirred
up the devout and prominent women and the
chief men of the city, [a]raised up persecution
against Paul and Barnabas, and expelled them
from their region. 51 [a]But they shook off the
dust from their feet against them, and came to
Iconium. 52 And the disciples [a]were filled with
joy and [b]with the Holy Spirit.

### *AT ICONIUM*

**14** Now it happened in Iconium that they went
together to the synagogue of the Jews, and
so spoke that a great multitude both of the Jews
and of the [a]Greeks believed. 2 But the unbelieving
Jews stirred up the Gentiles and poisoned their
minds against the brethren. 3 Therefore they
stayed there a long time, speaking boldly in the
Lord, [a]who was bearing witness to the word of
His grace, granting signs and [b]wonders to be
done by their hands.
4 But the multitude of the city was [a]divided:
part sided with the Jews, and part with the [b]apos-
tles. 5 And when a violent attempt was made by
both the Gentiles and Jews, with their rulers, [a]to
abuse and stone them, 6 they became aware of it
and [a]fled to Lystra and Derbe, cities of Lycaonia,
and to the surrounding region. 7 And they were
preaching the gospel there.

### *IDOLATRY AT LYSTRA*

8 [a]And in Lystra a certain man without
strength in his feet was sitting, a cripple from
his mother's womb, who had never walked. 9 *This*
man heard Paul speaking. Paul, observing him
intently and seeing that he had faith to be healed,
10 said with a loud voice, [a]"Stand up straight on
your feet!" And he leaped and walked. 11 Now when
the people saw what Paul had done, they raised
their voices, saying in the Lycaonian *language,*
[a]"The gods have come down to us in the likeness of
men!" 12 And Barnabas they called Zeus, and Paul,
Hermes, because he was the chief speaker. 13 Then
the priest of Zeus, whose temple was in front of
their city, brought oxen and garlands to the gates,
[a]intending to sacrifice with the multitudes.
14 But when the apostles Barnabas and Paul
heard this, [a]they tore their clothes and ran in
among the multitude, crying out 15 and saying,
"Men, [a]why are you doing these things? [b]We
also are men with the same nature as you, and
preach to you that you should turn from [c]these
useless things [d]to the living God, [e]who made
the heaven, the earth, the sea, and all things
that are in them, 16 [a]who in bygone generations
allowed all nations to walk in their own ways.
17 [a]Nevertheless He did not leave Himself with-
out witness, in that He did good, [b]gave us rain
from heaven and fruitful seasons, filling our
hearts with [c]food and gladness." 18 And with
these sayings they could scarcely restrain the
multitudes from sacrificing to them.

### *STONING, ESCAPE TO DERBE*

19 [a]Then Jews from Antioch and Iconium
came there; and having persuaded the multi-
tudes, [b]they stoned Paul *and* dragged *him* out of
the city, supposing him to be [c]dead. 20 However,
when the disciples gathered around him, he rose
up and went into the city. And the next day he
departed with Barnabas to Derbe.

### *STRENGTHENING THE CONVERTS*

21 And when they had preached the gos-
pel to that city [a]and made many disciples,
they returned to Lystra, Iconium, and Anti-
och, 22 strengthening the souls of the disciples,

**13:41** [a] Hab. 1:5 [1] Habakkuk 1:5 **13:42** [1] Or *And when they went out of the synagogue of the Jews;* NU-Text reads *And when they went out, they begged.* **13:43** [a] Acts 11:23 [b] Titus 2:11 **13:45** [a] 1 Pet. 4:4 **13:46** [a] Rom. 1:16 [b] Ex. 32:10 [c] Acts 18:6 **13:47** [a] Is. 42:6; 49:6 [1] Isaiah 49:6 **13:48** [a] [Acts 2:47] **13:50** [a] 2 Tim. 3:11 **13:51** [a] Matt. 10:14 **13:52** [a] John 16:22 [b] Acts 2:4; 4:8, 31; 13:9 **14:1** [a] Acts 18:4 **14:3** [a] Heb. 2:4 [b] Acts 5:12 **14:4** [a] Luke 12:51 [b] Acts 13:2, 3 **14:5** [a] 2 Tim. 3:11 **14:6** [a] Matt. 10:23 **14:8** [a] Acts 3:2 **14:10** [a] [Is. 35:6] **14:11** [a] Acts 8:10; 28:6 **14:13** [a] Dan. 2:46 **14:14** [a] Matt. 26:65 **14:15** [a] Acts 10:26 [b] James 5:17 [c] 1 Cor. 8:4 [d] 1 Thess. 1:9 [e] Rev. 14:7 **14:16** [a] Ps. 81:12 **14:17** [a] Rom. 1:19, 20 [b] Deut. 11:14 [c] Ps. 145:16 **14:19** [a] Acts 13:45, 50; 14:2–5 [b] 2 Cor. 11:25 [c] [2 Cor. 12:1–4] **14:21** [a] Matt. 28:19

[a]exhorting *them* to continue in the faith, and
*saying,* [b]"We must through many tribulations
enter the kingdom of God." 23 So when they had
[a]appointed elders in every church, and prayed
with fasting, they commended them to the Lord
in whom they had believed. 24 And after they had
passed through Pisidia, they came to Pamphyl-
ia. 25 Now when they had preached the word in
Perga, they went down to Attalia. 26 From there
they sailed to Antioch, where they had been
commended to the grace of God for the work
which they had completed.

27 Now when they had come and gathered the
church together, [a]they reported all that God had
done with them, and that He had [b]opened the
door of faith to the Gentiles. 28 So they stayed
there a long time with the disciples.

### CONFLICT OVER CIRCUMCISION

**15** And [a]certain *men* came down from Judea
and taught the brethren, [b]"Unless you are
circumcised according to the custom of Moses,
you cannot be saved." 2 Therefore, when Paul
and Barnabas had no small dissension and
dispute with them, they determined that [a]Paul
and Barnabas and certain others of them should
go up to Jerusalem, to the apostles and elders,
about this question.

3 So, [a]being sent on their way by the church,
they passed through Phoenicia and Samaria,
[b]describing the conversion of the Gentiles; and
they caused great joy to all the brethren. 4 And
when they had come to Jerusalem, they were
received by the church and the apostles and
the elders; and they reported all things that God
had done with them. 5 But some of the sect of
the Pharisees who believed rose up, saying, "It is
necessary to circumcise them, and to command
*them* to keep the law of Moses."

### THE JERUSALEM COUNCIL

6 Now the apostles and elders came together
to consider this matter. 7 And when there had been
much dispute, Peter rose up *and* said to them:
[a]"Men *and* brethren, you know that a good while
ago God chose among us, that by my mouth the
Gentiles should hear the word of the gospel and
believe. 8 So God, [a]who knows the heart, acknowl-
edged them by [b]giving them the Holy Spirit, just as
*He did* to us, 9 [a]and made no distinction between us
and them, [b]purifying their hearts by faith. 10 Now
therefore, why do you test God [a]by putting a yoke
on the neck of the disciples which neither our
fathers nor we were able to bear? 11 But [a]we believe
that through the grace of the Lord Jesus Christ[1]
we shall be saved in the same manner as they."

12 Then all the multitude kept silent and
listened to Barnabas and Paul declaring how
many miracles and wonders God had [a]worked
through them among the Gentiles. 13 And after
they had become silent, [a]James answered, say-
ing, "Men *and* brethren, listen to me: 14 [a]Simon
has declared how God at the first visited the
Gentiles to take out of them a people for His
name. 15 And with this the words of the prophets
agree, just as it is written:

16 'After[a] this I will return
And will rebuild the tabernacle of David,
which has fallen down;
I will rebuild its ruins,
And I will set it up;
17 So that the rest of mankind may seek the
LORD,
Even all the Gentiles who are called by My
name,
Says the LORD who does all these things.'[1]

18 "Known to God from eternity are all His
works.[1] 19 Therefore [a]I judge that we should not
trouble those from among the Gentiles who [b]are
turning to God, 20 but that we [a]write to them to
abstain [b]from things polluted by idols, [c]*from* sex-
ual immorality,[1] [d]*from* things strangled, and *from*
blood. 21 For Moses has had throughout many
generations those who preach him in every city,
[a]being read in the synagogues every Sabbath."

### THE JERUSALEM DECREE

22 Then it pleased the apostles and elders,
with the whole church, to send chosen men of
their own company to Antioch with Paul and
Barnabas, *namely,* Judas who was also named
[a]Barsabas,[1] and Silas, leading men among the
brethren.

23 They wrote this *letter* by them:

The apostles, the elders, and the brethren,

To the brethren who are of the Gentiles in
Antioch, Syria, and Cilicia:

Greetings.

24 Since we have heard that [a]some who went
out from us have troubled you with words,
[b]unsettling your souls, saying, "*You must*
be circumcised and keep the law"[1]—to
whom we gave no *such* commandment—
25 it seemed good to us, being assembled
with one accord, to send chosen men to
you with our beloved Barnabas and Paul,

**14:22** [a] Acts 11:23 [b] [2 Tim. 2:12; 3:12] **14:23** [a] Titus 1:5 **14:27** [a] Acts 15:4, 12 [b] 2 Cor. 2:12 **15:1** [a] Gal. 2:12 [b] Phil. 3:2 **15:2** [a] Gal. 2:1 **15:3** [a] Rom. 15:24 [b] Acts 14:27; 15:4, 12 **15:7** [a] Acts 10:20 **15:8** [a] Acts 1:24 [b] Acts 2:4; 10:44, 47 **15:9** [a] Rom. 10:12 [b] Acts 10:15, 28 **15:10** [a] Matt. 23:4 **15:11** [a] Rom. 3:4; 5:15 [1] NU-Text and M-Text omit *Christ.* **15:12** [a] Acts 14:27; 15:3, 4 **15:13** [a] Acts 12:17 **15:14** [a] Acts 15:7 **15:16** [a] Amos 9:11, 12 **15:17** [1] Amos 9:11, 12 **15:18** [1] NU-Text (combining with verse 17) reads *Says the Lord, who makes these things known from eternity (of old).* **15:19** [a] Acts 15:28; 21:25 [b] 1 Thess. 1:9 **15:20** [a] Acts 21:25 [b] [1 Cor. 8:1; 10:20, 28] [c] [1 Cor. 6:9] [d] Lev. 3:17 [1] Or *fornication* **15:21** [a] Acts 13:15, 27 **15:22** [a] Acts 1:23 [1] NU-Text and M-Text read *Barsabbas.* **15:24** [a] Titus 1:10, 11 [b] Gal. 1:7; 5:10 [1] NU-Text omits *saying, "You must be circumcised and keep the law."*

ACTS 15:1–21

## THE JERUSALEM COUNCIL

53

STORY OF SCRIPTURE

### WHAT'S GOING ON?

This passage describes a pivotal moment in the early church: a gathering of church leaders known as the Jerusalem Council. This council addressed a crucial question: Must Gentile converts to Christianity be required to follow the Jewish law, specifically circumcision? In other words, does a Gentile's journey of faith to Christianity pass through Judaism? After respectful but intense deliberation, the apostles and elders, led by James (the half-brother of Jesus), concluded Gentiles didn't need to adhere to the Jewish practices; salvation was by faith in Jesus alone.

The council's decision highlights the triumph of grace over legalism. Just as the Jews could not earn their way to salvation by any work of the law, neither can the believer. Salvation has always been a gift and always will be.

### WHAT DOES THIS MEAN FOR ME?

The early church leaders came together, debated, and reached a consensus on a contentious issue. Some disagreed, but they worked through the differing opinions and came to a God-honoring agreement. This story reminds us of the need and possibility of Christian unity. Reasonable and Jesus-loving people can disagree but still come together as one in the end.

### DID YOU CATCH THE PATTERN?

Although the Bible emphasizes equality and dignity among all people, it also includes a common theme of someone appointed "first among equals." These were people appointed to lead a group and help guide them into God-honoring decisions. For the Israelites, it was often prophets and kings. For the Jerusalem Council, it was James. For the modern church, it is often pastors and elders. These individuals are never more important than others, but God has placed them in a special position to serve, help, and guide His people.

*For the next* Story of Scripture *reading and devotion, turn to Acts 16:11–40 on page 1127.*

26 [a]men who have risked their lives for the name of our Lord Jesus Christ. 27 We have therefore sent Judas and Silas, who will also report the same things by word of mouth. 28 For it seemed good to the Holy Spirit, and to us, to lay upon you no greater burden than these necessary things:
29 [a]that you abstain from things offered to idols, [b]from blood, from things strangled, and from [c]sexual immorality.[1] If you keep yourselves from these, you will do well.

Farewell.

### CONTINUING MINISTRY IN SYRIA

30 So when they were sent off, they came to Antioch; and when they had gathered the multitude together, they delivered the letter.
31 When they had read it, they rejoiced over its encouragement. 32 Now Judas and Silas, themselves being [a]prophets also, [b]exhorted and strengthened the brethren with many words.
33 And after they had stayed *there* for a time, they were [a]sent back with greetings from the brethren to the apostles.[1]

34 However, it seemed good to Silas to remain there.[1] 35 [a]Paul and Barnabas also remained in Antioch, teaching and preaching the word of the Lord, with many others also.

### DIVISION OVER JOHN MARK

36 Then after some days Paul said to Barnabas, "Let us now go back and visit our brethren in every city where we have preached the word of the Lord, *and see* how they are doing." 37 Now Barnabas was determined to take with them [a]John called Mark. 38 But Paul insisted that they should not take with them [a]the one who had departed from them in Pamphylia, and had not gone with them to the work. 39 Then the contention became so sharp that they parted from one another. And so Barnabas took Mark and sailed to [a]Cyprus; 40 but Paul chose Silas and departed, [a]being commended by the brethren to the grace of God. 41 And he went through Syria and Cilicia, [a]strengthening the churches.

**15:26** [a] Acts 13:50; 14:19 **15:29** [a] Acts 15:20; 21:25 [b] Lev. 17:14 [c] Col. 3:5 [1] Or *fornication* **15:32** [a] Eph. 4:11 [b] Acts 14:22; 18:23 **15:33** [a] Heb. 11:31 [1] NU-Text reads *to those who had sent them.* **15:34** [1] NU-Text and M-Text omit this verse. **15:35** [a] Acts 13:1 **15:37** [a] Acts 12:12, 25 **15:38** [a] Acts 13:13 **15:39** [a] Acts 4:36; 13:4 **15:40** [a] Acts 11:23; 14:26 **15:41** [a] Acts 16:5

### *TIMOTHY JOINS PAUL AND SILAS*

**16** Then he came to [a]Derbe and Lystra. And be-
hold, a certain disciple was there, [b]named
Timothy, [c]*the* son of a certain Jewish woman who
believed, but his father *was* Greek. 2 He was well
spoken of by the brethren who were at Lystra and
Iconium. 3 Paul wanted to have him go on with
him. And he [a]took *him* and circumcised him
because of the Jews who were in that region, for
they all knew that his father was Greek. 4 And as
they went through the cities, they delivered to
them the [a]decrees to keep, [b]which were deter-
mined by the apostles and elders at Jerusalem.
5 [a]So the churches were strengthened in the faith,
and increased in number daily.

### *THE MACEDONIAN CALL*

6 Now when they had gone through Phrygia
and the region of [a]Galatia, they were forbidden by
the Holy Spirit to preach the word in Asia. 7 After
they had come to Mysia, they tried to go into Bi-
thynia, but the Spirit[1] did not permit them. 8 So
passing by Mysia, they [a]came down to Troas. 9 And
a vision appeared to Paul in the night. A [a]man of
Macedonia stood and pleaded with him, saying,
"Come over to Macedonia and help us." 10 Now
after he had seen the vision, immediately we
sought to go [a]to Macedonia, concluding that the
Lord had called us to preach the gospel to them.

### *LYDIA BAPTIZED AT PHILIPPI*

11 Therefore, sailing from Troas, we ran a
straight course to Samothrace, and the next *day*
came to Neapolis, 12 and from there to [a]Philippi,
which is the foremost city of that part of Mace-
donia, a colony. And we were staying in that city
for some days. 13 And on the Sabbath day we went
out of the city to the riverside, where prayer was
customarily made; and we sat down and spoke to
the women who met *there.* 14 Now a certain woman
named Lydia heard *us.* She was a seller of purple
from the city of [a]Thyatira, who worshiped God.
[b]The Lord opened her heart to heed the things
spoken by Paul. 15 And when she and her house-
hold were baptized, she begged *us,* saying, "If you
have judged me to be faithful to the Lord, come to
my house and stay." So [a]she persuaded us.

### *PAUL AND SILAS IMPRISONED*

16 Now it happened, as we went to prayer,
that a certain slave girl [a]possessed with a spirit
of divination met us, who brought her masters
[b]much profit by fortune-telling. 17 This girl fol-
lowed Paul and us, and cried out, saying, "These
men are the servants of the Most High God, who
proclaim to us the way of salvation." 18 And this
she did for many days.

But Paul, [a]greatly annoyed, turned and said
to the spirit, "I command you in the name of
Jesus Christ to come out of her." [b]And he came
out that very hour. 19 But [a]when her masters
saw that their hope of profit was gone, they
seized Paul and Silas and [b]dragged *them* into
the marketplace to the authorities.

20 And they brought them to the magistrates,
and said, "These men, being Jews, [a]exceedingly
trouble our city; 21 and they teach customs which
are not lawful for us, being Romans, to receive or
observe." 22 Then the multitude rose up together
against them; and the magistrates tore off their
clothes [a]and commanded *them* to be beaten with
rods. 23 And when they had laid many stripes on
them, they threw *them* into prison, command-
ing the jailer to keep them securely. 24 Having
received such a charge, he put them into the
inner prison and fastened their feet in the stocks.

### *THE PHILIPPIAN JAILER SAVED*

25 But at midnight Paul and Silas were pray-
ing and singing hymns to God, and the prisoners
were listening to them. 26 [a]Suddenly there was
a great earthquake, so that the foundations of
the prison were shaken; and immediately [b]all
the doors were opened and everyone's chains
were loosed. 27 And the keeper of the prison,
awaking from sleep and seeing the prison doors
open, supposing the prisoners had fled, drew his
sword and was about to kill himself. 28 But Paul
called with a loud voice, saying, "Do yourself no
harm, for we are all here."

29 Then he called for a light, ran in, and fell
down trembling before Paul and Silas. 30 And he
brought them out and said, [a]"Sirs, what must I
do to be saved?"

31 So they said, [a]"Believe on the Lord Jesus
Christ, and you will be saved, you and your
household." 32 Then they spoke the word of the
Lord to him and to all who were in his house.
33 And he took them the same hour of the night
and washed *their* stripes. And immediately he
and all his *family* were baptized. 34 Now when he
had brought them into his house, [a]he set food
before them; and he rejoiced, having believed
in God with all his household.

### *PAUL REFUSES TO DEPART SECRETLY*

35 And when it was day, the magistrates sent
the officers, saying, "Let those men go."

36 So the keeper of the prison reported these
words to Paul, saying, "The magistrates have
sent to let you go. Now therefore depart, and
go in peace."

37 But Paul said to them, "They have beaten
us openly, uncondemned [a]Romans, *and* have

**16:1** [a] Acts 14:6 [b] Rom. 16:21 [c] 2 Tim. 1:5; 3:15 **16:3** [a] [Gal. 2:3; 5:2] **16:4** [a] Acts 15:19–21 [b] Acts 15:28, 29 **16:5** [a] Acts 2:47; 15:41 **16:6** [a] Gal. 1:1, 2 **16:7** [1] NU-Text adds *of Jesus.* **16:8** [a] 2 Cor. 2:12 **16:9** [a] Acts 10:30 **16:10** [a] 2 Cor. 2:13 **16:12** [a] Phil. 1:1 **16:14** [a] Rev. 1:11; 2:18, 24 [b] Luke 24:45 **16:15** [a] Gen. 19:3; 33:11; Judg. 19:21; Luke 24:29; [Heb. 13:2] **16:16** [a] Lev. 19:31; 20:6, 27; Deut. 18:11; 1 Sam. 28:3, 7; 2 Kin. 21:6; 1 Chr. 10:13; Is. 8:19 [b] Acts 19:24 **16:18** [a] Mark 1:25, 34 [b] Mark 16:17 **16:19** [a] Acts 16:16; 19:25, 26 [b] Matt. 10:18 **16:20** [a] 1 Kin. 18:17; Acts 17:8 **16:22** [a] 2 Cor. 6:5; 11:23, 25; 1 Thess. 2:2 **16:26** [a] Acts 4:31 [b] Acts 5:19; 12:7, 10 **16:30** [a] Luke 3:10; Acts 2:37; 9:6; 22:10 **16:31** [a] [John 3:16, 36; 6:47; Acts 13:38, 39; Rom. 10:9–11; 1 John 5:10] **16:34** [a] Matt. 5:4; Luke 5:29; 19:6 **16:37** [a] Acts 22:25–29

ACTS 16:11–40

## THE CHURCH EXPANDS

54

STORY OF SCRIPTURE

### WHAT'S GOING ON?

Paul and Silas arrived in Philippi, a leading city of Macedonia, where they experienced fruitful ministry, catastrophe, persecution, and miracles, showcasing the power of and challenges to the faith. First, they met Lydia, a dealer in purple cloth, who believed in Jesus and helped start the Philippian church. All seemed well for Paul and this new church until a sinister spirit shouted apparent mockery through a slave girl who followed Paul and Silas. Paul exorcised the demon in the name of Jesus, but her masters became outraged at the loss of her income and had the two missionaries beaten and imprisoned.

Paul and Silas were locked in a cell; but instead of wallowing in self-pity, they began praying and singing. Their worship was interrupted by an earthquake, which broke the foundations of the prison and freed Paul and Silas. Instead of running, they stayed, preserving the jailer's life and leading to his conversion, along with his family's.

### WHAT DOES THIS MEAN FOR ME?

This passage reminds us of the importance of steadfast faith and worship amid trials. Paul and Silas sang hymns and prayed in prison, showing their unwavering trust in God even in the bleakest circumstances. Worship certainly is more difficult when we're suffering, confused, or empty, but it is always a sweet aroma to Christ and He often will use it to carry us through whatever we are facing.

### DID YOU CATCH THE PATTERN?

This wasn't the first time worship was used as an act of warfare and defense. In 2 Chronicles 20, a procession of musicians and worship leaders led the charge into battle, proclaiming the victory of the Lord. Just like Paul and Silas were freed from prison, the people of Israel were delivered from their enemy.

*For the next* Story of Scripture *reading and devotion, turn to 1 Corinthians 2:1–5 on page 1168.*

thrown *us* into prison. And now do they put us
out secretly? No indeed! Let them come them-
selves and get us out."
38 And the officers told these words to the
magistrates, and they were afraid when they
heard that they were Romans. 39 Then they
came and pleaded with them and brought
*them* out, and [a]asked *them* to depart from the
city. 40 So they went out of the prison [a]and en-
tered *the house of* Lydia; and when they had
seen the brethren, they encouraged them and
departed.

### *PREACHING CHRIST AT THESSALONICA*

17 Now when they had passed through Am-
phipolis and Apollonia, they came to
[a]Thessalonica, where there was a synagogue
of the Jews. 2 Then Paul, as his custom was, [a]went
in to them, and for three Sabbaths [b]reasoned
with them from the Scriptures, 3 explaining and
demonstrating [a]that the Christ had to suffer and
rise again from the dead, and *saying,* "This Jesus
whom I preach to you is the Christ." 4 [a]And some
of them were persuaded; and a great multitude
of the devout Greeks, and not a few of the leading
women, joined Paul and [b]Silas.

### *ASSAULT ON JASON'S HOUSE*

5 But the Jews who were not persuaded, be-
coming [a]envious,[1] took some of the evil men
from the marketplace, and gathering a mob,
set all the city in an uproar and attacked the
house of [b]Jason, and sought to bring them out
to the people. 6 But when they did not find them,
they dragged Jason and some brethren to the
rulers of the city, crying out, [a]"These who have
turned the world upside down have come here
too. 7 Jason has harbored them, and these are
all acting contrary to the decrees of Caesar,
[a]saying there is another king—Jesus." 8 And
they troubled the crowd and the rulers of the
city when they heard these things. 9 So when
they had taken security from Jason and the rest,
they let them go.

**16:39** [a] Matt. 8:34 **16:40** [a] Acts 16:14 **17:1** [a] Acts 17:11, 13; 20:4; 27:2; Phil. 4:16; 1 Thess. 1:1; 2 Thess. 1:1; 2 Tim. 4:10 **17:2** [a] Luke 4:16; Acts 9:20; 13:5, 14; 14:1; 16:13; 19:8 [b] 1 Thess. 2:1–16 **17:3** [a] Luke 24:26, 46; Acts 18:5, 28; Gal. 3:1 **17:4** [a] Acts 28:24 [b] Acts 15:22, 27, 32, 40 **17:5** [a] Acts 13:45 [b] Rom. 16:21 [1] NU-Text omits *who were not persuaded;* M-Text omits *becoming envious.* **17:6** [a] [Acts 16:20] **17:7** [a] 1 Pet. 2:13

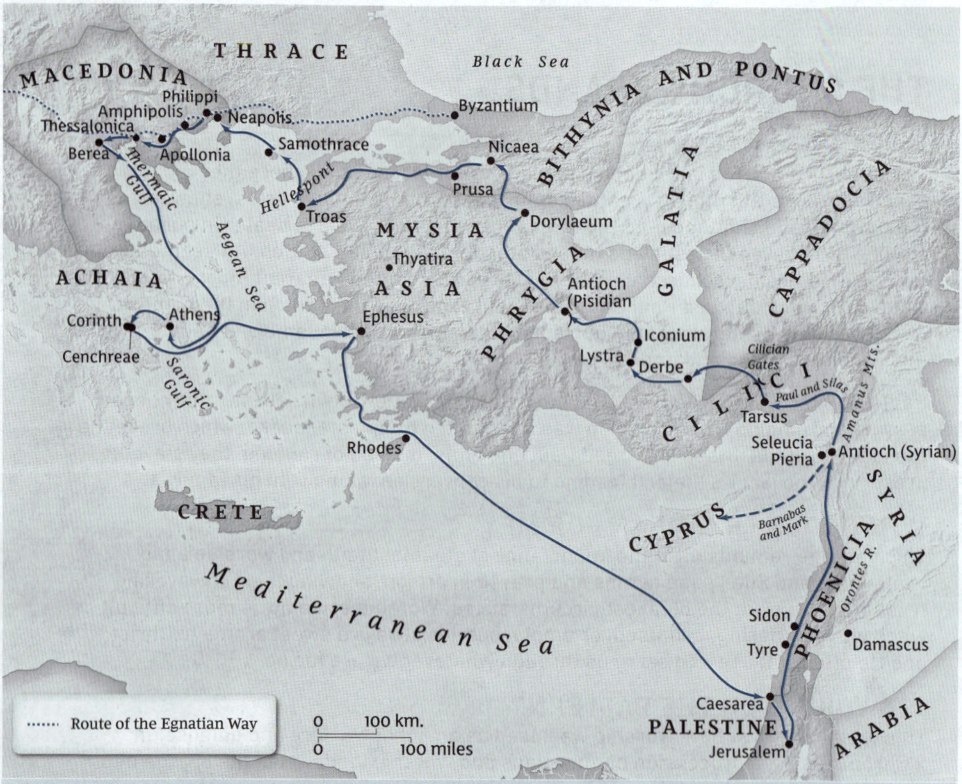


## PAUL'S SECOND MISSIONARY JOURNEY
ACTS 15:36—18:22 (C. AD 49–52)

### *MINISTERING AT BEREA*

[10] Then [a]the brethren immediately sent
Paul and Silas away by night to Berea. When
they arrived, they went into the synagogue of
the Jews. [11] These were more fair-minded than
those in Thessalonica, in that they received
the word with all readiness, and [a]searched the
Scriptures daily *to find out* whether these things
were so. [12] Therefore many of them believed,
and also not a few of the Greeks, prominent
women as well as men. [13] But when the Jews
from Thessalonica learned that the word of
God was preached by Paul at Berea, they came
there also and stirred up the crowds. [14] [a]Then
immediately the brethren sent Paul away, to go
to the sea; but both Silas and Timothy remained
there. [15] So those who conducted Paul brought
him to Athens; and [a]receiving a command for
Silas and Timothy to come to him with all speed,
they departed.

### *THE PHILOSOPHERS AT ATHENS*

[16] Now while Paul waited for them at Ath-
ens, [a]his spirit was provoked within him when
he saw that the city was given over to idols.
[17] Therefore he reasoned in the synagogue with
the Jews and with the *Gentile* worshipers, and in
the marketplace daily with those who happened
to be there. [18] Then[1] certain Epicurean and Stoic
philosophers encountered him. And some said,
"What does this babbler want to say?"

Others said, "He seems to be a proclaimer
of foreign gods," because he preached to them
[a]Jesus and the resurrection.

[19] And they took him and brought him to
the Areopagus, saying, "May we know what this
new doctrine *is* of which you speak? [20] For you
are bringing some strange things to our ears.
Therefore we want to know what these things
mean." [21] For all the Athenians and the foreigners
who were there spent their time in nothing else
but either to tell or to hear some new thing.

### *ADDRESSING THE AREOPAGUS*

[22] Then Paul stood in the midst of the Ar-
eopagus and said, "Men of Athens, I perceive
that in all things you are very religious; [23] for
as I was passing through and considering the

17:10 [a] Acts 9:25; 17:14 17:11 [a] John 5:39 17:14 [a] Matt. 10:23 17:15 [a] Acts 18:5 17:16 [a] 2 Pet. 2:8 17:18 [a] 1 Cor. 15:12

[1] NU-Text and M-Text add *also*.

**17:23** In the sixth century BC, it was said that a poet from Crete named Epimenides turned aside a horrible plague from the people of Athens by appealing to a god of whom the people had never heard. An **altar** was built to honor this **unknown god**, and its **inscription** caught Paul's attention. Knowing the Athenians had no background in the Old Testament Scriptures unlike the Jews in the synagogues, Paul began his discourse with what they were already familiar with: their own legends and observation.

objects of your worship, I even found an altar with this inscription:

TO THE UNKNOWN GOD.

Therefore, the One whom you worship without knowing, Him I proclaim to you: 24 [a]God, who made the world and everything in it, since He is [b]Lord of heaven and earth, [c]does not dwell in temples made with hands. 25 Nor is He worshiped with men's hands, as though He needed anything, since He [a]gives to all life, breath, and all things. 26 And He has made from one blood[1] every nation of men to dwell on all the face of the earth, and has determined their preappointed times and [a]the boundaries of their dwellings, 27 [a]so that they should seek the Lord, in the hope that they might grope for Him and find Him, [b]though He is not far from each one of us; 28 for [a]in Him we live and move and have our being, [b]as also some of your own poets have said, 'For we are also His offspring.' 29 Therefore, since we are the offspring of God, [a]we ought not to think that the Divine Nature is like gold or silver or stone, something shaped by art and man's devising. 30 Truly, [a]these times of ignorance God overlooked, but [b]now commands all men everywhere to repent, 31 because He has appointed a day on which [a]He will judge the world in righteousness by the Man whom He has ordained. He has given assurance of this to all by [b]raising Him from the dead."

32 And when they heard of the resurrection of the dead, some mocked, while others said, "We will hear you again on this *matter.*" 33 So Paul departed from among them. 34 However, some men joined him and believed, among them Dionysius the Areopagite, a woman named Damaris, and others with them.

**17:24** [a] Acts 14:15 [b] Matt. 11:25 [c] Acts 7:48–50 **17:25** [a] Is. 42:5 **17:26** [a] Deut. 32:8 [1] NU-Text omits *blood.* **17:27** [a] [Rom. 1:20] [b] Jer. 23:23, 24 **17:28** [a] [Heb. 1:3] [b] Titus 1:12 **17:29** [a] Is. 40:18, 19 **17:30** [a] [Rom. 3:25] [b] [Titus 2:11, 12] **17:31** [a] Acts 10:42 [b] Acts 2:24

KNOW THE TRUTH

## THE DOCTRINE OF GOD

### PART 18: THE IMMANENCE OF GOD

**17:27** Two of the few ways to "get close" to the Greek and Romans gods were building and visiting temples and making and worshiping idols. In the middle of temple-saturated, idol-infested Athens, Paul proclaimed a God with a unique attribute: the true God who is "not far" from each person. Instead of being far from God, we live, move, and have being *in* Him.

God is immanent, meaning He is present in creation in a personal and intimate way. His immanence differs from His omnipresence. Gravity is omnipresent on earth. We're affected by it, but we don't relate to it in a personal way. Because God is immanent, we're not merely affected by His presence, but we can also intimately relate to Him through faith in Jesus Christ. God's immanence works with His transcendence, not against it. He is present within His creation without being part of it or corrupted by it.

The endgame of the Bible's overarching story is God with His people (see Rev. 21:3). Presently, God's immanence is most marvelously displayed in two main ways. First, by **the incarnation of Jesus**, *Immanuel* ("God with us"). God was among His people—seen, heard, touched, and related to—through Jesus. Second, by **the dwelling of the Spirit** within born again believers. Through the Holy Spirit, God is in us and always among us to relate with us until we're face-to-face with Him.

*For* **THE DOCTRINE OF GOD: PART 19: THE TRANSCENDENCE OF GOD,** *turn to Psalm 97:9 on page 593.*

**18:1 Athens** was known for its beautiful buildings and schools. Alexandria was known for its library and museum. **Corinth**, on the other hand, was known for its immorality. Located in southern Greece, about fifty miles from Athens, Corinth was the site of a temple for Aphrodite, the goddess of love. The temple housed one thousand priestesses, who worked as prostitutes.

### *MINISTERING AT CORINTH*

**18** After these things Paul departed from Ath-
ens and went to Corinth. 2 And he found
a certain Jew named [a]Aquila, born in Pontus,
who had recently come from Italy with his wife
Priscilla (because Claudius had commanded all
the Jews to depart from Rome); and he came to
them. 3 So, because he was of the same trade, he
stayed with them [a]and worked; for by occupation
they were tentmakers. 4 [a]And he reasoned in the
synagogue every Sabbath, and persuaded both
Jews and Greeks.

5 [a]When Silas and Timothy had come from
Macedonia, Paul was [b]compelled by the Spirit,
and testified to the Jews *that* Jesus *is* the Christ.
6 But [a]when they opposed him and blasphemed,
[b]he shook *his* garments and said to them, [c]"Your
blood *be* upon your *own* heads; [d]I *am* clean. [e]From
now on I will go to the Gentiles." 7 And he departed
from there and entered the house of a certain *man*
named Justus,[1] *one* who worshiped God, whose
house was next door to the synagogue. 8 [a]Then
Crispus, the ruler of the synagogue, believed on
the Lord with all his household. And many of the
Corinthians, hearing, believed and were baptized.

9 Now [a]the Lord spoke to Paul in the night by
a vision, "Do not be afraid, but speak, and do not
keep silent; 10 [a]for I am with you, and no one will
attack you to hurt you; for I have many people in
this city." 11 And he continued *there* a year and six
months, teaching the word of God among them.

12 When Gallio was proconsul of Achaia, the
Jews with one accord rose up against Paul and
brought him to the judgment seat, 13 saying,
"This *fellow* persuades men to worship God
contrary to the law."

14 And when Paul was about to open *his*
mouth, Gallio said to the Jews, "If it were a matter
of wrongdoing or wicked crimes, O Jews, there
would be reason why I should bear with you.
15 But if it is a [a]question of words and names
and your own law, look *to it* yourselves; for I do
not want to be a judge of such *matters*." 16 And
he drove them from the judgment seat. 17 Then
all the Greeks[1] took [a]Sosthenes, the ruler of the
synagogue, and beat *him* before the judgment
seat. But Gallio took no notice of these things.

### *PAUL RETURNS TO ANTIOCH*

18 So Paul still remained a good while. Then
he took leave of the brethren and sailed for Syria,
and Priscilla and Aquila *were* with him. [a]He had
*his* hair cut off at [b]Cenchrea, for he had taken a
vow. 19 And he came to Ephesus, and left them
there; but he himself entered the synagogue
and reasoned with the Jews. 20 When they asked
*him* to stay a longer time with them, he did not
consent, 21 but took leave of them, saying, [a]"I
must by all means keep this coming feast in
Jerusalem;[1] but I will return again to you, [b]God
willing." And he sailed from Ephesus.

22 And when he had landed at [a]Caesarea,
and gone up and greeted the church, he went
down to Antioch. 23 After he had spent some time
*there*, he departed and went over the region of
[a]Galatia and Phrygia in order, [b]strengthening
all the disciples.

### *MINISTRY OF APOLLOS*

24 [a]Now a certain Jew named Apollos, born
at Alexandria, an eloquent man *and* mighty in
the Scriptures, came to Ephesus. 25 This man
had been instructed in the way of the Lord; and
being [a]fervent in spirit, he spoke and taught
accurately the things of the Lord, [b]though he
knew only the baptism of John. 26 So he began
to speak boldly in the synagogue. When Aquila
and Priscilla heard him, they took him aside
and explained to him the way of God more
accurately. 27 And when he desired to cross to
Achaia, the brethren wrote, exhorting the dis-
ciples to receive him; and when he arrived, [a]he
greatly helped those who had believed through
grace; 28 for he vigorously refuted the Jews
publicly, [a]showing from the Scriptures that
Jesus is the Christ.

### *PAUL AT EPHESUS*

**19** And it happened, while [a]Apollos was at
Corinth, that Paul, having passed through
[b]the upper regions, came to Ephesus. And find-
ing some disciples 2 he said to them, "Did you
receive the Holy Spirit when you believed?"

So they said to him, [a]"We have not so much
as heard whether there is a Holy Spirit."

3 And he said to them, "Into what then were
you baptized?"

So they said, [a]"Into John's baptism."

4 Then Paul said, [a]"John indeed baptized
with a baptism of repentance, saying to the

**18:2** [a] 1 Cor. 16:19 **18:3** [a] Acts 20:34 **18:4** [a] Acts 17:2 **18:5** [a] Acts 17:14, 15 [b] Acts 18:28 **18:6** [a] Acts 13:45 [b] Neh. 5:13 [c] 2 Sam. 1:16 [d] [Ezek. 3:18, 19] [e] Acts 13:46–48; 28:28 **18:7** [1] NU-Text reads *Titius Justus.* **18:8** [a] 1 Cor. 1:14 **18:9** [a] Acts 23:11 **18:10** [a] Jer. 1:18, 19 **18:15** [a] Acts 23:29; 25:19 **18:17** [a] 1 Cor. 1:1 [1] NU-Text reads *they all.* **18:18** [a] Acts 21:24 [b] Rom. 16:1 **18:21** [a] Acts 19:21; 20:16 [b] 1 Cor. 4:19 [1] NU-Text omits *I must* through *Jerusalem.* **18:22** [a] Acts 8:40 **18:23** [a] Gal. 1:2 [b] Acts 14:22; 15:32, 41 **18:24** [a] Titus 3:13 **18:25** [a] Rom. 12:11 [b] Acts 19:3 **18:27** [a] 1 Cor. 3:6 **18:28** [a] Acts 9:22; 17:3; 18:5 **19:1** [a] 1 Cor. 1:12; 3:5, 6 [b] Acts 18:23 **19:2** [a] 1 Sam. 3:7 **19:3** [a] Acts 18:25 **19:4** [a] Matt. 3:11

KNOW THE TRUTH

## THE DOCTRINE OF SCRIPTURE

### PART 9: THE CANONIZATION OF SCRIPTURE

**18:27–28** To prove Jesus is God's promised Messiah, Apollos used the Scriptures—the Old Testament (OT) in this case. He didn't choose other religious or secular writings, for they lacked the authority of Scripture to prove his point. Rather, he relied on the OT canon alone. *Canon* is a term describing the collection of approved writings that constitute God's holy Scriptures. Because we place great importance on the Scriptures, both the OT and New Testament (NT), it's critical to know what makes up the canon of Scripture and how this canon was determined.

The most important factor in determining the canon of Scripture is that each book included is God-breathed (see 2 Tim. 3:15–17). Each book bears evidence of being the very words of God. Other factors included the reliability of the author (a prophet, an apostle, or a close associate of either), truthfulness (containing no errors), acceptance by Israel (OT) and the church (NT), and use in worship.

Genesis through Malachi make up the OT, although the order of these books has changed throughout history. It's generally accepted that the OT was officially canonized in fourth century BC. Matthew through Revelation make up the NT, although, again, the order of these books has changed. The NT was officially canonized in the early fourth century AD. While other historically important and helpful writings exist, the sixty-six books of the canon of Scripture are unique in that they alone are the very words of God.

*For* **THE DOCTRINE OF SCRIPTURE: PART 10: THE TRANSLATION OF SCRIPTURE**, *turn to Colossians 4:16 on page 1218.* • • •

people that they should believe on Him who
would come after him, that is, on Christ Jesus."
[5]When they heard *this,* they were baptized [a]in
the name of the Lord Jesus. [6]And when Paul had
[a]laid hands on them, the Holy Spirit came upon
them, and [b]they spoke with tongues and proph-
esied. [7]Now the men were about twelve in all.
[8][a]And he went into the synagogue and spoke
boldly for three months, reasoning and persuad-
ing [b]concerning the things of the kingdom of
God. [9]But [a]when some were hardened and did
not believe, but spoke evil [b]of the Way before the
multitude, he departed from them and withdrew
the disciples, reasoning daily in the school of
Tyrannus. [10]And [a]this continued for two years,
so that all who dwelt in Asia heard the word of
the Lord Jesus, both Jews and Greeks.

### *MIRACLES GLORIFY CHRIST*

[11]Now [a]God worked unusual miracles by the
hands of Paul, [12][a]so that even handkerchiefs or
aprons were brought from his body to the sick,
and the diseases left them and the evil spirits
went out of them. [13][a]Then some of the itinerant
Jewish exorcists [b]took it upon themselves to call
the name of the Lord Jesus over those who had
evil spirits, saying, "We[1] exorcise you by the Jesus
whom Paul [c]preaches." [14]Also there were seven
sons of Sceva, a Jewish chief priest, who did so.
[15]And the evil spirit answered and said,
"Jesus I know, and Paul I know; but who are you?"
[16]Then the man in whom the evil spirit was
leaped on them, overpowered[1] them, and pre-
vailed against them,[2] so that they fled out of
that house naked and wounded. [17]This became
known both to all Jews and Greeks dwelling
in Ephesus; and [a]fear fell on them all, and the
name of the Lord Jesus was magnified. [18]And
many who had believed came [a]confessing and
telling their deeds. [19]Also, many of those who
had practiced magic brought their books togeth-
er and burned *them* in the sight of all. And they
counted up the value of them, and *it* totaled fifty
thousand *pieces* of silver. [20][a]So the word of the
Lord grew mightily and prevailed.

### *THE RIOT AT EPHESUS*

[21][a]When these things were accomplished,
Paul [b]purposed in the Spirit, when he had passed
through [c]Macedonia and Achaia, to go to Jeru-
salem, saying, "After I have been there, [d]I must
also see Rome." [22]So he sent into Macedonia two
of those who ministered to him, [a]Timothy and
[b]Erastus, but he himself stayed in Asia for a time.

**19:5** [a] Acts 8:12, 16; 10:48 **19:6** [a] Acts 6:6; 8:17 [b] Acts 2:4; 10:46 **19:8** [a] Acts 17:2; 18:4 [b] Acts 1:3; 28:23 **19:9** [a] 2 Tim. 1:15 [b] Acts 9:2; 19:23; 22:4; 24:14 **19:10** [a] Acts 19:8; 20:31 **19:11** [a] Mark 16:20 **19:12** [a] Acts 5:15 **19:13** [a] Matt. 12:27 [b] Mark 9:38 [c] 1 Cor. 1:23; 2:2 [1] NU-Text reads *I.* **19:16** [1] M-Text reads *and they overpowered.* [2] NU-Text reads *both of them.* **19:17** [a] Luke 1:65; 7:16 **19:18** [a] Matt. 3:6 **19:20** [a] Acts 6:7; 12:24 **19:21** [a] Rom. 15:25 [b] Acts 20:22 [c] Acts 20:1 [d] Rom. 1:13; 15:22–29 **19:22** [a] 1 Tim. 1:2 [b] Rom. 16:23

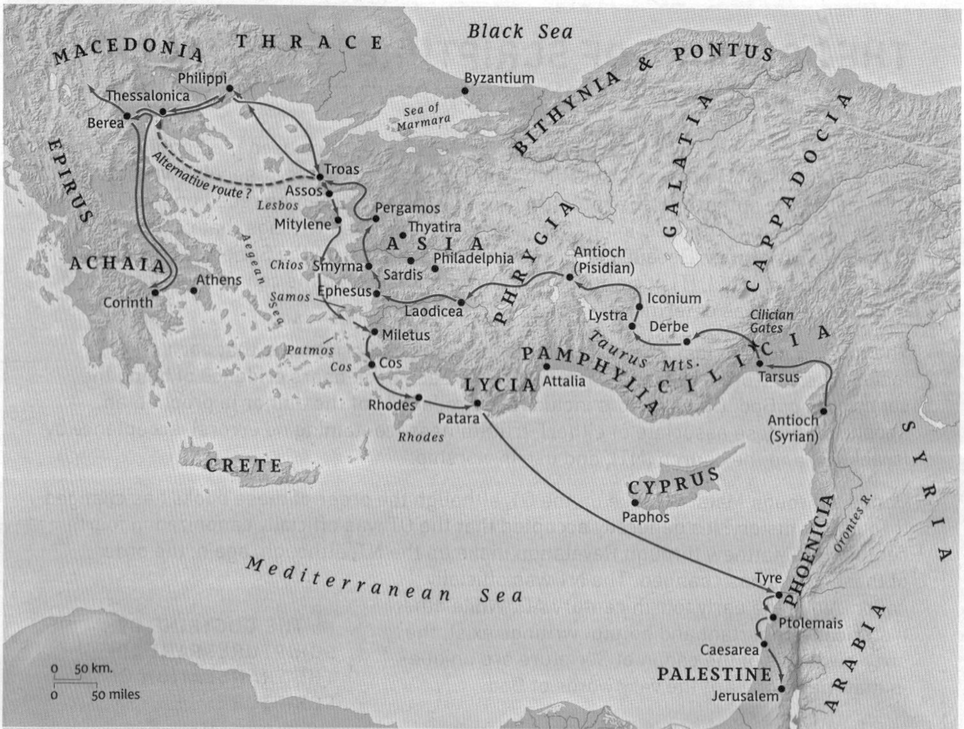


## PAUL'S THIRD MISSIONARY JOURNEY
ACTS 18:23—21:16 (C. AD 53–57)

23 And [a]about that time there arose a great
commotion about [b]the Way. 24 For a certain man
named Demetrius, a silversmith, who made
silver shrines of Diana,[1] brought [a]no small profit
to the craftsmen. 25 He called them together with
the workers of similar occupation, and said:
"Men, you know that we have our prosperity by
this trade. 26 Moreover you see and hear that not
only at Ephesus, but throughout almost all Asia,
this Paul has persuaded and turned away many
people, saying that [a]they are not gods which are
made with hands. 27 So not only is this trade of
ours in danger of falling into disrepute, but
also the temple of the great goddess Diana may
be despised and her magnificence destroyed,[1]
whom all Asia and the world worship."

28 Now when they heard *this,* they were full
of wrath and cried out, saying, "Great *is* Diana
of the Ephesians!" 29 So the whole city was filled
with confusion, and rushed into the theater with
one accord, having seized [a]Gaius and [b]Aristar-
chus, Macedonians, Paul's travel companions.
30 And when Paul wanted to go in to the people,
the disciples would not allow him. 31 Then some
of the officials of Asia, who were his friends,
sent to him pleading that he would not venture
into the theater. 32 Some therefore cried one
thing and some another, for the assembly was
confused, and most of them did not know why
they had come together. 33 And they drew Al-
exander out of the multitude, the Jews putting
him forward. And [a]Alexander [b]motioned with
his hand, and wanted to make his defense to
the people. 34 But when they found out that he
was a Jew, all with one voice cried out for about
two hours, "Great *is* Diana of the Ephesians!"
35 And when the city clerk had quieted the
crowd, he said: "Men of Ephesus, what man is
there who does not know that the city of the

**19:35** The Greek goddess Artemis had a different Roman name—**Diana**. The **temple** built in her honor in **Ephesus** was one of the seven wonders of the ancient world. The temple boasted more than one hundred columns, each five stories tall. Inside the temple was an image of Diana, carved into a stone that many scholars believe was a meteorite. Worshipers of the goddess claimed the stone had been sent from heaven by **Zeus**, the god of gods.

**19:23** [a] 2 Cor. 1:8 [b] Acts 9:2 **19:24** [a] Acts 16:16, 19 [1] Greek *Artemis* **19:26** [a] Is. 44:10–20 **19:27** [1] NU-Text reads *she be deposed from her magnificence.* **19:29** [a] Rom. 16:23 [b] Col. 4:10 **19:33** [a] 1 Tim. 1:20; 2 Tim. 4:14 [b] Acts 12:17

Ephesians is temple guardian of the great goddess Diana, and of the *image* which fell down from Zeus? 36 Therefore, since these things cannot be denied, you ought to be quiet and do nothing rashly. 37 For you have brought these men here who are neither robbers of temples nor blasphemers of your[1] goddess. 38 Therefore, if Demetrius and his fellow craftsmen have a case against anyone, the courts are open and there are proconsuls. Let them bring charges against one another. 39 But if you have any other inquiry to make, it shall be determined in the lawful assembly. 40 For we are in danger of being called in question for today's uproar, there being no reason which we may give to account for this disorderly gathering." 41 And when he had said these things, he dismissed the assembly.

### JOURNEYS IN GREECE

**20** After the uproar had ceased, Paul called the disciples to *himself,* embraced *them,* and [a]departed to go to Macedonia. 2 Now when he had gone over that region and encouraged them with many words, he came to [a]Greece 3 and stayed three months. And [a]when the Jews plotted against him as he was about to sail to Syria, he decided to return through Macedonia. 4 And Sopater of Berea accompanied him to Asia—also [a]Aristarchus and Secundus of the Thessalonians, and [b]Gaius of Derbe, and [c]Timothy, and [d]Tychicus and [e]Trophimus of Asia. 5 These men, going ahead, waited for us at [a]Troas. 6 But we sailed away from Philippi after [a]the Days of Unleavened Bread, and in five days joined them [b]at Troas, where we stayed seven days.

> **20:6** The Feast of **Unleavened Bread** was part of the annual Passover celebration. When Moses and the Israelites left Egypt, they were in a hurry. There was no time for them to prepare food or to wait for bread to rise, thus they made "unleavened bread," or bread without yeast. Today unleavened bread is called matzo.

### MINISTERING AT TROAS

7 Now on [a]the first *day* of the week, when the disciples came together [b]to break bread, Paul, ready to depart the next day, spoke to them and continued his message until midnight. 8 There were many lamps [a]in the upper room where they[1] were gathered together. 9 And in a window sat a certain young man named Eutychus, who was sinking into a deep sleep. He was overcome by sleep; and as Paul continued speaking, he fell down from the third story and was taken up dead. 10 But Paul went down, [a]fell on him, and embracing *him* said, [b]"Do not trouble yourselves, for his life is in him." 11 Now when he had come up, had broken bread and eaten, and talked a long while, even till daybreak, he departed. 12 And they brought the young man in alive, and they were not a little comforted.

### FROM TROAS TO MILETUS

13 Then we went ahead to the ship and sailed to Assos, there intending to take Paul on board; for so he had given orders, intending himself to go on foot. 14 And when he met us at Assos, we took him on board and came to Mitylene. 15 We sailed from there, and the next *day* came opposite Chios. The following *day* we arrived at Samos and stayed at Trogyllium. The next *day* we came to Miletus. 16 For Paul had decided to sail past Ephesus, so that he would not have to spend time in Asia; for [a]he was hurrying [b]to be at Jerusalem, if possible, on [c]the Day of Pentecost.

### THE EPHESIAN ELDERS EXHORTED

17 From Miletus he sent to Ephesus and called for the elders of the church. 18 And when they had come to him, he said to them: "You know, [a]from the first day that I came to Asia, in what manner I always lived among you, 19 serving the Lord with all humility, with many tears and trials which happened to me [a]by the plotting of the Jews; 20 how [a]I kept back nothing that was helpful, but proclaimed it to you, and taught you publicly and from house to house, 21 [a]testifying to Jews, and also to Greeks, [b]repentance toward God and faith toward our Lord Jesus Christ. 22 And see, now [a]I go bound in the spirit to Jerusalem, not knowing the things that will happen to me there, 23 except that [a]the Holy Spirit testifies in every city, saying that chains and tribulations await me. 24 But [a]none of these things move me; nor do I count my life dear to myself,[1] [b]so that I may finish my race with joy, [c]and the ministry [d]which I received from the Lord Jesus, to testify to the gospel of the grace of God.

25 "And indeed, now I know that you all, among whom I have gone preaching the kingdom of God, will see my face no more. 26 Therefore I testify to you this day that I *am* [a]innocent of the blood of all *men.* 27 For I have not shunned to declare to you [a]the whole counsel of God. 28 [a]Therefore take heed to yourselves and to all the flock, among which the Holy Spirit [b]has made you overseers, to shepherd the church of

**19:37** [1] NU-Text reads *our.* **20:1** [a] 1 Cor. 16:5; 1 Tim. 1:3 **20:2** [a] Acts 17:15; 18:1 **20:3** [a] Acts 9:23; 23:12; 25:3; 2 Cor. 11:26 **20:4** [a] Acts 19:29; Col. 4:10 [b] Acts 19:29 [c] Acts 16:1 [d] Eph. 6:21; Col. 4:7; 2 Tim. 4:12; Titus 3:12 [e] Acts 21:29; 2 Tim. 4:20 **20:5** [a] 2 Cor. 2:12; 2 Tim. 4:13 **20:6** [a] Ex. 12:14, 15 [b] Acts 16:8; 2 Cor. 2:12; 2 Tim. 4:13 **20:7** [a] 1 Cor. 16:2; Rev. 1:10 [b] Acts 2:42, 46; 20:11; 1 Cor. 10:16 **20:8** [a] Acts 1:13 [1] NU-Text and M-Text read *we.* **20:10** [a] 1 Kin. 17:21; 2 Kin. 4:34 [b] Matt. 9:23, 24; Mark 5:39 **20:16** [a] Acts 18:21; 19:21; 21:4 [b] Acts 24:17 [c] Acts 2:1; 1 Cor. 16:8 **20:18** [a] Acts 18:19; 19:1, 10; 20:4, 16 **20:19** [a] Acts 20:3 **20:20** [a] Acts 20:27 **20:21** [a] Acts 18:5; 19:10 [b] Mark 1:15 **20:22** [a] Acts 19:21 **20:23** [a] Acts 21:4, 11 **20:24** [a] Acts 21:13 [b] 2 Tim. 4:7 [c] Acts 1:17 [d] Gal. 1:1 [1] NU-Text reads *But I do not count my life of any value or dear to myself.* **20:26** [a] Acts 18:6 **20:27** [a] Luke 7:30 **20:28** [a] 1 Pet. 5:2 [b] 1 Cor. 12:28

LIVE THE TRUTH

## SERVING OTHERS

**20:18–21** Serving is a huge part of what it means to be a Christian. Jesus said it's the path to leadership and lasting kingdom work (see Luke 22:24–27). Of course, Jesus was the greatest servant the world has ever seen; therefore, service must be something we value too. To serve is to give of yourself—resources, time, and energy—to others. It's not done out of selfish ambition or vain conceit (see Phil. 2:5–11), but rather out of deep gratitude for what our Savior has done for us.

Here, as Paul recounted his time in Ephesus, he provided a blueprint for service. What Paul did, he did for the Lord, not himself. He served with humility, even when it was difficult. He gave more than was expected, holding nothing back. And most importantly, all his service was done with the gospel in mind. Basically, he served in the footsteps of Jesus. We can do many things to serve—and they all should be done. But as we serve, we must never forget to point people to the ultimate Servant, Jesus. Whenever we give of ourselves, it's because the gospel is alive in us.

God[1] [c]which He purchased [d]with His own blood.
29 For I know this, that after my departure [a]sav-
age wolves will come in among you, not sparing
the flock. 30 Also [a]from among yourselves men
will rise up, speaking perverse things, to draw
away the disciples after themselves. 31 Therefore
watch, and remember that [a]for three years I
did not cease to warn everyone night and day
with tears.
32 "So now, brethren, I commend you to God
and [a]to the word of His grace, which is able [b]to
build you up and give you [c]an inheritance among
all those who are sanctified. 33 I have coveted no
one's silver or gold or apparel. 34 Yes,[1] you your-
selves know [a]that these hands have provided for
my necessities, and for those who were with me.
35 I have shown you in every way, [a]by laboring
like this, that you must support the weak. And
remember the words of the Lord Jesus, that He
said, 'It is more blessed to give than to receive.'"
36 And when he had said these things, he
knelt down and prayed with them all. 37 Then
they all [a]wept freely, and [b]fell on Paul's neck and
kissed him, 38 sorrowing most of all for the words
which he spoke, that they would see his face no
more. And they accompanied him to the ship.

### *WARNINGS ON THE JOURNEY TO JERUSALEM*

21 Now it came to pass, that when we had
departed from them and set sail, running
a straight course we came to Cos, the following
*day* to Rhodes, and from there to Patara. 2 And
finding a ship sailing over to Phoenicia, we went
aboard and set sail. 3 When we had sighted Cy-
prus, we passed it on the left, sailed to Syria, and
landed at Tyre; for there the ship was to unload
her cargo. 4 And finding disciples,[1] we stayed
there seven days. [a]They told Paul through the
Spirit not to go up to Jerusalem. 5 When we had
come to the end of those days, we departed and
went on our way; and they all accompanied us,
with wives and children, till *we were* out of the
city. And [a]we knelt down on the shore and prayed.
6 When we had taken our leave of one another,
we boarded the ship, and they returned [a]home.
7 And when we had finished *our* voyage from
Tyre, we came to Ptolemais, greeted the brethren,
and stayed with them one day. 8 On the next *day* we
who were Paul's companions[1] departed and came
to [a]Caesarea, and entered the house of Philip [b]the
evangelist, [c]who was *one* of the seven, and stayed
with him. 9 Now this man had four virgin daughters
[a]who prophesied. 10 And as we stayed many days,
a certain prophet named [a]Agabus came down
from Judea. 11 When he had come to us, he took
Paul's belt, bound his *own* hands and feet, and
said, "Thus says the Holy Spirit, [a]'So shall the Jews
at Jerusalem bind the man who owns this belt,
and deliver *him* into the hands of the Gentiles.'"
12 Now when we heard these things, both we
and those from that place pleaded with him not
to go up to Jerusalem. 13 Then Paul answered,
[a]"What do you mean by weeping and breaking
my heart? For I am ready not only to be bound,
but also to die at Jerusalem for the name of the
Lord Jesus."
14 So when he would not be persuaded, we
ceased, saying, [a]"The will of the Lord be done."

### *PAUL URGED TO MAKE PEACE*

15 And after those days we packed and went
up to Jerusalem. 16 Also some of the disciples
from Caesarea went with us and brought with

20:28 [c] Eph. 1:7, 14 [d] Heb. 9:14 [1] M-Text reads *of the Lord and God.* 20:29 [a] Matt. 7:15 20:30 [a] 1 Tim. 1:20 20:31 [a] Acts 19:8, 10; 24:17 20:32 [a] Heb. 13:9 [b] Acts 9:31 [c] [Heb. 9:15] 20:34 [a] Acts 18:3 [1] NU-Text and M-Text omit *Yes.* 20:35 [a] Rom. 15:1 20:37 [a] Acts 21:13 [b] Gen. 45:14 21:4 [a] [Acts 20:23; 21:12] [1] NU-Text reads *the disciples.* 21:5 [a] Acts 9:40; 20:36 21:6 [a] John 1:11 21:8 [a] Acts 8:40; 21:16 [b] Eph. 4:11 [c] Acts 6:5 [1] NU-Text omits *who were Paul's companions.* 21:9 [a] Joel 2:28 21:10 [a] Acts 11:28 21:11 [a] Acts 20:23; 21:33; 22:25 21:13 [a] Acts 20:24, 37 21:14 [a] Luke 11:2; 22:42

them a certain Mnason of Cyprus, an early dis-
ciple, with whom we were to lodge.
17 [a]And when we had come to Jerusalem, the
brethren received us gladly. 18 On the following
*day* Paul went in with us to [a]James, and all the
elders were present. 19 When he had greeted
them, [a]he told in detail those things which
God had done among the Gentiles [b]through
his ministry. 20 And when they heard *it,* they
glorified the Lord. And they said to him, "You
see, brother, how many myriads of Jews there
are who have believed, and they are all [a]zealous
for the law; 21 but they have been informed about
you that you teach all the Jews who are among
the Gentiles to forsake Moses, saying that they
ought not to circumcise *their* children nor to
walk according to the customs. 22 What then?
The assembly must certainly meet, for they will[1]
hear that you have come. 23 Therefore do what
we tell you: We have four men who have taken a
vow. 24 Take them and be purified with them, and
pay their expenses so that they may [a]shave *their*
heads, and that all may know that those things
of which they were informed concerning you are
nothing, but *that* you yourself also walk orderly
and keep the law. 25 But concerning the Gentiles
who believe, [a]we have written *and* decided that
they should observe no such thing, except[1] that
they should keep themselves from *things* offered
to idols, from blood, from things strangled, and
from sexual immorality."

### *ARRESTED IN THE TEMPLE*

26 Then Paul took the men, and the next
day, having been purified with them, [a]entered
the temple [b]to announce the expiration of the
days of purification, at which time an offering
should be made for each one of them.
27 Now when the seven days were almost
ended, [a]the Jews from Asia, seeing him in the
temple, stirred up the whole crowd and [b]laid
hands on him, 28 crying out, "Men of Israel, help!
This is the man [a]who teaches all *men* everywhere
against the people, the law, and this place; and
furthermore he also brought Greeks into the
temple and has defiled this holy place." 29 (For
they had previously[1] seen [a]Trophimus the Ephe-
sian with him in the city, whom they supposed
that Paul had brought into the temple.)
30 And [a]all the city was disturbed; and the
people ran together, seized Paul, and dragged
him out of the temple; and immediately the
doors were shut. 31 Now as they were [a]seeking to
kill him, news came to the commander of the
garrison that all Jerusalem was in an uproar.
32 [a]He immediately took soldiers and centurions,
and ran down to them. And when they saw the
commander and the soldiers, they stopped
beating Paul. 33 Then the [a]commander came
near and took him, and [b]commanded *him* to be
bound with two chains; and he asked who he was
and what he had done. 34 And some among the
multitude cried one thing and some another.
So when he could not ascertain the truth
because of the tumult, he commanded him to
be taken into the barracks. 35 When he reached
the stairs, he had to be carried by the soldiers
because of the violence of the mob. 36 For the
multitude of the people followed after, crying
out, [a]"Away with him!"

### *ADDRESSING THE JERUSALEM MOB*

*(Acts 9:1–19; 26:12–18)*

37 Then as Paul was about to be led into the
barracks, he said to the commander, "May I speak
to you?"
He replied, "Can you speak Greek? 38 [a]Are you
not the Egyptian who some time ago stirred up
a rebellion and led the four thousand assassins
out into the wilderness?"
39 But Paul said, [a]"I am a Jew from Tarsus, in
Cilicia, a citizen of no mean city; and I implore
you, permit me to speak to the people."
40 So when he had given him permission,
Paul stood on the stairs and [a]motioned with
his hand to the people. And when there was a
great silence, he spoke to *them* in the [b]Hebrew
language, saying,

**22** "Brethren[a] and fathers, hear my defense
before you now." 2 And when they heard
that he spoke to them in the [a]Hebrew language,
they kept all the more silent.
Then he said: 3 [a]"I am indeed a Jew, born in
Tarsus of Cilicia, but brought up in this city [b]at
the feet of [c]Gamaliel, taught [d]according to the
strictness of our fathers' law, and [e]was zealous
toward God [f]as you all are today. 4 [a]I persecuted
this Way to the death, binding and delivering
into prisons both men and women, 5 as also
the high priest bears me witness, and [a]all the
council of the elders, [b]from whom I also received
letters to the brethren, and went to Damascus
[c]to bring in chains even those who were there
to Jerusalem to be punished.
6 "Now [a]it happened, as I journeyed and
came near Damascus at about noon, suddenly a
great light from heaven shone around me. 7 And
I fell to the ground and heard a voice saying to
me, 'Saul, Saul, why are you persecuting Me?'
8 So I answered, 'Who are You, Lord?' And He
said to me, 'I am Jesus of Nazareth, whom you
are persecuting.'

**21:17** [a]Acts 15:4 **21:18** [a]Gal. 1:19; 2:9 **21:19** [a]Rom. 15:18, 19 [b]Acts 1:17; 20:24 **21:20** [a]Acts 15:1; 22:3 **21:22** [1]NU-Text reads *What then is to be done? They will certainly.* **21:24** [a]Acts 18:18 **21:25** [a]Acts 15:19, 20, 29 [1]NU-Text omits *that they should observe no such thing, except.* **21:26** [a]Acts 21:24; 24:18 [b]Num. 6:13 **21:27** [a]Acts 20:19; 24:18 [b]Acts 26:21 **21:28** [a]Acts 6:13; 24:6 **21:29** [a]Acts 20:4 [1]M-Text omits *previously.* **21:30** [a]Acts 16:19; 26:21 **21:31** [a]2 Cor. 11:23 **21:32** [a]Acts 23:27; 24:7 **21:33** [a]Acts 24:7 [b]Acts 20:23; 21:11 **21:36** [a]John 19:15 **21:38** [a]Acts 5:36 **21:39** [a]Acts 9:11; 22:3 **21:40** [a]Acts 12:17 [b]Acts 22:2 **22:1** [a]Acts 7:2 **22:2** [a]Acts 21:40 **22:3** [a]2 Cor. 11:22 [b]Deut. 33:3 [c]Acts 5:34 [d]Acts 23:6; 26:5 [e]Gal. 1:14 [f][Rom. 10:2] **22:4** [a]1 Tim. 1:13 **22:5** [a]Acts 23:14; 24:1; 25:15 [b]Luke 22:66 [c]Acts 9:2 **22:6** [a]Acts 9:3; 26:12, 13

9 "And [a]those who were with me indeed saw
the light and were afraid,[1] but they did not hear
the voice of Him who spoke to me. 10 So I said,
'What shall I do, Lord?' And the Lord said to me,
'Arise and go into Damascus, and there you will
be told all things which are appointed for you
to do.' 11 And since I could not see for the glory
of that light, being led by the hand of those who
were with me, I came into Damascus.
12 "Then [a]a certain Ananias, a devout man
according to the law, [b]having a good testimony
with all the [c]Jews who dwelt *there,* 13 came to
me; and he stood and said to me, 'Brother Saul,
receive your sight.' And at that same hour I
looked up at him. 14 Then he said, [a]'The God of
our fathers [b]has chosen you that you should
[c]know His will, and [d]see the Just One, [e]and hear
the voice of His mouth. 15 [a]For you will be His
witness to all men of [b]what you have seen and
heard. 16 And now why are you waiting? Arise and
be baptized, [a]and wash away your sins, [b]calling
on the name of the Lord.'
17 "Now [a]it happened, when I returned to
Jerusalem and was praying in the temple, that
I was in a trance 18 and [a]saw Him saying to me,
[b]'Make haste and get out of Jerusalem quickly,
for they will not receive your testimony con-
cerning Me.' 19 So I said, 'Lord, [a]they know that
in every synagogue I imprisoned and [b]beat
those who believe on You. 20 [a]And when the
blood of Your martyr Stephen was shed, I also
was standing by [b]consenting to his death,[1] and
guarding the clothes of those who were killing
him.' 21 Then He said to me, 'Depart, [a]for I will
send you far from here to the Gentiles.' "

### *PAUL'S ROMAN CITIZENSHIP*

22 And they listened to him until this word,
and *then* they raised their voices and said, [a]"Away
with such a *fellow* from the earth, for [b]he is not
fit to live!" 23 Then, as they cried out and tore
off *their* clothes and threw dust into the air,
24 the commander ordered him to be brought
into the barracks, and said that he should be
examined under scourging, so that he might
know why they shouted so against him. 25 And
as they bound him with thongs, Paul said to
the centurion who stood by, [a]"Is it lawful for
you to scourge a man who is a Roman, and
uncondemned?"
26 When the centurion heard *that,* he went
and told the commander, saying, "Take care
what you do, for this man is a Roman."
27 Then the commander came and said to
him, "Tell me, are you a Roman?"
He said, "Yes."

> **22:28** Roman **citizenship** was originally limited to free Romans, but later it was offered to many others in the empire, either as a reward for outstanding service, or in exchange for a high price. Because Paul's father was a Roman citizen, Paul **was born a citizen**. Ultimately, God used Paul's Roman citizenship to spread the gospel in Rome.

28 The commander answered, "With a large
sum I obtained this citizenship."
And Paul said, "But I was born *a citizen.*"
29 Then immediately those who were about to
examine him withdrew from him; and the com-
mander was also afraid after he found out that
he was a Roman, and because he had bound him.

### *THE SANHEDRIN DIVIDED*

30 The next day, because he wanted to know
for certain why he was accused by the Jews, he
released him from *his* bonds, and commanded
the chief priests and all their council to appear,
and brought Paul down and set him before them.

**23** Then Paul, looking earnestly at the coun-
cil, said, "Men *and* brethren, [a]I have lived
in all good conscience before God until this day."
2 And the high priest Ananias commanded those
who stood by him [a]to strike him on the mouth.
3 Then Paul said to him, "God will strike you,
*you* whitewashed wall! For you sit to judge me
according to the law, and [a]do you command me
to be struck contrary to the law?"
4 And those who stood by said, "Do you revile
God's high priest?"
5 Then Paul said, [a]"I did not know, brethren,
that he was the high priest; for it is written, [b]'You
shall not speak evil of a ruler of your people.' "[1]
6 But when Paul perceived that one part were
Sadducees and the other Pharisees, he cried out
in the council, "Men *and* brethren, [a]I am a Phar-
isee, the son of a Pharisee; [b]concerning the hope
and resurrection of the dead I am being judged!"
7 And when he had said this, a dissension
arose between the Pharisees and the Sadducees;
and the assembly was divided. 8 [a]For Sadducees
say that there is no resurrection—and no angel
or spirit; but the Pharisees confess both. 9 Then
there arose a loud outcry. And the scribes of the
Pharisees' party arose and protested, saying,
[a]"We find no evil in this man; but [b]if a spirit or
an angel has spoken to him, [c]let us not fight
against God."[1]

**22:9** [a] Acts 9:7 [1] NU-Text omits *and were afraid.* **22:12** [a] Acts 9:17 [b] Acts 10:22 [c] 1 Tim. 3:7 **22:14** [a] Acts 3:13; 5:30 [b] Acts 9:15; 26:16 [c] Acts 3:14; 7:52 [d] 1 Cor. 9:1; 15:8 [e] Gal. 1:12 **22:15** [a] Acts 23:11 [b] Acts 4:20; 26:16 **22:16** [a] Heb. 10:22 [b] Rom. 10:13 **22:17** [a] Acts 9:26; 26:20 **22:18** [a] Acts 22:14 [b] Matt. 10:14 **22:19** [a] Acts 8:3; 22:4 [b] Matt. 10:17 **22:20** [a] Acts 7:54—8:1 [b] Luke 11:48 [1] NU-Text omits *to his death.* **22:21** [a] Acts 9:15 **22:22** [a] Acts 21:36 [b] Acts 25:24 **22:25** [a] Acts 16:37 **23:1** [a] 2 Tim. 1:3 **23:2** [a] John 18:22 **23:3** [a] Lev. 19:35; Deut. 25:1, 2; John 7:51 **23:5** [a] Lev. 5:17, 18 [b] Ex. 22:28; Eccl. 10:20; 2 Pet. 2:10 [1] Exodus 22:28 **23:6** [a] Acts 26:5; Phil. 3:5 [b] Acts 24:15, 21; 26:6; 28:20 **23:8** [a] Matt. 22:23; Mark 12:18; Luke 20:27 **23:9** [a] Acts 25:25; 26:31 [b] John 12:29; Acts 22:6, 7, 17, 18 [c] Acts 5:39
[1] NU-Text omits last clause and reads *what if a spirit or an angel has spoken to him?*

10 Now when there arose a great dissen-
sion, the commander, fearing lest Paul might
be pulled to pieces by them, commanded the
soldiers to go down and take him by force
from among them, and bring *him* into the
barracks.

### THE PLOT AGAINST PAUL

11 But [a]the following night the Lord stood
by him and said, "Be of good cheer, Paul; for as
you have testified for Me in [b]Jerusalem, so you
must also bear witness at [c]Rome."
12 And when it was day, [a]some of the Jews
banded together and bound themselves under
an oath, saying that they would neither eat nor
drink till they had [b]killed Paul. 13 Now there were
more than forty who had formed this conspiracy.
14 They came to the chief priests and [a]elders,
and said, "We have bound ourselves under a
great oath that we will eat nothing until we have
killed Paul. 15 Now you, therefore, together with
the council, suggest to the commander that he
be brought down to you tomorrow,[1] as though
you were going to make further inquiries con-
cerning him; but we are ready to kill him before
he comes near."
16 So when Paul's sister's son heard of their
ambush, he went and entered the barracks and
told Paul. 17 Then Paul called one of the centu-
rions to *him* and said, "Take this young man to
the commander, for he has something to tell
him." 18 So he took him and brought *him* to the
commander and said, "Paul the prisoner called
me to *him* and asked *me* to bring this young
man to you. He has something to say to you."
19 Then the commander took him by the
hand, went aside, and asked privately, "What is
it that you have to tell me?"
20 And he said, [a]"The Jews have agreed to
ask that you bring Paul down to the council
tomorrow, as though they were going to inquire
more fully about him. 21 But do not yield to them,
for more than forty of them lie in wait for him,
men who have bound themselves by an oath
that they will neither eat nor drink till they have
killed him; and now they are ready, waiting for
the promise from you."
22 So the commander let the young man
depart, and commanded *him*, "Tell no one that
you have revealed these things to me."

### SENT TO FELIX

23 And he called for two centurions, say-
ing, "Prepare two hundred soldiers, seventy
horsemen, and two hundred spearmen to go to
[a]Caesarea at the third hour of the night; 24 and
provide mounts to set Paul on, and bring *him*
safely to Felix the governor." 25 He wrote a letter
in the following manner:

26 Claudius Lysias,

To the most excellent governor Felix:

Greetings.

27 [a]This man was seized by the Jews and
was about to be killed by them. Coming
with the troops I rescued him, having
learned that he was a Roman. 28 [a]And
when I wanted to know the reason they
accused him, I brought him before
their council. 29 I found out that he was
accused [a]concerning questions of their
law, [b]but had nothing charged against him
deserving of death or chains. 30 And [a]when
it was told me that the Jews lay in wait for
the man,[1] I sent him immediately to you,
and [b]also commanded his accusers to
state before you the charges against him.

Farewell.

31 Then the soldiers, as they were command-
ed, took Paul and brought *him* by night to An-
tipatris. 32 The next day they left the horsemen
to go on with him, and returned to the barracks.
33 When they came to [a]Caesarea and had de-
livered the [b]letter to the governor, they also
presented Paul to him. 34 And when the gover-
nor had read *it*, he asked what province he was
from. And when he understood that *he was* from
[a]Cilicia, 35 he said, [a]"I will hear you when your
accusers also have come." And he commanded
him to be kept in [b]Herod's Praetorium.

### ACCUSED OF SEDITION

24 Now after [a]five days [b]Ananias the high
priest came down with the elders and
a certain orator *named* Tertullus. These gave
evidence to the governor against Paul.
2 And when he was called upon, Tertullus be-
gan his accusation, saying: "Seeing that through
you we enjoy great peace, and prosperity is being
brought to this nation by your foresight, 3 we
accept *it* always and in all places, most noble
Felix, with all thankfulness. 4 Nevertheless, not
to be tedious to you any further, I beg you to
hear, by your courtesy, a few words from us. 5 [a]For
we have found this man a plague, a creator of
dissension among all the Jews throughout the
world, and a ringleader of the sect of the Naz-
arenes. 6 [a]He even tried to profane the temple,
and we seized him,[1] and wanted [b]to judge him

**23:11** [a] Acts 18:9; 27:23, 24 [b] Acts 21:18, 19; 22:1–21 [c] Acts 28:16, 17, 23 **23:12** [a] Acts 23:21, 30; 25:3 [b] Acts 9:23, 24; 25:3; 26:21; 27:42; 1 Thess. 2:15 **23:14** [a] Acts 4:5, 23; 6:12; 22:5; 24:1; 25:15 **23:15** [1] NU-Text omits *tomorrow*. **23:20** [a] Acts 23:12 **23:23** [a] Acts 8:40; 23:33 **23:27** [a] Acts 21:30, 33; 24:7 **23:28** [a] Acts 22:30 **23:29** [a] Acts 18:15; 25:19 [b] Acts 25:25; 26:31 **23:30** [a] Acts 23:20 [b] Acts 24:8; 25:6 [1] NU-Text reads *there would be a plot against the man.* **23:33** [a] Acts 8:40 [b] Acts 23:26–30 **23:34** [a] Acts 6:9; 21:39 **23:35** [a] Acts 24:1, 10; 25:16 [b] Matt. 27:27 **24:1** [a] Acts 21:27 [b] Acts 23:2, 30, 35; 25:2 **24:5** [a] 1 Pet. 2:12, 15 **24:6** [a] Acts 21:28 [b] John 18:31 [1] NU-Text ends the sentence here and omits the rest of verse 6, all of verse 7, and the first clause of verse 8.

according to our law. 7 [a]But the commander
Lysias came by and with great violence took *him*
out of our hands, 8 [a]commanding his accusers
to come to you. By examining him yourself you
may ascertain all these things of which we accuse
him." 9 And the Jews also assented,[1] maintaining
that these things were so.

### THE DEFENSE BEFORE FELIX

10 Then Paul, after the governor had nodded
to him to speak, answered: "Inasmuch as I know
that you have been for many years a judge of
this nation, I do the more cheerfully answer
for myself, 11 because you may ascertain that
it is no more than twelve days since I went up
to Jerusalem [a]to worship. 12 [a]And they neither
found me in the temple disputing with anyone
nor inciting the crowd, either in the synagogues
or in the city. 13 Nor can they prove the things of
which they now accuse me. 14 But this I confess
to you, that according to [a]the Way which they
call a sect, so I worship the [b]God of my fathers,
believing all things which are written in [c]the
Law and in the Prophets. 15 [a]I have hope in God,
which they themselves also accept, [b]that there
will be a resurrection of *the* dead,[1] both of *the* just
and *the* unjust. 16 [a]This *being* so, I myself always
strive to have a conscience without offense
toward God and men.

17 "Now after many years [a]I came to bring
alms and offerings to my nation, 18 [a]in the midst
of which some Jews from Asia found me [b]puri-
fied in the temple, neither with a mob nor with
tumult. 19 [a]They ought to have been here before
you to object if they had anything against me.
20 Or else let those who are *here* themselves say if
they found any wrongdoing[1] in me while I stood
before the council, 21 unless *it is* for this one
statement which I cried out, standing among
them, [a]'Concerning the resurrection of the dead
I am being judged by you this day.' "

### FELIX PROCRASTINATES

22 But when Felix heard these things, hav-
ing more accurate knowledge of *the* [a]Way, he
adjourned the proceedings and said, "When
[b]Lysias the commander comes down, I will make
a decision on your case." 23 So he commanded
the centurion to keep Paul and to let *him* have
liberty, and [a]told him not to forbid any of his
friends to provide for or visit him.

24 And after some days, when Felix came
with his wife Drusilla, who was Jewish, he
sent for Paul and heard him concerning the
[a]faith in Christ. 25 Now as he reasoned about
righteousness, self-control, and the judgment
to come, Felix was afraid and answered, "Go
away for now; when I have a convenient time
I will call for you." 26 Meanwhile he also hoped
that [a]money would be given him by Paul, that
he might release him.[1] Therefore he sent for him
more often and conversed with him.

27 But after two years Porcius Festus suc-
ceeded Felix; and Felix, [a]wanting to do the Jews
a favor, left Paul bound.

### PAUL APPEALS TO CAESAR

25 Now when Festus had come to the prov-
ince, after three days he went up from
[a]Caesarea to Jerusalem. 2 [a]Then the high priest[1]
and the chief men of the Jews informed him
against Paul; and they petitioned him, 3 asking
a favor against him, that he would summon him
to Jerusalem—[a]while *they* lay in ambush along
the road to kill him. 4 But Festus answered that
Paul should be kept at Caesarea, and that he
himself was going *there* shortly. 5 "Therefore,"
he said, "let those who have authority among
you go down with *me* and accuse this man, to
see [a]if there is any fault in him."

6 And when he had remained among them
more than ten days, he went down to Caesarea.
And the next day, sitting on the judgment seat,
he commanded Paul to be brought. 7 When he
had come, the Jews who had come down from
Jerusalem stood about [a]and laid many serious
complaints against Paul, which they could not
prove, 8 while he answered for himself, [a]"Nei-
ther against the law of the Jews, nor against the
temple, nor against Caesar have I offended in
anything at all."

9 But Festus, [a]wanting to do the Jews a favor,
answered Paul and said, [b]"Are you willing to go
up to Jerusalem and there be judged before me
concerning these things?"

10 So Paul said, "I stand at Caesar's judgment
seat, where I ought to be judged. To the Jews
I have done no wrong, as you very well know.
11 [a]For if I am an offender, or have committed
anything deserving of death, I do not object to
dying; but if there is nothing in these things of
which these men accuse me, no one can deliver
me to them. [b]I appeal to Caesar."

12 Then Festus, when he had conferred with
the council, answered, "You have appealed to
Caesar? To Caesar you shall go!"

### PAUL BEFORE AGRIPPA

13 And after some days King Agrippa and Ber-
nice came to Caesarea to greet Festus. 14 When

**24:7** [a] Acts 21:33; 23:10 **24:8** [a] Acts 23:30 **24:9** [1] NU-Text and M-Text read *joined the attack.* **24:11** [a] Acts 21:15, 18, 26, 27; 24:17 **24:12** [a] Acts 25:8; 28:17 **24:14** [a] Acts 9:2; 24:22 [b] 2 Tim. 1:3 [c] Acts 26:22; 28:23 **24:15** [a] Acts 23:6; 26:6, 7; 28:20 [b] [Dan. 12:2] [1] NU-Text omits *of the dead.* **24:16** [a] Acts 23:1 **24:17** [a] Rom. 15:25–28 **24:18** [a] Acts 21:27; 26:21 [b] Acts 21:26 **24:19** [a] [Acts 23:30; 25:16] **24:20** [1] NU-Text and M-Text read *say what wrongdoing they found.* **24:21** [a] [Acts 23:6; 24:15; 28:20] **24:22** [a] Acts 9:2; 18:26; 19:9, 23; 22:4 [b] Acts 23:26; 24:7 **24:23** [a] Acts 23:16; 27:3; 28:16 **24:24** [a] [Rom. 10:9] **24:26** [a] Ex. 23:8 [1] NU-Text omits *that he might release him.* **24:27** [a] Acts 12:3; 23:35; 25:9, 14 **25:1** [a] Acts 8:40; 25:4, 6, 13 **25:2** [a] Acts 24:1; 25:15 [1] NU-Text reads *chief priests.* **25:3** [a] Acts 23:12, 15 **25:5** [a] Acts 18:14; 25:18 **25:7** [a] Mark 15:3; Luke 23:2, 10; Acts 24:5, 13 **25:8** [a] Acts 6:13; 24:12; 28:17 **25:9** [a] Acts 12:2; 24:27 [b] Acts 25:20 **25:11** [a] Acts 18:14; 23:29; 25:25; 26:31 [b] Acts 26:32; 28:19

> **25:11** If a Roman citizen thought he was not getting justice in a provincial court, he could **appeal** to the emperor himself. If the appeal was declared valid, all other proceedings in the lower courts ceased and the prisoner was sent to Rome for the disposition of his case. Because he was a Roman citizen by birth, Paul had the right to appeal his case all the way to the Roman emperor Nero.

they had been there many days, Festus laid Paul's
case before the king, saying: [a]"There is a certain
man left a prisoner by Felix, 15 [a]about whom the
chief priests and the elders of the Jews informed
*me,* when I was in Jerusalem, asking for a judg-
ment against him. 16 [a]To them I answered, 'It is
not the custom of the Romans to deliver any
man to destruction[1] before the accused meets
the accusers face to face, and has opportunity
to answer for himself concerning the charge
against him.' 17 Therefore when they had come
together, [a]without any delay, the next day I sat
on the judgment seat and commanded the man
to be brought in. 18 When the accusers stood
up, they brought no accusation against him
of such things as I supposed, 19 [a]but had some
questions against him about their own religion
and about a certain Jesus, who had died, whom
Paul affirmed to be alive. 20 And because I was
uncertain of such questions, I asked whether
he was willing to go to Jerusalem and there be
judged concerning these matters. 21 But when
Paul [a]appealed to be reserved for the decision
of Augustus, I commanded him to be kept till I
could send him to Caesar."

22 Then [a]Agrippa said to Festus, "I also would
like to hear the man myself."

"Tomorrow," he said, "you shall hear him."

23 So the next day, when Agrippa and Berni-
ce had come with great pomp, and had entered
the auditorium with the commanders and the
prominent men of the city, at Festus' command
[a]Paul was brought in. 24 And Festus said: "King
Agrippa and all the men who are here present
with us, you see this man about whom [a]the
whole assembly of the Jews petitioned me, both
at Jerusalem and here, crying out that he was
[b]not fit to live any longer. 25 But when I found
that [a]he had committed nothing deserving of
death, [b]and that he himself had appealed to Au-
gustus, I decided to send him. 26 I have nothing
certain to write to my lord concerning him.
Therefore I have brought him out before you,
and especially before you, King Agrippa, so
that after the examination has taken place I
may have something to write. 27 For it seems to
me unreasonable to send a prisoner and not to
specify the charges against him."

### *PAUL'S EARLY LIFE*

**26** Then Agrippa said to Paul, "You are per-
mitted to speak for yourself."

So Paul stretched out his hand and answered
for himself: 2 "I think myself [a]happy, King Agrip-
pa, because today I shall answer [b]for myself
before you concerning all the things of which
I am [c]accused by the Jews, 3 especially because
you are expert in all customs and questions
which have to do with the Jews. Therefore I beg
you to hear me patiently.

4 "My manner of life from my youth, which
was spent from the beginning among my own
nation at Jerusalem, all the Jews know. 5 They
knew me from the first, if they were willing to
testify, that according to [a]the strictest sect of our
religion I lived a Pharisee. 6 [a]And now I stand
and am judged for the hope of [b]the promise
made by God to our fathers. 7 To this *promise*
[a]our twelve tribes, earnestly serving *God* [b]night
and day, [c]hope to attain. For this hope's sake,
King Agrippa, I am accused by the Jews. 8 Why
should it be thought incredible by you that God
raises the dead?

9 [a]"Indeed, I myself thought I must do many
things contrary to the name of [b]Jesus of Naza-
reth. 10 [a]This I also did in Jerusalem, and many
of the saints I shut up in prison, having received
authority [b]from the chief priests; and when they
were put to death, I cast my vote against *them.*
11 [a]And I punished them often in every synagogue
and compelled *them* to blaspheme; and being
exceedingly enraged against them, I persecuted
*them* even to foreign cities.

### *PAUL RECOUNTS HIS CONVERSION*

*(Acts 9:1–19; 22:6–16)*

12 [a]"While thus occupied, as I journeyed to
Damascus with authority and commission from
the chief priests, 13 at midday, O king, along the
road I saw a light from heaven, brighter than
the sun, shining around me and those who jour-
neyed with me. 14 And when we all had fallen to
the ground, I heard a voice speaking to me and
saying in the Hebrew language, 'Saul, Saul, why
are you persecuting Me? *It is* hard for you to
kick against the goads.' 15 So I said, 'Who are You,
Lord?' And He said, 'I am Jesus, whom you are
persecuting. 16 But rise and stand on your feet; for
I have appeared to you for this purpose, [a]to make
you a minister and a witness both of the things
which you have seen and of the things which I
will yet reveal to you. 17 I will deliver you from the

**25:14** [a] Acts 24:27 **25:15** [a] Acts 24:1; 25:2, 3 **25:16** [a] Acts 25:4, 5 [1] NU-Text omits *to destruction,* although it is implied. **25:17** [a] Matt. 27:19; Acts 25:6, 10 **25:19** [a] Acts 18:14, 15; 23:29 **25:21** [a] Acts 25:11, 12 **25:22** [a] Acts 9:15 **25:23** [a] Acts 9:15 **25:24** [a] Acts 25:2, 3, 7 [b] Acts 21:36; 22:22 **25:25** [a] Acts 23:9, 29; 26:31 [b] Acts 25:11, 12 **26:2** [a] [1 Pet. 3:14; 4:14] [b] [1 Pet. 3:15, 16] [c] Acts 21:28; 24:5, 6 **26:5** [a] Phil. 3:5 **26:6** [a] Acts 23:6 [b] Acts 13:32 **26:7** [a] James 1:1 [b] 1 Thess. 3:10 [c] Phil. 3:11 **26:9** [a] 1 Tim. 1:12, 13 [b] Acts 2:22; 10:38 **26:10** [a] Acts 8:1–3; 9:13 [b] Acts 9:14 **26:11** [a] Acts 22:19 **26:12** [a] Acts 9:3–8; 22:6–11; 26:12–18 **26:16** [a] Acts 22:15

*Jewish* people, as well as *from* the Gentiles, [a]to
whom I now[1] send you, 18 [a]to open their eyes, *in*
*order* [b]to turn *them* from darkness to light, and
*from* the power of Satan to God, [c]that they may
receive forgiveness of sins and [d]an inheritance
among those who are [e]sanctified by faith in Me.'

### PAUL'S POST-CONVERSION LIFE

19 "Therefore, King Agrippa, I was not dis-
obedient to the heavenly vision, 20 but [a]declared
first to those in Damascus and in Jerusalem, and
throughout all the region of Judea, and *then* to
the Gentiles, that they should repent, turn to
God, and do [b]works befitting repentance. 21 For
these reasons the Jews seized me in the temple
and tried to kill *me.* 22 Therefore, having obtained
help from God, to this day I stand, witnessing
both to small and great, saying no other things
than those [a]which the prophets and [b]Moses said
would come— 23 [a]that the Christ would suffer,
[b]that He would be the first to rise from the dead,
and [c]would proclaim light to the *Jewish* people
and to the Gentiles."

### AGRIPPA PARRIES PAUL'S CHALLENGE

24 Now as he thus made his defense, Festus
said with a loud voice, "Paul, [a]you are beside
yourself! Much learning is driving you mad!"

25 But he said, "I am not mad, most noble
Festus, but speak the words of truth and rea-
son. 26 For the king, before whom I also speak
freely, [a]knows these things; for I am convinced
that none of these things escapes his attention,
since this thing was not done in a corner. 27 King
Agrippa, do you believe the prophets? I know
that you do believe."

28 Then Agrippa said to Paul, "You almost
persuade me to become a Christian."

29 And Paul said, [a]"I would to God that not
only you, but also all who hear me today, might
become both almost and altogether such as I
am, except for these chains."

30 When he had said these things, the king
stood up, as well as the governor and Bernice
and those who sat with them; 31 and when they
had gone aside, they talked among themselves,
saying, [a]"This man is doing nothing deserving
of death or chains."

32 Then Agrippa said to Festus, "This man
might have been set [a]free [b]if he had not appealed
to Caesar."

### THE VOYAGE TO ROME BEGINS

27 And when [a]it was decided that we should
sail to Italy, they delivered Paul and some
other prisoners to *one* named Julius, a centurion
of the Augustan Regiment. 2 So, entering a ship
of Adramyttium, we put to sea, meaning to sail
along the coasts of Asia. [a]Aristarchus, a Macedo-
nian of Thessalonica, was with us. 3 And the next
*day* we landed at Sidon. And Julius [a]treated Paul
kindly and gave *him* liberty to go to his friends
and receive care. 4 When we had put to sea from
there, we sailed under *the shelter of* Cyprus, be-
cause the winds were contrary. 5 And when we
had sailed over the sea which is off Cilicia and
Pamphylia, we came to Myra, *a city* of Lycia.
6 There the centurion found [a]an Alexandrian
ship sailing to Italy, and he put us on board.

7 When we had sailed slowly many days, and
arrived with difficulty off Cnidus, the wind not
permitting us to proceed, we sailed under *the*
*shelter of* [a]Crete off Salmone. 8 Passing it with
difficulty, we came to a place called Fair Havens,
near the city *of* Lasea.

### PAUL'S WARNING IGNORED

9 Now when much time had been spent, and
sailing was now dangerous [a]because the Fast was
already over, Paul advised them, 10 saying, "Men,
I perceive that this voyage will end with disaster
and much loss, not only of the cargo and ship,
but also our lives." 11 Nevertheless the centurion
was more persuaded by the helmsman and the
owner of the ship than by the things spoken by
Paul. 12 And because the harbor was not suitable
to winter in, the majority advised to set sail from
there also, if by any means they could reach
Phoenix, a harbor of Crete opening toward the
southwest and northwest, *and* winter *there.*

### IN THE TEMPEST

13 When the south wind blew softly, sup-
posing that they had obtained *their* desire,
putting out to sea, they sailed close by Crete.
14 But not long after, a tempestuous head wind
arose, called Euroclydon.[1] 15 So when the ship was
caught, and could not head into the wind, we let
*her* drive. 16 And running under *the shelter of* an
island called Clauda,[1] we secured the skiff with
difficulty. 17 When they had taken it on board,
they used cables to undergird the ship; and fear-
ing lest they should run aground on the Syrtis[1]
*Sands,* they struck sail and so were driven. 18 And
because we were exceedingly tempest-tossed,
the next *day* they lightened the ship. 19 On the
third *day* [a]we threw the ship's tackle overboard
with our own hands. 20 Now when neither sun
nor stars appeared for many days, and no small
tempest beat on *us,* all hope that we would be
saved was finally given up.

21 But after long abstinence from food, then
Paul stood in the midst of them and said, "Men,
you should have listened to me, and not have

**26:17** [a] Acts 22:21 [1] NU-Text and M-Text omit *now.* **26:18** [a] Is. 35:5; 42:7, 16 [b] 1 Pet. 2:9 [c] Luke 1:77 [d] Col. 1:12 [e] Acts 20:32 **26:20** [a] Acts 9:19, 20, 22; 11:26 [b] Matt. 3:8 **26:22** [a] Rom. 3:21 [b] John 5:46 **26:23** [a] Luke 24:26 [b] 1 Cor. 15:20, 23 [c] Luke 2:32 **26:24** [a] [1 Cor. 1:23; 2:13, 14; 4:10] **26:26** [a] Acts 26:3 **26:29** [a] 1 Cor. 7:7 **26:31** [a] Acts 23:9, 29; 25:25 **26:32** [a] Acts 28:18 [b] Acts 25:11 **27:1** [a] Acts 25:12, 25 **27:2** [a] Acts 19:29 **27:3** [a] Acts 24:23; 28:16 **27:6** [a] Acts 28:11 **27:7** [a] Acts 2:11; 27:12, 21; Titus 1:5, 12 **27:9** [a] Lev. 16:29–31; 23:27–29; Num. 29:7 **27:14** [1] NU-Text reads *Euraquilon.* **27:16** [1] NU-Text reads *Cauda.* **27:17** [1] M-Text reads *Syrtes.* **27:19** [a] Jon. 1:5

sailed from Crete and incurred this disaster
and loss. 22 And now I urge you to take heart,
for there will be no loss of life among you, but
only of the ship. 23 [a]For there stood by me this
night an angel of the God to whom I belong and
[b]whom I serve, 24 saying, 'Do not be afraid, Paul;
you must be brought before Caesar; and indeed
God has granted you all those who sail with you.'
25 Therefore take heart, men, [a]for I believe God
that it will be just as it was told me. 26 However,
[a]we must run aground on a certain island."
27 Now when the fourteenth night had come,
as we were driven up and down in the Adriatic
*Sea,* about midnight the sailors sensed that they
were drawing near some land. 28 And they took
soundings and found *it* to be twenty fathoms;
and when they had gone a little farther, they took
soundings again and found *it* to be fifteen fath-
oms. 29 Then, fearing lest we should run aground
on the rocks, they dropped four anchors from
the stern, and prayed for day to come. 30 And
as the sailors were seeking to escape from the
ship, when they had let down the skiff into the
sea, under pretense of putting out anchors from
the prow, 31 Paul said to the centurion and the
soldiers, "Unless these men stay in the ship, you
cannot be saved." 32 Then the soldiers cut away
the ropes of the skiff and let it fall off.
33 And as day was about to dawn, Paul im-
plored *them* all to take food, saying, "Today is the
fourteenth day you have waited and continued
without food, and eaten nothing. 34 Therefore
I urge you to take nourishment, for this is for
your survival, [a]since not a hair will fall from the
head of any of you." 35 And when he had said
these things, he took bread and [a]gave thanks to
God in the presence of them all; and when he
had broken *it* he began to eat. 36 Then they were
all encouraged, and also took food themselves.
37 And in all we were two hundred and seventy-
six [a]persons on the ship. 38 So when they had
eaten enough, they lightened the ship and threw
out the wheat into the sea.

### SHIPWRECKED ON MALTA

39 When it was day, they did not recognize the
land; but they observed a bay with a beach, onto
which they planned to run the ship if possible.
40 And they let go the anchors and left *them* in
the sea, meanwhile loosing the rudder ropes;
and they hoisted the mainsail to the wind and
made for shore. 41 But striking a place where two
seas met, [a]they ran the ship aground; and the
prow stuck fast and remained immovable, but
the stern was being broken up by the violence
of the waves.
42 And the soldiers' plan was to kill the pris-
oners, lest any of them should swim away and
escape. 43 But the centurion, wanting to save
Paul, kept them from *their* purpose, and com-
manded that those who could swim should jump
*overboard* first and get to land, 44 and the rest,
some on boards and some on *parts* of the ship.
And so it was [a]that they all escaped safely to land.

### PAUL'S MINISTRY ON MALTA

28 Now when they had escaped, they then
found out that [a]the island was called
Malta. 2 And the [a]natives showed us unusual
kindness; for they kindled a fire and made us
all welcome, because of the rain that was falling
and because of the cold. 3 But when Paul had
gathered a bundle of sticks and laid *them* on
the fire, a viper came out because of the heat,
and fastened on his hand. 4 So when the natives
saw the creature hanging from his hand, they
said to one another, "No doubt this man is a
murderer, whom, though he has escaped the

27:23 [a] Acts 18:9; 23:11; 2 Tim. 4:17 [b] Dan. 6:16; Rom. 1:9; 2 Tim. 1:3 27:25 [a] Luke 1:45; Rom. 4:20, 21; 2 Tim. 1:12 27:26 [a] Acts 28:1 27:34 [a] 1 Kin. 1:52; [Matt. 10:30; Luke 12:7; 21:18] 27:35 [a] 1 Sam. 9:13; Matt. 15:36; Mark 8:6; John 6:11; [1 Tim. 4:3, 4] 27:37 [a] Acts 2:41; 7:14; Rom. 13:1; 1 Pet. 3:20 27:41 [a] 2 Cor. 11:25 27:44 [a] Acts 27:22, 31 28:1 [a] Acts 27:26 28:2 [a] Col. 3:11

APPLY THE TRUTH

## NATURAL DISASTERS

**27:13–38** Some things happen in our world that often cause us to scratch our heads and wonder. If God is so good, why do terrible things happen? Maybe we can wrap our heads around these things when sinful people are involved, like murder, injustice, unfairness, or mistreatment. But what about things that have no human involvement, like freak accidents and natural disasters? How do we process devastating earthquakes, tsunamis, floods, and fires? The Bible's big story follows a very clear pattern: creation and commission, rebellion and redemption, new creation and commission. When humanity rebelled, it didn't just corrupt our relationship with God; it affected all of creation. The whole earth is broken and longs for redemption (see Rom. 8:20–22).

The Bible also teaches God can use natural disasters as a tool to get people to turn to Him. They can get someone's attention like nothing else. In this passage, God shows us even difficult things can work out for people's good and for the furthering of the gospel. God is in control of everything, even the storms of earth and the storms of life. When you experience a storm, look to God for peace and protection.

sea, yet justice does not allow to live." 5 But he
shook off the creature into the fire and [a]suffered
no harm. 6 However, they were expecting that
he would swell up or suddenly fall down dead.
But after they had looked for a long time and
saw no harm come to him, they changed their
minds and [a]said that he was a god.

7 In that region there was an estate of the lead-
ing citizen of the island, whose name was Publius,
who received us and entertained us courteously
for three days. 8 And it happened that the father
of Publius lay sick of a fever and dysentery. Paul
went in to him and [a]prayed, and [b]he laid his hands
on him and healed him. 9 So when this was done,
the rest of those on the island who had diseases
also came and were healed. 10 They also honored
us in many [a]ways; and when we departed, they
provided such things as were [b]necessary.

### *ARRIVAL AT ROME*

11 After three months we sailed in [a]an Alex-
andrian ship whose figurehead was the Twin
Brothers, which had wintered at the island.
12 And landing at Syracuse, we stayed three days.
13 From there we circled round and reached Rhe-
gium. And after one day the south wind blew;
and the next day we came to Puteoli, 14 where we
found [a]brethren, and were invited to stay with
them seven days. And so we went toward Rome.
15 And from there, when the brethren heard
about us, they came to meet us as far as Appii
Forum and Three Inns. When Paul saw them,
he thanked God and took courage.

16 Now when we came to Rome, the centu-
rion delivered the prisoners to the captain of
the guard; but [a]Paul was permitted to dwell
by himself with the soldier who guarded him.

### *PAUL'S MINISTRY AT ROME*

17 And it came to pass after three days that
Paul called the leaders of the Jews together. So
when they had come together, he said to them:
"Men *and* brethren, [a]though I have done noth-
ing against our people or the customs of our
fathers, yet [b]I was delivered as a prisoner from
Jerusalem into the hands of the Romans, 18 who,
[a]when they had examined me, wanted to let *me*
go, because there was no cause for putting me
to death. 19 But when the Jews[1] spoke against *it,*
[a]I was compelled to appeal to Caesar, not that
I had anything of which to accuse my nation.
20 For this reason therefore I have called for you,
to see *you* and speak with *you,* because [a]for the
hope of Israel I am bound with [b]this chain."

21 Then they said to him, "We neither received
letters from Judea concerning you, nor have any
of the brethren who came reported or spoken
any evil of you. 22 But we desire to hear from you
what you think; for concerning this sect, we know
that [a]it is spoken against everywhere."

23 So when they had appointed him a day,
many came to him at *his* lodging, [a]to whom he
explained and solemnly testified of the kingdom
of God, persuading them concerning Jesus [b]from
both the Law of Moses and the Prophets, from
morning till evening. 24 And [a]some were persuad-
ed by the things which were spoken, and some
disbelieved. 25 So when they did not agree among
themselves, they departed after Paul had said one
word: "The Holy Spirit spoke rightly through Isa-
iah the prophet to our[1] fathers, 26 saying,

> [a]'Go to this people and say:
> "Hearing you will hear, and shall not
> understand;

**28:5** [a] Mark 16:18 **28:6** [a] Acts 12:22; 14:11 **28:8** [a] [James 5:14, 15] [b] Mark 5:23; 6:5; 7:32; 16:18 **28:10** [a] Matt. 15:6 [b] [Phil. 4:19] **28:11** [a] Acts 27:6 **28:14** [a] Rom. 1:8 **28:16** [a] Acts 23:11; 24:25; 27:3 **28:17** [a] Acts 23:29; 24:12, 13; 26:31 [b] Acts 21:33 **28:18** [a] Acts 22:24; 24:10; 25:8; 26:32 **28:19** [a] Acts 25:11, 21, 25 [1] That is, the ruling authorities **28:20** [a] Acts 26:6, 7 [b] Eph. 3:1; 4:1; 6:20 **28:22** [a] [1 Pet. 2:12; 3:16; 4:14, 16] **28:23** [a] Luke 24:27 [b] Acts 26:6, 22 **28:24** [a] Acts 14:4; 19:9 **28:25** [1] NU-Text reads *your.* **28:26** [a] Is. 6:9, 10; Jer. 5:21; Ezek. 12:2; Matt. 13:14, 15; Mark 4:12; Luke 8:10; John 12:40, 41; Rom. 11:8

APPLY THE TRUTH

## IDOLS AND HERO WORSHIP

**28:1–6** We all crave role models and tend to put people on a pedestal. This is because it makes our goals seem achievable. If *they* did it, surely, *we* can too! The problem is our role models can easily go from being those we admire to those we worship. This happens when we look at them not for motivation, but for emulation; it happens when we attempt to shape our whole life after that person. The problem is all people are deeply flawed. What we love about them one day can become a source of agitation under a different light. If we place too much trust in people, we are bound to be disappointed or led astray.

In this passage, Paul dealt with the extremes of human opinion. In one moment, the people of Malta thought he was a murderer, deserving death (v. 4). The next minute, they thought he was a god, deserving worship (v. 6). We can avoid these extremes and help others do the same by always looking to Jesus as the greatest one we admire and emulate. Jesus is the only one worthy of trust and worship because He is the only one truly perfect. He will never disappoint or lead us astray.

And seeing you will see, and not
perceive;
27 For the hearts of this people have grown
dull.
*Their* ears are hard of hearing,
And their eyes they have closed,
Lest they should see with *their* eyes and
hear with *their* ears,
Lest they should understand with *their*
hearts and turn,
So that I should heal them." '[1]

28 "Therefore let it be known to you that the
salvation of God has been sent [a]to the Gentiles,
and they will hear it!" 29 And when he had said
these words, the Jews departed and had a great
dispute among themselves.[1]

30 Then Paul dwelt two whole years in his
own rented house, and received all who came
to him, 31 [a]preaching the kingdom of God and
teaching the things which concern the Lord
Jesus Christ with all confidence, no one forbidding him.

28:27 [1] Isaiah 6:9, 10 28:28 [a] Is. 42:1, 6; 49:6; Matt. 21:41; Luke 2:32; Rom. 11:11 28:29 [1] NU-Text omits this verse. 28:31 [a] Acts 4:31; Eph. 6:19

*Introduction to*

# THE EPISTLES AND THE BOOK OF APOCALYPSE

The Epistles, or letters, were written by several leaders in the early church to local churches and individuals. Paul wrote most of these letters, which is why they are often divided into two categories: the Pauline Epistles and the General Epistles. Paul's letters are grouped together in order from longest (**Romans**) to shortest (**Philemon**) and with letters to the churches coming before letters to individuals. The Epistles generally begin by identifying the writer and recipient followed by a greeting, the body of the letter, individual greetings, and a closing.

When reading the Epistles, keep in mind their audience, time frame, and purposes. For this reason, while reading one of Paul's letters, you might find it helpful to turn to the Book of Acts to read the backstory of the church or individual he was writing to. It's also a good idea to remember that the primary audience of these letters was always believers. This is important to consider as you come across the many promises made in them. They're not promises to all people but to those who have trusted in Christ.

The Book of **Revelation** is technically an epistle, but it's generally classified as a book of apocalypse, or prophecy, its main emphasis. When reading this book, recognize that it's a mixture of literal and figurative language. For example, the appearance of Jesus to John on Patmos is literal, but the description of Jesus is figurative, using various Old Testament symbols and images to describe Him. Because of this mixture, Revelation can be one of the more challenging books to read. Yet that doesn't mean it shouldn't be read, or that it cannot be understood. Read slowly and carefully, look for Old Testament connections, and keep the main idea of the book in mind—Jesus will return in victory one day.

ROMANS • 1–2 CORINTHIANS • GALATIANS
EPHESIANS • PHILIPPIANS • COLOSSIANS
1–2 THESSALONIANS • 1–2 TIMOTHY • TITUS
PHILEMON • HEBREWS • JAMES • 1–2 PETER
1–3 JOHN • JUDE • REVELATION

## THE EPISTLES (IN CHRONOLOGICAL ORDER)

| Book | Author | Primary Audience | Date | Theme |
|---|---|---|---|---|
| **Galatians** | Paul | Churches in Galatia | c. AD 40–56 | Freedom |
| **James** | James | Jewish Christians | c. AD 44–49 | Faith |
| **1 Thessalonians** | Paul | Church in Thessalonica | c. AD 51 | Anticipation |
| **2 Thessalonians** | Paul | Church in Thessalonica | c. AD 51–52 | Diligence |
| **1 Corinthians** | Paul | Church in Corinth | c. AD 55–56 | Godliness |
| **2 Corinthians** | Paul | Church in Corinth | c. AD 55–56 | Perseverance |
| **Romans** | Paul | Church in Rome | c. AD 56–57 | Righteousness |
| **Ephesians** | Paul | Church in Ephesus | c. AD 60–62 | Identity |
| **Philippians** | Paul | Church in Philippi | c. AD 60–62 | Joy |
| **Colossians** | Paul | Church in Colosse | c. AD 60–62 | Supremacy |
| **Philemon** | Paul | Philemon | c. AD 60–62 | Unity |
| **1 Peter** | Peter | Christians | c. AD 62–65 | Endurance |
| **1 Timothy** | Paul | Timothy | c. AD 62–66 | Doctrine |
| **Titus** | Paul | Titus | c. AD 62–66 | Holiness |
| **2 Timothy** | Paul | Timothy | c. AD 66–67 | Faithfulness |
| **2 Peter** | Peter | Christians | c. AD 67–68 | Purity |
| **Hebrews** | Unknown | Jewish Christians | c. AD 67–69 | Superiority |
| **Jude** | Jude | Christians | c. AD 68–70 | Contend |
| **1 John** | John | Christians | c. AD 90–95 | Confidence |
| **2 John** | John | Elect Lady or Christians | c. AD 90–95 | Discernment |
| **3 John** | John | Gaius | c. AD 90–95 | Hospitality |

## THE BOOK OF APOCALYPSE

| Book | Author | Audience | Date | Theme |
|---|---|---|---|---|
| **Revelation** | John | Seven Churches in Asia | c. AD 94–96 | Triumph |

*The Epistle of Paul the Apostle to the*

# ROMANS

| AUTHOR | KEY VERSES | READING TIME |
|---|---|---|
| Paul | Romans 1:16–17 | 1 hour 15 minutes |

The church in Rome was well-known (Rom. 1:8) and established several years before Paul wrote a letter to them. The believers were probably numerous, evidently meeting in several places (16:1–16). The historian Tacitus even referred to the Christians who were persecuted there under Nero in AD 64 as an "immense multitude." The gospel apparently filled a gap left by the practically defunct polytheism of Roman religion. Paul recognized the importance of the church in this city, and he wanted to ensure it was built on the right foundation of the gospel. Using a question-and-answer format, Paul recorded perhaps the most systematic presentation of the doctrine of salvation in the Bible. Romans is more than a book of theology, though. It is also a book of practical exhortation. The good news of Jesus Christ is more than facts to be believed; it is also a transformation to be experienced. The gospel sparks a new way of life—one of righteousness befitting the person "justified freely by [God's] grace through the redemption that is in Christ Jesus" (3:24).

**Occasion:** Paul wrote Romans near the end of his third missionary journey, most likely from Corinth during a three-month stay in Greece (Acts 20:3–6).

**Main Point:** The righteousness of God has been made known in Christ.

**Big Ideas:** All people are sinful and in need of salvation. Jesus is the only way for a person to be saved. All who trust in Jesus are saved of their sins. As those who have been saved by Jesus, our lives should look different.

## OUTLINE:

I. The Need for God's Righteousness (chs. 1–3)
II. The Demonstration of God's Righteousness (chs. 4–8)
III. The Vindication of God's Righteousness (chs. 9–11)
IV. The Application of God's Righteousness (chs. 12–16)

**c. AD 34**
Paul is converted

**c. AD 47–49**
Paul's first missionary journey

**AD 49**
Claudius expels the Jews from Rome

**c. AD 50**
The Jerusalem Council

**c. AD 50–53**
Paul's second missionary journey

**AD 52–60**
Felix is procurator of Judea

**c. AD 53–57**
Paul's third missionary journey

**AD 54–68**
Nero is Roman emperor

**c. AD 56–57**
**Romans written**

**c. AD 58**
Paul is arrested in Jerusalem

**AD 60–62**
Festus is procurator of Judea

**c. AD 60–62**
Paul is imprisoned in Rome

**AD 64**
Great Fire of Rome; first Roman mass persecution of Christians

**c. AD 67**
Peter and Paul are executed

**AD 70**
The Romans, led by Titus, destroy the temple

**AD 79**
Pompeii and Herculaneum destroyed by eruption of Mount Vesuvius

### GREETING

**1** Paul, a bondservant of Jesus Christ, [a]called *to be* an apostle, [b]separated to the gospel of God 2 [a]which He promised before [b]through His prophets in the Holy Scriptures, 3 concerning His Son Jesus Christ our Lord, who was [a]born of the seed of David according to the flesh, 4 *and* [a]declared *to be* the Son of God with power according [b]to the Spirit of holiness, by the resurrection from the dead. 5 Through Him [a]we have received grace and apostleship for [b]obedience to the faith among all nations [c]for His name, 6 among whom you also are the called of Jesus Christ;

> **SEEING JESUS IN THE SCRIPTURE**
>
> **1:4** The resurrection fulfilled prophecy, affirming Jesus' identity as the Savior of the world (see Ps. 16:10).

7 To all who are in Rome, beloved of God, [a]called *to be* saints:

[b]Grace to you and peace from God our Father and the Lord Jesus Christ.

### DESIRE TO VISIT ROME

8 First, [a]I thank my God through Jesus Christ for you all, that [b]your faith is spoken of throughout the whole world. 9 For [a]God is my witness, [b]whom I serve with my spirit in the gospel of His Son, that [c]without ceasing I make mention of you always in my prayers, 10 making request if, by some means, now at last I may find a way in the will of God to come to you. 11 For I long to see you, that [a]I may impart to you some spiritual gift, so that you may be established— 12 that is, that I may be encouraged together with you by [a]the mutual faith both of you and me.

13 Now I do not want you to be unaware, brethren, that I often planned to come to you (but [a]was hindered until now), that I might have some [b]fruit among you also, just as among the other Gentiles. 14 I am a debtor both to Greeks and to barbarians, both to wise and to unwise. 15 So, as much as is in me, *I am* ready to preach the gospel to you who are in Rome also.

### THE JUST LIVE BY FAITH

16 For [a]I am not ashamed of the gospel of Christ,[1] for [b]it is the power of God to salvation for everyone who believes, [c]for the Jew first and also for the Greek. 17 For [a]in it the righteousness of God is revealed from faith to faith; as it is written, [b]"The just shall live by faith."[1]

> **1:17 Faith** is at the beginning of the salvation process, and it's the goal as well. Paul had faith that **God**, through the Holy Spirit, could and would build true **righteousness** in him. For the believer this means honest self-examination, prayer to love and obey God more, and careful response to those inner nudges that prompt us to live more like Christ.

### GOD'S WRATH ON UNRIGHTEOUSNESS

18 [a]For the wrath of God is revealed from heaven against all ungodliness and [b]unrighteousness of men, who suppress the truth in unrighteousness, 19 because [a]what may be known of God is manifest in them, for [b]God has shown *it* to them. 20 For since the creation of the world [a]His invisible *attributes* are clearly seen, being understood by the things that are made, *even* His eternal power and Godhead, so that they are without excuse, 21 because, although they knew God, they did not glorify *Him* as God, nor were thankful, but [a]became futile in their thoughts, and their foolish hearts were darkened. 22 [a]Professing to be wise, they became fools, 23 and changed the glory of the [a]incorruptible [b]God into an image made like corruptible man—and birds and four-footed animals and creeping things.

24 [a]Therefore God also gave them up to uncleanness, in the lusts of their hearts, [b]to dishonor their bodies [c]among themselves, 25 who exchanged [a]the truth of God [b]for the lie, and worshiped and served the creature rather than the Creator, who is blessed forever. Amen.

26 For this reason God gave them up to [a]vile passions. For even their women exchanged the natural use for what is against nature. 27 Likewise also the men, leaving the natural use of the woman, burned in their lust for one another, men with men committing what is shameful, and receiving in themselves the penalty of their error which was due.

28 And even as they did not like to retain God in *their* knowledge, God gave them over to a debased mind, to do those things [a]which are not fitting; 29 being filled with all unrighteousness, sexual immorality,[1] wickedness, covetousness, maliciousness; full of envy, murder, strife, deceit, evil-mindedness; *they are* whisperers, 30 backbiters, haters of God, violent, proud, boasters, inventors of evil things, disobedient to parents, 31 undiscerning, untrustworthy, unloving, unforgiving,[1] unmerciful; 32 who,

**1:1** [a] 1 Tim. 1:11 [b] Acts 9:15; 13:2 **1:2** [a] Acts 26:6 [b] Gal. 3:8 **1:3** [a] Gal. 4:4 **1:4** [a] Acts 9:20; 13:33 [b] [Heb. 9:14] **1:5** [a] Eph. 3:8 [b] Acts 6:7 [c] Acts 9:15 **1:7** [a] 1 Cor. 1:2, 24 [b] 1 Cor. 1:3 **1:8** [a] 1 Cor. 1:4 [b] Rom. 16:19 **1:9** [a] Rom. 9:1 [b] Acts 27:23 [c] 1 Thess. 3:10 **1:11** [a] Rom. 15:29 **1:12** [a] Titus 1:4 **1:13** [a] [1 Thess. 2:18] [b] Phil. 4:17 **1:16** [a] Ps. 40:9, 10 [b] 1 Cor. 1:18, 24 [c] Acts 3:26 [1] NU-Text omits *of Christ.* **1:17** [a] Rom. 3:21; 9:30 [b] Hab. 2:4 [1] Habakkuk 2:4 **1:18** [a] [Acts 17:30] [b] 2 Thess. 2:10 **1:19** [a] [Acts 14:17; 17:24] [b] [John 1:9] **1:20** [a] Ps. 19:1–6 **1:21** [a] Jer. 2:5 **1:22** [a] Jer. 10:14 **1:23** [a] 1 Tim. 1:17; 6:15, 16 [b] Deut. 4:16–18 **1:24** [a] Eph. 4:18, 19 [b] 1 Cor. 6:18 [c] Lev. 18:22 **1:25** [a] 1 Thess. 1:9 [b] Is. 44:20 **1:26** [a] Lev. 18:22 **1:28** [a] Eph. 5:4 **1:29** [1] NU-Text omits *sexual immorality.* **1:31** [1] NU-Text omits *unforgiving.*

[a]knowing the righteous judgment of God, that
those who practice such things [b]are deserving
of death, not only do the same but also [c]approve
of those who practice them.

### GOD'S RIGHTEOUS JUDGMENT

2 Therefore you are [a]inexcusable, O man, who-
ever you are who judge, [b]for in whatever you
judge another you condemn yourself; for you
who judge practice the same things. 2 But we
know that the judgment of God is according to
truth against those who practice such things.
3 And do you think this, O man, you who judge
those practicing such things, and doing the
same, that you will escape the judgment of God?
4 Or do you despise [a]the riches of His goodness,
[b]forbearance, and [c]longsuffering, [d]not knowing
that the goodness of God leads you to repen-
tance? 5 But in accordance with your hardness
and your impenitent heart [a]you are treasuring
up for yourself wrath in the day of wrath and
revelation of the righteous judgment of God,
6 who [a]"will render to each one according to
his deeds":[1] 7 eternal life to those who by pa-
tient continuance in doing good seek for glory,
honor, and immortality; 8 but to those who are
self-seeking and [a]do not obey the truth, but obey
unrighteousness—indignation and wrath, 9 trib-
ulation and anguish, on every soul of man who
does evil, of the Jew [a]first and also of the Greek;
10 [a]but glory, honor, and peace to everyone who
works what is good, to the Jew first and also to
the Greek. 11 For [a]there is no partiality with God.
12 For as many as have sinned without law
will also perish without law, and as many as have
sinned in the law will be judged by the law 13 (for
[a]not the hearers of the law *are* just in the sight
of God, but the doers of the law will be justified;
14 for when Gentiles, who do not have the law, by
nature do the things in the law, these, although
not having the law, are a law to themselves,
15 who show the [a]work of the law written in their
hearts, their [b]conscience also bearing witness,
and between themselves *their* thoughts accusing
or else excusing *them*) 16 [a]in the day when God
will judge the secrets of men [b]by Jesus Christ,
[c]according to my gospel.

### THE JEWS GUILTY AS THE GENTILES

17 Indeed[1] [a]you are called a Jew, and [b]rest
on the law, [c]and make your boast in God, 18 and
[a]know *His* will, and [b]approve the things that are
excellent, being instructed out of the law, 19 and
[a]are confident that you yourself are a guide to
the blind, a light to those who are in darkness,
20 an instructor of the foolish, a teacher of babes,
[a]having the form of knowledge and truth in the
law. 21 [a]You, therefore, who teach another, do you
not teach yourself? You who preach that a man
should not steal, do you steal? 22 You who say,
"Do not commit adultery," do you commit adul-
tery? You who abhor idols, [a]do you rob temples?
23 You who [a]make your boast in the law, do you
dishonor God through breaking the law? 24 For
[a]"the name of God is [b]blasphemed among the
Gentiles because of you,"[1] as it is written.

### CIRCUMCISION OF NO AVAIL

25 [a]For circumcision is indeed profitable
if you keep the law; but if you are a breaker of

**1:32** [a] [Rom. 2:2] [b] [Rom. 6:21] [c] Hos. 7:3 **2:1** [a] [Rom. 1:20] [b] [Matt. 7:1–5] **2:4** [a] [Eph. 1:7, 18; 2:7] [b] [Rom. 3:25] [c] Ex. 34:6 [d] Is. 30:18 **2:5** [a] [Deut. 32:34] **2:6** [a] Ps. 62:12; Prov. 24:12 [1] Psalm 62:12; Proverbs 24:12 **2:8** [a] [2 Thess. 1:8] **2:9** [a] 1 Pet. 4:17 **2:10** [a] [1 Pet. 1:7] **2:11** [a] Deut. 10:17 **2:13** [a] [James 1:22, 25] **2:15** [a] 1 Cor. 5:1 [b] Acts 24:25 **2:16** [a] [Matt. 25:31] [b] Acts 10:42; 17:31 [c] 1 Tim. 1:11 **2:17** [a] John 8:33 [b] Mic. 3:11 [c] Is. 48:1, 2 [1] NU-Text reads *But if.* **2:18** [a] Deut. 4:8 [b] Phil. 1:10 **2:19** [a] Matt. 15:14 **2:20** [a] [2 Tim. 3:5] **2:21** [a] Matt. 23:3 **2:22** [a] Mal. 3:8 **2:23** [a] Rom. 2:17; 9:4 **2:24** [a] Ezek. 16:27 [b] Is. 52:5; Ezek. 36:22 [1] Isaiah 52:5; Ezekiel 36:22 **2:25** [a] [Gal. 5:3]

APPLY THE TRUTH

## JUDGING OTHERS

**2:1–2** What would happen if you put on glasses not made for your prescription? You wouldn't see very clearly, would you? Or, what if you stood on a scale that wasn't weighing correctly? Your weight would be wrong. To get accurate results, we need an accurate standard of measurement. You can't compare apples and oranges, and you can't say someone has bad eyesight if she is wearing the wrong prescription. Only when we have a set standard can we make such claims. The same is true when it comes to judging.

Paul explains people make poor judges because we lack a perfect standard of judgment. We're quick to judge others for failing to keep standards we can't keep ourselves. We judge in hypocrisy. When we fall short, we want grace. But when others fall short, we want them punished. We lower the bar for ourselves and raise it for others. God, however, is the perfect judge. He judges all people consistently and with a perfect standard of truth. He is likewise just as consistent in pouring out His perfect grace. This is why we should leave the judging to Him. Our job isn't to judge, but rather to point people to the perfect Judge.

the law, your circumcision has become uncir-
cumcision. 26 Therefore, [a]if an uncircumcised
man keeps the righteous requirements of the
law, will not his uncircumcision be counted as
circumcision? 27 And will not the physically un-
circumcised, if he fulfills the law, [a]judge you who,
*even* with *your* written *code* and circumcision,
*are* a transgressor of the law? 28 For [a]he is not a
Jew who *is one* outwardly, nor *is* circumcision
that which *is* outward in the flesh; 29 but *he is* a
Jew [a]who *is one* inwardly; and [b]circumcision *is*
*that* of the heart, [c]in the Spirit, not in the letter;
[d]whose praise *is* not from men but from God.

## GOD'S JUDGMENT DEFENDED

3 What advantage then has the Jew, or what *is*
the profit of circumcision? 2 Much in every
way! Chiefly because [a]to them were committed
the oracles of God. 3 For what if [a]some did not
believe? [b]Will their unbelief make the faith-
fulness of God without effect? 4 [a]Certainly not!
Indeed, let [b]God be true but [c]every man a liar.
As it is written:

[d]"That You may be justified in Your words,
And may overcome when You are
judged."[1]

5 But if our unrighteousness demonstrates
the righteousness of God, what shall we say?
*Is* God unjust who inflicts wrath? [a](I speak as
a man.) 6 Certainly not! For then [a]how will God
judge the world?

7 For if the truth of God has increased
through my lie to His glory, why am I also still
judged as a sinner? 8 And *why* not *say*, [a]"Let us
do evil that good may come"?—as we are slan-
derously reported and as some affirm that we
say. Their condemnation is just.

## ALL HAVE SINNED

*(Ps. 14:1–3; 53:1–4)*

9 What then? Are we better *than they?* Not at
all. For we have previously charged both Jews
and Greeks that [a]they are all under sin.
10 As it is written:

[a]"There is none righteous, no, not one;
11 There is none who understands;
There is none who seeks after God.
12 They have all turned aside;
They have together become unprofitable;
There is none who does good, no, not
one."[1]
13 "Their[a] throat *is* an open tomb;
With their tongues they have practiced
deceit";[1]
[b]"The poison of asps *is* under their lips";[2]
14 "Whose[a] mouth *is* full of cursing and
bitterness."[1]
15 "Their[a] feet *are* swift to shed blood;
16 Destruction and misery *are* in their ways;
17 And the way of peace they have not
known."[1]
18 "There[a] is no fear of God before their
eyes."[1]

19 Now we know that whatever [a]the law says, it
says to those who are under the law, that [b]every
mouth may be stopped, and all the world may
become guilty before God. 20 Therefore [a]by the
deeds of the law no flesh will be justified in His
sight, for by the law *is* the knowledge of sin.

## GOD'S RIGHTEOUSNESS THROUGH FAITH

21 But now [a]the righteousness of God apart
from the law is revealed, [b]being witnessed by the
Law [c]and the Prophets, 22 even the righteousness
of God, through faith in Jesus Christ, to all and
on all[1] who believe. For [a]there is no difference;
23 for [a]all have sinned and fall short of the glory
of God, 24 being justified freely [a]by His grace
[b]through the redemption that is in Christ Jesus,
25 whom God set forth [a]*as* a propitiation [b]by
His blood, through faith, to demonstrate His
righteousness, because in His forbearance God
had passed over [c]the sins that were previously

THE ROMANS ROAD 1

## THE PROBLEM: SIN

**3:23** In His essence, God, who is three Persons in one, is relational. He made us to be likewise relational—to know, love, and worship Him and to know and love one another. This is what it means, at least in part, to be made in God's image. We can connect with Him on a deep level no one else can, not even the angels.

But we *all* have a problem, and that problem is called *sin*. To sin is to disobey God in what we think, say, or do. It's to rebel against our Maker and determine to go our own way and do our own thing.

*Now, turn to Romans 6:23.*

**2:26** [a][Acts 10:34] **2:27** [a]Matt. 12:41 **2:28** [a][Gal. 6:15] **2:29** [a][1 Pet. 3:4] [b]Phil. 3:3 [c]Deut. 30:6 [d][1 Cor. 4:5] **3:2** [a]Deut. 4:5–8 **3:3** [a]Heb. 4:2 [b][2 Tim. 2:13] **3:4** [a]Job 40:8 [b][John 3:33] [c]Ps. 62:9 [d]Ps. 51:4 [1]Psalm 51:4 **3:5** [a]Gal. 3:15 **3:6** [a][Gen. 18:25] **3:8** [a]Rom. 5:20 **3:9** [a]Gal. 3:22 **3:10** [a]Ps. 14:1–3; 53:1–3; Eccl. 7:20 **3:12** [1]Psalms 14:1–3; 53:1–3; Ecclesiastes 7:20 **3:13** [a]Ps. 5:9 [b]Ps. 140:3 [1]Psalm 5:9 [2]Psalm 140:3 **3:14** [a]Ps. 10:7 [1]Psalm 10:7 **3:15** [a]Prov. 1:16; Is. 59:7, 8 **3:17** [1]Isaiah 59:7, 8 **3:18** [a]Ps. 36:1 [1]Psalm 36:1 **3:19** [a]John 10:34 [b]Job 5:16 **3:20** [a][Gal. 2:16] **3:21** [a]Acts 15:11 [b]John 5:46 [c]1 Pet. 1:10 **3:22** [a][Col. 3:11] [1]NU-Text omits *and on all.* **3:23** [a]Gal. 3:22 **3:24** [a][Eph. 2:8] [b][Heb. 9:12, 15] **3:25** [a]Lev. 16:15 [b]Col. 1:20 [c]Acts 14:16; 17:30

committed, [26] to demonstrate at the present time His righteousness, that He might be just and the justifier of the one who has faith in Jesus.

> **3:25–26 Propitiation** means to placate or appease. Here, it reveals that God accepts the death of Christ as the complete and satisfying sacrifice for human sin. The Bible never describes people appeasing God for their salvation. God is a loving God, but He is also a God of justice. So out of His love, God provided justice for our sins—the substitutionary death of His Son Jesus Christ.

### BOASTING EXCLUDED

[27][a]Where *is* boasting then? It is excluded. By what law? Of works? No, but by the law of faith. [28] Therefore we conclude [a]that a man is justified by faith apart from the deeds of the law. [29] Or *is He* the God of the Jews only? *Is He* not also the God of the Gentiles? Yes, of the Gentiles also, [30] since [a]*there is* one God who will justify the circumcised by faith and the uncircumcised through faith. [31] Do we then make void the law through faith? Certainly not! On the contrary, we establish the law.

### ABRAHAM JUSTIFIED BY FAITH

*(Gen. 17:10)*

**4** What then shall we say that [a]Abraham our [b]father has found according to the flesh?[1] [2] For if Abraham was [a]justified by works, he has *something* to boast about, but not before God. [3] For what does the Scripture say? [a]"Abraham believed God, and it was accounted to him for righteousness."[1] [4] Now [a]to him who works, the wages are not counted as grace but as debt.

### DAVID CELEBRATES THE SAME TRUTH

[5] But to him who [a]does not work but believes on Him who justifies [b]the ungodly, his faith is accounted for righteousness, [6] just as David also [a]describes the blessedness of the man to whom God imputes righteousness apart from works:

[7] "Blessed[a] *are those* whose lawless deeds are forgiven,
And whose sins are covered;
[8] Blessed *is the* man to whom the LORD shall not impute sin."[1]

### ABRAHAM JUSTIFIED BEFORE CIRCUMCISION

[9] *Does* this blessedness then *come* upon the circumcised *only*, or upon the uncircumcised also? For we say that faith was accounted to Abraham for righteousness. [10] How then was it accounted? While he was circumcised, or uncircumcised? Not while circumcised, but while uncircumcised. [11] And [a]he received the sign of circumcision, a seal of the righteousness of the faith which *he had while still* uncircumcised, that [b]he might be the father of all those who believe, though they are uncircumcised, that righteousness might be imputed to them also, [12] and the father of circumcision to those who not only *are* of the circumcision, but who also walk in the steps of the faith which our father [a]Abraham *had while still* uncircumcised.

### THE PROMISE GRANTED THROUGH FAITH

[13] For the promise that he would be the [a]heir of the world *was* not to Abraham or to his seed through the law, but through the righteousness of faith. [14] For [a]if those who are of the law *are* heirs, faith is made void and the promise made of no effect, [15] because [a]the law brings about wrath; for where there is no law *there is* no transgression.

[16] Therefore *it is* of faith that *it might be* [a]according to grace, [b]so that the promise might be sure to all the seed, not only to those who are of the law, but also to those who are of the faith of Abraham, [c]who is the father of us all [17] (as it is written, [a]"I have made you a father of many nations"[1]) in the presence of Him whom he believed—God, [b]who gives life to the dead and calls those [c]things which do not exist as though they did; [18] who, contrary to hope, in hope believed, so that he became the father of many nations, according to what was spoken, [a]"So shall your descendants be."[1] [19] And not being weak in faith, [a]he did not consider his own body, already dead (since he was about a hundred years old), [b]and the deadness of Sarah's womb. [20] He did not waver at the promise of God through unbelief, but was strengthened in faith, giving glory to God, [21] and being fully convinced that what He had promised [a]He was also able to perform. [22] And therefore [a]"it was accounted to him for righteousness."[1]

[23] Now [a]it was not written for his sake alone that it was imputed to him, [24] but also for us. It shall be imputed to us who believe [a]in Him who raised up Jesus our Lord from the dead, [25][a]who was delivered up because of our offenses, and [b]was raised because of our justification.

> **SEEING JESUS IN THE SCRIPTURE**
>
> **4:25** Jesus died to pay our sin penalty (see Is. 53:4). He then rose from the grave so we might have new life.

**3:27** [a][1 Cor. 1:29] **3:28** [a]Gal. 2:16 **3:30** [a][Gal. 3:8, 20] **4:1** [a]Is. 51:2 [b]James 2:21 [1]Or *Abraham our (fore)father according to the flesh has found?* **4:2** [a]Rom. 3:20, 27 **4:3** [a]Gen. 15:6 [1]Genesis 15:6 **4:4** [a]Rom. 11:6 **4:5** [a][Eph. 2:8, 9] [b]Josh. 24:2 **4:6** [a]Ps. 32:1, 2 **4:7** [a]Ps. 32:1, 2 **4:8** [1]Psalm 32:1, 2 **4:11** [a]Gen. 17:10 [b]Luke 19:9 **4:12** [a]Rom. 4:18–22 **4:13** [a]Gen. 17:4–6; 22:17 **4:14** [a]Gal. 3:18 **4:15** [a]Rom. 3:20 **4:16** [a][Rom. 3:24] [b][Gal. 3:22] [c]Is. 51:2 **4:17** [a]Gen. 17:5 [b][Rom. 8:11] [c]Rom. 9:26 [1]Genesis 17:5 **4:18** [a]Gen. 15:5 [1]Genesis 15:5 **4:19** [a]Gen. 17:17 [b]Heb. 11:11 **4:21** [a][Heb. 11:19] **4:22** [a]Gen. 15:6 [1]Genesis 15:6 **4:23** [a]Rom. 15:4 **4:24** [a]Acts 2:24 **4:25** [a]Is. 53:4, 5 [b][1 Cor. 15:17]

### *FAITH TRIUMPHS IN TROUBLE*

5 Therefore, [a]having been justified by faith,
we have[1] [b]peace with God through our Lord
Jesus Christ, 2 [a]through whom also we have ac-
cess by faith into this grace [b]in which we stand,
and [c]rejoice in hope of the glory of God. 3 And
not only *that,* but [a]we also glory in tribulations,
[b]knowing that tribulation produces persever-
ance; 4 [a]and perseverance, character; and char-
acter, hope. 5 [a]Now hope does not disappoint,
[b]because the love of God has been poured out in
our hearts by the Holy Spirit who was given to us.

### *CHRIST IN OUR PLACE*

6 For when we were still without strength,
in due time [a]Christ died for the ungodly. 7 For
scarcely for a righteous man will one die; yet
perhaps for a good man someone would even
dare to die. 8 But [a]God demonstrates His own
love toward us, in that while we were still sinners,
Christ died for us. 9 Much more then, having now
been justified [a]by His blood, we shall be saved
[b]from wrath through Him. 10 For [a]if when we were
enemies [b]we were reconciled to God through
the death of His Son, much more, having been
reconciled, we shall be saved [c]by His life. 11 And
not only *that,* but we also [a]rejoice in God through
our Lord Jesus Christ, through whom we have
now received the reconciliation.

### *DEATH IN ADAM, LIFE IN CHRIST*
*(Gen. 3:1–19)*

12 Therefore, just as [a]through one man sin
entered the world, and [b]death through sin, and
thus death spread to all men, because all sinned—
13 (For until the law sin was in the world, but [a]sin
is not imputed when there is no law. 14 Neverthe-
less death reigned from Adam to Moses, even
over those who had not sinned according to the

THE ROMANS ROAD 3

## THE SOLUTION: JESUS

**5:8** Do you see the glimmer of hope at the end of the last verse and this one? While we're sinners and our sin has earned us death, there's a way—one single way—we can have eternal life. That way is through Jesus Christ.

Jesus is the Son of God who obeyed God perfectly, not sinning even once. Then, He gave up His life—dying in our place as our perfect substitute—to pay the penalty of sin we owed. Death was owed and death was paid. On the third day, however, Jesus rose from the dead proving God the Father accepted His sacrifice and showing He has conquered sin and death.

*Now, turn to Romans 10:13.*
*To begin the Romans Road, turn to Romans 3:15.*

**5:13–14 Imputed** means to charge to one's account, as by an entry made into a ledger. In other words, **sin** was present **in the world** from Adam to Moses, but God didn't keep an account of sins before the giving of the **law** because there was no revealed law to obey or disobey. Those before Moses didn't break the law then, but we know they sinned because **death reigned**. Sin produced death and they all died.

**5:1** [a] Is. 32:17 [b] [Eph. 2:14] [1] Another ancient reading is, *let us have peace.* **5:2** [a] [Eph. 2:18; 3:12] [b] 1 Cor. 15:1 [c] Heb. 3:6 **5:3** [a] Matt. 5:11, 12 [b] James 1:3 **5:4** [a] [James 1:12] **5:5** [a] Phil. 1:20 [b] 2 Cor. 1:22 **5:6** [a] [Rom. 4:25; 5:8; 8:32] **5:8** [a] [John 3:16; 15:13] **5:9** [a] Eph. 2:13 [b] 1 Thess. 1:10 **5:10** [a] [Rom. 8:32] [b] 2 Cor. 5:18 [c] John 14:19 **5:11** [a] [Gal. 4:9] **5:12** [a] [1 Cor. 15:21] [b] Gen. 2:17 **5:13** [a] 1 John 3:4

APPLY THE TRUTH

## EVIL

**5:12, 17** God is on a mission to rid the world of evil. When we look out at our world, we see injustice, selfishness, pride, and disobedience. When we look within ourselves, we see we're capable of the same evil. If God is going to rid the world of evil, then He'd have to rid the world of us. Or so it seems.

We can trace the root of evil back to the original sin of pride and disobedience in Eden. Through Adam's disobedience, evil flooded into the world. We all have sinned and contributed to this evil. As a result, we all deserve death. God will vanquish *all* evil. But His plan to do so allows for us to be saved through one Man's righteous act. Sin and death came to all through the act of Adam; Grace and life came to all through the act of Jesus. God's way of healing the world is by healing individuals through their faith in Jesus Christ. Evil persists. But when we allow ourselves to be transformed by God, we push back against the darkness with the light of God's love.

likeness of the transgression of Adam, [a]who is a
type of Him who was to come. 15 But the free gift
*is* not like the offense. For if by the one man's of-
fense many died, much more the grace of God and
the gift by the grace of the one Man, Jesus Christ,
abounded [a]to many. 16 And the gift *is* not like *that*

**SEEING JESUS IN THE SCRIPTURE**

**5:15** Adam disobeyed and brought death to humanity (see Gen. 3:19); Jesus obeyed and brought life to all who trust in Him.

*which came* through the one who sinned. For the
judgment *which came* from one *offense resulted* in
condemnation, but the free gift *which came* from
many offenses *resulted* in justification. 17 For if by
the one man's offense death reigned through the
one, much more those who receive abundance of
grace and of the gift of righteousness will reign
in life through the One, Jesus Christ.)

18 Therefore, as through one man's offense
*judgment came* to all men, resulting in condem-
nation, even so through [a]one Man's righteous
act *the free gift came* [b]to all men, resulting in
justification of life. 19 For as by one man's disobe-
dience many were made sinners, so also by [a]one
Man's obedience many will be made righteous.

**5:18 Justification** is a legal term used for a favorable verdict in a trial. The word depicts a courtroom setting with God as the Judge determining the faithfulness of each person to His law. It's clear that no one can withstand God's **judgment** (Rom. 3:23). To remedy this inescapable situation, God sent His son to die for our sins, in our place. When we believe in Jesus, God pronounces us justified. God is both a righteous Judge and our gracious Justifier.

20 Moreover [a]the law entered that the of-
fense might abound. But where sin abounded,
grace [b]abounded much more, 21 so that as sin
reigned in death, even so grace might reign
through righteousness to eternal life through
Jesus Christ our Lord.

### *DEAD TO SIN, ALIVE TO GOD*

**6** What shall we say then? [a]Shall we continue in
sin that grace may abound? 2 Certainly not!
How shall we who [a]died to sin live any longer in it?
3 Or do you not know that [a]as many of us as were
baptized into Christ Jesus [b]were baptized into
His death? 4 Therefore we were [a]buried with Him
through baptism into death, that [b]just as Christ was
raised from the dead by [c]the glory of the Father,
[d]even so we also should walk in newness of life.

5 [a]For if we have been united together in the
likeness of His death, certainly we also shall be
*in the likeness* of *His* resurrection, 6 knowing this,
that [a]our old man was crucified with *Him,* that
[b]the body of sin might be done away with, that
we should no longer be slaves of sin. 7 For [a]he
who has died has been freed from sin. 8 Now [a]if
we died with Christ, we believe that we shall also
live with Him, 9 knowing that [a]Christ, having been
raised from the dead, dies no more. Death no
longer has dominion over Him. 10 For *the death*
that He died, [a]He died to sin once for all; but
*the life* that He lives, [b]He lives to God. 11 Likewise
you also, reckon yourselves to be [a]dead indeed
to sin, but [b]alive to God in Christ Jesus our Lord.

**6:6** Simply put, a believer is not the same person he or she was before conversion. A believer is a new creation in Christ (2 Cor. 5:17).

12 [a]Therefore do not let sin reign in your mor-
tal body, that you should obey it in its lusts. 13 And
do not present your [a]members *as* instruments of
unrighteousness to sin, but [b]present yourselves
to God as being alive from the dead, and your
members *as* instruments of righteousness to
God. 14 For [a]sin shall not have dominion over
you, for you are not under law but under grace.

### *FROM SLAVES OF SIN TO SLAVES OF GOD*

15 What then? Shall we sin [a]because we are not
under law but under grace? Certainly not! 16 Do you
not know that [a]to whom you present yourselves
slaves to obey, you are that one's slaves whom
you obey, whether of sin *leading* to death, or of
obedience *leading* to righteousness? 17 But God be
thanked that *though* you were slaves of sin, yet you
obeyed from the heart [a]that form of doctrine to
which you were delivered. 18 And [a]having been set
free from sin, you became slaves of righteousness.
19 I speak in human *terms* because of the weakness
of your flesh. For just as you presented your mem-
bers *as* slaves of uncleanness, and of lawlessness
*leading* to *more* lawlessness, so now present your
members *as* slaves *of* righteousness for holiness.
20 For when you were [a]slaves of sin, you were
free in regard to righteousness. 21 [a]What fruit
did you have then in the things of which you
are now ashamed? For [b]the end of those things

**5:14** [a] [1 Cor. 15:21, 22] **5:15** [a] [Is. 53:11] **5:18** [a] [1 Cor. 15:21, 45] [b] [John 12:32] **5:19** [a] [Phil. 2:8] **5:20** [a] John 15:22 [b] 1 Tim. 1:14 **6:1** [a] Rom. 3:8; 6:15 **6:2** [a] [Gal. 2:19] **6:3** [a] [Gal. 3:27] [b] [1 Cor. 15:29] **6:4** [a] Col. 2:12 [b] 1 Cor. 6:14 [c] John 2:11 [d] [Gal. 6:15] **6:5** [a] Phil. 3:10 **6:6** [a] Gal. 2:20; 5:24; 6:14 [b] Col. 2:11 **6:7** [a] 1 Pet. 4:1 **6:8** [a] 2 Tim. 2:11 **6:9** [a] Rev. 1:18 **6:10** [a] Heb. 9:27 [b] Luke 20:38 **6:11** [a] [Rom. 6:2; 7:4, 6] [b] [Gal. 2:19] **6:12** [a] Ps. 19:13 **6:13** [a] Col. 3:5 [b] 1 Pet. 2:24; 4:2 **6:14** [a] [Gal. 5:18] **6:15** [a] 1 Cor. 9:21 **6:16** [a] 2 Pet. 2:19 **6:17** [a] 2 Tim. 1:13 **6:18** [a] John 8:32 **6:20** [a] John 8:34 **6:21** [a] Rom. 7:5 [b] Rom. 1:32

APPLY THE TRUTH

## SOCIAL MEDIA

**6:16–18** Social media can be a poisonous trap; it's easy to make social media our whole lives. From doom scrolling at night, overthinking who is—and isn't—liking our posts, and being unable to be without our phones in fear of missing something, social media pulls us right in. When we fall for its trap, we miss being present with others, we become self-conscience about our image, and we compare our "real lives" to everyone else's "plastic" highlight reels. Social media easily makes us feel down about ourselves and we return to it to try to feel good again. It's a vicious cycle.

But social media can also be a powerful tool. It all depends on how we use it. We have unique opportunities to build community, meet interesting people, and even share the message of Jesus on social media platforms. People it took days, weeks, months, or even years to reach with the gospel can be reached instantly. But this requires self-control and refusing to become slaves to our profiles. These verses warn us how easily we can become slaves to something—even things that aren't sin on their own. So use caution, set boundaries, and become an influencer for the gospel. Use the powerful tool of social media to bring the message of Jesus to the world.

*is* death. 22 But now [a]having been set free from
sin, and having become slaves of God, you have
your fruit to holiness, and the end, everlasting
life. 23 For [a]the wages of sin *is* death, but [b]the gift
of God *is* eternal life in Christ Jesus our Lord.

### *FREED FROM THE LAW*

7 Or do you not know, brethren (for I speak to
those who know the law), that the law has do-
minion over a man as long as he lives? 2 For [a]the
woman who has a husband is bound by the law to
*her* husband as long as he lives. But if the husband
dies, she is released from the law of *her* husband.
3 So then [a]if, while *her* husband lives, she marries
another man, she will be called an adulteress; but
if her husband dies, she is free from that law, so
that she is no adulteress, though she has married
another man. 4 Therefore, my brethren, you also
have become [a]dead to the law through the body
of Christ, that you may be married to another—
to Him who was raised from the dead, that we
should [b]bear fruit to God. 5 For when we were in
the flesh, the sinful passions which were aroused
by the law [a]were at work in our members [b]to bear
fruit to death. 6 But now we have been delivered
from the law, having died to what we were held
by, so that we should serve [a]in the newness of the
Spirit and not *in* the oldness of the letter.

### *SIN'S ADVANTAGE IN THE LAW*

7 What shall we say then? *Is* the law sin? Cer-
tainly not! On the contrary, [a]I would not have
known sin except through the law. For I would not
have known covetousness unless the law had said,
[b]"You shall not covet."[1] 8 But [a]sin, taking opportu-
nity by the commandment, produced in me all
*manner of evil* desire. For [b]apart from the law sin
*was* dead. 9 I was alive once without the law, but
when the commandment came, sin revived and
I died. 10 And the commandment, [a]which *was* to
*bring* life, I found to *bring* death. 11 For sin, taking
occasion by the commandment, deceived me,
and by it killed *me*. 12 Therefore [a]the law *is* holy,
and the commandment holy and just and good.

THE ROMANS ROAD 2

## THE RESULT: DEATH

**6:23** Few, if anyone, would deny they do bad things from time to time. It's not hard to admit we lose our temper, look at things we shouldn't look at, aren't always totally truthful, and perhaps have stolen a candy bar or something like that. But hardly anyone would see himself or herself as a "bad" person, as a "sinner." We aren't mass murderers or evil dictators, right? Surely God cannot be too upset with us like He should be with them.

While we aren't as bad as we could be, neither are we as good as we need to be. God is holy and perfect. His standard for us is the same. And because of that, our sin—whatever it is—has earned us death, separation from Him forever.

*Now, turn to Romans 5:8.*

*To begin the Romans Road, turn to Romans 3:15.*

**6:22** [a] Rom. 6:18; 8:2 **6:23** [a] Gen. 2:17 [b] 1 Pet. 1:4 **7:2** [a] 1 Cor. 7:39 **7:3** [a] [Matt. 5:32] **7:4** [a] Gal. 2:19; 5:18 [b] Gal. 5:22 **7:5** [a] Rom. 6:13 [b] James 1:15 **7:6** [a] Rom. 2:29 **7:7** [a] Rom. 3:20 [b] Ex. 20:17; Deut. 5:21 [1] Exodus 20:17; Deuteronomy 5:21 **7:8** [a] Rom. 4:15 [b] 1 Cor. 15:56 **7:10** [a] Lev. 18:5 **7:12** [a] Ps. 19:8

### LAW CANNOT SAVE FROM SIN

13 Has then what is good become death to me? Certainly not! But sin, that it might appear sin, was producing death in me through what is good, so that sin through the commandment might become exceedingly sinful. 14 For we know that the law is spiritual, but I am carnal, [a]sold under sin. 15 For what I am doing, I do not understand. [a]For what I will to do, that I do not practice; but what I hate, that I do. 16 If, then, I do what I will not to do, I agree with the law that *it is* good. 17 But now, *it is* no longer I who do it, but sin that dwells in me. 18 For I know that [a]in me (that is, in my flesh) nothing good dwells; for to will is present with me, but *how* to perform what is good I do not find. 19 For the good that I will *to do,* I do not do; but the evil I will not *to do,* that I practice. 20 Now if I do what I will not *to do,* it is no longer I who do it, but sin that dwells in me.

21 I find then a law, that evil is present with me, the one who wills to do good. 22 For I [a]delight in the law of God according to [b]the inward man. 23 But [a]I see another law in [b]my members, warring against the law of my mind, and bringing me into captivity to the law of sin which is in my members. 24 O wretched man that I am! Who will deliver me [a]from this body of death? 25 [a]I thank God—through Jesus Christ our Lord!

So then, with the mind I myself serve the law of God, but with the flesh the law of sin.

### FREE FROM INDWELLING SIN

8 *There is* therefore now no condemnation to those who are in Christ Jesus,[1] [a]who do not walk according to the flesh, but according to the Spirit. 2 For [a]the law of [b]the Spirit of life in Christ Jesus has made me free from [c]the law of sin and death. 3 For [a]what the law could not do in that it was weak through the flesh, [b]God *did* by sending His own Son in the likeness of sinful flesh, on account of sin: He condemned sin in the flesh, 4 that the righteous requirement of the law might be fulfilled in us who [a]do not walk according to the flesh but according to the Spirit. 5 For [a]those who live according to the flesh set their minds on the things of the flesh, but those *who live* according to the Spirit, [b]the things of the Spirit. 6 For [a]to be carnally minded *is* death, but to be spiritually minded *is* life and peace. 7 Because [a]the carnal mind *is* enmity against God; for it is not subject to the law of God, [b]nor indeed can be. 8 So then, those who are in the flesh cannot please God.

9 But you are not in the flesh but in the Spirit, if indeed the Spirit of God dwells in you. Now if anyone does not have the Spirit of Christ, he is not His. 10 And if Christ *is* in you, the body *is* dead because of sin, but the Spirit *is* life because of righteousness. 11 But if the Spirit of [a]Him who raised Jesus from the dead dwells in you, [b]He who raised Christ from the dead will also give life to your mortal bodies through His Spirit who dwells in you.

### SONSHIP THROUGH THE SPIRIT

12 [a]Therefore, brethren, we are debtors—not to the flesh, to live according to the flesh. 13 For [a]if you live according to the flesh you will die; but if by the Spirit you [b]put to death the deeds of the body, you will live. 14 For [a]as many as are led by the Spirit of God, these are sons of God. 15 For [a]you did not receive the spirit of bondage again [b]to fear, but you received the [c]Spirit of adoption by whom we cry out, [d]"Abba, Father." 16 [a]The Spirit Himself bears witness with our spirit that we are children of God, 17 and if children, then [a]heirs—heirs of God and joint heirs with Christ, [b]if indeed we suffer with *Him,* that we may also be glorified together.

### FROM SUFFERING TO GLORY

18 For I consider that [a]the sufferings of this present time are not worthy *to be compared* with the glory which shall be revealed in us. 19 For [a]the earnest expectation of the creation eagerly waits for the revealing of the sons of God. 20 For [a]the creation was subjected to futility, not willingly, but because of Him who subjected *it* in hope; 21 because the creation itself also will be delivered from the bondage of corruption into the glorious [a]liberty of the children of God. 22 For we know that the whole creation [a]groans and labors with birth pangs together until now. 23 Not only *that,* but we also who have [a]the firstfruits of the Spirit, [b]even we ourselves groan [c]within ourselves, eagerly waiting for the adoption, the [d]redemption of our body. 24 For we were saved in this hope, but [a]hope that is seen is not hope; for why does one still hope for what he sees? 25 But if we hope for what we do not see, we eagerly wait for *it* with perseverance.

26 Likewise the Spirit also helps in our weaknesses. For [a]we do not know what we should pray for as we ought, but [b]the Spirit Himself makes intercession for us[1] with groanings which cannot be uttered. 27 Now [a]He who searches the hearts knows what the mind of the Spirit *is,* because He makes intercession for the saints [b]according to *the will of* God.

28 And we know that all things work together for good to those who love God, to those [a]who are the called according to *His* purpose. 29 For whom [a]He foreknew, [b]He also predestined [c]*to be* conformed to the image of His Son, [d]that He might be the firstborn among many brethren.

**7:14** [a] 2 Kin. 17:17 **7:15** [a] [Gal. 5:17] **7:18** [a] [Gen. 6:5; 8:21] **7:22** [a] Ps. 1:2 [b] [2 Cor. 4:16] **7:23** [a] [Gal. 5:17] [b] Rom. 6:13, 19 **7:24** [a] [1 Cor. 15:51, 52] **7:25** [a] 1 Cor. 15:57 **8:1** [a] Gal. 5:16 [1] NU-Text omits the rest of this verse. **8:2** [a] Rom. 6:18, 22 [b] [1 Cor. 15:45] [c] Rom. 7:24, 25 **8:3** [a] Acts 13:39 [b] [2 Cor. 5:21] **8:4** [a] Gal. 5:16, 25 **8:5** [a] John 3:6 [b] [Gal. 5:22–25] **8:6** [a] Gal. 6:8 **8:7** [a] James 4:4 [b] 1 Cor. 2:14 **8:11** [a] Acts 2:24 [b] 1 Cor. 6:14 **8:12** [a] [Rom. 6:7, 14] **8:13** [a] Gal. 6:8 [b] Eph. 4:22 **8:14** [a] [Gal. 5:18] **8:15** [a] Heb. 2:15 [b] 2 Tim. 1:7 [c] [Is. 56:5] [d] Mark 14:36 **8:16** [a] Eph. 1:13 **8:17** [a] Acts 26:18 [b] Phil. 1:29 **8:18** [a] 2 Cor. 4:17 **8:19** [a] [2 Pet. 3:13] **8:20** [a] Gen. 3:17–19 **8:21** [a] [2 Cor. 3:17] **8:22** [a] Jer. 12:4, 11 **8:23** [a] 2 Cor. 5:5 [b] 2 Cor. 5:2, 4 [c] [Luke 20:36] [d] Eph. 1:14; 4:30 **8:24** [a] Heb. 11:1 **8:26** [a] Matt. 20:22 [b] Eph. 6:18 [1] NU-Text omits *for us.* **8:27** [a] 1 Chr. 28:9 [b] 1 John 5:14 **8:28** [a] 2 Tim. 1:9 **8:29** [a] 2 Tim. 2:19 [b] Eph. 1:5, 11 [c] [2 Cor. 3:18] [d] Heb. 1:6

KNOW THE TRUTH

# THE DOCTRINE OF SALVATION

## PART 8: THE COMPLETION OF SALVATION

**8:28–30** This passage, sometimes called "the golden chain of redemption," shows the beautiful progression of God's plan of salvation from before creation to its completion. Each link is vital and is fused with the others by the inseparable bond of God's power.

Before God created, He **foreknew** us. In His omniscience, He intimately knew every person He would create. No one is an accident. Everyone is made on purpose, for purpose. God also foreknew we would rebel against Him, leading to sin and death. Therefore, He **predestined** us to be saved. God initiated the plan through Christ to pay the price due for sin and make a way for people to be forgiven and be born again as His sons and daughters. God has thus **called** on us to repent of our sins and believe in Jesus to receive forgiveness and new life. Those who believe in the heart and confess with the mouth Jesus as Lord are **justified**, or declared "not guilty" and completely righteous before God. One day, Jesus will return and all who've been justified by Him will be **glorified**. Like Jesus who was raised first, believers will be resurrected into glorified bodies to live with God and His people in perfection forevermore.

*For* **THE DOCTRINE OF THE CHURCH: PART 1: OVERVIEW OF THE DOCTRINE OF THE CHURCH**, *turn to Acts 4:21–37 on page 1109.*

30 Moreover whom He predestined, these He also
[a]called; whom He called, these He also [b]justified;
and whom He justified, these He also [c]glorified.

### *GOD'S EVERLASTING LOVE*

31 What then shall we say to these things?
[a]If God *is* for us, who *can be* against us? 32 [a]He
who did not spare His own Son, but [b]delivered
Him up for us all, how shall He not with Him
also freely give us all things? 33 Who shall bring
a charge against God's elect? [a]*It is* God who jus-
tifies. 34 [a]Who *is* he who condemns? *It is* Christ
who died, and furthermore is also risen, [b]who is
even at the right hand of God, [c]who also makes
intercession for us. 35 Who shall separate us from
the love of Christ? *Shall* tribulation, or distress,
or persecution, or famine, or nakedness, or peril,
or sword? 36 As it is written:

> [a]"For Your sake we are killed all day long;
> We are accounted as sheep for the
> slaughter."[1]

37 [a]Yet in all these things we are more than
conquerors through Him who loved us. 38 For I
am persuaded that neither death nor life, nor
angels nor [a]principalities nor powers, nor things
present nor things to come, 39 nor height nor
depth, nor any other created thing, shall be able
to separate us from the love of God which is in
Christ Jesus our Lord.

**8:39** Christ created all things, "in heaven and . . . on earth, visible and invisible," and He was "before all things, and in Him all things consist" (Col. 1:16–17). If God, who was from the beginning, is *for* us, then no **created thing** can **separate us from** His **love**. Our security in Him is absolute.

### *ISRAEL'S REJECTION OF CHRIST*

9 I [a]tell the truth in Christ, I am not lying, my
conscience also bearing me witness in the Holy
Spirit, 2 [a]that I have great sorrow and continual grief
in my heart. 3 For [a]I could wish that I myself were
accursed from Christ for my brethren, my country-
men[1] according to the flesh, 4 who are Israelites, [a]to
whom *pertain* the adoption, [b]the glory, [c]the cov-
enants, [d]the giving of the law, [e]the service *of God,*
and [f]the promises; 5 [a]of whom *are* the fathers and
from [b]whom, according to the flesh, Christ *came,*
[c]who is over all, *the* eternally blessed God. Amen.

### *ISRAEL'S REJECTION AND GOD'S PURPOSE*

*(Gen. 25:19–23)*

6 [a]But it is not that the word of God has taken
no effect. For [b]they *are* not all Israel who *are* of
Israel, 7 [a]nor *are they* all children because they
are the seed of Abraham; but, [b]"In Isaac your
seed shall be called."[1] 8 That is, those who *are* the

**8:30** [a] [1 Pet. 2:9; 3:9] [b] [Gal. 2:16] [c] John 17:22 **8:31** [a] Num. 14:9 **8:32** [a] Rom. 5:6, 10 [b] [Rom. 4:25] **8:33** [a] Is. 50:8, 9 **8:34** [a] John 3:18 [b] Mark 16:19 [c] Heb. 7:25; 9:24 **8:36** [a] Ps. 44:22 [1] Psalm 44:22 **8:37** [a] 1 Cor. 15:57 **8:38** [a] [Eph. 1:21] **9:1** [a] 2 Cor. 1:23 **9:2** [a] Rom. 10:1 **9:3** [a] Ex. 32:32 [1] Or *relatives* **9:4** [a] Ex. 4:22 [b] 1 Sam. 4:21 [c] Acts 3:25 [d] Ps. 147:19 [e] Heb. 9:1, 6 [f] [Acts 2:39; 13:32] **9:5** [a] Deut. 10:15 [b] [Luke 1:34, 35; 3:23] [c] Jer. 23:6 **9:6** [a] Num. 23:19 [b] [Gal. 6:16] **9:7** [a] [Gal. 4:23] [b] Gen. 21:12 [1] Genesis 21:12

children of the flesh, these *are* not the children of
God; but [a]the children of the promise are counted
as the seed. 9 For this *is* the word of promise: [a]"At
this time I will come and Sarah shall have a son."[1]
10 And not only *this,* but when [a]Rebecca also
had conceived by one man, *even* by our father
Isaac 11 (for *the children* not yet being born, nor
having done any good or evil, that the purpose
of God according to election might stand, not of
works but of [a]Him who calls), 12 it was said to her,
[a]"The older shall serve the younger."[1] 13 As it is writ-
ten, [a]"Jacob I have loved, but Esau I have hated."[1]

> **9:10–13** In the Old Testament, the oldest male child in a family received a larger inheritance than the other children. **Jacob** was a famous exception to that rule. Jacob and his brother **Esau** were twins, but Esau was born first. God, however, chose to bless Jacob, whom He later called Israel. The twelve tribes of Israel were descendants of Jacob's twelve sons.

### *ISRAEL'S REJECTION AND GOD'S JUSTICE*

14 What shall we say then? [a]*Is there* unrigh-
teousness with God? Certainly not! 15 For He says
to Moses, [a]"I will have mercy on whomever I
will have mercy, and I will have compassion on
whomever I will have compassion."[1] 16 So then *it*
*is* not of him who wills, nor of him who runs, but
of God who shows mercy. 17 For [a]the Scripture
says to the Pharaoh, [b]"For this very purpose I
have raised you up, that I may show My power
in you, and that My name may be declared in all
the earth."[1] 18 Therefore He has mercy on whom
He wills, and whom He wills He [a]hardens.
19 You will say to me then, "Why does He still
find fault? For [a]who has resisted His will?" 20 But
indeed, O man, who are you to reply against God?
[a]Will the thing formed say to him who formed
*it,* "Why have you made me like this?" 21 Does
not the [a]potter have power over the clay, from
the same lump to make [b]one vessel for honor
and another for dishonor?
22 *What* if God, wanting to show *His* wrath
and to make His power known, endured with
much longsuffering [a]the vessels of wrath [b]pre-
pared for destruction, 23 and that He might make
known [a]the riches of His glory on the vessels of
mercy, which He had [b]prepared beforehand for
glory, 24 even us whom He [a]called, [b]not of the
Jews only, but also of the Gentiles?

25 As He says also in Hosea:

[a]"I will call them My people, who were not
My people,
And her beloved, who was not
beloved."[1]
26 "And[a] it shall come to pass in the place
where it was said to them,
'*You are* not My people,'
There they shall be called sons of the
living God."[1]

27 Isaiah also cries out concerning Israel:[1]

[a]"Though the number of the children of
Israel be as the sand of the sea,
[b]The remnant will be saved.
28 For He will finish the work and cut *it* short
in righteousness,
[a]Because the LORD will make a short work
upon the earth."[1]

29 And as Isaiah said before:

[a]"Unless the LORD of Sabaoth[1] had left us a
seed,
[b]We would have become like
Sodom,
And we would have been made like
Gomorrah."[2]

### *PRESENT CONDITION OF ISRAEL*

30 What shall we say then? [a]That Gentiles,
who did not pursue righteousness, have at-
tained to righteousness, [b]even the righteous-
ness of faith; 31 but Israel, [a]pursuing the law of
righteousness, [b]has not attained to the law of
righteousness.[1] 32 Why? Because *they did* not
*seek it* by faith, but as it were, by the works of
the law.[1] For [a]they stumbled at that stumbling
stone. 33 As it is written:

[a]"Behold, I lay in Zion a stumbling stone
and rock of offense,
And [b]whoever believes on Him will not be
put to shame."[1]

> **SEEING JESUS IN THE SCRIPTURE**
>
> **9:33** Jesus is the prophesied stumbling block for those who reject Him, but for those who believe, He is our righteousness (see Is. 28:16).

**9:8** [a] Gal. 4:28 **9:9** [a] Gen. 18:10, 14 [1] Genesis 18:10, 14 **9:10** [a] Gen. 25:21 **9:11** [a] [Rom. 4:17; 8:28] **9:12** [a] Gen. 25:23 [1] Genesis 25:23 **9:13** [a] Mal. 1:2, 3 [1] Malachi 1:2, 3 **9:14** [a] Deut. 32:4 **9:15** [a] Ex. 33:19 [1] Exodus 33:19 **9:17** [a] Gal. 3:8 [b] Ex. 9:16 [1] Exodus 9:16 **9:18** [a] Ex. 4:21 **9:19** [a] 2 Chr. 20:6 **9:20** [a] Is. 29:16 **9:21** [a] Prov. 16:4 [b] 2 Tim. 2:20 **9:22** [a] [1 Thess. 5:9] [b] [1 Pet. 2:8] **9:23** [a] [Col. 1:27] [b] [Rom. 8:28–30] **9:24** [a] [Rom. 8:28] [b] Rom. 3:29 **9:25** [a] Hos. 2:23 [1] Hosea 2:23 **9:26** [a] Hos. 1:10 [1] Hosea 1:10 **9:27** [a] Is. 10:22, 23 [b] Rom. 11:5 [1] Isaiah 10:22, 23 **9:28** [a] Is. 10:23; 28:22 [1] NU-Text reads *For the LORD will finish the work and cut it short upon the earth.* **9:29** [a] Is. 1:9 [b] Is. 13:19 [1] Literally, in Hebrew, *Hosts* [2] Isaiah 1:9 **9:30** [a] Rom. 4:11 [b] Rom. 1:17; 3:21; 10:6 **9:31** [a] [Rom. 10:2–4] [b] [Gal. 5:4] [1] NU-Text omits *of righteousness.* **9:32** [a] [1 Cor. 1:23] [1] NU-Text reads *by works.* **9:33** [a] Is. 8:14; 28:16 [b] Rom. 5:5; 10:11 [1] Isaiah 8:14; 28:16

### ISRAEL NEEDS THE GOSPEL

**10** Brethren, my heart's desire and prayer to
God for Israel[1] is that they may be saved.
2 For I bear them witness [a]that they have a zeal
for God, but not according to knowledge. 3 For
they being ignorant of [a]God's righteousness, and
seeking to establish their own [b]righteousness,
have not submitted to the righteousness of God.
4 For [a]Christ *is* the end of the law for righteous-
ness to everyone who believes.
5 For Moses writes about the righteousness
which is of the law, [a]"The man who does those
things shall live by them."[1] 6 But the righteous-
ness of faith speaks in this way, [a]"Do not say in
your heart, 'Who will ascend into heaven?' "[1] (that
is, to bring Christ down *from above*) 7 or, [a]" 'Who
will descend into the abyss?' "[1] (that is, to bring
Christ up from the dead). 8 But what does it say?
[a]"The word is near you, in your mouth and in
your heart"[1] (that is, the word of faith which we
preach): 9 that [a]if you confess with your mouth
the Lord Jesus and believe in your heart that
God has raised Him from the dead, you will be
saved. 10 For with the heart one believes unto
righteousness, and with the mouth confession
is made unto salvation. 11 For the Scripture says,
[a]"Whoever believes on Him will not be put to
shame."[1] 12 For [a]there is no distinction between
Jew and Greek, for [b]the same Lord over all [c]is
rich to all who call upon Him. 13 For [a]"whoever
calls [b]on the name of the LORD shall be saved."[1]

## THE ROMANS ROAD 4

## THE RESPONSE: FAITH

**10:13** Is that it? Does that mean we're forgiven of our sins, we've escaped death, and we have eternal life? Not quite. Salvation is now available, but it's not automatic. There's one thing we must do: place our faith in Jesus, basically accepting the gift He has offered.

To have faith in Jesus means we acknowledge our own sin, want to turn away from it (which is called repentance), believe who Jesus is and what He did, and trust in Him alone for salvation. That's it. There's nothing else we can do. We cannot obey our way to salvation. We cannot religion our way to salvation. We can only be saved by faith in Jesus. Period.

*Now, turn to Romans 12:1.*
*To begin the Romans Road, turn to Romans 3:15.*

10:1 [1] NU-Text reads *them.* 10:2 [a] Acts 21:20 10:3 [a] [Rom. 1:17] [b] [Phil. 3:9] 10:4 [a] [Gal. 3:24; 4:5] 10:5 [a] Lev. 18:5 [1] Leviticus 18:5 10:6 [a] Deut. 30:12–14 [1] Deuteronomy 30:12 10:7 [a] Deut. 30:13 [1] Deuteronomy 30:13 10:8 [a] Deut. 30:14 [1] Deuteronomy 30:14 10:9 [a] Luke 12:8 10:11 [a] Is. 28:16 [1] Isaiah 28:16 10:12 [a] Rom. 3:22, 29 [b] Acts 10:36 [c] Eph. 1:7 10:13 [a] Joel 2:32 [b] Acts 9:14 [1] Joel 2:32

## KNOW THE TRUTH

## THE DOCTRINE OF SALVATION

### PART 5: THE MOMENT OF SALVATION

**10:8–17** According to Romans 10:8–17, at least three things must occur for a person to be saved: communication of the gospel, conviction in the heart, and confession with the mouth.

First, a person must receive **communication** of the good news about Jesus by reading, hearing, or both. This message of the good news concerns who Jesus is, what He has done, and what a person must do to be saved from sin.

Second, a person must experience **conviction** concerning the gospel message they've heard or read. Conviction is a work of the Holy Spirit to clarify one's hopeless spiritual condition, clarify Christ as the only Lord and Savior, and convince one of his or her need to repent and trust in Jesus alone.

Third, one must **confess** what the gospel says. To *confess* is to agree with God, namely about the message of the gospel. But confession goes beyond mere intellectual belief. It's to place one's faith, or trust, in Jesus, repent of sin, and want to live for God's glory. Upon confession, a person moves from unforgiven sinner to forgiven child of God and can be confident of being spared from sin's penalty and power, and the coming wrath of God.

*For* **THE DOCTRINE OF SALVATION: PART 6: THE RESULT OF SALVATION,** *turn to 1 John 2:3–5 on page 1277.*

### *ISRAEL REJECTS THE GOSPEL*

14 How then shall they call on Him in whom
they have not believed? And how shall they
believe in Him of whom they have not heard?
And how shall they hear [a]without a preacher?
15 And how shall they preach unless they are
sent? As it is written:

> [a]"How beautiful are the feet of those who
> preach the gospel of peace,[1]
> Who bring glad tidings of good things!"[2]

16 But they have not all obeyed the gospel. For
Isaiah says, [a]"LORD, who has believed our re-
port?"[1] 17 So then faith *comes* by hearing, and
hearing by the word of God.

> **SEEING JESUS IN THE SCRIPTURE**
>
> **10:16** Salvation is granted only to those who trust in Jesus. Isaiah foretold of the lack of belief in Jesus as Messiah (see Is. 53:1).

18 But I say, have they not heard? Yes indeed:

> [a]"Their sound has gone out to all the earth,
> And their words to the ends of the world."[1]

19 But I say, did Israel not know? First Moses
says:

> [a]"I will provoke you to jealousy by *those who*
> *are* not a nation,
> I will move you to anger by a [b]foolish
> nation."[1]

20 But Isaiah is very bold and says:

> [a]"I was found by those who did not seek Me;
> I was made manifest to those who did not
> ask for Me."[1]

21 But to Israel he says:

> [a]"All day long I have stretched out My hands
> To a disobedient and contrary people."[1]

### *ISRAEL'S REJECTION NOT TOTAL*

11 I say then, [a]has God cast away His people?
[b]Certainly not! For [c]I also am an Israelite,
of the seed of Abraham, *of* the tribe of Benjamin.
2 God has not cast away His people whom [a]He
foreknew. Or do you not know what the Scripture
says of Elijah, how he pleads with God against
Israel, saying, 3 [a]"LORD, they have killed Your
prophets and torn down Your altars, and I alone
am left, and they seek my life"?[1] 4 But what does
the divine response say to him? [a]"I have reserved
for Myself seven thousand men who have not
bowed the knee to Baal."[1] 5 [a]Even so then, at this
present time there is a remnant according to the
election of grace. 6 And [a]if by grace, then *it is* no
longer of works; otherwise grace is no longer
grace.[1] But if *it is* of works, it is no longer grace;
otherwise work is no longer work.
7 What then? [a]Israel has not obtained what
it seeks; but the elect have obtained it, and the
rest were [b]blinded. 8 Just as it is written:

> [a]"God has given them a spirit of stupor,
> [b]Eyes that they should not see
> And ears that they should not hear,
> To this very day."[1]

9 And David says:

> [a]"Let their table become a snare and a trap,
> A stumbling block and a recompense to
> them.
> 10 Let their eyes be darkened, so that they do
> not see,
> And bow down their back always."[1]

### *ISRAEL'S REJECTION NOT FINAL*

11 I say then, have they stumbled that they
should fall? Certainly not! But [a]through their fall,
to provoke them to [b]jealousy, salvation *has come*
to the Gentiles. 12 Now if their fall *is* riches for the
world, and their failure riches for the Gentiles,
how much more their fullness!
13 For I speak to you Gentiles; inasmuch as
[a]I am an apostle to the Gentiles, I magnify my
ministry, 14 if by any means I may provoke to
jealousy *those who are* my flesh and [a]save some
of them. 15 For if their being cast away *is* the rec-
onciling of the world, what *will* their acceptance
*be* [a]but life from the dead?
16 For if [a]the firstfruit *is* holy, the lump *is* also
*holy;* and if the root *is* holy, so *are* the branches.
17 And if [a]some of the branches were broken off,
[b]and you, being a wild olive tree, were grafted in
among them, and with them became a partaker
of the root and fatness of the olive tree, 18 [a]do not
boast against the branches. But if you do boast,
*remember that* you do not support the root, but
the root *supports* you.
19 You will say then, "Branches were broken
off that I might be grafted in." 20 Well *said.* Be-
cause of [a]unbelief they were broken off, and you
stand by faith. Do not be haughty, but fear. 21 For

**10:14** [a] Titus 1:3 **10:15** [a] Is. 52:7; Nah. 1:15 [1] NU-Text omits *preach the gospel of peace, Who.* [2] Isaiah 52:7; Nahum 1:15 **10:16** [a] Is. 53:1 [1] Isaiah 53:1 **10:18** [a] Ps. 19:4 [1] Psalm 19:4 **10:19** [a] Deut. 32:21 [b] Titus 3:3 [1] Deuteronomy 32:21 **10:20** [a] Is. 65:1 [1] Isaiah 65:1 **10:21** [a] Is. 65:2 [1] Isaiah 65:2 **11:1** [a] Jer. 46:28 [b] 1 Sam. 12:22 [c] 2 Cor. 11:22 **11:2** [a] [Rom. 8:29] **11:3** [a] 1 Kin. 19:10, 14 [1] 1 Kings 19:10, 14 **11:4** [a] 1 Kin. 19:18 [1] 1 Kings 19:18 **11:5** [a] Rom. 9:27 **11:6** [a] Rom. 4:4 [1] NU-Text omits the rest of this verse. **11:7** [a] Rom. 9:31 [b] 2 Cor. 3:14 **11:8** [a] Is. 29:10, 13 [b] Deut. 29:3, 4 [1] Deuteronomy 29:4; Isaiah 29:10 **11:9** [a] Ps. 69:22, 23 **11:10** [1] Psalm 69:22, 23 **11:11** [a] Is. 42:6, 7 [b] Rom. 10:19 **11:13** [a] Acts 9:15; 22:21 **11:14** [a] 1 Cor. 9:22 **11:15** [a] [Is. 26:16–19] **11:16** [a] Lev. 23:10 **11:17** [a] Jer. 11:16 [b] [Eph. 2:12] **11:18** [a] [1 Cor. 10:12] **11:20** [a] Heb. 3:19

if God did not spare the natural branches, He
may not spare you either. 22 Therefore consider
the goodness and severity of God: on those who
fell, severity; but toward you, goodness,[1] [a]if you
continue in *His* goodness. Otherwise [b]you also
will be cut off. 23 And they also, [a]if they do not
continue in unbelief, will be grafted in, for God
is able to graft them in again. 24 For if you were
cut out of the olive tree which is wild by nature,
and were grafted contrary to nature into a cul-
tivated olive tree, how much more will these,
who *are* natural *branches,* be grafted into their
own olive tree?

25 For I do not desire, brethren, that you
should be ignorant of this mystery, lest you
should be [a]wise in your own opinion, that [b]blind-
ness in part has happened to Israel [c]until the
fullness of the Gentiles has come in. 26 And so
all Israel will be saved,[1] as it is written:

[a]"The Deliverer will come out of Zion,
And He will turn away ungodliness from
Jacob;
27 For [a]this *is* My covenant with them,
When I take away their sins."[1]

## SEEING JESUS IN THE SCRIPTURE

**11:26** The hope for Israel—and the entire world—always has been, always will be, and only can be the only Deliverer: Jesus (see. Is. 59:20).

28 Concerning the gospel *they are* enemies
for your sake, but concerning the election *they*
*are* [a]beloved for the sake of the fathers. 29 For
the gifts and the calling of God *are* [a]irrevocable.
30 For as you [a]were once disobedient to God,
yet have now obtained mercy through their
disobedience, 31 even so these also have now
been disobedient, that through the mercy shown
you they also may obtain mercy. 32 For God has
committed them [a]all to disobedience, that He
might have mercy on all.

33 Oh, the depth of the riches both of the wis-
dom and knowledge of God! How unsearchable
*are* His judgments and His ways past finding out!

34 "For who has known the [a]mind of the
LORD?
Or [b]who has become His
counselor?"[1]
35 "Or [a] who has first given to Him
And it shall be repaid to him?"[1]

36 For [a]of Him and through Him and to Him
*are* all things, [b]to whom *be* glory forever. Amen.

THE ROMANS ROAD 5

## THE CHANGE: LIFE

**12:1** Placing your faith in Jesus and being saved from sin isn't the end of the story; it's only the beginning. Remember, we aren't here to escape death, but to *live*, truly and fully. And this new life starts today. Right now, in Christ, we can experience life to the fullest and be the image-bearers of God He made us to be. We can grow to know Him more, love Him more, and worship Him more. A big part of that happens probably by what you're thinking: reading the Bible, praying, and singing. But worship is far more than that.

We can worship God in how we live every minute of every day. What we do in our homes, at school, on the ball field, at a part time job, online, and everywhere else can be done to celebrate who God is and help others to come to know Him too. This is our purpose. This is our worship. This is our joy.

*To begin the Romans Road, turn to Romans 3:15.*

### *LIVING SACRIFICES TO GOD*

**12** I [a]beseech you therefore, brethren, by
the mercies of God, that you present your
bodies [b]a living sacrifice, holy, acceptable to God,
*which is* your reasonable service. 2 And [a]do not
be conformed to this world, but [b]be transformed
by the renewing of your mind, that you may
[c]prove what *is* that good and acceptable and
perfect will of God.

**12:1** In the Old Testament sacrificial system, the "job" of the sacrificial lamb was ended with its death. An individual or household selected an animal according to the dictated forms, and it was sacrificed to cover sins. Since Christ became the final atonement for sin, we no longer need the old system. But Paul called believers to consider their whole lives as a sacrifice dedicated to God and His purposes, **a living sacrifice**, both **holy** and single-minded.

**11:22** [a] 1 Cor. 15:2 [b] [John 15:2] [1] NU-Text adds *of God.* **11:23** [a] [2 Cor. 3:16] **11:25** [a] Rom. 12:16 [b] 2 Cor. 3:14 [c] Luke 21:24 **11:26** [a] Is. 59:20, 21 [1] Or *delivered* **11:27** [a] Is. 27:9 [1] Isaiah 59:20, 21 **11:28** [a] Deut. 7:8; 10:15 **11:29** [a] Num. 23:19 **11:30** [a] [Eph. 2:2] **11:32** [a] [Gal. 3:22] **11:34** [a] Is. 40:13; Jer. 23:18 [b] Job 36:22 [1] Isaiah 40:13; Jeremiah 23:18 **11:35** [a] Job 41:11 [1] Job 41:11 **11:36** [a] Heb. 2:10 [b] Heb. 13:21 **12:1** [a] 2 Cor. 10:1–4 [b] Heb. 10:18, 20 **12:2** [a] 1 John 2:15 [b] Eph. 4:23 [c] [1 Thess. 4:3]

### SERVE GOD WITH SPIRITUAL GIFTS

3 For I say, [a]through the grace given to me,
to everyone who is among you, [b]not to think
*of himself* more highly than he ought to think,
but to think soberly, as God has dealt [c]to each
one a measure of faith. 4 For [a]as we have many
members in one body, but all the members
do not have the same function, 5 so [a]we, *being*
many, are one body in Christ, and individually
members of one another. 6 Having then gifts
differing according to the grace that is [a]given to
us, *let us use them:* if prophecy, *let us* [b]*prophesy* in
proportion to our faith; 7 or ministry, *let us use it*
in *our* ministering; [a]he who teaches, in teaching;
8 [a]he who exhorts, in exhortation; [b]he who gives,
with liberality; [c]he who leads, with diligence; he
who shows mercy, [d]with cheerfulness.

### BEHAVE LIKE A CHRISTIAN

9 [a]*Let* love *be* without hypocrisy. [b]Abhor
what is evil. Cling to what is good. 10 [a]*Be* kindly
affectionate to one another with brotherly love,
[b]in honor giving preference to one another;
11 not lagging in diligence, fervent in spirit, serv-
ing the Lord; 12 [a]rejoicing in hope, [b]patient in
tribulation, [c]continuing steadfastly in prayer;
13 [a]distributing to the needs of the saints, [b]given
to hospitality.

14 [a]Bless those who persecute you; bless and
do not curse. 15 [a]Rejoice with those who rejoice,
and weep with those who weep. 16 [a]Be of the same
mind toward one another. [b]Do not set your mind
on high things, but associate with the humble.
Do not be wise in your own opinion.

17 [a]Repay no one evil for evil. [b]Have re-
gard for good things in the sight of all men.
18 If it is possible, as much as depends on you,
[a]live peaceably with all men. 19 Beloved, [a]do
not avenge yourselves, but *rather* give place to
wrath; for it is written, [b]"Vengeance *is* Mine, I
will repay,"[1] says the Lord. 20 Therefore

> [a]"If your enemy is hungry, feed
> him;
> If he is thirsty, give him a drink;
> For in so doing you will heap coals of fire
> on his head."[1]

21 Do not be overcome by evil, but [a]overcome
evil with good.

### SUBMIT TO GOVERNMENT

13 Let every soul be [a]subject to the govern-
ing authorities. For there is no authority
except from God, and the authorities that exist
are appointed by God. 2 Therefore whoever
resists [a]the authority resists the ordinance of
God, and those who resist will bring judgment
on themselves. 3 For rulers are not a terror to
good works, but to evil. Do you want to be un-
afraid of the authority? [a]Do what is good, and
you will have praise from the same. 4 For he is
God's minister to you for good. But if you do
evil, be afraid; for he does not bear the sword
in vain; for he is God's minister, an avenger
to *execute* wrath on him who practices evil.
5 Therefore [a]*you* must be subject, not only be-
cause of wrath [b]but also for conscience' sake.
6 For because of this you also pay taxes, for they
are God's ministers attending continually to
this very thing. 7 [a]Render therefore to all their
due: taxes to whom taxes *are due,* customs to
whom customs, fear to whom fear, honor to
whom honor.

**12:3** [a]Gal. 2:9 [b]Prov. 25:27 [c][Eph. 4:7] **12:4** [a]1 Cor. 12:12–14 **12:5** [a][1 Cor. 10:17] **12:6** [a][John 3:27] [b]Acts 11:27 **12:7** [a]Eph. 4:11 **12:8** [a]Acts 15:32 [b][Matt. 6:1–3] [c][Acts 20:28] [d]2 Cor. 9:7 **12:9** [a]1 Tim. 1:5 [b]Ps. 34:14 **12:10** [a]Heb. 13:1 [b]Phil. 2:3 **12:12** [a]Luke 10:20 [b]Luke 21:19 [c]Luke 18:1 **12:13** [a]1 Cor. 16:1 [b]1 Tim. 3:2 **12:14** [a][Matt. 5:44] **12:15** [a][1 Cor. 12:26] **12:16** [a][Phil. 2:2; 4:2] [b]Jer. 45:5 **12:17** [a][Matt. 5:39] [b]2 Cor. 8:21 **12:18** [a]Heb. 12:14 **12:19** [a]Lev. 19:18 [b]Deut. 32:35 [1]Deuteronomy 32:35 **12:20** [a]Prov. 25:21, 22 [1]Proverbs 25:21, 22 **12:21** [a][Rom. 12:1, 2] **13:1** [a]1 Pet. 2:13 **13:2** [a][Titus 3:1] **13:3** [a]1 Pet. 2:14 **13:5** [a]Eccl. 8:2 [b][1 Pet. 2:13, 19] **13:7** [a]Matt. 22:21

APPLY THE TRUTH

## COMMUNITY

**12:4–6** What do you look for when you're choosing a new restaurant? Good food, obviously. Maybe a nice aesthetic or a convenient location. We usually figure all this out by looking at reviews. What do other people say? If others like it, we'll give it a shot. But a few bad reviews can mean we never try it. With so much of our lives built around reviews and having good experiences, it's easy to carry this consumer attitude into church and community. You can even find online reviews about churches! But church isn't about being a consumer, but rather being a contributor—an active participant.

This passage tells us God has given us different gifts by His grace, and He gave those gifts so we can use them together to bless others. The church is at its best not when *someone* is doing *everything*, but when *everyone* is doing *something*. That's why the church is called "a body" (see also 1 Cor. 12:12–31; Eph. 4:7–16). Every part matters. We each have a role to play both when we gather and when we scatter, and each of our roles is important. Together, we're better. That's what community is all about.

APPLY THE TRUTH

## POLITICS

**13:1–7** Politics have always been a hot topic, even in Jesus' day. At one point, a group of people came to Jesus to test Him, asking if it was lawful to pay taxes to Caesar (Matt. 22:17–21). Caesar wasn't just the leader of the Roman empire; He was also viewed as a god. (Those who refused to confess him as a god could be severely punished. This would give rise to Rome's persecution of the early church.) Jesus responded by pointing to Caesar's face on the Roman currency and saying to give to Caesar what was Caesar's and to God what is God's. In other words, politics have their place, but they should never take God's place. We're to reconcile politics with our Christian faith, not reconcile Christian faith with our politics.

In Romans, we're instructed to obey civil authorities because obeying governing authorities becomes a way to practice obeying God. But when the government does something contrary to what the Bible teaches, it's our responsibility to obey God instead. Sometimes that will mean disobeying, like we see in Acts 5:29. More often, it will mean working within the system to expand the gospel, like we see in Acts 22:25. Either way, we move forward with humility, being clear of our intention to make much of Jesus.

### LOVE YOUR NEIGHBOR

*(cf. Mark 12:31; James 2:8)*

8 Owe no one anything except to love one another, for [a]he who loves another has fulfilled the law. 9 For the commandments, [a]"You shall not commit adultery," "You shall not murder," "You shall not steal," "You shall not bear false witness,"[1] "You shall not covet,"[2] and if *there is* any other commandment, are *all* summed up in this saying, namely, [b]"You shall love your neighbor as yourself."[3] 10 Love does no harm to a neighbor; therefore [a]love *is* the fulfillment of the law.

### PUT ON CHRIST

11 And *do* this, knowing the time, that now *it is* high time [a]to awake out of sleep; for now our salvation *is* nearer than when we *first* believed. 12 The night is far spent, the day is at hand. [a]Therefore let us cast off the works of darkness, and [b]let us put on the armor of light. 13 [a]Let us walk properly, as in the day, [b]not in revelry and drunkenness, [c]not in lewdness and lust, [d]not in strife and envy. 14 But [a]put on the Lord Jesus Christ, and [b]make no provision for the flesh, to *fulfill its* lusts.

### THE LAW OF LIBERTY

14 Receive[a] one who is weak in the faith, *but* not to disputes over doubtful things. 2 For one believes he [a]may eat all things, but he who is weak eats *only* vegetables. 3 Let not him who eats despise him who does not eat, and [a]let not him who does not eat judge him who eats; for God has received him. 4 [a]Who are you to judge another's servant? To his own master he stands or falls. Indeed, he will be made to stand, for God is able to make him stand.

5 [a]One person esteems *one* day above another; another esteems every day *alike.* Let each be fully convinced in his own mind. 6 He who [a]observes the day, observes *it* to the Lord;[1] and he who does not observe the day, to the Lord he does not observe *it.* He who eats, eats to the Lord, for [b]he gives God thanks; and he who does not eat, to the Lord he does not eat, and gives God thanks. 7 For [a]none of us lives to himself, and no one dies to himself. 8 For if we [a]live, we live to the Lord; and if we die, we die to the Lord. Therefore, whether we live or die, we are the Lord's. 9 For [a]to this end Christ died and rose[1] and lived again, that He might be [b]Lord of both the dead and the living. 10 But why do you judge your brother? Or why do you show contempt for your brother? For [a]we shall all stand before the judgment seat of Christ.[1] 11 For it is written:

> [a]"*As* I live, says the LORD,
> Every knee shall bow to Me,
> And every tongue shall confess to God."[1]

12 So then [a]each of us shall give account of himself to God. 13 Therefore let us not judge one another anymore, but rather resolve this, [a]not to put a stumbling block or a cause to fall in *our* brother's way.

### THE LAW OF LOVE

14 I know and am convinced by the Lord Jesus [a]that *there is* nothing unclean of itself; but to him who considers anything to be unclean,

**13:8** [a] [Gal. 5:13, 14] **13:9** [a] Ex. 20:13–17; Deut. 5:17–21 [b] Lev. 19:18 [1] NU-Text omits *"You shall not bear false witness."* [2] Exodus 20:13–15, 17; Deuteronomy 5:17–19, 21 [3] Leviticus 19:18 **13:10** [a] [Matt. 7:12; 22:39, 40] **13:11** [a] [1 Cor. 15:34] **13:12** [a] Eph. 5:11 [b] [Eph. 6:11, 13] **13:13** [a] Phil. 4:8 [b] Prov. 23:20 [c] [1 Cor. 6:9] [d] James 3:14 **13:14** [a] Gal. 3:27 [b] [Gal. 5:16] **14:1** [a] [1 Cor. 8:9; 9:22] **14:2** [a] [Titus 1:15] **14:3** [a] [Col. 2:16] **14:4** [a] James 4:11, 12 **14:5** [a] Gal. 4:10 **14:6** [a] Gal. 4:10 [b] [1 Tim. 4:3] [1] NU-Text omits the rest of this sentence. **14:7** [a] [Gal. 2:20] **14:8** [a] 2 Cor. 5:14, 15 **14:9** [a] 2 Cor. 5:15 [b] Acts 10:36 [1] NU-Text omits *and rose.* **14:10** [a] 2 Cor. 5:10 [1] NU-Text reads *of God.* **14:11** [a] Is. 45:23 [1] Isaiah 45:23 **14:12** [a] 1 Pet. 4:5 **14:13** [a] 1 Cor. 8:9 **14:14** [a] 1 Cor. 10:25

to him *it is* unclean. 15 Yet if your brother is
grieved because of *your* food, you are no longer
walking in love. [a]Do not destroy with your food
the one for whom Christ died. 16 [a]Therefore do
not let your good be spoken of as evil; 17 [a]for
the kingdom of God is not eating and drinking,
but righteousness and [b]peace and joy in the
Holy Spirit. 18 For he who serves Christ in these
things[1] [a]*is* acceptable to God and approved
by men.

19 [a]Therefore let us pursue the things *which*
*make* for peace and the things by which [b]one
may edify another. 20 [a]Do not destroy the work
of God for the sake of food. [b]All things indeed
*are* pure, [c]but *it is* evil for the man who eats
with offense. 21 *It is* good neither to eat [a]meat
nor drink wine nor *do anything* by which your
brother stumbles or is offended or is made
weak.[1] 22 Do you have faith? Have[1] *it* to yourself
before God. [a]Happy *is* he who does not con-
demn himself in what he approves. 23 But he
who doubts is condemned if he eats, because
*he does* not *eat* from faith; for [a]whatever *is* not
from faith is sin.[1]

### *BEARING OTHERS' BURDENS*

15 We [a]then who are strong ought to bear with
the scruples of the weak, and not to please
ourselves. 2 [a]Let each of us please *his* neighbor
for *his* good, leading to edification. 3 [a]For even
Christ did not please Himself; but as it is writ-
ten, [b]"The reproaches of those who reproached
You fell on Me."[1] 4 For [a]whatever things were
written before were written for our learning,
that we through the patience and comfort of
the Scriptures might have hope. 5 [a]Now may
the God of patience and comfort grant you to
be like-minded toward one another, according
to Christ Jesus, 6 that you may [a]with one mind
*and* one mouth glorify the God and Father of
our Lord Jesus Christ.

> **SEEING JESUS IN THE SCRIPTURE**
>
> **15:3** The people rejecting Jesus and causing Him to suffer wasn't a surprise but rather a fulfillment of Scripture (see Ps. 69:9).

### *GLORIFY GOD TOGETHER*

7 Therefore [a]receive one another, just [b]as
Christ also received us,[1] to the glory of God.
8 Now I say that [a]Jesus Christ has become a
servant to the circumcision for the truth of God,
[b]to confirm the promises *made* to the fathers,
9 and [a]that the Gentiles might glorify God for
*His* mercy, as it is written:

[b]"For this reason I will confess to You
among the Gentiles,
And sing to Your name."[1]

10 And again he says:

[a]"Rejoice, O Gentiles, with His
people!"[1]

11 And again:

[a]"Praise the LORD, all you Gentiles!
Laud Him, all you peoples!"[1]

**14:15** [a] 1 Cor. 8:11 **14:16** [a] [Rom. 12:17] **14:17** [a] 1 Cor. 8:8 [b] [Rom. 8:6] **14:18** [a] 2 Cor. 8:21 [1] NU-Text reads *this.* **14:19** [a] Rom. 12:18 [b] 1 Cor. 14:12 **14:20** [a] Rom. 14:15 [b] Acts 10:15 [c] 1 Cor. 8:9–12 **14:21** [a] 1 Cor. 8:13 [1] NU-Text omits *or is offended or is made weak.* **14:22** [a] [1 John 3:21] [1] NU-Text reads *The faith which you have—have.* **14:23** [a] Titus 1:15 [1] M-Text puts Romans 16:25–27 here. **15:1** [a] [Gal. 6:1, 2] **15:2** [a] 1 Cor. 9:22; 10:24, 33 **15:3** [a] Matt. 26:39 [b] Ps. 69:9 [1] Psalm 69:9 **15:4** [a] 1 Cor. 10:11 **15:5** [a] 1 Cor. 1:10 **15:6** [a] Acts 4:24 **15:7** [a] Rom. 14:1, 3 [b] Rom. 5:2 [1] NU-Text and M-Text read *you.* **15:8** [a] Matt. 15:24 [b] 2 Cor. 1:20 **15:9** [a] John 10:16 [b] 2 Sam. 22:50; Ps. 18:49 [1] 2 Samuel 22:50; Psalm 18:49 **15:10** [a] Deut. 32:43 [1] Deuteronomy 32:43 **15:11** [a] Ps. 117:1 [1] Psalm 117:1

> LIVE THE TRUTH
>
> ## BEING A STUDENT
>
> **15:4** There's a difference between reading and studying. We should read God's Word, but we should study it carefully also. When we study the Scriptures, we diligently inspect it to go beyond understanding it to reach the point of living it. In studying Scripture, we commit it to memory, internalize its truths, apply it to our lives, and place our hope in it and its author. Only by studying the Bible will we truly receive its full blessing in our lives.
>
> Paul reminds us here that the Scriptures are a blessing. They inform us of what is true, especially when we need it. Life can be frustrating, but when we understand the full picture of God's plan and provision through Jesus, we can withstand the brokenness of this world. Study God's Word until it becomes part of the fabric of your life. Don't skip over the difficult parts—God purposefully included them for us. Lean on others who can help you with your study. Seek supplemental materials that can aide you in your learning. Above all else, never stop. You'll be surprised by what God shows you as you continue to be filled by His encompassing truths.

12 And again, Isaiah says:

> [a]"There shall be a root of Jesse;
> And He who shall rise to reign over the Gentiles,
> In Him the Gentiles shall hope."[1]

13 Now may the God of hope fill you with all
[a]joy and peace in believing, that you may abound
in hope by the power of the Holy Spirit.

### *FROM JERUSALEM TO ILLYRICUM*

14 Now [a]I myself am confident concerning
you, my brethren, that you also are full of good-
ness, [b]filled with all knowledge, able also to
admonish one another.[1] 15 Nevertheless, breth-
ren, I have written more boldly to you on *some*
points, as reminding you, [a]because of the grace
given to me by God, 16 that [a]I might be a minister
of Jesus Christ to the Gentiles, ministering the
gospel of God, that the [b]offering of the Gentiles
might be acceptable, sanctified by the Holy Spir-
it. 17 Therefore I have reason to glory in Christ
Jesus [a]in the things *which pertain* to God. 18 For
I will not dare to speak of any of those things
[a]which Christ has not accomplished through
me, in word and deed, [b]to make the Gentiles
obedient— 19 [a]in mighty signs and wonders,
by the power of the Spirit of God, so that from
Jerusalem and round about to Illyricum I have
fully preached the gospel of Christ. 20 And so I
have made it my aim to preach the gospel, not
where Christ was named, [a]lest I should build on
another man's foundation, 21 but as it is written:

> [a]"To whom He was not announced, they shall see;
> And those who have not heard shall understand."[1]

### *PLAN TO VISIT ROME*

22 For this reason [a]I also have been much
hindered from coming to you. 23 But now no
longer having a place in these parts, and [a]having
a great desire these many years to come to you,
24 whenever I journey to Spain, I shall come to
you.[1] For I hope to see you on my journey, [a]and
to be helped on my way there by you, if first
I may [b]enjoy your *company* for a while. 25 But
now [a]I am going to Jerusalem to minister to the
saints. 26 For [a]it pleased those from Macedonia
and Achaia to make a certain contribution for
the poor among the saints who are in Jerusa-
lem. 27 It pleased them indeed, and they are
their debtors. For [a]if the Gentiles have been
partakers of their spiritual things, [b]their duty
is also to minister to them in material things.
28 Therefore, when I have performed this and
have sealed to them [a]this fruit, I shall go by
way of you to Spain. 29 [a]But I know that when I
come to you, I shall come in the fullness of the
blessing of the gospel[1] of Christ.
30 Now I beg you, brethren, through the Lord
Jesus Christ, and [a]through the love of the Spirit,
[b]that you strive together with me in prayers to
God for me, 31 [a]that I may be delivered from those
in Judea who do not believe, and that [b]my service
for Jerusalem may be acceptable to the saints,
32 [a]that I may come to you with joy [b]by the will of
God, and may [c]be refreshed together with you.
33 Now [a]the God of peace *be* with you all. Amen.

### *SISTER PHOEBE COMMENDED*

16 I commend to you Phoebe our sister, who is
a servant of the church in [a]Cenchrea, 2 [a]that
you may receive her in the Lord [b]in a manner
worthy of the saints, and assist her in whatever
business she has need of you; for indeed she
has been a helper of many and of myself also.

### *GREETING ROMAN SAINTS*

3 Greet [a]Priscilla and Aquila, my fellow work-
ers in Christ Jesus, 4 who risked their own necks
for my life, to whom not only I give thanks, but
also all the churches of the Gentiles. 5 Likewise
*greet* [a]the church that is in their house.

> **16:3 Priscilla and Aquila** were originally from Rome. When the Emperor Claudius ordered all the Jews out of Rome, the couple moved to Corinth, a city in Greece, and worked with Paul there. Before they eventually moved back to Rome, they also helped Paul in Ephesus, a city across the Aegean Sea from Corinth.

Greet my beloved Epaenetus, who is [b]the
firstfruits of Achaia[1] to Christ. 6 Greet Mary, who
labored much for us. 7 Greet Andronicus and
Junia, my countrymen and my fellow prisoners,
who are of note among the [a]apostles, who also
[b]were in Christ before me.
8 Greet Amplias, my beloved in the Lord.
9 Greet Urbanus, our fellow worker in Christ, and
Stachys, my beloved. 10 Greet Apelles, approved
in Christ. Greet those who are of the *household*
of Aristobulus. 11 Greet Herodion, my country-
man.[1] Greet those who are of the *household* of
Narcissus who are in the Lord.

**15:12** [a] Is. 11:1, 10 [1] Isaiah 11:10 **15:13** [a] Rom. 12:12; 14:17 **15:14** [a] 2 Pet. 1:12 [b] 1 Cor. 1:5; 8:1, 7, 10 [1] M-Text reads *others.* **15:15** [a] Rom. 1:5; 12:3 **15:16** [a] Rom. 11:13 [b] [Is. 66:20] **15:17** [a] Heb. 2:17; 5:1 **15:18** [a] Acts 15:12; 21:19 [b] Rom. 1:5 **15:19** [a] Acts 19:11 **15:20** [a] [2 Cor. 10:13, 15, 16] **15:21** [a] Is. 52:15 [1] Isaiah 52:15 **15:22** [a] Rom. 1:13 **15:23** [a] Acts 19:21; 23:11 **15:24** [a] Acts 15:3 [b] Rom. 1:12 [1] NU-Text omits *I shall come to you* (and joins *Spain* with the next sentence). **15:25** [a] Acts 19:21 **15:26** [a] 1 Cor. 16:1 **15:27** [a] Rom. 11:17 [b] 1 Cor. 9:11 **15:28** [a] Phil. 4:17 **15:29** [a] [Rom. 1:11] [1] NU-Text omits *of the gospel.* **15:30** [a] Phil. 2:1 [b] 2 Cor. 1:11 **15:31** [a] 2 Tim. 3:11; 4:17 [b] 2 Cor. 8:4 **15:32** [a] Rom. 1:10 [b] Acts 18:21 [c] 1 Cor. 16:18 **15:33** [a] 1 Cor. 14:33 **16:1** [a] Acts 18:18 **16:2** [a] Phil. 2:29 [b] Phil. 1:27 **16:3** [a] Acts 18:2, 18, 26 **16:5** [a] 1 Cor. 16:19 [b] 1 Cor. 16:15 [1] NU-Text reads *Asia.* **16:7** [a] Acts 1:13, 26 [b] Gal. 1:22 **16:11** [1] Or *relative*

[12]Greet Tryphena and Tryphosa, who have
labored in the Lord. Greet the beloved Persis,
who labored much in the Lord. [13]Greet Rufus,
[a]chosen in the Lord, and his mother and mine.
[14]Greet Asyncritus, Phlegon, Hermas, Patrobas,
Hermes, and the brethren who are with them.
[15]Greet Philologus and Julia, Nereus and his
sister, and Olympas, and all the saints who are
with them.

[16][a]Greet one another with a holy kiss. The[1]
churches of Christ greet you.

### *AVOID DIVISIVE PERSONS*

[17]Now I urge you, brethren, note those
[a]who cause divisions and offenses, contrary
to the doctrine which you learned, and [b]avoid
them. [18]For those who are such do not serve
our Lord Jesus[1] Christ, but [a]their own belly,
and [b]by smooth words and flattering speech
deceive the hearts of the simple. [19]For [a]your
obedience has become known to all. Therefore
I am glad on your behalf; but I want you to be
[b]wise in what is good, and simple concerning
evil. [20]And [a]the God of peace [b]will crush Satan
under your feet shortly.

[c]The grace of our Lord Jesus Christ *be* with
you. Amen.

### *GREETINGS FROM PAUL'S FRIENDS*

[21][a]Timothy, my fellow worker, and [b]Luci-
us, [c]Jason, and [d]Sosipater, my countrymen,
greet you.

[22]I, Tertius, who wrote *this* epistle, greet
you in the Lord.

[23][a]Gaius, my host and *the host* of the whole
church, greets you. [b]Erastus, the treasurer of
the city, greets you, and Quartus, a brother.
[24][a]The grace of our Lord Jesus Christ *be* with
you all. Amen.[1]

### *BENEDICTION*

[25]Now [a]to Him who is able to establish you
[b]according to my gospel and the preaching of
Jesus Christ, [c]according to the revelation of
the mystery [d]kept secret since the world began
[26]but [a]now made manifest, and by the prophetic
Scriptures made known to all nations, according
to the commandment of the everlasting God, for
[b]obedience to the faith— [27]to [a]God, alone wise,
*be* glory through Jesus Christ forever. Amen.[1]

**16:13** [a] 2 John 1 **16:16** [a] 1 Cor. 16:20 [1] NU-Text reads *All the churches.* **16:17** [a] [Acts 15:1] [b] [1 Cor. 5:9] **16:18** [a] Phil. 3:19 [b] Col. 2:4 [1] NU-Text and M-Text omit *Jesus.* **16:19** [a] Rom. 1:8 [b] Matt. 10:16 **16:20** [a] Rom. 15:33 [b] Gen. 3:15 [c] 1 Cor. 16:23 **16:21** [a] Acts 16:1 [b] Acts 13:1 [c] Acts 17:5 [d] Acts 20:4 **16:23** [a] 1 Cor. 1:14 [b] Acts 19:22 **16:24** [a] 1 Thess. 5:28 [1] NU-Text omits this verse. **16:25** [a] [Eph. 3:20] [b] Rom. 2:16 [c] Eph. 1:9 [d] Col. 1:26; 2:2; 4:3 **16:26** [a] Eph. 1:9 [b] Rom. 1:5 **16:27** [a] Jude 25 [1] M-Text puts Romans 16:25–27 after Romans 14:23.

# *The First Epistle of Paul the Apostle to the*
# CORINTHIANS

| AUTHOR | KEY VERSE | READING TIME |
|---|---|---|
| Paul | 1 Corinthians 10:31 | 1 hour 12 minutes |

Corinth, the most important city in Greece during Paul's day, was a bustling hub of worldwide commerce, but it was also a city of degraded culture and idolatrous religion. In this center of unabashed sin, Paul taught the Word of God for eighteen months from AD 51 to AD 52 (Acts 18:1–17) before leaving Apollos in the city to continue preaching and teaching. When word of some problems in the Corinthian church reached Paul, he penned a letter to provide guidance. First Corinthians reveals the problems, pressures, and struggles of a church called out of a pagan society it still lives within. Paul addressed factions, lawsuits, immorality, questionable practices, abuse of the Lord's Supper, and misused spiritual gifts. In addition to words of correction, Paul shared words of counsel, answering several questions raised by the Corinthian believers.

**Occasion:** When Paul was in Ephesus during his third missionary journey, he became disturbed by reports of discord in the church of Corinth. First Corinthians is a record of Paul's initial response to these problems.

**Main Point:** Believers are to live rightly with God and one another in all situations.

**Big Ideas:** The church is to be unified by the gospel. Followers of Jesus should live differently from the people around them. We are given gifts to use in the church and each gift is important.

## OUTLINE:

I. Divisions in the Church (chs. 1–4)
II. Immorality in the Church (ch. 5)
III. Lawsuits and Impurity in the Church (ch. 6)
IV. Instructions Concerning Marriage (ch. 7)
V. Instructions Concerning Offerings to Idols (chs. 8–10)
VI. Instructions Concerning Worship (chs. 11–14)
VII. Instructions Concerning Resurrection (ch. 15)
VIII. Instructions Concerning Collections (ch. 16)

**c. AD 34**
Paul is converted

**c. AD 47–49**
Paul's first missionary journey

**c. AD 50**
The Jerusalem Council

**c. AD 50–53**
Paul's second missionary journey

**AD 52**
The church at Corinth is founded

**c. AD 53–57**
Paul's third missionary journey

**AD 54–68**
Nero is Roman emperor

**c. AD 55–56**
**1 Corinthians written**

**c. AD 58**
Paul is arrested in Jerusalem

**c. AD 60–62**
Paul is imprisoned in Rome

**AD 64**
Great Fire of Rome; first Roman mass persecution of Christians

**c. AD 67**
Peter and Paul are executed

### *GREETING*

**1** Paul, [a]called *to be* an apostle of Jesus Christ
[b]through the will of God, and [c]Sosthenes
*our* brother,

2 To the church of God which is at Corinth,
to those who [a]are sanctified in Christ Jesus,
[b]called *to be* saints, with all who in every place
call on the name of Jesus Christ [c]our Lord, [d]both
theirs and ours:

3 [a]Grace to you and peace from God our Fa-
ther and the Lord Jesus Christ.

### *SPIRITUAL GIFTS AT CORINTH*

4 [a]I thank my God always concerning you for
the grace of God which was given to you by Christ
Jesus, 5 that you were enriched in everything by
Him [a]in all utterance and all knowledge, 6 even
as [a]the testimony of Christ was confirmed in
you, 7 so that you come short in no gift, eagerly
[a]waiting for the revelation of our Lord Jesus
Christ, 8 [a]who will also confirm you to the end,
[b]*that you may be* blameless in the day of our
Lord Jesus Christ. 9 [a]God *is* faithful, by whom
you were called into [b]the fellowship of His Son,
Jesus Christ our Lord.

### *SECTARIANISM IS SIN*

10 Now I plead with you, brethren, by the
name of our Lord Jesus Christ, [a]that you all
speak the same thing, and *that* there be no di-
visions among you, but *that* you be perfectly
joined together in the same mind and in the
same judgment. 11 For it has been declared to
me concerning you, my brethren, by those of
Chloe's *household,* that there are contentions
among you. 12 Now I say this, that [a]each of you
says, "I am of Paul," or "I am of [b]Apollos," or "I
am of [c]Cephas," or "I am of Christ." 13 [a]Is Christ
divided? Was Paul crucified for you? Or were
you baptized in the name of Paul?

> **1:12 Apollos** was an important leader in the early Christian church. He was a gifted public speaker and an expert on Old Testament writings. He lived in Alexandria, Egypt. **Cephas** was another name for Peter.

14 I thank God that I baptized [a]none of you
except [b]Crispus and [c]Gaius, 15 lest anyone should
say that I had baptized in my own name. 16 Yes,
I also baptized the household of [a]Stephanas.
Besides, I do not know whether I baptized any
other. 17 For Christ did not send me to baptize,
but to preach the gospel, [a]not with wisdom of
words, lest the cross of Christ should be made
of no effect.

### *CHRIST THE POWER AND WISDOM OF GOD*

*(cf. Is. 29:14)*

18 For the message of the cross is [a]foolishness
to [b]those who are perishing, but to us [c]who are
being saved it is the [d]power of God. 19 For it is
written:

[a]"I will destroy the wisdom of the wise,
And bring to nothing the understanding
of the prudent."[1]

20 [a]Where *is* the wise? Where *is* the scribe?
Where *is* the disputer of this age? [b]Has not God
made foolish the wisdom of this world? 21 For
since, in the [a]wisdom of God, the world through
wisdom did not know God, it pleased God through
the foolishness of the message preached to save
those who believe. 22 For [a]Jews request a sign, and
Greeks seek after wisdom; 23 but we preach Christ
crucified, [a]to the Jews a stumbling block and to
the Greeks[1] [b]foolishness, 24 but to those who are
called, both Jews and Greeks, Christ [a]the power
of God and [b]the wisdom of God. 25 Because the
foolishness of God is wiser than men, and the
weakness of God is stronger than men.

### *GLORY ONLY IN THE LORD*

26 For you see your calling, brethren, [a]that
not many wise according to the flesh, not many
mighty, not many noble, *are called.* 27 But [a]God
has chosen the foolish things of the world to put
to shame the wise, and God has chosen the weak
things of the world to put to shame the things
which are mighty; 28 and the base things of the
world and the things which are despised God has
chosen, and the things which are not, to bring
to nothing the things that are, 29 that no flesh
should glory in His presence. 30 But of Him you
are in Christ Jesus, who became for us wisdom
from God—and [a]righteousness and sanctifica-
tion and redemption— 31 that, as it is written,
[a]"He who glories, let him glory in the LORD."[1]

### *CHRIST CRUCIFIED*

**2** And I, brethren, when I came to you, did
not come with excellence of speech or of
wisdom declaring to you the testimony[1] of God.
2 For I determined not to know anything among
you [a]except Jesus Christ and Him crucified. 3 [a]I
was with you [b]in weakness, in fear, and in much

**1:1** [a] Rom. 1:1 [b] 2 Cor. 1:1 [c] Acts 18:17 **1:2** [a] [Acts 15:9] [b] Rom. 1:7 [c] [1 Cor. 8:6] [d] [Rom. 3:22] **1:3** [a] Rom. 1:7 **1:4** [a] Rom. 1:8 **1:5** [a] [1 Cor. 12:8] **1:6** [a] 2 Tim. 1:8 **1:7** [a] Phil. 3:20 **1:8** [a] 1 Thess. 3:13; 5:23 [b] Col. 1:22; 2:7 **1:9** [a] Is. 49:7 [b] [John 15:4] **1:10** [a] 2 Cor. 13:11 **1:12** [a] 1 Cor. 3:4 [b] Acts 18:24 [c] John 1:42 **1:13** [a] 2 Cor. 11:4 **1:14** [a] John 4:2 [b] Acts 18:8 [c] Rom. 16:23 **1:16** [a] 1 Cor. 16:15, 17 **1:17** [a] [1 Cor. 2:1, 4, 13] **1:18** [a] 1 Cor. 2:14 [b] 2 Cor. 2:15 [c] [1 Cor. 15:2] [d] Rom. 1:16 **1:19** [a] Is. 29:14 [1] Isaiah 29:14 **1:20** [a] Is. 19:12; 33:18 [b] Job 12:17 **1:21** [a] Dan. 2:20 **1:22** [a] Matt. 12:38 **1:23** [a] Luke 2:34 [b] [1 Cor. 2:14] [1] NU-Text reads *Gentiles.* **1:24** [a] [Rom. 1:4] [b] Col. 2:3 **1:26** [a] John 7:48 **1:27** [a] Matt. 11:25 **1:30** [a] [2 Cor. 5:21] **1:31** [a] Jer. 9:23, 24 [1] Jeremiah 9:24 **2:1** [1] NU-Text reads *mystery.* **2:2** [a] Gal. 6:14 **2:3** [a] Acts 18:1 [b] [2 Cor. 4:7]

KNOW THE TRUTH

## THE DOCTRINE OF SALVATION

### PART 7: THE CONTINUATION OF SALVATION

**1:18** For the born-again believer, salvation is at once a completed event in the past, continual events in the present, and an anticipated event in the future. We *have been* saved. We *are being* saved. We *will be* saved. All three statements are wonderfully simultaneously true.

Salvation is a **past event** in that we've been entirely forgiven of sin, saved from God's wrath, and granted eternal life with God as His son or daughter. It is a completed work meaning our new standing is immediate and secure forevermore.

Salvation is a **present work** as day by day we're being delivered from the destructive and decaying power of sin, the schemes of the devil, and the evil actions of others. The Holy Spirit leads us out of bondage into freedom, trauma into healing, selfishness into love, and fear into faith, as He also provides comfort, encouragement, and wisdom for every trial, tragedy, and triumph we face.

Salvation is a **future promise** in that we have hope—confident expectation—Jesus is returning, and when He does, He will put an end to all evil, sin, and death. We will then live for eternity with Him and all other believers of all time as God originally intended for us to live—without any reference to sin, suffering and death.

*For* **THE DOCTRINE OF SALVATION: PART 8: THE COMPLETION OF SALVATION**, *turn to Romans 8:28–30 on page 1155.* • • •

trembling. 4 And my speech and my preaching
[a]*were* not with persuasive words of human[1]
wisdom, [b]but in demonstration of the Spirit
and of power, 5 that your faith should not be in
the wisdom of men but in the [a]power of God.

### *SPIRITUAL WISDOM*

6 However, we speak wisdom among those
who are mature, yet not the wisdom of this age,
nor of the rulers of this age, who are coming to
nothing. 7 But we speak the wisdom of God in a
mystery, the hidden *wisdom* which God ordained
before the ages for our glory, 8 which none of the
rulers of this age knew; for [a]had they known,
they would not have [b]crucified the Lord of glory.
9 But as it is written:

[a]"Eye has not seen, nor ear heard,
Nor have entered into the heart of man
The things which God has prepared for
those who love Him."[1]

10 But [a]God has revealed *them* to us through His
Spirit. For the Spirit searches all things, yes, the
deep things of God. 11 For what man knows the
things of a man except the [a]spirit of the man
which is in him? [b]Even so no one knows the
things of God except the Spirit of God. 12 Now we
have received, not the spirit of the world, but [a]the
Spirit who is from God, that we might know the
things that have been freely given to us by God.
13 These things we also speak, not in words
which man's wisdom teaches but which the
Holy[1] Spirit teaches, comparing spiritual things
with spiritual. 14 [a]But the natural man does not
receive the things of the Spirit of God, for they
are foolishness to him; nor can he know *them,*
because they are spiritually discerned. 15 But he
who is spiritual judges all things, yet he himself
is *rightly* judged by no one. 16 For [a]"who has
known the mind of the LORD that he may in-
struct Him?"[1] [b]But we have the mind of Christ.

### *SECTARIANISM IS CARNAL*

3 And I, brethren, could not speak to you as to
spiritual *people* but as to carnal, as to [a]babes
in Christ. 2 I fed you with [a]milk and not with solid
food; [b]for until now you were not able *to receive
it,* and even now you are still not able; 3 for you
are still carnal. For where *there are* envy, strife,
and divisions among you, are you not carnal and
behaving like *mere* men? 4 For when one says,
"I am of Paul," and another, "I *am* of Apollos,"
are you not carnal?

### *WATERING, WORKING, WARNING*

5 Who then is Paul, and who *is* Apollos, but
[a]ministers through whom you believed, as the

**2:4** [a] 2 Pet. 1:16 [b] Rom. 15:19 [1] NU-Text omits *human.* **2:5** [a] 1 Thess. 1:5 **2:8** [a] Luke 23:34 [b] Matt. 27:33–50 **2:9** [a] [Is. 64:4; 65:17] [1] Isaiah 64:4 **2:10** [a] Matt. 11:25; 13:11; 16:17 **2:11** [a] [James 2:26] [b] Rom. 11:33 **2:12** [a] [Rom. 8:15] **2:13** [1] NU-Text omits *Holy.* **2:14** [a] Matt. 16:23 **2:16** [a] Is. 40:13 [b] [John 15:15] [1] Isaiah 40:13 **3:1** [a] Heb. 5:13 **3:2** [a] 1 Pet. 2:2 [b] John 16:12 **3:5** [a] 2 Cor. 3:3, 6; 4:1; 5:18; 6:4

1 CORINTHIANS 2:1–5

## THE MAIN MESSAGE

55 STORY OF SCRIPTURE

### WHAT'S GOING ON?

This statement from Paul reflects the overall tone of the apostles and the message of Christ to the world. Paul emphasized that he didn't come to the church in Corinth with eloquence of speech or superior wisdom. Instead, he came in weakness, fear, and trembling. He knew the strength of the gospel wasn't found in persuasive speaking or lofty practices, but rather in a demonstration of the Spirit's power. This approach ensured the Corinthians' faith wouldn't rest on human persuasiveness—dependent on Paul—but rather on God's power.

Paul's method contrasted sharply with what a Greek audience expected. The Greeks valued eloquence and philosophy. Instead, Paul focused on the simple, yet profound, truth of Christ and Him crucified.

### WHAT DOES THIS MEAN FOR ME?

Paul's approach teaches us about the essence of the gospel message. It's not about complex theology or eloquent speeches but the simple, transformative power of Christ's sacrifice. It also reassures us that in sharing our faith, we don't need to rely on our eloquence or wisdom to convince others. Ultimately, that is the Holy Spirit's work. It's good that we study and prepare, but our inadequacies and weaknesses can actually be strengths in God's hands.

### DID YOU CATCH THE PATTERN?

Throughout the Bible, God used unlikely people in powerful ways. Moses was slow of speech, David was a shepherd boy, the disciples were mostly fishermen, and here, Paul, despite being educated, chose simplicity over complexity. This pattern shows God's preference for humble hearts over impressive human qualifications. It echoes Jesus' teachings in the Beatitudes, where the poor in spirit, the meek, and the pure in heart are blessed (see Matt. 5:3–10). Paul's message aligns with this beatitude-like humility, focusing not on human wisdom but on the power of God.

*For the next* Story of Scripture *reading and devotion, turn to 1 Timothy 1:15–16 on page 1229.*

Lord gave to each one? 6 [a]I planted, [b]Apollos wa-
tered, [c]but God gave the increase. 7 So then [a]neither
he who plants is anything, nor he who waters, but
God who gives the increase. 8 Now he who plants
and he who waters are one, [a]and each one will
receive his own reward according to his own labor.
9 For [a]we are God's fellow workers; you are
God's field, *you are* [b]God's building. 10 [a]According
to the grace of God which was given to me, as a
wise master builder I have laid [b]the foundation,
and another builds on it. But let each one take
heed how he builds on it. 11 For no other foun-
dation can anyone lay than [a]that which is laid,
[b]which is Jesus Christ. 12 Now if anyone builds on

### SEEING JESUS IN THE SCRIPTURE

**3:11** Jesus is the precious and sure foundation we build our lives upon, just as the Scriptures foretold (see Is. 28:16).

this foundation *with* gold, silver, precious stones,
wood, hay, straw, 13 each one's work will become
clear; for the Day [a]will declare it, because [b]it will
be revealed by fire; and the fire will test each one's
work, of what sort it is. 14 If anyone's work which he
has built on *it* endures, he will receive a reward.
15 If anyone's work is burned, he will suffer loss;
but he himself will be saved, yet so as through fire.
16 [a]Do you not know that you are the temple
of God and *that* the Spirit of God dwells in you?
17 If anyone defiles the temple of God, God will
destroy him. For the temple of God is holy, which
*temple* you are.

### *AVOID WORLDLY WISDOM*

18 [a]Let no one deceive himself. If anyone
among you seems to be wise in this age, let him
become a fool that he may become wise. 19 For
the wisdom of this world is foolishness with God.
For it is written, [a]"He catches the wise in their
*own* craftiness";[1] 20 and again, [a]"The LORD knows
the thoughts of the wise, that they are futile."[1]

**3:6** [a] Acts 18:4 [b] Acts 18:24–27 [c] [2 Cor. 3:5] **3:7** [a] [Gal. 6:3] **3:8** [a] Ps. 62:12 **3:9** [a] 2 Cor. 6:1 [b] [Eph. 2:20–22] **3:10** [a] Rom. 1:5 [b] 1 Cor. 4:15 **3:11** [a] Is. 28:16 [b] Eph. 2:20 **3:13** [a] 1 Pet. 1:7 [b] Luke 2:35 **3:16** [a] 2 Cor. 6:16 **3:18** [a] Prov. 3:7 **3:19** [a] Job 5:13 [1] Job 5:13 **3:20** [a] Ps. 94:11 [1] Psalm 94:11

LIVE THE TRUTH

## GROWING AND MATURING

**3:11–15** When we trust in Christ, we haven't arrived; we've just begun. To follow Jesus is to grow. It's to be changed by Him to look more like Him. It's about allowing God to shape us more into the image of Christ day by day. We grow in part by reading God's Word and doing what it says. As we do, we'll find it easier to read, understand, and obey. We'll find we gradually live more like Jesus. We'll still sin and make mistakes, but as we mature, we'll find we do that less often. We'll also discover we can handle and comprehend biblical truths that were once too difficult. We just need to be sure to grow the right way.

In 1 Corinthians 3, Paul addressed disunity in the Corinthian church. Some opposing leaders had come in and were teaching false "Christian" practices. We don't exactly know what they were, but because they were false, those who followed them weren't growing. They had the wrong foundation; therefore, the steps they took were worthless. The gospel, on the other hand, is a sure foundation allowing us to take steps that are like precious jewels. Our growth is valuable and lasting. We can't stay still. Be sure to grow but be extra sure to grow the right way.

21 Therefore let no one boast in men. For [a]all things are yours: 22 whether Paul or Apollos or Cephas, or the world or life or death, or things present or things to come—all are yours. 23 And [a]you *are* Christ's, and Christ *is* God's.

### STEWARDS OF THE MYSTERIES OF GOD

**4** Let a man so consider us, as [a]servants of Christ [b]and stewards of the mysteries of God. 2 Moreover it is required in stewards that one be found faithful. 3 But with me it is a very small thing that I should be judged by you or by a human court.[1] In fact, I do not even judge myself. 4 For I know of nothing against myself, yet I am not justified by this; but He who judges me is the Lord. 5 [a]Therefore judge nothing before the time, until the Lord comes, who will both bring to [b]light the hidden things of darkness and [c]reveal the counsels of the hearts. [d]Then each one's praise will come from God.

### FOOLS FOR CHRIST'S SAKE

6 Now these things, brethren, I have figuratively transferred to myself and Apollos for your sakes, that you may learn in us not to think beyond what is written, that none of you may be puffed up on behalf of one against the other. 7 For who makes you differ *from another?* And [a]what do you have that you did not receive? Now if you did indeed receive *it,* why do you boast as if you had not received *it?*

8 You are already full! [a]You are already rich! You have reigned as kings without us—and indeed I could wish you did reign, that we also might reign with you! 9 For I think that God has displayed us, the apostles, last, as men condemned to death; for we have been made a [a]spectacle to the world, both to angels and to men. 10 We *are* [a]fools for Christ's sake, but you *are* wise in Christ! [b]We *are* weak, but you *are* strong! You *are* distinguished, but we *are* dishonored! 11 To the present hour we both hunger and thirst, and we are poorly clothed, and beaten, and homeless. 12 [a]And we labor, working with our own hands. [b]Being reviled, we bless; being persecuted, we endure; 13 being defamed, we entreat. [a]We have been made as the filth of the world, the offscouring of all things until now.

### PAUL'S PATERNAL CARE

14 I do not write these things to shame you, but [a]as my beloved children I warn *you.* 15 For though you might have ten thousand instructors in Christ, yet *you do* not *have* many fathers; for [a]in Christ Jesus I have begotten you through the gospel. 16 Therefore I urge you, [a]imitate me. 17 For this reason I have sent [a]Timothy to you, [b]who is my beloved and faithful son in the Lord, who will [c]remind you of my ways in Christ, as I [d]teach everywhere [e]in every church.

18 [a]Now some are puffed up, as though I were not coming to you. 19 [a]But I will come to you shortly, [b]if the Lord wills, and I will know, not the word of those who are puffed up, but the power. 20 For [a]the kingdom of God *is* not in word but in [b]power. 21 What do you want? [a]Shall I come to you with a rod, or in love and a spirit of gentleness?

### IMMORALITY DEFILES THE CHURCH

**5** It is actually reported *that there is* sexual immorality among you, and such sexual immorality as is not even named[1] among the Gentiles—that a man has his father's [a]wife!

**3:21** [a] [2 Cor. 4:5] **3:23** [a] 2 Cor. 10:7 **4:1** [a] Col. 1:25 [b] Titus 1:7 **4:3** [1] Literally *day* **4:5** [a] Matt. 7:1 [b] Matt. 10:26 [c] 1 Cor. 3:13 [d] Rom. 2:29 **4:7** [a] John 3:27 **4:8** [a] Rev. 3:17 **4:9** [a] Heb. 10:33 **4:10** [a] Acts 17:18; 26:24 [b] 2 Cor. 13:9 **4:12** [a] Acts 18:3; 20:34 [b] Matt. 5:44 **4:13** [a] Lam. 3:45 **4:14** [a] 1 Thess. 2:11 **4:15** [a] Gal. 4:19 **4:16** [a] [1 Cor. 11:1] **4:17** [a] Acts 19:22 [b] 1 Tim. 1:2, 18 [c] 1 Cor. 11:2 [d] 1 Cor. 7:17 [e] 1 Cor. 14:33 **4:18** [a] 1 Cor. 5:2 **4:19** [a] Acts 19:21; 20:2 [b] Acts 18:21 **4:20** [a] 1 Thess. 1:5 [b] 1 Cor. 2:4 **4:21** [a] 2 Cor. 10:2 **5:1** [a] Lev. 18:6–8 [1] NU-Text omits *named.*

APPLY THE TRUTH

## PORNOGRAPHY

**5:1** It's easy to allow what goes on in the world to affect us as followers of Jesus. That's what happened in Corinth. The culture influenced the church. In fact, Paul said the culture wouldn't even permit the sexual immorality the church tolerated. Especially recently, pornography, a form of sexual immorality, has become widespread in the church with even pastors and leaders struggling with it. But just because pornography is common doesn't make it okay; it makes it even more dangerous. Out of shame or fear, we rarely talk about pornography, leaving far too many people struggling in silence and alone. Meanwhile, pornography continues to leave its trail of destruction in relationships, marriages, motivations, and social interactions.

If you're struggling with pornography, don't tolerate it. Instead, turn it over to Christ, basking in His love, forgiveness, and power, while you act in practical ways to protect yourself and find deliverance. **Confess.** Tell someone you trust about this struggle. You'll be surprised by how just getting it into the light begins to release its grip on you. **Create boundaries.** Notice the times, places, and emotions that lead to pornography and set boundaries that keep you from going there. **Check in.** Ask someone you trust and respect to check in on you regularly to help you overcome and live in the light.

2 [a]And you are puffed up, and have not rath-
er [b]mourned, that he who has done this deed
might be taken away from among you. 3 [a]For I
indeed, as absent in body but present in spirit,
have already judged (as though I were present)
him who has so done this deed. 4 In the [a]name
of our Lord Jesus Christ, when you are gathered
together, along with my spirit, [b]with the power
of our Lord Jesus Christ, 5 [a]deliver such a one to
[b]Satan for the destruction of the flesh, that his
spirit may be saved in the day of the Lord Jesus.[1]
6 [a]Your glorying *is* not good. Do you not
know that [b]a little leaven leavens the whole
lump? 7 Therefore purge out the old leaven,
that you may be a new lump, since you truly are
unleavened. For indeed [a]Christ, our [b]Passover,
was sacrificed for us.[1] 8 Therefore [a]let us keep
the feast, [b]not with old leaven, nor [c]with the
leaven of malice and wickedness, but with the
unleavened *bread* of sincerity and truth.

### IMMORALITY MUST BE JUDGED

9 I wrote to you in my epistle [a]not to keep
company with sexually immoral people. 10 Yet
*I* certainly *did* not *mean* with the sexually im-
moral people of this world, or with the covetous,
or extortioners, or idolaters, since then you
would need to go [a]out of the world. 11 But now I
have written to you not to keep company [a]with
anyone named a brother, who is sexually im-
moral, or covetous, or an idolater, or a reviler,
or a drunkard, or an extortioner—[b]not even to
eat with such a person.
12 For what *have* I *to do* with judging those
also who are outside? Do you not judge those
who are inside? 13 But those who are outside God
judges. Therefore [a]"put away from yourselves
the evil person."[1]

### DO NOT SUE THE BRETHREN

6 Dare any of you, having a matter against
another, go to law before the unrighteous,
and not before the [a]saints? 2 Do you not know
that [a]the saints will judge the world? And if the
world will be judged by you, are you unworthy
to judge the smallest matters? 3 Do you not know
that we shall [a]judge angels? How much more,
things that pertain to this life? 4 If then you have
judgments concerning things pertaining to this
life, do you appoint those who are least esteemed
by the church to judge? 5 I say this to your shame.
Is it so, that there is not a wise man among you,
not even one, who will be able to judge between
his brethren? 6 But brother goes to law against
brother, and that before unbelievers!
7 Now therefore, it is already an utter failure
for you that you go to law against one another.
[a]Why do you not rather accept wrong? Why do
you not rather *let yourselves* be cheated? 8 No, you
yourselves do wrong and cheat, and *you do* these
things *to your* brethren! 9 Do you not know that
the unrighteous will not inherit the kingdom of
God? Do not be deceived. [a]Neither fornicators,
nor idolaters, nor adulterers, nor homosexuals,[1]
nor sodomites, 10 nor thieves, nor covetous, nor
drunkards, nor revilers, nor extortioners will
inherit the kingdom of God. 11 And such were
[a]some of you. [b]But you were washed, but you were
sanctified, but you were justified in the name
of the Lord Jesus and by the Spirit of our God.

**5:2** [a] 1 Cor. 4:18 [b] 2 Cor. 7:7–10 **5:3** [a] Col. 2:5 **5:4** [a] [Matt. 18:20] [b] [John 20:23] **5:5** [a] 1 Tim. 1:20 [b] [Acts 26:18] [1] NU-Text omits *Jesus.* **5:6** [a] 1 Cor. 3:21 [b] Gal. 5:9 **5:7** [a] Is. 53:7 [b] John 19:14 [1] NU-Text omits *for us.* **5:8** [a] Ex. 12:15 [b] Deut. 16:3 [c] Matt. 16:6 **5:9** [a] 2 Cor. 6:14 **5:10** [a] John 17:15 **5:11** [a] Matt. 18:17 [b] Gal. 2:12 **5:13** [a] Deut. 13:5; 17:7, 12; 19:19; 21:21; 22:21, 24; 24:7 [1] Deuteronomy 17:7; 19:19; 22:21, 24; 24:7 **6:1** [a] Dan. 7:22 **6:2** [a] Ps. 49:14 **6:3** [a] 2 Pet. 2:4 **6:7** [a] [Prov. 20:22] **6:9** [a] Gal. 5:21 [1] That is, catamites **6:11** [a] [1 Cor. 12:2] [b] Heb. 10:22

### *GLORIFY GOD IN BODY AND SPIRIT*

12 [a]All things are lawful for me, but all things are not helpful. All things are lawful for me, but I will not be brought under the power of any. 13 [a]Foods for the stomach and the stomach for foods, but God will destroy both it and them. Now the body *is* not for [b]sexual immorality but [c]for the Lord, [d]and the Lord for the body. 14 And [a]God both raised up the Lord and will also raise us up [b]by His power.

15 Do you not know that [a]your bodies are members of Christ? Shall I then take the members of Christ and make *them* members of a harlot? Certainly not! 16 Or do you not know that he who is joined to a harlot is one body *with her?* For [a]"the two," He says, "shall become one flesh."[1] 17 [a]But he who is joined to the Lord is one spirit *with Him.*

18 [a]Flee sexual immorality. Every sin that a man does is outside the body, but he who commits sexual immorality sins [b]against his own body. 19 Or [a]do you not know that your body is the temple of the Holy Spirit *who is* in you, whom you have from God, [b]and you are not your own? 20 For [a]you were bought at a price; therefore glorify God in your body[1] and in your spirit, which are God's.

### *PRINCIPLES OF MARRIAGE*

**7** Now concerning the things of which you wrote to me:

[a]*It is* good for a man not to touch a woman. 2 Nevertheless, because of sexual immorality, let each man have his own wife, and let each woman have her own husband. 3 [a]Let the husband render to his wife the affection due her, and likewise also the wife to her husband. 4 The wife does not have authority over her own body, but the husband *does.* And likewise the husband does not have authority over his own body, but the wife *does.* 5 [a]Do not deprive one another except with consent for a time, that you may give yourselves to fasting and prayer; and come together again so that [b]Satan does not tempt you because of your lack of self-control. 6 But I say this as a concession, [a]not as a commandment. 7 For [a]I wish that all men were even as I myself. But each one has his own gift from God, one in this manner and another in that.

8 But I say to the unmarried and to the widows: [a]It is good for them if they remain even as I am; 9 but [a]if they cannot exercise self-control, let them marry. For it is better to marry than to burn *with passion.*

### *KEEP YOUR MARRIAGE VOWS*

10 Now to the married I command, *yet* not I but the [a]Lord: [b]A wife is not to depart from *her* husband. 11 But even if she does depart, let her remain unmarried or be reconciled to *her* husband. And a husband is not to divorce *his* wife.

12 But to the rest I, not the Lord, say: If any brother has a wife who does not believe, and she is willing to live with him, let him not divorce her. 13 And a woman who has a husband who does not believe, if he is willing to live with her, let her not divorce him. 14 For the unbelieving husband is sanctified by the wife, and the unbelieving wife is sanctified by the husband; otherwise [a]your children would be unclean, but now they are holy. 15 But if the unbeliever departs, let him depart; a brother or a sister is not under bondage in such *cases.* But God has called us [a]to peace. 16 For how do you know, O wife, whether you will [a]save *your* husband? Or how do you know, O husband, whether you will save *your* wife?

**6:12** [a] 1 Cor. 10:23 **6:13** [a] Matt. 15:17 [b] Gal. 5:19 [c] 1 Thess. 4:3 [d] [Eph. 5:23] **6:14** [a] 2 Cor. 4:14 [b] Eph. 1:19 **6:15** [a] Rom. 12:5 **6:16** [a] Gen. 2:24 [1] Genesis 2:24 **6:17** [a] [John 17:21–23] **6:18** [a] Heb. 13:4 [b] Rom. 1:24 **6:19** [a] 2 Cor. 6:16 [b] Rom. 14:7 **6:20** [a] 2 Pet. 2:1 [1] NU-Text ends the verse at *body.* **7:1** [a] 1 Cor. 7:8, 26 **7:3** [a] Ex. 21:10 **7:5** [a] Joel 2:16 [b] 1 Thess. 3:5 **7:6** [a] 2 Cor. 8:8 **7:7** [a] Acts 26:29 **7:8** [a] 1 Cor. 7:1, 26 **7:9** [a] 1 Tim. 5:14 **7:10** [a] Mark 10:6–10 [b] [Matt. 5:32] **7:14** [a] Mal. 2:15 **7:15** [a] Rom. 12:18 **7:16** [a] 1 Pet. 3:1

APPLY THE TRUTH

## SELF-HARM

**6:19** You're a temple of the living God. In the past, people encountered God's presence in a physical temple. The temple was a spectacular building designed by David, built by Solomon, rebuilt by the returning exiles, and renovated by Herod. Its furnishings were made of the finest metals: gold, silver, and bronze. People would come from all over the world just to see this building. But even the temple wasn't glorious enough to permanently house God's presence.

Now, because of the work of Jesus, the presence of God doesn't dwell in a temple, but rather in Christians. If you've trusted in Christ, God makes His home in *you*. Because of this astounding truth, Paul urged us to glorify God in our bodies. This means we should have a positive self-image of our bodies and we should take care of our bodies. The temple in all its beauty and perfection wasn't good enough to house the presence of God. *You*, however, are remarkable enough to be the very temple of the living God. What would it look like for you to view and treat your body the way God views and treats you?

APPLY THE TRUTH

## LONELINESS

**7:8** We *love* love. Our culture is obsessed with it. There are songs, stories, movies, and even gameshows about love. Few of us want to be single and miss out on falling in love. There's nothing wrong with that, of course, but there comes a point when love can become an idol. One sign is when dating apps, direct messages, and the desire for belly butterflies consume our lives. Another is if we believe our lives can have meaning and joy *only* if we're in a relationship. We don't feel "complete" or "whole" without someone else. Part of our obsession with romance stems from emotional dependency. But two broken people don't make a whole person.

Whether we're single or in a relationship, we've been called to live for Christ and find fullness in Him. Indeed, the Bible encourages singleness, like here. This is countercultural. Why would we *want* to be single? First, being single teaches you to depend on God instead of others and gives you the opportunity to do that. Second, being single allows you to serve God distraction free. You don't have to worry about pleasing a significant other, but simply pleasing Christ. Use a time of singleness not merely to wait for a relationship, but rather to pursue the things of God and be used by Him for His glory.

### *LIVE AS YOU ARE CALLED*

17 But as God has distributed to each one, as the Lord has called each one, so let him walk. And [a]so I ordain in all the churches. 18 Was anyone called while circumcised? Let him not become uncircumcised. Was anyone called while uncircumcised? [a]Let him not be circumcised. 19 [a]Circumcision is nothing and uncircumcision is nothing, but [b]keeping the commandments of God *is what matters.* 20 Let each one remain in the same calling in which he was called. 21 Were you called *while* a slave? Do not be concerned about it; but if you can be made free, rather use *it.* 22 For he who is called in the Lord *while* a slave is [a]the Lord's freedman. Likewise he who is called *while* free is [b]Christ's slave. 23 [a]You were bought at a price; do not become slaves of men. 24 Brethren, let each one remain with [a]God in that *state* in which he was called.

### *TO THE UNMARRIED AND WIDOWS*

25 Now concerning virgins: [a]I have no commandment from the Lord; yet I give judgment as one [b]whom the Lord in His mercy has made [c]trustworthy. 26 I suppose therefore that this is good because of the present distress—[a]that *it is* good for a man to remain as he is: 27 Are you bound to a wife? Do not seek to be loosed. Are you loosed from a wife? Do not seek a wife. 28 But even if you do marry, you have not sinned; and if a virgin marries, she has not sinned. Nevertheless such will have trouble in the flesh, but I would spare you.

29 But [a]this I say, brethren, the time *is* short, so that from now on even those who have wives should be as though they had none, 30 those who weep as though they did not weep, those who rejoice as though they did not rejoice, those who buy as though they did not possess, 31 and those who use this world as not [a]misusing *it.* For [b]the form of this world is passing away.

32 But I want you to be without care. [a]He who is unmarried cares for the things of the Lord—how he may please the Lord. 33 But he who is married cares about the things of the world—how he may please *his* wife. 34 There is[1] a difference between a wife and a virgin. The unmarried woman [a]cares about the things of the Lord, that she may be holy both in body and in spirit. But she who is married cares about the things of the world—how she may please *her* husband. 35 And this I say for your own profit, not that I may put a leash on you, but for what is proper, and that you may serve the Lord without distraction.

36 But if any man thinks he is behaving improperly toward his virgin, if she is past the flower of youth, and thus it must be, let him do what he wishes. He does not sin; let them marry. 37 Nevertheless he who stands steadfast in his

**7:26** First-century Rome was a dangerous place for Christians. The Emperor Claudius banished all Jews and Christians from Rome. In time, people throughout the entire Roman Empire turned against Christians. Believers were tortured and killed for their faith in Jesus. Paul knew firsthand about the persecution of Christians. Before he was called to be an apostle of Jesus, he was a notorious Christian hunter.

**7:17** [a] 1 Cor. 4:17 **7:18** [a] Acts 15:1 **7:19** [a] [Gal. 3:28; 5:6; 6:15] [b] [John 15:14] **7:22** [a] [John 8:36] [b] 1 Pet. 2:16 **7:23** [a] 1 Pet. 1:18, 19 **7:24** [a] [Col. 3:22–24] **7:25** [a] 2 Cor. 8:8 [b] 1 Tim. 1:13, 16 [c] 1 Tim. 1:12 **7:26** [a] 1 Cor. 7:1, 8 **7:29** [a] 1 Pet. 4:7 **7:31** [a] 1 Cor. 9:18 [b] [1 John 2:17] **7:32** [a] 1 Tim. 5:5 **7:34** [a] Luke 10:40 [1] M-Text adds *also.*

heart, having no necessity, but has power over his own will, and has so determined in his heart that he will keep his virgin,[1] does well. 38 [a]So then he who gives *her*[1] in marriage does well, but he who does not give *her* in marriage does better.

39 [a]A wife is bound by law as long as her husband lives; but if her husband dies, she is at liberty to be married to whom she wishes, [b]only in the Lord. 40 But she is happier if she remains as she is, [a]according to my judgment—and [b]I think I also have the Spirit of God.

## BE SENSITIVE TO CONSCIENCE

8 Now [a]concerning things offered to idols: We know that we all have [b]knowledge. [c]Knowledge puffs up, but love edifies. 2 And [a]if anyone thinks that he knows anything, he knows nothing yet as he ought to know. 3 But if anyone loves God, this one is known by Him.

4 Therefore concerning the eating of things offered to idols, we know that [a]an idol *is* nothing in the world, [b]and that *there is* no other God but one. 5 For even if there are [a]so-called gods, whether in heaven or on earth (as there are many gods and many lords), 6 yet [a]for us *there is* one God, the Father, [b]of whom *are* all things, and we for Him; and [c]one Lord Jesus Christ, [d]through whom *are* all things, and [e]through whom we *live.*

7 However, *there is* not in everyone that knowledge; for some, [a]with consciousness of the idol, until now eat *it* as a thing offered to an idol; and their conscience, being weak, is [b]defiled. 8 But [a]food does not commend us to God; for neither if we eat are we the better, nor if we do not eat are we the worse.

9 But [a]beware lest somehow this liberty of yours become [b]a stumbling block to those who are weak. 10 For if anyone sees you who have knowledge eating in an idol's temple, will not [a]the conscience of him who is weak be emboldened to eat those things offered to idols? 11 And [a]because of your knowledge shall the weak brother perish, for whom Christ died? 12 But [a]when you thus sin against the brethren, and wound their weak conscience, you sin against Christ. 13 Therefore, [a]if food makes my brother stumble, I will never again eat meat, lest I make my brother stumble.

## A PATTERN OF SELF-DENIAL

9 Am [a]I not an apostle? Am I not free? [b]Have I not seen Jesus Christ our Lord? [c]Are you not my work in the Lord? 2 If I am not an apostle to others, yet doubtless I am to you. For you are [a]the seal of my apostleship in the Lord.

3 My defense to those who examine me is this: 4 [a]Do we have no right to eat and drink? 5 Do we have no right to take along a believing wife, as *do* also the other apostles, [a]the brothers of the Lord, and [b]Cephas? 6 Or *is it* only Barnabas and I [a]*who* have no right to refrain from working? 7 Who ever [a]goes to war at his own expense? Who [b]plants a vineyard and does not eat of its fruit? Or who [c]tends a flock and does not drink of the milk of the flock?

8 Do I say these things as a *mere* man? Or does not the law say the same also? 9 For it is written in the law of Moses, [a]"You shall not muzzle an ox while it treads out the grain."[1] Is it oxen God is concerned about? 10 Or does He say *it* altogether for our sakes? For our sakes, no doubt, *this* is written, that [a]he who plows should plow in hope, and he who threshes in hope should be partaker of his hope. 11 [a]If we have sown spiritual things for you, *is it* a great thing if we reap your material things? 12 If others are partakers of *this* right over you, *are* we not even more?

[a]Nevertheless we have not used this right, but endure all things [b]lest we hinder the gospel of Christ. 13 [a]Do you not know that those who minister the holy things eat *of the things* of the [b]temple, and those who serve at the altar partake of *the offerings of* the altar? 14 Even so [a]the Lord has commanded [b]that those who preach the gospel should live from the gospel.

15 But [a]I have used none of these things, nor have I written these things that it should be done so to me; for [b]it *would be* better for me to die than that anyone should make my boasting void. 16 For if I preach the gospel, I have nothing to boast of, for [a]necessity is laid upon me; yes, woe is me if I do not preach the gospel! 17 For if I do this willingly, [a]I have a reward; but if against my will, [b]I have been entrusted with a stewardship. 18 What is my reward then? That [a]when I preach the gospel, I may present the gospel of Christ[1] without charge, that I [b]may not abuse my authority in the gospel.

## SERVING ALL MEN

19 For though I am [a]free from all *men,* [b]I have made myself a servant to all, [c]that I might win the more; 20 and [a]to the Jews I became as a Jew, that I might win Jews; to those *who are* under the law, as under the law,[1] that I might win those *who are* under the law; 21 [a]to [b]those *who are* without law, as without law [c](not being without law toward God,[1] but under law toward Christ[2]), that I might win those *who are* without law; 22 [a]to the weak I became as[1] weak, that I

**7:37** [1] Or *virgin daughter* **7:38** [a] Heb. 13:4 [1] NU-Text reads *his own virgin.* **7:39** [a] Rom. 7:2 [b] 2 Cor. 6:14 **7:40** [a] 1 Cor. 7:6, 25 [b] 1 Thess. 4:8 **8:1** [a] Acts 15:20 [b] Rom. 14:14 [c] Rom. 14:3 **8:2** [a] [1 Cor. 13:8–12] **8:4** [a] Is. 41:24 [b] Deut. 4:35, 39; 6:4 **8:5** [a] [John 10:34] **8:6** [a] Mal. 2:10 [b] Acts 17:28 [c] John 13:13 [d] John 1:3 [e] Rom. 5:11 **8:7** [a] [1 Cor. 10:28] [b] Rom. 14:14, 22 **8:8** [a] [Rom. 14:17] **8:9** [a] Gal. 5:13 [b] Rom. 14:13, 21 **8:10** [a] 1 Cor. 10:28 **8:11** [a] Rom. 14:15, 20 **8:12** [a] Matt. 25:40 **8:13** [a] Rom. 14:21 **9:1** [a] Acts 9:15 [b] 1 Cor. 15:8 [c] 1 Cor. 3:6; 4:15 **9:2** [a] 2 Cor. 12:12 **9:4** [a] [1 Thess. 2:6, 9] **9:5** [a] Matt. 13:55 [b] Matt. 8:14 **9:6** [a] Acts 4:36 **9:7** [a] 2 Cor. 10:4 [b] Deut. 20:6 [c] John 21:15 **9:9** [a] Deut. 25:4 [1] Deuteronomy 25:4 **9:10** [a] 2 Tim. 2:6 **9:11** [a] Rom. 15:27 **9:12** [a] [Acts 18:3; 20:33] [b] 2 Cor. 11:12 **9:13** [a] Lev. 6:16, 26; 7:6, 31 [b] Num. 18:8–31 **9:14** [a] Matt. 10:10 [b] Rom. 10:15 **9:15** [a] Acts 18:3; 20:33 [b] 2 Cor. 11:10 **9:16** [a] [Rom. 1:14] **9:17** [a] 1 Cor. 3:8, 14; 9:18 [b] Gal. 2:7 **9:18** [a] 1 Cor. 10:33 [b] 1 Cor. 7:31; 9:12 [1] NU-Text omits *of Christ.* **9:19** [a] 1 Cor. 9:1 [b] Gal. 5:13 [c] Matt. 18:15 **9:20** [a] Acts 16:3; 21:23–26 [1] NU-Text adds *though not being myself under the law.* **9:21** [a] [Gal. 2:3; 3:2] [b] [Rom. 2:12, 14] [c] [1 Cor. 7:22] [1] NU-Text reads *God's law.* [2] NU-Text reads *Christ's law.* **9:22** [a] Rom. 14:1; 15:1 [1] NU-Text omits *as.*

might win the weak. [b]I have become all things to all *men,* [c]that I might by all means save some. 23 Now this I do for the gospel's sake, that I may be partaker of it with *you.*

### STRIVING FOR A CROWN

24 Do you not know that those who run in a race all run, but one receives the prize? [a]Run in such a way that you may obtain *it.* 25 And everyone who competes *for the prize* is temperate in all things. Now they *do it* to obtain a perishable crown, but we *for* [a]an imperishable *crown.* 26 Therefore I run thus: [a]not with uncertainty. Thus I fight: not as *one who* beats the air. 27 [a]But I discipline my body and [b]bring *it* into subjection, lest, when I have preached to others, I myself should become [c]disqualified.

> **9:24–26** Paul's reference to running and boxing would have had special significance to the people of Corinth. Every two years, their city hosted the Isthmian Games, an ancient predecessor to the Summer Olympics. Fans traveled for miles to watch athletic contests of strength and skill.

### OLD TESTAMENT EXAMPLES

**10** Moreover, brethren, I do not want you to be unaware that all our fathers were under [a]the cloud, all passed through [b]the sea, 2 all were baptized into Moses in the cloud and in the sea, 3 all ate the same [a]spiritual food, 4 and all drank the same [a]spiritual drink. For they drank of that spiritual Rock that followed them, and that Rock was Christ. 5 But with most of them God was not well pleased, for *their bodies* [a]were scattered in the wilderness.

6 Now these things became our examples, to the intent that we should not lust after evil things as [a]they also lusted. 7 [a]And do not become idolaters as *were* some of them. As it is written, [b]"The people sat down to eat and drink, and rose up to play."[1] 8 [a]Nor let us commit sexual immorality, as [b]some of them did, and [c]in one day twenty-three thousand fell; 9 nor let us tempt Christ, as [a]some of them also tempted, and [b]were destroyed by serpents; 10 nor complain, as [a]some of them also complained, and [b]were destroyed by [c]the destroyer. 11 Now all[1] these things happened to them as examples, and [a]they were written for our admonition, [b]upon whom the ends of the ages have come.

12 Therefore [a]let him who thinks he stands take heed lest he fall. 13 No temptation has overtaken you except such as is common to man; but [a]God *is* faithful, [b]who will not allow you to be tempted beyond what you are able, but with the temptation will also make the way of escape, that you may be able to bear *it.*

### FLEE FROM IDOLATRY

14 Therefore, my beloved, [a]flee from idolatry. 15 I speak as to [a]wise men; judge for yourselves what I say. 16 [a]The cup of blessing which we bless, is it not the communion of the blood of Christ? [b]The bread which we break, is it not the communion of the body of Christ? 17 For [a]we, *though* many, are one bread *and* one body; for we all partake of that one bread.

18 Observe [a]Israel [b]after the flesh: [c]Are not those who eat of the sacrifices partakers of the altar? 19 What am I saying then? [a]That an idol is anything, or what is offered to idols is anything? 20 Rather, that the things which the Gentiles [a]sacrifice [b]they sacrifice to demons and not to God, and I do not want you to have fellowship with demons. 21 [a]You cannot drink the cup of the Lord and [b]the cup of demons; you cannot partake of the [c]Lord's table and of the table of demons. 22 Or do we [a]provoke the Lord to jealousy? [b]Are we stronger than He?

### ALL TO THE GLORY OF GOD

*(cf. Ps. 24:1)*

23 All things are lawful for me,[1] but not all things are [a]helpful; all things are lawful for me,[2] but not all things edify. 24 Let no one seek his own, but each one [a]the other's *well-being.*

25 [a]Eat whatever is sold in the meat market, asking no questions for conscience' sake; 26 for [a]"the earth *is* the LORD's, and all its fullness."[1]

27 If any of those who do not believe invites you *to dinner,* and you desire to go, [a]eat whatever is set before you, asking no question for conscience' sake. 28 But if anyone says to you, "This was offered to idols," do not eat it [a]for the sake of the one who told you, and for conscience' sake;[1] for [b]"the earth *is* the LORD's, and all its fullness."[2] 29 "Conscience," I say, not your own, but that of the other. For [a]why is my liberty judged by another *man's* conscience? 30 But if I partake with thanks, why am I evil spoken of for *the food* [a]over which I give thanks?

31 [a]Therefore, whether you eat or drink, or whatever you do, do all to the glory of God. 32 [a]Give no offense, either to the Jews or to the Greeks or to the church of God, 33 just [a]as I also

**9:22** [b] 1 Cor. 10:33 [c] Rom. 11:14 **9:24** [a] Gal. 2:2 **9:25** [a] James 1:12 **9:26** [a] 2 Tim. 2:5 **9:27** [a] [Rom. 8:13] [b] [Rom. 6:18] [c] Jer. 6:30 **10:1** [a] Ex. 13:21, 22 [b] Ex. 14:21, 22, 29 **10:3** [a] Ex. 16:4, 15, 35 **10:4** [a] Ex. 17:5–7 **10:5** [a] Num. 14:29, 37; 26:65 **10:6** [a] Num. 11:4, 34 **10:7** [a] 1 Cor. 5:11; 10:14 [b] Ex. 32:6 [1] Exodus 32:6 **10:8** [a] Rev. 2:14 [b] Num. 25:1–9 [c] Ps. 106:29 **10:9** [a] Ex. 17:2, 7 [b] Num. 21:6–9 **10:10** [a] Ex. 16:2 [b] Num. 14:37 [c] Ex. 12:23 **10:11** [a] Rom. 15:4 [b] Phil. 4:5 [1] NU-Text omits *all.* **10:12** [a] Rom. 11:20 **10:13** [a] 1 Cor. 1:9 [b] Ps. 125:3 **10:14** [a] 2 Cor. 6:17 **10:15** [a] 1 Cor. 8:1 **10:16** [a] Matt. 26:26–28 [b] Acts 2:42 **10:17** [a] 1 Cor. 12:12, 27 **10:18** [a] Rom. 4:12 [b] Rom. 4:1 [c] Lev. 3:3; 7:6, 14 **10:19** [a] 1 Cor. 8:4 **10:20** [a] Lev. 17:7 [b] Deut. 32:17 **10:21** [a] 2 Cor. 6:15, 16 [b] Deut. 32:38 [c] [1 Cor. 11:23–29] **10:22** [a] Deut. 32:21 [b] Ezek. 22:14 **10:23** [a] 1 Cor. 6:12 [1] NU-Text omits *for me.* [2] NU-Text omits *for me.* **10:24** [a] Phil. 2:4 **10:25** [a] [1 Tim. 4:4] **10:26** [a] Ps. 24:1 [1] Psalm 24:1 **10:27** [a] Luke 10:7, 8 **10:28** [a] [1 Cor. 8:7, 10, 12] [b] Ps. 24:1 [1] NU-Text omits the rest of this verse. [2] Psalm 24:1 **10:29** [a] Rom. 14:16 **10:30** [a] Rom. 14:6 **10:31** [a] Col. 3:17 **10:32** [a] Rom. 14:13 **10:33** [a] Rom. 15:2

**10:31** Here, Paul didn't just answer the Corinthians' question about eating meat from an animal that had been sacrificed to a pagan god, but he provided a principle that can relate to any circumstance a believer faces. As followers of Jesus, **whatever** we **do** is to be done for **the glory of God**. In times when there is no clear command or prohibition in Scripture, the question should be: "Would doing this glorify God or not?"

please all *men* in all *things,* not seeking my own profit, but the *profit* of many, that they may be saved.

**11** Imitate[a] me, just as I also *imitate* Christ.

### HEAD COVERINGS

[2]Now I praise you, brethren, that you remember me in all things and keep the traditions just as I delivered *them* to you. [3]But I want you to know that [a]the head of every man is Christ, [b]the head of woman *is* man, and [c]the head of Christ *is* God. [4]Every man praying or [a]prophesying, having *his* head covered, dishonors his head. [5]But every woman who prays or prophesies with *her* head uncovered dishonors her head, for that is one and the same as if her head were [a]shaved. [6]For if a woman is not covered, let her also be shorn. But if it is [a]shameful for a woman to be shorn or shaved, let her be covered. [7]For a man indeed ought not to cover *his* head, since [a]he is the image and glory of God; but woman is the glory of man. [8]For man is not from woman, but woman [a]from man. [9]Nor was man created for the woman, but woman [a]for the man. [10]For this reason the woman ought to have *a symbol of* authority on *her* head, because of the angels. [11]Nevertheless, [a]neither *is* man independent of woman, nor woman independent of man, in the Lord. [12]For as woman *came* from man, even so man also *comes* through woman; but all things are from God.

[13]Judge among yourselves. Is it proper for a woman to pray to God with her head uncovered? [14]Does not even nature itself teach you that if a man has long hair, it is a dishonor to him? [15]But if a woman has long hair, it is a glory to her; for *her* hair is given to her[1] for a covering. [16]But [a]if anyone seems to be contentious, we have no such custom, [b]nor *do* the churches of God.

### CONDUCT AT THE LORD'S SUPPER

[17]Now in giving these instructions I do not praise *you,* since you come together not for the better but for the worse. [18]For first of all, when you come together as a church, [a]I hear that there are divisions among you, and in part I believe it. [19]For [a]there must also be factions among you, [b]that those who are approved may be recognized among you. [20]Therefore when you come together in one place, it is not to eat the Lord's Supper. [21]For in eating, each one takes his own supper ahead of *others;* and one is hungry and [a]another is drunk. [22]What! Do you not have houses to eat and drink in? Or do you despise [a]the church of God and [b]shame those who have nothing? What shall I say to you? Shall I praise you in this? I do not praise *you.*

### INSTITUTION OF THE LORD'S SUPPER

*(Matt. 26:26–29; Mark 14:22–25; Luke 22:14–23)*

[23]For [a]I received from the Lord that which I also delivered to you: [b]that the Lord Jesus on the *same* night in which He was betrayed took bread; [24]and when He had given thanks, He broke *it* and said, "Take, eat;[1] this is My body which is broken[2] for you; do this in remembrance of Me." [25]In the same manner *He* also *took* the cup after supper, saying, "This cup is the new covenant in My blood. This do, as often as you drink *it,* in remembrance of Me."

[26]For as often as you eat this bread and drink this cup, you proclaim the Lord's death [a]till He comes.

**SEEING JESUS IN THE SCRIPTURE**

**11:26** In the Lord's Supper we remember Jesus' death on our behalf and His promise that we will eat it with Him one day (see Matt. 26:26–29).

### EXAMINE YOURSELF

[27]Therefore whoever eats [a]this bread or drinks *this* cup of the Lord in an unworthy manner will be guilty of the body and blood[1] of the Lord. [28]But [a]let a man examine himself, and so let him eat of the bread and drink of the cup. [29]For he who eats and drinks in an unworthy manner[1] eats and drinks judgment to himself, not discerning the Lord's[2] body. [30]For this reason many *are* weak and sick among you, and many sleep. [31]For [a]if we would judge ourselves, we would not be judged. [32]But when we are judged, [a]we are chastened by the Lord, that we may not be condemned with the world.

[33]Therefore, my brethren, when you [a]come together to eat, wait for one another. [34]But if anyone is hungry, let him eat at home, lest you come together for judgment. And the rest I will set in order when I come.

**11:1** [a] Eph. 5:1 **11:3** [a] Eph. 1:22; 4:15; 5:23 [b] Gen. 3:16 [c] John 14:28 **11:4** [a] 1 Cor. 12:10 **11:5** [a] Deut. 21:12 **11:6** [a] Num. 5:18 **11:7** [a] Gen. 1:26, 27; 5:1; 9:6 **11:8** [a] Gen. 2:21–23 **11:9** [a] Gen. 2:18 **11:11** [a] [Gal. 3:28] **11:15** [1] M-Text omits *to her.* **11:16** [a] 1 Tim. 6:4 [b] 1 Cor. 7:17 **11:18** [a] 1 Cor. 1:10–12; 3:3 **11:19** [a] 1 Tim. 4:1 [b] [Deut. 13:3] **11:21** [a] Jude 12 **11:22** [a] 1 Cor. 10:32 [b] James 2:6 **11:23** [a] 1 Cor. 15:3 [b] Matt. 26:26–28 **11:24** [1] NU-Text omits *Take, eat.* [2] NU-Text omits *broken.* **11:26** [a] John 14:3 **11:27** [a] [John 6:51] [1] NU-Text and M-Text read *the blood.* **11:28** [a] 2 Cor. 13:5 **11:29** [1] NU-Text omits *in an unworthy manner.* [2] NU-Text omits *Lord's.* **11:31** [a] [1 John 1:9] **11:32** [a] Ps. 94:12 **11:33** [a] 1 Cor. 14:26

KNOW THE TRUTH

## THE DOCTRINE OF THE CHURCH

### PART 7: THE ORDINANCES OF THE CHURCH

**11:23–34** Jesus commanded His church to participate in at least two regular practices, often called ordinances, which means order, decree, or command. The first ordinance is **baptism** (see Matt. 28:19). While churches disagree on who is baptized (believers or infants) and how one is baptized (immersion or sprinkling), some form of baptism is practiced signifying a person is part of a gospel community, as a profession of faith, or as the initial act of obedience of a new believer.

The second ordinance is the **Lord's Supper**, or communion. The Lord's Supper reminds believers of the power of Christ's suffering and death, communes believers with the strengthening presence of Jesus through the Holy Spirit, and focuses believers on the return of Jesus for His church. Like baptism, not every church practices the Lord's Supper the same way—some use wine while others use grape juice and some limit participation only to its members while others invite all believers to participate.

Laying on of hands and foot washing are two other ordinances practiced by churches. The first marks a transfer of God's blessing, power, and/or authority (see Acts 9:17; 13:3; 1 Tim. 4:14; James 5:14–15). The second is an act of humility and service, imitating Christ's character and activity on earth (see John 13:14).

*For* **THE DOCTRINE OF THE CHURCH: PART 8: THE LEADERSHIP OF THE CHURCH**, *turn to Ephesians 4:11–16 on page 1205.*

### *SPIRITUAL GIFTS: UNITY IN DIVERSITY*

12 Now [a]concerning spiritual *gifts*, brethren, I
do not want you to be ignorant: 2 You know
[a]that[1] you were Gentiles, carried away to these
[b]dumb idols, however you were led. 3 Therefore I
make known to you that no one speaking by the
Spirit of God calls Jesus accursed, and [a]no one can
say that Jesus is Lord except by the Holy Spirit.
4 [a]There are diversities of gifts, but [b]the same
Spirit. 5 [a]There are differences of ministries,
but the same Lord. 6 And there are diversities
of activities, but it is the same God [a]who works
all in all. 7 But the manifestation of the Spirit is
given to each one for the profit *of all:* 8 for to one
is given [a]the word of wisdom through the Spirit,
to another [b]the word of knowledge through the
same Spirit, 9 [a]to another faith by the same Spirit,
to another [b]gifts of healings by the same[1] Spirit,
10 [a]to another the working of miracles, to another
[b]prophecy, to another [c]discerning of spirits, to
another [d]*different* kinds of tongues, to another
the interpretation of tongues. 11 But one and the
same Spirit works all these things, [a]distributing
to each one individually [b]as He wills.

### *UNITY AND DIVERSITY IN ONE BODY*

*(cf. Eph. 4:1–16)*

12 For [a]as the body is one and has many mem-
bers, but all the members of that one body, being
many, are one body, [b]so also *is* Christ. 13 For [a]by one
Spirit we were all baptized into one body—[b]wheth-
er Jews or Greeks, whether slaves or free—and
[c]have all been made to drink into[1] one Spirit. 14 For
in fact the body is not one member but many.
15 If the foot should say, "Because I am not a
hand, I am not of the body," is it therefore not of
the body? 16 And if the ear should say, "Because I
am not an eye, I am not of the body," is it there-
fore not of the body? 17 If the whole body *were*
an eye, where *would be* the hearing? If the whole
*were* hearing, where *would be* the smelling? 18 But
now [a]God has set the members, each one of them,
in the body [b]just as He pleased. 19 And if they
were all one member, where *would* the body *be?*
20 But now indeed *there are* many members,
yet one body. 21 And the eye cannot say to the hand,
"I have no need of you"; nor again the head to the
feet, "I have no need of you." 22 No, much rather,
those members of the body which seem to be
weaker are necessary. 23 And those *members* of the
body which we think to be less honorable, on these
we bestow greater honor; and our unpresentable
*parts* have greater modesty, 24 but our presentable
*parts* have no need. But God composed the body,
having given greater honor to that *part* which lacks
it, 25 that there should be no schism in the body,
but *that* the members should have the same care
for one another. 26 And if one member suffers, all

**12:1** [a] 1 Cor. 12:4; 14:1, 37 **12:2** [a] Eph. 2:11 [b] Ps. 115:5 [1] NU-Text and M-Text add *when.* **12:3** [a] Matt. 16:17 **12:4** [a] Rom. 12:3–8 [b] Eph. 4:4 **12:5** [a] Rom. 12:6 **12:6** [a] 1 Cor. 15:28 **12:8** [a] 1 Cor. 2:6, 7 [b] Rom. 15:14 **12:9** [a] 2 Cor. 4:13 [b] Mark 3:15; 16:18 [1] NU-Text reads *one.* **12:10** [a] Mark 16:17 [b] Rom. 12:6 [c] 1 John 4:1 [d] Acts 2:4–11 **12:11** [a] Rom. 12:6 [b] [John 3:8] **12:12** [a] Rom. 12:4, 5 [b] [Gal. 3:16] **12:13** [a] [Rom. 6:5] [b] Col. 3:11 [c] [John 7:37–39] [1] NU-Text omits *into.* **12:18** [a] 1 Cor. 12:28 [b] Rom. 12:3

the members suffer with *it;* or if one member is
honored, all the members rejoice with *it.*
27 Now [a]you are the body of Christ, and [b]mem-
bers individually. 28 And [a]God has appointed these
in the church: first [b]apostles, second [c]prophets,
third teachers, after that [d]miracles, then [e]gifts of
healings, [f]helps, [g]administrations, varieties of
tongues. 29 *Are* all apostles? *Are* all prophets? *Are*
all teachers? *Are* all workers of miracles? 30 Do all
have gifts of healings? Do all speak with tongues?
Do all interpret? 31 But [a]earnestly desire the best[1]
gifts. And yet I show you a more excellent way.

### THE GREATEST GIFT

13 Though I speak with the tongues of men
and of angels, but have not love, I have
become sounding brass or a clanging cymbal.
2 And though I have *the gift of* [a]prophecy, and
understand all mysteries and all knowledge, and
though I have all faith, [b]so that I could remove
mountains, but have not love, I am nothing.
3 And [a]though I bestow all my goods to feed *the
poor,* and though I give my body to be burned,[1]
but have not love, it profits me nothing.
4 [a]Love suffers long *and* is [b]kind; love [c]does
not envy; love does not parade itself, is not
puffed up; 5 does not behave rudely, [a]does not
seek its own, is not provoked, thinks no evil;
6 [a]does not rejoice in iniquity, but [b]rejoices in
the truth; 7 [a]bears all things, believes all things,
hopes all things, endures all things.
8 Love never fails. But whether *there are*
prophecies, they will fail; whether *there are*
tongues, they will cease; whether *there is* knowl-
edge, it will vanish away. 9 [a]For we know in part
and we prophesy in part. 10 But when that which
is perfect has come, then that which is in part
will be done away.
11 When I was a child, I spoke as a child, I
understood as a child, I thought as a child; but
when I became a man, I put away childish things.
12 For [a]now we see in a mirror, dimly, but then
[b]face to face. Now I know in part, but then I shall
know just as I also am known.
13 And now abide faith, hope, love, these
three; but the greatest of these *is* love.

**13:1–13** The more we read 1 Corinthians 13, the more we must admit we don't naturally have this kind of **love** in us. The only way to get it is to get it from God. Love comes from God (1 John 4:7). It can be difficult because it means depending on God for what we cannot do by ourselves. It can be difficult because the objects of our love often act in unlovable ways, or they reject our love when we give it. It can be difficult because we have to keep coming back with more love, even when it is rejected.

**12:27** [a] Rom. 12:5 [b] Eph. 5:30 **12:28** [a] Eph. 4:11 [b] [Eph. 2:20; 3:5] [c] Acts 13:1 [d] 1 Cor. 12:10, 29 [e] 1 Cor. 12:9, 30 [f] Num. 11:17 [g] Rom. 12:8 **12:31** [a] 1 Cor. 14:1, 39 [1] NU-Text reads *greater.* **13:2** [a] 1 Cor. 12:8–10, 28; 14:1 [b] Matt. 17:20; 21:21 **13:3** [a] Matt. 6:1, 2 [1] NU-Text reads *so I may boast.* **13:4** [a] Prov. 10:12; 17:9 [b] Eph. 4:32 [c] Gal. 5:26 **13:5** [a] 1 Cor. 10:24 **13:6** [a] Rom. 1:32 [b] 2 John 4 **13:7** [a] Gal. 6:2 **13:9** [a] 1 Cor. 8:2; 13:12 **13:12** [a] Phil. 3:12 [b] [1 John 3:2]

KNOW THE TRUTH

## THE DOCTRINE OF THE CHURCH

### PART 9: THE NECESSITY OF THE CHURCH

**12:4–27** There are two primary necessities to consider when it comes to the church. First, for the church to grow, be healthy, and be effective, there's a necessity **for every member of the church to personally thrive and intentionally serve the rest of the body**. No part of the body can say it doesn't have need nor can it say it's not needed. Every person in the church is extremely valuable and indispensable. When the church healthily grows into the stature of Christ Jesus, it can minister His love and power to a world in need (see Eph. 4:11–16).

That leads to the second necessity: the necessity **for the church to shine and fulfill its mission from Christ to the world**. The church is called to witness to the gospel of Jesus Christ and then welcome all who repent and believe into a life-giving local community of believers—a local church (see Acts 11:19–26). Each believer must be discipled to Christ, learning his or her identity and position in Him and how to obey Him in everything, and be mentored to minister in fulfillment of the first necessity. The church is called to see lost people saved and disciples made by reaching neighbors, nations, and generations with the gospel until Christ returns for His Bride (see Matt. 24:14; 28:18–20; Luke 24:44–49).

*For* **THE DOCTRINE OF THE FUTURE: PART 1: OVERVIEW OF THE DOCTRINE OF THE FUTURE,** *turn to Daniel 12:1–3 on page 879.*

### *PROHECY AND TONGUES*

**14** Pursue love, and [a]desire spiritual *gifts,* [b]but especially that you may prophesy. 2 For he who [a]speaks in a tongue does not speak to men but to God, for no one understands *him;* however, in the spirit he speaks mysteries. 3 But he who prophesies speaks [a]edification and [b]exhortation and comfort to men. 4 He who speaks in a tongue edifies himself, but he who prophesies edifies the church. 5 I wish you all spoke with tongues, but even more that you prophesied; for[1] he who prophesies *is* greater than he who speaks with tongues, unless indeed he interprets, that the church may receive edification.

### *TONGUES MUST BE INTERPRETED*

6 But now, brethren, if I come to you speaking with tongues, what shall I profit you unless I speak to you either by [a]revelation, by knowledge, by prophesying, or by teaching? 7 Even things without life, whether flute or harp, when they make a sound, unless they make a distinction in the sounds, how will it be known what is piped or played? 8 For if the trumpet makes an uncertain sound, who will prepare for battle? 9 So likewise you, unless you utter by the tongue words easy to understand, how will it be known what is spoken? For you will be speaking into the air. 10 There are, it may be, so many kinds of languages in the world, and none of them *is* without significance. 11 Therefore, if I do not know the meaning of the language, I shall be a foreigner to him who speaks, and he who speaks *will be* a foreigner to me. 12 Even so you, since you are zealous for spiritual *gifts, let it be* for the edification of the church *that* you seek to excel.

13 Therefore let him who speaks in a tongue pray that he may [a]interpret. 14 For if I pray in a tongue, my spirit prays, but my understanding is unfruitful. 15 What is *the conclusion* then? I will pray with the spirit, and I will also pray with the understanding. [a]I will sing with the spirit, and I will also sing [b]with the understanding. 16 Otherwise, if you bless with the spirit, how will he who occupies the place of the uninformed say "Amen" [a]at your giving of thanks, since he does not understand what you say? 17 For you indeed give thanks well, but the other is not edified.

18 I thank my God I speak with tongues more than you all; 19 yet in the church I would rather speak five words with my understanding, that I may teach others also, than ten thousand words in a tongue.

### *TONGUES A SIGN TO UNBELIEVERS*

20 Brethren, [a]do not be children in understanding; however, in malice [b]be babes, but in understanding be mature.

21 [a]In the law it is written:

[b]"With *men of* other tongues and other lips
I will speak to this people;
And yet, for all that, they will not hear Me,"[1]

says the Lord.

22 Therefore tongues are for a [a]sign, not to those who believe but to unbelievers; but prophesying is not for unbelievers but for those who believe. 23 Therefore if the whole church comes together in one place, and all speak with tongues, and there come in *those who are* uninformed or unbelievers, [a]will they not say that you are out of your mind? 24 But if all prophesy, and an unbeliever or an uninformed person comes in, he is convinced by all, he is convicted by all. 25 And thus[1] the secrets of his heart are revealed; and so, falling down on *his* face, he will worship God and report [a]that God is truly among you.

### *ORDER IN CHURCH MEETINGS*

26 How is it then, brethren? Whenever you come together, each of you has a psalm, [a]has a teaching, has a tongue, has a revelation, has an interpretation. [b]Let all things be done for edification. 27 If anyone speaks in a tongue, *let there be* two or at the most three, *each* in turn, and let one interpret. 28 But if there is no interpreter, let him keep silent in church, and let him speak to himself and to God. 29 Let two or three prophets speak, and [a]let the others judge. 30 But if *anything* is revealed to another who sits by, [a]let the first keep silent. 31 For you can all prophesy one by one, that all may learn and all may be encouraged. 32 And [a]the spirits of the prophets are subject to the prophets. 33 For God is not *the author* of confusion but of peace, [a]as in all the churches of the saints.

34 [a]Let your[1] women keep silent in the churches, for they are not permitted to speak; but *they are* to be submissive, as the [b]law also

**14:34** This command is the subject of much debate. Some suggest Paul was addressing a particular problem in the Corinthian church, a group of **women** who were disruptive, but the prohibition is repeated at a different time to a different group of people (1 Tim. 2:11–12). Others interpret this verse as a prohibition on women interpreting prophecy, judging the prophets, or speaking in tongues. Others believe that women do prophesy and minister, but only to other women, or in a setting other than public church meetings, such as Priscilla and Aquila instructing Apollos (Acts 18:24–28).

**14:1** [a]1 Cor. 12:31; 14:39 [b]Num. 11:25, 29 **14:2** [a]Acts 2:4; 10:46 **14:3** [a]Rom. 14:19; 15:2 [b]1 Tim. 4:13 **14:5** [1]NU-Text reads *and.* **14:6** [a]1 Cor. 14:26 **14:13** [a]1 Cor. 12:10 **14:15** [a]Col. 3:16 [b]Ps. 47:7 **14:16** [a]1 Cor. 11:24 **14:20** [a]Ps. 131:2 [b][1 Pet. 2:2] **14:21** [a]John 10:34 [b]Is. 28:11, 12 [1]Isaiah 28:11, 12 **14:22** [a]Mark 16:17 **14:23** [a]Acts 2:13 **14:25** [a]Is. 45:14 [1]NU-Text omits *And thus.* **14:26** [a]1 Cor. 12:8–10; 14:6 [b][2 Cor. 12:19] **14:29** [a]1 Cor. 12:10 **14:30** [a][1 Thess. 5:19, 20] **14:32** [a]1 John 4:1 **14:33** [a]1 Cor. 11:16 **14:34** [a]1 Tim. 2:11 [b]Gen. 3:16 [1]NU-Text omits *your.*

says. 35 And if they want to learn something, let them ask their own husbands at home; for it is shameful for women to speak in church.

36 Or did the word of God come *originally* from you? Or *was it* you only that it reached? 37 [a]If anyone thinks himself to be a prophet or spiritual, let him acknowledge that the things which I write to you are the commandments of the Lord. 38 But if anyone is ignorant, let him be ignorant.[1]

39 Therefore, brethren, [a]desire earnestly to prophesy, and do not forbid to speak with tongues. 40 [a]Let all things be done decently and in order.

### THE RISEN CHRIST, FAITH'S REALITY

*(cf. Mark 16:9–20)*

15 Moreover, brethren, I declare to you the gospel [a]which I preached to you, which also you received and [b]in which you stand, 2 [a]by which also you are saved, if you hold fast that word which I preached to you—unless [b]you believed in vain.

3 For [a]I delivered to you first of all that [b]which I also received: that Christ died for our sins [c]according to the Scriptures, 4 and that He was buried, and that He rose again the third day [a]according to the Scriptures, 5 [a]and that He was seen by Cephas, then [b]by the twelve. 6 After that He was seen by over five hundred brethren at once, of whom the greater part remain to the present, but some have fallen asleep. 7 After that He was seen by James, then [a]by all the apostles. 8 [a]Then last of all He was seen by me also, as by one born out of due time.

9 For I am [a]the least of the apostles, who am not worthy to be called an apostle, because [b]I persecuted the church of God. 10 But [a]by the grace of God I am what I am, and His grace toward me was not in vain; but I labored more abundantly than they all, [b]yet not I, but the grace of God *which was* with me. 11 Therefore, whether *it was* I or they, so we preach and so you believed.

### THE RISEN CHRIST, OUR HOPE

*(cf. 1 Thess. 4:13–18)*

12 Now if Christ is preached that He has been raised from the dead, how do some among you say that there is no resurrection of the dead? 13 But if there is no resurrection of the dead, [a]then Christ is not risen. 14 And if Christ is not risen, then our preaching *is* empty and your faith *is* also empty. 15 Yes, and we are found false witnesses of God, because [a]we have testified of God that He raised up Christ, whom He did not raise up—if in fact the dead do not rise. 16 For if *the* dead do not rise, then Christ is not risen. 17 And if Christ is not risen, your faith *is* futile; [a]you are still in your sins! 18 Then also those who have fallen [a]asleep in Christ have perished. 19 [a]If in this life only we have hope in Christ, we are of all men the most pitiable.

### THE LAST ENEMY DESTROYED

20 But now [a]Christ is risen from the dead, *and* has become [b]the firstfruits of those who have fallen asleep. 21 For [a]since by man *came* death, [b]by Man also *came* the resurrection of the dead. 22 For as in Adam all die, even so in Christ all shall [a]be made alive. 23 But [a]each one in his own

**14:37** [a] 2 Cor. 10:7 **14:38** [1] NU-Text reads *if anyone does not recognize this, he is not recognized.* **14:39** [a] 1 Cor. 12:31 **14:40** [a] 1 Cor. 14:33 **15:1** [a] [Gal. 1:11] [b] [Rom. 5:2; 11:20] **15:2** [a] Rom. 1:16 [b] Gal. 3:4 **15:3** [a] 1 Cor. 11:2, 23 [b] [Gal. 1:12] [c] Ps. 22:15 **15:4** [a] Ps. 16:9–11; 68:18; 110:1 **15:5** [a] Luke 24:34 [b] Matt. 28:17 **15:7** [a] Acts 1:3, 4 **15:8** [a] [Acts 9:3–8; 22:6–11; 26:12–18] **15:9** [a] Eph. 3:8 [b] Acts 8:3 **15:10** [a] Eph. 3:7, 8 [b] Phil. 2:13 **15:13** [a] [1 Thess. 4:14] **15:15** [a] Acts 2:24 **15:17** [a] [Rom. 4:25] **15:18** [a] Job 14:12; Ps. 13:3 **15:19** [a] 1 Cor. 4:9; 2 Tim. 3:12 **15:20** [a] Acts 2:24; 1 Pet. 1:3 [b] Acts 26:23; 1 Cor. 15:23; Rev. 1:5 **15:21** [a] Gen. 3:19; Ezek. 18:4; Rom. 5:12; 6:23; Heb. 9:27 [b] John 11:25 **15:22** [a] [John 5:28, 29] **15:23** [a] [1 Thess. 4:15–17]

APPLY THE TRUTH

## THE EXISTENCE OF JESUS

**15:4–8** Imagine you misplaced your keys. You're looking everywhere for them, trying to retrace your steps. You wish someone could help you find them. Then suddenly, five-hundred people show up and say they saw exactly where you set them. You'd feel confident your search was over, right? Five-hundred eyewitnesses are more than enough to validate something. One or two witnesses, or even a few, can be doubtful, but five hundred makes it virtually indisputable.

Here, we're told there were over five-hundred eyewitnesses to the resurrected Jesus. This helps validate Jesus' existence and gives us great confidence in the most controversial aspect of His life: His resurrection. Many people try to dispute the existence of Jesus. But to dispute His existence you must deny the evidence. We have historical eyewitness biographies of His life, ancient artifacts that back up the biographies, and thousands of years of people who have claimed a personal relationship with the resurrected Jesus. There's also evidence through the countless lives transformed through a relationship with Jesus. Maybe that's your story. Think of who you were before Christ and now who you are because of your relationship with a living Savior. That's more than enough evidence, isn't it?

order: Christ the firstfruits, afterward those *who are* Christ's at His coming. 24 Then *comes* the end, when He delivers [a]the kingdom to God the Father, when He puts an end to all rule and all authority and power. 25 For He must reign [a]till He has put all enemies under His feet. 26 [a]The last enemy *that* will be destroyed *is* death. 27 For [a]"He has put all things under His feet."[1] But when He says "all things are put under *Him,*" *it is* evident that He who put all things under Him is excepted. 28 [a]Now when all things are made subject to Him, then [b]the Son Himself will also be subject to Him who put all things under Him, that God may be all in all.

### SEEING JESUS IN THE SCRIPTURE

**15:24** When Jesus returns, His kingdom will come in full and all other kingdoms will end, just as the Scriptures say (see Dan. 7:14, 27).

### *EFFECTS OF DENYING THE RESURRECTION*

29 Otherwise, what will they do who are baptized for the dead, if the dead do not rise at all? Why then are they baptized for the dead? 30 And [a]why do we stand in jeopardy every hour? 31 I affirm, by [a]the boasting in you which I have in Christ Jesus our Lord, [b]I die daily. 32 If, in the manner of men, [a]I have fought with beasts at Ephesus, what advantage *is it* to me? If *the* dead do not rise, [b]"Let us eat and drink, for tomorrow we die!"[1]

33 Do not be deceived: [a]"Evil company corrupts good habits." 34 [a]Awake to righteousness, and do not sin; [b]for some do not have the knowledge of God. [c]I speak *this* to your shame.

**15:29** Some of the Corinthians may have been **baptized** on behalf of others who had died without baptism. Paul didn't address whether this practice was right or wrong (although his use of **they** rather than **we** indicates he didn't participate) but made the point that their own actions were inconsistent with their beliefs. There would be no point in doing anything for the dead if there is no resurrection.

### *A GLORIOUS BODY*

35 But someone will say, [a]"How are the dead raised up? And with what body do they come?" 36 Foolish one, [a]what you sow is not made alive unless it dies. 37 And what you sow, you do not sow that body that shall be, but mere grain—perhaps wheat or some other *grain.* 38 But God gives it a body as He pleases, and to each seed its own body.

39 All flesh *is* not the same flesh, but *there is* one *kind of* flesh[1] of men, another flesh of animals, another of fish, *and* another of birds.

40 *There are* also celestial bodies and terrestrial bodies; but the glory of the celestial *is* one, and the *glory* of the terrestrial *is* another. 41 *There is* one glory of the sun, another glory of the moon, and another glory of the stars; for *one* star differs from *another* star in glory.

42 [a]So also *is* the resurrection of the dead. *The body* is sown in corruption, it is raised in incorruption. 43 [a]It is sown in dishonor, it is raised in glory. It is sown in weakness, it is raised in power. 44 It is sown a natural body, it is raised a spiritual body. There is a natural body, and there is a spiritual body. 45 And so it is written, [a]"The first man Adam became a living being."[1] [b]The last Adam *became* [c]a life-giving spirit.

46 However, the spiritual is not first, but the natural, and afterward the spiritual. 47 [a]The first man *was* of the earth, [b]*made* of dust; the second Man *is* the Lord[1] [c]from heaven. 48 As *was* the *man* of dust, so also *are* those *who are made* of dust; [a]and as *is* the heavenly *Man,* so also *are* those *who are* heavenly. 49 And [a]as we have borne the image of the *man* of dust, [b]we shall also bear[1] the image of the heavenly *Man.*

### *OUR FINAL VICTORY*

50 Now this I say, brethren, that [a]flesh and blood cannot inherit the kingdom of God; nor does corruption inherit incorruption. 51 Behold, I tell you a mystery: [a]We shall not all sleep, [b]but we shall all be changed— 52 in a moment, in the twinkling of an eye, at the last trumpet. [a]For the trumpet will sound, and the dead will be raised incorruptible, and we shall be changed. 53 For this corruptible must put on incorruption, and [a]this mortal *must* put on immortality. 54 So when this corruptible has put on incorruption, and this mortal has put on immortality, then shall be brought to pass the saying that is written: [a]"Death is swallowed up in victory."[1]

55 "O[a] Death, where *is* your sting?[1]
O Hades, where *is* your victory?"[2]

56 The sting of death *is* sin, and [a]the strength of sin *is* the law. 57 [a]But thanks *be* to God, who gives us [b]the victory through our Lord Jesus Christ.

**15:24** [a] [Dan. 2:44; 7:14, 27; 2 Pet. 1:11] **15:25** [a] Ps. 110:1; Matt. 22:44 **15:26** [a] [2 Tim. 1:10; Rev. 20:14; 21:4] **15:27** [a] Ps. 8:6 [1] Psalm 8:6 **15:28** [a] [Phil. 3:21] [b] 1 Cor. 3:23; 11:3; 12:6 **15:30** [a] 2 Cor. 11:26 **15:31** [a] 1 Thess. 2:19 [b] Rom. 8:36 **15:32** [a] 2 Cor. 1:8 [b] Eccl. 2:24; Is. 22:13; 56:12; Luke 12:19 [1] Isaiah 22:13 **15:33** [a] [1 Cor. 5:6] **15:34** [a] Rom. 13:11; Eph. 5:14 [b] [1 Thess. 4:5] [c] 1 Cor. 6:5 **15:35** [a] Ezek. 37:3 **15:36** [a] John 12:24 **15:39** [1] NU-Text and M-Text omit *of flesh.* **15:42** [a] [Dan. 12:3; Matt. 13:43] **15:43** [a] [Phil. 3:21; Col. 3:4] **15:45** [a] Gen. 2:7 [b] [Rom. 5:14] [c] John 5:21; 6:57; [Rom. 8:2; Phil. 3:21; Col. 3:4] [1] Genesis 2:7 **15:47** [a] John 3:31 [b] Gen. 2:7; 3:19 [c] John 3:13 [1] NU-Text omits *the Lord.* **15:48** [a] Phil. 3:20 **15:49** [a] Gen. 5:3 [b] Rom. 8:29 [1] M-Text reads *let us also bear.* **15:50** [a] [John 3:3, 5] **15:51** [a] [1 Thess. 4:15] [b] [Phil. 3:21] **15:52** [a] Matt. 24:31 **15:53** [a] 2 Cor. 5:4 **15:54** [a] Is. 25:8 [1] Isaiah 25:8 **15:55** [a] Hos. 13:14 [1] Hosea 13:14 [2] NU-Text reads *O Death, where is your victory? O Death, where is your sting?* **15:56** [a] [Rom. 3:20; 4:15; 7:8] **15:57** [a] [Rom. 7:25] [b] [1 John 5:4]

58 [a]Therefore, my beloved brethren, be stead-
fast, immovable, always abounding in the work
of the Lord, knowing [b]that your labor is not in
vain in the Lord.

### *COLLECTION FOR THE SAINTS*

**16** Now concerning [a]the collection for the
saints, as I have given orders to the church-
es of Galatia, so you must do also: 2 [a]On the first
*day* of the week let each one of you lay some-
thing aside, storing up as he may prosper, that
there be no collections when I come. 3 And when
I come, [a]whomever you approve by *your* letters
I will send to bear your gift to Jerusalem. 4 [a]But
if it is fitting that I go also, they will go with me.

### *PERSONAL PLANS*

*(cf. Acts 19:21)*

5 Now I will come to you [a]when I pass
through Macedonia (for I am passing through
Macedonia). 6 And it may be that I will remain,
or even spend the winter with you, that you may
[a]send me on my journey, wherever I go. 7 For I do
not wish to see you now on the way; but I hope
to stay a while with you, [a]if the Lord permits.

8 But I will tarry in Ephesus until [a]Pentecost.
9 For [a]a great and effective door has opened to
me, and [b]*there are* many adversaries.

10 And [a]if Timothy comes, see that he may
be with you without fear; for [b]he does the work
of the Lord, as I also *do.* 11 [a]Therefore let no one
despise him. But send him on his journey [b]in
peace, that he may come to me; for I am waiting
for him with the brethren.

12 Now concerning *our* brother [a]Apollos,
I strongly urged him to come to you with the
brethren, but he was quite unwilling to come at
this time; however, he will come when he has a
convenient time.

### *FINAL EXHORTATIONS*

13 [a]Watch, [b]stand fast in the faith, be brave,
[c]be strong. 14 [a]Let all *that* you *do* be done with
love.

15 I urge you, brethren—you know [a]the
household of Stephanas, that it is [b]the firstfruits
of Achaia, and *that* they have devoted them-
selves to [c]the ministry of the saints— 16 [a]that
you also submit to such, and to everyone who
works and [b]labors with *us.*

17 I am glad about the coming of Stephanas,
Fortunatus, and Achaicus, [a]for what was lacking
on your part they supplied. 18 [a]For they refreshed
my spirit and yours. Therefore [b]acknowledge
such men.

### *GREETINGS AND A SOLEMN FAREWELL*

19 The churches of Asia greet you. Aquila and
Priscilla greet you heartily in the Lord, [a]with the
church that is in their house. 20 All the brethren
greet you.

[a]Greet one another with a holy kiss.

21 [a]The salutation with my own hand—Paul's.

22 If anyone [a]does not love the Lord Jesus
Christ, [b]let him be accursed.[1] [c]O Lord, come![2]

23 [a]The grace of our Lord Jesus Christ *be*
with you. 24 My love *be* with you all in Christ
Jesus. Amen.

**15:58** [a] 2 Pet. 3:14 [b] [1 Cor. 3:8] **16:1** [a] Gal. 2:10 **16:2** [a] Acts 20:7 **16:3** [a] 2 Cor. 3:1; 8:18 **16:4** [a] 2 Cor. 8:4, 19 **16:5** [a] 2 Cor. 1:15, 16 **16:6** [a] Acts 15:3 **16:7** [a] James 4:15 **16:8** [a] Lev. 23:15–22 **16:9** [a] Acts 14:27 [b] Acts 19:9 **16:10** [a] Acts 19:22 [b] Phil. 2:20 **16:11** [a] 1 Tim. 4:12 [b] Acts 15:33 **16:12** [a] 1 Cor. 1:12; 3:5 **16:13** [a] Matt. 24:42 [b] Phil. 1:27; 4:1 [c] [Eph. 3:16; 6:10] **16:14** [a] [1 Pet. 4:8] **16:15** [a] 1 Cor. 1:16 [b] Rom. 16:5 [c] 2 Cor. 8:4 **16:16** [a] Heb. 13:17 [b] [Heb. 6:10] **16:17** [a] 2 Cor. 11:9 **16:18** [a] Col. 4:8 [b] Phil. 2:29 **16:19** [a] Rom. 16:5 **16:20** [a] Rom. 16:16 **16:21** [a] Col. 4:18 **16:22** [a] Eph. 6:24 [b] Gal. 1:8, 9 [c] Jude 14, 15 [1] Greek *anathema* [2] Aramaic *Maranatha* **16:23** [a] Rom. 16:20

# *The Second Epistle of Paul the Apostle to the*
# CORINTHIANS

| AUTHOR | KEY VERSES | READING TIME |
|---|---|---|
| Paul | 2 Corinthians 4:17–18 | 48 minutes |

Since Paul's first letter, false teachers had swayed the Corinthian church and stirred the people against Paul. They claimed Paul was fickle, arrogant, unimpressive in appearance and speech, and unqualified to be an apostle of Jesus Christ. Paul paid an unpleasant visit to the church (2 Cor. 2:1–4). He then sent another letter to them (7:8–12), a letter that has since been lost. Paul then sent Titus to Corinth to deal with these difficulties, and upon Titus's return, the apostle rejoiced to hear of the Corinthians' change of heart. Paul wrote 2 Corinthians to express his thanksgiving for the repentant majority and appeal to the rebellious minority to accept his authority. Throughout the book, Paul defended his conduct, character, and calling as an apostle of Jesus Christ.

**Occasion:** Paul wrote 2 Corinthians from Macedonia about a year after the first letter and sent it to the church with Titus and another believer (2 Cor. 8:16).

**Main Point:** Believers are called to persevere through trials and hardships knowing that God is always at work.

**Big Ideas:** As followers of Jesus, we are to be forgiving and united as much as possible. We can expect to suffer at times, knowing Jesus suffered for us. When we trusted in Christ, we became new creations.

**OUTLINE:**

I. The Ministry of Paul (chs. 1–7)
II. The Request of Paul (chs. 8–9)
III. The Apostleship of Paul (chs. 10–13)

**c. AD 34**
Paul is converted

**c. AD 47–49**
Paul's first missionary journey

**c. AD 50**
The Jerusalem Council

**c. AD 50–53**
Paul's second missionary journey

**AD 52**
The church at Corinth is founded

**c. AD 53–57**
Paul's third missionary journey

**AD 54–68**
Nero is Roman emperor

**c. AD 56**
1 Corinthians written

**c. AD 55–56**
**2 Corinthians written**

**c. AD 58**
Paul is arrested in Jerusalem

**c. AD 60–62**
Paul is imprisoned in Rome

**AD 64**
Great Fire of Rome; first Roman mass persecution of Christians

**c. AD 67**
Peter and Paul are executed

### GREETING

1 Paul, [a]an apostle of Jesus Christ by the will of God, and [b]Timothy *our* brother,

To the church of God which is at Corinth, [c]with all the saints who are in all Achaia:

2 [a]Grace to you and peace from God our Father and the Lord Jesus Christ.

### COMFORT IN SUFFERING

3 [a]Blessed *be* the God and Father of our Lord Jesus Christ, the Father of mercies and God of all comfort, 4 who [a]comforts us in all our tribulation, that we may be able to comfort those who are in any trouble, with the comfort with which we ourselves are comforted by God. 5 For as [a]the sufferings of Christ abound in us, so our consolation also abounds through Christ. 6 Now if we are afflicted, [a]*it is* for your consolation and salvation, which is effective for enduring the same sufferings which we also suffer. Or if we are comforted, *it is* for your consolation and salvation. 7 And our hope for you *is* steadfast, because we know that [a]as you are partakers of the sufferings, so also *you will partake* of the consolation.

### DELIVERED FROM SUFFERING

8 For we do not want you to be ignorant, brethren, of [a]our trouble which came to us in Asia: that we were burdened beyond measure, above strength, so that we despaired even of life. 9 Yes, we had the sentence of death in ourselves, that we should [a]not trust in ourselves but in God who raises the dead, 10 [a]who delivered us from so great a death, and does[1] deliver us; in whom we trust that He will still deliver *us,* 11 you also [a]helping together in prayer for us, that thanks may be given by many persons on our[1] behalf [b]for the gift *granted* to us through many.

### PAUL'S SINCERITY

12 For our boasting is this: the testimony of our conscience that we conducted ourselves in the world in simplicity and [a]godly sincerity, [b]not with fleshly wisdom but by the grace of God, and more abundantly toward you. 13 For we are not writing any other things to you than what you read or understand. Now I trust you will understand, even to the end 14 (as also you have understood us in part), [a]that we are your boast as [b]you also *are* ours, in the day of the Lord Jesus.

### SPARING THE CHURCH

15 And in this confidence [a]I intended to come to you before, that you might have [b]a second benefit— 16 to pass by way of you to Macedonia, [a]to come again from Macedonia to you, and be helped by you on my way to Judea. 17 Therefore, when I was planning this, did I do it lightly? Or the things I plan, do I plan [a]according to the flesh, that with me there should be Yes, Yes, and No, No? 18 But *as* God *is* [a]faithful, our word to you was not Yes and No. 19 For [a]the Son of God, Jesus Christ, who was preached among you by us—by me, [b]Silvanus, and [c]Timothy—was not Yes and No, [d]but in Him was Yes. 20 [a]For all the promises of God in Him *are* Yes, and in Him Amen, to the glory of God through us. 21 Now He who establishes us with you in Christ and [a]has anointed us *is* God, 22 who [a]also has sealed us and [b]given us the Spirit in our hearts as a guarantee.

23 Moreover [a]I call God as witness against my soul, [b]that to spare you I came no more to Corinth. 24 Not [a]that we have dominion over your faith, but are fellow workers for your joy; for [b]by faith you stand.

2 But I determined this within myself, [a]that I would not come again to you in sorrow. 2 For if I make you [a]sorrowful, then who is he who makes me glad but the one who is made sorrowful by me?

### FORGIVE THE OFFENDER

3 And I wrote this very thing to you, lest, when I came, [a]I should have sorrow over those from whom I ought to have joy, [b]having confidence in you all that my joy is *the joy* of you all. 4 For out of much affliction and anguish of heart I wrote to you, with many tears, [a]not that you should be grieved, but that you might know the love which I have so abundantly for you.

5 But [a]if anyone has caused grief, he has not [b]grieved me, but all of you to some extent—not to be too severe. 6 This punishment which *was inflicted* [a]by the majority *is* sufficient for such a man, 7 [a]so that, on the contrary, you *ought* rather to forgive and comfort *him,* lest perhaps such a one be swallowed up with too much sorrow. 8 Therefore I urge you to reaffirm *your* love to him. 9 For to this end I also wrote, that I might put you to the test, whether you are [a]obedient in all things. 10 Now whom you forgive anything, I also *forgive.* For if indeed I have forgiven anything, I have forgiven that one[1] for your sakes in the presence of Christ, 11 lest Satan should take advantage of us; for we are not ignorant of his devices.

### TRIUMPH IN CHRIST

12 Furthermore, [a]when I came to Troas to *preach* Christ's gospel, and [b]a door was opened to me by the Lord, 13 [a]I had no rest in my spirit,

**1:1** [a] 2 Tim. 1:1 [b] 1 Cor. 16:10 [c] Col. 1:2 **1:2** [a] Rom. 1:7 **1:3** [a] 1 Pet. 1:3 **1:4** [a] Is. 51:12; 66:13 **1:5** [a] 2 Cor. 4:10 **1:6** [a] 2 Cor. 4:15; 12:15 **1:7** [a] [Rom. 8:17] **1:8** [a] Acts 19:23 **1:9** [a] Jer. 17:5, 7 **1:10** [a] [2 Pet. 2:9] [1] NU-Text reads *shall.* **1:11** [a] Rom. 15:30 [b] 2 Cor. 4:15; 9:11 [1] M-Text reads *your behalf.* **1:12** [a] 2 Cor. 2:17 [b] [1 Cor. 2:4] **1:14** [a] 2 Cor. 5:12 [b] Phil. 2:16 **1:15** [a] 1 Cor. 4:19 [b] Rom. 1:11; 15:29 **1:16** [a] 1 Cor. 16:3–6 **1:17** [a] 2 Cor. 10:2; 11:18 **1:18** [a] 1 John 5:20 **1:19** [a] Mark 1:1 [b] 1 Pet. 5:12 [c] 2 Cor. 1:1 [d] [Heb. 13:8] **1:20** [a] [Rom. 15:8, 9] **1:21** [a] [1 John 2:20, 27] **1:22** [a] [Eph. 4:30] [b] [Eph. 1:14] **1:23** [a] Gal. 1:20 [b] 1 Cor. 4:21 **1:24** [a] [1 Pet. 5:3] [b] Rom. 11:20 **2:1** [a] 2 Cor. 1:23 **2:2** [a] 2 Cor. 7:8 **2:3** [a] 2 Cor. 12:21 [b] Gal. 5:10 **2:4** [a] [2 Cor. 2:9; 7:8, 12] **2:5** [a] [1 Cor. 5:1] [b] Gal. 4:12 **2:6** [a] 1 Cor. 5:4, 5 **2:7** [a] Gal. 6:1 **2:9** [a] 2 Cor. 7:15; 10:6 **2:10** [1] NU-Text reads *For indeed, what I have forgiven, if I have forgiven anything, I did it.* **2:12** [a] Acts 16:8 [b] 1 Cor. 16:9 **2:13** [a] 2 Cor. 7:6, 13; 8:6

because I did not find Titus my brother; but taking my leave of them, I departed for Macedonia. 14 Now thanks *be* to God who always leads us in triumph in Christ, and through us diffuses the fragrance of His knowledge in every place. 15 For we are to God the fragrance of Christ [a]among those who are being saved and [b]among those who are perishing. 16 [a]To the one *we are* the aroma of death *leading* to death, and to the other the aroma of life *leading* to life. And [b]who *is* sufficient for these things? 17 For we are not, as so many,[1] [a]peddling the word of God; but as [b]of sincerity, but as from God, we speak in the sight of God in Christ.

### CHRIST'S EPISTLE

*(cf. Jer. 31:31–34)*

**3** Do [a]we begin again to commend ourselves? Or do we need, as some *others*, [b]epistles of commendation to you or *letters* of commendation from you? 2 [a]You are our epistle written in our hearts, known and read by all men; 3 clearly you are an epistle of Christ, [a]ministered by us, written not with ink but by the Spirit of the living God, not [b]on tablets of stone but [c]on tablets of flesh, *that is,* of the heart.

> **3:2** Paul sometimes provided an **epistle**, or a letter, of recommendation for others (see Rom. 16:1; 1 Cor. 16:10; 2 Cor. 8:22; Col. 4:10), but he didn't need one for himself. The Corinthians served as his letter of recommendation. Paul's love for the Corinthians was known to all who were acquainted with him. One of the qualifications for ministry is love for people, both God's people and the lost.

### THE SPIRIT, NOT THE LETTER

4 And we have such trust through Christ toward God. 5 [a]Not that we are sufficient of ourselves to think of anything as *being* from ourselves, but [b]our sufficiency *is* from God, 6 who also made us sufficient as [a]ministers of [b]the new covenant, not [c]of the letter but of the Spirit;[1] for [d]the letter kills, [e]but the Spirit gives life.

### GLORY OF THE NEW COVENANT

7 But if [a]the ministry of death, [b]written *and* engraved on stones, was glorious, [c]so that the children of Israel could not look steadily at the face of Moses because of the glory of his countenance, which *glory* was passing away, 8 how will [a]the ministry of the Spirit not be more glorious? 9 For if the ministry of condemnation *had* glory, the ministry [a]of righteousness exceeds much more in glory. 10 For even what was made glorious had no glory in this respect, because of the glory that excels. 11 For if what is passing away *was* glorious, what remains *is* much more glorious.

12 Therefore, since we have such hope, [a]we use great boldness of speech— 13 unlike Moses, [a]*who* put a veil over his face so that the children of Israel could not look steadily at [b]the end of what was passing away. 14 But [a]their minds were blinded. For until this day the same veil remains unlifted in the reading of the Old Testament, because the *veil* is taken away in Christ. 15 But even to this day, when Moses is read, a veil lies on their heart. 16 Nevertheless [a]when one turns to the Lord, [b]the veil is taken away. 17 Now [a]the Lord is the Spirit; and where the Spirit of the Lord *is,* there *is* [b]liberty. 18 But we all, with unveiled face, beholding [a]as in a mirror [b]the glory of the Lord, [c]are being transformed into the same image from glory to glory, just as by the Spirit of the Lord.

> **SEEING JESUS IN THE SCRIPTURE**
>
> **3:14** As prophesied, faith in Jesus removes the veil of confusion and unbelief from those seeking salvation by the law (see Is. 29:10).

### THE LIGHT OF CHRIST'S GOSPEL

**4** Therefore, since we have this ministry, [a]as we have received mercy, we [b]do not lose heart. 2 But we have renounced the hidden things of shame, not walking in craftiness nor handling the word of God deceitfully, but by manifestation of the truth [a]commending ourselves to every man's conscience in the sight of God. 3 But even if our gospel is veiled, [a]it is veiled to those who are perishing, 4 whose minds [a]the god of this age [b]has blinded, who do not believe, lest [c]the light of the gospel of the glory of Christ, [d]who is the image of God, should shine on them. 5 [a]For we do not preach ourselves, but Christ Jesus the Lord, and [b]ourselves your bondservants for Jesus' sake. 6 For it is the God [a]who commanded light to shine out of darkness, who has [b]shone in our hearts to *give* the light of the knowledge of the glory of God in the face of Jesus Christ.

### CAST DOWN BUT UNCONQUERED

7 But we have this treasure in earthen vessels, [a]that the excellence of the power may be of God and not of us. 8 *We are* [a]hard-pressed on every side, yet not crushed; *we are* perplexed, but

**2:15** [a] [1 Cor. 1:18] [b] [2 Cor. 4:3] **2:16** [a] Luke 2:34 [b] [1 Cor. 15:10] **2:17** [a] 2 Pet. 2:3 [b] 2 Cor. 1:12 [1] M-Text reads *the rest.* **3:1** [a] 2 Cor. 5:12; 10:12, 18; 12:11 [b] Acts 18:27 **3:2** [a] 1 Cor. 9:2 **3:3** [a] 1 Cor. 3:5 [b] Ex. 24:12; 31:18; 32:15 [c] Ps. 40:8 **3:5** [a] [John 15:5] [b] 1 Cor. 15:10 **3:6** [a] 1 Cor. 3:5 [b] Jer. 31:31 [c] Rom. 2:27 [d] Gal. 3:10 [e] John 6:63 [1] Or *spirit* **3:7** [a] Rom. 7:10 [b] Ex. 34:1 [c] Ex. 34:29 **3:8** [a] [Gal. 3:5] **3:9** [a] [Rom. 1:17; 3:21] **3:12** [a] Eph. 6:19 **3:13** [a] Ex. 34:33–35 [b] [Gal. 3:23] **3:14** [a] Acts 28:26 **3:16** [a] Rom. 11:23 [b] Is. 25:7 **3:17** [a] [1 Cor. 15:45] [b] Gal. 5:1, 13 **3:18** [a] 1 Cor. 13:12 [b] [2 Cor. 4:4, 6] [c] [Rom. 8:29, 30] **4:1** [a] 1 Cor. 7:25 [b] 2 Cor. 4:16 **4:2** [a] 2 Cor. 5:11 **4:3** [a] [1 Cor. 1:18] **4:4** [a] John 12:31 [b] John 12:40 [c] [2 Cor. 3:8, 9] [d] [John 1:18] **4:5** [a] 1 Cor. 1:13 [b] 1 Cor. 9:19 **4:6** [a] Gen. 1:3 [b] 2 Pet. 1:19 **4:7** [a] 1 Cor. 2:5 **4:8** [a] 2 Cor. 1:8; 7:5

KNOW THE TRUTH

# THE DOCTRINE OF THE HOLY SPIRIT

## PART 6: THE HOLY SPIRIT'S WORK IN SANCTIFICATION

**3:17–18** *Sanctification* concerns setting something or someone apart for the use (or uses) intended by its designer or creator. The work of the Holy Spirit's sanctification takes place in our lives in two main ways. First, by **inner renovation**. The Holy Spirit sets us apart to know and serve Christ by renovating the way we think (see Rom. 12:1–2). He removes certain ways of thinking (e.g., selfishness, fear, pride) and replaces them with new ways of thinking (e.g., love, faith, humility). As Paul states in 2 Corinthians 3:17–18, the Spirit reveals more about Christ to us and progressively transforms us into being more like Christ in the way we think, speak, and act. He not only changes the way we think, but He also changes what we desire and therefore seek. Instead of living to fulfill our flesh's desires, He leads us to fulfill God's will (see Ps. 34:4–5; Gal. 5:16–25). Second, by **outer separation**. The Holy Spirit calls us out of the world's sinful ways of living (see 2 Cor. 6:16—7:1). He separates us from the lust and pride of the world's systems (see 1 John 2:15–17). At the same time, He separates us to God and God's purposes for our lives. Whatever believers "lose" as the Spirit sanctifies us is nothing compared to what we gain.

*For* **THE DOCTRINE OF THE HOLY SPIRIT: PART 7: THE FRUIT OF THE HOLY SPIRIT**, *turn to Galatians 5:22–25 on page 1199.*

not in despair; [9]persecuted, but not [a]forsaken;
[b]struck down, but not destroyed— [10][a]always
carrying about in the body the dying of the
Lord Jesus, [b]that the life of Jesus also may be
manifested in our body. [11]For we who live [a]are
always delivered to death for Jesus' sake, that
the life of Jesus also may be manifested in our
mortal flesh. [12]So then death is working in us,
but life in you.

[13]And since we have [a]the same spirit of faith,
according to what is written, [b]"I believed and
therefore I spoke,"[1] we also believe and therefore
speak, [14]knowing that [a]He who raised up the
Lord Jesus will also raise us up with Jesus, and
will present *us* with you. [15]For [a]all things *are* for
your sakes, that [b]grace, having spread through
the many, may cause thanksgiving to abound
to the glory of God.

**4:9** This literally happened to Paul (see Acts 14:19). In Lystra a crowd stoned and **struck down** Paul, leaving him for dead. But the Lord spared his life so he could continue to preach the gospel and testify to God's deliverance.

**4:9** [a][Heb. 13:5] [b]Ps. 37:24 **4:10** [a]Phil. 3:10 [b]Rom. 8:17 **4:11** [a]Rom. 8:36 **4:13** [a]2 Pet. 1:1 [b]Ps. 116:10 [1]Psalm 116:10 **4:14** [a][Rom. 8:11] **4:15** [a]Col. 1:24 [b]2 Cor. 1:11

LIVE THE TRUTH

# USING YOUR TALENTS

**4:7** God has purposefully and specifically given you gifts and abilities, also called talents. You may not yet realize why God has gifted you the way He has, but you can be sure He has. You can also know the general purpose of your talents: to glorify God and help build His kingdom. Every gift you have is thus to be leveraged for Jesus. They are all gifts *from* Him, so they all belong *to* Him. It makes sense, then, they are all to be used *for* Him. This is exciting because it means we have the incredible opportunity to steward our talents well and use them for an eternal effect.

This verse tells of the invaluable treasure of knowing God through Jesus, but it also teaches something about ourselves. Here on earth, we are fragile human beings dependent on God, but we contain powerful treasures within us. The main part of that treasure is Jesus, but it also includes the talents He has given us. It might not seem as if we have much to offer Jesus—our "earthen vessels"—but that's not the focus anyway. It's the talents He has given us that He wants to use through those earthen vessels. When we yield ourselves to Christ and allow Him to work through the talents He has given, we can bring glory to God.

### *SEEING THE INVISIBLE*

16 Therefore we [a]do not lose heart. Even
though our outward man is perishing, yet the
inward *man* is [b]being renewed day by day. 17 For
[a]our light affliction, which is but for a moment, is
working for us a far more exceeding *and* eternal
weight of glory, 18 [a]while we do not look at the
things which are seen, but at the things which
are not seen. For the things which are seen *are*
temporary, but the things which are not seen
*are* eternal.

### *ASSURANCE OF THE RESURRECTION*

**5** For we know that if [a]our earthly house, *this*
tent, is destroyed, we have a building from
God, a house [b]not made with hands, eternal in
the heavens. 2 For in this [a]we groan, earnest-
ly desiring to be clothed with our habitation
which is from heaven, 3 if indeed, [a]having been
clothed, we shall not be found naked. 4 For we
who are in *this* tent groan, being burdened, not
because we want to be unclothed, [a]but further
clothed, that mortality may be swallowed up
by life. 5 Now He who has prepared us for this
very thing *is* God, who also [a]has given us the
Spirit as a guarantee.

6 So *we are* always confident, knowing that
while we are at home in the body we are ab-
sent from the Lord. 7 For [a]we walk by faith, not
by sight. 8 We are confident, yes, [a]well pleased
rather to be absent from the body and to be
present with the Lord.

### *THE JUDGMENT SEAT OF CHRIST*

9 Therefore we make it our aim, whether
present or absent, to be well pleasing to Him.
10 [a]For we must all appear before the judgment
seat of Christ, [b]that each one may receive the
things *done* in the body, according to what he has
done, whether good or bad. 11 Knowing, therefore,
[a]the terror of the Lord, we persuade men; but
we are well known to God, and I also trust are
well known in your consciences.

### *BE RECONCILED TO GOD*

12 For [a]we do not commend ourselves again
to you, but give you opportunity [b]to boast on our
behalf, that you may have *an answer* for those
who boast in appearance and not in heart. 13 For
[a]if we are beside ourselves, *it is* for God; or if we
are of sound mind, *it is* for you. 14 For the love
of Christ compels us, because we judge thus:
that [a]if One died for all, then all died; 15 and He
died for all, [a]that those who live should live no
longer for themselves, but for Him who died for
them and rose again.

16 [a]Therefore, from now on, we regard no
one according to the flesh. Even though we
have known Christ according to the flesh, [b]yet
now we know *Him thus* no longer. 17 Therefore,
if anyone [a]*is* in Christ, *he is* [b]a new creation;
[c]old things have passed away; behold, all things
have become [d]new. 18 Now all things *are* of God,
[a]who has reconciled us to Himself through
Jesus Christ, and has given us the ministry of
reconciliation, 19 that is, that [a]God was in Christ
reconciling the world to Himself, not imputing
their trespasses to them, and has committed to
us the word of reconciliation.

20 Now then, we are [a]ambassadors for Christ,
as though God were pleading through us: we
implore *you* on Christ's behalf, be reconciled to
God. 21 For [a]He made Him who knew no sin *to
be* sin for us, that we might become [b]the righ-
teousness of God in Him.

> **SEEING JESUS IN THE SCRIPTURE**
>
> **5:21** Jesus didn't die because He sinned; Jesus died because He took our sin and its punishment upon Himself just as the Scriptures promised (see Is. 53:6, 9).

### *MARKS OF THE MINISTRY*

**6** We then, *as* [a]workers together *with Him* also
[b]plead with *you* not to receive the grace of
God in vain. 2 For He says:

> [a]"In an acceptable time I have heard you,
> And in the day of salvation I have helped
> you."[1]

Behold, now *is* the accepted time; behold, now
*is* the day of salvation.

3 [a]We give no offense in anything, that our
ministry may not be blamed. 4 But in all *things* we
commend ourselves [a]as ministers of God: in much
patience, in tribulations, in needs, in distresses,
5 [a]in stripes, in imprisonments, in tumults, in
labors, in sleeplessness, in fastings; 6 by purity, by
knowledge, by longsuffering, by kindness, by the
Holy Spirit, by sincere love, 7 [a]by the word of truth,
by [b]the power of God, by [c]the armor of righteous-
ness on the right hand and on the left, 8 by honor
and dishonor, by evil report and good report; as
deceivers, and *yet* true; 9 as unknown, and [a]*yet*
well known; [b]as dying, and behold we live; [c]as
chastened, and *yet* not killed; 10 as sorrowful, yet
always rejoicing; as poor, yet making many [a]rich;
as having nothing, and *yet* possessing all things.

**4:16** [a] 2 Cor. 4:1 [b] [Is. 40:29, 31] **4:17** [a] Rom. 8:18 **4:18** [a] [Heb. 11:1, 13] **5:1** [a] Job 4:19 [b] Mark 14:58 **5:2** [a] Rom. 8:23 **5:3** [a] Rev. 3:18 **5:4** [a] 1 Cor. 15:53 **5:5** [a] Rom. 8:23 **5:7** [a] Heb. 11:1 **5:8** [a] Phil. 1:23 **5:10** [a] Rom. 2:16; 14:10, 12 [b] Eph. 6:8 **5:11** [a] [Heb. 10:31; 12:29] **5:12** [a] 2 Cor. 3:1 [b] 2 Cor. 1:14 **5:13** [a] 2 Cor. 11:1, 16; 12:11 **5:14** [a] [Rom. 5:15; 6:6] **5:15** [a] [Rom. 6:11] **5:16** [a] 2 Cor. 10:3 [b] [Matt. 12:50] **5:17** [a] [John 6:63] [b] [Rom. 8:9] [c] Is. 43:18; 65:17 [d] [Rom. 6:3–10] **5:18** [a] Rom. 5:10 **5:19** [a] [Rom. 3:24] **5:20** [a] Eph. 6:20 **5:21** [a] Is. 53:6, 9 [b] [Rom. 1:17; 3:21] **6:1** [a] 1 Cor. 3:9 [b] 2 Cor. 5:20 **6:2** [a] Is. 49:8 [1] Isaiah 49:8 **6:3** [a] Rom. 14:13 **6:4** [a] 1 Cor. 4:1 **6:5** [a] 2 Cor. 11:23 **6:7** [a] 2 Cor. 7:14 [b] 1 Cor. 2:4 [c] 2 Cor. 10:4 **6:9** [a] 2 Cor. 4:2; 5:11 [b] 1 Cor. 4:9, 11 [c] Ps. 118:18 **6:10** [a] [2 Cor. 8:9]

KNOW THE TRUTH

## THE DOCTRINE OF SALVATION

### PART 3: THE MANNER OF SALVATION

**5:21** The manner by which God saves us from His wrath is reconciliation. *Reconciliation*, used five times in 2 Corinthians 5:18–20, has literal and figurative meanings that express one unifying idea: exchange. *Reconciliation* was often used to describe exchanging monetary currencies. If a foreign currency was worthless, it had to be exchanged (*reconciled*) for local currency that was of value. Our righteousness is of no value. Indeed, compared to God's flawless and boundless righteousness, our "righteousness" is like filthy rags (see Is. 64:6). Therefore, an exchange must be made. This exchange is described in 2 Corinthians 5:21.

God the Father placed our sins upon Jesus (without Jesus sinning) and Jesus became the sacrifice for our sins on the cross. The Father then by grace offers the righteousness of His Son to us in exchange. The penalty for our sin is paid by Christ the righteous One, God's holy wrath is satisfied, and Christ's perfect holiness is credited to. Reconciliation, then, is a wondrous exchange of our sinfulness for Christ's righteousness. We eternally belong in the holy presence of a righteous God because we've been made the righteousness of God in Christ.

*For* **THE DOCTRINE OF SALVATION: PART 4: THE PROCESS OF SALVATION**, *turn to Titus 3:4–7 on page 1240.* •••

### *BE HOLY*

[11]O Corinthians! We have spoken openly
to you, [a]our heart is wide open. [12]You are not
restricted by us, but [a]you are restricted by
your *own* affections. [13]Now in return for the
same [a](I speak as to children), you also be
open.

[14a]Do not be unequally yoked together with
unbelievers. For [b]what fellowship has righteousness with lawlessness? And what communion has light with darkness? [15]And what

> **6:14** This verse has most often been applied to the subject of marriage, warning believers not to bind themselves for life to one who doesn't love the Lord. It could also apply to other important unions.

accord has Christ with Belial? Or what part
has a believer with an unbeliever? [16]And what
agreement has the temple of God with idols?
For [a]you[1] are the temple of the living God. As
God has said:

[b]"I will dwell in them
And walk among *them*.
I will be their God,
And they shall be My
people."[2]

[17]Therefore

[a]"Come out from among them
And be separate, says the Lord.
Do not touch what is unclean,
And I will receive you."[1]

[18] "I [a]will be a Father to you,
And you shall be My [b]sons and daughters,
Says the LORD Almighty."[1]

**7** Therefore,[a] having these promises, beloved,
let us cleanse ourselves from all filthiness
of the flesh and spirit, perfecting holiness in
the fear of God.

### *THE CORINTHIANS' REPENTANCE*

[2]Open *your hearts* to us. We have wronged no
one, we have corrupted no one, [a]we have cheated
no one. [3]I do not say *this* to condemn; for [a]I have
said before that you are in our hearts, to die
together and to live together. [4a]Great *is* my boldness of speech toward you, [b]great *is* my boasting
on your behalf. [c]I am filled with comfort. I am
exceedingly joyful in all our tribulation.

[5]For indeed, [a]when we came to Macedonia,
our bodies had no rest, but [b]we were troubled
on every side. [c]Outside *were* conflicts, inside
*were* fears. [6]Nevertheless [a]God, who comforts
the downcast, comforted us by [b]the coming of
Titus, [7]and not only by his coming, but also by
the consolation with which he was comforted
in you, when he told us of your earnest desire,

**6:11** [a] 2 Cor. 7:3 **6:12** [a] 2 Cor. 12:15 **6:13** [a] 1 Cor. 4:14 **6:14** [a] 1 Cor. 5:9 [b] Eph. 5:6, 7, 11 **6:16** [a] [1 Cor. 3:16, 17; 6:19] [b] Ezek. 37:26, 27 [1] NU-Text reads *we*. [2] Leviticus 26:12; Jeremiah 32:38; Ezekiel 37:27 **6:17** [a] Is. 52:11 [1] Isaiah 52:11; Ezekiel 20:34, 41 **6:18** [a] 2 Sam. 7:14 [b] [Rom. 8:14] [1] 2 Samuel 7:14 **7:1** [a] [1 John 3:3] **7:2** [a] Acts 20:33 **7:3** [a] 2 Cor. 6:11, 12 **7:4** [a] 2 Cor. 3:12 [b] 1 Cor. 1:4 [c] Phil. 2:17 **7:5** [a] 2 Cor. 2:13 [b] 2 Cor. 4:8 [c] Deut. 32:25 **7:6** [a] Is. 49:13; 2 Cor. 1:3, 4 [b] 2 Cor. 2:13; 7:13

your mourning, your zeal for me, so that I rejoiced even more.

8 For even if I made you [a]sorry with my letter, I do not regret it; [b]though I did regret it. For I perceive that the same epistle made you sorry, though only for a while. 9 Now I rejoice, not that you were made sorry, but that your sorrow led to repentance. For you were made sorry in a godly manner, that you might suffer loss from us in nothing. 10 For [a]godly sorrow produces repentance *leading* to salvation, not to be regretted; [b]but the sorrow of the world produces death. 11 For observe this very thing, that you sorrowed in a godly manner: What diligence it produced in you, *what* [a]clearing *of yourselves, what* indignation, *what* fear, *what* vehement desire, *what* zeal, *what* vindication! In all *things* you proved yourselves to be [b]clear in this matter. 12 Therefore, although I wrote to you, *I did* not *do it* for the sake of him who had done the wrong, nor for the sake of him who suffered wrong, [a]but that our care for you in the sight of God might appear to you.

### THE JOY OF TITUS

13 Therefore we have been comforted in your comfort. And we rejoiced exceedingly more for the joy of Titus, because his spirit [a]has been refreshed by you all. 14 For if in anything I have boasted to him about you, I am not ashamed. But as we spoke all things to you in truth, even so our boasting to Titus was found true. 15 And his affections are greater for you as he remembers [a]the obedience of you all, how with fear and trembling you received him. 16 Therefore I rejoice that [a]I have confidence in you in everything.

### EXCEL IN GIVING

**8** Moreover, brethren, we make known to you the grace of God bestowed on the churches of Macedonia: 2 that in a great trial of affliction the abundance of their joy and [a]their deep poverty abounded in the riches of their liberality. 3 For I bear witness that according to *their* ability, yes, and beyond *their* ability, *they were* freely willing, 4 imploring us with much urgency that we would receive[1] the gift and [a]the fellowship of the ministering to the saints. 5 And not *only* as we had hoped, but they first [a]gave themselves to the Lord, and *then* to us by the [b]will of God. 6 So [a]we urged Titus, that as he had begun, so he would also complete this grace in you as well. 7 But as [a]you abound in everything—in faith, in speech, in knowledge, in all diligence, and in your love for us—*see* [b]that you abound in this grace also.

### CHRIST OUR PATTERN

8 [a]I speak not by commandment, but I am testing the sincerity of your love by the diligence of others. 9 For you know the grace of our Lord Jesus Christ, [a]that though He was rich, yet for your sakes He became poor, that you through His poverty might become [b]rich.

10 And in this [a]I give advice: [b]It is to your advantage not only to be doing what you began and [c]were desiring to do a year ago; 11 but now you also must complete the doing *of it;* that as *there was* a readiness to desire *it,* so *there* also *may be* a completion out of what *you* have. 12 For [a]if there is first a willing mind, *it is* accepted according to what one has, *and* not according to what he does not have.

> **8:10–11** The Christians in Jerusalem were experiencing some tough times. They had endured two earthquakes and a severe famine. Christian churches in other cities offered to give their own money to help their brothers and sisters in Christ. Paul and Barnabas were collecting the money and taking it to Jerusalem.

13 For *I do* not *mean* that others should be eased and you burdened; 14 but by an equality, *that* now at this time your abundance *may supply* their lack, that their abundance also may *supply* your lack—that there may be equality. 15 As it is written, [a]"He who *gathered* much had nothing left over, and he who *gathered* little had no lack."[1]

### COLLECTION FOR THE JUDEAN SAINTS

16 But thanks *be* to God who puts[1] the same earnest care for you into the heart of Titus. 17 For he not only accepted the exhortation, but being more diligent, he went to you of his own accord. 18 And we have sent with him [a]the brother whose praise *is* in the gospel throughout all the churches, 19 and not only *that,* but who was also [a]chosen by the churches to travel with us with this gift, which is administered by us [b]to the glory of the Lord Himself and *to show* your ready mind, 20 avoiding this: that anyone should blame us in this lavish gift which is administered by us— 21 [a]providing honorable things, not only in the sight of the Lord, but also in the sight of men.

22 And we have sent with them our brother whom we have often proved diligent in many things, but now much more diligent, because of the great confidence which *we have* in you. 23 If *anyone inquires* about [a]Titus, *he is* my partner and

**7:8** [a] 2 Cor. 2:2 [b] 2 Cor. 2:4 **7:10** [a] 2 Sam. 12:13; Ps. 32:10; Matt. 26:75 [b] Prov. 17:22 **7:11** [a] Eph. 5:11 [b] 2 Cor. 2:5–11 **7:12** [a] 2 Cor. 2:4 **7:13** [a] Rom. 15:32 **7:15** [a] 2 Cor. 2:9; Phil. 2:12 **7:16** [a] 2 Cor. 2:3; 8:22; 2 Thess. 3:4; Philem. 8, 21 **8:2** [a] Mark 12:44 **8:4** [a] Acts 11:29; 24:17; Rom. 15:25, 26; 1 Cor. 16:1, 3, 4; 2 Cor. 9:1 [1] NU-Text and M-Text omit *that we would receive,* thus changing text to *urgency for the favor and fellowship . . . .* **8:5** [a] [Rom. 12:1, 2] [b] [Eph. 6:6] **8:6** [a] 2 Cor. 8:17; 12:18 **8:7** [a] [1 Cor. 1:5; 12:13] [b] 2 Cor. 9:8 **8:8** [a] 1 Cor. 7:6 **8:9** [a] Matt. 8:20; Luke 9:58; Phil. 2:6, 7 [b] Rom. 9:23; [Eph. 1:7; Rev. 3:18] **8:10** [a] 1 Cor. 7:25, 40 [b] [Prov. 19:17; Matt. 10:42; 1 Tim. 6:18, 19; Heb. 13:16] [c] 1 Cor. 16:2; 2 Cor. 9:2 **8:12** [a] Mark 12:43, 44; Luke 21:3, 4; 2 Cor. 9:7 **8:15** [a] Ex. 16:18 [1] Exodus 16:18 **8:16** [1] NU-Text reads *has put.* **8:18** [a] 1 Cor. 16:3; 2 Cor. 12:18 **8:19** [a] 1 Cor. 16:3, 4 [b] 2 Cor. 4:15 **8:21** [a] Rom. 12:17 **8:23** [a] 2 Cor. 7:13, 14

fellow worker concerning you. Or if our brethren *are inquired about, they are* [b]messengers of the churches, the glory of Christ. 24 Therefore show to them, and[1] before the churches, the proof of your love and of our [a]boasting on your behalf.

### ADMINISTERING THE GIFT

9 Now concerning [a]the ministering to the saints, it is superfluous for me to write to you; 2 for I know your willingness, about which I boast of you to the Macedonians, that Achaia was ready a [a]year ago; and your zeal has stirred up the majority. 3 [a]Yet I have sent the brethren, lest our boasting of you should be in vain in this respect, that, as I said, you may be ready; 4 lest if *some* Macedonians come with me and find you unprepared, we (not to mention you!) should be ashamed of this confident boasting.[1] 5 Therefore I thought it necessary to exhort the brethren to go to you ahead of time, and prepare your generous gift beforehand, which *you had* previously promised, that it may be ready as *a matter of* generosity and not as a grudging obligation.

### THE CHEERFUL GIVER

6 [a]But this *I say:* He who sows sparingly will also reap sparingly, and he who sows bountifully will also reap bountifully. 7 *So let* each one *give* as he purposes in his heart, [a]not grudgingly or of necessity; for [b]God loves a cheerful giver. 8 [a]And God *is* able to make all grace abound toward you, that you, always having all sufficiency in all *things,* may have an abundance for every good work. 9 As it is written:

> [a]"He has dispersed abroad,
> He has given to the poor;
> His righteousness endures forever."[1]

10 Now may[1] He who [a]supplies seed to the sower, and bread for food, supply and multiply the seed you have *sown* and increase the fruits of your [b]righteousness, 11 while *you are* enriched in everything for all liberality, [a]which causes thanksgiving through us to God. 12 For the administration of this service not only [a]supplies the needs of the saints, but also is abounding through many thanksgivings to God, 13 while, through the proof of this ministry, they [a]glorify God for the obedience of your confession to the gospel of Christ, and for *your* liberal [b]sharing with them and all *men,* 14 and by their prayer for you, who long for you because of the exceeding [a]grace of God in you. 15 Thanks *be* to God [a]for His indescribable gift!

### THE SPIRITUAL WAR

10 Now [a]I, Paul, myself am pleading with you by the meekness and gentleness of Christ— [b]who in presence *am* lowly among you, but being absent am bold toward you. 2 But I beg *you* [a]that when I am present I may not be bold with that confidence by which I intend to be bold against some, who think of us as if we walked according to the flesh. 3 For though we walk in the flesh, we do not war according to the flesh. 4 [a]For the weapons [b]of our warfare *are* not carnal but [c]mighty in God [d]for pulling down strongholds, 5 [a]casting down arguments and every high thing that exalts itself against the knowledge of God, bringing every thought into captivity to the obedience of Christ, 6 [a]and being ready to punish all disobedience when [b]your obedience is fulfilled.

### REALITY OF PAUL'S AUTHORITY

7 [a]Do you look at things according to the outward appearance? [b]If anyone is convinced in himself that he is Christ's, let him again consider this in himself, that just as he *is* Christ's, even so [c]we *are* Christ's.[1] 8 For even if I should boast somewhat more [a]about our authority, which the Lord gave us[1] for edification and not for your destruction, [b]I shall not be ashamed— 9 lest I seem to terrify you by letters. 10 "For *his* letters," they say, "*are* weighty and powerful, but [a]*his* bodily presence *is* weak, and *his* [b]speech contemptible." 11 Let such a person consider this, that what we are in word by letters when we are absent, such *we will* also *be* in deed when we are present.

### LIMITS OF PAUL'S AUTHORITY

12 [a]For we dare not class ourselves or compare ourselves with those who commend themselves. But they, measuring themselves by themselves, and comparing themselves among themselves, are not wise. 13 [a]We, however, will not boast beyond measure, but within the limits of the sphere which God appointed us—a sphere which especially includes you. 14 For we are not overextending ourselves (as though *our authority* did not extend to you), [a]for it was to you that we came with the gospel of Christ; 15 not boasting of things beyond measure, *that is,* [a]in other men's labors, but having hope, *that* as your faith is increased, we shall be greatly enlarged by you in our sphere, 16 to preach the gospel in the *regions* beyond you, *and* not to boast in another man's sphere of accomplishment.

17 But [a]"he who glories, let him glory in the LORD."[1] 18 For [a]not he who commends himself is approved, but [b]whom the Lord commends.

**8:23** [b] Phil. 2:25 **8:24** [a] 2 Cor. 7:4, 14; 9:2 [1] NU-Text and M-Text omit *and.* **9:1** [a] Gal. 2:10 **9:2** [a] 2 Cor. 8:10 **9:3** [a] 2 Cor. 8:6, 17 **9:4** [1] NU-Text reads *this confidence.* **9:6** [a] Prov. 11:24; 22:9 **9:7** [a] Deut. 15:7 [b] Rom. 12:8 **9:8** [a] [Prov. 11:24] **9:9** [a] Ps. 112:9 [1] Psalm 112:9 **9:10** [a] Is. 55:10 [b] Hos. 10:12 [1] NU-Text reads *Now He who supplies . . . will supply . . . .* **9:11** [a] 2 Cor. 1:11 **9:12** [a] 2 Cor. 8:14 **9:13** [a] [Matt. 5:16] [b] [Heb. 13:16] **9:14** [a] 2 Cor. 8:1 **9:15** [a] [James 1:17] **10:1** [a] Rom. 12:1 [b] 1 Thess. 2:7 **10:2** [a] 1 Cor. 4:21 **10:4** [a] Eph. 6:13 [b] 1 Tim. 1:18 [c] Acts 7:22 [d] Jer. 1:10 **10:5** [a] 1 Cor. 1:19 **10:6** [a] 2 Cor. 13:2, 10 [b] 2 Cor. 7:15 **10:7** [a] [John 7:24] [b] 1 Cor. 1:12; 14:37 [c] 1 Cor. 3:23 [1] NU-Text reads *even as we are.* **10:8** [a] 2 Cor. 13:10 [b] 2 Cor. 7:14 [1] NU-Text omits *us.* **10:10** [a] Gal. 4:13 [b] 2 Cor. 11:6 **10:12** [a] 2 Cor. 5:12 **10:13** [a] 2 Cor. 10:15 **10:14** [a] 1 Cor. 3:5, 6 **10:15** [a] Rom. 15:20 **10:17** [a] Jer. 9:24 [1] Jeremiah 9:24 **10:18** [a] Prov. 27:2 [b] Rom. 2:29

### CONCERN FOR THEIR FAITHFULNESS

11 Oh, that you would bear with me in a little
[a]folly—and indeed you do bear with me.
2 For I am [a]jealous for you with godly jealou-
sy. For [b]I have betrothed you to one husband,
[c]that I may present *you* [d]*as* a chaste virgin to
Christ. 3 But I fear, lest somehow, as [a]the ser-
pent deceived Eve by his craftiness, so your
minds [b]may be corrupted from the simplicity[1]
that is in Christ. 4 For if he who comes preaches
another Jesus whom we have not preached, or
*if* you receive a different spirit which you have
not received, or a [a]different gospel which you
have not accepted—you may well put up with it!

### PAUL AND FALSE APOSTLES

5 For I consider that [a]I am not at all inferior
to the most eminent apostles. 6 Even though [a]*I*
*am* untrained in speech, yet *I am* not [b]in knowl-
edge. But [c]we have been thoroughly manifested[1]
among you in all things.
7 Did I commit sin in humbling myself that
you might be exalted, because I preached the
gospel of God to you [a]free of charge? 8 I robbed
other churches, taking wages *from them* to min-
ister to you. 9 And when I was present with you,
and in need, [a]I was a burden to no one, for what I
lacked [b]the brethren who came from Macedonia
supplied. And in everything I kept myself from be-
ing burdensome to you, and so I will keep *myself.*
10 [a]As the truth of Christ is in me, [b]no one shall stop
me from this boasting in the regions of Achaia.
11 Why? [a]Because I do not love you? God knows!
12 But what I do, I will also continue to do,
[a]that I may cut off the opportunity from those
who desire an opportunity to be regarded just
as we are in the things of which they boast. 13 For
such [a]*are* false apostles, [b]deceitful workers,
transforming themselves into apostles of Christ.
14 And no wonder! For Satan himself transforms
himself into [a]an angel of light. 15 Therefore *it is*
no great thing if his ministers also transform
themselves into ministers of righteousness,
[a]whose end will be according to their works.

### RELUCTANT BOASTING

16 I say again, let no one think me a fool. If
otherwise, at least receive me as a fool, that I also
may boast a little. 17 What I speak, [a]I speak not
according to the Lord, but as it were, foolishly, in
this confidence of boasting. 18 Seeing that many
boast according to the flesh, I also will boast. 19 For
you put up with fools gladly, [a]since you *yourselves*
are wise! 20 For you put up with it [a]if one brings
you into bondage, if one devours *you,* if one takes
*from you,* if one exalts himself, if one strikes you
on the face. 21 To *our* shame [a]I say that we were too
weak for that! But [b]in whatever anyone is bold—I
speak foolishly—I am bold also.

### SUFFERING FOR CHRIST

22 Are they [a]Hebrews? So *am* I. Are they Is-
raelites? So *am* I. Are they the seed of Abraham?
So *am* I. 23 Are they ministers of Christ?—I speak
as a fool—I *am* more: [a]in labors more abundant,
[b]in stripes above measure, in prisons more
frequently, [c]in deaths often. 24 From the Jews
five times I received [a]forty [b]*stripes* minus one.
25 Three times I was [a]beaten with rods; [b]once I
was stoned; three times I [c]was shipwrecked; a
night and a day I have been in the deep; 26 *in*
journeys often, *in* perils of waters, *in* perils of
robbers, [a]*in* perils of *my own* countrymen, [b]*in*
perils of the Gentiles, *in* perils in the city, *in* perils
in the wilderness, *in* perils in the sea, *in* perils
among false brethren; 27 in weariness and toil,
[a]in sleeplessness often, [b]in hunger and thirst, in
[c]fastings often, in cold and nakedness— 28 be-
sides the other things, what comes upon me
daily: [a]my deep concern for all the churches.
29 [a]Who is weak, and I am not weak? Who is made
to stumble, and I do not burn *with indignation?*

> **11:23** Paul acknowledged the silliness of such bragging. He knew only God had made his preaching and service effective. Paul's credentials were superior to those of the false teachers on every point of experience and background, but even so, his ministry had authority only because he received it from God.

30 If I must boast, [a]I will boast in the things
which concern my infirmity. 31 [a]The God and
Father of our Lord Jesus Christ, [b]who is blessed
forever, knows that I am not lying. 32 [a]In Da-
mascus the governor, under Aretas the king,
was guarding the city of the Damascenes with
a garrison, desiring to arrest me; 33 but I was let
down in a basket through a window in the wall,
and escaped from his hands.

### THE VISION OF PARADISE

12 It is doubtless[1] not profitable for me to
boast. I will come to [a]visions and [b]revela-
tions of the Lord: 2 I know a man [a]in Christ who
fourteen years ago—whether in the body I do not

**11:1** [a]2 Cor. 11:4, 16, 19 **11:2** [a]Gal. 4:17 [b]Hos. 2:19 [c]Col. 1:28 [d]Lev. 21:13 **11:3** [a]Gen. 3:4, 13 [b]Eph. 6:24 [1]NU-Text adds *and purity.* **11:4** [a]Gal. 1:6–8 **11:5** [a]2 Cor. 12:11 **11:6** [a][1 Cor. 1:17] [b][Eph. 3:4] [c][2 Cor. 12:12] [1]NU-Text omits *been.* **11:7** [a]1 Cor. 9:18 **11:9** [a]Acts 20:33 [b]Phil. 4:10 **11:10** [a]Rom. 1:9; 9:1 [b]1 Cor. 9:15 **11:11** [a]2 Cor. 6:11; 12:15 **11:12** [a]1 Cor. 9:12 **11:13** [a]Phil. 1:15 [b]Phil. 3:2 **11:14** [a]Gal. 1:8 **11:15** [a][Phil. 3:19] **11:17** [a]1 Cor. 7:6 **11:19** [a]1 Cor. 4:10 **11:20** [a][Gal. 2:4; 4:3, 9; 5:1] **11:21** [a]2 Cor. 10:10 [b]Phil. 3:4 **11:22** [a]Phil. 3:4–6 **11:23** [a]1 Cor. 15:10 [b]Acts 9:16 [c]1 Cor. 15:30 **11:24** [a]Deut. 25:3 [b]2 Cor. 6:5 **11:25** [a]Acts 16:22, 23; 21:32 [b]Acts 14:5, 19 [c]Acts 27:1–44 **11:26** [a]Acts 9:23, 24; 13:45, 50; 17:5, 13 [b]Acts 14:5, 19; 19:23; 27:42 **11:27** [a]Acts 20:31 [b]1 Cor. 4:11 [c]Acts 9:9; 13:2, 3; 14:23 **11:28** [a]Acts 20:18 **11:29** [a][1 Cor. 8:9, 13; 9:22] **11:30** [a][2 Cor. 12:5, 9, 10] **11:31** [a]1 Thess. 2:5 [b]Rom. 9:5 **11:32** [a]Acts 9:19–25 **12:1** [a]Acts 16:9; 18:9; 22:17, 18; 23:11; 26:13–15; 27:23 [b][Gal. 1:12; 2:2] [1]NU-Text reads *necessary, though not profitable, to boast.* **12:2** [a]Rom. 16:7

know, or whether out of the body I do not know,
God knows—such a one [b]was caught up to the
third heaven. 3 And I know such a man—whether
in the body or out of the body I do not know, God
knows— 4 how he was caught up into [a]Paradise
and heard inexpressible words, which it is not
lawful for a man to utter. 5 Of such a one I will
boast; yet of myself I will not [a]boast, except in my
infirmities. 6 For though I might desire to boast,
I will not be a fool; for I will speak the truth. But
I refrain, lest anyone should think of me above
what he sees me *to be* or hears from me.

### THE THORN IN THE FLESH

7 And lest I should be exalted above measure
by the abundance of the revelations, a [a]thorn in
the flesh was given to me, [b]a messenger of Satan
to buffet me, lest I be exalted above measure.

> **12:7** Many commentators interpret Paul's **thorn** as a physical ailment, perhaps it was eye trouble based on Galatians 4:15. It's also possible that **flesh** is a reference to the fallen human nature, in which case the thorn could be a temptation, or it could refer to persecution or opposition. Whatever the case, God permitted **Satan** to afflict Paul as he did Job (see Job 1–2).

8 [a]Concerning this thing I pleaded with the Lord
three times that it might depart from me. 9 And
He said to me, "My grace is sufficient for you,
for My strength is made perfect in weakness."
Therefore most gladly [a]I will rather boast in my
infirmities, [b]that the power of Christ may rest
upon me. 10 Therefore [a]I take pleasure in infir-
mities, in reproaches, in needs, in persecutions,
in distresses, for Christ's sake. [b]For when I am
weak, then I am strong.

> **SEEING JESUS IN THE SCRIPTURE**
>
> **12:9** True strength is found in our weakness and reliance on God in the pattern of Jesus, who humbled Himself and relied on the Father (see Phil. 2:5–11).

### SIGNS OF AN APOSTLE

11 I have become [a]a fool in boasting;[1] you have
compelled me. For I ought to have been com-
mended by you; for [b]in nothing was I behind the
most eminent apostles, though [c]I am nothing.
12 [a]Truly the signs of an apostle were accom-
plished among you with all perseverance, in
signs and [b]wonders and mighty [c]deeds. 13 For
what is it in which you were inferior to other
churches, except that I myself was not burden-
some to you? Forgive me this wrong!

### LOVE FOR THE CHURCH

14 [a]Now *for* the third time I am ready to come
to you. And I will not be burdensome to you;
for [b]I do not seek yours, but you. [c]For the chil-
dren ought not to lay up for the parents, but the
parents for the children. 15 And I will very gladly
spend and be spent [a]for your souls; though [b]the
more abundantly I love you, the less I am loved.
16 But be that *as it may,* [a]I did not burden
you. Nevertheless, being crafty, I caught you by
cunning! 17 Did I take advantage of you by any
of those whom I sent to you? 18 I urged Titus,
and sent our [a]brother with *him.* Did Titus take
advantage of you? Did we not walk in the same
spirit? Did *we* not *walk* in the same steps?
19 [a]Again, do you think[1] that we excuse our-
selves to you? [b]We speak before God in Christ.
[c]But *we do* all things, beloved, for your edifica-
tion. 20 For I fear lest, when I come, I shall not
find you such as I wish, and *that* [a]I shall be found
by you such as you do not wish; lest *there be* con-
tentions, jealousies, outbursts of wrath, selfish
ambitions, backbitings, whisperings, conceits,
tumults; 21 lest, when I come again, my God [a]will
humble me among you, and I shall mourn for
many [b]who have sinned before and have not
repented of the uncleanness, [c]fornication, and
lewdness which they have practiced.

### COMING WITH AUTHORITY

13 This *will be* [a]the third *time* I am coming
to you. [b]"By the mouth of two or three
witnesses every word shall be established."[1] 2 [a]I
have told you before, and foretell as if I were
present the second time, and now being absent
I write[1] to those [b]who have sinned before, and to
all the rest, that if I come again [c]I will not spare—
3 since you seek a proof of Christ [a]speaking in
me, who is not weak toward you, but mighty [b]in
you. 4 [a]For though He was crucified in weakness,
yet [b]He lives by the power of God. For [c]we also
are weak in Him, but we shall live with Him by
the power of God toward you.
5 Examine yourselves *as to* whether you are
in the faith. Test yourselves. Do you not know
yourselves, [a]that Jesus Christ is in you?—unless
indeed you are [b]disqualified. 6 But I trust that
you will know that we are not disqualified.

**12:2** [b] Acts 22:17 **12:4** [a] Luke 23:43 **12:5** [a] 2 Cor. 11:30 **12:7** [a] Ezek. 28:24 [b] Job 2:7 **12:8** [a] Matt. 26:44 **12:9** [a] 2 Cor. 11:30 [b] [1 Pet. 4:14] **12:10** [a] [Rom. 5:3; 8:35] [b] 2 Cor. 13:4 **12:11** [a] 2 Cor. 5:13; 11:1, 16; 12:6 [b] 2 Cor. 11:5 [c] 1 Cor. 3:7; 13:2; 15:9 [1] NU-Text omits *in boasting.* **12:12** [a] Rom. 15:18 [b] Acts 15:12 [c] Acts 14:8–10; 16:16–18; 19:11, 12; 20:6–12; 28:1–10 **12:14** [a] 2 Cor. 1:15; 13:1, 2 [b] [1 Cor. 10:24–33] [c] 1 Cor. 4:14 **12:15** [a] [2 Tim. 2:10] [b] 2 Cor. 6:12, 13 **12:16** [a] 2 Cor. 11:9 **12:18** [a] 2 Cor. 8:18 **12:19** [a] 2 Cor. 5:12 [b] [Rom. 9:1, 2] [c] 1 Cor. 10:33 [1] NU-Text reads *You have been thinking for a long time . . . .* **12:20** [a] 1 Cor. 4:21 **12:21** [a] 2 Cor. 2:1, 4 [b] 2 Cor. 13:2 [c] 1 Cor. 5:1 **13:1** [a] 2 Cor. 12:14 [b] Deut. 17:6; 19:15 [1] Deuteronomy 19:15 **13:2** [a] 2 Cor. 10:2 [b] 2 Cor. 12:21 [c] 2 Cor. 1:23; 10:11 [1] NU-Text omits *I write.* **13:3** [a] Matt. 10:20 [b] [1 Cor. 9:2] **13:4** [a] [1 Pet. 3:18] [b] [Rom. 1:4; 6:4] [c] [2 Cor. 10:3, 4] **13:5** [a] [Gal. 4:19] [b] 1 Cor. 9:27

KNOW THE TRUTH

# THE DOCTRINE OF GOD

## PART 20: THE TRIUNE NATURE OF GOD

**13:14** A grand mystery and truth about God is His triune nature. *Triune* means one God in three Persons. For example, Paul pronounced various blessings upon his readers from each of the three Persons of the Godhead: the Father, Son, and Holy Spirit. The triune nature of God is also often referred to as the *Trinity*.

While the Father, Son, and Holy Spirit are distinct Persons, all three Persons share one nature, essence, and substance. The Father *is* God, the Son *is* God, and the Spirit *is* God. But the Father *is not* the Son nor the Spirit, the Son *is not* the Father nor the Spirit, and the Spirit *is not* the Father nor the Son.

The three Persons of the Godhead work in unity to achieve their one shared purpose. We can see this in prayer. While we can pray to any Person of the Godhead, the traditional manner is to pray to the Father through the Son in the power of the Spirit. Likewise, we can see this in salvation. All who are drawn by the Spirit to believe in the Son are forgiven by the Father.

Because the triune nature of God is a mystery, many have suggested various analogies to aid our understanding (e.g., a three-leaf clover, the three parts of an egg, the three states of water). However, because all analogies lead to an incorrect understanding of the Trinity, it's best not to use any. Rather, rest in the glorious mystery of our triune God in faith.

*For* **THE DOCTRINE OF JESUS: PART 1: OVERVIEW OF THE DOCTRINE OF JESUS**, *turn to Mark 1:1 on page 1003.*

### *PAUL PREFERS GENTLENESS*

7 Now I[1] pray to God that you do no evil,
not that we should appear approved, but that
you should do what is honorable, though [a]we
may seem disqualified. 8 For we can do nothing
against the truth, but for the truth. 9 For we are
glad [a]when we are weak and you are strong.
And this also we pray, [b]that you may be made
complete. 10 [a]Therefore I write these things being
absent, lest being present I should use sharpness,
according to the [b]authority which the Lord has
given me for edification and not for destruction.

### *GREETINGS AND BENEDICTION*

11 Finally, brethren, farewell. Become com-
plete. [a]Be of good comfort, be of one mind, live
in peace; and the God of love [b]and peace will
be with you.
12 [a]Greet one another with a holy kiss.
13 All the saints greet you.
14 [a]The grace of the Lord Jesus Christ, and
the love of God, and [b]the communion of the
Holy Spirit *be* with you all. Amen.

**13:7** [a] 2 Cor. 6:9 [1] NU-Text reads *we.* **13:9** [a] 1 Cor. 4:10 [b] [1 Thess. 3:10] **13:10** [a] 1 Cor. 4:21 [b] 2 Cor. 10:8 **13:11** [a] Rom. 12:16, 18 [b] Rom. 15:33 **13:12** [a] Rom. 16:16 **13:14** [a] Rom. 16:24 [b] Phil. 2:1

# *The Epistle of Paul the Apostle to the*
# GALATIANS

| AUTHOR | KEY VERSE | READING TIME |
|---|---|---|
| Paul | Galatians 3:3 | 25 minutes |

The Galatians had begun their Christian journey by faith. Now, they seemed content to abandon that faith and chart a new course based on works instead. Paul's letter to the churches of Galatia is at once a vigorous attack against a gospel of works and a rigorous defense of the gospel of faith. The apostle began by presenting his credentials that supported the message from God that he shared: blessing comes from God by faith, not by the law. The law declares people guilty and imprisons them; God declares those with faith righteous and sets them free in Christ. But liberty is not license. Freedom in Christ means believers are free to produce the fruit of righteousness through a Spirit-led lifestyle, not live any way they please.

**Occasion:** Views differ on whether Paul wrote to the northern or southern Galatians. If Paul wrote to the southern Galatians, he would have written the epistle right after his first missionary journey and just before the Jerusalem council (Acts 15). If Paul wrote to the northern Galatians, he would have written the epistle later, sometime during his third missionary journey.

**Main Point:** The same faith that justifies sustains the believer through the Christian life.

**Big Ideas:** We are saved by God's gift of grace through our faith in Jesus. Nothing we do can save us, but our lives should look much different because we have been saved.

**OUTLINE:**

I. The Gospel of Grace Defended (chs. 1–2)
II. The Gospel of Grace Explained (chs. 3–4)
III. The Gospel of Grace Applied (chs. 5–6)

**c. AD 34**
Paul is converted

**c. AD 47–49**
Paul's first missionary journey

**c. AD 48**
**Galatians written**, if to southern Galatia

**c. AD 50**
The Jerusalem Council

**c. AD 50–53**
Paul's second missionary journey

**AD 52**
**Galatians written**, if to northern Galatia

**c. AD 53–57**
Paul's third missionary journey

**AD 54–68**
Nero is Roman emperor

**c. AD 58**
Paul is arrested in Jerusalem

**c. AD 60–62**
Paul is imprisoned in Rome

**AD 64**
Great Fire of Rome; first Roman mass persecution of Christians

**c. AD 67**
Peter and Paul are executed

### GREETING

**1** Paul, an apostle (not from men nor through man, but [a]through Jesus Christ and God the Father [b]who raised Him from the dead), 2 and all the brethren who are with me,

To the churches of Galatia:

3 Grace to you and peace from God the Father and our Lord Jesus Christ, 4 [a]who gave Himself for our sins, that He might deliver us [b]from this present evil age, according to the will of our God and Father, 5 to whom *be* glory forever and ever. Amen.

### ONLY ONE GOSPEL

6 I marvel that you are turning away so soon [a]from Him who called you in the grace of Christ, to a different gospel, 7 [a]which is not another; but there are some [b]who trouble you and want to [c]pervert the gospel of Christ. 8 But even if [a]we, or an angel from heaven, preach any other gospel to you than what we have preached to you, let him be accursed. 9 As we have said before, so now I say again, if anyone preaches any other gospel to you [a]than what you have received, let him be accursed.

10 For [a]do I now [b]persuade men, or God? Or [c]do I seek to please men? For if I still pleased men, I would not be a bondservant of Christ.

### CALL TO APOSTLESHIP

*(cf. Acts 9:1–25)*

11 [a]But I make known to you, brethren, that the gospel which was preached by me is not according to man. 12 For [a]I neither received it from man, nor was I taught *it,* but *it came* [b]through the revelation of Jesus Christ.

13 For you have heard of my former conduct in Judaism, how [a]I persecuted the church of God beyond measure and [b]*tried to* destroy it. 14 And I advanced in Judaism beyond many of my contemporaries in my own nation, [a]being more exceedingly zealous [b]for the traditions of my fathers.

15 But when it pleased God, [a]who separated me from my mother's womb and called *me* through His grace, 16 [a]to reveal His Son in me, that [b]I might preach Him among the Gentiles, I did not immediately confer with [c]flesh and blood, 17 nor did I go up to Jerusalem to those *who were* apostles before me; but I went to Arabia, and returned again to Damascus.

### CONTACTS AT JERUSALEM

*(cf. Acts 9:26–31)*

18 Then after three years [a]I went up to Jerusalem to see Peter,[1] and remained with him fifteen days. 19 But [a]I saw none of the other apostles except [b]James, the Lord's brother. 20 (Now *concerning* the things which I write to you, indeed, before God, I do not lie.)

21 [a]Afterward I went into the regions of Syria and Cilicia. 22 And I was unknown by face to the churches of Judea which [a]*were* in Christ. 23 But they were [a]hearing only, "He who formerly [b]persecuted us now preaches the faith which he once *tried to* destroy." 24 And they [a]glorified God in me.

### DEFENDING THE GOSPEL

*(cf. Acts 15:1–21)*

**2** Then after fourteen years [a]I went up again to Jerusalem with Barnabas, and also took Titus with *me.* 2 And I went up by revelation, and communicated to them that gospel which I preach

**1:1** [a]Acts 9:6 [b]Acts 2:24 **1:4** [a][Matt. 20:28] [b]Heb. 2:5 **1:6** [a]Gal. 1:15; 5:8 **1:7** [a]2 Cor. 11:4 [b]Gal. 5:10, 12 [c]2 Cor. 2:17 **1:8** [a]1 Cor. 16:22 **1:9** [a]Deut. 4:2 **1:10** [a]1 Thess. 2:4 [b]1 Sam. 24:7 [c]1 Thess. 2:4 **1:11** [a]1 Cor. 15:1 **1:12** [a]1 Cor. 15:1 [b][Eph. 3:3–5] **1:13** [a]Acts 9:1 [b]Acts 8:3; 22:4, 5 **1:14** [a]Acts 26:9 [b]Jer. 9:14 **1:15** [a]Is. 49:1, 5 **1:16** [a][2 Cor. 4:5–7] [b]Acts 9:15 [c]Matt. 16:17 **1:18** [a]Acts 9:26 [1]NU-Text reads *Cephas.* **1:19** [a]1 Cor. 9:5 [b]Matt. 13:55 **1:21** [a]Acts 9:30 **1:22** [a]Rom. 16:7 **1:23** [a]Acts 9:20, 21 [b]Acts 8:3 **1:24** [a]Acts 11:18 **2:1** [a]Acts 15:2

APPLY THE TRUTH

## CULTS

**1:8** A cult is a system of religious belief usually centered around extreme devotion to its leader. Often, cults separate their followers from their families and friends, forcing total reliance on the cults themselves. At times, cults use the Bible or portions of the Bible combined with other teachings to frame their beliefs. But partial truth isn't good enough. Partial truth isn't real truth. Here, the Bible makes a sharp distinction between true faith and any other system of beliefs, including cults. Following "any other gospel" than the true gospel of Jesus is grave error.

Not all faith is equal. Just because we believe something to be true and live with radical devotion, doesn't make it true. In this text, Paul makes a clear case for a singular gospel. There's only one way to have forgiveness of sins, access to God, and the hope of eternal life: through Jesus. One primary distinction between Christianity and all other beliefs is the Bible's teaching that God is the Creator and the re-Creator who rescues sinful humans. All other religions require people's good behavior to bring them to god. What makes the gospel of Jesus truly good news is it's a free gift to be received, not good advice that must be followed. Any other way isn't good news at all.

among the Gentiles, but [a]privately to those who
were of reputation, lest by any means [b]I might
run, or had run, in vain. 3 Yet not even Titus who
*was* with me, being a Greek, was compelled to
be circumcised. 4 And *this occurred* because of
[a]false brethren secretly brought in (who came in
by stealth to spy out our [b]liberty which we have
in Christ Jesus, [c]that they might bring us into
bondage), 5 to whom we did not yield submission
even for an hour, that [a]the truth of the gospel
might continue with you.

6 But from those [a]who seemed to be
something—whatever they were, it makes no
difference to me; [b]God shows personal favoritism
to no man—for those who seemed *to be something*
[c]added nothing to me. 7 But on the contrary, [a]when
they saw that the gospel for the uncircumcised
[b]had been committed to me, as *the gospel* for the
circumcised *was* to Peter 8 (for He who worked
effectively in Peter for the apostleship to the
[a]circumcised [b]also [c]worked effectively in me
toward the Gentiles), 9 and when James, Cephas,
and John, who seemed to be [a]pillars, perceived
[b]the grace that had been given to me, they gave
me and Barnabas the right hand of fellowship,
[c]that we *should go* to the Gentiles and they to the
circumcised. 10 *They desired* only that we should
remember the poor, [a]the very thing which I also
was eager to do.

### NO RETURN TO THE LAW

11 [a]Now when Peter[1] had come to Antioch,
I withstood him to his face, because he was to
be blamed; 12 for before certain men came from
James, [a]he would eat with the Gentiles; but
when they came, he withdrew and separated
himself, fearing those who were of the circum-
cision. 13 And the rest of the Jews also played the
hypocrite with him, so that even Barnabas was
carried away with their hypocrisy.

14 But when I saw that they were not straight-
forward about [a]the truth of the gospel, I said
to Peter [b]before *them* all, [c]"If you, being a Jew,
live in the manner of Gentiles and not as the
Jews, why do you[1] compel Gentiles to live as
Jews?[2] 15 [a]We *who are* Jews by nature, and not
[b]sinners of the Gentiles, 16 [a]knowing that a man
is not justified by the works of the law but [b]by
faith in Jesus Christ, even we have believed in
Christ Jesus, that we might be justified by faith
in Christ and not [c]by the works of the law; for by
the works of the law no flesh shall be justified.

17 "But if, while we seek to be justified by Christ,
we ourselves also are found [a]sinners, *is* Christ
therefore a minister of sin? Certainly not! 18 For
if I build again those things which I destroyed, I
make myself a transgressor. 19 For I [a]through the
law [b]died to the law that I might [c]live to God. 20 I
have been [a]crucified with Christ; it is no longer I
who live, but Christ lives in me; and the *life* which
I now live in the flesh [b]I live by faith in the Son of
God, [c]who loved me and gave Himself for me. 21 I do
not set aside the grace of God; for [a]if righteousness
*comes* through the law, then Christ died in vain."

**SEEING JESUS IN THE SCRIPTURE**

**2:20** Because Jesus gave up His life for us as sinners, we can now give up our lives for Him as those He loves (see Is. 53:12).

**2:2** [a] Acts 15:1–4 [b] Phil. 2:16 **2:4** [a] Acts 15:1, 24 [b] Gal. 3:25; 5:1, 13 [c] Gal. 4:3, 9 **2:5** [a] [Gal. 1:6; 2:14; 3:1] **2:6** [a] Gal. 2:9; 6:3 [b] Acts 10:34 [c] 2 Cor. 11:5; 12:11 **2:7** [a] Acts 9:15; 13:46; 22:21 [b] 1 Thess. 2:4 **2:8** [a] 1 Pet. 1:1 [b] Acts 9:15 [c] [Gal. 3:5] **2:9** [a] Matt. 16:18 [b] Rom. 1:5 [c] Acts 13:3 **2:10** [a] Acts 11:30 **2:11** [a] Acts 15:35 [1] NU-Text reads *Cephas.* **2:12** [a] [Acts 10:28; 11:2, 3] **2:14** [a] Gal. 1:6; 2:5 [b] 1 Tim. 5:20 [c] [Acts 10:28] [1] NU-Text reads *how can you.* [2] Some interpreters stop the quotation here. **2:15** [a] [Acts 15:10] [b] Matt. 9:11 **2:16** [a] Acts 13:38, 39 [b] Rom. 1:17 [c] Ps. 143:2 **2:17** [a] [1 John 3:8] **2:19** [a] Rom. 8:2 [b] [Rom. 6:2, 14; 7:4] [c] [Rom. 6:11] **2:20** [a] [Rom. 6:6] [b] 2 Cor. 5:15 [c] Eph. 5:2 **2:21** [a] Heb. 7:11

APPLY THE TRUTH

## RACISM

**2:11–16** Many things make people distinct. Differences such as upbringing, wealth, geography, and ethnicity aren't bad. They're part of what makes people so amazing. Diversity creates color and life in our world. But a far-too-common product of these differences is division, which certainly is bad. One way we often see this division is through racism, prejudice and mistreatment of others based on race. This is what was happening in this passage in Galatians. Peter was mistreating Gentiles simply because they were Gentiles and he wanted to impress the Jews. In response, Paul confronted Peter. Paul knew racism creates division in the beautiful tapestry that is the church of Jesus Christ.

The enemy wants to divide and conquer the church. He knows if people spend their time fighting with and mistreating one another, the kingdom can't advance like it should. Instead, the church must stand unified. We must share the same heart and mind so *together* we can represent Christ. This doesn't mean we ignore our differences; it means we embrace diversity as part of the beauty of the church. Our unity amid diversity becomes our strength and our sign to the world of the boundless power of Jesus Christ.

### JUSTIFICATION BY FAITH
*(cf. Rom. 4:1–25)*

3 O foolish Galatians! Who has bewitched you
that you should not obey the truth,[1] before
whose eyes Jesus Christ was clearly portrayed
among you[2] as crucified? 2 This only I want to
learn from you: Did you receive the Spirit by
the works of the law, [a]or by the hearing of faith?
3 Are you so foolish? [a]Having begun in the Spirit,
are you now being made perfect by [b]the flesh?
4 [a]Have you suffered so many things in vain—if
indeed *it was* in vain?

> **3:3** The Galatians were mistakenly trying to become **perfect** through their own efforts, especially through circumcision. They understood grace was necessary to come into salvation, but they didn't understand grace was just as needed within salvation.

5 Therefore He who supplies the Spirit to
you and works miracles among you, *does He do
it* by the works of the law, or by the hearing of
faith?— 6 just as Abraham [a]"believed God, and
it was accounted to him for righteousness."[1]
7 Therefore know that *only* [a]those who are of
faith are sons of Abraham. 8 And [a]the Scripture,
foreseeing that God would justify the Gentiles
by faith, preached the gospel to Abraham beforehand, *saying,* [b]"In you all the nations shall
be blessed."[1] 9 So then those who *are* of faith are
blessed with believing Abraham.

### THE LAW BRINGS A CURSE

10 For as many as are of the works of the law
are under the curse; for it is written, [a]"Cursed *is*
everyone who does not continue in all things
which are written in the book of the law, to do
them."[1] 11 But that no one is justified by the law
in the sight of God *is* evident, for [a]"the just shall
live by faith."[1] 12 Yet [a]the law is not of faith, but
[b]"the man who does them shall live by them."[1]
13 [a]Christ has redeemed us from the curse of
the law, having become a curse for us (for it is written, [b]"Cursed *is* everyone who hangs on a tree"[1]),
14 [a]that the blessing of Abraham might come upon
the [b]Gentiles in Christ Jesus, that we might receive
[c]the promise of the Spirit through faith.

### THE CHANGELESS PROMISE
*(cf. Gen. 12:1–3)*

15 Brethren, I speak in the manner of men:
[a]Though *it is* only a man's covenant, yet *if it is*

> **SEEING JESUS IN THE SCRIPTURE**
>
> **3:16** Jesus is the fulfillment of God's promise to Abraham, being the Seed who brought blessing to the entire word (see Gen. 22:18).

confirmed, no one annuls or adds to it. 16 Now to
Abraham and his Seed were the promises made.
He does not say, "And to seeds," as of many, but
as of [a]one, [b]"And to your Seed,"[1] who is [c]Christ.
17 And this I say, *that* the law, [a]which was four
hundred and thirty years later, cannot annul
the covenant that was confirmed before by God
in Christ,[1] [b]that it should make the promise of
no effect. 18 For if [a]the inheritance *is* of the law,
[b]*it is* no longer of promise; but God gave *it* to
Abraham by promise.

### PURPOSE OF THE LAW

19 What purpose then *does* the law *serve?* [a]It
was added because of transgressions, till the
[b]Seed should come to whom the promise was
made; *and it was* [c]appointed through angels
by the hand [d]of a mediator. 20 Now a mediator
does not *mediate* for one *only,* [a]but God is one.
21 *Is* the law then against the promises of God?
Certainly not! For if there had been a law given
which could have given life, truly righteousness
would have been by the law. 22 But the Scripture
has confined [a]all under sin, [b]that the promise by
faith in Jesus Christ might be given to those who
believe. 23 But before faith came, we were kept
under guard by the law, kept for the faith which
would afterward be revealed. 24 Therefore [a]the
law was our tutor *to bring us* to Christ, [b]that we
might be justified by faith. 25 But after faith has
come, we are no longer under a tutor.

> **3:23–25** Paul gave two different illustrations concerning the function of the **law** until Christ came (Gal. 4:4–5). The law acted as a jailor to hold people in custody until **faith** in Christ was **revealed**. But the law also served as a **tutor**. A tutor in ancient Greek culture would accompany the children in his care, instructing and disciplining them when necessary. The law was like a tutor because it both corrected and instructed the Israelites in God's ways until Christ was revealed and such a schoolmaster was no longer needed (Gal. 4:1–2).

**3:1** [1] NU-Text omits *that you should not obey the truth.* [2] NU-Text omits *among you.* **3:2** [a] Rom. 10:16, 17 **3:3** [a] [Gal. 4:9] [b] Heb. 7:16 **3:4** [a] Heb. 10:35 **3:6** [a] Gen. 15:6 [1] Genesis 15:6 **3:7** [a] John 8:39 **3:8** [a] Rom. 9:17 [b] Gen. 12:3; 18:18; 22:18; 26:4; 28:14 [1] Genesis 12:3; 18:18; 22:18; 26:4; 28:14 **3:10** [a] Deut. 27:26 [1] Deuteronomy 27:26 **3:11** [a] Hab. 2:4 [1] Habakkuk 2:4 **3:12** [a] Rom. 4:4, 5 [b] Lev. 18:5 [1] Leviticus 18:5 **3:13** [a] [Rom. 8:3] [b] Deut. 21:23 [1] Deuteronomy 21:23 **3:14** [a] [Rom. 4:1–5, 9, 16] [b] Rom. 3:29, 30 [c] Is. 32:15 **3:15** [a] Heb. 9:17 **3:16** [a] Gen. 22:18 [b] Gen. 12:3, 7; 13:15; 24:7 [c] [1 Cor. 12:12] [1] Genesis 12:7; 13:15; 24:7 **3:17** [a] Ex. 12:40 [b] [Rom. 4:13] [1] NU-Text omits *in Christ.* **3:18** [a] [Rom. 8:17] [b] Rom. 4:14 **3:19** [a] John 15:22 [b] Gal. 4:4 [c] Acts 7:53 [d] Ex. 20:19 **3:20** [a] [Rom. 3:29] **3:22** [a] Rom. 11:32 [b] Rom. 4:11 **3:24** [a] Rom. 10:4 [b] Acts 13:39

## BLENDED FAMILIES

APPLY THE TRUTH

**3:28** Nearly half of marriages end in divorce. Future remarriages result in almost 16 percent of children living in blended families. Depending on the situation, for a child this can be difficult, fun, or simply all that's ever been known. Being part of a blended family involves managing a lot of different personalities, navigating new and changing family dynamics, and adapting to new surroundings. Something as simple and joyful as celebrating holidays can become complex and even stressful. Did you realize Jesus came from a blended family of sorts? His Father is God, His mother is Mary, and His earthly father is Joseph. That means Jesus' brothers and sisters were half siblings. Jesus can relate to joys and challenges of blended-family life.

Even if you aren't part of a blended family in your home, we're all part of a blended family in the church. This passage describes how God created a way for people with all backgrounds to be united into one beautiful family. And like every other blended family, being part of our church family provides joys and challenges. The key is the same for both: focus on what unifies us as a family: Jesus. He won't make the challenges go away, but He will give you a way to get through them as one unified, amazing family.

### SONS AND HEIRS

26 For you [a]are all sons of God through
faith in Christ Jesus. 27 For [a]as many of you as
were baptized into Christ [b]have put on Christ.
28 [a]There is neither Jew nor Greek, [b]there is
neither slave nor free, there is neither male
nor female; for you are all [c]one in Christ
Jesus. 29 And [a]if you *are* Christ's, then you are
Abraham's [b]seed, and [c]heirs according to the
promise.

**4** Now I say *that* the heir, as long as he is a child,
does not differ at all from a slave, though
he is master of all, 2 but is under guardians and
stewards until the time appointed by the father.
3 Even so we, when we were children, [a]were in
bondage under the elements of the world. 4 But
[a]when the fullness of the time had come, God
sent forth His Son, [b]born[1] [c]of a woman, [d]born
under the law, 5 [a]to redeem those who were under
the law, [b]that we might receive the adoption
as sons.

### SEEING JESUS IN THE SCRIPTURE

**4:4** Jesus came to earth, born of a virgin, exactly when and how the Father desired (see Is. 7:14).

6 And because you are sons, God has
sent forth [a]the Spirit of His Son into your
hearts, crying out, "Abba, Father!" 7 Therefore
you are no longer a slave but a son,
[a]and if a son, then an heir of[1] God through
Christ.

### FEARS FOR THE CHURCH

8 But then, indeed, [a]when you did not know
God, [b]you served those which by nature are not
gods. 9 But now [a]after you have known God, or
rather are known by God, [b]how *is it that* you
turn again to [c]the weak and beggarly elements,
to which you desire again to be in bondage?
10 [a]You observe days and months and seasons
and years. 11 I am afraid for you, [a]lest I have
labored for you in vain.

12 Brethren, I urge you to become like me, for
I *became* like you. [a]You have not injured me at all.
13 You know that [a]because of physical infirmity I
preached the gospel to you at the first. 14 And my
trial which was in my flesh you did not despise
or reject, but you received me [a]as an angel of
God, [b]*even* as Christ Jesus. 15 What[1] then was the
blessing you *enjoyed?* For I bear you witness that,
if possible, you would have plucked out your own
eyes and given them to me. 16 Have I therefore
become your enemy because I tell you the truth?
17 They [a]zealously court you, *but* for no good;
yes, they want to exclude you, that you may be
zealous for them. 18 But it is good to be zealous
in a good thing always, and not only when I am
present with you. 19 [a]My little children, for whom I
labor in birth again until Christ is formed in you,
20 I would like to be present with you now and
to change my tone; for I have doubts about you.

### TWO COVENANTS

*(Gen. 21:8–21; Is. 54:1)*

21 Tell me, you who desire to be under the
law, do you not hear the law? 22 For it is written
that Abraham had two sons: [a]the one by a bondwoman,
[b]the other by a freewoman. 23 But he *who*

**3:26** [a] John 1:12 **3:27** [a] [Rom. 6:3] [b] Rom. 10:12; 13:14 **3:28** [a] Col. 3:11 [b] [1 Cor. 12:13] [c] [Eph. 2:15, 16] **3:29** [a] Gen. 21:10 [b] Rom. 4:11 [c] Rom. 8:17 **4:3** [a] Col. 2:8, 20 **4:4** [a] [Gen. 49:10] [b] [John 1:14] [c] Gen. 3:15 [d] Luke 2:21, 27 [1] Or *made* **4:5** [a] [Matt. 20:28] [b] [John 1:12] **4:6** [a] [Rom. 5:5; 8:9, 15, 16] **4:7** [a] [Rom. 8:16, 17] [1] NU-Text reads *through God* and omits *through Christ.* **4:8** [a] Eph. 2:12 [b] Rom. 1:25 **4:9** [a] [1 Cor. 8:3] [b] Col. 2:20 [c] Heb. 7:18 **4:10** [a] Rom. 14:5 **4:11** [a] 1 Thess. 3:5 **4:12** [a] 2 Cor. 2:5 **4:13** [a] 1 Cor. 2:3 **4:14** [a] Mal. 2:7 [b] [Luke 10:16] **4:15** [1] NU-Text reads *Where.* **4:17** [a] Rom. 10:2 **4:19** [a] 1 Cor. 4:15 **4:22** [a] Gen. 16:15 [b] Gen. 21:2

APPLY THE TRUTH

## ADOPTION

**4:5–7** Do you remember team captains at recess? Their job was to pick who they wanted on their teams. How did that usually go? Depending on your skill, height, or personality, you may have been picked early or perhaps not at all. We all know what it feels like to be chosen, and what it also feels like to be rejected. Some of us have experienced both these feelings in a powerful way in our families. We carry the pain of being rejected by our biological family while also experiencing the joy of being chosen by our adopted family.

The Bible makes it clear—like here in Galatians—no matter what your family background is, if you've trusted in Jesus, you've been adopted. God so loved broken and sinful people that He sent His only Son to rescue us and bring us into His family. The God who created and rules over everything, knows *you*, loves *you*, and has chosen *you*. And He will never reject you. We might have felt pain, sorrow, and the sting of rejection with our families on earth. Those feelings are real, and they are difficult. But remembering God has adopted you into His forever family can provide comfort, hope, and joy.

**4:23** Sarah, **the freewoman**, and Hagar, **the bondwoman**, both gave birth to a son of Abraham. But Sarah was Abraham's wife and Hagar was Sarah's slave. God had promised Abraham and Sarah they would have a son. Sarah believed she was too old to have a child, so she thought the next best thing would be for her servant to have Abraham's son. Hagar gave birth to a son named Ishmael. God, however, made it clear that Ishmael wasn't the son He had promised. Even though she was ninety years old, Sarah became pregnant and gave birth to a son named Isaac—the one God had promised.

*was* of the bondwoman [a]was born according to
the flesh, [b]and he of the freewoman through
promise, 24 which things are symbolic. For these
are the[1] two covenants: the one from Mount
[a]Sinai which gives birth to bondage, which is
Hagar— 25 for this Hagar is Mount Sinai in Ara-
bia, and corresponds to Jerusalem which now is,
and is in bondage with her children— 26 but the
[a]Jerusalem above is free, which is the mother
of us all. 27 For it is written:

[a]"Rejoice, O barren,
*You* who do not bear!
Break forth and shout,
You who are not in labor!
For the desolate has many more
children
Than she who has a husband."[1]

28 Now [a]we, brethren, as Isaac *was,* are [b]chil-
dren of promise. 29 But, as [a]he who was born
according to the flesh then persecuted him *who
was born* according to the Spirit, [b]even so *it is*
now. 30 Nevertheless what does [a]the Scripture
say? [b]"Cast out the bondwoman and her son,
for [c]the son of the bondwoman shall not be
heir with the son of the freewoman."[1] 31 So then,
brethren, we are not children of the bondwoman
but of the free.

### *CHRISTIAN LIBERTY*

5 [a]Stand fast therefore in the liberty by which
Christ has made us free,[1] and do not be entan-
gled again with a [b]yoke of bondage. 2 Indeed I,
Paul, say to you that [a]if you become circumcised,
Christ will profit you nothing. 3 And I testify
again to every man who becomes circumcised
[a]that he is a debtor to keep the whole law. 4 [a]You
have become estranged from Christ, you who
*attempt to* be justified by law; [b]you have fallen
from grace. 5 For we through the Spirit eagerly
[a]wait for the hope of righteousness by faith. 6 For
[a]in Christ Jesus neither circumcision nor uncir-
cumcision avails anything, but [b]faith working
through love.

### *LOVE FULFILLS THE LAW*

7 You [a]ran well. Who hindered you from
obeying the truth? 8 This persuasion does not
*come* from Him who calls you. 9 [a]A little leaven
leavens the whole lump. 10 I have confidence
in you, in the Lord, that you will have no other
mind; but he who troubles you shall bear his
judgment, whoever he is.
11 And I, brethren, if I still preach circum-
cision, [a]why do I still suffer persecution? Then

**4:23** [a] Rom. 9:7, 8 [b] Heb. 11:11 **4:24** [a] Deut. 33:2 [1] NU-Text and M-Text omit *the.* **4:26** [a] [Is. 2:2] **4:27** [a] Is. 54:1 [1] Isaiah 54:1 **4:28** [a] Gal. 3:29 [b] Acts 3:25 **4:29** [a] Gen. 21:9 [b] Gal. 5:11 **4:30** [a] [Gal. 3:8, 22] [b] Gen. 21:10, 12 [c] [John 8:35] [1] Genesis 21:10 **5:1** [a] Phil. 4:1 [b] Acts 15:10 [1] NU-Text reads *For freedom Christ has made us free; stand fast therefore.* **5:2** [a] Acts 15:1 **5:3** [a] [Rom. 2:25] **5:4** [a] [Rom. 9:31] [b] Heb. 12:15 **5:5** [a] Rom. 8:24 **5:6** [a] [Gal. 6:15] [b] 1 Thess. 1:3 **5:7** [a] 1 Cor. 9:24 **5:9** [a] 1 Cor. 5:6 **5:11** [a] 1 Cor. 15:30

[b]the offense of the cross has ceased. 12 [a]I could
wish that those [b]who trouble you would even
cut themselves off!
13 For you, brethren, have been called to lib-
erty; only [a]do not *use* liberty as an [b]opportunity
for the flesh, but [c]through love serve one another.
14 For [a]all the law is fulfilled in one word, *even* in
this: [b]"You shall love your neighbor as yourself."[1]
15 But if you bite and devour one another, beware
lest you be consumed by one another!

### *WALKING IN THE SPIRIT*

16 I say then: [a]Walk in the Spirit, and you shall
not fulfill the lust of the flesh. 17 For [a]the flesh
lusts against the Spirit, and the Spirit against
the flesh; and these are contrary to one another,
[b]so that you do not do the things that you wish.
18 But [a]if you are led by the Spirit, you are not
under the law.
19 Now [a]the works of the flesh are evident,
which are: adultery,[1] fornication, uncleanness,
lewdness, 20 idolatry, sorcery, hatred, conten-
tions, jealousies, outbursts of wrath, selfish am-
bitions, dissensions, heresies, 21 envy, murders,[1]
drunkenness, revelries, and the like; of which
I tell you beforehand, just as I also told *you* in
time past, that [a]those who practice such things
will not inherit the kingdom of God.
22 But [a]the fruit of the Spirit is [b]love, joy,
peace, longsuffering, kindness, [c]goodness,
[d]faithfulness, 23 gentleness, self-control. [a]Against
such there is no law. 24 And those *who are* Christ's
[a]have crucified the flesh with its passions and
desires. 25 [a]If we live in the Spirit, let us also walk
in the Spirit. 26 [a]Let us not become conceited,
provoking one another, envying one another.

### *BEAR AND SHARE BURDENS*

6 Brethren, if a man is overtaken in any tres-
pass, you who *are* spiritual restore such a one
in a spirit of [a]gentleness, considering yourself
lest you also be tempted. 2 [a]Bear one another's
burdens, and so fulfill [b]the law of Christ. 3 For [a]if
anyone thinks himself to be something, when
[b]he is nothing, he deceives himself. 4 But [a]let
each one examine his own work, and then he
will have rejoicing in himself alone, and [b]not in
another. 5 For [a]each one shall bear his own load.

### *BE GENEROUS AND DO GOOD*

6 [a]Let him who is taught the word share in
all good things with him who teaches.
7 Do not be deceived, God is not mocked; for
[a]whatever a man sows, that he will also reap.
8 For he who sows to his flesh will of the flesh
reap corruption, but he who sows to the Spirit
will of the Spirit reap [a]everlasting life. 9 And [a]let
us not grow weary while doing good, for in due
season we shall reap [b]if we do not lose heart.
10 [a]Therefore, as we have opportunity, [b]let us do
good to all, [c]especially to those who are of the
household of faith.

**5:11** [b][1 Cor. 1:23] **5:12** [a]Josh. 7:25 [b]Acts 15:1, 2 **5:13** [a]1 Cor. 8:9 [b]1 Pet. 2:16 [c]1 Cor. 9:19 **5:14** [a]Matt. 7:12; 22:40 [b]Lev. 19:18 [1]Leviticus 19:18 **5:16** [a]Rom. 6:12 **5:17** [a]Rom. 7:18, 22, 23; 8:5 [b]Rom. 7:15 **5:18** [a][Rom. 6:14; 7:4; 8:14] **5:19** [a]Eph. 5:3, 11 [1]NU-Text omits *adultery*. **5:21** [a]1 Cor. 6:9, 10 [1]NU-Text omits *murders*. **5:22** [a][John 15:2] [b][Col. 3:12–15] [c]Rom. 15:14 [d]1 Cor. 13:7 **5:23** [a]1 Tim. 1:9 **5:24** [a]Rom. 6:6 **5:25** [a][Rom. 8:4, 5] **5:26** [a]Phil. 2:3 **6:1** [a]Eph. 4:2 **6:2** [a]Rom. 15:1 [b][James 2:8] **6:3** [a]Rom. 12:3 [b][2 Cor. 3:5] **6:4** [a]1 Cor. 11:28 [b]Luke 18:11 **6:5** [a][Rom. 2:6] **6:6** [a]1 Cor. 9:11, 14 **6:7** [a][Rom. 2:6] **6:8** [a][Rom. 6:8] **6:9** [a]1 Cor. 15:58 [b][James 5:7, 8] **6:10** [a]Prov. 3:27 [b]Titus 3:8 [c]Rom. 12:13

KNOW THE TRUTH

## THE DOCTRINE OF THE HOLY SPIRIT

### PART 7: THE FRUIT OF THE HOLY SPIRIT

**5:22–25** Galatians 5:22–23 lists what we should want to be. At the end of your life, what more would you want to be known for than being "loving," "joyful," "kind," and "gentle"? We've been designed by God to desire and express these Christlike attributes. The point Paul makes in Galatians is that these characteristics of Christ aren't the fruit of hard work in our strength. Rather, they're the fruit of being led by the Holy Spirit. When we "walk in" (or, are constantly led by) the Spirit, He will produce Christ's character in and through us. When we walk in the "flesh" (doing things our own way in our own strength), the results are disastrous (see Gal. 5:16–21). We know we must love better. But where do we find such love? The love we need for God and others is available only through the Holy Spirit. We long for joy, but the world doesn't have it. Joy isn't us putting on a smile and trying to be more joyful. Joy is a glad, deep satisfaction only God gives. Day by day, the Spirit makes us more gentle, self-controlled, and patient as we're guided by Him to think, do, and say what His Word teaches.

*For* **THE DOCTRINE OF CREATION AND HUMANS: PART 1: OVERVIEW OF THE DOCTRINE OF CREATION AND HUMANS,** *turn to Colossians 1:16–17 on page 1215.*

### *GLORY ONLY IN THE CROSS*

11 See with what large letters I have written to you with my own hand! 12 As many as desire to make a good showing in the flesh, these *would* compel you to be circumcised, [a]only that they may not suffer persecution for the cross of Christ. 13 For not even those who are circumcised keep the law, but they desire to have you circumcised that they may boast in your flesh. 14 But God forbid that I should boast except in the [a]cross of our Lord Jesus Christ, by whom[1] the world has been crucified to me, and [b]I to the world. 15 For [a]in Christ Jesus neither circumcision nor uncircumcision avails anything, but a new creation.

### *BLESSING AND A PLEA*

16 And as many as walk according to this rule, peace and mercy *be* upon them, and upon the Israel of God.

**6:11** Many people in New Testament times used secretaries to write letters for them. Paul perhaps used a secretary because he had poor eyesight. Apparently, Paul had dictated this letter to a secretary, but then wrote the last paragraph in his own handwriting, so the churches in Galatia would know it really came from him.

17 From now on let no one trouble me, for I bear in my body the marks of the Lord Jesus.

18 Brethren, the grace of our Lord Jesus Christ *be* with your spirit. Amen.

**6:12** [a] Gal. 5:11 **6:14** [a] [1 Cor. 1:18] [b] [Gal. 2:20]; Col. 2:20 [1] Or *by which* (the cross) **6:15** [a] [Rom. 2:26, 28]; 1 Cor. 7:19; [Gal. 5:6]

# *The Epistle of Paul the Apostle to the* EPHESIANS

**AUTHOR**
Paul

**KEY VERSES**
Ephesians 4:1–3

**READING TIME**
24 minutes

Paul addressed Ephesians to a group of believers rich beyond measure in Jesus Christ yet living as beggars, ignorant of their true wealth. What God had declared to be true of them in Christ had not carried over to how they lived each day. In chapters 1–3, Paul began by describing the contents of the Christian's heavenly "bank account": adoption, acceptance, redemption, forgiveness, wisdom, inheritance, the seal of the Holy Spirit, life, grace, and citizenship—in short, every spiritual blessing. Then in chapters 4–6, he described a spiritual walk rooted in spiritual wealth. "For we are His workmanship, created in Christ Jesus [Eph. 1–3] for good works . . . that we should walk in them [chs. 4–6]" (Eph. 2:10). Paul's message was that the believers' goal is to live in a way that reflects the reality of their new identity in Christ.

**Occasion:** Paul wrote Ephesians during his first Roman imprisonment, perhaps around the same time as Philippians, Colossians, and Philemon.

**Main Point:** Believers are to live according to their heavenly calling in Christ.

**Big Ideas:** When we trust in Christ, we are given a new identity rooted in Him. Our new identity should guide us to a new way of thinking and living.

**OUTLINE:**

I. The Position of the Christian (chs. 1–3)
II. The Practice of the Christian (chs. 4–6)

**c. AD 34**
Paul is converted

**c. AD 47–49**
Paul's first missionary journey

**c. AD 50**
The Jerusalem Council

**c. AD 50–53**
Paul's second missionary journey

**AD 53**
The church at Ephesus is founded

**c. AD 53–57**
Paul's third missionary journey

**AD 54–68**
Nero is Roman emperor

**c. AD 54–56**
Paul's extended stay in Ephesus

**c. AD 58**
Paul is arrested in Jerusalem

**c. AD 60–62**
Paul is imprisoned in Rome

**c. AD 60–62**
**Ephesians written**

**AD 64**
Great Fire of Rome; first Roman mass persecution of Christians

**c. AD 67**
Peter and Paul are executed

### GREETING

1 Paul, an apostle of Jesus Christ by the will
of God,

To the saints who are in Ephesus, and faith-
ful in Christ Jesus:

2 Grace to you and peace from God our Fa-
ther and the Lord Jesus Christ.

### REDEMPTION IN CHRIST

3 [a]Blessed *be* the God and Father of our Lord
Jesus Christ, who has blessed us with every spir-
itual blessing in the heavenly *places* in Christ,
4 just as [a]He chose us in Him [b]before the foun-
dation of the world, that we should [c]be holy and
without blame before Him in love, 5 [a]having pre-
destined us to [b]adoption as sons by Jesus Christ
to Himself, [c]according to the good pleasure of
His will, 6 to the praise of the glory of His grace,
[a]by which He made us accepted in [b]the Beloved.
7 [a]In Him we have redemption through
His blood, the forgiveness of sins, according
to [b]the riches of His grace 8 which He made to
abound toward us in all wisdom and prudence,
9 [a]having made known to us the mystery of His
will, according to His good pleasure [b]which He
purposed in Himself, 10 that in the dispensation
of [a]the fullness of the times [b]He might gather
together in one [c]all things in Christ, both[1] which
are in heaven and which are on earth—in Him.
11 [a]In Him also we have obtained an inheritance,
being predestined according to [b]the purpose
of Him who works all things according to the
counsel of His will, 12 [a]that we [b]who first trusted
in Christ should be to the praise of His glory.
13 In Him you also *trusted,* after you heard
[a]the word of truth, the gospel of your salva-
tion; in whom also, having believed, [b]you were
sealed with the Holy Spirit of promise, 14 [a]who[1]
is the guarantee of our inheritance [b]until the
redemption of [c]the purchased possession, [d]to
the praise of His glory.

### PRAYER FOR SPIRITUAL WISDOM

15 Therefore I also, [a]after I heard of your faith
in the Lord Jesus and your love for all the saints,
16 [a]do not cease to give thanks for you, making
mention of you in my prayers: 17 that [a]the God of
our Lord Jesus Christ, the Father of glory, [b]may
give to you the spirit of wisdom and revelation
in the knowledge of Him, 18 [a]the eyes of your
understanding[1] being enlightened; that you may
know what is [b]the hope of His calling, what are
the riches of the glory of His inheritance in the
saints, 19 and what *is* the exceeding greatness of
His power toward us who believe, [a]according to
the working of His mighty power 20 which He
worked in Christ when [a]He raised Him from the
dead and [b]seated *Him* at His right hand in the
heavenly *places,* 21 [a]far above all [b]principality
and power and might and dominion, and every
name that is named, not only in this age but also
in that which is to come.
22 And [a]He put all *things* under His feet,
and gave Him [b]*to be* head over all *things* to the
church, 23 [a]which is His body, [b]the fullness of
Him [c]who fills all in all.

> **SEEING JESUS IN THE SCRIPTURE**
>
> **1:22** As its head, Jesus has all authority over the church, just as He said (see Matt. 28:18).

### BY GRACE THROUGH FAITH

2 And [a]you *He made alive,* [b]who were dead
in trespasses and sins, 2 [a]in which you once
walked according to the course of this world,
according to [b]the prince of the power of the air,
the spirit who now works in [c]the sons of disobedi-
ence, 3 [a]among whom also we all once conducted
ourselves in [b]the lusts of our flesh, fulfilling the
desires of the flesh and of the mind, and [c]were
by nature children of wrath, just as the others.
4 But God, [a]who is rich in mercy, because of His
[b]great love with which He loved us, 5 [a]even when
we were dead in trespasses, [b]made us alive togeth-
er with Christ (by grace you have been saved), 6 and
raised *us* up together, and made *us* sit together
[a]in the heavenly *places* in Christ Jesus, 7 that in
the ages to come He might show the exceeding
riches of His grace in [a]*His* kindness toward us in
Christ Jesus. 8 [a]For by grace you have been saved
[b]through faith, and that not of yourselves; [c]*it is*
the gift of God, 9 not of [a]works, lest anyone should
[b]boast. 10 For we are [a]His workmanship, created in
Christ Jesus for good works, which God prepared
beforehand that we should walk in them.

### BROUGHT NEAR BY HIS BLOOD

11 Therefore remember that you, once Gen-
tiles in the flesh—who are called Uncircumci-
sion by what is called [a]the Circumcision made in
the flesh by hands— 12 that at that time you were
without Christ, being aliens from the common-
wealth of Israel and strangers from the cov-
enants of promise, having no hope and without

**1:3** [a] 2 Cor. 1:3 **1:4** [a] Rom. 8:28 [b] 1 Pet. 1:2 [c] Luke 1:75 **1:5** [a] [Rom. 8:29] [b] John 1:12 [c] [1 Cor. 1:21] **1:6** [a] [Rom. 3:24] [b] Matt. 3:17 **1:7** [a] [Heb. 9:12] [b] [Rom. 3:24, 25] **1:9** [a] [Rom. 16:25] [b] [2 Tim. 1:9] **1:10** [a] Gal. 4:4 [b] 1 Cor. 3:22 [c] [Col. 1:16, 20] [1] NU-Text and M-Text omit *both.* **1:11** [a] Rom. 8:17 [b] Is. 46:10 **1:12** [a] 2 Thess. 2:13 [b] James 1:18 **1:13** [a] John 1:17 [b] [2 Cor. 1:22] **1:14** [a] 2 Cor. 5:5 [b] Rom. 8:23 [c] [Acts 20:28] [d] 1 Pet. 2:9 [1] NU-Text reads *which.* **1:15** [a] Col. 1:4 **1:16** [a] Rom. 1:9 **1:17** [a] John 20:17 [b] Col. 1:9 **1:18** [a] Acts 26:18 [b] Eph. 2:12 [1] NU-Text and M-Text read *hearts.* **1:19** [a] Col. 2:12 **1:20** [a] Acts 2:24 [b] Ps. 110:1 **1:21** [a] Phil. 2:9, 10 [b] [Rom. 8:38, 39] **1:22** [a] Ps. 8:6; 110:1 [b] Heb. 2:7 **1:23** [a] Rom. 12:5 [b] Col. 2:9 [c] [1 Cor. 12:6] **2:1** [a] Col. 2:13 [b] Eph. 4:18 **2:2** [a] Col. 1:21 [b] Eph. 6:12 [c] Col. 3:6 **2:3** [a] 1 Pet. 4:3 [b] Gal. 5:16 [c] [Ps. 51:5] **2:4** [a] Rom. 10:12 [b] John 3:16 **2:5** [a] Rom. 5:6, 8 [b] [Rom. 6:4, 5] **2:6** [a] Eph. 1:20 **2:7** [a] Titus 3:4 **2:8** [a] [2 Tim. 1:9] [b] Rom. 4:16 [c] [John 1:12, 13] **2:9** [a] Rom. 4:4, 5; 11:6 [b] Rom. 3:27 **2:10** [a] Is. 19:25 **2:11** [a] [Col. 2:11]

## APPLY THE TRUTH

### PURPOSE

**2:10** Your life is no accident. You were created on purpose for a purpose. In fact, the chances of you being alive are about 1 in $10^{2685000}$. That's a 1 with over two million zeroes after it. The probability of your life is like rolling that many dice and having every one of them land on the same number. Seems improbable, right? Yet here you are. Sure, you have struggles, doubts, and even pain. But those difficulties are reserved only for the living. As impressive as the odds are, your life is far more than an improbable outcome; it's an intentional design. God didn't rely on odds for you to be born, He created *you*, designed *you*, and chose *you* to live, breathe, and bring Him glory. As such, your life has infinite meaning and purpose, far beyond the measure of a 1 with over two million zeroes after it.

When you choose to follow Jesus, you're choosing to be this amazing person God made you to be in full. That decision sets you on the direction of all the good God has prepared for you. It doesn't mean life will be perfect. But it does mean even those imperfections have purpose. What would your life look like if you chose to embrace the miracle that is your life and walk in the plans God has for you?

God in the world. 13 But now in Christ Jesus you who once were far off have been brought near by the blood of Christ.

### CHRIST OUR PEACE

14 For He Himself is our peace, who has made both one, and has broken down the middle wall of separation, 15 having abolished in His flesh the enmity, *that is,* the law of commandments *contained* in ordinances, so as to create in Himself one [a]new man *from* the two, *thus* making peace, 16 and that He might [a]reconcile them both to God in one body through the cross, thereby [b]putting to death the enmity. 17 And He came and preached peace to you who were afar off and to those who were near. 18 For [a]through Him we both have access [b]by one Spirit to the Father.

**2:14** The temple area in Jerusalem was divided into a series of courts. The outermost court, which was called the Court of the Gentiles, was the only area of the temple that non-Jews were allowed to enter.

### CHRIST OUR CORNERSTONE

19 Now, therefore, you are no longer strangers and foreigners, but fellow citizens with the saints and members of the household of God, 20 having been [a]built [b]on the foundation of the [c]apostles and prophets, Jesus Christ Himself being [d]the chief corner*stone,* 21 in whom the whole building, being fitted together, grows into [a]a holy temple in the Lord, 22 [a]in whom you also are being built together for a [b]dwelling place of God in the Spirit.

### SEEING JESUS IN THE SCRIPTURE

**2:20** Jesus is the chief cornerstone, giving direction and stability to His church just as the Scriptures said (see Ps. 118:22).

### THE MYSTERY REVEALED

**3** For this reason I, Paul, the prisoner of Christ Jesus for you Gentiles— 2 if indeed you have heard of the dispensation of the grace of God [a]which was given to me for you, 3 [a]how that by revelation [b]He made known to me the mystery (as I have briefly written already, 4 by which, when you read, you may understand my knowledge in the mystery of Christ), 5 which in other ages was not made known to the sons of men, as it has now been revealed by the Spirit to His holy apostles and prophets: 6 that the Gentiles [a]should be fellow heirs, of the same body, and partakers of His promise in Christ through the gospel, 7 [a]of which I became a minister [b]according to the gift of the grace of God given to me by [c]the effective working of His power.

### PURPOSE OF THE MYSTERY

8 To me, [a]who am less than the least of all the saints, this grace was given, that I should preach among the Gentiles [b]the unsearchable riches of Christ, 9 and to make all see what *is* the fellowship[1] of the mystery, which from the beginning of the ages has been hidden in God who [a]created all things through Jesus Christ;[2] 10 [a]to the intent that now [b]the manifold wisdom of God might be made known by the church [c]to the principalities and powers in the heavenly *places,* 11 [a]according to

**2:15** [a] Gal. 6:15 **2:16** [a] [Col. 1:20–22] [b] [Rom. 6:6] **2:18** [a] John 10:9 [b] 1 Cor. 12:13 **2:20** [a] 1 Pet. 2:4 [b] Matt. 16:18 [c] 1 Cor. 12:28 [d] Ps. 118:22 **2:21** [a] 1 Cor. 3:16, 17 **2:22** [a] 1 Pet. 2:5 [b] John 17:23 **3:2** [a] Acts 9:15 **3:3** [a] Acts 22:17, 21; 26:16 [b] [Rom. 11:25; 16:25] **3:6** [a] Gal. 3:28, 29 **3:7** [a] Rom. 15:16 [b] Rom. 1:5 [c] Rom. 15:18 **3:8** [a] [1 Cor. 15:9] [b] [Col. 1:27; 2:2, 3] **3:9** [a] Heb. 1:2 [1] NU-Text and M-Text read *stewardship* (dispensation). [2] NU-Text omits *through Jesus Christ.* **3:10** [a] 1 Pet. 1:12 [b] [1 Tim. 3:16] [c] Col. 1:16; 2:10, 15 **3:11** [a] [Eph. 1:4, 11]

the eternal purpose which He accomplished in Christ Jesus our Lord, 12 in whom we have boldness and access [a]with confidence through faith in Him. 13 [a]Therefore I ask that you do not lose heart at my tribulations for you, [b]which is your glory.

### *APPRECIATION OF THE MYSTERY*

14 For this reason I bow my knees to the [a]Father of our Lord Jesus Christ,[1] 15 from whom the whole family in heaven and earth is named, 16 that He would grant you, [a]according to the riches of His glory, [b]to be strengthened with might through His Spirit in [c]the inner man, 17 [a]that Christ may dwell in your hearts through faith; that you, [b]being rooted and grounded in love, 18 [a]may be able to comprehend with all the saints [b]what *is* the width and length and depth and height— 19 to know the love of Christ which passes knowledge; that you may be filled [a]with all the fullness of God.

20 Now [a]to Him who is able to do exceedingly abundantly [b]above all that we ask or think, [c]according to the power that works in us, 21 [a]to Him *be* glory in the church by Christ Jesus to all generations, forever and ever. Amen.

### *WALK IN UNITY*

**4** I, therefore, the prisoner of the Lord, beseech you to [a]walk worthy of the calling with which you were called, 2 with all lowliness and gentleness, with longsuffering, bearing with one another in love, 3 endeavoring to keep the unity of the Spirit [a]in the bond of peace. 4 [a]*There is* one body and one Spirit, just as you were called in one hope of your calling; 5 [a]one Lord, [b]one faith, [c]one baptism; 6 [a]one God and Father of all, who *is* above all, and [b]through all, and in you[1] all.

### *SPIRITUAL GIFTS*

7 But [a]to each one of us grace was given according to the measure of Christ's gift. 8 Therefore He says:

[a]"When He ascended on high,
He led captivity captive,
And gave gifts to men."[1]

9 [a](Now this, "He ascended"—what does it mean but that He also first[1] descended into the lower parts of the earth? 10 He who descended is also the One [a]who ascended far above all the heavens, [b]that He might fill all things.)

11 And He Himself gave some *to be* apostles, some prophets, some evangelists, and some pastors and teachers, 12 for the equipping of the saints for the work of ministry, [a]for the edifying of [b]the body of Christ, 13 till we all come to the unity of the faith [a]and of the knowledge of the Son of God, to [b]a perfect man, to the measure of the stature of the fullness of Christ; 14 that we should no longer be [a]children, tossed to and fro and carried about with every wind of doctrine, by the trickery of men, in the cunning craftiness of [b]deceitful plotting, 15 but, speaking the truth in love, may grow up in all things into Him who is the [a]head—Christ— 16 [a]from whom the whole body, joined and knit together by what every joint supplies, according to the effective working by which every part does its share, causes growth of the body for the edifying of itself in love.

### *THE NEW MAN*

17 This I say, therefore, and testify in the Lord, that you should [a]no longer walk as the rest of[1] the Gentiles walk, in the futility of their mind, 18 having their understanding darkened, being alienated from the life of God, because of the ignorance that is in them, because of the [a]blindness of their heart; 19 [a]who, being past feeling, [b]have given themselves over to lewdness, to work all uncleanness with greediness.

20 But you have not so learned Christ, 21 if indeed you have heard Him and have been taught by Him, as the truth is in Jesus: 22 that you [a]put off, concerning your former conduct, the old man which grows corrupt according to the deceitful lusts, 23 and [a]be renewed in the spirit of your mind, 24 and that you [a]put on the new man which was created according to God, in true righteousness and holiness.

### *DO NOT GRIEVE THE SPIRIT*

25 Therefore, putting away lying, [a]"*Let* each one *of you* speak truth with his neighbor,"[1] for [b]we are members of one another. 26 [a]"Be angry, and do not sin":[1] do not let the sun go down on your wrath, 27 [a]nor give place to the devil. 28 Let him who stole steal no longer, but rather [a]let him labor, working with *his* hands what is good, that he may have something [b]to give him who has need. 29 [a]Let no corrupt word proceed out of your mouth, but [b]what is good for necessary edification, [c]that it may impart grace to the hearers. 30 And [a]do not grieve the Holy Spirit of God, by whom you were sealed for the day of redemption. 31 [a]Let all bitterness, wrath, anger, clamor, and [b]evil speaking be put away from you,

3:12 [a] Heb. 4:16; 10:19, 35 3:13 [a] Phil. 1:14 [b] 2 Cor. 1:6 3:14 [a] Eph. 1:3 [1] NU-Text omits *of our Lord Jesus Christ.* 3:16 [a] [Phil. 4:19] [b] Col. 1:11 [c] Rom. 7:22 3:17 [a] John 14:23 [b] Col. 1:23 3:18 [a] Eph. 1:18 [b] Rom. 8:39 3:19 [a] Eph. 1:23 3:20 [a] Rom. 16:25 [b] 1 Cor. 2:9 [c] Col. 1:29 3:21 [a] Rom. 11:36 4:1 [a] 1 Thess. 2:12 4:3 [a] Col. 3:14 4:4 [a] Rom. 12:5 4:5 [a] 1 Cor. 1:13 [b] Jude 3 [c] [Heb. 6:6] 4:6 [a] Mal. 2:10 [b] Rom. 11:36 [1] NU-Text omits *you;* M-Text reads *us.* 4:7 [a] [1 Cor. 12:7, 11] 4:8 [a] Ps. 68:18 [1] Psalm 68:18 4:9 [a] John 3:13; 20:17 [1] NU-Text omits *first.* 4:10 [a] Acts 1:9 [b] [Eph. 1:23] 4:12 [a] 1 Cor. 14:26 [b] Col. 1:24 4:13 [a] Col. 2:2 [b] 1 Cor. 14:20 4:14 [a] 1 Cor. 14:20 [b] Rom. 16:18 4:15 [a] Eph. 1:22 4:16 [a] Col. 2:19 4:17 [a] Eph. 2:2; 4:22 [1] NU-Text omits *the rest of.* 4:18 [a] Rom. 1:21 4:19 [a] 1 Tim. 4:2 [b] 1 Pet. 4:3 4:22 [a] Col. 3:8 4:23 [a] [Rom. 12:2] 4:24 [a] [Rom. 6:4; 7:6; 12:2] 4:25 [a] Zech. 8:16 [b] Rom. 12:5 [1] Zechariah 8:16 4:26 [a] Ps. 4:4; 37:8 [1] Psalm 4:4 4:27 [a] [Rom. 12:19] 4:28 [a] Acts 20:35 [b] Luke 3:11 4:29 [a] Col. 3:8 [b] 1 Thess. 5:11 [c] Col. 3:16 4:30 [a] Is. 7:13 4:31 [a] Col. 3:8, 19 [b] James 4:11

KNOW THE TRUTH

## THE DOCTRINE OF THE CHURCH

### PART 8: THE LEADERSHIP OF THE CHURCH

**4:11–16** The church has one head, one Chief Shepherd, one Lord: Jesus Christ (see Eph. 4:1–6; 1 Peter 5:1–4). Therefore, all leadership in the church must be a delegation of authority from Jesus and an extension of the servant-hearted, humble, truth-seeking, righteous, patient, pure, protective, gentle, and nurturing leadership He modeled. To see what Paul calls the "growth of the body" come about, Jesus calls and enables certain individuals to lead under His authority.

Throughout the New Testament church, there were numerous leaders who carried out various functions of leadership. In many local churches today, the most recognized leadership role is the elder, overseer, or bishop. These various titles appear interconnected in the New Testament, describing one office. Perhaps the most common term used today for this office is pastor. Pastors are responsible for equipping people for service, overseeing the worship activities of church gatherings, teaching God's Word, bringing rebuke and correction to those in the church opposing sound doctrine and practice, praying for the physically ill, being hospitable with one's home, and more.

*For* **THE DOCTRINE OF THE CHURCH: PART 9: THE NECESSITY OF THE CHURCH**, *turn to 1 Corinthians 12:4–27 on page 1177.* •••

[c]with all malice. 32 And [a]be kind to one another,
tenderhearted, [b]forgiving one another, even as
God in Christ forgave you.

### *WALK IN LOVE*

**5** Therefore[a] be imitators of God as dear [b]chil-
dren. 2 And [a]walk in love, [b]as Christ also has
loved us and given Himself for us, an offering
and a sacrifice to God [c]for a sweet-smelling
aroma.
3 But fornication and all [a]uncleanness or
[b]covetousness, let it not even be named among
you, as is fitting for saints; 4 [a]neither filthiness,
nor [b]foolish talking, nor coarse jesting, [c]which
are not fitting, but rather [d]giving of thanks.
5 For this you know,[1] that no fornicator, unclean
person, nor covetous man, who is an idolater,
has any [a]inheritance in the kingdom of Christ
and God. 6 Let no one deceive you with empty
words, for because of these things the wrath
of God comes upon the sons of disobedience.
7 Therefore do not be [a]partakers with them.

### *WALK IN LIGHT*

8 For you were once darkness, but now *you
are* [a]light in the Lord. Walk as children of light
9 (for [a]the fruit of the Spirit[1] *is* in all goodness,
righteousness, and truth), 10 [a]finding out what
is acceptable to the Lord. 11 And have [a]no fellow-
ship with the unfruitful works of darkness, but
rather expose *them.* 12 [a]For it is shameful even to
speak of those things which are done by them
in secret. 13 But [a]all things that are exposed are
made manifest by the light, for whatever makes
manifest is light. 14 Therefore He says:

[a]"Awake, you who sleep,
Arise from the dead,
And Christ will give you light."

**SEEING JESUS IN THE SCRIPTURE**

**5:14** Jesus is the light that gives life and direction to those who believe, just as the Scriptures promised (see Is. 60:1).

### *WALK IN WISDOM*

15 [a]See then that you walk circumspectly,
not as fools but as wise, 16 [a]redeeming the time,
[b]because the days are evil.
17 [a]Therefore do not be unwise, but [b]under-
stand [c]what the will of the Lord *is.* 18 And [a]do
not be drunk with wine, in which is dissipation;
but be filled with the Spirit, 19 speaking to one
another [a]in psalms and hymns and spiritual
songs, singing and making [b]melody in your
heart to the Lord, 20 [a]giving thanks always for
all things to God the Father [b]in the name of our

**4:31** [c] Titus 3:3 **4:32** [a] 2 Cor. 6:10 [b] [Mark 11:25] **5:1** [a] Luke 6:36 [b] 1 Pet. 1:14–16 **5:2** [a] 1 Thess. 4:9 [b] Gal. 1:4 [c] 2 Cor. 2:14, 15 **5:3** [a] Col. 3:5–7 [b] [Luke 12:15] **5:4** [a] Matt. 12:34, 35 [b] Titus 3:9 [c] Rom. 1:28 [d] Phil. 4:6 **5:5** [a] 1 Cor. 6:9, 10 [1] NU-Text reads *For know this.* **5:7** [a] 1 Tim. 5:22 **5:8** [a] 1 Thess. 5:5 **5:9** [a] Gal. 5:22 [1] NU-Text reads *light.* **5:10** [a] [Rom. 12:1, 2] **5:11** [a] 2 Cor. 6:14 **5:12** [a] Rom. 1:24 **5:13** [a] [John 3:20, 21] **5:14** [a] [Is. 26:19; 60:1] **5:15** [a] Col. 4:5 **5:16** [a] Col. 4:5 [b] Eccl. 11:2 **5:17** [a] Col. 4:5 [b] [Rom. 12:2] [c] 1 Thess. 4:3 **5:18** [a] Prov. 20:1; 23:31 **5:19** [a] Acts 16:25 [b] James 5:13 **5:20** [a] Ps. 34:1 [b] [1 Pet. 2:5]

**5:18** Just as a person who is **drunk** is under the control of alcohol, so a Spirit-filled believer is controlled by the **Spirit**. Filling is a step beyond the sealing of the Holy Spirit (see Eph. 1:13). Sealing is a one-time action God takes at our new birth. The tense of the Greek word translated **filled** indicates filling is a moment-by-moment repeatable action. To be **filled with the Spirit** is to be controlled by the Spirit and is, therefore, crucial to living the Christian life. The Spirit-filled person will exhibit the Christlike character described in Galatians 5:22–23 as the fruit of the Spirit. Any Christian may be transformed by the filling of the Spirit and possess these qualities.

Lord Jesus Christ, 21 [a]submitting to one another
in the fear of God.[1]

### *MARRIAGE—CHRIST AND THE CHURCH*

*(cf. Col. 3:18, 19)*

22 Wives, [a]submit to your own husbands, as
to the Lord. 23 For [a]the husband is head of the
wife, as also [b]Christ is head of the church; and
He is the Savior of the body. 24 Therefore, just as
the church is subject to Christ, so *let* the wives
*be* to their own husbands [a]in everything.
25 [a]Husbands, love your wives, just as Christ
also loved the church and [b]gave Himself for her,
26 that He might sanctify and cleanse her [a]with
the washing of water [b]by the word, 27 [a]that He
might present her to Himself a glorious church,
[b]not having spot or wrinkle or any such thing,
but that she should be holy and without blemish.
28 So husbands ought to love their own wives as
their own bodies; he who loves his wife loves
himself. 29 For no one ever hated his own flesh,
but nourishes and cherishes it, just as the Lord
*does* the church. 30 For [a]we are members of His
body,[1] of His flesh and of His bones. 31 [a]"For this
reason a man shall leave his father and mother
and be joined to his wife, and the [b]two shall
become one flesh."[1] 32 This is a great mystery,
but I speak concerning Christ and the church.
33 Nevertheless [a]let each one of you in particular
so love his own wife as himself, and let the wife
*see* that she [b]respects *her* husband.

### *CHILDREN AND PARENTS*

*(Ex. 20:12; Deut. 5:16)*

6 Children, [a]obey your parents in the Lord,
for this is right. 2 [a]"Honor your father and
mother," which is the first commandment with
promise: 3 "that it may be well with you and you
may live long on the earth."[1]
4 And [a]you, fathers, do not provoke your
children to wrath, but [b]bring them up in the
training and admonition of the Lord.

### *BONDSERVANTS AND MASTERS*

5 [a]Bondservants, be obedient to those who
are your masters according to the flesh, [b]with
fear and trembling, [c]in sincerity of heart, as to
Christ; 6 [a]not with eyeservice, as men-pleasers,
but as bondservants of Christ, doing the will of
God from the heart, 7 with goodwill doing ser-
vice, as to the Lord, and not to men, 8 [a]knowing
that whatever good anyone does, he will receive
the same from the Lord, whether *he is* a slave
or free.

**5:21** [a] [Phil. 2:3] [1] NU-Text reads *Christ.* **5:22** [a] Col. 3:18—4:1 **5:23** [a] [1 Cor. 11:3] [b] Col. 1:18 **5:24** [a] Titus 2:4, 5 **5:25** [a] Col. 3:19 [b] Acts 20:28 **5:26** [a] John 3:5 [b] [John 15:3; 17:17] **5:27** [a] Col. 1:22 [b] Song 4:7 **5:30** [a] Gen. 2:23 [1] NU-Text omits the rest of this verse. **5:31** [a] Gen. 2:24 [b] [1 Cor. 6:16] [1] Genesis 2:24 **5:33** [a] Col. 3:19 [b] 1 Pet. 3:1, 6 **6:1** [a] Col. 3:20 **6:2** [a] Deut. 5:16 **6:3** [1] Deuteronomy 5:16 **6:4** [a] Col. 3:21 [b] Gen. 18:19 **6:5** [a] [1 Tim. 6:1] [b] 2 Cor. 7:15 [c] 1 Chr. 29:17 **6:6** [a] Col. 3:22 **6:8** [a] Rom. 2:6

APPLY THE TRUTH

## MARRIAGE AND DIVORCE

**5:21–33** Marriage is difficult. Two broken people uniting doesn't make one whole person. It usually creates twice as much mess. This is why so many marriages end in divorce. Making a marriage work is difficult, but not impossible. God cares about marriage and wants us to be in wonderful, lasting, fruitful marriages, which is why He's given us ample directions in the Bible, like Song of Solomon and here. Partnership is at the heart of marriage, which is why this section begins with mutual submission. Husbands and wives are to respect and honor each other. The husband is to love his wife; the wife is to honor her husband. Difficulties and disagreements are inevitable in marriage, but when husbands and wives recognize they're on the same team, they stop fighting *with* each other and start fighting *for* each other.

God's plan for a man and woman marrying for a lifetime is possible. When we trust and obey God, we can experience lasting, happy marriages. The pattern we should aim for isn't what we see around us, but rather what is laid out for us in God's Word. Not all marriages are bad. Not all bad marriages have to end. God can protect and restore relationships when we seek His ways and His glory.

APPLY THE TRUTH

## TROUBLING PASSAGES

**6:5** One of the beauties of the Bible is it doesn't sugarcoat or shy away from difficult people or ideas. Even the heroes of the faith had messy storylines. Abraham was an idol worshipper. Sarah a doubter. Moses a murderer. David an adulterer. Solomon a womanizer. The list goes on and on! This reminds us that God is the main character of the Bible, not people. But with all its transparency, some of the Bible's subject matter can raise a few eyebrows, questions, and concerns. Like this one.

At first glance, this passage seems to approve of slavery. Other passages prompt questions of the value of women, role of government, and nature of human sexuality. But as always, context matters. When we dig into its context, we see the intent of this verse. This passage isn't talking about race-based chattel slavery; it addresses a system more like that of bosses and employees. When we understand that, it frames the meaning. There are clear and intelligent answers in the Bible for even the most complicated or confusing passages; we just have to investigate.

9 And you, masters, do the same things to
them, giving up threatening, knowing that your
own [a]Master also[1] is in heaven, and [b]there is no
partiality with Him.

### *THE WHOLE ARMOR OF GOD*

10 Finally, my brethren, be strong in the
Lord and in the power of His might. 11 [a]Put on
the whole armor of God, that you may be able
to stand against the wiles of the devil. 12 For
we do not wrestle against flesh and blood, but
against [a]principalities, against powers, against
[b]the rulers of the darkness of this age,[1] against
spiritual *hosts* of wickedness in the heavenly
*places.* 13 [a]Therefore take up the whole armor of
God, that you may be able to withstand [b]in the
evil day, and having done all, to stand.

**6:11** Roman foot soldiers wore **armor** and carried shields for protection. The armor was made of thick leather or metal. Helmets came in all shapes and sizes. Some covered the entire head with metal and provided a protective screen for the face.

14 Stand therefore, [a]having girded your waist
with truth, [b]having put on the breastplate of
righteousness, 15 [a]and having shod your feet with
the preparation of the gospel of peace; 16 above
all, taking [a]the shield of faith with which you
will be able to quench all the fiery darts of the
wicked one. 17 And [a]take the helmet of salvation,
and [b]the sword of the Spirit, which is the word
of God; 18 [a]praying always with all prayer and
supplication in the Spirit, [b]being watchful to
this end with all perseverance and [c]supplication
for all the saints— 19 and for me, that utterance
may be given to me, [a]that I may open my mouth
boldly to make known the mystery of the gospel,
20 for which [a]I am an ambassador in chains; that
in it I may speak boldly, as I ought to speak.

### *A GRACIOUS GREETING*

21 But that you also may know my affairs *and*
how I am doing, [a]Tychicus, a beloved brother
and [b]faithful minister in the Lord, will make all
things known to you; 22 [a]whom I have sent to you
for this very purpose, that you may know our
affairs, and *that* he may [b]comfort your hearts.
23 Peace to the brethren, and love with faith,
from God the Father and the Lord Jesus Christ.
24 Grace *be* with all those who love our Lord Jesus
Christ in sincerity. Amen.

**6:9** [a] Col. 4:1 [b] Rom. 2:11 [1] NU-Text reads *He who is both their Master and yours.* **6:11** [a] [2 Cor. 6:7] **6:12** [a] Rom. 8:38 [b] Luke 22:53 [1] NU-Text reads *rulers of this darkness.* **6:13** [a] [2 Cor. 10:4] [b] Eph. 5:16 **6:14** [a] Is. 11:5 [b] Is. 59:17 **6:15** [a] Is. 52:7 **6:16** [a] 1 John 5:4 **6:17** [a] 1 Thess. 5:8 [b] [Heb. 4:12] **6:18** [a] Luke 18:1 [b] [Matt. 26:41] [c] Phil. 1:4 **6:19** [a] Col. 4:3 **6:20** [a] 2 Cor. 5:20 **6:21** [a] Acts 20:4 [b] 1 Cor. 4:1, 2 **6:22** [a] Col. 4:8 [b] 2 Cor. 1:6

*The Epistle of Paul the Apostle to the*

# PHILIPPIANS

| AUTHOR | KEY VERSES | READING TIME |
|---|---|---|
| Paul | Philippians 4:4–5 | 17 minutes |

During Paul's second missionary journey, he experienced his "Macedonian call" in Troas, which led him to Philippi. Once there, the apostle helped start a church consisting of Lydia and others. Later, when Paul was in need, this church stepped forward to help, an act for which the apostle was deeply grateful. In response, Paul wrote a thank-you note to the believers at Philippi and used the occasion to provide instruction on Christian unity. His central argument was simple: Only in Christ are unity and joy possible. With Christ as the model of humility and service, believers can enjoy oneness of purpose, attitude, and work—a truth that Paul illustrated from his own life and one the Philippians desperately needed to hear. Within their ranks, workers in the Philippian church were at odds, hindering the work of proclaiming new life in Christ. Because of this, Paul exhorted the church to "stand fast . . . be of the same mind . . . rejoice in the Lord always . . . but in everything by prayer and supplication, with thanksgiving, let your requests be made known . . . and the peace of God, which surpasses all understanding, will guard your hearts and minds through Christ Jesus" (Phil. 4:1–2, 4, 6–7).

**Occasion:** As Paul wrote this letter, he evidently awaited the verdict of the imperial court with his life hanging in the balance (Phil. 2:20–26). Internal evidence suggests that Paul wrote the epistle from Rome (1:3; 4:22) at the same time he wrote Ephesians, Colossians, and Philemon. Some contend that Paul wrote from Caesarea or Ephesus instead.

**Main Point:** The believer is to live joyfully like Christ.

**Big Ideas:** God wants us to live in joy no matter what we face. We should imitate Jesus in everything we do, especially living humbly with others. We are to strive to think only on the things of God, that which is noble, right, pure, lovely, excellent, admirable, and praiseworthy.

## OUTLINE:

I. Encouragement for Living in Christ (ch. 1)
II. Examples of Living in Christ (chs. 2–3)
III. Empowerment for Living in Christ (ch. 4)

**c. AD 34**
Paul is converted

**c. AD 47–49**
Paul's first missionary journey

**c. AD 50**
The Jerusalem Council

**c. AD 50–53**
Paul's second missionary journey

**c. AD 53–57**
Paul's third missionary journey

**AD 54–68**
Nero is Roman emperor

**c. AD 56**
Paul revisits Philippi

**c. AD 58**
Paul is arrested in Jerusalem

**c. AD 60–62**
Paul is imprisoned in Rome

**c. AD 60–62**
**Philippians written**

**AD 64**
Great Fire of Rome; first Roman mass persecution of Christians

**c. AD 67**
Peter and Paul are executed

### GREETING

1 Paul and Timothy, bondservants of Jesus
Christ,

To all the saints in Christ Jesus who are in
Philippi, with the bishops[1] and [a]deacons:

2 Grace to you and peace from God our Fa-
ther and the Lord Jesus Christ.

### THANKFULNESS AND PRAYER

3 [a]I thank my God upon every remembrance
of you, 4 always in [a]every prayer of mine making
request for you all with joy, 5 [a]for your fellowship
in the gospel from the first day until now, 6 being
confident of this very thing, that He who has begun
[a]a good work in you will complete *it* until the day of
Jesus Christ; 7 just as it is right for me to think this of
you all, because I have you in my heart, inasmuch
as both in my chains and in the defense and con-
firmation of the gospel, you all are partakers with
me of grace. 8 For God is my witness, how greatly I
long for you all with the affection of Jesus Christ.

> **1:7** Paul lived under house arrest in Rome for two years while he waited for Caesar to hear his case. Soldiers guarded him day and night. These guards worked four-hour shifts, with at least one person always chained to Paul. Even though he was a prisoner, Paul was allowed to receive visitors. This gave him an opportunity to share the message of Christ not only with the people who came to see him, but with the soldiers as well.

9 And this I pray, that your love may abound
still more and more in knowledge and all dis-
cernment, 10 that you may approve the things
that are excellent, that you may be sincere and
without offense till the day of Christ, 11 being
filled with the fruits of righteousness [a]which *are*
by Jesus Christ, [b]to the glory and praise of God.

### CHRIST IS PREACHED

12 But I want you to know, brethren, that
the things *which happened* to me have actually
turned out for the furtherance of the gospel, 13 so
that it has become evident [a]to the whole palace
guard, and to all the rest, that my chains are in
Christ; 14 and most of the brethren in the Lord,
having become confident by my chains, are
much more bold to speak the word without fear.
15 Some indeed preach Christ even from envy
and strife, and some also from goodwill: 16 The
former[1] preach Christ from selfish ambition,
not sincerely, supposing to add affliction to my
chains; 17 but the latter out of love, knowing that
I am appointed for the defense of the gospel.
18 What then? Only *that* in every way, whether in
pretense or in truth, Christ is preached; and in
this I rejoice, yes, and will rejoice.

### TO LIVE IS CHRIST

19 For I know that [a]this will turn out for my
deliverance through your prayer and the supply
of the Spirit of Jesus Christ, 20 according to my
earnest expectation and hope that in nothing
I shall be ashamed, but [a]with all boldness, as
always, so now also Christ will be magnified in
my body, whether by life [b]or by death. 21 For to
me, to live *is* Christ, and to die *is* gain. 22 But if I
live on in the flesh, this *will mean* fruit from *my*
labor; yet what I shall choose I cannot tell. 23 For[1]
I am hard-pressed between the two, having a
[a]desire to depart and be with Christ, *which is*
[b]far better. 24 Nevertheless to remain in the flesh
*is* more needful for you. 25 And being confident
of this, I know that I shall remain and continue
with you all for your progress and joy of faith,
26 that [a]your rejoicing for me may be more abun-
dant in Jesus Christ by my coming to you again.

### STRIVING AND SUFFERING FOR CHRIST

27 Only [a]let your conduct be worthy of the
gospel of Christ, so that whether I come and
see you or am absent, I may hear of your affairs,
that you stand fast in one spirit, [b]with one mind
[c]striving together for the faith of the gospel,
28 and not in any way terrified by your adversar-
ies, which is to them a proof of perdition, but
to you of salvation,[1] and that from God. 29 For
to you [a]it has been granted on behalf of Christ,
[b]not only to believe in Him, but also to [c]suffer
for His sake, 30 [a]having the same conflict [b]which
you saw in me and now hear *is* in me.

### UNITY THROUGH HUMILITY

2 Therefore if *there is* any consolation in Christ,
if any comfort of love, if any fellowship of the
Spirit, if any [a]affection and mercy, 2 [a]fulfill my joy
[b]by being like-minded, having the same love, *being*
of [c]one accord, of one mind. 3 [a]*Let* nothing *be done*
through selfish ambition or conceit, but [b]in low-
liness of mind let each esteem others better than
himself. 4 [a]Let each of you look out not only for his
own interests, but also for the interests of [b]others.

### THE HUMBLED AND EXALTED CHRIST

5 [a]Let this mind be in you which was also in
Christ Jesus, 6 who, [a]being in the form of God, did

**1:1** [a] [1 Tim. 3:8–13] [1] Literally *overseers* **1:3** [a] 1 Cor. 1:4 **1:4** [a] Eph. 1:16; 1 Thess. 1:2 **1:5** [a] [Rom. 12:13] **1:6** [a] [John 6:29] **1:11** [a] [Eph. 2:10]; Col. 1:6 [b] John 15:8 **1:13** [a] Phil. 4:22 **1:16** [1] NU-Text reverses the contents of verses 16 and 17. **1:19** [a] Job 13:16, LXX **1:20** [a] Eph. 6:19, 20 [b] [Rom. 14:8] **1:23** [a] [2 Cor. 5:2, 8]; 2 Tim. 4:6 [b] [Ps. 16:11] [1] NU-Text and M-Text read *But.* **1:26** [a] 2 Cor. 1:14 **1:27** [a] Eph. 4:1 [b] Eph. 4:3 [c] Jude 3 **1:28** [1] NU-Text reads *of your salvation.* **1:29** [a] [Matt. 5:11, 12] [b] Eph. 2:8 [c] [2 Tim. 3:12] **1:30** [a] Col. 1:29; 2:1 [b] Acts 16:19–40 **2:1** [a] Col. 3:12 **2:2** [a] John 3:29 [b] Rom. 12:16 [c] Phil. 4:2 **2:3** [a] Gal. 5:26 [b] Rom. 12:10 **2:4** [a] 1 Cor. 13:5 [b] Rom. 15:1, 2 **2:5** [a] [Matt. 11:29] **2:6** [a] 2 Cor. 4:4

not consider it robbery to be equal with God, 7 [a]but
made Himself of no reputation, taking the form
[b]of a bondservant, *and* [c]coming in the likeness of
men. 8 And being found in appearance as a man,
He humbled Himself and [a]became [b]obedient to
*the point of* death, even the death of the cross.
9 [a]Therefore God also [b]has highly exalted Him
and [c]given Him the name which is above every
name, 10 [a]that at the name of Jesus every knee
should bow, of those in heaven, and of those on
earth, and of those under the earth, 11 and [a]*that*
every tongue should confess that Jesus Christ *is*
Lord, to the glory of God the Father.

> **2:8** Jesus willingly took the role of a servant; no one forced Him to do it. Although He never sinned and didn't deserve to die, He chose to die so the sins of the world could be charged to His account. Subsequently, He could credit His righteousness to the account of all who believe in Him (2 Cor. 5:21; Gal. 1:4). Paul describes the depths of Christ's humiliation by reminding his readers that Christ died by the cruelest form of capital punishment, crucifixion. The Jews viewed **death** on **a cross** as a curse from God (see Deut. 21:23; Gal. 3:13).

### *LIGHT BEARERS*

12 Therefore, my beloved, [a]as you have al-
ways obeyed, not as in my presence only, but
now much more in my absence, [b]work out your
own salvation with [c]fear and trembling; 13 for [a]it
is God who works in you both to will and to do
[b]for *His* good pleasure.
14 Do all things [a]without complaining and
[b]disputing, 15 that you may become blameless
and harmless, children of God without fault in
the midst of a crooked and perverse generation,
among whom you shine as [a]lights in the world,
16 holding fast the word of life, so that [a]I may
rejoice in the day of Christ that [b]I have not run
in vain or labored in [c]vain.
17 Yes, and if [a]I am being poured out *as a*
*drink offering* on the sacrifice [b]and service of
your faith, [c]I am glad and rejoice with you all.
18 For the same reason you also be glad and
rejoice with me.

### *TIMOTHY COMMENDED*

19 But I trust in the Lord Jesus to send [a]Timo-
thy to you shortly, that I also may be encouraged
when I know your state. 20 For I have no one
[a]like-minded, who will sincerely care for your
state. 21 For all seek their own, not the things
which are of Christ Jesus. 22 But you know his
proven character, [a]that as a son with *his* father
he served with me in the gospel. 23 Therefore I
hope to send him at once, as soon as I see how
it goes with me. 24 But I trust in the Lord that I
myself shall also come shortly.

### *EPAPHRODITUS PRAISED*

25 Yet I considered it necessary to send to
you [a]Epaphroditus, my brother, fellow worker,
and [b]fellow soldier, [c]but your messenger and
[d]the one who ministered to my need; 26 [a]since
he was longing for you all, and was distressed
because you had heard that he was sick. 27 For

2:7 [a] Ps. 22:6 [b] Is. 42:1 [c] [John 1:14] 2:8 [a] Matt. 26:39 [b] Heb. 5:8 2:9 [a] Heb. 2:9 [b] Acts 2:33 [c] Eph. 1:21 2:10 [a] Is. 45:23 2:11 [a] John 13:13 2:12 [a] Phil. 1:5, 6; 4:15 [b] John 6:27, 29 [c] Eph. 6:5 2:13 [a] Heb. 13:20, 21 [b] Eph. 1:5 2:14 [a] 1 Pet. 4:9 [b] Rom. 14:1 2:15 [a] Matt. 5:15, 16 2:16 [a] 2 Cor. 1:14 [b] Gal. 2:2 [c] 1 Thess. 3:5 2:17 [a] 2 Tim. 4:6 [b] Rom. 15:16 [c] 2 Cor. 7:4 2:19 [a] Rom. 16:21 2:20 [a] 2 Tim. 3:10 2:22 [a] 1 Cor. 4:17 2:25 [a] Phil. 4:18 [b] Philem. 2 [c] 2 Cor. 8:23 [d] 2 Cor. 11:9 2:26 [a] Phil. 1:8

LIVE THE TRUTH

## FELLOWSHIPPING WITH OTHERS

**2:1–4** Fellowship is the sense of unity or closeness we experience when gathered with other Christians. As believers, we may have many differences, but we all share one thing in common: a relationship with God through faith in Jesus Christ. As a marker of this common relationship, believers enjoy a special connection to one another, one that leads to Christian fellowship. It's both a calling and a privilege to gather with other believers regularly and be in fellowship together. Our connection is more than physical and proximal; it is spiritual as well. We gather to enjoy friendship, encourage one another, worship, and walk through life's difficulties together.

This doesn't mean it's always easy to get along with other Christians. We are all broken people, and we don't always navigate relationships perfectly. However, Christian fellowship is born out of the truth that we have more in common than not. Remembering this generates a spirit of grace and forgiveness within Christian fellowship. We can gather in worship, service, community, and life—no matter our differences—because Jesus has united us through His life, death, and resurrection. Jesus' love for us is to drive our love of fellowship with our Christian brothers and sisters.

indeed he was sick almost unto death; but God
had mercy on him, and not only on him but on
me also, lest I should have sorrow upon sorrow.
28 Therefore I sent him the more eagerly, that
when you see him again you may rejoice, and I
may be less sorrowful. 29 Receive him therefore
in the Lord with all gladness, and hold such
men in esteem; 30 because for the work of Christ
he came close to death, not regarding his life,
[a]to supply what was lacking in your service
toward me.

### *ALL FOR CHRIST*

**3** Finally, my brethren, [a]rejoice in the Lord.
For me to write the same things to you *is*
not tedious, but for you *it is* safe.
2 [a]Beware of dogs, beware of [b]evil workers,
[c]beware of the mutilation! 3 For we are [a]the
circumcision, [b]who worship God in the Spirit,[1]
rejoice in Christ Jesus, and have no confidence
in the flesh, 4 though [a]I also might have con-
fidence in the flesh. If anyone else thinks he
may have confidence in the flesh, I [b]more so:
5 circumcised the eighth day, of the stock of
Israel, [a]*of* the tribe of Benjamin, [b]a Hebrew of
the Hebrews; concerning the law, [c]a Pharisee;
6 concerning zeal, [a]persecuting the church;
concerning the righteousness which is in the
law, blameless.

> **3:2** In Paul's day, **dogs** weren't pets. Rather, wild, vicious canines roamed the ancient Near East, eating anything they could find—including garbage—and attacking people. "Dog" was a popular insulting name for a Gentile. Paul turned the insult around in this verse. The people he called dogs were those who insisted that circumcision (**mutilation**) was necessary for Christians.

7 But [a]what things were gain to me, these I
have counted loss for Christ. 8 Yet indeed I also
count all things loss [a]for the excellence of the
knowledge of Christ Jesus my Lord, for whom
I have suffered the loss of all things, and count
them as rubbish, that I may gain Christ 9 and be
found in Him, not having [a]my own righteous-
ness, which *is* from the law, but [b]that which *is*
through faith in Christ, the righteousness which
is from God by faith; 10 that I may know Him
and the [a]power of His resurrection, and [b]the
fellowship of His sufferings, being conformed

> **3:7–8 Loss** indicates something damaged or of no further use. Those things Paul thought to be important became unimportant after confronting the resurrected Christ. **Rubbish** means anything detestable or worthless. **All things** of this world are dung compared to **Christ**. Even our righteousness is like filthy rags (Is. 64:6).

to His death, 11 if, by any means, I may [a]attain to
the resurrection from the dead.

### *PRESSING TOWARD THE GOAL*

12 Not that I have already [a]attained, or am
already [b]perfected; but I press on, that I may
lay hold of that for which Christ Jesus has also
laid hold of me. 13 Brethren, I do not count my-
self to have apprehended; but one thing *I do,*
[a]forgetting those things which are behind and
[b]reaching forward to those things which are
ahead, 14 [a]I press toward the goal for the prize of
[b]the upward call of God in Christ Jesus.
15 Therefore let us, as many as are [a]mature,
[b]have this mind; and if in anything you think
otherwise, [c]God will reveal even this to you.
16 Nevertheless, to *the degree* that we have already
attained, [a]let us walk [b]by the same rule,[1] let us
be of the same mind.

### *OUR CITIZENSHIP IN HEAVEN*

17 Brethren, [a]join in following my example,
and note those who so walk, as [b]you have us
for a pattern. 18 For many walk, of whom I have
told you often, and now tell you even weep-
ing, *that they are* [a]the enemies of the cross of
Christ: 19 [a]whose end *is* destruction, [b]whose
god *is their* belly, and [c]*whose* glory *is* in their
shame—[d]who set their mind on earthly things.
20 For [a]our citizenship is in heaven, [b]from
which we also [c]eagerly wait for the Savior, the
Lord Jesus Christ, 21 [a]who will transform our
lowly body that it may be [b]conformed to His
glorious body, [c]according to the working by
which He is able even to [d]subdue all things to
Himself.

**4** Therefore, my beloved and [a]longed-for
brethren, [b]my joy and crown, so [c]stand fast
in the Lord, beloved.

### *BE UNITED, JOYFUL, AND IN PRAYER*

2 I implore Euodia and I implore Syntyche
[a]to be of the same mind in the Lord. 3 And[1] I urge

**2:30** [a] 1 Cor. 16:17 **3:1** [a] 1 Thess. 5:16 **3:2** [a] Gal. 5:15 [b] Ps. 119:115 [c] Rom. 2:28 **3:3** [a] Deut. 30:6 [b] Rom. 7:6 [1] NU-Text and M-Text read *who worship in the Spirit of God.* **3:4** [a] 2 Cor. 5:16; 11:18 [b] 2 Cor. 11:22, 23 **3:5** [a] Rom. 11:1 [b] 2 Cor. 11:22 [c] Acts 23:6 **3:6** [a] Acts 8:3; 22:4, 5; 26:9–11 **3:7** [a] Matt. 13:44 **3:8** [a] Jer. 9:23 **3:9** [a] Rom. 10:3 [b] Rom. 1:17 **3:10** [a] Eph. 1:19, 20 [b] [Rom. 6:3–5] **3:11** [a] Acts 26:6–8 **3:12** [a] [1 Tim. 6:12, 19] [b] Heb. 12:23 **3:13** [a] Luke 9:62 [b] Heb. 6:1 **3:14** [a] 2 Tim. 4:7 [b] Heb. 3:1 **3:15** [a] 1 Cor. 2:6 [b] Gal. 5:10 [c] Hos. 6:3 **3:16** [a] Gal. 6:16 [b] Rom. 12:16; 15:5 [1] NU-Text omits *rule* and the rest of the verse. **3:17** [a] [1 Cor. 4:16; 11:1] [b] Titus 2:7, 8 **3:18** [a] Gal. 1:7 **3:19** [a] 2 Cor. 11:15 [b] 1 Tim. 6:5 [c] Hos. 4:7 [d] Rom. 8:5 **3:20** [a] Eph. 2:6, 19 [b] Acts 1:11 [c] 1 Cor. 1:7 **3:21** [a] [1 Cor. 15:43–53] [b] 1 John 3:2 [c] Eph. 1:19 [d] [1 Cor. 15:28] **4:1** [a] Phil. 1:8 [b] 2 Cor. 1:14 [c] Phil. 1:27 **4:2** [a] Phil. 2:2; 3:16 **4:3** [1] NU-Text and M-Text read *Yes.*

APPLY THE TRUTH

## POVERTY

**4:12** Does anyone like waiting? Standing in line, waiting for a video to load, or not having free next-day shipping can feel like torture. But in the waiting, we can find godliness. Not getting everything when we want it requires patience, and more importantly, trust in God's timing. The same is true of learning contentment. If we had everything at the snap of our fingers, we wouldn't need to be content, and we would miss out on what it means to rely on God. That's why Paul says he learned the secret to contentment by having nothing and by having more than enough. It's recognizing things come and go, but true, lasting satisfaction goes beyond any material possession.

Poverty is a real problem in our world with millions of people living without the basic commodities many of us take for granted. God has called His church to be the hands and feet of Christ and help provide for the poor. To do that, we must have learned contentment, so we don't cling to an abundance of possessions. Contentment is the key to letting go, going without, and delighting in meeting someone else's needs. It's to see we have all we need and could ever want in Christ and are satisfied in Him.

you also, true companion, help these women
who [a]labored with me in the gospel, with Clem-
ent also, and the rest of my fellow workers, whose
names *are* in [b]the Book of Life.
4 [a]Rejoice in the Lord always. Again I will
say, rejoice!
5 Let your gentleness be known to all men.
[a]The Lord *is* at hand.
6 [a]Be anxious for nothing, but in everything
by prayer and supplication, with [b]thanksgiving,
let your requests be made known to God; 7 and
[a]the peace of God, which surpasses all under-
standing, will guard your hearts and minds
through Christ Jesus.

### SEEING JESUS IN THE SCRIPTURE

**4:7** Jesus is the peace of God, comforting us in all our afflictions just as He promised (see John 14:27).

### *MEDITATE ON THESE THINGS*

8 Finally, brethren, whatever things are
[a]true, whatever things *are* [b]noble, whatever
things *are* [c]just, [d]whatever things *are* pure,
whatever things *are* [e]lovely, whatever things
*are* of good report, if *there is* any virtue and if
*there is* anything praiseworthy—meditate on
these things. 9 The things which you learned
and received and heard and saw in me,
these do, and [a]the God of peace will be with
you.

### *PHILIPPIAN GENEROSITY*

10 But I rejoiced in the Lord greatly that now
at last [a]your care for me has flourished again;
though you surely did care, but you lacked op-
portunity. 11 Not that I speak in regard to need,
for I have learned in whatever state I am, [a]to be
content: 12 [a]I know how to be abased, and I know
how to abound. Everywhere and in all things I
have learned both to be full and to be hungry,
both to abound and to suffer need. 13 I can do
all things [a]through Christ[1] who strengthens me.
14 Nevertheless you have done well that [a]you
shared in my distress. 15 Now you Philippians
know also that in the beginning of the gospel,
when I departed from Macedonia, [a]no church
shared with me concerning giving and receiving
but you only. 16 For even in Thessalonica you sent
*aid* once and again for my necessities. 17 Not that I
seek the gift, but I seek [a]the fruit that abounds to
your account. 18 Indeed I have all and abound. I
am full, having received from [a]Epaphroditus the
things *sent* from you, [b]a sweet-smelling aroma, [c]an
acceptable sacrifice, well pleasing to God. 19 And
my God [a]shall supply all your need according to
His riches in glory by Christ Jesus. 20 [a]Now to our
God and Father *be* glory forever and ever. Amen.

### *GREETING AND BLESSING*

21 Greet every saint in Christ Jesus. The
brethren [a]who are with me greet you. 22 All the
saints greet you, but especially those who are
of Caesar's household.
23 The grace of our Lord Jesus Christ be with
you all.[1] Amen.

**4:3** [a] Rom. 16:3 [b] Luke 10:20 **4:4** [a] Rom. 12:12 **4:5** [a] [James 5:7–9] **4:6** [a] Matt. 6:25 [b] [1 Thess. 5:17, 18] **4:7** [a] [John 14:27] **4:8** [a] Eph. 4:25 [b] 2 Cor. 8:21 [c] Deut. 16:20 [d] 1 Thess. 5:22 [e] 1 Cor. 13:4–7 **4:9** [a] Rom. 15:33 **4:10** [a] 2 Cor. 11:9 **4:11** [a] 2 Cor. 9:8; 1 Tim. 6:6, 8; Heb. 13:5 **4:12** [a] 1 Cor. 4:11 **4:13** [a] John 15:5 [1] NU-Text reads *Him who.* **4:14** [a] Phil. 1:7 **4:15** [a] 2 Cor. 11:8, 9 **4:17** [a] Titus 3:14 **4:18** [a] Phil. 2:25 [b] Heb. 13:16 [c] Rom. 12:1; 2 Cor. 9:12 **4:19** [a] Ps. 23:1; 2 Cor. 9:8 **4:20** [a] Rom. 16:27 **4:21** [a] Gal. 1:2 **4:23** [1] NU-Text reads *your spirit.*

# *The Epistle of Paul the Apostle to the* COLOSSIANS

| AUTHOR | KEY VERSES | READING TIME |
|---|---|---|
| Paul | Colossians 1:17–18 | 16 minutes |

On Paul's third missionary journey, he devoted almost three years to an Asian ministry centered in Ephesus (Acts 19:10; 20:31). Epaphras probably came to Christ during this time and then carried the gospel to cities like Colosse in the Lycus valley. It is evident from Colossians 1:4–8 and 2:1 that Paul had never visited the church at Colosse. Later, when Epaphras visited Paul in prison (Col. 4:12), his report concerning the church in Colosse prompted this epistle. Paul's purpose was to show that Christ is preeminent—first and foremost in everything—and the Christian's life should reflect that priority. Because believers are rooted in Christ, alive in Him, hidden in Him, and complete in Him, it is inconsistent for them to live without Him. Clothed with His love, with His peace ruling in their hearts, believers are equipped to make Christ first in every area of life.

**Occasion:** Paul wrote Colossians during his first Roman imprisonment, perhaps around the same time as Ephesians, Philippians, and Philemon.

**Main Point:** Christ is supreme over everything.

**Big Ideas:** Christ is our greatest treasure. We are to practice our faith every day in everything we do. Our attitudes and actions should reflect who we now are in Christ.

## OUTLINE:

I. The Supremacy of Christ (chs. 1–2)
II. The Submission to Christ (chs. 3–4)

**c. AD 34**
Paul is converted

**c. AD 47–49**
Paul's first missionary journey

**c. AD 50**
The Jerusalem Council

**c. AD 50–53**
Paul's second missionary journey

**c. AD 53–57**
Paul's third missionary journey

**c. AD 54–56**
The Church at Colosse is founded

**AD 54–68**
Nero is Roman emperor

**c. AD 58**
Paul is arrested in Jerusalem

**c. AD 60–62**
Paul is imprisoned in Rome

**c. AD 60–62**
**Colossians written**

**AD 64**
Great Fire of Rome; first Roman mass persecution of Christians

**c. AD 67**
Peter and Paul are executed

### GREETING

**1** Paul, [a]an apostle of Jesus Christ by the will of God, and Timothy our brother,

2 To the saints [a]and faithful brethren in Christ *who are* in Colosse:

[b]Grace to you and peace from God our Father and the Lord Jesus Christ.[1]

### THEIR FAITH IN CHRIST

3 [a]We give thanks to the God and Father of our Lord Jesus Christ, praying always for you, 4 [a]since we heard of your faith in Christ Jesus and of [b]your love for all the saints; 5 because of the hope [a]which is laid up for you in heaven, of which you heard before in the word of the truth of the gospel, 6 which has come to you, [a]as *it has* also in all the world, and [b]is bringing forth fruit,[1] as *it is* also among you since the day you heard and knew [c]the grace of God in truth; 7 as you also learned from [a]Epaphras, our dear fellow servant, who is [b]a faithful minister of Christ on your behalf, 8 who also declared to us your [a]love in the Spirit.

> **1:7 Epaphras** was a Gentile who became a Christian, probably because of Paul's teaching. He then returned to his native city of Colosse to tell others about Jesus and start a church. During the two years Paul was under house arrest, Epaphras visited him, cheering up the apostle with stories about the good things that were happening in the church at Colosse.

### PREEMINENCE OF CHRIST

9 [a]For this reason we also, since the day we heard it, do not cease to pray for you, and to ask [b]that you may be filled with [c]the knowledge of His will [d]in all wisdom and spiritual understanding; 10 [a]that you may walk worthy of the Lord, [b]fully pleasing *Him,* [c]being fruitful in every good work and increasing in the [d]knowledge of God; 11 [a]strengthened with all might, according to His glorious power, [b]for all patience and longsuffering [c]with joy; 12 [a]giving thanks to the Father who has qualified us to be partakers of [b]the inheritance of the saints in the light. 13 He has delivered us from [a]the power of darkness [b]and conveyed *us* into the kingdom of the Son of His love, 14 [a]in whom we have redemption through His blood,[1] the forgiveness of sins.

15 He is [a]the image of the invisible God, [b]the firstborn over all creation. 16 For [a]by Him all things were created that are in heaven and that are on earth, visible and invisible, whether thrones or [b]dominions or principalities or powers. All things were created [c]through Him and for Him. 17 [a]And He is before all things, and in Him [b]all things consist. 18 And [a]He is the head of the body, the church, who is the beginning, [b]the firstborn from the dead, that in all things He may have the preeminence.

### RECONCILED IN CHRIST

19 For it pleased *the Father that* [a]in Him all the fullness should dwell, 20 and [a]by Him to reconcile [b]all things to Himself, by Him, whether things on earth or things in heaven, [c]having made peace through the blood of His cross.

> **1:15–20** These verses are thought to be an early Christian hymn celebrating the supremacy of Christ. **Firstborn** could denote a priority in time or in rank. The word doesn't describe Christ as the first being *created* in time because the hymn proclaims that all things were **created by Him** and that **He is before all things**. Being firstborn referred more to rank and privilege than to order of birth.

21 And you, [a]who once were alienated and enemies in your mind [b]by wicked works, yet now He has [c]reconciled 22 [a]in the body of His flesh through death, [b]to present you holy, and blameless, and above reproach in His sight— 23 if indeed you continue [a]in the faith, grounded and steadfast, and are [b]not moved away from the hope of the gospel which you heard, [c]which was preached to every creature under heaven, [d]of which I, Paul, became a minister.

### SACRIFICIAL SERVICE FOR CHRIST

24 [a]I now rejoice in my sufferings [b]for you, and fill up in my flesh [c]what is lacking in the afflictions of Christ, for [d]the sake of His body, which is the church, 25 of which I became a minister according to [a]the stewardship from God which was given to me for you, to fulfill the word of God, 26 [a]the mystery which has been hidden from ages and from generations, [b]but now has been revealed to His saints. 27 [a]To them God willed to make known what are [b]the riches of

**1:1** [a] Eph. 1:1 **1:2** [a] 1 Cor. 4:17 [b] Gal. 1:3 [1] NU-Text omits *and the Lord Jesus Christ.* **1:3** [a] 1 Cor. 1:4; Eph. 1:16; Phil. 1:3 **1:4** [a] Eph. 1:15 [b] [Heb. 6:10] **1:5** [a] [1 Pet. 1:4] **1:6** [a] Matt. 24:14 [b] John 15:16 [c] Eph. 3:2 [1] NU-Text and M-Text add *and growing.* **1:7** [a] Col. 4:12; Philem. 23 [b] 1 Cor. 4:1, 2; 2 Cor. 11:23 **1:8** [a] Rom. 15:30 **1:9** [a] Eph. 1:15–17 [b] 1 Cor. 1:5 [c] [Rom. 12:2]; Eph. 5:17 [d] Eph. 1:8 **1:10** [a] Eph. 4:1 [b] 1 Thess. 4:1 [c] Heb. 13:21 [d] 2 Pet. 3:18 **1:11** [a] [Eph. 3:16; 6:10] [b] Eph. 4:2 [c] [Acts 5:41] **1:12** [a] [Eph. 5:20] [b] Eph. 1:11 **1:13** [a] Eph. 6:12 [b] 2 Pet. 1:11 **1:14** [a] Eph. 1:7 [1] NU-Text and M-Text omit *through His blood.* **1:15** [a] 2 Cor. 4:4 [b] Rev. 3:14 **1:16** [a] Heb. 1:2, 3 [b] [Eph. 1:20, 21] [c] Heb. 2:10 **1:17** [a] [John 17:5] [b] Heb. 1:3 **1:18** [a] Eph. 1:22 [b] Rev. 1:5 **1:19** [a] John 1:16 **1:20** [a] Eph. 2:14 [b] 2 Cor. 5:18 [c] Eph. 1:10 **1:21** [a] [Eph. 2:1] [b] Titus 1:15 [c] 2 Cor. 5:18, 19 **1:22** [a] 2 Cor. 5:18 [b] [Eph. 5:27] **1:23** [a] Eph. 3:17 [b] [John 15:6] [c] Col. 1:6 [d] Col. 1:25 **1:24** [a] 2 Cor. 7:4 [b] Eph. 3:1, 13 [c] [2 Cor. 1:5; 12:15] [d] Eph. 1:23 **1:25** [a] Gal. 2:7 **1:26** [a] [1 Cor. 2:7] [b] [2 Tim. 1:10] **1:27** [a] 2 Cor. 2:14 [b] Rom. 9:23

KNOW THE TRUTH

## THE DOCTRINE OF CREATION AND HUMANS

### PART 1: OVERVIEW OF THE DOCTRINE OF CREATION AND HUMANS

**1:16–17** The Godhead—Father, Son, and Holy Spirit—is uncreated, eternal, and immutable (unchanging). Everything else has been created by God, including heaven (the spiritual realm of God's throne and unrestrained manifest presence), angels, the cosmos, and humanity. Paul told the Colossians because Jesus Christ is Creator, He has preeminence over creation. He is responsible for both the first creation and *re*creation, when everything will be made right once again.

In the beginning, when God created everything, He declared everything to be "good" (Gen. 1:31). But things would not remain good. Given freewill by the Creator to love and obey Him, people instead used it to reject His perfect rule, rebel against Him, and pursue self-rule. This historical act is often called *the Fall*.

The Fall's result was separation from our sinless Creator and every person being corrupted with sin, evil, sickness, disease, death, and more. In time, the perfect Creator stepped into His fallen creation. Living a sinless life, paying the price for humanity's sin on the cross, and rising from dead, Jesus inaugurated the restoration of creation. Soon, God will make a new heaven and new earth filled with spiritually renewed, eternally purified people in resurrected bodies living in His presence, free of all sin, evil, and death without end.

*For* **THE DOCTRINE OF CREATION AND HUMANS: PART 2: THE CREATION OF EVERYTHING**, *turn to Psalm 33:6 on page 551.*

the glory of this mystery among the Gentiles:
which[1] is [c]Christ in you, [d]the hope of glory. 28 Him
we preach, [a]warning every man and teaching
every man in all wisdom, [b]that we may present
every man perfect in Christ Jesus. 29 To this *end*
I also labor, striving according to His working
which works in me [a]mightily.

### *NOT PHILOSOPHY BUT CHRIST*

**2** For I want you to know what a great [a]conflict
I have for you and those in Laodicea, and *for*
as many as have not seen my face in the flesh,
2 that their hearts may be encouraged, being
knit together in love, and *attaining* to all riches
of the full assurance of understanding, to the
knowledge of the mystery of God, both of the
Father and[1] of Christ, 3 [a]in whom are hidden all
the treasures of wisdom and knowledge.

**2:1** Built on the banks of the Lycus River in what is now known as Turkey, **Laodicea** was known for its wealth in New Testament times. Other passages in the Bible seem to suggest that the Christians in Laodicea had lost their enthusiasm for, and commitment to, the things of God.

4 Now this I say [a]lest anyone should deceive
you with persuasive words. 5 For [a]though I am
absent in the flesh, yet I am with you in spirit,
rejoicing to see [b]your *good* order and the [c]stead-
fastness of your faith in Christ.
6 [a]As you therefore have received Christ
Jesus the Lord, so walk in Him, 7 [a]rooted and
built up in Him and established in the faith,
as you have been taught, abounding in it[1] with
thanksgiving.
8 Beware lest anyone cheat you through phi-
losophy and empty deceit, according to [a]the tra-
dition of men, according to the [b]basic principles
of the world, and not according to Christ. 9 For
[a]in Him dwells all the fullness of the Godhead
bodily; 10 and you are complete in Him, who is
the [a]head of all principality and power.

### *NOT LEGALISM BUT CHRIST*

11 In Him you were also [a]circumcised with
the circumcision made without hands, by [b]put-
ting off the body of the sins[1] of the flesh, by the
circumcision of Christ, 12 [a]buried with Him in
baptism, in which you also were raised with *Him*
through [b]faith in the working of God, [c]who raised
Him from the dead. 13 And you, being dead in
your trespasses and the uncircumcision of your
flesh, He has made alive together with Him,
having forgiven you all trespasses, 14 [a]having

**1:27** [c] [Rom. 8:10, 11] [d] 1 Tim. 1:1 [1] M-Text reads *who.* **1:28** [a] Acts 20:20 [b] Eph. 5:27 **1:29** [a] Eph. 3:7 **2:1** [a] Phil. 1:30 **2:2** [1] NU-Text omits *both of the Father and.* **2:3** [a] 1 Cor. 1:24, 30 **2:4** [a] Rom. 16:18 **2:5** [a] 1 Thess. 2:17 [b] 1 Cor. 14:40 [c] 1 Pet. 5:9 **2:6** [a] 1 Thess. 4:1 **2:7** [a] Eph. 2:21 [1] NU-Text omits *in it.* **2:8** [a] Gal. 1:14 [b] Gal. 4:3, 9, 10 **2:9** [a] [John 1:14] **2:10** [a] [Eph. 1:20, 21] **2:11** [a] Deut. 10:16 [b] Rom. 6:6; 7:24 [1] NU-Text omits *of the sins.* **2:12** [a] Rom. 6:4 [b] Eph. 1:19, 20 [c] Acts 2:24 **2:14** [a] [Eph. 2:15, 16]

APPLY THE TRUTH

## THE OCCULT

**2:8** We live in a spiritual age. Many people believe in signs, stars, and miracles. But just because someone is spiritual doesn't mean they're godly. Often, the signs, stars, and miracles people believe in are rooted in the cosmos, themselves, or some other external power apart from God. The stars aren't in control of our lives. Neither are our ancestors, magic, or nature. Wishing upon a star, heeding the instructions of your zodiac sign, or having crystals won't make everything work out the way you want.

In this passage, Paul warns of the dangers of falling for spiritual things not of Christ—what can be called the occult. God hasn't hidden the truth of Himself or spirituality in the stars; He has revealed it in the person of Jesus and the pages of His Word. This is why Paul says anyone who leads us toward the occult rather than Christ is cheating us; they're robbing us of the answers we long for. Only God can work all things together for good, and only He can reveal His plans for our lives. Refuse to look anywhere else but to Him to find the answers you seek.

wiped out the handwriting of requirements that
was against us, which was contrary to us. And
He has taken it out of the way, having nailed it
to the cross. 15 [a]Having disarmed [b]principalities
and powers, He made a public spectacle of them,
triumphing over them in it.

**2:15** In the days of the Roman Empire, when a Roman general returned home after a successful military campaign, he was honored with a special ceremony called a "triumph." A parade was thrown in his honor, with the general leading the way in his chariot and prisoners of war following behind. Those prisoners were then divided into two groups: those who would be executed and those who would become slaves of the Roman Empire.

16 So let no one [a]judge you in food or in drink,
or regarding a festival or a new moon or sab-
baths, 17 [a]which are a shadow of things to come,
but the substance is of Christ. 18 Let no one cheat
you of your reward, taking delight in *false* humil-
ity and worship of angels, intruding into those
things which he has not[1] seen, vainly puffed up
by his fleshly mind, 19 and not holding fast to [a]the
Head, from whom all the body, nourished and
knit together by joints and ligaments, [b]grows
with the increase *that is* from God.
20 Therefore,[1] if you [a]died with Christ from
the basic principles of the world, [b]why, as *though*
living in the world, do you subject yourselves to
regulations— 21 [a]"Do not touch, do not taste, do
not handle," 22 which all concern things which
perish with the using—[a]according to the com-
mandments and doctrines of men? 23 [a]These
things indeed have an appearance of wisdom
in self-imposed religion, *false* humility, and
neglect of the body, *but are* of no value against
the indulgence of the flesh.

### NOT CARNALITY BUT CHRIST

**3** If then you were [a]raised with Christ, seek
those things which are above, [b]where Christ
is, sitting at the right hand of God. 2 Set your
mind on things above, not on things on the
[a]earth. 3 [a]For you died, [b]and your life is hidden
with Christ in God. 4 [a]When Christ *who is* [b]our
life appears, then you also will appear with Him
in [c]glory.
5 [a]Therefore put to death [b]your members
which are on the earth: [c]fornication, unclean-
ness, passion, evil desire, and covetousness,
[d]which is idolatry. 6 [a]Because of these things
the wrath of God is coming upon [b]the sons of
disobedience, 7 [a]in which you yourselves once
walked when you lived in them.
8 [a]But now you yourselves are to put off all
these: anger, wrath, malice, blasphemy, filthy
language out of your mouth. 9 Do not lie to one
another, since you have put off the old man
with his deeds, 10 and have put on the new *man*
who [a]is renewed in knowledge [b]according to
the image of Him who [c]created him, 11 where
there is neither [a]Greek nor Jew, circumcised
nor uncircumcised, barbarian, Scythian, slave
*nor* free, [b]but Christ *is* all and in all.

### CHARACTER OF THE NEW MAN

12 Therefore, [a]as *the* elect of God, holy and
beloved, [b]put on tender mercies, kindness, hu-
mility, meekness, longsuffering; 13 [a]bearing with

**2:15** [a] [Is. 53:12] [b] Eph. 6:12 **2:16** [a] Rom. 14:3 **2:17** [a] Heb. 8:5; 10:1 **2:18** [1] NU-Text omits *not.* **2:19** [a] Eph. 4:15 [b] Eph. 1:23; 4:16 **2:20** [a] Rom. 6:2–5 [b] Gal. 4:3, 9 [1] NU-Text and M-Text omit *Therefore.* **2:21** [a] 1 Tim. 4:3 **2:22** [a] Titus 1:14 **2:23** [a] 1 Tim. 4:8 **3:1** [a] Col. 2:12 [b] Eph. 1:20 **3:2** [a] [Matt. 6:19–21] **3:3** [a] [Rom. 6:2] [b] [2 Cor. 5:7] **3:4** [a] [1 John 3:2] [b] John 14:6 [c] 1 Cor. 15:43 **3:5** [a] [Rom. 8:13] [b] [Rom. 6:13] [c] Eph. 5:3 [d] Eph. 4:19; 5:3, 5 **3:6** [a] Rom. 1:18 [b] [Eph. 2:2] **3:7** [a] 1 Cor. 6:11 **3:8** [a] Eph. 4:22 **3:10** [a] Rom. 12:2 [b] [Rom. 8:29] [c] [Eph. 2:10] **3:11** [a] Gal. 3:27, 28 [b] Eph. 1:23 **3:12** [a] [1 Pet. 1:2] [b] 1 John 3:17 **3:13** [a] [Mark 11:25]

**3:9–10** The **old man** and the **new man** don't refer to the Christian's fleshly and spiritual natures. Instead, Paul describes our former unredeemed life as the "old man" and our life as God's child as the "new man." The new man has the image of the new creation in Christ, just as the old man bears the image of our fallen nature. The old man is under an old master, Satan, while the new man has a new master, the Spirit of God living within.

one another, and forgiving one another, if any-
one has a complaint against another; even as
Christ forgave you, so you also *must do.* 14[a]But
above all these things [b]put on love, which is
the [c]bond of perfection. 15 And let [a]the peace of
God rule in your hearts, [b]to which also you were
called [c]in one body; and [d]be thankful. 16 Let the
word of Christ dwell in you richly in all wisdom,
teaching and admonishing one another [a]in
psalms and hymns and spiritual songs, singing
with grace in your hearts to the Lord. 17 And
[a]whatever you do in word or deed, *do* all in the
name of the Lord Jesus, giving thanks to God
the Father through Him.

### THE CHRISTIAN HOME
*(cf. Eph. 5:21—6:9)*

18[a]Wives, submit to your own husbands, [b]as
is fitting in the Lord.

19[a]Husbands, love your wives and do not be
[b]bitter toward them.

20[a]Children, obey your parents [b]in all things,
for this is well pleasing to the Lord.

21[a]Fathers, do not provoke your children,
lest they become discouraged.

22[a]Bondservants, obey in all things your
masters according to the flesh, not with eye-
service, as men-pleasers, but in sincerity of heart,
fearing God. 23[a]And whatever you do, do it heart-
ily, as to the Lord and not to men, 24[a]knowing
that from the Lord you will receive the reward of
the inheritance; [b]for[1] you serve the Lord Christ.
25 But he who does wrong will be repaid for what
he has done, and [a]there is no partiality.

4 Masters,[a] give your bondservants what is
just and fair, knowing that you also have a
Master in heaven.

### CHRISTIAN GRACES

2[a]Continue earnestly in prayer, being vigi-
lant in it [b]with thanksgiving; 3[a]meanwhile pray-
ing also for us, that God would [b]open to us a door
for the word, to speak [c]the mystery of Christ, [d]for
which I am also in chains, 4 that I may make it
manifest, as I ought to speak.

5[a]Walk in [b]wisdom toward those *who are*
outside, [c]redeeming the time. 6 *Let* your speech
always *be* [a]with grace, [b]seasoned with salt, [c]that
you may know how you ought to answer each
one.

### FINAL GREETINGS
*(cf. Eph. 6:21, 22)*

7[a]Tychicus, a beloved brother, faithful min-
ister, and fellow servant in the Lord, will tell you
all the news about me. 8[a]I am sending him to you
for this very purpose, that he[1] may know your

**3:14** [a] 1 Pet. 4:8 [b] [1 Cor. 13] [c] Eph. 4:3 **3:15** [a] [John 14:27] [b] 1 Cor. 7:15 [c] Eph. 4:4 [d] [1 Thess. 5:18] **3:16** [a] Eph. 5:19 **3:17** [a] 1 Cor. 10:31 **3:18** [a] 1 Pet. 3:1 [b] [Eph. 5:22—6:9] **3:19** [a] [Eph. 5:25] [b] Eph. 4:31 **3:20** [a] Eph. 6:1 [b] Eph. 5:24 **3:21** [a] Eph. 6:4 **3:22** [a] Eph. 6:5 **3:23** [a] [Eccl. 9:10] **3:24** [a] Eph. 6:8 [b] 1 Cor. 7:22 [1] NU-Text omits *for.* **3:25** [a] Rom. 2:11 **4:1** [a] Eph. 6:9 **4:2** [a] Luke 18:1 [b] Col. 2:7 **4:3** [a] Eph. 6:19 [b] 1 Cor. 16:9 [c] Eph. 3:3, 4; 6:19 [d] Eph. 6:20 **4:5** [a] Eph. 5:15 [b] [Matt. 10:16] [c] Eph. 5:16 **4:6** [a] Eccl. 10:12 [b] Mark 9:50 [c] 1 Pet. 3:15 **4:7** [a] 2 Tim. 4:12 **4:8** [a] Eph. 6:22 [1] NU-Text reads *you may know our circumstances and he may.*

APPLY THE TRUTH

## SCHOOL

**3:23** Sometimes it feels like we have two lives. One is our "spiritual life"; the other is our "regular life." Our spiritual life is praying, going to church, reading the Bible, or listening to worship music. Our regular life is everything else, including school. But God doesn't want part of our lives (the "spiritual" part); He wants our *whole* lives. Every aspect of our lives can and should be part of our Christian life. It isn't about having "spiritual things" in one area and "regular things" in another. It's about offering everything to God for His glory.

This verse tells us to do *everything* "as to the Lord." This means even what we do in school can be done for God just like how we read our Bibles or listen to worship music. How we act in class and how we study can be worship. We do this by closing the gap in our minds between what is spiritual and what is regular. We recognize God's presence everywhere and invite Him into everything we say and do. When we do that, we'll see school can be a great place to honor God. We can learn, grow, challenge ourselves, and be the best student we can be for God's glory and fame. It's also a prime mission field, ripe for harvest.

KNOW THE TRUTH

## THE DOCTRINE OF SCRIPTURE

### PART 10: THE TRANSLATION OF SCRIPTURE

**4:16** Paul's epistles (letters) and the rest of the New Testament (NT) was written in Koine Greek, the primary language of the day. The Old Testament (OT) was written almost entirely in Hebrew, with a few parts in Aramaic. However, most OT quotations in the NT, including many by Jesus, came from a Greek translation of the OT called the Septuagint (translated about 130 BC). This OT translation was what the Berean Jews likely read carefully to confirm Paul's claims (Acts 17:10–12).

Throughout church history, Bible translation has been crucial for spreading the gospel. The Bible was translated into Syriac in the second century AD, Latin in 382, old English in the 730s, Middle English in 1382, Hungarian and Bohemian in 1435, German in 1534, and Common English in the 1530s, eventually resulting in the King James Version in 1611. Today, the Bible has been translated into nearly 700 different languages with over 2,500 translation projects advancing toward completion. Using the massive number of highly reliable manuscripts (handwritten copies of the Bible's original writings), trustworthy translations are being produced to give all people on earth the Scriptures in their languages.

*For* **THE DOCTRINE OF GOD: PART 1: OVERVIEW OF THE DOCTRINE OF GOD**, *turn to Deuteronomy 4:24–40 on page 181.* •••

circumstances and comfort your hearts, 9 with
[a]Onesimus, a faithful and beloved brother, who
is *one* of you. They will make known to you all
things which *are happening* here.
10 [a]Aristarchus my fellow prisoner greets
you, with [b]Mark the cousin of Barnabas (about
whom you received instructions: if he comes
to you, welcome him), 11 and Jesus who is called
Justus. These *are my* only fellow workers for the
kingdom of God who are of the circumcision;
they have proved to be a comfort to me.
12 [a]Epaphras, who is *one* of you, a bondservant
of Christ, greets you, always [b]laboring fervently for
you in prayers, that you may stand [c]perfect and
complete[1] in all the will of God. 13 For I bear him
witness that he has a great zeal[1] for you, and those
who are in Laodicea, and those in Hierapolis.
14 [a]Luke the beloved physician and [b]Demas greet
you. 15 Greet the brethren who are in Laodicea, and
Nymphas and [a]the church that *is* in his[1] house.

### *CLOSING EXHORTATIONS AND BLESSING*

16 Now when [a]this epistle is read among you,
see that it is read also in the church of the La-
odiceans, and that you likewise read the *epistle*
from Laodicea. 17 And say to [a]Archippus, "Take
heed to [b]the ministry which you have received
in the Lord, that you may fulfill it."
18 [a]This salutation by my own hand—Paul.
[b]Remember my chains. Grace *be* with you. Amen.

4:9 [a] Philem. 10 4:10 [a] Acts 19:29; 20:4; 27:2 [b] 2 Tim. 4:11 4:12 [a] Philem. 23 [b] Rom. 15:30 [c] Matt. 5:48 [1] NU-Text reads *fully assured.* 4:13 [1] NU-Text reads *concern.* 4:14 [a] 2 Tim. 4:11 [b] 2 Tim. 4:10 4:15 [a] Rom. 16:5 [1] NU-Text reads *Nympha . . . her house.* 4:16 [a] 1 Thess. 5:27 4:17 [a] Philem. 2 [b] 2 Tim. 4:5 4:18 [a] 1 Cor. 16:21 [b] Heb. 13:3

*The First Epistle of Paul the Apostle to the*

# THESSALONIANS

**AUTHOR**
Paul

**KEY VERSES**
1 Thessalonians 3:12–13

**READING TIME**
14 minutes

Paul planted the church in Thessalonica during his second missionary journey and quickly grounded it in Christian doctrine. The church's faith, hope, love, and perseverance in the face of persecution were exemplary. Paul's labors as a spiritual parent to the fledgling church had been richly rewarded, and his affection is visible in every line of his letter. The only problem that had arisen concerned the return of Christ. Paul wrote to encourage the Thessalonians that the Lord's return should bring hope and comfort to them. As they waited for this glorious day, however, the church was to keep living as they had: to excel in their faith, to increase in their love for one another, and to rejoice, pray, and give thanks always.

**Occasion:** Paul wrote this epistle while he was in Corinth with Silvanus and Timothy (1:1; Acts 18:5) in response to Timothy's good report regarding the Thessalonian church.

**Main Point:** Believers are to be steadfast and holy while waiting for the return of Christ.

**Big Ideas:** We don't know when Jesus will return, but we know He will. We are forgiven and have no reason to fear Jesus' return. We cannot take advantage of God's grace and live however we please; we should strive to be holy and obedient as we wait for Jesus' return.

**OUTLINE:**

I. Personal Reflections on the Church (chs. 1–3)
II. Practical Instructions to the Church (chs. 4–5)

**c. AD 34**
Paul is converted

**c. AD 47–49**
Paul's first missionary journey

**c. AD 50**
The Jerusalem Council

**c. AD 50–53**
Paul's second missionary journey

**c. AD 51**
The church at Thessalonica is founded

**c. AD 50–54**
**1 Thessalonians written**

**c. AD 53–57**
Paul's third missionary journey

**AD 54–68**
Nero is Roman emperor

**c. AD 58**
Paul is arrested in Jerusalem

**c. AD 60–62**
Paul is imprisoned in Rome

**AD 64**
Great Fire of Rome; first Roman mass persecution of Christians

**c. AD 67**
Peter and Paul are executed

### GREETING

**1** Paul, [a]Silvanus, and Timothy,

To the church of the [b]Thessalonians in God the Father and the Lord Jesus Christ:

Grace to you and peace from God our Father and the Lord Jesus Christ.[1]

### THEIR GOOD EXAMPLE

2 [a]We give thanks to God always for you all, making mention of you in our prayers, 3 remembering without ceasing [a]your work of faith, [b]labor of love, and patience of hope in our Lord Jesus Christ in the sight of our God and Father, 4 knowing, beloved brethren, [a]your election by God. 5 For [a]our gospel did not come to you in word only, but also in power, [b]and in the Holy Spirit [c]and in much assurance, as you know what kind of men we were among you for your sake.

6 And [a]you became followers of us and of the Lord, having received the word in much affliction, [b]with joy of the Holy Spirit, 7 so that you became examples to all in Macedonia and Achaia who believe. 8 For from you the word of the Lord [a]has sounded forth, not only in Macedonia and Achaia, but also [b]in every place. Your faith toward God has gone out, so that we do not need to say anything. 9 For they themselves declare concerning us [a]what manner of entry we had to you, [b]and how you turned to God from idols to serve the living and true God, 10 and [a]to wait for His Son from heaven, whom He raised from the dead, *even* Jesus who delivers us [b]from the wrath to come.

### PAUL'S CONDUCT

*(cf. Acts 17:1–9)*

**2** For you yourselves know, brethren, that our coming to you was not in vain. 2 But even[1] after we had suffered before and were spitefully treated at [a]Philippi, as you know, we were [b]bold in our God to speak to you the gospel of God in much conflict. 3 [a]For our exhortation *did* not *come* from error or uncleanness, nor *was it* in deceit.

4 But as [a]we have been approved by God [b]to be entrusted with the gospel, even so we speak, [c]not as pleasing men, but God [d]who tests our hearts. 5 For [a]neither at any time did we use flattering words, as you know, nor a cloak for covetousness—[b]God *is* witness. 6 [a]Nor did we seek glory from men, either from you or from others, when [b]we might have [c]made demands [d]as apostles of Christ. 7 But [a]we were gentle among you, just as a nursing *mother* cherishes her own children. 8 So, affectionately longing for you, we were well pleased [a]to impart to you not only the gospel of God, but also [b]our own lives, because you had become dear to us. 9 For you remember, brethren, our [a]labor and toil; for laboring night and day, [b]that we might not be a burden to any of you, we preached to you the gospel of God.

> **2:9** Church leaders in New Testament times often took second jobs to support themselves and their families. Paul's second job was making tents, a skill he may have learned as a boy in Cilicia, which was known for exporting a special kind of cloth made from goat's hair—a cloth used to make tents.

10 [a]You *are* witnesses, and God *also,* [b]how devoutly and justly and blamelessly we behaved ourselves among you who believe; 11 as you know how we exhorted, and comforted, and charged[1] every one of you, as a father *does* his own children, 12 [a]that you would walk worthy of God [b]who calls you into His own kingdom and glory.

### THEIR CONVERSION

13 For this reason we also thank God [a]without ceasing, because when you [b]received the word of God which you heard from us, you welcomed *it* [c]not *as* the word of men, but as it is in truth, the word of God, which also effectively [d]works in you who believe. 14 For you, brethren, became imitators [a]of the churches of God which are in Judea in Christ Jesus. For [b]you also suffered the same things from your own countrymen, just as they *did* from the Judeans, 15 [a]who killed both the Lord Jesus and [b]their own prophets, and have persecuted us; and they do not please God [c]and are contrary to all men, 16 [a]forbidding us to speak to the Gentiles that they may be saved, so as always [b]to fill up *the measure of* their sins; [c]but wrath has come upon them to the uttermost.

### LONGING TO SEE THEM

17 But we, brethren, having been taken away from you for a short time [a]in presence, not in heart, endeavored more eagerly to see your face with great desire. 18 Therefore we wanted to come to you—even I, Paul, time and again—but [a]Satan hindered us. 19 For [a]what *is* our hope, or joy, or [b]crown of rejoicing? *Is it* not even you in the [c]presence of our Lord Jesus Christ [d]at His coming? 20 For you are our glory and joy.

**1:1** [a] 1 Pet. 5:12 [b] Acts 17:1–9 [1] NU-Text omits *from God our Father and the Lord Jesus Christ.* **1:2** [a] Rom. 1:8 **1:3** [a] John 6:29 [b] Rom. 16:6 **1:4** [a] Col. 3:12 **1:5** [a] Mark 16:20 [b] 2 Cor. 6:6 [c] Heb. 2:3 **1:6** [a] 1 Cor. 4:16; 11:1 [b] Acts 5:41; 13:52 **1:8** [a] Rom. 10:18 [b] Rom. 1:8; 16:19 **1:9** [a] 1 Thess. 2:1 [b] 1 Cor. 12:2 **1:10** [a] [Rom. 2:7] [b] Rom. 5:9 **2:2** [a] Acts 14:5; 16:19–24 [b] Acts 17:1–9 [1] NU-Text and M-Text omit *even.* **2:3** [a] 2 Cor. 7:2 **2:4** [a] 1 Cor. 7:25 [b] Titus 1:3 [c] Gal. 1:10 [d] Prov. 17:3 **2:5** [a] 2 Cor. 2:17 [b] Rom. 1:9 **2:6** [a] 1 Tim. 5:17 [b] 1 Cor. 9:4 [c] 2 Cor. 11:9 [d] 1 Cor. 9:1 **2:7** [a] 1 Cor. 2:3 **2:8** [a] Rom. 1:11 [b] 2 Cor. 12:15 **2:9** [a] Acts 18:3; 20:34, 35 [b] 2 Cor. 12:13 **2:10** [a] 1 Thess. 1:5 [b] 2 Cor. 7:2 **2:11** [1] NU-Text and M-Text read *implored.* **2:12** [a] Eph. 4:1 [b] 1 Cor. 1:9 **2:13** [a] 1 Thess. 1:2, 3 [b] Mark 4:20 [c] [Gal. 4:14] [d] [1 Pet. 1:23] **2:14** [a] Gal. 1:22 [b] Acts 17:5 **2:15** [a] Acts 2:23 [b] Matt. 5:12; 23:34, 35 [c] Esth. 3:8 **2:16** [a] Luke 11:52 [b] Gen. 15:16 [c] Matt. 24:6 **2:17** [a] 1 Cor. 5:3 **2:18** [a] Rom. 1:13; 15:22 **2:19** [a] 2 Cor. 1:14 [b] Prov. 16:31 [c] Jude 24 [d] 1 Cor. 15:23

### CONCERN FOR THEIR FAITH

**3** Therefore, when we could no longer endure it, we thought it good to be left in Athens alone, 2 and sent [a]Timothy, our brother and minister of God, and our fellow laborer in the gospel of Christ, to establish you and encourage you concerning your faith, 3 [a]that no one should be shaken by these afflictions; for you yourselves know that [b]we are appointed to this. 4 [a]For, in fact, we told you before when we were with you that we would suffer tribulation, just as it happened, and you know. 5 For this reason, when I could no longer endure it, I sent to know your faith, [a]lest by some means the tempter had tempted you, and [b]our labor might be in vain.

### ENCOURAGED BY TIMOTHY

6 [a]But now that Timothy has come to us from you, and brought us good news of your faith and love, and that you always have good remembrance of us, greatly desiring to see us, [b]as we also *to see* you— 7 therefore, brethren, in all our affliction and distress [a]we were comforted concerning you by your faith. 8 For now we live, if you [a]stand fast in the Lord.

9 For what thanks can we render to God for you, for all the joy with which we rejoice for your sake before our God, 10 night and day praying exceedingly that we may see your face [a]and perfect what is lacking in your faith?

### PRAYER FOR THE CHURCH

11 Now may our God and Father Himself, and our Lord Jesus Christ, [a]direct our way to you. 12 And may the Lord make you increase and [a]abound in love to one another and to all, just as we *do* to you, 13 so that He may establish [a]your hearts blameless in holiness before our God and Father at the coming of our Lord Jesus Christ with all His saints.

### PLEA FOR PURITY

**4** Finally then, brethren, we urge and exhort in the Lord Jesus [a]that you should abound more and more, [b]just as you received from us how you ought to walk and to please God; 2 for you know what commandments we gave you through the Lord Jesus.

3 For this is [a]the will of God, [b]your sanctification: [c]that you should abstain from sexual immorality; 4 [a]that each of you should know how to possess his own vessel in sanctification and honor, 5 [a]not in passion of lust, [b]like the Gentiles [c]who do not know God; 6 that no one should take advantage of and defraud his brother in this matter, because the Lord [a]*is* the avenger of all such, as we also forewarned you and testified. 7 For God did not call us to uncleanness, [a]but in holiness. 8 [a]Therefore he who rejects *this* does not reject man, but God, [b]who has also given[1] us His Holy Spirit.

### A BROTHERLY AND ORDERLY LIFE

9 But concerning brotherly love you have no need that I should write to you, for [a]you yourselves are taught by God [b]to love one another; 10 and indeed you do so toward all the brethren who are in all Macedonia. But we urge you, brethren, [a]that you increase more and more; 11 that you also aspire to lead a quiet life, [a]to mind your own business, and [b]to work with your own hands, as we commanded you, 12 [a]that you may walk properly toward those who are outside, and *that* you may lack nothing.

**3:2** [a] Rom. 16:21 **3:3** [a] Eph. 3:13 [b] Acts 9:16; 14:22 **3:4** [a] Acts 20:24 **3:5** [a] 1 Cor. 7:5 [b] Gal. 2:2 **3:6** [a] Acts 18:5 [b] Phil. 1:8 **3:7** [a] 2 Cor. 1:4 **3:8** [a] Phil. 4:1 **3:10** [a] 2 Cor. 13:9 **3:11** [a] Mark 1:3 **3:12** [a] Phil. 1:9 **3:13** [a] 2 Thess. 2:17 **4:1** [a] 1 Cor. 15:58 [b] Phil. 1:27 **4:3** [a] [Rom. 12:2] [b] Eph. 5:27 [c] [1 Cor. 6:15–20] **4:4** [a] Rom. 6:19 **4:5** [a] Col. 3:5 [b] Eph. 4:17, 18 [c] 1 Cor. 15:34 **4:6** [a] 2 Thess. 1:8 **4:7** [a] Lev. 11:44 **4:8** [a] Luke 10:16 [b] 1 Cor. 2:10 [1] NU-Text reads *who also gives.* **4:9** [a] [Jer. 31:33, 34] [b] Matt. 22:39 **4:10** [a] 1 Thess. 3:12 **4:11** [a] 2 Thess. 3:11 [b] Acts 20:35 **4:12** [a] Rom. 13:13

LIVE THE TRUTH

## BEING CHASTE

**4:4** God calls His followers to live in a way different from the world around us. One of those commands is to be sexually pure—to live with chastity. Simply put, *chastity* is refraining from all sexual contact outside of marriage. Sexual temptation makes living with chastity difficult and the world's ethics make it unpopular. But chastity is right, important, and wise; sex outside of marriage is full of negative consequences. It comes with an emotional, physical, and spiritual toll. Sex is a powerful gift inside of marriage; it can be an uncontrollable fire outside of marriage, destroying everything in its path.

Your body is the temple of the Holy Spirit. Therefore, it belongs not to you, but rather to God. That may sound strange but consider this: God created you (and your body), and as your Maker and the Owner of everything in the universe, He has every right to command how you are to live. But God isn't an unloving authoritarian. He is a loving Father. And as such, His commands to be holy, or set apart, in all areas of life, including sexuality, are for His glory *and* your good. Practicing self-control and living with chastity now *will* pay off now and in the future. More importantly, obeying God always brings you closer to Him.

### *THE COMFORT OF CHRIST'S COMING*

13 But I do not want you to be ignorant, breth-
ren, concerning those who have fallen asleep,
lest you sorrow [a]as others [b]who have no hope.
14 For [a]if we believe that Jesus died and rose
again, even so God will bring with Him [b]those
who sleep in Jesus.[1]

> **4:14** Some believe **sleep** here indicates that departed Christians are unconscious until the second coming. But the Bible indicates that to be absent from our body is to be present with the Lord Jesus (see 2 Cor. 5:8; Phil. 1:23; 1 Thess. 5:10).

15 For this we say to you [a]by the word of the
Lord, that [b]we who are alive *and* remain until
the coming of the Lord will by no means precede
those who are asleep. 16 For [a]the Lord Himself
will descend from heaven with a shout, with the
voice of an archangel, and with [b]the trumpet
of God. [c]And the dead in Christ will rise first.
17 [a]Then we who are alive *and* remain shall be
caught up together with them [b]in the clouds
to meet the Lord in the air. And thus [c]we shall
always be with the Lord. 18 [a]Therefore comfort
one another with these words.

> **SEEING JESUS IN THE SCRIPTURE**
>
> **4:17** Paul reminded the Thessalonians that one day Jesus will return to take His people home (see Rev. 21–22).

### *THE DAY OF THE LORD*

5 But concerning [a]the times and the seasons,
brethren, you have no need that I should write
to you. 2 For you yourselves know perfectly that
[a]the day of the Lord so comes as a thief in the
night. 3 For when they say, "Peace and safety!" then
[a]sudden destruction comes upon them, [b]as labor
pains upon a pregnant woman. And they shall not
escape. 4 [a]But you, brethren, are not in darkness, so
that this Day should overtake you as a thief. 5 You
are all [a]sons of light and sons of the day. We are
not of the night nor of darkness. 6 [a]Therefore let
us not sleep, as others *do,* but [b]let us watch and be
sober. 7 For [a]those who sleep, sleep at night, and
those who get drunk [b]are drunk at night. 8 But let
us who are of the day be sober, [a]putting on the
breastplate of faith and love, and *as* a helmet the
hope of salvation. 9 For [a]God did not appoint us to
wrath, [b]but to obtain salvation through our Lord
Jesus Christ, 10 [a]who died for us, that whether we
wake or sleep, we should live together with Him.
11 Therefore comfort each other and edify
one another, just as you also are doing.

**4:13** [a] Lev. 19:28 [b] [Eph. 2:12] **4:14** [a] 1 Cor. 15:13 [b] 1 Cor. 15:20, 23 [1] Or *those who through Jesus sleep* **4:15** [a] 1 Kin. 13:17; 20:35 [b] 1 Cor. 15:51, 52 **4:16** [a] [Matt. 24:30, 31] [b] [1 Cor. 15:52] [c] [1 Cor. 15:23] **4:17** [a] [1 Cor. 15:51–53] [b] Acts 1:9 [c] John 14:3; 17:24 **4:18** [a] 1 Thess. 5:11 **5:1** [a] Matt. 24:3 **5:2** [a] [2 Pet. 3:10] **5:3** [a] Is. 13:6–9 [b] Hos. 13:13 **5:4** [a] 1 John 2:8 **5:5** [a] Eph. 5:8 **5:6** [a] Matt. 25:5 [b] [1 Pet. 5:8] **5:7** [a] [Luke 21:34] [b] Acts 2:15 **5:8** [a] Eph. 6:14 **5:9** [a] Rom. 9:22 [b] [2 Thess. 2:13] **5:10** [a] 2 Cor. 5:15

KNOW THE TRUTH

## THE DOCTRINE OF THE FUTURE

### PART 2: THE RETURN OF JESUS

**5:23** An astounding number of fulfilled prophecies are recorded throughout the Bible and no one has fulfilled more of them than Jesus. His birthplace (Mic. 5:2), family lineage (Is. 9:6–7), Spirit-empowered ministry (Is. 11:1–2; 61:1–3), suffering (Is. 52:13—53:12), crucifixion (Zech. 12:10), and resurrection (Ps. 16:9–11) were all foretold and fulfilled. These fulfilled prophecies and others throughout the Bible give us tremendous confidence that the Bible is true and the prophecies yet to be fulfilled will surely come to pass. One such promise from Jesus is His return (see Mark 13:24–27).

While debate centers on *when* and *how* Christ will return, what is certain is He *will* return. His return will be both physical and visible (see Luke 21:27). It will initiate the first resurrection, the raising of all God's people into glorified bodies that cannot die (see 1 Cor. 15:20–58; 1 Thess. 4:14–18), and bring about a series of final acts of divine judgment resulting in the ultimate defeat and unending destruction of all evil (see Rev. 19:1—20:15). His return will be followed by the creation of a new heaven and new earth where God and His people will dwell together forever (see Rev. 21:1—22:5).

*For* **THE DOCTRINE OF THE FUTURE: PART 3: THE RESURRECTION OF THE DEAD,** *turn to John 6:39–40 on page 1078.*

### *VARIOUS EXHORTATIONS*

12 And we urge you, brethren, [a]to recognize
those who labor among you, and are over you
in the Lord and admonish you, 13 and to esteem
them very highly in love for their work's sake.
[a]Be at peace among yourselves.

**SEEING JESUS IN THE SCRIPTURE**

**5:12–13** Living in peace with other believers is obedience to Christ and can be done only in His power (see Mark 9:50).

14 Now we exhort you, brethren, [a]warn those
who are unruly, [b]comfort the fainthearted, [c]uphold
the weak, [d]be patient with all. 15 [a]See that no one
renders evil for evil to anyone, but always [b]pursue
what is good both for yourselves and for all.
16 [a]Rejoice always, 17 [a]pray without ceasing,
18 in everything give thanks; for this is the will
of God in Christ Jesus for you.
19 [a]Do not quench the Spirit. 20 [a]Do not de-
spise prophecies. 21 [a]Test all things; [b]hold fast
what is good. 22 Abstain from every form of evil.

### *BLESSING AND ADMONITION*

23 Now may [a]the God of peace Himself [b]sanc-
tify you completely; and may your whole spirit,
soul, and body [c]be preserved blameless at the
coming of our Lord Jesus Christ. 24 He who calls
you *is* [a]faithful, who also will [b]do *it*.
25 Brethren, pray for us.
26 Greet all the brethren with a holy kiss.
27 I charge you by the Lord that this epistle
be read to all the holy[1] brethren.
28 The grace of our Lord Jesus Christ *be* with
you. Amen.

**5:12** [a] 1 Cor. 16:18 **5:13** [a] Mark 9:50 **5:14** [a] 2 Thess. 3:6, 7, 11 [b] Heb. 12:12 [c] Rom. 14:1; 15:1 [d] Gal. 5:22 **5:15** [a] Lev. 19:18 [b] Gal. 6:10 **5:16** [a] [2 Cor. 6:10] **5:17** [a] Eph. 6:18 **5:19** [a] Eph. 4:30 **5:20** [a] 1 Cor. 14:1, 31 **5:21** [a] 1 John 4:1 [b] Phil. 4:8 **5:23** [a] Phil. 4:9 [b] 1 Thess. 3:13 [c] 1 Cor. 1:8, 9 **5:24** [a] [1 Cor. 10:13] [b] Phil. 1:6 **5:27** [1] NU-Text omits *holy*.

*The Second Epistle of Paul the Apostle to the*

# THESSALONIANS

| AUTHOR | KEY VERSE | READING TIME |
| --- | --- | --- |
| Paul | 2 Thessalonians 3:5 | 8 minutes |

Since Paul's first letter to the Thessalonians, the seeds of false doctrine were sown among the Thessalonians, causing them to waver in their faith. Paul wrote to remove these destructive seeds and replant seeds of truth. He began by commending the believers because of their faithfulness amid persecution. He reminded them that their present sufferings would be repaid with future glory. Paul then addressed the central matter of his letter: the misunderstanding spawned by the false teachers regarding the coming day of the Lord. Despite reports to the contrary, that day had not yet come. Certain events must first take place. Paul encouraged the Thessalonians to continue laboring for the gospel while they waited.

**Occasion:** Paul wrote this letter a few months after 1 Thessalonians while he was still in Corinth with Silvanus and Timothy (2 Thess. 1:1; cf. Acts 18:5).

**Main Point:** Believers can wait for the Lord's return with hope and confidence but are not to be passive while waiting.

**Big Ideas:** No one will miss Jesus' return. We should work hard to fulfill the mission Jesus gave us as we wait, using our time wisely. We need to stay strong in our faith and not be swayed by other ideas.

## OUTLINE:

I. Encouragement in Persecution (ch. 1)
II. Explanation of the Day of the Lord (ch. 2)
III. Exhortation to the Church (ch. 3)

**c. AD 34**
Paul is converted

**c. AD 47–49**
Paul's first missionary journey

**c. AD 50**
The Jerusalem Council

**c. AD 50–53**
Paul's second missionary journey

**c. AD 51**
The church at Thessalonica is founded

**c. AD 50–54**
1 Thessalonians written

**c. AD 50–54**
**2 Thessalonians written**

**c. AD 53–57**
Paul's third missionary journey

**AD 54–68**
Nero is Roman emperor

**c. AD 58**
Paul is arrested in Jerusalem

**c. AD 60–62**
Paul is imprisoned in Rome

**AD 64**
Great Fire of Rome; first Roman mass persecution of Christians

**c. AD 67**
Peter and Paul are executed

### GREETING

**1** Paul, Silvanus, and Timothy,

To the church of the Thessalonians in God our Father and the Lord Jesus Christ:

2 [a]Grace to you and peace from God our Father and the Lord Jesus Christ.

> **1:1 Paul** was in the middle of a very busy missionary journey when he wrote this second letter to the church in Thessalonica. Apparently, Paul wrote from Corinth, where he was staying after preaching in Athens, Berea, and Thessalonica. **Silvanus** (better known as Silas) and **Timothy** are mentioned because they were with Paul when he started the church in Thessalonica.

### GOD'S FINAL JUDGMENT AND GLORY

3 We are bound to thank God always for you, brethren, as it is fitting, because your faith grows exceedingly, and the love of every one of you all abounds toward each other, 4 so that [a]we ourselves boast of you among the churches of God [b]for your patience and faith [c]in all your persecutions and tribulations that you endure, 5 *which is* [a]manifest evidence of the righteous judgment of God, that you may be counted worthy of the kingdom of God, [b]for which you also suffer; 6 [a]since *it is* a righteous thing with God to repay with tribulation those who trouble you, 7 and to *give* you who are troubled [a]rest with us when [b]the Lord Jesus is revealed from heaven with His mighty angels, 8 in flaming fire taking vengeance on those who do not know God, and on those who do not obey the gospel of our Lord Jesus Christ. 9 [a]These shall be punished with everlasting destruction from the presence of the Lord and [b]from the glory of His power, 10 when He comes, in that Day, [a]to be [b]glorified in His saints and to be admired among all those who believe,[1] because our testimony among you was believed.

11 Therefore we also pray always for you that our God would [a]count you worthy of *this* calling, and fulfill all the good pleasure of *His* goodness and [b]the work of faith with power, 12 [a]that the name of our Lord Jesus Christ may be glorified in you, and you in Him, according to the grace of our God and the Lord Jesus Christ.

### THE GREAT APOSTASY

**2** Now, brethren, [a]concerning the coming of our Lord Jesus Christ [b]and our gathering together to Him, we ask you, 2 [a]not to be soon shaken in mind or troubled, either by spirit or by word or by letter, as if from us, as though the day of Christ[1] had come. 3 Let no one deceive you by any means; for *that Day will not come* [a]unless the falling away comes first, and [b]the man of sin[1] is revealed, [c]the son of perdition, 4 who opposes and [a]exalts himself [b]above all that is called God or that is worshiped, so that he sits as God[1] in the temple of God, showing himself that he is God.

5 Do you not remember that when I was still with you I told you these things? 6 And now you know what is restraining, that he may be revealed in his own time. 7 For [a]the mystery of lawlessness is already at work; only He[1] who now restrains *will do so* until He[2] is taken out of the way. 8 And then the lawless one will be revealed, [a]whom the Lord will consume [b]with the breath of His mouth and destroy [c]with the brightness of His coming. 9 The coming of the *lawless one* is [a]according to the working of Satan, with all power, [b]signs, and lying wonders, 10 and with all unrighteous deception among [a]those who perish, because they did not receive [b]the love of the truth, that they might be saved. 11 And [a]for this reason God will send them strong delusion, [b]that they should believe the lie, 12 that they all may be condemned who did not believe the truth but [a]had pleasure in unrighteousness.

### STAND FAST

13 But we are bound to give thanks to God always for you, brethren beloved by the Lord, because God [a]from the beginning [b]chose you for salvation [c]through sanctification by the Spirit and belief in the truth, 14 to which He called you by our gospel, for [a]the obtaining of the glory of our Lord Jesus Christ. 15 Therefore, brethren, [a]stand fast and hold [b]the traditions which you were taught, whether by word or our epistle.

16 Now may our Lord Jesus Christ Himself, and our God and Father, [a]who has loved us and given *us* everlasting consolation and [b]good hope by grace, 17 comfort your hearts [a]and establish you in every good word and work.

### PRAY FOR US

**3** Finally, brethren, [a]pray for us, that the word of the Lord may run *swiftly* and be glorified, just as *it is* with you, 2 and [a]that we may be delivered from unreasonable and wicked men; [b]for not all have faith.

**1:2** [a] 1 Cor. 1:3 **1:4** [a] 2 Cor. 7:4; [1 Thess. 2:19] [b] 1 Thess. 1:3 [c] 1 Thess. 2:14 **1:5** [a] Phil. 1:28 [b] 1 Thess. 2:14 **1:6** [a] Rev. 6:10 **1:7** [a] Rev. 14:13 [b] Jude 14 **1:9** [a] Phil. 3:19 [b] Deut. 33:2 **1:10** [a] Matt. 25:31 [b] John 17:10 [1] NU-Text and M-Text read *have believed.* **1:11** [a] Col. 1:12 [b] 1 Thess. 1:3 **1:12** [a] [Col. 3:17] **2:1** [a] [1 Thess. 4:15–17] [b] Matt. 24:31 **2:2** [a] Matt. 24:4 [1] NU-Text reads *the Lord.* **2:3** [a] 1 Tim. 4:1 [b] Dan. 7:25; 8:25; 11:36 [c] John 17:12 [1] NU-Text reads *lawlessness.* **2:4** [a] Is. 14:13, 14 [b] 1 Cor. 8:5 [1] NU-Text omits *as God.* **2:7** [a] 1 John 2:18 [1] Or *he* [2] Or *he* **2:8** [a] Dan. 7:10 [b] Is. 11:4 [c] Heb. 10:27 **2:9** [a] John 8:41 [b] Deut. 13:1 **2:10** [a] 2 Cor. 2:15 [b] 1 Cor. 16:22 **2:11** [a] Rom. 1:28 [b] 1 Tim. 4:1 **2:12** [a] Rom. 1:32 **2:13** [a] Eph. 1:4 [b] 1 Thess. 1:4 [c] [1 Pet. 1:2] **2:14** [a] 1 Pet. 5:10 **2:15** [a] 1 Cor. 16:13 [b] 1 Cor. 11:2 **2:16** [a] [Rev. 1:5] [b] 1 Pet. 1:3 **2:17** [a] 1 Cor. 1:8 **3:1** [a] Eph. 6:19 **3:2** [a] Rom. 15:31 [b] Acts 28:24

3 But [a]the Lord is faithful, who will establish
you and [b]guard *you* from the evil one. 4 And
[a]we have confidence in the Lord concerning
you, both that you do and will do the things we
command you.
5 Now may [a]the Lord direct your hearts into
the love of God and into the patience of Christ.

### *WARNING AGAINST IDLENESS*

6 But we command you, brethren, in the
name of our Lord Jesus Christ, [a]that you with-
draw [b]from every brother who walks [c]disorderly
and not according to the tradition which he[1]
received from us. 7 For you yourselves know
how you ought to follow us, for we were not
disorderly among you; 8 nor did we eat anyone's
bread free of charge, but worked with [a]labor and
toil night and day, that we might not be a bur-
den to any of you, 9 not because we do not have
[a]authority, but to make ourselves an example
of how you should follow us.
10 For even when we were with you, we
commanded you this: If anyone will not work,
neither shall he eat. 11 For we hear that there
are some who walk among you in a disorderly
manner, not working at all, but are [a]busybodies.
12 Now those who are such we command and
exhort through our Lord Jesus Christ [a]that they
work in quietness and eat their own bread.
13 But *as for* you, brethren, [a]do not grow wea-
ry *in* doing good. 14 And if anyone does not obey
our word in this epistle, note that person and
[a]do not keep company with him, that he may be
ashamed. 15 [a]Yet do not count *him* as an enemy,
[b]but admonish *him* as a brother.

### *BENEDICTION*

16 Now may [a]the Lord of peace Himself give
you peace always in every way. The Lord *be*
with you all.
17 [a]The salutation of Paul with my own hand,
which is a sign in every epistle; so I write.
18 [a]The grace of our Lord Jesus Christ *be* with
you all. Amen.

**3:17** Apparently, impostors had been sending out letters full of false teachings that they had signed Paul's name on. To make sure the people in Thessalonica knew this was a genuine letter, Paul signed his name to it.

**3:3** [a] 1 Cor. 1:9 [b] John 17:15 **3:4** [a] 2 Cor. 7:16 **3:5** [a] 1 Chr. 29:18 **3:6** [a] Rom. 16:17 [b] 1 Cor. 5:1 [c] 1 Thess. 4:11 [1] NU-Text and M-Text read *they.* **3:8** [a] 1 Thess. 2:9 **3:9** [a] 1 Cor. 9:4, 6–14 **3:11** [a] 1 Tim. 5:13; 1 Pet. 4:15 **3:12** [a] Eph. 4:28; 1 Thess. 4:11, 12 **3:13** [a] 2 Cor. 4:1; Gal. 6:9 **3:14** [a] Matt. 18:17 **3:15** [a] Lev. 19:17 [b] Titus 3:10 **3:16** [a] John 14:27; Rom. 15:33; Phil. 4:9 **3:17** [a] 1 Cor. 16:21 **3:18** [a] Rom. 16:20, 24; 1 Thess. 5:28

*The First Epistle of Paul the Apostle to*

# TIMOTHY

| AUTHOR | KEY VERSE | READING TIME |
|---|---|---|
| Paul | 1 Timothy 4:16 | 19 minutes |

Timothy was the son of a Greek father and Jewish mother, Eunice, who with her mother, Lois, were both known for their faith (Acts 16:1; 2 Tim. 1:5). If Timothy did not come to faith through his mother and grandmother, he did through Paul's ministry (1 Tim. 1:2, 18; 1 Cor. 4:17; 2 Tim. 1:2). Timothy then became one of the apostle's traveling companions, going with him to his hometown of Lystra on the second missionary journey (Acts 16:1–3), as well as Berea (Acts 17:14), Athens (Acts 17:15), and Corinth (Acts 18:5; 2 Cor. 1:19), before accompanying him on his trip to Jerusalem (Acts 20:4). Paul often used Timothy as his representative (Acts 19:22; 1 Cor. 4:17; 16:10; 2 Cor. 1:19; Phil. 2:19; 1 Thess. 3:2), and Timothy was with Paul during his first Roman imprisonment. Then after Paul's release, Timothy went to Philippi (Phil. 2:19–23). Now, the young pastor was facing a heavy burden of responsibility in the church at Ephesus (1 Tim. 1:3), prompting the older apostle to provide guidance. The task was challenging. False doctrine had to be purged, public worship safeguarded, and mature leadership developed. In addition, Timothy needed to be on his guard lest his youthfulness turn from being an asset into a liability to the gospel.

**Occasion:** Paul likely wrote 1 Timothy from Macedonia while Timothy was serving as his representative in Ephesus.

**Main Point:** The church must be built on the foundation of sound doctrine.

**Big Ideas:** We must hold to sound doctrine, not straying from the gospel of Jesus. Even if you're young, you can set a godly example for others in what you say and do. Be careful not to be taken in by the love of money.

## OUTLINE:

I. The Damage of False Doctrines (ch. 1)
II. The Directions for Public Worship (chs. 2–3)
III. The Defense against False Teachers (ch. 4)
IV. The Duties Toward Believers (ch. 5)
V. The Danger of Money (ch. 6)

**c. AD 34**
Paul is converted

**c. AD 47–49**
Paul's first missionary journey

**c. AD 50**
The Jerusalem Council

**c. AD 50–53**
Paul's second missionary journey

**c. AD 50**
Timothy joins Paul and Silas in Lystra

**c. AD 53–57**
Paul's third missionary journey

**c. AD 54**
Timothy again joins Paul's entourage

**AD 54–68**
Nero is Roman emperor

**c. AD 58**
Paul is arrested in Jerusalem

**c. AD 60–62**
Paul is imprisoned in Rome

**c. AD 62**
Paul is released

**c. AD 62–66**
**1 Timothy written**

**AD 64**
Great Fire of Rome; first Roman mass persecution of Christians

**c. AD 67**
Peter and Paul are executed

### GREETING

1 Paul, an apostle of Jesus Christ, by the com-
mandment of God our Savior and the Lord
Jesus Christ, our hope,

2 To Timothy, a [a]true son in the faith:

[b]Grace, mercy, *and* peace from God our Fa-
ther and Jesus Christ our Lord.

### NO OTHER DOCTRINE

3 As I urged you [a]when I went into Macedo-
nia—remain in Ephesus that you may charge
some [b]that they teach no other doctrine, 4 [a]nor
give heed to fables and endless genealogies,
which cause disputes rather than godly edifi-
cation which is in faith. 5 Now [a]the purpose of
the commandment is love [b]from a pure heart,
*from* a good conscience, and *from* sincere faith,
6 from which some, having strayed, have turned
aside to [a]idle talk, 7 desiring to be teachers of
the law, understanding neither what they say
nor the things which they affirm.
8 But we know that the law *is* [a]good if one
uses it lawfully, 9 knowing this: that the law is
not made for a righteous person, but for *the*
lawless and insubordinate, for *the* ungodly and
for sinners, for *the* unholy and profane, for mur-
derers of fathers and murderers of mothers, for
manslayers, 10 for fornicators, for sodomites, for
kidnappers, for liars, for perjurers, and if there
is any other thing that is contrary to sound doc-
trine, 11 according to the glorious gospel of the
[a]blessed God which was [b]committed to my trust.

### GLORY TO GOD FOR HIS GRACE

*(cf. Acts 8:1–3; 9:1–19)*

12 And I thank Christ Jesus our Lord who has
[a]enabled me, [b]because He counted me faithful,
[c]putting *me* into the ministry, 13 although [a]I was
formerly a blasphemer, a persecutor, and an
insolent man; but I obtained mercy because [b]I
did *it* ignorantly in unbelief. 14 [a]And the grace
of our Lord was exceedingly abundant, [b]with
faith and love which are in Christ Jesus. 15 [a]This
*is* a faithful saying and worthy of all acceptance,
that [b]Christ Jesus came into the world to save
sinners, of whom I am chief. 16 However, for
this reason I obtained mercy, that in me first
Jesus Christ might show all longsuffering, as a
pattern to those who are going to believe on Him
for everlasting life. 17 Now to [a]the King eternal,
[b]immortal, [c]invisible, to God [d]who alone is wise,[1]
[e]*be* honor and glory forever and ever. Amen.

**SEEING JESUS IN THE SCRIPTURE**

**1:15** Jesus' purpose on earth was to save sinners; our purpose is to point others to Him to be saved (see Matt. 9:13).

### FIGHT THE GOOD FIGHT

18 This charge I commit to you, son Tim-
othy, according to the prophecies previously
made concerning you, that by them you may
wage the good warfare, 19 having faith and a
good conscience, which some having rejected,
concerning the faith have suffered shipwreck,
20 of whom are [a]Hymenaeus and [b]Alexander,
whom I delivered to Satan that they may learn
not to [c]blaspheme.

### PRAY FOR ALL MEN

2 Therefore I exhort first of all that supplica-
tions, prayers, intercessions, *and* giving of
thanks be made for all men, 2 [a]for kings and [b]all
who are in authority, that we may lead a quiet
and peaceable life in all godliness and reverence.
3 For this *is* [a]good and acceptable in the sight
[b]of God our Savior, 4 [a]who desires all men to
be saved [b]and to come to the knowledge of the
truth. 5 [a]For *there is* one God and [b]one Mediator
between God and men, *the* Man Christ Jesus,

**2:4** God **desires all** people **to be saved**, although this doesn't mean He will force this to happen. Only those who believe in Christ will receive salvation (see Rom. 1:16–17; 3:21–26; 5:17).

6 [a]who gave Himself a ransom for all, to be tes-
tified in due time, 7 [a]for which I was appointed
a preacher and an apostle—I am speaking the
truth in Christ[1] *and* not lying—[b]a teacher of the
Gentiles in faith and truth.

**SEEING JESUS IN THE SCRIPTURE**

**2:5–6** Jesus is the Mediator bridging God and people, the one Job longed for (see Job 9:33).

### MEN AND WOMEN IN THE CHURCH

8 I desire therefore that the men pray [a]every-
where, [b]lifting up holy hands, without wrath
and doubting; 9 in like manner also, that the
[a]women adorn themselves in modest apparel,

**1:2** [a]Titus 1:4 [b]Gal. 1:3 **1:3** [a]Acts 20:1, 3 [b]Gal. 1:6, 7 **1:4** [a]Titus 1:14 **1:5** [a]Rom. 13:8–10 [b]Eph. 6:24 **1:6** [a]1 Tim. 6:4, 20 **1:8** [a]Rom. 7:12, 16 **1:11** [a]1 Tim. 6:15 [b]1 Cor. 9:17 **1:12** [a]1 Cor. 15:10 [b]1 Cor. 7:25 [c]Col. 1:25 **1:13** [a]Acts 8:3 [b]John 4:21 **1:14** [a]Rom. 5:20 [b]2 Tim. 1:13; 2:22 **1:15** [a]2 Tim. 2:11 [b]Matt. 1:21; 9:13 **1:17** [a]Ps. 10:16 [b]Rom. 1:23 [c]Heb. 11:27 [d]Rom. 16:27 [e]1 Chr. 29:11 [1]NU-Text reads *to the only God.* **1:20** [a]2 Tim. 2:17, 18 [b]2 Tim. 4:14 [c]Acts 13:45 **2:2** [a]Ezra 6:10 [b][Rom. 13:1] **2:3** [a]Rom. 12:2 [b]2 Tim. 1:9 **2:4** [a]Ezek. 18:23, 32 [b][John 17:3] **2:5** [a]Gal. 3:20 [b][Heb. 9:15] **2:6** [a]Mark 10:45 **2:7** [a]Eph. 3:7, 8 [b][Gal. 1:15, 16] [1]NU-Text omits *in Christ.* **2:8** [a]Luke 23:34 [b]Ps. 134:2 **2:9** [a]1 Pet. 3:3

1 TIMOTHY 1:15–16

## GRACE ALONE

STORY OF SCRIPTURE 56

### WHAT'S GOING ON?

Paul wrote to Timothy, acknowledging his own past as a blasphemer, persecutor, and violent man. Despite his history, he received God's mercy because he had acted in ignorance and unbelief. Paul's statement, "Christ Jesus came into the world to save sinners, of whom I am chief," is a powerful declaration of God's boundless grace. Paul viewed his transformation as a display of Christ's perfect patience, serving as an example to those who would believe in Him for eternal life.

This statement also fits into the story of Scripture as a concise declaration of the gospel. Christ came to save sinners, and although we'll continue to struggle in this life, it's all for a greater purpose.

### WHAT DOES THIS MEAN FOR ME?

Paul's statement wasn't just a personal confession, but it also communicated a fundamental of maturing in the Christian faith: the longer we follow Jesus, the more aware of our sins we become. It's critical we recognize and acknowledge our sinfulness before coming to Christ and our desperate need of Jesus. But how we view our sins after coming to Christ is also important. Paul saw himself *as* "chief" among sinners, not that he *was*. He knew he continued to sin. But he also knew God gave him mercy and grace through Jesus. Maturing in Christ is not to think we don't sin, neither is it believing we are defined by our sins. It's realizing how hopeless we are without Christ and a yearning for His return when sin will be no more.

### DID YOU CATCH THE PATTERN?

Grace and mercy didn't begin in the New Testament. Throughout the Old Testament, God showered grace and mercy on His people. He blessed Abraham, Isaac, Jacob, Moses, David, and so many others despite their failures. The reason is that grace and mercy are fundamental parts of God's perfect nature.

*For the next* Story of Scripture *reading and devotion, turn to Hebrews 11:1–40 on page 1255.*

with propriety and moderation, not with braided
hair or gold or pearls or costly clothing, 10 [a]but,
which is proper for women professing godliness,
with good works. 11 Let a woman learn in silence
with all submission. 12 And [a]I do not permit a
woman to teach or to have authority over a man,
but to be in silence. 13 For Adam was formed first,
then Eve. 14 And Adam was not deceived, but the
woman being deceived, fell into transgression.
15 Nevertheless she will be saved in childbearing
if they continue in faith, love, and holiness, with
self-control.

### *QUALIFICATIONS OF OVERSEERS*

3 This *is* a faithful saying: If a man desires the
position of a bishop,[1] he desires a good work.
2 A bishop then must be blameless, the husband
of one wife, temperate, sober-minded, of good
behavior, hospitable, able to teach; 3 not given
to wine, not violent, not greedy for money,[1] but
gentle, not quarrelsome, not covetous; 4 one who
rules his own house well, having *his* children in
submission with all reverence 5 (for if a man does
not know how to rule his own house, how will he
take care of the church of God?); 6 not a novice,
lest being puffed up with pride he fall into the
*same* condemnation as the devil. 7 Moreover he
must have a good testimony among those who
are outside, lest he fall into reproach and the
[a]snare of the devil.

**3:2** The idea of **blameless** isn't that **a bishop** is sinless, but rather that he displays consistent mature Christian conduct that gives no reason for anyone to accuse him of wrongdoing. What a **husband of one wife** means is debated. Many feel it means "a one-woman kind of man," indicating a lifestyle of fidelity. Others feel it's more specific and prohibits a divorced and remarried man from this position. Certainly, it is an exclusion of anyone who is sexually immoral or a polygamist.

**2:10** [a] 1 Pet. 3:4 **2:12** [a] 1 Cor. 14:34 **3:1** [1] Literally *overseer* **3:3** [1] NU-Text omits *not greedy for money.* **3:7** [a] 2 Tim. 2:26

### QUALIFICATIONS OF DEACONS

8 Likewise deacons *must be* reverent, not
double-tongued, [a]not given to much wine, not
greedy for money, 9 holding the mystery of the

> **3:8 Deacons** fill a second leadership position in the local assembly. The Greek word for *deacon* means "servant."

faith with a pure conscience. 10 But let these also
first be tested; then let them serve as deacons,
being *found* blameless. 11 Likewise, *their* wives
*must be* reverent, not slanderers, temperate,
faithful in all things. 12 Let deacons be the hus-
bands of one wife, ruling *their* children and their
own houses well. 13 For those who have served
well as deacons [a]obtain for themselves a good
standing and great boldness in the faith which
is in Christ Jesus.

### THE GREAT MYSTERY

14 These things I write to you, though I hope
to come to you shortly; 15 but if I am delayed, *I
write* so that you may know how you ought to
conduct yourself in the house of God, which
is the church of the living God, the pillar and
ground of the truth. 16 And without controversy
great is the mystery of godliness:

[a]God[1] was manifested in the
flesh,
[b]Justified in the Spirit,
[c]Seen by angels,
[d]Preached among the Gentiles,
[e]Believed on in the world,
[f]Received up in glory.

### THE GREAT APOSTASY

4 Now the Spirit expressly says that in latter times
some will depart from the faith, giving heed
[a]to deceiving spirits and doctrines of demons,
2 [a]speaking lies in hypocrisy, having their own
conscience [b]seared with a hot iron, 3 forbidding
to marry, *and commanding* to abstain from foods
which God created to be received with thanks-
giving by those who believe and know the truth.
4 For every creature of God *is* good, and nothing
is to be refused if it is received with thanksgiving;
5 for it is sanctified by the word of God and prayer.

### A GOOD SERVANT OF JESUS CHRIST

6 If you instruct the brethren in these things,
you will be a good minister of Jesus Christ, [a]nour-
ished in the words of faith and of the good doctrine
which you have carefully followed. 7 But [a]reject pro-
fane and old wives' fables, and [b]exercise yourself
toward godliness. 8 For [a]bodily exercise profits a
little, but godliness is profitable for all things, [b]hav-
ing promise of the life that now is and of that which
is to come. 9 This *is* a faithful saying and worthy of
all acceptance. 10 For to this *end* we both labor and
suffer reproach,[1] because we trust in the living God,
[a]who is *the* Savior of all men, especially of those
who believe. 11 These things command and teach.

### TAKE HEED TO YOUR MINISTRY

12 Let no one despise your youth, but be an
[a]example to the believers in word, in conduct, in
love, in spirit,[1] in faith, in purity. 13 Till I come, give
attention to reading, to exhortation, to doctrine.
14 [a]Do not neglect the gift that is in you, which was
given to you by prophecy [b]with the laying on of
the hands of the eldership. 15 Meditate on these
things; give yourself entirely to them, that your
progress may be evident to all. 16 Take heed to
yourself and to the doctrine. Continue in them,

**3:8** [a] Ezek. 44:21 **3:13** [a] Matt. 25:21 **3:16** [a] [John 1:14; 1 Pet. 1:20; 1 John 1:2; 3:5, 8] [b] [Matt. 3:16; Rom. 1:4] [c] Matt. 28:2 [d] Acts 10:34; Rom. 10:18 [e] Rom. 16:26; 2 Cor. 1:19; Col. 1:6, 23 [f] Luke 24:51 [1] NU-Text reads *Who*. **4:1** [a] 2 Tim. 3:13; Rev. 16:14 **4:2** [a] Matt. 7:15 [b] Eph. 4:19 **4:6** [a] 2 Tim. 3:14 **4:7** [a] 2 Tim. 2:16; Titus 1:14 [b] Heb. 5:14 **4:8** [a] 1 Cor. 8:8 [b] Ps. 37:9 **4:10** [a] Ps. 36:6 [1] NU-Text reads *we labor and strive*. **4:12** [a] Phil. 3:17; Titus 2:7; 1 Pet. 5:3 [1] NU-Text omits *in spirit*. **4:14** [a] 2 Tim. 1:6 [b] Acts 6:6; 1 Tim. 5:22

APPLY THE TRUTH

## PHYSICAL HEALTH

**4:8** Bodily exercise only profits a little because it isn't eternal. This body isn't supposed to last forever. We get old, we get sick, or we experience things beyond our control. We aren't created for this earth. We are created for eternity.

That doesn't mean we shouldn't take care of ourselves to the best of our ability. God cares about our spiritual, mental, *and* physical health. The amazing thing is, God views us a whole person: mind, body, and spirit. He invites us into bringing our whole self to Him as a form of worship and praise.

So, hit the gym. Go for a walk. Set a fitness goal and accomplish it. Learn to place your whole life—mind, body, and spirit—on the altar to God as your way of doing all things as unto Him. You may find new ways to encounter your Creator when you live like this. But be careful not to make your fitness your primary identity. Remember, bodily exercise only profits a *little*. We must remember first and foremost we are children of God. All other things are activities, not our identity.

for in doing this you will save both yourself and those who hear you.

### *TREATMENT OF CHURCH MEMBERS*

**5** Do not rebuke an older man, but exhort *him* as a father, younger men as brothers, 2 older women as mothers, younger women as sisters, with all purity.

### *HONOR TRUE WIDOWS*

3 Honor widows who are really widows. 4 But if any widow has children or grandchildren, let them first learn to show piety at home and [a]to repay their parents; for this is good and[1] acceptable before God. 5 Now she who is really a widow, and left alone, trusts in God and continues in supplications and prayers [a]night and day. 6 But she who lives in pleasure is dead while she lives. 7 And these things command, that they may be blameless. 8 But if anyone does not provide for his own, [a]and especially for those of his household, [b]he has denied the faith [c]and is worse than an unbeliever.

> **5:3** Here, Paul's was repeating the law God had given Moses centuries earlier. A **widow** usually lived with her husband's family or with one of her children. However, if she had no family to live with, the church was responsible for taking care of her.

9 Do not let a widow under sixty years old be taken into the number, *and not unless* she has been the wife of one man, 10 well reported for good works: if she has brought up children, if she has lodged strangers, if she has washed the saints' feet, if she has relieved the afflicted, if she has diligently followed every good work.

11 But refuse *the* younger widows; for when they have begun to grow wanton against Christ, they desire to marry, 12 having condemnation because they have cast off their first faith. 13 And besides they learn *to be* idle, wandering about from house to house, and not only idle but also gossips and busybodies, saying things which they ought not. 14 Therefore I desire that *the* younger *widows* marry, bear children, manage the house, give no opportunity to the adversary to speak reproachfully. 15 For some have already turned aside after Satan. 16 If any believing man or[1] woman has widows, let them relieve them, and do not let the church be burdened, that it may relieve those who are really widows.

### *HONOR THE ELDERS*

17 Let the elders who rule well be counted worthy of double honor, especially those who labor in the word and doctrine. 18 For the Scripture says, [a]"You shall not muzzle an ox while it treads out the grain,"[1] and, [b]"The laborer *is* worthy of his wages."[2] 19 Do not receive an accusation against an elder except [a]from two or three witnesses. 20 Those who are sinning rebuke in the presence of all, that the rest also may fear.

21 I charge *you* before God and the Lord Jesus Christ and the elect angels that you observe these things without [a]prejudice, doing nothing with partiality. 22 Do not lay hands on anyone hastily, nor [a]share in other people's sins; keep yourself pure.

23 No longer drink only water, but use a little wine for your stomach's sake and your frequent infirmities.

24 Some men's sins are [a]clearly evident, preceding *them* to judgment, but those of some *men* follow later. 25 Likewise, the good works *of some* are clearly evident, and those that are otherwise cannot be hidden.

### *HONOR MASTERS*

**6** Let as many [a]bondservants as are under the yoke count their own masters worthy of all honor, so that the name of God and *His* doctrine may not be blasphemed. 2 And those who have believing masters, let them not despise *them* because they are brethren, but rather serve *them* because those who are benefited are believers and beloved. Teach and exhort these things.

### *ERROR AND GREED*

3 If anyone teaches otherwise and does not consent to [a]wholesome words, *even* the words of our Lord Jesus Christ, [b]and to the doctrine which accords with godliness, 4 he is proud, knowing nothing, but is obsessed with disputes and arguments over words, from which come envy, strife, reviling, evil suspicions, 5 useless wranglings[1] of men of corrupt minds and destitute of the truth, who suppose that godliness is a *means of* gain. From [a]such withdraw yourself.[2]

6 Now godliness with [a]contentment is great gain. 7 For we brought nothing into *this* world, *and it is* [a]certain[1] we can carry nothing out. 8 And having food and clothing, with these we shall be [a]content. 9 But those who desire to be rich fall into temptation and a snare, and *into* many foolish and harmful lusts which drown men in destruction and perdition. 10 For the love of money is a root of all *kinds of* evil, for

> **6:10** Money, in and of itself, is not a problem. The **love of money** is. Christians can be so blinded by greed that they no longer see the need for holy living. A life focused on material things brings only pain.

**5:4** [a] Gen. 45:10 [1] NU-Text and M-Text omit *good and.* **5:5** [a] Acts 26:7 **5:8** [a] Is. 58:7; 2 Cor. 12:14 [b] 2 Tim. 3:5 [c] Matt. 18:17 **5:16** [1] NU-Text omits *man or.* **5:18** [a] Deut. 25:4 [b] Luke 10:7 [1] Deuteronomy 25:4 [2] Luke 10:7 **5:19** [a] Deut. 17:6; 19:15 **5:21** [a] Deut. 1:17 **5:22** [a] Eph. 5:6, 7 **5:24** [a] Gal. 5:19–21 **6:1** [a] Eph. 6:5 **6:3** [a] 2 Tim. 1:13 [b] Titus 1:1 **6:5** [a] 2 Tim. 3:5 [1] NU-Text and M-Text read *constant friction.* [2] NU-Text omits this sentence. **6:6** [a] Heb. 13:5 **6:7** [a] Job 1:21 [1] NU-Text omits *and it is certain.* **6:8** [a] Prov. 30:8, 9

which some have strayed from the faith in their
greediness, and pierced themselves through
with many sorrows.

### THE GOOD CONFESSION

11 But you, O man of God, flee these things
and pursue righteousness, godliness, faith, love,
patience, gentleness. 12 Fight the good fight of
faith, lay hold on eternal life, to which you were
also called and have confessed the good confes-
sion in the presence of many witnesses. 13 I urge
you in the sight of God who gives life to all things,
and *before* Christ Jesus [a]who witnessed the good
confession before Pontius Pilate, 14 that you keep
*this* commandment without spot, blameless
until our Lord Jesus Christ's appearing, 15 which
He will manifest in His own time, *He who is* the
blessed and only Potentate, the King of kings
and Lord of lords, 16 who alone has immortality,
dwelling in [a]unapproachable light, [b]whom no
man has seen or can see, to whom *be* honor and
everlasting power. Amen.

### INSTRUCTIONS TO THE RICH

17 Command those who are rich in this pres-
ent age not to be haughty, nor to trust in uncer-
tain [a]riches but in the living God, who gives us
richly all things [b]to enjoy. 18 *Let them* do good,
that they be rich in good works, ready to give,
willing to share, 19 [a]storing up for themselves a
good foundation for the time to come, that they
may lay hold on eternal life.

### GUARD THE FAITH

20 O Timothy! [a]Guard what was committed
to your trust, [b]avoiding the profane *and* idle
babblings and contradictions of what is falsely
called knowledge— 21 by professing it some have
strayed concerning the faith.

Grace *be* with you. Amen.

**6:13** [a] John 18:36, 37 **6:16** [a] Dan. 2:22 [b] John 6:46 **6:17** [a] Jer. 9:23; 48:7 [b] Eccl. 5:18, 19 **6:19** [a] [Matt. 6:20, 21; 19:21] **6:20** [a] [2 Tim. 1:12, 14] [b] Titus 1:14

*The Second Epistle of Paul the Apostle to*

# TIMOTHY

| AUTHOR | KEY VERSE | READING TIME |
|---|---|---|
| Paul | 2 Timothy 1:12 | 14 minutes |

Someone in prison is the last person one would expect to write a letter of encouragement, but that is what Paul did. The apostle was in a cold Roman prison cell (2 Tim. 4:13) without hope of acquittal despite the success of his initial defense. Fearing for their own lives, the Asian believers had failed to support Paul during this second Roman imprisonment, leaving him feeling abandoned (1:15; 4:16). Yet, when Paul wrote to Timothy, his message was not one of despair but rather one of hope. Paul began by assuring Timothy of his continuing love and prayers before reminding him of his spiritual heritage and responsibilities. The one who perseveres—whether as a soldier, athlete, farmer, or minister of Jesus Christ—will reap the reward. Paul warned Timothy that sound teaching would come under attack as people deserted the truth for words their itching ears desired (4:3). But Timothy had Paul's example to guide him and God's Word to fortify him as he faced growing opposition and pursued gospel opportunities in the last days.

**Occasion:** Paul wrote this epistle from a prison in Rome, hoping Timothy would be able to visit him before the approaching winter (2 Tim. 4:21).

**Main Point:** No matter what the obstacle or how hard the situation, believers are to continue in the faith.

**Big Ideas:** We know the Bible is true because it is inspired by God. People will always oppose the gospel, often outside the church but sometimes inside it too. We can be strong in our faith because God has given us a spirit of power.

## OUTLINE:

I. Faithfulness in Ministry (ch. 1)
II. Patterns of Ministry (ch. 2)
III. Challenges to Ministry (ch. 3)
IV. Encouragement for Ministry (ch. 4)

**c. AD 34**
Paul is converted

**c. AD 47–49**
Paul's first missionary journey

**c. AD 50**
The Jerusalem Council

**c. AD 50–53**
Paul's second missionary journey

**c. AD 50**
Timothy joins Paul and Silas in Lystra

**c. AD 53–57**
Paul's third missionary journey

**c. AD 54**
Timothy again joins Paul's entourage

**AD 54–68**
Nero is Roman emperor

**c. AD 58**
Paul is arrested in Jerusalem

**c. AD 60–62**
Paul is imprisoned in Rome

**c. AD 62**
Paul is released

**c. AD 62–66**
1 Timothy written

**AD 64**
Great Fire of Rome; first Roman mass persecution of Christians

**c. AD 67**
Paul is imprisoned again in Rome

**c. AD 67**
**2 Timothy written**

**c. AD 67**
Peter and Paul are executed

### GREETING

**1** Paul, an apostle of Jesus Christ[1] by the will of God, according to the [a]promise of life which is in Christ Jesus,

[2] To Timothy, a [a]beloved son:

Grace, mercy, *and* peace from God the Father and Christ Jesus our Lord.

### TIMOTHY'S FAITH AND HERITAGE

[3] I thank God, whom I serve with a pure conscience, as *my* [a]forefathers *did,* as without ceasing I remember you in my prayers night and day, [4] greatly desiring to see you, being mindful of your tears, that I may be filled with joy, [5] when I call to remembrance [a]the genuine faith that is in you, which dwelt first in your grandmother Lois and [b]your mother Eunice, and I am persuaded is in you also. [6] Therefore I remind you [a]to stir up the gift of God which is in you through the laying on of my hands. [7] For [a]God has not given us a spirit of fear, [b]but of power and of love and of a sound mind.

### NOT ASHAMED OF THE GOSPEL

[8] [a]Therefore do not be ashamed of [b]the testimony of our Lord, nor of me [c]His prisoner, but share with me in the sufferings for the gospel according to the power of God, [9] who has saved us and called *us* with a holy calling, [a]not according to our works, but [b]according to His own purpose and grace which was given to us in Christ Jesus [c]before time began, [10] but [a]has now been revealed by the appearing of our Savior Jesus Christ, *who* has abolished death and brought life and immortality to light through the gospel, [11] [a]to which I was appointed a preacher, an apostle, and a teacher of the Gentiles.[1] [12] For this reason I also suffer these things; nevertheless I am not ashamed, [a]for I know whom I have believed and am persuaded that He is able to keep what I have committed to Him until that Day.

**SEEING JESUS IN THE SCRIPTURE**

**1:8** Jesus suffered on our behalf to provide forgiveness of sin and to be an example for our lives (see Is. 53:5; John 16:33).

### BE LOYAL TO THE FAITH

[13] [a]Hold fast [b]the pattern of [c]sound words which you have heard from me, in faith and love which are in Christ Jesus. [14] That good thing which was committed to you, keep by the Holy Spirit who dwells in us.

[15] This you know, that all those in Asia have turned away from me, among whom are Phygellus and Hermogenes. [16] The Lord grant mercy to the [a]household of Onesiphorus, for he often refreshed me, and was not ashamed of my chain; [17] but when he arrived in Rome, he sought me out very zealously and found *me.* [18] The Lord [a]grant to him that he may find mercy from the Lord [b]in that Day—and you know very well how many ways he [c]ministered *to me*[1] at Ephesus.

**1:15 Asia** was the name of a Roman province located in what is now Turkey. At the time Paul wrote this letter, Nero, the Roman emperor, was increasing his persecution of Christians throughout the empire.

### BE STRONG IN GRACE

**2** You therefore, [a]my son, [b]be strong in the grace that is in Christ Jesus. [2] And the things that you have heard from me among many witnesses, commit these to faithful men who will be able to teach others also. [3] You therefore must [a]endure[1] hardship [b]as a good soldier of Jesus Christ. [4] [a]No one engaged in warfare entangles himself with the affairs of *this* life, that he may please him who enlisted him as a soldier. [5] And also [a]if anyone competes in athletics, he is not crowned unless he competes according to the rules. [6] The hard-working farmer must be first to partake of the crops. [7] Consider what I say, and may[1] the Lord [a]give you understanding in all things.

[8] Remember that Jesus Christ, [a]of the seed of David, [b]was raised from the dead [c]according to my gospel, [9] [a]for which I suffer trouble as an evildoer, [b]*even* to the point of chains; [c]but the word of God is not chained. [10] Therefore [a]I endure all things for the sake of the elect, [b]that they also may obtain the salvation which is in Christ Jesus with eternal glory.

[11] *This is* a faithful saying:

For [a]if we died with *Him,*
We shall also live with *Him.*
12 [a]If we endure,
We shall also reign with *Him.*
[b]If we deny *Him,*
He also will deny us.
13 If we are faithless,
He remains faithful;
He [a]cannot deny Himself.

**1:1** [a] Titus 1:2 [1] NU-Text and M-Text read *Christ Jesus.* **1:2** [a] 1 Tim. 1:2; 2 Tim. 2:1; Titus 1:4 **1:3** [a] Acts 24:14 **1:5** [a] 1 Tim. 1:5; 4:6 [b] Acts 16:1 **1:6** [a] 1 Tim. 4:14 **1:7** [a] John 14:27; Rom. 8:15; 1 John 4:18 [b] [Acts 1:8] **1:8** [a] [Mark 8:38; Luke 9:26; Rom. 1:16]; 2 Tim. 1:12, 16 [b] 1 Tim. 2:6 [c] Eph. 3:1; 2 Tim. 1:16 **1:9** [a] [Rom. 3:20]; Eph. 2:8, 9 [b] Rom. 8:28 [c] Rom. 16:25; Eph. 1:4; Titus 1:2 **1:10** [a] Eph. 1:9 **1:11** [a] Acts 9:15 [1] NU-Text omits *of the Gentiles.* **1:12** [a] 1 Pet. 4:19 **1:13** [a] 2 Tim. 3:14; Titus 1:9 [b] Rom. 2:20; 6:17 [c] 1 Tim. 6:3 **1:16** [a] 2 Tim. 4:19 **1:18** [a] Matt. 6:4; Mark 9:41 [b] 2 Thess. 1:10 [c] Heb. 6:10 [1] *To me* is from the Vulgate and a few Greek manuscripts. **2:1** [a] 1 Tim. 1:2 [b] Eph. 6:10 **2:3** [a] 2 Tim. 4:5 [b] 1 Cor. 9:7; 1 Tim. 1:18 [1] NU-Text reads *You must share.* **2:4** [a] [2 Pet. 2:20] **2:5** [a] [1 Cor. 9:25] **2:7** [a] Prov. 2:6 [1] NU-Text reads *the Lord will give you.* **2:8** [a] Rom. 1:3, 4 [b] 1 Cor. 15:4 [c] Rom. 2:16 **2:9** [a] Acts 9:16 [b] Eph. 3:1 [c] Acts 28:31 **2:10** [a] Eph. 3:13 [b] 2 Cor. 1:6 **2:11** [a] Rom. 6:5, 8 **2:12** [a] [Rom. 5:17; 8:17] [b] Matt. 10:33 **2:13** [a] Num. 23:19

### APPROVED AND DISAPPROVED WORKERS

14 Remind *them* of these things, [a]charging *them* before the Lord not to strive about words to no profit, to the ruin of the hearers. 15 [a]Be diligent to present yourself approved to God, a worker who does not need to be ashamed, rightly dividing the word of truth. 16 But shun profane *and* idle babblings, for they will increase to more ungodliness. 17 And their message will spread like cancer. [a]Hymenaeus and Philetus are of this sort, 18 who have strayed concerning the truth, [a]saying that the resurrection is already past; and they overthrow the faith of some. 19 Nevertheless [a]the solid foundation of God stands, having this seal: "The Lord [b]knows those who are His," and, "Let everyone who names the name of Christ[1] depart from iniquity."

20 But in a great house there are not only [a]vessels of gold and silver, but also of wood and clay, some for honor and some for dishonor. 21 Therefore if anyone cleanses himself from the latter, he will be a vessel for honor, sanctified and useful for the Master, [a]prepared for every good work. 22 [a]Flee also youthful lusts; but pursue righteousness, faith, love, peace with those who call on the Lord out of a pure heart. 23 But avoid foolish and ignorant disputes, knowing that they generate strife. 24 And [a]a servant of the Lord must not quarrel but be gentle to all, [b]able to teach, [c]patient, 25 [a]in humility correcting those who are in opposition, [b]if God perhaps will grant them repentance, [c]so that they may know the truth, 26 and *that* they may come to their senses *and* [a]*escape* the snare of the devil, having been taken captive by him to *do* his will.

### PERILOUS TIMES AND PERILOUS MEN

**3** But know this, that [a]in the last days perilous times will come: 2 For men will be lovers of themselves, lovers of money, boasters, proud, blasphemers, disobedient to parents, unthankful, unholy, 3 unloving, unforgiving, slanderers, without self-control, brutal, despisers of good, 4 [a]traitors, headstrong, haughty, lovers of pleasure rather than lovers of God, 5 [a]having a form of godliness but [b]denying its power. And [c]from such people turn away! 6 For [a]of this sort are those who creep into households and make captives of gullible women loaded down with sins, led away by various lusts, 7 always learning and never able [a]to come to the knowledge of the truth. 8 [a]Now as Jannes and Jambres resisted Moses, so do these also resist the truth: [b]men of corrupt minds, [c]disapproved concerning the faith; 9 but they will progress no further, for their folly will be manifest to all, [a]as theirs also was.

### THE MAN OF GOD AND THE WORD OF GOD

10 [a]But you have carefully followed my doctrine, manner of life, purpose, faith, longsuffering, love, perseverance, 11 persecutions, afflictions, which happened to me [a]at Antioch, [b]at Iconium, [c]at Lystra—what persecutions I endured. And [d]out of *them* all the Lord delivered me. 12 Yes, and [a]all who desire to live godly in

> **3:11** As far as city authorities were concerned, Paul overstayed his welcome in each city he visited. When people began responding to the message Paul preached in **Antioch**, city officials ran him out of town. His next stop was **Iconium**. When the people there started converting to Christianity, Paul was forced to leave out of fear for his life. His next stop was **Lystra**, Timothy's hometown.

**2:14** [a]Titus 3:9 **2:15** [a]2 Pet. 1:10 **2:17** [a]1 Tim. 1:20 **2:18** [a]1 Cor. 15:12 **2:19** [a][1 Cor. 3:11] [b][Nah. 1:7] [1]NU-Text and M-Text read *the Lord.* **2:20** [a]Rom. 9:21 **2:21** [a]2 Tim. 3:17 **2:22** [a]1 Tim. 6:11 **2:24** [a]Titus 3:2 [b]Titus 1:9 [c]1 Tim. 3:3 **2:25** [a]Gal. 6:1 [b]Acts 8:22 [c]1 Tim. 2:4 **2:26** [a]1 Tim. 3:7 **3:1** [a]1 Tim. 4:1 **3:4** [a]2 Pet. 2:10 **3:5** [a]Titus 1:16 [b]1 Tim. 5:8 [c]2 Thess. 3:6 **3:6** [a]Matt. 23:14 **3:7** [a]1 Tim. 2:4 **3:8** [a]Ex. 7:11, 12, 22; 8:7; 9:11 [b]1 Tim. 6:5 [c]Rom. 1:28 **3:9** [a]Ex. 7:11, 12; 8:18; 9:11 **3:10** [a]1 Tim. 4:6 **3:11** [a]Acts 13:44–52 [b]Acts 14:1–6, 19 [c]Acts 14:8–20 [d]Ps. 34:19 **3:12** [a][Ps. 34:19]

LIVE THE TRUTH

## BEING PURE

**2:22** Purity simply means staying free of sin. We often use it to refer to sexual purity, but it's not limited to that area of our lives. God wants us to stay pure of sin in every area of our lives, including our thoughts and desires. Anything we desire that's of the world and not of God will lead us to sin, brokenness, and impurity. Here, Paul reminds us that young people especially should take care to avoid the world's temptations, but believers of all ages should strive for purity.

God knows keeping a pure heart, mind, and body protects us from all manner of temptation, hurt, and pain. But He also tells us the path to true fulfillment and joy. Purity gets us halfway—it protects and preserves us from evil—but we aren't called to live neutrally. We're called to live like Jesus. Rather than pursuing evil, impure desires, we are to pursue righteousness, faith, love, and peace. Purity safeguards room in our minds, hearts, and conduct to be filled by these godly characteristics.

Christ Jesus will suffer persecution. 13 [a]But evil men and impostors will grow worse and worse, deceiving and being deceived. 14 But you must [a]continue in the things which you have learned and been assured of, knowing from whom you have learned *them,* 15 and that from childhood you have known [a]the Holy Scriptures, which are able to make you wise for salvation through faith which is in Christ Jesus.

**SEEING JESUS IN THE SCRIPTURE**

**3:15** All Scripture points to Jesus and salvation found only in Him, just as He said (see John 5:39).

16 [a]All Scripture *is* given by inspiration of God, [b]and *is* profitable for doctrine, for reproof, for correction, for instruction in righteousness, 17 [a]that the man of God may be complete, [b]thoroughly equipped for every good work.

### *PREACH THE WORD*

**4** I [a]charge *you* therefore before God and the Lord Jesus Christ, [b]who will judge the living and the dead at[1] His appearing and His kingdom: 2 Preach the word! Be ready in season *and* out of season. [a]Convince, [b]rebuke, [c]exhort, with all longsuffering and teaching. 3 [a]For the time will come when they will not endure [b]sound doctrine, [c]but according to their own desires, *because* they have itching ears, they will heap up for themselves teachers; 4 and they will turn *their* ears away from the truth, and [a]be turned aside to fables. 5 But you be watchful in all things, [a]endure afflictions, do the work of [b]an evangelist, fulfill your ministry.

### *PAUL'S VALEDICTORY*

6 For [a]I am already being poured out as a drink offering, and the time of [b]my departure is at hand. 7 [a]I have fought the good fight, I have finished the race, I have kept the faith. 8 Finally, there is laid up for me [a]the crown of righteousness, which the Lord, the righteous [b]Judge, will give to me [c]on that Day, and not to me only but also to all who have loved His appearing.

### *THE ABANDONED APOSTLE*

9 Be diligent to come to me quickly; 10 for [a]Demas has forsaken me, [b]having loved this present world, and has departed for Thessalonica—Crescens for Galatia, Titus for Dalmatia. 11 Only Luke is with me. Get [a]Mark and bring him with you, for he is useful to me for ministry. 12 And [a]Tychicus I have sent to Ephesus. 13 Bring the cloak that I left with Carpus at Troas when you come—and the books, especially the parchments.

14 [a]Alexander the coppersmith did me much harm. May the Lord repay him according to his works. 15 You also must beware of him, for he has greatly resisted our words.

**3:13** [a] 2 Thess. 2:11 **3:14** [a] 2 Tim. 1:13 **3:15** [a] John 5:39 **3:16** [a] [2 Pet. 1:20] [b] Rom. 4:23; 15:4 **3:17** [a] 1 Tim. 6:11 [b] 2 Tim. 2:21 **4:1** [a] 1 Tim. 5:21 [b] Acts 10:42 [1] NU-Text omits *therefore* and reads *and by* for *at.* **4:2** [a] Titus 2:15 [b] 1 Tim. 5:20 [c] 1 Tim. 4:13 **4:3** [a] 2 Tim. 3:1 [b] 1 Tim. 1:10 [c] 2 Tim. 3:6 **4:4** [a] 1 Tim. 1:4 **4:5** [a] 2 Tim. 1:8 [b] Acts 21:8 **4:6** [a] Phil. 2:17 [b] [Phil. 1:23] **4:7** [a] 1 Cor. 9:24–27 **4:8** [a] James 1:12 [b] John 5:22 [c] 2 Tim. 1:12 **4:10** [a] Col. 4:14 [b] 1 John 2:15 **4:11** [a] Acts 12:12, 25; 15:37–39 **4:12** [a] Acts 20:4 **4:14** [a] 1 Tim. 1:20

KNOW THE TRUTH

## THE DOCTRINE OF SCRIPTURE

### PART 5: THE INSPIRATION OF SCRIPTURE

**3:14–17** The phrase "is given by inspiration of God" in verse 16 is one word in Greek. This one word could also be translated "God-breathed." It means what's written in the Bible doesn't come from a person's imagination. All that's in the Bible comes from the mind of God alone. Or, put another way, the Bible is of divine origin, not human origin.

Second Peter 1:20–21 explains the writers of Scripture were "moved by the Spirit" as they wrote. In other words, the writers faithfully wrote down what the Holy Spirit guided them to write. This is why the Bible's writers repeatedly refer to Scripture's words as being from God. Moses (e.g., Deut. 1:3), the psalmists (e.g., Ps. 119:16), the prophets (e.g., Is. 55:11; Jer. 30:1–3; Ezek. 34:1–3), Jesus (e.g., Mark 7:8–13) and the New Testament writers (e.g., Heb. 4:12) all called Scripture God's words. The Bible's absolute authority is based on it being from God alone. The Bible's every word is inspired by the Holy Spirit of God. When we obey the Word of God, we are obeying the God of the Word.

*For* **THE DOCTRINE OF SCRIPTURE: PART 6: THE INERRANCY OF SCRIPTURE,** *turn to Ezekiel 11:19–20 on page 822.*

**4:13** New Testament documents weren't written in book form; they were written on long pieces of paper or leather called **parchments**, or scrolls. Because scrolls could be twenty-five feet long or more, the best way to store them was to roll them around a wooden rod.

[16] At my first defense no one stood with me, but all forsook me. [a]May it not be charged against them.

## *THE LORD IS FAITHFUL*

[17] [a]But the Lord stood with me and strengthened me, [b]so that the message might be preached fully through me, and *that* all the Gentiles might hear. Also I was delivered [c]out of the mouth of the lion. [18] [a]And the Lord will deliver me from every evil work and preserve *me* for His heavenly kingdom. [b]To Him *be* glory forever and ever. Amen!

## *COME BEFORE WINTER*

[19] Greet [a]Prisca and Aquila, and the household of [b]Onesiphorus. [20] [a]Erastus stayed in Corinth, but [b]Trophimus I have left in Miletus sick.

[21] Do your utmost to come before winter.

Eubulus greets you, as well as Pudens, Linus, Claudia, and all the brethren.

## *FAREWELL*

[22] The Lord Jesus Christ[1] be with your spirit. Grace be with you. Amen.

**4:16** [a] Acts 7:60 **4:17** [a] Acts 23:11 [b] Acts 9:15 [c] 1 Sam. 17:37 **4:18** [a] Ps. 121:7 [b] Rom. 11:36 **4:19** [a] Acts 18:2 [b] 2 Tim. 1:16 **4:20** [a] Rom. 16:23 [b] Acts 20:4; 21:29 **4:22** [1] NU-Text omits *Jesus Christ.*

*The Epistle of Paul the Apostle to*

# TITUS

**AUTHOR**
Paul

**KEY VERSE**
Titus 3:8

**READING TIME**
8 minutes

Titus was one of Paul's Gentile converts, or at least a protégé (Titus 1:4; Gal. 2:3). Paul gave Titus the difficult assignment of representing him in Corinth (2 Cor. 2:13; 7:6–7, 13–15; 8:6, 16–17), and the two later visited Crete between Paul's imprisonments. Paul would leave Titus behind on that island to look after the church there. Titus's task was unenviable. He needed to set the church in order and help it handle a sinful society all around it. Later, Paul wrote telling Titus to appoint elders, men of proven spiritual character, to oversee the church's work. But elders were not the only ones in the church who were required to excel spiritually. Men and women, young and old, all had vital functions to fulfill in the church if it was to live as an example of the gospel it professed. Throughout his letter to Titus, Paul stressed the necessary, practical working out of salvation in the daily lives of both the elders and the congregation. Good works were desirable, profitable, and necessary for all believers.

**Occasion:** Paul wrote this letter, perhaps from Corinth, taking advantage of the journey of Zenas and Apollos (Titus 3:13), whose destination would take them by way of Crete.

**Main Point:** Believers are to maintain godly living even in challenging settings.

**Big Ideas:** God has given leaders to safeguard, care for, and guide the church. Every believer has an important role to play in the church. Because God has given us the gift of salvation, we are to live with self-control and do what is right.

## OUTLINE:

I. The Church's Leaders (ch. 1)
II. The Church's Behavior (ch. 2)
III. The Church's Power (ch. 3)

**c. AD 34**
Paul is converted

**c. AD 47–49**
Paul's first missionary journey

**c. AD 50**
The Jerusalem Council

**c. AD 50–53**
Paul's second missionary journey

**c. AD 53–57**
Paul's third missionary journey

**AD 54–68**
Nero is Roman emperor

**c. AD 58**
Paul is arrested in Jerusalem

**c. AD 60–62**
Paul is imprisoned in Rome

**c. AD 62**
Paul is released

**c. AD 62–66**
**Titus written**

**AD 64**
Great Fire of Rome; first Roman mass persecution of Christians

**c. AD 67**
Peter and Paul are executed

### GREETING

**1** Paul, a bondservant of God and an apostle of Jesus Christ, according to the faith of God's elect and [a]the acknowledgment of the truth [b]which accords with godliness, 2 in hope of eternal life which God, who [a]cannot lie, promised before time began, 3 but has in due time manifested His word through preaching, which was committed to me according to the commandment of God our Savior;

4 To [a]Titus, a true son in *our* common faith:

Grace, mercy, *and* peace from God the Father and the Lord Jesus Christ[1] our Savior.

### QUALIFIED ELDERS

5 For this reason I left you in Crete, that you should [a]set in order the things that are lacking, and appoint elders in every city as I commanded you— 6 if a man is blameless, the husband of one wife, [a]having faithful children not accused of dissipation or insubordination. 7 For a bishop[1] must be blameless, as a steward of God, not self-willed, not quick-tempered, [a]not given to wine, not violent, not greedy for money, 8 but hospitable, a lover of what is good, sober-minded, just, holy, self-controlled, 9 holding fast the faithful word as he has been taught, that he may be able, by sound doctrine, both to exhort and convict those who contradict.

**1:5 Crete** is an island in the Mediterranean Sea, southeast of Greece. Paul **left** Titus behind in Crete to organize the new church he had started on his final missionary journey.

### THE ELDERS' TASK

10 For there are many insubordinate, both idle [a]talkers and deceivers, especially those of the circumcision, 11 whose mouths must be stopped, who subvert whole households, teaching things which they ought not, [a]for the sake of dishonest gain. 12 [a]One of them, a prophet of their own, said, "Cretans *are* always liars, evil beasts, lazy gluttons." 13 This testimony is true. [a]Therefore rebuke them sharply, that they may be sound in the faith, 14 not giving heed to Jewish fables and [a]commandments of men who turn from the truth. 15 [a]To the pure all things are pure, but to those who are defiled and unbelieving nothing is pure; but even their mind and conscience are defiled. 16 They profess to [a]know God, but [b]in works they deny *Him,* being abominable, disobedient, [c]and disqualified for every good work.

**SEEING JESUS IN THE SCRIPTURE**

**1:16** Just as Jesus warned, not all who claim faith in Jesus are following Him (see Matt. 7:21).

### QUALITIES OF A SOUND CHURCH

**2** But as for you, speak the things which are proper for sound doctrine: 2 that the older men be sober, reverent, temperate, sound in faith, in love, in patience; 3 the older women likewise, that they be reverent in behavior, not slanderers, not given to much wine, teachers of good things— 4 that they admonish the young women to love their husbands, to love their children, 5 *to be* discreet, chaste, [a]homemakers, good, [b]obedient to their own husbands, [c]that the word of God may not be blasphemed.

6 Likewise, exhort the young men to be sober-minded, 7 in all things showing yourself *to be* [a]a pattern of good works; in doctrine *showing* integrity, reverence, [b]incorruptibility,[1] 8 sound speech that cannot be condemned, that one who is an opponent may be ashamed, having nothing evil to say of you.[1]

9 *Exhort* [a]bondservants to be obedient to their own masters, to be well pleasing in all *things,* not answering back, 10 not pilfering, but showing all good fidelity, that they may adorn the doctrine of God our Savior in all things.

### TRAINED BY SAVING GRACE

11 For [a]the grace of God that brings salvation has appeared to all men, 12 teaching us that, denying ungodliness and worldly lusts, we should live soberly, righteously, and godly in the present age, 13 [a]looking for the blessed [b]hope and glorious appearing of our great God and Savior Jesus Christ, 14 [a]who gave Himself for us, that He might redeem us from every lawless deed [b]and purify for Himself [c]*His* own special people, zealous for good works.

**SEEING JESUS IN THE SCRIPTURE**

**2:14** Jesus purifies us from sin so we can live for Him, just as the Scriptures promised (see Mal. 3:3).

15 Speak these things, [a]exhort, and rebuke with all authority. Let no one despise you.

**1:1** [a] 2 Tim. 2:25 [b] [1 Tim. 3:16] **1:2** [a] Num. 23:19 **1:4** [a] 2 Cor. 2:13; 8:23 [1] NU-Text reads *and Christ Jesus.* **1:5** [a] 1 Cor. 11:34 **1:6** [a] 1 Tim. 3:2–4 **1:7** [a] Lev. 10:9 [1] Literally *overseer* **1:10** [a] James 1:26 **1:11** [a] 1 Tim. 6:5 **1:12** [a] Acts 17:28 **1:13** [a] 2 Cor. 13:10 **1:14** [a] Is. 29:13 **1:15** [a] 1 Cor. 6:12 **1:16** [a] Matt. 7:20–23; 25:12 [b] [2 Tim. 3:5, 7] [c] Rom. 1:28 **2:5** [a] 1 Tim. 5:14 [b] 1 Cor. 14:34 [c] Rom. 2:24 **2:7** [a] 1 Tim. 4:12 [b] Eph. 6:24 [1] NU-Text omits *incorruptibility.* **2:8** [1] NU-Text and M-Text read *us.* **2:9** [a] 1 Tim. 6:1 **2:11** [a] [Rom. 5:15] **2:13** [a] 1 Cor. 1:7 [b] [Col. 3:4] **2:14** [a] Gal. 1:4 [b] [Heb. 1:3; 9:14] [c] Ex. 15:16 **2:15** [a] 2 Tim. 4:2

KNOW THE TRUTH

# THE DOCTRINE OF SALVATION

## PART 4: THE PROCESS OF SALVATION

**3:4–7** Here, we see the progression of God's plan of saving people and making us into completely new, eternal co-heirs with His Son.

First, **sinful people don't love God** nor seek salvation. God alone initiated the plan of salvation out of His great love for us and His desire to help us by sending Jesus to be our Savior. God loved us *way* before we loved Him.

Second, **no sinful person did anything righteous to earn salvation**. God's basis for saving us is solely His unimaginably powerful mercy and grace, His desire to spare us what we deserve and give us what we don't deserve.

Third, when we place our trust in Jesus, **the Holy Spirit comes into our lives to wash away all that is old and sinful and make us completely new** people in Christ. The initial and progressive work of the Spirit in our lives isn't small nor insubstantial, but abundant and remarkably noticeable.

Fourth, the **long list of wrongs we've committed against God and are accountable for is wiped clean.** By grace we are declared "not guilty" and completely righteous by a holy God.

Finally, **we're made Christ's coheirs** of eternal life with our Heavenly Father.

*For* **THE DOCTRINE OF SALVATION: PART 5: THE MOMENT OF SALVATION,** *turn to Romans 10:8–17 on page 1157.*

### *GRACES OF THE HEIRS OF GRACE*

**3** Remind them [a]to be subject to rulers and au-
thorities, to obey, [b]to be ready for every good
work, 2 to speak evil of no one, to be peaceable,
gentle, showing all humility to all men. 3 For [a]we
ourselves were also once foolish, disobedient,
deceived, serving various lusts and pleasures,
living in malice and envy, hateful and hating
one another. 4 But when [a]the kindness and the
love of [b]God our Savior toward man appeared,
5 [a]not by works of righteousness which we have
done, but according to His mercy He saved us,
through [b]the washing of regeneration and re-
newing of the Holy Spirit, 6 [a]whom He poured
out on us abundantly through Jesus Christ our
Savior, 7 that having been justified by His grace
[a]we should become heirs according to the hope
of eternal life.

8 [a]This is a faithful saying, and these things
I want you to affirm constantly, that those who
have believed in God should be careful to main-
tain good works. These things are good and
profitable to men.

### *AVOID DISSENSION*

9 But [a]avoid foolish disputes, genealogies,
contentions, and strivings about the law; for

**3:9** Paul's reference to **genealogies** has to do with some Jewish leaders obsessed with being able to trace their family tree back to Abraham.

they are unprofitable and useless. 10 [a]Reject a
divisive man after the first and second admo-
nition, 11 knowing that such a person is warped
and sinning, being self-condemned.

### *FINAL MESSAGES*

12 When I send Artemas to you, or [a]Tychicus,
be diligent to come to me at Nicopolis, for I have
decided to spend the winter there. 13 Send Zenas
the lawyer and [a]Apollos on their journey with
haste, that they may lack nothing. 14 And let our
*people* also learn to maintain good works, to *meet*
urgent needs, that they may not be unfruitful.

### *FAREWELL*

15 All who *are* with me greet you. Greet those
who love us in the faith.
Grace *be* with you all. Amen.

**3:1** [a] 1 Pet. 2:13 [b] Col. 1:10 **3:3** [a] 1 Cor. 6:11 **3:4** [a] Titus 2:11 [b] 1 Tim. 2:3 **3:5** [a] [Rom. 3:20]; Eph. 2:4–9 [b] John 3:3 **3:6** [a] Ezek. 36:26 **3:7** [a] [Matt. 25:34]; Mark 10:17; [Rom. 8:17, 23, 24; Titus 1:2] **3:8** [a] 1 Tim. 1:15 **3:9** [a] 1 Tim. 1:4; 2 Tim. 2:23 **3:10** [a] Matt. 18:17 **3:12** [a] Acts 20:4; Eph. 6:21; Col. 4:7; 2 Tim. 4:12 **3:13** [a] Acts 18:24; 1 Cor. 16:12

*The Epistle of Paul the Apostle to*

# PHILEMON

| AUTHOR | KEY VERSES | READING TIME |
|---|---|---|
| Paul | Philemon vv. 17–18 | 4 minutes |

Onesimus had been a slave in Philemon's household until he fled to Rome. There, he met Paul and became a brother in Christ. While Paul wanted Onesimus to stay with him in Rome to help with his work, he knew that the way Onesimus had left Philemon may have caused problems they needed to resolve. As a result, Paul sent Onesimus back to Philemon, but he did not send him empty-handed. The apostle wrote a brief letter to Philemon, his beloved brother and fellow worker, on behalf of Onesimus. With tact and tenderness, Paul asked Philemon to receive Onesimus back with the same gentleness with which he would receive Paul himself. Any debt Onesimus might have owed Paul promised to make good. Knowing Philemon, Paul was confident that brotherly love and unity would carry the day.

**Occasion:** Paul wrote Philemon during his first Roman imprisonment, perhaps around the same time as Ephesians, Philippians, and Colossians.

**Main Point:** Believers are to be united in Christ no matter what.

**Big Ideas:** We are one in Christ. Our identity as brothers and sisters in Christ is more important than any other identity.

## OUTLINE:

I. Paul's Prayer (vv. 1–7)
II. Paul's Plea (vv. 8–16)
III. Paul's Promise (vv. 17–25)

**c. AD 34**
Paul is converted

**c. AD 47–49**
Paul's first missionary journey

**c. AD 50**
The Jerusalem Council

**c. AD 50–53**
Paul's second missionary journey

**c. AD 53–57**
Paul's third missionary journey

**AD 54–68**
Nero is Roman emperor

**c. AD 58**
Paul is arrested in Jerusalem

**c. AD 60–62**
Paul is imprisoned in Rome

**c. AD 60–62**
**Philemon written**

**AD 64**
Great Fire of Rome; first Roman mass persecution of Christians

**c. AD 67**
Peter and Paul are executed

## GREETING

Paul, a [a]prisoner of Christ Jesus, and Timothy
*our* brother,

To Philemon our beloved *friend* and fellow
laborer, 2 to the beloved[1] Apphia, [a]Archippus our
fellow soldier, and to the church in your house:

3 Grace to you and peace from God our Father
and the Lord Jesus Christ.

## PHILEMON'S LOVE AND FAITH

4 [a]I thank my God, making mention of you
always in my prayers, 5 [a]hearing of your love
and faith which you have toward the Lord Jesus
and toward all the saints, 6 that the sharing
of your faith may become effective [a]by the
acknowledgment of [b]every good thing which
is in you[1] in Christ Jesus. 7 For we have[1] great
joy[2] and consolation in your love, because
the hearts of the saints have been refreshed
by you, brother.

## THE PLEA FOR ONESIMUS

8 Therefore, though I might be very bold in
Christ to command you what is fitting, 9 *yet* for
love's sake I rather appeal *to you*—being such
a one as Paul, the aged, and now also a prisoner
of Jesus Christ— 10 I appeal to you for my son
[a]Onesimus, whom I have begotten *while* in my

> **v. 10** In the Roman Empire, slaves were considered to be nothing more than property. They were bought, sold, and used as their masters saw fit. The punishment for a runaway slave was a severe beating or, in some cases, crucifixion.

chains, 11 who once was unprofitable to you, but
now is profitable to you and to me.
12 I am sending him back.[1] You therefore
receive him, that is, my own heart, 13 whom I
wished to keep with me, that on your behalf
he might minister to me in my chains for the
gospel. 14 But without your consent I wanted to
do nothing, [a]that your good deed might not be
by compulsion, as it were, but voluntary.
15 For perhaps he departed for a while for
this *purpose,* that you might receive him for-
ever, 16 no longer as a slave but more than a
slave—a beloved brother, especially to me but
how much more to you, both in the [a]flesh and
in the Lord.

## PHILEMON'S OBEDIENCE ENCOURAGED

17 If then you count me as a partner, receive
him as *you would* me. 18 But if he has wronged
you or owes anything, put that on my account.

1 [a] Eph. 3:1 2 [a] Col. 4:17 [1] NU-Text reads *to our sister Apphia.* 4 [a] Eph. 1:16; 1 Thess. 1:2; 2 Thess. 1:3 5 [a] Eph. 1:15; Col. 1:4; 1 Thess. 3:6 6 [a] Phil. 1:9; [Col. 1:9; 3:10; James 2:14–17] [b] [1 Thess. 5:18] [1] NU-Text and M-Text read *us.* 7 [1] NU-Text reads *had.* [2] M-Text reads *thanksgiving.* 10 [a] Col. 4:9 12 [1] NU-Text reads *back to you in person, that is, my own heart.* 14 [a] 2 Cor. 9:7 16 [a] Col. 3:22

KNOW THE TRUTH

## THE DOCTRINE OF THE CHURCH

### PART 3: THE NATURE OF THE CHURCH

**v. 2** The Greek word translated into English as "church" primarily refers to the people assembling, not the place of assembly. The church isn't a place; it's a people. The church is the people Jesus Christ has saved and called together to serve Him, one another, and the world in His name. Therefore, wherever followers of Jesus gather, the church is there. The church is the assembly of the saved but it's so much more.

The church is called the "**body of Christ**," receiving life, healing, power, and direction from its "head," Jesus (see 1 Cor. 12:12–27; Eph. 1:22–23). The church is a "**holy priesthood**," which means followers of Jesus bring people to God in prayer, bring God to people through service, and offer sacrifices of praise and thanksgiving to the Father and the Son (see 1 Pet. 2:5). The church is the **bride of Christ**, the community to whom Christ has pledged an eternity of love (see Eph. 5:22–33). The church is **Christ's flock** whom He protects, directs, feeds, and nurtures (see Ps. 23:1–6; John 10:1–16). The church is God's "**own special people**" whom He created, redeemed, called together, and will glorify with His Son forever (see 1 Pet. 2:9; cf. Rev. 21:22—22:5). No demonic or human scheme can triumph against the advance of Christ's church (see Matt. 16:18–19).

*For* **THE DOCTRINE OF THE CHURCH: PART 4: THE UNIVERSAL AND LOCAL CHURCH**, *turn to Acts 2:47 on page 1107.*

**v. 18** Onesimus may have stolen something from Philemon to enable his escape. This accounting imagery reminds us of the theological truth that our sins were charged over to Christ even though He had not "earned" them. Forgiveness is costly (see Is. 53:6).

19 I, Paul, am writing with my own [a]hand. I will
repay—not to mention to you that you owe me
even your own self besides. 20 Yes, brother, let
me have joy from you in the Lord; refresh my
heart in the Lord.
21 [a]Having confidence in your obedience,
I write to you, knowing that you will do even
more than I say. 22 But, meanwhile, also prepare
a guest room for me, for [a]I trust that [b]through
your prayers I shall be granted to you.

### *FAREWELL*

23 [a]Epaphras, my fellow prisoner in Christ
Jesus, greets you, 24 *as do* [a]Mark, [b]Aristarchus,
[c]Demas, [d]Luke, my fellow laborers.
25 [a]The grace of our Lord Jesus Christ *be* with
your spirit. Amen.

**19** [a] 1 Cor. 16:21 **21** [a] 2 Cor. 7:16 **22** [a] Phil. 1:25; 2:24 [b] 2 Cor. 1:11 **23** [a] Col. 1:7; 4:12 **24** [a] Acts 12:12, 25; 15:37–39 [b] Acts 19:29; 27:2 [c] Col. 4:14 [d] 2 Tim. 4:11 **25** [a] 2 Tim. 4:22

*The Epistle to the*

# HEBREWS

| AUTHOR | KEY VERSE | READING TIME |
|---|---|---|
| Unknown, perhaps Barnabas, Luke, or Apollos | Hebrews 10:10 | 55 minutes |

Many Jewish believers who had left Judaism to embrace Christianity wanted to reverse their course to escape persecution by their people. The writer of Hebrews exhorted them instead to "go on to perfection" (Heb. 6:1). He based his appeal on the superiority of Christ over all that Judaism could offer. Christ is better than the angels, for they worship Him. He is better than Moses, for He created him. He is better than the Aaronic priesthood, for His sacrifice was once for all time. He is better than the law, for He mediates a better covenant. In short, there is more to be gained in Christ than to be lost. Pressing on in Christ produces tested faith, self-discipline, and a visible love seen in good works.

**Occasion:** Uncertainty plagues not only this book's authorship but also its date and its readership. The present tense used to refer to the temple operations suggests it was written before its destruction in AD 70. One common view is that the writer of Hebrews was addressing some Jewish believers, perhaps former priests, who were considering abandoning the faith and returning to Judaism.

**Main Point:** Jesus is superior to the old covenant, which pointed to Him.

**Big Ideas:** The Old Testament points to Jesus. Following Jesus is worth any hardship we might face. We can find encouragement in following Jesus from others who kept the faith before us.

## OUTLINE:

I. The Superiority of Jesus (chs. 1–4)
II. The Superiority of the Gospel (chs. 5–10)
III. The Superiority of Faith (chs. 10–13)

**c. AD 50**
The Jerusalem Council

**AD 54–68**
Nero is Roman emperor

**c. AD 58**
Paul is arrested in Jerusalem

**c. AD 60–62**
Paul is imprisoned in Rome

**AD 64**
Great Fire of Rome; first Roman mass persecution of Christians

**c. AD 67–69**
**Hebrews written**

**c. AD 67**
Peter and Paul are executed

**AD 70**
The Romans, led by Titus, destroy the temple

## GOD'S SUPREME REVELATION
*(cf. John 1:1–4)*

1 God, who at various times and [a]in various
ways spoke in time past to the fathers by the
prophets, 2 has in these last days spoken to us
by *His* Son, whom He has appointed heir of all
things, through whom also He made the worlds;
3 [a]who being the brightness of *His* glory and the
express [b]image of His person, and [c]upholding
all things by the word of His power, [d]when He
had by Himself[1] purged our[2] sins, [e]sat down at
the right hand of the Majesty on high, 4 having
become so much better than the angels, as [a]He
has by inheritance obtained a more excellent
name than they.

## THE SON EXALTED ABOVE ANGELS

5 For to which of the angels did He ever say:

[a]"You are My Son,
Today I have begotten You"?[1]

And again:

[b]"I will be to Him a Father,
And He shall be to Me a Son"?[2]

6 But when He again brings [a]the firstborn
into the world, He says:

[b]"Let all the angels of God worship Him."[1]

7 And of the angels He says:

[a]"Who makes His angels spirits
And His ministers a flame of fire."[1]

8 But to the Son *He says:*

[a]"Your throne, O God, *is* forever and ever;
A scepter of righteousness *is* the scepter
of Your kingdom.
9 You have loved righteousness and hated
lawlessness;
Therefore God, Your God, [a]has anointed
You
With the oil of gladness more than Your
companions."[1]

10 And:

[a]"You, LORD, in the beginning laid the
foundation of the earth,
And the heavens are the work of Your hands.
11 [a]They will perish, but You remain;
And [b]they will all grow old like a garment;
12 Like a cloak You will fold them up,
And they will be changed.
But You are the [a]same,
And Your years will not fail."[1]

13 But to which of the angels has He ever said:

[a]"Sit at My right hand,
Till I make Your enemies Your footstool"?[1]

14 [a]Are they not all ministering spirits sent forth
to minister for those who will [b]inherit salvation?

## DO NOT NEGLECT SALVATION

2 Therefore we must give the more earnest
heed to the things we have heard, lest we drift
away. 2 For if the word [a]spoken through angels
proved steadfast, and [b]every transgression and
disobedience received a just reward, 3 [a]how shall
we escape if we neglect so great a salvation,
[b]which at the first began to be spoken by the Lord,
and was [c]confirmed to us by those who heard
*Him,* 4 [a]God also bearing witness [b]both with signs
and wonders, with various miracles, and [c]gifts
of the Holy Spirit, [d]according to His own will?

## THE SON MADE LOWER THAN ANGELS
*(cf. Ps. 8:1–9)*

5 For He has not put [a]the world to come, of
which we speak, in subjection to angels. 6 But
one testified in a certain place, saying:

[a]"What is man that You are mindful of him,
Or the son of man that You take care of him?
7 You have made him a little lower than the
angels;
You have crowned him with glory and
honor,[1]
And set him over the works of Your hands.
8 [a]You have put all things in subjection
under his feet."[1]

For in that He put all in subjection under him,
He left nothing *that is* not put under him. But
now [b]we do not yet see all things put under
him. 9 But we see Jesus, [a]who was made a little
lower than the angels, for the suffering of death
[b]crowned with glory and honor, that He, by the
grace of God, might taste death [c]for everyone.

**SEEING JESUS IN THE SCRIPTURE**

**1:9** Jesus is the anointed one, the Messiah promised throughout the Old Testament who makes us glad (see Is. 61:1, 3).

**1:1** [a] Num. 12:6, 8 **1:3** [a] John 1:14 [b] 2 Cor. 4:4 [c] Col. 1:17 [d] [Heb. 7:27] [e] Ps. 110:1 [1] NU-Text omits *by Himself.* [2] NU-Text omits *our.* **1:4** [a] [Phil. 2:9, 10] **1:5** [a] Ps. 2:7 [b] 2 Sam. 7:14 [1] Psalm 2:7 [2] 2 Samuel 7:14 **1:6** [a] [Rom. 8:29] [b] Deut. 32:43, LXX, DSS; Ps. 97:7 [1] Deuteronomy 32:43 (Septuagint, Dead Sea Scrolls); Psalm 97:7 **1:7** [a] Ps. 104:4 [1] Psalm 104:4 **1:8** [a] Ps. 45:6, 7 **1:9** [a] Is. 61:1, 3 [1] Psalm 45:6, 7 **1:10** [a] Ps. 102:25–27 **1:11** [a] [Is. 34:4] [b] Is. 50:9; 51:6 **1:12** [a] Heb. 13:8 [1] Psalm 102:25–27 **1:13** [a] Ps. 110:1 [1] Psalm 110:1 **1:14** [a] Ps. 103:20 [b] Rom. 8:17 **2:2** [a] Acts 7:53 [b] Num. 15:30 **2:3** [a] Heb. 10:28 [b] Matt. 4:17 [c] Luke 1:2 **2:4** [a] Mark 16:20 [b] Acts 2:22, 43 [c] 1 Cor. 12:4, 7, 11 [d] Eph. 1:5, 9 **2:5** [a] [2 Pet. 3:13] **2:6** [a] Ps. 8:4–6 **2:7** [1] NU-Text and M-Text omit the rest of verse 7. **2:8** [a] Matt. 28:18 [b] 1 Cor. 15:25, 27 [1] Psalm 8:4–6 **2:9** [a] Phil. 2:7–9 [b] Acts 2:33; 3:13 [c] [John 3:16]

### *BRINGING MANY SONS TO GLORY*

10 For it was fitting for Him, [a]for whom *are*
all things and by whom *are* all things, in bring-
ing many sons to glory, to make the captain of
their salvation [b]perfect through sufferings. 11 For
[a]both He who sanctifies and those who are being
sanctified [b]*are* all of one, for which reason [c]He
is not ashamed to call them brethren, 12 saying:

[a]"I will declare Your name to My brethren;
In the midst of the assembly I will sing
praise to You."[1]

> **2:10 Captain** here means "leader" or "originator." The word describes a pioneer or pathfinder. Jesus' endurance of **sufferings** on this earth makes Him our leader. He not only endured them but also triumphed over sin, death, and Satan through them.

13 And again:

[a]"I will put My trust in Him."[1]

And again:

[b]"Here am I and the children whom God
has given Me."[2]

14 Inasmuch then as the children have
partaken of flesh and blood, He [a]Himself like-
wise shared in the same, [b]that through death
He might destroy him who had the power of
[c]death, that is, the devil, 15 and release those who
[a]through fear of death were all their lifetime
subject to bondage. 16 For indeed He does not
give aid to angels, but He does give aid to the
seed of Abraham. 17 Therefore, in all things He
had [a]to be made like *His* brethren, that He might
be [b]a merciful and faithful High Priest in things
*pertaining* to God, to make propitiation for the
sins of the people. 18 [a]For in that He Himself has
suffered, being tempted, He is able to aid those
who are tempted.

> **SEEING JESUS IN THE SCRIPTURE**
>
> **2:17** Jesus is the faithful and eternal High Priest, promised by God to make atonement for sin (see 1 Sam. 2:35).

### *THE SON WAS FAITHFUL*

3 Therefore, holy brethren, partakers of the
heavenly calling, consider the Apostle and
High Priest of our confession, Christ Jesus,
2 who was faithful to Him who appointed Him,
as [a]Moses also *was faithful* in all His house. 3 For
this One has been counted worthy of more glory

**2:10** [a] Col. 1:16 [b] Heb. 5:8, 9; 7:28 **2:11** [a] Heb. 10:10 [b] Acts 17:26 [c] Matt. 28:10 **2:12** [a] Ps. 22:22 [1] Psalm 22:22 **2:13** [a] 2 Sam. 22:3; Is. 8:17 [b] Is. 8:18 [1] 2 Samuel 22:3; Isaiah 8:17 [2] Isaiah 8:18 **2:14** [a] John 1:14 [b] Col. 2:15 [c] 2 Tim. 1:10 **2:15** [a] [Luke 1:74] **2:17** [a] Phil. 2:7 [b] [Heb. 4:15; 5:1–10] **2:18** [a] [Heb. 4:15, 16] **3:2** [a] Num. 12:7

KNOW THE TRUTH

## THE DOCTRINE OF SALVATION

### PART 1: OVERVIEW OF THE DOCTRINE OF SALVATION

**2:9–15** *Salvation* in Hebrews 2:10 has to do with preserving someone or something from eventual decay or delivering someone or something from impending danger. Salting a piece of meat to preserve it from rotting or saving an animal from falling off a cliff are examples of *salvation*. Christians are saved from sin in both senses of this word. Sin corrupts and ruins everything about us. Its allure is tempting, but its fruit is rancid. The ultimate fruit sin produces is eternal separation from God.

Apart from Christ, we are slaves to sin and have no alternative except to practice sin as a lifestyle until we die. Christ saves us from this power of sin by forgiving our sins, cleansing us, and giving us the Holy Spirit to dwell within us. In Christ, we have the power to say no to sin, and thus its rotting effects, and yes to being sanctified, growing into Christ's image.

Another thing we're saved from is the blinding and binding works of the devil (see 2 Cor. 4:3–6; 1 John 3:8). Because of Christ's victory on the cross, His followers are given authority and power to resist and overcome demonic resistance. The ultimate salvation Jesus provides, though, is from God's wrath against sin. Christ saves us from eternal separation from God.

*For* **THE DOCTRINE OF SALVATION: PART 2: THE NEED OF SALVATION,** *turn to Acts 10:42–43 on page 1118.*

than Moses, inasmuch as [a]He who built the house
has more honor than the house. 4 For every house
is built by someone, but [a]He who built all things
*is* God. 5 [a]And Moses indeed *was* faithful in all
His house as [b]a servant, [c]for a testimony of those
things which would be spoken *afterward,* 6 but
Christ as [a]a Son over His own house, [b]whose
house we are [c]if we hold fast the confidence and
the rejoicing of the hope firm to the end.[1]

### SEEING JESUS IN THE SCRIPTURE

**3:5** Moses's faithful obedience to God pointed to the perfect obedience of Jesus (see Ex. 40:16).

### *BE FAITHFUL*

*(Ps. 95:7–11)*

7 Therefore, as [a]the Holy Spirit says:

[b]"Today, if you will hear His voice,
8 Do not harden your hearts as in the
rebellion,
In the day of trial in the wilderness,
9 Where your fathers tested Me, tried Me,
And saw My works forty years.
10 Therefore I was angry with that
generation,
And said, 'They always go astray in *their*
heart,
And they have not known My ways.'
11 So I swore in My wrath,
'They shall not enter My rest.' "[1]

12 Beware, brethren, lest there be in any of
you an evil heart of unbelief in departing from
the living God; 13 but exhort one another daily,
while it is called "Today," lest any of you be hard-
ened through the deceitfulness of sin. 14 For we
have become partakers of Christ if we hold the
beginning of our confidence steadfast to the
end, 15 while it is said:

[a]"Today, if you will hear His voice,
Do not harden your hearts as in the
rebellion."[1]

### *FAILURE OF THE WILDERNESS WANDERERS*

16 [a]For who, having heard, rebelled? Indeed,
*was it* not all who came out of Egypt, *led* by
Moses? 17 Now with whom was He angry forty
years? *Was it* not with those who sinned, [a]whose
corpses fell in the wilderness? 18 And [a]to whom
did He swear that they would not enter His rest,
but to those who did not obey? 19 So we see that
they could not enter in because of [a]unbelief.

### *THE PROMISE OF REST*

4 Therefore, since a promise remains of en-
tering His rest, [a]let us fear lest any of you
seem to have come short of it. 2 For indeed the
gospel was preached to us as well as to them;
but the word which they heard did not profit
them,[1] not being mixed with faith in those who
heard *it.* 3 For we who have believed do enter
that rest, as He has said:

[a]"So I swore in My wrath,
'They shall not enter My rest,' "[1]

although the works were finished from the foun-
dation of the world. 4 For He has spoken in a
certain place of the seventh *day* in this way:
[a]"And God rested on the seventh day from all
His works";[1] 5 and again in this *place:* [a]"They
shall not enter My rest."[1]

6 Since therefore it remains that some *must*
enter it, and those to whom it was first preached
did not enter because of disobedience, 7 again
He designates a certain day, saying in David,
"Today," after such a long time, as it has been
said:

[a]"Today, if you will hear His voice,
Do not harden your hearts."[1]

8 For if Joshua had [a]given them rest, then
He would not afterward have spoken of anoth-
er day. 9 There remains therefore a rest for the
people of God. 10 For he who has entered His
rest has himself also ceased from his works as
God *did* from His.

### *THE WORD DISCOVERS OUR CONDITION*

11 [a]Let us therefore be diligent to enter that
rest, lest anyone fall according to the same

**3:14** The Book of Hebrews was apparently written to Jewish Christians who were being persecuted for their beliefs. As Jews, they had been safe because Judaism was recognized by the empire as a legitimate religion and was, therefore, protected under the law. When those Jews became Christians, however, they put themselves in danger. Christianity was not a recognized religion. As a result, new Christians faced harassment from other Jews who were upset with them for leaving the Jewish faith. Apparently, some Jewish Christians were frightened enough to consider leaving their Christian faith and returning to Judaism.

**3:3** [a] Zech. 6:12, 13 **3:4** [a] [Eph. 2:10] **3:5** [a] Heb. 3:2 [b] Ex. 14:31 [c] Deut. 18:15, 18, 19 **3:6** [a] Heb. 1:2 [b] [1 Cor. 3:16] [c] [Matt. 10:22] [1] NU-Text omits *firm to the end.* **3:7** [a] Acts 1:16 [b] Ps. 95:7–11 **3:11** [1] Psalm 95:7–11 **3:15** [a] Ps. 95:7, 8 [1] Psalm 95:7, 8 **3:16** [a] Num. 14:2, 11, 30 **3:17** [a] Num. 14:22, 23 **3:18** [a] Num. 14:30 **3:19** [a] 1 Cor. 10:11, 12 **4:1** [a] Heb. 12:15 **4:2** [1] NU-Text and M-Text read *profit them, since they were not united by faith with those who heeded it.* **4:3** [a] Ps. 95:11 [1] Psalm 95:11 **4:4** [a] Gen. 2:2 [1] Genesis 2:2 **4:5** [a] Ps. 95:11 [1] Psalm 95:11 **4:7** [a] Ps. 95:7, 8 [1] Psalm 95:7, 8 **4:8** [a] Josh. 22:4 **4:11** [a] 2 Pet. 1:10

example of disobedience. 12 For the word of
God *is* [a]living and powerful, and [b]sharper than
any [c]two-edged sword, piercing even to the
division of soul and spirit, and of joints and
marrow, and is [d]a discerner of the thoughts
and intents of the heart. 13 [a]And there is no
creature hidden from His sight, but all things
*are* [b]naked and open to the eyes of Him to
whom we *must give* account.

### *OUR COMPASSIONATE HIGH PRIEST*

14 Seeing then that we have a great [a]High
Priest who has passed through the heavens,
Jesus the Son of God, [b]let us hold fast *our* con-
fession. 15 For [a]we do not have a High Priest
who cannot sympathize with our weaknesses,
but [b]was in all *points* tempted as *we are*, [c]*yet*
without sin. 16 [a]Let us therefore come boldly to
the throne of grace, that we may obtain mercy
and find grace to help in time of need.

**SEEING JESUS IN THE SCRIPTURE**

**4:15** On earth, Jesus was tempted but didn't sin, proving He is the worthy Savior and becoming our example (see Luke 4:1–13).

### *QUALIFICATIONS FOR HIGH PRIESTHOOD*

5 For every high priest taken from among men
[a]is appointed for men in things *pertaining* to
God, that he may offer both gifts and sacrifices
for sins. 2 He can have compassion on those
who are ignorant and going astray, since he
himself is also subject to [a]weakness. 3 Because
of this he is required as for the people, so also
for [a]himself, to offer *sacrifices* for sins. 4 And no
man takes this honor to himself, but he who is
called by God, just as [a]Aaron *was*.

### *A PRIEST FOREVER*

5 [a]So also Christ did not glorify Himself to
become High Priest, but *it was* He who said to
Him:

> [b]"You are My Son,
> Today I have begotten You."[1]

6 As *He* also says in another *place*:

> [a]"You *are* a priest forever
> According to the order of Melchizedek";[1]

7 who, in the days of His flesh, when He had
[a]offered up prayers and supplications, [b]with
vehement cries and tears to Him [c]who was able
to save Him from death, and was heard [d]because

**4:12** [a] Ps. 147:15 [b] Is. 49:2 [c] Eph. 6:17 [d] 1 Cor. 14:24, 25 **4:13** [a] Ps. 33:13–15; 90:8 [b] Job 26:6 **4:14** [a] Heb. 2:17; 7:26 [b] Heb. 10:23 **4:15** [a] Is. 53:3–5 [b] Luke 22:28 [c] 2 Cor. 5:21 **4:16** [a] [Eph. 2:18] **5:1** [a] Heb. 2:17; 8:3 **5:2** [a] Heb. 7:28 **5:3** [a] Lev. 9:7; 16:6 **5:4** [a] Ex. 28:1 **5:5** [a] John 8:54 [b] Ps. 2:7 [1] Psalm 2:7 **5:6** [a] Ps. 110:4 [1] Psalm 110:4 **5:7** [a] Matt. 26:39, 42, 44 [b] Ps. 22:1 [c] Matt. 26:53 [d] Matt. 26:39

KNOW THE TRUTH

## THE DOCTRINE OF JESUS

### PART 3: THE HUMANITY OF JESUS

**4:14–16** Jesus of Nazareth being a real person of history is scarcely challenged by fair-minded researchers. What's often challenged is His deity, not His humanity. However, in the first few centuries AD, Jesus' deity was relatively unquestioned. His miracles, resurrection, and the strangely explosive numerical growth of His followers left little doubt of His divinity. His humanity, though, was the issue of great debate. People wondered, *How could the holy God become like sinful people and remain the holy God?* The answer is found in Hebrews 4:15.

While Jesus was tempted in every way as we are, He never yielded to temptation and He committed no sin (see Matt. 4:1). He was fully human, yet He remained completely holy. The eternal Son of God became a literal, physical human being (see John 1:14). Jesus needed protection and provision as a child (see Matt. 1:13–15). He physically grew and developed through childhood, adolescence, and into adulthood (see Luke 2:40, 52). He experienced hunger and thirst (see Matt. 4:2; John 19:28). He experienced physical weariness and required sleep (see Mark 4:38; John 4:6). Jesus knew sorrow and joy, weeping and laughing, rejection and friendship, betrayal and loyalty, and physical death and physical resurrection. He became like us in all ways, except sin, and can help us in all ways against sin.

*For* **THE DOCTRINE OF JESUS: PART 4: THE CHARACTER OF JESUS**, *turn to 1 Peter 2:22 on page 1268.*

### SEEING JESUS IN THE SCRIPTURE

**5:6** Jesus isn't a priest according to Aaron, but rather according to the king-priest Melchizedek, just as the Scriptures foretold (see Ps. 110:4).

of His godly fear, 8 though He was a Son, *yet* He learned [a]obedience by the things which He suffered. 9 And [a]having been perfected, He became the author of eternal salvation to all who obey Him, 10 called by God as High Priest [a]"according to the order of Melchizedek," 11 of whom [a]we have much to say, and hard to explain, since you have become [b]dull of hearing.

## SPIRITUAL IMMATURITY

12 For though by this time you ought to be teachers, you need *someone* to teach you again the first principles of the oracles of God; and you have come to need [a]milk and not solid food. 13 For everyone who partakes *only* of milk *is* unskilled in the word of righteousness, for he is [a]a babe. 14 But solid food belongs to those who are of full age, *that is,* those who by reason of use have their senses exercised [a]to discern both good and evil.

## THE PERIL OF NOT PROGRESSING

**6** Therefore, [a]leaving the discussion of the elementary *principles* of Christ, let us go on to perfection, not laying again the foundation of repentance from [b]dead works and of faith toward God, 2 [a]of the doctrine of baptisms, [b]of laying on of hands, [c]of resurrection of the dead, [d]and of eternal judgment. 3 And this we will[1] do if God permits.

4 For *it is* impossible for those who were once enlightened, and have tasted [a]the heavenly gift, and [b]have become partakers of the Holy Spirit, 5 and have tasted the good word of God and the powers of the age to come, 6 if they fall away,[1] to renew them again to repentance, [a]since they crucify again for themselves the Son of God, and put *Him* to an open shame.

7 For the earth which drinks in the rain that often comes upon it, and bears herbs useful for those by whom it is cultivated, [a]receives blessing from God; 8 [a]but if it bears thorns and briers, *it is* rejected and near to being cursed, whose end *is* to be burned.

## A BETTER ESTIMATE

9 But, beloved, we are confident of better things concerning you, yes, things that accompany salvation, though we speak in this manner. 10 For [a]God *is* not unjust to forget [b]your work and labor of[1] love which you have shown toward His name, *in that* you have [c]ministered to the saints, and do minister. 11 And we desire that each one of you show the same diligence [a]to the full assurance of hope until the end, 12 that you do not become sluggish, but imitate those who through faith and patience [a]inherit the promises.

## GOD'S INFALLIBLE PURPOSE IN CHRIST

13 For when God made a promise to Abraham, because He could swear by no one greater, [a]He swore by Himself, 14 saying, [a]"Surely blessing I will bless you, and multiplying I will multiply you."[1] 15 And so, after he had patiently endured, he obtained the [a]promise. 16 For men indeed swear by the greater, and [a]an oath for confirmation *is* for them an end of all dispute. 17 Thus God, determining to show more abundantly to [a]the heirs of promise [b]the immutability of His counsel, confirmed *it* by an oath, 18 that by two immutable things, in which it *is* impossible for God to [a]lie, we might[1] have strong consolation, who have fled for refuge to lay hold of the hope [b]set before *us.*

**6:18** In ancient times, six towns in Israel were set aside as cities of **refuge**. "An eye for an eye" was the rule of the day. If a person killed someone—even accidentally—legally, he could be killed in retaliation. That's why cities of refuge were important. If a person accidentally killed another person, he could run to the nearest city of refuge to escape vengeance-seeking family members of the person he killed. Once a person reached a city of refuge, safety was assured until a fair trial could be conducted. If the killing was found to be accidental, the person on trial was allowed to live in the city of refuge with full protection from those who wanted to kill him.

19 This *hope* we have as an anchor of the soul, both sure and steadfast, [a]and which enters the *Presence* behind the veil, 20 [a]where the forerunner has entered for us, *even* Jesus, [b]having become High Priest forever according to the order of Melchizedek.

## THE KING OF RIGHTEOUSNESS

*(Gen. 14:17–20)*

**7** For this [a]Melchizedek, king of Salem, priest of the Most High God, who met Abraham returning from the slaughter of the kings and blessed him, 2 to whom also Abraham gave a

**5:8** [a] Phil. 2:8 **5:9** [a] Heb. 2:10 **5:10** [a] Ps. 110:4 **5:11** [a] [John 16:12] [b] [Matt. 13:15] **5:12** [a] 1 Cor. 3:1–3 **5:13** [a] Eph. 4:14 **5:14** [a] Is. 7:15 **6:1** [a] Heb. 5:12 [b] [Heb. 9:14] **6:2** [a] Acts 19:3–5 [b] [Acts 8:17] [c] Acts 17:31 [d] Acts 24:25 **6:3** [1] M-Text reads *let us do.* **6:4** [a] [John 4:10] [b] [Gal. 3:2, 5] **6:6** [a] Heb. 10:29 [1] Or *and have fallen away* **6:7** [a] Ps. 65:10 **6:8** [a] Is. 5:6 **6:10** [a] Rom. 3:4 [b] 1 Thess. 1:3 [c] Rom. 15:25 [1] NU-Text omits *labor of.* **6:11** [a] Col. 2:2 **6:12** [a] Heb. 10:36 **6:13** [a] Gen. 22:16, 17 **6:14** [a] Gen. 22:16, 17 [1] Genesis 22:17 **6:15** [a] Gen. 12:4; 21:5 **6:16** [a] Ex. 22:11 **6:17** [a] Heb. 11:9 [b] Rom. 11:29 **6:18** [a] Num. 23:19 [b] [Col. 1:5] [1] M-Text omits *might.* **6:19** [a] Lev. 16:2, 15 **6:20** [a] [Heb. 4:14] [b] Heb. 3:1; 5:10, 11 **7:1** [a] Gen. 14:18–20

tenth part of all, first being translated "king of
righteousness," and then also king of Salem,
meaning "king of peace," 3 without father, with-
out mother, without genealogy, having neither
beginning of days nor end of life, but made like
the Son of God, remains a priest continually.
4 Now consider how great this man *was,* to
whom even the patriarch Abraham gave a tenth
of the spoils. 5 And indeed [a]those who are of the
sons of Levi, who receive the priesthood, have a
commandment to receive tithes from the people
according to the law, that is, from their brethren,
though they have come from the loins of Abra-
ham; 6 but he whose genealogy is not derived from
them received tithes from Abraham [a]and blessed
[b]him who had the promises. 7 Now beyond all
contradiction the lesser is blessed by the better.
8 Here mortal men receive tithes, but there he
*receives them,* [a]of whom it is witnessed that he
lives. 9 Even Levi, who receives tithes, paid tithes
through Abraham, so to speak, 10 for he was still in
the loins of his father when Melchizedek met him.

> **7:8–10 Melchizedek** wasn't only superior to Abraham, but he was also superior to the Levitical priesthood. In a sense, **Levi paid tithes** to Melchizedek **through** the tithe **Abraham** gave. Because he was descended from Abraham, he is counted as having paid tithes to Melchizedek. The lesser tithes to the greater, thus Levi would be lesser than Melchizedek.

### *NEED FOR A NEW PRIESTHOOD*
*(Ps. 110:4)*

11 [a]Therefore, if perfection were through the
Levitical priesthood (for under it the people re-
ceived the law), what further need *was there* that
another priest should rise according to the order
of Melchizedek, and not be called according to
the order of Aaron? 12 For the priesthood being
changed, of necessity there is also a change
of the law. 13 For He of whom these things are
spoken belongs to another tribe, from which
no man has officiated at the altar.
14 For *it is* evident that [a]our Lord arose from
[b]Judah, of which tribe Moses spoke nothing
concerning priesthood.[1] 15 And it is yet far more
evident if, in the likeness of Melchizedek, there
arises another priest 16 who has come, not ac-
cording to the law of a fleshly commandment,
but according to the power of an endless life.
17 For He testifies:[1]

[a]"You *are* a priest forever
According to the order of Melchizedek."[2]

> **SEEING JESUS IN THE SCRIPTURE**
>
> **7:17** Jesus isn't a priest according to Aaron, but rather according to the king-priest Melchizedek, just as the Scriptures foretold (see Ps. 110:4).

18 For on the one hand there is an annulling
of the former commandment because of [a]its
weakness and unprofitableness, 19 for [a]the law
made nothing perfect; on the other hand, *there is
the* bringing in of [b]a better hope, through which
[c]we draw near to God.

### *GREATNESS OF THE NEW PRIEST*

20 And inasmuch as *He was* not *made priest*
without an oath 21 (for they have become priests
without an oath, but He with an oath by Him
who said to Him:

[a]"The LORD has sworn
And will not relent,
'You *are* a priest forever'[1]
According to the order of Melchizedek' "),[2]

22 by so much more Jesus has become a surety
of a [a]better covenant.
23 Also there were many priests, because
they were prevented by death from continuing.
24 But He, because He continues forever, has an
unchangeable priesthood. 25 Therefore He is also
[a]able to save to the uttermost those who come
to God through Him, since He always lives [b]to
make intercession for them.
26 For such a High Priest was fitting for us,
[a]*who is* holy, harmless, undefiled, separate from
sinners, [b]and has become higher than the heav-
ens; 27 who does not need daily, as those high
priests, to offer up sacrifices, first for His [a]own
sins and then for the people's, for this He did once
for all when He offered up Himself. 28 For the law
appoints as high priests men who have weakness,
but the word of the oath, which came after the law,
*appoints* the Son who has been perfected forever.

### *THE NEW PRIESTLY SERVICE*

8 Now *this is* the main point of the things
we are saying: We have such a High Priest,
[a]who is seated at the right hand of the throne of
the Majesty in the heavens, 2 a Minister of [a]the
sanctuary and of [b]the true tabernacle which the
Lord erected, and not man.
3 For [a]every high priest is appointed to offer
both gifts and sacrifices. Therefore [b]*it is* neces-
sary that this One also have something to offer.
4 For if He were on earth, He would not be a
priest, since there are priests who offer the gifts

**7:5** [a] Num. 18:21–26 **7:6** [a] Gen. 14:19, 20 [b] [Rom. 4:13] **7:8** [a] Heb. 5:6; 6:20 **7:11** [a] Heb. 7:18; 8:7 **7:14** [a] Is. 1:1 [b] Matt. 1:2 [1] NU-Text reads *priests.* **7:17** [a] Ps. 110:4 [1] NU-Text reads *it is testified.* [2] Psalm 110:4 **7:18** [a] [Rom. 8:3] **7:19** [a] [Acts 13:39] [b] Heb. 6:18, 19 [c] Rom. 5:2 **7:21** [a] Ps. 110:4 [1] NU-Text ends the quotation here. [2] Psalm 110:4 **7:22** [a] Heb. 8:6 **7:25** [a] Jude 24 [b] Rom. 8:34 **7:26** [a] Heb. 4:15 [b] Eph. 1:20 **7:27** [a] Lev. 9:7; 16:6 **8:1** [a] Col. 3:1 **8:2** [a] Heb. 9:8, 12 [b] Heb. 9:11, 24 **8:3** [a] Heb. 5:1; 8:4 [b] [Eph. 5:2]

according to the law; 5 who serve [a]the copy and [b]shadow of the heavenly things, as Moses was divinely instructed when he was about to make the tabernacle. For He said, [c]"See *that* you make all things according to the pattern shown you on the mountain."[1] 6 But now [a]He has obtained a more excellent ministry, inasmuch as He is also Mediator of a [b]better covenant, which was established on better promises.

### A NEW COVENANT
*(Jer. 31:31–34)*

7 For if that [a]first *covenant* had been faultless, then no place would have been sought for a second. 8 Because finding fault with them, He says: [a]"Behold, the days are coming, says the LORD, when I will make a new covenant with the house of Israel and with the house of Judah— 9 not according to the covenant that I made with their fathers in the day when I took them by the hand to lead them out of the land of Egypt; because they did not continue in My covenant, and I disregarded them, says the LORD. 10 For this *is* the covenant that I will make with the house of Israel after those days, says the [a]LORD: I will put My laws in their mind and write them on their hearts; and [b]I will be their God, and they shall be My people. 11 [a]None of them shall teach his neighbor, and none his brother, saying, 'Know the [b]LORD,' for all shall know Me, from the least of them to the greatest of them. 12 For I will be merciful to their unrighteousness, [a]and their sins and their lawless deeds[1] I will remember no more."[2]

**SEEING JESUS IN THE SCRIPTURE**

**8:8–9** Jesus is the fulfillment of the New Covenant, the everlasting covenant that would provide salvation for all people (see Jer. 31:31–34).

13 [a]In that He says, "A new *covenant*," He has made the first obsolete. Now what is becoming obsolete and growing old is ready to vanish away.

### THE EARTHLY SANCTUARY
*(cf. Ex. 25:10–40)*

9 Then indeed, even the first *covenant* had ordinances of divine service and [a]the earthly sanctuary. 2 For a tabernacle was prepared: the first *part,* in which *was* the lampstand, the table, and the showbread, which is called the sanctuary; 3 [a]and behind the second veil, the part of the tabernacle which is called the Holiest of All, 4 which had the [a]golden censer and [b]the ark of the covenant overlaid on all sides with gold, in which *were* [c]the golden pot that had the manna, [d]Aaron's rod that budded, and [e]the tablets of the covenant; 5 and [a]above it were the cherubim of glory overshadowing the mercy seat. Of these things we cannot now speak in detail.

### LIMITATIONS OF THE EARTHLY SERVICE

6 Now when these things had been thus prepared, [a]the priests always went into the first part of the tabernacle, performing the services. 7 But into the second part the high priest *went* alone [a]once a year, not without blood, which he offered for [b]himself and *for* the people's sins *committed* in ignorance; 8 the Holy Spirit indicating this, that [a]the way into the Holiest of All was not yet made manifest while the first tabernacle was still standing. 9 It *was* symbolic for the present time in which both gifts and sacrifices are offered [a]which cannot make him who performed the service perfect in regard to the conscience— 10 *concerned* only with [a]foods and drinks, [b]various washings, [c]and fleshly ordinances imposed until the time of reformation.

### THE HEAVENLY SANCTUARY

11 But Christ came *as* High Priest of [a]the good things to come,[1] with the greater and more perfect tabernacle not made with hands, that is, not of this creation. 12 Not [a]with the blood of goats and calves, but [b]with His own blood He entered the Most Holy Place [c]once for all, [d]having obtained eternal redemption. 13 For if [a]the blood of bulls and goats and [b]the ashes of a heifer, sprinkling the unclean, sanctifies for the purifying of the flesh, 14 how much more shall the blood of Christ, who through the eternal Spirit offered Himself without spot to God, [a]cleanse your conscience from [b]dead works [c]to serve the living God? 15 And for this reason [a]He is the Mediator of the new covenant, by means of death, for the redemption of the transgressions under the first covenant, that [b]those who are called may receive the promise of the eternal inheritance.

### THE MEDIATOR'S DEATH NECESSARY

16 For where there *is* a testament, there must also of necessity be the death of the testator. 17 For [a]a testament *is* in force after men are dead, since it has no power at all while the testator lives. 18 [a]Therefore not even the first *covenant* was dedicated without blood. 19 For when Moses had spoken every precept to all the people according to the law, [a]he took the blood of calves and goats, [b]with water, scarlet wool, and hyssop,

**8:5** [a] Heb. 9:23, 24 [b] Col. 2:17 [c] Ex. 25:40 [1] Exodus 25:40 **8:6** [a] [2 Cor. 3:6–8] [b] Heb. 7:22 **8:7** [a] Ex. 3:8; 19:5 **8:8** [a] Jer. 31:31–34 **8:10** [a] Jer. 31:33 [b] Zech. 8:8 **8:11** [a] Is. 54:13 [b] Jer. 31:34 **8:12** [a] Rom. 11:27 [1] NU-Text omits *and their lawless deeds.* [2] Jeremiah 31:31–34 **8:13** [a] [2 Cor. 5:17] **9:1** [a] Ex. 25:8 **9:3** [a] Ex. 26:31–35; 40:3 **9:4** [a] Lev. 16:12 [b] Ex. 25:10 [c] Ex. 16:33 [d] Num. 17:1–10 [e] Ex. 25:16; 34:29 **9:5** [a] Lev. 16:2 **9:6** [a] Num. 18:2–6; 28:3 **9:7** [a] Ex. 30:10 [b] Heb. 5:3 **9:8** [a] [John 14:6] **9:9** [a] Heb. 7:19 **9:10** [a] Col. 2:16 [b] Num. 19:7 [c] Eph. 2:15 **9:11** [a] Heb. 10:1 [1] NU-Text reads *that have come.* **9:12** [a] Heb. 10:4 [b] Eph. 1:7 [c] Zech. 3:9 [d] [Dan. 9:24] **9:13** [a] Lev. 16:14, 15 [b] Num. 19:2 **9:14** [a] 1 John 1:7 [b] Heb. 6:1 [c] Luke 1:74 **9:15** [a] Rom. 3:25 [b] Heb. 3:1 **9:17** [a] Gal. 3:15 **9:18** [a] Ex. 24:6 **9:19** [a] Ex. 24:5, 6 [b] Lev. 14:4, 7

and sprinkled both the book itself and all the
people, 20 saying, [a]"This *is* the [b]blood of the
covenant which God has commanded you."[1]
21 Then likewise [a]he sprinkled with blood both
the tabernacle and all the vessels of the ministry.
22 And according to the law almost all things are
purified with blood, and [a]without shedding of
blood there is no remission.

### GREATNESS OF CHRIST'S SACRIFICE

23 Therefore *it was* necessary that [a]the copies
of the things in the heavens should be purified
with these, but the heavenly things themselves
with better sacrifices than these. 24 For [a]Christ
has not entered the holy places made with hands,
*which are* copies of [b]the true, but into heaven
itself, now [c]to appear in the presence of God for
us; 25 not that He should offer Himself often, as
[a]the high priest enters the Most Holy Place every
year with blood of another— 26 He then would
have had to suffer often since the foundation of
the world; but now, once at the end of the ages, He
has appeared to put away sin by the sacrifice of
Himself. 27 [a]And as it is appointed for men to die
once, [b]but after this the judgment, 28 so [a]Christ
was [b]offered once to bear the sins [c]of many. To
those who [d]eagerly wait for Him He will appear
a second time, apart from sin, for salvation.

> **SEEING JESUS IN THE SCRIPTURE**
>
> **9:26** Jesus' sacrifice was better than those made under the Mosaic covenant; His one sacrifice completed the work of salvation (see Ex. 30:10).

### ANIMAL SACRIFICES INSUFFICIENT

**10** For the law, having a [a]shadow of the good
things to come, *and* not the very image of the
things, [b]can never with these same sacrifices, which
they offer continually year by year, make those who
approach perfect. 2 For then would they not have
ceased to be offered? For the worshipers, once
purified, would have had no more consciousness
of sins. 3 But in those *sacrifices there is* a reminder
of sins every year. 4 For [a]*it is* not possible that the
blood of bulls and goats could take away sins.

### CHRIST'S DEATH FULFILLS GOD'S WILL

*(cf. Ps. 40:6–8)*

5 Therefore, when He came into the world,
He said:

[a]"Sacrifice and offering You did not desire,
But a body You have prepared for Me.

> **SEEING JESUS IN THE SCRIPTURE**
>
> **10:5** Jesus came as a priest not to offer sacrifices, but to become the sacrifice for sin just as the Scriptures promised (see Ps. 40:6–8).

6 In burnt offerings and *sacrifices* for sin
You had no pleasure.
7 Then I said, 'Behold, I have come—
In the volume of the book it is written
of Me—
To do Your will, O God.'"[1]

8 Previously saying, "Sacrifice and offering,
burnt offerings, and *offerings* for sin You did
not desire, nor had pleasure *in them*" (which
are offered according to the law), 9 then He said,
"Behold, I have come to do Your will, O God."[1] He
takes away the first that He may establish the
second. 10 [a]By that will we have been sanctified
[b]through the offering of the body of Jesus Christ
once *for all*.

### CHRIST'S DEATH PERFECTS THE SANCTIFIED

11 And every priest stands [a]ministering daily
and offering repeatedly the same sacrifices,
which can never take away sins. 12 [a]But this Man,
after He had offered one sacrifice for sins for-
ever, sat down [b]at the right hand of God, 13 from
that time waiting [a]till His enemies are made His
footstool. 14 For by one offering He has perfected
forever those who are being sanctified.
15 But the Holy Spirit also witnesses to us;
for after He had said before,
16 [a]"This *is* the covenant that I will make with
them after those days, says the LORD: I will put
My laws into their hearts, and in their minds I
will write them,"[1] 17 *then He adds,* [a]"Their sins and
their lawless deeds I will remember no more."[1]
18 Now where there is remission of these, *there
is* no longer an offering for sin.

### HOLD FAST YOUR CONFESSION

19 Therefore, brethren, having [a]boldness to
enter [b]the Holiest by the blood of Jesus, 20 by
a new and [a]living way which He consecrated
for us, through the veil, that is, His flesh, 21 and
*having* a High Priest over the house of God, 22 let
us [a]draw near with a true heart [b]in full assurance
of faith, having our hearts sprinkled from an evil
conscience and our bodies washed with pure
water. 23 Let us hold fast the confession of *our*
hope without wavering, for [a]He who promised

**9:20** [a] [Matt. 26:28] [b] Ex. 24:3–8 [1] Exodus 24:8 **9:21** [a] Ex. 29:12, 36 **9:22** [a] Lev. 17:11 **9:23** [a] Heb. 8:5 **9:24** [a] Heb. 6:20 [b] Heb. 8:2 [c] Rom. 8:34 **9:25** [a] Heb. 9:7 **9:27** [a] Gen. 3:19 [b] [2 Cor. 5:10] **9:28** [a] Rom. 6:10 [b] 1 Pet. 2:24 [c] Matt. 26:28 [d] Titus 2:13 **10:1** [a] Heb. 8:5 [b] Heb. 7:19; 9:9 **10:4** [a] Mic. 6:6, 7 **10:5** [a] Ps. 40:6–8 **10:7** [1] Psalm 40:6–8 **10:9** [1] NU-Text and M-Text omit *O God.* **10:10** [a] John 17:19 [b] [Heb. 9:12] **10:11** [a] Num. 28:3 **10:12** [a] Col. 3:1 [b] Ps. 110:1 **10:13** [a] Ps. 110:1 **10:16** [a] Jer. 31:33, 34 [1] Jeremiah 31:33 **10:17** [a] Jer. 31:34 [1] Jeremiah 31:34 **10:19** [a] [Eph. 2:18] [b] Heb. 9:8, 12 **10:20** [a] John 14:6 **10:22** [a] Heb. 7:19; 10:1 [b] Eph. 3:12 **10:23** [a] 1 Cor. 1:9; 10:13

**10:22** The **conscience** can be cleansed through the blood of Christ (see Heb. 9:14). Just as the high priest **washed** before entering the Most Holy Place (see Lev. 16:3–4), believers are cleansed before they come before the Holy One.

*is* faithful. 24 And let us consider one another
in order to stir up love and good works, 25 [a]not
forsaking the assembling of ourselves together,
as *is* the manner of some, but exhorting *one*
*another,* and [b]so much the more as you see [c]the
Day approaching.

### THE JUST LIVE BY FAITH

26 For [a]if we sin willfully [b]after we have re-
ceived the knowledge of the truth, there [c]no
longer remains a sacrifice for sins, 27 but a cer-
tain fearful expectation of judgment, and [a]fiery
indignation which will devour the adversaries.
28 Anyone who has rejected Moses' law dies
without mercy on *the testimony of* two or three
[a]witnesses. 29 [a]Of how much worse punishment,
do you suppose, will he be thought worthy who
has trampled the Son of God underfoot, [b]count-
ed the blood of the covenant by which he was
sanctified a common thing, [c]and insulted the
Spirit of grace? 30 For we know Him who said,
[a]"Vengeance is Mine, I will repay,"[1] says the Lord.[2]
And again, [b]"The LORD will judge His people."[3]
31 [a]It is a fearful thing to fall into the hands of
the living God.
32 But [a]recall the former days in which,
after you were illuminated, you endured a
great struggle with sufferings: 33 partly while
you were made [a]a spectacle both by reproaches
and tribulations, and partly while [b]you be-
came companions of those who were so treat-
ed; 34 for you had compassion on me[1] [a]in my
chains, and [b]joyfully accepted the plundering
of your goods, knowing that [c]you have a better
and an enduring possession for yourselves in
heaven.[2] 35 Therefore do not cast away your
confidence, [a]which has great reward. 36 [a]For
you have need of endurance, so that after you
have done the will of God, [b]you may receive
the promise:

37 "For [a]yet a little while,
*And* [b]He[1] who is coming will come and
will not tarry.
38 Now [a]the[1] just shall live by faith;
But if *anyone* draws back,
My soul has no pleasure in
him."[2]

**10:25** [a]Acts 2:42 [b]Rom. 13:11 [c]Phil. 4:5 **10:26** [a]Num. 15:30 [b]2 Pet. 2:20 [c]Heb. 6:6 **10:27** [a]Zeph. 1:18 **10:28** [a]Deut. 17:2–6; 19:15 **10:29** [a][Heb. 2:3] [b]1 Cor. 11:29 [c][Matt. 12:31] **10:30** [a]Deut. 32:35 [b]Deut. 32:36 [1]Deuteronomy 32:35 [2]NU-Text omits *says the Lord.* [3]Deuteronomy 32:36 **10:31** [a][Luke 12:5] **10:32** [a]Gal. 3:4 **10:33** [a]1 Cor. 4:9 [b]Phil. 1:7 **10:34** [a]2 Tim. 1:16 [b]Matt. 5:12 [c]Matt. 6:20 [1]NU-Text reads *the prisoners* instead of *me in my chains.* [2]NU-Text omits *in heaven.* **10:35** [a]Matt. 5:12 **10:36** [a]Luke 21:19 [b][Col. 3:24] **10:37** [a]Luke 18:8 [b]Hab. 2:3, 4 [1]Or *that which* **10:38** [a]Rom. 1:17 [1]NU-Text reads *My just one.* [2]Habakkuk 2:3, 4

KNOW THE TRUTH

## THE DOCTRINE OF THE CHURCH

### PART 6: THE FUNCTIONS OF THE CHURCH

**10:19–25** Three of the church's main functions are reaching up toward God, reaching in toward one another, and reaching out toward the world. The most basic action required to fulfill these functions is gathering. As the writer of Hebrews exhorts, the church must come together to function together and stir one another to love and good works.

When the church gathers, it **reaches up toward God** through corporate prayer and praise (see Ps. 34; Acts 12:5; Heb. 13:15). Petition, lament, gratitude, and adoration are spoken and sung by the gathered saints.

The church **reaches in toward one another** through praying for each other, equipping each other for the work of ministry, serving and caring for each other, using God-given gifts to help each other, teaching the Word to one another, and making disciples of each other (see Acts 6:5–7; 16:11–15; Rom. 12:3–13; 1 Cor. 11:23–34; Eph. 4:11–16; 1 Tim. 4:1–16).

The church **reaches out toward the world** through the ministries of evangelism, compassionate care for those in need, and planting local churches so all who believe can have a community to grow and thrive in (see Matt. 9:35–38; Acts 8:4–13; 11:19–26).

*For* **THE DOCTRINE OF THE CHURCH: PART 7: THE ORDINANCES OF THE CHURCH**, *turn to 1 Corinthians 11:23–34 on page 1176.*

39 But we are not of those [a]who draw back to perdition, but of those who [b]believe to the saving of the soul.

### BY FAITH WE UNDERSTAND

11 Now faith is the substance of things hoped for, the evidence [a]of things not seen. 2 For by it the elders obtained a *good* testimony.

3 By faith we understand that [a]the worlds were framed by the word of God, so that the things which are seen were not made of things which are visible.

### FAITH AT THE DAWN OF HISTORY

*(Gen. 4:1–16; 5:18–24; 6:5—8:22)*

4 By faith [a]Abel offered to God a more excellent sacrifice than Cain, through which he obtained witness that he was righteous, God testifying of his gifts; and through it he being dead still [b]speaks.

5 By faith Enoch was taken away so that he did not see death, [a]"and was not found, because God had taken him";[1] for before he was taken he had this testimony, that he pleased God. 6 But without faith *it is* impossible to please *Him,* for he who comes to God must believe that He is, and *that* He is a rewarder of those who diligently seek Him.

7 By faith [a]Noah, being divinely warned of things not yet seen, moved with godly fear, [b]prepared an ark for the saving of his household, by which he condemned the world and became heir of [c]the righteousness which is according to faith.

### FAITHFUL ABRAHAM

*(Gen. 15:1–6; 21:1–7)*

8 By faith [a]Abraham obeyed when he was called to go out to the place which he would receive as an inheritance. And he went out, not knowing where he was going. 9 By faith he dwelt in the land of promise as *in* a foreign country, [a]dwelling in tents with Isaac and Jacob, [b]the heirs with him of the same promise; 10 for he waited for [a]the city which has foundations, [b]whose builder and maker *is* God.

11 By faith [a]Sarah herself also received strength to conceive seed, and [b]she bore a child[1] when she was past the age, because she judged Him [c]faithful who had promised. 12 Therefore from one man, and him as good as [a]dead, were born *as many* as the [b]stars of the sky in multitude—innumerable as the sand which is by the seashore.

### THE HEAVENLY HOPE

13 These all died in faith, [a]not having received the [b]promises, but [c]having seen them afar off were assured of them,[1] embraced *them* and [d]confessed that they were strangers and pilgrims on the earth. 14 For those who say such things [a]declare plainly that they seek a homeland. 15 And truly if they had called to mind [a]that *country* from which they had come out, they would have had opportunity to return. 16 But now they desire a better, that is, a heavenly *country.* Therefore God is not ashamed [a]to be called their God, for He has [b]prepared a city for them.

### THE FAITH OF THE PATRIARCHS

*(Gen. 22:1–14; 48:8–16; 50:22–25)*

17 By faith Abraham, [a]when he was tested, offered up Isaac, and he who had received the promises offered up his only begotten *son,* 18 of whom it was said, [a]"In Isaac your seed shall be called,"[1] 19 concluding that God [a]*was* able to raise *him* up, even from the dead, from which he also received him in a figurative sense.

**SEEING JESUS IN THE SCRIPTURE**

**11:17–19** Isaac was figuratively raised from the dead being spared at the last moment, foreshadowing Jesus being literally raised from the dead (see Gen. 21:12).

20 By faith [a]Isaac blessed Jacob and Esau concerning things to come.

21 By faith Jacob, when he was dying, [a]blessed each of the sons of Joseph, and worshiped, *leaning* on the top of his staff.

22 By faith [a]Joseph, when he was dying, made mention of the departure of the children of Israel, and gave instructions concerning his bones.

### THE FAITH OF MOSES

*(Ex. 2:1–10; 12:31–51)*

23 By faith [a]Moses, when he was born, was hidden three months by his parents, because they saw *he was* a beautiful child; and they were not afraid of the king's [b]command.

24 By faith [a]Moses, when he became of age, refused to be called the son of Pharaoh's daughter, 25 choosing rather to suffer affliction with the people of God than to enjoy the passing pleasures of sin, 26 esteeming [a]the reproach of Christ greater riches than the treasures in[1] Egypt; for he looked to the [b]reward.

27 By faith [a]he forsook Egypt, not fearing the wrath of the king; for he endured as seeing Him who is invisible. 28 By faith [a]he kept the

**10:39** [a] 2 Pet. 2:20 [b] Acts 16:31 **11:1** [a] Rom. 8:24 **11:3** [a] Ps. 33:6 **11:4** [a] Gen. 4:3–5 [b] Heb. 12:24 **11:5** [a] Gen. 5:21–24 [1] Genesis 5:24 **11:7** [a] Gen. 6:13–22 [b] 1 Pet. 3:20 [c] Rom. 3:22 **11:8** [a] Gen. 12:1–4 **11:9** [a] Gen. 12:8; 13:3, 18; 18:1, 9 [b] Heb. 6:17 **11:10** [a] [Heb. 12:22; 13:14] [b] [Rev. 21:10] **11:11** [a] Gen. 17:19; 18:11–14; 21:1, 2 [b] Luke 1:36 [c] Heb. 10:23 [1] NU-Text omits *she bore a child.* **11:12** [a] Rom. 4:19 [b] Gen. 15:5; 22:17; 32:12 **11:13** [a] Heb. 11:39 [b] Gen. 12:7 [c] John 8:56 [d] Ps. 39:12 [1] NU-Text and M-Text omit *were assured of them.* **11:14** [a] Heb. 13:14 **11:15** [a] Gen. 11:31 **11:16** [a] Ex. 3:6, 15; 4:5 [b] [Rev. 21:2] **11:17** [a] James 2:21 **11:18** [a] Gen. 21:12 [1] Genesis 21:12 **11:19** [a] Rom. 4:17 **11:20** [a] Gen. 27:26–40 **11:21** [a] Gen. 48:1, 5, 16, 20 **11:22** [a] Gen. 50:24, 25 **11:23** [a] Ex. 2:1–3 [b] Ex. 1:16, 22 **11:24** [a] Ex. 2:11–15 **11:26** [a] Heb. 13:13 [b] Rom. 8:18 [1] NU-Text and M-Text read *of.* **11:27** [a] Ex. 10:28 **11:28** [a] Ex. 12:21

HEBREWS 11:1–40

## HEROES OF FAITH

57

STORY OF SCRIPTURE

### WHAT'S GOING ON?

This chapter is often called the "Hall of Faith"—a play on the Hall of Fame. It showcases men and women who lived by faith even when it was difficult, and they couldn't see the outcome of God's promises. From Abel who offered a better sacrifice, to Abraham who was willing to sacrifice his son Isaac, and to Moses who led the Israelites out of Egypt, each person exemplified faith in action. Their stories collectively affirm that faith is the assurance of things hoped for, the conviction of unseen realities.

However, there are some strange additions to the Hall of Faith, like Samson, who was more known for his pride and impulsiveness than his faithfulness (see Judg. 13–15). The presence of "heroes" like Samson presents a paradox. They serve as a reminder that God can do great things even with just the smallest, clumsiest amount of faith. This, in essence, encapsulates the story of Scripture—imperfect people loved by a perfect God.

### WHAT DOES THIS MEAN FOR ME?

This chapter encourages us to view our trials and challenges as opportunities to demonstrate faith, following the examples of those who came before us. We can rely on God even when things look bleak.

This passage also comforts us that we are part of a long lineage of believers who have faced difficulties, persecutions, and even death without losing faith in God's promises. Our faith connects us to a grand narrative of God's redemptive history.

### DID YOU CATCH THE PATTERN?

Salvation has always been by faith and faith is what God has always desired from His people. Abel's sacrifice, Noah's ark, Abraham's journey, and Moses's leadership are not just isolated incidents of belief but are interconnected stories highlighting faith as a response to God's promises. These stories culminate in Jesus, the pioneer and perfecter of our faith (Heb. 12:2).

*For the next* Story of Scripture *reading and devotion, turn to James 5:1–20 on page 1264.*

Passover and the sprinkling of blood, lest he
who destroyed the firstborn should touch them.
29 By faith [a]they passed through the Red Sea
as by dry *land, whereas* the Egyptians, attempt-
ing to do so, were drowned.

### *BY FAITH THEY OVERCAME*

30 By faith [a]the walls of Jericho fell down
after they were encircled for seven days. 31 By
faith [a]the harlot Rahab did not perish with those
who did not believe, when [b]she had received the
spies with peace.
32 And what more shall I say? For the time
would fail me to tell of [a]Gideon and [b]Barak and
[c]Samson and [d]Jephthah, also *of* [e]David and
[f]Samuel and the prophets: 33 who through faith
subdued kingdoms, worked righteousness, ob-
tained promises, [a]stopped the mouths of lions,
34 [a]quenched the violence of fire, escaped the
edge of the sword, out of weakness were made
strong, became valiant in battle, turned to flight
the armies of the aliens. 35 [a]Women received
their dead raised to life again.
Others were [b]tortured, not accepting deliver-
ance, that they might obtain a better resurrection.
36 Still others had trial of mockings and scourg-
ings, yes, and [a]of chains and imprisonment.
37 [a]They were stoned, they were sawn in two, were
tempted,[1] were slain with the sword. [b]They wan-
dered about [c]in sheepskins and goatskins, being
destitute, afflicted, tormented— 38 of whom the
world was not worthy. They wandered in deserts
and mountains, [a]*in* dens and caves of the earth.
39 And all these, [a]having obtained a good
testimony through faith, did not receive the
promise, 40 God having provided something
better for us, that they should not be [a]made
perfect apart from us.

**11:29** [a] Ex. 14:22–29 **11:30** [a] Josh. 6:20 **11:31** [a] Josh. 2:9; 6:23 [b] Josh. 2:1 **11:32** [a] Judg. 6:11; 7:1–25 [b] Judg. 4:6–24 [c] Judg. 13:24—16:31 [d] Judg. 11:1–29; 12:1–7 [e] 1 Sam. 16; 17 [f] 1 Sam. 7:9–14 **11:33** [a] Dan. 6:22 **11:34** [a] Dan. 3:23–28 **11:35** [a] 1 Kin. 17:22 [b] Acts 22:25 **11:36** [a] Gen. 39:20 **11:37** [a] 1 Kin. 21:13 [b] 2 Kin. 1:8 [c] Zech. 13:4 [1] NU-Text omits *were tempted.* **11:38** [a] 1 Kin. 18:4, 13; 19:9 **11:39** [a] Heb. 11:2, 13 **11:40** [a] Heb. 5:9

### *THE RACE OF FAITH*

**12** Therefore we also, since we are surrounded
by so great a cloud of witnesses, [a]let us lay
aside every weight, and the sin which so easily
ensnares *us,* and [b]let us run [c]with endurance the
race that is set before us, 2 looking unto Jesus,
the author and finisher of *our* faith, [a]who for the
joy that was set before Him [b]endured the cross,
despising the shame, and [c]has sat down at the
right hand of the throne of God.

> **SEEING JESUS IN THE SCRIPTURE**
>
> **12:2** Jesus endured the shame we deserve on our behalf, just as was prophesied (see Ps. 69:7, 19).

### *THE DISCIPLINE OF GOD*

*(Prov. 3:11, 12)*

3 [a]For consider Him who endured such hos-
tility from sinners against Himself, [b]lest you
become weary and discouraged in your souls.
4 [a]You have not yet resisted to bloodshed, striv-
ing against sin. 5 And you have forgotten the
exhortation which speaks to you as to sons:

[a]"My son, do not despise the chastening of
the LORD,
Nor be discouraged when you are rebuked
by Him;
6 For [a]whom the LORD loves He chastens,
And scourges every son whom He receives."[1]

7 [a]If[1] you endure chastening, God deals with
you as with sons; for what [b]son is there whom a
father does not chasten? 8 But if you are without
chastening, [a]of which all have become par-
takers, then you are illegitimate and not sons.
9 Furthermore, we have had human fathers who
corrected *us,* and we paid *them* respect. Shall we
not much more readily be in subjection to [a]the
Father of spirits and live? 10 For they indeed for
a few days chastened *us* as seemed *best* to them,
but He for *our* profit, [a]that *we* may be partakers
of His holiness. 11 Now no chastening seems to be
joyful for the present, but painful; nevertheless,
afterward it yields [a]the peaceable fruit of righ-
teousness to those who have been trained by it.

### *RENEW YOUR SPIRITUAL VITALITY*

*(Gen. 25:29–34; 27:30–40)*

12 Therefore [a]strengthen the hands which
hang down, and the feeble knees, 13 and make
straight paths for your feet, so that what is lame
may not be dislocated, but rather be healed.
14 [a]Pursue peace with all *people,* and holiness,
[b]without which no one will see the Lord: 15 look-
ing carefully lest anyone [a]fall short of the grace
of God; lest any [b]root of bitterness springing up
cause trouble, and by this many become defiled;
16 lest there *be* any [a]fornicator or profane person
like Esau, [b]who for one morsel of food sold
his birthright. 17 For you know that afterward,
when he wanted to inherit the blessing, he was
[a]rejected, for he found no place for repentance,
though he sought it diligently with tears.

### *THE GLORIOUS COMPANY*

18 For you have not come to [a]the mountain
that[1] may be touched and that burned with fire,
and to blackness and darkness[2] and tempest,
19 and the sound of a trumpet and the voice

**12:1** [a] Col. 3:8 [b] 1 Cor. 9:24 [c] Rom. 12:12 **12:2** [a] Luke 24:26 [b] Phil. 2:8 [c] Ps. 110:1 **12:3** [a] Matt. 10:24 [b] Gal. 6:9 **12:4** [a] [1 Cor. 10:13] **12:5** [a] Prov. 3:11, 12 **12:6** [a] Rev. 3:19 [1] Proverbs 3:11, 12 **12:7** [a] Deut. 8:5 [b] Prov. 13:24; 19:18; 23:13 [1] NU-Text and M-Text read *It is for discipline that you endure; God . . . .* **12:8** [a] 1 Pet. 5:9 **12:9** [a] [Job 12:10] **12:10** [a] Lev. 11:44 **12:11** [a] James 3:17, 18 **12:12** [a] Is. 35:3 **12:14** [a] Ps. 34:14 [b] Matt. 5:8 **12:15** [a] Heb. 4:1 [b] Deut. 29:18 **12:16** [a] [1 Cor. 6:13–18] [b] Gen. 25:33 **12:17** [a] Gen. 27:30–40 **12:18** [a] Deut. 4:11; 5:22 [1] NU-Text reads *to that which.* [2] NU-Text reads *gloom.*

> **APPLY THE TRUTH**
>
> **PAIN AND SUFFERING**
>
> **12:1–8** What's the farthest you've run? Maybe a mile at school? Perhaps a 5K? Something longer, like a 10K, half-marathon, or a full marathon—26.2 miles of nothing but you and your feet? For some people, running long distances brings pleasure; for most of us, it brings only pain and suffering. That doesn't mean the former are exempt from pain. The difference is they have a goal in mind, prepare themselves as best they can, and endure the pain, knowing it has a purpose.
>
> These verses compare a life of faith to a race. It can be challenging and painful at times, but when our motivation is like Jesus', we can make it through. Jesus endured unimaginable pain when He went to the cross. Notice, though, He did so with *joy.* He was able to find joy amid pain because He knew it was for the Father's glory and our salvation. In the same way, we can turn our pain and suffering over to God and find joy in our race, knowing it's all for Jesus, the one who suffered for us and suffers with us. We can endure great pain and suffering in this life because Jesus is with us and has gone before us.

of words, so that those who heard *it* [a]begged
that the word should not be spoken to them
anymore. 20(For they could not endure what
was commanded: [a]"And if so much as a beast
touches the mountain, it shall be stoned[1] or
shot with an arrow."[2] 21And so terrifying was
the sight *that* Moses said, [a]"I am exceedingly
afraid and trembling."[1])

22But you have come to Mount Zion and to
the city of the living God, the heavenly Jeru-
salem, to an innumerable company of angels,
23to the general assembly and church of [a]the
firstborn [b]*who are* registered in heaven, to God
[c]the Judge of all, to the spirits of just men [d]made
perfect, 24to Jesus [a]the Mediator of the new
covenant, and to [b]the blood of sprinkling that
speaks better things [c]than *that of* Abel.

### HEAR THE HEAVENLY VOICE

25See that you do not refuse Him who
speaks. For [a]if they did not escape who refused
Him who spoke on earth, much more *shall we*
*not escape* if we turn away from Him who *speaks*
from heaven, 26whose voice then shook the
earth; but now He has promised, saying, [a]"Yet
once more I shake[1] not only the earth, but also
heaven."[2] 27Now this, "Yet once more," indicates
the [a]removal of those things that are being shak-
en, as of things that are made, that the things
which cannot be shaken may remain.

28Therefore, since we are receiving a king-
dom which cannot be shaken, let us have grace,
by which we may[1] [a]serve God acceptably with
reverence and godly fear. 29For [a]our God *is* a
consuming fire.

### CONCLUDING MORAL DIRECTIONS

13 Let [a]brotherly love continue. 2[a]Do not for-
get to entertain strangers, for by so *doing*
[b]some have unwittingly entertained angels.
3[a]Remember the prisoners as if chained with
them—those who are mistreated—since you
yourselves are in the body also.

> **13:2** This is a reference to people in the Old Testament who encounter heavenly beings. These people included Abraham (Gen. 18), Lot (Gen. 19), and Gideon (Judg. 6). The idea is that, when you practice hospitality, you may be helping a messenger of God without realizing it.

4[a]Marriage *is* honorable among all, and the
bed undefiled; [b]but fornicators and adulterers
God will judge.

5*Let your* conduct *be* without covetousness;
*be* content with such things as you have. For He

**12:19** [a] Ex. 20:18–26 **12:20** [a] Ex. 19:12, 13 [1] NU-Text and M-Text omit the rest of this verse. [2] Exodus 19:12, 13 **12:21** [a] Deut. 9:19 [1] Deuteronomy 9:19 **12:23** [a] [James 1:18] [b] Luke 10:20 [c] Ps. 50:6; 94:2 [d] [Phil. 3:12] **12:24** [a] Heb. 8:6; 9:15 [b] Ex. 24:8 [c] Gen. 4:10 **12:25** [a] Heb. 2:2, 3 **12:26** [a] Hag. 2:6 [1] NU-Text reads *will shake.* [2] Haggai 2:6 **12:27** [a] [Is. 34:4; 54:10; 65:17] **12:28** [a] Heb. 13:15, 21 [1] M-Text omits *may.* **12:29** [a] Ex. 24:17 **13:1** [a] Rom. 12:10 **13:2** [a] Matt. 25:35 [b] Gen. 18:1–22; 19:1 **13:3** [a] Matt. 25:36 **13:4** [a] Prov. 5:18, 19 [b] 1 Cor. 6:9

KNOW THE TRUTH

## THE DOCTRINE OF GOD

### PART 17: THE IMMUTABILITY OF GOD

**13:8** Life is full of change. No two days—no two moments—are the same. Weather, societies, economies, science, and people all change all the time. In contrast, the writer of Hebrews exhorted his readers to establish, or make firm, their hearts upon good doctrine by focusing on the Unchangeable One: Jesus Christ. The Godhead (Father, Son, and Holy Spirit) is *immutable*, meaning unchanging. Everything God is, He always has been exactly as He is and always will be. Nothing about His essence intensifies, weakens, ages, or alters.

When Moses asked God who he should say sent him to Pharaoh and Israel, God's reply was, "I AM WHO I AM" (Ex. 3:14). The name *I AM* comes from a Hebrew verb meaning "to be." It means timeless existence. God was telling Moses He is who He is, who He always has been, and who He always will be.

In James 1:17, the apostle James contrasts God's immutability with the sun and moon. As the earth rotates around the sun and the moon rotates around the earth, all kinds of shifting shadows are created on our planet. To the contrary, the generous nature of God is changeless. He always does what He's always done because He always is who He's always been. Whatever may change, God won't.

*For* **THE DOCTRINE OF GOD: PART 18: THE IMMANENCE OF GOD**, *turn to Acts 17:27 on page 1129.* • • •

Himself has said, [a]"I will never leave you nor
forsake you."[1] 6 So we may boldly say:

> [a]"The LORD *is* my helper;
> I will not fear.
> What can man do to me?"[1]

### CONCLUDING RELIGIOUS DIRECTIONS

7 Remember those who rule over you, who
have spoken the word of God to you, whose
faith follow, considering the outcome of *their*
conduct. 8 Jesus Christ *is* [a]the same yesterday,
today, and forever. 9 Do not be carried about[1]
with various and strange doctrines. For *it is* good
that the heart be established by grace, not with
foods which have not profited those who have
been occupied with them.

10 We have an altar from which those who
serve the tabernacle have no right to eat. 11 For
the bodies of those animals, whose blood is
brought into the sanctuary by the high priest for
sin, are burned outside the camp. 12 Therefore
Jesus also, that He might sanctify the people
with His own blood, suffered outside the gate.
13 Therefore let us go forth to Him, outside the
camp, bearing [a]His reproach. 14 For here we have
no continuing city, but we seek the one to come.
15 [a]Therefore by Him let us continually offer [b]the
sacrifice of praise to God, that is, [c]the fruit of *our*
lips, giving thanks to His name. 16 [a]But do not
forget to do good and to share, for [b]with such
sacrifices God is well pleased.

17 [a]Obey those who rule over you, and be
submissive, for [b]they watch out for your souls,
as those who must give account. Let them do
so with joy and not with grief, for that would be
unprofitable for you.

### PRAYER REQUESTED

18 [a]Pray for us; for we are confident that we
have [b]a good conscience, in all things desiring
to live honorably. 19 But I especially urge *you* to
do this, that I may be restored to you the sooner.

### BENEDICTION, FINAL EXHORTATION, FAREWELL

20 Now may [a]the God of peace [b]who brought
up our Lord Jesus from the dead, [c]that great
Shepherd of the sheep, [d]through the blood of the
everlasting covenant, 21 make you complete in
every good work to do His will, [a]working in you[1]
what is well pleasing in His sight, through Jesus
Christ, to whom *be* glory forever and ever. Amen.

**SEEING JESUS IN THE SCRIPTURE**

**13:20–21** The resurrection of Jesus happened just as prophesied (see Hos. 6:2). God raised Jesus so we can follow Him for His glory.

22 And I appeal to you, brethren, bear with
the word of exhortation, for I have written to you
in few words. 23 Know that *our* brother Timothy
has been set free, with whom I shall see you if
he comes shortly.

24 Greet all those who rule over you, and all
the saints. Those from Italy greet you.

25 Grace *be* with you all. Amen.

13:5 [a] Deut. 31:6, 8; Josh. 1:5 [1] Deuteronomy 31:6, 8; Joshua 1:5 13:6 [a] Ps. 27:1; 118:6 [1] Psalm 118:6 13:8 [a] Heb. 1:12 13:9 [1] NU-Text and M-Text read *away.* 13:13 [a] 1 Pet. 4:14 13:15 [a] Eph. 5:20 [b] Lev. 7:12 [c] Hos. 14:2 13:16 [a] Rom. 12:13 [b] Phil. 4:18 13:17 [a] Phil. 2:29 [b] Ezek. 3:17 13:18 [a] Eph. 6:19 [b] Acts 23:1 13:20 [a] Rom. 5:1, 2, 10; 15:33 [b] Rom. 4:24 [c] 1 Pet. 2:25; 5:4 [d] Zech. 9:11 13:21 [a] Phil. 2:13 [1] NU-Text and M-Text read *us.*

# *The Epistle of* JAMES

| AUTHOR | KEY VERSE | READING TIME |
|---|---|---|
| James | James 2:17 | 19 minutes |

"Faith without works is dead" (James 2:26), and a dead faith is worse than no faith at all. Faith must work. Faith must produce. Faith must be visible, or it is not faith. Internal faith is not enough, nor is verbal faith. These aspects of faith must be present, but more is needed. Faith must prompt action. These are the thoughts that James had in mind when he wrote to Jewish believers. Faith in Christ is by grace, but that does not mean that works do not matter. Works do not lead *into* faith, but they will flow *from* faith. Throughout his epistle, James proclaimed the excellencies of true faith in Christ. Faith endures trials. Faith resists temptations. Faith obeys the Word. Faith produces doers. Faith harbors no prejudice. Faith rejects favoritism. Faith responds to the promises of God. Faith controls the tongue. Faith acts wisely. Faith produces separation from the world and submission to God. Faith provides us with the ability to resist the devil and humbly draw near to God. Faith waits patiently for the coming of the Lord. Faith is the start of a person's salvation, and it sustains that person in his salvation.

**Occasion:** James wrote to the scattered Jewish believers encouraging them to live out the faith in Christ that they profess.

**Main Point:** Faith without works is dead.

**Big Ideas:** Salvation is based on faith in Jesus alone. True faith in Jesus leads to living like Jesus. Every area of our lives should reveal we are followers of Christ.

## OUTLINE:

I. The Test of Faith (ch. 1)
II. The Characteristics of Faith (chs. 2–4)
III. The Triumph of Faith (ch. 5)

**c. AD 30**
Jesus' crucifixion and resurrection

**c. AD 30–35**
Pentecost; the early church in Jerusalem

**c. AD 37**
Jewish historian Josephus is born

**AD 37–41**
Caligula is Roman emperor

**AD 41–54**
Claudius is Roman emperor

**c. AD 44**
James is mentioned in a church leadership role

**c. AD 44–49**
**James written**

**c. AD 50**
The Jerusalem Council

**AD 54–68**
Nero is Roman emperor

**c. AD 62**
James is executed

### GREETING TO THE TWELVE TRIBES

**1** James, [a]a bondservant of God and of the Lord Jesus Christ,

To the twelve tribes which are scattered abroad:

Greetings.

### PROFITING FROM TRIALS

2 My brethren, [a]count it all joy [b]when you fall into various trials, 3 [a]knowing that the testing of your faith produces patience. 4 But let patience have *its* perfect work, that you may be perfect and complete, lacking nothing. 5 [a]If any of you lacks wisdom, [b]let him ask of God, who gives to all liberally and without reproach, and [c]it will be given to him. 6 [a]But let him ask in faith, with no doubting, for he who doubts is like a wave of the sea driven and tossed by the wind. 7 For let not that man suppose that he will receive anything from the Lord; 8 *he is* [a]a double-minded man, unstable in all his ways.

### THE PERSPECTIVE OF RICH AND POOR

9 Let the lowly brother glory in his exaltation, 10 but the rich in his humiliation, because [a]as a flower of the field he will pass away. 11 For no sooner has the sun risen with a burning heat than it withers the grass; its flower falls, and its beautiful appearance perishes. So the rich man also will fade away in his pursuits.

### LOVING GOD UNDER TRIALS

12 [a]Blessed *is* the man who endures temptation; for when he has been approved, he will receive [b]the crown of life [c]which the Lord has promised to those who love Him. 13 Let no one say when he is tempted, "I am tempted by God"; for God cannot be tempted by evil, nor does He Himself tempt anyone. 14 But each one is tempted when he is drawn away by his own desires and enticed. 15 Then, [a]when desire has conceived, it gives birth to sin; and sin, when it is full-grown, [b]brings forth death.

16 Do not be deceived, my beloved brethren. 17 [a]Every good gift and every perfect gift is from above, and comes down from the Father of lights, [b]with whom there is no variation or shadow of turning. 18 [a]Of His own will He brought us forth by the [b]word of truth, [c]that we might be a kind of firstfruits of His creatures.

### QUALITIES NEEDED IN TRIALS

19 So then,[1] my beloved brethren, let every man be swift to hear, [a]slow to speak, [b]slow to wrath; 20 for the wrath of man does not produce the righteousness of God.

### DOERS—NOT HEARERS ONLY

21 Therefore [a]lay aside all filthiness and overflow of wickedness, and receive with meekness the implanted word, [b]which is able to save your souls.

22 But [a]be doers of the word, and not hearers only, deceiving yourselves. 23 For [a]if anyone is a hearer of the word and not a doer, he is like a man observing his natural face in a mirror; 24 for he observes himself, goes away, and immediately forgets what kind of man he was. 25 But [a]he who looks into the perfect law of liberty and continues *in it,* and is not a forgetful hearer but a doer of the work, [b]this one will be blessed in what he does.

> **1:22** Believers who hear the Word of God (v. 19) must receive it with a teachable spirit (v. 21), applying it to their daily lives. To hear and not obey is to be deceived.

26 If anyone among you[1] thinks he is religious, and [a]does not bridle his tongue but deceives his own heart, this one's religion *is* useless. 27 [a]Pure and undefiled religion before God and the Father is this: [b]to visit orphans and widows in their trouble, [c]*and* to keep oneself unspotted from the world.

### BEWARE OF PERSONAL FAVORITISM

**2** My brethren, do not hold the faith of our Lord Jesus Christ, [a]*the Lord* of glory, with [b]partiality. 2 For if there should come into your assembly a man with gold rings, in fine apparel, and there should also come in a poor man in filthy clothes, 3 and you pay attention to the one wearing the fine clothes and say to him, "You sit here in a good place," and say to the poor man, "You stand there," or, "Sit here at my footstool," 4 have you not shown partiality among yourselves, and become judges with evil thoughts?

5 Listen, my beloved brethren: [a]Has God not chosen the poor of this world *to be* [b]rich in faith and heirs of the kingdom [c]which He promised to those who love Him? 6 But [a]you have dishonored the poor man. Do not the rich oppress you [b]and drag you into the courts? 7 Do they not blaspheme that noble name by which you are [a]called?

8 If you really fulfill *the* royal law according to the Scripture, [a]"You shall love your neighbor as yourself,"[1] you do well; 9 but if you show partiality, you commit sin, and are convicted by the

**1:1** [a] Acts 12:17 **1:2** [a] Acts 5:41 [b] 1 Pet. 1:6 **1:3** [a] Rom. 5:3–5 **1:5** [a] 1 Kin. 3:9 [b] Matt. 7:7 [c] Jer. 29:12 **1:6** [a] [Mark 11:23, 24] **1:8** [a] James 4:8 **1:10** [a] Job 14:2 **1:12** [a] James 5:11 [b] [1 Cor. 9:25] [c] Matt. 10:22 **1:15** [a] Job 15:35 [b] [Rom. 5:12; 6:23] **1:17** [a] John 3:27 [b] Num. 23:19 **1:18** [a] John 1:13 [b] [1 Pet. 1:3, 23] [c] [Eph. 1:12, 13] **1:19** [a] Prov. 10:19; 17:27 [b] Prov. 14:17; 16:32 [1] NU-Text reads *Know this* or *This you know.* **1:21** [a] Col. 3:8 [b] Acts 13:26 **1:22** [a] Matt. 7:21–28 **1:23** [a] Luke 6:47 **1:25** [a] James 2:12 [b] John 13:17 **1:26** [a] Ps. 34:13 [1] NU-Text omits *among you.* **1:27** [a] Matt. 25:34–36 [b] Is. 1:17 [c] [Rom. 12:2] **2:1** [a] 1 Cor. 2:8 [b] Lev. 19:15 **2:5** [a] 1 Cor. 1:27 [b] Luke 12:21 [c] Ex. 20:6 **2:6** [a] 1 Cor. 11:22 [b] Acts 13:50 **2:7** [a] 1 Pet. 4:16 **2:8** [a] Lev. 19:18 [1] Leviticus 19:18

APPLY THE TRUTH

## TEMPTATION

**1:13–15** Have you ever known the right thing to do and done the wrong thing anyway? We all have. Each of us has given in to temptation and gone the wrong way. Temptation is a huge part of the human experience. While temptation isn't a sin, it can be extremely dangerous. It pulls us away from God's good plans and the abundant living Jesus promised and draws us toward sin and a poor substitute that never delivers. Quite simply, temptation is a liar. This is why God is never the source of temptation; it's always from Satan, the broken world around us, or our sinful desires.

The way to resist temptation is first through endurance. Temptation often makes everything seem urgent—we must act right away, or we'll miss out. Be patient instead. Wisdom, strength, and guidance will come. Second, fight the lure of temptation from your identity. You are a child of God and have access to His victory and strength. Know who you are and what God has given you. Third, fight temptation with faith. Believe whatever God has for you is ultimately best and will bring you true, lasting joy.

law as [a]transgressors. 10 For whoever shall keep the whole law, and yet [a]stumble in one *point,* [b]he is guilty of all. 11 For He who said, [a]"Do not commit adultery,"[1] also said, [b]"Do not murder."[2] Now if you do not commit adultery, but you do murder, you have become a transgressor of the law. 12 So speak and so do as those who will be judged by [a]the law of liberty. 13 For [a]judgment is without mercy to the one who has shown [b]no [c]mercy. [d]Mercy triumphs over judgment.

**SEEING JESUS IN THE SCRIPTURE**

**2:10** Jesus is the only one to obey the law perfectly (see Matt. 5:11). Salvation is only found in His completed work.

### *FAITH WITHOUT WORKS IS DEAD*

*(cf. Gen. 22; Josh. 2)*

14 [a]What *does it* profit, my brethren, if someone says he has faith but does not have works? Can faith save him? 15 [a]If a brother or sister is naked and destitute of daily food, 16 and [a]one of you says to them, "Depart in peace, be warmed and filled," but you do not give them the things which are needed for the body, what *does it* profit? 17 Thus also faith by itself, if it does not have works, is dead.

18 But someone will say, "You have faith, and I have works." [a]Show me your faith without your[1] works, [b]and I will show you my faith by my[2] works. 19 You believe that there is one God. You do well. Even the demons believe—and tremble! 20 But do you want to know, O foolish man, that faith without works is dead?[1] 21 Was not Abraham our father justified by works [a]when he offered Isaac his son on the altar? 22 Do you see [a]that faith was working together with his works, and by [b]works faith was made perfect? 23 And the Scripture was fulfilled which says, [a]"Abraham believed God, and it was accounted to him for righteousness."[1] And he was called [b]the friend of God. 24 You see then that a man is justified by works, and not by faith only.

**2:19** Although they **believe**, the **demons** don't love Jesus (see Matt. 8:29). Their kind of belief doesn't lead to love, submission, and obedience; instead, it leads to hatred, rebellion, and disobedience.

**2:22** **Faith** and **works** should be **together**; there is a close relationship between the two. Faith produces works; and works make faith **perfect**, meaning "mature" or "complete."

25 Likewise, [a]was not Rahab the harlot also justified by works when she received the messengers and sent *them* out another way? 26 For as the body without the spirit is dead, so faith without works is dead also.

### *THE UNTAMABLE TONGUE*

3 My brethren, [a]let not many of you become teachers, [b]knowing that we shall receive a stricter judgment. 2 For [a]we all stumble in many things. [b]If anyone does not stumble in word, [c]he

**2:9** [a] Deut. 1:17 **2:10** [a] Gal. 3:10 [b] Deut. 27:26 **2:11** [a] Ex. 20:14; Deut. 5:18 [b] Ex. 20:13; Deut. 5:17 [1] Exodus 20:14; Deuteronomy 5:18 [2] Exodus 20:13; Deuteronomy 5:17 **2:12** [a] James 1:25 **2:13** [a] Job 22:6 [b] Prov. 21:13 [c] Mic. 7:18 [d] Rom. 12:8 **2:14** [a] Matt. 7:21–23, 26; 21:28–32 **2:15** [a] Luke 3:11 **2:16** [a] [1 John 3:17, 18] **2:18** [a] Heb. 6:10 [b] James 3:13 [1] NU-Text omits *your.* [2] NU-Text omits *my.* **2:20** [1] NU-Text reads *useless.* **2:21** [a] Gen. 22:9, 10, 12, 16–18 **2:22** [a] Heb. 11:17 [b] John 8:39 **2:23** [a] Gen. 15:6 [b] 2 Chr. 20:7 [1] Genesis 15:6 **2:25** [a] Heb. 11:31 **3:1** [a] [Matt. 23:8] [b] Luke 6:37 **3:2** [a] 1 Kin. 8:46 [b] Ps. 34:13 [c] [Matt. 12:34–37]

*is* a perfect man, able also to bridle the whole body. 3 Indeed,[1] [a]we put bits in horses' mouths that they may obey us, and we turn their whole body. 4 Look also at ships: although they are so large and are driven by fierce winds, they are turned by a very small rudder wherever the pilot desires. 5 Even so [a]the tongue is a little member and [b]boasts great things.

See how great a forest a little fire kindles! 6 And [a]the tongue *is* a fire, a world of iniquity. The tongue is so set among our members that it [b]defiles the whole body, and sets on fire the course of nature; and it is set on fire by hell.

**3:6** The Greek word translated **hell** literally means "Hinnom Valley." The Hinnom Valley is a deep ravine located south of Jerusalem that was used as an ancient garbage dump. All kinds of waste material and dead animals were taken to Hinnom Valley to be burned. Eventually, the place came to be used as a symbol of judgment and sorrow.

7 For every kind of beast and bird, of reptile and creature of the sea, is tamed and has been tamed by mankind. 8 But no man can tame the tongue. *It is* an unruly evil, [a]full of deadly poison. 9 With it we bless our God and Father, and with it we curse men, who have been made [a]in the similitude of God. 10 Out of the same mouth proceed blessing and cursing. My brethren, these things ought not to be so. 11 Does a spring send forth fresh *water* and bitter from the same opening? 12 Can a [a]fig tree, my brethren, bear olives, or a grapevine bear figs? Thus no spring yields both salt water and fresh.[1]

### HEAVENLY VERSUS DEMONIC WISDOM

13 [a]Who *is* wise and understanding among you? Let him show by good conduct *that* his works *are done* in the meekness of wisdom. 14 But if you have [a]bitter envy and self-seeking in your hearts, [b]do not boast and lie against the truth. 15 [a]This wisdom does not descend from above, but *is* earthly, sensual, demonic. 16 For [a]where envy and self-seeking *exist,* confusion and every evil thing *are* there. 17 But [a]the wisdom that is from above is first pure, then peaceable, gentle, willing to yield, full of mercy and good fruits, [b]without partiality [c]and without hypocrisy. 18 [a]Now the fruit of righteousness is sown in peace by those who make peace.

### PRIDE PROMOTES STRIFE

**4** Where do wars and fights *come* from among you? Do *they* not *come* from your *desires for* pleasure [a]that war in your members? 2 You lust and do not have. You murder and covet and cannot obtain. You fight and war. Yet[1] you do not have because you do not ask. 3 [a]You ask and do not receive, [b]because you ask amiss, that you may spend *it* on your pleasures. 4 Adulterers and[1] adulteresses! Do you not know that [a]friendship with the world is enmity with God? [b]Whoever therefore wants to be a friend of the world makes himself an enemy of God. 5 Or do you think that the Scripture says in vain, [a]"The Spirit who dwells in us yearns jealously"?

6 But He gives more grace. Therefore He says:

[a]"God resists the proud,
But gives grace to the humble."[1]

### HUMILITY CURES WORLDLINESS

7 Therefore submit to God. [a]Resist the devil and he will flee from you. 8 [a]Draw near to God and He will draw near to you. [b]Cleanse *your* hands, *you* sinners; and [c]purify *your* hearts, *you* double-minded. 9 [a]Lament and mourn and weep! Let your laughter be turned to mourning and *your* joy to gloom. 10 [a]Humble yourselves in the sight of the Lord, and He will lift you up.

### DO NOT JUDGE A BROTHER

11 [a]Do not speak evil of one another, brethren. He who speaks evil of a brother [b]and judges his brother, speaks evil of the law and judges the law. But if you judge the law, you are not a doer of the law but a judge. 12 There is one Lawgiver,[1] [a]who is able to save and to destroy. [b]Who[2] are you to judge another?[3]

### DO NOT BOAST ABOUT TOMORROW

13 Come now, you who say, "Today or tomorrow we will[1] go to such and such a city, spend a year there, buy and sell, and make a profit"; 14 whereas you do not know what *will happen* tomorrow. For what *is* your life? [a]It is even a vapor that appears for a little time and then vanishes away. 15 Instead you *ought* to say, [a]"If

**4:13** The problem here isn't the plan itself or the concept of planning; it's leaving God out of the plan (v. 15).

**3:3** [a] Ps. 32:9 [1] NU-Text reads *Now if.* **3:5** [a] Prov. 12:18; 15:2 [b] Ps. 12:3; 73:8 **3:6** [a] Prov. 16:27 [b] [Matt. 12:36; 15:11, 18] **3:8** [a] Ps. 140:3 **3:9** [a] Gen. 1:26; 5:1; 9:6 **3:12** [a] Matt. 7:16–20 [1] NU-Text reads *Neither can a salty spring produce fresh water.* **3:13** [a] Gal. 6:4 **3:14** [a] Rom. 13:13 [b] Rom. 2:17 **3:15** [a] Phil. 3:19 **3:16** [a] 1 Cor. 3:3 **3:17** [a] 1 Cor. 2:6, 7 [b] James 2:1 [c] Rom. 12:9 **3:18** [a] Prov. 11:18 **4:1** [a] Rom. 7:23 **4:2** [1] NU-Text and M-Text omit *Yet.* **4:3** [a] Job 27:8, 9 [b] [Ps. 66:18] **4:4** [a] 1 John 2:15 [b] Gal. 1:4 [1] NU-Text omits *Adulterers and.* **4:5** [a] Gen. 6:5 **4:6** [a] Prov. 3:34 [1] Proverbs 3:34 **4:7** [a] [Eph. 4:27; 6:11] **4:8** [a] 2 Chr. 15:2 [b] Is. 1:16 [c] 1 Pet. 1:22 **4:9** [a] Matt. 5:4 **4:10** [a] Job 22:29 **4:11** [a] 1 Pet. 2:1–3 [b] [Matt. 7:1–5] **4:12** [a] [Matt. 10:28] [b] Rom. 14:4 [1] NU-Text adds *and Judge.* [2] NU-Text and M-Text read *But who.* [3] NU-Text reads *a neighbor.* **4:13** [1] M-Text reads *let us.* **4:14** [a] Job 7:7 **4:15** [a] Acts 18:21

LIVE THE TRUTH

## CONFESSING SIN

**4:1–6** It isn't easy to admit when you're wrong, but it's at the heart of the gospel. Confession is admitting, owning, and turning from wrongdoing. It's taking responsibility for our sin, being honest with God about it, and wanting never to sin again. Confession can be painful, but the beautiful part is Jesus stands in the gap between where we are and perfection. God promises if we confess our sin to Him, He is faithful and just to forgive it and cleanse us from all unrighteousness (1 John 1:9). Because of what Jesus has done on the cross, we can be forgiven of our wrongdoing and declared righteous, but only if we acknowledge we are hopeless without Him.

Here, James tells us the source of our sin: our own selfish desires. But James's message contains an unbelievable encouragement. God freely gives grace to those who admit their mistakes. If we are prideful and refuse to own our sinfulness, we basically say we don't need Jesus. Ultimately, we're rejecting Jesus and remain enemies of God. However, if we confess our sins and accept Jesus' provision, we receive undeserved and ultimate forgiveness. Confess your sins to God, and others. When we humbly admit our shortcomings and struggles, God provides what we need both in the moment and eternally.

the Lord wills, we shall live and do this or that."
16 But now you boast in your arrogance. [a]All such
boasting is evil.
17 Therefore, [a]to him who knows to do good
and does not do *it,* to him it is sin.

### *RICH OPPRESSORS WILL BE JUDGED*

5 Come now, *you* [a]rich, weep and howl for your
miseries that are coming upon *you!* 2 Your
[a]riches are corrupted, and [b]your garments are
moth-eaten. 3 Your gold and silver are corroded,
and their corrosion will be a witness against
you and will eat your flesh like fire. [a]You have
heaped up treasure in the last days. 4 Indeed
[a]the wages of the laborers who mowed your
fields, which you kept back by fraud, cry out;
and [b]the cries of the reapers have reached the
ears of the Lord of Sabaoth.[1] 5 You have lived
on the earth in pleasure and luxury; you have
fattened your hearts as[1] in a day of slaughter.
6 You have condemned, you have murdered the
just; he does not resist you.

### *BE PATIENT AND PERSEVERING*

7 Therefore be patient, brethren, until the
coming of the Lord. See *how* the farmer waits for
the precious fruit of the earth, waiting patiently
for it until it receives the early and latter rain.
8 You also be patient. Establish your hearts, for
the coming of the Lord is at hand.
9 Do not grumble against one another, breth-
ren, lest you be condemned.[1] Behold, the Judge
is standing at the door! 10 [a]My brethren, take the
prophets, who spoke in the name of the Lord, as
an example of suffering and [b]patience. 11 Indeed
[a]we count them blessed who [b]endure. You have
heard of [c]the perseverance of Job and seen [d]the
end *intended by* the Lord—that [e]the Lord is very
compassionate and merciful.
12 But above all, my brethren, [a]do not swear,
either by heaven or by earth or with any other
oath. But let your "Yes" be "Yes," and *your* "No,"
"No," lest you fall into judgment.[1]

### *MEETING SPECIFIC NEEDS*

*(cf. 1 Kin. 18:41–46)*

13 Is anyone among you suffering? Let him
[a]pray. Is anyone cheerful? [b]Let him sing psalms.
14 Is anyone among you sick? Let him call for
the elders of the church, and let them pray
over him, [a]anointing him with oil in the name
of the Lord. 15 And the prayer of faith will save
the sick, and the Lord will raise him up. [a]And
if he has committed sins, he will be forgiven.
16 Confess *your* trespasses[1] to one another, and
pray for one another, that you may be healed.
[a]The effective, fervent prayer of a righteous

**5:12–13** James isn't forbidding a believer from taking an **oath** in court or invoking God as witness to some significant statement (see 1 Thess. 2:5). Instead, he is prohibiting the ancient practice of appealing to a variety of different objects, such as the temple or the altar, to confirm the truthfulness of one's statement. Our word should stand on its own.

**4:16** [a] 1 Cor. 5:6 **4:17** [a] [Luke 12:47] **5:1** [a] [Luke 6:24] **5:2** [a] Matt. 6:19 [b] Job 13:28 **5:3** [a] Rom. 2:5 **5:4** [a] Lev. 19:13 [b] Deut. 24:15 [1] Literally, in Hebrew, *Hosts* **5:5** [1] NU-Text omits *as.* **5:9** [1] NU-Text and M-Text read *judged.* **5:10** [a] Matt. 5:12 [b] Heb. 10:36 **5:11** [a] [Ps. 94:12] [b] [James 1:12] [c] Job 1:21, 22; 2:10 [d] Job 42:10 [e] Num. 14:18 **5:12** [a] Matt. 5:34–37 [1] M-Text reads *hypocrisy.* **5:13** [a] Ps. 50:14, 15 [b] Eph. 5:19 **5:14** [a] Mark 6:13; 16:18 **5:15** [a] Is. 33:24 **5:16** [a] Num. 11:2 [1] NU-Text reads *Therefore confess your sins.*

JAMES 5:1–20

# CHRISTIAN LIVING

58

STORY OF SCRIPTURE

## WHAT'S GOING ON?

The Book of James offers blunt but encouraging truths for Christian living. James, the half-brother of Jesus, knew Jesus' character more than most. In this chapter, James shows a contrast between how the world lives and how the believer, imitating Jesus, should live. While the world exploits others, we live generously (vv. 1–6). While the world grows impatient, we wait on the Lord (vv. 7–8). While the world complains and fights, we endure with patience and compassion (vv. 9–10). While the world is wishy-washy, we are decisive and act with conviction (v.12). While the world lives selfishly, we look out for each other and pray for each other (vv.13–18). While the world writes us off for our mistakes, we seek the wanderer out aiming for restoration (vv. 19–20). This is what faith in action looks like, a faith that is living and not dead (see James 2:14–26).

## WHAT DOES THIS MEAN FOR ME?

This passage, and the rest of the Book of James, offers many relatable applications for how we live each day. James challenges us to consider our priorities and the effect our lives have on others. He calls into question the pursuit of wealth for its own sake and instead invites us to invest in what endures: righteousness, patience, and prayerful reliance on God.

## DID YOU CATCH THE PATTERN?

Throughout the Bible, a clear distinction is made between earthly and spiritual wealth. Jesus warned against storing up treasures on earth, where moth and rust destroy (see Matt. 6:19–21). Earlier, the prophets condemned injustice and called for care for the oppressed, mirroring James's admonitions (see Mic. 6:8).

*For the next* Story of Scripture *reading and devotion, turn to Revelation 19:6–21 on page 1307.*

man avails much. 17 Elijah was a man [a]with a
nature like ours, and [b]he prayed earnestly that
it would not rain; and it did not rain on the land
for three years and six months. 18 And he prayed
[a]again, and the heaven gave rain, and the earth
produced its fruit.

### *BRING BACK THE ERRING ONE*

19 Brethren, if anyone among you wanders
from the truth, and someone [a]turns him back,
20 let him know that he who turns a sinner from
the error of his way [a]will save a soul[1] from death
and [b]cover a multitude of sins.

5:17 [a] Acts 14:15 [b] 1 Kin. 17:1; 18:1 5:18 [a] 1 Kin. 18:1, 42 5:19 [a] Gal. 6:1 5:20 [a] Rom. 11:14 [b] [1 Pet. 4:8] [1] NU-Text reads *his soul.*

# *The First Epistle of the Apostle*

# PETER

| AUTHOR | KEY VERSES | READING TIME |
| --- | --- | --- |
| Peter | 1 Peter 2:11–12 | 20 minutes |

Persecution can produce bitterness, or it can lead to growth. How a person responds to persecution determines which it will be. In writing to Jewish believers struggling through persecution, Peter encouraged them to conduct themselves courageously for the Person and program of Christ. Both their character and conduct were to be above reproach. Having been born again to a living hope, they were to imitate the Holy One who had called them. The fruit of that character would be conduct rooted in submission and honor: citizens to government, servants to masters, wives to husbands, husbands to wives, and Christians to one another. Christians are not to "think it strange concerning the fiery trial which is to try you, as though some strange thing happened to you" (1 Pet. 4:12), but are to rejoice as partakers of the suffering of Christ. That response to life is truly the climax of one's submission to the good hand of God.

**Occasion:** Peter wrote his epistle from Babylon (1 Pet. 5:13), which could mean literally from Mesopotamia or symbolically from Rome. Peter wrote to encourage believers to live in faith through persecution.

**Main Point:** Believers are called to endure suffering with faith, and in doing so, they will testify to Jesus, whose suffering brought about their salvation.

**Big Ideas:** Jesus never promised that His followers would be free from difficulties and suffering. As believers, we are to respond differently to suffering and hardship than those around us. We are citizens of Christ's kingdom first and foremost.

## OUTLINE:

I. The Salvation of the Believer (ch. 1)
II. The Submission of the Believer (chs. 2–3)
III. The Suffering of the Believer (chs. 4–5)

**c. AD 27**
Andrew brings his brother Simon Peter to Jesus

**c. AD 29**
Peter witnesses the transfiguration

**c. AD 30**
Jesus' crucifixion and resurrection

**c. AD 30–35**
Pentecost; the early church in Jerusalem

**c. AD 37**
Jewish historian Josephus is born

**c. AD 41**
Peter takes the gospel to Gentiles

**c. AD 50**
The Jerusalem Council

**AD 54–68**
Nero is Roman emperor

**c. AD 64–65**
**1 Peter written**

**c. AD 67**
Peter and Paul are executed

### *GREETING TO THE ELECT PILGRIMS*

1 Peter, an apostle of Jesus Christ,

To the pilgrims [a]of the Dispersion in Pontus,
Galatia, Cappadocia, Asia, and Bithynia, 2 [a]elect
[b]according to the foreknowledge of God the
Father, [c]in sanctification of the Spirit, for [d]obedi-
ence and [e]sprinkling of the blood of Jesus Christ:

[f]Grace to you and peace be multiplied.

### *A HEAVENLY INHERITANCE*

3 [a]Blessed *be* the God and Father of our Lord
Jesus Christ, who [b]according to His abundant
mercy [c]has begotten us again to a living hope
[d]through the resurrection of Jesus Christ from
the dead, 4 to an inheritance incorruptible and
undefiled and that does not fade away, [a]reserved
in heaven for you, 5 [a]who are kept by the power
of God through faith for salvation ready to be
revealed in the last time.

6 [a]In this you greatly rejoice, though now
[b]for a little while, if need be, [c]you have been
grieved by various trials, 7 that [a]the genuineness
of your faith, *being* much more precious than
gold that perishes, though [b]it is tested by fire,
[c]may be found to praise, honor, and glory at the
revelation of Jesus Christ, 8 [a]whom having not
seen[1] you love. [b]Though now you do not see *Him*,
yet believing, you rejoice with joy inexpressible
and full of glory, 9 receiving the end of your
faith—the salvation of *your* souls.

> **1:7 Gold** is rarely found by itself. Usually, it's mined with other rocks and substances. Whatever was mined was placed in a large container over a very hot **fire**. As the objects heated, the impurities could be separated from the gold and scraped off. This purifying process resulted in pure and costly gold.

10 Of this salvation the prophets have inquired
and searched carefully, who prophesied of the
grace *that would come* to you, 11 searching what, or
what manner of time, [a]the Spirit of Christ who was
in them was indicating when He testified before-
hand the sufferings of Christ and the glories that
would follow. 12 To them it was revealed that, not
to themselves, but to us[1] they were ministering
the things which now have been reported to you
through those who have preached the gospel to
you by the Holy Spirit sent from heaven—things
which [a]angels desire to look into.

### *LIVING BEFORE GOD OUR FATHER*

13 Therefore gird up the loins of your mind,
be sober, and rest *your* hope fully upon the
grace that is to be brought to you at the revela-
tion of Jesus Christ; 14 as obedient children, not
[a]conforming yourselves to the former lusts, *as*
in your ignorance; 15 [a]but as He who called you

**1:1** [a] James 1:1 **1:2** [a] Eph. 1:4 [b] [Rom. 8:29] [c] 2 Thess. 2:13 [d] Rom. 1:5 [e] Heb. 10:22; 12:24 [f] Rom. 1:7 **1:3** [a] Eph. 1:3 [b] Gal. 6:16 [c] [John 3:3, 5] [d] 1 Cor. 15:20 **1:4** [a] Col. 1:5 **1:5** [a] John 10:28 **1:6** [a] Matt. 5:12 [b] 2 Cor. 4:17 [c] James 1:2 **1:7** [a] James 1:3 [b] Job 23:10 [c] [Rom. 2:7] **1:8** [a] 1 John 4:20 [b] John 20:29 [1] M-Text reads *known*. **1:11** [a] 2 Pet. 1:21 **1:12** [a] Eph. 3:10 [1] NU-Text and M-Text read *you*. **1:14** [a] [Rom. 12:2] **1:15** [a] [2 Cor. 7:1]

KNOW THE TRUTH

## THE DOCTRINE OF JESUS

### PART 8: THE RESURRECTION OF JESUS

**1:3–5** Jesus rose from the dead for at least four reasons. First, His resurrection **verifies everything He claimed is true**. Under threat of torture and death, Jesus was asked if He was the Christ (heir to King David's throne) and God's Son (and thus God Himself). Jesus boldly asserted in Mark 14:62, "I am." Jesus made other shocking claims about being the only way to salvation, the Lord of the Sabbath, and more. His death brought all those claims into question. His resurrection proved every claim true; Jesus is exactly who He claims to be. Second, Christ's resurrection **shows His supremacy over the power of death**. No matter how impressive one's life may be, every person loses the battle with death. But not Jesus. If Jesus can overcome death's power over Him, He can overcome death's power over others. Third, Jesus' resurrection **guarantees those who call on Him will be saved**. The living have no contact with the dead. What good is a dead savior to a living sinful person? But Jesus isn't dead; He's alive. A living person can confidently call on the living Savior and be saved. Finally, Jesus' resurrection **enables our resurrection**. Because Jesus rose, we will rise. When we rise, we will be like Him and with Him forever.

*For* **THE DOCTRINE THE HOLY SPIRIT: PART 1: OVERVIEW OF THE DOCTRINE OF THE HOLY SPIRIT**, *turn to Judges 6:34–35 on page 248.*

**1:10–12** Peter indicates the Old Testament **prophets** knew of the gracious salvation we would one day receive and, as a result, studied it carefully and intensively. They, however, didn't experience the fullness of this salvation during their lives. Just as these prophets surely would have loved to understand the gospel message they shared in part, so do the **angels** long to understand it more fully. Angels understand the gospel, but they will never know what it's like to experience it.

*is* holy, you also be holy in all *your* conduct,
16 because it is written, [a]"Be holy, for I am holy."[1]

## SEEING JESUS IN THE SCRIPTURE

**1:15–16** In Christ, we have indeed been made holy and can thus live in holiness as God commands (see Lev. 11:44).

17 And if you call on the Father, who [a]without
partiality judges according to each one's work,
conduct yourselves throughout the time of your
stay *here* in fear; 18 knowing that you were not re-
deemed with corruptible things, *like* silver or gold,
from your aimless conduct *received* by tradition
from your fathers, 19 but [a]with the precious blood of
Christ, [b]as of a lamb without blemish and without
spot. 20 [a]He indeed was foreordained before the
foundation of the world, but was manifest [b]in these
last times for you 21 who through Him believe in
God, [a]who raised Him from the dead and [b]gave
Him glory, so that your faith and hope are in God.

### *THE ENDURING WORD*

22 Since you [a]have purified your souls in obey-
ing the truth through the Spirit[1] in sincere [b]love
of the brethren, love one another fervently with a
pure heart, 23 [a]having been born again, not of cor-
ruptible seed but incorruptible, [b]through the word
of God which lives and abides forever,[1] 24 because

[a]"All flesh *is* as grass,
And all the glory of man[1] as the flower of
the grass.
The grass withers,
And its flower falls away,
25 [a]But the word of the LORD endures forever."[1]

[b]Now this is the word which by the gospel was
preached to you.

2 Therefore, [a]laying aside all malice, all deceit,
hypocrisy, envy, and all evil speaking, 2 [a]as
newborn babes, desire the pure [b]milk of the
word, that you may grow thereby,[1] 3 if indeed you
have [a]tasted that the Lord *is* gracious.

### *THE CHOSEN STONE AND HIS CHOSEN PEOPLE*

*(Ps. 118:22; Is. 28:16)*

4 Coming to Him *as to* a living stone, [a]re-
jected indeed by men, but chosen by God *and*
precious, 5 you also, as living stones, are being
built up a spiritual house, a holy priesthood,
to offer up spiritual sacrifices acceptable to
God through Jesus Christ. 6 Therefore it is also
contained in the Scripture,

[a]"Behold, I lay in Zion
A chief cornerstone, elect, precious,
And he who believes on Him will by no
means be put to shame."[1]

7 Therefore, to you who believe, *He is* pre-
cious; but to those who are disobedient,[1]

[a]"The stone which the builders rejected
Has become the chief cornerstone,"[2]

8 and

[a]"A stone of stumbling
And a rock of offense."[1]

[b]They stumble, being disobedient to the word,
[c]to which they also were appointed.
9 But you *are* a chosen generation, a roy-
al priesthood, a holy nation, His own special
people, that you may proclaim the praises of
Him who called you out of [a]darkness into His
marvelous light; 10 [a]who once *were* not a peo-
ple but *are* now the people of God, who had
not obtained mercy but now have obtained
mercy.

### *LIVING BEFORE THE WORLD*

11 Beloved, I beg *you* as sojourners and pil-
grims, abstain from fleshly lusts [a]which war
against the soul, 12 [a]having your conduct honor-
able among the Gentiles, that when they speak
against you as evildoers, [b]they may, by *your*
good works which they observe, glorify God in
the day of visitation.

### *SUBMISSION TO GOVERNMENT*

*(cf. Rom. 13:1–5)*

13 [a]Therefore submit yourselves to every
ordinance of man for the Lord's sake, whether

**1:16** [a] Lev. 11:44, 45; 19:2; 20:7 [1] Leviticus 11:44, 45; 19:2; 20:7 **1:17** [a] Acts 10:34 **1:19** [a] Acts 20:28 [b] Ex. 12:5 **1:20** [a] Rom. 3:25 [b] Gal. 4:4 **1:21** [a] Acts 2:24 [b] Acts 2:33 **1:22** [a] Acts 15:9 [b] Heb. 13:1 [1] NU-Text omits *through the Spirit.* **1:23** [a] John 1:13 [b] James 1:18 [1] NU-Text omits *forever.* **1:24** [a] Is. 40:6–8 [1] NU-Text reads *all its glory.* **1:25** [a] Is. 40:8 [b] [John 1:1] [1] Isaiah 40:6–8 **2:1** [a] Heb. 12:1 **2:2** [a] [Matt. 18:3; 19:14] [b] 1 Cor. 3:2 [1] NU-Text adds *up to salvation.* **2:3** [a] Heb. 6:5 **2:4** [a] Ps. 118:22 **2:6** [a] Is. 28:16 [1] Isaiah 28:16 **2:7** [a] Ps. 118:22 [1] NU-Text reads *to those who disbelieve.* [2] Psalm 118:22 **2:8** [a] Is. 8:14 [b] 1 Cor. 1:23 [c] Rom. 9:22 [1] Isaiah 8:14 **2:9** [a] [Acts 26:18] **2:10** [a] Hos. 1:9, 10; 2:23 **2:11** [a] James 4:1 **2:12** [a] Phil. 2:15 [b] Matt. 5:16; 9:8 **2:13** [a] Matt. 22:21

to the king as supreme, 14 or to governors, as to those who are sent by him for the punishment of evildoers and *for the* praise of those who do good. 15 For this is the will of God, that by doing good you may put to silence the ignorance of foolish men— 16 [a]as free, yet not [b]using liberty as a cloak for vice, but as bondservants of God. 17 Honor all *people.* Love the brotherhood. Fear [a]God. Honor the king.

### *SUBMISSION TO MASTERS*

*(Is. 53:7–9)*

18 [a]Servants, *be* submissive to *your* masters with all fear, not only to the good and gentle, but also to the harsh. 19 For this *is* [a]commendable, if because of conscience toward God one endures grief, suffering wrongfully. 20 For [a]what credit *is it* if, when you are beaten for your faults, you take it patiently? But when you do good and suffer, if you take it patiently, this *is* commendable before God. 21 For [a]to this you were called, because Christ also suffered for us,[1] [b]leaving us[2] an example, that you should follow His steps:

22 "Who[a] committed no sin,
Nor was deceit found in His mouth";[1]

23 [a]who, when He was reviled, did not revile in return; when He suffered, He did not threaten, but [b]committed *Himself* to Him who judges righteously; 24 [a]who Himself bore our sins in His own body on the tree, [b]that we, having died to sins, might live for righteousness—[c]by whose stripes you were healed. 25 For [a]you were like sheep going astray, but have now returned [b]to the Shepherd and Overseer[1] of your souls.

> **SEEING JESUS IN THE SCRIPTURE**
>
> **2:24–25** Jesus died to save us from sin (see Is. 53:4). We aren't free to live in sin, but rather to live in righteousness.

### *SUBMISSION TO HUSBANDS*

**3** Wives, likewise, *be* [a]submissive to your own husbands, that even if some do not obey the word, [b]they, without a word, may [c]be won by the conduct of their wives, 2 [a]when they observe your chaste conduct *accompanied* by fear. 3 [a]Do not let your adornment be *merely* outward—arranging the hair, wearing gold, or putting on *fine* apparel— 4 rather *let it be* [a]the hidden person of the heart, with the incorruptible *beauty* of a gentle and quiet spirit, which is very precious in the sight of God. 5 For in this manner, in former times, the holy women who trusted in God also adorned themselves, being submissive to their own husbands, 6 as Sarah obeyed Abraham, [a]calling him lord, whose daughters you are if you do good and are not afraid with any terror.

**2:16** [a] Rom. 6:14, 20, 22 [b] Gal. 5:13 **2:17** [a] Prov. 24:21 **2:18** [a] Eph. 6:5–8 **2:19** [a] Matt. 5:10 **2:20** [a] Luke 6:32–34 **2:21** [a] Matt. 16:24 [b] [1 John 2:6] [1] NU-Text reads *you.* [2] NU-Text and M-Text read *you.* **2:22** [a] Is. 53:9 [1] Isaiah 53:9 **2:23** [a] Is. 53:7 [b] Luke 23:46 **2:24** [a] [Heb. 9:28] [b] Rom. 7:6 [c] Is. 53:5 **2:25** [a] Is. 53:5, 6 [b] [Ezek. 34:23] [1] Greek *Episkopos* **3:1** [a] Eph. 5:22 [b] 1 Cor. 7:16 [c] Matt. 18:15 **3:2** [a] 1 Pet. 2:12; 3:6 **3:3** [a] 1 Tim. 2:9 **3:4** [a] Rom. 2:29 **3:6** [a] Gen. 18:12

KNOW THE TRUTH

## THE DOCTRINE OF JESUS

### PART 4: THE CHARACTER OF JESUS

**2:22** Jesus lived free of sin. While He was tempted in all the ways we are, He chose not to follow temptation and He committed no sin (see Heb. 4:14–16). The word *sin* has to do with missing the mark of what God wants for us. It's living our way instead of God's way. Sometimes we sin by commission (intentionally doing something we ought *not* to do) and other times we sin by omission (intentionally *not* doing something we ought to do). Jesus did something no other person has done or will do: He never sinned by commission or omission, instead choosing only righteousness. His life on earth perfectly fulfilled God's moral law.

Jesus' perfect life makes Him the perfect candidate for two things. First, **He's the perfect sacrifice for our sins.** He is the perfect, sinless Savior who died in the place of imperfect, sinful people. Believers in Jesus become the righteousness of God because Jesus died in our place (see 2 Cor. 5:21). Second, **He's the best person to help us with temptation.** Christ gives us His Holy Spirit to lead us. As we're led by the Spirit, the fruit of Christ's character (faithfulness, self-control, etc.) is produced in us. What's true of Christ's life becomes true of our own as we're led by the Spirit.

*For* **THE DOCTRINE OF JESUS: PART 5: THE MIRACLES OF JESUS,** *turn to John 20:30–31 on page 1101.*

### A WORD TO HUSBANDS

7 [a]Husbands, likewise, dwell with *them* with understanding, giving honor to the wife, [b]as to the weaker vessel, and as *being* heirs together of the grace of life, [c]that your prayers may not be hindered.

### CALLED TO BLESSING

8 Finally, all *of you be* of one mind, having compassion for one another; love as brothers, *be* tenderhearted, *be* courteous;[1] 9 [a]not returning evil for evil or reviling for reviling, but on the contrary [b]blessing, knowing that you were called to this, [c]that you may inherit a blessing. 10 For

[a]"He who would love life
And see good days,
[b]Let him refrain his tongue from evil,
And his lips from speaking deceit.
11 Let him [a]turn away from evil and do good;
[b]Let him seek peace and pursue it.
12 For the eyes of the LORD *are* on the righteous,
[a]And His ears *are open* to their prayers;
But the face of the LORD *is* against those who do evil."[1]

### SUFFERING FOR RIGHT AND WRONG

13 [a]And who *is* he who will harm you if you become followers of what is good? 14 [a]But even if you should suffer for righteousness' sake, *you are* blessed. [b]"And do not be afraid of their threats, nor be troubled."[1] 15 But sanctify the Lord God[1] in your hearts, and always [a]*be* ready to *give* a defense to everyone who asks you a reason for the [b]hope that is in you, with meekness and fear; 16 [a]having a good conscience, that when they defame you as evildoers, those who revile your good conduct in Christ may be ashamed. 17 For *it is* better, if it is the will of God, to suffer for doing good than for doing evil.

**3:17** Peter isn't encouraging believers to seek out situations in which they will **suffer**. Instead, he's saying believers should make certain that when they suffer, it is the result of having been faithful to God and done **good** rather than because they have been unfaithful and done **evil** (1 Pet. 2:19).

### CHRIST'S SUFFERING AND OURS

18 For Christ also suffered once for sins, the just for the unjust, that He might bring us[1] to God, being put to death in the flesh but made alive by the Spirit, 19 by whom also He went and preached to the spirits in prison, 20 who formerly were disobedient, when once the Divine longsuffering waited[1] in the days of Noah, while *the* ark was being prepared, in which a few, that is, eight souls, were saved through water. 21 [a]There is also an antitype which now saves us—baptism [b](not the removal of the filth of the flesh, [c]but the answer of a good conscience toward God), through the resurrection of Jesus Christ, 22 who has gone into heaven and [a]is at the right hand of God, [b]angels and authorities and powers having been made subject to Him.

4 Therefore, since Christ suffered for us[1] in the flesh, arm yourselves also with the same mind, for he who has suffered in the flesh has ceased from sin, 2 that he no longer should live the rest of *his* time in the flesh for the lusts of men, [a]but for the will of God. 3 For we *have spent* enough of our past lifetime[1] in doing the will of the Gentiles—when we walked in lewdness, lusts, drunkenness, revelries, drinking parties, and abominable idolatries. 4 In regard to these, they think it strange that you do not run with *them* in the same flood of dissipation, speaking evil of *you.* 5 They will give an account to Him who is ready [a]to judge the living and the dead. 6 For this reason [a]the gospel was preached also to those who are dead, that they might be judged according to men in the flesh, but [b]live according to God in the spirit.

### SERVING FOR GOD'S GLORY

7 But [a]the end of all things is at hand; therefore be serious and watchful in your prayers. 8 And above all things have fervent love for one another, for [a]"love will cover a multitude of sins."[1] 9 [a]*Be* hospitable to one another [b]without grumbling. 10 [a]As each one has received a gift, minister it to one another, [b]as good stewards of [c]the manifold grace of God. 11 [a]If anyone speaks, *let him speak* as the oracles of God. If anyone ministers, *let him do it* as with the ability which God supplies, that [b]in all things God may be glorified through Jesus Christ, to whom belong the glory and the dominion forever and ever. Amen.

### SUFFERING FOR GOD'S GLORY

12 Beloved, do not think it strange concerning the fiery trial which is to try you, as though some strange thing happened to you; 13 but rejoice [a]to the extent that you partake of Christ's sufferings, that [b]when His glory is revealed, you may also be glad with exceeding joy. 14 If you are reproached

**3:7** [a][Eph. 5:25] [b]1 Cor. 12:23 [c]Job 42:8 **3:8** [1]NU-Text reads *humble.* **3:9** [a][Prov. 17:13] [b]Matt. 5:44 [c]Matt. 25:34 **3:10** [a]Ps. 34:12–16 [b]James 1:26 **3:11** [a]Ps. 37:27 [b]Rom. 12:18 **3:12** [a]John 9:31 [1]Psalm 34:12–16 **3:13** [a]Prov. 16:7 **3:14** [a]James 1:12 [b]Is. 8:12 [1]Isaiah 8:12 **3:15** [a]Ps. 119:46 [b][Titus 3:7] [1]NU-Text reads *Christ as Lord.* **3:16** [a]Heb. 13:18 **3:18** [1]NU-Text and M-Text read *you.* **3:20** [1]NU-Text and M-Text read *when the longsuffering of God waited patiently.* **3:21** [a]Eph. 5:26 [b][Titus 3:5] [c][Rom. 10:10] **3:22** [a]Ps. 110:1 [b]Rom. 8:38 **4:1** [1]NU-Text omits *for us.* **4:2** [a]John 1:13 **4:3** [1]NU-Text reads *time.* **4:5** [a]Acts 10:42 **4:6** [a]1 Pet. 1:12; 3:19 [b][Rom. 8:9, 13] **4:7** [a]Rom. 13:11 **4:8** [a][Prov. 10:12] [1]Proverbs 10:12 **4:9** [a]Heb. 13:2 [b]2 Cor. 9:7 **4:10** [a]Rom. 12:6–8 [b]1 Cor. 4:1, 2 [c][1 Cor. 12:4] **4:11** [a]Eph. 4:29 [b][1 Cor. 10:31] **4:13** [a]James 1:2 [b]2 Tim. 2:12

for the name of Christ, [a]blessed *are you,* for the
Spirit of glory and of God rests upon you.[1] On
their part He is blasphemed, [b]but on your part
He is glorified. 15 But let none of you suffer as a
murderer, a thief, an evildoer, or as a busybody
in other people's matters. 16 Yet if *anyone suffers*
as a Christian, let him not be ashamed, but let
him glorify God in this matter.[1]

**SEEING JESUS IN THE SCRIPTURE**

**4:14** The church was already being persecuted in Peter's day and it would only intensify, just as Jesus foretold (see John 15:20).

17 For the time *has come* [a]for judgment to
begin at the house of God; and if *it begins* with
us first, [b]what will *be* the end of those who do
not obey the gospel of God? 18 Now

[a]"If the righteous one is scarcely saved,
Where will the ungodly and the sinner
appear?"[1]

19 Therefore let those who suffer according to
the will of God [a]commit their souls *to Him* in
doing good, as to a faithful Creator.

### *SHEPHERD THE FLOCK*

**5** The elders who are among you I exhort, I
who am a fellow elder and a [a]witness of the
sufferings of Christ, and also a partaker of the
[b]glory that will be revealed: 2 [a]Shepherd the
flock of God which is among you, serving as
overseers, [b]not by compulsion but willingly,[1] [c]not
for dishonest gain but eagerly; 3 nor as [a]being
lords over [b]those entrusted to you, but [c]being
examples to the flock; 4 and when [a]the Chief
Shepherd appears, you will receive [b]the crown
of glory that does not fade away.

### *SUBMIT TO GOD, RESIST THE DEVIL*

5 Likewise you younger people, submit
yourselves to *your* elders. Yes, [a]all of *you* be
submissive to one another, and be clothed with
humility, for

[b]"God resists the proud,
But [c]gives grace to the humble."[1]

6 Therefore humble yourselves under the mighty
hand of God, that He may exalt you in due time,
7 casting all your care upon Him, for He cares
for you.
8 Be sober, be vigilant; because[1] your adversary the devil walks about like a roaring lion,
seeking whom he may devour. 9 Resist him,

**5:8 The devil** is our avowed enemy. He never ceases from being hostile toward us; he is constantly accusing us before God (see Job 1:9—2:7; Zech. 3:1; Luke 22:31; Rev. 12:10). Satan is both cunning and cruel. He attacks when least expected and desires to destroy completely those whom he attacks.

**4:14** [a] Matt. 5:11 [b] Matt. 5:16 [1] NU-Text omits the rest of this verse. **4:16** [1] NU-Text reads *name.* **4:17** [a] Is. 10:12 [b] Luke 10:12 **4:18** [a] Prov. 11:31 [1] Proverbs 11:31 **4:19** [a] 2 Tim. 1:12 **5:1** [a] Matt. 26:37 [b] Rom. 8:17, 18 **5:2** [a] Acts 20:28 [b] 1 Cor. 9:17 [c] 1 Tim. 3:3 [1] NU-Text adds *according to God.* **5:3** [a] Ezek. 34:4 [b] Ps. 33:12 [c] Phil. 3:17 **5:4** [a] Heb. 13:20 [b] 2 Tim. 4:8 **5:5** [a] Eph. 5:21 [b] Prov. 3:34 [c] Is. 57:15 [1] Proverbs 3:34 **5:8** [1] NU-Text and M-Text omit *because.*

**LIVE THE TRUTH**

## SETTING PRIORITIES

**4:7** We have many responsibilities to juggle in life. If you haven't felt that tension yet, you surely will. It can be difficult knowing what your most important task of the day is, or sometimes even of the moment. There's so much competing for our time and attention, many of which are good and important. Thankfully, God's Word helps us organize our priorities. We first focus on God and our relationship with Him. Then, other people are our priority. Finally there's everything else. It's what God consistently commands in Scripture, and we see it clearly in Jesus' teaching and ministry.

Here, Peter provides the reason behind those top two priorities: life is short and eternity is upon us. The next life is infinitely longer than our time on earth. In this life, we must focus on what carries over into the next. Be serious in prayer as you seek God's presence and direction in your life. Pour into others for their salvation, sanctification, and encouragement. Love without ceasing, so the world can see God's grace through you. Serve, so others can benefit and experience God through you. If you prioritize what God points you toward, it will give you great direction as you seek to organize your life for lasting effect each day.

steadfast in the faith, knowing that the same
sufferings are experienced by your brother-
hood in the world. 10 But may[1] the God of all
grace, [a]who called us[2] to His eternal glory by
Christ Jesus, after you have suffered a while,
perfect, establish, strengthen, and settle *you.*
11 [a]To Him *be* the glory and the dominion forever
and ever. Amen.

### FAREWELL AND PEACE

12 By [a]Silvanus, our faithful brother as I con-
sider him, I have written to you briefly, exhorting
and testifying [b]that this is the true grace of God
in which you stand.

13 She who is in Babylon, elect together with
*you,* greets you; and *so does* [a]Mark my son.
14 Greet one another with a kiss of love.

Peace to you all who are in Christ Jesus.
Amen.

5:10 [a] 1 Cor. 1:9 [1] NU-Text reads *But the God of all grace . . . will perfect, establish, strengthen, and settle you.* [2] NU-Text and M-Text read *you.* 5:11 [a] Rev. 1:6 5:12 [a] 2 Cor. 1:19 [b] Acts 20:24 5:13 [a] Acts 12:12, 25; 15:37, 39

# *The Second Epistle of the Apostle*
# PETER

**AUTHOR**
Peter

**KEY VERSE**
2 Peter 2:1

**READING TIME**
12 minutes

First Peter deals with problems from outside the church; 2 Peter deals with threats from inside it. Peter wrote to warn believers about false teachers who were peddling damaging doctrine. He began by urging the church to keep a close watch on their lives. The Christian life demands diligence in pursuing moral excellence, knowledge, self-control, perseverance, godliness, brotherly kindness, and selfless love. By contrast, the false teachers were sensual, arrogant, greedy, and covetous. They scoffed at the thought of future judgment and lived as if the present was the pattern for the future. Peter reminded the church that although God may be patient in sending judgment, ultimately judgment would come. Given this promise, believers should strive to be godly, blameless, and steadfast.

**Occasion:** Peter wrote this epistle just before his death (2 Pet. 1:14), probably from Rome.

**Main Point:** False teachers in the church must be exposed and rejected.

**Big Ideas:** There is only one true gospel of Jesus Christ. We must be diligent to know the truth and reject any false teaching we hear.

**OUTLINE:**

I. Growing in Christ (ch. 1)
II. Rejecting False Teachers (ch. 2)
III. Hoping in Christ's Return (ch. 3)

**c. AD 27**
Andrew brings his brother Simon Peter to Jesus

**c. AD 29**
Peter witnesses the transfiguration

**c. AD 30**
Jesus' crucifixion and resurrection

**c. AD 30–35**
Pentecost; the early church in Jerusalem

**c. AD 37**
Jewish historian Josephus is born

**c. AD 41**
Peter takes the gospel to Gentiles

**c. AD 50**
The Jerusalem Council

**AD 54–68**
Nero is Roman emperor

**c. AD 64–65**
1 Peter written

**c. AD 66–67**
**2 Peter written**

**c. AD 67**
Peter and Paul are executed

### GREETING THE FAITHFUL

1 Simon Peter, a bondservant and [a]apostle of
Jesus Christ,

To those who have obtained [b]like precious
faith with us by the righteousness of our God
and Savior Jesus Christ:

2 [a]Grace and peace be multiplied to you in
the knowledge of God and of Jesus our Lord,
3 as His [a]divine power has given to us all things
that *pertain* to life and godliness, through the
knowledge of Him [b]who called us by glory and
virtue, 4 [a]by which have been given to us ex-
ceedingly great and precious promises, that
through these you may be [b]partakers of the
divine nature, having escaped the corruption
*that is* in the world through lust.

### FRUITFUL GROWTH IN THE FAITH

5 But also for this very reason, [a]giving all
diligence, add to your faith virtue, to virtue
[b]knowledge, 6 to knowledge self-control, to
self-control perseverance, to perseverance
godliness, 7 to godliness brotherly kindness,
and [a]to brotherly kindness love. 8 For if these
things are yours and abound, *you* will be nei-
ther barren [a]nor unfruitful in the knowledge
of our Lord Jesus Christ. 9 For he who lacks
these things is [a]shortsighted, even to blindness,
and has forgotten that he was cleansed from
his old sins.
10 Therefore, brethren, be even more diligent
[a]to make your call and election sure, for if you
do these things you will never stumble; 11 for so
an entrance will be supplied to you abundantly
into the everlasting kingdom of our Lord and
Savior Jesus Christ.

### PETER'S APPROACHING DEATH

12 For this reason [a]I will not be negligent to
remind you always of these things, [b]though you
know and are established in the present truth.
13 Yes, I think it is right, [a]as long as I am in this
tent, [b]to stir you up by reminding *you*, 14 [a]know-
ing that shortly I *must* put off my tent, just as
[b]our Lord Jesus Christ showed me. 15 Moreover
I will be careful to ensure that you always have
a reminder of these things after my decease.

### THE TRUSTWORTHY PROPHETIC WORD

*(Matt. 17:5; Mark 9:7; Luke 9:35)*

16 For we did not follow [a]cunningly devised
fables when we made known to you the [b]power
and [c]coming of our Lord Jesus Christ, but were
[d]eyewitnesses of His majesty. 17 For He received
from God the Father honor and glory when
such a voice came to Him from the Excellent
Glory: [a]"This is My beloved Son, in whom I am
well pleased." 18 And we heard this voice which
came from heaven when we were with Him on
[a]the holy mountain.

#### SEEING JESUS IN THE SCRIPTURE

**1:17** The message the Father declared over the Son is the same message we proclaim to the world until His return (see Rev. 19:5).

19 And so we have the prophetic word con-
firmed,[1] which you do well to heed as a [a]light that
shines in a dark place, [b]until [c]the day dawns and
the morning star rises in your [d]hearts; 20 know-
ing this first, that [a]no prophecy of Scripture is of
any private interpretation,[1] 21 for [a]prophecy never

**1:1** [a] Gal. 2:8 [b] Eph. 4:5 **1:2** [a] Dan. 4:1 **1:3** [a] 1 Pet. 1:5 [b] 1 Thess. 2:12 **1:4** [a] 2 Cor. 1:20; 7:1 [b] [2 Cor. 3:18] **1:5** [a] 2 Pet. 3:18 [b] 2 Pet. 1:2 **1:7** [a] Gal. 6:10 **1:8** [a] [John 15:2] **1:9** [a] 1 John 2:9–11 **1:10** [a] 1 John 3:19 **1:12** [a] Phil. 3:1 [b] 1 Pet. 5:12 **1:13** [a] [2 Cor. 5:1, 4] [b] 2 Pet. 3:1 **1:14** [a] [2 Tim. 4:6] [b] John 13:36; 21:18, 19 **1:16** [a] 1 Cor. 1:17 [b] [Eph. 1:19–22] [c] [1 Pet. 5:4] [d] Matt. 17:1–5 **1:17** [a] Matt. 17:5 **1:18** [a] Matt. 17:1 **1:19** [a] [John 1:4, 5, 9] [b] Prov. 4:18 [c] Rev. 2:28; 22:16 [d] [2 Cor. 4:5–7] [1] Or *We also have the more sure prophetic word.* **1:20** [a] [Rom. 12:6] [1] Or *origin* **1:21** [a] [2 Tim. 3:16]

LIVE THE TRUTH

## MAINTAINING SELF-CONTROL

**1:5–9** Everyone is controlled by something. We can be swayed by the crowd, pushed by our families, or felled by temptation. God, however, wants us to be controlled by His Spirit and to live according to His nature, not our human nature. Self-control is a huge aspect of godliness because it means we have the discipline to resist external and internal temptations and act based on God's Word instead. Thus, self-control is really God-control.

Here, we see self-control is a result of truly understanding who God is and embracing what He has done for us. When we are centered on who Jesus says we are, and we pursue the new life He has called us into, we find the calls and pressures of the world will leave a bitter taste in our mouths. We'll see them for what they really are. We must live based on what God says more than what we experience, think, or feel. We must be controlled by God's laws over all else. Self-control isn't easy, but it's fruitful. Through it, we avoid rash mistakes and spiteful words. Even better, living a self-controlled life brings the blessings that come with obedience to God.

came by the will of man, [b]but holy men of God[1] spoke *as they were* moved by the Holy Spirit.

> **1:20** Although some have taken this verse to mean no individual Christian has the right to interpret **prophecy** for himself or herself, the context and the Greek word for **interpretation** indicate another meaning. The word can also mean "origin." In the context of verse 21, Peter is speaking of **Scripture**'s "origin" from God Himself and not the credentials of the one who interprets it. There's no **private** source for the Bible; the prophets didn't supply their own solutions or explanations to the mysteries of life. Rather, God spoke through them; He alone is responsible for what is written in Scripture.

### *DESTRUCTIVE DOCTRINES*

**2** But there were also false prophets among the people, even as there will be [a]false teachers among you, who will secretly bring in destructive heresies, even denying the Lord who bought them, *and* bring on themselves swift destruction. 2 And many will follow their destructive ways, because of whom the way of truth will be blasphemed. 3 By covetousness they will exploit you with deceptive words; for a long time their judgment has not been idle, and their destruction does[1] not slumber.

### *DOOM OF FALSE TEACHERS*

4 For if God did not spare the angels who sinned, but cast *them* down to hell and delivered *them* into chains of darkness, to be reserved for judgment; 5 and did not spare the ancient world, but saved Noah, *one of* eight *people*, a preacher of righteousness, bringing in the flood on the world of the ungodly; 6 and turning the cities of [a]Sodom and Gomorrah into ashes, condemned *them* to destruction, making *them* an example to those who afterward would live ungodly; 7 and [a]delivered righteous Lot, *who was* oppressed by the filthy conduct of the wicked 8 (for that righteous man, dwelling among them, [a]tormented *his* righteous soul from day to day by seeing and hearing *their* lawless deeds)— 9 *then* [a]the Lord knows how to deliver the godly out of temptations and to reserve the unjust under punishment for the day of judgment, 10 and especially [a]those who walk according to the flesh in the lust of uncleanness and despise authority. [b]*They are* presumptuous, self-willed. They are not afraid to speak evil of dignitaries, 11 whereas [a]angels, who are greater in power and might, do not bring a reviling accusation against them before the Lord.

> **2:4** There are two main interpretations of this passage. Some think Peter is referring to the "sons of God" in Genesis 6:2. According to this interpretation, the "sons of God" were **angels** who rebelled against God and their role in creation. They began to engage in forbidden practices with the daughters of men. Their conduct was met with immediate **judgment**. A second group balks at the suggestion of sexual relations between angels and women. They believe this is a reference to those angels who fell with Satan.

### *DEPRAVITY OF FALSE TEACHERS*

12 But these, [a]like natural brute beasts made to be caught and destroyed, speak evil of the things they do not understand, and will utterly perish in their own corruption, 13 [a]*and* will receive the wages of unrighteousness, *as* those who count it pleasure [b]to carouse in the daytime. [c]*They are* spots and blemishes, carousing in their own deceptions while [d]they feast with you, 14 having eyes full of adultery and that cannot cease from sin, enticing unstable souls. [a]They have a heart trained in covetous practices, *and are* accursed children. 15 They have forsaken the right way and gone astray, following the way of [a]Balaam the *son* of Beor, who loved the wages of unrighteousness; 16 but he was rebuked for his iniquity: a dumb donkey speaking with a man's voice restrained the madness of the prophet.

17 [a]These are wells without water, clouds[1] carried by a tempest, for whom is reserved the blackness of darkness forever.[2]

### *DECEPTIONS OF FALSE TEACHERS*

18 For when they speak great swelling *words* of emptiness, they allure through the lusts of the flesh, through lewdness, the ones who have actually escaped[1] from those who live in error. 19 While they promise them liberty, they themselves are slaves of corruption; [a]for by whom a person is overcome, by him also he is brought into bondage. 20 For if, after they [a]have escaped the pollutions of the world through the knowledge of the Lord and Savior Jesus Christ, they are [b]again entangled in them and overcome, the latter end is worse for them than the beginning. 21 For [a]it would have been better for them not to have known the way of righteousness, than having known *it*, to turn from the

1:21 [b]2 Sam. 23:2 [1]NU-Text reads *but men spoke from God.* 2:1 [a]1 Tim. 4:1, 2 2:3 [1]M-Text reads *will not.* 2:6 [a]Gen. 19:1–26 2:7 [a]Gen. 19:16, 29 2:8 [a]Ps. 119:139 2:9 [a]Ps. 34:15–19 2:10 [a]Jude 4, 7, 8 [b]Jude 8 2:11 [a]Jude 9 2:12 [a]Jude 10 2:13 [a]Phil. 3:19 [b]Rom. 13:13 [c]Jude 12 [d]1 Cor. 11:20, 21 2:14 [a]Jude 11 2:15 [a]Num. 22:5, 7 2:17 [a]Jude 12, 13 [1]NU-Text reads *and mists.* [2]NU-Text omits *forever.* 2:18 [1]NU-Text reads *are barely escaping.* 2:19 [a]John 8:34 2:20 [a]Matt. 12:45 [b][Heb. 6:4–6] 2:21 [a]Luke 12:47

holy commandment delivered to them. 22 But
it has happened to them according to the true
proverb: [a]"A dog returns to his own vomit,"[1]
and, "a sow, having washed, to her wallowing
in the mire."

### *GOD'S PROMISE IS NOT SLACK*

*(Gen. 6:5—8:22)*

**3** Beloved, I now write to you this second
epistle (in *both of* which [a]I stir up your pure
minds by way of reminder), 2 that you may
be mindful of the words [a]which were spoken
before by the holy prophets, [b]and of the com-
mandment of us,[1] the apostles of the Lord and
Savior, 3 knowing this first: that scoffers will
come in the last days, [a]walking according to
their own lusts, 4 and saying, "Where is the
promise of His coming? For since the fathers
fell asleep, all things continue as *they were*
from the beginning of [a]creation." 5 For this they
willfully forget: that [a]by the word of God the
heavens were of old, and the earth [b]standing
out of water and in the water, 6 [a]by which the
world *that* then existed perished, being flooded
with water. 7 But [a]the heavens and the earth
*which* are now preserved by the same word,
are reserved for [b]fire until the day of judgment
and perdition of ungodly men.

8 But, beloved, do not forget this one thing,
that with the Lord one day *is* as a thousand years,
and [a]a thousand years as one day. 9 [a]The Lord
is not slack concerning *His* promise, as some
count slackness, but [b]is longsuffering toward
us,[1] [c]not willing that any should perish but [d]that
all should come to repentance.

### *THE DAY OF THE LORD*

10 But [a]the day of the Lord will come as a thief
in the night, in which [b]the heavens will pass away
with a great noise, and the elements will melt
with fervent heat; both the earth and the works
that are in it will be burned up.[1] 11 Therefore, since
all these things will be dissolved, what manner
*of persons* ought you to be [a]in holy conduct
and godliness, 12 [a]looking for and hastening
the coming of the day of God, because of which
the heavens will [b]be dissolved, being on fire,
and the elements will [c]melt with fervent heat?
13 Nevertheless we, according to His promise,
look for [a]new heavens and a [b]new earth in which
righteousness dwells.

### *BE STEADFAST*

14 Therefore, beloved, looking forward to
these things, be diligent [a]to be found by Him
in peace, without spot and blameless; 15 and
consider *that* [a]the longsuffering of our Lord *is*
salvation—as also our beloved brother Paul, ac-
cording to the wisdom given to him, has written
to you, 16 as also in all his [a]epistles, speaking in
them of these things, in which are some things
hard to understand, which untaught and unsta-
ble *people* twist to their own destruction, as *they*
*do* also the [b]rest of the Scriptures.

17 You therefore, beloved, [a]since you know
*this* beforehand, [b]beware lest you also fall from
your own steadfastness, being led away with the
error of the wicked; 18 [a]but grow in the grace and
knowledge of our Lord and Savior Jesus Christ.
[b]To Him *be* the glory both now and forever.
Amen.

**2:22** [a] Prov. 26:11 [1] Proverbs 26:11 **3:1** [a] 2 Pet. 1:13 **3:2** [a] 2 Pet. 1:21 [b] Jude 17 [1] NU-Text and M-Text read *commandment of the apostles of your Lord and Savior* or *commandment of your apostles of the Lord and Savior.* **3:3** [a] 2 Pet. 2:10 **3:4** [a] Gen. 6:1–7 **3:5** [a] Gen. 1:6, 9 [b] Ps. 24:2; 136:6 **3:6** [a] Gen. 7:11, 12, 21–23 **3:7** [a] 2 Pet. 3:10, 12 [b] [2 Thess. 1:8] **3:8** [a] Ps. 90:4 **3:9** [a] Hab. 2:3 [b] Is. 30:18 [c] Ezek. 33:11 [d] [Rom. 2:4] [1] NU-Text reads *you.* **3:10** [a] Rev. 3:3; 16:15 [b] Ps. 102:25, 26 [1] NU-Text reads *laid bare* (literally *found*). **3:11** [a] 1 Pet. 1:15 **3:12** [a] 1 Cor. 1:7, 8 [b] Ps. 50:3 [c] Mic. 1:4 **3:13** [a] Is. 65:17; 66:22 [b] Rev. 21:1 **3:14** [a] 1 Cor. 1:8; 15:58 **3:15** [a] Rom. 2:4 **3:16** [a] 1 Cor. 15:24 [b] 2 Tim. 3:16 **3:17** [a] Mark 13:23 [b] Eph. 4:14 **3:18** [a] Eph. 4:15 [b] 2 Tim. 4:18

LIVE THE TRUTH

## BEING PATIENT

**3:8–9** It's difficult to be patient. When we want something, we tend to want it *now.* Because of our impatience, we can become frustrated when we see the brokenness of the world around us. Why hasn't Jesus returned to fix all the wrongs of the world, execute justice, and end the pain that sin caused? We don't know. But we do know we can trust God's wisdom and timing. We can have patience, even amid the most discouraging situations, because of the faithfulness of our God.

Peter reminds us God hasn't forgotten His promises, nor is He slow to act. There's a purpose in His waiting. He wants to give more people the opportunity to repent and place their faith in Christ. In God's perfect provision, it isn't time for Jesus to return yet, and that's a good thing. Just as God isn't idle as He waits, neither should we be. We wait *and* work. We share the gospel with others and pray for them to believe in Jesus. We strive toward godliness and anticipate heaven. We glorify and praise God, even when we don't have the answers. As we practice patience, we trust God has everything under control. He always does.

# *The First Epistle of the Apostle* JOHN

| AUTHOR | KEY VERSE | READING TIME |
|---|---|---|
| John | 1 John 5:13 | 20 minutes |

False teachers who denied Christ (1 John 2:22) were sowing doubt and confusion within the church, leaving many believers struggling to know if they had been saved. John, the elder statesman of the church, responded by writing a letter of encouragement. There was no need to doubt. Christ indeed came as God in the flesh and lived a sinless life. He indeed died and rose again. All one must do is trust in Jesus to be saved. There was no secret knowledge; there is only Jesus. As John wrote to comfort the church, he reminded them that he had been an eyewitness to Jesus—he had seen, heard, and touched Jesus. Even though the recipients of John's letter had not done the same, they could have equal confidence in Jesus because the testimony of John and the others who had was true. John then provided several doctrinal and ethical tests to identify false teachers: Did they view Christ and sin rightly? Were they part of Christian fellowship? Did they live in love? Did they hope in Christ? Through it all, John's intention was not to cause additional doubt in true believers but rather to strengthen the hope and confidence they had in Christ.

**Occasion:** John probably wrote this epistle, along with the other two, from Ephesus after writing the Gospel of John.

**Main Point:** All who have placed faith in Christ can have confidence in their salvation.

**Big Ideas:** Jesus is the Son of God who came to earth in the flesh. If you have trusted in Jesus, you have been forgiven of your sin and you can rest in your salvation. Because God is love, we are to live in love.

## OUTLINE:

I. The Basis of Christian Fellowship (chs. 1–2)
II. The Result of Christian Fellowship (chs. 3–5)

**c. AD 27**
Jesus calls John the son of Zebedee to follow Him

**c. AD 30**
Jesus' crucifixion and resurrection

**c. AD 30–35**
Pentecost; the early church in Jerusalem

**c. AD 37**
Jewish historian Josephus is born

**c. AD 50**
The Jerusalem Council

**AD 54–68**
Nero is Roman emperor

**c. AD 67**
Peter and Paul are executed; John lives in Ephesus

**AD 70**
The Romans, led by Titus, destroy the temple

**AD 79**
Pompeii and Herculaneum destroyed by eruption of Mount Vesuvius

**c. AD 80–90**
John written

**c. AD 90**
John is exiled to the island of Patmos

**c. AD 90–95**
**1 John written**

**c. AD 95**
Revelation written

### *WHAT WAS HEARD, SEEN, AND TOUCHED*

*(John 1:1–5)*

**1** That [a]which was from the beginning, which we have heard, which we have [b]seen with our eyes, [c]which we have looked upon, and [d]our hands have handled, concerning the [e]Word of life— 2 [a]the life [b]was manifested, and we have seen, [c]and bear witness, and declare to you that eternal life which was [d]with the Father and was manifested to us— 3 that which we have seen and heard we declare to you, that you also may have fellowship with us; and truly our fellowship *is* [a]with the Father and with His Son Jesus Christ. 4 And these things we write to you [a]that your[1] joy may be full.

### *FELLOWSHIP WITH HIM AND ONE ANOTHER*

5 [a]This is the message which we have heard from Him and declare to you, that [b]God is light and in Him is no darkness at all. 6 [a]If we say that we have fellowship with Him, and walk in darkness, we lie and do not practice the truth. 7 But if we [a]walk in the light as He is in the light, we have fellowship with one another, and [b]the blood of Jesus Christ His Son cleanses us from all sin. 8 If we say that we have no sin, we deceive ourselves, and the truth is not in us. 9 If we [a]confess our sins, He is [b]faithful and just to forgive us *our* sins and to [c]cleanse us from all unrighteousness. 10 If we say that we have not sinned, we [a]make Him a liar, and His word is not in us.

> **1:8–9** To **confess** is to agree with God, to admit we are sinners in need of His mercy. If a person confesses his or her sins to God, He will **cleanse** them **from all unrighteousness**. Forgiveness and cleansing are guaranteed because God is faithful to His promises. Those promises are sure because God is just. God can maintain His perfect character and yet forgive us because of the perfect and righteous sacrifice of Jesus, His own Son (see 1 John 2:2).

**2** My little children, these things I write to you, so that you may not sin. And if anyone sins, [a]we have an Advocate with the Father, Jesus Christ the righteous. 2 And [a]He Himself is the propitiation for our sins, and not for ours only but [b]also for the whole world.

### *THE TEST OF KNOWING HIM*

3 Now by this we know that we know Him, if we keep His commandments. 4 He who says, "I know Him," and does not keep His commandments, is a [a]liar, and the truth is not in him. 5 But [a]whoever keeps His word, truly the love of God is perfected [b]in him. By this we know that we are in Him. 6 [a]He who says he abides in Him [b]ought himself also to walk just as He walked.

**1:1** [a] [John 1:1] [b] John 1:14 [c] 2 Pet. 1:16 [d] Luke 24:39 [e] [John 1:1, 4, 14] **1:2** [a] John 1:4 [b] Rom. 16:26 [c] John 21:24 [d] [John 1:1, 18; 16:28] **1:3** [a] 1 Cor. 1:9 **1:4** [a] John 15:11; 16:24 [1] NU-Text and M-Text read *our.* **1:5** [a] 1 John 3:11 [b] [1 Tim. 6:16] **1:6** [a] [1 John 2:9–11] **1:7** [a] Is. 2:5 [b] [1 Cor. 6:11] **1:9** [a] Prov. 28:13 [b] [Rom. 3:24–26] [c] Ps. 51:2 **1:10** [a] 1 John 5:10 **2:1** [a] Heb. 7:25; 9:24 **2:2** [a] [Rom. 3:25] [b] John 1:29 **2:4** [a] Rom. 3:4 **2:5** [a] John 14:21, 23 [b] [1 John 4:12] **2:6** [a] John 15:4 [b] 1 Pet. 2:21

KNOW THE TRUTH

## THE DOCTRINE OF SALVATION

### PART 6: THE RESULT OF SALVATION

**2:3–5** Multiple nouns and verbs in the New Testament describe God's marvelous work of transforming us from sinful people into His sons and daughters. To be *converted* is to be made new in both identity and conduct. It's to be spared from sin's judgment and enabled to pursue godly living (see Acts 3:19). *New birth* means to be born from above by the Holy Spirit into God's family and as a result to live increasingly like our Heavenly Father (see John 1:11–13; 3:3–16; Eph. 5:1). *Regeneration* has to do with being made new, both one time and continually throughout our lives (see Titus 3:4–7).

Notice these terms share something in common: an extreme change in who we are, how we live, and whom we obey. To be saved isn't just deliverance from God's wrath against sin, it's also a daily deliverance from sin's dominating and destructive power so we can live differently. We're empowered to say no to sin and yes to God's good and loving commands. According to John, the clearest change in our life is who we obey. The fruit of being saved and knowing God is our devotion to keeping God's commands. A changed life produces changed living.

*For* **THE DOCTRINE OF SALVATION: PART 7: THE CONTINUATION OF SALVATION**, *turn to 1 Corinthians 1:18 on page 1167.*

7 Brethren,[1] I write no new commandment
to you, but an old commandment which you
have had [a]from the beginning. The old com-
mandment is the word which you heard from
the beginning.[2] 8 Again, [a]a new commandment
I write to you, which thing is true in Him and
in you, [b]because the darkness is passing away,
and [c]the true light is already shining.

9 [a]He who says he is in the light, and hates
his brother, is in darkness until now. 10 [a]He who
loves his brother abides in the light, and [b]there
is no cause for stumbling in him. 11 But he who
[a]hates his brother is in darkness and [b]walks in
darkness, and does not know where he is going,
because the darkness has blinded his eyes.

### THEIR SPIRITUAL STATE

12 I write to you, little children,
Because [a]your sins are forgiven you for
His name's sake.
13 I write to you, fathers,
Because you have known Him *who is*
[a]from the beginning.
I write to you, young men,
Because you have overcome the wicked
one.
I write to you, little children,
Because you have [b]known the Father.
14 I have written to you, fathers,
Because you have known Him *who is*
from the beginning.
I have written to you, young men,
Because [a]you are strong, and the word of
God abides in you,
And you have overcome the wicked one.

### DO NOT LOVE THE WORLD

15 [a]Do not love the world or the things in
the world. [b]If anyone loves the world, the love
of the Father is not in him. 16 For all that *is* in
the world—the lust of the flesh, [a]the lust of the
eyes, and the pride of life—is not of the Father
but is of the world. 17 And [a]the world is passing
away, and the lust of it; but he who does the will
of God abides forever.

> **2:15 World** here is the morally evil system opposed to all that God is and holds dear. In this sense, the "world" is the satanic system opposing Christ's kingdom on this earth (see John 12:31; Eph. 6:11–12; James 4:4; 1 John 2:16; 3:1; 4:4; 5:19). *World* can also mean the people of the world, whom God loves (see John 3:16), or the physical planet He created.

### DECEPTIONS OF THE LAST HOUR

18 [a]Little children, [b]it is the last hour; and as
you have heard that [c]the[1] Antichrist is coming,
[d]even now many antichrists have come, by which
we know [e]that it is the last hour. 19 [a]They went
out from us, but they were not of us; for [b]if they
had been of us, they would have continued with
us; but *they went out* [c]that they might be made
manifest, that none of them were of us.

20 But [a]you have an anointing [b]from the
Holy One, and [c]you know all things.[1] 21 I have
not written to you because you do not know
the truth, but because you know it, and that no
lie is of the truth.

22 [a]Who is a liar but he who denies that [b]Jesus
is the Christ? He is antichrist who denies the
Father and the Son. 23 [a]Whoever denies the Son
does not have the [b]Father either; [c]he who ac-
knowledges the Son has the Father also.

### LET TRUTH ABIDE IN YOU

24 Therefore let that abide in you [a]which you
heard from the beginning. If what you heard
from the beginning abides in you, [b]you also
will abide in the Son and in the Father. 25 [a]And
this is the promise that He has promised us—
eternal life.

26 These things I have written to you con-
cerning those who *try to* deceive you. 27 But the
[a]anointing which you have received from Him
abides in you, and [b]you do not need that anyone
teach you; but as the same anointing [c]teaches you
concerning all things, and is true, and is not a lie,
and just as it has taught you, you will[1] abide in Him.

### THE CHILDREN OF GOD

28 And now, little children, abide in Him, that
when[1] He appears, we may have [a]confidence and
not be ashamed before Him at His coming. 29 [a]If you
know that He is righteous, you know that [b]every-
one who practices righteousness is born of Him.

3 Behold [a]what manner of love the Father has
bestowed on us, that [b]we should be called
children of God![1] Therefore the world does not
know us,[2] [c]because it did not know Him. 2 Be-
loved, [a]now we are children of God; and [b]it has
not yet been revealed what we shall be, but we
know that when He is revealed, [c]we shall be
like Him, for [d]we shall see Him as He is. 3 [a]And
everyone who has this hope in Him purifies
himself, just as He is pure.

**2:7** [a] 1 John 3:11, 23; 4:21 [1] NU-Text reads *Beloved.* [2] NU-Text omits *from the beginning.* **2:8** [a] John 13:34; 15:12 [b] Rom. 13:12 [c] [John 1:9; 8:12; 12:35] **2:9** [a] [1 Cor. 13:2] **2:10** [a] [1 John 3:14] [b] 2 Pet. 1:10 **2:11** [a] [1 John 2:9; 3:15; 4:20] [b] John 12:35 **2:12** [a] [1 Cor. 6:11] **2:13** [a] John 1:1 [b] [Rom. 8:15–17] **2:14** [a] Eph. 6:10 **2:15** [a] [Rom. 12:2] [b] James 4:4 **2:16** [a] [Eccl. 5:10, 11] **2:17** [a] 1 Cor. 7:31 **2:18** [a] John 21:5 [b] 1 Pet. 4:7 [c] 2 Thess. 2:3 [d] 2 John 7 [e] 1 Tim. 4:1 [1] NU-Text omits *the.* **2:19** [a] Deut. 13:13 [b] Matt. 24:24 [c] 1 Cor. 11:19 **2:20** [a] 2 Cor. 1:21 [b] Acts 3:14 [c] [John 16:13] [1] NU-Text reads *you all know.* **2:22** [a] 2 John 7 [b] 1 John 4:3 **2:23** [a] John 15:23 [b] John 5:23 [c] 1 John 4:15; 5:1 **2:24** [a] 2 John 5, 6 [b] John 14:23 **2:25** [a] John 3:14–16; 6:40; 17:2, 3 **2:27** [a] [John 14:16; 16:13] [b] [Jer. 31:33] [c] [John 14:16] [1] NU-Text reads *you abide.* **2:28** [a] 1 John 3:21; 4:17; 5:14 [1] NU-Text reads *if.* **2:29** [a] Acts 22:14 [b] 1 John 3:7, 10 **3:1** [a] [1 John 4:10] [b] [John 1:12] [c] John 15:18, 21; 16:3 [1] NU-Text adds *And we are.* [2] M-Text reads *you.* **3:2** [a] [Rom. 8:15, 16] [b] [Rom. 8:18, 19, 23] [c] Rom. 8:29 [d] [Ps. 16:11] **3:3** [a] 1 John 4:17

### SIN AND THE CHILD OF GOD

4 Whoever commits sin also commits lawlessness, and [a]sin is lawlessness. 5 And you know [a]that He was manifested [b]to take away our sins, and [c]in Him there is no sin. 6 Whoever abides in Him does not sin. Whoever sins has neither seen Him nor known Him.

> **3:5–6** Habitually sinful conduct indicates an absence of fellowship with Christ. Thus, if we claim to be a Christian but sin is our way of life, our status as children of God can legitimately be questioned. This doesn't mean we won't struggle with sin or even repeat the same sins. Rather, it means a person will sin on an ongoing basis without conviction or repentance.

7 Little children, let no one deceive you. He who practices righteousness is righteous, just as He is righteous. 8 [a]He who sins is of the devil, for the devil has sinned from the beginning. For this purpose the Son of God was manifested, [b]that He might destroy the works of the devil. 9 Whoever has been [a]born of God does not sin, for [b]His seed remains in him; and he cannot sin, because he has been born of God.

### THE IMPERATIVE OF LOVE

*(Matt. 22:39)*

10 In this the children of God and the children of the devil are manifest: Whoever does not practice righteousness is not of God, nor *is* he who does not love his brother. 11 For this is the message that you heard from the beginning, [a]that we should love one another, 12 not as [a]Cain *who* was of the wicked one and murdered his brother. And why did he murder him? Because his works were evil and his brother's righteous.

13 Do not marvel, my brethren, if [a]the world hates you. 14 We know that we have passed from death to life, because we love the brethren. He who does not love *his* brother[1] abides in death. 15 [a]Whoever hates his brother is a murderer, and you know that [b]no murderer has eternal life abiding in him.

### THE OUTWORKING OF LOVE

16 [a]By this we know love, [b]because He laid down His life for us. And we also ought to lay down *our* lives for the brethren. 17 But [a]whoever has this world's goods, and sees his brother in need, and shuts up his heart from him, how does the love of God abide in him?

18 My little children, [a]let us not love in word or in tongue, but in deed and in truth. 19 And by this we know[1] [a]that we are of the truth, and shall assure our hearts before Him. 20 [a]For if our heart condemns us, God is greater than our heart, and knows all things. 21 Beloved, if our heart does not condemn us, [a]we have confidence toward God. 22 And [a]whatever we ask we receive from Him, because we keep His commandments [b]and do those things that are pleasing in His sight. 23 And this is His commandment: that we should believe on the name of His Son Jesus Christ [a]and love one another, as He gave us[1] commandment.

### THE SPIRIT OF TRUTH AND THE SPIRIT OF ERROR

24 Now [a]he who keeps His commandments [b]abides in Him, and He in him. And [c]by this we know that He abides in us, by the Spirit whom He has given us.

4 Beloved, do not believe every spirit, but [a]test the spirits, whether they are of God; because [b]many false prophets have gone out into the world. 2 By this you know the Spirit of God: [a]Every spirit that confesses that Jesus Christ has come in the flesh is of God, 3 and every spirit that does not confess that[1] Jesus Christ has come in the flesh is not of God. And this is the *spirit* of the Antichrist, which you have heard was coming, and is now already in the world.

> **4:2** This test seems to be aimed at the Docetists, who taught Christ didn't have a physical body. The test may also be aimed at the followers of Cerinthus who claimed Jesus and "the Christ" were two separate beings, one physical and the other spiritual. In this letter, John is careful to use the name and the title of **Jesus Christ** together to express the complete union of the two titles in one person.

4 You are of God, little children, and have overcome them, because He who is in you is greater than [a]he who is in the world. 5 [a]They are of the world. Therefore they speak *as* of the world, and [b]the world hears them. 6 We are of God. He who knows God hears us; he who is not of God does not hear us. [a]By this we know the spirit of truth and the spirit of error.

**3:4** [a] Rom. 4:15 **3:5** [a] 1 John 1:2; 3:8 [b] John 1:29 [c] [2 Cor. 5:21] **3:8** [a] Matt. 13:38 [b] Luke 10:18 **3:9** [a] John 1:3; 3:3 [b] 1 Pet. 1:23 **3:11** [a] [John 13:34; 15:12] **3:12** [a] Gen. 4:4, 8 **3:13** [a] [John 15:18; 17:14] **3:14** [1] NU-Text omits *his brother.* **3:15** [a] Matt. 5:21 [b] [Gal. 5:20, 21] **3:16** [a] [John 3:16] [b] John 10:11; 15:13 **3:17** [a] Deut. 15:7 **3:18** [a] Ezek. 33:31 **3:19** [a] John 18:37 [1] NU-Text reads *we shall know.* **3:20** [a] [1 Cor. 4:4, 5] **3:21** [a] [1 John 2:28; 5:14] **3:22** [a] Ps. 34:15 [b] John 8:29 **3:23** [a] Matt. 22:39 [1] M-Text omits *us.* **3:24** [a] John 14:23 [b] John 14:21; 17:21 [c] Rom. 8:9, 14, 16 **4:1** [a] 1 Cor. 14:29 [b] Matt. 24:5 **4:2** [a] 1 Cor. 12:3 **4:3** [1] NU-Text omits *that* and *Christ has come in the flesh.* **4:4** [a] John 14:30; 16:11 **4:5** [a] John 3:31 [b] John 15:19; 17:14 **4:6** [a] [1 Cor. 2:12–16]

### *KNOWING GOD THROUGH LOVE*
*(cf. John 3:16)*

7 [a]Beloved, let us love one another, for love
is of God; and everyone who [b]loves is born of
God and knows God. 8 He who does not love
does not know God, for God is love. 9 [a]In this
the love of God was manifested toward us, that
God has sent His only begotten [b]Son into the
world, that we might live through Him. 10 In this
is love, [a]not that we loved God, but that He loved
us and sent His Son [b]*to be* the propitiation for
our sins. 11 Beloved, [a]if God so loved us, we also
ought to love one another.

### *SEEING GOD THROUGH LOVE*

12 [a]No one has seen God at any time. If we
love one another, God abides in us, and His love
has been perfected in us. 13 [a]By this we know
that we abide in Him, and He in us, because He
has given us of His Spirit. 14 And [a]we have seen
and testify that [b]the Father has sent the Son *as*
Savior of the world. 15 [a]Whoever confesses that
Jesus is the Son of God, God abides in him, and
he in God. 16 And we have known and believed
the love that God has for us. God is love, and
[a]he who abides in love abides in God, and God
[b]in him.

### *THE CONSUMMATION OF LOVE*

17 Love has been perfected among us in this:
that [a]we may have boldness in the day of judg-
ment; because as He is, so are we in this world.
18 There is no fear in love; but perfect love casts
out fear, because fear involves torment. But he
who fears has not been made perfect in love.
19 [a]We love Him[1] because He first loved us.

### *OBEDIENCE BY FAITH*

20 [a]If someone says, "I love God," and hates
his brother, he is a liar; for he who does not
love his brother whom he has seen, how can[1] he
love God [b]whom he has not seen? 21 And [a]this
commandment we have from Him: that he who
loves God *must* love his brother also.

**5** Whoever believes that [a]Jesus is the Christ
is [b]born of God, and everyone who loves
Him who begot also loves him who is begotten
of Him. 2 By this we know that we love the chil-
dren of God, when we love God and [a]keep His
commandments. 3 [a]For this is the love of God,
that we keep His commandments. And [b]His
commandments are not burdensome. 4 For
[a]whatever is born of God overcomes the world.
And this is the victory that [b]has overcome the
world—our[1] faith. 5 Who is he who overcomes

**4:7** [a] 1 John 3:10, 11, 23 [b] 1 Thess. 4:9 **4:9** [a] Rom. 5:8 [b] John 3:16 **4:10** [a] Titus 3:5 [b] 1 John 2:2 **4:11** [a] Matt. 18:33
**4:12** [a] John 1:18 **4:13** [a] John 14:20 **4:14** [a] John 1:14 [b] John 3:17; 4:42 **4:15** [a] [Rom. 10:9] **4:16** [a] [1 John 3:24] [b] [John 14:23]
**4:17** [a] 1 John 2:28 **4:19** [a] 1 John 4:10 [1] NU-Text omits *Him.* **4:20** [a] [1 John 2:4] [b] 1 John 4:12 [1] NU-Text reads *he cannot.*
**4:21** [a] [Matt. 5:43, 44; 22:39] **5:1** [a] 1 John 2:22; 4:2, 15 [b] John 1:13 **5:2** [a] John 15:10 **5:3** [a] John 14:15 [b] Matt. 11:30; 23:4
**5:4** [a] John 16:33 [b] 1 John 2:13; 4:4 [1] M-Text reads *your.*

KNOW THE TRUTH

## THE DOCTRINE OF GOD
### PART 11: THE LOVE OF GOD

**4:8** Perhaps nothing is desired more yet misunderstood more than love. People have made endless attempts to explain what love is, but John takes a remarkably different approach by describing *who* love is: God is love. John didn't say God *is loving*, though that's certainly true. John didn't say God *has love*, though He absolutely does. Instead, John defined God *as* love, which, in turn, defines love.

The word for *love* here carries the idea of a free, unconditional, self-giving, sacrificial commitment to another's greatest benefit without concern of repayment. This love seeks the highest possible good of another. This love was most clearly manifested in the Father sending His Son to be a bruised, broken, and bloodied sacrifice for sinful people who don't love Him. God loves us in this way, not eying what we might be able to return for it (we have nothing to offer), but rather based solely on what He wants to give us: relationship with Him.

John expands his definition of love to include three standards: love is who God is (1 John 4:8), love is whatever God does (1 John 4:9–10), and love is whatever God's will for us is (1 John 5:2–3). In Galatians 5:22, Paul tells us how we can express this divine love in our lives toward others: by being led by the Holy Spirit who leads us to say and do what is loving.

*For* **THE DOCTRINE OF GOD: PART 12: THE GRACE AND MERCY OF GOD**, *turn to 2 John v. 3 on page 1283.*

LIVE THE TRUTH

## LOVING OTHERS

**5:2–3** God is love (1 John 4:16). We can only understand what love is, then, when we look to God. Love is made plain when we consider what Jesus did: He chose to serve people who didn't deserve it. Jesus sacrificed Himself for those who sinned against Him. *That's* love. When we experience this amazing love, it moves us to act. More precisely, Jesus' love for us compels us to love others.

Our love for others is one of the biggest markers of our love for God. We cannot claim to love God and refuse to love others. Nor can we love others the way they deserve apart from God's love channeled through us. This is why God commanded us to love. It's not a feeling we might experience, but an attitude we have and actions we take. Loving others might not always be easy, but it isn't painful and doesn't weigh us down. Despite what the world tells us about living God's way, the truth is it's exactly what we were made to do. When we love God, love others, and obey God's commands, we experience abundant living and find we've never been freer. Love has changed your eternity; let it change the way you live today.

### SEEING JESUS IN THE SCRIPTURE

**5:3** We cannot keep God's commands in our own power, but we can when we're filled with love from and for Jesus (see Deut. 6:5).

the world, but [a]he who believes that Jesus is
the Son of God?

### *THE CERTAINTY OF GOD'S WITNESS*

6 This is He who came [a]by water and blood—
Jesus Christ; not only by water, but by water and
blood. [b]And it is the Spirit who bears witness,
because the Spirit is truth. 7 For there are three
that bear witness in heaven: the Father, [a]the
Word, and the Holy Spirit; [b]and these three are
one. 8 And there are three that bear witness on
earth:[1] [a]the Spirit, the water, and the blood; and
these three agree as one.
9 If we receive [a]the witness of men, the
witness of God is greater; [b]for this is the wit-
ness of God which[1] He has testified of His Son.
10 He who believes in the Son of God [a]has the
witness in himself; he who does not believe
God [b]has made Him a liar, because he has not
believed the testimony that God has given of
His Son. 11 And this is the testimony: that God
has given us eternal life, and this life is in His
Son. 12 [a]He who has the Son has life; he who
does not have the Son of God does not have
life. 13 These things I have written to you who
believe in the name of the Son of God, that
you may know that you have eternal life,[1] and
that you may *continue to* believe in the name
of the Son of God.

### *CONFIDENCE AND COMPASSION IN PRAYER*

14 Now this is the confidence that we have in
Him, that [a]if we ask anything according to His
will, He hears us. 15 And if we know that He hears
us, whatever we ask, we know that we have the
petitions that we have asked of Him.
16 If anyone sees his brother sinning a sin
*which does* not *lead* to death, he will ask, and
[a]He will give him life for those who commit
sin not *leading* to death. [b]There is sin *leading* to
death. [c]I do not say that he should pray about
that. 17 [a]All unrighteousness is sin, and there is
sin not *leading* to death.

### *KNOWING THE TRUE—REJECTING THE FALSE*

18 We know that [a]whoever is born of God does
not sin; but he who has been born of God [b]keeps
himself,[1] and the wicked one does not touch
him.
19 We know that we are of God, and [a]the whole
world lies *under the sway of* the wicked one.
20 And we know that the [a]Son of God has
come and [b]has given us an understanding, [c]that
we may know Him who is true; and we are in
Him who is true, in His Son Jesus Christ. [d]This
is the true God [e]and eternal life.
21 Little children, keep yourselves from idols.
Amen.

**5:5** [a] 1 Cor. 15:57 **5:6** [a] John 1:31–34; [Eph. 5:26, 27] [b] [John 14:17] **5:7** [a] [John 1:1] [b] John 10:30 **5:8** [a] John 15:26 [1] NU-Text and M-Text omit the words from *in heaven* (verse 7) through *on earth* (verse 8). Only four or five very late manuscripts contain these words in Greek. **5:9** [a] John 5:34, 37; 8:17, 18 [b] [Matt. 3:16, 17]; John 5:32, 37 [1] NU-Text reads *God, that.* **5:10** [a] [Rom. 8:16]; Gal. 4:6; Rev. 12:17 [b] John 3:18, 33; 1 John 1:10 **5:12** [a] [John 3:15, 36; 6:47; 17:2, 3] **5:13** [1] NU-Text omits the rest of this verse. **5:14** [a] [1 John 2:28; 3:21, 22] **5:16** [a] Job 42:8 [b] [Matt. 12:31] [c] Jer. 7:16; 14:11 **5:17** [a] 1 John 3:4 **5:18** [a] [1 Pet. 1:23]; 1 John 3:9 [b] James 1:27 [1] NU-Text reads *him.* **5:19** [a] John 12:31; 17:15; Gal. 1:4 **5:20** [a] 1 John 4:2 [b] Luke 24:45 [c] John 17:3; Rev. 3:7 [d] Is. 9:6 [e] 1 John 5:11, 12

# *The Second Epistle of the Apostle*
# JOHN

| AUTHOR | KEY VERSE | READING TIME |
|---|---|---|
| John | 2 John v. 9 | 2 minutes |

"Let him who thinks he stands take heed lest he fall" (1 Cor. 10:12). These words of the apostle Paul could serve as a fitting subtitle for John's second epistle. John's recipients were standing. They were walking in truth and remaining faithful to the commandments they had received from the Father. John was pleased to be able to commend them, but he took nothing for granted. Because falling was always a danger, he issued an important reminder: "Love one another" (2 John v. 5). This was not new revelation, but John knew it was sufficiently important to repeat. Loving one another, he stressed, was equivalent to walking according to God's commandments. John indicated, however, that this love was to be discerning. It was not a naive, unthinking, open-to-anything kind of love. Such an undiscerning love was foolish and dangerous. False teachers abounded who did not acknowledge Christ as having come in the flesh. Opening the door to their false teachings was false charity. Believers must have fellowship with God. They must have fellowship with one another. But they must not have fellowship with false teachers.

**Occasion:** John probably wrote this epistle, along with the other two, from Ephesus after writing the Gospel of John.

**Main Point:** False teachers are to be rejected.

**Big Ideas:** Followers of Jesus are to live in God's truth and love. We are also to be careful about who they fellowship with.

## OUTLINE:

I. Practice the Truth (vv. 1–6)
II. Protect the Truth (vv. 7–13)

**c. AD 27**
Jesus calls John the son of Zebedee to follow Him

**c. AD 30**
Jesus' crucifixion and resurrection

**c. AD 30–35**
Pentecost; the early church in Jerusalem

**c. AD 37**
Jewish historian Josephus is born

**c. AD 50**
The Jerusalem Council

**AD 54–68**
Nero is Roman emperor

**c. AD 67**
Peter and Paul are executed; John lives in Ephesus

**AD 70**
The Romans, led by Titus, destroy the temple

**AD 79**
Pompeii and Herculaneum destroyed by eruption of Mount Vesuvius

**c. AD 80–90**
John written

**c. AD 90**
John is exiled to the island of Patmos

**c. AD 90–95**
1 John written

**c. AD 90–95**
**2 John written**

**c. AD 95**
Revelation written

### *GREETING THE ELECT LADY*

The Elder,

To the elect lady and her children, whom I
love in truth, and not only I, but also all those
who have known [a]the truth, 2 because of the
truth which abides in us and will be with us
forever:

3 [a]Grace, mercy, *and* peace will be with you[1]
from God the Father and from the Lord Jesus
Christ, the Son of the Father, in truth and love.

### *WALK IN CHRIST'S COMMANDMENTS*

4 I [a]rejoiced greatly that I have found *some*
of your children walking in truth, as we received
commandment from the Father. 5 And now I
plead with you, lady, not as though I wrote a
new commandment to you, but that which we
have had from the beginning: [a]that we love one
another. 6 [a]This is love, that we walk according to
His commandments. This is the commandment,
that [b]as you have heard from the beginning, you
should walk in it.

### *BEWARE OF ANTICHRIST DECEIVERS*

7 For [a]many deceivers have gone out into
the world [b]who do not confess Jesus Christ *as*
coming in the flesh. [c]This is a deceiver and an
antichrist. 8 [a]Look to yourselves, [b]that we[1] do
not lose those things we worked for, but *that*
we[2] may receive a full reward.

9 [a]Whoever transgresses[1] and does not abide
in the doctrine of Christ does not have God. He
who abides in the doctrine of Christ has both the
Father and the Son. 10 If anyone comes to you
and [a]does not bring this doctrine, do not receive
him into your house nor greet him; 11 for he who
greets him shares in his evil deeds.

### *JOHN'S FAREWELL GREETING*

12 [a]Having many things to write to you, I did
not wish *to do so* with paper and ink; but I hope
to come to you and speak face to face, [b]that our
joy may be full.

13 [a]The children of your elect sister greet
you. Amen.

**v. 7** The **deceivers** John warned about may have been Gnostics, a group of false teachers who plagued the early Christian church. The Gnostics believed all physical matter was evil, so they refused to accept that Jesus was God in human form.

1 [a] Col. 1:5 3 [a] Rom. 1:7; 1 Tim. 1:2 [1] NU-Text and M-Text read *us.* 4 [a] 1 Thess. 2:19, 20; 3 John 3, 4 5 [a] [John 13:34, 35; 15:12, 17]; 1 John 3:11; 4:7, 11 6 [a] John 14:15; 1 John 2:5; 5:3 [b] 1 John 2:24 7 [a] 1 John 2:19; 4:1 [b] 1 John 4:2 [c] 1 John 2:22 8 [a] Mark 13:9 [b] Gal. 3:4 [1] NU-Text reads *you.* [2] NU-Text reads *you.* 9 [a] John 7:16; 8:31; 1 John 2:19, 23, 24 [1] NU-Text reads *goes ahead.* 10 [a] 1 Kin. 13:16; Rom. 16:17; 2 Thess. 3:6, 14; Titus 3:10 12 [a] 3 John 13, 14 [b] John 17:13 13 [a] 1 Pet. 5:13

KNOW THE TRUTH

## THE DOCTRINE OF GOD

### PART 12: THE GRACE AND MERCY OF GOD

**v. 3** It's common for New Testament letters to begin with a pronouncement of grace and mercy from God upon the recipients. The concepts of grace and mercy only exist because of God's character. He is gracious and merciful. The word for *grace* John used has to do with God's undeserved favor and goodwill toward people and the free gifts He gives us from His goodwill toward us. *Mercy* has to do with God's deep feeling of compassion and longing to help people in our need. It's been said God's grace sees Him giving us what we *don't* deserve (good gifts) while His mercy sees Him not giving us what we *do* deserve (judgment).

An astounding truth about God is He's perfectly righteous and just while being eternally gracious and merciful. The ultimate expression of God's righteousness and justice meeting His grace and mercy is the cross. The person who trusts in Jesus is forgiven of sin, saved from wrath, and freely given an eternal inheritance in Christ. Meanwhile, the person who rejects Jesus receives what is justly due: judgment. While God will judge people for sin, His disposition is to show us mercy and grace through His gracious gift, His Son.

*For* **THE DOCTRINE OF GOD: PART 13: THE RIGHTEOUSNESS AND JUSTNESS OF GOD**, *turn to Psalm 89:14 on page 587.*

# *The Third Epistle of the Apostle*
# JOHN

| AUTHOR | KEY VERSE | READING TIME |
|---|---|---|
| John | 3 John v. 8 | 2 minutes |

In 1 John, the apostle discussed fellowship with God. In 2 John, he warned of fellowship with false teachers. Finally, in 3 John, the apostle encouraged fellowship with fellow Christians. John shared his joy over Gaius's persistent walk in truth and how he extended hospitality and supported the missionaries who had come to his church. But then John acknowledged that not everyone in the church felt the same way. Diotrephes's heart was one hundred and eighty degrees removed from Gaius's heart. He did not live in love. Pride took precedence in his life. Diotrephes had refused a letter John had written for the church, fearing that his authority might be superseded by the apostle's. He instead accused John of evil words. Diotrephes had also refused to accept missionaries and forbidden others to do so—even having expelled from the church those who had disobeyed him. While John used this negative example of Diotrephes to encourage Gaius to continue his hospitality, he also used a positive one. Demetrius had a good testimony and may have even been one of those Diotrephes had turned away. He was widely known for his good character and loyalty to the truth. John commended him well.

**Occasion:** John probably wrote this epistle, along with the other two, from Ephesus after writing the Gospel of John.

**Main Point:** Believers are to practice hospitality to one another to help advance the gospel.

**Big Ideas:** Followers of Christ are to work together. We are always to do what is good and never imitate what is evil.

**OUTLINE:**

I. The Good Example of Gaius (vv. 1–8)
II. The Evil Example of Diotrephes (vv. 9–11)
III. The Praise of Demetrius (vv. 12–14)

**c. AD 27**
Jesus calls John the son of Zebedee to follow Him

**c. AD 30**
Jesus' crucifixion and resurrection

**c. AD 30–35**
Pentecost; the early church in Jerusalem

**c. AD 37**
Jewish historian Josephus is born

**c. AD 50**
The Jerusalem Council

**AD 54–68**
Nero is Roman emperor

**c. AD 67**
Peter and Paul are executed; John lives in Ephesus

**AD 70**
The Romans, led by Titus, destroy the temple

**AD 79**
Pompeii and Herculaneum destroyed by eruption of Mount Vesuvius

**c. AD 80–90**
John written

**c. AD 90**
John is exiled to the island of Patmos

**c. AD 90–95**
1 John written

**c. AD 90–95**
2 John written

**c. AD 90–95**
**3 John written**

**c. AD 95**
Revelation written

### GREETING TO GAIUS

The Elder,

To the beloved Gaius, [a]whom I love in truth:

2 Beloved, I pray that you may prosper in
all things and be in health, just as your soul
prospers. 3 For I [a]rejoiced greatly when brethren
came and testified of the truth *that is* in you, just
as you walk in the truth. 4 I have no greater [a]joy
than to hear that [b]my children walk in truth.[1]

### GAIUS COMMENDED FOR GENEROSITY

5 Beloved, you do faithfully whatever you do for
the brethren and[1] for strangers, 6 who have borne
witness of your love before the church. *If* you send
them forward on their journey in a manner worthy
of God, you will do well, 7 because they went forth
for His name's sake, [a]taking nothing from the
Gentiles. 8 We therefore ought to [a]receive[1] such,
that we may become fellow workers for the truth.

### DIOTREPHES AND DEMETRIUS

9 I wrote to the church, but Diotrephes, who
loves to have the preeminence among them,
does not receive us. 10 Therefore, if I come, I will
call to mind his deeds which he does, [a]prating
against us with malicious words. And not content with that, he himself does not receive the
brethren, and forbids those who wish to, putting
*them* out of the church.

11 Beloved, [a]do not imitate what is evil, but
what is good. [b]He who does good is of God, but[1]
he who does evil has not seen [c]God.
12 Demetrius [a]has a *good* testimony from
all, and from the truth itself. And we also bear
witness, [b]and you know that our testimony is
true.

### FAREWELL GREETING

13 [a]I had many things to write, but I do not
wish to write to you with pen and ink; 14 but
I hope to see you shortly, and we shall speak
face to face.

Peace to you. Our friends greet you. Greet the friends by name.

**v. 6** In the Bible, the word **church** refers to a group of Christ's followers in a certain area. Church buildings as we know them today—places set aside specifically for Christian worship and Bible study—weren't common until the third century. Before then, people met in homes to study Scripture and pray. Traveling teachers and missionaries moved from city to city, relying on the kindness of local Christians for food, housing, and other necessities.

1 [a] 2 John 1 3 [a] 2 John 4 4 [a] 1 Thess. 2:19, 20; 2 John 4 [b] [1 Cor. 4:15] [1] NU-Text reads *the truth.* 5 [1] NU-Text adds *especially.* 7 [a] 1 Cor. 9:12, 15 8 [a] Matt. 10:40; Rom. 12:13; Heb. 13:2; 1 Pet. 4:9 [1] NU-Text reads *support.* 10 [a] Prov. 10:8, 10 11 [a] Ps. 34:14; 37:27; Rom. 14:19; 1 Thess. 5:15; 1 Tim. 6:11; 2 Tim. 2:22 [b] [1 John 2:29; 3:10] [c] [1 John 3:10] [1] NU-Text and M-Text omit *but.* 12 [a] Acts 6:3; 1 Tim. 3:7 [b] John 19:35; 21:24 13 [a] 2 John 12

APPLY THE TRUTH

## THE EXISTENCE OF GOD

**v. 11** Can we know without a doubt that God exists? The Bible tells us creation points to a Creator. It's been said you would never examine the intricate details of a premium wristwatch without recognizing it was made by a watchmaker. It's not here by random chance. The same is true of the world. This is what John may have had in mind when he wrote those who do evil haven't seen God. Their hearts are so hardened, they fail to recognize the obvious truth that a Creator brought all things into existence.

Creation moves us toward God's existence, but it only hints at the specifics of who He is, what He is like, what He wants, and how we can know Him. That's where the Bible comes in. God has given us the Scriptures to answer these questions. The Bible doesn't tell us everything we might want to know, but it tells us everything we need to know. It teaches us God is one and He is good, loving, powerful, and just. It tells us He wants to have a relationship with us, and it tells us how we can do that through Jesus. You can be sure God exists. Just look at the amazing world around you and in His Word.

*The Epistle of*

# JUDE

| AUTHOR | KEY VERSE | READING TIME |
|---|---|---|
| Jude | Jude v. 3 | 5 minutes |

As Jude began his letter, he shared a desire to focus on the believers' common salvation. But that desire gave way to Jude feeling compelled to call on the church to contend for the faith. The danger was real. False teachers had crept into the church, turning God's grace into unbounded license to do as they pleased. Jude reminded the church of God's past dealings with unbelieving Israel, disobedient angels, and wicked Sodom and Gomorrah. In the face of such danger, Christians were not to be caught off guard. The challenge was great, but so was the God who could keep them from stumbling.

**Occasion:** Jude's location when he wrote this epistle is unknown, as is his audience, but what is known is his desire to stand against false teachers.

**Main Point:** Believers are to contend for the faith.

**Big Ideas:** The gospel is most important. As believers, we need to fight for the faith at times, protecting it from false teachings.

## OUTLINE:

I. Identifying False Teachers (vv. 1–16)
II. Contending against False Teachers (vv. 17–25)

**c. AD 30**
Jesus' crucifixion and resurrection

**c. AD 30–35**
Pentecost; the early church in Jerusalem

**c. AD 37**
Jewish historian Josephus is born

**c. AD 50**
The Jerusalem Council

**AD 54–68**
Nero is Roman emperor

**c. AD 62**
James is executed

**c. AD 67**
Peter and Paul are executed

**c. AD 68–70**
**Jude written**

**AD 70**
The Romans, led by Titus, destroy the temple

### GREETING TO THE CALLED

Jude, a bondservant of Jesus Christ, and [a]brother of James,

To those who are [b]called, sanctified[1] by God the Father, and [c]preserved in Jesus Christ:

2 Mercy, [a]peace, and love be multiplied to you.

> **SEEING JESUS IN THE SCRIPTURE**
>
> **v. 2** We experience peace from Jesus now in part; when He returns, we will experience it in full (see Rev. 21:4).

### CONTEND FOR THE FAITH

3 Beloved, while I was very diligent to write to you [a]concerning our common salvation, I found it necessary to write to you exhorting [b]you to contend earnestly for the faith which was once for all delivered to the saints. 4 For certain men have crept in unnoticed, who long ago were marked out for this condemnation, ungodly men, who turn the grace of our God into lewdness and deny the only Lord God[1] and our Lord Jesus Christ.

### OLD AND NEW APOSTATES

5 But I want to remind you, though you once knew this, that [a]the Lord, having saved the people out of the land of Egypt, afterward destroyed those who did not believe. 6 And the angels who did not keep their proper domain, but left their own abode, He has reserved in everlasting chains under darkness for the judgment of the great day; 7 as [a]Sodom and Gomorrah, and the cities around them in a similar manner to these, having given themselves over to sexual immorality and gone after strange flesh, are set forth as an example, suffering the vengeance of eternal fire.

8 [a]Likewise also these dreamers defile the flesh, reject authority, and [b]speak evil of dignitaries. 9 Yet Michael the archangel, in contending with the devil, when he disputed about the body of Moses, dared not bring against him a reviling accusation, but said, [a]"The Lord rebuke you!" 10 [a]But these speak evil of whatever they do not know; and whatever they know naturally, like brute beasts, in these things they corrupt themselves. 11 Woe to them! For they have gone in the way [a]of Cain, [b]have run greedily in the error of Balaam for profit, and perished [c]in the rebellion of Korah.

> **v. 9** Jude's description here is probably taken from an apocryphal book called *The Assumption of Moses*, written in the first century AD. There's no record in the Bible of the **archangel . . . contending with the devil**, nor a detailed account of what happened to **the body of Moses**.

> **v. 11** Despite God's warning, when his brother, Abel, received God's approval for his worship, **Cain** got jealous and killed Abel. **Balaam** tried to curse Israel, God's chosen people. **Korah** led a rebellion against Moses, God's chosen leader of the Israelites.

### APOSTATES DEPRAVED AND DOOMED

12 These are spots in your love feasts, while they feast with you without fear, serving *only* themselves. *They are* clouds without water, carried about[1] by the winds; late autumn trees without fruit, twice dead, pulled up by the roots; 13 [a]raging waves of the sea, [b]foaming up their own shame; wandering stars [c]for whom is reserved the blackness of darkness forever.

14 Now Enoch, the seventh from Adam, prophesied about these men also, saying, "Behold, the Lord comes with ten thousands of His saints, 15 to execute judgment on all, to convict all who are ungodly among them of all their ungodly deeds which they have committed in an ungodly way, and of all the [a]harsh things which ungodly sinners have spoken against Him."

### APOSTATES PREDICTED

16 These are grumblers, complainers, walking according to their own lusts; and they [a]mouth great swelling *words*, [b]flattering people to gain advantage. 17 [a]But you, beloved, remember the words which were spoken before by the apostles of our Lord Jesus Christ: 18 how they told you that [a]there would be mockers in the last time who would walk according to their own ungodly lusts. 19 These are sensual persons, who cause divisions, not having the Spirit.

### MAINTAIN YOUR LIFE WITH GOD

20 But you, beloved, [a]building yourselves up on your most holy faith, [b]praying in the Holy Spirit, 21 keep yourselves in the love of God, [a]looking for the mercy of our Lord Jesus Christ unto eternal life.

1 [a] Acts 1:13 [b] Rom. 1:7 [c] John 17:11, 12 [1] NU-Text reads *beloved.* 2 [a] 1 Pet. 1:2; 2 Pet. 1:2 3 [a] Titus 1:4 [b] Phil. 1:27
4 [1] NU-Text omits *God.* 5 [a] Ex. 12:51; 1 Cor. 10:5–10; Heb. 3:16 7 [a] Gen. 19:24 8 [a] 2 Pet. 2:10 [b] Ex. 22:28 9 [a] Zech. 3:2
10 [a] 2 Pet. 2:12 11 [a] Gen. 4:3–8 [b] 2 Pet. 2:15 [c] Num. 16:1–3, 31–35 12 [1] NU-Text and M-Text read *along.* 13 [a] Is. 57:20 [b] [Phil. 3:19]
[c] 2 Pet. 2:17 15 [a] 1 Sam. 2:3 16 [a] 2 Pet. 2:18 [b] Prov. 28:21 17 [a] 2 Pet. 3:2 18 [a] [1 Tim. 4:1] 20 [a] Col. 2:7 [b] [Rom. 8:26]
21 [a] Titus 2:13

KNOW THE TRUTH

# THE DOCTRINE OF CREATION AND HUMANS

## PART 7: THE PURPOSE OF HUMANS

**vv. 24–25** According to Jude, all God does in us is on purpose and for a purpose: holy living, being with God, and glorifying Him. We see God has created us for at least three primary and grand purposes. First, God created us to **know Him** (see John 17:3). Jesus came from heaven to make sinful people into God's sons and daughters who will spend eternity with Him (see John 14:2–3). Knowing God personally, intimately, and deeply is the highest privilege imaginable and a primary purpose for which we exist.

Second, God created us to **serve in His plans**. Humans were created to have communion with God and authority over the earth. Under God's perfect rule and reign, we're called to rule and reign (see Gen. 1:26–27; Rev. 20:4). We're created to assist God in His perfect plans for creation. In this age, those plans include sharing the gospel, making disciples, and serving the needs of others in Christ's name. There's a special part in God's plans for each person.

Finally, God created us to **worship and glorify Him**. The human soul can find no deeper satisfaction and no greater sense of significance than speaking and singing praise to God, worshiping Him through Spirit-empowered excellent work, and living in a way that honors His holy majesty.

*For* **THE DOCTRINE OF CREATION AND HUMANS: PART 8: THE FALL OF HUMANS**, *turn to Genesis 5:1–5 on page 11.*

22 And on some have compassion, making a distinction;[1] 23 but [a]others save with fear, [b]pulling *them* out of the fire,[1] hating even [c]the garment defiled by the flesh.

### *GLORY TO GOD*

24 [a]Now to Him who is able to keep you[1] from
stumbling,
And [b]to present *you* faultless
Before the presence of His glory with
exceeding joy,
25 To God our Savior,[1]
Who alone is wise,[2]
*Be* glory and majesty,
Dominion and power,[3]
Both now and forever.
Amen.

22 [1] NU-Text reads *who are doubting* (or *making distinctions*). 23 [a] Rom. 11:14 [b] Amos 4:11 [c] [Zech. 3:4, 5] [1] NU-Text adds *and on some have mercy with fear* and omits *with fear* in first clause. 24 [a] [Eph. 3:20] [b] Col. 1:22 [1] M-Text reads *them.* 25 [1] NU-Text reads *To the only God our Savior.* [2] NU-Text omits *Who . . . is wise* and adds *Through Jesus Christ our Lord.* [3] NU-Text adds *Before all time.*

*The*

# REVELATION

*of Jesus Christ*

| AUTHOR | KEY VERSES | READING TIME |
|---|---|---|
| John | Revelation 22:12–13 | 1 hour 33 minutes |

Just as Genesis is the book of beginnings, Revelation is the book of consummation. In Genesis, God's divine program of redemption began; in Revelation, it comes to fruition. God's holy name will be vindicated before all creation. Although there are numerous prophecies in the Gospels and Epistles, Revelation is the only New Testament book that focuses primarily on prophetic events. Its title means "unveiling" or "disclosure." Thus, the book is an unveiling of God's redemptive program. Penned by John during his exile on the island of Patmos, Revelation centers around visions and symbols of the resurrected Christ, who alone has authority to judge the earth, to remake it, and to rule it in righteousness.

**Occasion:** John wrote this book in exile on the island of Patmos as severe persecution of Christians began near the end of the emperor Domitian's reign (AD 81–96).

**Main Point:** Jesus is victorious.

**Big Ideas:** Jesus came the first time as a Suffering Servant, but He will return as a conquering King. Jesus will return and make all things right. Evil will be punished and destroyed; all who have trusted in Jesus will experience abundant life with Him forevermore.

## OUTLINE:

I. A Vision of Jesus (ch. 1)
II. Letters to the Churches (chs. 2–3)
III. The Judge (chs. 4–5)
IV. The Tribulation (chs. 6–18)
V. The Second Coming (ch. 19)
VI. The Millennium (ch. 20)
VII. The New Jerusalem (chs. 21–22)

**c. AD 27**
Jesus calls John the son of Zebedee to follow Him

**c. AD 30**
Jesus' crucifixion and resurrection

**c. AD 30–35**
Pentecost; the early church in Jerusalem

**c. AD 37**
Jewish historian Josephus is born

**c. AD 50**
The Jerusalem Council

**AD 54–68**
Nero is Roman emperor

**c. AD 67**
Peter and Paul are executed; John lives in Ephesus

**AD 70**
The Romans, led by Titus, destroy the temple

**AD 79**
Pompeii and Herculaneum destroyed by eruption of Mount Vesuvius

**c. AD 80–90**
John written

**c. AD 90**
John is exiled to the island of Patmos

**c. AD 90–95**
1–3 John written

**c. AD 95**
**Revelation written**

**c. AD 96**
Clement, bishop of Rome, dies

**c. AD 107**
Ignatius is executed in Rome

## *INTRODUCTION AND BENEDICTION*

**1** The Revelation of Jesus Christ, [a]which God
gave Him to show His servants—things
which must shortly take place. And [b]He sent
and signified *it* by His angel to His servant John,
2 [a]who bore witness to the word of God, and to
the testimony of Jesus Christ, to all things [b]that
he saw. 3 [a]Blessed *is* he who reads and those
who hear the words of this prophecy, and keep
those things which are written in it; for [b]the
time *is* near.

## *GREETING THE SEVEN CHURCHES*

4 John, to the seven churches which are in Asia:

Grace to you and peace from Him [a]who is
and [b]who was and who is to come, [c]and from
the seven Spirits who are before His throne,
5 and from Jesus Christ, [a]the faithful [b]witness,
the [c]firstborn from the dead, and [d]the ruler over
the kings of the earth.

To Him [e]who loved us [f]and washed[1] us from
our sins in His own blood, 6 and has [a]made us
kings[1] and priests to His God and Father, [b]to Him
*be* glory and dominion forever and ever. Amen.
7 Behold, He is coming with [a]clouds, and
every eye will see Him, even [b]they who pierced
Him. And all the tribes of the earth will mourn
because of Him. Even so, Amen.
8 [a]"I am the Alpha and the Omega, *the* Be-
ginning and *the* End,"[1] says the Lord,[2] [b]"who is
and who was and who is to come, the [c]Almighty."

## *VISION OF THE SON OF MAN*

9 I, John, both[1] your brother and [a]companion
in the tribulation and [b]kingdom and patience
of Jesus Christ, was on the island that is called
Patmos for the word of God and for the testi-
mony of Jesus Christ. 10 [a]I was in the Spirit on
[b]the Lord's Day, and I heard behind me [c]a loud
voice, as of a trumpet, 11 saying, "I am the Alpha
and the Omega, the First and the Last," and,[1]
"What you see, write in a book and send *it* to the
seven churches which are in Asia:[2] to Ephesus,

> **1:9** At this time, Christianity was an illegal religion. Tradition has it, the apostle **John** was sentenced to live on the **island** of **Patmos** for eighteen months because he refused to stop preaching about Jesus. While there, John would have been forced to work in mines and quarries.

to Smyrna, to Pergamos, to Thyatira, to Sardis,
to Philadelphia, and to Laodicea."
12 Then I turned to see the voice that spoke with
me. And having turned [a]I saw seven golden lamp-
stands, 13 [a]and in the midst of the seven lampstands
[b]*One* like the Son of Man, [c]clothed with a garment
down to the feet and [d]girded about the chest with
a golden band. 14 His head and [a]hair *were* white like
wool, as white as snow, and [b]His eyes like a flame
of fire; 15 [a]His feet *were* like fine brass, as if refined

> **1:13–14 Son of Man** echoes Daniel 7:13. Comparisons of these two passages, along with Jesus' common use of the name "Son of Man" for Himself, indicate He is the subject of verses 12–18. The **white** appearance is parallel to the description of the "Ancient of Days" in Daniel 7:9, and of Christ on the Mount of Transfiguration (see Matt. 17:2). The similarity of descriptions demonstrates the purity and eternality of both God the Father and God the Son. Overcoming believers will also be "clothed in white garments" (see Rev. 3:5; 19:8) in Christ's presence, symbolizing purity.

in a furnace, and [b]His voice as the sound of many
waters; 16 [a]He had in His right hand seven stars,
[b]out of His mouth went a sharp two-edged sword,
[c]and His countenance *was* like the sun shining in
its strength. 17 And [a]when I saw Him, I fell at His

> **SEEING JESUS IN THE SCRIPTURE**
>
> **1:16** Jesus depicted with a sharp sword coming from His mouth fulfills prophecy (see Is. 49:2).

feet as dead. But [b]He laid His right hand on me,
saying to me,[1] "Do not be afraid; [c]I am the First
and the Last. 18 [a]I *am* He who lives, and was dead,
and behold, [b]I am alive forevermore. Amen. And
[c]I have the keys of Hades and of Death. 19 Write[1]
the things which you have [a]seen, [b]and the things
which are, [c]and the things which will take place
after this. 20 The mystery of the seven stars which
you saw in My right hand, and the seven golden
lampstands: The seven stars are [a]the angels of the
seven churches, and [b]the seven lampstands which
you saw[1] are the seven churches.

**1:1** [a]John 3:32 [b]Rev. 22:6 **1:2** [a]1 Cor. 1:6 [b]1 John 1:1 **1:3** [a]Luke 11:28 [b]James 5:8 **1:4** [a]Ex. 3:14 [b]John 1:1 [c][Is. 11:2] **1:5** [a]John 8:14 [b]Is. 55:4 [c][Col. 1:18] [d]Rev. 17:14 [e]John 13:34 [f]Heb. 9:14 [1]NU-Text reads *loves us and freed;* M-Text reads *loves us and washed.* **1:6** [a]1 Pet. 2:5, 9 [b]1 Tim. 6:16 [1]NU-Text and M-Text read *a kingdom.* **1:7** [a]Matt. 24:30 [b]Zech. 12:10–14 **1:8** [a]Is. 41:4 [b]Rev. 4:8; 11:17 [c]Is. 9:6 [1]NU-Text and M-Text omit *the Beginning and the End.* [2]NU-Text and M-Text add *God.* **1:9** [a]Phil. 1:7 [b][2 Tim. 2:12] [1]NU-Text and M-Text omit *both.* **1:10** [a]Acts 10:10 [b]Acts 20:7 [c]Rev. 4:1 **1:11** [1]NU-Text and M-Text omit *I am* through third *and.* [2]NU-Text and M-Text omit *which are in Asia.* **1:12** [a]Ex. 25:37 **1:13** [a]Rev. 2:1 [b]Ezek. 1:26 [c]Dan. 10:5 [d]Rev. 15:6 **1:14** [a]Dan. 7:9 [b]Dan. 10:6 **1:15** [a]Ezek. 1:7 [b]Ezek. 1:24; 43:2 **1:16** [a]Rev. 1:20; 2:1; 3:1 [b]Is. 49:2 [c]Matt. 17:2 **1:17** [a]Ezek. 1:28 [b]Dan. 8:18; 10:10, 12 [c]Is. 41:4; 44:6; 48:12 [1]NU-Text and M-Text omit *to me.* **1:18** [a]Rom. 6:9 [b]Rev. 4:9 [c]Ps. 68:20 **1:19** [a]Rev. 1:9–18 [b]Rev. 2:1 [c]Rev. 4:1 [1]NU-Text and M-Text read *Therefore, write.* **1:20** [a]Rev. 2:1 [b]Zech. 4:2 [1]NU-Text and M-Text omit *which you saw.*

### THE LOVELESS CHURCH

**2** "To the angel of the church of Ephesus write, 'These things says [a]He who holds the seven stars in His right hand, [b]who walks in the midst of the seven golden lampstands: 2 [a]"I know your works, your labor, your patience, and that you cannot bear those who are evil. And [b]you have tested those [c]who say they are apostles and are not, and have found them liars; 3 and you have persevered and have patience, and have labored for My name's sake and have [a]not become weary. 4 Nevertheless I have *this* against you, that you have left your first love. 5 Remember therefore from where you have fallen; repent and do the first works, [a]or else I will come to you quickly and remove your lampstand from its place—unless you repent. 6 But this you have, that you hate the deeds of the Nicolaitans, which I also hate.

7 [a]"He who has an ear, let him hear what the Spirit says to the churches. To him who overcomes I will give [b]to eat from [c]the tree of life, which is in the midst of the Paradise of God." '

### THE PERSECUTED CHURCH

8 "And to the angel of the church in Smyrna write,

'These things says [a]the First and the Last, who was dead, and came to life: 9 "I know your works, tribulation, and poverty (but you are [a]rich); and *I know* the blasphemy of [b]those who say they are Jews and are not, [c]but *are* a synagogue of Satan. 10 [a]Do not fear any of those things which you are about to suffer. Indeed, the devil is about to throw *some* of you into prison, that you may be tested, and you will have tribulation ten days. [b]Be faithful until death, and I will give you [c]the crown of life.

11 [a]"He who has an ear, let him hear what the Spirit says to the churches. He who overcomes shall not be hurt by [b]the second death." '

### THE COMPROMISING CHURCH

12 "And to the angel of the church in Pergamos write,

'These things says [a]He who has the sharp two-edged sword: 13 "I know your works, and where you dwell, where Satan's throne *is.* And you hold fast to My name, and did not deny My faith even in the days in which Antipas *was* My faithful martyr, who was killed among you, where Satan dwells. 14 But I have a few things against you, because you have there those who hold the doctrine of [a]Balaam, who taught Balak to put a stumbling block before the children of Israel, [b]to eat things sacrificed to idols, [c]and to commit sexual immorality. 15 Thus you also have those who hold the doctrine of the Nicolaitans, which thing I hate.[1] 16 Repent, or else I will come to you quickly and [a]will fight against them with the sword of My mouth.

17 "He who has an ear, let him hear what the Spirit says to the churches. To him who overcomes I will give some of the hidden [a]manna to eat. And I will give him a white stone, and on the stone [b]a new name written which no one knows except him who receives *it.*" '

### THE CORRUPT CHURCH

18 "And to the angel of the church in Thyatira write,

'These things says the Son of God, [a]who has eyes like a flame of fire, and His feet like fine brass: 19 [a]"I know your works, love, service, faith,[1] and your patience; and *as* for your works, the last *are* more than the first. 20 Nevertheless I have a few things against you, because you allow[1] that woman[2] [a]Jezebel, who calls herself a prophetess, to teach and seduce[3] My servants [b]to commit sexual immorality and eat things sacrificed to idols. 21 And I gave her time [a]to repent of her sexual immorality, and she did not repent.[1] 22 Indeed I will cast her into a sickbed, and those who commit adultery with her into great tribulation, unless they repent of their[1] deeds. 23 I will kill her children with death, and all the churches shall know that I am He who [a]searches the minds and hearts. And I will give to each one of you according to your works.

24 "Now to you I say, and[1] to the rest in Thyatira, as many as do not have this doctrine, who have not known the [a]depths of Satan, as they say, [b]I will[2] put on you no other burden. 25 But hold fast [a]what you have till I come. 26 And he who overcomes, and keeps [a]My works until the end, [b]to him I will give power over the nations—

27 'He[a] shall rule them with a rod of iron;
They shall be dashed to pieces like the
potter's vessels'[1]—

**SEEING JESUS IN THE SCRIPTURE**

**2:26–27** Jesus is the ruler of all nations, just as the Old Testament promised, and will rule in full upon His return (see Ps. 2:8–9).

**2:1** [a] Rev. 1:16 [b] Rev. 1:13 **2:2** [a] Ps. 1:6 [b] 1 John 4:1 [c] 2 Cor. 11:13 **2:3** [a] Gal. 6:9 **2:5** [a] Matt. 21:41 **2:7** [a] Matt. 11:15; Rev. 2:11, 17; 3:6, 13, 22; 13:9 [b] [Rev. 22:2, 14] [c] [Gen. 2:9; 3:22] **2:8** [a] Rev. 1:8, 17, 18 **2:9** [a] Luke 12:21 [b] Rom. 2:17 [c] Rev. 3:9 **2:10** [a] Matt. 10:22 [b] Matt. 24:13 [c] James 1:12 **2:11** [a] Rev. 13:9 [b] [Rev. 20:6, 14; 21:8] **2:12** [a] Is. 49:2; Rev. 1:16; 2:16 **2:14** [a] Num. 31:16 [b] Num. 25; Acts 15:29; [1 Cor. 10:20]; Rev. 2:20 [c] 1 Cor. 6:13 **2:15** [1] NU-Text and M-Text read *likewise* for *which thing I hate.* **2:16** [a] Is. 11:4; 2 Thess. 2:8; Rev. 19:15 **2:17** [a] Ex. 16:33, 34; [John 6:49, 51] [b] Is. 56:5; 62:2; 65:15; Rev. 3:12 **2:18** [a] Rev. 1:14, 15 **2:19** [a] Rev. 2:2 [1] NU-Text and M-Text read *faith, service.* **2:20** [a] 1 Kin. 16:31; 21:25; 2 Kin. 9:7, 22, 30 [b] Ex. 34:15 [1] NU-Text and M-Text read *I have against you that you tolerate.* [2] M-Text reads *your wife Jezebel.* [3] NU-Text and M-Text read *and teaches and seduces.* **2:21** [a] Rom. 2:5; Rev. 9:20; 16:9, 11 [1] NU-Text and M-Text read *time to repent, and she does not want to repent of her sexual immorality.* **2:22** [1] NU-Text and M-Text read *her.* **2:23** [a] Ps. 7:9; 26:2; 139:1; Jer. 11:20; 17:10; Matt. 16:27; Luke 16:15; Acts 1:24; Rom. 8:27 **2:24** [a] 2 Tim. 3:1–9 [b] Acts 15:28 [1] NU-Text and M-Text omit *and.* [2] NU-Text and M-Text omit *will.* **2:25** [a] Rev. 3:11 **2:26** [a] [John 6:29] [b] [Matt. 19:28] **2:27** [a] Ps. 2:8, 9; Rev. 12:5; 19:15 [1] Psalm 2:9

# THE SEVEN CHURCHES OF REVELATION

The Book of Revelation contains special messages directed to churches in seven specific cities throughout the Roman province of Asia, modern-day Turkey. These cities were important trade and communication centers, which were connected by major roads in New Testament times. John addressed the churches in an upside-down "u," beginning with Ephesus and ending with Laodicea. Each letter may have been intended to be a circular letter read by all the churches.

## 1. EPHESUS (2:1–7)

Ephesus was the most important city of 250,000 people in Asia Minor when Revelation was written. It was the center of the worship of Artemis (or Diana; Acts 19:28), a goddess of fertility. It was a strategic commercial center and a great seaport. The apostle Paul had started a church in Ephesus, and the apostle John had worked in the city for almost thirty years before being shipped off to Patmos.

**Potential Church History Period:** The Apostolic Church (AD 30–300)
**Commendation:** (1) Rejecting evil; (2) Patient; (3) Labor; (4) Testing false apostles; (5) Perseverance
**Condemnation:** Lost their love for Jesus
**Correction:** (1) Remember; (2) Repent; (3) Do the first works
**Judgment:** Removal of lampstand
**Reward:** Access to the tree of life

## 2. SMYRNA (2:8–11)

Smyrna, a large harbor city about thirty-five miles north of Ephesus, was the home of a temple built to honor the emperor Tiberius. The city became a center of emperor worship. Christians who chose not to join the pagan worship were severely persecuted.

**Potential Church History Period:** The Martyr Church (AD 100–313)
**Commendation:** Enduring suffering and poverty
**Condemnation:** None
**Correction:** None
**Judgment:** None
**Reward:** The crown of life

### 3. PERGAMOS (2:12–17)

Pergamos was the ancient capital of the province of Asia and was about fifty miles north of Smyrna. It was said to be the place where parchment was first used. It had a library of about 200,000 volumes and a famous medical center. The city also offered a wide variety of pagan worship opportunities. In addition to its three temples dedicated to the Roman emperors, Pergamos was home to temples for the goddess, Athena, and the god, Zeus.

**Potential Church History Period:** The State-Sanctioned Church (AD 314–590)
**Commendation:** Faithfulness to Christ, even in the face of martyrdom
**Condemnation:** Tolerated immorality, idolatry, and heresies
**Correction:** Repent
**Judgment:** The sword of Christ's mouth
**Reward:** (1) Hidden manna; (2) A white stone; (3) A new name

### 4. THYATIRA (2:18–29)

Thyatira was a city with a large military detachment about thirty miles southeast of Pergamos. Recognized for its wool and dye industries, the city was also noted for its trade guilds.

**Potential Church History Period:** The Catholic Church (AD 590–1517)
**Commendation:** (1) Love; (2) Service; (3) Faith; (4) Patience
**Condemnation:** Tolerance of Jezebel and her wickedness
**Correction:** Repent
**Judgment:** Casting of Jezebel into great tribulation and killing her children
**Reward:** (1) Ruler over nations; (2) Possession of the morning star

### 5. SARDIS (3:1–6)

Sardis, located thirty miles southeast of Thyatira, had been the capital of Lydia. Sardis was destroyed by an earthquake in AD 17. The Roman emperor Tiberius helped rebuild the city. The citizens were so grateful they built temples in his honor and made Sardis one of the centers for emperor worship in the ancient Near East.

**Potential Church History Period:** The Reformation Church (1517–1700)
**Commendation:** Few who have remained faithful
**Condemnation:** Deadness despite reputation for life
**Correction:** (1) Repent; (2) Strengthen what remains
**Judgment:** Approach of Christ Himself
**Reward:** (1) Clothed in white garments; (2) Permanent listing in the Book of Life; (3) Confession of name before the Father

### 6. PHILADELPHIA (3:7–13)

Philadelphia, which means "brotherly love," was located about seventy-five miles east of Ephesus. Like Sardis, Philadelphia was damaged by an earthquake in AD 17. Its location, vineyards, and wine production made it wealthy and commercially important.

**Potential Church History Period:** The Revival Church (1700–1900)
**Commendation:** Faithfulness
**Condemnation:** None
**Correction:** None
**Judgment:** None
**Reward:** (1) An open door; (2) Deliverance from great tribulation; (3) A new name

### 7. LAODICEA (3:14–22)

Laodicea was forty-five miles southeast of Philadelphia and ninety miles east of Ephesus. It was a wealthy city with thriving banks, a textile industry, and a medical school. The city was also known for its sparse water supply. The city survived until the Middle Ages when it was destroyed by during the Crusades.

**Potential Church History Period:** The Modern Church (1900–present)
**Commendation:** None
**Condemnation:** (1) Indifference; (2) Overestimate of status before God
**Correction:** (1) Repent; (2) Seek genuine spiritual riches
**Judgment:** Expulsion from the mouth of the Lord
**Reward:** Sharing Christ's throne

as I also have received from My Father; 28 and I will give him [a]the morning star.

29 "He who has an ear, let him hear what the Spirit says to the churches." '

### THE DEAD CHURCH

3 "And to the angel of the church in Sardis write,

'These things says He who [a]has the seven Spirits of God and the seven stars: "I know your works, that you have a name that you are alive, but you are dead. 2 Be watchful, and strengthen the things which remain, that are ready to die, for I have not found your works perfect before God.[1] 3 [a]Remember therefore how you have received and heard; hold fast and [b]repent. [c]Therefore if you will not watch, I will come upon you [d]as a thief, and you will not know what hour I will come upon you. 4 You[1] have [a]a few names even in Sardis who have not [b]defiled their garments; and they shall walk with Me [c]in white, for they are worthy. 5 He who overcomes [a]shall be clothed in white garments, and I will not [b]blot out his name from the [c]Book of Life; but [d]I will confess his name before My Father and before His angels.

6 [a]"He who has an ear, let him hear what the Spirit says to the churches." '

### THE FAITHFUL CHURCH

7 "And to the angel of the church in Philadelphia write,

'These things says [a]He who is holy, [b]He who is true, [c]"He who has the key of David, [d]He who opens and no one shuts, and [e]shuts and no one opens":[1] 8 [a]"I know your works. See, I have set before you [b]an open door, and no one can shut it;[1] for you have a little strength, have kept My word, and have not denied My name. 9 Indeed I will make [a]*those* of the synagogue of Satan, who say they are Jews and are not, but lie—indeed [b]I will make them come and worship before your feet, and to know that I have loved you. 10 Because you have kept My command to persevere, [a]I also will keep you from the hour of trial which shall come upon [b]the whole world, to test those who dwell [c]on the earth. 11 Behold,[1] [a]I am coming quickly! [b]Hold fast what you have, that no one may take [c]your crown. 12 He who overcomes, I will make him [a]a pillar in the temple of My God, and he shall [b]go out no more. [c]I will write on him the name of My God and the name of the city of My God, the [d]New Jerusalem, which [e]comes down out of heaven from My God. [f]And *I will write on him* My new name.

13 [a]"He who has an ear, let him hear what the Spirit says to the churches." '

### THE LUKEWARM CHURCH

14 "And to the angel of the church of the Laodiceans[1] write,

[a]'These things says the Amen, [b]the Faithful and True Witness, [c]the Beginning of the creation of God: 15 [a]"I know your works, that you are neither cold nor hot. I could wish you were cold or hot. 16 So then, because you are lukewarm, and neither cold nor hot,[1] I will vomit you out of My mouth. 17 Because you say, [a]'I am rich, have become wealthy, and have need of nothing'—and do not know that you are wretched, miserable, poor, blind, and naked— 18 I counsel you [a]to buy from Me gold refined in the fire, that you may be rich; and [b]white garments, that you may be clothed, *that* the shame of your nakedness may not be revealed; and anoint your eyes with eye salve, that you may see. 19 [a]As many as I love, I rebuke and [b]chasten. Therefore be zealous and repent. 20 Behold, [a]I stand at the door and knock. [b]If anyone hears My voice and opens the door, [c]I will come in to him and dine with him, and he with Me. 21 To him who overcomes [a]I will grant to sit with Me on My throne, as I also overcame and sat down with My Father on His throne.

22 [a]"He who has an ear, let him hear what the Spirit says to the churches." ' "

**SEEING JESUS IN THE SCRIPTURE**

**3:20** Jesus is the master who knocks on the door, wanting those within to open to Him and experience blessing (see Luke 12:36–37).

### THE THRONE ROOM OF HEAVEN

*(Is. 6:1–3)*

4 After these things I looked, and behold, a door *standing* [a]open in heaven. And the first voice which I heard *was* like a [b]trumpet speaking with me, saying, "Come up here, and I will show you things which must take place after this."

2 Immediately [a]I was in the Spirit; and behold, [b]a throne set in heaven, and *One* sat on the throne. 3 And He who sat there was[1] [a]like a jasper and a sardius stone in appearance; [b]and *there was* a rainbow around the throne,

**2:28** [a] 2 Pet. 1:19; Rev. 22:16 **3:1** [a] Rev. 1:4, 16 **3:2** [1] NU-Text and M-Text read *My God.* **3:3** [a] 1 Tim. 6:20 [b] Rev. 3:19 [c] Matt. 24:42, 43; Luke 12:39 [d] [Rev. 16:15] **3:4** [a] Acts 1:15 [b] [Jude 23] [c] Rev. 4:4; 6:11 [1] NU-Text and M-Text read *Nevertheless you have a few names in Sardis.* **3:5** [a] [Rev. 19:8] [b] Ex. 32:32 [c] Phil. 4:3 [d] Luke 12:8 **3:6** [a] Rev. 2:7 **3:7** [a] Acts 3:14 [b] 1 John 5:20 [c] Is. 9:7; 22:22 [d] [Matt. 16:19] [e] Job 12:14 [1] Isaiah 22:22 **3:8** [a] Rev. 3:1 [b] 1 Cor. 16:9 [1] NU-Text and M-Text read *which no one can shut.* **3:9** [a] Rev. 2:9 [b] Is. 45:14; 49:23; 60:14 **3:10** [a] 2 Pet. 2:9 [b] Luke 2:1 [c] Is. 24:17 **3:11** [a] Phil. 4:5 [b] Rev. 2:25 [c] [Rev. 2:10] [1] NU-Text and M-Text omit *Behold.* **3:12** [a] 1 Kin. 7:21 [b] Ps. 23:6 [c] [Rev. 14:1; 22:4] [d] [Heb. 12:22] [e] Rev. 21:2 [f] [Rev. 2:17; 22:4] **3:13** [a] Rev. 2:7 **3:14** [a] 2 Cor. 1:20 [b] Rev. 1:5; 3:7; 19:11 [c] [Col. 1:15] [1] NU-Text and M-Text read *in Laodicea.* **3:15** [a] Rev. 3:1 **3:16** [1] NU-Text and M-Text read *hot nor cold.* **3:17** [a] Hos. 12:8 **3:18** [a] Is. 55:1 [b] 2 Cor. 5:3 **3:19** [a] Job 5:17 [b] Heb. 12:6 **3:20** [a] Song 5:2 [b] Luke 12:36, 37 [c] [John 14:23] **3:21** [a] Matt. 19:28 **3:22** [a] Rev. 2:7 **4:1** [a] Ezek. 1:1 [b] Rev. 1:10 **4:2** [a] Rev. 1:10 [b] Is. 6:1 **4:3** [a] Rev. 21:11 [b] Ezek. 1:28 [1] M-Text omits *And He who sat there was* (which makes the description in verse 3 modify the throne rather than God).

in appearance like an emerald. 4 [a]Around the
throne *were* twenty-four thrones, and on the
thrones I saw twenty-four elders sitting, [b]clothed
in white robes; and they had crowns[1] of gold on
their heads. 5 And from the throne proceeded
[a]lightnings, thunderings, and voices.[1] [b]Seven
lamps of fire *were* burning before the throne,
which are [c]the[2] seven Spirits of God.
6 Before the throne *there was*[1] [a]a sea of glass,
like crystal. [b]And in the midst of the throne, and
around the throne, *were* four living creatures
full of eyes in front and in back. 7 [a]The first living
creature *was* like a lion, the second living crea-
ture like a calf, the third living creature had a face
like a man, and the fourth living creature *was* like
a flying eagle. 8 *The* four living creatures, each

> **4:7** The Old Testament prophet Ezekiel saw a very similar vision. Each of the four creatures looks like one of the most powerful creatures on earth—a **lion**, a bull, a **man**, and an **eagle**. The lion is the king of the jungle. Humans rule over every creature on earth. Bulls are the strongest tame animals. Eagles are the strongest birds.

having [a]six wings, were full of eyes around and
within. And they do not rest day or night, saying:

[b]"Holy, holy, holy,[1]
[c]Lord God Almighty,
[d]Who was and is and is to come!"

9 Whenever the living creatures give glory and
honor and thanks to Him who sits on the throne,
[a]who lives forever and ever, 10 [a]the twenty-four
elders fall down before Him who sits on the throne
and worship Him who lives forever and ever, and
cast their crowns before the throne, saying:

11 "You[a] are worthy, O Lord,[1]
To receive glory and honor and power;
[b]For You created all things,
And by [c]Your will they exist[2] and were
created."

### THE LAMB TAKES THE SCROLL

5 And I saw in the right *hand* of Him who sat
on the throne [a]a scroll written inside and on
the back, [b]sealed with seven seals. 2 Then I saw a
strong angel proclaiming with a loud voice, [a]"Who
is worthy to open the scroll and to loose its seals?"
3 And no one in heaven or on the earth or under the
earth was able to open the scroll, or to look at it.
4 So I wept much, because no one was found
worthy to open and read[1] the scroll, or to look
at it. 5 But one of the elders said to me, "Do not
weep. Behold, [a]the Lion of the tribe of [b]Judah,
[c]the Root of David, has [d]prevailed to open the
scroll [e]and to loose[1] its seven seals."

> **SEEING JESUS IN THE SCRIPTURE**
>
> **5:5** The tribe of Judah was chosen to be Israel's line of kings (see Gen. 49:10). Jesus, the King of kings, came from this royal family.

6 And I looked, and behold,[1] in the midst of the
throne and of the four living creatures, and in the
midst of the elders, stood [a]a Lamb as though it had
been slain, having seven horns and [b]seven eyes,
which are [c]the seven Spirits of God sent out into all
the earth. 7 Then He came and took the scroll out
of the right hand [a]of Him who sat on the throne.

### WORTHY IS THE LAMB

8 Now when He had taken the scroll, [a]the
four living creatures and the twenty-four elders
fell down before the Lamb, each having a harp,
and golden bowls full of incense, which are the
[b]prayers of the saints. 9 And [a]they sang a new
song, saying:

[b]"You are worthy to take the scroll,
And to open its seals;
For You were slain,
And [c]have redeemed us to God [d]by Your
blood
Out of every tribe and tongue and people
and nation,
10 And have made us[1] [a]kings[2] and [b]priests to
our God;
And we[3] shall reign on the earth."

11 Then I looked, and I heard the voice of
many angels around the throne, the living crea-
tures, and the elders; and the number of them
was ten thousand times ten thousand, and thou-
sands of thousands, 12 saying with a loud voice:

"Worthy is the Lamb who was slain
To receive power and riches and wisdom,
And strength and honor and glory and
blessing!"

**4:4** [a] Rev. 11:16 [b] Rev. 3:4, 5 [1] NU-Text and M-Text read *robes, with crowns.* **4:5** [a] Rev. 8:5; 11:19; 16:18 [b] Ex. 37:23 [c] [Rev. 1:4] [1] NU-Text and M-Text read *voices, and thunderings.* [2] M-Text omits *the.* **4:6** [a] Rev. 15:2 [b] Ezek. 1:5 [1] NU-Text and M-Text add *something like.* **4:7** [a] Ezek. 1:10; 10:14 **4:8** [a] Is. 6:2 [b] Is. 6:3 [c] Rev. 1:8 [d] Rev. 1:4 [1] M-Text has *holy* nine times. **4:9** [a] Rev. 1:18 **4:10** [a] Rev. 5:8, 14; 7:11; 11:16; 19:4 **4:11** [a] Rev. 1:6; 5:12 [b] Gen. 1:1 [c] Col. 1:16 [1] NU-Text and M-Text read *our Lord and God.* [2] NU-Text and M-Text read *existed.* **5:1** [a] Ezek. 2:9, 10 [b] Is. 29:11 **5:2** [a] Rev. 4:11; 5:9 **5:4** [1] NU-Text and M-Text omit *and read.* **5:5** [a] Gen. 49:9 [b] Heb. 7:14 [c] Is. 11:1, 10 [d] Rev. 3:21 [e] Rev. 6:1 [1] NU-Text and M-Text omit *to loose.* **5:6** [a] [John 1:29] [b] Zech. 3:9; 4:10 [c] Rev. 1:4; 3:1; 4:5 [1] NU-Text and M-Text read *I saw in the midst . . . a Lamb standing.* **5:7** [a] Rev. 4:2 **5:8** [a] Rev. 4:8–10; 19:4 [b] Rev. 8:3 **5:9** [a] Rev. 14:3 [b] Rev. 4:11 [c] John 1:29 [d] [Heb. 9:12] **5:10** [a] Ex. 19:6 [b] Is. 61:6 [1] NU-Text and M-Text read *them.* [2] NU-Text reads *a kingdom.* [3] NU-Text and M-Text read *they.*

13 And [a]every creature which is in heaven and on the earth and under the earth and such as are in the sea, and all that are in them, I heard saying:

[b]"Blessing and honor and glory and power
*Be* to Him [c]who sits on the throne,
And to the Lamb, forever and ever!"[1]

14 Then the four living creatures said, "Amen!" And the twenty-four[1] elders fell down and worshiped Him who lives forever and ever.[2]

### FIRST SEAL: THE CONQUEROR

6 Now [a]I saw when the Lamb opened one of the seals;[1] and I heard [b]one of the four living creatures saying with a voice like thunder, "Come and see." 2 And I looked, and behold, [a]a white horse. [b]He who sat on it had a bow; [c]and a crown was given to him, and he went out [d]conquering and to conquer.

### SECOND SEAL: CONFLICT ON EARTH

3 When He opened the second seal, [a]I heard the second living creature saying, "Come and see."[1] 4 [a]Another horse, fiery red, went out. And it was granted to the one who sat on it to [b]take peace from the earth, and that *people* should kill one another; and there was given to him a great sword.

### THIRD SEAL: SCARCITY ON EARTH

5 When He opened the third seal, [a]I heard the third living creature say, "Come and see." So I looked, and behold, [b]a black horse, and he who sat on it had a pair of [c]scales in his hand. 6 And I heard a voice in the midst of the four living creatures saying, "A quart[1] of wheat for a denarius,[2] and three quarts of barley for a denarius; and [a]do not harm the oil and the wine."

> **6:6** Because bread was served at almost every Jewish meal, **wheat** was considered a necessity of life. Only slaves and poor people ate **barley**, which was normally used as feed for livestock.

### FOURTH SEAL: WIDESPREAD DEATH ON EARTH

7 When He opened the fourth seal, [a]I heard the voice of the fourth living creature saying, "Come and see." 8 [a]So I looked, and behold, a pale horse. And the name of him who sat on it was Death, and Hades followed with him. And power was given to them over a fourth of the earth, [b]to kill with sword, with hunger, with death, [c]and by the beasts of the earth.

### FIFTH SEAL: THE CRY OF THE MARTYRS

9 When He opened the fifth seal, I saw under [a]the altar [b]the souls of those who had been slain [c]for the word of God and for [d]the testimony which they held. 10 And they cried with a loud voice, saying, [a]"How long, O Lord, [b]holy and true, [c]until You judge and avenge our blood on those who dwell on the earth?" 11 Then a [a]white robe was given to each of them; and it was said to them [b]that they should rest a little while longer, until both *the number of* their fellow servants and their brethren, who would be killed as they *were,* was completed.

### SIXTH SEAL: COSMIC DISTURBANCES

12 I looked when He opened the sixth seal, [a]and behold,[1] there was a great earthquake; and [b]the sun became black as sackcloth of hair, and the moon[2] became like blood. 13 [a]And the stars of heaven fell to the earth, as a fig tree drops its late figs when it is shaken by a mighty wind. 14 [a]Then the sky receded as a scroll when it is rolled up, and [b]every mountain and island was moved out of its place. 15 And the [a]kings of the earth, the great men, the rich men, the commanders,[1] the mighty men, every slave and every free man, [b]hid themselves in the caves and in the rocks of the mountains, 16 [a]and said to the mountains and rocks, "Fall on us and hide us from the face of Him who [b]sits on the throne and from the wrath of the Lamb! 17 For the great day of His wrath has come, [a]and who is able to stand?"

### THE SEALED OF ISRAEL

7 After these things I saw four angels standing at the four corners of the earth, [a]holding the four winds of the earth, [b]that the wind should not blow on the earth, on the sea, or on any tree. 2 Then I saw another angel ascending from the east, having the seal of the living God. And he cried with a loud voice to the four angels to whom it was granted to harm the earth and the sea, 3 saying, [a]"Do not harm the earth, the sea, or the trees till we have sealed the servants of our God [b]on their foreheads." 4 [a]And I heard the number of those who were sealed. [b]One hundred

**5:13** [a] Phil. 2:10 [b] 1 Chr. 29:11 [c] Rev. 4:2, 3; 6:16; 20:11 [1] M-Text adds *Amen.* **5:14** [1] NU-Text and M-Text omit *twenty-four.* [2] NU-Text and M-Text omit *Him who lives forever and ever.* **6:1** [a] [Rev. 5:5–7, 12; 13:8] [b] Rev. 4:7 [1] NU-Text and M-Text read *seven seals.* **6:2** [a] Zech. 1:8; 6:3 [b] Ps. 45:4, 5, LXX [c] Zech. 6:11 [d] Matt. 24:5 **6:3** [a] Rev. 4:7 [1] NU-Text and M-Text omit *and see.* **6:4** [a] Zech. 1:8; 6:2 [b] Matt. 24:6, 7 **6:5** [a] Rev. 4:7 [b] Zech. 6:2, 6 [c] Matt. 24:7 **6:6** [a] Rev. 7:3; 9:4 [1] Greek *choinix;* that is, approximately one quart [2] This was approximately one day's wage for a worker. **6:7** [a] Rev. 4:7 **6:8** [a] Zech. 6:3 [b] Ezek. 5:12, 17; 14:21; 29:5 [c] Lev. 26:22 **6:9** [a] Rev. 8:3 [b] [Rev. 20:4] [c] Rev. 1:2, 9 [d] 2 Tim. 1:8 **6:10** [a] Zech. 1:12 [b] Rev. 3:7 [c] Rev. 11:18 **6:11** [a] Rev. 3:4, 5; 7:9 [b] Heb. 11:40 **6:12** [a] Matt. 24:7 [b] Joel 2:10, 31; 3:15 [1] NU-Text and M-Text omit *behold.* [2] NU-Text and M-Text read *the whole moon.* **6:13** [a] Rev. 8:10; 9:1 **6:14** [a] Is. 34:4 [b] Rev. 16:20 **6:15** [a] Ps. 2:2–4 [b] Is. 2:10, 19, 21; 24:21 [1] NU-Text and M-Text read *the commanders, the rich men.* **6:16** [a] Luke 23:29, 30 [b] Rev. 20:11 **6:17** [a] Zeph. 1:14 **7:1** [a] Dan. 7:2 [b] Rev. 7:3; 8:7; 9:4 **7:3** [a] Rev. 6:6 [b] Rev. 22:4 **7:4** [a] Rev. 9:16 [b] Rev. 14:1, 3

**7:4** Those **sealed** are all **the children of Israel**, fulfilling the promise that when the "fullness of the Gentiles has come in" all Israel will be saved (see Rom. 11:25–27).

*and* forty-four thousand [c]of all the tribes of the
children of Israel *were* sealed:

5 of the tribe of Judah twelve thousand *were* sealed;[1]
of the tribe of Reuben twelve thousand *were* sealed;
of the tribe of Gad twelve thousand *were* sealed;
6 of the tribe of Asher twelve thousand *were* sealed;
of the tribe of Naphtali twelve thousand *were* sealed;
of the tribe of Manasseh twelve thousand *were* sealed;
7 of the tribe of Simeon twelve thousand *were* sealed;
of the tribe of Levi twelve thousand *were* sealed;
of the tribe of Issachar twelve thousand *were* sealed;
8 of the tribe of Zebulun twelve thousand *were* sealed;
of the tribe of Joseph twelve thousand *were* sealed;
of the tribe of Benjamin twelve thousand *were* sealed.

### A MULTITUDE FROM THE GREAT TRIBULATION

9 After these things I looked, and behold, [a]a
great multitude which no one could number,
[b]of all nations, tribes, peoples, and tongues,
standing before the throne and before the
Lamb, [c]clothed with white robes, with palm
branches in their hands, 10 and crying out with
a loud voice, saying, [a]"Salvation *belongs* to our
God [b]who sits on the throne, and to the Lamb!"
11 [a]All the angels stood around the throne and
the elders and the four living creatures, and fell
on their faces before the throne and [b]worshiped
God, 12 [a]saying:

"Amen! Blessing and glory and wisdom,
Thanksgiving and honor and power and might,
*Be* to our God forever and ever.
Amen."

13 Then one of the elders answered, saying
to me, "Who are these arrayed in [a]white robes,
and where did they come from?"
14 And I said to him, "Sir,[1] you know."
So he said to me, [a]"These are the ones who
come out of the great tribulation, and [b]washed
their robes and made them white in the blood
of the Lamb. 15 Therefore they are before the
throne of God, and serve Him day and night
in His temple. And He who sits on the throne
will [a]dwell among them. 16 [a]They shall neither
hunger anymore nor thirst anymore; [b]the sun
shall not strike them, nor any heat; 17 for the
Lamb who is in the midst of the throne [a]will
shepherd them and lead them to living foun-
tains of waters.[1] [b]And God will wipe away every
tear from their eyes."

### SEVENTH SEAL: PRELUDE TO THE SEVEN TRUMPETS

8 When[a] He opened the seventh seal, there
was silence in heaven for about half an hour.
2 [a]And I saw the seven angels who stand before
God, [b]and to them were given seven trumpets.
3 Then another angel, having a golden censer,
came and stood at the altar. He was given much
incense, that he should offer *it* with [a]the prayers
of all the saints upon [b]the golden altar which
was before the throne. 4 And [a]the smoke of the
incense, with the prayers of the saints, ascended
before God from the angel's hand. 5 Then the
angel took the censer, filled it with fire from
the altar, and threw *it* to the earth. And [a]there
were noises, thunderings, [b]lightnings, [c]and an
earthquake.
6 So the seven angels who had the seven
trumpets prepared themselves to sound.

### FIRST TRUMPET: VEGETATION STRUCK

7 The first angel sounded: [a]And hail and
fire followed, mingled with blood, and they
were thrown [b]to the earth.[1] And a third [c]of the
trees were burned up, and all green grass was
burned up.

### SECOND TRUMPET: THE SEAS STRUCK

8 Then the second angel sounded: [a]And
*something* like a great mountain burning with
fire was thrown into the sea, [b]and a third of the
sea [c]became blood. 9 [a]And a third of the living
creatures in the sea died, and a third of the ships
were destroyed.

### THIRD TRUMPET: THE WATERS STRUCK

10 Then the third angel sounded: [a]And a great
star fell from heaven, burning like a torch, [b]and

**7:4** [c] Gen. 49:1–27 **7:5** [1] In NU-Text and M-Text *were sealed* is stated only in verses 5a and 8c; the words are understood in the remainder of the passage. **7:9** [a] Rom. 11:25 [b] Rev. 5:9 [c] Rev. 3:5, 18; 4:4; 6:11 **7:10** [a] Ps. 3:8 [b] Rev. 5:13 **7:11** [a] Rev. 4:6 [b] Rev. 4:11; 5:9, 12, 14; 11:16 **7:12** [a] Rev. 5:13, 14 **7:13** [a] Rev. 7:9 **7:14** [a] Rev. 6:9 [b] [Heb. 9:14] [1] NU-Text and M-Text read *My lord.* **7:15** [a] Is. 4:5, 6 **7:16** [a] Is. 49:10 [b] Ps. 121:6 **7:17** [a] Ps. 23:1 [b] Rev. 21:4 [1] NU-Text and M-Text read *to fountains of the waters of life.* **8:1** [a] Rev. 6:1 **8:2** [a] [Matt. 18:10] [b] 2 Chr. 29:25–28 **8:3** [a] Rev. 5:8 [b] Ex. 30:1 **8:4** [a] Ps. 141:2 **8:5** [a] Rev. 11:19; 16:18 [b] Rev. 4:5 [c] 2 Sam. 22:8 **8:7** [a] Ezek. 38:22 [b] Rev. 16:2 [c] Rev. 9:4, 15–18 [1] NU-Text and M-Text add *and a third of the earth was burned up.* **8:8** [a] Jer. 51:25 [b] Ex. 7:17 [c] Ezek. 14:19 **8:9** [a] Rev. 16:3 **8:10** [a] Is. 14:12 [b] Rev. 14:7; 16:4

# COMMON VIEWS OF THE BOOK OF REVELATION

| Element | References | Amillennial Viewpoint | Premillennial Viewpoint | Postmillennial Viewpoint |
|---|---|---|---|---|
| **Overview** | | There will be no literal thousand-year reign of Christ on earth proceeding the eternal state. | Christ will return, usher in a millennial age, and rule on earth. Beginning with Revelation 4, the events described belong to a future age. They present, through prophecy, God's plan for the consummation of the age. | Christ will return at the end of the millennial age. Meanwhile, the world will progress under the missionary success of the church. |
| **Twenty-four elders** | Revelation 4:4, 10; 5:9, 14 | Represent all the redeemed. | Represent the saints gathered together in heaven as the family of God. | Represent all the redeemed. |
| **The 144,000** | Revelation 7:4–8 | The redeemed on earth who are protected from God's wrath. | Jews who will be converted during the Tribulation. | The redeemed people of God. |
| **The Great Tribulation** | Revelation 7:14 | Persecution of Christians in John's time representative of tribulation throughout history. | A seven-year exhibition of the wrath and judgment of God in final preparation for the return of the Lord. | Symbolic of tribulation suffered throughout history. |
| **Forty-two months or 1,260 days** | Revelation 11:2–3 | An indefinite time of evil influence. | Half of the seven-year Tribulation. | Indefinite period of time of pagan desolation. |
| **The Woman** | Revelation 12:1–6 | True people of God under the old and new covenants. | Israel, not the church. | True people of God under the old and new covenants. |
| **The 1,260 days** | Revelation 12:6 | An indefinite time period. | The first half of the seven-year Tribulation period. | Indefinite time period. |
| **The seven heads** | Revelation 13:1 | Roman emperors. | A revival of the ancient Roman Empire greatly expanded. | Roman emperors. |
| **The ten horns** | Revelation 13:1 | A symbol of power. | Ten powers that will combine to make the federation of nations of a new Rome. | A symbol of power. |
| **Babylon** | Revelation 17:5 | Historic Rome. | Resurgence of the apostate church. | Representing evil. |
| **The wife** | Revelation 19:7 | All the redeemed. | The church (no Old Testament or Tribulation saints). | All the redeemed. |

## COMMON VIEWS OF THE BOOK OF REVELATION

| Element | References | Amillennial Viewpoint | Premillennial Viewpoint | Postmillennial Viewpoint |
|---|---|---|---|---|
| **Armageddon** | Revelation 19:19–21 | Not literally at the end of time, but symbolizing power of God's Word in overcoming evil. | A literal bloody battle at the valley of Megiddo at the end of the Great Tribulation between kings of the East and the federation of nations of new Rome; they are all defeated by Christ. The millennium then begins. | Representing power of God's Word overcoming evil forces. |
| **The Millennium** | Revelation 20:2–6 | A symbolic reference to the period from Christ's Incarnation to His return. | A literal, thousand-year period during which Christ rules with His people on earth before the final state. | A lengthy period of expansion and spiritual prosperity brought about by preaching the gospel. |



it fell on a third of the rivers and on the springs
of water. 11 [a]The name of the star is Wormwood.
[b]A third of the waters became wormwood, and
many men died from the water, because it was
made bitter.

### *FOURTH TRUMPET: THE HEAVENS STRUCK*

12 [a]Then the fourth angel sounded: And a
third of the sun was struck, a third of the moon,
and a third of the stars, so that a third of them
were darkened. A third of the day did not shine,
and likewise the night.
13 And I looked, [a]and I heard an angel[1] fly-
ing through the midst of heaven, saying with a
loud voice, [b]"Woe, woe, woe to the inhabitants
of the earth, because of the remaining blasts of
the trumpet of the three angels who are about
to sound!"

### *FIFTH TRUMPET: THE LOCUSTS FROM THE BOTTOMLESS PIT*

9 Then the fifth angel sounded: [a]And I saw a
star fallen from heaven to the earth. To him
was given the key to [b]the bottomless pit. 2 And
he opened the bottomless pit, and smoke arose
out of the pit like the smoke of a great furnace.
So the [a]sun and the air were darkened because
of the smoke of the pit. 3 Then out of the smoke
locusts came upon the earth. And to them was
given power, [a]as the scorpions of the earth have
power. 4 They were commanded [a]not to harm
[b]the grass of the earth, or any green thing, or

> **9:3 Locusts** travel in swarms large enough to blot out the sun in the sky. An average-size swarm of locusts, numbering in the millions, can strip a field completely bare—down to its last leaf—within minutes.

any tree, but only those men who do not have
[c]the seal of God on their foreheads. 5 And they
were not given *authority* to kill them, [a]but to
torment them *for* five months. Their torment
*was* like the torment of a scorpion when it strikes
a man. 6 In those days [a]men will seek death and
will not find it; they will desire to die, and death
will flee from them.
7 [a]The shape of the locusts was like horses
prepared for battle. [b]On their heads were crowns
of something like gold, [c]and their faces *were* like
the faces of men. 8 They had hair like women's
hair, and [a]their teeth were like lions' *teeth*. 9 And
they had breastplates like breastplates of iron,
and the sound of their wings *was* [a]like the sound
of chariots with many horses running into battle.
10 They had tails like scorpions, and there were
stings in their tails. Their power *was* to hurt men
five months. 11 And they had as king over them
[a]the angel of the bottomless pit, whose name
in Hebrew *is* Abaddon, but in Greek he has the
name Apollyon.
12 [a]One woe is past. Behold, still two more
woes are coming after these things.

**8:11** [a] Ruth 1:20 [b] Ex. 15:23 **8:12** [a] Is. 13:10 **8:13** [a] Rev. 14:6; 19:17 [b] Rev. 9:12; 11:14; 12:12 [1] NU-Text and M-Text read *eagle.* **9:1** [a] Rev. 8:10 [b] Luke 8:31 **9:2** [a] Joel 2:2, 10 **9:3** [a] Judg. 7:12 **9:4** [a] Rev. 6:6 [b] Rev. 8:7 [c] Rev. 7:2, 3 **9:5** [a] [Rev. 9:10; 11:7] **9:6** [a] Jer. 8:3 **9:7** [a] Joel 2:4 [b] Nah. 3:17 [c] Dan. 7:8 **9:8** [a] Joel 1:6 **9:9** [a] Joel 2:5–7 **9:11** [a] Eph. 2:2 **9:12** [a] Rev. 8:13; 11:14

### *SIXTH TRUMPET: THE ANGELS FROM THE EUPHRATES*

13 Then the sixth angel sounded: And I heard a voice from the four horns of the [a]golden altar which is before God, 14 saying to the sixth angel who had the trumpet, "Release the four angels who are bound [a]at the great river Euphrates." 15 So the four angels, who had been prepared for the hour and day and month and year, were released to kill a [a]third of mankind. 16 Now [a]the number of the army [b]of the horsemen *was* two hundred million; [c]I heard the number of them. 17 And thus I saw the horses in the vision: those who sat on them had breastplates of fiery red, hyacinth blue, and sulfur yellow; [a]and the heads of the horses *were* like the heads of lions; and out of their mouths came fire, smoke, and brimstone. 18 By these three *plagues* a third of mankind was killed—by the fire and the smoke and the brimstone which came out of their mouths. 19 For their power[1] is in their mouth and in their tails; [a]for their tails *are* like serpents, having heads; and with them they do harm.

20 But the rest of mankind, who were not killed by these plagues, [a]did not repent of the works of their hands, that they should not worship [b]demons, [c]and idols of gold, silver, brass, stone, and wood, which can neither see nor hear nor walk. 21 And they did not repent of their murders [a]or their sorceries[1] or their sexual immorality or their thefts.

### *THE MIGHTY ANGEL WITH THE LITTLE BOOK*

**10** I saw still another mighty angel coming down from heaven, clothed with a cloud. [a]And a rainbow *was* on [b]his head, his face *was* like the sun, and [c]his feet like pillars of fire. 2 He had a little book open in his hand. [a]And he set his right foot on the sea and *his* left *foot* on the land, 3 and cried with a loud voice, as *when* a lion roars. When he cried out, [a]seven thunders uttered their voices. 4 Now when the seven thunders uttered their voices,[1] I was about to write; but I heard a voice from heaven saying to me,[2] [a]"Seal up the things which the seven thunders uttered, and do not write them."

5 The angel whom I saw standing on the sea and on the land [a]raised up his hand[1] to heaven 6 and swore by Him who lives forever and ever, [a]who created heaven and the things that are in it, the earth and the things that are in it, and the sea and the things that are in it, [b]that there should be delay no longer, 7 but [a]in the days of the sounding of the seventh angel, when he is about to sound, the mystery of God would be finished, as He declared to His servants the prophets.

### *JOHN EATS THE LITTLE BOOK*

8 Then the voice which I heard from heaven spoke to me again and said, "Go, take the little book which is open in the hand of the angel who stands on the sea and on the earth."

9 So I went to the angel and said to him, "Give me the little book."

And he said to me, [a]"Take and eat it; and it will make your stomach bitter, but it will be as sweet as honey in your mouth."

10 Then I took the little book out of the angel's hand and ate it, [a]and it was as sweet as honey in my mouth. But when I had eaten it, [b]my stomach became bitter. 11 And he[1] said to me, "You must prophesy again about many peoples, nations, tongues, and kings."

### *THE TWO WITNESSES*

**11** Then I was given [a]a reed like a measuring rod. And the angel stood,[1] saying, [b]"Rise and measure the temple of God, the altar, and those who worship there. 2 But leave out [a]the court which is outside the temple, and do not measure it, [b]for it has been given to the Gentiles. And they will [c]tread the holy city underfoot *for* [d]forty-two months. 3 And I will give *power* to my two [a]witnesses, [b]and they will prophesy [c]one thousand two hundred and sixty days, clothed in sackcloth."

> **11:3 Sackcloth** was a coarse, uncomfortable material made from camel or goat hair, worn during times of sorrow and mourning.

4 These are the [a]two olive trees and the two lampstands standing before the God[1] of the earth. 5 And if anyone wants to harm them, [a]fire proceeds from their mouth and devours their enemies. [b]And if anyone wants to harm them, he must be killed in this manner. 6 These [a]have power to shut heaven, so that no rain falls in the days of their prophecy; and they have power over waters to turn them to blood, and to strike the earth with all plagues, as often as they desire.

### *THE WITNESSES KILLED*

7 When they [a]finish their testimony, [b]the beast that ascends [c]out of the bottomless pit [d]will make war against them, overcome them, and kill them. 8 And their dead bodies *will lie* in the street of [a]the great city which spiritually is called Sodom and Egypt, [b]where also our[1] Lord

**9:13** [a]Rev. 8:3 **9:14** [a]Rev. 16:12 **9:15** [a]Rev. 8:7–9; 9:18 **9:16** [a]Dan. 7:10 [b]Ezek. 38:4 [c]Rev. 7:4 **9:17** [a]Is. 5:28, 29 **9:19** [a]Is. 9:15 [1]NU-Text and M-Text read *the power of the horses.* **9:20** [a]Deut. 31:29 [b]1 Cor. 10:20 [c]Dan. 5:23 **9:21** [a]Rev. 21:8; 22:15 [1]NU-Text and M-Text read *drugs.* **10:1** [a]Rev. 4:3 [b]Rev. 1:16 [c]Rev. 1:15 **10:2** [a]Matt. 28:18 **10:3** [a]Ps. 29:3–9 **10:4** [a]Dan. 8:26; 12:4, 9 [1]NU-Text and M-Text read *sounded.* [2]NU-Text and M-Text omit *to me.* **10:5** [a]Dan. 12:7 [1]NU-Text and M-Text read *right hand.* **10:6** [a]Rev. 4:11 [b]Rev. 16:17 **10:7** [a]Rev. 11:15 **10:9** [a]Jer. 15:16 **10:10** [a]Ezek. 3:3 [b]Ezek. 2:10 **10:11** [1]NU-Text and M-Text read *they.* **11:1** [a]Ezek. 40:3—42:20 [b]Num. 23:18 [1]NU-Text and M-Text omit *And the angel stood.* **11:2** [a]Ezek. 40:17, 20 [b]Ps. 79:1 [c]Dan. 8:10 [d]Rev. 12:6; 13:5 **11:3** [a]Rev. 20:4 [b]Rev. 19:10 [c]Rev. 12:6 **11:4** [a]Zech. 4:2, 3, 11, 14 [1]NU-Text and M-Text read *Lord.* **11:5** [a]2 Kin. 1:10–12 [b]Num. 16:29 **11:6** [a]1 Kin. 17:1 **11:7** [a]Luke 13:32 [b]Rev. 13:1, 11; 17:8 [c]Rev. 9:1, 2 [d]Dan. 7:21 **11:8** [a]Rev. 14:8 [b]Heb. 13:12 [1]NU-Text and M-Text read *their.*

was crucified. 9[a]Then *those* from the peoples, tribes, tongues, and nations will see their dead bodies three-and-a-half days, [b]and not allow[1] their dead bodies to be put into graves. 10[a]And those who dwell on the earth will rejoice over them, make merry, [b]and send gifts to one another, [c]because these two prophets tormented those who dwell on the earth.

### THE WITNESSES RESURRECTED

11[a]Now after the three-and-a-half days [b]the breath of life from God entered them, and they stood on their feet, and great fear fell on those who saw them. 12And they[1] heard a loud voice from heaven saying to them, "Come up here." [a]And they ascended to heaven [b]in a cloud, [c]and their enemies saw them. 13In the same hour [a]there was a great earthquake, [b]and a tenth of the city fell. In the earthquake seven thousand people were killed, and the rest were afraid [c]and gave glory to the God of heaven.

14[a]The second woe is past. Behold, the third woe is coming quickly.

### SEVENTH TRUMPET: THE KINGDOM PROCLAIMED

15Then [a]the seventh angel sounded: [b]And there were loud voices in heaven, saying, [c]"The kingdoms[1] of this world have become *the kingdoms* of our Lord and of His Christ, [d]and He shall reign forever and ever!" 16And [a]the twenty-four elders who sat before God on their thrones fell on their faces and [b]worshiped God, 17saying:

"We give You thanks, O Lord God
Almighty,
The One [a]who is and who was and who is
to come,[1]
Because You have taken Your great power
[b]and reigned.
18 The nations were [a]angry, and Your wrath
has come,
And the time of the [b]dead, that they
should be judged,
And that You should reward Your servants
the prophets and the saints,
And those who fear Your name, small and
great,
And should destroy those who destroy the
earth."

19Then [a]the temple of God was opened in heaven, and the ark of His covenant[1] was seen in His temple. And [b]there were lightnings, noises, thunderings, an earthquake, [c]and great hail.

### THE WOMAN, THE CHILD, AND THE DRAGON

12 Now a great sign appeared in heaven: a woman clothed with the sun, with the moon under her feet, and on her head a garland of twelve stars. 2Then being with child, she cried out [a]in labor and in pain to give birth.

3And another sign appeared in heaven: behold, [a]a great, fiery red dragon having seven heads and ten horns, and seven diadems on his heads. 4[a]His tail drew a third [b]of the stars of heaven [c]and threw them to the earth. And the dragon stood [d]before the woman who was ready to give birth, [e]to devour her Child as soon as it was born. 5She bore a male Child [a]who was to rule all nations with a rod of iron. And her Child was [b]caught up to God and His throne. 6Then [a]the woman fled into the wilderness, where she has a place prepared by God, that they should feed her there [b]one thousand two hundred and sixty days.

**SEEING JESUS IN THE SCRIPTURE**

**12:4–5** Jesus is the child the dragon tried to devour through Herod's actions (see Matt. 2:16–18).

### SATAN THROWN OUT OF HEAVEN

7And war broke out in heaven: [a]Michael and his angels fought [b]with the dragon; and the dragon and his angels fought, 8but they did not prevail, nor was a place found for them[1] in heaven any longer. 9So [a]the great dragon was cast out, [b]that serpent of old, called the Devil and Satan, [c]who deceives the whole world; [d]he was cast to the earth, and his angels were cast out with him.

10Then I heard a loud voice saying in heaven, [a]"Now salvation, and strength, and the kingdom of our God, and the power of His Christ have come, for the accuser of our brethren, [b]who accused them before our God day and night, has been cast down. 11And [a]they overcame him by

**12:11** The heavenly defeat of Satan (vv. 7–9) is followed by reference to his earthly setbacks, including the crucifixion of Christ, the verbal witness of believers, and the martyrdom of some of the believers. That these witnesses were willing to die for **their testimony** showed they knew Christ had defeated **death**.

**11:9** [a]Rev. 17:15 [b]Ps. 79:2, 3 [1]NU-Text and M-Text read *nations see . . . and will not allow.* **11:10** [a]Rev. 12:12 [b]Esth. 9:19, 22 [c]Rev. 16:10 **11:11** [a]Rev. 11:9 [b]Ezek. 37:5, 9, 10 **11:12** [a]Is. 14:13 [b]Acts 1:9 [c]2 Kin. 2:11, 12 [1]M-Text reads *I.* **11:13** [a]Rev. 6:12; 8:5; 11:19; 16:18 [b]Rev. 16:19 [c]Rev. 14:7; 16:9; 19:7 **11:14** [a]Rev. 8:13; 9:12 **11:15** [a]Rev. 8:2; 10:7 [b]Is. 27:13 [c]Rev. 12:10 [d]Ex. 15:18 [1]NU-Text and M-Text read *kingdom . . . has become.* **11:16** [a]Rev. 4:4 [b]Rev. 4:11; 5:9, 12, 14; 7:11 **11:17** [a]Rev. 16:5 [b]Rev. 19:6 [1]NU-Text and M-Text omit *and who is to come.* **11:18** [a]Ps. 2:1 [b]Dan. 7:10 **11:19** [a]Rev. 4:1; 15:5, 8 [b]Rev. 8:5 [c]Rev. 16:21 [1]M-Text reads *the covenant of the Lord.* **12:2** [a]Is. 26:17; 66:6–9 **12:3** [a]Rev. 13:1; 17:3, 7, 9 **12:4** [a]Rev. 9:10, 19 [b]Rev. 8:7, 12 [c]Dan. 8:10 [d]Rev. 12:2 [e]Matt. 2:16 **12:5** [a]Ps. 2:9 [b]Acts 1:9–11 **12:6** [a]Rev. 12:4, 14 [b]Rev. 11:3; 13:5 **12:7** [a]Dan. 10:13, 21; 12:1 [b]Rev. 20:2 **12:8** [1]M-Text reads *him.* **12:9** [a]John 12:31 [b]Gen. 3:1, 4 [c]Rev. 20:3 [d]Rev. 9:1 **12:10** [a]Rev. 11:15 [b]Zech. 3:1 **12:11** [a]Rom. 16:20

the blood of the Lamb and by the word of their testimony, [b]and they did not love their lives to the death. 12 Therefore [a]rejoice, O heavens, and you who dwell in them! [b]Woe to the inhabitants of the earth and the sea! For the devil has come down to you, having great wrath, [c]because he knows that he has a short time."

### THE WOMAN PERSECUTED

13 Now when the dragon saw that he had been cast to the earth, he persecuted [a]the woman who gave birth to the male *Child*. 14 [a]But the woman was given two wings of a great eagle, [b]that she might fly [c]into the wilderness to her place, where she is nourished [d]for a time and times and half a time, from the presence of the serpent. 15 So the serpent [a]spewed water out of his mouth like a flood after the woman, that he might cause her to be carried away by the flood. 16 But the earth helped the woman, and the earth opened its mouth and swallowed up the flood which the dragon had spewed out of his mouth. 17 And the dragon was enraged with the woman, and he went to make war with the rest of her offspring, who keep the commandments of God and have the testimony of Jesus Christ.[1]

### THE BEAST FROM THE SEA

13 Then I[1] stood on the sand of the sea. And I saw [a]a beast rising up out of the sea, [b]having seven heads and ten horns,[2] and on his horns ten crowns, and on his heads a [c]blasphemous name. 2 Now the beast which I saw was like a leopard, his feet were like *the feet of* a bear, and his mouth like the mouth of a lion. The [a]dragon gave him his power, his throne, and great authority. 3 And I saw one of his heads [a]as if it had been mortally wounded, and his deadly wound was healed. And [b]all the world marveled and followed the beast. 4 So they worshiped the dragon who gave authority to the beast; and they worshiped the beast, saying, [a]"Who *is* like the beast? Who is able to make war with him?"

5 And he was given [a]a mouth speaking great things and blasphemies, and he was given authority to continue[1] for [b]forty-two months. 6 Then he opened his mouth in blasphemy against God, to blaspheme His name, [a]His tabernacle, and those who dwell in heaven. 7 It was granted to him [a]to make war with the saints and to overcome them. And [b]authority was given him over every tribe,[1] tongue, and nation. 8 All who dwell on the earth will worship him, [a]whose names have not been written in the Book of Life of the Lamb slain [b]from the foundation of the world.

9 [a]If anyone has an ear, let him hear. 10 [a]He who leads into captivity shall go into captivity; [b]he who kills with the sword must be killed with the sword. [c]Here is the patience and the faith of the saints.

### THE BEAST FROM THE EARTH

11 Then I saw another beast [a]coming up out of the earth, and he had two horns like a lamb and spoke like a dragon. 12 And he exercises all the authority of the first beast in his presence, and causes the earth and those who dwell in it to worship the first beast, [a]whose deadly wound was healed. 13 [a]He performs great signs, [b]so that he even makes fire come down from heaven on the earth in the sight of men. 14 [a]And he deceives those[1] who dwell on the earth [b]by those signs which he was granted to do in the sight of the beast, telling those who dwell on the earth to make an image to the beast who was wounded by the sword [c]and lived. 15 He was granted *power* to give breath to the image of the beast, that the image of the beast should both speak [a]and cause as many as would not worship the image of the beast to be killed. 16 He causes all, both small and great, rich and poor, free and slave, [a]to receive a mark on their right hand or on their foreheads, 17 and that no one may buy or sell except one who has the mark or[1] [a]the name of the beast, [b]or the number of his name.

18 [a]Here is wisdom. Let him who has [b]understanding calculate [c]the number of the beast, [d]for it is the number of a man: His number *is* 666.

> **13:18** No one knows exactly what this number means. It's the **number of the beast**, and **the number of a man**, so the beast is merely a man, not a god. We can be sure that this "man's number" will someday be understood in relation to the number **666**, and that when the people who are living at the time of the fulfillment of the prophecies in this book need to understand this clearly, the Lord will make it plain. In the meantime, the warning is enough for all who will hear.

### THE LAMB AND THE 144,000

14 Then I looked, and behold, a[1] [a]Lamb standing on Mount Zion, and with Him [b]one hundred *and* forty-four thousand, having[2] His Father's name [c]written on their foreheads. 2 And I heard a voice from heaven, [a]like the voice of many waters, and like the voice of loud thunder.

**12:11** [b] Luke 14:26 **12:12** [a] Ps. 96:11 [b] Rev. 8:13 [c] Rev. 10:6 **12:13** [a] Rev. 12:5 **12:14** [a] Ex. 19:4 [b] Rev. 12:6 [c] Rev. 17:3 [d] Dan. 7:25; 12:7 **12:15** [a] Is. 59:19 **12:17** [1] NU-Text and M-Text omit *Christ*. **13:1** [a] Dan. 7:2, 7 [b] Rev. 12:3 [c] Rev. 17:3 [1] NU-Text reads *he*. [2] NU-Text and M-Text read *ten horns and seven heads*. **13:2** [a] Rev. 12:3, 9; 13:4, 12 **13:3** [a] Rev. 13:12, 14 [b] Rev. 17:8 **13:4** [a] Rev. 18:18 **13:5** [a] Dan. 7:8, 11, 20, 25; 11:36 [b] Rev. 11:2 [1] M-Text reads *make war*. **13:6** [a] [Col. 2:9] **13:7** [a] Dan. 7:21 [b] Rev. 11:18 [1] NU-Text and M-Text add *and people*. **13:8** [a] Ex. 32:32 [b] Rev. 17:8 **13:9** [a] Rev. 2:7 **13:10** [a] Is. 33:1 [b] Gen. 9:6 [c] Rev. 14:12 **13:11** [a] Rev. 11:7 **13:12** [a] Rev. 13:3, 4 **13:13** [a] Matt. 24:24 [b] 1 Kin. 18:38 **13:14** [a] Rev. 12:9 [b] 2 Thess. 2:9 [c] 2 Kin. 20:7 [1] M-Text reads *my own people*. **13:15** [a] Rev. 16:2 **13:16** [a] Rev. 7:3; 14:9; 20:4 **13:17** [a] Rev. 14:9–11 [b] Rev. 15:2 [1] NU-Text and M-Text omit *or*. **13:18** [a] Rev. 17:9 [b] [1 Cor. 2:14] [c] Rev. 15:2 [d] Rev. 21:17 **14:1** [a] Rev. 5:6 [b] Rev. 7:4; 14:3 [c] Rev. 7:3; 22:4 [1] NU-Text and M-Text read *the*. [2] NU-Text and M-Text add *His name and*. **14:2** [a] Rev. 1:15; 19:6

And I heard the sound of [b]harpists playing their
harps. 3 They sang as it were a new song before
the throne, before the four living creatures, and
the elders; and no one could learn that song
[a]except the hundred *and* forty-four thousand
who were redeemed from the earth. 4 These
are the ones who were not defiled with women,
[a]for they are virgins. These are the ones [b]who
follow the Lamb wherever He goes. These [c]were
redeemed[1] from *among* men, [d]*being* firstfruits
to God and to the Lamb. 5 And [a]in their mouth
was found no deceit,[1] for [b]they are without fault
before the throne of God.[2]

### THE PROCLAMATIONS OF THREE ANGELS

6 Then I saw another angel [a]flying in the
midst of heaven, [b]having the everlasting gospel
to preach to those who dwell on the earth—[c]to
every nation, tribe, tongue, and people— 7 saying
with a loud voice, [a]"Fear God and give glory to
Him, for the hour of His judgment has come;
[b]and worship Him who made heaven and earth,
the sea and springs of water."

8 And another angel followed, saying, [a]"Baby-
lon[1] is fallen, is fallen, that great city, because
[b]she has made all nations drink of the wine of
the wrath of her fornication."

9 Then a third angel followed them, saying
with a loud voice, [a]"If anyone worships the beast
and his image, and receives *his* [b]mark on his
forehead or on his hand, 10 he himself [a]shall
also drink of the wine of the wrath of God, which
is [b]poured out full strength into [c]the cup of
His indignation. [d]He shall be tormented with
[e]fire and brimstone in the presence of the holy
angels and in the presence of the Lamb. 11 And
[a]the smoke of their torment ascends forever and
ever; and they have no rest day or night, who
worship the beast and his image, and whoever
receives the mark of his name."

> **14:10 Brimstone** is another name for sulfur, a fast-burning, disgusting-smelling rock. Ancient armies sometimes used burning sulfur as ammunition in their catapults, launching it over city walls to set fire to the buildings inside.

12 [a]Here is the patience of the saints; [b]here
*are* those[1] who keep the commandments of God
and the faith of Jesus.

13 Then I heard a voice from heaven saying
to me,[1] "Write: [a]'Blessed *are* the dead [b]who die
in the Lord from now on.' "

"Yes," says the Spirit, [c]"that they may rest
from their labors, and their works follow [d]them."

### REAPING THE EARTH'S HARVEST

14 Then I looked, and behold, a white cloud,
and on the cloud sat *One* like the Son of Man,
having on His head a golden crown, and in His
hand a sharp sickle. 15 And another angel [a]came
out of the temple, crying with a loud voice to
Him who sat on the cloud, [b]"Thrust in Your
sickle and reap, for the time has come for You[1]
to reap, for the harvest [c]of the earth is ripe." 16 So
He who sat on the cloud thrust in His sickle on
the earth, and the earth was reaped.

### REAPING THE GRAPES OF WRATH

17 Then another angel came out of the temple
which is in heaven, he also having a sharp sickle.

18 And another angel came out from the
altar, [a]who had power over fire, and he cried
with a loud cry to him who had the sharp sickle,
saying, [b]"Thrust in your sharp sickle and gather
the clusters of the vine of the earth, for her
grapes are fully ripe." 19 So the angel thrust his
sickle into the earth and gathered the vine of
the earth, and threw *it* into [a]the great winepress
of the wrath of God. 20 And [a]the winepress was
trampled [b]outside the city, and blood came out
of the winepress, [c]up to the horses' bridles, for
one thousand six hundred furlongs.

### PRELUDE TO THE BOWL JUDGMENTS

15 Then [a]I saw another sign in heaven, great
and marvelous: [b]seven angels having the
seven last plagues, [c]for in them the wrath of
God is complete.

2 And I saw *something* like [a]a sea of glass
[b]mingled with fire, and those who have the
victory over the beast, [c]over his image and over
his mark[1] *and* over the [d]number of his name,
standing on the sea of glass, [e]having harps of
God. 3 They sing [a]the song of Moses, the servant
of God, and the song of the [b]Lamb, saying:

[c]"Great and marvelous *are* Your works,
Lord God Almighty!
[d]Just and true *are* Your ways,
O King of the saints![1]
4 [a]Who shall not fear You, O Lord, and
glorify Your name?
For *You* alone *are* [b]holy.

**14:2** [b] Rev. 5:8 **14:3** [a] Rev. 5:9 **14:4** [a] [2 Cor. 11:2] [b] Rev. 3:4; 7:17 [c] Rev. 5:9 [d] James 1:18 [1] M-Text adds *by Jesus.* **14:5** [a] Ps. 32:2 [b] Eph. 5:27 [1] NU-Text and M-Text read *falsehood.* [2] NU-Text and M-Text omit *before the throne of God.* **14:6** [a] Rev. 8:13 [b] Eph. 3:9 [c] Rev. 13:7 **14:7** [a] Rev. 11:18 [b] Neh. 9:6 **14:8** [a] Is. 21:9 [b] Jer. 51:7 [1] NU-Text reads *Babylon the great is fallen, is fallen, which has made;* M-Text reads *Babylon the great is fallen. She has made.* **14:9** [a] Rev. 13:14, 15; 14:11 [b] Rev. 13:16 **14:10** [a] Ps. 75:8 [b] Rev. 18:6 [c] Rev. 16:19 [d] Rev. 20:10 [e] 2 Thess. 1:7 **14:11** [a] Is. 34:8–10 **14:12** [a] Rev. 13:10 [b] Rev. 12:17 [1] NU-Text and M-Text omit *here are those.* **14:13** [a] Eccl. 4:1, 2 [b] 1 Cor. 15:18 [c] Heb. 4:9, 10 [d] [1 Cor. 3:11–15; 15:58] [1] NU-Text and M-Text omit *to me.* **14:15** [a] Rev. 16:17 [b] Joel 3:13 [c] Jer. 51:33 [1] NU-Text and M-Text omit *for You.* **14:18** [a] Rev. 16:8 [b] Joel 3:13 **14:19** [a] Rev. 19:15 **14:20** [a] Is. 63:3 [b] Heb. 13:12 [c] Is. 34:3 **15:1** [a] Rev. 12:1, 3 [b] Rev. 21:9 [c] Rev. 14:10 **15:2** [a] Rev. 4:6 [b] [Matt. 3:11] [c] Rev. 13:14, 15 [d] Rev. 13:17 [e] Rev. 5:8 [1] NU-Text and M-Text omit *over his mark.* **15:3** [a] Ex. 15:1–21 [b] Rev. 15:3 [c] Deut. 32:3, 4 [d] Ps. 145:17 [1] NU-Text and M-Text read *nations.* **15:4** [a] Ex. 15:14 [b] Lev. 11:44

For [c]all nations shall come and worship
before You,
For Your judgments have been
manifested."

5 After these things I looked, and behold,[1] [a]the
temple of the tabernacle of the testimony in heav-
en was opened. 6 And out of the temple came the
seven angels having the seven plagues, [a]clothed in
pure bright linen, and having their chests girded
with golden bands. 7 [a]Then one of the four living
creatures gave to the seven angels seven golden
bowls full of the wrath of God [b]who lives forever
and ever. 8 [a]The temple was filled with smoke
[b]from the glory of God and from His power, and
no one was able to enter the temple till the seven
plagues of the seven angels were completed.

16 Then I heard a loud voice from the temple
saying [a]to the seven angels, "Go and pour
out the bowls[1] [b]of the wrath of God on the earth."

### FIRST BOWL: LOATHSOME SORES

2 So the first went and poured out his bowl
[a]upon the earth, and a foul and [b]loathsome
sore came upon the men [c]who had the mark of
the beast and those [d]who worshiped his image.

### SECOND BOWL: THE SEA TURNS TO BLOOD

3 Then the second angel poured out his bowl
[a]on the sea, and [b]it became blood as of a dead
*man;* [c]and every living creature in the sea died.

### THIRD BOWL: THE WATERS TURN TO BLOOD

4 Then the third angel poured out his bowl [a]on
the rivers and springs of water, [b]and they became
blood. 5 And I heard the angel of the waters saying:

[a]"You are righteous, O Lord,[1]
The One [b]who is and who was and who is
to be,[2]
Because You have judged these things.
6 For [a]they have shed the blood [b]of saints
and prophets,
[c]And You have given them blood to drink.
For[1] it is their just due."

7 And I heard another from[1] the altar saying,
"Even so, [a]Lord God Almighty, [b]true and righ-
teous *are* Your judgments."

### FOURTH BOWL: MEN ARE SCORCHED

8 Then the fourth angel poured out his bowl
[a]on the sun, [b]and power was given to him to
scorch men with fire. 9 And men were scorched
with great heat, and they [a]blasphemed the name
of God who has power over these plagues; [b]and
they did not repent [c]and give Him glory.

### FIFTH BOWL: DARKNESS AND PAIN

10 Then the fifth angel poured out his bowl
[a]on the throne of the beast, [b]and his kingdom
became full of darkness; [c]and they gnawed their
tongues because of the pain. 11 They blasphemed
the God of heaven because of their pains and
their sores, and did not repent of their deeds.

### SIXTH BOWL: EUPHRATES DRIED UP

12 Then the sixth angel poured out his bowl
[a]on the great river Euphrates, [b]and its water was
dried up, [c]so that the way of the kings from the
east might be prepared. 13 And I saw three un-
clean [a]spirits like frogs *coming* out of the mouth
of [b]the dragon, out of the mouth of the beast,
and out of the mouth of [c]the false prophet. 14 For
they are spirits of demons, [a]performing signs,
*which* go out to the kings of the earth and[1] of
[b]the whole world, to gather them to [c]the battle
of that great day of God Almighty.
15 [a]"Behold, I am coming as a thief. Blessed
*is* he who watches, and keeps his garments, [b]lest
he walk naked and they see his shame."

**SEEING JESUS IN THE SCRIPTURE**

**16:15** Jesus' return is sure, but the hour when it will happen is unknown; we must live always ready (see Matt. 24:43).

16 [a]And they gathered them together to the
place called in Hebrew, Armageddon.[1]

**16:16 Armageddon** means "hill of Megiddo." In Old Testament times, Megiddo, which was located in the Carmel Mountain range, was a popular spot for military battles.

### SEVENTH BOWL: THE EARTH UTTERLY SHAKEN

17 Then the seventh angel poured out his bowl
into the air, and a loud voice came out of the
temple of heaven, from the throne, saying, [a]"It is
done!" 18 And [a]there were noises and thunderings

15:4 [c] Is. 66:23 15:5 [a] Num. 1:50 [1] NU-Text and M-Text omit *behold.* 15:6 [a] Ex. 28:6 15:7 [a] Rev. 4:6 [b] 1 Thess. 1:9 15:8 [a] Ex. 19:18; 40:34 [b] 2 Thess. 1:9 16:1 [a] Rev. 15:1 [b] Rev. 14:10 [1] NU-Text and M-Text read *seven bowls.* 16:2 [a] Rev. 8:7 [b] Ex. 9:9–11 [c] Rev. 13:15–17; 14:9 [d] Rev. 13:14 16:3 [a] Rev. 8:8; 11:6 [b] Ex. 7:17–21 [c] Rev. 8:9 16:4 [a] Rev. 8:10 [b] Ex. 7:17–20 16:5 [a] Rev. 15:3, 4 [b] Rev. 1:4, 8 [1] NU-Text and M-Text omit *O Lord.* [2] NU-Text and M-Text read *who was, the Holy One.* 16:6 [a] Matt. 23:34 [b] Rev. 11:18 [c] Is. 49:26 [1] NU-Text and M-Text omit *For.* 16:7 [a] Rev. 15:3 [b] Rev. 13:10; 19:2 [1] NU-Text and M-Text omit *another from.* 16:8 [a] Rev. 8:12 [b] Rev. 9:17, 18 16:9 [a] Rev. 16:11 [b] Dan. 5:22 [c] Rev. 11:13 16:10 [a] Rev. 13:2 [b] Rev. 8:12; 9:2 [c] Rev. 11:10 16:12 [a] Rev. 9:14 [b] Jer. 50:38 [c] Is. 41:2, 25; 46:11 16:13 [a] 1 John 4:1 [b] Rev. 12:3, 9 [c] Rev. 13:11, 14; 19:20; 20:10 16:14 [a] 2 Thess. 2:9 [b] Luke 2:1 [c] Rev. 17:14; 19:19; 20:8 [1] NU-Text and M-Text omit *of the earth and.* 16:15 [a] Matt. 24:43 [b] 2 Cor. 5:3 16:16 [a] Rev. 19:19 [1] M-Text reads *Megiddo.* 16:17 [a] Rev. 10:6; 21:6 16:18 [a] Rev. 4:5

and lightnings; [b]and there was a great earthquake, such a mighty and great earthquake [c]as had not occurred since men were on the earth. 19 Now [a]the great city was divided into three parts, and the cities of the nations fell. And [b]great Babylon [c]was remembered before God, [d]to give her the cup of the wine of the fierceness of His wrath. 20 Then [a]every island fled away, and the mountains were not found. 21 And great hail from heaven fell upon men, *each hailstone* about the weight of a talent. Men blasphemed God because of the plague of the hail, since that plague was exceedingly great.

### THE SCARLET WOMAN AND THE SCARLET BEAST

**17** Then [a]one of the seven angels who had the seven bowls came and talked with me, saying to me,[1] "Come, [b]I will show you the judgment of [c]the great harlot [d]who sits on many waters, 2 [a]with whom the kings of the earth committed fornication, and [b]the inhabitants of the earth were made drunk with the wine of her fornication."

3 So he carried me away in the Spirit [a]into the wilderness. And I saw a woman sitting [b]on a scarlet beast *which was* full of [c]names of blasphemy, having seven heads and ten horns. 4 The woman [a]was arrayed in purple and scarlet, [b]and adorned with gold and precious stones and pearls, [c]having in her hand a golden cup [d]full of abominations and the filthiness of her fornication.[1] 5 And on her forehead a name *was* written:

[a]MYSTERY, BABYLON THE GREAT,
THE MOTHER OF HARLOTS
AND OF THE ABOMINATIONS
OF THE EARTH.

6 I saw [a]the woman, drunk [b]with the blood of the saints and with the blood of [c]the martyrs of Jesus. And when I saw her, I marveled with great amazement.

### THE MEANING OF THE WOMAN AND THE BEAST

7 But the angel said to me, "Why did you marvel? I will tell you the mystery of the woman and of the beast that carries her, which has the seven heads and the ten horns. 8 The beast that you saw was, and is not, and [a]will ascend out of the bottomless pit and [b]go to perdition. And those who [c]dwell on the earth [d]will marvel, [e]whose names are not written in the Book of Life from the foundation of the world, when they see the beast that was, and is not, and yet is.[1]

9 [a]"Here *is* the mind which has wisdom: [b]The seven heads are seven mountains on which the woman sits. 10 There are also seven kings. Five have fallen, one is, *and* the other has not yet come. And when he comes, he must [a]continue a short time. 11 The [a]beast that was, and is not, is himself also the eighth, and is of the seven, and is going to perdition.

12 [a]"The ten horns which you saw are ten kings who have received no kingdom as yet, but they receive authority for one hour as kings with the beast. 13 These are of one mind, and they will give their power and authority to the beast. 14 [a]These will make war with the Lamb, and the Lamb will [b]overcome them, [c]for He is Lord of lords and King of kings; [d]and those *who are* with Him *are* called, chosen, and faithful."

15 Then he said to me, [a]"The waters which you saw, where the harlot sits, [b]are peoples, multitudes, nations, and tongues. 16 And the ten horns which you saw on[1] the beast, [a]these will hate the harlot, make her [b]desolate [c]and naked, eat her flesh and [d]burn her with fire. 17 [a]For God has put it into their hearts to fulfill His purpose, to be of one mind, and to give their kingdom to the beast, [b]until the words of God are fulfilled. 18 And the woman whom you saw [a]is that great city [b]which reigns over the kings of the earth."

### THE FALL OF BABYLON THE GREAT

**18** After[a] these things I saw another angel coming down from heaven, having great authority, [b]and the earth was illuminated with his glory. 2 And he cried mightily[1] with a loud voice, saying, [a]"Babylon the great is fallen, is fallen, and [b]has become a dwelling place of demons, a prison for every foul spirit, and [c]a cage for every unclean and hated bird! 3 For all the nations [a]have drunk of the wine of the wrath of her fornication, the kings of the earth have committed fornication with her, [b]and the merchants of the earth have become rich through the abundance of her luxury."

4 And I heard another voice from heaven saying, [a]"Come out of her, my people, lest you share in her sins, and lest you receive of her plagues. 5 [a]For her sins have reached[1] to heaven, and [b]God has remembered her iniquities. 6 [a]Render to her just as she rendered to you,[1] and repay her double according to her works; [b]in the cup which she has mixed, [c]mix double for her. 7 [a]In the measure that she glorified herself and lived luxuriously, in the same measure give her torment and sorrow; for she says in her heart, 'I sit *as* [b]queen, and am no widow, and will not

**16:18** [b] Rev. 11:13 [c] Dan. 12:1 **16:19** [a] Rev. 14:8 [b] Rev. 17:5, 18 [c] Rev. 14:8; 18:5 [d] Is. 51:17 **16:20** [a] Rev. 6:14; 20:11 **17:1** [a] Rev. 1:1; 21:9 [b] Rev. 16:19 [c] Nah. 3:4 [d] Jer. 51:13 [1] NU-Text and M-Text omit *to me.* **17:2** [a] Rev. 2:22; 18:3, 9 [b] Jer. 51:7 **17:3** [a] Rev. 12:6, 14; 21:10 [b] Rev. 12:3 [c] Rev. 13:1 **17:4** [a] Rev. 18:12, 16 [b] Dan. 11:38 [c] Jer. 51:7 [d] Rev. 14:8 [1] M-Text reads *the filthiness of the fornication of the earth.* **17:5** [a] 2 Thess. 2:7 **17:6** [a] Rev. 18:24 [b] Rev. 13:15 [c] Rev. 6:9, 10 **17:8** [a] Rev. 11:7 [b] Rev. 13:10; 17:11 [c] Rev. 3:10 [d] Rev. 13:3 [e] Rev. 13:8 [1] NU-Text and M-Text read *and shall be present.* **17:9** [a] Rev. 13:18 [b] Rev. 13:1 **17:10** [a] Rev. 13:5 **17:11** [a] Rev. 13:3, 12, 14; 17:8 **17:12** [a] Dan. 7:20 **17:14** [a] Rev. 16:14; 19:19 [b] Rev. 19:20 [c] 1 Tim. 6:15 [d] Jer. 50:44 **17:15** [a] Is. 8:7 [b] Rev. 13:7 **17:16** [a] Jer. 50:41 [b] Rev. 18:17, 19 [c] Ezek. 16:37, 39 [d] Rev. 18:8 [1] NU-Text and M-Text read *saw, and the beast.* **17:17** [a] 2 Thess. 2:11 [b] Rev. 10:7 **17:18** [a] Rev. 11:8; 16:19 [b] Rev. 12:4 **18:1** [a] Rev. 17:1, 7 [b] Ezek. 43:2 **18:2** [a] Is. 13:19; 21:9 [b] Is. 13:21; 34:11, 13–15 [c] Is. 14:23 [1] NU-Text and M-Text omit *mightily.* **18:3** [a] Rev. 14:8 [b] Is. 47:15 **18:4** [a] Is. 48:20 **18:5** [a] Gen. 18:20 [b] Rev. 16:19 [1] NU-Text and M-Text read *have been heaped up.* **18:6** [a] Ps. 137:8 [b] Rev. 14:10 [c] Rev. 16:19 [1] NU-Text and M-Text omit *to you.* **18:7** [a] Ezek. 28:2–8 [b] Is. 47:7, 8

see sorrow.' 8 Therefore her plagues will come [a]in one day—death and mourning and famine. And [b]she will be utterly burned with fire, [c]for strong *is* the Lord God who judges[1] her.

### THE WORLD MOURNS BABYLON'S FALL

9 [a]"The kings of the earth who committed fornication and lived luxuriously with her [b]will weep and lament for her, [c]when they see the smoke of her burning, 10 standing at a distance for fear of her torment, saying, [a]'Alas, alas, that great city Babylon, that mighty city! [b]For in one hour your judgment has come.'

11 "And [a]the merchants of the earth will weep and mourn over her, for no one buys their merchandise anymore: 12 [a]merchandise of gold and silver, precious stones and pearls, fine linen and purple, silk and scarlet, every kind of citron wood, every kind of object of ivory, every kind of object of most precious wood, bronze, iron, and marble; 13 and cinnamon and incense, fragrant oil and frankincense, wine and oil, fine flour and wheat, cattle and sheep, horses and chariots, and bodies and [a]souls of men. 14 The fruit that your soul longed for has gone from you, and all the things which are rich and splendid have gone from you,[1] and you shall find them no more at all. 15 The merchants of these things, who became rich by her, will stand at a distance for fear of her torment, weeping and wailing, 16 and saying, 'Alas, alas, [a]that great city [b]that was clothed in fine linen, purple, and scarlet, and adorned with gold and precious stones and pearls! 17 [a]For in one hour such great riches came to nothing.' [b]Every shipmaster, all who travel by ship, sailors, and as many as trade on the sea, stood at a distance 18 [a]and cried out when they saw the smoke of her burning, saying, [b]'What *is* like this great city?'

19 [a]"They threw dust on their heads and cried out, weeping and wailing, and saying, 'Alas, alas, that great city, in which all who had ships on the sea became rich by her wealth! [b]For in one hour she is made desolate.'

20 [a]"Rejoice over her, O heaven, and *you* holy apostles[1] and prophets, for [b]God has avenged you on her!"

### FINALITY OF BABYLON'S FALL

21 Then a mighty angel took up a stone like a great millstone and threw *it* into the sea, saying, [a]"Thus with violence the great city Babylon shall be thrown down, and [b]shall not be found anymore. 22 [a]The sound of harpists, musicians, flutists, and trumpeters shall not be heard in you anymore. No craftsman of any craft shall be found in you anymore, and the sound of a millstone shall not be heard in you anymore. 23 [a]The light of a lamp shall not shine in you anymore, [b]and the voice of bridegroom and bride shall not be heard in you anymore. For [c]your merchants were the great men of the earth, [d]for by your sorcery all the nations were deceived. 24 And [a]in her was found the blood of prophets and saints, and of all who [b]were slain on the earth."

### HEAVEN EXULTS OVER BABYLON

**19** After these things [a]I heard[1] a loud voice of a great multitude in heaven, saying, "Alleluia! [b]Salvation and glory and honor and power *belong* to the Lord[2] our God! 2 For [a]true and righteous *are* His judgments, because He has judged the great harlot who corrupted the earth with her fornication; and He [b]has avenged on her the blood of His servants *shed* by her." 3 Again they said, "Alleluia! [a]Her smoke rises up forever and ever!" 4 And [a]the twenty-four elders and the four living creatures fell down and worshiped God who sat on the throne, saying, [b]"Amen! Alleluia!" 5 Then a voice came from the throne, saying, [a]"Praise our God, all you His servants and those who fear Him, [b]both[1] small and great!"

6 [a]And I heard, as it were, the voice of a great multitude, as the sound of many waters and as the sound of mighty thunderings, saying, "Alleluia! For [b]the[1] Lord God Omnipotent reigns! 7 Let us be glad and rejoice and give Him glory, for [a]the marriage of the Lamb has come, and His wife has made herself ready." 8 And [a]to her it was granted to be arrayed in fine linen, clean and bright, [b]for the fine linen is the righteous acts of the saints.

9 Then he said to me, "Write: [a]'Blessed *are* those who are called to the marriage supper of the Lamb!' " And he said to me, [b]"These are the true sayings of God." 10 And [a]I fell at his feet to worship him. But he said to me, [b]"See *that you do* not *do that!* I am your [c]fellow servant, and of your brethren [d]who have the testimony of Jesus. Worship God! For the [e]testimony of Jesus is the spirit of prophecy."

### CHRIST ON A WHITE HORSE

11 [a]Now I saw heaven opened, and behold, [b]a white horse. And He who sat on him *was* called [c]Faithful and True, and [d]in righteousness He judges and makes war. 12 [a]His eyes *were* like a flame of fire, and on His head *were* many crowns. [b]He had[1] a name written that no one knew except Himself. 13 [a]He *was* clothed with a robe dipped in

**18:8** [a] Rev. 18:10 [b] Rev. 17:16 [c] Jer. 50:34 [1] NU-Text and M-Text read *has judged.* **18:9** [a] Ezek. 26:16; 27:35 [b] Jer. 50:46 [c] Rev. 19:3 **18:10** [a] Is. 21:9 [b] Rev. 18:17, 19 **18:11** [a] Ezek. 27:27–34 **18:12** [a] Rev. 17:4 **18:13** [a] Ezek. 27:13 **18:14** [1] NU-Text and M-Text read *been lost to you.* **18:16** [a] Rev. 17:18 [b] Rev. 17:4 **18:17** [a] Rev. 18:10 [b] Is. 23:14 **18:18** [a] Ezek. 27:30 [b] Rev. 13:4 **18:19** [a] Josh. 7:6 [b] Rev. 18:8 **18:20** [a] Jer. 51:48 [b] Luke 11:49 [1] NU-Text and M-Text read *saints and apostles.* **18:21** [a] Jer. 51:63, 64 [b] Rev. 12:8; 16:20 **18:22** [a] Jer. 7:34; 16:9; 25:10 **18:23** [a] Jer. 25:10 [b] Jer. 7:34; 16:9 [c] Is. 23:8 [d] 2 Kin. 9:22 **18:24** [a] Rev. 16:6; 17:6 [b] Jer. 51:49 **19:1** [a] Rev. 11:15; 19:6 [b] Rev. 4:11 [1] NU-Text and M-Text add *something like.* [2] NU-Text and M-Text omit *the Lord.* **19:2** [a] Rev. 15:3; 16:7 [b] Deut. 32:43 **19:3** [a] Is. 34:10 **19:4** [a] Rev. 4:4, 6, 10 [b] 1 Chr. 16:36 **19:5** [a] Ps. 134:1 [b] Rev. 11:18 [1] NU-Text and M-Text omit *both.* **19:6** [a] Ezek. 1:24 [b] Rev. 11:15 [1] NU-Text and M-Text read *our.* **19:7** [a] [Matt. 22:2; 25:10] **19:8** [a] Ezek. 16:10 [b] Ps. 132:9 **19:9** [a] Luke 14:15 [b] Rev. 22:6 **19:10** [a] Rev. 22:8 [b] Acts 10:26 [c] [Heb. 1:14] [d] 1 John 5:10 [e] Luke 24:27 **19:11** [a] Rev. 15:5 [b] Rev. 6:2; 19:19, 21 [c] Rev. 3:7, 14 [d] Is. 11:4 **19:12** [a] Rev. 1:14 [b] Rev. 2:17; 19:16 [1] M-Text adds *names written, and.* **19:13** [a] Is. 63:2, 3

### SEEING JESUS IN THE SCRIPTURE

**19:13** Jesus returning wearing a robe dipped in blood marks His coming judgment and fulfills Scripture (see Is. 63:2–3).

blood, and His name is called [b]The Word of God.
14 [a]And the armies in heaven, [b]clothed in fine
linen, white and clean,ˈ followed Him on white
horses. 15 Now [a]out of His mouth goes a sharpˈ
sword, that with it He should strike the nations.
And [b]He Himself will rule them with a rod of
iron. [c]He Himself treads the winepress of the
fierceness and wrath of Almighty God. 16 And [a]He
has on *His* robe and on His thigh a name written:

[b]KING OF KINGS AND
LORD OF LORDS.

### *THE BEAST AND HIS ARMIES DEFEATED*

17 Then I saw an angel standing in the sun;
and he cried with a loud voice, saying to all the
birds that fly in the midst of heaven, [a]"Come and
gather together for the supper of the great God,ˈ
18 [a]that you may eat the flesh of kings, the flesh
of captains, the flesh of mighty men, the flesh of
horses and of those who sit on them, and the flesh
of all *people,* freeˈ and slave, both small and great."
19 [a]And I saw the beast, the kings of the earth,
and their armies, gathered together to make war
against Him who sat on the horse and against His
army. 20 [a]Then the beast was captured, and with
him the false prophet who worked signs in his
presence, by which he deceived those who received
the mark of the beast and [b]those who worshiped
his image. [c]These two were cast alive into the lake
of fire [d]burning with brimstone. 21 And the rest
[a]were killed with the sword which proceeded from
the mouth of Him who sat on the horse. [b]And all
the birds [c]were filled with their flesh.

### *SATAN BOUND 1,000 YEARS*

20 Then I saw an angel coming down from
heaven, [a]having the key to the bottomless
pit and a great chain in his hand. 2 He laid hold
of [a]the dragon, that serpent of old, who is *the*

**19:13** [b] [John 1:1, 14] **19:14** [a] Rev. 14:20 [b] Matt. 28:3 ˈ NU-Text and M-Text read *pure white linen.* **19:15** [a] Is. 11:4 [b] Ps. 2:8, 9 [c] Is. 63:3–6 ˈ M-Text adds *two-edged.* **19:16** [a] Rev. 2:17; 19:12 [b] Dan. 2:47 **19:17** [a] Ezek. 39:17 ˈ NU-Text and M-Text read *the great supper of God.* **19:18** [a] Ezek. 39:18–20 ˈ NU-Text and M-Text read *both free.* **19:19** [a] Rev. 16:13–16 **19:20** [a] Rev. 16:13 [b] Rev. 13:8, 12, 13 [c] Dan. 7:11 [d] Rev. 14:10 **19:21** [a] Rev. 19:15 [b] Rev. 19:17, 18 [c] Rev. 17:16 **20:1** [a] Rev. 1:18; 9:1 **20:2** [a] 2 Pet. 2:4

REVELATION 19:6–21

## THE HERO AND THE GROOM

59

STORY OF SCRIPTURE

### WHAT'S GOING ON?

This is the dramatic and majestic climax of Revelation, showcasing Jesus' final victory over the forces of evil. This passage is divided into two distinct sections: a celebration in heaven, marked by a chorus of alleluias and marriage supper of the Lamb (vv. 6–10), and the earth-shattering return of Jesus, described with powerful imagery of warfare and divine judgment (vv. 11–21).

Jesus is both a hero, riding atop a horse to defeat the forces of darkness, and a groom, welcoming in His bride, the church. This image of Jesus contrasts sharply with His first coming, when He appeared in humility as the Suffering Servant. His return as conquering King will be marked by power and glory, His robe dipped in blood, not in weakness but as the mighty Word of God leading the heavenly armies.

### WHAT DOES THIS MEAN FOR ME?

God is a God of love and justice. He is your comforter, friend, and companion, but He is also the Hero of heaven and vanquisher of evil. Approaching God with this understanding that He is both a fierce judge and fiercely in love with us, gives us a balanced prayer life and relationship with Him marked by both adoration and respect for Him.

### DID YOU CATCH THE PATTERN?

The marriage supper of the Lamb was foreshadowed in an unlikely place—the Last Supper. During the Last Supper, Jesus welcomed His disciples into a covenant bond with Him, one founded upon the blood He would soon after shed on the cross. This permanent joining can be thought of as the wedding ceremony while the feast depicted in Revelation 19 is the celebratory wedding banquet.

*For the next* Story of Scripture *reading and devotion, turn to Revelation 22:1–21 on page 1311.*

Devil and Satan, and bound him for a thousand
years; 3 and he cast him into the bottomless pit,
and shut him up, and [a]set a seal on him, [b]so
that he should deceive the nations no more
till the thousand years were finished. But after
these things he must be released for a little
while.

### THE SAINTS REIGN WITH CHRIST 1,000 YEARS

4 And I saw [a]thrones, and they sat on them,
and [b]judgment was committed to them. Then *I
saw* [c]the souls of those who had been beheaded
for their witness to Jesus and for the word of
God, [d]who had not worshiped the beast [e]or his
image, and had not received *his* mark on their
foreheads or on their hands. And they [f]lived and
[g]reigned with Christ for a[1] thousand years. 5 But
the rest of the dead did not live again until the
thousand years were finished. This *is* the first
resurrection. 6 Blessed and holy *is* he who has
part in the first resurrection. Over such [a]the
second death has no power, but they shall be
[b]priests of God and of Christ, [c]and shall reign
with Him a thousand years.

### SATANIC REBELLION CRUSHED

*(cf. Ezek. 38; 39)*

7 Now when the thousand years have ex-
pired, Satan will be released from his prison
8 and will go out [a]to deceive the nations which
are in the four corners of the earth, [b]Gog and
Magog, [c]to gather them together to battle, whose
number *is* as the sand of the sea. 9 [a]They went
up on the breadth of the earth and surrounded
the camp of the saints and the beloved city.
And fire came down from God out of heaven
and devoured them. 10 The devil, who deceived
them, was cast into the lake of fire and brim-
stone [a]where[1] the beast and the false prophet
*are.* And they [b]will be tormented day and night
forever and ever.

### THE GREAT WHITE THRONE JUDGMENT

11 Then I saw a great white throne and Him
who sat on it, from whose face [a]the earth and
the heaven fled away. [b]And there was found no
place for them. 12 And I saw the dead, [a]small and
great, standing before God,[1] [b]and books were
opened. And another [c]book was opened, which
is *the Book* of Life. And the dead were judged
[d]according to their works, by the things which
were written in the books. 13 The sea gave up
the dead who were in it, [a]and Death and Hades
delivered up the dead who were in them. [b]And
they were judged, each one according to his
works. 14 Then [a]Death and Hades were cast into
the lake of fire. [b]This is the second death.[1] 15 And
anyone not found written in the Book of Life
[a]was cast into the lake of fire.

20:3 [a] Dan. 6:17 [b] Rev. 12:9; 20:8, 10 20:4 [a] Dan. 7:9 [b] [1 Cor. 6:2, 3] [c] Rev. 6:9 [d] Rev. 13:12 [e] Rev. 13:15 [f] John 14:19 [g] Rom. 8:17 [1] M-Text reads *the.* 20:6 [a] [Rev. 2:11; 20:14] [b] Is. 61:6 [c] Rev. 20:4 20:8 [a] Rev. 12:9; 20:3, 10 [b] Ezek. 38:2; 39:1, 6 [c] Rev. 16:14 20:9 [a] Ezek. 38:9, 16 20:10 [a] Rev. 19:20; 20:14, 15 [b] Rev. 14:10 [1] NU-Text and M-Text add *also.* 20:11 [a] 2 Pet. 3:7 [b] Dan. 2:35 20:12 [a] Rev. 19:5 [b] Dan. 7:10 [c] Ps. 69:28 [d] Matt. 16:27 [1] NU-Text and M-Text read *the throne.* 20:13 [a] Rev. 1:18; 6:8; 21:4 [b] Rev. 2:23; 20:12 20:14 [a] 1 Cor. 15:26 [b] Rev. 21:8 [1] NU-Text and M-Text add *the lake of fire.* 20:15 [a] Rev. 19:20

KNOW THE TRUTH

## THE DOCTRINE OF THE FUTURE

### PART 4: THE FINAL JUDGMENT

**20:11–15** Heaven and hell are often misunderstood. It's common to believe "good people" who live "good lives" go to heaven while "bad people" who live "bad lives" go to hell. That isn't what the Bible teaches though. Rather, heaven is the eternal destination for those who trust in Christ and submit to His loving, perfect rule; hell is the eternal destination for those who don't. There are no "good" people compared to the flawless, endless, shocking perfection of God. Therefore, no "good" people go to heaven. There is only One who is good and has done good: Jesus. He alone is the Judge of the living and the dead (2 Tim. 4:1).

While every person deserves to spend eternity in hell because of sin, all who repent of sin, regardless of its quantity or nature, and call out to Jesus for salvation will be saved (Rom. 10:13). This act alone determines a person's eternal destination. Those who have trusted in Jesus will be judged by that faith and will spend eternity in perfect fellowship with Christ and His people. Those who refuse to turn to Jesus will be judged for their lifetime of rebellion and spend eternity apart from God and all that is good (see Rev. 20:11–15).

*For* **THE DOCTRINE OF THE FUTURE: PART 5: THE NEW HEAVEN AND NEW EARTH,** *turn to Revelation 21:1 on page 1309.*

### *ALL THINGS MADE NEW*

21 Now [a]I saw a new heaven and a new earth,
[b]for the first heaven and the first earth
had passed away. Also there was no more sea.
2 Then I, John,[1] saw [a]the holy city, New Jerusa-
lem, coming down out of heaven from God,
prepared [b]as a bride adorned for her husband.
3 And I heard a loud voice from heaven saying,
"Behold, [a]the tabernacle of God *is* with men, and
He will dwell with them, and they shall be His
people. God Himself will be with them *and be*
their God. 4 [a]And God will wipe away every tear
from their eyes; [b]there shall be no more death,
[c]nor sorrow, nor crying. There shall be no more
pain, for the former things have passed away."

> **SEEING JESUS IN THE SCRIPTURE**
>
> **21:4** When Jesus returns, He will remove every evidence of brokenness from the world as the Scriptures promised (see Is. 25:8).

5 Then [a]He who sat on the throne said, [b]"Be-
hold, I make all things new." And He said to me,[1]
"Write, for [c]these words are true and faithful."
6 And He said to me, [a]"It is done![1] [b]I am the
Alpha and the Omega, the Beginning and the
End. [c]I will give of the fountain of the water of life
freely to him who thirsts. 7 He who overcomes
shall inherit all things,[1] and [a]I will be his God
and he shall be My son. 8 [a]But the cowardly,

> **21:6 Alpha** and **Omega** are the first and last letters of the Greek alphabet.

unbelieving,[1] abominable, murderers, sexually
immoral, sorcerers, idolaters, and all liars shall
have their part in [b]the lake which burns with
fire and brimstone, which is the second death."

### *THE NEW JERUSALEM*
*(cf. Ezek. 48:30–35)*

9 Then one of [a]the seven angels who had the
seven bowls filled with the seven last plagues
came to me[1] and talked with me, saying, "Come,
I will show you [b]the bride, the Lamb's wife."[2]
10 And he carried me away [a]in the Spirit to a
great and high mountain, and showed me [b]the
great city, the holy[1] Jerusalem, descending out
of heaven from God, 11 [a]having the glory of God.
Her light *was* like a most precious stone, like
a jasper stone, clear as crystal. 12 Also she had
a great and high wall with [a]twelve gates, and
twelve angels at the gates, and names written on
them, which are *the names* of the twelve tribes
of the children of Israel: 13 [a]three gates on the
east, three gates on the north, three gates on the
south, and three gates on the west.
14 Now the wall of the city had twelve foun-
dations, and [a]on them were the names[1] of the
twelve apostles of the Lamb. 15 And he who talked
with me [a]had a gold reed to measure the city,
its gates, and its wall. 16 The city is laid out as a

**21:1** [a] [2 Pet. 3:13] [b] Rev. 20:11 **21:2** [a] Is. 52:1 [b] 2 Cor. 11:2 [1] NU-Text and M-Text omit *John*. **21:3** [a] Lev. 26:11 **21:4** [a] Is. 25:8 [b] 1 Cor. 15:26 [c] Is. 35:10; 51:11; 65:19 **21:5** [a] Rev. 4:2, 9; 20:11 [b] Is. 43:19 [c] Rev. 19:9; 22:6 [1] NU-Text and M-Text omit *to me*. **21:6** [a] Rev. 10:6; 16:17 [b] Rev. 1:8; 22:13 [c] John 4:10 [1] M-Text omits *It is done*. **21:7** [a] Zech. 8:8 [1] M-Text reads *overcomes, I shall give him these things*. **21:8** [a] 1 Cor. 6:9 [b] Rev. 20:14 [1] M-Text adds *and sinners*. **21:9** [a] Rev. 15:1 [b] Rev. 19:7; 21:2 [1] NU-Text and M-Text omit *to me*. [2] M-Text reads *I will show you the woman, the Lamb's bride*. **21:10** [a] Rev. 1:10 [b] Ezek. 48 [1] NU-Text and M-Text omit *the great* and read *the holy city, Jerusalem*. **21:11** [a] Rev. 15:8; 21:23; 22:5 **21:12** [a] Ezek. 48:31–34 **21:13** [a] Ezek. 48:31–34 **21:14** [a] Eph. 2:20 [1] NU-Text and M-Text read *twelve names*. **21:15** [a] Ezek. 40:3

KNOW THE TRUTH

## THE DOCTRINE OF THE FUTURE
### PART 5: THE NEW HEAVEN AND NEW EARTH

**21:1** The Bible has one continuous, overarching storyline. Its books don't detail multiple plots moving toward many conclusions. Instead, God is writing one story with one definitive conclusion. That destination is, perhaps surprisingly, the beginning. God is working to redeem a people for Himself and will one day place those people within a new heaven and new earth to live with Him and one another forever, just as He intended in Eden.

When people rebelled against God, sin destroyed our relationship with Him and tarnished creation (see Rom. 8:20–22). Thus, it's not good enough for God to redeem a people to live forever in a broken world; He will repair that world too. There are two views of how God will do this. The first sees God **destroying** the present heavens and earth and creating a new heavens and earth from scratch, as He did the first time. The second sees God **renovating** the present heavens and earth and restoring them to perfection. *New*, in this sense, isn't a matter of timing, but rather one of quality. Either way, all who trust in Jesus have hope we will live forever as perfect people in a perfect heaven and earth in God's perfect presence. The story's end is this new creation for God's forever family of new creations.

square; its length is as great as its breadth. And he measured the city with the reed: twelve thousand furlongs. Its length, breadth, and height are equal. 17 Then he measured its wall: one hundred *and* forty-four cubits, *according* to the measure of a man, that is, of an angel. 18 The construction of its wall was *of* jasper; and the city *was* pure gold, like clear glass. 19 [a]The foundations of the wall of the city *were* adorned with all kinds of precious stones: the first foundation *was* jasper, the second sapphire, the third chalcedony, the fourth emerald, 20 the fifth sardonyx, the sixth sardius, the seventh chrysolite, the eighth beryl, the ninth topaz, the tenth chrysoprase, the eleventh jacinth, and the twelfth amethyst. 21 The twelve gates *were* twelve [a]pearls: each individual gate was of one pearl. [b]And the street of the city *was* pure gold, like transparent glass.

### THE GLORY OF THE NEW JERUSALEM

22 [a]But I saw no temple in it, for the Lord God Almighty and the Lamb are its temple. 23 [a]The city had no need of the sun or of the moon to shine in it,[1] for the glory[2] of God illuminated it. The Lamb *is* its light. 24 [a]And the nations of those who are saved[1] shall walk in its light, and the kings of the earth bring their glory and honor into it.[2] 25 [a]Its gates shall not be shut at all by day [b](there shall be no night there). 26 [a]And they shall bring the glory and the honor of the nations into it.[1] 27 But [a]there shall by no means enter it anything that defiles, or causes[1] an abomination or a lie, but only those who are written in the Lamb's [b]Book of Life.

### THE RIVER OF LIFE

**22** And he showed me [a]a pure[1] river of water of life, clear as crystal, proceeding from the throne of God and of the Lamb. 2 [a]In the middle of its street, and on either side of the river, *was* [b]the tree of life, which bore twelve fruits, each *tree* yielding its fruit every month. The leaves of the tree *were* [c]for the healing of the nations. 3 And [a]there shall be no more curse, [b]but the throne of God and of the Lamb shall be in it, and His [c]servants shall serve Him. 4 [a]They shall see His face, and [b]His name *shall be* on their foreheads. 5 [a]There shall be no night there: They need no lamp nor [b]light of the sun, for [c]the Lord God gives them light. [d]And they shall reign forever and ever.

> **22:2 The tree of life** in the original creation was in the middle of the garden of Eden (see Gen. 2:9), from which Adam and Eve were banished after their rebellion (Gen. 3:22–24). Ezekiel's apocalyptic vision included trees bearing fruit every month with medicinal leaves (Ezek. 47:12). Because only one tree of life is mentioned here, even though it is on both sides of the **river**, it's probably meant as a parallel to Genesis 2, implying a new, better, and everlasting Eden has come.

### THE TIME IS NEAR

6 Then he said to me, [a]"These words *are* faithful and true." And the Lord God of the holy[1] prophets [b]sent His angel to show His servants the things which must [c]shortly take place.

7 [a]"Behold, I am coming quickly! [b]Blessed *is* he who keeps the words of the prophecy of this book."

8 Now I, John, saw and heard[1] these things. And when I heard and saw, [a]I fell down to worship before the feet of the angel who showed me these things.

9 Then he said to me, [a]"See *that you do* not *do that.* For[1] I am your fellow servant, and of your brethren the prophets, and of those who keep the words of this book. Worship God." 10 [a]And he said to me, "Do not seal the words of the prophecy of this book, [b]for the time is at hand. 11 He who is unjust, let him be unjust still; he who is filthy, let him be filthy still; he who is righteous, let him be righteous[1] still; he who is holy, let him be holy still."

### JESUS TESTIFIES TO THE CHURCHES

12 "And behold, I am coming quickly, and [a]My reward *is* with Me, [b]to give to every one according to his work. 13 [a]I am the Alpha and the Omega, *the* Beginning and *the* End, the First and the Last."[1]

> **SEEING JESUS IN THE SCRIPTURE**
>
> **22:12** Jesus promised to return and reward the faithful for their work on His behalf, a promise God made in the days of Isaiah (see Is. 40:10).

14 [a]Blessed *are* those who do His commandments,[1] that they may have the right [b]to the tree

**21:19** [a] Is. 54:11 **21:21** [a] Matt. 13:45, 46 [b] Rev. 22:2 **21:22** [a] John 4:21, 23 **21:23** [a] Is. 24:23; 60:19, 20 [1] NU-Text and M-Text omit *in it.* [2] M-Text reads *the very glory.* **21:24** [a] Is. 60:3, 5; 66:12 [1] NU-Text and M-Text omit *of those who are saved.* [2] M-Text reads *the glory and honor of the nations to Him.* **21:25** [a] Is. 60:11 [b] Is. 60:20 **21:26** [a] Rev. 21:24 [1] M-Text adds *that they may enter in.* **21:27** [a] Joel 3:17 [b] Phil. 4:3 [1] NU-Text and M-Text read *anything profane, nor one who causes.* **22:1** [a] Ezek. 47:1 [1] NU-Text and M-Text omit *pure.* **22:2** [a] Ezek. 47:12 [b] Gen. 2:9 [c] Rev. 21:24 **22:3** [a] Zech. 14:11 [b] Ezek. 48:35 [c] Rev. 7:15 **22:4** [a] [Matt. 5:8] [b] Rev. 14:1 **22:5** [a] Rev. 21:23 [b] Rev. 7:15 [c] Ps. 36:9 [d] Dan. 7:18, 27 **22:6** [a] Rev. 19:9 [b] Rev. 1:1 [c] Heb. 10:37 [1] NU-Text and M-Text read *spirits of the prophets.* **22:7** [a] [Rev. 3:11] [b] Rev. 1:3 **22:8** [a] Rev. 19:10 [1] NU-Text and M-Text read *am the one who heard and saw.* **22:9** [a] Rev. 19:10 [1] NU-Text and M-Text omit *For.* **22:10** [a] Dan. 8:26 [b] Rev. 1:3 **22:11** [1] NU-Text and M-Text read *do right.* **22:12** [a] Is. 40:10; 62:11 [b] Rev. 20:12 **22:13** [a] Is. 41:4 [1] NU-Text and M-Text read *the First and the Last, the Beginning and the End.* **22:14** [a] Dan. 12:12 [b] [Prov. 11:30] [1] NU-Text reads *wash their robes.*

REVELATION 22:1–21

## THE PROMISE OF HEAVEN

60

STORY OF SCRIPTURE

### WHAT'S GOING ON?

The Book of Revelation (and the Bible) ends by tying the biblical narrative back to its beginning, reminding us of God's sovereignty from creation to culmination. The declaration "It is done!" (v. 6) echoes the completion of creation in Genesis when God rested (see Gen. 2:1–3) and marks the fulfillment of God's redemptive plan through Jesus, who declared "It is finished!" from the cross (John 19:30).

The new heavens and new earth are described like Eden, only this time we have a more excellent representative than Adam at the helm. We have Jesus. Revelation 21:1—22:5 restores what was broken in Genesis 3. The rest of Revelation 22 then promises Jesus is coming back sooner than we might think. This is both a promise of hope to those who love Him and a warning to those who reject Him.

### WHAT DOES THIS MEAN FOR ME?

Revelation is a complicated book, but at its core, we find a clear message of hope and strength. Whoever believes in Jesus will share in His glorious victory. Precisely how and when this comes to pass have been debated for centuries, but that it will come to pass has never been in doubt. Rest in the known rather than being confused by the unknown.

### DID YOU CATCH THE PATTERN?

This is our final glimpse of the pattern of God's presence throughout Scripture. First, it was in the garden of Eden. Then, it was with Abraham's family. Then, it was in the tabernacle and temple. After that, it was the presence of Jesus on earth, followed by the indwelling of the Holy Spirit. God's desire has always been to dwell among people. The new heaven and new earth is the final thread in the grand tapestry of God's desire to dwell with us in love and harmony.

of life, [c]and may enter through the gates into the
city. 15 But[1] [a]outside *are* [b]dogs and sorcerers and
sexually immoral and murderers and idolaters,
and whoever loves and practices a lie.

16 [a]"I, Jesus, have sent My angel to testify
to you these things in the churches. [b]I am the
Root and the Offspring of David, [c]the Bright
and Morning Star."

17 And the Spirit and [a]the bride say, "Come!"
And let him who hears say, "Come!" [b]And let him
who thirsts come. Whoever desires, let him take
the water of life freely.

### *A WARNING*

18 For[1] I testify to everyone who hears the
words of the prophecy of this book: [a]If anyone
adds to these things, God will add[2] to him the
plagues that are written in this book; 19 and
if anyone takes away from the words of the
book of this prophecy, [a]God shall take away[1]
his part from the Book[2] of Life, from the holy
city, and *from* the things which are written in
this book.

### *I AM COMING QUICKLY*

20 He who testifies to these things says,
"Surely I am coming quickly."

Amen. Even so, come, Lord Jesus!

21 The grace of our Lord Jesus Christ *be* with
you all.[1] Amen.

**22:14** [c] Rev. 21:27 **22:15** [a] 1 Cor. 6:9 [b] Phil. 3:2 [1] NU-Text and M-Text omit *But.* **22:16** [a] Rev. 1:1 [b] Rev. 5:5 [c] Num. 24:17 **22:17** [a] [Rev. 21:2, 9] [b] Is. 55:1; Rev. 21:6 **22:18** [a] Deut. 4:2; 12:32; Prov. 30:6 [1] NU-Text and M-Text omit *For.* [2] M-Text reads *may God add.* **22:19** [a] Ex. 32:33 [1] M-Text reads *may God take away.* [2] NU-Text and M-Text read *tree of life.* **22:21** [1] NU-Text reads *with all;* M-Text reads *with all the saints.*

# TABLE OF MONIES, WEIGHTS, AND MEASURES

The Hebrews probably first used coins in the Persian period (500–350 BC). However, minting began around 700 BC in other nations. Prior to this, precious metals were weighed, not counted as money. Thus, some units appear as both measures of money and measures of weights with the naming of these coins deriving from their weight. For example, the shekel was a weight long before it became the name of a coin. It is helpful to relate biblical monies to current values, but exact equivalents cannot be made. The fluctuating value of money's purchasing power is difficult to determine in our own day. It is even harder to evaluate currencies used two- to three-thousand years ago. Therefore, it is best to choose a value meaningful over time, such as a common laborer's daily wage. One day's wage corresponds to the ancient Jewish system (a silver shekel is four days' wages) as well as to the Greek and Roman systems (the drachma and the denarius were each coins representing a day's wage). The monies chart below takes a current day's wage as thirty-two dollars. Though there are differences of economies and standards of living, this measure will help us apply meaningful values to the monetary units in the chart and in the biblical text.

## MONIES

| Unit | Monetary Value | Equivalents | Translations |
|---|---|---|---|
| **Jewish** | | | |
| Talent | gold—$5,760,000[1]<br>silver—$384,000 | 3,000 shekels; 6,000 bekas | talent |
| Shekel | gold—$1,920<br>silver—$128 | 4 days' wages; 2 bekas; 20 gerahs | shekel |
| Beka | gold—$960<br>silver—$64 | ½ shekel; 10 gerahs | bekah |
| Gerah | gold—$96<br>silver—$6.40 | 1/20 shekel | gerah |
| **Persian** | | | |
| Daric | gold—$1,280[2]<br>silver—$64 | 2 days' wages; ½ Jewish silver shekel | daric, drachma |
| **Greek** | | | |
| Tetradrachma (Stater) | $128 | 4 drachmas | piece of money |
| Didrachma | $64 | 2 drachmas | tribute |
| Drachma | $32 | 1 day's wage | piece of silver, coin |
| Lepton | $0.25 | ½ of a Roman kodrantes | mite |
| **Roman** | | | |
| Aureus | $800 | 25 denarii | gold |
| Denarius | $32 | 1 day's wage | denarius |
| Assarius | $2 | 1/16 of a denarius | copper coin |
| Kodrantes | $0.50 | ¼ of an assarius | penny |

**[1] Value of gold is fifteen times the value of silver. [2] Value of gold is twenty times the value of silver.**

## WEIGHTS

| Unit | Monetary Value | Equivalents | Translations |
|---|---|---|---|
| **Jewish** | | | |
| Talent | c. 75 pounds for common talent, c. 150 pounds for royal talent | 60 minas; 3,000 shekels | talent |
| Mina | 1.25 pounds | 50 shekels | mina |
| Shekel | c. 0.4 ounce (11.4 grams) for common shekel, c. 0.8 ounce for royal shekel | 2 bekas; 20 gerahs | shekel |
| Beka | c. 0.2 ounce (5.7 grams) | ½ shekel; 10 gerahs | half a shekel |
| Gerah | c. 0.02 ounce (0.57 grams) | 1/20 shekel | gerah |
| **Roman** | | | |
| Litra | 12 ounces | | pound |

## MEASURES OF LENGTH

| Unit | Length | Equivalents | Translations |
|---|---|---|---|
| Day's journey | c. 20 miles | | day's journey |
| Roman mile | 4,854 feet | 8 stadia | mile |
| Sabbath day's journey | 3,637 feet | 6 stadia | Sabbath day's journey |
| Stadion | 606 feet | ⅛ Roman mile | furlong |
| Rod | 9 feet (10.5 feet in Ezekiel) | 3 paces; 6 cubits | measuring reed, reed |
| Fathom | 6 feet | 4 cubits | fathom |
| Pace | 3 feet | ⅓ rod; 2 cubits | pace |
| Cubit | 18 inches | ½ pace; 2 spans | cubit |
| Span | 9 inches | ½ cubit; 3 handbreadths | span |
| Handbreadth | 3 inches | ⅓ span; 4 fingers | handbreadth |
| Finger | 0.75 inches | ¼ handbreadth | finger |

## DRY MEASURES

| Unit | Measure | Equivalents | Translations |
|---|---|---|---|
| Homer | 6.52 bushels | 10 ephahs | homer |
| Kor | 6.52 bushels | 1 homer; 10 ephahs | kor, measure |
| Lethech | 3.26 bushels | ½ kor | half homer |
| Ephah | 0.65 bushel, 20.8 quarts | 1/10 homer | ephah |
| Modius | 7.68 quarts | | bushel |
| Seah | 7 quarts | ⅓ ephah | measure |
| Omer | 2.08 quarts | 1/10 ephah; 1 ⅘ kab | omer |
| Kab | 1.16 quarts | 4 logs | kab |
| Choenix | 1 quart | | measure |
| Xestes | 1 1/16 pints | | pot |
| Log | 0.58 pint | ¼ kab | log |

## LIQUID MEASURES

| Unit | Measure | Equivalents | Translations |
|---|---|---|---|
| Kor | 60 gallons | 10 baths | kor |
| Metretes | 10.2 gallons | | gallon |
| Bath | 6 gallons | 6 hins | measure, bath |
| Hin | 1 gallon | 2 kabs | hin |
| Kab | 2 quarts | 4 logs | kab |
| Log | 1 pint | ¼ kab | log |

# THE JEWISH CALENDAR

The Jews used two kinds of calendars:
A *Civil Calendar*, the official calendar of kings, childbirth, and contracts.
A *Sacred Calendar*, from which the dates of festivals were computed.

| Names of Months | Corresponds with | Number of Days | Month of Civil Year | Month of Sacred Year |
|---|---|---|---|---|
| **Tishri** | September–October | 30 | 1st | 7th |
| **Heshvan** | October–November | 29 or 30 | 2nd | 8th |
| **Chislev** | November–December | 29 or 30 | 3rd | 9th |
| **Tebeth** | December–January | 29 | 4th | 10th |
| **Shebat** | January–February | 30 | 5th | 11th |
| **Adar** | February–March | 29 | 6th | 12th |
| **Nisan** | March–April | 30 | 7th | 1st |
| **Iyar** | April–May | 29 | 8th | 2nd |
| **Sivan** | May–June | 30 | 9th | 3rd |
| **Tammuz** | June–July | 29 | 10th | 4th |
| **Ab** | July–August | 30 | 11th | 5th |
| ***Elul** | August–September | 29 | 12th | 6th |

* Hebrew months were alternately 29 and 30 days long, meaning their year had 354 days. Every three years (seven times in 19 years), an extra 20-day-month, Veadar, was added between Adar and Nisan.

| The Jewish day was from sunset to sunset, in eight equal parts: | |
|---|---|
| **First Watch** | Sunset to 9 pm |
| **Second Watch** | 9 pm to Midnight |
| **Third Watch** | Midnight to 3 am |
| **Fourth Watch** | 3 am to Sunrise |
| **First Watch** | Sunrise to 9 am |
| **Second Watch** | 9 am to Noon |
| **Third Watch** | Noon to 3 pm |
| **Fourth Watch** | 3 pm to Sunset |

# 30 DAYS OF GETTING TO KNOW GOD

In less than five minutes each day, you will be better able to know who God is, what He is like, and what He does.

| Day | Reading | Passage |
|---|---|---|
| 1 | God is Creator of everything | Genesis 1:1–31 |
| 2 | God is eternal | Psalms 90:1–4; 102:24–27; Isaiah 40:28 |
| 3 | God is all-powerful | Genesis 18:9–14; Jeremiah 32:26–35; Luke 2:34–38; Mark 10:25–27 |
| 4 | God is all-knowing | Job 37:16; Psalm 139:1–6; Matthew 10:29–30; 1 John 3:19–20 |
| 5 | God is present everywhere | Psalm 139:7–12; John 4:23–24 |
| 6 | God is above His creation | Isaiah 55:8–9; 57:15; Ezekiel 1:25–28 |
| 7 | God is active in His creation | Romans 1:18–20; Colossians 1:15–17; Hebrews 1:1–3 |
| 8 | God is personal | Genesis 3:8–9; Joshua 1:1–9; Psalm 8:1–9 |
| 9 | God is good | 2 Chronicles 5:13–14; Psalms 34:8; 100:1–5; 145:9; Luke 18:18–19; James 1:17 |
| 10 | God is holy | Exodus 3:1–5; 15:11; Isaiah 6:1–3; 1 John 1:5–7 |
| 11 | God is love | Romans 5:6–8; 1 John 4:7–21 |
| 12 | God is wise | Job 9:1–4; Psalm 104:24; Romans 16:27; 1 Corinthians 1:18–31 |
| 13 | God is righteous | Deuteronomy 32:4; Psalm 19:7–11; Jeremiah 9:23–26 |
| 14 | God is just | Genesis 2:16–17; Job 34:12; Amos 5:21–27; Romans 6:23 |
| 15 | God is true | 1 Samuel 15:29; Proverbs 30:5–6; Titus 1:2; Hebrews 6:16–20 |
| 16 | God is faithful | Numbers 23:19; 2 Samuel 7:27–29; 2 Corinthians 1:18–22; 1 Thessalonians 5:24 |
| 17 | God is forgiving | Exodus 34:6–7; Numbers 14:17–20; Psalms 86:15–17; 103:8–13; 145:8; Jonah 4:2; Nahum 1:3 |
| 18 | God is abundant in grace | Exodus 33:18–23; Romans 3:23–24; Ephesians 1:5–8; 2:1–10 |
| 19 | God is abundant in compassion | Exodus 3:7–8; 2 Samuel 24:14; Mark 6:34–35 |
| 20 | God is jealous about His glory | Exodus 20:3–5; 34:14; Deuteronomy 4:24; Isaiah 48:11 |
| 21 | God is worthy of praise | 1 Chronicles 16:31–36; Psalm 150:1–6; Revelation 4:1—5:14 |
| 22 | God is mighty King | Psalm 47:1–9; Philippians 2:9–11; 1 Timothy 1:17; Revelation 19:16 |
| 23 | God is loving Father | Psalm 68:4–6; Isaiah 63:16; Romans 8:14–19; 2 Corinthians 6:17–18 |
| 24 | God is faithful Friend | Exodus 33:11; John 15:13–15; James 2:23 |
| 25 | God is the Good Shepherd | Psalm 23:1–6; Isaiah 40:11; John 10:1–17 |
| 26 | God is the generous Provider | Matthew 5:44–45; Acts 14:17; Philippians 4:19 |
| 27 | God is in control | Psalm 115:1–3; Romans 8:28; Philippians 3:20–21 |
| 28 | God is Redeemer | Psalm 18:1–20; Zephaniah 3:17; Romans 8:1–2; Titus 2:11–14 |
| 29 | God is the destroyer of death | Isaiah 25:6–9; 1 Corinthians 15:22–28; 2 Timothy 1:8–10; Revelation 21:1–4 |
| 30 | God is the Giver of life | Matthew 22:23–33; John 3:13–17 |

# 60 DAYS WITH PAUL

Averaging about thirty-four verses a day, you will be able to read through the writings of the apostle Paul in the order they appear in Scripture.

| Date | Reference | Date | Reference |
|---|---|---|---|
| 1 | Romans 1:1–32 | 31 | 2 Corinthians 7:1—8:24 |
| 2 | Romans 2:1–29 | 32 | 2 Corinthians 9:1—10:18 |
| 3 | Romans 3:1–31 | 33 | 2 Corinthians 11:1–33 |
| 4 | Romans 4:1–25 | 34 | 2 Corinthians 12:1—13:14 |
| 5 | Romans 5:1–21 | 35 | Galatians 1:1—2:21 |
| 6 | Romans 6:1–23 | 36 | Galatians 3:1–29 |
| 7 | Romans 7:1–25 | 37 | Galatians 4:1–31 |
| 8 | Romans 8:1–39 | 38 | Galatians 5:1—6:18 |
| 9 | Romans 9:1–33 | 39 | Ephesians 1:1—2:22 |
| 10 | Romans 10:1–21 | 40 | Ephesians 3:1–21 |
| 11 | Romans 11:1–36 | 41 | Ephesians 4:1–32 |
| 12 | Romans 12:1—13:14 | 42 | Ephesians 5:1–33 |
| 13 | Romans 14:1–26 | 43 | Ephesians 6:1–24 |
| 14 | Romans 15:1–33 | 44 | Philippians 1:1–30 |
| 15 | Romans 16:1–25 | 45 | Philippians 2:1–30 |
| 16 | 1 Corinthians 1:1–31 | 46 | Philippians 3:1—4:23 |
| 17 | 1 Corinthians 2:1—3:23 | 47 | Colossians 1:1–29 |
| 18 | 1 Corinthians 4:1–21 | 48 | Colossians 2:1–23 |
| 19 | 1 Corinthians 5:1—6:20 | 49 | Colossians 3:1—4:18 |
| 20 | 1 Corinthians 7:1–40 | 50 | 1 Thessalonians 1:1—2:20 |
| 21 | 1 Corinthians 8:1—9:27 | 51 | 1 Thessalonians 3:1—4:18 |
| 22 | 1 Corinthians 10:1–33 | 52 | 1 Thessalonians 5:1–28 |
| 23 | 1 Corinthians 11:1–34 | 53 | 2 Thessalonians 1:1—3:18 |
| 24 | 1 Corinthians 12:1—13:13 | 54 | 1 Timothy 1:1—2:14 |
| 25 | 1 Corinthians 14:1–40 | 55 | 1 Timothy 3:1—4:16 |
| 26 | 1 Corinthians 15:1–48 | 56 | 1 Timothy 5:1—6:25 |
| 27 | 1 Corinthians 16:1–24 | 57 | 2 Timothy 1:1—2:26 |
| 28 | 2 Corinthians 1:1—2:17 | 58 | 2 Timothy 3:1—4:22 |
| 29 | 2 Corinthians 3:1—4:18 | 59 | Titus 1:1—3:15 |
| 30 | 2 Corinthians 5:1—6:18 | 60 | Philemon 1:1–25 |

# 90 DAYS THROUGH THE GOSPELS CHRONOLOGICALLY

Reading about forty verses a day, you will be able to follow the life and ministry of Jesus as it happened in chronological order. Each day's reading attempts to preserve the narrative flow as much as possible, thus some readings may be noticeably shorter or longer than the average. Daily readings separated with a slash (/) follow one another chronologically. Readings within parentheses separated by semicolons are parallel passages.

## PROLOGUE

| Day | Reference |
|---|---|
| 1 | John 1:1–18 / Matthew 1:1–17 / Luke 3:23–38 |
| 2 | Luke 1:1–38 |
| 3 | Luke 1:39–80 |

## BIRTH & CHILDHOOD (C. 5 BC–AD 8)

| Day | Reference |
|---|---|
| 4 | Matthew 1:18–25 / Luke 2:1–38 |
| 5 | Matthew 2:1–18 / (Matthew 2:19–23; Luke 2:39) / Luke 2:40–52 |

## JOHN'S MINISTRY (AD 25–27)

| Day | Reference |
|---|---|
| 6 | (Matthew 3:1; Mark 1:1; Luke 3:1–2; John 1:19–25) / (Matthew 3:2–10; Mark 1:2–6; Luke 3:3–14) / (Matthew 3:11–12; Mark 1:7–8; Luke 3:15–18; John 1:26–28) |

## JESUS' MINISTRY BEGINS (AD 27)

| Day | Reference |
|---|---|
| 7 | (Matthew 3:13–17; Mark 1:9–11; Luke 3:21–23; John 1:29–34) / (Matthew 4:1–11; Mark 1:12–13; Luke 4:1–13) |
| 8 | John 1:35—2:25 |
| 9 | John 3:1–36 / (Matthew 4:12; Mark 1:14; Luke 4:14; John 4:1–4) |
| 10 | John 4:5–52 / (Mark 1:15; Luke 4:15; John 4:43–45) |

## GALILEAN MINISTRY (AD 27–29)

| Day | Reference |
|---|---|
| 11 | John 4:46–54 / Luke 4:16–30 / Matthew 4:13–17 / (Matthew 4:18–22; Mark 1:16–20; Luke 5:1–11) |
| 12 | (Mark 1:21–28; Luke 4:31–37) / (Mark 1:29–34; Luke 4:38–41) / Matthew 8:14–17 / (Matthew 4:23–25; Mark 1:35–39; Luke 4:42–44) |
| 13 | (Matthew 8:1–4; Mark 1:40–45; Luke 5:12–16) / (Matthew 9:1–8; Mark 2:1–12; Luke 5:17–26) |
| 14 | (Matthew 9:9–13; Mark 2:13–17; Luke 5:27–32) / (Matthew 9:14–17; Mark 2:18–22; Luke 5:33-39) |
| 15 | John 5:1–47 |

| Day | Reference |
|---|---|
| 16 | (Matthew 12:1–8; Mark 2:23–28; Luke 6:1–5) / (Matthew 12:9–14; Mark 3:1–6; Luke 6:6–11) |
| 17 | (Matthew 12:15–21; Mark 3:7–12; Luke 6:17–19) / (Mark 3:13–19; Luke 6:12–16) |
| 18 | (Matthew 5:1–48; Luke 6:20–36) |
| 19 | Matthew 6:1–34 |
| 20 | (Matthew 7:1–29; Luke 6:37–49) |
| 21 | (Matthew 8:5–13; Luke 7:1–10) / Luke 7:11–17 |
| 22 | (Matthew 11:2–19; Luke 7:18–35) / Matthew 11:20–30 |
| 23 | Luke 7:36–50 / Luke 8:1–3 / (Matthew 12:22–37; Mark 3:20–30; Luke 11:14–23) |
| 24 | (Matthew 12:38–45; Luke 11:24–26, 29–36) / (Matthew 12:46–50; Mark 3:31–35; Luke 8:19–21) |
| 25 | (Matthew 13:1–23; Mark 4:1–25; Luke 8:4–18) |
| 26 | (Matthew 13:24–52; Mark 4:26–34) |
| 27 | (Matthew 8:23–27; Mark 4:35–41; Luke 8:22–25) / (Matthew 8:28–34; Mark 5:1–20; Luke 8:26–39) |
| 28 | (Matthew 9:18–26; Mark 5:21–43; Luke 8:40–56) |
| 29 | Matthew 9:27–31 / Matthew 9:32–34 / (Matthew 13:53–58; Mark 6:1–6) |
| 30 | (Matthew 9:35—10:15; Mark 6:7–11; Luke 9:1–5) |
| 31 | (Matthew 10:16—11:1; Mark 6:12–13; Luke 9:6) |
| 32 | (Matthew 14:1–12; Mark 6:14–29; Luke 3:19–20; 9:7–9) |
| 33 | (Matthew 14:13–21; Mark 6:30–44; Luke 9:10–17; John 6:1–14) |
| 34 | (Matthew 14:22–33; Mark 6:45–52; John 6:15–21) / (Matthew 14:34–36; Mark 6:53–56) |
| 35 | John 6:22–71 |
| 36 | (Matthew 15:1–20; Mark 7:1–23; John 7:1) |
| 37 | (Matthew 15:21–28; Mark 7:24–30) / (Matthew 15:29–31; Mark 7:31–37) / (Matthew 15:32–39; Mark 8:1–9) |
| 38 | (Matthew 16:1–4; Mark 8:10–13) / (Matthew 16:5–12; Mark 8:14–26) / (Matthew 16:13–20; Mark 8:27–30; Luke 9:18–21) |
| 39 | (Matthew 16:21–26; Mark 8:31–38; Luke 9:22–25) / (Matthew 16:17–28; Mark 9:1; Luke 9:26–27) |
| 40 | (Matthew 17:1–13; Mark 9:2–13; Luke 9:28–36) |
| 41 | (Matthew 17:14–21; Mark 9:14–29; Luke 9:37–41) / (Matthew 17:22–23; Mark 9:30–32; Luke 9:43–45) / Matthew 17:24–27 |
| 42 | (Matthew 18:1–14; Mark 9:33–50; Luke 9:46–50) |
| 43 | (Matthew 18:15–35; Luke 9:51–63) |
| 44 | John 7:2–9 / (Matthew 19:1; Luke 9:51–56; John 7:10) / (Matthew 8:18–22; Luke 9:57–62) |

## LATE JUDEAN AND PEREAN MINISTRY (AD 29–30)

| Day | Reference |
|---|---|
| 45 | John 8:12–59 |
| 46 | John 9:1–41 |
| 47 | John 10:1–21 |
| 48 | Luke 10:1–42 |
| 49 | Luke 11:1–54 |
| 50 | Luke 12:1–59 |
| 51 | Luke 13:1–21 |
| 52 | John 10:22–42 |
| 53 | Luke 13:22—14:35 |
| 54 | Luke 15:1–32 |

| Day | Reference |
|---|---|
| 55 | Luke 16:1—17:10 |
| 56 | John 11:1-54 |
| 57 | Luke 17:11—18:14 |
| 58 | (Matthew 19:1-12; Mark 10:1-12) / (Matthew 19:13-15; Mark 10:13-16; Luke 18:15-17) |
| 59 | (Matthew 19:16-30; Mark 10:17-31; Luke 18:18-30) |
| 60 | Matthew 20:1-16 / (Matthew 20:17-19; Mark 10:32-34; Luke 18:31-34) / (Matthew 20:20-28; Mark 10:35-45) |
| 61 | (Mark 10:36-52; Luke 18:35-43) / Luke 19:1-27 / John 11:55—12:1 / John 12:9-11 |

## THE CRUCIFIXION AND RESURRECTION (AD 30)

### *Sunday*

| Day | Reference |
|---|---|
| 62 | (Matthew 21:1-9; Mark 11:1-11; Luke 19:28-44; John 12:12-19) |

### *Monday*

| Day | Reference |
|---|---|
| 63 | (Matthew 21:10-19; Mark 11:12-18; Luke 19:45-48) / John 12:20-50 |

### *Tuesday*

| Day | Reference |
|---|---|
| 64 | (Matthew 21:20-22; Mark 11:19-26) / (Matthew 21:23-46; Mark 11:27—12:12; Luke 20:1-19) |
| 65 | Matthew 22:1-14 / (Matthew 22:15-22; Mark 12:13-17; Luke 20:20-26) |
| 66 | (Matthew 22:23-33; Mark 12:18-27; Luke 20:27-40) |
| 67 | (Matthew 22:34-40; Mark 12:28-34) / (Matthew 22:41-46; Mark 12:35-37; Luke 20:41-44) |
| 68 | (Matthew 23:1-39; Mark 12:38-40; Luke 20:45-47) |
| 69 | (Mark 12:41-44; Luke 21:1-4) / (Matthew 24:1-14; Mark 13:1-13; Luke 21:5-19) |
| 70 | (Matthew 24:15-31; Mark 13:14-27; Luke 21:20-27) |
| 71 | (Matthew 24:32-51; Mark 13:28-37; Luke 21:28-36) |
| 72 | Matthew 25:1-46 |
| 73 | (Matthew 26:1-5; Mark 14:1-2; Luke 22:1-2) / (Matthew 26:6-13; Mark 14:3-9; John 12:2-8) / (Matthew 26:14-16; Mark 14:10-11; Luke 22:3-6) |

### *Thursday*

| Day | Reference |
|---|---|
| 74 | (Matthew 26:17-19; Mark 14:12-16; Luke 22:7-13) / (Matthew 26:20; Mark 14:17; Luke 22:14-16, 24-30) / John 13:1-20 |
| 75 | (Matthew 26:21-25; Mark 14:18-21; Luke 22:21-23; John 13:21-30) / (Matthew 26:31-35; Mark 14:27-31; Luke 22:31-38; John 13:31-38) / (Matthew 26:26-29; Mark 14:22-25; Luke 22:17-20) |
| 76 | (John 14:1—15:27) |
| 77 | (John 16:1—17:26) |
| 78 | (Matthew 26:30, 36-46; Mark 14:26, 32-42; Luke 22:39-46; John 18:1) |

### *Friday*

| Day | Reference |
|---|---|
| 79 | (Matthew 26:47-56; Mark 14:43-52; Luke 22:47-53; John 18:2-12) |
| 80 | John 18:13-14, 19-23 / (Matthew 26:57, 59-68; Mark 14:53, 55-65; Luke 22:54, 63-64; John 18:24) |
| 81 | (Matthew 26:58, 69-75; Mark 14:54, 66-72; Luke 22:54-62; John 18:15-18, 25-27) / (Matthew 27:1; Mark 15:1; Luke 22:66-71) |
| 82 | Matthew 27:3-10 / (Matthew 27:2, 11-14; Mark 15:1-5; Luke 23:1-7; John 18:28-38) / Luke 23:6-12 / (Matthew 27:15-26; Mark 15:6-15; Luke 23:13-25; John 18:39—19:15) |

| Day | Reference |
|---|---|
| 83 | (Matthew 27:27–30; Mark 15:16–19) |
| 84 | (Matthew 27:31–34; Mark 15:20–23; Luke 23:26–32; John 19:16–17) / (Matthew 27:35–44; Mark 15:24–32; Luke 23:33–43; John 19:18–27) |
| 85 | (Matthew 27:45–50; Mark 15:33–37; Luke 23:44–46; John 19:28–30) / (Matthew 27:51–56; Mark 15:38–41; Luke 23:45, 47–49) |
| 86 | (Matthew 27:57–60; Mark 15:42–46; Luke 23:50–54; John 19:31–42) / (Matthew 27:61–66; Luke 23:55–56) / Mark 15:47 |

### *Resurrection Sunday Morning*

| Day | Reference |
|---|---|
| 87 | (Matthew 28:1–10; Mark 16:1–8; Luke 24:1–11) / (Luke 24:12; John 20:1–10) / (Mark 16:9–11; John 20:11–18) / Matthew 28:9–15 |

### *Resurrection Sunday Afternoon*

| Day | Reference |
|---|---|
| 88 | (Mark 16:12–13; Luke 24:13–35) |

### *Resurrection Sunday Evening*

| Day | Reference |
|---|---|
| 89 | (Luke 24:36–43; John 20:19–25) |

## OVER THE NEXT FORTY DAYS

| Day | Reference |
|---|---|
| 90 | John 20:26—21:25 / (Matthew 28:16–20; Mark 16:14–18; Luke 24:44–49) / (Mark 16:19–20; Luke 24:50–53) |

# 365 DAYS THROUGH THE BIBLE CHRONOLOGICALLY

Using this plan, you will read the entire Bible in chronological order. The plan seeks to preserve the chronological narrative of Scripture as much as possible, while also seeking to keep chapters intact to improve the reading experience (with the notable exception in the Gospels). Individual psalms are placed chronologically when possible and thematically when not.

| Day | Reference |
|---|---|
| 1 | Genesis 1–3 |
| 2 | Genesis 4–7 |
| 3 | Genesis 8–11 |

### THE PATRIARCHS

| Day | Reference |
|---|---|
| 4 | Genesis 12–15 |
| 5 | Genesis 16–18 |
| 6 | Genesis 19–21 |
| 7 | Genesis 22–24 |
| 8 | Genesis 25–26 |
| 9 | Genesis 27–29 |
| 10 | Genesis 30–31 |
| 11 | Genesis 32–34 |
| 12 | Genesis 35–37 |
| 13 | Genesis 38–40 |
| 14 | Genesis 41–42 |
| 15 | Genesis 43–45 |
| 16 | Genesis 46–47 |
| 17 | Genesis 48–50 |
| 18 | Job 1–5 |
| 19 | Job 6–9 |
| 20 | Job 10–13 |
| 21 | Job 14–16 |
| 22 | Job 17–20 |
| 23 | Job 21–23 |
| 24 | Job 24–28 |
| 25 | Job 29–31 |
| 26 | Job 32–34 |
| 27 | Job 35–37 |
| 28 | Job 38–39 |
| 29 | Job 40–42 |

### THE EXODUS & WANDERING

| Day | Reference |
|---|---|
| 30 | Exodus 1–3 |
| 31 | Exodus 4–6 |
| 32 | Exodus 7–9 |
| 33 | Exodus 10–12 |
| 34 | Exodus 13–15 |
| 35 | Exodus 16–18 |
| 36 | Exodus 19–21 |
| 37 | Exodus 22–24 |
| 38 | Exodus 25–27 |
| 39 | Exodus 28–29 |
| 40 | Exodus 30–32 |
| 41 | Exodus 33–35 |
| 42 | Exodus 36–38 |
| 43 | Exodus 39–40 |
| 44 | Leviticus 1–4 |
| 45 | Leviticus 5–7 |
| 46 | Leviticus 8–10 |
| 47 | Leviticus 11–13 |
| 48 | Leviticus 14–15 |
| 49 | Leviticus 16–18 |
| 50 | Leviticus 19–21 |
| 51 | Leviticus 22–23 |
| 52 | Leviticus 24–25 |
| 53 | Leviticus 26–27 |
| 54 | Numbers 1–2 |
| 55 | Numbers 3–4 |
| 56 | Numbers 5–6 |
| 57 | Numbers 7–8 |
| 58 | Numbers 9–10 |
| 59 | Numbers 11–13 |
| 60 | Numbers 14–15 |
| 61 | Numbers 16–17 |
| 62 | Numbers 18–20 |
| 63 | Numbers 21–22 |
| 64 | Numbers 23–25 |
| 65 | Numbers 26–27 |
| 66 | Numbers 28–30 |
| 67 | Numbers 31–32 |
| 68 | Numbers 33–34 |
| 69 | Numbers 35–36 |
| 70 | Deuteronomy 1–2 |
| 71 | Deuteronomy 3–4 |
| 72 | Deuteronomy 5–7 |
| 73 | Deuteronomy 8–10 |
| 74 | Deuteronomy 11–13 |
| 75 | Deuteronomy 14–16 |
| 76 | Deuteronomy 17–20 |
| 77 | Deuteronomy 21–23 |
| 78 | Deuteronomy 24–27 |
| 79 | Deuteronomy 28–29 |
| 80 | Deuteronomy 30–31 |
| 81 | Deuteronomy 32–34; Psalms 90–91 |

## THE CONQUEST & JUDGES

82 Joshua 1–4

83 Joshua 5–8

84 Joshua 9–11

85 Joshua 12–15

86 Joshua 16–18

87 Joshua 19–21

88 Joshua 22–24

89 Judges 1–2

90 Judges 3–5

91 Judges 6–7

92 Judges 8–9

93 Judges 10–12

94 Judges 13–15

95 Judges 16–18

96 Judges 19–21

97 Ruth 1–4

98 1 Samuel 1–3

99 1 Samuel 4–8

## THE UNITED KINGDOM

100 1 Samuel 9–12

101 1 Samuel 13–15

102 Psalm 23; 1 Samuel 16–17

103 1 Samuel 18–20; Psalm 59

104 1 Samuel 21; Psalms 34; 56

105 1 Samuel 22–23; Psalms 52; 54; 63

106 1 Samuel 24–25; Psalms 57; 142

107 1 Samuel 26–30; 1 Chronicles 12:19–22

108 1 Samuel 31; 1 Chronicles 10; 2 Samuel 1; Psalm 18

109 2 Samuel 2–4

110 2 Samuel 5; 1 Chronicles 11:1—12:18, 23–40

111 2 Samuel 6–7; 1 Chronicles 13; 17

112 1 Chronicles 14–16

113 Psalms 8; 19; 29; 32

114 Psalms 39; 62; 65; 68

115 Psalms 103; 108; 138

116 2 Samuel 8–9; 1 Chronicles 18; Psalm 60

117 2 Samuel 10; 1 Chronicles 19–20

118 2 Samuel 11:1—12:14; Psalm 51

119 2 Samuel 12:15—14:33

120 2 Samuel 15–17; Psalms 3; 7

121 2 Samuel 18–20

122 2 Samuel 21–23

123 1 Kings 1:1—2:9; 2 Samuel 24; 1 Chronicles 21

124 Psalms 2; 4–6; 9

125 Psalms 10–14

126 Psalms 16–17; 20–22

127 Psalms 25–28; 31

128 Psalms 35–38; 40

129 Psalms 41; 53; 55; 58; 61

130 Psalms 64; 69–71; 86

131 Psalms 93–95; 97–98

132 Psalms 99; 101–102; 109–110

133 Psalms 139–141; 143–144

134 1 Chronicles 22–25; Psalm 30

135 Psalms 15; 24; 42–46

136 Psalms 47–49; 84–85; 87

137 1 Chronicles 26–29

138 1 Kings 2:10—3:28; 2 Chronicles 1; Psalm 72

139 Proverbs 1–3

140 Proverbs 4–6

141 Proverbs 7–9

142 Proverbs 10–12

143 Proverbs 13–15

144 Proverbs 16–18

145 Proverbs 19–21

146 Proverbs 22–24

147 Song of Solomon 1–8

148 1 Kings 4–6; 2 Chronicles 2–3

149 1 Kings 7; 2 Chronicles 4

150 1 Kings 8; 2 Chronicles 5

151 2 Chronicles 6–7

152 Psalms 50; 73–77

153 Psalms 78–83

154 Psalms 88; 96; 105–106

155 1 Kings 9; 2 Chronicles 8

156 Proverbs 25–26

157 Proverbs 27–29

158 Proverbs 30–31

159 Ecclesiastes 1–4

160 Ecclesiastes 5–8

161 Ecclesiastes 9–12

162 1 Kings 10–11; 2 Chronicles 9

## THE DIVIDED KINGDOM

163 1 Kings 12–14

164 2 Chronicles 10–12

165 1 Kings 15; 2 Chronicles 13–16

166 1 Kings 16; 2 Chronicles 17

167 1 Kings 17–19

168 1 Kings 20–21

169 1 Kings 22; 2 Chronicles 18

170 2 Chronicles 19–23

171 2 Kings 1–4

172 2 Kings 5–8

173 2 Kings 9–11

174 2 Kings 12–13; 2 Chronicles 24

175 Psalm 137; Obadiah

176 Joel 1–3

177 2 Kings 14; 2 Chronicles 25

178 Jonah 1–4

179 2 Kings 15; 2 Chronicles 26–27

180 Isaiah 1–4

181 Isaiah 5–8

182 Amos 1–5

183 Amos 6–9

184 Hosea 1–7

185 Hosea 8–14

186 Isaiah 9–12

187 Micah 1–7
188 2 Chronicles 28; 2 Kings 16–17
189 Isaiah 13–15
190 Isaiah 16–18
191 Isaiah 19–21
192 Isaiah 22–24
193 Isaiah 25–27
194 2 Kings 18; 2 Chronicles 29–31
195 Isaiah 28–30
196 Isaiah 31–34
197 Isaiah 35–36
198 Isaiah 37–39
199 Isaiah 40–43
200 Isaiah 44–48
201 2 Kings 19
202 Isaiah 49–53
203 Isaiah 54–58
204 Isaiah 59–63
205 Isaiah 64–66
206 2 Kings 20–21
207 2 Chronicles 32–33
208 Nahum 1–3
209 2 Kings 22–23; 2 Chronicles 34–35
210 Zephaniah 1–3
211 Psalms 33; 66–67; 100
212 Jeremiah 1–3
213 Jeremiah 4–6
214 Jeremiah 7–9
215 Jeremiah 10–13
216 Jeremiah 14–17
217 Jeremiah 18–22
218 Jeremiah 23–25
219 Jeremiah 26–29
220 Jeremiah 30–31
221 Jeremiah 32–34
222 Jeremiah 35–37
223 Jeremiah 38–40
224 2 Kings 24–25; 2 Chronicles 36

## THE CAPTIVITY

225 Habakkuk 1–3
226 Jeremiah 41–45
227 Jeremiah 46–48
228 Jeremiah 49–50
229 Jeremiah 51–52
230 Lamentations 1–2
231 Lamentations 3–5
232 Daniel 1–4
233 Ezekiel 1–4
234 Ezekiel 5–8
235 Ezekiel 9–12
236 Ezekiel 13–15
237 Ezekiel 16–17
238 Ezekiel 18–20
239 Ezekiel 21–22
240 Ezekiel 23–24
241 Ezekiel 25–27
242 Ezekiel 28–30
243 Ezekiel 31–32
244 Ezekiel 33–36
245 Ezekiel 37–39
246 Ezekiel 40–42
247 Ezekiel 43–45
248 Ezekiel 46–48
249 Daniel 5–6
250 Daniel 7–9
251 Daniel 10–12

## RETURN FROM EXILE

252 Ezra 1–4
253 Ezra 5:1; Haggai 1–2; Zechariah 1–3
254 Zechariah 4–6
255 Zechariah 7–8; Ezra 5:2—6:22
256 1 Chronicles 1–3
257 1 Chronicles 4–6
258 1 Chronicles 7–9
259 Ezra 7–10
260 Nehemiah 1–4
261 Nehemiah 5–7
262 Nehemiah 8–10; Psalms 1; 91
263 Psalm 119:1–88
264 Psalm 119:89–176
265 Nehemiah 11–12
266 Psalms 120–134
267 Psalms 104; 107; 111–113
268 Psalms 114–118; 135–136
269 Psalms 145–150
270 Nehemiah 13; Psalm 92
271 Zechariah 9–11
272 Zechariah 12–14
273 Esther 1–5
274 Esther 6–10
275 Malachi 1–4

## THE LIFE AND MINISTRY OF JESUS

276 John 1:1–18; Matthew 1:1–17; Luke 3:23–38; Luke 1
277 Matthew 1:18–25; Luke 2:1–38; Matthew 2:1–21
278 Luke 2:39—3:18; Matthew 2:22—3:12; Mark 1:1–8; John 1:19–28
279 John 1:29–34; Matthew 3:13—4:11; Mark 1:9–13; Luke 3:21–22; 4:1–13
280 John 1:35—3:36
281 John 4:1–45; Matthew 4:12–22; Mark 1:14–20; Luke 4:14–30
282 Mark 1:21–45; Luke 4:31—5:16; Matthew 4:23–25; 8:1–4, 14–17
283 Matthew 9:1–17; 12:1–14; Mark 2:1—3:6; Luke 5:17—6:11
284 Matthew 12:15–21; Mark 3:7–19
285 Matthew 5–7; Luke 6:12–49; 11:1–13; 12:22–34
286 Matthew 8:5–13; 11:2–19; Luke 7; John 4:46–54
287 Matthew 12:22—13:52; Mark 3:20—4:34; Luke 8:1–21; 11:14–36; 13:18–21

288 Matthew 8:23–34; Mark 4:35—5:20; Luke 8:22–39
289 Matthew 9:18–34; 13:53–58; Mark 5:21—6:6; Luke 8:40–56; John 5
290 Matthew 9:35—11:1; 14:1–12; Mark 6:7–29; Luke 3:19–20; 9:1–9
291 Matthew 14:13–36; Mark 6:30–56; Luke 9:10–17; John 6
292 Matthew 15; Mark 7:1—8:10
293 Matthew 16:1—17:13; Mark 8:11—9:13; Luke 9:18–36
294 Matthew 17:14—18:9; Mark 9:14–50; Luke 9:37–50
295 John 7–8
296 John 9:1—10:21; Matthew 8:18–22; Luke 9:51–62
297 Matthew 11:20–30; Luke 10; 11:37—12:12
298 Luke 12:13–21; 12:35—13:17; 13:22—14:24
299 Luke 14:25–35; Matthew 18:10–14; Luke 15–16
300 Matthew 18:15–35; Luke 17; 18:1–14
301 Matthew 19; Mark 10:1–31; Luke 18:15–30
302 Matthew 20:1–16; John 10:22—11:57
303 Matthew 20:17–34; Mark 10:32–52; Luke 18:31—19:27; John 12:1–11
304 Matthew 21:1–17; Mark 11:1–19; Luke 19:28–48; John 12:12–19
305 Matthew 21:18—22:14; Mark 11:20—12:12; Luke 20:1–19
306 Matthew 22:15–46; Mark 12:13–37; Luke 20:20–44
307 Matthew 23:1—24:35; Mark 12:38—13:31; Luke 20:45—21:33
308 Matthew 24:36—26:16; Mark 13:32—14:11; Luke 21:34—22:6; John 12:20–50
309 Matthew 26:17–29; Mark 14:12–25; Luke 22:7–30; John 13:1–35
310 Matthew 26:30–35; Mark 14:26–31; Luke 22:31–38; John 13:36—16:33
311 John 17:1—18:11; Matthew 26:36–56; Mark 14:32–52; Luke 22:39–53
312 Matthew 26:57–75; Mark 14:53–72; Luke 22:54–71; John 18:12–27
313 Matthew 27:1–26; Mark 15:1–15; Luke 23:1–25; John 18:28–40
314 Matthew 27:27–56; Mark 15:16–41; John 19:1–37; Luke 23:26–49
315 Matthew 27:57—28:15; Mark 15:42—16:11; Luke 23:50—24:12; John 19:38—20:18
316 Mark 16:12–20; Luke 24:13–53; John 20:19—21:25; Matthew 28:16–20

## THE BIRTH AND MINISTRY OF THE CHURCH

317 Acts 1–2
318 Acts 3–5
319 Acts 6–7
320 Acts 8–9; Galatians 1
321 Acts 10–12
322 Acts 13–14
323 Acts 15; Galatians 2–3
324 Galatians 4–6
325 James 1–5
326 Acts 16–18
327 1 Thessalonians 1–5
328 2 Thessalonians 1–3; Acts 19
329 1 Corinthians 1–3
330 1 Corinthians 4–7
331 1 Corinthians 8–11
332 1 Corinthians 12–16
333 2 Corinthians 1–4
334 2 Corinthians 5–9
335 2 Corinthians 10–13
336 Romans 1–3
337 Romans 4–7
338 Romans 8–10
339 Romans 11–13
340 Romans 14–16
341 Acts 20–21
342 Acts 22–24
343 Philippians 1–4
344 Acts 25–26
345 Acts 27–28; Philemon
346 Colossians 1–4
347 Ephesians 1–3
348 Ephesians 4–6
349 1 Timothy 1–6
350 Titus 1–3
351 2 Timothy 1–4
352 1 Peter 1–5
353 Jude; 2 Peter 1–3
354 Hebrews 1–3
355 Hebrews 4–6
356 Hebrews 7–10
357 Hebrews 11–13
358 1 John 1–5; 2 John; 3 John

## THE CONSUMMATION OF THE AGE

359 Revelation 1–3
360 Revelation 4–5
361 Revelation 6–9
362 Revelation 10–13
363 Revelation 14–16
364 Revelation 17–19
365 Revelation 20–22

# THE PROPHECIES OF JESUS

partial list presented in their order of fulfillment

| PROPHETIC SCRIPTURE | SUBJECT | FULFILLED |
|---|---|---|
| **Genesis 3:15**<br>"And I will put enmity between you and the woman, and between your seed and her Seed; He shall bruise your head, and you shall bruise His heel." | **seed of a woman** | **Galatians 4:4**<br>"But when the fullness of the time had come, God sent forth His Son, born of a woman, born under the law." |
| **Genesis 12:3**<br>"I will bless those who bless you, and I will curse him who curses you; and in you all the families of the earth shall be blessed." | **descendant of Abraham** | **Matthew 1:1**<br>"The book of the genealogy of Jesus Christ, the Son of David, the Son of Abraham." |
| **Genesis 17:19**<br>"Then God said, 'No, Sarah your wife shall bear you a son, and you shall call his name Isaac; I will establish My covenant with him for an everlasting covenant, and with his descendants after him.'" | **descendant of Isaac** | **Luke 3:34**<br>"the son of Jacob, the son of Isaac, the son of Abraham, the son of Terah, the son of Nahor." |
| **Numbers 24:17**<br>"I see Him, but not now; I behold Him, but not near; a Star shall come out of Jacob; a Scepter shall rise out of Israel, and batter the brow of Moab, and destroy all the sons of tumult." | **descendant of Jacob** | **Matthew 1:2**<br>"Abraham begot Isaac, Isaac begot Jacob, and Jacob begot Judah and his brothers." |
| **Genesis 49:10**<br>"The scepter shall not depart from Judah, nor a lawgiver from between his feet, until Shiloh comes; and to Him shall be the obedience of the people." | **from the tribe of Judah** | **Luke 3:33**<br>"the son of Amminadab, the son of Ram, the son of Hezron, the son of Perez, the son of Judah." |
| **Isaiah 9:7**<br>"Of the increase of His government and peace there will be no end, upon the throne of David and over His kingdom, to order it and establish it with judgment and justice from that time forward, even forever. The zeal of the LORD of hosts will perform this." | **heir to the throne of David** | **Luke 1:32–33**<br>"He will be great, and will be called the Son of the Highest; and the Lord God will give Him the throne of His father David. And He will reign over the house of Jacob forever, and of His kingdom there will be no end." |

| PROPHETIC SCRIPTURE | SUBJECT | FULFILLED |
|---|---|---|
| **Psalm 45:6–7**<br>"Your throne, O God, is forever and ever; a scepter of righteousness is the scepter of Your kingdom. You love righteousness, and hate wickedness; therefore God, Your God, has anointed You with the oil of gladness more than Your companions."<br>**Psalm 102:25–27**<br>"Of old You laid the foundation of the earth, and the heavens are the work of Your hands. They will perish, but You will endure; yes, they will all grow old like a garment; like a cloak You will change them, and they will be changed. But You are the same, and Your years will have no end." | **anointed and eternal** | **Hebrews 1:8–12**<br>"But to the Son He says: 'Your throne, O God, is forever and ever; a scepter of righteousness is the scepter of Your kingdom. You have loved righteousness and hated lawlessness; therefore God, Your God, has anointed You with the oil of gladness more than Your companions.' And: 'You, LORD, in the beginning laid the foundation of the earth, and the heavens are the work of Your hands. They will perish, but You remain; and they will all grow old like a garment; like a cloak You will fold them up, and they will be changed. But You are the same, and Your years will not fail.'" |
| **Micah 5:2**<br>"But you, Bethlehem, Ephrathah, though you are little among the thousands of Judah, yet out of you shall come forth to Me the One to be Ruler in Israel, whose goings forth are from of old, from everlasting." | **born in Bethlehem** | **Luke 2:4–5, 7**<br>"And Joseph also went up from Galilee, out of the city of Nazareth, into Judea, to the city of David, which is called Bethlehem, because he was of the house and lineage of David, to be registered with Mary, his betrothed wife, who was with child. . . . And she brought forth her firstborn Son, and wrapped Him in swaddling cloths, and laid Him in a manger, because there was no room for them in the inn." |
| **Daniel 9:25**<br>"Know therefore and understand, that from the going forth of the command to restore and build Jerusalem until Messiah the Prince, there shall be seven weeks, and sixty-two weeks; the street shall be built again, and the wall, even in troublesome times." | **time for His birth** | **Luke 2:1–2**<br>"And it came to pass in those days that a decree went out from Caesar Augustus that all the world should be registered. This census first took place while Quirinius was governing Syria." |
| **Isaiah 7:14**<br>"Therefore the Lord Himself will give you a sign: behold, the virgin shall conceive and bear a Son, and shall call His name Immanuel." | **to be born of a virgin** | **Luke 1:26–27, 30–31**<br>"Now in the sixth month the angel Gabriel was sent by God to a city of Galilee named Nazareth, to a virgin betrothed to a man whose name was Joseph, of the house of David. The virgin's name was Mary. . . . Then the angel said to her, 'Do not be afraid, Mary, for you have found favor with God. And behold, you will conceive in your womb and bring forth a Son, and shall call His name JESUS.'" |

| PROPHETIC SCRIPTURE | SUBJECT | FULFILLED |
|---|---|---|
| **Jeremiah 31:15**<br>"Thus says the LORD: 'A voice was heard in Ramah, lamentation, and bitter weeping, Rachel weeping for her children, refusing to be comforted for her children, because they are no more.'" | **slaughter of children** | **Matthew 2:16–18**<br>"Then Herod, when he saw that he was deceived by the wise men, was exceedingly angry; and he sent forth and put to death all the male children who were in Bethlehem and in all its districts, from two years old and under, according to the time which he had determined from the wise men. Then was fulfilled what was spoken by Jeremiah the prophet, saying: 'A voice was heard in Ramah, lamentation, weeping, and great mourning, Rachel weeping for her children, refusing to be comforted, because they are no more.'" |
| **Hosea 11:1**<br>"When Israel was a child, I loved him, and out of Egypt I called My son." | **flight to Egypt** | **Matthew 2:14–15**<br>"When he arose, he took the young Child and His mother by night and departed for Egypt, and was there until the death of Herod, that it might be fulfilled which was spoken by the Lord through the prophet, saying, 'Out of Egypt I called My Son.'" |
| **Isaiah 40:3–5**<br>"The voice of one crying in the wilderness: 'Prepare the way of the LORD; make straight in the desert a highway for our God. Every valley shall be exalted, and every mountain and hill brought low; the crooked places shall be made straight and the rough places smooth; the glory of the LORD shall be revealed, and all flesh shall see it together; for the mouth of the LORD has spoken.'" | **the way prepared** | **Luke 3:3–6**<br>"And he went into all the region around the Jordan, preaching a baptism of repentance for the remission of sins, as it is written in the book of the words of Isaiah the prophet, saying: 'The voice of one crying in the wilderness: "Prepare the way of the LORD; make His paths straight. Every valley shall be filled and every mountain and hill brought low; the crooked places shall be made straight and the rough ways smooth; and all flesh shall see the salvation of God."'" |
| **Malachi 3:1**<br>"'Behold, I send My messenger, and he will prepare the way before Me. And the Lord, whom you seek, will suddenly come to His temple, even the Messenger of the covenant, in whom you delight. Behold, He is coming,' says the LORD of hosts." | **preceded by a forerunner** | **Luke 7:24, 27**<br>"When the messengers of John had departed, He began to speak to the multitudes concerning John: 'What did you go out into the wilderness to see? A reed shaken by the wind? . . . This is he of whom it is written: "Behold, I send My messenger before Your face, who will prepare Your way before You."'" |

| PROPHETIC SCRIPTURE | SUBJECT | FULFILLED |
|---|---|---|
| **Malachi 4:5–6**<br>"Behold, I will send you Elijah the prophet before the coming of the great and dreadful day of the LORD. And he will turn the hearts of the fathers to the children, and the hearts of the children to their fathers, lest I come and strike the earth with a curse." | **preceded by Elijah** | **Matthew 11:13–14**<br>"For all the prophets and the law prophesied until John. And if you are willing to receive it, he is Elijah who is to come." |
| **Psalm 2:7**<br>"I will declare the decree: the LORD has said to Me, 'You are My Son, today I have begotten You.'" | **declared the Son of God** | **Matthew 3:17**<br>"And suddenly a voice came from heaven, saying, 'This is My beloved Son, in whom I am well pleased.'" |
| **Isaiah 9:1–2**<br>"Nevertheless the gloom will not be upon her who is distressed, as when at first He lightly esteemed the land of Zebulun and the land of Naphtali, and afterward more heavily oppressed her, by the way of the sea, beyond the Jordan, in Galilee of the Gentiles. The people who walked in darkness have seen a great light; those who dwelt in the land of the shadow of death, upon them a light has shined." | **Galilean ministry** | **Matthew 4:13–16**<br>"And leaving Nazareth, He came and dwelt in Capernaum, which is by the sea, in the regions of Zebulun and Naphtali, that it might be fulfilled which was spoken by Isaiah the prophet, saying: 'The land of Zebulun and the land of Naphtali, by the way of the sea, beyond the Jordan, Galilee of the Gentiles: The people who sat in darkness have seen a great light, and upon those who sat in the region and shadow of death light has dawned.'" |
| **Psalm 78:2–4**<br>"I will open my mouth in a parable; I will utter dark sayings of old, which we have heard and known, and our fathers have told us. We will not hide them from their children, telling to the generation to come the praises of the LORD, and His strength and His wonderful works that He has done." | **speaks in parables** | **Matthew 13:34–35**<br>"All these things Jesus spoke to the multitude in parables; and without a parable He did not speak to them, that it might be fulfilled which was spoken by the prophet, saying: 'I will open My mouth in parables; I will utter things kept secret from the foundation of the world.'" |
| **Deuteronomy 18:15**<br>"The LORD your God will raise up for you a Prophet like me from your midst, from your brethren. Him you shall hear." | **a prophet** | **Acts 3:20, 22**<br>"And that He may send Jesus Christ, who was preached to you before, . . . For Moses truly said to the fathers, 'The LORD your God will raise up for you a Prophet like me from your brethren. Him you shall hear in all things, whatever He says to you.'" |
| **Isaiah 61:1–2**<br>"The Spirit of the Lord GOD is upon Me, because the LORD has anointed Me to preach good tidings to the poor; He has sent Me to heal the brokenhearted, to proclaim liberty to the captives, and the opening of the prison to those who are bound; to proclaim the acceptable year of the LORD, and the day of vengeance of our God; to comfort all who mourn." | **to bind up the brokenhearted** | **Luke 4:18–19**<br>"The Spirit of the LORD is upon Me, because He has anointed Me to preach the gospel to the poor; He has sent Me to heal the brokenhearted, to proclaim liberty to the captives, and recovery of sight to the blind, to set at liberty those who are oppressed; to proclaim the acceptable year of the LORD." |

| PROPHETIC SCRIPTURE | SUBJECT | FULFILLED |
|---|---|---|
| **Isaiah 53:3**<br>"He is despised and rejected by men, a Man of sorrows and acquainted with grief. And we hid, as it were, our faces from Him; He was despised, and we did not esteem Him." | **rejected by His own people, the Jews** | **John 1:11**<br>"He came to His own, and His own did not receive Him."<br>**Luke 23:18**<br>"And they all cried out at once, saying, 'Away with this Man, and release to us Barabbas.'" |
| **Psalm 110:4**<br>"The LORD has sworn and will not relent, 'You are a priest forever according to the order of Melchizedek.'" | **priest after order of Melchizedek** | **Hebrews 5:5–6**<br>"So also Christ did not glorify Himself to become High Priest, but it was He who said to Him: 'You are My Son, today I have begotten You.' As He also says in another place: 'You are a priest forever according to the order of Melchizedek.'" |
| **Zechariah 9:9**<br>"Rejoice greatly, O daughter of Zion! Shout, O daughter of Jerusalem! Behold, your King is coming to you; He is just and having salvation, lowly and riding on a donkey, a colt, the foal of a donkey." | **triumphal entry** | **Mark 11:7, 9, 11**<br>"Then they brought the colt to Jesus and threw their clothes on it, and He sat on it. . . . Then those who went before and those who followed cried out, saying: 'Hosanna! Blessed is He who comes in the name of the LORD!' . . . And Jesus went into Jerusalem and into the temple. So when He had looked around at all things, as the hour was already late, He went out to Bethany with the twelve." |
| **Psalm 8:2**<br>"Out of the mouth of babes and nursing infants You have ordained strength, because of Your enemies, that You may silence the enemy and the avenger." | **adored by infants** | **Matthew 21:15–16**<br>"But when the chief priests and scribes saw the wonderful things that He did, and the children crying out in the temple and saying, 'Hosanna to the Son of David!' they were indignant and said to Him, 'Do You hear what these are saying?' And Jesus said to them, 'Yes. Have you never read, "Out of the mouth of babes and nursing infants You have perfected praise"?'" |
| **Isaiah 53:1**<br>"Who has believed our report? And to whom has the arm of the LORD been revealed?" | **not believed** | **John 12:37–38**<br>"But although He had done so many signs before them, they did not believe in Him, that the word of Isaiah the prophet might be fulfilled, which he spoke: 'LORD, who has believed our report? And to whom has the arm of the LORD been revealed?'" |

| PROPHETIC SCRIPTURE | SUBJECT | FULFILLED |
|---|---|---|
| **Psalm 41:9**<br>"Even my own familiar friend in whom I trusted, who ate my bread, has lifted up his heel against me." | **betrayed by a close friend** | **Luke 22:47–48**<br>"And while He was still speaking, behold, a multitude; and he who was called Judas, one of the twelve, went before them and drew near to Jesus to kiss Him. But Jesus said to him, 'Judas, are you betraying the Son of Man with a kiss?'" |
| **Psalm 35:11**<br>"Fierce witnesses rise up; they ask me things that I do not know." | **accused by false witnesses** | **Mark 14:57–58**<br>"Then some rose up and bore false witness against Him, saying, 'We heard Him say, "I will destroy this temple made with hands, and within three days I will build another made without hands."'" |
| **Isaiah 53:7**<br>"He was oppressed and He was afflicted, yet He opened not His mouth; He was led as a lamb to the slaughter, and as a sheep before its shearers is silent, so He opened not His mouth." | **silent to accusations** | **Mark 15:4–5**<br>"Then Pilate asked Him again, saying, 'Do You answer nothing? See how many things they testify against You!' But Jesus still answered nothing, so that Pilate marveled." |
| **Isaiah 50:6**<br>"I gave My back to those who struck Me, and My cheeks to those who plucked out the beard; I did not hide My face from shame and spitting." | **spat on and struck** | **Matthew 26:67**<br>"Then they spat in His face and beat Him; and others struck Him with the palms of their hands." |
| **Psalm 35:19**<br>"Let them not rejoice over me who are wrongfully my enemies; nor let them wink with the eye who hate me without a cause." | **hated without reason** | **John 15:24–25**<br>"If I had not done among them the works which no one else did, they would have no sin; but now they have seen and also hated both Me and My Father. But this happened that the word might be fulfilled which is written in their law, 'They hated Me without a cause.'" |
| **Isaiah 53:5**<br>"But He was wounded for our transgressions, He was bruised for our iniquities; the chastisement for our peace was upon Him, and by His stripes we are healed." | **vicarious sacrifice** | **Romans 5:6, 8**<br>"For when we were still without strength, in due time Christ died for the ungodly. . . . But God demonstrates His own love toward us, in that while we were still sinners, Christ died for us." |
| **Isaiah 53:12**<br>"Therefore I will divide Him a portion with the great, and He shall divide the spoil with the strong. Because He poured out His soul unto death, and He was numbered with the transgressors, and He bore the sin of many, and made intercession for the transgressors." | **crucified with malefactors** | **Mark 15:27–28**<br>"With Him they also crucified two robbers, one on His right and the other on His left. So the Scripture was fulfilled which says, 'And He was numbered with the transgressors.'" |

| PROPHETIC SCRIPTURE | SUBJECT | FULFILLED |
|---|---|---|
| **Zechariah 12:10**<br>"And I will pour on the house of David and on the inhabitants of Jerusalem the Spirit of grace and supplication; then they will look on Me whom they pierced. Yes, they will mourn for Him as one mourns for his only son, and grieve for Him as one grieves for a firstborn." | **pierced through hands and feet** | **John 20:27**<br>"Then He said to Thomas, 'Reach your finger here, and look at My hands; and reach your hand here, and put it into My side. Do not be unbelieving, but believing.'" |
| **Psalm 22:7–8**<br>"All those who see Me ridicule Me; they shoot out the lip, they shake the head, saying, 'He trusted in the LORD, let Him rescue Him; let Him deliver Him, since He delights in Him!'" | **sneered and mocked** | **Luke 23:35**<br>"And the people stood looking on. But even the rulers with them sneered, saying, 'He saved others; let Him save Himself if He is the Christ, the chosen of God.'" |
| **Psalm 69:9**<br>"Because zeal for Your house has eaten me up, and the reproaches of those who reproach You have fallen on me." | **was reproached** | **Romans 15:3**<br>"For even Christ did not please Himself; but as it is written, 'The reproaches of those who reproached You fell on Me.'" |
| **Psalm 109:4**<br>"In return for my love they are my accusers, but I give myself to prayer." | **prayer for His enemies** | **Luke 23:34**<br>"Then Jesus said, 'Father, forgive them, for they do not know what they do.' And they divided His garments and cast lots." |
| **Psalm 22:17–18**<br>"I can count all My bones. They look and stare at Me. They divide My garments among them, and for My clothing they cast lots." | **soldiers gambled for His clothing** | **Matthew 27:35–36**<br>"Then they crucified Him, and divided His garments, casting lots, that it might be fulfilled which was spoken by the prophet: 'They divided My garments among them, and for My clothing they cast lots.' Sitting down, they kept watch over Him there." |
| **Psalm 22:1**<br>"My God, My God, why have You forsaken Me? Why are You so far from helping Me, and from the words of My groaning?" | **forsaken by God** | **Matthew 27:46**<br>"And about the ninth hour Jesus cried out with a loud voice, saying, 'Eli, Eli, lama sabachthani?' that is, 'My God, My God, why have You forsaken Me?'" |
| **Psalm 34:20**<br>"He guards all his bones, not one of them is broken." | **no bones broken** | **John 19:32–33, 36**<br>"Then the soldiers came and broke the legs of the first and of the other who was crucified with Him. But when they came to Jesus and saw that He was already dead, they did not break His legs. . . . For these things were done that the Scripture should be fulfilled, 'Not one of His bones shall be broken.'" |

| PROPHETIC SCRIPTURE | SUBJECT | FULFILLED |
|---|---|---|
| **Zechariah 12:10**<br>"And I will pour on the house of David and on the inhabitants of Jerusalem the Spirit of grace and supplication; then they will look on Me whom they have pierced. Yes, they will mourn for Him as one mourns for his only son, and grieve for Him as one grieves for a firstborn." | **His side pierced** | **John 19:34**<br>"But one of the soldiers pierced His side with a spear, and immediately blood and water came out." |
| **Isaiah 53:9**<br>"And they made His grave with the wicked—but with the rich at His death, because He had done no violence, nor was any deceit in His mouth." | **buried with the rich** | **Matthew 27:57–60**<br>"Now when evening had come, there came a rich man from Arimathea, named Joseph, who himself had also become a disciple of Jesus. This man went to Pilate and asked for the body of Jesus. Then Pilate commanded the body to be given to him. When Joseph had taken the body, he wrapped it in a clean linen cloth, and laid it in his new tomb which he had hewn out of the rock; and he rolled a large stone against the door of the tomb, and departed." |
| **Psalm 16:10**<br>"For You will not leave my soul in Sheol, nor will You allow Your Holy One to see corruption."<br>**Psalm 49:15**<br>"But God will redeem my soul from the power of the grave, for He shall receive me. Selah" | **to be resurrected** | **Mark 16:6–7**<br>"But he said to them, 'Do not be alarmed. You seek Jesus of Nazareth, who was crucified. He is risen! He is not here. See the place where they laid Him. But go, tell His disciples—and Peter—that He is going before you into Galilee; there you will see Him, as He said to you.'" |
| **Psalm 68:18**<br>"You have ascended on high. You have led captivity captive; You have received gifts among men; even from the rebellious, that the LORD God might dwell there." | **His ascension to God's right hand** | **Mark 16:19**<br>"So then, after the Lord had spoken to them, He was received up into heaven, and sat down at the right hand of God."<br>**1 Corinthians 15:4**<br>"And that He was buried, and that He rose again the third day according to the Scriptures."<br>**Ephesians 4:8**<br>"Therefore He says: 'When He ascended on high, He led captivity captive, and gave gifts to men.'" |

# THE MIRACLES OF JESUS

| MIRACLE | MATTHEW | MARK | LUKE | JOHN |
|---|---|---|---|---|
| 1. Man with Leprosy | 8:2–4 | 1:40–42 | 5:12–13 | |
| 2. Centurion's Servant | 8:5–13 | | 7:1–10 | |
| 3. Peter's Mother-in-Law | 8:14–15 | 1:30–31 | 4:38–39 | |
| 4. Calming the Storm | 8:23–27 | 4:37–41 | 8:22–25 | |
| 5. Gadarenes Demoniac | 8:28–34 | 5:1–15 | 8:27–35 | |
| 6. Paralyzed Man | 9:2–7 | 2:3–12 | 5:18–25 | |
| 7. Raising of Jairus's Daughter | 9:18–19, 23–25 | 5:22–24, 35–42 | 8:41–42, 49–56 | |
| 8. Hemorrhaging Woman | 9:20–22 | 5:25–34 | 8:43–48 | |
| 9. Two Blind Men | 9:27–31 | | | |
| 10. Mute and Possessed Man | 9:32–34 | | | |
| 11. Man with a Withered Hand | 12:9–14 | 3:1–6 | 6:6–11 | |
| 12. Blind, Mute, and Possessed Man | 12:22–32 | | 11:14–23 | |
| 13. Feeding of over Five Thousand | 14:15–21 | 6:35–44 | 9:12–17 | 6:5–14 |
| 14. Walking on Water | 14:25–32 | 6:48–51 | | 6:19–21 |
| 15. Gentile Woman's Daughter | 15:21–28 | 7:24–30 | | |
| 16. Feeding of over Four Thousand | 15:32–38 | 8:1–9 | | |
| 17. Demon-Possessed Boy | 17:14–18 | 9:14–29 | 9:38–43 | |
| 18. Coin in Fish's Mouth | 17:24–27 | | | |
| 19. The Blind Men | 20:29–34 | 10:46–52 | 18:35–43 | |
| 20. Fig Tree Withered | 21:18–22 | 11:12–14, 20–25 | | |
| 21. Possessed Man in Synagogue | | 1:23–26 | 4:33–35 | |
| 22. Deaf and Mute | | 7:31–37 | | |
| 23. Blind Man at Bethsaida | | 8:22–26 | | |
| 24. First Catch of Fish | | | 5:1–11 | |
| 25. Raising Widow's Son at Nain | | | 7:11–15 | |
| 26. Crippled Woman | | | 13:10–13 | |
| 27. Man with Dropsy | | | 14:1–4 | |
| 28. Ten Lepers | | | 17:11–19 | |
| 29. High Priest's Servant | | | 22:50–51 | |

| MIRACLE | MATTHEW | MARK | LUKE | JOHN |
|---|---|---|---|---|
| 30. Water to Wine | | | | 2:1–11 |
| 31. Nobleman's Son | | | | 4:46–54 |
| 32. Sick Man at Pool of Bethesda | | | | 5:1–9 |
| 33. Man Born Blind | | | | 9:1–41 |
| 34. Raising of Lazarus | | | | 11:1–44 |
| 35. Second Catch of Fish | | | | 21:1–14 |

# THE PARABLES OF JESUS

| PARABLE | MATTHEW | MARK | LUKE |
|---|---|---|---|
| 1. Lamp Under a Basket | 5:14–16 | 4:21–22 | 8:16–17; 11:33–36 |
| 2. The House Built on Rock and the House Built on Sand | 7:24–27 | | 6:47–49 |
| 3. New Cloth on an Old Garment | 9:16 | 2:21 | 5:36 |
| 4. New Wine in Old Wineskins | 9:17 | 2:22 | 5:37–38 |
| 5. The Sower | 13:3–9, 18–23 | 4:3–9, 14–20 | 8:4–9, 11–15 |
| 6. The Tares | 13:24–30, 36–43 | | |
| 7. The Mustard Seed | 13:31–32 | 4:30–32 | 13:18–19 |
| 8. The Leaven | 13:33 | | 13:20–21 |
| 9. The Hidden Treasure | 13:44 | | |
| 10. The Pearl of Great Price | 13:45–46 | | |
| 11. The Dragnet | 13:47–50 | | |
| 12. The Lost Sheep | 18:12–14 | | 15:3–7 |
| 13. The Unforgiving Servant | 18:23–35 | | |
| 14. The Laborers in the Vineyard | 20:1–16 | | |
| 15. The Two Sons | 21:28–32 | | |
| 16. The Wicked Vinedressers | 21:33–45 | 12:1–12 | 20:9–19 |
| 17. The Wedding Feast | 22:2–14 | | |
| 18. The Fig Tree | 24:32–36 | 13:28–32 | 21:29–33 |
| 19. The Wise and Foolish Virgins | 25:1–13 | | |
| 20. The Talents | 25:14–30 | | |
| 21. The Growing Seed | | 4:26–29 | |
| 22. The Absent Householder | | 13:33–37 | |
| 23. The Creditor and the Two Debtors | | | 7:41–43 |
| 24. The Good Samaritan | | | 10:30–37 |
| 25. A Friend in Need | | | 11:5–13 |
| 26. The Rich Fool | | | 12:16–21 |
| 27. The Faithful Servant | | | 12:35–40 |
| 28. The Faithful and Wise Steward | | | 12:42–48 |
| 29. The Barren Fig Tree | | | 13:6–9 |
| 30. The Great Supper | | | 14:16–24 |
| 31. Building a Tower and a King Making War | | | 14:25–35 |
| 32. The Lost Coin | | | 15:8–10 |
| 33. The Prodigal Son | | | 15:11–32 |
| 34. The Unjust Steward | | | 16:1–13 |

| PARABLE | MATTHEW | MARK | LUKE |
|---|---|---|---|
| 35. The Rich Man and Lazarus | | | 16:19–31 |
| 36. Unprofitable Servants | | | 17:7–10 |
| 37. The Persistent Widow | | | 18:1–8 |
| 38. The Pharisee and the Tax Collector | | | 18:9–14 |
| 39. The Minas | | | 19:11–27 |

# FEATURES INDEX

## SEEING JESUS NOTES


Genesis 3:15
Genesis 3:21
Genesis 12:3
Genesis 14:18
Genesis 17:7
Genesis 17:19
Genesis 21:12
Genesis 22:18
Genesis 26:4
Genesis 28:10–12
Genesis 49:10
Genesis 50:20
Exodus 1:15
Exodus 3:14
Exodus 12:14
Exodus 13:2
Exodus 17:5–6
Exodus 20:13
Exodus 26:33
Leviticus 11:44
Leviticus 16:22
Leviticus 18:5
Leviticus 19:18
Leviticus 25:10
Leviticus 26:11
Numbers 9:12
Numbers 11:7–9
Numbers 21:8
Numbers 24:17
Deuteronomy 6:4–5
Deuteronomy 8:3
Deuteronomy 11:16–17
Deuteronomy 12:7
Deuteronomy 18:15
Joshua 1:1–2
Joshua 6:17
Joshua 10:24
Joshua 22:4–5
Judges 2:16
Judges 13:5
Ruth 1:16–17
Ruth 4:9–11
1 Samuel 2:35
1 Samuel 14:45
1 Samuel 17:34–35
1 Samuel 19:6
2 Samuel 7:12
2 Samuel 9:7
2 Samuel 12:18
2 Samuel 22:3–4
2 Samuel 24:17
1 Kings 10:4–5
1 Kings 17:17–24
1 Kings 19:20
2 Kings 2:11
2 Kings 4:42–44
2 Kings 5:3
2 Kings 20:2–6
1 Chronicles 13:9–10
1 Chronicles 17:11
1 Chronicles 21:17
1 Chronicles 22:10
1 Chronicles 29:1–3
2 Chronicles 1:11
2 Chronicles 7:14
2 Chronicles 21:7
2 Chronicles 26:20
2 Chronicles 30:15
2 Chronicles 31:20
Ezra 1:1–4
Ezra 4:6
Ezra 6:20
Ezra 10:10–11
Nehemiah 1:3–4
Nehemiah 2:5
Nehemiah 9:17
Nehemiah 9:26–27
Nehemiah 13:8
Esther 4:11
Esther 6:10–11
Esther 7:10
Job 4:7
Job 9:33
Job 11:6
Job 12:4
Job 13:20–21
Job 14:13–14
Job 16:10
Psalm 2:1–2
Psalm 8:2
Psalm 15:1–2
Psalm 16:10
Psalms 22:1
Psalm 27:12
Psalm 34:20
Psalm 35:19
Psalm 41:9
Psalm 49:15
Psalm 69:21
Psalm 72:1–2
Psalm 78:2
Psalm 91:11–12
Psalm 98:9
Psalm 102:16
Psalm 109:3–5
Psalm 110:4
Psalm 118:22–23
Psalm 118:26
Psalm 126:1–3
Proverbs 1:10
Proverbs 2:13–14
Proverbs 6:16–19
Proverbs 8:23
Proverbs 25:21–22
Ecclesiastes 2:11
Ecclesiastes 3:11
Ecclesiastes 9:7–9
Ecclesiastes 12:13
Song of Solomon 8:6
Isaiah 2:3
Isaiah 6:9–10
Isaiah 7:14
Isaiah 8:14
Isaiah 9:6–7
Isaiah 11:2
Isaiah 25:8
Isaiah 26:19
Isaiah 28:16
Isaiah 35:5–6
Isaiah 40:3
Isaiah 42:1–4
Isaiah 49:6
Isaiah 50:6
Isaiah 52:13
Isaiah 53:1–12
Isaiah 55:5
Isaiah 59:20
Isaiah 60:3
Isaiah 61:1
Isaiah 63:2–3
Isaiah 65:2
Jeremiah 7:11
Jeremiah 23:5–8
Jeremiah 30:9

Jeremiah 31:15
Lamentations 3:28–30
Ezekiel 16:60
Ezekiel 34:23
Ezekiel 37:25
Daniel 2:44
Daniel 3:25
Daniel 7:14
Daniel 9:25
Hosea 3:2–3
Hosea 6:2
Hosea 11:1–2
Joel 2:28
Amos 8:9
Amos 9:11–12
Jonah 1:17
Micah 1:3–4
Micah 5:2
Micah 7:6
Micah 7:20
Nahum 3:6
Habakkuk 2:4
Zephaniah 3:15
Haggai 2:9
Zechariah 3:8
Zechariah 6:12
Zechariah 8:7–8
Zechariah 9:9
Zechariah 11:12–13
Zechariah 12:10
Zechariah 13:7
Malachi 3:1
Malachi 4:6
Matthew 1:1, 6
Matthew 1:18
Matthew 2:5–6
Matthew 3:2–3
Matthew 5:8
Matthew 7:23
Matthew 8:11
Matthew 8:16–17
Matthew 11:10
Matthew 12:40
Matthew 13:14
Matthew 14:27
Matthew 16:18
Matthew 17:23
Matthew 20:28
Matthew 21:5
Matthew 26:15
Matthew 26:47–57
Matthew 26:74–75
Matthew 27:57–60
Matthew 28:16–17
Mark 1:2
Mark 3:6
Mark 7:6–7
Mark 9:7
Mark 11:9
Mark 12:10
Mark 13:26
Mark 14:18
Mark 15:5
Mark 15:38
Mark 16:6
Luke 1:31
Luke 2:22–24
Luke 3:31
Luke 4:15
Luke 7:22
Luke 8:10
Luke 9:61–62
Luke 11:30
Luke 12:32
Luke 13:35
Luke 19:14
Luke 20:17
Luke 22:37
Luke 23:2–3
Luke 24:51
John 1:23
John 2:17
John 3:14–17
John 4:25
John 6:4–5
John 6:45
John 7:14
John 8:58–59
John 10:11
John 12:3, 7
John 13:18
John 14:16
John 16:13
John 17:8
John 18:22
John 19:23–24
John 19:36
John 20:17
Acts 1:11
Acts 2:3–4
Acts 4:11
Acts 7:37
Acts 8:32–33
Acts 10:40–41
Acts 13:22–23
Romans 1:4
Romans 4:25
Romans 5:15
Romans 9:33
Romans 10:16
Romans 11:26
Romans 15:3
1 Corinthians 3:11
1 Corinthians 11:26
1 Corinthians 15:24
2 Corinthians 3:14
2 Corinthians 5:21
2 Corinthians 12:9
Galatians 2:20
Galatians 3:16
Galatians 4:4
Ephesians 1:22
Ephesians 2:20
Ephesians 5:14
Philippians 4:7
1 Thessalonians 4:17
1 Thessalonians 5:12–13
1 Timothy 1:15
1 Timothy 2:5–6
2 Timothy 1:8
2 Timothy 3:15
Titus 1:16
Titus 2:14
Hebrews 1:9
Hebrews 2:17
Hebrews 3:5
Hebrews 4:15
Hebrews 5:6
Hebrews 7:17
Hebrews 8:8–9
Hebrews 9:26
Hebrews 10:5
Hebrews 11:17–19
Hebrews 12:2
Hebrews 13:20–21
James 2:10
1 Peter 1:14–16
1 Peter 2:24–25
1 Peter 4:14
2 Peter 1:17
1 John 5:3
Jude 1:2
Revelation 1:16
Revelation 2:26–27
Revelation 3:20
Revelation 5:5
Revelation 12:4–5
Revelation 16:15
Revelation 19:13
Revelation 21:4
Revelation 22:12

## THE STORY OF SCRIPTURE DEVOTIONALS


1. **Light, Order, and Life** . . . Genesis 1:1–5 . . . 5
2. **A Promise of Redemption** . . . Genesis 3:1–24 . . . 8
3. **Brothers at War** . . . Genesis 4:1–8 . . . 10
4. **Stepping Out in Faith** . . . Genesis 12:1–9 . . . 17
5. **The Test** . . . Genesis 22:1–19 . . . 27
6. **Wrestling with God** . . . Genesis 32:22–32 . . . 39
7. **From the Prison to the Palace** . . . Genesis 41:37–57 . . . 49
8. **Drawn from Water** . . . Exodus 1:8—2:10 . . . 61
9. **God Is Near** . . . Exodus 3:1–22 . . . 63
10. **The Blood of the Lamb** . . . Exodus 12:1–32 . . . 71
11. **God Parts the Sea** . . . Exodus 13:17—14:31 . . . 75
12. **Sky Bread and Stone Water** . . . Exodus 16:1—17:7 . . . 78
13. **Promises and Covenants** . . . Exodus 19:16—20:21 . . . 81
14. **The Spirit and the Tabernacle** . . . Exodus 35:30-35 . . . 100
15. **Rest Sets Us Free** . . . Leviticus 25:1–34 . . . 130
16. **The Bronze Serpent** . . . Numbers 21:4–9 . . . 159
17. **God's Special People** . . . Deuteronomy 6:1—7:26 . . . 185
18. **The Scarlet Cord** . . . Joshua 2:18–19 . . . 218
19. **Crossing the Jordan** . . . Joshua 3:1–17 . . . 219
20. **Israel's Spiral of Sin** . . . Judges 2:11–23 . . . 243
21. **Samson's Death Brings Life** . . . Judges 16:23–31 . . . 259
22. **Ruth's Legacy** . . . Ruth 4:11–22 . . . 270
23. **Self-Rule** . . . 1 Samuel 10:1–27 . . . 282
24. **David and Goliath** . . . 1 Samuel 17:1–50 . . . 290
25. **God's Covenant with David** . . . 2 Samuel 7:1–17 . . . 311
26. **The Wake of David's Sin** . . . 1 Chronicles 21:1–5 . . . 415
27. **The Temple** . . . 1 Kings 6:1–28 . . . 339
28. **Solomon's Fall** . . . 1 Kings 11:1–9 . . . 348
29. **A Divided Kingdom** . . . 1 Kings 12:1–33 . . . 350
30. **Elijah's Battle and God's Victory** . . . 1 Kings 18:17–40 . . . 357
31. **Israel's Fall** . . . 2 Kings 17:5–23 . . . 383
32. **Judah's Fall** . . . 2 Chronicles 36:11–21 . . . 456
33. **The Temple Is Rebuilt** . . . Ezra 6:13–18 . . . 465
34. **God's Silent Hand** . . . Esther 9:1–32 . . . 494
35. **God Promises Hope** . . . Jeremiah 29:1–14 . . . 775
36. **The Breath of God** . . . Ezekiel 37:1–14 . . . 849
37. **The Lesson of the Lions** . . . Daniel 6:1–28 . . . 871
38. **The Prophecy of Jonah** . . . Jonah 2:1–10 . . . 911
39. **Refiner's Fire** . . . Malachi 3:1–7 . . . 950
40. **Jesus, the Word and the Light** . . . John 1:1–5 . . . 1069
41. **Jesus, God with Us** . . . Matthew 1:18–24 . . . 962
42. **Jesus, the Beloved Son** . . . Matthew 3:1–17 . . . 964
43. **Jesus, the Storm Calmer** . . . Mark 4:35—5:20 . . . 1009
44. **Jesus, the Savior of All** . . . Luke 4:16–30 . . . 1036
45. **Jesus, the Christ** . . . Matthew 16:13–23 . . . 982
46. **Jesus, the Life Giver** . . . John 11:38–44 . . . 1088
47. **The Crucifixion** . . . Mark 15:6–39 . . . 1026
48. **The Resurrection** . . . Luke 24:1–35 . . . 1066
49. **The Great Commission** . . . Matthew 28:16–20 . . . 1000
50. **The Church Is Born** . . . Acts 1:1—2:4 . . . 1105
51. **Saul's Conversion** . . . Acts 9:1–31 . . . 1116
52. **Paul's Mission** . . . Acts 13:4–52 . . . 1122
53. **The Jerusalem Council** . . . Acts 15:1–21 . . . 1125
54. **The Church Expands** . . . Acts 16:11–40 . . . 1127

55. **The Main Message** . . . 1 Corinthians 2:1–5 . . . 1168
56. **Grace Alone** . . . 1 Timothy 1:15–16 . . . 1229
57. **Heroes of Faith** . . . Hebrews 11:1–40 . . . 1255
58. **Christian Living** . . . James 5:1–20 . . . 1264
59. **The Hero and the Groom** . . . Revelation 19:6–21 . . . 1307
60. **The Promise of Heaven** . . . Revelation 22:1–21 . . . 1311

## KNOW THE TRUTH ARTICLES

### *The Doctrine of Scripture*

Part 1: **Overview of the Doctrine of Scripture** . . . Nehemiah 8:7–12 . . . 479
Part 2: **The Purpose of Scripture** . . . Deuteronomy 31:9–13 . . . 208
Part 3: **The Content of Scripture** . . . John 5:39 . . . 1077
Part 4: **The Authority of Scripture** . . . Matthew 5:17–18 . . . 966
Part 5: **The Inspiration of Scripture** . . . 2 Timothy 3:14–17 . . . 1236
Part 6: **The Inerrancy of Scripture** . . . Ezekiel 11:19–20 . . . 822
Part 7: **The Illumination of Scripture** . . . Matthew 23:8–10 . . . 991
Part 8: **The Transmission of Scripture** . . . Jeremiah 36:32 . . . 786
Part 9: **The Canonization of Scripture** . . . Acts 18:27–28 . . . 1131
Part 10: **The Translation of Scripture** . . . Colossians 4:16 . . . 1218

### *The Doctrine of God*

Part 1: **Overview of the Doctrine of God** . . . Deuteronomy 4:24–40 . . . 181
Part 2: **God the Creator** . . . Genesis 2:4 . . . 7
Part 3: **God the Spirit** . . . John 4:24 . . . 1075
Part 4: **The Eternality of God** . . . Isaiah 40:28 . . . 716
Part 5: **The Infinity of God** . . . Luke 1:37 . . . 1031
Part 6: **The Omnipotence of God** . . . Jeremiah 32:27 . . . 781
Part 7: **The Omniscience of God** . . . Psalm 147:5 . . . 622
Part 8: **The Omnipresence of God** . . . Proverbs 15:3 . . . 638
Part 9: **The Sovereignty of God** . . . Psalm 115:3 . . . 605
Part 10: **The Holiness of God** . . . Isaiah 6:1–7 . . . 684
Part 11: **The Love of God** . . . 1 John 4:8 . . . 1280
Part 12: **The Grace and Mercy of God** . . . 2 John 1:3 . . . 1283
Part 13: **The Righteousness and Justness of God** . . . Psalm 89:14 . . . 587
Part 14: **The Goodness and Benevolence of God** . . . Exodus 34:6–7 . . . 97
Part 15: **The Faithful and Truthfulness of God** . . . Deuteronomy 32:3–4 . . . 209
Part 16: **The Perfection of God** . . . Psalm 18:30 . . . 541
Part 17: **The Immutability of God** . . . Hebrews 13:8 . . . 1257
Part 18: **The Immanence of God** . . . Acts 17:27 . . . 1129
Part 19: **The Transcendence of God** . . . Psalm 97:9 . . . 593
Part 20: **The Triune Nature of God** . . . 2 Corinthians 13:14 . . . 1192

### *The Doctrine of Jesus*

Part 1: **Overview of the Doctrine of Jesus** . . . Mark 1:1 . . . 1003
Part 2: **The Deity of Jesus** . . . Mark 14:61–62 . . . 1025
Part 3: **The Humanity of Jesus** . . . Hebrews 4:14–16 . . . 1248
Part 4: **The Character of Jesus** . . . 1 Peter 2:22 . . . 1268
Part 5: **The Miracles of Jesus** . . . John 20:30–31 . . . 1101
Part 6: **The Teachings of Jesus** . . . John 7:37–46 . . . 1081
Part 7: **The Sacrifice of Jesus** . . . Isaiah 53:4–12 . . . 731
Part 8: **The Resurrection of Jesus** . . . 1 Peter 1:3–5 . . . 1266

### *The Doctrine of the Holy Spirit*

Part 1: **Overview of the Doctrine of the Holy Spirit** . . . Judges 6:34–35 . . . 248
Part 2: **The Deity of the Holy Spirit** . . . Zechariah 4:6–9 . . . 938
Part 3: **The Holy Spirit's Work in Christ's Life** . . . Isaiah 11:1–5 . . . 690
Part 4: **The Holy Spirit's Work in Revelation** . . . John 14:26 . . . 1092

Part 5: **The Holy Spirit's Work in Salvation** .................. John 16:7–15 . . .1094
Part 6: **The Holy Spirit's Work in Sanctification** ........ 2 Corinthians 3:17–18 . . .1185
Part 7: **The Fruit of the Holy Spirit** ..............................Galatians 5:22–25 . . .1199

*The Doctrine of Creation and Humans*

Part 1: **Overview of the Doctrine of Creation and Humans**......Colossians 1:16–17 . . .1215
Part 2: **The Creation of Everything** .............................. Psalm 33:6 . . . .551
Part 3: **The Creation of Angels** .......................... Psalm 103:20–21 . . . .596
Part 4: **The Creation of Satan and Demons**........................ Mark 3:22–27 . . .1006
Part 5: **The Creation of Humans** ..................... Psalm 139:13–18 . . . .618
Part 6: **The Image of God in Humans** ...............................Genesis 9:6–7 . . . . .15
Part 7: **The Purpose of Humans** .......................................Jude 1:24–25 . . .1288
Part 8: **The Fall of Humans** ..............................................Genesis 5:1–5 . . . . .11
Part 9: **The Sin and Evil in Humans** ..................................Genesis 6:5 . . . . .12
Part 10: **The Death of Humans** ..........................................Job 19:25–26 . . . .512

*The Doctrine of Salvation*

Part 1: **Overview of the Doctrine of Salvation** .............. Hebrews 2:9–15 . . .1246
Part 2: **The Need of Salvation** ........................................Acts 10:42–43 . . .1118
Part 3: **The Manner of Salvation**............................... 2 Corinthians 5:21 . . .1187
Part 4: **The Process of Salvation** ....................................... Titus 3:4–7 . . .1240
Part 5: **The Moment of Salvation** ................................Romans 10:8–17 . . .1157
Part 6: **The Result of Salvation**............................................ 1 John 2:3–5 . . .1277
Part 7: **The Continuation of Salvation** ........................ 1 Corinthians 1:18 . . .1167
Part 8: **The Completion of Salvation** ...............................Romans 8:28–30 . . .1155

*The Doctrine of the Church*

Part 1: **Overview of the Doctrine of the Church** ...................... Acts 4:21–37 . . .1109
Part 2: **The Kingdom of God**............................................... John 3:3–5 . . .1073
Part 3: **The Nature of the Church**........................................Philemon 1:2 . . .1242
Part 4: **The Universal and Local Church** ................................. Acts 2:47 . . .1107
Part 5: **The Purpose of the Church** .....................................Acts 11:19–26 . . .1119
Part 6: **The Functions of the Church** ............................ Hebrews 10:19–25 . . .1253
Part 7: **The Ordinances of the Church** .................... 1 Corinthians 11:23–24 . . .1176
Part 8: **The Leadership of the Church** ..........................Ephesians 4:11–16 . . .1205
Part 9: **The Necessity of the Church** ....................... 1 Corinthians 12:4–27 . . .1177

*The Doctrine of the Future*

Part 1: **Overview of the Doctrine of the Future**................ Daniel 12:1–3 . . . .879
Part 2: **The Return of Jesus**............................... 1 Thessalonians 5:23 . . .1222
Part 3: **The Resurrection of the Dead**.................................. John 6:39–40 . . .1078
Part 4: **The Final Judgment**.....................................Revelation 20:11–15 . . .1308
Part 5: **The New Heaven and New Earth** ..........................Revelation 21:1 . . .1309

## APPLY THE TRUTH ARTICLES

**Abuse**.......................................................... Exodus 22:22–24 . . . . .85
**Acceptance and Belonging** .........................................Jeremiah 1:5 . . . .745
**Adoption**......................................................Galatians 4:5–7 . . .1198
**Anger**......................................................Numbers 20:7–13 . . . .157
**Archeological Finds** ...................................... Matthew 27:11–16 . . . .998
**Authority** ......................................................Numbers 27:20 . . . .167
**Betrayal** ............................................................... Hosea 1:2 . . . .881
**Bible's Reliability, The** .............................................. Matthew 12:40 . . . .976
**Blended Families** ..................................................Galatians 3:28 . . .1197
**Bullying** ......................................................Genesis 16:1–6 . . . . .21
**Community** .....................................................Romans 12:4–6 . . .1160
**Conflict**............................................................. Psalm 35:1 . . . .552
**Crime**.......................................................... Exodus 20:2–17 . . . . .82

**Cults** . . . . Galatians 1:8 . . 1194
**Dating** . . . . Ruth 3:1–18 . . 269
**Deception** . . . . Joshua 9:1–27 . . . 225
**Depression** . . . . Job 3:1–26 . . . 500
**Disappointment** . . . . Psalm 42:11 . . . 558
**Discouragement** . . . . Psalm 73:1–28 . . . 576
**Doubt** . . . . Matthew 14:25–31 . . . 980
**Emotional Health** . . . . Psalm 40:1–17 . . . 556
**Entertainment** . . . . Psalm 46:10 . . . 561
**Environment, The** . . . . Psalm 24:1–10 . . . 545
**Evangelism** . . . . Isaiah 52:7 . . . 729
**Evil** . . . . Romans 5:12, 17 . . . 1151
**Existence of God, The** . . . . 3 John 1:11 . . . 1285
**Existence of Jesus, The** . . . . 1 Corinthians 15:4–8 . . . 1179
**Failure** . . . . Proverbs 24:16 . . . 648
**Fame** . . . . Matthew 10:40–41 . . . 973
**Fear** . . . . 2 Kings 6:16 . . . 371
**Freedom** . . . . Psalm 16:1–11 . . . 539
**Gender and Sexuality** . . . . Matthew 19:1–6 . . 986
**Greed** . . . . 1 Kings 21:1–29 . . . 361
**Grief** . . . . 2 Samuel 18:19–33 . . . 324
**Guilt and Shame** . . . . Psalm 32:1–11 . . . 550
**Heartache** . . . . Isaiah 65:17–25 . . . 742
**Human Trafficking** . . . . Genesis 37:25–27 . . . 44
**Hunger** . . . . Matthew 15:32–39 . . 981
**Hypocrisy** . . . . 2 Samuel 12:1–7 . . . 316
**Idols and Hero Worship** . . . . Acts 28:1–6 . . . 1142
**Judging Others** . . . . Romans 2:1–2 . . . 1148
**Loneliness** . . . . 1 Corinthians 7:8 . . . 1172
**Marriage and Divorce** . . . . Ephesians 5:21–33 . . . 1206
**Materialism** . . . . Ecclesiastes 5:10 . . . 662
**Mental Health** . . . . 1 Kings 19:4–10 . . . 358
**Morality and Ethics** . . . . Psalm 119:159–160 . . . 611
**Natural Disasters** . . . . Acts 27:13–38 . . . 1141
**Occult, The** . . . . Colossians 2:8 . . . 1216
**Pain and Suffering** . . . . Hebrews 12:1–8 . . . 1256
**Peer Pressure** . . . . Psalm 1:1–6 . . . 531
**Physical Health** . . . . 1 Timothy 4:8 . . . 1230
**Pluralism** . . . . Matthew 7:13–14 . . . 969
**Politics** . . . . Romans 13:1–7 . . . 1161
**Pornography** . . . . 1 Corinthians 5:1 . . . 1170
**Poverty** . . . . Philippians 4:12 . . . 1212
**Pride** . . . . Daniel 4:28–34 . . . 868
**Purpose** . . . . Ephesians 2:10 . . . 1203
**Racism** . . . . Galatians 2:11–16 . . . 1195
**Rebellion** . . . . Isaiah 14:12–15 . . . 693
**Relationships** . . . . Proverbs 27:17 . . . 651
**Religions** . . . . 1 Samuel 5:1–12 . . . 277
**School** . . . . Colossians 3:23 . . . 1217
**Science** . . . . Psalm 19:1–6 . . . 542
**Self-Harm** . . . . 1 Corinthians 6:19 . . . 1171
**Selfishness** . . . . Judges 14:1–3 . . . 256
**Social Media** . . . . Romans 6:16–18 . . . 1153
**Substance Abuse** . . . . Isaiah 5:11 . . . 683
**Temptation** . . . . James 1:13–15 . . . 1261

**Trial and Tribulations** .......... Genesis 39:19–23 .... 46
**Troubling Passages** .......... Ephesians 6:5 ... 1207
**Truth** .......... John 17:17 ... 1096
**War** .......... Exodus 15:3 .... 76
**Worldviews** .......... Deuteronomy 18:9 .... 196
**Worry** .......... Matthew 6:25–34 .... 968

## LIVE THE TRUTH ARTICLES

**Being a Good Friend** .......... Leviticus 19:18 .... 124
**Being a Student** .......... Romans 15:4 ... 1162
**Being Alone** .......... Luke 5:16 ... 1038
**Being Chaste** .......... 1 Thessalonians 4:4 ... 1221
**Being Compassionate** .......... 2 Kings 5:3 .... 369
**Being Content** .......... Mark 10:17–30 ... 1017
**Being Courageous** .......... Numbers 13:30 .... 150
**Being Engaged at Home** .......... Joshua 24:14–15 .... 239
**Being Frugal** .......... Luke 12:13–21 ... 1050
**Being Grateful** .......... Luke 17:11–19 ... 1055
**Being Humble** .......... John 13:2–5 ... 1091
**Being Joyful** .......... John 15:11 ... 1093
**Being Kind** .......... 2 Samuel 9:1–13 .... 313
**Being On Mission** .......... Mark 16:15 ... 1028
**Being Patient** .......... 2 Peter 3:8–9 ... 1275
**Being Pure** .......... 2 Timothy 2:22 ... 1235
**Caring for Others** .......... Zechariah 7:9–10 .... 940
**Celebrating God** .......... Ezra 3:10 .... 462
**Confessing Sin** .......... James 4:1–6 ... 1263
**Doing What Is Best** .......... Jonah 1:10–16 .... 910
**Doing What Is Right** .......... Daniel 11:1 .... 877
**Fasting** .......... Joel 2:12 .... 894
**Fellowshipping with Others** .......... Philippians 2:1–4 ... 1210
**Forgiving Others** .......... Matthew 18:21–35 .... 985
**Fulfilling Your Purpose** .......... Jeremiah 11:1–5 .... 758
**Growing and Maturing** .......... 1 Corinthians 3:11–15 ... 1169
**Growing in Faith** .......... Habakkuk 2:4 .... 926
**Having Character** .......... Proverbs 22:1 .... 646
**Having the Right Attitude** .......... Acts 5:1–11 ... 1110
**Helping Others** .......... Micah 6:8 .... 918
**Holding on to Hope** .......... Matthew 11:2–6 .... 974
**Honoring Parents** .......... Deuteronomy 5:16 .... 184
**Knowing Who You Are** .......... Psalm 100:1–3 .... 594
**Knowing Your Identity** .......... Mark 9:7 ... 1015
**Loving Others** .......... 1 John 5:2–3 ... 1281
**Maintaining Integrity** .......... Proverbs 11:1 .... 633
**Maintaining Self-Control** .......... 2 Peter 1:5–9 ... 1273
**Making Wise Decisions** .......... Proverbs 3:5–6 .... 627
**Managing Time Wisely** .......... Psalm 90:4–6 .... 589
**Meditating on God's Word** .......... Psalm 77:12 .... 579
**Persevering** .......... Mark 6:48–52 ... 1011
**Praying** .......... 1 Samuel 12:23 .... 284
**Respecting Others** .......... Luke 10:25–37 ... 1047
**Resting in God's Approval** .......... 2 Samuel 6:14 .... 310
**Seeking True Success** .......... Luke 19:1–10 ... 1057
**Serving Others** .......... Acts 20:18–21 ... 1134
**Serving Your Community** .......... Matthew 25:35–40 .... 995

**Setting Goals** ........ Mark 8:36 . . .1014
**Setting Priorities** ........ 1 Peter 4:7 . . .1270
**Submitting to Authority** ........ John 12:49 . . .1090
**Using Silence Wisely** ........ Ecclesiastes 3:6–7 . . . .660
**Using Your Talents** ........ 2 Corinthians 4:7 . . .1185
**Valuing Siblings** ........ Proverbs 17:17 . . .640
**Valuing Who You Are** ........ Job 31:15 . . . .520
**Valuing Your Words** ........ Proverbs 18:20 . . . .642
**Worshiping God** ........ Psalm 146:1–2 . . . .621

## CHARTS, ILLUSTRATIONS, AND MAPS

**Appearances of the Risen Christ, The** ........ 1100
**Book of Apocalypse, The** ........ 1145
**Books of History, The** ........ 215
**Books of Poetry and Wisdom, The** ........ 497
**Books of Prophecy, The** ........ 677
**Books of the Law, The** ........ 3
**Christ in the Jewish Feasts** ........ 122
**Christ in the Levitical Sacrifices** ........ 108
**Christ in the Psalms** ........ 533
**Common Views of the Book of Revelation** ........ 1298
**Covenants in the Bible** ........ 411
**Epistles, The** ........ 1145
**Events of Jesus' Final Week** ........ 1019
**Exile of the Northern Kingdom, The** ........ 384
**Exile of the Southern Kingdom, The** ........ 393
**Exodus, The** ........ 73
**Gospels and the Book of History, The** ........ 959
**Herod's Temple** ........ 992
**Jewish Sects, The** ........ 956
**Kings of Israel and Judah, The** ........ 432
**Paul's First Missionary Journey** ........ 1121
**Paul's Second Missionary Journey** ........ 1128
**Paul's Third Missionary Journey** ........ 1132
**Return from Exile, The** ........ 460
**Returns of the Exiles** ........ 459
**Seven Churches of Revelation, The** ........ 1292
**Seven "I Am" Statements in John, The** ........ 1082
**Seven Signs in John, The** ........ 1071
**Solomon's Temple and Temple Furnishings** ........ 340
**Tabernacle and Tabernacle Furnishings, The** ........ 88
**Ten Commandments Throughout Scripture, The** ........ 183
**Wilderness Wanderings, The** ........ 158
**Zerubbabel's Temple** ........ 464

# TOPICAL INDEX


**Abortion:** Exodus 21:22–25; Psalms 127:3–5; 139:13–16; Isaiah 46:3; 49:1; Jeremiah 1:5; Luke 1:41; Galatians 1:15

**Abuse of Authority:** Numbers 20:10–13; Psalms 9:9; 82:3; 1 Corinthians 9:18; 1 Peter 5:3

**Abuse, Physical:** Exodus 2:11–12; Judges 16:21; Psalms 9:9; 82:3; 1 Corinthians 6:19–20

**Abuse, Sexual:** Genesis 19:5–9, 31–38; Psalms 9:9; 82:3; 1 Corinthians 6:19–20

**Abuse, Substance:** Proverbs 20:1; 23:21, 29–35; 31:4–5; John 8:36; Romans 12:1; Philippians 4:13; 1 Corinthians 6:19–20; 10:13; Ephesians 5:18; 1 Peter 4:7 (*see also* Self-Care)

**Acceptance of God:** Genesis 4:7; John 6:37; Romans 15:7; 1 Thessalonians 2:4

**Acceptance of Others:** Matthew 7:1–5; Romans 15:7; Galatians 1:10; 1 Thessalonians 2:4

**Advice:** 1 Kings 12:6–11; Proverbs 11:14; 12:15; 19:20; 24:6

**Alcohol:** Ecclesiastes 9:7; Psalm 104:14–15; Proverbs 20:1; Isaiah 5:11, 22; Luke 21:34; Romans 13:11–14; Galatians 5:19–21; Ephesians 5:18; 1 Timothy 5:23; 1 Peter 4:3 (*see also* Abuse, Substance)

**Ambition, Improper:** Matthew 18:1–6; 20:20–28; Mark 12:38–40; Luke 9:25; 1 Corinthians 3:3–8; Philippians 1:14–17; 2:3

**Ambition, Proper:** Matthew 6:33; Romans 15:17–20; 1 Corinthians 12:31; 2 Corinthians 5:9–10; Philippians 3:12–14

**Anger:** Psalm 37:8; Proverbs 12:16; 14:17, 29; 15:1; 22:24–25; 29:22; Ecclesiastes 7:9; Matthew 5:22–24; Galatians 5:19–20; Ephesians 4:26–27, 31–32; Colossians 3:8; James 1:19–20 (*see also* Forgiving Others; Hatred)

**Anorexia:** *See* Self-Care

**Anxiety:** Psalm 94:18–19; Isaiah 45:5–7; Luke 12:26–29; Philippians 4:6

**Appearance, Physical:** 1 Samuel 16:7; Psalm 139:14; Proverbs 31:30; Matthew 6:25–33; 1 Timothy 2:9–10; 1 Peter 3:3–4

**Arrogance:** 1 Samuel 2:3; Proverbs 8:13; 27:2; Isaiah 13:11; Romans 12:3; James 4:16 (*see also* Pride; Vanity)

**Asking Questions:** Deuteronomy 4:29; Matthew 7:7; 1 Corinthians 13:12; 14:33

**Assurance of Salvation:** Psalm 37:23–24; Jeremiah 32:40–41; Luke 18:18–30; John 5:24; 10:27–30; Romans 8:33–39; 2 Timothy 1:12; 1 John 5:13

**Authority, Human:** Exodus 20:12; Proverbs 29:2; Acts 5:29; Romans 13:1–2; Titus 3:1; Hebrews 13:17; 1 Peter 2:13

**Baptism:** Matthew 28:19–20; Mark 16:15–16; Acts 2:38; Romans 6:3–4; Ephesians 4:5

**Blessings:** Leviticus 26:3–5; Numbers 6:24–26; Psalms 5:12; 24:3–6; James 1:17, 25

**Bullying:** Leviticus 19:18; Deuteronomy 31:6; Proverbs 21:23; Matthew 5:43–48; Luke 10:25–37; Romans 12:18–20; Ephesians 4:29; 2 Timothy 1:7

**Burdens:** Psalm 55:22; Matthew 11:28–29; Galatians 6:2; Philippians 4:6

**Career:** Genesis 2:15; Psalm 90:17; Proverbs 13:22; 16:3; 18:9; 22:29; Ecclesiastes 3:12–13; 1 Corinthians 10:31; Ephesians 4:28; Colossians 3:17, 23; James 1:5 (*see also* Work)

**Choices:** *See* Decisions

**Comfort:** *See* God's Comfort

**Compassion:** Exodus 34:6; Matthew 15:32; Mark 1:40–45; 6:30–44; Luke 8:40–56; 10:25–37; Ephesians 4:32; Colossians 3:12–14; 1 John 3:16–20

**Complaining:** Philippians 2:14; 1 Thessalonians 5:18; James 5:9; 1 Peter 4:9

**Confidence:** Psalm 20:7; Proverbs 3:26; Isaiah 32:15–17; Romans 8:38–39; 2 Corinthians 3:4–5; Hebrews 10:35; 13:6

**Contentment:** Proverbs 15:16; Luke 12:15; 2 Corinthians 12:10; Philippians 4:11–13; 1 Timothy 6:6–8; Hebrews 13:5

**Courage:** Deuteronomy 31:6; Joshua 1:9; 1 Samuel 17:34–37; Esther 4:15–16; Psalms 16:8; 27:1–14; 31:24; 46:1–3; Proverbs 3:24–26; 28:1; Isaiah 41:10; John 16:33; Romans 8:35–39; Ephesians 6:10; 2 Timothy 1:7; 1 John 4:18

**Creation Care:** Genesis 1:26–28; 2:15; Leviticus 25:23–24; Nehemiah 9:6; Psalms 24:1–2; 89:11; Isaiah 24:4–6; Luke 12:6; John 1:3; Romans 8:18–22; 1 Corinthians 4:2; Colossians 1:16–17; James 3:7

**Cutting:** *See* Self-Care

**Death, Fear of:** *See* Fear of Death

**Decisions:** Joshua 24:14–15; Nehemiah 1:4; Psalms 37:5; 119:105; Proverbs 3:5–6, 13–18; 16:1–3; 18:15; Jeremiah 33:3; John 15:16; Philippians 4:6–7; 2 Timothy 3:14; James 1:5; 4:17

**Depression:** Psalms 34:17–18; 42:5–11; 43:5; 143:7–8; Proverbs 12:25; Isaiah 40:31; 41:10; Jonah 2:2; Mark 10:27; John 10:10; Philippians 4:6–7; 2 Thessalonians 2:16–17; 1 Peter 5:6–7 (*see also* Self-Care)

**Disabilities:** Genesis 1:26–27; 2 Samuel 9:1–13; Isaiah 35:3–6; Matthew 20:29–34; John 5:1–18; 9:1–12; 1 Corinthians 15:51–53; 2 Corinthians 12:7–9; Philippians 3:20–21

**Discernment:** 1 Kings 3:9; Psalm 119:125; Hosea 14:9; John 7:24; Acts 17:11; Philippians 1:9–10; 1 Thessalonians 5:21–22; 2 Timothy 2:7; Hebrews 4:12; 5:14; James 1:5; 1 John 4:1, 6

**Discipline, Corrective:** Deuteronomy 8:5; Job 5:17; Psalm 94:12–13; Proverbs 6:23; 10:17; 12:1; 15:5; Hebrews 12:11; Revelation 3:19

**Discipline, Personal:** Proverbs 22:6; 25:28; 1 Corinthians 9:24–27; 1 Timothy 4:7–11; Titus 1:8; 1 Peter 5:8

**Discouragement:** Deuteronomy 31:8; Psalm 142:1–7; John 16:33; Romans 8:31; 15:13; 1 Corinthians 15:58; 2 Corinthians 12:9; Galatians 6:9; 1 Peter 5:10

**Discrimination:** Malachi 3:5; Acts 10:34; Galatians 3:26–28; 5:14; Colossians 3:25; James 2:1–9

**Diversity:** Psalm 117:1–2; Daniel 7:14; Matthew 28:19–20; Romans 12:4–8; 1 Corinthians 12:12–30; Revelation 7:9–10

**Divorce:** *See* Marriage and Divorce

**Doing the Right Thing:** Matthew 5:16; Romans 12:21; Galatians 6:9; Ephesians 2:10; 5:15–16; Colossians 3:23; Titus 2:11–12; 1 Peter 1:14–15; 1 John 3:7; 3 John v. 11

**Doubt:** Proverbs 3:5–8; Isaiah 41:10; Matthew 14:31; 21:21; Mark 9:24; Luke 24:36–43; John 20:24–29; Hebrews 11:1; James 1:6; Jude vv. 20–22 (*see also* Faith)

**Dreams:** Genesis 37:1–11; 40:8; Numbers 12:6; Ecclesiastes 5:7; Daniel 1:17; Joel 2:28; Matthew 2:13; 27:19; Acts 2:17; 1 John 4:1

**Drinking/Drunkenness:** *See* Abuse, Substance; Alcohol

**Drugs:** *See* Abuse, Substance; Self-Care

**Eating Disorders:** *See* Self-Care

**Education:** Deuteronomy 6:6–9; Psalm 32:8; Proverbs 1:1–7; 9:9; 18:15; 22:6; Daniel 1:17; John 14:26; Ephesians 4:14–15; 6:4; Colossians 3:16; 2 Timothy 3:16; Titus 2:1

**Encouragement:** Psalm 31:24; Proverbs 12:18; John 16:33; Acts 9:31; 11:23–24; Romans 8:28; 15:4; Ephesians 4:29; 1 Thessalonians 5:11; 2 Thessalonians 2:16–17; Hebrews 3:13; 10:24–25

**Enemies:** Exodus 14:14; Deuteronomy 31:6; Proverbs 16:7; 24:17; 25:21–22; Matthew 5:43–48; Luke 6:27–36; 23:34; Romans 12:14; James 4:4

**Entertainment:** Psalm 101:2–3; 1 Corinthians 10:31; Philippians 4:8; Colossians 3:17

**Environment, the:** *See* Creation Care

**Envy:** Job 5:2; Psalm 37:1–4; Proverbs 14:30; Romans 13:13; 1 Corinthians 13:4; Galatians 5:26; 1 Timothy 6:4; James 3:14–15; 1 Peter 2:1 (*see also* Contentment; Jealousy)

**Eternal Life:** Matthew 7:13–14; John 3:15–16; 5:28–29; 11:25; 14:6; 17:3; Romans 6:23; 8:38–39; Titus 3:7; 1 John 2:25

**Evil:** Psalms 5:4; 23:4; 34:14; Proverbs 6:16–19; 8:13; Isaiah 5:20; Matthew 6:13; Romans 12:9, 21; 1 Corinthians 4:5; Ephesians 6:12; 1 Thessalonians 5:22; 1 Peter 3:12; 3 John v. 11

**Fairness:** Leviticus 19:15; Psalms 98:8–9; 106:3; Proverbs 16:11; 31:9; Matthew 5:45; Romans 2:11; James 2:1–5

**Faith:** Genesis 15:6; Habakkuk 2:4; Matthew 17:20; 21:21; Mark 9:24; 11:23; Luke 17:6; Romans 10:17; 2 Corinthians 5:7; Galatians 2:20; Ephesians 2:8–9; Hebrews 11:1, 6; James 1:6; 2:17–18

**Family:** Genesis 1:28; 2:24; Exodus 20:12; Deuteronomy 6:6–7; Psalms 127:3–5; 128:3; Proverbs 1:8; 6:20; 11:29; 12:4; 22:6; Luke 12:51–53; Ephesians 5:22—6:9; Colossians 3:18—4:1; 1 Timothy 5:8 (*see also* Marriage and Divorce; Parents; Parents, Honoring)

**Fear:** Deuteronomy 31:6; Joshua 1:9; 2 Chronicles 20:15; Psalms 23:4; 27:1; 34:4; 46:1–3; 56:3, 11; 112:4–8; Proverbs 29:25; Isaiah 41:10; Jeremiah 46:27; Matthew 10:28; John 14:27; Romans 8:15; 2 Timothy 1:7; Hebrews 13:6; 1 John 4:18 (*see also* Courage)

**Fear of Death:** Psalms 23:4; 116:1–15; John 5:24; 11:25; 14:27; Romans 6:9; 8:38–39; 1 Corinthians 15:54; 2 Corinthians 5:6–8; Philippians 4:6–7; 1 Thessalonians 4:13–18; Hebrews 2:14–15; 1 John 4:18; Revelation 21:4

**Fear of the Lord:** Job 28:28; Psalms 25:12–15; 111:10; Proverbs 1:7; 19:23; Ecclesiastes 12:13; Luke 1:50

**Forgiveness, God's:** *See* God's Forgiveness
**Forgiving Others:** Genesis 50:15–23; Proverbs 10:12; 17:9; 19:11; Matthew 5:22–24, 44; 6:14–15; 18:21–35; Mark 11:25–26; Luke 6:37; Ephesians 4:32; Colossians 3:12–13
**Friendship:** Exodus 33:11; 1 Samuel 18:1–3; 19:1–7; Job 2:11–13; 6:14; Proverbs 12:26; 17:9, 17; 18:24; 27:6, 17; Ecclesiastes 4:9–12; John 15:13–15; 1 Corinthians 15:33
**Gender:** Genesis 1:27; Deuteronomy 22:5; Mark 10:6
**Generosity:** Deuteronomy 15:10–11; Proverbs 11:25; Matthew 6:1–4; Mark 12:41–44; Luke 6:38; Acts 2:44–47; 20:35; 2 Corinthians 9:6–8; 1 Timothy 6:17–19 (*see also* Giving)
**Gentleness:** 1 Kings 19:11–13; Proverbs 15:1; Zechariah 9:9; Matthew 11:29; Ephesians 4:1–2; Galatians 5:22–23; Philippians 4:5; Colossians 3:12; 1 Peter 3:15
**Getting High:** *See* Abuse, Substance
**Gifts and Talents:** Exodus 31:3–5; Proverbs 22:29; Daniel 1:17; Romans 12:3–8; 1 Corinthians 12:1–27; Ephesians 4:7–16; 1 Peter 4:10–11
**Giving:** Exodus 35:22; 2 Chronicles 31:4; Proverbs 3:9; Haggai 2:8; Malachi 3:10; Matthew 6:1–4; 23:23; Acts 2:44–47; 2 Corinthians 9:6–7 (*see also* Generosity)
**Glory:** *See* God's Glory
**God's Comfort:** 1 Kings 19:11–18; Psalms 23:4; 34:18; 147:3; Isaiah 49:13; Matthew 5:4; 11:28–30; John 16:22; 2 Corinthians 1:3–5; 2 Thessalonians 2:16–17; Revelation 21:4
**God's Faithfulness:** Numbers 23:19; Deuteronomy 7:9; Psalms 36:5; 89:1; 119:90; Lamentations 3:22–23; 2 Thessalonians 3:3; Hebrews 10:23; 1 John 1:9
**God's Forgiveness:** Psalms 32:5; 86:5–7; Nehemiah 9:17; Isaiah 1:18; Ezekiel 37:23; Luke 23:26–43; Acts 13:38–39; Ephesians 1:6–7; Colossians 1:13–14; 3:12–13; Hebrews 8:12; 1 John 1:9
**God's Glory:** Exodus 40:34–35; Psalm 19:1–3; Isaiah 6:3; Ezekiel 43:2; Habakkuk 2:14; John 1:14; 11:40; Romans 1:20; 2 Corinthians 3:18; Hebrews 1:3; Revelation 21:23
**God's Grace:** Genesis 6:8; Exodus 34:6; Psalm 84:11; John 1:17; Acts 15:11; Romans 3:23–24; 5:1–2; 2 Corinthians 12:9; Ephesians 2:8–9; 2 Timothy 1:9; Titus 2:11–12; Hebrews 4:16
**God's Guidance:** Exodus 15:13; Psalms 18:28; 23:3; 25:4–5, 9; 32:8; 48:14; 119:105; 139:9–10; Proverbs 3:5–6; 16:9; Luke 1:79; John 16:13; Romans 8:14
**God's Judgment:** Psalm 9:7–8; Ecclesiastes 12:14; Ezekiel 7:3–4; Obadiah v. 15; Malachi 3:5; Matthew 12:36–37; 2 Corinthians 5:10; Hebrews 9:27; Revelation 20:11–15
**God's Justice:** Deuteronomy 32:4; Psalm 33:5; Isaiah 30:18
**God's Love:** Psalms 86:15; 136:26; Jeremiah 31:3; Zephaniah 3:17; John 3:16–17; Romans 5:8; 8:35–39; Galatians 2:20; Ephesians 2:4–5; 3:19; 5:1–2; 1 John 3:1; 4:7–12, 16, 19
**God's Mercy:** 1 Kings 8:23; Psalms 13:5–6; 103:8; 106:1; 107:1; 145:8; Isaiah 54:10; Lamentations 3:22–23; Luke 6:36; Ephesians 2:4–5; Hebrews 4:16
**God's Power:** Exodus 14:14; 1 Chronicles 29:11; Jeremiah 10:12; Matthew 19:26; Romans 1:16, 20; 1 Corinthians 6:14; Ephesians 3:20; 6:10; Colossians 1:16
**God's Presence:** Exodus 33:14; Psalms 16:11; 73:23–24; 139:7–9; 145:18; Matthew 28:18–20; Acts 3:20–21; Revelation 21:3–4
**God's Promises:** Deuteronomy 15:6; 2 Corinthians 1:20; 1 Thessalonians 5:24; Hebrews 6:13–15; 10:23, 36; 2 Peter 3:9
**God's Protection:** Genesis 15:1; Deuteronomy 31:6; Psalms 3:3; 4:8; 5:11–12; 28:7; 46:1; 118:6–9; Proverbs 1:33; 2:8; 18:10; Isaiah 41:10; 54:17; Nahum 1:7; Romans 8:31; Ephesians 6:10–18; 2 Thessalonians 3:3; Hebrews 13:6; 1 John 5:18
**God's Provision:** Genesis 9:3; Psalms 23:1–6; 65:9; 68:10; 145:15–17; Malachi 3:10; Matthew 6:8, 25–26, 31–33; 7:7, 11; Romans 8:32; 2 Corinthians 9:8; Philippians 4:19; 1 Timothy 6:17; James 1:17
**Gossip:** Exodus 23:1; Leviticus 19:16; Proverbs 4:24; 11:13; 16:28; 18:8; 20:19; 26:20, 22; Romans 1:29; 2 Corinthians 12:20; Ephesians 4:29; 1 Timothy 5:13; James 1:26
**Grace:** *See* God's Grace
**Greed:** Psalm 10:3; Proverbs 1:18–19; 28:25; 1 Corinthians 6:9–11; Ephesians 4:19 (*see also* Contentment; Generosity; Selfishness)
**Grief:** Job 2:13; Psalms 30:11; 34:18; 73:26; 147:3; Isaiah 40:1–31; Jeremiah 33:6; Lamentations 3:32; Matthew 5:4; 26:38; John 11:17–44; 16:22, 33; 2 Corinthians 1:3–11; 1 Thessalonians 4:14–18; Revelation 21:3–4
**Guidance:** *See* God's Guidance
**Guilt:** Psalms 19:12–13; 38:1–16; 51:1–10; Romans 8:1; Ephesians 2:8; 1 John 1:9 (*see also* God's Forgiveness)

**Happiness:** 1 Samuel 2:1; Psalms 16:11; 32:11; 37:4; 100:2; 118:24; Proverbs 15:30; 17:22; Ecclesiastes 3:12–13; Isaiah 12:3; 51:11; Habakkuk 3:18; Romans 15:13; Galatians 5:22; Philippians 4:4; 1 Thessalonians 2:19 (*see also* Joy)

**Hatred:** Leviticus 19:17; Proverbs 10:12, 18; 26:24–26; Matthew 5:43–45; Romans 12:9; Ephesians 4:31; 1 John 2:9–11; 4:20 (*see also* Anger)

**Heaven:** 1 Kings 8:30; 2 Kings 2:11; Isaiah 25:8; 66:1; Matthew 3:16–17; 6:19–21; Luke 24:51; John 14:1–3; 2 Corinthians 5:1; Philippians 3:20; Colossians 1:5; Hebrews 11:16; 2 Peter 3:13; Revelation 7:15–17; 21:4; 22:1–5

**Hell:** Psalms 9:17; 86:13; Daniel 12:2; Matthew 8:12; 10:28; 13:50; 25:46; Luke 16:19–31; 2 Thessalonians 1:9; Hebrews 9:27; 2 Peter 2:4; Revelation 20:10–15; 21:8

**Helping Others:** Proverbs 3:27; 21:13; Micah 6:8; Matthew 5:42; 25:37–40; Galatians 6:2; Philippians 2:4; Hebrews 13:16; 1 John 3:17

**Homosexuality:** Genesis 19:1–29; Leviticus 18:22; 20:13; Judges 19:22; Romans 1:26–27; 1 Corinthians 6:9–11; 1 Timothy 1:9–10; Jude v. 7 (*see also* Gender)

**Honesty:** Exodus 20:16; Leviticus 19:35–36; Psalm 34:13; Proverbs 11:3; 12:17, 22; Ezekiel 45:10–11; Ephesians 4:15, 25 (*see also* Integrity; Truth)

**Hope:** 2 Samuel 22:7; Psalms 9:18; 33:18, 22; 43:5; Proverbs 24:14; Isaiah 40:31; Lamentations 3:21–22; Romans 8:24–25, 28; 15:13; 2 Thessalonians 2:16–17; Titus 1:1–2; Hebrews 11:1; 1 Peter 1:3

**Humility:** Proverbs 11:2; 18:12; 22:4; Micah 6:8; Zephaniah 2:3; Matthew 16:24; 18:4; Luke 14:11; Romans 12:3, 16; Philippians 2:1–11; Colossians 3:12; James 4:8–10

**Hurt:** *See* Pain and Suffering

**Hypocrisy:** Proverbs 11:9; Isaiah 29:13; 58:3–7; Jeremiah 7:8–11; Matthew 7:1–5; Luke 6:46; Romans 2:3; Titus 1:16; James 1:26; 1 John 4:20 (*see also* Integrity)

**Identity:** Genesis 1:27; Psalm 139:13–15; Luke 12:6–7; John 15:15; Acts 17:28; Romans 8:15; 14:8; 1 Corinthians 12:27; 2 Corinthians 5:17; Galatians 2:20; 3:28; Ephesians 2:10; 1 Peter 2:9; 1 John 3:1

**Idolatry:** Exodus 20:3–6; Leviticus 19:4; Deuteronomy 4:23–24; Psalm 106:19–21, 36–43; Isaiah 31:6–7; 44:9–20; Jeremiah 10:2–8; 1 Corinthians 10:14; Galatians 4:8; Colossians 3:5; 1 John 5:21

**Integrity:** 2 Chronicles 26:4; Job 1:1; Psalms 25:21; 78:70–72; Proverbs 10:9; 11:3; 19:1; 28:6; Daniel 6:4–5; 2 Corinthians 8:21; Colossians 3:23; 1 Peter 3:16 (*see also* Honesty; Truth)

**Intimidation:** Deuteronomy 31:6; Psalm 91:14; Isaiah 41:10; Romans 8:31; Philippians 4:13; 1 Timothy 4:12; 2 Timothy 1:7

**Jealousy:** Genesis 37:1–36; Proverbs 14:30; 23:17; 24:1; 1 Corinthians 13:4; Galatians 5:26; 1 Peter 2:1; James 3:16 (*see also* Contentment; Envy)

**Joy:** Ezra 3:10–13; Nehemiah 8:10; Psalms 16:11; 118:24; Proverbs 15:30; Isaiah 51:11; 62:5; Habakkuk 3:18; Zephaniah 3:17; John 16:24; Romans 12:12; 15:13; Galatians 5:22; Philippians 4:4; 1 Thessalonians 2:19; James 1:2 (*see also* Happiness)

**Judging Others:** Numbers 12:1–3; 2 Chronicles 19:7; Proverbs 31:9; Matthew 7:1–5; Luke 6:37; John 7:24; Romans 14:13; James 4:11–12

**Judgment:** *See* God's Judgment

**Justice:** *See* God's Justice; Social Justice

**Kindness:** Ruth 3:10; 2 Samuel 9:1–13; 2 Kings 4:1–7; Proverbs 11:17; Zechariah 7:9–10; 1 Corinthians 13:4; Galatians 6:10; Ephesians 4:32; Colossians 3:12

**Knowing God:** Exodus 3:1–22; Proverbs 8:17; Jeremiah 9:23–24; John 14:6; 17:3; Philippians 3:10; James 4:8; 1 John 1:5–6; 4:12

**Knowing God's Will:** Psalm 119:10, 105; Proverbs 3:5–6; 8:17; 19:21; Micah 6:8; Matthew 6:33; Romans 12:2; 1 Timothy 2:3–4; 1 Thessalonians 4:3–5; 5:18; 1 Peter 2:15

**Laziness:** Genesis 2:15; Proverbs 6:6–11; 10:4; 12:24; 13:4; 18:9; 19:15; Ecclesiastes 9:10; Colossians 3:23; 2 Thessalonians 3:10–12 (*see also* Work)

**Leadership:** Exodus 18:21; 2 Samuel 8:15; 2 Kings 15:2–5; 23:3; 2 Chronicles 19:5–7; Esther 10:3; Proverbs 11:14; Matthew 20:26–28; John 13:12–15; Philippians 2:3; 1 Timothy 3:1–7; 4:12; Titus 1:7–9

**Learning:** *See* Education

**Listening:** Psalm 46:10; Proverbs 1:33; 18:13; 25:12; James 1:19, 22

**Loneliness:** Deuteronomy 31:6; Psalms 25:16; 38:9–15; 68:6; 145:18; Isaiah 41:10; Ecclesiastes 4:10–11; Haggai 1:13; Matthew 28:20; John 14:18; Hebrews 13:5; James 4:8 (*see also* God's Presence)

**Love:** Romans 12:9; 1 Corinthians 13:4–8, 13; Colossians 3:14; 1 Peter 4:8; 1 John 4:18 (*see also* God's Love)

**Loving God:** Deuteronomy 6:5; Psalm 18:1–3; Ecclesiastes 12:1; Jeremiah 9:23–24; Matthew 22:37; John 21:15–19; 1 John 4:20–21

**Loving Others:** Leviticus 19:18; Proverbs 10:12; Matthew 5:43–44; Luke 10:25–37; John 13:34–35; 15:13; Acts 9:20–31; 11; 1 Corinthians 16:14; Ephesians 5:1–2; 29–30; James 2:8; 1 Peter 4:8; 1 John 4:7–12, 19–21

**Lust:** 2 Samuel 11:1–4; Job 31:1; Proverbs 6:25; 11:6; Matthew 5:28; Romans 6:12; 13:13; Galatians 5:16–22; 1 Thessalonians 4:3–5; 2. Timothy 2:22; James 1:14–15; 1 Peter 2:11; 1 John 2:16 (*see also* Purity, Sexual; Self-Control)

**Lying:** Genesis 3:1–5; Exodus 20:16; 23:1; Leviticus 19:16; Proverbs 4:24; 6:16–19; 12:19, 22; 17:4; Luke 8:17; John 8:44; Ephesians 4:25; Colossians 3:9 (*see also* Honesty)

**Marriage and Divorce:** Genesis 2:18–24; Deuteronomy 24:5; Proverbs 19:4; 21:9; 31:10; Song of Solomon 8:6–7; Malachi 2:16; Matthew 5:32; 19:2–9; Luke 16:18; 1 Corinthians 7:10–11, 15; Ephesians 5:22–33; Colossians 3:18–19; Hebrews 13:4; 1 Peter 3:1–7

**Materialism:** *See* Greed

**Maturity:** Proverbs 9:9; Luke 2:41–52; 1 Corinthians 13:11; 14:20; Ephesians 4:13–15; Colossians 1:10; 4:12; Hebrews 5:12–14; James 1:4; 1 Peter 2:2; 2 Peter 3:18

**Mercy:** 1 Samuel 24:1–15; Proverbs 3:3–4; 11:17; 14:31; Micah 6:8; Matthew 5:7; 9:13; Luke 6:36–37 (*see also* God's Mercy)

**Money:** Proverbs 3:9; 13:11; 22:1; Ecclesiastes 5:10, 19; Matthew 6:19–21, 24; Mark 10:17–24; Luke 16:13; Acts 2:42–45; 1 Timothy 6:9–10, 17–19; Hebrews 13:5

**Murder:** Genesis 9:6; Exodus 20:13; Deuteronomy 5:17; Proverbs 6:16–17; Matthew 5:21–22; 1 John 3:12, 15

**Obedience:** Exodus 20:1–17; Deuteronomy 26:18; 1 Samuel 15:22–23; Psalm 119:101; Proverbs 13:13; 29:18; Jeremiah 11:7; 42:6; Ezekiel 36:26–27; Matthew 28:19–20; Luke 11:28; John 8:31–32; 14:15, 21; Ephesians 6:1–4; Colossians 3:20; Hebrews 13:17; 1 John 5:2–3

**Occult, the:** Exodus 22:18; Leviticus 19:26, 31; 20:27; Numbers 23:23; Isaiah 8:19; Acts 8:9–24; 19:19

**Pain and Suffering:** Psalms 12:5; 34:18; Isaiah 33:2; 40:9–11; Jeremiah 15:18; Romans 5:3–5; 8:18; 2 Timothy 4:7–8; Hebrews 12:3; James 1:2–3; 1 Peter 4:12–19; 5:10; Revelation 7:17

**Parents:** Deuteronomy 6:1–9; 1 Chronicles 28:8; Psalm 127:3; Proverbs 22:6; 23:13; Ephesians 6:4; Colossians 3:20–21 (*see also* Family)

**Parents, Honoring:** Exodus 20:12; Deuteronomy 5:16; Proverbs 1:8–9; 3:1–2; 6:20; 23:22; Ephesians 6:1–3; Colossians 3:20

**Partying:** Ecclesiastes 10:17; Daniel 5:1–30; Matthew 14:1–12; Luke 15:22–32; John 2:7–11; Romans 13:13–14

**Patience:** Psalms 27:14; 37:5–9; 40:1; Proverbs 14:29; 16:32; Luke 2:25–38; Romans 8:25; 12:12; Galatians 5:22; 6:9; Ephesians 4:2; 1 Thessalonians 5:14; 2 Thessalonians 3:5; 1 Timothy 6:11; James 1:4; 5:7–8

**Peace:** Numbers 6:24–26; Psalms 4:8; 29:11; Isaiah 26:3; Luke 2:14; John 14:27; 16:33; Romans 5:1; 12:17–18; Galatians 5:22; Philippians 4:6–7; Colossians 3:15; 2 Thessalonians 3:16

**Peer Pressure:** Exodus 23:2; Psalm 1:1–2; Proverbs 1:10; 4:14–15; 13:20; Isaiah 51:7–8; Romans 12:2; 1 Corinthians 10:13; 15:33; Galatians 1:10; Colossians 3:23–24; James 1:12–15

**Perseverance:** 1 Samuel 1:1–28; 1 Chronicles 16:11; Mark 13:13; Luke 18:1–8; Romans 5:3–4; 8:25; 2 Corinthians 4:16–18; Galatians 6:9–10; 1 Timothy 4:15–16; Hebrews 6:11–12; 12:1; James 1:2–4, 12; 5:11

**Pornography:** *See* Lust; Purity

**Power:** *See* God's Power; Strength

**Prayer:** Nehemiah 2:3–5; Psalms 17:6; 145:18; Proverbs 15:29; Jeremiah 29:7; 33:3; Matthew 5:44; 6:6, 9–13; Mark 11:24–25; Luke 6:12; 11:9; John 16:23–24; 17:1–26; Romans 8:26; 2 Corinthians 12:7–10; Ephesians 6:18; Philippians 4:6–7; Colossians 4:2; 1 Thessalonians 5:16–18; James 4:3; 5:16; 1 Peter 3:12

**Pride:** 2 Chronicles 26:16–23; 32:25; Psalm 59:12; Proverbs 8:13; 11:2; 13:10; 16:18; 21:4; 29:23; Isaiah 13:11; Jeremiah 50:32; Obadiah vv. 3–4; Luke 18:14; Romans 12:16; Philippians 2:3; James 4:6; 1 John 2:16 (*see also* Arrogance; Vanity)

**Procrastination:** Psalm 119:60; Proverbs 13:4; 18:9; 27:1; Ecclesiastes 9:10; Luke 9:59–62; 12:40; John 9:4; Galatians 6:9; Ephesians 5:15–17

**Promises, Keeping:** Numbers 30:2; Psalm 89:34; Ecclesiastes 5:4–5 (*see also* God's Promises)

**Protection:** *See* God's Protection

**Provision:** *See* God's Provision

**Purity, Sexual:** Psalms 101:2–4; 119:1–20; Proverbs 6:32; Matthew 5:28; Romans 6:11–14; 13:14; 1 Corinthians 6:13, 18–19; 10:13; Colossians 3:5; 1 Thessalonians 4:1–8; 1 Timothy 4:12; 5:22; 2 Timothy 2:22; Titus 1:15–16; Hebrews 13:4

**Purpose:** Genesis 1:27–28; Esther 4:14; Proverbs 16:3; Ecclesiastes 3:9–15; 12:13; Isaiah 43:7; Micah 6:8; Mark 16:14–18; Romans 8:28; 1 Corinthians 10:31; 12:12–27; Ephesians 2:10; 1 Peter 2:9

**Questions:** *See* Asking Questions

**Rebellion:** Nehemiah 9:17; Job 34:37; Psalm 68:6; Proverbs 17:11; Isaiah 1:20; 65:2; John 14:15; Acts 5:29; Romans 13:1–2; Ephesians 6:1–3

**Recycling:** *See* Creation Care

**Regret:** Ecclesiastes 7:10; Romans 8:28; 2 Corinthians 7:10; Philippians 3:13

**Relationships:** Genesis 2:18; Proverbs 17:17; 27:17; Ecclesiastes 4:9–12; John 13:34; 15:13; 1 Corinthians 1:10; 2 Corinthians 6:14; 1 Thessalonians 5:11; 1 Peter 1:22; 4:8 (*see also* Friendship; Marriage and Divorce)

**Repentance:** Psalm 51:1–7; Proverbs 28:13; Ezekiel 18:32; Joel 2:13; Zechariah 1:3; Matthew 3:8; 4:17; Luke 5:32; 13:3–5; 15:7; Acts 3:19; 17:30; Romans 2:4; 2 Corinthians 7:10; 2 Peter 3:9

**Reputation:** Proverbs 10:7; 20:11; 22:1; Ecclesiastes 7:1; Matthew 5:16; Philippians 1:27; 4:5; 1 Peter 2:12

**Respect:** Exodus 3:5; 20:12; Leviticus 19:3, 32; Proverbs 31:28; Matthew 7:12; Romans 12:10; 13:1–7; 1 Thessalonians 5:12–13; 1 Peter 2:17

**Responsibility:** Proverbs 6:6–8; Ezekiel 18:20; Matthew 5:33–37; 25:14–29; Luke 16:10; Romans 14:12; Galatians 6:5; 1 Timothy 5:8

**Rest:** Genesis 2:2–3; Exodus 20:8–11; Psalms 3:5; 4:8; 23:1–2; 127:2; Matthew 11:28–30; Mark 6:31; Hebrews 4:9–11 (*see also* Work)

**Revenge:** Leviticus 19:18; Deuteronomy 32:35; 1 Samuel 24:12; Proverbs 20:22; 24:29; Matthew 5:38–39; Romans 12:17–21; Colossians 3:25; 1 Thessalonians 5:15; 1 Peter 3:9 (*see also* Forgiving Others)

**Sadness:** Psalms 30:11–12; 34:17–18; 42:5–6; 147:3; Proverbs 14:13; Ecclesiastes 3:4; Matthew 5:4; 26:37–38; John 11:35; 16:20; Romans 12:15; Philippians 4:7; James 5:13; Revelation 21:3–4

**Salvation:** 2 Samuel 22:2, 47–48; Psalms 3:8; 27:1; Joel 2:32; John 3:16–18; 14:6; Acts 2:37–38; 4:12; Romans 1:16; 10:8–10; Ephesians 2:8–9; 1 Thessalonians 5:9; 1 Timothy 2:3–4; Titus 3:5; 1 Peter 1:18–19

**Second Coming of Jesus:** Matthew 16:27; 24:20–31, 36–44; John 14:1–3; Acts 1:10–11; Colossians 3:4; 1 Thessalonians 4:16–17; 5:2; Hebrews 9:28; 10:24–25; 2 Peter 3:10; Revelation 1:7; 22:12, 20

**Self-Control:** 1 Samuel 24:1–22; 26:1–25; Proverbs 25:28; 29:11; Daniel 1:8–16; 1 Corinthians 9:24–27; Galatians 5:22–25; Titus 1:8; 2:11–12; 2 Peter 1:5–7; James 1:19, 26

**Self-Care:** Psalms 8:5; 139:13–14; Proverbs 25:16; Luke 12:6–7; Romans 12:2; 1 Corinthians 3:16–17; 6:19–20; 12:27; Ephesians 2:10; Philippians 4:8–9; 13; James 5:13–16; 3 John v. 2

**Self-Esteem:** *See* Identity

**Self-Harm:** *See* Self-Care

**Selfishness:** Psalm 119:36; Ezekiel 33:31; Haggai 1:9; Luke 14:7–14; Romans 2:8; 1 Corinthians 10:24; 2 Corinthians 12:20–21; Galatians 5:19–20; Philippians 2:4; Titus 2:12; James 3:16; 4:1–3; 1 John 3:17 (*see also* Greed)

**Serving God:** Deuteronomy 13:4; 1 Samuel 12:24; Psalm 100:2; Malachi 3:18; Matthew 6:24; Mark 10:45; Luke 4:8; Romans 12:1; 1 Corinthians 15:58; Colossians 3:23–24

**Sex:** Genesis 1:28; 2:24–25; 9:1; Proverbs 5:15–19; Song of Solomon 1:2; 7:6–13; 8:4; Mark 10:6–9; 1 Corinthians 7:3–5; Hebrews 13:4 (*see also* Purity, Sexual)

**Shame:** Genesis 3:10; Psalms 25:1–22; 34:4–5; 44:15; 71:1; Proverbs 3:35; 11:2; Isaiah 50:7; 54:4; Mark 8:38; Romans 1:16; 10:11; 1 John 2:28 (*see also* Acceptance of God)

**Sickness:** Psalms 41:3; 147:3; Proverbs 17:22; Jeremiah 17:14; Matthew 9:35; 10:27; Acts 10:38; James 5:14–16; 3 John v. 2; Revelation 21:4

**Sin:** Genesis 4:7; 1 Kings 8:46; 2 Chronicles 6:24–25; Psalm 51:5; Proverbs 28:13; Ezra 9:6; Isaiah 53:6; Jeremiah 16:17; Matthew 5:48; Mark 7:20–23; Romans 3:9–18, 23; 6:23; James 1:15; 4:17; 1 John 1:8–10 (*see also* God's Forgiveness)

**Social Justice:** Leviticus 19:15; 24:22; Numbers 15:15–16; Deuteronomy 1:16–18; Psalm 33:5; Proverbs 6:16–19; Isaiah 1:17; Amos 5:24; Micah 6:8; Habakkuk 1:4; Zechariah 7:9–10; Malachi 2:17; James 1:27; 2:1–9

**Strength:** Exodus 15:2; Deuteronomy 31:6; Joshua 1:9; 1 Chronicles 16:11; Job 17:9; Psalms 18:32; 27:14; 31:24; 46:1; 68:35; 73:26; Isaiah 12:2; 30:15; 40:29–31; 41:10; 2 Corinthians 12:9–10; Ephesians 6:10; Philippians 4:13; Jude v. 24

**Stress:** *See* Anxiety

**Success:** Genesis 39:2; Deuteronomy 8:10–18; Joshua 1:8; 1 Chronicles 22:11–13; 2 Chronicles 12:1; Psalms 20:4; 37:4; Proverbs 3:1–4; 16:3; Ecclesiastes 10:10; Matthew 16:26; Luke 16:10–11; Philippians 4:13

**Suffering:** *See* Pain and Suffering

**Suicide:** *See* Identity; Self-Care

**Swearing:** *See* Words, Profane

**Talents:** *See* Gifts and Talents

**Temptation:** Proverbs 2:10–14; 7:1–5; Matthew 4:1–11; 6:13; Mark 14:38; 1 Corinthians 10:13; Ephesians 4:27; 6:11; 2 Timothy 2:22; Hebrews 2:18; 4:15–16; James 1:12–16; 4:7

**Thankfulness:** 1 Chronicles 16:34; Ezra 3:10–13; Psalms 100:4; 107:1–3; 136:1–26; 138:1–8; Luke 17:11–19; Ephesians 5:19–20; Philippians 4:6; Colossians 3:17; 4:2; 1 Thessalonians 5:18

**Thoughts:** Psalm 19:14; Proverbs 4:23; 16:3; Isaiah 55:8–9; Romans 8:5–6; 12:2; 2 Corinthians 10:5; Ephesians 4:22–24; Philippians 4:8; Colossians 3:2; Hebrews 4:12

**Tithing:** *See* Giving

**Trials:** Job 14:1; Nahum 1:7; John 16:33; Romans 5:3–5; 8:28, 35–39; 12:12; 2 Corinthians 4:16–18; Philippians 4:6–7; James 1:2–4, 12; 1 Peter 1:6; 4:12–13; 5:10

**Trust:** Deuteronomy 9:23; 2 Samuel 22:31; Psalms 37:3, 5; 56:3, 11; 62:8; Proverbs 3:5–6; 28:25–26; 29:25; Isaiah 26:4; Jeremiah 17:7; 1 Timothy 4:10; Hebrews 10:23 (*see also* Faith)

**Truth:** 1 Samuel 12:24; Psalms 25:5; 86:11; 119:160; 145:18; John 1:14; 4:24; 8:31–32; 14:6; 17:17; Ephesians 4:15; 6:14; 1 John 3:18 (*see also* Honesty)

**Vanity:** 1 Samuel 16:7; Proverbs 31:30 (*see also* Arrogance; Pride)

**Wisdom:** 1 Kings 3:9; Job 28:28; Psalm 111:10; Proverbs 1:5, 7; 4:5–7; 8:12–14; 9:9–11; 10:1; 19:20; 24:3–5; Ecclesiastes 2:26; Hosea 14:9; 1 Corinthians 1:20–25; 2:1–16; Ephesians 1:17; 5:15–16; Colossians 1:9–10; 1 Timothy 1:17; James 1:5; 3:17

**Witnessing:** 1 Chronicles 16:24; Matthew 5:16; 28:16–20; Acts 1:8; 18:9–10; Romans 1:16; 10:14–15; 1 Corinthians 9:22; 2 Corinthians 5:18–21; Colossians 4:6; 1 Peter 3:15

**Words:** Psalms 12:6; 19:14; 119:11; Proverbs 10:19; 13:3; 15:1; 16:24; 25:11; Matthew 12:36–37; Ephesians 4:29; Colossians 4:6; James 1:19

**Words, Profane:** Exodus 20:7; Psalm 34:13; Matthew 12:36; Ephesians 5:4; Colossians 3:8; James 3:10

**Work:** Genesis 2:15; Psalm 104:23; Proverbs 22:29; Ecclesiastes 5:19; 9:10; 1 Corinthians 10:31; Ephesians 4:28; 6:5–9; Colossians 3:23; 1 Thessalonians 4:11; 2 Thessalonians 3:10–12 (*see also* Career; Rest)

**Works, Good:** Proverbs 16:3; Matthew 5:16; Romans 12:21; 1 Corinthians 15:58; Galatians 6:9; Ephesians 2:4–10; Philippians 2:13; James 2:14–17, 26; 3 John v. 11

**Worry:** *See* Anxiety

**Worship:** Exodus 34:14; 2 Samuel 22:4; 1 Chronicles 16:29, 34; 2 Chronicles 7:1–22; Ezra 3:11; Psalms 5:7; 29:1–2; 67:3; 95:1–6; 100:1–5; 106:1; 145:2–3; 149:5; 150:6; Isaiah 12:5; 25:1; 66:2; John 4:23–24; Romans 12:1–2; Ephesians 5:19; Philippians 2:9–11; Colossians 3:16; Hebrews 13:15; 1 Peter 2:9; Revelation 4:11; 5:13–14; 15:4

**Worship, False:** *See* Idolatry

**Youth:** Exodus 20:12; Deuteronomy 6:7; 1 Samuel 3:1–21; Psalms 119:9; 127:3–5; Proverbs 1:8–9; 17:6; 20:11; 22:6; 29:17; Ecclesiastes 11:9; Matthew 18:10; 19:13–15; 21:15–16; Luke 2:41–52; Ephesians 6:1–4; Colossians 3:20; 1 Timothy 4:12; 2 Timothy 2:22

# DICTIONARY-CONCORDANCE

This dictionary-concordance defines about 700 words, phrases, people, and places in the Bible and identifies about 1,250 verses where they are mentioned. Help pronouncing each word and name is also provided.

Words and phrases are followed by a definition and then the concordance listing. In the concordance listing, only the first letter of the word is used, and it is bolded and italicized, such as ***l*** for *love*. The references give you the name of the Bible book, chapter, and verse or verses. Luke 24:30ff, for example, would be Luke chapter 24 verse 30 and the verses that follow. You can find the abbreviations for each Bible book in the front of this Bible.

People, places, and names and titles that help identify God are followed by information and facts with Bible references for each in parenthesis.

## A

**Aaron** [EH·ruhn] *person* older brother of Moses (Ex. 6:20; 7:7); spokesman for Moses (Ex. 7:1); brings on plagues with his rod (Ex. 7:10—8:17); the class of priests in Israel descend from him (Ex. 29:9); makes atonement and stops a plague (Num. 16:41–50); his rod buds (Num. 17:1–11).

**Abba** [AB·uh] *identity* Aramaic for "father" used to describe God; Aramaic was a common language spoken late in Old Testament times into New Testament times (Mark 14:36; Rom. 8:15; Gal. 4:6).

**Abed-Nego** [uh·BEHD·nee·go] *person* Babylonian name given to Azariah, one of Daniel's companions (Dan. 1:7); refuses to eat unclean foods (Dan. 1:3ff); saved in fiery furnace (Dan. 3:8ff).

**Abel** [AY·buhl] *person* son of Adam and Eve, murdered by his brother Cain (Gen. 4:2–12); described as righteous (Matt. 23:35; 1 John 3:12); first one mentioned in heroes of faith (Heb. 11:4).

**abhor** [uhb·HOR] *verb* to hate or despise.

I hate and ***a*** lying . . . . . . . . . . . . Ps. 119:163
Nations will ***a*** him . . . . . . . . . . . Prov. 24:24
***A*** what is evil . . . . . . . . . . . . . . Rom. 12:9

**abide** [uh·BIDE] *verb* to live in, accept, or tolerate.

He shall ***a*** before God . . . . . . . . . . Ps. 61:7
***A*** in Me, and I in you. . . . . . . . . . John 15:4
does the love of God ***a*** . . . . . . . . 1 John 3:17

**abomination** [uh·baa·muh·NAY·shun] *noun* something that is not acceptable or agreeable at all; something disgusting and loathsome.

an ***a*** to the LORD . . . . . . . . . . . . Deut. 27:15
Wickedness is an ***a*** . . . . . . . . . . . Prov. 8:7
is an ***a*** in the sight of God . . . . . . Luke 16:15

**Abram**; **Abraham** [AY·bruhm; AY·bruh·ham] *person* chosen by God to begin His new people from which Jesus would come (Gen. 12:1–3); God makes a covenant with him (Gen. 15:7–21); name changes to Abraham (Gen. 17:5); father of Isaac (Gen. 21:1–7); God tests his faith (Gen. 22:1–19); stands as the father of all the faithful (Gal. 3:7).

**Absalom** [AB·suh·luhm] *person* third son of David (2 Sam. 3:3); turns the people against his father but is defeated and killed by Joab, causing David much sadness and grief (2 Sam. 13:20—19:10).

**abstain** [uhb·STAYN] *verb* to choose not to do something; not to participate in something.

we write to them to ***a***. . . . . . . . . . Acts 15:20
***A*** from every form . . . . . . . . . 1 Thess. 5:22
and commanding to ***a*** . . . . . . . . . 1 Tim. 4:3

**accursed** [uh·KURST] *adjective* being under a curse or judgment.

he who is hanged is ***a*** . . . . . . . . Deut. 21:23
regarding the ***a*** things . . . . . . . . . . Josh. 7:1
let him be ***a***. . . . . . . . . . . . . . . . . Gal. 1:8

**Adam** [AH·duhm] *person* the first man, made perfect and in the image of God (Gen. 1:26–27); all people descend from Eve and him (Gen. 1:26–28; 2:21–24); along with Eve, commits the first sin (Gen. 3:1–8); judged for sin (Gen. 3:9–19).

**admonish** [ad·MAA·nish] *verb* to remind others of their responsibilities; to encourage and advise.

and I will ***a*** you . . . . . . . . . . . . . . Ps. 81:8
also to ***a*** one another. . . . . . . . . . Rom. 15:14
***a*** him as a brother . . . . . . . . . . 2 Thess. 3:15

**adoption** [uh·DAAP·shun] *noun* to make someone your child; God adopts as His children all who trust in Jesus.

received the Spirit of ***a***. . . . . . . . . . Rom. 8:15
we might receive the ***a*** . . . . . . . . . . . Gal. 4:5
***a*** as sons by Jesus . . . . . . . . . . . . . Eph. 1:5

**adversary** [AD·ver·sair·ee] *noun* an opponent or enemy; Satan is the adversary of God and His people.
in the way as an ***a*** . . . . . . . . . . . . . Num. 22:22
how long will the ***a*** . . . . . . . . . . . . . . . Ps. 74:10
your ***a*** the devil walks . . . . . . . . . . . 1 Pet. 5:8
**advocate** [AD·vuh·kuht] *noun* one who speaks in defense of another; Christ is the believer's advocate.
we have an ***A*** with the . . . . . . . . . . 1 John 2:1
**affliction** [uh·FLIK·shun] *noun* major trouble, distress, pain, or adversity.
God has seen my ***a*** . . . . . . . . . . . . Gen. 31:42
***a*** take hold of me . . . . . . . . . . . . . . . Job 30:16
For our light ***a*** . . . . . . . . . . . . . . . . . 2 Cor. 4:17
**Ahab** [AY·hab] *person* evil king of the northern kingdom of Israel in the time of Elijah (1 Kin. 16:29–30); marries Jezebel and together they lead the people further into idolatry (1 Kin. 16:31—22:40).
**Ahasuerus** [Ah·HAS·oo·ER·uhs] *person* also known as Xerxes I, the Persian king who marries Esther (Esth. 1–2).
**alien** [AY·lee·uhn] *noun* a foreigner; someone who comes from a different land.
give it to the ***a*** . . . . . . . . . . . . . . . . Deut. 14:21
I am an ***a*** in their . . . . . . . . . . . . . . Job 19:15
who turn away an ***a*** . . . . . . . . . . . . . . Mal. 3:5
**alleluia** [a·leh·LOO·yuh] *noun* expression that means "praise the Lord."
saying, "***A***! Salvation and glory . . . . . Rev. 19:1
Again they said, "***A*** . . . . . . . . . . . . . Rev. 19:3
saying "Amen! ***A*** . . . . . . . . . . . . . . . Rev. 19:4
**Almighty** [aal·MY·tee] *identity* describes God's power; usually appears as God Almighty and Almighty God (Gen. 17:1; Ex. 6:3; Rev. 4:8).
**alms** [AALMZ] *noun* gifts given to help the poor.
But rather give ***a*** . . . . . . . . . . . . . . Luke 11:41
you have and give ***a*** . . . . . . . . . . . . Luke 12:33
I came to bring ***a*** . . . . . . . . . . . . . . Acts 24:17
**Alpha and Omega** [AL·fuh; oh·MEH·guh] *identity* describes Jesus' eternality; alpha is the first letter of the Greek alphabet and omega is the last, so this can be understood as the first and the last or the beginning and the end (Rev. 1:8, 11; 21:6; 22:13).
**altar** [AAL·tr] *noun* a place of sacrifice.
Noah built an ***a*** Gen. 8:20
it to you upon the ***a*** . . . . . . . . . . . . . Lev. 17:11
your gift to the ***a*** . . . . . . . . . . . . . . . Matt. 5:23
**amen** [ay·MEN] *noun* an expression of agreement; often used to end a prayer; means "so be it."
shall say, "***A***, so be it . . . . . . . . . . . . Num. 5:22
and the glory forever. ***A*** . . . . . . . . . Matt. 6:13
I am coming quickly." ***A*** . . . . . . . . . . Rev. 22:20
**amend** [uh·MEND] *verb* to repair or fix.
"***A*** your ways and your . . . . . . . . . . . Jer. 7:3
***a*** your ways and your doings . . . . . . Jer. 26:13
from his evil way, ***a*** . . . . . . . . . . . . Jer. 35:15
**Amos** [AY·mus] *person* prophet who tells of the sins and coming downfall of the northern kingdom of Israel (Amos 1–9). The Book of Amos is the third of the twelve Minor Prophets.
**Ananias** [an·uh·NIGH·uhs] 1. *person* man in Jerusalem; loses his life for lying about how much he and his wife, Sapphira, had given to God (Acts 5:1–10).
2. *person* man in Damascus; helps Paul when he becomes a Christian (Acts 9:10–17; 22:12–16).
3. *person* Jewish high priest; Paul is tried before him in Jerusalem (Acts 23:2; 24:1).
**Ancient of Days** [AYN·chent; DAYZ] *identity* describes God as judge (Dan. 7:9, 13, 22).
**Andrew** [AN·droo] *person* apostle; disciple of John the Baptist (John 1:35–40); becomes one of Jesus' twelve apostles (John 1:35–40); brings his brother Simon Peter to Jesus (John 1:41–42); brings a boy with fish and bread to Jesus (John 6:8–9).
**angel** [AYN·jel] *noun* created being who serves God primarily as a messenger; Gabriel and Michael are angels named in the Bible.
an ***a*** spoke to me . . . . . . . . . . . . 1 Kin. 13:18
a little lower than the ***a*** . . . . . . . . . . . . Ps. 8:5
the ***a*** Gabriel was sent . . . . . . . . . . . Luke 1:26
**Angel of the Lord** [AYN·jel; LORD] *identity* angel who speaks and acts like God; commands Hagar (Gen. 16:7–12); makes promises to Abraham (Gen. 22:11–13, 15–18); appears to Moses in a burning bush (Ex. 3:2); confronts Balaam (Num. 22:22–35); corrects the people of Israel (Judg. 2:1–4); calls Gideon (Judg. 6:11–24); tells of Samson's birth (Judg. 13:2ff).
**anoint** [uh·NOYNT] *verb* to pour oil over someone or something to show that it belongs to God or is special to Him; for healing; as a sign of love, respect, and value.
***a*** my head with oil . . . . . . . . . . . . . . . Ps. 23:5
to ***a*** My body . . . . . . . . . . . . . . . . . Mark 14:8
You did not ***a*** . . . . . . . . . . . . . . . . . . Luke 7:46
**antichrist** [AN·tee·krighst] *noun* a person or attitude that is against Christ; a specific enemy of Jesus.
heard that the ***A*** . . . . . . . . . . . . . . . 1 John 2:18
He is ***a*** who denies . . . . . . . . . . . . . 1 John 2:22
deceiver and an ***a*** . . . . . . . . . . . . . . 2 John 1:7
**Antioch** [AN·tee·ock] 1. **Antioch in Syria** [SEER·ee·uh] *place* the name "Christian" was first used here (Acts 11:26).
2. **Antioch in Pisidia** [pih·SIH·dee·uh] *place* visited by Paul and Barnabas (Acts 13:14–52).
**Apollos** [uh·PAA·lowz] *person* well-educated Jew who knows the Old Testament well and teaches others (Acts 18:24–25); learns more about God's ways from Aquila and Priscilla (Acts 18:26); becomes leader in Corinth (1 Cor. 1:12; 3:4–6, 22; 4:6).
**apostle** [uh·PAA·sul] *noun* one of the twelve main disciples chosen by Jesus (Matt. 10:2–4); an early Christian leader.

names of the twelve ***a*** . . . . . . . . . . . Matt. 10:2
called to be an ***a*** . . . . . . . . . . . . . . . Rom. 1:1
the signs of an ***a*** were . . . . . . . . . 2 Cor. 12:12

**appoint** [uh·POYNT] *verb* to set apart someone for ministry or to establish.

***a*** me ruler over the . . . . . . . . . . 2 Sam. 6:21
***a*** elders in every church . . . . . . . . .Acts 14:23
***a*** elders in every city . . . . . . . . . . . . Titus 1:5

**Aquila** [uh·KWIL·uh] *person* Jewish Christian who lives in Rome with his wife, Priscilla, until the emperor orders all Jewish people to leave; moves to Corinth (Acts 18:1–3); travels with Paul to Syria (Acts 18:18–19); instructs Apollos (Acts 18:26).

**archangel** [ARK·ayn·jel] *noun* angel of the highest order.

the voice of an ***a*** . . . . . . . . . . . . 1 Thess. 4:16
Michael the ***a*** . . . . . . . . . . . . . . . . . . . Jude 1:9

**ark** [ARK] *noun* a ship or floating vessel; most often, the ship God commands Noah to construct, which saves him and his family from the Flood.

Make yourself an ***a*** . . . . . . . . . . . . . . Gen. 6:14
she took an ***a*** of bulrushes . . . . . . . . . . .Ex. 2:3
Noah entered the ***a*** . . . . . . . . . . . . Matt. 24:38

**ark of the Testimony** [ARK; TES·tih·mow·nee] *noun* chest that held the two stone tablets on which were inscribed the Ten Commandments; also called the ark of the covenant; placed in the Most Holy Place within the tabernacle and, later, the temple.

in the ***a*** you shall put . . . . . . . . . . . .Ex. 25:21
"Cross over before the ***a*** . . . . . . . . . . Josh. 4:5
***a*** of God was captured . . . . . . . . . 1 Sam. 4:19

**Armageddon** [ar·muh·GEH·dun] *place* meaning "mountain of Megiddo," according to prophecy the place where the last battle of this age will be fought between the forces of good and evil (Rev. 16:14–16); Barak and Deborah defeat Canaanites here (Judg. 5:19).

**Artaxerxes** [ar·tack·SERK·seez] *person* son of Xerxes I, Persian king who allows Ezra (Ezra 7) and Nehemiah (Neh. 2; 13) to return to Jerusalem.

**Asherah** [ah·SHER·uh] *noun* false Canaanite goddess who was said to be the wife of Baal and whose image was placed on top of wooden poles in places of worship; Gideon destroys one wooden image beside the altar (Judg. 6:25); Asa removes an image (1 Kin. 15:13); Manasseh places an image in the temple (2 Kin. 21:7); Josiah removes images from the temple (2 Kin. 23:4, 7).

**Asia** [AY·zhuh] *place* Roman province in the western part of what we call Asia Minor, or modern-day Turkey; Paul is prohibited from going (Acts 16:6); believers settle in (1 Pet. 1:1); John writes letters to seven churches in (Rev. 1:4; 2:1—3:22).

**assuredly, I say to you** *phrase* the way Jesus makes it clear that what He is about to say is important.

"***A***, among those born of . . . . . . . . Matt. 11:11
"***A***, I will no longer . . . . . . . . . . . . Mark 14:25
"Most ***a***, unless one is born . . . . . . . John 3:3

**Assyria** [uh·SEER·ee·uh] *place* powerful kingdom between the ninth and seventh centuries BC; conquers the northern kingdom of Israel in 722 BC and takes the people into captivity (2 Kin. 17:3–6; 18:9–11); Jonah preaches to (Jon. 3–4); attacks southern kingdom of Judah in 701 BC but fails (2 Kin. 19:35).

**at the right hand** *phrase* place of honor and authority.

Son of Man sitting ***a*** . . . . . . . . . . . . Matt. 26:64
Jesus standing ***a*** of God . . . . . . . . . . Acts 7:55
sat down ***a*** of the Majesty . . . . . . . . . Heb.1:3

**Athens** [A·thens] *place* capital city of the ancient Greeks where Paul preaches a sermon at the Areopagus (Acts 17:15—18:1).

**atonement** [uh·TONE·mehnt] *noun* being right with another after wrong has been done; what is required to right a wrong that has been done.

a year he shall make ***a*** . . . . . . . . . . . Ex. 30:10
what shall I make ***a*** . . . . . . . . . . . 2 Sam. 21:3
I provide you an ***a*** . . . . . . . . . . . . Ezek. 16:63

# B

**Baal** [BAYL] *noun* false god or gods of the Canaanites; the people of Israel worship (Num. 25:1–9; Judg. 2:11–14; 3:7; 10:10–14; 1 Kin. 16:31–32; 2 Kin. 21:3); Gideon tears down altar to (Judg. 6:24–32); Elijah confronts worship of (1 Kin. 18); Jehu stops worship of (2 Kin. 10:28); Jehoiada tears down temple of (2 Kin. 11:18); Josiah removes idols of from the temple (2 Kin. 23:4–5).

**Babel** [BAY·buhl] *place* site where people disobey God and build a tall tower (Gen. 11:1–9).

**Babylon** [BA·buh·laan] *place* capital of the Babylonian Empire that conquers the southern kingdom of Judah, destroying Jerusalem and the temple and taking the people into exile in 586 BC (2 Kin. 24–25).

**baptism** [BAP·tih·zum] *noun* an ordinance of the church commanded by Jesus (Matt. 28:18–20) that demonstrates a person is part of the community of faith.

coming to his ***b*** . . . . . . . . . . . . . . . . Matt. 3:7
from the ***b*** of John . . . . . . . . . . . . . .Acts 1:22
Lord, one faith, one ***b*** . . . . . . . . . . . . Eph. 4:5

**Barabbas** [buh·RA·buhs] *person* robber whom the people choose to free, leading Pilate to condemn Jesus to death (Matt. 27:20–26; Mark 15:7–15; Luke 23:18–25; John 18:39–40).

**Barnabas** [BAR·nuh·buhs] *person* name (which means "Son of Encouragement") that the apostles give to Joses (Acts 4:36); gives generous gift to the church (Acts 4:37); brings Paul to the apostles (Acts 9:27); sent to Antioch (Acts 11:22–30); travels with Paul on missionary journey (Acts 13:2ff); attends Jerusalem Council (Acts 15); parts ways with Paul and Silas (Acts 15:36–40).

**Bartholomew** [bar·THAWL·uh·myoo] *person* apostle; may have been another name for Nathanael (John 1:45–51; 21:2).

**Bathsheba** [bath·SHEE·buh] *person* also called Bathshua, wife of Uriah the Hittite; David sins against and marries her (2 Sam. 11); becomes mother of Solomon (1 Chr. 3:5); ensures Solomon becomes king after David (1 Kin. 1).

**bear fruit** *phrase* way to describe a person's actions, which can be either pleasing to God (good fruit) or not (bad fruit).

bring forth branches, ***b*** . . . . . . . . . . Ezek. 17:8
***b*** worthy of repentance . . . . . . . . . . . Matt. 3:8
branch cannot ***b*** of itself . . . . . . . . . John 15:4

**Beelzebub** [bee·EL·zuh·buhb] *noun* false god that Jesus refers to as Satan (Matt. 10:25; 12:24–26; Mark 3:22–23; Luke 11:15, 18).

**believe** [buh·LEEV] *verb* to trust that something is true and place one's faith in—namely, in Jesus and the gospel.

Repent, and ***b*** . . . . . . . . . . . . . . . Mark 1:15
to those who ***b*** . . . . . . . . . . . . . . John 1:12
the Lord Jesus and ***b*** . . . . . . . . . . . Rom. 10:9

**Benjamin** [BEHN·juh·mihn] *person* favored and youngest son of Jacob (Gen. 42:4, 36); born to Rachel (Gen. 35:16–20).

**beseech** [buh·SEECH] *verb* to ask urgently.

Return, we ***b*** You . . . . . . . . . . . . . . Ps. 80:14
***b*** you therefore . . . . . . . . . . . . . . . Rom. 12:1
of the Lord, ***b*** you to . . . . . . . . . . . . Eph. 4:1

**besiege** [buh·SEEJ] *verb* to attack a city by surrounding it.

went up and ***b*** Samaria . . . . . . . . . . 2 Kin. 6:24
army ***b*** Jerusalem . . . . . . . . . . . . . . Jer. 32:2
to Jerusalem and ***b*** it. . . . . . . . . . . . Dan. 1:1

**Bethany** [BETH·uh·nee] *place* small village east of Jerusalem by the Mount of Olives; Jesus makes triumphal entry from here (Mark 11:1–11); home of Simon the leper (Matt. 26:6; Mark 14:3); home of Lazarus, Mary, and Martha (John 11:1–44); Jesus leaves His disciples from (Luke 24:50–51).

**Bethel** [BETH·uhl] *place* city fourteen miles north of Jerusalem; Abram builds altar here (Gen. 12:8; 13:3–4); Jacob's name changes to Israel here (Gen. 35:10–15); the ark of the Testimony rests here (Judg. 20:18–28); Jeroboam makes it a place of idolatry (1 Kin. 12:29—13:32).

**Bethlehem** [BETH·luh·hem] *place* town about six miles southwest of Jerusalem; David from here (1 Sam. 16:1–13); Naomi and Ruth live here (Ruth 1:19); Jesus born here (Matt. 2:1–16; Luke 2:4–15).

**betroth** [bih·TROTH] *verb* to promise to marry; to become engaged.

"You shall ***b*** a wife . . . . . . . . . . . . Deut. 28:30
"I will ***b*** you to Me. . . . . . . . . . . . . . Hos. 2:19
Mary was ***b*** to Joseph . . . . . . . . . . . Matt. 1:18

**birthright** [BURTH·rite] *noun* privilege of the firstborn son of a family that entitles him to a double portion of the family inheritance and leadership of the family upon the father's death.

Esau despised his ***b*** . . . . . . . . . . . . Gen. 25:34
according to his ***b*** . . . . . . . . . . . . . Gen. 43:33
of food sold his ***b*** . . . . . . . . . . . . . Heb. 12:16

**bishop** [BIH·shuhp] *noun* title used in the New Testament for an elder or pastor.

the position of a ***b*** . . . . . . . . . . . . . 1 Tim. 3:1
A ***b*** then must be blameless . . . . . . 1 Tim. 3:2
***b*** must be blameless . . . . . . . . . . . . Titus 1:7

**blameless** [BLAYM·luhs] *adjective* to be right with God.

walk before Me and be ***b*** . . . . . . . . . Gen. 17:1
a ***b*** and upright man . . . . . . . . . . . . . Job 1:8
you holy, and ***b*** . . . . . . . . . . . . . . . . . Col. 1:22

**blasphemy** [BLAS·fuh·mee] *noun* to insult, speak against, or claim to be God.

trouble and rebuke and ***b*** . . . . . . . . . . Is. 37:3
not stone You, but for ***b*** . . . . . . . . . John 10:33
mouth in ***b*** against God . . . . . . . . . . . Rev. 13:6

**blessing** [BLEH·sihng] *noun* something good given by God to people; words of praise, goodness, and favor said to a person; words of worship said to God.

and you shall be a ***b*** . . . . . . . . . . . . . Gen. 12:2
with every spiritual ***b*** . . . . . . . . . . . . Eph. 1:3
same mouth proceed ***b*** . . . . . . . . . James 3:10

**blot** [BLAWT] *verb* to remove or mark out.

***b*** me out of Your book . . . . . . . . . . . Ex. 32:32
from my sins, and ***b*** . . . . . . . . . . . . . . Ps. 51:9
and I will not ***b*** . . . . . . . . . . . . . . . . . Rev. 3:5

**Boaz** [BOW·az] *person* wealthy man from Bethlehem who marries Ruth (Ruth 2:1—4:13); becomes great-grandfather of David (Ruth 4:18–22).

**bondservant** [BAAND·sur·vihnt] *noun* someone who is bound to work for another, usually without pay.

Paul, a ***b*** of Jesus Christ . . . . . . . . . Rom. 1:1
James, a ***b*** of God and of . . . . . . . . James 1:1
Simon Peter, a ***b*** and . . . . . . . . . . . . 2 Pet. 1:1

**Book of Life** [BUK; LIFE] *noun* expression for all those who have been saved by God through Jesus.

whose names are in the ***B*** . . . . . . . . . . Phil. 4:3
out his name from the ***B*** . . . . . . . . . . Rev. 3:5
written in the Lamb's ***B*** . . . . . . . . . . Rev. 21:27

**bottomless pit** [BAA·tuhm·luhs PIT] *noun* location from which locust-like creatures and a beast, Abaddon, come (Rev. 9:1–11; 11:7; 17:8); Satan bound in (Rev. 20:1–3).

the key to the ***b*** . . . . . . . . . . . . . . . . . . Rev. 9:1
ascend out of the ***b*** . . . . . . . . . . . . . . Rev. 17:8

cast him into the ***b***. . . . . . . . . . . . . . Rev. 20:3

**breaking of bread** *phrase* to eat a meal together, which is part of the early church's celebration of the Lord's Supper.

known to them in the ***b*** . . . . . . . . Luke 24:35
fellowship, in the ***b***. . . . . . . . . . . . . . Acts 2:42
***b*** from house to . . . . . . . . . . . . . . . . Acts 2:46

# C

**Caesar** [SEE·zuhr] *noun* title for the Roman emperors; Augustus Caesar (31 BC–AD 14) decrees census that brings Joseph and Mary to Bethlehem (Luke 2:1); Tiberius Caesar (AD 14–37) rules during Jesus' ministry (Matt. 22:17–21; Luke 3:1–23; John 19:12); Claudius Caesar (AD 41–54) banishes Jews from Rome (Acts 11:28; 18:2); Nero Caesar (AD 54–68) hears Paul's case (Acts 25:8–12; Phil. 4:22; 2 Tim. 4:16–18).

**Cain** [KAYN] *person* son of Adam; murders his brother Abel (Gen. 4:2ff); represents wicked people (1 John 3:12; Jude v. 11).

**calamity** [kuh·LA·muh·tee] *noun* an event that causes major distress.

for the day of their ***c***. . . . . . . . . . . . Deut. 32:35
***c*** shall come suddenly . . . . . . . . . . Prov. 6:15
If there is ***c*** in a. . . . . . . . . . . . . . . . . Amos 3:6

**Caleb** [KAY·lehb] *person* one of the two spies sent into the Promised Land to give a good report (Num. 13:2, 6, 27, 30; 14:5–9, 24–38); allowed by God to enter the land (Num. 26:65); inherits Hebron (Josh. 14:6–15); conquers his territory with Othniel's help (Josh. 15:13–19).

**Calvary** [KAL·vuh·ree] *place* meaning "skull," location outside Jerusalem where Jesus is crucified (Luke 23:33); also known by the Hebrew name, *Golgotha* (Matt. 27:33; Mark 15:22; John 19:17).

**Canaan** [KAY·nuhn] *place* region along the Mediterranean Sea that connects Africa, Asia, and Europe that God gives to Abraham and his descendants (Gen. 11:31; 13:1–18; 15:1–21); Jacob removes family from (Gen. 46); spies return with a bad report of (Num. 13–14); Joshua leads the people back into (Josh. 3ff); Assyrians and Babylonians exile people from (2 Kin. 17:3–6; 18:9–11; 24:1—25:30); exiles return to (Ezra; Nehemiah).

**Capernaum** [kuh·PER·nay·uhm] *place* city on the Sea of Galilee; Jesus lives here (Mark 2:1); home of Peter and Andrew (Matt. 8:5, 14); Jesus heals a man with an unclean spirit (Mark 1:21–28) and a paralytic here (Mark 2:1–12); discussions about true greatness (Mark 9:33–37) and paying the temple tax here (Matt. 17:24–27).

**cavalry** [KA·vuhl·ree] *noun* army that travels on horses.

and cities for his ***c*** . . . . . . . . . . . . . . 1 Kin. 9:19
on a horse with the ***c*** . . . . . . . . . . . 1 Kin. 20:20
their ***c*** comes from afar. . . . . . . . . . . Hab. 1:8

**census** [SEN·suhs] *noun* counting of a people.

When you take the ***c*** of . . . . . . . . . . Ex. 30:12
the ***c*** in which David. . . . . . . . . . 2 Chr. 2:17
***c*** first took place while . . . . . . . . . . Luke 2:2

**centurion** [sen·CHUR·ee·uhn] *noun* Roman military officer who commanded one hundred soldiers.

***c*** came to Him, pleading . . . . . . . . Matt. 8:5
when the ***c*** saw what . . . . . . . . . . Luke 23:47
Cornelius the ***c***, a just . . . . . . . . . . Acts 10:22

**chasten** [CHAY·sin] *verb* to discipline or punish.

***C*** your son while there. . . . . . . . . . Prov. 19:18
a father does not ***c***. . . . . . . . . . . . . Heb. 12:7
I love, I rebuke and ***c*** . . . . . . . . . . . . Rev. 3:19

**cherubim** [CHER·uh·bihm] *noun* winged creatures, statues of which were placed atop the mercy seat of the ark of the Testimony.

and He placed ***c*** . . . . . . . . . . . . . . . Gen. 3:24
two ***c*** of gold . . . . . . . . . . . . . . . . . . . Ex. 25:18
fire from among the ***c*** . . . . . . . . . . . . Ezek. 10:2

**Christ** [KRIGHST] *identity* meaning "anointed one," describes Jesus as the one God promised to send to rescue people from sin (Gen. 3:15; Matt. 1:1); Greek version of the Jewish word *messiah*.

**Christians** [KRIS·chihns] *noun* followers of Christ.

first called ***C*** in Antioch . . . . . . . . . Acts 11:26

**church** [CHERCH] *noun* all followers of Jesus; a local group of believers.

I will build My ***c***. . . . . . . . . . . . . . . Matt. 16:18
Christ is head of the ***c*** . . . . . . . . . . . Eph. 5:23
head of the body, the ***c***. . . . . . . . . . . Col. 1:18

**clean** [KLEEN] *adjective* free from defilement; under the Old Testament law, certain animals were declared clean, meaning they could be eaten, and others unclean, meaning they could not be eaten (Lev. 11:1–47; Deut. 14:3–21).

seven each of every ***c***. . . . . . . . . . . . . Gen. 7:2
all who are ***c*** may eat of it . . . . . . . . . Lev. 7:19
all things are ***c*** . . . . . . . . . . . . . . . . Luke 11:41

**Colosse** [ko·LAW·see] *place* city in Asia Minor (modern-day Turkey); Paul writes to Christians here (Col. 1:2).

**commandment** [kuh·MAND·mehnt] *noun* instruction or rule, notably those given by God; more specifically at times, one of the Ten Commandments (Ex. 20:1–17; Deut. 5:6–21).

shall keep every ***c*** which . . . . . . . . Deut. 11:8
which is the great ***c*** . . . . . . . . . . . . Matt. 22:36
you love Me, keep My ***c*** . . . . . . . . . . John 14:15

**commend** [kuh·MEND] *verb* to speak good things about; to recommend.

I ***c*** you to God and to the . . . . . . . . Acts 20:32
begin again to ***c*** ourselves. . . . . . . . 2 Cor. 3:1
those who ***c*** themselves . . . . . . . . 2 Cor. 10:12

**communion** [kuh·MYOON·yehn] *noun* unity; fellowship; oneness.

bless, is it not the ***c*** . . . . . . . . . . . . 1 Cor. 10:16
***c*** has light with. . . . . . . . . . . . . . . . . 2 Cor. 6:14
***c*** of the Holy Spirit . . . . . . . . . . . . 2 Cor. 13:14

**condemn** [kuhn·DEHM] *verb* to declare guilty; to sentence to death.
who is he who will *c*. . . . . . . . . . . . . . . Is. 50:9
world to *c* the world . . . . . . . . . . . . John 3:17
is he who does not *c* . . . . . . . . . . . Rom. 14:22
**confess** [kuhn·FEHS] *verb* to admit sin as part of repentance; to acknowledge Jesus as Lord.
*c* that he has sinned. . . . . . . . . . . . . . Lev. 5:5
*c* Me before men . . . . . . . . . . . . . Matt. 10:32
that if you *c* with. . . . . . . . . . . . . . Rom. 10:9
**consecrate** [KAAN·suh·krayt] *verb* to set something apart as special and holy.
"*C* to Me all the . . . . . . . . . . . . . . . Ex. 13:2
*c* himself this day. . . . . . . . . . . . . 1 Chr. 29:5
*c* their gain to the. . . . . . . . . . . . . . Mic. 4:13
**consolation** [kaan·suh·LAY·shun] *noun* comfort and reassurance.
waiting for the *C*. . . . . . . . . . . . . . . Luke 2:25
if there is any *c*. . . . . . . . . . . . . . . . Phil. 2:1
given us everlasting *c* . . . . . . . . . 2 Thess. 2:16
**contrite** [kuhn·TRITE] *adjective* showing sorrow and regret, notably of sin.
a broken and a *c*. . . . . . . . . . . . . . . . Ps. 51:17
with him who has a *c*. . . . . . . . . . . . . Is. 57:15
poor and of a *c* spirit . . . . . . . . . . . . . Is. 66:2
**converted** [kuhn·VUR·tuhd] *adjective* having a changed spiritual state—namely, a sinner who is now forgiven by God.
sinners shall be *c*. . . . . . . . . . . . . . . Ps. 51:13
unless you are *c*. . . . . . . . . . . . . . . . Matt. 18:3
Repent therefore and be *c*. . . . . . . . . Acts 3:19
**convicted** [kuhn·VICK·tuhd] *adjective* having an awareness of, and being sorry for, one's sins.
*c* by their conscience . . . . . . . . . . . . . John 8:9
he is *c* by all . . . . . . . . . . . . . . . 1 Cor. 14:24
sin, and are *c* by the law . . . . . . . . . . James 2:9
**Corinth** [KOR·inth] *place* important, wealthy, and sinful city of ancient Greece; Paul stays with Pricilla and Aquilla here (Acts 18:1–3); Paul, Silas, and Timothy share the gospel for eighteen months here (Acts 18:5–11); Paul writes letters to the church here (1 Cor. 1:2; 2 Cor. 1:1).
**Cornelius** [kor·NEE·lee·uhs] *person* Roman centurion stationed in Caesarea who was the first recorded Gentile to become a Christian (Acts 10:1–33).
**cornerstone** [KOR·ner·stohwn] *noun* important stone placed at the corner of two walls; used as a symbol of Jesus' importance in God's plans
has become the chief *c*. . . . . . . . . . . Ps. 118:22
stone, a precious *c*. . . . . . . . . . . . . . Is. 28:16
Himself being the chief *c* . . . . . . . . . . Eph. 2:20
**council** [KOWN·sihl] *noun* group of leaders and advisors.
a prominent *c* member . . . . . . . . . . . Mark 15:43
Pharisees gathered a *c* . . . . . . . . . . . John 11:47
all the *c* of the elders. . . . . . . . . . . . . Acts 22:5
**countenance** [KOWN·tuh·nuhns] *noun* expression on someone's face.
The LORD lift up His *c* . . . . . . . . . . . Num. 6:26
hypocrites, with a sad *c*. . . . . . . . . . Matt. 6:16
sword, and His *c*. . . . . . . . . . . . . . . . . Rev. 1:16
**covenant** [KUH·vuh·nuhnt] *noun* binding agreement; initiated by God with people, such as God and Noah (Gen. 9:8–17), God and Abraham (Gen. 12:1–3; 15:9–21), God and the Israelites (Ex. 24:3–8; Josh 24:1–33; Jer. 31:31–40), and God and David (2 Sam. 7:1–29; 1 Kin. 8:17ff); initiated between two people, such as between Abraham and Eliezer (Gen. 24:2–3, 9, 41), Abimelech and Isaac (Gen. 26:28–30), David and Jonathan (1 Sam 18:3–4), David and Abner (2 Sam. 3:12–21), Solomon and Shimei (1 Kin. 2:42–46), Solomon and Hiram (1 Kin. 5:12), and Jehoiada and the royal guard (2 Kin. 11:4).
the LORD made a *c* . . . . . . . . . . . . . Gen. 15:18
My blood of the new *c* . . . . . . . . . . . Mark 14:24
cup is the new *c* . . . . . . . . . . . . . . 1 Cor. 11:25
**creation** [kree·AY·shun] *noun* what God has made.
the beginning of the *c* . . . . . . . . . . . . Mark 10:6
since the *c* of the world . . . . . . . . . . . Rom. 1:20
Christ, he is a new *c* . . . . . . . . . . . . 2 Cor. 5:17
**Creator** [kree·AY·ter] *identity* describes God as the maker of everything (Eccl. 12:1; Is. 40:28; Rom. 1:25; 1 Pet. 4:19).
**cross** [KRAWS] *noun* upright post and crossbeam on which the Romans executed the most severe of criminals; a symbol of the gospel and forgiveness of sin.
come down from the *c*. . . . . . . . . . . . Matt. 27:40
lest the *c* of Christ . . . . . . . . . . . . . 1 Cor. 1:17
boast except in the *c* . . . . . . . . . . . . . Gal. 6:14
**crown** [KROWN] *noun* headpiece, usually made of gold and jewels, worn by kings and leaders or a wreath worn by athletic victors; faithful believers will receive the crown of righteousness (2 Tim. 4:8) and the crown of life (James 1:12; Rev. 2:10); faithful elders will receive the crown of glory (1 Pet. 5:4); Paul mentions a crown of rejoicing (1 Thess. 2:19); Jesus wore a crown of thorns (Matt. 27:29).
obtain a perishable *c*. . . . . . . . . . . 1 Cor. 9:25
laid up for me the *c* . . . . . . . . . . . . . 2 Tim. 4:8
cast their *c* before the throne . . . . . Rev. 4:10
**crucify** [KROO·suh·figh] *verb* to put someone to death by using a cross.
out again, "*C* Him. . . . . . . . . . . . . . Mark 15:13
"Shall I *c* your King . . . . . . . . . . . . John 19:15
since they *c* again. . . . . . . . . . . . . . . . Heb. 6:6
**curse** [KERS] 1. *verb* to call for harm to come on someone else, including through God's punishment.
*c* him who curses you . . . . . . . . . . . . Gen. 12:3
*C* God and die . . . . . . . . . . . . . . . . . . Job 2:9
bless those who *c* you . . . . . . . . . . . . Luke 6:28
2. *noun* harm or misfortune that comes upon someone; the sinful state of the universe because of the fall.

your *c* be on me, my son . . . . . . . . Gen. 27:13
us from the *c* of the law. . . . . . . . . . Gal. 3:13
there shall be no more *c* . . . . . . . . . . Rev. 22:3

**Cyrus** [SIGH·ruhs] *person* king of Persia known as "Cyrus the Great" (559–530 BC); allows the exiles to return from Babylon to Jerusalem in 536 BC (2 Chr. 36:22–23; Ezra 1:1–4; Is. 45:1); encourages the rebuilding of the temple (Ezra 3:7; 4:3; Is. 44:28).

# D

**Damascus** [duh·MAS·kuhs] *place* capital of Aramean kingdom and then Syria; Paul converted here (Acts 9:1–22).

**Daniel** [DAN·yuhl] *person* prophet exiled in Babylon; serves in the palace and given the name Belteshazzar (Dan. 1:1–7); becomes governor (Dan. 2:48); interprets dreams (Dan. 2:1–45) and the handwriting on the wall (Dan. 5:17–30); saved by God from the lions (Dan. 6:16–24); shares visions given by God (Dan. 7–12).

**Darius** [duh·RIGH·uhs] 1. **Darius the Mede** [MEED] *person* Babylonian ruler; succeeds Belshazzar (Dan. 5:30–31); co-ruler with Cyrus (Dan. 6:28); made king of Chaldeans (Dan. 9:1).
2. **Darius Hystaspes** [hih·STAS·pes] *person* Persian king (522–486 BC); temple work resumes during his reign (Ezra 4:5, 24); confirms Cyrus's royal edict (Ezra 6:1–14).
3. **Darius II Ochus** [O·kus] *person* Persian ruler (423–404 BC); priestly records kept during his reign (Neh. 12:22).

**David** [DAY·vihd] *person* second king over Israel; youngest son of Jesse (1 Sam. 17:12, 14); defeats Goliath (1 Sam. 17:41–50); friend of Jonathan (1 Sam. 19:1—20:42); fugitive from Saul's wrath (1 Sam. 21–27; 30); king of Judah (2 Sam. 1:1—5:5); king of Israel (2 Sam. 3:6—1 Kin. 2:11); brings the ark of the Testimony to Jerusalem (2 Sam. 6:1–17); sins against God, Bathsheba, and Uriah (2 Sam. 11); confesses and repents of his sins (2 Sam. 12; Ps. 51); son Absalom rebels (2 Sam. 14–18); names Solomon, his son, to succeed him (1 Kin. 1:11—2:12).

**Day of Atonement** [DAY; uh·TOHN·ment] *noun* annual fast day ordained in the law as a day of making amends for sins (Lev. 16:1–34; 23:26–32).

**day of the Lord** [DAY; LORD] *noun* the day when God punishes evil (Amos 5:18–20) through great disaster (Is. 2:5–22; 13:1–22; 24:1–23; Zeph. 1:7–18; 2:2–3; 3:8) and judgment (1 Cor. 4:5; 5:5; 1 Thess. 5:2; Rev. 16:14).
the great and awesome *d* . . . . . . . . Joel 2:31
the great and dreadful *d* . . . . . . . . . Mal. 4:5
*d* will come as a thief. . . . . . . . . . . 2 Pet. 3:10

**deacon** [DEE·kuhn] *noun* servant-leader in a local church who assists the pastors and/or elders.
with the bishops and *d* . . . . . . . . . . Phil. 1:1
*d* must be reverent, not . . . . . . . . . 1 Tim. 3:8
*d* be the husbands . . . . . . . . . . . . . 1 Tim 3:12

**Dead Sea** [DED SEE] *place* salty lake at the mouth of the Jordan River; also called the Salt Sea (Gen. 14:3; Num. 34:3), the Sea of the Arabah (Deut. 3:17), and the eastern sea (Joel 2:20).

**death** [DETH] 1. *noun* losing one's physical life.
valley of the shadow of *d* . . . . . . . . . Ps. 23:4
swallow up *d* forever . . . . . . . . . . . . . . Is. 25:8
who shall not taste *d* . . . . . . . . . . Matt. 16:28
2. *noun* final state of the unsaved, also called the "second death."
he shall never see *d* . . . . . . . . . . . . . John 8:51
the wages of sin is *d* . . . . . . . . . . Rom. 6:23
Over such the second *d* . . . . . . . . . . Rev. 20:6
3. *noun* sin's power over people.
Nevertheless *d* reigned . . . . . . . . . . Rom. 5:14
*D*, where is your sting . . . . . . . . . 1 Cor. 15:55
*d* is working in us . . . . . . . . . . . . . 2 Cor. 4:12

**Deborah** [DEH·bruh] *person* fourth judge of Israel; encourages Barak to oppose the Canaanites (Judg. 4:6–7); goes with Barak to face the Canaanites (Judg. 4:8–10); celebrates victory (Judg. 5:2–31).

**deceiver** [deh·SEE·ver] *noun* one who lies and misleads another.
"But cursed be the *d* . . . . . . . . . . . . . Mal. 1:14
both idle talkers and *d* . . . . . . . . . . . Titus 1:10
This is a *d* and an . . . . . . . . . . . . . . 2 John 1:7

**decree** [duh·KREE] *noun* official declaration, statement, or order given by a king or other leader.
King Cyrus issued a *d* to . . . . . . . . . Ezra 5:13
let a *d* be written that they . . . . . . . . Esth. 3:9
in those days that a *d* . . . . . . . . . . . . Luke 2:1

**defile** [dih·FIGHL] *verb* to make something unclean or impure.
to *d* My sanctuary and profane . . . . . Lev. 20:3
the heart, and they *d* . . . . . . . . . . . Matt. 15:18
also these dreamers *d* . . . . . . . . . . . . Jude 1:8

**Delilah** [dih·LIE·luh] *person* woman who betrays Samson to the Philistines (Judg. 16:4–22).

**deliverer** [dih·LIH·ver·er] *noun* one who provides rescue; God is said to be the deliverer of His people.
the Lord raised up a *d* . . . . . . . . . . . . Judg. 3:9
You are my help and my *d* . . . . . . . . . Ps. 40:17
*D* will come out of . . . . . . . . . . . . . Rom. 11:26

**demon** [DEE·muhn] *noun* evil spirit.
offer their sacrifices to *d* . . . . . . . . . . Lev. 17:7
when the *d* was cast out . . . . . . . . . Matt. 9:33
Even the *d* believe . . . . . . . . . . . . . James 2:19

**despise** [duh·SPIZE] *verb* to look down on someone or something; to see something as worthless.
if you *d* My statutes . . . . . . . . . . . . . Lev. 26:15
but fools *d* wisdom . . . . . . . . . . . . . . . Prov. 1:7
Let no one *d* your youth . . . . . . . . . 1 Tim. 4:12

**detestable** [deh·TEH·stuh·bul] *adjective* strongly disliked; loathsome.
not eat any ***d*** thing . . . . . . . . . . . . . Deut. 14:3
their ***d*** and abominable idols . . . . . Jer. 16:18
nor with their ***d*** things . . . . . . . . . Ezek. 37:23
**devil** [DEH·vul] *noun* chief demon, also called Satan.
to be tempted by the ***d*** . . . . . . . . . . . . Matt. 4:1
of your father the ***d*** . . . . . . . . . . . . John 8:44
***d***, who deceived them . . . . . . . . . . Rev. 20:10
**devout** [deh·VOWT] *adjective* very committed, faithful, or religious.
man was just and ***d*** . . . . . . . . . . . . . Luke 2:25
***d*** men carried Stephen . . . . . . . . . . . . Acts 8:2
***d*** proselytes followed Paul . . . . . . . . Acts 13:43
**diligence** [DIH·luh·jins] *noun* good and lasting effort to get something done.
your heart with all ***d*** . . . . . . . . . . . . Prov. 4:23
he who leads, with ***d*** . . . . . . . . . . . . Rom. 12:8
of your love by the ***d*** . . . . . . . . . . . 2 Cor. 8:8
**discern** [dih·SURN] *verb* to detect or recognize.
Can I ***d*** between the . . . . . . . . . . 2 Sam. 19:35
Then you shall again ***d*** . . . . . . . . . . . Mal. 3:18
***d*** the face of the sky . . . . . . . . . . . Matt. 16:3
**disciple** [dih·SIGH·pul] *noun* learner; follower, particularly one who follows Jesus Christ; sometimes references the twelve apostles in the Gospels.
called His twelve ***d*** to . . . . . . . . . . . . Matt. 10:1
he cannot be My ***d*** . . . . . . . . . . . . . Luke 14:26
the ***d*** were first called . . . . . . . . . . . Acts 11:26
**Dispersion** [dis·PURR·zhun] *noun* meaning to "spread out," the scattering of Jews outside ancient Palestine from the time of the exile into New Testament times.
intend to go to the ***D*** . . . . . . . . . . . . . John 7:35
the pilgrims of the ***D*** . . . . . . . . . . . . 1 Pet. 1:1
**dissipation** [dih·si·PAY·shun] *noun* being wasteful; acting without caution or restraint.
which is ***d***; but be filled . . . . . . . . . . . Eph. 5:18
not accused of ***d*** . . . . . . . . . . . . . . . . Titus 1:6
in the same flood of ***d*** . . . . . . . . . . . . 1 Pet. 4:4
**divine** [deh·VINE] 1. *verb* to determine what will happen in the future or an action to take based on methods apart from asking God, including by sinful means.
futility and who ***d*** . . . . . . . . . . . . . . Ezek. 13:9
and her prophets ***d*** . . . . . . . . . . . . . . Mic. 3:11
2. *adjective* related to God or godliness.
what does the ***d*** response say . . . . Rom. 11:4
***d*** service and the . . . . . . . . . . . . . . . . . Heb. 9:1
***d*** power has given . . . . . . . . . . . . . . . 2 Pet. 1:3
**doctrine** [DAAK·truhn] *noun* teaching or instruction about God and His ways, but there can also be false doctrines.
idol is a worthless ***d*** . . . . . . . . . . . . . Jer. 10:8
with every wind of ***d*** . . . . . . . . . . . . . . Eph. 4:14
is contrary to sound ***d*** . . . . . . . . . . . 1 Tim. 1:10
**dominion** [duh·MIN·yuhn] *noun* power or authority.
let them have ***d*** . . . . . . . . . . . . . . . . Gen. 1:26
made him to have ***d*** . . . . . . . . . . . . . . . . Ps. 8:6
sin shall not have ***d*** . . . . . . . . . . . . . Rom. 6:14
**double-minded** [DUH·buhl MINE·dehd] *adjective* being indecisive; acting in two different ways.
I hate the ***d*** . . . . . . . . . . . . . . . . . . Ps. 119:113
he is a ***d*** man . . . . . . . . . . . . . . . . . James 1:8
your hearts, you ***d*** . . . . . . . . . . . . . . James 4:8
**dreadful** [DRED·fuhl] *adjective* greatly feared; terrible.
a fourth beast, ***d*** and terrible . . . . . . Dan. 7:7
They are terrible and ***d*** . . . . . . . . . . . Hab. 1:7
***d*** day of the LORD Mal. 4:5

## E

**earnestly** [UR·nuhst·lee] *adverb* something done with seriousness, intensity, and conviction.
if you ***e*** obey My . . . . . . . . . . . . . . Deut. 11:13
He prayed more ***e*** . . . . . . . . . . . . . . Luke 22:44
you to contend ***e*** . . . . . . . . . . . . . . . . Jude 1:3
**ears to hear** *phrase* expression telling people to pay close attention to what is being said.
eyes to see and ***e*** . . . . . . . . . . . . . . . Deut. 29:4
***e*** but does not hear . . . . . . . . . . . . . Ezek. 12:2
He who has ***e*** . . . . . . . . . . . . . . . . . . Matt. 11:15
**Eden** [EE·dehn] *place* area where God plants a garden for Adam and Eve to live in (Gen. 2:8); after sinning, Adam and Eve removed from (Gen. 3:22–24); some form of restoration promised (Is. 51:3).
**edification** [eh·duh·fuh·KAY·shun] *noun* instruction and encouragement for believers to grow spiritually and morally.
his good, leading to ***e*** . . . . . . . . . . . . Rom. 15:2
things be done for ***e*** . . . . . . . . . . . 1 Cor. 14:26
rather than godly ***e*** . . . . . . . . . . . . . . 1 Tim. 1:4
**Edom** [EE·duhm] *place* country to the south of ancient Moab; home to descendants of Esau (Gen. 36:1); Israelites not allowed to pass through the land (Num. 20:14–21); Saul fights against (1 Sam. 14:47); David fights against (2 Sam. 8:13–14); cursed by God (Is. 34:5–6).
**Egypt** [EE·jihpt] *place* powerful African nation; Abraham lives here (Gen. 12:10–20); Joseph taken here (Gen. 37:28, 36); Joseph governor over (Gen. 41:37—47:26); the Israelites servants here (Ex. 1:1—12:36); the exodus out of (Ex. 12:37—14:31); Jesus taken here (Matt. 2:13).
**elders** [EL·derz] 1. *noun* older and mature civil and religious leaders over Israel.
seventy of the ***e*** of Israel . . . . . . . . . . Ex. 24:9
called for the ***e*** of Israel . . . . . . . . . Josh. 24:1
tradition of the ***e*** . . . . . . . . . . . . . . . Matt. 15:2
2. *noun* leaders of the local church.
appointed ***e*** in every . . . . . . . . . . . . Acts 14:23
the ***e*** who rule well . . . . . . . . . . . . . 1 Tim. 5:17
Let him call for the ***e*** . . . . . . . . . . . James 5:14
**elect** [uh·LEKT] *noun* chosen ones.
whom I uphold, My ***E*** . . . . . . . . . . . . . . Is. 42:1

gather together His ***e*** . . . . . . . . . . . Matt. 24:31
***e*** according to the . . . . . . . . . . . . . . 1 Pet. 1:2
**Eli** [EE·lie] *person* priest who takes in Samuel as a boy (1 Sam. 1–4).
**Elijah** [uh·LIE·juh] *person* prophet to the northern kingdom of Israel; proclaims drought and fed by ravens (1 Kin. 17:1–6); raises widow's son (1 Kin. 17:17ff); confronts prophets of Baal on Mount Carmel (1 Kin. 18:20ff); taken to heaven without dying (2 Kin. 2:11); appears with Moses at Jesus' transfiguration (Matt. 17:3–4; Mark 9:4–5).
**Elisha** [uh·LIE·shuh] *person* prophet to northern kingdom of Israel; successor to Elijah (2 Kin. 2:14–24); raises woman's son (2 Kin. 4:8–37); purifies deadly stew (2 Kin. 4:38–41); heals Naaman's leprosy (2 Kin. 5:1–19); makes ax head float (2 Kin. 6:1–7); captures Syrians (2 Kin. 6:8ff); contact with his bones revives a dead man (2 Kin. 13:20–21).
**Elizabeth** [ih·LIZ·uh·beth] *person* relative of Mary, wife of Zacharias, and mother of John the Baptist (Luke 1:5–66).
**Emmaus** [uh·MAY·uhs] *place* village near Jerusalem; on the day of His resurrection, Jesus teaches two disciples on road to (Luke 24:13–29).
**enmity** [EN·muh·tee] *noun* strong feelings against; hatred.
And I will put ***e*** . . . . . . . . . . . . . . . . Gen. 3:15
the carnal mind is ***e*** . . . . . . . . . . . . . . Rom. 8:7
with the world is ***e*** . . . . . . . . . . . . . . James 4:4
**Enoch** [EE·naak] *person* father of Methuselah, the longest living person recorded in the Bible (Gen. 5:21); walks with God (Gen. 5:22); taken to heaven without dying (Gen. 5:24).
**entreat** [in·TREET] *verb* to ask urgently; to plead.
"***E*** me not to leave you . . . . . . . . . . Ruth 1:16
"But now ***e*** God's favor . . . . . . . . . . . Mal. 1:9
being defamed, we ***e*** . . . . . . . . . . . 1 Cor. 4:13
**Ephesus** [EFF·uh·sus] *place* seaport city in Asia (modern-day Turkey); Paul visits on his second missionary journey (Acts 18:19–21); Paul visits on his third missionary journey (Acts 19); riot at (Acts 19:21–41); Paul writes letter to (Eph. 1:1); Jesus writes letter to through John (Rev. 2:1–7).
**ephod** [EH·faad] *noun* item of clothing worn by the high priest.
a breastplate, an ***e*** . . . . . . . . . . . . . . . Ex. 28:4
was wearing an ***e*** . . . . . . . . . . . . . . 1 Sam. 14:3
was wearing a linen ***e*** . . . . . . . . . . 2 Sam. 6:14
**Ephraim** [EE·free·im] *person* younger son of Joseph; adopted by Jacob (Gen. 48).
**epistle** [uh·PIH·suhl] *noun* letter; specifically, the letters written by the apostles that are included in the New Testament.
You are our ***e*** written . . . . . . . . . . . . 2 Cor. 3:2
by word or our ***e*** . . . . . . . . . . . . . 2 Thess. 2:15
is a sign in every ***e*** . . . . . . . . . . . 2 Thess. 3:17
**Esau** [EE·saw] *person* Jacob's older twin brother and son of Isaac and Rebekah; trades his birthright to Jacob for a bowl of stew (Gen. 25:22–34); his blessing stolen by Jacob (Gen. 27:1–40); forgives Jacob (Gen. 32–33).
**Esther** [EH·stir] *person* Jewish woman who becomes the queen of the Persian king Ahasuerus (Esth. 2:17); reveals Haman's evil plan to the king (Esth. 5:1–8; 7:1–10); saves the Jews (Esth. 8); Feast of Purim celebrates her actions (Esth. 9:18–29).
**eternal** [ee·TUR·nuhl] *adjective* everlasting, ongoing, without end; God is eternal in that He has no beginning or end; people are eternal in that they have a beginning but will exist forever; when the Bible speaks of eternal life, it means existing forever with God, but unbelievers will exist forever apart from Him.
that I may have ***e*** life . . . . . . . . . . . Matt. 19:16
the gift of God is ***e*** life . . . . . . . . . . Rom. 6:23
and of ***e*** judgment . . . . . . . . . . . . . . . . Heb. 6:2
**Euphrates** [you·FRAY·tees] *place* longest river in western Asia and one of the two major rivers in Mesopotamia.
**evangelist** [ih·VAN·juh·lehst] *noun* one who shares the good news about Jesus Christ with others.
house of Philip the ***e*** . . . . . . . . . . . . Acts 21:8
some prophets, some ***e*** . . . . . . . . . Eph. 4:11
do the work of an ***e*** . . . . . . . . . . . . 2 Tim. 4:5
**Eve** [EEV] *person* the first woman, made perfect and in the image of God (Gen. 2:18–25); all people descend from Adam and her (Gen. 1:26–28; 2:21–24); along with Adam, commits the first sin (Gen. 3:1–8); judged for sin (Gen. 3:9–16).
**everlasting** [eh·vur·LA·stihng] *adjective* ongoing, without end; all people, believers and unbelievers, are everlasting, but only those who believe in Jesus will have everlasting life with God.
for an ***e*** covenant . . . . . . . . . . . . . . . Gen. 17:7
away into ***e*** punishment . . . . . . . . Matt. 25:46
not perish but have ***e*** . . . . . . . . . . . . John 3:16
**evil** [EE·vuhl] 1. *noun* sinfulness, wickedness; slanderous or injurious actions.
knowledge of good and ***e*** . . . . . . . . . Gen. 2:9
I will fear no ***e*** . . . . . . . . . . . . . . . . . . Ps. 23:4
root of all kinds of ***e*** . . . . . . . . . . . 1 Tim. 6:10
2. *adjective* quality of being sinful and wicked.
rebellious and ***e*** city . . . . . . . . . . . . Ezra 4:12
turn from his ***e*** way . . . . . . . . . . . . . . . Jon. 3:8
envy, and all ***e*** speaking . . . . . . . . . . 1 Pet. 2:1
**evil one** [EE·vhul WUHN] *noun* Satan.
But deliver us from the ***e*** . . . . . . . . Matt. 6:13
keep them from the ***e*** . . . . . . . . . . . John 17:15
guard you from the ***e*** . . . . . . . . . . 2 Thess. 3:3
**exalt** [ehg·ZAALT] *verb* to praise; to raise someone or something to higher authority or honor.

God, and I will ***e*** . . . . . . . . . . . . . . . . . . . . . . . .Ex. 15:2
***E*** the LORD our God. . . . . . . . . . . . . . . . .Ps. 99:5
He may ***e*** you in due time . . . . . . . . 1 Pet. 5:6

**exhort** [ehg·ZORT] *verb* to urge strongly; to give important advice to; to warn; to call to action.
we command and ***e*** . . . . . . . . . . 2 Thess. 3:12
Convince, rebuke, ***e*** . . . . . . . . . . . . 2 Tim. 4:2
***e*** one another. . . . . . . . . . . . . . . . . . . . Heb. 3:13

**exile** [EG·zile] *noun* one who is forced to leave his or her home and live elsewhere.
and also an ***e*** from . . . . . . . . . . . 2 Sam. 15:19
And let My ***e*** go free. . . . . . . . . . . . . . Is. 45:13
The captive ***e*** hastens . . . . . . . . . . . . Is. 51:14

**Ezekiel** [eh·ZEE·kee·uhl] *person* prophet exiled in Babylon; receives vision from God (Ezek. 1:4–28); given a parable of the two eagles and the vine (Ezek. 17); tells of the fall of Jerusalem (Ezek. 24); prophesies about other nations (Ezek. 25–32).

**Ezra** [EZ·ruh] *person* priest and scribe who returns to Jerusalem from exile (Ezra 7:7); helps with efforts to rebuild the temple (Ezra 7:17–20; 8:1–15); begins spiritual reforms (Ezra 9–10); reads the law to the people after Jerusalem's walls are rebuilt (Neh. 8).

# F

**faith** [FAYTH] *noun* belief or trust that something is true—namely, in Jesus and the gospel.
shall live by his ***f*** . . . . . . . . . . . . . . . . . Hab. 2:4
***f*** is the substance. . . . . . . . . . . . . . . . Heb. 11:1
***f*** without works is dead . . . . . . . . . .James 2:20

**false prophet** [FAALS PRAA·fuht] *noun* one who claims to be a prophet of God but who is not.
Beware of ***f***, who come to . . . . . . . . Matt. 7:15
But there were also ***f*** . . . . . . . . . . . . 2 Pet. 2:1
many ***f*** have gone out . . . . . . . . . . . 1 John 4:1

**fast** [FAST] 1. *verb* to go without food for the purpose of confession, humility, or drawing closer to God.
they ***f***, I will not hear . . . . . . . . . . . . Jer. 14:12
believed God, proclaimed a ***f*** . . . . . . .Jon. 3:5
"Moreover, when you ***f*** . . . . . . . . . . . Matt. 6:16
2. *adjective* hold on to firmly.
"But you who held ***f*** to the. . . . . . . . .Deut. 4:4
For he held ***f*** to the LORD . . . . . . . . 2 Kin. 18:6
hold ***f*** the confession . . . . . . . . . . . Heb. 10:23

**Father** [FAA·thur] *identity* God the Father, First Person of the Trinity, along with God the Son and God the Spirit; describes God's loving, fatherly care (Rom. 8:15); the name Jesus called upon (Matt. 5:16); believers are to be baptized in His name, along with the Son and Holy Spirit (Matt. 28:19).

**fear of the LORD** [FEER; LORD] *noun* worship of and reverence for God; to fear God is not to be afraid of Him with terror but to know and respect Him as the all-powerful, holy Creator who judges sin.
The ***f*** is the beginning of . . . . . . . . . . Prov. 1:7
His delight is in the ***f*** . . . . . . . . . . . . . . Is. 11:3
And walking in the ***f***. . . . . . . . . . . . . . Acts 9:31

**feast** [FEEST] *noun* religious celebration of joy and thanksgiving, usually remembering a work of God. Those mentioned in Scripture:

1. **Feast of Dedication** [deh·duh·KAY·shun] or **Hanukkah** [HAA·nuh·kuh] eight-day festival observing the victories of Judas Maccabeus and the purification and rededication of the temple that takes place between the events of Malachi and Jesus' birth (John 10:22).
2. **Feast of Purim** [POOR·em] celebrates how God used Esther to rescue His people from being killed (Esth. 9:20–28).
3. **Feast of Tabernacles** [TA·buhr·na·kulz] celebrates how God provided for His people in the wilderness after they left Egypt; the people live in tents or booths for seven days (Lev. 23:34–36; Deut. 16:13–15; John 7:2).
4. **Feast of Trumpets** [TRUHM·puhts] or **Rosh Hashanah** [RAASH huh·SHAA·nuh] celebrates the beginning of the Jewish new year (Lev. 23:23–25; Num. 29:1–6).
5. **Feast of Unleavened Bread** [uhn·LEH·vend BRED] or **Passover** [PA·sow·vuhr] celebrates how God rescued His people from captivity in Egypt (Ex. 12:1–30; Lev. 23:4–14; Deut. 16:1–8; Matt. 26:17–29).
6. **Feast of Weeks** [WEEKS] or **Pentecost** [PEHN·tuh·kaast] is celebrated fifty days after Passover to thank God for the summer harvest that He provided (Ex. 34:22; Lev. 23:15–22; Num. 28:26–31; Deut. 16:9–12; Acts 2:1).

**fellowship** [FEH·low·ship] *noun* companionship and friendship; a group of people who share a common interest.
doctrine and ***f*** . . . . . . . . . . . . . . . . . .Acts 2:42
And have no ***f*** with the . . . . . . . . . . . Eph. 5:11
we say that we have ***f*** . . . . . . . . . . 1 John 1:6

**fervent** [FUR·vuhnt] *adjective* intense, passionate, sincere.
***f*** desire I have desired . . . . . . . . . . Luke 22:15
and being ***f*** in spirit . . . . . . . . . . . .Acts 18:25
***f*** prayer of a . . . . . . . . . . . . . . . . .James 5:16

**filled with the Holy Spirit** *phrase* to be controlled and guided by the Holy Spirit.
and Elizabeth was ***f*** . . . . . . . . . . . . . Luke 1:41
Peter, ***f***, said to them . . . . . . . . . . . . .Acts 4:8
who also is called Paul, ***f*** . . . . . . . . .Acts 13:9

**firmament** [FUR·muh·muhnt] *noun* sky; heavens.
Thus God made the ***f*** . . . . . . . . . . . . . Gen. 1:7
***f*** shows His handiwork . . . . . . . . . . . .Ps. 19:1
brightness of the ***f*** . . . . . . . . . . . . . . Dan. 12:3

**First and the Last** [FURST; LAST] *identity* describes God's everlasting control, majesty, and power (Is. 41:4; 44:6; 48:12); describes the lordship of Jesus Christ (Rev. 1:11, 17; 2:8; 22:13).

**firstborn; firstfruits** [FURST·born; FURST·froots] *noun* eldest son or animal born, or earliest fruits harvested, that are to be set apart for God.

"Consecrate to Me all the *f*. . . . . . . . . Ex. 13:2
the *f* of your harvest to . . . . . . . . . Lev. 23:10
brought forth her *f* Son . . . . . . . . . . . Luke 2:7

**fleshly** [FLESH·lee] *adjective* worldly and sinful; not godly or of God.

*f* wisdom but by the . . . . . . . . . . . . 2 Cor. 1:12
law of a *f* commandment . . . . . . . . Heb. 7:16
*f* lusts which war against . . . . . . . 1 Pet. 2:11

**follow** [FAA·low] *verb* to walk after; to live according to the ways of another.

If the LORD is God, *f*. . . . . . . . . . . . 1 Kin. 18:21
"*F* Me, and I will make . . . . . . . . . . . Matt. 4:19
that you should *f* . . . . . . . . . . . . . 1 Pet. 2:21

**forefathers** [FOR·faa·therz] *noun* ancestors; those who came before; often refers to the patriarchs of the Old Testament.

*f* who refused to hear . . . . . . . . . . . Jer. 11:10
and oppressed our *f*. . . . . . . . . . . . . Acts 7:19
conscience, as my *f* . . . . . . . . . . . . . 2 Tim. 1:3

**foreign gods** [FOR·uhn GAADZ] *noun* false gods and idols normally worshiped by others than the Israelites and Christians, but sometimes by them as well.

"Put away the *f*. . . . . . . . . . . . . . . . Gen. 35:2
So they put away the *f* . . . . . . . . . Judg. 10:16
to be a proclaimer of *f*. . . . . . . . . . . Acts 17:18

**forgive** [for·GIV] *verb* to pardon others for wrongs they have done; to show mercy.

if You will *f* their sin. . . . . . . . . . . . . Ex. 32:32
Who can *f* sins but God . . . . . . . . . . . Mark 2:7
*f* us our sins and to . . . . . . . . . . . . . . 1 John 1:9

**forsake** [for·SAYK] *verb* to turn away from; to abandon or leave; to quit.

And does not *f* His saints . . . . . . . . . Ps. 37:28
worthless idols *f* . . . . . . . . . . . . . . . . . Jon. 2:8
never leave you nor *f*. . . . . . . . . . . . . Heb. 13:5

**frontlets** [FRUHNT·luhts] *noun* small containers holding portions of Scripture that are worn on the forehead.

on your hand and as *f* . . . . . . . . . . . Ex. 13:16
and they shall be as *f*. . . . . . . . . . . . . Deut. 6:8
and they shall be as *f*. . . . . . . . . . . Deut. 11:18

**fruitful** [FROOT·fuhl] *adjective* producing fruit; often used to describe people being productive.

them, saying, "Be *f* . . . . . . . . . . . . . Gen. 1:22
heaven and *f* seasons . . . . . . . . . . . . Acts 14:17
pleasing Him, being *f*. . . . . . . . . . . . . . Col. 1:10

# G

**Gabriel** [GAY·bree·ul] *noun* angel of high rank; appears to Daniel (Dan. 8:16; 9:21); announces upcoming birth of John (Luke 1:19); announces upcoming birth of Jesus (Luke 1:26).

**Galatia** [guh·LAY·shee·uh] *place* region and Roman province in Asia Minor, or modern-day Turkey. Paul visits on his first missionary journey (Acts 13:14; 14:24); Paul visits on his second missionary journey (Acts 16:1–5); Paul writes letter to the churches of (Gal. 1:2).

**Galilee** [GA·luh·lee] *place* northern region of ancient Palestine, including the Sea of Galilee, that was important for agriculture and trade; also called "land of Gennesaret" (Matt. 14:34; Mark 6:53); Jesus calls first disciples here (Matt. 4:12–22); Jesus shares Sermon on the Mount here (Matt. 5–7); Jesus feeds more than five thousand here (John 6:1–13); Jesus gives Great Commission here (Matt. 28:16–20).

**Gamaliel** [guh·MAY·lee·uhl] *person* famous member of the Jewish Sanhedrin and a teacher of the law; speaks on behalf of Peter and the apostles (Acts 5:33–39); teaches Paul in Jerusalem (Acts 22:3).

**Gaza** [GAH·zuh] *place* one of the five main cities of the Philistines; Old Testament prophets condemn (Amos 1:6; Zeph. 2:4; Zech. 9:5); Philip shares the gospel with an Ethiopian on road to here (Acts 8:26–40).

**genealogy** [jee·nee·AA·luh·jee] *noun* listing of the people in a family going back many generations.

This is the *g* of Noah . . . . . . . . . . . . . Gen. 6:9
The book of the *g* . . . . . . . . . . . . . . . . Matt. 1:1
mother, without *g*. . . . . . . . . . . . . . . . Heb. 7:3

**Gentiles** [JEN·tilez] *noun* non-Jews; those who are not part of Abraham's family.

The *G* shall see your . . . . . . . . . . . . . . Is. 62:2
all these things the *G*. . . . . . . . . . . . Matt. 6:32
a light to the *G* . . . . . . . . . . . . . . . . Acts 13:47

**Gethsemane** [geth·SEH·muh·nee] *place* garden on the Mount of Olives east of Jerusalem; Jesus prays and is betrayed here (Matt. 26:36; Mark 14:32).

**Gideon** [GID·ee·un] *person* judge who delivers the people of Israel from the Midianites (Judg. 6–8); destroys the altar of Baal (Judg. 6:28–35); asks for a sign of the fleece (Judg. 6:36–40); leads an army of three hundred (Judg. 7:1—8:21); refuses being named king (Judg. 8:22–28).

**Gilead** [GI·lee·uhd] *place* a rugged, mountainous region east of the Jordan River; David flees here (2 Sam. 17:21–22); David fights against Absalom here (2 Sam. 18:6).

**Gilgal** [GIL·gal] 1. *place* city area near Jericho; after crossing the Jordan River, the Israelites camp here (Josh. 4:19–20); the Gibeonites deceive Joshua here (Josh. 9:6); Ehud delivers the Israelites near here (Judg. 3:12–30); Saul becomes king here (1 Sam. 11:14–15); Samuel rebukes Saul here (1 Sam. 15).

2. *place* area north of Bethel; Elijah leaves here when he is about to be taken into heaven (2 Kin. 2:1); Elisha purifies deadly stew here (2 Kin. 4:38–41).

**gird** [GURD] *verb* to make something secure; to fasten; to prepare.
*G* Your sword upon Your . . . . . . . . . . Ps. 45:3
and another will *g* . . . . . . . . . . John 21:18
Therefore *g* up the . . . . . . . . . . 1 Pet. 1:13
**glad tidings** [GLAD TIE·dihngz] *noun* good news, specifically the gospel.
Who brings *g* of good things . . . . . . . . . . Is. 52:7
and bring you these *g* . . . . . . . . . . Luke 1:19
we declare to you *g* . . . . . . . . . . Acts 13:32
**glorify** [GLOR·uh·figh] *verb* to make much of; to honor or praise; to magnify.
My altar, and I will *g* . . . . . . . . . . Is. 60:7
Father, *g* Your name . . . . . . . . . . John 12:28
therefore *g* God in . . . . . . . . . . 1 Cor. 6:20
**glory of the Lord** *phrase* describes God's holy and majestic presence.
*g* filled the tabernacle . . . . . . . . . . Ex. 40:34
They shall see the *g* . . . . . . . . . . Is. 35:2
the *g* shone around them . . . . . . . . . . Luke 2:9
**godliness** [GAAD·lee·nuhs] *noun* characteristics and actions that please God.
*g* is profitable . . . . . . . . . . 1 Tim. 4:8
having a form of *g* . . . . . . . . . . 2 Tim. 3:5
pertain to life and *g* . . . . . . . . . . 2 Pet. 1:3
**Golgotha** [GOL·goth·uh] *place* site of Jesus' crucifixion (Matt. 27:33; Mark 15:22; John 19:17).
**Goliath** [guh·LIE·uhth] *person* Philistine giant and champion; taunts the Israelites (1 Sam. 17:8–11); defeated by David (1 Sam. 17:12–51).
**Gomer** [GO·mer] *person* unfaithful wife of the prophet Hosea; forgiven and restored to Hosea to picture God's relationship with the Israelites (Hos. 3).
**Gomorrah** [guh·MOR·uh] *place* wicked city destroyed by the Lord (Gen. 19:24–28).
**good** [GUD] 1. *adjective* meets God's standard and design; pleasing to God.
God saw that it was *g* . . . . . . . . . . Gen. 1:10
tidings of *g* things . . . . . . . . . . Is. 52:7
No one is *g* but One . . . . . . . . . . Matt. 19:17
2. *noun* person, action, or thing that meets God's standard and design.
Shall we indeed accept *g* . . . . . . . . . . Job 2:10
Learn to do *g* . . . . . . . . . . Is. 1:17
love your enemies, do *g* . . . . . . . . . . Luke 6:35
**gospel** [GAA·spuhl] *noun* good news, specifically the message of salvation through Jesus.
and believe in the *g* . . . . . . . . . . Mark 1:15
not ashamed of the *g* . . . . . . . . . . Rom. 1:16
of truth, the *g* . . . . . . . . . . Eph. 1:13
**grace** [GRACE] *noun* God's favor; undeserved good things that God gives, specifically forgiveness of sin.
But Noah found *g* . . . . . . . . . . Gen. 6:8
*g* you have been saved . . . . . . . . . . Eph. 2:8
But He gives more *g* . . . . . . . . . . James 4:6
**guarantee** [gair·uhn·TEE] *noun* a pledge given that something will be done; a down payment or deposit.
in our hearts as a *g* . . . . . . . . . . 2 Cor. 1:22
us the Spirit as a *g* . . . . . . . . . . 2 Cor. 5:5
who is the *g* of our . . . . . . . . . . Eph. 1:14

# H

**Habakkuk** [huh·BACK·kuk] *person* prophet of Judah; the Old Testament book that bears his name is the eighth of the twelve Minor Prophets.
**Hades** [HAY·deez] *place* the place of the dead.
being in torments in *H* . . . . . . . . . . Luke 16:23
not leave my soul in *H* . . . . . . . . . . Acts 2:27
*H* were cast into the . . . . . . . . . . Rev. 20:14
**Hagar** [HAY·gaar] *person* servant of Sarah, Abraham's wife; mother of Abraham's son Ishmael (Gen. 16).
**Haggai** [HA·gee·igh] *person* prophet to the Israelites after the exile; encourages the rebuilding of the temple (Ezra 5:1—6:22; Hag. 1:1–4); the Old Testament book that bears his name is the tenth of the twelve Minor Prophets.
**hallowed** [HA·lowd] *adjective* sacred; holy; set apart.
the Sabbath day and *h* . . . . . . . . . . Ex. 20:11
but I will be *h* . . . . . . . . . . Lev. 22:32
heaven, *h* be Your name . . . . . . . . . . Matt. 6:9
**Hannah** [HA·nuh] *person* mother of the judge and prophet Samuel; heavyhearted because of being childless (1 Sam. 1:5–7); promises God that she would dedicate a son to Him (1 Sam. 1:8–18); gives birth to Samuel and dedicates him to God (1 Sam. 1:19–28); prays to God with joy and gratitude (1 Sam. 2:1–10).
**Haran** [HEH·ruhn] *place* city of northern Mesopotamia; Abraham and his father, Terah, are from here (Gen. 11:31–32; 12:4–5); Jacob marries Leah and Rachel here (Gen. 28:10; 29:4–6).
**hated** [HAY·tuhd] *verb* to have had a strong dislike for; at times used to describe something that was not chosen.
they *h* knowledge . . . . . . . . . . Prov. 1:29
world has *h* them . . . . . . . . . . John 17:14
but Esau I have *h* . . . . . . . . . . Rom. 9:13
**haughty** [HAA·tee] 1. *adjective* proud; overbearing.
my heart is not *h* . . . . . . . . . . Ps. 131:1
*h* spirit before a fall . . . . . . . . . . Prov. 16:18
traitors, headstrong, *h* . . . . . . . . . . 2 Tim. 3:4
2. *noun* someone who is proud or overbearing.
Your eyes are on the *h* . . . . . . . . . . 2 Sam. 22:28
the *h* will be humbledIs. 10:33
**heart** [HAART] *noun* part of the person that represents the center of the will and emotions.
A broken and a contrite *h* . . . . . . . . . . Ps. 51:17
Blessed are the pure in *h* . . . . . . . . . . Matt. 5:8
always go astray in their *h* . . . . . . . . . . Heb. 3:10
**heathen** [HEE·then] *noun* someone who does not believe in God.
repetitions as the *h* . . . . . . . . . . Matt. 6:7

him be to you like a ***h*** . . . . . . . . . . . Matt. 18:17

**heaven; heavens** [HEH·vin; HEH·vinz] 1. *place* sky.

He adorned the ***h*** . . . . . . . . . . . . . . . Job 26:13

***h*** declare the glory of God . . . . . . . . . . Ps. 19:1

saw ***h*** opened and . . . . . . . . . . . . . . Acts 10:11

2. *place* where God dwells and where believers go upon death.

Elijah into ***h*** by a . . . . . . . . . . . . . . . . 2 Kin. 2:1

"***H*** is My throne. . . . . . . . . . . . . . . . Is. 66:1

Now I saw a new ***h*** . . . . . . . . . . . . . . . Rev. 21:1

**Hebrews** [HEE·brooz] *noun* Israelites or Jews; those who are part of Abraham's family.

not eat food with the ***H*** . . . . . . . . . Gen. 43:32

one of the ***H*** children . . . . . . . . . . . . . . Ex. 2:6

complaint against the ***H*** . . . . . . . . . . . Acts 6:1

**Hebron** [HEE·bruhn] *place* city south of Jerusalem; Sarah, Abraham, Isaac, Rebekah, Leah, and Jacob buried here (Gen. 23:17–19; 25:9–10; 49:29–32; 50:12–13); David anointed king here (2 Sam. 2:4); David reigns from here (2 Sam. 2:1—5:5).

**hell** [HEL] *noun* place of the unbelieving dead.

go down alive into ***h*** . . . . . . . . . . . . . Ps. 55:15

be in danger of ***h*** fire . . . . . . . . . . . . Matt. 5:22

power to cast into ***h*** . . . . . . . . . . . . . Luke 12:5

**Hellenists** [HEL·uh·nists] *noun* Jews who accepted Greek culture in Israel.

against the Hebrews by the ***H*** . . . . . . Acts 6:1

disputed against the ***H*** . . . . . . . . . . . Acts 9:29

spoke to the ***H***, preaching . . . . . . . . Acts 11:20

**Helper** [HEL·pur] *identity* title for the Holy Spirit; describes His ministry in guiding and encouraging believers (John 14:26; 15:26; 16:7).

**heresies** [HAIR·uh·seez] *noun* false teachings and doctrines that deny the truth about God and Jesus Christ.

selfish ambitions, dissensions, ***h*** . . . Gal. 5:20

secretly bring in destructive ***h*** . . . . 2 Pet. 2:1

**Herod** [HAIR·uhd] 1. **Herod the Great** [GRAYT] *person* territorial ruler under the Romans (37–4 BC); sends the wise men to search for Jesus (Matt. 2:1–9).

2. **Herod Antipas** [AN·tuh·puhs] *person* territorial ruler under the Romans (4 BC–AD 39); puts John the Baptist in prison (Matt. 14:1–5); has John the Baptist killed (Matt. 14:6–12); hears Jesus' trial (Luke 23:6–12).

3. **Herod Agrippa I** [uh·GRI·puh] *person* territorial ruler under the Romans (AD 37–44); has the apostle James killed (Acts 12:1–2); arrests Peter (Acts 12:3–4).

4. **Herod Agrippa II** [uh·GRI·puh] *person* territorial ruler under the Romans (AD 48–93); hears Paul's defense (Acts 25–26).

**Herodians** [heh·ROW·dee·uhns] *noun* group that supports the Herods as rulers.

with the ***H***, saying. . . . . . . . . . . . . Matt. 22:16

plotted with the ***H*** . . . . . . . . . . . . . . Mark 3:6

Pharisees and the ***H*** . . . . . . . . . . . Mark 12:13

**Hezekiah** [heh·zuh·KIGH·uh] *person* fourteenth king of Judah (715–687 BC); good king (2 Kin. 18:2–8); gives silver and gold from the temple to Assyria (2 Kin. 18:13–16); becomes ill and prays to God (2 Kin. 20:1–11).

**high places** [HIGH PLAY·suhz] *noun* sites of worship, usually of false gods.

him up to the ***h*** of Baal . . . . . . . . . Num. 22:41

and sets me on my ***h*** . . . . . . . . . 2 Sam. 22:34

Him to anger with their ***h*** . . . . . . . . . Ps. 78:58

**high priest** [HIGH PREEST] *noun* chief priest who performs the regular priestly duties but also serves as the mediator between Israel and God on the Day of Atonement.

'He who is the ***h*** . . . . . . . . . . . . . . . Lev. 21:10

Caiaphas, being ***h*** that. . . . . . . . . . John 11:49

a merciful and faithful ***H*** . . . . . . . . . . Heb. 2:17

**Hittites** [HIH·tites] *noun* a people of the ancient world who lived in Asia Minor between 1900 and 1200 BC; spread into northern Syria and later into the land promised to Abraham; driven out by Israel under Joshua (Ex. 3:8, 17; Deut. 7:1; Judg. 3:5); most famous Hittite is Uriah, the husband of Bathsheba. David has Uriah killed in battle so he can marry Bathsheba (2 Sam. 11).

**holy** [HO·lee] *adjective* set apart; devoted; dedicated; without sin.

Where you stand is ***h*** . . . . . . . . . . . . . . Ex. 3:5

the LORD your God am ***h*** . . . . . . . . . . Lev. 19:2

it is written, "Be ***h*** . . . . . . . . . . . . . 1 Pet. 1:16

**Holy Spirit** [HO·lee SPEER·uht] *identity* Third Person of the Trinity, along with God the Father and God the Son; also called the Spirit of the Lord, Spirit of God; indwells believers (John 14:16–17; Rom 8:11); guarantees salvation of believers (2 Cor. 1:22; 5:5; Eph. 1:13–14; 4:30); fills, empowers, and guides believers (Luke 1:15–17; John 16:13; Acts 1:4–5); teaches believers (Luke 12:12; John 14:26); prays on behalf of believers (Rom. 8:26–27); makes believers more like Jesus (Rom. 8:2–17; 2 Thess. 2:13); produces fruit in believers (Gal. 5:22–23); gives gifts to believers (Rom. 12:6–8; 1 Cor. 12:4–11; Eph. 4:11; 1 Pet. 4:11).

**honor** [AA·nuhr] 1. *verb* to respect; to esteem.

"***H*** your father and your . . . . . . . . . Ex. 20:12

before ***h*** is humility . . . . . . . . . . . . Prov. 15:33

***h*** the Son just as they . . . . . . . . . . . John 5:23

2. *noun* respect; esteem.

both riches and ***h*** . . . . . . . . . . . . . . 1 Kin. 3:13

***H*** and majesty are . . . . . . . . . . . . . . . . Ps. 96:6

is not without ***h*** . . . . . . . . . . . . . . . . Matt. 13:57

**hope** [HOHP] 1. *verb* to trust something will happen; Christian hope is more of a confident expectation.

I ***h*** in Your word . . . . . . . . . . . . . . . Ps. 119:147

good that one should ***h*** . . . . . . . . . . Lam. 3:26

***h*** that is seen is . . . . . . . . . . . . . . . . Rom. 8:24

2. *noun* confident expectation of what will happen; trust.

My ***h*** is in You . . . . . . . . . . . . . . . . . . . . Ps. 39:7

*h* does not disappoint . . . . . . . . . . . Rom. 5:5
Jesus Christ, our *h* . . . . . . . . . . . 1 Tim. 1:1
**hosanna** [hoh·ZAA·nuh] *noun* cry that means "save us"; shouted when part of the Psalms are read.
*H* in the highest . . . . . . . . . . . . . . Matt. 21:9
"*H*! Blessed is He. . . . . . . . . . . . . . Mark 11:9
"*H*! Blessed is He. . . . . . . . . . . . . . John 12:13
**Hosea** [hoh·ZAY·uh] *person* prophet of Israel; the Old Testament book that bears his name is the first of the twelve Minor Prophets.
**host of heaven** [HOHST; HEH·vin] 1. *noun* sun, moon, and stars.
the stars, all the *h* . . . . . . . . . . . . Deut. 4:19
worshiped all the *h* . . . . . . . . . . . 2 Kin. 17:16
the moon and all the *h* . . . . . . . . . . . Jer. 8:2
2. *noun* mighty army in God's service, including the angels.
and all the *h* standing by . . . . . . . 1 Kin. 22:19
and all the *h* standing on. . . . . . . 2 Chr. 18:18
**house** [HOWS] 1. *noun* dwelling place; home.
not covet your neighbor's *h*. . . . . . . . Ex. 20:17
dwell in the *h* of the LORD. . . . . . . . . . Ps. 23:6
Father's *h* are many mansions . . . . John 14:2
2. *noun* family; group; nation.
But as for me and my *h* . . . . . . . . . Josh. 24:15
'Set your *h* in order . . . . . . . . . . . . 2 Kin. 20:1
*h* divided against . . . . . . . . . . . . . . Matt. 12:25
**humility** [hyoo·MIL·uh·tee] *noun* thinking properly and not too highly of oneself.
righteousness, seek *h*. . . . . . . . . . . . Zeph. 2:3
the Lord with all *h* . . . . . . . . . . . . . Acts 20:19
mercies, kindness, *h* . . . . . . . . . . . . Col. 3:12
**hypocrite** [HIH·puh·krit] *noun* someone who pretends to be what he or she is not; the word comes from the ancient Greek theater where an actor would wear a mask to play a role on stage.
For everyone is a *h*. . . . . . . . . . . . . . Is. 9:17
not be like the *h*. . . . . . . . . . . . . . . . Matt. 6:5
also played the *h* . . . . . . . . . . . . . . Gal. 2:13

## I

**I AM** [I AM] *identity* meaning "to be," describes God's timeless existence; name God uses for Himself when speaking with Moses (Ex. 3:14); Jesus uses to defend His identity (John 8:58).
**idol** [I·duhl] *noun* false god; image or figure regarded as an object of worship.
'Do not turn to *i* . . . . . . . . . . . . . . . . Lev. 19:4
a wooden *i* is a worthless . . . . . . . . . Jer. 10:8
keep yourselves from *i* . . . . . . . . . 1 John 5:21
**image** [IH·muhj] *noun* likeness of either God or an idol.
make man in Our *i* . . . . . . . . . . . . . . Gen. 1:26
since he is the *i* . . . . . . . . . . . . . . . 1 Cor. 11:7
the beast and his *i* . . . . . . . . . . . . . . Rev. 14:9
**imitate** [IH·muh·tayt] *verb* to copy; to do what another does.
I urge you, *i* me . . . . . . . . . . . . . . . 1 Cor. 4:16
as I also *i* Christ . . . . . . . . . . . . . . 1 Cor. 11:1
*i* those who through. . . . . . . . . . . . . Heb. 6:12
**Immanuel** [ih·MAN·yoo·ehl] *identity* Hebrew name meaning "God with us"; describes how God is with His people; Isaiah uses to speak of Christ's coming (Is. 7:14; 8:8); what Jesus is called (Matt. 1:23).
**impute** [ihm·PYOOT] *verb* to credit to another.
guilt of bloodshed shall be *i* . . . . . . . Lev. 17:4
the LORD does not *i*. . . . . . . . . . . . . . Ps. 32:2
righteousness might be *i* . . . . . . . . Rom. 4:11
**iniquity** [ih·NI·kwuh·tee] *noun* sin; wickedness.
God, visiting the *i* of the. . . . . . . . . . Ex. 20:5
O LORD, pardon my *i* . . . . . . . . . . . . . Ps. 25:11
all you workers of *i* . . . . . . . . . . . . Luke 13:27
**inspiration** [in·spur·AY·shun] *noun* God's guidance of the writers of the Bible to record what He desired.
is given by *i* of God . . . . . . . . . . . . . 2 Tim. 3:16
**intercession** [in·tur·SEH·shun] *noun* prayer for someone; plea on behalf of another.
of many, and made *i*. . . . . . . . . . . . . . Is. 53:12
Spirit Himself makes *i*. . . . . . . . . . . Rom. 8:26
always lives to make *i* . . . . . . . . . . . Heb. 7:25
**Isaac** [I·zuhk] *person* promised son of Abraham and Sarah; God tests Abraham concerning (Gen. 22:1–19); husband of Rebekah (Gen. 24); father of Jacob and Esau (Gen. 25:19–28); tricked by Jacob (Gen. 27:1–29).
**Isaiah** [I·ZAY·uh] *person* prophet of Israel and writer of the Book of Isaiah.
**Ishmael** [ISH·may·el] *person* son of Abraham and Hagar; Abraham and Sarah send away with Hagar (Gen. 21:8–16); God promises to make a great nation (Gen. 21:17–21).
**Israel** [IZ·ree·uhl] 1. *person* Jacob; name given to him after overnight struggle (Gen. 32:22–30).
2. *noun* people descended from Jacob also called the children of Israel, the Israelites, the Hebrews, and, after the exile, the Jews.
Then the children of *I* groaned . . . . . . Ex. 2:23
spoke to all *I* . . . . . . . . . . . . . . . . . Deut. 1:1
which God does for *I* . . . . . . . . . . 1 Sam. 2:32
3. *noun* northern kingdom during the period of the divided monarchy.
made him king over all *I* . . . . . . . . 1 Kin. 12:20
Judah was defeated by *I* . . . . . . . . 2 Kin. 14:12
king of Assyria carried *I* . . . . . . . . 2 Kin. 18:11

## J

**Jacob** [JAY·kuhb] *person* Esau's younger twin brother and son of Isaac and Rebekah; trades a bowl of stew for Esau's birthright (Gen. 25:22–34); steals Esau's blessing by tricking Isaac (Gen. 27:1–40); flees from Esau (Gen. 27:41–46); hears from God in a dream (Gen. 28:10–22); marries Leah and Rachel (Gen. 29:1–30); fathers twelve sons (Gen. 29:31—30:24); wrestles with God and renamed Israel (Gen. 32:22–32); restored with Esau (Gen. 33:1–17); takes family to Egypt (Gen. 46:1–7).

**James** [JAYMZ] 1. **James the son of Zebedee** [ZEH·buh·dee] *person* apostle (Matt. 10:2); brother of John (Matt. 4:21); fisherman (Mark 1:20); at Jesus' transfiguration (Matt. 17:1); requests place of honor (Mark 10:35–37); with Jesus as He prays in Gethsemane (Matt. 26:37); Herod Agrippa puts to death (Acts 12:1–2).

2. **James the son of Alphaeus** [AL·fee·uhs] *person* apostle; also called "James the Less" (Mark 15:40).

3. **James the brother of the Lord** [LORD] *person* brother of Jesus (Matt. 13:55); did not believe in Jesus during His lifetime (John 7:1–5); resurrected Jesus appears to (1 Cor. 15:7); in upper room (Acts 1:14); becomes leader of the Jerusalem church (Acts 12:17); leader at Jerusalem Council (Acts 15:13); writes epistle of James (James 1:1).

**Jeremiah** [jeh·ruh·MIGH·uh] *person* priest and prophet (c. 626–580 BC); prophesies against Jerusalem (Jer. 2); receives visions of almond branch and boiling pot (Jer. 1:11–19), the potter's wheel (Jer. 18:2–10), and the good and bad figs (Jer. 24:1–10); laments over Jerusalem (Jer. 4:1–4; Lam. 1:1—4:22); scroll he writes is destroyed (Jer. 36:20–26); scroll is rewritten (Jer. 36:27–32); imprisoned (Jer. 37:11–21); freed (Jer. 39:11–18); taken to Egypt (Jer. 43).

**Jericho** [JEHR·ih·koh] *place* city in the south of the Jordan valley; falls to Joshua's army (Josh. 6:1–21); Rahab spared from (Josh. 2:1–24; 6:22–25)

**Jeroboam** [jehr·uh·BOW·uhm] 1. *person* **Jeroboam** (c. 922–901 BC); rebels against Solomon (1 Kin. 11:26–40); rebels against Rehoboam and becomes first king of northern kingdom (1 Kin. 12:1–24); makes golden calves for worship (1 Kin. 12:25–33).

2. *person* **Jeroboam II** (c. 786–747 BC); son of Joash; evil king of Israel (2 Kin. 14:23–29).

**Jerusalem** [jeh·ROO·suh·luhm] *place* important city of ancient Palestine; David captures and makes capital (2 Sam. 5:6–9; 1 Chr. 11:4–8); David brings ark of the Testimony here (2 Sam. 6:1–17); Solomon builds the temple and other buildings here (1 Kin. 5–7); captured by Nebuchadnezzar (Jer. 39); Zerubbabel, Ezra, and Nehemiah rebuild (Ezra 1–10; Neh. 1–13); Jesus presented at temple here (Luke 2:22–38); Jesus talks with Nicodemus here (John 2:23; 3:1–21); Jesus spends week leading up to the cross here (Matt. 21:1—28:20; Mark 11:1—16:20; Luke 19:28—24:53; John 12:12—21:25); church begins here (Acts 1–2).

**Jesse** [JEH·see] *person* grandson of Boaz and Ruth (Ruth 4:17, 22); father of David (1 Sam. 16:1–13; 17:12ff).

**Jesus** [JEE·suhs] *identity* personal name of the Son of God that He took on when He came to earth; often referred to as Jesus Christ (Matt. 1:1), Christ Jesus (Acts 19:4), Lord Jesus (Acts 1:21), and Jesus of Nazareth (Acts 6:14) to distinguish from others named Jesus (Col. 4:11); born to Mary (Matt. 1:18–25; Luke 2:1–20); baptized by John (Matt. 3:13–17); turns water into wine (John 2:1–12); gives Sermon on the Mount (Matt. 5:1—7:29); stills a storm (Mark 4:35–41); sends unclean spirits into the swine (Mark 5:1–20); feeds over five thousand (Matt. 14:13–21); walks on water (Matt. 14:22–33); feeds over four thousand (Matt. 15:32–39); transfigured (Matt. 17:1–8); triumphally enters Jerusalem (Matt. 21:1–11); raises Lazarus from the dead (John 11:1–44); shares the Lord's Supper (Matt. 26:26–29); arrested (Matt. 26:47–56); tried (Matt. 27:11–14); crucified and buried (Matt. 27:32–61); is raised back to life and ascends to heaven (Matt. 28; Mark 16; Luke 24; John 20–21).

**Jews** [JOOZ] *noun* Hebrews or Israelites; those who are part of Abraham's family; name used after the exile.

the elders of the ***J*** build . . . . . . . . . . Ezra 6:7
You the King of the ***J*** . . . . . . . . . . . Matt. 27:11
whether ***J*** or Greeks . . . . . . . . . 1 Cor. 12:13

**Jezebel** [JEH·zuh·bel] *person* idolatrous wife of Ahab (1 Kin. 16:31); kills God's prophets (1 Kin. 18:4); chases after Elijah (1 Kin. 19:1–2); has Naboth killed and takes his vineyard (1 Kin. 21:1–16); used as a symbolic name of false teachers (Rev. 2:20).

**Job** [JOBE] *person* upright man whom God allowed Satan to test; loses his children and possessions (Job 1:13–22); loses his health (Job 2:1–10); debates three friends on the cause of his suffering (Job 3–31); confronted by Elihu (Job 32–37); confronted by God (Job 38–41); repents and is restored (Job 42).

**Joel** [JO·ehl] *person* prophet; son of Pethuel; the Old Testament book that bears his name is the second of the twelve Minor Prophets.

**John** [JAAN] 1. **John the Baptist** [BAP·tuhst] *person* son of Elizabeth and Zacharias (Luke 1:5–25, 57–66); prophet, called the forerunner of Jesus (John 1:15–28); baptizes Jesus (Matt. 3:13–17); imprisoned by Herod and put to death (Matt. 14:3–12).

2. **John the son of Zebedee** [ZEH·buh·dee] *person* apostle; brother of James (Matt. 4:21–22; Mark 1:19–20; Luke 5:10); fisherman (Mark 1:20); disciple of John the Baptist (John 1:35–40); at Jesus' transfiguration (Matt. 17:1); requests place of honor (Mark 10:35–37); with Jesus as He prays in Gethsemane (Matt. 26:37); refers to himself as the "disciple whom [Jesus] loved" in his Gospel (John 19:26); exiled on Patmos where he writes Revelation (Rev. 1:9).

3. **John Mark** [JAAN MAARK] *person See* Mark.

**Jonah** [JO·nuh] *person* prophet sent to Nineveh; tries to run from God's call (Jon. 1:1–9); thrown into the sea and swallowed by a great fish (Jon. 1:10—2:10); preaches to Nineveh (Jon. 3); becomes angry when Nineveh repents (Jon. 4); the Old Testament book that bears his name is the fifth of the twelve Minor Prophets.

**Jonathan** [JAAN·uh·thun] *person* oldest son of Saul; befriends David (1 Sam. 18:1–4); makes covenant with David (1 Sam. 20:1–23); warns David to flee (1 Sam. 20:35–42); killed by Philistines in battle (1 Sam. 31:2).

**Jordan River** [JOR·dun RIH·vuhr] *place* main river in ancient Palestine, flowing from the slopes of Mount Hermon through the Sea of Galilee into the Dead Sea; waters miraculously stop for the Israelites to cross (Josh. 3:14—4:24); John baptizes Jesus here (Matt. 3:13).

**Joseph** [JO·sef] 1. **Joseph, son of Jacob** [JAY·kuhb] *person* favored son of Jacob (Gen. 37:3); brothers sell him to traders and taken to Egypt (Gen. 37:18–36); imprisoned on false accusations (Gen. 39:7–23); interprets Pharaoh's dreams (Gen. 41:1–36); becomes administrator of Egypt (Gen. 41:37—50:26); restored with his brothers (Gen. 42–45); forgives his brothers (Gen. 50).

2. **Joseph, husband of Mary** [MAIR·ee] *person* descended from David (Matt. 1:16–25); raises Jesus as His human father (John 1:45).

3. **Joseph of Arimathea** [ehr·uh·muh·THEE·uh] *person* devout Jew (Luke 23:50–51); member of the Sanhedrin (Mark 15:43); secret follower of Jesus (John 19:38); buries Jesus' body (Matt. 27:57–60).

**Joshua** [jaa·SHOO·ah] *person* originally named Hoshea (Num. 13:8); Moses's primary helper (Num. 11:28); spies out Promised Land (Num. 13:16); with Caleb, brings back good report (Num. 14:6–9); becomes the Israelites' leader after Moses (Josh. 1); leads the Israelites into the Promised Land (Josh. 3ff); prays for the sun to stand still (Josh. 10).

**Josiah** [jo·SIGH·uh] *person* good king of Judah; son of Amon and grandson of Manasseh (2 Kin. 21:18, 24); becomes king at the age of eight (1 Kin. 22:1); finds the Book of the Law while the house of the Lord was being repaired (2 Chr. 34:14); reads the book to the inhabitants of Judah (2 Chr. 34:29–32), which prompts repentance and reform (2 Kin. 23:1–25).

**Jubilee** [joo·buh·LEE] *noun* fiftieth-year celebration by the Israelites in which rented lands are returned to their original owners.

cause the trumpet of the *J* . . . . . . . . Lev. 25:9
his field after the *J*, then . . . . . . . . . Lev. 27:18
the *J* of the children. . . . . . . . . . . . . .Num. 36:4

**Judah** [JOO·duh] *person* fourth son of Jacob by Leah (Gen. 29:31, 35); convinces his brothers to sell Joseph to traders instead of killing him (Gen. 37:26–27); offers to remain in Egypt instead of Benjamin (Gen. 44:18–33); ancestor of the tribe of Judah.

**Judas** [JOO·duhs] 1. **Judas, brother of Jesus** [JEE·suhs] *person* brother of Jesus (Matt. 13:55) and writer of the Book of Jude (Jude v. 1).

2. **Judas Iscariot** [ihs·KEHR·ee·uht] *person* apostle; greedy and a thief (John 12:5–6); betrays Jesus (Matt. 26:20–25, 47–50).

3. **Judas, son of James** [JAYMZ] *person* apostle (Luke 6:16). Also called Thaddaeus.

4. **Judas Barsabas** [BAHR·suh·buhs] *person* Jewish Christian and prophet who carried the Jerusalem Council's letter to Antioch (Acts 15:22, 27, 32).

**Jude** [JOOD] *person* brother of James and Jesus (Jude v. 1); also called Judas.

**Judea** [joo·DEE·uh] *place* area of ancient southern Palestine, also called Judah, which was the center of government and religious life; Jesus born here (Matt. 2:5); John the Baptist preaches here (Matt. 3:1); more hostile toward Jesus (John 7:1; 11:7–8); starting point of the church's growth (Acts 1:8).

**judge** [JUHJ] 1. *verb* to determine right and wrong, innocence and guilt.

Moses sat to *j* the people . . . . . . . . Ex. 18:13
Arise, O God, *j* the earth . . . . . . . . . . .Ps. 82:8
the saints will *j* the world . . . . . . . . 1 Cor. 6:2

2. *noun* one who declares the guilt or innocence of another.

you a prince and a *j* over us . . . . . . . .Ex. 2:14
you to the *j* . . . . . . . . . . . . . . . . . . . Matt. 5:25
"Man, who made Me a *j* . . . . . . . . Luke 12:14

3. *noun* military and political leader who God raises to rescue His people in the Book of Judges.

the LORD raised up *j* . . . . . . . . . . . . Judg. 2:16
the LORD was with the *j* . . . . . . . . .Judg. 2:18
when the *j* was dead . . . . . . . . . . . .Judg. 2:19

4. *identity* God; Christ.

Rise up, O *J* of the . . . . . . . . . . . . . . .Ps. 94:2
Lord, the righteous *J* . . . . . . . . . . . . 2 Tim. 4:8
heaven, to God the *J* . . . . . . . . . . . . Heb. 12:23

**judgment** [JUHJ·muhnt] *noun* the decision of a person's guilt or innocence; the discipline or punishment given to the guilty.

Teach me good *j*. . . . . . . . . . . . . . . . .Ps. 119:66
the righteous *j* of God . . . . . . . . . . . Rom. 1:32
the hour of His *j* has come . . . . . . . . . Rev. 14:7

**justified** [JUH·stuh·fide] *adjective* declared forgiven, acceptable, and righteous by God through faith in Jesus Christ.

having been *j* by . . . . . . . . . . . . . . . . . Rom. 5:1
these He also *j*. . . . . . . . . . . . . . . . . . Rom. 8:30
but you were *j*. . . . . . . . . . . . . . . . . . 1 Cor. 6:11

# K

**Kidron** [KIHD·ruhn] *place* a stream and valley that runs east of Jerusalem; Nehemiah inspects the broken-down walls of Jerusalem here (Neh. 2:13–15); site of a burial ground (2 Kin. 23:6); dumping ground for ashes of idols (1 Kin. 15:13; 2 Kin. 23:4; 2 Chr. 29:16; 30:14); Jesus crosses to pray in the Garden of Gethsemane (John 18:1).

**kingdom of God; kingdom of heaven** [KING·duhm of GAAD; KING·duhm of HEH·vin] *noun* God's rule over His creation; experienced in part now as God rules through His people and will be experienced in full when Jesus returns to rule perfectly over the new heavens and earth.

"Repent, for the ***k***. . . . . . . . . . . . . . . . Matt. 3:2
the ***k*** is at hand. . . . . . . . . . . . . . . . . . . . Mark 1:15
will not inherit the ***k*** . . . . . . . . . . . . 1 Cor. 6:9

# L

**Laban** [LAY·ben] *person* brother of Rebekah and father of Leah and Rachel; tricks Jacob into marrying Leah (Gen 29:15–25); gives Rachel to Jacob (Gen. 29:26–30); makes covenant with Jacob (Gen. 31).

**Lamb** [LAM] *identity* title for Jesus identifying how He became the sacrifice for the sins of the world.

"Behold! The ***L*** of God . . . . . . . . . . . . John 1:29
stood a ***L*** as though it had . . . . . . . . . . Rev. 5:6
***L*** will overcome them . . . . . . . . . . . Rev. 17:14

**lamentation** [la·muhn·TAY·shun] *noun* cry of deep pain, distress, and mourning.

with this ***l*** over Saul and . . . . . . . . 2 Sam. 1:17
***l*** in the daughter of Judah. . . . . . . . . Lam. 2:5
and made great ***l*** . . . . . . . . . . . . . . . . . . Acts 8:2

**lampstand** [LAMP·stand] *noun* object used to hold up a lamp for lighting an area; particularly, the seven-branched lampstand in the tabernacle and temple and the symbolic ones mentioned in Revelation.

make a ***l*** of pure gold. . . . . . . . . . . . . . Ex. 25:31
not to be set on a ***l***. . . . . . . . . . . . . . Mark 4:21
I saw seven golden ***l*** . . . . . . . . . . . . . . Rev. 1:12

**last days** [LAST DAYZ] *noun* days that will come in the future; particularly, the time when Christ returns and judges the world and redeems believers.

shall befall you in the ***l*** . . . . . . . . . . Gen. 49:1
come to pass in the ***l*** . . . . . . . . . . . . . Acts 2:17
in the ***l*** perilous times . . . . . . . . . . . 2 Tim. 3:1

**laver** [LAY·ver] *noun* basin made of bronze in which priests washed their hands for purification purposes while serving at the altar of the tabernacle or temple.

also make a ***l*** of bronze . . . . . . . . . . . Ex. 30:18
and the ***l*** and its base . . . . . . . . . . . . Lev. 8:11
***l*** contained forty baths. . . . . . . . . . 1 Kin. 7:38

**law** [LAW] *noun* rules of how people are to live; particularly, the rules given by God to Moses explaining how the Israelites were to live and worship Him.

and the ***l*** and commandments . . . . . Ex. 24:12
The ***l*** of the LORD is. . . . . . . . . . . . . . . Ps. 19:7
hang all the ***L*** and the . . . . . . . . . . Matt. 22:40

**laying on of (hands)** *phrase* the act of placing hands on someone for blessing, healing, or dedication.

***l*** the apostles' hands . . . . . . . . . . . . . Acts 8:18
the ***l*** my hands . . . . . . . . . . . . . . . . . 2 Tim. 1:6
of ***l*** hands, of resurrection . . . . . . . . Heb. 6:2

**Lazarus** [LAZ·er·uhs] 1. **Lazarus the beggar** [BEH·guhr] *person* character mentioned by Jesus in a parable (Luke 16:19–31).

2. **Lazarus, brother of Mary and Martha** [MAIR·ee; MAR·thuh] *person* raised from the dead by Jesus (John 11:1–44; 12:1–11).

**Leah** [LEE·uh] *person* oldest daughter of Laban; marries Jacob (Gen. 29:15–25); unloved by Jacob (Gen. 29:30–31); mother of Reuben, Simeon, Levi, Judah, Issachar, Zebulun, and Dinah (Gen. 29:31–35; 30:17–21).

**leaven** [LEH·vin] *noun* yeast or other ingredient that makes bread rise; at times used as an image for the effects of sin.

day you shall remove ***l***. . . . . . . . . . . . Ex. 12:15
and beware of the ***l*** . . . . . . . . . . . . . Matt. 16:6
know that a little ***l*** . . . . . . . . . . . . . 1 Cor. 5:6

**Lebanon** [LEH·buh·nuhn] *place* nation just north of ancient Palestine; wood from cedar trees that grew here used in building the temple (1 Kin. 5:14) and palace (1 Kin. 7:2–5).

**leprosy** [LEH·pruh·see] *noun* number of similar skin diseases and conditions that made a person ceremonially unclean.

This is the law of ***l*** . . . . . . . . . . . . . . Lev. 14:57
he would heal him of his ***l***. . . . . . . . 2 Kin. 5:3
Immediately the ***l*** left him. . . . . . . . . Luke 5:13

**Levi** [LEE·vie] *person* third son of Jacob and Leah (Gen. 29:31, 34); ancestors of the tribe of Levi were charged with the care of the tabernacle and the temple.

**lord** [LORD] 1. **lord** *noun* person who has authority over another or over a group of people.

my ***l*** being old also. . . . . . . . . . . . . Gen. 18:12
who is ***l*** over us . . . . . . . . . . . . . . . . . . Ps. 12:4
and hid his ***l*** money . . . . . . . . . . . . Matt. 25:18

2. **Lord** *identity* name for God in the Old Testament and title used of Jesus in the New Testament to recognize that He is the Son of God.

***L*** GOD, how shall I know. . . . . . . . . . Gen. 15:8
who is Christ the ***L***. . . . . . . . . . . . . . . Luke 2:11
and the ***L*** Jesus Christ . . . . . . . . . . . Rom. 1:7

3. **LORD** *identity* name of God as the supreme authority that is based on the original Hebrew name *Yahweh*.

The ***L*** God of your fathers . . . . . . . . . Ex. 3:15
'Prepare the way of the ***L*** . . . . . . . . . Mark 1:3
'The ***L*** said to my Lord . . . . . . . . . . . . Acts 2:34

**Lord of hosts** [LORD; HOSTS] *identity* name of God that describes Him as Creator and Warrior.
to the ***L*** in Shiloh . . . . . . . . . . . . . . . 1 Sam. 1:3
The ***L***, He is the King . . . . . . . . . . . . Ps. 24:10
The zeal of the ***L***. . . . . . . . . . . . . . . . . Is. 9:7
**Lord of lords** [LORD; LORDZ] *identity* name of God that describes His absolute authority and rule over all.
give thanks to the ***L*** . . . . . . . . . . . . . Ps. 136:3
King of kings and ***L*** . . . . . . . . . . . . 1 Tim. 6:15
KING OF KINGS AND ***L*** . . . . . . . . Rev. 19:16
**Lord's Day** [LORDZ DAY] *noun* Sunday, the first day of the week on which Jesus raised from the dead and on which Christians tend to worship.
in the Spirit on the ***L*** Rev. 1:10
**Lot** [LAAT] *person* nephew of Abraham; comes with Abraham to Canaan (Gen. 11:27–31); settles in Sodom (Gen. 13:12); captured and rescued by Abraham (Gen. 14:1–17); saved from Sodom's destruction (Gen. 19); wife turns into a pillar of salt (Gen. 19:26).
**lots** [LAATZ] *noun* a method of casting or throwing an object to make a decision.
***l*** causes contentions . . . . . . . . . . . Prov. 18:18
garments, casting ***l*** . . . . . . . . . . . . Mark 15:24
And they cast their ***l***. . . . . . . . . . . . . . Acts 1:26
**love** [LUHV] 1. *noun* deep affection; devotion.
***l*** covers all sins . . . . . . . . . . . . . . . Prov. 10:12
Greater ***l*** has no one . . . . . . . . . . . John 15:13
greatest of these is ***l*** . . . . . . . . . . 1 Cor. 13:13
2. *verb* to have deep affection and a devotion for someone or something.
***l*** your neighbor as . . . . . . . . . . . . . Lev. 19:18
***l*** the LORD your God . . . . . . . . . . . . . Deut. 6:5
to ***l*** one another . . . . . . . . . . . . . . . . Rom. 13:8
**Lucifer** [LOO·suh·fuhr] *noun* name used for Satan.
O ***L***, son of the morning. . . . . . . . . . . . Is. 14:12
**Luke** [LEWK] *person* author of the Books of Luke and Acts; physician (Col. 4:14); accompanies Paul on parts of the second and third missionary journeys and the journey to Rome (2 Tim. 4:11; Philem. v. 24).
**Lydia** [LIH·dee·uh] *person* prosperous businesswoman from the city of Thyatira in Asia Minor (modern-day Turkey); seller of purple cloth (Acts 16:14); hears Paul preach about Jesus and becomes a Christian (Acts 16:14–15).
**Lystra** [LIGH·struh] *place* city of Lycaonia in Asia Minor (modern-day Turkey); home of Timothy (Acts 16:1–2); on his first missionary journey, Paul preaches and heals here (Acts 14:8–10); Paul and Barnabas called Zeus and Hermes here (Acts 14:11–18); Paul stoned and left for dead here (Acts 14:19–20); Paul returns and encourages believers here (Acts 14:21–23); on his second missionary journey, Paul meets Timothy here (Acts 16:1–3).

# M

**Macedonia** [ma·suh·DOE·nee·uh] *place* country north of Greece; Paul visits on his missionary journeys after receiving his "Macedonian call" (Acts 16:9).
**majesty** [MA·juh·stee] *noun* power, authority, dignity, and splendor, especially of a king or queen.
Honor and ***m*** are before . . . . . . . 1 Chr. 16:27
with God is awesome ***m***. . . . . . . . . . . Job 37:22
wise, be glory and ***m*** . . . . . . . . . . . . Jude 1:25
**Malachi** [MAL·uh·kigh] *person* prophet; the Old Testament book that bears his name is the final of the twelve Minor Prophets.
**malice** [MA·luhs] *noun* the desire to cause someone harm.
away from you, with all ***m*** . . . . . . . . . Eph. 4:31
wrath, ***m***, blasphemy. . . . . . . . . . . . . . Col. 3:8
laying aside all ***m*** . . . . . . . . . . . . . . . 1 Pet. 2:1
**Manasseh** [muh·NA·suh] 1. **Manasseh, son of Joseph** [JO·sef] *person* Joseph's eldest son, born in Egypt (Gen. 41:50–51); receives lesser blessing from Jacob (Gen. 48:14–20).
2. **Manasseh, king of Judah** [JOO·duh] *person* reigns longer than any of the Israelite kings but is the most wicked (2 Kin. 21:1–18); rebuilds the altars to idols that had been destroyed by King Hezekiah and makes sacrifices to false gods (2 Chr. 33:2–9); sent to Babylon, where he repents (2 Chr. 33:11–13); tries to turn God's people back to Him but fails (2 Chr. 33:14–17).
**manifest** [MA·nuh·fest] *verb* to make known; to recognize by the senses, such as sight.
***m*** Myself to him . . . . . . . . . . . . . . . John 14:21
that I may make it ***m***, as I . . . . . . . . . . Col. 4:4
was ***m*** in these last times . . . . . . 1 Pet. 1:20
**manna** [MA·nuh] *noun* bread from heaven that God provides to feed the Israelites as they wander in the wilderness; literally means "What is it?"
of Israel ate ***m*** . . . . . . . . . . . . . . . . . Ex. 16:35
the ***m*** was like coriander. . . . . . . . . Num. 11:7
of the hidden ***m*** . . . . . . . . . . . . . . . . . Rev. 2:17
**Mark** [MAARK] *person* also called John Mark, the author of the Gospel of Mark; Christians gather in the house of his mother, Mary (Acts 12:12); possible cousin of Barnabas (Col. 4:10); travels with Paul and Barnabas to Antioch (Acts 12:25); participates in first missionary journey (Acts 12:25); returns to Jerusalem before Paul and Barnabas (Acts 13:13); his early departure causes a dispute (Acts 15:36–41); later reconciles with Paul (2 Tim. 4:11).
**marriage** [MAIR·ij] *noun* union designed by God of one man and one woman; used as an illustration of Christ's relationship with the church.
join in ***m*** with the people . . . . . . . . Ezra 9:14
nor are given in ***m*** . . . . . . . . . . . . . . Matt. 22:30
the ***m*** of the Lamb has . . . . . . . . . . . Rev. 19:7

**Martha** [MAR·thuh] *person* sister of Mary and Lazarus; becomes distracted in serving Jesus (Luke 10:38–42); demonstrates faith in Jesus at Lazarus's death (John 11:19–28); serves supper to Jesus and others (John 12:1–3).

**martyr** [MAR·ter] *noun* one who is a witness; one who suffers or dies because of his or her witness to Christ.

*m* Stephen was shed . . . . . . . . . . . . . Acts 22:20
was My faithful *m*. . . . . . . . . . . . . . . . . Rev. 2:13
the blood of the *m* . . . . . . . . . . . . . . . Rev. 17:6

**marvel** [MAR·vuhl] 1. *verb* to be in wonder, awe, or amazement.

do not *m* at the matter . . . . . . . . . . . Eccl. 5:8
Do not *m* that I said to you . . . . . . . . John 3:7
I *m* that you are turning. . . . . . . . . . . . Gal. 1:6

2. *noun* something that causes wonder, awe, or amazement; miracles.

I will do *m* such as . . . . . . . . . . . . . . . . Ex. 34:10

**Mary** [MAIR·ee] 1. **Mary, mother of Jesus** [JEE·suhs] *person* told by an angel that she would have a son (Luke 1:26–38); gives birth to Jesus (Luke 2:1–7); prompts Jesus to perform miracle at wedding (John 2:1–11); witnesses Jesus' crucifixion (John 19:25–27); in the upper room in Jerusalem (Acts 1:14).

2. **Mary Magdalene** [MAG·duh·lehn] *person* Galilean follower of Jesus who supports His ministry (Matt. 27:55–56); healed of evil spirits (Luke 8:2); witnesses Jesus' crucifixion (Matt. 27:56); speaks to Jesus after His resurrection (John 20:11–18).

3. **Mary, sister of Martha and Lazarus** [MAR·thuh; LAZ·er·uhs] *person* sits at Jesus' feet as He teaches (Luke 10:38–42); demonstrates faith in Jesus at Lazarus's death (John 11:28–32); anoints Jesus' feet (John 12:1–3).

4. **Mary, mother of James and Joses (Joseph)** ([JAYMZ; JO·sus] *person* witnesses Jesus' crucifixion (Matt. 27:56, 61) and resurrection (Matt. 28:1–8; Luke 24:1–10).

5. **Mary, mother of John Mark** [JAAN MAARK] *person* provides her house for believers to meet in (Acts 12:12).

**master** [MA·stihr] *noun* owner; person in authority; one who controls someone or something.

of Abraham his *m*. . . . . . . . . . . . . . . . Gen. 24:9
can serve two *m* . . . . . . . . . . . . . . . . Luke 16:13
is not greater than his *m*. . . . . . . . John 13:16

**Matthew** [MATH·yoo] *person* apostle (Matt. 10:3); also called Levi (Mark 2:14); tax collector (Luke 5:27–28); holds feast for Jesus (Mark 2:15–17).

**mediator** [MEE·dee·ay·tor] *noun* one who acts as a go-between in making an agreement between two parties.

Nor is there any *m* between us. . . . . Job 9:33
one *M* between God and men . . . . . 1 Tim. 2:5
He is the *M* of the new covenant. . . Heb. 9:15

**meditate** [MEH·dih·tate] *verb* to study; to contemplate; to think deeply about.

he *m* day and night . . . . . . . . . . . . . . . Ps. 1:2
who *m* on His name . . . . . . . . . . . . . . Mal. 3:16
*m* on these things . . . . . . . . . . . . . . . Phil. 4:8

**meek** [MEEK] 1. *adjective* humble; gentle.

A *m* and humble people . . . . . . . . . Zeph. 3:12

2. *noun* those who are humble and gentle.

But the *m* shall inherit the . . . . . . . . Ps. 37:11
with equity for the *m* . . . . . . . . . . . . . Is. 11:4
Blessed are the *m* . . . . . . . . . . . . . . . . Matt. 5:5

**Megiddo** [mee·GIH·doe] *place* fortified, walled city at the foot of the Carmel mountain range in ancient northern Palestine; the Israelites fail to remove Canaanites from (Josh. 17:11–12); Solomon rebuilds (1 Kin. 9:15); King Josiah dies here (2 Kin. 23:29–30).

**Melchizedek** [mehl·KIHZ·eh·dehk] *person* king of Salem and priest of God Most High (Gen. 14:18); blesses Abraham (Gen. 14:19–20); accepts tithe from Abraham (Gen. 14:20); Jesus called a priest according to him (Ps. 110:4; Heb. 5:6–11; 6:20—7:21).

**Mephibosheth** [meh·FIHB·oh·shehth] *person* son of Jonathan and grandson of King Saul who was injured in both feet (2 Sam. 4:4); receives kindness from King David (2 Sam. 9); spared by King David (2 Sam. 21:7).

**merciful** [MUR·suh·fuhl] 1. *adjective* forgiving; withholding punishment from someone.

your God is a *m* God. . . . . . . . . . . . . Deut. 4:31
He is ever *m* . . . . . . . . . . . . . . . . . . . . Ps. 37:26
Therefore be *m*, just as . . . . . . . . . . Luke 6:36

2. *noun* those who are forgiving.

"With the *m* You will show. . . . . 2 Sam. 22:26
With the *m* You will show. . . . . . . . . . Ps. 18:25
Blessed are the *m* . . . . . . . . . . . . . . . . Matt. 5:7

**mercy** [MUR·see] *noun* forgiveness; not punishing someone for something he or she has done.

His *m* endures forever. . . . . . . . . . . . Ezra 3:11
they shall obtain *m* . . . . . . . . . . . . . . . Matt. 5:7
God, who is rich in *m*. . . . . . . . . . . . . Eph. 2:4

**mercy seat** [MUR·see SEET] *noun* lid of the ark of the Testimony; literally means "covering."

"You shall make a *m* . . . . . . . . . . . . . Ex. 25:17
incense may cover the *m*. . . . . . . . . Lev. 16:13
glory overshadowing the *m*. . . . . . . . Heb. 9:5

**merry** [MAIR·ee] *adjective* joyous; happy.

*m* heart makes a cheerful. . . . . . . Prov. 15:13
voice of those who make *m*. . . . . . . Jer. 30:19
eat, drink, and be *m*. . . . . . . . . . . . . . Luke 12:19

**Meshach** [MEE·shack] *person* Babylonian name given to Mishael, of one of Daniel's companions (Dan. 1:7); refuses to eat unclean foods (Dan. 1:3ff); saved in fiery furnace (Dan. 3:8ff).

**Mesopotamia** [meh·suh·puh·TAY·mee·uh] *place* region between the Tigris and Euphrates Rivers in the modern-day countries of Iraq and Syria and traditional site of the Garden of

Eden; Abraham from here (Acts 7:2); Isaac's wife found here (Gen. 24); some people at Pentecost from here (Acts 2:9).

**Messiah** [muh·SIGH·uh] *identity* literally, "anointed one," the Hebrew term for "Christ" in Greek (John 4:25); describes how Jesus is God's chosen Savior of the world (Dan. 9:25–26; John 1:41).

**Methuselah** [meh·THOO·suh·luh] *person* Noah's grandfather; lived for 969 years, the oldest person mentioned in the Bible (Gen. 5:27).

**Micah** [MY·kuh] *person* prophet and contemporary of Isaiah (Jer. 26:18; Mic. 1:1); the Old Testament book that bears his name is the sixth of the twelve Minor Prophets.

**ministry** [MIH·nuh·stree] *noun* acts of service to God or to others for God.

the garments of ***m*** . . . . . . . . . . . . . . . Ex. 31:10
to the ***m*** of the word. . . . . . . . . . . . . . Acts 6:4
***m*** of reconciliation . . . . . . . . . . . . 2 Cor. 5:18

**miracle** [MIHR·uh·kuhl] *noun* something done by God or through a person that is beyond the natural laws and that only God can do. Miracles in the Old Testament include the ten plagues on Egypt (Ex. 7:14—12:30), the parting of the Red Sea (Ex. 14:21–31), manna from heaven (Ex. 16:14–35), the walls of Jericho falling (Josh. 6:1–21), strength given to Samson (Judg. 14:1—16:30), Elijah taken into heaven by a whirlwind (2 Kin. 2:11), Elisha reviving a dead child (2 Kin. 4:18–37), three men saved from a fiery furnace (Dan. 3:19–27), Daniel saved from lions (Dan. 6:16–23), and Jonah saved in a fish (Jon. 1:10—2:10). Miracles in the New Testament include Jesus healing a leper (Matt. 8:2–3), Jesus healing a centurion's servant (Matt. 8:5–13), Jesus calming a storm (Matt. 8:23–26), Jesus casting demons into swine (Matt. 8:28–32), Jesus healing a demoniac (Matt. 9:32–33), Jesus feeding more than five thousand people (Matt. 14:15–21), Jesus walking on the water (Matt. 14:25–27), Jesus feeding more than four thousand people (Matt. 15:32–38), Jesus healing ten lepers (Luke 17:11–19), Jesus changing water into wine (John 2:1–11), Jesus raising Lazarus from the dead (John 11:38–44), Jesus' resurrection (John 20:1–18), the apostles speaking in unknown tongues (Acts 2:4–11), Peter healing a man who could not walk (Acts 3:1–8), Peter raising Tabitha (Acts 9:36–41), Peter being delivered from prison (Acts 12:5–10), Paul casting out demons and healing people (Acts 19:11–12), Paul raising Eutychus (Acts 20:9–12), and Paul unharmed by a viper (Acts 28:3–6).

saying, 'Show a ***m*** . . . . . . . . . . . . . . . . Ex. 7:9
no one who works a ***m*** . . . . . . . . . . . Mark 9:39
with various ***m*** . . . . . . . . . . . . . . . . . Heb. 2:4

**Miriam** [MIHR·ee·uhm] *person* sister of Aaron and Moses (Num. 26:59); prophet (Ex. 15:20); punished for rebellion (Num. 12).

**money changers** [MUH·nee CHAYN·jerz] *noun* bankers who exchanged one nation's currency for another, often taking advantage of people by charging too much for this service.

overturned the tables of the ***m*** . . . Matt. 21:12
overturned the tables of the ***m*** . . . . Mark 11:15
and the ***m*** doing business . . . . . . . . John 2:14

**Mordecai** [MOR·duh·kigh] *person* cousin and adopted father of Esther (Esth. 2:7); overhears plot against Persian king (Esth. 2:19–22); refuses to bow before Haman, prompting the leader's evil plan (Esth. 3:2); encourages Esther to intervene for her people (Esth. 4:13–14); leads Jews to defeat their opponents (Esth. 9); promoted to an official position (Esth. 10).

**mortal** [MOR·tuhl] *adjective* human; subject to sin and death; fleshly.

'Can a ***m*** be more righteous . . . . . . . Job 4:17
sin reign in your ***m*** . . . . . . . . . . . . . . Rom. 6:12
and this ***m*** must put. . . . . . . . . . . 1 Cor. 15:53

**Moses** [MO·zuhs] *person* great deliverer and lawgiver of Israel; born during the oppression of the Israelites in Egypt (Ex. 1:22—2:2); raised in Pharaoh's house (Ex. 2:5–10); flees to Midian where he lives forty years (Ex. 2:15–25); called by God from a burning bush (Ex. 3:2–5); leaves Egypt with the Israelites after a series of ten plagues (Ex. 7:14—12:32); receives the Ten Commandments from God (Ex. 20); leads the Israelites through the wilderness for forty years (Num. 14:26–35); sins by striking a rock (Num. 20:1–13); sees the Promised Land from afar (Deut. 34:1–4); appears at Jesus' transfiguration (Matt. 17:1–4); author of Genesis, Exodus, Leviticus, Numbers, and Deuteronomy.

**Most High** [MOST HIGH] *identity* name used of God describing His authority and power.

When the ***M*** divided . . . . . . . . . . . . Deut. 32:8
the ***M*** rules in . . . . . . . . . . . . . . . . . Dan. 4:25
the ***M*** does not dwell . . . . . . . . . . . Acts 7:48

**Most Holy Place** [MOST HO·lee PLACE] *noun* innermost part of the tabernacle and temple where God's presence dwells over the ark of the covenant.

sanctuary, as the ***M*** . . . . . . . . . . . . 1 Kin. 6:16
to me, "This is the ***M*** . . . . . . . . . . Ezek. 41:4
blood He entered the ***M*** . . . . . . . . . . Heb. 9:12

**Mount Ararat** [MOWNT EH·rr·at] *place* mountain on which Noah's ark comes to rest after the Flood (Gen. 8:4).

**Mount Carmel** [MOWNT KAR·mel] *place* mountain range in ancient northern Palestine; Elijah confronts the prophets of Baal here (1 Kin. 18:20–40); Elisha journeys here (2 Kin. 2:25); Shunammite woman comes to Elisha here (2 Kin. 4:25).

**Mount Ebal** [MOWNT EE·bul] *place* mountain in ancient northern Palestine opposite Mount Gerizim that becomes known as the Mount of Cursing (Deut. 11:29); Joshua builds an altar here (Josh. 8:30).

**Mount Gerizim** [MOWNT geh·RIH·zim] *place* mountain in ancient northern Palestine opposite Mount Ebal that becomes known as the Mount of Blessing (Deut. 11:29); Jacob's well, where Jesus talks with the Samaritan woman, is situated here (John 4:14); Samaritan's sacred mountain (John 4:20–21).

**Mount Gilboa** [MOWNT gil·BO·ah] *place* mountain on the eastern edge of the valley of Jezreel; Saul and his sons killed in battle here (1 Sam. 31:1–8).

**Mount Gilead** [MOWNT GIH·lee·uhd] *place* mountainous region of the Transjordan; Gideon divides his army here (Judg. 7:3); David flees here (2 Sam. 17:21–22); medicines made from trees here (Jer. 8:22; 46:11).

**Mount Hermon** [MOWNT HUR·man] *place* snowcapped mountain in ancient northern Palestine; regarded as a sacred mountain (Judg. 3:3; 1 Chr. 5:23).

**Mount Hor** MOWNT HOR] *place* mountain on border of Edom; God speaks to Moses and Aaron here (Num. 20:23); Aaron dies here (Num. 20:25–28).

**Mount Horeb** [MOWNT HOR·ehb] *place* sacred mountain of God that may be the same as Mount Sinai; Moses experiences the burning bush here (Ex. 3); the children of Israel strip themselves of ornaments here (Ex. 33:6).

**Mount Moriah** [MOWNT muh·RIGH·uh] *place* mountain in ancient Palestine; Abraham told to sacrifice Isaac here (Gen. 22:2); Solomon builds the temple here (2 Chr. 3:1).

**Mount Nebo** [MOWNT NEE·bo] *place* mountain east of where the Jordan River empties into the Dead Sea; Moses looks into the Promised Land from here (Deut. 32:49).

**Mount of Olives** [MOWNT; AA·luhvz] *place* mountain overlooking Jerusalem; Jesus weeps over Jerusalem from here (Luke 19:37–41); Jesus prays in a garden and is arrested here (John 18); Jesus ascends to heaven from here (Luke 24:51; Acts 1:9–12).

**Mount Sinai** [MOWNT SIGH·nigh] *place* mountain in ancient Palestine that may be the same as Mount Horeb; Moses receives the Ten Commandments here (Ex. 19–20).

**Mount Tabor** [MOWNT TAY·buhr] *place* mountain east of Nazareth; location of Baal worship (Deut. 33:19); Deborah sends Barak to defeat the Canaanites here (Judg. 4:6–14).

**Mount Zion** [MOWNT ZIGH·uhn] *place* mountain on which Jerusalem is built; used as another name for Jerusalem at times (Pss. 14:7; 48:2); used in reference to the temple at times (Ps. 20:2; Is. 18:7); used as another name for the New Jerusalem (Rev. 14:1).

**mourn** [MORN] *verb* to grieve a loss, especially by death.

a time to ***m*** . . . . . . . . . . . . . . . . . . . Eccl. 3:4
to comfort all who ***m*** . . . . . . . . . . . . . Is. 61:2
are those who ***m*** . . . . . . . . . . . . . . . . Matt. 5:4

**mysteries** [MIH·stihr·eez] *noun* things that were previously hidden and not understood but have been revealed by God.

to you to know the ***m*** . . . . . . . . . . . Matt. 13:11
and understand all ***m*** . . . . . . . . . . . 1 Cor. 13:2
the spirit he speaks ***m*** . . . . . . . . . . 1 Cor. 14:2

# N

**Naaman** [NAW·muhn] *person* commander of the Syrian army and a leper healed by Elisha (2 Kin. 5); Jesus refers to as evidence of God's care for Gentiles (Luke 4:27).

**Nahum** [NAY·hum] *person* prophet; the Old Testament book that bears his name is the seventh of the twelve Minor Prophets.

**name** [NAYM] *noun* word by which a person, place, or thing is called; in biblical times, a person's name often revealed something about his or her character, which is why God changed people's names at times.

***n*** of the LORD your God in vain . . . . . . . Ex. 20:7
How excellent is Your ***n*** . . . . . . . . . . . . Ps. 8:1
ask the Father in My ***n*** . . . . . . . . . . John 15:16

**Naomi** [NAY·oh·mee] *person* mother-in-law of Ruth; after her husband and two sons die, returns to Bethlehem with Ruth (Ruth 1:16–17); convinces Ruth to approach Boaz and ask him to become a kinsman redeemer (Ruth 3–4).

**Nathan** [NAY·thuhn] *person* prophet during the reign of David and Solomon; tells David that he would not build the temple in Jerusalem (1 Chr. 17:1–15); confronts David about his sins against Bathsheba and Uriah (2 Sam. 12:9–15); intercedes for Solomon (1 Kin. 1).

**nation** [NAY·shun] *noun* group of people joined by family, history, or leadership.

make you a great ***n*** . . . . . . . . . . . . . Gen. 12:2
priests and a holy ***n*** . . . . . . . . . . . . . .Ex. 19:6
***n*** will rise against ***n*** . . . . . . . . . . . . . Matt. 24:7

**Nazareth** [NAZ·uhr·eth] *place* town in Galilee; Jesus raised here (Luke 1:26; 2:4–5, 39, 51); Jesus comes from here to be baptized (Mark 1:9); Jesus' message rejected here (Mark 6:1).

**Nazirite** [NAZ·uhr·ite] *noun* person who takes a vow to be separated from the world and completely dedicated to God, which includes promising not to touch strong drink, shave or cut their hair, or touch or go near a dead body (Num. 6:1–12; Prov. 20:1; Eph. 5:17–18).

to take the vow of a ***N*** . . . . . . . . . . . .Num. 6:2
the child shall be a ***N*** . . . . . . . . . . . .Judg. 13:5
your young men as ***N*** . . . . . . . . . . . Amos 2:11

**Nebuchadnezzar** [neh·byoo·kuhd·NEHZ·er] *person* king of Babylonia (605–562 BC); conquers Jerusalem and takes its people into captivity (2 Kin. 24:20—25:21).

**Nehemiah** [nee·huh·MIGH·uh] *person* Jewish cupbearer to Persian king Artaxerxes I (Neh. 1:11); given permission to return to Jerusalem to rebuild the city walls (Neh. 2:1–10); leads a building project that takes fifty-two days (Neh. 6:15).

**new covenant** [NOO KUH·vuh·nehnt] *noun* covenant established by God that is based on Jesus' sacrifice for sin rather than animal sacrifices.

I will make a ***n*** with . . . . . . . . . . . . Jer. 31:31
this is My blood of the ***n*** . . . . . . . . Matt. 26:28
the Mediator of the ***n*** . . . . . . . . . . . Heb. 12:24

**new man** [NOO MAN] *noun* another term for believers in Jesus Christ who have become new people, fully forgiven and righteous in Him.

create in Himself one ***n*** . . . . . . . . . . Eph. 2:15
that you put on the ***n*** . . . . . . . . . . . . Eph. 4:24
and have put on the ***n*** . . . . . . . . . . . . Col. 3:10

**Nicodemus** [nih·kuh·DEE·muhs] *person* wealthy, educated, and respected Pharisee and member of the Sanhedrin; visits Jesus at night to learn more about His teachings (John 3:1–21); tells Sanhedrin it should hear from Jesus (John 7:50–51); purchases one hundred pounds of spices for Jesus' burial and assists with the burial (John 19:39–40).

**Nineveh** [NIHN·eh·veh] *place* capital of Assyria; Jonah sent to preach here (Jon. 1:2; 3:2); Nahum prophesies its fall (Nah. 1:1).

**Noah** [NO·uh] *person* builder of the ark who escapes the Flood (Gen. 6–9); ancestor of Jesus (Luke 3:36); follower of God (Gen. 6:9); receives grace from God (Gen. 6:8); faith is praised (Heb. 11:7).

# O

**oath** [OWTH] *noun* a binding promise usually made before witnesses.

two of them swore an ***o*** . . . . . . . . . Gen. 21:31
themselves under an ***o*** . . . . . . . . . . Acts 23:12
or with any other ***o*** . . . . . . . . . . . . James 5:12

**Obadiah** [oh·buh·DIGH·uh] *person* prophet; the Old Testament book that bears his name is the fourth of the twelve Minor Prophets.

**offense** [uh·FENCE] *noun* something that is displeasing or causes anger or harm to another; sin.

one man's ***o*** many died . . . . . . . . . . Rom. 5:15
Give no ***o***, either to . . . . . . . . . . . 1 Cor. 10:32
the ***o*** of the cross . . . . . . . . . . . . . . . Gal. 5:11

**offering** [AA·fuhr·ihng] *noun* something given as an act of worship. The Old Testament describes three main types of offerings:

1. **grain offering** [GRAYN] unleavened bread, cakes, wafers, or grain mixed with salt and, except when a sin offering, with olive oil (Lev. 2:1–16; 5:11; 6:14–23; Num. 15:4, 6, 9); sometimes accepted from the poor as a sin offering in place of the burnt offering (Lev. 5:11–13).
2. **drink offering** [DRINK] wine used with the grain and burnt offerings, except in the sin and trespass offerings (Num. 6:17; 15:5, 10).
3. **animal offering** [A·nuh·muhl] or **sacrifice** [SA·kruh·fise] cattle, sheep, goats, doves, or pigeons that are free from blemish (Lev. 1:3). Four types of animal offerings are given: a. **burnt offering** [BURNT] male lamb, ram, goat, bull, dove, or pigeon entirely consumed on the altar (Lev. 1; 6:9–13); b. **sin offering** [SIN] bull, male or female goat, female lamb, dove, or pigeon (Lev. 4; 5:7; 6:25–30); c. **trespass offering** [TREHS·pass] ram or lamb (Lev. 5:6, 15; 6:6; 7:1–8; 14:12, 21); d. **peace offering** [PEES] any animal, except birds, without blemish (Lev. 3; 7:11–27).

not respect Cain and his ***o*** . . . . . . . . . Gen. 4:5
you shall bring your ***o*** . . . . . . . . . . . . . Lev. 1:2
out as a drink ***o*** . . . . . . . . . . . . . . . . Phil. 2:17

**old man** [OHLD MAN] *noun* another term for a person before he or she becomes a believer in Jesus Christ; still sinful, unrighteous, and in need of forgiveness.

our ***o*** was crucified . . . . . . . . . . . . . . Rom. 6:6
the ***o*** which grows corrupt . . . . . . . . Eph. 4:22
put off the ***o*** with his . . . . . . . . . . . . . Col. 3:9

**omnipotent** [aam·NIH·puh·tent] *adjective* all-powerful; one of God's "all" attributes, along with omniscience (all-knowing) and omnipresence (all-present).

For the Lord God ***O*** . . . . . . . . . . . . . . Rev. 19:6

**Onesimus** [oh·NEH·sih·muhs] *person* servant of Philemon; meets Paul in Rome and becomes a follower of Jesus (Philem. vv. 10, 16); sent back to Philemon (Philem. v. 12); carries Paul's letters to Philemon in Colosse (Col. 4:7–9).

**only begotten Son** [OWN·lee buh·GAA·tuhn SON] *identity* title for Jesus that describes His uniqueness, without meaning that the Son of God was created.

The ***o***, who is in the . . . . . . . . . . . . John 1:18
world that He gave His ***o*** . . . . . . . . . John 3:16
God has sent His ***o*** . . . . . . . . . . . . . . 1 John 4:9

**oracles** [OR·uh·kulz] *noun* messages from God.

received the living ***o*** . . . . . . . . . . . . . Acts 7:38
were committed the ***o*** . . . . . . . . . . . . . Rom. 3:2
principles of the ***o*** . . . . . . . . . . . . . . Heb. 5:12

**ordain** [or·DAYN] *verb* to establish or appoint; to order; to make a law.

the stars, which You have ***o*** . . . . . . . . . . Ps. 8:3
***o*** you a prophet . . . . . . . . . . . . . . . . . . Jer. 1:5
the Man whom He has ***o*** . . . . . . . . . Acts 17:31

**ordinance** [OR·duh·nuhns] *noun* a law or rule.

shall you walk in their ***o*** . . . . . . . . . Lev. 18:3
according to Your ***o*** . . . . . . . . . . . . . Ps. 119:91
contained in ***o*** . . . . . . . . . . . . . . . . . . Eph. 2:15

**overcome** [oh·vuhr·KUHM] *verb* to be victorious; to remain faithful.
of God ***o*** the world . . . . . . . . . . . . . 1 John 5:4
***o*** I will give to eat . . . . . . . . . . . . . .Rev. 2:7
***o*** shall inherit all . . . . . . . . . . . . . . .Rev. 21:7
**overseer** [OH·vuhr·see·ur] *noun* one who supervises others; elder; pastor.
Then he made him ***o*** . . . . . . . . . . Gen. 39:4
Holy Spirit has made you ***o*** . . . . . .Acts 20:28
to the Shepherd and ***O*** . . . . . . . . . . 1 Pet. 2:25

# P

**pagan** [PAY·guhn] *noun* one who does not believe in God; unbelieving Gentiles.
have taken ***p*** wives from . . . . . . . . . Ezra 10:2
have begotten ***p*** children. . . . . . . . . . Hos. 5:7
priests with the ***p*** priests . . . . . . . . .Zeph. 1:4
**parable** [PAIR·uh·bull] *noun* short story that helps teach an important truth, often about the kingdom of God. Jesus' parables include the lamp under a basket (Matt. 5:14–16), the unshrunk cloth on an old garment (Matt. 9:16–17), the weeds among wheat (Matt. 13:24–30), the mustard seed (Matt. 13:31–32), the lost sheep (Matt. 18:12–14), the laborers in a vineyard (Matt. 20:1–16), the wise and foolish virgins (Matt. 25:1–13), the talents (Matt. 25:14–30), the two debtors (Luke 7:41–50), the good Samaritan (Luke 10:30–37), the prodigal son (Luke 15:11–32), the Pharisee and the tax collector (Luke 18:9–14), and the shepherd and the sheep (John 10:1–30).
open my mouth in a ***p*** . . . . . . . . . . . .Ps. 78:2
learn this ***p*** from the fig. . . . . . . . . Matt. 24:32
rest it is given in ***p*** . . . . . . . . . . . . . Luke 8:10
**paralytic** [pair·uh·LIH·tehk] *noun* one who cannot walk.
demon-possessed, epileptics, and ***p***. .Matt. 4:24
then He said to the ***p*** . . . . . . . . . . . .Matt. 9:6
on which the ***p*** was lying . . . . . . . . . Mark 2:4
**pardon** [PAAR·duhn] *verb* to forgive.
***p*** your transgressions . . . . . . . . . . . . .Ex. 23:21
not ***p*** my transgression . . . . . . . . . . . Job 7:21
***p*** all their iniquities . . . . . . . . . . . . . . Jer. 33:8
**partiality** [paar·shee·AL·uh·tee] *noun* favoritism.
You shall not show ***p*** . . . . . . . . . . . .Deut. 1:17
For there is no ***p***. . . . . . . . . . . . . . . .Rom. 2:11
but if you show ***p*** . . . . . . . . . . . . . . .James 2:9
**Passover** [PA·so·vuhr] *noun* seven-day Jewish festival held in March or April that remembers God sparing the Israelites from the death of the firstborn in Egypt by placing the blood of a lamb around the door (Ex. 12); the sacrificial lamb of the Passover (Ex. 12:11, 21, 27).
It is the LORD's ***P*** . . . . . . . . . . . . . . . . .Ex. 12:11
And they kept the ***P*** . . . . . . . . . . . . . .Num. 9:5
Christ, our ***P***, was sacrificed . . . . . . . 1 Cor. 5:7
**Patmos** [PAT·mos] *place* small, rocky island off the coast of Asia Minor (modern-day Turkey); John receives visions from the Lord and records the Book of Revelation here (Rev. 1:9–11).
**Paul** [PAWL] *person* also called Saul, a rigorous Pharisee and persecutor of the early church (Acts 8:3; Gal. 1:13–14); encounters Jesus on the road to Damascus and becomes a follower (Acts 9:1–9); goes on first missionary journey (Acts 13–14); participates in Jerusalem Council (Acts 15:1–29); goes on second missionary journey (Acts 15:36—18:23); goes on third missionary journey (Acts 19:1—21:16); arrested in Jerusalem (Acts 21:26—22:30); discovers plot against him and transferred to prison in Caesarea (Acts 23:1—24:27); appeals to Caesar and taken to Rome (Acts 25:1—28:31); writer of Romans, 1 and 2 Corinthians, Galatians, Ephesians, Philippians, Colossians, 1 and 2 Thessalonians, 1 and 2 Timothy, Titus, and Philemon.
**peace** [PEES] 1. *noun* freedom from turmoil and conflict with God.
sacrifice of a ***p*** offering . . . . . . . . . . . Lev. 3:1
we have ***p*** with God . . . . . . . . . . . . . .Rom. 5:1
having made ***p*** through the blood. . . Col. 1:20
2. *noun* internal sense of calm; state of wholeness.
lie down in ***p*** . . . . . . . . . . . . . . . . . . . . .Ps. 4:8
"There is no ***p*** . . . . . . . . . . . . . . . . . . . Is. 57:21
My ***p*** I give to you . . . . . . . . . . . . . . John 14:27
3. *noun* freedom from turmoil, conflict, and war with others.
men are at ***p*** with us . . . . . . . . . . . Gen. 34:21
I will give ***p*** in the land. . . . . . . . . . . .Lev. 26:6
accept your offer of ***p***. . . . . . . . . . . .Deut. 20:11
**Pentecost** [PEN·tih·kaast] *noun* festival fifty days after Passover; also called Feast of Weeks (Lev. 23:15–16); observed by the church as the day on which the gift of the Holy Spirit was given (Acts 2:1–33).
Day of ***P*** had fully come . . . . . . . . . . . .Acts 2:1
if possible, on the Day of ***P*** . . . . . .Acts 20:16
tarry in Ephesus until ***P***. . . . . . . . . 1 Cor. 16:8
**perdition** [pur·DIH·shun] *noun* judgment; destruction.
except the son of ***p***. . . . . . . . . . . . . John 17:12
to them a proof of ***p*** . . . . . . . . . . . . . Phil. 1:28
day of judgment and ***p***. . . . . . . . . . . 2 Pet. 3:7
**perish** [PAIR·ish] *verb* to die; to be destroyed.
way of the ungodly shall ***p***. . . . . . . . . . .Ps. 1:6
believes in Him should not ***p***. . . . . . John 3:16
"Your money ***p*** with you . . . . . . . . . . .Acts 8:20
**persecute** [PUR·suh·kyoot] *verb* to attack, harm, or kill, particularly for one's faith.
***p*** me as God does. . . . . . . . . . . . . . . . Job 19:22
when they revile and ***p***. . . . . . . . . . . . Matt. 5:11
Bless those who ***p*** . . . . . . . . . . . . . . . Rom. 12:14
**Peter** [PEE·tuhr] *person* apostle; originally named Simon (Mark 3:16); fisherman along with his

brother, Andrew, and friends James and John (Luke 5:10; 6:14); becomes follower of Jesus (Matt. 4:18–20); among the closest to Jesus (Mark 5:37); leader among the apostles (Matt. 16:16–19); often speaks and acts boldly (Matt. 14:28–29; 16:16, 22; 17:4; Mark 14:29–31; John 18:10; 21:7); denies Jesus (Matt. 26:69–75); Jesus restores (John 21:15–19); preaches Christ at Pentecost (Acts 2:14–39); performs miracles (Acts 3:1–10; 5:15–16; 9:32–43); arrested for his faith (Acts 4:1–22); placed on trial (Acts 5:22–40); has a vision concerning the Gentiles (Acts 10:9–48); imprisoned again and freed (Acts 12:5–19); participates in the Jerusalem Council (Acts 15:1–29); writer of 1 and 2 Peter (1 Pet. 1:1; 2 Pet. 1:1).

**Pharaoh** [FEHR·oh] *noun* title used as a name, or before a name, of the king of Egypt.
And ***P*** called Abram . . . . . . . . . . . . Gen. 12:18
***P*** commanded the taskmasters . . . . . . Ex. 5:6
***P*** Necho king of Egypt . . . . . . . . . 2 Kin. 23:29

**Pharisees** [FEHR·uh·seez] *noun* strict Jewish group in New Testament times that closely follow the Mosaic law and their own traditions; seen by the people as righteous, but by Jesus as hypocritical; oppose Jesus because He did not follow their rules as they wanted.
you ***P*** make the outside . . . . . . . . . Luke 11:39
of the ***P*** named Nicodemus . . . . . . . . . John 3:1
concerning the law, a ***P*** . . . . . . . . . . . Phil. 3:5

**Philemon** [fuh·LEE·muhn] *person* Christian from Colosse; Paul encourages him to accept back his runaway slave, Onesimus (Philemon).

**Philip** [FIH·luhp] 1. **Philip, the apostle** [uh·PAA·sul] *person* brings Nathanael to Jesus (John 1:45–51); tested by Jesus before miraculous feeding (John 6:5–6); asks Jesus to show the apostles the Father (John 14:8).
2. **Philip, the evangelist** [ih·VAN·juh·lehst] *person* chosen to serve tables (Acts 6:1–6); preaches in Samaria (Acts 8:4–8); preaches to an Ethiopian (Acts 8:26–40).

**Philippi** [FIH·lih·pie] *place* ancient city of Macedonia where Paul establishes the first Christian congregation in Europe (Acts 16:11–15); Paul and Silas imprisoned and released by an earthquake here (Acts 16:16–34); Paul writes a letter to the believers who live here (Phil. 1:1).

**Philistines** [FIH·lih·steenz] *noun* people who live along the southern coast of ancient Palestine who are often at war with the Israelites.
six hundred men of the ***P*** . . . . . . . . Judg. 3:31
Then the ***P*** took the ark . . . . . . . . . . 1 Sam. 5:1
the ***P*** went up to search . . . . . . . . 2 Sam. 5:17

**Phoenicia** [fuh·NIH·she·uh] *place* ancient country on the coast of the Mediterranean Sea with the chief cities of Tyre and Sidon; supplies for building the temple and palace from here (2 Sam. 5:11; 1 Kin. 5:1–12; 2 Chr. 2:13–16); Ahab marries Jezebel, who is from here (1 Kin. 16:30–31); Jesus spends time here (Mark 7:24–31); the gospel brought here (Acts 11:19; 15:3).

**phylacteries** [fuh·LACK·tuh·reez] *noun* small boxes containing parts of Scripture worn on the arm or head.
They make their ***p*** . . . . . . . . . . . . Matt. 23:5

**pilgrims** [PIL·gruhmz] *noun* travelers to foreign lands.
we are aliens and ***p*** . . . . . . . . . 1 Chr. 29:15
were strangers and ***p*** . . . . . . . . . . Heb. 11:13
as sojourners and ***p*** . . . . . . . . . . . 1 Pet. 2:11

**pledge** [PLEJ] *noun* promise; a token, deposit, or down payment that guarantees a promise.
give me a ***p*** till you send . . . . . . . Gen. 38:17
shakes hands in a ***p***, and . . . . . . . . Prov. 17:18
on clothes taken in ***p*** . . . . . . . . . . . . Amos 2:8

**Pontius Pilate** [PAWN·chuhs PIE·luht] *person* Roman governor of Judea (AD 26–36); serves as judge in the trial and execution of Jesus (Matt. 27:1–26).

**praise the Lord** *phrase* expression of worship and gratitude toward God.
with cymbals, to ***p*** . . . . . . . . . . . . . Ezra 3:10
that has breath ***p*** . . . . . . . . . . . . . . . Ps. 150:6
"***P***, all you Gentiles . . . . . . . . . . . . Rom. 15:11

**prayer** [PREHR] *noun* talking with God, either silently or out loud.
***p*** made in this place . . . . . . . . . . . 2 Chr. 7:15
things you ask in ***p*** . . . . . . . . . . . . Matt. 21:22
but in everything by ***p*** . . . . . . . . . . . . Phil. 4:6

**preach the gospel** *phrase* to tell the good news of salvation found in Jesus Christ.
into all the world and ***p*** . . . . . . . . Mark 16:15
the feet of those who ***p*** . . . . . . . . . Rom. 10:15
who ***p*** should live from . . . . . . . . . 1 Cor. 9:14

**precept** [PREE·sept] *noun* rule, command, or principle to follow or obey.
***p*** must be upon ***p*** . . . . . . . . . . . . . Is. 28:10
walked by human ***p*** . . . . . . . . . . . . Hos. 5:11
***p*** to all the people . . . . . . . . . . . . . Heb. 9:19

**predestine** [pree·DEH·stuhn] *verb* to determine or choose beforehand.
He foreknew, He also ***p*** . . . . . . . . . . Rom. 8:29
having ***p*** us to . . . . . . . . . . . . . . . . . Eph. 1:5
inheritance, being ***p*** . . . . . . . . . . . . Eph. 1:11

**preeminence** [pree·EH·muh·nuhns] *noun* superiority; of the highest rank, value, or importance.
He may have the ***p*** . . . . . . . . . . . . . Col. 1:18
loves to have the ***p*** . . . . . . . . . . . . 3 John 1:9

**priest** [PREEST] *noun* intercessor or mediator between God and His people who performs sacrifices for the people and leads in worship; Jesus is the High Priest; God has intended for all His people to act as priests in bringing others to Him.
The sons of Aaron the ***p*** . . . . . . . . . . Lev. 1:7
the ***p*** and the prophet . . . . . . . . . . . . Is. 28:7
and faithful High ***P*** . . . . . . . . . . . . . Heb. 2:17

**principalities** [prin·suh·PA·luh·teez] *noun* powers and authorities; governments and monarchs.
nor ***p*** nor powers . . . . . . . . . . . . . . . Rom. 8:38
and blood, but against ***p*** . . . . . . . . . Eph. 6:12
dominions or ***p*** or powers . . . . . . . . . . Col. 1:16

**Priscilla** [pruh·SIH·luh] *person* Jewish Christian who lives in Rome with her husband, Aquilla; moves to Corinth when the emperor orders all Jewish people to leave Rome (Acts 18:1–3); travels with Paul to Syria (Acts 18:18–19); instructs Apollos (Acts 18:26).

**proclaim** [prow·KLAYM] *verb* to declare; to say officially.
***p*** the name of the LORD . . . . . . . . . . Deut. 32:3
to ***p*** liberty to the captives . . . . . . . . . . Is. 61:1
drink this cup, you ***p*** . . . . . . . . . . 1 Cor. 11:26

**prodigal** [PRAA·duh·guhl] *adjective* wasteful; reckless; without control.
with ***p*** living . . . . . . . . . . . . . . . . . Luke 15:13

**profane** [pro·FAYN] 1. *verb* to treat something that is holy and sacred in the wrong way.
nor shall you ***p*** the name . . . . . . . . Lev. 19:12
"But you ***p*** it . . . . . . . . . . . . . . . . . . Mal. 1:12
tried to ***p*** the temple . . . . . . . . . . . . . Acts 24:6
2. *adjective* unholy; impure.
and offered ***p*** fire . . . . . . . . . . . . . . . . Lev. 10:1
and priest are ***p*** . . . . . . . . . . . . . . . . Jer. 23:11
***p*** person like Esau . . . . . . . . . . . . . . Heb. 12:16

**prophecy** [PRAA·fuh·see] *noun* messages given by God through a person called a prophet, who shares it with others; in the New Testament, one of the spiritual gifts.
he pronounced this ***p*** . . . . . . . . . . . . . Neh. 6:12
miracles, to another ***p*** . . . . . . . . . 1 Cor. 12:10
for ***p*** never came by . . . . . . . . . . . . . 2 Pet. 1:21

**prophet** [PRAA·fuht] *noun* person called by God to share messages from Him to His people.
raise up for you a ***P*** . . . . . . . . . . . . Deut. 18:15
***p*** is not without honor . . . . . . . . . . . Matt. 13:57
no ***p*** is accepted in his . . . . . . . . . . . Luke 4:24

**propitiation** [pro·pih·shee·AY·shn] *noun* payment or atonement for sin that brings removal of guilt and God's wrath.
set forth as a ***p*** . . . . . . . . . . . . . . . . Rom. 3:25
to God, to make ***p*** . . . . . . . . . . . . . . . Heb. 2:17
He Himself is the ***p*** . . . . . . . . . . . . . 1 John 2:2

**proselyte** [PRAA·suh·lite] *noun* new convert to a religion or the Christian faith.
and sea to win one ***p*** . . . . . . . . . . . . Matt 23:15
Nicolas, a ***p*** from Antioch . . . . . . . . . . Acts 6:5
Jews and devout ***p*** . . . . . . . . . . . . . . . Acts 13:43

**proverb** [PRAA·verb] *noun* short, meaningful saying, generally about the nature of people and life.
an astonishment, a ***p*** . . . . . . . . . . . Deut. 28:37
The ***p*** of Solomon the . . . . . . . . . . . . . . Prov. 1:1
to the true ***p*** . . . . . . . . . . . . . . . . . . . 2 Pet. 2:22

**prudence** [PROO·dens] *noun* good judgment; good reason; caution.
son, endowed with ***p*** . . . . . . . . . . . 2 Chr. 2:12
To give ***p*** to the . . . . . . . . . . . . . . . . . Prov. 1:4
us in all wisdom and ***p*** . . . . . . . . . . . . Eph. 1:8

**psalm** [SAHM] *noun* song or hymn to be sung as part of worship.
and the sound of a ***p*** . . . . . . . . . . . . . . Ps. 98:5
each of you has a ***p*** . . . . . . . . . . . 1 Cor. 14:26
to one another in ***p*** . . . . . . . . . . . . . . Eph. 5:19

**Purim** [POOR·em] *noun* festival celebrating the deliverance of the Jews from massacre as described in the Book of Esther.
called these days ***P*** . . . . . . . . . . . . . Esth. 9:26
second letter about ***P*** . . . . . . . . . . . . Esth. 9:29
confirm these days of ***P*** . . . . . . . . . . Esth. 9:31

# Q

**quench** [KWENCH] *verb* to satisfy; to put out; to end.
so that no one can ***q*** . . . . . . . . . . . . . . Jer. 4:4
***q*** all the fiery . . . . . . . . . . . . . . . . . . . . Eph. 6:16
Do not ***q*** the Spirit . . . . . . . . . . . 1 Thess. 5:19

# R

**Rabbi** [RA·bie] *noun* master; teacher.
be called by men, '***R*** . . . . . . . . . . . . . Matt. 23:7
"***R***, is it I . . . . . . . . . . . . . . . . . . . Matt. 26:25
They said to Him, "***R*** . . . . . . . . . . . . . John 1:38

**Rachel** [RAY·chul] *person* younger daughter of Laban; Jacob's second wife (Gen. 29:17–20, 26–30); mother of Joseph (Gen. 30:22–24) and Benjamin (Gen. 35:16–19).

**Rahab** [RAY·hab] *person* woman from Jericho; hides and protects two Israelite spies (Josh. 2:1–7); asks the Israelites to spare her and her family (Josh. 2:8–21); spared from Jericho's destruction (Josh. 6:17); becomes part of the Israelite community (Josh. 6:22–25); part of Jesus' family (Matt. 1:5); her faith praised (Heb. 11:31; James 2:25).

**reap** [REEP] *verb* to gather crops; to obtain.
"You shall sow, but not ***r*** . . . . . . . . . . Mic. 6:15
they neither sow nor ***r*** . . . . . . . . . . . . Matt. 6:26
in Your sickle and ***r*** . . . . . . . . . . . . . . Rev. 14:15

**Rebekah** [rih·BEH·kuh] *person* sister of Laban; marries Isaac (Gen. 24); becomes mother of Esau and Jacob (Gen. 25:21–26); favors Jacob (Gen. 25:28); encourages Jacob to trick Isaac (Gen. 27:5–17); encourages Jacob to run away (Gen. 27:42–46).

**rebuke** [reh·BYOOK] *verb* to correct strongly; to disapprove of strongly.
better to hear the ***r*** . . . . . . . . . . . . . . . Eccl. 7:5
sins against you, ***r*** . . . . . . . . . . . . . . . Luke 17:3
As many as I love, I ***r*** . . . . . . . . . . . . . . Rev. 3:19

**recompense** [REH·kuhm·pens] 1. *verb* to pay for; to return.
Let Him ***r*** him . . . . . . . . . . . . . . . . . . . Job 21:19
not say, "I will ***r*** . . . . . . . . . . . . . . . Prov. 20:22
He shall ***r*** her . . . . . . . . . . . . . . . . . . . Jer. 51:6
2. *noun* payment.
He will accept no ***r*** . . . . . . . . . . . . . . Prov. 6:35
The days of ***r*** have come . . . . . . . . . . . Hos. 9:7

stumbling block and a *r* . . . . . . . . . Rom. 11:9
**reconcile** [REH·kuhn·sile] *verb* to restore; to resolve conflict; to make up with another.
what could he *r* himself. . . . . . . . . 1 Sam. 29:4
and that He might *r* . . . . . . . . . . Eph. 2:16
*r* all things to . . . . . . . . . . . . . . . . . . Col. 1:20
**Redeemer** [rih·DEE·muhr] *noun* one who buys back, rescues, or ransoms; particularly Jesus as the Redeemer who has rescued people from sin and death.
For I know that my *R* . . . . . . . . . . . Job 19:25
Most High God their *R* . . . . . . . . . . Ps. 78:35
*R* will come to Zion . . . . . . . . . . . . . Is. 59:20
**redemption** [rih·DEMP·shn] *noun* the act of redeeming; particularly the rescue from sin and death that Jesus has provided.
*r* is yours to buy it . . . . . . . . . . . . . Jer. 32:7
In Him we have *r* . . . . . . . . . . . . . . . Eph. 1:7
obtained eternal *r* . . . . . . . . . . . . . . Heb. 9:12
**refined** [rih·FIND] *adjective* purified; freed from impurities.
where gold is *r* . . . . . . . . . . . . . . . . . Job 28:1
Behold, I have *r* you, but . . . . . . . . . . Is. 48:10
from Me gold *r* in the fire . . . . . . . . . Rev. 3:18
**refrain** [rih·FRAYN] *verb* to keep from doing; to restrain; to stop oneself.
*R* from meddling with . . . . . . . . 2 Chr. 35:21
who have no right to *r* . . . . . . . . 1 Cor. 9:6
good days, let him *r* . . . . . . . . . . . 1 Pet. 3:10
**refuge** [REH·fyooj] *noun* shelter; place of protection.
six cities of *r* . . . . . . . . . . . . . . . . . . Num. 35:6
but the LORD is his *r* . . . . . . . . . . . . . Ps. 14:6
who have fled for *r* . . . . . . . . . . . . . . Heb. 6:18
**regeneration** [ree·jeh·nuh·RAY·shun] *noun* the process of giving new life.
to you, that in the *r* . . . . . . . . . . . Matt. 19:28
the washing of *r* . . . . . . . . . . . . . . . . . Titus 3:5
**Rehoboam** [ree·huh·BO·uhm] *person* son of Solomon; becomes king after Solomon (1 Kin. 11:43); refuses to ease up on the people (1 Kin. 12:1–15); ten tribes revolt against him (1 Kin. 12:16–24); does evil (2 Chr. 12:14–16).
**relent** [ree·LENT] *verb* to lessen discipline or punishment; to become less severe.
sworn and will not *r* . . . . . . . . . . . . Ps. 110:4
if He will turn and *r* . . . . . . . . . . . . . Joel 2:14
sworn and will not *r* . . . . . . . . . . . . . Heb. 7:21
**religion** [rih·LIH·juhn] *noun* beliefs and practices; the Christian faith or the faith practices of others.
about their own *r* . . . . . . . . . . . . . . Acts 25:19
in self-imposed *r* . . . . . . . . . . . . . . . . Col. 2:23
and undefiled *r* . . . . . . . . . . . . . . . . James 1:27
**remission** [rih·MIH·shun] *noun* stopping; setting something aside; giving relief.
repentance for the *r* . . . . . . . . . . . . . . Mark 1:4
Jesus Christ for the *r* . . . . . . . . . . . . Acts 2:38
where there is *r* . . . . . . . . . . . . . . . . Heb. 10:18
**remnant** [REM·nuhnt] *noun* small part of a larger group that survives or lasts when others do not.
would be no *r* or survivor . . . . . . . . Ezra 9:14
"Yet I will leave a *r* . . . . . . . . . . . . . . . Ezek. 6:8
time there is a *r* . . . . . . . . . . . . . . . . . Rom. 11:5
**render** [REN·duhr] *verb* to give; to pay.
What shall I *r* to the . . . . . . . . . . . . Ps. 116:12
"*R* therefore to Caesar . . . . . . . . . Matt. 22:21
*r* to each one according . . . . . . . . . . . Rom. 2:6
**repent** [rih·PENT] *verb* to change one's mind, desires, and actions; to turn from; particularly, to turn from sin.
I abhor myself, and *r* . . . . . . . . . . . . . Job 42:6
"*R*, for the kingdom . . . . . . . . . . . . . . Matt. 3:2
*R* therefore and be . . . . . . . . . . . . . . . Acts 3:19
**reproach** [rih·PROWCH] *noun* shame; disapproval; discredit.
has taken away my *r* . . . . . . . . . . . . Gen. 30:23
we may no longer be a *r* . . . . . . . . . Neh. 2:17
the camp, bearing His *r* . . . . . . . . . . Heb. 13:13
**reproof** [rih·PROOF] *noun* correction; rebuke.
*R* of instruction are the way . . . . . . Prov. 6:23
for doctrine, for *r* . . . . . . . . . . . . . . 2 Tim. 3:16
**resurrection** [reh·zuh·RECK·shun] *noun* rising from the dead; return to life; particularly, the rising of Jesus Christ from the dead.
to her, "I am the *r* . . . . . . . . . . . . . . John 11:25
and the power of His *r* . . . . . . . . . . . . Phil. 3:10
This is the first *r* . . . . . . . . . . . . . . . . Rev. 20:5
**Reuben** [ROO·bin] *person* firstborn son of Jacob; born to Leah (Gen. 29:32); convinces his brothers not to kill Joseph (Gen. 37:21–22).
**revelation** [reh·vuh·LAY·shun] *noun* something made known that had previously been unknown or hidden; particularly, what God has chosen to share about Himself and His ways.
was no widespread *r* . . . . . . . . . . . 1 Sam. 3:1
it came through the *r* . . . . . . . . . . . . . Gal. 1:12
The *R* of Jesus Christ . . . . . . . . . . . . . Rev. 1:1
**reverence** [REHV·rehns] *noun* honor; respect.
to be held in *r* Ps. 89:7
submission with all *r* . . . . . . . . . . . . 1 Tim. 3:4
God acceptably with *r* . . . . . . . . . . Heb. 12:28
**revile** [rih·VILE] *verb* to speak against; to abuse verbally.
shall not *r* God . . . . . . . . . . . . . . . . Ex. 22:28
are you when they *r* . . . . . . . . . . . . . Matt. 5:11
evildoers, those who *r* . . . . . . . . . . . 1 Pet. 3:16
**revive** [rih·VIVE] *verb* to bring back to consciousness or life; to restore.
*r* me according to Your . . . . . . . . . Ps. 119:25
*r* the spirit of the . . . . . . . . . . . . . . . . Is. 57:15
two days He will *r* . . . . . . . . . . . . . . . . Hos. 6:2
**reward** [rih·WARD] 1. *verb* to pay for something done, particularly, God's blessings upon the obedient and punishment upon the wicked.
*r* me evil for good . . . . . . . . . . . . . . . Ps. 35:12
and the LORD will *r* . . . . . . . . . . . . . Prov. 25:22
*r* them for their deeds . . . . . . . . . . . . . Hos. 4:9
2. *noun* what is given for something done.
behold, His *r* is with . . . . . . . . . . . . . . Is. 40:10

for great is your *r* . . . . . . . . . . . . . . . Matt. 5:12
cheat you of your *r* . . . . . . . . . . . . . . . Col. 2:18

**righteous** [RIGH·chuhs] 1. *adjective* right with God; aligning God's will and ways.
"You are more *r* . . . . . . . . . . . . . 1 Sam. 24:17
receive a *r* man's reward . . . . . . . . Matt. 10:41
*r* are Your judgments . . . . . . . . . . . . . Rev. 16:7
2. *noun* those who are right with God.
me die the death of the *r* . . . . . . . . Num. 23:10
LORD, will bless the *r* . . . . . . . . . . . . . Ps. 5:12
*r* will shine forth as . . . . . . . . . . . Matt. 13:43

**righteousness** [RIGH·chuhs·nes] *noun* right actions; aligning with God's will and ways.
in the paths of *r* . . . . . . . . . . . . . . . . . Ps. 23:3
hunger and thirst for *r* . . . . . . . . . . . . . Matt. 5:6
grace might reign through *r* . . . . . . Rom. 5:21

**rock** [RAAK] *identity* symbol or title for God that describes His strength, stability, and protection.
Of the *R* who begot you . . . . . . . . . Deut. 32:18
any *r* like our God . . . . . . . . . . . . . . 1 Sam. 2:2
The LORD is my *r* . . . . . . . . . . . . . . . . . . Ps. 18:2

**Rome** [ROWM] *place* capital of the Roman Empire; controls Israel in New Testament times (John 11:48); some people at Pentecost from here (Acts 2:10); Paul desires to go here (Acts 19:21); God promises Paul would preach here (Acts 23:11); Paul goes here (Acts 27–28); Paul writes a letter to believers who live here (Rom. 1:7).

**Ruth** [ROOTH] *person* Moabite woman; travels to Bethlehem with Naomi (Ruth 1:6–17); works in the fields to provide for her and Naomi (Ruth 2:1–3); meets and marries Boaz (Ruth 2:4—4:12); great-grandmother of King David (Ruth 4:21–22); part of Jesus' family (Matt. 1:5).

# S

**sabbath** [SA·buhth] *noun* seventh day of the week, on which God commanded Israel to rest.
"Remember the *S* day . . . . . . . . . . . . . Ex. 20:8
a *s* of solemn rest for you . . . . . . . . Lev. 16:31
*S* was made for man . . . . . . . . . . . . . Mark 2:27

**sackcloth** [SAK·klaath] *noun* rough fabric worn in times of mourning, distress, or repentance.
I have sewn *s* over my . . . . . . . . . . . . Job 16:15
a fast, and put on *s* . . . . . . . . . . . . . . . . Jon. 3:5
repented long ago in *s* . . . . . . . . . . . Matt. 11:21

**sacrifice** [SA·kruh·fyce] 1. *verb* to make an offering to God as part of worship.
you shall *s* the Passover . . . . . . . . . Deut. 16:2
Let them *s* . . . . . . . . . . . . . . . . . . . . . Ps. 107:22
But I will *s* to You . . . . . . . . . . . . . . . . . Jon. 2:9
2. *noun* offering given to God; particularly, animal sacrifices in the Old Testament and Jesus Himself in the New Testament.
is a *s* of a peace offering . . . . . . . . . . Lev. 3:1
your bodies a living *s* . . . . . . . . . . . . Rom. 12:1
He had offered one *s* . . . . . . . . . . . . Heb. 10:12

**Sadducees** [SA·dyoo·seez] *noun* aristocratic and wealthy Jewish group in New Testament times that closely aligns with Rome to maintain their authority in Israel; control most of the Sanhedrin and oppose Jesus as a threat to their power.
Pharisees and *S* coming . . . . . . . . . . Matt. 3:7
leaven of the Pharisees and the *S* . Matt. 16:6
*S* say that there is no resurrection . . Acts 23:8

**saints** [SAYNTS] *noun* holy ones; set-apart ones; believers.
*s* who are on the earth . . . . . . . . . . . . . Ps. 16:3
Christ with all His *s* . . . . . . . . . . 1 Thess. 3:13
all delivered to the *s* . . . . . . . . . . . . . . Jude 1:3

**Salome** [suh·LO·mee] *person* woman who ministers to Jesus; present at crucifixion (Mark 15:40–41); present at empty tomb (Mark 16:1).

**salvation** [sal·VAY·shun] *noun* deliverance from evil, danger, or trouble; particularly, God's gift of rescue from sin and death through Jesus Christ.
*S* belongs to the LORD . . . . . . . . . . . . . Ps. 3:8
raised up a horn of *s* . . . . . . . . . . . . Luke 1:69
the power of God to *s* . . . . . . . . . . . . Rom. 1:16

**Samaria** [suh·MAIR·ee·uh] 1. *place* in Old Testament times, capital city of the northern kingdom of Israel; founded by King Omri (1 Kin. 16:23–24); falls to the Assyrians in 722–721 BC (2 Kin. 17:6).
2. *place* in New Testament times, region between Judea and Galilee with residents who are part Jewish and part Gentile; Jesus visits and meets a woman at a well here (John 4); Jesus tells parable of the good Samaritan (Luke 10:30–37); Jesus commands His disciples to take the gospel here (Acts 1:8); Philip preaches here (Acts 8:4–8).

**Samson** [SAM·suhn] *person* judge known for his great strength; the Angel of the LORD tells of his birth (Judg. 13); kills a lion with his hands (Judg. 14:5–6); sets the Philistines' fields on fire (Judg. 15:3–5); kills one thousand Philistines with the jawbone of a donkey (Judg. 15:14–17); betrayed by Delilah (Judg. 16:1–22); defeats the Philistines in his death (Judg. 16:23–30); mentioned in "Hall of Faith" (Heb. 11:32).

**Samuel** [SAM·yoo·uhl] *person* prophet and last judge of Israel; his birth is an answer to prayer (1 Sam. 1); hears from the Lord as a boy (1 Sam. 3); the Israelites go to him to demand a king (1 Sam. 8); anoints Saul as king (1 Sam. 9–10); anoints David as king (1 Sam. 16:11–13).

**sanctify** [SANGK·tuh·fygh] *verb* to set apart as holy; to protect only for specific use; to make holy.
seventh day and *s* it . . . . . . . . . . . . . . Gen. 2:3
*S* them by Your . . . . . . . . . . . . . . . . John 17:17
*s* by the Holy Spirit . . . . . . . . . . . . . Rom. 15:16

**sanctuary** [SANGK·choo·ehr·ee] *noun* place set apart for worship; particularly, in the Old Testament, the tabernacle (Ex. 25:8) or the temple (1 Chr. 22:19); place of security.
let them make Me a ***s*** . . . . . . . . . . . . . Ex. 25:8
I went into the ***s*** . . . . . . . . . . . . . . . . Ps. 73:17
and the earthly ***s*** . . . . . . . . . . . . . . . . Heb. 9:1

**Sapphira** [suh·FIGH·ruh] *person* woman in Jerusalem; loses her life for lying about how much she and her husband, Ananias, had given to God (Acts 5:1–10).

**Sarai; Sarah** [SEHR·igh; SEHR·uh] *person* wife of Abraham; God changes her name from Sarai (Gen. 17:15–16); laughs when an angel says she will have a son (Gen. 18:11–12); gives birth to Isaac (Gen. 21:1–7).

**Satan** [SAY·tuhn] *noun* the devil; the adversary of God.
***S*** also came among them . . . . . . . . . . Job 1:6
forty days, tempted by ***S*** . . . . . . . . . Mark 1:13
***S*** will be released from . . . . . . . . . . . Rev. 20:7

**Saul** [SAAL] 1. **King Saul** [KING] *person* first king of Israel; Samuel anoints to be king (1 Sam. 9–10); early victory (1 Sam. 11); makes an unlawful sacrifice to God (1 Sam. 13); disobeys God and is rejected as king (1 Sam. 15); troubled by spirit (1 Sam. 16:14–23); resents David's fame (1 Sam. 18:1–16); chases and tries to kill David (1 Sam. 19–20); life spared by David (1 Sam 24); life spared by David a second time (1 Sam. 26); killed in battle (1 Sam. 31).
2. **Saul of Tarsus** [TAAR·suhs] *person* apostle. *See* Paul.

**savior** [SAY·vyr] *identity* one who rescues or delivers; particularly, Jesus Christ, the One who delivers people from sin and death.
my refuge; my ***S*** . . . . . . . . . . . . . . 2 Sam. 22:3
Christ, the ***S*** of the world . . . . . . . . John 4:42
***S***, the Lord Jesus Christ . . . . . . . . . . Phil. 3:20

**scourge** [SKURJ] *verb* to beat with a whip, often with pieces of metal, bone, or rock tied to it.
when he had ***s*** Jesus . . . . . . . . . . . Matt. 27:26
They will ***s*** Him . . . . . . . . . . . . . . . . Luke 18:33
***s*** a man who is a Roman . . . . . . . . . Acts 22:25

**scribes** [SKRIBEZ] *noun* teachers of the law; in New Testament times, often partner with the Pharisees.
the families of the ***s*** . . . . . . . . . . . 1 Chr. 2:55
"Beware of the ***s*** . . . . . . . . . . . . . . Mark 12:38
the ***s*** of the Pharisees' . . . . . . . . . . . Acts 23:9

**Scripture** [SKRIP·chur] *noun* writings, generally of a religious nature; particularly, the Bible.
what is noted in the ***S*** . . . . . . . . . . . Dan. 10:21
All ***S*** is given by . . . . . . . . . . . . . . . 2 Tim. 3:16
that no prophecy of ***S*** . . . . . . . . . . . . 2 Pet. 1:20

**Sea of Galilee** [SEE; GA·lih·lee] *place* large lake on the Jordan River; also called "Chinnereth" (Num. 34:11), "Chinneroth" (Josh. 12:3), "Gennesaret" (Luke 5:1), and "Tiberias" (John 6:1); Jesus calls Peter and Andrew as followers here (Matt. 4:18); great catch of fish here (Luke 5:1–11); Jesus stills the waters here (Matt. 8:23–26); Jesus walks on the water here (Matt. 14:25–27).

**second death** [SEH·kund DETH] *noun* final judgment of unbelievers.
not be hurt by the ***s*** . . . . . . . . . . . . . Rev. 2:11
Over such the ***s*** has no . . . . . . . . . . Rev. 20:6
brimstone, which is the ***s*** . . . . . . . . . Rev. 21:8

**sect** [SEKT] *noun* religious group with beliefs that are somewhat different from those held by others who share similar beliefs; a party or faction within a major religious community.
which is the ***s*** of the Sadducees . . . . Acts 5:17
of the ***s*** of the Pharisees . . . . . . . . . Acts 15:5
of the ***s*** of the Nazarenes . . . . . . . . Acts 24:5

**Seth** [SETH] *person* third son of Adam and Eve; born after Cain kills Abel (Gen. 4:25); part of Jesus' family (Luke 3:38).

**Shadrach** [SHAD·rack] *person* Babylonian name given to Hananiah, one of Daniel's companions (Dan. 1:7); refuses to eat unclean foods (Dan. 1:3ff); saved in fiery furnace (Dan. 3:8ff).

**Sheol** [shee·OL] *place* domain of the dead; the grave; sometimes used symbolically for death.
down to the gates of ***S*** . . . . . . . . . . . Job 17:16
not leave my soul in ***S*** . . . . . . . . . . . Ps. 16:10
the belly of ***S*** I cried . . . . . . . . . . . . . . Jon. 2:2

**Shiloh** [SHY·lo] *place* ancient city north of Jerusalem; division of Promised Land decided here (Josh. 18:1, 10); center of worship (Judg. 18:31); ark of the covenant taken from here (1 Sam. 4:3–11).

**signs and wonders** *phrase* miracles that reveal God's identity, power, and character.
LORD showed ***s*** . . . . . . . . . . . . . . . . Deut. 6:22
"Unless you people see ***s*** . . . . . . . . John 4:48
bearing witness both with ***s*** . . . . . . . Heb. 2:4

**Silas** [SIGH·luhs] *person* missionary; also called Silvanus (2 Cor. 1:19); carries letter from Jerusalem Council (Acts 15:22–29); encourages the church in Antioch (Acts 15:30–35); travels with Paul on second missionary journey (Acts 15:40—18:5).

**Siloam** [sih·LOW·uhm] *place* pool and tunnel that serve as a water supply for Jerusalem; in use in time of King David (2 Sam. 5:8); changed or expanded in time of King Hezekiah (2 Chr. 32:30); Jesus tells a blind man to wash here (John 9:7).

**Simeon** [SIH·mee·uhn] 1. **Simeon, son of Jacob** [JAY·kuhb] *person* second son of Jacob, by Leah (Gen. 29:33); bound in Egypt (Gen. 42:24).
2. **Simeon, a devout man** [duh·VOWT MAAN] *person* faithful man in Jerusalem; blesses the infant Jesus (Luke 2:25–35).

**Simon** [SIGH·muhn] 1. **Simon Peter** [PEE·tuhr] *person* apostle. *See* Peter.
2. **Simon the Zealot** [ZEH·luht] *person* apostle (Luke 6:15).
3. **Simon the Pharisee** [FEHR·uh·see] *person* Pharisee in whose home Jesus is anointed (Luke 7:36–50).
4. **Simon the leper** [LEH·puhr] *person* leper in whose home Jesus was anointed by Mary (Mark 14:3–9).
5. **Simon of Cyrene** [sigh·REE·nee] *person* man forced to carry Jesus' cross (Matt. 27:32).
6. **Simon the sorcerer** [SOR·suh·rer] *person* former sorcerer who offers money to Peter and John for the power of the Holy Spirit (Acts 8:9–24).

**sin** [SIHN] 1. *verb* to act or think in a way that goes against God and His ways; to disobey God; to rebel against God.
is no one who does not ***s*** . . . . . . . . . 1 Kin. 8:46
***S*** no more, lest a . . . . . . . . . . . . . . . . John 5:14
Shall we ***s*** because we . . . . . . . . . . . . Rom. 6:15
2. *noun* an action or thought that is against God and His ways; disobedience; rebellion.
our ***s*** testify against us . . . . . . . . . . . Is. 59:12
takes away the ***s*** of . . . . . . . . . . . . . John 1:29
the wages of ***s*** is death . . . . . . . . . . Rom. 6:23

**sinful** [SIHN·fuhl] *adjective* wicked; full of iniquity; disobedient; unforgiven.
***s*** nation, a people laden . . . . . . . . . . . . Is. 1:4
from me, for I am a ***s*** . . . . . . . . . . . . . Luke 5:8
in the likeness of ***s*** flesh . . . . . . . . . Rom. 8:3

**sinner** [SIH·ner] *noun* one who commits sin; one who acts in ways against God; one who is disobedient; one who is unforgiven.
***s*** does evil a hundred. . . . . . . . . . . . Eccl. 8:12
***s*** who repents than . . . . . . . . . . . . . . Luke 15:7
the ungodly and the ***s*** . . . . . . . . . . 1 Pet. 4:18

**slanderers** [SLAN·der·ehrs] *noun* those who say false things of others to harm them.
Let not a ***s*** be established . . . . . . . . . Ps. 140:11
be reverent, not ***s*** . . . . . . . . . . . . . . 1 Tim. 3:11
in behavior, not ***s*** . . . . . . . . . . . . . . . . Titus 2:3

**Sodom** [SAA·duhm] *place* wicked city destroyed by the Lord (Gen. 19:24–28).

**sojourner** [SO·juhr·nur] *noun* one who stays for a short time in another land.
are strangers and ***s*** . . . . . . . . . . . . . . Lev. 25:23
land where you are ***s*** . . . . . . . . . . . . . . Jer. 35:7
I beg you as ***s*** . . . . . . . . . . . . . . . . . . 1 Pet. 2:11

**Solomon** [SAA·luh·muhn] *person* third king of Israel; son of David and Bathsheba (2 Sam. 12:24); noted for his wisdom (1 Kin. 3:16–28); builds temple (1 Kin. 6); builds palace (1 Kin. 7:1–8); marries many women and turns from God (1 Kin. 11:1–13); writer of much of Proverbs and all of Song of Solomon and Ecclesiastes.

**Son of God** [SON; GAAD] *identity* Jesus Christ, the Second Person of the Trinity; declared as such by God the Father (Matt. 3:17); questioned as such by Satan (Matt. 4:1–11); recognized as such by demons (Matt. 8:29); declared as such by Peter (Matt. 16:16).

**son of man** [SON; MAN] 1. *noun* a human.
a ***s***, that He should repent . . . . . . . Num. 23:19
a ***s***, who is a worm . . . . . . . . . . . . . . Job 25:6
***s*** that You visit him . . . . . . . . . . . . . . . Ps. 8:4
2. *identity* messianic title that Jesus often uses for Himself.
the ***S*** has nowhere to . . . . . . . . . . . . Matt. 8:20
that the ***S*** has power . . . . . . . . . . . . Luke 5:24
One like the ***S*** . . . . . . . . . . . . . . . . . . Rev. 1:13

**sons of God** [SONZ; GAAD] 1. *noun* angels.
***s*** came to present . . . . . . . . . . . . . . . Job 1:6
***s*** came to present . . . . . . . . . . . . . . . Job 2:1
all the ***s*** shouted for. . . . . . . . . . . . . Job 38:7
2. *noun* Christians; believers.
for they shall be called ***s*** . . . . . . . . . . Matt. 5:9
Spirit of God, these are ***s*** . . . . . . . . . Rom. 8:14
For you are all ***s*** . . . . . . . . . . . . . . . . Gal. 3:26

**sorcery** [SOR·suh·ree] *noun* evil magic.
"For there is no ***s*** . . . . . . . . . . . . . Num. 23:23
who previously practiced ***s*** . . . . . . . . . Acts 8:9
idolatry, ***s***, hatred . . . . . . . . . . . . . . . Gal. 5:20

**soul** [SOL] *noun* nonphysical essence of a person; some see this as the same as a person's spirit.
with all your ***s*** . . . . . . . . . . . . . . . . . Deut. 6:5
destroy both ***s*** and body . . . . . . . . Matt. 10:28
which war against the ***s*** . . . . . . . . . 1 Pet. 2:11

**sow** [SO] *verb* to plant seed; to cause something to happen.
***s*** in tears shall reap in joy . . . . . . . . Ps. 126:5
they neither ***s*** nor reap . . . . . . . . . Luke 12:24
man ***s***, that he will also reap. . . . . . . . . Gal. 6:7

**spirit** [SPEER·uht] *noun* nonphysical essence of a person; some see this to be the same as a person's soul.
Into Your hand I commit my ***s*** . . . . . . . Ps. 31:5
The ***s*** indeed is willing Matt. 26:41
yielded up His ***s*** . . . . . . . . . . . . . . . Matt. 27:50

**splendor** [SPLEN·duhr] *noun* greatness; majesty; wonderfulness.
Like the ***s*** of the meadows . . . . . . . . Ps. 37:20
the ***s*** of old men is their . . . . . . . . Prov. 20:29
of Zion all her ***s*** . . . . . . . . . . . . . . . . Lam. 1:6

**stature** [STA·chur] *noun* height; size.
child Samuel grew in ***s*** . . . . . . . . . 1 Sam. 2:26
add one cubit to his ***s*** . . . . . . . . . . . Matt. 6:27
the measure of the ***s*** . . . . . . . . . . . . . Eph. 4:13

**statute** [STA·choot] *noun* law; rule.
It shall be a ***s*** forever to . . . . . . . . . . Ex. 27:21
For this is a ***s*** for Israel . . . . . . . . . . . Ps. 81:4
to establish a royal ***s*** . . . . . . . . . . . . . Dan. 6:7

**steadfast** [STED·fast] *adjective* determined; not giving up; fixed.
O God, my heart is ***s***. . . . . . . . . . . . . . . Ps. 57:7
faith, grounded and ***s*** . . . . . . . . . . . . . Col. 1:23
Resist him, ***s*** in the . . . . . . . . . . . . . . 1 Pet. 5:9

**Stephen** [STEE·vuhn] *person* early believer; chosen to serve tables (Acts 6:1–7); accused of blasphemy (Acts 6:8–15); offers defense of the faith (Acts 7:1–53); becomes first Christian martyr (Acts 7:54–60).

**steward** [STOO·urd] *noun* one who manages a household or property that belongs to another.
faithful and wise ***s*** . . . . . . . . . . . Luke 12:42
***s*** of the mysteries of God . . . . . . . . 1 Cor. 4:1
***s*** of the manifold grace of God . . . . 1 Pet. 4:10

**stiff-necked** [stif·NEKT] *adjective* stubborn; arrogant.
you are a ***s*** people . . . . . . . . . . . . . . Ex. 33:3
Now do not be ***s*** . . . . . . . . . . . . . . 2 Chr. 30:8
"You ***s*** and uncircumcised . . . . . . . . . Acts 7:51

**stone** [STOWN] *verb* to put someone to death by throwing stones at him or her.
***s*** Stephen as he was . . . . . . . . . . . . Acts 7:59
once I was ***s*** . . . . . . . . . . . . . . . . 2 Cor. 11:25
They were ***s*** . . . . . . . . . . . . . . . . . . Heb. 11:37

**strife** [STRIGHF] *noun* conflict; dissension; disagreement.
let there be no ***s*** . . . . . . . . . . . . . . . Gen. 13:8
Hatred stirs up ***s*** . . . . . . . . . . . . . Prov. 10:12
which come envy, ***s*** . . . . . . . . . . . . 1 Tim. 6:4

**stumbling block** [STUM·bling BLOK] *noun* obstacle; something that causes another difficulty.
I lay a ***s*** before him. . . . . . . . . . . . . Ezek. 3:20
***s*** and a recompense . . . . . . . . . . . . Rom. 11:9
to the Jews a ***s*** . . . . . . . . . . . . . . . 1 Cor. 1:23

**subdue** [sub·DOO] *verb* to control; to conquer; to rule over.
fill the earth and ***s*** it . . . . . . . . . . . . Gen. 1:28
***s*** our iniquities . . . . . . . . . . . . . . . . Mic. 7:19
***s*** all things to . . . . . . . . . . . . . . . . . Phil. 3:21

**submission** [sub·MIH·shun] *noun* recognizing another's authority; obedience; subordination.
pretend ***s*** to Him . . . . . . . . . . . . . . . . Ps. 81:15
not yield ***s*** even for . . . . . . . . . . . . . . . Gal. 2:5
his children in ***s*** . . . . . . . . . . . . . . . . 1 Tim 3:4

**sufficient** [suh·FIH·shunt] *adjective* enough; ample.
one witness is not ***s*** . . . . . . . . . . . . Num. 35:30
***S*** for the day is its . . . . . . . . . . . . . Matt. 6:34
Not that we are ***s*** . . . . . . . . . . . . . . 2 Cor. 3:5

**supplication** [suh·plih·KAY·shun] *noun* humble and urgent requests; what is asked for of another.
LORD has heard my ***s*** . . . . . . . . . . . . . . . Ps. 6:9
They will make ***s*** . . . . . . . . . . . . . . . . Is. 45:14
with all prayer and ***s*** . . . . . . . . . . . . Eph. 6:18

**surety** [SHUR·uh·tee] *noun* pledge or deposit that guarantees full payment to be made in the future.
Be ***s*** for Your servant . . . . . . . . . . . Ps. 119:122
one who hates being ***s*** . . . . . . . . . . . Prov. 11:15
Jesus has become a ***s*** . . . . . . . . . . . . . Heb. 7:22

**swear** [SWEHR] *verb* to declare under oath; to make a binding promise.
not ***s*** by My name falsely . . . . . . . . . Lev. 19:12
***s*** oaths by the LORD. . . . . . . . . . . . . . Zeph. 1:5
my brethren, do not ***s*** . . . . . . . . . . . James 5:12

**synagogue** [SIH·nuh·gaag] *noun* building where Jewish religious services, schools, and other meetings are held.
teaching in their ***s*** . . . . . . . . . . . . . . . Matt. 4:23
He went into the ***s*** . . . . . . . . . . . . . . . Luke 4:16
in the ***s*** every Sabbath . . . . . . . . . . . . Acts 18:4

# T

**tabernacle** [TA·ber·na·kel] *noun* the "tent of meeting" in which God meets and lives with His people; the portable shelter used by the Hebrews as a place of worship beginning in the wilderness journey.
you shall make the ***t*** . . . . . . . . . . . . . . Ex. 26:1
I will abide in Your ***t*** . . . . . . . . . . . . . Ps. 61:4
the true ***t*** which the Lord. . . . . . . . . . Heb. 8:2

**tablets** [TA·bluhts] *noun* flat stones with writing engraved on them; particularly, the tablets of the Ten Commandments.
two ***t*** of the Testimony . . . . . . . . . . . Ex. 31:18
write them on the ***t*** . . . . . . . . . . . . . . Prov. 3:3
God, not on ***t*** of stone. . . . . . . . . . . . 2 Cor. 3:3

**Tarsus** [TAR·suhs] *place* city of Cilicia, a province in Asia Minor (modern-day Turkey); Paul was from here (Acts 9:11).

**tax collector** [TACKS kuh·LEK·tuhr] *noun* despised profession in New Testament times; work for Rome, collecting taxes that support their occupation; allowed to collect any amount above Rome's requirement.
Matthew the ***t*** . . . . . . . . . . . . . . . . . . Matt. 10:3
a friend of ***t*** and sinners . . . . . . . . . Matt. 11:19
saw a ***t*** named Levi . . . . . . . . . . . . . . Luke 5:27

**teacher** [TEE·cher] *noun* rabbi; one who instructs others—namely, in the law and ways of God; particularly used by some as a title for Jesus.
your ***T***, the Christ . . . . . . . . . . . . . Matt. 23:8, 10
trouble the ***T*** . . . . . . . . . . . . . . . . . . Mark 5:35
call Me ***T*** and Lord . . . . . . . . . . . . . . John 13:13

**temperate** [TEM·puhr·uht] *adjective* moderate; not extreme or excessive; disciplined.
for the prize is ***t*** in all . . . . . . . . . . . 1 Cor. 9:25
husband of one wife, ***t*** . . . . . . . . . . . 1 Tim. 3:2
reverent, ***t***, sound in faith . . . . . . . . . . Titus 2:2

**temple** [TEM·puhl] *noun* building that replaced the tabernacle; where God meets and dwells among His people; site of worship, including where sacrifices are made; the First Temple is built by Solomon and destroyed by the Assyrians; the Second Temple is built by returning exiles and is remodeled during Jesus' life but is later destroyed by the Romans.
So Solomon built the ***t*** . . . . . . . . . . . 1 Kin. 6:14
laid the foundation of the ***t*** . . . . . . . Ezra 3:10
One greater than the ***t*** . . . . . . . . . . . Matt. 12:6

**temptation** [tem·TAY·shun] *noun* something that causes a person to want to do something wrong; enticement.

do not lead us into *t* . . . . . . . . . . . . Matt. 6:13
*t* has overtaken you . . . . . . . . . . . 1 Cor. 10:13
the man who endures *t* . . . . . . . . . James 1:12

**testimony** [TEH·stuh·mow·nee] *noun* witness; precisely, the law as a witness to God in the Old Testament and believers as witnesses to Christ in the New Testament.
law and to the *t* . . . . . . . . . . . . . . . . . Is. 8:20
know that his *t* is true . . . . . . . . . . John 21:24
to the *t* of Jesus Christ . . . . . . . . . . . . Rev. 1:2

**Thaddaeus** [THA·dee·uhs] *person* apostle; also called Lebbaeus (Matt. 10:3) and probably Judas (Luke 6:16).

**Theophilus** [thee·AH·fih·luhs] *person* the recipient of Luke's Gospel (Luke 1:3) and the Book of Acts (Acts 1:1).

**Thessalonica** [theh·suh·lo·NIGH·kuh] *place* city in Macedonia; Paul visits on his second missionary journey (Acts 17:1–10); people from here follow Paul to Berea to oppose him (Acts 17:13); Paul writes two letters to the church here (1 Thess. 1:1; 2 Thess. 1:1).

**Thomas** [TAW·muhs] *person* apostle; also called "the Twin" (John 11:16); willing to go with Jesus to Bethany (John 11:16); admits not knowing where Jesus was to go (John 14:3–5); wants to see and touch Jesus' wounds to confirm the resurrection (John 20:24–29).

**thresh** [THRESH] *verb* to separate the parts of grain that can be eaten from the parts that cannot.
he does not *t* it . . . . . . . . . . . . . . . . . Is. 28:28
"Arise and *t* . . . . . . . . . . . . . . . . . . . . Mic. 4:13
and he who *t* in hope . . . . . . . . . . 1 Cor. 9:10

**Timothy** [TIH·muh·thee] *person* companion of Paul; joins Paul and Silas on second missionary journey (Acts 16:1–5); remains in Macedonia with Silas (Acts 17:1–15); rejoins Paul in Corinth (Acts 18:5); sent by Paul to the church in Thessalonica (1 Thess. 3:1–2); with Paul before the apostle's trip to Jerusalem (Acts 20:4); serves in Ephesus (1 Tim. 1:3); with Paul as the apostle was in prison (Phil. 1:1); Paul asks for (2 Tim. 4:9, 21); imprisoned at some point (Heb. 13:23); Paul writes the epistles of 1 Timothy (1 Tim. 1:2) and 2 Timothy (2 Tim. 1:2) to him.

**tithe** [TITHE] *noun* tenth of one's possessions or income given for the work of ministry.
And he gave him a *t* . . . . . . . . . . . . . Gen. 14:20
shall bring out the *t* . . . . . . . . . . . . . Deut. 14:28
For you pay *t* of mint . . . . . . . . . . Matt. 23:23

**Titus** [TIE·tuhs] *person* companion of Paul; travels to Jerusalem with Paul (Gal. 2:1); reports to Paul about the church in Corinth (2 Cor. 7:5–7, 13–16); Paul leaves on Crete to set the church in order (Titus 1:5); travels to Dalmatia (2 Tim. 4:10); Paul writes the epistle of Titus (Titus 1:4) to him.

**tore his clothes** *phrase* display of great sadness, grief, and distress.
Then Joshua *t*, and fell . . . . . . . . . . Josh. 7:6
he *t* and put on sackcloth . . . . . . . . Esth. 4:1
Then the high priest *t* . . . . . . . . . Mark 14:63

**tradition** [truh·DIH·shun] *noun* mostly spoken beliefs and practices handed down; particularly, those of the Pharisees and scribes during the time of the Gospels and those of the apostles during the early church.
holding the *t* of the elders . . . . . . . . . Mark 7:3
according to the *t* . . . . . . . . . . . . . . . . Col. 2:8
*t* which he received . . . . . . . . . . . 2 Thess. 3:6

**transfigure** [trans·FIH·gyur] *verb* change in appearance; particularly, Jesus' glorious and radiant change witnessed by three disciples.
He was *t* before them . . . . . . . . . . . . . Mark 9:2

**transgression** [trans·GREH·shun] *noun* an action or thought that is against God and His ways; disobedience; rebellion.
forgiving iniquity and *t* . . . . . . . . . . . . Ex. 34:7
who blots out your *t* . . . . . . . . . . . . . Is. 43:25
of the *t* of Adam . . . . . . . . . . . . . . . . Rom. 5:14

**treacherous** [TREH·chuh·ruhs] *adjective* deceptive; likely to betray; dangerous.
The *t* dealers have dealt . . . . . . . . . . Is. 24:16
yet her *t* sister Judah did . . . . . . . . . . Jer. 3:8
are insolent, *t* . . . . . . . . . . . . . . . . . . Zeph. 3:4

**tree of life** [TREE; LIFE] *noun* tree in the Garden of Eden that Adam and Eve could eat from at first but then could not after the fall.
The *t* was also in the midst . . . . . . . . Gen. 2:9
and take also of the *t* . . . . . . . . . . . Gen. 3:22
have the right to the *t* . . . . . . . . . . Rev. 22:14

**trespass** [TREHS·pas] *noun* an action or thought that is against God and His ways; disobedience; rebellion.
he shall bring his *t* offering . . . . . . . . . Lev. 5:6
forgive the *t* of your . . . . . . . . . . 1 Sam. 25:28
a man is overtaken in any *t* . . . . . . . . . Gal. 6:1

**tribe** [TRIBE] *noun* family; smaller portion of a larger people.
a man from every *t* . . . . . . . . . . . . . . . Num. 1:4
belongs to another *t* . . . . . . . . . . . . . Heb. 7:13
the Lion of the *t* . . . . . . . . . . . . . . . . . . Rev. 5:5

**tribulation** [trih·byuh·LAY·shun] *noun* strong and intense suffering; distress; opposition and persecution.
deliver me out of all *t* . . . . . . . . 1 Sam. 26:24
when *t* or persecution . . . . . . . . . . Matt. 13:21
and you will have *t* . . . . . . . . . . . . . . . Rev. 2:10

**trust** [TRUHST] 1. *verb* to have or put confidence in someone or something.
'We *t* in the LORD our . . . . . . . . . . 2 Kin. 18:22
*T* in the LORD . . . . . . . . . . . . . . . . . . . . . Ps. 37:3
those who *t* in riches . . . . . . . . . . . Mark 10:24
2. *noun* confidence in someone or something.
In You, O LORD, I put my *t* . . . . . . . . . . Ps. 71:1
such *t* through Christ . . . . . . . . . . . . 2 Cor. 3:4
committed to your *t* . . . . . . . . . . . . . 1 Tim. 6:20

**Tyre and Sidon** [TIE·er; SIGH·duhn] *place* Phoenician cities; Jesus withdraws here (Matt. 15:21–29); people come to hear Jesus preach from here (Mark 3:7–12); Jesus says these cities would have repented rather than Chorazin and Bethsaida (Matt. 11:20–24).

## U

**unbelief** [uhn·buh·LEEF] *noun* doubt; determining something is not true; particularly, the gospel.
help my ***u*** . . . . . . . . . . . . . . . . . . . Mark 9:24
promise of God through ***u*** . . . . . . . . Rom. 4:20
you an evil heart of ***u*** . . . . . . . . . . Heb. 3:12

**unclean** [uhn·KLEEN] *adjective* defiled; under the Old Testament law, certain animals are declared clean, meaning they can be eaten, and others unclean, meaning they cannot be eaten (Lev. 11:1–47; Deut. 14:3–21).
of animals that are ***u*** . . . . . . . . . . . Gen. 7:2
person touches any ***u*** thing . . . . . . . . . Lev. 5:2
Do not touch what is ***u*** . . . . . . . . . 2 Cor. 6:17

**ungodly** [uhn·GAAD·lee] 1. *adjective* displeasing to God; unlike or against God and His ways.
my cause against an ***u*** . . . . . . . . . . . . Ps. 43:1
***u*** man digs up evil . . . . . . . . . . . . Prov. 16:27
all their ***u*** deeds . . . . . . . . . . . . . . . . . Jude 1:15
2. *noun* characteristics and actions that displease God.
delivered me to the ***u*** . . . . . . . . . . . Job. 16:11
***u*** shall not stand . . . . . . . . . . . . . . . . . . Ps. 1:5
Christ died for the ***u*** . . . . . . . . . . . . . Rom. 5:6

**unjust** [uhn·JUHST] 1. *adjective* not acting or being in a way that is right according to God.
the deceitful and ***u*** man . . . . . . . . . . . Ps. 43:1
commended the ***u*** steward . . . . . . . . . Luke 16:8
For God is not ***u*** . . . . . . . . . . . . . . . . Heb. 6:10
2. *noun* something that is not right according to the identity and ways of God.
***u*** knows no shame . . . . . . . . . . . . . . . Zeph. 3:5
on the just and on the ***u*** . . . . . . . . . . Matt. 5:45
the just for the ***u*** . . . . . . . . . . . . . . 1 Pet. 3:18

**unleavened bread** [uhn·LEH·vuhnd BRED] *noun* bread made without yeast or leaven, which causes it to be flat instead of rising.
roasted in fire, with ***u*** . . . . . . . . . . . . . Ex. 12:8
the meat and the ***u*** . . . . . . . . . . . . . . Judg. 6:20
***u*** of sincerity and truth . . . . . . . . . . 1 Cor. 5:8

**unrighteousness** [uhn·RIGH·chuhs·ness] *noun* wrong actions; not aligning with God's will and ways.
and there is no ***u*** . . . . . . . . . . . . . . . . Ps. 92:15
Is there ***u*** with God . . . . . . . . . . . . . . Rom. 9:14
cleanse us from all ***u*** . . . . . . . . . . . . . 1 John 1:9

**Uriah** [yoo·RIGH·uh] *person* Hittite warrior; one of King David's mighty men (2 Sam. 23:8, 39); sent to his death by David (2 Sam. 11:6–17).

**Uzziah** [yoo·ZIGH·uh] *person* king of Judah also called Azariah; good king, although he does not remove places of pagan worship (2 Kin. 15:3–4); leads building projects (2 Chr. 26:9–10); God gives him leprosy (2 Kin. 15:5; 2 Chr. 26:16–23).

## V

**vanity** [VA·nih·tee] *noun* futility; emptiness; pointlessness.
"***V*** of ***v***, all is ***v*** . . . . . . . . . . . . . . . . . . Eccl. 1:2
iniquity with cords of ***v*** . . . . . . . . . . . . Is. 5:18
surely they are ***v*** . . . . . . . . . . . . . . . . Hos. 12:11

**veil** [VAYL] 1. *noun* face covering.
she took a ***v*** and covered . . . . . . . . Gen. 24:65
he put a ***v*** on his face . . . . . . . . . . . . . . Ex. 34:33
Moses, who put a ***v*** . . . . . . . . . . . . . 2 Cor. 3:13
2. *noun* curtains in the tabernacle and temple.
The ***v*** shall be a divider for . . . . . . . . . Ex. 26:33
***v*** of the temple was . . . . . . . . . . . . . Matt. 27:51
because the ***v*** is taken . . . . . . . . . . . . . 2 Cor. 3:14

**vengeance** [VEN·jehns] *noun* revenge; punishment for a harm done.
***V*** is Mine . . . . . . . . . . . . . . . . . . . . . . . . . Deut. 32:35
it is the day of the LORD's ***v*** . . . . . . . . . . Is. 34:8
are the days of ***v*** . . . . . . . . . . . . . . . . Luke 21:22

**vision** [VIH·zhuhn] *noun* supernatural experience that is like a dream; particularly, God revealing something to a person who sees it in a way that is not normal.
came to Abram in a ***v*** . . . . . . . . . . . . Gen. 15:1
young men shall see ***v*** . . . . . . . . . . . . . Joel 2:28
in a ***v*** he has seen a man . . . . . . . . . . Acts 9:12

**vow** [VOW] *noun* binding promise.
to take the ***v*** of a Nazirite . . . . . . . . . Num. 6:2
not to ***v*** than to ***v*** . . . . . . . . . . . . . . . . . . Eccl. 5:5
men who have taken a ***v*** . . . . . . . . . Acts 21:23

## W

**wages** [WAY·juhz] *noun* payment for work done; what is earned.
I will give you your ***w*** . . . . . . . . . . . . . . . Ex. 2:9
be content with your ***w*** . . . . . . . . . . . Luke 3:14
the ***w*** of sin is death . . . . . . . . . . . . . . Rom. 6:23

**walk** [WAAK] *verb* at times used in a way to mean how a person lives.
people, who ***w*** in a way . . . . . . . . . . . . Is. 65:2
***w*** humbly with your God . . . . . . . . . . . . Mic. 6:8
Let us ***w*** properly . . . . . . . . . . . . . . . Rom. 13:13

**whitewashed** [WITE·waasht] *adjective* used to describe walls that have been whitened through a cleaning process; also used to describe people who might look good on the outside but who have not dealt with who they are on the inside.
you are like ***w*** tombs . . . . . . . . . . . . Matt. 23:27
strike you, you ***w*** wall . . . . . . . . . . . . Acts 23:3

**wicked** [WIK·id] 1. *adjective* sinful; evil.
turn from their ***w*** ways . . . . . . . . . . . 2 Chr. 7:14
heart that devises ***w*** plans . . . . . . . . Prov. 6:18
with this ***w*** generation . . . . . . . . . . . Matt. 12:45
2. *noun* something or someone that is sinful and evil.
Why do the ***w*** live and . . . . . . . . . . . . . Job 21:7
***w*** forsake his way . . . . . . . . . . . . . . . . . . Is. 55:7
separate the ***w*** from . . . . . . . . . . . . . Matt. 13:49

**will** [WIL] *noun* when used of a person, his or her desire to do something or for something to happen; when used of God, His plans and purposes.
I delight to do Your ***w*** . . . . . . . . . . . . . . Ps. 40:8
***w*** be done on earth as . . . . . . . . . . . Matt. 6:10
what the ***w*** of the Lord is . . . . . . . . . Eph. 5:17
**wise** [WIZE] *adjective* having good judgment; knowing how to live rightly and best.
tree desirable to make one ***w*** . . . . . . Gen. 3:6
Do not be ***w*** in your . . . . . . . . . . . . . Prov. 3:7
to God who alone is ***w*** . . . . . . . . . 1 Tim. 1:17
**with one accord** *phrase* togetherness; in agreement.
Joshua and Israel ***w*** . . . . . . . . . . . . . . Josh. 9:2
to serve Him ***w*** . . . . . . . . . . . . . . . . . . Zeph. 3:9
These all continued ***w*** . . . . . . . . . . . . Acts 1:14
**witness** [WIT·nuhs] *noun* person who has experienced something; a person or an object that helps prove something is true; a reminder of something that is true.
a true and faithful ***w*** . . . . . . . . . . . . . . Jer. 42:5
For you will be His ***w*** . . . . . . . . . . . . Acts 22:15
who bore ***w*** to the word . . . . . . . . . . . . Rev. 1:2
**woe** [WOH] *noun* deep grief, distress, or suffering.
***W*** to the wicked . . . . . . . . . . . . . . . . . . . . Is. 3:11
***W*** to you, O Jerusalem . . . . . . . . . . . . Jer. 13:27
But ***w*** to you, scribes . . . . . . . . . . . Matt. 23:13
**Word** [WURD] *identity* title used of Christ.
the ***W*** was God . . . . . . . . . . . . . . . . . . . . John 1:1
concerning the ***W*** of life . . . . . . . . . 1 John 1:1
is called The ***W*** of God . . . . . . . . . . . . Rev. 19:13
**word of God** [WURD; GAAD] *noun* messages from God; God's revealed will; the Scriptures.
***w*** came to Nathan . . . . . . . . . . . . . . . 1 Chr. 17:3
alone, but by every ***w*** . . . . . . . . . . . . . . Luke 4:4
spoke the ***w*** with boldness . . . . . . . . . Acts 4:31
**world** [WURLD] 1. *noun* the earth; the universe.
the ***w*** is Mine, and all . . . . . . . . . . . . . Ps. 50:12
since the beginning of the ***w*** . . . . . . . . . Is. 64:4
famine throughout all the ***w*** . . . . . . . Acts 11:28
2. *noun* the things of the world; the ungodly systems of the world.
He shall judge the ***w*** . . . . . . . . . . . . . . . . Ps. 9:8
conformed to this ***w*** . . . . . . . . . . . . . . Rom. 12:2
Do not love the ***w*** . . . . . . . . . . . . . . 1 John 2:15
3. *noun* the people of the world.
"You are the light of the ***w*** . . . . . . . . Matt. 5:14
God so loved the ***w*** . . . . . . . . . . . . . . . John 3:16
Son as Savior of the ***w*** . . . . . . . . . . 1 John 4:14
**worship** [WUR·shuhp] *verb* to celebrate; to praise; to honor; to express the worth of something or someone.
you shall ***w*** no other god . . . . . . . . . . . Ex. 34:14
Oh come, let us ***w*** . . . . . . . . . . . . . . . . . . Ps. 95:6
***w*** the LORD your God . . . . . . . . . . . . . . Matt. 4:10
**wrath** [RATH] *noun* punishment; great anger.
soft answer turns away ***w*** . . . . . . . . . Prov. 15:1
For the ***w*** of God is . . . . . . . . . . . . . . . Rom. 1:18
for the ***w*** of man does . . . . . . . . . . . . James 1:20

# Y

**yoke** [YOHK] *noun* object used for work; an animal yoke joins two animals at the neck so they can work together to pull an object such as a plow; a person's yoke is placed over the shoulders to carry two loads of equal weight.
"Your father made our ***y*** . . . . . . . . 1 Kin. 12:4
Take My ***y*** upon you . . . . . . . . . . . . Matt. 11:29
not be unequally ***y*** together . . . . . . 2 Cor. 6:14

# Z

**Zacchaeus** [za·KEE·uhs] *person* chief tax collector; climbs tree to see Jesus (Luke 19:1–4); Jesus stays at his house (Luke 19:5–7); gives back what he had taken from others (Luke 19:8–10).
**Zacharias** [za·kuh·RIGH·uhs] *person* priest; angel tells of the birth of John the Baptist (Luke 1:13–17); questions the angel and left unable to speak (Luke 1:18–22); son born to him (Luke 1:57–58); agrees to name his son John and can speak again (Luke 1:59–66); prophesies about his son (Luke 1:67–79).
**zeal** [ZEEL] *noun* eagerness; great desire for something.
The ***z*** of the LORD of . . . . . . . . . . . . . 2 Kin. 19:31
He shall stir up His ***z*** . . . . . . . . . . . . . . Is. 42:13
that they have a ***z*** . . . . . . . . . . . . . . . . . Rom. 10:2
**Zealot** [ZEH·luht] *noun* person who is a part of a group of radical Jews who want to rebel against Roman rule.
and Simon called the ***Z*** . . . . . . . . . . . Luke 6:15
and Simon the ***Z*** . . . . . . . . . . . . . . . . . . Acts 1:13
**Zebedee** [ZEH·beh·dee] *person* father of the apostles James and John (Matt. 4:21); owner of a fishing business (Mark 1:20).
**Zebulun** [ZEH·byoo·luhn] *person* tenth son of Jacob, the sixth by Leah (Gen. 30:19–20).
**Zechariah** [zeh·kuh·RIGH·uh] 1. **Zechariah, the priest** [PREEST] *person* warns the people in the days of King Joash (2 Chr. 24:20); put to death (2 Chr. 24:21).
2. **Zechariah, the prophet** [PRAA·fuht] *person* with Haggai, urges the people to rebuild the temple (Ezra 5:1; 6:14); the Old Testament book that bears his name is the eleventh of the twelve Minor Prophets.
**Zedekiah** [zeh·duh·KIGH·uh] *person* last king of Judah (c. 597–586 BC); originally named Mattaniah (2 Kin. 24:17); rebels against the king of Babylon (2 Kin. 24:20); defeated by Babylon (2 Kin. 25:1–21); taken to Babylon in captivity (2 Kin. 25:7).
**Zephaniah** [zeh·fuh·NIGH·uh] *person* prophet; the Old Testament book that bears his name is the ninth of the twelve Minor Prophets.

**Zerubbabel** [zeh·RUH·buh·behl] *person* the governor of Judah; descendant of David (1 Chr. 3:1–19); part of the family of Jesus (Matt. 1:12); leader of returning Jewish exiles (Neh. 7:6–7; Hag. 2:21–23); rebuilds the temple (Ezra 3:1–10; Zech. 4:1–14).

**Zion** [ZIGH·uhn] *place* eastern hills of Jerusalem; used of the city (Pss. 14:7; 48:2); used of the Temple Mount (Pss. 20:2; 125:1; Is. 18:7; Joel 3:17); used of God's city (Heb. 12:22); used of the New Jerusalem (Rev. 14:1); also called Sion (Deut. 4:48).

### *A NOTE REGARDING THE TYPE*

This Bible was set in the Thomas Nelson NKJV Typeface, commissioned by Thomas Nelson Publishers and designed in Aarhus by Klaus Krogh and Heidi Rand Sørensen of 2K/DENMARK. The letter forms take inspiration from a distinctive typeface found in an early Thomas Nelson *Novum Testamentum*, printed in 1844 in Edinburgh—which in turn reflects the Scotch Roman typefaces created by the celebrated English punchcutter Richard Austin for the type foundry of William Miller, circa 1808–1813.

Just as the NKJV translation inherits the tradition and literary beauty of the King James Bible while updating the language for today's readers, so Thomas Nelson's custom NKJV font family builds on classic letter forms of the past while reflecting cutting-edge typographical design. The result is a type design that is at once beautiful and efficient, traditional and modern—ideal for presenting the sacred words of ancient Scripture to readers today.

# INDEX TO MAPS

References are to the map number in **bold**, followed by the letter and number coordinates that correspond to the margin markings.


## A

Abel Shittim **2** D3
Abilene **6** D8
Acco **3** B2; **4** B4
Achaia **6** C4
Adriatic Sea **6** B3
Aegean Sea **1** A1; **6** C5
Africa **6** D1
Ai **1** C3; **2** C3
Aleppo **1** D2; **4** C1; **6** D8
Altar **7** C3
Ammon **2** D2; **3** D4; **4** C4
Amphipolis **6** B5
Antioch **6** D8
Antioch in Pisidia **6** C7
Antonia Fortress **7** C2
Aphek **3** B4
Apollonia **6** B5
Appii Forum **6** B3
Arabia **1** D3; **6** E8
Aram **3** D1; **4** C3
Aramean (Syrian) Desert **4** D3
Araxes (Aras) River **1** F1
Arnon River **2** D3; **3** C5
Aroer **3** C5
Arvad **4** B2
Ashdod **3** A4; **4** A4
Asher **3** B2
Ashkelon **3** A4
Ashtaroth **3** D2; **4** B4
Asia **6** C6
Asshur **1** E2
Assos **6** C5
Athens **6** C5
Attalia **6** C7
Azekah **2** C3

## B

Babylon **1** E3
Babylonians **1** E3
Bashan **2** D2
Beautiful Gate **7** D3
Beersheba **1** C3; **2** C3; **3** B5; **4** B5
Benjamin **3** B4
Berea **6** B5
Berothah **4** C3
Berothai **4** C3
Besor Valley **2** C3
Beth Horon **2** C3
Beth Shean **3** C3; **4** B4
Beth Shemesh **3** B4
Bethabara beyond the Jordan **5** C3, C5
Bethany **5** B5
Bethel **1** C3; **2** C3; **3** B4
Bethesda Pool **7** C2
Bethlehem **3** B4; **5** B5
Bethsaida **5** C2
Bezer **3** D4
Bithynia & Pontus **6** B6
Black Sea **1** C1; **6** A7
Bridge **7** C3
Brook of Egypt **2** C3; **4** A5
Byblos **1** C3; **4** B3

## C

Cabul **3** B2
Caesarea **5** A3; **6** E8
Caesarea Philippi (Panias) **5** C1
Cana of Galilee **5** B3
Canaan **2** D2
Capernaum **5** C2
Caphtor **1** A2
Cappadocia **6** C8
Carchemish **1** D2
Carmel, Mt. **3** B2
Caspian Sea **1** F1
Cenchrea **6** C5
Chios **6** C5
Chorazin **5** C2
Cilicia **6** C8
Clauda **6** D5
Cnidus **6** D6
Colosse **6** C6
Commagene **6** C8
Coos **6** D6
Corinth **6** C5
Corsica **6** B2
Crete **1** A2; **6** D5
Cyprus (island) **1** C2; **4** A2; **6** D7
Cyrenaica **6** E5

## D

Dacia **6** A5
Dalmatia **6** A4
Damascus **1** D3; **3** D1; **4** C3; **6** D8
Dan (town) **3** C2; **4** B3
Dan (tribe) **3** B4
Debir **2** C3
Decapolis **5** D3
Delphi **6** C5
Derbe **6** C7
Dibon **2** D3; **3** C5
Dophkah **2** C5
Dor **3** B3
Dothan **1** C3

## E

Eastern Desert **4** C5
Ebal, Mt. **3** B3
Ebla **1** D2
Edom **2** D4; **3** C6; **4** B5
Edrei **2** D2; **3** D3; **4** B4
Eglon **2** C3; **3** B4
Egypt **2** A3; **6** F6
Egyptians **1** C3
Ekron **3** B4
Elim **2** B4
Emmaus (Nicopolis) **5** A5
En Gedi **3** C5
Ephesus **6** C6
Ephraim **3** B4
Epirus **6** C4
Erech **1** E3
Essene Gate **7** A5
Essene Quarter **7** A5
Euphrates River **1** E3; **4** D1; **6** C8
Ezion Geber **2** C4; **4** B6

## F

Fair Havens **6** D5
First Wall **7** B4
Fish Gate **7** B2

## G

Gad **3** C4
Gadara **5** C3
Galatia **6** B7
Galilee **5** B2
Galilee, Sea of **2** D2; **3** C2; **4** B4; **5** C2

Gallia **6** A1
Gath **3** B4; **4** B4
Gaza **3** A5; **4** A5
Gebal (Byblos) **1** C3; **4** B3
Gennath Gate **7** A4
Gentiles, Court of **7** C3
Gerar **1** C3; **3** A5
Gerasa **5** C4
Gergesa (Kursi) **5** C2
Gerizim, Mt. **3** B3; **5** B4
Germania **6** A4
Gethsemane **7** D2
Gezer **3** B4; **4** B4
Gibeah **4** B4
Gibeon **2** C3; **3** B4
Gihon Spring **7** D5
Gilboa, Mt. **2** D2; **4** B4
Gilgal **2** D3; **3** C4
Golan **3** C2
Golden Gate **7** D3
Golgotha **7** A3
Gordon's Calvary and Garden Tomb **7** B1
Goshen **2** A3
Great Bitter Lake **2** B4
Gulf of Aqaba **2** C4; **4** B6
Gulf of Suez **2** B4

## H

Hamath (region) **4** D2
Hamath (town) **4** C2
Haran **1** D2
Hattusa **1** C1
Hazeroth **2** C5
Hazor **1** C3; **2** D2; **3** C2; **4** B3
Hebron **1** C3; **2** C3; **3** B5; **4** B5
Hermon, Mt. **3** C1; **4** B3; **5** C1
Herod Antipas' Palace **7** B4
Herod's Palace **7** A4
Heshbon **2** D3; **3** C4
Hezekiah's Tunnel **7** C5
High Priest's House **7** A5
Hinnom Valley **7** B6
Hippicus, Tower of **7** A4
Hittites **1** C1
Hormah **3** B5
Hulda Gates **7** C4

## I

Iconium **6** C7
Idumea **5** B6
Ije Abarim **2** D3
Ijon **3** C1
Inner Court **7** C3
Ionian Sea **6** C4
Israel, Court of **7** C3
Issachar **3** C3
Issus **6** C8
Italia **6** B2

## J

Jabbok River **3** C3; **5** C4
Jabesh Gilead **3** C3
Jahaz **2** D3
Jarmuth **2** C3
Jazer **3** C4
Jebel Musa **2** C5
Jericho **2** D3; **3** C4; **5** B5
Jerusalem **2** C3; **3** C4; **4** B4; **5** B5; **6** E8
Jezreel **3** C3
Joppa **3** B4; **4** B4
Jordan River **2** D2; **3** C3; **4** B4; **5** C4; **6** E8
Judah **3** B5
Judea **5** B5; **6** E8

## K

Kadesh Barnea **1** C3; **2** C4; **4** A5
Kedesh (on the Orontes) **4** C2
Kedesh **2** D2; **3** C2; **4** B3
Kidron Valley **7** D5
Kir Hareseth **4** B5
Kirjath Jearim **3** B4
Kishon River **3** B2
Kittim **1** C2; **4** A2
Knossos **1** A2

## L

Lachish **2** C3; **3** B4
Laodicea **6** C6
Lasea **6** D5
Libnah **2** C3
Litani River **3** C1; **4** B3
Lower City **7** B5
Lycaonia **6** C7
Lycia **6** C6
Lydia **6** C6
Lystra **6** C7

## M

Macedonia **6** B4
Machaerus **5** C6
Magdala **5** C2
Mahanaim **3** C3; **4** B4
Makkedah **2** C3
Malta **6** D3
Manasseh, East **3** D2
Manasseh, West **3** B3
Marah **2** B4
Mari **1** D2
Mariamne, Tower of **7** A4
Medeba **4** B4
Mediterranean Sea (The Great Sea) **1** B3; **2** B2; **3** A2; **4** A2; **5** A2; **6** D3
Megiddo **1** C3; **3** B3; **4** B4
Menzaleh, Lake **2** A3
Merom **2** D2; **3** C2
Midian **2** C5
Miletus **6** C6
Mitylene **6** C6
Mizpah **3** B4
Moab **2** D3; **3** C5; **4** B5
Moesia **6** A6
Moreh, Mt. **3** C3
Mycenae **1** A2
Myra **6** D6
Mysia **6** C6

## N

Nain **5** B3
Naphtali **3** C2
Nazareth **5** B3
Neapolis **6** B5
Nebo, Mt. **2** D3; **3** C4
New Quarter **7** B3
Nile River **1** C4; **2** A4; **6** F7
Nineveh **1** E2
Nippur **1** E3
Noph (Memphis) **1** C4; **2** A4
Numidia **6** D1
Nuzi **1** E2

## O

Oboth **2** C4
Olives, Mt. of **5** B5; **7** D3
Olympus, Mt. **6** B5
On (Heliopolis) **1** C4; **2** A4
Orontes River **4** C1

## P

Padan Aram **1** D2
Pamphylia **6** C7
Paphos **6** D7
Paran, Wilderness of **2** C4
Patara **6** D6
Patmos **6** C6
Perea **5** C4
Perga **6** C7
Pergamos **6** C6
Persian Gulf **1** F4
Pharpar River **3** D1

Phasael, Tower of **7** A4
Philadelphia **6** C6
Philippi **6** B5
Philistia **2** C3; **4** A4
Phoenicia **4** B3; **5** B1; **6** D8
Phoenix **6** D5
Pinnacle of the Temple **7** D4
Pisidia **6** C6
Pithom **2** B4
Ptolemais (Acco) **5** B2; **6** E8
Punon **2** D3
Puteoli **6** B3

## Q

Qatna **4** C2

## R

Raamses **2** A3
Rabbah (Amman) **3** D4; **4** B4
Ramoth Gilead **3** D3; **4** B4
Red Sea **1** C4; **2** C6; **6** F8
Rephidim **2** C5
Reuben **3** C4
Rhegium **6** C3
Rhodes **6** D6
Rimmon **3** C2
Robinson's Arch **7** C4
Rome **6** B2
Royal Porch **7** C4

## S

Salamis **6** D7
Salim **5** C3
Salmone **6** D6
Salt Sea (Dead Sea) **2** D3; **3** C4; **4** B5; **5** C6
Samaria (region) **5** B3
Samaria (town) **3** B3
Samos **6** C6
Samothrace **6** B5
Sardinia **6** B1
Sardis **6** C6
Second Wall **7** B2
Seleucia Pieria **6** D8
Serpent Pool **7** A5
Shechem **1** C3; **2** C2; **3** B3; **4** B4
Sheep Gate **7** C2
Sheep's Pool **7** C2
Shiloh **2** C3; **3** B4
Shur, Wilderness of **2** B4
Sicily **6** C3
Sidon **4** B3; **6** D8
Siloam Pool **7** C6
Simeon **3** B5
Sin, Wilderness of **2** B4
Sinai **1** C4; **2** B4; **4** A5
Sinai, Mt. **2** C5
Smyrna **6** C6
Sparta **6** C5
Stairs **7** C4
Succoth **1** C3; **2** A3; **3** C3
Sychar **5** B4
Syracuse **6** C3
Syria **6** D8

## T

Taanach **3** B3; **4** B4
Tabor, Mt. **2** D2; **3** C3; **5** B3
Tadmor **1** D2; **4** D2
Tamar **4** B5
Tarsus **6** C8
Taurus Mountains **1** C2
Temple **7** C3
Theater **7** B5
Thessalonica **6** B5
Thrace **6** B5
Three Inns **6** B2
Thyatira **6** C6
Tiberias **5** C2
Tigris River **1** E2
Tiphsah **4** D1
Tirzah **3** C3
Tower Pool **7** A3
Tripolitania **6** E3
Troas **6** C5
Troy **1** A1
Tyre **3** B2; **4** B3; **5** B1; **6** E8
Tyropoeon Valley **7** B2, C5
Tyrrhenian Sea **6** B2

## U

Ugarit **1** C2
Upper City **7** B4
Upper Room **7** A5
Ur **1** F3
Urmia, Lake **1** E2

## V

Valley Gate **7** C4

## W

Water Gate **7** C6
Wilson's Arch **7** B3
Women, Court of **7** C3

## Y

Yarmuk River **3** C3; **5** C3

## Z

Zebulun **3** B2
Zered Brook **2** D3; **3** C6
Ziklag **3** A5; **4** A5
Zin, Wilderness of **2** C3
Zoan (Tanis) **1** C3
Zoar **1** C3

## Map 1: WORLD OF THE PATRIARCHS

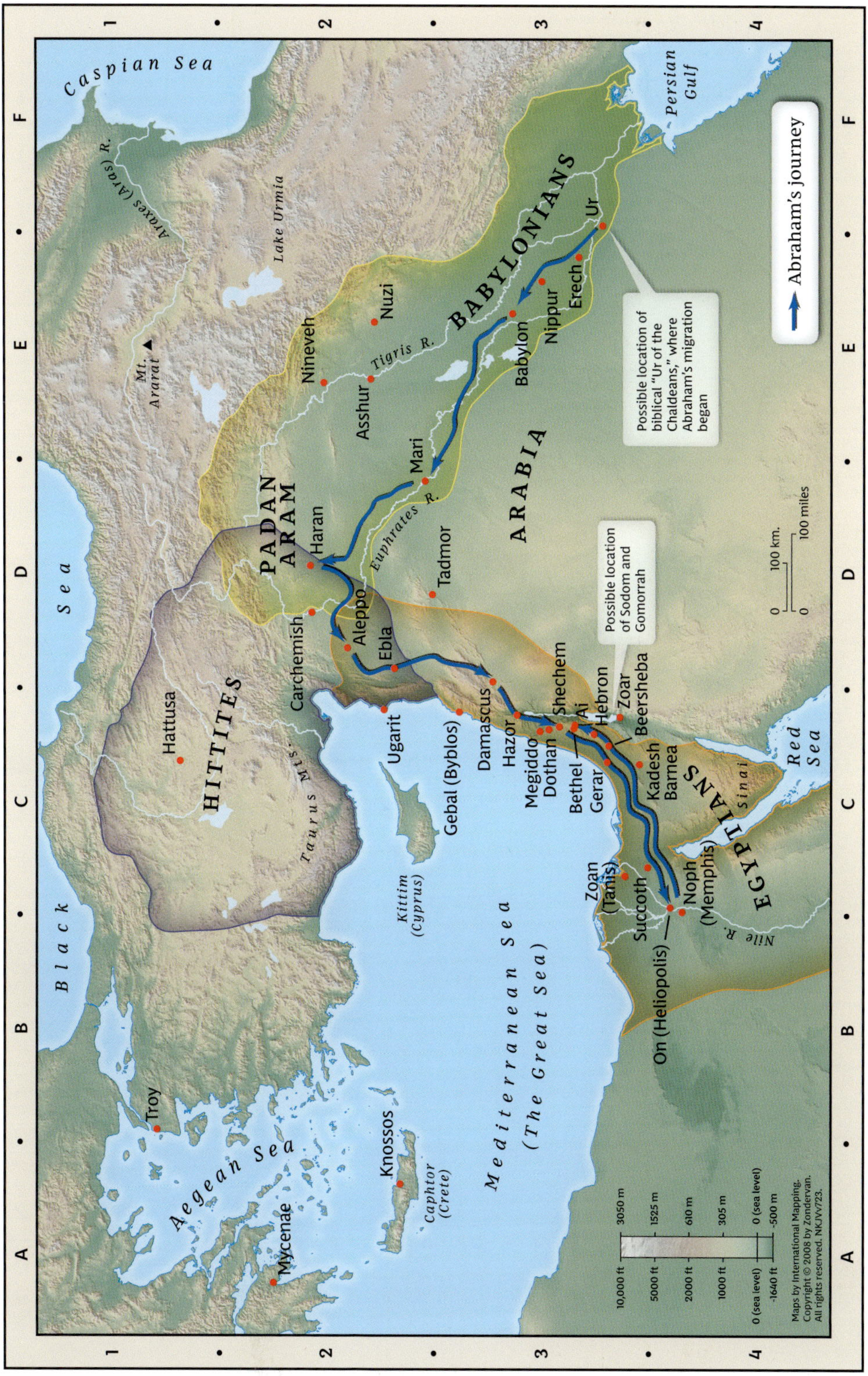

## Map 2: EXODUS AND CONQUEST OF CANAAN

## Map 3: LAND OF THE TWELVE TRIBES

## Map 4: KINGDOM OF DAVID AND SOLOMON

## Map 5: JESUS' MINISTRY

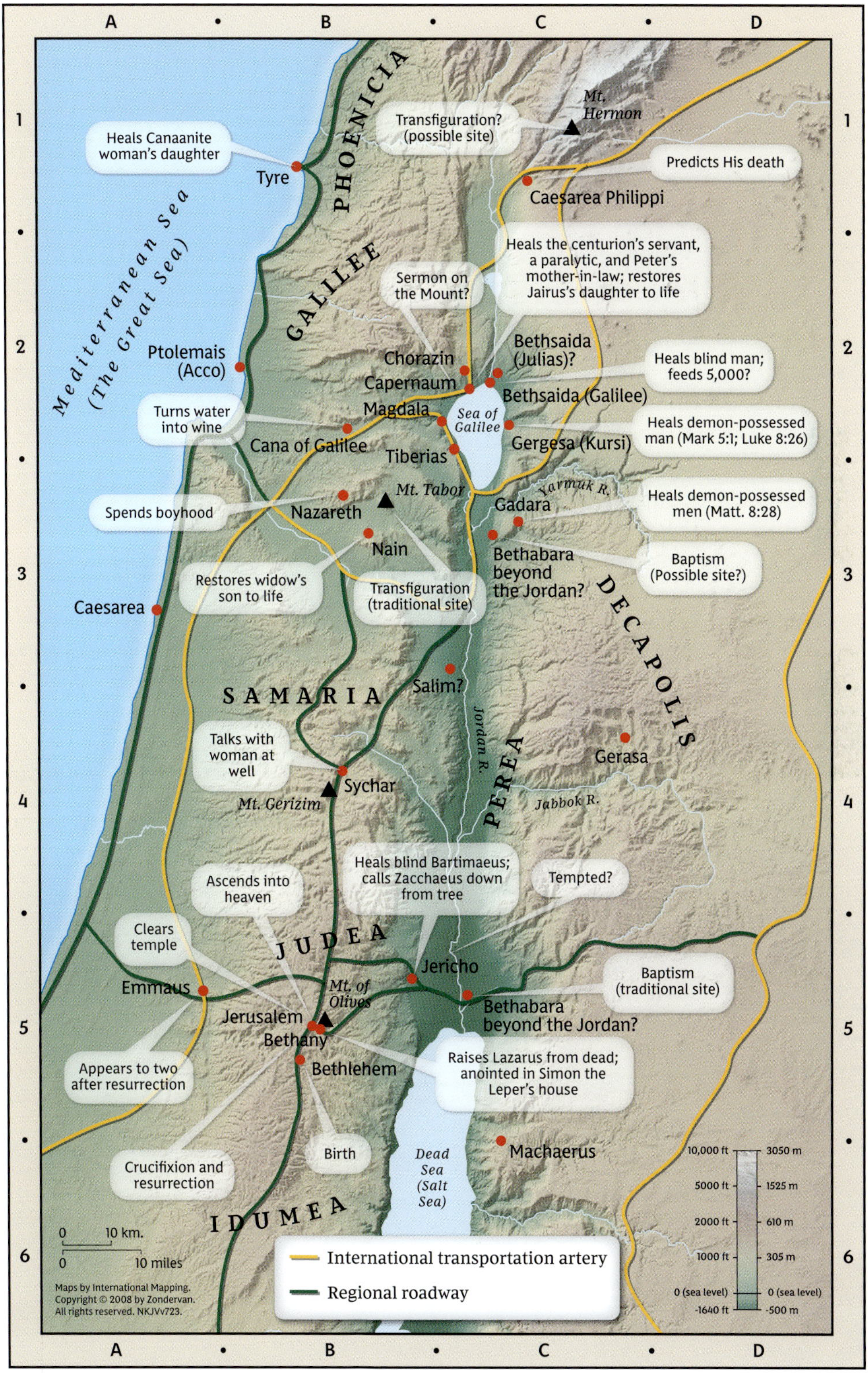

## Map 6: PAUL'S MISSIONARY JOURNEYS

DACIA
MOESIA
THRACE
Black Sea
10,000 ft
5000 ft
2000 ft
1000 ft
0 (sea level)
-1640 ft
3050 m
1525 m
610 m
305 m
0 (sea level)
-500 m
ONIA
Amphipolis
Thessalonica
Philippi
Neapolis
Samothrace
Apollonia?
BITHYNIA & PONTUS
Mt. Olympus
Troas
Assos
Mitylene
Aegean Sea
MYSIA
ASIA
Pergamos
Thyatira
GALATIA
CAPPADOCIA
Chios
LYDIA
Sardis
Delphi
Smyrna
Ephesus
LYCAONIA
Antioch (Pisidian)
Philadelphia
PISIDIA
COMMAGENE
Iconium
Athens
Samos
Laodicea
Colosse
PAMPHYLIA
Derbe
Euphrates R.
Cenchrea
Corinth
Miletus
Lystra
CILICIA
Patmos
Sparta
LYCIA
Attalia
Tarsus
Issus
SYRIA
Cos
Cnidus
Seleucia Pieria
Aleppo
Patara
Myra
Crete
Rhodes
Perga
Antioch (Syrian)
Phoenix
Salmone
Cyprus
Lasea
Salamis
Clauda
Fair Havens
Paphos
ABILENE
PHOENICIA
Sidon
Mediterranean Sea
(The Great Sea)
Tyre
Damascus
Ptolemais
Caesarea
JUDEA
Jordan R.
Jerusalem
Dead Sea
(Salt Sea)
ENAICA
ARABIA
EGYPT
Nile R.
0
200 km.
0
200 miles
Red Sea
5
6
7
8
A
B
C
D
E
F

## Map 7: JERUSALEM IN THE TIME OF JESUS

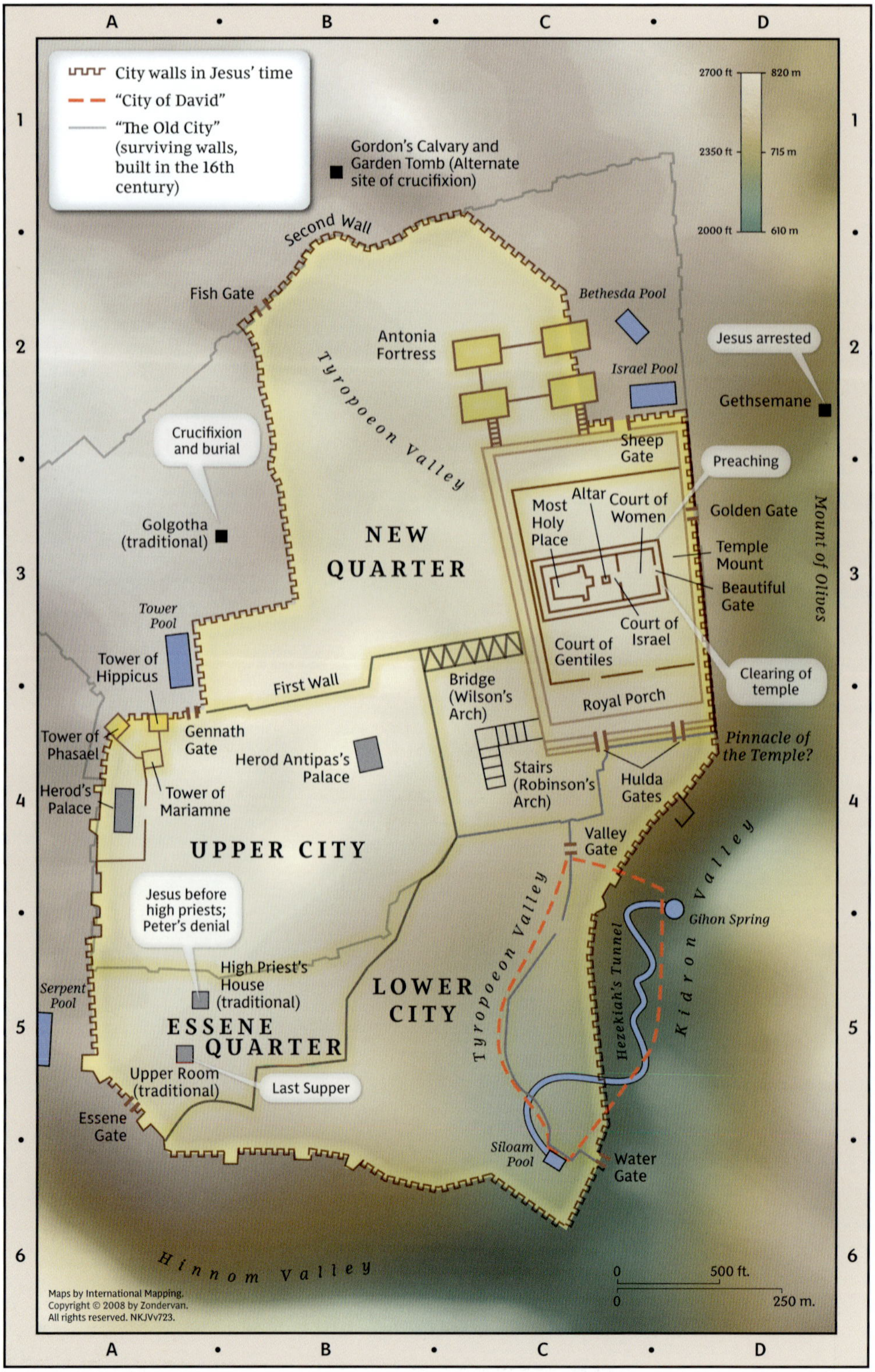